DICTIONARY OF THE BIBLE

DICTIONARY
OF THE
BIBLE

EDITED BY

JAMES HASTINGS

REVISED EDITION BY

FREDERICK C. GRANT

AND

H. H. ROWLEY

A CHARLES SCRIBNER'S SONS BOOK
MACMILLAN PUBLISHING COMPANY
NEW YORK

The Publishers are indebted to the Division of Christian Education, National Council of Churches, for permission to use Scripture quotations from the Revised Standard Version of the Bible, copyrighted 1946 and 1952

Macmillan Publishing Company
866 Third Avenue, New York, NY 10022
Collier Macmillan Canada, Inc.

Library of Congress Catalog Card Number 77-088224
ISBN 0-684-15556-7

First Scribner / Macmillan Hudson River Edition 1988

10 9 8 7 6 5 4 3

Printed in the United States of America

PREFACE

For more than fifty years James Hastings' one volume *Dictionary of the Bible* has been a valued work of reference in many libraries, both public and private. During that time much new knowledge has been acquired. The spade of the archaeologist has brought exciting new material into our hands, and our knowledge of the Biblical languages is fuller than it was half a century ago. Moreover, Biblical research has not stood still, and we have not rested in the positions of those days. In textual criticism there is greater caution to-day than there was, while interest in worship and in Biblical theology occupies a larger place in our study than it did formerly. It therefore seemed desirable to issue a revised edition of this Dictionary.

Not everything has been rewritten, but every entry has been read by a competent scholar. Some entries have been passed as needing no change; some have been partly modified; some have been wholly rewritten. Every effort has been made to ensure that the information here given is accurate and in line with present-day knowledge. Where no material change has been made in an article the initials of the original author stand alone at the end. Similarly, where an article has been completely rewritten the initials of the new author stand alone. Where part of the old article has been retained and part supplied by the reviser, the initials of the original author are followed by those of the reviser. The editors express their thanks to all who have collaborated with them in this revision.

The old edition was based on the Revised Version of the Bible, and head entries were in the forms found in that version, with frequent cross-references from Authorized Version forms. The present edition is based on the Revised Standard Version, and Biblical quotations and head entries are, by permission, normally in agreement with that version, with cross-references from both Authorized Version and Revised Version forms. The number of cross references is therefore substantially larger than in the former edition, with the result that it is possible to use the Dictionary with any one of these versions. The New Testament of the New English Bible appeared while this Dictionary was in the press, and therefore too late to be used in its preparation.

In addition to a greater number of cross-references there are many new entries, sometimes dealing with new sources of knowledge, such as the Dead Sea Scrolls, and sometimes with Biblical terms which were not included in the old edition, though of comparable character with others which were. At the same time every effort has been made to keep the over-all length of the Dictionary as close as possible to that of the original edition.

The maps have been prepared by Messrs. Thos. Nelson & Sons, Ltd., and are identical with those which appear in the new edition of Peake's *Commentary on the Bible*.

In sending out this edition the Editors express the hope that it may be found useful to a further generation of Biblical students, giving not alone factual information about obscure and familiar Biblical persons and places, but mediating the fruits of Biblical scholarship and offering guidance on the significance of the Biblical revelation.

F. C. Grant.

H. H. Rowley.

ABBREVIATION OF BIBLICAL BOOKS

Old Testament

Gn = Genesis.
Ex = Exodus.
Lv = Leviticus.
Nu = Numbers.
Dt = Deuteronomy.
Jos = Joshua.
Jg = Judges.
Ru = Ruth.
1 S, 2 S = 1 and 2 Samuel.
1 K, 2 K = 1 and 2 Kings.
1 Ch, 2 Ch = 1 and 2 Chronicles.
Ezr = Ezra.
Neh = Nehemiah.
Est = Esther.
Job.
Ps = Psalms.
Pr = Proverbs.
Ec = Ecclesiastes.
Ca = Canticles.
Is = Isaiah.
Jer = Jeremiah.
La = Lamentations.
Ezk = Ezekiel.
Dn = Daniel
Hos = Hosea.
Jl = Joel.
Am = Amos.
Ob = Obadiah.
Jon = Jonah.
Mic = Micah.
Nah = Nahum.
Hab = Habakkuk.
Zeph = Zephaniah.
Hag = Haggai.
Zec = Zechariah.
Mal = Malachi.

Apocrypha

1 Es, 2 Es = 1 and 2 Esdras.
Ad. Est = Additions to Esther.
Wis = Wisdom.
Sir = Sirach or Ecclesiasticus.
Bar = Baruch.
Ep. Jer = Letter of Jeremiah (Bar 6).
Three = Song of the Three Children.
To = Tobit.
Jth = Judith.
Sus = Susanna.
Bel = Bel and the Dragon.
Pr. Man = Prayer of Manasses.
1 Mac, 2 Mac = 1 and 2 Maccabees.

New Testament

Mt = Matthew.
Mk = Mark.
Lk = Luke.
Jn = John.
Ac = Acts.
Ro = Romans.
1 Co, 2 Co = 1 and 2 Corinthians.
Gal = Galatians.
Eph = Ephesians.
Ph = Philippians.
Col = Colossians.
1 Th, 2 Th = 1 and 2 Thessalonians.
1 Ti, 2 Ti = 1 and 2 Timothy.
Tit = Titus.
Phn = Philemon.
He = Hebrews.
Ja = James.
1 P, 2 P = 1 and 2 Peter.
1 Jn, 2 Jn, 3 Jn = 1, 2, and 3 John.
Jd = Jude.
Rev = Revelation.

ABBREVIATIONS

I. General

Aq. = Aquila.
Arab. = Arabic.
Aram. = Aramaic.
Assyr. = Assyrian.
ARV = American Revised Version.
AS = Anglo-Saxon.
ASV = American Standard Version.
AV = Authorized Version.
Bab. = Babylonian.
c = *circa*.
cf = compare.
D = Deuteronomist.
E = Elohist.
EV = English Versions.
fl. = *floruit*.
H = Holiness Code.
J = Yahwist.
LXX = Septuagint; LXX^B = Codex Vaticanus; LXX^L = Recension of Lucian.
MT = Massoretic Text.
NT = New Testament.
OL = Old Latin.
OS = Old Syriac.
OT = Old Testament.
Onk. or Onq. = Targum of Onkelos (Onqelos).
P = Priestly Code.
Pesh. = Peshitta.
Ps.-Jn. = Pseudo-Jonathan.
RSV = Revised Standard Version.
RV = Revised Version.
Sah. = Sahidic.
Sam. = Samaritan.
sc. = *scilicet*.
Symm. = Symmachus.
Syr^c = Curetonian Syriac.
Syr^s or Syr.-Sin. = Sinaitic Syriac.
Targ. = Targum.
Theod. = Theodotion.
TR = Textus Receptus.
v.l. = varia lectio.
VSS = Versions.
Vulg. = Vulgate.
WH = Westcott and Hort's text.
Y″ = Yahweh.

II. For the Literature

AASOR = *Annual of the American Schools of Oriental Research*.
Ab. = *Pirke Aboth*.
AJSL = *American Journal of Semitic Languages and Literatures*.
ANEP = *The Ancient Near East in Pictures* (J. B. Pritchard).
ANET = *Ancient Near Eastern Texts relating to the Old Testament* (ed. by J. B. Pritchard).
APEF = *Annual of the Palestine Exploration Fund*.
Apoc. Bar. = *Apocalypse of Baruch*.
APOT = *Apocrypha and Pseudepigrapha of the Old Testament* (ed. by R. H. Charles).
Appian, *Bell. Civ.* = *Bella Civilia*.
  Syr. = *Syriakē*.
ARI = *Archaeology and the Religion of Israel* (W. F. Albright).
Ascens. Is. = *Ascension of Isaiah*.
ATD = *Das Alte Testament Deutsch*.
ATR = *Anglican Theological Review*.
BA = *Biblical Archaeologist*.
Barn. = *Epistle of Barnabas*.
BASOR = *Bulletin of the American Schools of Oriental Research*.
BC = *Beginnings of Christianity* (Foakes-Jackson and Lake).
BDB = Brown-Driver-Briggs, *Hebrew and English Lexicon*.
Bell. Afr. = *Bellum Africum*.
Berak. = *Berakhoth*.
Bi. Or. = *Bibliotheca Orientalis*.
BJRL = *Bulletin of the John Rylands Library*.
BRL = *Biblisches Reallexikon* (K. Galling).
CD or CDC = Zadokite Work.
Cent B = Century Bible.
Cicero, *De Nat. Deor.* = *De Natura Deorum*.
  Philipp. = *Philippicae*.
CIG = *Corpus Inscriptionum Graecarum*.
CIL = *Corpus Inscriptionum Latinarum*.
CIS = *Corpus Inscriptionum Semiticarum*.
1 Clem or Clem. *Cor.* = Clement, *Epistle to the Corinthians*.
Clem. Alex. *Strom.* = Clement of Alexandria, *Stromata*.
C.S.C.O. = *Corpus Scriptorum Christianorum Orientalium*.
Cyprian, *ep.* = *Epistula*.
Cyril of Jerusalem, *Cat.* = *Catecheses*.
DAC = *Dictionary of the Apostolic Church* (ed. by J. Hastings).
DB = *Dictionary of the Bible*, 4 vols. and Extra Vol. (ed. by J. Hastings).
DCG = *Dictionary of Christ and the Gospels* (ed. by J. Hastings).
Did. = *Didache*.
DLZ = *Deutsche Literaturzeitung*.
DSD = *Manual of Discipline* from Qumrân Cave 1.
DSH = *Hymns Scroll* from Qumrân Cave 1.
EBi = *Encyclopaedia Biblica*.
EBrit. = *Encyclopaedia Britannica*.
Eccles. R. = *Ecclesiastes Rabbah*.
EGT = *Expositor's Greek Testament* (ed. by W. Robertson Nicoll).
Einl. = *Einleitung*.
Epiphanius, *Haer.* = *Haereses*.
ERE = *Encyclopaedia of Religion and Ethics* (ed. by J. Hastings).
E(xp)T = *Expository Times*.
Eusebius, *HE* = *Historia Ecclesiastica*.
  Mart. Pal. = *Martyrs of Palestine*.
  Praep. Ev. = *Praeparatio Evangelica*.
  Onom. = *Onomasticon*.
Ev. Ver. = *Evangelium Veritatis*.
FIRA = *Fontes Iuris Romani Antejustiniani*.
FSAC = *From the Stone Age to Christianity* (W. F. Albright).
GAP = *Geographie des alten Palästina* (F. Buhl).
GJV = *Geschichte des Jüdischen Volkes* (E. Schürer).
GVI = *Geschichte des Volkes Israel*.
Grafton, *Chron.* = *Chronicle*.
HAT = *Handbuch zum Alten Testament*.
Heb. Arch. = *Hebräische Archäologie* (I. Benzinger).
Hermas, *Vis.* = *Visiones*.
  Sim(il). = *Similitudines*.
  Mand. = *Mandata*.
HGHL = *Historical Geography of the Holy Land* (G. A. Smith).
HJP = *History of the Jewish People* (E. Schürer).
HPN = *Hebrew Proper Names* (G. B. Gray).
Hum. Marr. = *History of Human Marriage* (E. Westermarck).
IB = *Interpreter's Bible*.

ABBREVIATIONS

ICC=*International Critical Commentary.*
IEJ=*Israel Exploration Journal.*
IG=*Inscriptiones Graecae.*
Ignatius, *Eph.*=*ad Ephesios.*
Mag.=*ad Magnesios.*
Trall.=*ad Trallianos.*
Ro.=*ad Romanos.*
ad Polyc. or *Pol.*=*ad Polycarpum.*
Smyr.=*ad Smyrnaeos.*
IOT=*Introduction to the Old Testament* (R. H. Pfeiffer).
Irenaeus, *Haer.*=*Adversus omnes haereses.*
Isidore, *Etym.*=*Etymologiae.*
JAOS=*Journal of the American Oriental Society.*
JBL=*Journal of Biblical Literature.*
JBR=*Journal of Bible and Religion.*
JE=*Jewish Encyclopedia.*
Jer. Talm.=Jerusalem Talmud.
Jerome, *adv. Pelag.*=*Dialogi contra Pelagianos.*
de viris illus.=*de Viris illustribus.*
Ep. Paul.=*Epistola ad Paulam.*
Quaest. Gen.=*Liber Hebraicarum quaestionum in Genesim.*
JNES=*Journal of Near Eastern Studies.*
Jos. Ant.=Josephus, *Antiquitates Judaicae.*
BJ=*Bellum Judaicum.*
c.Ap(ion).=*contra Apionem.*
Vit.=*Vita.*
JQR=*Jewish Quarterly Review.*
JSS=*Journal of Semitic Studies.*
JThSt=*Journal of Theological Studies.*
JTVI=*Journal of the Transactions of the Victoria Institute.*
Jub=*Jubilees.*
Jud. Pal.=*Le Judaïsme palestinien* (J. Bonsirven).
Justin, *Dial.* or *Dial. Tryph.*=*Dialogus cum Tryphone.*
Ap(ol).=*Apologiae.*
KAT=*Die Keilinschriften und das Alte Testament* (E. Schrader; 3rd ed. by H. Zimmern and H. Winckler).
KB=Koehler-Baumgartner, *Lexicon in Veteris Testamenti libros.*
Ker.=*Kerithoth.*
KIB=*Keilinschriftliche Bibliothek* (E. Schrader).
Kidd.=*Kiddushin.*
Krit.exeg.K.u.d.NT=*Kritischexegetischer Kommentar über das Neuen Testament* (Meyer).
Livy, *Epit.*=*Epitomae.*
LOT=*Introduction to the Literature of the Old Testament* (S. R. Driver).
LT=*The Life and Times of Jesus the Messiah* (A. Edersheim).
Mart.Pol.=*Martyrdom of Polycarp.*
Midd.=*Middoth.*
Milton, *PL*=*Paradise Lost.*
Mod. Egyp.=*Modern Egyptians* (E. W. Lane).
Nidd.=*Niddah.*
NSI=*Handbook of North-Semitic Inscriptions* (G. A. Cooke).
OED=*Oxford English Dictionary.*
OGIS=*Orientis Graecae Inscriptiones Selectae.*
Origen, *de Orat.*=*de Oratione.*
OTJC=*The OT in the Jewish Church* (W. R. Smith).
Ovid, *Ars Amat.*=*Ars Amatoria.*
Oxf. Heb. Lex.=*Hebrew and English Lexicon* (Brown-Driver-Briggs).
Oxyr. Pap.=*Oxyrhynchus Papyri.*
PEF(Q)St.=*Palestine Exploration Fund* (*Quarterly*) *statement.*
PEQ=*Palestine Exploration Quarterly.*
Pes.=*Pesachim.*
Philo, *de spec. legg.*=*de specialibus legibus.*
Quis rer.div.her.=*Quis rerum divinarum heres.*
Vit. Mos.=*de Vita Mosis.*
Gig.=*de Gigantibus.*
In Flacc.=*in Flaccum.*
de Sept.=*de Septenario.*
PJB=*Palästina-Jahrbücher.*
PL=*Patrologia, Series Latina* (ed. Migne).
Pliny, *Ep(p).*=*Epistula(e).*
NH or *HN*=*Historia Naturalis.*

Plutarch, *de def. Orac.*=*de defectu Oraculorum.*
Pollux, *Onom.*=*Onomasticon.*
Polycarp, *Phil.*=*ad Philippenses.*
PRE=*Protestantische Reallexikon für Theologie und Kirche* (Herzog-Hauck).
Prudentius, *Peristeph.*=*Peristephanon.*
PSBA=*Proceedings of the Society for Biblical Archaeology.*
Ps. Sol.=*Psalms of Solomon.*
QDAP=*Quarterly of the Department of Antiquities of Palestine.*
4 Q Florilegium=*Florilegium* from Qumrân Cave 1.
1 Q H=*Hymns Scroll* from Qumrân Cave 1.
1 Q Isa[a]=*Isaiah A* scroll from Qumrân Cave 1.
1 Q M=*War Scroll* from Qumrân Cave 1.
1 Q P H=*Habakkuk Pesher* from Qumrân Cave 1.
1 Q S=*Manual of Discipline* from Qumrân Cave 1.
1 Q Sa=*Rule of the Community* (appendix) from Qumrân Cave 1.
4 Q Sam[a]=*Samuel A* text from Qumrân Cave 4; Sam[b]=*Samuel B* text.
1 Q Sb=*Benedictions* text from Qumrân Cave 1.
RB=*Revue Biblique.*
REJ=*Revue des Études juives.*
Reste arab. Heid.=*Reste arabischen Heidentums* (J. Wellhausen).
RHPR=*Revue d'histoire et de philosophie religieuses.*
RHR=*Revue de l'histoire des religions.*
RLA=*Reallexikon für Assyriologie.*
RQ=Redequelle.
RS=*Religion of the Semites* (W. R. Smith).
SB=Strack-Billerbeck, *Kommentar zum Neuen Testament aus Talmud und Midrasch.*
SBOT=*Sacred Books of the Old Testament* (ed. by P. Haupt).
Semit. Or.=*Semitic Origins* (G. A. Barton).
Shab.=*Shabbath.*
Shebi.=*Shebiith.*
Sib. Or(ac).=*Sibylline Oracles.*
SP=*Sinai and Palestine* (A. P. Stanley).
Spenser, *FQ*=*Faerie Queene.*
SS=*Šḥr and Šlm* text from Râs Shamra.
Suetonius, *Tib.*=*Tiberius.*
Sylloge Inscr. Gr.=*Sylloge inscriptionum graecarum* (ed. by W. Dittenberger).
Tacitus, *Ann.*=*Annales.*
Hist.=*Historiae.*
Ter. *Eun.*=Terence, *Eunuchus.*
Tertullian, *ad Mart.*=*ad Martyres.*
adv. Jud.=*adversus Judaeos.*
adv. Marc.=*adversus Marcionem.*
de Bapt.=de Baptismo.
de Pr. Haer.=*de praescriptione Haereticorum.*
de Spect.=*de Spectaculis.*
res. carn.=*de Resurrectione carnis.*
Scorp.=*Scorpiace.*
Test. Dan=Testament of Dan.
Test. Levi=Testament of Levi.
Test.XII Pat.=*Testaments of the Twelve Patriarchs.*
Th Z=*Theologische Zeitschrift.*
Theophilus of Antioch, *Aut(ol).*=*ad Autolycum.*
Theophrastus, *de lapid.*=*de Lapidibus.*
ThWB=*Theologisches Wörterbuch zum Neuen Testament* (ed. by G. Kittel).
TLZ—Theologische Literaturzeitung.
Trench, *Syn.*=*Synonyms of the NT.*
TSBA=*Transactions of the Society of Biblical Archaeology.*
TU=*Texte und Untersuchungen.*
VT=*Vetus Testamentum.*
VTS=Supplements to *Vetus Testamentum.*
WC=Westminster Commentaries.
Wright, *BA*=G. E. Wright, *Biblical Archaeology.*
Wright, *Synopsis*=A. Wright, *Synopsis of the Gospels in Greek.*
Zahn, *Apg.*=*Die Apostelgeschichte des Lucas.*
ZAW=*Zeitschrift für die alttestamentliche Wissenschaft.*
ZDPV=*Zeitschrift der Deutschen Palästina-Vereins.*
ZNW=*Zeitschrift für die neutestamentliche Wissenschaft.*

AUTHORS OF ARTICLES

IN THE FIRST EDITION

Rev. Walter Frederick Adeney, D.D., Principal of the Lancashire College, Manchester.
Rev. John S. Banks, D.D., Professor of Theology in the Headingley College, Leeds.
Rev. George A. Barton, A.M., Ph.D., Professor of Biblical Literature and Semitic Languages in Bryn Mawr College.
Rev. William Henry Bennett, D.D., Litt.D., Professor of Old Testament Exegesis in Hackney College and New College, London.
Rev. George Ricker Berry, D.D., Professor of Semitic Languages in Colgate University, New York.
Rev. A. W. F. Blunt, M.A., Fellow of Exeter College, Oxford.
Rev. George Herbert Box, M.A., Late Hebrew Master at Merchant Taylors' School, London, Incumbent of Linton, Ross.
Rev. William F. Boyd, M.A., Ph.D., Minister at Methlick, Aberdeenshire.
Rev. A. E. Burn, M.A., D.D., Rector and Rural Dean of Handsworth, Birmingham, and Prebendary of Lichfield.
Rev. Ernest De Witt Burton, D.D., Professor of New Testament Interpretation in the University of Chicago.
Rev. George G. Cameron, D.D., Professor of Hebrew in the United Free Church College, Aberdeen.
Rev. John S. Clemens, B.A., D.D., Principal of Ranmoor College, Sheffield.
Rev. William F. Cobb, D.D., Rector of the Church of St. Ethelburga the Virgin, London.
Rev. H. F. B. Compston, M.A., Hebrew Lecturer and Tutor in King's College, London; Member of the Theological Board of Studies in the University of London.
Rev. James A. Craig, D.D., Professor of Old Testament Interpretation in the University of Michigan.
Rev. T. Witton Davies, B.A., Ph.D., Professor of Hebrew in Bangor College.
Rev. W. T. Davison, M.A., D.D., Professor of Theology in Richmond Theological College, Surrey.
Adolf Deissmann, D.Th., D.D., Ord. Professor of New Testament Exegesis in the University of Berlin.
Rev. S. R. Driver, D.D., Litt.D., Professor of Hebrew in the University of Oxford, and Canon of Christ Church.
Rev. E. A. Edghill, M.A., B.D., College of St. Saviour, Southwark.
Rev. Cyril W. Emmet, M.A., Vicar of West Hendred, Steventon.
Rev. W. Ewing, M.A., Minister at Edinburgh.
Rev. Robert A. Falconer, D.Litt., D.D., President of the University of Toronto.
Rev. George G. Findlay, M.A., D.D., Professor of Biblical Literature in the Headingley College, Leeds.
Rev. Henry Thatcher Fowler, D.D., Professor of Biblical Literature and History in Brown University, Providence.
Rev. Kemper Fullerton, D.D., Professor of Old Testament Language and Literature in Oberlin College, Ohio.
Rev. Alfred E. Garvie, M.A., D.D., Principal of New College, London.
Rev. Owen H. Gates, Ph.D., Librarian and Instructor in Hebrew in Andover Theological Seminary.
Rev. James Gilroy, D.D., Professor of Hebrew in the University of Aberdeen.
Rev. G. Buchanan Gray, M.A., D.D., Professor of Hebrew in Mansfield College, Oxford.
Rev. S. W. Green, M.A., Professor of Hebrew in Regent's Park College, London.
Rev. Charles T. P. Grierson, M.A., B.D., Canon of Down, and Rector of Seapatrick, Banbridge.
F. Ll. Griffith, M.A., F.S.A., Reader in Egyptology in the University of Oxford.
Rev. H. M. Gwatkin, M.A., D.D., Dixey Professor of Ecclesiastical History in the University of Cambridge.
Rev. G. H. Gwilliam, B.D., Rector of Remenham, Henley.
Rev. D. A. Hayes, Ph.D., S.T.D., LL.D., Professor of New Testament Exegesis in Garrett Biblical Institute, Northwestern University, Evanston, Ill.
Rev. W. J. Henderson, B.A., Principal of Bristol College.
G. F. Hill, M.A., Assistant Keeper of the Department of Coins and Medals in the British Museum, London.
Rev. A. E. Hillard, M.A., D.D., High Master of St. Paul's School, London.
Rev. F. R. Montgomery Hitchcock, B.D., Rector of Kinnitty, King's County.
Rev. C. H. W. Johns, M.A., Fellow of Queens' College, Cambridge.
Rev. D. M. Kay, M.A., D.D., Professor of Hebrew in the University of St. Andrews.
Rev. James A. Kelso, D.D., Professor of Old Testament Exegesis in the Western Theological Seminary, Allegheny.
Rev. A. R. S. Kennedy, D.D., Professor of Hebrew in the University of Edinburgh.
F. G. Kenyon, M.A., D.Litt., Ph.D., of the Department of Manuscripts in the British Museum, London, Late Fellow of Magdalen College, Oxford.
Leonard W. King, M.A., F.S.A., of the Department of Egyptian and Assyrian Antiquities in the British Museum, London.
Rev. G. A. Frank Knight, M.A., F.R.S.E., Minister at Perth.
Nicholas Koenig, M.A., University Fellow in Semitic Languages, Columbia University, New York.
Rev. J. C. Lambert, M.A., D.D., Fenwick, Assistant Editor of the *Dictionary of Christ and the Gospels.*
Rev. H. C. O. Lanchester, M.A., Fellow of Pembroke College, Cambridge.
R. A. Stewart Macalister, M.A., F.S.A., Director of Excavations for the Palestine Exploration Fund.

AUTHORS OF ARTICLES

Rev. J. FREDERIC McCURDY, Ph.D., LL.D., Professor of Oriental Languages in the University of Toronto.
Rev. WILLIAM M. MACDONALD, M.A., Minister at Foveran, Aberdeenshire.
Rev. GEORGE M. MACKIE, M.A., D.D., Chaplain to the Church of Scotland at Beirut, Syria.
Rev. HUGH R. MACKINTOSH, M.A., D.Phil., D.D., Professor of Systematic Theology in New College, Edinburgh.
Right Rev. ARTHUR JOHN MACLEAN, M.A., D.D., Bishop of Moray and Ross.
Rev. A. H. McNEILE, B.D., Fellow and Dean of Sidney Sussex College, Cambridge.
Rev. D. S. MARGOLIOUTH, M.A., D.Litt., Laudian Professor of Arabic in the University of Oxford.
Rev. JOHN T. MARSHALL, M.A., D.D., Principal of the Baptist College, Manchester.
E. W. GURNEY MASTERMAN, M.D., F.R.G.S., Jerusalem, Syria.
Rev. J. HOWARD B. MASTERMAN, M.A., Professor of History in the University of Birmingham, and Hon. Canon of Birmingham.
Rev. SHAILER MATHEWS, D.D., Professor of Theology and Dean of the Divinity School in the University of Chicago.
Rev. J. H. MAUDE, M.A., Rector of Hilgay, Downham Market.
Rev. R. WADDY MOSS, M.A., D.D., Professor of Systematic Theology in Didsbury College, Manchester.
Rev. JAMES HOPE MOULTON, M.A., D.Litt., Greenwood Professor of Hellenistic Greek in the Victoria University of Manchester.
Rev. WILFRID J. MOULTON, M.A., Professor of Old Testament Languages and Literature in Headingley College, Leeds.
Rev. T. ALLEN MOXON, M.A., Vicar of Alfreton, Derbyshire.
Rev. HENRY S. NASH, D.D., Professor in the Episcopal Theological School, Cambridge, Mass.
Rev. W. M. NESBIT, M.A., B.D., Fellow of Drew Theological Seminary.
THEODOR NÖLDEKE, Ph.D., LL.D., Professor Emeritus in the University of Strassburg.
Rev. W. O. E. OESTERLEY, D.D., Organizing Secretary to the Parochial Missions to the Jews, and Lecturer to the Palestine Exploration Fund.
Rev. JAMES ORR, D.D., Professor of Apologetics and Theology in the United Free Church College, Glasgow.
Rev. WILLIAM P. PATERSON, D.D., Professor of Divinity in the University of Edinburgh.
Rev. JAMES PATRICK, M.A., B.D., B.Sc., Minister at Edinburgh.
T. G. PINCHES, LL.D., M.R.A.S., Lecturer in Assyrian at University College, London.
Rev. IRA M. PRICE, M.A., B.D., Ph.D., Professor of Semitic Languages and Literature in the University of Chicago.
Rev. H. A. REDPATH, M.A., Litt.D., Rector of St. Dunstan's in the East, London.
Rev. FRANK EDWARD ROBINSON, B.A., Professor of Hebrew and Church History in the Baptist College, Bristol.
Rev. GEORGE L. ROBINSON, Ph.D., D.D., Professor of Old Testament Literature in McCormick Theological Seminary, Chicago.
Miss ETHEL G. ROMANES, Lady Margaret Hall, Oxford.
Rev. A. H. SAYCE, D.D., Litt.D., LL.D., Professor of Assyriology in the University of Oxford.
Rev. C. ANDERSON SCOTT, M.A., Professor of New Testament Literature in Westminster College, Cambridge.
Rev. JAMES G. SIMPSON, M.A., Principal of the Clergy School, Leeds.
Rev. JOHN SKINNER, M.A., D.D., Principal of Westminster College, Cambridge.
Rev. DAVID SMITH, M.A., D.D., Minister at Blairgowrie.
Rev. HENRY P. SMITH, M.A., D.D., LL.D., Professor of Old Testament Literature in Meadville Theological School.
Rev. JOHN MERLIN POWIS SMITH, D.D., Professor in the University of Chicago.
W. TAYLOR SMITH, B.A., Sevenoaks, Kent.
ALEXANDER SOUTER, M.A., Litt.D., Professor of New Testament Exegesis in Mansfield College, Oxford.
Rev. J. H. STEVENSON, D.D., Professor in Vanderbilt University, Nashville.
Rev. MORLEY STEVENSON, M.A., Principal of Warrington Training College, and Canon of Liverpool.
Rev. ALEXANDER STEWART, M.A., D.D., Principal of St. Mary's College, and Professor of Systematic Theology in the University of St. Andrews.
Rev. ROBERT H. STRACHAN, M.A., Minister at Elie.
Rev. A. W. STREANE, D.D., Formerly Dean and Hebrew and Divinity Lecturer in Corpus Christi College, Cambridge.
Rev. JOHN G. TASKER, D.D., Professor of Biblical Literature and Exegesis in Handsworth College, Birmingham.
Rev. JOHN TAYLOR, M.A., D.Litt., Vicar of Winchcombe.
Rev. R. BRUCE TAYLOR, M.A., Minister of St. John's Wood Presbyterian Church, London.
Rev. MILTON SPENCER TERRY, D.D., LL.D., Professor of Christian Doctrine in the Garrett Biblical Institute, Northwestern University, Evanston, Ill.
Rev. W. H. GRIFFITH THOMAS, D.D., Principal of Wycliffe Hall, Oxford.
Rev. G. W. WADE, D.D., Professor and Senior Tutor in St. David's College, Lampeter.
Rev. A. C. WELCH, M.A., B.D., Minister at Glasgow.
Rev. H. L. WILLETT, D.D., Dean of the Disciples' Divinity House in the University of Chicago.
Rev. J. R. WILLIS, B.D., Rector of Preban and Moyne, Co. Wicklow.
HERBERT G. WOOD, M.A., Fellow of Jesus College, Cambridge.
Rev. F. H. WOODS, B.D., Rector of Bainton, Late Fellow and Theological Lecturer of St. John's College, Oxford.

AUTHORS OF ARTICLES

IN THE REVISED EDITION

Rev. PETER R. ACKROYD, M.A., M.Th., Ph.D., Samuel Davidson Professor of Old Testament Studies, University of London King's College.

D. R. AP-THOMAS, M.A., B.D., Lecturer in Hebrew and Biblical Studies, University College, Bangor, North Wales.

Rev. FRANK K. BALCHIN, B.A., B.D., Th.D., Professor of Biblical Theology and New Testament, Trinity Theological College, Singapore.

DENIS BALY, B.A., Chairman, Department of Religion, Kenyon College, Gambier, Ohio.

Rev. ROBIN S. BARBOUR, M.A., B.D., S.T.M., Lecturer in New Testament Language, Literature, and Theology, New College, Edinburgh.

Rev. R. A. BARCLAY, M.A., B.D., Senior Lecturer in Old Testament Studies and Biblical Hebrew and in the History of Religion, University of Leeds.

Rev. ALLAN BARR, M.A., D.D., Professor of New Testament Language, Literature, and Exegesis, United Free Church of Scotland College, Edinburgh.

Rev. JAMES BARR, M.A., B.D., W. H. Green Professor of Old Testament Literature, Princeton Theological Seminary, Princeton, N.J.

WILLIAM A. BEARDSLEE, Ph.D., Professor of Bible, Emory University, Atlanta, Georgia.

J. CHRISTIAAN BEKER, B.D., Ph.D., S.T.M., Associate Professor of Biblical Theology, Pacific School of Religion, Berkeley, California.

Rev. E. F. F. BISHOP, M.A., Sometime Principal of the Newman School of Missions in Jerusalem and Lecturer in the University of Glasgow.

Rev. JOHN BOWMAN, M.A., B.D., D.Phil., Professor of Semitic Studies, University of Melbourne.

Rev. JOHN BRIGHT, Ph.D., Hon.D.D., Professor of Hebrew and the Interpretation of the Old Testament, Union Theological Seminary, Richmond, Virginia.

Rev. LYLE O. BRISTOL, M.A., B.D., S.T.M., Th.D., Senior Minister, First Baptist Church, Medford, Massachusetts.

Rev. L. H. BROCKINGTON, M.A., B.D., Senior Lecturer in Aramaic and Syriac, University of Oxford.

Rev. Professor WILLIAM H. BROWNLEE, B.A., Th.M., Ph.D., D.D., Claremont Graduate School, Claremont, California.

F. F. BRUCE, M.A., D.D., Rylands Professor of Biblical Criticism and Exegesis, University of Manchester.

RUDOLF BULTMANN, D., Dr. Phil. h.c., D.D., D.S.Th., Emeritus Professor of Theology, University of Marburg.

Rev. MILLAR BURROWS, Ph.D., D.D., Emeritus Professor of Biblical Theology, Yale University.

Rev. GEORGE B. CAIRD, M.A., D.Phil., D.D., Senior Tutor, Mansfield College, Oxford.

Rev. Canon HENRY CHADWICK, D.D., Mus.B., F.B.A., Regius Professor of Divinity, University of Oxford.

Professor EDMOND LA B. CHERBONNIER, M.A., Ph.D., D.D., Chairman of the Department of Religion, Trinity College, Hartford, Connecticut.

LEONARD W. CLARKE, M.A., F.R.A.S., Senior Narrator, The London Planetarium.

Rev. HENRI CLAVIER, Dr. Th., Hon. D.D., Professeur de Nouveau Testament, Faculté de Théologie Protestante, University of Strasbourg.

ROBERT GREENHILL COCHRANE, M.D., F.R.C.P., D.T.M. & H., Adviser in Leprosy to the Ministry of Health, Late Principal and Director, Christian Medical College, Vellore, South India.

†Rabbi SAMUEL S. COHON, D.D., Emeritus Professor of Jewish Theology, Hebrew Union College, Cincinnati, Ohio.

ERNEST CADMAN COLWELL, B.D., Ph.D., Litt.D., LL.D., S.T.D., President and Professor of New Testament, Southern California School of Theology, Claremont, California.

Rev. PAUL E. DAVIES, Ph.D., D.D., Professor of New Testament Greek and Exegesis, McCormick Theological Seminary, Chicago, Illinois.

Rev. W. D. DAVIES, M.A., D.D., Edward Robinson Professor of Biblical Theology, Union Theological Seminary, New York City.

ERICH DINKLER, D., Dr., Professor of New Testament Theology, University of Bonn.

G. R. DRIVER, M.A., Hon. D.D., Hon. D.Litt., F.B.A., M.C., C.B.E., Fellow of Magdalen College and Professor of Semitic Philology, University of Oxford.

Rev. S. IFOR ENOCH, M.A., Professor of Greek and New Testament, United Theological College, Aberystwyth.

MORTON S. ENSLIN, A.B., Th.D., D.D., Craig Professor of Biblical Languages and Literature, St. Lawrence University, Canton, New York.

H. W. FAIRMAN, M.A., Brunner Professor of Egyptology, University of Liverpool.

Rev. WILLIAM R. FARMER, M.A., B.D., Th.D., Associate Professor of New Testament, Perkins School of Theology, Southern Methodist University, Dallas, Texas.

Rev. FLOYD V. FILSON, Th.D., D.D., Dean and Professor of New Testament Literature and History, McCormick Theological Seminary, Chicago, Illinois.

Rev. T. FISH, M.A., Ph.D., Emeritus Professor of Mesopotamian Studies, University of Manchester; Vicar of Rostherne, Cheshire.

WERNER FÖRSTER, D.Theol., Ord. Professor für Neues Testament, University of Münster.

Rev. DAVID NOEL FREEDMAN, A.B., Th.B., Ph.D., James A. Kelso Professor of Hebrew and Old Testament Literature, Pittsburgh Theological Seminary, Pittsburgh, Pennsylvania.

Rev. STANLEY BRICE FROST, B.D., M.Th., Dr. Phil., Professor of Old Testament and Dean of the Faculty of Theology, McGill University, Montreal, Quebec.

Rev. REGINALD H. FULLER, M.A., S.T.D., Professor of New Testament Literature and Language, Seabury-Western Theological Seminary, Evanston, Illinois.

AUTHORS OF ARTICLES

Rev. Percival Gardner-Smith, B.D., Fellow of Jesus College, University of Cambridge.

Rev. Henry S. Gehman, M.A., Ph.D., S.T.D., Litt.D., Emeritus Professor of Old Testament Literature and Chairman of the Department of Biblical Studies, Princeton Theological Seminary, and formerly Lecturer in Semitic Languages, Princeton University, Princeton, New Jersey.

Rev. S. MacLean Gilmour, Ph.D., D.D., Norris Professor of New Testament, Andover Newton Theological School, Newton Centre, Massachusetts.

F. Wilbur Gingrich, A.M., Ph.D., Professor of Greek, Albright College, Reading, Pennsylvania.

Rev. Eugene Van Ness Goetchius, M.A., B.D., M.S., Ph.D., Associate Professor of the New Testament, Episcopal Theological School, Cambridge, Massachusetts.

Hymie Gordon, B.Sc., M.D., M.R.C.P., Senior Lecturer in Medicine, University of Cape Town.

Rev. Norman K. Gottwald, A.B., Th.B., B.D., Ph.D., Lowry Professor of Old Testament, Andover Newton Theological School, Newton Centre, Massachusetts.

Rev. Holt H. Graham, M.A., Th.D., S.T.D., Professor of New Testament, Protestant Episcopal Theological Seminary in Virginia, Alexandria, Virginia.

Rev. Frederick Clifton Grant, Th.D., D.S.Litt., D.C.L., Litt.D., L.H.D., S.T.D., D.D., Emeritus Professor of Biblical Theology, Union Theological Seminary, New York.

Robert M. Grant, Th.D., Professor of New Testament, The Divinity School, University of Chicago.

Rev. John Gray, M.A., B.D., Ph.D., Lecturer in Hebrew and Biblical Criticism, University of Aberdeen.

Heinrich Greeven, D.Theol., Ord. Professor für Neues Testament und Sozialethik, University of Kiel.

Rev. James C. G. Greig, M.A., B.D., S.T.M., Professor of New Testament, Westminster College, Cambridge.

Kendrick Grobel, B.D., D.Theol., Professor of New Testament, Vanderbilt University, Nashville, Tennessee.

Ernst Haenchen, D., Dr., Emeritus Professor in the University of Münster.

Rev. Edward R. Hardy, Ph.D., S.T.D., Professor of Church History, Berkeley Divinity School, New Haven, Connecticut.

Rev. Walter J. Harrelson, B.D., Th.D., Professor of Old Testament, Vanderbilt University, Nashville, Tennessee.

Rev. H. St. J. Hart, B.D., Fellow, Dean, and Hebrew Lecturer, Queens' College, Cambridge.

Rev. Johannes Hempel, D., Dr., Emeritus Professor, University of Göttingen.

Rev. Arthur S. Herbert, M.A., B.D., Professor of Old Testament Literature and Religion, Selly Oak Colleges, Birmingham.

Jean Héring, D.Th., Agregé ès Lettres, Emeritus Professor, University of Strasbourg.

S. H. Hooke, M.A., D.D., F.S.A., Emeritus Professor of Old Testament Studies, University of London.

Rev. Siegfried H. Horn, Ph.D., Professor of Archaeology and History of Antiquity, Andrews University, Berrien Springs, Michigan.

Harold H. Hutson, A.B., B.D., Ph.D., LL.D., President and Professor of Religion, Greensboro College, Greensboro, North Carolina.

Rev. J. Philip Hyatt, M.A., B.D., Ph.D., Professor of Old Testament, Vanderbilt University, Nashville, Tennessee.

Rev. Gerhard Iber, Dr., Studentenpfarrer, Mannheim, Germany.

William A. Irwin, M.A., B.D., Ph.D., L.H.D., Emeritus Professor of Old Testament Literature and Languages, University of Chicago, and Southern Methodist University, Dallas, Texas.

†Rev. Arthur Jeffery, M.A., Ph.D., Professor of Semitic Languages, Columbia University, New York.

Rev. Aubrey R. Johnson, Ph.D., Hon. D.D., F.B.A., Professor of Semitic Languages, University College of South Wales and Monmouthshire, Cardiff.

Rev. Sherman E. Johnson, Ph.D., D.D., S.T.D., Dean of the Church Divinity School of the Pacific, Berkeley, California.

Rev. George Johnston, M.A., B.D., Ph.D., D.D., Professor of New Testament in McGill University and Principal of United Theological College, Montreal, Canada.

Rev. Douglas Rawlinson Jones, M.A., Lecturer in Theology, University of Durham.

Rev. J. N. D. Kelly, M.A., D.D., Hon. D.D., Principal of St. Edmund Hall, University of Oxford.

Rev. J. Spencer Kennard, Jr., Ph.D., D.Théol., Litt.D., Kendall Park, New Jersey.

Kathleen M. Kenyon, C.B.E., D.Lit., F.B.A., F.S.A., Lecturer in Palestinian Archaeology, Institute of Archaeology, University of London, and Director, British School of Archaeology in Jerusalem.

Thomas S. Kepler, A.B., Ph.D., S.T.D., D.D., Professor of New Testament Language and Literature, Graduate School of Theology, Oberlin College, Oberlin, Ohio.

Very Rev. Walter Conrad Klein, Ph.D., Th.D., S.T.D., President and Dean, Nashotah House, Nashotah, Wisconsin.

Rev. John Knox, Ph.D., Baldwin Professor of Sacred Literature, Union Theological Seminary, New York City.

Rev. Emil G. Kraeling, Ph.D., Retired Professor in Union Theological Seminary and Columbia University, New York City.

Rev. Charles Franklin Kraft, B.D., Ph.D., Professor of Old Testament Interpretation and Director of Graduate Studies, Garrett Theological Seminary, Northwestern University Campus, Evanston, Illinois.

Samuel Laeuchli, Th.D., Professor of Patristics, Garrett Theological Seminary, Evanston, Illinois.

Rev. G. W. H. Lampe, D.D., Ely Professor of Divinity, University of Cambridge.

†Very Rev. John Lowe, M.A., D.D., LL.D., Dean of Christ Church, Oxford.

Rev. Canon H. K. Luce, B.D., Durham.

S. Vernon McCasland, A.M., Ph.D., John B. Cary Memorial Professor of Religion, University of Virginia, Charlottesville, Virginia.

Rev. William Duff McHardy, D.Phil., D.D., Regius Professor of Hebrew and Student of Christ Church, University of Oxford.

Rev. A. G. MacLeod, M.A., Professor of Old Testament Studies, Westminster College, Cambridge.

Rev. John Macquarrie, M.A., B.D., Ph.D., Lecturer in Systematic Theology, University of Glasgow.

Rev. John Marsh, M.A., D.Phil., D.D., Principal of Mansfield College, Oxford.

Rev. John Mauchline, M.A., D.D., Professor of Old Testament Language and Literature, University of Glasgow.

Theophile J. Meek, B.A., D.D., Ph.D., F.R.S.C., Emeritus Professor of Near Eastern Studies, University College, University of Toronto.

Rev. Bruce M. Metzger, Ph.D., D.D., L.H.D., Professor of New Testament Language and Literature, Princeton Theological Seminary, Princeton, New Jersey.

Rev. C. Leslie Mitton, B.A., M.Th., Ph.D., Principal and Tutor in New Testament Studies, Handsworth College, Birmingham.

Rev. James Muilenburg, M.A., Ph.D., L.H.D., D.D., S.T.D., Davenport Professor of Hebrew and Cognate Languages, Union Theological Seminary, New York City.

Rev. Christopher R. North, D.Litt, D.D., Emeritus Professor of Hebrew, University College of North Wales, Bangor, North Wales.

Merrill M. Parvis, A.B., B.D., Ph.D., Litt.D., Professor of New Testament, Emory University, Atlanta, Georgia.

Rev. John Paterson, M.A., B.D., Ph.D., D.D., Emeritus Professor of Hebrew and Old Testament Exegesis, Drew University, Madison, New Jersey.

AUTHORS OF ARTICLES

Rev. Otto A. Piper, Th.D., D.D., LL.D., Professor of New Testament Literature and Exegesis, Princeton Theological Seminary, Princeton, New Jersey.

Rev. W. Norman Pittenger, S.T.D., Professor of Apologetics, General Theological Seminary, New York City.

James B. Pritchard, B.D., Ph.D., S.T.D., Professor of Religious Thought and Curator in the University Museum, University of Pennsylvania.

A. C. Purdy, A.B., Ph.D., LL.D., D.D., Visiting Professor of Religion, Earlham College, Richmond, Indiana.

Howard L. Ramsey, B.A.., B.D., Ph.D., Associate Professor of Religion, Lycoming College, Williamsport, Pennsylvania.

Rev. William L. Reed, B.A., B.D., Ph.D., Professor of Old Testament, College of the Bible, Lexington, Kentucky.

Rev. J. Howard W. Rhys, D.Th., Associate Professor of New Testament, University of the South, Sewanee, Tennessee.

Rev. Canon Alan Richardson, M.A., D.D., Professor of Theology, University of Nottingham.

Rev. Cyril C. Richardson, Th.D., D.D., Washburn Professor of Church History, Union Theological Seminary, New York City.

Harald Riesenfeld, T.D., F.M., Professor of Biblical Exegesis, University of Uppsala.

Rev. Corwin C. Roach, Ph.D., S.T.D., Director, Fargo School of Religion, Fargo, North Dakota.

Rev. B. J. Roberts, M.A., D.D., Professor of Hebrew and Biblical Studies, University College of North Wales, Bangor, North Wales.

James M. Robinson, D.Theol., Th.D., Professor of Theology and New Testament, Southern California School of Theology, Claremont, California.

Rev. Elwyn R. Rowlands, M.A., Lecturer in Semitic Languages, University College of South Wales and Monmouthshire, Cardiff.

Rev. Harold H. Rowley, M.A., D.D., B.Litt., Hon. Theol.D., Hon. LL.D., Hon. D.D., F.B.A., Emeritus Professor of Hebrew Language and Literature, University of Manchester.

Rev. E. T. Ryder, M.A., B.D., Lecturer in the Department of Semitic Languages, University College of South Wales and Monmouthshire, Cardiff.

Rev. J. Coert Rylaarsdam, B.A., Ph.D., D.D., Professor of Old Testament Theology, University of Chicago.

Rabbi Samuel Sandmel, Ph.D., Provost and Professor of Bible and Hellenistic Literature, Hebrew Union College-Jewish Institute of Religion, Cincinnati, Ohio.

John H. Scammon, A.B., B.D., S.T.M., Th.D., Professor of Hebrew and Old Testament, Andover Newton Theological School, Newton Centre, Massachusetts.

William R. Schoedel, M.A., Department of Religious Studies, Brown University, Providence, Rhode Island.

Rev. Charles H. H. Scobie, B.D., S.T.M., Ph.D., Minister, Clark Memorial Church of Scotland, Largs, Ayrshire.

William Scott, M.A., B.D., S.T.M., Th.D., Emeritus Professor of Religion, Randolph-Macon Woman's College, Lynchburg, Virginia.

Rev. Oscar J. F. Seitz, Th.D., Bedell Professor of New Testament, Bexley Hall, Kenyon College, Gambier, Ohio.

Rev. Massey H. Shepherd, Jr., Ph.D., S.T.D., D.D., Litt.D., Professor of Liturgics, Church Divinity School of the Pacific, Berkeley, California.

A. N. Sherwin-White, M.A., F.B.A., Fellow of St. John's College, Oxford.

Rev. Henry M. Shires, A.B., B.D., Th.D., Professor of New Testament, Episcopal Theological School, Cambridge, Massachusetts.

Marcel Simon, Docteur ès-Lettres, Professor and Dean of the Faculty of Arts, University of Strasbourg.

Very Rev. C. A. Simpson, M.A., D.D., D.Th., D.C.L., Dean of Christ Church, Oxford; formerly Professor of Old Testament Literature, General Theological Seminary, New York, and Regius Professor of Hebrew, University of Oxford.

Rev. Norman Henry Snaith, M.A., D.D., Litt.D., formerly Principal, Wesley College, Leeds.

Rev. H. F. D. Sparks, D.D., F.B.A., Oriel Professor of the Interpretation of Holy Scripture, University of Oxford, and Fellow of Oriel College.

Rev. W. D. Stacey, M.A., Chaplain of Queen's College, Taunton, Somerset.

Raymond T. Stamm, A.B., B.D., Ph.D., Professor in the Department of New Testament, Lutheran Theological Seminary, Gettysburg, Pennsylvania.

Rev. William F. Stinespring, M.A., Ph.D., Professor of Old Testament and Semitics in the Divinity School, Duke University, Durham, North Carolina.

Rev. G. M. Styler, M.A., S.T.M., Fellow of Corpus Christi College and University Lecturer in Divinity, University of Cambridge.

Sydney Temple, B.A., B.D., Ph.D., University of Massachusetts, Amherst, Massachusetts.

Rev. S. L. Terrien, B.A., B.D., S.T.M., Th.D., Auburn Professor of Old Testament, Union Theological Seminary, New York City.

T. W. Thacker, M.A., Professor of Semitic Philology, Durham.

Rev. Burton H. Throckmorton, Jr., B.D., Ph.D., Hayes Professor of New Testament Language and Literature, Bangor Theological Seminary, Bangor, Maine.

Rev. Nigel Turner, Ph.D., M.Th., B.D.

Rev. W. C. van Unnik, Dr. Theol., D.D. Professor of New Testament, University of Utrecht.

Rev. Luther A. Weigle, Ph.D., D.D., Litt.D., S.T.D., L.H.D., LL.D., J.U.D., Dean and Sterling Professor Emeritus, Yale Divinity School, New Haven, Connecticut.

Rev. Cecil J. Mullo Weir, M.A., D.Phil., D.D., Professor of Hebrew and Semitic Languages, University of Glasgow.

P. Wernberg-Møller, Cand. Theol., D.Phil., Lecturer in Semitic Languages and Literatures, University of Manchester.

Rev. John William Wevers, B.A., B.D., Th.D., Associate Professor of Near Eastern Studies, University College, University of Toronto.

Allen Wikgren, A.B., M.A., Ph.D., Associate Professor of New Testament and Early Christian Literature, University of Chicago.

Amos N. Wilder, Ph.D., L.H.D., D.D., Hollis Professor of Divinity, Harvard Divinity School, Cambridge, Massachusetts.

†Rev. C. S. C. Williams, M.A., Chaplain, Fellow, and Senior Tutor, Merton College, Oxford.

Daniel Day Williams, B.D., Ph.D., Roosevelt Professor of Systematic Theology, Union Theological Seminary, New York City.

Rev. Ronald J. Williams, M.A., B.D., Ph.D., Professor of Near Eastern Studies, University College, University of Toronto.

†Rev. Harold Rideout Willoughby, A.M., Ph.D., D.Litt., D.D., Emeritus Professor of New Testament, University of Chicago.

KEY TO CONTRIBUTORS' INITIALS

P. R. A. =P. R. Ackroyd.
W. F. A. =W. F. Adeney
D. R. Ap-T. =D. R. Ap-Thomas
F. B. =F. Balchin
A. D. B. =A. D. Baly
J. S. B. =J. S. Banks
R. S. B. =R. S. Barbour
R. A. B. =R. A. Barclay
A. B. =A. Barr
J. Ba. =J. Barr
G. A. B. =G. A. Barton
W. A. B. =W. A. Beardslee
J. C. B. =J. C. Beker
W. H. Be. =W. H. Bennett
G. R. B. =G. R. Berry
E. F. F. B. =E. F. F. Bishop
A. W. B. B. =A. W. F. Blunt
J. Bo. =J. Bowman
G. H. B. =G. H. Box
W. F. B. =W. F. Boyd
J. Br. =J. Bright
L. O. B. =L. O. Bristol
L. H. B. =L. H. Brockington
W. H. Br. =W. H. Brownlee
F. F. B. =F. F. Bruce
R. B. =R. Bultmann
A. E. B. =A. E. Burn
M. B. =M. Burrows
E. de W. B. =E. de Witt Burton
G. B. C. =G. B. Caird
R. G. C. =R. G. Cameron
H. C. =H. Chadwick
E. L. C. =E. La B. Cherbonnier
L. C. =L. Clarke
H. Cl. =H. Clavier
J. S. C. =J. S. Clemens
W. F. C. =W. F. Cobb
R. G. C. =R. G. Cochrane
S. S. C. =S. S. Cohon
E. C. C. =E. C. Colwell
H. F. B. C. =H. F. B. Compston
J. A. C. =J. A. Craig
P. E. D. =P. E. Davies
T. W. D. =T. Witton Davies
W. D. D. =W. D. Davies
W. T. D. =W. T. Davison
A. D. =A. Deissmann
E. D. =E. Dinkler
G. R. D. =G. R. Driver
S. R. D. =S. R. Driver
E. A. E. =E. A. Edghill
C. W. E. =C. W. Emmet
S. I. E. =S. I. Enoch
M. S. E. =M. S. Enslin
W. E. =W. Ewing
H. W. F. =H. W. Fairman
R. A. F. =R. A. Falconer
W. R. F. =W. R. Farmer
F. V. F. =F. V. Filson
G. G. F. =G. G. Findlay
T. F. =T. Fish
W. F. =W. Förster
H. T. F. =H. T. Fowler
D. N. F. =D. N. Freedman
S. B. F. =S. B. Frost
R. H. F. =R. H. Fuller
K. F. =K. Fullerton
P. G.-S. =P. Gardner-Smith
A. E. G. =A. E. Garvie
O. H. G. =O. H. Gates
H. S. G. =H. S. Gehman
S. M. G. =S. M. Gilmour
J. Gi. =J. Gilroy
F. W. G. =F. W. Gingrich
E. G. =E. Goetchius
H. Go. =H. Gordon
N. K. G. =N. K. Gottwald
H. H. G. =H. H. Graham
F. C. G. =F. C. Grant
R. M. G. =R. M. Grant
G. B. G. =G. B. Gray
J. Gr. =J. Gray
S. W. G. =S. W. Green
H. G. =H. Greeven
J. C. G. G. =J. C. G. Greig
C. T. P. G. =C. T. P. Grierson
F. Ll. G. =F. Ll. Griffith
K. G. =K. Grobel
H. M. G. =H. M. Gwatkin
G. H. G. =G. H. Gwilliam
E. H. =E. Haenchen
E. R. H. =E. R. Hardy
W. J. Ha. =W. J. Harrelson
H. St. J. H. =H. St. J. Hart
D. A. H. =D. A. Hayes
J. H. =J. Hempel
W. J. He. =W. J. Henderson
A. S. H. =A. S. Herbert
J. He. =J. Héring
G. F. H. =G. F. Hill
A. E. H. =A. E. Hillard
F. R. M. H. =F. R. M. Hitchcock
S. H. He. =S. H. Hooke
S. H. Hn. =S. H. Horn
H. H. H. =H. H. Hutson
J. P. H. =J. P. Hyatt
G. I. =G. Iber
W. A. I. =W. A. Irwin
A. J. =A. Jeffery
C. H. W. J. =C. H. W. Johns
A. R. J. =A. R. Johnson
S. E. J. =S. E. Johnson
G. J. =G. Johnston
D. R. J. =D. R. Jones
D. M. K. =D. M. Kay
J. N. D. K. =J. N. D. Kelly
J. A. K. =J. A. Kelso
J. S. K. =J. S. Kennard
A. R. S. K. =A. R. S. Kennedy
F. G. K. =F. G. Kenyon
K. M. K. =K. M. Kenyon
T. S. K. =T. S. Kepler

KEY TO CONTRIBUTORS' INITIALS

L. W. K. =L. W. King
W. C. K. =W. C. Klein
G. A. F. K. =G. A. F. Knight
J. K. =J. Knox
N. K. =N. Koenig
E. G. K. =E. G. Kraeling
C. F. K. =C. F. Kraft
S. L. =S. Laeuchli
J. C. L. =J. C. Lambert
G. W. H. L. =G. W. H. Lampe
H. C. O. L. =H. C. O. Lanchester
J. L. =J. Lowe
H. K. L. =H. K. Luce
R. A. S. M. =R. A. S. Macalister
S. V. McC. =S. V. McCasland
J. F. McC. =J. F. McCurdy
W. M. McD. =W. M. Macdonald
W. D. McH. =W. D. McMcHardy
G. M. M. =G. M. Mackie
H. R. M. =H. R. Mackintosh
A. J. M. =A. J. Maclean
A. G. McL. =A. G. MacLeod
A. H. McN. =A. H. McNeile
J. Macq. =J. Macquarrie
D. S. M. =D. S. Margoliouth
J. Mar. =J. Marsh
J. T. M. =J. T. Marshall
E. W. G. M. =E. W. G. Masterman
J. H. B. M. =J. H. B. Masterman
S. M. =S. Mathews
J. Ma. =J. Mauchline
J. H. Ma. =J. H. Maude
T. J. M. =T. J. Meek
B. M. M. =B. M. Metzger
C. L. M. =C. L. Mitton
R. W. M. =R. W. Moss
J. H. Mo. =J. H. Moulton
W. J. M. =W. J. Moulton
T. A. M. =T. A. Moxon
J. Mu. =J. Muilenburg
H. S. N. =H. S. Nash
W. M. N. =W. M. Nesbit
Th. N. =Th. Nöldeke
C. R. N. =C. R. North
W. O. E. O. =W. O. E. Oesterley
J. O. =J. Orr
M. M. P. =M. M. Parvis
J. Pn. =J. Paterson
W. P. P. =W. P. Paterson
J. Pk. =J. Patrick
T. G. P. =T. G. Pinches
O. A. P. =O. A. Piper
W. N. P. =W. N. Pittenger
I. M. P. =I. M. Price
J. B. P. =J. B. Pritchard
A. C. P. =A. C. Purdy
H. L. R. =H. L. Ramsey
H. A. R. =H. A. Redpath
W. L. R. =W. L. Reed
J. H. W. R. =J. H. W. Rhys
A. R. =A. Richardson
C. C. Ri. =C. C. Richardson
H. R. =H. Riesenfeld
C. C. Ro. =C. C. Roach
B. J. R. =B. J. Roberts
F. E. R. =F. E. Robinson
G. L. R. =G. L. Robinson
J. M. R. =J. M. Robinson
E. G. R. =E. G. Romanes
E. R. R. =E. R. Rowlands
H. H. R. =H. H. Rowley
E. T. R. =E. T. Ryder
J. C. R. =J. C. Rylaarsdam
S. S. =S. Sandmel
A. H. S. =A. H. Sayce
J. H. Sc. =J. H. Scammon
W. R. S. =W. R. Schoedel
C. H. H. S. =C. H. H. Scobie
C. A. Sc. =C. A. Scott
W. S. =W. Scott
O. J. F. S. =O. J. F. Seitz
M. H. S. =M. H. Shepherd, Jr.
A. N. S.-W. =A. N. Sherwin-White
H. M. S. =H. M. Shires
M. Si. =M. Simon
C. A. Si. =C. A. Simpson
J. G. S. =J. G. Simpson
J. S. =J. Skinner
D. S. =D. Smith
H. P. S. =H. P. Smith
J. M. P. S. =J. M. P. Smith
W. T. S. =W. T. Smith
N. H. S. =N. H. Snaith
A. So. =A. Souter
H. F. D. S. =H. F. D. Sparks
W. D. S. =W. D. Stacey
R. T. S. =R. T. Stamm
J. H. St. =J. H. Stevenson
M. St. =M. Stevenson
A. St. =A. Stewart
W. F. S. =W. F. Stinespring
R. H. S. =R. H. Strachan
A. W. S. =A. W. Streane
G. M. S. =G. M. Styler
J. G. T. =J. G. Tasker
J. T. =J. Taylor
R. B. T. =R. B. Taylor
S. T. =S. Temple, Jr.
S. L. T. =S. L. Terrien
M. S. T. =M. S. Terry
T. W. T. =T. W. Thacker
W. H. G. T. =W. H. G. Thomas
B. H. T. =B. H. Throckmorton
N. T. =N. Turner
W. C. v. U. =W. C. van Unnik
G. W. W. =G. W. Wade
L. A. W. =L. A. Weigle
C. J. M. W. =C. J. Mullo Weir
A. C. W. =A. C. Welch
P. W.-M. =P. Wernberg-Møller
J. W. W. =J. W. Wevers
A. P. W. =A. P. Wikgren
A. N. W. =A. N. Wilder
H. L. W. =H. L. Willett
C. S. C. W. =C. S. C. Williams
D. D. W. =D. D. Williams
R. J. W. =R. J. Williams
J. R. W. =J. R. Willis
H. R. W. =H. R. Willoughby
H. G. W. =H. G. Wood
F. H. W. =F. H. Woods

DICTIONARY OF THE BIBLE

A

AALAR, 1 Es 5^{36} (AV).—See Allar.

AARON.—In examining the Biblical material concerning Aaron, it is important to attempt to distinguish between various strands of tradition, since the picture which may be drawn from different sources is by no means simple, and the Aaron of post-exilic material is a vastly more complex and developed figure than that of pre-exilic sources. The name Aaron is obscure, possibly of Egyptian origin ; the meaning 'oracle-giver' has also been suggested.

1. It is worth noting at the outset that Aaron appears only in Mic 6^{4} in the prophetic books, together with Moses and Miriam as agents of deliverance in the Exodus. Similar references may be seen in Jos 24^{5}, 1 S 12$^{6, 8}$, Ps 77^{20}. Greater elaboration is traceable in Ps 99^{6} (Moses and Aaron as 'among his priests') and further in 105^{26} 106^{16} where prominence is given to the position of Aaron. Other Psalm references are to the 'house of Aaron' (115$^{10, 12}$ 118^{3} 135^{19}) and to 'Aaron's beard' (133^{2}) where the anointing of the high priest is a metaphor of Divine blessing to the whole people.

2. Jg 20^{28} associates the family of Aaron with the sanctuary at Bethel (the Mosaic priesthood of the sanctuary at Dan may be compared; cf also Eleazar's burial in the hill country of Ephraim in Jos 24^{33}), though Jos 21$^{13-19}$ assigns cities in the south to the descendants of Aaron.

3. Deuteronomy refers to Aaron in connexion with the story of the Golden Calf (9$^{13-21}$) as saved from destruction by Moses' prayer. It also preserves two traditions of his death : in 10^{6} at Moserah (cf the itinerary in Nu 33^{30f}), and in 32^{50} at Mount Hor (cf Nu 33^{37} 'on the edge of the land of Edom').

4. The distinction between J and E is not always sufficiently clear for a coherent picture to be drawn. It has been doubted whether Aaron appeared at all in J : certainly his position can have been only subordinate in the narrative. He was sent to meet Moses in the wilderness and together they performed signs before the people (4$^{27-31}$). He is also mentioned as spokesman for Moses in 4$^{13-16}$ (prob. E) though the description of him as Levite is peculiar, since Moses was also of the tribe of Levi. The term seems here to have become a technical one, and the reference may belong to a later time when priestly descent was traced from Aaron. Moses and Aaron demanded release from Pharaoh, and on his refusal the people murmured (ch. 5). In the plague narratives (mainly J), Aaron is a silent figure, merely summoned with Moses four times when Pharaoh entreats for the removal of the plagues (8$^{8, 25}$ 9^{27} 10^{16}). In each case Moses alone answers and in the last three he alone departs. In 10^{3} Moses and Aaron went in to announce the plague, but Moses alone 'turned and went out' (v.^{6}). The occurrence of Aaron's name seems likely in these passages to be due to later redaction, perhaps designed to assimilate the older plague narratives to those of P.

Aaron is brother of Miriam in 15^{20} (? J or E) : in 17 he and Hur held up Moses' hands at Rephidim to ensure Joshua's victory over the Amalekites. In 18^{12} (E) Aaron is included with the elders in the sacrificial meal with Jethro. He alone is permitted to go up into the mountain with Moses (Ex 19^{24}), though in 24$^{1, 9}$ they appear to be accompanied by Nadab and Abihu and seventy elders : here Moses alone actually goes up into the mountain. With Hur he is to act as deputy for Moses during the latter's absence (24^{14}). E has the story of the making of the golden calf during Moses' absence (Ex 32$^{1-24}$: the narrative is now not in a simple form, and has some connexion with the story of 1 K 12$^{26-30}$, for Jeroboam's words appear here in the mouth of Aaron). J appears to have a different tradition of rebellion in Ex 32$^{25-29}$ where Aaron is said to 'have let them break loose, to their shame among their enemies' : the story provides a basis for the consecration of the Levites (cf the parallel for the priesthood of Aaron in Nu 25$^{7-13}$ and other traditions of the Levites in Nu 3$^{44-46}$ 8$^{5-19}$).

In Nu 12, Aaron is involved with Miriam in a protest against Moses' marriage to a Cushite woman, though the real basis of their protest seems to be their claim that they too had received Divine revelation. Punishment fell in the form of leprosy upon Miriam alone, but Aaron intercedes with Moses and after Miriam has been excluded from the camp for seven days, order is restored : the halting of the people on the march for this period seems to indicate that Miriam's sin involves more than herself and Aaron.

5. In P, Aaron stands beside Moses, with Moses occupying much more the position of secular leader, while Aaron is his religious vice-gerent. Aaron plays a considerable part in the narrative of the Exodus—as spokesman to Pharaoh (7^{1}) in whose presence he changed his rod into a serpent (7$^{8-13}$; the word is *tannîn* = dragon, a primeval monster : in 4^{3} (J) *nāḥāsh* = snake is used). In P's narrative of the plagues, Aaron is conspicuous. Aaron as well as Moses suffered from the murmurings of the people (Ex 16^{2}, Nu 14^{2} 16$^{3, 41}$ 20^{2}) : both were consulted by the people (Nu 9^{6} 15^{33}) ; and many of God's commands were addressed to both (Ex 9$^{8-10}$ 12$^{1, 43}$, Lv 11^{1} 13^{1} 14^{33} 15^{1}, Nu 2^{1}). Aaron stayed a plague by offering incense (Nu 16$^{46-48}$) [on the combined narratives in Nu 16, 17 see Aaron's Rod, Korah]. At Meribah-Kadesh he, with Moses, sinned against Yahweh (Nu 20$^{1-13}$), but the nature of his sin is obscure ; he was consequently forbidden to enter Canaan and died on Mount Hor aged 123, Eleazar his son being clothed in priestly garments (Nu 20$^{22-29}$ 33^{38f} ; cf Dt 32^{50}).

The prominence of Aaron in P may in part be

accounted for by the supposition that there were traditions concerning Aaron already in existence—as indicated in JE—with perhaps some elements which allowed of Aaron being viewed as a wonder-worker, now incorporated with later presentation (*e.g.* 7[1-13]). But a very important factor in the shaping of the traditions appears to be the changing situation in the Jerusalem priesthood. The priesthood at Jerusalem was, from the time of Solomon at least, of Zadokite descent (1 K 1[39] 2[27]); this position appears to have lasted until the exile, and Ezekiel envisages a continuance of it in his ideal state (Ezk 43[19] 44[15ff]). When local sanctuaries were abolished at Josiah's reform and the country priests came up to Jerusalem to seek a livelihood (cf Dt 18[6-8]), the Zadokite priests charged them with idolatry and allowed them only an inferior position as servants (2 K 23[9], Ezk 44[9-15]; cf 1 S 2[36]). It is probable that many of these country priests traced their descent to Aaron. With the exile, the Jerusalem priests were presumably carried away (cf 2 K 24[14] 25[11]) or put to death (2 K 25[18-21]). Since it is unlikely that all religious observance ceased during the exile, priests of Aaronite descent may well have replaced the Zadokites. Some scholars think that the religious centre shifted to Mizpah or Bethel. After the exile, the return of a Zadokite priesthood (cf Jeshua ben Jozadak, Ezr 3[2], etc.) must have created a difficult situation. Some compromise was perhaps effected in which the Zadokite priests re-established their superiority and claimed Aaronic descent: others, tracing their ancestry by Ithamar, younger son of Aaron, could be regarded as inferior. Sixteen priestly courses were traced back to Eleazar and eight to Ithamar (1 Ch 24). Priests who could not claim a proper genealogy were evidently excluded (Ezr 2[61-63]).

Reference must be made to other articles for Aaron's consecration, his purely priestly functions and his relation to the Levites (see Priests and Levites, Sacrifice, Tabernacle).

6. In the NT, Elizabeth is of the family of Aaron (Lk 1[5]): Stephen refers to the Golden Calf narrative (Ac 7[40]): Aaron's priestly calling is mentioned (He 5[4]) but shown to be inadequate (7[11]). Cf also Aaron's Rod.

A. H. McN.—**P. R. A.**

AARON'S ROD.—In a very complicated section (Nu 16–18) which deals with the various revolts against authority in the wilderness period, the exclusive right of the tribe of Levi to the duties and privileges of the priesthood is miraculously attested (Nu 17[1-11]). Twelve rods, representing the twelve tribes, each inscribed with the name of the leader of the tribe, Aaron's being upon that of the tribe of Levi, were deposited 'in the tent of meeting before the testimony,' and the man chosen by Yahweh was to be the one whose rod sprouted. Aaron's rod was found the next day to have 'put forth buds, and produced blossoms, and it bore ripe almonds' (v.[8]). The rod was thereafter to be put back 'before the testimony, to be kept as a sign for the rebels' (v.[10]). The story has parallels in that of Joseph of Arimathaea at Glastonbury, and in the sprouting of Hercules' club and Romulus' spear. He 9[4], no doubt following later Jewish tradition, describes the rod as within the Ark, along with the tables of the covenant and the golden urn containing the manna. Aaron's rod also appears prominently in the plague narratives of Ex 7–9, notably in 7[8-12] where it swallows the rods of the Egyptian magicians, and probably also in Nu 20[1-13] in the narrative of the giving of the waters of Meribah from a rock at Kadesh. Later Rabbinical tradition identifies Aaron's rod with Moses' staff, and preserves much legend concerning it and its nature. It appears in Christian writings as the type of the Cross, and is also glorified in Islamic legend.

A. R. S. K.—**P. R. A.**

AB.—See Time.

ABACUC (2 Es 1[40] AV, RV).—A form of the name **Habakkuk** (so RSV).

ABADDON.—A Hebrew word meaning 'destruction.' The RSV transliterates all six occurrences in the Bible. Five are found in the later OT Wisdom literature: as a general term for destruction, Job 31[12]; a parallel to **Sheol** (q.v.), Job 26[6], Pr 15[11] 27[20]; to death, Job 28[22]; and the grave, Ps 88[11]. In the only NT reference, Rev 9[11], the personification is complete: Abaddon is angel of the abyss and king over the destroying locusts. His name in Greek is **Apollyon** (q.v.), destroyer. In the later Jewish literature Abaddon is the lowest place of Gehenna, hell.

C. C. Ro.

ABADIAS (1 Es 8[35] AV, RV).—See Obadiah, **6.**

ABAGTHA (Est 1[10]).—One of the seven chamberlains or eunuchs sent by Ahasuerus (q.v.) to fetch Queen Vashti to his banquet.

ABANA (AV, RSV; RV **Abanah**).—One of the two rivers of Damascus mentioned by Naaman, 2 K 5[12]. It is identified with the mod. *Nahr Baradā*, which rises in the Anti-Lebanon and runs first southward, then westward, towards Damascus. After dividing fan-wise into a number of branches, it skirts the northern wall of the city and flows into the Meadow Lake. The Greeks called it Chrysorrhoas (Strabo, xvi. ii. 16), the 'golden stream.'

ABANAH, 2 K 5[12] (RV).—See Abana.

ABARIM.—Name meaning 'parts beyond' given to the heights E. of Jordan (including Mt Nebo, q.v.) as viewed from the W. side. From there the land beyond Jordan rises as a mountain chain to a height of 3000 feet and more from the Jordan valley. Hence Abarim is joined with 'mountain' (Nu 27[12], Dt 32[49]; cf Nu 33[47]), and in Jer 22[20] is mentioned with Lebanon and Bashan. See also Iye-Abarim. In Ezk 39[11] we should probably read 'Abarim' (AV 'passengers,' RV 'them that pass through,' RSV 'travellers').

ABBA, which occurs only in Mk 14[36], Ro 8[15], Gal 4[6], is an Aramaic word meaning 'father.' In Levantine Aramaic of NT times it could mean 'father,' 'the father,' or 'my father,' and both Chrysostom and Theodoret, who were Syrians by birth, state that children there commonly addressed their father as *Abbā*. Jesus so uses it of God in Mt 14[36], and it is highly probable that in many cases in the Gospels where in the words of Jesus we have *patēr*, *patēr mou*, *ho patēr*, *ho patēr mou*, the underlying Aramaic was simply *Abbā*. It is used of God only very rarely and uncertainly in Jewish Palestinian documents, this usage being an innovation of Jesus to whom God was always 'my Father.' The following *ho patēr* in Mt 14[36] would seem to be an addition by the evangelist, translating the Aramaic, as he does in 5[41] 7[11, 34], and using the Greek article to represent the Aramaic emphatic case. It is also followed by *ho patēr* in the Epistles, Paul apparently having received the saying in that form.

A. J.

ABDA ('servant' *sc* of the Lord).—**1.** Father of Adoniram, master of Solomon's forced levy (1 K 4[6]). **2.** A Levite (Neh 11[17]) who returned with Zerubbabel; called **Obadiah** in 1 Ch 9[16].

ABDEEL.—Father of Shelemiah (Jer 36[26]), one of those ordered by Jehoiakim to arrest Jeremiah and Baruch.

ABDI ('my servant,' or for 'servant of Y″').—**1.** Grandfather of Ethan, 1 Ch 6[44]. **2.** Father of the Levite, Kish, 2 Ch 29[12]. **3.** A Jew who had married a foreign wife, Ezr 10[26]; cf Es 9[27] (AV **Aedias,** RV **Oabdius**).

ABDIAS (2 Es 1[39] AV, RV).—See Obadiah (so RSV) the prophet.

ABDIEL ('servant of God').—Son of Guni, 1 Ch 5[15].

ABDON ('servile').—**1.** The last of the minor judges, Jg 12[13-15]. **2.** A family of Benjamites, 1 Ch 8[23]. **3.** A Gibeonite family, 1 Ch 8[30] 9[36]. **4.** A courtier of Josiah, 2 Ch 34[20]; called **Achbor,** 2 K 22[12, 14], Jer 26[22] 36[12]. **5.** A Levitical city of Asher, Jos 21[30], 1 Ch 6[74], mod. *Khirbet 'Abdeh*, E. of Achzib on the hills.

ABEDNEGO.—Name given by Nebuchadnezzar's chief eunuch to **Azariah,** one of Daniel's companions, Dn 1^{7}, who refused to worship the king's image, Dn 3^{12}. The name is probably a corruption of Abed-nebo, 'servant of Nebo.'

ABEL.—The second son of Adam (Gn 4^{2ff}). The Yahwist does not give a meaning to the name, as he usually does. The word *hebhel* means 'breath,' (tr. 'vanity' in Ec 1^{1}). It is improbable that the name was given to Abel on account of his brief span of life. Neither is the derivation from Akkadian *aplu,* 'son' now accepted. A more probable suggestion connects it with the name Jabal (4^{20}), the ancestor of nomadic shepherds. The name Abel in 2 S 20^{18}, and in several compound names of places is from a different Hebrew root.

The Yahwist's story of Cain and Abel rests upon sources other than those from which he has drawn the narratives of the Creation and the Fall. This is manifest from the fact that the story assumes the existence of other people on the earth ; Cain says, 'whosoever finds me will slay me.' Moreover, the story is made up of two independent strands : one in vv.$^{1-15}$, dealing with the killing of Abel, and the other in vv.$^{16-26}$, dealing with the genealogy and traditions of the Kenite clan, of which Cain is the eponymous ancestor.

The Yahwist has used the tradition to develop the theme of the consequences of the breach between man and God described in the story of the Fall. The first result is the break-up of the family, brother slays brother, and man flees from the presence of God and builds up a godless civilization. But underlying the story in the form in which we have it now are several layers of tradition. The original tradition seems to represent a ritual slaying intended to secure fertility for the crops whose failure is implied by the rejection of Cain's offering. The ritual slaying is followed by the flight of the slayer who is protected by a mark which indicates his sacred character. But in the course of transmission the story had acquired other meanings. It had become an aetiological myth intended to explain the origin of the age-long feud between the nomad and the agriculturalist, although a distortion of the tradition is apparent in the fact that it is the agriculturalist who slays the pastoralist. Then, by a further transformation, the story assumed the form of an aetiological myth intended to explain the origin of the blood-feud. The suggestion that the story was intended to explain Yahweh's preference for animal sacrifices must be rejected, since both kinds of offering are prescribed in the Levitical code. He 11^{4} gives 'faith' as the reason. In He 12^{24} the 'sprinkled blood' 'speaks more graciously than the blood of Abel,' in that the latter cried for vengeance (Gn 4^{10}).

In Mt 23^{35} ∥ Lk 11^{51} Abel is named as the first of the true martyrs whose blood had been shed during the period covered by the OT, the last being Zechariah (see Zechariah, **35**). In Jn 8^{44} it is possible that Jesus was thinking of the story of Abel when He spoke of the devil as 'a murderer from the beginning,' *i.e.* the instigator of murder as he is of lies. A. H. McN.—**S. H. He.**

ABEL.—A word meaning 'meadow' and entering as an element into several place-names. In 1 S 6^{18} a reference in AV to 'Abel' is corrected in RV, RSV to 'great stone.' Elsewhere in place-names Abel is found only in combination with another word.

ABEL-BETH-MAACHAH.—The AV spelling of **Abel beth-Maacah.** See Abel (of) Beth-Maacah.

ABEL (OF) BETH-MAACAH.—Where Sheba took refuge from Joab (2 S 20$^{14-18}$) ; it was captured by Ben-hadad (1 K 15^{20}), and by Tiglath-pileser (2 K 15^{29}) ; corresponding to the modern *Tell Abil,* W. of *Tell el-Qâḍi* (Dan), and N. of Lake Huleh.

ABEL-CHERAMIM, Jg 11^{33} (RV).—See Abel-Keramim.

ABEL-KERAMIM (RSV ; RV **Abel-cheramim** ; 'meadow of the vineyards' (cf AV)).—The limit of Jephthah's pursuit of the Midianites (Jg 11^{33}) ; site uncertain, possibly modern *Na'ûr,* NE. of Nebo.

ABEL-MAIM ('meadow of waters').—An alternative name for **Abel of Beth-maacah** (q.v.), found in 2 Ch 16^{4}, which corresponds to 1 K 15^{20}.

ABEL-MEHOLAH ('meadow of the dance').—A place in the Jordan valley, the limit of Gideon's pursuit of the Midianites (Jg 7^{22}) ; in the administrative district of Taanach and Megiddo under Solomon (1 K 4^{12}) ; native place of Adriel, husband of Merab, Saul's daughter (1 S 18^{19}), and of Elisha (1 K 19^{16}) ; the location is uncertain (Westminster Atlas, *Tell el-Maqlûb* ; Grollenberg's Atlas, possibly *Tell Abû Sifri*).

ABEL-MIZRAIM ('meadow of the Egyptians').—The scene of the mourning for Jacob (Gn 50^{11}) at the threshing-floor of Atad. There is a play on words with *'ābhēl,* 'meadow,' and *'ēbhel,* 'mourning.' The location was beyond Jordan, but is unknown.

ABEL-SHITTIM ('meadow of acacias').—In the plains of Moab (Nu 33^{49}) ; also called Shittim ; the last trans-Jordanic stage where the Israelites encamped (Jos 3^{1}), and the scene of the offence of Baal-peor (Nu 25^{1}). From here Joshua sent the spies (Jos 2^{1}). Prob. mod. *Tell el-Ḥammâm,* S. of *Tell Kefrein.*

ABEZ, Jos 19^{20} (AV).—See Ebez.

ABI.—The name of Hezekiah's mother (2 K 18^{2}), called **Abijah** in 2 Ch 29^{1}.

ABIAH.—1. 1 Ch 6^{28} (AV) ; see Abijah, **2. 2.** 1 Ch 2^{24} (AV) ; see Abijah, **6.**

ABI-ALBON.—See Abiel, **2.**

ABIASAPH ('father has gathered').—Son of Korah (Ex 6^{24}), called **Ebiasaph** in 1 Ch 6$^{23, 37}$ 9^{19}, who gave his name to a division of the Korahite Levites, mentioned only in the genealogies of P and the Chronicler. A section of the division acted as doorkeepers (1 Ch 9^{19} 26^{1} ; in the latter passage read Ebiasaph for Asaph).

ABIATHAR.—Son of Ahimelech and descendant of Eli. In the days of Saul, the family were priests at the shrine of Nob, and in charge of the Ephod. When the sanctuary priests were murdered at Saul's command he fled to David at Keilah, bringing the oracular ephod with him (1 S 22^{20}—23^{14} 30^{7f}). He accompanied David during his days of outlawry and, with Zadok, occupied an important priestly position when David became king of all Israel. (At 2 S 8^{17} the names of father and son have been transposed, cf 1 Ch 18^{16} 24^{6}.) During the revolt of Absalom, Abiathar and Zadok supported David. Whatever element of personal loyalty is indicated by this, it was of great importance since by this action David was assured of the approval of traditional Yahwism. At the end of David's reign, Abiathar supported Adonijah (1 K 1$^{7, 19, 25}$), was degraded by Solomon and relegated to Anathoth (1 K 2^{26}), where apparently he and his descendants continued their priesthood until the days of Jeremiah (Jer 1^{1}) ; but his association with the sacral kingship was broken by Solomon. This appears as the fulfilment of the prophecy against Eli's household in 1 S 2$^{27-36}$. The reference to Abiathar as High-Priest at Mk 2^{26} is due to a mistaken memory of the incidents of David's life ; it is omitted in the Matthaean and Lukan parallels and, apparently by way of correction, in the Western text of Mark. A. S. H.

ABIB (the 'green ear' month, Ex 13^{4} etc.).—See Time.

ABIDA ('father hath knowledge').—A son of Midian (Gn 25^{4} [AV **Abidah**], 1 Ch 1^{33}).

ABIDAN ('father is judge').—Representative of the tribe of Benjamin at the census (Nu 1^{11} 2^{22}), who brought offerings (Nu 7$^{60, 65}$) and led the tribe (Nu 10^{24}).

ABIEL ('father is El').—**1.** Father of Kish and Ner, and grandfather of Saul (1 S 9^{1} 14^{51}). The latter passage should read, 'Kish, the father of Saul, and Ner, the father of Abner, were sons of Abiel.' In 1 Ch 8^{33} 9^{39} the father of Kish is called Ner, prob. in error. **2.** One of David's heroes (1 Ch 11^{32}), from Beth-arabah (q.v.). **Abi-albon** (2 S 23^{31}) is a copyist's error, the eye having fallen on *albon* below ; some LXX MSS have Abiel.

ABIEZER (' father is help ').—**1.** The son of Hammolecheth, sister of Machir, the son of Manasseh (1 Ch 7[18]). His descendants formed one of the smallest clans belonging to the Gileadite branch of the tribe of Manasseh, from which Gideon sprang (Jg 6[11, 15]). According to Jg 6[24] they were settled at Ophrah (q.v.); they were the first to answer the summons of Gideon to fight against the Midianites (Jg 6[34]). In Nu 26[30] the name stands in the abbreviated form **Iezer** (RV, RSV; AV **Jeezer**). **2.** One of David's heroes (2 S 23[27], 1 Ch 27[12]), from Anathoth, who commanded the army in the ninth month.

ABIGAIL (' father is joyful ').—**1.** Wife of Nabal (1 S 25[14]), who dissuaded David from avenging himself on the surly farmer, and after the latter's death married David (1 S 25[39-42]), and accompanied him to Gath and Ziklag (1 S 27[3] 30[5, 18]). At Hebron she bore him a son, called Chileab (2 S 3[3]) or Daniel (1 Ch 3[1]). In 1 S 25[32] the name stands in the Hebrew as **Abigal**. **2.** Step-sister of David, mother of Amasa (1 Ch 2[16f]; in 2 S 17[25] **Abigal** in Hebrew, and so RV, RSV).

ABIGAL.—See ABIGAIL.

ABIHAIL (' father is might ').—The name of a man or a woman. **1.** Father of Zuriel, a Levite of the family of Merari (Nu 3[35]). **2.** Wife of Abishur, of the family of Jerahmeel (1 Ch 2[29]). **3.** Son of Huri, a Gadite of the land of Bashan (1 Ch 5[14]). **4.** Mother of Rehoboam's wife, Mahalath, and daughter of Eliab, David's eldest brother (2 Ch 11[18]). **5.** Father of Esther and uncle of Mordecai (Est 2[15] 9[29]).

ABIHU (' he is father ').—Second son of Aaron (Ex 6[23], Nu 3[2]); he accompanied Moses to the top of Sinai (Ex 24[1, 9]), and was admitted to the priest's office (Ex 28[1]), but was later struck by fire with his brother Nadab for offering strange fire (Lv 10[1, 2], Nu 3[4] 26[61]).

ABIHUD (' father is majesty ').—A Benjamite (1 Ch 8[3]).

ABIJAH.—**1.** Son and successor of Rehoboam, 2 Ch 13[1]; also called **Abijam,** 1 K 14[31]. The accounts of him in the Books of Kings and Chronicles are discrepant. The difference begins with the name of his mother, which 2 Ch gives as **Micaiah,** daughter of Uriel of Gibeah, while 1 K makes her to have been **Maacah,** daughter of Abishalom. As the latter is also the name of Asa's mother (1 K 15[10], 2 Ch 15[16]), there is probably some confusion in the text. Beyond this, the Book of Kings tells us only that he reigned three years, that he walked in the sins of his father, and that he had war with Jeroboam, king of Israel. **2.** Samuel's second son, 1 S 8[2], 1 Ch 6[28] (AV **Abiah**). **3.** A son of Jeroboam I. who died in childhood, 1 K 14. **4.** One of the ' heads of fathers' houses ' of the sons of Eleazar, who gave his name to the eighth of the twenty-four courses of priests, 1 Ch 24[3, 10], 2 Ch 8[14]. To this course Zechariah, the father of John the Baptist, belonged, Lk 1[5]. The name occurs also in the lists of priests who ' went up with Zerubbabel,' Neh 12[4], and of those who set their seal to the covenant in the time of Nehemiah, Neh 10[7]. **5.** A son of Becher, son of Benjamin, 1 Ch 7[8]. **6.** Wife of Hezron, eldest son of Perez, son of Judah, 1 Ch 2[24] (AV **Abiah**; but RSV reads ' Caleb went in to Ephrathah, the wife of Hezron his father '). **7.** Wife of Ahaz, and mother of Hezekiah, 2 Ch 29[1]; named **Abi** in 2 K 18[2]. H. P. S.—**P. W.-M.**

ABIJAM.—See ABIJAH.

ABILENE.—Mentioned in Lk 3[1], and also in several passages in Josephus, as a tetrarchy of Lysanias (q.v.). It was situated in the Anti-Lebanon and, its capital was Abila, a town whose ruins are found to-day on the northern bank of the river Baradā, near a village called *Sûq Wâdī Baradā*. It is one of the most picturesque spots on the railroad to Damascus. The ancient name is to-day preserved in a Latin inscription on a deep rock-cutting high up above the railway. It was a political entity until A.D. 37. E. W. G. M.—**E. G. K.**

ABILITY.—In the Bible ' ability ' is either *material capacity* (Lv 27[8], Ezr 2[69], Ac 11[29]) or *technical skill* (Ex 31[3] 35[25], Dn 1[4], Mt 25[15]). The modern meaning (' mental power ') is not found in the Bible.

ABIMAEL (? ' father is God ').—One of the sons of Joktan (q.v.), or S. Arabians (Gn 10[28], 1 Ch 1[22]). This form of name (with medial *m*) is found in S. Arabian (*Abmi-'athtar*), and in Akkadian *Ili-ma-abi* is found.

ABIMELECH (' the father is king ').—**1.** King of Gerar. According to Gn 20 he took Sarah into his harem quite innocently, but on learning through a vision that she was Abraham's wife restored her to him uninjured and made ample amends. Subsequently he entered into a covenant of friendship with Abraham (21[22ff]). A variant of the same tradition is recorded in Gn 26 as having taken place with Isaac. Apparently the stories were variants of Beersheba traditions. **2.** A son of Gideon by a Shechemite concubine (Jg 8[31]), who made an illstarred attempt at becoming king of Shechem. After his father's death he with the help of a band of outlaws murdered all but one of his half-brothers and was accepted as king by the mixed Canaanite and Israelite populace of the Shechem area. The young brother, Jotham, who had escaped, was able to sow dissension among the subjects who after three years revolted under Gaal son of Ebed. Abimelech by ruthless action was able to defeat the Shechemites and raze their city. Thereupon he attacked Thebez but he was mortally wounded by a woman while assaulting the tower of that city. The account of the fortunes of this precursor of the monarchy is told in Jg 9. **3.** A son of Abiathar the priest according to 1 Ch 18[16]. This should be corrected to Ahimelech; cf. 2 S 8[17]. **4.** In the title of Ps 34; apparently this is intended to refer to Achish, king of Gath; cf 1 S 21[10-15]. J. T.—**J. W. W.**

ABINADAB (' father is generous ').—**1.** The second son of Jesse (1 S 16[8] 17[13], 1 Ch 2[13]). **2.** Son of Saul slain in the battle of Mount Gilboa (1 S 31[2], 1 Ch 10[2]). **3.** Owner of the house whither the Ark was brought by the men of Kiriath-jearim (1 S 7[1]), whence it was later taken by David to Jerusalem (2 S 6[3], 1 Ch 13[7]). **4.** In 1 K 4[11], for ' the son of Abinadab ' (AV) RV, RSV have **Ben-abinadab** (q.v.).

ABINOAM (' father is pleasantness ').—Father of Barak (Jg 4[6, 12] 5[12]).

ABIRAM (' father is the Exalted One ').—**1.** A Reubenite, who conspired with Dathan against Moses (Nu 16[1], Dt 11[6], Ps 106[17]). See KORAH. **2.** The first-born son of Hiel the Bethelite, who died when his father rebuilt Jericho (1 K 16[34]).

ABISEI, 2 Es 1[2] (AV).—See ABISHUA, **1.**

ABISHAG (? ' father has wandered ').—A beautiful young Shunammitess, who attended upon David in old age (1 K 1[2ff, 15]). After David's death, Adonijah desired to marry her, but the request cost him his life (1 K 2[13-25]).

ABISHAI.—Son of Zeruiah, David's step-sister (1 S 26[6], 2 S 2[18], 1 Ch 2[16]). His brothers were Joab and Asahel (2 S 2[18]). He was a hot-tempered, ruthless soldier. Accompanying David into Saul's camp, he would fain have killed the sleeper (1 S 26[8]). He is associated with Joab in the blood-revenge taken on Abner (2 S 2[24] 3[30]). During the campaign against the Ammonites, he shared the command of the army with Joab (2 S 10[10]), while at the time of Absalom's uprising he was in charge of one-third of the army, the other two commanders being Joab and Ittai the Gittite (2 S 18[2]). The text of 2 S 23[18], 1 Ch 11[20] is emended to read " thirty " for " three " (see RSV), and so assumes that Abishai was commander of the famous thirty. He is credited with the slaughter of 300 foes (2 S 23[18]), and David once owed his life to Abishai's interposition (2 S 21[17]). Notwithstanding their relationship and their usefulness, there was a natural antipathy between king David and the two brothers Joab and Abishai (2 S 3[39]). J. T.—**E. R. R.**

ABISHALOM.—See Absalom.

ABISHUA (' father is salvation ' or ' rich ').—**1.** Son of Phinehas and father of Bukki (1 Ch $6^{4f.}$, ^{50f}, Ezr 7^5, 1 Es 8^2 (AV **Abisum,** RV **Abisue**), 2 Es 1^2 (AV **Abisei,** RV **Abissei**). **2.** A Benjamite (1 Ch 8^4; cf Nu 26^{38ff}).

ABISHUR (' father is a wall ').—A Jerahmeelite (1 Ch 2^{28f}).

ABISSEI, 2 Es 1^2 (RV).—See Abishua, **1.**

ABISUE, 1 Es 8^2 (RV).—See Abishua, **1.**

ABISUM, 1 Es 8^2 (AV).—See Abishua, **1.**

ABITAL (' father is dew ').—Wife of David and mother of Shephatiah (2 S 3^4, 1 Ch 3^3).

ABITUB (' father is good ').—A Benjamite (1 Ch 8^{11}).

ABIUD (*i.e.* Abihud).—An ancestor of Jesus, Mt 1^{13}.

ABJECT.—In Ps 35^{15} (AV, RV) ' abject ' occurs as a noun, as in Herbert's *Temple*—' Servants and abjects flout me ' ; RSV has ' cripples.'

ABNER.—Saul's cousin (1 S 9^1 14^{51}) and commander-in-chief (1 S 17^{55} 26^5). He set Ish-bosheth on his father's throne, and fought long and bravely against David's general, Joab (2 S 2). After a severe defeat, he killed Asahel in self-defence (2 S 2^{23}). He behaved arrogantly towards the puppet-king, especially in taking possession of one of Saul's concubines (2 S 3^7). Resenting bitterly the remonstrances of Ish-bosheth, he entered into negotiations with David (2 S 3^{8-12}), and then, on David's behalf, with the elders of Israel (2 S 3^{17}). Dreading the loss of his own position, and thirsting for revenge for Asahel's murder, Joab murdered him at Hebron (2 S 3^{26f}). David gave him a public funeral, dissociated himself from Joab's act (2 S 3^{31-37}), and afterwards charged Solomon to avenge it (1 K 2^5). Abner was destitute of all lofty ideas of morality or religion (2 S $3^{8, 16}$), but was the only capable person on the side of Saul's family. J. T.

ABOMINATION.—Four Hebrew words from three different roots are rendered by ' abomination ' and, occasionally, ' abominable thing.' In almost all cases *tō'ēbhāh* has reference to objects and practices abhorrent to Y″, and opposed to the moral requirements and ritual of His religion (for exceptions cf Gn 43^{32} 46^{34}, ' an abomination to the Egyptians '). Among the objects so described are heathen deities such as Milcom, the ' abomination ' of the Ammonites (2 K 23^{13}) ; images and other paraphernalia of the forbidden cults (Dt 7^{25} 27^{15}, and often in Ezk). Some of the practices that are an ' abomination unto Y″ ' are the worship of heathen deities and of the heavenly bodies (Dt 13^{14} 17^4 and oft), the practice of witchcraft and kindred arts (Dt 18^{12}), gross acts of immorality (Lv $18^{22, 26ff}$), falsification of weights and measures (Pr 11^1), and ' evil devices ' generally (Pr 15^{26}). The word *sheḳeṣ* is a technical term for the flesh of animals ritually taboo (Lv 11^{10ff} ; see Clean and Unclean). Another word, *piggûl*, is a technical term for stale sacrificial flesh, which has not been eaten within the prescribed time (Lv 7^{18} 19^7, Ezk 4^{14} [RSV ' foul flesh '], Is 65^4). The fourth word, *shiḳḳûṣ*, is used particularly of objects connected with idolatry, or as a contemptuous term for heathen deities (Jer 4^1 7^{30}, 1 K $11^{5, 7}$ [Milcom, Chemosh], 2 K 23^{13} (Ashtoreth [Astarte], Chemosh) ^{24}, Is 66^3, Zec 9^7). This last word is frequently rendered ' detestable thing ' in EV. A. R. S. K.—**H. H. R.**

ABOMINATION OF DESOLATION (RSV ' desolating sacrilege ').—The phrase occurs in Mk 13^{14} and in the parallel passage of Mt 24^{15}. In form it is a quotation from the Book of Daniel (9^{27} 11^{31} 12^{11}) where it refers to the heathen altar set up in 168 B.C. by Antiochus Epiphanes on the altar of burnt offering in the Temple at Jerusalem. The Book of Daniel, supposed to be a prophecy of the future, had much influence on the development of apocalyptic ideas among Jews and Christians, and the striking phrase was variously interpreted. Mark's use of it is remarkable for the masculine participle ' standing ' instead of a neuter participle agreeing with the neuter word translated ' abomination,' which strict grammar would require. This would seem to mean that he had in mind a person rather than a thing, and most modern commentators suppose that he was influenced by the belief in Antichrist whose coming was expected by later Judaism (cf 2 Th 2^{3f}). Just as the power of God would be finally revealed in the coming of the Messiah, so the power of evil would be manifested in the appearance of Antichrist, whom the Messiah would destroy. Mark reflects the belief, founded on Daniel, that Antichrist would stand in the Temple at Jerusalem, and that this would be the signal for the final tribulation (Mk 13^{19}).

Whether Mark, or his source, connected this expectation with any particular historical situation is uncertain, but the words ' let him that readeth understand ' suggest that he did, and some commentators believe that we have here a reflection of the excitement aroused by Caligula's abortive attempt to have his statue erected in the Temple in A.D. 40, which Jewish Christians may have thought to mark the beginning of the end.

Matthew, though clearly using Mark, introduces several modifications ; he substitutes a neuter participle for ' standing,' changes ' where it ought not to be ' into ' in the holy place,' and makes express reference to Daniel. This last seems to suggest that he is still interpreting the Abomination of Desolation of Antichrist, and if so the neuter participle is no more than a grammatical correction. Luke departs more widely from Mark and interprets the passage with reference to the fall of Jerusalem in A.D. 70 : ' When you see Jerusalem surrounded by armies, then know that its desolation has come near ' (21^{20}). Luke may be drawing on an independent source, but it is more likely that he is eliminating ideas and phrases that would have been obscure to Gentile readers and giving what he believes to be the sense of the passage. P. G.-S.

ABRAHAM.—*Abram* and *Abraham* are the two forms in which the name of the first patriarch was handed down in Hebrew tradition. The change of name recorded in Gn 17^5 (P) represents an attempt to give a theological explanation of this double tradition of the name, and involves a popular etymology of the latter of the two forms. Actually, *Abram* and *Abraham* seem to be dialectal or orthographic variations of a name of ancient type found in Babylonian (and perhaps also Egyptian) texts of the Patriarchal Age in the forms *Abarama*, *Abamrama*, etc., the West Semitic (and Hebrew) form of which is *Abiram*. Its meaning is ' My (Divine) Father is Exalted.' The history of Abraham (Gn 11^{27}–25^{18}) consists of a number of originally separate traditions which have been brought together into a semblance of biographical continuity. These narratives (with the exception of ch. 14, which is assigned to a special source) are apportioned by critics to the three main documents of Genesis, J, E, and P ; analysis shows that the biographic arrangement is not due solely to the compiler of the Pentateuch, but existed in the separate sources and, no doubt, in the oral tradition behind them. We can recognize, amidst much diversity, the outlines of a fairly solid and consistent tradition, which may be assumed to have taken shape at different centres where the traditions were handed down, such as the sanctuaries of Hebron and Beersheba.

1. *The account of J* opens with the divine call to Abraham, in obedience to which he separates himself from his kindred and migrates to Canaan (12^{1-8}).

In all streams of the tradition Abraham's migration was from Harran in Upper Mesopotamia, but in 11^{28ff} (cf 15^7) we find the further tradition that he had come originally from Ur of the Chaldees in S. Babylonia. Since both Ur and Harran were centres of the moon-cult, a migration from one to the other is not implausible. But the mention of Ur is not textually certain. Many scholars seek Abraham's home farther to the north.

Arrived in Canaan, Abraham builds altars at Shechem, where he received the first promise of the land, and Bethel, where the separation from Lot takes place ;

after which Abraham resumes his southern journey and takes up his abode at Hebron (ch. 13). J thereafter depicts Abraham for the most part either as residing at Hebron, or as leading a semi-nomadic life in the Negeb. It is possible, though not certain, that we have to do with two originally separate strata or cycles of tradition. To the latter belong the episode of Abraham's stay in Egypt, which breaks the connexion in chs. 12f, and the story of Hagar's flight and the prophecy regarding Ishmael in ch. 16. Chs. 18f have their locale in Hebron. Abraham in a theophany receives the promise of a son to be born to Sarah, and also an intimation of the doom impending over the guilty cities of the Plain. The destruction of Sodom and Gomorrah, and the deliverance of Lot, are graphically described in ch. 19, which closes with an account of the shameful origins of Moab and Ammon. Passing over some fragmentary notices in ch. 21, which have been amalgamated with the fuller narrative of E, we come to the last scene of J's record, the mission of Abraham's servant to seek a bride for Isaac, told with such dramatic power in ch. 24. It would seem that the death of Abraham, of which J's account has nowhere been preserved, must have taken place before the servant returned. A note is appended in 25[1ff] as to the descent of various Arabian tribes from Abraham and Keturah.

2. Of *E's narrative* the first traces appear in ch. 15, a composite and difficult chapter, whose kernel probably belongs rather to this document than to J. In its present form it narrates the renewal to Abraham of the two great promises on which his faith rested—the promise of a seed and of the land of Canaan—and the confirmation of the latter by an impressive ceremony in which God entered into a covenant with the patriarch. The main body of Elohistic tradition, however, is found in chs. 20–22. We have here a notice of Abraham's arrival in the Negeb, followed by a sojourn in Gerar, where Sarah's honour is compromised by the deliberate concealment of the fact that she is married (ch. 20)—a variant form of the Yahwistic account of 12[10-20]. The expulsion of Hagar, recorded in 21[9-21] is an equally obvious parallel to J's account of the flight of Hagar in ch. 16, although in E the incident follows, while in J it precedes, the births of both Ishmael and Isaac. The latter part of ch. 21 is occupied with the narrative of Abraham's adventures in the Negeb—especially his covenant with Abimelech of Gerar—which leads up to the consecration of the sanctuary of Beersheba to the worship of Yahweh. Here the narrative has been supplemented by extracts from a Yahwistic recension of the same tradition. To E, finally, we are indebted for the fascinating story of the sacrifice of Isaac in ch. 22, which may be fairly described as the gem of this collection.

3. *In P* the biography of Abraham is mostly reduced to a chronological epitome, based on the narrative of J, and supplying some gaps left by the compiler in the older document. There are just two places where the meagre chronicle expands into elaborately circumstantial description. The first is the account, in ch. 17, of the institution of circumcision as the sign of the covenant between God and Abraham, round which are gathered all the promises which in the earlier documents are connected with various experiences in the patriarch's life. The second incident is the purchase of the cave of Machpelah after the death of Sarah, recorded at great length in ch. 23; this is peculiar to P but, as the fact that the transaction takes place in accordance with the ancient Hittite law shows, it rests, like so much in P, on very old tradition.

4. Such is, in outline, the history of Abraham as transmitted through the major strands of the national tradition. What is the historical value of these traditions? There has been no agreed answer to the question. The tendency has been widespread, while not denying that the traditions might contain some nucleus of fact, to doubt that documents so far removed in time from the events of which they tell could contain much of historical worth. Some have even denied that the Patriarchs ever actually existed. But it is evident to-day that a more positive verdict is required. While archaeological discoveries have cast only indirect light on the patriarchal narratives and have not proved them true in any detail, they have shown that they reflect authentically the situation of the first half of the 2nd millennium B.C. and not that of any later period. We must assume, therefore, that the documents as we read them rest on an unbroken stream of tradition reaching back to the age of Israel's origins. Since in the course of transmission the traditions were subjected to selection, expansion, combination, and refraction, it is impossible to reconstruct from them a biography of Abraham in the modern sense of the word. As is usual in epic material, the figure of the individual patriarch often masks the movements of a sizeable clan. But there is no reason whatever to doubt that Abraham (and Isaac and Jacob) was an individual who actually lived. In the early 2nd millennium Palestine was receiving an influx of North-west-Semitic ('Amorite' or Aramaean) clans, while similar groups were to be found all over Upper Mesopotamia. We may suppose that Abraham, whose stories fit perfectly in this context, was the chief of just such a clan. In one place (14[13]) he is called a 'Hebrew,' which in this context may refer to a class of people (Khapiru, Ḫabiru, 'Apiru) who appear in texts of the day as rootless folk without fixed status, at times wandering adventurers, at times brigands, at times slaves. The religion of Abraham as described in Genesis is likewise of an ancient type. The God of the Patriarchs was the patron Deity of the clan and its unseen head. It is probable that the note of promise of land and posterity, as well as that of a contractual relationship (covenant) between clan-father and Deity, is an authentic feature of this type of religion. If so, the patriarchal religion was, as one scholar (A. Alt) has happily put it, a 'schoolmaster' to Moses. A precise date for Abraham cannot be given. If the Amraphel of ch. 14 could be identified with Hammurabi (*c* 1728–1686 B.C.), Abraham could be placed in the 18th–17th cents. But although this date is probably not far wrong, the identification cannot be carried through.

5. From the religious point of view, the life of Abraham has a surprising inner unity as a record of the progressive trial and strengthening of faith. It is a life of unclouded earthly prosperity, broken by no reverse of fortune; yet it is rooted in fellowship with the unseen. 'He goes through life,' it has been well said, 'listening for the true *tōrā*, which is not shut up in formal precepts, but revealed from time to time to the conscience; and this leaning upon God's word is declared to be in Yahweh's sight a proof of genuine righteousness.' He is the Father of the faithful, and the Friend of God. And that inward attitude of spirit is reflected in a character of singular loftiness and magnanimity, an unworldly and disinterested disposition which reveals no moral struggle, but is nevertheless the fruit of habitual converse with God. The few narratives which present the patriarch in a less admirable light only throw into bolder relief those ideal features of character in virtue of which Abraham stands in the pages of Scripture as one of the noblest types of Hebrew piety. J. S.—**J. Br.**

ABRAHAM'S BOSOM.—To Jews of NT times the place to which souls went to await the final judgment had compartments, mutually visible but decisively separated, where evil souls endured torment, while righteous souls enjoyed comfort. In Lk 16[19ff] Jesus calls the latter 'Abraham's Bosom,' picturing Lazarus there, while Dives calls to him from torment. 'Bosom' as a place of rest was a common figure, *e.g.* the bosom of mother earth; so in Jn 1[18] the Son is 'in the bosom of the Father.' The connexion with paternal tenderness is obvious, and so. since Abraham was the 'father' of the Jews (Lk 3[8]), being 'gathered to the fathers' (Jg 2[10]) was to go to the Patriarchs (4 Mac 13[17]; *Gittin* 57b), and in particular to Abraham's bosom (Buber's *Eka rabbati*, I, 43a; *Pesiqta rabbati* 180b; *Qiddushin* 72b).

The phrase was widely used in Christian literature as a synonym for the intermediate state or for Paradise. A. J.

ABRAM.—See Abraham.

ABRECH (AVm, RVm).—See Abrek.

ABREK (RSVm).—A word of doubtful signification, translated ' Bow the knee ' in EV (Gn 41^{43}). This rests on an improbable Hebrew derivation. An Assyrian etymology has been proposed, viz. *abarakku*, the title of one of the highest officials in the Assyrian empire, but no such borrowings from Assyria are shown in Egypt. It is more probable that it is of Egyptian origin. Two possible Egyptian explanations have been offered: (1) ' Praise! ' but the word is rare and doubtful; (2) *abrak*, apparently meaning ' Attention! ' ' Have a care! ' (Spiegelberg). The latter seems the least improbable. F. Ll. G.

ABRON.—A brook mentioned in Jth 2^{24} (AV, RV **Arbonai**); its identification is unknown.

ABRONAH.—A station in the journeyings in the wilderness (Nu 33^{34f}); poss. *'Ain ed-Defiyeh*, near Ezion-geber.

ABSALOM, ABISHALOM (' (my) father is Shalom,' *i.e.* ' Peace,' a divine name or title associated particularly with Jerusalem, cf ' Solomon ').—Third son of David, by Maacah, dtr of Talmai, king of Geshur (2 S 3^{3}). His history is told in 2 S 13–19. He murdered his half-brother Amnon for the rape of Tamar his sister, fled to his grandfather for three years, returned when Joab engineered the royal assent thereto, but being still excluded from court, set himself with his undoubted address (2 S 14^{25}) and egotism to win support for his bid to supplant David as king (2 S 15$^{1-6}$). Four (not ' forty ') years after his return he set up the standard of rebellion at Hebron, his birthplace and the former capital. The rest of Judah, too, seems to have supported him, possibly being aggrieved at David's ' pan-Israel ' politics. As an assertion of his claim to the throne Absalom appropriates the members of the royal harem left in Jerusalem by the fleeing David; but having lost his precious military initiative owing to the insidious advice of Hushai, Absalom's army is beaten in the field by David's veteran troops at Mahanaim. Against the king's express injunction, Joab personally kills Absalom, who has become entangled in a tree. There may be some mythological traits mixed up with his history, *e.g.* his burial and pillar (2 S 18^{17f}), his excessive growth of hair (about 5 lb. per annum, 14^{26})—though hair cutting, especially of royalty, is subject to many taboos in all primitive societies. More credence is usually given to 18^{18}, which makes him sonless, than to 14^{27} which gives him four children. Rehoboam's favourite wife was a (grand-) daughter of Absalom (2 Ch 11^{20f}). The ' house of Absalom ' in DSH i, 13 can have no more than an allegorical reference to the above. J. T.—**D. R. Ap-T.**

ABSALOM (in Apocr).—**1.** The father of Mattathias, one of the captains who stood by Jonathan at Hazor (1 Mac 11^{70}=Jos *Ant.* xiii. v. 7 [161]). It is perhaps the same Absalom whose son Jonathan was sent by Simon to secure Joppa (1 Mac 13^{11}=Jos *Ant.* xiii. vi. 4 [202]). **2.** An envoy sent by the Jews to Lysias (2 Mac 11^{17}).

ABUBUS.—Father of Ptolemy, the murderer of Simon the Maccabee (1 Mac 16$^{11, 15}$).

ABYSS.—A Greek adjective meaning ' very deep ' or ' bottomless ' is used in the LXX, mainly as a translation of the Hebrew *t^{e}hôm* (Gn 1^{2}, etc.), and signifying therefore the primeval deep upon which the earth rests. It was then applied to the subterranean abode of the dead and came to have the meaning of dwelling place for the evil spirits or their fiery prison house. This latter view is present already in Enoch. The word is found nine times in the NT, the RV transliterating all nine, the RSV reverting to the AV ' bottomless pit ' in all Rev. passages. Ro 10^{7} uses it for the place of the dead; Lk 8^{31} and Rev 9$^{1, 2, 11}$ 11^{7} 17^{8} 20$^{1, 3}$, refer to the abode of the demons, questionably as a place of punishment. C. C. Ro.

ACACIA.—See Shittah Tree.

ACATAN, 1 Es 8^{38} (AV).—See Hakkatan.

ACCABA, 1 Es 5^{30} (RV).—See Hagab.

ACCAD.—See Akkad.

ACCEPTANCE denotes the being in favour with anyone. In EV the noun is found only in Is 60^{7}, but ' accept ' and ' acceptable ' are used frequently both in OT and NT to express the acceptance of one man with another (Gn 32^{20}, Lk 4^{24}), but above all the acceptance of man with God. In OT the conditions of acceptance with God are sometimes ceremonial (Ex 28^{38}, Ps 20^{3}). But of themselves these are insufficient (Gn 4$^{5, 7}$, Am 5^{22}, Jer 6^{20} 14$^{10, 12}$), and only moral uprightness (Pr 21^{3}, Job 42^{8f}) and the sacrifices of a sincere heart (Ps 19^{14} 119^{108}; cf 40^{6ff} 51^{15ff}) are recognized as truly acceptable with God. In NT the grounds of the Divine acceptance are never ceremonial, but always spiritual (Ro 12^{1}, Ph 4^{18}, 1 P 2^{5}). Jesus Christ is the type of perfect acceptance (Mk 1^{11} ||, He 10^{5ff}). In Him as ' the Beloved,' and through Him as the Mediator, men secure their religious standing and fundamental acceptance with God (Eph 1^{6}). In serving Him (Ro 14^{18}), and following His example (1 P 2$^{20, 21}$), they become morally acceptable in the Father's sight. J. C. L.

ACCESS (Gr. *prosagōgē*).—The word occurs only in Zec 3^{7}, Ro 5^{2}, Eph 2^{18} 3^{12}, and the question (regarding which commentators are much divided) is whether it ought to be understood in the transitive sense as ' introduction,' the being brought near by another, or in the intransitive sense as ' access ' or personal approach. The transitive sense is most in keeping with the ordinary use of the verb *prosagō* in classical Gr. (cf its use in 1 P 3^{18} ' that he might bring us to God ')—the idea suggested being that of a formal introduction into a royal presence. ' Access,' moreover, does not so well express the fact that we cannot approach God in our own right, but need Christ to introduce us; cf ' by [RV, RSV ' through '] whom ' (Ro 5^{2}), ' through him ' (Eph 2^{18}), ' in whom ' (3^{12}). The word ' access ' does not occur in Hebrews, but the writer has much to say on the subject of our approach to God through Christ, especially for the purpose of prayer (4^{14ff}) and worship (10^{19ff}). J. C. L.

ACCHO, Jg 1^{31} (AV).—See Acco.

ACCO.—Jg 1^{31} (AV **Accho**). See Ptolemais.

ACCOS.—Grandfather of one of the envoys sent to Rome by Judas Maccabaeus in 161 b.c. (1 Mac 8^{17}). Accos represents the Hebrew **Hakkoz** (q.v.), the name of a priestly family (1 Ch 24^{10}, Ezr 2^{61}).

ACCOZ, 1 Es 5^{38} (AV).—See Hakkoz, **1.**

ACCURSED.—See Ban.

ACELDAMA, Ac 1^{19} (AV).—See Akeldama.

ACHAIA.—This name was originally applied to a strip of land on the N. coast of the Peloponnese. On annexing Greece and Macedonia as a province in 146 b.c., the Romans applied the name Achaia to the whole of that country. In 27 b.c. two provinces were formed, Macedonia and Achaia; and the latter included Thessaly, Aetolia, Acarnania, and some part of Epirus, with Euboea and most of the Cyclades. A Senatorial province since Caligula, it was governed by a proconsul of the second grade, with headquarters at Corinth (Ac 18^{12}). ' Hellas ' (Ac 20^{2}) is the native Greek name corresponding to the Roman ' Achaia.' There were Jewish settlements in this province, at Corinth, Athens, etc. (Ac 17^{17} 18$^{4, 7}$), and the work of St. Paul began amongst them and was carried on by Apollos (1 and 2 Co *passim*, Ac 17$^{16ff.}$ 18. 19^{1}). A. So.

ACHAICUS.—The name of a member of the Church at Corinth. He was with Stephanas and Fortunatus (1 Co 16^{17f}) when they visited St. Paul at Ephesus and ' refreshed his spirit.' Nothing more is certainly known of him. As slaves were often named from the country of their birth, it is a probable conjecture that he was a slave, born in Achaia. J. G. T.

ACHAN.—Son of Carmi, of the tribe of Judah (Jos 7[1]). After the defeat at Ai, Joshua resorted to the sacred lot to find out who had transgressed by retaining some of the spoil of Jericho, which had been placed under the ban (q.v.), and Achan was singled out (Jos 7[16ff]). He confessed his guilt, and according to the usage of the times, he and his family were stoned, and their dead bodies burned—the latter an even more terrible punishment in the eyes of ancient Israel. The sentence was carried out in the valley of **Achor** (Jos 7[24]), whose name (' trouble ') is connected with the ' trouble ' Achan had brought on Israel and on himself (Jos 7[25f]). In 1 Ch 2[7] his name is given as **Achar,** as also in LXX^B in Jos 7. Koehler thinks this was the original form of the name.
W. O. E. O.—**H. H. R.**

ACHAR.—See Achan.

ACHBOR (' mouse ' or ' jerboa ').—**1.** An Edomite (Gn 36[38]). **2.** A courtier under Josiah, son of Micaiah (2 K 22[12, 14]), and father of Elnathan (Jer 26[22]; omitted in LXX, 36[12]). Called **Abdon** (q.v.) in 2 Ch 34[20].

ACHIACHARUS, To 1[21] (AV, RV).—Form of the name **Ahikar** (q.v.), which stands in RSV.

ACHIAS, 2 Es 1[2] (AV, RV).—An ancestor of Ezra, omitted in Ezr and 1 Es ; RSV **Ahijah** (q.v.).

ACHIM (perhaps a shortened form of **Jehoiachim**), an ancestor of our Lord (Mt 1[14]).

ACHIOR (' brother of light ').—A general of the Ammonites (Jth 5[5], etc.), afterwards converted to Judaism (14[10]).

ACHIPHA, 1 Es 5[31] (RV).—See Hakupha.

ACHISH.—The king of Gath to whom David fled for refuge after the massacre of the priests at Nob (1 S 21[10]). In 1 S 27[2] he is called ' the son of Maoch ' (possibly = ' son of Maacah,' 1 K 2[39]). He received David with his band of 600 men, and assigned him the city of Ziklag in the S. of Judah. Despite the wishes of Achish, the other Phil. princes refused to let David take part in the final campaign against Saul. [' Achish ' should be read for ' Abimelech ' in Ps 34 (title).]

ACHITOB, 1 Es 8[2], 2 Es 1[1] (AV).—See Ahitub, **3.**

ACHMETHA, Ezr 6[2] (AV, RV).—See Ecbatana.

ACHOR (' grief ').—In this valley **Achan** (q.v.), with his family, was stoned to death. It lay on the boundary between Judah and Benjamin (Jos 15[7]), but its exact location is unknown. The *Wâdī Qelt*, a tremendous gorge which breaks down from the mountain W. of Jericho, has been suggested. In prophetic visions of the future it was to become a ' door of hope ' (Jos 2[15]) and a place of pasture (Is 65[10]).

ACHSA, 1 Ch 2[49] (AV).—See Achsah.

ACHSAH (' anklet ').—The daughter of Caleb, Jos 15[16], Jg 1[12], 1 Ch 2[40] (AV **Achsa**). Her father promised her in marriage to the man who should capture Debir or Kiriath-sepher—a feat accomplished by Othniel, the brother of Caleb. Her dowry was increased by the grant of ' the upper springs and the lower springs ' (Jos 15[16-19], Jg 1[11-15]).

ACHSHAPH.—A city of Asher (Jos 19[25]), whose king joined Jabin's confederacy, which was defeated by Joshua, the ruler of Achshaph being amongst the slain (Jos 11[1] 12[20]); or possibly these were two separate cities. The location is unknown ; suggested identifications include *El-Kesâf, c* 17 miles E. of Tyre, *Tell Kīsân*, SE. of Acre, and *et-Tell* on the *Nahr Mefshuḥ*.

ACHZIB.—**1.** A town in Asher (Jos 19[29]), from which the natives could not be dislodged (Jg 1[31]) ; it lay on the coast between Acre and Tyre, modern **Ez-Zib.** In NT times it was called *Ekdippa*. **2.** A town in the S. of the Shephelah (Jos 15[44]), near Mareshah. Mic 1[14] predicts that Achzib shall become ' a deceitful thing ' (*'akhzābh*), *i.e.* failing those who trust it. Possibly modern *Tell el-Beiḍâ*.

ACIPHA, 1 Es 5[31] (AV).—See Hakupha.

ACITHO, Jth 8[1] (AV).—See Ahitub, **4.**

ACRA.—See Citadel.

ACRABA (Jth 7[18]).—Apparently the town of *'Akrabeh*, E. of Shechem, the capital of Akrabattene (AV, RV **Ekrebel**).

ACRE.—See Weights and Measures.

ACROSTIC.—An acrostic poem is one so arranged that the initial letters of a sequence of literary units (single lines, two lines, three lines, etc., as the case may be) follow a definite arrangement or spell out a significant word or words. There are fourteen such poems in the OT: Nah 1 ; Pss 9–10, 25, 34, 37, 111, 112, 119, 145 ; Pr 31[10-31] ; La 1, 2, 3, 4 ; another instance is Sir 51[13-30]. All these are of a similar type, and are so planned that the initials recurring at fixed intervals follow the order of the Hebrew alphabet ; thus the first unit of the poem begins with the first letter of the Hebrew alphabet, the second unit with the second letter, and so on down to the last letter. Pss 111, 112 represent the one-line unit ; in Pss 25, 34, 145, Pr 31[10-31], Sir 51[13-30], and in the fragment, which does not clearly extend beyond the thirteenth letter, contained in Nah 1, the unit is two lines ; in La 4 it is two longer lines, in chs. 1 and 2 it is three longer lines ; in Pss 9 and 10 (a single continuous poem) and in Ps 37, it is four lines. In La 3, where the unit is three lines, each line of each three-line unit begins with the appropriate letter ; in Ps 119, where the unit is sixteen lines, each alternate line within the unit begins with the appropriate letter.

Certainly in La 2, 3, 4 and, according to the order of the verses in LXX, in Pr 31, probably also in Ps 34 (where the sense seems to require the transposition of vv. [15] and [16]) and in Ps 9, the sixteenth and seventeenth letters of the Hebrew alphabet occupy respectively the seventeenth and sixteenth places in the acrostic scheme. The reason for this is unknown.

Comparatively few of these poems have come down to us intact. They have suffered from accidental errors of textual transmission, and probably also from editorial alterations. In some cases an entire strophe has dropped out of the text ; thus the sixth strophe (of two lines) has fallen out between v. [6] and v. [7] in Ps. 34, and the fourteenth between v. [13] and v. [14] in Ps. 145, although in the latter case is still stood in the Hebrew MS from which the Greek version was made. Occasionally lines have been inserted, as, apparently, in more than one place in Ps 37 and in Nah 1[2]. But such corruption of the text is really serious only in Pss 9–10, Nah 1, and Sir 51[13-30].

The earliest of these fifteen poems are probably La 2 and 4, which may have been written in the earlier half of the 6th cent. B.C. ; but the custom of writing such poems may have been much more ancient. Perhaps the latest of the poems is Sir 51[13-30] (*c* 180 B.C.), but the Jews continued to compose such poems long after that.

The English reader will find the strophes clearly distinguished and the initial letters with their names in English letters indicated, in the RV of Ps 119. Unfortunately the RV does not give the initials in the other poems ; but they will be found, in the case of the Psalms, in (for example) Kirkpatrick's *Psalms* and other commentaries ; for Lamentations, in Gottwald's *Studies in the Book of Lamentations* ; for Nahum, in Stonehouse's *Nahum* or Driver's *Nahum*. Common though it is in other literatures and with such mediaeval Jewish poets as Ibn Ezra, no decisive instance of the type of acrostic in which the initial letters compose a name has been found in the OT, though some have detected the name Simeon thus given in Ps 110. Pss 25 and 34 contain each an additional strophe at the close of the alphabetic strophes ; in each case the first word of the verse is a part of the Hebrew verb *pādhāh*, ' to redeem,' and it has been suggested that the author or a copyist has thus left us a clue to his name—*Pedahel* ; but interesting as this suggestion is, it remains doubtful. G. B. G.—**J. Ma.**

ACTS OF THE APOSTLES.—See LUKE, GOSPEL ACCORDING TO.

ACUA, 1 Es 5[30] (AV).—See AKKUB, **3.**

ACUB, 1 Es 5[31] (AV, RV).—See BAKBUK.

ACUD, 1 Es 5[30] (RV).—See AKKUB, **3.**

ADADAH.—A city of Judah in the Negeb (Jos 15[22]), perhaps a corrupt reading for **Ararah,** to be identified with Aroer, **2** (q.v.).

ADAH.—**1.** One of the two wives of Lamech, and mother of Jabal and Jubal (Gn 4[19f]). The name possibly means 'brightness' (cf Arab. *ghadāt*), Lamech's other wife being named Zillah ('shadow'). **2.** Daughter of Elon, a Hittite, and one of the wives of Esau (Gn 36[2]). In Gn 26[34] Elon's daughter is named **Basemath** (q.v.).

ADAIAH ('Y″ has adorned').—**1.** The maternal grandfather of Josiah, 2 K 22[1]. **2.** A Levite, 1 Ch 6[41], called **Iddo** (q.v.) in v.[21]. **3.** A son of Shimei (in v.[13] Shema) the Benjamite, 1 Ch 8[21]. **4.** The son of Jeroham, a priest, and head of a family in Jerusalem, 1 Ch 9[12]. **5.** The father of Maaseiah, a captain who helped to overthrow the usurpation of Athaliah, 2 Ch 23[1]. **6.** One of the family of Bani, who took a foreign wife during the Exile, Ezr 10[29], 1 Es 9[30] (AV, RV **Jedeus**). **7.** Another of a different family of Bani, who had committed the same offence, Ezr 10[39]. **8.** A descendant of Judah by Perez, Neh 11[5]. **9.** A Levite of the family of Aaron, Neh 11[12]; probably the same as No. **4.**

ADALIA.—The fifth of the sons of Haman (Est 9[8]), put to death by the Jews.

ADAM.—The derivation of this word is doubtful. Some derive it from a root signifying 'red' (cf *Edom*, Gn 25[30]). The Biblical writer (Gn 2[7]) explains it by a play on the word *'ᵃdhāmāh*, 'ground'; but that is itself derived from the same root 'red.' The word itself occurs in the Hebrew thirty-one times in Gn 1[5]–5[5]. In most of these it is not a proper name, and the RSV and RV have rightly substituted 'man' or 'the man' in some verses where AV has 'Adam.' Since the name signifies 'mankind,' *homo*, *Mensch*, not 'a man,' *vir*, *Mann* (see 5[2]), the narrative appears to be a description, not of particular historical events in the life of an individual, but of the beginnings of human life (ch. 2), human sin (ch. 3), human genealogical descent (4[1, 25] 5[1-5]). In a few passages, the writer slips into the use of Adam as a proper name, but only in 5[3-5] does it stand unmistakably for an individual.

For the Babylonian affinities with the story of Adam, see CREATION, EDEN. A. H. McN.—**J. W. W.**

ADAM (city).—A city in the Jordan valley, 'beside Zarethan' (Jos 3[16]), where the waters were held back for the crossing of the river; modern *Tell ed-Dâmiyeh*. A cryptic reference stands in Hos 6[7] (RSV 'at Adam'; AV 'like men,' RV 'like Adam'). In 1 K 7[46] some read 'at the ford of Adamah' for EV 'in the clay ground,' and it may be that Hiram had his furnace here (note that it was near Zarethan, though 2 Ch 4[17] has Zeredah).

ADAM IN THE NT.—A. In the Gospels.—**1.** In Mt 19[4-6] || Mk10[6-8] Jesus refers to Gn 1[27] (5[2]) and 2[24] to support the view that the provision made for divorce in the Mosaic law (Dt 24[1]) was only a concession to men's perversity ('hardness of heart'). The truer and deeper view of marriage is to be based upon the primaeval nature of man and woman, as shown in the Creation story (see also Eph 5[28-31]).

2. In Lk 3[38] the ancestry of Jesus is traced back to Adam. As a Gentile writing for Gentiles, Luke took occasion to emphasize the universalism of the gospel. Jesus is not, as in Matthew's genealogy, a descendant of Abraham only (Mt 1[2]), but of Adam, the ancestor of all mankind. Moreover, not only is Jesus 'the Son of God' in a very special sense (Lk 1[35]), but, by the closing words of the genealogy, Luke claims that the first man, and hence every human being, is a 'son of God.' As Jesus is both human and divine, so all mankind partake of this twofold nature.

B. In the Epistles.—The truth taught by Luke is treated in its redemptive aspect by Paul.

1. 1 Co 15[22]. The solidarity of mankind in their physical descent from Adam and their spiritual union with Christ involves respectively universal death and eternal life as a consequence of Adam's sin (Gn 3) and of Christ's redemptive work.

2. In Ro 5[12-21] this theme is treated more fully.—(*a*) vv.[12-14]. *There is a parallelism between Adam and Christ.* Both had a universal effect upon mankind. Adam transmitted sin and therefore death; even those who lived before Moses received the Law sinned and were subject to death, though their sin cannot be held against them, since they were without the guidance of the Law. The Apostle, without attempting fully to reconcile them, places side by side the hereditary transmission of guilt ('original sin') and moral responsibility: 'and so death spread to all men *because all men sinned.*' —(*b*) vv.[15-17]. *The contrast is far greater than the similarity*; in quality (v.[15]), in quantity (v.[16]), in character and consequences (v. [17]).—(*c*) vv.[18-21]. *Summary.* Men are now to be evaluated not in the light of Adam but in the light of Christ. The Law (Torah, probably meaning here the entire OT revelation) made sin worse because it showed a better way; but the grace of God in Christ became all the more abundant in its saving power. (See K. Barth, *Christ and Adam*, for further implications.)

3. 1 Co 15[35-50]. In the foregoing passages Paul deals with the practical moral results of union with Adam and Christ respectively. This passage (*a*) goes deeper, showing that there is a radical difference between their two natures; and (*b*) it looks forward to show that this difference has a vital bearing on the question of man's resurrection.

(*a*) vv.[35-41]. It is shown, by illustrations from nature, that it is reasonable to believe man to exist in two different states, one far higher than the other.

(*b*) vv.[42-50]. Paul utilizes Gn 2[7], 'man became a living soul' (Hebrew *nephesh*, Greek *psychē*; RSV 'being'), deriving the doctrine that the body of the first man (Adam) was 'psychical' (so the Greek; AV 'natural,' RSV 'physical'), and thus equating the words ordinarily translated 'soul' in English with the carnal and the transitory. Since 'the last Adam became a life-giving spirit' (v.[45]), 'soul' and 'spirit' are set in contrast, contrary to popular understanding in our day, but in accord with Greek usage in NT times.

As the living soul or being (*psychē*) preceded the life-giving spirit (*pneuma*), so it is with the development of mankind (v.[46]). The first man had a nature in conformity with his origin from clay, while the Second has His origin 'from heaven' (v.[47]); thus the nature of some men remains earthy, while that of others has become heavenly (v.[48]). Moreover, in his present state man is the exact counterpart of the first man because of his corporate union with him; but the time is coming when we shall become the exact counterpart of the Second Man (cf Gn 1[26f]), because of our spiritual union with Him (v.[49]).

4. In Ph 2[5-6] there is an implied contrast between 'Christ Jesus, who . . . did not count equality with God a thing to be grasped,' and Adam, who took fruit from the tree of knowledge of good and evil, an act which God said had made him 'like one of us' (Gn 3[22]).

5. On 1 Ti 2[13f] see EVE; and on Jd [14] see ENOCH.

A. H. McN.—**W. F. S.**

ADAMAH.—**1.** A fortified city of Naphtali, Jos 19[36]; its situation is unknown, and the identification with *ed-Dâmiyeh*, 5 miles SW. of Tiberias (see ADAMI-NEKEB) is thought improbable. **2.** See ADAM.

ADAMANT.—In Ezk 3[9], Zec 7[12] EV use the word to render *shāmîr*, which is elsewhere rendered either 'brier' (Is 5[6] 7[23ff] and elsewhere) or 'diamond' (Jer 17[1]). 'Diamond,' which arose from 'adamant' by a variety of spelling ('adamant' or 'adimant,' then 'diamant' or 'diamond') has displaced 'adamant' as the name of the precious stone, ' adamant ' being now used rhetorically to express extreme hardness. LXX has ' adamant ' for ' plumbline ' in Am 7^{7f}, where Hebrew word is different; but few follow. See also JEWELS AND PRECIOUS STONES (*sub* **Diamond**).

ADAMI-NEKEB.—A place on the border of Naphtali, mentioned in Jos 19^{36} (AV Adami, Nekeb, taking as two places; so *Westminister Atlas*); modern *Khirbet ed-Dâmiyeh,* 5 miles SW. of Tiberias. See ADAMAH, **1.**

ADAR, Jos 15^{3} (AV).—See ADDAR.

ADAR.—See TIME.

ADASA.—A town near Bethhoron (1 Mac $7^{40, 45}$, Jos. *Ant.* XII. x. 5 [408]), now the ruin *'Adaseh* near Gibeon. See Map 10.

ADBEEL (? ' God disciplines ').—Third son of Ishmael (Gn 25^{13}, 1 Ch 1^{29}), eponym of the North Arabian tribe, which appears in cuneiform inscriptions as *Idibi'lu*, and which had its settlements SW. of the Dead Sea.

ADDAN.—A place in Babylonia from which some returned with Zerubbabel, who were unable to prove their Israelite descent by showing to what clan or family they belonged (Ezr 2^{59}; also 1 Es 5^{36} RSV, where AV has Charaathalar and RV Charaathalan, q.v.). The name does not appear in the later lists in Ezr 10, Neh 10. In Neh 7^{61} it appears as **Addon.**

ADDAR.—**1.** A town on the border of Judah south of Beersheba, Jos 15^{3} (AV **Adar**); Hezron and Addar, which appear to be distinct here, probably together constitute **Hazar-addar** (q.v.) in Nu 34^{4}. **2.** See ARD.

ADDER.—See SERPENT.

ADDI.—An ancestor of Jesus, Lk 3^{28}.

ADDO, 1 Es 6^{1} (AV, RV).—See IDDO, **7.**

ADDON, Neh 7^{61}.—See ADDAN.

ADDUS.—**1.** One whose sons returned with Zerubbabel, 1 Es 5^{34}; omitted in the parallel lists in Ezr 2, Neh 7. **2.** 1 Es 5^{38} (AV); see JADDUS.

ADER, 1 Ch 8^{15} (AV).—See EDER, **4.**

ADIDA.—A city in the Shephelah (Jos. *Ant.* XIII. vi. 5 [203]) fortified by Simon the Hasmonaean (1 Mac 12^{38} 13^{13}); probably identical with **Hadid** (q.v.).

ADIEL (' El is an ornament ').—**1.** A Simeonite prince, 1 Ch 4^{36}. **2.** A priest, 1 Ch 9^{12}. **3.** The father of Azmaveth, David's treasurer, 1 Ch 27^{25}.

ADIN.—One whose descendants returned with Zerubbabel to the number of 454 (Ezr 2^{15}, 1 Es 5^{14} ([RV **Adinu**]) or 655 (Neh 7^{20}). A second party of 51 (Ezr 8^{6}), or 250 (1 Es 8^{32}) accompanied Ezra. They are mentioned among ' the chiefs of the people ' who sealed the covenant (Neh 10^{16}).

ADINA.—A Reubenite chief, 1 Ch 11^{42}.

ADINO, 2 S 23^{8} (AV, RV).—The Hebrew text of this verse is corrupt, the true reading being preserved in the parallel passage 1 Ch 11^{11}, which is restored here in RSV.

ADINU, 1 Es 5^{14} (RV).—See ADIN.

ADINUS, 1 Es 9^{48} (AV).—See JAMIN, **3.**

ADITHAIM.—A city of Judah in the Shephelah, Jos 15^{36}; location uncertain.

ADLAI (? ' Y″ is just ').—The father of Shaphat, one of David's herdsmen, 1 Ch 27^{29}.

ADMAH.—A city near Sodom (Gn 10^{19} $14^{2, 8}$), whose overthrow is not recorded in the account of the destruction of Sodom and Gomorrah (Gn 19), but is linked with them in Dt 29^{23}, Hos 11^{8}.

ADMATHA.—One of the seven counsellors of Ahasuerus (Est 1^{14}), who were granted admittance to the king's presence (cf 2 K 25^{19}).

ADMIRATION.—This word in AV means no more than *wonder*, as Rev 17^{6} ' I wondered with great admiration ' (RV ' with a great wonder,' RSV ' I marvelled greatly ').

ADNA (' pleasure ').—**1.** A contemporary of Ezra, who married a foreign wife, Ezr 10^{30}. **2.** The head of the priestly house of Harim, Neh 12^{15}.

ADNAH.—**1.** A Manassite officer of Saul's who deserted to David at Ziklag, 1 Ch 12^{20}. **2.** An officer in Jehoshaphat's army, 2 Ch 17^{14}.

ADONI-BEZEK.—A king of Bezek (see BEZEK, **1**), who was defeated by Simeon and Judah. The mutilation inflicted upon him—the cutting off of the thumbs and great toes—was in order to render him harmless, while retaining him as a trophy; but he died on reaching Jerusalem. Adoni-bezek boasted of having mutilated seventy kings in a similar manner. The passage which speaks of Adoni-bezek (Jg 1^{5-7}) does not appear to be intact; the original form probably gave more details. The name Adoni-bezek is perhaps a corrupted form of Adoni-zedek (Jos 10^{1}), with which cf Melchizedek (Gn 14^{10}), also of Jerusalem.

ADONIJAH (' Jah is Lord ').—**1.** The fourth of the six sons of David who were born in Hebron; his mother was Haggith, a name which is possibly of Phoenician origin (2 S 3^{4}). The story of Adonijah (typical of many an oriental court intrigue) is recorded in 1 K 1^{1}–2^{36} at the end of the court history of David, which may be acclaimed as probably the first and certainly among the greatest of all the historical narratives of antiquity. Apart from the disputed passage 2^{1-9}, the story is a unity, and marked by a strong sense of inevitable tragedy. Its main theme and interest is the succession to the Davidic throne and the necessity of ensuring that, in a kingdom so dependent on the personality of its founder, a successor of similar calibre may be chosen.

David's marriage with Saul's daughter Michal had proved childless. After the death of Absalom, Amnon and Chileab also being dead, Adonijah became the obvious heir to the throne. The old Israelite custom was that the first-born son took precedence without regard to the position of the mother in the hierarchy of the father's wives. 1 K 2^{15} suggests that the general populace expected Adonijah to succeed his father. He is described as ' very handsome,' but spoiled by his father who had failed to discipline him. But his succession was not taken for granted by everyone, since there was already a strong party in favour of Solomon, son of Bathsheba. It seems that the succession finally depended on the decision of David and, fatally, David postponed decision. Adonijah sought support from the immediate entourage of David; and Joab, one of David's generals, together with Abiathar, priest of the Jerusalem sanctuary, adhered to his cause. There was an opposition party including Benaiah (a rival of Joab), Zadok (the other priest of the royal sanctuary), and, the leading mind, the court prophet Nathan. That Nathan should support the son of Bathsheba, the circumstances of whose marriage with David he had so strongly denounced, and that he should enter into a plot with her to induce David to decide in Solomon's favour, probably means that Nathan regarded Adonijah as a totally inadequate and unsuitable personality for the royal office. Thus Adonijah may be said to have come under unfavourable prophetic judgment.

The course of events is straightforward. Adonijah arranged an accession festival to which he invited all the men of note, except those who supported Solomon, and mention is made of ' all the men of Judah.' It appears that Adonijah tried to play upon the jealousy which still existed between the North and the South, as Absalom had done. His sacrificial act at the stone of Zoheleth proclaimed his kingship. But it also gave timely warning to his enemies. These, now on the alert, represented the gathering to the aged David as an attempt to usurp the throne while he was still alive. Bathsheba reminded David of his promise that Solomon should succeed him, and this is the first statement of the royal intention. It is possible that David thought it politic to prefer a Jerusalem-born son to those born at Hebron, as the best means of preserving the unity of North and South.

However that may be, David, guided by the influential Bathsheba who played her part with consummate tact, decisively named Solomon as his successor.

It was now the turn of Adonijah and his party to be caught by surprise. Adonijah took sanctuary. Solomon granted him his life, provided he behaved like 'a gentleman,' and dismissed him to private life. Tragically the prince then had the misfortune to fall in love with Abishag the Shunammite, the maiden who was brought to David in his old age. It is made clear that she was not the king's wife; otherwise, of course, Bathsheba would not have dared to support his suit to the king. Adonijah was probably moved by passion rather than by ambition for the throne (though this remains a matter of dispute). But so long as Adonijah was alive, however loyal he might be, he was a potential centre of disaffection. Solomon therefore seized his opportunity, interpreted Adonijah's suit as concealed conspiracy, condemned him and ordered Benaiah to execute him the same day.

2. One of the leading laymen who sealed the covenant in Neh 10[16] (probably=**Adonikam** Ezr 2[13]).

3. One of the Levites sent in the third year of Jehoshaphat to teach the Law in the cities of Judah (2 Ch 17[7-9]). W. O. E. O.—**D. R. J.**

ADONIKAM ('my Lord has arisen').—The head of a Jewish family after the Exile, Ezr 2[13] 8[13], Neh 7[18], 1 Es 5[14] 8[39]; apparently called **Adonijah** in Neh 10[16].

ADONIRAM, ADORAM ('my Lord is exalted').—An official who superintended the levies employed in the public works during the reigns of David, Solomon, and Rehoboam, 2 S 20[24], 1 K 4[6] 5[14] 12[18]. He was stoned to death by the rebellious Israelites when sent to them by Rehoboam. The shorter form of the name (2 S 20[24], 1 K 12[18]) is probably a corruption of the longer. In 2 Ch 10[18] he is called **Hadoram.**

ADONIS.—The Greek form of Semitic *'ādōn*, meaning 'lord.' Adonis was the Syrian deity of vegetation which wilted with the summer sun. The death of the god was mourned by the women of Phoenicia, particularly by the river Adonis (modern *Nahr Ibrahim*) near Beirut. The cult was known in Greece also, where Plato mentions Adonis-gardens (*Phaedrus*), pots of herbs, which were used in rites of imitative magic during the seven-day ascendancy of the Dog-star. There is a conceivable reference to this rite in *niṭ'ê na'ᵃmānîm* ('plantings of Adonis,' AV; cf RSV 'pleasant plants') mentioned in Is 17[10], the title of Adonis being *na'ᵃmān* ('pleasant'). See also TAMMUZ. J. Gr.

ADONI-ZEDEC (AV).—See ADONI-ZEDEK.

ADONI-ZEDEK ('my Lord is Zedek').—King of Jerusalem (AV **Adoni-zedec**) at the time of the invasion of Canaan by the Israelites under Joshua. After the Gibeonites had made a league with Israel, he induced four other kings to unite with him against the invaders. Joshua came unexpectedly upon them and routed them. They were captured in a cave at Makkedah, and brought to Joshua, who had them slain. Their bodies were hung up until the evening, when they were taken down and flung into the cave where they had hidden themselves. The mouth of the cave was filled up with great stones (Jos 10[1-27]). Some have identified Adoni-zedek with Adoni-bezek (q.v.). For the divine name, **Zedek,** associated with Jerusalem, cf MELCHIZEDEK.

ADOPTION.—The term 'adoption' is found four times in the undoubted Pauline letters (Ro 8[15, 23] 9[4], Gal 4[5]), once in Eph 1[5], which may be Pauline, and not elsewhere in the NT. In Ro 9[4] the Apostle refers to the privileged position of the Jews as the chosen people, the allusion no doubt being to Ex 4[22] where God calls Israel his first-born son. The other passages describe the privileges of the Christian, who is no longer under bondage to the Law, to sin and to death, but has the freedom of a son in the household. The free Christian is contrasted with the slave, and also with the heir who has not yet reached his majority, but is under guardians and trustees.

St. Paul's metaphor of adoption is usually traced to Roman law, but it has OT overtones as well. Adoption was of course a common feature of the ancient Nuzi law; cf Gen 15[2-4] where Abraham's household slave, Eliezer, is his heir. In Ex 2[10] Moses became the son of Pharaoh's daughter, and in Jer 3[19] the idea of adoption is applied to Israel's relation to Yahweh; see W. H. Rossell, *JBL*, lxxi (1952), 233 f.

The evidence of the Synoptic Gospels shows that Jesus taught His followers to think of themselves as sons of God. The disciples become God's sons in the true sense by loving their enemies, for their Father does the same (Mt 5[44-48], Lk 6[35f]) and those who do the will of God are Jesus' brother and sister and mother (Mk 3[35]). It is significant that Jesus is represented as using the word *Abba* in prayer to God (Mk 14[36]) and that this word probably underlies the *pater* of the Lord's Prayer (Lk 11[2]). According to St. Paul, the mark of the Christian's new sonship is that the spirit of God's Son (Gal 4[6]) or the spirit of adoption (Ro 8[15]) impels him to cry *Abba*.

Sir W. M. Ramsay attempted to identify peculiarities of Syro-Greek law in Gal 4, but the idea of adoption was very common in the whole Graeco-Roman world. The word *huiothesia* is very common in inscriptions and frequently occurs in the phrase *kath' huiothesian*; it occurs occasionally in literature, *e.g.* Diog. Laert. iv. 9 (53), but is not found in the LXX. St. Paul may have had Roman law specifically in mind. The form of *adoptio*, in which the person to be adopted was still subject to the *patria potestas* of his father or grandfather, seems to be the type more closely corresponding to what the Apostle had in mind. In ancient times this was effected by emancipation *per aes et libram* and surrender to the adoptive father by the legal form called *in jure cessio*. The Law of the XII Tables provided that if a father sold his son thrice the son would be free from his father; thus a triple sale was necessary, with two manumissions in between, after which the adopter by an action before the Praetor claimed the son as his own. In later times a simpler form was used whereby a declaration was made before the Praetor at Rome or the governor in the provinces; see S. Buss, *Roman Law and History in the NT* (London, 1901), pp. 271–82. The important point is that in Roman law the adopted son became a member of the new family just as if he had been born of the blood of the adopter. He was in all respects a real son: he underwent a change of family and *potestas*, of name and domicile, and acquired all the privileges and responsibilities of sonship; and he did not participate in the worship of the old family but in the *sacra privata* of the new. W. E. Ball (*Contemp. Review*, 1891) argued that the work of the Spirit as witness (Ro 8[16]) is parallel to the place of the five witnesses in the Roman process of adoption, but this analogy may not be in St. Paul's mind.

St. Paul speaks of adoption as both present (Ro 8[15]) and future (v.[23]). With Pfleiderer it is appropriate to distinguish three moments in adoption. It involves, here and now, freedom from the Law, and the possession of the spirit of adoption which enables the Christian to address God as Father. Adoption will be completed by the redemption of the body. 'Believers have this blessing (adoption) already, but only in an inward relation and as Divine right, with which, however, the objective and real state does not yet correspond' (Meyer on Ro 8[23]). It is the 'first-fruits' of the Spirit that Christians now possess.

In St. Paul's thought, 'adoption' does not represent believers as children of God by nature but only by grace which they accept. But it would be a mistake to press the term as giving a complete account of St. Paul's views of the relation of God to man; it is only one metaphor among many and subject to the imperfection of analogies and metaphors. The usage of the Synoptic Gospels shows that in Jesus' teaching the relation of sonship has only to be claimed to be made effective and that it is not just a status but a moral relationship always intended by God. See, further, INHERITANCE. S. E. J.

ADORA (1 Mac 13^{20}).—The same as **Adoraim.**

ADORAIM.—A city of Judah fortified by Rehoboam on the SW. of his kingdom, 2 Ch 11^{9}; modern *Dûrā*, W. of Hebron. In 1 Mac 13^{20} called **Adora.**

ADORAM.—See ADONIRAM.

ADORATION.—The word is not found in AV or RV, and even for the verb RV substitutes 'worship' in Bel^{4}; but both the idea and its expression in act are frequent.

Amongst the Hebrews the postures and gestures expressive of adoration underwent slight change in the course of time. Kissing the statue of a god (1 K 19^{18}, Hos 13^{2}; cf Job 31^{27}) was an early Arab custom, and became a technical meaning of *adoratio* amongst the Romans; but in this usage the sense is identical with that of worship. Adoration proper was expressed by prostration to the ground, or even by lying prone with the face touching the ground (Gn 17^{3}, Jos 5^{14}, Job 1^{20}, Ps 95^{6} 99^{5}, Dn 3^{5}). Primarily this posture was confined to man's approach to God, but it was adopted towards sacred persons; mysterious strangers (Gn 18^{2}), kings (2 S 14^{4}, Est 8^{3}), the son and heir of a king (1 S 20^{41}), a 'man of God' (2 K 4^{37}). In Gn 33^{3} Jacob has a special desire to conciliate Esau, but the 'seven times' brings the ceremony within the realm of the magico-religious. 'Divine' honours were accorded to kings, and Mt 18^{26} is an extension of this. 'Sat before the Lord' (2 S 7^{18}) may refer to a special and solemn mode of sitting, as in 1 K 18^{42}; the Arabs are said to have sat during a part of their worship in such a way that the head could easily be bent forward and made to touch the ground.

Outside the Christian sphere, prostration continued in the East to be a mark of submission and homage, rendered to such men as were for any reason or even by convention invested in thought with Divine qualities or powers. The NT, by example and less frequently by precept, confines this fullest mode of worship to God, and protests against its use towards men. Jairus' act (Mk 5^{22}, Lk 8^{41}) was prompted by intense yearning, a father's self-abandonment in the sore sickness of his child, and must not be taken as implying a full recognition of Christ's Divinity. Like Mary's posture at Bethany (Jn 11^{32}), it was a preparation for the attitude of the disciples after their visit to the empty tomb (Mt 28^{9}). Whatever Cornelius intended (Ac 10^{25f}), Peter found an opportunity to lay down the rule that no man under any circumstances is an appropriate object of adoration; and John repeats that rule twice not far from the end of Scripture (Rev 19^{10} 22^{8f}). The attempt to alienate from God His peculiar honours is a work of Satan (Mt 4^{9}); and adoration naturally follows a conviction of the presence of God (1 Co 14^{25}). R. W. M.—**N. H. S.**

ADRAMMELECH.—**1.** Adrammelech and Anammelech (q.v.), the gods of Sepharvaim to whom the colonists, brought to Samaria from Sepharvaim, burnt their children in the fire, 2 K 17^{31}. The divine name *Adad-milki* has been found in an inscription from *Tell Ḥalâf* (Gozan), where it figures as part of a proper name (cf Pohl, *Biblica*, xxii, 1941, 35). **2.** Adrammelech and Sharezer (q.v.) are given in 2 K 19^{37} as the sons of Sennacherib who murdered their father (the *Kᵉthîbh* omits 'his sons'). The Babylonian Chronicle says: 'On the 20th of Tebet, Sennacherib, king of Assyria, was killed by his son in an insurrection'; and all other native sources agree in ascribing the murder to one son, but do not name him. The sons of Sennacherib known to us are Ashur-nādin-shum, king of Babylon, 700–694 B.C.; Esarhaddon (q.v.), who succeeded his father, 681 B.C.; Ardi-Bēlit, Crown Prince, 694 B.C.; Ashur-shum-ushabshi, for whom Sennacherib built a palace in Tarbisi; Ashur-ilu-muballitsu, for whom Sennacherib built a palace in Ashur; and Shar-eṭir-Ashur. Possibly Ardi-Bēlit is intended. C. W. H. J.—**H. H. R.**

ADRAMYTTIUM.—A town of Mysia (in the Roman province of Asia) on the Adramyttene Gulf, originally a native State, and only later Hellenized by the Delians, who had been driven from their home by the Athenians (422 B.C.). In Roman times it was a place of considerable importance both politically and intellectually. It possessed a harbour, and a ship belonging to the place carried St. Paul from Caesarea by Sidon and Cyprus to Myra (Ac 27^{2-6}). Money belonging to the Jews of that place was confiscated 62–61 B.C. by Gnaeus Domitius, legate of Flaccus (Cicero, *Pro Flacco*, 28). A. So.—**E. G. K.**

ADRIA (more correctly *Hadria*).—The name was at first confined to the northern part of what we call the Adriatic Sea, or to a stretch of land near that, and was derived from a once important Etruscan city, Atria, situated at the mouth of the Po. The rest of what we call the Adriatic Sea appears to have been at that time included in the term Ionian Sea or Ionian Gulf. It was only later, with the growth of the Syracusan colonies on the coasts of Italy and Illyria, that the name 'Hadria' came to include the whole Adriatic, and even then, at first, it was the practice to call the southernmost part the Ionian Sea. When the name 'Ionian Sea' was transferred to the Sicilian Sea in the W. of Greece, the term 'Hadria' was improperly extended to include the Tarentine Gulf, the Sicilian Sea, the Corinthian Gulf, and even the waters between Crete and Malta, as in Ac 27^{27} and Josephus, *Vita*, 3 (15). A. So.—**E. G. K.**

ADRIEL ('my help is El').—Son of Barzillai, the Meholathite. He married Merab, the eldest daughter of Saul, who should have been given to David as the slayer of Goliath, 1 S 18^{19}, 2 S 21^{8} (AV, RV here read 'Michal,' with Hebrew; RSV corrects to 'Merab,' with two Hebrew MSS and LXX^{L}).

ADUEL.—An ancestor of Tobit, To 1^{1}; a variant form of **Adiel,** 1 Ch 4^{36}.

ADULLAM.—A city in the Shephelah, assigned to Judah, Jos 15^{35}, named between Jarmuth and Soco; formerly a Canaanite royal city, Jos 12^{15}. Rehoboam fortified it, 2 Ch 11^{7}, and the children of Judah returned to it after the Exile, Neh 11^{30}. It is identified with *Tell esh-Sheikh-Madhkûr*. The **Cave of Adullam,** the refuge of David (1 S 22^{1}, 2 S 23^{13}, 1 Ch 11^{15}) must have been in the adjoining valley. **Adullamite** (Gn 38^{1}) is an inhabitant of Adullam.

ADULTERY.—See CRIMES, MARRIAGE.

ADUMMIM, THE ASCENT OF.—This is the steep pass in which the road ascends from Jericho to Jerusalem, named in Jos 15^{7} 18^{7}. In this pass, notorious for robberies and murders, is the traditional 'inn' of Lk 10^{34}. Its modern name, *Tal'at ed-Damm*, 'the ascent of blood' or 'red,' is most probably due to the red marl which is so distinctive a feature of the pass.

ADVENT.—See PAROUSIA.

ADVERSARY.—See SATAN.

ADVERTISE.—In Ru 4^{4} (AV), 'I thought to advertise thee,' *i.e.* inform (RSV 'tell'); so Nu 24^{14} (AV, RV).

ADVOCATE.—See COUNSELLOR.

AEDIAS (1 Es 9^{27} AV, RV).—One of those who agreed to put away their 'strange' wives. The name is probably a corruption for **Elijah** of Ezr 10^{26} (so RSV).

AENEAS.—The name of a paralytic at Lydda who was cured by Peter (Ac $9^{33, 34}$).

AENON.—Jn 3^{23}, meaning 'springs'; a site near Salim (q.v.).

AESORA (Jth 4^{4}).—An unknown Samaritan town, possibly modern *'Aṣireh*, NE. of Shechem.

AGABA, 1 Es 5^{30} (AV).—See HAGAB.

AGABUS.—A Christian prophet of Jerusalem (Ac 11^{27ff} 21^{10f}), whose prediction of a famine over the (civilized) world occasioned the sending of alms from Antioch to Jerusalem. The famine happened, not simultaneously in all countries, in Claudius' reign (Suetonius, Tacitus). Agabus also foretold St. Paul's imprisonment, by binding his feet and hands with the Apostle's girdle (cf Jer 13^{1ff}). A. J. M.

AGADE.—A city of Northern Babylonia and the capital of Sargon, the founder of the first Semitic empire (*c* 2850 B.C.). As was first discovered by George Smith, Agade was the Semitic Akkad(u) (see AKKAD). It stood near **Sippar** (see SEPHARVAIM, **2**), and may have been in later times a suburb of that town.

AGAG.—1. In Nu 24^{7} the meaning of 'his king shall be higher than Agag' is uncertain. **2.** A king of Amalek, whom Saul defeated and spared, but who was slain by Samuel (1 S 15). Whether he met his death defiantly, cheerfully, or timidly cannot be determined from the text (v. ^{32}).

AGAGITE.—The designation of Haman, Est 3$^{1, 10}$ 8$^{3, 5}$ 9^{24}. The land of Agag is mentioned in Akkadian texts and was probably in Media. Josephus (*Ant.* XI. vi. 5 [209]) calls Haman an Amalekite, doubtless to link him with Agag (1 S 15). The author may have chosen the epithet here to indicate that, as Agag was Saul's enemy, so Haman was the foe of this other Benjamite, Mordecai.

AGAIN.—The English word 'again' means in AV either 'a second time,' as Ph 4^{16}, 'you sent once again'; or 'back,' as in Mt 11^{4} (AV) 'go and show John again those things which ye do hear' (*i.e.* 'go back and show John').

AGAPE.—See LOVE FEAST.

AGAR.—Greek form of the name **Hagar** (q.v.) found in Bar 3^{23} (RV; RSV Hagar; AV 'the Agarenes' for 'the sons of Agar')—where 'the sons of Hagar' may mean the **Hagrites** (q.v.)—and Gal 4^{24f} (AV; RV, RSV Hagar).

AGARENES, Bar 3^{23} (AV).—See AGAR.

AGATE.—See JEWELS AND PRECIOUS STONES.

AGE, AGED, OLD AGE.—In the OT advancing age is represented by words of different root-meanings. The aged man is *zāḳēn*, perhaps 'grey-bearded' (Gn 48^{10}, 2 S 19^{32}, Job 12^{20} 32^{9}, Ps 71^{18}, Jer 6^{11}); 'old age' is also *śêbhāh*, *i.e.* 'hoary-headedness' (Gn 15^{15}, 1 K 14^{4}; cf Gn 42^{38}, Ps 71^{18}). According to the Mishnah (*Ab.* v. 21) the latter word implies a greater age (70) than the former (60). But in Job 15^{10} (cf 29^{8}) *yāshîsh*, *i.e.* 'very aged,' marks a further advance in years, of which the sign is a *withering* of strength. Ps 90^{10} is the only passage in which a definite period is fixed for human life (apart from Gn 6^{3}, which is in a mythological context). The idea that 'ripe old age' (*kelaḥ*) is a blessing is expressed in Job 5^{26}; the contrast is furnished by the gloomy picture (30^{2}) of the 'fathers' whose age lacks vigour.

The wisdom of the old was proverbial (Job 12^{12} 32^{7}), though there were exceptions (Job 32^{9}, Ps 119^{100}). The experience of the older men fitted them for positions of trust and authority; hence by a natural transition of thought 'elders' became an official title (Ex 3^{16}, Ac 11^{30}). Respect is to be shown to the old (Lv 19^{32}, Pr 23^{22}), and the decay of reverence for age is an evil omen (Dt 28^{50}, 1 K 12^{8}, Is 47^{6}). It was to the grandmother of Obed that the Hebrew women said 'he shall be . . . a nourisher of your old age' (Ru 4^{15}); the dutiful affection of children's children illumined the gracious message of Israel's God: 'even to old age I am He, and to gray hairs I will carry you' (Is 46^{4}). J. G. T.

AGEE (? 'fugitive').—The father of Shammah, one of David's 'three mighty men,' 2 S 23^{11}.

AGGABA, 1 Es 5^{29} (AV, RV).—See HAGABAH.

AGGAEUS.—The Greek form or **Haggai** (q.v.) used in AV and RV in 1 Es 6^{1} 7^{3}, 2 Es 1^{40}; RSV has Haggai.

AGIA.—1. Wife of Jaddus (AV Addus), 1 Es 5^{38} (AV, RV **Augia**). **2.** 1 Es 5^{34} (RV); see HATTIL.

AGONY (Lk 22^{44}) is not a translation but a transliteration of the Greek *agōnia*, equivalent to St. Matthew's 'sorrowful and troubled' (26^{37}) and St. Mark's 'greatly distressed and troubled' (14^{33}). The word does not mean 'agony' in the English sense. *Agōn* was 'a contest,' and *agōnia* the trepidation of a combatant about to enter the lists. Christ's Agony in Gethsemane was the horror which overwhelmed Him as He faced the final ordeal. D. S.

AGRAPHA.—Since Jesus' sayings are known to us only through writing, the term *Agrapha* (Körner, 1776), *i.e.* 'unwritten,' is inept; nevertheless it has become current as a convenient abbreviation for 'words somewhere ascribed to Jesus but *not written* in the best MSS of the canonical Gospels.' The earliest Agrapha themselves are proof that the writing of the canonical Gospels did not once for all freeze the stream of living tradition of words believed to have been uttered by Jesus of Nazareth. This continuing oral stream is valuable historical testimony to the specific views of its custodians. Here and there it may even (rarely) preserve genuine words of Jesus not otherwise recorded. But he who turns to the Agrapha for any significant supplement to his knowledge of the historical Jesus is bound to be either disappointed or deluded. Even so, the study of the Agrapha is rewarding in what they reveal of either didactic or polemic alteration (whether of canonical sayings or of unwritten folk-memories) and invention of words of Jesus, usually with polemic tendency. The polemic may be inner-Christian (against an opposing faction), or against non-Christians or heretics, but may also come from the opposite direction: from heretics or non-Christians, as anti-Christian propaganda.

1. In secondary recensions of the canonical Gospels.—(*a*) Those contained in TR (and hence in AV) but relegated to the margin of most or all modern critical Greek texts. The most important are: Mt 6^{13b} 17^{21}, Mk 9^{49b} 16$^{15-18}$, Lk 9^{55f} 11^{2b} 23^{34}, Jn 7^{53}–8^{11}. All of these except Lk 23^{34} are omitted from the text of RSV; all likewise, with the same exception and the additional exception of the two long passages, from RV. (*b*) Those not in TR (and hence in no historic English version) but found in some MS or MSS. The most striking of them is offered by Codex D in place of Lk 6^{5} (this displaced verse then appears between vv.^{10} and ^{11}):

'The same day seeing a man working on the sabbath, he said to him, " Man, if you know what you are doing you are blessed; but if you do not know, you are accursed and a transgressor of the law." '

The same MS joined by several ancient versions offers an independent parallel to Lk 14$^{8-10}$ after Mt 20^{28}: 'As for you, seek to increase from [being] little and (not, syr^{c}) to be smaller from [being] greater. When you come in and are urged to dine, sit not in the raised places lest one in higher esteem than you also enter and the host approach and say to you, " Move farther down," and you be put to shame. But if you sit in the least place and one less than you come in, the host will say to you, " Advance higher up," and it will be to your advantage.' Another surplus of words of Jesus is contained in the Freer Logion (Codex W), a third variant for the end of Mark in addition to the two previously known. The exclusion of both classes (*a*) and (*b*) from the NT is purely a matter of the genuine text of the Gospels; it does not in itself preclude the possibility that each group may contain authentic tradition.

2. In the rest of the NT.—1 Co 11^{24f} as a whole is an Agraphon independent of Mk 14, Mt 26 and is the probable source of the later Lk 22^{19b-20} (omitted by RSV), particularly of the additional saying, 'Do this [as often as you drink it] in remembrance of me.' Also 'It is more blessed to give than to receive,' Ac 20^{35}. The sayings within Ac 1, as words of the Risen Christ, probably should not be included here; nor is it clear in what sense or how much of 1 Th 4$^{15-17}$ is a 'word of the Lord' (Jesus on earth? the exalted Christ? God?). The parenetic passages in Paul, especially Ro 12, abound in similarities to sayings later written down in the Gospels as uttered by Jesus, but Paul does not ascribe them to Jesus nor do they verbally agree with sayings in the Gospels. Rev 16^{15} is an enigma. Ja 5^{12}, though not explicitly quoted, may well be a more primary form of the saying in Mt 5^{37} (Dibelius).

3. In the Apostolic Fathers.—In the sober judgment of the compilers of *The NT in the Apostolic Fathers*, all of these works show clear acquaintance with the synoptic *tradition*, either directly by the oral stream or indirectly through now lost documents, while only Ignatius alludes with reasonable clarity to any particular Gospel. The one direct quotation which Ignatius ascribes to Jesus (Smyr 3^{2}) comes, according to Jerome, from a Jewish apocryphal gospel known to him. The most interesting allusions in the Apostolic Fathers are the collections of sayings of Jesus that seem to be echoes of widely scattered canonical passages but because of their divergences must be agrapha: Did. 1^{3-6} (no attribution to Jesus, no formula of quotation), 1 Clem 13^{2}, Polycarp 2^{3}. 2 Clem 5^{2-4} is probably from the Gospel of the Egyptians.

4. In Apocryphal Gospels.—See APOCRYPHAL NEW TESTAMENT.

5. In the Fathers.—Of the many alleged agrapha in the Fathers many have turned out to be quotations of apocryphal gospels. Others presumably are from unidentified gospels. Among them are: Clement of Alex. (*Strom.* i. 28, 177), ‘ Be approved bankers ’ (related to Mt 25^{14-30} and 1 Th 5^{21}?); Didascalia ii. 8, ‘ A man that is not tempted is not approved ’; Acts of Philip, 140, ‘ Unless you change your “ down ” to “ up ” [and “ up ” to “ down ” and “ right ” to “ left ”] and “ left ” to “ right,” you shall not enter my kingdom [of heaven] ’ (cf Mt 18^{3}).

6. In Papyri.—Among the many Oxyrhynchus Papyri discovered in 1897, 1903, and 1908 at least four (nos. 1, 654, 655, and 1224) contain words ascribed to Jesus. The most important can be consulted in *Gospel Parallels*, p. V; M. R. James, *Apocryphal NT*, pp. 25–30; and Evelyn White, *The Sayings of Jesus from Oxyrhynchus*. According to White the first three papyri are extracts from the Gospel according to the Hebrews, but according to Preuschen from the Gospel of the Egyptians. There are also Coptic papyri (James, pp. 30–32), and *Pistis Sophia* contains many fantastic agrapha. It is probable that Gnostic sources contained many such sayings. The discovery of Coptic texts of the *Gospel of Thomas* and the *Gospel of Philip*, among the collection found at Nag Hammadi in Upper Egypt in 1947, supports this view. (See APOCRYPHAL NEW TESTAMENT.)

7. In Heretical and non-Christian writings.—(*a*) *Gnostic.* Certain of the apocryphal gospels (see **4**, above) show tendentious distortion of canonical sayings in a Gnostic direction; for unbridled invention of sayings of Jesus, see Acts of John 94–96 (James, pp. 253 f) and *Pistis Sophia*, *passim*. The newly discovered *Gospel of Truth* has no professed quotation of Jesus, yet it surely cites Lk 15^{3-7}, which it allegorizes by identifying the parable's shepherd with Jesus: “ He is the Shepherd who ‘ abandoned the ninety-nine lambs who had not strayed. He went in search of the one that had strayed. He rejoiced when he found it ’ ” (*Ev. Ver.*, 31^{35ff}). (*b*) The uncensored editions of the *Talmud* and related literature contain various references to Jesus, usually veiled, but rarely quote him (cf the explicit alleged quotation, *Abodah Zarah* 16b, 17a, which first quotes Mic 1^{7} and adds as Jesus' comment: ‘ From filth it came, to the place of filth shall it go ’—probably spun out of Mk 7^{18f}). The most interesting agrapha here—(probably all parodies) concern neighbouring verses of Mt 5^{13} ‘ If the salt have lost its savour wherewith shall it be salted? ’ (*Berak.* 8b, but with only the subtlest reference to Jesus, if any. Is it perhaps a proverb in both Jesus' and the Rabbi's mouth ?). V.^{17} ‘ Not to subtract from the Law of Moses did I [gloss: the Gospel] come, nor [var. lect: but] to add to the Law of Moses did I come ’ (*Shab.* 116b, but no mention of Jesus). V.^{16} (?) ‘ Let your light shine as a lamp ’ (*ibid.*, again no mention of Jesus). V.^{15} (by a punning allusion): ‘ The ḤMR came and stamped the lamp out ’ (*ibid.*, the Aramaic word can mean 1. bushel [*i.e. homer*], 2. lampstand, 3. ass; the pun involves double meaning of 3. and one of the others.) (*c*) *Manichaean. A Manichaean Psalm-book* (ed. Allberry, 1938) contains a long explicit composite quotation from Jesus (pp. 39–41) consisting both of nearly canonical sayings and unknown agrapha. Among the latter are:

AGRAPHA

‘ Repent, that I may forgive you your sins ’; ‘ I am near to you, like the clothing of your body ’; ‘ Pray for thine enemies, bless them that revile thee (Lk 6^{27f}), that thou mayest be good (*agathos*) like thy Father who is in [heaven] ’ (cf Lk 6^{36}); ‘ The fire that dwells in the body, its affair is eating and drinking; but the soul thirsts for the Word of God always ’ (gnosticized version of Mt $6^{31ff}+5^{6}$?). In other psalms: ‘ The will that is in heaven shall be upon the earth, the kingdom shall come which not many have known ’ (p. 156—from the Lord's prayer !); ‘ You received my name, but you did not do my works ’ (in a strange version of the Wise and Foolish Virgins, p. 191); ‘ He that dies shall live, he that humbles himself shall be exalted ’ (p. 93). (*d*) *Mandaean.* Both *Ginza* and *Book of Jahja* contain many transparently polemic inventions as words of Jesus or of Christ. Yet cf the following (Christ speaks): ‘ In whose name did you clothe with clothes and wrap with wraps, pay ransoms, and grant alms and benefits ? ’ (Mt 25 ? *Ginza*, p. 187). ‘ That which is above is heaven, that which is below is earth; Jesus Christ am I, the Holy Spirit is here ’ (*ibid.*). ‘ I am the true God whom my Father sent hither. I am the first, I am the last Ambassador; I am the Father, I am the Son, I am the Holy Spirit, I who set forth from the city of Nazareth ’ (*Ginza* 50^{26}; cf 29^{29}). ‘ Behold how my glory has dawned upon the world ’ (*ibid.*). ‘ John, baptize me with thy baptism, and speak over me the name you are wont to speak. If I show myself to be your disciple, I will remember you in my book; if I prove a failure as a disciple, wipe out my name from off your page ’ (*Jahja*, p. 103). (*e*) *Mohammedan.* The Koran contains many sayings, some long, attributed to Jesus. Some are allusions to known apocryphal gospels (Sura 3, 43 from *Infancy* Gospel of Thomas), some to presumed Jewish-Christian apocrypha or dim recollections of oral tradition preserved by Jewish and Arabic Christians whom Mohammed had encounted in Arabia; most are polemic inventions. The infant Jesus is made to say, ‘ Verily, I am the servant of God; He hath given me the Book, and He hath made me a prophet; and He hath made me blessed wherever I may be, and hath enjoined me prayer and almsgiving so long as I shall live; and to be duteous to her that bare me: and he hath not made me proud, depraved. And the peace of God was on me the day I was born, and will be the day I shall die, and the day I shall be raised to life ’ (Sura 19, 32—from some apocryphon ?). ‘ Now am I come to you with wisdom; and a part of those things about which ye are at variance I will clear up to you; fear ye God therefore and obey me. Verily, God is my Lord and your Lord; wherefore worship ye him: this is a right way ’ (Sura 43, 63; the last sentence in several other places). Jesus prays: ‘ O God, our Lord ! send down a table to us out of Heaven [the Eucharist !] that it may become a recurring festival to us, to the first of us and to the last of us, and a sign from thee; and do thou nourish us, for thou art the best of nourishers ’ (Sura 5, 114). Perhaps by a pun on ‘ Paraclete ’ Jesus is made to predict and approve Ahmad-Mohammed: ‘ O children of Israel ! of a truth I am God's apostle to you to confirm the law which was given before me, and to announce an apostle [the *Parakletos* ?] that shall come after me whose name shall be Ahmad [=Glorified; *periklytos*=glorified] ’ (Sura 61, 6). ‘ Jesus ’ is also made to deny the Trinity; see Sura 5, 116 and cf 4, 169. Some forty-eight of the extra-Koranic Mohammedan agrapha collected by D. S. Margoliouth in the *Expository Times*, 1893–94, are reprinted in Hastings' *Dictionary of the Bible*, Extra Volume, pp. 350 ff; many of them are not unworthy of the Jesus of the Synoptics. A curious additional one is furnished by the syncretist Emperor Akbar: in the gateway of the Great Mosque in his deserted capital, Fatehpur Sikri (near Agra), is the inscription, ‘ Jesus, on whom be peace, hath said, “ This world is but a bridge; pass over, but build not thy dwelling there.” ’ This is probably a quotation from *Historia Christi*, the earliest Jesus-novel, written for

Akbar in Persian by Jerome Xavier, 1602. Akbar's Christian instructor, Jerome Xavier, must have been the mediator of this Spanish agraphon. It has been traced back to a converted Spanish rabbi, Moise Sephardi (d. *c* 1140; Christian name, Petrus Alphonsi), whose *Disciplina Clericalis*, however, is full of Oriental wisdom. Consequently this saying must have a still earlier history in Jewish or Islamic tradition. K. G.

AGRICULTURE.—Throughout the whole period of their national existence, agriculture was the principal occupation of the Hebrews. According to the priestly theory, the land was the property of Y″; His people enjoyed the usufruct (Lv 25[23]). In actual practice, the bulk of the land was owned by the towns and village communities, each free husbandman having his allotted portion of the common lands. The remainder included the Crown lands and the estates of the nobility, at least under the monarchy. Husbandry—the Biblical term for agriculture (2 Ch 26[10])—was highly esteemed, and was regarded as dating from the earliest times (Gn 4[2]). It was Y″ Himself who taught the husbandman his art (Is 28[26]).

Of the wide range of topics embraced by agriculture in the wider significance of the term, some of the more important will be treated in separate articles, such as Cart, Flax, Food, Garden, Olive, Ox, Thorns, Vine, etc. The present article will deal only with the more restricted field of the cultivation of the principal cereals. These were, in the first rank, wheat and barley; less important were the crops of millet and spelt, and those of the pulse family—lentils, beans, and the like.

1. The agricultural year began in the latter half of October, with the advent of the early rains, which softened the ground baked by the summer heat. Then the husbandman began to prepare his fields for the winter seed by means of the **plough**. From the details given in post-Biblical literature, it is evident that the Hebrew plough differed but little from its modern Syrian counterpart (see *PEFSt*, 1891). The essential part or ' body ' of the latter, corresponding in position to the modern plough-tail or ' stilt,' consists of a piece of tough wood bent and pointed at the foot to receive an iron sheath or share (1 S 13[20]), the upper end being furnished with a short cross-piece to serve as a handle. The pole is usually in two parts: one stout and curved, through the lower end of which the ' body ' is passed just above the share; at the other end is attached the lighter part of the pole, through the upper end of which a stout pin is passed to serve as attachment for the yoke. The plough was usually drawn by two or more oxen (Am 6[12]), or by asses (Is 30[24]), but the employment of one of each kind was forbidden (Dt 22[10]). The **yoke** is a short piece of wood—the **bar** of Lv 26[13] (RV, RSV)—fitted with two pairs of converging pegs, the lower ends connected by thongs, to receive the necks of the draught animals. Two smaller pegs in the middle of the upper side hold in position a ring of willow, rope, or other material, which is passed over the end of the pole and kept in position by the pin above mentioned. As the ploughman required but one hand to guide the plough, the other was free to wield the **ox-goad,** a light wooden pole shod at one end with an iron spike wherewith to prick the oxen (cf Ac 26[14]), and having at the other a small spade with which to clean the plough-share. Gardens, vineyards (Is 5[6] RV, RSV), and parts too difficult to plough were worked with the hoe or mattock (Is 7[25]).

The prevailing mode of **sowing** was by hand, as in the parable of the Sower, the seed being immediately ploughed in. It was possible, however, to combine both operations by fixing a seed-box to the plough-tail. The seed passed through an aperture at the bottom of the box and was conducted by a pipe along the tail. It thus fell into the drill behind the share and was immediately covered in. The patriarch Abraham was credited by Jewish legend with the invention of this form of seeding-plough (Book of Jubilees 11[23ff]). There is no evidence that **harrows** were used for covering in the seed.

2. During the period of growth the crops were exposed to a variety of risks, such as the delay or scanty fall of the spring rains (the ' latter rain ' of the OT, Am 4[7]), blasting by the hot sirocco wind, mildew, hail—these three are named together in Hag 2[17]; cf Dt 28[22], Am 4[9]—and worst of all a visitation of locusts. The productiveness of the soil naturally varied greatly (cf Mt 13[8]). Under favourable conditions, as in the Haurân, wheat is said to yield a hundredfold return.

3. Owing to the wide range of climatic conditions in Palestine, the time of the **harvest** was not uniform, being earliest in the semi-tropical Jordan valley, and latest in the uplands of Galilee. The average harvest period, reckoned by the Hebrew legislation (Lv 23[15], Dt 16[9]) to cover seven weeks, may be set down as from the middle of April to the beginning of June, the barley ripening about a fortnight sooner than the wheat.

The standing corn was reaped with the **sickle** (Dt 16[9] RV, RSV), the stalks being cut considerably higher up than with us. The handfuls of ears were gathered into sheaves, and these into heaps (not into shocks) for transportation to the threshing-floor. The **corners** of the field were left to be reaped, and the fallen ears to be gleaned, by the poor and the stranger (Lv 19[9f], Dt 24[19], Ru 2[2ff]).

For small quantities the ears were stripped by beating with a stick (Ru 2[17], Jg 6[11] RV, RSV), otherwise the threshing was done at the village **threshing-floor.** This was a large, specially prepared (Jer 51[33] RV, RSV) space on an elevated situation. Hither the corn was brought on asses or on a cart (Am 2[13]), and piled in heaps. Enough sheaves were drawn out to form a layer, 6 to 8 ft. wide, all round the heap. Over this layer several oxen, unmuzzled according to the law (Dt 25[4]), and harnessed together as represented on the Egyptian monuments, might be driven. More effective work, however, was got from the **threshing-drag** and the **threshing-wagon,** both still in use in the East, the former being the favourite in Syria, the latter in Egypt. The former consists of two or three thick wooden planks held together by a couple of cross-pieces, the whole measuring from 5 to 7 ft. in length by 3 to 4 ft. in breadth. The underside of the drag is set with sharp pieces of hard stone (cf Is 41[15]), which strip the ears as the drag, on which the driver sits or stands, is driven over the sheaves, and at the same time cut up the stalks into small lengths. The threshing-wagon is simply a wooden frame containing three or more rollers set with parallel metal discs, and supporting a seat for the driver. The former instrument was used by Araunah the Jebusite (2 S 24[22]), while the latter is probably referred to in ' the threshing wheel ' of Pr 20[26] (RV, RSV). Both are mentioned together in the original of Is 28[27].

After the threshing came the **winnowing.** By means of a five- or six-pronged fork, the **' fan '** of the OT and NT, the mass of grain, **chaff,** and chopped straw is tossed into the air in the western evening breeze. The chaff is carried farthest away (Ps 1[4]), the light morsels of straw to a shorter distance, while the heavy grains of wheat or barley fall at the winnower's feet. After being thoroughly sifted with a variety of **sieves** (Am 9[9], Is 30[28]), the grain was stored in jars for immediate use, and in cisterns (Jer 41[8]), or in specially constructed granaries, the **' barns '** of Mt 6[26].

4. Of several important matters, such as irrigation, the terracing of slopes, manuring of the fields, the conditions of lease, etc., there is little direct evidence in Scripture. On these Vogelstein's treatise *Die Landwirtschaft in Palästina* is a mine of information for the Roman period. Cf also Dalman's *Arbeit und Sitte in Palästina*, 6 vols., 1928–39, especially vol. i, 1 and 2, 1928, where a detailed account of the year's work is outlined, with innumerable and interesting parallels with Arab customs. (In view of the rapidly changing customs of modern agriculture in Israel, this survey by Dalman is invaluable for OT study.) Agriculture, as is natural, bulks largely in the legislative codes of the Pentateuch. Some of the provisions have already been cited. To these may be added the solemn injunction against removing a neighbour's ' landmarks,' the upright stones marking the boundaries of his fields (Dt 19[14] 27[17]), the humanitarian provision regarding strayed cattle (Ex 23[4], Dt 22[1ff]), the law that every field must lie fallow for one year in seven (Ex 23[10f]; see, for later development, SABBATICAL YEAR), the law forbidding the breeding of hybrids and the sowing of a field with two kinds of seed (Lv 19[19] RV, RSV), and the far-reaching provision as to the inalienability of the land (Lv 25[8ff]).

The fact that no department of human activity has enriched the language of Scripture, and in consequence the language of the spiritual life in all after ages, with so many appropriate figures of speech, is a striking testimony to the place occupied by agriculture in the life and thought of the Hebrew people. A. R. S. K. —**B. J. R.**

AGRIPPA.—See HEROD, **6, 7.**

AGUE.—See MEDICINE.

AGUR.—Son of Jakeh and author of the whole or part of Pr 30, one of the latest sections of the book. His name may mean 'hireling' or 'assembler'; cf Vulg. 'Verba *Congregantis filii Vomentis*.' The word *massā'* (AV 'the prophecy,' RV 'the oracle') is either out of place here, or is the name of his country (so RSV; cf. Gn 25[14]).

AHAB.—1. Son of Omri, and the most noted member of his dynasty, king of Israel from about 875 to about 853 B.C. The account of him in our Book of Kings is drawn from two separate sources, one of which views him more favourably than the other. From the secular point of view he was an able and energetic prince; from the religious point of view he was a dangerous innovator, and a patron of foreign gods. His alliance with the Phoenicians was cemented by his marriage with Jezebel, daughter of Ethbaal, king of Tyre (1 K 16[31]), who was also, if we may trust Josephus, priest of Astarte. At a later date Ahab entered into alliance with Judah, giving his daughter Athaliah in marriage to Jehoram, son of Jehoshaphat (2 K 8[18]). His wealth is indicated by the ivory palace which he built (1 K 21[1] 22[39]).

The reign of Ahab was marked by frequent wars with the Syrian kingdom of Damascus. Benhadad, the king of that country, was so successful that he claimed suzerainty over Israel—a claim which Ahab was at first disposed to admit (1 K 20[2ff]). But when Benhadad went so far as to threaten Samaria with indiscriminate plunder, Ahab resisted. In two campaigns he defeated the invaders, even taking their haughty leader prisoner. Contrary to the advice of the prophetic party, he treated his captive magnanimously, and concluded an alliance with him, stipulating only that the cities formerly taken from Israel should be restored. The alliance was one for trade and commerce, each party having bazaars assigned him in the capital of the other (1 K 20[34]). It is not improbable also that common measures of defence were planned against the Assyrians, who were showing hostile intentions in the region of the Lebanon. In the battle of Qarqar, which was fought against these invaders in the year 854, Ahab was present with ten thousand troops. This we learn from the Assyrian inscriptions.

The religious innovation for which Ahab is held responsible by the Hebrew writers, was the introduction of the Phoenician Baal as one of the gods of Israel. It is clear that Ahab had no idea of displacing Yahweh altogether, for he gave his children names which indicated his devotion to Him. But to please his wife he allowed her to introduce and foster the worship of her own divinities. Her thought was that with the religion of her own country she would introduce its more advanced civilization. The champion of Yahweh's exclusive right to the worship of Israel was Elijah. This prophet, by his bold challenge to the priests of Baal, roused the anger of Jezebel, and was obliged to flee the country (1 K 17–19). Other prophets do not seem to have been disturbed, for we find them at the court of Ahab in the last year of his life (22[6]). These, however, were subservient to the crown, while Elijah was not only a protestant against religious changes, but the champion of the common people, whose rights were so signally violated in the case of Naboth.

Ahab died fighting for his people. The Syrian war had again broken out—apparently because Benhadad had not kept his agreement. Ahab therefore tried to recover Ramoth-gilead, being assisted by Jehoshaphat of Judah. In the first encounter Ahab was slain, his reputation for courage being vindicated by the direction of his adversary to his soldiers—'Fight neither with small nor with great, but only with the king of Israel' (1 K 22[31]).

2. A false prophet 'roasted in the fire' by the king of Babylon (Jer 29[21f]). H. P. S.

AHARAH.—See AHIRAM.

AHARHEL.—A descendant of Judah, 1 Ch 4[8].

AHASAI, Neh 11[13] (AV).—See AHZAI.

AHASBAI.—Father of Eliphelet (2 S 23[34]) and a member of the family of Maacah, settled at Beth-maacah (20[14]), or a native of the Syrian kingdom of Maacah (10[6, 8]).

AHASUERUS, old Persian *Khshayārshā*, Hebrew *'Ahashwērôsh*, Greek *Xerxes* (486–465 B.C.), mentioned briefly in Ezr 4[6] as receiving an accusation against the Jews. He figures prominently in the Book of Esther. Dn 9[1] mentions an Ahasuerus, father of Darius; To 14[15] uses Ahasuerus for Cyaxares the king of the Medes in the late 7th cent. B.C. The Daniel passage may contain a similar erroneous identification. The name was used in late Jewish tradition for the 'wandering Jew.' P. R. A.

AHAVA.—A settlement in Babylonia lying along a stream of the same name, probably a large canal near the Euphrates. None of the conjectures as to the exact locality can be verified. It was here that Ezra mustered his people before their departure for Jerusalem (Ezr 8[15, 21, 31]). Some district north or north-west of Babylon, near the northern boundary of Babylonia, is most probable. It is called **Theras** in 1 Es 8[41].

AHAZ.—1. Son and successor of Jotham as king of Judah *c* 735 B.C. His full name, Joahaz, appears in Tiglath-pileser's list of vassal kings. Early in his reign, he was threatened with invasion from the league formed by Pekah of Israel and Rezin of Syria (2 K 16[5], Is 7 f). Behind this attack lies the expansionist policy of Assyria. The two kings were in revolt against their overlord, and it was a military necessity for them to have the support or assured neutrality of Judah. They therefore proposed to replace Ahaz with a Syrian, 'the son of Tabeel.' The attack was initially successful, and Ahaz, in spite of the assurance given by Isaiah, took desperate measures to ensure his safety. He sacrificed his son as a burnt offering in order to obtain Yahweh's protection; and he offered himself as a vassal to the Assyrian king, accompanying the offer with a gift of gold and silver from the palace and Temple treasures. Tiglath-pileser quelled the revolt, and the threat to Judah's territorial integrity was removed. But Ahaz, with other kings, had to pay homage to the Assyrian at Damascus. As a mark of his submission he was compelled to replace at the Jerusalem shrine the worship of Yahweh with that of the Assyrian deities (1 K 16[10ff]). A further result was that Edom regained independence.

A carnelian seal of this period has been discovered, bearing the inscription, 'to Ushna, servant of Ahaz.'

2. The name Ahaz also appears at 1 Ch 8[35] 9[41] as a great-grandson of Jonathan. A S. H.

AHAZIAH.—Two kings of this name are mentioned in the OT, one in each of the Israelite kingdoms.

1. Ahaziah of Israel was the son of Ahab, and ruled after him only two years or parts of years. He is said to have been a worshipper of Baal, that is, to have continued the religious policy of his father. By a fall from a window of his palace he was seriously injured, and, after lingering awhile, died from the accident. The Moabites, who had been subject to Israel, took this opportunity to revolt. Ahaziah is accused of sending messengers to inquire of the celebrated oracle at Ekron, and is said unexpectedly to have received his answer from Elijah (2 K 1).

2. Ahaziah of Judah was son of Jehoram and grandson of Jehoshaphat. Under the influence of his mother, who was a daughter of Ahab (and Jezebel), it is not surprising to read that he walked in the ways of Ahab. All that we know of him is that he continued the league with Israel, and that, going to visit his uncle Jehoram in Jezreel, he was involved in his fate at the revolt of Jehu (2 K 9^{27}). See JEHOAHAZ, **3.** H. P. S.

AHBAN (' brother of a prudent one ').—A Judahite, son of Abishur, 1 Ch 2^{29}.

AHER (' another ').—A Benjamite, 1 Ch 7^{12}.

AHI (' brother,' perhaps for ' brother is Y" ').—**1.** A Gadite, 1 Ch 5^{15}. **2.** An Asherite, 1 Ch 7^{34} (AV, RV) ; but RSV takes as a common noun, ' his brother.'

AHIAH.—A layman who sealed Nehemiah's covenant, Neh 10^{26} (AV **Ahijah**). See also AHIJAH, **1, 6.**

AHIAM.—One of David's heroes, the son of Sharar (2 S 23^{33}) or Sachar (1 Ch 11^{35}).

AHIAN (' fraternal ').—A Manassite, son of Shemida, 1 Ch 7^{19}. It is improbable that an individual is meant, however ; note in the context Shechem and Abiezer.

AHIEZER (' brother is help ').—**1.** Son of Ammishaddai, one of the tribal leaders representing Dan at the census in the wilderness and on other occasions, Nu 1^{12} 2^{25} $7^{66, 71}$ 10^{25}. **2.** The chief of the Benjamite archers who deserted to David at Ziklag, 1 Ch 12^{1-3}.

AHIHUD (' brother is majesty ').—**1.** The leader of the tribe of Asher, Nu 34^{27}. **2.** A Benjamite, 1 Ch 8^{7}.

AHIJAH.—**1.** 1 S $14^{3, 18}$ (AV **Ahiah**), a priest, son of Ahitub, who had charge of the oracular ephod and consulted it for Saul [read ' ephod ' for ' ark ' at v.^{18}]. Ahijah is probably to be identified with Ahimelech (21^{1}), but they may have been brothers. **2.** 1 K 4^{3}, one of Solomon's secretaries, who conducted the king's correspondence and wrote out his decrees. His father, Shisha or Shavsha (cf 1 Ch 18^{16}), seems to have held the same office under David. **3.** 1 K 11^{29f} 12^{15}, 2 Ch 10^{15}, a prophet of Shiloh who foretold and apparently favoured the division of the kingdom and the elevation of Jeroboam. Subsequently he broke with Jeroboam and announced the overthrow of his house (1 K 14^{2ff}). **4.** 1 K $15^{27, 33}$, father of Baasha. **5.** 1 Ch 2^{25} has an Ahijah, son of Jerahmeel. But the text is difficult and various emendations are suggested. **6.** 1 Ch 8^{7} (AV **Ahiah**), son of Ehud, a Benjamite ; at v.^{4} **Ahoah**, but LXX *Ahijah*. **7.** 1 Ch 11^{36}, one of David's heroes, the ' Pelonite.' But the text is corrupt. The parallel list in 2 S 23^{24ff} reads another name. **8.** 1 Ch 26^{20}, a Levite, overseer of the Temple treasures. But we ought probably to substitute the words ' their brethren ' with LXX. **9.** Neh 10^{26} (AV) ; see AHIAH. **10.** An ancestor of Ezra, 2 Es 1^{2} (AV, RV **Achias**). J. T.—**J. Br.**

AHIKAM (' my brother has arisen ').—One of the deputation sent by King Josiah to Huldah the prophetess, 2 K $22^{12, 14}$, 2 Ch 34^{20}. Later he used his influence to protect Jeremiah from the violence of the populace during the reign of Jehoiakim, Jer 26^{24}. His son Gedaliah (q.v.) became governor for Nebuchadrezzar after the fall of Jerusalem (2 K 25^{22}) until he was murdered.

AHIKAR, BOOK OF.—An Oriental Wisdom book, which survives in Syriac, Arabic, Armenian, and other languages. Its antiquity was proved by the rediscovery of portions of an Old Aramaic version among the Elephantine Papyri (q.v.) of the 5th cent. B.C. It must have arisen in Mesopotamia and may ultimately be Assyrian in origin. Knowledge of the story of Ahikar is reflected in the Book of Tobit (1^{21f} 2^{10} 10^{17} 14^{10f}), a work of the early 2nd cent. B.C. The book purports to give the wise saws and fables which Ahikar ' a wise and ready scribe ' and vizier of Sennacherib king of Assyria gave his adopted son Nadin by way of instruction. He brought Nadin to Esarhaddon, who soon advanced him to his father's position, thus enabling Ahikar to retire to his country estates. Nadin falsely accuses Ahikar of plotting against the king, who orders the sage's execution. He is saved by the executioners and later is proved innocent. See R. H. Charles, *APOT* ii (1913), 715–784. J. B. Pritchard, *ANET* (1950), 427 f. E. G. K.

AHILUD (? ' my brother is born ').—**1.** Father of Jehoshaphat, the chronicler under David and Solomon, 2 S 8^{16} 20^{24}, 1 K 4^{3}, 1 Ch 18^{15}. **2.** Father of Baana, one of Solomon's twelve commissariat officers, 1 K 4^{12}.

AHIMAAZ.—**1.** Saul's father-in-law (1 S 14^{50}). **2.** Son of Zadok. He and Jonathan, son of Abiathar (2 S 15^{27}), were stationed outside Jerusalem to learn Absalom's plans ; after an adventurous journey they succeeded in warning David (2 S $15^{27, 36}$ 17^{17-21}). Ahimaaz was eager to carry the tidings of Absalom's defeat ; but Joab preferred to send by an Ethiopian slave the unwelcome news of the prince's death. Obtaining leave to follow, Ahimaaz outstripped this man, was recognized by the watchman through the style of his running, but left the Ethiopian to disclose the worst (2 S 18^{19-32}). It may be the same person who appears later as Solomon's son-in-law and commissioner in Naphtali (1 K 4^{15}). J. T.—**R. A. B.**

AHIMAN (' my brother is a gift ').—**1.** One of the sons of Anak who terrified the spies at Hebron, Nu 13^{22}. The three clans, of which this was one, were either destroyed by Judah (Jg 1^{10}) or expelled by the clan Caleb (Jos 15^{14}). **2.** A family of Levites who had charge of that gate of the Temple through which the King entered, 1 Ch 9^{17f}.

AHIMELECH (' my brother is Melekh,' *i.e.* ' King,' a divine title).—**1.** Son of Ahitub, and grandson of Phinehas. He either succeeded his brother Ahijah in the priesthood, or was the same person under another name (1 S $14^{3, 18}$). For his fate see DOEG. **2.** Grandson of **1,** if 1 Ch $24^{3, 31}$ are correct, for in 2 S 8^{17} and 1 Ch 18^{16} 24^{6} the names of Abiathar and Ahimelech may have been transposed. **3.** A Hittite who joined David when a fugitive (1 S 26^{6}). D. R. Ap.-T.

AHIMOTH (' my brother is death ').—A Kohathite Levite, 1 Ch 6^{25}. Cf MAHATH, **1.**

AHINADAB (' my brother is noble ').—Son of Iddo, one of Solomon's twelve commissariat officers, 1 K 4^{14}.

AHINOAM (' my brother is delight ').—**1.** Daughter of Ahimaaz and wife of Saul, 1 S 14^{50}. **2.** A Jezreelitess whom David married after Michal had been taken from him. She was the mother of David's firstborn, Amnon (q.v.), 1 S 25^{43} 27^{3} 30^{5}, 2 S 2^{2} 3^{2}, 1 Ch 3^{1}.

AHIO (' fraternal ').—**1.** Son of Abinadab, **3,** and brother of Uzzah. He helped to drive the cart on which the Ark was brought from Abinadab's house to Jerusalem, 2 S 6^{3f}, 1 Ch 13^{7}. **2.** A son of Jeiel, and brother of Kish, the father of Saul, 1 Ch 8^{31} 9^{37}. **3.** A Benjamite, 1 Ch 8^{14}.

AHIRA (' my brother is evil ').—Tribal leader representing Naphtali at the census in the wilderness and on other occasions, Nu 1^{15} 2^{29} $7^{78, 83}$ 10^{27}.

AHIRAM.—The eponym of a Benjamite family, the Ahiramites, Nu 26^{38}. The name occurs in the corrupt forms **Ehi** (Gn 46^{21}) and **Aharah** (1 Ch 8^{1}).

AHISAMACH (' my brother has supported ').—A Danite, father of Oholiab, Ex 31^{6} 35^{34} 38^{23}.

AHISHAHAR (' brother of the dawn ').—A Benjamite, 1 Ch 7^{10}.

AHISHAR (? ' my brother has sung ').—Superintendent of Solomon's household, 1 K 4^{6}.

AHITHOPHEL.—David's counsellor (2 S 15^{12}, 1 Ch 27^{33}), whose advice was deemed infallible (2 S 16^{23}). Being perhaps Bathsheba's grandfather (see ELIAM, **2**), he may have been alienated by David's conduct (11^{3} 23^{34}), and so readily joined Absalom (15^{12}). Ahithophel advised the prince to take possession of the royal harem, thus declaring his father's deposition, and begged for a body of men with whom he might at once overtake and destroy the fugitive monarch (17^{1-3}). Hushai thwarted this move (17^{11}). Disgusted at the collapse of his influence, and foreseeing that this lack of enterprise meant the failure of the insurrection, Ahithophel withdrew, set his affairs in order, and hanged himself (17^{23}).

AHITOB, 1 Es 8^{2}, 2 Es 1^{1} (RV).—See Ahitub, **3.**

AHITUB (' my brother is goodness ').—**1.** Son of Phinehas and grandson of Eli, the father of Ahijah or Ahimelech, the priest who was put to death by Saul, 1 S 14^{3} 22$^{9, 20}$. **2.** According to 2 S 8^{17}, 1 Ch 18^{16} the father, according to 1 Ch 9^{11}, Neh 11^{11} the grandfather, of Zadok the priest, who was contemporary with David and Solomon. It is very doubtful, however, whether this has not arisen from a copyist's error. The text of 2 S 8^{17} should probably run: ' And Zadok and Abiathar the son of Ahimelech, the son of Ahitub.' See Zadok, **1. 3.** Even more doubt attaches to another Ahitub, father of another Zadok, 1 Ch 6^{11f}; cf 1 Es 8^{2}, 2 Es 1^{1}, in both of which AV has **Achitob** and RV **Ahitob. 4.** An ancestor of Judith, Jth 8^{1} (AV **Acitho**).

AHLAB.—A city of Asher, Jg 1^{31}. Possibly Ahlab and Helbah in this verse are to be identified with one another and with **Mahalab** (q.v.).

AHLAI (? ' O! Would that! ').—**1.** The daughter of Sheshan, of the tribe of Judah, 1 Ch 2^{31}, cf v. ^{34}. **2.** The father of Zabad, one of David's heroes, 1 Ch 11^{41}.

AHOAH.—A Benjamite, son of Bela, 1 Ch 8^{4}; but LXX^{B} has Ahijah (see Ahijah, **6**). The patronymic **Ahohite** occurs in 2 S 23^{9} (AV, RV; but RSV has ' son of Ahohi ') v. ^{28}, 1 Ch 11$^{12, 29}$ 27^{4}.

AHOHI.—In 2 S 23^{9} RSV renders ' son of Ahohi,' where AV has ' the Ahohite ' and RV ' the son of an Ahohite.' AV rendering is here to be preferred. See Ahoah.

AHOLAH, AHOLIAB, AHOLIBAH, AHOLIBAMAH.—The AV forms of the correct RV and RSV Oholah, Oholiab, Oholibah, Oholibamah (q.v.).

AHUMAI.—A descendant of Judah, 1 Ch 4^{2}.

AHUZAM, 1 Ch 4^{6} (AV).—See Ahuzzam.

AHUZZAM (' possessor ').—A man of Judah, 1 Ch 4^{6} (AV **Ahuzam**).

AHUZZATH (' possession ').—The friend of Abimelech, the Philistine of Gerar, mentioned on the occasion when the latter made a league with Isaac at Beersheba, Gn 26^{26}. The position of ' king's friend ' may possibly have been an official one, and the title a technical one (cf 1 K 4^{5}, 1 Ch 27^{33}). The rendering of LXX gives a different conception, that of *pronubus*, or friend of the bridegroom.

AHZAI (' Y″ hath grasped ').—A priest, Neh 11^{13} (AV **Ahasai**); called **Jahzerah,** 1 Ch 9^{12}.

AI.—**1.** A place between which and Bethel Abraham camped before (Gn 12^{8}) and after (13^{3}) his sojourn in Egypt. The repulse of the Israelite attempt on the place (Jos 7$^{2-5}$) led to the exposure of the crime of Achan, which being expiated, Ai was taken by a ruse and destroyed (8$^{1-28}$). It is perhaps the **Aiath** of Isaiah's description of the advance of the Assyrians (10^{28}), and the **Aija** mentioned in Nehemiah's account of the resettlement of Benjamites after the restoration from Exile (11^{31}, Ezr 2^{28}), though these places may be identified with *Kh. Ḥayyân*, about a mile from Ai. Located ' to the E. of Bethel ' (Gn 12^{8}), with which it is generally associated (*e.g.* Jos 12^{9}), it is probably to be identified with *et-Tell*, meaning, like Heb. *hā-ʿay*, ' the ruined mound.' Here excavations by Mme Marquet-Krause established that the place flourished, with palace, sanctuary, and impressive fortifications, in the Early Bronze Age (3rd millennium B.C.), when it had contacts with Egypt of the Pyramid Age, but lay derelict from *c* 2000 to *c* 1150. This raises the problem of the authenticity of the Hebrew tradition regarding the capture of Ai (Jos 8$^{1-23}$), which can only be solved by supposing that the men of Bethel occupied the derelict site to resist the Hebrews advancing up the pass from Jericho. The account in Jos 7^{3} suggests that Ai was not a formidable obstacle.

2. A wholly distinct place, mentioned in a prophecy against the Ammonites, Jer 49^{3} (where it is possibly a scribal error for *Ar*, or more probably *shôdhēdh ʿālāh*, ' the plunderer is gone up ' should be read for MT *shuddᵉdhāh ʿai*, ' Ai is plundered ').

R. A. S. M.—**J. Gr.**

AIAH (' falcon ').—**1.** A Horite, son of Zibeon, Gn 36^{24}, 1 Ch 1^{40}. **2.** Father of Rizpah, Saul's concubine, 2 S 3^{7} 21$^{8, 10f}$.

AIATH, Is 10^{28}; **AIJA,** Neh 11^{31}.—See Ai, **1.**

AIJALON.—**1.** A town allotted to, but not occupied by, Dan (Jos 19^{42}, Jg 1^{35}). It was assigned to the Levites (Jos 21^{24}) and is named as a city of refuge in Ephraim. After the Disruption of the Kingdom it was fortified by Rehoboam as a frontier post (2 Ch 11^{10}) and was later taken by the Philistines (2 Ch 28^{18}).

Aijalon is mentioned in the Amarna Tablets and the list of Sheshonk's conquests in Palestine, and is to be identified with *Yâlō* in the Valley of Aijalon at the lower end of the Pass of Beth-horon, 3 miles N. of the old Jerusalem-Jaffa road and 14 miles W. of Jerusalem. Late Bronze Age remains are found on the village mound, and at the adjacent mound *Tell el-Qōqaʿ* occupation is carried back to *c* 2000 B.C.

2. The burial-place of the Judge Elon in Zebulun (Jg 12^{12}), and possibly identical with Elon, which is named with Sered and Jahleel (Gn 46^{14} and Nu 26^{26}) as a family of Zebulun. The fact that Sered and Jahleel are also place-names suggests that Elon (or Aijalon) was also a place-name. *Khirbet el-Lôn*, a Late Bronze Age site in the Plain of the *Baṭṭûf*, may be Aijalon of Zebulun. Alternatively, on the assumption that Aijalon is a broken plural of *'ēlôn*, ' terebinth-tree,' the site may be located at *Tell el-Buṭmeh* (' mound of the terebinth '), also in the *Baṭṭûf*. W. E.—**J. Gr.**

AIJELETH (HASH)-SHAHAR, Ps 22 title (AV, RV).—See Psalms, **2.**

AIN.—**1.** A town in the neighbourhood of Riblah (Nu 34^{11}); the site is unknown. **2.** A town in Judah, Jos 15^{32}, 1 Ch 4^{32}, where Ain and Rimmon should be taken together, see En-Rimmon. **3.** A Levitical city, Jos 21^{16}; but we should probably read **Ashan** (q.v.), with 1 Ch 6^{59}.

AIN.—The sixteenth letter of the Hebrew alphabet, and so used to introduce the sixteenth part of Ps 119, every verse of which begins with this letter.

AIRUS, 1 Es 5^{31} (AV).—See Reaiah, **3.**

AKAN.—A descendant of Esau, Gn 36^{27}; in 1 Ch 1^{42} called **Jaakan** (AV Jakan).

AKATAN, 1 Es 8^{38} (RV).—See Hakkatan.

AKELDAMA (AV **Aceldama**).—The name of the field allegedly bought by Judas Iscariot and the scene of his suicide (Ac 1^{19}). It is quite correctly interpreted there as ' field of blood ' (Aramaic *ḥᵃkal dᵉmāʾ*). The name is given only in translated form in Mt 27^{3}, where the field is bought by the Temple authorities with the discarded blood-money and devoted to the burial of strangers. Matthew seems to know that it was once a potter's field and connects therewith the prophetic passage Zech 11$^{12-13}$, wrongly attributing it to Jeremiah. Antoninus (*c* 570) describes Akeldama as near the pool of Siloam; Arculf, a century later, as a place south of Jerusalem's western ridge (wrongly called Sion in Christian history), where corpses were still cast in his day. Since the Crusades a definite place has been pointed out on the E. side of the *Wâdī er-Rabābi*, and the remains of a charnel house of those days still exist there. It is called *ḥaqq ed-Damm* in Arabic, *i.e.* ' field of blood.' The connexion of the Aramaic name with the actions reported in Matthew and Acts cannot be regarded as certain. E. G. K.

AKHENATEN (*c* 1366–50 B.C.), later name of Amenophis IV., son and successor of Amenophis III. He initiated a religious reform that led eventually to the banning of the old gods of Egypt and the substitution of a single god, the Aten or Sun's Disk. It is probable, though still disputed, that he had a co-regency of nine or eleven years with his father. His wife was Nefertiti, by whom he had six daughters. In his fifth or sixth year he moved his capital to a new city, Akhetaten, 'the Horizon of the Disk' (the modern *Tell el-Amarna*), began the systematic elimination of the name of Amun from the monuments and changed his own name to Akhenaten, 'It is well with the Disk.' In the ninth year of the reign the movement became even more intolerant and extremist, but about the fourteenth year Akhenaten quarrelled with Nefertiti, probably because even he now realized that some compromise with the old religion was necessary, and banished her to a palace to the extreme north of Akhetaten. Akhenaten appointed his half-brother Smenkhkare as co-regent, married him to his eldest daughter Meritaten, and sent him to Thebes where in the next two or three years he effected some slight restoration of the old religion. Akhenaten himself married his third daughter, Ankhesenpaaten, and before his death in his seventeenth year had had a daughter by her. On his death Nefertiti seized power, installed on the throne Tutankhaten, another half-brother (?) of Akhenaten and married him to Ankhesenpaaten. Within about three years Tutankhaten abandoned Amarna, returned to Thebes and the old religion and changed his name to Tutankhamun.

The old views that Akhenaten was a man far in advance of his time, that Atenism was the first real monotheism and due to foreign or Semitic influence are all untenable. In origin and outlook Atenism was Egyptian, except in its intolerance. The movement was fundamentally political in origin, the culmination of a century long struggle to curb the power of the state priesthoods. Atenism was a form of the old solar cult, emphasizing the life-giving power of the sun graphically depicted by descending rays ending in hands that offer the sign of life. King and Aten are very intimately linked, they share the same regnal years and jubilees, the King is high priest and sole intermediary between men and Aten. But having swept away the old religion, Akhenaten had created a vacuum which he did not or could not fill: he produced a beautiful hymn, but no teaching, philosophy or ethic, and because Atenism thus gave the people nothing, it gained no hold and failed. H. W. F.

AKKAD (ACCAD), AKKADIANS.—*Akkad(u)* is the Semitic equivalent of the Sumerian **Agadê** (q.v.), the capital of the founder of the first Semitic empire. It was probably in consequence of this that it gave its name to Northern Babylonia, the Semitic language of which came to be known as *Akkadu* or 'Akkadian.' In the early days of cuneiform decipherment 'Akkadian' was the name usually applied to the non-Semitic language of primitive Babylonia now known to be Sumerian. When Babylonia became a united monarchy, its rulers took the title of 'kings of Sumer and Akkad' in Semitic, 'Kengi and Uri' in Sumerian. In Gn 10^{10} Accad is the city, not the country to which it gave its name.
A. H. S.—**C. J. M. W.**

AKKOS, 1 Es 5^{38} (RV).—See Hakkoz, **1.**

AKKUB ('cunning').—**1.** A son of Eloenai and descendant of David, 1 Ch 3^{24}. **2.** A Levite, one of the porters at the E. gate of the Temple; the eponym of a family that returned from the Exile, 1 Ch 9^{17}, Ezr 2^{42}, Neh 7^{45} 11^{19} 12^{25}, 1 Es 5^{28} (AV **Dacobi,** RV **Dacubi**). **3.** The name of a family of Nethinim (q.v.) who returned with Zerubbabel, Ezr 2^{45}, 1 Es 5^{30} (AV **Acua,** RV **Acud**). Omitted in Neh 7. **4.** A Levite who helped to expound the Law, Neh 8^{7}, 1 Es 9^{48} (AV, RV **Jacubus**).

AKRABATTENE (1 Mac 5^{3}).—The region in Idumaea near Akrabbim (AV **Arabattine,** RV **Akrabattine**). See Map 10.

AKRABATTINE, 1 Mac 5^{3} (RV).—See Akrabattene.

AKRABBIM, ASCENT OF.—This name, 'ascent of the scorpions' was given to a pass in a very barren region on the south side of the Dead Sea, Nu 34^{4}, Jos 15^{3} (AV **Maaleh-acrabbim**), Jg 1^{36}; modern *Naqb eṣ-Ṣafā.*

ALABASTER.—See Jewels and Precious Stones.

ALAMETH, 1 Ch 7^{8} (AV).—See Alemeth, **1.**

ALAMOTH, Ps 46 title, 1 Ch 15^{20}.—See Psalms, **2.**

ALBEIT.—Albeit is a contraction for 'all be it,' and means 'although it be.' It occurs in Ezk 13^{7} (AV, RV), Phn ^{19} (AV), and in the Apocrypha (AV, RV).

ALCIMUS (the Greek for 'valiant' suggested by the Hebrew *Eliakim,* 'God sets up') was son or nephew of Jose ben-Joeser, pupil to Antigonus of Soco (190 B.C.). Antiochus v. (Eupator), king of Syria, appointed him high priest (162 B.C.). Either because he was not of high-priestly family (though of the stock of Aaron, 1 Mac 7^{14}), or, more probably, from his Hellenizing tendencies, his appointment was stoutly opposed by Judas Maccabaeus, and received but scanty recognition at Jerusalem. Demetrius Soter, cousin and successor to Antiochus, in response to Alcimus's solicitations, reinstated him by the means of Nicanor, the Syrian general. He now received, moreover, considerable local support from the Hellenizing party. It was not, however, till the defeat and death of Judas at Elasa that he was in a position to commence his Hellenizing measures, and shortly afterwards he died of paralysis (160 B.C.). A. W. S.

ALCOVE.—RVm in Nu 25^{8} for RV 'pavilion,' AV 'tent,' RSV 'inner room.' See Pavilion.

ALEMA.—A city in Gilead, 1 Mac 5^{26}; possibly **Helam** (q.v.).

ALEMETH.—**1.** A son of Becher, a Benjamite, 1 Ch 7^{8} (AV **Alameth**). **2.** A descendant of Saul and son of Jehoaddah (1 Ch 8^{36}) or of Jarah (1 Ch 9^{42}). **3.** A Levitical city of Benjamin, 1 Ch 6^{60} (RV **Allemeth**); called **Almon** in Jos 21^{18}; modern *'Almît.*

ALEPH.—First letter of Hebrew alphabet, and so used to introduce the first part of Ps 119, every verse of which begins with this letter.

ALEXANDER.—**1.** Son of Simon of Cyrene; like his brother Rufus, evidently a well-known man (Mk 15^{21} only). **2.** One of the high-priestly family (Ac 4^{6}). **3.** The would-be spokesman of the Jews in the riot at Ephesus, which endangered them as well as the Christians (Ac 19^{33}); not improbably the same as the coppersmith (2 Ti 4^{14}) who did St. Paul 'great harm,' and who was probably an Ephesian Jew; possibly the same as the Alexander of 1 Ti 1^{20} (especially if 2 Ti preceded 1 Ti, as B. S. Easton held), in which case we may regard him as an apostate Christian who had relapsed into Judaism. (See Hymenaeus.) A. J. M.—**F. C. G.**

ALEXANDER BALAS.—A low-born youth called Balas, living in Smyrna, was put forward by the enemies of Demetrius i. as son of Antiochus iv., king of Syria. In their struggle for the throne the rivals sought to outbid each other for the support of Jonathan the Maccabee, who elected to side with Alexander, and was appointed high priest by him (153 B.C.). Jonathan defeated Apollonius, one of the generals of Demetrius, and received still further honours (1 Mac 10). But Alexander Balas cared more for sensual pleasures than for kingly duties: his father-in-law Ptolemy turned against him, and Alexander, fleeing to Arabia, was assassinated there (1 Mac 11^{17}). J. T.

ALEXANDER THE GREAT.—Alexander iii. of Macedonia (356–323 B.C.) was the son of Philip ii. and Olympias of Epirus. His tutor was Aristotle, whose influence on the young prince is hard to estimate. Certainly there were some things in the philosopher's teaching (*e.g.* the nature of barbarians, who were born to be slaves) which Alexander had to unlearn (see W. W. Tarn, *Alexander the Great,* 54 f), and some which he should have unlearned but did not (*e.g.* the king as 'god' among men). Alexander succeeded to the throne in 336 and two years later began his invasion of the Persian empire. His first objective was the liberation of the Greek cities in Asia Minor, after which he moved farther east and defeated the Persians at Issus (October 333), near the NE. corner of the Mediterranean; then he

 ALEXANDRIA

turned southward to Egypt, then NE. toward Mesopotamia, where he finally defeated the Persian Great King, Darius III., at Gaugamela in October 331. After the conquest of Babylon his eastward march continued through Media, Parthia, Bactria, and Sogdiana, and then down the Indus to the sea and thence back to Babylon, where he died in June 323. His impact upon the Near and Middle East began a new era in history, the 'Alexandrine' or better the 'Hellenistic' age, when Greek language, commodities, art, customs, and ideas, including religious and theological conceptions, penetrated the whole inhabited world of western Asia; by the same route Asiatic ideas penetrated the West and affected the whole development of civilization from the 4th cent. B.C. onwards. His claim to divinity was partly, perhaps largely, political; for he aimed to succeed and not merely to supplant both the Persian Great King and also the Egyptian Pharaoh (the latter was always known as a son of a god, Amon Rē). This claim marked a stage in the development of the Hellenistic ruler cult, and was eventually reflected in Roman emperor worship, which was the political-religious cultus offered the 'divine' world-ruler.

His reputed interest in Judaism and his supposed visit to Jerusalem were a subject of later speculation and fancy. A Jewish legend reported by Josephus and the Talmud, relates that while the renowned Macedonian conqueror was besieging Tyre (333 B.C.), rival embassies from the Jews and the Samaritans solicited his protection. At the close of the siege he set out for Jerusalem, and was met outside by the entire population, with the high priest at their head. Recognizing the latter as the person who had appeared to him in a dream and promised him victory, the king prostrated himself. He then entered the city, offered sacrifice, was shown the passages in Daniel relating to himself, granted the people unmolested use of their customs, promised to befriend their eastern settlements, and welcomed Jews to his army (*Ant.* XI. viii. 4 ff [321 ff]). The objections to this story are: (1) that although there are references to Alexander and his successors in Daniel (2^{40ff} 7^{7} $8^{5, 8, 21}$ 11^{3f}), they were not written till the 2nd cent. B.C.; and (2) that the accounts given by Arrian and Quintus Curtius do not mention these events. It is also most likely that when Josephus declares that Alexander gave to the Jews in Alexandria equal privileges with the Macedonians (*c. Ap.* ii. 4 [35]), he is anticipating by some years what happened under the Ptolemies.

The deep impression made by Alexander's successes is shown by numerous other legends connected with his name in later Jewish literature. But his real importance to the Biblical student consists in this—his conquest of the Near and Middle East brought the Jews, along with all the other nations from the Mediterranean to the Indus, into contact with Greek literature and thought; and his inauguration of the new era of Hellenism, in this area, became the most important feature in the world-wide *praeparatio evangelica*. Perhaps his next greatest achievement was the foundation of the city of Alexandria, at the mouth of the Nile: a city which provided a centre for the dissemination of Hellenistic culture for over six centuries (see Map 16). **J. T.—F. C. G.**

ALEXANDRIA was founded (332 B.C.) by Alexander the Great after his conquest of Egypt. Recognizing the inconvenience caused by the want of a harbour for 600 miles along the shore, he selected as the site of a new port the village of Rhacotis, lying in the extreme west of the Nile delta on a strip of land between Lake Mareotis and the sea. This he united to the little island of Pharos by a huge mole about a mile long, and thus he formed two splendid havens, which speedily became the commercial meeting-place of Africa, Asia, and Europe. The city was laid out in shape like the outspread cloak of a Macedonian soldier; in circumference about 15 miles; and it was divided into quarters by a magnificent street nearly 5 miles long and 100 feet wide, running from E. to W., and crossed by another of somewhat lesser dimensions from N. to S. In the great palace area the corpse of Alexander was given a tomb by Ptolemy, after he took it from Perdiccas. The Ptolemies, who succeeded to the Egyptian portion of Alexander's divided empire, made Alexandria their capital, and by their extensive building operations rendered the city famous for the magnificence and beauty of its public edifices. The city had five quarters named after the first five letters of the alphabet. The Jews lived in the quarter of the Macedonians ('*Delta*') in Josephus' time. Beside the Royal Palace the Royal Mausoleum, the Temple of Neptune, the Great Theatre, the Gymnasium, the Hippodrome (3 Mac 4^{11} 5^{46}), and the vast Necropolis, Alexandria possessed three other structures for which it was celebrated. (1) The *Museum*, which was not a place where collections were laid out for instruction, but a spot where the fine arts, science, and literature were studied. The Museum of Alexandria became in course of time practically the centre of the intellectual life of the world. It answered very largely to what we associate with the idea of a great modern university. It had its staff of State-paid professors, its professorial dining-hall, its shaded cloisters, where eager students from all parts of the world walked about, listening to lectures from men like Euclid, Eratosthenes, and Hipparchus. (2) The *Library*, which was the greatest treasure of the city, was founded by the first Ptolemy. His successors increased the number of volumes till the collection embraced upwards of 700,000 MSS, in which were inscribed the intellectual efforts of Greece, Rome, Asia Minor, Palestine, and even India. The value of this unrivalled collection was immense. The Library was in two portions; and, in the siege of Alexandria by Julius Caesar, the part stored in the Museum was burned, a loss, however, which was largely made up by the presentation to Cleopatra, by Mark Antony, of the Royal Library of Pergamum. The other portion was stored in the Serapeum, which in 1895 was discovered to have been situated where 'Pompey's Pillar' now stands. Historians are uncertain whether this celebrated Library was destroyed in A.D. 391 by Bishop Theophilus or in A.D. 641 by the Caliph Omar. (3) The third structure which attracted the attention of the world to Alexandria was the *Pharos* (Lighthouse), erected by Ptolemy II. Philadelphus, on the island which had been joined to the mainland by Alexander. Rising in storeys of decreasing dimensions to a height of 450–490 feet, adorned with white marble columns, balustrades, and statues, it was justly reckoned one of the 'Seven Wonders of the World.' Though it was destroyed by an earthquake in A.D. 1303, it has nevertheless exercised a permanent influence on mankind. The idea of humanity to the mariner which it embodied was accepted by almost every civilized nation, and the thousands of lighthouses throughout the world to-day can all be traced to the erection of this first Pharos.

In its times of greatest prosperity, Alexandria had a population of between 800,000 and 1,000,000. Trade, amusement, and learning attracted to it inhabitants from every quarter. It was an amalgam of East and West. The alertness and versatility of the Greeks were here united with the gravity, conservatism, and dreaminess of the Orientals. Alexandria became, next to Rome, the largest and most splendid city in the world. Amongst its polyglot community, the Jews formed no inconsiderable portion. Jewish colonists had settled in Egypt in large numbers after the destruction of Jerusalem (Jer 42^{14}), and during the Persian period their numbers greatly increased. The Ptolemies, with one exception, favoured them, and assigned a special quarter of the city to them. More than an eighth of the population of Egypt was Jewish. Their business instincts brought to them the bulk of the trade of the country. They practically controlled the vast export of wheat. Some had great ships with which they traded over all the Mediterranean. St. Paul twice sailed in a ship of Alexandria (Ac 27^{6} 28^{11}). The Jews were under their own ethnarch, who was called 'Alabarch,' and observed their own domestic and religious customs. Their great central synagogue was an immense and most imposing structure, where all the trade guilds sat together, and the seventy elders were accommodated in seventy splendidly jewelled chairs of state.

It was in Alexandria that one of the most important events in the history of religion took place, when the Hebrew Scriptures were translated into the Greek tongue. The *Letter of Aristeas*, written 130–100 B.C., gives a legendary account of this undertaking. But it is undisputed that during the reigns of the earlier Lagidae (somewhere between 250 and 132 B.C.) the 'Septuagint' made its appearance. It is certainly not the product of a syndicate of translators working harmoniously, as Jewish tradition asserted. The work is of very unequal merit, the Pentateuch (q.v.) being the best done, while some of the later books are wretchedly translated. The translation was regarded by the Jews with mingled feelings—execrated by one section as a desecration of the holy oracles, extolled by another section as the means by which the truth and beauty of the Law and the Prophets could be appreciated for the first time by the Greek-speaking Gentile world. The LXX became a most valuable preparation for Christianity. It familiarized the heathen nations with the God of righteousness as He had been revealed to the Jews. It diluted some Semitic ideas with more acceptable Greek ones. It formed the Bible of the early Church. In the Eastern Church to-day it is the only orthodox text of the OT.

The wars of the Ptolemies with the Seleucids at Antioch are described in Dn 11. Ptolemy II. *Philadelphus* left his mark on Palestine in the cities of Philadelphia (=Rabbath-ammon, Dt 3^{11}), Ptolemais (Ac 21^{7}=Acco, Jg 1^{31}), Philoteria, etc. Under Ptolemy III. *Euergetes* I. (247–222 B.C.) the famous 'stele of Canopus' was inscribed. With Ptolemy IV. *Philopator* the dynasty began to decline, and his alleged oppressions of the Jews are narrated in 3 Maccabees. Under Ptolemy V. *Epiphanes* the Alexandrian supremacy over Palestine was exchanged 198 B.C. for that of Antiochus III. *the Great* (Dn 11^{14-17}). The ten succeeding Ptolemies were distinguished for almost nothing but their effeminacy, folly, luxury, and cruelty. The city increased in wealth, but sank more and more in political power. Julius Cæsar stormed Alexandria in 47 B.C., and after a brief spell of false splendour under Cleopatra, it fell after the battle of Actium (31 B.C.) into the hands of the Romans, and its fortunes were henceforth merged with those of the Empire. Egypt as a whole became the private possession of the emperor.

But while its political power was thus passing away, it was developing an intellectual greatness destined to exercise a profound influence through succeeding centuries. Among its Jewish population there had arisen a new school which sought to amalgamate Hebrew tradition and Greek philosophy, and to make the OT yield up Platonic and Stoic doctrines. This attempted fusion of Hebraism and Hellenism was begun by Aristobulus, and reached its climax in Philo, a contemporary of Jesus Christ. The Jews found in the Gentile writings many beautiful and inspiring thoughts. They could logically defend their own proud claim to be the sole depositaries and custodians of Divine truth only by asserting that every rich and luminous Greek expression was borrowed from their Scriptures. Plato and Pythagoras, they declared, were deeply in debt to Moses. The Greeks were merely reproducers of Hebrew ethics, of Hebrew religious and moral conceptions. The next step was to re-write their own Scriptures in terms of Greek philosophy, and the most simple way of doing this was by an elaborate system of allegory. Philo carried the allegorizing of the OT to such an extent that he was able to read philosophy into the most matter-of-fact narratives of the patriarchs and their wives. This allegorical method of interpretation was destined to have a large influence in Christian Church history. We read of a 'synagogue of the Alexandrians' in Jerusalem, furiously hostile to St. Stephen with his plain declaration of facts (Ac 6^{9}). Apollos of Alexandria (Ac 18^{24-28}) needed to be 'more accurately instructed' in Christian doctrine, though we have no direct evidence that he was a disciple of Philo. The Epistle to the Hebrews shows traces of Alexandrian influence, and there are evidences that St. Paul was not unfamiliar with Alexandrian hermeneutics and terminology (cf Gal 4^{24-31}). But there is no proof that St. Paul ever visited Alexandria. He seems to have refrained from going thither because the gospel had already reached the city (cf Ro 15^{20}). Eusebius credits St. Mark with the introduction of Christianity into Egypt—a legend which survived for centuries. In the 2nd and 3rd cents. Alexandria was the intellectual capital of Christendom. The Alexandrian school of theology was made lustrous by the names of Pantaenus, Clement, and especially Origen, who, while continuing the allegorical tradition, strove to show that Christian doctrine enshrined and realized the dreams and yearnings of Greek philosophy. The Gnostics (q.v.), Basilides, and Valentinus also flourished here. Alexandria became more and more the stronghold of the Christian faith. Here Athanasius defended *contra mundum* the true Divinity of Christ in the Nicene controversy, and the city's influence on Christian theology has been profound. In A.D. 641, Alexandria was occupied by the Caliph Omar's general Amr ibn el-Asi. Omar did not permit it to be a seat of government any longer, but established a more easily controlled one at Fosṭaṭ (Old Cairo). Alexandria now began to decline, and the discovery in 1497 of the new route to the East *via* the Cape of Good Hope almost destroyed its trade. At the beginning of the 19th cent. Alexandria was a mere village. To-day it is again a large and flourishing city, with a population of 928,237 (1956), and its port is one of the busiest on the Mediterranean shore. G. A. F. K.—**E. G. K.**

ALGUM.—See ALMUG.

ALIAH.—A chief of Edom, 1 Ch 1^{51}; called **Alvah,** Gn 36^{40}.

ALIAN.—An Edomite, son of Shobal, 1 Ch 1^{40}; called **Alvan,** Gn 36^{23}.

ALIEN.—See NATIONS, STRANGER.

ALLAMMELECH.—A town of Asher, Jos 19^{26}; site unknown.

ALLAR.—Name given to one of the leaders of the Jews who could not show their pedigree at the return under Zerubbabel, 1 Es 5^{36} (RV; AV **Aalar**). But 'Charaathalan (q.v.) leading them, and Allar' is due to some perversion of the original, and RSV reads 'Cherub, Addan and Immer,' as in Ezr 2^{59} (cf Neh 7^{16}); these are three places from which Jews returned.

ALLEGORY.—See PARABLE.

ALLELUIA.—See HALLELUJAH.

ALLEMETH, 1 Ch 6^{60} (RV).—See ALEMETH, **3.**

ALLIANCE.—During the patriarchal age Abraham is pictured as making an alliance of friendship with Abimelech (Gn 21^{22ff}) at Beersheba; this is probably a popular aetiology on the name Beersheba ('well of swearing an oath'). The pact between Jacob and Laban may be similarly explained (cf Galeed—'heap of witness,' Gn 31^{44ff}). Abraham stood in tribal alliance with certain Canaanites (Eshcol and Aner, 14^{13}).

Formal alliances between nations appear under the monarchy. Such was Solomon's treaty with Hiram (1 K 5^{1-12}; cf 9^{10-14}). His marriage with Pharaoh's daughter undoubtedly had political implications as well (3^{1}; cf 9^{16}). Such a policy of treaty through inter-marriage is apparent in Ahab's marriage with Jezebel of the Sidonian royal house (16^{31}). A marriage alliance between the house of David and that of the Omrids is also attested (2 K 8^{16-18}). Both kingdoms sought alliance with Benhadad of Damascus at one time (1 K 15^{19}), and later Ahab was in league with him (20^{34}). The later kings of these states, Pekah and Rezin respectively, made an alliance against Judah (2 K 16^{5}, Is 7^{1}) as a coalition against the Assyrians.

During the Assyrian Empire period both the Northern and the Southern Kingdoms sought to ward off Assyrian domination through alliance with Damascus and/or

Egypt. This led to the quick destruction of the Northern state (2 K 17$^{1-6}$), while the Judaean state miraculously survived. Reliance on Egypt on Judah's part was of little help, however (a ' broken reed of a staff '), as far as the Assyrians were concerned (18$^{21-24}$). The prophets were unanimously opposed to such alliances (Dt 17^{16}, Hos 8^{9}, Is 20. 30, Jer 2$^{18, 36}$), advocating throughout a policy of isolation and reliance on Yahweh alone.

After the loss of national independence alliance with foreign states were of course impossible until the period of resurgent independence under the Maccabees, when alliances with Rome were made (1 Mac 8^{17}, 15^{16}). Cf also COVENANT. J. W. W.

ALLOM, 1 Es 5^{34} (AV).—See AMI.

ALLON.—1. A Simeonite, 1 Ch 4^{37}. **2.** Head of a family of Solomon's servants, 1 Es 5^{34} (RV ; AV **Allom**) ; RSV has **Ami** (q.v.). **3.** Jos 19^{33} (AV) ; see ZAANANNIM.

ALLON-BACHUTH, Gn 35^{8} (AV).—See ALLON-BACUTH.

ALLON-BACUTH (' oak of weeping ').—The place where Deborah, Rebekah's nurse, was buried, Gn 35^{8} (AV **Allon-bachuth**) ; it was near Bethel, but the site is unknown.

ALLOW.—To ' allow ' generally means in AV ' to approve,' as Ro 7^{15} ' that which I do I allow not.' But in Ac 24^{15} it has the modern sense, *admit*. In RSV the word bears its modern meaning.

ALLOY, Is 1^{25} (RSV, RVm ; AV, RV ' tin ').—See MINING AND METALS.

ALL TO BRAKE, Jg 9^{53} (AV).—Phrase meaning ' altogether broke ' (RSV ' crushed).' The ' all ' is for ' altogether,' as in 1 K 14^{10}, ' until it is all gone ' ; and the ' to ' is not the sign of the infin., but an adverb like German *zer*, meaning ' thoroughly.' Cf Chaucer, *Knight's Tale*, 2759 : ' His breast to-broken with his sadil bowe.'

ALMIGHTY is the regular rendering of *Shaddai*, a term which occurs forty-five times in the OT, six times qualifying *El* (God) and thirty-nine times (thirty-one of these in Job) standing by itself. In the Hexateuch its use is almost wholly confined to P, according to which source it is the name by which Yahweh revealed himself to the patriarchs (Ex 6^{3}, cf Gn 17^{1} 35^{11}) ' God Almighty ' AV, RV, RSV). LXX usually renders by *Pantokratōr* (' ruler of all ') but six times it renders by the rather fanciful ' he who is sufficient.' But in Genesis *El Shaddai* is always represented in LXX by a pronoun, ' my (or thy) God ' : in Ezk 10^{5} it is merely transliterated. Other suggested renderings are ' The Destroyer,' *i.e.* ' the Storm-God,' ' the Pourer,' *i.e.* ' the Rain-God,' ' the Mountain ' (cf ' Rock ' as a divine title in Dt 32$^{4, 18, 30, 31}$), or ' Lord.' The ' Mountain ' seems most probable and Albright judges this ' explanation of the name inexpugnable ' (*FSAC*, p. 326). In Babylon ' the Great Mountain ' (*Shadu rabu*) is a common title of Bel : *El Shaddai* would thus be equivalent to Akkadian *Ilu-shadu-ni*, ' El is my mountain.' ' The symbol of a mountain was often used in antiquity to point to the might and awe-inspiring majesty of a particular deity ' (G. E. Wright, *BA*, p. 52). In composition the word occurs in two personal names, Zurishaddai (Nu 1^{6}) and Ammishaddai (Nu 1^{12}), and perhaps also in Shedeur (Nu 1^{5}).

In the NT, with exception of 2 Co 6^{18} (quoted from 2 S 7^{14}) the name is confined to the Apocalypse. That it renders *Shaddai* rather than *Sabaoth* seems proved (in spite of the echo of Is 6^{3} present in Rev 4^{8}) by the fact that it always either stands alone or qualifies ' God,' never ' Lord.' The writer loves to pile up the titles and attributes of God, and among them is that ancient title which carries him back to the patriarchal period, the title *El Shaddai*. H. C. O. L.—**J. Pn.**

AL-MODAD.—Eldest son of Joktan (q.v.), mentioned in Gn 10^{26}, 1 Ch 1^{20}. From the position of the name in the list of ' sons,' he would seem to be located in the south of the Arabian peninsula, but the name cannot be connected with any known region.

ALMON.—A Levitical city of Benjamin, Jos 21^{18} ; modern *'Almît*, between Geba and Anathoth ; called **Alemeth** (q.v.) in 1 Ch 6^{60}.

ALMOND.—The fruit is mentioned in Gn 43^{11}, Ex 25^{33f} 37^{19f} ; the tree in Jer 1^{11}, Ec 12^{5}. The almond (*Amygdalus communis*) is in Palestine the earliest harbinger of spring, bursting into beautiful white blossom late in January in Jerusalem, before its leaves appear. Hence its name and symbolism : *shāḳēdh* (almond) is from a root meaning ' waken ' or ' watch,' and in Jer 1^{11f} there is a play on the name and *shōḳēdh* (' watching '). Probably the whiteness of the blossom from a distance—the delicate pink at the bases of the petals being visible only on closer inspection—suggested its comparison to the white hair of age (Ec 12^{5}). The fruit is a great favourite. It is eaten green before the shell hardens, especially by children, and the ripe kernels are eaten by themselves or made into sweetmeats with sugar. A present of Palestine almonds would be appreciated in Egypt (Gn 43^{11}), as they did not then grow in the latter country. In Gn 30^{37} a different word is used for ' almond ' (AV ' hazel ' is wrong) ; this is the word *lûz*, which is modern Arabic for ' almond.' Luz, the ancient name of Bethel, may be due to the abundance of almond trees in the district in ancient times.

E. W. G. M.—**H. H. R.**

ALMON-DIBLATHAIM.—A station in the journeyings, Nu 33^{46f} ; probably identical with **Beth-diblathaim** (q.v.), mentioned in Jer 48^{22}. Site unknown, possibly modern *Khirbet Deleilât esh-Sherqîyeh*.

ALMS, ALMSGIVING.—' An alms ' (Ac 3^{3}) is something freely given, in money or in kind, to the needy, from motives of love and pity for the recipient, and of gratitude to the Giver of all. Much might be said of the humane spirit which pervades the whole of the Hebrew legislation, and in particular the legislation of Deuteronomy, of which, in this respect, 15^{11} may be taken as the epitome : ' You shall open wide your hand to your brother, to the needy and to the poor, in the land.' The writings of the prophets, also, are full of generous advocacy of the rights of the poor. In the later pre-Christian centuries almsgiving became one of the most prominent of religious duties (Ps 112^{9}, Pr 14^{21} 19^{17} 31^{20}, Job 29^{12f}). The sentiment of the 2nd cent. B.C.—by which time it is significant that the Hebrew word for ' righteousness ' had acquired the special sense of almsgiving as in the true text of Mt 6^{1} (see RSV)—is fully reflected in Sirach (7^{10} 17^{22} 29^{11ff}) and Tobit (see especially 4$^{7-11}$). From this time onwards, indeed, almsgiving was considered to possess an atoning or redemptive efficacy (Sir 3^{30} to 4^{10} 12^{9}, ' almsgiving delivers from death,' cf Dn 4^{27}). After the cessation of sacrifice, almsgiving appears to have ranked among the Jews as the first of religious duties, more meritorious even than prayer and fasting. Arrangements were made by Jewish authorities for the systematic collection and distribution of the alms of the people. An offertory for the poor also formed a recognized part of the synagogue service.

In sectarian circles like the Qumrân group, the practice of almsgiving took a more radical form : when a member was received into the sect, he abandoned to it all that he owned. Almsgiving thus became the foundation of community goods. The group as such undertook the support of its members, with a tendency to restrict the concept of ' poor ' or ' neighbour ' within the limits of the sect.

Almsgiving occupies a prominent place in the teaching of our Lord, who rebukes the ostentatious charity of His day (Mt 6$^{1-4}$), emphasizes the blessedness of giving (Ac 20^{35}), its opportunities (Mt 25^{35ff}), and its highest motive, ' in my name ' (Mk 9^{41}). In the early Christian community of Jerusalem the needs of the poor were effectively supplied, for its members ' had everything in common . . . and there was not a needy person among them ' (Ac 4$^{32, 34}$). Concern for the careful distribution of the Church's alms led to the appointment of special officers (Ac 6^{1ff}). The provision of a poor fund for the aid of the mother Church was much in the thoughts of the Apostle Paul (1 Co 16^{1ff}, 2 Co 9^{1ff}), and until a period within living memory the care of God's poor has continued to be in some countries the almost exclusive privilege of the Christian Church.

A. R. S. K.—**M. Si.**

ALMUG.—A tree mentioned 1 K10^{11f}, imported from Ophir. In 2 Ch 9^{10f} it is called the **algum** tree, while in 2 Ch 2^{8} the algum is mentioned as imported from Lebanon. Both are commonly identified with the red sandalwood (*Pterocarpus santalinus*). Moldenke (*Plants of the Bible*, 188, 209) thinks the almug tree was native in Ophir, and was the red sandalwood, while the algum tree was the eastern savin (*Sabina excelsa*), which is native to Lebanon. This would involve correcting the text in 2 Ch 9^{10f}.

ALNATHAN, 1 Es 8^{44} (AV).—See Elnathan, **3.**

ALOES.—An odoriferous tree, *'ahālîm* Pr 7^{17}, *'ahālôth* Ps 45^{8}, Ca 4^{14}. This is not the bitter aloes of medicine, but the eaglewood (*Aquilaria agallocha*), a lofty tree, native to Cochin-China, Malaya, and Northern India. The fragrant parts are those which are diseased, and the odoriferous qualities are due to the infiltration with resin. The development of this change in the wood is hastened by burying it in the ground. In Nu 24^{6} (RSV ' aloes ' ; AV, RV ' **lign aloes** ') it is unlikely that this tree is meant, since it was not native to the region. A slight emendation of the text would yield ' terebinths,' which some would read.

In Jn 19^{39}, where the word is *aloē*, it is possible that bitter aloes (*Aloe succotrina*) may be meant (so Moldenke, *Plants of the Bible*, 35, 47) ; this was used by the Egyptians in embalming. E. W. G. M.—**H. H. R.**

ALOTH, 1 K 4^{16} (AV).—See Bealoth, **2.**

ALPHA AND OMEGA.—A title of God in Rev 1^{8} 21^{6}, of Jesus in 22^{13} [its presence in 1^{11} AV is not justified by the MSS]. Alpha was the first and Omega the last letter of the Greek alphabet, as Aleph and Taw were the first and last of the Hebrew. In the Talmud, ' From Aleph to Taw ' meant ' From first to last,' including all between. Cf *Shabb.* 55a (on Ezk 9^{6}) : ' Do not read " My Sanctuary," but " My Saints," who are the sons of men who have kept the whole Law from Aleph to Taw.'

This explains the title. In each instance the seer defines it. Rev 1^{8} ' I am the Alpha and the Omega,' says the Lord God, ' who is and who was and who is to come, the Almighty ' (cf 1^{4} 4^{8}), *i.e.* the Eternal, the Contemporary of every generation. Rev 21^{6} ' I am the Alpha and the Omega, the beginning and the end ' (cf 3^{14} ; 22^{13} ' I am the Alpha and the Omega, the first and the last [cf 1^{17}, Is 41^{4} 44^{6} 48^{12}], the beginning and the end,' *i.e.* He who comprehends and embraces all things, from whom all come and to whom all return, the *fons et clausula*, the starting point and the goal of history (cf Ro 11^{36}, Col 1^{17}).

Though the antecedents of this use of the first and last letters of the alphabet lie in Judaism, analogous practice is to be found among the Greeks (Martial, v. 26). We also find the thought that Zeus is the beginning, the middle, and the end of all things (Plato, Pausanias). What is especially striking in the book of Revelation as in Isaiah is the I-style of the divine revelation and the liturgical context suggested. Our MSS uniformly present the Alpha as a word written out but the Omega only as the letter Ω.

Aurelius Prudentius (A.D. 348–410) makes fine use of the title in his hymn on *The Lord's Nativity* (' Corde natus ex parentis '), thus rendered by J. M. Neale :

' Of the Father's love begotten
Ere the worlds began to be,
He is Alpha and Omega,
He the source, the ending He,
Of the things that are, that have been,
And that future years shall see,
Evermore and evermore.'

D. S.—**A. N. W.**

ALPHABET.—See Writing.

ALPHAEUS.—**1.** The father of Levi according to Mk 2^{14} (cf Lk 5^{27}). We know nothing more of him than his name. Matthew's identification of Levi with the apostle Matthew (Mt 9^{9} 10^{3}) and the reading of some manuscripts in Mk 2^{14} (which identify Levi with James the son of Alphaeus) appear to be attempts to bring Levi within the circle of the twelve apostles. **2.** The father of James the apostle (Mt 10^{3}, Mk 3^{18}, Lk 6^{15}, Ac 1^{13}). The attempts to relate Alphaeus the father of James with Alphaeus the father of Levi rest on the insufficient manuscript evidence referred to above and late tradition which asserts that both Matthew and James had been tax collectors (Chrysostom). More frequent has been the identification of this James with James the younger whose mother was Mary and whose brother was Joses (Mk 15^{40}, Mt 27^{56}). This Mary is then identified with Mary the wife of Clopas mentioned in Jn 19^{25}. If this is so, Clopas and Alphaeus are one and the same person and it is pointed out that either name may be derived from the Aramaic name Chalphai (cf 1 Mac 11^{70}). Finally, some follow out the suggestion of Hegesippus that Clopas was a brother of Joseph (which was perhaps inferred from what appears to be a misunderstanding of Jn 19^{25}) and thus introduce further complications into the picture. But none of this can be proved. For the names Mary and James are much too common to make identification certain and there is some evidence that Alphaeus and Clopas are not derived from the same Aramaic name. These identifications are made all the less likely since they are arrived at through an arbitrary combination of references from the Synoptic Gospels and John.

W. R. S.

ALTANEUS, 1 Es 9^{33} (AV).—See Mattenai, **1.**

ALTAR.—A place where animals were slaughtered in sacrifice to a deity, then by extension a place where offerings of any kind were presented to him (Heb. *mizbēaḥ*, Gr. *thusiastērion*).

1. Varieties of altar.—A suitable rock might be used for the purpose, or a heap of stones, which in the earliest times must be unhewn (Ex 20^{25}), or of turf (' an altar of earth,' Ex 20^{24}). A good example of a natural rock-altar is that on which Gideon placed the ' present ' which he brought for the angel of Yahweh (Jg 6^{20}) or that on which Manoah offered up a kid and a cereal offering to Yahweh (Jg 13^{19}). Another is the outcrop of rock on the Temple hill at Jerusalem which to this day gives its name to the ' Dome of the Rock ' erected upon it. The ' great stone ' on which Saul's followers slaughtered their oxen after defeating the Philistines at Michmash was not strictly an altar, as these oxen do not appear to have been offered in sacrifice ; the altar which Saul built to Yahweh on that occasion was evidently distinct from the great stone (1 S 14^{33ff}).

More elaborate altars might be made of bronze, like that of Ex 27^{1ff} (constructed on a wooden framework) or the great altar of Solomon's Temple (1 K 8^{64}). When Solomon's Temple was dedicated, the bronze altar was inadequate for the great number of sacrifices, and so Solomon ' consecrated the middle of the court that was before the house of Yahweh ' (1 K 8^{64})—a reference, probably, to the outcrop of rock—to serve as a more spacious place of sacrifice. Both these bronze altars were equipped with ' horns,' as were also the altar at the Ark-shrine in Jerusalem before Solomon's Temple was founded (1 K 1^{50} 2^{28}) and the altar in Ezekiel's vision of the post-exilic Temple (Ezk 43$^{15, 20}$). Altars with four horns have been recovered from Megiddo, belonging to the 10th and 9th centuries B.C., and horned altars and shrines, of varying stages of development from the Early to the Late Bronze Age have been discovered at Beycesultan in Anatolia.

2. Cosmic features.—Ezekiel's altar (Ezk 43^{13ff}) has features of recognizably cosmic significance, taken over probably from the altar in the Jerusalem Temple which he knew. It was a stepped structure in three stages. The lowest stage rested on a base or foundation-platform (lit. 'the bosom of the earth'), set in the pavement and surrounded by a border or 'rim.' The topmost stage is the *har'ēl*, conventionally rendered 'altar-hearth'; W. F. Albright, however, takes *har'ēl* ('hill of God') to reflect a popular etymology of Akk. *arallu*, which means both 'underworld' and 'mountain of the gods,' the significance here being 'underworld.' Since the foundation-platform also has an Akkadian counterpart in *irat erṣiti* ('bosom of the earth'), used of the foundation-platforms of the royal palace and the temple-tower of Etemenanki in Babylon, Albright takes the altar to have the same cosmic significance as the ziggurat (the summit of which was also equipped with four 'horns'). Further cosmic significance is recognized in the *kiyyôr* or bronze platform on which Solomon stood in front of the altar when he prayed to Yahweh at the dedication of his Temple (2 Ch 6^{12f}, not mentioned in the parallel account of 1 K 8). Solomon's standing on this *kiyyôr* is illustrated by Albright from Syrian representations of a king or priest standing on a chest or tub-shaped vessel in the attitude of prayer. He derives the term *kiyyôr* (which elsewhere denotes a portable laver) from a Sumerian word meaning 'foundation of the earth' (again with cosmic significance). The details were no doubt the work of the Phoenician architects and builders whom Solomon employed, but in the Jerusalem Temple they were regarded (together with the cosmic symbolism of the structure as a whole) as representing Yahweh's enthronement as sole ruler over the cosmos.

3. Location of altars.—In early Israel, as even earlier in the patriarchal period, an altar was regularly erected wherever Yahweh manifested his presence among men, like Abraham's at Shechem (Gn 12^{7}), Isaac's at Beersheba (Gn 26^{24f}), Jacob's at Bethel (Gn 35^{7}), Gideon's at Ophrah (Jg 6^{24}) and David's on Mount Moriah (2 S 24^{25}). With this practice may be compared the promise associated with the command to make 'an altar of earth' (Ex 20^{24}): 'In every place where I cause my name to be remembered I will come to you and bless you.' There are also records of altar-building where no theophany is expressly mentioned, from Noah's altar (Gn 8^{20}) to Elijah's on Carmel (1 K 18^{31f})—although Elijah's action was the repairing of an old altar of Yahweh which had fallen into ruins (v.^{30}). From Josiah's reformation onwards, however, the Deuteronomic principle of one altar only for the nation was enforced—the one altar being that at the central sanctuary in Jerusalem. The altar on Gerizim was not intended to conflict with this principle, since the Samaritans believed that Gerizim was the true central sanctuary intended in Dt 12^{5}. The altar in the Jewish temple of Elephantine in Egypt (cf Is 19^{19}?) was technically an infraction of the Deuteronomic principle, although it was built at a time when the Jerusalem Temple lay derelict (during the exile). But the law of Deuteronomy does not envisage Israelites living in Egypt, and it is plain that the Jewish colony at Elephantine was largely uninfluenced by Josiah's reformation. The altar in the Leontopolis temple (*c* 160 B.C.–A.D. 73), founded by Onias IV., was equally irregular, but it was founded in the conviction that the legitimacy of the Jerusalem cultus had lapsed with the supersession of the Zadokite high priesthood there.

In Israel's earliest legislation altars provided **sanctuary** for fugitives from vengeance (Ex 21^{14}); the altar at David's Ark-shrine in Jerusalem was so used (1 K 1^{50} 2^{28}).

4. Pagan altars.—The altar which Ahaz saw at Damascus and which so attracted him that he installed a replica in the Jerusalem Temple (2 K 16^{10ff}) may have been a Damascene altar or one brought by Tiglath-pileser III. to establish the Assyrian cultus in what was now to be the capital of an Assyrian province. In the latter case, the installation of a replica in Jerusalem would be a token of Ahaz's vassalage to Assyria.

The 'abomination of desolation' which was erected upon the altar of burnt-offering in the second Temple under Antiochus IV. in December, 167 B.C., was a smaller altar dedicated to the worship of Olympian Zeus (1 Mac $1^{54, 59}$; cf Dn 8^{13} 9^{27} 11^{31} 12^{11}); see under IDOLATRY. Three years later a new altar of unhewn stones was dedicated in place of the altar defiled by the pagan installation (1 Mac 4^{47})—an event commemorated in Israel by the festival of Hanukkah.

Altars of incense (Hebrew *ḥammānîm*), stands or braziers for the burning of incense, go back at least to the 2nd millennium B.C. A Canaanite incense-altar of basalt has been discovered at Hazor, and Megiddo supplies a limestone sample from *c* 1000 B.C. In earlier times they were commonly made of pottery. Whether incense-altars of metal were called by the same name is doubtful; in OT *ḥammān* is reserved for Canaanite or at least idolatrous installations, and other expressions are used for the golden incense-altars of the wilderness tabernacle (Ex 30^{1}) and Solomon's Temple (1 K 6^{22} 7^{48}, 2 Ch 26^{16}).

5. In NT.—Greek *bōmos*, the common classical word for 'altar,' is used once in NT—appropriately, for the Athenian altar 'To an unknown god' (Ac 17^{23}).

No Christian altar in the material sense appears in NT. In He 13^{10} 'we have an altar' refers by metonymy to the sacrifice of Christ, from which Christians derive their holy status and their spiritual sustenance, and in response to which they present to God the sacrifices of praise and charity of vv.^{15f}. The altar of Rev 6^{9} 8^{3} belongs to the heavenly temple; it is the eternal reality of which the incense-altar in the earthly temple was a material copy.

F. F. B.

AL-TASCHITH, Pss 57, 58, 59, 75 titles (AV).—See AL-TASHHETH.

AL-TASHHETH, Pss 57, 58, 59, 75 titles (RV).—RSV translates, 'Do not destroy.' See PSALMS, **2.**

ALUSH.—A station in the journeyings, Nu 33^{13f}, near Dophkah (q.v.); site unknown, but possibly modern *Wâdi el-'Eshsh*.

ALVAH.—A chief of Edom, Gn 36^{40}; called **Aliah,** 1 Ch 1^{51}.

ALVAN.—An Edomite, son of Shobal, Gn 36^{23}; called **Alian,** 1 Ch 1^{40}.

AMAD.—A city of Asher, Jos 19^{26}; site unknown.

AMADATHUS, Ad. Est 12^{6} $16^{10, 17}$ (AV, RV).—See HAMMEDATHA (so RSV).

AMAL ('toil').—A descendant of Asher, 1 Ch 7^{35}.

AMALEK, AMALEKITES.—A tribe which roamed from the days of the Exodus till the time of king Saul, over the region from the southern boundary of Judah to the Egyptian frontier and the peninsula of Sinai. They are not counted among the kindred of the Israelites and probably were among the inhabitants of the region whom the Hebrew immigrants found already in the land. With this agrees the statement of a poem quoted in Nu 24^{20} 'Amalek was the first of the nations.'

Israel first met with the Amalekites in the region near Sinai, when Amalek naturally tried to prevent the entrance of a new tribe into the region (cf Ex 17^{8-16}). The battle which ensued produced such a profound impression, that one of the few things which the Pentateuch claims that Moses wrote is the ban of Yahweh upon Amalek (Ex 17^{14}). It appears from Dt 25^{17-19} that Amalek made other attacks upon Israel, harassing her rear. On the southern border of Palestine the Amalekites also helped at a later time to prevent Israel's entrance from Kadesh (Nu 13^{29} 14^{25}).

During the period of the Judges, Amalekites aided the Moabites in raiding Israel (Jg 3^{13}), and at a later time they helped the Midianites to do the same thing ($6^{3, 33}$ 7^{12}). This kept alive the old enmity. King Saul attempted to shatter their force, and captured their king, whom Samuel afterwards slew (1 S 15). Although Saul is said to have taken much spoil, the Amalekites were still there for David to raid during that part of Saul's reign when

David was an outlaw (1 S 27⁸). The boundaries of the *habitat* of the Amalekites at this time are said to have been from Telem, one of the southern cities of Judah (Jos 15²⁴), to Shur on the way to Egypt (1 S 15⁴). Most modern critics also read *Telem* for *Havilah* in 1 S 15⁷, and for '*of old*' in 1 S 27⁸.

It was formerly supposed, on the basis of Jg 5¹⁴ and 12¹⁵, that there was at one time a settlement of Amalekites farther north, in the hill country of Ephraim. That is, however, improbable, for both passages contain textual difficulties. Individual Amalekites, nevertheless, sojourned in Israel (2 S 1⁸, ¹³).

In 1 Ch 4⁴²ᶠᶠ there is a remarkable statement that a remnant of the Amalekites had escaped and dwelt in Edom, and that 500 Simeonites attacked and smote them. Perhaps this accounts for the genealogies which make Amalek a descendant of Esau and a subordinate Edomite tribe (cf Gn 36¹², ¹⁶ and 1 Ch 1³⁶). Perhaps here we learn how the powerful Amalek of the earlier time faded away.

According to Arab historians *Amálik* (*sic*) was a primitive 'Cushite' race which became extinct (Montgomery, *The Bible and Arabia*, Philadelphia, 1934, p. 20, n. 37). G. A. B.—**S. H. Hn.**

AMAM.—A city of Judah, Jos 15²⁶, S. of Beersheba; site unknown.

AMAN.—**1.** The ungrateful foster-son of Ahikar, To 14¹⁰ (AV, RV); RSV **Nadab** (see NADAB, **4**). **2.** Form of the name **Haman** (q.v.) found in Ad. Est 12⁶ 16¹⁰, ¹⁷ (AV, RV; RSV Haman).

AMANA.—One of the mountains near the river Abana (which is called Amana in a variant reading in 2 K 5¹²), mentioned with Lebanon and Hermon in Ca 4⁸.

AMARIAH ('Y″ said').—**1.** Zeph 1¹, a great-grandfather of the prophet Zephaniah, and son of a Hezekiah, who may possibly be the king of that name. **2.** 1 Ch 6⁷, ⁵², grandfather of Zadok the priest. **3.** 1 Ch 23¹⁹ 24²³, a Levite, descendant of Kohath, in the time of David. **4.** 1 Ch 6¹¹, Ezr 7³, 1 Es 8² (AV, RV **Amarias**), 2 Es 1² (AV, RV **Amarias**), son of Azariah, who is said to have ministered in Solomon's Temple. It is stated that Ezra belonged to the same family. The lists in which **2** and **4** occur are very uncertain, and the name may refer to the same person in both. **5.** 2 Ch 19¹¹, a high priest in the reign of Jehoshaphat, and appointed to have charge of 'matters of the Lord,' while Zebadiah was in charge of the 'king's matters.' **6.** 2 Ch 31¹⁵, a Levite in the time of Hezekiah, and one of the six assistants to Kore, who was 'keeper of the east gate.' These assistants helped to 'distribute the portions to their brethren.' **7.** Neh 12², ¹³ 10³, a priestly clan which returned to Jerusalem, and sealed the covenant under Nehemiah (probably the same as **Immer**, 1 Ch 24¹⁴, Ezr 2³⁷ 10²⁰, Neh 7⁴⁰, 1 Es 5²⁴ (AV **Meruth**, RV **Emmeruth**). **8.** Ezr 10⁴², 1 Es 9³⁴ (AV **Zambis**, RV **Zambri**), a Judahite, one of the sons of Bani (v.³⁴, 1 Ch 9⁴) who had taken strange wives. **9.** Neh 11⁴, a Judahite, who offered to dwell in Jerusalem. **10.** Neh 12¹², where **Meraiah** is probably a corruption of Amariah (so Syr. and LXXᴸ). A. H. McN.—**E. R. R.**

AMARIAS, 1 Es 8², 2 Es 1² (AV, RV).—See AMARIAH, **4.**

AMASA.—**1.** The son of Ithra an Ishmaelite, and of Abigal (in 1 Ch 2¹⁶ᶠ Abigail) the sister of king David. He commanded the army of the rebel Absalom (2 S 17²⁵); but was completely routed by Joab in the forest of Ephraim (18⁶⁻⁸). David not only pardoned him, but, probably to placate the Judahites, gave him the command of the army in place of Joab (19¹³). He was treacherously slain by Joab (2 S 20⁹⁻¹²). **2.** An Ephraimite who opposed the bringing into Samaria of the Jewish prisoners, whom Pekah, king of Israel, had taken in his campaign against Ahaz (2 Ch 28¹²).

AMASAI.—**1.** A Kohathite, 1 Ch 6²⁵, ³⁵; the eponym of a family, 2 Ch 29¹². **2.** One of the priests who blew trumpets when David brought the Ark to Jerusalem, 1 Ch 15²⁴. **3.** One of David's officers at Ziklag, 1 Ch 12¹⁸; possibly to be identified with Amasa, **1.**

AMASHSAI.—A priest of the family of Immer, Neh 11¹³ (AV **Amashai**).

AMASIAH.—One of Jehoshaphat's commanders, 2 Ch 17¹⁶.

AMATHEIS, 1 Es 9²⁹ (AV).—See EMATHIS.

AMAW.—The name of a country, found only in Nu 22⁵ (RSV). AV and RV follow MT and render 'the land of the children of his people,' instead of 'the land of Amaw.' Samaritan Pentateuch, Peshitta, and Vulgate read 'the land of the children of Ammon.' Some scholars find the same name in Ex 15¹⁴ (where RSV has 'the peoples') standing parallel to Philistia, cf Egyptian *ꜣmw* = (Asiatic) or (Syrian).

AMAZIAH.—**1.** Son of Jehoash of Judah. He came to the throne after the assassination of his father. It is recorded in his favour (2 K 14⁶) that although he put the murderers of his father to death he spared their children —something unheard of up to that time, we infer. Our sources know of a successful campaign of his against Edom, and an unsuccessful one against Israel. In this he seems to have been the aggressor; and after refusing to hear the advice of Jehoash, whom he had challenged to a trial of strength, he had the mortification of seeing his own capital plundered. The conspiracy by which he perished may have been prompted by his conduct in this war. In the matter of religion he received qualified praise from the author of Kings (2 K 14³ᶠ), while the Chronicler accuses him of gross apostasy (2 Ch 25¹⁴ᶠᶠ). **2.** The priest at Bethel who opposed the prophet Amos (Am 7¹⁶ᶠᶠ). **3.** A Simeonite (1 Ch 4³⁴). **4.** A Merarite (1 Ch 6⁴⁵). H. P. S.

AMBASSADOR.—As diplomatic agents of sovereigns or other persons in high authority, ambassadors are frequently mentioned in the OT and Apocrypha from the time of Moses to the Maccabees (1 Mac 9⁷⁰ 11⁹ 14²¹ 15¹⁷) as they are in the diplomatic archives of the kings of the ancient Near East. Insult to their persons was a sufficient *casus belli* (2 S 10⁴ᶠᶠ). In several passages (*e.g.* Nu 20¹⁴ 21²¹, Dt 2²⁶, Jg 11¹², ¹⁹, 2 S 5¹¹, 2 K 19⁹) the 'messengers' of RSV are practically 'ambassadors,' as the Hebrew word is elsewhere rendered (Is 18², Ezk 17¹⁵) or 'envoys' (2 Ch 32³¹ 35²¹, Is 30⁴ 33⁷). In NT the word is used only metaphorically (2 Co 5²⁰, Eph 6²; cf Phn ⁹ RSV).

AMBER, Ezk 1⁴, ²⁷ 8² (AV, RV).—This translation of *ḥashmal* is much questioned, and it is more probable that a metallic substance is meant, perhaps brass; RSV renders 'bronze.' There is no evidence that amber was imported into Palestine as early as the time of Ezekiel.

AMBUSH.—See WAR.

AMEN.—A Hebrew form of affirmation usually translated in the LXX by an equivalent Greek expression (Nu 5²², Dt 27¹⁵ 'so be it,' Jer 28⁶ (35⁶) 'truly,' but sometimes transliterated (1 Ch 16³⁶) as in English. It is an indication of solemn assent, chiefly in prayer, to the words of another, on the part either of an individual (Nu 5²²) or of an assembly (Dt 27¹⁵); sometimes reduplicated (Ps 41¹³), sometimes accompanied by a rubrical direction (Ps 106⁴⁸). In Is 65¹⁶ it is rendered 'truth' in the phrase 'the God of truth.' From the synagogue the word passed into the liturgical use of Christian congregations, and is so referred to in 1 Co 14¹⁶—'the (customary) Amen to your thanksgiving' (? Eucharist). The use peculiar to the NT is that ascribed to our Lord in the Gospels, where the word—'truly' (AV, RV 'verily') followed by 'I say'—introduces statements which He desires to invest with special authority (Mt 5¹⁸, Mk 3²⁸, Lk 4²⁴ etc.) as worthy of unquestioning trust. The Fourth Gospel reduplicates —a form which, though Christ may Himself have varied the phrase in this manner, is nevertheless stereotyped by this Evangelist (Jn 1⁵¹ and twenty-four other places), and marks the peculiar solemnity of the utterances it introduces. The impression created by this idiom may have influenced the title of ' the Amen ' given to the Lord in the Epistle to Laodicea (Rev 3^{14}). A strikingly similar phrase is used by St. Paul in 2 Co 1^{20}—' we utter the Amen through Him ' (*i.e.* Jesus Christ)—the seal of God's promises. Its use in doxologies is frequent.

J. G. S.—**H. H. R.**

AMETHYST.—See Jewels and Precious Stones.

AMI.—Head of a family of Solomon's servants, Ezr 2^{57}, 1 Es 5^{34} (AV **Allom** ; RV **Allon**) ; called **Amon** in Neh 7^{59}.

AMINADAB, Mt 1^4 (AV).—See Amminadab, **1.**

AMITTAI (' true ').—Father of the prophet Jonah, 2 K 14^{25}, Jon 1^1.

AMMAH.—A hill near Giah, in the wilderness of Gibeon, 2 S 2^{24} ; site unknown.

AMMI (' my people ').—The name to be applied to Israel in the time of restoration, Hos 2^1 (AV, RV ; RSV ' my people '). It is to take the place of Lo-ammi (' not my people '), the name given by Hosea to Gomer's third child (Hos 1^8).

AMMIDIANS.—One of the families that returned with Zerubbabel, 1 Es 5^{20} (AV **Ammidoi** ; RV **Ammidioi** ; omitted in the parallel lists in Ezr 2, Neh 7.

AMMIDIOI, 1 Es 5^{20} (RV).—See Ammidians.

AMMIDOI, 1 Es 5^{20} (AV).—See Ammidians.

AMMIEL (' kinsman is El ').—**1.** Son of Gemalli, and spy from the tribe of Dan, Nu 13^{12}. **2.** Father of Machir (see Machir, **2**), 2 S 9^{4f} 17^{27}. **3.** The sixth son of Obed-edom, who with his family constituted one of the courses of door-keepers in the time of David ; to them was allotted charge of the S. gate of the Temple, and the storehouse, 1 Ch $26^{5, 15}$. **4.** Father of Bathsheba (here called Bath-shua), according to 1 Ch 3^5 ; called **Eliam,** 2 S 11^3 ; see Eliam, **1.**

AMMIHUD (' kinsman is majesty ').—**1.** An Ephraimite, father of Elishama, Nu 1^{10} 2^{18} $7^{48, 53}$ 10^{22}. **2.** A Simeonite, father of Shemuel, Nu 34^{20}. **3.** A Naphtalite, father of Pedahel, Nu 34^{28}. **4.** Father of Talmai, king of Geshur, 2 S 13^{37} (AV, RSV with *Ḳ^{e}rê* ; RV **Ammihur** with *K^{e}thîbh*). **5.** Son of Omri and father of Uthai, 1 Ch 9^4.

AMMIHUR, 2 S 13^{37} (RV).—See Ammihud, **4.**

AMMINADAB (' kinsman is noble ').—**1.** Son of Ram and father of Nahshon, Nu 1^7 2^3 7^{12} 10^{14}, Ru 4^{19f}, 1 Ch 2^{10}, Mt 1^4 ; father-in-law of Aaron, Ex 6^{23}. **2.** Son of Kohath and father of Korah, 1 Ch 6^{22}. **3.** A chief of a Levitical house, 1 Ch 15^{10f}.

AMMINADIB.—Occurs in an obscure passage, Ca 6^{12} (AV, RVm), where AVm and RV render ' my willing (AVm ; RV ' princely ') people,' and RSV ' my prince.'

AMMISHADDAI (' kinsman is Shaddai ').—A Danite, father of Ahiezer, Nu 1^{12} 2^{25} $7^{66, 71}$ 10^{25}.

AMMIZABAD (' kinsman hath bestowed ').—Son of Benaiah, 1 Ch 27^6.

AMMON, AMMONITES.—A people inhabiting the Transjordanian territory within the bend of the upper course of the river Jabbok, between the tribe of Gad and the Arabian desert. Rabbah (modern *ʽAmmân*) was its capital and centre.

The narrative of Gn 19 tells the story of the origin of the Ammonites from Ben-Ammi and through him from Lot, explaining also their relationship with the Moabites. They are regularly called ' children of Ammon,' or ' Ammonites ' in the OT, twice simply ' Ammon ' (1 S 11^{11}, Ps 83^7). The Hebrew expression *b^{e}nê ʽAmmōn* in the Syro-Palestinian usage corresponds to the *Bīt-Ammānu,* the name for the Ammonite state used in Assyrian inscriptions (Noth, *ZDPV*, lxviii [1951], 37). The story of Gn 19 reveals furthermore a consciousness on the part of the Israelites that the Ammonites were their kindred. The proper names of individual Ammonites, so far as they are known to us, confirm this view.

In Dt 2^{20} the Ammonites are said to have displaced the Zamzummim, a prehistoric people, of whom we know nothing. An Aramaic apocryphon to Genesis found among the Dead Sea scrolls mentions the Zamzummim among the people defeated by the four northern kings of Gn 14 instead of the Zuzim of the Massoretic text. It is still uncertain at what time the Ammonites settled in their country as a sedentary people. N. Glueck concluded from the absence of Middle or Late Bronze-Age pottery in the Ammonite territory that they had not settled before the 13th cent. B.C. (*BASOR*, 68 [1937], 16–20). However, the recent discoveries of Middle-Bronze Age tomb groups at Mount Nebo, Naur and ʽAmmân, a Middle to Late Bronze-Age temple at ʽAmmân, and a Late Bronze to Early Iron-Age tomb at Mâdebā, seem to indicate that a sedentary life in this area existed before the 13th cent. B.C. (Harding, *PEQ*, xc [1958], 12).

At the time of the conquest the Israelites did not disturb the Ammonites (Nu 21^{24}, Dt 2^{37}), or attempt to conquer their territory. During the period of the judges the Ammonites assisted Eglon of Moab in his invasion of Israel (Jg 3^{13}), and later attempted to conquer Gilead, but were driven back by Jephthah the judge ($11^{4-9, 30-36}$ 12^{1-3}). In the 11th cent. B.C., Nahash, their king, oppressed the town of Jabesh in Gilead, but Saul's victory over them delivered Jabesh from the Ammonites and established the liberator as Israel's king (1 S 11). Saul and Nahash thus became enemies. Consequently, later, Nahash befriended David, apparently to weaken the growing power of Israel. When David succeeded Saul in power, Hanun, the son of Nahash, provoked him to war, with the result that Rabbah, the Ammonite capital, was stormed and taken, the Ammonites were reduced to vassalage, and terrible vengeance was wreaked upon them (2 S 10–12). Afterwards, during Absalom's rebellion, a son of Nahash rendered David assistance at Mahanaim (2 S 17^{27}). Zelek, an Ammonite, was among David's heroes (2 S 23^{37}). These friendly relations continued through the reign of Solomon. He took as one of his wives the Ammonite princess Naamah, who became the mother of Rehoboam, the next king (1 K 11^1 $14^{21, 31}$). After the reign of Solomon the Ammonites appear to have gained their independence.

In the reign of Ahab, Ba'sa, son of Ruḫubi, King of Ammon, was a member of the confederacy which opposed the progress of Shalmaneser III. of Assyria into the West (*ANET*, p. 279a). According to 2 Ch $20^{1, 10}$, the Ammonites joined with Moab and Edom in invading Judah in the reign of Jehoshaphat. Before the reign of Jeroboam II. the Ammonites had made another attempt to get possession of Gilead, and their barbarities in warfare excited the indignation of the prophet Amos (Am 1^{13-15}). Chronicles represents them as paying tribute to Uzziah of Judah, and as beaten by his son Jotham (2 Ch 26^8 27^5). Tiglath-pileser III. of Assyria received tribute from Sanipu, King of the Ammonites (*ANET*, p. 282a), Esarhaddon from King Puduil (*ANET*, p. 291b), and Ashurbanipal from King Amminadbi (*ANET*, p. 294a). The name of the last-mentioned Ammonite king appears on two ancient seals found at ʽAmmân (*BA* xvi [1953], 4). When next we hear of the Ammonites, Nebuchadnezzar of Babylon is employing them to harass the refractory Judaean king Jehoiakim (2 K 24^2). Perhaps it was at this period that the Ammonites occupied the territory of Gad (Jer 49^{1ff}). Later, the domination of the Babylonians compelled Ammon and Judah to become friends, for Ammon conspired with king Zedekiah against Nebuchadrezzar (Jer 27^3). The Babylonian king regarded both Ammon and Judah as rebels, for Ezekiel represents him as casting lots to see whether he should first attack Rabbah or Jerusalem (Ezk 21^{20ff}, cf Zeph $2^{8, 9}$). During the Babylonian invasion of Palestine many Judaeans seem to have migrated to Ammon (Jer 40^{11}).

After the destruction of Jerusalem, Baalis, king of Ammon, sent a man to assassinate Gedaliah, whom Nebuchadrezzar had made governor of Judah (Jer 40^{14}).

Again, 140 years later, the Ammonites did everything in their power to prevent the rebuilding of the walls of Jerusalem by Nehemiah (Neh 2^{10, 19} 4^{3, 7}). Nehemiah and Ezra fomented this enmity by making illegal the marriages of Ammonitish women with citizens of Judah (Neh 13^{23}).

Between the time of Nehemiah and Alexander the Great the country east of the Jordan was overrun by the Nabataeans. Perhaps the Ammonites lost their identity at this time; for, though their name appears later, many scholars think it is used of these Arabs. Thus in 1 Mac 5^{6ff} Judas Maccabaeus is said to have defeated the Ammonites; while Justin Martyr (*Dial. Tryph.*, 19) says the Ammonites were numerous in his day. As Josephus (*Ant.* I. xi. 5 [206]) uses the same language of the Moabites and Ammonites, though elsewhere (XIV. i. 4 [18]) he seems to call them Arabians, it is possible that the Ammonites had lost their identity at the time of the Nabataean invasion. Their capital, Rabbah, was rebuilt in the Greek style by Ptolemy II Philadelphus of Egypt in the 3rd cent. B.C. and named Philadelphia. Its ruins amid the modern city of ʿAmmân are impressive. The God of the Ammonites is called in the OT **Milcom,** a variation of *Melekh*, 'king,' also **Molech,** to whom Solomon dedicated a sanctuary at Jerusalem (1 K 11^{7}).
G. A. B.—**S. H. Hn.**

AMNON ('faithful').—**1.** Eldest son of David by Ahinoam the Jezreelitess; he dishonoured his half-sister Tamar, and was on that account slain by her brother Absalom, 2 S 3^{2} 13^{1f}, 1 Ch 3^{1}. **2.** Son of Shimon, 1 Ch 4^{20}.

AMOK.—A priestly family in the time of Zerubbabel and of Joiakim, Neh 12^{7, 20}.

AMOMUM.—See SPICE.

AMON ('master workman').—**1.** Son and successor of Manasseh, king of Judah, who reigned for two years and followed the way of his father. He was killed in a palace conspiracy, but the assassins were punished by the populace, who put Josiah on the throne, 2 K 21^{19ff}. Some have connected his name with the Egyptian sun-god (see next article). **2.** A governor of Samaria, 1 K 22^{26}, 2 Ch 18^{25}. **3.** Head of a family of Solomon's servants, Neh 7^{59}; called **Ami** in Ezr 2^{57}.

AMON (Gr. *Ammōn*, Egyp. *Amūn*).—An Egyptian deity who was originally a fertility god and therefore often depicted with the head of a ram. He first comes into prominence with the rise of Thebes (whose local deity he was) after the expulsion of the Hyksos. In the 18th Dynasty, when Thebes was the capital of Egypt, he became the national god. As such he was often identified with the sun god Rēʿ and called Amūn-rēʿ 'the king of the gods.' His supremacy lasted as long as Thebes remained the capital, but when, in the 21st and subsequent Dynasties, the centre of gravity shifted to Lower Egypt, he relapsed into the status of god of the South and of Nubia, yielding place to Osiris in the North. Only once in the 500 years that he was the supreme God of Egypt was his position challenged: this was during the reign of the reformer king Akhenaton, who moved the capital to Tell el-Amarna and substituted the worship of Aton, the sun's disc, for that of Amūn. During the 18th and 19th Dynasties enormous temples, richly endowed, were built for Amūn, especially at Thebes, from the wealth which poured into Egypt as a result of the Asiatic campaigns. Their ruins are amongst the most impressive remains of ancient Egypt. T. W. T.

AMORITES.—An ancient people, called *'ᵉmōrî* in Hebrew, *Amurru* in Akkadian, and *'Imur* in Egyptian texts, who frequently appear in the early books of the Bible as one of the aboriginal tribes of Canaan.

The history of the Amorites is somewhat obscure since they have left no historical records in their own language, and those left by them in Akkadian cover only short periods or reigns of a few individual rulers like those of Hammurabi of Babylon or of Zimri-Lim of Mari. The first word about the Amorites comes from Sumeria. Shu-Sin, one of the last kings of the 3rd dynasty of Ur, records the building of a wall against the Amorites. This shows that they must have been on the move and posed a threat for the lower Euphrates valley. Shortly afterwards all of Syria and Palestine was simply called *Amurru* by the Babylonians, which may be an indication that they came from that area. During the period of the dynasties of Isin and Larsa two kings of Larsa appear with Amorite names in the 19th cent. B.C. The rule of these kings was not more than an intermezzo, but by the end of the 19th cent. B.C. Amorites were found firmly entrenched as kings and rulers throughout the Mesopotamian valley. They founded the 1st dynasty of Babylon whose famous 6th ruler, Hammurabi, built an empire that reached from the Persian Gulf to the Mediterranean Sea. Also the powerful kingdom of Mari in whose capital city French excavations have discovered a large palace archive, was of Amorite origin. Other Amorite Kingdoms mentioned in the records of that time are those of *Yamḫad* (Aleppo) and *Qaṭna* in Syria. The rule of the Amorites in Mesopotamia was brought to an end in the 16th cent. B.C. by the invasions of the Hittites and the Kassites.

The Amorites must have taken over Syria and Palestine towards the end of the 3rd millennium B.C., for the majority of cities in those countries were in the hands of Amorite rulers during the time of the powerful 12th dynasty of Egypt (1991–*c* 1780 B.C.). Many of their names are mentioned in the Egyptian execration texts by means of which the Egyptians attempted to curb the power of these dangerous princes. In the Amarna period (14th cent. B.C.) *Amurru* was the name of a kingdom in inland Syria, a vassal state of Egypt. Taking advantage of Egypt's political weakness at that time this state carried out an active warfare against many Syrian and Phoenician city states whose rulers were like the king of Amurru vassals of Egypt.

The Amorite language is not well known, since only a few Amorite phrases in Akkadian texts so far have come to light. Hence, most of our knowledge of that language is based on the personal names of Amorites. This evidence reveals that Amorite was a Semitic language, closely related to the West-Semitic tongues. That it differed only dialectically from Canaanite ('Sidonian'), which is also Hebrew, is revealed by Dt 3^{9}. In the Table of Nations the Amorites are listed among the Hamites (Gn 10^{6}) probably more for religious than for ethnological or linguistic reasons.

Biblical tradition attests that the Amorites were in possession of large parts of Palestine during the patriarchal period. They are said to have lived at Hebron in Abraham's time, whose confederates they became (Gn 14^{13}). In Gn 15^{16} they are simply synonymous with the population of the whole country, and Jacob is said to have taken a certain section of Canaan by sword and bow from the Amorites (Gn 48^{22}). They are also quite regularly mentioned in the lists of nations whom the Israelites were supposed to drive out from Canaan (Gn 15^{21}, Ex 3^{8}, Dt 7^{1}, etc.). At the time of the Exodus the Amorites are described as being in possession of the hill country of western Palestine and of two large areas in Transjordania (Nu 13^{29}, Dt 1^{19, 20, 44}, Nu 21^{26-30}). The invading Hebrews defeated Amorite armies on several occasions and took much of their territory from them (Nu 21^{25, 31, 32}, Jos 10^{5, 6, 28-43}). However, strong remnants of these people remained in the country, and they kept many of their cities and territories (Jg 1^{35} 3^{5}). In Samuel's time they lived in peace with the Israelites and did not side with their enemies, the Philistines (1 S 7^{14}). Solomon incorporated all Amorites who were still found in his kingdom into his forced labour corps (1 K 9^{20, 21}, 2 Ch 8^{7}). From that time on they disappear from view.
G. A. B.—**S. H. Hn.**

AMOS.—1. The man.—Amos, the earliest of the prophets whose utterances are preserved for us in the Bible, lived and prophesied in the 8th cent. B.C., at some time during the long and almost precisely contemporaneous reigns of Uzziah in Judah (*c* 783–42) and Jeroboam II. (*c* 786–46) in Israel (1^{1}). The further notice placing his ministry two years before the great eathquake of Uzziah's reign (cf Zec 14^{5}) is, unfortunately, of no help to us, since we do not know in what year this catastrophe took place. His activity, however, fell well along in Jeroboam's reign after that king's victorious campaigns had been completed (6^{13f}). Of Amos himself we know almost nothing. His home was Tekoa, a village on the edge of the Judaean wilderness some six miles south of Bethlehem. He is said to have been a herdsman (1^{1} 7^{14}). Though some have argued that this term designated a cultic functionary, the probability is that it means just what it seems to mean : a small sheep-farmer. He is also said to have been 'a dresser of sycamore trees' : *i.e.* one who nipped or bruised the coarse sycamore fig in order to hasten its ripening. Though it may be that something of the spiritual experience which led Amos to the prophetic office is reflected in such passages as 3^{1-8} or 7^{1-9}, we do not know how his call came to him. He expressly denied that he had been a member of one of the prophetic guilds, asserting simply (7^{14f}) that the word of Yahweh had come to him commanding him to speak. Though a Judahite, Amos' public ministry was, so far as we know, carried out entirely in the northern Kingdom. But although this may have lasted over a period of years and taken him to various of the cities of Israel, we know of but one incident relating to it (7^{10-17}). Amos had come to Bethel, the official state shrine of the northern kingdom, and there had pronounced doom on the nation and on the royal house. Amaziah the priest, thinking him to be one of 'the sons of the prophets' stirring up revolution, as such prophets had often done before (*e.g.* 1 K 9^{1ff}), silenced him, contemptuously bidding him betake himself to Judah and earn his living prophesying there. Amos, indignantly denying that he was a professional prophet, cursed Amaziah and pronounced doom on him for interfering with the word of Yahweh which he had been commanded to speak. Whether this ended Amos' ministry in Israel or not, we do not know ; but one gains the impression that he continued to speak—though perhaps no longer at the royal shrine.

2. The time in which he lived.—When Amos spoke, Israel and Judah were stronger and more prosperous than they had been since Solomon. In the preceding century, internally weakened by Jehu's purge of the house of Omri (842 B.C.), Israel had suffered severely at the hands of the Aramaean kingdom of Damascus, losing all of her territory east of the Jordan (2 K 10^{32f}, cf Am 1^{3}) and probably more besides (2 K 12^{17}), and becoming ultimately a dependency of the Aramaean king (2 K 13^{7}). At the end of the 9th cent., however, Assyrian invasions crippled Damascus while leaving Israel relatively untouched. Then the Assyrians withdrew and for some fifty years, busied with internal problems and with campaigns elsewhere, did not march into Syria and Palestine at all. This gave Israel her chance. Under Jehoash (*c* 801–786), and then under Jeroboam II., she won back all her lost territories and enlarged her borders considerably at the expense of her neighbours (2 K $14^{25, 28}$). Judah meanwhile pursued a similarly aggressive policy. By the mid-8th cent. the two nations between them held a domain very nearly as large as that of Solomon.

The prosperity which accompanied this resurgence is reflected in every line of Amos. But it is equally evident that Israel was internally sick. The tribal structure of her society had long since disintegrated, leaving wide gaps between rich and poor. Covenant law, in which all social obligation had once been based, had largely ceased to have any real meaning. The rich took advantage of the poor at every opportunity (2^{6f} 5^{11}), amassing wealth by dishonest means and without regard for the rights of the weaker brother (8^{4-6}). Their womenfolk, 'cows of Bashan,' were equally guilty with them (4^{1}). Since the judges were venal, the poor had no recourse (5^{10f}). The shrines were busy and well supported (4^{4f} 5^{21-24}) ; but immorality and pagan practices were rife (2^{7f} 5^{26}), together with the pagan notion that religious obligation could be discharged by external observance. Religion had divorced itself from morality. The clergy, being servants of the existing order, could neither utter criticism of it nor tolerate any (7^{10-13}). The nation, nevertheless, was optimistic, proud of its strength (6^{13}), unconcernedly enjoying its luxuries without thought of the sickness of society (6^{1-6}), confident that Yahweh would always protect His people and at 'the Day of Yahweh' (5^{18-20}) intervene in their behalf to make all His promises actual.

3. Contents of the book.—The book of Amos is not a connected treatise written by Amos, but a collection of his utterances, or fragments of utterances, which were delivered orally, remembered and subsequently written down. Over a period of time these, and other utterances attributed to Amos, were brought together into the book as we know it. The book falls into three major sections.

(1) 1^{2}–2^{16}. A single connected discourse. Amos denounces Israel's neighbours for their crimes, all of which have shocked the common conscience of the day, and declares that Yahweh will surely punish. Then, having gained his hearers' agreement, he turns on Israel also and pronounces the righteous judgment of Yahweh upon her for her crimes of injustice and oppression of the poor.

(2) Ch 3–6. A series of oracles or fragments of oracles without original connexion with one another, but all with the theme of the national sin. Most of them are introduced by 'Hear (this word) !,' 'Woe——!' and the like.

(3) 7^{1}–9^{10}. A series of five visions interspersed with oracles and interrupted (7^{10-17}) by the account of Amaziah's attempt to silence Amos. The visions are : locusts (7^{1-3}), drought (7^{4-6}), the plumb-line (7^{7-9}), the basket of summer fruit (8^{1-3}), the sanctuary smitten at Yahweh's command (9^{1-4}).

In striking contrast to the rest of the book is 9^{11-15}. It speaks of promise for the future, which elsewhere in Amos is barely implicit (5^{14f}). Most scholars regard this as a later addition to the prophecy. This is very possibly correct, although there is nothing here that is inconsonant with prophetic theology. The further opinion that the passage comes from a time as late as the Exile should be received with caution, for the hopes expressed in it were popular ones of a sort that could be relatively old.

The fact that Amos was a countryman of humble background must not lead us to suppose that he was ignorant or rude in speech. His utterances are couched in an excellent, at times polished, Hebrew. His imagery is vivid, most of it drawn from nature. He displays wide knowledge of his world and of contemporary events ; he is aware of the history of his nation's relationship with its neighbours, and also knows something of the history of neighbouring nations (*e.g.* that the Philistines had migrated from Caphtor and the Aramaeans from Kir : 9^{7}). He was, in short, an intelligent man who was above all a keen observer of conditions in his own country, which he knew well.

4. The Theology of Amos.—The message of Amos is on the surface terrifyingly simple, and one that gives classic expression to a theme which recurs in all the great prophets. It is essentially an attack upon the sins of society as sins against Yahweh, and a warning of the coming judgment. Amos singles out those powerful ones who have crowded their weaker brothers (2^{6f}), gained wealth dishonestly (8^{4-6}), and so corrupted the courts by bribery that a poor man can get no justice ($5^{7, 10-12}$). He scores the irresponsible wealthy class (6^{1-6}) and their womenfolk (4^{1-3}), who enjoy every luxury but are unconcerned over the plight of the less fortunate. He declares that the worship of such people is a sin (4^{4f}), a thing hateful to Yahweh (5^{21-24}), whose first demand is just behaviour. Amos likened Israel to a tottering wall which Yahweh will pull down (7^{7-9}) ; she will be left like a sheep that a lion has torn (3^{12}) ; she is already as good as dead (5^{2}). While he called for repentance (5^{14f}) and extended hope on that condition, it appears that he expected none. His undisputed sayings point only to Israel's doom.

Amos was, then, primarily concerned to proclaim the justice of Yahweh. But he does not do this as one expounding a loftier idea of God, or as one who is concerned with teachings about the nature of God at all. To understand the prophets in this light is to misunderstand them, for they represented essentially a reform movement in the mainstream of Israel's historic faith. Amos, though his originality is unquestioned, propounded no fundamentally new doctrine. His preaching is based on the notion of covenant, a basic stipulation of which was that Israel obey covenant law in all dealings with the brother upon pain of divine displeasure. Concern for social righteousness, especially toward the weak, is prominent in the Book of the Covenant (*e.g.* Ex 22^{21ff}), which reflects legal practice of pre-monarchial days. One sees it also in Nathan's rebuke of David (2 S 12^{1ff}) and Elijah's denunciation of Ahab (1 K 21). Amos' preaching thus carried forward an ancient tradition. The people whom he addressed had perverted the notion of covenant and imagined that the bond between Yahweh and Israel was one based on nature and eternal, requiring of them at most attention to sacrifice and ritual. It is this paganized notion of covenant which Amos attacks. He reminded the people of the gracious acts of Yahweh toward them in the past (2^{9-12}), in the light of which their sins are sins against grace. He insisted that the righteous demands of Yahweh do not exempt Israel (chs. 1–2), for Yahweh (9^7) has no 'pet' people: election leads not to privilege only, but to double responsibility (3^2).

Because Israel had violated covenant, Amos pronounced doom on her. But he did not, like earlier prophets, attempt to purge the state by revolution. He was suspected of this, it is true, but his denial (7^{10-17}) is borne out by the facts: the classical prophets, however much they sought to influence the policies of state, never indulged in revolutionary action. They believed that the state was under the judgment of Yahweh, Who would himself execute sentence. Amos therefore declared that the expected Day of Yahweh, the day of His definitive intervention in history, would be a day of judgment for sinful Israel (5^{18-20}). J. Br.

AMOZ ('strong').—Father of the prophet Isaiah, 2 K 19^2, Is 1^1; the name (*'āmôṣ*) is to be distinguished from that of the prophet Amos (*'āmôs*).

AMPHIPOLIS.—A town in a part of Macedonia formerly reckoned to Thrace, on the river Strymon, about three miles from its mouth, where the harbour Eion was situated. It was founded by the Athenians, 436 B.C., and was a place of great strategic and mercantile importance. It underwent various vicissitudes, but retained its importance based on its abundant supplies of excellent wine, figs, oil, and wood, its silver and gold mines, its woollen fabrics. The Romans raised it to the rank of a free town and the chief town of the first district of the province Macedonia; through it the Via Egnatia passed. The verb in the Greek (Ac 17^1) seems to indicate that St. Paul passed through it without preaching there. A. So.

AMPLIATUS (AV **Amplias**).—Greeted by St. Paul (Ro 16^8), perhaps of the Imperial household (Lightfoot on Ph 4^{22}), and a prominent Christian (Sanday-Headlam). The name, a common slave designation, is found inscribed in the catacombs. A. J. M.

AMRAM ('kinsman is exalted').—**1.** A Levite, son of Kohath and grandson of Levi, Nu 3^{17-19}, 1 Ch $6^{2f, 18}$); he married Jochebed, his father's sister, by whom he begat Aaron and Moses (Ex 6^{18-20}) and Miriam (Nu 26^{59}, 1 Ch 6^3). The **Amramites** are mentioned in Nu 3^{27}, 1 Ch 26^{23}. **2.** A son of Bani, who had contracted a foreign marriage, Ezr 10^{34}, 1 Es 9^{34} (AV **Omaerus,** RV **Ismaerus**) **3.** 1 Ch 1^{41} (AV). See HAMRAN.

AMRAPHEL.—King of Shinar (Gn 14^1). Head of the league of four kings who invaded Canaan in the time of Abraham. The old identification of Amraphel with Hammurabi, the 6th king of the 1st Amorite dynasty in Babylon, is now generally rejected. While Shinar is used by the Yahwist to denote Babylon in Gn 10^{10} 11^2, there is another region mentioned in Egyptian and cuneiform documents which can be transliterated as Shinar and which cannot be Babylonia. Moreover, the Mari documents have shown that there were several kings bearing the name Hammurabi. Hence, even if the doubtful equation of Amraphel were accepted, it would still be uncertain whether Hammurabi of Babylon is the king referred to. No satisfactory solution has yet been proposed. S. H. He.

AMULETS AND CHARMS.—The terms are almost synonymous but also of loose definition. However, we may speak of them in general as signifying objects, commonly worn on the person but sometimes installed in a home, to protect or induce welfare. The origins of such practices are lost in far antiquity, quite evidently so remote in the Stone Ages that we may conclude they have characterized human life almost from its earliest evidences; and it persists into the present of even sophisticated societies, where, however, faith in its efficacy varies from sincerity to an amused concession to common 'superstition.'

From ancient Egypt we have a great variety of small religious objects; miniature figures of gods, some carved into real art pieces, are familiar in museums; and 'Horus eyes,' symbols of the mythical activity of Isis in restoring Osiris to life, are regular designs on coffins and mummies but also as independent trinkets. They are frequent in Palestinian archaeological excavation, as are also scarabs, miniature beetles in stone or faience with a religious design or a name on the under, flat surface. However this is merely a sampling of what our evidence shows to have been a pervasive mood of the entire ancient East; again for illustration one may mention the divine symbols on Babylonian boundary stones, or more relevant, the immense number of personal seals, engraved as they are with mythical symbols.

With Palestine geographically central in the cultures of the Biblical world, it is not surprising that such objects and beliefs are richly attested in archaeological discovery there. Typical of the land, however, as distinct from the import of foreign objects or impulses, are the clay figurines of Astarte with gross exaggeration of sex features. The guess is so obvious as to have won general acceptance that they were believed to assist in pregnancy and birth. A number of objects have been classed as children's toys; it is quite possible, though they may at the same time have been thought to have provided some sort of protection for the child—and in the deficiency of sanitation and medical skill, they needed it!

Doubtless the clearest reference to amulets in the OT is the legislation for 'tassels' (Dt 22^{12}), 'signs,' 'frontlets,' and the 'writing on the doorposts' (Dt 6^{8-9}); or rather we should say the allusion is to a popular use of amulets which the Deuteronomist here sublimates into a religious practice of high meaning. Indeed the word 'phylactery,' commonly applied to these 'frontlets' means a protective object, though the Hebrew word has no such value. A similar exalted interpretation of popular superstitions is to be recognized in the official robe of the High Priest, with its pomegranates and bells and its ornate 'breastpiece' (Ex 28^{33} 39^{25}). Clear mention of the popular use, so richly attested in archaeology and by later evidence, is rare in the Bible. It is plausibly believed that the 'earrings,' still more the 'crescents and the pendants' and the camels' 'collars' taken by Gideon from the pagan Midianites (Jg 8^{25}) were really amulets (cf Gn 35^4). A similar guess relates to some items of women's finery listed in Is 3^{18-21}. Indeed RSV uses the word 'amulets'; it is highly probable, for the Hebrew word means 'charms.' Here again we have come upon the overlapping of decorative with magical purpose.

The 'sacred tokens' (2 Mac 12^{40}) found by Judas Maccabaeus on the bodies of his soldiers were heathen charms against death in battle, the peculiar Greek word being a translation of the Aramaic word for 'amulet.'
A. R. S. K.—**W. A. I.**

AMUSEMENTS.—See GAMES.

AMZI ('strong' or 'strong is Y″').—**1.** A Merarite, 1 Ch 6^{46}. **2.** A priest in the second Temple, Neh 11^{12}.

ANAB.—A city in the hill country of Judah, once inhabited by Anakim, Jos 11^{21} 15^{50}; modern *Khirbet 'Anâb* near Debir.

ANAEL.—Brother of Tobit and father of Ahikar (To 1^{21}).

ANAH.—**1.** A son (so RSV, with LXX, Sam., Pesh.; AV, RV 'daughter' with Hebrew) of Zibeon, and mother of Oholibamah, one of Esau's wives, Gn $36^{2, 14, 18, 25}$, 1 Ch 1^{40f}; he is said to be a Hivite, but we should perhaps read 'Horite.' **2.** A Horite chief, brother of Zibeon, Gn $36^{20, 29}$, 1 Ch 1^{38}. It is possible that Anah is an eponym and these two are to be identified. In regard to **1** the note is appended: 'he is the Anah who found the hot springs (so RV, RSV with Vulg.; AV wrongly 'mules') in the wilderness, as he pastured the asses of Zibeon his father,' Gn 36^{24}.

ANAHARATH.—A city of Issachar, mentioned with Shion and Rabbith, Jos 19^{19}: possibly modern *en-Na'ūrah*, in the Valley of Jezreel.

ANAIAH ('Y″ hath answered').—**1.** A Levite, Neh 8^{4}, 1 Es 9^{43} (AV, RV **Ananias**). **2.** One of those who sealed the covenant, Neh 10^{22}.

ANAK, ANAKIM.—Early inhabitants of the southern hill country of Judah, whom tradition credited with extraordinary height. The word *'Anaḳ* is properly a race-name, and, being often used with the article, it is really an appellative, probably meaning 'the necklace-wearing (people)' (Noth, *Joshua*, p. 63). They are possibly attested in the Egyptian execration texts of the Middle Kingdom (Dussaud, *Syria*, xxi, 175). In the genealogizing narrative of Jos $15^{13, 14}$ there were three sons or clans of Anak with Aramaic names: Sheshai, Ahiman, and Talmai. These were all driven out by Caleb (cf Jg 1^{20}). Jos 11^{21} gives them a wider *habitat*, as scattered over the hill-country of Palestine generally, whence they were exterminated by Joshua. In Gaza, Gath, and Ashdod some remnants were found after Joshua's time (11^{22}).
J. F. McC.—**S. H. Hn.**

ANAMIM.—A people not yet identified, named among the descendants of Egypt, Gn 10^{13}, 1 Ch 1^{11}.

ANAMMELECH.—A god worshipped by captives transplanted from Sepharvaim to Samaria by the Assyrians, 2 K 17^{24}; human sacrifice (v.^{31}) was the most prominent rite connected with the god's worship. The name probably stands for *Anu-milki* and means 'Anu is prince' (cf Albright, *AJSL*, xli, 86 f.). See also ADRAMMELECH.

ANAN.—**1.** One of those who sealed the covenant, Neh 10^{26}. **2.** Eponym of a family of Temple servants, 1 Es 5^{30} (AV, RV; RSV **Hana**); called **Hanan** in Ezr 2^{46}, Neh 7^{49}.

ANANI.—A son of Elioenai, 1 Ch 3^{24}.

ANANIAH.—**1.** The father of Maaseiah and grandfather of Azariah, who took part in rebuilding the walls of Jerusalem, Neh 3^{23}. **2.** A town inhabited by Benjamites after the return from exile, Neh 11^{32}; possibly modern *el-'Azarîyeh* (Bethany).

ANANIAS.—This name occurs frequently in the Septuagint where it is used for a variety of closely related Hebrew names, the most common of which is Hananiah. It is the name of three persons in the NT. **1.** A member of the early Church in Jerusalem who, according to Ac 5^{1-11}, died with his wife Sapphira for dishonesty in financial matters. **2.** A 'devout man according to the law' at Damascus, a disciple who instructed and baptized Paul after his conversion, restoring to him his sight by the imposition of hands (Ac 9^{1-19} 22^{4-16} 26^{9-18}). **3.** A Jewish high priest and a Sadducee, son of Nedebaeus, who held office from A.D. 47 to 59. He is mentioned several times by Josephus. In A.D. 52 he was sent to Rome by the legate of Syria because of a dispute with the Samaritans. With the aid of Agrippa II. he regained his freedom and returned to Palestine. Even after his high priesthood came to an end he exercised a despotic authority because of his wealth and his friendship with the Romans. He was finally murdered by the *sicarii* as a friend of the Romans at the beginning of the Jewish war (A.D. 66 or 67). He is mentioned twice in the NT. In Ac 23^{1-5} he plays an active role in the trial of Paul before the Sanhedrin. In Ac 24^{1} he is said to have gone down to Caesarea along with others to accuse Paul before Felix. **4.** 1 Es 9^{43} (AV, RV); see ANAIAH, **1.** **5.** 1 Es 5^{16} (AV); see ANNIAS. **6.** 1 Es 9^{21} (AV, RV); see HANANI, **4.**
W. R. S.

ANANIEL.—One of the ancestors of Tobit (To 1^{1}).

ANASIB.—A family that returned with Zerubbabel, 1 Es 5^{24} (AV, RV **Sanasib**).

ANATH.—The father of Shamgar, one of the minor Judges, Jg 3^{31} 5^{6}. The name is that of a goddess of war worshipped at Ugarit (see RAS SHAMRA), on whom cf Gordon, *The Loves and Wars of Anat* (1943); in the Elephantine Papyri (q.v.) we find reference to **Anath-yahu** in the Jewish Temple. On this goddess cf also Albright, *AJSL* xli, 73 ff.

ANATHEMA.—See BAN.

ANATHOTH.—**1.** A Levitical city in Benjamin, Jos 21^{18}; to it Abiathar went when dismissed by Solomon (1 K 2^{26}), and it was the home of Jeremiah (Jer 1^{1} $11^{21, 23}$); after the Exile it was reoccupied, Ezr 2^{23}, Neh 7^{27}; modern *Râs el-Kharrûbeh*, near *'Anâta*. The name is derived from that of the Semitic goddess **Anath** (see ANATH). **2.** A Benjamite, son of Becher, 1 Ch 7^{8}. **3.** One of those who sealed the covenant, Neh 10^{19}.

ANCESTOR WORSHIP.—The question of the existence of a cult of the ancestors among the ancient Israelites is bound up with the interpretation of their burial and mourning customs. In the first place it must be recognized that the early Hebrew attitude towards the dead is ambivalent, and in the second place it is clear that as the uniqueness of Yahweh became more sharply emphasized through the work of the 8th and 7th cent. prophets, the conception of the relation between the dead and the living underwent a change.

On the one hand, as Pedersen has said (*Israel*, ii, 486), 'The early Israelite relation to the dead shows that in older times there was no gulf between the divine and the human.' The ancestors were thought of as still part of the collective personality which was Israel; they continued to be the source of the vitality of the community and of the *b^{e}rākhāh* upon which its life and prosperity depended. The graves of the ancestors were sacred places, and there is some evidence that cultic rites may have been connected with the dead, *e.g.* in Dt 26^{14} the bringer of tithes has to declare, 'I have not offered any of it to the dead.' Moreover, although the mourning customs of rending the clothes, shaving the head, and gashing the face, may have had their origin in the fear of the dead and in the attempt to prevent the dead from recognizing the living and harming them, it is possible that at a later time such customs may have been intended to express sorrow and the wish to honour the dead. Thus, as Pedersen says, 'the mourning rites acquired the character of a cult; the deceased was honoured by them' (op. cit. 484). This tendency is most clearly seen in the ritual burning for the kings of Judah (Jer 34^{5}, 2 Ch 16^{14} 21^{19}), which it is difficult to regard as unconnected with the sacral character of the kingship in Israel.

On the other hand, there are aspects of the Israelite attitude towards death and the dead which point in a different direction: (*a*) Everything connected with death and the dead is unclean. In Nu 19 we have the torah o uncleanness, where it is laid down that any kind of contact with a dead person caused ritual uncleanness. Even open vessels in the tent where death had occurred became unclean. The most efficacious method of defiling the places where idolatrous worship had been practised was by scattering dead men's bones upon them (2 K 23[14] *et al.*). By Ezekiel's time even the nearness of the royal tombs to the Temple in Jerusalem was to be regarded as defiling (Ezk 43[7]). (*b*) The grave, which is identified in Hebrew thought with Sheol, the dwelling place of the dead, lies beyond the domain of Yahweh; 'for in death there is no remembrance of thee; in Sheol who can give thee praise?' (Ps 6[5]); 'for Sheol cannot thank thee, those who go down to the pit cannot hope for thy faithfulness' (Is 38[18]). The state of the dead in Sheol is a pale shadow of their life on earth; they are 'shades' (Heb. *r^ephā'îm*, 'powerless ones'); they cannot, like the Babylonian *etimmu*, harm the living.

But there is a third aspect of the relation between the living and the dead in Israel, namely the practice, old and deep-rooted, of resorting to the dead in times of crisis for counsel. As evidence for the existence of this practice we have the classic case of Saul and the witch of Endor (1 S 28[8ff]), the stringent prohibitions of the practice in Lv 19[26] and Dt 18[11], where it is stated that it was a Canaanite custom; and the passage in Is 8[19], where the people are represented as saying that in a time of crisis it is necessary for them to 'consult the dead on behalf of the living,' and use the term *'^elōhîm* to describe the dead. That the practice had survived as late as the 8th cent. shows how deep-seated it was; but the prohibitions in Leviticus and Deuteronomy, and the prophetic comment in Is 8, show also that such practices were coming to be regarded as an invasion of the realm which belonged to Yahweh alone, 'the secret things belong unto the Lord our God' (Dt 29[29]).

One more feature of early Israelite practice has been appealed to as evidence of the existence of the cult of the ancestors, namely the existence of sacred objects called *t^erāphîm*. We are told that when Jacob fled from Laban, Rachel stole her father's *t^erāphîm*, and Laban refers to them as his 'gods' (Gn 31[30, 34]); they are mentioned among the sacred objects in Micah's household shrine (Jg 17[5]); and in Ho 3[4] the prophet says that Israel is to be deprived of 'ephod and teraphim' for a long period of time. But we do not know what they were like, and apart from the fact that they were connected with the household cult, there is nothing to connect them with a cult of the ancestors.

From these various references it is possible to draw the following conclusions: (*a*) it is clear that when the Israelites came into Canaan, they found the inhabitants of the land practising a cult of the ancestors, and also that they adopted the practice themselves, possibly in connexion with the graves of the patriarchs and the kings of Judah; (*b*) the practice of consulting the dead, also borrowed from the Canaanites, although condemned by the prophets and the codes, cannot strictly be called ancestor-worship; (*c*) that, as the unique character of Yahweh came to dominate the religious outlook of Israel, the powers of the dead tended to recede into obscurity; (*d*) as the holiness of Yahweh became more strongly realized, the idea of the uncleanness of death and the dead replaced the idea of honour done to the dead in the old Canaanite mourning customs, although those customs probably had their origin, during the animistic stage of Canaanite religion, in the fear of the dead. S. H. He.

ANCHOR.—See Ships and Boats, **2** (2).

ANCIENT OF DAYS occurs three times in Daniel (7[9, 13, 22]) as a title of God in His capacity as Judge of the world. In the Vision of the Great Assizes He is depicted as a very old and majestic figure, with white hair and white raiment, seated on a fiery throne, and having the books of the records of man opened before Him. The picture is no doubt suggested by the contrast between the Eternal God (Ps 55[19]) and the new-fangled deities which were from time to time introduced (Jg 5[8], Dt 32[17]), rather than, as Hippolytus (quoted by Behrmann, *Das Buch Daniel*, p. 46) suggests, by the idea of God as making the ages old without turning old Himself. In the troublous times which are represented by the Book of Daniel, it was at once a comfort and a warning to remember that above the fleeting phases of life there sat One who remained eternally the same (Ps 90[1-3] 102[24-27]). At the same time it is worth remembering that the phrase in itself has no mystical significance, but, by an idiom common in Hebrew as in other languages, is merely a paraphrase for 'an old man.' H. C. O. L.

ANDREW.—One of the twelve apostles. According to Jn 1[40-44] he was a brother of Simon Peter and a native of Bethsaida. The evangelist further relates that Andrew had been a disciple of John the Baptist before he became a follower of Jesus (Jn 1[35-40]). The Synoptic Gospels likewise indicate that Andrew was the brother of Simon Peter (Mt 10[2], Lk 6[14]), and add that they lived together, apparently in Capernaum (Mk 1[29]), and were fishermen on the sea of Galilee (Mt 4[18], Mk 1[16]). In one place Andrew is linked with the inner circle of disciples made up of Peter, James, and John (Mk 13[3]). According to Eusebius he evangelized Scythia, and later tradition adds that he was crucified at Patrae.

Andrew is a good Greek name, but is used of a Jew in Dio Cassius lxviii. 32. 2. W. R. S.

ANDRONICUS.—**1.** An officer of Antiochus Epiphanes who was instrumental in the removal of the legitimate high priest in Jerusalem shortly before the war of the Maccabees (2 Mac 4[30-38]). **2.** An officer of Antiochus Epiphanes mentioned in 2 Mac 5[23] usually distinguished from the Andronicus mentioned above. **3.** A Christian greeted by Paul in Ro 16[7]. From this passage we learn that he was a 'kinsman' of Paul, *i.e.* a fellow-countryman (cf Ro 9[3] 16[11, 21]), that he had suffered imprisonment at some unknown time with Paul, that Paul regarded him as an 'apostle,' and that he had been a Christian before Paul's own conversion. It has been suggested, therefore, that Andronicus along with Junias played a significant role in the establishment of the Roman church (G. A. Barton) or of the Ephesian church (B. W. Bacon). W. R. S.

ANEM.—A Levitical city of Issachar, mentioned with Ramoth, 1 Ch 6[73]. The parallel list in Jos 21[29] has **En-gannim** (q.v.). Perhaps modern *Khirbet 'Anîn*.

ANER.—**1.** One of the three Amorite chieftains, the others being Mamre and Eshcol, who were in covenant with Abraham, Gn 14[13f]. As Mamre is an old name for Hebron (Gn 23[19]), and Eshcol is the name of a valley near Hebron (Nu 13[23]), it is natural to suppose that Aner was also the name of a locality that gave its name to a clan. **2.** A Levitical city of Manasseh, W. of Jordan, 1 Ch 6[70]; site unknown.

ANETHOTHITE, 2 S 23[27] (AV), **ANETOTHITE,** 1 Ch 27[12] (AV)=man of **Anathoth** (q.v.).

ANGEL OF THE LORD (YAHWEH), also called 'Angel of God.'—He plays the leading role among the angels, both in heaven (*e.g.* Zec 3[1ff]) and on earth (*e.g.* Jg 6[11ff]), as Yahweh's personal representative. Cf Is 63[9], EV 'the angel of his presence,' or, with due recognition of Hebrew idiom, 'his personal messenger' (unless we should follow LXX and render by 'No envoy or messenger but he himself saved them'). He frequently appears, sometimes in seemingly human form, as the envoy through whom Yahweh communicates with mankind (*e.g.* Gn 16[7-13] 22[11ff], Ex 3[2], Nu 22[22ff], Jg 6[11ff] 13[3ff], 2 K 1[3, 15]) and keeps himself informed of conditions upon the earth (Zec 1[11f]). He also has what may be called civil and military responsibilities, for it is his task, not only to pronounce the Divine judgment (Zec 3[1ff]: cf 2 S 14[17] 19[27]) and, when necessary, inflict suitable punishment (2 S 24[16]: cf Nu 22[22ff]), but also to defend the faithful (2 K 19[35], Ps 34[7] 35[5f]). In fact his powers are so wide that, from first to last, he is virtually indistinguishable from Yahweh (*e.g.* Gn 16[7-13], Zec 3[1ff]); and to see him is thought to be as dangerous as seeing Yahweh himself (*e.g.* Jg 6^{22f} 13^{21f}). The way in which he thus figures in the OT, *i.e.* at one moment identified with Yahweh and, at another moment, treated as quite distinct (*e.g.* Gn 16$^{7-13}$ 22^{11f}, Jg 6^{11ff}, Zec 3^{1ff}: cf Gn 48^{15f}, Hos 12^{4}, Zec 12^{8}) is not to be explained in terms of a *growing* emphasis upon the transcendence of Yahweh. It can be properly understood only by bearing in mind the Hebrew conception of ‘ corporate personality,’ specifically the part played by any member of a social body, particularly one of its leading figures, as an ‘ extension ’ of the personality of its founder or head (cf A. R. Johnson, *The One and the Many in the Israelite Conception of God*, 2nd edit. [1961], pp. 28 ff). A. R. J.

ANGELS.—Throughout the Near East, from comparatively ancient times, there was belief in the existence of beings, inferior in power and dignity to the great gods, but nevertheless potencies whose activity might affect human life for good or ill. Some of these were local deities, some were associated with the great forces of nature, others were less awesome powers whose activities might be concerned with the upper world, or the underworld, as well as with this world of man's habitation. At times these beings seemed benevolent, at others malevolent. Some groups, indeed, were thought of as generally benevolent, while others were in general malevolent. A great deal of the magic practised both in Egypt and in Mesopotamia was concerned with attracting the benevolence or avoiding the malevolence of these beings in the unseen world around men. We still preserve the distinction between angels and DEMONS (q.v.), the former generally benevolent and associated with the upper world, the latter generally malevolent and associated with the underworld.

Our word ‘ angel ’ derives from another ancient belief, namely, that the great gods commonly used these beings of lesser rank as agents, envoys, and messengers. As human potentates extended the range of their power and influence by envoys and agents, so it was to be expected that in the unseen world, usually thought of as monarchically organized, the great powers would have a similar arrangement. Where henotheism, and later monotheism, emerged, such lesser deities and spirits as continued to survive in the religion were commonly thought of as attendants on, or holding some subordinate position to, the Supreme God, in a court where they had their ranks and grades, held only delegated authority, and functioned at the bidding of their Lord.

In the OT the common word for ‘ angel ’ is *mal'ākh*, and in the NT *angelos*. Both words mean ‘ messenger ’ and are used for messengers sent by human potentates as well as for messengers, celestial or human, sent by God—precisely as *mal'ak* in Ugaritic texts from Râs Shamra, and *angelos* in ancient Greek texts, may be used of messengers sent by kings as well as of those sent by the gods. In the OT these celestials are referred to as ‘ divine beings ’ (*'^{e}lōhîm*, Ps 8$^{6\,(5)}$ 82$^{1,\,6}$ 97^{7} 138^{1}), ‘ sons of divine beings ’ (*b^{e}nê '^{e}lōhîm*, Gn 6$^{2,\,4}$, Job 1^{6} 2^{1} 38^{7}; *b^{e}nê 'ēlîm*, Ps 29^{1} 89$^{7\,(6)}$), ‘ mighty ones ’ (*'abbîrîm*, Ps 78^{25}), ‘ holy ones ’ or ‘ saints (*ḳ^{e}dhōshîm*, Job 5^{1}, Ps 89$^{6\,(5)}$, Zec 14^{5}, Dn 4$^{14\,(17)}$ 8^{13}). They are ‘ the host of heaven ’ (1 K 22^{19}), the ‘ host of the height ’ (Is 24^{21}), the ‘ host of Yahweh ’ (Jos 5$^{14,\,15}$), who form a courtly assembly around God (1 K 22$^{19-22}$, Job 1^{6} 2^{1}, Ps 89$^{7\,(6)}$) much as the *ilm*, the *bn ilm* and the *bn qds* formed an assembly around El in the Ugaritic texts. This assembly, though subject to God, who as ‘ Lord of Hosts ’ held supreme position, was not entirely submissive to Him, so that He had to preserve peace among them (Job 25^{2} 21^{22}, cf Is 24^{21}), and some who revolted against Him became the fallen angels (Gn 6$^{2-4}$ with Jd ^{6}, 2 P 2^{4}, and cf Is 27^{1} 34$^{4,\,5}$).

Certain classes of celestials were recognized, for we read of Watchers (*'îrîn*, Dn 4$^{14\,(17)}$), Seraphim (Is 6$^{2,\,6}$), Cherubim (Ps 18$^{11\,(10)}$, Ezk 9^{3}). Perhaps rank was also recognized, for in Jos 5^{14} one calls himself the ‘ captain ’ (*śar*) of Yahweh's host, the same word used in Dn 10$^{20,\,21}$ of Michael and the angel ‘ princes ’ of Greece and Persia. In particular there is one exalted figure, the ‘ angel of the Lord ’ (*mal'akh Yahweh*) who, though an angel messenger, is yet greater than any angel and at times indistinguishable from Yahweh Himself (Gn 16$^{7-13}$ 21^{7} 31$^{11-13}$, Ex 3$^{2-6}$, Jg 2$^{1-5}$). Possibly he was thought of in early days as a theophany, but in later writings is certainly only an angel, though one with superior authority (Zec 1–6). It was after the Jewish people had come more closely into contact with other cultures that we find a particular development in their angelology. With a growing sense of the transcendence of God came a stress on the activities of these celestial attendants, creatures whom He had created (Neh 9^{6}) before the creation of the earth (Job 38$^{6,\,7}$), who acted as His agents, envoys, and intermediaries. Their normal abode was heaven (Gn 28^{12}, 1 K 22^{19}, Job 2^{7}, Neh 9^{6}, and cf Dt 17^{3} where the ‘ host ’ may be the stars as celestial beings), but they came down freely to earth (Gn 32$^{2\,(1)}$, Ex 14^{9} 23$^{20,\,23}$, Job 1^{7}, Is 6^{6}, Zec 4^{1}, Dn 10$^{10,\,11}$). Normally they are invisible beings of a spiritual and fiery nature (Ps 104^{4}, Jg 13^{20}, 2 K 6^{17} Dn 10^{6}), of superhuman power (Ps 103^{20}, Gn 19$^{10,\,11}$, Jg 6$^{20,\,21}$, Zec 12^{8}, Dn 10^{5ff}) and wisdom (2 S 14$^{17,\,20}$, Dn 10^{21}), though they are by no means perfect (Job 4^{18}). When they are seen in vision, or come down to perform tasks on earth, they are in human form (Gn 19^{1ff}, Jos 5^{3}, Jg 6^{11}, Dn 8^{15}) and can be spoken of as men (Gn 18$^{2,\,16,\,22}$ 32$^{25\,(24)}$, Jg 13^{6ff}, Ezk 40$^{3,\,4}$, Zec 1^{8}, Dn 3^{25} 10$^{16,\,18}$), for they speak in human fashion (Jos 5^{15}, Jg 6^{12} 13$^{3,\,11}$, 1 K 19^{5}, Zec 4$^{1,\,5}$), stand or sit (Dn 8^{16}, Jg 6^{11}), walk about (Gn 32$^{2\,(1)}$, Job 2^{2}, Zec 1$^{10,\,11}$), eat (Gn 18^{8}), wear clothes (Ezk 9^{2}, Dn 10^{5}), brandish weapons (Nu 22^{23}, Jos 5^{13}, 1 Ch 21$^{16,\,30}$, Ezk 9^{2}), and even ride horses (Zec 1^{8} 6^{1ff}, cf Rev 9^{16}).

Their functions are many. In heaven they worship God (Neh 9^{6}, Ps 103$^{20,\,21}$ 29$^{1,\,2}$ 97^{7} 148^{2}, Is 6^{3}) and stand ready to do His will (Ps 103^{20}, Is 45^{12}, 1 Ch 21^{27}). They may report to the heavenly court the doings of men on earth (Job 1^{6ff,} 2^{1ff}, Zec 1^{11}), but more particularly they are the messengers of God to men, bringing instruction (Nu 22^{35}, Jos 5^{14}, Jg 13^{12ff}, Job 33^{23}, Zec 1^{9}, Dn 8^{16} 9^{22}), transmitting revelation to the prophets (Dn10^{11}, Ezk 40^{4}, Zec 4$^{1-7}$, 1 K 13^{18}, 2 K 1^{3}), and announcing coming events, *e.g.* the destruction of Sodom (Gn 19^{13}), the birth of Isaac (Gn 18^{10ff}), the birth of Samson (Jg 13^{3ff}). They accompany God as His attendants when He appears on earth (Dt 32^{2}, Job 38^{7}). They may be sent as God's guardians over a people (Ex 32^{34} 33^{2}, Nu 20^{16}), whence later we find angels designated as the patrons of different national groups (Dn 10$^{13,\,20,\,21}$). Or they may be guardians over places, as over Bethel (Gn 31$^{11,\,13}$), or Jerusalem (Zec 12^{8}), over individuals, *e.g.* Hagar (Gn 16^{7ff,} 21^{17ff}), Isaac (Gn 22^{11ff}), Jacob (Gn 48$^{15,\,16}$), the three children (Dn 3^{28}), Elijah (1 K 19^{5ff}, 2 K 1^{15}), and over the righteous in general (Ps 91^{11} 34$^{8\,(7)}$, Is 63^{9} and cf Job 5^{1}). They are sent to guide both communities (Ex 14^{19} 23$^{20,\,23}$) and individuals (Gn 24$^{7,\,40}$). They are very numerous (Dt 32^{2}, Job 25^{3} 33^{23}, Ps 68$^{18\,(17)}$, Dn 7^{10}), and are normally good (1 S 29^{9}, 2 S 19$^{28\,(27)}$). So awesome were they that men were inclined to offer them that worship which should be offered only to God (Jos 5^{14}, Zeph 1^{5}, Jer 8^{2} and Jer 4^{19} where the stars as angels are meant, cf Neh 9^{6}). They may also, however, be the agents of God's testing, as when Satan tested Job, or of His wrath, thwarting (Nu 22$^{22-35}$) or bringing chastisement on evil men, as on Sodom (Gn 19^{11ff}), on Egypt (Ps 78^{49}), on Meroz (Jg 5^{23}), on Israel (2 S 24$^{16,\,17}$, 1 Ch 21^{12ff}), on the Assyrian host (2 K 19^{35}, 2 Ch 32^{21}), or on evil doers in general (Ps 35$^{5,\,6}$).

As the celestial agents who execute God's judgments among men are acting against men and not for them, *i.e.* are seemingly maleficent rather than beneficent, they are referred to as ‘ evil angels ’ (Ps 78^{49}, cf Job 33^{22}). So the troubling spirit which visited Saul is called an evil spirit from the Lord (1 S 16$^{14-23}$), and the spirit with the message persuading Ahab to go up to Ramoth-Gilead is ‘ a lying spirit in the mouth of all his prophets ’ (1 K 22$^{20-23}$). Similarly Satan, who in Job 1^{6} 2^{1} is one of the *b^enê 'elōhîm*, because he is hostile to such pious servants as Job and the high-priest Joshua (Zec 3[1,2]), came to be regarded as an instigator to evil (1 Ch 21[1] compared with 2 S 24[1]), and was later identified with the serpent of the Eden story (Wis 2[24], Rev 12[9]). Here a moral distinction has developed between powers working for good and those working for evil. This fitted in with popular memory of ancient cosmic myths about the dark forces of chaos which at creation fought against the introduction of order, some reminiscences of which are found in the OT (*e.g.* Ps 74[12ff] 89[9 (8)], Job 26[12], Is 51[9,10]), and the already mentioned belief that the celestial powers are at times not completely submissive to God. In Dn 10[20] there is reference to strife among the celestial powers, among whom God has to keep peace (Job 25[2]). That He was not completely successful is suggested by the story in Gn 6[2-4]. These unsubmissive powers came to be regarded as concerned with wickedness on earth, and ultimately God will have to deal with all such recalcitrant powers (Is 27[1] 24[21,22], Ps 82[1] and cf Jd [6]).

It has often been noted that there is a development of thought in the OT with regard to angels. In the earlier passages they are rarely called angels, and though always in attendance on God are limited in their relations with mankind, and no stress is laid on their moral character. Even Satan, though an ' adversary ', is still subject to the will of God. It was as the sense of God's uniqueness became clearer that there was on the one hand a tendency to emphasize the position of angels as intermediaries between Him and mankind, so that things formerly attributed to His action were attributed to the action of angels (cf 2 S 24[11ff] with 1 Ch 21[18]), or on the other hand to ignore, if not deny, the existence of such intermediaries. The writer of the priestly document P does not mention angels, and in such books as Proverbs, Esther, Ecclesiastes they receive little or no attention. Ezekiel would seem to belong to the period of transition. In some places the Lord speaks directly to him (44[2]), but in others it is an angel who instructs him (40[4]). Ezekiel does not use the word ' angel,' generally referring to them as men, but on the other hand he names various groups of celestials, the Seraphim, Cherubim, Ōphannim (wheels), Ḥayyôth (living beings), and a certain Spirit (2[2] 3[12] 9[5,24]). In still later books such as Daniel and Zechariah we find even fuller development, and certain important angelic beings are given personal names, *e.g.* Michael and Gabriel.

In the Intertestamental period as reflected in the Apocrypha and some Pseudepigrapha, we find again the two tendencies. Such books as Ecclesiasticus, Wisdom, Judith, Maccabees, Psalms of Solomon rarely mention angels whereas in Tobit, Jubilees, Fourth Ezra, the Testaments, and the Enoch literature, there is a considerable development of angelology. This tallies with early statements that some groups, such as the Sadducees, were sceptical about the activity of angels (Ac 23[8]), while other groups, such as the Essenes, made much of them (Jos. *BJ* II. viii. 7 [142]). They figure prominently in the Dead Sea Scrolls of the Qumrân community. The angelology of this period continues that of the later books of the OT but develops it. Angels were thought of as very numerous (Enoch 40[1] 60[1] 71[8], Apoc. Bar 48[10] 56[14] 59[11], Jub 2[18]). They still are busy praising and blessing the Lord (To 8[15], Enoch 61[7], Three 36), and are the instruments of Divine aid to men (2 Mac 11[6] 15[23], 3 Mac 6[18], Bel 34–39, To 3[17], Jub 4[21]), guiding them as Raphael guides Tobit, guarding individuals (Jub 35[17], 2 Mac 10[29,30]), places (4 Mac 4[10]) and nations (Bar 6[7], Jub 15[31]), and giving instruction (Jub 4[15] 32[21], 4 Ezr 5[31ff], 7[1ff], To 6[3ff] 12[6ff]). But they are also the instruments of punishment (Enoch 53[3-5] 56[1] 62[11] 63[1], Test. Levi 3[2]). In this period the ' sons of God ' in the story of Gn 6[2-4] have become clearly identified with a group of fallen angels (Enoch 6–15, Jub 5[1] 7[21], Apoc. Bar 56[11-13]), whose chief is Satan (=Belial=Mastema), so that the good angels (To 5[21], 2 Mac 11[6]) are carefully distinguished from the demons (To 6[14], Jub 10[3], Enoch 99[7]). The angelic organization also now appears more clearly. We find reference to **archangels** (Test. Levi 3[5(a)]; cf To 12[15], Enoch 20[1-8] 40[2-10])—Raphael, Uriel, and others are named along with Michael and Gabriel; there is a clearer distinction of classes of angels (Enoch 61[10] 71[7]), and a definite assignment of angels to have charge of the phenomena of nature (Jub 2[2], Enoch 60[14-21], 4 Ezr 8[22]); and we find angels regarded as intercessors with God for mankind (Enoch 9[3] 15[2] 40[6] 99[3] 104[1], To 12[12,15], Test. Dan 6[2], Test. Levi 5[6]).

The NT teaching concerning angels is not very different from this. It also marks clearly the distinction between good and evil angels (Rev 12[7], cf Mt 25[41]). The good angels, who are fiery spiritual beings (He 1[7]), dwell normally in heaven, where they glorify God and attend on Him (Mt 18[10], Lk 1[19] 2[13-15] 12[8,9], Jn 1[51], Rev 5[11]), and form the armies of the Most High (Rev 7[12] 19[14]). They come down to earth (Mt 28[2], Lk 2[9], Ac 10[3], Rev 18[1]) as instruments of divine aid to Jesus (Mt 4[11] 26[53], Lk 22[43]), or to men in general (Jn 5[4], Ac 5[19] 12[7ff], He 1[14]). They come also as messengers from God communicating to men (Mt 1[20] 2[13] 28[5ff], Lk 1[11,28] 2[10ff], Ac 8[26ff] 10[3-7,30-32] 27[23-26], Rev 21[9]), and as such are concerned with revelation (Rev 1[1] 14[6] 22[16], Ac 7[53], Gal 1[8], He 2[2]). They are men's guardians (Mt 18[10], Ac 12[15]), are interested in men's salvation (Lk 15[10], cf 1 Ti 5[21]), present their prayers before God (Rev 8[3,4]), and at death convey their souls to rest (Lk 16[22]). They may also be the instruments of chastisement (Mt 13[49,50], Rev 9[15] 16[1] 21[9]). When they appear in dream or on earth they usually appear in human form, even though more radiant than ordinary human beings (Mt 28[3], Lk 2[9], Ac 1[10] 10[30], Rev 18[1]). They wear garments (Lk 24[4], Jn 20[12], Rev 19[14]), and speak like human persons (Mt 1[20] 2[19,20], Jn 12[29], Rev 7[2]), and are of limited knowledge (Mt 24[36], Mk 13[32]). There are ranks and grades amongst them, for we read of archangels (Jd [9], 1 Th 4[16]), and of celestial groups called dominions, principalities, and powers (Col 1[16], Eph 1[21] 3[10], 1 P 3[22]), whom some were inclined to worship (Col 2[18], cf Rev 19[10] 22[8,9]). There is an angel set over the bottomless pit (Rev 9[11]), and angels are in charge of the phenomena of nature (Rev 7[1] 14[18] 16[5] 19[17]). In the events of the Last Day angels will have an important share (Matt 13[39ff] 16[27] 24[31], 2 Th 1[7-10]). On that Day there will be a judgment also on the fallen angels (2 P 2[4] Jd [6]) with their principalities and powers (1 Co 15[24] Eph 6[12]), and their ruler Satan (Rev 12[7] 20[1-3,10]). A. J.

ANGELS OF THE SEVEN CHURCHES.—The author of Revelation views each of the churches named in chs. 2 and 3 as having its angelic guardian: Ephesus, Smyrna, Pergamum, Sardis, Philadelphia, Thyatira, and Laodicea. In viewing these seven angels as seven stars, he is resorting to a view common in his day: the stars in their heavenly wonder were esteemed as gods or living beings, and out of this awesome feeling arose star-worship. Jewish cosmology personalized the stars (Jg 5[20], Job 38[7], Enoch 21[6]). The personalized stars were thus akin to angels.

Several views have been held regarding the angels of the seven churches: **1.** Each angel is a bishop or presbyter of a church who acts as a messenger of God (cf Hag 1[13], Mal 2[7] 3[1]). But the Greek word for angel or messenger (*angelos*) has no such use elsewhere in the NT. It is doubtful if each church at the time of Revelation had its particular monarchical bishop with responsibilites as assigned to an angel. **2.** Each angel is a heavenly representative to act as a guardian of a church. In Persian religion each person had his guardian angel (*fravashi*); Tobit on his journey to Ragae is protected by his guardian angel Raphael (To 5[4-21]); Peter's guardian angel will descend from heaven on the last days (Ascension of Isaiah 3[15], written about the same time as Revelation); the success or failure of a nation agrees with that of a nation's guardian angel. **3.** Each angel is a representative sent by a church from Asia Minor to John on the Isle of Patmos. This view, however, has little weight. **4.** Each angel is a personification of a church, in which the life of the church finds embodiment. In apocalyptic thought angels were active in the waters, the abyss, the fire, the winds (cf Rev 9^{11} 16^{5} 7^{1} 14^{18}); each of the elements symbolized the life or personality of an angel.

The most probable view is one which sees a close correlation between each church and its angel, both the angel and the church sharing equally in the life of the community. In an age which held to the apocalyptic views of angelology, an angel was a special protector of each person or nation (or in this case, a church). In the seven churches of Revelation each angel is an immanent guardian sharing in the life of the church, not a transcendent heavenly creature. T. S. K.

ANGER.—In OT 'anger' represents about a dozen Hebrew roots, which occur as nouns, verbs (once 'angered' is used transitively, Ps 106^{32}), and adjectives. By far the most frequent words are *'ānaph* (literally 'to snort') and its derivative noun *'aph*, which is used of the anger both of men (Gn 27^{45} 30^{2}, Ex 11^{8} 32^{9}, etc.) and God (Ex 4^{14} 32^{22}, Ps 6^{1} 7^{6}, etc.). In NT 'anger' is of much less frequent occurrence, and represents only two roots: (1) the noun *orgē* (which, however, is usually translated 'wrath'), the verb *orgizomai*, the adjective *orgilos* (only in Tit 1^{7}, RSV 'quick tempered'), and the transitive verb *parorgizō* (Ro 10^{19}, the only case of a transitive use of 'anger' in NT); (2) the verb *cholaō* (literally 'to be full of bile,' from *cholē*, 'bile'), used only in Jn 7^{23} to express the bitter anger of 'the Jews' against Jesus. With regard to the distinction between *orgē* and the synonym *thymos*, it is to be noted that while *orgē* is very often translated 'wrath,' *thymos* is never translated 'anger,' and when the two words occur together, *thymos* in each case is 'wrath' (Ro 2^{8}, RSV) 'fury' (Eph 4^{31}, Col 3^{8}) and *orgē* 'anger' (Eph 4^{31}, Col 3^{8}) or 'wrath' (Ro 2^{8} RSV). *Thymos* is the more violent word, denoting anger as a strong passion or emotion, while *orgē* points rather to a settled moral indignation. Thus *orgē* is used of the sorrowful anger of Jesus (Mk 3^{5}); *thymos* of the rage of His enemies (Lk 4^{28}; cf Ac 19^{28}). And, outside of the Apocalypse, *thymos* is applied almost exclusively to the wrath of men (the only exception being Ro 2^{8}) while *orgē* in the great majority of cases (Mt 3^{7}, Jn 3^{36}, Ro 1^{18}, etc.) denotes the righteous indignation of God. J. C. L.

ANGER (WRATH) OF GOD.—It might seem that the idea of the Divine anger, manifesting itself in judgments of destruction, belongs to an early and anthropomorphic stage of religion. Yet, on the whole, the Biblical conception will be found consistent and profoundly ethical. God is *holy*—a term which seems to unite all the unapproachable perfections of Deity, especially His majesty and awful purity. He is the 'Holy One of Israel,' in covenant relation with a nation to whom He has revealed Himself as holy, and whom He will fashion with slow redemptive purpose into 'a holy people.' Moreover, God is *righteous*, a moral governor and lawgiver, demanding obedience and punishing transgression of His commands. The Divine holiness is not an element in an abstract conception of Deity: it is not a passive perfection, but an active attribute of a self-revealing and redeeming God. It follows that one side of this activity is necessarily a reaction against, a repudiation of, what is unholy and unrighteous in His creatures. This disposition towards sin is the anger or wrath of God. In the history of Israel it appears as a terrible factor in the discipline of the nation to righteousness: the ungrateful, the rebellious, and especially the idolatrous, are destroyed by fire and sword, pestilence and famine (Ps 78, Dt 32^{15-43}). So 'jealous' is God for His holiness, that even accidental profanation of its symbol, the Ark, is visited by extreme penalty (1 S $6^{19, 20}$, 2 S 6^{7}). But the anger of the Lord, though fierce, is also just: it is 'provoked' by moral causes and for moral ends, and is averted by penitence and moral acquiescence in the righteousness of His judgments (Ex 32, Lv 10^{6}, Nu 25^{11}, Dt 13^{17}). Psalmist and Prophet dwell upon the subordination of the Divine anger to the Divine mercy. God is 'slow to anger' (Ps 103^{8} 145^{8}, Jl 2^{13}, Jon 4^{2}, Nah 1^{3}), and His anger passes away (Ps 30^{5}, Is 12^{1}, Jer 3^{12}, Mic 7^{19}).

Yet the wrath of God remains an essential element of His revelation through the prophets, a real Divine attribute, complementary, not antithetic to the Divine mercy (Is 1^{18-20} 5^{25} 42^{25} 54^{8}). In the NT, although the stress has shifted to the love of God revealed to the world in Jesus Christ, the anger of God still holds place. The teaching of Jesus, while refusing to see in all physical ills the Divine displeasure against sin (Lk 13^{1-5}, Jn 9^{3}), contains impressive warning of the terrible reality of God's judgments (Lk 13^{3-5}, Mt $25^{30, 41}$, Lk 12^{5}). In St. Paul's writings this conception of judgment, held in reserve against unrepentant sin, is expressed in the phrase 'the wrath of God,' or, more simply, 'the wrath' (Ro 1^{18}, Eph 5^{6}, Col 3^{6}, Ro 2^{8} 5^{9}). There is a coming 'day of wrath' (Ro 2^{5}; cf Mt 3^{7}); sinful man unredeemed by Christ is necessarily a 'vessel of wrath,' a 'child of wrath' (Ro 9^{22}, Eph 2^{3}).

It is true that the NT references to God's anger are mainly eschatological and contain figurative elements (see especially Rev 6^{16} 'the wrath of the Lamb,' 11^{18} 14^{10} 16^{19} 19^{15}). But for the significance of the Divine wrath as an ethical necessity in God, though His fundamental attribute is love, it may be noted that (1) the writer through whom the revelation of the Divine love attains its culminating expression ('God *is* love,' 1 Jn 4^{8}) declares also of him that obeys not the Son, 'the wrath of God rests upon him' (Jn 3^{36}). (2) The Epistle which shows how in Christ the aloofness and terror of Israel's worship are done away in favour of full and free access to a 'throne of grace,' has, as the climax to its glowing description of Christian privilege, the solemn warning 'our God is a consuming fire' (He 4^{16} 12^{18-29}). S. W. G.

ANGLE.—Is 19^{8}, Hab 1^{15} (AV, RV), where RSV has 'hook.' The same word in Job 41^{1} is rendered 'hook' in AV, and 'fishhook' in RV, RSV.

ANIAM ('lament of people' or 'I am kinsman').—A Manassite, 1 Ch 7^{19}.

ANIM.—A town of Judah, in the mountains near Eshtemoh, Jos 15^{50}; possibly modern *Khirbet Ghuwein et-Taḥtā*.

ANISE (RV, RSV 'dill,' Mt 23^{23}) is the familiar plant *Anethum graveolens*, one of the Umbelliferae. It is indigenous in Palestine, and is extensively used both in cooking and in the form of 'dill water' as a domestic remedy for flatulence. It is expressly stated in Jewish writers that the dill was subject to tithe (*Maaseroth* 4^{5}). E. W. G. M.

ANKLE-CHAINS, ANKLETS.—See Ornaments, **4.**

ANNA (the Greek form of Hebrew *Hannah*, which means 'grace').—The name of an aged prophetess (Lk 2^{36-38}), one of the godly remnant in Israel who in the dark days which preceded the Messiah's advent were looking for the dayspring from on high and waiting for the consolation of Israel. She was the daughter of Phanuel, and belonged to the ancient tribe of Asher, whose women were celebrated for their beauty, which fitted them for wedding with high priests and kings. She had attained the age of eighty-four (see RSV). She had given herself to a life of devotion, frequenting the Temple and 'worshiping with fasting and prayer night and day' (cf 1 Ti 5^{5}). At the Presentation of the Infant Messiah (Lk 2^{22-24}) she entered the sacred court, and, hearing Simeon's benediction and prophecy, took up the refrain of praise to God, and talked about the Holy Child to 'all who were looking for the redemption of Jerusalem.' D. S.—F. C. G.

ANNAAS, 1 Es 5^{23} (AV).—See Senaah.

ANNAN.—Father of one who agreed to put away his foreign wife, 1 Es 9^{32} (AV, RV **Annas**); perhaps the **Harim** of Ezr 10^{31}.

ANNAS.—1. High priest from A.D. 6 to 15. He is mentioned in three passages of the NT. In Lk 3^{2} the

beginning of John the Baptist's ministry is dated ' in the high priesthood of Annas and Caiaphas.' In Ac 4[6ff] Annas is introduced as playing a role in the trial of Peter and John. In Jn 18[12-24] Jesus is brought to trial before him. In all these passages Annas appears as high priest (or as one of the high priests). In actual fact Caiaphas was sole high priest from A.D. 18 to 36 when these events took place. The confusion in the NT is usually explained as stemming from Annas' influence which continued long after the end of his high priesthood. The influence is attested among other things by the fact that five of his sons became high priests. John also asserts that Caiaphas was his son-in-law (Jn 18[13]). The name Annas (or Hannas) is an abbreviated form of Hananus (=Hananiah) which is given as the name of this high priest in Josephus. **2.** Annas (or Hannas) appears in the Septuagint (1 Es 9[32]=Ezr 10[31]) for the Hebrew name Harim (RSV in 1 Es 9[32], **Annan**).
W. R. S.

ANNIAS.—The eponym of a family that returned with Zerubbabel, 1 Es 5[16] (AV **Ananias** ; RV **Annis**). Omitted in the lists in Ezr and Neh.

ANNIS, 1 Es 5[16] (RV).—See ANNIAS.

ANNIUTH.—A Levite who expounded the Law, 1 Es 9[48] (AV **Anus** ; RV **Annus**) ; in Neh 8[7] called **Bani** (q.v.).

ANNUNUS.—A Levite, 1 Es 8[48] (AV, RV **Annuus**) ; not mentioned in Ezr 8[19].

ANNUS, 1 Es 9[48] (RV).—See ANNIUTH.

ANNUUS, 1 Es 8[48] (AV, RV).—See ANNUNUS.

ANOINTING, ANOINTED.—1. The Hebrews distinguished between anointing with oil in the sense of its application to the body in ordinary life (*sûkh*), and anointing by pouring sacred oil on the head as a rite of consecration (*māshaḥ*). As regards the former, olive oil, alone or mixed with perfumes, was largely used in the everyday toilet of the Hebrews, although among the poor its use would be reserved for special occasions (Ru 3[3]). To abstain from anointing in this sense was one of the tokens of mourning (2 S 14[2]), its resumption a sign that mourning was at an end (12[20]). Honour was shown to a guest by anointing his head with oil (Ps 23[5], Lk 7[46]), and still more by anointing his feet (Lk 7[38]). For medicinal anointing see OIL.

2. Anointing as a religious rite was applied to both persons and things. **Kings** in particular were consecrated for their high office by having oil poured upon their heads. Though first met with in OT in the case of Saul (1 S 10[1], cf David, 2 S 2[4] 5[3], Solomon, 1 K 1[39], etc.), similar rites were practised in Canaan and in other lands of the ancient world long before the Hebrew conquest. By the pouring of the consecrated oil upon the head (see 2 K 9[3]), there was thought to be effected a transference to the person anointed of part of the essential holiness and virtue of the deity in whose name and by whose representative the rite was performed. By the Hebrews the rite was also believed to impart a special endowment of the spirit of Y″ (1 S 16[13], cf Is 61[1]). Hence the sacrosanct character of the king as ' the Lord's anointed ' (Hebrew *m^eshîaḥ* [*Yahweh*] which became in Greek *messias* or, translated, *christos*—both ' Messiah ' and ' Christ,' therefore signifying ' the anointed '). The application of this honorific title to kings alone in the oldest literature makes it probable that the similar consecration of the **priesthood** (Ex 29[7] 40[13-15], Lv 8[1-12]) was a later extension of the rite. Only one exceptional instance is recorded of the anointing of a **prophet** (1 K 19[16]). Whether the speaker in Is 61[1] is the Servant of Yahweh or the prophet is disputed ; the usage, however, is metaphorical.

In the case of inanimate objects, we find early mention of the primitive and widespread custom of anointing **sacred stones** (Gn 31[13], etc., see PILLAR), and in the Priests' Code the **tabernacle** and its furnishings were similarly consecrated (Ex 30[25ff] 40[9]). For 2 S 1[21] see WAR. See also MARY, No. **2.** A. R. S. K.—**J. Br.**

ANON.—A contraction for ' in one (moment),' ' anon ' means *at once*, as Mt 13[20] ' he that received the seed into stony places, the same is he that heareth the word, and anon (RV ' straightway,' RSV ' immediately ') with joy receiveth it.'

ANOS, 1 Es 9[34] (AV, RV).—See VANIAH.

ANSWER.—An answer is (1) an apology or defence, as 2 Ti 4[16] AV ' at my first answer (RV, RSV ' defence ') no man stood by me ' ; so perhaps 1 P 3[21] AV ' the answer (RV ' interrogation,' RSV ' appeal ') of a good conscience ' ; (2) oracle, Divine response, as Ro 11[4] AV, RV ' what saith the answer (RSV ' reply ') of God ? '

ANT.—Ants are mentioned only twice in the Bible, as a model of industry and requiring no overseer or ruler and, though having no strength, able to lay in a good store of food in the summer (Pr 6[6-8] 30[25]), presumably for use in winter. This practice has been disputed, on the two grounds that the ant is carnivorous and that it hibernates ; these objections are partly true and partly false. All ants eat flesh, but they eat also many other things, *e.g.* more or less fruit, seeds and meal, cake and sweetmeats ; they also abstract quantities of grain from threshing floors and granaries and put them away in their nests. Further, Arab peasants say that they feed on the grain during the season of non-production ; that they begin by eating off the heads is not so much due to a conscious intention to prevent germination but rather because this is the softest part of the grain and the most accessible, not being protected by the silicious envelope. The stores of seeds collected by ants have been found so great that the Mishnah lays down rules regarding the ownership of them : if discovered in a field before reaping, they belong to the owner ; if afterwards, they go all or in part to the poor. Ants also derive an important part of their sustenance from the sweet juice which aphides secrete and for which they keep flocks and herds of these creatures ; they further collect the eggs and larvae of these aphides, keep them with their own during their long hibernation that they may be hatched in spring and again supply them with their favourite food. This behaviour affords ' a case of prudence unexampled in the animal kingdom.' That they are ' exceeding wise ' is seen also in their nests, which are marvels of construction, some composed of chambers and galleries underground, others built as mounds or huts above ground ; these are grouped in towns connected by surface-roads, sometimes arched over at places, and by subterranean tunnels. They also divide their labour suitably amongst themselves. Finally, ants make organized raids on other hives and seize their eggs, larvae and pupae, which they rear as slaves to do their work for them ; and some 584 other species of insects are found in association with ants, serving them in various ways. These small creatures are exceedingly abundant all over Palestine, where they perform the functions of earth-worms in other countries, continually changing the surface of the soil by their operations. E. W. G. M.—**G. R. D.**

ANTELOPE.—What the Hebrew *t^e'ô, tô'* denotes is uncertain ; for the root is unknown and the word itself does not occur in the cognate languages. It is translated in the older versions (LXX, Aq., Symm., Theod., Vulg.) ' oryx,' *i.e.* a white antelope with straight pointed horns (*antelope leucoryx*, Tristram) found in the Belqâ and Ḥaurân and in Arabia. This is preferable to the wild ' ox ' of the later versions (Targ., Onq., and Ps-Jn). It is mentioned only twice in the OT, in a list of clean animals (Dt 14[5]) and in the comparison of Jerusalem's sons ' lying at the top of all the streets, like an antelope in a net ' (Is 51[20]). G. R. D.

ANTHOTHIJAH.—A Benjamite, 1 Ch 8[24] (AV **Antothijah**).

ANTICHRIST.—The great opponent and counterpart of Christ, by whom he is finally to be conquered. The word appears only in the NT (1 Jn 2[18-22] 4[3], 2 Jn [7]), where, when used in the plural, it describes those who oppose the true Christian message and display in the present the spirit of the eschatological Antichrist. But the idea was present in Judaism and developed with the growth of the Messianic hope.

1. The origin of the conception.—While the precise term 'Antichrist' is lacking in Jewish literature, the idea of an opponent, who persecutes God's people and is ultimately to be conquered by the Messiah, is an integral part of that general hope, born in Prophetism, which developed into Messianism in the NT period. As in the case of so many elements of Messianism, the beginning of the 'opponent' idea may fairly be said to have been Dn 11[36] (cf also Zec 12–14), where the reference is to Antiochus IV.; but it would be a mistake to see in the Antichrist conception of the Johannine literature an unprecedented description of distinct personalities. There seems to have been rather a gradually developing anti-Messianic scheme, which at many points duplicated the developing Messianic hope. This general conception, which played an important role in early Christianity, was probably due to the synthesis of various factors, among which the following three deserve special mention.

(*a*) *The historical opponents of the Jews*, such as Antiochus IV., Pompey, and the Roman Empire in general (cf the rôle of Gog in Prophetic thought). These naturally aroused the most intense hatred on the part of important sections of the Jewish people. Their hostility was regarded as extending not only to the Jews as a nation, but, as heathen, to Yahweh Himself, and particularly to His plans for the Jewish people. This political hatred entered into the Antichrist expectation, just as the political hope of the Jews contributed to the Messianic programme. Both alike tended to grow transcendental.

(*b*) *The dualism of Babylonia and Persia, especially as it was expressed by the dragon*, between whom and the agents of righteousness there was to be a fight to the death. This dragon conception may with much probability be seen not only in the identification of the serpent of the Temptation with the devil, but also in the beast of the Johannine Apocalypse, the great opponent of the Christ, and in the sea monster of Rabbinism.

(*c*) *The Beliar* (or *Belial) myth*, which underlies NT thought (cf 2 Co 6[15]) as well as Jewish fears. The first reference to Beliar seems to have been in Jub 1[20], but the myth is not unlike that of the Babylonian *Tiamat*, queen of the abyss, who was conquered by Marduk. Subsequently he was identified with Satan, who was also identified with the dragon (cf Ascens. Is 4[3], Rev 12[10]). This identification was the first step towards the fully developed expectation in the Talmud of a conflict between God and the devil.

2. Synthesis of the elements.—These various elements, though independent in origin, possess so much in common that it was inevitable that they should be combined in the figure of the Satanic opponent whom the Christ would utterly destroy as a pre-condition of establishing His Kingdom of God. A study of the Book of Revelation, as well as of other NT writings (*e.g.* 2 Th 2[1–12], 2 Co 6[15], 1 Jn 2[18–22] 4[3], 2 Jn [7], Rev 11[4–13] 13[1–18] 17. 19[11–21], Mk 13[14–20]) will show that there was always present in the minds of the writers of the NT a superhuman figure, Satanic in power and character, who was to head the opposition both to the people of Christ and to the Christ Himself. This person is represented in *Assumption of Moses* (ch. 8), *Ascension of Isaiah* (ch. 4), as well as in other Jewish writings, as one who possessed the Satanic supremacy over the army of devils. He was not a general tendency, but a definite personality. As such it was easy to see his counterpart or incarnation in historical characters. Indeed, the entire anti-Messianic programme was employed to characterize historical situations. In the Dead Sea Scrolls, the wicked priest, as opposed to the teacher of righteousness, plays a part not unlike that of the eschatological Antichrist, whose action withholds the instauration of the Kingdom, *versus* Christ and His faithful. We must think similarly of the use of 'the man of lawlessness' of St. Paul (2 Th 2[3]; see MAN OF SIN) and the various opponents of Christ in the Apocalypse. Transcendental pictures and current eschatology set forth the Christian's fear on the one hand of the Roman Emperor or Empire as a persecuting power, and on the other of Jewish fanaticism. Just which historical persons were in the mind of the writers it is now impossible to say with accuracy, but Nero and Domitian are very likely. Belief in the return from death of the persecuting Emperor Nero seems to have been widely diffused throughout the Roman Empire in the latter part of the first Christian century (*Sib. Or.* iv. 119–150, v. 363 ff.). This expectation lies behind the figures of Rev 13, 16, and 17. He is apparently to return with the kings of Parthia, but he is also, in Rev 17[8–11], identified with the beast of the abyss (cf *Sib. Or.* v. 28–34). Similarly the legends developed around the figure of Simon Magus seem to have been widely diffused in Christian circles, and Simon Magus (q.v.) became the typical (Jewish) false prophet and magician who opposed Christianity.

In the Patristic period the eschatological aspects of the anti-Messianic hope were developed, but again as a mystical picture of historical conditions either existing or expected. In Ephraem Syrus the fall of the Roman Empire is attributed to Antichrist. He is also, by the early Church writers, sometimes identified with the false Jewish Messiah, who was to work miracles, rebuild the Temple, and establish a great empire with demons as his agents. Under the inspiration of the two Witnesses (Elijah and Enoch or, more probably, Moses) the Messianic revolt against the Antichrist was to begin—the Book of Revelation being interpreted literally at this point. The saints were to be exposed to the miseries that the book describes, but the Messiah was to slay Antichrist with the breath of His mouth, hold the Last Judgment, and establish the conditions of eternity.

Thus in Christian literature the fusion of those elements of the Antichrist idea which were present in Judaism and later Christianity is completed by the addition of the traits of the false prophet, and extended under the influence of the current polemic against Jewish Messianism. The figure of Antichrist, which is Satanic, Neronic, falsely prophetic, the enemy of God and His kingdom, moves out into theological history, to be identified by successive ages with nearly every great opponent of the Church and its doctrines, whether persecutor or heretic. See MAN OF SIN. S. M.—**M. Si.**

ANTILEBANON.—Jth 1[7] (AV, RV **Antilibanus**); see LEBANON.

ANTILIBANUS, Jth 1[7] (AV, RV).—See ANTILEBANON.

ANTIMONY.—Is 54[11] (RVm, RSV; AV, RV 'fair colours'), 1 Ch 29[2] (RSV; AV 'glistering stones,' RV 'stones for inlaid work'). See also EYE.

ANTIOCH (Syrian).—By his victory in the battle of Ipsus (301 B.C.), Seleucus Nicator (312–280 B.C.) secured the rule over most of Alexander the Great's Asiatic empire, which stretched from the Hellespont and the Mediterranean on the one side to the Jaxartes and Indus on the other. The Seleucid dynasty, which he founded, lasted for 247 years. He founded no fewer than thirty-seven cities, of which four are mentioned in the NT—(1) Antioch of Syria (Ac 11[19]), (2) Seleucia (Ac 13[4]), *i.e.* Seleucia Pieria, (3) Antioch of Pisidia (Ac 13[14] 14[21], 2 Ti 3[11]), and (4) Laodicea (Col 4[13–16], Rev 1[11] 3[14]). The most famous of the sixteen Antiochs, which he built and named after his father Antiochus, was Antioch on the Orontes in Syria. The spot was carefully chosen, and religious sanction given to it by the invention of a story that sacred birds had revealed the site while he watched their flight from a neighbouring eminence. It was politically of advantage that the seat of empire should be removed from Seleucia, near the present Baghdad, to a locality nearer the Mediterranean. The new city lay in the deep bend of the Levant, about 300 miles N. of Jerusalem. Though fourteen miles from the sea, the navigable river Orontes, on whose left bank it was built, united it with Seleucia Pieria and its splendid harbour. Connected thus by the main caravan roads with the commerce of Babylon, Persia, and India, and with a seaport keeping it in touch with the great world to the west, Antioch speedily fell heir to that vast trade which had once been the monopoly of Tyre. Its seaport Seleucia was a great fortress, like Gibraltar or Sebastopol. Seleucus attracted to his new capital thousands of Jews, by offering them equal rights of citizenship with all the other inhabitants. The citizens were divided into eighteen wards, and each commune attended to its own municipal affairs.

His successor, Antiochus I., *Soter* (280–261 B.C.), introduced an abundant water supply into the city, so that every private house had its own pipe, and every public spot its graceful fountain. He further strove to render Antioch the intellectual rival of Alexandria, by inviting to his court scholars such as Aratus the astronomer, and by superintending the translation into Greek of learned works in foreign tongues. In this way the invaluable history of Babylon by Berosus, the Chaldaean priest was preserved for posterity.

The succession of wars which now broke out between the Seleucids and the Ptolemies is described in Dn 11. The fortunes of the war varied greatly. Under the next king but one, Seleucus II., *Callinicus* (246–225 B.C.), Ptolemy Euergetes captured Seleucia, installed an Egyptian garrison in it, and harried the Seleucid empire as far as Susiana and Bactria, carrying off to Egypt an immense spoil. Worsted on the field, Callinicus devoted himself to the embellishment of his royal city. As founded by Seleucus Nicator, Antioch had consisted of a single quarter. Antiochus I., *Soter*, had added a second, but Callinicus now included a third, by annexing to the city the island in the river and connecting it to the mainland by five bridges. In this new area the streets were all at right angles, and at the intersection of the two principal roads the way was spanned by a tetrapylon, a covered colonnade with four gates. The city was further adorned with costly temples, porticoes, and statues. But the most remarkable engineering feat begun in this reign was the excavation of the great dock at Seleucia, the building of the protecting moles, and the cutting of a canal inland through high masses of solid rock. The canal is successively a cutting and a tunnel, the parts open to the sky aggregating in all 1869 feet, in some places cut to the depth of 120 feet, while the portions excavated as tunnels (usually 24 feet high) amount in all to 395 feet.

With Antiochus III., *the Great* (223–187 B.C.), the fortunes of the city revived. He drove out the Egyptian garrison from Seleucia, ended the Ptolemaic sovereignty over Judaea, reduced all Palestine and nearly all Asia Minor to his sway, until his might was finally shattered by the Romans in the irretrievable defeat of Magnesia (190 B.C.). After the assassination of his son Seleucus IV., *Philopator* (187–175 B.C.), who was occupied mostly in repairing the financial losses his kingdom had sustained, Antiochus IV., *Epiphanes* (175–163 B.C.), succeeded to the throne. He promoted both Greek architecture and Greek culture. In his dreams Antioch was to be a metropolis second to none for beauty, and Greek art and Greek religion were to be the uniform rule throughout all his dominions. To the three quarters already existing he added a fourth, which earned for Antioch the title 'Tetrapolis.' Here he erected a Senate House, a temple to Jupiter Capitolinus on one of the eminences of Mount Silpius, and a strong citadel on another spur of the mountains that surround the city. From E. to W. of Antioch he laid out a splendid street with double colonnades, which ran for five miles in a straight line. In wet weather the populace could walk from end to end under cover. Trees, flowers, and fountains adorned the promenade; and poets sang of the beauty of the statue of Apollo and of the Nymphaeum which he erected near the river. To avert the anger of the gods during a season of pestilence, he ordered the sculptor Leios to hew Mount Silpius into one vast statue of Charon, the ferryman of Hades. It frowned over the city, and was named the Charonium. Epiphanes' policy of Hellenizing Judaea evoked the determined opposition of the Maccabees (q.v.). Succeeding rulers exercised only a very moderate influence over the fortunes of Palestine, and the palmy days of Antioch as a centre of political power were gone for ever.

The city was the scene of many a bloody conflict in the years of the later Seleucids, as usurper after usurper tried to wade through blood to the throne, and was shortly after overcome by some rival. In several of these struggles the Jews took part, and as the power of Antioch waned, the strength and practical independence of the Jewish Hasmonaean princes increased. In 83 B.C. all Syria passed into the hands of Tigranes, king of Armenia, who remained master of Antioch for fourteen years. When Tigranes was overwhelmed by the Romans, Pompey put an end to the Seleucid dynasty, and the line of Antiochene monarchs expired in 64 B.C. The strong *Pax Romana* gave new vigour to the city. Antioch was made a free city, and became the seat of the prefect and the capital of the Roman province of Syria. Mark Antony ordered the release of all the Jews in it enslaved during the recent disturbances, and the restoration of their property. As a reward for Antioch's fidelity to him, Julius Caesar built a splendid basilica, the *Caesareum*, and gave, besides, a new aqueduct, theatre, and public baths. Augustus, Agrippa, Herod the Great, Tiberius, and, later, Antoninus Pius, all greatly embellished the city, contributing many new and striking architectural features. The ancient walls were rebuilt to the height of 50–60 feet, with a thickness at the top of 8 feet, and surmounted by gigantic towers. The vast rampart was carried across ravines up the mountain slope to the very summit of the hills which overlook the city. Antioch seemed thus to be defended by a mountainous bulwark, seven miles in circuit. Earthquakes have in later ages demolished these walls, though some of the Roman castles are still standing.

When Christianity reached Antioch, it was a great city of over 500,000 inhabitants, called the 'Queen of the East,' the 'Third Metropolis of the Roman Empire.' In 'Antioch the Beautiful' there was to be found everything which Italian wealth, Greek aestheticism, and Oriental luxury could produce. The ancient writers, however, are unanimous in describing the cosmopolitan city as one of the most depraved in the world. Licentiousness, superstition, quackery, indecency, every fierce and base passion, were displayed by the populace; their skill in coining scurrilous verses was notorious, their sordid, fickle, turbulent, and insolent ways rendered the name of Antioch a byword. Their brilliance and energy, so praised by Cicero, were balanced by an incurable levity and shameless disregard for the principles of morality. So infamous was the grove of Daphne, five miles out of the city, filled with shrines to Apollo, Venus, Isis, etc., and crowded with theatres, baths, taverns, and dancing saloons, that soldiers detected there were punished and dismissed from the Imperial service. 'Daphnic morals' became a proverb. Juvenal could find no more forcible way of describing the pollutions of Rome than by saying, 'The Orontes has flowed in the Tiber.' In this Vanity Fair the Jews were resident in large numbers, yet they exerted little or no influence on the morals of the city. We hear in the NT of one Nicolas, a proselyte of Antioch (Ac 6^{5}). But after the death of St. Stephen, Christian fugitives from persecution fled as far north as Antioch, began to preach to the Greeks there (Ac 11^{19}), and a great number believed. So great was the work that Jerusalem Church sent Barnabas to assist, who, finding that more help was needed, sought out and brought Saul from Tarsus. There they continued a year, and built up a strong Church. Antioch had the honour of being the birthplace of (1) the name 'Christian' (Ac 11^{26}), and (2) of foreign missions. From the city Paul and Barnabas started on their first missionary journey (Ac 13^{1-4}), and to Antioch they returned at the end of the tour (Ac 14^{26}). The second journey was begun from and ended at Antioch (Ac 15^{25-41} 18^{22}); and the city was again the starting-point of the third tour (Ac 18[23]). The Antiochene Church contributed liberally to the poor saints in Jerusalem, during the famine (Ac 11[27-30]). Here also the dispute regarding the circumcision of Gentile converts broke out (Ac 15[1-22]), and here Paul withstood Peter for his inconsistency (Gal 2[11-21]). A gate still bears the name of 'St. Paul's Gate.' It was from Antioch that Ignatius set out on his journey to martyrdom at Rome. The city claimed as its natives John Chrysostom, Ammianus Marcellinus, Evagrius, and Libanius. From A.D. 252–380 Antioch was the scene of ten Church Councils. The Patriarch of Antioch took precedence of those of Rome, Constantinople, Jerusalem, and Alexandria. Antioch was captured in A.D. 260 by Shapur of Persia; in A.D. 538 it was burned by Chosroes; rebuilt by Justinian, it again fell before the Saracens in A.D. 635. Nicephorus Phocas recovered it in A.D. 969, but in A.D. 1084 it fell to the Seljuk Turks. The first Crusaders retook it in 1098 after a celebrated siege, signalized by the 'invention of the Holy Lance'; but in 1268 it passed finally into the hands of the Turks. Earthquakes have added to the ruining hand of man. Those of 184 B.C., A.D. 37, 115, 457, and especially 526 (when 200,000 persons perished), 528, 1170, and 1872 have been the most disastrous. The once vast city still bears the name of *Antaki* (Turkish) or *Antakiyah* (Arabic). Its inhabitants have increased to nearly 40,000 in recent years. G. A. F. K.—**E. G. K.**

ANTIOCH (Pisidian).—The expression 'Antioch of Pisidia' or 'Antioch in Pisidia' is inexact as the town was not in Pisidia. Its official title was 'Antioch near Pisidia,' and as it existed for the sake of Pisidia, the adjective 'Pisidian' was sometimes loosely attached to it. It was actually in the ethnic district of Phrygia, and in the Roman province of Galatia (that region of it called Phrygia Galatica). Founded by the inhabitants of Magnesia, it was made a free town by the Romans, and a *colonia* was established there by the emperor Augustus to keep the barbarians of the neighbourhood in check. The municipal government became Roman and the official language Latin. St. Paul visited it at least three times (Ac 13[14] 14[21] 16[6]), and it is one of the churches addressed in the Epistle to the Galatians. A. So.

ANTIOCHIANS (2 Mac 4[9, 19]).—The efforts of Antiochus Epiphanes to spread Greek culture and Greek customs throughout his dominions were dilgently furthered by a section of the Jews. The leader of this Hellenizing party, Jason, brother of the high priest Onias III., offered a large sum of money to Antiochus to induce the king to allow him to 'enrol the men of Jerusalem as citizens of Antioch.' Antiochus acceded to the proposal, and shortly afterwards a party of 'Antiochians' from Jerusalem was sent by him with a contribution of money for the festival of Heracles at Tyre.

ANTIOCHIS (2 Mac 4[30]).—A concubine of Antiochus Epiphanes, who assigned to her the revenues of the two Cilician cities, Tarsus and Mallus.

ANTIOCHUS (1 Mac 12[16] 14[22]; cf Jos. *Ant.* XIII. v. 8 [169]).—The father of Numenius, who was one of the envoys sent (*c* 144 B.C.) by Jonathan the Maccabee to renew the covenant made by Judas with the Romans, and to enter into friendly relations with the Spartans.

ANTIOCHUS.—A name borne by a number of the kings of Syria subsequent to the period of Alexander the Great.

1. Antiochus I. (280–261 B.C.) was the son of Seleucus Nicator, the chiliarch under Perdiccas who was regent immediately after the death of Alexander. On the murder of his father he came into possession of practically the entire region of Asia Minor as far east as the provinces beyond Mesopotamia. The most important fact of his reign was his defeat of the Celts, who, after devastating Macedonia and Thrace, swarmed into Asia Minor and established a kingdom which was subsequently known as Galatia. The date and place of the victory are unknown, but it won him the name of *Sōtēr* ('Saviour'). His capital was Antioch in Syria, but he was never able to bring his vast empire into complete subjection. He was a friend of literature and art, and it is thought possible that under him a beginning was made in the Greek translation of the Pentateuch.

2. Antiochus II., *Theos* (261–246 B.C.).—Son of the foregoing, essentially a warrior, carrying on interminable struggles both with the free Greek cities of his own territory, to which he finally gave something like democratic rights, and with Ptolemy Philadelphus of Egypt. Under him, however, the Jews of Asia Minor gained many civic rights.

3. Antiochus III., *the Great.*—He ascended the throne when only 15 years of age, and he reigned from 223 to 187 B.C. Along with Antiochus I. and Antiochus II. he may be referred to in the early portions of Dn 11. His reign, like that of most of his contemporaries, was one of constant war, particularly with Egypt. In the course of these wars he gained possession of Palestine through the battle of Panion (198 B.C.), and established the Syrian administration over Judaea, although for a time he ruled the province jointly with Ptolemy Epiphanes of Egypt. Like Antiochus I., he was a great colonizer, and induced 2000 Jewish families to go from Mesopotamia into Lydia and Phrygia, thus laying the foundation for the influential Jewish Dispersion in those regions. So warlike a monarch could not fail to come into conflict sooner or later with Rome. He was defeated in the battle of Magnesia in 190 B.C., and three years later was killed, according to some authorities while plundering a temple at Elymais in Persia.

4. Antiochus IV., *Epiphanes* ('the Illustrious'; also nicknamed *Epimanes*, 'the Madman').—The son of the preceding, who had been sent as a hostage to Rome. In 175 B.C. he seized the Syrian throne, and began a series of conquests which bade fair to rival his father's. While in Egypt, however, he was ordered by the Romans to leave that country, and thus found himself forced to limit his energies to Syria. In the course of his conflict with Egypt he had become suspicious of Judaea, and determined to force that country into complete subjection to his will. His motives were probably more political than religious, but as a part of his programme he undertook to compel the Jews to worship heathen gods as well as, if not in place of, Yahweh. His plans were first put into active operation probably towards the end of 170 B.C., when he returned from Egypt, although the chronology at this point is very obscure and it may have been a couple of years later. He plundered the Temple of many of its treasures (1 Mac 1[21-24]). He also placed a garrison in the citadel of Jerusalem, and set about the complete Hellenizing of Judaea. Circumcision and the observance of the Sabbath were forbidden under penalty of death. Pagan sacrifices were ordered in every town in Judaea, and every month a search was made to discover whether any Jew possessed a copy of the Law or had circumcised his children. In December 168 B.C. a pagan altar, probably to Olympian Zeus (identified with *Baal Shamayim*; Zeus Shamayim was parodied as *shikkûṣîm m*ᵉ*shōmēm*, the 'desolating sacrilege' of 1 Mac 1[54], Dn 9[27]), was erected on the altar of burnt-offering, and the entire Jewish worship seemed threatened with extinction. This probability was increased by the apostasy of the high priest.

This excess of zeal on the part of Antiochus led to the reaction which, under the Hasideans and Mattathias, the founder of the Maccabaean house, ultimately brought about the release of Judaea from Syrian control. The events of this period of persecution are related in detail—though with a large element of legend—in 2 Maccabees, and reference is to be found to them also in Dn 11[21-45]. Antiochus finally died on an expedition against the Parthians in 164 B.C. (For an account of the struggle of Mattathias and Judas against Antiochus, see MACCABEES).

5. Antiochus V., *Eupator.*—Son of the preceding; began to reign at the death of his father, when a mere boy of 9 (or 12) years. He was left by his father under the control of Lysias, his chief representative in Palestine, and with him was present at the victory of Beth-zechariah, 163 B.C., when Judas Maccabaeus was defeated (1 Mac 6^{32-47}). The complete conquest of Judaea was prevented by the rise of the pretender Philip, who, however, was conquered. In the midst of their success, both young Antiochus and Lysias were assassinated by Demetrius I. (162 B.C.). Their death reacted favourably on the circumstances surrounding the rising Maccabaean house.

6. Antiochus VI.—Son of Alexander Balas (q.v.), Trypho, one of the generals of Alexander Balas, at first championed the cause of this boy after his father had been killed in Arabia. After a few months, however, he caused the assassination of Antiochus by the physicians of the court, and reigned in his stead (1 Mac 13^{31f}).

7. Antiochus VII., *Sidetes* (138–128 B.C.), the last of the energetic Seleucid monarchs, came to the throne during the imprisonment of Demetrius II. After defeating Trypho, he undertook to establish his sovereignty over the Jews. Simon partially won his favour by presents and by furnishing auxiliary troops, but at last refused to meet his excessive demands for permitting such independence as Judaea had come to enjoy under the weak predecessor of Antiochus. Thereupon Antiochus sent his generals into Judaea, but they were defeated by the sons of Simon (1 Mac 15, 16). He himself came during the first year of John Hyrcanus (135–134), and after devastating Judaea shut up Hyrcanus in Jerusalem. He was about to capture the city through starvation when he unexpectedly made terms with Hyrcanus, probably because of the intervention of the Romans. These terms laid very heavy demands upon the Jews, and included the destruction of the fortifications of the city. Until 129–128 B.C. Judaea was again subject to the Syrian kingdom, but at the end of that year Antiochus was killed in a campaign against the Parthians, and Hyrcanus was enabled to reassert his independence. See MACCABEES, 5. S. M.—F. C. G.

ANTIPAS.—**1.** See HEROD, No. **3.**—**2.** A martyr of the church of Pergamum, mentioned only in Rev 2^{13}, unless some credit is to be given to the late accounts of his martyrdom. According to these, he was roasted to death in a brazen bowl in the days of Domitian. Cures of toothache were believed to be accomplished at his tomb.

ANTIPATER.—Son of Jason, one of two ambassadors sent by Jonathan to the Romans and to the Spartans to renew 'the friendship and the confederacy' (1 Mac 12^{16} 14^{22}).

ANTIPATRIS.—The place to which St. Paul was conducted in the night and from which he then was escorted to Caesarea (Ac 23^{31}). The town was founded by Herod the Great and named in honour of his father, Antipater. Josephus speaks of it as on the road from Lydda to Caesarea. It thus was at an important road intersection. It is held to be identical with *Râs el-ʿAin* at the head of the stream called *el-ʿAujeh*. E. G. K.

ANTONIA.—See CITADEL.

ANTOTHIJAH, 1 Ch 8^{24} (AV).—See ANTHOTHIJAH.

ANTOTHITE, 1 Ch 11^{28} 12^{3} (AV) = man of **Anathoth** (q.v.).

ANUB.—A man of Judah, 1 Ch 4^{8}.

ANUS, 1 Es 9^{48} (RV).—See ANNIUTH.

ANVIL.—See ARTS AND CRAFTS, **2.**

APACE.—Means 'at a quick pace'; cf Ps 68^{12} 'did flee apace' (AV), 2 S 18^{25} 'he came apace' (AV, RV, RSV) Jer 48^{16} 'hastens apace' (RSV).

APAME.—Daughter of Bartacus, and concubine of Darius I. (1 Es 4^{29}).

APE.—Apes were imported from Ophir (q.v.) by Solomon, 1 K 10^{22}, 2 Ch 9^{21}. The Hebrew name for this animal, *ḳôph*, is probably from Sanskrit *kapi*, though not necessarily derived directly. The apes may have come from India, or from S. Arabia, or from Africa. No kind of monkey is indigenous in Palestine. In importing monkeys Solomon imitated the custom of Assyrian and Egyptian monarchs.

APELLES.—The name of a Christian who is greeted by St. Paul in Ro 16^{10}, and who is described as the 'approved in Christ.' It was the name borne by a distinguished tragic actor, and by members of the imperial household.

APHAEREMA, 1 Mac 11^{34} (RV).—See APHAIREMA.

APHAIREMA.—A district taken from Samaria and added to Judaea by Demetrius Soter (*Ant.* XIII. iv. 9 [127]), 1 Mac 11^{34} (AV **Apherema,** RV **Aphaerema**). See EPHRAIM, **1.**

APHARSACHITES.—See next article.

APHARSATHCHITES.—A colony of the Assyrians in Samaria, Ezr 4^{9} (AV, RV); probably the same as the Apharsachites, Ezr 5^{6} 6^{6} (AV, RV). Some scholars regard the word as an official title, rather than as a gentilic; so RSV, which renders 'governors.'

APHARSITES.—One of the colonies transported to Samaria by the Assyrians, Ezr 4^{9} (AV, RV). Some scholars hold them to be Persians, and so RSV; others find here an official title, 'secretaries.'

APHEK.—**1.** A Canaanite city in the plain of Sharon, Jos 12^{18}; the Philistines gathered here, 1 S 4^{1} 29^{1}; probably the same as **Antipatris** (q.v.) of Ac 23^{31}; probably modern *Râs el-ʿAin.* **2.** A city of Asher, Jos 19^{30}; the tribe failed to take it, Jg 1^{31} (**Aphik**); probably modern *Tell Kurdâneh.* **3.** A city on the border between Canaanites and Amorites, Jos 13^{4}; possibly modern *Afqa*, E. of Byblos. **4.** The place where Ahab defeated Ben-hadad, 1 K $20^{26, 30}$ (cf 2 K 13^{17}); possibly modern *Fîq*, E. of the Sea of Galilee.

APHEKAH.—A city of Judah, Jos 15^{53}; possibly modern *Khirbet Kanaʿan*, SW. of Hebron.

APHEREMA, 1 Mac 11^{34} (AV).—See APHAIREMA.

APHERRA.—One whose descendants returned with Zerubbabel, 1 Es 5^{34}; omitted in the parallel lists in Ezra and Nehemiah.

APHIAH.—One of Saul's ancestors, 1 S 9^{1}.

APHIK.—See APHEK, **2.**

APHRAH, Mic 1^{10} (AV).—See BETH-LE-APHRAH.

APHSES, 1 Ch 24^{15} (AV).—See HAPPIZZEZ.

APIS.—See MEMPHIS.

APOCALYPSE.—See REVELATION [BOOK OF].

APOCALYPTIC LITERATURE. — See PSEUDEPIGRAPHA.

APOCRYPHA.—The word 'Apocrypha' is of Greek derivation and signifies books that are 'hidden away.' From the point of view of those who approved of these books, they were 'hidden' or withdrawn from general use because they were deemed to contain mysterious or esoteric teaching, too profound to be communicated to any except the initiated. From another point of view, however, it was held that such books deserved to be 'hidden,' because they were spurious and/or heretical. Such books frequently bore, as their alleged authors, the names of notable personages in Hebrew history. These names were not sufficient, however, to carry the books over into the canonical collection of the Bible (see article CANON OF THE OLD TESTAMENT).

Traditionally there are fourteen or fifteen books of the Apocrypha. As regards literary type, they may be classified as follows:

1. *Historical*: First and Second Maccabees, and First Esdras (Third Esdras in the Vulgate).
2. *Legendary*: Additions to Esther, Prayer of Azariah and the Song of the Three Young Men, Susanna, Bel and the Dragon, Tobit, and Judith.
3. *Prophetical*: Baruch, Letter of Jeremiah (in AV and RV this is ch. 6 of Baruch), and Prayer of Manasseh.
4. *Apocalyptic*: Second Esdras (Fourth Esdras in the Vulgate).
5. *Didactic*: Ecclesiasticus and Wisdom of Solomon.

In the 4th cent., when Jerome made his revision of the Old Latin Bible (which contained the Apocryphal books as carried over from the Greek Septuagint), he was careful to indicate by means of Prefaces those books and parts of books not found in the Hebrew canon. Subsequently, however, copyists of the manuscripts of the Latin Vulgate frequently omitted the Prefaces, and thus facilitated confusion as to the limits of the Hebrew canon. Consequently many of the Church Fathers made no distinction in quoting from both kinds of books. It is true, however, that from the time of Jerome down to the Reformation a succession of the more learned theologians in the West maintained the distinctive and unique authority of the books of the Hebrew canon. It was not until the Council of Trent (April 8, 1546) that the Roman Catholic Church set its seal of authority upon eleven of the Apocryphal books (or parts of books) and decreed an anathema upon any who would not receive the old Latin Vulgate Bible, with all its books and parts, as sacred and canonical. Thus Roman Catholic Bibles now contain the following mingled with the OT Books: Tobit, Judith, Additions to Esther, Wisdom of Solomon, Ecclesiasticus, Baruch (including the Epistle of Jeremiah), three Additions to Daniel, 1 and 2 Maccabees. The official Latin Vulgate Bible prints the Prayer of Manasseh and 1 and 2 Esdras (called 3 and 4 Esdras) in an Appendix after the NT. At the time of the Reformation Luther, Calvin, Zwingli, and other Reformers revived the ancient view that only the books of the Hebrew canon were to be regarded as authoritative, and in most Protestant editions of the Bible the Apocryphal books were gathered into a separate section, printed either between the OT and the NT, or at the close of the NT. It was included in the first edition of the AV in 1611, but not long after it began to be omitted from some copies and editions. In 1957 the Revised Standard Version of the Apocrypha was issued, being the first translation of these books which was prepared by a committee of American scholars.

The general character, contents, and date of the fifteen books of the Apocrypha are as follows:

1. The First Book of Esdras (Third Esdras in the Vulgate) is the canonical book of Ezra (and part of Nehemiah) in Greek, which in reconstructed form tells the story of the decline and fall of the kingdom of Judah from the time of Josiah. It recites the overthrow of Jerusalem, the Babylonian exile, the return under Zerubbabel, and Ezra's part in the reorganization of the Jewish State. Of special interest in the book is the section (3^{1}—4^{63}) which tells how it came about that the Jews were permitted to resume the work of rebuilding the walls of Jerusalem and the Temple. A contest of wits was held among three courtiers of Darius's bodyguard, and to the winner, Zerubbabel, Darius granted money and authorization to finish the work of construction. The date and author of the book are unknown. Most scholars date it between about 150 B.C. and A.D. 50.

2. The Second Book of Esdras [Vulg. Fourth Esdras. If *First* Esdras is the reconstructed Ezra, and the canonical Ezra and Nehemiah are taken as one book, then this is *Third* Esdras (as in the Septuagint). If Ezra and Nehemiah are left out of account, this book is *Second* Esdras (as in the Apocrypha of AV, RV, and RSV). If, as in the Vulgate, Ezra is reckoned as *First* Esdras, and Nehemiah as *Second* Esdras, and the reconstructed Ezra as *Third* Esdras, then this book is *Fourth* Esdras]. The literary form of 2 Esdras is known as an apocalypse, that is, a ' revelation ' of the future. Like other Jewish and Christian apocalypses, the author makes use of many symbols, some of which are explained while others are not. The religious concern of the book centres in the problem of justifying the ways of God in dealing with His people, good and bad alike. The main part of the book (chs. 3–14 purports to record seven revelations granted to Ezra in Babylon during the 6th cent. B.C. The author of these chapters was an unknown Jew who probably wrote in Aramaic near the end of the 1st cent. A.D. During the following century an unknown Christian author prefixed an introduction (which is now chs. 1 and 2), and sometime in the 3rd cent. another Christian author appended what is now chs. 15 and 16, a tiny fragment of which has been found in Greek. From the Aramaic form of chs. 3–14 several Oriental versions were made, including Syriac, Coptic, Ethiopic, Arabic (two independent versions), Armenian, and Georgian. In the West the entire book (chs. 1–16) circulated in several Old Latin versions. A later Latin translation stands in the appendix to the NT of the Roman Catholic Vulgate Bible.

3. Tobit is a romantic story of the time of Israel's captivity. Tobit is a pious son of Naphtali who becomes blind. He sends his son Tobias to Rages in Media to collect a debt. An angel leads him to Ecbatana, where he marries a widow who was still a virgin though she had had seven husbands. Each of the seven had been slain on their wedding-day by Asmodaeus, an evil spirit. On the inspiration of the angel, Tobias marries the widow, and, by burning the inner parts of a fish, puts the spirit to flight by the offensive smoke. The blindness of Tobit is healed by using the gall of the fish, the burning of whose entrails had saved the life of Tobias. The lesson inculcated by this widely read book of pious fiction is that, though God permits calamities to befall the righteous, he exercises special care for them during their suffering and grants them a happy ending to their trials. Its popularity is attested by the multiplicity of forms in which it circulated, including several versions each in Hebrew, Greek, Latin, and Syriac. An Aramaic recension has been found at Qumrân. The date of its composition is uncertain, though it probably appeared sometime before the beginning of the 1st cent. B.C.

4. Judith is a thrilling tale of how Judith, a Jewish widow, secured the confidence of Holofernes, an Assyrian commander who was besieging Bethulia. With courage and cunning in the night she approached him in his tent, where he was already overcome with heavy drinking, took his own scimitar and cut off his head, and fled with it to the besieged city. This valorous act saved the distressed Israelites. The story bristles with absurdities in names, dates, and geographical details. It seems to have imitated in one respect Jael's murder of Sisera (Jg 4^{17-22}). Its unknown author may have written some time about 100 B.C., so long after the life of Nebuchadnezzar as to have made him king of Nineveh, instead of Babylon. Because the extant Greek text preserves many Semitisms, scholars generally believe that the original composition was in Hebrew (or Aramaic). The Greek version is preserved in three different forms or recensions. The Latin Vulgate text was made by Jerome from an Aramaic text (which is no longer extant). The religious teaching of the book culminates in ch. 8, where man's dependence upon God, who is absolutely sovereign, is emphasized and in ch. 9, which records Judith's sublime prayer.

5. Additions to Esther.—Sometime in the 2nd or 1st cent. B.C. a certain Lysimachus (11^{1}) translated the Hebrew text of the OT Book of Esther into Greek. At six different places in the Greek narrative he or someone else added substantial episodes not in the Hebrew, totalling 107 verses. Though the canonical Book of Esther makes no reference to God, all but one of the additions contain the name of God. The literary style of the Greek continuator tends to be wordy and occasionally bombastic. Moreover, at several places the additions contradict the Hebrew text.

6. The Wisdom of Solomon appears to have been composed in Greek with several kinds of readers in view. The author attempts to rekindle in lukewarm and apostate Jews a genuine zeal for God and his law (chs. 1–5). Other Jews, loyal to their ancestral faith but perplexed and disheartened by persecutions, would find in this book encouragement in faith and practice (chs. 10–12 and 16–19). With an eye upon possible Gentile readers, the author argues for the truth of Judaism and the folly of idolatry (chs. 6–9 and 13–15). In supplying historical incidents illustrative of his doctrine he limits himself to those recorded in the Pentateuch. Though purporting to be Solomon, the unknown author probably was an Alexandrian Jew who lived sometime between 100 B.C. and A.D. 50. He was a man of a certain degree of genius and piety; his philosophical and religious character is witnessed by expressions of belief in immortality. Parts of the book are characterized by a high rhetorical skill, while others degenerate into mere bombast. In its present form it ends abruptly, and apparently is incomplete.

7. Ecclesiasticus, or, **The Wisdom of Jesus the Son of Sirach,** is one of the most highly esteemed of the non-canonical books. Resembling the canonical books of Proverbs, Job, and Ecclesiastes, it is the only Apocryphal book the author of which is known. It was composed in Hebrew about 180 B.C. by a Jew of Palestine named Jesus [Hebrew, Joshua; Aramaic, Jeshua] the son of Sirach (50^{27}). About fifty years later the author's grandson took a copy of this work to Egypt, where he translated it into Greek for the large Jewish population at Alexandria. In modern times sizeable fragments of the Hebrew text of Ecclesiasticus have been discovered, and the entire work is extant in Greek, Latin, Syriac, Coptic, Ethiopic, Armenian, Georgian, Arabic, and Old Slavonic. The book embodies what the author was accustomed to teach in his academy for Jewish boys, and touches upon a wide variety of social relationships and religious duties. It is one of the most important sources for our knowledge of orthodox Jewish piety and customs in the 2nd cent. B.C.

8. Baruch.—This is a pseudepigraphic book attributed to Baruch, the scribe of Jeremiah. Its purpose seems to have been (1) to quiet the souls of the Jews in exile by telling them that they would soon return to their native land; and (2) to admonish them to flee the idolatry that was everywhere prevalent in Babylonia. On stylistic grounds it appears that this book is a composite work of two or more authors, the latest of whom may have lived just before or just after the beginning of the Christian era. Though parts of the book may have been written in Hebrew, to-day Baruch is extant in Greek, from which several ancient versions were made (in Latin, Syriac, Coptic, Armenian, Ethiopic, and Arabic).

9. The Letter of Jeremiah is ostensibly a letter of that prophet warning the Babylonian exiles against the sinful folly of worshiping idols. Who the author was and when and where he lived are unknown. In several ancient Greek and Syriac manuscripts the Letter stands after the OT Book of Lamentations. In other Greek and Syriac manuscripts, as well as the Latin version, it is attached to the book of Baruch (as ch. 6); consequently most English translations of the Apocrypha have printed it as part of that book. Since, however, the Letter is really quite independent of Baruch, the RSV prints it as a separate book.

10. The addition to Daniel called **The Prayer of Azariah and the Song of the Three Young Men** appears in Greek and Latin versions between vv.^{23} and ^{24} of Dn 3. The addition may have been composed in Hebrew sometime within the 2nd or 1st cent. B.C. The Song of the Three Young Men came to be widely used in the liturgy of the early and mediaeval Church, from which it has passed into modern liturgies (where it is commonly called the 'Benedicite').

11. The book of **Susanna** is a spirited detective story of how Daniel discovered and exposed the malicious slander of two lustful elders who had plotted against the beautiful wife of a prominent Jew of Babylon. In many Greek manuscripts this account is prefixed to the canonical Book of Daniel; in the Latin Vulgate it follows the last chapter of Daniel. Who composed the story is not known, nor can its date be fixed more exactly than some time during the two centuries preceding the Christian era.

12. Bel and the Dragon is a melodramatic detective story in which Daniel unmasks the chicanery of the priests of Bel. Later, having slain the dragon that the Babylonians venerated as a god, Daniel is thrown (a second time) into the lions' den. Here he is fed with food brought miraculously from Judaea by the prophet Habakkuk. When and where the unknown author lived cannot be determined with certainty.

13. The Prayer of Manasseh is attributed to the King of Judah of that name when he was a captive of Ashurbanipal in the city of Babylon (2 Ch $33^{12, 13}$). It probably originated in some of the legends current regarding this notable king, and may have been intended for insertion in the narrative of 2 Ch 33^{13}. Its original is Greek. It is not a part of the Latin Vulgate Bible adopted at the Council of Trent, but is in the appendix thereof.

14. The First Book of the Maccabees is an historical work of considerable value recounting the heroic exploits of Judas Maccabaeus and his family during the struggle of the Jews for religious and political liberty during the 2nd cent. B.C. Beginning with the accession of Antiochus Epiphanes in 175 B.C., the book carries on the narrative of the Syrian invasions and religious persecutions to the death of Simon, the last of Judas's brothers (about 134 B.C.). The author of this stirring account is unknown, but was probably a Jew of Palestine who wrote in Hebrew about 100 B.C. or soon thereafter. Copies of the original Hebrew circulated until at least the time of Jerome (end of 4th cent.), but to-day the book is extant only in Greek and in versions made from the Greek (including two Latin translations and two Syriac translations).

15. The Second Book of the Maccabees is an abridgment of a five-volume work by Jason of Cyrene (2^{23}). It is prefaced by two letters said to have been sent from the Jews of Jerusalem to their brethren in Egypt. This book deals with the history of the Jews from the reign of Seleucus IV. (175 B.C.) to the death of Nicanor (160 B.C.). The multiplication of the marvellous and miraculous in the narrative discounts the value of the material as a source of historical data. The book was written some time between 125 B.C. and the fall of Jerusalem in A.D. 70 It is extant in Greek and in several versions made from the Greek, including Latin, Syriac, Coptic, and Armenian.

The influence of the Apocrypha has extended far and wide. Though no NT writer quotes explicitly from these fifteen non-canonical books, the NT contains several striking instances of parallels and/or allusions to words, phrases, or whole sections in the Apocryphal literature. It is probable that the Apostle Paul had at some time read and was impressed by the Wisdom of Solomon; cf Ro $1^{20-23, 26, 29-31}$ with Wis $13^{1, 5, 8}$ 12^{24} 14^{24-27}, and Ro 9^{20-23} with Wis $12^{12, 20}$ 15^{7}. Jesus' invitation in Mt 11^{28-30} is couched in language that is reminiscent of Sir $51^{23, 26, 27}$ (cf also Sir 6^{24-25} and 24^{19-22}), In later ages many Church Fathers regarded Bar 3^{36-37} as a witness to the Incarnation and Wis 2^{12-20} and 14^{7} as predictive of Christ's Passion. In modern times many artists, poets, hymn-writers, and novelists have drawn upon the Apocrypha both directly and indirectly. Even Christopher Columbus was encouraged to set sail westward by what he understood 2 Es 6^{42} to imply with regard to the limited extent of the seas.

In addition to these fifteen Apocryphal books, there is an ever-increasing list of works that scholars call pseudepigrapha (q.v.). These were written at various periods, but mainly just before, during, and just after the time of Christ. Many of them deal with the doctrinal discussions of their day, and present revelations to the author under strange and even weird conditions. These writers attached to their books as a rule the name of some famous personage, not by way of deception, but to court favour for the views set forth. See PSEUDEPIGRAPHA.

I. M. P.—**B. M. M.**

APOCRYPHAL GOSPELS.—See APOCRYPHAL NEW TESTAMENT.

APOCRYPHAL NEW TESTAMENT.—The word 'apocryphal,' meaning properly 'hidden' or 'secret,' applied originally to books which were kept from the general public and reserved for initiates, or for a special sect. Because of the nature of such works, however, it gradually came to acquire the meaning 'false' or 'spurious.' (See APOCRYPHA.) Frequently the word is

APOCRYPHAL NEW TESTAMENT

used as the equivalent of 'non-canonical.' We shall here describe various works which were not included in the NT, but which claimed to be genuine Gospels, Acts, Epistles, or Revelations. These were often written under the names of NT writers, and purported to give information about the life and teaching of Jesus and the apostles. This literature is voluminous, but far the greater part of it was written later than the NT period and is 'apocryphal' in the bad sense. The NT Apocrypha, quite rightly, never attained to the importance of the OT Apocrypha, and have never been accepted by any orthodox branch of the Church.

This literature has come down to us in various ways. (1) Some works have survived by being copied through the centuries, and manuscripts exist in the original Greek or Latin, or else in translations made into languages such as Syriac, Coptic, or Ethiopic. (2) Others are known only through quotations or references given in early writers. In this way parts even of heretical works are preserved in the writings of Church Fathers who attacked the heresies involved. (3) Many books are mentioned by name in lists of canonical and non-canonical books issued by the Church. These include the *Gelasian Decree* (6th cent.), the *List of the Sixty Books* (7th cent.), and the *Stichometry of Nicephorus* (in its present form, 9th cent., but possibly as old as the 4th cent.). The last work gives the size of the books it mentions. (4) Apocryphal works have also come to light as the result of manuscript discoveries in modern times. Interesting finds were made by Grenfell and Hunt at Oxyrhynchus, in Egypt, at the end of last century and the beginning of the present century. The most valuable single find has been the discovery of the remains of a Gnostic library at Nag Hammadi, in Upper Egypt, in 1945.

The literature which makes up the apocryphal NT is diverse in character, but for the most part it originated: (a) *From the continuing tradition of the Church.* According to Lk 1^{1-4}, there were a number of written accounts of the life and teachings of Jesus in circulation in the 1st cent. Some of these, but not necessarily all of them, were used by the writers of the canonical Gospels. Similarly, earlier sources lie behind the book of Acts, and some of them may have survived separately. In addition, traditions about Jesus and the apostles must have continued to circulate orally. But the amount of genuine tradition which has been preserved in the apocryphal works is very small indeed. (*b*) *From the homiletic tendency* which has always given rise to stories like the Haggadah of Judaism. Works of this kind undertake to complete the accounts of the lives of Jesus and the apostles by supplying fictitious incidents, and in them the legend-making processes were given free scope. (*c*) *From the desire to support various heresies*, such as Docetism and asceticism, and especially to further the ends of the various Gnostic sects.

Even the most superficial reader of these works recognizes their inferiority to the NT, not merely in point of literary style, but also in general soberness of view. In the entire literature there are only one or two incidents, and a number of sayings (see AGRAPHA) which may be considered authentic. For the most part the narratives and teachings are either a working up of canonical material, or else pure inventions. In some cases it is not impossible that current pagan legends and folk-stories were taken over and attached, *e.g.* to Jesus or Mary. In spite of this, many of these works have enjoyed a considerable popularity and have had their effect on Christian art and literature. They have even influenced the development of doctrine in the Roman Church, particularly in the case of legends about the birth, girlhood, and death of Mary, although certain infancy gospels were declared by Leo XIII., in 1884, to be 'impure sources of tradition.'

None of these works has been unjustly excluded from the NT, as has sometimes been implied. M. R. James, in whose *Apocryphal New Testament* (Oxford, 1924) may be found English translations of all the main works, sums up well (pp. xi f.): 'It will very quickly be seen that there is no question of any one's having excluded them from the New Testament: they have done that for themselves.'

The main apocryphal Gospels, Acts, Epistles, and Revelations may now be mentioned.

I. GOSPELS. (A) Full Gospels. **1. An Unknown Gospel (Papyrus Egerton 2).**—This Gospel is known only through three papyrus fragments, written in Greek, purchased by the British Museum in 1934. Enough is preserved to discern the broad outlines, if not all the details, of four incidents.

1. A Conversation with the Rulers of the People. Jesus is engaged in a controversy with the lawyers and the rulers of the people. He turns to them and says, 'Search the scriptures, in which you think you have life; these are they that bear witness of me. Think not that I came to accuse you to my Father; there is one that accuses you, even Moses, on whom you have set your hope.' The hearers are then chided for their unbelief. At the top of the other side of this leaf, there is what was probably the conclusion of this incident, the account of an attempt to stone Jesus. The rulers lay hands on him in order to hand him over to the multitude. But 'the hour of his betrayal was not yet come,' and so 'he himself, even the Lord, going forth out of their hands, departed from them.'

2. The Healing of a Leper. A leper comes to Jesus and says, 'Master Jesus, journeying with lepers and eating with them in the inn, I myself also became a leper. If therefore thou wilt, I am made clean.' Jesus then heals the man, telling him to go and show himself to the priests.

3. The Question of the Tempters. Some people ask Jesus, in order to tempt him, about the duty of men to secular rulers, 'Is it lawful to render to kings those things which pertain to their rule?' Jesus discerns their motives and replies, 'Why do you call me with your mouth Master, when you do not hear what I say? Well did Isaiah prophesy of you saying, "This people honour me with their lips, but their heart is far from me."'

4. A Miracle by the Jordan. This incident is only very partially preserved. It begins with a question asked by Jesus; then, as he stands on the edge of the Jordan a miracle of some kind is performed. The only phrases in the description of the miracle that can definitely be made out are, 'he sprinkled it,' 'the water that was sprinkled,' and 'brought forth fruit.' Probably a nature miracle of some kind is narrated, connected with the saying of Jesus with which the incident opens.

The papyrus fragments date, on palaeographical evidence, from about the middle of the 2nd cent., so that the original gospel must have been written at an early date. Although there are resemblances to the canonical Gospels, the fragments are neither a copy, nor a harmony, of the canonical Gospels, for the story of the miracle by the Jordan has no parallel, while the other incidents, though they have resemblances to canonical stories, are told in a quite independent way. There are some sayings which recall parts of the Fourth Gospel; these may show that the author of the Unknown Gospel used John, or both writers may have drawn from a common source. The fact that the Gospel shows no heretical tendency, and is comparatively free from exaggeration confirms that it is to be dated in the early 2nd cent., or perhaps even the late 1st cent.

2. The Gospel according to the Hebrews.—Several early Christian writers mention a Gospel according to the Hebrews. Clement of Alexandria quotes it twice; Origen quotes from this gospel—'if anyone accepts it,' he adds. Eusebius also refers to it several times, and states (*HE* iii. 25) that it belongs to that class which was accepted in some parts of the Empire and rejected in others. Jerome obtained from the Syrian Christians a copy of this Gospel, which was written in Aramaic, and which he claims to have translated into Greek and Latin; he also calls it, 'The Gospel of the Nazarenes.'

APOCRYPHAL NEW TESTAMENT

Variant readings found in some manuscripts of Matthew and ascribed to the 'Jewish Gospel' may come from the Gospel according to the Hebrews.

Evidently this gospel stood in a close relationship to the Gospel of Matthew. Jerome thought that the Aramaic version he knew was in fact the original of Matthew's Gospel, but later he rejected this view. Comparison of the surviving quotations with the First Gospel show that they are on the whole later and of a secondary nature. For example, Jesus' reluctance to be baptized (cf Mt 3[14]) is carried a stage further; and the temptation story, which has Jesus being carried by the Holy Spirit by one of his hairs, has been enlarged under the influence of Ezk 8[3] and Bel [36]. On the other hand, some of the quotations suggest that the author had access to genuine early tradition. This is so in the case of the resurrection appearance to James, which is confirmed by 1 Co 15[7], and in some of the sayings such as, 'Never rejoice, except when you have looked upon your brother in love,' which may be regarded as being on the same level as the canonical sayings. The original Gospel must have been written some time in the first half of the 2nd cent.; it expands the Gospel of Matthew, though not in the interests of any heresy, and incorporates some early traditions not found in the canonical Gospels.

The Gospel contains an account of the baptism, in which Jesus is reluctant to be baptized, saying to his family, 'What sin have I done, that I should go and be baptized by him ?—unless perchance this very thing that I have said is a sin of ignorance' (Jerome, *adv. Pelag.* iii. 2).

There is a version, differing slightly from the canonical one, of the story of the Rich Young Ruler. When Jesus spoke to him, 'the rich man began to scratch his head, and it pleased him not. And the Lord said to him, "How do you say, I have kept the Law and the Prophets, since it is written in the Law, Thou shalt love thy neighbour as thyself; and behold, many of your brothers, sons of Abraham, are clad in filth, dying of hunger, and your house is full of good things, and nothing at all goes out from it to them"' (Origen, *in Matt.* xv. 14). According to Jerome (*in Matt.* 12[13]), the man with the withered hand was a mason, who prayed to Jesus for help in these words: 'I was a mason seeking a livelihood with my hands; I pray you, Jesus, to restore me my health, that I may not beg meanly for my food.' The Gospel also had a variant version of the Parable of the Pounds, according to Eusebius.

When Simon asked if a brother must indeed be forgiven seven times in a day, Jesus replied, 'Yes, I say unto you, until seventy times seven; for with the prophets also, after they were anointed with the Holy Spirit, the word of sin was found' (Jerome, *adv. Pelag.* iii. 2). Clement of Alexandria quotes a saying, also found in Oxyrhynchus Papyrus 654: 'He who seeks shall not stop until he finds, and when he has found he shall wonder, and when he has wondered he shall reign, and when he has reigned, he shall rest' (Clement of Alexandria, *Strom.* II. ix. 45).

The Gospel tells of how Jesus, after his resurrection, appeared to James. 'For James had taken an oath that he would not eat bread from that hour in which he had drunk the cup of the Lord, until he should see him rising from them that sleep.' Jesus called for a table and for bread, and 'he took the bread, and blessed, and brake, and gave to James the Just, and said to him, "My brother, eat your bread, for the Son of Man has risen from them that sleep"' (Jerome, *de Vir. Illus.* ii).

3. The Gospel of the Egyptians.—This gospel is mentioned by Clement of Alexandria, and later by Hippolytus, Origen, and other writers. It would appear that it originally circulated without incurring the hostility of the Church, but by the end of the 2nd cent. it was used by at least one Gnostic sect, and was condemned as heretical. The name suggests an Egyptian origin, and the gospel must have been written some time in the first half of the 2nd cent.

Most of the surviving quotations are part of a dialogue between Jesus and Salome, and show that the gospel was of an ascetic character and discouraged the bearing of children. 'When Salome asked how long death should have power,' the Lord said, 'As long as you women bear' (Clem. of Alex. *Strom.* III. vi. 45). Jesus said, 'I come to destroy the works of the female' (Clem. of Alex. *Strom.* III. ix. 63). 'When Salome inquired when those things should be concerning which she asked, the Lord said, 'when you trample on the garment of shame, and when the two shall be one, and the male with the female, neither male nor female' (Clem. of Alex. *Strom.* III. xiii. 92). The 'garment of shame' evidently means the physical body.

A fragment discovered by Grenfell and Hunt, Oxyrhynchus Papyrus 655, may be part of the Gospel of the Egyptians. On one side of the leaf is a discourse on anxiety similar to that in the Sermon on the Mount; in what can be made out of the rest, Jesus appears to answer questions put to him by his disciples. Traces of Gnosticism and of sexual asceticism, and also the dialogue form, suggest a connexion with the Gospel of the Egyptians. If the fragment is not a part of this Gospel, then all that can be said is that it comes from a 2nd cent. Egyptian Gnostic gospel of a similar type.

Two versions of a Gospel of the Egyptians, also called the Book of the Great Invisible Spirit, were found at Nag Hammadi.

4. An Unknown Gospel (Oxyrhynchus Papyrus 840).—Discovered by Grenfell and Hunt, and published in 1908, this single leaf contains part of an otherwise unknown gospel.

The fragment begins with the conclusion of an exhortation by Jesus to avoid the example of certain evildoers. There then follows an almost complete incident in which a Pharisee, a chief priest, encounters Jesus in the Temple and demands why He and His disciples are walking in 'this place of purification' and looking at the holy vessels, when they are unclean. Jesus asks if the priest is clean and the priest replies that he is, having washed in the pool of David and put on clean, white clothes. Jesus gives a crushing reply contrasting outward cleanness with inward purity. Jesus and His followers have been 'dipped in the waters of eternal life.'

The references to Jewish customs have caused much debate, some holding that the writer shows gross ignorance of the Judaism of Jesus' day. But the fragment has also been defended on this score, and although it probably uses the Fourth Gospel, it may not be later than the mid 2nd cent.

5. The Gospel according to Peter.—This Gospel is mentioned by Eusebius (*HE* vi. 12) as having been rejected by Serapion, bishop of Antioch, in the last decade of the 2nd cent. He found it in circulation among the Syrian Christians, and at first did not oppose it, but after having studied it further, condemned it as Docetic. Origen in his Commentary on Matthew (Book x. 17, and occasionally elsewhere) mentions it, or at least shows an acquaintance with it. Eusebius (*HE* iii. 3, 25) rejects it as heretical, as does Jerome (*de Vir. Illus.* i.).

In 1886 a fragment of this Gospel was discovered by M. Bouriant, and published with a translation in 1892. It relates in some detail the death, burial, and resurrection of Jesus. It is particularly interesting as indicating how canonical material could be elaborated and changed in the interests of the Docetic heresy. Thus the words of Jesus on the cross, 'My God, my God, why hast thou forsaken me ?' are made to read, 'My power, my power, thou hast forsaken me,' while it is said that when He was being crucified He kept silence, 'as one feeling no pain.' At the time of the resurrection the soldiers are said to have seen how 'three men came forth from the tomb, and two of them supported one, and the cross followed them; and of the two the head reached unto the heavens, but the head of him that was led by them overpassed the heavens; and they heard a

APOCRYPHAL NEW TESTAMENT

voice from the heavens saying, 'Thou hast preached unto them that sleep.' And a response was heard from the cross, 'Yea.' The Gospel was probably written about the middle of the 2nd cent.

6. The Gospel of the Ebionites.—This gospel comes down to us only in quotations from Epiphanius (*Haer.* xxx. 13–26, 22). It uses Matthew and Luke, and part of it is narrated by the disciples in the first person plural. Jesus is represented as saying, 'I come to put an end to sacrifices, and unless you cease from sacrificing, anger will not cease from you'; and some of the gospel stories are altered to suit the adoptianist Christology and vegetarianism of the sect in which the gospel originated. It is possible that this work is to be identified with a Gospel of the Twelve Apostles mentioned by Origen, Ambrose, and Jerome. The date may be late 2nd or early 3rd cent.

(B) Infancy Gospels. **1. The Book of James.**—This book, also known as the Protevangelium, is referred to by Origen and Epiphanius, and has survived in various versions.

It purports to be an account of the birth of Mary and of her early life in the Temple, whither she was brought by her parents when she was three years of age, and where at twelve years of age she was married to Joseph, then an old man with children. It includes also an account of the Annunciation and the visit of Mary to Elizabeth, of the trial by ordeal of Joseph and Mary on the charge of having been secretly married, of the birth of Jesus in a cave, and accompanying miracles of the most extravagant sort. The writing closes with an account of the martyrdom of Zechariah and the death of Herod.

The work as it now stands is probably composite. The writer betrays ignorance of Jewish customs, but is dependent both on the canonical gospels and on the OT. Clement of Alexandria and Justin Martyr both refer to incidents connected with the birth of Jesus which are related in the Book of James, but they may have derived the information from independent tradition. Probably the work is to be dated some time in the second half of the 2nd cent.

The author is a not unaccomplished story-teller and his work was used in the later Gospel of Pseudo-Matthew and the Arabic Gospel of the Infancy. The book is of no historical value, but is important as it shows an insistence in the 2nd cent. upon the miraculous birth of Jesus, and shows also the growing importance and the growing veneration of the Virgin Mary.

2. The Gospel according to Thomas.—Hippolytus quotes from a Gospel according to Thomas which was being used by the Naassenes. The Gospel was also known to Origen and to Eusebius, who classes it with the heretical writings. It was subsequently held in high regard by the Manichaeans. It exists to-day in Greek, Latin, and Syriac versions, which, however, do not altogether agree, and all of which are apparently abbreviated recensions of the original Gospel.

The Gospel of Thomas is an account of the childhood of Jesus, and consists largely of stories of His miraculous power and knowledge, the most interesting of the latter being the account of Jesus' visit to a school, and of the former, the well-known story of His causing twelve sparrows of clay to fly.

The book is undoubtedly of Gnostic origin, and its chief motive seems to be to show that Jesus was possessed of Divine power before His baptism. The original Gospel of Thomas, the nature of which is, however, very much in dispute, may have been in existence in the middle of the 2nd cent. Its present form is later than the 6th cent.

3. The History of Joseph the Carpenter, which may date from the 5th cent., has survived in various versions. Written to glorify Joseph, it was probably intended to be recited on his feast day. Other infancy gospels are of later date. The *Arabic Gospel of the Infancy* is a compilation which uses as its main sources the Book of James and the Gospel of Thomas. It can hardly be earlier than the 7th or 8th cent. The *Gospel of Pseudo-Matthew* also draws upon the two earlier infancy gospels. It contains many details, such as the ox and the ass in the birth story, which have influenced Christian art and literature. It may date from the 8th or 9th cent. Other late infancy gospels include the *Gospel of the Birth of Mary* and the *Armenian Gospel of the Infancy*.

(C) Other Gospels. **1.** Some gospels deal only with the narrative of the Passion. **The Gospel of Nicodemus,** also known as the **Acts of Pilate,** consists of two parts, a narrative of the Passion, and an account of the descent into Hades. Some such Acts are referred to by Tertullian, Eusebius, and Epiphanius, but it is very uncertain as to whether any of these are to be identified with this work which has survived in a variety of versions. The first part of the Gospel abounds in anecdotes concerning Jesus and his trial, in which the question of the legitimacy of Jesus' birth is established by twelve witnesses of the marriage of Mary and Joseph. It relates also that at the trial of Jesus a number of persons, including Nicodemus and Veronica, appeared to testify on His behalf. The accounts of the crucifixion are clearly based upon Lk 23. The story of the burial is further elaborated by the introduction of a number of Biblical characters, who undertake to prove the genuineness of the resurrection. This work belongs to the 4th or 5th cent. The second part, probably somewhat later in date, contains an elaborate account of Jesus' descent into Hades, related by two men, Karinus and Leucius, who reveal how Christ vanquished Satan and released Adam and all the saints. The Gospel of Nicodemus cannot be regarded as having any historical value, yet it has exercised considerable influence on the thought of the Church.

Various other works have come to be associated with the Gospel of Nicodemus. These include the **Letter of Pilate** which seeks to lay the blame for the crucifixion solely on the Jews. There are two versions of the **Report of Pilate.** The **Delivering up of Pilate** recounts how Pilate appeared before Caesar, and was beheaded. These and other similar works are all of a late date.

2. There are a number of gospels which, in content, are theological treatises rather than narratives of the life of Jesus. Various Gnostic sects produced gospels of this type which sometimes used the period after the resurrection of Jesus, of which the canonical Gospels say little, for accounts of special doctrines revealed by Christ to select disciples. These gospels can tell us nothing of the life and teachings of Jesus, but are of value for the study of the history of Gnosticism.

Such gospels include the **Gospel of Truth,** mentioned by Irenaeus, and recovered in the Nag Hammadi library; it is of the first importance for the study of Valentinian Gnosticism, and must have been written in the middle of the 2nd cent. The **Gospel of Philip,** referred to by Irenaeus, contained special revelations supposed to have been given by Christ to Philip. This work has been found at Nag Hammadi. Jerome mentions a **Gospel of Bartholomew.** There does exist a work known as the **Questions of Bartholomew,** which may incorporate parts of this gospel. A **Gospel** or **Traditions of Matthias** is mentioned by various writers, and Hippolytus connects it with the Gnostics, Basilides and Isidore. It is probably identical with a work found at Nag Hammadi. From Nag Hammadi also come several versions of the **Apocryphon of John,** purporting to contain special doctrines revealed by Christ to the Apostle John.

3. The Gospel of Thomas (not to be confused with the Infancy Gospel of the same name), which was found in the Nag Hammadi library, is of a unique kind, consisting of over 100 sayings of Jesus (it is also known as *The Secret Sayings of Jesus*). Its beginning coincides with Oxyrhynchus Papyrus 654, discovered by Grenfell and Hunt in 1903. Many of the sayings have a Gnostic ring, but others are of the Synoptic type and may preserve genuine tradition. The gospel is probably a collection of quotations from the Gospel according to the Hebrews, the Gospel of the Egyptians and other works, and was compiled in the 2nd cent.

4. Many other gospels are known to us practically only by name. These include Gospels of *Andrew, Apelles, Barnabas, Bartholomew, Basilides, Cerinthus, Eve, Judas Iscariot, Thaddaeus,* and *Valentinus.* The **Gospel of Marcion,** although lost, we know as a probable re-working of Luke by the omission of the Infancy section and other material that in any way favoured the Jewish-Christian conceptions which Marcion opposed. The **Fayoum Gospel Fragment** contains the words of Christ to Peter at the Last Supper in a different form from that of the canonical Gospels, but may be merely a loose quotation rather than part of a lost gospel.

II. Acts.—The canonical Acts were not originally a separate book, but rather the second part of a two-volume work, the first half of which was the Gospel of Luke. With the appearance of other Gospels, however, Luke's Gospel came to be classed along with them, while Acts thus became separated, and so served as a model for later compositions. Of these apocryphal Acts, the earliest and most important are five in number. These five were used by the Manichaeans ; they are described and condemned as heretical by Photius (9th cent.). But references and quotations in earlier writers show that some are as old as the 2nd cent. The motive of the authors of these Acts was largely to commend Gnostic doctrines, but also merely to expand what little was known about the lives of the apostles by means of highly imaginative and almost entirely mythical additions. However, it is possible that in a few cases genuine early traditions have been preserved. These works were very popular and the existence of different versions may be attributed to the fact that orthodox revisions were made of heretical works. In several cases the passion narratives of the various apostles circulated separately. The five main Acts are as follows :

1. The Acts of John date from the mid 2nd cent., and probably about two-thirds of the original work survives. It is attributed to Leucius, who is said to have been a companion of the Apostle John. (According to Photius, this Leucius was the author of all five Acts, but a common authorship for all these works is quite impossible.)

2. The Acts of Paul were composed in the second half of the 2nd cent. by a presbyter in Asia, who was condemned for producing this fictitious work, although it alone of these Acts is not heretical. Part of it survives as the **Acts of Paul and Thecla,** which contain an interesting description of Paul, uncomplimentary enough to suggest that it may preserve a true tradition—' A man of little stature, thin-haired upon the head, crooked in the legs . . . with eyebrows joining, and nose somewhat hooked. . . .'

3. The Acts of Peter are modelled on the Acts of John, and may date from around A.D. 200. Much of the narrative describes the struggles between Peter and Simon the Magician. Part of this work is preserved separately as the *Martyrdom of Peter,* which includes the well-known *Quo Vadis* legend.

4. The Acts of Andrew, dating probably from the 3rd cent., are the least well preserved.

5. The Acts of Thomas have survived in their entirety, and form a work of considerable length. The date of composition is uncertain.

Numerous other Acts are known, although many of them survive only in fragmentary form or even only in name. For the most part they are later than and inferior to the ones listed above. The following may be mentioned : *The Acts of Philip, The Acts of Andrew and Matthew,* and *The Acts of Peter and Andrew.*

III. Epistles.—The apocryphal epistles are of a wholly fictitious character. Eusebius is the first to refer to the correspondence of **Christ and Abgar,** the latter being a king of Edessa who writes asking Christ to come and heal him. A supposed correspondence between **Paul and Seneca,** consisting of fourteen letters, has survived ; it is first mentioned by Jerome. We know from Col 4^{16} that Paul wrote to the Laodiceans, and an apocryphal **Epistle to the Laodiceans** has survived, as also has a ' third ' **Epistle to the Corinthians,** which was probably originally part of the Acts of Paul. **The Epistle of the Apostles,** purporting to have been written by the apostles to all Christians, may be as old as the 2nd cent. The **Letter of James** and the **Epistle of Peter to Philip** are Gnostic works found at Nag Hammadi.

IV. Revelations.—The most important of these is the **Revelation of Peter,** dating from the early 2nd cent., which is referred to by several early writers, and which survives in Ethiopic. A Greek fragment was discovered at Akhmim in 1884, attached to the Gospel of Peter. It contains a description of heaven, and of the many torments which the wicked endure in hell. The **Revelation of Paul** dates from the 4th cent., although earlier sources are incorporated in it. Other revelations are those of *Thomas,* of *the Virgin,* of *Stephen,* and of *Bartholomew.* Two *Revelations of James,* and *Revelations of Paul and of Peter* were found at Nag Hammadi. C. H. H. S.

APOLLONIA (Ac 17^{1}).—Paul and Silas passed through this town on the way from Amphipolis to Thessalonica. It was on the important Egnatian road which ran between Dyrrhachium (modern *Durazzo*) and Thessalonica. It was about half-way between Amphipolis and Thessalonica, and lay between the rivers Axius and Strymon. To-day *Pollina.* A. So.—**E. G. K.**

APOLLONIUS.—1. A governor of Coele-Syria and Phoenicia under Seleucus IV. (2 Mac 4^{4}), who suggested the abortive attempt of Heliodorus on the Temple-treasury. To this he perhaps owed the title *mysarches* (2 Mac 5^{24}), which the Vulgate renders *odiosum principem,* AV ' detestable ringleader,' RV ' lord of pollutions.' But RSV reads, ' the captain of the Mysians.' In 168–167 B.C. he was sent to Hellenize Jerusalem, and he initiated the great persecution with a cruel massacre on the Sabbath (2 Mac 5^{24-26}). Judas Maccabaeus defeated and slew him, wearing his sword ever after (1 Mac 3^{10ff}, Jos. *Ant.* XII. vii. 1 [287]). **2.** An envoy sent to Egypt by Antiochus IV., 173 B.C. (2 Mac 4^{21}). Some MSS identify this man with the preceding, describing each as ' son of Menestheus.' **3.** An official under Antiochus V. who molested the Jews (2 Mac 12^{2}). **4.** A governor of Coele-Syria who fought against the Jews (147 B.C.) on the side of Demetrius (1 Mac 10^{69-85} ; Jos. *Ant.* XIII. iv. 3 f [86 ff] is in error). From Jamnia he sent a pompous defiance to Jonathan who, however, captured Joppa and defeated Apollonius. J. T.—**F. C. G.**

APOLLOPHANES (2 Mac 10^{37}).—A Syrian killed at the taking of Gazara by Judas Maccabaeus.

APOLLOS (a pet name, abbreviated from Apollonios, which appears in the D text of Ac 18^{24}, or from Apollodoros or Apollonides), was according to Ac 18^{24-28} and 1 Co 1^{12} 3^{4-8} 4^{6} 16^{12} an Alexandrian Jew and Christian missionary, who preached effectively at Ephesus, Corinth (where his disciples formed a close group) and again at Ephesus. His picture in Ac 18^{25f} is not quite clear : was he then a Jew with fervent messianic expectations, baptized by John, or already a Christian? The story told in Acts seems to be a compromise between these two views. That he used Philonic allegory is only a guess. Probably he was neither an adherent of the Jewish baptist movement nor a follower of St. Paul, but an independent Christian missionary. The old conjecture that he wrote the Wisdom of Solomon before, and the letter to the Hebrews after, his conversion has now been abandoned. Concerning Tit 3^{13}, see Pastoral Epistles. E. H.

APOLLYON (' the Destroyer ').—The Greek equivalent in Rev 9^{11} of **Abaddon,** the angel of the bottomless pit, who was also the king of the locusts (see Abaddon). The word does not appear in its Greek form in later Rabbinic writings, and only here in the NT. As an angel, Apollyon seems to have been regarded as equivalent to Asmodaeus, king of demons, in Judaistic mythology ; but our data are too few to warrant precise statements. S. M.

APOPLEXY.—See MEDICINE.

APOSTASY.—A defection from the tenets of some religious community. In Ac 21^{21} it describes the charge brought against St. Paul by the Jews, viz., that he taught that the Jews should abandon the Law of Moses. In 2 Th 2^{3} (RSV 'the rebellion') it describes the defection of Christians which was to accompany the 'man of lawlessness'—*i.e.* the Antichrist. This expectation is an illustration of what seems to have been a common belief—that the return of Christ to establish His Kingdom would be preceded by violent activity on the part of His superhuman opponent, and that this would result in an abandonment of Christian faith by many nominal Christians. The seriousness of the act is reflected in He 6^{6} where, probably as a result of persecution, some have defected and thus 'crucify the Son of God on their own account' (RSV). It is equally reflected in the Jewish prayer, Shemoneh Esreh (§ 12), where a malediction was pronounced against the apostates. Such persons had undoubtedly denounced their fellows, friends, and relatives to the authorities, thus virtually handing them over to torture and death. S. M.—**F. C. G.**

APOSTLES.—The New Testament word *apostolos* has a meaning which bears little relation to the almost uniform classical usage of the word, where it has for the most part a nautical flavour. Possibly its NT connotation of 'authorized agent,' 'a commissioned person,' 'one designated as envoy,' emphasizing not only the one sent but the one sending, is related to the Rabbinical legal term *shālîaḥ*, which has the same meaning but which is difficult to date as to early usage. Some scholars, on the other hand, find its beginnings in a pre-Christian Gnosticism. Or possibly the NT sense of the word is Christian in origin, although Herodotus (alone of classical authors) uses it in the sense of 'envoy.' The Talmud says, 'The one whom a man sends is the equivalent of himself' (*Berakhoth*, v. 5), *i.e.* so far as that particular commission is concerned. The term was applied, especially in Luke–Acts, to the twelve disciples whom Jesus attached to Himself to aid Him in His ministry and to be trained by the discipline of His example and precept for carrying it on after His departure (Lk 6^{13}, etc., and often in Ac, Mk 6^{30}, Mt 10^{2}). Thus Jesus was regarded as the sender, and the twelve as the Gospel bearers.

By and by, when Jesus was setting out on His last journey to Jerusalem, He 'appointed seventy others, and sent them on ahead of him,' *i.e.* as His agents (Lk 10^{1}; 'sent' is the verb cognate to 'apostle').

Later on the Twelve (the Eleven plus Matthias) were regarded as the Apostles *par excellence* (cf Ac 6$^{2, 6}$). They were the men who had been with Jesus, and their peculiar function was to testify of Him, and especially of His resurrection (Ac 1^{21f}; cf v.^{8} and Lk 24^{48}). But soon they were not the only Apostles. The title was given to Barnabas (Ac 14$^{4, 14}$, 1 Co 9$^{5, 6}$), perhaps to Andronicus and Junias (Ro 16^{7}), and possibly to others (see 1 Co 15$^{5, 7}$). Why was it withheld from one like Timothy (2 Co 1^{1}, Col 1^{1})? If Barnabas, as Eusebius declares (*HE* i. 12) and Andronicus and Junias (the possibility is raised by Origen: *ad Romanos*, xvi) belonged to the Seventy, it is just possible that the great majority of those others besides the Twelve who were styled 'Apostles' were of the Seventy. It is true that the title is given to James the Lord's brother (Gal 1^{19}) and to Paul, who belonged neither to the Twelve nor to the Seventy. But it was natural that James, who was recognized as the head of the Church at Jerusalem, should be called an 'Apostle,' as well for the great piety which tradition ascribes to him, as for his relationship to Jesus. As for Paul, his Apostolic title was bitterly contested, but he triumphantly defended it (1 Co 9$^{1, 2}$, 2 Co 12^{12}). Perhaps it was his example that emboldened others outside the ranks of the Twelve (and perhaps of the Seventy) to claim Apostleship on the score of Apostolic gifts, real or supposed (2 Co 11^{13}, Rev 2^{2}).

The application of the term 'Apostle' to Jesus (He 3^{1}) carries the general connotation of one who is an authorized agent. See also DISCIPLES. D. S.—**J. H. Sc.**

APOTHECARY.—This word is found eight times in AV, but should be rendered 'perfumer'; it is so rendered in RV in Ex 30$^{25, 35}$ 37^{29}, Ec 10^{1}, and in RVm in Neh 3^{8}, but RV retains 'apothecary' in 2 Ch 16^{14}, Neh 3^{8}, Sir 38^{8} 49^{1}; RSV renders by 'perfumer' in all cases save Sir 38^{8}, where it has 'pharmacist.' See PERFUMER.

APPAIM ('nostrils').—A man of Judah, 1 Ch 2^{30f}.

APPAREL.—See DRESS.

APPARITION.—In RV of Mt 14^{26} and Mk 6^{49} for AV 'spirit.' The Greek word (*phantasma*) differs from the usual word for 'spirit' (*pneuma*); it occurs only in these passages. RSV uses 'ghost' here and in Is 29^{4}. See GHOST.

APPEAL.—See JUSTICE.

APPHIA.—A Christian lady of Colossae, a member o the household of Philemon, probably his wife (Phn ^{2}).

APPHUS (1 Mac 2^{5}).—The surname of Jonathan the Maccabee. The name is usually thought to mean 'dissembler'; and some suppose that it was given to Jonathan for his stratagem against the tribe of the Jambri, who had killed his brother John (1 Mac 9$^{37-41}$).

APPII FORUM.—Ac 28^{15} AV; RV 'The Market of Appius.' See next article.

APPIUS, FORUM OF.—A market-town (without city rights) on the Appian Way, 43 miles from Rome, and about 10 miles from *Tres Tabernae* (Three Taverns), near the modern railway station, Foro Appio. As the Appian Way was the main road from Rome to the south and east under the Roman Empire, it was traversed by nearly all travellers from or to those parts (Ac 28^{15}). A. So.

APPLE.—That the apple (*tappuaḥ*) of the OT is the fruit known by that name to-day is extremely doubtful. It is true that the tree in size and foliage would answer to the reference in Ca 8^{5}, Jl 1^{12}; the fruit too in its sweetness (Ca 2^{3}) and its smell (Ca 7^{8}) is very appropriate. It is also suggestive that Hebrew *tappuaḥ* closely resembles the Arabic for 'apple,' *tuffâḥ*. On the other hand, it is a substantial difficulty that the apple does not grow well in Palestine proper, as distinguished from the Lebanon. The native fruit is small and wanting in sweetness; almost all eatable apples are imported from the North. In consequence of this, several fruits which to-day are found in Palestine have been suggested. The *citron*, a favourite with the Jews on account of its smell and golden colour, is certainly a more recent introduction. The *apricot*, suggested by Tristram, which flourishes in parts of Palestine in greater profusion than any other fruit, would seem to answer to the references well. It is deliciously sweet, with a pleasant smell, and, when ripe, of a brilliant golden colour. The tree is one of the most beautiful in the land, and when loaded with its golden fruit might well suggest the expression 'apples of gold in pictures of silver' (Pr 25^{11}). Unfortunately there is considerable doubt whether this tree, a native of China, was known in Palestine much before the Christian era. A fourth fruit has been suggested, namely, the *quince*. This is certainly a native of the land, and is common all over Palestine. The fruit, when ripe, though smelling pleasantly, is not 'sweet' according to our ideas, but even to-day is much appreciated. It is a great favourite when cooked, and is extensively used for making a delicious confection. The quince, along with the true apple, was sacred to Aphrodite, the goddess of love. E. W. G. M.

APPLE OF THE EYE.—A figure for that which is most precious and most carefully guarded. It represents three different expressions in Hebrew: the 'little man of the eye' in Dt 32^{10}, Pr 7^{2}; 'the daughter of the eye' in La 2^{18} (AV, RV); 'the gate of the eye' in Zec 2^{8}. In Ps 17^{8} the first two of these are combined. It is used of God's care of His people in Dt 32^{10}, Ps 17^{8}, Zec 2^{8}, and of the preciousness of the Divine law in Pr 7^{2}. In La 2^{18}, where RSV has simply 'your eyes,' it is the source of tears.

APRON.—See DRESS.

AQUILA AND PRISCILLA.—The names of a married couple mentioned in Ac $18^{2f, 18, 26}$, Ro 16^{3-5}, 1 Co 16^{19}, 2 Ti 4^{19}. From the fact that only in 1 Co and Ac 18^{2} is Aquila mentioned first, Harnack concluded that Priscilla (a diminutive; St. Paul calls her Prisca) was a more effective missionary than Aquila. The statement of Chrysostom (i. 306 D, 177 A; iii. 176 B, C) that Prisca was able to instruct Apollos, probably was an inference too.

Aquila was a Jew of Pontus. He lived (as a leather-merchant) with Prisca in Rome until they were driven out by the edict of Claudius (A.D. 49). Possibly they were already Christians when they came to Corinth; it is not said that St. Paul converted them. When he left Corinth after 18 months (A.D. 51), he followed them to Ephesus. There they remained; they are mentioned honourably in Ro 16^{3}: this chapter was probably a letter to the Christians at Ephesus, where as in 2 Ti 4^{19} Aquila and Prisca are supposed to be. E. H.

AQUILA'S VERSION.—See GREEK VERSIONS OF OT, **15.**

AR.—A city or district of Moab in the region of the Arnon, the border between Moab and the Amorites, Nu 21^{15}, Dt $2^{9, 18, 29}$, Is 15^{1}; possibly modern *el-Miṣna'*. It is called Ar of Moab in Nu 21^{28}; this may be the same as 'the city of Moab' (Nu 22^{36}), 'Ar' and 'city' being consonantally the same in Hebrew. If this is the capital city, **Kir-hareseth** (q.v.) may be meant.

ARA.—A descendant of Asher, 1 Ch 7^{38}.

ARAB.—A city of Judah in the mountains, near Dumah, Jos 15^{52}; possibly modern *Khirbet er-Râbiyeh.*

ARABAH.—The name given by the Hebrews to the whole of the great depression from the Sea of Galilee to the Gulf of 'Aqaba, *e.g.* 2 S 4^{7}, where it refers to the Jordan Valley east of Bethshan (see JORDAN). The 'Brook of the Arabah' (RV), named by Amos (6^{14}) as the southern boundary of Israel may be the *Wâdî Nimrîn*, which flows into the Jordan from the east 7 miles N. of the Dead Sea, but here the Hebrew *'ᵃrābhāh* may mean 'willows' (cf Is 15^{7}, of the same region). The name in Ezk 47^{8} applied to the desert W. of the Dead Sea, is now applied only to the southern part, extending from a line of white cliffs that cross the valley a few miles S. of the Dead Sea. The floor of the valley, about 10 miles broad at the north end, gradually rises towards the S., until at a height of *c* 2000 feet above the Dead Sea (*Jebel er-Rîsheh*) it narrows considerably and drops to the Gulf of 'Aqaba at an average width of 6 miles. The surface is formed of loose gravel, stones and sand (*raml*), and patches of mud-pans (*qa'a*). There is sparse seasonal herbage, confined mainly to watercourses, with occasional acacia trees. The escarpment of the great limestone plateau, *et-Tih*, the Wilderness of Paran, forms the western boundary, and the Edomite escarpment the eastern. Here copper ores were worked by the Egyptians in the Pyramid Age (3rd millennium), and were later more extensively exploited under Solomon. Traces of ancient mining and smelting, and fortified camps for slave-miners have been explored by Glueck, who, further, excavated *Tell el-Kheleifeh* at the head of the Gulf of 'Aqaba and found the remains of a refinery with possible evidence of ship-building of the Solomonic age. According to OT tradition Israel traversed the Arabah when they went to Kadesh-Barnea, and again when they returned to the south in their detour past Edom (Nu 20^{21} 21^{4}, Dt 2^{8}). W. E.—**J. Gr.**

ARABATTINE, 1 Mac 5^{3} (AV).—See AKRABATTENE.

ARABIA, ARABS.—Historians use the name Arabia sometimes with a wider, sometimes with a narrower connotation, but the Arabia of the Bible is the whole of that large, and somewhat barren, peninsula jutting out from south-west Asia just before it joins on to Africa. Geologically it is part of the great land mass stretching from Turkestan to the African Sahara. The great rift which formed the Red Sea cut it off from its western connexion, and a similar depression, now partially filled by Mesopotamia and the Persian Gulf, separated it on the east. Cut off by depressions of quite a different nature, the Mediterranean border to the north and the Indian Ocean to the south, it was left an almost rectangular peninsula, about twice as long as it is broad, set obliquely to normal longitude and latitude. It is for the most part a plateau whose steep escarpment is to the west, so that from the Red Sea it presents a mountainous appearance, but slopes gently eastwards, though not without interruptions, to the basin of Mesopotamia and the Persian Gulf. The western escarpment rises sharply in the south to the mountains of Yemen, and to the south-east there is a similar sharp rise to the highlands of Oman. This plateau is intersected by innumerable valleys, in which are many scattered oases, and has two large desert bulges, one to the north, the Nefud, and one to the south, the famous Empty Quarter. Save in the mountainous areas of Yemen and Oman, which catch some of the monsoon rains, the rainfall is scarce and uncertain, and the characteristic fauna and flora are consequently of the desert type. Continuous cultivation is possible only in the south and in the oases. This limited fertility, added to the fact that though the coast line is extensive it has very few practicable harbours, has prevented the development of settlements of any size and made the typical life of the country that of the nomad. Before the effective domestication of the camel the people were ass nomads, but in Biblical times their characteristic beast of burden was the camel. Horses are a relatively late importation, and are still in the nature of a luxury.

In early times there was no common name for the whole of this area, nor a common name for its inhabitants, who were known by local, or clan names, as Sabaeans, Amalekites, Midianites, Dedanians, Ishmaelites, Hagarenes, or even 'sons of the East.' The earliest inhabitants were not of a single racial stock, as is evident from an examination of even the few ancient skeletal remains so far brought to light, but it would seem that the cultural unity in which the Semitic family of languages arose was first attained on this plateau. There seems, however, to have been a marked feeling of distinction between peoples of the south and those of the north, a feeling which has survived into modern days. The word *'arab* means 'nomad,' and has connexions both with the Hebrew *'erebh* 'mixed multitude' and *'ᵃrābhāh* 'desert land,' much as the Arabic *badawī* (from whose plural comes our familiar *bedouin*) has with *bādiya*, the 'steppe land.' It occurs with this meaning of 'nomad' in Egyptian texts as early as the 13th Dynasty, as well as in both cuneiform and South Arabian inscriptions, and in the Qur'ān. This would seem to be its meaning in the OT in such passages as 'No Arab will pitch his tent there' (Is 13^{10}), 'like an Arab in the wilderness' (Jer 3^{2}), for the prophets doubtless mean 'nomad' rather than any particular ethnic group. Similarly the 'kings of Arabia' (1 K 10^{15}, Jer 25^{24}) would be nomad chiefs just as those Arabians who attacked Judas Maccabaeus are expressly called 'nomads' (2 Mac 12^{10-12}). In the Behistun inscription of Darius I., however, *Arbāya* is the province lying between Assyria and Egypt. Likewise in Greek writers from Herodotus onwards *Arabia* is the name for this area, so that in Is 21^{13}, Ezk 30^{5}, the reference could be to the geographical area in which the nomads roam. Similarly 'Arabs' as an ethnic name for the inhabitants of this area occurs both in the Old Persian inscriptions and in Herodotus, as indeed in the earliest occurrence of the word in Greek (Aeschylus, *Persae*, 316). It is so used in 2 Ch 21^{16}, Neh 4^{7}.

In the genealogical tables of the OT many names included among the descendants of Cush (Gn 10^{7}), of Eber (Gn 10^{25-30}), of Abraham by Keturah (Gn 25^{1-4}), and by Hagar (Gn 25^{13-16}), can be related to persons and places in Arabia, several being names which appear also in accounts of Arabian contacts in Assyrian annals. Gn 21[20, 21] pictures Ishmael as dwelling in the desert country and places his ' sons ' in the wilderness area stretching from near the Egyptian border across to Mesopotamia (Gn 25[13ff], Jth 2[23]). This is North Arabia, but the Joctanid genealogy in Gn 10[26–30] contains names which have good South Arabian correspondences. Saba, the land of rich merchandise, hard by Ethiopia (Is 43[3] 45[14]), belonged to this South Arabia the true greatness of whose civilization is only now beginning to be appreciated. The South Arabians were particularly interested in the incense and luxury trade, in the interests of which they established trade centres in the north. Possibly the Sheba which appears beside Saba in Gn 10[7], Ps 72[10] may refer to these North Arabian settlements (cf Job 1[15], Jer 6[20]), and the queen of Sheba who visited Solomon (1 K 10[1–13]) may have been a chieftainess from some such centre, since we know nothing of reigning queens in South Arabia.

The Ishmaelites in the Joseph story (Gn 37[25, 28]) appear as traders leading caravans between North Arabia and Egypt, which suggests they were a camel people, and in 1 Ch 27[30] the overseer of David's camels was an Ishmaelite and his chief herdsman a Hagarene. In Gn 37[28, 31] these Ishmaelites are equated with the Midianites (cf Jg 8[24], Jth 2[23, 26]), whom the prophets also knew as traders who brought to Palestine goods of the South Arabian trade (Is 60[6]), but who in the Moses story are a pastoral people (Ex 2[15ff]). The nomads are still frequently both. They were a people who dwelt in tents (Jg 6[5] 8[11], Ps 83[7 (6)]), as did the Qedar, the Bene Qedem (sons of the East) and other North Arabian peoples (Ps 120[5], Jer 49[29, 31], Ezk 38[11], Ca 1[5], 1 Ch 5[10]), who supplied Israel with small cattle (Is 60[7], Ezk 27[21], 2 Ch 17[11]), and were middlemen in the luxury trade (Jer 6[20], Ezk 27[20, 22], 1 K 10[15], 2 Ch 9[14]).

There was also, however, a tradition of hostility between the children of Israel and these nomadic Arabs. Ps 83 lists the Ishmaelites, the Hagarenes, and the Midianites among the traditional enemies. It was the Amalekites who harrassed them as they came up from Egypt (Ex 17[8–16], Dt 25[17–19], Nu 14[45]), the Midianites who troubled them during the desert wandering (Nu 22–25), and Amalekites, Midianites, and Bene Qedem were the enemies with whom Gideon had to deal (Jg 6[2–7, 33] 7[12]), and some of whom were still a source of trouble during the monarchy (1 S 15[7ff] 30[1ff], 2 Ch 21[16f] 22[1] 26[17]). It was Sabaeans who raided Job's cattle (Job 1[15]), and when Nehemiah commenced rebuilding Jerusalem after the ' exile,' a certain ' Geshem the Arab,' whose name has recently appeared in inscriptional evidence, was prominent among his opponents (Neh 6[1–6]).

In the Intertestamental period it was the **Nabataeans** who dominated the North Arabian scene. They were Arabs, and were still nomads when they first appear in history. By the 3rd cent. B.C., however, they had begun to settle down in places to agricultural life, proving themselves highly expert irrigators, and also came to control the caravan trade of North Arabia. From their chief centre at Petra they built up a kingdom extending from the Red Sea and the Egyptian border across to the head of the Persian Gulf, most of the caravan cities, even Damascus at times, being largely under their control. As their language of cultural expression they used Aramaic, and eagerly absorbed Hellenistic culture. Their earliest known king, Aretas I., became involved in Jewish affairs through the adventures of the High Priest Jason (2 Mac 5[6–8]), and they were the Arabs with whom the early Maccabees had friendly relations (1 Mac 5[24f] 9[35]), though the Hasmonaeans quarrelled with them. The Arabians who were present in Jerusalem on the Day of Pentecost (Ac 2[11]) would have been Jews from some Nabataean settlement, possibly in the area of Arabia beyond Damascus to which Paul withdrew after his conversion (Gal 1[17]). It was the ethnarch at Damascus of the Nabataean ruler Aretas IV. from whom Paul had to make a hurried escape (2 Co 11[32, 33]). This is the last Biblical reference to Arabia or the Arabs. See ARETAS. A. J.

ARABIC VERSIONS OF OT.—See GREEK VERSIONS OF OT, **11.**

ARAD.—1. A city in the Negeb, the king of which provoked Israel (Nu 21[1] 33[40]) and was slain by Joshua (Jos 12[14]); in its vicinity the Kenites settled, Jg 1[16]; probably modern *Tell 'Arâd*, 16 miles south of Hebron. **2.** A Benjamite, 1 Ch 8[15].

ARADUS.—Name of the city of **Arvad** (q.v.), found in 1 Mac 15[23].

ARAH.—1. A descendant of Asher, 1 Ch 7[39]. **2.** Head of a family of exiles who returned with Zerubbabel, Ezr 2[5], Neh 6[18] 7[10], 1 Es 5[10] (AV, RV **Ares**). The numbers of those who returned are variously given as 775 (Ezr 2[5]), 652 (Neh 7[10]), and 756 (1 Es 5[10]). **3.** See MEARAH.

ARAM.—1. A grandson of Nahor, Gn 22[21]. **2.** An Asherite, 1 Ch 7[34]. **3.** Mt 1[3f] (AV); see RAM. **4.** Lk 3[33] (AV); see ARNI. **5.** Fifth son of Shem, Gn 10[22f], 1 Ch 1[17], eponymous ancester of the Aramaeans; see next article.

ARAM, ARAMAEANS (often in AV and RV **' Syrians '**).—A number of scattered but kindred tribes which made their appearance in the Euphrates valley about 2000 B.C. Their chief *habitat* stretched from Harran, east of the Euphrates, south-westward to the Ḥaurân in Transjordania. The north-eastern part of this region was called ' Aram of the rivers ' (**Aram-naharaim,** Ps 60, title). The Aramaeans are first mentioned in Akkadian texts, possibly in *c* 2250 B.C., but certainly about 2000 B.C., and seem to have become rather important before the 17th cent. as the Mari texts indicate. They are also mentioned in the texts from Ugarit of the 14th cent. and in the Amarna Letters of the same time. Tiglath-pileser I. (*c* 1100 B.C.) mentions Aramaeans (*ANET*, p. 275a) in the region of Palmyra, east of the Euphrates, and in this same area they were later (883–824 B.C.) encountered by Ashurnasirpal II. and Shalmaneser III. Many of them continued to live in the Euphrates valley where their language spread to such an extent that, in the reign of Tiglath-pileser III., Aramaic glosses begin (729 B.C.) to make their appearance on Babylonian contracts. In Nippur many similar documents from the Persian period have been found. They indicate that the use of Aramaic was spreading among the common people of Babylonia. It probably came into general use here, as the Babylonian Talmud is written in it.

The Aramaeans pushed into Syria in large numbers shortly after 1300 B.C. In course of time they occupied Hamath, Damascus, and a part of the country to the south as far as the Ḥaurân, founding several city states. Damascus became the leading Aramaean State (cf Am 1[5] and Is 7[8]), but other independent Aramaean kingdoms were **Aram-Geshur,** and **Aram-Maacah** in the Ḥaurân to the north of Bashan (Dt 3[14], Jos 13[13]); **Aram-Zobah,** farther north, apparently lying to the west of Damascus; and **Aram-Rehob,** which has not been identified although it seems to have been located near the town of Dan, now *Tell el-Qâḍî* (Nu 13[21], Jg 18[28], 2 S 10[6]).

King David married a daughter of the king of Geshur and she became the mother of Absalom (2 S 3[3]), who afterwards fled thither (13[38]). Damascus was conquered by David (8[6]), who also made Zobah, Rehob, and Maacah tributary (ch. 10). Zobah is mentioned by Ashurbanipal three centuries later as *Subatu* (*ANET*, p. 298a).

After the death of David, Damascus regained its independence. In the reigns of Baasha and Asa it was an ally now of Israel and now of Judah (1 K 15[18]). During the century from Ahab to Jehoash of Israel, Damascus and Israel were frequently at war, and Damascus held much of Israel's trans-Jordanic territory. After this the Aramaean kingdom became weaker, but in the reign of Ahaz it attempted to force Judah to become its ally, probably against Assyria (Is 7). It was finally subdued by Tiglath-pileser III. of Assyria in 732 B.C.

The Aramaeans continued to form the basis of the population in the region from Aleppo to the Euphrates and beyond. Early in the Christian era this region became Christian, and in that Aramaic dialect called Syriac a large Christian literature exists.
G. A. B.—**S. H. Hn.**

ARAMAIC is found in the OT at Gn 31^{47} (two words), Jer 10^{11}, Ezr 4^{8}–6^{18} 7^{12-26}, Dn 2^{4b}–7^{28}, and elsewhere as 'Aramaisms.' It was the language of the Aramaeans (*e.g.* 2 S 8^{5} 10^{16}—EV, 'Syrians') which, widely diffused at an early period, gained international currency in the Near East from the 7th cent. B.C. (cf 2 K 18^{26}) and thereafter was officially used in the western part of the Persian empire. Its many dialects grouped as eastern (Syriac, Babylonian Talmudic, and Mandaean) and western (Palmyrene, Nabataean, Samaritan, Targumic, Palestinian Christian, and Egyptian Aramaic) corresponded to its geographical sphere of influence—from Italy to India and Asia Minor to Egypt. It was from the beginning a component of Hebrew, and after the Exile, by reason of its syntactical flexibility and its capacity for absorbing foreign elements, it gradually ousted Hebrew from popular usage, even as, by its much simpler script, it had previously triumphed over Akkadian. The Aramaic of Ezra and Daniel is of the western variety and was current in Palestine between the 4th and 1st cents. B.C. E. T. R.

ARAM-GESHUR.—See ARAM.

ARAMITESS.—A feminine gentilic, found in AV and RV in 1 Ch 7^{14}, for the elsewhere frequent term Syrian. RSV has 'his Aramaean concubine' for 'his concubine the Aramitess.'

ARAM-MAACAH, ARAM-NAHARAIM, ARAM-REHOB, ARAM-ZOBAH.—See ARAM.

ARAN (? 'wild goat').—Son of Dishan (q.v.) the Horite and descendant of Esau, Gn 36^{28}, 1 Ch 1^{42}.

ARARAH.—See ADADAH.

ARARAT (Gn 8^{4}, 2 K 19^{37} [|| Is 37^{27}], Jer 51^{27}) is the Hebrew form of the Assyrian *Urarṭu*, which on the monuments from the 9th cent. downwards designates a kingdom in the N. of the later **Armenia.** The extension of the name naturally varied with the political limits of this State; but properly it seems to have denoted a small district on the middle Araxes, of which the native name *Ayrarat* is thought to be preserved in the *Alarodioi* of Herodotus (iii. 94, vii. 79). Jerome describes it as 'a level region of Armenia, through which the Araxes flows, of incredible fertility, at the foot of the Taurus range, which extends thus far.' The Araxes (or *Aras*), on its way to the Caspian Sea, forms a great elbow to the S.; and at the upper part of this, on the right (or SW.) bank of the river, the lofty snowclad summit of Massis (called by the Persians the 'mountain of Noah') rises to a height of nearly 17,000 feet above sea-level. This is the traditional landing-place of the Ark; and, through a misunderstanding of Gn 8^{4} ('in [one of] the mountains of Ararat'), the name was transferred from the surrounding district to the two peaks of this mountain, Great Ararat and Little Ararat—the latter about 7 miles distant and 4000 feet lower.

Whether this is the site contemplated by the writer in Genesis (P) is not quite certain. The Syrian and Moslem tradition places it at *Jebel Jûdî*, a striking mountain considerably S. of Lake Van, commanding a wide view over the Mesopotamian plain. It is just possible that this might be included among the 'mountains of Ararat' in the wider sense of the term. This seems the view of Josephus (*Ant.* I. iii. 5, 6 [89 ff]), who is unconscious of any discrepancy between 'Armenia' and the 'Kordyaean' mountain of Berosus. His statement about relics of the Ark being shown in his time appears to be borrowed from Berosus, and applies to whatever mountain that writer had in mind—possibly *Jebel Jûdî*! The Targums and Peshiṭta, however, which are influenced by this tradition, read *Ḳardû* (Kurdistan), in verbal agreement with Berosus. The cuneiform Flood-legend puts it much farther S., at the 'mountain of Niṣir, probably in one of the ranges E. of the Tigris and S. of the Lesser Zab. This, of course, is quite beyond any imaginable extension of the name Ararat. Assuming, therefore, that the Biblical and Babylonian narratives have a common origin, the landing-place of the Ark would seem to have been pushed gradually northward, the natural tendency of such a tradition being to attach itself to the highest mountain known at the time. On this principle the ultimate selection of the imposing Mount Massis would be almost inevitable; and it is *probable* that this is the view of Gn 8^{4}, although the alternative hypothesis that *Jebel Jûdî* is meant has still some claim to be considered. The suggestion of Nöldeke, that Ararat is a late substitution for Kardû in the original text of Genesis, has nothing to recommend it. J. S.

ARARITE, 2 S 23^{33} (RV).—See HARARITE, **2.**

ARATHES, 1 Mac 15^{22} (RV).—See ARIARATHES.

ARAUNAH.—A Jebusite whose threshing-floor David bought in order to erect an altar to Y″, because the plague which followed the numbering of the people was halted there, 2 S 24^{18}. He is called **Ornan** in 1 Ch 21^{15} (cf 2 Ch 3^{1}), where the price paid to him by David is given as 600 shekels of gold (1 Ch 21^{25}), as against the figure of 50 shekels of silver in 2 S 24^{24}.

ARBA is assumed as the founder of Kiriath-arba, later Hebron (q.v.). It is stated that he was the father of the giants (Jos 14^{15} 15^{13} 21^{11}), who were traditionally associated with Hebron in pre-Israelite days. *Arbaʿ* means 'four,' and probably refers to four originally distinct settlements which became the later Hebron.

ARBAH, CITY OF, Gn 35^{27} (AV).—See KIRIATH-ARBA.

ARBATHITE.—A gentilic meaning 'a man of Beth-arabah' (q.v.), 2 S 23^{31}.

ARBATTA.—A district of Palestine, mentioned in 1 Mac 5^{23}; perhaps to be identified with **Arubboth** (q.v.).

ARBELA.—The discrepancy between 1 Mac 9 and Jos. *Ant.* XII. xi. 1 [421], our only authorities, makes uncertain the route of Bacchides in his march on Jerusalem. Josephus makes him pitch his camp at Arbela in Galilee: 1 Maccabees brings him 'by the road which leads to Gilgal,' where he encamped against 'Mesaloth in Arbela.' His course thence points to *Jiljilia* as Gilgal, about 5 miles N. of *Bîr ez-Zeit*, where the battle was fought with Judas. **Mesaloth** might then be sought in *Meselieh*, about 3 miles SE. of Dothan. But no name resembling Arbela, either of town or district, is found in the neighbourhood; although Eusebius (*Onomasticon*) seems to have known an Arbela not far from Lejjun. On the other hand, Arbela in Galilee survives in the modern *Irbil* or *Irbid*, a ruin on the S. lip of the gorge, *Wâdī Ḥamām*, which breaks westward from Gennesaret. There is, however, no trace of a Mesaloth here, unless indeed Robinson's ingenious suggestion is right, that it may be the Hebrew *mesillîth*, referring to the famous caverned cliffs in the gorge, whence Bacchides extirpated the refugees. W. E.

ARBITE.—A gentilic found only in 2 S 23^{35}, where LXX has 'Archite (q.v.); perhaps from **Arab** (q.v.). In the parallel passage in 1 Ch 11^{37} we find 'the son of Ezbai,' which some MSS of LXX have in 2 S 23^{35}.

ARBONAI, Jth 2^{24} (AV, RV).—See ABRON.

ARCH.—It is usually stated that the Hebrews were unacquainted with the architectural principle of the arch, but in view of the extreme antiquity of the arch in Babylonian mason work, as *e.g.* at Nippur, of the discovery of early arches by modern explorers, and of the vaulted roofs of later Jewish tombs, this view is now seen to be erroneous, although the arch is not mentioned in Scripture. The word 'arch' occurs in AV and RV of Ezk 40[16ff], but this is an error for 'vestibule' (so RSV). See TEMPLE.

ARCHAEOLOGY.—1. Definition and limitations.—Archaeology can best be defined as a study of the material remains of the past. In this definition, some of its limitations are immediately apparent. In most conditions, only certain materials survive; for instance, only very rarely do organic materials such as wood and textiles survive. The picture of any settlement as recovered by archaeology is therefore an incomplete one. Secondly, ideas, social organization and many other aspects of the human element, can sometimes be inferred, but rarely proved. Thirdly, unless, exceptionally, inscriptional material is found, the actors on the archaeological scene remain anonymous.

2. Functions.—Archaeology has two main functions. For the period before written history, it must serve as a substitute in establishing, as far as its limitations allow, the sequence of events and the way men lived. Once these events are available from written documents, it can both fill in details and provide the background by showing how the common man, in whom history is often not interested, lived. Between the two extremes of prehistory and a full historical record, it can serve a combination of these purposes, and also help to unravel the complexities of an incomplete or confused historical record. In Palestine, the full historical record begins approximately with the establishment of the United Monarchy. From that time on, the course of events can be satisfactorily traced from the historical works of the Bible; archaeology provides the background of how the common people lived, and suggests an explanation for many obscure details. The period covered by the entry of the Israelites into Palestine and the times of the Judges is within the stage of written history, but a history for the most part compiled from orally-transmitted tradition. Such history must be confirmed and elucidated by archaeology. This applies with greater force to the earlier phase of the times of the Patriarchs, the Descent into Egypt and the Exodus. Written history thus begins to touch Palestine at a date probably in the 18th or 17th cent. B.C., but detailed contemporary records are not available until about the 10th cent. Before the 18th cent., Palestine itself is prehistoric, though an occasional gleam of light is thrown upon events there from the literate civilization of Egypt, and from the written records of Egypt and Mesopotamia the general course of events in the region can be established. For everything earlier than the 3rd millennium, archaeology is the only source.

3. Chronology.—As will be described in a subsequent paragraph, archaeology can establish a sequence, but not as a rule an exact chronology.

Calendars were developed in Egypt and Mesopotamia in the 4th and 3rd millennia. In both countries, king lists exist from early in the 3rd millennium. Reasonably accurate dates for rulers in Egypt can be established from that date, though there is not yet complete agreement between scholars; dates given for the beginning of the 1st dynasty vary between *c* 3200 B.C. and *c* 2900 B.C. In Mesopotamia, dating is not so close, and there is still uncertainty as late as the beginning of the 2nd millennium.

In non-literate countries, such as Palestine in the 3rd and 2nd millennia, an exact chronology can only be established by relating events, or points in an archaeologically fixed sequence, to one of the countries, usually Egypt, with a calendar which can be related to our own. For instance, major political events such as the end of the Old Empire in Egypt, can often be correlated with events in adjoining areas. Historically recorded campaigns of Egyptian rulers can sometimes be correlated with destructions of Palestinian towns. Alternatively, recognizable and datable Egyptian objects found in a Palestinian or Syrian context may suggest a date for that context, or Palestinian and Syrian objects found in a datable deposit in Egypt can suggest a date for the material with which these objects are ordinarily found in their native lands.

Very recently the radio-active carbon method of dating has been developed. This method is invaluable for the older archaeological sites, and all dates earlier than *c* 3000 B.C. (*e.g.* Jericho, q.v.) are dependent on it. It is less useful for later periods, since the dating cannot usually be exact within a margin of three hundred years and later sites can usually be dated more closely by other methods.

4. The archaeological sequence.—An archaeological sequence is established by the study of the types of common objects found in any settlement. The most useful material is pottery, or, for the pre-ceramic period, the flint industry. The building-up of a reliable corpus of information on these objects is a slow business, and, as far as Palestine is concerned is still in progress; a reliable sequence only began to be established in the period between the two wars. As far as flint industries are concerned, most of the basic work was done by M. René Neuville, and a reliable sequence was mainly the result of Professor Dorothy Garrod's work on the Mount Carmel caves between 1929 and 1934. The first beginnings of a pottery sequence were made by Sir Flinders Petrie in his excavations at Tell el-Ḥesī in 1890. He observed that recognizably different types of pottery appeared at successive levels in the mound. Some of these, and also scarabs, he recognized as associated with phases in Egyptian history. His classification was very broad, and his actual dating was wrong owing to his inflated Egyptian chronology, but a beginning was made.

It can now be said that for Palestine there is a reasonably accurate and complete sequence from the end of the 4th millennium onwards. For the earlier periods there are gaps. The material is still small and not very coherent for the 4th millennium and the early 3rd millennium. For periods earlier than that we are still dependent on a few sites, notably Jericho. But each year, new information is being secured, and the picture will soon be filled in.

5. Excavation methods.—The value of all finds is enormously increased if they are found on scientifically conducted excavations. The dawn of scientific excavation in Palestine came with Petrie's excavations at Tell el-Ḥesī, already mentioned. Petrie recognized that tells are built up by the construction of successive buildings on the same site, each rising on the ruins of its predecessor. The depth in the mound at which an object was found therefore gave a broad indication of its antiquity. Petrie accordingly recorded his finds in foot-levels with reference to some datum point. This was a beginning, but it represents a very elementary method of stratigraphy.

To obtain a true interpretation of stratification, it is necessary actually to observe and record all layers of soil. Floors of buildings, occupation levels, destruction or decay levels, pits, trenches sunk to dig out the stones of a wall, must all be observed while excavation is in progress, the finds correctly attributed to them, and the deposits correctly interpreted. In this way the relation of the structures to the finds can be established, and they can be dated by the finds, either relatively by the flint or pottery sequence, or absolutely by coins or epigraphic material.

Though Petrie first introduced stratigraphical methods to Palestine over sixty years ago, progress has been slow, largely owing to the temptation to dig with a far larger labour force than would allow of accurate observation by those in charge. The results of many of the earlier excavations are therefore unreliable, though in some cases the records are sufficiently detailed to enable revised conclusions to be drawn in the light of modern knowledge.

6. Archaeology and Biblical Studies.—The extent of the help which archaeology has given in tracing the history of Palestine is well illustrated by a comparison of the article on *Palestine* in this edition and that in the first. In the latter, Professor R. A. C. Macalister could write 'The earliest dawn of history in Palestine has left no trace in the country itself. . . . About 3000 B.C. we first reach a period where excavation in Palestine has some information to give.' Actually, most of the information has to be corrected in the light of modern knowledge.

The greatest advance has of course come in knowledge of the earlier periods. An outline history can now be provided back to the beginnings of settled life soon after 8000 B.C., and something is known of the Palaeolithic hunters who inhabited Palestine for hundreds of thousands of years before that.

The information obtained by archaeology which can throw light on the Bible can be grouped under four headings: (1) the culture and organization of the country as found by the Israelites on their entry; (2) the problems of the chronology and character of the beginnings of Israelites settlement; (3) the culture and background of the Israelites in the historical period; (4) the culture and background of the inhabitants in NT times.

As regards the first heading, we can now give a fairly complete picture. Palestine of the Middle Bronze Age, the period within which the wanderings of the Patriarchs probably fell, is well known. The excavations at Jericho, Tell Beit Mirsim, and elsewhere have provided a picture of the towns. The culture was individually Palestinian, with a traceable combination of Amorite and Canaanite elements (see PALESTINE); there was some slight Egyptian influence, and some Egyptian political control. Through this country of little towns and agricultural communities the Patriarchs journeyed as pastoralists.

This was still essentially the picture of the country into which the Israelites penetrated as settlers. Archaeology has unfortunately not provided conclusive chronological evidence of the entry. The latest Bronze Age occupation of Jericho apparently came to an end in the second half of the 13th cent. B.C., a date which does not fit the views either of the proponents of a date for the entry into Palestine *c* 1400 B.C., or of those of a later date, *c* 1260 B.C. Archaeological evidence for Ai is even more unsatisfactory, for it was not apparently occupied after *c* 2300 B.C.; either the story of its capture is aetiological, or the site was confused with another, perhaps Bethel. Hazor seems to have been destroyed early in the 13th cent., but the excavations are still (1958) in progress, and all the evidence is not yet available. Archaeological evidence is, however, emphatic that there was no major cultural break until after 1200 B.C. Archaeology would therefore support the view that there was a gradual infiltration in comparatively small numbers, and only a gradual assertion of supremacy over the Canaanites. This would reflect the impression which can be derived from the Book of Judges, and the fact that it was not until *c* 1000 B.C. that the first Jewish kingdom emerged.

For the kaleidoscopic history of the Jewish kingdoms, archaeology produces comparatively little evidence. The towns suffer a series of destructions, but archaeological dating is not yet sufficiently refined to enable them to be related with known campaigns. Of the magnificence of the kingdom of Solomon, there is almost no evidence. The probability is that it was all concentrated at Jerusalem, too destroyed and too buried to provide evidence. The evidence of Phoenician masonry and Phoenician art at Samaria and Megiddo in the later kingdom of Israel does, however, give some indication of what Jerusalem may have been.

The inhabitants of OT Palestine were undoubtedly simple folk. Excavations at Beth Shemesh, Tell Beit Mirsim, Lachish, Tell Naṣbeh (Mizpah?), and other places, show small towns with unpretentious houses and simple equipment. The prevalence of fertility figurines and Canaanite cult objects, particularly in the 8th cent., are evidence of the heathen practices against which the prophets preached.

Of Jerusalem in the time of Christ, almost nothing is known, for it was almost completely destroyed, and obliterated by Aelia Capitolina. Prolonged research has failed to produce conclusive evidence as to the authenticity of the site of the Holy Sepulchre by establishing the line of the north wall of the city in the 1st cent. A.D. A number of excavations have, however, given a picture of what the appearance of other towns, notably of Samaria and of Gerasa (Jerash) in the Decapolis. Both these towns were dominated by buildings in a classical style which is a combination of Roman and Hellenistic traditions. Samaria was largely rebuilt in the time of Herod, with grandiose public buildings, and was renamed Sebaste.

7. Epigraphic material.—From time to time excavations produce material which is of the greatest importance culturally, linguistically, and epigraphically. The two most important finds bearing on the first aspect are those at Râs Shamra and Mari. The former provides evidence of the Canaanite pantheon and religion. The latter gives vivid evidence of the Hurrian social structure, and shows to what a large extent the customs and laws of the ancestors of the Israelites were influenced by their contacts with the Hurrians.

Archaeology is gradually building up evidence of the development of the Hebrew script. Finds such as the Samaria ostraca, the Lachish letters and stamped jar handles from known archaeological contexts have given much help to epigraphists in dating the development of the script. The most recent finds, the Dead Sea Scrolls, have not only helped in this, but also throw much light on the history of the books of the OT. K. M. K.

ARCHANGEL.—See ANGEL.

ARCHELAUS.—Mt 2[22]. See HEROD, **2.**

ARCHER.—See ARMOUR, ARMY.

ARCHEVITES, Ezr 4[9] (AV, RV).—See ERECH.

ARCHI, Jos 16[2] (AV).—See ARCHITE.

ARCHIPPUS (Phn[2], Col 4[17]) has usually been thought of as a member of the household of Philemon of Colossae, probably his son. He shared his spirit, since St. Paul, referring doubtless to his aid in missionary operations in those parts, styles him 'our fellow-soldier.' He had been entrusted with some important office, a 'service' or 'ministry,' in the Church, whether at Colossae, or, as Lightfoot, in view of the preceding context, more probably supposes, at the neighbouring town of Laodicea; and, considering the spiritual atmosphere of the place (Rev 3[14-19]), one is not surprised that the Apostle should have thought it needful to exhort him to zeal in his ministry. In another more recent view, Archippus' 'service' was to secure the release for Paul's use of the slave Onesimus. See PHILEMON. D. S.—**J. K.**

ARCHITE.—A gentilic of unknown derivation, given to Hushai (2 S 15[32]). See also ARBITE. In Jos 16[2] the Archites (AV wrongly 'Archi') are located on the N. border of Benjamin.

ARCHITECTURE.—The Hebrews never developed a native style of architecture. The genius of the people lay elsewhere. Alike in civil, religious, and funerary architecture, they were content to follow alien models. In domestic architecture there was little symmetry, and houses were fitted into available space as best could be done. Large buildings from the period of the Judges have been found at Bethel and Beth-shemesh, consisting of two storeys of rooms round open courtyards. Houses of the period of the monarchy have walls of rubble, with stone pillars to support the ceiling or upper storey. David's palace in Jerusalem was a more ambitious building, and it is significant that workmen, plans, and decorative material were all Phoenician (2 S 5[11]). The palace and Temple of Solomon were likewise the work of Phoenician architects, and the former doubtless supplied the model for the more ambitious private buildings erected under the monarchy. Late Egyptian influence has been traced in the tombs in the Valley of Jehoshaphat, but the prevailing influence from the beginning of the 3rd cent. was undoubtedly Greek (cf 1 Mac 1[14], 2 Mac 4[12]). The many magnificent buildings of Herod, for example, including the colonnades and gates of the Temple, were entirely built in the prevailing Graeco-Roman style. See, further, FORTIFICATION, PALACE, TEMPLE, TOMB. A. R. S. K.—H. H. R.

ARCHIVES.—The 'house of the archives' is mentioned in Ezr 6^{1} (AV 'house of the rolls'), and in Ezr 5^{17} (where AV, RV have 'the king's treasure house' for 'the royal archives').

ARCTURUS.—See STARS.

ARD.—A son of Benjamin in Gn 46^{21}, but his grandson in Nu 26^{40} and 1 Ch 8^{3} (here called **Addar**); patronymic **Ardites,** Nu 26^{40}.

ARDAT.—A 'field' in an unknown situation, 2 Es 9^{26} (AV **Ardath**).

ARDATH, 2 Es 9^{26} (AV).—See ARDAT.

ARDITES.—See ARD.

ARDON.—A son of Caleb, 1 Ch 2^{18}.

ARELI.—A son of Gad, Gn 46^{16}, Nu 26^{17}. Patronymic **Arelites,** Nu 26^{17}.

AREOPAGUS.—Really the *Areios pagos,* 'Hill of Ares,' or Mars Hill—Ares being the Greek god of war corresponding to Roman Mars. The hill is a rocky knoll 380 feet high, lying NW. of the Acropolis and separated from the latter by a connecting ridge or saddle. From early times this was the place where a court known as 'Council from the Areopagus' met to try cases of murder. By the time of St. Paul's visit to Athens this court had greatly extended its functions. Cicero already speaks of the state of the Athenians as led by the Areopagus, thus implying political activities. One of its new functions was the supervision of education. This would imply a right to control the introduction of new philosophical or religious teachings, and would require the propagandists of such to appear before the council. Some have held that the council would not have held sessions on Mars Hill itself. The latter was certainly not suitable for audibility to a surrounding crowd, as presupposed in Ac 17$^{19, 22}$. According to a recent theory the council may have met on the ridge extending SE. to the Acropolis, where there would be enough room for the public to gather. One member of the Council was even persuaded of Paul's teaching—Dionysius the Areopagite (17^{34}), whose name was used and made famous by a Neo-Platonic Christian mystic of A.D. 500.
E. G. K.

ARES, 1 Es 5^{10} (AV, RV).—See ARAH.

ARETAS.—This is the Greek form of the name *Harithah,* borne by four known rulers of the Nabataean kingdom, whose capital in Biblical times was Petra, the ancient 'Sela,' to the S. of the Dead Sea. These **Nabataeans** were mainly of Arab stock though they used Aramaic as their language of cultural expression. The first Aretas must have been reigning *c* 169 B.C., for in 2 Mac 5^{8} he is mentioned as the *tyrannus* of the Arabs with whom Jason attempted to find refuge, and was doubtless the ruler of those Nabataeans with whom Judas Maccabaeus had friendly relations (1 Mac 5^{25}, 9^{35}). It was Aretas II. who sought to aid Gaza in 96 B.C. when it was menaced by Alexander Jannaeus (Jos. *Ant.* XIII. xii. 3 [358]). Aretas III., called Philhellene, the greatest of all known Nabataean rulers (87–62 B.C.), was the one who supported Hyrcanus II. against Aristobulus II., when Hyrcanus took refuge with him at Petra (Jos. *Ant.* XIV. i. 4 [14]; ii. 1–3 [19 ff]; *BJ* I. vi. 2–4 [123 ff]). Aretas IV., called Philodemos (9 B.C.–A.D. 40), aided the Roman legate Varus against Herod Antipas (Jos. *Ant.* XVII. x. 9 [287]; *BJ* II. v. 1 [68]), in revenge for Herod's having married and then repudiated his sister. He apparently regained some control in Damascus, which Aretas III. had held in 85 B.C. but had lost, for he is the Aretas whose ethnarch in Damascus sought to apprehend Paul (2 Co 11^{32f}).
A. J.

ARGOB.—**1.** Argob and Arieh were guards of Pekahiah, 2 K 15^{25}, who fell by the hands of Pekah along with their master. RSV omits, as probably misplaced from the list of places in v.^{29} (cf RSVm). **2.** A district in the kingdom of Og, abounding in strong cities and unwalled towns. It was subdued by 'Jair son of Manasseh,' and became the possession of his tribe (Dt 3$^{3, 13}$, 1 K 4^{15}, etc.). It is called 'the Argob (Dt 3^{13}). This, together with the fact that *ḥebhel,* 'measured area,' always precedes the name, seems to indicate a definitely marked district. This would apply admirably to the great lava field of *el-Lejā,* NW. of *Jebel Ḥaurân.* Within this forbidding tract the names of more than seventy ruined sites are found. Had Gesenius rightly translated 'a heap of stones,' the identification would be almost certain. But the name seems to mean 'arable land' (*reghebh*='clod,' Job 21^{33} 38^{38}). Argob must therefore be sought elsewhere. The W. slopes of the mountain (now *Jebel ed-Drûz*) would always form a clearly defined district. They abound in ruins of antiquity; while the rich soil, now turned to good account by the Druzes, would amply justify the name of Argob.
W. E.

ARIARATHES (AV, Vulgate, Rahlfs following Sinaiticus) or **ARATHES** (RV and Swete, following Alexandrinus etc.) was king of Cappadocia 163–130 B.C. In 139 B.C. the Romans wrote letters to Ariarathes V. and other eastern sovereigns in favour of the Jews (1 Mac 15^{22}). In 130 B.C. he joined the consul P. Licinius Crassus in the attack on Aristonicus the son of Eumenes II. of Pergamum, who claimed the kingdom despite Attalus III.'s bequest of it to Rome. They were totally defeated.
F. C. G.

ARIDAI.—Ninth son of Haman, put to death by the Jews, Est 9^{9}.

ARIDATHA.—Sixth son of Haman, put to death by the Jews, Est 9^{8}.

ARIEH ('lion').—Mentioned in 2 K 15^{25}. See ARGOB, **1.**

ARIEL.—**1.** One of Ezra's chief men, Ezr 8^{16}. **2.** The name of a Moabite, according to RV of 2 S 23^{20}, 1 Ch 11^{22}, whose two sons were slain by Benaiah. AV has 'two lion-like men,' and RSV 'two ariels,' adding in margin that the meaning is unknown. **3.** A name given to Jerusalem by Isaiah (29^{1ff}). The word probably means 'altar-hearth,' and it is found on the Moabite Stone (see MESHA). It is perhaps used for Jerusalem here, since the altar of Y″ was there; cf Is 31^{9}, Ezk 43^{15ff}. It has been suggested that in Is 29^{1} we should read *Uriel* ('city of God'), as a word-play on *Urusalim,* the ancient form of the name 'Jerusalem.' But this does not fit the other occurrences.

ARIMATHEA (Mt 27^{57}, Mk 15^{43}, Lk 23^{51}, Jn 19^{38}).—A place known only in connexion with Joseph. It was probably near Lydda. See Map 15.

ARIOCH.—The name of one of the four kings who raided Canaan in the time of Abraham (Gn 14^{1}). He is called king of Ellasar. The identification of Ellasar with Larsa, and of Arioch with Warad-Sin, who reigned in Larsa (1997–1986 B.C.), is now abandoned. The name Ariukki occurs as a Hurrian name in the Nuzi tablets. It seems most probable that the name is not that of some unidentified king of Larsa, contemporary with Hammurabi, but the name of a Hurrian prince whose city may possibly be identified with Telassar in 2 K 19^{12}.
S. H. He.

ARISAI.—Eighth son of Haman, put to death by the Jews, Est 9^{9}.

ARISTARCHUS.—One of St. Paul's companions in travel. He was 'a Macedonian of Thessalonica' (Ac 19^{29} 27^{2}), but according to Col 4^{10f} a Jew. From 'Greece' (probably Corinth) he accompanied Paul on his last journey to Jerusalem (Ac 20^{4}); he was one of the representatives of the Pauline communities which sent a collection to the poor of the community at Jerusalem. He also embarked with Paul on his voyage to Rome (27^{2}). In Col 4^{19} he is called St. Paul's 'fellow-prisoner' (cf Phn ^{23}). The expression may mean the voluntary sharing of Paul's captivity by Aristarchus. At Ephesus, Aristarchus and Gaius were seized by the crowd and brought to the theatre; but that would not justify the expression 'fellow-prisoner' (Ac 19^{29}).
E. H.

ARISTOBULUS.—1. The name of a son and of a grandson of Herod the Great. The grandson lived as a private individual at Rome, and was a friend of the Emperor Claudius ; those greeted by St. Paul in Ro 16^{10} were probably some of his slaves. If he was then dead, they might have become members of the Imperial household, but would still retain Aristobulus' name. **2.** The teacher of Ptolemy (2 Mac 1^{10}). It was also a Maccabaean name. See MACCABEES.

ARIUS (1 Mac $12^{7, 20}$).—A king of Sparta, grandson and successor of Cleomenes II. His reign lasted from 309 to 265 B.C., and he was contemporary with the high priest Onias I., the successor of Jaddua. Friendly letters were interchanged between Arius and Onias (probably about 300 B.C.) ; and Jonathan Maccabaeus refers to these communications in a letter which he sent by his ambassadors to Sparta (*c* 144 B.C.), 1 Mac $12^{7ff, 19ff}$. The AV reading, **Darius** (in v.^{7}), is that of the Greek codices ; Fritzsche corrected it from Jos. *Ant.* XII. iv. 10 [225].

ARK.—This word, from Latin *arca*, ' a chest,' is the rendering of two Hebrew words, of which one (*tēbhāh*, probably a loan-word) is applied both to the basket of bulrushes in which the infant Moses was exposed, and to the Ark built by Noah (see DELUGE). The other (*'ᵃrōn*, the native word for box or chest, 2 K 12^{10f}), is used for a mummy-case or coffin (Gn 50^{26}), and in particular for the sacred Ark of the Hebrews.

Ark of the Covenant.—1. *Names of the Ark.*—Apart from the simple designation ' the ark ' found in all periods of Hebrew literature, the names of the Ark, more than twenty in number, fall into three groups, which are characteristic (*a*) of the oldest literary sources, viz. Samuel and the traditions of the Hexateuch designated by the symbols J and E ; (*b*) of Deuteronomy and the writers influenced by Deuteronomy ; and (*c*) of the priestly tradition of the Hexateuch (P) and subsequent writings. In (*a*) we find chiefly ' the ark of Y",' doubtless the oldest name of all, and ' the ark of God ' ; in (*b*) the characteristic title is ' the ark of the covenant '—alone or with the additions ' of Y",' ' of God,' etc.—a contraction for ' the ark or chest containing the tables of the covenant ' (Dt 9^{9ff}), and therefore practically ' the ark of the Decalogue ' ; in (*c*) the same conception of the Ark prevails (see below), but as the Decalogue is by P termed ' the testimony,' the Ark becomes ' the ark of the testimony.' All other designations are expansions or modifications of one or other of the above.

2. History of the Ark.—The oldest Pentateuch traditions (J, E) are now silent as to the origin of the Ark, but since the author of Dt 10^{1-6} was doubtless acquainted with these traditions, it may be assumed that its construction was there also assigned to Moses in obedience to a Divine command. It certainly played an important part in the wanderings (Nu 10^{33ff} 14^{44}), and in the conquest of Canaan (Jos 3^{3ff} 6^{6f}), and finally found a resting-place in the temple of Shiloh under the care of a priestly family claiming descent from Moses (1 S 3^{3}). After its capture by the Philistines and subsequent restoration, it remained at Kiriath-jearim (1 S 4^{1}–7^{1}), until removed by David, first to the house of Obed-edom, and thereafter to a specially erected tent in his new capital (2 S 6^{10ff}). Strangely enough, there is no further mention of the Ark in the historical books. Whether it was among ' the treasures of the house of the Lord ' (1 K 14^{26}) carried off by Shishak (*c* 950 B.C.), or whether it was still in its place in the days of Jeremiah (3^{16f}) and was ultimately destroyed by the soldiers of Nebuchadrezzar (586 B.C.), it is impossible to say. There was no ark in the Temples of Zerubbabel and Herod.

3. The significance of the Ark.—In attempting a solution of this difficult problem, we must, as in the foregoing section, leave out of account the late theoretical conception of the Ark to be found in the Priestly tradition (P ; see TABERNACLE), and confine our attention to the oldest sources. In these the Ark—a chest of acacia wood, according to Dt 10^{3}—is associated chiefly with the operations of war, in which it is the sign of the presence of Y", the God of the armies of Israel, or His actual representative. Its presence on the field of battle is the warrant of victory (1 S 4^{3ff}, cf 2 S 11^{11}), as its absence is the explanation of defeat (Nu 14^{44}). Its issue to and return from battle are those of Y" Himself (Nu 10^{35f}). This virtual identification of the Ark with the personal presence of Y" in the oldest narratives (see, besides the above 1 S 6^{20}, 2 S $6^{7f, 14}$) has been explained in numerous ways. It has been suggested that the original Ark was a box containing sacred stones in which the Deity was conceived to dwell. Attention has also been called to the use by certain bedouin tribes of Arabia of an elaborate saddle-structure, often in the form of a tent, sacred to the tribe, and of particular significance in time of battle as the sign of the active presence of the tribal deity.

Considerable archaeological evidence has been adduced to support yet another hypothesis. Since later tradition clearly depicts the Ark as a throne-seat upon which the invisible Deity was conceived to be enthroned, especially upon the great holy days (see 2 S 6^{2}), it has been proposed that such an understanding of the Ark may be more nearly correct than that found in Dt 10^{1ff}. Numerous representations of deities and kings, seated upon thrones supported by mythological beasts, have been unearthed. It is argued, therefore, that the Ark of the wilderness period may have been such a throne-seat borne in battle and during the wanderings of the Israelites, representing the seat of the invisible Y", from which He guided His people and gave victory over His enemies. It has also been proposed that the Ark played a highly significant part in the ceremonies and processional acts associated with the celebration of the New Year and the renewal of the Israelite covenant (2 S 6^{12-19}, Ps 132 ; see also Jos 24. 8^{30-35}, Dt 11^{26-32} 27). Thus the Ark, rather than representing a primitive stage in the development of the religious understandings of early Israel, may have been a cult object well suited to the expression of the religious understandings associated with the figure and work of Moses : Y" was a God active in history ; He accompanied his people on their wanderings ; gave deliverance in battle. Yet He was not to be represented in any form, nor could He always be counted upon to save simply because His throne had been carried into battle (1 S 4^{10-11}). A. R. S. K.—**W. J. Ha.**

ARKITE is used (Gn 10^{17}, 1 Ch 1^{15}) for the people of Arka, modern *Tell 'Arqa*, a town and district of Phoenicia about 12 miles north of Tripolis. It was taken by Tiglath-pileser III. in 738 B.C. As the birthplace of the Emperor Alexander Severus, it was later called Caesarea Libani. It is probably mentioned in the Amarna letters under the form *Irkata*, and in 15th cent. Egyptian under the form *'rqt*.

ARM.—The Hebrew word for arm occurs some ninety times in the OT ; the corresponding Greek word occurs three times in the NT and in each instance in an allusion to an OT passage. The verb ' to take into one's arms ' occurs at Mk 9^{36} 10^{16}, Lk 2^{28}. The Hebrew word is used of animals (Nu 6^{19}, Dt 18^{3} ' shoulder '), of man (Jg 15^{14} 16^{12}) and of God (Ex 6^{6} 15^{16}). About one-fifth of the occurrences are quite literal, and mean the forearm or the whole arm. Predominantly, however, the term is used in a psycho-physical sense to mean ' strength ' either of body or soul. The fact that the arm of the labourer or warrior obviously expresses the energy of his life, makes this usage natural (cf Is 17^{5}, 2 S 22^{35}). Thus a man who displays vigour is ' a man of arm ' (Job 22^{8}) ; and the arm will be the vital energy of an individual or a society (1 S 2^{31}, Ps 10^{15} 44^{3} 83^{8}) ; it is by the arm bared for action that the soul manifests itself. It may thus display tyranny or cruelty (Job 38^{15}, Ps 10^{15}, Ezk 30^{21-25}) ; alternatively if the soul is weak, so the arm will be ineffective (Job 26^{2}, 2 Ch 32^{8}, Jer 48^{25}). By a natural extension, the forces of a nation engaged in war, are the ' arms ' of the nation (Dn $11^{15, 22, 31}$), not in our English sense of ‘ weapons ’ for which a quite different word is used.

It is this psychical usage, rather than anthropomorphism, which enables the word to be used of God’s activity on behalf of His people, and this usage accounts for some two-fifths of the occurrences of ‘ arm ’ in the OT. In the early ritual word of Ex 15^{1-18}, the thought of Yahweh as the mighty warrior subduing the foes of Israel with His great strength is presented (v.^{16}), but normally the word is used in the sense of Yahweh’s effective power to judge and save, cf Dt 4^{34}, Ps $89^{10, 13, 21}$, Is 40^{10}. It is this usage that appears in the NT (Lk 1^{51}, Ac 13^{17}). The word has become part of the salvation terminology (Is 59^{16} 63^{5}). Finally the word is used of God’s creative activity (Job 40^{8}, Jer 27^{5}, Is 51^{9}). The last passage suggests that there is an allusion to an ancient Canaanite creation myth, although the ideas originally expressed have been assimilated into Yahweh worship. Thus the arm of the Lord is Yahweh Himself, active to effect His righteousness and salvation, and to create and maintain His world. A. S. H.

ARMAGEDDON (RV **Har-Magedon**).—The name of the place in which, according to Rev 16^{16}, the kings of the lower world are to be gathered together by the Dragon, the Beast and the false prophet, to make war upon God. The most generally accepted location makes this to be the mountains of **Megiddo**, that is to say, those surrounding the plain of Megiddo, in which so many great battles of the past were fought. The difficulty with this explanation is that one would expect the plain rather than the mountains to be chosen as a battle-field. Another explanation finds in the word a survival of the name of the place in which the gods of Babylonia were believed to have defeated the dragon Tiāmat and the other evil spirits. Such a view, however, compels a series of highly speculative corrections of the text, as well as various critical suppositions regarding the structure of the Book of Revelation. While the reference is apocalyptic, it seems probable on the whole that the word perpetuates Megiddo as the synonym of the battle-field—whether above the earth or in the under world—on which the final victory over evil was to be won. S. M.—F. C. G.

ARMENIA.—See Ararat.

ARMENIAN VERSION OF OT.—See Greek Versions of OT, **11.**

ARMLET.—See Ornaments, **4**, Tablet, **2.**

ARMONI.—Son of Saul by Rizpah ; he was hanged by the Gibeonites, 2 S 21^{8}.

ARMOUR, ARMS.—The soldier’s arms, offensive and defensive, are never so termed in our EV ; **‘ armour,’** ‘ whole armour ’ (Eph 6^{11} [Gr. *panoplia*], the ‘harness’ of 2 Mac 15^{28}, RV and RSV ‘ full armour ’), and more frequently **‘ weapons of war ’** are the terms employed. In RV and RSV **‘ harness ’** in this sense has in most cases given place to ‘ armour.’

1. *Offensive arms.*—In a familiar representation from an Egyptian tomb of date *c* 1895 B.C., a band of Semitic nomads are depicted with the primitive arms of their race—the short spear, the bow, and the throw-stick—the last perhaps the **handstaves** (RSV **handpikes**) of Ezk 39^{9}. In OT the principal arms of attack are the sword, the spear, the javelin, the bow, and the sling. (*a*) The **spear** claims precedence as an older weapon than the sword. The normal Hebrew form, the *ḥ^anith*, had a stout wooden shaft with a flint, bronze, or iron (1 S 13^{19}) head, according to the period. Like the spear of the modern Bedouin sheikh, it figures as a symbol of leadership in the case of Saul (1 S 22^{6} 26^{7}, cf 18^{10ff} RV and RSV). The *rōmaḥ* appears to have been a lighter form of spear, a **lance,** and to have largely supplanted the heavier spear or pike in later times (Neh $4^{13, 16}$, Jl 3^{10}). Both are rendered ‘ spear ’ in EV. (*b*) The *kîdhôn* was shorter and lighter than either of the above, and was used as a missile, and may be rendered **javelin** (Jos $8^{18, 26}$ RV and RSV, Job 41^{29} RV and RSV ‘ the rushing of the javelin ’) or **dart.** The latter term is used as the rendering of several missile weapons, of which the precise nature is uncertain. For a new interpretation of *kîdhôn* see below, **3.**

(*c*) The **sword** had a comparatively short, straight blade of iron (1 S 13^{21}, Is 2^{4}), and was occasionally two-edged (Ps 149^{6}, He 4^{12}). Ehud’s weapon, only 18 inches long, was rather a **dagger** (Jg 3^{16} AV ; RV and RSV ‘ sword ’). The sword was worn on the left side in a leather or metal **sheath** (1 S 17^{51}), attached to a waist-belt or girdle (1 S 17^{51} 25^{13}, 2 S 20^{8} RV). It occurs frequently in symbol and metaphor in both OT and NT. It is appropriately the symbol of war, as the ploughshare is of peace (Is 2^{4}, Mic 4^{3}, Jl 3^{10}). In NT the word of God is described as a two-edged sword (He 4^{12}), and by St. Paul as the ‘ sword of the Spirit ’ (Eph 6^{17}).

(*d*) The **bow** is common to civil (Gn 21^{20}) and military life, and vies in antiquity with the spear. It was made of tough, elastic wood, sometimes mounted with bronze (Ps 18^{34} [RV, RSV] Job 20^{24}). Horn also was used for **bows** in ancient times, and those with the double curve seem to have been modelled on the horns of oxen. The bow-string was usually of ox-gut, the **arrows** of reed or light wood tipped with flint, bronze, or iron. The **battle bows** (Zec 9^{10} 10^{4}), at least, must have been of considerable size—the Egyptian bow measured about 5 feet —since they were strung by pressing the foot on the lower end, while the upper end was bent down to receive the string into a notch. Hence the Hebrew expressions ‘ to tread (=string) the bow,’ and ‘ bow-treaders ’ for **archers** (Jer $50^{14, 29}$). The arrows, ‘ the sons of the quiver ’ (La 3^{13} AV ; RV **shafts,** RSV ‘ arrows ’), were carried in the **quiver,** which was either placed on the back or slung on the left side by a belt over the right shoulder. Another type of bow, the composite bow, was well known in antiquity. The earliest representations come from the era of the Dynasty of Akkad (24th cent. B.C.) ; from there the bow moved west, and was apparently brought to Egypt in the time of the Hyksos, though the first examples come from New Kingdom. The best of these were found in the tomb of Tut-ankh-amun (cf Howard Carter, *The Tomb of Tut-ankh-amen*, iii. [1933], 138 ff). The bow was made of strips of horn and wood glued together and then bound with bark, thus producing an extremely tough and powerful weapon. For discussion of the composite bow, see W. F. Albright and G. E. Mendenhall, *JNES* i. (1942), 227–29 ; also Y. Sukenik (Yadin), *BASOR*, No. 107 (1947), 11–15.

(*e*) The **sling** was the shepherd’s defence against wild beasts (1 S 17^{40}), as well as a military weapon (2 K 3^{25} and often). The Hebrew sling, like those of the Egyptians and Assyrians, doubtless consisted of a long narrow strip of leather, widening in the middle to receive the stone, and tapering to both ends. At one end was a loop by which the sling was held as the slinger swung it round his head, while the other end was released as the stone was thrown. The Benjamites were specially noted for the accuracy of their aim (Jg 20^{16}).

(*f*) The **battle axe** (Jer 51^{20} AV ; RV **maul,** RSV ‘ hammer ’ ; cf Pr 25^{18} where RSV has **war club**), literally ‘ shatterer ’ (no doubt identical with the ‘ weapon of his shattering,’ Ezk 9^{2} [RVm ‘ battle axe ’]), was probably, as the etymology suggests, a club or mace of hard wood, studded with iron spikes, such as was carried by the Assyrians in the army of Xerxes (Herod. vii. 63). See Rich, *Dict. of Ant.*, *s.v.* ‘ Clava.’

2. *Defensive arms.*—(*a*) First among the arms of defence must be placed the **shield,** of which two main varieties are common to all periods, the small shield or **buckler** (*māghēn*), and the large shield (*ṣinnāh*), the **target** of 1 K 10^{16ff} (AV, RV ; RSV ‘ large shields ’). The distinction between these is rarely preserved in our EV (*e.g.* Jer 46^{3}—in Ps 35^{2}, Ezk 23^{24} they are reversed), but the relative sizes of the two kinds may be seen in the passage of 1 Kings just cited, where the targets or large shields each required four times as much gold as the smaller buckler. These, however, were only for state processions and the like (14^{28}, but cf 1 Mac 6^{39}). The *māghēn* was the ordinary light round shield of the ancient world, the Roman *clypeus*; the *ṣinnāh* was the *scutum* or large oblong shield which more effectively protected its bearer against the risks of battle. The normal type of both was most probably made of layers of leather stretched on a frame of wood or wickerwork, since 'both the shields and the bucklers' might be burned (Ezk 39⁹). The shield, as a figure of God's protecting care, is a favourite with the religious poets of Israel (Psalms, *passim*). St. Paul also in his great military allegory introduces the large Graeco-Roman shield (Eph 6[16]).

(*b*) Of the shapes of the Hebrew **helmets** we have no information. Kings and other notables wore helmets of bronze (1 S 17[5, 38]), but those prepared by Uzziah for 'all the host' (2 Ch 26[14] RV) were more probably of leather, such as the monuments show to have been worn by the rank and file of other armies until supplanted in the Greek age by bronze, for the *élite* of the infantry at least (1 Mac 6[35]).

(*c*) The same difference of material—bronze for the leaders, leather for the common soldier—holds good for the cuirass or **coat of mail** (1 S 17[5, 38]). The latter term takes the place in RV and RSV of the antiquated **habergeon** (2 Ch 26[14], Neh 4[16]), and **brigandine** (Jer 46[4] 51[3]). The cuirass, which protected both back and front, is also intended by the **breastplate** of Is 59[17] (RVm 'coat of mail'), 1 Mac 3[3], 1 Th 5[8], Eph 6[14]. Goliath's coat of mail was composed of scales of bronze, and probably resembled the Egyptian style of cuirass described and illustrated by Wilkinson (*Anc. Egyp.* [1878] i. 219 ff). This detail is not given for Saul's cuirass (1 S 17[38]). Ahab's '**harness**' (AV, RV) consisted of a cuirass which ended in 'tassels' or flaps, the 'lower armour' (cf RVm, RSV) of 1 K 22[34]. The Syrian war-elephants were protected by breastplates (1 Mac 6[43]), and probably also the horses of the Egyptian cavalry (Jer 46[4]).

(*d*) **Greaves** of bronze to protect the legs are mentioned only in connexion with Goliath (1 S 17[6]). The military **boot** is perhaps referred to in Is 9[5] (RVm, RSV).

The **armourbearer** is met with as early as the time of Abimelech (Jg 9[54]), and later in connexion with Jonathan, Saul, and Goliath, and with Joab, who had several (2 S 18[15]). This office was held by a young man, like the squire of mediaeval knighthood, who carried the shield (1 S 17[7]), cuirass, the reserve of darts (2 S 18[14]), and other weapons of his chief, and gave the *coup de grâce* to those whom the latter had struck down (1 S 14[13]).

An **armoury** for the storage of material of war is mentioned by Nehemiah (3[19]), but that this was built by David can scarcely be inferred from the difficult text of Ca 4[4]. Solomon's armoury was 'the house of the forest of Lebanon' (1 K 10[17], Is 22[8]). The Temple also seems to have been used for this purpose (2 K 11[10]). See further the articles Army, Fortification and Siegecraft, War.

3. In the War Scroll from Qumrân there is a detailed description of the different weapons used by the army of the Sons of Light in its eschatological struggle with the Sons of Darkness. In spite of the theological and apocalyptic tone of the document, the discussion of arms is entirely practical. As Y. Yadin has shown conclusively (cf *The Scroll of the War of the Sons of Light against the Sons of Darkness* [Hebrew 1955], ch. vi, pp. 106–30), the weapons (along with military organization and tactics) correspond closely to those of the Roman army, specifically during the latter part of the 1st cent. B.C. (but not earlier or later periods, or to those of the Hellenistic kingdoms of the Near East). Yadin argues that the Scroll reflects the contemporary pattern of the Jewish army, which in turn was based upon that of the Roman legions and their auxiliaries. Since the weapons described bear the same names as those of the OT, and undoubtedly reflect some continuity in usage, the Scroll in effect serves as a 1st cent. B.C. commentary on the military terminology of the Bible. While great caution must be exercised in applying the new information to earlier periods, we may reasonably expect help in interpreting difficult passages, and describing the different weapons. In at least one case (the *kîdhôn*), the traditional interpretation, 'javelin,' appears to be wrong, since in the Scroll the weapon is plainly a sword. Passages like Jos 8[18, 26], Job 41[29], etc., need to be revised accordingly. A sampling of the weapons listed in the Scroll follows: The *mgn* or shield was rectangular and convex in shape, 115 × 69 cm. It was used by the heavy infantry and corresponded to the Roman *scutum.* The cavalry used a round shield (*mgny 'glh*), corresponding to the Roman *parma* or *clypeus.* In addition, the horsemen wore body armour, including helmet, breastplate, and greaves (also in accord with Roman practice). The *kîdhôn* was a straight sword, 69 cm. long, 6 cm. wide, corresponding to the Roman *gladius.* (G. Molin, however, has argued that it was really a **scimitar**; cf *JSS* i [1956], 334–335; so also Dupont-Sommer, *RHR* cxlviii [1955], 143 n.) There were a variety of spears, including the following: the *zrḳ* (plural *zrḳwt*), also called *šlṭ*, were used by specified units of light infantry, with seven of these javelins being assigned to each soldier; this may be equivalent to the Roman *iaculum.* The *ḥᵃnîth* corresponds to the Roman *pilum* (about 2 m. in length). There were two types of *rmḥ* 'spear'; the one used by the heavy infantry was 3.21 m. in length, while the cavalry spear was somewhat longer (3.60 m.). Slings and bows are also included in the catalogue of weapons. A. R. S.K.—D. N. F.

ARMOURBEARER, ARMOURY.—See Armour.

ARMY.—1. In default of a strong central authority, an army in the sense of a permanently organized and disciplined body of troops was an impossibility among the Hebrews before the establishment of the monarchy. During the period of the Judges, the army of the Confederation consisted of military units supplied by the several tribes. From various traditions in the Book of Judges, and the census lists in Numbers 1 and 26 (specifically described as military roll calls), it is possible to recover the general pattern and some of the details of early Israelite military organization. Each tribe was responsible to the amphictyony for its levy of men, who were chosen from among the eligible population, and served under the tribal chieftain or *nāśî'*. The twelve chieftains, referred to repeatedly in Numbers, constituted the council of war, while the charismatic judge (*shōphēṭ*) acted as commander-in-chief of a particular expedition. The levies presumably served for the duration of a campaign and then returned to civilian life. For a detailed discussion of the early Israelite army, see G. E. Mendenhall, *JBL* lxxvii (1958), 52–66. In his judgment the *'ᵃlāphîm* were not originally, 'thousands,' but population units from which the levies were drawn. The result is an army of approximately 6000 men for the period of the amphictyony, though in practice the number of troops available was probably smaller. Steps toward a more permanent arrangement were taken by Saul in his operations against the Philistines (1 S 13[2], cf 14[52]). David, however, was the first to establish the nucleus of a standing army, by retaining as a permanent **bodyguard** 600 'mighty men' (their official title) who had gathered round him in his exile (1 S 23[13] 30[9], 2 S 10[7] 16[6]). To these were added the mercenary corps of the Cherethites and Pelethites (q.v.), and a company of 600 Gittites (2 S 15[18]). Apart from these, David attempted to create a truly national army, based upon a regular federal census or military enrolment of all eligible citizens (2 S 24). The resentment of the people, and theological condemnation of this procedure (following the outbreak of a plague), show that David had undertaken a drastic shift from traditional methods. Solomon's organization of his kingdom into administrative districts (1 K 4[7ff]) doubtless included matters of army administration (cf v.[28] 9[19] 10[26]).

2. The organization of the Hebrew army was by units of thousands, originally associated with the civil divisions of the same name, with subdivisions of hundreds, fifties, and tens (1 S 8[12] 17[18] 22[7], 2 K 1[9ff], 11[4]), an arrangement which continued into the Maccabaean period (1 Mac 3^{55}). Each of these divisions had its special **'captain.'** The whole was under the supreme command of the 'captain of the host.' The relative positions and duties of the *shōṭᵉrîm* (EV 'officers') and other military officials are quite uncertain. The former appear to have been charged with keeping and checking the lists of the quotas to be furnished by the various districts (Dt 20^{5ff}).

3. The army was composed in early times entirely, and at all times chiefly, of infantry, the bulk of whom were armed with the spear or pike and the large shield or target (see ARMOUR). The **archers** carried a sword and buckler (1 Ch 5^{18}), and with the **slingers** (2 Ch 26^{14}) made up the light infantry. Chariots, although long before a vital part of the forces of the surrounding nations, were first introduced into the Hebrew army by Solomon (1 K 4^{26} 9^{22} 10^{26ff}; see CHARIOT, HORSE).

4. The period during which a citizen was liable for military service extended from his twentieth (Nu 1^{3}, 2 Ch 25^{5}) to his fiftieth year (Jos. *Ant.* III. xii. 4 [288]). Exemption was granted in the cases specified in Dt 20^{5ff}, at least under the Maccabees (1 Mac 3^{56}), and to the members of the priestly caste (Nu 2^{33}).

5. As regards maintenance, each city and district had doubtless to supply its own quota with provisions, in so far as these were not drawn from the enemy's country. The soldier's recompense consisted in his share of the loot, the division of which was regulated by the precedent of 1 S 30^{24}. The first mention of regular pay is in connexion with the army of Simon Maccabaeus (1 Mac 14^{32}). Foreign mercenaries figure largely in the armies of the later Maccabaean princes and of Herod. No reference has been made to the numbers of the Hebrew armies, since these have in so many cases been greatly corrupted in transmission.

6. Extensive information about army organization and practice in the intertestamental period is provided by the Dead Sea scrolls, especially the War Scroll (1QM). The regulations are based upon the relevant passages in Numbers and Deuteronomy, but the details reflect in large measure the recent and current practice of the Jewish commonwealth. Even though the War Scroll is apocalyptically oriented, and focuses attention on the final war between the children of light and the children of darkness, nevertheless it shows considerable knowledge of the practical details of military order. Thus the army consists of infantry (28,000) and cavalry (6000), each group being divided into principal (heavy) and auxiliary (light) units. The older, more experienced men (ages 40–50) serve in the main units, the younger men (30–45) in the light forces; and the apprentices (25 up) are organized into service units. The heavy infantry, which constitutes the backbone of the army, is equipped with shield, spear, and sword; while different units of the light infantry are supplied with slings-and-stones, lances, shields, etc. Various tactical formations are described, including the 'tower,' a self-protecting rectangle of heavy infantry. More attention is allotted, however, to the trumpets and banners, all of which bear religious inscriptions of different kinds, and which serve a bewildering variety of functions. In addition the banners bear the names of the unit commanders, in descending order until the banner of the smallest unit carries the names of all the men enrolled. Of prime importance is the role of the chief priest and his aides; sample prayers for all possible occasions are given. For a comprehensive treatment of the scroll and its military features see Y. Yadin, *The War of the Children of Light and the Children of Darkness* (Hebrew: Jerusalem, 1955; English: Oxford, 1962).

For methods of mobilization, tactics, etc., see WAR, also FORTIFICATION AND SIEGECRAFT; and for the Roman army in NT times see LEGION. A. R. S. K.—**D. N. F.**

ARNA.—An ancestor of Ezra, 2 Es 1^{2}, corresponding apparently to **Zerahiah,** Ezr 7^{4}, and **Zaraias,** 1 Es 8^{2} (AV, RV; RSV omits).

ARNAN.—A descendant of David, 1 Ch 3^{21}.

ARNI.—An ancestor of Jesus, Lk 3^{33} (RV, RSV; AV **Aram**); called **Ram** in Mt 1^{3f} (RV, RSV; AV **Aram**); cf Ru 4^{19}, 1 Ch 2^{9f}.

ARNON.—A valley with a swiftly flowing stream in its bed, now called *Wâdī el-Môjib*, which gathers the waters from many tributary vales—the wadis (AV 'brooks'; RV, RSV 'valleys') of Arnon (Nu 21^{14})—as it flows westward to the Dead Sea. It was the N. border of Moab, cutting it off from the land of the Amorites in ancient times (Nu 21^{13}), and later, from that of the Eastern tribes (Jos 12^{1}). Near its entry into the Dead Sea it flows between high, perpendicular rocks. Is 16^{2} refers to the 'fords of Arnon.' On the Moabite Stone (see MOAB) Mesha records that he fortified Aroer (modern *ʿArâʿir*) and built a road by the Arnon. This road probably followed the line of the Roman road, traces of which still remain, with indications of a bridge, some distance W. of Aroer, which stands on the N. bank. W. E.—**H. H. R.**

AROD.—A son of Gad, Nu 26^{17}; called **Arodi** in Gn 46^{16}. Patronymic **Arodites,** Nu 26^{17}.

AROER (? juniper).—**1.** A city on the N. bank of the Arnon (q.v.), modern *ʿArâʿir*, Dt 2^{36}. In such a position it necessarily became a frontier town (cf Dt 2^{36}, 2 K 10^{33}). It was captured by Sihon, king of the Amorites (Dt 2^{36} 4^{48}, Jos 12^{2}); when captured by Israel it was assigned to Reuben (Dt 3^{12}) but is said to have been rebuilt by the Gadites (Nu 32^{34}); it was the starting point of David's census (2 S 24^{5}); later it was taken by Hazael, king of Syria (2 K 10^{33}). Mesha, the king of Moab, tells on the Moabite Stone (see MOAB) that he fortified it, and in a later age it apparently still belonged to Moab (Jer 48^{19}). **2.** A city of Judah, 1 S 30^{28}; probably the same as **Adadah,** Jos 15^{22} (where we should probably read **Ararah;** see ADADAH); modern *ʿArʿarah*, 12 miles E. of Beersheba. **3.** A city of Gad near Rabbah (modern *ʿAmmân*), Jos 13^{25}, Jg 11^{33}; its site is unknown. **4.** In Is 17^{2} AV and RV mention an Aroer, which apparently belongs to Damascus, but RSV follows LXX in reading 'her cities will be deserted for ever' instead of 'the cities of Aroer shall be forsaken.'

AROM.—Father of some of the exiles who returned with Zerubbabel, 1 Es 5^{16}. The name has no parallel in the lists in Ezra and Nehemiah.

ARPACHSHAD.—According to Gn 10^{22} the third son of Shem, and according to Gn 11^{10} the second in the line of descent from Shem to Abraham. Gn 10^{22ff} is an enumeration of peoples descended from Shem; or countries inhabited by them, from which Babylonia is absent. It has been suggested that Arpachshad is a combination of two once separate words: *Arpach*, a region SW. of Assyria, and *Kasdim* (Chaldeës), and that the mistaken reading was then the basis of Gn 11^{10ff}. This does not seem very probable. Alternative suggestions are that Arpachshad is the *Arrapachitis* of the Greek geographer Ptolemy (VI. i. 2), between Urmia and Lake Van, or the Assyrian city of *Arrapkha* (modern *Kirkûk*); cf Unger, *RLA* i (1932), 154. But these also are doubtful.

ARPAD.—A city of Syria NW. of Aleppo, 2 K 18^{34} 19^{13}, Is 10^{9} 36^{19} 37^{13}, Jer 49^{23}; modern *Tell Erfâd*.

ARPHAXAD.—**1.** A King of the Medes who figures in the story of Judith, and who is said to have reigned in Ecbatana, Jth 1^{1ff}; he was defeated and slain by Nebuchadnezzar, King of Nineveh—an Assyrian king unknown to history. **2.** The AV spelling of **Arpachshad** (q.v.) in Gn $10^{22,\,24}$ 11^{10}, 1 Ch 1^{17}, and in AV, RV, and RSV in Lk 3^{36}.

ARROW.—See ARMOUR, and MAGIC, DIVINATION, AND SORCERY.

ARROWSNAKE.—Is 34^{15} (RV), probably rightly; AV 'great owl,' RSV **'owl'** (q.v.).

ARSACES.—A king of Parthia (known also as Mithridates I.). When opposed by Demetrius Nicator, who thought the people would rise in his favour and afterwards assist him against Tryphon, he deceived Demetrius by a pretence of negotiations, and in 138 B.C. took him prisoner (1 Mac 14[1-3] ; Justin, xxxvi. 1). In 1 Mac 15[22] Arsaces is mentioned among the kings to whom was sent an edict from Rome forbidding the persecution of the Jews.

ARSIPHURITH, 1 Es 5[16] (RV).—See JORAH.

ART.—The Hebrews were not distinguished in the ancient world for their contributions in art ; both the Bible and archaeological discovery support the view that they had little native genius in this area. The products of their artisans seem to have had utility rather than artistic excellence as their goal (see ARTS and CRAFTS). There was little, if any, pursuit of art for art's sake.

In **architecture,** the most famous building was the Temple of Solomon in Jerusalem (see TEMPLE). This was erected, however, by Phoenician architects and skilled artisans, with Hebrews furnishing largely the unskilled labour. Biblical statements to this effect (1 K 5[1-18]) are borne out by study of archaeological parallels ; *e.g.* the closest parallels to the floor-plan have been found at *Tell Tainat* (Syria) and Late Bronze Age Hazor. That the Hebrews were able to erect public buildings that were both sturdy and attractive is shown by the palaces of Omri and Ahab at Samaria. The city walls and gates built in the era of Solomon at Megiddo, Hazor, Ezion-geber and elsewhere show excellent workmanship.

In **sculpture** there are no large objects to which we may refer. Numerous figurines of clay or bronze, either whole or fragmentary, have been discovered. Some of these are of human form, others animal. These may in some instances represent deities, but it is seldom possible to determine what specific deity is intended. Nearly every excavation in Palestine has yielded 'Astarte figurines,' little clay representations of the mother-goddess. These are sometimes ugly and crude, and few show artistic sense. They were probably mass-produced in moulds, for the most part, and the use to which they were put did not demand artistic excellence.

Perhaps the finest works of art produced in Palestine are the carved ivories that have been found at Megiddo, Samaria, Hazor, and several other sites. Those at Megiddo are from the pre-Israelite Canaanite period, but those at Samaria and Hazor are from the 9th and 8th cent. B.C. These ivories exhibit several different techniques : some were carved in the round, some are in pierced relief, and some are in low relief. Many were decorated with insets of lapis lazuli, or coloured pastes or glass. These ivories were apparently used as inlays for furniture, boxes, wood-panelling, and the like ; some cosmetic items were made entirely of ivory. They illustrate the 'houses of ivory' of 1 K 22[39] and Am 3[15]—houses filled with ivories such as these. The themes they employed are borrowed mainly from Egypt and Syria. It is not certain whether they were of native Hebrew workmanship or not. Many scholars believe they were made by Syrian artisans, because of the similarity to ivories found at *Arslân Ṭâsh* (Syria), *Nimrûd* (Assyria), and elsewhere. The presence in the Samaria excavation of unworked tusks speaks for native workmanship, or at least for the importation of Syrian workmen into the city.

Almost as artistic as the carved ivories, and more likely to be of native workmanship, are the examples of **glyptic art** found on personal seals. While some of these bear only names, many have carved figures of animals, plants, and the like (see SEALS).

No examples of **painting** have come down to us from OT times. It is possible that the representations referred to in Ezk 23[14f] 8[10] were wall frescoes. From the Chalcolithic Age come the polychrome frescoes of *Teleilât el-Ghassûl,* and from the 3rd cent. A.D. the synagogue paintings of *Dura Europos.*

In **music** there can be no doubt that the Hebrews had much talent. The OT contains many references to music, both sacred and secular. It is possible for us to study the musical instruments from their representation on various types of monuments ; but, since no musical scores have survived, we can say virtually nothing about the nature of Hebrew tunes, except as they may have survived in the music of the synagogue and early Christian church (see MUSIC).

Many conjectures have been made as to the reasons why the Hebrews were not distinguished as artists. Reference is often made to the prohibition in the Second Commandment (Ex 20[4]). Yet it is difficult to determine just how this was interpreted. If it was interpreted to mean that no representation of deity was to be made, we can say that no discovery has ever been made of a representation of Yahweh (the inscription on a coin which was formerly thought to be YHW should be read YHD—*i.e.* 'Judah'). Yet representations have been found of various male and female deities, especially of the mother-goddess, referred to above. Strictly interpreted, the Second Commandment seems to prohibit any kind of representational art ; yet the Hebrews did represent plants, animals, and even human beings in various ways. It is probable that the commandment was interpreted in different ways at various times. For example, coins of the Maccabaean period never represent human portraits, but those of the Herodian period do. Also, it has been observed that the personal seals of Judah more often contain only the name, without any representation. Judah was generally more orthodox and less open to foreign influence than North Israel.

Another possible type of explanation involves the nature of Palestine, and the Hebrew form of society. Palestine is a land which is relatively poor in natural resources. Hebrew society put emphasis—at least ideally—upon brotherhood and democracy. The arts flourish best in an economy where there is leisure, and where a wealthy class exists that can patronize and encourage the arts. Such conditions did not often exist in ancient Israel.

Perhaps it is best simply to say that the Hebrews lacked artistic 'genius.' Their special talents lay in other directions. Yet, they did not lack artistic sensitivity, as is shown by their importation of foreign artisans and *objets d'art,* and in some cases their adaptation of foreign techniques and themes for their own purposes. J. P. H.

ARTAXERXES is the Greek form of the Old Persian *Artakhshatra,* Hebrew *'Artaḥshast(ā).* The identification of the Artaxerxes of the Bible is not completely certain. Neh 2[1] 5[14] 13[6] refer to Artaxerxes I. Longimanus (465–424 B.C.), son of Xerxes (Bibl. Ahasuerus). Ezr 7[1ff.] 8[1] imply that the same ruler is intended, but the overlapping of the activities of Ezra and Nehemiah raises historical difficulties, some of which are resolved if Ezra's mission is placed in the reign of Artaxerxes II. Mnemon (404–358 B.C.). The events narrated in Ezr 4[7-23] are also assigned to the reign of Artaxerxes. The section is clearly misplaced (note its different position in 1 Es 2[16-30]). Artaxerxes might be an error for some other name ; but more probably, the passage refers to events early in the reign of Artaxerxes I., before the mission of Nehemiah (cf Neh 1[3]). P. R. A.

ARTEMAS.—A trusted companion of St. Paul, in the later part of his life (as represented in Ti 3[12]). There is no evidence for the statements of Dorotheus (*Bibl. Maxima,* Lugd. 1677, iii. p. 429) that he had been one of the 70 disciples, and was afterwards bishop of Lystra.

ARTEMIS, the Greek goddess of the wild, the hunt, and also of fertility and childbearing. The name 'Diana' is entirely erroneous, due to late Roman identification of Greek and Roman gods, though it has now become popularized (in English) almost beyond the possibility of correction. The true name of the goddess, as in the NT, was Artemis. There were two conceptions of Artemis in ancient times : (1) the Greek, perhaps originally Minoan, maiden huntress, sister of Apollo : to this conception corresponds the Italian Diana ; (2) the mother goddess, the emblem of fertility, the fountain of nourishment, an Anatolian divinity, Hellenized under the name of Artemis : this is the goddess referred to in Acts and she has nothing to do with Diana, representing in fact a contrary idea. While the Greek maiden Artemis was represented in art attired as a huntress, with bow and arrows, the Anatolian maternal Artemis was represented with many breasts (*multimammia*), though sometimes still accompanied by two stags. In this form she was worshipped over the whole of Lydia, before Greeks ever settled there, and the same divine power of reproduction was worshipped under other names over most of the peninsula of Asia Minor. The rude idol or fetish (' secret stone,' RSV) preserved in her great temple at Ephesus was said to have fallen from heaven (this is the real meaning of *diopetēs*, Ac 19^{35}), a not uncommon idea in ancient times, which suggests that such images were sometimes meteoric stones. The chief priest, who bore a Persian title (*Essēn*), had under him a large company of priestesses. There was also a large body of priests (*megabyzoi*, also a Persian word), each appointed for a year, who seem also to have been city officials ; and there were other bodies of ministers.

The epithet ' great ' (Ac 19^{34f}) is proved by inscriptions to have been characteristically applied to the goddess, and the exclamation in Acts may have been really an invocation. The ' silver shrines ' (Ac 19^{24}), were small representations of the goddess within her shrine, were purchased by the rich ; the poor bought replicas in terra cotta or marble. Both classes dedicated them as offerings to the goddess, in whose temple they would be hung up. When the accumulation became too great, the priests cleared them away, throwing the terra cotta or marble ones on the rubbish heap, or into a hole, but reserving the others for the melting pot. Those which survive are naturally the terra cotta or marble. The goddess had so many worshippers that the manufacture of silver shrines must have been very profitable (Ac 19^{27}).

A. So.—**H. R. W.**

ARTIFICER.—See ARTS AND CRAFTS.

ARTILLERY.—Used in 1 S 20^{40} in AV in obsolete sense, of Jonathan's bow and arrows (RV, RSV have ' weapons ') ; also in AV of 1 Mac 6^{51} of Antiochus's siege works (RV ' mounds,' RSV ' siege towers ').

ARTS AND CRAFTS.—One of the most characteristic distinctions between the Hebraic and the Hellenic views of life is found in the attitude of the two races to manual labour. By the Greek it was regarded as unworthy of a free citizen ; by the Jew it was held in the highest esteem, as many Talmudic aphorisms bear witness. The general term in OT for **craftsman** (2 K 24^{14}, Jer 24^{1}, 1 Ch 29^{5} [AV, RV **artificer**]), or skilled artisan, is *hārāsh* from a root meaning ' to cut.' Most frequently, however, it is qualified by the name of the material. This suggests the following divisions :

1. *Workers in wood.*—Palestine was relatively poor in trees, and the best wood, cedar, was imported from Lebanon. The productions of the **carpenter** (1 Ch 22^{15}, Mt 13^{55}, Mk 6^{3}) probably surpassed in variety those of any other craftsman, for they comprised not only those of the modern carpenter and cabinetmaker, but also of the ploughwright, woodcarver, and other specialized arts and crafts of to-day. Examples of tools which have been discovered in excavations may be seen in Wright, *Biblical Archaeology*, p. 92, Fig. 57 (cf p. 195), and in the respective articles in Galling, *Biblisches Reallexikon*. Egyptian carpenters at work are depicted on the wall of the tomb of Ti at Sakkarah (*ANEP*, No. 123). Various **axes** are named in OT. For one variety the text distinguishes between the iron head and the wooden handle (Dt 19^{5}). Another is from the context probably an adze (Jer 10^{3}), while a third appears as a **hatchet** in Ps 74^{6} RSV. The carpenter's **hammer** (Jer 10^{4}) was made with a head of stone or metal (iron or bronze) ; it may have been on occasion a wooden mallet (Jg 4^{21} 5^{26}). The **saw** (Is 10^{15}) was single-handed ; saws of flint and of metal have been discovered by archaeologists (the former even from the Iron Age). Holes were bored with a drill worked by a bow and string, as in the present day and as represented on Egyptian monuments (Galling, *op. cit.*, cols. 283–5). In Is 44^{13}, which describes the work of a Babylonian idol-maker, are further named the **measuring line** (AV ' rule '), the **pencil** or *stylus* for outlining the work, the **planes** (which may rather have been chisels), and the **compass.** A few nails of bronze have been excavated.

2. *Workers in metal.*—The principal metals of OT times are enumerated in Nu 31^{22}. The ' brass ' of some English versions of OT is probably always bronze, *i.e* copper with an alloy of tin, except where pure copper is intended, as Dt 8^{9}. Iron was introduced into Palestine for the making of weapons and jewellery in the 12th cent. B.C., but was not used for agricultural implements until about 1000 B.C. The Philistines introduced the metal and for a time had a monopoly of its manufacture (1 S 13^{19-21}) ; the Hebrews learned to work iron by the 10th cent. However, bronze continued in use for a long time. Exploration and excavation have shown that extensive mines of both iron and copper were exploited in the Arabah, south of the Dead Sea, and that Ezion-geber was devoted largely to the smelting of ore and the manufacture of metal objects, particularly in the reign of Solomon. Mining operations are described in Job 28^{1-11}, and the processes of smelting and refining are referred to in Ezk 22^{17-22} and Jer 6^{27-30}. For the more artistic handling of copper the Hebrews were at first dependent on Phoenician craftsmen (1 K 7^{13ff}), but in time the Israelites became expert metalworkers. The tools of the smith were the **hammer** (Is 44^{12}), the **anvil** (Is 41^{7}, Sir 38^{28}), the **tongs** (Is 6^{6}), and the **bellows** (Jer 6^{29}). The last-named object is depicted as being carried on the back of an ass in the famous tomb painting of Beni-Hasan, of about 1900 B.C. (*ANEP*, No. 3) ; in fact, it has been conjectured that the Semites depicted there were travelling smiths or tinkers. Some metal objects were cast in moulds (*ibid.*, No. 135) ; smelting furnaces have been found at some sites in Palestine, most notably at Tell Qasîle, near Tell Aviv (*ibid.*, No. 134). For the goldsmith and silversmith see MINING AND METALS, *s.vv.* ' Gold ' and ' Silver.' The **smiths** carried away by Nebuchadnezzar (2 K 24^{14}, Jer 24^{1}) were probably those specially skilled in the manufacture of weapons of war.

3. *Workers in stone.*—From the far-off palaeolithic days man has been a ' worker in stone,' a term used in the OT mostly for those who cut and dressed stone for building purposes (1 Ch 22^{15}). The usual rendering is **masons** (2 S 5^{11}, 1 Ch 14^{1}). In Palestine there is an abundance of soft limestone which could easily be worked, and provided an excellent building material. The finest buildings were those in Jerusalem and Megiddo of Solomonic times, and the palaces of Omri and Ahab in Samaria ; these, however, may have all been built by Phoenician workmen. There are references in OT to various processes, such as the quarrying out of the stones in the **quarry** (1 K 5^{17} 6^{7}), the hewing of wine-vats (Is 5^{2}) and of tombs (22^{16}) in the solid rock, and the cutting and dressing of ' hewn stones ' for various constructions (Ex 20^{25}, 1 K 5^{17}, Am 5^{11}). The **builders** (Ps 118^{22}) worked from a prepared **pattern** or plan (Ex 25^{9}, 1 Ch 28^{11}), using the **measuring-reed** (Ezk 40^{3}) and the **plumb line** (Am 7^{7}) or **plummet** (2 K 21^{13}, Zec 4^{10}). The large **hammer** used in quarrying (Jer 23^{29}) was different from the smaller hammer of the stone-cutter (1 K 6^{7}). The **axe** of the last passage is rather the pick-axe or adze for stone cutting and dressing, and was the tool used in cutting the Siloam tunnel, as the workmen tell us in their famous inscription. On a bronze relief from the time of Shalmaneser III., Assyrian stonemasons are depicted carving a royal image with chisel and hammer (*ANEP*, No. 364). For the ' engraver in stone,' or jeweller, of Ex 28^{11}, see SEALS.

4. *Workers in clay.*—Clay, not stone, was the ordinary building material among the Hebrews (see HOUSE). **Brickmaking,** however, was apparently too simple an operation to attain the dignity of a special craft in OT times, as was also **' plastering '** with clay or lime (Lv 14^{42}, Dn 5^{5} ; cf Ezk 13^{10-16}, Mt 23^{27}, Ac 23^{3}). There are excellent illustrations of brickmaking in Egypt (*e.g.*

ANEP, No. 115; see Heaton, *Everyday Life in Old Testament Times*, pp. 131–34). In Egypt at least some of the brickmaking was done by captives; we may note that David compelled Ammonite captives to 'toil at the brick-kilns' (2 S 12³¹). For the **potter** and his work, perhaps the oldest of all crafts, see POTTERY.

5. *Workers in leather*.—First among these is the **tanner** (Ac 9⁴³), who prepared the leather from the skins of domestic and other animals (Ex 25⁵ 26¹⁴, 2 K 1⁸). Little is known of the actual method by which leather was made; presumably the hair was removed by means of lime, or the acrid juices of plants, applied to the skins after they had been soaked in water, and then they were dried and tanned. Owing to their uncleanly accompaniments, the tanner and his trade were regarded by the Jews with much disfavour. Like the fuller, he was forbidden to carry on his work within the city; this partly explains the situation of Simon's tannery 'by the sea side' (Ac 10³²). In early times the tanner not only supplied the material but probably actually manufactured the leather shields, helmets, quivers, etc., required by soldiers, while the making of sandals, girdles, and other articles of leather (Lv 13⁴⁸), and the preparation of skins for water, wine, and milk (see BOTTLE) were long matters of purely domestic economy. In late OT times skins, prepared as leather or parchment, began to be used as writing material; *e.g.* most of the scrolls and fragments found at Qumrân were of animal skins.

6. *Trades connected with dress*.—The ordinary dress of the Hebrews was made in the home (cf 1 S 2¹⁹). The **tailor** first appears in the Mishnah. Certain of the processes, however, gradually developed into separate crafts, such as that of the **weaver** (Ex 35³⁵, 1 S 17⁷; see SPINNING AND WEAVING), the **embroiderer** (Ex 35³⁵), whose designs were sewed upon the finished fabric, the **dyer** and the **fuller**. The wool was usually dyed before or after being spun (Ex 35²⁵). Both animal and vegetable dyes were employed (see COLOURS). The work of the fuller (Is 7³, Mal 3², Mk 9³) was of two kinds, according as he dealt with the web fresh from the loom, or with soiled garments that had already been worn. The latter he cleaned by steeping and treading in water mixed with an alkaline substance (rendered **soap** in Mal 3²) and fuller's earth. The new web—the 'unshrunk cloth' of Mt 9¹⁶, Mk 2²¹ RSV—on the other hand, after being thoroughly steeped in a similar mixture, was stamped and felted, then bleached with fumes of sulphur, and finally pressed in the fuller's press. Fulling, like tanning, was carried on outside the town, but the situation of the 'fuller's field' of Isaiah's day (7³) is uncertain. Here may be mentioned the **barber** (Ezk 5¹) and the **perfumer**, for whom see HAIR and PERFUMER respectively.

7. *Employments connected with food*.—**Cooks**, as a special class, were to be found only in the houses of the wealthy (see FOOD). The Hebrew name shows that they killed as well as cooked the animals. The **shambles** of 1 Co 10²⁵, however, are not, as in modern English, the slaughter-house, but the provision-market of Corinth, where meat and other provisions were sold (RSV 'meat market'). The **bakers** were numerous enough to give their name to a street of the capital in Jeremiah's day (37²¹); for their work see BREAD. Public mills employing **millers** appear late, but are implied in the rendering 'great millstone' of Mt 18⁶ RSV (see MILL). The well-known Tyropoeon or **Cheesemakers'** valley in Jerusalem received its name from the industry carried on there (Jos. *BJ* v. iv. 1 [140]).

8. *Employments connected with the land*.—Most of these are noticed in other connexions; see AGRICULTURE, SHEEP, VINE, etc. The prophet Amos describes himself as 'a dresser of sycamore trees' (Am 7¹⁴), for which see AMOS.

9. *Miscellaneous employments*.—If to the above there be added the **tentmaker**, representing the craft (RSV 'trade') of St. Paul and his friends Aquila and Priscilla (Ac 18³, see TENT), and the **fisherman** (see NETS), no trade or manual employment of importance will, it is hoped, have been overlooked. Most of the remaining employments will be found under their own (*e.g.* RECORDER, SCRIBE) or kindred titles, as 'merchant' under TRADE, 'physician' under MEDICINE, etc.

10. *Two general characteristics*.—This article may fitly close with a brief reference to two characteristics of all the more important handicrafts and employments. The first is that certain towns were largely given over to specific crafts, or the members of a single craft were grouped in one street or quarter of a town, to which they gave their name. Examples of the former are pre-exilic Debir, where the discovery of numerous loom weights and dye-vats proved that the principal industry of the town was dyeing and weaving; and Solomonic Ezion-geber, which was an important centre for the refining of metals and manufacture of metal objects. As for the latter, we find in Jerusalem, as has been noted, 'the bakers' street,' 'the fullers' field,' and 'the cheese-makers' valley,' to which should perhaps be added 'the valley of craftsmen' (Neh 11³⁵). Josephus mentions a smiths' bazaar, a wool-market, and a clothes-market in the Jerusalem of his day (*BJ* v. viii. 1 [331]).

The second point to be noted is the evidence that the members of the various crafts had already formed themselves into associations or guilds. Thus we read in Nehemiah of a 'son of the perfumers,' *i.e.* a member of the guild of perfumers (3⁸), and of 'a son of the goldsmiths' (3³¹). Cf Ezr 2⁴² 'the sons of the gatekeepers' and the familiar 'sons of the prophets.' In 1 Ch 4²¹ᶠᶠ there is mention of similar associations of linenweavers and potters. The expression 'sons of' to denote membership of an association may go back to the days when trades were hereditary in particular families. A guild of silversmiths is attested for Ephesus (Ac 19²⁵). For the probable earnings of artisans among the Jews see WAGES.

A. R. S. K.—**J. P. H.**

ARUBBOTH.—A place in Solomon's third district, 1 K 4¹⁰ (AV **Aruboth**); its site is unknown, but it was near Hepher and Soco (q.v.), the former being in Manasseh, and the latter probably being modern *Tell er-Rās*, WNW. of Samaria.

ARUBOTH, 1 K 4¹⁰ (AV).—See ARUBBOTH.

ARUMAH.—Abimelech's place of refuge, Jg 9⁴¹; possibly modern *Khirbet el-ʿOrmah*, 6 miles SE. of *Nâblus* (Shechem).

ARVAD.—The most important of the northern cites of Phoenicia. It was built on an island 70 miles N. of *Beirût*—a sort of second Tyre, with another town on the mainland opposite. In Ezk 27⁸, ¹¹ it is named as furnishing oarsmen for the galleys of Tyre and warriors for its defence. In the ethnological list of Gn 10¹⁸, 1 Ch 1¹⁶, the **Arvadites** are mentioned amongst the Canaanites or Phoenicians. Throughout antiquity it was a place of renown for trade and general enterprise, ranking next to Tyre and Sidon. Sennacherib records its submission to him in his prism inscription. In 1 Mac 15²³ it is called **Aradus**. J. F. McC.—**H. H. R.**

ARZA.—Prefect of the palace at Tirzah, in whose house King Elah was assassinated during a carouse by Zimri, who seized the throne, 1 K 16⁹.

ARZARETH (2 Es 13⁴⁵).—A region beyond the river from which the ten tribes are to return. It became the subject of many later Jewish legends concerning the Sabbatic River beyond which the lost tribes were to be found—variously identified with the Oxus and the Ganges. Arzareth is not a true geographical name, but is probably Hebrew *'ereṣ 'aḥereth*, 'another land' (RSVm; cf Dt 29²⁸ [Heb 27]). E. G. K.

ASA.—1. The third king of Judah after the disruption, succeeding Abijah. Since his mother's name is given as the same as that of Abijah's mother, some have supposed the two kings to have been brothers. But there may be some mistake in the text. Asa is praised by the Biblical writer for his religious zeal, which led him to reform the worship, and even to depose his mother from her place of influence at court because of her idolatrous practices. Politically he took a mistaken course when he submitted to Benhadad of Damascus to secure his aid against Baasha of Israel, who had captured Ramah. The Temple treasures were sent to Benhadad, who thereupon invaded Israel, and Baasha was compelled to evacuate the threatening fortress (1 K 15^{9ff}). Asa was, however, able to extend his territory northwards at the expense of the Northern Kingdom and to use Baasha's materials to fortify Geba and Mizpah. The Chronicler (2 Ch 14^{9ff}) credits Asa with a victory over an enormous force of Ethiopians. **2.** A Levite (1 Ch 9^{16}). H. P. S.—**A. S. H.**

ASADIAS, Bar 1^{1} (AV, RV).—See HASADIAH.

ASAEL, To 1^{1} (AV).—See ASIEL, **3.**

ASAHEL.—**1.** The youngest son of Zeruiah, David's sister, and the brother of Joab and Abishai. He was famous for his swiftness of foot, a much valued gift in ancient times. He was one of David's thirty heroes, probably the third of the second three (2 S 23^{24}). He was also commander of a division in David's army (1 Ch 27^{7}). He was slain by Abner (2 S 2^{18-23}), and this gave rise to a blood feud which ended in the killing of Abner by Joab (2 S 3^{27}). **2.** A Levite, who taught the people in the reign of Jehoshaphat (2 Ch 17^{8}). **3.** A subordinate collector of offerings and tithes in the reign of Hezekiah (2 Ch 31^{13}). **4.** Father of Jonathan, who opposed Ezra's action in connexion with the divorce of foreign wives (Ezr 10^{15}); cf 1 Es 9^{14} (AV, RV **Azael**).

ASAHIAH, 2 K $22^{12f\ 14}$ (AV).—See ASAIAH, **1.**

ASAIAH ('Y″ made').—**1.** One of the deputation sent by Josiah to consult Huldah the prophetess, 2 K $22^{12, 14}$ (AV **Asahiah**), 2 Ch 34^{20}. **2.** One of the Simeonite princes who attacked the shepherds of Gedor, 1 Ch 4^{36}. **3.** A **Merarite** who took part in bringing the Ark to Jerusalem, 1 Ch 6^{30} $15^{6, 11}$. **4.** The firstborn of the Shilonites, 1 Ch 9^{5}; probably called **Maaseiah** in Neh 11^{5}. See MAASEIAH, **9.**

ASAIAS.—One of the sons of Annan (AV, RV Annas) who agreed to put away his foreign wife, 1 Es 9^{32} (AV, RV **Aseas**); perhaps the **Isshijah** of Ezr 10^{31}.

ASANA, 1 Es 5^{31} (AV, RV).—See ASNAH.

ASAPH ('gatherer').—**1.** The father of Joah, the 'recorder' or chronicler (*mazkîr*, literally 'one who reminds,' possibly according to Egyptian analogies one of three very high-ranking officials—cf 2 K $18^{18, 37}$, the others being the one over the household and the secretary—who had *inter alia* the ordering of palace ceremonial and the arranging of audiences, and the making of royal or state proclamations, *i.e.* the herald royal in the fullest possible sense) at the court of Hezekiah. **2.** The 'keeper of the king's forest,' to whom king Artaxerxes addressed a letter directing him to supply Nehemiah with timber, Neh 2^{8}. **3.** A Korahite (1 Ch 26^{1}), same as **Abiasaph** (q.v.). **4.** The eponym of one of the three guilds (the others being Heman and Ethan = Jeduthun) which conducted the musical services of the Temple in the time of the Chronicler, 1 Ch 15^{16f}, etc. The Chronicler traces this arrangement to the appointment of David, in whose reign Asaph, who is called 'the seer' (2 Ch 29^{30}), is supposed to have lived. At first the Asaphites alone seem to have formed the Temple choir, and in the time of Ezra and Nehemiah (wherever we have the memoirs of the latter in their original form) they are not yet reckoned among the *Levites*; cf, *e.g.* Ezr 2^{41} 7^{7}, Neh 12^{47}. At a later period they share the musical service with the 'sons of Korah' (see KORAHITES). Pss 50 and 73–83 have the superscription *le- 'Asaph*, which means in all probability that they once belonged to the hymn-book of the Asaphite choir (see PSALMS).

ASARA, 1 Es 5^{31} (RV).—See HASRAH, **2.**

ASARAMEL (AV **Saramel**).—An expression 'in Asaramel,' in 1 Mac 14^{28} in the inscription upon the memorial pillar of Simon Maccabaeus. A place-name is indicated by the Greek text. This reading, however, is unsuitable, and it is best to assume, as has been proposed, that there was originally written a Hebrew title of Simon, additional to 'the high-priest,' meaning 'prince of the people of God' (*Sar-'am-'ēl*). So RSVm. For other explanations see *Exp T* Aug. 1900, pp. 523 ff. J. F. McC.

ASAREEL, 1 Ch 4^{16} (AV).—See ASAREL.

ASAREL.—A son of Jehallelel, 1 Ch 4^{16} (AV **Asareel**).

ASARELAH, 1 Ch 25^{2} (AV).—See ASHARELAH.

ASBASARETH, 1 Es 5^{69} (RV).— A corrupt form of **Esarhaddon** (q.v.; so RSV).

ASCALON.—The Greek form of the name **Ashkelon,** Jth 2^{28} (AV, RV, RSV), 1 Mac 10^{86} 11^{60} 12^{33} (AV, RV; RSV **Askalon**).

ASCENSION.—The Ascension of our Lord is not related as an event in the Synoptic Gospels. There is no reference to it in Matthew. In the appendix to Mark (16^{9-20}, RSVm) the words in which it is stated are rather the formula of a creed than the narrative of an event. Lk 24^{50-53} specifies only that 'he parted from them' (though many ancient authorities add, 'and was carried up into heaven,' RSVm) after having 'led them out as far as Bethany' (v.^{50}). The context dates the parting on the Resurrection day ($24^{13, 33, 36}$). However, if the additional words referred to are ignored, vv.$^{50-53}$ refer to an appearance of the risen Lord, and the words 'he parted from them' need not refer to the Ascension (cf 24^{13}).

The only narrative of the Ascension as a separate event is found in Ac 1^{6-11}, where we find the words, 'he was lifted up, and a cloud took him out of their sight,' 'they were gazing into heaven as he went,' and 'who was taken up from you into heaven' (cf 1^{22}). The preceding paragraph dates the event forty days after the passion (v.^{3}); the following one locates it on the mount called Olivet (v.^{12}).

The Gospels contain statements compatible with this conception of the Ascension. In Lk 9^{31} Moses and Elijah speak of 'his departure (*exodos*) which he was to accomplish at Jerusalem,' and Lk 9^{51} reads, 'When the days drew near for him to be received up, he set his face to go to Jerusalem.' It is probable that the Ascension is here delicately blended with the crucifixion, as in Jn 12^{32}. In Jn 6^{62} the question is asked, 'Then what if you were to see the Son of man ascending where he was before?'; and in Jn 20^{17} Mary is told, 'Do not hold me, for I have not yet ascended to the Father; but go to my brethren and say to them, I am ascending to my Father and your Father, to my God and your God.' The latter reference stands in the narrative between the account of the resurrection and that of the appearances of the risen Lord and the gift of the Spirit.

References to the exaltation of Christ occur in three types of passages. First, there are a number in which the exaltation or heavenly session is directly connected with the resurrection (Ro 8^{34}, Eph 1^{20}, Ac 2^{32-33} 5^{30-31}, 1 P 1^{21} 3^{21-22}), and four others where such a connexion is implied (1 Co 15^{4-5}, 2 Co 4^{14}, Col 3^{1-4}, Ph 2^{8-9}). Resurrection and exaltation are theologically distinct, however: the former asserts that Jesus was raised from the dead, the latter that he shares in the sovereignty of God. Both affirmations are made in the earliest preaching as reported in Acts and in the NT generally; and each has its own imagery linked to OT proof-texts (*e.g.* Ps 16^{8-10} for the former, Ps 110^{1} for the latter).

Second, there are the more numerous passages which refer to the exaltation of Christ without alluding either to the Resurrection or to the Ascension: he is exalted (Ac 5^{31}); he is highly exalted (Ph 2^{9}); he entered heaven (He 6^{20} 9^{12} 9^{24}); he sat down at the right hand of the Father (Eph 1^{20}, 1 P 3^{22}, He 1^{3} 4^{14} 8^{1} 10^{12} 12^{2}); he goes to the Father (1 P 3^{22}). The last expression (using the verbs *aperchomai*, *metabainō*, *poreuomai*, and *hypagō*) is characteristic of the Fourth Gospel, where it occurs fourteen times in chs. 7–16.

As noted above, the Fourth Gospel also contains two passages using the language of ascent and descent. This is the third type of usage, to be found in 1 Th 4[16], in the quotations in Eph 4[8] and 1 Ti 3[16], and in passages referring to the coming of the Son of Man on the clouds (Mk 14[62], Mt 24[30] 26[64], Rev 1[7]). It should be observed, however, that there are fifteen references to the *parousia* using the words 'revealing,' 'appearing,' and 'coming' without reference to a descent.

The imagery of ascension suggests assumption-stories (*e.g.* 2 K 2[11ff], Enoch 39[3]), but the restraint of the Acts narrative, the lack of interest in the psychological effects, and the fact that no earthly element (cloud, wind) effects an elevation, mark it off from such. The connexion of such imagery with the expectation of the *parousia*, together with the words of the two angels, suggests that the original pericope was an assurance of the second coming but a refusal to date it. The narrative as it stands serves to mark the end of the Resurrection-appearances and provides a transition from the Jerusalem appearances to the invisible lordship of the exalted Christ. Further, the Ascension, in Acts, like the glorification of the Son in the Fourth Gospel (see especially chs. 14–16), is the precondition of the gift of the Spirit and the new mode of Jesus' presence with his own. What is precarious about the narrative in Acts is the suggestion that the Ascension is a distinct event separable from the Resurrection, and the placing of it in the sequence of events.

We observe that the actual recession of Jesus into the upper air is not described (as His Resurrection is not), and that the cloud is suggestive of a theophany as in the Transfiguration narrative. This suggests a vision of the (already) exalted Lord, in harmony with the appearance to the disciples in the Fourth Gospel. On the other hand, the language of ascent is used, but without the anti-docetic motivation of the Fourth Gospel to account for it. It appears, then, that the Acts narrative is a statement of the exaltation of Christ, the imagery of which is derived from the language used to affirm the *parousia*. H. H. G.

ASCENSION OF ISAIAH.—See PSEUDEPIGRAPHA, **6.**

ASCENT OF BLOOD, Jos 15[7] (AV).—See ADUMMIM.

ASCENTS, SONGS OF.—See PSALMS, **2.**

ASEAS, 1 Es 9[32] (AV, RV).—See ASAIAS.

ASEBEBIA, 1 Es 8[47] (AV).—See SHEREBIAH.

ASEBEBIAS, 1 Es 8[47] (RV).—See SHEREBIAH.

ASEBIA, 1 Es 8[48] (AV).—See HASHABIAH, **7.**

ASEBIAS, 1 Es 8[48] (RV).—See HASHABIAH, **7.**

ASENATH.—Daughter of Potiphera, priest of On (q.v.), wife of Joseph and mother of Ephraim and Manasseh (Gn 41[45, 50] 46[20]). The name, like the other Egyptian names in the story of Joseph, is of a well-known type, prevalent during the Late Period (*c* 1075–663 B.C.). To be vocalized *Esneit*, it represents Egyptian *ns-Nit* (the initial *n* had disappeared by 670 B.C.) or *iw.s-n-Nit*, meaning 'belonging to Neith' or 'she belongs to Neith' respectively. Neith was the goddess of Saïs, and her name was especially popular in names from the 26th (Saïte) dynasty (*c* 663–525 B.C.).

Asenath is the heroine of a remarkable Jewish and Christian romance, in which she renounces her false gods before her marriage with Joseph; it can be traced back to the 5th cent. A.D., and is probably a good deal earlier. F. Ll. G.—**R. J. W.**

ASER, Lk 2[36], Rev 7[6] (AV) = the tribe of **Asher** (q.v.).

ASERER, 1 Es 5[32] (AV).—See SISERA, **2.**

ASH.—This tree is mentioned only in AV and RVm in Is 44[14], where it renders Hebrew *'ōren*. This is probably some species of **laurel.** It is rendered **fir** in RV, while RSV follows an alternative reading *'erez* and renders **cedar.**

ASHAN.—A town of Judah, Jos 15[42]. It is uncertain whether it is to be identified with the Ashan of Simeon in Jos 19[7], 1 Ch 4[32] 6[59], which is called **Ain** (q.v.) in Jos 31[16], and is to be identified with **Bor-ashan,** 1 S 30[30] (AV Chor-ashan, RV Cor-ashan); probably modern *Khirbet 'Asan.*

ASHARELAH.—An Asaphite, 1 Ch 25[2] (AV **Asarelah**); called **Jesharelah** in v.[14].

ASHBEA.—See BETH-ASHBEA.

ASHBEL (? 'having a long upper lip').—The second son of Benjamin, 1 Ch 8[1], Nu 26[38]; but cf Gn 46[21]. The patronymic **Ashbelite** occurs in Nu 26[38].

ASHDOD.—Modern *Esdûd*, called in Apocrypha and NT by its Greek name **Azotus,** a city of the Anakim not captured by Joshua; although it was allotted along with its villages to the tribe of Judah, it was never occupied by Judah, for it soon became one of the five cities of the Philistines (Jos 11[22] 13[3] 15[47]). It was to the temple of Dagon in Ashdod that the Philistines first brought the Ark of Yahweh after they captured it from the Israelites (1 S 5[1f]). Uzziah attacked Ashdod, dismantled its walls and established Jewish settlements in its neighbourhood (2 Ch 26[6]). It probably became tributary to Assyria under Tiglath-pileser III. In 711 B.C. it revolted against Sargon II. at the instigation of a Greek whom the Ashdodites chose in preference to the Assyrian nominee; the crushing of this revolt is mentioned in Is 20[1]. Mitinti, king of Ashdod, remained loyal to Sennacherib when Hezekiah and others revolted, and was rewarded by receiving portions of Hezekiah's territory. Judgment is pronounced on Ashdod by Hebrew prophets both before and after the exile (cf Am 1[8], Zeph 2[4], Jer 25[20], Zec 9[6]). (In Am 3[9] read 'Assyria' with LXX; so RSV.)

Ashdod was the capital of a district under the Persian Empire; Nehemiah was indignant at hearing its dialect spoken by Jewish children whose fathers had married women from there (Neh 13[23f]). It was captured by Judas Maccabaeus (1 Mac 5[68]) and his brother Jonathan (1 Mac 10[84]), and burned by John Hyrcanus (1 Mac 16[10]). It was given the status of a free city by Pompey in 63 B.C. Herod the Great bequeathed it to his sister Salome, who bequeathed it in turn to the Empress Livia (A.D. 10).

In NT Philip visits it after his meeting with the Ethiopian eunuch (Ac 8[40]). R. A. S. M.—**F. F. B.**

ASHDOTH-PISGAH.—AV for RV and RSV 'slopes of Pisgah' in Dt 3[17], Jos 12[3] 13[20]. In Dt 4[49] AV has 'springs of Pisgah'; cf AVm at 3[17], Jos 12[3] 13[20] and RVm at Dt 3[17] 4[49], Jos 13[20].

ASHER.—**1.** A town in Manasseh, apparently in the N. of the tribal territory (Jos 17[7]). This is located by the early pilgrims and the *Onomasticon* on the Roman road from *Nâblus* to Scythopolis (*Beisân*), 15 Roman miles from the former, a location which would suggest the modern village of *Teyasir*, some 9 miles NE. of *Nâblus*. **2.** To 1[2]; see HAZOR, **1.** J. Gr.

ASHER.—The eighth son of Jacob by Leah's maid Zilpah, and named by Leah 'Happy' (Gn 30[13]). This 'popular etymology' dominates J's thought in the 'Blessing of Jacob' (Gn 49[20]) and in the 'Blessing of Moses' (Dt 33[24]). Asher's territory was especially fertile, and the well-watered western escarpment of Galilee is still renowned for its olives. The district of Asher is said to have reached from the Carmel range E. of *Haifa* to the confines of Tyre and included the coastal plain of *'Akkâ* (Jos 19[24–30]), but this claim is drastically modified in Jg 1[31ff], from which it is obvious that the Hebrew settlement in western Galilee was achieved rather by infiltration than by conquest, the Canaanite element predominating. Thus Asher played no part in the conflict against Sisera (Jg 5[17ff]), though they are assigned a part in Gideon's campaign against the Midianites (Jg 6[35] 7[23]). The tribe is said to have gone 40,000 strong to support David in Hebron (1 Ch 12[36]) and to have numbered 41,500 males at Sinai and 53,400 in the Plains of Moab (Nu 1[41] 26[47]). Though this is obvious exaggeration, not uncommon in P, it reflects the large population in the district of Asher. The political insignificance of Asher, however, is indicated by the fact that in 1 Ch 27[16ff], where the tribes are enumerated under their respective leaders under David, Asher is not

mentioned. The mention of *Asaru* as a place-name in Palestine in Egyptian records of the 14th cent. may indicate either that the settlement of the tribe of Asher was earlier than the decisive phase of the Israelite settlement at the end of the 13th cent., a view which may be supported by the tradition that Asher was one of the older, or Leah, tribes, or it may indicate that the Hebrews who settled here took the name of Asher from the district. It may even be that Asher signifies the name of a Canaanite deity, the male counterpart of Ashera, the Canaanite mother-goddess, well known from the OT, the Amarna Tablets, and now the Râs Shamra texts. The tradition of Asher's birth from the concubine Zilpah indicates a certain doubt about the purity of the stock of Asher. In the publication of one of the legends from Râs Shamra (*Keret*) it was claimed that Asher was mentioned as a folk-element in Galilee. A more critical appraisal of the text has exploded this theory.
J. A. C.—**J. Gr.**

ASHERAH (plur. usually *Asherim*, masc. and once *Asheroth*, fem.).—The AV following Vulg. (and LXX) mistakenly rendered the Hebrew word as **grove.** The word is the Hebrew equivalent for the Canaanite goddess Ashirtu or Ashratu as she is known in the Amarna tablets. In Ugaritic literature Lady Athirat is the mother of the gods, the female counterpart to El, and she is thus given the title 'Mistress Athirat of the Sea, the Creatress of the Gods' (*ḳnyt ẻlm*).

1. In the OT the term is sometimes used to designate this Canaanite goddess. She as well as Baal had her prophets (four hundred) in Israel during the time of Ahab (1 K 18^{19}). Sacred vessels for her cult were removed from the Jerusalem Temple at Josiah's command and then destroyed (2 K 23^{4}). 'Hangings' were woven for her in the houses of the sacred prostitutes within the Temple (v.^{7}), and an 'abominable image' of Asherah was reverenced by king Asa's mother (1 K 15^{13}, 2 Ch 15^{16}). The goddess is once referred to in the plural (Jg 3^{7}) along with Baalim as illegitimate objects of worship for the Israelites, but this word is commonly emended (for insufficient reasons?) to Ashtaroth in view of 2^{13}.

2. The word is sometimes used for the image of the goddess. The 'graven image of Asherah' which Manasseh erected in the Temple (2 K 21^{7}) is simply referred to as an Asherah in 2 K 23^{6}. Apparently the Asherah set up by Ahab in the Baal temple at Samaria (1 K 16^{33}; cf 2 K 10^{26}) was such an image. Though destroyed, it reappeared in Samaria during the reign of Jehoahaz, Jehu's son (13^{6}).

3. Sacred trees or poles erected as symbols of the goddess. Since these symbols were 'planted' (Dt 16^{21}), and were to be cut down (Ex 34^{13}, etc.), and burnt (Dt 12^{3}, etc.), they were obviously wooden, and therefore archaeological remains do not exist. In the Early Bronze sanctuary at Ai, however, there was found a four-foot piece of carbonized wood lying between two incense burners. It was probably originally a tree trunk with its branches lopped off. This has been suggested as possibly having been an Asherah.

The worship of Asherah and the erection of such sacred symbols of the goddess of fertility were strictly forbidden to the Israelites. The popularity of the Asherah particularly in the Northern Kingdom under the Omrids and afterwards was 'evil in the sight of Yahweh,' incurring his wrath and according to the prophetic historian contributed to the eventual destruction of the Kingdom (cf 2 K 17^{7ff}).
A. R. S. K.—**J. W. W.**

ASHES.—Ashes on the head formed one of the ordinary tokens of mourning for the dead (see MOURNING CUSTOMS) as of private (2 S 13^{19}) and national humiliation (Neh 9^{1}, 1 Mac 3^{47}). The penitent and the afflicted might also sit (Job 2^{8}, Jon 3^{6}) or even wallow in ashes (Jer 6^{26}, Ezk 27^{30}). In 1 K $20^{38, 41}$ we must, with RV, read 'headband' (q.v.; RSV 'bandage') for 'ashes.'

In a figurative sense the term 'ashes' is often used to signify evanescence, worthlessness, insignificance (Gn 18^{27}, Job 30^{19}). 'Proverbs of ashes' (13^{12}) is Job's equivalent for the modern 'rot.' For the use of ashes in the priestly ritual see RED HEIFER.

ASHHUR.—The 'father' of Tekoa, 1 Ch 2^{24} 4^{5} (AV **Ashur**).

ASHIMA(H).—Deity worshipped by the men of Hamath who were settled in Samaria (2 K 17^{30}). The name is probably to be equated with the deity mentioned in Am 8^{14} (RSV), and related to the first element in Ishumbethel found in an Aramaic papyrus from Elephantine of 419 or 400 B.C.
J. B. P.

ASHKELON.—Modern *Khirbet 'Asqalân*, Greek *Askalon*; a city on the Mediterranean seaboard of Palestine, mentioned in Egyptian texts of the 11th dynasty and in the Amarna correspondence. Rameses II. reduced it *c* 1280 B.C. According to Jg 1^{18} it was taken by the tribe of Judah, but this occupation can have been temporary at best, for it is listed in Jos 13^{3} with the other cities of the Philistine pentapolis as unconquered by Israel. It figures in the Samson story as the place where he procured the thirty festal garments to pay his wager when his riddle was discovered (Jg 14^{19}); it is mentioned in the account of the returning of the Ark (1 S 6^{17}) and in David's dirge over Saul and Jonathan (2 S 1^{20}). It became tributary to Assyria under Tiglath-pileser III. (738 B.C.); an attempt at revolt in Sennacherib's reign was quickly put down, and the rebel king Sidqia carried captive to Assyria (701 B.C.). It was taken and destroyed by the Babylonians under Nebuchadrezzar in December, 604 B.C., having presumably held out against him in hope of aid from Egypt. An Aramaic letter in which a Palestinian king named Adon urgently begs Neco for help against the Babylonians may have come from Ashkelon (although E. Vogt [*VT* Supplements iv, 1957, 87] argues to the contrary). Doom is pronounced on Ashkelon by pre-exilic and post-exilic prophets (Am 1^{8}, Zeph 2^{7}, Jer 25^{20} $47^{5, 7}$, Zec 9^{5}). Here Jonathan Maccabaeus was honourably received (1 Mac 10^{86} 11^{60}). In 104 B.C. it became a free city with authority to strike its own coins and reckon by its own era. It was the birthplace of Herod the Great (74 B.C.) and was greatly embellished by him. It was captured by the Crusaders in 1153, but retaken by the Muslims after the battle of Hattin (1187).

Considerable quantities of 'Philistine' pottery (Early Iron imitations of Mycenaean and Aegean ware) have been found on the site. Sample soundings have revealed a thick layer of ashes from the Late Bronze or Early Iron Age.
R. A. S. M.—**F. F. B.**

ASHKENAZ.—A son of Gomer (q.v.) in the table of the nations, Gn 10^{3}, 1 Ch 1^{6}. This means apparently that the name represents a people akin to the Cimmerians an Indo-European people who made trouble for the Assyrians in and about Armenia in the 7th cent. B.C. In Jer 51^{27} Ashkenaz is coupled with Ararat and Minni. Some connect the name with Akkadian *Ishkuzai*, Old Persian **Skûča*, a tribe akin to the Cimmerians, and with Greek *Skythoi*=Scythians (cf E. Herzfeld, *A New Inscription of Darius from Hamadan*, 1928, p. 4). Others, with less probability, connect it with the Greek *Ascanioi*, or Phrygians. Mediaeval Jews groundlessly connected the name with Germany, and German Jews are known as Ashkenazim.
J. F. McC.—**H. H. R.**

ASHNAH.—Two cities of Judah. **1.** Jos 15^{43}, possibly modern *Idhna*. **2.** Jos 15^{33}, near Zorah; site unknown.

ASHPENAZ.—The chief of Nebuchadnezzar's eunuchs, Dn 1^{3}. The name is perhaps of Persian derivation; it is found on an incantation text from Nippur.

ASHRIEL, 1 Ch 7^{14} (AV).—See ASRIEL.

ASHTAROTH.—This city (plural of *Ashtoreth*, q.v.), originally held by Og, king of Bashan (Dt 1^{4}, Jos 9^{10} 12^{4} $13^{12, 31}$), later captured by the Israelites and by them awarded to the Gershonites (Jos 21^{27} **Be-eshterah,** 'dwelling [or temple] of Ashtoreth'; cf ‖ 1 Ch 6^{56}, which reads *Ashtaroth*), might, without contradicting

Biblical records, be identified with Ashteroth-karnaim (q.v.). However, a statement found in Eusebius' *Onomasticon* favours the view that the names designate two localities. Eusebius relates that there were at his time two villages of the same name, separated by a distance of 9 miles lying between Adara (Edrei) and Abila; viz., (1) Ashtaroth, the ancient city of Og, 6 miles from Abila, and (2) Karnaim Ashtaroth, a village in the corner of Bashan, where Job's village is shown (cf Book of Jubilees, 29^{10}). Eusebius' Karnaim Ashtaroth evidently lay in the corner or angle formed by the rivers *Nahr er-Ruqqâd* and *Sharî'at el-Manâdireh*, in which vicinity tradition places Uz, Job's fatherland. At long. 36° E., lat. 32° 50′ N., on the Bashan plateau, stands *Tell 'Ashtarah*, whose strategical value, as shown by the ruins, was recognized in the Middle Ages. Its base is watered by the *Moyet en-Nebî Ayyûb* (' stream of the prophet Job '). Following this rivulet's course for 2½ miles NNE., passing through the *Ḥammam Ayyûb* (' Job's bath '), is found its source, a spring said to have welled forth when Job in his impatience stamped upon the ground. In the immediate vicinity towards the S., Job's grave is shown. Furthermore, upon the hill, at whose base these two places are situated, lies the village of *Sa'dîyeh* or *Sheikh Sa'd*, whose mosque contains the *Sakhret Ayyûb*, a large basalt boulder against which Job is said to have leaned while receiving his friends. Indeed, ¾ of a mile S. of *Sa'dîyeh*, at *el-Merkez*, another grave (modern) of Job is shown, and a *Deir* (' monastery ') *Ayyûb*, according to tradition built by the Ghassanide Amr I., is known to have existed. Eusebius' Ashtaroth must then have been in the proximity of *Muzeirîb*, 9½ miles S. of *Sa'dîyeh*, and 8 miles NW. of Adara, almost the distance of the *Onomasticon*. Even *Tell Ash'ari*, 4½ miles S. of *Tell 'Ashtarah*, protected on the one side by the Yarmuk, on the second by a chasm, and showing evidence of having been fortified by a triple wall on the third, is admirably situated for a royal stronghold.

None of these modern place-names, with the exception of *Tell 'Ashtarah*, is linguistically related to the ' Ashtaroth and 'Ashteroth-karnaim of the Bible and the *Onomasticon*. The description of 'Ashteroth-karnaim (2 Mac 12^{21f}, cf 1 Mac 5^{43}) as a place hard to besiege and difficult of access because of numerous passes leading to it, in whose territory a temple was situated, is applicable to *Sa'dîyeh* or to *Tell 'Ashtarah* or even to *Tell Ash'ari*, whose double peak at the S. summit is partly responsible for the translation of the name ' Ashtaroth of (near) the double peak.' The similarity of name between *Tell 'Ashtarah* and *'Ashteroth-karnaim*, even though *Tell 'Ashtaroh* does not lie directly between Adara and Abila, and lacks, with the other places, narrow passes, would favour the identification of 'Ashteroth-karnaim with *Tell 'Ashtarah*, and hence, according to the distances of Eusebius, the location of 'Ashtaroth near *Muzeirîb*. However, until the ancient name of *Mazeirîb* is known, and the various sites excavated, a definite determination of the location of these cities, and even of the difference between them, must remain impossible. N. K.

ASHTERATHITE (1 Ch 11^{44}).—An inhabitant of **Ashtaroth** (q.v.).

ASHTEROTH-KARNAIM.—The scene of Chedorlaomer's defeat of the Rephaim, Gn 14^{5}. It is perhaps mentioned in Am 6^{13} (RSV **Karnaim**; AV, RV ' horns '). It is identical with **Carnaim** (q.v.) or **Carnion,** after whose capture in 164 B.C., Judas Maccabaeus destroyed the temple of Atargatis (q.v.), whither the inhabitants had fled for refuge (2 Mac 12^{21f}, cf 1 Mac 5^{43f}). For interpretation of name see ASHTORETH, and for location, ASHTAROTH.

ASHTORETH.—The Hebrew form of the name of a Canaanite goddess Ashtart (Astarte), or Ashtereth. The name is vocalized with the vowels of the word *bōsheth*, ' shame,' after the analogy of Mephi-bosheth (1 S 9^{6}), for Merib-baal (1 Ch 8^{33}). The name first occurs in the plural Ashtaroth in Jg 10^{6}, where it is coupled with Baalim, ' the baals.' In Jg 3^{7} we have in a similar context the form Asheroth, although two MSS and Vulg. have Ashtaroth. In 1 K 11^{5} Ashtoreth is named as the goddess of the Sidonians, worshipped by Solomon. In 1 S 31^{10} we are told that the Philistines put Saul's armour and weapons as spoils of war in the temple of Ashtaroth (probably read Ashtoreth) in Ashkelon, from which it would appear that the non-Semitic Philistines had adopted the cult of the Semitic and Canaanite goddess. The OT gives us no particulars about any special characteristics of this goddess, and it is clear that the plural of the name had become a generic term for all the local Canaanite female deities associated with Canaanite fertility cults. In Jer 7^{18} 44$^{17, 18}$ we are told that the women of Jerusalem, with the connivance of their husbands, had been in the habit of worshipping an unnamed goddess, whom they call ' the queen of heaven '; it is possible that this goddess may have been Astarte, or Ashtoreth.

The Ugaritic texts have now thrown fresh light on the nature of the Canaanite Ashtoreth, and have provided a possible explanation of the confusion in the OT between Ashtoreth and **Asherah** (q.v.). In these texts there is frequent mention of a goddess Athirat (*'aṯrt*), who is the consort of the high god El. She has many titles, among which are ' mistress of the gods ' (*rbt êlm*), and 'Athirat, mistress of the sea ' (*rbt 'aṯrt ym*). She evidently occupied a place in the Ugaritic pantheon corresponding to that of ' the queen of heaven ' mentioned in Jeremiah. There is also another female deity mentioned in the Keret text whose name is Ashtoreth (*'aṯtrt*), and who appears to be the consort of Baal; she is characterized by the epithet Ashtoreth-name-of-Baal (*'aṯtrt-šm-b'l*), ' a title designed to describe her as a manifestation of Baal whose consort she has become ' (G. R. Driver, *Canaanite Myths and Legends*, p. 5, n. 2). It seems clear that in the Ugaritic texts the two names designate two different female deities. There is the same philological difference between the names in Ugaritic as there is in Hebrew, but in the latter the names have become confused.

In the Tell el-Amarna Letters we have the name Abd-ashirta, giving further evidence for the existence of the cult of Ashtoreth in Canaan in the 14th cent. B.C. The OT place-names Ashteroth-karnaim (Gn 14^{5}), and Ashtaroth (Dt 1^{4}) in Bashan, have the same significance. In the Mesha Stele it is recorded that the king of Moab dedicated his prisoners to Ashtar-Chemosh, suggesting that in Moab Ashtart was worshipped as the consort of Chemosh. In a Phoenician inscription we have also the title *'štrt-šm-b'l* (Cooke, NSI 5 : 8), corresponding to the title already mentioned as occurring in the Ugaritic texts.

Behind these various forms of the Semitic female deity lies the archetypal figure of the Babylonian and Assyrian goddess Ishtar who occupies so large a place in Sumerian and Babylonian mythology. Her Sumerian name was Innina, and at an early date she ousted Anu's legitimate consort, the colourless figure Antu, from her place, and became herself the consort of the high god Anu. She gradually absorbed into herself the attributes of most of the other female deities, and was known as ' the goddess ' *par excellence*, so much so that the plural *ishtarâti* came to be a generic term for all the goddesses, just as in the OT ' the ashtoreths ' became a generic term for foreign goddesses. The influence of the Ishtar cult made itself felt indirectly on the religion of Israel through that aspect of the cult in which Ishtar was worshipped as the goddess of love and procreation. As such the Canaanite *ḳ^{e}dēshôth*, or hierodules, were the priestesses of Ashtoreth, and the Pentateuchal legislation directed against this institution shows that it existed among the early Israelite settlers in Canaan. The other aspect of Ishtar, prominent in Assyria, as goddess of war, does not seem to have influenced Canaanite religion.

Asherah is mentioned as a goddess in 1 K 18^{19} and

elsewhere, and as we have already seen, occurs in Jg 3[7] in the plural as a generic term; but it is unlikely that in the OT she is to be regarded as a different goddess from Ashtoreth. S. H. He.

ASHUR, 1 Ch 2[24] 4[5] (AV).—See Ashhur.

ASHURBANIPAL.—Son and successor of Esarhaddon on the throne of Assyria, 668–626 B.C. He is usually identified with Osnappar, Ezr 4[10] (AV 'Asnapper'). He included Manasseh of Judah among his tributaries, and kept an Assyrian garrison at Gezer. See Assyria, Osnappar.

ASHURITES.—One of the tribes over whom Ishbosheth ruled, 2 S 2[9]. Neither the Assyrians (*Asshur*) nor the Arabian tribe of *Asshurim* (Gn 25[3]) can be intended. The Pesh. and Vulg. read 'the Geshurites' (see Geshur), whose territory bordered on Gilead; but against this is the fact that Geshur was an independent kingdom at this time (cf 2 S 3[3] 13[27]). Many editors therefore read *hā-'Ashērî*=' the Asherites,' *i.e.* the tribe of Asher (cf Jg 1[32]).

ASHVATH.—An Asherite, 1 Ch 7[33].

ASIA.—A geographical term of uncertain origin, used quite broadly by early Greek writers, and later usually synonymous with the Persian or Seleucid empires. In the Books of the Maccabees we still find this usage. The Romans formed a province called Asia, when they took over the Kingdom of Pergamum in 133 B.C. The regions of Mysia, Lydia, and Caria were included in it, and western Phrygia was subsequently added. In Ac 2[9–10] Phrygia receives separate mention, and so it seems probable that in this book Asia has the narrower meaning (Ac 16[6f] 19[10, 22, 26f] 20[4, 16, 18] 21[27] 24[18] 27[2]). Paul refers to the Roman province of his day when he uses the term (Ro 16[5], 1 Co 16[19], 2 Co 1[8]). See also 2 Ti 1[15], 1 P 1[1], Rev 1[4]. Asia was one of the richest provinces of the empire and was governed by the Senate's appointees—a proconsul with three legati. It was much exploited until a new and better era of peaceful development began in the time of Augustus (31 B.C.). In 24 B.C. earthquakes destroyed Laodicea and Thyatira, Chios, and Tralles; in A.D. 17 twelve cities were similarly destroyed, including Sardis and Philadelphia. A provincial assembly was founded to nurture the new cult of emperor-worship (q.v.). Domitian, demanding worship of himself while yet alive, created a perilous situation for the Christians of Asia. The letters to the seven churches in Rev 1–3 mention leading cities, of which Ephesus, Smyrna and Pergamum were the largest. E. G. K.

ASIARCH.—The form of the word is parallel with *Lyciarch, Bithyniarch*, etc., but the signification is by no means certain. The title of Asiarch could be held in conjunction with any civil office, and with the high priesthood of a particular city, but the high priest of Asia and the Asiarch were probably not identical; for there was only one high priest of Asia at a time, but there were a number of Asiarchs, as Ac 19[31] shows, even in one city. The honour lasted one year, but re-election was possible. The Asiarchs constituted the *Koinon* of the province which was patterned after the Greek amphictyonies. It was a religious organization with certain political tasks, especially the regulation of the cult of 'Roma' and the Emperor in the form of a yearly festival and public games. A. So.—**J. C. B.**

ASIBIAS (1 Es 9[26]).—One of the sons of Phoros or Parosh who agreed to put away his 'strange' wife; answering to **Malchijah** (2°) in Ezr 10[25]. See Malchijah, **5.**

ASIEL.—**1.** Great-grandfather of Jehu, a Simeonite 'prince,' 1 Ch 4[35]. **2.** One of five scribes employed by Ezra to transcribe the Law, 2 Es 14[24]. **3.** An ancestor of Tobit, To 1[1] (AV **Asael**).

ASIPHA, 1 Es 5[29] (AV, RV).—See Hasupha.

ASKALON.—The form of the name **Ashkelon** found in RSV in 1 Mac 10[86] 11[60] 12[33] (AV, RV **Ascalon**).

ASKELON.—The form of the name **Ashkelon** found in AV in Jg 1[18], 1 S 6[17], 2 S 1[20] (RV, RSV **Ashkelon**).

ASMODAEUS is the evil demon who afflicts Sarah, in the book of Tobit (3[17]), and has to be bound by an angel. The Tobit story has Median connexions and it is hardly possible to explain *Ashmedai* otherwise than as a reflection of the Iranian demon of wrath *Aēshmā daēva*, who in the Avesta is the foe of the righteous and must be stayed, while in the Pahlavi texts he is the sower of discord among men. In later Jewish legend he became the king of all *shēdhîm*, was the demon who took Solomon's place upon his throne, and who daily mounts to the heavens to listen for anything he may use to deceive men. A. J.

ASNAH.—The head of a family of Nethinim (q.v.), which returned with Zerubbabel, Ezr 2[50], 1 Es 5[31] (AV, RV **Asana**).

ASNAPPER, Ezr 4[10] (AV).—See Osnappar.

ASOM, 1 Es 9[33] (AV, RV).—See Hashum, **1.**

ASP.—See Serpent.

ASPALATHUS (Sir 24[15]).—The name of an aromatic plant associated with cinnamon in the passage cited, but impossible to identify. It is probable that there were two or more plants, and more than one vegetable product, known by this name. RSV reads 'camel's thorn.'

ASPATHA.—Third son of Haman, put to death by the Jews, Est 9[7].

ASPHALT.—See Bitumen.

ASPHAR (1 Mac 9[33]).—A pool in the desert of Tekoa, or Jeshimon, where Jonathan and Simon the Maccabees encamped. The site is not known with certainty, although it may plausibly be identified with the modern *Bîr Selhûb*, a reservoir 6 miles WSW. of Engedi.

ASPHARASUS, 1 Es 5[8] (AV, RV).—See Mispar.

ASRIEL.—A Manassite, Jos 17[2], Nu 26[31], 1 Ch 7[14] (AV **Ashriel**). The patronymic **Asrielite** occurs in Nu 26[31].

ASS (*ḥamôr*); 'she-ass,' *'āthôn* (Gr. *onos* of both sexes); 'young ass' or 'colt,' *'ayir* (Gr. *pōlos*); 'wild ass,' *pere'* and *'ārôdh*).—The ass (Arabic *ḥimâr*) is the general utility animal in the Bible's domestic scene, as it was until, in modern times, some of its tasks have been taken over by mechanized forms of transport and of agricultural implements. The ass is used for riding (Nu 22[22], Jg 1[14], 2 S 17[23] 19[26], etc.) by both men and women (Jos 15[18]); it was also the beast of burden for carrying corn (Gn 42[26]), firewood (Gn 22[3]), provisions (1 S 16[20] 25[18]), and harvest produce (Neh 13[15]). Riding a tawny ass (RV 'white') is a mark of wealth (Jg 5[10]). The she-ass (Arabic *'atân*) was preferred (Nu 22[21–33], 1 S 9[3], 2 K 4[22–24], 1 Ch 27[30]) because quieter and more easily left tied up. The common ass (*ḥamôr*) is brown, sometimes almost black or grey. The male ass, uncontrollable at times, is noted for its bray on sight of the female ass. The idea of the stupidity of the ass is skilfully used in the Balaam story (Nu 22[21ff]; cf Job 11[12]). Skeletons of asses were a not uncommon sight by the side of the highroad and the jawbone, so easily found (Jg 15[15]), proved a good weapon (Jg 15[16], where there is a play on the word 'ass' [*ḥamôr*] and 'heap' [*ḥamôr*]). Although the ass was forbidden food to the Jews, we read (2 K 6[25]) 'an ass's head was sold for eighty shekels of silver' in the severe famine in beseiged Samaria. Dt 22[10] forbade ploughing 'with an ox and an ass together,' a custom practised by modern *fellahin*.

The young ass (Is 30[6, 24] RV) or colt (Job 11[12], Zec 9[9], Lk 19[33], etc.), the Arabic *jaḥsh*, is referred to several times. Little colts of very tender age trot beside their mothers, and soon have small burdens put on them. They should not be regularly ridden for three years. The young asses in the Bible are all apparently old enough for riding or burden-bearing.

Wild asses are not to-day found in Palestine, though, it is said, plentiful in the deserts to the East (Job 24[5]), where they roam in herds and run with extraordinary fleetness (Job 39[5]). The tame ass likewise can cover ground rapidly at a pace more comfortable than that of an ordinary horse ; it is also very sure-footed. Ishmael is compared in his wildness and freedom to a wild ass (Gn 16[12]), while Issachar is a wild ass subdued (49[14, 15]).

The importance of the ass is noted in the Decalogue (Ex 20[17]) ; a neighbour's ass is not to be coveted. An interesting phrase has been noted in the Mari tablets, where ' to kill an ass ' seems to mean to make a peace treaty. E. W. G. M.—**R. A. B.**

ASSABIAS, 1 Es 1[9] (AV).—See Hashabiah, **6.**

ASSALIMOTH, 1 Es 8[36] (AV).—See Shelomith, **5.**

ASSAMIAS, 1 Es 8[54] (RV).—See Hashabiah, **8.**

ASSANIAS, 1 Es 8[54] (AV).—See Hashabiah, **8.**

ASSAPHIOTH, 1 Es 5[33] (RV).—See Hassophereth.

ASSASSINS, THE.—In the time of Felix a band of robbers so named disturbed Judaea. They are mentioned in Ac 21[38] (*sicarii*, AV ' murderers '). Josephus says that at Felix's suggestion they murdered Jonathan son of Ananus, the high priest (*Ant.* xx. viii. 5 [163 f]). They took a leading part in the Jewish War. See article Egyptian [The]. A. J. M.

ASSEMBLY.—See Congregation.

ASSHUR.—See Assyria.

ASSHURIM.—The Asshurim, Letushim, and Leummim were Arabian tribes, supposed to be descended from Abraham and Keturah through Dedan, Gn 25[3] (also in Vulg. in 1 Ch 1[32]) ; possibly the *A'shur* mentioned on Minaean inscriptions.

ASSIDEANS, 1 Mac 2[42] (AV).—See Hasidaeans.

ASSIR.—**1.** A son of Korah, Ex 6[24], 1 Ch 6[22]. **2.** A son of Ebiasaph, 1 Ch 6[23, 37]. **3.** A son of Jeconiah, 1 Ch 3[17] (AV, RVm ; RV, RSV ' the captive ').

ASSOS.—A town over half a mile from the Gulf of Adramyttium (in Mysia, province of Asia), in a splendid position on a hill about 770 feet high at its highest point. The fortifications are amongst the most excellent and best preserved of their kind, the greater part of them dating from the 4th cent. B.C. It passed through various hands before it was from 334–241 B.C. under Alexander the Great and his successors, and from 241–133 B.C. under the Pergamene dynasty. At the last date it became Roman (see Asia). It was the birth-place of the Stoic Cleanthes. St. Paul went from Troas to Assos by the land-route on his last visit to Asia (Ac 20[13f]). A. So.—**E. G. K.**

ASSUMPTION OF MOSES.—See Pseudepigrapha, **4.**

ASSUR, 1 Es 5[31] (AV).—See Asur.

ASSURANCE.—The assurance which the NT writers affirm in their declaration of the Gospel refers to the possibility of man's absolute trust in God's forgiveness, which is the ground of his salvation. Thus assurance refers both to the signs which God himself gives of His power and mercy and to the knowledge and trust with which the believer receives the offer of salvation. When Paul declares at Athens (Ac 17[31]) that God has appointed Christ to judge the world, and has ' given assurance ' (*pistin*) of this to all men by raising Him from the dead, he points to God's act as the ground for confidence in the Gospel. The assurance which the believer experiences is his personal reception of this offer of salvation and his discovery of a released and joyful confidence in the Divine mercy and power. In 2 Ti 3[14], Timothy's assurance (' confident belief '—cf RSV) in the things he has learned of the Gospel is connected with the authority of the person from whom he has learned them ; but the confidence is his own personal response to the Gospel. Thus assurance is given by God but it implies a new state of the believer, as in the OT, Is 32[17], where assurance (AV and RSV) is portrayed as the effect of the righteousness which the Spirit will pour out upon the world. In the NT assurance (*plērophoria*) is an accompaniment and result of confrontation with the Gospel. There is a full assurance of understanding (Col 2[2]), a full assurance of faith (He 10[22] ; cf 2 Ti 1[12]) and a full assurance of hope (He 6[11]). In He 11[1] faith is itself spoken of as the ground or assurance (*hypostasis*) of hope (AV ' substance,' RSV ' assurance '). The Johannine letters speak of deeds of love as constituting a way to the reassurance of the heart in the midst of its self-condemnation (1 Jn 3[19]).

It is this relationship between the grace of God which comes to man and his act of laying hold upon grace which has given rise to the far-reaching discussion of ' assurance ' in the history of the church. Different views have been taken on the question of whether the assurance to which faith testifies can be directly confirmed in the experience of the believer. Many theologians have asserted that while there is an objective and unshakeable ground of assurance in the message of salvation, this must not be made dependent upon the moral, intellectual, and emotional state of the person, for experience can never of itself provide a complete and unthreatened security. Yet the discovery that God is gracious and merciful does create within the person a release from self-centredness and an outgoing confidence in God which does not require subjective proofs of worthiness. Thus what the NT speaks of as assurance is a reality in Christian experience ; but it involves the profound mystery of man's dependence upon God even for the perfecting of his faith in Him. D. D. W.

ASSYRIA AND BABYLONIA.—I. Assyria.—**1. Natural features and Civilization.**—Geographically speaking, Assyria was a small district bounded by the Tigris valley on the W., the mountains of Armenia and Kurdistan on the N. and E., and the Lower Zab on the S., but historically its dominion gradually extended to include the whole of the Fertile Crescent from the Persian Gulf to the Egyptian border, with parts of Asia Minor and Egypt. The land took its name from Asshur, its capital from the earliest times to the 7th cent. B.C., a city on the W. bank of the Tigris, about midway between the Upper and the Lower Zab. For the most part hilly, with well watered valleys and a wide plain along the Tigris, Assyria was fertile and populous. Of the chief cities, Calah, near the mouth of the Upper Zab, and Nineveh, further N., lay in the Tigris valley. Dur-Sharrukin (modern *Khorsabad*) was NE. of Nineveh. In the E. of the country lay Arbela.

The climate was temperate. The slopes of the hills were well wooded with oak, plane, and pine ; the plains and valleys produced figs, olives, and vines. Wheat, barley, and millet were cultivated. In the days of the Empire the orchards were stocked with trees, among which have been recognized date palms, orange, lemon, pomegranate, apricot, mulberry, and other fruits. A great variety of vegetables were grown in the gardens, including beans, peas, cucumbers, onions, lentils. The hills furnished plenty of excellent building stone, the soft alabaster specially lent itself to the decoration of halls with sculptures in low relief, while fine marbles, hard limestone, conglomerate and basalt were worked into stone vessels, pillars, altars, etc. Iron, lead, and copper were obtainable in the mountains near. The lion and wild ox, the boar, deer, gazelle, goat, and hare were hunted. The wild ass, mountain sheep, bear, fox, jackal, and many other less easily recognized animals are named. The eagle, bustard, crane, stork, wild goose, various ducks, partridge, plover, the dove, raven, swallow, are named, besides many other birds. Fish were plentiful. The Assyrians had domesticated oxen, asses, sheep, goats, and dogs. Camels and horses were introduced from abroad.

The Assyrians belonged largely to the North Semitic group, being closely akin to the Aramaeans, Phoenicians, and Hebrews, but contained a large non-Semitic and non-Indo-European element akin to modern Caucasian peoples. Assyria early came under the predominating influence of Babylonia. The Assyrians of historic times were more robust, warlike, ' fierce ' (Is 33[19]), than the mild, industrial Babylonians. This may have been due partly to the influence of climate and incessant warfare ; but it also indicates the difference in race. The culture

ASSYRIA AND BABYLONIA

and religion of Assyria were essentially Babylonian, save for the predominance of the national god Ashur. The king was a despot at home, general of the army abroad, and he rarely missed an annual expedition to exact tribute or plunder some State. The whole organization of the State was essentially military. The literature was largely borrowed from Babylonia, and to the library of the last great king, Ashurbanipal, we owe most of the Babylonian classics. The Assyrians were historians more than the Babylonians, and they invented a chronology which is the basis of all dating for Western Asia. They were a predatory race, and amassed the spoils of all Mesopotamia in their treasure-houses, but they at least learned to value what they had stolen. The enormous influx of manufactured articles from abroad and the military demands prevented a genuinely native industrial development, but the Assyrians made splendid use of foreign talent. In later times, the land became peopled by captives, while the drain upon the Assyrian army to conquer, garrison, colonize, and hold down the vast Empire probably robbed the country of resisting power.

2. Chronology.—(*a*) *Eponym lists.*—The Assyrians named each year after a particular official, calling it his *limmu* or eponymy. Originally he was selected by lot but later a fixed order was followed, namely, the king, the Tartan (generalissimo), the chief of the levy, various other officials, then the governors of the provincial cities. As the empire extended, the governors of such distant places as Carchemish, Razappa, Kummuh, and even Samaria became eponyms. Surviving lists of these officials in their actual order of succession, known as the Eponym lists, are complete from 892–668 B.C. and they can be restored for some earlier periods and down to 648 B.C.

(*b*) *King lists.*—Assyrian king lists give the names of the rulers of Assyria, with in most cases their father's name and the length of their reign, from about 1900 B.C. to the fall of Assyria. There are however, small errors and mutual divergencies in the lists. Babylonian dynastic lists classify under their city names the rulers of Babylonian cities back to prehistoric times, stating the number of kings in each dynasty, its duration in years, the names of the kings in chronological order and the length of each reign. Large sections of the lists, however, are defective. Errors and inconsistencies also occur and for the earliest dynasties the reigns are impossibly long. No indication, moreover, is given that some dynasties overlap. Some of the early names appear in Babylonian mythology as gods and some kings are omitted whose actual contemporary records have survived. The general reliability of the lists to the middle of the 3rd millennium is, however, confirmed by extant historical inscriptions in which a king mentions his father, grandfather and other ancestors.

(*c*) *Synchronistic lists.*—Synchronisms can sometimes be established between Assyrian and Babylonian kings through the mention by one of another in his inscriptions. There are also a fragmentary synchronistic history and some synchronistic king lists and chronicles from both countries which are particularly useful between the 11th and 9th cent. In some cases, Babylonian dynasties can be synchronized as far back as the middle of the 3rd millennium by royal and other inscriptions.

(*d*) *Chronological statements.*—Royal inscriptions sometimes cite the number of years since an earlier king's reign and although some of these figures are unreliable others accord with information from other sources. Thus Shalmaneser I. states that Erishum built the temple of Ashur in Asshur which Shamshi-Adad rebuilt 159 years later but which was destroyed 580 years later by a fire and built afresh by him. Esarhaddon also states that the temple was built by Erishum, restored by Shamshi-Adad and again by Shalmaneser 434 years later and again by himself. Sennacherib's Bavian inscription states that he recovered the gods of Ekallate which had been carried away by Marduk-nādin-ahhē, king of Akkad, in the days of Tiglath-pileser 418 years before. This dates both Marduk-nādin-ahhē and Tiglath-pileser I. at about 1107. Tiglath-pileser tells us that he rebuilt the temple of Ashur and Adad which had been pulled down by his great-grandfather, Ashur-dān, sixty years before and had then stood 641 years since its foundation by Shamshi-Adad, son of Ishme-Dagān. This puts Shamshi-Adad about 1810 (rather early ?) and Ashur-dān about 1170. Nabonidus states that he restored a temple in Sippar which had not been restored since Shagarakti-Shuriash ; this puts that king about 1350 (a little too early). It is evident that all such dates are vague.

(*e*) *Year-names.*—From as early as the dynasty of Akkad in the middle of the 3rd millennium various cities of Babylonia gave each year an individual designation which usually included the king's name. Thus the names of the first four years of Hammurabi are (1) ' the year in which Hammurabi became king ' ; (2) ' the year in which Hammurabi the king established justice in the land ' ; (3) ' the year in which Hammurabi the king established the throne for the main dais of Nanna in Babylon ' ; (4) ' the year in which the wall of the holy precinct was built.' The date-formula was fixed early in the year and was circulated to the principal districts. Until a new formula was fixed, the year was dated in terms of the preceding year as ' the year after.' Thus the third year of Hammurabi would be called ' the year after that in which Hammurabi the king established justice in the land.' A record of these dates was kept and long lists of year-names has been preserved, each recording some event, usually domestic, religious or military. Other year-names have been recovered from legal documents. The kings of Larsa developed an era in which the years were called the first, second, etc., up to the thirtieth, ' after the capture of Isin.' The Kassite dynasty introduced the method of dating according to the regnal year of the reigning king. If a king died in the twentieth year of his reign he was said to have reigned twenty years, the remainder of the year being described as the ' accession year ' of his successor, and his own ' first year ' began on the 1st Nisan after his accession. Thus over a long series of years the sum of the regnal years is accurately the duration in years except for a margin at the beginning and end ; it is exact to a year.

(*f*) *Astronomical data.*—A series of astrological tablets gives the dates of the rising and setting of the planet Venus for the twenty-one years of the reign of Ammi-zaduga of Babylon, so that this king's reign can be definitely located in one of a few definite periods, although there are unfortunately some slight divergences between different copies of the tablets.

(*g*) *The Canon of Ptolemy*, an Egyptian document of the second Christian century, begins with Nabonassar, king of Babylonia, and gives the names and regnal years of all the Babylonian kings down to Nabonidus, then the Achaemenids to Alexander the Great, the Ptolemies and Romans, so connecting with well-known dates ; it also mentions three Assyrian kings and can thus be coordinated with Assyrian history. Its accuracy is corroborated by the mention in the Assyrian eponym canon of a total solar eclipse in the ninth year of Ashur-dān which can be proved to be 763 B.C. The use of the Assyrian *limmu* lists enables Assyrian dates to be fixed back to 912 B.C. and before that date the Assyrian king lists, in so far as they are reliable, give a chronological framework back to about 1750 B.C. A possible margin of error of about fifty years must be allowed, however, throughout the 2nd millennium. The fragmentary nature of the Babylonian king lists renders it impossible at the present time to date Babylonian kings exactly before 747 B.C., since the exact duration of many of the reigns is unknown and established synchronisms with Assyrian kings are few. The contemporaneous deaths of Adad-shum-nazir of Babylonia and Enlil-kudurra-uzur of Assyria (*c* 1206 B.C.) enable, however, exact provisional dates to be assigned to a number of Babylonian kings before and after that date since the Babylonian king lists for that period are intact. Since, however, they are not entirely in accord at this point with the evidence of the Assyrian lists, some adjustment has to be made. For the earlier part of the 2nd millennium, the known synchronism of Hammurabi with Shamsi-adad I. is very important, but there is divergence among scholars about the date of Hammurabi. The dates usually suggested for his accession are 1792, or 1728, or 1704 B.C., but some scholars would date it as early as 1848 B.C., and various intermediate datings have also been proposed. For earlier dates back to the dynasty of Akkad (c 2300 B.C.) the margin of error is scarcely larger.

The following list of dates is based largely on the views of Cornelius who adopts 1728 B.C. as the date for Hammurabi's accession and accepts the tradition of the Assyrian king lists as substantially trustworthy. He assigns, however, sixteen years to the reign of Mutakkil-Nusku of Assyria, thus raising his dates for Assyrian

kings before 1131 B.C. about twenty years higher than some would favour. The first Elamite dynasty, 1163–1156 B.C., is not included in any Babylonian king list but there seem to be sound reasons for assuming it. In order to harmonize the Babylonian with the Assyrian king lists, Adad-shum-iddin is here placed after Adad-shum-nazir although there is perhaps stronger evidence for putting him immediately before him. Regnal years of Babylonian kings prior to 747 B.C. are, when known, entered in brackets after the royal name ; where such evidence is lacking no attempt at exact dating has been made but the names are arranged in chronological order. Synchronisms (prior to 747 B.C.) validated by historical inscriptions which mention two kings as contemporaries are indicated by = with the addition, where appropriate, of square brackets. ' S ' and ' B ' represent respectively ' son of ' and ' brother of ' the preceding king.

B.C.	KINGS OF BABYLONIA.		KINGS OF ASSYRIA.	B.C.
	FIRST DYNASTY OF BABYLON.			
1830	Sumu-abum (14)		Puzur-Ashur I.	c 1830
			Shallim-ahhē, S	
			Ilu-shūma, S	
1816	Sumu-la-ilum (36)		Erishum I. S	c 1817
			Ikunum, S	
1780	Zabum, S (14)		Sharru-kīn (Sargon) I. S	
1766	Apil-Sîn, S (18)		Puzur-Ashur II. S	
			Narām-Sîn, S	
1748	Sîn-muballit, S (20)		Erishum II. S	
1728	Hammu-rabi, S (43)	=	Shamshi-Adad I.	1750
			Ishme-Dagān I. S	1717
			?	1697
1686	Samsu-ilūna, S (38)		Puzur-Sîn	1697
			Ashur-dugul	1677
			Ashur-apla-īdi	1676
			Nāzir-Sîn	1675
			Sîn-nāmir	1674
			Ipki-Ishtar	1673
			Adad-zalulu	1672
			Adasi	1671
			Bēlu-bani	1671
			Libāya, S or B	1660
1648	Abi-eshuh, S (28)		Sharma-Adad I. S or B	1643
			Iptar-Sîn, S or B	1631
1620	Ammi-ditāna, S (37)		Bazāya	1619
			Lullāya	1591
1583	Ammi-zadūga, S (21 ?)		Kidin-Ninua	1585
			Sharma-Adad II. S or B	1571
1562	Samsu-ditāna, S (31 ?)		Erishum III. B	1568
			Shamshi-Adad II. S or B	1555
			Ishme-Dagān II. S	1549
	KASSITE DYNASTY.			
c 1530	Agum II.		Shamshi-Adad III. S	1533
			Ashur-nirāri I. B	1517
	Burna-Buriash I.	=	Puzur-Ashur III. S	1491
	Kashtiliash II. S		Enlil-nāzir I. S	1478
			Nūr-ili, S or B	1465
	Ulam-Buriash, B		Ashur-shadūni, S or B	1453
			Ashur-rabi I.	1452
			Ashur-nādin-ahhē I. S or B	1444
	Agum III.		Enlilnāzir II. B (?)	1444
			Ashur-nirāri II. B	1438
	Kara-Indash II.	=	Ashur-bēl-nishēshu, S	1431
	Kadashman-Harbe I. S		Ashur-rīm-nishēshu, B	1422
	Kurigalzu I.		Ashur-nādin-ahhē II. S or B	1414
			Erība-Adad I. B	1404
c 1360	Burna-Buriash II. (25)	=	Ashur-uballit I. S	1377
	Kadashman-Harbe II.			
1341	Nazibugash			
1341	Kurigalzu II. (23)			
1318	Nazi-Maruttash, S (26)	=	Enlil-nirāri, S	1341
1292	Kadashman-Turgu, S (17)		Arik-dēn-ili, S	1331
1275	Kadashman-Enlil II. S (6)	=	Adad-nirāri I. S	1319
1269	Kudur-Enlil II. S (9)		Shulmānu-asharid (Shalmaneser) I. S	1287
1260	Shagarakti-Shuriash, S (13)			

	Kassite Dynasty—*contd.*		Kings of Assyria—*contd.*	
1247	Kashtiliash III. S (8)	=	Tukulti-Ninurta I. S	1257
1239	Enlil-nādin-shumi (1½)		Ashur-nādin-apli, S	1220
1238	Kadashman-Harbe III. (1½)		Ashur-nirāri III.	1217
1236	Adad-shum-nāzir (30)	=	Enlil-kudurra-uzur	1211
1206	Adad-shum-iddin (6)		Ninurta-apil-ēkur	1206
1199	Melishipak (15)			
1183	Marduk-apla-iddin (Merodach-baladan) I. (13)			
1169	Zabāba-shum-iddin (1)	=	Ashur-dān I. S	1193
1167	Enlil-nādin-ahhē (3)			
	First Elamite Dynasty.			
1163	Shutruk-Nahhunte (or Kutir-Nahhunte)			
	Dynasty of Isin (Pa-she).			
1156	Marduk-kabit-ahhēshu (18)	=	Ninurta-tukulti-Asshur, S	1147
1137	Itti-Marduk-balātu (8)		Mutakkil-Nusku, B	1147
1128	Ninurta-nādin-shumi (6)	=	Ashur-rēsha-īshi I. S	1131
1121	Nabu-kudurra-uzur (Nebuchadrezzar) I. (22) S			
1098	Enlil-nādin-apli (4) S	=	Tukulti-apil-esharra (Tiglath-pileser) I. S	1113
1091	Marduk-nādin-ahhē (18)		Asharid-apil-ēkur, S	1074
1073	Marduk-shāpik-zēri (13)	=	Ashur-bēl-kāla, S	1072
1060	Adad-apla-iddin (22)		Erība-Adad II. S	1054
			Shamshi-Adad IV.	1052
1037	Marduk-ahhē-erība (1½)		Ashur-nāzir-apli (Ashurnazirpal) I. S	1048
1034	Marduk-zēr-[ibni (?)] (12)		Shulmānu-asharid (Shalmaneser) II. S	1029
1021	Nabu-shum-lībur (8)		Ashur-nirāri IV. S	1017
	Maritime Dynasty.			
1012	Shimbar-Shipak (18)		Ashur-rabi II.	1011
993	Ea-mukīn-shumi (5/12)			
991	Kashshu-nādin-ahhē (3)			
	Dynasty of Shashi (Bazu).			
987	Eulmash-shākin-shumi (17)			
969	Ninurta-kudurra-uzur I. (3)		Ashur-rēsha-īshi II. S	970
965	Shiriktu-Shukamūna (¼)			
	Second Elamite Dynasty.			
964	Marbīti-apla-uzur (6)		Tukulti-apil-esharra (Tiglath-pileser) II.	965
	Dynasty 'H.'			
957	Nabu-mukīn-apli (36)			
920	Ninurta-kudurra-uzur II. S		Ashur-dān II. S	933
	Marbīti-aha-iddin, B			
	Shamash-mudammik	=	Adad-nirāri II.	910
	Nabu-shum-ukīn I. S		Tukulti-Ninurta II. S	889
	Nabu-apla-iddin, S	=	Ashur-nāzir-apli (Ashurnazirpal) II. S	883
	Marduk-zākir-shumi I. S		Shulmānu-asharid (Shalmaneser) III. S	858
	Marduk-balatsu-ikbi, S	=	Shamshi-Adad V. S	823
	Bau-aha-iddin	=	Adad-nirāri III. S	810
	Nabu-mukīn-zēri			
	Marduk-bēl-zēri			
	Marduk-apla-uzur		Shulmānu-asharid (Shalmaneser) IV. S	782
	?			
	?			
	?			
	Erība-Marduk		Ashur-dān III. B	772
	Marduk-apla-iddin I.			
	Nabu-shum-ishkun, S		Ashur-nirāri V. B	754
747	Nabu-nāzir (Nabonassar)		Tukulti-apil-esharra (Tiglath-pileser) III. B (?)	744
733	Nabu-nādin-zēri, S			
732	Nabu-shum-ukīn II.			
	Dynasty 'J.' (Period of Assyrian domination.)			
731	Ukīn-zēra (Mukīn-zēri)			
728	Pulu (Tiglath-pileser III.)			
726	Ululāia (Shalmaneser V.), S		Shulmānu-asharid (Shalmaneser) V. S	726
721	Marduk-apla-iddin (Merodach-baladan) II.		Sharru-kīn (Sargon) II. B (?)	721
709	Sharru-kīn (Sargon) II.			
704	Sīn-ahhē-erība (Sennacherib), S		Sīn-ahhē-erība (Sennacherib), S	704
703	Marduk-zākir-shumi II.			
703	Marduk-apla-iddin (Merodach-baladan) II. (*again*)			
702	Bēl-ibni			

DYNASTY 'J'—*contd.*

699	Ashur-nādin-shumi
693	Nergal-ushēzib
691	Mushēzib-Marduk
687	Sīn-ahhē-erība (Sennacherib) (*again*)
680	Ashur-aha-iddina (Esar-haddon), S
668	Shamash-shum-ukīn, S
648	Kandalānu

CHALDAEAN DYNASTY.

626	Nabu-apla-uzur (Nabopolassar)
605	Nabu-kudurra-uzur (Nebuchadrezzar) II. S
561	Amēl-Marduk (Evil-Merodach), S
560	Nergal-sharra-uzur (Nergal-sharezer)
556	Labāshi-Marduk, S
555	Nabu-nāid (Nabonidus)
539	*End of Babylonian kingdom*

ASSYRIA AND BABYLONIA

KINGS OF ASSYRIA—*contd.*

Ashur-aha-iddina (Esar-haddon), S	680
Ashur-bān-apli (Ashurbanipal), S	668
(Sīn-sharra-ishkun?), S	(627?)
Ashur-ētil-ilāni, B	*c* 626
(Sīn-shum-līshir?)	?
Ashur-uballit II.	612 (?)
End of Assyrian kingdom	606

3. History. (*a*) *Sources.*—Excavations have recovered a great mass of cuneiform documents from Assyria and Babylonia which can be used for the reconstruction of the history. Besides this primary source of information, chiefly contemporaneous with the events it records, there are scattered incidental notices in the historical and prophetical books of the OT giving an important external view and some records in the Greek and Latin classics mostly too late and uncritical to be of direct value.

The bulk of the history is derived from the inscriptions of the kings themselves. Here there is an often remarked difference between Assyrian and Babylonian usage. The former are usually very full concerning the wars of conquest, the latter almost entirely concerned with temple buildings or domestic affairs, such as palaces, walls, canals, etc. Many Assyrian kings arrange their campaigns in chronological order, forming what are called Annals. Others are content to sum up their conquests in a list of lands subdued. We rarely have anything like Annals from Babylonia.

The value to be attached to these inscriptions is very various. They are contemporary, and for geography invaluable. A king would hardly boast of conquering a country which did not exist. The historical value is more open to question. A 'conquest' meant little more than a raid successful in exacting tribute. The Assyrians, however, gradually learnt to consolidate their conquests. They planted colonies of Assyrian people, endowing them with conquered lands. They transplanted the people of a conquered State to some other part of the Empire, allotting them lands and houses, vineyards and gardens, even cattle, and so endeavoured to destroy national spirit and produce a blended population of one language and one civilization. The weakness of the plan lay in the heavy taxation which prevented loyal attachment. The population of the Empire had no objection to the substitution of one master for another. The demands on the subject States for men and supplies for the incessant wars weakened all without attaching any. The population of Assyria proper was insufficient to officer and garrison so large an empire, and every change of monarch was the signal for rebellion in all outlying parts. A new dynasty usually had to reconquer most of the Empire. Civil war occurred several times, and always led to great weakness, finally rendering the Empire an easy prey to the invader.

(*b*) *Earliest period.*—Neolithic settlements from the 5th or 4th millennium have been excavated at Nineveh and elsewhere in Assyria. Later cultures, using copper, had affinities, sometimes close, with those of Iran and Babylonia. Probably as early as the beginning of the 3rd millennium, Asshur was the most important town in the area and it continued to be so, with few interruptions, to the end of Assyrian history. Late king lists preserve the names of its early rulers, who probably owed allegiance to successive Babylonian city-states, from at least as early as the dynasty of Akkad (*c* 2300 B.C.) and its buildings and associated objects show from that time onwards Sumerian cultural influence. Most of the early rulers have Semitic, though not Akkadian, names but some are non-Semitic and the population probably already included the large Subaraean element characteristic of later periods. The first seventeen kings are described in the lists as 'dwelling in tents' but the sixteenth, Ushpia, who dates probably from the time of the 3rd dynasty of Ur (*c* 2000 B.C.), built a temple to Ashur, the city-god, and is reputed to have founded a dynasty that lasted until displaced by Kik(k)ia, the twenty-eighth ruler and builder of the city-wall. From Puzur-Ashur I., founder of another long dynasty extending to the death of Erishum II. (*c* 1830 B.C.), all but a few of the Assyrian rulers bore Akkadian names. With Shallim-ahhē, his son, royal inscriptions begin. From the time of Erishum I. until the reign of Shamshi-Adad I. a wealthy Assyrian trading colony flourished at Kanesh in Cappadocia. Under Erishum and his successors, Ikunum and Sharru-kīn I., the prosperity and influence of Asshur increased, but the dynasty ended when Erishum II. was displaced from the throne (*c* 1750 B.C.) by Shamshi-Adad I., an Amorite usurper from the West, many of whose letters have been excavated at Mari. During Shamshi-Adad's long reign Assyrian influence extended far to the N. and W. and although in his closing years both Asshur and Nineveh seem to have owed allegiance to Hammurabi of Babylon, Ishme-Dagān I., owing perhaps to the Kassite invasion of Babylonia, restored Assyrian independence. After a succession of usurpers had occupied the throne for brief periods, a dynasty founded in 1671 B.C. by Adasi or his son Bēlu-bani continued in power for half a century. A new dynasty was established by Kidin-Ninua, 1585 B.C., but during its régime there is little to record except the buildings of such kings as Ishme-Dagān II., Shamshi-Adad III., and Ashurnirāri I. which attest the city's growing prosperity. The dynasty was displaced by Ashur-rabi I. in 1452.

(*c*) *Relations with Egypt, Babylonia, and the Hittites.*—During the 17th and 16th cent. there were large racial movements in Western Asia from E. to W. and from N. to S. By 1530 the Kassites, infiltrating westward across the Tigris, had gained control of Babylonia, and by about the same time the Hurrians, expanding SW. from the region of Lake Van in Armenia, had established the powerful military state of Mitanni (later called Hanigalbat) in upper Mesopotamia between the Assyrians and the Hittites, becoming a thorn in the flesh to both people and sitting astride the trade-routes into Asia Minor. Assyria suffered a severe defeat from them about the time of Ashur-rabi I. Egypt was also interesting itself in Western Asia; Thothmes I. (*c* 1525 B.C.) had advanced as far as upper Mesopotamia and Thothmes III. (1504–1450 B.C.) made a punitive expedition across the Euphrates into Mitanni and received gifts from Babylonia and the Hittites as well as from

Enlil-nāzir I. of Assyria. At this time there were chronic petty wars between Assyria and its nearest neighbours. Puzur-Ashur III. (1491–1478 B.C.) made a boundary-treaty with Burna-Buriash I. of Babylonia. Mitanni was now however becoming a more dangerous foe. The international situation is illustrated by the El-Amarna letters which show that while Egypt had control of Palestine under Amenophis III. (1416–1379 B.C.) a precarious balance of power farther N. was maintained by a succession of temporary alliances between Egypt and one or more of the kingdoms of Assyria, Babylonia, Mitanni, and the Hittites, with the object of keeping both Mitanni and the Hittites in check. Diplomatic marriages were also sometimes arranged between the royal families, and gifts were exchanged. Ashur-bēl-nishēshu of Assyria, after being obliged to pay tribute to Mitanni, took part in a defensive alliance with Kara-Indash II. of Babylonia and Amenophis III., although this did not interrupt the friendly relationship between Egypt and Mitanni. After the death of Amenophis III. Egypt began to move out of Asia and a throne-dispute in Mitanni enabled Ashur-uballit I., in alliance with the Hittites, to assert his independence of Mitanni. A daughter of Ashur-uballit was married to the son of Burna-Buriash II. of Babylonia after whose death the Assyrian king helped Kadashman-Harbe II., his own grandson, to ascend the Babylonian throne. When Kadashman-Harbe was murdered, Ashur-uballit assisted Kurigalzu II. to secure the kingship but subsequently a frontier war was waged between Kurigalzu and Ashur-uballit's son and successor, Enlil-nirari.

Toward the end of the 14th cent. movements of Mediterranean peoples (the same factor as that which brought the Philistines into Palestine) weakened the power of Mitanni and the Hittites. At the same time, bedouin Aramaean groups, especially Ahlamē and Sutē, began to move in large numbers into both Babylonia and Hanigalbat (Mitanni). Ark-dēn-ili, the earliest Assyrian monarch to record systematically his campaigns, had to overcome their pressure on his W. frontier. His successor, Adad-nirāri I., subdued the W. regions as far as Carchemish and extracted tribute from them, with the Hittites powerless to prevent it. He also led conquering expeditions eastward into the Zagros mountains and, after a war with Nazi-Maruttash of Babylonia, adjusted his southern frontier in Assyria's favour. In Asshur he rebuilt the royal palace, some temples, and the city walls. His son, Shalmaneser I., had to repel an attack from the Hurrian peoples of Urartu (Ararat), or Nairi, in Armenia, and to suppress serious revolts, fomented by the Hittites, in Hanigalbat, but he considerably extended the eastern border among the Zagros foothills. He also built the fortress-city of Calah, about midway between Asshur and Nineveh.

Tukulti-Ninurta I. (1257–1220 B.C.) firmly consolidated Assyrian power in the N. and W. and his renewed eastward expansion led to a war with Babylonia in which he captured its king, Kashtiliash III., and plundered his capital, thus becoming ruler of an empire from Carchemish to the Persian Gulf. He built a new residence-city, Kar-tukulti-Ninurta, but was killed seven years later in a revolt by his son. Babylon then regained its independence and Assyria entered upon a long period of weakness and decline. Ashur-nirāri III. and Enlil-kudurra-uzur owed allegiance to the Babylonian king, Adad-shum-nāzir, and although Assyria partly revived under Ninurta-apil-ēkur and Ashur-dān I., their successors, Ninurta-tukulti-Asshur and Mutakkil-Nusku, became vassals of Babylonia, where the Kassites had just been replaced by the dynasty of Isin. Assyrian fortunes began to rise again under Ashur-rēsha-īshi I. (1131–1113 B.C.) who repelled a Babylonian incursion by Nebuchadrezzar I. and fought victorious campaigns against the Aramaeans to the W.

(*d*) *Tiglath-pileser I. and his successors.*—Tiglath-pileser I. (1113–1074 B.C.) has left very full accounts of his long reign and his abundant conquests. His successes were gained chiefly in upper Mesopotamia along the base of the Caucasus, in Armenia (the Nairi lands), and W. through Syria to the NE. corner of the Mediterranean where he received tribute from Arvad, Gebal (Byblos), and Sidon. Invading bedouin Ahlamē were driven back across the Euphrates. The Babylonian king, Marduk-nādin-ahhē, attacked Assyria but after two years North Babylonia was ravaged and his capital was taken and sacked. Tiglath-pileser carried out extensive building operations in his own country and acclimatized useful trees and garden plants. After his death, however, Assyrian power relapsed. Ashur-bēl-kāla had to subdue a rebellion in Nairi. He entered into a treaty of friendship with Marduk-shāpik-zēri of Babylonia, probably in face of the common Aramaean threat, but after the Aramaeans, infiltrating into S. Babylonia, dethroned the Babylonian king he married the daughter of the new Aramaean ruler, Adad-apla-iddin. During the following century the Aramaeans gradually increased their pressure on N. Mesopotamia and eventually established there a series of independent kingdoms, even penetrating into the Assyrian homeland. Both Assyria and Babylonia entered on a long period of decline about which little is known, but Assyrian revival began under Ashur-dān II. (933–910 B.C.). Adad-nirāri II. warred with Shamash-mudammik and Nabu-shum-ukīn I. of Babylonia; Tukulti-Ninurta II. continued the subjugation of the mountaineers N. of Assyria, gradually winning back the Empire of Tiglath-pileser I.

With Ashur-nāzir-apli II. began a fresh tide of Assyrian conquest, 883 B.C. He rebuilt Calah, and made it his capital. The small Aramaean State of Bīt-Adīni, between the Balih and Euphrates, held out against him, but he conquered, in the N., Kutmuh and Kirruri and, in the E., Zamua. Carchemish and Unki (ʿAmk) or Hattina on the Orontes were raided, and the army reached the Lebanon. Tyre, Sidon, Gebal, Arvad, etc., were fain to buy off the conqueror. Ashur-nāzir-apli had invaded the Babylonian sphere of influence, and Nabū-apla-iddina sent his brother Zabdānu to support his allies. Ashur-nāzir-apli took Zabdānu and 3000 troops prisoners.

(*e*) *Shalmaneser III., etc.*—The reign of Shalmaneser III., his son and successor, was one long campaign. He began to annex his conquests by placing governors over the conquered districts. The Armenian Empire now began to bar Assyria's progress north. Assyria now first appeared on Israel's horizon as a threatening danger. Shalmaneser's celebrated bronze doors at Balâwat and the Black Obelisk give us pictures of scenes in his reign. They represent ambassadors from Gilzān near Lake Urmia, from Ja'ua (Jehu) of Israel, from Musri, from Suhi, and from Hattina. This Musri is NE. of Cilicia (1 K 10[28]), whence Solomon brought his horses. Shalmaneser invaded Kuē in Cilicia, and Tabal (Tubal), where he annexed the silver, salt, and alabaster works. He reached Tarzi (Tarsus, the birthplace of St. Paul). To the NE. he penetrated Parsūa, the original Persia. In Babylonia, Nabū-apla-iddina was followed by his son, Marduk-zākir-shumi I., against whom arose his brother Marduk-bēl-usāte, who held the southern States of the Sealand, already peopled by the Chaldaeans. Shalmaneser invaded Babylonia, and, passing to the E., besieged Marduk-bēl-usāte, drove him from one stronghold to another, and finally killed him and all his partisans. In the role of a friend of Babylon, Shalmaneser visited the chief cities and sacrificed to the gods, captured most of the southern States, and laid them under tribute.

Shalmaneser's campaign against Hamath on the Orontes took place in 853 B.C. The fall of Bīt-Adīni had roused all N. Syria to make a stand. At Ḳarḳar the Assyrian army had against them a truly wonderful combination.

	Chariots.	Horsemen.	Foot.
Adad-idri of Damascus	1200	1200	20,000
Irhuleni of Hamath .	700	700	10,000
Ahabbu of Sir'il . .	2000	..	10,000
The Guī (Kuē) . . .	..	..	500
Musri	..	..	1,000

ASSYRIA AND BABYLONIA

	Chariots.	Horsemen.	Foot.
Irkanati	10	..	10,000
Matinu-ba'il of Arvad	..	..	200
Usanati	..	..	200
Adunu-ba'il of Shiana	30	..	10,000
Ba'sa of Ammon	..	..	1,000
Gindibu the Arab	1000 Camels.		

The presence of Ahab in this battle in which Shalmaneser claims to have won the victory is most interesting. The battle was not productive of any settled results, as Shalmaneser had to fight the same foes in 849 B.C. and again in 846 B.C. In 842 B.C. Shalmaneser defeated Hazael, besieged him in Damascus, and carried off the spoils of his residence. At this time he received tribute from Tyre, Sidon, and Jehu, 'of the house of Omri.' Jehu's tribute includes silver, gold, a golden bowl, a golden vase, golden goblets and buckets, and tin.

Shalmaneser's last years were clouded by the rebellion of his son Ashur-dānin-apli, who alienated more than half the Empire, and was not subdued by the successor to the throne, his brother Shamshi-Adad v., until the second year of his reign. Shamshi-Adad had to fight the Babylonian kings Marduk-balatsu-ikbi and Bau-aha-iddin. Adad-nirāri III, fought in Media and in the W. From the upper part of the Euphrates to Tyre, Sidon, the land of Omri (Israel), Udumu (Edom), and Palastu (Philistia), to the Mediterranean, he exacted tribute. He besieged Mari, king of Damascus, in his capital, captured it and carried off rich spoil.

(*f*) *Tiglath-pileser III.*—Armenia was steadily rising in power, and under Shalmaneser IV. Assyria lost all its northern conquests in Upper Mesopotamia; Tiglath-pileser III., who was perhaps a usurper, came to the throne in 744 B.C. The world of small States had given way to a few strong kingdoms; the Chaldaeans were strongly forcing their way into lower Babylonia; in the N., Armenia was powerful and ready to threaten W. Syria; Egypt was soon to awaken and interfere in Palestine. Assyria and Babylonia bade fair to fall a prey to stronger nations, when Tiglath-pileser III. roused the old energy. The Aramaeans were pouring into Babylonia, filled the Tigris basin from the lower Zab to the Uknu, and held some of the most celebrated cities of Akkad. Tiglath-pileser scourged them into subjection, and deported multitudes to the NE. hills. The Medes were set in order, and then Tiglath-pileser turned to the W. The new kingdom of Arpad was strongly supported by Armenia, and Tiglath-pileser swept into Kummuh, and took the Armenians in the rear. He crushed them, and for the time was left to deal with the W. Arpad took three years to reduce: then gradually all N. Syria came into Assyrian hands, 740 B.C. Hamath allied itself with Azrija'u of Ja'udi (not to be confused with Azariah of Judah) and Panammu of Sam'al. Tiglath-pileser broke up the coalition, devastated Hamath, and made the district an Assyrian province. The Southern States hastened to avoid invasion by paying tribute. Menahem of Israel, Zabibi of Arabia, Rahianu (Rezon) of Damascus, Hiram of Tyre are noteworthy; but Gebal, Carchemish, Hamath, Milidia, Tabal, Kullāni (Calno, Is 10[9]) also submitted, 734 B.C. Hanno of Gaza was defeated. In 732 B.C. Damascus was besieged and taken, Israel was invaded, the whole of Naphtali taken, and Pekah had to pay heavy toll. In 732 B.C. he was murdered, and Tiglath-pileser acknowledged Hoshea as successor. Ammon, Moab, Ashkelon, Edom, and Ahaz of Judah paid tribute. Samsi, queen of the Arabians, was defeated and the Sabaeans sent presents. This Tiglath-pileser is the **Pul** of 2 K 15[19f], who, after defeating the Chaldaean Ukīn-zēr, who had ascended the Babylonian throne, was crowned king of Babylon, as Pulu.

(*g*) *Sargon.*—Shalmaneser v. seems to have been the son of Tiglath-pileser. He was king of Babylonia as Ululai, and succeeded to Tiglath-pileser's empire. In 724 B.C. he began the siege of Samaria, but we have no annals of his reign. Sargon II., his successor, may have founded a new dynasty or was perhaps a brother of Shalmaneser v. Samaria fell almost immediately (721 B.C.), and the flower of the nation, to the number of 27,290 persons, was deported and settled about Halah on the Habur, in the province of Gozan, and in Media (2 K 17[6]), being replaced by Babylonians and Syrians. **Merodach-baladan II.**, a king of Bīt Iakin, a Chaldaean state in S. Babylonia, who had been tributary to Tiglath-pileser III., had made himself master of Babylon, and was supported there by Elam. Sargon met the Elamites in a battle which he claimed as a victory, but he had to leave Merodach-baladan alone as king in Babylon for twelve years. This failure roused the West under Iaubidi of Hamath, who secured Arpad, Simirra, Damascus, and Samaria as allies, supported by Hanno of Gaza. Sargon in 720 B.C. set out to recover his power here. At Ḳarḳar, Iaubidi was defeated and captured, and the southern branch of the confederacy was crushed at Raphia. Hanno was carried to Assyria, 9000 people deported, Sibu (Sewe, So), the Tartan of Egypt, fled, the Arabians submitted and paid tribute. Azuri of Ashdod, who began to intrigue with Egypt, was deposed and replaced by his brother, Ahimiti. A rebellion in Ashdod led to a pretender being installed, but Sargon sent his Tartan to Ashdod (Is 20[1]), the pretender fled, and Ashdod and Gath were reduced to Assyrian provinces. Judah, Edom, and Moab staved off vengeance by heavy toll. Sargon's heaviest task was the reduction of Armenia. Rusa I. was able to enlist all Upper Mesopotamia, including Mita of Mushki, and it took ten years to subdue the foe. Sargon's efforts were clearly aided by the incursions of the Gimirrai (Gomer, Cimmerians) into N. Armenia. Having triumphed everywhere else, Sargon turned his veterans against Babylonia. The change of kings in Elam was a favourable opportunity for attacking Merodach-baladan, who was merely holding down the country by Chaldaean troops. Sargon marched down the Tigris, seized the chief posts on the east, screened off the Elamites and threatened Merodach-baladan's rear. He therefore abandoned Babylon and fell on Sargon's rear, but, meeting no support, retreated S. to his old kingdom and fortified it strongly. Sargon entered Babylon, welcomed as a deliverer, and in 709 B.C. became king of Babylon. The army stormed Bīt Iakin, but Merodach-baladan escaped over sea. Sargon then restored the ancient cities of Babylonia. Dilmun, an island far down the Persian Gulf, did homage. Sargon founded a magnificient city, Dur-Sharrukin, modern Khorsabad, to the NE. of Nineveh. He died a violent death, but how or where is now uncertain.

(*h*) *Sennacherib.*—Sennacherib soon had to put down rebellion in the SE. and NW., but his Empire was very well held together, and his chief wars were to meet the intrigues of his neighbours, Elam and Egypt. Babylonia was split up into semi-independent States, peopled by Aramaeans, Chaldaeans, and kindred folk, all restless and ambitious. Merodach-baladan seized the throne of Babylon from Marduk-zākir-shumi, Sargon's viceroy, 704 B.C. The Aramaeans and Elam supported him. Sennacherib defeated him at Kish, 703 B.C., and drove him out of Babylon after nine months' reign. Sennacherib entered Babylon, spoiled the palace, swept out the Chaldaeans from the land, and carried off 208,000 people as captives. On the throne of Babylon he set Bēl-ibni, of the Babylonian seed royal, but educated at his court. Merodach-baladan had succeeded in stirring the W., where Tyre had widely extended its power, and Hezekiah of Judah had grown wealthy and ambitious, to revolt. Ammon, Moab, Edom, the Arabians joined the confederacy, and Egypt encouraged. Padi, king of Ekron, a faithful vassal of Assyria, was overthrown by a rebellion in his city and sent in chains to Hezekiah. Sennacherib, early in 701 B.C., appeared on the Mediterranean coast, received the submission of the Phoenician cities, isolated Tyre, and had tribute from Ammon, Moab, and Edom. Tyre he could not capture, so he made Ethbaal of Sīdon overlord of Phoenicia, and assailed Tyre with the allied fleet. Its king escaped to Cyprus, but the city held out. Sennacherib meanwhile passed down the coast, reduced

Ashkelon, but was met at Eltekeh by the Arabians and Egyptians. He gained an easy victory, and captured Eltekeh, Timnath, and Ekron. Then he concentrated his attention upon Judah, captured forty-six fortified cities, deported 200,150 people, and shut up Hezekiah, 'like a bird in a cage,' in Jerusalem. He assigned the Judaean cities to the kings of Ashdod, Ekron, and Gaza, imposed fresh tribute, and received of Hezekiah thirty talents of gold, eight hundred talents of silver, precious stones, antimony, precious woods, his daughters, his palace women, male and female singers, etc., an enormous spoil, which was carried to Nineveh. His siege of Lachish is depicted on his monuments. Sennacherib continued South but suddenly changed his plans and returned to Babylonia, probably because the Egyptian army was advancing to meet him or because he had heard that Merodach-baladan had again appeared in Babylon. Biblical and Greek evidence also suggest that his army suffered a disaster, probably an outbreak of bubonic plague. If the year was 700 B.C. an eclipse of the sun may have led him to abandon his campaign.

In Babylonia, Bēl-ibni proved unfaithful and was recalled. Ashur-nādin-shumi, Sennacherib's son, was installed as king, and reigned six years. Sennacherib devastated Bīt Iakin. He then employed Phoenician shipbuilders and sailors to build ships at Til-barsip, on the Euphrates, and at Nineveh, on the Tigris. He floated his fleets down to the mouth of the rivers, shipped his army, and landed at the mouth of the Karūn, where the Chaldaeans had taken refuge, 695 B.C. He sent the captives by ship to Assyria, and marched his army into S. Elam. The king of Elam, however, swooped down on Babylon and carried off Ashur-nādin-shumi to Elam. Nergal-ushēzib was raised to the throne, and, aided by Elamite troops, proceeded to capture the Assyrian garrisons and cut off the southern army. Sennacherib moved to Erech and awaited Nergal-ushēzib, who had occupied Nippur. He was defeated, captured, and taken to Assyria, 693 B.C. A revolution in Elam tempted Sennacherib to invade that country, perhaps in hope of rescuing his son. He swept all before him, the Elamite king retreating to the mountains, but the severe winter forced Sennacherib to retreat, 692 B.C. Mushēzib-Marduk and the Babylonians opened the treasury of Marduk to bribe the Elamites for support. A great army of Elamites, Aramaeans, Chaldaeans, and Babylonians barred Sennacherib's return at Halūle, on the E. of the Tigris, 691 B.C. Sennacherib claimed the victory, but had no power to do more, and left Mushēzib-Marduk alone for the time. He came back to Babylonia in 690 B.C., and the new Elamite king being unable to assist, Babylon was taken. Mushēzib-Marduk was deposed and sent to Nineveh. Babylon was then sacked, fortifications and walls, temples and palaces razed to the ground, the inhabitants massacred, the canals turned over the ruins, 689 B.C. Sennacherib made Babylonia an Assyrian province, and was king himself till his death (681 B.C.).

Sennacherib chose Nineveh, which had become a second-rate city, as his capital, and, by his magnificent buildings and great fortifications, made it a formidable rival to Calah, Asshur, and even Babylon before its destruction. His last few years are in obscurity, but he was murdered by his son or sons. See ADRAMMELECH.

(*i*) *Esarhaddon* came to the throne (680 B.C.), after a short struggle with the murderers of his father and their party, and he rebuilt Babylon. He had to repel an incursion of the Cimmerians in the beginning of his reign, and then defeated the Medes. In 677 B.C. Sidon was in revolt, but was taken and destroyed, a new city called Kar-Esarhaddon being built to replace it and colonized with captives from Elam and Babylonia (Ezr 4[2]). In 676 B.C., Esarhaddon marched into Arabia and conquered the eight kings of Bazu and Hazu (Buz and Huz of Gn 22[21]). In 674 B.C. he invaded Egypt and again in 673. In 670 B.C. he made his great effort to conquer Egypt, drove back the Egyptian army from the frontier to Memphis, winning three severe battles. Memphis surrendered, Tirhakah fled to Thebes, and Egypt was made an Assyrian province. In 668 B.C. it revolted, and on the march to reduce it Esarhaddon died. He divided the Empire between his two sons, Ashurbanipal being king of Assyria and the Empire, while Shamash-shum-ukīn was king of Babylon as a vassal of his brother.

(*j*) *Ashurbanipal* at once prosecuted his father's reduction of Egypt to submission. Tirhakah had drawn the Assyrian governors, some of them native Egyptians, as Neco, into a coalition against Assyria. Some remained faithful, and the rising was suppressed ; Tirhakah was driven back to Ethiopia, where he died (664 B.C.). Tanutamon, the son of Tirhakah, invaded Egypt and Ashurbanipal in 662 B.C. again suppressed a rising, drove the Ethiopian out, and captured Thebes. Ashurbanipal besieged Ba'al, king of Tyre, and although unable to capture the city, obtained its submission and that of Arvad, Tabal, and Cilicia. Gyges, king of Lydia, exchanged embassies, and sent Ashurbanipal two captive Cimmerians, but he afterwards allied himself with Psammetichus, son of Neco, and assisted him to throw off the Assyrian yoke. The Mannai had been restless, and Ashurbanipal next reduced them. Elam was a more formidable foe. Allying himself with the Aramaeans and Chaldaeans, Urtaku, king of Elam, invaded Babylonia, but died and his throne was seized by Teumman. Ashurbanipal took advantage of the accession dispute to invade Elam and capture Susa ; and after killing Teumman put Ummanigash and Tammaritu, two sons of Urtaku, on the thrones of two districts of Elam. He then took vengeance on the Aramaeans, E. of the Tigris. His brother, Shamash-shum-ukīn, now began to plot for independence. He enlisted the Chaldaeans, Aramaeans, and Ummanigash of Elam, Arabia, and Egypt. A simultaneous rising took place, and Ashurbanipal seemed likely to lose his Empire. He invaded Babylonia. In Elam, Tammaritu put to death Ummanigash and all his family, but was defeated by Indabigash, and had to flee to Assyria. Ashurbanipal defeated his opponents and laid siege to Babylon, Borsippa, Sippar, and Cutha, capturing one after the other. Shamash-shum-ukīn burnt his palace over his head, and Babylon surrendered (648 B.C.). The conquest of S. Babylonia and Chaldaea was followed by campaigns against Elam, culminating in the capture of Susa and its destruction in 639 B.C. The last years of his reign are in obscurity.

(*k*) *Fall of Assyria.*—Ashurbanipal was succeeded by Ashur-etil-ilāni, his son. Another son, Sīn-sharra-ishkun, and a general, Sīn-shum-līshir, seem to have disputed the succession and perhaps both held the throne for a time. Sin-sharra-ishkun may have become king after Ashur-ētil-ilāni's death. Under these kings, the western provinces were occupied by the Scythians, and Nabopolassar, an Aramaean, achieved the independence of Babylonia with the help of Cyaxares the Mede. The Medes, after being kept at bay for a time by the Assyrians, with the aid of the Scythians and of Psammetichus I. of Egypt, destroyed Asshur in 614 B.C. and Nineveh in 612 B.C. Ashur-uballit II., a general of perhaps royal lineage, retreated westwards with the army to Harran but the Medes captured it in 608 B.C. and in 606 B.C. the Assyrian kingdom came to an end.

II. BABYLONIA.—**1. Natural features.**—Babylonia is the name given to the great alluvial plain between the Tigris and the Euphrates S. of the point where the rivers come closest together, about the latitude of modern Baghdad. There were also extensions NW. up the Euphrates and NE. in the Diyâlā valley. In ancient times the Persian Gulf penetrated much farther inland, and as the sea receded vast marshy tracts with islands were left which gradually came to be cultivated as the land dried. An elaborate system of irrigation was necessary and the need to control it led early to a strong government by city-states and to frequent wars between them. The smaller, northern part of the country came to be called Akkad and was mainly populated by Semites ; the larger, southern part was named Sumer and its population was chiefly Sumerian. The central cities of

Akkad were Kish, Kuta, Sippar (Sepharvaim), and Akkad; to the NE. lay Akshak and Eshnunna and to the NW., on the Euphrates, Mari. In the SE. were Babylon, the city of the god Marduk, and its sister city, Borsippa where Nebo was worshipped. The oldest city in Sumer was Eridu, on the Persian Gulf, the seat of the cult of Ea; a little to the N. lay Ur, whose patron was Sin, the moon-god. To the N. lay Larsa with its temple of Shamash, the sun-god, Uruk (Erech), whose chief god was Anu, and Lagash, with its shrine of Ningirsu. Farther N. were Umma, Adab and Shuruppak and beyond that the cities of Nippur, the abode of Enlil, the earth-god, and Isin. Great commercial rivalry existed between the states, and at one time or another several exercised in turn lordship over the greater part of Babylonia.

2. History.—(*a*) *Prehistoric period.*—Three successive chalcolithic cultures have been distinguished in Babylonia in the 4th and 3rd millennia, centred respectively at 'Ubaid (near Ur), Uruk (in Sumer), and at modern *Jemdet Nasr* (in Akkad). The first and third are related to the painted pottery cultures of Iran (Susa, etc.) and N. Mesopotamia (*Tell Halâf*, etc.) and the second may also be. Building (with mud bricks), agriculture, cattle-breeding, fishing, weaving, brewing, metal-working, and decorative arts were practised. As early as the Uruk period, when writing first appears, the Sumerians entered the country, settling among Subaraeans, Semites, and perhaps others.

(*b*) *The city-states.*—What is called the early dynastic period began soon after 3000 B.C. when many city-states existed under their several kings. Babylonian king-lists classify these in dynasties named after the cities but of most of the earliest kings nothing more is known. A few, however, such as Ziusudra of Shuruppak, Dumuzi (Tammuz) of Bad-tibira, Etana of Kish, and Gilgamish of Uruk occur also in legend or mythology; some of these were later worshipped as gods. The earliest are described as ruling 'before the flood' but of this event nothing is known; floods were common in early Babylonia. Some notable names and some powerful dynasties known from early cuneiform sources are not included in the king-lists. The earliest royal inscriptions are perhaps those of Mesilim of Kish (*c* 2600 B.C.?), who included in his dominions Lagash and Umma, and of his contemporary, Iku-Shamash of Mari. History virtually begins with the 1st dynasty of Ur (*c* 2450–2300 B.C.) founded by Mesannipadda and noted for its 'royal cemetery' with its evidences of human sacrifice and its wealth of gold jewellery. During this dynasty, Lagash, though apparently subject to Ur, was ruled by notable kings such as Ur-Nanshe, Eannatum, and Enannatum I. and II. Supremacy passed for brief periods to various cities until Lugalzaggisi of Uruk, after defeating Urukagina of Lagash and Ur-Zababa of Kish, was overcome by Sargon of Akkad (*c* 2300 B.C.) who founded the Semitic dynasty of Akkad, uniting all Babylonia under his rule and conducting campaigns as far as Asia Minor. Akkad flourished under his successors, Rimush, Manishtusu, and Narâm-Sin, but in the reign of Sharkalisharri (*c* 2150 B.C.) its power declined. Soon after his death Babylonia passed under the rule of barbarian invaders from Gutium, a district E. of the Tigris, but in spite of this domination Sumerian culture reached a lofty height at Lagash under its ruler Gudea. Deliverance from Gutium came through Utuhegal of Uruk but dominion then almost immediately passed (*c* 2050 B.C.) to Ur-Nammu, founder of the brilliant 3rd dynasty of Ur during which the Sumerian civilization reached its zenith. His son, Shulgi (or Dungi?), and the succeeding kings, Bur-Sīn and Shu-Sīn (or Gimil-Sīn?) exacted tribute from Elam and Assyria, but the fifth king, Ibbi-Sīn, was defeated and captured by the Elamites (*c* 1960 B.C.) and supreme power in Babylonia was then shared between Isin and Larsa under dynasties recently founded by Ishbi-Erra and Naplānum respectively, Amorite leaders who had infiltrated with their troops from the Euphrates region to the NW. In NE. Babylonia Eshnunna maintained its independence under an Akkadian dynasty. Isin at first dominated the scene and its earliest kings, like the latter kings of the preceding Ur dynasty, received divine worship. The fifth king was Lipit-Ishtar whose law-code has been recovered from the excavations. He was displaced, however, by a usurper, Ur-Ninurta, and from that time Larsa began to contest with some measure of success for the leading place, under Gungunum, its fifth king, and his successors, Abisare and Sumuilum.

(*c*) *The Hammurabi dynasty.*—Meanwhile, another Amorite dynasty, the 1st dynasty of Babylon, led by Sumu-abum, took possession (*c* 1830 B.C.) of the hitherto unimportant town of Babylon, and under his successors, Sumu-la-ilum, Zabum, Apil-Sīn, and Sīn-muballit, its power rapidly grew. In the reign of Zabum of Babylon, Kudur-Mabug, an Elamite, conquered Larsa, appointing as king his elder son, Warad-Sīn, and after the latter's death, his second son, Rīm-Sīn. Rīm-Sīn dethroned Damik-ilishu of Isin and assumed for a time rule over most of Babylonia but in the sixtieth year of his reign (*c* 1698 B.C.) he was himself defeated by Hammurabi of Babylon who united all Babylonia under his dominion. The Amorites adopted the Akkadian language and accepted into their pantheon the chief gods of Babylonia, but the Sumerian language and much of the Sumerian culture were soon extinguished and Babylonia became a Semitic country, with Marduk, the god of Babylon, as its principal deity. Under Hammurabi's wise and firm administration, the land grew very wealthy. Great attention was paid to irrigation and commerce, and science and letters flourished. Hammurabi's code of laws was based partly on earlier codes. Much light has been thrown on Amorite history and culture (and perhaps on the origins of the Hebrews) by the great hoard of documents, especially letters, found at Mari, an important city-state on the Euphrates, N. of Babylon, whose king, Zimri-lim, was subdued by Hammurabi. Even Asshur and Nineveh acknowledged Hammurabi as overlord, but after his death the power of Babylon declined. In the ninth year (*c* 1677 B.C.) of his successor, Samsu-ilūna, great parts of Babylonia fell under the rule of invading Kassites (perhaps the Cush of Gn 10[8]), coming from Iran under their leader Gandash.

(*d*) *Kassite supremacy and the rise of Assyria.*—During Samsu-ilūna's reign a rival, but effete, 'Maritime' dynasty was inaugurated (*c* 1658 B.C.) by Iluma-ilum in the S. of Babylonia, but the Hammurabi dynasty continued to rule most of the country until the sack of Babylon by the Hittite king, Mursilis I. (*c* 1531 B.C.), which ended the reign of its last king, Samsu-ditāna. Agum II., the Kassite king, took advantage of this event to assume control of the whole of Babylonia. The Kassites gave to Babylonia the name Kar-duniash, and although they adopted the Babylonian language and the Babylonian gods their earliest kings bore Kassite names. Burna-Buriash I. (*c* 1485) was a contemporary of Puzur-Ashur III. of Assyria, with whom he had a boundary dispute. The Maritime dynasty was brought to an end by Ulam-Buriash (*c* 1453 B.C.). Kara-Indash II. concluded a frontier agreement with Ashur-bēl-nishēshu of Assyria, and his daughter was married to Amenophis III. of Egypt. Three letters of his son, Kadashman-Harbe I., to Amenophis and two replies are found among the El-Amarna correspondence, and the Egyptian king appears to have married his sister. Kurigalzu I., the next king, declined to join a Canaanite coalition against Amenophis. In an expedition into Elam, he captured Susa, its capital, and on his N. frontier he built a fortified city, Dur-Kurigalzu (modern *Aqarqûf*), as a defence against Assyria. Burna-Buriash II. (*c* 1360) was allied with Amenophis IV. of Egypt against Suppiluliuma the Hittite king, Mitanni, Egypt's former ally, being now in decline. His son married a daughter of Ashur-uballit I. of Assyria, and after Kadashman-Harbe II., the offspring of this union, was killed in a revolt led by a pretender, Nazibugash, the Assyrian king helped Kurigalzu II., a son of Burna-buriash II., to gain the throne. Later, however, frontier wars developed between Kurigalzu and Enlil-nirāri of Assyria and afterwards between his son,

ASSYRIA AND BABYLONIA

Nazi-Maruttash, and the Assyrian king Adad-nirāri I. Kadashman-Turgu and Kadashman-Enlil II. were allied with the Hittite king Hattusilis III. against Assyria, but in the next reign Kashtiliash III. was taken captive by Tukulti-Ninurta I. and his capital was plundered. The next kings of Babylonia owed allegiance to Assyria and the land was raided by the Elamites, but after the murder of Tukulti-Ninurta Adad-shum-nāzir gained the upper hand over his northern neighbour. Ashur-nirāri III. of Assyria and his son Enlil-kudurra-uzur became in turn his vassals until, in an Assyrian rising, Enlil-kudurra-uzur and he both lost their lives in the same battle. The reigns of Melishipak and Merodach-baladan I. were comparatively peaceful, but Zabāba-shum-iddin (1169–1167 B.C.) was besieged in his capital by Ashur-dān I. of Assyria. The dynasty was brought to an end, however, through the defeat of Enlil-nādin-ahhē by Shutruk-nahhunte I. of Elam, who seems to have appointed his son, Kutur-nahhunte, to rule in his place as king of Babylonia.

(*e*) *The dynasty of Isin and its successors.*—Independence for Babylonia was shortly afterwards regained under Marduk-kābit-ahhēshu, an Aramaean prince of Isin, who founded a new dynasty. His reign and those of his two successors seem to have been prosperous and the next king, Nebuchadrezzar I., although fighting indecisively with Ashur-rēsha-ishi I. of Assyria, had a signal victory over the Elamites. Marduk-nādin-ahhē, however, after routing an Assyrian army was decisively defeated and lost his life when Tiglath-pileser I. of Assyria retaliated by ravaging Babylonia. Marduk-shāpik-zēri had amicable relations with Ashur-bēl-kāla of Assyria, to whom his successor, Adad-apla-iddin, married his daughter after a preliminary conflict. Of the remainder of this dynasty and the next four dynasties practically nothing is known. The Aramaean migration swallowed up Mesopotamia and drove back both Assyria and Babylonia. The Chaldaeans followed the old route from Arabia by Ur, and established themselves firmly in the S. of Babylonia. Akkad was plundered by the Sūtē. Thus cut off from the West, the absence of Babylonian power allowed the rise of Philistia ; Israel consolidated, Phoenicia grew into power. Hamath, Aleppo, Sam'al became independent States. Damascus became an Aramaean power. Egypt also was split up, and could influence Palestine but little. When Assyria revived under Adad-nirāri III., the whole West was a new country and had to be reconquered. Babylonia had no hand in it. She was occupied in suppressing the Chaldaeans and Aramaeans on her borders ; and had to call for Assyrian assistance in the time of Shalmaneser IV. Finally, Tiglath-pileser III. became master of Babylonia, and after him it fell into the hands of the Chaldaean Merodach-baladan, till Sargon drove him out. Under Sennacherib it was a mere dependency of Assyria, till he destroyed Babylon. Under Esarhaddon and Ashurbanipal Babylonia revived somewhat, and under Nabopolassar, a Chaldaean, found in the weakness of Assyria and the fall of Nineveh a chance to recover.

Nabopolassar reckoned his reign from 625 B.C., but during the early years of his rule some Southern Babylonian cities such as Erech continued to acknowledge Sīn-sharra-ishkun, but he allied himself with the Medes who devastated Mesopotamia and captured Nineveh. The Medes made no attempt to hold Mesopotamia, and Pharaoh Neco, who was advancing from Egypt to take Syria, was defeated at Carchemish (605 B.C.) by Nebuchadrezzar II. So Babylonia succeeded to the W. part of the Assyrian Empire. Nebuchadrezzar attacked Egypt itself in 601 B.C. but retired after a battle in which both sides suffered severely. In 597 B.C., however, he occupied Jerusalem and in 586 B.C., after a further siege, he destroyed it. After a thirteen years' siege he captured Tyre in 573 B.C., but various conflicts with Egypt ended indecisively.

Nebuchadrezzar's inscriptions hardly mention anything but his buildings. He fortified Babylon, enriched it with temples and palaces ; restored temples at Sippara, Larsa, Ur, Dilbat, Erech, Kutha, Marad, and other cities ; cleaned out and walled with quays the Arahtu canal which ran through Babylon, and dug a canal N. of Sippar.

Amēl-Marduk (Evil-Merodach), his son, was not acceptable to the priests, and was murdered by his brother-in-law Neriglissar, who had married a daughter of Nebuchadrezzar. He, too, was occupied chiefly with the temples of his land. Neriglissar was succeeded by his son Labāshi-Marduk, a ' bad character,' whom the priests deposed, setting up Nabonidus, a Babylonian. He rebuilt many of the oldest Babylonian temples, and in exploring their ruins found records which have helped to date early kings. Partly owing to his unpopularity with the Babylonian priesthood and partly in order to strengthen his western defences he spent the later years of his reign at Harran in N. Mesopotamia and eventually at Teima (Tema) in N. Arabia, leaving the command of the army in Babylonia to his son Belshazzar. Meanwhile, Cyrus, king of Anshan in Persia, by his overthrow of Astyages the Mede, became king of Persia and then conquered Croesus of Lydia. He began to threaten Babylonia and in 539 B.C. Nabonidus returned to Babylon, but when Cyrus marched against it, it opened its gates and in October 539 B.C. Cyrus entered without resistance. Nabonidus was spared and sent to Karmania ; Belshazzar was probably killed. Cyrus was acceptable to the Babylonians, worshipped at the ancient shrines, glorified the gods who had given him leadership over their land and people, made Babylon a royal city, and took the old native titles, but the sceptre had departed from the Semitic world.

3. Literature.—Babylonia was very early in possession of a form of writing. The earliest specimens of which we know are little removed from pictorial writing ; but the use of flat pieces of soft clay, afterwards dried in the sun or baked hard in a furnace, as writing material, and strokes of a triangular reed, soon led to conventional forms of characters in which the curved lines of a picture were replaced by one or more short marks on the line. These were gradually reduced in number until the resultant group of strokes bore little resemblance to the original. The short pointed wedge-shaped ' dabs ' of the reed have given rise to the name ' cuneiform.' The necessities of the engraver on stone led him to reproduce these wedges with an emphasized head that gives the appearance of nails, but all such graphic varieties make no essential difference. The signs denoted primarily concrete objects, such as a man's head, but from the Sumerian and the Semitic words for ' head ' (*sag, reshu*) were derived syllabic values, *shak, rish*, etc., which were used in spelling out words syllabically. From the concrete objects were also developed ideas ; the picture of a bull's head symbolized power, courage, and greatness. The picture of a star denoted the sky, the supreme god (Anu) and the ideas of divinity and loftiness ; and from the Sumerian word *an*, ' sky,' and the Semitic word *ilu*, ' god,' were derived the phonetic values *an* and *il*. Thus many signs have several ideographic and phonetic values. The script, containing over six hundred signs and first used by the Sumerians, was adopted by the Assyrians and Babylonians to write their own language (Akkadian), which superseded Sumerian early in the 2nd millennium except for some liturgical and literary purposes. The earliest inscriptions date back to the late 4th or early 3rd millennium and come from temple archives, and relate to offerings to the gods or gifts to the temples. From very early times, however, contracts such as deeds of sale, dispositions of property, marriage settlements, etc., were preserved in the archives, together with large quantities of deeds, letters, business accounts, etc., and we have enormous collections in our museums of material relating to the private life and customs of the people at almost all periods of the history.

The Babylonians early drew up codes of laws, hymns, ritual texts, and mythology. The supposed influence of the heavenly bodies led to works associating celestial phenomena with terrestrial events—the so-called astrological texts which recorded astronomical observations from very early dates. A wonderful collection of extraordinary events, as births of monsters or abnormal beings, were regarded as ominous, and an attempt was made to connect them with events in national or private history. These 'omen tablets' also deal with morals, attaching to human acts consequences evincing royal or Divine displeasure. Evil conduct was thus placed under a ban, and the punishment of it was assigned to the 'hand of God or the king.' It was a very high morality that was so inculcated: to say yea with the lips and nay in the heart, to use false weights, to betray a friend, to estrange relations, to slander or backbite, are all forbidden. The conduct of a good king, of a good man, of a faithful son of his god, are set out with great care, and culminate in the precept, 'To him that does thee wrong do no evil; recompense thine adversary with good.' Medicine was extensively written upon, and the number of cases prescribed for is very great. We are not able, as a rule, to recognize either the ailment or the prescription; but magical spells were often used to drive out the demon supposed to be the cause of the disease.

The Babylonians had some acquaintance with mathematics, so far as necessary for the calculation of areas, and they early drew up tables of squares and cubes, as well as of their measures of surface and capacity. To them we owe the division of time into hours, minutes, and seconds. See WEIGHTS AND MEASURES.

The Babylonian Literature was extensive, and much of it has striking similarities to portions of the Bible (see CREATION, DELUGE, etc.). It also seems to have had influence upon classical mythology.

4. Religion.—The religion of Babylonia was a syncretic result of the union of a number of city and local cults. Consequently Shamash the sun-god; Sin the Moon-god; Ishtar, Venus; Marduk the god of Babylon, Nabū of Borsippa, Enlil of Nippur, Nergal the god of pestilence, Nusku the new-moon crescent, and a host of others, were worshipped with equal reverence by both kings and people. Most men, however, were specially devoted to one god, determined for them by hereditary cult, or possibly personal choice: a man was 'son of his god' and the god was his 'father.' In the course of time almost every god absorbed much of the attributes of every other god, so that, with the exception of such epithets as were peculiarly appropriate to him, Shamash could be addressed or hymned in much the same words as Marduk or Sin. By some teachers all the gods were said to be Marduk in one or other manifestation of his Divine activity. The whole pantheon became organized and simplified by the identification of deities originally distinct, as a result of political unification or theological system. The ideal of Divinity was high and pure, often very poetic and beautiful, but the Babylonian was tolerant of other gods, and indisposed to deny the right of others to call a god by another name than that which best summed up for him his own conception.

Magic entered largely into the beliefs and practices of life, invading religion in spite of spiritual authority. The universe was peopled with spirits, good and bad, who had to be appeased or propitiated. Conjurations, magic spells, forecasts, omens were resorted to in order to bind or check the malign influences of demons. The augurs, conjurers, magicians, soothsayers were a numerous class, and were usually called in whenever disease or fear suggested occult influence. The priest was devoted to the service of his god, and originally every head of a family was priest of the local god, the right to minister in the temple descending in certain families to the latest times. The office was later much subdivided, and as the temple became an overwhelming factor in the city life, its officials and employees formed a large part of the population. A temple corresponded to a monastery in the Middle Ages, having lands, houses, tenants, and a host of dependants, as well as enormous wealth, which it employed on the whole in good deeds, and certainly threw its influence on the side of peace and security. Although distinct classes, the judges, scribes, physicians, and even skilled manufacturers were usually attached to the temple, and priests often exercised these functions. Originally the god, and soon his temple, were the visible embodiment of the city life. The king grew out of the high priest. He was the vicegerent of the god on earth, and retained his priestly power to the last, but he especially represented its external aspect. He was ruler, leader of the army, chief judge, supreme builder of palaces and temples, guardian of right, defender of the weak and oppressed, accessible to the meanest subject. The expansion of city territory by force of arms, the growth of kingdoms and rise of empires, led to a military caste, rapacious for foreign spoils, and domestic politics became a struggle for power between the war party of expansion and conquest and the party of peace and consolidation. C. H. W. J.—**C. J. M. W.**

ASTAD, 1 Es 5[13] (RV).—See AZGAD.

ASTATH, 1 Es 8[38] (AV, RV).—See AZGAD.

ASTROLOGY, ASTRONOMY.—See MAGIC, etc.

ASTYAGES (Bel [1]) was the last king of Media. He was defeated and dethroned by Cyrus the Great in 550 B.C.

ASUPPIM.—Asuppim is mentioned in 1 Ch 26[15, 17] (AV); RV, RSV 'the storehouse' is to be preferred.

ASUR (AV **Assur**), 1 Es 5[31].—His sons returned among the Temple servants under Zerubbabel; called **Harhur,** Ezr 2[51], Neh 7[53].

ASYLUM.—See ALTAR, KIN [NEXT OF], REFUGE [CITIES OF].

ASYNCRITUS (Ro 16[14]).—A Christian greeted by St. Paul with four others 'and the brethren who are with them,' perhaps members of the same small community. The name occurs in Roman inscription *CIL* vi. 12,565, of a freedman of Augustus.

ATAD.—A threshing-floor in Transjordan on the road to Hebron, Gn 50[10f]; the site is unknown. See ABEL-MIZRAIM.

ATAR, 1 Es 5[28] (RV).—See ATER, **1.**

ATARAH ('crown').—Wife of Jerahmeel and mother of Onam, 1 Ch 2[26].

ATARGATIS (RV less correctly **Atergatis**).—In addition to the sanctuary of this goddess (also known in Gr. as Derceto) at Carnion (2 Mac 12[26]; see ASHTAROTH, ASHTEROTH-KARNAIM), other shrines were situated at Hierapolis and Askalon (=Ashkelon, q.v.). Here sacred fish were kept, and at the latter place the goddess was represented as a mermaid, resembling the supposed form of the Philistine Dagon (q.v.). Some expositors, because of the ancient name of Carnion, *i.e.*, Ashteroth-Karnaim, have identified the goddess with Astarte. The name, however, a compound of *'Athar* (=Phoen. 'Ashtart, Heb. 'Ashtoreth [q.v.]) and of *'Atti* or *'Attah*, which latter term appears as a god's name upon inscriptions, shows her to be Astarte who has assimilated the functions of 'Atti. This etymology, together with her mermaid form and the fact that fish were sacred to her, apparently makes her a personification of the fertilizing powers of water.

Atargatis was so prominently a Syrian goddess that Greek and Latin authors habitually referred to her as *Dea Syria* or, in one word, *Deasura*. Nevertheless the Atargatis cult was extensively disseminated all over the Mediterranean world and even as far to the west and north as the island of Britain. As a rule, her cults were located in seaport towns. Far-travelling Syrian merchants were her highly effective missionaries.

At present her best known sanctuary is the inland Nabataean temple that crowns *Khirbet et-Tannûr* in *Wâdī Ḥesā*, east of the southern end of the Dead Seat It has been fully excavated and the results published in very dependable fashion. N. K.—**H. R. W.**

ATAROTH.—**1.** A town not far from Dibon, rebuilt by the Gadites, Nu 32[3, 34]; modern *Khirbet 'Aṭṭārûs*,

NW. of *Dhībân*. On the Moabite stone (see MOAB) Mesha says the Gadites had long dwelt there. **2.** A town on the S. border of the territory of the children of Joseph, Jos 16[2]; it is called **Ataroth-addar** in Jos 16[5] 18[13]; probably modern *Khirbet ʿAṭṭāra*, near *Tell en-Naṣbeh* (? Mizpah). **3.** Another town on the same border, Jos 16[7]; possibly modern *Tell Sheik edh-Dhiâb*. **4.** 1 Ch 2[54] (AV 'Ataroth, the house of Joab'); see ATROTH-BETH-JOAB.

ATAROTH-ADDAR.—See ATAROTH, **2.**

ATER.—1. Eponym of a guild of porters who returned with Zerubbabel, Ezr 2[16, 42], Neh 7[21, 45], 1 Es 5[28] (AV **Jatal,** RV **Atar**). **2.** Another whose sons returned with Zerubbabel, Ezr 2[16], 1 Es 5[15] (AV **Aterezias**). The numbers are variously given as 98 (Ezr) and 92 (1 Es).

ATEREZIAS, 1 Es 5[15] (AV).—See ATER, **2.**

ATERGATIS.—See ATARGATIS.

ATETA, 1 Es 5[28] (RV).—See HATITA.

ATHACH.—Town in S. of Judah, 1 S 30[30]; the site is unknown, but possibly to be identified with **Ether, 2** (q.v.).

ATHAIAH.—A Judahite who lived in Jerusalem in the time of Nehemiah, Neh 11[4].

ATHALIAH.—1. The only queen who occupied the throne of Judah. She was the daughter of Ahab and Jezebel, and was married to Jehoram, son of Jehoshaphat. On the accession of her son Ahaziah she became queen-mother, second only to the king in power and influence. When Ahaziah was slain by Jehu, she could not bring herself to take an inferior position, and seized the throne for herself, making it secure, as she supposed, by slaying all the male members of the house of David so far as they were within her reach. One infant was preserved, and was successfully concealed in the Temple six years. The persons active in this were Jehosheba, sister of Ahaziah, and her husband Jehoiada, the chief priest. The story of the young prince's coronation by the body-guard is one of the most dramatic in Hebrew history. The death of Athaliah at the hands of the guard forms the logical conclusion of the incident. The destruction of the temple of Baal, which is spoken of in the same connexion, indicates that Athaliah was addicted to the worship of the Phoenician Baal, introduced by her mother into Israel (2 K 11). **2.** See GOTHOLIAH. **3.** A Benjamite (1 Ch 8[26]). H. P. S.

ATHARIAS, 1 Es 5[40] (AV).—See ATTHARIAS.

ATHARIM.—A place mentioned in Nu 21[1] 'the way of Atharim.' The place is unknown, unless with some editors we assume a corruption of the text and identify with **Tamar** = **Hazazon-tamar** (qq.v.), near the Dead Sea. The rendering of AV 'the way of the spies' follows Pesh., Targ., and Vulg., and is due to the resemblance between *tārîm* and *'ᵃthārîm*. The suggestion that we should render 'the way of tracks,' *i.e.* the caravan route, rests on an improbable connexion with an Arabic word.

ATHENOBIUS (1 Mac 15[28–36]).—A friend of Antiochus VII. Sidetes. He was sent to Jerusalem to remonstrate with Simon Maccabaeus for the occupation of Joppa, Gazara, the citadel of Jerusalem, and certain places outside Judaea. Simon refused the terms proposed, and Athenobius was obliged to return in indignation to the king.

ATHENS.—In the earliest times, Athens, on the Gulf of Aegina, consisted of two settlements, the town on the plain and the citadel on the hill above, the Acropolis, where the population fled from invasion. Its name and the name of its patron-goddess Athene (Athenaia), to whom was dedicated the glorious Parthenon, are inextricably connected. She was the maiden goddess, the warlike defender of her people, the patroness of the arts. The city lies about three miles from the seacoast on a large plain. When Greece was free, Athens was the capital of the district Attica, and developed a unique history in Greece (q.v.). It first gained distinction by the repulse of the Persian invasions in 490 and 480 B.C. It was burned by the Persians in the latter year. Themistocles provided it with a new wall embracing a larger area. The city now had a brilliant career of political, commercial, literary, and artistic supremacy. It was in the 5th cent. B.C. the greatest of Greek democracies, and produced the greatest sculptures and literary works the world has ever seen. In the same century Socrates lived and taught there, as did later Plato (q.v.) and Aristotle. The conflict with Sparta, the effects of the Macedonian invasion, and ultimately the Roman conquest of Greece (146 B.C.) which became a Roman province under the name 'Achaia' (q.v.), lessened the political importance of Athens, but as a State it received from Rome a position of freedom and consideration worthy of its undying merits. Athens remained supreme in philosophy and the arts, and in St. Paul's time (Ac 17[15]–18[1], 1 Th 3[1]) was still the intellectual centre of the world. It was also noted for its piety (Ac 17[22], Jos. *c. Ap.* ii. 11 [130]). On the altar to the Unknown God, see UNKNOWN GOD. The market where Paul argued (Ac 17[17]) lay north of the Areopagus (q.v.).

A. So.—**E. G. K.**

ATHLAI.—A Jew who had married a foreign wife, Ezr 10[28]; called **Emathis** in 1 Es 9[29] (AV **Amatheis, RV Ematheis**).

ATHLETE.—This word stands in RSV in 1 Co 9[25] (AV, RV 'every man that striveth'), 2 Ti 2[5] (AV 'if a man strive for masteries'; RV 'if a man contend in the games'). See GAMES II.

ATIPHA, 1 Es 5[32] (AV, RV).—See HATIPHA.

ATONEMENT.—1. General. The word 'atone' etymologically is 'to make at one,' and the nearest equivalent perhaps to 'atonement' taken in this sense is 'reconciliation.' In the translations of the Bible however 'atonement' appears predominantly for a Heb. root which means not reconciliation but expiation, not the bringing together of persons separated but the removal of sin and its accompanying uncleanness. In more general theological usage the 'Atonement' is the work of Christ both in removing sin and in bringing together or reconciling God and man. For the details of the Biblical term which is translated 'atonement' or 'expiation,' see EXPIATION; and likewise articles on related Biblical terms, *e.g.* PROPITIATION, RECONCILIATION. It is impossible however to keep these various terms completely apart, since especially in the NT they are interlocked to form a composite pattern. The purpose of this article is to bring together some of the aspects of reconciliation and removal of sin in a wider perspective, and to discuss their more general relations, leaving the details of the Biblical terms to the relevant articles.

2. In the Old Testament. The terms 'atonement' or 'expiation' in the OT have their setting predominantly in the sacrificial system. Their evaluation for Biblical theology however presents certain problems.

It is characteristic of the codes which frame the sacrificial system that for the most part they present a formal and external outline of procedure rather than a theological account of the way in which the sacrifices have their effect. It should not however be assumed because of the formal expression of the laws that Israel held a mechanical view of the efficacy of sacrifice. Sacrificial thinking should not be classified under 'magic,' nor did the Hebrews have the clear hard understanding of 'cause and effect' by which one would interpret the sacrifice as a cause which once set in motion could not fail to effect the good will of God. Even those abuses in sacrificial worship which the prophets criticized were not so much 'mechanical' as syncretistic, un-Yahwistic, and separated from the ethical traditions of the covenant. Along with the sacrificial laws we should take sections of the Psalter as the sung liturgy which accompanied the sacrificial service. Here we find the reception of sacrifice a matter of prayer (*e.g.* Ps 20[3]); the need of inward worship is emphasized (4[5], etc.), and it is proclaimed that sacrifice is not something needed by God (Pss 40, 50). Inward cleanliness is asked by God, and sacrifices are not a substitute for it (Ps 51^{15-17}); the paradox of the ending of Ps 51 should not be too easily evaded by assigning the last two verses to a redactor. All this hardly amounted to a theology of sacrifice; but it indicated that expiation and cleansing depended on the mercy of God (Ps 65^{4} 78^{38} 79^{9}—in all of which the Heb. *kippēr* ‘expiate, remove sin’ appears, RSV ‘forgive’).

It need not be doubted, then, that the sense of need for expiation was set deeply in the Israelite consciousness from early times, and that although it may have been increased by the Exile it was not, as was formerly suggested quite often, largely a product of that catastrophe. Expiation and propitiation are after all prominent parts of Babylonian religion in a much more developed civilization and yet at an earlier date.

On the other hand it is clear that the sacrificial concepts cover only a limited sector of the religious tradition in Israel. The great events of the so-called ‘history of salvation’ such as the Exodus are not called sacrifices or expiations. Their interpretation is more characteristically put in the terms of ransom or redemption. The characteristic situation is that of the first-born, whose life is forfeit to the Lord and must therefore be returned to Him by killing or alternatively be redeemed by a substitution or payment; or the man who has become enslaved (normally for debt) and has to be ransomed by his kin; or the piece of land which is in danger of alienation from the family and can be ‘redeemed’ for restoration to the family. For the interpretation of the Exodus in this way, see Ex 4^{22-23}.

The importance of this for the Atonement is firstly its place as background for certain central NT affirmations, *e.g.* Mk 10^{45}, ‘to give his life as a ransom for many,’ but secondly and no less important that it brings into prominence the history and life of the people of God and not only an external transaction between them and God. The choosing of Israel can itself be seen as a ransom (Is 43^{3}); the other nations are the price which God pays for the choice and redemption of His people. The history of Israel from a theological standpoint is the living out by the people of this special position in interaction with the other nations.

The characteristics of God which are involved in the atonement conceptions are among the most fundamental of the God of Israel. In particular we may mention the holiness of God. This appears in the priestly-sacrificial line of thought as marking out a realm which must not be violated by men and for violations of which the necessary expiation is inexorably demanded. In the prophetic and historical tradition God's holiness is manifested in His acts of judgment and mercy (*e.g.* Is 5^{16}). We should however not speak of God's holiness in the abstract, for in action it is the holiness of God in His covenant with His people. When sin appears within the covenant relationship atonement is the question of the preservation of the covenant in spite of what Israel has done. Of this the classic instance is immediately after the Sinai covenant, when Israel worships the golden calf (Ex 32–34, especially 32^{30}). Ex 33 meditates mainly on the question of how God can go with this rebellious people.

In such situations a visitation of the Divine anger often follows, commonly in the form of plague (Ex 32^{35}, Nu 25^{8}, etc.). We may ask how far the anger of God is important for the understanding of atonement. The visitation can clearly be understood as punishment (Ex 32^{35}). Though the technical terminology of expiation is not used of such punishment as a rule, we do have expiation by retribution for murder in Nu 35^{33}, and Is 40^{2} implies the same for the sufferings of Israel, which in this case have exceeded their deserts. Against this Divine anger we may have in certain mainly early sources the idea of appeasing or propitiation (see PROPITIATION), but this seems to apply more to mysterious or arbitrary Divine visitations than to anger that reacts against plain disobedience; and the sacrificial technical terminology seems to refer to expiation of sin rather than appeasement of God. But since unexpiated sin brings the anger of God swiftly upon the people, it is difficult to make a clear distinction here, and the expiation of sin is done with an evident apotropaic intent in cases like Nu 16^{41-50}, 25^{6-13}.

Mention must also be made of the place of intercession in the removal of sin, although it is rather too much to describe intercession as itself expiatory. In 2 S 21^{14}, 24^{25} (both ending passages of allied content) the expression ‘heeded supplication’ or ‘let himself be supplicated’ goes back to a form of intercession by sacrifice. In both these cases an apotropaic sense is involved; famine or plague is to be averted. This however is not simple intercession; such does appear however in the case of Moses, Ex 32^{30} 34^{9}. Jer 15^{1-4} suggests that one might have expected the intercession of a Moses or a Samuel to avert disaster sent by God. The basis for all such intercession is the sense of the freedom of God, the knowledge that even in His wrath He is not tied legalistically to a precise penalty which He is forced by His own nature to exact, or a procedure which He cannot but follow. Something like this is expressed in Ex 33^{19}.

It is probably along this line of intercession that the OT comes to an idea of vicarious suffering. Ex 32^{32} is not so much an idea that Moses by perishing might save his people, but rather an expression that though himself not implicated in their idolatry he would wish to perish with them if they cannot be forgiven. The figure of Moses may lie behind the Suffering Servant of Is 53; and in any case the Servant is intercessor (v.^{12}) as well as bearing the sin of ‘many.’

It may be reasonably said that, much as the OT contributes to the understanding of sin and atonement, it hardly makes known a final basis of atonement. The Servant of Is 53 is after all a rather isolated figure in the OT. The last resort in the OT is the faithfulness of God to His covenant with His people, His will to sustain it from His side even where Israel betrays it.

3. In the New Testament. Classical theological treatments of the atonement have correctly seen how atonement and incarnation, or atonement and Christology, must be handled together; for with Christ occupying the centre of atonement and drawing into Himself the lines and figures of OT thinking, so much comes to depend on the person of Christ, and the way in which He was one with God and one with His fellow-men. Along with this goes the problem of His self-presentation to men, the methods by which and the order in which He made Himself known. For He did not simply state the truths of Christology and the purpose of atonement and having stated them openly proceed to act them out. In the gospel story the Christological claim, the task of atonement, and the making known of these to men, are all unfolded together through the historical movement of the life and mission of Christ, with a climax in the Easter and Ascension narrative. The rather different presentation of these in the Epistles is because these take a post-resurrection position and are not trying to reconstruct the presentation of Jesus as it was in fact made before the fullest disclosures were given.

If we were right in saying that the ultimate ground of atonement in the OT was the faithful will of God to sustain His covenant with man (though the OT left it somewhat uncertain how sin was indeed destroyed or absorbed on such a basis), we may say that now Christ is a living embodiment of this covenant, as One who in His body holds together by His faithfulness God and man. If this is so, then it is worth pointing out that this bond of faithfulness is to be seen not only in the death of Christ but in all His life and work, although the times of greatest trial show forth most clearly the deep love and suffering involved.

It seems likely that the thought of sacrificial expiation came into the church through the mind of Christ Himself. Most scholars (with some important exceptions) have seen in this the influence of Is 53. For the theme of sacrificial expiation in most forms the centre is the crucifixion. This is not, however, an arbitrarily imposed means of satisfying a divine command. Jesus here takes upon Himself the sins of the world, by His complete identification with men at the same time as they most completely reject Him, and in His death brings sin to death. We thus have an objective and final act of atonement where the OT for its final ground could only refer us to the covenant will of God. We must add that in the crucifixion we have a complete identification with the will of God at the same time as God leaves Him to His dereliction and suffering. Such a statement may help us to avoid a misuse of the propitiation idea which would suggest a changing of God's mind by the sacrifice of Jesus or a conflict between holiness and love in God. The identification of Christ with men follows in some respects the sacrificial rituals, *e.g.* Lv 16^{21-22}. More broadly however it can be understood by the NT term 'reconciliation,' 2 Co 5^{18-21}. In either case the place of the resurrection of Christ must not be neglected. By it God displays that Christ, in identifying Himself with sinful man and in suffering dereliction by His Father, was indeed doing the will of God; the Resurrection is thus His justification or vindication. It also makes clear that the atonement of the Cross is not only a willing expiation of sin but is a triumph over sin; sin brought Jesus to His death and grave, but it was sin that perished, and He rose again victorious.

A rather different development of sacrificial expiation is that given by the letter to the Hebrews, modelled on the Day of Atonement. Christ makes expiation, however, not in the earthly tabernacle but in the heavenly sanctuary which He enters with His own expiatory blood. This places an emphasis on the Ascension as the climactic moment of atonement.

The element of intercessory atonement appears in the NT as in the OT, He 7^{25}, Ro 8^{34}. It would be too harsh to separate this intercession from atonement proper and regard it as subsidiary; Jesus' identification with God and with man together means a continual service of intercession by Him for man, summed up at the crucifixion in the prayer 'Father, forgive them' (Lk 23^{34}). Cf also at length the Johannine 'high-priestly' prayer, Jn 17.

The thought of ransom or release is also prominent in the NT, and appears in one of the earliest statements about the atonement in the synoptic tradition, Mk 10^{45}. Ransom and redemption are interlaced with sacrificial expiatory terms in Ro 3^{24-25}, 1 P 1^{18-19}. We do not need to construe the ransom primarily as a money payment or a price of that kind, for the oldest practice of 'redemption' is that where the life of the first-born belongs to God and can be redeemed only by the giving of a life in its place as substitute.

One or two ways must be mentioned in which the atonement is related to the history of the divine economy of salvation. Firstly, the interaction of Jew and Gentile is one of the main themes of the Passion Narrative—their hostility to each other, yet their need of each other to take responsibility for the rejection of Christ. It is in the letter to the Ephesians in particular that the atonement is expounded as the overcoming of the opposition of Jew and Gentile, itself once founded in God's plan of salvation, and thus as the basis for a church of Jew and Gentile together (Eph 2). Secondly, the atonement is related in a similar way to the Law, its works, its domination, and its penalties—so Gal 3^{10-14}, Col 2^{13-15}, Eph 2^{15}.

Lastly we may mention the relation of the Church to the atonement; we saw how in the OT the ransom or redemption idea is not external to the history of the people of God but is worked out in their life. The NT is emphatic about the uniqueness and the finality of the atonement made by Christ. On the other hand passages like Col 1^{24} envisage the apostle filling up something lacking in the sufferings of Christ. It seems wiser not to say that the sufferings of the Church are themselves atoning, but that it is of the nature of the atoning suffering of Christ that it should be accompanied by the suffering of His people. This may include not only the suffering of the Church but the suffering of the Jews; cf the children of Bethlehem who suffered for their association with Jesus although they knew nothing of Him, Mt 2^{16-18}. J. Ba.

ATONEMENT, DAY OF.—The Day of Atonement, with its unique and impressive ritual, is the culmination and crown of the sacrificial worship of the OT. The principal details are given in Lv 16, supplemented by 23^{26-32}, Nu 29^{7-11}, Ex 30^{10}, all from the Priests' Code which, however, as we shall see, has combined various rituals, some of them of the greatest antiquity. The date was the 10th day of the seventh month (Tishri) reckoning from evening to evening (Lv 16^{29} 23^{27ff}). Not only was this day a 'sabbath of solemn rest,' on which no work of any sort was to be done, but its unique place among the religious festivals of the OT was emphasized by the strict observance of a fast. The rites peculiar to 'the Day' (*Yômā*), as it is termed in later literature, may be conveniently grouped in five stages.

(*a*) In the preparatory stage (Lv 16^{3-10}), after the special morning sacrifices had been offered (Nu 29^{7-11}), the high priest selected the appointed sin- and burnt-offerings for himself and 'his house,' *i.e.* the priestly caste, then laid aside his usual ornate vestments, bathed, and robed in a simple white linen tunic and girdle. He next selected two he-goats and a ram for the people's offerings, and proceeded to 'cast lots upon the two goats; one lot for Yahweh, and the other lot for Azazel' (AV 'scapegoat,' see AZAZEL). These preparations completed, the proper expiatory rites were begun, and were accomplished in three successive stages.

(*b*) In the first stage (vv.$^{11-14}$) the high priest made atonement for himself and the priesthood. After slaying the bullock of the sin-offering, he took a censer filled with live charcoal from the altar of burnt-offering and a handful of incense, and entered the Most Holy Place. Here he cast the incense on the coals, producing a cloud of smoke, by which the dwelling-place of the Most High between the Cherubim was hidden from mortal gaze (see Ex 33^{20}). This done, he returned to the court, to enter immediately, for the second time, the inner sanctuary, carrying a basin with the blood of the bullock, which he sprinkled on the front of the mercy-seat once, and seven times on ground before the Ark.

(*c*) In the second stage (vv.$^{15-19}$) atonement was made in succession for the Most Holy Place, the Holy Place, and the outer court. The goat on which the lot 'for Yahweh' had fallen was slain by the high priest who then once again entered the Most Holy Place with its blood, which he manipulated as before. On his return through the Holy Place a similar ceremony was performed (v.^{33}, cf Ex 30^{10}), after which he proceeded, as directed in vv.^{18f}, to 'cleanse and hallow' the altar of burnt-offering, which stood in the outer court (or the altar of incense, as others believe: cf Ex 30^{10}).

(*d*) These all led up to the culminating rite in the third stage (vv.$^{20-22}$). Here the high priest, placing both hands on the head of the goat allotted to Azazel, made solemn confession—the tenor of which may still be read in the Mishnic treatise *Yômā*—of all the nation's sins. By this ceremony these sins were conceived as not only symbolically but actually transferred to the head of the goat (vv.^{21f}, see below), which was solemnly conducted into the wilderness, the supposed abode of the mysterious Azazel. In NT times the goat was led to a lofty precipice in the wilderness about 12 miles E. of Jerusalem over which it was thrown backwards, to be dashed in pieces on the rocks below (*Yômā*, vi. 6 ff).

(*e*) We now reach the concluding stage of 'the Day's' ceremonial (vv.$^{23-28}$). The fact that the essential part was now accomplished was strikingly shown by the high priest's retiring into the Holy Place to put off 'the holy garments' (vv.$^{23, 32}$), bathe, and resume his ordinary high-priestly vestments. Returning to the court, he offered the burnt-offerings for himself and the people, together with the fat of the sin-offering. The remaining verses ($^{26-28}$) deal with details, the characteristic significance of which will be discussed presently.

Though we have no evidence for the practice of the ritual described above prior to the Exile (the first clear reference to it is probably Sir 50^{5}—*i.e.* *c* 180 B.C.), and though all directives regarding it come from P, the latest of the Pentateuchal documents, it is inconceivable that rites such as these should be of late origin. It is probable that in Lv 16 various originally separate rites are combined, of which at least two—that of Azazel, and that of the purification of the Ark and the sanctuary—must go back to earliest times. The fact that these were originally purely priestly transactions, in which the community did not participate, may explain why older bodies of law do not mention them. P seems to have taken these ceremonies, plus one (vv.^{12f}) involving incense, and drawn them together into a single ritual in which the people (vv.^{29ff}) participated actively, if indirectly. In the post-Exilic period, when older features of the New Year celebration had lost relevance, and when a heightened sense of sin and need of purification had impressed itself on the Jewish spirit, the ritual of atonement became the most important event of the ecclesiastical year. In NT it is referred to as 'the Fast' (Ac 27^{9}) and so occasionally by Josephus. To this day it remains the most solemn and most largely attended religious celebration of the Jewish year.

The dominating thought of Lv 16 is the awful reality and contagion of sin, which affects not only priest and people, but the sanctuary itself. Its correlate is the intense realization of the need of cleansing and propitiation, as the indispensable condition of right relations with a holy God. The details of the ritual by which these relations were periodically renewed are of surpassing interest, as showing how the loftiest religious thought may be associated with ritual elements belonging to the most primitive stages of religion. Thus, in the case before us, the efficacy of the blood, the universal medium of purification and atonement, is enhanced by cessation from labour and complete abstinence from food—the latter the outward accompaniment of inward penitence—and by the high priest's public and representative confession of the nation's sins. Yet alongside of these we find the antique conception of holiness and uncleanliness as something material, and of the fatal consequences of unguarded contact with the one or the other. It is only on this plane of thought that one understands the need of the cleansing of the sanctuary, infected by the 'uncleannesses' of the people among whom it dwelt (16^{16} RV, RSV, cf Ezk 45^{18ff}). The same primitive idea of the contagion of holiness underlies the prescribed change of garments on the part of the high priest. The 'holy garments' in which the essential parts of the rite were performed had to be deposited in the Holy Place; those who had been brought into contact with the sacrosanct animals (vv.^{26ff}) must bathe and wash their clothes, lest, as Ezekiel says in another connexion, 'they communicate holiness to the people with their garments' (44^{19} RSV), *i.e.* lest the mysterious contagion pass to the people with disastrous results. The most striking illustration of this transmissibility, however, is seen in the central rite by which the nation's sins are transferred to the head of 'the goat for Azazel,' the demonic spirit of the wilderness (cf the similar rite, Lv 14^{6f}).

These survivals from the earlier stages of the common Semitic religion should not blind the modern student to the profound conviction of sin to which the institution bears witness, nor to the equally profound sense of the need of pardon and reconciliation, and of uninterrupted approach to God. By its emphasis on these perennial needs of the soul the Day of Atonement played no unimportant part in the preparation of Judaism for the perfect atonement through Jesus Christ. The author of the Epistle to the Hebrews in a familiar passage contrasts the propitiatory work of the Jewish high priest on this day with the great propitiation of Him who, by virtue of His own atoning blood, 'entered once for all into the holy place' (He 9^{12} RSV), even 'into heaven itself,' where He remains, our great High Priest and Intercessor (7^{25f}).
A. R. S. K.—**J. Br.**

ATROTH, Nu 32^{35} (AV).—See ATROTH-SHOPHAN.

ATROTH-BETH-JOAB.—The name of a family descended from Salma, 1 Ch 2^{54} (AV 'Ataroth, the house of Joab').

ATROTH-SHOPHAN.—A city of Gad, near Jogbehah, Nu 32^{35} (AV 'Atroth, Shophan'); the site is unknown.

ATTAI.—**1.** A Jerahmeelite, 1 Ch 2^{35f}. **2.** A Gadite who joined David at Ziklag, 1 Ch 12^{11}. **3.** A son of Rehoboam, 2 Ch 11^{20}.

ATTAIN.—In Ac 27^{12} 'attain' has the literal meaning of *reach* a place (sc RV, RSV). Elsewhere it has the figurative sense still in use.

ATTALIA (modern *Adalia*).—A town on the coast of Pamphylia, not far from the mouth of the river Catarrhactes, founded and named by Attalus II. of Pergamum. It was besieged in 79 B.C. by P. Servilius Isauricus, when in possession of the pirates. In the Byzantine period it was of great importance. It has the best harbour on the coast. Paul and Barnabas came on there from Perga, and took ship for Antioch (Ac 14^{25}). Remains of the old walls and towers still exist.
A. So.—**E. G. K.**

ATTALUS.—King of Pergamum (q.v.) (159–138 B.C.) and a prominent figure in Near Eastern politics. He was one of the kings to whom the Roman Senate is said to have written in support of the Jews in the time of Simon the Maccabee (1 Mac 15^{22}). He was Attalus II.

ATTENDANCE.—In 1 Mac 15^{32} (AV) 'attendance' is used for a king's *retinue* (RSV 'magnificence'); while in 1 Ti 4^{13} it is used in the obsolete sense of *attention*: 'Till I come give attendance (RV 'heed,' RSV 'attend') to reading.'

ATTHARATES.—Apparently a proper name in 1 Es 9^{49}, but really a corruption of the Pers. title *tirshatha* (cf Neh 8^{9} AV, RV; RSV 'governor'). See TIRSHATHA.

ATTHARIAS.—Apparently a proper name in 1 Es 5^{40} (AV **Atharias**), but really a corruption of the title *tirshatha* (cf Ezr 2^{63} AV, RV; RSV 'governor'). See TIRSHATHA.

ATTIRE.—See DRESS.

ATTUS, 1 Es 8^{29} (RV).—See HATTUSH, **2.**

AUDIENCE.—From Lat. *audientia*; 'audience' means in AV the act of *hearing*, as Lk 20^{45} 'in the audience of all the people.' Now it means the people gathered to hear. RSV 'in the hearing.'

AUGIA, 1 Es 5^{38} (AV, RV).—See AGIA, **1.**

AUGURY.—See MAGIC, DIVINATION, AND SORCERY.

AUGUSTAN COHORT (RSV), **AUGUSTAN BAND** (RV), **AUGUSTUS' BAND** (AV).—See BAND.

AUGUSTUS.—This name is Latin, and was a new name conferred (16th Jan. 27 B.C.) by the Roman Senate on Gaius Octavius, who, after his adoption by the dictator Gaius Julius Caesar, bore the names Gaius Julius Caesar Octavianus. The word means 'worthy of reverence' (as a god), and was represented in Greek by *Sebastos*, which has the same signification. Doubtless to avoid this impiety, the title is transliterated instead of translated in Lk 2^{1}; but the cognate adjective, *sebastē* for 'Augustan,' is used in Ac 27^{1}. In official documents Augustus appears as 'Imperator Caesar Augustus.' He was born 63 B.C., was the first Roman emperor from 27 B.C., and died in A.D. 14. He was equally eminent as soldier and administrator, and the Empire was governed for centuries very much on the lines laid down by him. In Lk 2^{1} he is mentioned as having issued a decree that all inhabitants of the Roman Empire should be enrolled (for purposes of taxation). There is evidence for a 14-year cycle of enrolment in the Roman province of Egypt.
A. So.—**E. R. H.**

AUL.—See Awl.

AURANUS.—A man 'advanced in years and no less advanced in folly,' who endeavoured to suppress a tumult in Jerusalem provoked by the sacrileges of Lysimachus, brother of the apostate high priest Menelaus, 2 Mac 4^40; (RV **Hauran**).

AUTEAS, 1 Es 9^48 (AV, RV).—See Hodiah, **2.**

AUTHORITY.—The capability, liberty, and right to perform what one wills. The word implies also the physical and mental ability for accomplishing the end desired. Authority refers especially to the right one has, by virtue of his office, position, or relationship, to command obedience. The centurion was 'a man under authority,' who knew what it meant to be subject to others higher in authority than himself, and who also himself exercised authority over the soldiers placed under him (Mt 8^8f). In like manner 'Herod's jurisdiction' (Lk 23^7) was his authority over the province which he ruled. Hence the authority of any person accords with the nature of his office or position, so that we speak of the authority of a husband, a parent, an apostle, a judge, or of any civil ruler. The magistrates who are called in Ro 13^1 'the higher powers,' are strictly the highly exalted and honoured authorities of the State (so RSV 'governing authorities'), who are to be obeyed in all that is right, and reverenced as the 'ministers of God for good.' God is Himself the highest authority in heaven and on earth, but He has also given to His Son 'authority on earth to forgive sins' (Mt 9^6) and to execute judgment (Jn 5^27). After His resurrection Jesus Himself declared: 'All authority in heaven and on earth has been given to me' (Mt 28^18). In the plural the word is used in Eph 2^2 3^10 6^12, Col 1^16 2^15, to denote good and evil angels, who are supposed to hold various degrees and ranks of authority. See Dominion, Power. **M. S. T.—F. W. G.**

AUTHORIZED VERSION.—See English Versions, **30.**

AVA, AVITES, 2 K 17^24, 31 (AV).—See Avva.

AVARAN ('pale'?).—Surname of Eleazar, a brother of Judas Maccabaeus (1 Mac 2^5 6^43)

AVEN.—An insulting pointing in the Hebrew, followed by AV, RV, in Ezk 30^17, for **On** (q.v.; so RSV).

AVEN.—This stands for Beth-aven (q.v.) in Hos 10^8.

AVENGER OF BLOOD.—The practice of blood-revenge has been very widely spread among societies in a certain stage of civilization, where there has been no central authority to enforce law and order, and where the certainty of retaliation has been the only guarantee for security of life. Among the Semites the custom was in full force from the earliest times, and it is still the only basis of order in Arabia. It depends for its maintenance upon the solidarity of the clan or tribe. All the members of the tribe, whatever may be the immediate parental relationship, are counted as being of one blood; a wrong done to one is a wrong done to all, to be avenged if necessary by all the offended clan upon all the clan of the offender. The phrase used by the Arabs is, 'Our blood has been shed.'

Of the form of blood-revenge that involved the whole clan or tribe in the murder of a single individual there are still traces in the OT (Jos 7^24, 2 K 9^26). Naturally, however, the duty of avenging the shedding of blood fell primarily upon him who was nearest of kin to the slaughtered man. This next of kin was called the *gō'ēl*. The word in Hebrew law was used in a wide sense for him whose duty it was to redeem the property or the person of an impoverished or enslaved relative (Lv 25^25, 47–49, Ru 4^1ff), but it came to be used specially of the man who had to perform this most tragic duty of kinship. The steady effort of Hebrew law was to limit this ancient custom so as to ensure that a blood feud should not perpetuate itself to the ruin of a whole clan, and that deliberate murder and accidental homicide should not come under the same penalty. It is possible to trace with some definiteness the progress of this sentiment by which the *gō'ēl* was gradually transformed from being the irresponsible murderer of a possibly blameless manslayer to being practically the executioner of a carefully considered sentence passed by the community. See Kin [Next of].

R. B. T.

AVIM, AVIMS, AVITES.—The AV spellings of **Avvim** (q.v.), **Avvites** (see Avva).

AVITH.—An Edomite city, Gn 36^35; the site is unknown.

AVOID.—This verb is used intransitively in 1 S 18^11 (AV, RV), 'David avoided out of his presence twice' (RSV 'evaded him'). So Coverdale translates Mt 16^23 'Auoyde fro me, Sathan.'

AVOUCH.—This word, found in Dt 26^17f (AV, RV), is now obsolete except in legal phrases; RSV 'declare.'

AVVA.—A city from which the Assyrian king brought settlers to the Samaritan cities, 2 K 17^24 (AV **Ava**); probably to be identified with **Ivvah** (q.v.). The people are called **Avvites** in 2 K 17^31 (AV **Avites**).

AVVIM.—1. The name of primitive inhabitants of SW. Palestine, near Gaza, who were absorbed by immigrants from Caphtor (q.v.), *i.e.* the Philistines, Dt 2^23 (AV **Avims**); cf Jos 13^3 (AV **Avites**). **2.** A Benjamite town, Jos 18^23 (AV **Avim**); possibly to be identified with **Ai, 1.**

AWAY WITH.—This phrase is used idiomatically with the force of a verb in Is 1^13 (AV, RV). 'I cannot away with' = RSV 'I cannot endure.'

AWE.—RSV uses 'awe' more frequently than AV or RV in passages where this word has a more appropriate nuance; cf 1 Ch 16^25 ('to be held in awe'; AV, RV 'to be feared'), Mt 17^6 27^54, Mk 4^41 5^26 ('were filled with awe'; AV, RV 'were sore afraid,' 'feared greatly or exceedingly,' 'were filled with fear'), Ro 11^20 ('stand in awe'; AV, RV 'fear'), He 12^28 ('awe,' so also RV; AV 'godly fear'). See Fear.

AWL.—A boring instrument, named only in connexion with the ceremony whereby a slave was bound to perpetual servitude, Ex 21^6, Dt 15^17 (AV 'aul').

AWNING.—Correctly given by RV, RSV in Ezk 27^7 as translation of Hebrew *mikhsēkh* ('your awning'), corrected from *m^ekhassēkh* (AV 'that covereth thee').

AX, AXE.—See Arts and Crafts, **1, 3.**

AXLE (AV, RV **Axletree**).—See Wheel.

AYEPHIM.—Unknown place mentioned in 2 S 16^14, according to RVm; AV, RV, RSV render 'weary.'

AYYELETH HASH-SHARAR.—See Psalms, **2.**

AZAEL.—1. 1 Es 9^14 (AV, RV); see Asahel, **4. 2.** One of those who put away foreign wives, 1 Es 9^34 (AV, RV **Azaelus**).

AZAELUS, 1 Es 9^34 (AV, RV).—See Azael, **2.**

AZAL, Zec 14^5 (AV).—See Azel, **2.**

AZALIAH.—Father of Shaphan the scribe, 2 K 22^3, 2 Ch 34^8.

AZANIAH.—A Levite who signed the covenant, Neh 10^7.

AZAPHION, 1 Es 5^33 (AV).—See Hassophereth.

AZARA, 1 Es 5^31 (AV).—See Hasrah, **2.**

AZARAIAS.—1. 1 Es 8^1 (RV); see Seraiah, **2. 2.** 2 Es 4^1 (RV); see Azariah, **9.**

AZAREL.—1. A Korahite follower of David at Ziklag, 1 Ch 12^6. **2.** A son of Heman, 1 Ch 25^18; called **Uzziel** in v.^4. **3.** A prince of the tribe of Dan, 1 Ch 27^22. **4.** A son of Bani, who had married a foreign wife, Ezr 10^41, 1 Es 9^34 (AV **Esril**, RV **Ezril**). **5.** A priest, Neh 11^13. **6.** A Levite, Neh 12^36.

AZARIAH.—1. King of Judah; see Uzziah. **2.** 2 Ch 22^6 (AV, RV), an error for **Ahaziah** (RSV); cf v.^1 (see Ahaziah, **2**). **3.** A prophet, son of Oded, who met Asa's victorious army at Mareshah, and urged them to undertake a religious reform, 2 Ch 15^1–8. **4.** Son of

Zadok and high priest in the reign of Solomon, 1 K 4^{2}. **5.** A descendant of Aaron and father of Johanan, 1 Ch 6^{10}. **6.** Another descendant of Aaron, the son of Johanan and father of Amariah, 1 Ch 6^{10f}, Ezr 7^{3}, 2 Es 1^{2} (AV, RV **Aziei**). **7.** High priest in the reign of Uzziah, 2 Ch 26^{16-20}; he withstood the king when he attempted to usurp the priests' office. **8.** High priest in the reign of Hezekiah, 2 Ch $31^{10, 13}$. **9.** A son of Hilkiah the high priest, 1 Ch 6^{13f}, Ezr 7^{1}, 1 Es 8^{1} (AV **Ezerias,** RV **Zechrias**), 2 Es 1^{1} (AV **Azarias,** RV **Azaraias**). **10.** A priest who had married a foreign wife, 1 Es 9^{21} (AV, RV **Azarias**); he is called **Uzziah** in Ezr 10^{21}. **11.** A son of Nathan who was ' over the officers,' 1 K 4^{5}. **12.** A son of the Ethan whose wisdom was surpassed by that of Solomon (1 K 4^{31}), mentioned in 1 Ch 2^{8}. **13.** A Judahite, 1 Ch 2^{38}; he had Egyptian blood in his veins, v.^{34}. **14.** A Korahite Levite, 1 Ch 6^{36}; called **Uzziah** in v.^{24}. **15, 16.** Two of the sons of Jehoshaphat, 2 Ch 21^{2}. **17, 18.** Two of the five ' commanders of hundreds ' who assisted Jehoiada in the restoration of Joash, 2 Ch 23^{1}. **19.** An Ephraimite who supported the prophet Oded when he rebuked the army of Israel for purposing to enslave the captives of Judah, 2 Ch 28^{12}. **20, 21.** Two Levites, a Kohathite and a Merarite, 2 Ch 29^{12}. **22.** One of those who repaired the wall of Jerusalem, Neh 3^{23}. **23.** One of the twelve leaders of Israel who returned with Zerubbabel, Neh 7^{7}; called **Seraiah** in Ezr 2^{2}, 1 Es 5^{8} (AV **Zacharias,** RV **Zaraias**). **24.** One of those who helped to explain the law to the people, Neh 8^{7}, 1 Es 9^{48} (AV, RV **Azarias**), and who signed the covenant, Neh 10^{3}. **25.** One of those who stood on Ezra's right hand at the reading of the law 1 Es 9^{43} (AV, RV **Azarias**). **26.** A priest, the son of Hilkiah, 1 Ch 9^{11}; called **Seraiah** in Neh 11^{11}. **27.** Son of Hoshaiah (the Maacathite, Jer 40^{8}), Jer 42^{1} (AV, RV **Jezaniah**) 43^{2}; called **Jezaniah** in 40^{8}, and **Jaazaniah** in 2 K 25^{23}. He was one of the ' captains of the forces ' who joined Gedaliah at Mizpah. **28.** A captain of Judas Maccabæus, 1 Mac $5^{18, 56, 60}$ (AV, RV **Azarias**). **29.** The Hebrew name of Abednego, Dn $1^{6f. 11, 19}$ 2^{17}.

AZARIAS.—1. 1 Es 9^{21} (AV, RV); see Azariah, **10. 2.** 1 Es 9^{43} (AV, RV); see Azariah, **25. 3.** 1 Es 9^{48} (AV, RV); see Azariah, **24. 4.** 2 Es 1^{1} (AV); see Azariah, **9. 5.** 1 Mac $5^{18, 56, 60}$ (AV, RV); see Azariah, **28. 6.** Name assumed by the angel Raphael, To 5^{12} $6^{6, 13}$ 7^{8} 9^{2}.

AZARU.—Ancestor of a family which returned with Zerubbabel, 1 Es 5^{15}. His name is omitted from the parallel lists in Ezra and Nehemiah.

AZAZ.—A Reubenite, 1 Ch 5^{8}.

AZAZEL.—The name in Hebrew and in RV and RSV of the desert spirit to whom one of the two goats was sent, laden with the sins of the people, in the ritual of the Day of Atonement (Lv $16^{8, 10, 26}$ RV, RSV, see Atonement [Day of]). Etymology, origin and significance are still matters of conjecture. The AV designation **scapegoat** (*i.e.* the goat that is allowed to escape, which goes back to the *caper emissarius* of the Vulg.) obscures the fact that the word *Azazel* is a proper name in the original, and in particular the name of a powerful spirit or demon supposed to inhabit the wilderness or ' solitary land ' (16^{22} RV, RSV). The most plausible explanation of this strange element in the rite is that which connects Azazel with the illicit worship of field-spirits or satyrs (lit. ' he-goats ') of which mention is made in Lv 17^{7} (AV ' devils,' RV ' he-goats '), Is 13^{21} (AV, RV, RSV ' satyrs '). It may have been the intention of the authors of Lv 16 in its present form to strike at the roots of this popular belief and practice by giving Azazel, probably regarded as the prince of the satyrs, a place in the recognized ritual. Christianity itself can supply many analogies to such a proceeding. The belief that sin, disease and the like can be removed by being transferred to living creatures, beasts or birds, is not confined to the Semitic races, and has its analogy in Hebrew ritual, in the ceremony of the cleansing of the leper (Lv 14^{53}). In the Book of Enoch (see Pseudepigrapha, **1**) Azazel appears as the prince of the fallen angels, the offspring of the unions described in Gn 6^{1ff}. A. R. S. K.

AZAZIAH.—1. A Levite who played on the lyre, 1 Ch 15^{21}. **2.** Father of Hoshea the Ephraimite leader, 1 Ch 27^{20}. **3.** A Temple overseer under Hezekiah, 2 Ch 31^{13}.

AZBAZARETH, 1 Es 5^{69} (AV).—A corrupt form of **Esarhaddon** (q.v.; so RSV), derived from Vulg.

AZBUK.—Father of Nehemiah, who took part in rebuilding the walls of Jerusalem, Neh 3^{16}.

AZEKAH.—A city in the ' lowland ' (Shephelah) of Judah (Jos 15^{33-35}), identified with modern *Tell Zakarîyeh*, overlooking the ' valley of Elah ' (1 S 17^{1f}). It marked the limits of Joshua's pursuit of the five kings after his victory near Gibeon (Jos 10^{10f}). It was fortified by Rehoboam (2 Ch 11^{9}). With the exception of Lachish, it was the last Judaean stronghold to be captured by Nebuchadrezzar before the fall of Jerusalem in 586 B.C. (Jer 34^{7}). In Lachish Letter 4, reference is apparently made to the cessation of fire-signals from Azekah, presumably an indication of its fall while Lachish still held out. Azekah and its villages were reoccupied by Jews after the exile (Neh 11^{30}). F. F. B.

AZEL.—1. A descendant of Jonathan, 1 Ch 8^{37f} 9^{43f}. **2.** An unknown place in the neighbourhood of Jerusalem according to RV of Zec 14^{5} (AV **Azal**); but RSV renders ' the side of it.'

AZEM, Jos 15^{29} 19^{3} (AV).—See Ezem.

AZEPHURITH, 1 Es 5^{16} (AV).—See Jorah.

AZETAS.—Ancestor of a family which returned with Zerubbabel, 1 Es 5^{15}. His name is omitted from the parallel lists in Ezra and Nehemiah.

AZGAD.—One whose descendants returned with Zerubbabel. The numbers vary in the different lists: 1222 in Ezr 2^{12}, 2322 in Neh 7^{17}, 1322 (3222 in AV) in 1 Es 5^{13} (AV **Sadas,** RV **Astad**). A second detachment of 110 returned under Ezra, Ezr 8^{12}, 1 Es 8^{38} (AV, RV **Astath**). An Azgad appears among the leaders who sealed the covenant, Neh 10^{15}.

AZIA, 1 Es 5^{31} (AV).—See Uzza, **2.**

AZIEI, 2 Es 1^{2} (AV, RV).—See Azariah, **6.**

AZIEL.—A Levite, 1 Ch 15^{20}; called **Jaaziel** (q.v.) in v.^{18}.

AZIZA.—A Jew who had married a foreign wife, Ezr 10^{27}; called **Zerdaiah** in 1 Es 9^{28} (AV **Sardeus,** RV **Zardeus**).

AZMAVETH.—1. A descendant of Saul, 1 Ch 8^{36}. **2.** One of David's heroes, 2 S 23^{31}, 1 Ch 11^{33}; probably the same as the Azmaveth of 1 Ch 12^{3} 27^{25}, whose sons joined David at Ziklag, and who was ' over the treasuries.' **3.** A Benjamite town, Ezr 2^{24}, Neh 7^{28} (**Beth-azmaveth**) 12^{29}; called **Beth-asmoth** in 1 Es 5^{18}; probably modern *Ḥizmeh*, N. of Anathoth.

AZMON.—A place on the border of Judah, Nu 34^{4}, Jos 15^{4}; possibly modern *Qeṣeimah.*

AZNOTH-TABOR.—The lower slopes of Mt. Tabor, marking the SW. corner of the portion of Naphtali, Jos 19^{34}; possibly modern *Umm Jebeil.*

AZOR.—An ancestor of Jesus (Mt 1^{13f}).

AZOTUS.—See Ashdod.

AZRIEL (' El is my help ').—**1.** Head of a ' father's house ' in the E. half of the tribe of Manasseh, 1 Ch 5^{24}. **2.** A Naphtalite, 1 Ch 27^{19}. **3.** Father of Seraiah, Jer 36^{26}.

AZRIKAM (' my help has arisen ').—**1.** Son of Neariah, 1 Ch 3^{23}. **2.** A descendant of Jonathan, 1 Ch 8^{38} 9^{44}. **3.** A Levite, 1 Ch 9^{14}, Neh 11^{15}. **4.** The ' commander of the palace ' under Ahaz, 2 Ch 28^{7}.

AZUBAH (' forsaken ').—**1.** Wife of Caleb, 1 Ch 2^{18f}. **2.** Mother of Jehoshaphat, 1 K 22^{42}, 2 Ch 20^{31}.

AZZAN.—Father of Paltiel, Nu 34^{26}.

AZZUR.—1. One of those who sealed the covenant, Neh 10^{17}. **2.** Father of Hananiah the false prophet, Jer 28^{1}. **3.** Father of Jaazaniah, one of the princes of the people, Ezk 11^{1}.

B

BAAL (BAALI, BAALIM).—Used generally, the word *baʿal* means 'possessor,' 'inhabitant,' 'controller.' Thus, a married man is called 'possessor of a woman' (2 S 11^{26}), a ram, 'possessor of horns,' and the citizens of a locality are denoted by this word (Jg 9^2 20^5, 1 S 23^{11f}, 2 S 21^{12}). With a similar meaning, it is applied to numerous Canaanite local deities (plural *beʿālîm*, Jg 2^{11} 3^7 8^{33} 10^{10}, 1 S 7^1 12^{10}, 1 K 18^{18}, most of which may be local manifestations of the *Baʿal* par excellence, the fertility-god of Canaan); cf BAAL-GAD, BAALATH-BEER. These local gods were supposed to manifest themselves in the fertility, or in some startling natural formation, of the locality where they were worshipped. Such an animistic conception is evident from the fact that they were worshipped in high places and in groves, where such rites as prophetic ecstasy (Jer 22^{13}), self-mutilation (1 K 18^{28}), child-sacrifice (Jer 19^5), and fornication (Jer 7^9) were practised, the last as a rite of imitative magic.

Any local god could be so designated (*e.g.* Dagon is termed the *baʿal* of a devotee who set up a stele to him at Râs Shamra), and Baal-berith ('Lord of the Covenant'), the god worshipped at Shechem, may have been Yahweh. Jg 8^{33} does not suggest this, but in view of the late revision of the Book of Judges, the significance of Baal-berith may be misunderstood, especially if the worship of Yahweh had been contaminated by the local fertility-cult. Baal, however, was specifically the title of the Amorite god of winter rain and storm, otherwise known from Mesopotamian texts as Adad and in Canaan as Hadad ('thunderer') see also HADAD, RIMMON, and HADADRIMMON. Hadad is known from Egyptian execration texts to have been worshipped in Palestine from at least as early as *c* 1800 B.C., and several centuries later the Râs Shamra texts comprise a large complex of myths pertaining to Baal as the champion of Cosmos against Chaos in Nature and as the dying and rising vegetation-deity in annual conflict with Drought and Sterility. He is known from sculpture and figurines from Syria and Palestine as a warrior-god, striding into action with thunderbolt-spear and mace uplifted. His power of fertility is expressed by his association with the bull, the horns of which he wears on his helmet. In Aramaean sculpture he is shown standing on a bull, and Albright suggests that the bulls of Bethel and Dan in Israelite times may have served similarly as pedestals for the invisible Yahweh. Baal's stock epithet in the Râs Shamra texts is 'he who mounteth the clouds' (*rkb bʿrpt*) an epithet of Yahweh also in Dt 33^{26} and Ps 68^5 104^3.

The theme of the Canaanite myth of Baal's victory over the unruly waters and his assumption of kingship was adapted by the Hebrews as the expression of their faith in Providence, but that of the vicissitudes of Baal as a vegetation-deity, in spite of Israel's appropriation of seasonal rituals connected with it, did not seriously influence Hebrew thought, though the imagery of the Canaanite myth was freely used in Hebrew poetry. From the references in Judges to repeated lapses to the cult of *Baalim* and *Ashtaroth* we may infer that in the early days of the settlement the Hebrews tended to assimilate the Baal-cult without adapting it, and at various crises in Hebrew history, *e.g.* under Ahab and Jezebel (1 K 16^{32}), there was a recrudescence of Baal-worship in its native form in Israel, and Yahweh was apparently given the title as well as the attributes of Baal. Thus Saul, a zealous worshipper of Yahweh, names one of his sons *Eshbaal* (1 Ch 8^{33}); cf also *Meribbaal* (1 Ch 9^{40}) and *Jerubbaal* (Jg 8^{35}). Fiscal dockets from the time of Jeroboam II. from the palace of Samaria show many such theophoric names compounded with *Baal* as well as *Yahweh.* The prophets, especially Hosea, who demanded that (2^{16}) that Yahweh be no more called *Baʿalî* ('my Baal'), but *'Îshî* ('my husband') inveigh against this materialistic nature-cult and the licentious rites by which it was practised, and, though Hezekiah and Josiah suppressed it (2 K 18^4 23), it is mentioned as the cult of Tammuz, the dying and rising vegetation-deity, in the early days of the Exile and in Zec 12^{11} in a passage probably from the 2nd cent. B.C.

The final triumph of orthodoxy is indicated in the OT by the substitution of *bōsheth* ('shame') for *Baal* in proper names, not only when it denoted the Canaanite deity (Hos 9^{19}, Jer 3^{24} 11^{13}), but also in some of the above names, where it had really referred to Yahweh.

J. Gr.

BAAL.—**1.** A Reubenite, 1 Ch 5^5. **2.** A Gibeonite, related to Saul, 1 Ch 8^{30} 9^{36}. **3.** A place mentioned in 1 Ch 4^{33}; see BAALATH-BEER.

BAALAH.—**1.** A city on the border of Judah, Jos 15^{9f}, 1 Ch 13^6; identical with **Kiriath-jearim** (q.v.). **2.** A city in the Negeb, assigned to Judah, Jos 15^{29}; identical with **Balah** (q.v.) and **Bilhah** (q.v.).

BAALAH, MOUNT.—A site between Ekron and Jabneel, Jos 15^{11}; its location is unknown.

BAALATH.—**1.** A town of Dan, Jos 19^{44}. **2.** An unknown town mentioned in 1 K 9^{18}, 2 Ch 8^6.

BAALATH-BEER.—A city of Simeon in the Negeb, Jos 19^8; called **Baal** in 1 Ch 4^{33}.

BAAL-BERITH ('lord of the covenant').—The god of Shechem, where he had a temple, Jg 8^{33} 9^4; called also **El-berith**, 9^{46} (AV 'the god Berith'). The 'covenant' may be that amongst the Canaanite peoples or that between Shechemites and Israelites (cf Gn 34); or the title may be parallel to **Zeus Horkios**, the god who presides over covenants.

BAALE, 2 S 6^2 (AV).—See BAALE-JUDAH.

BAALE-JUDAH.—A place mentioned in 2 S 6^2 (AV **Baale of Judah**); probably to be identified with **Baalah, 1** (q.v.) and **Kiriath-jearim** (q.v.).

BAAL-GAD (? 'lord of fortune').—A place under Hermon, in the valley of the Lebanon, referred to only as the northern limit of the country conquered by Joshua, Jos 11^{17} 12^7 13^5. Its location is uncertain, possibly modern *Ḥāṣbeiyah.*

BAAL-HAMON.—The site of Solomon's vineyard, Ca 8^{11}; its location is unknown.

BAAL-HANAN ('Baal is gracious').—**1.** A King of Edom, Gn 36^{38f}, 1 Ch 1^{49f}. **2.** A Gederite of the time of David, 1 Ch 27^{28}.

BAAL-HAZOR ('lord of a court').—A place where Absalom's sheep shearers were when Amnon was killed, 2 S 13^{23}; probably modern *Jebel el-ʿAṣûr*, a mountain 4960 feet above the sea NE. of *Beitîn* (Bethel).

BAAL-HERMON.—A place on the slopes of Mount Hermon (q.v.), Jg 3^3; it marked the border of the territory of Manasseh in Transjordan, 1 Ch 5^{23}; its exact site is unknown.

BAALIS.—King of Ammon in the time of Gedaliah, Jer 40^{14}.

BAAL-MEON.—A city of Moab assigned to Reuben, Nu 32^{38}; mentioned also 1 Ch 5^8, Ezk 25^9; it is called **Beth-baal-meon** in Jos 13^{17}, and **Beth-meon** in Jer 48^{23}, while in Nu 32^3 it is called **Beon.** The names Baal-meon and Beth-baal-meon are found on the Moabite Stone (see Moab). It is identified with modern *Maʿîn*, about 5 mile SW. of Medeba.

BAAL-PEOR (' Baal of Peor ').—The local deity of Mount Peor, Dt 4[3], Nu 25[3, 5], Ps 106[28]. In Dt 4[3], Hos 9[10] it appears to be the name of a place, perhaps to be identified with **Beth-peor** (q.v.).

BAAL-PERAZIM.—A place near Jerusalem where David defeated the Philistines, 2 S 5[20], 1 Ch 14[11] (cf ' Mt. Perazim,' Is 28[21]); perhaps modern *Râs en-Nâdir* or *Sheikh Bedr*.

BAALSAMUS.—One of those who stood on the right hand of Ezra at the reading of the Law, 1 Es 9[43] (AV **Balasamus**); called **Maaseiah** in Neh 8[4]; see Maaseiah, **6.**

BAAL-SHALISHA, 2 K 4[42] (AV).—See Baal-Shalishah.

BAAL-SHALISHAH.—A place mentioned in 2 K 4[42] (AV **Baal-shalisha**); probably modern *Kefr Thilth*.

BAAL-TAMAR.—An unidentified site near Bethel and Gibeah, Jg 20[33].

BAALZEBUB, BEELZEBUL.—Baalzebub appears as the name of a Philistine god worshipped at Ekron (2 K 1[2, 3, 6, 16]) while Beelzebul (so RSV; AV and RV Beelzebub) is the name applied to the prince of demons in Mt 10[25] 12[24], Mk 3[22], Lk 11[15, 18, 19]. The older commentators took the form Baalzebub, ' lord of flies,' as original, indicating a deity with the power to send or avert plagues of flies. This was supposed to have been changed by the Jews to the offensive form, Beelzebul, ' lord of filth.' But if such a view were correct it would be hard to understand why a minor local deity should become such an important figure in later demonology. The finding of the form ' Baalzebul ' in the Râs Shamra tablets favours a different and more plausible explanation. According to this, Baalzebul, ' lord of the mansion ' or ' lord of the lofty dwelling ' was the original form (preserved in the NT) and would refer not to a local deity but to the great Baal of Syria who would have a local shrine at Ekron. The form Baalzebub is then to be explained as a perversion, made either to ridicule the god or because to a pious Jew the title ' lord of the lofty dwelling ' would seem to be appropriate only to Yahweh. This line of explanation derives some support from the title ' master of the house ' applied to Beelzebul in Mt 10[25]. Other explanations suggest that the name means ' the enemy ' or have sought to represent Zebul as a place-name, but without much plausibility. If we accept the most plausible among these explanations, we can understand why Beelzebul came to be regarded as a major demonic power, and his name became interchangeable with that of Satan.
J. Macq.

BAAL-ZEPHON.—Apparently a shrine of ' Baal of the north,' near the spot where the Israelites crossed the Red Sea, Ex 14[2, 9], Nu 33[7]; its site is unknown. The corresponding goddess ' Baalit of the north ' is named along with the god of Kesem (Goshen) in an Egyptian papyrus of the New Kingdom, as worshipped at Memphis.
F. Ll. G.

BAANA.—**1. 2.** Two of Solomon's commissariat officers, 1 K 4[12, 16]. **3.** Father of Zadok, one of those who rebuilt the wall, Neh 3[4]. **4.** One of those who returned with Zerubbabel, 1 Es 5[8] (AV, RV), possibly identical with the preceding, and with **Baanah, 3.**

BAANAH.—**1.** One of the murderers of Ishbosheth, 2 S 4[2, 5, 6, 9]. **2.** A Netophathite, 2 S 23[29], 1 Ch 11[30]. **3.** One of those who returned with Zerubbabel, Ezr 2[2], Neh 7[7], 1 Es 5[8] (AV, RV **Baana**). **4.** One of those who sealed the covenant, Neh 10[27].

BAANI, 1 Es 9[34] (RV).—See Bani, **9.**

BAANIAS, 1 Es 9[26] (AV).—See Benaiah, **3.**

BAARA.—Wife of a Benjamite, 1 Ch 8[8].

BAASEIAH.—A Kohathite, 1 Ch 6[40]; perhaps a textual error for **Maaseiah** (q.v.).

BAASHA.—An officer of the army under Nadab, son of Jeroboam i., who assassinated the king while the army was besieging Gibbethon, and became the third king of Israel. Thereafter he slew the whole house of Jeroboam (1 K 15[27–29]). He captured and fortified Ramah, and this led Asa to form an alliance with Benhadad, of Damascus, and this in turn led to Baasha's withdrawal to Tirzah (1 K 15[17–21]). Although Baasha died in his bed after a reign of twenty-four years, his dynasty was extinguished two years after his death, as foretold by the prophet Jehu (1 K 16[1–6]).

BABBLER.—Ac 17[18] ' What will (RSV ' would ') this babbler say? ' The Gr. word translated ' babbler ' means literally ' seed-picker," applied first to such birds as the rook, and then, symbolically, to men who make their living by picking up scraps in the market-place (from Demosthenes to Eustathius). Goodspeed ' rag-picker '; Moffatt ' the fellow . . . with his scraps of learning.'
F. W. G.

BABE.—See Child.

BABEL, TOWER OF.—See Tongues, Confusion of.

BABI, 1 Es 8[37] (AV, RV).—See Bebai.

BABYLON.—*Bābel* is the Hebrew form of the native name *Bāb-ilim*, ' Gate of God,' a popular etymology of a pre-Semitic name. It was also *Tin-tir*, ' Grove of life.' According to the Hebrew tradition (Gn 10[10]), it was as old as Erech, Akkad, and Calneh. Excavations show that there was a prehistoric settlement here. The first historical reference to Babylon occurs in a year formula of the Agade dynasty, *c* 2200 b.c. It lay on the E. bank of the Euphrates, part of its site being now occupied by Hillah, about 50 miles S. of Baghdad. The ruins extend for 5 miles N. to S. Bābil, the N. ruin, covers 120,000 sq. ft. and is still 90 ft. high. It covers the remains of the celebrated Esagila temple. The shape and form of Babylon as revealed by fourteen years' excavation is that of Nabopolassar and Nebuchadrezzar. The description given by Herodotus and Ctesias is that of Persian times. The Kasr contains the ruins of Nebuchadrezzar's palace, along whose E. side ran the sacred procession street, decorated with enamelled tiles representing the dragon and the bull, to the Ishtar-gate at the SE. corner. The whole was enclosed within an irregular triangle, formed by two lines of ramparts and the river, an area of about 8 sq. miles. The city crossed the river to the W., where are remains of a palace of Neriglissar. In later times it became coterminous with many other large cities, and Herodotus ascribes to it a circuit of 55 miles.

From the very earliest times the kings and rulers of Babylonia worked at the building of its temples, palaces, walls, bridges, quays, etc. Hammurabi first raised it to be the capital of all Babylonia. It was sacked by Sennacherib in 689 b.c., the chief palaces, temples, and city walls levelled with the ground, and the waters of the Euphrates turned over it. Esarhaddon began to rebuild it, and it stood another long siege under his son, Ashurbanipal. Nabopolassar began its restoration; Nebuchadrezzar raised it to its height of glory. Cyrus took it without resistance, and held his court there. Darius Hystaspis besieged, took it, and destroyed its walls. Xerxes plundered it. Alexander the Great planned to restore it. Antiochus Soter actually began the restoration of its great temple. The foundation of Seleucia robbed it of its population, but the temple services continued to 29 b.c., at least. See, further, Assyria and Babylonia.
C. H. W. J.—T. F.

BABYLON (in NT).—Babylon was apparently used by the early Church as a symbol for Rome. **1.** In Rev (14[8] 16[19] 17[5] 18[2, 10, 21]) its destruction is foretold, because of its sins, and particularly because of its persecution of the Christians. Such identification is, however, somewhat uncertain, and rests ultimately on the improbability that the word in the connexion in which it appears can refer to the city of Mesopotamia (the word is so used in Mt 1[11] 12[17], Ac 7[43]). This probability is supported by the fact that Babylon is called ' mystery ' in Rev 17[5], is said to be seated on seven mountains (v.[9]), and to be a centre of commerce and authority (18[3-19] 17. 14[8]). Rome is apparently called Babylon in *Sib. Or.* v. 143, 158 ; 2 Es ; Apoc. Baruch.

This identification of Babylon in Revelation with Rome dates at least from the time of Jerome. The attempt has been made to identify it with Jerusalem ; but this conflicts with Rev 11[8]. The fact that Revelation utilized Jewish apocalyptic material makes it imperative that the term symbolize a power which stood related both to Christians and Jews, in a way parallel with the relation of Babylon to the ancient Hebrew nation.

2. The reference to Babylon in 1 P 5[13] has had three interpretations : (*a*) Babylon in Egypt, mentioned by Strabo and Epiphanius ; (*b*) Babylon on the Euphrates ; and (*c*) Rome. In view of the symbolic use of the word 'Babylon,' as mentioned above, the last seems the most probable. Eusebius (*HE* ii. 15) so interprets the reference, and, in view of the ancient and persistent tradition, partly literary, partly archaeological, there is nothing improbable in St. Peter's having been in Rome. This probability is strengthened by the reference to the persecution to which Christians were being subjected. Assyrian Babylon in the second half of the 1st cent. was in decay. Even if pseudonymous, the presumed authorship of 1 P would be most appropriate if the epistle was written from Rome, where persecution took place under Nero and Domitian. S. M.—**F. C. G.**

BABYLONISH GARMENT, Jos 7[21] (AV).—See SHINAR, MANTLE FROM.

BABYLONISH MANTLE, Jos 7[21] (RV).—See SHINAR, MANTLE FROM.

BACA, VALLEY OF.—An allegorical place-name, found only in Ps 84[6] (AV, RSV), where RV renders 'Valley of Weeping.' Most probably it is no more an actual locality than is the 'Valley of the Shadow of Death' in Ps 23[4].

BACCHIDES.—Governor of Mesopotamia under Demetrius Soter ; sent to establish Alcimus (q.v.) in the priesthood ; defeated and killed Judas the Maccabee, and at a later period besieged Jonathan in the fortress of Bethbasi ; was finally compelled to entertain proposals for peace (1 Mac 7[8-20] 9[1-72] 10[12] ; Jos. *Ant.* XII. x. 1 [389]–XIII. i. 6 [34]).

BACCHURUS, 1 Es 9[24] (AV, RV).—See ZACCUR, **7.**

BACCHUS.—See DIONYSUS.

BACENOR.—An officer of Judas Maccabaeus (2 Mac 12[35]).

BADGER or **ROCK BADGER** (*shāphān*).—The *Hydrax syriacus*, a small rabbit-like animal, with short ears and a mere stump of a tail. It has stiff greyish-brown hair, with softer, lighter-coloured hair on the belly ; it is nocturnal in its habits, and lives in holes in the rocks. Rock badgers are very plentiful along the rocky shores of the Dead Sea, and also in the Lebanon, especially above Sidon ; they can, however, be seen as a rule only between sunset and sunrise. They are gregarious in their habits, and disappear into their rocky fastnesses (Ps 104[18], Pr 30[26] where RSV has 'badgers' and AV, RV 'conies') with the greatest rapidity on the slightest approach of danger. The Bedouin, when hunting them, lie hidden for many hours during the night close to their holes. They feed on grass and sweet-smelling herbs, and their flesh is esteemed for eating by the Bedouin ; they do not actually 'chew the cud' (Lv 11[5], Dt 14[7] where RSV has 'rock badger' and AV, RV '**coney**'), though they work their jaws in a way that resembles a ruminant. E. W. G. M.

BADGERS' SKINS.—This rendering of AV in Ex 25[5] 26[14] etc. (RV 'sealskins,' RVm 'porpoise-skins,' RSV 'goatskins') and Ezk 16[10] (RV 'sealskin,' RVm 'porpoise-skin,' RSV 'leather') is a mistranslation. Badgers' skins are not suitable for the covering of the Tabernacle or for making sandals. See PORPOISE.

BAEAN.—The name of an unknown tribe destroyed by Judas Maccabaeus (1 Mac 5[4]).

BAG, PURSE, WALLET.—Several kinds of bags, etc., may be distinguished. (*a*) The shepherd's and traveller's wallet for carrying one or more days' provisions. Like most of the other OT bags, it was made of skin, generally undressed, and was slung across the shoulder. This is the scrip of Mt 10[10] and parallels (RV 'wallet' ; RSV 'bag'). The former is retained by RV (but RSV 'wallet') to render a unique word, which had to be explained even to Hebrew readers by the gloss 'the shepherd's bag' (1 S 17[40]). (*b*) A more finished article, the leather satchel which served as a **purse** (Lk 10[4] 12[33] AV here 'bag'). For illust. see Rich, *Dict. of Antiq.* 217. The purse of Mt 10[9], Mk 6[8], however, was merely the folds of the girdle (RSV 'belt'). (*c*) The merchant's bag, in which he kept his stone weights (Dt 25[13]), also served as a purse (Pr 1[14]). (*d*) The favourite bag of money and valuables—hence the beautiful figure 1 S 25[29], where 'the bundle of life' = life's jewel-case—was one which could be tied with a string (2 K 12[10], Pr 7[20], also Gn 42[35] EV 'bundle'). If required, a seal could be put on the knot (Job 14[17]). (*e*) Another word is used both for a large bag, capable of holding a talent of silver (2 K 5[23]), and for the dainty lady's **satchel** (Is 3[22] RV ; RSV 'handbags' ; AV **crisping pins**). (*f*) The 'bag' which Judas carried (Jn 12[6] 13[29]) was rather a small box (RSV 'money box'), originally used for holding the mouth-pieces of wind-instruments. See also VESSEL.

A. R. S. K.—**F. W. G.**

BAGO, 1 Es 8[40] (AV, RV).—See BIGVAI, **1.**

BAGOAS.—A eunuch in the service of Holofernes (Jth 12[11, 13, 15] 13[3] 14[14]).

BAGOI, 1 Es 5[14] (AV, RV).—See BIGVAI, **1.**

BAGPIPE.—See MUSIC and DULCIMER.

BAHARUM.—An unknown place found only in the gentilic *Baharumite* in 1 Ch 11[33] (AV, RV ; RSV 'of **Baharum**') ; 2 S 23[31] has **Barhumite** (AV, RV). In both places we should probably read 'of **Bahurim**' (so RSV in 2 S 23[31]). See BAHURIM.

BAHARUMITE, 1 Ch 11[33] (AV, RV).—See BAHURIM.

BAHURIM.—The town where Paltiel, son of Laish, was ordered to relinquish Michal, 2 S 3[16] ; where Shimei lived, who cursed and stoned David in his flight, 2 S 16[5], 1 K 2[8] ; where Ahimaaz and Jonathan hid in the well from Absalom, 2 S 17[18f] ; and the home of Azmaveth, one of David's mighty men, 1 Ch 11[33] (AV, RV **Baharumite** ; RSV 'of Baharum'), 2 S 23[31], where **Barhumite** is incorrectly written (so AV, RV ; RSV 'of Bahurim') for **Bahurimite**. It was in the tribe of Benjamin between Jerusalem and the Jordan River, according to the reports of David's flight and that of Ahimaaz and Jonathan. *Râs eṭ-Ṭmîm*, NE. of the Mount of Olives, about one mile from Jerusalem and near the ancient road from Jerusalem to Jericho, best fits the topographical allusions in the references cited above ; Israelite, Hellenistic, and Roman sherds have been found there (cf E. E. Voigt, 'Bahurim,' *AASOR*, v, 1925, 67–76). R. A. S. M.—**W. L. R.**

BAITERUS.—The head of a family which returned with Zerubbabel, 1 Es 5[17] (AV **Meterus**).

BAJITH, Is 15[2] (AV).—See BAYITH.

BAKBAKKAR.—A Levite, 1 Ch 9[15].

BAKBUK.—The ancestor of certain Nethinim (q.v.), who returned with Zerubbabel, Ezr 2[51], Neh 7[53], 1 Es 5[31] (AV, RV, **Acub**).

BAKBUKIAH.—**1.** A Levite, Neh 11[17]. **2.** A porter, Neh 12[25].

BAKEMEATS, BAKER.—See BREAD.

BAKING.—See BREAD.

BAKING-PAN.—Lv 2[5] 6[21] 7[9] (RV) ; see HOUSE, **9.**

BALAAM is the subject of a remarkable and intricate narrative in Nu 22–24, connected with the arrival of Israel on the plains of Moab. He was a soothsayer of Pethor on the Euphrates, called by Balak king of Moab to curse the invaders. At first God refused him permission to go, but, when Balak sent a larger and more honourable embassy, permission to go was granted to Balaam but only on condition that he spoke as God directed him. As Balaam journeyed to Moab on his ass, the angel of the Lord thrice stood in the way but was visible only to the ass which refused to proceed. Three times Balaam beat his animal, which at last spoke and reproached its master, and then Balaam's eyes were opened and he saw the angel. In the face of the Divine disapproval Balaam offered to go back, but he was allowed to proceed on condition that he spoke as God directed him. Balak met Balaam at the frontier and took him first to Bamoth-baal at Kiriath-huzoth, then to the field of Zophim, to the top of Pisgah, and finally to the top of Peor. Though the three successive sites are regarded by Balak as increasingly favourable for his purpose of obtaining a curse on Israel, Balaam each time pronounces a eulogy in the form of a poem expressing thoughts favourable to Israel. In anger Balak dismisses the soothsayer, who before he goes recites a poem or poems on the destruction of Moab and Edom at the hands of a future ruler of Israel:

> a star shall come forth out of Jacob,
> and a sceptre shall rise out of Israel;
> it shall crush the forehead of Moab,
> and break down all the sons of Sheth.
> Edom shall be dispossessed. (24^{17f})

followed by three short pieces on the fate of Amalek, the Kenites, Asshur, and Eber.

Those chapters are usually regarded as compiled from the sources J and E. The composite nature of the narrative is deduced from the doublets (cf 22^{2a} and v.^{4b}, 22^{3a} and v.^{3b}) and the divergent traditions about Balaam's home (cf 22^{5} [MT] with v.^{5} [MSS, Sam., Pesh., Vulg.]), but especially from the inconsistency between 22^{22-35} and the surrounding verses. In 22^{22-34} (v.^{35} is an editorial link) Balaam seems to have set out without the Divine approval and he is accompanied by two servants; in vv.^{20f} Balaam has God's permission for his journey and he is escorted by the embassy sent by Balak. J is thought to be the source of 22^{22-34} (cf the episode of the speaking serpent in Gn 3, also from J; for another example of an ass speaking, see M. R. James, *Apocryphal New Testament*, p. 383) and most of 24, with perhaps other odd verses; the rest is from E.

But the poems have also been treated as separate compositions, distinct from the prose framework. Thus while von Gall argues for a post-Exilic date for the poems and regards them as Messianic, G. B. Gray favours a theory of their antiquity because of 'the feeling of national confidence, success, prosperity, and contentment which pervades them, and in virtue of which they are most closely connected with the ancient poems known as 'the blessing of Jacob' (Gn 49) and 'the blessing of Moses' (Dt 33). W. F. Albright has argued that the composition of the poems should be dated in the 13th or 12th cent. B.C. and their original writing down in or near the 10th cent. B.C. (*JBL*, lxiii. [1944], 207 ff).

The first poem 23^{7-10} is independent of its context for it is an intelligible unit and it is inconsistent with its framework, which regards the poem as a blessing of Israel whereas it is not. The contents suggest that it is a poetic version of the Balaam story (cf Jg 5 with Jg 4), and probably it is an ancient song from an alternative tradition.

The second poem 23^{18-24} may contain in vv. $^{22, 24}$ Balaam's blessing in an early form; the remainder of the poem represents a theocratic viewpoint and so is later, though not necessarily post-Exilic.

Similarly, it can be argued that the third, 24^{3-9}, though the text has suffered, may be pre-Exilic and even as early as the time of the United Monarchy. The fourth, a composite piece, is outside the plan of the story and must be a later incorporation, less certainly early. If v.^{17} is Messianic as the later Jews, the early Church (cf Rev 22^{16}), and some recent scholars hold, then the poem may be Exilic or later; but the argument is less strong if vv.^{17f} refer to David. It may be noted that Bar Koseba, the Jewish leader in the Second Revolt against Rome (A.D. 132–135) was called Bar Kochba 'Son of the star' (24^{17}). The Qumrân Community makes use of this verse both in the *War of the Sons of Light and Sons of Darkness* and in the *Zadokite Document*.

In Nu $31^{8, 16}$ (cf Jos 13^{22}), assigned to the Priestly document (P), there is recorded Balaam's death at the hands of the Israelites, because he led Israel into sin. Cf Rev 2^{14}: 'the teaching of Balaam, who taught Balak to put a stumbling block before the sons of Israel, that they might eat food sacrificed to idols and practice immorality.' Jd ^{11} brackets Balaam with Cain and Korah as examples of evil men, and the epithet 'wicked' is regularly applied to him (cf *Aboth* v. 19). Because Balaam, like Samuel and Ahijah, received a fee (Dt 23^{4}), he has been accused of avarice; cf 2 P 2^{15}: 'they have followed the way of Balaam, the son of Beor, who loved gain from wrongdoing.' Cf also Philo, *De Vita Mosis*, i. 48; Jos. *Ant.* IV. vi. 5 f (118, 126). But there is nothing in the story in Numbers to support this view. That Balak sent a second embassy with the message: 'Whatever you say to me I will do' (22^{17}) reveals not Balaam's greed but the king's need. And though the P source links Balaam's death (31^{16}) with the events of 25^{1-5}, the earlier traditions, properly understood, know nothing against Balaam's character. W. D. McH.

BALAC, Rev 2^{14} (AV) = **Balak** (q.v.).

BALADAN.—See MERODACH-BALADAN.

BALAH.—A city of Simeon in the Negeb, Jos 19^{3}; called **Baalah** in Jos 15^{29}, where it is assigned to Judah (see BAALAH, **2**) and **Bilhah** in 1 Ch 4^{29}.

BALAK.—The king of Moab who hired Balaam, Nu 22–24; mentioned also in Jos 24^{9}, Jg 11^{25}, Mic 6^{5}, Rev 2^{14}. See BALAAM.

BALAMON.—A town near Dothaim (Jth 8^{3}).

BALANCE.—The Hebrew balances probably differed but little from those in use in Egypt (see illustration in *BRL*, p. 178). The main parts were the **beam** with its support, and the **scales** which were hung by cords from the ends of the equal arms of the beam. The 'pair of scales' is used in OT by a figure for the balance as a whole; only once is the beam so used (Is 46^{6}). The **weights** were originally of stone and are always so termed. The moral necessity of a just balance and true weights and the iniquity of false ones are frequently emphasized by the prophets, moral teachers, and legislators of Israel; see Am 8^{5}, Mic 6^{11}, Pr 11^{1} 16^{11} ('a just balance and scales are the LORD's') 20^{23}, Lv 19^{36}, Dt 25^{13ff}. A. R. S. K.

BALASAMUS, 1 Es 9^{43} (AV).—See BAALSAMUS.

BALBAIM (Jth 7^{3}).—See BELMAIN.

BALD LOCUST (Lv 11^{22}).—See LOCUST.

BALDNESS.—See CUTTINGS IN THE FLESH, HAIR.

BALLAD.—See PARABLE.

BALM.—Nothing is known for certain about the nature of this substance (Heb. *ṣᵒrî*), but it is usually supposed to be some kind of aromatic gum or resin. It was a product of Gilead (Gn 37^{25}, Jer 8^{22} 46^{11}), an important article of commerce (Gn 37^{25}, Ezk 27^{17}), suitable for a gift (Gn 43^{11}), and celebrated for its healing properties (Jer 8^{22} 46^{11} 51^{8}). There is now no plant in Gilead which yields any characteristic product of this nature. The so-called 'balm of Gilead' of commerce and the substance sold by the monks of Jericho to-day (the latter a product of the *zakkûm* tree) are neither of them serious claimants to be the article referred to in the Bible. Many consider that *ṣᵒrî* was mastic (so RVm in Gn 37^{25}), a gum which exudes from the bark of the *Pistacia lentiscus* and much used by the Arabs for flavouring coffee, sweets, etc., and as a chewing gum. This has been credited with medicinal properties. See also SPICE.
E. W. G. M.—**H. H. R.**

BALNUUS, 1 Es 9^{31} (AV, RV).—See Belnuus.

BALSAM.—See Spice.

BALSAM TREES.—Heb. *bᵉkhā'îm*, 2 S 5^{23f}, 1 Ch 14^{14f} (AV, RV **mulberry trees**). These trees have on philological grounds been supposed to be a variety of balsam (so RSV), and on grounds of appropriateness to the story (2 S 5^{23f}) to be poplars, whose leaves readily quiver with the slightest breath of air. Their identity is, however, quite uncertain. Mulberries they cannot be ; for though to-day plentiful in Palestine, and still more so in the Lebanon, these trees were introduced into the land later than OT times. See Sycamine.

E. W. G. M.

BALTASAR.—The Greek form of *Belteshazzar* and of *Belshazzar* (qq.v.). In Bar 1^{11f} (RV ; AV **Balthasar)** it stands for Belshazzar (RSV).

BALTHASAR.—See Baltasar.

BAMAH.—The ordinary word for **high place** (q.v.), retained only in Ezk 20^{29} in its Hebrew form (as the word *manna* in the parallel case in Ex 16^{15}) on account of the word-play : 'What (*māh*) is the *bāmāh* to which you go (*bā*)?'

BAMOTH, BAMOTH-BAAL.—Bamoth is mentioned in Nu 21^{19f} as a station in the journey of Israel from the Arnon to the Jordan. It is probably identical with Bamoth-baal of Nu 22^{41} (RVm, RSV ; AV, RV 'the high places of Baal'), to which Balaam was led by Balak. Bamoth-baal is listed as a Reubenite city in Jos 13^{17}, and is perhaps mentioned on the Moabite Stone (see Moab) as Beth-bamoth. It is possibly to be identified with *Khirbet Quweiqiyeh*.

BAN.—The ban is an institution from remote antiquity, which still survives in the Jewish and Christian Churches. On its origin and early history cf C. H. W. Brekelmans, *De Ḥerem in het OT*, 1959. The original idea, common to all the Semitic languages, is that of withdrawing something from common use and setting it apart for the exclusive use of a deity. In Hebrew the verbal root acquired the more specialized meaning of devoting to Y″ His enemies and their belongings by means of fire and sword, and is usually rendered 'utterly destroy' (RVm adds 'Heb. *devote*'), while the cognate noun (*ḥērem*, Gr. *anathema*) is '**accursed** (AV) *or* **devoted** (RV, RSV) **thing.**' In this brief treatment of a large subject we propose to distinguish between the war ban, the justice ban, and the private ban.

1. The *war ban*, clearly the oldest form of the institution, shows various degrees of severity. The war ban of the first degree, as it may be termed, involved the destruction not only of every man, woman, and child of the enemy, but also of their entire property of every description (see Dt 13^{16}). The treatment of the Amalekites in 1 S 15 is a familiar example. The case of Achan, after the ban and capture of Jericho, affords a striking illustration of the early ideas associated with the ban. Every 'devoted thing,' as henceforth the inviolate property of Y″, and therefore taboo, became infected with the deadly contagion of holiness (note Lv 27^{28} 'most holy,' literally 'holy of holies'). Hence by retaining part of the 'devoted thing' (*ḥērem*) in his tent Achan infected the whole 'camp of Israel,' with disastrous results (Jos 6^{18} 7^{11f}, cf Dt 7^{26}). More frequently we meet with a relaxed form of the war ban, which may be called the ban of the second degree. In this case only the men, women, and children of the doomed city were devoted, while the cattle and the rest of the spoil became the property of the victors (Dt 2^{34f} 3^{6f} 7^{2}, Jos 11^{14}). A still further relaxation, a ban of the third degree, is contemplated by the law of Dt 20^{10ff}, by which only the males are put to the ban, the women and children being spared as the perquisites of the besiegers. On the other hand, only virgins were to be spared in Nu 31^{17f} and Jg 21^{11ff}, for special reasons in the latter case.

2. The *justice ban* differs from the other in being applicable only to members of the theocratic community. It appears in the oldest legislation as the punishment of the apostate Israelite (Ex 22^{20}), and is extended in the Deuteronomic code to the idolatrous city (Dt 13^{12ff}). Here only the ban of the first degree was admissible. An important modification of the judicial ban is first met with in Ezr 10^{8}, where recalcitrant members of the community, instead of being put to death, are excommunicated, and only their 'substance forfeited' (RVm 'devoted') to the Temple treasury. This modified *ḥērem* became the starting-point of a long development. For these later Jewish and Christian bans see Excommunication.

3. The attenuated form of ban found in the late passage Lv 27^{28} may be termed the *private ban*. The cases contemplated—'man or beast or field'—are evidently those of unusually solemn and inalienable dedications by private persons for religious purposes (cf Nu 18^{14}, Ezk 44^{27}, and the NT 'corban'), as opposed to the redeemable dedications of the preceding verses. the latter are holy while the former are 'most holy.' The following verse, on the contrary, must refer to the justice ban.

The ban was an institution of earlier date than the Hebrew conquest, and was practised by the Moabites in its most rigorous form (see Mesha's inscription, lines 11–17), perhaps also by the Ammonites (2 Ch 29^{23}). Instances of similar practices among many half-civilized races are noted by the anthropologists. The original motive of the ban is probably reflected in Nu 21^{2f}, where it is represented as the return made to Y″ for help against the enemy vouchsafed in terms of a preceding vow (cf *devotio* from *devoveo*). This has to be interpreted in the light of the primitive solidarity between a god and his clan. Even in Israel the wars of the Hebrews were the 'wars of Y″' (Nu 21^{14}). 'The religious element is found in the complete renunciation of any profit from the victory, and this renunciation is an expression of gratitude for the fact that the war-God has delivered the enemy, who is His enemy also, into the hands of the conqueror' (Kautzsch in Hastings' *DB* Ext. Vol. 619^{b}). The ban was thus the outcome of religious zeal in an age when the moral sense was less advanced than the religious.

With regard to the wholesale application of the war ban in the Deuteronomic sections of Joshua, modern criticism has taught us to see in these the ideal generalizations of the exilic age. The Hebrews of the conquest were in truth the children of their age, but such a stupendous holocaust as is implied in such passages as Jos $11^{11,14}$ must not be placed to their credit. The legislation of Dt., it must further be remembered, is the outcome of several centuries' experience of Canaanite heathenism, the true character of which the soil of Palestine is only now revealing, and of its baneful influence on the religion of Y″. In this legislation the antique institution of the ban was retained as a means of protecting the community against a serious menace to its religious life. Nevertheless the enactment of Dt 13^{12ff} remained a dead letter till the age of the Maccabees (1 Mac 5^{5ff}).

A. R. S. K.

BAN, 1 Es 5^{37} (AV, RV).—See Tobiah, **1.**

BANAIAS, 1 Es 9^{35} (AV, RV).—See Benaiah **3.**

BAND.—This spelling represents three distinct though ultimately related English words, used in AV and RSV for various Hebrew and Greek words : (1) that which binds, *e.g.* Lv 26^{13} (RSV here 'bars,' elsewhere often 'bonds'), Dn $4^{15,23}$, Hos 11^{4} ; (2) a strip or ribbon, *e.g.* Ex 28^{8} RSV, Ezk $13^{18,20}$ RSV, Ex 39^{23} AV ; (3) a group of men bound for a common purpose, more or less informally, as a band of prophets (1 S 10^{5} RSV), raiders (2 K 24^{2}), soldiers (Ezr 8^{22}). In NT, AV uses 'band' for *speira*, the Greek equivalent of Roman *cohors* (for Roman Army in the NT period, see Legion). Cohort is approximately 'regiment,' as a division of the legion or as an infantry unit of the auxiliary forces—which alone were regularly stationed in a minor province such as Judaea. The auxiliary cohorts were (nominally) 500 or 1000 strong, commanded by a prefect or military tribune, in Greek called *chiliarchos* ('commander of 1000'), rendered in AV as 'captain' or 'chief captain,' in RSV as 'tribune' (Ac 21[31], etc.). RSV renders *speira* by 'band' when used informally, for the guards who accompanied Judas (Jn 18[3, 12]), 'garrison' when it refers to the soldiers present at Jerusalem (Mt 27[27], Mk 15[16]), 'cohort' when used strictly technically. The auxiliaries were normally recruited from provincials, but a few units of Roman citizens were raised in emergencies. The Italian Cohort of Ac 10[1] would have been such, very likely the *cohors II Italica* known to have been in Syria in A.D. 88 (CIL xvi. 35). 'Augustan' ('Emperor's Own') was a title of honour, hence not distinctive. The Greek is *sebastē*, which has tempted scholars to connect the Augustan Cohort of Ac 27[1] with Samaria (Gr. *Sebastē*, 'Augusta'), troops from which were stationed at Caesarea at this time. But this would call for a different Greek form, *sebastēnē* or *Sebastēnōn*. E. R. H.

BANI ('Y" built').—**1.** A Gadite, one of David's heroes, 2 S 23[36] (cf HAGRI). **2. 3. 4.** Levites, 1 Ch 6[46]; Neh 3[17]; Neh 8[7] (in 1 Es 9[48] called **Anniuth**; in AV Anus, RV Annus) 9[4f] 10[13] 11[22] (called **Binnui** in Ezr 8[33], Neh 10[9]). **5.** A Judahite, 1 Ch 9[4]. **6.** Head of a family that returned with Zerubbabel, Ezr 2[10], 1 Es 5[12]; called **Binnui** in Neh 7[15]. **7.** One of those who sealed the covenant, Neh 10[14]. **8.** One of those whose sons had married foreign wives, Ezr 10[29], 1 Es 9[30] (AV, RV **Mani**). **9.** Another whose sons had married foreign wives, Ezr 10[34], 1 Es 9[34] (AV **Maani**, RV **Baani**). See BINNUI. **10.** Ancestor of Shelomith, who returned with Ezra, 1 Es 8[36] (AV **Banid**, RV **Banias**).

BANIAS, 1 Es 8[36] (RV).—See BANI, **10.**

BANID, 1 Es 8[36] (AV).—See BANI, **10.**

BANISHMENT.—See CRIMES AND PUNISHMENTS, **11.**

BANK.—**1.** A mound of earth in siegecraft, see FORTIFICATION AND SIEGECRAFT. **2.** The table of a money-changer or banker, see MONEY-CHANGERS.

BANNAIA, 1 Es 9[33] (AV).—See ZABAD, **6.**

BANNAS.—A Levite who returned with Zerubbabel, 1 Es 5[26] (AV **Banuas**).

BANNEAS, 1 Es 9[26] (RV).—See BENAIAH, **3.**

BANNER, ENSIGN, STANDARD. — That the Hebrews, like the Egyptians, Assyrians, and other ancient nations, possessed military ensigns is a safe inference from Nu 2[2]. Nothing certain, however, is known regarding them. In the above passage a distinction seems to be made between the 'ensigns' (literally 'signs'; cf Ps 74[4] which, on the assumption of a Maccabaean date, may be alluded to in *DSH* (vi. 4 f) of the 'fathers' houses,' and the standards of the four great divisions of the Hebrew tribes in the wilderness, according to the artificial theory of the priestly writer.

Equally uncertain is the relation of these to the *nēs*, the wooden pole (Nu 21[8f], Is 30[17]), set up on an eminence as a signal for the mustering of the troops. This word is of frequent occurrence both in the original sense and in the figurative sense of a rallying point, in the prophetic announcements of the future (Is 5[26] 11[10], Jer 4[21], and often). A. R. S. K.—**P. W.-M.**

BANNUS, 1 Es 9[34] (AV, RV).—See BINNUI.

BANQUET.—In OT the Hebrew or Aramaic expression rendered 'banquet' or 'banqueting house' means literally 'drinking' (*mishteh*) or 'house of drinking' (*bêth mishteh*), since wine was an important element of such feasts; so Ca 2[4], Dn 5[10]. In the book of Esther the term is rendered by AV and RV 'feast' in Es 1[3, 5, 9] 2[18] 8[17] and 'banquet' in 5[4, 5, 6, 8, 12] 6[14] 7[1, 2, 7], while RSV reverses these save in 5[12] 6[14] 7[1] 8[17] where it agrees with them, 5[4, 5, 8] where it has 'dinner,' and 4[6] 7[2] where it has 'drinking wine' for 'banquet of wine.' There are many passages where all EV render *mishteh* by 'feast.' In Job 41[6] (Heb. 40[30]) AV 'make a banquet' is a mistranslation of the verb *kārāh*, 'make trade of' (RV 'make traffic of,' RSV 'bargain over'). In Am 6[7] *mirzaḥ* is rendered 'banquet' in AV (but 'mourning' in Jer 16[5]; so RV, RSV), where RV, RSV have 'revelry'; the word really indicates a cultic feast. In NT RSV has 'banquet' for Gr. *deipnon* in Mk 6[21], Lk 14[16, 17, 24] where AV, RV have supper.' In 1 P 4[3] AV 'banquetings' renders Gr. *potos*, literally 'drinkings' (RV, RSV 'carousing'), the normal LXX rendering of *mishteh*. See also MEALS. H. H. R.

BANUAS, 1 Es 5[26] (AV).—See BANNAS.

BAPTISM.—This term, which designates a NT rite, is confined to the vocabulary of the NT. It does not occur in the LXX, neither is the verb with which it is connected ever used of an initiatory ceremony. This verb is derivative from one which means 'to dip' (Jn 13[26], Rev 19[13]), but itself has a wider meaning, ='to wash' whether the whole or part of the body, whether by immersion or by the pouring of water (Mk 7[4], Lk 11[38]). The substantive is used (*a*) of Jewish ceremonial washings (Mk 7[4], He 9[10]); (*b*) in a metaphorical sense (Mk 10[38], Lk 12[50]; cf 'plunged in calamity'); and (*c*) most commonly in the technical sense of a religious ceremony of initiation. Remarkable are also the synonyms for *baptisma*, viz. *sphragis*, *sēmeion*, *onoma*, *stigma*, *charagma*.

1. The earliest use of the word 'baptism' to describe a religious and not merely ceremonial observance is in connexion with the preaching of *John the Baptist*, and the title which is given to him is probably an indication of the novelty of his procedure (Mt 3[1], Mk 8[28], Lk 7[20]; cf Mk 6[14, 24], where he is called 'the Baptizer'). He preached 'a baptism of repentance for the remission (RSV 'forgiveness') of sins' (Mk 1[4]), *i.e.* the result of his preaching was to induce men to seek baptism as an outward sign and pledge of inward repentance on their part, and of their forgiveness on the part of God. Thus one may say: 'Baptism is related to repentance as the outward act in which the inward change finds expression.' And insofar as by immersion not only outward cleansing but also the purifying of man's heart is effected, we must define baptism with John as already a sacramental act, not merely as a symbol, although the effect is not an immediate one, but a promise for the future. The baptism of proselytes, practised by the Jewish community, must be viewed as mere ceremonial cleansing without sacramental meaning; it is found at the end of the 1st cent., but probably was older. The texts of Qumrân (the Dead Sea Scrolls) give further insight into ceremonial washings, also non-sacramental. As far as we know, John was the first to employ baptism as a means of religious purification promising forgiveness of sin and an initiation into the eschatological congregation of God. But, according to the gospel record, John himself recognized the incomplete and provisional character of the baptism administered by him: 'I have baptized you with water; but he will baptize you with the Holy Spirit' (Mk 1[8]).

2. *Jesus* Himself accepted baptism at the hands of John (Mk 1[9]). There is no reason to question this record; if non-historical it would have been omitted (*lectio difficilior*) because it involves difficulty with the early Christian belief that the divinity of Jesus was revealed already in his supernatural birth. That Jesus himself baptized is nowhere suggested in the Synoptic Gospels, and is expressly denied in the Fourth Gospel (Jn 4[2]). Neither do we have reliable accounts of Jesus' disciples baptizing during his lifetime. On the other hand, one must acknowledge that immediately after the death and Resurrection of Jesus baptism was practised —appearing as if spontaneously—as the indispensable condition for membership in the Christian congregation. It seems to be the earliest Christian sacrament.

While the Lord's Supper was observed because it was traced back to the historical Jesus, whether as a Passover meal or not, and is explained by the account of Jesus' own words (Mk 14[22-24] and parallels; 1 Co 11[23-25]), baptism is never commanded in the NT as an institution ascribed to Jesus Himself. In order to prove Him its founder one generally refers to passages like Mk 16[15f], Jn 3[5], Mt 28[19f]. Yet are these sayings

BAPTISM

historically trustworthy? The Marcan verses belong to a section (Mk 16^{9-20}) regarded in textual and literary criticism as a later addition—it is not found in the manuscripts א, B, or the Syriac and Armenian versions. The Johannine verse is a typical symbolic interpretation of an early Christian liturgical practice. The passage quoted as chief witness, Mt 28^{19f}, gives a word of the *risen* Lord, and combines the commandment of mission and of baptism, to be done 'in the name of the Father and of the Son and of the Holy Spirit.' It thus takes up an early Christian liturgical formula which was not used before the second half of the 1st cent. It is hardly possible to harmonize the universal aspect with the historical Jesus, and it is impossible to assume the trinitarian formula for the teaching in his life-time. One must conclude that Christian baptism has no anchorage in an institution by Jesus but presupposes His Crucifixion and Resurrection, *i.e.* the institution was by the risen Lord.

3. In order to rediscover *the earliest statements on Christian baptism* we must turn to *Paul* and concentrate on passages where the apostle cites common tradition: *e.g.* Ro 10^{9}, 1 Co 6^{11}; and also Ro 8^{29f}. In Ro 6^{3} and 1 Co 12^{13} Paul presupposes that all Christians, Jewish as well as Gentiles, are baptized. Over and again in his letters he refers to baptism as a constitutive act, and derives from this his ethical imperatives. Characteristic of this is Gal 5^{25}: 'If we live by the Spirit, let us also walk by the Spirit.' The deeper meaning is understood only when we recognize that 'the Spirit' here and elsewhere refers to baptism. One may paraphrase the words: Since we are baptized and have the Spirit, let us also walk as those who are moved and marked by the Spirit! Over against the teaching and practice of John the Baptist, this connexion of baptism with the gift of the Holy Spirit is a new feature. In 1 Co 6^{11} Paul, after picturing their sinful past, reminds the Christians of their newness of life: "But you were washed, you were sanctified, you were justified in the name of the Lord Jesus Christ and in the Spirit of our God.' The three verbs used here describe the sacramental purification, the remission of sins, and the new element in life: the eschatological seal given in the Spirit of God—for Paul the Spirit of God is identical with the Spirit of Christ (see the remarkable changes in Ro 8^{9-11}). Different from the post-apostolic and later Christian liturgical praxis, which is marked by the trinitarian formula of Mt 28^{19} (see *Did.* VII. i. 3; Just. *Apol.* LXI. 3, 11, 13) the primitive Church baptized 'in' or 'into the name of Jesus' (or 'Jesus Christ,' or 'the Lord Jesus; see 1 Co $1^{13, 15}$; Ac 8^{16} 19^{5}; *Did.* ix. 5). The calling of a name effected—according to primitive belief—the presence of the divine person (or demon). Thus the spoken formula, 'in the name of Jesus,' effected the presence of the risen Lord and gave the baptized into His possession and protection. In this context the verb 'to seal' or the noun 'the seal' is often used (2 Co 1^{22}; perhaps also Ro 4^{11}; cf Eph 1^{13} and Rev 7^{3ff}). In all these passages, which obviously set forth the earliest traditions, the connexion of baptism with Christ's person and work is inherent. On the ground of this practice Paul can say: 'For as many of you as were baptized into Christ have put on Christ' (Gal 3^{27}). Referring in these words to 'rebirth' with Christ's resurrection, Paul presupposes that 'all of us who have been baptized into Christ Jesus were baptized into his death' (Ro 6^{3}). The old 'Adam of our sinful past has died in baptism, and the 'new life' appeared when we 'put on Christ.' Thus baptism is no longer, as with John, only a cleansing from sins committed in the past, but is the act which sanctifies the present life and guarantees eschatological bliss.

4. The further development was not uniform, as we see in *Acts*. Here most of the Pauline elements are present but there is an inconsistency with regard to the liturgical performance. On the one hand baptism precedes the gift of the Holy Spirit, which is administered by a particular act, the laying on of hands (*e.g.* Ac 8^{14ff}); on the other hand baptism concludes God's work, the Spirit being already present with the believer in his very decision for faith in Christ (Ac 10^{44-48} 11^{15-18}). This inconsistency seems to reflect geographical as well as theological differences of the second half of the 1st century. It makes clear the danger that baptism might break up into two acts: (*a*) a sacramental rite of cleansing, effected by immersion and relating to the past, and (*b*) a sacramental imparting of the Holy Spirit, effected by the laying on of hands and relating to the present and the future life. If this took place, it would be possible to administer the two acts separately, at different times and by different persons.

5. *The external form of baptism* was *immersion* in flowing water, which is presupposed in Ac 8^{36}, He 10^{22} and expressly prescribed in *Did.* vii. 1–3. The passage in *Did.* permits—in emergency cases only—the head of the baptized to be sprinkled with water. It seems as if *a profession of faith in Christ* had to be made prior to baptism, at least at the end of 1st cent. The 'good confession in the presence of many witnesses' in 1 Ti 6^{12} obviously points to the baptismal profession of faith, and the phrase often occurring in the context with baptism, 'What prevents [namely the baptism]?' (Ac 8^{36} 10^{47} 11^{17}, Mt 3^{14}) still reminds us of the liturgical procedure (O. Cullmann).—As far as one can see, *the laying on of hands* is an early part of baptism, probably connected with the *acclamation of the name Jesus Christ.* It is probable that *a catechetical instruction* preceded baptism, where the ethical obligations, the demand of being and becoming 'holy' were taught, and special elements of the Holiness-code (Lv 17 ff) were included (Ph. Carrington). *The administration of baptism* was in general left to the local officers of the congregation and did not require a special charisma or quality; it was not a duty of the Apostle, and Paul could write 'for Christ did not send me to baptize but to preach the gospel' (1 Co 1^{17}). In the earliest stage of Christianity only *adults* were baptized. As to the controversial question of *infant-baptism* the NT gives no explicit answer; it must be inferred from the theological meaning of baptism (cf § **9**).

6. *The theological meaning* of baptism is complex and contains various elements, sometimes separate, sometimes intermingling. One aspect is common in all NT writings, namely that baptism is neither a magic tool, nor a symbolic action, but *a sacrament*; *i.e.* divine forces work with man through a this-worldly action; certain presupposed special rites are performed in orderly fashion, and the requirements set before the participant are fulfilled (repentance, true faith, personal decision for Jesus as Lord). When Paul refers (1 Co 15^{29}) to the practice of Gnostic Christians in Corinth, allowing themselves to be baptised on behalf of the dead, it is clear that he himself acknowledges the sacramental meaning of baptism but rejects the magical misuse as found in the Greek mysteries.

The *various elements* may be summarized as follows: (*a*) *The remission of sins* (Ac 2^{38}, 1 Co 6^{11}; cf He 10^{22}, 1 P 3^{21}, 2 P 1^{9} and Hermas *Mand.* IV. iii. 1, Just. *Apol.* lxi. 10), referring of course to sins of the past. (*b*) *The calling of the name* of the Lord is an element concurrent with immersion. Its meaning is twofold, namely (1) to 'seal' the baptized in Christ's possession and protection (see § **7**) and (2) apotropaic, to ban evil spirits (Co 1^{13}, cf Barn 16^{7}). (*c*) *The gift of the Holy Spirit* as an effect of baptism is presupposed by Paul (1 Co 12^{13}, 2 Co 1^{22}; also Eph 1^{13}, 4^{30}) and is an early feature of Christian baptism distinguishing it from pre-Christian rites and from the practice of John the Baptist (Ac 19^{1-8}; cf Mk 1^{8}). In Jn 3^{5} we read, 'Unless one is born of water and the Spirit, he cannot enter the kingdom of God'; the same is said in Barn 16^{9-11} (cf Hermas, *Simil.* ix. 13). (*d*) In connexion with the last two elements must be viewed *the participation in Christ's death and resurrection*, which is brought about through baptism (best stated in Ro 6^{2ff}). This aspect seems to be introduced by Paul, who received it from Gentile Christians; it does not occur in Jewish-Christian writings of the NT. Yet while the participation in Christ's death is stated in the aorist tense, and thus interpreted as a reality of the Christian present, the participation in Christ's resurrection is given in the future tense and thus interpreted as a hope and an eschatological gift. Especially in this interpretation, Paul decisively corrects the view which would identify it with magical initiation of mystery-cults.

Yet one must recognize that with regard to the eschatological gift—the *arrabōn* ('down-payment') of the Spirit—the baptized knows that he is already a 'new creation' and rejoices with Paul: 'The old has passed away, behold the new has come' (2 Co 5^{17}). It is this awareness and self-understanding of the Christian which sets forth the characteristic interrelation of being and becoming, of baptism and ethics, linked together by a fundamental eschatological hope. This hope is no mere horizon of future events but is realized in the idea of the Church as the one body of Christ (1 Co 12^{13}), into which baptism has conferred incorporation.

7. Baptism in the NT, though a genuine Christian sacrament, has been nourished by pre-Christian concepts cf § **1**). We have not yet mentioned a particular OT feature, taken up and transformed into a Christian thought of great importance: the idea of the '*holy remnant*.' It is first found in the story of Elijah in the 9th cent. B.C. (1 K 19^{18}), then in Isaiah, Zephaniah, and Ezekiel (Ezk 9^{4}). The idea of an eschatological remnant is connected with *the rite of sealing or branding*. This eschatological concept played a great role in Judaism (Zadokite Fragments, B-text, 9^{10-12}, Odes Solom. 15^{6-9}; cf Rev 13^{16f} 14^{9} 16^{2} 20^{4}), and was taken up by the early Christians, for whom 'to seal' meant 'to baptize,' namely for the kingdom of God. This is the realization of the 'holy remnant' (cf Ro 9–11). When Hellenistic Christianity interpreted the 'holy remnant' or the 'true Israel' as the sacramental *sōma Christou,* being the eschatological congregation of God and Christ, the sealing practice became a natural part of baptism as a sign of membership (1 Co 12^{12-27}; cf Hermas, *Simil.* VIII. vi. 3; IX. xvi. 2 ff; xvii. 4; and 2 Clem 7^{6} 8^{6}). Possibly even the saying of Jesus in Mk 8^{34} and ‖ had this sealing idea in the background.

8. Form-critical analysis has shown that baptism—its preparation as well as administration, in the widest meaning—forms a primary source—perhaps the most significant one—for the *confessional formulas* in the NT writings (cf R. Bultmann). Ro 10^{9} contains a baptismal confession, Eph 5^{14} gives a (fragmentary?) baptismal acclamation. 1 Co 10 and 11 bring sacramental formulas of the Eucharist ('cup of blessing,' 'Lord's Supper') but include also the typological passage concerning baptism (1 Co 10^{1-6}); 1 Co 6^{11} and He 6^{4} take up baptismal formulas and Ro 8^{29f} contains a hymnic fragment rooted in baptism. The 'turn' or conversion to a new life rooted in baptism is set forth in sayings like Ac 26^{18}, Col 1^{13}, 1 P 2^{9}, 1 Jn 3^{14}, and seems to be in the background of Ro 6^{4f}. Further we must reckon with Christian adaptation of pre-Christian formulas, as *e.g.* in hymns like Col 1^{15-20} (E. Käsemann). The *Sitz im Leben* of all these quotations or allusions is early Christian liturgical praxis. Here baptism has a place as *primus inter pares* because of the theological neighbourhood or even correlation of baptism with Christ's crucifixion and resurrection as outlined in Ro 6 (cf § 6 (*d*)), a section of the greatest importance for the further development of Christian thought and for the iconography of early Christian art in the Roman catacombs as well as in the baptistry of Dura-Europos (3rd cent.).

9. Parallelism between *baptism and circumcision* cannot be assumed. In Col 2^{11} the word circumcision is used as a metaphor for baptism, but this single verse cannot be used as a basis for generalizations. The religious distinction of the father of a family is not taken up by the earliest Christianity, which emphasized instead the individual person before God and in Christ and thus opened the door for a new social and religious recognition of women. Male *and* female persons were baptized from the earliest time, and their equality in principle is stated in Gal 3^{8}. The question of children is mentioned in 1 Co 7^{14}: they are 'holy' because of their parents' faith. It is possible—at least it is not excluded—that Paul's remark concerns baptism. Yet neither here nor in sentences like 'Lydia was baptized with her household' is any explicit word said about the legitimacy of *infant baptism.* We may conclude that the question was not yet urgent, because of the expectation of the immediacy of Christ's parousia.

When the Church of the 2nd cent. began to carry out the practice of infant baptism, this was not felt to be an unauthorized innovation. One justification for this usage was found in the postponement of Christ's imminent return. Further, there was the general tendency towards sacramentalism, in which the eschatological future was anticipated. The salvation through baptism has already taken place, the 'riches of his glorious inheritance' (Eph 1^{18}) are present, the forgiveness of sins and the possession of righteousness have been assured to the believers as members of Christ's body (Ti 3^{5}, 1 P 3^{21}, Barn 11^{11} cf 2 Clem 1^{4} 2^{7} 3^{3} 9^{2-5}, etc.). And since natural death before Christ's parousia was now regarded as a law of nature, infant baptism became sanctioned. It was seen as the sacramental door opening in a way which had to be traversed in fulfilment of the credal and ethical demands of the Church. Thus baptism started a process—it was not the result of a development.

10. NT scholarship has reached the result that no longer can we present a uniform Biblical Theology. The NT canon contains a plurality of concepts which must be taken into account. Baptism greatly differs with John the Baptist, the Pre-pauline and Pauline usage, and the Synoptic writers. Though the evidences in Luke's Book of Acts may go back to earlier levels of tradition, they picture a later stage of liturgical development, as also do the Pastorals and the Book of Revelation. Divergences in these documents originating from different times and local traditions cannot be overlooked. What can be shown are the constant features, on the one side, and variant accents on the other. *Constant* is the sacramental meaning of baptism ever since the time of John the Baptist. From here baptism entered into the earliest Christianity after Christ's crucifixion and resurrection. The new situation after Easter Day is marked by the step from the work and word of Jesus to the faith in the crucified and risen Christ. In the following period, increasing missionary demands and the obvious delay of Christ's parousia brought out new features which may be evaluated as *variant* accents. The sacramental meaning is no longer exclusively dependent on the faith of the participant but attains a quality in itself as a magically operative rite. This development begins as early as the time of Luke's Acts and is influenced in general by Gnostic-Christian practice. It is openly stated in Hermas *Vis.* III. iii. 5. Faith in Christ is no longer the only *conditio sine qua non* but is seen as an outcome of baptism. As soon as this was acknowledged, infant baptism had its dogmatic justification. The possible magical misunderstanding of 'faith' was excluded, because the Christian in the course of his life had to confess his faith repeatedly in order to preserve the sacramental gift of baptism. E. D.

BAR.—Aramaic word for 'son'; used, especially in NT times, as the first component of personal names, such as Bar-abbas, Bar-jesus, Bar-jonah, etc. The word stands in Ps 2^{12}, where AV, RV have 'kiss the son,' where an Aramaic word is out of place (the normal Hebrew word stands in v.^{7}), and where the text should probably be emended to read 'kiss his feet' with RSV.

BARABBAS.—A revolutionist and a murderer according to the Synoptic Gospels; a robber according to John (Mt 27^{15-26}, Mk 15^{6-15}, Lk 23^{18-23}, Jn 18^{39-40}). The Evangelists relate that Pilate at the time of the Passover offered to release either Jesus or Barabbas and that the Jews chose Barabbas. The whole proceeding is explicitly regarded as resting upon a Jewish custom. There is, however, no other evidence of such a practice. This fact, along with the obvious function which the story plays in the narrative, has rendered it suspect historically in the eyes of many critics. The name Barabbas is probably a patronymic meaning ' son of Abbas.' According to an ancient reading of Mt 27^{17} supported by Origen, his surname was Jesus. Many textual critics believe that this was the original reading and that it disappeared from the majority of the manuscripts since some were offended that the name of the murderer should be the same as that of Christ.

BARACHEL.—Father of Elihu, Job $32^{2,6}$.

BARACHIAH.—See Zechariah.

BARAK (' lightning ').—The son of Abinoam; he lived at a time when the Canaanite kingdom of Hazor, having recovered from its overthrow by Joshua (Jos 11^{10-15}), was taking vengeance by oppressing Israel. He is called from his home in Kedesh-naphtali by Deborah to deliver Israel. He gathers an army of 10,000 men from the tribes of Naphtali and Zebulun. With this force, accompanied by Deborah, without whom he refuses to go forward, he encamps on Mt. Tabor, while the enemy under Sisera lies in the plain on the banks of the Kishon. At the word of Deborah, Barak leads his men down to battle, and completely defeats Sisera. The latter flees; Barak pursues him, but on reaching his hiding-place finds that he has been already slain by Jael, the wife of Heber. The glory of the victory, therefore, does not lie with Barak, but with Deborah, who was his guiding spirit, and with Jael who slew the enemy's leader (Jg 4, 5). W. O. E. O.

BARBARIAN.—The English word is used in Ac $28^{2,4}$ (RSV ' native '), Ro 1^{14}, 1 Co 14^{11} (RSV ' foreigner '), Col 3^{11} to translate a Greek word which does not at all connote savagery, but means simply ' foreign,' ' speaking an unintelligible language.' The expression first arose among the Greeks in the days of their independence, and was applied by them to all who could not speak Greek. When Greece became subject to Rome, it was then extended to mean all except the Greeks and Romans. There may be a touch of contempt in St. Luke's use of it, but St. Paul uses it simply in the ordinary way; see especially 1 Co 14^{11}. A. So.

BARBER.—See Hair.

BARCHUS, 1 Es 5^{32} (RV).—See Barkos.

BARHUMITE, 2 S 23^{31} (AV, RV).—See Bahurim.

BARIAH.—A son of Shemaiah, 1 Ch 3^{22}.

BAR-JESUS.—The name of ' a certain magician, a Jewish false prophet ' (Ac 13^{6}), probably an astrologer, in the retinue of Sergius Paulus, the Roman proconsul of Cyprus. The title *Elymas* (v.^{8}) seems to be derived from the Arabic word *'alîm*, signifying ' wise,' and to be equivalent to Magus. Because Bar-Jesus feared the loss of his influence on the proconsul, he opposed the preaching of St. Paul. According to Ac 13^{11} he was punished by temporary blindness. Josephus mentions (*Ant.* xx. vii. 2 [142]) a Jew of Cyprus and magician named Atomos or Hetoimos who helped the procurator Felix to win Drusilla (Ac 24^{24}), the wife of king Aziz of Emesa. Perhaps it was the same person (Zahn, *Apg.* 419). E. H.

BAR-JONA(H).—See Bar, and John, **6.**

BARKOS.—Ancestor of certain Nethinim (q.v.) who returned with Zerubbabel, Ezr 2^{53}, Neh 7^{55}, 1 Es 5^{32} (AV **Charcus**, RV **Barchus**).

BARLEY (*śᵉʿôrāh*).—As in ancient times, so to-day barley (Arab. *shaʿîr*) is the most plentiful cereal of Palestine. It is the chief food of horses (1 K 4^{28}), mules, and donkeys, oats being practically unknown. It is still used by the poor for making bread (Jg 7^{13}, Jn $6^{9,13}$ etc.) in the villages, but not in the cities. Barley was the special ritual offering for jealousy (Nu 5^{15}). The barley harvest (Ru 1^{22}) precedes that of wheat: it begins around Jericho as early as March, and in Jerusalem and the neighbourhood at the end of May. E. W. G. M.

BARN.—Several words are rendered ' barn ' in AV. **1.** *'āsām* in Dt 28^{8} (AV ' storehouses,' AVm, RV, RSV ' barns '), Pr 3^{10} (AV, RV, RSV ' barns '), from verb meaning ' to store.' **2.** *gōren* in 2 K 6^{27}, Job 39^{12} means ' threshing floor ' (so RV, RSV). **3.** *mᵉghûrāh* in Jl 1^{17} (AV, RV ' barns,' RSV ' granaries '), Hag 2^{19} (AV, RV, RSV ' barn '), probably from the verb *'āghar*, ' to gather food.' **4.** *apothēkē* in Mt 6^{26} 13^{30}, Lk $12^{18,24}$ (AV, RV, RSV), meaning ' storehouse ' or ' granary '; rendered ' garner ' in Mt 3^{12}, Lk 3^{17} (AV, RV; RSV ' granary ').

BARNABAS was an important and widely known Christian missionary, who appears in Ac 4^{36f} 9^{27} $11^{22-26,30}$ 12^{25} 13^{1}–15^{39}. A Levite, Joseph of Cyprus, sold his estate and gave the money to the community. He was given the surname Barnabas (' son of comfort ') by the apostles, to whom he introduced the converted Saul. He was sent to inspect the new community at Antioch. From Tarsus he brought Saul there and worked together with him a whole year. Then both delivered a collection to the brethren at Jerusalem. From there they brought with them John Mark, a cousin of Barnabas (Col 4^{10}). Barnabas, Paul, and John Mark made a missionary voyage to Cyprus; then John went home. Barnabas and Paul founded communities at Antioch of Pisidia, Lystra, Iconium, and Derbe. After their return to Antioch they were sent to the Jerusalem conference (see Gal 2^{1-10}). Later on there arose between them ' a sharp contention ' concerning John and ' they separated from each other.' Finally Barnabas and Mark ' sailed away to Cyprus ' (Ac 15^{36-39}).

Some critics have made out that Barnabas means ' son of Nebo,' and also that the scene in Ac 9^{27} becomes meaningless if St. Paul came to Jerusalem three years after his conversion (Gal 1^{18}). Possibly Barnabas was one of the ' men of Cyprus ' (Ac 11^{20}) who founded the community at Antioch. Later on Barnabas withdrew from fellowship with St. Paul and the Gentile Christians, when ' certain men came from James ' (Gal 2^{12f}). But the way in which Paul speaks of Barnabas in 1 Co 9^{6} points to a reconciliation. E. H.

BARODIS.—A name occurring in 1 Es 5^{34} (omitted in Ezra and Nehemiah).

BARRACKS.—This word stands in RSV in Ac $21^{34,37}$ 22^{24} $23^{10,16,32}$, where AV and RV have ' castle ' in all cases. See Praetorium; also Citadel.

BARREL.—Hebrew *kadh* is rendered ' barrel ' in AV, RV 1 K $17^{12,14,16}$ 18^{33}, but ' jar ' in ARV, RSV. It is a large earthenware jar used for fetching water from the well, storing grain, etc., and is elsewhere rendered **pitcher** (*e.g.* Ec 12^{6}).

BARRENNESS.—See Child.

BARSABAS.—AV form of **Barsabbas** (q.v.).

BARSABBAS.—See Joseph (in NT), **5,** and Judas (in NT), **6.**

BARTACUS.—Father of Apame (1 Es 4^{29}).

BARTHOLOMEW.—One of the Twelve, mentioned only in the lists of the Apostles (Mt 10^{3} = Mk 3^{18} = Lk 6^{14}). Jerome says that he wrote a Gospel, preached to the Indians, and died at Albanopolis in Armenia. Bartholomew is really not a name, but a patronymic—*Bar Talmai* = ' son of Talmai ' (cf 2 S 13^{37}). See Nathanael. D. S.

BARTIMAEUS.—A blind man whom Jesus, on His way to the last Passover, healed at the gate of Jericho (Mk 10^{46-52}). The order of events is somewhat different in Luke (18^{35-43}) and the blind man's name is not given. In Matthew's account (20^{29-34}) two unnamed blind men appear. Bartimaeus is probably a patronymic meaning ' son of Timaeus ' (=Timai) as Mark suggests (10^{46}). But the explanation is made in a manner contrary to Mark's usual practice and may be a scribal gloss. W. R. S.

BARUCH (' blessed ').—**1.** Son of Neriah, the son of Mahseiah and brother of Seraiah (Jer 51^{59}); known from Jer 36, 45, 32^{12-16} $43^{3,6}$; by Jeremiah's side in the conflict with Jehoiakim (604 B.C.), again during the last siege of Jerusalem (587–586 B.C.), and again amongst the Judaeans left behind after the Second Captivity. 'Baruch' the scribe, named in Jer 36^{26} along with 'Jeremiah the prophet,' is already the recognized attendant and amanuensis of the latter; he seems to have rendered the prophet over twenty years of devoted service. He belonged to the order of 'princes,' among whom Jeremiah had influential friends (26^{16} 36^{25}); Baruch's rank probably secured for Jeremiah's objectionable 'roll' (ch. 36) the hearing that was refused to his spoken words. When he cast in his lot with Jeremiah, Baruch made a heavy sacrifice; he might have 'sought great things' for himself, and is warned against his natural ambition (45^{3-5}). The promise that Baruch's life shall be given him 'as a prize' wherever he goes, placed where it is (45^{5}), suggests that he survived his master, to act as his literary executioner. The Book of Jeremiah (q.v.) owes much to this loyal secretary, though the final arrangement of the materials is far from satisfactory. Tradition adds nothing of any certainty to the references of Scripture; see, however, Jos. *Ant.* x. ix. 1, 6 (158, 179). For the Apocryphal writings attached to his name, see APOCRYPHA and PSEUDEPIGRAPHA. **2.** One of the wall-builders (Neh 3^{20}). **3.** A signatory to the covenant (10^{6}). **4.** A Judahite (11^{5}). G. G. F.

BARZILLAI.—**1.** The name of a chieftain of Gilead who brought supplies to David and his army at Mahanaim (2 S 17^{27ff}). After the death of Absalom, Barzillai went across Jordan with the king, but declined to go to court (19^{31ff}). On his deathbed David charged Solomon to 'deal loyally with (AV, RV 'show kindness to') the sons of Barzillai' (1 K 2^{7}). His descendants are mentioned in Ezr 2^{61}, Neh 7^{63}, 1 Es 5^{38} (AV **Berzelus,** RV **Zorzelleus**). One of his daughters, named **Agia** (q.v.), married **Jaddus** (q.v.). **2.** The Meholathite whose son Adriel received Merab (1 S 18^{19}), Saul's daughter in marriage. She bore five sons (2 S 21^{8}, where Hebrew reads *Michal,* so AV, RV). J. G. T.—**R. A. B.**

BASALOTH, 1 Es 5^{31} (AV, RV).—See BAZLUTH.

BASCAMA, 1 Mac 13^{23} (AV, RV).—See BASKAMA.

BASE.—To be base is in modern English to be morally bad, but in AV it sometimes means to be of humble birth or lowly position. In RV, RSV the word is normally used in the sense of morally low, mean.

BASEMATH.—**1.** Daughter of Elon the Hittite and wife of Esau, Gn 26^{34}; called **Adah** in Gn 36^{2}. **2.** Daughter of Ishmael and sister of Nebaioth, who became Esau's wife, Gn 36^{3}; called **Mahalath** in Gn 28^{9}. **3.** Daughter of Solomon and wife of Ahimaaz, one of the king's officers, 1 K 4^{15} (AV **Basmath**).

BASHAN.—The name of the territory east of the Sea of Tiberias. It was the kingdom of Og, the Rephaite opponent of Israel, and with his name the country is almost invariably associated (Nu 21^{33}, Dt 29^{7}, Neh 9^{22}, etc.). The territory was given to the half-tribe of Manasseh, with a reservation of two cities, Golan and Be-eshterah (Ashtaroth in 1 Ch 6^{71}), for the Gershonite Levites (Jos 21^{27}). In the time of Jehu the country was smitten by Hazael (2 K 10^{33}). It was noted for mountains (Ps 68^{15}), lions (Dt 33^{22}), oak trees (Is 2^{13}, Ezk 27^{6}, Zec 11^{2}), and especially cattle, both rams (Dt 32^{14}) and bullocks (Ezk 39^{18}); the bulls and kine of Bashan are typical of cruelty and oppression (Ps 22^{12}, Am 4^{1}). The extent of the territory denoted by this name cannot be exactly defined till some important identifications can be established, such as the exact meaning of the 'the region of Argob' (q.v.; included in the kingdom of Og, Dt 3^{4}, etc.), where were threescore great cities with walls and brazen bars, administered for Solomon by Ben-geber of Ramoth-gilead (1 K 4^{13}). It included Salecah (*Salkhad,* on the borders of the desert), Edrei (*Derʿā*), Ashtaroth (*Tell ʿAshtarah*), and Golan, one of the cities of refuge, the name of which may be preserved in the *Saḥem el-Jōlân,* the region immediately east of the Sea of Tiberias. R. A. S. M.

BASHEMATH.—AV form of **Basemath, 1, 2** (q.v.).

BASILISK.—See SERPENT.

BASIN (AV, RV 'bason').—Chiefly the large bowl (Heb. *mizrāḳ*) of bronze used by the priests to receive the blood of the sacrificial victims (Ex 27^{3}, 1 K 7^{45}, etc.). Similar bowls or basins of silver, filled with flour mingled with oil, were presented by the princes of the congregation (Nu 7^{13ff}), while golden ones were prepared for use in Solomon's Temple (1 K 7^{50}) or for the second Temple (Neh 7^{70}). The same term is found only once for a vessel for secular use (Am 6^{6}, where EV render 'bowl'). A different term (Heb. *saph*) is used in Ex 12^{22} for the basin containing the blood of the Passover lamb, and in 2 K 12^{14} for Temple vessels and 1 K 7^{50} (AV 'bowls'; RV, RSV 'cups') for vessels for ordinary use. Jesus used a basin (Gr. *niptēr*) for washing the disciples' feet (Jn 13^{5}).

BASKAMA.—An unknown town of Gilead, 1 Mac 13^{23} (AV, RV **Bascama**).

BASKET.—The names of a round score of baskets in use in NT times are known from the Mishnah (see Krengel, *Das Hausgerät in der Mishnah*, pp. 39–45). They were made of willow, rush, palm-leaf, and other materials, and used in an endless variety of ways, for purely domestic purposes, in agriculture, in gathering and serving fruit, and for collecting the alms in kind for the poor, etc. Some had handles, others lids, some had both, others had neither. In OT times the commonest basket was the *sal*, made, at least in later times, of peeled willows or palm-leaves. It was large and flat like the Roman *canistrum*, and like it, was used for carrying bread (Gn 40^{16ff}) and other articles of food (Jg 6^{19}), and for presenting the meal-offerings at the sanctuary (Ex 29^{3}). Another (*dûdh*), also of wicker-work, probably resembled the *calathus*, which tapered towards the bottom, and was used in fruit-gathering (Jer 24^{1}). In what respect it differed from Amos' 'basket of summer fruit' (Am 8^{1}) (*keluâbh ḳayiṣ*) is unknown. A fourth and larger variety *ṭene'* was employed for carrying home the produce of the fields (Dt 28^{5} 'blessed shall be your basket and your kneading-trough'), and for presenting the first-fruits (26^{2}). The basket (*tēbhāh*) in which Moses was put (Ex $2^{3, 5}$; RV 'ark') was of papyrus reeds.

In NT interest centres in the two varieties of basket distinguished consistently by the Evangelists in their accounts of the feeding of the 5000 and the 4000 respectively, the *kophinos* and the *sphyris*. The *kophinos* (Mt 14^{20}) is probably to be identified with the exceedingly popular *ḳuppāh* of the Mishnah, which 'was provided with a cord for a handle by means of which it was usually carried on the back' (Krengel), with provisions, etc., and which, therefore, the disciples would naturally have with them. The Jews of Juvenal's day carried such a provision basket (*cophinus*). The *sphyris* or *spyris* (Mt 15^{37}, Mk 8^{8}), from its use in St. Paul's case (Ac 9^{25}), must have been considerably larger than the other. The *sarganē* (2 Co 11^{33}) in which St. Paul was let down was either of rope net-work or a mat-basket, 'hamper.' A. R. S. K.—**R. A. B.**

BASMATH, 1 K 4^{15} (AV).—See BASEMATH, 3.

BASON.—See BASIN.

BASSA, 1 Es 5^{16} (AV).—See BEZAI, 2.

BASSAI, 1 Es 5^{16} (RV).—See BEZAI, 2.

BASTAI, 1 Es 5^{31} (AV).—See BESAI.

BASTARD.—**1.** Hebrew *mamzēr*, Dt 23^{2} (AV, RV, RSV), Zec 9^{6} (AV, RV; RSV 'mongrel'). According to rabbinical tradition this does not mean, as with us, one born out of wedlock, but the offspring of an incestuous union, or of a marriage within the prohibited degrees of affinity, and this is probably right. Cf Driver, *Deuteronomy*, p. 260. In Zec 9^{6} it appears to mean one of racially mixed origin.

2. Greek *nothos*, He 12^{8} (AV, RV; RSV 'illegitimate children'). Here the meaning is 'born out of wedlock.'

BASTHAI, 1 Es 5^{31} (RV).—See BESAI.

BAT (*ᵃṭallēph*, Lv 11^{19}, Dt 14^{18}).—The 'bat' (LXX, Vulg.) is added at the end of the list of birds (cf Bar 6^{22}, where it heads a list) because it was regarded as half-way between beasts and birds (cf Aristotle *de partibus animalium* iv. 13, 697b). It is mostly an insectivorous creature as are all the seventeen species found in Palestine except one (the *xantharpaeia*, which eats fruit), modified for flying and ranging from the size of a mouse to that of a rat. Bats flit about on noiseless wings on warm evenings in summer and haunt ruins, old tombs, and dark recesses of caves (cf Is 2^{20}), in great numbers all over Palestine. They are considered unclean from their habit of bespattering walls with ordure as they fly, the overpowering mousy odour of their homes, and because their flesh is quite uneatable.
E. W. G. M.—**G. R. D.**

BATH.—A liquid measure; see WEIGHTS AND MEASURES.

BATH, BATHING.—The latter term is most frequently used in our EV in connexion with purification from ceremonial defilement—contact with holy things, with the dead, etc. (see CLEAN AND UNCLEAN)—and in this sense denotes the washing of the body *with* water, not necessarily the total immersion of the body *in* water. Bathing in the modern and non-religious sense is rarely mentioned (Ex 2^5 Pharaoh's daughter, 2 S 11^2 (RV, RSV) Bathsheba, and the curious case 1 K 22^{38}). Egyptian-style bathrooms, assigned to the early half of the 2nd millennium B.C., have been discovered in the palaces of the rulers of *Tell el-ʿAjjûl* (Gaza), one such example (also with simple toilet facilities) measuring 2.50 metres × 2 metres and having a plastered, sloping floor with a waste-pipe—bathing having been done by pouring. Belonging to the latter half of the same millennium, a bathing place (possibly used also for washing clothes) has similarly come to light in a courtyard at Megiddo. W. F. Albright, *The Archaeology of Palestine*, 1949, 139 f., mentions 'a built-in basin for washing' in what may have been the 'official guest-house' of *Tell Beit Mirsim* (Debir, Kiriath-sepher) at the time of the late Divided Monarchy. The buildings in Gezer, thought by R. A. S. Macalister to have been a bathing establishment, are now considered to have been used for dyeing. Public baths are met with in the Greek period—they were included in the 'gymnasium' (1 Mac 1^{14})—and remains of such buildings from the Roman period are fairly numerous, with rooms for changing and chambers of different temperature. Especially celebrated at this time were the mineral and thermal springs of the Dead Sea, Tiberias, Gadara, and Callirrhoë. The therapeutic aspect of bathing receives mention at 2 K 5^{10}, Jn 5^{2ff}. Facilities for ceremonial ablution were provided at the synagogues in the form of pitchers and basins. The foot-bath placed before the warrior victoriously returned from battle, cf Ps 60^8 and note A. F. Kirkpatrick, *The Psalms*, 1902, 342, may be illustrated by the oval tub discovered in Samaria, having (besides an outlet pipe and four handles moulded near the rim, for ease of carrying) a low foot-shaped platform in the middle. Open cisterns entered by wide steps, which have been discovered at *Khirbet Qumrân*, may have been used for ritual or ordinary bathing; cf Millar Burrows, *More Light on the Dead Sea Scrolls*, 1958, 371 f.

The Hebrews were well acquainted with the use of mineral and vegetable alkalis for increasing the cleansing properties of water (Jer 2^{22}, RSV 'lye,' 'soap,' cf Job 9^{30} 'lye'). In Sus v.^{17} 'oil and ointments' for bathing suggest a similarity to the practice in Hellenistic-Roman times of anointing the body at the baths. For further details relating to several of the foregoing items cf K. Galling, *BRL*, 1937. Art. 'Bad und Baden.'
A. R. S. K.—E. T. R.

BATH-RABBIM.—The name of a gate of Heshbon, near which were pools, to which the Shulammite's eyes are compared (Ca 7^4).

BATHSHEBA (1 Ch 3^5 **Bathshua**: this may be a mere textual error).—Wife of Uriah the Hittite, seduced by David (2 S 11$^{2-4}$), and afterwards married to him (v.^{27}). The child died (12^{18}), but another son, Solomon, was subsequently born (12^{24}). Bathsheba, instigated and supported by Nathan, successfully combated Adonijah's attempt to secure the throne (1 K 1$^{11-53}$). Acting as Adonijah's intercessor in the matter of Abishag, she was most respectfully received by Solomon, but her unwise request was refused (1 K 2$^{13-25}$). J. T.

BATHSHUA.—**1.** See BATHSHEBA. **2.** See SHUA.

BATH-ZACHARIAS, 1 Mac 6^{32f} (AV).—See BETH-ZECHARIAH.

BATTALION.—This word is found in RSV in Mt 27^{27}, Mk 15^{16}, here AV and RV have 'band.' See BAND and LEGION.

BATTERING-RAM.—See FORTIFICATION AND SIEGE-CRAFT.

BATTLE.—See WAR.

BATTLE AXE.—See ARMOUR, **1** (*f*).

BATTLE BOW.—See ARMOUR, **1** (*d*).

BATTLEMENT.—See HOUSE.

BAVVAI.—The son of Henadad (Neh 3^{18}; AV **Bavai**); rebuilt a portion of the wall of Jerusalem; called in v.^{24} **Binnui.**

BAY.—See COLOURS, **3.**

BAYITH ('house').—Occurs as a proper name in Is 15^2 (RV; AV **Bajith**); but the sense is uncertain and RSV reads *bath* ('daughter').

BAY-TREE.—This word, found in Ps 37^{35} (AV) is probably a mistranslation. For 'green bay tree' (Heb. *'ezrāḥ raʿᵃnān*) RV has 'a green tree in its native soil.' RSV emends the Hebrew to read *'erez lᵉbhānôn* and renders 'a cedar of Lebanon.'

BAZAAR.—Found only in 1 K 20^{34} (RSV; AV, RV 'street'), where it has its original, oriental meaning of a trading quarter.

BAZLITH.—See BAZLUTH.

BAZLUTH.—Founder of a family of Nethinim (q.v.) who returned with Zerubbabel, Ezr 2^{52}, 1 Es 5^{31} (AV, RV **Basaloth**); called **Bazlith** in Neh 7^{54}.

BDELLIUM.—The Assyrian *budulḫu, biderḫu* is given in a botanical list between storax and ladanum and is therefore a gum-resin; and the Heb. *bᵉdhōlah*, which is derived from it, is 'bdellium' according to most ancient authorites (Aq., Symm., Theod., Vulg.) This, a fragrant yellow resinous gum of the tree known scientifically as *balsamodendron mukul*, was obtained from Arabia (Galen), Babylonia, Media, Bactria, and India (Pliny) and the word is perhaps derived from the Sanskrit *udūkhala* (cf Gr. *bdellion bolchon*; *madelkon* and Lat. *maldacon, bidellium, bidella, bdella, vidella*) 'bdellium.' It is described as one of the choicest products of the land of Havilah (Gn 2^{12}), being much valued as a spice in antiquity (Josephus); and manna is aptly compared to it in colour, if this is rightly identified with the dirty-yellowish exudation with which the *tamarix gallica* or *mannifera* oozes by night during the season. G. R. D.

BE.—To be is to exist, as in 'To be, or not to be, that is the question.' This primary meaning is found in Gn 5^{24} 'Enoch walked with God; and he was not'; He 11^6 'he that cometh to God must believe that he is' (AV, RV; RSV 'exists'). In 1611 'be' and 'are' were interchangeable auxiliary forms in the present indicative plural, as Ps 107^{30} 'Then are they glad because they be quiet' (AV, RV; RSV 'were glad . . . had quiet').

BEALIAH ('Y″ is lord').—A Benjamite who joined David at Ziklag, 1 Ch 12^5.

BEALOTH.—**1.** A town in the Negeb, Jos 15^{24}; perhaps the same as **Baalath-beer** (q.v.). **2.** A town in Solomon's 9th district, 1 K 4^{16} (RV, RSV), in the north; AV reads 'in **Aloth.**'

BEAM.—**1.** A tree roughly trimmed serving as support of the flat roof of an Eastern house (2 K 6$^{2, 5}$

(AV, RV; RSV 'log'), Ezr 6^{11} (RV RSV; AV 'timber'), Mt 7^{3ff}, Lk 6^{41f} (AV, RV; RSV 'log'). Sometimes it was elaborately decorated (2 Ch 3^{7} 34^{11} (AV 'floor'), Ca 1^{17}). See HOUSE, **5**, MOTE. **2.** The weaver's beam (Jg 16^{14} (AV, RV; RSV 'loom'), 1 S 17^{7}, 2 S 21^{19}, 1 Ch 11^{23} 20^{5}), (see SPINNING AND WEAVING). **3.** Beam of a balance. See BALANCE.

BEANS (*pôl*, Arab. *fûl*).—A very common and popular vegetable in Palestine, used from ancient times; they are the seeds of the *vicia faba*. The bean plant, which is sown in October or November, is in blossom in early spring, when its sweet perfume fills the air. Beans are gathered young and eaten, pod and seed together, cooked with meat; or the fully mature beans are cooked with fat or oil. As the Israelites took little meat, such leguminous plants were a necessary ingredient of their diet. In Ezk 4^{9} we read of beans as being mixed with barley, lentils, millet, and fitches to make bread.

E. W. G. M.

BEAR (*dōbh*).—The Syrian bear (*Ursus syriacus*, Arab. *dubb*) is still fairly common in Hermon and the Anti-Lebanon, and is occasionally found in the Lebanon and east of the Jordan; it is practically extinct in Palestine. It is smaller and of a lighter colour than the brown bear (*Ursus arctos*). It is a somewhat solitary animal, eating vegetables, fruit, and honey, but, when hungry, attacking sheep (1 S 17^{34-36}) and occasionally, but very rarely, to-day at any rate, human beings (2 K 2^{24}). The fierceness of a bear robbed of her whelps (2 S 17^{8}, Pr 17^{12}, Hos 13^{8}) is well known. Next to the lion, the bear was considered the most dangerous of animals to encounter (Pr 28^{15}), and that it should be subdued was to be one of the wonders of the Messiah's kingdom (Is 11^{7}).

E. W. G. M.

BEARD.—See HAIR.

BEAST.—**1.** In OT (1) *bᵉhēmāh*, used for a quadruped as distinguished from man, Gn 6^{7}, Ex 9^{9}, etc., also used specifically for domestic animals and translated 'animal' Gn 7^{2}, or 'cattle' Lv 1^{2}. (2) *ḥayyāh*, used of animals in general but specially 'wild beasts,' see Gn 7^{14} 8^{1} 9^{2}, etc. (3) *bᵉʿîr*, sometimes translated 'beasts' and sometimes 'cattle,' see Gn 45^{17}, Ex 22^{5}, etc. (4) *zîz*, 'wild beasts' (AV and RV), Ps 50^{11} 80^{13}; RSV, 'all that move.'

2. In NT (1) *thērion*: Mk 1^{13}, Ac 28^{4} (a viper), Ti 1^{12}, He 12^{20}, Ja 3^{7}, and over thirty times in Revelation. (2) *zōon*, of the 'beasts' (AV), or 'living creatures' (RV and RSV), round about the throne (Rev $5^{6, 8, 11}$, etc.).

E. W. G. M.—**L. H. B.**

BEAST (in Apocalypse).—In Revelation, particularly ch. 13, are symbolic pictures of two beasts who are represented as the arch-opponents of the Christians. The first beast demands worship, and is said to have as his number 666—a numerical symbol most easily referred to the Emperor Nero, or the Roman Empire. In the former case the reference would be undoubtedly to the myth of Nero *redivivus*, and this is, on the whole, the most probable interpretation.

If instead of 666 we read with Zahn, O. Holtzmann, Spitta, and Erbes, 616 (a variant reading known to Irenaeus—see v. xxx. 1), the number would be the equivalent of Gaius Cæsar, who in A.D. 39 ordered the procurator Petronius to set up his statue in the Temple of Jerusalem. This view is, in a way, favoured not only by textual variations, but by the fact that Revelation has used so much Jewish apocalyptic material. However this may be, it seems more probable that the reference in Rev 17^{10-11}, as re-edited by the Christian writer, refers to Nero *redivivus*, the incarnation of the persecuting Roman Empire, the two together standing respectively as the Antichrist and his kingdom over against the Messiah and His kingdom. As in all apocalyptic writings, a definite historical ruler is a representative of an empire. Until the Messiah comes His subjects are at the mercy of His great enemy. E. Stauffer maintains that Rev 13 refers to actual historical circumstances surrounding the arrival and cultic worship of the imperial image in the harbour of Ephesus and identifies the name of the beast as concealed in the cipher 666 with Domitian's official name 'autokrator KAIsar DOMETianos SEBastos GErmanikos.'

The present difficulty in making the identification is due not only to the process of redaction, but also to the highly complex and, for the modern mind, all but unintelligible fusion of the various elements of the Antichrist belief (see ANTICHRIST, DOMITIAN). S. M.—**J. C. B.**

BEATING.—See CRIMES AND PUNISHMENTS **9.**

BEATITUDES.—This word comes from the Latin *beatitudo*, used in Vulg. of Ro 4^{6}, where David is said to pronounce the beatitude of the forgiven soul. Since the time of Ambrose the term has been used to describe the particular collection of sayings (cast in the form of which Ps 32^{1} is an OT specimen) in which Christ depicts the qualities to be found in members of His kingdom—as an introduction to the discourse known as the Sermon on the Mount (Mt 5^{3-12}=Lk 6^{20-23}). The only thing is, that quite clearly the blessings which Jesus here promises are far superior to those of the OT psalms, and are more in line with those spoken of in the writings of the inter-testamental period; they are qualities of the mind and heart, for the most part.

Each of these sayings follows the form 'Blessed are . . . for . . .' Matthew records eight of these general declarations, with a special application of the last of them; Luke has only four, to which are added four corresponding Woes. It is possible that in other parts of the NT we have quotations from sayings of the same kind. Thus 1 P 4^{14}, Ja 1^{12}, Rev 14^{13} might easily be supposed to rest on words of Christ. Moreover, even in Matthew apparently there are other beatitudes (13^{16} 24^{46}).

The Beatitudes are thought to belong to a common Greek source, 'Q,' used by both Matthew and Luke, and that in their original form they were in Aramaic. But Luke does not seem to follow the same version of the Beatitudes as Matthew, and there may have been two slightly different recensions of the common source. Putting aside Nos. 3, 5, 6, 7 in Matthew, which have no counterparts in Luke, we see the following main lines of difference—(1) Luke's are in the second person, Matthew's in the third, except in the verses which apply No. 8 ($5^{11, 12}$); (2) Luke's are apparently external: the poor, the hungry, those that weep, receive felicitation as such, instead of the commiseration ('Woe') which the world would give them. But since in Luke disciples are addressed, the divergence does not touch the real meaning. A theodicy is proclaimed in which the hardships of the present, sanctified to the disciple as precious discipline, will be transformed into abiding blessedness. Such a reversal of the order of this life involves here, as elsewhere, the casting down of those whom men count happy (cf Is $65^{13, 14}$, Lk $1^{52, 53}$ 16^{25}, Jn 16^{20}, Ja $1^{9, 10}$). The paradoxical form of the sayings in Luke produces a strong impression of originality, suggesting that here, as often elsewhere, Matthew has interpreted the words which Luke has transcribed unchanged. Matthew has arranged them according to the form of Heb. parallelism: observe how the first and last have the same refrain, the poem beginning and ending on the same note—cf Ps 8. His No. 8 sums up in the form of the other Beatitudes the principle of the appendix vv.^{11f}, which Lk 6^{22f} shows to be original: he then inserts this as a comment, much as he appends a sentence of comment to the Lord's Prayer (6^{14-15}). It may perhaps be doubted whether the Beatitudes peculiar to Matthew are in their original context. No. 3, proclaiming the triumph of those who do not 'struggle to survive,' is quoted from Ps 37^{11}; No. 5 is found as early as Clement of Rome, in the form 'Show mercy, that mercy be shown to you'; No. 6 reproduces the sense of Ps 24^{4}; No. 7, echoed in Ja 3^{18}, may have been altered in form to fit the appropriate context. We seem to be justified in conjecturing that Luke inserts all the Beatitudes he found in his source under the same context, and that he faithfully preserved the words as they stood; the Woes likewise belonged to the same discourse. (Note the support given to them

by Ja 5^{1}, and the use of the commercial technical term 'have received,' so characteristic of the Sermon; cf Mt $6^{2,5,16}$). The gloss with which Matthew interprets the blessing on the poor was not apparently known to St. James (2^{5}), whose very clear allusion to the Beatitude in its Lukan form determines the exegesis. The rich man could bring himself within the range of the blessing by accepting the humiliation that Christian discipleship brought (Ja 1^{10}); so that Matthew's interpretation is supported by the writer, who shows us most clearly that the exact words have not been preserved by him. In No. 2 Matthew seems to have slightly altered the original (Lk 6^{21}), under the influence of Is 61^{1}. It should be observed however that all attempts to ascertain the original form of sayings of Jesus have at best a large subjective element. Moreover, we must always allow for the probability that modifications introduced by Matthew or Luke may often rest on early traditions, so that elements not included in the principal Gospel sources may nevertheless be derived from first-hand authority.
N. T.

BEAUTIFUL GATE.—See Temple.

BEBAI.—**1.** The eponym of a family of returning exiles (Ezr 2^{11} 8^{11} 10^{28}, Neh 7^{16} 10^{15}, 1 Es 5^{13} 8^{37} (AV RV **Babi**) 9^{29}. **2.** A place mentioned in Jth 15^{4}; the site is unknown.

BECHER.—**1.** Son of Ephraim, Nu 26^{35}=1 Ch 7^{20} where the name appears as **Bered.** Patronymic in Nu 26^{35} **Becherites** (AV Bachrites). **2.** Son of Benjamin, Gn 46^{21}, 1 Ch $7^{6,8}$.

BECORATH.—One of Saul's ancestors, 1 S 9^{1}.

BECTILETH (Jth 2^{21}).—A plain between Nineveh and Cilicia. Perhaps the *Bactiali* of the Peutinger Tables, 21 miles from Antioch.

BED, BEDCHAMBER.—See House, **8.**

BEDAD.—An Edomite king, father of Hadad, Gn 36^{35}, 1 Ch 1^{46}.

BEDAN.—**1.** Mentioned with Jerubbaal (Gideon), Jephthah, and Samuel as one of the deliverers of Israel, 1 S 12^{11} (AV, RV). The name does not occur in Judges, and it is probably a corruption for **Barak,** which RSV reads, following LXX and Pesh. Chronologically Barak should precede Gideon, but the order cannot be pressed. **2.** A Manassite, 1 Ch 7^{17}.

BEDEIAH.—One of those who had married foreign wives, Ezr 10^{35}, 1 Es 9^{34} (AV **Pelias, RV Pedias**).

BEE (*debhōrāh*).—The species commonly found in Palestine (*Apis fasciata*) is beautifully striped but is smaller than that common in England (*Apis mellifica*). They are very active and are noted for their short temper and irritability. They are found wild, hiving in hollow trees and rock crevices, and their honey is collected by the Arabs for sale. Bee-keeping is also widely practised, with hives of varying shape. It is well known that in OT times there were bees in Palestine (Dt 1^{44}) and that their honey was eaten (Jonathan in 1 S 14^{27}) and regarded as a delicacy (Sir 11^{3}), but it is not clear whether the honey with which the land flowed (Ex 3^{8} etc.) was bees' honey or fruit juice (syrup) which bore the same name (see Honey). The mention of hissing for bees in Is 7^{8} suggests that bee-keeping was practised in Isaiah's day and that the bees could be induced to swarm in that way. They were clearly as aggressive in those days as they are to-day so that the way they chased a man became proverbial, Dt 1^{44}, cf Ps 118^{12}. The story of the swarm of bees found in the carcase of the lion by Samson (Jg 14^{8}) is familiar to all: the improbability of such a thing happening lends point to the story. In the LXX there is an addition to Pr 6^{8} in which the bee is, like the ant, commended for her diligence and wisdom.
E. W. G. M.—**L. H. B.**

BEELIADA (' Baal knows '.—A son of David, 1 Ch 14^{7}; called **Eliada** (' El knows ') in 2 S 5^{16}.

BEELSARUS, 1 Es 5^{8} (AV, RV).—See Bilshan.

BEELTETHMUS, 1 Es $2^{16,25}$ (AV, RV).—See Beltethmus.

BEELZEBUB, BEELZEBUL.—See Baalzebub.

BEER (' a well ').—**1.** A station in the journey from the Arnon to the Jordan, mentioned Nu 21^{16}, with a poetical extract commemorating the digging of a well at this spot. The context indicates the neighbourhood, but further identification is wanting; it was probably in the *Wâdī eth-Themed.* Perhaps the words translated 'and from the wilderness,' which immediately follow this extract (Nu 21^{18}), should be translated (following the LXX) 'and from Beer,' or 'the well.' It is generally identified with **Beer-elim** (' well of mighty men '?), mentioned Is 15^{8}, but without strong reason. **2.** The place to which Jotham ran away after uttering his parable (Jg 9^{21}). Its position is unknown; possibly *Kh. el-Bîreh.*

BEERA.—A man of Asher, son of Zophah, 1 Ch 7^{37}.

BEERAH.—A Reubenite who was carried captive by Tiglath-pileser, 1 Ch 5^{6}.

BEER-ELIM.—Mentioned only in Is 15^{8}; commonly identified with **Beer, 1,** but with little reason.

BEERI.—**1.** A Hittite whose daughter became one of Esau's wives, Gn 26^{34}. **2.** The father of the prophet Hosea, Hos 1^{1}.

BEER-LAHAI-ROI (' Well of the Living One who sees me ').—A well between Kadesh and Bered, where the fleeing Hagar was turned back (Gn 16^{14}), where Isaac met his bride (24^{62}), and where he dwelt after Abraham's death (25^{11}). Its site is unknown.

BEEROTH (' wells ').—A Gibeonite city, usually coupled in enumeration with Chephirah and Kiriath-jearim (Jos 9^{17}, Ezr 2^{25}, Neh 7^{29}, 1 Es 5^{19} (AV, RV **Beroth**)); assigned to the tribe of Benjamin (Jos 18^{25}, 2 S 4^{2}); the home of Rechab, murderer of Ish-bosheth (2 S 4^{2}), and of Naharai, armour-bearer of Joab (2 S 23^{37}). *El-Bîreh,* about 10 miles from Jerusalem on the main road to the north, is the usual identification, and there seems no special reason for objecting thereto. The circumstances and date of the flight of the **Beerothites** to Gittaim (2 S 4^{3}) are not recorded. R. A. S. M.

BEEROTH-BENE-JAAKAN.—A halting-place in the Israelite wanderings, between Moseroth and Hor-haggidgad, Nu 33^{31f} (where it is called simply **Bene-jaakan**), Dt 10^{6}; probably wells in the territory of some nomad Horite tribe (cf Gn 36^{27}, 1 Ch 1^{42}), the *Benê Ja'aḳān.* It is perhaps modern *Birein.*

BEERSHEBA.—A halting-place of Abraham (Gn 21^{31}), where Hagar was sent away (Gn 21^{14}), and where he made a covenant with Abimelech, from which the place is alleged to take its name (' well of the covenant,' according to one interpretation). Isaac after his disputes with the 'Philistines' settled here (26^{23}), and discovered the well **Shibah,** another etymological speculation (v.^{33}). Hence Jacob was sent away (28^{10}), and returned and sacrificed on his way to Egypt (46^{1}). It was assigned to the tribe of Judah (Jos 15^{28}), but set apart for the Simeonites (19^{2}). Here Samuel's sons were judges (1 S 8^{2}), and hither Elijah fled before Jezebel (1 K 19^{3}). Zibiah, the mother of Joash, belonged to Beersheba (2 K 12^{1}). It was an important holy place: here Abraham planted a sacred tree (Gn 21^{33}), and theophanies were vouchsafed to Hagar (v.^{17}), to Isaac (26^{24}), to Jacob (46^{2}), and to Elijah (1 K 19^{5}). Amos couples it with the shrines of Bethel and Gilgal (Am 5^{5}), and oaths by its *numen* are denounced (8^{14}). The fact that this shrine was a centre of pilgrimage for North Israel suggests that it was the religious centre of the tribe of Simeon, once located at Shechem (Gn 34^{25-31}). It is recognized as the southern boundary of the settled land in the frequent phrase 'from Dan to Beersheba' (Jg 20^{1} etc.). The place was resettled by Jews after the Exile (Neh 11^{30}), though it was not in the Persian administrative district of Yehud, but Arabia. Seven ancient wells exist here, and it has been suggested that these gave its name to the locality. The name persists. Several Chalcolithic sites have been recently discovered in the vicinity, and the modern site was occupied by a Byzantine town, the Biblical Beersheba being probably at *Tell es-Sebaʿ*, about two miles to the E. In recent times a poor market village for Bedouin, it was rebuilt in Turkish times, served as an administrative centre then and during the British Mandate, when it was the seat of a tribal court, and has now expanded as the capital of the Negeb in the state of Israel. R. A. S. M.—**J. Gr.**

BE-ESHTERAH.—A Levitical city, Jos 21^{27}; the same as **Ashtaroth** (q.v.).

BEETLE, Lv 11^{22} (AV).—See Cricket.

BEHEADING.—See Crimes and Punishments, **10.**

BEHEMOTH.—Commonly identified with the hippopotamus (Job 40^{15}), as leviathan (41^{1}) as the crocodile; but cf G. R. Driver, *Studi orientalistici in onore di G. Levi della Vida*, i, 1956, 234, where textual corruption is found in 40^{15} and the first creature is identified with the crocodile and the second with the whale. It has been suggested that the ancient Babylonian Creation-myth underlies the poet's description of the two animals (Gunkel, *Schöpf. u. Chaos*, 61ff). This is doubtful, but the myth undoubtedly reappears in later Jewish literature: 'And in that day will two monsters be separated, a female named Leviathan to dwell in the abyss over the fountains of waters. But the male is called Behemoth, which occupies with its breast [?] an immeasurable desert named Dendain' (1 En 60$^{7, 8}$; cf 2 Es 6$^{49-51}$, Apoc. Bar 29^{4}, *Baba bathra* 74*b*). *Behemoth* is rendered by 'beasts' in Is 30^{6}. This may be correct, but the oracle which follows says nothing about the 'beasts of the south'; either the text is corrupt or the title may have been prefixed because Rahab, another name for the chaos-monster, occurs in v.^{7}. The psalmist confesses, '*Behemoth* was I with thee' (Ps 73^{22}). The LXX understood this to be an abstract noun, 'Beast-like was I with thee'; others substitute the singular, and render 'a beast,' etc.
J. T.—**A. S. H.**

BEKA (AV **Bekah**).—See Weights and Measures.

BEL.—Originally used of the Sumerian deity Enlil, the god of Nippur, the name Bel was later identified with the Babylonian god Marduk (Merodach), whose temple was called E-sagila. The Biblical occurrences of the name (Jer 50^{2} 51^{44}, Is 46^{1}, Ep. Jer 6^{4f}, Bel 1^{3}+) all refer to the Babylonian god. See also Assyria and Babylonia, Apocrypha, **12** (Bel and the Dragon).

BELA.—**1.** A king of Edom, Gn 36^{32f}, 1 Ch 1^{43f}. The close resemblance of this name to that of 'Balaam the son of Beor,' the seer (Nu 21^{5}), is noteworthy, and it gave rise to the Targ. of Pseudo-Jonathan reading 'Balaam the son of Beor' in Gn 36^{32}. **2.** The eldest of the sons of Benjamin, Gn 46^{21} (AV **Belah**), Nu 26^{38}, 1 Ch 7^{6} 8$^{1, 3}$; the patronymic **Belaites** occurs in Nu 26^{38}. **3.** A Reubenite who was a dweller in Moabite territory. It is noteworthy that this Bela, like Balaam (Nu 21^{5}), seems to have been traditionally connected with the Euphrates (1 Ch 5^{9}). **4.** A name of the city Zoar, Gn 14$^{2, 8}$. See Plain, Cities of the.

BELAH, Gn 46^{21} (AV).—See Bela, **3.**

BELEMUS, 1 Es 2^{16} (AV, RV).—See Bishlam.

BELIAL (BELIAR).—The etymology of the word is uncertain. The most probable view is that it originates from the Hebrew *b^{e}lî*=without and *ʿālāh*=to go up, to return, and means 'land without return,' like Sheol. In the OT it takes on the sense of 'worthlessness' or 'wickedness' and is generally found in combination with a noun: 1 S 1^{16} 'daughter of wickedness' (RSV a 'base woman'; cf Dt 13^{13} 15^{9}, Jg 20^{13}). RSV translates 'evil' (Jg 9^{22}), 'worthless' (1 S 2^{12} 10^{27}), 'ill-natured' (1 S 25$^{17, 25}$). As 'perdition' it is found in Ps 18^{4} (cf 2 S 22^{5}); see also Ps 41^{8} and Nah 1^{11} (villainy). Nah 1^{15}—an exception in the OT—gives an independent use: 'the wicked one' (RSV). The intertestamental literature uses it often as a proper noun (cf Test. XII Patr., Reuben 4^{7} 6^{3}; *Sib. Or.* iii. 63; 1*QS* ii. 5, 19) and thus prepares for its usage by Paul in 2 Co 6^{15}, 'Beliar'; the change from *l* to *r* is due to dissimilation.
J. C. B.

BELIEF.—It is usual in modern English to take faith in God to mean something more than belief in God, faith meaning a personal trust and commitment, belief only an intellectual or impersonal acceptance or credence, or a traditional dogmatic statement. The verb corresponding to 'faith' is, however, 'believe,' unless one wishes to emphasize the personal relation by using 'trust.' 'Belief' occurs in English translations sporadically, *e.g.* 2 Th 2^{13}, and probably indicates the translators to have supposed a kind of credal assent to be intended. Only one Greek word, however, is used, and all usages are therefore to be found under Faith. J. Ba.

BELL.—Bells are rarely mentioned in the Bible. **1.** The word *paʿ^{a}mōn* (from the *beat*) is used of the bells of gold (Ex 28^{34} 39^{25}), which alternated with pomegranates on the skirt of the high priest's robe (28$^{33f.}$ 39^{25f}). Their purpose is stated in 28^{35}. Small bronze bells, both of the ordinary shape with clapper and of the 'ball and slit' form, have been found by archaeologists, and the high priest's bells were doubtless of one or other of these forms. **2.** The word *m^{e}ṣillāh* (from the *tinkling* sound) is used of the bells of the horses in Zec 14^{20}. This word is from the same root as the word for 'cymbals.' Whether these ornaments were really bells, or as is sometimes supposed, small metal discs (cf the 'crescents' of Jg 8^{21} [RV, RSV; cf AVm]) is uncertain. A. R. S. K.—**H. H. R.**

BELLOWS.—See Arts and Crafts, **2.**

BELMAIN, Jth 4^{4} (AV **Belmen,** RV **Belmaim**); cf Balbaim, Jth 7^{3} (AV, RV **Belmaim**).—It seems to have lain south of Dothan, but the topography of Judith is very difficult. Bileam in Manasseh lay farther N. than Dothan.

BELMEN, Jth 4^{4} (AV).—See Belmain.

BELNUUS.—One of the returning exiles, 1 Es 9^{31} (AV, RV **Balnuus**); called **Binnui** (q.v.) in Ezr 10^{30}.

BELOVED.—(*a*) *In the OT.* Solomon is said to have been beloved of his God (Neh 13^{26}), in the sense of *loved by*; the word occurs in the erotic sense in the Song of Solomon (1$^{13, 14, 16}$, 2$^{3, 8}$, etc.) and in Hosea (3^{1}): all these are from the Hebrew root *'hb, to love.* Rendering the Hebrew adjective *yādhîdh* (*beloved*) are Dt 33^{12} (Benjamin stands in this relationship with God), Ps 60^{5}, 108^{6} (Israel to God), 127^{2} (the Israelite to God), Jer 11^{15} (Judah to God). From the Hebrew noun *maḥmādh* (*desirable thing*) is Hos 9^{16} (of children). From the Hebrew *y^{e}dhîdhûth* (*beloved*) is Jer 12^{7} (Judah to God). From the Hebrew *ḥ^{a}mûdhôth* is Dan 9^{23}, 10$^{11, 19}$ (Daniel to God). Very important, because of its connexion with the NT, is the occurrence of 'beloved' in Is 5^{1} (*dôdh*): 'Let me sing for my beloved a love song concerning his vineyard: My beloved had a vineyard on a very fertile hill.' Cf under (*b*).

(*b*) *In the NT.* The Greek word is *agapētos*, the weakened verbal adjective of *agapaō* (for the meaning of which in Jewish and Christian Greek circles, cf the article on Love). There is not general agreement as to the fundamental or earliest meaning of *agapētos*. The idea of *uniqueness* is certainly implied in at least the contexts in which the word is used, if not in the word itself. Not everyone would agree that an adequate translation is *only* or even *unique* in any of the contexts. Certainly, in the language of the Pauline and later Christian epistles the word is parallel in meaning with *agapē*, Christian *love*, and the contexts make it clear that *beloved* is the only possible meaning. The question is, was this alleged Christianization of the word already present in the minds of the writers of the Gospels? In other words, is the voice at the Baptism saying 'This is my beloved Son,' or 'This is my unique son'? (Mk 1^{11}, Mt 3^{17}, Lk 3^{22}, 2 P 1^{17}). The same problem arises with the voice at the Transfiguration (Mk 9^{7}, Mt 17^{5}), and in the parable of the Vineyard (Mk 12^{6}, Lk 20^{13}). Bu this parable must stand in close relationship with the parable in Is 5, where *agapētos* clearly renders the Hebrew *beloved*; and the evangelists must have viewed the passage messianically. It was this that they had in mind, rather than the passage concerning Abraham's *only* son (Gn 22[2]), and there is no reason why they should have understood *agapētos* differently in the Baptism voice. The message of that voice appears to be based on the following OT passages in the LXX: Ps 2[7] (' You are my son '), Is 5[1] (' my beloved '), 42[1] (' my servant . . . my chosen, in whom my soul delights '), 44[2] (' my servant, Jeshurun, whom I have chosen ' RSV; *ēgapēmenos* in LXX), Jer 38(31)[20] (' my dear son '; *agapētos* in LXX), as well as Gn 22[2] (' only son '). John the Baptist's mission is to prepare the way for the Messiah and the purpose of the voice is to show that the messianic prophecies are fulfilled; one would therefore suppose that *agapētos* here was understood as in the Messianic passage Is 5[1ff]. Moreover, the author of 2 P 1[17] is able to quote the baptismal voice in an epistle in which he also uses *agapētos* in the undoubted sense of *beloved* (2 P 3[15]).

The use of the word in the LXX was with a two-fold meaning. (1) *Only*, of an only child, in Gn 22[2, 12, 16], Jer 6[26], Am 8[10], Zec 12[10], rendering *yāḥîdh*. (2) *Beloved*, in Is 5[1] (*dôdhî*), Jer 38 (31)[20] (*yaḳḳîr*), Ps 44(45)[tit] 59(60)[5] 83(84)[1] 107(108)[6] 126(127)[2], rendering *yādhîdh*; and Sir 15[13], Is 26[17], To 3[10]S 10[13]B, Bar 4[16], Sus [63] (*sine Heb. aequ.*). The later versions confine themselves to the meaning *beloved*, correcting the LXX where necessary. The close similarity of the Hebrew words *yādhîdh* and *yāḥîdh* may have caused confusion in the minds of the translators of Genesis, Jeremiah, and Minor Prophets; or perhaps the requirement of the particular contexts suggested the need of a word more affectionate in content than *monogenēs*, and the LXX equivalent of *yādhîdh* came readily to hand. It is significant that when Paul alludes to Gn 22[2] he avoids the LXX word *agapētos* (Ro 8[31]), although the LXX version of Genesis was known to him.

To argue that in the Gospels *agapētos* must be a synonym of *monogenēs* (*only*), because John uses the latter in his Prologue, is weak. Jn 1[18] is in no sense a parallel to the voice at the Baptism; we are more likely to find this in 1[34], where in fact he uses neither word according to the best reading, but where according to a ' noteworthy rejected reading ' of WH he has *eklektos* (*electus*, Old Latin), and if that is correct the evangelist did not regard *only* as the true interpretation of *agapētos*.

Apart, then, from this doubt in the case of the Gospels, the NT use is always *beloved*—of children, Christian brethren, with proper names (*e.g.* Ro 16[12]), and alone (*e.g.* 3 Jn[2]). Even so, it is not used of Christ; when He is described as Beloved (Eph 1[6]) it is the participle *ēgapēmenos* which is used. N. T.

BELSHAZZAR.—Son of Nebuchadnezzar, last king of Babylon before its capture by Cyrus (Dn 5[1]). The name is given as **Baltasar** in LXX and Theodotion in Daniel (so RV in Bar 1[11f]; AV **Balthasar**, RSV Belshazzar). There is no doubt that Bēl-shar-uṣur, son of Nabonidus, is meant. He was regent in Babylon during most of his father's reign. It is probable that he was in command of Babylon on its surrender.

C. H. W. J.

BELTESHAZZAR.—The name conferred on the youthful Daniel by Nebuchadnezzar, Dn 1[7]. The Babylonian form would be *balâṭsu-uṣur* (' protect his life '). Since in 4[8] this name is said to be in accordance with the name of Nebuchadnezzar's god, its full form should be *Bêl-bâlâṭsu-uṣur*. The LXX and Theodotion employ **Baltasar** both for it and for Belshazzar (ch. 5); and pseudo-Epiphanius repeats a legend that Nebuchadnezzar wished to make the two men co-heirs.

BELTETHMUS.—An officer of Artaxerxes in Palestine; 1 Es 2[16, 25] (AV, RV **Beeltethmus**). It is not a proper name, but a title of Rehum, the name immediately preceding it in 2[16] (cf Ezr 4[9]). It is a corruption of *be'ēl ṭe'ēm*=' lord of command,' and is rendered ' commander ' (AV, RV ' chancellor ') in Ezr 4[9]; in 1 Es 2[17] it is translated ' recorder ' (AV, RV ' storywriter '), while in 1 Es 2[25] it is doubly represented as ' the recorder (AV, RV ' storywriter ') Beltethmus.'

BEN (' son ').—A Levite, 1 Ch 15[18] (AV, RV). The name is omitted in LXX, and by both MT and LXX in v.[20]. RSV accordingly omits it in v.[18].

BEN TREE.—In Is 44[4] RV has ' They shall spring up among the grass ' (cf AV), where RSV emends the text to yield ' They shall spring up like grass amid waters.' It is probable that the word *bên* is here not ' among,' but the name of a species of *moringa*, and should be rendered ' the ben tree ' (Arab. *bân*). The verse should then be rendered ' They shall spring up as the green ben tree ' (cf J. M. Allegro, *ZAW* lxiii, 1951, 154ff). The ben tree is tall and erect, and noted for the intense greenness of its leaves.

BEN-ABINADAB.—One of Solomon's commissariat officers, 1 K 4[11]; AV has ' the son of Abinadab.'

BENAIAH (Y'' hath built).—**1.** A brave soldier from Kabzeel in Judah (2 S 23[20ff]), captain of David's bodyguard (8[18] 20[23]). He became a partisan of Solomon's and carried ' the mighty men,' ' the Cherethites and Pelethites,' with him (1 K 1[8, 38]). He played an important rôle in the young king's coronation (vv.[38, 44]), and was subsequently ordered to dispatch Joab, whose place as commander-in-chief he then filled (2[28–35]). **2.** One of the thirty who formed the second class of David's heroes (2 S 23[22]). He came from Pirathon in Mount Ephraim (2 S 23[30], cf Jg 12[15]). 1 Ch 27[14] assigns to him the command of the course for the eleventh month, with twenty-four thousand Ephraimites under him. **3.** Some ten obscure persons of this name appear in 1 Ch 4[36] 15[18, 20, 24] 16[5f], 2 Ch 20[14] 31[13], Ezr 10[25] (=1 Es 9[26] [AV **Baanias**, RV **Banneas**]), [30, 35] (=**Mamdai,** 1 Es 9[34] [AV **Mabdai**]), [43] (=1 Es 9[35] [AV, RV **Banaias**]), Ezk 11[1, 13]. J. T.

BEN-AMMI (' son of my father's kinsman ').—The son of Lot's younger daughter as the fruit of her incestuous union with her father, Gn 19[38]. The story is intended to explain the name Ammon. Incestuous unions were held in abhorrence in Israel, but by some peoples have been accepted without shame. Here the story is intended to express the contempt of the writer for the Ammonites (and Moabites).

BEN-DEKER.—One of Solomon's twelve commissariat officers, 1 K 4[9] (AV ' son of Dekar ').

BENE-BERAK.—A town in the territory of Dan, Jos 19[45]; mentioned by Sennacherib in his account of the campaign of 701 B.C. (*Banai-barḳa*). It is identified with modern *Ibn Ibrâq* about 5 miles E. of Jaffa.

BENEFACTOR.—Lk 22[25] only, ' those in authority over them (the Gentiles) are called benefactors.' The word is an exact translation of the Greek *Euergetēs*, a title of honour borne by two of the Greek kings of Egypt before Christ's day, Ptolemy III. (246–221 B.C.) and Ptolemy VII. (IX.) (145–116 B.C.). Hence RV spells with a capital, ' Benefactors '; but an explicit reference to the Ptolemies is questionable, and RSV uses lower case.

BENE-JAAKAN.—A station in the journeyings, Nu 33[31f]; called **Beeroth-bene-jaakan** (q.v.) in Dt 10[6].

BEN-GEBER.—One of Solomon's twelve commissariat officers, 1 K 4[13] (AV ' son of Geber ').

BEN-HADAD.—The name of three kings of Syria in the 9th cent. B.C.

1. Benhadad I., the son of Tab-rimmon of Damascus. At the instance of Asa, king of Judah, he intervened against Baasha of Israel and took from him valuable territory on his northern border. For this service Ben-hadad received from Asa costly treasures from the Temple and the royal palace (1 K 15[17–20]).

2. Ben-hadad II. In the days of this Ben-hadad war with Israel was common, he being usually successful. But Ahab was more fortunate in the campaigns of 856 and 855 B.C., which were followed by a treaty of peace with concessions to Israel (1 K 20). Ben-hadad was the leader of a confederacy of western princes who successfully opposed the attempts of Shalmaneser II. of Assyria to conquer southern Syria; at the battle of Ḳarḳar in 854 B.C. he had Ahab as one of his chief allies. On the resumption of hostilities between Syria and Israel soon thereafter, Ben-hadad was victorious (1 K 22). He was assassinated by the usurper Hazael about 843 B.C. (2 K 8[15]). 1 K 20[34] states that this Ben-hadad was a son of the preceding one and should, therefore, be designated Ben-hadad II.; but some scholars believe that Ben-hadad I. was still alive at the time of the events just mentioned and that the second Ben-hadad came to the throne of Syria some years later.

3. Ben-hadad III., son of Hazael, probably the same as the Mari' of the Assyrian inscriptions. Under him Damascus lost his father's conquests in Palestine (2 K 13[24f]), and he also suffered heavily from the Assyrians.

J. F. McC.—**J. Ma.**

BEN-HAIL (' son of might ').—A prince sent by Jehoshaphat to teach in the cities of Judah, 2 Ch 17[7].

BEN-HANAN (' son of a gracious one ').—A Judahite, 1 Ch 4[20].

BEN-HESED (' son of kindness ').—One of Solomon's twelve commissariat officers, who had charge of a district in Judah, 1 K 4[10] (AV ' son of Hesed ').

BEN-HINNOM.—Found only in RSV in Jer 19[2, 6], where AV and RV have ' the son of Hinnom.' See HINNOM.

BEN-HUR.—One of Solomon's twelve commissariat officers, who had charge of a district of Ephraim, 1 K 4[8] (AV ' son of Hur ').

BENINU.—One of those who sealed the covenant, Neh 10[13].

BENJAMIN.—1. The youngest son of Jacob by Rachel, and the only full brother of Joseph (Gn 30[22ff] [JE] 35[17] [J] 35[24] [P]). He alone of Jacob's sons was held to have been born in Palestine. J (Gn 35[16]) puts his birth near Ephrath in Benjamin. A later interpolation identifies Ephrath with Bethlehem, but cf 1 S 10[2]. P, however (Gn 35[22-26]), gives Paddan-Aram as the birth-place of all Jacob's children. His mother, dying soon after he was born, named him **Ben-oni** (' son of my sorrow '). Jacob changed this ill-omened name to the more auspicious one **Benjamin,** which is usually interpreted ' son of my right hand,' the right hand being the place of honour (cf Gn 48[14]). He was eventually taken down with Jacob's sons to Egypt for famine relief on the insistence of Joseph. Throughout the earlier documents Benjamin is a tender youth, the idol of his father and brothers. A late editor of P (Gn 46[21]) makes him, when he entered Egypt, the father of ten sons, that is more than twice as many as any of Jacob's other sons except Dan, who had seven.

What is the historical significance of these various traditions? It seems scarcely a coincidence that Benjamin (' son(s) of the right hand,' *i.e.* South) was the southernmost of the northern tribes in Palestine, and this would suggest that the name really originated after the settlement. The narrow wedge of stony hill-land between Judah and Ephraim suggests that Benjamin came last to Palestine, a fact which may be reflected in the tradition that he was the youngest son of Jacob, *i.e.* the last folk-element to be incorporated in the Israelite confederacy and that too in Palestine; hence the tradition that Benjamin was born in the land. Apart from the tradition that Benjamin was the brother of Joseph, there are certain facts which indicate that Benjamin was an offshoot of Joseph, *e.g.* Bethel, which was later reckoned in the territory of Benjamin (Jos 18[22]) is stated to have been taken by Joseph (Jg 1[22]), and the Benjamite Shimei claims to be ' of the house of Joseph ' (1 S 19[20]). It has been suggested that Ben-oni may be connected with On or Ono, a locality near Lydda named in the account of the restoration of the Jews in Ezr 2[33], Neh 7[37], 1 Ch 8[12]. This locality, however, was beyond the district of Benjamin in pre-Exilic times, but it is not so far beyond it as to preclude the possibility that it may have been so named by some element related to the tribe of Benjamin.

The limits of the tribal territory are given in the late source in Jos 18[11-28]. Within it lay Bethel (elsewhere assigned to Ephraim), Ophrah, Geba, Gibeon, Ramah, Mizpah, Gibeah, of which Bethel and Gibeon were certainly primitive seats of Canaanite worship and important centres in the cultus of Israel (*e.g.* Bethel, Ai 7[10ff], Gibeon, 1 K 3[4]). Jericho, where in early times there may have been a cult of the moon-god (*yārēaḥ*), and Jerusalem are also assigned to Benjamin. Jerusalem, however, was neutral territory until taken under David and retained as a crown possession and capital of Judah. Dt 33[12] (' he will dwell between his (Benjamin's) shoulders ') apparently refers to Yahweh's dwelling at Jerusalem, which is overlooked from the NE. and NW. by the heights of Benjamin, like the neck between the shoulders. Anathoth, the home of Jeremiah, also lay in Benjamin (Jos 21[18]). In the Blessing of Jacob (Gn 49[27]), which has the appearance of *vaticinium post eventum*, a fierce and warlike character is ascribed to Benjamin. The rugged and poor nature of the tribal territory doubtless conditioned the character of the Benjamites, so that Saul and his tribesmen, in a new military order, became a fitting striking-force against the Philistines. The tribe participated in the campaign against Sisera (Jg 5[14]). A late and composite story is found in Jg 19–21 of an almost complete annihilation of Benjamin by the rest of the tribes. It had in Asa's army, according to the exaggerated statement of 2 Ch 14[8], 280,000 picked warriors. This statement is significant confirmation of the martial character of Benjamin and is important as suggesting that the affinities of Benjamin soon after the disruption of the kingdom were with Judah. Benjamin, under Sheba, a kinsman of Saul, led in the revolt against David when the quarrel provoked by David's partisanship broke out between Judah and the northern tribes (2 S 20[1ff]). The tribe was naturally loyal to the house of Saul and violently opposed to David (cf 2 S 16[5] 20[2]). In the revolt against Rehoboam it joined with the northern tribes (1 K 12[20]). A variant account joins it with Judah (12[21ff]), but this is only a reflexion of later times. Jerusalem lay in the extreme north of the proper territory of Judah, it was imperative for the kings of Judah to extend their territory northwards, and so most of Benjamin was eventually incorporated in the southern Kingdom. The history of the tribe is unimportant after David. Besides Saul and Jeremiah, St. Paul also traced descent to this tribe (Ph 3[5]). See also TRIBES.

2. A great-grandson of Benjamin (1 Ch 7[10]). **3.** One of those who had married a foreign wife (Ezr 10[32]; probably also Neh 3[23] 12[34]).

J. A. C.—**J. Gr.**

BENJAMIN GATE.—See TEMPLE, **6** (*a*), and JERUSALEM (GATES OF).

BENO (' his son ').—Apparently a proper name in 1 Ch 24[26f]; but the text reads strangely since Beno is said to be the ' sons ' of Jaaziah. Hence it has been suggested that the passage should be rendered ' of Jaaziah *his son*, even the sons of Merari by Jaaziah *his son* ' (*Oxf. Heb. Lex. s.v.*).

BENONI.—See BENJAMIN, **1.**

BEN-ZOHETH.—A Judahite, 1 Ch 4[20].

BEON.—A city mentioned in Nu 32[3]; see BAAL-MEON.

BEOR.—1. Father of Balaam, Nu 22[5] 24[3, 15]; mentioned also Nu 31[8], Dt 23[4], Jos 13[22] 24[9], Mic 6[5], 2 P 2[15] (AV, RVm **Bosor**). **2.** Father of Bela, king of Edom, Gn 36[32], 1 Ch 1[43].

BERA.—King of Sodom at the time of Chedorlaomer's invasion, Gn 14[2].

BERACAH (' blessing ').—**1.** One of Saul's kinsmen who joined David at Ziklag, 1 Ch 12[3] (AV **Berachah**). **2.** A valley where Jehoshaphat gave thanks (2 Ch 20[26];

AV **Berachah**) for victory over the Ammonites, Moabites, and Edomites, who had marched from Engedi to Tekoa (vv.$^{2, 20}$); probably modern *Bereikût*, between Tekoa and Engedi.

BERACHAH.—The AV spelling of **Beracah** (q.v.).

BERACHIAH, 1 Ch 6^{39} (AV).—See Berechiah.

BERAIAH.—A Benjamite, 1 Ch 8^{21}.

BEREA (1 Mac 9^{4}).—See Beroea, **3.**

BERECHIAH.—**1.** Father of Asaph (1 Ch 6^{39}, AV **Berachiah**). **2.** Son of Zerubbabel (1 Ch 3^{20}). **3.** Father of Meshullam, one of Nehemiah's chiefs (Neh $3^{4, 30}$ 6^{13}). **4.** A Levite gatekeeper for the Ark in David's reign (1 Ch 15^{23}), probably the same as the Levite descended from Elkanah of the Netophathites (1 Ch 9^{16}). **5.** Father of the prophet Zechariah (Zec 1^{1}). **6.** An Ephraimite chief (2 Ch 28^{12}).

BERED.—**1.** An unknown place, mentioned only in Gn 16^{14} as an indication fixing the site of Beer-lahai-roi. **2.** Son of Ephraim, 1 Ch 7^{20}; called **Becher** (q.v.) in Nu 26^{35}.

BERENICE.—See Bernice.

BERI.—An Asherite, son of Zophah, 1 Ch 7^{36}.

BERIAH.—**1.** Son of Asher, Gn 46^{17}, Nu 26^{44f}, 1 Ch 7^{30f}. The patronymic **Beriites** occurs in Nu 26^{44}. **2.** Son of Ephraim, begotten in the days of mourning occasioned by the death of Ephraim's four sons, who were killed by the men of Gath whilst cattle-raiding; hence the false etymology, *b^erā'âh*, 'in affliction,' 1 Ch 7^{23}. **3.** A Benjamite of Aijalon, who with Shema put the Gittites to flight (cf **2**), 1 Ch $8^{13, 16}$. **4.** A Levite, son of Shimei, 1 Ch 23^{10f}.

BERITES, 2 S 20^{14} (AV, RV).—See Bichri.

BERNICE or **BERENICE.**—Sister of Agrippa II. (Ac $25^{13, 23}$ 26^{30}), married to her uncle Herod, king of Chalcis.

BERODACH-BALADAN.—See Merodach-baladan.

BEROEA.—**1.** A town in the district of Macedonia called Emathia. The earliest certain reference to it occurs in an inscription of the end of the 4th cent. B.C. After the battle of Pydna (168 B.C.) in which the Romans destroyed the Macedonian kingdom, it was the first city which surrendered to the Romans. In winter 49–48 B.C. it was the headquarters of Pompey's infantry. In St. Paul's time there was a Jewish community there to which he preached the gospel with success (Ac $17^{10, 13}$ [Sopater, a native] 20^{4}). It was a populous city, and is in modern times called *Verria* by Greeks, *Karaferia* by Turks, and *Ber* by Slavs.

2. The place where Antiochus Eupator caused Menelaus, the ex-high priest, to be put to death (2 Mac 13^{4}). It is now the well-known *Ḥaleb* or *Aleppo*, with about 450,000 inhabitants.

3. Mentioned 1 Mac 9^{4} (**Berea**). Some MSS have Beërzath (cf Jos. *Ant.* XII. xi. 1 [422]), which suggests Birzaith. See Birzaith, **2.** A. So.—**E. G. K.**

BEROTH, 1 Es 5^{19} (AV, RV).—See Beeroth. **Berothite** in 1 Ch 11^{39} (AV, RV) is for **Beerothite** (RSV 'of Beeroth'); cf 2 S 23^{37}.

BEROTHAH.—City named by Ezekiel as a limiting point in his ideal restoration of the Kingdom, Ezk 47^{16}. Ezekiel places it between Hamath and Damascus; possibly modern *Bereitân*.

BEROTHAI.—A city of Syria, despoiled by David, 2 S 8^{8}. In the parallel 1 Ch 18^{8} it is replaced by **Cun** (AV **Chun**). Possibly Berothai is identical with Berothah.

BERYL.—See Jewels and Precious Stones.

BERZELUS, 1 Es 5^{38} (AV).—See Barzillai, **1.**

BESAI.—Father of some Nethinim (q.v.) who returned with Zerubbabel, Ezr 2^{49}, Neh 7^{52}, 1 Es 5^{31} (AV **Bastai**, RV **Basthai**).

BESCASPASMYS, 1 Es 9^{31}.—See Mattaniah, **6.**

BESODEIAH.—Father of Meshullam who took part in repairing the Old Gate, Neh 3^{6}.

BESOM.—Occurs only in Is 14^{23} (AV, RV) in figurative use, 'I will sweep it with the besom (RSV 'broom') of destruction.'

BESOR.—A torrent-valley, S. or SW. of Ziklag, 1 S $30^{9f, 21}$; possibly modern *Wâdī Ghazzeh.*

BESTIALITY.—See Crimes and Punishments, **3.**

BETAH.—Place mentioned only in 2 S 8^{8}. The parallel 1 Ch 18^{8} has **Tibhath** (q.v.).

BETANE, Jth 1^{9} (AV, RV).—A place apparently south of Jerusalem (RSV **Bethany**). It may be the same as **Beth-anoth.**

BETEN.—A town of Asher, near Achshaph, Jos 19^{25}. In the 4th cent. it was shown eight Roman miles E. of Ptolemais. It is possibly modern *Abṭûn.*

BETH.—The second letter of Hebrew alphabet, and so used to introduce the second part of Ps 119, every verse of which begins with this letter.

BETHABARA.—Mentioned once only, Jn 1^{28}, as the scene of John's baptism; the principal codices, followed by the RV and RSV, here read Bethany (q.v.). Perhaps Bethabara is to be connected with the Beth-barah of Jg 7^{24} (q.v.). Others would seek it at a ford named *'Abārah*, about twelve miles south of the outlet of the Sea of Galilee. R. A. S. M.—**E. G. K.**

BETH-ANATH.—A town of Naphtali, Jos 19^{38}, Jg 1^{33}; perhaps modern *el-Ba'neh.*

BETH-ANOTH.—A town in the hill country of Judah, near Gedor, Jos 15^{59}; possibly modern *Beit 'Ainûn*, N. of Hebron. See also Betane.

BETHANY (Greek *Bethania*, probably Hebrew *Beth-aniah*, the second element a contracted form of the personal name Ananiah).—A village about 15 *stadia* (2910 yards or about 1⅝ mile) from Jerusalem (Jn 11^{18}) on the road from Jericho, close to Bethphage and on the Mount of Olives (Mk 11^{1}, Lk 19^{29}). It was the lodging-place of Jesus when in Jerusalem (Mk 11^{11}). Here lived Lazarus and Martha and Mary (Jn 11^{1}), and here He raised Lazarus from the dead (Jn 11). Here also He was entertained by Simon the leper, at the feast where the woman made her offering of ointment (Mt 26^{6}, Mk 14^{3}). From Bethany also took place the Ascension (Lk 24^{50}). In this case the topographical indications agree exceptionally with the constant tradition which fixes Bethany at the village of *el-'Azarîyeh*, on the SE. of the Mount of Olives beside the Jericho road. The tomb of Lazarus and the house of Martha and Mary are pointed out in the village, but of course without any historical authority. Traces of ancient occupation have been found at the village.

The Bethany that replaces Bethabara (q.v.) in the best manuscripts of Jn 1^{28} is only seemingly the same name. It may be from Aramaic *Beth-'enayyā* 'house of springs,' though no such town-name is reported from this area. See also Betane. R. A. S. M.—**E. G. K.**

BETH-ARABAH.—A place in the Jericho plain, on the boundary between Judah and Benjamin, Jos $15^{6, 61}$ 18^{18} (RSV; AV, RV 'against the Arabah)^{22}; possibly modern *'Ain el-Gharabeh*, in the *Wâdī Qelt.*

BETH-ARAM, Jos 13^{17} (AV).—See Beth-haram.

BETH-ARBEL.—A place mentioned only in Hos 10^{14}, where it is said to have been destroyed 'in the day of battle' by Shalman (q.v.). It is probably modern *Irbid*, E. of the Jordan, in Gilead.

BETH-ASHBEA.—Found in 1 Ch 4^{21}; if a place name it is unknown, or if Ashbea is the name of a man (AV, RV 'house of Ashbea'), he is otherwise unknown.

BETH-ASMOTH.—A Benjamite town, 1 Es 5^{18}; called **Beth-azmaveth** in Neh 7^{28} and **Azmaveth** (q.v.) in Ezr 2^{24}, Neh 12^{29}.

BETH-AVEN ('house of iniquity').—A place close to Ai (Jos 7^{2}), by the wilderness (18^{12}), NW. of Michmash (1 S 13^{5}), and on the way to Aijalon (14^{23}), still inhabited in the 8th cent. B.C. (Hos 5^{8}). The 'calf of Beth-aven' (Hos 10^{5}) was probably that at **Bethel,** but Bethel is distinguished from Beth-aven in Jos 7^{2}. Bethel is probably meant by Beth-aven in Hos 4^{15} 5^{8} (cf Am 5^{5}), and by **Aven** in Hos 10^{8}.

BETH-AZMAVETH.—A Benjamite town, Neh 7^{28}; also called **Azmaveth** (q.v.).

BETH-BAAL-MEON.—A city mentioned in Jos 13^{17}; see BAAL-MEON.

BETH-BARAH.—A place in the Jordan valley near the valley of Jezreel, Jg 7^{24}. Its location is unknown.

BETHBASI (1 Mac $9^{62, 64}$).—Josephus reads Bethhoglah. The name has not been recovered.

BETH-BIREI, 1 Ch 4^{31} (AV).—See BETH-BIRI.

BETH-BIRI.—A town of Simeon, 1 Ch 4^{31} (AV **Beth-birei**). In the parallel list in Jos 19^{6} it is replaced by **Beth-lebaoth.** Its site is unknown.

BETH-CAR (' house of a lamb ').—A place mentioned as the terminus of the pursuit of the Philistines under Samuel's guidance, 1 S 7^{11}. Its site is unknown, save that it must have been near Jerusalem, on the west.

BETH-DAGON (' house of Dagon ').—**1.** A city of Judah, in the Shephelah, Jos 15^{41}. It is possibly *Kh. Dajûn.* **2.** A border city of Asher, Jos 19^{27}. It is mentioned by Sennacherib in the account of his campaign of 701 B.C. The site is unknown.

BETH-DIBLATHAIM (' house of two fig-cakes ').—Moabite city, Jer 48^{22}; probably identical with **Almon-diblathaim** (q.v.), a station in the journeyings, Nu 33^{46f}; mentioned on the Moabite Stone.

BETH-EDEN.—A place or district connected politically with Damascus, Am 1^{5} (AV, RV ' house of Eden '). Its situation is unknown. There is a *Bît Adini* mentioned in Assyrian inscriptions, but it is too far from Damascus to be suitable. See EDEN.

BETH-EKED.—A place at which Jehu, on his way from Jezreel to Samaria, met and slew the brethren of Ahaziah, king of Judah, 2 K $10^{12, 14}$ (AV, RV **the shearing house**). It is perhaps modern *Beit Qâd*, near to *Jenîn.*

BETHEL.—**1.** Modern *Beitîn*, just E. of the Great North Road of Palestine (Jordan) about 12 miles from Jerusalem, a village of some 600 inhabitants. Four springs furnish good water, and in ancient times they were supplemented by a reservoir hewn in the rock, S. of the town. Originally named Luz, it was later known as Bethel, tradition referring this name specifically to the stone which Jacob set up and anointed as the symbol of God's presence after his theophany (Gn 28^{22}). In Christian times this spot was located about a mile E. of *Beitîn*, and was the site of a church and monastery, remains of which are possibly those to be seen at *Burj Beitîn.* There were earlier religious associations. Abraham, according to Hebrew tradition, sacrificed here (Gn 12^{8}). From an eminence to the E. almost the whole of the plains of Jericho is visible, and this may have been the scene of Lot's selfish choice (13).

Excavations at Bethel by Albright and Kelso established continuous occupation from *c* 2000 B.C. till Christian times. Bethel, a royal Canaanite city (Jos 12^{16}), fell to Benjamin in the division of the land (18^{22}), but he did not immediately succeed in making good his possession. It was finally taken by the men of Joseph (Jg 1^{22}, 1 Ch 7^{28}). The above-mentioned excavations demonstrate that Bethel was destroyed at the end of the 14th or the beginning of the 13th cent. B.C., which is before the final phase of the Hebrew settlement, so older elements from the hill-country of Ephraim may have been responsible rather than the mass of the invaders. Hither the Ark was brought from Gilgal (Jg 20^{18} LXX), and Bethel was a place of sacrifice in the time of Saul (1 S 10^{3}). The prophetess Deborah lived in the vicinity of Bethel (Jg 4^{5}). In judging Israel Samuel is said to have gone forth from year to year in circuit to Bethel (1 S 7^{10}). No doubt the ancient sanctity of the place, as well as its location on the road southwards at the border of Israel and Judah led Jeroboam I. to choose Bethel as the site of a rival shrine to the Temple in Jerusalem (1 K 12^{26f}), and it became the great sanctuary of the Northern Kingdom. The ' calf ' of Jeroboam, though probably serving only as a pedestal for the presence of Yahweh, indicates an adaptation of the fertility-cult of the local Canaanite Baal, whose cult-animal was the bull. Elements of this local cult which retained undue prominence were apparently the reason for the violent denunciations of Amos (3^{14} 4^{4} 5^{5} etc.) and Hosea (4^{15} 5^{8}). At Bethel Jeroboam was denounced by the man of God out of Judah (13^{1ff}) and it was the scene of Amos' famous encounter with the priest Amaziah in his denunciation of the house of Jeroboam II. A guild of dervishes (' sons of the prophets ') in sympathy with Elijah flourished there (2 K 2^{2f}). After the fall of Samaria it was the seat of the priest who was sent by the king of Assyria to teach the mixed population of military colonists the worship of the God of the land (2 K 17^{29f}). Bethel was reoccupied by the returning exiles (Ezr 2^{28}, 1 Es 5^{21} [AV **Betolius,** RV **Betolion**]). In 161 B.C. it was taken by the Seleucid general Bacchides (1 Mac 9^{50}) in his strategy of sealing off and keeping watch on Jerusalem, and in pursuance of the same policy it was taken by Vespasian before the fall of Jerusalem (Jos. *BJ* iv. ix. 9 [551]).

2. A town in the SE. of Judah, not identified, called in different places **Bethul** (Jos 19^{4}), Bethel (1 S 30^{27}), and **Bethuel** (1 Ch 4^{30}). See also CHESIL.

W. E.—**J. Gr.**

BETH-EMEK (' house of the valley ').—A town of Asher, apparently not far from Cabul, Jos 19^{27}. It is possibly the modern *Tell Mīmâs.*

BETHER.—A city belonging to Judah, mentioned in Jos 15^{59} in LXX, but not in the Hebrew. It is the modern *Bittîr*, SW. of Jerusalem. This place was celebrated for the resistance to the Romans during the revolt of Bar Cochba in A.D. 135. In Ca 2^{17} there is a reference to the ' mountains of Bether ' in AV, RV; but the meaning is doubtful. RVm suggests that the spice **malobathron** (q.v.) is meant (cf Ca 4^{6}) or else ' mountains of separation,' while RSV renders ' rugged mountains.' The word *bether* means ' cleaving.'

BETHESDA (RSV Bethzatha).—A pool mentioned in Jn 5^{2}. The latter name is no doubt derived from that of the new suburb north of the city, which Josephus calls Bezatha. The meaning of the name is not certain. It could be Aramaic *Bē-zaitā* ' Olive place ' or *beza'tā* ' section.' The reading Bethesda probably is from Aramaic *Beth-ḥisdā* ' house of mercy,' and may be a name given the pool by Christians owing to the incident of Jn 5. Some MSS contain information about the periodic disturbance of the water referred to in v.^{7} and the popular explanation of this phenomenon. The RSV has relegated this material to the margin. The Virgin's Fountain (ancient Gihon), which sent its water to the pool of Siloam, is still intermittent, but whether the same thing was true of a reservoir in the north is doubtful. That item could suggest transfer of the story. The localization of Bethesda by the Sheep-gate necessitates seeking it north of the city. Two pools between and around which ran porticoes have been located and painstakingly explored by Schick, Vincent, and Van der Vliet. As they are in the proper area they probably represent ancient Bethesda. E. G. K.

BETH-EZEL.—A place mentioned only in Mic 1^{11} along with Shaphir and Zaanan. It is perhaps modern *Deir el-'Aṣal*, SW. of Hebron. Some have supposed it was identical with **Azel** (q.v.).

BETH-GADER.—A place mentioned with Bethlehem and Kiriath-jearim in 1 Ch 2^{51}. Its site is unknown. Some have thought it to be identical with **Geder** or **Gedor, 1** (qq.v.).

BETH-GAMUL.—A place in Moab, mentioned with Dibon, Nebo, and Kiriathaim, Jer 48^{23}. It is modern *Kh. Jumeil*, E. of Dibon.

BETH-GILGAL.—A place mentioned in Neh 12^{29} (AV ' house of Gilgal '); perhaps identical with **Gilgal, 1.**

BETH-HACCEREM.—The AV spelling of **Beth-haccherem** (q.v.).

BETH-HACCHEREM (' place of the vineyard ').—A city of Judah, mentioned with Tekoa, Jer 6^{1}. It was the chief town of a district, Neh 3^{14}. It appears to have had a commanding position for a beacon or ensign (Jer 6^{1}). It is perhaps identical with **Karem** (q.v.).

BETH-HAGGAN (' place of the garden ').—A place mentioned only in 2 K 9^{27} (AV, RV ' the garden house '). It is possibly the same as **En-gannim, 2** (q.v.).

BETH-HARAM.—A city of Gad, in the Jordan valley, Jos 13^{27} (AV **Beth-aram**) ; called **Beth-haran** in Nu 32^{36}. It was rebuilt and fortified by Herod Antipas when he became tetrarch, and in honour of the Roman empress was called Livias or Libias. Merrill (*East of the Jordan*, p. 383) gives reasons for believing that it was in the palace here that Herod celebrated his birthday by the feast recorded (Mt 14$^{6-12}$, Mk 6$^{21-28}$), and that the Baptist's head was brought hither from Machaerus, some 20 miles south. It is identified with *Tell Iktanû*, E. of *Tell er-Râmeh*.

BETH-HARAN.—See BETH-HARAM.

BETH-HOGLA, Jos 15^{6} (AV).—See BETH-HOGLAH.

BETH-HOGLAH (' place of the partridge ').—A city of Benjamin, Jos 18^{21}, on the border between Judah and Benjamin (15^{6} (AV **Beth-hogla**) 18^{19}). It is the modern *'Ain Ḥajlah*, SE. of Jericho.

BETH-HORON.—The upper and nether, two towns represented by the villages *Beit 'Ûr el-fôqā* and *Beit 'Ûr et-taḥta*. The nether Beth-horon is the larger and more important site, with remains going back to the Late Bronze Age. Their position, as commanding the ancient high-road from the maritime plain into the heart of the mountains of Benjamin, made these places of great importance, and several celebrated battles occurred in their neighbourhood. Here Joshua defeated the Canaanites (Jos 10$^{10-14}$). Solomon fortified both these cities (2 Ch 8^{5}, 1 K 9^{17}). Here Judas Maccabaeus defeated the Syrian general Seron (1 Mac 3$^{13-24}$) and five years afterwards Nicanor (7$^{39-50}$) ; more than 200 years later the Jews at the same place beat back a Roman force under Cestius Gallus. In few places in Palestine can we with greater precision set history in its geographical setting ; the whole ancient road, with abundant traces of Roman work, can be followed throughout, and the two *Beit 'Ûrs*, less than two miles apart, stand sentinel above the road as the two Beth-horons did in ancient times. The Beth-horons were on the frontier between Benjamin and Ephraim (Jos 16$^{3-5}$ and 18^{13f}). They belonged to the latter (Jos 21^{22}), and followed the Northern Kingdom. Post-exilic resettlement of the place is reflected in 1 Ch 7^{24}. Possibly Sanballat the Horonite (Neh 2^{10}) was from here.
E. W. G. M.—**E. G. K.**

BETH-JESHIMOTH (' place of the desert ').—The S. limit of the encampment on ' the plains of Moab ' at the close of the journeyings, Nu 33^{49} (AV **Beth-Jesimoth**). In Jos 12^{3} it is said to be in the S. of the Arabah, towards the Dead Sea. In 13^{20} it is assigned to Reuben, but later, in Ezk 25^{9} it is mentioned as belonging to Moab. Eusebius places it 10 miles S. of Jericho. It is probably modern *Tell el-'Azeimeh*.

BETH-JESIMOTH, Nu 33^{49} (AV).—See BETH-JESHIMOTH.

BETH-LE-APHRAH.—A town apparently in Philistine territory, whose site is unknown, Mic 1^{10} (AV ' house of Aphrah '). In the words ' in Beth-le-aphrah roll yourselves in the dust ' there is a double play upon words, *'aphrāh* containing a punning allusion to *'āphār* (dust), and *hithpallāshî* (roll yourself) to *Pelishtî* (Philistine).

BETH-LEBAOTH (' house of lionesses ').—A town of Simeon, near Sharuhen, Jos 19^{6}. In the parallel list in 1 Ch 4^{31} its place is taken by **Beth-biri** (AV **Beth-birei**). It is probably identical with **Lebaoth,** Jos 15^{32}. Its site is unknown.

BETHLEHEM.—The name of two places in Palestine. **1.** Bethlehem of Judah, now represented by the town of *Beit Laḥm*, 5 miles S. of Jerusalem. On the way thither Rachel was buried according to post-exilic Jewish belief, as expressed in the glosses in Gn 35^{19} 48^{7}. However the Ephrath referred to there originally meant a place N. of Jerusalem. But Ephrath(ah) was also the name of the district in which Bethlehem lay. From Bethlehem came the Levite whose adventures are related in Jg 17. It was the home of Elimelech, the father-in-law of Ruth (Ru 1^{1}), and here Ruth settled and became the ancestress of the family of David, whose connexion with Bethlehem is emphasized throughout his history (1 S 16$^{1-18}$ 17^{12} 20^{6} etc). The Philistines had here a garrison during David's outlawry (2 S 23^{14}, 1 Ch 11^{16}). Here Asahel was buried (2 S 2^{32}), and hence came Elhanan, one of the mighty men (2 S 23^{24}, cf 21^{19}). Rehoboam fortified it (2 Ch 11^{6}), and here (Jer 41^{17}) the Egypt-bound fugitives who took Jeremiah along with them tarried. Its area (Ephrath) was potentially one where the Ark might have been kept (Ps 132^{6}). The birth of the Messiah there is prophesied in Mic 5^{2} (quoted Mt 2^{6}, Jn 7^{42}), a prophecy fulfilled by the birth of Christ (Mt 2$^{1, 5}$, Lk 2$^{4, 15}$). Here Herod sent to seek the new-born Christ, and not finding Him ordered the massacre of the infants of the city (Mt 2$^{8, 16}$). The modern town, containing about 20,000 inhabitants, is Christian and comparatively prosperous. Within it stands the basilica of the Nativity, founded by Constantine (about 330), and restored by Justinian (about 550) and many later emperors. Within it is shown the grotto of the Nativity. The antiquity of the tradition makes this a venerable place, though there is no way of knowing what information led Constantine's advisers to seek the birth-place of Jesus there.
2. Bethlehem of Zebulun, a place named but once (Jos 19^{15}), in enumerating the towns of that tribe. It is identified with *Beit Laḥm*, 7 miles NW. of Nazareth. It was the home of Ibzan, the judge (Jg 12$^{8-10}$).
R. A. S. M.—**E. G. K.**

BETH-LOMON, 1 Es 5^{17} (AV, RV).—For **Bethlehem, 1** (so RSV).

BETH-MAACAH.—A descriptive epithet of Abel (2 S 20^{14}), where we should read with RSV ' Abel of Beth-maacah ' instead of AV ' Abel *and* B,' which the Hebrew has (cf v.^{15}). In 1 K 15^{20}, 2 K 15^{29} AV, RV, and RSV have Abel-beth-m. See ABEL (OF) BETH-MAACAH.

BETH-MAACHAH.—The AV spelling of **Beth Maacah** (q.v.).

BETH-MARCABOTH (' place of chariots ').—A city of Simeon in the southern plains, near Ziklag, Jos 19^{5}, 1 Ch 4^{31}. Its site is unknown. See MADMANNAH.

BETH-MEON.—A city mentioned in Jer 48^{23} ; see BAAL-MEON.

BETH-MERHAK.—A place mentioned only in RV in 2 S 15^{17}. It is improbable that it is a place-name at all. AV translates ' a place that was afar off ' and RSV ' the last house.'

BETH-MILLO.—**1.** A place near Shechem, mentioned only in Jg 9$^{6, 20}$ (AV, RV ' the house of Millo '). The site is unknown. See MILLO. **2.** An unknown place, apparently in Judah, mentioned only in 2 K 12^{20} (so AVm ; AV, RV, RSV ' the house of Millo '). See MILLO.

BETH-NIMRAH (' place of the leopard ').—A town E. of the Jordan in the territory of Gad, Jos 13^{27}, Nu 32^{36}. It is called **Nimrah** in Nu 32^{3}, and some think it is identical with **Nimrim** (q.v.) in Is 15^{6}. It is the modern *Tell el-Bileibil*, near *Tell Nimrîn*.

BETH-PALET, Jos 15^{27} (AV).—See BETH-PELET.

BETH-PAZZEZ.—A town of Issachar near En-gannim and En-haddah, Jos 19^{21} The site is unknown.

BETH-PELET.—A town of Judah, S. of Beersheba, Jos 15[27] (AV **Beth-palet**), Neh 11[26] (AV **Beth-phelet**). The gentilic **Paltite** is found in 2 S 23[26] (cf 1 Ch 11[27], where the same person is called a **Pelonite**). The site is unknown.

BETH-PEOR.—A city belonging to Reuben, Jos 13[20]; the Israelites encamped opposite to it (Dt 3[29] 4[46]), and Moses was buried there (Dt 34[6]). It is perhaps to be identified with **Baal-peor** (q.v.), and with modern *Khirbet esh-Sheikh-Jâyil.*

BETHPHAGE (Heb. *Bêth-pâghê*).—Hardly 'house of figs,' but rather 'house of the country districts' (Lat. *pagi*). Here Jesus, coming from Jericho, sent His disciples to fetch the ass (Mt 21[1], Mk 11[1], Lk 19[29]). It is mentioned in the Rabbinic sources as the easternmost point in Jerusalem's territory. It must have lain E. of the summit of the Mount of Olives proper (*eṭ-Ṭur*) and N. of Bethany. Jesus coming from the latter place would have crossed the summit via Bethphage. To-day *Abū Dīs.* R. A. S. M.—**E. G. K.**

BETH-PHELET, Neh 11[26] (AV).—See Beth-pelet.

BETH-RAPHA ('house of the giant'?).—A Judahite, or an else unknown place belonging to the tribe, 1 Ch 4[12].

BETH-REHOB.—An Aramaean district near Laish (Jg 18[28]), whose inhabitants joined the Ammonites against David (2 S 10[6]); called **Rehob** in 10[8]. Probably Rehob in Nu 13[21], which marked the limit of the journey of the spies, is the same place. Its site is unknown.

BETHSAIDA.—A place on the shore of the Sea of Galilee, whither Jesus went after feeding the five thousand (Mk 6[45], cf Lk 9[10]), and where He healed a blind man (Mk 8[22]); the home of Philip, Andrew, and Peter (Jn 1[44] 12[21]). Along with Chorazin (q.v.) it was denounced for its failure to respond to the gospel (Mt 11[21], Lk 10[13]). The town was advanced by Philip the tetrarch to the dignity of a city, and named Julias, in honour of Caesar's daughter. The situation is disputed, and, indeed, authorities differ as to whether or not there were two places of the same name, one E., one W. of the Jordan. However, it seems probable that the old fishing village lay on the shore at *Khirbet al-'Araj*, E. of the mouth of the Jordan, and that Julias was built further inland. The mound of *et-Tell*, also E. of the Jordan, must mark the site. R. A. S. M.—**E. G. K.**

BETH-SHEAN, BETH-SHAN.—The site of this ancient stronghold, allotted to Manasseh, although in the territory of Issachar (Jos 17[11ff], Jg 1[27]), is marked by the great mound of *Tell el-Ḥuṣn* ('Mound of the Fortress') by the former Arab village of *Beisân* (Israeli *Bethshan*) where the Valley of Jezreel narrows and dips to the Jordan Valley. Bethshan never seems to have been integrated into the life of Israel. Here the Philistines hung the bodies of Saul and his sons on the wall after the battle of Gilboa (1 S 31[7ff]). Excavations have shown that the site was occupied from long before 3000 B.C. to the Arab period. In the period of Egyptian domination from the 15th to the 13th cent. there were several temples under Egyptian patronage to local deities, including Mekal ('Consumer'), or Reshef the god of pestilence, Anat, the sister of the fertility-god Baal, and doubtless Baal himself. There is evidence that the place was occupied by the 'Sea-peoples,' including the Philistines, probably as mercenaries of Egypt, though in the time of Saul they may have been occupying Bethshan on their own account. It was incorporated with other Canaanite towns into the realm of Solomon in the fiscal district of Baanah (1 K 4[12]), but plays no part in the history of Israel. During the Greek period it was known as Scythopolis and also as Nyssa, but the ancient name reappeared in the Arab period as *Beisân*, the name of the adjacent Arab village. After changes of fortune in the struggles of the Hasmonaeans and in the succeeding period, it attained considerable prosperity as a member of the Decapolis (1 Mac 12[40], Jos. *Ant.* XIV. v. 3 [88], *BJ* III. ix. 7 [446], etc), a federation of free cities interested in trade, of which Bethshan was the only member W. of the Jordan. There must always have been a strong admixture of heathen inhabitants (Jos. *Vita* 6 [26]; *Abodah Zarah* i. 4). W. E.—**J. Gr.**

BETH-SHEMESH ('house' or 'temple of the sun'). —**1.** A town in Judah (Jos 15[10] etc., called **Ir-Shemesh** in Jos 19[41]) allotted to the children of Aaron (Jos 21[16]). Hither the Ark was brought when sent back by the Philistines, and the inhabitants were smitten for their profane curiosity (1 S 6). Here Amaziah was defeated and captured by Jehoash, king of Israel (2 K 14[11, 13]). It was one of the cities of Judah taken by the Philistines in time of Ahaz (2 Ch 28[18]). The name is preserved in *'Ain Shems*, a Byzantine site on the S. slope of the *Wâdī eṣ-Ṣarâr* (Vale of Sorek), 15 miles W. of Jerusalem, the Hebrew site being *Tell er-Rumeileh*, slightly further W. Excavations by Mackenzie and later by Fisher and Grant show occupation from before 3000 till its destruction by Nebuchadrezzar. Casemate walls of the early Iron Age probably indicate David's fortification of the place as a frontier post against the Philistines. **2.** A city in Issachar (Jos 19[22]) not certainly identified, but possibly at *'Ain esh-Shemsîyeh*, 7 miles S. of Bethshan. **3.** A city in Naphtali (Jos 19[38], Jg 1[33]), mentioned with certain localities in Upper Galilee. The site has so far not been identified, but Abel suggests that it may be located at *Ḥāris* in this locality, SW. of *Tibnîn*. *Ḥeres* in Hebrew is a synonym of *shemesh* ('sun'). **4.** A city in Egypt, a seat of heathen idolatry (Jer 43[13]), identified with the ancient Heliopolis, locally called once *'Ain Shems.* E. W.—**J. Gr.**

BETH-SHITTAH ('place of the acacia').—A place mentioned in Jg 7[22]. It was in the neighbourhood of Abel-meholah; possibly *Shaṭṭah*, N. of Beth-shan.

BETHSURA.—See Beth-zur.

BETHSURON, 2 Mac 11[5] (RV).—See Beth-zur.

BETH-TAPPUAH ('place of apples').—A town of Judah in the Hebron mountains, Jos 15[53] (see Tappuah, **1**); modern *Taffûḥ*, W. of Hebron.

BETH-TOGARMAH.—A place which traded with Tyre in horses and mules, Ezk 27[14] 38[6] (AV, RV 'house of **Togarmah**'). See Togarmah.

BETHUEL.—**1.** The son of Nahor and Milcah, nephew of Abraham, and father of Laban and Rebekah (Gn 22[23] 24[15, 24, 47, 50] 25[20] 28[2, 5]). In Gn 28[5] (P) he is called 'Bethuel the Aramaean.' **2.** A place in Judah, mentioned in 1 Ch 4[30]; called **Bethul** in Jos 19[4]. See Bethel, **2.**

BETHUL.—See Bethel, **2.**

BETHULIA.—The place besieged by Holofernes in the Book of Judith (Jth 4[6f] etc.). The form of the name follows the Vulg.; LXX has *Betuloua* or *Baitouloua.* The name suggests Bethel, but this does not fit the topography. The old notion that it was a cryptic name for Jerusalem is impossible (that city being named in the story), and Shechem does not fit either. The topographical indications would best suit some point in the vicinity of the villages of *Jebaʻ*, *Fendaqūmiyeh*, and *Sīlet eḍ-Ḍahr*, between the city of Samaria and the plain of Esdraelon. The corruption of the names by Greek copyists and the fictitious nature of the book as such make the search for Bethulia and Betomastaim (q.v.) rather useless. E. G. K.

BETH-ZACHARIAS, 1 Mac 6[32f] (RV).—See Beth-zechariah.

BETH-ZAITH.—An unknown site, apparently near Jerusalem, 1 Mac 7[19] (AV, RV **Bezeth**).

BETH-ZATHA.—See Bethesda.

BETH-ZECHARIAH (1 Mac 6[32, 33]).—A village on the mountain pass, S. of Jerusalem and W. of Bethlehem (AV **Bathzacharias,** RV **Bethzacharias**), now the ruin *Beit Sakaria.* It was the scene of the defeat of Judas Maccabaeus by Lysias.

BETH-ZUR ('house of rock').—A town of Judah in the Hebron mountains, Jos 15[58] (cf 1 Ch 2[45]). It was fortified by Rehoboam (2 Ch 11[7]), and still important after the Captivity (Neh 3^{16}). (According to LXX^B David sent spoils from Ziklag to Beth-zur, 1 S 30^{27}, but the Hebrew followed by EV, has Bethel.) In the Maccabaean period it was an important strategic position, and it is frequently mentioned in 1 and 2 Mac (AV, RV **Bethsura**; in 2 Mac 11^5 RV has **Bethsuron**). Here Judas Maccabaeus defeated the Greeks under Lysias in 165 B.C., 1 Mac 4^{29}. It is the modern *Kh. eṭ-Ṭubeiqah.*

BETOLION, 1 Es 5^{21} (RV).—See BETHEL, **1.**

BETOLIUS, 1 Es 5^{21} (AV).—See BETHEL, **1.**

BETOMASTHAIM (Jth 15^4, AV **Betomasthem**); **Betomesthaim** (4^6, AV **Betomestham**).—Apparently N. of Bethulia (q.v.), and facing Dothan.

BETONIM.—A town of Gad, mentioned Jos 13^{26}; modern *Kh. Baṭneh.*

BETROTHING.—See MARRIAGE.

BEULAH (' married ' [of a wife]).—An allegorical name applied to Israel in Trito-Isaiah, Is 62^4. She was no longer to be a wife deserted by God, as she had been during the Captivity, but married (1) to God, (2) by a strange application of the figure, to her own sons (v.^{5}).

BEWITCH.—See MAGIC.

BEWRAY.—To bewray (from Anglo-Saxon prefix *be* and *wregan*, to accuse) is not the same as to betray (from *be* and Latin *tradere* to deliver). To bewray, now obsolete, means in AV and RV to make known, reveal, as Mt 26^{73} ' thy speech bewrayeth thee.' Adams (*Works*, ii. 328) distinguishes the two words thus : ' he . . . will not bewray his disease, lest he betray his credit.' Sometimes, however, bewray is used in an evil sense, and is scarcely distinguishable from betray. RSV uses ' betray ' and ' betrays.' Cf **bewrayer** in 2 Mac 4^1 AV ' a bewrayer of the money, and of his country ' ; RSV ' who had informed about the money against his own country.'

BEZAANANNIM, Jos 19^{33} (RVm).—See ZAANANNIM.

BEZAI.—**1.** One of those who sealed the covenant, Neh 10^{18}. **2.** The eponym of a family that returned with Zerubbabel, Ezr 2^{17}, Neh 7^{23}, 1 Es 5^{16} (AV **Bassa,** RV **Bassai**).

BEZALEL.—**1.** The chief architect of the Tabernacle. The name occurs only in P and in the Book of Chronicles (1 Ch 2^{20}, 2 Ch 1^5). It signifies ' in the shadow (*i.e.* under the protection) of El.' According to P's representation, Bezalel was expressly called by Y″ (Ex 31^2) to superintend the erection of the ' tent of meeting ' and the Ark of the testimony (v.^{7}), and endowed with the special gifts required for the proper execution of his task (vv.$^{3, 5}$). He was also charged with the construction of the furniture for court and Tabernacle, as well as with the preparation of the priestly garments, and of the necessary oil and incense. Among the gifts thus bestowed upon him, not the least was the gift of teaching the arts of which he was himself a master, to his subordinates (Ex 35^{34}), the chief of whom was Oholiab (Ex 31^6 35^{34} etc.). **2.** One of the sons of Pahath-moab who had married foreign wives (Ezr 10^{30}); called **Sesthel** in 1 Est 9^{31}.

A. R. S. K.

BEZEK.—Two places of this name are to be distinguished in the OT. **1.** Jg 1^5, a place attacked by Judah after Joshua's death, possibly *Bezqā*, 4 miles NE. of Gezer, though this was in the foothills of Ephraim. **12.** S 11^8, where Saul gathered Israel before advancing on Jabesh-Gilead. The most probable location is the ruined site of *Ibzîq*, 12 miles NE. of *Nâblus*, opposite Jabesh-Gilead. This is the site identified in the *Onostmaicon* 17 Roman miles from Neapolis (*Nâblus*) on the hill-road to Bethshan (Scythopolis). J. Gr.

BEZER (' fortress ').—**1.** An Asherite (1 Ch 7^{37}). **2.** A city of Reuben, allotted as a city of refuge, situated ' in the wilderness on the tableland ' (Dt 4^{43}, Jos 20^8). It was a Levitical city assigned to the Merarites (Jos 21^{36}, whence 1 Ch 6^{78}). Mesha mentions it on the Moabite Stone (see MOAB) as being in ruins in his day, and as having been rebuilt by him, after his revolt from Israel and the expulsion of the Israelites from the territory N. of the Arnon. From its being described as ' in the wilderness ' it may be inferred that it lay towards the E. border of the Moabite tableland. Its site is unknown. It is possible that it is identical with **Bozrah, 2** (q.v.).

BEZETH, 1 Mac 7^{19} (AV, RV).—See BETH-ZAITH.

BIATAS, 1 Es 9^{48} (AV).—See PELAIAH, **2.**

BIBLE.—**1. The Name.**—The word ' Bible ' strictly employed is the title of the Jewish and Christian Scriptures, though occasionally by a loose usage of the term it is applied to the sacred writings of pagan religions. It is derived from a Greek word *Biblia*—originating in *biblos* (*byblos*), the inner bark of the papyrus plant (whence our word paper)—literally meaning ' Little Books ' ; but since the diminutive had come into common use in late popular Greek apart from its specific signification, the term really means simply ' books.' It is the Greek translation of the Hebrew word for ' books,' which is the oldest designation for the Jewish Scriptures as a collection (see Dn 9^2). The title ' Holy Books '—equivalent to our ' Holy Scripture '—came later among the Jews (1 Mac 12^9, Ro 1^2, 2 Ti 3^{15}). The Greek word *Biblia* is first met with in this connexion in the introduction to Sirach, written in 132 B.C. by the grandson of Sirach, the phrase ' the rest of the books ' implying that the Law and the Prophets previously named, as well as those books subsequently known specially as ' the Writings,' are included. It is used in the Hebrew sense, for the OT, by the unknown author of the Christian homily in the 2nd cent. designated *The Second Epistle of Clement* (xiv. 2). It does not appear as a title of the whole Christian Scriptures before the 5th cent., when it was thus employed by Greek Church writers in lists of the canonical books. Thence it passed over into the West, and then the Greek word *Biblia*, really a neuter plural, came to be treated as a Latin singular noun, a significant grammatical change that pointed to the growing sense of the unity of Scripture. The word cannot be traced in Anglo-Saxon literature, and we first have the English form of it in the 14th cent. It occurs in *Piers Plowman* and Chaucer. Its adoption by Wycliffe secured it as the permanent English name for the Scriptures, as Luther's use of the corresponding German word fixed that for Continental Protestants.

2. Contents and Divisions.—The Jewish Bible is the OT ; the Protestant Christian Bible consists of the OT and the NT, but with the Apocrypha included in some editions ; the Roman Catholic Bible contains the OT and NT, and also the Apocrypha, the latter authoritatively treated as Scripture since the Council of Trent in 1546. The main division is between the Jewish Scriptures and those which are exclusively Christian. These are known respectively as the OT and the NT. The title ' Testament ' is unfortunate, since it really means a will. It is derived from the Latin word *testamentum*, ' a will,' which is the translation of the Greek word *diathēkē*, itself in the classics also meaning ' a will.' But the LXX employs this Greek word as the translation of the Hebrew *berîth*, a word meaning ' covenant.' Therefore ' testament ' in the Biblical sense really means ' covenant,' and the two parts of our Bible are the ' Old Covenant ' and the ' New Covenant.' When we ask why the Greek translators used the word meaning ' will ' while they had ready to hand another word meaning ' covenant ' (viz. *synthēkē*), the answer has been proposed that they perceived the essential difference between God's covenants with men and men's covenants one with another. The latter are arranged on equal terms. But God's covenants are made and offered by God and accepted by men only on God's terms. A Divine covenant is like a will in which a man disposes of his property on whatever terms he thinks fit. On the other hand, however, it may be observed that the word *diathēkē* is also used for a covenant between man and man (*e.g.* Dt 7^2). The origin of this term as applied by Christians to the two main divisions of Scripture is Jeremiah's promise of a New Covenant (Jer 31^{31}), endorsed by Christ (Mk 14^{24}, 1 Co 11^{25}), and enlarged upon in NT teaching (*e.g.* Gal 4^{24}, He 8^6).

Here, however, the reference is to the Divine arrangements and pledges, not to the books of Scripture, and it is by a secondary usage that the books containing the two covenants have come to be themselves designated Testaments, or Covenants.

The Jewish division of the OT is into three parts known as (1) the Law, (2) the Prophets, and (3) the Writings, or the Sacred Writings (*Hagiographa*). The 'Law' consisted of the first five books of our Bible (Genesis, Exodus, Leviticus, Numbers, Deuteronomy), ascribed to Moses; and it was treated as peculiarly sacred, the most holy and authoritative portion of Scripture. It was the only part of the Hebrew Scriptures accepted by the Samaritans, who worshipped the very document containing it almost as a fetish. But the name 'Law' (Heb. *Tôrāh*, Gr. *Nomos*) is sometimes given to the whole Jewish Bible (*e.g.* Jn 10^{34}). The 'Prophets' (*Nᵉbhî'îm*) included not only the utterances ascribed to inspired teachers of Israel, but also the chief historical books later than the Pentateuch. There were reckoned to be 8 books of the Prophets (*Nᵉbhî'îm*), divided into the 'Former' or earlier (Joshua, Judges, Samuel, Kings) and the 'Latter' or later (Isaiah, Jeremiah, Ezekiel, the Twelve Minor Prophets). Usage by the Chronicler (*c* 250 B.C.) and the reference in Sirach (132 B.C.) would indicate the acceptance of this collection as Scripture sometime within that period. The Hagiographa (*Kᵉthûbhîm*) were the poetical books (Psalms, Proverbs, Job), the 5 *Mᵉghillôth* ('rolls') which came to be associated with various festivals (Song of Songs, Ruth, Lamentations, Ecclesiastes, Esther), and 3 late, narrative books (Daniel, Ezra-Nehemiah, Chronicles). This total group of 11 writings did not find complete acceptance until near the end of the 1st cent. A.D. Thus there were in all 24 books by Jewish reckoning. Josephus, however, counted 22 (the number of letters in the Hebrew alphabet), probably joining Ruth to Judges and Lamentations to Jeremiah, and in this he was followed by a few Christian fathers, *e.g.* Origen and Jerome. Our total of 39 books comes from counting the Minor Prophets individually and following a division of Samuel, Kings, Ezra-Nehemiah, and Chronicles into two books each in accordance with the usage of the Greek OT or Septuagint (LXX) and the Latin Vulgate.

The books now known as the Apocrypha were not in the Hebrew Bible, and were not used in the Palestinian synagogues. They were found in the LXX, which represents the enlarged Greek Canon of Alexandria. From this they passed into the Latin versions, and so into Jerome's revision, the Vulgate, which in time became the authorized Bible of the Roman Catholic Church. They were not accepted by the Protestants as Divinely inspired, but were printed in some Protestant Bibles between the OT and the NT, not in their old places in the Septuagint and Vulgate versions, where they were interspersed with the OT books as though forming part of the OT itself. The Apocrypha consists of 15 books or writings (1 and 2 Esdras, Tobit, Judith, Additions to Esther, The Wisdom of Solomon, Ecclesiasticus or the Wisdom of Jesus the Son of Sirach, Baruch, The Letter of Jeremiah, The Prayer of Azariah and the Song of the Three Young Men, Susanna, Bel and the Dragon, The Prayer of Manasseh, 1 and 2 Maccabees. But certain books, notably 2 Esdras (not found in Greek) and The Prayer of Manasseh, are sometimes excluded; and in early MSS other books like 3 and 4 Maccabees are sometimes added. See APOCRYPHA; ENGLISH VERSIONS.

The NT like the OT was a collection of collections and was also gradually formed, although over a much briefer period of time. The Four Gospels, originally of local origin and use, were collected early in the 2nd cent. and were being used as Scripture by the middle of the century, as is witnessed by Justin Martyr (who called them 'The Memoirs of the Apostles') and by Tatian's use of them interwoven into a continuous narrative, the *Diatessaron*. Towards the end of the century a collection of St. Paul's letters was also being so used. This apparently consisted of an original gathering of 10 letters made a century earlier, augmented by the 3 'Pastoral' epistles and by Hebrews, which, though anonymous and only slowly admitted in the West, had come to circulate with the Pauline corpus. The Acts of the Apostles, separated from its companion volume, Luke, was attached to the epistles, and to this group the seven so-called 'general' or 'catholic' epistles were added as time went on, local variation continuing here well into the 4th and 5th cents. Thus there came to be two volumes known as 'The Gospel' and 'The Apostle,' corresponding respectively in primacy of honour to the Law and the Prophets among the Jews. The Apocalypse of John, early accepted only in the West, usually stood by itself in the manuscript period, or even circulated with non-canonical books. Thus the collection was formed which we know, consisting of 27 books, viz. Four Gospels, Acts, 13 Epistles of Paul, Hebrews, James, 2 Epistles of St. Peter, 3 of St. John, Jude, Revelation. See CANON.

Within the books of the Bible there were originally no divisions, except in the case of the Psalms, which were always indicated as separate poems, and elsewhere in the case of definite statements of differences of contents, such as the Song of Miriam, the Song of Deborah, 'the words of Agur,' and 'the words of King Lemuel' (in Proverbs). A division of the Pentateuch into sense units (each a *pārāshāh*) was probably made soon after its canonization, and was later introduced into the Prophets. It is found in the Qumrân scroll of Isaiah. A somewhat different division into sections was devised for convenience of reading in the synagogue. These in Palestine were known as the *sēdher* in the Torah (Babylonian, *pārāshāh*), and in both schools as the *haphtārāh* in the Prophets. The present chapter division, however, was taken over eventually from Christian usage (see below). Verse division marks appeared somewhat later, but are presupposed in the Talmudic prescriptions regarding liturgical use of the Scriptures. Babylonian and Palestinian systems differed, a standardization being first achieved by ben Asher in the 10th cent. Our modern usage, however, was devised by Rabbi Nathan in the 15th cent., first being printed in 1524, and coming into Christian usage also through Pagninus' Latin Bible of 1528. The first indications of divisions in the NT are marginal insertions ascribed to Tatian in the 2nd cent. A system of paragraphs was early developed for the Gospels and known as 'Titles' (*Titloi*), after the descriptive headings to each section, or as 'Chapters' (*Kephalaia*). Eusebius devised a large number of sections as the basis for a 'harmony' of the Gospels, which he presented in the form of tables and marginal numbers. Because this was supposedly based on an earlier division by Ammonius of Alexandria in the early 3rd cent., they were known as the 'Ammonian sections.' In Matthew there were 68 'titles' and 355 'sections,' in Mark, 48 and 233 (later 241), in Luke, 83 and 342, and in John, 18 and 232 respectively. A system of divisions found only in codices Vaticanus and Zacynthius is carried through Acts and the Epistles in Vaticanus to where this breaks off in Hebrews. Otherwise in the Apostolos there came into general use a division into chapters (*kephalaia*) ascribed to Euthalius of Alexandria (5th cent.), which correspond in length to the Gospel 'titles.' Thus there were 40 in Acts, 19 in Romans, 10 in 1 Corinthians, etc. In Acts and Paul another system, called 'lessons' (*anagnōseis* or *anagnōsmata*), also came into use and is ascribed to Euthalius. In the late 5th cent. Archbishop Andreas of Cappadocian Caesarea divided the Apocalypse into 72 *kephalaia*.

A still smaller division of the books of Scripture was that of the *stichoi*, or lines, a word used for a line of poetry, and then for a similar length of prose, marked off for the payment of copyists. Subsequently it was employed for the piece of writing which a reader was supposed to render without taking breath, and the marks of the *stichoi* would be helps for the reader, indicating where he might pause. In Matthew there were 2560 *stichoi*; the same Gospel has 1071 modern verses. Scrivener calculates 19,241 *stichoi* for the 7959 modern verses of the whole NT—giving an average of nearly 2½ *stichoi* per verse. Cardinal Hugo de Sancto Caro is credited with having made our present chapter divisions about A.D. 1248 when preparing a Bible index. But it may be that he borrowed these divisions from an earlier scholar, possibly Lanfranc or Stephen Langton, archbishops of Canterbury in the early 11th and early 12th cent. respectively. Henry Stephens states that his father Robert Stephens made verse divisions in the NT during the intervals of a journey on horseback from Paris to Lyons. Whether he actually invented these arrangements or copied them from some predecessor, they were first published in Stephens' Greek Testament of 1551.

3. Historical Origin.—The Bible is not only a library, the books of which come from various writers in different periods of time; many of these books may be said to be composed of successive literary strata, so that the authors of the most ancient parts of them belong to much earlier times than their final redactors. All the OT writers, and also all those of the NT with one exception (St. Luke), were Jews. The OT was nearly all written in the Holy Land; the only exceptions being in the case of books composed in the valley of the Euphrates during the Exile (Ezekiel, possibly Lamentations, Deutero-Isaiah, or part of it, perhaps some of the Psalms, a revision of the Law). The NT books were written in many places; most of the Epistles of St. Paul can be located; the Gospel and Epistles of St. John probably come from Ephesus or its neighbourhood, St. Mark from Rome, and St. Matthew from Antioch or its vicinity; but the place of origin of the other books is doubtful.

Probably the oldest book of the Bible is Amos, written about 750 B.C. A little later in the great 8th cent. we come to Hosea, Isaiah, and Micah. The 7th cent. gives us Nahum, Zephaniah, Jeremiah, and Habakkuk among the prophets, also Deuteronomy, and at the beginning of this century we have the earliest complete historical books, Samuel and Judges. The end of this century or beginning of the 6th cent. gives us Kings. In the 6th cent. also we have Obadiah (?), Ezekiel, part, if not all, of Deutero-Isaiah (40–55). Haggai, Zechariah (1–8), and most of Lamentations. The 5th cent. gives us the completed Pentateuch—or rather the Hexateuch, Joshua going with the five books of the Law—perhaps part of Deutero-Isaiah (56–66), Malachi, Books 1 and 2 of the Psalter, and Ruth. The 4th cent. has Proverbs, Job, Book 3 of the Psalter, and the prophets Joel and Jonah. From the 3rd cent. we have Chronicles, Ezra and Nehemiah, Zechariah (9–14), Ecclesiastes, and the Song of Songs. Lastly, the 2nd cent. is credited with Esther, Daniel, and Books 4 and 5 of the Psalter. Several of these dates are conjectural and refer, unless otherwise noted, to the substantial completion of the works. But since many are composite in nature they may contain elements which are much earlier or much later than the periods indicated. When we look to the analysis of the books, and inquire as to the dates of their constituent parts, we are carried back to pre-literary ages.

A long period of oral transmission of traditions and narratives which assumed relatively fixed forms preceded written documents. The earliest writings probably consisted of ballads, such as the Song of Deborah (*c* 1200 B.C.), law codes such as are reflected in parts of the Book of the Covenant in Ex 20–23, and epic narratives such as the Joseph saga in Genesis. The law code of the Babylonian king Hammurabi, a thousand years earlier than Moses, shows points of striking similarity to the Mosaic code. As time went on other kinds of tradition (oracular, proverbial, prophetic, liturgical, annalistic, historical, etc.) were no doubt at least in part reduced to writing. But, with few exceptions, there is no general agreement regarding documentary sources immediately related to our OT books until we come to the so-called Graf-Wellhausen theory concerning the Hexateuch. This posits four basic sources or strands of writing known as J (the Yahwistic prophetic narrative, *c* 850 B.C.), E (the Elohistic prophetic narrative, *c* 750 B.C.), D (Deuteronomy and Deuteronomic notes elsewhere (*c* 600 B.C.), and P (the Priestly Code, represented especially in Leviticus and in reformulations elsewhere, *c* 400 B.C.). J and E, often difficult to distinguish, were supposedly combined *c* 700 B.C., and the Deuteronomic and Priestly addition and revision followed. In this theory, still widely held, there have been various proposed modifications in terms of subdivision of the proposed sources, additional written and oral traditions, and further revision. See PENTATEUCH.

Aside from the more primitive sources of the Hexateuch, the earliest of the prophetic writings (8th cent. B.C.) were the first complete books actually to exist essentially as we have them. But even here there is evidence of a process of combination of various sources, oral and written, and of editorial work carried on over a number of years and sometimes centuries. Similar developments are clear among the Hagiographa, notably in the Psalter and Proverbs. See OLD TESTAMENT and articles on the books of the Bible.

There is much less range of question for the dates of the NT books. The earliest date possible for any of them is A.D. 44 for James, but its canonical history and other factors make a 2nd-cent. origin more likely. Our earliest books are then the Pauline letters, beginnning probably with 1 Thessalonians (*c* A.D. 50) and ending with the imprisonment epistles (*c* A.D. 62). The latest Book is 2 Peter, which must be assigned to the middle of the 2nd cent. With the probable exception of the Pastorals as we have them, which with Jude appear to belong to the 2nd cent., all of the remaining books were possibly written before the end of the first. As in the case of certain OT books, a process of development is discernible in several of the compositions, especially in the Gospels and the early chapters of Acts. Oral tradition in the form of brief recollections of the acts and teachings of Jesus preceded written documents (see FORM CRITICISM). Then appeared such written accounts as the Passion narrative and those more extensive compilations of materials which served as the immediate sources of our Gospels (q.v.). The oral Gospel coloured all of this, and itself received documentary representation in the speeches of Acts. Thus we have a period of about 100 years for the composition of the NT writings, most of them coming in the second half of the 1st cent. A.D. See articles on the individual books.

4. Original Languages.—The bulk of the OT was written in Hebrew, and without vowel points. Hebrew is the Israelite dialect of the Canaanite language, which belongs to the Semitic family, and is closely allied to Aramaic. Some portions of the OT (viz. documents in Ezr 4^{7}–6^{18} and 7^{12-26}, Dn 2^{4}–7^{28} and a few scattered words and phrases elsewhere) are in Aramaic, the language of Syria, which was widely known, being found in Babylonia, Egypt, and Arabia. After the Exile, since Aramaic then became the everyday language of the Jews, Hebrew was relegated to a position of honourable neglect as the language of literature and the Law, and Aramaic came into general use. Certain of the sources, oral and written, used by our Gospels were doubtless in this language. When Papias says that Matthew wrote 'the oracles of the Lord in the Hebrew dialect,' he would seem to mean Aramaic. Since Jesus taught in Aramaic, it is likely that His discourses were preserved in oral and perhaps written collections in their original form before being translated into Greek. But, however far we may go in detecting Aramaic writings beneath and behind our Gospels, it cannot be held that any of these Gospels, or any other NT books, are translations from that language. Matthew, the most Jewish of the Gospels, contains quotations from the LXX as well as direct translations from the Hebrew OT, which shows that while its author—or at all events the author of one of its sources—knew Hebrew, the Gospel itself was a

Greek composition. The NT documents, as we have them, appear to have been written originally in Greek for a Greek-reading public. It was long held that this Greek was a peculiar dialect, but the discovery of contemporary inscriptions and papyri shows that the colloquial Greek, used in commerce and popular intercourse all round the Mediterranean during the 1st cent., has the same peculiar forms that we meet with in the NT, many of which had been attributed to Semitic influences. It must still be admitted that a certain amount of Hebrew influence is felt in the NT style. This is most apparent in the Gospels, especially Matthew and above all the earlier chapters of Luke (except the Preface), and also in the Apocalypse. An overuse of possible but uncommon Greek locutions corresponding to Semitic idiom explains much of what we find. The influence of LXX phraseology, especially in Luke, was also important. A style of Greek more like the classical is found in the Preface to Luke, Hebrews, James, 1 Peter, and the latter half of Acts. St. Paul's writings and the other books occupy an intermediate position. The Fourth Gospel is written in good Greek; but the structure of the sentences indicates a mind accustomed to think in Hebrew or Aramaic. Nevertheless, in spite of these differences, it remains true that the grammar and style of the NT are in the main those of contemporary Greek throughout the Roman Empire, *i.e.* the *Koine* or common dialect.

5. Translations.—The OT was first translated into Greek, for the benefit of Jews residing in Egypt, in the version known as the Septuagint (LXX), which was begun under Ptolemy II. (285–247 B.C.), and almost, if not quite, completed before the commencement of the Christian era. Another Greek version is ascribed to Aquila, who is said to have been a disciple of the famous Rabbi Akiba. This version, commonly dated about A.D. 130, was remarkable for its pedantic literalness, and was popular for a long time among Jews. On the other hand, about the end of the 2nd cent. A.D., Symmachus, who, according to Epiphanius, was a Samaritan turned Jew, although Eusebius calls him an Ebionite, produced a version the aim of which was to render the original text into idiomatic Greek of good style, with the result, however, that in some places it became a paraphrase rather than a translation. Lastly may be mentioned the version of Theodotion, variously identified as a Jewish proselyte or as an Ebionite. This is really a revision of the LXX to bring it closer to the Hebrew text, and was made about A.D. 185. It was popular with the Christians, and in Daniel replaced the LXX version. While only fragments of Aquila and Symmachus remain, Theodotion's Daniel has survived to this day. Other versions, known from Origen and others as *Quinta*, *Sexta*, and *Septima*, are little more than names to us, especially the last.

Oral paraphrases, the Targums ('interpretations,' 'translations'), were made in Aramaic for the benefit of Palestinian Jews when Hebrew was no longer understood. Tradition carries this back to the time of Ezra (Neh 8[8]). Our earliest written Targums are associated with the rabbinic schools of Jerusalem and Babylonia and date from the 2nd to 7th cent. A.D. While the official Babylonian Targum to the Pentateuch (Babli) attributed to Onkelos (Aquila?) is generally regarded as the earliest of these, a Palestinian form, extant in recensions known as Pseudo-Jonathan or the Jerusalem Targum, and the Old Palestinian Targum, contains a large element of earlier interpretative materials, some of which have been traced back as far as the 2nd cent. B.C. These were largely purged from the official version to bring it close to the Hebrew text. The Prophetic Targum survives mainly in the official form, ascribed also to Jonathan, a pupil of Hillel, and representing as we have it a Babylonian revision of the 4th or 5th cent. A.D. A fragmentary Palestinian form of later date is also extant. The Targums to the Hagiographa are likewise mostly later in date in their present forms. See TARGUMS.

Of the other early translations of the OT, the Syriac and Latin were made apparently from the Hebrew. The former, which may be as early as the 1st cent. A.D., was subject to various revisions, in some of which the influence of the LXX is clear, until the text was more or less standardized in the 5th-cent. Peshitta revision attributed to Rabbula, bishop of Edessa. A Latin translation appeared first in North Africa in the 2nd cent., where Latin was commonly used at a time when Greek was still the language of Christian literature at Rome. This version, in both OT and NT, is reflected in Tertullian, Cyprian, and others of the period. Soon new translations were made also in Italy, the end result being a confusion of texts which induced Damasus, bishop of Rome, to commit to Jerome (A.D. 382) the task of preparing a reliable Latin version of the Bible. This came to be known as the Vulgate, *i.e.* common version. For it served as the Bible of the western church for 1000 years, and, since the Council of Trent it has been honoured as an officially correct rendering of the Scriptures. The other versions, Gothic, Armenian, Georgian, Coptic, Ethiopic, Slavonic, Arabic, which range in date from the 4th to the 10th cent., generally depend in their earliest forms upon the Greek text. See TEXT CRITICISM and TEXT, VERSIONS, AND LANGUAGES OF THE OT.

The oldest Versions of the NT are the Syriac and the Latin, both of which may be traced back in some form to the 2nd cent. A.D. Representing the Syriac of this period we have two fragmentary versions of the Gospels discovered in the 19th cent., viz. the Curetonian, edited by Cureton in 1858, and the Sinaitic, found in the monastery of St. Catherine on Mount Sinai in 1892. The MSS themselves, however, are probably both from the 5th cent. A distinct though somewhat related text made in the 2nd cent. is Tatian's *Diatessaron*, which was used in eastern churches down to the 5th cent. but now survives only in translation. Revision and standardization of text resulted in the definitive form known as the Peshitta ('simple') version, which became dominant in the 5th cent. Finally we may mention the literalistic Harclean version of the early 7th cent., representing a revision by Thomas of Harkel (Heraclea) of a 6th cent. Jacobite translation, and the so-called Palestinian Syriac of the 6th cent., found mainly in lectionaries and extant in the Gospels and in parts of other books. The story of the Latin NT is like that of the OT recounted above. However, we know more about the various types of Old Latin texts and can reconstruct a complete version, whereas in the OT, including the Apocrypha, fewer than a dozen books are completely extant. In Egypt the NT was early translated into Coptic, and it appeared in several dialects of that language. Chief of these were the Sahidic of upper Egypt, originating in the 3rd cent. or earlier, and the Bohairic of lower Egypt, somewhat later in date. The latter, in which alone the NT is completely extant, became the dominant form and has been used ecclesiastically by the Copts down to modern times. Several books and a large number of fragments are also found in three or four dialects of the areas about Akhmim and the Fayyum. A Gothic version was made by Ulfilas in the 4th cent. This survives mainly in fragmentary Gospels, and is also the earliest extant literary product in a Teutonic language. The 5th cent. saw the production of Armenian, Georgian, and Ethiopic translations; and subsequently there appeared Slavonic (9th cent.), Arabic (10th cent.), and, fragmentarily at first, the early vernacular versions of modern Europe. The Reformation period, from Wycliffe onwards saw complete editions of the last; and the 19th and 20th cents., under the stimulus of biblical scholarship, the missionary enterprise and the work of Bible societies, have made the Scriptures available, in whole or in part, in well over a thousand languages and dialects. See also TEXT OF THE NT; ENGLISH VERSIONS. W. F. A.—**A. P. W.**

BIBLICAL THEOLOGY.—Biblical Theology arose among German Protestant theologians after 1650 in opposition against the *Theologia Dogmatica* which used biblical utterances merely as *dicta probantia* (proving sayings) for the Lutheran or the Reformed system. It has three main presuppositions:

1. Biblical Theology describes the *history* of the religious ideas and institutions in both Testaments by reconstructing the individual forms of faith and piety set forth by the various speakers and writers. The 'theology' of Amos or Jeremiah is not the same as that of the eschatological Book of Daniel nor as that of Jesus or Paul. Consequently Biblical Theology demonstrates the differences between the OT and the NT; within the OT, *e.g.* those existing between the older sagas in the Pentateuch and the 'ethical monotheism' of the prophets; within the NT those between Jesus Himself and the gospels (especially John) or between the Judaistic and the Hellenistic tendencies. These individual forms were arranged according to the generally assumed line of human development from the simpler to the more complicated. The rich and strictly regulated Israelite cult in the work of the Priestly Code in Exodus, Leviticus, and Numbers, or the Christology of Ephesians and Colossians had to be the latest stages in their respective fields.

2. This development of the biblical ideas and institutions is an indissoluble part of the *history of religion* in the old oriental and the Hellenistic world. The first chapters of Genesis cannot be separated from the Babylonian epics of the creation and the flood (*Enuma Elish, Gilgamesh*). Behind the faith of the NT lies the Judaism of the intertestamental period, which differs from the OT especially in the most important field of apocalyptic eschatology. The Christology was influenced not only by the messianic hopes of the OT but also by the expectation of a *Sōter* ('saviour') in Hellenism, and the term 'Son of Man' not only by Dn 7. Perhaps there were Persian influences at work upon the dualistic tendencies in Judaism and in the NT (as also in the Qumrân texts), or upon the belief in a personal immortality. Myth being one of the forms most often used to express religious ideas and facts in antiquity, the problem arose of 'demythologizing' the faith of the NT, *e.g.* the eschatology, or the belief in the Resurrection of Christ, in order to make it easier for the 'modern' man to grasp the meaning of the main contents of the Bible.

3. But side by side with the differences between the Biblical writers and the similarities with foreign religions, there is an *inner unity* in the faith of both Testaments which is independent of their religious environment: the belief in words and actions of the One living God in history, fulfilling the promises he gave to Abraham and to David by liberating Israel from Egypt, by giving to the people of his election and covenant the land of Canaan as their homeland, and by sending Christ as His 'Servant' and Messiah. Both Testaments confess the holiness of this God who punishes evildoers and transgressors of His commandments, from the expulsion of the first couple from the Garden of God until the Last Judgment, but also forgiving sins where He finds repentance and sacrifice—in the NT the sacrifice of Christ for the salvation of mankind according to the will of His Father. In both Testaments the main content of God's commandments is the right attitude towards one's brother, including servants and foreigners, in accordance with His 'Love' for His people—a view inherited by the Christian community.

4. At present Biblical Theology manifests a strong effort (sometimes at the expense of sound historical interpretation) to demonstrate that this inner unity is not only the result of human development but is also the truth about God as revealed in the words of the prophets, in Jesus' sayings and deeds, and in the apostolic preaching under the guiding influence of the Holy Spirit. J. H.

BICHRI.—Father of Sheba, a Benjamite, 2 S 20^{1ff}. In 2 S 20^{14} where MT has **Berites** (so AV, RV), we should probably read the patronymic **Bichrites** (so RSV), which the sense demands. Some support for this reading is offered by LXX.

BIDKAR.—An officer of Ahab and afterwards of Jehu, who cast the body of King Joram on the plot of ground that belonged to Naboth, 2 K 9^{25}.

BIER.—See MOURNING CUSTOMS.

BIGTHA.—One of the seven eunuch chamberlains of Ahasuerus, Est 1^{10}.

BIGTHAN (Est 2^{21}) or **BIGTHANA** (Est 6^{2}).—One of the eunuchs of Ahasuerus who plotted with Teresh against the king's life. The plot was exposed by Mordecai.

BIGVAI.—**1.** A companion of Zerubbabel, Ezr 2^{2}, Neh 7^{7}; cf Ezr 2^{14} 8^{14}, Neh 7^{19}, 1 Es 5^{14} (AV, RV **Bagoi**) 8^{40} (AV, RV **Bago**). **2.** A signatory to the covenant, Neh 10^{16}. **3.** See NAHAMANI. **4.** See ENENEUS.

BILDAD.—See JOB.

BILEAM.—A Levitical city of Manasseh, 1 Ch 6^{70}. In the parallel Jos 21^{25} **Gath-rimmon** stands instead of Bileam, perhaps by a scribal error (cf v.^{24}). Bileam is called **Ibleam** (q.v.) in Jos 17^{11}, Jg 1^{27}, 2 K 9^{27}.

BILGAH ('cheerfulness').—Head of the 15th course of priests in the time of David, 1 Ch 24^{11}. **2.** A priest who returned with Zerubbabel, Neh $12^{5,\ 18}$.

BILGAI.—A priest who sealed the covenant, Neh 10^{8}.

BILHAH.—**1.** A slave-girl given to Rachel by Laban (Gn 29^{29}), and by her to Jacob as a concubine (Gn 30^{3f}); mother of Dan and Naphtali (Gn 30^{5-8} 35^{25} 46^{24f}, 1 Ch 7^{13}). She was guilty of incest with Reuben (Gn 35^{22}). These narratives and genealogies probably embody early traditions as to the origin and mutual relations of the tribes. Tribes are traced to a concubine ancestress, because they were a late accession to Israel. It should be noted, however, that the custom for a childless wife to provide her husband with a slave concubine is reflected in marriage contracts from Nuzi in the 2nd millennium B.C. **2.** A city of Simeon, 1 Ch 4^{29}; called **Balah** in Jos 19^{3}, and **Baalah** in Jos 15^{29}, where it is assigned to Judah (see BAALAH, **2**).

BILHAN.—**1.** A Horite chief, the son of Ezer, Gn 36^{27}, 1 Ch 1^{42}. **2.** A Benjamite, son of Jediael, and father of seven sons who were heads of houses in their tribe, 1 Ch 7^{10}.

BILL.—**1.** In the parable of the Unjust Steward (Lk 16^{6f} AV, RSV) 'bill' (RV **bond**) renders the Greek *grammata*, the equivalent of the contemporary Hebrew legal term *shᵉṭār* (literally 'writing'), an acknowledgment of goods or money received written and signed by the debtor himself (*Baba bathra* x. 8). Edersheim's statement (*Life and Times of Jesus*, ii. 272) that the Greek word was adopted into Hebrew is based on a false reading. See, further, DEBT. **2.** Bill of divorce; see MARRIAGE.

BILSHAN.—A companion of Zerubbabel, Ezr 2^{2}, Neh 7^{7}, 1 Es 5^{8} (AV, RV **Beelsarus**).

BIMHAL ('son of circumcision').—An Asherite, 1 Ch 7^{33}.

BINDING AND LOOSING.—See KEYS, POWER OF THE.

BINEA.—A descendant of Jonathan, 1 Ch 8^{37} 9^{43}.

BINNUI ('buildings').—**1.** Head of a family that returned with Zerubbabel, Neh 7^{15}; called **Bani** (q.v.) in Ezr 2^{10}. **2.** A Levite, Ezr 8^{33}, 1 Es 8^{63} (AV **Saban**, RV **Sabannus**), Neh 10^{9} (called **Bani**, q.v., in Neh 8^{7}; **Anniuth**, q.v., in 1 Es 9^{48}; **Bunni**, q.v., in Neh 9^{4}) 12^{8}. **3.** A son of Pahath-moab, Ezr 10^{30} (called **Belnuus**, q.v., in 1 Es 9^{31}). **4.** One whose sons had married foreign wives, Ezr 10^{38}, 1 Es 9^{34} (AV, RV **Bannus**). **5.** The son of Henadad, who repaired part of the wall, Neh 3^{24} (called **Bavvai** in v.^{18}). There appears to be much confusion amongst these names.

BIRD.—**1.** In OT: (1) *'ôph*, translated 'birds' or 'fowl,' usually joined with 'of heaven' or 'of the air': see Gn $1^{21,\ 30}$, Lv 17^{13}, 2 S 21^{10}, Jer 4^{25}, Ezk $31^{6,\ 13}$;

(2) *'ayiṭ*, usually translated 'fowls' (AV) and 'birds of prey' (RV, RSV): Gn 15[11], Job 28[7], Is 18[6], Ezk 39[4]; (3) *ṣippôr* (Arab. *'uṣfûr*), small birds like sparrows which twitter: Gn 7[14], Lv 14[6], Ps 84[3] etc.; (4) *ba'al kānāph*, 'possessor of a wing,' Pr 1[17]. **2.** In NT: (1) *peteina*, Mt 13[4], Lk 13[19] etc. (2) *ornea*, 'birds of prey,' Rev 18[2] 19[17, 21].

Birds abound in Palestine, and evidently did so in ancient times. They were sympathetically watched and studied; we read, for example, of their migrations (Jer 8[7] etc.), their care of their young (Dt 32[11], Mt 23[37] etc.), the helplessness of their young (Pr 27[8], Is 16[2] etc.), their nesting (Ps 104[12, 17]); indeed, every phase of bird life is touched upon. There are many references to the snares of the fowler (see SNARES). Birds are divided into clean and unclean. In some cases they were allowed as sacrificial offerings (Lv 1[14–17] 14[4–53]). It is a curious thing that the duck is not apparently (unless, as some think, in 1 K 4[23], under the 'fatted fowl'—*barbūrîm 'ᵃbhûsîm*; KB, however, identifies here with a species of cuckoo) mentioned in the OT, although a beautifully modelled clay duck of an early period, certainly earlier than the OT records, was found during excavations in Gezer. All birds mentioned by name in the Bible are dealt with in separate articles. E. W. G. M.

BIRSHA ('ugly').—King of Gomorrah at the time of Chedorlaomer's invasion, Gn 14[2].

BIRTH.—See CHILD, CLEAN AND UNCLEAN, 1.

BIRTHDAY.—Birthday celebrations are mentioned only in connexion with royalty, viz. Pharaoh's birthday (Gn 40[20]), the monthly celebration of that of Antiochus Epiphanes (2 Mac 6[7]), and the birthday feast given by Herod Antipas (Mt 14[6], Mk 6[21]). The 'day of our king,' to which Hosea refers (7[5]), may have been the anniversary either of the King's birth or of his accession. In Job 1[4] the feasts in the houses of Job's sons 'each on his day' probably means every seventh day, and not once a year in each house. Some authorities (*e.g.* Edersheim, *Life and Times of Jesus*, i. 672) regard Herod's feast as celebrating the anniversary of his accession—a view based on a mistaken exegesis of the Talmudic passage *Abodah zarah* 1[3] (see the full discussion in Schürer, *GJV*[3] i. 438–441). A. R. S. K.

BIRTHRIGHT.—See FIRSTBORN.

BIRZAITH.—**1.** A 'son' of Asher, 1 Ch 7[31] (AV **Birzavith**). Possibly a town of Asher is indicated. **2.** According to Josephus the village where Judas Maccabaeus pitched his last camp (*Ant.* XII. xi. 1 [422]); modern *Bîr ez-Zeit*, about 15 miles N. of Jerusalem.

BIRZAVITH, 1 Ch 7[31] (AV).—See BIRZAITH, 1.

BISHLAM.—An officer of Artaxerxes in Palestine at the time of the return from captivity under Zerubbabel, Ezr 4[7], 1 Est 2[16] (AV, RV **Belemus**). The word '*bishlām*' could be rendered 'in peace' and is so rendered by LXX in Ezr 4[7], and since Bishlam is not mentioned later in the chapter, it has been held that instead of 'Bishlam, Mithredath,' we should read 'with the approval of Mithredath.'

BISHOP (Gr. *episkopos*, Lat. *episcopus*, Ital. *vescovo*, Fr. *évêque*, Germ. *Bischof*), **ELDER** (Gr. *presbyteros*, Lat. *presbyterus*, Fr. *prêtre*, Eng. *priest*).—The two words are so closely connected in the NT that they must be taken together here.

1. The terms.—The Greek word for 'bishop' is common in the general sense of an *overseer*, and in particular of sundry municipal officers. In LXX it is used in Is 60[17] of taskmasters, in Neh 11[19] of minor officials, and in 1 Mac 1[51] of the commissioners of Antiochus who enforced idolatry. But, so far as we can see, it was not the common name for the treasurers of private associations.

In the NT the word is found five times. In Ac 20[28] St. Paul reminds the elders of Ephesus that the Holy Spirit has made them bishops over the flock; in Ph 1[1] he sends a greeting to the saints at Philippi 'with the bishops and deacons'; in 1 Ti 3[2] he tells Timothy that 'a bishop must be above reproach,' etc.; in Tit 1[7] he gives a similar charge to Titus. (1 P 2[25] 'the shepherd and bishop of your souls' is in RSV 'the Shepherd and Guardian,' Gr. *episkopon*.)

In the OT the word 'elder' is used from early times of an official class having jurisdiction both civil and religious, so that when synagogues were built, the elders of the city would naturally be the elders of the synagogue, with the right of regulating the services and excluding offenders.

In NT times the idea would be carried over to the churches. The first clear trace of Christian elders is at Jerusalem. In Ac 11[30] (A.D. 44) they receive the offerings from Barnabas and Saul; in 15[6] (A.D. 50) they take part in the Conference; in 21[18] (A.D. 58) they join in the welcome to St. Paul. To the post-apostolic period belong Ja 5[14], where the word seems to denote officials, the Pastoral Epistles and 1 Peter.

It has been often maintained that bishops and elders in the NT and for some time later were substantially identical. For (1) bishops and elders are never joined like bishops and deacons, as distinct classes of officials. (2) Ph 1[1] is addressed 'to bishops and deacons.' So 1 Ti 3 ignores the elders, though (5[17]) there were elders at Ephesus, and had been (Ac 20[17]) for some time. Conversely, Tit 1[5–7] describes elders instead, and nearly in the same words. (3) The bishop described to Timothy, the elders of Ac 20, those of 1 Ti 5[17], those described to Titus, and those of 1 P 5[2], all seem to hold a subordinate position, and to have pastoral duties rather than what we should call episcopal. (4) The same persons are called elders and bishops (Ac 20[17, 28]). The words may be also synonymous in Clement of Rome. Ignatius is the first writer who makes a single bishop ruler of a Church. But he pleads no Apostolic command for this position.

It may be, however, that bishops (and possibly deacons) were elders who exercised specific functions of oversight and service with respect to the churches' worship and charity. Thus not every elder would be a bishop, *i.e.* an appointed overseer, but every bishop would be counted among the number of elders and be associated with them in the general government of the local churches. In communities with more than one congregation, there might have been a bishop acting as overseer in each congregation. How the monarchical episcopate developed, as represented in Ignatius, is nowhere discussed in extant sources. But it is generally believed to have come about through the need of centralizing authority to meet the crises of heresy within and persecution without the Church.

2. Appointment.—At first popular election and Apostolic institution seem to have gone together. The Seven (Ac 6[5, 6]) are chosen by the people and instituted by the Apostles with prayer and laying-on of hands. In the case of the Lycaonian elders (Ac 14[23]) the Apostles 'appointed' them with prayer and fastings. Similarly the elders in Crete (Tit 1[5]) are 'appointed' by Titus, and apparently the bishops at Ephesus by Timothy. In these cases popular election and laying-on of hands are not mentioned; but neither are they excluded. 1 Ti 5[22] does not refer to ordination at all, nor He 6[2] to ordination only. The one is of the laying-on of hands in restoring offenders, while the other takes in all occasions of laying-on hands. But in any case Timothy and Titus would have to approve the candidate before instituting him, so that the description of his qualifications is no proof that they had to select him in the first instance. Conversely, popular election is very prominent (Clement, and *Didache*) in the next age; but neither does this exclude formal approval and institution. The elders are already attached (1 Ti 4[14]) to the Apostles in the conveyance of special gifts; and when the Apostles died out, they might act alone in the institution to local office. The development of an episcopate is a further question, and very much a question of words if the bishop (in the later sense) was gradually developed upward from the elders. But the next stage after this was that, while the bishop instituted his own elders, he was himself instituted by the neighbouring bishops, or in still later times by the bishops of the civil province or by a metropolitan. The outline of the process is always the same. First popular election, then formal approval by authority and institution by prayer, with (at least commonly) its symbolic accompaniments of laying-on of hands and fasting.

3. Duties.—(1) *General superintendence*: Elders in Ac 20[28], 1 Ti 5[17], 1 P 5[2, 3] (ruling badly); bishops in 1 Ti 3[5]. Indicated *possibly* in 1 Co 12[28] 'helpers, administrators': more distinctly in Eph 4[11] 'pastors and teachers,' in pointed contrast to 'apostles, prophets, and evangelists,' whose office was not local. So 1 Th 5[12] 'those who are over you,' Ro 12[8] 'he who gives aid,' and He 13[7, 17, 24] 'your leaders,' remind us of the bishops and elders who rule (1 Ti 3[4] 5[17]). So, too, the 'rulers' in Clement must be bishops or elders, for these bishops plainly have no earthly superior, so that they must be themselves the rulers.

Under this head we may place the share taken by the elders: (*a*) at Jerusalem (Ac 15[6]) in the deliberations of the Apostolic Conference, and (Ac 21[18]) in the reception held by James; (*b*) elsewhere (1 Ti 4[14]) in the laying-on of hands on Timothy, whether that corresponds to ordination or to something else.

(2) *Teaching*: 1 Th 5[12] rulers admonishing in the Lord; 1 Ti 3[2] the bishop apt to teach; 5[17] double honour to the elders who rule well, especially those who toil in word and teaching; Tit 1[9] the elder or bishop must be able to teach, and to convince the gainsayers. Yet 1 Ti 5[17] seems to imply that elders might rule well who toiled in other duties than word and teaching; and if so, these were not the sole work of all elders.

Preaching is rather connected with the non-local ministry of apostles, prophets, and evangelists; but in their absence the whole function of public worship would devolve on the local ministry of bishops and deacons. This becomes quite plain in the *Didache* and in Clement.

(3) *Pastoral care*: This is conspicuous everywhere. To it we may also refer: (*a*) visiting of the sick (Ja 5[14]) with a view to anointing and cure—not as a *viaticum* at the approach of death; (*b*) care of strangers and *a fortiori* of the poor (1 Ti 3[2], Tit 1[8], the bishop to be a lover of strangers). H. M. G.—**M. H. S.**

BISHOP'S BIBLE.—See ENGLISH VERSIONS, **28.**

BIT, BRIDLE.—The Hebrews were doubtless well acquainted with the *bit*, but there is no clear mention of it as distinct from the *bridle*, the words for which in Greek and Latin include bit, headstall, and reins. (*a*) Heb. *methegh* is rendered *bit* in RSV in 2 K 19[28], Is 37[29] (AV, RV 'bridle' in both cases), Ps 32[9] (so AV, RV); and *bridle* in Pr 26[3] (so AV, RV). (*b*) Heb. *resen* is rendered *bridle* in RSV in Ps 32[9], Is 30[28] (so AV, RV in both cases), and *restraint* in Job 30[11] (AV, RV 'bridle'). In Job 41[13] 'double bridle' (AV, RV) is sometimes taken to refer to the double jaws of Leviathan; but this is doubtful and RSV renders 'who can penetrate his double coat of mail' (reading *siryōnô* for *risnô*). (*c*) Heb. *maḥsôm* (literally 'muzzle'; cf Dt 25[4] where the same root is used) is rendered *bridle* in AV, RV, and RSV in Ps 39[1]. (*d*) Gr. *chalinos* is rendered *bit* in AV and RSV in Ja 3[3] (RV 'bridle'), and *bridle* in AV, RV, and RSV in Rev 14[20], while the verb *chalinagōgeō* is rendered *bridle* in AV, RV, RSV in Ja 1[26] 3[2]. A. R. S. K.—**H. H. R.**

BITHIAH ('daughter of Y″').—The daughter of a Pharaoh, who became the wife of Mered, a descendant of Judah, 1 Ch 4[18] (RSV v.[17]). Whether Pharaoh is to be taken here as the Egyptian royal title or as a Hebrew proper name, it is difficult to determine.

BITHRON ('cleaving').—This word is taken as the name of a place in 2 S 2[29] (AV, RV). Some have understood it to mean 'the gorge' that led to Mahanaim. RSV renders 'the forenoon' (*i.e.* the symmetrical half [of the day]), following W. F. Arnold (*AJSL* xxviii, 1911–12, 274 ff).

BITHYNIA.—A district in the NW. of Asia Minor, which had been a Roman province since 74 B.C. For administrative purposes it was generally united with the province of Pontus, which bounded it on the E., under one governor. The province was senatorial till about A.D. 165, and was governed by a proconsul. The younger Pliny governed it from A.D. 111–113 by a special commission from the emperor Trajan. Paul and Silas were prevented by the Spirit from preaching in Bithynia (Ac 16[7]), and the beginnings of Christianity there are unknown. That there were churches there after St. Paul's time is certain from the address of the First Epistle of Peter (q.v.). A. So.

BITTER HERBS (*m*ᵉ*rôrîm*, Ex 12[8], Nu 9[11]).—These were commanded to be eaten with the Passover meal, perhaps as a symbol of the bitterness of the Egyptian bondage (so Rashi). Various herbs have been used by Jews for this purpose. The Mishnah (Pesaḥim 2[6]) mentions five kinds of herbs which might be used: lettuce, chicory, pepperwort, snakeroot, and dandelion (H. Danby, *The Mishnah*, p. 138).

BITTERN.—The Hebrew *ḳippōdh* has been thought to be the 'porcupine' (Arab. *qunfuḏ* 'porcupine') or the 'bittern' (*botaurus stellaris*). RV renders 'porcupine,' RSV once 'porcupine' and twice 'hedgehog,' AV 'bittern.' The porcupine (*hystrix cristata*), though common enough in Palestine, cannot be meant; for the statement that 'the porcupine shall lodge in the chapiters thereof,' *sc.* of the ruins of Nineveh (Zeph 2[14] RV), is absurd, since it cannot live on the tops of pillars or columns, even if they are lying on the ground. The bittern haunts watery places and is possible in reference to Babylon (Is 14[23]), improbable in the case of Edom (Is 34[11]) and impossible in Nineveh, if it is parched and wasted (Zeph 2[14]); nor is the interpretation philologically suitable. The root of the noun is connected with the Hebrew *ḳippōdh* 'rolled up,' the Syriac *'eṯpqaḏ* 'was bunched up' and the Arabic *qafida* 'had a big flaccid neck'; these suggest a creature with a bunched-up neck, such as the 'bustard,' of which 'the neck, especially of the male in the breeding season, is thick.' It is a shy bird, found almost always on waste ground, open plains or the desert edge: and three varieties occur in Palestine. The *ḳippōdh* is perhaps the 'ruffed bustard,' while *ḥarabh* (as the MT's *ḥōrebh* 'drought' in the same passage ought perhaps to be read) will be the 'great' and 'little bustard' (Arab. *ḥarbu* 'male bustard'), which frequent the plains. G. R. D.

BITTERNESS, WATER OF.—Nu 5[18] (RV, RSV; AV 'bitter water'); see JEALOUSY.

BITTER WATER, Nu 5[18] (AV).—See BITTERNESS, WATER OF.

BITUMEN, asphalt, or mineral pitch is an inflammable viscous substance, composed of hydrocarbons of the same series as those which constitute mineral oil or petroleum. It is formed by the distillation or evaporation of petroleum and may vary in consistency from a solid to a semi-liquid condition. It occurs both in Mesopotamia and Palestine. The springs at Hit, on the Euphrates, 150 miles above Babylon, are mentioned by Herodotus (i. 179). In Palestine it is found at Ḥāṣbeyah, near Mount Hermon, and in the neighbourhood of the Dead Sea (hence called *Asphaltitis Limnē* by Josephus [*BJ* IV. viii. 4 (476)] and *Lacus Asphaltites* by Pliny [*HN* v. xv. 15]). Some of the limestone strata in the last-named locality are highly bituminous, and masses of bitumen are known to float on the Dead Sea itself after earthquakes. In the OT there are three Hebrew words which denote some form of this substance.

In the Flood-story *kōpher* (LXX *asphaltos*, bitumen, EV 'pitch') is used in the construction of the ark (Gn 6[14]). *Ḥēmār* (bitumen; AV and RV 'slime') was the mortar employed by the early Babylonian builders (Gn 11[3], LXX *asphaltos*). Bitumen pits or wells, into which the pitchy liquid (LXX *asphaltos*) oozed from the earth, are mentioned as occurring in the Valley of Siddim, *i.e.* the Dead Sea basin (Gn 14[10]). This is quite

in keeping with the nature of the region, though such wells are not now found in it. In Ex 2^{3} *ḥēmār* is one of the substances with which the ark of bulrushes was made watertight, the other being *zepheth* (EV ' pitch '). LXX includes both in the general rendering *asphaltopissa*, and they probably denote the more solid and the more liquid varieties of bitumen respectively. *Zepheth* also occurs twice in Is 34^{9} (LXX *pissa*, EV ' pitch '). The context makes it probable that the reference is again to bitumen.
J. Pk.—**C. J. M. W.**

BIZIOTHIAH.—Apparently a town near Beersheba according to the Hebrew text, Jos 15^{28} (AV **Bizjothjah**) ; but we should probably follow LXX and read *bᵉnôthêhā*, ' and her villages ' (cf Neh 11^{27}).

BIZTHA.—One of the seven eunuch chamberlains of Ahasuerus, Est 1^{10}.

BLACK.—See Colours, **2.**

BLAIN.—An inflammatory swelling on the body, Ex 9^{9f} (AV, RV ; RSV **sores**). See Botch, Medicine.

BLASPHEMY.—The modern use of this word is more restricted in its range than that of either the OT or the NT. **1.** In the former it is narrower in its scope than in the latter, being almost universally confined to language or deeds (1 Mac 2^{6}) derogating from the honour of God and His claims to the over-lordship of men (Lv 24$^{10-16}$, cf 1 K 21$^{10, 13}$, 2 K 19^{6}, etc.). Contemptuous scorn for sacred places was regarded as blasphemy (see 1 Mac 2^{6} 7^{28}, cf Ac 6^{13}), as was also the light and irresponsible utterance of the sacred Name (Is 52^{5}, Ezk 36^{20}, Dt 5^{11}), the degradation of the worship of Yahweh by conformity to pagan rites (Ezk 20^{27}), and the continued wilful transgression of Divine commands and despising of ' the word of the Lord ' (Nu 15^{30f}). The incident of the man gathering sticks on the Sabbath seems to be a concrete example of blasphemy (Nu 15^{32f}). The legal punishment for blasphemy was death.

2. When we come to the NT, the word is found more frequently, and is employed in a manner more nearly allied to the usage of classical writings. The EV have accordingly translated it often as ' railing ' or slanderous talk generally (Mt 15^{19} = Mk 7^{22}, Eph 4^{31}, Col 3^{8}, 1 Ti 6^{4}, Jd ^{9}), looked at, however, on its ethical and religious side. The cognate verb, too, is treated in the same way (Mk 15^{29} = Mt 27^{39}, Lk 22^{65} 23^{39}, Ro 3^{8} 14^{16}, 1 Co 4^{13} 10^{30}, Tit 3^{2}, 1 P 4$^{4, 14}$, 2 P 2$^{2, 10, 12}$, Jd $^{8, 10}$), as is also the derived adjective (2 Ti 3^{2}, 2 P 2^{11}).

According to the Synoptic Gospels, the principal charge brought by the Jews against Jesus was that of blasphemy, and when we inquire into the meaning of the accusation, we find that it was His claim to Divine authority or prerogatives (Mk 2^{7} = Mt 9^{3}, Mk 14^{64} = Mt 26^{65}, cf also Jn 10$^{33, 36}$). On the other hand, the NT writers regarded the unreasoning attitude of the Jews to the claims and teaching of Jesus as blasphemous (Mk 15^{29} = Mt 27^{39}, Lk 22^{65} 23^{39}, Ac 13^{45} 18^{6}). As is the case also in wider considerations, the data on blasphemy in Rabbinic literature are in conflict with those of the NT. It is interesting also to notice that this is the word put by the author of the Acts into the mouth of the town-clerk of Ephesus when he was appeasing the riotous mob who were persuaded that St. Paul and his companions had insulted the local deity (Ac 19^{37}). Evidently the term had a wider use than as it is technically defined (cf Mk 4$^{28-30}$). In the Passion narrative, the accusation of blasphemy is the basis on which the Jewish opponents of Jesus base their demand for his death. The proto-martyr Stephen lost his life too on a charge of blasphemy (Ac 6^{13}, 7^{58}). In both cases it is difficult, even impossible, to reach a level of sound historical reliability. On the ' blasphemy against the Holy Spirit,' see article Sin, iii. **1.**
J. R. W.—**S. S.**

BLASTING.—See Mildew.

BLASTUS.—A chamberlain of Agrippa i., through whose intervention the people of Tyre and Sidon secured a hearing at Caesarea (Ac 12^{20}). The name is common in the inscriptions and papyri.

BLEMISH.—See Medicine.

BLESSEDNESS.—With its customary dislike for more abstract words the Bible does not use the noun ' blessedness.' The nearest approach to it is in the noun meaning ' a declaration of blessing ' (Ro 4$^{6, 9}$, Gal 4^{15}). ' Blessed ' and ' happy ' are found in both OT and NT as translations for the same Hebrew or Greek word, with ' blessed ' being used more frequently.

The blessedness described in the Bible is limited to the religious situation of the person who is blessed. In the OT there is an emphasis on the material blessings of long life, wealth, many children, outward peace and prosperity. Too often these are seen as the direct result of trust in God (Ps 1) without a recognition that the righteous do not always prosper. Some Psalms (*e.g.* 22, 73) and Job face the problem of innocent suffering in its relation to blessedness.

In the NT the emphasis is on the *spiritual content* of blessedness, which may flourish even in the face of adverse earthly conditions (Mt 5$^{10, 11}$, Lk 6^{22}, Ja 1^{12}). The thought of future reward occurs here and there (Lk 6$^{20-26}$), but this reward is clearly only the consummation of a blessedness already attained by the poor in spirit, the meek, etc. In the teaching of Jesus the *summum bonum* is related to the Kingdom of God (Mt 25^{34}, Mk 10$^{17, 23}$) or to eternal life (Jn 3$^{3-5}$ 4^{14}), and these are present possessions (Lk 17^{20f}, Jn 3^{36}).

In the Johannine writings, eternal life is described as personal union with Christ, the Son of God, by trust and fellowship (Jn 17^{3}, 1 Jn 5$^{11-20}$). Thus man through Christ becomes a sharer of the life of Him who is Himself the ' blessed God ' (1 Ti 1^{11} 6^{15}). S. W. G.—**L. O. B.**

BLESSING AND CURSE.—Blessing in the experience of ancient Israel might be subjective or objective, the ultimate subject being God and the object the individual, community, race, or animals, plants, or land. A general term expressing this experience of God's blessing would be ' gift ' or ' endowment.' The virtue of the grape, for instance, is said to be its ' blessing ' (Is 65^{8}) and the ascendancy over the creatures is the peculiar ' blessing ' of man (Gn 1^{28}). Success in life or what we should term good fortune is regarded as the manifestation of the possession of the blessing as in the cases of David and his house or Joseph in Egypt.

This blessing conditions a man's whole life, giving him a moral assurance which predisposes the successful issue of his undertakings. It also affects favourably all associated with him. This is often regarded as happening automatically, as in the case of Jacob's blessing in which Laban shared (Gn 30^{27ff}), or the prosperity of Joseph's Egyptian master Potiphar (Gn 39$^{2-5}$). When the King enjoys God's blessing this is reflected in the material prosperity and in the spiritual state of his land and subjects (Ps 72). The curse, on the other hand, signifies in one Hebrew root (*ḳll*, literally ' to lighten ') the deprivation of the capacity to enjoy fulness of life, and the person conscious of being thus affected labours under a moral burden which impairs all his efforts and frustrates his enterprises, *e.g.* Saul, who is not actually said to be cursed, but who opposes David, who manifestly has the blessing. This principle is applied in the curse in ancient Hebrew law in oaths of purgation in cases of adultery, for instance (Nu 5^{11ff}). The curse, like the blessing, was ' infectious,' extending even to the land, which would be polluted if the corpse of a criminal were not immediately removed (Dt 21^{22f}). So after Cain is cursed he is banished to the desert lest his curse infect the sown land (Gn 4^{11}). The breach of a taboo imposed with the sanction of a curse, involved the whole community and impaired their efficiency, *e.g.* the cases of Achan (Jos 6^{17ff}) and Jonathan (1 S 14^{24ff}). For this reason the associates of a man whose misfortunes were anciently held to be the result of a curse held aloof from him, a theme often expressed in Psalms of Lamentation (*e.g.* Ps 31^{11f} 69^{8} $88^{8, 18}$ 142^{4}, etc. ; cf Jer 30^{14}, Job 19^{13-19}). The curse, so potent in its effect, was an effective sanction of ancient law and is so employed in the public declaration and homologation of Hebrew law (Dt 28^{15-68}) and in the Babylonian Code of Hammurabi.

The blessing, manifested in obvious, if often materialistic, tokens of Divine favour, as well as automatically affecting others, may be consciously transmitted, the oral blessing being occasionally accompanied by a simple ritual, *e.g.* lifting up or laying on of hands (Gn 48^{14}), a kiss (Gn 27^{27}), which is still used in the blessing of greeting in the East, or by contact with the staff of the person who blesses (*e.g.* that of Elisha, 2 K 4^{29}). The moral advantage of the blessing thus communicated may be materialized by palpable gifts, such as the land and springs which Caleb gave to his daughter (Jos 15^{19}, Jg 1^{15}) or the flocks given by Jacob to Esau (Gn 33^{11}). Thus the Hebrew word for blessing may often mean ' present,' *e.g.* the provisions which Abigail, the wife of Nabal, gave David (1 S 25^{18ff}) though in all such cases the present symbolizes the fellowship which it is desired to communicate or to enjoy.

The undoubted moral effect of the blessing and the curse in ancient Israel derived from the firm belief in the efficacy of imitative magic. That which was brought to the notice of the deity in graphic ritual or striking utterance was held *ipso facto* to have substance. Blessings, therefore, and usually curses, were thought to operate automatically, hence Isaac's distress that his blessing of Jacob could not be revoked in Esau's favour (Gn 27^{25ff}). Apparently a curse could be revoked, however (*e.g.* the case of Jonathan, 1 S 14^{24ff}). This was most effectively done when countermanded by the blessing of the imprecator (*e.g.* the mother of Micah the Ephraimite, Jg 17^{2}).

An application of the blessing and the curse as the creative word was the prophetic oracle, given as a reassurance, *e.g.* ' Go up to Ramoth-gilead and triumph ' (1 K 22^{12}) and in similar oracles in royal psalms, *e.g.* Ps 2, 110, or as oracles designed to cripple the power of the enemy, as Balaam was expected to do to Israel (Nu 22 ff). The so-called ' burdens ' of the canonical prophets on the foreign nations are by their title and content fundamentally of this nature. Such curses or invocations could also be used against private individuals, and many Mesopotamian incantations are of this nature, the detailed and circumstantial list of desired calamities indicating ritual practices of witchcraft. Counter-incantations consist in a careful unravelling of the spell with the repetition of the same details. The ancient Israelite had not quite divested himself of the belief that misfortune was the result of the curse of malicious persons, and the details of sufferings are a regular feature of the Hebrew Plaint of the Sufferer. Certain psalms and portions of psalms of this type are devoted to detailed cursing of those held to have caused the suffering of the psalmist or those who used his text, *e.g.* Ps 109^{1-20} 129^{5ff} 35^{26} 40^{15} 55^{15-23} 83^{10} 137.

Blessings or auspicious words were given in prospect at crises of individual or communal life, such as departure or a journey (Gn 24^{60}), marriage (Gn 24^{60}, Ru 3^{11-12}), birth (Ru 3^{14-15}), death, when the blessing of the dying man is transmitted with his status and estate to his heir (Gn 27^{27} $48^{15ff, 20ff}$), and, of course, when one man meets another and by his greeting indicates his fellowship, as his silence indicates his enmity. At the conclusion of a cultic occasion, *e.g.* the installation of the Ark in Jerusalem, David materializes his blessing in the distribution of cakes to the community (2 S 6^{18}), and at the selection of Saul as King at Mizpah the fellowship of King and community is symbolized by material presents (literally ' blessings ') to the King (1 S 10^{27}). J. Gr.

BLINDNESS.—See MEDICINE.

BLOOD.—The blood was regarded by the Israelites with sanctity and awe, because they understood it to be the life or soul (***nephesh***) of flesh (Lv 17^{14}). ' Flesh and blood ' accordingly is mankind, a designation used in late Judaism and the NT. Because it is the life, the blood belongs specially to God. Therefore though animals may be slaughtered for human food by the Noachic covenant (Gn 9^{1-7}) the blood is not to be consumed ; where the slaughter is at the altar, the blood goes to God at the altar ; otherwise it is poured out. The application of blood as life to the altar is a powerful expiatory measure ; it is part of all animal sacrifices, but the blood ritual is especially elaborate in the expiatory sacrifice called the sin offering, and most of all in the Day of Atonement. Most (though not absolutely all) rituals to which the term *kipper* ' expiate ' is attached include the use of blood (He 9^{22}). The blood does not expiate as representing death as a penalty paid on behalf of the offerer, but as life liberated and returned to God. The killing of the victim may be done by a layman, but the blood manipulation requires a priest.

The shedding of human blood, however, is not permitted by the Noachic law, which prescribes rather a divine search and retribution ; the slayer will also have his blood shed, and only thus can expiation be made (Gn 9^{6}, Nu 35^{33}). Unexpiated blood cries to God for revenge (Gn 4^{10}) and where the slayer is unknown special rituals are used in order to ' burn away the innocent blood,' *e.g.* Dt 21^{1-9}. The retribution for blood is normally taken by the kinsman, the ' redeemer of blood.' ' Blood ' in the plural is a normal Hebrew expression for punishment or compensation, and for the bloodguilt which is thus repaid ; *e.g.* Ex 22^{2} discusses whether there is bloodguilt, and therefore revenge or compensation for the family, when a thief is killed. The phrase can also be used of purely monetary compensation, or price.

In the NT references to the blood of Christ are interpretations of His work as sacrificial and expiatory ; the wine of the last Supper is related especially to the blood of the covenant, Ex 24. Bloodguilt appears in cases like the killing of the prophets, Mt 23^{34-36} ; $27^{1-10, 24-26}$ relate to guilt for the slaying of Jesus. J. Ba.

BLOOD, AVENGER OF.—See AVENGER OF BLOOD, and KIN [NEXT OF].

BLOOD, FIELD OF.—See AKELDAMA.

BLOOD, ISSUE OF.—See MEDICINE.

BLOODY FLUX, BLOODY SWEAT.—See MEDICINE.

BLUE.—See COLOURS, **5.**

BOANERGES (Mk 3^{17}), ' Sons of Thunder.'—The Master's appellation of James and John. The etymology (Hebrew or Aramaic) is uncertain. Jerome takes it as a reference to their fiery eloquence. Others derive it rather from their fiery disposition in early days (cf Lk 9^{52-56}). It would thus be a playful yet serious sobriquet, constantly reminding them of their besetting sin and warning them to overcome it. D. S.—**J. C. B.**

BOAR.—The wild boar (Heb. *ḥᵃzîr*, Arab. *khinzîr*) is quite common in the Jordan Valley, especially in the reed thickets near the Dead Sea. It is also found on Mt. Tabor. It is noted for its destructiveness, Ps 80^{13}. The same Hebrew word is elsewhere rendered **swine** (q.v.).

BOAT.—See SHIPS AND BOATS.

BOAZ.—A wealthy Bethlehemite, who became the second husband of Ruth, when the nearer kinsman refused to marry her (Ru 4^{1-10}). This marriage was clearly not strictly a levirate marriage (see MARRIAGE, **4**), but indicates that in the absence of a brother-in-law a more distant kinsman might undertake the duty. By this marriage Boaz became the ancestor of David and thus of our Lord (Ru 4^{21f}, 1 Ch 2^{12}, Mt 1^{5f}, Lk 3^{32}). See RUTH.

BOAZ.—See JACHIN AND BOAZ, TEMPLE.

BOCCAS, 1 Es 8^{2} (AV, RV).—See BUKKI, **2.**

BOCHERU.—A descendant of Jonathan, 1 Ch 8^{38} 9^{44}.

BOCHIM (' weepers ').—The place where the angel rebuked Israel, Jg $2^{1, 5}$. The LXX reads **Bethel.** Some think it may be the same as **Allon-bacuth** (q.v.), which was near Bethel.

BODY in OT represents various Hebrew words, especially that for 'flesh' (q.v.). In Ex 24^{10} AV, there is no personification; prefer RSV, 'the very heaven.' In the OT, RSV often substitutes 'body' for AV 'flesh,' when required by modern idiom. In NT, though the body may be the seat of sin and death (Ro 6^{6} 7^{24}), it is never treated with contempt (Ro 12^{1}, 1 Co 6$^{13, 19}$); Ph 3^{21} is a well-known mistranslation; prefer RSV, 'our lowly body.' Accordingly the body could be used metaphorically of the Church, Christ being sometimes the Head, sometimes the Body itself. No trace of the ancient Orphic, Neo-Pythagorean, or Manichaean view of the body is to be found in the Bible. See FLESH.
C. W. E.—**F. C. G.**

BODY-GUARD.—See ARMY, **1**, GUARD.

BOHAIRIC VERSIONS.—See GREEK VERSIONS OF OT, **11**, and TEXT (OT and NT).

BOHAN.—The son of Reuben, Jos 15^{6} 18^{17}. The stone of Bohan, mentioned in these passages, marked the division between Judah and Benjamin. It is possibly modern *Ḥajar el-Aṣbaḥ*.

BOILS.—See MEDICINE.

BOLLED.—The boll of a plant is its seed-vessel or pod. Cf Fitzherbert, 'The bolles of flaxe . . . made drye with the son to get out the sedes.' Thus Ex 9^{31} 'the flax was bolled' (AV, RV), means that it had reached the seed stage. But the Hebrew means only that it was in flower. RSV reads 'the flax was in bud.'

BOLSTER.—This word, which appears six times in AV (1 S 19$^{13, 16}$ 26$^{7, 11, 12, 16}$) as the rendering of a Hebrew word signifying 'the place at the head,' 'head-place,' has rightly disappeared from RV and RSV, which gives 'head' throughout.

BOLT.—See HOUSE, **6.**

BOND.—**1.** See BAND. **2.** See BILL. **3.** See CHAIN.

BONDAGE, BONDMAID, BONDMAN, etc.—See SLAVE, SLAVERY.

BONES is used widely in OT as a synonym for the body, living or dead, or the person (Ps 42^{10} 51^{8}). As the solid framework of the body, the bones are the seat of health and strength, so that breaking, rottenness, dryness of the bones are frequent figures for sickness or moral disorder (Pr 14^{30} 17^{22}, Ps 6^{2} 22^{14}). 'Bone of my bone' answers to the English phrase 'of the same blood'; but the concluding words of Eph 5^{30} (AV), 'of his flesh and of his bones,' should be omitted (with RV, RSV). In Lk 24^{39} the unique expression seems to emphasize the nature of the Resurrection body, as different from the ordinary 'flesh and blood.' See Gibson, *Thirty-Nine Articles*, p. 188.
C. W. E.

BONNET.—**1.** This is the AV designation of the special headdress of the rank and file of the priesthood (*mighbāʿāh*: Ex 28^{40} 29^{9} 39^{28}, Lv 8^{13}, and *pᵉʾēr*: Ezk 44^{18}), as distinct from the high priest's mitre (Ex 28^{4}). RV translates by **head-tire** and RSV by **cap.** It was of fine white linen wound round the head (Ex 29^{9}) to form a conical-shaped tall headdress. Josephus (*Ant.* III. vii. 3 [157]) confuses the tall cap of the ordinary priests and the **turban** (AV mitre) of the high priest. A late-Roman fresco from Syria shows a picture of a conical-shaped priest's headdress (Galling, *BRL*, 1937, s.v. Priesterkleidung, p. 430).

2. The headdress (RSV) of a lady in Isaiah's time, Is 3^{20} (AV bonnet).
L. H. B.

BOOK.—**1.** A roll of papyrus or parchment; see WRITING. **2.** A sacred or canonical document (Dn 9^{2}); see CANON OF OT. **3.** 'Book of life,' etc.; see next article and ESCHATOLOGY.

BOOK OF LIFE is the Divine record in which the righteous and their deeds are inscribed. It grows out of the Hebrew custom of registering the citizens, especially the priests (Jer 22^{30}, Neh 7$^{5, 64}$ 12^{23} and see *DSD* vii. 3). God has such a book in which he inscribes the citizens of Zion Ps 87^{6}, their life-span Ps 139^{16}, their sorrows Ps 56^{8}. The term referred to the members of the theocratic community, present or imminent (Ex 32^{32f}, Is 4^{3}, Ezr 9^{4} 13^{9} and for the reverse idea of those blotted out of the book, see also Ps 69^{28}). In Dn 12^{2}, Mal 3^{16} the phrase has a more definite eschatological reference to future blessedness. This is true in the later apocalyptic and pseudepigraphic literature, *e.g.* 1 En 47^{3} and *passim.* The thought of a second book for death and punishment is also introduced, see 1 En 81^{4} and *passim.* Jub 30^{20ff}, 36^{10}, Apoc. Bar 24^{1}, but also Is 65^{6}, Dn 7^{10}, and Rev 20^{12}. The other NT citations are to the book of life Ph 4^{3}, Rev 3^{5} and *passim*, also variously referred to as 'names written in heaven,' He 12^{23}, 'book of life of the Lamb,' Rev 13^{8} 21^{27}, 'his share in the tree of life,' Rev 22^{19}.
C. C. Ro.

BOOT.—See ARMOUR, **2** (*d*), DRESS, **6.**

BOOTH.—The Hebrew *sukkāh* (note Gn 33^{17} RVm) was a simple structure made of the branches of trees, which the peasant erected for rest and shelter in his field or vineyard (Is 1^{8} RV, RSV; AV 'lodge'). In EV it is variously rendered **booth, cottage, hut, pavilion, tabernacle, tent.** The booth was also a convenient shelter for cattle (Gn 33^{17}) and for the army in the field (2 S 11^{11} RV, RSV; AV 'tents').

BOOTHS, FEAST OF.—See TABERNACLES, FEAST OF.

BOOTY.—See WAR. Cf BAN.

BOOZ, Mt 1^{5}, Lk 3^{32} (AV) = **Boaz** (q.v.).

BOR-ASHAN.—A place mentioned in 1 S 30^{30} (AV **Chor-ashan,** RV **Cor-ashan**), to be identified with **Ashan** (q.v.).

BORDER (OF GARMENT).—See FRINGES.

BORITH.—An ancestor of Ezra, 2 Es 1^{2}; called **Bukki** in 1 Ch 6$^{5, 51}$, Ezr 7^{4}, 1 Es 8^{2} (AV, RV **Boccas**).

BORROWING.—See DEBT.

BOSCATH, 2 K 22^{1} (AV).—See BOZKATH.

BOSOR.—**1.** A town in Gilead, 1 Mac 5$^{26, 36}$; modern *Buṣr el-Ḥarîrî.* **2.** 2 P 2^{15} (AV, RVm); see BEOR, **1.**

BOSORA, 1 Mac 5$^{26, 28}$ (AV, RV).—See BOZRAH, **3.**

BOSS.—Only Job 15^{26} (AV, RV; RSV 'bossed'). The word properly means 'back,' and it here refers to the curved projection of the shield. The same word occurs in 13^{12} (AV 'bodies'; RV, RSV 'defences') where *ICC* (p. 123) takes it to have the same meaning, and to indicate that the friends' bosses are useless, since made of clay instead of iron. Dhorme (*Job*, 1926, p. 169) derives it from a different root and finds the meaning to be 'answers.'

BOTCH.—A swelling or eruption of the skin, Dt 28^{27} (AV; RV, RSV **boil**). Cf Milton *PL* xii. 180, 'Botches and blaines must all his flesh imboss.'

BOTTLE.—Although glass was not unknown in Palestine in Bible times, most of the words rendered by 'bottle' in the Bible denote receptacles of skin. (*a*) Hebrew *nōʾdh* is the *skin* of a domestic animal, especially the goat, used for wine or milk (Jg 4^{19}). It is always rendered by 'bottle' in AV (Jos 9$^{4, 13}$, Jg 4^{19}, 1 S 16^{20}, Ps 56^{8} 119^{83}), and so in RV, save in Jos 9$^{4, 13}$ where 'wineskins' is used. RSV has 'skin' or 'wineskin' in all cases except Ps 56^{8}, where 'bottle' is retained. In Ps 33^{7}, where the Hebrew has *nēdh* (AV, RV 'heap'), RSV finds the same Hebrew word and renders 'bottle.' (*b*) Hebrew *ḥēmath* means *waterskin.* In Gn 21$^{14, 15, 19}$ it is rendered 'bottle' in AV, RV, and 'skin' in RSV. The same word is rendered 'bottle' in AV in Hab 2^{15}, but here another word of the same spelling should be read (RV 'venom,' RSV 'wrath'). (*c*) Hebrew *nēbhel* may mean a *skin* or a *jar.* It is rendered 'bottle' in AV and RV in 1 S 1^{24} 10^{3} 25^{18}, 2 S 16^{1}, Jer 13^{12}, but 'skin' in RSV in all of these save Jer 13^{12}, where 'jar' is used. In other passages the context indicates that an earthenware vessel is intended. AVm has 'bottle' in Is 30^{14} (RV, RSV 'vessel'), and AV, RV have 'bottles' in Jer 48^{12} (RSV 'jars'). In Is 22^{24} AV, RV, RSV have 'flagons,' and in La 4^{2} AV, RV 'pitchers' and RSV 'pots.' (*d*) Hebrew *baḳbūḳ* is an onomatopoeic word meaning *flask.* In Jer 19$^{1, 10}$ it is said to be of earthenware, but is rendered 'bottle' by AV, RV, and 'flask' by RSV. In 1 K 14^{3} AVm has 'bottle,' AV and RV have 'cruse' and RSV 'jar.' (*e*) Greek *askos*, rendered 'bottle' in AV in Mt 9^{17} ||, is a *skin* as RV, RSV recognize.

A. R. S. K.—**H. H. R.**

BOTTOMLESS PIT.—See ABYSS.

BOUGAEAN.—A descriptive epithet applied to Haman in Ad. Est 12^{6} (RV **Bugean**; AV has 'Agagite'). *Bougaios* occurs in Homer (*Il.* xiii. 824, *Od.* xviii. 79) as a term of reproach = 'bully' or 'braggart.' Whether the LXX intended it in this sense, or as a gentilic adjective, is wholly uncertain.

BOW, BATTLE BOW.—See ARMOUR, **1** (*d*).

BOWELS.—The bowels are in Biblical language the seat of emotions. Hence Ps 40^{8} 'Thy law is in the midst of my bowels' (see AVm), *i.e.* the object of my deepest affection (EV 'within my heart'); Jer 4^{19} 'My bowels, my bowels!' (AV, RV), where RSV has 'My anguish, my anguish!'; Ph 2^{1} 'if any bowels and compassions' (AV), where RV has 'tender mercies' and RSV 'affection.'

BOWL.—It is impossible to distinguish with certainty between the numerous words rendered, somewhat indiscriminately, 'cup,' 'basin,' and 'bowl.' The wandering Bedouin of to-day make little use, for obvious reasons, of the fragile products of the potter's art, preferring vessels of skin, wood, and copper. The 'lordly bowl' with which Sisera was served (Jg 5^{25}) was doubtless of wood; so too, perhaps, Gideon's bowl (6^{38}) which bears the same name. For ordinary domestic purposes bowls of glazed or unglazed earthenware were preferred, of which specimens in endless variety have been unearthed (see POTTERY). Among the wealthier classes silver and even gold (1 K 10^{21}) were employed. Of one or other of these were doubtless the large bowls—the word elsewhere used for the sacrificial basins (q.v.)—from which the nobles of Samaria quaffed their wine (Am 6^{6}). Similar, probably, were the large wine-bowls, distinguished from the smaller cups, to which Jeremiah refers (Jer 35^{5} RV; RSV 'pitchers'; AV 'pots').

From the above are to be distinguished the bowl or reservoir for the oil of the 'candlestick' (Zec 4^{2f}), the golden cup-like ornaments of the Tabernacle lampstand (Ex 25^{31} AV 'bowls'; RV, RSV 'cups'), and the 'bowls of the chapiters' (2 Ch 4^{12f} RV and RSV; AV '**pommels**'). See, further, CUP, BASIN, VIAL.

For an important ritual use of bowls and lamps, see HOUSE, **3.** A. R. S. K.

BOX.—**1.** Hebrew *pakh*, 'flask' or 'vial,' is rendered 'box' in AV in 2 K 9$^{1, 3}$ (RV 'vial', RSV 'flask'), but 'vial' in AV, RV, RSV in 1 S 10^{1}. This appears to have corresponded to the 'horn' elsewhere referred to in connexion with anointing oil. **2.** Hebrew *'argaz*, 'box' or 'chest' is rendered 'box' in RSV in 1 S 6$^{8, 11, 15}$ (AV, RV 'coffer'). Here it was the chest in which the Philistine gifts to appease Y″ were placed. **3.** Hebrew *bāttê hannephesh*, literally 'houses of soul,' is rendered 'perfume boxes' in RV, RSV in Is 3^{20} (AV 'tablets'). There is nothing to indicate their nature, or the material from which they were made. **4.** Greek *alabastron* is clearly a container made of alabaster. It is rendered 'alabaster box' in AV of Mt 26^{7}, Mk 14^{3} (RV 'alabaster cruse,' RSV 'alabaster jar'), Lk 7^{37} (RV 'alabaster cruse,' RSV 'alabaster flask'). See JEWELS AND PRECIOUS STONES. **5.** Greek *glōssokomon* is rendered 'bag' in AV, RV in Jn 12^{6} 13^{29} (RVm, RSV 'box'). It is uncertain whether this was a bag or a box. See BAG.

A. R. S. K.—**H. H. R.**

BOX-TREE.—Whether the Hebrew *t^{e}'ashshûr* was the box-tree (*Buxus longifolia*) or the *sherbîn*, modern Arabic for the cypress (*Cupressus sempervirens*), or, as others propose, a kind of juniper, is quite unsettled. AV has the first in Is 41^{19} 60^{13} and so RV, with RVm 'cypress' in 41^{19}, while RSV has 'pine' in both. So good an authority as Post rejects 'box' as improbable. In Ezk 27^{6}, where AV has 'company of Ashurites,' we should probably read *bith^{e}'ashshûrîm* for *bath'^{a}shûrîm* (RV 'boxwood,' RSV 'pines').

E. W. G. M.—**H. H. R.**

BOY.—See CHILD, FAMILY.

BOZEZ.—A rocky crag on one side of the Michmash gorge, opposite Seneh, 1 S 14^{4}.

BOZKATH.—A town of Judah, in the plain near Lachish, Jos 15^{39}; home of Josiah's mother, 2 K 22^{1} (AV **Boscath**). The site is unknown.

BOZRAH ('fortress').—**1.** An Edomite city known only as the place of origin of Jobab, son of Zerah, one of the Edomite kings (Gn 36^{33}, 1 Ch 1^{44}). It was, however, of such importance in the Kingdom of Edom that it is coupled with the name of the latter in poetic parallelisms (*e.g.* the denunciation in Is 34^{6}; cf Jer 49$^{13, 22}$, Am 1^{12}). The reference to 'crimsoned garments' from Bozrah in Is 63^{1} may indicate an industry for which it was noted. In Mic 2^{12} read 'like sheep in a fold' (so RSV) for 'as the sheep of Bozrah' (AV, RV). The site is probably to be identified with *Buṣeirah*, SE. of the Dead Sea. **2.** A Moabite city denounced by Jeremiah (48^{24}); possibly identical with **Bezer, 2** (q.v.). **3.** A city E. of the Sea of Galilee, 1 Mac 5$^{26, 28}$ (AV, RV **Bosora**); modern *Buṣrā Eski-Shâm*.

BRACELETS.—See ORNAMENTS, **4.**

BRAMBLE.—See THORNS.

BRAN.—The burning of bran for incense is mentioned in Bar 6^{43} (=Letter of Jeremiah) as an accompaniment of the idolatrous worship of the women of Babylon.

BRANCH.—**1.** The great variety of Hebrew words rendered by the English 'branch' may be gathered from the following list of passages, in each of which a different term is used: Gn 40^{10}, Ex 25^{33}, Nu 13^{23}, Is 16^{8} 27^{10}, Jer 11^{16}, Zec 4^{12}, Ps 104^{12}, Job 15^{32} 18^{16}. In the following verses RV (or RVm) and RSV add or substitute another word: Is 18^{5} ('spreading branches') 25^{5} ('song'), Ezk 17$^{3, 22}$ ('top,' 'lofty top'), Ps 80^{15} ('Heb. *son*': RVm of Gn 49^{22} in like manner has 'Heb. *daughters*'), Pr 11^{28} ('leaf,' RSV 'green leaf'), Job 8^{16} ('shoot,' so RSV). In the NT four Greek words are translated 'branch,' but RVm points out that 'layers of leaves' are meant at Mk 11^{8} (RSV 'leafy branches'), and at Jn 12^{13} *palm*-branches are in question. **2.** 'Branch' is used figuratively for human offspring (Job 15^{32}), especially for the scion of a royal house (Dn 11^{7}); also for persons in lofty station (Is 9^{14}). The Hebrew *nêṣer*, properly signifying 'sprout' or 'shoot,' but rendered 'branch' (Is 11^{1}), is a designation of the Messianic king; not improbably this was in the Evangelist's mind when he wrote Mt 2^{23}. We have the same English term at Jer 23^{5} 33^{15}, where another word *ṣemaḥ*, is a title for the Messianic king, intimating that this 'shoot' should arise of 'the low estate' of the restored remnant. Zec 3^{8} 6^{12}, following Jeremiah, actually makes *Ṣemaḥ* a proper name, and seems to identify with Zerubbabel. The Targ. of Jeremiah and Zechariah unhesitatingly substitutes for it 'the Messiah.' J. T.—**E. R. R.**

BRASIER.—See COAL and FIREPAN.

BRASS.—The Hebrew *nāḥāsh* means 'copper' rather than 'brass,' since it is mined and smelted (Dt 8^{2}, Job 28^{2}) and also is used for primitive tools and weapons (Gn 4^{22}); and weapons of copper have been found at Tell el-Ḥesī (*c* 1500 B.C.). Palestine itself has no copper, but several neighbouring places are known to have produced it in varying quantities (Cyprus, the *māt Nuḫašše* 'land of copper' near Aleppo, Antilebanon, Feinân and Ezion-geber, Serâbiṭ el-Khâdim in Sinai, where traces of ancient workings are still visible, and Madiama off the SE. end of the Gulf of 'Aqaba). Copper was commonly alloyed with tin to harden it, thus yielding bronze, which is commonly meant when *nāḥāsh* denotes worked metal, *e.g.* weapons (1 S 17^{5}; cf Homer *Il.* xviii. 474). Copper or perhaps bronze, commonly mistranslated 'brass' in the English Bible, is often mentioned for its value (Is 60[7]) or as money (Mt 10[9]) and as a symbol of dazzling heat or brilliance (Dt 28[23], Dn 10[6]), hardness or strength (Is 45[2], Ps 107[16], Job 6[12] 40[18] 41[27], 1 Co 13[1]). The Hebrew *nᵉḥōsheth muṣhābh* 'bright brass' (Ezr 8[27], RV) of some of the vessels from the Temple means literally 'copper of ruddy ore,' perhaps 'orichalc,' an alloy of copper held by some to have been a form of brass. Lastly, the Hebrew *ḥashmal* 'amber' (Ezk 1[4, 28], AV and RV) could not have been that, since it would have perished in the fire; it was probably the Assyrian *elmēšu* 'brass' (Thompson), rather than 'electrum' (Forbes), and perhaps also the Egyptian *ḥsmn* 'bronze.' Brass has been found in excavations of the third Semitic period (*c* 1400–1100) in Palestine and in Rhodes of the 6th cent. B.C., and several classical writers speak of smelting it (Aristotle, Strabo, Pliny). Ezekiel, therefore, in describing 'the sparkle of brass like the appearance of fire, having a covering about it' seems to be referring to the Assyrian brass-founder's furnace with a dome over it, such as he may actually have seen. G. R. D.

BRAVERY.—In Is 3[18] (AV) 'the bravery of their tinkling ornaments' (RV 'the bravery of their anklets') bravery means splendour, ostentation (RSV 'the finery of the anklets').

BRAY.—In AV and RV of Pr 27[22] 'bray' has the obsolete sense of 'crush' (so RSV).

BRAZEN SEA.—See TEMPLE.

BRAZEN SERPENT.—See SERPENT [BRAZEN].

BRAZIER.—See COAL and FIREPAN.

BREACH.—'Breach' is a literal translation of the Hebrew in AV of 2 S 6[8], 1 Ch 13[11] 'the Lord had made a breach upon Uzzah' (RV, RSV 'had broken forth'), and Job 16[14] 'He breaketh me with breach upon breach' (so RV, RSV). The word is used in these passages figuratively of an outburst of wrath.

BREAD.—The pre-eminence of bread in Hebrew diet is shown by the frequent use in OT from Gn 3[19] onwards, of 'bread' for food in general. It was made chiefly from wheat, barley, and, according to Ezk 4[9], beans, lentils, millet, and spelt—probably any millable grain which could be baked in time of scarcity. Whether or not there was a class distinction between eaters of barley and wheaten bread is not certain.

Bread was made from the sifted grain, rubbed, pounded or ground (Nu 11[8]) into flour, and the great number of millstones found on most archaeological sites in Palestine show that the custom was universal, and suffered but little change over the centuries. Two qualities of flour are distinguished, a coarse sort obtained by the usual crushing methods (*ḳemaḥ*), and a fine meal for honoured guests (Gn 18[6]) or the king's table (1 K 4[22]) (*sōleth*). The flour was mixed with water and kneaded in a wooden basin or **kneading bowl** (Ex 8[3] 12[34]), and in the emergency of the Exodus from Egypt was at once made into **cakes** and baked, and consequently became the prototype of the *maṣṣôth*, the unleavened bread, which was alone permitted for the altar celebration, during Passover and the immediately following Feast of Unleavened Bread (Ex 13). The Râs Shamra tablets, however, show that this feast was an ancient Canaanite agricultural rite. On ordinary occasions, a small lump of the previous day's baking, which had been kept for the purpose, was broken down and mixed with dough. The whole was then set aside for a few hours till thoroughly leavened (see LEAVEN).

Three modes of firing bread are found in OT, as in the East at the present day. (*a*) The first is represented by Elijah's 'cake baked on the hot stones' (1 K 19[6]). A few flat stones are gathered together, and a fire lighted upon them. When the stones are sufficiently heated, the embers are raked aside, the cakes are laid on the stones and covered with the embers. After a little the ashes are again removed. the cake is turned (Hos 7[8]) and once more covered. Presently the cake is ready. (*b*) In Syria and Arabia to-day a convex iron plate is much used, especially among the Bedouin. It is placed over a small fire-pit with the convex side uppermost, on which the cakes of dough are laid and fired. The Hebrew **'baking-pan'** (Lv 2[5] 7[9] or griddle) must have resembled this species of iron 'griddle.' (*c*) The settled population, however, chiefly made use of one or other of the various kinds of **oven,** then as now called *tannûr*. In one form, which may be termed the bowl-oven, since it consists of a large clay bowl inverted, with a movable lid, the heat is applied by heaping cattle dung, etc., on the *outside*. The cakes are baked on the heated stones covered by the oven. In other parts of the country the jar-oven is used. This is really a large earthenware jar which is heated by fuel, consisting of stubble (Mal 4[1]), grass (Mt 6[30]), dry twigs (1 K 17[12]) and the like, placed in the bottom of the jar. When the latter is thoroughly heated, the cakes are applied to the inside walls. From this type was developed the pit-oven, which was formed partly in the ground, partly built up of clay and plastered throughout, narrowing from the bottom upwards. Many of these pit-ovens have been discovered in recent excavations. It is to the smoke issuing from one of these, while being heated, that the smoke of the ruined cities of the plain is compared in Gn 19[28] (EV **furnace,** an often unnecessary rendering for 'oven'). Such no doubt were the ovens of the professional bakers in the street named after them in Jerusalem (Jer 37[21]).

Bread-making was at all times the special charge of the women of the household. Even when, as we have just seen, baking became a recognized industry, a large part of the baker's work had been, as now in the East, merely to fire the bread baked by the women at home.

A considerable variety of **bakemeats** (Gn 40[17], literally 'food, the work of the baker') is met with in OT, but only in a few cases is it possible to identify their nature or form. The ordinary cake—the **loaf** of OT and NT—was round and fairly thick; such at least was the rolling 'cake of barley bread' of Jg 7[13]. These cakes were always broken by the hand, never cut. A cake frequently used for ritual purposes (Ex 29[2] and often) seems, from its name, to have been pierced with holes like the modern Passover-cakes. The precise nature of the **cracknels** of 1 K 14[3] (ARV 'cakes') is unknown. The **wafer,** often named in ritual passages (cf also Ex 16[31]), was evidently a very thin species of cake.

A. R. S. K.—**B. J. R.**

BREAD OF THE PRESENCE.—See SHOWBREAD.

BREAKFAST.—See MEALS.

BREASTPLATE.—See ARMOUR, **2** (*c*), BREASTPIECE.

BREASTPIECE (of the High Priest).—In the directions for the official dress of the high priest, as laid down by the Priestly writer, a prominent place is occupied by the breastpiece (AV, RV **breastplate**) or pectoral. The fuller designation 'the breastpiece of judgment' (Ex 28[15], Sir 45[10]) is significant of its purpose; it had pouches in which were kept the sacred lots, Urim and Thummim (q.v.) by means of which judgment was given. The special directions for the making of the breastpiece are given in Ex 28[13-30] (cf 39[8-21]). It was made of an oblong piece of richly wrought linen, which, folded in two, formed a square of half a cubit, or nine inches, in the side. Attached to the outer side were four rows of precious stones in gold settings, twelve in all each stone having engraved upon it the name of a tribe 'to bring them to continual remembrance before the Lord' 28[29]). The breastpiece was kept in position by means of 'twisted chains like cords, of pure gold,' by which it was attached to 'two settings of filigree' on the shoulder pieces of the ephod, while the lower part was fastened to the ephod by a 'face of blue' at each corner (28[22, 25, 28]). A. R. S. K.—**J. Ma.**

BREECHES.—Rather short drawers of white linen ordered to be worn by the priests on the grounds of modesty (Ex 28[42] 39[28], Lv 6[10] 16[4], Ezk 44[18], Sir 45[8]). Josephus describes those worn in his time in *Ant.* III.

vii. 1 (152). The modern trousers are represented in AV and RV by **hosen** (q.v.).

BRETHREN OF THE LORD.—Jesus was Mary's first-born (Lk 2[7]), and she subsequently bore to Joseph four sons, James, Joseph (Mt 13[55] reads *Joses* [so AV], which in Rabbinic literature stands for the same name), Judas and Simon, and several daughters (Mt 13[55-56] = Mk 6[3]. The first two were perhaps sons of another Mary). During His ministry the Lord's brethren did not believe in Him. They sneered at Him (Jn 7[3-5]), and once they concluded that He was mad, and wished to arrest Him and convey Him away from Capernaum (Mk 3[21, 31]). After the Resurrection, however, convinced by so tremendous a demonstration, they joined the company of the believers (Ac 1[14]). Paul says of them that they took their wives along on their missionary journeys as the other apostles had done (1 Co 9[5]). James became one of the ' pillars ' of the church of Jerusalem (Gal 2[9], Ac 15[13]) after he had received a revelation of the risen Christ (1 Co 15[7]); Paul went to visit him on his last visit (Ac 21[18]) and his church was later on named the ' seat of James ' (*Cathedra Jacobi*). Josephus refers to him as ' brother of the one who is called Christ.'

In the early days, partly at least in the interests of the notion of Mary's perpetual virginity, two theories were promulgated in regard to the ' Brethren of the Lord.' (*a*) They were supposed to be *sons of Joseph by a former marriage*, having thus no blood-relationship with Jesus. So Origen, Clement of Alexandria, Epiphanius. (*b*) They were held to be His *cousins, sons of Mary, the wife of Alphaeus* (Mt 27[56] = Mk 15[40]); ' brother ' here implying merely kinship, as Abraham calls himself and his nephew Lot ' brethren ' (Gn 13[8]), and Laban calls Jacob, his sister's son, his ' brother ' (29[15]). So Jerome and Augustine. That Mary, the wife of Alphaeus and mother of James the Little, was a sister of Mary the mother of Jesus, is an inference from Jn 19[25], where it is supposed that only three women are mentioned: (1) His mother, (2) His mother's sister, viz., Mary, the wife of Clopas (= Alphaeus), and (3) Mary Magdalene. But there are probably four: (1) His mother, (2) her sister Salome, the mother of the sons of Zebedee (cf Matthew = Mark), (3) Mary, the wife of Clopas, and (4) Mary Magdalene. It is very unlikely that two sisters should have been named Mary; and moreover, James, the son of Alphaeus, was an Apostle (Mt 10[3] = Mk 3[18] = Lk 6[15]), and none of the Lord's brethren was an Apostle in His life-time (cf Ac 1[13-14]). D. S.—**S. L.**

BRIBERY.—See Crimes and Punishments, **5.**

BRICK.—The use of sun-dried bricks in the period of the OT, beside lime-stone, is attested both by Scripture and by excavations (see House, **1**); their use was due partly to cheapness, especially in districts where stone was scarce, and partly to the lack of adequate tools, at any rate in the early period, for working stone. The process of making bricks is more or less the same everywhere. Suitable mud or clay is thoroughly moistened and reduced to uniform consistency by treading and kneading (Nah 3[14] and 2 S 12[31], where these tasks and handling the brick-mould are imposed on captives); this is then carried in baskets to the brick-moulder, who puts the right quantity in his mould, an open woven frame with one of its four sides prolonged as a handle, and wipes off the superfluous clay with his hand; the mould is removed and the brick left on the ground to be dried by the sun. In Egypt, where bricks were used also for paving (Jer 43[9]), the consistency of the clay was increased by mixing chopped straw and refuse with it; indeed, bricks made without this, as found at Pithom, are rare in Egypt (Ex 5[7-19]). An expert moulder in Egypt to-day is said to be able to turn out some 3000 bricks a day. Egyptian bricks resembled our own in shape, while Babylonian bricks were generally as broad as they were long; the earliest Palestinian bricks are said to have followed the Babylonian model, but bricks of very varying shapes have been found. The burning of bricks in a kiln was a foreign practice to the Hebrews (Gn 11[3]); for fire-burnt bricks have very rarely been found in Palestine, being used only for plinths and paving, and glazed bricks are practically unknown. In low-lying districts the houses were structures of mud-brick, faced with jambs and lintels of stone, and the rain-fall was absorbed by grass growing on the roof (Ps 129[6]); consequently, they would have to be regularly repaired every autumn against the coming rains. The ritual use of bricks as incense-altars may also be noted (Is 65[3]). Clay-bricks were used also for writing, as the letters found at Tell el-Amarna (*c* 1400 B.C.) and the library found at Ugarit or Râs Shamra (*c* 1400–1350 B.C.) prove; the practice was Babylonian and did not long survive in the west, since it required a specially fine clay which was not readily available there. Thousands of Babylonian and Assyrian, Hittite and Hurrian (Horite), documents written on clay-bricks have been recovered by archaeologists; and these include maps and plans, which illustrate the command to the prophet to draw a plan of Jerusalem on a ' tile ' or rather a ' brick ' (Ezk 4[1], where the Hebrew word is the same as the Babylonian word for a building brick).

A. R. S. K.—**G. R. D.**

BRIDE, BRIDEGROOM.—See Marriage.

BRIDGE.—Only 2 Mac 12[13] AV, where RV reads the proper name *Gephyrun* (RSV appears to render by ' earthworks '). The Greek text may be corrupt. See RVm and RSVm. For the extreme antiquity of the arch see Arch.

BRIDLE.—See Bit.

BRIER.—See Thorns.

BRIGANDINE.—The ' brigand ' was originally simply a light-armed irregular foot soldier, and the coat of mail which he wore was called a ' brigandine.' The word is used in AV in Jer 46[4] 51[3] (RV, RSV ' coat of mail ').

BRIMSTONE.—Hebrew *gophrîth*, probably connected with Hebrew *kōpher*, ' pitch.' It is the same as sulphur, one of the chemical elements. It is found in volcanic regions, in solid and in gaseous form. Its first occurrence in the Bible is in the story of the destruction of Sodom and Gomorrah (Gn 19[24f]). We are there told that the Lord ' rained upon Sodom and Gomorrah brimstone and fire '; the words which follow, ' from the Lord out of heaven,' are usually regarded as a gloss. What happened has been explained as an eruption of petroleum caused by an earthquake, an explanation which attempts to combine the Genesis account with the word ' overthrow ' (Heb. *mahpēkhāh*), which is frequently used in the OT to describe the catastrophe, and which implies an earthquake. But this ignores the difficulties which are raised by the story if it is taken as historical. In the first place, it is clear that the story is one form of the myth of the destruction of mankind, as is shown by Gn 19[31], where it is implied that Lot and his daughters are the only survivors of the catastrophe. In the second place, we are told in Gn 13[10] that the whole ' circle ' of the Jordan where Lot settled, was a well-watered plain, like ' the garden of the Lord,' before the act of divine judgment turned it into a salt and desolate waste. But geological evidence shows that the Jordan has flowed into the Dead Sea as it is now from long before historical times. Hence it is probable that the Sodom-legend may have arisen, as Gunkel suggests, in a region where the volcanic features of the description would be more applicable, and may have been transferred to the Dead Sea valley to serve as an aetiological myth explaining the origin of the Dead Sea. It has been pointed out that there is no mention of the Dead Sea in the legend, and it is clear from Gn 13–14 that in the Hebrew tradition the Dead Sea did not exist before the catastrophe. The story is frequently referred to in later Hebrew literature, and is mentioned in the NT (cf Dt 29[23], Is 1[9] 13[19], Jer 20[16] 50[40], Am 4[11], Lk 17[29]). The element of fire and brimstone has passed into the

imagery of the Apocalypse in the picture of 'the lake that burneth with fire and brimstone (Rev 20^{10})
S. H. He.

BROAD PLACE.—See CITY.

BROID.—To broid or to braid is to plait. Both spellings are used in AV, 1 Ti 2^{9} 'with broided hair' (Gr. 'in plaits'; RV, RSV 'braided'), and Jth 10^{3} 'braided the hair of her head' (so RV; RSV 'combed').

BROIDER.—This English word has no connexion with *broid.* It means to adorn cloth with needlework. The modern form is *embroider.* 'Broider' occurs in AV in Ex 28^{4} (RV, RSV 'of chequer work') and in AV and RV in Ezk $16^{10, 13, 18}$ 26^{16} $27^{7, 16, 24}$ (RSV 'embroider'). See EMBROIDERY.

BRONZE.—See BRASS.

BROOCH.—Ex 35^{22} RV and RSV, for AV 'bracelets.' See ORNAMENTS, **5.**

BROOK.—The Hebrew words thus rendered are: **1.** *'ăphîḳ*, meaning the actual bed of the stream, Ps 42^{1} (AV, RV; RSV 'stream'); translated also by 'stream' and 'river.' RSV renders by 'brook' only in Jl 1^{20}. **2.** *ye'ôr*—almost always used of the Nile and water-trenches of Egypt. It is rendered by 'brook' in AV only in Is 19^{6-8} (RV, RSV 'Nile'). In AV of Job 28^{10} it is rendered 'rivers' (RV, RSV 'channels'); in Is 33^{21} it is rendered 'stream' (AV, RV, RSV); in Dn 12^{5f} (AV, RV 'river'; RSV 'stream') it stands for the Tigris. **3.** *mîkhāl*, a word of uncertain meaning, found only in 2 S 17^{20} (AV, RV, RSV 'brook'). **4.** *naḥal* is the most usual word for 'brook' in EV. It is the exact equivalent of the Arabic *wâdî*, which means a valley containing a stream of water. It may be applied to the valley (Nu 21^{12}, etc.), or to the water-course alone (Dt 9^{21}, etc.), which is still 'the wady,' even after it has escaped from the valley. **4.** In Jer 15^{18} (RV, RSV) 'as a deceitful brook' follows LXX in reading *k^eme*, 'as waters of' for MT *k^emô*, 'as' (AV 'as a liar').

The slopes of the mountain range of Western Palestine are deeply furrowed by a succession of great wadys. The sides of the mountains that dip into the Jordan Valley are far steeper than those to the W., and the streams flowing eastward plunge down through awful chasms, worn deep with the lapse of ages. In the longer descent westward the valleys frequently open into beautiful and fertile glades. For the most part the brooks, fed only by the rain, dry up in the summertime, and the mills along their banks fall silent, waking to fresh activity again only with the music of the rushing storm. There are, however, streams fed by perennial springs, such as *el-'Aujā* and the Kishon, W. of Jordan, and the Yarmuk and the Jabbok on the E. W. E.—**H. H. R.**

BROOM.—A tree (Heb. *rōthem*) mentioned in 1 K 19^{5f}, Job 30^{4}, Ps 120^{4} (always **juniper** in AV, and **broom** in RSV; 'broom' in RV in Job 30^{4} and in RVm in the other passages). It is undoubtedly the Arabic *ratam*, a species of broom very common in desert places in Palestine and Sinai. This broom (*Retama retem*) is in many such places the only possible shade; it sometimes attains a height of 7 to 8 feet (1 K 19^{5}). The root is still burned to furnish charcoal (Ps 120^{4}). In Job 30^{4} mention is made of the roots being cut up for food. As they are bitter and nauseous and contain very little nourishment, this vividly pictures the severity of the famine in the wilderness. E. W. G. M.

BROTHER.—See FAMILY, and BRETHREN OF THE LORD.

BROTHERLY LOVE.—*Philadelphia* is 'brother-love,' the love one has for brothers and sisters; in the NT it is used in the larger sense of 'love of the brethren' (so 1 Th 4^{9}, 1 P 1^{22}; and Ro 12^{10}, He 13^{1}, and 2 P 1^{7} might well have been so translated for the sake of consistency). The adjective in 1 P 3^{8} is also correctly rendered, 'have love of the brethren.' This adjective appears in classical Greek in its primary (family) sense, as the designation, *e.g.* of the Graeco-Egyptian king Ptolemy *Philadelphus*, and of Attalus II. of Pergamum, founder of Philadelphia (Rev 1^{11}, etc.) which was named after this king. Jews called each other 'brethren' as being 'sons of the family of Abraham' (Ac 13^{26}). First occurring in its Christian sense in 1 Th 4^{9}, its elements lie in the teaching of Jesus. 'Call no man your father on earth, for you have one Father, who is in heaven,' for 'you are all brethren' (Mt 23^{8f}; cf 6^{9}); the love of the natural household is transferred, with a deepened sense, to 'the household of faith' (see Gal 6^{10}; cf Eph 2^{19}). This sentiment is formed in the community gathered around Christ its 'first-born,' the family of the 'sons' and 'heirs of God and fellow heirs with Christ' (Ro $8^{14-17, 29}$). 'Go to my brethren,' the Risen Christ had said, 'and say to them, "I am ascending to my Father and your Father"' (Jn 20^{17}; cf Mt 12^{49f} 28^{10}); He required them to cherish toward each other the love He showed toward them, making this the mark of discipleship (Jn 13^{34f} 15^{12f}, 1 Jn 2^{7f} 3^{11} 4^{20f}, 2 Jn ^{5}, 1 Co 8^{11}, etc.). The body to which this love belongs is called 'the brotherhood' in 1 P 2^{17} (cf 5^{9}), where love is associated with respect for humanity and fear of God as a fundamental Christian instinct (cf 1 Th 4^{9}, Col 3^{14}, 1 Co 13, etc.). St. Paul describes this affection as the mutual 'care' of 'members' of 'one body' (1 Co 12^{12-27}); it forbids envy, unkindness, schism; it animates, and virtually includes, all services and duties of Christians toward each other (1 Co 13, Gal 5^{13-15}); it is the first 'fruit of the Spirit' (Gal 5^{22}, cf 4^{6f} 5^{6}), the fruit of God's love to us and the test of our love to God (1 Jn 4^{11-21}), 'the fulfilling of the law' (Ro 13^{8-10}), and the crown of Christian purity (1 P 1^{22}); the Cross supplies its model and its inspiration Eph (4^{31}–5^{2}, 1 Jn 3^{16}). When St Paul speaks of 'love,' he means 'brother-love' in the first place, but not exclusively (Gal 6^{10}, 1 Th 5^{15}, Ro 12^{18-21}; cf Mt 5^{43-48}, etc.). Among the manifestations of *philadelphia*, hospitality (*philoxenia*) is conspicuous (He 13^{1f}, 1 P 4^{8-10}, 3 Jn $^{5-8}$); also sharing and contributing to the needs of the saints (Ro 12^{13} 15^{25}, He 6^{10} 13^{16}, 1 Jn 3^{17f}). The prominence and strangeness to the world of this feature of primitive Christianity are strikingly attested by the *Epistle to Diognetus*, §1; Tertullian's *Apol.*, §39; and (from outside) Lucian's *de Morte Peregrini*, §§12 and 16 (Loeb Classical Library); and Julian's *Epist.*, xxii (Loeb). G. G. F.—**J. H. Sc.**

BROWN.—See COLOURS, **2.**

BRUIT.—A bruit (pronounced as *brute*) is a rumour or report (Fr. *bruit*, from *bruire* 'to roar.' The word stands in AV in Jer 10^{22} (RV, RSV 'rumour'), in AV and RV in Nah 3^{19} (RSV 'news'), and in AV and RV in 2 Mac 4^{39} (RSV 'report').

BUCKET.—See HOUSE, **9.**

BUCKLE.—See ORNAMENTS, **5.**

BUCKLER.—See ARMOUR, **2**(*a*).

BUGEAN, Ad. Est 12^{6} (RV).—See BOUGAEAN.

BUGLE.—In 1 Co 14^{8} RSV renders *salpinx* by 'bugle' (AV, RV **trumpet**). Elsewhere (*e.g.* Mt 24^{31}, 1 Co 15^{52}, 1 Th 4^{16}, He 12^{19}) RSV renders the same word by 'trumpet,' as AV and RV (save 1 Th 4^{16}, where they have 'trump'). See MUSIC AND MUSICAL INSTRUMENTS.

BUILDER.—See ARTS AND CRAFTS, **3.**

BUKKI.—**1.** Son of Jogli, a prince of the tribe of Dan, and one of the ten men entrusted with the task of dividing the land of Canaan among the tribes of Israel, Nu 34^{22}. **2.** Son of Abishua and father of Uzzi, fifth in descent from Aaron in the line of the high priests through Phinehas, 1 Ch $6^{5, 51}$, Ezr 7^{4}, 1 Es 8^{2} (AV, RV **Boccas**); called **Borith** in 2 Es 1^{2}.

BUKKIAH.—A Levite of the sons of Heman, and leader of the sixth band or course in the Temple service, 1 Ch $25^{4, 13}$.

BUL.—1 K 6^{38}, the Canaanite name for the month which the Babylonians termed **Marcheshvan.** See TIME.

BULL, BULLOCK.—See OX.

BULRUSH.—See Reed.

BULWARK.—This is a defensive structure built to reinforce the walls of a city. One of the words so translated is *ḥêl*, Is 26¹ (AV, RV, RSV), Ps 48¹³ (AV, RV; RSV '**ramparts**'). The same word is elsewhere rendered 'rampart' in RV and RSV; so 2 S 20¹⁵ (AV 'trench'), La 2⁸, Nah 3⁸ (AV 'rampart'). In 1 K 21²³ RSV has '**bounds**' (AV 'wall,' RV 'rampart'). It denotes an outer wall, of less height than the main wall. At Tell Sandaḥannah—probably Mareshah—there were found two walls of the same period, the outer being in some places fifteen feet in advance of the inner. Jerusalem was latterly fenced on the N. and NW. by three walls. A different word is rendered 'rampart' in Nah 2¹ (AV, RV '**munition**').

In Dt 20²⁰, Ec 9¹⁴ AV and RV have 'bulwarks' for what is clearly an offensive construction, and RSV better renders by '**siegeworks**'.

In 1 Ti 3¹⁵ RSV uses 'bulwark' as a metaphor for the Church (AV, RV 'ground').

BUNAH ('intelligence').—A man of Judah, a Jerahmeelite, 1 Ch 2²⁵.

BUNCH.—Besides meaning *bundle* (of hyssop, Ex 12²², Hebrew something *tied* together) and *cluster* (of raisins, 2 S 16¹ [AV, RSV; RV 'cluster'], 1 Ch 12⁴⁰ [AV; RV, RSV 'cluster'], Hebrew 'something *dried*'), bunch is also used in AV and RV in Is 30⁶ for the hump of a camel (RSV 'hump'). Cf Shakespeare's *Richard III*. I. iii. 248—'This pois'nous bunch-back'd toad.'

BUNDLE.—A bundle of money is spoken of in Gn 42³⁵, of myrrh in Ca 1¹³ (AV, RV; RVm, RSV 'bag'), of barley in Ru 2¹⁶ (RV, RSV; AV 'handfuls'), of brushwood in RSV in Jg 9⁴⁸ᶠ (AV, RV 'bough'), of life in 1 S 25²⁹ (RSV 'bundle of the living'); also in RVm and RSV in Jer 10¹⁷ of a bundle for a journey (AV, RV 'wares'); and in NT of tares, Mt 13³⁰, and of sticks, Ac 28³.

BUNNI.—**1.** A Levite, Neh 9⁴; see Binnui. **2.** Another Levite, Neh 11¹⁵; but 1 Ch 9¹⁴ has 'of the sons of Merari' for 'son of Bunni.' **3.** One who sealed the covenant, Neh 10¹⁵ (but perhaps a repetition of Bani).

BURDEN.—The word so rendered in the OT is derived from a root which means to 'lift' or 'carry.' It has the two senses of an actual burden and a prophetic utterance. Instances of the former are 2 K 5¹⁷, Neh 13¹⁹. Related usages are frequent; in Is 22²⁵ the word suggests the pressure of something hanging on a peg, in Nu 11¹¹ the responsibility and in Hos 8¹⁰ (AV, RV) the privilege of government (RSV follows LXX), in Ps 38⁴ the responsibility for sin. The second sense is that of a solemn utterance, and RVm and RSV 'oracle' (Is 14²⁸ *et al.*) is to be preferred. It was customary to explain this use of the word as due to the threatening character of the utterance; but many of the utterances are not threatening (cf Zec 12 9¹, ⁹⁻¹⁷), and the word-play in Jer 23³³ᶠᶠ involves a reproof of the men who were disposed to regard the oracle of God as literally a burden. Most utterances of the prophets, moreover, were of necessity from their occasion minatory. 'Burden' in this second usage denotes simply something taken up solemnly upon the lips, both weighty in itself and weighty in its communication. It is not used of merely human utterances, but always carries with it the suggestion of Divine inspiration, actual or falsely assumed (La 2¹⁴). In Pr 30¹ 31¹, where AV has 'prophecy' and RV 'oracle' (with RVm 'burden'), RSV takes the word as a place name 'Massa' (cf RVm).

In the NT, Ac 21³ (RSV 'cargo') is an instance of the literal use. The figures are easy. The word is used for the ordinances of the Law as interpreted by the Pharisees (Mt 23⁴, Lk 11⁴⁶), for the prohibitions of the Apostolic decree (Ac 15²⁸; cf Rev 2²⁴), for the pressure and load of life (Mt 20¹²), for an exacting or even legitimate charge upon others (2 Co 11⁹ 12¹³ᶠ), for the imagined difficulties of following Christ (Mt 11³⁰). Two other kind of burdens with their right treatment are contrasted. Other men's errors and sorrows must be shared in sympathy (Gal 6²); though in the service of Christ there can be no transfer of obligations, but each man must carry his own kit and do his own duty (Gal 6⁵; RSV 'load'). R. W. M.—**H. H. R.**

BURGLARY.—See Crimes and Punishments, **6.**

BURIAL.—See Mourning Customs, Tomb.

BURLAP.—A coarse canvas made of hemp. It is found only in Sir 40⁴ 'clothed in burlap' (AV 'a linen frock,' RV 'a hempen frock'). See Frock.

BURNING.—See Crimes and Punishments, **11.**

BURNING BUSH.—See Bush.

BURNT-OFFERING.—See Sacrifice.

BUSH (*seneh*), Ex 3²⁻⁴, Dt 33¹⁶).—The 'burning bush' has traditionally been supposed to be a kind of bramble (*Rubus*), of which Palestine has several varieties, but one of the thorny shrubs of Sinai of the acacia family would seem more probable. The article 'the' is used five times with *seneh* in Ex 3²⁻⁴, and *seneh* is used only of this bush. Some scholars suggest *seneh* (Dt 33¹⁶) echoes the name 'Sinai.' Mk 12²⁶, Lk 20³⁷ 'in the passage about the bush' (AV 'in (or at) the bush'; RV 'in *the place concerning* the bush'). E. W. G. M.—**R. A. B.**

BUSHEL.—See Weights and Measures.

BUSTARD.—See Bittern.

BUTLER.—See Cupbearer.

BUTTER.—See Food, **5**, Milk.

BUZ.—**1.** The second son of Nahor and Milcah, and nephew of Abraham, Gn 22²¹. Elihu, one of the friends of Job, Job 32², is called a **Buzite**, and may have belonged to a tribe of that name against which judgments are denounced by Jeremiah, Jer 25²³. **2.** A man of the tribe of Gad, 1 Ch 5¹⁴.

BUZI.—The father of the prophet Ezekiel (1³) and consequently a member of the priestly house of Zadok. Of the man himself nothing is known. Jewish writers were led to identify him with Jeremiah, partly by a supposed connexion of the name with a verb meaning 'despise,' and partly by a theory that when the father of a prophet is named it is to be understood that he also was a prophet.

BUZITE.—See Buz.

BUZZARD.—In Dt 14¹³ RSV has 'buzzard' (AV, RV **glede**) for Hebrew *rā'āh*, for which *dā'āh* should be read with Sam. and LXX. Probably a species of **kite** was indicated.

BY.—In the AV *of* is generally used for the agent and *by* for the instrument. Thus Mt 1²² 'that it might be fulfilled which was spoken of (RV 'by') the Lord by (RV 'through') the prophet' (RSV 'what the Lord had spoken by the prophet').

In 1 Co 4⁴ 'I know nothing by myself,' *by* means *contrary to, against* (so RV), as in Hamilton's *Catechism*, 1559 (the Tabil), 'Jugis quhilk fur lufe of rewardis dois ony thing by the ordour of justice'; also fol. vii, 'cursit ar thai quhilk gangis by ye commondis of God.' RSV reads 'I am not aware of anything against myself.'

BY AND BY.—In AV 'by and by' means *immediately*, not as now *after some time*. Thus Lk 21⁹ 'the end is not by and by' (RV 'immediately'; RSV 'will not be at once').

BYWAY.—See Roads.

C

CAB.—See Weights and Measures.

CABBON.—A town of Judah near Eglon, Jos 15^{40}; perhaps the same as **Machbenah** (q.v.); possibly modern *Kh. Hebrah.*

CABIN.—The English word 'cabin' is now chiefly confined to an apartment in a ship, but was formerly used of any small room. It occurs in AV for the cell (which is the word in AVm, RV, and RSV) in which Jeremiah was confined (Jer 37^{16}). Cf Spenser, *FQ* I. vi. 23:

> 'So long in secret cabin there he held
> Her captive to his sensual desire.'

CABUL.—A town of Asher on the border of Zebulun, Jos 19^{27} (RSV **Kabul**). The district was ceded by Solomon to Tyre, 1 K 9^{13}. Probably modern *Kābûl*, E. of Acco.

CADDIS, 1 Mac 2^{2} (AV).—See Gaddi, **2.**

CADMIEL, 1 Es $5^{26, 58}$ (AV).—See Kadmiel.

CAESAR.—This is the *cognomen* or surname of the *gens Julia*, which was borne, for example, by its most illustrious representative, Gaius Julius Caesar. The emperor Augustus (q.v. 27 B.C. to A.D. 14) had it by adoption, and was officially named 'Imperator Caesar Augustus.' His stepson, the emperor Tiberius (q.v.), officially 'Tiberius Caesar Augustus' (A.D. 14–37), had it through his adoption by Augustus. It was borne also, amongst other less important persons, by the emperor Gaius (q.v.) Caesar Germanicus (A.D. 37–41), who was a son of Germanicus, the adopted son of the emperor Tiberius. These alone among the Roman emperors had it as a family name, but regularly the emperors bore it as a title, and hence we find it continued in the titles *Kaiser* and *Czar*. The beginning of this use is seen in the NT. There the name is found always, except twice (Lk 2^{1} 3^{1}), by itself, simply equal to 'the Emperor.' The remaining emperors of the 1st cent. are Claudius (q.v.) (41–54), Nero (q.v.) (54–68), Galba (June 9, 68–Jan. 15, 69), Otho (Jan. 15–Apr. 69), Vitellius (Jan. 2–Dec. 20 [?], 69), Vespasian (q.v.) (69–79), Titus (q.v.) (79–81), Domitian (q.v.) (81–96), Nerva (96–98), Trajan (q.v.) (98–117). A. So.—**E. R. H.**

CAESAR'S HOUSEHOLD.—In Ph 4^{22} 'those of Caesar's household' send special greetings to the Philippians. St. Paul wrote from Rome, where he was in semi-captivity, and some of the Christians in Rome belonged to the efficient and talented body of slaves and freedmen who worked in the Imperial palace and performed varied service for the emperor Nero. The number of these servants was very large, and amongst them were accountants, administrators, secretaries, stewards, etc., as well as a great many officials concerned with humbler duties. They were persons of influence and often of considerable wealth, drawn from all nations within the Empire. The testimony of inscriptions shows that among 'those of Caesar's household' were many names such as those that occur in Ro 16. A. So.—**E. R. H.**

CAESAREA (modern *Qaiṣāriyeh*).—A city rebuilt by Herod the Great on the site of Straton's Tower, on the coast of Palestine, between Joppa and Dora. Its special features were—a large harbour protected by a huge mole and by a wall with ten lofty towers and colossi; a promenade round the port, with arches where sailors could lodge; a temple of Augustus raised on a platform, and visible far out at sea, containing two colossal statues of Rome and the Emperor; a system of drainage whereby the tides were utilized to flush the streets; walls embracing a semicircular area stretching for a mile along the sea-coast; two aqueducts, one of them 8 miles in length; a hippodrome; an amphitheatre capable of seating 20,000 persons; a theatre; a court of justice, and many other noble structures. The city took 12 years to build, and Herod celebrated its completion (10–9 B.C.) with sumptuous games and entertainments. Herod used the port for his frequent voyages. Here he condemned to death his two sons Alexander and Aristobulus. After the banishment of Herod's successor Archelaus, Caesarea became the official residence of the Roman procurators of Palestine (broken only by the brief interval during which it was under the independent rule of Herod Agrippa I., who died here in A.D. 44 [Ac 12^{20-23}]). The fifth of these, Pontius Pilate, ordered a massacre in the hippodrome of Caesarea of those Jews who had flocked to implore the removal from Jerusalem of the profane eagle standards and images of the Emperor recently introduced. Only on their baring their necks for death and thus refusing to submit, did Pilate revoke the order, and direct the ensigns to be removed. Christianity early found its way here, Philip probably being the founder of the Church (Ac 8^{40}), while Paul passed through after his first visit to Jerusalem (Ac 9^{30}). Caesarea was the scene of the baptism of Cornelius (Ac 10). Here also the Holy Spirit for the first time fell on heathen, thus inaugurating the Gentile Pentecost (v.^{44}). Paul may have passed through Caesarea (Ac 18^{22}) at the time when numbers of Jewish patriots, captured by Cumanus, had here been crucified by Quadratus, legate of Syria. It was at Caesarea that Paul's arrest in Jerusalem was foretold by Agabus (Ac 21^{8-14}). Here he was imprisoned for two years under Felix (Ac 23^{23-35}). During that time a riot broke out between Greeks and Jews as to their respective rights, and Felix ordered a general massacre of the Jews to be carried out in the city. On the recall of Felix, Nero sent Porcius Festus, who tried Paul (Ac 25^{6}) and also allowed him to state his case before Herod Agrippa II. and Bernice (Ac 25^{23}–26^{32}). Under the last procurator, Gessius Florus, the Jews revolted, and began the Jewish war of A.D. 66–70. A riot in Caesarea led to a massacre in Jerusalem, and simultaneously 20,000 of the Jewish population of Caesarea were slaughtered. During the war, Caesarea was used as the base for operations, first by Vespasian, who was here proclaimed Emperor by his soldiers (A.D. 69), and later by his son Titus, who completed the destruction of Jerusalem. Titus celebrated the birthday of his brother Domitian by forcing 2500 Jews to fight with beasts in the arena at Caesarea. The city was made into a Roman colony, renamed *Colonia Prima Flavia Augusta Caesariensis*, released from taxation, and recognized as the capital of Palestine.

Several Church Councils were held at Caesarea. It was from A.D. 200 to 451 the residence of the Metropolitan bishop of Palestine. Origen taught here, and Eusebius was its bishop from A.D. 313 to 340. It was the birthplace of Procopius, the historian. In A.D. 548 the Christians were massacred by the Jews and Samaritans. In 638 it surrendered to the Muslims under Abu ʿObeida. It was recovered in 1102 by Baldwin I., who massacred the Saracens in the mosque, once the Christian cathedral. The loot contained the so-called 'Holy Grail' of mediaeval legend. Saladin recaptured Caesarea in 1187, but it was retaken by Richard I. in 1192. The city, however, was so ruined that when restored it covered only one-tenth of the original ground. In 1251 Louis IX. fortified it strongly. In 1265 it was stormed by Sultan Bibars, who utterly demolished it. Sand dunes gradually covered it and the district became malarial. Excavations

are being carried on there by the Department of Antiquities of the state of Israel.
G. A. F. K.—**E. G. K.**

CAESAREA PHILIPPI.—A place near the scene of Jesus' charge to Peter (Mk 8[27], Mt 16[13-20]). Here was a sanctuary of Pan and the city of Paneas (to-day still *Bāniyās*), first mentioned in connexion with the victory of Antiochus III. over the Egyptians in 198 B.C. When Herod the Great received the territory from Augustus in 20 B.C., he erected a temple here. His son Philip refounded the city, and changed its name from Paneas to *Caesarea* in honour of Augustus—adding his own name to distinguish the town from the similarly named city founded by his father on the sea-coast. (The common assumption that it was named in honour of Tiberius is based on a vague remark of Josephus; but the *era* of the city began 3–2 B.C., under Augustus.) It was rebuilt by Herod Agrippa II. and named Neronias in honour of Nero, but ultimately the old name came once more to the surface and ousted the others. Here Titus celebrated with gladiatorial shows the capture of Jerusalem. It was captured by the Crusaders in 1130, and finally lost by them to the Muslims in 1165. It lies 1150 ft. above the sea in a recess of the Hermon mountains, and is well watered. Under the ancient castle of the Crusaders a copious stream formerly issued from a cave, where was the shrine of Pan. The cave has collapsed in modern times. The modern village is small, and the remains of the Roman city meagre. R. A. S. M.—**E. G. K.**

CAGE.—Birds were taken to market in a cage or coop of wicker work (Jer 5[27]; RSV 'basket'); a similar cage might hold a decoy-bird in fowling (Sir 11[30]). One of Ashurbanipal's hunting scenes shows a cage of strong wooden bars from which a lion is being let loose (cf Ezk 19[9] RV, RSV). In Rev 18[2] render, with RSV, 'haunt' (RV 'hold,' RVm 'prison') for AV 'cage.'

CAIAPHAS.—Joseph Caiaphas, the son-in-law of Annas (Jn 18[13]), was high priest between A.D. 18 and 36. He was a Sadducee and co-operated successfully with Pontius Pilate. He figures thrice in the NT; (1) In Jn 11[49ff] he is said to have advised the chief and priests the Pharisees to let Jesus die for the people. (2) When Jesus was tried before the Sanhedrin (Mt 26[57-68] || Mk 14[53-65] || Lk 22[66-71]), the high priest Caiaphas put the decisive question to Jesus: 'Are you the Christ, the Son of the Blessed?' (Jn 18[13f, 19] makes the high priest Annas question Jesus, and only mentions briefly in 18[24, 28] the trial before Caiaphas). (3) Caiaphas took part in the trial of Peter and John, Ac 4[6], and (though not mentioned by name) in the trial of the apostles in Ac 5[17, 27ff]. E. H.

CAIN.—In Gn 4[1] the name (*Ḳayin*) is connected with *ḳānāh*, 'procure.' This is linguistically impossible. Actually it is derived from a root signifying to 'forge' in metal and means 'smith' (cf Arab. *ḳain*). Kenan (Gn 5[9ff]) is another form of the same name.

Gn 4[1f], introducing the story of Cain and Abel, represents them as the first two sons of Adam and Eve; it is clear however that the story was originally told in quite another context. The intent of vv.[3-12, 16] is to account for the wretched mode of life of some subnomad group, which it represents as being due to their ancestor having offered an unacceptable sacrifice and then in jealousy having murdered his brother. For this he was condemned to be 'a fugitive and a wanderer on the earth,' that is to a life without culture and without security. The name Cain (=smith) suggests that the reference may be to a group like the low-caste tribes described by Doughty in *Arabia Deserta* who, forbidden by the precept of their patriarch to own cattle, live by hunting and by doing smith work for the cattle-owning bedouin, who treat them with contempt. Thus the story may well have originated in the desert. It is however impossible that such a depressed group could have maintained the custom of seven-fold blood revenge reflected in vv.[13-15], even under the protection of the taboo alluded to as 'a mark on Cain.' These verses therefore would seem to come from another tradition, possibly that of the Kenites, who claimed Cain as their (eponymous) ancestor. If so, it may be inferred that the story had in course of time come to be interpreted as the story of the origin of the Kenite tribes, and that vv.[13-15] were added to it in an attempt to modify the impression of cultural degradation conveyed by the tale in its primary form. The present context of the story suggests an explanation for its inclusion in the primeval history of mankind: the story of the garden of Eden leaves the first man as a tiller of the ground (Gn 3[23]). But there was another tradition, preserved in 4[20ff], which represented nomadism, not agriculture, as the first step in man's economic development. The author of the J document, wishing to include both these traditions in his narrative, reconciled them by means of the story in 4[3-12, 16], which in this context told how the human race was reduced from tilling the ground to a cultureless existence, from which it began to rise with Jubal and his brothers, the 'fathers' of nomadism (vv.[20-22]). While the intrusion of the Kenite tradition, vv.[13-15], somewhat obscured the significance J had attached to the story, it did not affect the deeper meaning its new context had given it: that of the terrible effects of the Fall; Cain is more hardened than Adam, and his guilt is greater but he feels no shame. The story teaches also the sacredness of human life, the moral holiness of God, and the truth that a result of sin is a liability to succumb to further sin (v.[7b]).

Once it is recognized that the story in its origin had no connexion with the story of Adam and Eve, the casual reference to Cain's wife in v.[17] is explained. It is, however, unlikely that so skilled a writer as J would have left unanswered the question as to her identity to which the representation of Cain as the son of the first man inevitably gave rise. Here the fact that in the tradition preserved in Gn 5[1ff] (P) Kenan (=Cain) appears not as the son but as the great-grandson of Adam may be relevant. It is not impossible that J in his ordering of the traditional material with which he was working also represented Cain as the son of Enosh (cf 4[26]), and that the representation of him as the son of Adam is due to the redactor who conflated the J narrative with that of P.

The reference to Cain as the (first) builder of a city (v.[17b]) is from a tradition other than that which treats him as a fugitive and wanderer on the earth. Vv.[18-24] continue v.[17a]. It may be noted that although the poem quoted in vv.[23f] implicitly refers back to v.[15], it does so in terms which suggest that the Cain who 'is avenged seven-fold' is not the ancestor of Lamech but his enemy.

In the NT Cain is referred to in He 11[4], Jd [11], 1 Jn 3[12]. The meaning of the last passage is (cf vv.[9f]) that Cain was a child of the devil and murdered his brother because he was a child of God.
A. H. McN.—**C. A. Si.**

CAIN, Jos 15[57] (AV).—See KAIN.

CAINAN.—1. The son of Enos and father of Mahalaleel (Lk 3[37]). See KENAN. **2.** The son of Arphaxad (Lk 3[36], which follows LXX of Gn 10[24] 11[12]). The name is wanting in the Hebrew text of the last two passages.

CAKE.—See BREAD.

CALAH.—The *Kalaḥ* of the inscriptions, one of the great fortresses which after the fall of Nineveh (cf Jon 4[11] and the Greek writers) were supposed to make up that city. Both Nineveh and Calah were, however, always separate in structure and in administration. Calah lay on the site of the great modern mounds of *Nimrûd*, as was first proved by the explorer Layard. In Gn 10[11f] it is said to have been founded by Nimrod, and, along with Nineveh and other cities, to have formed part of 'the great city.' It was the capital, or at least the chief royal residence, under several of the greatest Assyrian kings, whose palaces have been excavated by modern explorers. Here also was found the famous black obelisk of Shalmaneser III.
J. F. McC.—**C. J. M. W.**

CALAMOLALUS, 1 Es 5[22] (AV, RV).—A corrupt place-name, probably due to a conglomeration of the two names Lod and Hadid in Ezr 2[33] (cf Neh 7[37]); RSV reads Elam.

CALAMUS.—See REED.

CALCOL.—A Judahite, a descendant of Zerah (1 Ch 2[6]), otherwise described in 1 K 4[31] (where AV has **Chalcol**) as a son of Mahol, famous for wisdom, but surpassed by Solomon.

CALDRON.—See HOUSE, **9.**

CALEB.—According to Nu 13[6] he was one of the twelve sent by Moses to spy out the land of Canaan. He is there said to be the son of Jephunneh, of the tribe of Judah. In Nu 32[12] he is described as a Kenizzite. In Jos 14[6–15] Joshua gives him Hebron as his possession in Canaan as a reward for his faithfulness at the time of the spying out of the land. He is the eponymous ancestor of the Calebites (the 'house of Caleb') who occupied part of the Negeb south of Hebron (cf 1 S 25[1–3] 30[14]). The Calebites, Kenizzites, and Kenites, were a group of clans or tribes, originally semi-nomadic inhabitants of the indeterminate region of steppe-land south of the 'hill-country' of Judah, and were ultimately absorbed into the tribe of Judah. The name Caleb in Hebrew means 'dog,' and this has been interpreted as evidence of the existence of totemism as an element in the early religion of the Hebrews, but this view is now generally rejected. S. H. He.

CALEB-EPHRATHAH.—Named in 1 Ch 2[24] (RV; AV **Caleb-ephratah**) as the place where Hezron died. We should probably read, however, with RSV: 'after the death of Hezron, Caleb went in to Ephrathah, the wife of Hezron his father.'

CALENDAR.—See TIME.

CALF, GOLDEN.—The incident of 'the golden calf' is related in detail in Ex 32 (cf Dt 9[7–21]), a chapter which belongs to the composite Prophetic source of the Pentateuch (JE). At the request of the people, who had begun to despair of Moses' return from the mount, Aaron consented to make a god who should go before them on the journey to Canaan. From the golden ear-rings of their wives and children he fashioned an image of a young bull; this, rather than 'calf,' is the rendering of the Hebrew word in the present connexion. The view that 'calf is diminutive and sarcastic for bull' is precluded by the use of the word elsewhere to denote the young but mature animal. A 'feast to Y″' was proclaimed for the following day, and an altar erected on which sacrifice was offered. The sequel tells of Moses' return, of the destruction of the image, and finally of Moses' call to his tribesmen, the sons of Levi, to prove their zeal for the pure worship of Y″ by taking summary vengeance on the backsliders, 3000 of whom fell by their swords.

Two to three centuries later, **bull images** again emerge in the history of Israel. Among the measures taken by Jeroboam I. for the consolidation of his new kingdom was one which was primarily designed to secure its independence of the rival kingdom of the South in the all-important matter of public worship. With this end in view, perhaps also with the subsidiary purpose of reconciling the priesthood of the local sanctuaries to the new order of things, Jeroboam set up two golden 'calves,' one at Bethel and the other at Dan, the two most important sanctuaries, geographically and historically, in his realm (1 K 12[26–33], 2 Ch 11[14f]). Of the workmanship of Jeroboam's 'calves,' as of that of Aaron, it is impossible to speak with certainty. The former probably, the latter possibly (cf Ex 32[20]), consisted of a wooden core overlaid with gold. The view that the Hebrew term necessarily implies that the images were small, has been shown above to be groundless.

With regard to the religious significance of this action on the part of Jeroboam, it is now admitted on all hands that the bulls are to be recognized as symbols of Y″. He, and He alone, was worshipped both in the wilderness (see Ex 32[5] 'a feast to Y″') and at Bethel and Dan under the symbol of the golden bull. It is possible, however, that the bull was not itself regarded as an image of Y″, but as the pedestal on which His image stood. That it became popularly treated as an image can scarcely be doubted. For the source of this symbolism we must not look to Egypt, as did the scholars of former days, but to the primitive religious conceptions of the Semitic stock to which the Hebrews belonged. Evidence, both literary and monumental, has accumulated in recent years, showing that among their Semitic kin the bull was associated with various deities as the symbol of vital energy and strength. In particular, the Râs Shamra (Ugarit) tablets make it clear that El, the High God of Canaan, was worshipped in the form of a bull. He is regularly called Shor-El (Bull-El). Jeroboam, therefore, may be regarded as having merely given official sanction to a symbolism with which the Hebrews had been familiar, if not from time immemorial, at least since their association with the Canaanites.

A comparison of Ex 32[8] with 1 K 12[28] shows that the two narratives have a literary connexion, of which more than one explanation is possible. In the opinion of most recent scholars, the author or editor of Ex 32 has adapted the traditional material on which he worked so as to provide a polemic, in the spirit of Hosea, against the established worship of the Northern Kingdom, which is here represented as condemned in advance by Y″ Himself (Ex 32[7f]). The attitude of Amos to this feature of the established worship at Bethel is not so evident as might have been expected, but of the attitude of Hosea there can be no doubt. It is one of profound scorn and bitter hostility (see 8[5f] 10[5] 13[2]—the last passage gives the interesting detail that the bulls were kissed like the black stone in the Kaaba at Mecca). In the same spirit, and in harmony with the true character of the religion of Y″, as revealed through the prophets who succeeded Hosea, the Deuteronomic editor of the Books of Kings repeatedly characterizes the introduction of the bull images into the cult of Y″ as the sin wherewith Jeroboam made Israel to sin (1 K 14[16] 15[26] etc.). A. R. S. K.—**N. H. S.**

CALITAS, 1 Es 9[23, 48] (AV, RV).—See KELAIAH.

CALLISTHENES (2 Mac 8[33]).—A Syrian, captured by the Jews in a small house, where he had taken refuge after the great victory over Nicanor and Gorgias, in 165 B.C. (cf 1 Mac 4[1–35]). At a festival in celebration of the victory, the Jews burnt Callisthenes to death, because he had set fire to the portals of the Temple (cf 1 Mac 4[38]).

CALNEH.—**1.** Calneh is associated in Gn 10[10] (AV, RV) with Babylon, Erech, and Accad as the earliest cities of Shinar. All attempts to identify the city, from the Talmudic assertion that 'Calneh means Nippur,' to the present have failed; but a convincing solution to the problem has been proposed by W. F. Albright (*JNES*, iii [1944], 254–55). He reads the word *klnh* as *kullānāh* 'all of them,' and so RSV. **2.** Calneh, linked with Hamath and Gath in Am 6[2], is probably the *Kullania* (*Kullani*) associated with Arpad and Hadrach, Syrian cities, in the Assyrian 'tribute' lists. It is perhaps to be identified with modern *Kullan Köy* some 10 miles SE. of Arpad, but Abel (*Géographie*, ii [1933], 101) rejects this view. C. H. W. J.—**D. N. F.**

CALNO.—A city of N. Syria compared with Carchemish in Is 10[9], probably to be identified with **Calneh, 2** (q.v.).

CALPHI, 1 Mac 11[70] (AV).—See CHALPHI.

CALVARY (Lk 23[33] AV).—See GOLGOTHA.

CALVES OF THE LIPS.—Hos 14[2] (AV 'so will we render the calves of our lips'; RV '. . . [as] bullocks [the offering of] our lips'), an obscure passage. A very slight change of the MT yields the LXX and Pesh. rendering 'the *fruit* of our lips' (so RSV).

CAMEL.—The bones of camels are found among the remains of the earliest Semitic civilization at Gezer, 3000 B.C. or earlier, and to-day camels are among the most common and important of domesticated animals in Palestine. The date of the effective domestication of the camel in the Arabian peninsula is much debated, however. It may best be fixed in the last centuries of the 2nd millennium B.C., since widespread camel-nomadism is not attested in the Near East until the end of the 2nd and the beginning of the 1st millennium. The first camel raid reported in our sources is the Midianite attack on Israel, which was repelled by Gideon and his band (Jg 6–8). Thus in spite of occasional references to camels in Genesis, it is certain that the Patriarchs were not camel-nomads, but semi-nomads, using asses for travel and transport, keeping flocks and herds, and living on the edge of the desert within easy reach of water and pasture. This picture is confirmed by the evidence for ass-nomadism in the Mari archives, cf J.-R. Kupper, *Les nomades en Mésopotamie au temps des rois de Mari* (1957); camels are not mentioned at all. With regard to the famous Tell Ḥalâf orthostate representing a man riding on a camel, the dates assigned by scholars range from the 3rd millennium to the 1st millennium B.C.; the most probable view is that of Albright and O'Callaghan, placing it in the 10th cent. (cf Albright, *Archaeology of Palestine* [rev. ed., 1956], pp. 206 f; R. T. O'Callaghan, *Aram Naharaim* [1948], pp. 114–16, with plate; for an excellent photograph see J. B. Pritchard, *ANEP*, Pl. 188). For a detailed discussion of the problem, see R. Walz, *ZDMG*, ci (1951), 29–51, and *Akten des* 4. *Int. Kong. für Anthropologie und Ethnologie*, iii (1956), 190–204; also W. G. Lambert, *BASOR*, 160 (Dec. 1960), 42 f.

Two species of camel are known: the one-humped *Camelus dromedarius*, by far the more common in Bible lands; and the Bactrian, two-humped *Camelus bactrianus*, which comes from the plateau of Central Asia. This latter is to-day kept in considerable numbers by Turkomans settled in the *Jaulân*, and long caravans of these magnificent beasts may sometimes be encountered coming across the Jordan into Galilee or on the Jericho-Jerusalem road. The *C. dromedarius* is kept chiefly for burden-bearing, and enormous are the loads of corn, wood, charcoal, stone, furniture, etc., which these patient animals carry: 600 to 800 lbs. are quite average loads. Their owners often ride on the top of the load, or on the empty baggage-saddle when returning; Moslem women and children are carried in a kind of palanquin—the camel's 'furniture' of Gn 31[34] (AV, RV). For swift travelling a different breed of camel known as *hajîn* is employed. Such a camel will get over the ground at eight to ten miles an hour, and keep going eighteen hours in the twenty-four. These animals are employed near Beersheba, and also regularly to carry the mails across the desert from Damascus to Baghdad. They may be the 'dromedaries' of Est 8[10] (AV; but cf RV, RSV).

Camels are bred by countless thousands in the lands to the E. of the Jordan, where they form the most valuable possessions of the Bedouin, as they did of the Midianites and Amalekites of old (Jg 7[12]). The Bedouin live largely upon the milk of camels (Gn 32[15]) and also occasionally eat their flesh, which was forbidden to the Israelites (Dt 14[7], Lv 11[4]). They also ride them on their raids, and endeavour to capture the camels of hostile clans. The *fellāhîn* use camels for ploughing and harrowing.

The camel is a stupid and long-enduring animal, but at times, especially in certain months, he occasionally 'runs amok,' and then he is very dangerous. His bite is almost always fatal. The camel's hair which is used for weaving (Mk 1[6], Mt 3[4]) is specially taken from the back, neck, and neighbourhood of the hump: over the rest of the body the ordinary camel has his hair worn short. His skin is kept anointed with a peculiar smelling composition to keep off parasites. The special adaptation of the camel to its surroundings lies in its compound stomach, two compartments of which, the *rumen* and the *reticulum*, are specially constructed for the storage of a reserve supply of water; its hump, which though useful to man for attachment of burdens and saddles, is primarily a reserve store of fat; and its wonderful fibrous padded feet adapted to the softest sandy soil. The camel is thus able to go longer without food and drink than any other burden-bearing animal, and is able to traverse deserts quite unadapted to the slender foot of the horse and the ass. On slippery soil, rock or mud, the camel is, however, a helpless flounderer. The camel's food is chiefly *tibn* (chopped straw), *kursenneh*, beans, oil-cake, and occasionally some grain. There seems, however, to be no thorn too sharp for its relish.

In the NT references to the camel it is more satisfactory to take the expressions 'swallow a camel' (Mt 23[24]) and 'It is easier for a camel to go through the eye of a needle,' etc. (Mt 19[24]‖), as types of ordinary Oriental proverbs (cf the Talmudic expression 'an elephant through a needle's eye') than to weave fancied and laboured explanations. The present writers agree with Post that the gate called the 'needle's eye' is a fabrication.

E. W. G. M.—**D. N. F.**

CAMEL'S HAIR.—See CAMEL, DRESS, **1.**

CAMON, Jg 10[5] (AV).—See KAMON.

CAMP.—See WAR.

CAMPHIRE, Ca 1[14] 4[13] (AV).—See HENNA.

CANA,—A Galilaean village mentioned only in John; here Jesus turned water into wine (Jn 2[1]) and healed with a word a nobleman's son who lay sick at Capernaum (4[46]). Nathanael was a native of this place (21[2]). Late tradition identified it with *Kufr Kenna*, NE. of Nazareth. But Cana is mentioned by Josephus and from his account it is clear that it lay at *Khirbet Qāna* on the north side of the *el-Baṭṭōf* plain. It was evidently called Cana of Galilee to differentiate it from the Cana (Kanah) near Tyre (Jos 19[28]). E. G. K.

CANAAN.—See next article; HAM, PALESTINE.

CANAANITES.—The early inhabitants of Canaan (later Palestine and Syria). Their settlement goes back to at least 3000 B.C., as evidenced by the excavations of important sites such as Jericho, Ai, Gezer, Megiddo, Beth-shan, Byblos, and Hamath. They settled where water was available, and hence largely on the plains and in the valleys. During the subsequent 2000 years Canaan was the bridge between Egypt and the nations to the east. At first the country was rather thinly populated, and even by the time of the Berlin Execration Texts in the 20th cent. there were comparatively few towns, and none evidently of great size. In contrast, the Brussels Execration Texts of the following century list a great many towns, showing a decided increase in the population. It was about this time that the Canaanites as far north as Byblos and Ugarit came under the suzerainty of Egypt's vigorous 12th Dynasty (*c* 1992–1779 B.C.), but there was little interference with the political organization of the Canaanites, which consisted of city-states, each with its own king. With the fall of the 12th Dynasty the power of Egypt sank to a low ebb, and the whole of the west was overrun by the Hyksos (*c* 1720–1550 B.C.). With the wane of Hyksos power Egypt regained her suzerainty over the Canaanites and remained more or less in control until *c* 1225 B.C. During this time the population became increasingly mixed, as we learn from Jos 9[1] and other references. Among the intruders mentioned are Hittites from Asia Minor, Horites (also apparently known as Hivites) from northern Mesopotamia, and Amorites, who had begun infiltrating into the country as early as 2000 B.C. From the 16th cent. onwards the Canaanites were becoming weaker, as indicated by the fact that the excavations show a gradual deterioration in the arts and crafts. The feudal system was breaking down, and by 1150 B.C. the nation had become the prey of many invaders, the Sea Peoples invading the south and the north from the sea, the Aramaeans from the north-east, and the Hebrews from the south and east. Ugarit was destroyed by the Sea Peoples, never again to be rebuilt. Sidon seems to have fallen *c* 1194 B.C., and Tyre somewhat earlier, but it was rebuilt a few years later, apparently by Sidonians. Tiglath-pileser I. of Assyria (1116–1078 B.C.) held the land for a brief period, but it was lost shortly after his death. By these several invasions the Canaanites were sent reeling back into the Lebanon mountains and the narrow coastal strip which these protected. Confined to this restricted area, they cut down trees with their newly-invented iron axes, built ships, and took to the sea, and in time they became the great traders of the world, indicated among other things by the fact that one of the words in Hebrew for 'trader' is 'Canaanite.' They established trading colonies in Cyprus, Sardinia, and North Africa, and as far west as Spain. This brought them in contact with the Greeks, by whom they were known as Phoenicians. In the later period their chief city was Tyre, and it was the assistance of Hiram I. of Tyre (969–936 B.C.) in the form of materials and craftsmen that made possible the building of Solomon's Temple. Some indication of the impact that the Canaanites made upon the world is to be found in the fact that Canaanite loan-words appear in every important language of the ancient Near East.

The Canaanites were one of the great nations of the ancient world. It is with Canaanites working for the Egyptians in the mines of the Sinaitic peninsula that we have our first alphabetic writing, c 1500 B.C. Once the alphabet was invented it spread rapidly into South Arabia and throughout Palestine and Syria (ancient Canaan). In the far north of Canaan writing was affected by the cuneiform of Mesopotamia, and at Ugarit a cuneiform alphabet was used in the 14th cent. to produce the so-called Râs Shamra texts. From the Phoenicians the alphabet passed to the Greeks some time in the 8th cent., and then presently throughout the whole world.

In general culture the Canaanites are no less remarkable, and not a little of that culture was taken over by the Hebrews. That the latter had much to learn from the Canaanites is shown by the excavation of Israelite sites; there is a marked inferiority on the Hebrew levels in contrast with those on the preceding Canaanite levels. The Hebrews were not great builders, nor very apt in the arts and crafts. As a result they had to rely heavily on the Canaanites in this field, and in others as well.

Whatever language the Hebrews spoke before settling in Palestine, it was a dialect of Canaanite that became their language after the settlement. As a result their literature was much affected in style and diction. In fact, it is now generally thought that Ps 29 was originally a hymn to the Canaanite storm-god Baal, and the Song of Songs in its original form may have been a fertility cult liturgy of the Canaanites. The Canaanites described creation as a battle between Baal, king of the gods, and the primordial dragon of chaos, to which there are a number of allusions in the OT (cf Ps 74¹³f 89¹⁰, Job 3⁸ 41, Is 27¹ 51⁹, Am 9³). A number of the titles of Canaanite gods, such as 'el, ba'al, 'adon, 'elyon, and 'rider of the clouds' have been appropriated by the Hebrews for their own God, and the more enlightened of the population had a difficult time to win their people away from the worship of Canaanite deities such as Baal, Astarte, Asherah, and Anath. Some parts of Hebrew ritual came from the Canaanites, and much of Hebrew music. Hence it is not surprising that the musical guilds of later Israel traced their origin back to families with Canaanite names. All in all it was no small contribution that the Canaanites made to the Hebrews, but what the Hebrews borrowed they sublimated and ethicized in the end, forever improving what they borrowed.   T. J. M.

CANAL.—Found only in RVm and RSV in Ex 7¹⁹ 8⁵ (AV 'rivers'; RV 'streams'), Is 19⁶ (AV 'brooks'; RV 'streams'); cf Is 7¹⁸, where RSV has 'streams' in a similar phrase. The word is used in the singular of the river Nile, and here it refers to the watercourses or canals through which its waters flowed.

CANANAEAN or CANAANITE (AV).—See ZEALOT.

CANDACE.—A dynastic name, like Pharaoh or Caesar, borne by the queens, or queen-mothers of Meroe, a small kingdom in southern Nubia, in the land known to the ancients as Ethiopia. A eunuch, treasure-guard for one of these rulers, as he returned from a visit to Jerusalem, was met by Philip, who converted and baptized him (Ac 8²⁶⁻³⁹).   A. J.

CANDLE.—See LAMP.

CANDLESTICK.—See HOUSE, **8.**

CANE.—See REED.

CANKERWORM.—RSV uses a variety of terms for this AV, RV name; 'hopping locust' Jl 1⁴, 'hopper' 2²⁵, 'locust' Nah 3¹⁵f, Jer 51¹⁴ (AV 'caterpillers'), 'young locusts' Ps 105³⁴ (AV 'caterpillers'). See LOCUST.

CANNEH.—A town named with Haran and Eden having trade relations with Tyre, Ezk 27²³. Many scholars have supposed **Calneh** (see CALNEH, **2**) to be meant, but it is more probable that the unidentified Akkadian *Kannu* is intended. It has been suggested that we should read *b^enê* for Canneh, when the passage would refer to the 'sons of Eden,' as in 2 K 19¹². See EDEN.

CANON OF THE OLD TESTAMENT.—**1. The term 'Canon.'** 'Canon' is the English equivalent of the Greek *kanōn*, which in turn corresponds to the Hebrew *kāneh* = 'reed.' Because a reed was employed in measuring the word came to be used in the sense of 'measuring-rod' or 'ruler'; and this use was gradually extended to cover all kinds of 'rules' or 'standards,' such as a 'model' of proportion in plastic art, a 'general rule' or 'paradigm' in grammar, and a 'table' of dates or 'system' of chronology in astronomy. As a technical term applied to a 'list' or 'catalogue' of scriptural books the word seems to have been first used by Origen († c A.D. 250), but this use did not become general till more than a century after his death. 'Canon' is thus a Christian, not a Jewish, term. By the Jews the idea of canonicity was expressed by the phrase 'defile the hands' (probably to be understood in the sense that the books so described were so sacred that touching them necessitated a ceremonial washing of the hands afterwards).

2. Circulation, Collection, and Canonization.—These three concepts should be clearly distinguished. Failure to distinguish can only result in confusion and misinterpretation of the evidence. By 'circulation' is meant the introduction of a book of the OT to such reading public as there was, its general acceptance as a book worth reading, and the consequent multiplication of copies of it. By 'collection' is meant the grouping together of individual books, usually similar in character, to form a corpus (*e.g.* the Prophets). By 'canonization' is meant the official designation of an individual book, or a group of books, as 'canonical'—*i.e.* as religiously authoritative through inclusion in a 'canon' or list of sacred books. The three concepts are, of course, interrelated; but they are by no means identical. Nor, indeed, are they so closely related as is sometimes thought. For example, it is inconceivable that a book could ever have been canonized without being previously in circulation, and to that extent we may say that 'circulation' was the first step along the road to 'canonization.' But it does not follow from this (as we know very well) that all books that were at any time in circulation were eventually canonized. To put the point thus bluntly may seem unnecessary. Yet there are many students who approach the evidence under the illusion that any book, or group of books, that is mentioned with respect by a later writer (much less accorded authority of any kind) was *ipso facto* regarded by that writer as 'scripture' and universally accepted by his contemporaries as 'canonical.' It cannot be too strongly emphasized that, so far as the OT is concerned, 'canonization' in the strict sense is a very late development. Varying degrees of authority were certainly accorded to various books at quite an early stage in Israel's history, and constantly thereafter. But that is not 'canonization' as properly understood. It may be argued, and sometimes is, that bit by bit an unofficial

CANON OF THE OLD TESTAMENT

'canon' was formed, and that all that officialdom ultimately did was to give official sanction to what was already unofficially agreed. Even if this were true, it would still also be true that it was the official sanction that crystallized the unofficial agreement by the promulgation of the official canon. In point of fact, however, there is far less evidence of agreement than is often supposed. Neither mention with respect of a book in circulation, nor appreciative reference to a collection however ancient, is in itself evidence of 'canonization.'

3. The Palestinian Jewish Canon, I (*The Evidence of the OT itself*).—From time to time the OT itself gives us a glimpse into the earliest stages in the development of the Canon by referring to the authority accorded certain books in certain concrete situations. Thus, after the giving of the Law on Mount Sinai, it is recorded that 'Moses came and told the people all the words of the Lord and all the ordinances. . . . And Moses wrote all the words of the Lord. . . . Then he took the book of the covenant, and read it in the hearing of the people, and they said, "All that the Lord has spoken we will do, and we will be obedient"' (Ex 24^{3-7}). Again, Josiah's religious reformation is said to have been inspired by 'the book of the law' found in the Temple by Hilkiah: this book was read first by the Temple authorities, then to Josiah, and then finally to 'all the men of Judah and all the inhabitants of Jerusalem, and the priests and the prophets, all the people, both small and great,' who thereupon entered into a solemn covenant 'to perform the words . . . that were written in this book' (2 K 22^{8}–23^{3}). And, after the Exile, Ezra's public reading of 'the book of the law of Moses which the Lord had given to Israel' is said to have been the occasion of the first popular observance of the Feast of Tabernacles since the days of Joshua—'they kept the feast seven days; and on the eighth day there was a solemn assembly, according to the ordinance' (Neh 8^{1-18}). We cannot, of course, be certain that in any one of these cases we are in possession of an exact historical record of what actually took place—the later historians may very well have 'written up' the records in the light of their own presuppositions and attributed a part in the proceedings to the discovery and reading of law books which they did not in fact play. Nor, if law books did play a part in the proceedings, can we do more than conjecture what was the relation of these books to the Pentateuch as we know it. Yet, taken as a whole, the evidence of the OT itself suggests that, in post-exilic times at least, collections of laws of Moses were known and circulated as books, and that such books were recognized as religiously authoritative, even though they may have been very far from identical with the Five Books of Moses as finally canonized.

4. The Palestinian Jewish Canon, II (*The Evidence from outside the OT*).—The first clear evidence for the existence of the Pentateuch as we know it comes from the Samaritans. This heterodox group established a rival sanctuary on Mount Gerizim in opposition to the Jerusalem Temple, with a separate ritual and organization. Disagreement between Samaritans and the more orthodox Jews of Jerusalem is apparent in the days of Nehemiah (*c* 440 B.C.; cf especially Neh 13^{28f}); but it is probable that the separation was not complete until more than a century later. At all events, the Samaritans were at one with the Jerusalem Jews in knowing, and accepting, the Pentateuch, which they still preserve and reverence as 'scripture'—they would hardly have accepted it from their hated opponents *after* the final schism. We may infer, therefore, that by 300 B.C., at the very latest, the Pentateuch was in circulation in Palestinian Judaism, that it was generally accepted as the permanent embodiment of 'the Law,' and that for this reason it was accorded something very like the same authority that was certainly accorded it after it was subsequently canonized. Concurrently with the acceptance of the Pentateuch collections of other books were being made, and the time was to come when they too were accorded authority. Ben-Sira's well-known catalogue of Famous Men (Sir 44–49), written about 200 B.C., shows that he knew and respected, not merely the Pentateuch, but also the historical and prophetical books in approximately (if not exactly) their present form (cf especially his reference to 'the Twelve Prophets'—treated apparently as one book—at Sir 49^{10}), and probably some of the other books as well (*e.g.* Psalms and Proverbs, Sir 44^{5}); and even if the terms of the assertion of his grandson, who translated his work into Greek, that Ben-Sira had 'much given himself to the reading of the Law, and the prophets, and the other books of our fathers' belong, strictly speaking, to the history of the Canon of the Dispersion, there is no reason to doubt that they reflect Palestinian usage, and that the threefold division into Law, Prophets, and 'the rest,' was customary in Palestine also, and may well have been so for some time. The Maccabaean revolt (167 B.C.) undoubtedly gave an impetus to the collection and preservation of traditional Jewish literature (cf 2 Mac 2^{14}), and the circumstances which occasioned the revolt necessarily tended to increase the reverence felt for it (cf 1 Mac 1^{41-64}). It is about this time that we first come across 'quotation-formulae'—*i.e.* such phrases as 'even as it is written' used to introduce a quotation or a reference. This is a sure sign that anyone using these phrases regarded his quotations or references as coming from what we should call 'scripture.' An example may probably be found at Sir 48^{10} (quoting Mal $4^{5,6}$): others are at 1 Es 1^{11} and To 1^{6}; and, although all three of these passages are in Greek books, the Greek texts are in each case translations of Palestinian Hebrew or Aramaic originals, and there are no grounds for supposing that the translators have tampered seriously with the sense of the originals. The same situation is reflected in the Qumrân documents. Members of 'the Community' were under obligation to study 'the Law' without ceasing (*DSD* vi. 7); whole sections of the non-biblical documents are little more than centos of biblical quotations and allusions (*e.g. CD* i. 1–12); and explicit quotations are not infrequently introduced by 'quotation-formulae' (*e.g. DSD* viii. 14). All the books in our present OT (except, apparently, Esther) were to be found in the Qumrân library. Furthermore, the many fragments of commentaries that have survived prove that the community accorded authority, not only to 'the Law,' but also to 'the Prophets,' and (of 'the rest') at least to the Psalms. If, then, those acholars who regard the Qumrân documents as pre-Christian are right, we can gain from them a very clear indication of the extent of 'scripture,' and of the attitude towards it, which obtained in a particular (even if heterodox) section of Palestinian Judaism at the close of the pre-Christian period.

5. The Palestinian Jewish Canon, III (*The Fixing of the Canon*).—If we may neglect the evidence of the NT here, since it may legitimately be held that this evidence very largely reflects the ideas of the Dispersion and may be coloured by Christian presuppositions, the earliest explicit Jewish statement about the extent and authority of 'scripture' comes from Josephus (*c. Ap.* i. 8 [38–42]). Although written in Rome, *c* A.D. 100, when the author was an old man, the statement obviously embodies the Palestinian tradition in which he had been brought up. It runs as follows:

'We do not possess myriads of inconsistent books, conflicting with each other,' he says, contrasting the Jewish books with those of other peoples, 'Our books, those which are justly accredited, are but two and twenty, and contain the record of all time. Of these, five are the books of Moses. . . . From the death of Moses until Artaxerxes . . . the prophets subsequent to Moses wrote the history of the events of their own time in thirteen books. The remaining four books contain hymns to God and precepts for the conduct of human life. . . . We have given practical proof of our reverence for our scriptures. For, although such long ages have now passed, no one has ventured either to add, or to remove, or to alter a syllable; and it is an instinct with every Jew, from the day of his birth, to regard them as the decrees of God, to abide by them, and, if need be, cheerfully to die for them.'

This statement gives clear expression to the authority attached to the books, as also to their threefold division. What is not clear is the identity of the twenty-two books mentioned. From the Mishnah (2nd cent. A.D.) it appears that in the 1st cent. A.D. there was vigorous debate about the acceptance of certain books (particularly about those in the third division) and that in some quarters doubts persisted even into the 2nd cent. But the language used by such men as Rabbi Akiba († *c* A.D. 135) implies that an official decision had by then been made—in other words, that a 'canon' had been fixed, and that it was the same Canon as that attested by our Hebrew Bibles to-day, consisting of three divisions ('Law,' 'Prophets,' 'Writings'). This fixing of the Canon is usually (and most reasonably) attributed to a council of Rabbis held at Jamnia, near Joppa, about A.D. 90, at which we know the 'canonicity' of both the Song of Songs and Ecclesiastes was discussed and agreed upon—'All Holy Scriptures defile the hands: the Song and Ecclesiastes defile the hands.' At all events, after A.D. 100 there was no serious dispute.

6. The Canon of the Jewish Dispersion.—Whether we have any right properly to speak of a 'Canon' of the Dispersion at all is doubtful. The evidence shows that the books circulating in Palestine circulated also in the Dispersion (usually in Greek translation), that they were increasingly recognized as 'scripture,' and that the division of them into three separate sections was also known. There is, however, no hint anywhere of an official canon having been either discussed or accepted, either before or after Jamnia. So far as we can tell, the situation in the Dispersion after A.D. 100 remained essentially what it was before. We may say, then, that the Judaism of the Dispersion differed from Palestinian Judaism in never having an official canon. There was also a further difference—namely, that more books circulated in the Dispersion than in Palestine, and some of them sometimes in some places seem to have been accorded almost as much respect as those in the third division of the Palestinian Canon. Yet these differences can easily be exaggerated. It is probable that the majority of the Jews in the Dispersion accepted the decision of Jamnia, even if there is no evidence that they did; while the respect accorded the additional 'fringe' books may not have been so great as is sometimes made to appear. The true situation is best illustrated by Philo of Alexandria († *c* A.D. 50). For Philo the Law is manifestly in the highest degree inspired and authoritative. He quotes also from other books which eventually became part of the Palestinian Canon, often introducing quotations with quotation-formulae: but there are books in this Canon from which he does not quote (Ezk, Dn, Ec, Ca, Est, Ru, La), whether by accident or by design. On the other hand, he shows knowledge of, and respect for, books which did not get into the Canon, though he never associates quotation-formulae with them. Summing up, the situation in the Dispersion seems to have been much more fluid than it was in Palestine.

7. The Christian Canon.—The NT has its roots partly in the Palestinian tradition and partly in that of the Dispersion, and it is impossible to separate the two. In the NT quotation-formulae are frequent: the inspiration of 'scripture' is asserted (2 Ti 3[16]): the threefold division of the books is recognized (Lk 24[44]); and all the books of the Palestinian Canon are quoted, or referred to, except the Song, Ecclesiastes, and Esther. Other books were certainly known, and no doubt reverenced, but the only direct quotation from these books is the quotation of 1 Enoch 1[9] at Jd [14, 15]. Where Jude led the way, others soon followed; and it became customary in the Church, not only to quote some of these books (*e.g.* Baruch, Ecclesiasticus, Wisdom) alongside the 'canonical' books as of equal authority, but also to copy them, intermingled with the 'canonical' books, in manuscripts of the complete OT. From time to time voices were raised in protest—in particular, Jerome, in the 4th cent., showed himself a doughty champion of the Palestinian Jewish Canon on the ground that only those books with an extant Hebrew original had any claim to recognition. But such protests went unheeded. Athanasius's Easter Letter, written in A.D. 367, gives a list of OT books and draws special attention to those additional books which Christians were accustomed to recognize outside the Jewish Canon; and a similar list was ratified by a synod at Carthage in A.D. 397. Thus, from A.D. 400 onwards the Church accepted officially a longer Canon than the Jews. At the Reformation the wisdom of this acceptance was questioned and the objections raised by Jerome were revived. The Protestant bodies rejected the so-called 'Apocryphal books' outright and reverted to the shorter Jewish Canon: at the Council of Trent (1546) the Church of Rome reasserted the validity of the traditional Christian longer Canon (a reassertion repeated at the Vatican Council in 1870); while the Church of England, in her *Articles of Religion*, listed the books of the shorter Canon as those 'of whose authority there was never any doubt in the Church' and added a list of 'the other books' from the longer Canon, which 'the Church doth read for example of life and instruction of manners, but yet doth it not apply them to establish any doctrine.' H. F. D. S.

CANON OF THE NEW TESTAMENT.—1. Title.—The Greek word 'canon,' meaning originally a 'rod' and so a 'rule for measuring,' is used in a variety of senses by Patristic writers, among the most familiar instances being the expressions 'rule of truth' and 'rule of faith' for the doctrinal teaching officially recognized by the bishops. Hence, since we meet with the phrase 'canonical books' in Origen, as rendered by Rufinus' translation, before we see the substantive 'canon' applied to the list of NT books, it has been argued that the adjective was first used in the sense of 'regulative,' so that the phrase means 'the books that regulate faith or morals.' But the substantive must mean the 'list' of books, and in Athanasius we have a passive participle in the phrase '*canonized* books,' *i.e.* books belonging to the Canon; soon after which the actual word 'canon' is applied to the books of the NT by Amphilochius, the bishop of Iconium (end of 4th cent. A.D.). The NT Canon, then, is the list of NT books, and this simple meaning, rather than 'the regulative books,' is the more likely interpretation of the expression to have occurred to people who were in the habit of using the term for lists of officials, lists of festivals, etc. The question of the Canon differs from questions of the authenticity, genuineness,. historicity, inspiration, value, and authority of the several NT books in concerning itself simply with their acceptance in the Church. Primarily the question was as to what books were read in the churches at public worship. Those so used became in course of time the Christian Scriptures. Then, having the value of Scripture gradually associated with them, they came to be treated as authoritative. The first stage is that of use in the form of Church lessons; the second that of a standard of authority to be employed as the basis of instruction, and to be appealed to in disputed cases of doctrines or discipline.

2. The Formation of the Canon in the 2nd Century.—The very earliest reading of NT books in the churches must have occurred in the case of epistles addressed to particular churches, which of course were read in those churches; next come the circular letters (*e.g.* Ephesians, 1 Peter), which were passed round a group of churches (see also Col 4[16]).

During the sub-Apostolic age, such writers as Clement of Rome, Ignatius, Polycarp, and 'Barnabas' quote from or allude to several of the Pauline Epistles. The first explicit reference to a collection of NT books involves the heretic Marcion, who about A.D. 140 issued a canon of Scripture consisting of a mutilated Gospel of St. Luke and ten Epistles of Paul (the three Pastoral Epistles being omitted). There has been much

CANON OF THE NEW TESTAMENT

debate among scholars as to whether this was the first collection of NT books. The fact that the Fathers consistently represent Marcion as having *rejected* certain books makes it probable that the church's canon preceded Marcion's rival canon. Support for this opinion is afforded by the recently discovered *Evangelium Veritatis*, a work thought to be by Valentinus (the Gnostic teacher from Egypt who taught at Rome about A.D. 135–160), which, though not quoting any NT book explicitly, shows acquaintance with the Synoptic Tradition, John, many of the Pauline Epistles, Hebrews, and Revelation. This information confirms Tertullian's contrast between Marcion and Valentinus in their treatment of Scripture: while Marcion had eliminated what did not suit his purpose, Valentinus 'seems to use the entire Testament (*integro instrumento*),' though he actually distorts the Scriptures by imposing on them his own fantastic system (*de Praescrip. Haer.* xxxviii, 7 ff). What is important here is that apparently Tertullian regarded Valentinus's NT to be the same in extent as his own.

The earliest reference to a liturgical use of NT books dates from the middle of the 2nd cent., when Justin Martyr, describing a Sunday service of worship at Rome (I *Apol.* lxvii), indicates that 'the memoirs of the Apostles [*i.e.* the Gospels] or the writings of the prophets are read.' A little later Justin's disciple Tatian prepared his *Diatessaron*, or Harmony of the four Gospels, for use in the church at Edessa.

When we come to Irenaeus, bishop of Lyons and Vienne in Gaul (*c* A.D. 180), we seem to be in another world. Irenaeus freely cites as authoritative most of the books of the NT (though not Philemon, James, 2 Peter, 3 John, or Jude; whether he knew Hebrews has been disputed). In discussing the grounds of determining the canonicity of a document, Irenaeus lays stress on apostolicity and ecclesiastical tradition. Though the designation *New* Testament for the whole complex of these writings does not appear until the following century, Irenaeus calls them 'Scripture' because they have the same character of inspiration as the writings of the OT.

The growth and recognition of the canon of the NT is one of the most important developments in the thought and practice of the Church; yet history is absolutely silent as to how, when, and by whom it was brought about. In the absence of all extant contemporary references to so great a movement, not a few conjectures have been proposed. Thus, Harnack supposed that bishops of Asia Minor in agreement with the Church at Rome deliberately drew up and settled the Canon, although we have no historical record of so significant an event. It is more likely, however, that the formation of the Canon was an instinctive act of the Christian society, resting upon the general confession of the Churches (Westcott). That is, the canonical books, by their intrinsic merit, came to be separated from the others by the intuitive insight of devout believers, and were later approved by synodical bodies as the authoritative standard of appeal in controversies.

The most ancient extant list of NT books in the Old Catholic Church is the 'Muratorian Fragment,' which is named after its discoverer Muratori, who found it in a 7th or 8th cent. monk's common-place book in the Ambrosian Library at Milan, and published it in 1740. The fragment is a mutilated extract of a list of NT books made at Rome probably before the end of the 2nd cent., since the author refers to the episcopate of Pius as recent (*nuperrime temporibus nostris*), and Pius I., who died in A.D. 157, is the only bishop of Rome of that name in the early age to which unquestionably, as internal evidence indicates, the original composition must be assigned. The fragment begins in the middle of a sentence which appears to allude to St. Peter's connexion with our Second Gospel, and goes on to mention Luke as the Third Gospel and John as the Fourth. Therefore it evidently acknowledged the Four Gospels. Then it has Acts, which it ascribes to Luke, and it acknowledges Thirteen Epistles of Paul—admitting the Pastorals, but excluding Hebrews, though it subsequently refers to 'an Epistle to the Laodiceans,' and another 'to the Alexandrians forged under the name of Paul,' as well as 'many others' which are not received in the Catholic Church 'because gall ought not to be mixed with honey.' Further, this Canon includes Jude, 2 Epistles of John, and the Apocalypse, which it ascribes to John. It also has the Book of Wisdom, which it says was 'written by the friends of Solomon in his honour,' and the Apocalypse of Peter, although acknowledging that there is a minority which rejects the latter work, for we read 'we receive moreover the Apocalypses of John and Peter only, which [latter] some of our body will not have read in the church.' This indicates that the author's church as a whole acknowledges the Apocalypse of Peter, and that he associates himself with the majority of his brethren in so doing, while he candidly admits that there are some dissentients. Lastly, the Canon admits Hermas for private reading, but not for use in the church services. We have here, then, most of our NT books; but, on the one hand, Hebrews, 1 and 2 Peter, James, and one of the Three Epistles of John are not mentioned. They are not named to be excluded, like the forged works referred to above; possibly the author did not know of their existence. At all events he did not find them used in his church. On the other hand, Wisdom, without question, and the Apocalypse of Peter, though rejected by some, are included in this canon, and Hermas is added for private reading.

Passing on to the 3rd cent. we come upon another anonymous writing, an anti-gambling tract called 'Concerning Dice-players' (*de Aleatoribus*), which Harnack attributed to Victor of Rome (A.D. 189–198), but which Koch attributed to a bishop of North Africa after Cyprian's time, perhaps toward A.D. 300. In this tract the *Shepherd of Hermas* and the *Didache* are both quoted as 'Scripture.' The author refers to three divisions of Scripture: (1) Prophetic writings—the OT Prophets, the Apocalypse, Hermas; (2) the Gospels; (3) the Apostolic Writings—Paul, 1 John, Hebrews.

Neither of these Canons can be regarded as authoritative either ecclesiastically or scientifically, since we are ignorant of their sources. But they both indicate a crystallizing process that was tending towards our NT, though with some curious variations. The writings of the Fathers of this period agree in the main with Irenaeus in their citations from most of the NT books as authoritative—a condition very different from that in Justin's writings half a century earlier. Two influences may be recognized as bringing this result about: (1) use in churches at public worship, (2) authoritative appeals against heresy—especially Gnosticism. It was necessary to settle what books should be read in church and what books should be appealed to in discussion. The former was the primary question. The books used at their services by the churches, and therefore admitted by them as having a right to be so employed, were the books to be appealed to in controversy.

Turning to the East, we find Clement of Alexandria (*c* A.D. 150–215) acknowledging the Four Gospels and Acts, and Fourteen Epistles of Paul (Hebrews being included), and quoting 1 and 2 John, 1 Peter, Jude, and the Apocalypse. He makes no reference to James, 2 Peter, or 3 John, any of which he may perhaps have known, as we have no list of NT books from his hand, for he does not name these books to reject them. Still, the probability as regards some, if not all, of them is that he did not know them. In the true Alexandrian spirit, Clement has a wide and comprehensive idea of inspiration, and therefore no very definite conception of Scriptural exclusiveness or fixed boundaries to the Canon. Thus he quotes Barnabas, Clement of Rome, Hermas, the Preaching of Peter, the Apocalypse of Peter, and the Sibylline Writings as in some way authoritative. He was a literary eclectic who delighted to welcome Christian truth in unexpected places. Origen (A.D. 184–253), who was a more critical scholar, treated questions of canonicity

CANON OF THE NEW TESTAMENT

more scientifically. Having travelled extensively he had opportunity of acquiring information as to what works were held to be canonical in many parts of the Church. According to a list quoted by Eusebius (*HE* vi. 25) he acknowledged as canonical the Four Gospels, Acts, Fourteen Epistles of Paul (including Hebrews; his statement, 'Who wrote this Epistle, in truth, [only] God knows,' probably refers to the unknown amanuensis employed by Paul), 1 Peter, 1 John, and Revelation. He mentions that 2 Peter and 2 and 3 John are of doubtful authorship. Elsewhere Origen quotes not infrequently from James and Jude as Holy Scripture, but occasionally alludes to their lack of general recognition. Furthermore, he refers to the Epistle of Barnabas, the Shepherd of Hermas, and the Teaching of the Twelve Apostles (the *Didache*) as canonical. It is a significant fact, however, that though an indefatigable commentator he apparently wrote no commentaries on any of those books which are not included in our NT.

3. The Settlement of the Canon in the Fourth and Fifth Centuries.—An important step towards the settlement of the Canon on historical and scientific lines was taken by Eusebius, who, with his wide reading and the great library of Pamphilus to resort to, also brought a fair and judicious mind to face the problems involved. Eusebius saw clearly that it is not always possible to give a definite affirmative or negative answer to the question whether a certain book should be in the Canon. Therefore he drew up three lists of books—(1) The books that are admitted by all, (2) the books which he is disposed to admit although there are some who reject them, (3) the books that he regards as spurious. A fourth class, which really does not come into the competition for a place in the Canon, consists of heretical works which 'are to be rejected as altogether absurd and impious' (*HE* iii. 25). The *first* class, consisting of the books universally acknowledged, contains the Four Gospels; Acts; the Epistles of Paul—which he reckons (iii. 3) to be fourteen, and therefore to include Hebrews; 1 Peter; 1 John; and Revelation (doubtfully). The *second* class, consisting of books widely accepted, though disputed by some (but apparently all admitted by Eusebius himself), contains James; Jude; 2 Peter (regarded in iii. 3 as spurious); 2 and 3 John. The *third* class, consisting of spurious works, contains the Acts of Paul; the Shepherd of Hermas; the Apocalypse of Peter; the Didache; and perhaps, according to some, the Revelation. Under the orders of Constantine, Eusebius had fifty copies of the Scriptures sumptuously produced on vellum for use in the churches of Constantinople. Of course these would correspond to his own Canon and so help to fix it and spread its influence. After this the fluctuations that we meet with are very slight. Athanasius in one of his *Festal Letters* (A.D. 367) undertakes to set forth in order the books that are canonical and handed down and believed to be Divine. His NT exactly agrees with our Canon, as does the NT of Epiphanius († A.D. 403). Cyril of Jerusalem († A.D. 386) gives a list of 'Divine Scriptures' which contains all the NT except the Revelation; and Amphilochius, Bishop of Iconium († after A.D. 394) has a versified catalogue of the Biblical books, in which also all our NT books appear except the Revelation, which he regards as spurious; Amphilochius refers to doubts concerning Hebrews and to a question as to whether the number of Catholic Epistles is seven or three. Even Chrysostom († A.D. 407) never alludes to the Revelation or the last four Catholic Epistles. But then he gives no list of the Canon. One of the *Apostolical Canons* (No. 85), which stand as an appendix to the eighth book of the *Apostolical Constitutions* (ch. 47), and cannot be dated earlier than the 4th cent. in their present form, gives a list of the books of Scripture. Sirach is here placed between the OT and the NT with a special recommendation to 'take care that your young persons learn the wisdom of the very learned Sirach.' Then follow the NT books—the Four Gospels, Fourteen Epistles of Paul (Hebrews therefore included in this category), two Epistles of Peter, three of John, James, Jude, two Epistles of Clement, the eight books of the *Constitutions*, Acts. Thus, while Clement and even the *Apostolical Constitutions* are included, the Revelation is left out, after a common custom in the East. Manifestly this is an erratic Canon.

Returning to the West, at this later period we have an elaborate discussion on the Canon by Augustine († A.D. 430), who lays down rules by which the canonicity of the several books claimed for the NT may be determined. (1) There are the books received and acknowledged by all the churches, which should therefore be treated as canonical. (2) There are some books not yet universally accepted. With regard to these, two tests are to be applied: (*a*) such as are received by the majority of the churches are to be acknowledged, and (*b*) such as are received by the Apostolic churches are to be preferred to those received only by a smaller number of churches and these of less authority, *i.e.* not having been founded by Apostles. In case (*a*) and (*b*) conflict, Augustine considers that 'the authority on the two sides is to be looked upon as equal' (*Christian Doctrine*, II. viii. 12). Thus the tests are simply Church reception, though with discrimination as to the respective authority of the several churches. The application of these tests gives Augustine just our NT.

Jerome († *c* A.D. 420) also accepts our NT, saying concerning Hebrews and the Revelation that he adopts both on the authority of ancient writers, not on that of present custom. He is aware that James has been questioned; but he states that little by little in course of time it has obtained authority. Jude was even rejected by most people because it contained quotations from Apocryphal writings. Nevertheless he himself accepts it. He notes that 2 and 3 John have been attributed to a presbyter whose tomb at Ephesus is still pointed out. The immense personal influence of Augustine and the acceptance of Jerome's Vulgate as the standard Bible of the Christian Church gave fixity to the Canon, which was not disturbed for a thousand years. No General Council had pronounced on the subject. The first Council claiming to be Ecumenical which committed itself to a decision on the subject was as late as the 16th cent. (the Council of Trent). We may be thankful that the delicate and yet vital question of determining the Canon was not flung into the arena of ecclesiastical debate to be settled by the triumph of partisan churchmanship, but was allowed to mature slowly and come to its final settlement under the twofold influences of Christian experience and honest scholarship. There were indeed local councils that dealt with the question; but their decisions were binding only on the provinces they represented, although, in so far as they were not disputed, they would be regarded as more or less normative by those other churches to which they were sent. As representing the East we have a Canon attributed to the Council of Laodicea (A.D. 363). There is a dispute as to whether this is genuine. It is given in the MSS variously as a 60th canon and as part of the 59th appended in red ink. Half the Latin versions are without it; so are the Syriac versions, which are much older than our oldest MSS of the canons. It closely resembles the Canon of Cyril of Jerusalem, from which Westcott supposed that it was inserted into the canons of Laodicea by a Latin hand. Its genuineness was defended by Hefele and Davidson. Jülicher regards it as probably genuine. This Canon contains the OT with Baruch and the Epistle of Jeremy, and all our NT *except* the Revelation. Then in the West we have the 3rd Council of Carthage (A.D. 397), which orders that 'besides the Canonical Scriptures nothing be read in the Church under the title of Divine Scriptures,' and appends a list of the books thus authorized in which we have the OT, the Apocrypha, and just our NT books. Here we have a whole province speaking for those books; when we add the great authority of Augustine, who belongs to this very province, and the influence of the Vulgate, we can well understand how the Canon should now be considered fixed and inviolable. Thus the matter rested for ten centuries in the West.

Among the Eastern churches, however, several diversities in the Canon have existed. During the first six centuries the Syrian churches were content with a NT Canon of twenty-two books (our NT except for 2 Peter, 2 and 3 John, Jude, and Revelation). It was not until the last quarter of the 10th cent. that the Book of Revelation was translated into Georgian. In fact, this book has never been included in the lectionary system of the Greek Orthodox Church. On the other hand, the Ethiopic Church had thirty-five books in the NT—our twenty-seven plus the eight books of canon law (the so-called Apostolic Constitutions). Furthermore, St. Ephraem the Syrian († *c* A.D. 378) wrote a commentary on the Third Epistle of Paul to the Corinthians, an Epistle which is also preserved in several mediaeval Armenian manuscripts.

4. Treatment of the Canon at the Renaissance and the Reformation.—The question of the Canon was revived by the Renaissance and the Reformation, the one movement directing critical, scholarly attention to what was essentially a literary question, the other facing it in the interest of religious controversy. Erasmus writes: 'The arguments of criticism estimated by the rules of logic, lead me to disbelieve that the Epistle to the Hebrews is by Paul or Luke, or that the Second of Peter is the work of that Apostle, or that the Apocalypse was written by the Evangelist John. All the same, I have nothing to say against the contents of these books, which seem to me to be in perfect conformity with the truth. If, however, the Church were to declare the titles they bear to be canonical, then I would condemn my doubt, for the opinion formulated by the Church has more value in my eyes than human reasons, whatever they may be'—a most characteristic statement, revealing the scholar, the critic, the timid soul—and the satirist (?). Within the Church of Rome even Cardinal Cajetan—Luther's opponent at Augsburg—freely discusses the Canon, doubting whether Hebrews is St. Paul's work, and whether, if it is not, it can be canonical. He also mentions doubts concerning the five General Epistles, and gives less authority to 2 and 3 John and Jude than to those books which he regards as certainly in the Holy Scriptures.

The Reformation forced the question of the authority of the Bible to the front, because it set that authority in the place of the old authority of the Church. While this chiefly concerned the book as a whole, it could not preclude inquiries as to its contents and the rights of the several parts to hold their places there. The general answer as to the authority of Scripture is an appeal to 'the testimony of the Holy Spirit.' Calvin especially works out this conception very distinctly. The difficulty was to apply it to particular books of the Bible so as to determine in each case whether they should be allowed in the Canon. Clearly a further test was requisite here. This was found in the 'analogy of faith' (*Analogia fidei*), which was more especially Luther's principle, while the testimony of the Holy Spirit was Calvin's. With Luther the Reformation was based on justification by faith. This truth Luther held to be confirmed (*a*) by its necessity, nothing else availing, and (*b*) by its effects, since in practice it brought peace, assurance, and the new life. Then those Scriptures which manifestly supported the fundamental principle were held to be *ipso facto* inspired, and the measure of their support of it determined the degree of their authority. Thus the doctrine of justification by faith is not accepted because it is found in the Bible; but the Bible is accepted because it contains this doctrine. Moreover, the Bible is sorted and arranged in grades according as it does so more or less clearly, and to Luther there is 'a NT within the NT,' a kernel of all Scripture, consisting of those books which he sees most clearly set forth the gospel. Thus he wrote: 'John's Gospel and his First Epistle, the Epistles of Paul, especially Romans, Galatians, Ephesians, and 1 Peter—these are the books which show thee Christ, and teach all that it is needful and blessed for thee to know even if you never see or hear any other book. . . . Therefore is the Epistle of James a mere epistle of straw (*eine rechte stroherne Epistel*) compared with them, since it has no character of the gospel in it' (Preface to NT[1], 1522; the passage was omitted from later editions). Luther places Hebrews, James, Jude, and the Apocalypse at the end of his translation, after the other NT books, which he designates 'the true and certain capital books of the NT, for these have been regarded in former times in a different light.' He regards Jude as 'indisputably an extract or copy from 2 Peter.' Nevertheless, while thus discriminating between the values of the several books of the NT, he includes them all in his translation. In fact, Luther concluded his Preface to the Epistle of James with the statement, 'I cannot place it among the right canonical works, but I do not wish thereby to prevent any one from so placing it and extolling it as seems good to him, for there are many good sayings in it.' Luther's friend Carlstadt has a curious arrangement of Scripture in three classes, viz. (1) The Pentateuch and the Four Gospels, as being 'the clearest luminaries of the whole Divine truth; (2) The Prophets 'of Hebrew reckoning' and the acknowledged Epistles of the NT, viz. Thirteen of Paul, 1 Peter, 1 John; (3) the Hagiographa of the Hebrew Canon, and the seven disputed books of the NT. Westcott suggested that the omission of Acts was owing to its being included with Luke.

Calvin is more conservative with regard to Scripture than the Lutherans. Still in his Commentaries he passes over 2 and 3 John and the Revelation without notice, and he refers to 1 John as 'the Epistle of John,' and expresses doubts as to 2 Peter; but he adds, with regard to the latter, 'Since the majesty of the Spirit of Christ exhibits itself in every part of the Epistle, I feel a scruple in rejecting it wholly, however much I fail to recognize in it the genuine language of Peter' (*Comm.* on *II Peter*, Argument). Further, Calvin acknowledges the existence of doubts with respect both to James and to Jude; but he accepts them both. He allows full liberty of opinion concerning the authorship of Hebrews; but he states that he has no hesitation in classing it among Apostolical writings. In spite of these varieties of opinion, the NT Canon remained unaltered. At the Council of Trent (1546) for the first time the Roman Catholic Church made an authoritative statement on the Canon, uttering an anathema ('*anathema sit*') on anyone who did not accept in their integrity all the books contained in the Vulgate. Thus the Apocrypha is treated as equally canonical with the OT books; but the NT Canon is the same in Roman Catholic and Protestant Canons. Translations of the Bible into the vernacular of various languages laid the question of the Canon to rest again, by familiarizing readers with the same series of books in all versions and editions.

5. The Canon in Modern Criticism.—In the 18th cent. the very idea of a Canon was attacked by the Deists and Rationalists (Toland, Diderot, etc.); but the critical study of the subject began with Semler (1771–1775), who pointed out the early variations in the Canon and attacked the very idea of a Canon as an authoritative standard, while he criticised the usefulness and theological value of the several books of the NT. Subsequent controversy has dealt less with the Canon as such than with the authenticity and genuineness of the books that it contains. In the view of extreme negative criticism canonicity as such has no meaning except as a historical record of Church opinion. On the other hand, those who accept a doctrine of inspiration in relation to the NT do not connect this very closely with critical questions in such a way as to affect the Canon. Thus doubts as to the authorship of the Pastoral Epistles, 2 Peter, James, etc., have not given rise to any serious proposal to remove these books from the NT. The Canon rests mainly on tradition and usage. But the justification for it when this is sought is usually found (1) in the Apostolic authorship of most of the NT books; (2) in the Apostolic atmosphere and association of the remaining books; (3) in the general acceptance and continuous use of them in the churches for centuries as a test of their value; (4) in their inherent worth to-day as realized in Christian experience. It cannot be said that these four tests would give an indefeasible right to every book to claim a place in the Canon if it were not already there—*e.g.* the small Epistle of Jude; but they throw the burden of proof on those who would disturb the Canon by a serious proposal to eject any of its contents; and in fact no such proposal—as distinct from critical questions of the dates, authorship, historicity, etc., of the several books—is now engaging the attention of scholars or churches. See INSPIRATION, REVELATION.

W. F. A.—**B. M. M.**

CANOPY.—A loan-word from the Greek *kōnōpeion*, a mosquito-net. It is used to render this word in the description of the bed of Holofernes with its mosquito-curtain (Jth 10[21], etc.); also in Is 4[5] (RV, RSV; AV 'defence') for Hebrew *ḥuppāh* in the sense of a protective covering. This Hebrew word is becoming naturalized in English to denote the canopy under which a Jewish bridegroom and bride stand while the wedding ceremony is being performed. A. R. S. K.

CANTICLES.—See SONG OF SONGS.

CAP.—See DRESS, **5** (*a*).

CAPER-BERRY (Heb. *'ᵃbhiyyônāh*).—Ec 12[5] RV; AV, RSV 'desire.' The RV translation is supported by the LXX, Pesh., and the Mishnah. The caper-berry is the fruit of *Capparis sicula*, a common Palestine plant, which, largely on account of its habit of growing out of crevices in walls, has been identified with the **hyssop** (q.v.). Various parts of the caper plant are extensively used as medicine by the *fellāhîn*. The familiar capers of commerce are the flower buds. The 'failure' of the caper-berry in old age may have been its ceasing to act as a stimulant, either as an aphrodisiac or a stomachic. E. W. G. M.

CAPERNAUM.—The headquarters of Jesus in His Galilaean ministry (Mt 4[13], Jn 2[12]). Here He healed the centurion's servant (Mt 8[5-13], Lk 7[2-10], Jn 4[46-54]), provided the half-shekel for the Temple tribute (Mt 17[24]), taught in the synagogue (Mk 1[21], Lk 4[31], Jn 6[59]), performed many miracles (Mk 1[23]–2[12], Lk 4[33-41]), taught His disciples (Mk 9[33]). For its unbelief He denounced the city (Mt 11[23], Lk 10[15]). Capernaum undoubtedly lay at *Tell Ḥûm*, where there are extensive ruins, including those of a fine 3rd cent. synagogue, which may stand on the very site of the one that Jesus attended. The town is mentioned in an inscription found at *el-Ḥammeh* near the mouth of the Yarmuk river as *Kephar Naḥum*.

R. A. S. M.—**E. G. K.**

CAPH or **KAPH.**—Eleventh letter of Hebrew alphabet, and so used in Ps 119 to introduce the 11th part, every verse of which begins with this letter.

CAPHARSALAMA.—Here Nicanor fought an engagement with Judas Maccabaeus (1 Mac 7[31]). The story gives no clue as to his line of march, so it is uncertain where it should be sought. E. G. K.

CAPHENATHA, 1 Mac 12[37] (AV).—See CHAPHENATHA.

CAPHIRA, 1 Es 5[19] (AV, RV).—See CHEPHIRAH.

CAPHTHORIM, 1 Ch 1[12] (AV)=people of **Caphtor** (q.v.).

CAPHTOR.—The region whence the Philistines came to Palestine (Am 9[7], Jer 47[4]). Hence in Dt 2[23] Caphtorim means Philistines (cf Gn 10[14]). It is generally accepted that Caphtor signifies Crete (cf CHERETHITES), a view which is confirmed by the mention of *Kptr* in the cuneiform tablets from *Râs Shamra* (ancient Ugarit) as a place overseas, regarded, with Egypt, as the home of the arts, with which Ugaritic merchants had sea-borne intercourse. The Biblical tradition deriving the Philistines from Crete is correct only in so far as the Philistines were not natives of Crete, but, with kindred peoples from the N. and W., destroyed the local Minoan civilization (*c* 1400 B.C.) before settling on the Asiatic mainland in the early 12th cent.

J. F. McC.—**J. Gr.**

CAPITAL.—See KNOP.

CAPPADOCIA.—A large district in the mid-eastern part of Asia Minor, formed into a Roman province in A.D. 17. It was administered by a *procurator* sent out by the reigning emperor, being regarded as an unimportant district. In A.D. 70 Vespasian united it with Armenia Minor, and made the two together a large and important frontier province, to be governed by an ex-consul, under the title of *legatus Augusti pro praetore*, on the emperor's behalf. The territory to the N. and W. of Cilicia, the kingdom of the client-king Antiochus of Commagene, was incorporated in it at the time, and it afterwards received various accessions of territory. Jews from Cappadocia are mentioned in Ac 2[9]. That such were already settled there (*c* 139 B.C.) is implied in 1 Mac 15[22] where a letter in their favour is addressed by the Roman Senate to king Ariarathes (q.v.). Cappadocia was not visited by St. Paul, probably as insufficiently Hellenized, but it was one of the provinces to which 1 Peter was addressed. A. So.—**E. G. K.**

CAPTAIN.—In the AV this word translates thirteen different Hebrew terms that denote a wide variety of leadership. *Śar* is the most frequent: in AV more often translated 'prince' and frequently 'chief' or 'ruler'; rendered 'captain,' it designates in the era of the Judges the head of a tribe or clan and thereafter usually a military officer who may be in command of from 50 to 1000 men or even of an entire army. The RSV usually substitutes 'commander.' Saul created a standing army of 3000 (1 S 13[2]; cf 24[2]), many of whom like the 'worthless fellows' of Jg 11[3] may already have looked to fighting as a vocation. David as brigand chief (1 S 22[2ff]) commanded a disciplined corps that later may have provided the officers for his expanded army. Among his high court functionaries was the commander (AV 'captain') of the royal bodyguard (2 S 8[18], 20[23]). The so-called captains (AV) of Ex 14[7] 15[4] were élite troops; elsewhere this term *shālîsh* designates the third in rank or battalion commander. As used in Lk 22[4, 52], Ac 4[1] 5[24, 26], a 'captain' commanded the gendarmerie which policed the Judaean Temple (see POLICE). In Jn 18[12], Rev 19[18] the Greek term means 'commander of a thousand'; in RSV elsewhere it is rendered 'tribune' in Ac 21[31f] and 'generals' in Rev 6[15]. J. S. K.

CAPTIVITY.—See ISRAEL, I. **22.**

CARABASION (1 Es 9[34]).—A corrupt name of one of those who put away their 'strange' wives. It seems to correspond to **Meremoth** in Ezr 10[36].

CARAVAN.—See TRADE AND COMMERCE.

CARBUNCLE.—See JEWELS AND PRECIOUS STONES.

CARCAS, Est 1[10] (AV, RV).—See CARKAS.

CARCHEMISH was an important city as it commanded the principal ford of the Euphrates on the right bank, and was therefore indispensable to travel and commerce in Northern Syria. Mentioned from the beginning of the 2nd millennium B.C. it came under Hittite influence in the 14th cent. B.C. After the fall of the Hittite empire (*c* 1200 B.C.) Carchemish became the most important of the Hittite city-states, so that the Assyrians regarded it as the Hittite capital. It paid tribute to Ashurnasirpal II. and to Shalmaneser III. in the 9th cent. B.C., and was frequently involved in wars with the Assyrians, until Sargon II. conquered it in 717 B.C. (cf Is 10[9]), after which it became the capital of an Assyrian province. Here Nebuchadnezzar defeated Pharaoh-neco in 605 B.C., and thus ended the latest native Egyptian *régime* in Asia (Jer 46[2], 2 Ch 35[20]). The site is marked by a mound called *Jerablus*. Successful excavations were carried out there for the British Museum from 1876–1879 and from 1912–1914. Many Hittite hieroglyphic inscriptions came to light.

J. F. McC.—**S. H. Hn.**

CAREFULNESS.—*Careful* and *carefulness* do not express approbation in the English of the AV as they do now. To be careful is to be too anxious, to worry. 'Be careful for nothing,' says St. Paul (Ph 4[6]), and 'I would have you without carefulness' (1 Co 7[32]). Latimer says: 'Consider the remedy against carefulness, which is to trust in God.' Again, to be *careless* is not blameworthy, meaning simply to be without apprehension, to feel safe, as Jg 18[7] 'they dwelt careless, after the manner of the Zidonians, quiet and secure.'

CARIA (a region in SW. Asia Minor) is mentioned only in 1 Mac 15[23] as one of the districts to which the Roman Senate sent a letter in favour of the Jews in 139–138 B.C. It was free at that date, with its inland States federated. The more important states, Rhodes, etc., are separately named. A. So.

CARITES occurs in the *Kᵉthîbh* of the Hebrew text and in RVm in 2 S 20[23], where the *Ḳᵉrê* has *Cherethites* (so EV), and in 2 K 11[4], where RV, RSV have Carites and AV 'captains' (RVm 'executioners'). The Carites were possibly Philistine mercenaries from Caria, as the Cherethites may have been from Crete.

CARKAS.—One of the seven eunuchs or chamberlains of King Ahasuerus Est 1[10] (AV, RV **Carcas**).

CARMANIANS, 2 Es 15[30] (AV).—See CARMONIANS.

CARME, 1 Es 5[25] (AV).—See HARIM, 2.

CARMEL.—**1.** An inhabited place in Judah (Jos 15[55], 1 S 30[29] LXX), identified with *el-Kirmil*, 7 miles S. of Hebron. Here Saul set up a memorial of his conquest of the Amalekites (1 S 15[12]), and here Nabal had his estate (1 S 25[2]). It was the home of Hezrai (Hezro), one of David's thirty heroes (2 S 23[25], 1 Ch 11[37]). In 2 Ch 26[10], where AV (following LXX) says that Uzziah had farmers and vinedressers here, the word is treated as a common noun by RV ('fruitful fields') and RSV ('fertile lands').

2. A hilly promontory, rising to over 1800 feet, by which the sea-coast of Palestine is broken, forming the south side of the Bay of Acre (modern *Jebel Kurmul, Jebel Mâr Elyâs*). It continues as a ridge running in a SE. direction, bordering the plain of Jezreel on the south. On this ridge was Jokneam, reduced by Joshua (Jos 12[22]). The promontory was included in the territory assigned to Asher (Jos 19[26]). Elijah chose Carmel as the scene of the trial of strength between Yahweh and Baal, possibly because it was so near Phoenicia, Jezebel's homeland. His sacrifice (1 K 18) is located by tradition at the SE. extremity of the ridge. Elisha had his headquarters at Carmel for a time, and it was a place of festal resort for Israelites (2 K 2[25], 4[25]). Its beauty and fruitfulness were proverbial (Is 33[9] 35[2], Am 1[2]); it was well-wooded (Mic 7[14]) and was therefore a good hiding-place (Am 9[3]). A maiden's head is compared to Carmel (Ca 7[5]).

Caves at the foot of Mount Carmel have yielded human remains representing apparently an intermediate or hybrid stage between palaeanthropic man (*Homo neanderthalensis*) and neanthropic man (*Homo sapiens*). From early times it was a holy place. In lists of Palestinian place-names in the records of Thothmes III. and later Egyptian kings it is probably Carmel that is meant by Rôsh Qâdesh ('holy headland'). There was a sanctuary of Yahweh there before Elijah's time, for he repaired Yahweh's ruined altar (1 K 18[30]); there was probably an ancient Baal-sanctuary there too (whether of Baal-Shamem or the Tyrian Melkart is disputed; perhaps they were identified at Carmel), and this, in addition to its geographical situation, made it an eminently suitable place for the ordeal. Its pagan sanctity persisted for long. In Greek times it was sacred to Zeus; a stone foot was discovered in the vicinity a few years ago dedicated to 'Zeus Heliopoleitēs Karmēlos.' Strabo (*c* A.D. 20) knew it as a place of asylum; Vespasian (A.D. 69) sacrificed here on the altar of the god 'Carmel' and obtained favourable auspices for his imperial ambitions; Iamblichus (c A.D. 330) describes the mountain as 'sacred above all mountains and not to be trodden (*abaton*) by the vulgar.' In later times the mountain gave its name to the order of Carmelite friars (founded 1156). R. A. S. M.—**F. F. B.**

CARMI.—**1.** A Judahite, the father of Achan (Jos 7[1, 18], 1 Ch 2[7]). **2.** The Carmi of 1 Ch 4[1] should probably be corrected to **Chelubai**, *i.e.* Caleb (cf 1 Ch 2[9, 18]). **3.** The eponym of a Reubenite family (Gn 46[9], Ex 6[14], 1 Ch 5[3]), the **Carmites** of Nu 26[6].

CARMONIANS (2 Es 15[30], AV **Carmanians**).—A people occupying an extensive district (Kermān) N. of the Persian Gulf, W. of Gedrosia. They are said to have resembled the Medes and Persians in customs and language. The name survives in the present town and district of *Kirman*. In the above verse the reference is probably to Sapor I. (A.D. 240–273), the founder of the Sassanid dynasty, who, after defeating Valerian, overran Syria, and destroyed Antioch.

CARNAIM.—A city mentioned in 1 Mac 5[26, 43f], 2 Mac 12[21, 26] (AV, RV **Carnion**); probably the same as **Ashteroth-Karnaim** (q.v.).

CARNELIAN.—See JEWELS AND PRECIOUS STONES.

CARNION, 2 Mac 12[21, 26] (AV, RV).—See CARNAIM.

CAROB (Lk 15[16] RVm; RSV 'pods').—See PODS.

CARPENTER.—See ARTS AND CRAFTS, **1.**

CARPUS.—An inhabitant of Troas, with whom St. Paul stayed, perhaps on his last journey to Rome (2 Ti 4[13]). The name is Greek, but we have no means of proving his nationality.

CARRIAGE.—This word is always used in the AV in the literal sense of 'something carried,' never in the modern sense of a vehicle used for carrying. Thus Ac 21[15] 'we took up our carriages' (RV 'baggage'; RSV 'we made ready').

CARSHENA.—One of the wise men or counsellors of king Ahasuerus (Est 1[14]).

CART, WAGON.—The cart, like the chariot, is an Asiatic invention. The earliest wheeled carts show a light framework set upon an axle with solid wheels (illustrated in Wilkinson, *Anc. Egyp.* [1878] i. 249). The type of cart in use under the Hebrew monarchy may be seen in the Assyrian representation of the siege of Lachish (Layard, *Monuments of Nineveh*, ii, pl. 23), where women captives and their children are shown in wagons with a low wooden body (cf 1 S 6[14]), furnished with wheels of six and eight spokes. They were drawn by a pair of oxen (Nu 7[3, 7f])—exceptionally by two cows (1 S 6[7, 10])—yoked to a pole which passed between them, and were used for the transport of persons (Gn 45[19ff]) and goods (Nu *l.c.*), including sheaves of grain to the threshing-floor (Am 2[13]). The rendering 'covered wagons' (Nu 7[3]) is doubtful. For the threshing-wagon, see AGRICULTURE, **3.** A. R. S. K.

CASEMENT.—Only Pr 7[6] (AV; RV, RSV 'lattice,' as AV, RV, RSV in Jg 5[28], where the same Hebrew word is used). Cf also the Hebrew text of Sir 42[11] (omitted in Greek and in EV); 'In the room where she (*i.e.* thy daughter) dwells let there be no lattice.' See, further, HOUSE, **7.**

CASIPHIA.—A settlement in the neighbourhood of Ahava (q.v.) in North Babylonia (Ezr 8[17]), whose site has not been identified.

CASLEU, 1 Mac 1[54] 4[59], 2 Mac 1[9, 18] 10[5] (AV).—See CHISLEV.

CASLUHIM.—A name occurring in Gn 10[14], 1 Ch 1[12] in connexion with the names of other peoples there spoken of as descended from Mizraim, especially the Caphtorim and Philistines. The name is not otherwise known.

CASPHOR, 1 Mac 5[26, 36] (AV, RV).—See CHASPHO.

CASPIN.—See CHASPHO.

CASPIS, 2 Mac 12[13] (AV).—See CHASPHO.

CASSIA.—**1.** *Ḳiddāh*, Ex 30[24], Ezk 27[19]. **2.** *Ḳᵉṣîʿôth*,

Ps 45[8]. 3. *Kinnamōmon*, Sir 24[15] (RSV; AV, RV **cinnamon**, q.v., as RSV in Rev 18[13]). All these words apparently refer to some kind of cassia wood. The cassia bark from the *Cinnamomum cassia* is very similar in smell and properties to cinnamon (q.v.).

CASTANET.—See MUSIC AND MUSICAL INSTRUMENTS, **4** (3) (*b*).

CASTLE.—**1.** In Gn 25[16], Nu 31[10], 1 Ch 6[54], an obsolete, if not erroneous, rendering in AV of a word denoting a nomad 'encampment' (so RV, RSV, save 1 Ch 6[54] where RSV has 'settlements').

2. In 1 Ch 11[5, 7] AV speaks of the 'castle' of Zion, the citadel or acropolis of the Jebusite city, but RV and RSV render as in 2 S 5[7, 9] 'stronghold' (AV 'fort' in v.[9]). A different word (*bîrāh*) is used of the castle or fortress (AV 'palace') which in Nehemiah's day defended the Temple (Neh 2[8] 7[2]), and of the fortified royal residence of the Persian kings at Susa (Neh 1[1], Est 1[2] etc.; AV, RV '**palace**,' RVm 'castle'; RSV '**capital**'). The fortress in Jerusalem to which the authors of the books of Maccabees and Josephus give the name of Acra, is termed 'the castle' in 2 Mac 4[27] (RSV 4[28]) 5[5] 10[20] AV, where RV throughout has '**citadel**' (so RSV, save 10[20] where it has 'towers'), as also in 1 Mac 1[33] (so RSV; AV 'strong hold') and elsewhere. See further, CITADEL.

3. See BARRACKS. A. R. S. K.—**H. H. R.**

CASTOR AND POLLUX.—See DIOSCURI.

CAT.—This animal is mentioned only in the Apocr. (Ep. Jer v.[22] [Gr. [21]].) Perhaps sacred (temple) cats; but the text has been questioned: Syr. reads 'weasels.' F. C. G.

CATARACTS.—See WATERSPOUTS.

CATERPILLAR.—See LOCUST.

CATHOLIC EPISTLES.—The title of 'Catholic' was given by the early Church to the seven Epistles which bear the names of James, Peter, John, and Jude. There is much uncertainty as to the meaning of the title. Perhaps the most probable explanation is that this group of Epistles was looked upon as addressed to the Church generally, while the Pauline Epistles were written to particular churches and were called forth by local circumstances.

CATHUA (1 Es 5[30]).—One of the heads of families of Temple servants who returned with Zerubbabel from captivity. It appears to correspond to **Giddel** in Ezr 2[47]; cf Neh 7[49].

CATTLE.—The word commonly used in OT is *miḳneh*, meaning primarily possessions or wealth—oxen, camels, sheep, and goats being the only wealth of peoples in a nomadic stage of civilization. It includes sometimes horses and asses, *e.g.* Ex 9[3], Job 1[3] (AVm, RVm; RSV leaves untranslated). The word is also sometimes rendered 'possessions' (*e.g.* Ec 2[7]), 'flocks' (Ps 78[48]), and 'herds' (Gn 47[18]). For other words rendered in EV 'cattle,' see BEAST. See also OX, SHEEP, SHEPHERD, etc. E. W. G. M.

CAUDA (AV wrongly **Clauda**; now *Gaudho*) is an island off the S. coast of Crete. St. Paul's ship, sailing from Myra to Rome, shortly after rounding Cape Matala was making in a WNW. direction, when a sudden strong wind coming from ENE. (see EURAQUILO) drove it along at a rapid rate for about 23 miles, till it got under the lee of Cauda (Ac 27[16]). Such a change of wind is frequent there at the present day. A. So.

CAUL.—The English word 'caul' is not used in RSV. It stands in AV and RV (1) in Is 3[18] (*shābhîs*) for a gold or silver headband (RSV 'headband'); (2) in Ex 29[13], Lv 3[4, 10, 15] 4[9] 7[4] 8[16, 25] 9[10, 19] (*yōthereth*) for the fatty mass (RSV 'appendage') at the opening of the liver (q.v.); (3) in Hos 13[8] (*seghôr*) for the pericardium, literally 'the enclosure of the heart' (RSV renders freely 'breast').

CAULDRON.—See HOUSE, 9.

CAUSEY.—This English word was used in the original edition of AV in 1 Ch 26[16, 18] (RV 'causeway,' RSV 'road'), and in the margin of Pr 15[19], Is 7[3] (RV, RSV 'highway'). It is now found only in Pr 15[19]m, being changed in modern editions in the other places into **causeway.** The Hebrew word is literally 'a raised way,' and is used of a public road, but never of a street in a city. The word 'causey' is still used in Scotland for the raised footpath by the side of a road or street.

CAVE.—The soft limestone hills of Palestine abound in caves, natural and artificial; and these attracted attention from the earliest antiquity. A remarkable series of stone age cultures has been found in caves near the NW. shore of the Sea of Galilee, in a ravine of Mt. Carmel, and elsewhere (cf C. C. McCown, *The Ladder of Progress in Palestine*). Lot (Gn 19[30]) and David (1 S 22[1] etc.) dwelt for a time in caves; and their use as places of hiding and refuge is illustrated by many passages, *e.g.* Jos 10[16], Jg 6[2], 1 K 18[4] etc. The Judaean Wilderness W. of the **Dead Sea** was especially famous for its caves (1 S 23[14, 24] 24, 2 S 17[9], 1 Mac 2[29–36]). In the 2nd cent. B.C. the **Essenes** found a haven there and at the time of the first Jewish revolt against **Rome** (A.D. 68–70) abandoned their scrolls in the caves near Khirbet Qumrân. At the time of the second Jewish revolt (A.D. 132–135) the warriors of Simon ben Kosibah (alias Bar Cochba) used several large caves of *Wâdī Murabbaʿât* as an outpost, where they likewise abandoned important documents, including letters from ben Kosibah himself. An even larger collection of such documents (together with well preserved artifacts) has been found in caves near En-gedi (P. Benoit, J. T. Milik, R. de Vaux, *Discoveries in the Judaean Desert*, ii; and Y. Yadin, *BA* xxiv, 1961). See also DEAD SEA SCROLLS.

Caves were also used at all periods in the history of Palestine for sepulture, as in the case of **Machpelah** (Gn 23). A remarkable series of caves are the great labyrinths tunnelled in the hills around *Beit Jibrîn*; one of these, in *Tell Sandaḥannah*, contains sixty chambers, united by doors and passages, and groups containing fourteen or fifteen chambers are quite common in the same hill. Another artificial cave near *Beit Jibrîn* contains a hall 80 ft. high and 400 ft. long; it has now fallen in. Other groups of caves, only less extensive, occur in various parts of Palestine on both sides of the Jordan. Little or nothing is known about the history of these great excavations. R. A. S. M.—**W. H. Br.**

CEDAR (*'erez*).—The finest of the trees of Lebanon, the principal constituent of its 'glory' (Is 35[2] 60[13]); it was noted for its strength (Ps 29[5]), its height (2 K 19[23]), and its majesty (1 K 4[33], 2 K 14[9], Zec 11[1f]). Its wood was full of resin (Ps 104[16]), and, largely on that account, was one of the most valuable kinds of timber for building, especially for internal fittings. It was exceedingly durable, being not readily infected with worms, and took a high polish (cf 1 K 10[27], Ca 1[17], Jer 22[14]). It was suitable, too, for carved work (Is 44[14f]). In all these respects the 'cedar of Lebanon' (*Cedrus Libani*) answers the requirements (but Koehler [*ZAW* lv (1937), 163–65] maintains that *Abies Cilicia* better fits some of the references). Though but a dwarf in comparison with the Indian cedar, *Cedrus Libani* is the most magnificent tree in Syria; it attains a height of from 80 to 100 feet, and spreads out its branches horizontally so as to give a beautiful shade (Ezk 31[3]); it is evergreen, and has characteristic egg-shaped cones. The great region of this cedar is now the Cilician Taurus Mountains beyond Mersina, but small groves survive in places in the Lebanon. The most famous of these is that at *Kadisha*, where there are upwards of 400 trees, some of great age. In a few references *'erez* does not mean the *Cedrus Libani*, but some other conifer. This is specially the case where 'cedarwood' is used in the ritual of cleansing after defilement by contact with a leper (Lv 14[4]) or a dead body (Nu 19[6]). Probably *'erez* here is a species of juniper, *Juniperus Sabina*, which grows in the wilderness. The reference in Nu 24[6] to 'cedar trees beside the waters' can hardly apply to the Lebanon cedar, which flourishes best on bare mountain slopes. E. W. G. M.—**H. H. R.**

CEDRON.—1. 1 Mac 15[39, 41] (AV); see KEDRON. **2.** Jn 18[1] (AV); see KIDRON, THE BROOK.

CEILAN, 1 Es 5[15] (AV).—See KILAN.

CEILED, CEILING.—The latter occurs only 1 K 6[9] (AV, RV 'covered') [15] (AV, RV 'ceiling'), where it has its modern signification. The verb, on the other hand, which is found only in AV, RV, should everywhere be rendered **'panelled'** (2 Ch 3[5] RSV 'lined'; Jer 22[14] RSV 'panelling'; Ezk 41[16], Hag 1[4] RSV 'panelled'), the reference being to the panels of cedar or other costly wood with which the inner walls were lined. See HOUSE, **4.**

CELLAR.—See HOUSE, **4.**

CENCHREAE (AV **Cenchrea** is wrong) was the southern harbour of Corinth, on the Saronic Gulf about 7 miles E. of Corinth. It was a mere village, and existed solely for the transit of goods to and from Corinth. Thence St. Paul set sail for Syria (Ac 18[18]). Phoebe, the woman commended for her service to the church here (Ro 16[1]), probably carried St. Paul's Epistle to Rome. A. So.—**E. G. K.**

CENDEBEUS (RV **Cendebaeus**).—A general of Antiochus VII. Sidetes, who was given the command of the sea-coast, and sent with an army into Palestine in order to enforce the claims of Antiochus against Simon Maccabaeus. In a battle which took place in a plain not far from Modin the Jews gained a complete victory over Cendebeus, and pursued the Syrians as far as Kedron and the neighbourhood of Azotus (1 Mac 15[38]–16[9]; cf Jos. *Ant.* XIII. vii. 3 [225–227]).

CENSER.—See FIREPAN, INCENSE.

CENSUS.—See QUIRINIUS.

CENTURION.—A Roman military officer, corresponding in number of infantry commanded by him (100) to the modern 'captain,' but in his status like our non-commissioned officers. The Capernaum centurion (Mt 8[5-13], Lk 7[2-10]) perhaps belonged to the army of Herod, and he may have been a Jew. Some of the captains mentioned in the NT were on special service in command of their units, and separated from the cohorts or legions of which they formed a part. See CAPTAIN. A. So.—**J. S. K.**

CEPHAS.—See PETER.

CERAS, 1 Es 5[29] (AV).—See KEROS.

CETAB, 1 Es 5[30] (AV).—See KETAB.

CHABRIS.—One of the three rulers of Bethulia (Jth 6[14] 8[10] 10[6]).

CHADIAS, 1 Es 5[20] (AV).—See CHADIASANS.

CHADIASAI, 1 Es 5[20] (RV).—See CHADIASANS.

CHADIASANS (AV 'they of **Chadias**; RV **Chadiasai**), 1 Es 5[20].—They and the Ammidians are mentioned as returning to the number of 422, with Zerubbabel. There are no corresponding names in the lists of Ezra and Nehemiah.

CHAEREAS (AV **Chereas**) held command at the fortress of Gazara, *i.e.* probably Jazer (OT Gezer) in the trans-Jordanic territory (see 1 Mac 5[6-8]). He was slain upon the capture of Gazara by Judas Maccabaeus (2 Mac 10[32-38]).

CHAFF.—See AGRICULTURE, **3.**

CHAIN is used in two different senses. **1.** Chains for securing prisoners are denoted by a variety of words in OT and NT, which are also rendered by **'bonds'** or **'fetters,'** although the monuments show that ropes were more generally used for this purpose. **2.** A chain of precious metal was worn as a sign of rank, as by Joseph and Daniel, or purely as an ornament. See ORNAMENTS, **2.** A. R. S. K.

CHALCEDONY.—See JEWELS AND PRECIOUS STONES.

CHALCOL, 1 K 4[31] (AV).—See CALCOL.

CHALDAEA, CHALDAEANS.—The Hebrew *Kaśdîm* is generally rendered 'Chaldees' (Gn 11[28]), and in Jer 50[10] 51[24] 24[5] 25[12], and often, is used for 'Babylonian.' The word is derived from the Babylonian *[māt]Kaldī*, the district in the SE. of Babylonia, and eventually limited to the sea-coast. From 1100 B.C. onwards, Aramaean nomadic tribes pushed into the country. Ukîn-zēr, a Chaldaean, became the first king of the 9th Babylonian dynasty which included Merodach-baladan II. (721–700 B.C.): cf Is 39, 2 K 20[12ff]. Nabopolassar, a Chaldaean, founded the Chaldaean kingdom (625 B.C.).

The name as applied since Jerome to the Aramaic portions of Daniel and Ezra is incorrect. The use of the term 'Chaldaean' (Dn 1[4] and often) to denote a class of astrologers is not found in native sources, but arose from a transfer of a national name to the Babylonians in general, and occurs in Strabo, Diodorus, etc. It can hardly be older than Persian times. C. H. W. J.—**T. F.**

CHALK-STONES (Is 27[9] only).—The expression is of much interest, as showing that the practice of burning limestone and slaking with water was followed in Palestine in OT times.

CHALLENGE.—To 'challenge' in the language of AV is to *claim*, as in Golding's translation of Calvin's *Job*, p. 578; 'Iob neuer went about to challenge such perfection, as to haue no sinne in him.' The word occurs in Ex 22[9] (RV, RSV 'one says, This is it'), in the heading of Is 45 'By his omnipotency he challengeth obedience,' and in Job 3[5] AVm (AV 'stain'; RV, RSV 'claim').

CHALPHI (AV **Calphi**).—The father of Judas, one of the two captains of Jonathan Maccabaeus who stood firm in a battle fought against the Syrians at Hazor in N. Galilee (1 Mac 11[70]).

CHAMBER.—Now obsolescent, is used by EV in a variety of connexions where modern usage employs 'room,' as *e.g.* 'bed-chamber,' 'upper chamber,' etc. See, generally, HOUSE. For the Temple chambers, see TEMPLE.

CHAMBERLAIN.—In OT the word occurs in 2 K 23[11] and repeatedly in AV and RV in Esther, where the original is *sārîs*, 'eunuch' (so RSV); but it is generally believed that this name is not to be taken always in a literal sense, and hence it is often rendered by the word 'officer.' In Esther, however, the chamberlain evidently belongs to that class of persons who are entrusted with the watchful care of the harems of Oriental monarchs. In NT at Ac 12[20] it is said that the people of Tyre and Sidon sought the favour of Herod Agrippa through the mediation of Blastus 'the king's chamberlain,' showing that the office was one of considerable influence. The word occurs again in AV in Ro 16[23], but is rendered in RV and RSV more accurately 'city treasurer.'

CHAMBERS OF THE SOUTH.—See STARS.

CHAMELEON.—The chameleon (*Chamoeleon vulgaris*) is a very common Palestine lizard. It may be found on hot days clinging with its bird-like feet and prehensile tail to the trees, or passing with slow and deliberate walk over the ground. It is remarkable for its marvellous protective gift of changing the colour of its skin to resemble its surroundings, and for its eyes which, moving independently, one looking backwards while the other looks to the front, give it an unusual range of vision. Even to-day it is supposed by the ignorant, as in olden times, to live upon air. In reality it lives on small insects, catching them by means of its long sticky tongue, which it can protrude and withdraw with extraordinary quickness. Two words in Lv 11[30] are rendered 'chameleon' in EV. In the AV *kōaḥ* is so translated, but RV and RSV have **'land crocodile'** (see LIZARD); while in RV and RSV *tinshemeth* is rendered 'chameleon' (AV 'mole'). See MOLE. E. W. G. M.

CHAMOIS (*zemer*).—The translation of *zemer* in AV and RV in Dt 14[5] as 'chamois' and in LXX as 'camelopard,' *i.e.* giraffe, is certainly incorrect, as neither of these animals occurs in Palestine. Tristram suggests the wild sheep, *Ovis tragelaphus*, an animal about 3 feet high with long curved horns, well known to the Bedouin. RSV renders '*mountain-sheep*.' E. W. G. M.

CHAMPAIGN.—This spelling in modern editions of AV has replaced *champion* (Dt 11^{30} [RV, RSV 'Arabah'], Jth 5^1 [RV, RSV 'plains']) and *champian* (Ezk 37^2) of the 1611 edition of AVm. The word means an open plain.

CHANAAN, Ac 7^{11} 13^9 (AV)=**Canaan** (q.v.).

CHANCELLOR.—See BELTETHMUS and REHUM.

CHANGES OF RAIMENT.—Gn 45^{22}, Jg 14^{12f}, 2 K 5^5 (AV, RV). A literal translation of a Hebrew expression which not merely denotes a change of garments in the modern sense, but implies that the 'changes' are superior, in material or texture or both, to those ordinarily worn. Hence 'gala dresses,' 'festal robes,' or the like, may be taken as a fair equivalent. RSV renders '**festal garments.**' Gifts of such gala robes have always been common in the East as special marks of favour or distinction. Cf DRESS, **7.** A. R. S. K.

CHANNUNEUS, 1 Es 8^{48} (AV).—See HANANIAH, **11.**

CHANUNEUS, 1 Est 8^{48} (RV).—See HANANIAH, **11.**

CHAPHENATHA (AV **Caphenatha**), 1 Mac 12^{37}.—Close to Jerusalem on the east. Unknown.

CHAPITER.—An architectural term for the capital of a column, found a number of times in AV and RV (Ex 36^{38} $38^{17, 19, 28}$, 1 K 7^{16}, 2 K 25^{17}, 2 Ch 4^{12f}, Jer 52^{22}, Am 9^1, Zeph 2^{14}); RSV in all these cases has '**capital.**'

CHAPMAN.—A chapman is a trader, the word being still used in some places for a travelling merchant. It occurs in AV and RV in 2 Ch 9^{14}, and in RV in 1 K 10^{15} (AV 'merchantmen'); RSV has 'trader' in both places.

CHARAATHALAN (AV **Charaathalar**), 1 Es 5^{36}.—A name given to a leader of certain families who returned under Zerubbabel. But 'Charaathalan leading them and Allar' is due to some perversion of the original, which has 'Cherub, Addan, Immer' (so RSV), three names of *places* in Babylonia, *from which* the return was made (Ezr 2^{59}; cf Neh 7^{61}).

CHARACA, 2 Mac 12^{17} (AV).—See CHARAX.

CHARASHIM, 1 Ch 4^{14} (AV).—See GE-HARASHIM.

CHARAX (2 Mac 12^{17}, AV 'to Characa').—East of Jordan, and apparently in the land of Tob. Unknown.

CHARCOAL.—Found only in RSV in Pr 26^{21}, Jn 18^{18} 21^9, in all of which AV and RV have 'coals.' See COAL.

CHARCUS, 1 Es 5^{32} (AV).—See BARKOS.

CHAREA, 1 Es 5^{32}=**Harsha,** Ezr 2^{52}, Neh 7^{54}.

CHARGER.—An obsolete word for a large flat dish on which meat was served, Nu $7^{13, 19, 25}$ etc. (AV, RV; RSV 'plate'), Mt 14^8, Mk 6^{25} (AV, RV; RSV 'platter').

CHARIOT.—The original home of the chariot was Western Asia, from which it passed to Egypt and other countries. The earliest models and representations come from pre-dynastic and early dynastic Ur (cf Sir Leonard Woolley, *Ur Excavations, IV. The Early Periods* [1955]). In OT chariots are associated mainly with war-like operations, although they also appear not infrequently as the 'carriages,' so to say, of kings, princes, and high dignitaries (Gn 50^9, 2 K 5^9, Jer 17^{25}; cf Ac 8^{28ff} the case of the Ethiopian eunuch) in times of peace. When royal personages drove in state, they were preceded by a body of 'runners' (2 S 15^1, 1K 1^5).

The war chariot appears to have been introduced among the Hebrews by David (2 S 8^4 LXX), but it did not become part of the organized military equipment of the State till the reign of Solomon. This monarch is said to have organized a force of 1400 chariots (1 K 10^{26}, 2 Ch 1^{14}), which he distributed among the principal cities of his realm (1 K 9^{19} 10^{26}). At this time, also, a considerable trade sprang up in connexion with the importation of chariots and horses. The nature of this trade has been clarified by W. F. Albright, who renders the crucial passage, 1 K 10^{28f}, as follows: 'And Solomon's horses were exported from Cilicia: the merchants of the king procured them from Cilicia at the current price; and a chariot was exported from Egypt at the rate of 600 shekels of silver, and a horse from Cilicia at 150; and thus (at this rate) they delivered them by their agency to all the kings of the Hittites and the kings of Aram' (*ARI*, p. 135). Solomon apparently controlled the trade in horses and chariots between Egypt and the north, delivering the famed Cilician horses to Egypt, and the equally famous Egyptian chariots to the Hittites and Aramaeans, while reaping a middleman's profit for himself and his merchants. Chariot-making had been brought to a peak of craftsmanship in Egypt; the best examples, from an earlier period, are the elaborate state chariots found in the tomb of Tut-ankh-amun (cf Howard Carter, *The Tomb of Tut-ankh-amen*, Vol. II. [1927], ch. iv. and plates).

Until the Macedonian period, when we first hear of chariots armed with scythes (2 Mac 13^2), the war chariot of antiquity followed one general type, alike among the Assyrians and the Egyptians, the Hittites and the Syrians. It consisted of a light wooden body, which was always open behind. The axle, fitted with stout wheels with six or eight spokes (for the Hebrew terms see 1 K 7^{33}), was set as far back as possible for the sake of greater steadiness, and consequently a surer aim. The pole was fixed into the axle, and after passing beneath the floor of the chariot was bent upwards and connected by a band of leather to the front of the chariot. The horses, two in number, were yoked to the pole. Traces were not used. In Assyrian representations a third horse sometimes appears, evidently as a reserve. The body of the chariot naturally received considerable decoration, for which, and for other details, reference may be made to J. B. Pritchard, *ANEP*, *s.v.* 'chariot,' where numerous illustrations are given. The 'chariots of iron' of the ancient Canaanites (Jos 17^{16}, Jg 1^{19} 4^3) were chariots of which the woodwork was strengthened by metal plates.

In Egypt and Assyria the normal number of the occupants of a war chariot was two—the driver, who was often armed with a whip, and the combatant, an archer whose bow-case and quiver were usually attached to the right-hand side of the car. Egyptian representations of Hittite chariots, however, show three occupants, of whom the third carries a shield to protect his comrades. This was almost certainly the practice among the Hebrews also, since a frequently recurring military term, *shālish*, signifies 'the third man,' presumably in such a chariot.

Mention may be made, finally, of the chariots set up at the entrance to the Temple at Jerusalem, which were destroyed by Josiah. They were doubtless dedicated originally to Y″, although they are termed by the Hebrew historian 'chariots of the sun' (2 K 23^{11}), their installation having been copied from the Babylonian custom of representing Shamash, the sun-god, riding in a chariot. A. R. S. K.—**D. N. F.**

CHARITY.—The word 'charity' never occurs in AV in the sense of *almsgiving*, but always with the meaning of *love*. It comes from the Vulg. *caritas*, which was frequently used to translate the Greek *agapē*, probably because *amor* had impure associations, and because *dilectio* (which is sometimes so used) was scarcely strong enough. Wycliffe followed the Vulg., as did afterwards the Rhemish translators. Tyndale and the Genevan Version preferred 'love'; but in the Bishops' Bible 'charity' was again often used, and the AV followed the Bishops in this. In the RV, however, 'charity' never occurs, the Greek *agapē* being everywhere rendered 'love.' RSV has one occurrence (Ac 9^{36}).

For **Feast of Charity** (Jd 12 AV) see LOVE FEAST.

CHARM.—See AMULETS AND CHARMS; and MAGIC, DIVINATION, AND SORCERY.

CHARME, 1 Es 5^{25} (RV).—See HARIM, **2.**

CHARMIS.—Son of Melchiel, one of three rulers or elders of Bethulia (Jth 6^{15} 8^{10} 10^6).

CHASE.—See Hunting.

CHASEBA, 1 Es 5^{31} (AV, RV).—See Chezib.

CHASM.—See Gulf.

CHASPHO.—Unknown site near a large lake in Gilead, 1 Mac $5^{26, 36}$ (AV, RV **Casphor**); called **Caspin** in 2 Mac 12^{13} (AV **Caspis**).

CHASTITY.—See Crimes and Punishments, **3**, and Marriage.

CHEBAR.—A canal in Babylonia (Ezk 1^{1ff}) beside which the principal colony of the first Exile of Judah was planted. It has been identified by the Pennsylvania expedition with the canal *Kabaru*, named in cuneiform documents of the time of Artaxerxes i. It apparently lay to the E. of Nippur. The name means 'great.' Hence for 'the river Chebar' we may read 'the Grand Canal.' J. F. McC.

CHECKER WORK.—A designation applied in 1 K 7^{17} to the net-ornament on the pillars before the Temple, and in Ex $28^{4, 39}$ (RV 'chequer work'; AV 'broidered,' 'embroider') of the embroidery of the priestly garments.

CHEDORLAOMER.—King of Elam (Gn 14^{1}), and one of the four kings who raided Canaan in the time of Abraham. It is generally accepted that the name represents the Elamite form Kudur-lagamar. Similar forms, *e.g.* Kudur-mabug, are known from the Elamite king-lists, but the name Kudur-lagamar is not found there. The Elamite kingdom, lying in the mountains to the E. of the Tigris-Euphrates valley, had been an important factor in the politics of Babylonia from very early times, and it is not impossible that in the time of Abraham the Elamites played a part in the struggles of the Amorite princes which may have involved all the states from the valley of the Orontes to the E. of the Tigris. S. H. He.

CHEEK.—The seat of health and beauty (Ca 1^{10} 5^{13}). To be smitten on the cheek was the climax of insult and violence (1 K 22^{24}, Job 16^{10}, Ps 3^{7}). That the command in Mt 5^{39} is not to be interpreted literally is shown by Christ's own protest in Jn 18^{23}. C. W. E.

CHEESE.—See Milk.

CHELAL.—One who had married a foreign wife, Ezr 10^{30}.

CHELCIAS.—AV for Hilkiah in Bar $1^{1, 7}$, Sus $^{2, 29}$; see Hilkiah, **3, 9, 10.**

CHELLIANS.—Probably the inhabitants of the town Chelous (q.v.). Cf Jth 1^{9} 2^{23}.

CHELLUS, Jth 1^{9} (AV, RV).—See Chelous.

CHELOUS.—From the text of Jth 1^{9} (AV, RV **Chellus**), this place is supposed to have been situated SW. of Jerusalem near Betane and N. of Kadesh and the 'river of Egypt,' *i.e.* the *Wâdī-el-ʿArîsh*; but any certain identification is impossible.

CHELOD.—Jth 1^{6b} RSV reads, not as AV and RV 'many nations of the sons of Chelod assembled themselves to battle,' but 'many nations joined the forces of the Chaldeans.' It is not quite certain whether the 'many nations' are allies of Nebuchadrezzar or of Arphaxad, or whether they come to help or to fight the 'sons of Cheleoud.' Probably v.^{6b} summarizes v.^{6a}; hence 'sons of Cheleoud' should be Nebuchadrezzar's army. But he is, in Judith, king of Assyrians, not Chaldaeans. No probable conjecture as to an Aramaic original has been made. F. C. G.

CHELUB.—**1.** A descendant of Judah, 1 Ch 4^{11}. **2.** The father of Ezri, one of David's superintendents, 1 Ch 27^{26}.

CHELUBAI (1 Ch 2^{9}).—Another form of **Caleb**. Cf 1 Ch $2^{18, 42}$, and see Caleb, and Carmi, **2.**

CHELUHI.—One of the sons of Bani who had married a foreign wife, Ezr 10^{35}.

CHEMARIM.—This word is found only in Zeph 1^{4} (RV; AV 'Chemarims'; RSV 'idolatrous priests'); but the original of which it is the transliteration is used also at 2 K 23^{5} and Hos 10^{5}, and in both instances *Chemarim* is placed in the margin of AV and RV. *Kōmer*, of which *kᵉmārîm* is the plural, is of Aramaic origin, and when used in Syriac carries no unfavourable connotation. In the Hebrew of the OT, however, *kᵉmārîm* always has a bad sense; it is applied to the priests who conducted the worship of the calves (2 K 23^{5}, Hos 10^{5}), and to those who served the Baalim (Zeph 1^{4}). Ḳimḥi believed the original significance of the verbal form was 'to be black,' and explained the use of the noun by the assertion that the idolatrous priests wore black garments. Others take the root to mean, 'to be sad,' the *kōmer* being a sad, ascetic person; or 'be excited,' the *kōmer* being 'the excited one.'

CHEMOSH.—The national god of the Moabites, Nu 21^{29}. On the Moabite Stone (see Moab) Mesha attributes his victory over Israel to the help of Chemosh. It was for this 'abomination of Moab' that Solomon erected a temple (1 K 11^{7}), later destroyed by Josiah (2 K 23^{13}). We read of a king of Moab sacrificing his heir to Chemosh in a national emergency (2 K 3^{27}). In Jg 11^{24} 'Chemosh' is probably a scribal error for 'Milcom' (q.v.), who was the national god of the Ammonites.

CHENAANAH.—**1.** A Benjamite, 1 Ch 7^{10}. **2.** The father of Zedekiah the false prophet in the reign of Ahab, 1 K $22^{11, 24}$, 2 Ch $18^{10, 23}$.

CHENANI.—A Levite, Neh 9^{4}.

CHENANIAH.—Leader of the Levites in music at the removal of the Ark from the house of Obed-edom, 1 Ch $15^{22, 27}$; named among the officers and judges over Israel, 26^{29}.

CHEPHAR-AMMONI ('village of the Ammonites').—A town of Benjamin, Jos 18^{24} (AV **Chephar-haammonai**); situation unknown.

CHEPHAR-HAAMMONAI, Jos 18^{24} (AV).—See Chephar-Ammoni.

CHEPHIRAH ('village').—One of four Hivite cities which made peace with the Hebrews (Jos 9^{17}), incorporated in the tribe of Benjamin (18^{26}); repeopled after the Captivity, Ezr 2^{25}, Neh 7^{29}, 1 Es 5^{19} (AV, RV **Caphira**); modern *Tell Kephîreh*, SW. of Gibeon.

CHEQUER WORK.—See Checker Work.

CHERAN.—One of the children of Dishon, the son of Seir, the Horite, Gn 36^{26}, 1 Ch 1^{41}.

CHERETHITES AND PELETHITES.—These were mercenary soldiers, who probably began to attach themselves to David whilst he was an outlaw (2 S 22^{2}, etc.), and subsequently became the king's bodyguard and the nucleus of his army (2 S 8^{18} 15^{18} $20^{7, 23}$, 1 K $1^{38, 44}$, 1 Ch 18^{17}). Benaiah, whom Josephus calls 'captain of the guard' (*Ant.* vii. xi. 8 [293]), was their commander. They accompanied David in his retreat from Jerusalem (2 S 15^{18}), fought against Absalom (2 S $20^{7, 23}$), and acted as Solomon's bodyguard at his coronation (1 K $1^{38, 44}$). The Cherethites apparently lived in Philistine territory (1 S 30^{14}), dwelling with the Philistines on the coast (Ezk 25^{16}, Zeph 2^{5}); and the name *Pelethites* may have been a corrupt form of *Philistines*. Unwillingness to believe that foreigners stood so near the national hero led certain Jewish scholars to assert that the two clans were Israelites. The appellation 'Cherethite' seems to be connected with Crete, and there is good ground (but see Caphtor) for the belief that Caphtor, from which Am 9^{7} says the Philistines came, is to be identified with Crete. The LXX of Ezk 25^{16}, Zeph 2^{5} used *Cretans* as the equivalent of *Cherethites*. The *Kᵉthîbh* of 2 S 20^{23} reads Carites in the Massoretic text (see Carites). J. T.—**S. H. Hn.**

CHERITH.—The 'brook' by which Elijah lived (1 K $17^{3, 5}$) was on the E. of Jordan; possibly *Wâdī Yâbis.*

CHERUB.—One of the places in Babylonia, from which certain families who returned with Zerubbabel failed to prove their register as genuine branches of the Israelite people (Ezr 2^{59}, Neh 7^{61}; also 1 Es 5^{36} RSV, where AV has **Charaathalar** and RV **Charaathalan,** q.v.).

CHERUBIM.—These creatures were connected with the Holy of Holies and are therefore closely associated with the presence of God in OT religion and worship. By inheritance from the OT they also figure in the background of Christian worship as giving constant utterance to the praises of God. In fulfilment of their functions as guardians of the approach to Yahweh or as bearers of His throne or chariot, they serve as a barrier or screen between God and man and help to enhance His aloofness, His holiness, and His majesty.

They were creatures of the imagination, an imagination probably fed by representations of winged creatures in ancient art. Being such, there is no clear and constant description of them in the OT. Each writer who mentioned them might conceive them in the way that best suited his idea of their purpose and duties. They are spoken of as winged creatures with faces, but beyond that agreement almost ceases. In one place (Ezk 41^{18}) they are said to have two faces, one of a man and one of a lion, but in another place (Ezk 10^{14}) they have four, those of a cherub, a man, a lion, and an eagle. They stood on their feet, presumably upright, as men do (2 Ch 3^{13}). According to Ezekiel (10^{8}) they had hands under their wings. They were identified by Ezekiel (10^{15}) with the living creatures that he saw by the river Chebar (ch. 1). These creatures had four wings and four faces, man, lion, ox, and eagle, and under their wings on their four sides they had human hands. In Ezekiel's vision there were four of these creatures, matching the four points of the compass and signifying ability to move in all directions, but in Exodus (25^{18}) there were two, one on either side of the Ark. There is no indication of their size in Ezekiel's description, but in Exodus they are commensurate with the Ark and its cover (mercy-seat) and of one piece with it (Ex 25^{10ff}). The Ark was 2½-cubits long and 1½ broad and high. In Solomon's Temple, on the other hand, the two cherubim were colossal figures of olive wood, 10-cubits high (1 K 6^{23}).

They seem to have been Assyrian in origin, both in conception and in name. The Akkadian word *karibu* means 'one who prays,' 'an intercessor.' This is the function of secondary gods called *lamassu* or *šedu* who are represented as winged creatures with human faces. They guarded the entrance to temples and palaces and were commissioned to intercede for men. Two of these may be seen in the British Museum. One of them once guarded the doorway to the palace of Ashurnasirpal at Nimrud; the other also came from Nimrud. One has the body of a bull, the other that of a lion, but otherwise they are very similar, having the wings and breast feathers of an eagle and the head of a man. They stand about 12 feet high. Assyrian sculptures offer several examples of winged creatures of one kind or another. These, or similar representations, may well have fired the imagination of the Hebrew writers.

If it was these Assyrian temple guardians and intercessors upon which the Hebrews were dependent for their idea of the cherubim it is not without interest that they already, as intercessors, had some spiritual significance which the Hebrews, true to their genius, greatly enriched when they enthroned Yahweh upon them. There were three more or less distinct functions of the cherubim as they appear in the Bible. **1.** They were guardians to the Garden of Eden (Gn 3^{24}, Ezk 28$^{14, 16}$). The cherubim in 1 K 6$^{23-28}$ 8^{7} may be regarded as guardians of the Ark and of the inner shrine.

2. They are bearers of Yahweh, or of the throne of Yahweh. Ps 18^{10} (=2 S 22^{11}) speaks of Yahweh 'riding upon a cherub' (where the singular may be collective in force). This may be simply a conventional representation of the storm clouds, for in Ps 104^{3} the clouds are his chariot, but it may be intended to represent the chariot itself as a kind of movable throne borne upon these creatures. Chariot and cherubim are closely linked in 1 Ch 28^{18}. In Ezekiel the cherubim clearly act as the bearers of Yahweh who is seated in person above them (10^{1ff}). This conception of the throne of Yahweh carried by the (two) winged creatures became conventionalized in the representation of the Ark in the inner sanctuary surmounted by its covering (mercy-seat) and guarded by the cherubim, at the very heart of the sanctuary, the abode of Yahweh (Ex 25^{18ff}, cf He 9^{5}). It was here that Yahweh would meet with Moses (Ex 25^{22}) and speak to him (Nu 7^{89}). The Ark itself was almost certainly at one time thought of as the earthly throne of Yahweh and we may imagine Him as invisibly enthroned there. At some point in the development of the idea of the cherubim as bearers of Yahweh to that of guardians of His throne the phrase was probably coined 'The Lord of Hosts who is enthroned on the cherubim'; it occurs seven times, viz.: 1 S 4^{4}, 2 S 6^{2}, 2 K 19^{15}, 1 Ch 13^{6}, Ps 80^{1} 99^{1}, Is 37^{16}. The throne and the Ark were almost certainly associated with one another at some time and it is possible that the cover (AV and RV 'mercy-seat') may have taken the place of the throne. **3.** The third function of the cherubim was as decoration motifs on the walls and doors of the Temple (1 K 6$^{29, 32, 35}$), on the panels of the bases (1 K 7$^{29, 36}$), on the curtains (Ex 26^{1} 36^{8}), and on the veil (Ex 26^{31} 36^{35}). They occur in association with lions and oxen, palm trees and open flowers, but the significance of the connexion is not certain. The palm trees occur again in association with cherubim in Ezk 41^{18}, a representation which 'recalls the winged genii who fertilize the palm trees on the walls of Ashurnasirpal's palace at Nimrud' (G. A. Cooke, *Ezekiel* (ICC), p. 451).

In later literature cherubim rank among the higher orders of angels (cf 1 En 20^{7}) and appear in Rev 4^{6ff} as the living creatures who give perpetual praise to God. (For a discussion of their nature and function see the article, 'Les Chérubin,' by P. Dhorme and L. H. Vincent, in *Revue Biblique* 1926, pp. 328–358 and 481–495, and for pictures of winged creatures see *ANEP*, 1954.)

L. H. B.

CHESALON.—A town of Judah, near Kiriath-jearim, Jos 15^{10}; modern *Keslā*.

CHESED.—One of the sons of Nahor and Milcah, Gn 22^{22}. The form of the name might suggest that he is the eponymous ancestor of the Kasdim, or Chaldaeans. But it is doubtful whether these are the Chaldaeans of S. Babylonia (Gn 11^{31}). It is more probable that the nomadic tribe mentioned in 2 K 24^{2}, Job 1^{17} is meant.

CHESIL.—A town of Judah, Jos 15^{30} (LXX *Bethel*). In the parallel passage, Jos 19^{4}, the name *Bethul* stands, and in 1 Ch 4^{30} *Bethuel*. Possible modern *Kh. er-Râs*.

CHESNUT TREE, Gn 30^{37}, Ezk 31^{8} (AV).—See Plane Tree.

CHESULLOTH.—A town of Issachar, Jos 19^{18}; probably to be identified with **Chisloth-tabor,** 19^{12}, and so on the border of Zebulun; modern *Iksâl* at the foot of the Nazareth hills.

CHETH.—See Ḥeth.

CHETTIIM, 1 Mac 1^{1} (AV).—See Kittim.

CHEZIB.—**1.** A place mentioned Gn 38^{5}; possibly the same as **Achzib, 2** (q.v.). **2.** Head of a family of Temple servants, 1 Es 5^{31} (AV, RV **Chaseba**). There is no corresponding name in the parallel Ezr 2^{47}, Neh 7^{50}.

CHIDON.—The name of the threshing floor where Uzzah died, 1 Ch 13^{9}; called **Nacon** in 2 S 6^{6} (AV **Nachon**).

CHIEF OF ASIA.—Ac 19^{31}; RV 'chief officers of Asia'; RSV 'Asiarchs.' See Asiarch.

CHIEF MUSICIAN.—See Psalms, **2.**

CHILD, CHILDREN.—**1. Value set on the possession of children.**—Throughout the Bible a noteworthy characteristic is the importance and happiness assigned to the possession of children, and, correspondingly, the intense sorrow and disappointment of childless parents. Children were regarded as Divine gifts (Gn 4[1] 33[5]), pledges of God's favour, the heritage of the Lord (Ps 127[3]). It followed naturally that **barrenness** was looked upon as a reproach, *i.e.* a punishment inflicted by God, and involving, for the woman, disgrace in the eyes of the world. Thus Sarah was despised by her more fortunate maid Hagar (Gn 16[4]); Rachel in envy of Leah cried, 'Give me children or I shall die!' (Gn 30[1]); Hannah's rival taunted her to make her irritated, because the Lord had closed her womb (1 S 1[6]); Elizabeth rejoiced when the Lord took away her 'reproach among men' (Lk 1[25]). 'He gives the barren woman a home, making her the joyous mother of children' (Ps 113[9]) cries the Psalmist as the climax of his praise. The reward of a man who fears the Lord shall be a wife like a fruitful vine, and children like olive shoots around his table (Ps 128[3]). Jesus refers to a woman's 'joy that a child (Gr. 'human being') is born into the world' (Jn 16[21]). An apostle, reflecting on the effect of Eve's transgression, writes, 'Yet woman will be saved through bearing children' (1 Ti 2[15]). Not only is natural parental affection set forth in these and similar passages, but also a strong sense of the worldly advantages which accompanied the condition of parentage. A man who was a father, especially of sons, was a rich man; his position was dignified and influential; his possessions were secured to his family, and his name perpetuated. 'Be fruitful and multiply, and fill the earth and subdue it' (Gn 1[28]) was the blessing desired by every married couple, for fatherhood involved expansion of property and increase in importance and wealth.

2. The parent-child relationship.—The position of children was one of complete subordination to their parents. That the father had powers of life and death over his children is indicated by many references to child sacrifice (Gn 22[1–14], Lv 18[21] 20[2–5], Dt 12[31] 18[10], Jg 11[30–40], 1 K 16[34], 2 K 3[27] 21[6] 23[10], Jer 7[31] 19[5] 32[35], Ezk 16[20–21] 20[26, 31] 23[37, 39], Mic 6[7]). However, these powers over children were limited (Dt 21[18–21]). Several passages urge care, even to severity, in the rearing of children (Pr 3[12] 13[24] 22[6, 15] 23[13] 29[15]) including constant religious nurture and parental justice (Dt 6[6f.] 11[19] 21[15–17] 24[16], Pr 22[6]). Children must be reverent and obedient to their parents (Ex 20[12], Lv 19[3], Pr 1[8], Eph 6[1], Col 3[20]). Any one striking or cursing his father or mother was to be put to death (Ex 21[15, 17]). Any one who was disrespectful to his parents was accursed (Dt 27[16]). Irreverence on the part of children towards the prophet Elisha was the occasion for a striking instance of Divine judgment (2 K 2[23f]). The outcome of this dependence of children upon their parents, and of their subordination to them, was an intensely strong sense of the closeness of the filial bond, and a horror of any violation of it. A son who could bring himself to defy his father and break away from his home life was indeed no longer worthy to be called a son (Lk 15[19]). The disobedience of Israel was bewailed in penitence by the prophet because it appeared to him like the most heinous crime, the rebellion of children against a loving father: 'Sons have I reared and brought up, but they have rebelled against me' (Is 1[2]). 'In his love and in his pity he redeemed them; . . . But they rebelled and grieved his holy spirit' (Is 63[9f]; cf Is 30[1], Ezk 20[21]). Children were expected to follow in the footsteps of their parents and to resemble them (Mal 4[6]). Hence such expressions as 'Abraham's children' (Jn 8[39]), which carried the notion of resemblance in character. Hence also the figurative use of the word 'children': 'children of transgression' (Is 57[4]), 'sons of disobedience' (Eph 2[2] 5[6]). Phrases like these are closely connected with others in which the words 'children' or 'sons' are used in a spiritual sense conveying the ideas of love and trust and obedience: 'my son Mark' (1 P 5[13]); 'my little children,' used by the apostle Paul in touching anxiety for the spiritual welfare of the Galatians (Gal 4[19]), and the frequent intimate form of address in the First Letter of John (1 Jn 2[1, 12, 28] 3[7, 18] 4[4] 5[21]).

3. The feeling for childhood.—Tenderness towards child life, appreciation of the simplicity, the helplessness, of children, affection of parents for their children, and children for their parents: all these are features of the Bible which the most superficial reader cannot fail to observe. There are many touching and vivid examples of and references to parental love. All the sons and daughters of Jacob rose up to comfort him for the loss of Joseph, but he refused to be comforted (Gn 37[35]). 'If I am bereaved of my children, I am bereaved' (43[14]) is his despairing cry when Benjamin also is taken from him—Benjamin, 'the child of his old age, . . . and his father loves him' (44[20]). Hannah dedicated her little son to the service of the Lord in gratitude for his birth; and then 'used to make for him a little robe and take it to him each year' (1 S 2[19]). David fasted and lay all night upon the ground praying for the life of his sick child (2 S 12[16]). The brief account of the death of the Shunammite's boy is a passage of restrained and pathetic beauty (2 K 4[18ff]). Isaiah's feeling for the weakness and helplessness of children is displayed in the mention of the words first articulated by his own son (Is 8[4]). The description of the time when the earth shall be full of the knowledge of the Lord pictures little children, still dependent for life and protection upon their mother's care, without fear of harm on her part, being allowed to play among wild beasts and handle the asp and the adder (11[6–9]). Zechariah envisioned the happy time when Jerusalem shall be full of boys and girls playing in the streets (Zec 8[5]). The beauty of a child's humble simplicity was acknowledged by the Psalmist who likened his own soul to 'a child quieted at its mother's breast (Ps 131[2]). Thus was anticipated the spirit of One, greater than he, who said that only those who become like children will ever enter the kingdom of heaven (Mt 18[3]), who gave thanks to His Father for revealing the things of God to 'babes' (Mt 11[25]), and who, despite the disciples' objections to His bothering with children, 'took them in his arms and blessed them, laying his hands upon them' (Mk 10[16]).

For customs on child-bearing, inheritance, and training see articles on CLEAN AND UNCLEAN, 1, FAMILY, FIRSTBORN, and INHERITANCE. E. G. R.—C. F. K.

CHILDREN [SONS] OF GOD.—In a few passages in the OT the term 'sons of God' is applied to divine beings, demigods or angels, members of the heavenly council (Gn 6[1–4], Job 1[6] 2[1] 38[7], Ps 29[1] 89[6] RVm, Heb. 'sons of gods,' RSV 'heavenly beings'; Dn 3[25] 'son of the gods'). According to one tradition (Dt 32[8] LXX) certain 'sons of God' were delegated authority by God to rule over the respective nations, while He reserved Israel for Himself. According to another (Ps 82[6]) some of these immortal 'gods, children (AV; RSV 'sons') of the Most High,' were divine judges (interpreted in Jn 10[34] as human rulers) held responsible for abetting human wickedness. Thus in these cases the 'children of God,' usually called 'sons of God,' were the family of divine beings of whom God was apparently the physical father.

With these exceptions the terms 'children of God' or 'sons of God,' with the correlative term 'Father,' designate the relation of men to God and of God to men, with varying fulness of meaning. It is obvious that the use of such a figure has wide possibilities. To call God 'Father' may imply little more than that He is creator and ruler of men (cf 'Zeus, father of gods and men'); or it may connote some phase of His providence towards a favoured individual or nation; or, again, it may assert that a father's love at its highest is the truest symbol we can frame of God's essential nature and God's disposition towards all men. Similarly, men may conceivably be styled 'children of God' from mere dependence, from special privilege, from moral likeness, or finally from a full and willing response to the Divine Fatherhood in filial love, trust, and obedience.

It is, therefore, not surprising that the Bible presents a varying and changing conception of God as Father and of men as His children.

I. In the OT.—The most characteristic use of the figure is in connexion with God's election of and providential dealings with His people Israel. That favoured nation as a whole is His 'son,' He their 'Father': it is because *this* tie is violated by Israel's ingratitude and apostasy that the prophets rebuke and appeal; it is when after Israel's repentance the tie is renewed that the prophets promise restoration. Thus Hosea declared that God loved Israel and called His 'son' out of Egypt (Hos 11[1]; cf Ex 4[22] 'Israel is my first-born son,' Sir 36[12], Ad. Est 16[16]). Thus the divine rejection of Israel (Hos 1[9] *Lo-ammi* 'Not my people'), and thus further the prophecy that it shall be said to them, 'Sons of the living God' (Hos 1[10]). So too Isaiah: 'Sons have I reared and brought up, but they have rebelled against me. . . . Israel does not know, my people does not understand' (1[2f]). In Deuteronomy the same figure is used of God's care for His people (1[31]), His discipline (8[5]), and His rejection of pagan mourning rites as violation of the body which is God's creation (14[1]). In the Song of Moses (Dt 32) God is the 'Father' of Israel whom He 'created' (v.[6]), 'begat,' 'gave birth' (v.[18]) by delivering them from Egypt; when in the wilderness 'His sons and daughters' (v.[19]) whom He has nourished and established 'are a perverse generation, children in whom is no faithfulness' (v.[20]), 'they are no longer His children' (v.[5]); therefore He 'will stir them to jealousy with those who are no people' (v.[21]), *i.e.* use enemy nations as instruments of judgment on His faithless chosen children (but cf Ro 10[19] 11[11]).

The relation between God the Father and Israel the son, then, is one of mutual intimacy and responsibility. As God is His people's Redeemer, the Divine Fatherhood is manifested in protecting and redeeming love. It involves the Divine faithfulness, to which His truly repentant people may make appeal in their extremity in the confident expectation of being gathered to their inheritance (Jer 31[9, 18–20], cf 3[4, 19], Is 43[6]). Thus the Lord, who has been His people's Saviour in all their affliction (Is 63[8f]) is their Father for all time (Is 63[16]; cf To 13[4]). However, the Father's offer of redemption carries with it the son's obligation of loyal filial response (Is 63[8]). 'A son honours his father . . . If then I am a father, where is my honour?' (Mal 1[6]). But such response is, of necessity, not only national, but also, and first, individual. Malachi's famous query, 'Have we not all one father? Has not one God created us?' (2[10]) refers not only to the nation, but also to faithful individuals (cf Mal 3[17], Wis 2[16] 5[5], Sir 23[1, 4]). This requirement of individual faithfulness to the Father opens the way for a conception of God as Father of every man, and of all men as at least potentially 'children of God.'

One might expect that a clear conception of such universal Fatherhood of God would naturally find utterance in the Psalms, in which we have at once the devoutest expression of the personal religious consciousness and the chosen vehicle of the worship of the congregation. But the dominating conception is of God as King and of man as His servant. In several passages the term ' on of God' is used of the Israelite king as the Divine King's adopted son (Ps 2[7] 89[26–29]; cf Ps 110[1–3], Sir 51[10]), for the Lord was the Father of the Davidic dynasty (2 S 7[14], cf He 1[5]), and the rule was a theocracy, whether the ruler be a reigning son of David in Jerusalem or a coming Messiah to be born of his line. In the Psalms the Divine care for man and the Divine help are set forth under a wealth of imagery: God is shield, rock, fortress, refuge, shepherd, light, salvation, but seldom Father (cf Wis 14[3]). But one Psalmist especially sensitive to the closeness of his relationship to God speaks to Him of 'the generation of Thy children' (Ps 73[15]). Two other psalms speak of the Divine Father in similes describing His tender mercies: He is 'Father of the fatherless' (Ps 68[5]); 'As a father pities his children, so the Lord pities those who fear him' (103[13]; with the allusion to the womb in the Hebrew verb translated 'pities,' cf the mother love of God in Is 66[13]).

Thus in the OT the doctrine of men as 'children of God' refers primarily to Israel as chosen and adopted sons of the redeemer God. However, the sense, on the one hand, of the filial responsibility of the faithful Israelite son as an individual and, on the other, of the tender mercy of the Father to the fatherless individual, together with the evangelistic zeal of a Second Isaiah for Israel's role in bringing 'light to the nations' (Is 49[6]) may have provided occasion for expansion of the concept. Central in such expansion was the realization of the common creaturehood of man as God's creation. Mal 2[10], easily the springboard for the ideal of a common brotherhood of all mankind under a common Fatherhood of God, and Is 45[11], which clearly refers to Gentiles as 'my children,' both are concerned with the creativs work of God (cf Is 64[8]). True, the concept of man ae created 'in the image of God' (Gn 1[27]), while seemingly implying man's universal sonship, is not explicitly interpreted as such in the OT. Nevertheless, God's Fatherhood, especially seen in His acts of grace to faithful Israel and to be made available through Israel to mankind beyond, is clearly affirmed in the OT. Thus the groundwork is laid for what is sometimes erroneously regarded as a uniquely NT doctrine of the 'children of God.' S. W. G.—**C. F. K.**

II. In the NT.—The outstanding fact is that in the self-revelation of Jesus Christ, as well as in His teaching, the *characteristic* name for God is 'Father.' He enters into full inheritance of the OT conception of the Divine power and transcendence, proclaims a Kingdom of God, and develops its meaning for His disciples; but the King is also Father, and the stress of Christ's teaching on this side is not on the Kingship but on the Fatherhood of God. In what *unique* sense He knew God as 'His own Father,' Himself as 'Son of God,' we do not here inquire (see Christology), noting only how simply, in the deepest experiences of joy or trouble, His faith uttered itself in the name 'Father' (Mt 11[25] 26[39], Lk 23[46]). But there was that in His religious consciousness which He could freely share with His disciples as 'children of God': the faint and halting analogy of the OT became through Him a clear and steadfast revelation of the Divine Fatherhood, and of sonship, in its fullest sense, as the possible and indeed normal relation of human to Divine.

1. The Synoptic Gospels.—The essential and universal Fatherhood of God appears in such sayings as that of Mt 5[43–48], and, supremely, in the parable of the Prodigal Son. Even when, as generally, it is in discourse to the disciples that the term 'your Father' is used, it still connotes what is in God, awaiting in man that obedient recognition which is sonship. It is the appeal of Christ to His disciples against hypocrisy, unforgivingness, lack of faith (Mt 6[1, 15, 26]); it stands as symbol of the Divine providence, forgiveness, redemption—in a word, of the Divine love (Lk 6[36] 11[13], Mk 11[25]), and hence it gives the ground and manner of all access to God,—'When you pray, say, Father' (Lk 11[2]).

If with Jesus the Fatherhood of God lies in His disposition towards men, not in the mere fact that He created them, so the filial relationship is ethical. God *is* Father, men must *become* children. In the Synoptic Gospels the term implying generation—'child (children) of God'— is not used, and the references to 'sons of God' are few, though sufficient to emphasize the moral conditions of sonship. Thus, the peacemakers 'shall be called sons of God' (Mt 5[9]): love to one's enemies has for its motive 'that you may be sons of your Father who is in heaven' (Mt 5[45]; cf Lk 6[35]). But since sonship is virtually identical with membership of the Kingdom of God, these direct references must be supplemented by the many sayings in which the conditions of entrance into the Kingdom are laid down: it is the *righteous* (and what the term means is set forth in the

Sermon on the Mount) who 'will shine like the sun in the kingdom of their Father' (Mt 13[43]).

2. The Gospel (and 1 Ep.) of St. John.—In the Fourth Gospel (considered here rather than in its chronological sequence, for the sake of comparison with the Synoptics) certain elements in our Lord's revelation of the Father receive new emphasis.

(*a*) The *unique* Sonship of Jesus is the prevailing theme (Jn 1[14, 18] 20[31]). Hence the Synoptic phrase 'your Father' all but disappears. What it implies is not absent, but is to be reached through a rich unfolding of, and fellowship with, the personal religious consciousness of Jesus Himself, under the terms 'my Father' and, especially, 'the Father.' Only once does He speak to the disciples of 'your Father,' when, after His resurrection, He links them with Himself as 'brethren' in the message, 'I am ascending to my Father and your Father, to my God and your God' (Jn 20[17], cf 14[20]).

(*b*) The sonship of the disciples is to be attained *through Jesus Christ*: 'No one comes to the Father, but by me' (Jn 14[6]). What is exceptional in the Synoptics (Mt 11[25], Lk 10[22]) becomes the normal teaching of the Fourth Gospel: to see, know, believe, love, confess the Son, is the one way of access to the Father (Jn 14–17, 1 Jn 2[23]). Moreover, the impulse of attraction to Christ is itself from the Father (Jn 6[44, 65]), and the Divine initiative, as well as the completeness of the break required with 'the world' and 'the flesh' (1 Jn 2[16], Jn 3[6]), is described as being 'born anew,' 'born of the Spirit,' 'born of God' (Jn 3[3–8] 1[13], 1 Jn 3[9]). In 1 John the moral fruits of this new birth are set forth—righteousness, incapability to sin, love, faith in the Son of God, victory over the world (1 Jn 2[29] 3[9] 4[7] 5[1, 4]).

These are the elements which combine in the conception of sonship in the Johannine writings: the actual phrase 'children (not 'sons') of God' occurs Jn 1[12] 11[52], 1 Jn 3[1f, 10] 5[2].

3. The Epistles of St. Paul.—St. Paul speaks both of 'children of God' and of 'sons of God.' His doctrine comprises the mystical and the ethical elements already noted, while it is enriched and developed by additional features. In his speech at Athens (Ac 17[28]) he for a moment adopts the Greek point of view, and regards all men as the 'offspring' of God. Apart from this, he—like the Fourth Gospel, but in his own way—connects sonship with faith in Christ: it is part of his doctrine of redemption, a status and privilege conferred by God upon men through faith in Christ, attested by the indwelling Spirit and His fruits. 'For in Christ Jesus you are all sons of God, through faith' (Gal 3[26]); 'It is the Spirit himself bearing witness with our spirit, that we are children of God' (Ro 8[16]); 'For all who are led by the Spirit of God are sons of God' (Ro 8[14]). It is as 'children of God' that his converts have a moral mission to the world (Ph 2[15]).

The idea of sonship as a Divinely conferred status is expressed by St. Paul under the figure (derived from Roman custom) of 'adoption' (q.v.), by which a stranger could be legally adopted as 'son' and endowed with all the privileges of the 'child' by birth (Eph 1[5–14], cf Ro 8[29]). The figure suggests fresh points of analogy. To the Romans, St. Paul makes moral appeal on the grounds that in exchange for the 'spirit of slavery' they had received the 'spirit of sonship' so that they could cry, 'Abba! Father!' (Ro 8[15]). In the passage Gal 3[23]–4[7] he likens the state of the faithful under the Law to that of 'children' needing a 'custodian'; 'heirs,' yet, because under guardians, differing nothing from 'slaves.' The Law as 'custodian' has led them to Christ, in whom they are now 'sons of God'; Christ has 'redeemed' them from the bondage of Law that they might 'receive adoption as sons,' and, because they are sons, 'God has sent the Spirit of his Son into [our] hearts, crying, "Abba! Father!"' This spiritual sonship, open to all believers, should be no stumbling-block to Israel, though to them specially belonged 'the sonship' (Ro 9[4]). It fulfils the typical distinction within Israel itself of 'children of the flesh' and 'children of the promise': by Divine election alone men become 'children of God,' 'sons of the living God' (Gal 4[28], Ro 9[8, 26]).

St. Paul further conceives of sonship as looking forward for its full realization. We are waiting 'for adoption as sons, the redemption of our bodies' (Ro 8[23]). As Christ was Son of God, yet was by His resurrection 'designated Son of God in power' (Ro 1[4]), so will deliverance from the 'bondage to decay' reveal the 'sons of God,' and all creation shall share in 'the glorious liberty of the children of God' (Ro 8[18–25]). This ultimate realization of sonship is 'to be conformed to the image of his Son, in order that he might be the first-born among many brethren' (Ro 8[29], cf 1 Jn 3[2]). Finally, the greatness and the certainty of the future glory are set forth under the thought of the son as 'heir' (Ro 8[17], Gal 4[1–7]; cf Eph 1[14–18]).

4. Other NT writers.—The opening chapters of the *Epistle to the Hebrews* emphasize the greatness and finality of a revelation through the Son, who in stooping to redeem men is not ashamed to call them 'brethren'; they are 'children' whose nature He shares, 'sons' who through Him are brought to glory (He 2[9–18]). And at the close of the Epistle the readers are exhorted to regard suffering as the Divine chastening, which marks them out as 'sons' and comes from 'the Father of spirits' (12[4–13]).

If the *Epistle of St. James* suggests a universal view of the Fatherhood of God in the phrases 'God and *the* Father,' '*the* Lord and Father,' '*the* Father of lights' (Ja 1[27] 3[9] 1[17]), it also endorses the deeper spiritual sonship under the figure, 'Of his own will he brought us forth by the word of truth' (1[18]). The same metaphor of spiritual birth is used by *St. Peter*. In 1 P 1[23] this birth, as in James, is through the 'word' of God; in 1[3] it is attributed to the resurrection of Jesus Christ, and is joined with the Pauline thought of an inheritance yet to be fully revealed. The name 'Father' appears as the distinctively Christian name for God—'if you invoke as Father him who judges . . .' (1[17]). But the idea of sonship is not developed: the thought does not occur in the enumeration of Christian privileges in 2[1–10], where the phrase 'sons of the living God' is absent from the reference to Hosea, though found in the corresponding reference by St. Paul (cf 1 P 2[10] with Ro 9[25f]).

Finally, in *Revelation* we meet with this figure of sonship, with emphasis on its ethical side, in the vision of the new heaven and the new earth: 'He who conquers shall have this heritage, and I will be his God and he shall be my son' (Rev 21[7], cf v.[8]). S. W. G.—**W. D. S.**

CHILDREN, SONG OF THE THREE.—See Apocrypha, **10.**

CHILEAB.—David's second son by Abigail, 2 S 3[3]; called **Daniel** in 1 Ch 3[1].

CHILIARCH (Rev 19[18] RVm; RSV 'captains').—See Band.

CHILIASM.—Otherwise known as Millenarianism, this is an extremist eschatological doctrine which was popular in the early Church and has been revived from time to time since the 16th cent. Based on a literalist exegesis of Scripture, it teaches that at the end of the world Christ will be visibly manifested and will reign among His saints for a thousand years (hence the name: Gr. *chilia* and Lat. *mille* = 1000). According to the primitive form of the doctrine, this earthly reign of Christ will fall between the first resurrection, which is reserved for the righteous, and the second, in which the wicked will be raised and which will be followed by the general judgment. In Christ's kingdom the elect will enjoy every kind of material and spiritual blessing.

The roots of Chiliasm can be traced to the late Jewish expectation, discernible also in the prophets, of an earthly reign of the Messiah prior to the final consummation. 2 Es 7[28] envisaged it as lasting 400 years, but some rabbis preferred 1000 years; they taught that human history down to the coming of the Messiah would last 6000 years, corresponding to the six days of creation, and the Messiah's 1000-year reign would correspond to the Sabbath. These ideas passed from

Judaism to Christianity by way of the Book of Revelation (cf especially Rev 20). They enjoyed a great vogue in the 2nd cent., being reproduced in vivid detail, for example, by 'Barnabas' (cf 15^{4-9}). If the heretic Cerinthus dwelt on the sensual satisfactions which the saints would enjoy, orthodox teachers like Papias were not much behind him. The Montanists were extreme chiliasts, but both Justin and Irenaeus were positive that the millenarian doctrine was an essential item in the Church's faith. In the 3rd cent., however, it began to come under heavy fire, Origen with his allegorical method of exegesis being its deadliest critic. In the 4th cent. the Cappadocians in the East and Jerome in the West condemned it, and Augustine dealt it a fatal blow by identifying the visible Church with the earthly kingdom spoken of by the Apocalyptist.

Augustine's views remained to the fore throughout the Middle Ages, but a revival of chiliastic conceptions came with the Reformation, when attention was again focused on the NT. The more enthusiastic reforming sects looked for the speedy establishment of Christ's reign on earth, and in 1534 the Anabaptists at Münster-i-W. actually began to set up a Kingdom of Zion, involving the sharing of women and property, as a prelude to Christ's kingdom. Both the Augsburg and the Helvetic Confessions, however, condemned Chiliasm, and the leading Reformers, while believing in the Lord's speedy return, did not attempt to literalize it.

In the 17th and 18th cents. the Pietist Movement encouraged the revival of millenarian ideas in Germany, while in the 19th cent. they found support both in the U.S.A. and in Great Britain amongst the Irvingites, the Mormons, and the Adventists. About the same time certain Roman Catholic theologians advanced a moderate form of the doctrine, especially in connexion with their interpretation of Revelation, but even this greatly 'mitigated Millenarianism' came under the condemnation of the Holy Office in 1944. At the present day chiliastic ideas are out of favour, being confined to a few unrepresentative sects and a number of individual revivalist evangelists; but they are always liable to come into their own again where a simple, fundamentalist piety holds sway. J. N. D. K.

CHILION ('wasting away').—Son of Elimelech and Naomi (Ru 1^2), who married Orpah (1^4 4^{10}), a Moabitess, and after a sojourn of ten years in Moabite territory died there.

CHILMAD.—Named in Ezk 27^{23} in a list of nations that traded with Tyre. Its location is unknown. Amongst the suggestions made is the identification with *Charmandē*, on the Euphrates, mentioned by Xenophon (*Anab.* I. v. 10). George Smith identified it with *Kalwâdha*, near Baghdad. Neither of these is probable.

CHIMHAM.—Probably the son (cf 1 K 2^7) of Barzillai the Gileadite, who returned with David from beyond Jordan to Jerusalem after the death of Absalom (2 S 19^{31f}). See, further, GERUTH-CHIMHAM.

CHIMNEY.—See HOUSE, 7.

CHINNERETH.—A city of Naphtali (Dt 3^{17}, Jos 11^2 [in latter **Chinneroth**] 19^{35}, 1 K 15^{20} [in latter **Chinneroth**; AV **Cinneroth**], which gave its name to the **Sea of Chinnereth** (Nu 34^{11}, Jos 12^3 [in latter **Chinneroth**] 13^{27}), the OT designation of the Sea of Galilee; modern *Tell el-'Oreimeh.*

CHIOS.—An island in the Aegean Sea opposite the Ionian peninsula in Asia Minor. In the 5th cent. B.C. the inhabitants were the richest of all the Greeks. The city was distinguished in literature also, and claimed to be the birth-place of Homer. Up to the time of Vespasian it was, under the Roman Empire, a free State. The chief city was also named Chios. St. Paul passed it on his last voyage in the Aegean Sea (Ac 20^{15}). A. So.

CHISLEU, Neh 1^1, Zec 7^1 (AV).—See CHISLEV.

CHISLEV.—Neh 1^1, Zec 7^1 (AV **Chisleu**), 1 Mac 1^{54} 4^{59}, 2 Mac $1^{9, 18}$ 10^5 (AV **Casleu**); see TIME.

CHISLON ('confidence'?).—Father of Elidad, Benjamin's representative for dividing the land, Nu 34^{21}.

CHISLOTH-TABOR.—See CHESULLOTH.

CHITHLISH, Jos 15^{40} (RV).—See CHITLISH.

CHITLISH.—A town of Judah, in the Shephelah, Jos 15^{40} (AV **Kithlish,** RV **Chithlish**); possibly modern *Kh. el-Makhaz.*

CHITTIM, Dn 11^{30}, Nu 24^{24}, Ezk 27^6 (AV), 1 Mac 1^1 8^5 (RV).—See KITTIM.

CHIUN, Am 5^{26} (AV, RV).—See KAIWAN.

CHLOE (mentioned only in 1 Co 1^{11}).—St. Paul had been informed of the dissensions at Corinth probably by some of her Christian slaves. Chloe herself may have been either a Christian or a heathen, and may have lived either at Corinth or at Ephesus. In favour of the latter is St. Paul's usual tact, which would not suggest the invidious mention of his informants' names, if they were members of the Corinthian Church.

CHOBA, Jth 4^4 15^{4f} (AV, RV **Chobai** in the latter), noticed with Damascus.—Perhaps the land of Hobah (q.v.).

CHOIR (Neh 12^8 RVm).—See PRAISE.

CHOIRMASTER.—See PSALMS, **2.**

CHOLA, Jth 15^4 (RV).—See KOLA.

CHOLER is used in Sir 31^{20} 37^{30} in the sense of a disease, 'perhaps cholera, diarrhoea'—*Oxf. Eng. Dict.* (RV 'colic'; RSV 'colic,' 'nausea'); and in Dn 8^7 11^{11} in the sense of bitter anger. Both meanings are old, and belonged indeed to the Latin *cholera* as early as the 3rd and 4th cents.

CHOR-ASHAN, 1 S 30^{30} (AV).—See BOR-ASHAN.

CHORAZIN.—Mentioned only in the woe pronounced by Jesus (Mt 11^{21}, Lk 10^{13}). The name survives at the ruins of *Kerāzeh*, N. of Capernaum. Here there are remains of a synagogue of the 3rd cent. A.D., probably standing on the site of the one which Jesus may have visited. Of particular interest is a *cathedra Mosis* (Mt 23^2) bearing an inscription in Aramaic honouring the man who had paid for the portico and stairway. E. G. K.

CHORBE (AV **Corbe**), 1 Es 5^{12}=**Zaccai,** Ezr 2^9, Neh 7^{14}.

CHOSAMAEUS (1 Es 9^{32}).—It is not improbable that the Greek reading is due to a copyist's error, especially seeing that the three proper names that follow Shimeon in the text of Ezr 10^{31} are omitted in 1 Esdras.

CHOZEBA, 1 Ch 4^{22} (AV).—See COZEBA.

CHRIST.—See CHRISTOLOGY, JESUS CHRIST, and MESSIAH.

CHRISTIAN.—**1. Usage.**—In the NT, this name is found only thrice (Ac 11^{26} 26^{28}, 1 P 4^{16}). In the Apostolic Fathers, too, it seldom occurs. It is found only in the letters of Ignatius (Eph 11^2, Mag 4^1, Trall 6^1, Ro 3^2, Pol 7^3), the Martyrdom of Polycarp (3^2 10^1 12^{1f}) and the Didache (12^4). This usage contrasts strongly with the many other self-designations used by the early Christians such as 'disciples,' 'brethren,' 'saints,' 'righteous,' 'poor,' 'believers,' 'those being saved,' 'elect,' 'those of the Way,' etc.

2. Origin of the Name.—According to Luke (Ac 11^{26}), who in that context probably follows an Antiochian source, the name 'Christian' originated in Antioch, probably early in the forties. Until recently it was held that the designation was given to the followers of Jesus by the mob of that city, who only superficially understood the public teaching of Paul and Barnabas and thus thought that the Christ or Chrestos whom they proclaimed was the founder of the new religion. Other scholars surmised that the designation was a taunt-name (the 'oily ones'). But the early history of the name demands a different explanation.

It has been pointed out by several scholars (*e.g.* Parabeni, Bikermann, E. Peterson) that the ending *-anoi* of the Greek designation *christianoi* does not agree with Hellenistic usage but rather points to Latin origin. In the Greek language of that time, the followers or supporters of a man would designate themselves by adding to his name the ending *-eioi* or *-esioi*. In connexion with a proper name, the Latin ending *-anus* indicates the followers of a party head, or the clients of an influential person. The most plausible explanation of the anomalous formation of the word *christianos* in the Greek-speaking world would be that Roman people of great influence had given it, and that swayed by their authority the Hellenistic population adopted the strangely coined word. Its non-Greek character furnishes the strongest argument against the view that the Greek-speaking populace of Antioch had invented it. Furthermore the verb *chrēmatizein* used by Luke in Ac 11^{26} is a legal term, and the correct rendering would not be 'the disciples were called Christians' (RSV) but rather 'the disciples received the legal designation "Christians".' Similarly the temporal adverb *prōtōs* belongs to legal language and indicates a legal precedent. Thus the statement in Luke-Acts points to a contact which followers of Jesus had with the Roman authorities, probably on account of a litigation, in the course of which it was established that these people had an identity of their own and did not belong to the Jewish commonwealth, and that therefore while no longer subject to Jewish jurisdiction they had no share in the Jewish religious privileges, either. The lack of an extensive bureaucracy in the Roman Empire would explain the fact that the proconsul Gallio dismissed the charges which the Jews had brought against Paul on the ground that this was an intra-Jewish matter (Ac 18^{14f}). The proper name which is used in the first half of the title is best explained as being adopted from the Christian self-designation 'those of Christ' (1 Co 1^{12} 3^{23}, 2 Cor 10^7; cf Mk 9^{41}, 1 Cor 11^3). Thus the designation Christian would characterize these people as the household or the clientèle of Christ. It is doubtful, however, whether the term goes back to the persecution of the Jewish Christians by Herod Agrippa, who claimed jurisdiction over them, so that the name would have been formed in analogy to that of the Herodians. More likely the latter title, too, was given to the supporters of the Herodian family by Romans. The legal character of the designation is reflected in the way in which reference is made to 'the name'; so probably Ac 5^{41}, unless the reference is here, as in Ph 2^9 and 3 Jn 7, to the title 'Lord' pertaining to Jesus; and certainly in 2 Clem $13^{1,4}$, Ignatius, Eph 3^1 7^1; Hermas, Vis III. ii. 1; Sim. VIII. x. 3, IX. xiii. 2, xxviii. 3 and 5.

Anyone who confessed that this designation applied to him would automatically be subject to the rules and laws dealing with this group. Hence the frequent expression 'suffering for the name.'

3. The Spread of the Name.—Since 'Christian' was not originally a self-designation of the followers of Jesus, it is not surprising that it is so rarely found in the NT. The usage in 1 P 4^{16} points clearly to the hostile environment by which the term was used. In Ac 26^{28} King Agrippa employs the title in an ironical way in the presence of a Roman magistrate. The correct rendering of his statement is probably: 'You almost persuade me to play the Christian.' Outside of the Church, however, the designation must have been commonly accepted, for Tacitus reports that in A.D. 64 the mob in Rome understood clearly who was meant when the blame for the burning of Rome was put upon 'the Christians' (*Ann.* xv. 44). He witnesses also to an equally important fact, viz. that in the popular view the name 'Christian' was associated with all kinds of detestable crimes. This, too, is a common feature of political propaganda, and the author of 1 Peter obviously refers to it, when he admonishes his readers (4^{15}) not to suffer for the things which for the populace were implied in the name 'Christian,' *e.g.* as 'a murderer, thief, wrongdoer [better 'malicious magician'], or mischief-maker [probably 'unfaithful treasurer,' or, according to W. Ramsay, 'people who stir up strife between servants and master']. While in Nero's time these alleged crimes had served as a pretext for occasional persecution, conditions changed radically in the days of Trajan (*c* A.D. 111–113), as is evidenced by Pliny the Younger's inquiry (Pliny, *Epist.* x. 27 f). For lack of administrative experience he requests the Emperor to send him instructions for dealing with the great many Christians living in his province. He wants to know, whether the 'name' by itself is punishable. The Emperor's reply is positive in principle, though he insists on strictly legal procedure. The 'name' itself, *i.e.* admitted or obvious membership in the Church, is considered a crime by the Roman authorities, apart from any other transgression of the laws.

The documents of the ancient Church show that the new designation was originally not popular with the people to whom it was given. Luke's own statement (Ac 11^{26}) simply records the fact that the name originated in Antioch. Obviously he presupposes readers who have already come across the designation. But it is hardly by accident that he refrains from using the name in narrative as a self-designation of the believers. The situation has changed, however, when we come to Ignatius. In his letters (*c* A.D. 110–115) he accepts the charge brought against him by the authorities and proudly calls himself a Christian (Eph 11^2, Mag 4^1, Ro 3^2, Pol 7^3), and so does Polycarp (Mart. Pol. 3^2 10^1 12^{1f}). As so often in the history of the Church, a nickname or taunting epithet was transformed by the people concerned into a title of honour. The adjectival use of the name ('Christian food,' Trall 6^1) points to a familiarity with this self-designation. Thus its adoption was not occasioned by the trial of Ignatius but must have preceded it. The fact that in the Didache, too, 'Christian' is employed as a self-designation (12^4) without any special reference to persecution bears witness to the general adoption of the name, at least by the Christians in Syria, at the outset of the 2nd cent.; for Asia Minor the Christian usage is corroborated by the Mart. Pol., probably A.D. 156. The Apologists used the term, but perhaps only because they realized that they were known under this name to the people whom they addressed (cf Justin, Ap. i. 4: 'we are accused of being Christians'). It is absent from 1 and 2 Clem, Barnabas, Hermas, the Pseudo-Clementine Homilies and Tatian. By the end of the 2nd cent. it seems to have been accepted generally as a self-designation by the members of the Church.

4. The Meaning of the Name.—The Roman authorities, who first designated the disciples of Jesus as Christians, attempted thereby to characterize them as a political group or party, held together by their loyalty to the party head, *Christos*. While originally the title was given for juridical convenience without implying a derogatory sense, the pagan mob must at a very early time have associated it with heinous crimes and vices, as Tacitus' reports and the reference in 1 P 4^{15} show. However, the way in which the crowd of heathen and Jews in the arena of Smyrna reacted to Polycarp's confession, would be an indication that by that time the designation had acquired a specifically religious character. For the mob shouts: 'This is the teacher of Asia, the father of the Christians, who has made it his business to destroy our gods, and who instructs multitudes not to offer sacrifices or to take part in the official worship' (Mart. Pol. 12^2). In other words, the designation 'Christian' already implies the charge of 'atheism.'

The Christian interpretation of the title is expressed very clearly in Ignatius' letter to Polycarp, when he writes: 'A Christian has no power over himself, but rather owes all his time to God' (Ignatius, Pol 7^3). The first half of the statement is obviously an allusion to the phrase 'belonging to Christ,' and the second half indicates the kind of action resulting from the lordship of Christ. In the Didache (12^{4-5}) the somewhat obscure contrast between a genuine Christian and a *Christemporos* (probably a person who seeks to derive profit from his being a Christian) is best interpreted in the light of the fact that everyone who comes in the name of the Lord, is to be granted hospitality (12[1]). The expression ' in the name ' indicates allegiance, and thus the semi-political character of the self-designation is implied. As others consider an earthly ruler as their head, so the Christians consider Christ. It is therefore not surprising, when Polycarp, enjoined ' to swear by the genius of Caesar,' replied to the Roman proconsul that he was unable to do so because he was a Christian (Mart. Pol. 10[1]). Ignatius is also anxious to underscore the fact that the designation ' Christian ' implies a special honour. Unlike other people who call themselves after another person, the Christians as clients of Christ or members of His household are by His name designated as people living in communion with a God (Mag 10[2]; cf Ro 3[3]).

It should be kept in mind, however, that this development took place on Hellenistic soil. Not too much emphasis should be placed, therefore, upon the etymology of *christos*. Though literally meaning the ' Anointed One,' *i.e.* the Messiah, the title soon lost its original denotation and became a personal name in the Greek-speaking church. Thus when used as a self-designation, the name ' Christian ' does not imply that its bearers considered themselves as anointed ones. Rather by means of it those who called themselves Christians wanted to emphasize the fact that they were not only different from the rest of the Jews as well as the Gentiles, but also that their differentia was rooted in their personal allegiance to Christ, and that as His clients or partisans they claimed a privileged position in the political set-up of the Roman state. This element of defiance, about which Pliny complains and which is so conspicuous in Polycarp's martyrdom, must have dominated the adoption of the title as a self-designation. By calling themselves after the originator of their religion, the members of the ancient Church established it as a public corporation, which had received its charter from its master and which therefore cared little whether or not the worldly authorities recognized them.

While it is true that down to the 4th cent., *e.g.* in Codex Sinaiticus, the spelling *chrestianos* occurs, not too much weight should be put on this orthographic peculiarity. In Hellenistic Greek, *ē* and *i* were both pronounced *ee*, and wrong spelling is a very frequent phenomenon. Since *Chrestos* was a common name, meaning the ' gracious one,' whereas *Christos* as a proper name made sense to Christians only, it is not unlikely that the Roman authorities were of the opinion that behind the movement was a certain Chrestos. The Roman historian Suetonius (*Claudius*, ch. 25) reports, *e.g.*, that the Emperor Claudius (*c* A.D. 50) expelled the Jews from Rome ' who under the instigation of Chrestus were in a continuous uproar.' Many scholars believe that Suetonius—who had not much knowledge of the facts—is here referring to dissensions between orthodox and Christian Jews in Rome. But when Ignatius and Tertullian, playing upon this orthographic blunder, find in the name an allusion to the graciousness (*chrēstotēs*) of the Christians, just as Peter was thereby reminded of the graciousness of Jesus (1 P 2[3]; cf Ignatius, Mag 10[1]), the rhetorical device should not be mistaken for historical information. O. A. P.

CHRISTIANITY.—What we call Christianity, was in the ancient Church usually designated as the ' Way ' (*e.g.* Ac 9[2] 19[2f] etc.), and qualified as the ' Way of the Lord ' (Ac 18[25]), the ' Way of Truth ' (2 P 2[2]), the ' Way of Salvation ' (Ac 6[17]), and the ' Way of Righteousness ' (2 P 2[21]). Ignatius, who probably was the first Christian to accept that name as a self-designation (see preceding article), was probably the author of the term *christianismos*, too (Mag 10[1, 3], Philad 6[1]; cf also Mart. Pol. 10[1]). The ending *-ismos* is used to place the Christian faith on a parallel with the philosophical schools of Hellenism and thus to proclaim it as having its own organizing principle. Incidentally that feature is used in order to state that Christianity is independent of Judaism. Ignatius emphasizes the fact that Christ is the Teacher, whom all Christians follow. Christianity is a way of life, however (Mag 10[1], Philad 6[1]), not an abstract philosophy; but, as Polycarp points out to the proconsul who tries him, it has a rational or reasonable foundation (Mart. Pol 10[1]). Christians live ' according to the *Christianismos*,' not, as the Stoics taught, ' according to nature.' The Christian system goes back to Jesus, who is the Teacher, and to live as a Christian makes one a member of God's people.

The term does not occur in any other of the Apostolic writers or in the Apologists, but became popular again in the 4th cent. A.D., then still denoting the practice of the Christian life or the profession of the right doctrine. Our term ' Christianity ' goes back to Latin *Christianitas*, which is the latinized form of *Christianismos*. But unlike the latter expression, *Christianitas* denoted both the Christian way of life and the community practising this life. O. A. P.

CHRISTOLOGY.—Christology has been called the despairing attempt of theologians to interpret the Person of Christ. From the earliest times it has been the preoccupation of the Church. It has given rise to long and bitter controversies, and some of the divisions to which it has led have never been healed. It is not the purpose of the present article to examine and compare later christologies, but to make some study of the NT Scriptures in order to discover how Christians of the 1st cent. regarded their Lord. It has been the claim of all later theologies to be founded upon the most certain warranty of Holy Scripture, and although it can no longer be assumed that all the writers of the NT reflect precisely the same point of view, together they provide invaluable testimony to the faith of the earliest Christian Church.

1. The Synoptic Gospels.—The first three gospels are not the earliest Christian documents, for all the genuine epistles of St. Paul were almost certainly written before the Gospel of St. Mark, which in turn provided the foundation for St. Matthew and St. Luke. But the first three gospels together reveal what was believed in the 1st cent. about the life and ministry of Jesus, and it is therefore necessary to examine them in order to discover how the Person of Jesus was regarded during His lifetime on earth, what claims He made, and how those claims were received by the disciples, by the populace, and by the Jewish authorities.

But here we meet a challenge from some who do not allow that the gospels have any great historical value. Early in the 20th cent. scholars of the school of Adolf Harnack, which was then dominant in Germany and influential throughout the world, believed that the critical study of the gospels yielded a portrait of Jesus of Nazareth who, though not indeed the supernatural figure of later Christian devotion, yet stood forth as the Jesus of History, Captain of the souls of men. There has been a widespread reaction against this ' Liberal Protestant ' view. On the one hand, it has been urged that the ' liberal ' conception of the Person of Christ was inadequate to provide a basis for the Christian faith or to account for the rise of the Christian Church; on the other hand, the criticism of the gospels has entered into a more radical and sceptical phase, leading some scholars to the conclusion that practically nothing can be known about the life and teaching of Jesus. If a christology is possible to-day it must be founded upon the inspired witness of St. Paul and other NT writers, and it must be accepted by faith, for the Jesus of History is for ever hidden from our sight.

This is not the place to enter into a discussion of the method of Form-Criticism (see CRITICISM, BIBLICAL, **4**) which has led scholars like Rudolf Bultmann to adopt this sceptical attitude towards the gospels as historical documents; it is enough to say that many critics, while admitting the value of the new methods, do not admit that so negative a conclusion is necessary. Even if it be allowed that most of the material of which the gospels were composed took shape in churches which had never heard or seen the original witnesses, yet it remains improbable that the corporate memory of the earliest

Church had ceased to exercise any control over the development of tradition by the middle of the 1st cent. Stories may have grown with the telling, legends and misinterpreted allegories may have found their way into the stream of tradition; but to suppose that the evangelists had no reliable information to use in the composition of the gospels is to make an assumption which does less than justice to the impression made by Jesus upon the minds of His followers, and which credits the early Christians with a faculty of invention that we have no reason to think they possessed. It may be granted that the purpose of the evangelists was theological, rather than historical in the modern sense; but it does not follow that they had no genuine historical material on which to work. The beliefs of Christians in the second half of the 1st cent. are ascertainable from other sources, and they are by no means identical with those reflected in the gospel narratives. There is little or no 'Paulinism' in the gospels, none of the distinctive theology of Hebrews, and the theology of the Fourth Gospel is hardly anticipated in the other three. The synoptic gospels may still be examined to discover what were the actual facts of the life of Jesus and what was the teaching He gave to His disciples and to the crowds.

Before proceeding to particulars we may learn something from the form of the gospel narratives. All give an account of the ministry of Jesus in Galilee and Judaea; but all allow a disproportionate amount of space to the narrative of the Passion at Jerusalem, leading up to the climax of the Resurrection. Only two of the four gospels have anything to tell of the birth of Jesus, and in both cases the nativity stories are loosely integrated with the rest of the gospel. This can only mean that in the regard of the Church and of the evangelists the death and resurrection of Jesus possessed a significance greater than his other actions and greater than his birth, concerning which little seems to have been known. It is to the final chapters that the gospels are obviously intended to lead, and the fact has christological significance. Jesus wrought many 'signs' as the Fourth Evangelist says, but His death and resurrection lay at the centre of the Church's message to the world. His death was no ordinary death because Jesus was no ordinary man. How then is His Person presented by the synoptic writers.

(*a*) THE MESSIAHSHIP OF JESUS.—In the first place they assume His humanity. As depicted in the first three gospels the life of Jesus was a real human life, and His death a real human death. He could hunger and thirst. He could feel joy, sorrow, love, pity, and even anger. He prayed to God like any other man, specially in the crises of His life. He was tempted. He shrank from the prospect of death. He asked questions, not rhetorically, but to elicit information. He confessed ignorance, and He shared the popular beliefs of his age. This is not the picture of the docetic Christ imagined by the heretics of the 2nd cent., nor indeed is it the picture on which some later Christian devotion has dwelt. It is the picture of a man.

But of no ordinary man. Jesus was the Christ. Central to St. Mark's gospel is the confession of Peter, 'You are the Christ' (8^{29}). Others might speculate as to His identity, moved as they were by His mighty works and prophetic power; but for Peter He was more than John the Baptist or one of the prophets; He was the Messiah, and Matthew adds 'the Son of the living God' (16^{16}). Mark does not add, as Matthew does, the commendation of Peter, 'Blessed are you, Simon Bar-Jona! For flesh and blood has not revealed this to you, but my Father who is in heaven'; but Mark implies that Jesus accepted the title, for he writes, 'And he charged them to tell no one about him.'

Here then we encounter the second element in the Church's christology as reflected in the synoptic gospels. Jesus was the Messiah, and from the rapidity with which the title passed into general use, so that by the time of the Pauline epistles 'Christ' had become virtually a proper name, it may be inferred that the Messiahship of Jesus was never questioned in the early Church.

But at this point difficult questions arise. What conceptions of the Messiah existed among the Jews in the 1st cent.? How did the early Christians interpret the title? Did Jesus quite certainly claim to be the Christ? and if so, in what sense?

It is only possible here to glance at the history of the Jewish hope in the coming of 'the Anointed One.' Amid the disasters that preceded the exile, the prophets of Israel, while admitting the inevitability of the overthrow of the national life, never lost hope of its eventual restoration. The dynasty of David, to which Judah had been faithful so long, would in God's own time be restored (Is 11^1, Jer 33^{15} etc.). This expectation of the restoration of the kingdom with its anointed king supported the Jews through many dark days; and although the post-exilic prophets conceived of the coming kingdom more as a theocracy, and laid little stress on the hope of a Messiah, the hope of a personal deliverer never died. In the later apocalyptic literature the Messiah is conceived as a supernatural figure, the agent of God in a wholly miraculous restoration of Israel. The assumption is sometimes made that all Jews in the 1st cent. accepted the apocalyptic picture of a Messiah coming with clouds of glory, smiting the nations with a rod of iron, and establishing in Jerusalem the eternal kingdom of the saints. But there is no evidence for this. Conceptions seem to have differed, and while some may have luxuriated in such fanciful pictures as are found in Enoch and the Apocalypse of Baruch, there were others who, while treasuring the age-long hope of Israel, held a quieter, saner faith. It is only necessary to remember the Psalms of Solomon (*c* 40 B.C.) and the outburst of the aged Simeon recorded in Lk 2^{29-32}. It may be dangerous to quote the *Nunc Dimittis* as the *ipsissima verba* of Simeon, but the whole chapter is intensely Jewish in tone and undoubtedly reflects a type of contemporary Jewish piety.

The more primitive conception of the Messiah has left its mark in certain passages of the gospels. Matthew's story of the alarm of Herod the Great at the arrival of the Wise Men presupposes a conception of the Messiah as a Jewish monarch destined to supplant the dynasty of the Herods. In Luke the first part of the Angel's message to Mary at the Annunciation rests upon similar hopes: 'You will conceive in your womb and bear a son, and you shall call his name Jesus. He will be great and will be called the Son of the Most High; and the Lord God will give to him the throne of his father David, and he will reign over the house of Jacob for ever; and of his kingdom there will be no end.' The rest of the Angel's message may embody other ideas, but vv.$^{30-33}$ of Lk 1 give expression to the old messianic hope of the restoration of the Davidic line which dates back to the 8th cent. B.C. There is no trace of apocalyptism here, nor even of later Christian ideas of the Christ. That this political conception of the Messiah persisted even among the followers of Jesus is evident from Lk 24^{21ff}: 'We had hoped that he was the one to redeem Israel.'

(*b*) THE WITNESS OF JOHN.—The witness of John the Baptist to current messianic hopes is difficult to interpret because the gospels do not give a clear and consistent picture of the nature of his mission. The Christian Church regarded him mainly as the herald of Christ, and in the Fourth Gospel little stress is laid on any other aspect of his ministry: 'He . . . came to bear witness to the light' (Jn 1^7). But other evidence makes it clear that he was more than a conscious forerunner. Mark has 'John the Baptist appeared in the wilderness preaching a baptism of repentance for the forgiveness [remission, AV] of sins' (1^4), and Luke records his advice to various classes among his hearers. Thus John appears primarily as a moral reformer, and this agrees with the testimony of Josephus. But all the evangelists mention an eschatological element in his preaching. According to Mt 3^2, he cried 'Repent, for the kingdom of heaven is at hand,' and Luke records the words, 'Even now the axe is laid to the root of the trees; every tree therefore that does not bear fruit is cut down and thrown into the fire' (Lk 3[9]). Such words imply the imminence of the messianic judgment, and it is in that connexion that the coming of 'one mightier than I' must be interpreted. The 'mightier one' can hardly be other than the Messiah, shortly to appear in judgment. John says no more of him except 'I have baptized you with water, but he will baptize you with Holy Spirit' (Mk 1[8]); but both Matthew and Luke add 'and with fire,' and it may be that the mention of 'fire' is more original than the reference to Spirit. Holy Spirit expresses the difference between John's baptism and that of the Christian Church, a subject of controversy in the early days; but John's concern was with the fire of judgment.

It seems probable therefore that John's message concerned the coming of the Messiah in judgment to inaugurate the Kingdom, but whether he identified Jesus as the Christ is much more doubtful. Two events recorded in the gospels are relevant, the baptism of Jesus by John, and the message sent by John to Jesus recorded in Mt 11[2ff] and Lk 7[18ff]. All the synoptists describe the baptism of Jesus, although it seems to have caused the church some embarrassment. Why should the mightier one, the Messiah, seek baptism from his humbler predecessor? Matthew introduces a protest on the part of John (Mt 3[14]), Luke hurries past the incident with an aorist participle (Lk 3[21]), and John omits it altogether. But it held its place in the synoptic tradition because it was the occasion of the descent of the Spirit upon Jesus (Mk 1[10f]). No event is more certainly historical, for the early Church, engaged as it seems to have been in controversy with the followers of John, would never have invented it. If Mark's were the only account it might be inferred that immediately after His baptism Jesus became conscious of the descent of the Spirit upon Himself, and of a divine assurance that He was God's beloved Son. It is possible, however, to take 'John' as the subject of the verb 'saw' in Mk 1[10], and to understand that the voice from heaven was audible to the bystanders. This is the interpretation of Matthew (3[16f]), who changes the words 'Thou art my beloved Son' into 'This is my beloved Son'—a declaration to all present. Luke merely states that 'the Holy Spirit descended upon him,' but by adding 'in bodily form, as a dove' he implies that this was more than a subjective experience on the part of Jesus. This is a good example of the way in which a story may be unconsciously modified, but if the Marcan account be accepted, there was nothing in the incident to impress the Baptist or convince him that Jesus was 'the mightier one.'

The action of the Baptist in sending messengers at a later time to enquire 'Are you he who is to come, or shall we look for another?' (Mt 11[3], Lk 7[19]) has generally been understood to betoken a failure of faith; but if the evidence is inconclusive that John had previously recognized Jesus as 'the mightier one' his inquiry may with more reason be taken to signify a growing understanding. Jesus betrays no resentment, but commends John in the highest terms.

It may therefore be necessary to discount the belief of the evangelists that John had recognized Jesus as the Christ, and to reserve that discovery for Peter.

(*c*) THE CONFESSION OF PETER.—Whatever different ideas the Jews may have had concerning the coming Messiah, they certainly did not conceive of him as a wandering prophet, and therefore Peter's declaration (Mk 8[29]) was in every way remarkable. His conception of messiahship may still have needed correction, but that he should have thought of Jesus as in any sense the Anointed One of prophecy reveals a depth of insight that can only be explained as the result of months of close intercourse with Jesus. The evidence of the synoptists does not suggest that the common people had any such idea, and perhaps Mark introduced his theory of 'the messianic secret' to explain what seemed to him a perplexing fact. Jesus was not recognized because He did not wish to be. He silenced the demons who knew Him (1[25] 3[12]); He charged those who had profited by His messianic power to 'tell no man' (1[44] 5[43]); He enjoined silence on the witnesses of the Transfiguration (9[9]); and He spoke in parables to avoid the premature disclosure of the secret of the Kingdom (4[11f]). Whatever else may be said about this theory, it acknowledges the fact that Jesus did not publicly assume the role of Messiah in the days of the ministry. Unexpected confirmation of this conclusion is found in Matthew's account of the triumphal entry into Jerusalem. The evangelist evidently regarded this as a fulfilment of messianic prophecy and remembered Zec 9[9]. But it is not certain that the multitudes so regarded the scene, and Matthew adds to his account 'and when he entered Jerusalem, all the city was stirred, saying, "Who is this?" And the crowds said, "This is the prophet Jesus from Nazareth of Galilee"' (Mt 21[10]). Nor do the glad Hosannas as reported in Mk 11[9f] imply that Jesus was regarded as the Messiah: 'Hosanna! Blessed be he who comes in the name of the Lord! Blessed be the kingdom of our father David that is coming! Hosanna in the highest!' A messianic movement was afoot, but that does not necessarily imply that Jesus was the Messiah.

Yet there were rumours of such a claim. Mark's account of the trial of Jesus before the High Priest makes it clear that the authorities suspected that Jesus regarded Himself as the Messiah. The High Priest's question is direct, and so is Jesus' answer: 'Are you the Christ, the Son of the Blessed?' And Jesus said, 'I am,' a declaration which the High Priest, according to Mark, considered blasphemous (14[61ff]). Although it may be doubted whether any follower of Jesus was present in court to report the exact words used, we have no reason to question the firm tradition that as a result of the High Priest's examination the Jewish authorities were convinced that Jesus claimed to be the Messiah and were thus able to present a case to Pilate. To Pilate's first question 'Are you the King of the Jews?' Jesus answered evasively, but He did not deny it (Mk 15[2]).

We conclude that from an early date in the ministry Jesus accepted the role of Messiah, but He made little use of the title and discouraged its employment, probably because of its nationalistic associations. The conviction that He was the Christ grew among His disciples, and in the end the claim reached the ears of the Sanhedrin, thence to be imparted to Pilate and broadcast to the multitude.

(*d*) 'THE SON OF MAN.'—The gospels bear abundant testimony to the frequent use by Jesus of the term 'Son of Man.' In Mark alone it occurs some fourteen times, and it is most remarkable that whereas Jesus is called 'Christ' in the rest of the NT and never 'Son of Man' (Ac 7[56] is the only exception, apart from Rev 1[13] and 14[14] where the reference is to Dn 7[13]), in the gospels the position is reversed. The conclusion follows that 'Son of Man' was a term used by Jesus, but that after the resurrection the early believers, perhaps at a loss to understand it, substituted 'Christ,' which was more easily understood—or misunderstood. Why did Jesus choose this title? In the OT the phrase 'Son of Man' occurs in the Psalms, where it means 'man,' as it should in Semitic usage, and it is frequent in Ezekiel, where it signifies the prophet. Both these uses may have influenced Jesus. But many critics suppose that its use in the gospels goes back to Dn 7[13], 'Behold, with the clouds of heaven there came one like a son of man.' There the phrase stands for a personification of the saints of the Most High (*i.e.* the Jews) who are to receive 'dominion and glory and a kingdom' after the destruction of the world powers signified by the various 'beasts' (7[18]). But in the *Similitudes of Enoch* (Enoch 37–71) and in other apocalyptic literature (*e.g.* 4 Ezr 13) 'the Son of Man' has become a superhuman being, the Elect One, destined to appear in judgment as the messianic ruler of the Kingdom of God. The evidence is not altogether satisfactory (cf C. H. Dodd, *Interpretation of the Fourth Gospel*, pp. 241 f), but many critics, particularly since the publication of Schweitzer's *Quest of the Historical Jesus*, have supposed that Jesus was much influenced by such apocalyptic ideas, and that by using the title ' Son of Man ' He wished to imply that He was indeed the Messiah, not yet revealed, but destined before long to appear with clouds of heaven. That such beliefs were treasured by the early Church is undeniable, for they find expression in the Epistles to the Thessalonians, the Revelation of St. John, and elsewhere ; but that they represent the mind of Jesus is much less certain. They seem to be implied in some sayings recorded in the synoptic gospels, but other passages reveal quite different ideas, and it is at least possible that the apocalyptism of the early Church, though actually derived from other sources, was read back into the teaching of Jesus.

The literature on this subject is extensive, and within the limits of this article no adequate discussion can be attempted ; but certain considerations may be advanced to serve as a warning against any hasty conclusion. In the first place, it may be argued that the recorded teaching of Jesus is predominantly religious and ethical, and although it has a strong eschatological element, eschatology is not the same thing as apocalyptic. Futurist expectations which might be called ' apocalyptic ' are mostly concentrated in a few chapters of the synoptic gospels, notably in Mark 13 and the parallels in Matthew and Luke. Moreover, the contention that all the ethical teaching in the gospels may be described as *Interimsethik*, intended to serve only during a brief period before the final consummation, is a theory that does little justice to its roots in the OT or to its relevance to human life in all ages. Experience shows that apocalyptic convictions, once admitted, generally become an obsession ; but when the teaching of Jesus is regarded as a whole, those parts which might naturally be related to such expectations are few and far between. The works of C. H. Dodd and J. Jeremias on the parables of Jesus do not support the theory that most of them have an apocalyptic undertone ; and Mark 13, ' the Little Apocalypse,' has long been recognized as an artificial composition, perhaps incorporated by the evangelist from an earlier source. Even so, the first eight verses of this chapter have reference to political upheavals culminating in the destruction of Jerusalem, vv.[9-13] refer to persecution, vv.[14-23] again refer to political tribulation, and only in vv.[24-27] is a genuinely apocalyptic element introduced. Vv.[26f], ' Then they will see the Son of Man coming in clouds with great power and glory ; and then he will send out the angels, and gather his elect from the four winds, from the ends of the earth to the ends of heaven,' have been described as ' a pastiche of Old Testament allusions ' (J. A. T. Robinson). It is significant that the last sentence is a quotation from the LXX, not the Hebrew, of Zec 2[6], which suggests that it was a discovery of the early Church. It is highly doubtful whether the saying is authentic. ' The whole impression of these verses is of a secondary composition on which it is impossible to rely for any fresh light on how Jesus himself thought ' (J. A. T. Robinson, *Jesus and His Coming*, p. 57).

That the early Church was capable of reading into the tradition of the sayings of Jesus its own apocalyptic ideas is made clear by a comparison of Mark with the later synoptists. For example, in Mk 13[3], after the prophecy of the destruction of the Temple, Peter, James, John, and Andrew asked him privately, ' Tell us, when will this be, and what will be the sign when these things are all to be accomplished ? ' But Mt 24[3] reads, ' Tell us, when will this be, and what will be the sign of your coming and of the close of the age ? '—a clear indication that it was the later evangelist, not Jesus, who connected the fall of Jerusalem with the Parousia. Again, the Marcan saying (Mk 9[1]) reads in Lk 9[27], ' I tell you truly, there are some standing here who will not taste of death before they see the kingdom of God,' whereas in Mt 16[28] it reads, ' Truly, I say to you, there are some standing here who will not taste death before they see the Son of Man coming in his kingdom.' If such changes could be made by one evangelist in order to introduce unmistakable references to a future Parousia, it is very probable that the process of editing the sayings of Jesus in accordance with current ideas had begun long before the gospels were written.

In the second place, a careful examination of all the passages in which Jesus uses the phrase ' Son of Man ' establishes the fact that in most cases He did not mean by it the Messiah, present or to come, and when He did use it in that sense (as in Mk 8[31]) He was deliberately substituting for ' the Christ ' a term free from political implications. But if He did wish to avoid nationalism, it does not seem likely that He would encourage apocalyptism, which was nationalism writ large.

An exhaustive examination of passages in which the phrase occurs has been made by various scholars (Vincent Taylor, T. W. Manson, C. J. Cadoux, G. S. Duncan, J. A. T. Robinson, and many more), from which it appears that one interpretation of the title ' Son of Man ' is not appropriate in every case. Sometimes there may have been a mistranslation of the Aramaic, and the true sense is ' man ' (*e.g.* ' Man is lord even of the sabbath '). In other and more numerous passages the meaning seems to be simply ' I.' In others again there are undertones, ' I, the Christ,' or ' I, the Son of God.' Only a minority of recorded sayings appear to reflect apocalyptic expectations, and the authenticity of some of these may fairly be doubted. The variety of use is in any case perplexing, and it suggests either that Jesus deliberately chose a term the vagueness of which left room for speculation, or that at some stage in the transmission of His teaching the use of phraseology was very loose, and the title was introduced into sayings to which it did not properly belong.

Unanimity among scholars is not to be expected, for the precise meaning of the phrase ' Son of Man ' is admittedly difficult to determine ; but the most probable view is that Jesus chose the title as an alternative to ' Christ ' partly to avoid exciting false hopes of a nationalist character, and partly because, though it had some messianic associations, it allowed the introduction of ideas foreign to current conceptions of the Messiah. In His words ' the Son of Man ' means ' the Christ,' but a suffering Christ, such as Jewish messianism could not conceive.

Some scholars think that the true origin of the term ' Son of Man ' as used by Jesus is to be found in Ezekiel rather than in Daniel, concluding that Jesus thought of Himself primarily as a prophet, the vehicle of the Spirit of God. If that were so, apocalyptism would be remote from His teaching and the presence of apocalyptic sayings in the gospels could only be explained as the product of the enthusiastic faith of the early Church which, misled by the use of the term ' Son of Man ' in some late Jewish literature, introduced into the traditions of the teaching of Jesus an element foreign to his authentic utterances. The objection that the large place of apocalyptism in the theology of the early Church is inexplicable unless it had some basis in the teaching of Jesus Himself is serious but not conclusive. It must be remembered that the Fourth Gospel, now increasingly regarded as resting upon a tradition independent of the synoptists, has hardly a trace of apocalyptism. There was more than one interpretation of the teaching and Person of Jesus current in the 1st cent. It is not difficult to imagine why such ideas as find expression most strongly in St. Matthew's Gospel, in the Epistles to the Thessalonians, and in the Revelation of St. John, spread rapidly among primitive believers ; but it does not follow that they dominated the minds of all Christians, or that they represented the mind of Jesus Himself.

(*e*) ' THE SON OF GOD.'—The title ' Son of God ' has influenced later Christian thought more deeply than ' Son of Man,' or even ' Christ.' It is not of frequent occurrence in the synoptic gospels, but in Mark it appears in the cries of demoniacs (3^{11} 5^7), in the question of the High Priest (14^{61}), and in the centurion's confession—but without the definite article (15^{39}). In 1^{11} the Divine voice speaks to 'My Son, the beloved' (RSVm), and the same words in the third person occur in the account of the Transfiguration (9^7). In Q passages 'Son of God' (with no article) is used in the story of the Temptation, and in Mt 11^{27} and Lk 10^{22} 'the Son' is contrasted with 'the Father.' In matter peculiar to Matthew or Luke 'Son of God' occurs in Mt 14^{33}, 16^{16}, $27^{40, 43}$ 28^{19} and Lk1^{35}, from which it may be inferred that the title is rooted in very early tradition. Whether Jesus used it of Himself is doubtful, depending in no small measure on the authenticity of the saying recorded in Mt 11^{27}=Lu 10^{22}, 'All things have been delivered to me by my Father; and no one knows the Son except the Father, and no one knows the Father except the Son and any one to whom the Son chooses to reveal him.' If this 'bolt from the Johannine blue' be accepted as an utterance of Jesus, similar sayings from the Fourth Gospel cannot be ruled out. But there is no agreement among scholars. On the one hand it is urged that the words, if derived from Q, come to us with the authority of what is probably our earliest source; while on the other hand it is objected that a saying so unlike other synoptic utterances cannot be ascribed to Jesus with any probability. However that may be, the presence of the saying in Q is at least evidence of a 'Sonship' christology at a very early date, and the fact must not be overlooked that the passage does not stand quite alone. Mk 13^{32}, 'Of that day or that hour no one knows, not even the angels in heaven, nor the Son, but only the Father' is not easily explained as a Christian invention; and the Marcan parable of the Vineyard (12^{1-11}) rests on a description of the last messenger as 'still one other, a beloved son.' The purpose of this parable was not to teach christology, but to lay stress on the responsibility of Israel and its leaders; nevertheless, the unique status of the final messenger is implicit in the story.

If it be allowed as probable that Jesus did refer to Himself as 'Son of God,' Semitic idiom must be borne in mind. In the OT 'son of God' is used in several senses. In Gn 6^2 we read of 'the sons of God' who took wives of the daughters of men, and presumably it is mythical angelic beings which are referred to. In Job 38^7 'all the sons of God' are said to have shouted for joy at the creation, and here some court of heaven is conceived (cf Job 1^6). In various passages Israel is referred to as 'God's son,' and in others the righteous are thus described (Ex 4^{22}, Hos 11^1, Sir 4^{10} etc.). In Semitic usage 'sonship' is a conception somewhat loosely employed to denote moral rather than physical or metaphysical relationship. Thus 'sons of Belial (Jg 19^{22} etc.) are wicked men, not descendants of Belial; and in the NT the 'children of the bridechamber' are wedding guests. So a 'son of God' is a man, or even a people, who reflect the character of God. There is little evidence that the title was used in Jewish circles of the Messiah, and a sonship which implied more than a moral relationship would be contrary to Jewish monotheism.

In the Hellenistic world the idea of Divine sonship was much more familiar and more literally interpreted, for the line between the human and the Divine was less clearly drawn. Kings and emperors liked to think of themselves as descended from the gods, and temples were erected to their honour. It is not surprising, therefore, that some critics, while denying that Jesus ever called Himself the Son of God, suppose that the title was borrowed by the Church from pagan usage. This is an easy explanation, but further consideration makes it improbable. It is partly a question of date. The NT as a whole provides evidence that Sonship titles were in use at a very early period (*e.g.* 1 Th 1^{10}), and it is highly improbable that the Church in the first twenty years of its history, when it was still largely Jewish, would have borrowed either its ideas or its terminology from the heathen world.

For the same reason the attempt of Bultmann to find the origin of the idea of Sonship in Gnosticism must be no less decisively rejected. It is incredible that the primitive Christians at Jerusalem knew anything about Gnostic 'redeemers' who descended from the spiritual world of light to release the prisoners of matter; and it is no less incredible that if they had heard of such fancies they would have applied them to Jesus. It is far more probable that the term 'Son of God' was of Hebraic origin, that it was used of Jesus by the first generation of believers, and that it must be interpreted in relation to Hebraic thought. If Jesus did refer to Himself as 'Son of God' the term implies His consciousness of standing in a relationship to God unique in its intimacy. More than that we cannot say.

(*f*) 'LORD.'—In recent years much discussion has centred round the title 'Lord' as applied to Jesus. It does not occur frequently in the synoptic gospels, and in most cases it is no more than a polite form of address, probably translating 'Rabbi'; but in the rest of the NT 'Lord' has become the regular title of Jesus, either in the phrase 'the Lord Jesus Christ,' or simply 'the Lord.' The inference is that 'Lord' is a post-resurrection title, hardly used, if at all, in the days of the ministry. It is a testimony to the historical reliability of the synoptists that, despite the undoubted usage of the early Church, 'the Lord' is not found in any Q passage and there is only one doubtful example in Mark and Matthew (Mk 11^3, Mt 21^3). But Mk 12^{36f} records that Jesus, with reference to the Messiah, quoted Ps 110^1 'The Lord said unto my Lord, Sit at my right hand,' adding, 'David himself calls him Lord; so how is he his son?', a saying which seems to mean that the Christ is Lord and therefore more than a scion of the house of David.

Unlike Matthew and Mark, Luke introduces the title of Lord with some frequency, using it fifteen times in the body of the gospel and twice in the nativity stories. In most cases it is clearly editorial (*e.g.* 'the Lord said'), and only once does it appear in a saying—'the Lord has risen indeed' (24^{34}). There can be no doubt that Luke is using the terminology of the early Church, and Vincent Taylor is right in his conclusion 'It is highly improbable that this title was in use in the lifetime of Jesus. It is as the risen and ascended "Lord" that he is *ho kyrios*' (*The Names of Jesus*, p. 43).

This conclusion is supported by a study of the Acts and Epistles, where the title occurs with great frequency, indicating that it was from a very early time the most common way of referring to Jesus in both Jewish and Gentile communities. It was not the invention of St. Paul, who in such passages as Ro 10^9 and 1 Cor 12^3 implies that the confession 'Jesus is Lord' was a kind of primitive creed, the watchword of the Christians. St. Paul refers to the Eucharist as 'the Lord's Supper,' and the phrase *Marana tha* (Our Lord come!) in 1 Co 16^{22} (cf *Didache* 10) proves that the title was in use in the original Aramaic-speaking communities.

Since Bousset published his well-known work *Kyrios Christos* the suggestion has often been made that the title 'Lord' was borrowed from the world of Hellenistic religion, where it was freely employed. This contention must be dismissed as offending against every canon of probability. The first Christians were Jews, and as we have seen with reference to the title 'Son of God,' it is quite incredible that they turned to heathenism, which they despised and detested, to find expression for their reverence for the risen Christ. As Bishop Rawlinson has said, 'The phrase *Marana tha* is the Achilles Heel of the theory of Bousset' (*N.T. Doctrine of Christ*, p. 235). One or two generations later Hellenistic ideas and expressions may have influenced the development of Christian terminology, but the recognition of Jesus as 'Lord' occurred long before Christian theology was subjected to pagan influences, when the Church hardly extended beyond the boundaries of Judaea.

How then is it to be explained? The main factor was the tremendous impact of the belief in the resurrection.

During the ministry the disciples, conscious of a numinous element in His Person, groped their way towards faith in Jesus as the Messiah; but their faith was insecure, and ideas as to the meaning of messiahship were ill-defined (Lk 24^{21}). After the resurrection their whole attitude was changed. The Jesus whom they had known was unmistakably revealed as a supernatural Being; in the words of St. Paul, he was 'declared to be Son of God in power' (Ro 1^{4}), worthy not only of love and reverence, but of worship too. In prayer, in fellowship, in eucharist, and in daily life, believers knew that the exalted Jesus was with them, and how else could they think of Him but as 'Lord'? In the LXX the word is constantly used to render the name of God, and that fact cannot have been without influence among Greek-speaking Christians; but the Lordship of Jesus was recognized earlier than the spread of Christianity to Greek world.

Connected with the impact of the resurrection faith, and springing from it, was the rapidly developing Christian cultus. That Jesus should have been offered worship by Jewish Christians is indeed surprising, for the attribution of Divine honours to a man was contrary to Jewish monotheism. But the fact remains; as Rawlinson has said, 'The cult of the Lord Jesus was inherent in Christianity from the beginning.' Such worship is a measure of the impression made by His Person, life, death, and resurrection upon the earliest Church. Yet this stage had not been reached in the days of the ministry, and the synoptic gospels are true to history in their reticence in presenting Jesus as an object of worship before the resurrection. In the words of C. V. Jones (*Christology and Myth in the New Testament*, p. 90) 'Of the later belief that Jesus was God Himself in the flesh there is no trace in the synoptic gospels'; but that very shortly after the resurrection He was regarded as a divine being, and the proper object of worship, is apparent from the rest of the NT, and this faith is summarized in the title 'Lord.'

(*g*) SUMMARY.—To sum up the evidence of the synoptic gospels: they make it clear that in the Church of the 1st cent. Jesus was believed to be the promised Messiah, and the evidence is strong that this belief was current among His followers during the ministry; the claim was suspected by the Jewish authorities and reported to the Roman Governor; Jesus Himself did not refuse the title, but He gave it a meaning that only partly corresponded with Jewish expectations, and during the ministry He did not proclaim His messiahship; He preferred the title 'Son of Man,' enriching it with a content not altogether understood by the disciples, but certainly including ideas derived from the picture of the Suffering Servant in Is 53. As to how far Jesus drew on the expectations of contemporary apocalyptism the opinions of scholars differ, but there can be no doubt that the early Church treasured such hopes. For the early believers, after the resurrection, Jesus was 'the Lord,' and they found in the symbolism of the apocalypses a way of expressing their faith in the certain triumph of their crucified and risen Master. The Kingdom preached and inaugurated in Galilee would be consummated at the Parousia of the Son of God.

2. Acts.—The date of Acts is still a matter of controversy, but if, as can hardly be denied, it is by the same author as the Third Gospel and a sequel to the earlier work, it must belong to the last quarter of the 1st cent. It therefore reflects the theology of the same period as saw the appearance of Matthew and Luke; but the author clearly made use of much earlier sources, and, as compared with the Epistles of St. Paul and the Johannine writings, the book is remarkably primitive in its theology. B. H. Streeter wrote of its 'pre-Pauline Gentile Christianity' (*The Four Gospels*, p. 556).

The Christology of Acts, which Harnack described as 'absolutely primitive,' is largely expressed in the speeches of St. Peter in the earlier chapters, and in the missionary addresses of St. Paul. Here the foundation is an unquestioning belief in the humanity of Jesus. In 2^{22} Peter speaks of 'Jesus of Nazareth, a man attested to you by God with mighty works and wonders and signs which God did through him in your midst'; and in 10^{38} Peter describes Jesus as one who 'went about doing good, and healing all that were oppressed by the devil, for God was with him.' Such language seems to date from a time when it was still considered proper to think of Jesus as 'the prophet of Nazareth' whatever other designations were in use, and in two passages (3^{22} 7^{37}) He is identified with 'the prophet' of Dt 18^{18}. Yet that this was not the only way in which the earliest Church thought of Jesus is manifest from other passages in Peter's sermons: thus 2^{24}, 'But God raised him up, having loosed the pangs of death, because it was not possible for him to be held by it'; and 2^{33} 'Being therefore exalted at the right hand of God, and having received from the Father the promise of the Holy Spirit, he has poured out this which you see and hear.' This is not language that could be used of a mere prophet.

The Messiahship of Jesus receives more emphasis in Acts than in the gospels, but it is not taken for granted as it is in St. Paul's Epistles. It is reckoned that the title 'the Christ,' in the strict sense of 'the Messiah,' occurs at least twelve times in Acts, although it has no political implications. As we have seen, the evidence of the gospels points to a certain reserve on the part of Jesus in claiming to be the Messiah, and He preferred the title 'Son of Man'; but after the Resurrection the Church had no doubt as to the messiahship, and, abandoning the designation 'Son of Man,' referred to Jesus constantly as 'the Christ,' so constantly, indeed, that the title soon became a proper name. It is a remarkable testimony to the primitive character of many passages in Acts that this latter stage has not been reached, and the emphasis still falls on the fulfilment of messianic prophecy in the Person of Jesus. 'Every day the Apostles in the temple and at home did not cease teaching and preaching Jesus as the Christ' (5^{42}); 'Saul increased all the more in strength, and confounded the Jews who lived in Damascus by proving that Jesus was the Christ' (9^{22}); and there are other passages.

That Jesus was 'the Servant of the Lord' of prophecy is a conviction which appears in Acts, if not for the first time, at least with new emphasis. The word used in $3^{13, 26}$ $4^{27, 30}$ is not *doulos* (slave) but *pais* (servant, or son) which is the word used in the LXX of Second Isaiah. Several passages affirm that 'it was necessary for the Christ to suffer' (*e.g.* 17^{3}), so that even apart from the incident of Philip and the eunuch (8^{26-40}), in which Is 53 is quoted at length, Acts leaves no doubt that the Servant prophecies were already in the mind of the Church. It is surprising that this element in the early christology seems to have largely dropped out at the stage represented by the later books of the NT.

Taking Acts as a whole we find that the title 'Lord' is applied to Jesus more frequently than any other, and here the contrast with the synoptic gospels is most marked. The Jesus of the synoptic gospels, the man who went about doing good, is not forgotten, but He is recognized unmistakably as a heavenly Being, the object of worship, the Lord. We see the impact of the resurrection faith, for the resurrection had shown Him to be 'both Lord and Christ' (2^{36}). So Stephen could pray, 'Lord Jesus, receive my spirit' (7^{59}), and Saul could meet Him on the road to Damascus. He is 'the Author of life' (3^{15}), and 'there is no other name under heaven, given among men, by which we must be saved' (4^{12}). Such language does not suggest an adoptianist christology, although the title 'Son of God' is not found in Acts. The vocabulary of the Church took time to develop, but the convictions it came to express were primitive.

3. St. Paul.—The Pauline Epistles are the earliest Christian writings that have survived. Thirteen epistles of St. Paul appear in the Canon of the NT, apart from the Epistle to the Hebrews, and although many modern scholars have serious doubts as to the authenticity of some of these, notably 2 Thessalonians, Ephesians, and the Pastoral Epistles, the genuineness of the rest is seldom questioned.

(*a*) St. Paul and the Primitive Church.—Although it cannot be supposed that St. Paul's theology, taken as a whole, was typical of the doctrine of the Christian Church in the first thirty years of its life, it reveals much of the common stock of the early Church. He himself, while claiming at times direct inspiration, could yet refer to 'that which I also received' (1 Co 15^3). Thus, for instance, he accepted the belief of all Christians at the time of his conversion that Jesus was the Messiah and was bringing in the messianic kingdom. But the Apostle's chief interest was in soteriology, and he had no concern with Jewish nationalistic aims. Yet he accepted the apocalyptic hopes which soon gained currency in the early Church, evidently regarding them as part of the faith he now professed. In some of his epistles apocalyptism is more prominent than in the gospels, and it is a legitimate matter for speculation how this type of thought had so quickly come to the front. Perhaps it is not difficult to reconstruct the current of thought. Jesus was the Christ, vindicated by the resurrection; but from a Jewish point of view a suffering Messiah was almost a contradiction in terms; however conceived, the Messiah was a glorious and triumphant figure, and, since Jesus had submitted to a shameful death, the glory must be manifested in the future. So the Church accepted a transmuted Jewish apocalyptism. Angels, the clouds of heaven, the judgment seat, the sound of the trumpet—these things were indeed appropriate to the manifestation of the Anointed One; but since His earthly life had been marked by humility and suffering, the true revelation of His glory must be still to come. Thus the apocalyptism of later Judaism became attached to Christianity, and the harassed believers found consolation in their trials by living in daily expectation of a miraculous deliverance.

St. Paul's general outlook is characterized by what has been aptly called 'sanctified common sense,' and it is perhaps surprising that he accepted so readily the fantastic imaginings of apocalyptism. Yet that he did so is obvious from almost all his epistles. He never became obsessed by such hopes, as do weaker minds, but the confident expectation of the *Parousia* is an undertone in all he writes. In 1 Thessalonians 'the Day of the Lord' is expected at any moment, 'like a thief in the night'; and although in his later epistles St. Paul realizes that his own death is probable before the end, he can still tell the Philippians that 'the Lord is at hand,' and he takes comfort in the hope that his converts may be 'pure and blameless for the day of Christ' (Ph 1^{10}).

Whatever may be said of St. Paul's eschatology, it throws much light upon his christology. The Lord who is to descend from heaven 'with a cry of command, with the archangel's call, and with the sound of the trumpet of God' (1 Th 4^{16}) is evidently a heavenly being, and it is not surprising that his majesty overshadows the memory of Jesus of Nazareth. St. Paul must have known something of the traditions of the ministry, and he was evidently acquainted with the ethical teaching of Jesus; but his mind was too full of the thought of Christ, risen and exalted, for him to dwell much upon the history of the earthly life of Jesus. His determination, expressed in 2 Co 5^{16}, no longer to regard Christ from a human point of view (or 'after the flesh'), may be variously explained, and perhaps he means 'as the Messiah of Judaism'; but in any case it is obvious that the Apostle was not much interested in the traditions of the life of Jesus except in so far as they concerned the crucifixion and resurrection, to which he attributed cosmic significance.

(*b*) Paul's Jewish Background.—Before proceeding further in the examination of St. Paul's thought it is necessary to glance at his background, and to appreciate the fundamental convictions from which he started. We have it on his own testimony that his education had been strictly Jewish. A Hebrew of pure Hebrew stock, he was 'a Pharisee, a son of Pharisees' (Ac 23^6), and according to Ac 22^3 he had been brought up at the feet of Gamaliel. There is some evidence that Gamaliel represented a liberal and enlightened Pharisaism, and although his pupil Saul was far from liberal at the time of the persecution that arose about Stephen, it may be that the master's influence remained dormant in the young zealot and contributed to the later development of his thought. (See Paul.)

Little is known about contemporary Pharisaism, but there can be no doubt that the main interest of the sect lay in the meticulous observance of the Mosaic Law. Thus the young Saul—as he said later—'advanced in Judaism beyond many of my own age among my people, so extremely zealous was I for the traditions of my fathers' (Gal 1^{14}). As a good Jew his predominating interest was in the question 'How is man to be justified in the sight of God?', and in his early years he did not doubt that the answer lay in the Jewish faith, 'through keeping the Law revealed to Moses.' Whether St. Paul's later dissatisfaction with the soteriology of Judaism was subconsciously present in his mind before his critical experience on the road to Damascus it is difficult to say. Knowing as we do the earnestness and sensitivity of the Apostle's nature, we may suspect that the faith of the followers of Jesus had already exerted an attraction on his mind which he was unwilling to admit. St. Paul was a good man at all times, and a good man does not take pleasure in persecution even when fanaticism drives him to make havoc of those whose convictions seem mistaken and dangerous. It is not unlikely that the martyrdom of Stephen had left a deep impression on the mind of the 'young man named Saul,' and although he took a leading part in the persecution that followed, he was kicking against the goads.

According to Gal 1^{16f} the converted Saul 'conferred not with men, neither went he up to Jerusalem to them that were apostles before him; but he went away into Arabia, and again returned to Damascus.' The journey to Arabia and the subsequent residence in Damascus covered a period of three years, and although by the end of that time he was already known as a preacher of the faith (Gal 1^{23}), it is reasonable to suppose that much of it was spent in thinking out his position. When in Ac 9^{20} Luke says that after his conversion Saul immediately in the synagogues proclaimed Jesus, saying 'He is the Son of God,' there may be a foreshortening of the chronology; but we have no reason to doubt that, when he did begin to preach, the substance of his message was the exaltation and Divine status of the Jesus who had appeared to him. From that time his outlook was wholly Christocentric. His own experience had proved the Jewish way of attaining justification to be a failure, and Jesus must provide the true and only alternative. Henceforth his life and thought were dominated by the conviction that 'Jesus is Lord'—St. Paul's creed in its simplest form (Ro 10^9, 1 Co 12^3, Ph 2^{11}).

(*c*) St. Paul and Hellenism.—Some modern writers describe the conception of the Messiah as a heavenly Being as 'mythology' and believe that St. Paul accepted without question the 'mythological' outlook and beliefs found in contemporary thought. That his convictions were in some ways similar may be allowed. For instance, St. Paul assumes the pre-existence of Christ in the heavenly sphere. The *locus classicus* is Ph 2^{5ff}: 'Christ Jesus, who, though he was in the form of God, did not count equality with God a thing to be grasped, but emptied himself, taking the form of a servant, being born in the likeness of men.' Wilhelm Bousset thought that such a passage removes Jesus entirely from 'the ethical historical picture,' identifying him with the Gnostic 'Anthropos,' the Heavenly Man. So, according to Bousset and his followers, the great christological passages in the epistles, and still more the theology of the Fourth Gospel, are based upon the presuppositions of Hellenism and incipient Gnosticism. Bultmann regards the prologue of the Fourth Gospel as a Gnostic redemption myth.

These contentions have been put forward by a number

of modern scholars with great learning and persuasive ingenuity, but nothing can conceal their intrinsic improbability. St. Paul was born and bred a Jew, and many passages in his epistles testify to his remaining a Jew in outlook and sympathy to the end of his life. He was deeply versed in the OT scriptures, he was proud of Jewish privileges, he could wish to be ' anathema from Christ ' for his brethren's sake. He never doubted the revelation of the old dispensation, and he was no admirer of the Gentile world (Ro 1[20ff]), despite his lifelong labours to bring to the Gentiles the gospel of salvation. He never quotes Greek thinkers except—according to Ac 17[28]—on the occasion at Athens, when he wishes to conciliate the philosophers, and—according to 1 Co 15[33] —when he quotes a popular line from Menander. It is therefore in the highest degree unlikely that his conversion to Christ was in fact a conversion to hellenistic gnosticism, or that he immediately interpreted his new experience in terms of an alien theosophy. If St. Paul had been largely under the spell of the mystery religions he could hardly have avoided the term *Sōtēr* in speaking of Christ; yet avoid it he did, save in two passages, Ph 3[20] and Eph 5[23]—and the authorship of Ephesians is widely challenged. Indeed it may be argued that he consciously refrained from using a title which, though well suited to express his thought, might easily suggest pagan ideas to some of his readers.

It must, of course, be granted that St. Paul spent many years—between his conversion and the writing of his early epistles—at Tarsus, far removed from the centre of Jewish orthodoxy at Jerusalem; and although it is impossible to believe that he ever became a Hellenistic Gnostic, it is not impossible to suppose that he drew on some of the thought-forms of the Gentile world in seeking to formulate his christology. As he stood blinded on the road to Damascus he became convinced that the Jesus whom he persecuted was indeed a heavenly being, that though He had died upon the cross He was risen and glorified, the Redeemer from sin and from the wrath of God. How could these facts be interpreted, save in terms reminiscent of the pagan myths? But the resemblance is superficial. The pagan myths were myths and no more. The saviour-gods of the mysteries may have been represented as dying and coming to life again, but they were no more than nature-symbols, utterly unlike the living personal Christ who was the object of St. Paul's devotion. Nor is there any real similarity between the pagan ceremonies of initiation and communion and the Christian sacraments accepted by the Apostle. Initiation into the mysteries might assure the participant that he was *renatus in aeternum* (though the phrase is late); but baptism into Christ, with its death to sin and its rising again unto righteousness, belonged to a different world of ideas.

St. Paul never lost his foothold in history. He thought of Christ as a man, born of the seed of David according to the flesh, whose example and teaching established the ethical norm for His followers (Ro 1[3], Ph 2[5], Ac 20[35]). That this aspect of the Apostle's teaching is not prominent in his epistles is a fact to be borne in mind. It may be that he was content that others should instruct his followers concerning the earthly life of Jesus; it may be that he knew little of it himself; it is certainly true that it did not occupy a central place in his thought. Yet it is there. St. Paul knew that Jesus had lived the life of man at a definite time and in a definite place, and thus his christology is firmly anchored in history. In his interpretation of the crucifixion and resurrection, St. Paul starts from historical fact, and without that his soteriology would have had no point. Moreover, his intense personal devotion to Christ must not be forgotten: ' To me to live is Christ, and to die is gain ' . . . having a desire ' to depart and be with Christ, for that is far better ' (Ph 1[21, 23]). No man ever spoke of Mithras in such a manner, and although we have no reason to suppose that St. Paul ever saw Jesus in the flesh, an outburst such as this implies that he had in mind a real historical person. The love of which men are capable for a purely mythical being can easily be exaggerated.

Yet, as we have seen, it was not on the earthly life of Jesus that St. Paul's mind chiefly dwelt. He may speak of Jesus Christ as born of the seed of David, but it is only to add ' designated Son of God in power according to the Spirit of holiness by his resurrection from the dead ' (Ro 1[4]). If this passage stood alone it might be thought to suggest an adoptianist christology. Something depends on the exact meaning of the Greek word translated ' designated ' (RSV) ' declared ' (RV), or ' determined ' (RVm). Probably the meaning is that, although Jesus was always Son of God, His true nature was only revealed by the resurrection. Then, His work on earth done, He received the name that is above every name (Ph 2[9]). Raised from the dead, He was acclaimed Christ and Lord.

(*d*) PAUL'S CONCEPTION OF CHRIST.—Apart from its influence in dictating his apocalyptic expectations, the messiahship of Jesus does not figure largely in the thought of St. Paul. Of course Jesus was the Christ, but current conceptions of the Messiah were too much associated with Jewish nationalism to make much appeal to the Apostle to the Gentiles. Rather his interest was in Christ Jesus as the agent of God in bringing justification to men, and hence as the mediator of a new covenant of grace. His belief in the saving efficacy of Christ's death was central to his thought. Men, sinners all, children of Adam, subject to the wrath of God, are ' justified by his grace as a gift, through the redemption which is in Christ Jesus, whom God put forward as an expiation by his blood ' (Ro 3[24f]). He was ' put to death for our trespasses and raised for our justification ' (Ro 4[25]). ' While we were yet sinners Christ died for us ' (Ro 5[8]). ' Where sin increased, grace abounded all the more, so that, as sin reigned in death, grace also might reign through righteousness to eternal life through Jesus Christ our Lord ' (Ro 5[20f])' ' Christ redeemed us from the curse of the Law, having become a curse for us ' (Gal 3[13]).

This is not the place to attempt the elucidation of these tremendous claims, but we must ask, Who is this Christ Jesus whose death and resurrection have such power over the eternal destiny of men?—and not of men only, for ' the whole creation has been groaning in travail together until now ' (Ro 8[22]).

It is surprising that the great christological passages do not occur in Romans, where St. Paul describes at length the work of Christ, but in his later epistles, Philippians and Colossians. Yet in Romans the later teaching is adumbrated, if not assumed. He refers to Jesus as ' Christ,' ' Lord,' and ' Son of God,' and such a sentence as occurs in 1[7], ' Grace to you and peace from God our Father and the Lord Jesus Christ,' clearly implies that he thought of Jesus as belonging to the heavenly sphere, to be mentioned in the same breath as ' God our Father.' In 2[16] we read of the day when ' God judges the secrets of men by Christ Jesus,' a clear reference to the messianic judgment. But in Romans the Apostle is too intent on the exposition of his soteriological convictions to pause and explain his faith in the Person of Christ, or to expound the exact meaning of the title ' Son.' Only we learn that the relationship of the Son to the Father, though unique—God ' did not spare his own Son, but gave him up for us all ' (8[32])—yet foreshadows the relationship to God of all who are called according to His purpose, , For those whom he foreknew he also predestined to be conformed to the image of his Son, in order that he might be the firstborn among many brethren ' (8[29]).

The references to the pre-existence of Christ are not numerous, but they are decisive. Apart from Ph 2[5ff], St. Paul writes in 2 Co 8[9], ' You know the grace of our Lord Jesus Christ, that though he was rich, yet for your sake he became poor '; and almost equally unmistakable is Gal 4[4], ' When the time had fully come, God sent forth his Son, born of a woman, born under the Law.' These passages must be read in conjunction with those which emphasize the exaltation of Christ through the resurrection. ‘God has highly exalted him and bestowed on him the name which is above every name’ (Ph 2^{9}). and ‘He raised him from the dead and made him sit at his right hand in the heavenly places, far above all rule and authority and power and dominion’ (Eph 1^{20}, if we may quote it as Pauline). But the Apostle does not mean that such dignity was new and strange to the risen Christ, who in taking the form of a servant had humbled and emptied Himself (Ph 2^{6ff}).

Much has been written and continues to be written on the precise meaning of this ‘emptying,’ or *kenōsis.* St. Paul does not elaborate his thought. It is possible that in Philippians he is quoting from some hymn to Christ, and the conception is not strictly original; but at least, if Ph 2 may be read with Col 1^{15ff}, no doubt remains as to the Apostle's conviction that Christ was eternally Divine. ‘For in him all things were created, in heaven and on earth, visible and invisible . . . all things were created through him and for him. He is before all things, and in him all things hold together.’ This may be dismissed as ‘mythology,’ but it can only mean that to St. Paul Christ was pre-existent and eternal.

How then was it possible for the heavenly Christ to live and die as a man? It may be that St. Paul's preoccupation with the redemptive work of the Divine Son prevented him from realizing the difficulties that emerged in later centuries. He never asked whether the Ego of Christ was human or Divine, or how the Divine nature could persist under conditions of human life, or how two natures could coexist in a single Person. The later history of doctrine testifies to the embarrassment of the Church in proclaiming that one who was Son of God could suffer on the cross and die. Docetism was the earliest Christian heresy, but St. Paul betrays no sign of docetic tendencies. He believed in the humanity of Jesus, born of the seed of David, and he believed that He was the Son of God. To become subject to suffering and death He who was in the form of God had emptied Himself, that is, had laid aside His Divine immunity and prerogative. If it be asked what else He laid aside, His power, His knowledge, or His claim to the worship of men, St. Paul has no answer. Such questions he left for later theologians, but a strong degree of self-limitation is implied in his view of the resurrection whereby Jesus was designated Son of God in power. His thought is not alien to that of the Fourth Gospel, ‘And now, Father, glorify thou me in thy own presence with the glory which I had with thee before the world was made’ (Jn 17^{5}). The dividing line between voluntary humiliation with all that that implied and final glorification was the resurrection.

So St. Paul opened the way to the development of a christology which denies neither the divinity nor the full humanity of Christ. While not ceasing to be God, and so able to effect redemption for sinners, the pre-existent Son divested Himself of such qualities as would be altogether incompatible with the reality of human life. Looking back at such records of the ministry as are available we must admit that even the consciousness of Divine Sonship is not to be assumed. No text is more significant than Lk 2^{52}, where the evangelist writes that the young Jesus ‘increased in wisdom and in stature, and in favour with God and man.’

Many problems remain unsolved, but unless either the divinity or the humanity of Christ is to be denied some form of kenotic christology is inevitable, and it must be built on the foundation of Ph 2$^{5-11}$.

(*e*) Summary.—To summarize, then, the witness of St. Paul, it must be insisted again that his approach is soteriological, rather than dogmatic. The Jesus who had lived and died on earth, but who had appeared to him on the road to Damascus, was indeed Messiah and Son of God. His death and resurrection had been part of the Divine plan whereby sinners might be ‘justified’ by faith, and not by works of law. Now he was by God exalted, the object of worship, accessible in prayer. Before long the final consummation would be reached when the glorified Christ would appear to reward the faithful and sit on the throne of messianic judgment. Meanwhile the Church enjoys the gift of the Spirit, in the strength of which the ‘Christian’ life is possible. The precise relationship of Christ to the Spirit is a question which the Apostle is content to leave undetermined, although there are many passages in which he distinguishes the Spirit from Christ (Ro 8^{16f}, 1 Co 6^{11} 12^{3}, etc.). Here again he lays the foundation of later doctrinal development. In the words of Vincent Taylor, ‘The doctrine of the Trinity is not taught, but its presuppositions in Pauline teaching are laid bare’ (*The Person of Christ*, p. 55).

St. Paul does not seem to have been conscious of any threat to the traditional monotheism of the Jews involved in his ‘high’ christology. Perhaps his mind had been prepared by the exaltation of Wisdom in late Jewish literature. Certainly he is able to associate the Divine Lordship of Christ with an uncompromising assertion of the unity of God: ‘For although there may be so-called gods in heaven and on earth—as indeed there are many “gods” and many “lords”—yet for us there is one God, the Father, from whom are all things and for whom we exist, and one Lord, Jesus Christ, through whom are all things and through whom we exist’ (1 Co 8^{5f}).

An element of ‘subordinationism’ is clearly discernible in St. Paul's teaching. However exalted, Christ was in the Apostle's mind no supreme Saviour God, but the Son of the Father, and obedient to Him; He was God's agent in the work of redemption, but destined at last to surrender the kingdom that ‘God may be all in all’ (or RSV ‘everything to everyone’) (1 Co 15$^{24, 28}$). However St. Paul may link together Christ Jesus and God the Father (Ro 1^{7}, 1 Co 1^{3}, 2 Co 1^{2}, Gal 1^{3}, etc.), he always ascribes the initiative to the Father, who *sent* His Son in the likeness of flesh (Ro 8^{3}), who *raised* Him from the dead (Ro 4^{24} 8^{11}, 1 Co 15^{15}, Col 2^{12}, 1 Th 1^{10}), who *has highly exalted* Him, and *bestowed* on Him the Name (Ph 2^{9}). There is nothing here to support the Arian conception of an inferior essence, but the Apostle does not equate the Father and the Son in function.

4. The Epistle to Hebrews.—We must now glance more briefly at the christology of another writer, so long and so mistakenly identified with St. Paul. Of the identity of the *Auctor ad Hebraeos* nothing is known, and all that can be said is that he was probably an Alexandrian Christian who wrote in the latter part of the 1st cent. Whether he was himself a Jew, and whether his epistle is indeed addressed to ‘Hebrews’ remains open to question. It has been forcibly argued that his approach to Judaism is not that of a Jew, but rather of a Gentile who has derived his conception of Jewish religion from an intensive study of parts of the OT. He shows particular interest in the Levitical sacrificial system, which, even before the destruction of the Temple in A.D. 70, had become of secondary importance in comparison with the worship of the synagogue.

The main theme of the Epistle is the superiority of the new dispensation to the old. The new is founded upon a better covenant of which Christ is the mediator, and Christ is far greater than Moses. ‘Christ has obtained a ministry which is as much more excellent than the old as the covenant he mediates is better, since it is enacted on better promises’ (8^{6}; cf 9^{15} 12^{24}). Of this new dispensation Christ is the true and eternal High Priest, far superior to the high priests of the old covenant, and offering a better sacrifice than they (7$^{26-28}$); hence the privilege of Christians who have ‘an altar from which those who serve the tent have no right to eat’ (13^{10}).

It is evident that the argument rests upon the author's christology; only because he can assume the acceptance of his own view of the Person of Christ has it any force. That his was a ‘high’ christology is obvious, for none but a Divine being could fulfil the functions ascribed to Christ in the Epistle. Yet he was no docetist, and he never forgets the human life of Jesus. The ‘great salvation ' offered to Christians was ' declared at first by the Lord, and it was attested to us by those who heard him, while God also bore witness by signs and wonders and various miracles and by gifts of the Holy Spirit ' (2^{3f}). This suggests a knowledge of the gospel history not found in St. Paul. Moreover, the difficult verse (5^{7}), ' In the days of his flesh, Jesus offered up prayers and supplications, with loud cries and tears, to him who was able to save him from death, and he was heard for his godly fear,' seems to go beyond the gospel record in emphasizing the human weakness of Jesus and the reality of his sufferings. The next verse, ' Although he was a Son, he learned obedience through what he suffered,' is a daring statement, but it accords with the author's general view. The human virtues displayed by Jesus consort with His subordination to the Father; ' He was faithful to him who appointed him, just as Moses also was faithful in God's house ' (3^{2}). The voluntary character of Christ's suffering is no less strongly emphasized than its reality: ' Jesus suffered in order to sanctify the people through his own blood ' (13^{12}); and in all ' he has been tempted as we are, yet without sinning ' (4^{15}). Even spiritual progress was experienced, since ' he learned obedience through what he suffered ' and was made perfect (5^{8f}).

It is indeed remarkable that in spite of this ' vivid portraiture of the humanity of Jesus ' (Mackintosh) the author should be able to conceive the essential nature of ' the Son ' in terms which almost go beyond the declared christology of St. Paul. Christ, the ideal High Priest, of whom even Melchizedek is but an adumbration, now ' is seated at the right hand of the throne of the Majesty in heaven ' (8^{1}). The first paragraph of the Epistle declares Him to be ' a Son,' and as such contrasted not only with prophets but with angels: ' To what angel did God ever say, " Thou art my Son, this day I have begotten thee "? ' (1^{5}). The scriptural quotations in chapter 1, however uncritically applied, are of great significance as revealing the author's convictions. Christ is a Son whose relation to the Father is unique (v.^{5}). He is the object of worship by the angels (v.^{6}). His throne and sceptre are eternal (v.^{8}). He is at once the anointed of God and the agent of creation, though in no way sharing the transitory nature of the material world, for ' they will all grow old like a garment . . . but thou art the same, and thy years will never end ' (vv.$^{11, 12}$). Thus, as for St. Paul, the earthly life of Jesus was an act of condescension: ' Since therefore the children share in flesh and blood, he himself likewise partook of the same nature, that through death he might destroy him who has the power of death, that is, the devil ' (2^{14}); ' He had to be made like his brethren in every respect ' (2^{17}); ' Because he himself has suffered and been tempted, he is able to help those who are tempted ' (2^{18}).

The author thinks of the relationship of the Son to the Father as eternal; else how could the Son have been concerned with creation? (1^{10}). It is the Son who founded the earth in the beginning, who built the ' house ' of the Mosaic dispensation (3^{3}), and whose work as High Priest on earth and in heaven secures the salvation of men (10^{12-14}). He uses ' Christ ' and ' Son ' without clear distinction, and he teaches the pre-existence of Christ without ambiguity. There is no exposition of the incarnation so formal as that of Ph 2^{5-11} or the Prologue to the Fourth Gospel; but the fact is taken for granted.

Hebrews has been called ' the Epistle of Priesthood,' for it is on the Priesthood of Christ that the author's mind chiefly dwells. He looks at the OT mainly as embodying a sacerdotal system, centred in the Tabernacle, whereby the Levitical priests, by the blood of bulls and of goats, sought to make atonement for the sins of the people. Their sacrifices had no true validity, since they served as ' a copy and shadow of the heavenly sanctuary ' (8^{5}). Levitical priests were but men, constrained to offer daily the same sacrifices for themselves and for others, sacrifices which ' can never take away sins ' (10^{11}); but Christ, the one true High Priest, offered Himself, ' for all time a single sacrifice for sins,' and ' sat down at the right hand of God ' (10^{12}). Thus the whole of the old dispensation, with its covenant, its priests, and its sacrifices, is no more than an adumbration of the new, and ' what is becoming obsolete and growing old is ready to vanish away ' (8^{13}).

The author is no more concerned than was St. Paul to explore the relation of his christology to monotheism. The Son is indeed unique, reflecting the glory of God and bearing the very stamp of His nature (1^{3}), so that he may fittingly sit down at God's right hand; but however exalted, he is not identified with God, and the note of subordination is maintained throughout. The eternal work of the Son, His task fulfilled on earth, is to make intercession for those who draw near to God through Him (7^{25} 9^{24}).

On the whole it may be said that the christology of Hebrews rests on convictions that do not differ essentially from those of St. Paul. The manhood of Jesus is emphasized rather more strongly than in the Pauline Epistles, but the author is no less convinced of His divinity. Indeed, the close relationship of Christ to the Father is assumed throughout, and the author leaves no doubt of his belief both in the eternal pre-existence of Christ and of His present exaltation. There is some shift of emphasis from the resurrection to the crucifixion: ' We see Jesus, who for a little while was made lower than the angels, crowned with glory and honour because of the suffering of death, so that by the grace of God he might taste death for every one ' (2^{9}).

In Hebrews, Jewish messianism has almost disappeared, giving place to the conception of Jesus as the great High Priest. The author has his eschatology, but the apocalyptism of St. Paul is absent. He speaks of ' the end ' (3^{14}), and there are references to judgment. ' Eternal judgment ' is classed among those elementary doctrines from which mature Christians must advance (6^{1f}). He preaches the fear of such judgment, and the punishment of those who have spurned the Son of God (10^{29}). He does not doubt that Christ will appear a second time ' not to deal with sin, but to save those who are eagerly waiting for him ' (9^{28}). ' The Day ' is drawing near (10^{25}). But the realistic picture of the messianic judgment is lacking in Hebrews, and the expectation of the future is left vague: ' There remains a sabbath rest for the people of God; . . . let us strive to enter that rest ' ($4^{9, 11}$). ' Let us be grateful for receiving a kingdom that cannot be shaken ' (12^{28}); ' Here we have no lasting city, but we seek the city which is to come ' (13^{14}). The author's hope (10^{23}) does not differ essentially from that of earlier believers, and he does not doubt that judgment will be meted out to those who refuse salvation in Christ; but he is too good a Platonist to share the materialistic outlook of those whose antecedents were Jewish rather than Greek. Like St. Paul he lays stress upon the necessity of faith whereby the benefits of Christ are appropriated; but for him faith is the religious sense in its widest aspect, ' the assurance of things hoped for, the conviction of things not seen ' (11^{1}). Of St. Paul's distinctive use of the term to express personal surrender and acceptance of justification through the work of Christ the author of Hebrews has no idea. This is not surprising, in view of the neglect—or misunderstanding—of Paul's teaching in the period following his martyrdom. The specifically Pauline view was probably *sui generis* in the first century. See FAITH, **2**, *ad fin.*

5. First Peter.—The place of the first Epistle of Peter in the development of christology is not easy to determine. Those who accept it as a genuine work of the Apostle naturally compare its teaching with that of the early speeches in Acts to which it bears some resemblance; but the short epistle contains little that may not be said to belong to the commonly accepted doctrine of the Church. If, as probably the majority of scholars now believe, it is a pseudonymous work of the latter part of the 1st cent., it may be legitimate to recognize not only primitive elements, but also a certain amount of development as compared with the earlier apostolic teaching.

The author's interest centres more in soteriology than in christology, and for that reason his precise convictions are implied rather than stated. He never uses the name Jesus by itself, and for him 'Christ' is a proper name with little trace of Jewish messianic implications. Christians are such as have been sprinkled with the blood of Christ (1^{2}). They are 'ransomed from the futile ways inherited from [their] fathers . . . with the precious blood of Christ, like that of a lamb without blemish or spot' (1^{18f}). Not only was the suffering of Christ an example to those who are called (2^{21}), but it had a deeper significance, inasmuch as 'he himself bore our sins in his body on the tree, that we might die to sin and live to righteousness' (2^{24}; cf Col 3^{3}, Ro 6^{2ff}). 'Christ . . . died for sins once for all, the righteous for the unrighteous, that he might bring us to God, being put to death in the flesh but made alive in the spirit' (3^{18}). The author's use of the conception of the Spirit is obscure. In 1^{11} he writes of the prophets as inspired by 'the Spirit of Christ,' and this has been taken as implying a belief in the pre-existence of Christ; but it is more probable that he retains an OT idea of the Spirit of God, active throughout history, but specially manifest in Christ, so that it may be called the spirit of Christ even when operative centuries before his birth. Christ's earthly life in the flesh ended with the crucifixion, but His true spiritual life was uninterrupted, and even before the resurrection He went to preach to the spirits in prison (3^{19}). To the dead He imparted something of His spiritual power, that 'though judged in the flesh like men, they might live in the spirit like God' (4^{6}).

The prevailing sacrifice of Christ was in accordance with God's eternal plan; 'he was destined before the foundation of the world, but was made manifest at the end of the times for your sake' (1^{20}). Now He is exalted by God who raised Him from the dead (1^{21}), and by men should be reverenced 'as Lord' (3^{15}). As a Divine being Jesus Christ has gone into heaven and is at the right hand of God, sharing God's power, since angels, authorities, and powers are subject to Him (3^{22}).

The Epistle has a strong eschatological element, though no apocalyptism is developed. Salvation is 'ready to be revealed in the last time' when the constancy of those born anew to a living hope will enjoy 'an inheritance imperishable, undefiled, and unfading, kept in heaven for you' ($1^{4,5}$). Genuineness of faith will be rewarded by 'praise, glory, and honour at the revelation [" apocalypse "] of Jesus Christ' (1^{7}). 'Set your hope fully on the grace that is coming to you at the revelation of Jesus Christ' (1^{13}). 'The end of all things is at hand, therefore keep sane and sober for your prayers' (4^{7}). In such passages the author reflects a faith in the imminent messianic consummation differing from that of St. Paul only in its lack of elaboration.

It may be concluded that the author of this Epistle thinks of Christ as the author of salvation by His sacrificial death, exalted to the throne of God, now the object of religious veneration, and destined at no distant time to reward the steadfastness of the faithful with the gift of their imperishable inheritance. That he was much influenced by the Christian interpretation of Isaiah 53 is certain, but in most respects he reflects the simple faith of 1st.-cent. Christianity and makes no attempt at theological systematization. He does not call Christ 'the Son,' and only in the opening words of the Epistle does he refer to God as 'Father'; there he describes the exiles of the dispersion as 'chosen and destined by God the Father and sanctified by the Spirit for obedience to Jesus Christ' (1^{2}). Dean Selwyn was surely right when he said that the Epistle 'contains the roots of later Catholic doctrine, but not yet its flower, so far as conscious formulation is concerned' (E. G. Selwyn, *The First Epistle of Peter*, p. 249). There is no Trinitarianism in the strict sense, but the materials out of which it was later constructed may be found in the Epistle. Similarly, in 3^{18} the Person of Christ is looked at from two points of view, the human and the Divine. He was 'put to death in flesh, but made alive in [the] spirit,' which is at least a pointer to the later doctrine of the Two Natures. It is a great advance on the Petrine speeches in Acts.

6. The Apocalypse of John.—Whatever may be said about the influence of Jewish apocalyptism on the synoptic gospels and the epistles of St. Paul, there can be no doubt about its dominating place in the Revelation of St. John the Divine. Here, if anywhere, the Christian faith is 'mythologized,' and the modern reader, unfamiliar with the bizarre imagery of apocalyptic literature, may find himself at a loss to understand the meaning of the book.

Yet further study makes it plain that, however strange the mode of expression, the underlying intention of the author does not differ fundamentally from that of more prosaic writers. His mind is filled with the thought of the exaltation of the risen Christ, and although his interest centres on the heavenly station, rather than on the earthly work of Jesus, he does not forget that it is the Jesus who was crucified, 'the lamb who was slain,' who is worthy to receive 'blessing and honour and glory and might for ever and ever' (5^{12f}). Amid all the cosmic terrors in which the author delights it is 'the faith of Jesus' that the enduring saints will keep (14^{12}); 'Also I saw the souls of those who had been beheaded for their testimony to Jesus' (20^{4}). Even in the most fantastic passages the historical background is still there: of the 'two witnesses' it is said that 'their dead bodies will lie in the street of the great city which is allegorically called Sodom and Egypt, where their Lord was crucified' (11^{8}). The glorification of Jesus is associated with His death and resurrection throughout. Jesus Christ is 'the firstborn of the dead' (1^{5}); 'I died, and behold I am alive for evermore' (1^{18}); 'He who conquers, I will grant him to sit with me on my throne, as I myself conquered and sat down with my Father on his throne' (3^{21}).

The thought of the glorification of Christ colours all the author's imagery. He has 'the keys of Death and Hades' (1^{18}). He 'holds the seven stars in his right hand' (2^{1}). He rewards the conquerors with eternal life (2^{7}). He is the messianic Judge (1^{7} 14^{14ff} 22^{12}). He is Lord of Lords and King of Kings (17^{14} 19^{16}). He is the Son of God (2^{18}) who has received power from His Father to rule the nations (2^{27}). Like God Himself, He is the Alpha and the Omega, the beginning and the end (21^{6}). Once He is called 'the Logos of God' (19^{13}); but the rest of the passage describes the Rider upon the white horse as the One who 'is called Faithful and True, and in righteousness he judges and makes war. His eyes are like a flame of fire, and on his head are many diadems.' This has little in common with Jn 1^{1-14}.

The Christ of the Apocalypse sits with God on His throne (7^{17} 22^{3} 12^{5}), is worshipped as God (5^{12f}), and is described by many passages applied to God in the OT (1^{14f} etc.). Yet the author never calls Christ 'God,' or says, as does St. John, that God and Christ are one. It is God who is the Creator (4^{11} 14^{7}); Christ is 'the beginning of God's creation' (3^{14}). Subordination, rather than equality, is presupposed.

The title that appears most frequently in the Apocalypse is 'the Lamb,' and the Greek word is not the same as that used in Jn 1^{19}. It occurs about twenty-eight times, and, as Charles pointed out, it combines two conceptions. From Isaiah 53 comes the thought of the Lamb sacrificed, 'a lamb that is led to the slaughter'; 'Worthy is the Lamb who was slain' (5^{12}); 'They have conquered . . . by the blood of the Lamb' (12^{11}). From Jewish apocalyptic literature comes the contrasting idea of the Lamb as the Leader: 'For the Lamb in the midst of the throne will be their shepherd, and he will guide them to springs of living water' (7^{17}); the 144,000 'follow the Lamb wherever he goes' (14^{4}); and he, with seven horns and seven eyes (symbols of power), makes the saints 'a kingdom and priests to our God, and they shall reign on earth' (5^{10}). He is a military leader against whom the forces of the Beast will make war, and 'the Lamb will conquer them' (17^{14}). In 6^{16} occurs the striking phrase 'the wrath of the Lamb.' With such language may be compared 1 En 90^{38}, where the Messiah becomes a lamb, a great animal with great black horns on its head, and the *Testament of Joseph* 19^{8} and 17^{4}. These two conceptions are interwoven in the Apocalypse, so that one shades off into the other, and this accounts in some measure for the strange combination of Christian devotion and ferocious vindictiveness which characterizes the book. No doubt the author reflects the spirit of his age, which was an age of persecution. Martyrdom was heroically accepted, and the example of Christ was not forgotten; but at the same time the thought of vengeance by the all-conquering Messiah was treasured by way of consolation. A century later Tertullian found comfort in such an expectation (*de Spect.* 30).

The author has no clear doctrine of the Spirit, who in certain passages is vaguely identified with Christ. Thus, in the Letters to the Seven Churches occurs the phrase 'Let him that hath an ear hear what the Spirit says to the churches'; but the speaker is Christ.

The seer was no philosophic theologian, but his utterances reflect the main elements of the christology of the early Church. Jesus, the Messiah, who had lived and died and risen in triumph from the dead, is now exalted to the throne of God and is the object of worship in heaven and on earth. The future history of the world is in His hands, and He will establish the kingdom which is symbolized by the New Jerusalem coming down out of heaven from God, whose temple is the Lord God the Almighty and the Lamb (21^{22}).

7. The Fourth Gospel.—The christology of the NT may be said to reach its climax in the Johannine writings. That the Gospel and the First Epistle are by the same hand is perhaps less certain than it seemed a few years ago, but for our present purpose the question is of no great importance. Gospel and Epistle alike present a view of the Person of Christ which, though having much in common with the synoptic gospels, and reflecting ideas familiar in the Pauline Epistles, goes far beyond them in development and in systematic expression.

(*a*) JESUS THE 'SON OF GOD.'—Christology is the main interest of the evangelist; indeed it is his whole concern. Though the Gospel is cast in narrative form, it is in the main a portrayal of Jesus as the Son of God. Thus it concludes, 'Now Jesus did many signs in the presence of the disciples which are not written in this book; but these are written that you may believe that Jesus is the Christ, the Son of God, and that believing you may have life in his name.' 'Believing' is crucial, for salvation, which is life, is dependent upon the realization of the true nature of Jesus (cf 1 Jn 4^{15} 5^{5}).

That Jesus is the Messiah is assumed. Thus Andrew announces to Simon Peter, 'We have found the Messiah' (1^{41}); and in the first chapter of the Gospel messianic titles are multiplied. So far St. John follows the synoptic tradition, but he is constantly at pains to refute erroneous Jewish conceptions, and his understanding of the title has little in common with current Jewish messianism. Thus Jesus is indeed 'the King of Israel,' a fact which even Pilate admits (for 18^{33} is surely a declaration, not a question); but His kingdom is the kingdom of Truth, and everyone who is of the truth hears His voice (18^{37}). The most probable interpretation of the title 'Lamb of God' is that which associates it with the Messiah, one of whose functions was to abolish sin, and throughout the Gospel the writer shows himself well acquainted with Jewish ideas, even though he is frequently concerned to refute them. But, in the words of C. H. Dodd, 'It is the titles "Son of God" and "Son of Man" that the evangelist has selected to bear the weight of his interpretation of the Person of Christ' (*The Interpretation of the Fourth Gospel*, p. 230). Indeed, in many passages 'Christ' is simply the equivalent of 'Son of God.' When Martha exclaims, 'Lord, I believe that you are the Christ, the Son of God, he who is coming into the world' (11^{27}), she is not concerned with Jewish nationalistic expectations, but with the Divine source of eternal life; and Nathanael's confession, 'You are the Son of God, you are the King of Israel!' (1^{49}), is equally far removed from traditional ideas. Even in the section 7^{25-32} in which the question is debated, 'Can it be that the authorities really know that this is the Christ?' the answer is that Jesus has been sent from God, whom He knows, though the Jews do not know Him; that He will shortly go to Him who sent Him; that He has the water of life and is the vehicle of the Spirit. Whether He was descended from David or born at Bethlehem is irrelevant: 'No man ever spoke like this man.' Thus the title 'Christ' is taken up and comprehended in wider conceptions. Not even the transmuted messianism of earlier Christian apocalyptism finds a place in the Fourth Gospel. The author may still speak of 'the last day,' but it is broadly true that the coming of the Paraclete has taken the place of hopes of the Parousia.

To the Fourth Evangelist, Jesus is pre-eminently 'the Son of God' (eight times) or simply 'the Son' (sixteen times). Men who receive the Logos have power to become 'children of God,' but Jesus is 'Son' in a wholly different sense. He is the 'only begotten' ($1^{14, 18}$ AV; $3^{16, 18}$); as the *only* Son, who is in the bosom of the Father, He has made known the invisible God (1^{18}). In the synoptic gospels stress is laid on the Fatherhood of God, but St. John shifts the emphasis to the Sonship of Christ, and the relationship of Father and Son is elaborated theologically. Fundamentally, the Son is dependent on the Father; He is 'sent' by the Father and comes in His name (4^{34} 5^{43} $8^{16, 28}$ etc.); it is as the representative of the Father that the Son exercises all Divine authority, judges, and gives life (5^{21ff}). He is the resurrection and the life, the Bread of Life. He belongs wholly to the sphere of 'spirit,' which is the sphere of God, and not to this world (8^{23}). His Divine status is eternal. There is no hint of a virgin birth in the Fourth Gospel, such as is described by Matthew and Luke. Christ, as the beloved Son of God, existed with God from all eternity (17^{5}) and was 'sent' from God to do His will and to reveal His nature. 'The human career of Jesus is, as it were, a projection of the eternal relation (which is the divine 'love') upon the field of time. . . . The love of God, thus released in history, brings men into the same unity of which the relation of Father and Son is the eternal archetype' (Dodd, *Interpretation of the Fourth Gospel*, p. 262).

Thus the evangelist analyses and develops a term which had been in use by the Church from the earliest times and was taken for granted by St. Paul. St. Paul had felt no need to define the relationship between God and Christ, the Son; Jesus belonged to the heavenly order, and that was enough; but St. John conceived Sonship in a manner that could only be expressed in the Logos doctrine. St. Paul's interest was primarily soteriological; St. John is no less concerned with salvation as he conceives it, but he carries his thought into the realms of philosophy.

It follows from his more metaphysical approach that St. John does not give to the resurrection of Christ the central place it had in the thought of St. Paul. The Apostle had written that Jesus was designated Son of God by the resurrection from the dead, but in the Fourth Gospel Jesus is manifestly Son of God throughout His earthly life. The resurrection marks the end of certain limitations voluntarily accepted, but it adds nothing to the transparent dignity of His Person or the majesty of His status. Though He had become flesh, Jesus manifested at all times the glory and power of God. Any change is to be found in the apprehension of His followers, and it is remarkable that the evangelist only uses the title 'the Lord' after the resurrection. Here, at least, he respects early tradition.

(*b*) 'SON OF MAN' AND 'SERVANT.'—The retention of the title 'Son of Man' in the Fourth Gospel is at first sight surprising. As we have seen, the evidence points to the conclusion that the phrase was not in use in the early Church, but it occurs in the Fourth Gospel more than a dozen times. None of the synoptic sayings in which it is found occurs in the Fourth Gospel, but the title is introduced quite naturally, as though familiar in the evangelical tradition. It is too simple an explanation to say that the author's purpose is to safeguard the manhood of Jesus as against docetic tendencies. The Platonic background of the Gospel must be remembered. In Hebraic idiom 'Son of Man' means 'Man,' and to those familiar with the vague Platonism of the Hellenistic age Man means the ideal of humanity. So to the evangelist Jesus as Son of Man is both the representative of mankind and also in a corporate sense the sum of all humanity. The Johannine usage has contacts both with Jewish thought (*e.g.* Dn 7^{13} where 'a Son of Man'—or 'one like a son of man'—signifies Israel), and with Philo and the Hermetic writings, whose references to the Heavenly Man (*Anthropos*) provide numerous parallels to the Fourth Gospel (cf Dodd, *Interpretation*, 31 ff, 43, 243). Another influence is to be found in the Servant passages of the Second Isaiah. Thus, Is 49^{3} 'You are my servant, Israel, in whom I will be glorified' and 49^{5} 'I will be glorified before the Lord' (LXX) may be compared with Jn 13^{31} 'Now is the Son of Man glorified, and in him God is glorified.' In this passage of Isaiah, the Servant is Israel, given for a light to the Gentiles (v.^{6}); and so in John Christ is the Light of the World. 'The evangelist found in the Servant of the Lord an embodiment of the people of God, and applied what is said of him to the Son of Man, conceived as embodying collectively in himself redeemed humanity' (Dodd, *op. cit.*, p. 246).

In various passages the term 'Son of Man' is related to the condescension and exaltation of the divine Son: 'What if you were to see the Son of Man ascending where he was before' (6^{62}; cf 3^{13}); and particularly significant is the use of the title in connexion with the Passion, always regarded in this gospel as the supreme triumph of Jesus. In 13^{31}, when Judas has gone out and the action of the Passion has begun, Jesus says, 'Now is the Son of Man glorified.' In three passages (3^{14}, 8^{28}, 12^{34}) there are references to the 'lifting up of the Son of Man,' and it is clear that John has in mind the exaltation of the Son of Man in the crucifixion. We may compare Mk 8^{31} where Jesus, after Peter's confession, teaches that the Son of Man must suffer many things; His messianic glory will shine from the cross.

Again the influence of Isaiah is discernible. For instance, in Is 52^{13} we read, 'My servant . . . shall be exalted and lifted up, and shall be very high'; so for St. John the cross is the glorification of Jesus, the Servant of the Lord, the Son of Man, the representative of the whole human race. C. H. Dodd sums up a learned and suggestive discussion as follows: 'The Son of Man throughout this gospel retains the sense of one who incorporates in himself the people of God, or humanity in its ideal aspect. . . . In the Fourth Gospel there is never any doubt that the evangelist is speaking of a real person, that is, of a concrete historical individual of the human race, 'Jesus of Nazareth, the son of Joseph.' He labours, grows weary, thirsts, feels joy and sorrow, weeps, suffers, and dies . . . His glory is the transfiguration of a human life by a supreme act of self-sacrifice . . . And yet, says the evangelist, in all this he was much more than one individual among the many. He was the true self of the human race, standing in that perfect union with God to which others can attain only as they are incorporate in him' (*op. cit.*, pp. 248 f).

(*c*) 'THE LOGOS.'—The Fourth Gospel begins, not with a birth narrative like Matthew and Luke, but with a Prologue setting forth the doctrine of the Logos. In 1892 Adolf Harnack argued that this Prologue was no integral part of the gospel, but a mere preface written to secure the interest of philosophers in what was essentially an historical document. Further study has not supported this view, and it is now generally admitted that although the word Logos does not occur in the rest of the gospel (except in the ordinary sense of the spoken word), the ideas to which concise expression is given in the Prologue control the christology of the gospel throughout.

Much has been written concerning the antecedents of the Johannine Logos doctrine. Some recent scholars have thought that the use of the term can be adequately explained by comparison with Jewish thought. 'The word of the Lord' is a common phrase in the OT, and in some late Jewish literature 'Wisdom' and 'Word' are almost hypostasized. Logos is then the translation of *Memra* about which much is said in the rabbinic writings. No doubt Jewish thought and Jewish scriptures deeply influenced the Fourth Evangelist, but it is very doubtful whether by themselves they provide an explanation of his choice of the term. To mention a single point, how could the Evangelist write, 'The Logos was with God and the Logos was God,' if by Logos he meant no more than *Memra*?

On the other hand, the idea of Logos had a long history in Greek philosophy, being much used by the Stoics, and perhaps traceable to Heraclitus. It was by using a term that expressed man's highest attributes, reason, and speech, that Greek thinkers expressed their belief in the rationality of the universe, and it is not surprising that the Evangelist, who was certainly familiar with Hellenistic thought, chose to use it to express the divine Sonship of Jesus. There can be no serious doubt that the gospel reveals the influence of Philo, the Alexandrian Jew, who had already produced a synthesis of Hebrew and Greek thought, and who made use of the term 'Logos.' Philo combined the Greek notion of all-pervading Reason with Hebrew faith in divine Energy and Revelation, and so for him the universe, instinct with Reason, is, through the operation of the Logos, the projection and embodiment of God's will. The similarity of such teaching to that of the Prologue is unmistakable, and the substance of a Logos doctrine closely resembling that of Philo is present throughout the gospel.

(*d*) THE SOTERIOLOGY OF THE FOURTH GOSPEL.—Philo's soteriology is relevant to the christology of the Fourth Gospel. According to Philo the Logos is the agent of revelation, manifesting himself in the theophanies of the OT and speaking through the prophets; thus it is through him that men come to a knowledge of God, escape from the tyranny of passion, and embark upon the spiritual life. Saved from ignorance and sensuality they become 'sons of God' and are possessed of immortality. We are reminded of Jn 1^{12f}, and of other passages such as 8^{32}, 'You will know the truth, and the truth will make you free.' Almost every sentence describing the work of the Logos in Jn 1 can be paralleled in Philo, but the Prologue ends with an affirmation that Philo could never have made, 'The Logos became flesh and dwelt among us, full of grace and truth,' which is the theme of the Fourth Gospel (cf W. R. Inge in *Cambridge Biblical Essays*, p. 275).

That the gospel is presented in historical form is of great significance. However deeply the author may have been indebted to Philo, his purpose was entirely different. Philo was a speculative philosopher; St. John was an evangelist, who had constantly in mind the interpretation of the life of Jesus. After the first few words he displays no further interest in the cosmic significance of the Logos, for he has no wish to write a metaphysical treatise. He is concerned to depict Jesus as sent out from the Father as speech goes out from men, the revealing Word of God, the source of 'Light' and 'Life' for all who believe. 'God so loved the world that he gave his only Son, that whoever believes in him should not perish but have eternal life' (3^{16}). Because Jesus is the incarnate Logos He is able to reveal the Father for the salvation of the world.

(*e*) LATER INTERPRETATIONS.—What problems are inherent in the Johannine christology the controversies of later centuries reveal. What was the relationship of the eternal Logos to the human personality? How could the Divine and the human coexist in one Person? Did the Divine or the human will predominate? There is no reason to suppose that the author was conscious of the problem of the Two Natures in Christ. He does not argue, he affirms. The Divine power had manifested itself fully in a human person, and the glory of God had been revealed. Belief rather than intellectual understanding was required of those who would have life in his name.

It is significant that the Fourth Gospel was chiefly relied upon by those theologians who in later times tended to minimize or explain away the humanity of Christ. In the Gospel His humanity, though real, is not that of other men, and the contrast between the Jesus of the synoptists and the Christ of the Fourth Gospel is plain for all to see. His miracles are essentially 'signs' of His divinity, wrought to confirm belief rather than from motives of compassion. Not only is He omniscient (1^{48} 2^{25} 11^{11}), He is aloof and solitary, by no means the friend of publicans and sinners; and although He may call His disciples 'friends' He does so by an infinite condescension (15^{15}). Whether in life or death He is completely self-determined, His Divine dignity remains serene, and His enemies are powerless, save with His own consent (7^{30} 10^{18} 18^{6} 19^{11}). Most of all, in His speech Jesus reveals His divinity. His words are spirit and life ($6^{63, 68}$), and they have cleansing power (15^{3}). But they are not the words of the synoptic Jesus. Gone are the homely parables of the earlier gospels, gone is the simple moral teaching. His words disclose, not the ethics of the Kingdom, but the relation of the Son to the Father. They are christological.

That there is loss in St. John's subservience to christology can hardly be denied. In a sense he preserves the humanity of Jesus, but it is an ideal humanity, and the force of the human example is lost. There can be no moral struggle in His life, such as might encourage His followers in moments of temptation. There is no temptation in the wilderness, no agony in the garden, no bitter cry of dereliction on the cross. The sayings recorded by the synoptists which reveal Jesus as familiar with all the details of social and family life give place to 'vague and oracular utterances' (E. F. Scott), some of which, if authentic, might seem unduly egotistical. If the Fourth Gospel had stood alone Christ could never have become the ideal of human endeavour. Despite centuries of christological debate, it is Jesus of Nazareth, rather than the incarnate Logos, who remains the object of the Church's adoration.

But the Johannine interpretation must not be mistaken for the reality, in which St. John, like all the NT writers, had found the true revelation of God. He used the Logos doctrine as an explanation of the Divine quality that he found in Jesus; but his Lord was Jesus, not the Logos, and his grasp of the one was only partly obscured by the other. The Johannine theory of the Logos has value in providing testimony to the impression made by Jesus upon the early Church, conscious as it was of the numinous quality of His Person; but it needs to be supplemented, and indeed corrected, by the interpretations of other writers, some of whom stood nearer to the historic Christ. It may be true that it was through the Logos doctrine that the Greek world came to accept Christ, but after the early years of the 4th cent. it gave way to a more adequate conception of 'the Son.'

8. Other New Testament books.—Other books of the NT reflect the several aspects of the Church's christology in the 1st cent., but none make important original contributions. The essential elements of the faith of believers are contained in those books that we have examined. It would be a mistake to speak of a single christology underlying the whole of the NT, for Peter in Jerusalem did not speak of the incarnate Logos, St. Paul did not write of Jesus as the great High Priest of the order of Melchizedek, and St. John did not proclaim 'Jesus of Nazareth, a man attested to you by God with mighty works and wonders and signs which God did through him.' The several books reveal different types of thought and different lines of approach to the problem of interpreting the Person of Christ. Yet differences must not be exaggerated, for the NT as a whole witnesses to the great essentials of the Church's faith. Jesus was man; He was the Christ, for whose appearing the old dispensation had prepared; He was Revealer of God, Saviour and Judge of men; exalted and sharing the Father's throne He was the object of the Church's worship and devotion, and to Him the future had been delivered. He was the Lord. See also INCARNATION. P. G.-S.

CHRONICLES I. AND II.—1. Position in Canon.—It is quite clear from linguistic and other considerations that Chron.-Ezr.-Neh. originally formed one book. As the first part of this large work dealt with a period which was already covered by Samuel and Kings, it was omitted, to begin with, in the formation of the Canon; while the latter part of the book, dealing with the ecclesiastical life of Jerusalem after the Exile, was granted a place. Only as the liturgical and ritual interest became more and more strong was it seen that Chronicles contained matter of special importance from that point of view. Hence the book was included in the Canon after Ezra and Nehemiah, which had originally formed its second and concluding portion. In the English Bible, which follows the LXX, the original order has been restored, but Chronicles is the last book in the Hebrew canon. Its Hebrew name is *Dibhrê Hayyāmîm*, *i.e.* 'the Annals.' The LXX entitled it the *Paraleipomena*, or 'things left out,' a reference to the fact that Chronicles contains much not found in the earlier narratives of Samuel and Kings. Our word 'Chronicles' is the Anglicized form of *Chronicon*, the name given to the book by Jerome in translating *Dibhrê Hayyāmîm*.

2. Aim.—The key to the understanding and estimation of Chronicles lies in a clear grasp of its aim. It is not a political and social history of Israel and Judah of the same kind as 1 and 2 Kings, but it is an interpretation of that history. It might be called a history of the holy congregation. It is, therefore, concerned with Judah, and with all that has reference to the worship and the institutions of the second Temple. This determines the Chronicler's choice of matter, and the treatment of such facts as he selects. The Northern Kingdom, politically so much more important than the kingdom of Judah, hardly comes within his range of view, and is referred to only when the narrative absolutely necessitates it. In the time of the Chronicler (see **5** below) the Samaritans believed that they were the true descendants of the Israelites of the Northern Kingdom, and that their sanctuary at Shechem was of greater importance than that of Jerusalem. The genealogies at the beginning of 1 Chronicles are intended to convince the Jews that they are the true, lineal descendants of the Chosen People of God, and have a unique office.

3. Contents.—With this clue the contents of the book are easily grouped.

(i) 1 Ch 1–9, Adam to the death of Saul. These chapters are filled mainly with genealogical tables, but even in these the ecclesiastical interest is supreme. Judah and Levi have the greatest space given to them (2^{3}–4^{23} 6).

(ii) 1 Ch 10–29, from the death of Saul to the accession of Solomon.

(iii) 2 Ch 1–9, the reign of Solomon.

(iv) 2 Ch 10–36, from the division of the kingdom down to the fall of Jerusalem, and the restoration edict of Cyrus.

The material is most carefully chosen with the object of showing the importance of Judah, the greatness of the line of David, and the unique place of the Jerusalem sanctuary. It manifests great interest in the cult of that sanctuary, in the Levites, and in the singers. The Chronicler writes much in the spirit of the Pentateuchal Document P, which makes the tabernacle built by Moses the only one until the Jerusalem Temple was built in the time of King Solomon. The singers, who are the successors of the cultic prophets of pre-exilic days, are given by the Chronicler rights and privileges which even

CHRONICLES I. AND II.

the Document P does not know. The Chronicler, indeed, is more interested in the Temple music than in its sacrificial rites, and believes that since the time of David the singers accompanied the armies to battle (cf *e.g.* 2 Ch 20$^{1-30}$). A comparison of the narrative in Chronicles with the earlier narratives of Samuel and Kings will do more than anything else to convince the reader of the pragmatism of the Chronicler.

(*a*) *Omissions in Chronicles.*—The whole career of Samuel; the reign of Saul, except its close; the struggle David had to establish himself on the throne; the story of Uriah and Bathsheba; the story of Amnon and Tamar; Absalom's rebellion and David's flight; the characteristically Oriental intrigues attending Solomon's accession; his alliances with foreign women and his idolatries in later life; his struggle against disaffection and rebellion; practically the entire history of the Northern Kingdom;—all these sections are omitted, with the view of suppressing what might be held to be discreditable to the religious heroes.

(*b*) *The additions* to the narrative show how the Chronicler's thoughts ran. He gives, as we should have expected, full statistical lists (1 Ch 12); he describes at length matters that have to do with the gradual elevation of the sanctuary at Jerusalem (1 Ch 13, 15, 16); he details the ordering of the Temple ministry and the genealogies of its members (1 Ch 22–29). There is a large class of additions connected with ritual, and especially with musical matters, a fact which has led to the suggestion that the writer was perhaps one of the musicians (2 Ch 5^{12f} 7$^{1, 3, 6}$ 13$^{8-12}$ 17^{8f} 20$^{19, 21}$). He so handles historical events as to make them bear out his particular theory of the working of Providence. To love God is to be blessed; to sin against God is immediately to feel the pressure of His hand; the religious meaning of particular events is pointed out to the wrong-doers by prophets of the Lord (1 Ch 10^{13f}, 2 Ch 12^{2} 13$^{3-21}$ 15$^{1-15}$ 16$^{7-12}$ 20^{37} 21$^{10, 16-19}$). In 2 Ch 8^{11} the removal of the daughter of Pharaoh, whom Solomon had married, from the city of David to the house that he had built for her, is said to have been occasioned by the house of David having become too holy because of the coming of the Ark. The compiler of Kings assigns no such reason for the removal to the new house (1 K 3^{1} 7^{8} 9^{24}). It was a stumbling-block to the later writer that so bad a king as Manasseh should have enjoyed so long a reign, and so he is described as latterly a penitent, although Kings has no thought of any such change (cf 2 Ch 33$^{11-19}$ with 2 K 21 and Jer 15^{4}).

(*c*) *Alterations* have been made in the narrative with the view of removing what seemed offensive to the later age. Kings distinctly says that Asa and Jehoshaphat did not abolish the high places, although they did what was right in the sight of the Lord (1 K 15^{14}, 22^{43}). Such a conjunction of well-doing with idolatry is incredible to the Chronicler, so he says that the high places *were* abolished by these kings (2 Ch 14^{5} 17^{6}). He finds it necessary to change several narratives in the interests of the Levites, who were not assigned so important a place in matters of ritual under the monarchy as in the days when he was writing (cf 1 Ch 13^{15} with 2 S 6, 2 Ch 5^{4} with 1 K 8^{3}). According to the original account (2 K 11), Jehoiada was assisted in his rebellion against Athaliah by the foreign bodyguard. In 2 Ch 23 the bodyguard is replaced by the Levites. The rule of the second Temple did not allow aliens to approach so near to the sacred things.

4. Historicity.—It is thus evident that Chronicles is not to be considered as history, in the sense in which we now use the word. The events of the time with which the writer deals have been treated in a particular religious interest. Some facts have been stated not simply as they were in themselves, but as they appeared to one whose vision was influenced by his theological viewpoint. Other facts have been suppressed when they interfered with the conveying of the impression that David and Solomon were almost immaculate kings. To a past age were attributed the customs and ceremonial of the days in which the writer lived. The Priests' Code was supposed to have been recognized and observed by David even before the Temple was built. Again and again an anachronism has been committed that the Levites might have the place of honour in the record. Some special features of this method of writing history are:

(*a*) *Exaggerated numbers.*—Everyone has felt difficulty with regard to these numbers. The population of Palestine in the time of its greatest prosperity may have reached 2,000,000, but it never remotely approached so high a figure before the time of the Chronicler. But we read (2 Ch 13$^{3, 17}$) that Abijah with 400,000 men fought against Jeroboam with 800,000, and killed 500,000 of them. Asa (2 Ch 14^{8}) takes the field against Zerah the Ethiopian, who has 1,000,000 men, with 300,000 men of Judah, and 280,000 of Benjamin, the smallest of the tribes, which had previously been practically wiped out by the slaying of 25,000 men (Jg 20^{46}). It is said that the whole 1,000,000 Ethiopians 'fell until none remained alive' (2 Ch 14^{13}), but it is explicity stated that the victory was due to the reliance of Asa on God (cf v.^{11f}). When the numbers can be checked by the parallel passages in the older narrative, the tendency of the Chronicler to exaggerate is manifest. 1 Ch 18^{4} 19^{18} make David capture 7000 horsemen and slay 7000 chariotmen, while 2 S 8^{4} 10^{18} give 700 of each. According to 1 Ch 21^{25}, David pays 600 shekels of gold for Ornan's threshing-floor, while according to 2 S 24^{24} he gives only 50 shekels of silver. David gathers together for the building of the Temple, according to 1 Ch 22^{14}, 100,000 talents of gold and 1,000,000 talents of silver; but, according to 1 K 10^{14}, the whole revenue in gold of the kingdom, in the much richer days of Solomon, was only 666 talents of gold.

(*b*) *Anachronisms* creep in to show that the writer was carrying back to that earlier day the customs and names of his own time. 1 Ch 26^{18} states that one of the gates of the Temple—the first Temple—was called Parbar. There is here the double mistake of supposing that the Temple existed in David's time, and that one of the gates of the first Temple had a Persian name. 1 Ch 29^{7} speaks of the coin 'daric' or 'dram' as being current in the time of David. This coin was Persian, and was current in Palestine only after the Captivity.

(*c*) *The speeches* put into the mouths of the personages have not been taken from any ancient document, but bear on every line the characteristics of the very peculiar Hebrew style of the Chronicler.

5. Date.—The text of 1 Ch 3$^{17-24}$ is uncertain and confused; the Hebrew text seems to give seven generations after Zerubbabel, but LXX gives eleven (it may be that the genealogy survived only in fragmentary form in the Chronicler's day). The Hebrew text might seem to suggest a date *c* 350 B.C., and the LXX *c* 250 B.C. Evidence as to date is clearer from Nehemiah, which, as we have seen, was originally part of Chronicles. Neh 12^{11} speaks of Jaddua, who was, as we know from Josephus, a contemporary of Alexander the Great (333 B.C.). Neh 12^{22} mentions the reign of Darius the Persian, *i.e.* Darius III., who reigned 336–332 B.C. A date, therefore, *c* 300–250 B.C. might seem to be indicated. The fact that Ben Sira gives a place to Nehemiah in the rôle of the heroes of the Fathers (49^{13}), while he makes no mention of Ezra, has led some scholars to believe that such an omission of Ezra could never have been made by a writer of 190 B.C. if the work of the Chronicler had been before him. That is an important observation, but it may be that Ben Sira, whose interest was in wisdom, not in the cult, had little sympathy with the point of view of the Chronicler.

6. Sources.—Chronicles contains several additions to the narrative of Samuel and Kings—additions that have not been inserted because of any special ecclesiastical interest (2 Ch 11$^{9-12, 17, 23}$ 14$^{9-15}$ 20 25$^{6-10, 13}$ 26$^{6-15}$ 28$^{5-15}$). Does the Chronicler then preserve any fresh and original tradition, or does he merely work up older material? Apart from Samuel and Kings, his main authority was a work cited under a variety of different titles, 'the Book of the Kings of Israel and Judah' (2 Ch 27^{7} 35^{27} 36^{8}), 'the Book of the Kings of Judah and Israel' (2 Ch 16^{11}, 25^{26} 28^{26}). This book must have contained genealogical tables (1 Ch 9^{1}), as well as other particulars not mentioned in any book that has come down to us (2 Ch 27^{7} 33^{18}). Another source is the 'Midrash of the Book of Kings' (2 Ch 24^{27}). A *midrash* was an exposition of the religious lessons that could be drawn from a historical work; Chronicles itself is an excellent instance of a *midrash*, and this earlier *midrash* may have been the writer's model. He frequently refers to writings quoted under the name of prophets: 1 Ch 29^{29} (Samuel, Nathan, and Gad), 2 Ch 9^{29} (Nathan, Ahijah, and Iddo), 12^{15} (Shemaiah and Iddo), 13^{22} (Iddo), 26^{22} (Isaiah). As he never cites at the same time the 'Book of the Kings of Israel and Judah,' it is probable that these passages, connected with the various prophets, were only excerpts from that book. From the extracts that Chronicles preserves of this book it is probable that it was post-exilic, unless indeed the Chronicler in using it has thoroughly transformed its style and diction into his own.

Chronicles, then, so far from being a fresh source for the period of which it treats, is a *midrash* of Jewish order. The book is evidence not only of the condition of things under the monarchy, but of the religious belief and ceremonial observances of a time when national life had ceased, and when the people's interest was confined to the worship of the Temple. R. B. T.—**J. Ma.**

CHRONOLOGY OF THE NEW TESTAMENT.—In this article it is proposed first to examine the books of the NT, so as to determine as far as possible their relative chronology—that is, the length of time between the principal events narrated; and then to investigate the points of contact between the NT and secular history, and thus to arrive at the probable dates of the incidents in the former. It must, however, be remembered that the Gospels and Acts are not biographies or histories in the modern sense of the terms. The writers had a religious object; they wished to teach contemporary Christians to believe (Jn 20^{31}), and were not careful to chronicle dates for the benefit of posterity. Indeed it may be questioned if the precise recording of history formed any part of their purpose in writing, or that absolute historicity was then a generally held idea. They unhesitatingly adopt legend and popular tale (as in Mk 6$^{17-29}$). Even Lk 3^{1f} is only a general chronological datum—there is, for example, no mention of the month. As Sir William Ramsay pointed out (*St. Paul the Traveller and Roman Citizen*^{7}, 1903, p. 18), the lack of any chronological sense was a fault of the age; Tacitus in his *Agricola* is no better (until the last paragraph) than the sacred writers. It must also be noted that reckoning in ancient times was inclusive. Thus 'three years after' (Gal 1^{18}) means 'in the third year after' (cf Ac 19$^{8, 10}$ with 20^{31}); 'three days and three nights' (Mt 12^{40}) means 'from to-day to the day after to-morrow' (Mt 17^{23}). Cf also Gn 42^{17f}.

I. Relative Chronology: Internal Evidence.—**1. Interval between our Lord's birth and baptism.**—This is stated in Lk 3^{23} to have been 'about 30 years,' but the exact interval is uncertain. The RV translates: 'Jesus himself, when he began [literally was beginning] to teach [cf Mk 4^{1}], was about thirty years of age;' and so most moderns, translate it, though the word 'beginning,' standing by itself, is awkward. It perhaps denotes the real commencement of the Gospel, the chapters on the Birth and Childhood being introductory (Plummer). The difficulty of the phrase was felt at an early date, for the Old Syriac and the Peshitta Syriac omit the participle altogether, and Clement of Alexandria (*Strom*, i. 21) has merely 'Jesus was coming to his baptism, being about,' etc. The AV, following Irenaeus and also the Valentinians whom he was opposing, renders: 'began to be about 30 years of age,' which can mean only that Jesus was 29 years old. Irenaeus (*Haer.* ii. xxii. 4 f). says that Jesus was baptized 'being 30 years old,' having 'not yet completed his 30th year,' He 'then possessing the full age of a teacher.' The translation of AV is judged to be grammatically impossible, though it is odd that the Greek-speaking Irenaeus did not discover the fact, unless we are to suppose that his Latin translator misrepresents him. Let us, then, take the RSV translation: 'Jesus, when he began his ministry, was about thirty years of age.' But what is the meaning of 'about 30 years'? Turner (article 'Chronology of NT' in Hastings' *DB*), Plummer (*St. Luke, in loc.*), and others think that any age from 28 to 32 would suit; but Ramsay, who remarks that St. Luke's authority for his early chapters was clearly a very good one, and that he could not have been ignorant of the real age, thinks that the phrase must mean 30 plus or minus a few months. There seems to be some doubt as to the age when a Levite began his ministry at this time, as the age had varied; but we may follow Irenaeus in thinking that 30 was the full age when a public teacher began his work. On this point, then, internal evidence by itself leaves us a latitude of some little time, whether of a few months or even of a few years.

2. Duration of the ministry.—Very divergent views have been held on this subject. (*a*) Clement of Alexandria (*loc. cit.*), and other 2nd and 3rd cent. Fathers, the *Clementine Homilies* (xvii. 19, 'a whole year'), and the Valentinians (quoted by Irenaeus, ii. xxii. 1), applying the phrase, 'the acceptable year of the Lord' (Is 61^{2}; cf Lk 4^{18f}) literally to the ministry, made it last for one year only. The Valentinians believed that Jesus was baptized at the beginning, and died at the end, of His 30th year—a view which suggests astral interpretations. A one-year ministry was also advocated by von Soden (*E Bi*, article 'Chronology') and by Hort (see below). The latter excises 'the passover' from the text of Jn 6^{4}. This view is said to be that of the Synoptists, who, however, give hardly any indications of the passing of time. (*b*) The other extreme is found in Irenaeus (*loc. cit.*), who held, as against the Valentinians, that the ministry lasted for more than ten years. He takes the feast of Jn 5^{1} to be a Passover, but does not mention that of Jn 6^{4}. He considers, however, that the Passovers mentioned in John are not exclusive; that Jesus was a little less than 30 years old at His baptism, and over 40 when He died. This appears (he says) from Jn 8^{56f}, which indicates one who had passed the age of 40; and moreover, Jesus, who came to save all ages, must have 'passed through every age,' and in the decade from 40 to 50 'a man begins to decline towards old age.' He declares that this tradition came from 'John the disciple of the Lord' through 'those who were conversant in Asia with' him—*i.e.* probably Papias; and that the same account had been received from other disciples. But here Irenaeus almost certainly makes a blunder. For a 3rd cent. tradition that Jesus was born A.D. 9, was baptized A.D. 46, and died A.D. 58 at the age of 49, see Chapman in *JThSt* viii, 590 (July, 1907). (*c*) Eusebius (*HE* i. 10), followed as to his results provisionally by Ramsay (*Was Christ born at Bethlehem?*^{3}, p. 212 f.), makes the ministry last over three years ('not quite four full years'), and this till lately was the common view. Melito (*c* A.D. 165) speaks of Jesus working miracles for three years after His baptism (*Ante-Nic. Chr. Lib.* xxii, p. 135). (*d*) Origen and others followed by Turner (*op. cit.* p. 409 f), Sanday (article 'Jesus Christ' in Hastings' *DB*, p. 610 ff), and Hitchcock (article 'Dates' in Hastings' *DCG*, p. 415 f), allow a little more than two years for the ministry ('Judas did not spend even three years with Jesus,' *c. Cels.* ii. 12).

Indications of a ministry of more than a single year have been found in the Synoptics; *e.g.* Mk 2^{23} (harvest), 6^{39} (spring; 'green grass')—for the length of the journeys of 6^{56}–10^{32} shows that the spring of 6^{39} could not be that of the Crucifixion. Thus Mark, if we accept his arrangement of the material as chronological, implies at least a two years' ministry. In Luke also

CHRONOLOGY OF THE NT

have been seen traces of three periods in the ministry: (1) 3^{21}–4^{30}, the beginning of the ministry in Nazareth and Galilee, briefly recorded—but this is clearly a 'programmatic' revision of Mk 6$^{1-6}$; (2) 4^{31}–9^{50}, preaching in Galilee and the North, related at length; (3) 9^{51}–end, preaching in Central Palestine as far as Jerusalem. Each one of these 'periods' has been taken to represent a year. But Luke's arrangement of his sources is not a sound basis for a three-year chronology of the ministry of Jesus.

In John we have several indications of time: 2$^{13, 23}$ (Passover), 4^{35} (four months before harvest; harvest near), 5^{1} ('a feast' or 'the feast'), 6^{4} (Passover, but see below), 7^{2} (Tabernacles, autumn), 10^{22} (Dedication, winter). In two cases (5^{1} 6^{4}) there is a question of text; in 5^{1} the reading 'a feast' (RSV) is somewhat better attested, and is preferable on internal grounds, for 'the feast' might mean either Passover or Tabernacles, and since there would be this doubt, the phrase 'the feast' is an unlikely one. If so, we cannot use 5^{1} as an indication of time, as any minor feast would suit it. 'It seems that John introduces a feast simply in order to account for the presence of Jesus in Jerusalem' (C. K. Barrett, Comm. *ad loc.*). In 6^{4} Hort excises 'the passover' as 'perhaps a primitive interpolation' (Westcott-Hort, *NT in Greek*, *Int.*, App. pp. 77 ff). But this is against all MSS and Versions and rests only on the omission by Irenaeus (who, however, merely enumerates the Passovers when Jesus went up to Jerusalem; yet the mention of 6^{4} would have added to his argument), and probably on Origen (for him and for others adduced, see Turner *op. cit.* p. 408); on internal grounds the omission is very improbable, and does not in reality reconcile John and the Synoptics, for the latter when closely examined do, as we have seen, imply more than a single year's ministry. The note of time in Jn 4^{35} seems to point to (say) January ('There are yet four months, then comes the harvest'), while the spiritual harvest was already ripe ('the fields are already white for harvest'), though Origen and others less probably take the former clause to refer to the spiritual, the latter to the material, harvest, which lasted from the middle of April to the end of May. We may probably conclude then that in the ministry, as related in John, there were not fewer than three Passovers, and that it therefore lasted (at least) rather more than two years. But did the Fourth Evangelist mention all the Passovers of the ministry? Irenaeus thought that he mentioned only some of them; and though his chronology is clearly wrong, and based (as was that of his opponents) on a fanciful exegesis, some scholars have held that in this respect he may to a very limited extent be right. Turner, on the other hand, considered that the enumeration in John is exclusive, and that the notes of time in that Gospel were intended to correct a false chronology deduced from the Synoptics. But it now appears doubtful if John presupposed any knowledge of the Synoptics on the part of his readers. On the whole we can say only that the choice apparently lies between a ministry of rather over two years, and one of rather over three years; and that the probability of the former appears to be slightly the greater. But it must be noted that more recent studies of the Fourth Gospel have tended to invalidate the whole appeal to its (admittedly uncertain) chronology. For example, have considerations of use of the evangelic materials in the Christian church (in worship and preaching) influenced their location in the Gospel? (See JOHN, GOSPEL OF.) And is John more interested in the theological significance of the Jewish festivals, and their Christian reinterpretation, than in their chronological sequence or historical date in the ministry of Jesus?

3. The Interval between the Resurrection and the Conversion of St. Paul.—There is no positive internal evidence as to the length of this period. Such a general statement as the one in Ac 2^{46f} may imply either a long or a short time. We must include in this period the spread of the Church among the Hellenists, and as far afield as Damascus and the coastal plain; the various incidents recalled from the early days, possibly reported in more than one source, written or oral; the election of the Seven, and the death of Stephen, followed closely by St. Paul's conversion. For this period Ramsay allowed 2½ to 4 years, Harnack less than one year; but these views are no longer widely held (see II). It is quite probable that in the early chapters of Acts the author had not the same exact information that he had for St. Paul's travels, or even for his Gospel (see Lk 1^{2f}).

4. St. Paul's missionary career.—The relative chronology of St. Paul's Christian life may be determined by a study of Acts combined with Gal 1^{18} 2^{1}. Indications of time are found in Ac 11^{26} 18^{11} 19$^{8, 10}$ 20$^{6, 16, 31}$ 21$^{1-5, 27}$ 24$^{1, 11, 27}$ 25$^{1, 6}$ 27$^{9, 27}$ 28$^{7, 11-14, 17, 30}$. With these data we may endeavour to reconstruct the chronology; but there is room for uncertainty (1) as to whether the visit to Jerusalem in Gal 2^{1} was that of Ac 11^{30} or that of Ac 15^{4}, and whether the 'three years' and 'fourteen years' of Gal 1^{18} 2^{1} are consecutive (so Lightfoot, Rackham), or concurrent (so Ramsay, Turner, Harnack); (2) as to the length of the First Missionary Journey; and (3) as to possible later journeys after the Roman imprisonment. If the 'three years' and 'fourteen years' are consecutive, a total of about 16 years is required for the interval between the conversion and the visit of Gal 2^{1}. But as the interval at Tarsus is indeterminate, and the First Journey may have been anything from one to three years, all systems of relative chronology can be made to agree, except in small details, by shortening or lengthening these periods (see II, and article PAUL).

The following table, in which the year of St. Paul's conversion is taken as 1, gives the various events as set forth in the traditional (19th and early 20th cent.) chronology. Ramsay's calculation is taken as a basis, and the differences of opinion are noted in brackets [H=Harnack, T=Turner, R=Ramsay, L=Lightfoot]. For more recent reconstructions, see II, **8–12**.

1, 2. Conversion near Damascus, Ac 9^{3} 22^{5} 26^{12}; retirement to Arabia, Gal 1^{17}; preaching in Damascus, Ac 9$^{20-22}$ (?), Gal 1^{17}.

3. First visit to Jerusalem, Ac 9^{26}, Gal 1^{18}, 'three years after' his conversion.

4–11. At Tarsus and in Syria-Cilicia, Ac 9^{30}, Gal 1^{21} [so HR, but T gives two years less, L three years less].

12. To Antioch with Barnabas, Ac 11^{26}.

13. Second visit to Jerusalem, with alms 11^{30} [=Gal 2^{1}, R?].

14–16. First Missionary Journey, to Cyprus, 13^{4}; Pamphylia, and Southern Galatia (Pisidian Antioch, 13^{14}; Iconium, 13^{51}; Lystra, 14^{6}; Derbe, 14^{20}), and back by Attalia to Antioch, 14^{26} [so HR: TL give one year less].

17. Apostolic Council and third visit to Jerusalem, 15^{4} [=Gal 2^{1}, TL?; so Sanday and most commentators].

18–20. Second Missionary Journey, from Antioch through Syria-Cilicia to Derbe and Lystra, Ac 15^{41} 16^{1}; through the 'Phrygo-Galatic' region of the province Galatia to Troas, 16$^{6-8}$; to Macedonia, 16^{11}; Athens, 17^{15}; and Corinth, 18^{1}, where eighteen months are spent; thence by sea to Ephesus, 18^{19}; Jerusalem (fourth visit), 18^{22}; and Antioch, where 'some time' is spent, 18^{23}.

21–24. Third Missionary Journey, from Antioch by the 'Galatic region' and the 'Phrygian region,' 18^{23}, to Ephesus, 19^{1}, where two years and three months are spent, 19$^{8, 10}$; by Troas 2 Co 2^{12}, to Macedonia, Ac 20^{1}; and Corinth, 20^{2} (see 2 Co 13^{1}), where three months are spent; thence back by Macedonia to Troas, Miletus, and Caesarea, 20$^{4f. 15}$ 21^{8}; fifth visit to Jerusalem, 21^{17}; and arrest, 21^{33}; imprisonment at Caesarea, 23^{33}.

25. In Caesarea, 24^{27}.

26. Departure for Rome, autumn, 27^{1}; shipwreck off Malta, 28^{1}.

CHRONOLOGY OF THE NT

27. Arrival at Rome, 28[16].
28. (end) or 29 (early). Acquittal (?).
29–34. Later journeys (?) and death [so R; L gives one year less, T two years less].

II. External Data: Points of Contact with General History.—It will be useful to give the dates of the earlier emperors, and those of the procurators of Judaea. Some of the latter dates are approximate only; information as to them is derived from Josephus' *Antiquities*, and to some extent from his *Jewish War* (*BJ*).

Roman Emperors

Augustus	[31 B.C. (*a*)]–A.D. 14 (Aug. 19)
Tiberius	14–37 (Mar. 16)
Caligula (Gaius)	37–41 (Jan. 24)
Claudius	41–54 (Oct. 13)
Nero	54–68
Galba	68–69
Otho	69
Vitellius	69
Vespasian	69–79
Titus	79–81
Domitian	81–96
Nerva	96–98
Trajan	98–117
Hadrian	117–138
Antoninus Pius	138–161
Marcus Aurelius	161–180
Commodus	180–192
Septimius Severus	193–211

(*a*) *i.e.* the battle of Actium; Julius Caesar died 44 B.C., and Eusebius dates Augustus' reign from that year (*HE* i. 5, 9), as does also Irenaeus (*Haer.* III. xxi. 3).

Rulers of Judaea

Herod the Great, king (*a*)	37–4 B.C.
Archelaus, ethnarch (*b*)	4 B.C.–A.D. 6
Procurators: Coponius (*c*)	A.D. 6–9?
Marcus Ambivius (*d*)	9–12?
Annius Rufus (*e*)	12–15?
Valerius Gratus (*f*)	15–26
Pontius Pilate (*g*)	26–36
Marcellus (*h*)	36–37?
Marullus (*i*)	37–41?
Herod Agrippa, king (*j*)	41–44
Procurators: Cuspius Fadus (*k*)	44–46?
Tiberius Alexander (*l*)	46?–48
Cumanus (*m*)	48–52
Antonius Felix (*n*)	52–58 or 59?
Porcius Festus (*o*)	59?–61
Albinus (*p*)	61–65
Gessius Florus (*q*)	65–66

(*a*) He had been king *de jure* since 40 B.C. (*b*) Josephus, *Ant.* XVII. xi. 4 [317], xiii. 2 [342 ff]); he reigned over nine years. (*c*) *ib.*; XVIII. i. 1 [2]; he arrived with Quirinius at the time of the taxing, Ac 5[37]. (*d*) *ib.* ii. 2 [31]. (*e*) *ib.* [32]; in his time 'the second emperor of the Romans [Augustus] died.' (*f*) *ib.*; sent by Tiberius; he ruled eleven years. (*g*) *ib.* and iv. 2 [88 ff]; he ruled ten years and was deposed and sent to Rome, arriving there just after Tiberius' death. (*h*) *ib.* iv. 2 [89]; sent temporarily by Vitellius, governor of Syria. (*i*) *ib.* vi. 10 [237]; sent by Caligula on his accession. (*j*) *ib.* and XIX. v. 1 [274]; made king by Claudius on his accession, having been previously given the tetrarchies of Philip and Lysanias by Caligula. (*k*) *ib.* XIX. ix. 2 [363]; sent by Claudius on Agrippa's death. (*l*) *ib.* XX. v. 2 [100 ff]. (*m*) *ib.* (*n*) *ib.* vii. 1 [137 ff], viii. 9 [182]; brother of Pallas; sent by Claudius; in his time was the rebellion of one Theudas; recalled by Nero. (*o*) *ib.* viii. 9 [182 ff]. (*p*) *ib.* ix. 1 [197 ff]; sent by Nero on Festus' death; while he was on his way to Judaea, 'the brother of Jesus who was called Christ, whose name was James,' was stoned by the Jews [200]. (*q*) *ib.* xi. 1 [252 ff]; the last procurator; he was appointed through the influence of Poppaea; his bad government precipitated the Jewish War.—For the procurators see also *BJ* II. viii. 1 [117 ff]; ix. 4 [175 ff]; xii. 1 f [223 ff]; 8 [247 ff]; xiii. 7 [266 ff]; xiv. 1 f [271 ff], etc.

1. Date of the Nativity.—Early Christian chronology is in such confusion that it is very difficult to assign exact dates to the various events, and the early Fathers give us little or no guidance. Clement of Alexandria (*Strom.* i. 21) says that our Lord was born 194 years, 1 month, 13 days, before the death of Commodus [A.D. 192], in the 28th year of Augustus; but his dating of Commodus is wrong (see **4** below). The calculation of our Christian era, due to Dionysius Exiguus in the 6th cent., is obviously wrong by several years. Even the dating by the regnal years of emperors is open to considerable doubt, as it is not always certain from what epoch calculation is made; *e.g.* whether from the death of the predecessor, or from the association with the predecessor as colleague. For the birth of Christ indications have been found in the death of Herod, the Lucan census, and the Star of the Magi.

(*a*) *Death of Herod.*—This probably took place in the spring (March) of 4 B.C. His son Archelaus (Mt 2[22]), who succeeded him in part of his dominions (Judaea, Samaria Idumaea) with the title of ethnarch, was deposed (Dio Cassius lv. 27) in the consulship of Lepidus and Arruntius (A.D. 6), either in his ninth (so Josephus *BJ.* II. vii. 3 [111 ff]) or in his tenth year (so *Ant.* XVII. xiii. 2 [342]; and the *Life*, §1, speaks of his tenth year). This would give the above dates for Herod's death; for various considerations which make 4 B.C. the preferable date, see Turner, *op. cit.* p. 404. We must then place our Lord's birth at least one or two years before this date, for Herod massacred 'all the male children . . . who were two years old or under' (Mt 2[16]), and we have to allow for the sojourn in Egypt. Luke apparently assumed that both John and Jesus were born under Herod. (*b*) *The Lucan census* (Lk 2[1ff]) is too uncertain to use as a positive datum; see articles Luke-Acts, Quirinius, and modern commentaries, *e.g.* Creed, *St. Luke*, 28 ff. (*c*) *The Magi.* The astronomer Johann Kepler calculated the date of the Nativity from a conjunction of planets, which he believed the 'star in the east' to be. (See Star of the Magi.) But it is impossible to build chronological results on such a hypothetical basis.

The date arrived at by Ramsay from these considerations was 6 B.C. (summer); by Turner, 6 B.C. (spring), or 7 B.C. But these are still not absolutely certain dates. We must remain in ignorance of the day and month. The calculations which give December 25 and January 6 are both based on fanciful exposition and a wrong date for the Crucifixion, and were involved in the transition from Hellenistic paganism to Christianity in the 3rd and 4th centuries.

2. The Baptism of Our Lord.—According to Lk 3[1], the Baptist began to preach in the fifteenth year of Tiberius, Pontius Pilate being Procurator of Judaea. Eusebius (*HE* i. 10) says that Christ was baptized in the fourth year of Pilate's governorship, and (*HE* i. 9) that Pilate was appointed 'about the twelfth year of the reign of Tiberius'; the latter statement is quoted from Josephus (*Ant.* XVIII. ii. 2 [35]), but the former seems to be Eusebius' own deduction from St. Luke. But Pilate cannot have reached Palestine before A.D. 26 or 27, as his ten years ended shortly before Tiberius' death in A.D. 37, and no date later than A.D. 27 is possible for our Lord's baptism, if we take into account the date of the Nativity and St. Luke's statement of our Lord's age—though 'about thirty' may be only approximate. It is probable, therefore, that Pilate's accession to office and John's appearance as a preacher both belong to the same year, say A.D. 26. Does this, however, suit St. Luke's phrase, 'the 15th year of the reign ['hegemony'] of Tiberius,' for that is the exact phrase? The fifteenth year from the death of Augustus would be August A.D. 28 to August A.D. 29. Ramsay and others supposed that 'the reign of Tiberius' was dated from the granting to him by Augustus of a share in the government of the provinces, just before he celebrated his triumph over

CHRONOLOGY OF THE NT

the people of Pannonia and Dalmatia, *i.e.* January 16, A.D. 12; and this would bring us to *c* A.D. 25–26. This system of counting years is not found elsewhere, but it is quite a possible one. Turner inclined to the same supposition. Several more recent writers incline to take the fifteenth year to mean A.D. 28. Lake favoured 27 (*BC* v. 467), Goguel 27–28 or 28–29 (*Vie de Jésus*, 206).

3. The rebuilding of the Temple.—In Jn 2[20], at a Passover not long after the Baptism, the Jews say that the Temple had been forty-six years in building, which, since the Temple was hardly completed at the outbreak of the War (Josephus, *Ant.* xx. ix. 7 [219 ff]), can only mean that the rebuilding had begun forty-six years before the Passover in question. But this rebuilding began in Herod's eighteenth year *de facto* (from 37 B.C., not 40; *ib.* xv. xi. 1 [380]; for the computation of *BJ* I. xxi. 1 [401], see Turner, p. 405); *i.e.* the Passover of 19 B.C. would be that of the first year of the rebuilding, and therefore the Passover of A.D. 27 that of the forty-sixth year (cf Goguel, p. 210). This would agree with the result already reached.

4. Date of the Crucifixion.—The Fathers seem to have known nothing certainly as to the exact year of our Lord's death. Clement of Alexandria (*loc. cit.*), who believed in a one-year ministry, gives the sixteenth year of Tiberius, forty-two and a half years before the Destruction of Jerusalem (this would be A.D. 28), which was 128 years, 10 months, 3 days, before the death of Commodus (this would make the latter seven years too late). A common tradition (Tertullian, *adv. Jud.* 8) assigns the Crucifixion to the consulship of L. Rubellius Geminus and C. Fifius (?) Geminus—Hippolytus (*in Dan.* iv.) and the *Acts of Pilate* give the names as Rufus and Rubellio,—*i.e.* A.D. 29, or possibly A.D. 28. The latest possible year is A.D. 33 (so Eusebius, *HE* i. 10), for Josephus (*Ant.* XVIII. iv. 3 [90], 6 [106]) relates that Caiaphas was deposed just before he tells us of the death of Herod Philip, which occurred in the twentieth year of Tiberius, *i.e.* A. D. 33–34, reckoning from Augustus' death; Josephus' order has every appearance of being chronological.

Now, it is not certain on which day of the month Nisan the Friday of the Passion fell. We must put aside Westcott's suggestion that our Lord died on a Thursday, as contradicting entirely the Eastern idea of 'the third day' and 'after three days' (see above). But the Synoptics would suggest that our Lord ate the Passover with the disciples on 14th Nisan, and died on the 15th, while John would lead us to suppose that He died on 14th Nisan at the time of the killing of the lambs. The determination of this difficult question will only affect the chronological investigation if in a possible year of the Passion only Nisan 15 or only Nisan 14 can positively be said to have fallen on a Friday. But there is some uncertainty in the reckoning of Nisan. The Jewish months were lunar, and (in early times at least) the first day of the month was not that of the true new moon, but that on which it was first visible. This would be some thirty hours later than the true new moon. But it seems certain that the Jews at the time of the Gospel narrative had some sort of calendrical rules or some rough cycle to determine the first day of a lunar month; otherwise the Jews of the Dispersion would never have been sure of observing the Passover all on the same day, and the difference of a cloudy or of a bright sky on a particular day would introduce confusion. Thus we have to exercise great caution. (The theory that various calendars were in use in 1st cent. Palestine, and that the Galilaeans may have celebrated the Passover on a different day from the Judaeans, is difficult to accept.) A table of the true new moons, and of the days when the moon may be presumed to have been first visible, shows that in A.D. 27, 30, 33, 34, one or other of the two days Nisan 14 and 15 might have fallen on a Friday. But A.D. 29, which has the best traditional support, is also calendrically possible. Taking the equinox as March 21, Nisan 14 that year would be Sunday, April 18; the moon would have been first visible on Monday, April 4. But the equinox was not then, as now, accurately determined, and Turner (*op. cit.* p. 411 f) gave an argument for believing that Nisan in A.D. 29 was really the month before. In that case Nisan 14 would fall on one of the three days March 17–19, of which March 18 was a Friday. Thus A.D. 29 is admissible, and the choice almost certainly lies between it and A.D. 30; for A.D. 33 or 34 is hard to fit in with the calculation as to the Nativity, and no doubt that year was selected because of the dating of the 'fifteenth year' of Lk 3[1] from the death of Augustus. Of the two years, then, A.D. 30 is chosen by Lightfoot, Wieseler, Salmon, Goguel, and others; A.D. 29 by Turner, Ramsay, Sanday, Lake, and other more recent writers—though the statement that the crucifixion took place 'the day before the Sabbath' (Friday) is 'the one really certain fact' in the chronology *BC*, v, 467). Of the days of the month, Nisan 14 is upheld by Claudius Apollinarius (*c* A.D. 160), Clement of Alexandria, Hippolytus, Tertullian, Julius Africanus; and by many moderns, *e.g.* Sanday and Westcott. Nisan 15 is supported by Origen, pseudo-Cyprian, Ambrose, Chrysostom; and in modern times by Edersheim, Lewin, and others. But the choice between these days should be determined by internal evidence of the Gospels rather than by chronological investigation, which is too uncertain to be trustworthy.

5. Aretas and the occupation of Damascus.—Most of the chronological data in the NT are found in Acts, which also provides the most serious chronological problems, chiefly in the correlation of its data with the Pauline epistles. Ac 1–8 contains no references to contemporary history, such as might enable us to fix the date of the events recorded there. Quite possibly these chapters cover a more extended period than has often been assumed. The conversion of Paul (9[1–22]) can scarcely have taken place within a year or two of the Crucifixion, and it is not unlikely that it took place late in the A.D. 30's, rather than early. The reference to the Nabataean King Aretas (Hāritha IV.), in Paul's own account of his flight from Damascus (2 Co 11[32ff]; cf Ac 9[23ff]) requires a date before A.D. 40, when Aretas died. It is not improbable that Paul's flight took place betwen A.D. 37 and 40, as the emperor Gaius presented Damascus to the Nabataeans in A.D. 37. If so, his conversion must have taken place shortly (*i.e.* some months) before a date between A.D. 37 and 40—*i.e.* in A.D. 37, 38, or 39.

6. The world-wide famine under Claudius.—This is described (11[28]) as the background of the first collection for the relief of the Church in Jerusalem (presumably in A.D. 44). But it is a question if this can be identified with any particular year. Tacitus (*Ann.* xii. 43) describes a wide scarcity in the year A.D. 51. Suetonius (*Claudius* 18) describes a similar scarcity, which reduced the grain-tribute sent to Rome, but he does not give any year. Other ancient writers give various dates, from A.D. 48–50 (Claudius reigned A.D. 41–54); it is probable that there were repeated local crises during this period, rather than one year of universal famine. If the reference is chiefly to famine in Palestine (*i.e.* the province of Judaea), with only a background of partial but recurrent scarcity on a world-scale, we may assume that the date must have been A.D. 46–48 (see Jos. *Ant.* xx. v. 2 [101]; cf Ernst Haenchen, *Die Apostelgeschichte*, 1956, pp. 52 f; K. Lake in *Beginnings of Christianity*, vol V, 1933, p. 455). But the significance of this date is only general: the fulfilment of a prophecy, and the reason for the collection at Antioch of a fund for Jerusalem. There is no exact correlation.

7. The Death of Herod Agrippa I.—Another datum in Acts is the death of Herod Agrippa I. (12[23]). This was early in A.D. 44 (probably March 10), after a reign of seven years during which his realm had grown to include most of Palestine. The use made of this date in Acts is homiletical and apologetic; the theme is the one frequent in ancient Jewish and early Christian literature, 'the deaths of the persecutors.' Hence the relevance of the story, for the author of Acts, lies in the manner of the king's death, after persecuting the apostles (12[1–5])

CHRONOLOGY OF THE NT

and accepting a blasphemous acclamation by the mob (12²²), rather than its exact date.

8. Paul's Journeys.—The identification of Paul's journeys as described in Gal 1¹⁵–2¹⁰ with those in Acts is possible on three alternative hypotheses (see Haenchen, 56 f): (1) Ac 15²ff = Gal 2¹ff. In this case, Paul did not mention his visit to Jerusalem described in Ac 11²⁷ff, as it had nothing to do with his 'dependence' on the Apostles and elders there. (2) Ac 11²⁷ff = Gal 2¹ff. If so, the date of the Epistle to Galatians preceded the Apostolic Council (Ac 15), perhaps by some years, as Ramsay and Plooij held, if the journey in Gal 2¹ff took place in A.D. 46. (This was Lake's date for the Council: *BC*, 470.) But the Council may have been held even later, *e.g.* in A.D. 48 (Haenchen), and it has perhaps been idealized, as an ecumenical body issuing a decree affecting the whole Church (16⁴), whereas its authority was really limited to Palestine, Syria, and Cilicia (15²³; cf M. Dibelius, *Studies in Acts*, 1956, p. 99). (3) Ac 11²⁷ff and 15²ff are really two variant accounts of the same journey, and this is the one to which Paul referred in Gal 2¹ff. If so, the Apostolic Council must have been held in A.D. 43 or 44. But this would set Paul's conversion back seventeen years (Gal 1¹⁸, 3 years + Gal 2¹, 14 years) to A.D. 27, which is impossible. (Lake's early proposal to read 'four' for 'fourteen' is improbable.) Even taking the minimal or inclusive reckoning, often used in antiquity, 2+13=15 years is equally impossible to correlate with A.D. 43 or 44. A further uncertainty centres in the date A.D. 43–44; if the action or the authority of the council has been idealized by the author of Acts, he may have pushed it back too far in time (cf the 'programmatic' dating of Jesus' visit to Nazareth in the gospel, Lk 4¹⁶⁻³⁰), and it really belonged in A.D. 48—or later. The fact that Paul in writing Galatians totally disregarded the apostolic decree, taken with the fact that his experience in Damascus (Ac 9) presupposes the settled existence of the Church in that city, and also with the fact that his conversion was a surprise to 'the churches of Christ in Judea' (Gal 1²²), implies (*a*) that his conversion took place somewhat later than the above chronology assumes, and (*b*) that the date of the Council was considerably later than the author of Acts represents.

9. Sergius Paulus.—The reference to the Procurator Sergius Paulus in Ac 13 has been viewed as an additional chronological datum; but unfortunately the ancient sources do not enable us to fix a date for his term of office. (Lake favours a date *c* A.D. 45.)

10. The expulsion of the Jews from Rome in the time of Claudius (Ac 18¹f) is mentioned by Suetonius (*Claudius* 25), but it may have been no more than the expulsion of those guilty of causing a disturbance of the peace. The leader named, one *Chrēstus*, has been supposed to refer to Christ (cf Tacitus, *Ann.* xv. 44); but it is more likely that the word was taken as a Greek *nomen proprium* meaning 'gentle,' 'honest,' or 'good.' It is not, therefore, a reference to Christians in Rome, nor to all Jews in the capital. The date of the riot and its suppression was not improbably *c* A.D. 49.

11. Gallio.—The most important of all chronological data in Acts is in 18¹²⁻¹⁷, the Proconsulship of Gallio, brother of the philosopher Seneca. The famous inscription found at Delphi (see illustration in Deissmann's *Paul*; text in his *App.* and also in *BC* v., pp. 460–64; Dittenberger, *Sylloge Inscr. Gr.*³, II. 801) describes him as appointed Proconsul of Achaia at the 26th acclamation of Claudius as Emperor. This probably took place some time between January 25 and August 1 in the year A.D. 52 (possibly 51). Gallio's term of office (if limited to one year) probably began May 1, 52 (or possibly 51) and terminated twelve months later. Ac 18¹² does not state that the charge against Paul was made as soon as Gallio arrived; nor does 18¹⁸ state how much longer Paul remained in Corinth after the incident. Although we cannot be sure of the year, whether A.D. 51 or 52, a difference as slight as this, at a distance of over nineteen centuries, is excellent chronological reckoning, and we may say that the fortunate discovery of the fragmentary inscription at Delphi has provided one of the main anchors of the whole system of NT chronology.

It is possible that the conference which Acts describes as occurring on Paul's visit to Jerusalem in 15²ff actually occurred on the visit briefly mentioned in 18²¹f. If so, the chronology of Acts and of the life of Paul fit together somewhat more loosely—and more comfortably. We are not then driven to force identifications which do not really come together, and we can allow more time for the growth and expansion of the Church, for the spread of ideas and practices, doctrinal and charitable, and for the maturing of Paul's own thought as reflected in his epistles. It is clear from the location of the narrative in Acts (*i.e.* in ch. 9) that the author did not think Paul's conversion took place immediately after the Resurrection, but only some years later. (Cf 1 Co 15⁸, where *ektrōma* means 'untimely,' not 'too soon,' *i.e.* as an abortion; see Liddell and Scott, *s.v.*, and reff.) On this hypothesis, as advocated by John Knox (see his *Chapters in a Life of Paul*, 1950) and others, Paul's conversion must have occurred in A.D. 37, his first visit to Jerusalem in A.D. 40, his missionary work in Syria, Anatolia, Macedonia, and Greece in A.D. 40–51 (with no long blank period of seven or eight years in Cilicia prior to the year in Antioch, Ac 9³⁰–11²⁵f), his second visit to Jerusalem in A.D. 51, his collection of funds in Greece and Asia in A.D. 51–52, and finally his journey to Jerusalem to deliver the fund and his arrest in the Temple in A.D. 53. (Cf Haenchen, pp. 63–69.)

Paul's transfer to Caesarea for trial by the Procurator Felix (Ac 23²³ff), and his two years' imprisonment there (24²⁷) followed by his trial before Festus and his appeal to Caesar must have transpired during the years A.D. 53–55 or 55–57, depending upon the chronology adopted for the preceding events. (Jülicher, *Einl.*⁷, pp. 40 ff, even preferred A.D. 58–60.) According to Tacitus (*Ann.* xii. 54), Felix had 'long since' been Procurator of Judaea in the year A.D. 52; but this is contradicted by Josephus (*War* II. xii. 8 [247], *Ant.* xx. vii. 1 [137]), whose narrative has first claim to acceptance. It is not improbable that Felix arrived in Palestine not earlier than the summer of A.D. 53. If so, his two years in office ran from A.D. 53–55, when he was succeeded (in the summer of A.D. 55) by Festus. Paul's trial probably took place during the summer of A.D. 55 (see Ac 25¹· ⁶· ¹³), and his departure for Rome the following autumn (27⁵); his arrival in Rome (28¹¹⁻¹⁶) early in A.D. 56. But these final dates may need to be shifted to a somewhat later period (see G. A. Barrois in *Interpreter's Bible*, I, 1952, p. 150).

12. The Persecutions of Nero and Domitian.—(1) *Death of St. Peter and of St. Paul.*—There is no good reason for supposing that the two Apostles died on the same day or even in the same year, though we may probably conclude that they both were martyred under Nero. Paul, in prison, could hardly have been accused of incendiarism; it is more likely that he died soon after his arrival in Rome, and long before the fire of A.D. 64. Their joint commemoration is due to their bodies having been transferred to the Catacombs together on June 29, A.D. 258 (so the Philocalian calendar, A.D. 354). Clement of Rome (Cor 5³⁻⁷) mentions them in the same connexion as examples of patience; Ignatius, writing to the Romans (4³), says: 'I do not order you as Peter and Paul did'; Tertullian says that they were both martyred at Rome under Nero (*Scorp.* 15, *de Praescr.* 36), and so does Origen (Euseb. *HE* iii. 1); Dionysius of Corinth says 'about the same time' (Euseb. *HE* ii. 25); Caius (*c* A.D. 200) describes their graves near Rome (Euseb. *ib.*). Prudentius (*Peristeph.* xii. 5), in the 4th cent., is the first to say that they died on the same day. Eusebius puts their death at the very end of Nero's reign, *i.e.* not long before A.D. 68. The determining considerations are: (*a*) the connexion of their deaths with the fire at Rome in July A.D. 64; (*b*) the necessary interval after St. Paul's acquittal for his later travels, which would take some three years; and this, if we took Lightfoot's chronology (*Clement* i. 75 n.), would prevent us from fixing on A.D. 64 as the year of St. Paul's death; (*c*) the date of St. Peter's First Epistle, if a genuine work; and (*d*) the fact that St. Mark attended both Apostles, the suggestion being that he served St. Peter after St. Paul's death. The last consideration, if true, would make St. Peter's martyrdom the later of the two. The date of 1 Peter (q.v.) is a difficulty. It makes Christianity a crime (1 P 4[14]). At first Christians were accused of ill doing; at a later period they were put to death 'for the name,' *i.e. as Christians.* Sir Wm. Ramsay gave reasons for believing that the change was made by Nero, and developed in the interval A.D. 68–96 under the Flavian emperors (*Ch. in the Rom. Emp.*, pp. 245, 252 ff, 280). The fact of persecutions being mentioned makes it unlikely that 1 Peter was written before A.D. 64 (Lightfoot, *Clement*, ii. 498 ff) and its indebtedness to St. Paul's Epistles implies some interval after they were written. Dr. Charles Bigg, however (*Internat. Crit. Com.*), pleaded for a much earlier date; he believed that the persecutions mentioned were not from the State at all, but from the Jews. Dr. Ramsay, on the other hand, held that the provinces of Asia Minor cannot have been so fully evangelized as 1 Peter implies before A.D. 65, and that the Epistle was written *c* A.D. 80, soon after which date St. Peter died. But this is against all the Patristic testimony, which there is little reason to reject. Probably, then, we must date the death of both Apostles in Nero's reign. Two of the arguments mentioned above—on the one hand that the two martyrdoms must have been in close connexion with the Roman fire; and, on the other hand, that St. Mark can only have attended on the one Apostle after the other's death—appear to have little weight.

(2) *The Apocalypse.*—This work gives us our last chronological indications in NT. Like 1 Peter, it implies persecution 'for the name'; but, unlike 1 Peter, it implies emperor-worship. The tone of antagonism to the Empire is entirely different from that of St. Paul's Epistles and the Acts. The worship of Roma was greatly developed by Domitian, and was scarcely at all prominent in Nero's time. This feature in Revelation (q.v.), then, points to the scene being laid in the Domitianic persecution. Some of the older scholars (*e.g.* Lightfoot and Westcott) argued for a date during Nero's persecution, mainly because of the difference of style between Revelation and John, the latter being dated late in the century; but this argument assumes identity of authorship, for which the evidence seems quite inadequate. Other arguments for a Neronian date have been drawn from the number of the Beast, which is supposed to spell, in Hebrew letters, the name and title 'Nero Caesar' (though it can also be made to refer to Domitian), and from the indication as to the 'kings' (emperors) in 17[10] (but this may be due to the use of an earlier source). The earlier date was popular in the 19th cent., but at present the statement of Irenaeus is more widely accepted, viz. that the book was written (' the vision was seen ') towards the end of the reign of Domitian, who died A.D. 96 (Irenaeus, *Haer.* v. xxx. 3; Euseb. *HE* iii. 18). A. J. M.—F. C. G.

CHRONOLOGY OF THE OLD TESTAMENT.—The practical beginning of the political development of Israel, to judge from references in the Hebrew prophets, was the agglomeration of Aramaean tribes associated with Jacob. The traditions of the earlier patriarchs suggest the general situation known in Palestine from archaeology in the first half of the 2nd millennium, but the narrative of the Jacob-tribes from the first settlement near Shechem to the final settlement after the Exodus reflects folk-movements which agree in general with the history and ethnology of the Near East revealed in the records of the great powers of the Late Bronze Age (1600–1200 B.C.). The Amarna Tablets, in noting the activity of the *Habiru* (q.v.) near Shechem *c* 1400 B.C., may refer to Jacob's settlement there (Gn 34). The weight of the evidence of recent archaeology in Palestine and the political condition of the land known from Egyptian records together with the Biblical evidence suggest that the Exodus, to which the date of the final settlement of Israel in Palestine is relative, must be dated in the 19th dynasty (13th cent.) rather than two centuries earlier as suggested by the numerical statement of 1 K 6[1] (480 years before the building of the Temple), which is obviously the artificial reconstruction of a late pious antiquary, like such specific numbers in the P source of the Pentateuch.

In the Hebrew Monarchy there is more specific chronological detail, though the forty years assigned to David and to Solomon suggest approximation. The duration of the reigns of the kings of Israel and Judah are noted, with synchronizations, but in the Books of Kings these precise figures often confuse rather than clarify. In Assyrian history a firm chronology is possible, thanks to official eponym (*limmu*) lists, annals recording events in the eponym's year of office, royal annals with cross-references to *limmu*-annals, and nearly complete lists of kings with the duration of their reigns, and to the cardinal date of a solar eclipse on June 15, 763 B.C. This holds good for the time coinciding with the Hebrew Monarchy to 649 B.C., after which the chronology of antiquity is supplemented and continued by Ptolemy of Alexandria (A.D. 70–161) on the basis of official annals and astronomical observations until the Roman era. Within this chronological scheme of Assyrian, Babylonian, Persian, Ptolemaic, and Seleucid history the OT affords certain synchronisms.

In the Assyrian account of the Battle of Qarqar, for instance, in the sixth year of Shalmaneser III. (853 B.C.), Ahab of Israel is mentioned. Jehu is listed among Sennacherib's tributaries in his eighteenth year (841 B.C.). Now between Ahab and Jehu fell the reigns of Ahaziah and Joram, given respectively as 2 (1 K 22[51]) and 12 years (2 K 3[1]). Presuming that Judaean scribes, accustomed to reckoning a king's reign from the first New Year after his accession (accession-reckoning), added a year to the official Israelite figures for the reigns of Ahaziah and Joram, which had been given from their natural accession (non-accession reckoning), the interval between Ahab and Joram is 12 years, exactly the interval between the two events associated with Ahab and Jehu which we have cited from the Assyrian inscriptions. Ahab, then, must have died in 853 B.C. and Jehu's first year was in 841 B.C. Reckoning back from 853 B.C. on the basis of statements about the duration of the reigns in Israel and Judah, and allowing for the extra year allowed by Judaean scribes, we arrive at the date 931 B.C. for the accession of Jeroboam I. of Israel and the death of Solomon, whose son Rehoboam officially acceded as king of Judah in 930 B.C. at the Autumnal New Year in the month Tishri. This is the basis of E. R. Thiele's attempt at a reconstruction of OT chronology (*The Mysterious Numbers of the Hebrew Kings*, 1951), which the writer follows, not because it is fully adequate, but because it solves more difficulties than most efforts in this direction. Thiele has explained the many chronological discrepancies in the Books of Kings by recognizing that an event may be dated so long after a king's accession or, alternatively, after another event, *e.g.* Baasha of Israel died in the twenty-sixth year of Asa of Judah (1 K 16[6, 8]); Baasha raided Judah in the thirty-sixth year of Asa (2 Ch 16[6]). The first date is reckoned from Asa's accession; the second from the disruption of the kingdom. So too Omri's slaughter of Elah is dated (1 K 16[10]) from 885 B.C., when Omri ruled with a rival king Tibni. In 1 K 16[23] the reign of Omri is dated in 881 B.C., that is, when he became sole ruler. The dates relative to the reign of Pekah of Israel (*e.g.* 2 K 15[33]) are reckoned not from 740–739 B.C., when he became undisputed ruler, but from 750 B.C., his first abortive attempt to gain the throne, relatively to which the reign of Ahaz is dated (2 K 16). At this point there is notorious confusion in OT chronology, but the accession of Hezekiah may be dated by cross-reference to Assyrian history in 714 B.C. Similarly a date may be reckoned from the time that a prince became co-regent with his father, as occasionally happened, or, alternatively, from the date of his succession. Such co-regencies were those of Jeroboam II. of Israel and Azariah (Uzziah) of Judah, and Jotham.

At the end of the Jewish Monarchy and in the Exile there are more detailed synchronisms with Babylonian history, where chronology is fixed by Babylonian chronicles and by Ptolemy's canon. Accurate cross-references to the regnal years of Babylonian and, later, Persian kings in Jewish records apparently reflect the intense editorial activity in the Exile, when the Books of Kings, for instance, were finally edited, the last historical reference being to the accession of Awil-Marduk (2 K 25^{27}) in 561 B.C.

The restoration of the Jewish community in the Persian period is synchronized with the regnal years of the Achaemenid kings. Ezra refers to a royal directive regarding the restoration of the Temple in Cyrus' first year, that is, his first year as suzerain of Babylon (538 B.C.). The actual rebuilding was undertaken in the second year of Darius I., *i.e.* 520 B.C. (Hag 1$^{1,\,5}$) and finished in his sixth year in 516 B.C. From the first two chapters of Ezra it is not clear whether Zerubbabel and Joshua were among the first exiles to return in 538 B.C., but Ezr 3^{8ff} taken in conjunction with Haggai and Zechariah clearly implies that they returned in 522 B.C.

In the restoration of Jerusalem the activities of Nehemiah and Ezra are dated with reference to Persian chronology, Nehemiah's commission being dated in the twentieth year of Artaxerxes (Neh 2^{1}) and Ezra's journey in the seventh year of Artaxerxes (Ezr 7^{7f}). The internal evidence of Nehemiah and Ezra together with information in the Elephantine Papyri about personalities in Jerusalem indicates that Nehemiah's commission was in 444 B.C. in the reign of Artaxerxes I. and that of Ezra under Artaxerxes II. in 397 B.C.

The Book of Daniel, quite unreliable in its references to Babylonian chronology, is rich in allusions to Palestinian history under the Diadochi, especially to details of the career of Antiochus IV., Epiphanes (175–163 B.C.) down to his death in Ispahan in 163 B.C., to which Dan 11$^{44-45}$ probably alludes.

There are references in Zechariah to the Maccabaean conflict (*e.g.* Zec 9^{13ff}) and Zec 12$^{10-14}$ may refer to the tragic death of Simon in 135–134 B.C., which would be the last topical reference in the OT. J. Gr.

CHRYSOLITE.—See JEWELS AND PRECIOUS STONES.

CHRYSOLYTE, Rev 21^{20} (AV).—See CHRYSOLITE.

CHRYSOPRASE.—See JEWELS AND PRECIOUS STONES.

CHRYSOPRASUS, Rev 21^{20} (AV).—See CHRYSOPRASE.

CHUB, Ezk 30^{5} (AV).—See CUB.

CHUN, 1 Ch 18^{8} (AV).—See CUN.

CHURCH.—1. The word *ecclesia*, which in its Christian application is usually translated 'church,' was applied in ordinary Greek usage to the duly constituted gathering of the citizens in a self-governing city, and it is so used of the Ephesian assembly in Ac 19^{39}. It was adopted in the LXX to translate a Hebrew word, *ḳāhāl*, signifying the nation of Israel as assembled before God or considered in a religious aspect (Jg 21^{8}, 1 Ch 29^{1}, Dt 31^{30}, etc.). In this sense it is found twice in the NT (Ac 7^{38} RV 'church,' RSV **'congregation,'** He 2^{12} RV and RSV **'congregation'**). The term is practically equivalent to the familiar **'synagogue,'** which, however, was more frequently used to translate another Hebrew word, *'ēdhāh*. This will probably explain our Lord's words in Mt 18^{17}. For 'synagogue' was the name regularly applied after the Babylonian exile to local congregations of Jews formally gathered for common worship, and from them subsequently transferred to similar congregations of Hebrew Christians (Ja 2^{2}). 'Tell it to the *ecclesia*' can hardly refer directly to communities of Jesus' disciples, as these did not exist in the time of the Galilaean ministry, but rather to the Jewish congregation, or its representative court, in the place to which the disputants might belong. The renewal of the promise concerning binding and loosing in v.^{18} (cf 16^{19}) makes against this interpretation. And the assurance of Christ's presence in v.^{20} can have reference only to gatherings of disciples. But it may well be that these sayings were brought together by Matthew in view of the Christian significance of *ecclesia*. They were doubtless understood by his readers as referring to the Church in their own time, to which the Gospel was addressed—sometime late in the 1st cent., or after. There is no evidence that *ecclesia*, like 'synagogue,' was transferred from the congregation of Israel to the religious assemblies which were its local embodiment. But, though not the technical term, there would be no difficulty in applying it, without fear of misunderstanding, to the synagogue. And this would be the more natural because the term is usually applied to Israel in its historical rather than in its ideal aspect (see Hort, *Christian Ecclesia*, p. 12).

2. *Ecclesia* is used constantly with its Christian meaning in the Pauline Epistles. Its earliest use chronologically is probably in 1 Th 1^{1}. But the growth of its use is best studied by beginning with Acts. Here the term first occurs in 5^{11}, applied to the Christians of Jerusalem in their corporate capacity. In 1^{15} St. Peter is represented as standing up 'among the brethren.' Thus from the first Christians are a brotherhood or family, not a promiscuous gathering. That this family is considered capable of an ordered extension is evident (*a*) from the steps immediately taken to fill a vacant post of authority (1^{25}), and (*b*) from the way in which converts on receiving baptism are spoken of as added to a fellowship (2^{47} AV 'added to the church,' but see RSV) which continues in the Apostles' teaching, and the bond of a common table and united prayer (2$^{42,\,46}$). This community is now called 'the company of those who believed' (4^{32}), the word used, as compared with its employment elsewhere, suggesting not a throng or crowd but the whole body of the disciples. In Ex 12^{6} we have the phrase 'the whole assembly of the congregation (Gr. *synagōgē*) of Israel.' When, therefore, it became necessary to find a collective name for 'the believers,' *ecclesia*, the alternative to 'synagogue,' was not unnaturally chosen. For the disciples meeting in Jerusalem were, as a matter of fact, the true Israel (Gal 6^{16}), the little flock to whom was to be given the Messianic Kingdom (Lk 12^{32}). Moreover, they were a Christian synagogue, and, but for the risk of confusion, might have been so called. The name, therefore, as applied to the primitive community of Jesus, is on the one hand universal and ideal, on the other local and particular. In either case the associations are Jewish, and by these the subsequent history of the name is determined.

3. As Christianity spread, the local units of the brotherhood came to be called *ecclesiae* (Ac 9^{31} 13^{1} 14^{23} 15^{41} 20^{17} etc.), the original community being now distinguished as 'the *ecclesia* in Jerusalem' (8^{1}). Thus we reach the familiar use of the Pauline Epistles, *e.g.* the *ecclesia* of the Thessalonians (1 Th 1^{1}), of Laodicea (Col 4^{16}), of Corinth (1 Co 1^{2}); cf 1 P 5^{13}, Rev 2^{1} etc. They are summed up in the expression 'all the *ecclesiae* of Christ' (Ro 16^{16}). This language has doubtless given rise to the modern conception of 'the churches'; but it must be observed that the Pauline idea is territorial, the only apparent departure from this usage being the application of the name to sections of a local *ecclesia*, which met for worship in the houses of prominent disciples (Ro 16^{5}, 1 Co 16^{19} etc.). The existence of independent congregations of Christians within a single area, like the Hellenistic and Hebrew synagogues (see Ac 6$^{1,\,9}$), does not appear to be contemplated in the NT.

4. The conception of a Catholic Church in the sense of a constitutional federation of local Christian organizations in a universal community is post-Apostolic. The phrase is first found in Ignatius (*c* A.D. 115; see Lightfoot, *Apost. Fathers*, Pt. 2 ii, p. 310). But in the 1st cent. the Church of Jerusalem, as the seat of Apostolic authority (Ac 8$^{1,\,14}$), still exercises an influence upon the other communities, which continues during the period of transition to the world-wide society. At Jerusalem Saul receives the right hand of fellowship and recognition from the pillar Apostles (Gal 2^{9}). Thence Apostles go forth to confirm and consolidate the work of evangelists (Ac 8^{14}). Thither missionaries return with reports of newly founded Gentile societies and contributions for the poor saints (Ac 15^{2} 24^{17}, 1 Co 16^{1-3}). It is this community that promulgates decisions on problems created by the extension of Christianity (Ac 15^{22-29}). Till after the destruction of the city in A.D. 70 this Church continued, under the presidency of James the Lord's brother (Gal 2^{12}, Ac 12^{17} 15^{13} 21^{18}), and then of other members of the Christian 'royal family' (Euseb. *HE* iii. 11, 19, 20), to be the typical society of Jesus' disciples.

5. But already in the NT the ideal element is present, especially as seen in the Epistle to Ephesians and the Gospel of John. Such a passage as Mt 16^{17-19} is probably a consequence rather than a source of this exalted view; it is now thought by many scholars to be a reflection of the position actually held by Peter, for a time, either in Jerusalem or in Antioch. It can scarcely be thought that the words are historical, or if historical were familiar to the other apostles—especially Paul—or to the early Christian Church either in Palestine or in the larger Gentile world outside.

6. Much 19th cent. interpretation of the NT teaching on the Church and its relation to the Kingdom of God was vitiated by a failure to recognize this secondary element in the gospels, or by a misunderstanding—or misinterpretation—of the latter term, as the 'Kingdom of the Messiah.' Always, in Jewish and early Christian teaching, *God* is the King of the Kingdom, which is *His Reign*; in Jewish and early Christian thought, it is inconceivable that Christ should usurp the prerogatives of His Father. Likewise, the identification of the Church with the Kingdom of God is also questionable. Only late passages like Mt 13^{41} assume that the Kingdom and the Church are identical, and that Christ is the head of the Kingdom of God as he is of the Church.

Normally, the Kingdom of God is viewed as the final state of the universe when sin, suffering, and death shall have been done away, and when God shall be 'all in all' (1 Co 15^{28})—or 'everything to everyone' (RSV). Even Christ will then 'be subjected to him who put all things under him': the Son 'must reign until he has put all his enemies under his feet' (v.^{25}). As the King's Son, the Young Prince now leads the armies of the Lord against all His spiritual foes, earthly or heavenly, human or angelic, demonic or diabolical; in the end, when the victory has been won, the Son will take his place for ever 'at God's right hand.' The Church is the body of His followers, who must be prepared like Him to lay down their lives, if necessary, in the expectation of rising again and sharing His victory, His judgment, and His rule. The Church is not identical with the Kingdom; but it is very remote from the modern idea of a voluntary society of religious minded people who admire Jesus and wish to follow Him, or even the idea of a body of the elect who live and die in this world, certain of their salvation in the world to come, but solely as individuals, with no vital relation to Christ, the supernatural heavenly Lord, or his warring hosts, or the Church which is His 'Body.'

7. It is only in the theology of St. Paul that we find the Kingdom of the Gospels interpreted in terms of the actual experience of the Christian *ecclesia*. The extension of the fellowship beyond the limits of a single city has shown that the ideal Church cannot be identified *simpliciter* with any Christian community, while the idealization of the federated *ecclesiae*, natural enough in a later age is, in the absence of a wider ecclesiastical organization, not yet possible. It is still further from the truth to assert that St. Paul had the conception of an invisible Church, of which the local communities were at best typical. 'We have no evidence that St. Paul regarded membership of the universal *ecclesia* as invisible' (Hort, *Christian Ecclesia*, p. 169). It was the historical fact of the inclusion of the Gentiles (cf Eph 2^{13}) that provided Paul's starting-point. Those nations which under the old covenant were alien from the people of God (Eph 2^{12}) are now included in the vast citizenship or polity (v.^{13ff}) which membership in a local *ecclesia* involves. The Church has existed from all eternity as an idea in the mind of God (3^{3-11}), the heritage prepared for Christ (1^{10f}). It is the people of possession (1^{14}, cf 1 P 2^{9}, Tit 2^{14}), identified with the commonwealth of Israel (Eph 2^{12}), and as such the immediate object of redemption (5^{25}); but through the reconciliation of the Cross extended (2^{14}), and, as it were, reincorporated on a wider basis (v.^{15}), as the sphere of universal forgiveness (v.^{16}), the home of the Spirit (v.^{18}), and the one body of Christ (4^{12}, etc.), in which all have access to the Father (2^{18}). The interlaced figures of growth and building ($4^{12, 16}$), under which it is presented, witness to its organic and therefore not exclusively spiritual character. Baptism, administered by the local *ecclesiae* and resulting in rights and duties in respect of them, is yet primarily the method of entrance to the ideal community (Ro 6^{3f}, 1 Co 12^{13}, Gal 3^{27f}, Eph 4^{5}), to which also belong those offices and functions which, whether universal like the Apostolate (1 Co 12^{27f}) or particular like the presbyterate (Ac $20^{17, 28}$; cf 1 Co 12^{8-11}, Eph 4^{11}), are exercised only in relation to the local societies. It is the Church of God that suffers persecution in the persons of those who are of 'the Way' (1 Co 15^{9}, Ac 8^{3} 9^{1}); is profaned by misuse of sacred ordinances at Corinth (1 Co 11^{22}); becomes at Ephesus the pillar and ground of the truth (1 Ti 3^{15}).

That St. Paul, in speaking of the Church now in the local now in the universal sense, is not dealing with ideas connected only by analogy, is proved by the ease with which he passes from the one to the other use (Col 4^{15f}; cf $1^{18, 24}$ and Ephesians *passim*). The Church is essentially visible, the shrine of God (1 Co 3^{16f}), the body of Christ (Eph 1^{23} etc.); schism and party-strife involving a breach in the unity of the Spirit (4^{3}). Under another figure the Church is the bride of Christ (5^{25ff}), His complement of fulness (1^{23}), deriving its life from Him as He does from the Father (v.^{22}, 1 Co 11^{3}).

8. Thus the Biblical view of the Church differs alike from the materialized conception of Augustine, which identifies it with the constitutionally incorporated and ecumenical society of the Roman Empire, with its canon law and hierarchical jurisdiction, and from that Kingdom of Christ which Luther, as interpreted by Ritschl, regarded as 'the inward spiritual union of believers with Christ' (*Justification and Reconciliation*, English translation, p. 287). The principle of the Church's life is inward, so that 'the measure of the stature of the fulness of Christ' remains the object of Christian hope (Eph 4^{13}). But its manifestation is outward, and includes those ministries which, though marred, as history shows, by human failure and sin, are set in the Church for the building up of the body (v.^{11f}). Just as members of the legal Israel are recognized by our Lord as sons of the Kingdom (Mt 8^{12}), so the baptized are the called, the saints, the members of the body. There is no warrant in the NT for that sharp separation between membership in the legal worshipping Church and the Kingdom of God which is characteristic of Ritschlianism and other modern views.

9. The Church in its corporate capacity is the primary object of redemption. This truth, besides being definitely asserted (Eph $5^{25, 27}$, Ac 20^{28}, Tit 2^{14}), is involved in the conception of Christ as the second Adam (Ro 5^{12-21}, 1 Co 15^{20-22}), the federal head of a redeemed race; underlies the institutions of Baptism and the Eucharist; and is expressed in the Apostolic teaching concerning the two Sacraments (see above, also 1 Co 10^{16-18} 11^{20-34}). The Church is thus not a voluntary association of justified persons for purposes of mutual edification and common worship, but the body in which the individual believer normally realizes his redemption. Christ's love for the Church, for which He gave Himself (Eph 5^{25}), constituting a royal priesthood, a holy nation, a people of possession (1 P $2^{5, 9}$) through His blood (Eph 2^{13}), completes the parallel, or rather marks the identity, with the historical Israel. Membership in Abraham's covenanted race, of which circumcision was the sign (Gn 17^{9}), brought the Israelite into relation with Yahweh. The sacrifices covered the whole 'church in the wilderness' (Ac 7^{38}), and each worshipper approached God in virtue of his inclusion in the holy people. No foreigner might eat of the Passover (Ex 12^{45}). The ritual of the Day of Atonement was expressly designed for the consecration of the whole nation (Lv 16). So the sacrifice of the Cross is our Passover (1 Co 5^{7}). The worship of the Christian congregation is the Paschal feast (v.^{8}, cf He 13^{10-15}). In Christ those who are now fellow-citizens have a common access to the Father (Eph 2^{18}, He 10^{22}). Through the Mediator of a new covenant (12^{24}) those who are consecrated ($10^{14, 22}$) have come to the Church of the first-born (12^{23}), which includes the spirits of the perfected saints (*ib.*) in the fellowship of God's household (Eph 2^{19}, He 10^{21}). See also following article. J. G. S.—F. C. G.

CHURCH GOVERNMENT.—1. The general development seems fairly clear, though its later stages fall beyond NT times. The Apostles were founders of churches, and therefore regulated and supervised the first arrangements; then were added sundry local and unlocal rulers; then the unlocal died out, and the local settled down into the three permanent classes of bishops, elders, and deacons. The chief disputed questions concern the origin of the local ministry, its relation to the other, and the time and manner in which it settled down under the government of (monarchical) bishops.

2. Twice over St. Paul gives something like a list of the chief persons of the Church. In 1 Co 12^{28} he counts up—'first apostles, second prophets, third teachers, then workers of miracles, then healers, helpers, administrators, speakers in various kinds of tongues.' It will be noticed that all the words after the first two plainly describe functions, not offices. A few years later he—or the author of Ephesians (4^{11f})—tells us how the ascended Lord gave His gifts to the church, 'that some should be apostles, some prophets, some evangelists, some pastors and teachers, for the equipment of the saints, for the work of ministry (*diakonia*)'—they are all of them 'deacons' (*diakonoi*), whatever more they may be.

3. At the head of both lists is the **Apostle** (q.v.). The Apostles were not limited to the Eleven, or to the number twelve, though twelve was always the ideal number (1 Co 15^{5}, Rev 21^{14}; perhaps Ac 2^{14} 6^{2}). Whether Matthias *remained* an Apostle or not, Paul and Barnabas were certainly Apostles (*e.g.* Ac 14^{14}), and so was James the Lord's brother (Gal 1^{19}). The old disciples Andronicus and Junias (not Junia) were 'notable' Apostles (Ro 16^{7}). On the other hand, Timothy seems excluded by the greetings of several Epistles (*e.g.* 2 Corinthians), and Apollos by the evidence of Clement of Rome, who most likely knew the truth of the matter.

The Apostle's first qualification was to have seen the risen Lord (Ac 1^{22}, 1 Co 9^{5}), for his first duty was to bear witness of the Resurrection. This qualification seems never to have been relaxed in NT times. A direct call was also needed, for (1 Co 12^{28}, Gal 1^{1}, Eph 4^{11}) no human authority could choose an Apostle. The call of Barnabas and Saul was acknowledged (Ac 13^{3}) by a commission from the church at Antioch.

Therefore the Apostle was in no sense a local official. His work was not to serve tables, but to preach and to make disciples of all nations, so that he led a wandering life, settling down only in his old age, or in the sense of making, say, Ephesus or Corinth his centre for a while. The stories which divide the world among the Twelve are legends: the only division we know of was made (Gal 2^{9}) at the Conference, when it was resolved that the Three should go to the Jews, Paul and Barnabas to the Gentiles. With this preaching went the founding and general care of churches, though not their ordinary government. St. Paul interferes only in cases of gross error or *corporate* disorder. His point is not that the Galatians are mistaken, but that they are altogether falling away from Christ; not that the Corinthian is a bad offender, but that the church sees no great harm in the matter. He does not advise the Corinthians on further questions without plain hints (1 Co 6^{5} 10^{14} 11^{14}) that they ought to have settled most of them for themselves.

4. Next to the Apostle comes the shadowy figure of the **Prophet** (q.v.). He too sustained the Church, and shared with the apostle (Eph 2^{20} 3^{5}) the revelation of the mystery. He spoke 'in the Spirit' words of warning, of comfort, or it might be of prediction. He too received his commission from God and not from men, and was no local officer of a church, even if he dwelt in the city. But he was not an eye-witness of the risen Lord, and 'the care of all the churches' did not rest on him. Women also might prophesy (1 Co 11^{5}), like Philip's daughters (Ac 21^{9}) at Caesarea, or perhaps the mystic Jezebel (Rev 2^{20}) at Thyatira. Yet even in the Apostolic age prophecy (1 Th 5^{20}) is beginning to fall into discredit, and false prophets are flourishing (1 John, 2 Peter, Jude).

5. It will be seen that St. Paul's lists leave no place for a local ministry of office, unless it comes in under 'helpers and administrators' or 'pastors and teachers.' Yet such a ministry must have existed almost from the first. We have (1) the appointment of the Seven at Jerusalem (Ac 6); (2) elders at Jerusalem about the years 44, 50, 58 (11^{30} $15^{6, 22}$ 21^{18}), appointed by Paul and Barnabas in every church about 48 (14^{23}), mentioned Ja 5^{14}; at Ephesus (Ac 20^{17}), mentioned 1 P 5^{1}; (3) Phoebe a deaconess at Cenchreae (Ro 16^{1}), bishops and deacons at Philippi (Ph 1^{1}). Also in the Pastoral Epistles, Timothy at Ephesus is (1 Ti 3, 4) in charge of four orders: (1) bishops (or elders) (5^{1}); (2) deacons; (3) deaconesses (3^{11}) ('women' [in Greek without the article] cannot be wives of deacons); (4) widows. With Titus in Crete only bishops are mentioned (Tit 1^{5ff}). To these we add (5) the prominent *quasi*-episcopal positions of James at Jerusalem about 44 (Ac 12^{17}), in 50, and in 58; and (6) of Timothy and Titus at Ephesus and in Crete.

To these we must *not* add (1) the 'young men' (*neōteroi*) who carried out Ananias (Ac 5^{6}) [The tacit contrast with *presbyteroi* is of age, not office, for it is *neaniskoi* who bury Sapphira]; (2) the indefinite *proistamenoi* of 1 Th 5^{12} and Ro 12^{8}, and the equally indefinite *hēgoumenoi* of some unknown church shortly after 70 (He $13^{7, 17}$) [If these are officials, we can say no more than that there are several of them]; (3) the angels of the seven churches in Asia. [These cannot safely be taken literally.]

6. The questions before us may be conveniently grouped round the three later offices of Bishop, Elder, and Deacon. But *bishop* and *deacon* seem at first to have denoted functions of oversight and service rather than definite offices. The *elder* carries over a more official character from the synagogue; but in any case there is always a good deal of give and take among officials of small societies. If so, we shall not be surprised if we find neither definite institution of offices nor sharp distinction of duties.

(1) **Deacons** (q.v.). The traditional view, that the choice of the Seven in Ac 6 marks the institution of a permanent order of deacons, is open to serious doubt. The opinion of Cyprian and later writers is not worth much on a question of this kind, and even that of Irenaeus is far from decisive. The vague word *diakonia* (also used in the context of the Apostles themselves) is balanced by the avoidance of the word 'deacon' in the Acts (*e.g.* 21^{8} Philip the evangelist, one of the Seven). Since, however, Phoebe was a deaconess at Cenchreae, there were probably deacons there and at Corinth, though St. Paul does not mention any; and at Philippi we have bishops and deacons. In both cases, however, the doubt remains, how far the name has settled into a definite office.

(2) **Elders** (see BISHOP). Elders at Jerusalem receive the offerings in 44 from Saul and Barnabas. They are joined with the Apostles at the Conference (Ac 15^{4}), and with James (21^{18}). As Paul and Barnabas appoint elders in every city on their first missionary journey, and we find elders at Ephesus (Ac 20^{17}), we may infer that the

churches generally had elders, though there is no further certain mention of them till the Pastoral Epistles and 1 Peter. Possibly Ja 5^{14} is earlier, but there we cannot be sure that the word is official.

The difference of name between elders and bishops may point to some difference of origin or duties; but in NT (and in Clement of Rome) the terms often appear equivalent. Thus the elders of Ephesus are reminded (Ac 20^{28}) that they are bishops. In the Pastoral Epistles, Timothy appoints 'bishops and deacons'; Titus, 'elders and deacons,' though Timothy also (1 Ti 5^{17}) has elders under him. The qualifications of the elder, as described to Titus, are practically those of the bishop as given to Timothy, and it is added (Tit 1^{7}) that the elders must be such 'because the bishop, as God's steward, must be blameless,' etc.—which is decisive that the bishop's office was at least as wide as the elder's. Moreover, in both cases the duties implied are ministerial, not governmental. If the elder's duty is to rule (1 Ti 5^{17}), he does it subject to Timothy, much as a modern elder rules subject to his bishop.

(3) **Bishops.** See BISHOP. H. M. G.—M. H. S.

CHURCHES, ROBBERS OF.—This is in Ac 19^{37} an AV mistranslation (RV has 'robbers of temples'). Even the RV is inexact. The word ought to be translated simply 'sacrilegious persons,' that is, persons acting disrespectfully to the goddess of Ephesus. See RSV 'sacrilegious,' *i.e.* desecrators of the temple. In 2 Mac 4^{42} (RV 'author of the sacrilege') the expression is applied to Lysimachus, brother of Menelaus the high priest, who perished in a riot caused by sacrilege (170 B.C.). RSV reads 'temple robber.' See Ro 2^{22}, and Cicero, *De Nat. Deor.* i. 82, with note in edition of A. S. Pease.
A. So.—F. C. G.

CHURCHES, SEVEN.—See ANGELS OF THE SEVEN CHURCHES, REVELATION [BOOK OF], also the articles on EPHESUS, SMYRNA, etc.

CHUSHAN-RISHATHAIM.—AV form of **Cushan-rishathaim** (q.v.).

CHUSI (Jth 7^{18}), mentioned with Ekrebel (*'Akrabeh*), is possibly *Kuzah*, 5 miles S. of Shechem and 5 miles W. of 'Akrabeh (RSV 'Acraba').

CHUZA.—The steward of Herod Antipas. His wife Joanna (q.v.) was one of the women who ministered to our Lord and His disciples (Lk 8^{3}).

CIELED, CIELING.—See CEILED, CEILING.

CILICIA.—A district in the SE. corner of Asia Minor, which in NT times was divided into two portions. The Roman province Cilicia, which alone is referred to in the NT, stretched from a little E. of Corycus to Mt. Amanus, and from the Cilician Gates to the sea. For administrative purposes it was combined with Syria and Phoenicia. The sense of the unity of Syria and Cilicia is seen clearly in Gal 1^{21} (also in Ac $15^{23, 41}$). The capital of the province Cilicia was Tarsus (Ac 21^{39} 22^{3}). The other portion to which the name was applied was the client-kingdom of king Antiochus of Commagene, which was under the suzerainty of Rome, and included Cilicia Tracheia (Rugged Cilicia) to the W., as well as a belt surrounding the Roman province on the N. and E.
A. So.

CIMMERIANS.—The name, which has come to us through the Greek, of the people known as **Gomer** (q.v.) in the Bible, the *Gimirrai* of the cuneiform inscriptions.

CINNAMON (Ex 30^{23}, Pr 7^{17}, Ca 4^{14}, Rev 18^{13}; Sir 24^{10} [AV, RV; RSV **cassia**, q.v.]).—Almost without doubt the product of *Cinnamomum zeylanicum* of Ceylon. The inner bark is the part chiefly used, but oil is also obtained from the fruit. Cinnamon is still a favourite perfume and flavouring substance in Palestine.
E. W. G. M.

CINNEROTH, 1 K 15^{20} (AV).—See CHINNERETH.

CIRAMA, 1 Es 5^{20} (AV).—See RAMAH, 3.

CIRCUIT.—Occurs four times in AV: 1 S 7^{16} (according to which Samuel went on circuit to various high places), Job 22^{14} (RVm and RSV 'vault' [of heaven]), Ps 19^{6} (of the sun's course in the heavens), Ec 1^{6} (of the circuits of the wind). RV retains these instances and substitutes 'make a circuit' for AV 'fetch a compass' in 2 S 5^{23} (RSV 'go around'), 2 K 3^{9} (RSV 'made a circuitous march'), Ac 28^{13} (so RSV); see COMPASS. RSV further reads 'in complete circuit' in 1 Ch 11^{8} (AV, RV 'round about'), 'the circuit round Jerusalem' in Neh 12^{28} (AV 'plain country,' RV 'plain,' RVm 'circuit').

CIRCUMCISION.—1. The origins of this rite are wrapped in obscurity. Many scholars have thought in terms of African origin, and Egypt as the medium through which the practice spread to the Semites. Herodotus says the Phoenicians and Syrians learned it from the Egyptians, and Jos $3^{2-3, 8-9}$ suggests that Egyptian disdain of the uncircumcised was a motive for its introduction into Israel. On the other hand, the use of the term *ḥtn* in Ugaritic (=Heb. *ḥāthān* 'bridegroom' Ex 4^{26}='circumcised') suggests that circumcision played a part in West Semitic marriage ceremonial in the 2nd millennium. The use of a flint (Jos 5^{2-3}) attests the antiquity of the rite. The original motive seems to have been either to please the god by making a redemption-offering of the foreskin or to provide a sign of initiation into the clan. The hygienic motive, where it existed, was secondary. It was carried out variously at puberty (six to fourteen amongst the Egyptians), and before marriage (*i.e.* to make a boy a true adult); but the circumcision of infants was also practised. The rite was observed by Egyptians, Arabs, Phoenicians, Edomites, Ammonites, Moabites. The Philistines from Asia Minor were the only uncircumcised known to the ancient Israelites, before the appearance of the Assyrians in the 9th cent.

2. All this is reflected in the OT. Thus (*a*) the idea of the redemption-offering is plain in Lv 19^{23f}. (*b*) Circumcision at puberty is attested in the case of Ishmael at the age of thirteen (Gn 17^{25}). (*c*) It is a preparation for marriage in Ex 4^{26} ('A bridegroom of blood, because of the circumcision'), where also it is possible to detect the primitive tradition of a prophylactic against desert demons. (*d*) Jos $5^{2, 8f}$ is another pointer to primitive custom. At the pre-Israelite sanctuary of Gilgal, there was a 'hill of foreskins,' associated traditionally with the mass circumcision by Joshua of all the uncircumcised in Israel. In the earliest traditions, the connexion of circumcision with Yahwism is tenuous. There is no divine command. Moses apparently was and remained uncircumcised.

3. Firm evidence of the use of circumcision as a sign of membership of the covenant-community comes mainly from the 5th cent. In the priestly tradition (Gn 17^{1-27}), it is the primary, God-given sign of the covenant made with Abraham, and every male (whether foreigner or slave) is to be circumcised at eight days (cf Lv 12^{3}). In Ezekiel also it is the mark of initiation into the community, so that, even in Sheol, the uncircumcised has no right to be reunited with his people (Ezk 28^{10} 31^{18} 32^{18}). No doubt exilic contact with uncircumcised Babylonians and Persians made circumcision nationally and religiously distinctive. Along with the sabbath, circumcision assumed the status of a *confession.*

4. When circumcision had become a self-evident pre-supposition of Jewish life, it was given a spiritual interpretation. There is a deeper circumcision of the heart (Jer 4^{4}, Dt 10^{16} 30^{6}). The uncircumcised ear is the ear that does not perform its proper function of hearing (Jer 6^{10}). Uncircumcised lips cannot speak (Ex $6^{12, 30}$). So also in the thought of the Qumrân community, the wicked priest is one who 'did not circumcise the foreskin of his heart'; and the 'men of truth' are those who 'circumcise in unity the foreskin of impulse and a stiff neck.'

5. This is the background of the Pauline teaching that 'circumcision is that of the heart, in the spirit, not in the letter' (Ro 2^{29}). But St. Paul went further to declare that this inward circumcision alone is effective.

'He is not a Jew who is one outwardly' (v.^{28}). Circumcision of the heart is equivalent to forgiveness through Jesus Christ; and in Col 2^{11f} 'the circumcision of Christ' is baptism. Hence for the Christian Church the Jewish ordinance ceased to have importance. 'In Christ Jesus neither circumcision nor uncircumcision is of any avail' (Gal 5^{6}). St. Paul was involved in a critical conflict, in the early Church, with Jewish Christians who wished to insist on circumcision. This was settled, according to Ac 15^{3-21} on the principle that St. Peter should be the apostle of the Jews, St. Paul of the gentiles, without any requirement of circumcision. The missionary appeal was for faith leading to baptism, and henceforth the Christian Church was the true Israel. 'We are the circumcision' (Ph 3^{3}). D. R. J.

CIS, Ac 13^{21} (AV).—See KISH, **1.**

CISAI, Ad. Est 11^{2} (AV).—See KISH, **4.**

CISTERN.—In Palestine, the climate and geological formation of the country render the storage of water a prime necessity of existence. Hence cisterns, mostly hewn in the solid rock, were universal in Bible times, and even before the Hebrew conquest (Dt 6^{11}, Neh 9^{25}, where AV has 'wells'). Thus at Gezer it has been found that 'the rock was honeycombed with cisterns, one appropriated to each house [cf 2 K 18^{31}] or group of houses . . . (and) fairly uniform in character. A circular shaft, about 3 feet in diameter and 5 feet deep, cut through the rock, expands downwards into a chamber roughly square or circular in plan, about 13 to 25 feet in diameter and generally about 20 feet deep. . . . The wall is generally covered with coarse plaster' (*PEFSt*, 1903, 111 f).

A cistern might contain only rain water conveyed from the court or flat roof during the rainy season by gutters and pipes, or might be fed by a conduit led from a spring at a distance. The largest of the innumerable cisterns of Jerusalem, the 'great sea' in the Haram area, which is estimated to have held 3,000,000 gallons, derived its water-supply partly from surface drainage and partly from water brought by a conduit from Solomon's Pools near Bethlehem (Wilson).

The mouth of a cistern, through which the water was sometimes drawn by a wheel (Ec 12^{6}), was legally required to have a cover (Ex 21^{33}, cf Jos. *Ant.* IV. viii. 37 [283 f]). A disused or temporarily empty cistern formed a convenient place of detention, as in the case of Joseph (Gn 37^{20ff}) and of Jeremiah (Jer 38^{6ff}).

A. R. S. K.

CITADEL.—This word is found in RSV in 1 K 16^{18}, 2 K 15^{25} (AV '**palace,**' RV '**castle**'), where it denotes the fortified part of the king's palace, which served as a refuge from, and a last defence against, the enemy when the city itself had been stormed. In Ps $48^{3, 13}$ it is used of the city of Zion. Such a citadel was the '**strong tower**' of Thebez (Jg 9^{50}), and perhaps the '**tower**' of 2 K 9^{17} (though this may have been a watch-tower or gate tower; see FORTIFICATION). The most frequent designation in EV, however, is **hold** or **stronghold** (Jg $9^{46, 49}$, 2 S 5^{7}). In the later struggles with the Seleucids and the Romans, respectively, two Jerusalem forts played an important part: the **citadel** (so RV, RSV; AV 'strong hold') of 1 Mac 1^{33} 3^{45} etc. (*i.e.* the **Acra,** built by Antiochus IV.), and the castle of **Antonia,** on the site of the earlier fortress (so RSV; AV 'palace,' RV 'castle') of Nehemiah's day (Neh 2^{8}), and itself the **barracks** (AV, RV 'castle') of Ac 21^{34} 22^{24}.

CITHERNS.—1 Mac 4^{54} (AV; RV, RSV 'harps'); see MUSIC.

CITIES OF THE PLAIN.—See PLAIN [CITIES OF THE].

CITIMS, 1 Mac 8^{5} (AV).—See KITTIM.

CITIZENSHIP.—See PAUL, ROMAN PUBLIC LAW, **6,** ROME.

CITY.—1. In the OT 'city' translates both the very common *'îr* and the more poetic *ḳiryāh*. Neither term in any way connotes bigness or prestige; in size they varied in Canaanite times from the 5 acres of Chephirah (population 1250?), or less, to the 175 acres of Hazor (population 40,000?). Near the lower limit were *Tell en-Naṣbeh* (Mizpah?), and Jericho (now hailed as the earliest 'city' on earth) with areas of 8 and 9 acres respectively, then Shechem (11), Taanach and pre-Davidic Jerusalem (11); Megiddo covered about 15 acres, while pre-exilic Jerusalem was roughly double.

Four factors influenced the siting of Palestinian cities: defensibility, control of communications, food supply, and water; though, naturally, many cities owed their founding to one of these more than to others, *e.g.* Jerusalem was ideally sited for defence (2 S 5^{6}), but its water supply was a constant problem for centuries (2 K 20^{20}), and it was off the main highways; Bethshean controlled the important routes along the Jordan valley, and the best gateway to the west, and drew on a rich agricultural area. Among the few cities founded by the Israelites on virgin sites may be reckoned Samaria (1 K 16^{24}); but usually Israelite towns grew up near, or on, the sites of earlier Canaanite cities. Much of the building material being adobe, rather than stone, earthquake, or weathering following enemy conquest, would soon make a city uninhabitable, but then a shift in political fortune might raise a new city on the roughly levelled ruins of the old. At *Tell ed-Duweir*, 60 feet of debris have been built up by successive destructions of the city of Lachish, giving rise here as elsewhere to the typical sugar-loaf shape of mound referred to in Jos 11^{13}, Jer 30^{18} (Heb. *tillîm* = Arab. *tell*).

The city was the centre of authority and defence for the surrounding countryside with its mainly open villages (Heb. 'daughters,' Jos 15^{32} etc.). A city might be autonomous and ruled by a 'king' (Jos 2^{2f} etc.), or by a senate (Jos $9^{3, 11}$). Several cities might form a confederacy (Jos 9^{17}), or a miniature empire (Jos 11^{1-5}, Jg 1^{7}). Seven years after David's accession authority was centred in Jerusalem (2 S 5^{6}), but was later shared with Samaria as the ultimate capital of the northern portion (1 K 16^{24}), so that all other cities were demoted to provincial status (1 K 4^{7-19}).

For the structure of walls and gates see FORTIFICATION. Owing to its natural or artificial elevation **access** to the city was usually up an inclined ramp directly to the city gate, though there might be a space immediately outside, but more commonly inside, the gate, sufficiently spacious to merit—in contrast to the almost incredible congestion of houses and narrow alleyways usual 'down-town'—the title **square** (RV 'broad place,' Jer 5^{1}, Neh 8^{1}). Space was at such a premium, especially for the houses of the poor, that they might be built even up against the city wall (Jos 2^{15}); the dwellings of the rich, and *a fortiori* the king, naturally took up more space, the latter often inhabiting an additionally fortified **acropolis** [*'îr*, the common word for 'city,' originally had this connotation, 2 S 5^{7}], or **strong tower** (Jg 9^{51}), where a last stand could be made in case of need. But domestic architecture, at least of the early Israelite period (see HOUSE) was not, on the whole, impressive, nor cities sanitary, though sewers, or at least drains, were not uncommon on a small scale. Garbage was thrown into the street (2 S 22^{43}, Jer 14^{16}), or at best, dumped over the city wall or outside the gate (Job 2^{8}), and all water had to be fetched from the well (Gn 24^{11}), or drawn from the private or public cisterns constructed to hold rainwater (2 K 18^{31}, cf Mesha [q.v.] inscr. ll. 20–25).

The main meeting place for the inhabitants was the **gate** (Ru 4^{1}), *i.e.* either the restricted but shady passage through the city wall, or the open space within, see above. Here news and gossip were retailed (Ps 69^{12}), legal, civic, and private business transacted (Dt 22^{24}).

No city, finally, was without its **sanctuary** or **high place,** either within its own precincts, as in most cities of note (see HIGH PLACE), or on an adjoining height (1 S 9^{12ff}). With due religious rites, too, the city had been founded in far-off Canaanite, or even, as we now know, pre-Canaanite days, when the **foundation sacrifice** claimed its human victim (see HOUSE, **3**). A survival of this wide-spread custom has been recognized in connexion with the rebuilding of Jericho, the foundation of which was laid by Hiel the Bethelite, 'at the cost of Abiram his first-born,' and whose gates were set up, 'at the cost of his youngest son Segub' (1 K 16[34]).

2. In the NT period there was a sharp rise in the number of cities (*poleis*) in Palestine, owing to the eastward growth of Hellenism following the footsteps of Alexander the Great. Almost entirely in Trans-Jordan we have the confederacy of cities known as **Decapolis** (q.v.) (Mk 5[20]), some admittedly on ancient sites, but all now centres of Hellenic culture, and as such, shunned by the conservative among the Jews. New cities founded by the Herods were Caesarea Maritima and Tiberias; others were built in the coastal areas of ancient Philistia. Although under Roman suzerainty, these cities, like others of the Roman empire, had a certain degree of self-government, and their citizens often possessed a considerable civic pride (Ac 21[39]).

With the partial exception of Jerusalem, Jesus seems to have avoided the larger cities—perhaps because of their Hellenism—but this policy seems to have been reversed by the apostles as soon as it became evident that the conservative Jews had broken with Christianity (Ac 8[5]). Paul practically limited his mission to the chief cities of the north-eastern Mediterranean.

A. R. S. K.—**D. R. Ap-T.**

CLASPS.—See Taches.

CLAUDA.—See Cauda.

CLAUDIA.—A Roman Christian, perhaps wife of **Pudens** and mother of Linus (2 Ti 4[21]); but Lightfoot (*Clement*, i. 76) shows that this is improbable. The two former names are found in a sepulchral inscription near Rome, and a Claudia was wife of Aulus Pudens, friend of Martial. If these are identified, Claudia was a British lady of high birth; but this is very unlikely.

A. J. M.—**E. R. H.**

CLAUDIUS.—Claudius, the fourth Roman emperor, who bore the names Tiberius Claudius Caesar Augustus Germanicus, reigned from January (24) 25, A.D. 41 till his murder on October 13, A.D. 54. He was a son of Nero Claudius Drusus (the brother of the emperor Tiberius) and Antonia minor (a daughter of the triumvir Mark Antony and Octavia, sister of the emperor Augustus), and was born on August 1, 10 B.C. at Lyons. From childhood he was weakly, and a prey to disease, which affected his mind as well as his body. This caused him to be neglected and despised. He was, however, a man of considerable ability, both literary and administrative, as he showed when he was called to succeed his own nephew Gaius (Caligula) as emperor. He has been compared with James I. (VI. of Scotland) in both his weak and his strong points. It was in his reign that the first real occupation of Britain by the Romans took place. He is twice mentioned in Acts (11[28] and 18[2]). The great famine over the whole of the Roman world which Agabus foretold took place in his reign. The expulsion of Jews from Rome, due to dissensions amongst them, occurred in the year A.D. 50. This latter date is one of the few fixed points of chronology in the Book of Acts. The reign of Claudius was satisfactory to the Empire beyond the average. The government of the provinces was excellent, and a marked feature was the large number of public works executed under the emperor's supervision.

A. So.—**E. R. H.**

CLAUDIUS LYSIAS.—See Lysias.

CLAW.—In Dn 4[33] 'claw' means a bird's claw; but in AV in Dt 14[6] and Zec 11[16] it has the obsolete meaning of an animal's hoof (so RV, RSV).

CLAY.—See Pottery.

CLEAN AND UNCLEAN. — Introductory. — The words 'clean,' 'unclean,' 'purity,' 'purification,' have acquired in the process of religious development a spiritual connotation which obscures their original meaning. Their primitive significance is wholly ceremonial; the conceptions they represent date back to a very early stage of religious practice, so early indeed that it may be called pre-religious, in so far as any useful delimitation can be established between the epoch in which spell and magic predominated, and that at which germs of a rudimentary religious consciousness can be detected. In a conspectus of primitive custom, one of the most wide-spread phenomena is the existence of 'taboo.' Anthropology has yet to say the last word about it, and its general characteristics can be differently summarized. But, broadly speaking, taboo springs from the religion of fear. The savage met with much which he could not understand, which was supra-normal to his experience. Such phenomena appeared to him charged with a potency which was secret and uncanny, and highly energetic. They were therefore to be avoided with great care; they were 'taboo' to him. It would be rash to dogmatize about the origin of this notion; it most probably dates back to days prior to any conscious animistic beliefs, and may even be traceable ultimately to instincts which mankind shares with the higher animals. No doubt in later times the idea was artificially exploited in deference to the exigencies of ambition and avarice on the part of chiefs and priests, to the distrust of innovations (cf Ex 20[25], Dt 27[5f], Jos 8[31]), to the recommendations of elementary sanitation, etc. But originally the savage regarded as taboo certain persons, material substances, and bodily acts or states which he considered to possess a kind of transmissible electric energy with which it was very dangerous to meddle; and these taboos were jealously guarded by the sanctions of civil authority, and later of religious belief.

It seems probable that even at such an early epoch taboos could be viewed from two distinct points of view. A taboo might be either a blessing or a curse, according as it was handled by an expert or a layman. Thus blood produced defilement, but, properly treated, it might remove impurity. A chief or king was taboo, and to touch him produced the primitive equivalent of 'king's evil'; and yet his touch could remove the disease it created. The reasons for this twofold point of view are very obscure, and do not come within the scope of this article. But the differentiation seems to have existed in a confused way at the earliest era. Afterwards this notion crystallized into a very vital distinction. On the one hand we find the conception of holiness as expressing an official consecration and dedication to the Divine beings. A sanctuary, a season, a priest or chief, were set apart from common life and placed in a peculiar relation of intimacy to God or the gods; they were tabooed as holy. On the other hand, certain taboos were held to arise from the intrinsic repulsiveness of the object or condition, a repulsiveness which affected both God and man with dislike. Such taboos were due to the essential uncleanness of their object.

With the rise of animistic beliefs and practices this differentiation was reinforced by the dualism of benevolent and malignant spirits. Uncanny energy varied according as it arose from the one or the other class, and much care must be taken to propitiate the one and avert the power of the other. Thus on the one side we find sacrificial ritual, which has as its object to please the good demons, and on the other side we have a cathartic ritual, which aims at expelling evil demons from the vicinity (cf Lv 16, where the two notions are united in one ceremony). But even after the growth of such refinements, ideas and rules survived which can be explained only as relics of primitive and even primeval taboo customs. A still later stage is seen when rules of purity are attributed to the conscious command of God, and their motive is found in His own personal character (Lv 11[44]). The Jewish sacred books teem with references which demonstrate the survival of primitive taboos. Thus Frazer draws especial attention to the Nazirite vows (Nu 6[1-21]), to the Sabbath regulations (Ex 35[2f]), to the views as to death (Nu 19[11ff]), and childbirth (Lv 12). Similarly the origin of the conception of holiness may be seen in the idea that it is transmissible by contact (Ex 29[37] 30[29], Lv 6[27], Ezk 44[19]), or in the penalty for meddling with a holy object (1 S 6[19], 2 S 6[7]); whilst allusions to ritual uncleanness occur frequently in Ezekiel, and the legislation on the subject forms a large part of Leviticus and Deuteronomy. In some cases these ideas may have arisen in protest against historical developments of Hebrew custom. Thus it has been supposed that the Nazirite vows originated in the desire for a return to primitive simplicity by way of contrast to the habits of Palestinian Canaanites. But many of the regulations about uncleanness can be explained only by a reference to primitive ritualism, with its conceptions of objects charged with a secret energy which the ordinary man does well to shun.

The word ' clean,' it may be remarked, conveyed originally no positive idea. A clean object was one which was not under a taboo, which had contracted no ceremonial taint. And so again ' purification ' meant the removal of a ceremonial taint by ceremonial means, the unclean object being thus restored to a normal condition. Fire and liquids were the best media of purification. Similarly **' common,'** the opposite of ' holy,' merely meant ' undedicated to God,' and expressed no ethical or spiritual notion. In fact, when the conceptions of holiness and uncleanness had been definitely differentiated, the rule would be that, though the holy must be clean, the clean need in no way be holy. Later thought, however, confused the two ideas (cf Ac 10[14]).

I. Uncleanness in the OT.—The consequences of uncleanness and the methods of purification naturally differed in different races. But in the Jewish religion uncleanness was always held to disqualify a man for Divine worship and sacrifice. In practice a certain amount of laxity seems to have been tolerated (Ezk 22[26] 44[7]), though this did not pass without protest (Ezk 44[9], Is 52[1]). But, strictly, an unclean man was debarred from religious offices (Lv 7[19, 20]); and nobody could perform them in an unclean place, *e.g.* in any land but Palestine (2 K 5[17], Hos 9[3]).

The Jewish rules about uncleanness can be roughly classified under five main heads: sexual impurity, uncleanness due to blood, uncleanness connected with food, with death, and with leprosy. This division is not scientific; some rules are equally in place in more than one class; but at present none but a rough classification is possible.

1. Sexual impurity.—All primitive religions display great terror of any functions connected, however remotely, with the organs of reproduction. Sexual intercourse produced uncleanness; and later animism taught that demons watched over such periods and must be averted with scrupulous care. The time when marriage is consummated was especially dangerous, and this idea is clearly seen in To 8[1-3], though this instance is unique in Jewish sacred literature. But, apart from this, the Jews considered all intercourse to defile till evening, and to necessitate a purificatory bath (Lv 15[18]). Under certain circumstances, when cleanness was especially important, complete abstinence from women was required (Ex 19[15]). Thus, too, from 1 S 21[5] it appears as if soldiers on a campaign came under this regulation; perhaps because war was a sacred function, duly opened with religious rites (cf 2 S 11[11]), and this may also be the cause for a bridegroom's exemption from military service for a year after marriage (Dt 24[5]).

Uncircumcision was regarded as unclean. The reason for this is not obvious; rites of circumcision were performed by many primitive nations at the time of puberty (whether for decorative purposes, or in order to prepare a young man or woman for marriage, or for some other reason), and it is possible that among the Jews this custom had been thrown back to an earlier period of life. Or it may be that they regarded circumcision as imposing a distinct tribe-mark on the infant. The condition of uncircumcision might be held as unclean because it implied foreign nationality. Taboos on strangers are very common in savage nations.

Seminal emission made a man unclean till the evening, and necessitated bathing and washing of clothes (Lv 15[16f]).

Childbirth was universally regarded as a special centre of impurity, though among the Jews we find no evidence that the newborn child was subject to it as well as the mother. The mother was completely unclean for seven days; after that she was in a condition of modified impurity for thirty-three days, disqualified from entering the sanctuary or touching any hallowed thing. (These periods were doubled when the baby was a girl.) After this, in order to complete her purification, she must offer a lamb of the first year and a pigeon or turtle dove, though poorer people might substitute another pigeon or dove for the lamb (Lv 12, cf Lk 2[24]).

Analogous notions may perhaps be traced in the prohibition of any sexual impersonation (Dt 22[5]), any mingling of different species (Dt 22[9-11], Lv 19[19]), and in the disqualifications on eunuchs, bastards, and the Ammonites and Moabites, the offspring of an incestuous union (Dt 23[1-6]); though some of these rules look like the product of later refinement.

Human excreta were sources of uncleanness (Dt 23[12-14]); but the directions on this subject very possibly date from the epoch of magical spells, and arose from the fear lest a man's excrement might fall into an enemy's hands and be used to work magic against him.

The prohibition to priests of woollen garments which caused sweat, is possibly an extension of a similar notion (Ezk 44[17f]). Finally, the abstinence from eating the sinew of the thigh, which in Gn 32[32] is explained by a reference to the story of Jacob, may have originated in the idea that the thigh was the centre of the reproductive functions.

2. Uncleanness due to blood.—The fear of blood dates back in all probability to the most primeval times, and may be in part instinctive. Among the Jews it was a most stringent taboo, and their aversion from it was reinforced by the theory that it was the seat of life (Dt 12[23]). A clear instance of the all-embracing nature of its polluting power is seen in Dt 22[8]. The same idea would probably cause the abstinence from eating beasts of prey, carrion birds, and animals which had died without being bled (Ezk 4[14], Ex 22[31], Lv 17[15] 22[8]). To break this rule caused defilement (1 S 14[33], Ezk 33[25]). Such a taboo is so universal and ancient that it cannot reasonably be accounted for by the Jewish hatred for heathen offerings of blood.

The taboos on menstrual blood and abnormal issues must come under this category or that of sexual impurity. Menstruation was terribly feared. It was exceedingly dangerous for a man even to see the blood. The woman in such a condition was unclean for seven days, and her impurity was highly contagious (Lv 15[19-24]). Similarly, abnormal issues produced contagious uncleanness for seven days after they had stopped. The purification required was the offering of two turtle doves and two young pigeons. A man had also to bathe and wash his clothes, but we are not told that a woman was under the same necessity, though it is hardly credible that she was exempt (Lv 15[2-15, 25-30]).

3. Uncleanness connected with food.—Anthropology no longer explains all food taboos as survivals of totemism, though no doubt this explanation may account for some. It appears rather that ' theriolatry ' was the more general phenomenon. For reasons which cannot even be conjectured in many cases, certain animals were treated as sacred, and tabooed accordingly; it might be that the animal was very useful or very dangerous or very strange; the savage had no consistent theory of taboo. Some animals may be cases of sympathetic taboo; they were not eaten from the fear lest their qualities should be imparted to the consumer. In later times some animals might be tabooed from more elaborate motives. But food taboos cover so wide a range, and appear in many cases so inexplicable, that no single derivation of them can be adequate.

The Jews themselves dated the distinction between clean and unclean animals from an early antiquity (cf Gn 7[2] and 8[20]); Gn 9[3], however, appears to embody a theory of antediluvian vegetarianism.

The lists of clean and unclean beasts are given in Lv 11 and Dt 14[4ff]. It is impossible to give any certain explanation of the separate items. Clean animals are there classified as those which part the hoof, are cloven-footed, and chew the cud. But this looks like an attempt of later speculation to generalize regulations already existent. The criterion would exclude the ass, horse, dog, and beasts of prey, which are nowhere mentioned as unclean. The last class, as we have seen, would probably be so on different grounds. The horse and dog seem to have been connected with idolatrous rites (2 K 23[11], Is 66[3]), and so perhaps were forbidden. But Jg 6[4] appears to treat the ass as an ordinary article of diet. (The circumstances in 2 K 6[25] are exceptional.) The rule that a kid must not be seethed in its mother's milk (Ex 23[19] 34[26], Dt 14[21]) is difficult to account for. A magical conception appears to underlie the prohibition, and it has been suggested that some nations used to sprinkle the broth on the ground for some such purposes. In that case the taboo would be of great antiquity. But the matter is not at present satisfactorily explained. The taboo on the tree in Eden (Gn 3[3]) hardly calls for discussion. So far as we know, it had no subsequent history; and the general colouring of the story makes it improbable that the prohibition had any origin in Jewish custom.

4. Uncleanness connected with death.—Death, as well as birth, was a source of great terror to the savage. The animistic horror of ghosts and theories of a continued existence after death, gave a rationale for such terror; but it probably existed in pre-animistic days, and the precautions exercised with regard to dead bodies were derived partly from the intrinsic mysteriousness of death, partly from the value of a corpse for magical purposes. Among the Jews a corpse was regarded as exceptionally defiling (Hag 2[13]). Even a bone or a grave caused infectious uncleanness, and graves were whitened in order to be easily recognizable. He who touched a corpse was unclean for seven days (Nu 19[11ff]). Purification was necessary on the third and seventh days; and on the latter the unclean person also washed his clothes and bathed. A corpse defiled a tent and all open vessels in it. For similar reasons warriors needed purification after a battle (Nu 31[19-24]); a murderer defiled the land and had to flee to a city of refuge, where he must remain till the death of the high priest (Nu 35). It has been suggested that this provision was due to the notion that the high priest, the temporary representative of Yahweh, was regarded as suffering from the defilement of murder as God suffered, and as the land suffered (Dt 21[1]). It is singular that apparently a person who was unclean from touching a corpse might yet eat the Passover (Nu 9[6-12]).

The kinsmen of a dead man were usually also unclean; Hos 9[4] points to a similar idea among the Jews. Indeed, mourning customs were in origin probably warnings of such impurity. Some of the most common are prohibited in Dt 14[1] and Lv 19[28], perhaps because of their heathenish associations.

The ritual of purification from corpse-defilement, described in Nu 19, must be of high antiquity. The purifying medium was water, the blood and ashes of a red heifer, with cedar, hyssop, and scarlet. This was sprinkled over the unclean person on the third and seventh days, and the priest and attendants who performed the ceremony were themselves defiled by it till evening, and needed purification (cf Dt 21). The ritual thus unites the three great cathartic media, fire, water, and aromatic woods and plants. The last, perhaps, were originally considered to be efficacious in expelling the death-demons by their scent.

5. Uncleanness connected with leprosy.—Orientals considered leprosy the one specially unclean disease, which required not healing but cleansing (cf Nu 12[12]). The term covered a wide range of skin diseases, and Lv 13 gives directions for its diagnosis. If pronounced unclean, the leper was excluded from the community (cf 2 K 7[3]). He could not attend a synagogue service in a walled town, though in open towns a special part of the synagogue was often reserved for lepers. If he was cured, he must undergo an elaborate process of purificatory ritual (Lv 14), including (*a*) the sacrifice of one bird and the release of another, perhaps regarded as carrying away the demon; fragrant plants, water, and the blood of the dead bird were used at this stage; (*b*) the washing of clothes, shaving of the hair and bathing of the body; then (*c*) after seven days' interval this second process was repeated; and finally (*d*) on the eighth day sacrifices were offered, and the man ceremonially cleansed with the blood and oil of the sacrifice.

II. Uncleanness in the NT.—Legal casuistry carried the cathartic ritual to a high pitch of complexity, and Jesus came into frequent conflict with the Jewish lawyers over the point (cf Mk 7[1-5]). He denounced it energetically (Lk 11[38], Mt 15[10]), and, by insisting on the supreme importance of moral purity, threw ceremonial ideas into a subordinate position. The full force of this teaching was not at once realized (cf Ac 10[14]). The decree in Ac 15[29] still recommends certain taboos. But St. Paul had no illusions on the subject (cf Ro 14[14], 1 Co 6[13], Col 2[16, 20-22], Tit 1[15]). In practice he made concessions to the scruples of others (Ac 21[26], Ro 14[20]) as Jesus had done (Mk 1[44]); and it was recognized that a man who had scruples must not be encouraged to violate them. But it was inevitable that with the process of time and reflection, ceremonial prohibitions and ritualistic notions of cleanness should disappear before the Christian insistence on the internal elements in religion. There are certain survivals of such notions even now, and ceremonialism is not extirpated. But its scope is very narrow, and it is the custom to explain such ritual regulations as survive, on grounds that accord better with the spirit of Christianity and the ideas of civilized society. A. W. F. B.

CLEMENT.—The name of a fellow-worker with St. Paul (Ph 4[3]). There are no sufficient grounds for identifying him with Clement, bishop of Rome, the writer of the *Epistle to the Church of Corinth.*

CLEMENT.—A leader, traditionally third (or fourth) bishop, of the Roman Church, author of its *Letter to the Church of Corinth* (I Clement, about A.D. 96), a document of importance for the theology and church order of the post-apostolic age. Later other works were (fictionally) connected with him, as a typical figure of the period, a sermon (II Clement), several works in the field of church order, and the pious novels known as the Clementine *Recognitions* and *Homilies*. There seems little reason for identifying him with the Clement of Ph 4[3], a fellow-worker of St. Paul's, at Philippi apparently. The Christians named Clement may have been freedmen or dependents of the aristocratic Roman family of the same name. E. R. H.

CLEOPAS.—One of the disciples at Emmaus, Lk 24[18]; the name is probably the same as Clopas (Jn 19[25]), and Alphaeus (Mk 3[18] and parallels) may be used as a Greek equivalent; but any identification of the characters is merely conjectural. E. R. H.

CLEOPHAS, Jn 19[25] (AV).—See Clopas.

CLEOPATRA.—A daughter of Ptolemy Epiphanes. She married in 173 B.C. her own brother Ptolemy Philometor, and afterwards her second brother Ptolemy Physcon (Liv. xlv. 13, *Epit.* 59; Justin, xxxviii. 8). She greatly favoured the Jews in Egypt (Jos. *c. Apion.* ii. 5 [49]), and encouraged Onias IV. in the erection of the temple at Leontopolis (Jos. *Ant.* XIII. iii. 2 [69–71]). **2.** A daughter of Ptolemy Philometor. In 150 B.C. she was given in marriage by her father to Alexander Balas (1 Mac 10[57f]; Jos. *Ant.* XIII. iv. 1 [80–82]). When Balas was driven into Arabia she became (146 B.C.), at her father's bidding, the wife of his rival, Demetrius Nicator (1 Mac 11[12]; Jos. *Ant.* XIII. iv. 7 [110]; Liv. *Epit.* 52). **3.** Daughter of Antiochus III.—the first of the Cleopatras—married Ptolemy V. She is referred to in Dn 11[17].

CLIFF.—Found only in AV in 2 Ch 20[16] (AV, RV 'ascent'), Job 30[6] (RV 'cliffs'; RSV 'gullies'), in ARV twice in Job 39[28] (AV, RV 'rock' and 'crag of the rock'; RSV 'rock' and 'rocky crag'), and in RSV in Ca 2[14] (AV, RV 'rock'), Is 2[21] (AV, RV 'ragged rocks'), Ezk 38[20] (AV, RV 'steep places').

CLOAK (AV, RV 'cloke').—See DRESS, **4.**

CLOPAS (AV **Cleophas**) is named only in Jn 19[25]. See ALPHAEUS and BRETHREN OF THE LORD.

CLOSET.—The Greek word so rendered in NT properly denotes 'a storehouse' as Lk 12[24] RSV, then any inner or more private room as opposed to the living-room; so Lk 12[3] RSV 'private room.' Cf 1 K 20[30] 22[25], literally 'a chamber within a chamber,' and HOUSE, **2.** For Jl 2[16] see Driver, *Joel and Amos, in loc.*

A. R. S. K.—**F. W. G.**

CLOTHES, CLOTHING.—See DRESS.

CLOUD.—In Scripture, as with us, the clouds are the visible masses of aqueous vapour, darkening the heavens, sources of rain and fertility, telling the present state of the weather or indicating a coming change. They serve also for figures of instability and transitoriness (Hos 6[4]), calamity (La 2[1]), the gloom of old age (Ec 12[2]), great height (Job 20[6]), immensity (He 12[1]). The following points should be noted. **1.** The poetic treatment in Job. The waters are bound up securely in the clouds, so that the rain does not break through (26[8]); when the ocean issues from chaos like a new-born child, God wraps it in the swaddling-bands of clouds (38[9]); the laws of their movements are impenetrable mysteries (36[29] 37[16] 38[37]). **2.** The cloud indicates the presence of God, and at the same time veils the insufferable brightness of His glory (Ex 16[10] 19[9] etc.). Similarly the bright cloud betokens the Father's presence, and His voice is heard speaking from it (Mt 17[5]). But a dark cloud would effectually hide Him, and thus furnishes a figure for displeasure (La 3[44]). At Rev 10[1] the cloud is an angel's glorious robe. **3.** The **pillar of cloud and fire** directs and protects the journeyings of the Exodus (Ex 13[21], Ps 105[39]). This corresponds with the fact that armies and caravans have frequently been directed by signals of fire and smoke. **4.** The cloud alternates with the cherub as Yahweh's chariot (Ps 18[10], Is 19[1]). Indeed, the cherub is a personification of the thunder-cloud. The Messianic people and the Messiah Himself sweep through the heaven with clouds (Dn 7[13], Mk 14[62], Rev 1[7]), or on the clouds (Mt 26[64]): hence the later Jews identified Anani (='He of the clouds,' 1 Ch 3[24]) with the Messiah. The saints are to be caught up in the clouds (1 Th 4[17]). The Messiah's throne is a white cloud (Rev 14[14]). **5.** In the 'Cloud Vision' of Apoc. Bar 53–73, the cloud from which the twelve streams of water pour is 'the wide world which the Almighty created'—a very peculiar piece of imagery.

J. T.—**D. R. Ap.-T.**

CLOUT.—Jer 38[11f] 'old cast clouts' (AV, RV; RSV 'old rags'). The word is still used in Scotland for cloths (as in 'dish-clout'), but for clothes only contemptuously. Formerly there was no contempt in the word. Sir John Mandeville (*Travels*, Macmillan's edition p. 75) says, 'And in that well she washed ofttentime the clouts of her son Jesu Christ.' The verb 'to clout' occurs in Jos 9[5] (AV, RV; RSV 'patched') of shoes.

CLUB.—**1.** *tôthāḥ*, Job 41[29] (RV, RSV; AV '**dart**'). **2.** *mēphîṣ*, Pr 25[18] (RSV; AV, RV '**maul**'). **3.** The stout shepherd's club (*shēbheṭ*), with its thick end probably studded with nails, with which he defended his flock against wild beasts, is rendered by '**rod**' in Ps 23[4] and elsewhere. **4.** *Xylon*, Mt 26[47, 55], Mk 14[43, 48], Lk 22[52] (RSV; AV, RV 'staves').

CNIDUS.—A city of Caria, on Cape Crio (=Roman Triopium), in SW. of Asia Minor. It was the dividing point between the S. and W. coasts of Asia Minor, and at this point St. Paul's ship changed its course in the voyage to Rome (Ac 27[7]). It contained Jewish inhabitants as early as the 2nd cent. B.C. (1 Mac 15[23]), and had the rank of a free city.

A. So.

COAL.—Mineral coal was unknown in Bible times. Wherever 'coal' (or 'coals') is mentioned, therefore, we must in the great majority of cases understand wood or charcoal. Several species of wood used for heating purposes are named in Is 44[14–16], to which Ps 120[4] adds 'coals of the broom tree' (RSV, cf RVm; AV, RV 'coals of juniper'). In two cases, however, the 'live coal' (RSV 'burning coal') of Isaiah's vision (Is 6[6]) and the 'coals' (RSV 'hot stones') on which was 'a cake baken' for Elijah (1 K 19[6]), the Hebrew word denotes a hot stone (so, in both cases, RVm—see BREAD). The charcoal was generally burned in a **brazier** (Jer 36[22ff] RSV; RV 'brasier'; AV 'hearth') or chafing-dish, the 'pan of fire' of Zec 12[6] (RV; RSV 'blazing pot'; AV 'hearth of fire'). See, further, HOUSE, **7.**

Coal, or rather charcoal, supplies several Scripture metaphors, the most interesting of which is illustrated by the expression of the wise woman of Tekoa, 'thus shall they quench my coal that is left' (2 S 14[7]). By this she means, as shown by the following words, the death of her son and the extinction of her family, an idea elsewhere expressed as a putting out of one's lamp (Pr 13[9]).

A. R. S. K.—**H. H. R.**

COAST.—Coast, now confined to the shore of the sea, was formerly used of the border between two countries, or the neighbourhood of any place. When St. Paul 'passed through the upper coasts' (Ac 19[2] AV), he was in the interior of Asia Minor. Herod 'slew all the children that were in Bethlehem, and in all the coasts thereof' (Mt 2[16] AV).

COAT.—See DRESS, **2** (*d*), **4.**

COAT OF MAIL.—See ARMOUR, ARMS, **2** (*c*).

COCK.—Mt 26[34, 74], Mk 13[35] 14[30, 72], Lk 22[34, 60, 61], Jn 13[30] 18[27]. Cocks and hens were probably unknown in Palestine until from two to three centuries before Christ's time. In the famous painted tomb at Marissa (see MARESHAH), a work of about 200 B.C., we have the cock depicted. Cocks and hens were introduced from Persia. The absence of express mention of them from the Law, and the fact that it is a 'clean' bird, have made it possible for the Jews for many centuries to sacrifice these birds on the eve of the Day of Atonement—a cock for each male and a hen for each female in the household. Talmudic tradition finds references to the cock in Is 22[17], Job 38[36], and Pr 30[31], but all these are very doubtful. The '**cock-crowing**' was the name of the third watch of the night, just before the dawn, in the time of our Lord, the four night watches being, Late, Midnight, Cock-crowing, and Early. 'Before cock-crowing' may have had reference to the trumpet call which marked the end of the third watch.

E. W. G. M.—**S. T.**

COCKATRICE.—This word is used in AV only to render: **1.** Hebrew *ṣephaʿ*, Is 14[29] (RV 'basilisk': RSV 'adder'); **2.** *ṣiphʿōnî*, Pr 23[32] (AVm; AV, RV, RSV 'adder'), Is 11[8] 59[5], Jer 8[17] (all RV 'basilisk' and RSV 'adder'). See SERPENT.

COCKER.—Sir 30[9] (AV, RV) 'Cocker thy child, and he shall make thee afraid,' that is 'pamper' (RSV). Cf Shakespeare, *King John*, v. i. 70—

'Shall a beardless boy,
A cocker'd silken wanton, brave our fields?'

and Hull (1611), 'No creatures more cocker their young than the Asse and the Ape.' The word is not found earlier than the 15th cent. Its origin is obscure.

COCKLE.—Found only in Job 31[40] (AV, RV; AVm 'stinking weeds'; RVm 'noisome weeds'; RSV 'foul weeds'). The Hebrew is *bo'shāh*, from the root *b'sh*, 'stink.' G. Dalman identifies with **darnel**, *Lolium temulentum* (*Arbeit und Sitte* II, 248 f).

COELE-SYRIA.—The meaning and origin of the first part of the name are obscure. The traditional interpretation is that it means 'Hollow Syria' and applies properly to the great hollow running N. and S.

between the Lebanon and Anti-Lebanon ranges (1 Es 4^{48}; Strabo, xvi. 2). It then would correspond to the *Biqʿath hal-Lᵉbhānôn* of Jos 11^{17} etc. The first element of the latter name persists in the modern name of the valley S. of Baalbek, *el-Beqāʿ*. The Orontes drains the valley northward, and the *Līṭânī* southward, both rivers rising near Baalbek. The soil is rich, producing large crops of wheat, etc., while some of the finest vineyards in Syria clothe the adjoining slopes. But ' Coele-Syria ' came to have a wider significance, covering indeed, with Phoenicia, all the Seleucid territory S. of the River Eleutherus (2 Mac 3^{5}, etc.; Strabo, xvi. 753). In 1 Es 2^{17} etc., Coele-Syria and Phoenicia denote the whole Persian province, stretching from the Euphrates to the borders of Egypt. Josephus reckons the country E. of Jordan to Coele-Syria (*Ant.* I. xi. 5 [206], XIII. xiii. 2 f [355 ff], etc.), including in it Scythopolis, the only member of the Decapolis W. of the river. W. E.—**E. G. K.**

COFFER occurs only in 1 S $6^{8, 11, 15}$ (AV, RV; RSV ' box '), and the Hebrew term *'argaz*, of which it is the translation, is also found nowhere else. It appears to have been a small chest (*KB* suggests ' saddle-bag ') which contained the golden figures sent by the Philistines as a guilt-offering.

COFFIN.—Gn 50^{26} only ' of the disposal of Joseph's body in Egypt). Israelitish burial rites (see MOURNING CUSTOMS, TOMB) did not include the use of coffins.

COHORT.—See BAND, LEGION.

COINS.—See MONEY.

COLA, Jth 15^{4} (AV).—See KOLA.

COLEWORT.—See HERB, **4.**

COL-HOZEH (' seeing all ').—A Judahite, Neh 3^{15} 11^{5}.

COLIUS, 1 Es 9^{23} (AV, RV).—See KELAIAH.

COLLAR.—See ORNAMENTS, **2.**

COLLEGE.—This stands in AV (2 K 22^{14}, 2 Ch 34^{22}) for the Hebrew *mishneh*, which RV and RSV correctly render ' second quarter '—a quarter of the city lying to the north (Zeph 1^{10}), and possibly referred to in Neh 11^{9}, where EV have ' second over the city.' The idea of a ' college ' came from the Targum on 2 K 22^{14}, ' house of instruction.' J. T.

COLONY.—The word *colonia* is a pure Latin word, which is written in Greek letters in the only place where it occurs in the Bible (Ac 16^{12}), and expresses a purely Roman institution. It is a piece of Rome transported bodily out of Rome itself and planted somewhere in the Roman Empire. In other words, it is a body of Roman citizen-soldiers settled on a military road to keep the enemies of the Empire in check. These retained their citizenship of Rome and constituted the aristocracy of every town in which they were situated. Their constitution was on the model of Rome and the Italian States. Philippi became a *colonia* when Augustus settled there the former Italian supporters of Mark Antony. A number of places are mentioned in the NT which were really *coloniae*, but only one, Philippi, is so *named*, and the reason for this naming is perhaps that the author of Acts was proud of this city, with which he had some connexion. Pisidian Antioch, Lystra, Corinth, and Ptolemais, not to mention others, were *coloniae*. Sometimes these *coloniae* were merely settlements of veterans for whom their generals had to find a home. A. So.—**J. C. B.**

COLOSSAE was an ancient city of Phrygia (in the Roman province of Asia), at one time of great importance, but dwindling later as its neighbour Laodicea prospered. Xenophon's Ten Thousand had stopped here on their way to Babylon. In the days of its prosperity it shared in the wool industry; Strabo mentions the fine black wool of its sheep. It was situated in the upper part of the valley of the Lycus, a tributary of the Maeander, about 10 miles E. of Laodicea, and 13 SE. of Hierapolis. The three cities naturally formed a sphere of missionary labour for Epaphras (Epaphroditus), who lived at Colossae (Col 4^{12f}), Timothy (Col 1^{1}) and others. St. Paul himself never visited any of them (Col 2^{1}). It has been suggested with great probability that in Rev 1^{11} 3^{14} the single church of Laodicea must represent the other churches of the Lycus valley also. The church in Colossae had developed tendencies which St. Paul found it necessary to combat in the Epistle which has come down to us. If, as some scholars believe, ' the epistle from Laodicea ' (Col 4^{16}) is our ' Epistle to the Ephesians,' or, as others hold, the epistle to Philemon, it also was read in the church at Colossae. Probably both letters were carried from Rome by Tychicus, who was accompanied by Onesimus, whose master Philemon was an inhabitant of Colossae. See also following article. A. So.—**F. C. G.**

COLOSSIANS, EPISTLE TO THE.—1. Authenticity.—This Epistle is one of the ten Epistles of St. Paul included in Marcion's collection (A.D. 140). It appears to have been accepted without question as genuine both by Churchmen and by heretics, and is referred to by the Muratorian Fragment, by Irenaeus, and by Clement of Alexandria. Its authenticity remained undisputed till the early part of last century, and was then contested only on internal grounds of style and subject-matter.

As to the first objection, the Epistle is marked, to a greater degree than St. Paul's earlier writings, by ' a certain ruggedness of expression, a want of finish that borders on obscurity.' The vocabulary also differs in some respects from that of the earlier writings, but this is amply accounted for by the difference of subject. As a matter of fact, the resemblances in style to St. Paul's other writings are as marked as the differences; and in any case arguments from style in disproof of authenticity are very unreliable. The later plays of Shakespeare, as compared with those of his middle period, show just the same condensation of thought and want of fluency and finish.

The argument from subject-matter is more important. The Epistle was regarded by earlier German critics as presupposing a fully developed system of Gnostic teaching, such as belongs to the middle of the 2nd cent., and a correspondingly developed Christology. But a more careful study of the Epistle has shown that what St. Paul has in view is not a system of teaching, but rather a tendency. Words like *plērōma*, to which later Gnosticism gave a technical sense, are used in this Epistle with their usual non-technical signification. And our study of early Christian and Jewish thought has shown that Gnostic tendencies date from a much earlier time than the great Gnostic teachers of the 2nd cent., and are, indeed, older than Christianity. The Christology of the Epistle certainly shows an advance on that of St. Paul's earlier Epistles, especially in the emphasis laid on the cosmical activity of the pre-incarnate Christ. This may be accounted for in part by the special purpose of the Epistle (see below), and in part by a development in St. Paul's own Christological ideas. It is irrational to deny the authenticity of an Epistle claiming to be St. Paul's, merely because it shows that the mind of the Apostle had not remained stagnant during a period of imprisonment that must have given him special opportunities for thought. (See EPHESIANS.)

The great majority of scholars agree in accepting the Epistle as St. Paul's, although many, beginning with H. J. Holtzmann, would argue that the text of the original letter has been amended in various ways by later editors and scribes. The authenticity of the Epistle is sustained by its close relation to the Epistle to Philemon, the Pauline authorship of which is hardly seriously disputed. (On the relation of our Epistle to the Epistle to the Ephesians, see EPHESIANS.)

2. Occasion and Purpose.—Most of Paul's Epistles were written under some definite external stimulus. In the case of this Epistle two events seem to have led to its composition. (1) Epaphras, who had been the first evangelist of the Colossians, and who seems to have held at Colossae a position somewhat similar to that which Timothy is represented in the Pastoral Epistles as holding in Ephesus, had come to Paul bringing information as to the special needs and dangers of the Colossian Church. Paul was in prison at the time—whether at Rome, Caesarea, Ephesus, or elsewhere, we do not know, nor can we be sure at just what period in the Apostle's career this imprisonment occurred. Because Epaphras elected to remain with Paul and apparently shared for a time the Apostle's imprisonment (Phn 2^{3}), Tychicus was sent to Asia, taking with him this letter. (2) Onesimus, a slave from Colossae, had found his way to the city of the Apostle's imprisonment and had there come under the influence of Paul. The Apostle took advantage of Tychicus' journey to send Onesimus back to his master at Colossae, with a letter of commendation and appeal (see PHILEMON).

The special purpose of the Epistle, as distinct from its general purpose as a message of goodwill, was to warn the Colossian Christians against a danger of which Epaphras had no doubt informed Paul. The exact nature of the so-called Colossian heresy is a matter of some uncertainty. On its doctrinal side it was probably a blend of Jewish theosophical or Gnostic ideas with floating Oriental speculations. It appears to have denied the direct agency of God in the work of creation, and to have inculcated the worship of angels and other mysterious powers of the unseen world (2^{18}). On its practical side it combined rigorous asceticism (2^{23}) and strict observance of Jewish ceremonial (2^{16}) with an arrogant claim to special enlightenment in spiritual things (2^{18}). Its special danger lay in the fact that it tended to obscure, or even to deny, the unique grandeur of the ascended Lord, the one Mediator, through faith in whom the life of the Christian was lifted into the new atmosphere of liberty. On one side, therefore, this Epistle may be compared with He 1, where the supremacy of the Son over all angels is strongly insisted on, while on the other side it takes up the line of thought of the Epistle to the Galatians—the relation of the Christian life to external ordinances. The way in which Paul deals with the question can best be seen by a short summary of the Epistle.

3. Summary.—After the usual salutation, thanksgiving, and prayer, in which Paul associates Timothy with himself (perhaps because he was known personally to the Colossian Church), he plunges at once into a doctrinal statement (1^{13}–2^{3}) of the Person and Work of Christ, who is the image of the invisible God, the origin and goal of all created things, in whom all the fulness (*plērōma*) of the Godhead abides. After a personal reference to his own commission and to his sufferings for the Church, he passes to the directly controversial part of the Epistle (2^{4}–3^{4}), warning the Colossians against being led astray by strange philosophies. The fulness of the Godhead is in Christ; He is over all principalities and powers; the life of externally imposed ordinances—' Touch not, taste not, handle not '—is a life to which the Christian has died in Christ. He has risen to a new life whose centre and secret are in heaven. He must still mortify the deeds of the flesh, but from a new motive and in the power of a new life. The third section of the Epistle (3^{5}–4^{6}) applies this principle to various relations of life—the mutual relation of Christians, husbands and wives, children and fathers, slaves and masters; and lastly, to the relation of Paul to them, and to their relation with the world. The closing section (4^{7-18}) deals with personal matters—with the mission of Tychicus, with whom Paul tactfully associates Onesimus; with Mark's proposed visit, in connexion with which St. Paul writes a word of special commendation, showing how completely the former discord has been healed. Then follow a warm commendation of Tychicus, greetings from Luke and Demas, instructions for exchanging letters with the neighbouring Church of Laodicea, and a final message for Archippus (q.v.). J. H. B. M.—J. K.

COLOURS.—The colours named in OT and NT, as in other ancient literatures, are few in number, and of these several are used with considerable latitude.

1. White as the colour of snow in Is 1^{18}, of the teeth described as milk-white (Gn 49^{12}), and of horses (Zec 1^{8} $6^{3,6}$); also of wool (Rev 1^{14})—the prevailing colour of the Palestinian sheep being white (see Ca 4^{2} 6^{6})—and of garments (Ec 9^{8}, Mk 9^{3}). **Gray** (and **grey**) occurs only in the expression ' gray hairs,' while **grisled** (literally ' grey,' from French *gris*) apparently means black with white spots (Gn 31^{10}, Zec $6^{3,6}$; cf **6** below). **Green** is not a colour adjective (in Est 1^{6} read as RSV), but a noun signifying green plants and herbs, as *e.g.* in Gn 1^{30} and Mk 6^{39}. A kindred word rendered **greenish** (Lv 13^{49} 14^{37}) is probably a greenish **yellow,** since it is also used in Ps 68^{13} of ' yellow gold.'

2. The darker colours likewise merge into each other, black and brown, for example, not being clearly distinguished. **Black** is the colour of hair (Ca 5^{11} ' black as a raven '), of horses (Zec $6^{2,6}$, Rev 6^{5}), and of ink (2 Co 3^{3}). In Ca 1^{5} the same Hebrew word signifies dark-complexioned (AV ' black '). Laban's black sheep (Gn 30^{32ff} RV) were probably dark brown (AV **brown**).

3. Red is the colour of blood (2 K 3^{22}), and of grape juice (Is 63^{2}). The same word is used of the reddish-brown colour of the ' red heifer ' of Nu 19, and of the chestnut horse of Zechariah's vision (1^{8}, AV ' red '), although the precise colour distinction between the latter and his companion, the **sorrel** (AVm **bay**; in Zec 6^{3} for ' bay ' [AV, RV], RSV has ' dappled,' and in v.[7]. has ' red ') horse, is not clear. ' Red ' is used also of the sky (Mt 16^{2f}—literally ' of the colour of fire ').

4. Crimson and **scarlet** are shades of the same colour, and were both derived from the same insect, the *coccus ilicis* or cochineal, which ' attaches itself to the leaves and twigs of the *quercus coccifera* ' (Post), and is termed in Hebrew ' the scarlet worm.' Scarlet-coloured garments were regarded as a mark of distinction and prosperity (2 S 1^{24}, Pr 31^{21}), but in OT scarlet is most frequently mentioned as one of the four liturgical, or, as we should say, ecclesiastical colours (see below). **Vermilion** is mentioned as a pigment (Jer 22^{14}, Ezk 23^{14}).

5. Associated with scarlet in the Priests' Code of the Pentateuch are found two colours, *'argāmān* rendered purple and *t^ekhēleth* rendered blue. In reality these are two shades of purple, the red tone predominating in the former, the blue tone in the latter. Since blue predominates in our modern purple it would be well to drop the cumbrous terms red-purple or purple-red, and blue-purple or purple-blue in favour of the simpler terms **purple** and **violet** as in AVm of Est 8^{15} (RSV ' purple ') 1^{6} (RSV ' blue '). Both shades were obtained by the use, as a dye, of a colourless fluid secreted by the gland of a shell-fish (*murex trunculus*) found in great quantities on the Phoenician coast. Hence Tyre became the chief seat of the manufacture of the purple cloth for which Phoenicia was famous throughout the ancient world (cf Ezk $27^{7,16}$). Most probably the word *Canaan* originated from this industry and like the Greek term Phoenicia means ' the land of the purple.' Purple raiment was the mark of high rank (cf ' born to the purple ') and was generally worn by kings and nobles (Mk 15^{17}, Lk 16^{19}, Jn 19^{2}).

In the Priests' Code, as has been noted, from Ex 25 onwards, ' violet ' (AV, RSV ' blue '), ' purple,' and ' scarlet ' are used—and always in this order—to denote the fine linen thread, spun from yarn that had been dyed these colours (cf Ex 35^{25}), which, with the natural white thread, was employed in weaving the rich material for the hangings of the Tabernacle, and for certain parts of the priests' dress.

6. Jacob's small cattle ' striped (AV **' ring-straked '**), speckled, and spotted ' (Gn 30^{39}) showed white mixed with black or brown in the case of the sheep, and black mixed with white in the case of goats.

It may be added that the art of **dyeing** was one in which the Jews of later times excelled. In NT times, as may be gathered from the Mishnah, dyeing was a flourishing branch of native industry. The true Tyrian purple was always a monopoly and consequently imported: but many less costly dyes were known, such as the cochineal insect for scarlet, dyer's woad (*isatis*) for true blue, madder (Heb. *pû'āh*) and others. Archaeology has shown that certain cities seem to have been centres of the dyeing industry. The city of Debir (*Tell beit Mirsim*) seems to have been such a centre and may have held a monopoly of the industry. In the Philistine region Gezer seems to have played a similar rôle.

A. R. S. K.—**J. Pn.**

COLT is applied in the Bible not to the young horse, but to the young ass, and once (Gn 32^{15}) to the young camel. Outside the Bible it is not applied to the young of any animal but the horse.

COMFORT, from late Latin *confortare*, 'to strengthen.' 'reinforce,' denoted in old English (*a*) physical, or (*b*) mental refreshment of an active kind (*invigoration, encouragement*)—obsolete meanings. In modern use it denotes (*c*) mental refreshment of the softer kind (*consolation*). Sense (*a*) appears in Gn 18^{5}, Jg $19^{5, 8}$, Ca 2^{5}; (*c*) elsewhere in OT. In NT, 'comfort' usually represents a Greek verb and noun, common in Paul, which include any kind of animating address; in this connexion the sense (*b*) prevails, as in Ac 9^{31} 16^{40}, Ro 1^{12} 15^{4}, 2 Co 13^{11} etc.; the tenderer signification (*c*) appears in Mt 5^{4}, 2 Co 1^{3ff}, etc. For the above Greek *noun*, however, AV fourteen times writes **'consolation'** (interchanging 'comfort' and 'consolation' in 2 Co 1^{3-7}), alike in senses (*b*) and (*c*): this RSV replaces several times (in Paul) by 'comfort.' 'Comfort' is also in AV the rendering of a second and rarer group of Greek words denoting *consolation* (in sorrow): so in Jn $11^{19, 31}$, 1 Co 14^{3}, and Ph 2^{1} (RSV 'encouragement'), 1 Th 2^{11} 5^{14}; the original of 'comfort' (*soothing*) in Col 4^{11} is an isolated expression kindred to the last. 'Of good comfort' in Ph 2^{19} renders a fourth Greek word *in good heart, cheerful*; while 'of good comfort' in Mt 9^{22} ‖ =*of good cheer* in v.^{2} and elsewhere (RSV 'take heart' here, and in Mk 10^{49}).

For OT and NT, comfort has its source in the tender love of God for His people, and for the individual soul; it is mediated (in the NT) by the sympathy of Christ, the visitings of the Holy Spirit, the help of brethren, and the hope of glory; it counteracts the troubles of life, and the discouragement of work for God: see especially Jn 16^{33}, Ro 5^{2-5}, 2 Co 1^{3-7}.

G. G. F.—**F. W. G.**

COMFORTER.—See COUNSELLOR.

COMING OF CHRIST.—See PAROUSIA.

COMMANDMENTS.—See TEN COMMANDMENTS.

COMMENTARY.—Mentioned only in RV in 2 Ch 13^{22} 24^{27} (AV, RSV 'story'). The Hebrew word is *midhrāsh*, which does not mean exactly what we understand by a commentary. It is 'an imaginative development of a thought or theme suggested by Scripture, especially a didactic or homiletic exposition, or an edifying religious story' (Driver).

COMMERCE.—See TRADE AND COMMERCE.

COMMON.—In Ac 10^{14f} synonymous with 'ceremonially unclean' (cf Mk 7^{2}, and see CLEAN AND UNCLEAN).

COMMUNICATION.—While 'conversation' in AV means *manner of life* or *conduct*, '*communication*' usually means *conversation, talk*. So Col 3^{8} 'filthy communication' AV ('foul talk,' RSV) and elsewhere. RSV entirely abandons AV usages of 'communication,' adopting instead renderings less likely to be misunderstood; *e.g.* Mt 5^{37} ('what you say'), 1 Co 15^{33} ('company'), Phn ^{6} ('sharing'). Similarly the verb 'to communicate,' in AV frequently used with the general sense of making common cause with one, appears only twice in RSV, both times in the sense of 'to impart.'

H. L. R.

COMMUNION.—See FELLOWSHIP.

COMPASS.—A 'compass' is the space occupied by a circle, or the circle itself: Pr 8^{27} 'he set a compass upon the face of the deep' (AVm and RV 'a circle'; RSV 'drew a circle') usually explained of the horizon, which seems to be a circle resting on the ocean. To 'fetch a compass' (Nu 34^{5}, Jos 15^{3} [RV, RSV 'turn about'], 2 S 5^{23} [RV 'make a circuit; RSV 'go around'], 2 K 3^{9} [RV 'make a circuit'; cf RSV], Ac 28^{13} [RV, RSV 'make a circuit']) is to make a **circuit** (q.v.). The tool for making a circle is a compass, mentioned Is 44^{13}. See ARTS AND CRAFTS, **1.**

COMPASSION.—See PITY.

CONANIAH.—**1.** A Levite who had charge of the tithes and offerings in the time of Hezekiah, 2 Ch 31^{12f} (AV **Cononiah**). **2.** A chief of the Levites in Josiah's reign, 2 Ch 35^{9}; called in 1 Es 1^{9} **Jeconiah** (RSV; AV, RV **Jeconias**).

CONCISION.—A name applied contemptuously by St. Paul (Ph 3^{2} AV) to the merely fleshly circumcision (Gr. *katatomē*; the ordinary word for 'circumcision' is *peritomē*). Prefer RSV, 'those who mutilate the flesh.'

CONCORDANCES.—The Latin word *concordantiae*, for an alphabetical list of words of Scripture drawn up for purposes of reference to the places where they occur, was first used by Cardinal Hugh of St. Cher (†1263), who compiled a Concordance to the Vulgate in 1244. This was revised by Arbottus (1290), and became the basis of a Hebrew Concordance by Isaac Nathan (1437–45). Nathan's work was revised and enlarged by John Buxtorf, the elder, whose *Concordantiae Bibliorum Hebraicae* (1632) held the place of standard Concordance for two centuries, and served as the model for many others. John Taylor's *Hebrew Concordance adapted to the English Bible, disposed after the manner of Buxtorf* (2 vols. folio, Norwich, 1754–57), is another link in the succession. The first Concordance to the English Bible is that of John Marbeck (folio, London, 1550). The earliest Concordance to the Septuagint is Conrad Kircher's (1607). The first Greek NT Concordance was published at Basle by Sixt Birch (Xystus Betuleius) in 1546. In the use of the following lists it will be understood that, while the most recent works, other things being equal, are to be preferred, there is so much common material that many of the older works are by no means obsolete.

1. Hebrew.—Fuerst, *Libr. Sacrorum Vet. Test. Concordantiae Heb. atque Chald.* (1840); *The Englishman's Hebrew and Chaldee Concordance of OT* (2 vols., Bagster); B. Davidson, *A Concordance of the Hebrew and Chaldee Scriptures* (Bagster, 1876); Bagster's *Handy Hebrew Concordance* [an invaluable work]; Mandelkern, *Vet. Test. Concordantiae* (folio, Leipzig, 1896), and a smaller edition without quotations (Leipzig, 1897). A revised edition was produced by Herner, 1909, and another edition by F. Margolin. Since 1955 there have been three independent photo-lithographic reproductions.

Another work based on *Biblia Hebraica*^{3} is G. Lisowsky, *Concordantiae Veteris Testamenti Hebraicae atque Aramaicae*, 1958, exquisitely written by hand.

2. Greek.—(*a*) THE SEPTUAGINT.—Bagster's *Handy Concordance of the Septuagint*; Hatch-Redpath's *Concordance of the Septuagint and other Greek Versions of the OT*, with two supplemental fasciculi (Clarendon Press, 1892–97). This is the standard work, and its latest reprint is 1955.

(*b*) THE NT.—*The Englishman's Greek Concordance of the NT* (Bagster), 9th edition, 1903; C. F. Hudson, *Greek Concordance to NT*, revised by Ezra Abbot (do.); Schmoller, *Concordantiae manuales NT graeci* (1890), *Handkonkordanz zum griech. N.T.* (Nestle Text), 1949; Bruder, *Concordantiae omnium vocum. NT graeci*^{4} (1888). All these works are superseded by Moulton-Geden's *Concordance to the Greek Testament* (1897, which is now in the third edition (1926), reprinted 1957).

3. English.—Until recent times the standard work was Cruden's *Complete Concordance to the Holy Scriptures*

(1st edition, 1738. Cruden's is truly a marvellous work, and was frequently copied. Its latest revision, 1954, was reprinted in 1957). More recent works are Eadie's *Analytical Concordance*; Young's *Analytical Bible Concordance* (1879–84, 11th edition, 1936, reprinted 1956), with supplementary vol. by W. B. Stevenson; Strong's *Exhaustive Concordance* (1894); Thom's *Concordance to RV of NT* (1882). For the Roman (Douay) Bible, see N. Thompson and R. Stock, *Concordance to the Bible in the Douay Version*, 1953. For the best known of recent Bible translations the following concordances are available: M. C. Hazard, *A Complete Concordance to the American Standard Version* (1922); W. J. Grant, *The Moffatt Bible Concordance* (1950); J. W. Ellison, *Nelson's Complete Concordance of the Revised Standard Version*, 1957.

W. F. A. and J. S. B.—**B. J. R.**

CONCUBINE.—See FAMILY, MARRIAGE, 6.

CONCUPISCENCE.—Concupiscence is intense desire, always in a bad sense, so that it is unnecessary to say 'evil concupiscence' as in Col 3^{5} (AV). The reference is nearly always to sexual lust. RSV, 'evil desire.'

CONDUIT.—An aqueduct for bringing water into a city. In early Jerusalem a tunnel was cut from the spring outside the city into the hill and a shaft cut through the rock so that the people might draw water from the point to which it was led. (For the arrangements at Gibeon see GIBEON.) Later a conduit was made to bring the water from the spring into the lower part of the city, and this is the conduit referred to in Is 7^{3} and 2 K 18^{17}, Is 36^{2}. In 2 K 20^{20} (cf 2 Ch 32^{30}) the conduit prepared by Hezekiah is probably to be identified with the **Siloam** tunnel, leading to the pool of Siloam. See SILOAM.

CONEY.—See BADGER.

CONFECTION.—This word in AV (Ex 30^{35}) means 'perfume,' and 'confectionary' (1 S 8^{13}, AV, RV) means 'perfumer' (q.v.).

CONFESSION.—In the English Bible the words 'confess' and 'confession' in relation to the Hebrew OT and the Greek NT carry the sense of agreement, promise, pointed and open declaration, acknowledgment, and the developed sense of grateful praise. In reference to an object they may refer to an open acknowledgment of sin or a profession of religious faith.

1. Confession of faith.—(1) In the OT the use of the word 'confess' in this sense is rare: AV 1 K $8^{33, 35}$ = 2 Ch $6^{24, 26}$; RSV Is 48^{1}. But there are other references to 'confession,' and the idea of acknowledging God as God and declaring personal trust in Him is found frequently in the OT. The Psalms are a storehouse of confessional utterance (see 48^{14}).

(2) In the NT the word usually translated 'confess' sometimes carries the sense of grateful praise and acknowledgment to God. But usually the verb 'confess' in relation to faith reflects the lively proclamation of Jesus as Lord and the requirements of discipleship and trust in Him. Here the context of the early Church and its life should be kept in mind.

(*a*) *The meaning of confession.*—The NT literature was written under the prompting of faith in Jesus which began in personal commitment and went on to recognition of his true role as 'Messiah,' 'Son of God,' 'Son of man.' The Synoptic Gospels reach a climax and turning point in Peter's confession at Caesarea Philippi: 'You are the Christ' (Mk 8^{29}||). After the Resurrection the primitive community found its faith in Jesus as Messiah confirmed in power (Ro 1^{4}), for Jesus then was 'designated Son of God in power.' All that was at first demanded of converts was the confession, 'Jesus is Lord' (1 Co 12^{3}; cf Ph 2^{11}); a view that is confirmed by the fact of their being baptized 'in the name of the Lord' (Ac 8^{16} 10^{48} 19^{5}).

The Fourth Gospel from the opening chapter is a conscious defence of the confession that Jesus is the Christ, over against the Baptist (1^{20}) and the Jewish opposition (9^{22} 12^{42}). Thomas' confession in 20^{28}, 'My Lord and my God!' is a climax in this confessional Gospel.

The growth of heresy made more precise confession necessary. In the Johannine Epistles it is essential to confess, on the one hand, that 'Jesus Christ has come in the flesh' (1 Jn 4^{2f}, 2 Jn^{7}), and, on the other hand, that 'Jesus is the Son of God' (1 Jn 4^{15}). In the Fourth Gospel Jesus' true humanity is asserted over against current docetic tendencies. With this developed type of confession may be compared the gloss that has been attached to the narrative of the Ethiopian eunuch's baptism (Ac 8^{37}, see RSV footnote), probably representing a formula that had come to be employed as a baptismal confession. It was out of baptismal formulae like this that there gradually grew those formal 'Confessions' of the early Church which are known as the Apostles' and the Nicene Creeds.

(*b*) *The value of confession.*—In the Synoptic Gospels Jesus Himself lays great stress on open confession of Him. If we confess Him before men, He will confess us before His Father in heaven; if we deny Him, He will also deny us (Mt 10^{32f}||, Mk 8^{38}||). But confession of Him as Lord must be backed up by obedience to the will of the Father (Mt $7^{21, 22, 23}$). In the sequel to Peter's confession at Caesarea Philippi in the Gospel of Matthew, Jesus pronounced Peter blessed on the basis of his outspoken affirmation, and gave the assurance that against the Church so founded the gates of Hades should not prevail (Mt 16^{17-19}). This section may have been added by the evangelist, but it reflects the emphasis on confession in one section of the Church.

In the Epistles the value of confession is emphasized not less strongly. According to St. Paul, the spirit of faith must speak (2 Co 4^{13}), and confession of faith is necessary to salvation (Ro 10^{8-10}). And in 1 John 4^{2} a true confession of Christ is a sign of the presence of the Divine Spirit, a proof of the mutual indwelling of God in man and man in God (v.^{15}).

2. Confession of sin.—(1) This holds a prominent place in the OT. The Mosaic ritual makes provision for the confession of both individual (Lv 5^{1ff}, 26^{40}) and national (16^{21}) transgressions; and many examples may be found of humble acknowledgment of both classes of sin, for instance in the Penitential Psalms and in such prayers as those of Ezra (10^{1}), Nehemiah (1^{6f}), and Daniel ($9^{4ff, 20}$). It is fully recognized in the OT that confession is not only the natural expression of penitent feeling, but the condition of the Divine pardon (Lv 5^{5f}, Ps 32^{5}, Pr 28^{13}).

(2) In the NT 'confess' occurs but seldom to express acknowledgment of sin (Mt 3^{6} = Mk 1^{5}, Ac 19^{18}, 1 Jn 1^{9}). But the duty of confessing sin both to God and to man is constantly referred to, and the relation of confession to forgiveness is made plain (Lk 18^{10f}, 1 Jn 1^{9}).

(*a*) *Confession to God.*—This meets us at many points in our Lord's teaching—in His calls to repentance, in which confession is involved (Mt 4^{17} = Mk 1^{15}, Lk $11^{29, 32}$ 24^{47}), in the petition for forgiveness in the Lord's Prayer (Mt 6^{12}, Lk 11^{4}), in the parables of the Prodigal Son (Lk $15^{17, 18, 21}$) and the Pharisee and the Publican (Lk 18^{10f}). It has been noted that while He recognizes confession as a universal human need (Lk 11^{4}||), He never confesses sin on His own account.

(*b*) *Confession to man.*—Besides confession to God, Christ enjoins confession to the brother we have wronged, and He makes it plain that human as well as Divine forgiveness are related to readiness to confess (Lk 17^{4}). In Ja 5^{16} (RSV) we are told to confess our sins one to another. The sins here spoken of are undoubtedly sins against God as well as sins against man. But the confession referred to is plainly not to any official of the Church, much less to an official with the power of granting absolution, but a mutual unburdening of Christian hearts with a view to prayer 'one for another.'

J. C. L.—**P. E. D.**

CONFIRMATION.—The noun 'confirmation' is used only twice in AV and RSV (Ph 1^{7}, He 6^{16}), the reference in the first case being to the establishment of the truth of the gospel, and in the second to the ratification of a statement by an oath. The verb 'confirm,' however, is used in RSV to translate various Hebrew and Greek words which are used in a general and non-technical sense. Thus it renders *ḳûm* in Dt 27[26] where the Hebrew verb signifies 'confirm' the Law, or 'give one's solemn assent' to it, by carrying out its precepts. The same Hebrew word is used of God confirming His words, spoken through the prophets, by His acts in history (Is 44[26], Dn 9[12]). It also denotes legal attestation of a transaction (Ru 4[7]), and authoritative attestation by a royal letter (Est 9[29]). 'Confirm' also appears as the translation of *mālē'* in 1 K 1[14], where it signifies the act of confirming or attesting a story by the evidence of a second witness, and it renders both *ḥāzaḳ*, in the sense of 'strengthen' (2 K 15[19], Dn 11[1]), and *'āmadh* which means 'ratify' (1 Ch 16[17]). In the NT it is used for *bebaioō* in 1 Co 1[6], of the experience of the Corinthians which attested the truth of the gospel. The noun 'confirmation' renders *bebaiōsis* in the sense of 'establishment' (Ph 1[7]), and in the more formal or legal meaning of the attestation or guarantee furnished by an oath (He 6[16]). In AV 'confirm' is used more often as a translation of verbs denoting strengthening, establishing, securing, and ratifying, and represents a greater variety of Hebrew and Greek words.

There is no clear evidence in the NT that the part of the baptismal rite which, after it became detached from the rest of the rite of initiation, came to be known in the West as *confirmatio* (cf 1st Council of Orange, 441; Canon 2), that is, the imposition of hands and/or consignation with chrism of the newly baptized, was practised in NT times. Tertullian (*De bapt.* 8–10; cf *Res. carn.* 8) and Cyprian (*Ep.* lxxiii. 9; cf Firmilian ap. Cypr. *Ep.* lxxv. 8) find authority for the imposition of hands by the bishop immediately after the baptized have emerged from the font in the narratives recorded in Ac 8[17] 19[6]; but it is unlikely that these instances of the laying of the apostles' hands on the newly baptized represent a normal feature of Christian initiation in NT times. They seem rather to be connected with major turning points in the Church's mission when a renewal of the special Pentecostal gifts of tongues and prophesying took place. They do, however, represent a confirmation of baptism, albeit in exceptional circumstances. He 6[2] might be cited in support of the view that the baptismal rite already included an imposition of hands; but it is far from certain that the reference in this passage is to initiation. There is, in any case, no support in the NT for the theory of Tertullian and many later writers that the beginning of the Christian life in the power of the indwelling Spirit is to be associated with the laying on of hands, or consignation, rather than with baptism in water.

J. C. L.—**G. W. H. L.**

CONFISCATION.—See BAN, **2,**

CONFUSION OF TONGUES.—See TONGUES, CONFUSION OF.

CONGREGATION, ASSEMBLY.—In AV these terms are both employed to render either of the two important Hebrew words *'ēdhāh* and *ḳāhāl*, with a decided preference, however, in favour of 'congregation' for the former and 'assembly' for the latter. In RV, as we read in the Revisers' preface, an effort was made to secure much greater uniformity in the use of these words. This is also true of RSV. Of the two Hebrew words, *ḳāhāl* ('assembly') is the more widely distributed, although neither is frequent in pre-exilic literature; *'ēdhāh* ('congregation') is not used in the earlier sources of the Pentateuch, but is found at least 115 times in the Priestly Narrative, where it denotes *the theocratic community of Israel as a whole*, the church-nation in its relation to Y″. The full designation, as found in Nu 1[2] and a score of times elsewhere, is 'all the congregation of the people of Israel,' which is the equivalent of the Deuteronomic phrase 'all the assembly (*ḳāhāl*) of Israel' (Dt 31[30]). In the older and more secular writers a similar idea could be expressed by the phrase 'all the tribes of Israel,' as in 2 S 24[2].

It is doubtful if there is any valid ground for the attempts to find a distinction between the two expressions 'congregation' and 'assembly,' even with P itself. For in the very same verse P sometimes employs the two terms synonymously, as in Lv 4[13], Nu 16[3] RV and RSV, and in the priestly redaction of Jg 20[1f], the whole body of the people being intended in every case. The only two passages which seem to imply that the 'assembly' was a limited section of the 'congregation' viz. Ex 12[6] and Nu 14[5] ('all the assembly of the congregation'), clearly show conflate readings (cf LXX). What difference, finally, can be detected between 'the assembly of the LORD' in Nu 16[3] 20[4] (cf Dt 23[3]) and 'the congregation of the LORD' in 27[17] 31[16]—all P passages?

In the LXX *'ēdhāh* is in most cases rendered by *synagōgē*, *ḳāhāl* by *ekklēsia*, both Greek terms being used, according to Schürer, without essential distinction to signify the religious community of Israel, as in the original Hebrew. But later Judaism, as Schürer has shown, began to distinguish between *synagōgē* and *ekklēsia*, applying the former in an empirical, the latter in an ideal, sense: the one to signify the religious community in a particular place, the other 'the community of those called by God to salvation,' the ideal Israel. This Jewish usage explains how, while *synagōgē* is occasionally found in early Patristic literature in the sense of 'the Christian congregation,' the rival word finally gained the day in Christian usage. The Christian community saw itself as the ideal Israel, and thus called itself 'the Church' (*ekklēsia*), while its Jewish counterpart remained 'the Synagogue' (see under CHURCH, SYNAGOGUE).

The word translated 'assembly' in Dt 33[4] and Neh 5[7] is *ḳᵉhillāh*, a form related to *ḳāhāl*. *Mō'ēdh*, related to *'ēdhāh*, and usually meaning 'appointed time or place,' is translated 'assembly' in Nu 16[2] and La 1[15] RSV. In Ezk 13[9] the word *sōdh* (literally 'secret council') is used to designate the whole community (AV 'assembly,' RSV 'council'). Cf 'assembly' (*mōshābh*, literally 'a sitting') in Ps 107[32].

The expression **solemn assembly,** in which 'solemn' has its etymological, but now obsolete, sense of 'stated,' 'appointed' (literally 'yearly,' *sollemnis*), represents another Hebrew word, *'ᵃṣārāh* or *'ᵃṣereth*. This word was originally applicable to any religious gathering (Is 1[13], Jl 1[14], Am 5[21], 2 K 10[20]; Jer 9[1] (EV 9[2]), sarcastic, RSV 'company'), but was afterwards limited mostly to connexion with the seventh day of the Feast of Unleavened Bread (Dt 16[8]), or the eighth day of the Feast of Booths (Lv 23[36], Nu 29[35], Neh 8[18], 2 Ch 7[9]).

'Holy **convocation**' occurs nine times in Lv 23, and six times in Nu 28–29; but for the same original, RSV has 'holy assembly' in Ex 12[16]. Since *miḳrā'* comes from the verb meaning 'to call,' 'convocation' would seem the best possible rendering; yet AV, RV, ARV, and RSV all have 'assemblies' in Is 1[13] and 4[5].

The '**mount of assembly** (AV, RV 'of [the] congregation') in the far north' (Is 14[13] RSV) refers to the Babylonian or Canaanite mountain of the gods from which an aspiring lesser deity might be cast down. This mythological conception is probably also to be found in Ezk 28[16], Ps 48[2] and 82[1, 6].

For '**tabernacle of the congregation,**' now called the 'tent of meeting' see TABERNACLE, **2,** and TENT.

A. R. S. K.—**W. F. S.**

CONIAH.—See JEHOIACHIN.

CONONIAH, 2 Ch 31[12f] (AV).—See CONANIAH, **1.**

CONSCIENCE.—1. The term.—The Greek word for 'conscience,' which occurs thirty times in the NT, has a narrower meaning than the English term used to translate it. In the NT the 'conscience' is a judge of one's past acts rather than a moral guide. The term is borrowed by NT writers, especially Paul, from the ordinary Greek language of the time. The OT has no word for 'conscience'; there the sense of guilt and obligation is expressed in more general terms, *e.g.* 'David's heart smote him' 1 S 24[5], 2 S 24[10]; 'my heart does not reproach me' Job 27[6].

The word translated 'conscience' in the NT may have the general meaning 'consciousness.' (He 10[2] RSV, ASV 'consciousness of sin(s)' is preferable to AV 'conscience of sins'; 1 P 2[19] RSV 'mindful of God,' translated literally would be 'through consciousness of God'; this is preferable to AV, ASV 'for conscience toward God.') Generally, however, 'conscience' is a moral-religious term meaning the pain experienced when one has done wrong. Usually conscience is concerned with wrong acts (He 10[22]), and a 'good conscience' (Ac 23[1], 1 Ti 1[5, 19]), or a 'clear conscience' (Ac 24[16], 1 Ti 3[9], 2 Ti 1[3], He 13[18], 1 P 3[16, 21]) is good in the sense that it reports nothing wrong about one's actions (C. A. Pierce, *Conscience in the NT*, 1955). Generally also conscience is thought of as reacting to acts which have already taken place (2 Co 1[12]). It is not thought of as a 'guide' to direct one's path.

2. Conscience and obedience to God.—Paul and other NT writers adopt a term which then as now was often used without religious meaning, and they expect that men generally, whether believers or not, will have some sensitivity of conscience. But for the NT the sense of guilt and obligation which the common-sense language named 'conscience' is a sign that each man is responsible to God (Ac 24[16], Ro 2[15f] 13[5], 2 Co 1[12]). Conscience is an index of this responsibility, even though it still functions in men who do not recognize its source.

3. Its sphere.—The sphere of conscience is choice in all its aspects. The judgment of conscience may test a Christian's loyalty to his faith or to the specific vocation to which Christ has called him (Ac 23[1] 24[16], 1 Ti 3[9]; cf 1 Co 4[4], where 'I am not aware of anything against myself' represents the verb corresponding to the noun 'conscience'), or it may deal with a specific practice like eating food offered to idols (1 Co 8[1-13] 10[23-33]), or test right and wrong action in general. Thus Paul expects that God's judgment on each man—pagans included—will be confirmed inwardly by that man's conscience (Ro 2[15f] '. . . while their conscience also bears witness and their conflicting thoughts accuse or perhaps excuse them on that day when, according to my gospel, God judges the secrets of men by Christ Jesus.')

4. The limitations of conscience.—Paul discusses conscience at length in connexion with eating food offered to idols. He shows two weaknesses of conscience. (*a*) Not all consciences judge alike. One person may find it right to eat food offered to idols, while another may find it wrong (1 Co 8[7] 10[28f]). The judgments of conscience are shaped in large measure by social and religious environment; in this case, the impact of pagan worship. Thus Paul speaks of a 'weak conscience' (1 Co 8[7, 10, 12]), which will be thrown into turmoil by seeing another Christian doing something which it judges wrong, and may thereby be led to consent to an act which is wrong for it. But Paul does not give his principal attention to the means of educating these 'weak' consciences. He accepts the variety of judgments about moral and religious practices as a permanent feature of life in the Christian fellowship. (*b*) Rather he turns to a second weakness of conscience, its self-centredness. Though a more thoughtful Christian may not be disturbed in conscience by eating food offered to idols, he must learn that the silence of his own conscience does not mean that he is free to do what seems right to him. Far more important is the obligation to exercise his freedom in a way not hurtful to the faith of another, even though the other may not be as mature as he (1 Co 8[13] 10[28-31], cf Ro 14[1-23]). Thus conscience is too self-centred a test of action to be adequate for a Christian—it does not make room for love (q.v.).

The Pastoral Epistles point out that conscience may become so seared (or scarred) by persistent falsehood that it is in effect destroyed (1 Ti 4[2]) or corrupted (Tit 1[15]).

5. Conscience and the acts of others.—Though conscience in the NT usually refers to the acts of others only when they attract or affect one's own acts (as in eating food offered to idols), conscience may also evaluate the acts of others. Thus Paul appeals to the Corinthians that their consciences may test him, and that they may know that he is truly Christ's representative (2 Co 4[2] 5[11]). He believes that they can make an inner judgment of what is right that goes beyond their party-loyalties and personal preferences.

6. Conscience as the sense of responsibility.—In the NT 'conscience' usually has the restricted meaning of a faculty of judgment that causes pain when one has done wrong. The modern meaning of conscience, as a sense of obligation or responsibility which guides men towards what is right and restrains them from wrong, is represented in the NT not by the word 'conscience,' but in more general terms. Thus Paul says of the Gentiles that 'what the law requires is written on their hearts' (Ro 2[15]), and he speaks of God having made known in the creation his invisible nature (Ro 1[19f]). He expects that believers and non-believers will share many basic standards of right and wrong, both for instance recognizing the value of honest work (1 Th 4[12]), and with respect to the customs of dress and appearance he can speak of what 'nature teaches' (1 Co 11[14f]). He speaks of the 'inmost self' that delights in the law of God, although there is another element in personality that wars against this inmost self (Ro 7[21-25]). Likewise in the Gospels, Jesus appeals to the sense of responsibility and to an inner judgment between better and worse (*e.g.* Lk 10[36], Mt 12[9-12]). That conscience in this broader sense receives little attention in the NT is not the result of the fact that the Greek word available had a more restricted meaning. For where men believe that 'conscience,' as a sense of obligation which guides men to do right, can be an important or sufficient guide to the moral life, a word is quickly found, as 'conscience' was among some later Greek and Latin writers, and in some modern ethics. NT writers recognize the sense of obligation as the fundamental human quality, but they also see its limitations and failures so clearly that it cannot be for them the central guide to life. It has been shown above that conscience even in the narrow sense of a judge of past actions is limited by the fact that different consciences judge differently, since their moral background is different, and that its self-centred nature makes it inadequate for the Christian. These same limitations apply to conscience in the modern meaning of the sense of obligation. Furthermore, NT writers prefer to speak about obligation in ways which make it clear that man's obligation is to God, not simply to his better self or to his sense of duty. Since God has revealed Himself in His law and in Christ, the NT usually presents man's responsibility in terms of his response to these clearer demands of God (*e.g.* Lk 10[26], Jn 3[16], Ro 3[19], 1 Co 12[3]). But from the NT point of view the fundamental difficulty with the sense of obligation which modern men call conscience is that men do not follow their sense of obligation even to that degree to which it is clear to them. Paul states the situation in Romans. Men fail to respond to what they know is right, and this failure is a rejection of God who commands what is right (Ro 3[9-20]). Thus the sense of obligation, taken seriously in the presence of God, results in man's knowing his failure and sin (q.v.). Only a new action of God in Christ can set men free from their guilt and enable them to find new energy from God's presence, and thus make it possible for them to fulfil the demands which their own nature puts upon them (Ro 3[21-26] 5[1-11]). Then a new guide to action, the Spirit (q.v.) gives men power to do what is required of them (Ro 8[1-39]), and the sense of obligation finds its fulfilment, not in self-centred 'conscience,' but in love (Ro 12[1-21] 13[8-10]). Once this basic change in their relation to God has come about, men will, however, still need to train and develop their sense of responsibility, as the NT often recognizes, and a growing understanding of one's responsibility is a central feature of the Christian life (Ph 1[9f], Col 1[9], Ja 1[5]).

7. The NT and modern problems of conscience.—Two limitations of 'conscience,' as a sense of responsibility, are seen clearly in recent discussions. (*a*) Conscience varies with the setting in which it is trained. The insufficiency of 'let your conscience be your guide' is shown by the variety of moral judgments which conscientious men make. The NT also recognizes this limitation of the sense of obligation, and holds that responsibility must be trained by participation in the life of the Church, which bears witness to Christ and His will. Within the fundamental commitment to Christ and His will, however, there is room for genuine variety of opinion about what one ought to do. (*b*) Studies of the self have shown how powerful are the effects of conscience (as a sense of guilt) in limiting man's freedom by creating compulsions below the level of conscious choice. A NT perspective would admit that men may destroy themselves by trying to find a motivation simply in their own sense of obligation and by preoccupation with their failures to fulfil their responsibilities. Though many instances of preoccupation with guilt may so deprive a person of freedom that healing requires special (psychological or psychiatric) treatment, a NT perspective would hold that beyond the inward preoccupation with guilt lies the reality of man's inadequacy and guilt before the holiness of God. Just as love and acceptance may be powers which overcome the preoccupation with guilt, so in the presence of God the love and forgiveness of Christ manifested in the Cross enable the believer to be free of an 'evil conscience' (He 10[22]). Thus though preoccupation with one's failure to accept responsibility may be destructive, the sense of guilt (q.v.) is not an aberration but a proper response to man's real situation before God and a means through which he may be led to open himself to God's love. W. J. He.—**W. A. B.**

CONSECRATION.—See Clean and Unclean, Nazirite.

CONSOLATION.—See Comfort.

CONSUMPTION.—The Hebrew word (*kālāh*) which is translated 'consummation' in Dn 9[27] (AV, RV; RSV 'end') is rendered 'consumption' in Is 10[23] (AV; RV 'consummation'; RSV 'full end') 28[22] (AV; RV 'consummation'; RSV 'destruction'), these English words having formerly the same meaning. Cf Foxe, *Actes and Mon.*, 'Christ shall sit . . . at the right hand of God till the consumption of the world.' Consumption occurs also with the same meaning in Is 10[22] (AV, RV; RSV 'destruction'), where Hebrew has *killāyôn* (rendered 'failing' in Dt 28[65]). But in Lv 26[16], Dt 28[22] (AV, RV, RSV) 'consumption' (Heb. *shaḥepheth*) is used of a disease of the body. See Medicine.

CONTENTMENT.—**1.** The word does not occur in the OT, but the duty is implied in the Tenth Commandment (Ex 20[17]), and the wisdom of contentment is enforced in Pr 15[17] 17[1] by the consideration that those who seem most enviable may be worse off than ourselves. But the bare commandment 'Thou shalt not covet' may only stir up all manner of coveting (Ro 7[7f]); and though a man may sometimes be reconciled to his lot by recognizing a principle of compensation in human life, that principle is far from applying to every case. It is not by measuring ourselves with one another, but only by consciously setting ourselves in the Divine presence, that true contentment can ever be attained. Faith in God is its living root (cf Ps 16[6] with v.[5]; also Hab 3[17f]).

2. In the NT the grace of contentment is expressly brought before us. Our Lord inculcated it negatively by His warnings against covetousness (Lk 12[15-21]), positively by His teaching as to the Fatherhood of God (Mt 6[25-32]||) and the Kingdom of God (v.[33], cf v.[19f]). St. Paul (Ph 4[11-13]) claims to have 'learned the secret' of being content in whatsoever state he was. The word he uses is *autarkēs*, literally 'self-sufficient.' It was a characteristic word of the Stoic philosophy, implying an independence of everything outside of oneself. The Apostle's self-sufficiency was of a very different kind (see v.[13]), for it rested on that great promise of Christ, 'My grace is sufficient (*arkei*) for thee' (2 Co 12[9]). Christian contentment comes not from a Stoic narrowing of our desires, but from the sense of being filled with the riches of Christ's grace. For other NT utterances see 1 Ti 6[8], He 13[5]. J. C. L.

CONVENIENT.—This English word often has in AV its primary meaning of *befitting*, as Ro 1[28] 'God gave them over to a reprobate mind, to do those things which are not convenient' (RV 'fitting'; RSV 'improper conduct'). So in the translation of *Agrippa's Van Artes* (1684) 'She sang and danc'd more exquisitely than was convenient for an honest woman.'

CONVERSATION.—In EV the word is always used in the archaic sense of 'behaviour,' 'conduct.' In the OT, AV gives it twice (Ps 37[14] 50[23]), representing Hebrew *derekh*='way' (cf RV and RVm). In the NT it is used in AV to render three sets of words. (1) The noun *anastrophē*='behaviour' (Gal 1[13], Eph 4[22], 1 Ti 4[12], He 13[7], Ja 3[13], 1 P 1[15, 18] 2[12] 3[1, 2, 16], 2 P 2[7] 3[11]), RV substituting in each case 'manner of life,' 'manner of living,' 'life,' 'living,' or 'behaviour'; the verb *anastrephesthai*='to behave oneself' (2 Co 1[12], Eph 2[3]). (2) The noun *politeuma*='citizenship' or 'commonwealth' (Ph 3[20]); the verb *politeuesthai*='to act as a citizen' (Ph 1[27]). (3) *tropos*='manner,' 'character,' literally 'turning' (He 13[5]). Cf RV and RVm throughout. The main point to notice is that in every case 'conversation' in AV and RV refers not to speech merely, but to *conduct*. RSV has the word only twice (Jer 38[27], Lk 24[17]), both times in the modern sense of 'talk.' J. C. L.—**F. C. G.**

CONVERSION.—The noun occurs only in Ac 15[3] (*epistrophē*), but in AV 'convert' is found several times both in OT (Heb. *shûbh*) and NT (Gr. *epistrephō, strephō*) to denote a spiritual turning, RV in most cases substituting '**turn**.' 'Turn' is to be preferred because (1) in the English of AV 'convert' meant no more than 'turn'; (2) 'conversion' has come to be employed in a sense that often goes beyond the meaning of the originals. RV and RSV have further corrected AV by giving active 'turn' for passive 'be converted' in Mt 13[15] 18[3], Mk 4[12], Lk 22[32], Jn 12[40], Ac 3[19] 28[27], where the Greek verbs are reflexive in meaning. In OT *shûbh* is used to denote a turning, whether of the nation (Dt 30[10], 2 K 17[13] etc.) or of the individual (Ps 51[13], Is 55[7] etc.). In NT *epistrephō, strephō* are used especially of individuals, but sometimes in a sense that falls short of 'conversion' as the conscious change implied in becoming a Christian. Mt 18[3] was spoken to true disciples, and the 'conversion' demanded of them was a renunciation of their foolish ambitions (cf v.[1]). Lk 22[32] was addressed to the leader of the Apostles, and his 'conversion' was his return to his Master's service after his fall. In Acts and Epistles, however, 'convert' or 'turn' is employed to denote conversion in the full Christian sense (Ac 3[19] 9[35] 11[21] 14[15] [cf 15[3] 'conversion'], 2 Co 3[16], 1 Th 1[9]). Conversion as a spiritual fact comes before us repeatedly in the Gospels (Lk 7[47ff] 15[17ff] 19[8ff] 23[42f]) and in the history of the Apostolic Church (Ac 2[41, 47] 8[5f. 12] 9[3ff] etc.). RV and RSV bring out the fact that in the NT conversion (as distinguished from regeneration [q.v.]) is an activity of the soul itself, and not an experience imposed from above. This view of its nature is confirmed when we find repentance (Ac 3[19] 26[20]; cf Ezk 14[6] 18[30]) and faith (Ac 11[21]; cf 20[21]) associated with it as the elements that make up the moral act of turning from sin and self to God in Christ. J. C. L.—**F. C. G.**

CONVINCE.—Adams (*Serm.* ii. 38) says: 'Whatsoever is written is written either for our instruction or destruction; to convert us if we embrace it, to convince us if we despise it.' This is the meaning of 'convince' in the AV. It is what we now express by ***convict*** (so RSV). Thus Jd [15] 'to convince all that are ungodly among them of their ungodly deeds.' But RSV uses the word in Jn 16[8], Ac 28[23], 2 Ti 4[2], Jd [22] etc.

COOKING AND COOKING UTENSILS.—See House, **9.**

COPPER.—See BRASS, and MINING AND METALS.

COPPERSMITH (2 Ti 4[14]).—See ALEXANDER, **2,** ARTS AND CRAFTS, **2.**

COR.—See WEIGHTS AND MEASURES.

CORAL.—See JEWELS AND PRECIOUS STONES.

COR-ASHAN, 1 S 30[30] (RV).—See BOR-ASHAN.

CORBAN.—Hebrew *ḳorbān* is a technical term for sacrifice, found in Ezk 20[28] and the Priestly Code, and rendered 'offering' or 'oblation.' It means something brought near, *i.e.* to the altar, or to God. The word Corban stands in the NT at Mk 7[11], where Jesus condemns the evasion of duty to parents on the ground of a vow to offer to God what is owed to them. See SACRIFICE AND OFFERINGS, VOWS.

CORBE, 1 Es 5[12] (AV).—See ZACCAI.

CORD, ROPE.—Hebrew possesses a considerable number of words rendered, without any attempt at uniformity, by 'cord,' 'rope,' and a variety of other terms. It is difficult for the English reader to recognize the same original in the Psalmist's bow 'string' (Ps 11[2]) and the '**green withs**' (RV '**withes**'; RSV 'fresh **bowstrings**,' cf RVm) with which Samson was bound (Jg 16[7]); or again in the tent ropes of Is 33[20] (EV 'cords') and the ships' '**tacklings**' (AV, RV; RSV '**tackle**') of v.[23]. The former set were probably of animal sinews or gut, the latter of twisted flax. The stronger ropes were of three strands (Ec 4[12]). No doubt the fibres of the palm and, as at the present day, goats' hair were spun into ropes. The process of rope-making from leather thongs is illustrated on an Egyptian tomb, the '**wreathen work**' (literally 'rope-work') of Ex 28[14] (AV, RV; RSV 'twisted like cords'), where, however, gold wire is the material used. Ec 12[6] speaks also of a silver cord, and Job 41[2] of 'a rope of rushes' (see RVm; AV 'hook'). The Greek word for the cords of our Saviour's scourge (Jn 2[15]) and the ropes of Ac 27[23] also denoted originally such a rope.

The everyday use of cords for binding evil-doers suggested the metaphor of the wicked man 'holden with the cords of his sin' (Pr 5[22]; RSV 'toils'), while from the hunter's snares comes the figure of Ps 140[5]; also 'the cords of death' of Ps 116[3] (RV; AV 'sorrows of death'; RSV 'snares of death.')

A. R. S. K.—**H. H. R.**

CORE.—AV in Sir 45[18], Jd [11] has this form for RV, RSV **Korah** (q.v.).

CORIANDER SEED (*gadh*, Ex 16[31], Nu 11[7]).—A product of the *Coriandrum sativum*, a common cultivated plant all over the East. It has a carminative action on the stomach. It is a globular 'fruit' about twice the size of a hemp seed. E. W. G. M.

CORINTH was the capital of the Roman province of Achaia, and, in every respect except educationally (see ATHENS), the most important city in Greece in Roman times. It was also a most important station on the sea route between E. and W., the next station to it on the E. being Ephesus, with which it was in close and continual connexion. Its situation made it an important centre of Christianity. The city occupied a powerful position at the S. extremity of the narrow four-mile isthmus which connected the mainland of Greece with the Peloponnese. Its citadel rises 1800 feet above sea-level, and it was in addition defended by its high walls, which not only surrounded the city but also reached to the harbour Lechaeum, on the W. (1½ miles away). The other harbour, Cenchreae, on the E., on the Saronic Gulf, was about 8½ miles away. The view from the citadel is splendid. The poverty of the stony soil and the neighbourhood of two quiet seas made the Corinthians a maritime people. It was customary to haul ships across from the one sea to the other on a made track called the Diolkos. This method at once saved time and avoided the dangers of the voyage round Cape Malea (S. of the Peloponnese). Large ships could not, of course, be conveyed in this way, and in their case the goods must have been conveyed across and transhipped at the other harbour. In A.D. 67, under Nero, a canal was begun across the isthmus, but the project was abandoned. In 1893 a modern ship canal was opened, which saves 200 miles on the voyage from Italy to Piraeus. The place was always crowded with traders and other travellers, and we find Paul speaking of Gaius of Corinth as 'my host and of the whole Church' (Ro 16[23]). The moral conditions at Corinth, in ancient times, were notorious. It was virtually a seaport, a meeting place of all nationalities, and its devotion to Aphrodite encouraged prostitution. But it had many other shrines in addition to the famous temple of Aphrodite which crowned the height of Acro-Corinthus; there were temples to Isis and Sarapis, Helios, the Great Mother, the Fates, Demeter and Korē. Within the city was at least one Jewish synagogue, a fragment of whose inscribed lintel still bears the letters AGOGEEBR, obviously part of the title, 'Synagogue of the Hebrews.'

The Corinth of St. Paul was a new city. The old Corinth had been destroyed by the Romans in 146 B.C., but exactly a hundred years afterwards it was refounded by Julius Caesar as a *colonia*, under the name *Laus Julia Corinthus* (see COLONY). A number of Roman names in the NT are found in connexion with Corinth: Crispus, Titius Justus (Ac 18[7f]), Lucius, Tertius, Gaius, Quartus (Ro 16[21-23]), Fortunatus (1 Co 16[17]). The population would consist of (1) descendants of the Roman colonists of 46 B.C., the local aristocracy; (2) resident Romans, government officials, and business men; (3) a large Greek population; (4) other resident strangers, of whom Jews would form a large number (their synagogue Ac 18[4]). Of these some joined Paul (Ac 18[4-8], Ro 16[21], 1 Co 9[20]), and the consequent hatred against him led to a plot against his life. The church, however, consisted chiefly of non-Jews (see 1 Co 12[2]).

Paul did not at first intend to make Corinth a centre of work (Ac 18[1]), but a special revelation altered his plans (Ac 18[9f]), and he remained there at least eighteen months. The opposition he met in the Jewish synagogue made him turn to the Gentiles. Paul left the baptism of his converts almost entirely to his subordinates, and himself baptized only Stephanas (1 Co 16[15]), Gaius (Ro 16[23]), and Crispus, the ruler of the synagogue (1 Co 1[14-16]). Some weeks after his arrival in Corinth, Paul was joined by Silas and Timothy, returning from Macedonia. News brought by Timothy caused him to write there the First Epistle to the Thessalonians (1 Th 3[6]), and the Second was probably written there also, soon after the receipt of an answer to the First. While Paul was in Corinth, **Gallio** (q.v.) came there as proconsul of the second grade to govern Achaia, probably in the summer of the year A.D. 52. The Jews brought an action before him against Paul, but Gallio, rightly recognizing that his court could take no cognizance of a charge of the sort they brought, dismissed the action. Paul's preaching was thus declared to be in no way an offence against Roman law, and in future he may have relied more on his relation to the State, as he faced the growing enmity of the Jews. After the examination, Gallio permitted the populace to show their hatred to the Jews (Ac 18[17]). It was in Corinth that Paul became acquainted with Prisca and Aquila (Ac 18[2, 3, 18, 26]), and he lived in their house during all his stay. They worked at the same industry as himself, as leather workers or 'tent-makers,' and no doubt influenced his plans for later work. They also left for Ephesus with him.

Christianity grew fast in Corinth, but the inevitable dissensions occurred. Apollos had crossed from Ephesus to Corinth (Ac 18[27], 2 Co 3[1]) and done valuable work there (Ac 18[27f], 1 Co 1[12]). He unconsciously helped to bring about this dissension, as did also Cephas, if (but see next article **4**) he visited Corinth. The subject of these dissensions is, however, more appropriately dealt with under the following two articles. The Apostle wrote at least three, perhaps four, letters to the church; the

 CORINTHIANS, FIRST LETTER TO THE

first, which is lost (1 Co 5^{9}); the second, which we call First Corinthians, and which was probably carried by Titus (Timothy also visited Corinth at the instance of Paul, 1 Co 4^{17}); the third, our Second Corinthians, which was taken by Titus and Luke (2 Co 8^{16-18} 12^{18}). Some scholars view 2 Co 10–13 as part of the 'stern' or 'painful' letter which preceded 2 Co 1–9 (see Paul, **5**, and CORINTHIANS, SECOND). Paul spent three months in Greece, chiefly no doubt at Corinth, in the winter of A.D. 56–57. Whether the Corinthians actually contributed or not to Paul's collection for the poor Christians at Jerusalem must remain uncertain though most probable.

A. So.—F. C. G.

CORINTHIANS, FIRST LETTER TO THE.—**1. The Question of integrity.**—We have two letters to the Corinthians, but Paul himself refers to four. In 1 Co 5^{9} a former letter is mentioned (A) and in 2 Co $2^{3f.\,9}$ he speaks of a letter written 'with many tears' (C), which must be dated between 1 Co (B) and 2 Co (D). With regard to 2 Co the question has often been discussed, whether or not chs. 10–13 represent the in-between-letter (written with 'tears' C). With regard to 1 Co the question of integrity is less often discussed (yet see J. Weiss). It is improbable that the Christian congregation at Corinth lost or suppressed any letters of Paul. The literary analysis of the two existing letters leads to the further assumption that the four letters to Corinth were put together by the Corinthian congregation to form the two existing ones. Analysis shows that we can assume in

1 *Co* the letters A and B (A: 6^{12-20}, 9^{24}–10^{22}, 11^{2-34}, 12–14; B: 1^{1}–6^{11}, 7^{1}–9^{23}, 10^{23}–11^{1}, 15–16), and in
2 *Co* the letters C and D (C: 2^{14}–7^{4}, 9, 10–13; 6^{14}–7^{1} is debatable; D: 1^{1}–2^{13}, 7^{5-16}, 8).

This literary analysis is—with more or less agreement—supported by J. Weiss, H. Windisch, R. Bultmann, J. Héring, E. Dinkler, W. Schmithals; see also R. H. Strachan (in the Moffatt Comm.). Yet it must be noted that liberal scholars like H. Lietzmann and W. G. Kümmel think that the two canonical letters as a whole are integral, and that—as Lietzmann suggests—the breaks in the continuity of thought resulted from 'a sleepless night.' Among British and American scholars this view is also held by C. T. Craig, H. L. Goudge, A. H. McNeile, Allan Menzies, and others. Hans Windisch believed that 2 Co 10–13 belonged to a later letter than chs. 1–9. On the other hand, the majority of British and American scholars hold that 2 Co 10–13 was at least part of the 'stern' letter which preceded chs. 1–9, and that 6^{14}–7^{1} is perhaps a fragment of a still earlier letter. A lexicographical article can only hint at such possibilities and probabilities. We may proceed by presupposing that both 1 and 2 Corinthians are entities in themselves—though we have serious doubts on this point.

2. Outline and character of the letter.—1 Co as we have it before us may be outlined as follows:

1^{1-9}: Address and Prooemium.
1^{10}–4^{21}: The parties in Corinth.
5^{1-13}: Fornication.
6^{1-11}: Lawsuits.
6^{12-20}: Warning concerning prostitutes.
7^{1-40}: Marriage.
8^{1}–10^{12}: Meals offered to idols.
10^{23}–11^{1}: Practical behaviour.
11^{2-16}: The veiling of Women.
11^{16-34}: The Eucharist.
12^{1}–14^{40}: Spiritual Gifts.
15^{1-58}: The Resurrection of the Body.
16^{1-24}: Conclusion and final Greetings.

The outline demonstrates the variety of mostly ethical themes which are anchored in christological statements. With the exception of ch. 1^{1-9}, which probably was composed independently by Paul and later included, all the themes considered in the letter go back to specific questions coming from Corinth or to news concerning the Corinthian congregation which had reached Paul. It is difficult to construct an inner line leading up to one central idea which embraces or underlies all other subject-matters, be it 'love' or 'resurrection' (K. Barth, *e.g.*, sees in ch. 15 the theme of the letter as a whole). Yet even when assuming that our letter is a later combination of two earlier letters one must acknowledge that there is an actual centre, a red line running through the whole, namely the Christ-event, to which all the decisions of Paul refer. And this centre implies that we must read and interpret the letter as an eschatological proclamation. Each actual question is answered in the light of Christ's resurrection, which has opened the future for those who believe in Him and determines the existential being of men and all their ethical decisions.

3. The Occasion of the Letter.—Five years had elapsed since Paul's first evangelization of Corinth (Ac 18^{1-17}) when he addressed the present letter to the Christians in that great centre of commerce. Corinth was the capital of the Roman province Achaia, after 29 B.C., and had at the time of Paul a greater importance than Athens. The harbour-city was known as a vicious and pleasure-loving place, being a commercial bridge between Orient and Occident in the ancient world. No doubt there had already been frequent communications, especially during the Apostle's stay in Asia, for the journey between Corinth and Ephesus was relatively easy. These communications may have been by letter (1 Co 7^{1}) or by oral report, or perhaps by a lost correspondence. The household of Chloe is mentioned (1 Co 1^{11}) and may be his informant, or Stephanas, the first Christian of Achaia, who had been baptized by Paul (1 Co 16^{15} 1^{16}). Further we cannot say with certainty whether the words in 1^{2} 'together with all those who in every place call on the name of our Lord Jesus Christ . . .' refer to Christians in Achaia outside of Corinth (cf 2 Co 1^{1}). The occasion of the letter is a series of questions addressed to the Apostle by the congregation, and a private report which has reached him orally.

4. The state of the Corinthian Church.—The majority of the Christians at Corinth were Gentiles. The general Hellenistic atmosphere and Gnostic tendencies there led to most of the evils or misunderstandings for which Paul rebukes them. (The thesis of Schmithals, that Paul attacks Jewish Gnostics, probably coming from Palestine, is based upon an overexegesis and generalization of 2 Co 11^{22}.) During his second journey Paul travelled via Philippi, Thessalonica, and Beroea (Ac 16^{11}–17^{15}) to Athens (Ac 17^{16ff}), where he obviously had no great success. In Corinth he first worked alone, later Aquila and Priscilla helped him, and Silas and Timothy arrived from Macedonia (Ac 18^{2ff}). Paul stayed in Corinth one year and six months (Ac 18^{11}). Soon after the Jewish attack upon Paul, the seizure of Sosthenes, and the trial before Gallio, the Apostle left together with Aquila and Priscilla for Ephesus (Ac 18^{18ff}).

About the organization of the Corinthian Church it is difficult to form a clear judgment. We do not yet have a hierarchical order, because it is still an eschatological congregation, a 'congregational democracy.' This does not exclude regulations or a churchly order, as is made explicit in 1 Co 12^{4ff}. And in 12^{28} we read of apostles, prophets, and teachers (the term 'presbyter' does not occur), referring to offices which were not locally attached; local officers with various gifts are also mentioned, all being 'charismatic' officers.

The state of the Corinthian Church at the time of our first letter was marked by *party spirit* (chs. 1–4). Presumably this was the actual reason for the writing of 1 Co. In 1^{12} Paul says that 'each one of you says "I belong to Peter," or "I belong to Apollos," or "I belong to Cephas," or "I belong to Christ."' It is a question whether *three* parties are meant, since 'I belong to Christ' refers to the only legitimate answer, or whether the sentence refers to *four* existing parties in Corinth. The reference by Clement of Rome (*c* A.D. 95), 'To be sure, under the Spirit's guidance, he wrote to

CORINTHIANS, FIRST LETTER TO THE

you a letter about himself and Cephas and Apollos, because even then you had formed cliques' (1 Clem 47[3]), is obviously written in view of 1 Co, but it is an exegetical problem whether he quoted 3[22]—where we have *three* parties—or 1[12]—where we have *four*. The result is: we cannot say on the basis of later exegesis what the Pauline text really meant. It is possible that the text of the letter as a whole says what is meant. We know about Paul's theology; through him we know also about Cephas-Peter's theological thought; Apollos is mentioned and pictured in Ac 18[24ff]; he was an Alexandrian Jew, working at Ephesus and Corinth, mentioned also in 1 Co 3[4–8, 22] 4[6], later returning to Ephesus (16[12]). He obviously worked independently of Paul (his relation to John the Baptist is questionable). Yet all these names may be just examples of churchly officers which were or could be misunderstood as mystagogical heroes. The main point is, the content of our letter (and of 2 Co too) does not give evidence of three or four parties but points to only one opposition group, namely a primarily Hellenistic Gnostic one. This observation can only be proved here with regard to 1 Co by considering its various themes. The question arises whether or not this one heretical group is to be connected with missionaries coming from Peter. Or was its hero Apollos? We can only conclude at this point that Paul sets against all factions (or schisms?) the event of the cross: 'Jesus Christ and him crucified' (2[2]), 'a stumbling-block to Jews and folly to Gentiles' (1[23]), and proclaims this event as the grace coming 'from God' (4[5]—according to K. Barth 'the secret nerve of the whole paragraph'). This implies that men can never rely upon man's judgment or a humanly designed gospel, but have to search for the Christ-centred gospel which comes 'from God.' As clear as this is, it opens up the difficulty that we hear God's *Euangelion* through man's proclamation, and are faced with the task of discrimination. Further characteristics of the opposition may be found in the following paragraphs, but they cannot be derived from Acts.

5. Moral Scandals (ch. 5).—A Christian had married his (probably heathen) step-mother. We cannot say whether his father was still alive or not (2 Co 7[12] does not refer to this incident). According to both Jewish (Lv 18[7f.] 20[11]) and Roman law this was forbidden. The Corinthian Church did not condemn this action and presumably did not even mention it in their letter to Paul. The Apostle reproves them for tolerating such immorality 'of a kind that is not found even among pagans' (5[1]). He orders (altering the punctuation), 'When you are assembled in the name of the Lord Jesus, and my spirit is present, with the power of our Lord Jesus . . . to deliver this man to Satan for the destruction of the flesh . . .' This cannot mean simply excommunication, since Paul continues: 'that his spirit may be saved in the day of the Lord Jesus' (5[4f]). We note that Paul demands an action from the congregation as a whole, not a decision from one of the officers. And he will not punish in order to annihilate the offender as a person, but in order to save his inner self. Just this intention to save 'his spirit' excludes excommunication (5[13b] is quotation of Dt 17[7]). Paul probably thinks in terms of a punishment by death, as told in Ac 5[5, 10] (cf *Acta Thomae* 6; *Acta Johannis* 86; cf 1 Ti 1[20]). In the further context, especially 5[9ff], the relation of the Christians to the Gentiles is discussed and a misunderstanding corrected. The Apostle does not order Christians 'to go out of the world,' but to stay in a mixed society. What he demands is this: cleanness among brothers, *i.e.* the holiness of the Church, and therefore inner-churchly discipline.

6. Legal Scandals (6[1–11]).—Paul rebukes the Corinthians for litigiousness, and writes principally about the problem of law-suits among Christians. The connexion with the previous section is given by the verb 'to judge' (twice in 5[12f] and again in 6[1]). Two different answers are given. In vv.[1–6] he demands that law-suits should be settled in the midst of the congregation through arbitration (similarly as in the Jewish diaspora), with a Christian acting as arbiter. The civil law is not discussed and the idea of right is not defined. In vv.[7] and [8] Paul demands that they suffer injustice rather than seek their own rights, *i.e.* the idea of personal rights is simply put aside and self-denying love is demanded. According to Paul's other letters this position seems to be his primary one, because looking out for one's own rights is close to 'boasting.'—The interesting point of this section is that Paul connects his decision with a reference to baptism, in vv.[9–11]: 'The unrighteous will not inherit the kingdom of God' . . . 'but you were washed, you were sanctified, you were justified. . . .' This does not imply that Christians possess a new quality, but that their baptism includes a *task of becoming*, namely to become holy, righteous, good.—The case, of course, concerns 'civil law,' not 'criminal law,' yet this historical reference does not exclude other implications, since *all* legal and political decisions of a Christian should and must go back to his awareness of being a member of the body of Christ—of his being 'holy' in the sense of Lv 17–20. The new being in Christ is a down-payment and guarantee of the Christians becoming real members of Christ.

7. Questions of Marriage (6[12]–7[40]).—The modern chapter divisions (introduced by Stephen Langton in the 13th cent.) are not entirely satisfactory. A break should come after 6[11]. The following section (6[12–20]) contains an answer to a previous letter from Corinth. The correspondent had said, 'All things are lawful for me.' The apostle replies, 'but not all things are helpful.' 'Food is meant for the stomach and the stomach for food' was the thesis in Corinth, *i.e.* let us allow freedom for sexual expression, since God will ultimately destroy both food and stomach as belonging to the flesh. Paul's answer is: The body as a whole belongs to the Lord; therefore the stomach and the sexual organs cannot live their own life. Our bodies are members of Christ—therefore no relation to prostitutes is allowable. Obviously the Apostle is fighting against a libertinistic and gnostic concept. Yet his argumentation involves at the same time a prejudice against marriage as such, which comes up in ch. 7. It is usually thought that the Corinthians wished to extol asceticism, basing their views on words like Mt 19[11f], and that they suggested that celibacy was to be strongly encouraged in all. The Apostle gives an answer, which is conditioned by his expectation of the approaching parousia (7[26, 29]). It does not matter whether one marries or not—but it is better not to marry. A tendency towards asceticism is obvious (7[8]); marriage is a concession for those who 'cannot exercise self-control' (7[9]). In v.[26] Paul gives his own opinion concerning marriage: 'It is well for a person to remain as he is.' And in vv.[29–30] the Apostle sounds the key for all ethical decisions: 'I mean, brethren, the appointed time has grown very short; from now on, let those who have wives live as though they had none, and those who mourn as though they were not mourning, and those who rejoice as though they were not rejoicing, and those who buy as though they had no goods, and those who deal with the world as though they had no dealings with it. For the form of this world is passing away.' This passage has an importance for *Christian ethics* like no other word of Paul. Man's relation to the world is a dialectical and paradoxical one. His existence in this world is always 'as if not,' *i.e.* he participates in all affairs yet his main interest is the 'Reign of God.' Of course he *is* married, but he is aware that 'the form of this world is passing away' (7[31]).

8. Social Questions (8[1]–11[1]).—The whole section concerns the right understanding of Christian freedom. (*a*) *Food.*—The opening phrase: 'all of us possess gnosis' seems to be in tension with 8[7]: 'not all possess gnosis.' The tension is removed as soon as one recognizes that knowledge as such without love and humility is nothing. And the very knowledge which is inherent in faith, all do not possess. Often it is just those who boast about their gnosis who do not search for it in Christ. This thesis is exemplified by a discussion of the

 CORINTHIANS, FIRST LETTER TO THE

Corinthian food problem, *i.e.* whether Christians may eat meat which has previously been offered to idols, as most of the meat sold in Corinth would have been. Paul's answer may be paraphrased like this: 'The false gods are really non-existent; we have but one God; as there is no such thing really as an idol we are free to eat meats offered in idol temples.' But there are weaker brethren who would be scandalized. 'Meat will not commend us to God: it is indifferent.' But do not let your liberty cause others to fall (note the change of pronoun in v.^{8f}). The whole section is obviously directed against Gnostic Christians who think they possess the quality of holiness through baptism and participation in the Lord's Supper, and therefore mean to have all freedom, even to eat meat which was previously offered to idols, since it cannot infect the inner self of a believer. Against this Paul writes. Without mentioning the decree of Ac 15^{29} he stresses the principle of love: offence must not be given to the weaker brethren.

(*b*) *Idol Feasts* (8^{10-13} 10^{14}–11^{1}).—Paul allows freedom, yet not absolutely. He forbids eating at idol feasts, if a Christian member is shocked by the participation of a brother, who does it on the ground of his conscience. In principle 'we are no worse off if we do not eat, and no better off if we do' (8^{8}). Yet our behaviour has to follow the knowledge that Christ died for all of us and that 'sinning against your brethren and wounding their conscience' means to 'sin against Christ' (8^{12}). Paul further explains the actual incompatibility of pagan cult feasts and the Christian Eucharist: 'You cannot partake of the table of the Lord and the table of the demons. Shall we provoke the Lord to jealousy?' (10^{21f}). In the context Paul's words about the Lord's supper (10^{16f}) are significant, especially in comparison with 11^{23ff}.

(*c*) *Digression on Forbearance* (9^{1}–10^{13}).—Paul says that he habitually considers the rights of the others and does not press his own rights as an Apostle to the full; he implies that the Corinthians should not press their liberty so as to scandalize others. Obviously some opponents at Corinth had questioned Paul's authority or legitimacy as an Apostle, because he did not accept financial support. Paul announces his position as an Apostle, and the right of the Christian minister to live by the gospel, but he will not use his rights to the full (9^{18}). He teaches self-denial and consistency from the example of the Isthmian games (9^{24ff}). When Paul in 10^{1} speaks of 'our fathers,' he does not turn to the Jewish section of the Corinthian Church, but considers the whole Church as being the spiritual descendants of Israel. In this line the following typology has to be understood: Moses acting with the Israelites is the prototype of Christ's acting with the Christians. The example is given in order to warn against a dangerous self-security, as if a Christian already possessed full salvation as a sacramental possession. 'Therefore let any one who thinks that he stands take heed lest he fall' (10^{12}). In the background we again must assume Gnostic concepts.

9. Christian Worship (11^{2}–14^{40}).—(*a*) *The Veiling of Women.*—In reply (as it seems) to another question, Paul says that it is the Christian custom for men 'praying or prophesying' to have their heads uncovered, but for women to have theirs covered. This apparently trivial matter is an instance of the application of general principles to Christian ceremonial. Paul's injunction is based on the subordination of the woman to the man, and his advice is: Faith in Christ does not imply a revolution of our social order.

(*b*) *The Eucharist.*—The Corinthians joined together a social meal—somewhat later called an Agape or Love-feast—and the Eucharist, probably in imitation both of the Last Supper and of the Jewish and heathen meals taken in common. To this combination the name 'Lord's Supper' (only here in NT) is given. But the party-spirit, already spoken of, showed itself in this custom; the Corinthians did not eat the Lord's Supper, but their own, because of their factions. Paul therefore gives the narrative of our Lord's Institution as he himself had received it, strongly condemns those who make an unworthy communion as 'guilty of the body and the blood of the Lord,' and inculcates preparation by self-examination. It is chiefly this passage that has led some to think that Paul is quoting the Synoptic Gospels (see below, **11**), where we have the parallels in Mk 14^{22-25}, Mt 26^{26-29}, and Lk 22^{15-20}. The Lukan account, as we have it in our Bibles, namely the shorter text, is very like the Pauline. But the inference is very improbable. The greater probability is (J. Jeremias), that the Lukan passage contained at first only 22^{15-19}, while 22^{19b} and 20 were later added on the basis of 1 Co 11. In other words: the Lukan version has no independent value. In the main points—namely proclamation of the death of Christ, re-establishment of the Covenant, anticipation of the coming messianic meal—Paul agrees with the accounts of Mark and Matthew, although the Greek texts differ. The similarity is best understood when we recognize that Paul as well as the Evangelists go back to an Aramaic source.

(*c*) *Spiritual Gifts* (chs. 12–14).—Again Paul seems to answer questions raised by the Corinthians concerning the unity of the congregation. He emphasizes, on the one hand, 'You are the body of Christ and individually members of it' (12^{27}), taking up a Gnostic metaphor (cf Ro 12); on the other hand 'There are varieties of gifts, but the same Spirit . . . the same Lord . . . the same God' (12^{4f}). Since all Christians were 'baptized into one body' (12^{13}), the variety of gifts among them does not establish a difference of value. In the hymn-like digression of ch. 13, Paul points to 'a still more excellent way' and shows that of all spiritual gifts love is the greatest, that without it all other gifts are useless. Yet love is no moral ideal, no human quality; love is God's gift to man and an eschatological possibility. Therefore Paul concludes, 'So faith, hope, love, abide, these three; but the greatest of these is love.' Paul thus proclaims that spiritual gifts are means to an end, not an end in themselves; and he therefore upholds 'prophecy' (*i.e.* in this connexion, the interpretation of Scripture and of Christian teaching) as superior to speaking with tongues, because it edifies all who are present. The principle of freedom in the use of spiritual gifts at Christian worship requires self-discipline and order. 'For God is not a God of confusion but of peace' (14^{33}). In this context he writes, further, that women are to keep silence in the public assemblies (14^{34f}), following the line of thought in ch. 11.

10. The Resurrection of the Body (ch. 15).—This, the only doctrinal chapter of the letter, cites at the beginning the earliest tradition of our Lord's Resurrection. The words 'For I delivered to you . . . what I also received' show that the passage is pre-Pauline. Whether the formula goes from v.^{3b} to v.^{5} or to v.^{7} is difficult to decide. We are inclined to think that the earliest tradition closed with v.^{5} and that Paul himself added the other witnesses according to a chronological sequence. Apparently Gnostic Christians at Corinth felt a great difficulty in accepting the doctrine of the Resurrection of the body. Paul characterizes their position in v.^{13}, 'there is no resurrection of the dead'; but he complicates the picture by assuming in v.^{29} that they practised the vicarious baptism of the dead. It seems as if the Gnostics did not deny a spiritual Resurrection but a realistic physical one, and that they hoped for a liberation of man's self from the body at death (the passage must be read together with 2 Co 5^{1-5}). Paul replies that Christ has risen, as many still alive can testify, and that therefore the dead will rise. For the treatment of the question how to understand this miracle (15^{35ff}) see PAUL'S THEOLOGY, **8**, and RESURRECTION. The Corinthian scepticism does not seem to have died out at the end of the century, for Clement of Rome, writing to Corinth, strongly emphasizes the doctrine (1 Clem 24–26), though it had no longer the feature of Gnostic heresy.

11. Date and genuineness of the letter.—It is referred to as Paul's by Clement of Rome, *c* A.D. 95 (1 Clem 47), who speaks of the parties of Paul, Cephas, and Apollos, but omits the Christ-party (see above, **3**); we cannot infer from his phrase 'the epistle of the blessed Paul' that he knew only one Epistle to the Corinthians, as early usage shows (Lightfoot, *Clement*, ii, 143). There are other clear allusions in Clement. Ignatius (Eph. 18) refers to 1 Co 1[20, 23f.] 4[13] and probably 2[6]; Polycarp (§11) quotes 1 Co 6[2] as Paul's; references are also found in the 'Martyrdom of Polycarp,' in Justin Martyr, and in the Epistle to Diognetus; while Irenaeus, Clement of Alexandria, and Tertullian at the end of the 2nd cent. quote the Epistle fully. Of the 2nd cent. heretics, the Ophites and Basilides certainly knew it. Internal evidence fully bears out the external; no Epistle shows more clearly the mark of originality. It is in fact one of the 'generally accepted' letters of Paul and all arguments against its authenticity have died out. For the open question of the lliterary unity and integrity see above, **1**. We may then take the genuineness of the letter as being unassailable.

If so, when and where was it written? In 16[8] Paul writes: 'But I will stay in Ephesus until Pentecost.' With this coincide the plans of 16[3ff] and the remarks in 16[19]. Relatively to the rest of the Pauline chronology, the date can be approximately fixed. In the year of his arrest at Jerusalem, Paul had left Corinth in the early spring, after spending three months there (Ac 20[3, 6]). He must therefore have arrived there in late autumn or early winter. This seems to have been the visit to Corinth promised in 2 Co 13[1], which was the third visit. Two visits in all must therefore have preceded 2 Cor (some think also 1 Cor), and in any case an interval of some months between the two Epistles must be allowed for. In 1 Co 16[6] the Apostle had announced his intention of wintering in Corinth, and it is possible that the visit of Ac 20[3] is the fulfilment of this intention, though Paul certainly did not carry out all his plans at this time (2 Co 1[15f, 23]). If so, 1 Co would have been written from Ephesus in the spring of the year before St. Paul's arrest at Jerusalem. This date is favoured by the allusion of 5[7f], which suggests to many commentators that the Easter festival was being, or about to be, celebrated when Paul wrote. The absolute date will depend on our view of the rival schemes given in article CHRONOLOGY OF THE NT, I, **4**. We suggest the time as Easter A.D. 55. E. D.

CORINTHIANS, SECOND LETTER TO.—1. Circumstances of the Letter.—2 Co is generally viewed as one of the most personal letters of Paul, marked by apologetic and polemic (Jülicher). Nevertheless, we must not interpret the Letter primarily as a biographical document. Paul writes first of all as an Apostle, not as a private person, and he includes personal passages only in order to lay bare his apostolic authority. We may even say that the *theme* of the Letter is the apostolic office. In order to strengthen it, Paul asks for the obedience and confidence of the congregation (2[9] 7[12] 10[6–11] 13[2f]). While in 2[14]–6[10] the apostolic office appears as the explicit theme, in chs. 10–13 the discussion concerns the apostolic qualifications of Paul himself, which had been questioned by his opponents in Corinth. Paul's main argument for his legitimacy as an apostle is formulated in 4[5]: 'For what we preach is not ourselves, but Jesus Christ as Lord, with ourselves as your slaves for Jesus' sake'—pointedly repeated in 13[3]: 'Christ is speaking in me.' Recognizing this argument as Paul's primary concern, one may even say, with a slight change of accent, that the Letter's theme is given in the ministry of preaching, *i.e.* in *the work of proclaiming Christ Jesus* (cf **4**).

It is surprising that 2 Co does not take up the problems mentioned in 1 Co, *e.g.* the three (or four) parties (1 Co 1–4) or the problems of Christian worship, marriage, and social questions. The only recurring theme is the resurrection of the body (2 Co 5[1–10]), which appears in a different perspective. All the other topics circle around one point: the right relationship between the Christian congregation and its Apostle.

2. Paul and Corinth.—In order to recognize the differences between 1 and 2 Co more clearly, the events must be recalled which took place between the writing of the two letters. According to 1 Co the Apostle was in Corinth only once (cf Ac 18[1, 18]), namely when founding the Christian congregation there as the first in Achaia. According to 2 Co he had visited Corinth twice: 12[14] 'For the third time I am ready to come to you'; 13[1], 'This is the third time I am coming to you.' One must therefore conclude that Paul paid a visit to Corinth between writing 1 and 2 Co, a visit to which he also refers in 2 Co 2[1], 'For I made up my mind not to make you another painful visit' (cf 12[21]). The 'pain' (more precisely 'grief,' *lupē*) apparently was caused through an offence by a fellow Christian (2[5–11] 7[11f]). The visit mentioned cannot be the first one nor the one planned in 1 Co 16[5–9], according to which Paul intended to stay longer in Corinth (perhaps throughout the winter) in order to return from here—taking with him the collection —to Jerusalem. It cannot be so, because 2 Co was written from Macedonia after he had been in Ephesus (2[12f.] 7[5f]). In other words, the visit which took place between 1 and 2 Co was not yet intended when 1 Co was written.

Besides this 'in between' visit one must also assume an 'in between' letter. In 2 Co 2[3f] Paul mentions a letter written 'out of much affliction and anguish of heart and with many tears,' and in 2[9] he adds the purpose of this letter: 'This is why I wrote, that I might test you and know whether you are obedient in everything.' This letter 'with many tears' cannot be identical with 1 Co, but must have been written after the intervening visit caused by the previous offence. Therefore Paul says in 7[12], 'So although I wrote to you, it was not on account of the one who did the wrong, nor on account of the one who suffered the wrong, but in order that your zeal for us might be revealed to you in the sight of God.' This letter apparently was carried by Titus to Corinth because his return—at first waited for (2[13f.] 7[5]) —seems to have been the actual reason for the writing of 2 Co (7[6ff]). Titus has reported the success of the 'in between' letter. The congregation has proved obedient (2[5f]) and Paul rejoices: 'At every point you have proved yourselves guiltless in the matter' (7[11])

3. Integrity.—Another and independent reason for writing 2 Co was the activity of opponents—called 'false apostles' in 11[13]—who were raising a discussion about the true apostolate, which somehow isolates chs. 10–13. This observation, made long ago, has led to the assumption that this section should be considered as a 'four chapter letter,' identical with the severe letter mentioned in 2 Co 2[4]. As early as 1870 Hausrath demonstrated convincingly that 2 Co 10–13 cannot form an original unit with 2 Co 1–10. Since then some scholars have regarded the four chapters as the letter written between 1 and 2 Co. But more than that needs to be noted. Inside chs. 1–7 we recognize 2[14]–7[4] as a coherent unit, 2[13] being well connected with 7[5]. This agreed upon, literary analysis further recognizes the inner link between 1[1]–2[13] and 7[5–16] and the character of the latter as a concluding part (letter D); consequently 2[14]–7[4] plus 10–13 represents the 'in between' letter (C). The real difficulty is in ch. 8 and 9, which cannot originally have belonged together. Although conclusive proof is lacking, we suggest identifying ch. 9 with C and ch. 8 with D (see CORINTHIANS, FIRST LETTER TO THE, **1**.

4. Outline and character of the Letter.—We present the following outline of 2 Co without taking up the results of the literary analysis.

(1) 1[1–11]. Preface and prooemium: a personal introduction.

(2) 1[12]–2[13]. Paul and his relation to the Corinthian church (explanation of his change of plans; the offence of an opponent is forgiven).

(3) 2[14]–7[4]. The apostolic office.

- (A) 2[14]–4[6]. The openness (*parrēsia*) of Paul.
  - (*a*) 2[14]–3[6]. Paul's conception of his vocation as Apostle.

 CORINTHIANS, SECOND LETTER TO

(*b*) 3^{7-18}. The vocation gives the Apostle his openness.
(*c*) 4^{1-6}. Paul fulfils his office in proclaiming the 'open statement of the truth.'
(B) 4^{7}–6^{10}. The concealment and revelation of glory (*doxa*) and life (*zōē*).
(*a*) 4^{7}–5^{10}. The concealment of life in the shape of the old aeon.
(*b*) 5^{11}–6^{10}. The revelation of life in the proclamation of the gospel.
(C) 6^{11}–7^{4}. The quest for confidence.
6^{14}–7^{1}. *parenesis*.
(4) 7^{5-16}. Titus' arrival from Corinth with good news, strengthening Paul's confidence.
(5) 8^{1}–9^{15}. The collection for Jerusalem.
(6) 10^{1}–13^{10}. The Apostle and his opponents.
(7) 13^{11-13}. Greetings.

The *character* of 2 Co is marked by those sections which are listed under C. The theme is 'the apostolic office' and 'the word of proclamation,' *i.e.* the office of the preaching ministry; the revelation is 'the fragrance (*osmē*) of the knowledge of God' (2^{14}), 'the light of the knowledge of the glory of God in the face of Christ' (4^{6}). This light (*phōtismos*) is paralleled with the creation of light at the beginning of the world (4^{6}): the proclamation sets forth 'the new creation' (5^{17}). The preaching of the word is itself an eschatological event. It reveals itself as bestowing both death and life: 'to one a fragrance from death to death, to the other a fragrance from life to life' (2^{16}). This means no less than that in the proclamation of God's Word the ultimate judgment takes place for man.

How is this possible? It is because the apostolic proclamation sets forth *the* 'salvation-event' which occurred in the death and resurrection of Christ Jesus. This crucial event is not told like a story but proclaimed as *the* event of God's reconciliation with the world, *the* event which in its very proclamation becomes effective for the hearer. And in proclaiming the reconciliation the preacher actualizes it in his call: 'be reconciled to God' (5^{20}). Just because the preacher calls upon his congregation for decision, the proclamation is an inherent part of the 'salvation occurrence' itself, is itself an eschatological event. The preaching ministry is not an additional possibility for the Church, restricted to apostles only, but is given together with the 'once for all' Christ-event when God had founded the *diakonia tēs katallagēs* (ministry of reconciliation) and given it the *logos tēs katallagēs* (word of reconciliation, 5^{18f}). This implies for Paul, as the context proves, that Christ and God are present in the proclamation. Whenever the sermon commences and wherever Christians open their hearts to the proclamation, the *hēmera sōterias* (day of salvation) is present in the *nun* (now). 'Behold, now is the acceptable time; behold, now is the day of salvation' (6^{2}).

Paul thus lays before the readers of 2 Co the decisive paradox of Christianity, namely that a historical event—Christ's death and resurrection—is at the same time an eschatological occurrence, ultimately done for the sake of mankind. This theological qualification of the Christian ministry of proclamation presents the highlight of 2 Co, unique in the Pauline correspondence (though Paul everywhere presupposes the same understanding of it by his readers; *e.g.* see Ro 10^{14-17}). The very soteriological basis of this Pauline 'sacrament of proclamation' (*sacramentum audibile*) consists in God's action, namely that He gave Christ over to death and raised Him again. Thus He gave the old *aiōn* of the *sarx* over to death and opened up the possibility of a new life to all believers who put on Christ in baptism and thus participate in His death and resurrection. And because this eschatological occurrence has already taken place, Paul can rejoice: 'Therefore, if any one is in Christ, he is a new creation; the old has passed away, behold, the new has come' (5^{17}).

Before believing in Christ men had been 'enemies' of God (Ro 5^{10}). Now a man participating in the 'salvation-occurrence' is 'reconciled,' *i.e.* he has 'peace with God,' is 'righteous.' The office of the preaching ministry can be called both a 'ministry of righteousness' (3^{9}) and a 'ministry of reconciliation' (5^{18}). Its meaning does not consist in the effort of kindling man's activity in order to accomplish a human 'reconciliation,' but it proclaims God's own initiative. 'All this has its origin in God who through Christ reconciled us to himself' (5^{18}).

The living representative of the ministry of God's reconciliation with man is the Apostle. He is an authority because he works as an 'ambassador for Christ,' represents Christ and God to his hearers (5^{20}). His calling is a qualified one: 'God making his appeal through us'; he speaks 'on behalf of Christ' (5^{20}). Therefore the Apostle must claim obedience (2^{9} 7^{15}) and exposes himself to a possible misunderstanding, that of being a tyrant (1^{24}), although he is under the same Lordship as the believers. Yet it is only as the bringer of God's Word that the Apostle is an authority; he has no external proof of his legitimacy. In his person, the Christian paradox becomes visible insofar as in his own weakness and strength the crucified and risen Lord is reflected (13^{4}). Outwardly his weakness, the *astheneia* (weakness) of death, prevails; yet under this mask the *dynamis Christou* (power of Christ), the life of the risen Lord, is working decisively and effectively (4^{7ff} 6^{9}: 'as dying and behold we live'). The apostle thus exemplifies the whole Christian existence. It is not by chance that in chs. 3–5 the subject often changes back and forth between the Apostle and the congregation—who live in paradoxes: 'as having nothing and yet possessing everything' (6^{4-10}). This eschatological gift, to exist *hōs mē* (as if not) (see 1 Co 7^{29-31}), actualizes itself in the Christian 'openness' and 'freedom.' It gives to the believer the radical openness towards the future, the constant 'renewal day by day' (4^{16}), the unique 'change into his likeness from one degree of glory to another.' And this freedom exists wherever there is the Spirit of the Lord (3^{17}).

Clarifying or rather correcting 1 Co 15, Paul takes up again *the theme of eschatology* in 2 Co 5^{1-10}. Apparently he has learned that his Corinthian opponents did not totally deny the resurrection of the dead, but spiritualized its very essence in hoping for a 'nakedness' of the soul, in other words, an eternal existence without imprisonment by *sarx* (flesh) or *sōma* (body). Gnostic ideas of an eternal *gymnotēs* (nakedness), based on an identification of *sōma* with *sēma* (tomb) marked this their heretical belief. (Note: 5^{3} should read, with D* G it Marcion Chr etc., *ekdusamenoi*, 'even in putting it off.')

5. Authenticity.—The evidence for the text of the letter is, of course, practically the same as that for 1 Co. The real proofs of authenticity are internal, and are given in the character of the letter. Only a short section, the six verses in 6^{14}–7^{1}, seems questionable. Both its vocabulary and thought are strange. The whole paragraph probably goes back to a Jewish source. If ever it was Paul himself who 'Christianized' this Jewish *parenesis* in 6^{14}–7^{1}, it fits better in the context of 1 Co (in letter B, namely before 5^{9-11}).

A brief remark is needed regarding the so-called 3 *Corinthians*, which is now included in the apocryphal Acts of Paul and was first found with Ephrem the Syrian around A.D. 370. A Latin translation goes back to the 3rd cent. The letter represents itself as an answer to one which the Corinthians had sent to Paul, and speaks about Simon and Cleobius, who tried to introduce heretical doctrines: 'They say that we must not use the prophets, and that God is not almighty, and that there will be no resurrection of the flesh, and that man was not made by God, and that Christ did not come down in the flesh, neither was born of Mary, and that the world is not of God but of angels' (M. R. James, *The Apocryphal NT*, 1924, p. 289). Interesting as this heresy and its refutation are, there is no doubt about the non-Pauline origin of the letter. The text was probably written at the end of the 2nd cent. and was later incorporated in a Syrian collection of Paul's epistles, and thus for some time was regarded as authentic by the Armenian and Syrian Churches.

6. Date.—2 Co, written from Macedonia, dates probably from the same year as 1 Co. A short interval between them seems adequate, though the time cannot be given exactly. Perhaps the fall months of the year A.D. 55 may be assumed (for other dates see article CHRONOLOGY). E. D.

CORMORANT.—Renders two words in EV. **1.** *Shālākh*, Lv 11[17], Dt 14[17]; see OWL. **2.** *Ḳāʿath*, Zeph 2[14] (AV; RV 'pelican,' RSV 'vulture'), Is 34[11] (AV; RV 'pelican,' RSV 'hawk'). See HERON, OWL, PELICAN, VULTURE.

CORN.—This term may be taken to include—(1) Barley, (2) Wheat, (3) Fitches, (4) Lentils, (5) Beans, (6) Millet, (7) Rye, wrong translation for 'spelt,' (8) Pulse—for most of which see separate articles. Rye and Oats are not cultivated in Palestine.
E. W. G. M.

CORNELIUS.—A 'devout man' (Ac 10[1]), *i.e.* a 'God-fearer' who leaned toward Judaism, and not necessarily a proselyte, whose baptism was a step forward towards admitting Gentiles into the Church. He was a Roman centurion of the Italic cohort (see BAND). The name is a common one, as thousands of Sulla's freedmen took this as a family name. An inscription discovered near Vienna shows that an Italic cohort was stationed in Syria shortly before A.D. 69, and this makes St. Luke's statement (once said to be an anachronism) quite probable. If the presence of such an officer in Caesarea was not possible during the semi-independent rule of Agrippa (A.D. 41–44), we must date the episode before that; but we cannot assert such an impossibility. A. J. M.—**F. C. G.**

CORNER, CORNER-STONE.—There are two Hebrew words translated 'corner' in the OT: (*a*) *pēʾāh*, 'corner,' or 'side' (part cut off). This is found in the following connexions: Am 3[12], the corner (or side) of a divan; Ex 25[26] *et al.*, the four corners of the table of show-bread; Lv 19[9], the corners of a field, which are to be left unreaped at harvest-time for the benefit of the poor and the *gēr* (stranger). It has been suggested that this custom is a relic of an ancient tabu or sanctity attaching to the corner, but as the word also means 'side,' and there is no supporting evidence in the OT for such an idea, the suggestion may be rejected. The same holds good about the prohibition in Lv 19[27] against shaving the temples (corners of the head) and trimming the beard. Any notion of sanctity attaches, not to the 'corner' as such, but to the hair of the head and beard. Jer 9[25] refers to the Arab custom of shaving the head. The word is used in Ezk 41–48 and in P for the sides of the Temple and the land. It is used figuratively in Nu 24[17], 'smite through the corners of Moab.'

(*b*) *pinnāh*, from the verbal root meaning 'to turn.' It is used in Ex 27[2], the horns of the brazen altar of burnt-offering are to be placed on the four 'corners' of the altar. Here again the idea of sanctity, if any, attaches, not to the corners, but to the horns which, as in Crete and elsewhere, are connected with the symbol of the bull. It is used in Job 1[19] for the four corners of the house. It is also frequently used figuratively for the chiefs of the people, the heads of tribes, as the corner-stone binds the sides of the wall together. In Zec 10[4] the corner (stone) and the tent-peg, both symbols of that which holds the body politic firm, are said to come from Y″.

There is an important use of the corner-stone with a figurative, and possibly Messianic, sense in Ps 118[22] and Is 28[16], both of which passages are quoted in the NT with reference to Christ (cf Mt 21[42||], Ac 4[11], 1 P 2[4f]). The question has been raised whether the corner-stone of Scripture is a foundation-stone, or the stone which crowns the building. The answer would seem to be that both uses are found in both OT and NT. The passage in Is 28 is almost certainly a reference to a foundation-stone, while the Psalm quite certainly refers to a stone crowning the building. Similarly in the NT, Christ is referred to both as the foundation on which the Church is built, and the coping stone which crowns the building.
S. H. He.

CORNER GATE.—See JERUSALEM, GATES OF.

CORNET.—See MUSIC AND MUSICAL INSTRUMENTS.

CORRUPTION.—The Greek term underlying this word is translated in the RSV by a variety of English expressions such as 'decay,' 'corruption,' 'the perishable.' When all these are gathered together, four general meanings emerge in the NT. **1.** Sometimes corruption refers simply to dissolution in the world of nature (Col 2[22], 2 P 2[12a]) including the physical dissolution of man, *i.e.* death and the decay which follows upon death (Ac 2[27, 31] 13[34–37]). The contrast drawn in the latter passages between corruption and the resurrection of Christ does not yet yield the level of meaning to be discussed next. **2.** The adjective related to this noun may indicate what is mortal in contrast to what is immortal, namely, God (Ro 1[23]). In 1 Co 15[43–54] a similar contrast, which is here stated in terms of the antagonism between the man of dust (Adam) and the spiritual man (Christ), brings us close to a dualism between matter and spirit. In the last analysis, however, it appears that for Paul the weakness of man's flesh and death itself are a result of sin (1 Co 15[55–58], cf Ro 8[21]). So also the 'decay' to which the whole universe is subject was imposed upon it by God and is not the result of a natural antagonism between matter and spirit (Ro 8[21], cf Gn 3[17]). **3.** In Gal 6[8] the same word has an eschatological significance and refers to the destruction that will come upon those who are not fit for eternal life. This is also the meaning in 2 P 2[12b]. **4.** Corruption may refer to moral depravity (2 P 1[4] 2[19]). The verb related to this noun is also used in this sense (*e.g.* 1 Co 15[33], 2 Co 11[3], Eph 4[22]). W. R. S.

COS.—An island off the coast of Caria, SW. of Asia Minor, famous for its fertility and beauty. It was a Dorian colony, and a great seat of the worship of Aesculapius and of the study of medicine. Its position made it also an important place for trade, as it lay on the cross lines of traffic between Greece, Asia Minor, Syria, and Egypt. It is uncertain whether Cos, which had been a faithful ally of the Romans, was incorporated in the province of Asia in 139 B.C. (see CARIA), but it certainly was a part of it in the time of Augustus. Its trade connexion made it one of the Jewish centres of the Aegean. The Jews there were favoured by the Romans in 139–138 B.C. (1 Mac 15[23]). It was a place on the route of the Jewish pilgrims to Jerusalem (cf Ac 21[1]). Herod the Great was a benefactor of the people of Cos.
A. So.

COSAM.—An ancestor of Jesus (Lk 3[28]).

COSMOGONY.—See CREATION.

COSSAEANS.—A name adapted from the Greek form of Bab. *Kaššu*, a semi-barbarous people inhabiting the mountain region between Elam and Media proper. They answer to Cush (q.v.) in Gn 10[8] (and 2[13]? AV 'Ethiopia') as distinguished from the African Cush. They were a powerful people between the 18th and the 12th cent. B.C., during which time Babylonia was ruled by a Cossaean dynasty. J. F. McC.

COTTON is the better translation (so RVm, RSV) of *karpas*, which in AV and RV is translated 'green,' Est 1[6]. It was either muslin or calico. A different word is rendered 'cotton' in RVm and RSV in Is 19[9] (AV 'networks'; RV 'cloth'). This is elsewhere rendered by RSV 'linen' and 'flax.'

COUCH.—See HOUSE, **8**. The verb 'to couch' occurs in Dt 33[13] 'the deep that couches beneath.' The word means simply to *lie down*, but it is used almost exclusively of animals, as is the Hebrew word also. The subterranean deep, says Driver, is perhaps pictured as a gigantic monster.

COULTER.—Only 1 S 13[20f] (AV, RV; RSV 'mattock') for the word elsewhere rendered 'plowshare,' and so it should be here, as the Hebrew plough, like its Syrian representative to-day, had no coulter. See AGRICULTURE, 1.

COUNCIL.—See SANHEDRIN. For the Council of Ac 15, Gal 2, see PAUL, GALATIANS [EPISTLE TO], 3.

COUNSELLOR.—This is the spelling in modern editions of the AV. In the edition of 1611 it is 'counseller,' except in Ezr 8[25], Pr 12[20] 15[22], where the spelling is 'counsellour.' The word is used mostly of a king's counsellor, or more generally of one who gives counsel (*bouleutēs*). But in Dn 3[2f] it means a justice; and in Mk 15[43], Lk 23[50], it is used of Joseph of Arimathaea as a member of the Sanhedrin (RSV 'member of the council). In Dn 3[24, 27] 4[36] 6[7] the peculiar word rendered 'counsellor' in AV is hesitatingly translated by Driver 'minister'; RV, RSV retain 'counsellor.' In Jn 14[16, 26] 15[26] 16[7] RSV translates *Paraklētos* by 'Counsellor,' a meaning supported by the papyri.

COUNSELLOR (Gr. *paraklētos*).—The word occurs only in the writings of John: four times in his Gospel (14[16, 26] 15[26] 16[7]) of the Holy Spirit and once in his Epistle (2[1]) of Jesus. It is unfortunate that our English Versions have rendered it in the former 'Comforter' (RVm 'or *Advocate*, or *Helper*, Gr. *Paraclete*') and in the latter 'Advocate' (RVm 'or *Comforter*, or *Helper*, Gr. *Paraclete*'). The RSV reads 'Counsellor' except in 1 Jn 2[1] where 'Advocate' is retained.

'Comforter,' though a true designation of the Holy Spirit, is an impossible rendering. The Greek verb *parakalein* means either 'comfort' (Mt 5[4], 2 Cor 1[4] 7[6]) or 'call to one's side' (Ac 28[20]). *Paraklētos* is a passive form and thus denotes if the former meaning is retained 'one comforted'; the latter meaning, 'one called to stand beside', accords both with grammatical requirements and with the meaning of Paraclete in the Gospel according to John. In 1st cent. Greek, *Paraklētos* was a legal term used mainly of advocate, defender, or intercessor. True to its basic meaning one 'called out to stand beside, defend, advise or intercede,' it was used of legal counsel and witnesses alike. RSV 'Counsellor' embraces this variety of meanings and describes one who in adversity stands by one's side—truly a Comforter (especially in the Latin sense of *Confortator*, 'Strengthener'). It should be noted that 'comfortless' AV Jn 14[18] is a mistranslation (RV and RSV read 'desolate'—AV and RV margins literally 'orphans'). Singularly enough, the Greek-speaking Fathers mostly took the word in the impossible sense of 'Comforter,' influenced perhaps by the false analogy of *Menahem* (*Consolator*), a Jewish name for Messiah; cf Cyril of Jerusalem, *Cat.*, Or. xvi. 20: 'He is called *Paraklētos* because he comforts (*parakalei*) and consoles and helps our infirmity.'

During His earthly ministry Jesus had been God's Counsellor with men, pleading God's cause with them and seeking to win them for Him. He was going away and on the night in which He was betrayed He assured the Eleven that they would not be left without a Counsellor on the earth. 'I will pray the Father and He will give you another Counsellor, to be with you for ever, even the Spirit of truth.' Not received because unrecognized by the unspiritual world, the Counsellor would be recognized and welcomed by believers (Jn 14[15f. 25f]). He would testify to them about Jesus, the unseen Lord, and they would repeat His testimony to the world (15[26f]). He would make their testimony effective: 'when he comes he will convince the world regarding sin, righteousness, and judgment' (16[8-11]).

Jesus told the Eleven that it was 'to their advantage' that He should go away, since His departure was the condition of the advent of the Counsellor (16[7]); 1 Jn 2[1] furnishes a profound commentary on this declaration. Jesus in the days of His flesh was God's Counsellor on earth, pleading with men for God. The Holy Spirit had taken His place and performs this office. But Jesus is still a Counsellor. For He is the heavenly Advocate of sinners, pleading their cause with God and, in the language of St. Paul (Ro 8[34]), 'making intercession for them.'

There are three dispensations in the history of redemption, each richer and fuller than the last: (1) The OT dispensation under which men knew only God in high heaven; (2) that of the Incarnation under which the Father came near to men in Jesus Christ and by His gracious advocacy appealed to their hearts; (3) that of the Holy Spirit under which the Holy Spirit is the Father's Counsellor here and Jesus 'our advocate above, our friend before the throne of love.' See Bauer's *Lexicon*, s.v. *paraklētos*, with bibliography. D. S.—**S. I. E.**

COUNTERVAIL.—To countervail (Est 7[4], Sir 6[15] AV) is to make up for, give an equivalent, as in More's *Utopia*: 'All the goodes in the worlde are not liable to countervayle man's life.'

COURAGE.—Courage in the OT is the strength, directness and determination of the soul in face of obstacles and dangers. These might weaken the soul and its purpose, but God strengthens His servants and encourages them. The prime example is Joshua as he is deputed to lead the entry into Canaan (Dt 31[7], Jos 1[6]). It is not a virtue of the autonomous man but of the man properly strengthened by Yahweh. Even the stout-hearted man will lose his courage if Yahweh is acting against him (Am 2[16]). Courage is needed not only in military operations but in supporting hope in times of desolation (*e.g.* Is 35[3-4]) and in obeying the law of God (Jos 1[7]). In the NT the same lines are followed. The despairing are told to be of good courage (Mt 9[2] etc.); the servants of the Lord must be firm and courageous (1 Co 16[13]). Boldness in speaking the truth is based on confidence in God (2 Co 10[1-2] etc.). Courage as a general virtue hardly appears, for it is understood to go with obedience to Christ and not (as in much Greek thought) to be one of the main aspects of the autonomous ethical life. J. Ba.

COURIER.—See POST.

COURSE.—See PRIESTS AND LEVITES, 3 (*a*).

COURT.—See HOUSE, 2; JUSTICE; TABERNACLE; TEMPLE.

COUSIN.—Elizabeth is called Mary's 'cousin' in Lk 1[36], and the relationship is often understood in the modern sense of that word. But 'cousin' in the English of 1611 meant no more than kinsman or kinswoman. The relationship between Mary and Elizabeth is not known. RSV uses 'kinswoman' here. In other passages, both OT and NT, 'cousin' is used where the modern sense is clearly intended (*e.g.* Col 4[10], *anepsios*).

COUTHA, 1 Es 5[32] (AV).—See CUTHA.

COVENANT.—1. This very important term is a translation of the Hebrew word *b^erîth*. The etymology of the latter is much disputed, but is most probably to be connected with the Akkadian root of *birîtum*, 'space between,' in prepositional phrases 'between,' with reference to the rite of dividing an animal as in Gn 15[10, 17]. The semantic development has also been traced through Akkadian *berîtu*, 'fetter,' hence 'binding agreement,' and from Hebrew *bārāh*, 'eat.'

A *b^erîth* is an agreement between two parties in which they pledge themselves in loyalty to one another. It differs from the modern concept of contract in that there is not only an obligation to carry out some specific commitment externally, but a pledge of loyalty or community of soul. This spiritual content of a covenant, if we can so call it, the inward will which goes beyond outward conformity, is *ḥesedh* (RSV usually 'steadfast love'). Thus God in His covenant is 'the faithful God who keeps the covenant and the loyalty to those who love him' (Dt 7[9]).

Covenants between man and man are numerous in the OT. A few typical cases may be noted. In Gn 31[43-54] the covenant between Laban and Jacob is an ending of past differences, and a restoration therefore of harmony between them (the word *shālôm*, peace or harmony, is often used of covenants, though in fact not in this case);

it is also a kind of boundary treaty at the Gileadite frontier; and it includes or implies good treatment for Laban's daughters, for whose welfare the covenant is a witness, with an oath in which the covenant conditions are placed under God's vindication. Another notable covenant is between David and Jonathan, 1 S 18^{1-4} $20^{12-16, 42}$. It is an expression of the community of the soul in love. Here the covenant relation conflicts with Jonathan's natural solidarity with his father; convinced that the Lord is with David, he invokes the loyalty of the covenant to ensure the survival of his name and house in the time of David's success. In Jos 9^{15} a covenant entered into by the leaders is binding on the whole people, even though the leaders were deceived in agreeing to it. Political covenants also abound; in 1 S 11^{1-3} the covenant or treaty amounts to terms of surrender; in 1 K 5^{12} it expresses friendly relations with a commercial agreement; in Ezk 17^{13f} it is an allegiance of submission to Nebuchadrezzar. Such covenants include an element of promise or oath, have conditions the non-fulfilment of which constitute the breaking or annulment of the covenant, and inaugurate an intended period of *shālôm* or harmonious relations. The covenant of 2 K 11^{4} is an agreement among conspirators, but in 11^{17} it is a restoration and regulation of right relations between God, king, and people. Marriage too is a covenant, Mal 2^{14}.

The parties to a covenant may be equal but perhaps more commonly are not, or are unequal in their interest in some object specially concerned in the covenant. Solomon and Hiram are roughly equals. Jonathan is superior to David in being the king's son, but it is he who is specially drawn to David, and David becomes the senior partner in the relation because Jonathan believes in David's future success and is anxious to safeguard his descendants in the days to come. Laban is perhaps a greater than Jacob, but it is his daughters whom he is anxious to protect.

Covenants between men are not a matter of word only, nor are they guaranteed by a written agreement usually, but they have a material expression. Jonathan gave David his armour and clothes (1 S 18^{4}); Jacob built a cairn, offered sacrifice and ate a common meal with his kin (Gn 31^{43-54}). The common eating of salt led to the expression 'a covenant of salt' (Nu 18^{19} etc.). The verb for making a covenant is *kārath* 'to cut,' and goes back probably to the ritual of dividing an animal.

2. God's covenant with Israel.—The relation of Yahweh to Israel was probably from an early date understood as a covenant, and this tradition almost certainly goes back before the entry into Canaan and represents Israel's understanding of her own origins as a people. The centrality of the covenant belongs in all probability, as the Exodus tradition holds, to the formative events of Sinai and the work of Moses. But the possibility of God, normally present in the *berîth* as guarantor between man to man, also relating Himself in the *berîth* to men who willed to adhere to Him, may well be pre-Mosaic. A recent attempt to invoke the similarities of covenant presentations to the Hittite treaties of sovereignty (Mendenhall, *BA*, Sept. 1954) seems to the writer only to pick out points which might belong to any treaty supported by sacral sanctions, and not to explain more for the covenant in Israel than at most the form of certain more developed statements of it. In any case it seems likely that the tradition of a covenant with Abraham is old tradition and not merely a secondary extension back of the Mosaic covenant. A covenant was indigenous to the traditions both of the Mosaic period and of 'the fathers,' and neither completely overwhelmed the other.

In the old Abraham tradition the covenant is made by the division of animals (Gn 15); its content is mainly promise of the later possession of the land. The old Mosaic story (Ex 24) begins with the recital of the words spoken by God to Moses; when these are accepted by the people as obligation, we have sacrifice and the ritual of the blood of the covenant, and in v.^{11} a sacrificial meal in the presence of God. In the Shechem covenant of Jos 24 Joshua tells the story of God's acts for Israel and challenges the people to choose whether He should be their God; on their declaration He makes the covenant. The content of the covenant of God with the people was thus roughly 'I will be your God and you will be my people,' as Jer 31^{33} reiterates for the 'new covenant.' The covenant binds God and Israel in loyalty together. In entering this the initiative with God is infinitely greater, and it is not a two-sided contract; yet it leaves and demands freedom of choice on Israel's side. When the time comes for the covenant to be solemnly entered, Israel must choose to enter.

The understanding of the covenant idea, and the terminology connected with it, undergo certain interesting changes during the OT period. The old term 'to cut a covenant' appears in the early story of Gn 15^{18}. In Deuteronomy and the Deuteronomic historical literature this is still used, but more emphasis is laid on the covenant as *law*, and we hear of God 'telling' or 'commanding' the covenant (Dt 4^{13}). The tables of the law are the covenant, 1 K 8^{21}, and are contained by the Ark, whose name 'Ark of the covenant' is now understood in this way. Meanwhile it is noticeable that the classical prophets before Jeremiah use the covenant conception very little (cases occur Hos 6^{7} 8^{1}). This is probably not because it meant nothing to them, but because they emphasize the covenant virtues, the loyalty and faithfulness which are the interior of the covenant relationship. Jeremiah shows a renewed interest in the old covenant (11^{1-13}), but with it an understanding that it is irretrievably broken; and thus he envisages the new covenant (33^{31ff}) where the outward law is written inwardly and enjoys the loyalty of will the lack of which destroyed the old covenant.

The priestly narrative in the Pentateuch uses 'covenant' only of covenants with God, not with man, and the verb is now 'set up' or 'give,' emphasizing the Divine initiative (Gn 9^{9-17} 17^{1-21}) and the element of promise. A covenant is made with Noah, and therefore with all living men, since all men after the Flood were descended from him; it promises the continuance of the world, gives certain laws, and its sign is the rainbow which reminds God of His covenant. The great covenant, however, is that with Abraham, and its sign is the circumcision; it is not associated with law. The sabbath too, in the Mosaic period, is a 'perpetual covenant' or sign (Ex 31^{16f}).

Among the later prophets Ezekiel follows lines similar to those of Jeremiah (Ezk 34^{25} 37^{26}), and the covenant emphasis is moved to the future; so also Deutero-Isaiah where, however, the most important innovation is the mission of the servant of the Lord as a 'covenant to the people' (so RSV), a phrase which in its context clearly indicates the extension of covenant to the other nations (42^{6} 49^{8}).

In the reforming groups of late Judaism the Jeremiah passage about the new covenant had great influence, and the *Zadokite Documents*, for instance, can speak of the 'new covenant in the land of Damascus' (vi. 19 etc.); the *Habakkuk Commentary* shows the same expression, and the *Manual of Discipline* shows how this was no mere metaphor for the Qumrân sect, who had the most solemn covenant ceremonies, and who understood that loyalty, love, and truth were the inward content of a covenant in the last days, as the prophets had spoken.

The LXX translated covenant with *diathēkē*, which in Hellenistic Greek usage meant 'will or testament,' and which has this sense in He 9^{16f}, Gal 3^{15}, both of which, however, are fitted into arguments where the sense 'covenant' is proper. For the rest, the NT word 'covenant' is heavily coloured and determined by OT usage. Like the Qumrân community, the early Church saw itself as the community of the new covenant (2 Co 3^{6}, He 8^{13} 9^{15}). The OT covenants are remembered as a privilege of Israel (Ro 9^{4}) and it is possible to argue from the priority of covenant to law in the OT (Gal 3^{15-18}). NT usage, as expressed in the word *diathēkē*, and avoiding, in the steps of the LXX, *synthēkē* which is more a double-sided pact, seems to stand with that side of OT usage which emphasizes the sole action of God in the covenant as His dispostion or promise. On the other hand, the tradition of the ceremonies of initiation into the covenant, which involved the hearing of God's claims and the acceptance of Him by the people, was in the early Church as in the Qumrân community very much alive and was active especially in the initiatory ceremony of baptism. On the other hand the wine at the Last Supper is called ' my blood of the covenant ' (Mk 14^{24}) or ' the new covenant in my blood ' (1 Co 11^{25}). Into the intricate problems of this passage we cannot go. But it is clear that we have the understanding of the Supper as a covenant meal with OT reminiscences (especially Ex 24), and that the blood, which is an interpretation of Christ's death as sacrificial and expiatory, is here taking up the covenant blood of the same chapter. The repetition of the Eucharist may be related to the renewal of covenant in the OT (*e.g.* Dt 29^{1}).

With the understanding of the new covenant as established in Christ and His church comes an assertion of the finality of this covenant and its superiority to the temporary and imperfect ' first covenant ' (He 9^{1}). None the less the first covenant, even in the argument of Hebrews, continues to provide the forms and categories for the understanding of the new (He 9^{18ff}). Meanwhile this old covenant, in its written embodiment in the OT, is still read by Israel, but they have a veil which obstructs its understanding (2 Co 3^{14}). In Ro 11^{27} a reference to the covenant from Isaiah is used as a promise of the eventual salvation of Israel. J. Ba.

COVENANT, BOOK OF THE.—The oldest Hebrew laws which have come down to us are to be found in the code contained in Ex 20^{22}–23^{19}. It is composed of material derived from earlier codes and, with the parenetic peroration (23^{20-33}) now loosely attached to it, is called the Book of the Covenant in 24^{7}, the representation being that it had just been delivered to Moses (cf 20^{21f}) and that it laid down the conditions upon which Yahweh was making the covenant with Israel. There can be little doubt, however, that the author of 24^{3-8} in its original form represented the Decalogue (20^{2-17}) as the basis of the covenant. If so, then the Book of the Covenant was placed in its present position at a relatively late stage in the growth of the Pentateuch. Whether at an earlier stage it had been included in one of its component documents, or whether, having taken form independently, it was inserted here by a redactor, it is impossible to say. Some scholars have thought that it once came immediately before the account of the death of Moses and that it was moved from that position to make room for the more elaborate code of Deuteronomy.

1. Contents.—The code is composed of three different kinds of material :—(1) *mishpāṭîm* (rendered ' ordinances ' in 21^{1} 24^{3}). In early Semitic life justice was administered according to a series of *Tôrôth*, or judicial and priestly decisions, originally transmitted orally but gradually written down for more exact use as precedents, and to serve as a handbook for those who had to administer the law. The *mishpāṭîm* are decisions of this kind. Each one consists of a conditional sentence introduced by ' when ' (=in case that), which describes the possible situation in general terms ; this is usually followed by one or more sentences introduced by ' if ' or ' and/but if,' dealing with special circumstances ; *e.g.* 21^{28f} ' when an ox gores a man or a woman to death the ox shall be stoned . . . but the owner of the ox shall be clear. But if the ox has been accustomed to gore in time past . . . its owner shall be put to death.'

There are fifteen laws in the code formulated in this way (21^{2} should begin ' when a man buys,' cf ' his master ' in vv.$^{4, 6}$; and in $22^{1, 7, 10}$ the Hebrew word rendered ' if ' is that rendered ' when ' elsewhere in these laws) : $21^{2-6, 7-11, 18f, 20f, 22-24, 26f, 28-32, 33-36}$ $22^{1-4, 5, 6, 7f, 10-13, 14f, 16f}$. They deal with manumission of Hebrew slaves, the sale of a daughter into slavery, murder and homicide, bodily injury to men and women, injuries to animals, theft, damage to another's crops, property held in trust or on loan, seduction of an unbetrothed virgin. The only reference to Yahweh in these laws is in 22^{11}, where it is probably a substitution for an original ' God ' (cf 21^{6} 22^{8f}) ; nor is there anything specifically Israelite in their requirements. For this reason, and because the laws in the code of Hammurabi and the Assyrian and Hittite laws are cast in this precedent form, it has been suggested that they were derived ultimately from a Canaanite code which had been taken over by Israel—the word ' Hebrew ' in 21^{2} being an adaptation. Additional laws in this form are found in Deuteronomy, possibly going back to the same ancient code.

(2) Akin to the precedent laws in form are five laws beginning with ' whoever ' (rendering the Hebrew participle) and ending with the formula ' shall be put to death ' (*môth yûmath*) : 21^{12} against murder (expanded in vv.^{13f} in the style of the precedent laws), v.^{15} violence against one's parents, v.^{16} abduction, v.^{17} cursing one's parents, 22^{19} bestiality ; 22^{20}, forbidding the worship of other gods than Yahweh, begins with ' whoever ' but has a different conclusion—which may of course be the result of redactional alteration. The concluding formula ' shall be put to death ' is used in eleven laws in Leviticus : $20^{2a, 9, 10, 11, 12a, 13, 15, 16, 27}$ 24^{16} (cf Ex 22^{19}) ^{17} (cf 24^{21b}, Ex 21^{12}), against the worship of Molech, cursing one's parents, adultery, incest, sodomy, necromancy, blasphemy, murder. Of these only that against blasphemy (24^{16}) has the participial introduction, which is found again, together with the conclusion, in the law against Sabbath-breaking in Ex 31^{15b}. Nevertheless the use of the concluding formula may indicate that these laws have been derived from an earlier code. The formula *môth yûmath* is early, being found in Gn 26^{11} in a story which comes from the 11th cent. This lends weight to the possibility that at least the nucleus of this code is early—that is the laws against practices which appear to have been characteristic of Canaanite religion : bestiality, adultery, incest, sodomy, and necromancy. These laws may indeed have been decreed in the early days of the settlement, and reflect the revulsion with which desert Yahwism regarded the excesses of the fertility cults. The laws against murder, violence to one's parents, abduction, cursing one's parents (Ex 21^{12-17}) and blasphemy (Lv 24^{16}) may come from the same period, but those against the worship of Molech and Sabbath-breaking are more likely to have been later. Upon what principle the compiler of the Book of the Covenant made his selection from this code (supposing it existed) it is now impossible to determine ; we cannot indeed be sure that the covenant code has come down to us intact.

(3) *d^ebhārîm* (rendered ' words ' in Ex 24^{3}) or commands, in form akin to the commands of the Decalogue, being introduced by ' you shall ' or ' you shall not.' These fall into two groups, those which regulate relations between man and man and those which regulate man's relation to God. To the former group belong $22^{21-24, 25-27}$ $23^{1-3, 4f, 6-8, 9, 10}$, demanding fair treatment and kindness for the stranger, the widow, the orphan, the poor, justice in the courts, and neighbourliness towards an enemy in difficulties. Characteristic of much of this material is its hortatory tone ($22^{23f, 27}$ $23^{7f, 9}$), suggesting that in their present form at any rate these laws come from the prophetic period.

Most of the commands regulating men's relation to God, are found again, though sometimes expanded, in the so-called ritual Decalogue, Ex 34^{14-26} : 22^{29b-30} (=$34^{19-20b\alpha}$), the law of firstlings ; 23^{12} (=34^{21}), the Sabbath ; 23^{13} (=34^{14}), only Yahweh to be worshipped ; $23^{14, 17}$ (=34^{23f}), the three annual festivals ; 23^{15a} (=34^{18}), unleavened bread ; 23^{15b} (=$34^{20b\beta}$), none shall appear before Yahweh empty-handed ; 23^{16} (=34^{22}), feasts of harvest and ingathering ; 23^{18} (=34^{25}), of sacrifice ; 23^{19a} (=34^{26a}), first fruits ; 23^{19b} (=34^{26b}), a kid not to be boiled in its mother's milk. This material undoubtedly has a Canaanite foundation but it has been carefully adapted to Yahwism. There is no agreement among scholars as to whether these commands, derived from a common source, were placed here independently of Ex 34, or whether they were taken from Ex 34 and appended here by a redactor who wished to include them explicitly within the terms of the covenant.

The remaining religious commands are 20^{24-26} dealing with the construction of an altar; 22^{18} forbidding sorcery; 22^{28} against reviling God or the ruler; the first part of this is found in a slightly different form in Lv 24^{15} (cf 24^{16}); the second part has usually been regarded as late, but if the word rendered 'ruler' (*nāśî*) was, as some scholars have maintained, the title of certain officials in the pre-monarchical federation of the Israelite tribes, it may be early. 22^{29a}, probably (the Hebrew is very terse) commanding the offering of first fruits; 22^{31}, animals found torn in the field are not to be eaten.

The fact that the peroration (23^{20-33}) nowhere states that obedience to the laws just promulgated is a condition of the angel's presence strongly suggests that it was at one time independent of the code. Some scholars have thought that in its original form it was Moses' farewell charge, delivered just before his death, conveying Yahweh's promise that the guidance and counsel which He had provided for His people through Moses would, in the future, be otherwise mediated.

2. Date.—As to the date of the code of the Covenant there is no evidence save what the document itself affords us. Basically it reflects an agricultural society; the law of blood-revenge is just beginning to be modified (21^{24f}); a woman is still the property of her father (21^{22} 22^{16f}); sacrifice is emerging from its primitive domestic character (20^{24} 23^{18}); and the only possible reference to anything approaching to a State is in 22^{28}. Allowing for some late additions (*e.g.* 22^{23-26}) the code would seem to date from the early days of Israel's settlement in Palestine. R. B. T.—**C. A. Si.**

COVERT.—This word is used in AV in three senses. **1.**=a covered place; so 2 K 16^{13} (RV, RSV 'covered way'). **2.**=a shelter; so Is 4^{6} (so RV; RSV 'shelter'), 1 Mac 9^{38} (so RV; RSV 'cover'). **3.**=an animal's lair; so Jer 25^{38} (so RV and RSV). RV has 'covert' where AV has 'den' in Job 37^{8} (RSV 'lair'), Ps 10^{9} (RSV 'covert'). See also Den.

COVETOUSNESS.—Normally the translation of Hebrew *ḥ-m-d* (desire) and Greek *epithumeō* (set the heart upon), the word means 'to desire earnestly in order to appropriate to oneself.' In AV 'covet' is capable of a good sense (1 Co 12^{31} 14^{39}) but RV and RSV use it only in the now more normal bad sense. To desire intensely to possess something is not wrong, if the object is in itself good, and if to possess it does not wrongly deprive some other person. The sin which is forbidden in the Ten Commandments is that of selfish greed, and it is significant that that early formulation of ethical instruction singles out this one inner motivation for condemnation. The other commandments prohibit outward acts; the tenth prohibits a state of mind which unchecked gives rise to a whole way of wrong living (Ezk 33^{31}). Nor is this necessarily a case of a later addition to the code, for the disruption and injustice wrought by greed are plain to see in the most primitive communities (cf 2 S 12^{1f}). It is, moreover, a very common fault (Jer 6^{13}). Jesus warned His followers particularly of the dangers of covetousness (Lk 12^{15}, Mk 4^{19}) and Paul saw the whole Mosaic Law, the means whereby man's sinful nature is made apparent to him, as typified by the Tenth Commandment (Ro 7^{7}). Biblical teaching emphasises three points: (*a*) Only as men learn to discipline their desires can society function justly and happily; otherwise oppression and injustice are inevitable (Mic 2^{2}). (*b*) It is harmful to the individual also, since it dominates him (Pr 21^{26}, Hab 2^{5b}) and finally destroys him (Pr 1^{19}, Heb. *b-ṣ-ʿ*, RSV 'gain by violence'; Ja 1^{14f}). (*c*) Selfish desire or covetousness is a general sin in that it often breeds wrong sexual desires or lust (Mt 5^{28}), and also leads to idolatry, *i.e.* setting on material objects or human goals the values that should be reserved for God alone (Eph 5^{5}). Hence covetousness, sexual immorality and idolatry are frequently linked together (1 Co 6^{9-11}, Eph 5^{3}). The opposite to covetousness is to love one's neighbour as oneself (Ro 13^{8-10}), to accept gratefully what God has given to enjoy (Mt 6^{33}, Phn 4^{11-13}, He 13^{5}), to desire earnestly the higher gifts of the Spirit (1 Co 12^{31}), and to set the mind upon the things that are above (Col 3^{1}). S. B. F.

COZ, 1 Ch 4^{8} (AV).—See Koz, **1.**

COZBI.—The Midianitess slain by Phinehas, Nu $25^{15, 18}$.

COZEBA.—Place mentioned 1 Ch 4^{22} (AV **Chozeba**). Possibly=**Achzib, 2**; alternatively identified with *Kh. ed-Dibb*, NW. of Hebron.

CRACKNELS.—1 K 14^{3} (AV, RV); RSV has 'cakes'; see Bread.

CRAFT, in the sense of 'trade,' survives in RV only in Rev 18^{22}, and in RSV in Ex 31^{5} 35^{33} (where AV and RV have 'workmanship' or 'work'), Rev 18^{22} 'no craftsman of whatever craft.' In Ac 18^{3} $19^{25, 27}$ 'trade' or 'business' has been substituted for AV 'craft.' 'Craftsman' and 'craftsmen,' however, are retained. See list under Arts and Crafts. In Is 2^{16} RSV has 'craft' in the sense of 'ships' where RV has 'imagery' (AV 'pictures').

CRANE.—In Is 38^{14} and Jer 8^{7} *sûs* or *sîs* is rendered in AV 'crane,' RV and RSV correctly 'swallow' (q.v.). In the same passages *ʿāghûr* is rendered in AV 'swallow,' RV and RSV 'crane.' The crane (*Grus communis*) is the largest bird which visits W. Palestine; its length is four feet. They arrive in large flocks in the winter (Jer 8^{7}). Its trumpeting note is strangely described (in Is 38^{14} AV, RV; RSV 'clamour') as 'chattering,' and this makes the translation somewhat doubtful.

CRATES.—A deputy left in charge of the citadel at Jerusalem (Acra) when the regular governor, Sostratus, was summoned to Antioch by Antiochus Epiphanes, in consequence of a dispute with the high priest Menelaus (2 Mac 4^{29}). Crates was 'commander of the Cyprian troops': probably he was sent to Cyprus shortly afterwards, when, in 168 B.C., Antiochus obtained possession of the island.

CREATION—a word of Latin origin commonly applied to the beginnings of the universe and all that is in it. The relevant Hebrew verb—the abstract noun does not occur—is of indefinite meaning but devoid of evidence that it implies calling into being from nothingness. The earliest certain expression of this idea is in 2 Mac 7^{28}, but the somewhat later mention in He 11^{3} is more familiar. The great accounts of creation are those in Gn 1 and 2–3, but there are several others of more or less extent and completeness. It is apparent that Ps 104 and Job 38 treat the theme; Ps 74^{12-17} and Job 26^{10-13} are also cosmological allusions; then we recognize there are many others, some quite brief, though considerable importance must be assigned to Hab 3^{1-15}. It will be apparent on study that through this total there is considerable diversity from the Genesis narratives; also the theme of the primordial combat comes to light, though completely lacking from Gn 1–3. To it there are far more references (*e.g.* Job 9^{13}) than can profitably be listed here. The classic presentation of this phase of ancient thinking is the story of Marduk's fight with Tiamat in the Babylonian so-called *Epic of Creation* (Pritchard, *ANET*, 60 ff). More recently a group of Canaanite documents that deal with a comparable theme were discovered at Râs Shamra on the northerly coast of Lebanon (Pritchard, *op. cit.*, 129 ff). It becomes apparent that both sources are related to antitheses such as are prominent in Zoroastrian alleged dualism: light and darkness, good and bad, true and false, etc. Early speculation was evidently much impressed with the existence of opposites, which are so far-reaching that man's early adventures into understanding the mystery of the world were led to make it basic and to conclude that the principle of opposites was creative.

Whether this had its origin in the creative reality of the male-female principle, of which primitive man was keenly aware, we do not know. But certainly some mythologies make the inception of creation an act of generation. Further it is notable that most of these ideas were also components of the myth of the dying and rising god ; *i.e.* they were integral to the fertility cultus. This entails two other facts that are of the greatest importance for our understanding. All this thinking was not primarily speculative at all, but practical and ritualistic : practical in that it aimed at serving human need, specifically man's welfare and supply ; and ritualistic in the means employed to this end ; through certain liturgies, notably the re-enactment of the episodes of the myth, the triumph of the god in his creative and bountiful roles was renewed. The other fact here calling for emphasis is then implied, that creation was not some far off, primeval event accomplished once for all ; it was annually renewed in a liturgical presentation shared in variously by all the people under a sense of its profound reality. Our logic-obsessed minds will doubtless quibble that ancient man must surely have realized that the earth continued ; it was not renewed each year, but must have had a single beginning in some sort of process. But it is revealing to note the seeming inconsistency—really the full consistency with ancient thought—of Gn 2 ; for it starts even less than ch. 1 with a *creatio ex nihilo*, rather with a waste and desert earth on which the drama of creation was enacted. The latter, not the origin of the desert expanse, was the centre of social, hence religious, interest.

How far these ideas entered Hebrew religious thought and practice is disputed. But the declared character of Hab 3 as a psalm, and the fact that certain of the poems in the Psalter are cosmogonic, still more the recurrence of the cultic themes just now referred to throughout much of the Psalter, is cogent evidence that for Israel, as for its neighbours and contemporaries, creation was a repetitive experience in public worship, and that the stories in Genesis as well as the relevant psalms were used in some way as liturgies.

This is a matter of far-reaching significance. The victory of God was primeval and annual ; it was written deep in the nature of things, but also it was re-enacted for each year as the time came around. What an enhancement and assurance of faith it was to know and be reminded through liturgical participation that God is eternally triumphant ! Whatever foe might arise, whether Pharaoh, Sennacherib, or Antiochus Epiphanes —or, shall one add, Adolf Hitler?—his defeat was already accomplished, and God and his people were for ever victorious. The discerning reader can sense this in Hab 3, fitting as it does with the rest of the little book to make of it a brief classic of religious faith. Relevant as all this is for us as well, another and quite different merit is its deliverance of us from the futile undertaking to defend the scientific accuracy of Gn 1–3. The stories never were science at all except that the writers made use of the scientific ideas of their time—in reality the religious ideas—but their prime concern, as it should be with us in interpreting their work, was with religious faith. It is a distortion of their original and continuing function to use the narratives as scientific sources or as antithetic to the findings of modern science. Happily the sincere believer in Biblical revelation and inspiration is not required to insult his intelligence with an effort to assent to propositions which he knows to be inherently absurd.

Thus it is we gain, also, perspective to realize the exaltation and greatness of these narratives. In the total of man's wistful, age-long exploration of the all-encompassing mystery there is nothing to rival Gn 1 : the majesty of an all-powerful God who speaks and things spring into being ; the orderliness of His working ; His benign purpose ; and then the unique profundity of man's creation—he was ' made in the image and likeness of God ' ! There at the outset of the Bible we have its great insight that man is not a brute, nor yet a half-demon of ' total depravity ' ; his spirit's home is with God, and he is restless and ill at ease until he finds rest in Him. Although chs. 2–3 go on with the equally necessary truth that even so man is a sinner, it nowhere repudiates or modifies this exalted insight. On the contrary, it is echoed so often through the OT that we can accurately assert it to be the Hebraic understanding of man : a sinner capable of horrible brutalities, but yet in his true nature made in the image of God and partaking of the Divine mind and nature.

Yet the relations of chs. 1 and 2 call for some further comment. Professor Skinner well spoke of ' the existence side by side of two independent and mutually irreconcilable accounts of the creation.' They are just that : irreconcilable in their starting point, in their sequence of events, but most of all in their theology. Little attention to detail is needed to show that over against the transcendent God of ch. 1, the viewpoint of ch. 2 is highly anthropomorphic. There is no thought here of relative evaluation. Actually both approaches to an understanding of God are of immense worth ; here we are concerned only to recognize relevant facts.

The understanding of man differs also in the two accounts. In contrast to the unique origin described in ch. 1, the second story (which continues through ch. 3) tells how the race developed, as a result of human conduct, it is true, yet by Divine action, out of an otherwise unknown primeval condition to the status of its historic being, toilful, suffering, and sinning. It may seem a drab, even a pessimistic, view of man. Rather let us say it is realistic ; it gives us man as he is. The great feature, too commonly overlooked in excessive emphasis on his sinful nature, is that this man is possessed of ' the knowledge of good and evil ' which clearly is a prerogative of God himself, though arrogated by man in wilful disobedience of Divine prohibition. As well his further possibilities are hinted at ; he might eat from the ' tree of life,' with incredible results.

An immense literature of interpretation, much of it of high value, at least demonstrates that the story possesses implications apparently not exhausted by any single exposition. It may then be permissible to add one more, which in any case has the merit of drawing on ancient thinking, hence perhaps of gathering up something of the author's actual intent.

Early speculation was much attracted by the problem, Why and how is it that man is so like the animals and yet so different? From one point of view he is just another animal (Ec 3[18–21]) ; yet such easy conclusion will not convince, for equally he is more than animal ; but why?

A variety of answers was given, seeming to stress, however, by their common element, the pervasive belief that man is possessed of a Divine quality—it is that which sets him apart. It is convenient to turn for illustration away from the Orient and invoke instead one of the delightful myths with which the Greeks sought answer for their profound questions, the story of Prometheus, best known in the remnants surviving from the great trilogy of Aeschylus. This ancient god, in revolt against triumphant new-comers, stole fire from the gods and gave it to man. The result was, as Aeschylus sketches at some length, that this hitherto savage and degraded being learned to build houses, to make and wear clothes, to build ships, to work metals—in brief, he became civilized. So for the Greeks, man's superiority is due to an inherent divine ' fire.' Equally it was characteristic of Oriental thinking that this supra-mundane essence in humanity was divine knowledge. The important matter is not the difference but rather the agreement that in man's nature, as man, there is something that is not of the earth, earthy.

The parallels with Gn 3 are such that we must conclude we have here the Hebraic explanation of man's more than biological being, his innate relationship to God (which, it will be apparent, is but another approach to the great insight of ch. 1). For this privilege he suffers acutely. But is it the author's thought that, even so, the boon is worth the price? For thus man became a responsible moral being. Consciously he refused to remain a passive imprint of the Divine fiat. It was disobedience; it was sin; but through it he became man! He chose rather the hazardous way of self-reliance and free will. It is illuminating to recognize that such high estate was won, not by man's boldness, but through woman in her weakness and emotionalism. She 'saw that the tree was good' . . . and 'she took of its fruit and ate; and she also gave some to her husband,' who evidently in his smug superiority was content to remain forever in secure mediocrity! W. A. I.

CREATURE.—In AV 'creature' is used in the general (and original) sense of 'what is created.' Thus 2 Co 5[17] 'if any man be in Christ, he is a new creature'; 1 Ti 4[4] 'for every creature of God is good.' In Ro 8[19ff] it is not merely living creatures in the modern use of the word that wait for deliverance, but the whole creation of God (as AV itself has it in v.[22]). See RSV. F. C. G.

CREDITOR.—See DEBT.

CREED (AS. *creda*, from Lat. *credo* = 'I believe').—The technical term for a fixed formula summarizing the essential articles of Christian belief and enjoying the sanction of ecclesiastical authority. The three best-known creeds are the Apostles' Creed, which is an 8th cent. elaboration of the late 2nd cent. baptismal creed of the Roman Church, the so-called Nicene (more properly Niceno-Constantinopolitan) Creed, which is probably connected with the Council of Constantinople (A.D. 381) and is the only truly ecumenical creed, and the Athanasian Creed (often designated, from its opening words, the *Quicunque Vult*), which some attribute to St. Ambrose but which more probably dates from *c* A.D. 500. There are no traces of creeds in the strict sense in the apostolic age, but the NT points to the existence of (*a*) an apostolic preaching, or *kērygma*, with a fairly definite outline, and (*b*) a variety of brief, semi-stereotyped confessions with a credal ring. Some of these were Christological, the most important being the slogan 'Jesus is Lord' (cf 1 Co 12[3], Ph 2[11] etc.); others were dyadic, mentioning the Father and the Son (*e.g.* 1 Co 8[6], Ti 2[5f], 6[13f]), while yet others were triadic (*e.g.* Mt 28[19], 2 Co 13[14]). Formal creeds began to emerge in the 2nd cent. in connexion with the questions and answers about belief employed at baptism. The ancient Roman baptismal creed is preserved, in the form of interrogations, in Hippolytus's *Apostolic Tradition*. In the 3rd and 4th cents. Church councils adopted the practice of drafting creeds as expressions of orthodox belief and requiring the bishops present to sign them. The most famous example is the creed promulgated at the Council of Nicaea in A.D. 325. At a much later date creeds found their way into the public services of the Church, the Nicene Creed establishing itself in the Eucharist from the 6th cent. onwards and the Apostles' Creed in the offices from the 7th cent. onwards. J. N. D. K.

CREEPING THINGS.—In AV and RV this term is the translation of two distinct words, which have no etymological connexion, and in usage are not synonymous. The Hebrew words are *remeś* and *shereṣ*. It is unfortunate that the latter term is translated 'creeping thing,' for the root means to *swarm*. Hence RSV renders by 'swarming creatures,' or 'winged insects.' It includes both terrestrial and aquatic animals which appear in great swarms; in Gn 1[20] it refers to the creatures that teem in the waters, while in other passages it includes insects, as locusts, crickets, and grasshoppers (Lv 11[20-23]), together with the smaller quadrupeds as the weasel and mouse, as well as reptiles proper (Lv 11[29-31]). The verb is used of frogs (Ex 8[3]). Etymologically *remeś* signifies that which *glides* or *creeps*, and for its usage the two crucial passages are Gn 1[24] and 1 K 4[33]. In the latter the entire animal kingdom is popularly divided into four classes: beasts, birds, creeping things, and fishes (cf Hos 2[18]). In Gn 1[24] the land animals are put into three groups: cattle, creeping things, and beasts of the earth. By eliminating the first and third classes, which respectively include domesticated quadrupeds, and the wild animals, we see that the expression 'creeping things' is, roughly speaking, equivalent to our term 'reptiles,' exclusive of those which are aquatic. Delitzsch defines *remeś* as 'the smaller creeping animals that keep close to the earth'; Dillmann as creatures 'which move along the ground either without feet or with imperceptible feet.' From this discussion it is evident that the two are not interchangeable terms. *Remeś* has also a wider signification: in Ps 104[25] it is used of marine animals, in Gn 9[8] (EV 'moving thing') it includes all living creatures. See, further, the careful discussion by Professor Driver in Hastings' *DB* i. 517 f. J. A. K.

CRESCENS.—According to 2 Ti 4[10] a companion of Paul sent by him to Galatia, a name used at this time to designate both Galatia in Asia Minor and ancient Gaul. A few good Greek manuscripts of the NT support the latter interpretation by reading Gallia. A decision on this point rests upon one's conception of the situation out of which the Pastoral letters grew. To-day scholars generally regard this as a reference to the province in Asia Minor. The tradition that Crescens founded the churches of Mayence and Vienne in France is late and may have been suggested by this verse. Late tradition also regards Crescens as one of the seventy disciples of Christ. W. R. S.

CRESCENTS.—See AMULETS, and ORNAMENTS, 3.

CRETE, CRETANS.—Crete, the modern *Candia*, is an island 60 miles S. of Greece proper, about 150 miles long, and varying in breadth from 30 to 7 miles, with mountains as high as 7000 feet. It is about equidistant from Europe, Asia, and Africa. The researches of Sir Arthur J. Evans and others have revealed traces of a very ancient civilization, including an alphabet hitherto unknown, the famous linear B Script of *c* 1200 B.C. recently (1954) deciphered by Michael Ventris and recognized as early Greek, and an earlier linear A Script which seems to be Babylonian (C. H. Gordon). In later times it was famed for its archers, who were valued in the armies of Europe. It was conquered by Rome in 67 B.C., and became, in conjunction with the district Cyrenaica in North Africa, a Roman senatorial province governed by a proconsul. Jews were early to be found there, and were very numerous. Some were present at Pentecost in the year of the crucifixion (Ac 2[11]). St. Paul's ship, on the voyage to Rome, sailed along the Cretan coast close in (Ac 27[7]), and came to Fair Havens near Lasea. These places (q.v.) were on the S. coast, which had few harbours.

The epithets which a native of the island, the poet Epimenides (flourished 600 B.C.), flung at the Cretans, are quoted in a somewhat un-apostolic manner in the Epistle to Titus (1[12]). Epimenides styled them 'always liars, evil beasts of prey, lazy gluttons.' Such vituperation must not be taken too seriously. The ancients were much given to it, and it probably reveals as much of the taste and even character of the persons who used it as it does the nature of those they attacked. When and by whom Christianity was planted in Crete cannot be said. It is probable that it was well established there in the 1st cent. In the Epistle to Titus we find Titus introduced as having been left by St. Paul in charge of the churches. A. So.—**E. G. K.**

CRIB.—This is the modern **manger** (Lk 2[7]). It survives in RSV in Is 1[3], Job 39[9]. In AV and RV it is found also in Pr 14[4] (RSV 'there is no grain').

CRICKET.—The Hebrew *ḥargōl* is rendered 'cricket' in Lv 11[22] (RV, RSV; AV 'beetle') erroneously. The term denotes a kind of **locust** (q.v.).

CRIME.—In 1611 the word ' crime ' had not lost its early meaning of *accusation*, whence Ac 25^{16} ' the crime laid against him ' (RSV ' charge '). It is possible that in Job 31^{11} ' crime ' is used in the more modern sense; elsewhere it means ' charge.'

CRIMES AND PUNISHMENTS.—The term ' crimes' is here used loosely in the sense of punishable offences, including not merely crimes (*crimina*) in the sense of breaches of the criminal law in the modern sense, and torts (*delicta*) or breaches of the civil law, but also those offences in the sphere of religion and worship to which definite penalties were attached. Within the limits of this article it is possible to present only a summary of the more important and typical punishable offences recognized in the various Hebrew law-codes. The latter, indicated by the usual symbols, are: (1) BC, the oldest code, known as the Book of the Covenant, Ex 20^{22}–23^{33}, with which for convenience sake is joined the Decalogue of Ex 20^{2-17}; (2) D, the Deuteronomic Code, Dt 12–28; (3) H, the Holiness Code, Lv 17–26; and (4) P, the great collection of laws known as the Priestly Code, and comprising the rest of the legislative material of the Pentateuch. In the case of P alone will it be necessary to name the books (Exodus, Leviticus, or Numbers) to which reference is made.

The penal offences of the Pentateuch may be conveniently grouped under the three heads of crimes against Y″, against society (including property), and against the individual.

1. A. CRIMES AGAINST Y″, or offences in the sphere of religion and worship.—Although it is true that misdemeanours of every kind were in the last resort offences against Y″, who was regarded as the only fountain of law and justice, it will be convenient to group under this head those belonging to the special sphere of religious belief and its outward expression in worship. Among these the first place must be given to the **worship of heathen deities**—condemned in the strongest terms in BC (from 20^{3} onwards) and D—and of **the heavenly bodies,** D 17^{3} (cf 4^{19}). The penalty is death under the ban (BC 22^{20}, D 13^{12ff} [see BAN]), or by stoning (D 17^{5}). Inseparable from this form of apostasy is the crime of **idolatry,** entailing the curse of God (D 27^{15}). **Blasphemy,** or profanation of the Divine name, is forbidden in all the codes; the penalty is death by stoning (H 24^{13ff}). The **practice of magic,** wizardry, and similar black arts, exposes their adepts and those who resort to them to the same penalty (H 20^{27}).

2. The punishment for doing ' any **work on the Sabbath day** ' is death, but only in the later legislation (Ex 31^{15} [probably H] 35^{2} [P]; cf the very late Haggadic section, Nu 15^{32ff}). For neglect of ordinances, to use a familiar phrase, such as **failing to observe the fast** of the Day of Atonement (H 23^{29}), or to keep the Passover (Nu 9^{13} [P]), an offender was liable to be ' cut off from his people '; (see below). This was also the punishment prescribed for a number of offences that may be grouped under the head of **sacrilege,** such as partaking of blood (Lv 7^{27} [P]), and the unauthorized manufacture and use of the holy anointing oil (Ex 30^{32f} [P]).

3. B. CRIMES AGAINST SOCIETY.—As the family, according to Hebrew ideas, was the unit of society, the crimes that mar the sanctities of family life may be taken first. Such pre-eminently was **adultery,** severely condemned in all the codes, the punishment for both parties being death (D 22^{22}, H 20^{10}). In a case of **seduction** the man was required to marry her whom he had wronged, if her father gave consent (BC 22^{16f}), paying the latter a ' dowry,' *i.e.* the usual purchase price (see MARRIAGE), estimated in D 22^{29} at 50 shekels of silver. On the other hand, the penalty for **rape,** if the victim was betrothed, was death (D 22^{25ff}), as it was for unnatural crimes like **sodomy** (H 18^{22} 20^{13} ' thou shalt not lie with mankind as with womankind ') and **bestiality** (BC 22^{19}, H 20^{15f}). The **marriage of near kin** is forbidden in H 18^{6-18} under seventeen heads (see MARRIAGE). **Incest** with a stepmother or a daughter-in-law was punishable by the death of both parties (H 20^{11f}), while for a man to marry ' a wife and her mother ' was a crime that could be expiated only by the death of all three, and that, as many hold (see below), by being burnt alive (*ib.* v.^{14}). Ordinary **prostitution** is condemned by H 19^{29} (cf D 22^{21})—for a priest's daughter the punishment was even death by burning (21^{9})—while the wide-spread heathen practice of establishing religious prostitutes, male and female, at the local sanctuaries is specially reprobated in D 23^{17f}, where the male prostitute is to be recognized under the inexact term ' sodomite,' and the contemptuous ' dog.'

4. To carry **disrespect for** one's **parents** to the extent of smiting (BC 21^{15}), or cursing them (BC 21^{17}, H 20^{9}), or even of showing persistent contumacy (D 21^{18ff}), entailed the extreme penalty of death at the hands of the local authorities.

5. Everything that would tend to impair the impartial and effective administration of justice is emphatically condemned in the Hebrew codes, the giving and receiving of **bribes,** in particular, being forbidden even in the oldest legislation (BC 23^{8} ' for a gift blindeth them that have sight '). Against those who would defeat the ends of justice by **perjury** and **false witness,** the law is rightly severe (D 19^{15ff}). **Tale-bearing** (H 19^{16}), and the spreading of a report known to be false (BC 23^{1}), are condemned, while in the more heinous case of a man **slandering** his newly wedded wife, the elders of the city are to amerce him in an hundred shekels (D 22^{13-21}).

6. Property had also to be protected against **theft** (BC 20^{15}) and **burglary** (22^{2}), with which may be classed the crime of **removing the boundary-stones** of a neighbour's property to increase one's own (D 19^{14}), and the use of **false weights and measures** (D 25^{15ff}, H 19^{35ff}). The earliest code likewise deals with **trespass** (BC 22^{5}), and **arson** or wilful fire-raising (*ib.* v.^{6}), for which the penalty in either case was restitution.

7. C. CRIMES AGAINST THE INDIVIDUAL.—BC 21^{15-26} deals with various forms of **assault,** a crime to which the pre-Mosaic *jus talionis* (see below) was specially applicable. **Kidnapping** a freeman was a criminal offence involving the death penalty (BC 21^{16}, D 24^{17}). **Murder** naturally has a place in the penal legislation of all the codes from BC 20^{13} onwards. The legislators, as is well known, were careful to distinguish between murder deliberately planned and executed (BC 21^{14}, D 19^{11f}) and unpremeditated **homicide** or **manslaughter** (BC 21^{13}, D 19^{4ff}, and especially P, Nu 35^{9ff}). The former, with certain exceptions (BC 21^{20} 22^{2}), entailed capital punishment in accordance with the fundamental principle laid down in Gn 9^{6}; in the case of ' the man-slayer ' special provision was made for the mitigation of the ancient right of blood-revenge (see REFUGE [CITIES OF]).

8. PUNISHMENTS.—From the earliest period of which we have any record two forms of punishment prevailed among the Hebrews and their Semitic kinsfolk, viz. retaliation and restitution. **Retaliation,** the *jus talionis* of Roman law, received its classical expression in the oldest Hebrew code: ' then you shall give life for life, eye for eye, tooth for tooth, hand for hand, foot for foot, burn for burn, wound for wound, stripe for stripe ' (BC 21^{23f}). The *talio*, as has already been mentioned, was specially applicable in cases of injury from assault. When life had been taken, whether intentionally or unintentionally, the right of enforcing the *jus talionis* lay with the dead man's next of kin (see KIN [NEXT OF]).

In BC **restitution** varies from fivefold for an ox, and fourfold for a sheep that has been stolen and thereafter killed or sold, to twofold if the animal is still in the thief's possession (BC 22^{1-4}), and finally to a simple equivalent in the case of wilful damage to a neighbour's property (*ib.* v.^{5f}). **Compensation** by a money payment was admitted for loss of time through bodily injury (BC 21^{19}), for loss of property (v.$^{33-35}$), but not, in Hebrew law, for loss of life, except in the cases mentioned BC 21^{30}. The payments of 100 shekels and 50 shekels respectively ordained in D $22^{19,\,29}$ appear to the modern eye as **fines,** but fall in reality under the head of compensation paid to the father of the women in question.

9. In the penal code of the Hebrews there is a comparative lack of what may be termed intermediate penalties. **Imprisonment,** for example, has no place in the Pentateuch codes as an authorized form of punishment, although frequent cases occur in later times and apparently with legal sanction (see Ezr 7[26]). The use of the **stocks** also was known to the Jewish (Jer 20[2f]) as well as to the Roman authorities (Ac 16[24]). **Beating** with rods and **scourging** with the lash were also practised. The former seems intended in D 25[1ff], but later Jewish practice substituted a lash of three thongs, thirteen strokes of which were administered (cf 2 Co 11[24]). Many, however, would identify the punishment of this passage of D with the favourite Egyptian punishment of the bastinado. **Mutilation,** apart from the *talio*, appears only as the penalty for indecent assault (D 25[11f]).

10. The regular form of capital punishment was death by **stoning,** which is prescribed in the Pentateuch as the penalty for eighteen different crimes, including Sabbath-breaking. 'For only one crime—murder—is it the penalty in all the codes.' The execution of the criminal took place outside the city (H 24[14]), and according to D 17[7] the witnesses in the case cast the first stone (cf Jn 8[7]). In certain cases the dead body of the malefactor was **impaled** upon a stake; this, it can hardly be doubted, is the true rendering of D 21[22f] (EV 'hang him on a tree'), and of the same expression elsewhere. **Hanging** or strangulation is mentioned only as a manner of suicide (2 S 17[23], Mt 27[5]). **Crucifixion,** it need hardly be said, was a Roman, not a Jewish, institution. **Beheading** appears in Mt 14[10]||, Ac 12[2], Rev 20[4].

11. The meaning of the expression frequently found in P, 'to be cut off from his people, from Israel,' etc., is uncertain; most probably it denotes a form of **excommunication,** with the implication that the offender is handed over to the judgment of God, which also seems to be intended by the **banishment** of Ezr 7[26] (note RVm). A similar division of opinion exists as to the penalty of **burning,** which is reserved for aggravated cases of prostitution (H 21[9]) and incest (20[19]). Here the probability seems in favour of the guilty parties being burned alive (cf Gn 38[24]), although many scholars hold that they were first stoned to death. The most extreme form of punishment known to the codes, in that a whole community was involved, is that of total destruction under **the ban** of the first degree (see BAN) prescribed for the crime of apostasy (BC 22[20], more fully D 13[15-17]).

In recent years the emphasis on the importance of the cult in OT religion has brought with it a tendency to regard as cultic some of the legislation that was formerly regarded as secular. Indeed, Bentzen (*Introduction to the OT*, 1948, i, p. 218) says, 'when we regard the Israelite laws, the religious point of view must always be kept in mind. The distinction of Roman law between *jus* and *fas* cannot be carried through clearly in Israel nor in the Orient as a whole.' A similar view may be found in most discussions of this point. Moreover, the literary style and pattern of legislative writing has been examined (especially by Alt) during recent years, with interesting results. Individual laws have been classified according to three groups: (*a*) Hypothetical or casuistic, such as 'if (or 'when') a man does this or that thing, then such and such a punishment is imposed. (Cf Ex 21[7-11, 14, 20f, 22f], and a sub-division in 21[12, 15-17]; or yet again, Lv 20[6ff], literally 'The man who . . . shall be . . .') (*b*) Categorical, such as the commandments and prohibitions in the Decalogue and very frequently. (*c*) A mixture of (*a*) and (*b*), as in Ex 21[2-6] 23[4f]. Bentzen (op. cit., p. 226) ventures the view that the hypothetical forms are used for civil law and the categorical for sacral. It is to be noted, too, that the collections of laws within the Pentateuch, both in small units and larger, contain the above patterns without apparent distinction. A. R. S. K.—**B. J. R.**

CRIMSON.—The word *tôlā'*, translated in Is 1[18] 'crimson' and in La 4[5] 'purple' (RSV; AV, RV 'scarlet') is closely similar to the word *tôlē'āh, tôla'ath,* usually translated '**worm**' (q.v.), exactly as the Arabic *dūdeh,* the common word for 'worm,' is to-day also used in Palestine for the imported cochineal insect. The Palestine insect is the female *Coccus ilicis* of the same Natural Order as the American *C. cacti*; it feeds on the holm-oak.

CRISPING PINS.—Is 3[22] AV; RV has **satchels** and RSV 'handbags'; see BAG.

CRISPUS.—The 'ruler' of the Jewish synagogue at Corinth (Ac 18[8]). Convinced by the reasonings of Paul that Jesus was the Messiah, he believed with all his household. The Apostle mentions him (1 Co 1[14]) as one of the few persons whom he himself had baptized.

CRITICISM, BIBLICAL.—1. Lower and Higher.—Criticism of the Bible, as of any ancient literature, includes two branches: (1) Lower Criticism, which seeks to reach the most reliable approximation to the text of the author's Hebrew (or Aramaic) or Greek autograph (see TEXT OF THE NT), and (2) Higher Criticism, which on the basis of the most reliable text seeks discriminating insight into the questions of authorship, date, circumstances of origin, historicity, literary integrity, evidence for and isolation of sources, literary category, doctrinal tendency, and the like. The object upon which such discriminating observation is practised is the text itself and, secondarily, related texts within and without the Canon. The tools are the lexicography and grammar of the language involved and archaeology in the widest sense: history, antiquities, monuments, and the vast lore of the history of considered opinion (which may be valuable even when false). However, these branches are only the two poles, toward one or the other of which criticism tends, for countless decisions made in lower criticism are made on premises of higher criticism, while higher criticism is constantly reweighing alternatives presented and partially clarified by lower criticism.

The title of the second branch of criticism is open to misuse and misunderstanding. Because lower criticism is seldom heard of except among experts, while higher criticism is often publicly mentioned, the comparative in both names often escapes notice and the latter term is taken for arrogance on the part of certain scholars who thus seem to call themselves 'higher critics' in contempt for 'lower,' older, and more conservative scholars. 'Criticism' itself is also understood as carping or fault-finding, rather than as discrimination. Worse yet, criticism is still often regarded as merely negative, an attack upon the Bible—for the results of criticism that attract popular attention are usually those startling ones which shatter preconceived notions. But the uncritical do not readily distinguish between such notions and saving faith. Not that negative criticism with an anti-biblical animus has been, or is now, unknown! But there is also higher criticism that is thoroughly constructive and leaves faith deprived only of previous false supports, and now all the more firmly undergirded by the genuine supports. In itself higher criticism is neutral; it is a scientific process. Even the champions of long-accepted but now threatened views are compelled to use this very process against the 'higher critics' with whom they disagree. There is a tendency in this generation to drop the wider term and use instead the name of some subdivision of it, such as historical criticism, literary criticism, form criticism.

2. Its Origin.—Only a kind of historical myopia can hold that any valid higher criticism has existed only since the Reformation, or even, as some have asserted, during the two centuries since 1750. Unless it be held that the determination of the Canon was entirely the work of the Holy Spirit working independently of the judgment of human minds, the Canon itself is the oldest monument of higher criticism, an eminent piece of discrimination which the Church by and large has always approved. The whole tenor of ancient and mediaeval exegesis was not congenial to the development of conscious, systematic criticism, for this requires a freedom from mere tradition and hierarchic authority that could only slowly and painfully be won. Nevertheless it appeared at an early date in the consideration of individual questions. Origen was certainly practising it in his analysis of the non-Pauline style of Hebrews; so was Julius Africanus in his proof that Susanna was composed in Greek and hence is no part of the Hebrew-Aramaic Daniel. Theodore of Mopsuestia recognized the Song of Solomon as an erotic poem, and saw that the author of Job was not a Jew. The *canons* of St. Victor (12th cent.) assumed that the Wisdom of Solomon is not the work of Solomon and that the key to Dn 11 lies in 1 and 2 Maccabees. But this kind of thing was sporadic, not systematic.

Neither did Luther practise systematic criticism, though he did question the validity of the Canon as to the inclusion of four books of the NT; the order of the German NT and of some Lutheran versions in other languages still shows traces of his originally more drastic criticism. Perhaps Calvin cautiously agreed with him to the extent that of all the books of the NT Revelation alone was left without a commentary from his hand.

To the embarrassment of professional exegetes, it must be admitted that modern higher criticism was first systematically practised by non-theologians: the jurist and diplomat Grotius, the philosophers Hobbes and Spinoza, and the medical professor Jean Astruc. For the OT, at least, Hobbes' *Leviathan* (ch. 33) contains an embryonic ' introduction ' to the Bible such as our century knows. It is higher criticism nearly free from unquestioned tradition. Perhaps Spinoza's greatest ' sin ' was to bring to the light of day in universal Latin the esoteric Rabbinic critical lore which he knew from the hints in Ibn Ezra and Rashi. The works of both Hobbes and Spinoza were proscribed by the High Court of Holland, though neither had ventured to deal in the same way with the NT. Astruc was the father of modern source-criticism of the Pentateuch. As a pioneer he overdid his search for sources, finding some thirteen in Genesis alone; but for what validity they have, he discovered the E and J ' sources.'

Seventy-five years before Astruc's book a fellow Frenchman, Richard Simon, a Catholic priest of the Oratory, had published his *Histoire Critique du Vieux Testament*. It treated first textual criticism, then higher. Here his most important insight (to-day a truism, but we owe it to him) was that the historical books of the OT are the product of gradual compilation and much later redaction. In the 18th cent. both Simon and Astruc were translated into German, and it was in Germany that their work bore fruit.

In Christian Europe free investigation of the NT was more dangerous than that of the OT, all the more so if it dealt with the Gospels and Jesus Himself. So it is not surprising that the first brilliant work of this sort was written by a non-theologian and published not only anonymously but posthumously: *Vom Zwecke Jesu und seiner Jünger: Noch ein Fragment des Wolfenbüttelschen Ungenannten* (' On the Purpose of Jesus and His Disciples—One More Fragment by the Anonymous Writer of Wolfenbüttel '), published by G. E. Lessing in 1778. The answers offered by this violent and much-hated little book may all be wrong, but it raised the *right questions*—all the basic questions that are still the core of investigation on the Gospels. The author was that Reimarus with whom Albert Schweitzer began his *Quest of the Historical Jesus* (*Von Reimarus zu Wrede*, 1906).

From the end of the 18th cent. onward the names and works in biblical criticism for both Testaments become so numerous that it is necessary to schematize. By a great over-simplification one may say that the 18th cent. fought for and won the right of independent criticism even of the Bible; that the 19th cent. was most concerned with source criticism; and that the first half of the 20th cent. has had for its central advancing concern stylistic analysis and deductions derived therefrom (=form criticism). See below, **4.**

3. Source Criticism.—Following the pioneer steps of Simon and Astruc, a whole series of scholars worked out multiple sources for the Pentateuch, proceeding with a degree of confidence in the (often subjective) techniques of literary criticism which to-day seems naive but which was an inevitable consequence of the intellectual atmosphere of the century and probably a necessary transitional stage in the history of biblical criticism. Only their names can be mentioned here: Semler, Michaelis, Eichhorn, DeWette, Ewald, Hupfeld, Kuenen, and especially Graf and Wellhausen, after whom the ' classic ' 19th-cent. conception of the Pentateuch is usually named. This very source-criticism also brought the prophets into prominence as perhaps the earliest distinct figures in Hebrew religious history, since their predecessors are known only through the eyes of editors later than the 8th-7th cent. (Kuenen, Robertson Smith). Studies in the Mesopotamian languages and cultures, along with archaeology and comparative religion, were also characteristic of the period, frequently supplementing the prevailing literary-critical studies. In the NT field source-criticism centred around the Synoptics. Scholars at the end of the century came nearly unanimously to the Two-Source Theory, but only after travelling successive blind alleys: a lost gospel as common source to all three gospels (Lessing), little slips of written memoranda (Schleiermacher), direct and sole use of oral tradition (Gieseler), Mark digested from Matthew and Luke (Griesbach), and many others. The priority of Mark was first detected and defended by Lachmann, the classical and Germanistic philologist (1835). The direct father of the Two-Source Theory was H. J. Holtzmann (1863), though it was anticipated by C. H. Weisse and C. G. Wilke in 1838. Various addenda and modifications of this theory, that is multiple-source theories, have been proposed, of which the most successful, at least in English-speaking lands, is the Four-Source theory of B. H. Streeter. But world scholarship prefers the older, simpler theory. There was also much discussion of the sources of Acts, but it still has not come to any definite conclusion. Much more important was the related question of the relative value of Acts and the Pauline corpus as sources for historical knowledge of Paul (F. C. Baur and the Tübingen School). This necessitated a critical sifting of the Pauline corpus: what really comes from the hand of Paul? The Tübingen School (except for Dutch extremists) always maintained the authorship of Romans, 1 and 2 Corinthians, and Galatians by Paul, but doubted all the rest. Even severely critical scholars to-day add to the big four three others: 1 Thessalonians, Philippians, Philemon, while they hold in suspension 2 Thessalonians and Colossians, and assign Ephesians and the Pastorals to disciples of Paul.

4. Form Criticism.—Partly by fructification from secular studies in folk-literature, partly by reaction against the strait-jacket of pure literary criticism, there arose towards the end of the 19th cent. a new method of criticism which now is best known by the name Form Criticism, though this name dates only from 1919. The immediate founder of the method was H. Gunkel, though he acknowledges great debt to Herder and recognizes Holtzmann and the philologist Edward Norden as predecessors. The great folklorists from the Grimm brothers on (and especially the Dane, Oxel Olrik) also directly influenced the NT branch of the school. The advantage of this method is that it offers a way, where there had been none, of dealing with oral tradition. There are ' laws ' of folk-behaviour in passing on tradition. Gunkel discovered in the OT certain recurrent literary categories which exhibited related form, with a related style appropriate to each form. This led him to inquire after their *Sitz im Leben*—their actual functioning-place in the life of the group whose motivating tradition they were. But to many *Form Criticism* means the specific application of Gunkel's OT method to the NT by three of his pupils: Martin Dibelius, K. L. Schmidt, and Rudolf Bultmann. In the years 1919–21 all three published books on the Synoptics using this method. Perhaps the most fruitful insight here has been Dibelius's (and Bultmann's) recognition of the paradigm (pronouncement-story; Bultmann's apophthegm) as the most important vehicle of relatively reliable tradition from and about Jesus. Form Criticism frankly recognizes the active and creative part of the Community in shaping the pre-Marcan tradition; no other of its assertions has aroused so much resistance and contradiction as this one. Less controversial has been the acceptance of their contention that the pericopes were originally independent except in the passion-story. The method has also been applied to other areas of traditional material elsewhere in the NT: Acts, James, and the exhortations, confessional statements, and 'hymns' embedded in the epistles. See ORAL TRADITION, and GOSPELS, 4. W. F. A.—**K. G.**

CROCODILE.—1. *liwyāthān* is rendered 'crocodile' in RVm, RSVm in Job 41^{1}, but in the text here and elsewhere '**Leviathan**' (q.v.). **2.** *ḥayyath ḳāneh*, 'the beasts that dwell among the reeds' (RSV, cf RV; AV 'the company of spearmen'), is thought by some to be the crocodile or the hippopotamus as symbolizing Egypt. **3.** *tannîm* is rendered 'crocodile' in RVm in Jer 14^{6} (RV, RSV 'jackals'; AV 'dragons'). See DRAGON and JACKAL. **4.** *kōaḥ* is rendered 'land crocodile' in RV and RSV in Lv 11^{30} (AV 'chameleon'). See LIZARD.

The crocodile probably still exists in the *Nahr ez-Zerkā*, S. of Mount Carmel, called by Pliny the Crocodile River. It is supposed to have been brought there by some Egyptian settlers. A dead crocodile was brought from there to the late Rev. J. Zeller of Nazareth. Herr Schumacher reports that he saw one there, and fifty years ago a number of crocodile's eggs were brought from this river and sold in Jerusalem. A stuffed specimen is in the *PEF* museum, London.

E. W. G. M.—**H. H. R.**

CROCUS.—See ROSE.

CROOKBACKT.—See MEDICINE.

CROSS.—The cross in its literal sense is dealt with under CRUCIFIXION, but there are certain spiritual uses of the word in the NT that call for separate consideration. (1) It is *a symbol of self-sacrifice.*—According to the Gospels, Jesus on at least three occasions affirmed the necessity for those who would follow Him of taking up the cross (Mt 10^{38}; Mk 8^{34}=Mt 16^{24}=Lk 9^{23}; [Mk 10^{21} only in AV]; Lk 14^{27}). The words imply a prophetic anticipation of His own experience on Calvary; but even although on Christ's earliest use of them this special application was hidden from His disciples (cf Mt 16^{21f} 20^{17-19}), the figure of bearing one's cross would convey a quite intelligible meaning. In Galilee multitudes had been crucified after the rebellion under Judas the son of Hezekiah (Jos. *Ant.* XVII. x. 10 [295], *BJ* II. v. 2 [75]; in Jerusalem, as we see from the execution of two robbers side by side with Jesus, a crucifixion must have been an ordinary incident under the Roman administration (Jos. *BJ* II. xii. 6 [241], xiii. 2 [253], xiv. 9 [306], v. xi. 1 [449–451]). And as it was usual to compel a *cruciarius* to carry to the place of execution the transverse beam (*patibulum*) of his own cross, Christ's figure would have a meaning as plain as it was vivid. But, unlike the wretched *cruciarius*, His disciples of their own free will were to take up the cross and follow Him. Luke's addition of the word 'daily' draws attention away from the historic event to self-sacrifice as a permanent obligation (9^{23}; cf 1 Co 15^{31}).

(2) It is *a thing of shame.*—The author of Hebrews tells us how Jesus 'endured the cross, despising the shame' (12^{2}). Both to the Roman and the Jew, the death on the cross was the most shameful death a man could die —to the former because reserved by Roman usage for slaves, foreigners, or desperate criminals; to the latter because it came under the curse pronounced by the Jewish Law upon any one whose dead body hung upon a tree (Dt 21^{23}; cf Gal 3^{13}). To Jew and Gentile alike this was the great 'stumbling-block of the cross' (Gal 5^{11}, 1 Co 1^{23}). And even Paul himself regards 'death on a cross' as the very lowest point in Christ's long pathway of humiliation (Ph 2^{8}).

(3) There are certain theological uses of the word peculiar to the Pauline writings. Paul makes the cross *a summary of the gospel.* Thus for 'the preaching of the gospel' in 1 Co 1^{17} he substitutes in v.^{18} 'the word of the cross,' and in v.^{23} 'the preaching of Christ crucified' (cf 2^{2}). Again in Gal 6^{12} he speaks of suffering persecution 'for the cross of Christ,' where the meaning evidently is 'for the confession of faith in the Christian gospel.' And when he glories in 'the cross of our Lord Jesus Christ' (v.^{14}), the cross is used, as the clauses following show, to epitomize the saving work of Jesus both *for* us and *in* us.

(4) Further, in the Pauline theology the cross is set forth as *the great instrument of reconciliation.* It is 'by the blood of his cross' that Christ has effected a reconciliation between God and man (Col 1^{20ff}). He took out of the way the bond written in ordinances that was against us, 'nailing it to the cross' (2^{14}). It is 'through the cross' that He has reconciled the Gentile and the Jew, abolishing that 'law of commandments' which rose between them like a middle wall of partition (Eph 2^{14-16}). And there are glimpses of a still wider reconciliation accomplished by Jesus through His cross—a reconciliation of all things to God the Father, whether they are things on the earth or things in the heavens (Col 1^{20}, cf Eph 1^{10}).

(5) Once more, the cross is to Paul *the symbol of a mystical union with Christ Himself.* In the great figure of the Gospels (Mt 10^{38}||) cross-bearing stands for the imitation of Christ. Paul goes deeper, and sees in the cross a crucifixion with Christ from which there springs a possession of the indwelling life of Christ (Gal 2^{20}). The old man is crucified (Ro 6^{6}), that a new man may rise from the dead (cf v.^{4}). The flesh is crucified, with its passions and lusts (Gal 5^{24}), that the Christian may live and walk by the Spirit (v.^{25}). And yet this mysticism of the cross never causes the Apostle to lose sight of the cross as the means of an objective redemption. On the contrary, he regards the two ideas as inseparably connected; and, glorying in the cross of our Lord Jesus Christ, does so because through it (*a*) the world—the sphere of external ordinances—is crucified to him; and (*b*) he himself is crucified to the world (Gal 6^{14}). J. C. L.—**W. D. S.**

CROW occurs once in Apocrypha (Bar 6^{54}), where the helplessness of idols is illustrated by the remark that 'they are as crows between heaven and earth.' See also RAVEN.

CROWN.—1. In the OT.—The word represents several Hebrew terms with distinct meanings. (1) *zēr*, properly an edge or border, with the suggestion of a twisted or wreathed appearance. It occurs only in Ex (25^{11} and frequently). It is always of gold, and in the furniture of the Tabernacle surrounds the Ark, the table of show-bread and its border, the altar of incense. RVm gives as alternative renderings 'rim,' 'moulding,' and RSV has the latter. Its purpose seems to have been ornamental merely. (2) *nēzer*, properly 'mark of separation or consecration' (from *nāzar* 'to separate, consecrate'; whence *nāzîr*='Nazirite'). Originally it was no more than a fillet to confine hair that was worn long (W. R. Smith, *RS*^{2} p. 483). It is used of the crown set upon the forehead of the high priest (Ex 29^{6} etc.)—a plate of pure gold with the engraving 'Holy to Y″' (39^{30}, cf Lv 8^{9}), and also of the crown worn by Hebrew kings (2 S 1^{10}, 2 K 11^{12}). In both cases it was the symbol of consecration. (3) *kether*, similar in meaning to (2) but without the idea of consecration, is used in Est (1^{11} 2^{17} 6^{8}) to denote the **diadem** of a Persian king or queen. (4) *ʿaṭārāh*, the word that is most frequent and of the most general significance. It is applied to the crown worn by kings, whether Jewish (2 S 12^{30} etc.) or foreign (1 Ch 20^{2}, Est 8^{15} [cf 6^{8}]), to the wreath worn at banquets

(Is 28$^{1, 3}$, Ezk 23^{42}); but also in a figurative sense, as when, *e.g.* a virtuous woman is called her husband's crown (Pr 12^{4}), a hoary head the crown of old age (16^{31}), the Lord of hosts the crown of His people (Is 28^{5}). (5) *ḳodhḳōdh* is the crown or top of the head, as in the expression 'from the sole of his foot to the crown of his head' (Job 2^{7}); cf Gn 49^{26}, Dt 33^{20} etc.—The verb 'to crown' is comparatively rare in the OT: *'āṭar* (corresponding to (4) above) is found in Ps 8^{5} 65^{11} 103^{4}, Ca 3^{11}, Is 23^{8}; *kāthar* (corresponding to (3)) in Pr 14^{18}; *nāzar* (corresponding to (2)) in Nah 3^{17} (RSV 'princes'; the Hebrew should probably be read as 'your crowned ones.')

2. In the NT.—In AV 'crown' represents two Greek words: (1) *stephanos* (whence *stephanoō*, 'to crown'), (2) *diadēma*; the former being the badge of merit or victory, the latter (found only in Rev 12^{3} 13^{1} 19^{12}) the mark of royalty. This distinction, though not strictly observed in LXX, is properly maintained in RV and RSV where (2) is in each case rendered 'diadem.' The *stephanos* (properly 'wreath' = Lat. *corona*) was the **garland** given as a prize to the victors in the games (1 Co 9^{25} [RSV 'wreath']; cf 2 Ti 2^{5}). It is the word applied to our Lord's 'crown of thorns' (Mt 27^{29}, Mk 15^{17}, Jn 19$^{2, 5}$). It is used figuratively of 'the crown of righteousness' (2 Ti 4^{8}), 'of life' (Ja 1^{12}, Rev 2^{10}), 'of glory' (1 P 5^{4}). St. Paul applies it to his converts as being his joy and reward (Ph 4^{1}, 1 Th 2^{19}); and in Revelation it is employed in various symbolical connexions (4$^{4, 10}$ 6^{2} 9^{7} 12^{1} 14^{14}). J. C. L.

CRUCIBLE.—See Fine.

CRUCIFIXION.—**1. Its nature.**—Crucifixion denotes a form of execution in which the condemned person was affixed in one way or another to a cross (Lat. *crux*) and there left to die. The Greek term rendered 'cross' in the English NT is *stauros* (*stauroō* = 'crucify'), which has a wider application than we ordinarily give to 'cross,' being used of a single stake or upright beam as well as of a cross composed of two beams. The crucifixion of living persons is unknown in OT, though death by impaling is referred to in Ezr 6^{11} and by hanging in Est 7^{19}. The *stauroō* of LXX here renders the Hebrew *tālāh* = 'to hang'; but the hanging up of a dead body, especially on a tree, is familiar (Jos 10^{26}; cf 1 S 31^{10}, 2 S 4^{12} 21^{12}), and is sanctioned by the Law (Dt 21^{22}), with the proviso that a body thus hung, as something accursed, must be removed and buried before nightfall (v.^{23}). This enactment explains Jn 19^{31}, Gal 3^{13}, as well as the references in the NT to the cross as a tree (Ac 5^{30} 10^{39} 13^{29}, 1 P 2^{24}). See Cross.

2. Its origin and use.—The origin of crucifixion is traced to the Phoenicians, from whom it passed to many other nations, including both Greeks and Romans. Among the latter it was exceedingly common, but was confined almost exclusively to the punishment of slaves, foreigners, or criminals of the lowest class, being regarded as incompatible with the dignity of any Roman citizen (cf Cic. *in Verr.* i. 5 [13], ii. v. 61–67 [158–173]). This explains why, as tradition affirms, Paul was beheaded, while Peter and other Apostles, like the Master Himself, were put to death on the cross. The Jews in Palestine were familiar with the Roman penalty—see *e.g.* Josephus, *War* ii. v. 2 [75], where Varus's crucifixion of two thousand Jews is described.

3. Forms of the cross.—The primitive form was the *crux simplex*—a single post set upright in the earth, to which the victim was fastened; or a sharp stake on which he was impaled. The Roman cross was more elaborate, consisting of two beams, which, however, might be put together in different ways. Three shapes are distinguished: (1) The *crux commissa* (T), shaped like a capital T, and commonly known as St. Anthony's cross; (2) the *crux immissa* (†), the form with which we are most familiar; (3) the *crux decussata* (X), shaped like the letter X, and known as St. Andrew's cross. Early Christian tradition affirms that it was on (2) that Jesus died (*e.g.* Iren. *Haer.* ii. 24, § 4; Justin, *Trypho*, 91); and this is confirmed by the statements of the Gospels as to the 'title' that was set above His head (Mt 27^{37}, Mk 15^{26}, Lk 23^{38}, Jn 19^{19f}).

4. Method and accompaniments of crucifixion.—These are very fully illustrated in the Gospel narratives of the death of Jesus. Immediately after being condemned to the cross, a prisoner was brutally scourged. [In the case of Jesus the scourging appears to have taken place before His condemnation (Jn 19^{1}), and to have been intended by Pilate as a compromise with the Jews between the death sentence and a verdict of acquittal (Lk 23^{22})]. The cross-beam (*patibulum*), not the whole cross, was then laid on his shoulders, and borne by him to the place of execution, while his *titulus* (Jn 19^{19f}, Greek *titlos*, English 'title' (q.v.) or tablet of accusation hung around his neck, or was carried before him by a herald. If it was only the *patibulum* that Jesus carried, the probable failure of His strength by the way, leading to the incident of Simon the Cyrenian (Mk 15^{21} ||), must be attributed not to the weight of His burden, but to sheer physical exhaustion aggravated by loss of blood through scourging, as well as to the anguish that pressed upon His soul.

Arrived at the place of execution, which both with the Romans and the Jews was outside of the city (see article Golgotha), the condemned was stripped of his clothing by the soldiers detailed to carry out the sentence, who immediately appropriated it as their lawful booty (Mk 15^{24} ||). He was then laid on the ground, the cross-beam was thrust beneath his shoulders, and his hands were fastened to the extremities, sometimes with cords, but more usually, as in the case of Jesus (Jn 20^{25}, Lk 24^{39f}; cf Col 2^{14}), with nails. The beam was next raised into position and securely fixed to the upright already planted in the ground. On the upright was a projecting peg (*sedile*) astride of which the victim was made to sit, thereby relieving the strain on the pierced hands, which might otherwise have been torn away from the nails. Finally the feet were fastened to the lower part of the upright, either with nails (Lk 24^{39f}) or with cords.

The cross was not a lofty erection—much lower than it is usually represented in Christian art (cf Mt 27^{48} ||). Hanging thus quite near the ground, Jesus, in the midst of His last agonies, was all the more exposed to the jeers and insults of the bystanders and passers-by. It was a custom in Jerusalem to provide some alleviation for the physical tortures and mental sufferings of the crucified by giving him a stupefying draught. This was offered to Jesus before He was nailed to the cross; but He refused to take it (Mk 15^{23} ||). He would drink every drop of the cup that His Father had given Him, and go on to death with an unclouded consciousness.

In crucifixion the pains of death were protracted long—sometimes for days (cf Jos. *BJ* v. xi. 1 [449–451], *Life*, 75 [420]). Even when the victims were nailed and not merely tied to the cross, it was hunger and exhaustion, not loss of blood, that was the direct cause of death. Sometimes an end was put to their sufferings by the *crurifragium*—the breaking of their legs by hammer-strokes. It is not likely that in ordinary circumstances the Jews would induce a Roman governor to pay any attention to the law of Dt 21^{22f}. But, as the day following our Lord's crucifixion was not only a Sabbath, but the Sabbath of Passover week, Pilate was persuaded to give orders that Jesus and the two robbers crucified along with Him should be despatched by the *crurifragium* and their bodies removed (Jn 19^{31}). The soldiers broke the legs of the robbers first, but when they came to Jesus they found that He was already dead. One of them, either in sheer brutality or to make sure of His death, ran a spear into His side. The blood and water that gushed out (Jn 19^{34}, cf 1 Jn 5$^{6, 8}$) have been held by some medical authorities to justify the opinion that the Saviour died of a broken heart; but their significance in John is more probably as proof of the reality of Jesus' physical body, against the Docetic theory of a phantom which resembled Him. His death being certified, Joseph of Arimathaea, who had begged the body from Pilate, removed it from the cross and laid it in his own sepulchre (Mk 15[42ff] ||).

J. C. L.—F. C. G.

CRUELTY.—The word 'cruelty' has nearly disappeared from our Bibles. RV and RSV have introduced 'violence' (Gn 49[5], Jg 9[24], Ps 74[20]), 'harshness' (Ezk 34[4] [RSV]), and 'rigour' (Ezk 34[4] [RV]), but RV retains 'cruelty' in Ps 27[12] (RSV 'violence') and RSV has 'inflicted cruelties' in 2 Ch 16[10] (AV, RV 'oppressed'). However, many instances of cruelty remain in the OT records, and some of these seem to have the sanction of Scripture. Such passages as Dt 20[17] and Jos 6[21] no longer trouble the devout student of the Bible as they once did. He now recognizes the fact that in the Bible we have a faithful record of the slow evolution of spiritual ideals, and that the revelation of the NT brands as unchristian and inhuman many things that were written by the ancient scribes and some things that were done by ancient saints. The spirit of Elijah may not be the spirit of Christ (Lk 9[55]). Cruelty is unchristian; kindness is the law of the Christian life. D. A. H.

CRUSE.—See House, **9**.

CRYSTAL.—See Jewels and Precious Stones.

CUB.—This place, mentioned in Ezk 30[5] (RV; AV **Chub**), is almost certainly a corruption of *Lub*, *i.e.* **Libya** (so RSV), as was read by LXX. The 'Libya' of AV is a misrendering of *Put* (so RV, RSV). Cf Nah 3[9], where Libyans are mentioned along with Cush (Ethiopia), Egypt, and Put, as here; also 2 Ch 12[3] 16[8].

CUBIT.—See Weights and Measures.

CUCKOW, Lv 11[16], Dt 14[15] (AV).—See Owl.

CUCUMBERS.—Two varieties of cucumber are very common in Palestine. The *Cucumis sativus* (Arab. *khyār*), a smooth-skinned, whitish cucumber of delicate flavour, is a prime favourite with the Arabs. It is cool and juicy, but for cultivation requires abundant water. The second (*C. chate*, Arab. [in Jerusalem] *faqqūs*, [in Syria] *qiththā*) is a long slender cucumber, less juicy than the former. The reference in Nu 11[5] is probably to the latter, which is an Egyptian plant. The 'lodge in a cucumber field' (Is 1[8]) is the rough booth erected by the owner, raised, as a rule, high upon poles, from which he may keep guard over his ripening vegetables. When the harvest is over, the 'lodge' is not taken down but is allowed to drop to pieces. It is a dreary ruin of poles and dried branches during more than half the year.

E. W. G. M.

CUMI.—See Talitha Cumi.

CUMMIN.—The seed of an umbelliferous plant, the *Cuminum cyminum* (*syriacum*), widely cultivated in and around Palestine. It is used to flavour dishes, and, more particularly, bread; in flavour and appearance it resembles carraway; it has long been credited with medicinal properties; it certainly is a carminative. It is even now beaten out with rods (Is 28[27]). Tithes of cummin were paid by the Jews (Mt 23[23]). E. W. G. M.

CUN.—A city of Syria, despoiled by David, 1 Ch 18[8] (AV **Chun**). In the parallel 2 S 8[8] it is replaced by **Berothai.** Possibly Cun is to be located at *Râs Baʿalbek*.

CUNNING.—As a substantive 'cunning' in AV means either *skill* or *knowledge*; as an adjective either *skilful* or *wise* (we cannot say *knowing*, for that adjective has also degenerated). It is the present participle of the Anglo-Saxon verb *cunnan*, which meant both 'to know' and 'to be able.' In the Preface to the Wycliffite version of 1388 we read of 'the Holy Spyrit, author of all wisdom and cunnynge and truth.'

CUP.—**1.** In OT the rendering of various words, the precise distinction between which, either as to form or use, is unknown to us. The usual word is *kōs*, the ordinary drinking-vessel of rich (Gn 40[11, 13, 21]) and poor (2 S 12[3]) alike, the material of which varied, no doubt, with the rank and wealth of the owner. Joseph's divining cup (*gābhîaʿ*, Gn 44[2ff]) was of silver, and, we may infer, of elaborate workmanship, since the same word is used for the **bowls** (AV) or cups (RV and RSV), *i.e.* the flower-shaped ornamentation on the candlestick of the Tabernacle. That the *gābhîaʿ*, was larger than the *kōs* is clear from Jer 35[5]. The *kᵉśāwôth* of 1 Ch 28[17] were more probably **flagons**, as RV and RSV in Ex 25[29] 37[16] (but Nu 4[7] RV 'cups,' RSV 'flagons'). The *'aggān* (Is 22[24]) was rather a **basin**, as Ex 24[6], than a cup (EV).

In NT *potērion* is the corresponding name of the ordinary drinking-cup (water Mt 10[42] etc., wine 23[25] etc.). The 'cup of blessing' (1 Co 10[16]) is so named from the *kōs habbᵉrākhāh* of the Jewish Passover (q.v., also Eucharist).

2. The word 'cup' has received an extended figurative application in both OT and NT. (*a*) As in various other literatures, 'cup' stands, especially in Psalms, for the happy fortune or experience of one's earthly lot, mankind being thought of as receiving this lot from the hand of God, as the guest receives the wine-cup from the hand of his host (Ps 16[5] 23[5] etc.). But also, conversely, for the bitter lot of the wicked, Ps 11[6] 75[8] (cf (*c*) below), and in particular for the sufferings of Jesus Christ, Mt 20[22f], Mk 10[38f] 14[36], Lk 22[42], Jn 18[11]. (*b*) Another figure is the 'cup of salvation' (literally 'of deliverances'), Ps 116[13]. The reference is to the wine of the thank-offerings, part of the ritual of which was the festal meal before Y″ (cf vv.[14, 17ff]). (*c*) By a still bolder figure the punitive wrath of the offended Deity is spoken of as a cup which the guilty, Israelites and heathen alike, must drain to the dregs. So Jer 25[15ff] (the wine-cup [of] wrath), Ezk 23[32–34], Is 51[17ff] ('the cup of trembling,' RV and RSV 'staggering'), Zec 12[2] (RV and RSV 'cup of reeling'), Ps 75[8], Rev 14[10] 16[19] 18[6], for all which see the commentaries. (*d*) Lastly, we have 'the cup of consolation' offered to the mourners after the funeral-rites, Jer 16[7] (cf Pr 31[6]).

CUPBEARER.—An officer of considerable importance at Oriental courts, whose duty it was to serve the wine at the table of the king. The first mention of this officer is in the story of Joseph (Gn 40[1–15]), where the term rendered **butler** in EV is the Hebrew word which is rendered in other passages 'cupbearer.' The holder of this office was brought into confidential relations with the king, and must have been thoroughly trustworthy, as part of his duty was to guard against poison in the king's cup. In some cases he was required to taste the wine before presenting it. The position of Nehemiah as cupbearer to Artaxerxes Longimanus was evidently high. Herodotus (iii. 34) speaks of the office at the court of Cambyses, king of Persia, as 'an honour of no small account,' and the narrative of Nehemiah shows the high esteem of the king, who is so solicitous for his welfare that he asks the cause of his sadness (2[2]). The cupbearers among the officers of king Solomon's household (1 K 10[5]) impressed the queen of Sheba, and they are mentioned among other indications of the grandeur of his court, which was modelled upon courts of other Oriental kings.

CUPBOARD (1 Mac 15[32] AV and RV).—A 'sideboard' (RSV) used for the display of gold and silver plate. This is the earliest meaning of 'cupboard'; cf Greene (1592), 'Her mistress . . . set all her plate on the cubboorde for shew.'

CURDS.—See Milk.

CURSE.—See Blessing and Curse, Ban, and Excommunication.

CURTAIN.—See Tabernacle, **5** (*a*).

CUSH.—A personal name found only in the title of Ps 7. He is described as a Benjamite, and was probably a follower of Saul who opposed David.

CUSH in OT designates **Ethiopia** (q.v.), and is the only name used there for that region. It is the same as the Egyptian *Kôsh*. Broadly speaking, it answers to the modern Nubia. More specifically, the Egyptian *Kôsh* extended southwards from the first Cataract at Syene (Ezk 29[10]), and in the periods of widest extension of the empire it embraced a portion of the Sudan. A rich source of gold, it attracted the lucrative caravan trade of

Egypt from early times. It was conquered and annexed by Egypt under the 12th dynasty (*c* 1991–1786 B.C.) and remained normally a subject country. After the decline of the 22nd (Libyan) dynasty, the Cushites became powerful and gradually encroached on northern Egypt, so that at length an Ethiopian dynasty was established (the 25th, 715–656 B.C.), which was overthrown by the Assyrians. Within this period falls the attempt of Tirhakah, king of Cush, to defeat Sennacherib of Assyria in Palestine (2 K 19^{9}).

In Gn 10^{6} Cush is a son of Ham, though his descendants as given in v.^{7} are mostly peoples of central and southern Arabia. Surprising also is the statement in 2 Ch 14^{9ff} that Zerah the Cushite invaded Judah in the days of Asa, at a time when the Cushites had no power in Egypt. An attempt has been made to solve these and other difficulties by the assumption of a second Cush in Arabia (cf 2 Ch 21^{16}). Instructive references to the Cushite country and people are found in Am 9^{7}, Is 18^{1f}, Jer 13^{23}. Cushites were frequent in Palestine, probably descendants of slaves; see 2 S 18^{21ff}, Jer 36^{14} 38^{7ff}. These were, however, possibly Arabian Cushites. For the explanation of the Cush of Gn 10^{8ff}, and possibly of 2^{13}, as the Kassites, see COSSAEANS. See also ETHIOPIA.

J. F. McC.—**R. J. W.**

CUSHAN.—A tribe near Midian, Hab 3^{7}; perhaps the Arabian **Cush** (q.v.).

CUSHAN-RISHATHAIM.—King of Mesopotamia, or Aram-naharaim, first of the oppressors of Israel, from whom Othniel, son of Kenaz, delivered them after eight years (Jg 3^{8-10}). It has been conjectured that he was a king of the Mitanni, whose territory once covered the district between the Euphrates and Habor, or—more probably—that 'Aram' is a mistake for Edom (with 'naharaim' a later addition). 'Rishathaim' ('two wickednesses') is doubtless a corruption, perhaps deliberate, of his name; Rêsh-hattêmānî, 'chief of the Temanites,' has been suggested. The name has not yet received any monumental explanation, and its nationality is unknown. C. H. W. J.—**H. H. R.**

CUSHI, CUSHITE.—The word *Kûshî* occurs with the article in Nu 12^{1}, 2 S 18^{21}; without the article in Jer 36^{14}, Zeph 1^{1}. **1.** With the article it is probably merely an expression of nationality, 'the Cushite' (see CUSH). It was looked upon as a disgrace that Moses should have married a Cushite. **2.** Without the article the word is used merely as a proper name. It is borne by (*a*) the great-grandfather of Jehudi, the latter one of Jehoiakim's courtiers (Jer 36^{14}); (*b*) the father of the prophet Zephaniah (Zeph 1^{1}).

CUSHION.—See PILLOW.

CUSHITE WOMAN.—See ETHIOPIAN WOMAN.

CUSTOM(S) (Mt 17^{25}, Ro 13^{7}): 'receipt of custom' (Mt 9^{9}, Mk 2^{14}, Lk 5^{27}), RSV 'toll,' 'revenue,' 'tax.'—This is to be carefully distinguished from 'tribute' (q.v.). The customs ('dues' or 'duties') were paid on the value of goods, in Galilee and Peraea to the Herods, but in the Roman province of Judaea to the procurator as agent of the Roman government. The 'receipt of custom' was the collector's office. A. So.

CUTH, CUTHAH.—One of the cities from which Sargon brought colonists to take the place of the Israelites whom he had deported from Samaria, 721 B.C. (2 K $17^{24, 30}$). These colonists intermingled with the Israelite inhabitants who were left by Sargon; and their descendants, the Samaritans, were in consequence termed by the Jews 'Cuthaeans.' According to the old Arabic geographers, Cuthah was situated not far from Babylon. This view is borne out by the Assyrian inscriptions, from which we learn that *Kutū* was a city of Middle-Babylonia. It has now been identified with the modern *Tell Ibrāhîm*, NE. of Babylon, where remains of the temple of Nergal (cf v.^{30}) have been discovered.

CUTHA (1 Es 5^{32}).—His sons were among the Temple servants who returned from Babylon with Zerubbabel.

CUTTING OFF FROM THE PEOPLE.—See CRIMES AND PUNISHMENTS, **11.**

CUTTINGS IN THE FLESH.—The phrase itself occurs only in Lv 19^{28} 21^{5}, but a similar prohibition is found in Dt 14^{1}. The reference is to a custom widespread among primitive peoples of gashing the body as part of mourning rites (Jer 16^{6}). The possible original reason may have been to make mourners unrecognisable to the departed, who would thus cease to haunt them; or to provide blood for the departed, who might thus be enabled to live again. In any case, the original rationale had long since been forgotten and the practice had become a ritual custom. The extravagance which often accompanies grief led to this practice being extended to other occasions of urgent need, *e.g.* lamenting before a deity in time of famine or defeat (Hos 7^{14} RVm, RSV; Jer 41^{5} 47^{5}). The practice also became a feature of the ecstatic phenomena exhibited by the more primitive prophets (1 K 18^{28}, Zech 13^{6}). The practice began to be condemned, at least from the time of Deuteronomy, because of undesirable religious associations rather than from ethical or aesthetic reasons. It was not Yahwistic and therefore to be abhorred. Shaving the whole head (Ezk 44^{20}) or the frontal area (Dt 14^{1}) or the temples (Jer 9^{26}) and shaping the beard were likewise forbidden, together with tattooing (Lv 19^{28}) because they were characteristic of non-Yahweh cults. Yet circumcision, a particular instance of cuttings in the flesh, was enjoined; it was a later custom to shave the head at the conclusion of the period of a vow (Nu 6^{1-21}, Ac 18^{18} 21^{24}); and tattooing is mentioned favourably at least twice (Is 44^{5} RVm, RSV; Rev 3^{12}). In both these last instances, however, the monogram definitely marks the bearer as a worshipper of the true God. Thus it was the pagan associations rather than the practices themselves which were condemned.

S. B. F.

CYAMON, Jth 7^{3} = **Jokneam** (q.v.).

CYLINDER.—Ca 5^{14} (RVm) for AV, RV 'ring' (RSV 'rounded'). See RING.

CYMBAL.—See MUSIC AND MUSICAL INSTRUMENTS.

CYPRESS.—**1.** *b*^{e}*rôsh* is rendered 'fir tree' in AV and RV, but 'cypress' in RVm in 2 S 6^{5} and elsewhere. RSV has 'fir' in Ezk 27^{5} 31^{8}, Ps 104^{17} (also in RSVm 2 S 6^{5}), but elsewhere 'cypress' (*e.g.* 1 K $5^{8, 10}$, Is 41^{19} 55^{13}, Ho 14^{8}, Zec 11^{2}), probably rightly. See FIR. In Palestine to-day cypresses are extensively planted, especially in cemeteries. **2.** *tirzāh* is rendered 'cypress' in AV in Is 44^{14}, but '**holm tree**' in RV, RSV. It is an unknown species of tree with very hard wood, the root meaning in Arabic *to be hard.* 'Holm oak' is the rendering of OL. This is the *Quercus ilex*, a tree now rare W. of the Jordan, but still found in Gilead and Bashan. **3.** *t*^{e}*'ashshūr* is rendered 'cypress' in RVm in Is 41^{19}, but here and in Is 60^{13} AV and RV have 'box' and RSV 'pine' (cf Ezk 27^{6}, where AV has 'Ashurites'). See BOX-TREE.

CYPRUS.—An island in the NE. corner of the Mediterranean Sea, about 40 miles W. of the coast of Syria and 60 miles S. of Turkey, whose mountains are visible on a clear day. Third largest of the islands of the Mediterranean (after Sicily and Sardinia), Cyprus has an area of 3572 square miles with 486 miles of coast line which is characterized by a few small harbours and long sandy beaches. Its greatest length is 140 miles, breadth 60 miles. In configuration it consists of a long plain shut in on the N. and the SW. by mountain ranges, Mount Olympus (Troodos) being the highest peak at 6406 feet; at the NE. it tapers into a narrow strip of land about 6 miles wide and 46 miles long, terminating in Cape Andreas. Once covered by extensive forests which are gradually being restored in modern times, the island has been coveted by great world powers since the dawn of history because of its natural resources and its strategic importance for the political and military control of the Middle East.

In the AV of the OT the name 'Cyprus' does not occur. The RSV has 'Cyprus' in four passages (Is 23[1, 12]; Jer 2[10], Ezk 27[6]) where it is a translation of the Hebrew *Kittîm* (Gr. *Kition* and *Chettion*). The contexts of these passages, with their references to wood from **Kittim** (q.v.) and implying proximity to the Phoenician cities of Tyre and Sidon, make it probable that Cyprus is mentioned. The name *Kittîm*, which is the same as the name of the Phoenician town Kition, now the city of Larnaka in Cyprus, was also used to designate a larger region of the Mediterranean and its peoples. In Gn 10[4] Kittim is spoken of as a son of Javan together with Elishah, Tarshish, and Dodanim. This probably implies that the earliest population of Cyprus was akin to the pre-Hellenic population of Greece. But the name Kittim is also used in the OT of the West generally, as in Dn 11[30] of the Romans (cf Dead Sea Scroll *Habakkuk Commentary*, col. iia, 12), and in Nu 24[24] where the context does not make clear whether the name refers to Cyprus or the Mediterranean countries generally.

In the early records of the Egyptian, Hittite, and Mesopotamian rulers, the island is mentioned under various names such as 'Asi' (records of the military campaigns of Thut-mose III.), 'Alashiya' (Journey of Wen-Amon to Phoenicia, War of Rameses III. against the Sea Peoples, and Hittite ritual texts) and 'Iadanana' (Inscriptions of Sargon II. and Sennacherib). The evidence pertaining to these early names for the island is summarized by R. Dussaud (cf C. Schaeffer, *Enkomi-Alasia*, I. (1952).

The name 'Cyprus' is a transliteration of the Greek *Kypros* (see 1 Mac 15[23], 2 Mac 4[29] 10[13] 12[2]) which is also the Greek word for 'copper,' the mineral which was mined in quantities in ancient times and exported to other regions of the Mediterranean. A Hittite ritual text refers to copper and bronze brought from Mount Taggata in Cyprus (Alasiya); copper was exported to Europe as late as the Middle Ages. In the NT, Cyprus (Gr. *Kypros*, *Kyprios*) is mentioned only in connexion with the missionary journeys of Paul and Barnabas (see below).

The history of Cyprus can be traced, not only through literary references to the island in ancient Near Eastern texts, but also through other results of archaeological work beginning during the period of Turkish domination and continuing in the 20th cent. under British control. Excavations have been conducted under the auspices of Swedish, British, and American institutions, and by the Department of Antiquities with headquarters in Nicosia, the capital of the island (see P. Dikaios, *A Guide to the Cyprus Museum*, 1953). Human occupation has been traced back to the Neolithic (New Stone) age, about 3700 B.C., when large communities existed near springs or rivers, some animals were domesticated, flint and bone implements were used, and the presence of obsidian blades suggests a contact with Asia Minor. Copper was apparently first used about 3200 B.C. (the beginning of the Chalcolithic period), although stone implements continued to be used during the period. The demand for copper in other parts of Asia Minor doubtless encouraged commercial relationships with Cyprus.

It was once thought that copper was first exported by Phoenicians, who early founded Kition and other towns in Cyprus, and introduced the worship of the Syrian Aphrodite who became known to the Greeks as the 'Cyprian goddess.' However, recent excavations have uncovered material remains of the early Bronze Age (also called Early Cypriot Age, *c* 2400–2000 B.C.) and of the Middle Bronze Age (also called Middle Cypriot Age, *c* 2000–1550 B.C.) which indicate commercial relationships with Anatolia, Minoan Crete, and Egypt, as well as with the peoples of the Syrian coast. The Late Bronze (or Late Cypriot) Age (*c* 1550–1050 B.C.) was a very significant one, witnessing as it did, further contacts with the Syro-Palestinian areas, and also the arrival of Mycenaean settlers, military occupation by the Egyptians under Thut-mose III., and waves of Achaean colonists following the Trojan War. During this period Cyprus became an island link between the lands of the East and the West; excavations reveal considerable wealth and a high degree of culture.

Although Cyprus did not develop as a strong independent power, some degree of independence was maintained under Cypriot kings during the Iron Age (*c* 1050–950 B.C.). Commercial relationships with Phoenicia were strong, but it was not until about 800 B.C. that Phoenician penetration reached its height, especially at the Tyrian city of Kition. In 709 B.C. Assyrian control of the island began, as recorded in the inscription of Sargon II. at Kition, and later Assyrian kings report tribute received from Cyprus. The prism of Esar-haddon (673 B.C.) refers to ten kings from Cyprus (Iadnana) who were, among others, subject to him. Shortly thereafter, Assyrian domination of Cyprus came to an end, and there was almost a century of independence which was characterized by much activity in the building of palaces, ships and homes, and advances in ceramic art and poetry. About 560 B.C. Amasis of Egypt conquered the island, and it passed with Egypt to Cambyses of Persia in 525 B.C., although Cypriot kings continued in power and minted their own coinage under the Persian kings. In 500 B.C. the Greek cities of the island joined in the Ionic revolt against the Persians, but Kition and probably other Phoenician cities on the island remained loyal to Persia. During the 5th cent. the island remained subject to Persia and in 480 B.C. supplied 150 ships for the fleet of Xerxes. Athens made repeated attempts to secure the island, but the mixed population prevented any strong Hellenic movement, and it only passed definitely into Greek hands by submission to Alexander the Great after the battle of Issus in 333 B.C. On the division of his empire it fell to the Ptolemies of Egypt, until it was annexed by Rome in 57 B.C. It was made a separate province after the battle of Actium in 31 B.C., becoming at first an 'imperial' province, but was, in 22 B.C. transferred to 'senatorial' government, so that in Ac 13[7] Luke rightly describes the governor as the proconsul, Sergius Paulus. An inscription found near Paphos about A.D. 1870 and dated about A.D. 55 mentions a Paulus who was proconsul, although scholars do not agree that this is the same individual mentioned in Ac 13[7].

Jews first settled in Cyprus under the Ptolemies, and their numbers there were considerable before the time of the Apostles. Barnabas is described as a 'Levite, a native of Cyprus' (Ac 4[36]). When he and Paul started from Antioch on the First Missionary Journey, they first of all passed through Cyprus (Ac 13[4-12]). They landed at Salamis, then a Greek port flourishing with Syrian trade (as demonstrated by modern excavations); the city now deserted—with its harbour silted up—is three miles from Famagusta. Here they preached in the synagogue, where their message was probably not entirely new (Ac 11[19]), and then journeyed through 'the whole island' (Ac 13[6], RSV) to New Paphos in the W.—a three or four days' journey, even if they preached nowhere on the way. New Paphos, like Old Paphos, was the seat of the worship of Aphrodite (see PAPHOS), and was at this time the Roman capital. (For the incidents connected with the proconsul and the *magus*, see articles SERGIUS PAULUS and BAR-JESUS.)

Besides Barnabas we have mention of Mnason, 'an early disciple' (RSV), as coming from Cyprus (Ac 21[16]), but little information is available regarding the fortunes of the Christian community under later centuries of Roman rule. The Jews of Cyprus took part in the great revolt in A.D. 117 (when Trajan was busy with Parthia) which was participated in by Jews of Egypt and Cyrene, and they are said to have massacred 240,000 of the Gentile population on Cyprus. Hadrian, who later became emperor, put down the revolt and expelled all Jews from the island.

Following the division of the Roman empire in A.D. 395 Cyprus was ruled from Constantinople by the Byzantine emperors. The Christians enjoyed a degree of autonomy having been granted the right to elect and consecrate their own bishops and archbishop by the councils of Ephesus

(A.D. 431) and Trullan (A.D. 692). During the following centuries Cyprus was often the scene of conflict involving Moslem and Byzantine forces. Seized in 1191 by Richard Coeur de Lion (Richard I.), it was sold to the Knights Templars, and it became a bastion of the Crusaders after defeats in Syria and Palestine. In 1373 Italian forces from Genoa were able to seize the port of Famagusta and assume control of the government and commerce for almost a century. In the 15th cent. Cyprus became a part of the Mediterranean empire ruled from Venice. After three centuries of Turkish rule it passed under British rule in 1878, by a convention requiring continued payment of tribute to the Sultan.

In 1914 Cyprus became a British crown colony and its people, a mixture of Greek and Turkish communities, enjoyed a period of peace and increasing prosperity. Following World War II. and the expulsion of British military forces from Egypt and Jordan, Cyprus became a strong British base in the eastern Mediterranean. This development coincided with a renewal of the demand by segments of the Greek population for union (*enosis*) with Greece. The Turkish population reacted against this movement, and the 1950's were characterized by violence and bloodshed caused by extremists in both segments of the population. In spite of this situation, the tourist trade and commerce increased. New roads were built, harbour installations were improved at Famagusta and Larnaka with the construction of piers, although Limassol remained an open roadstead where large ships must be loaded and unloaded by means of lighters. A modern airport near Nicosia served to link the island with Greece, Italy, Turkey, and the countries of the Middle East. The copper mines, which made Cyprus famous in ancient times but were neglected from the Roman occupation until the 19th cent., became in modern times the source of cupreous pyrites; other minerals being mined include iron pyrites, asbestos, chrome ore, and gypsum.

In 1960 Cyprus became an independent sovereign state with a Greek Cypriot President and a Turkish Cypriot Vice-President. It continues to belong to the British Commonwealth. Two areas of the island where there are military bases remain under United Kingdom sovereignty. A. E. H.—**W. L. R.**

CYRENE.—Capital of Libya (Tripoli) in N. Africa (Ac 2[10]), the home of numerous Jews who with the 'Libertines' (freedmen from Rome?) and Alexandrians had a synagogue of their own at Jerusalem (Ac 6[9]). Many of these became Christians, as Simon and his sons (doubtless), Mk 15[21]; Lucius, Ac 13[1]; and those in Ac 11[20] who preached to the 'Greeks' (*v.l.* 'Hellenists'). A. J. M.

CYRENIUS.—See QUIRINIUS.

CYRUS (Pers. *Kurush*, Bab. *Kurash*, Heb. *Kōresh*, possibly in origin an Elamite throne name meaning 'shepherd').—Cyrus the Great, founder of the Persian empire, was son of Cambyses I. of the Achaemenid family. He describes his ancestors as 'kings of Anshan,' formerly an Elamite province with its capital at Susa, and a vassal state of the Median empire. He himself became king in 559 B.C., but rebelled in 553 B.C. and defeated the Median king Astyages. Cyrus then termed himself 'king of the Persians,' and he soon made himself master of the whole Median empire. He was then faced with an alliance of Croesus of Lydia, Nabonidus of Babylon, and Amasis of Egypt, but defeating Croesus in 546 B.C., he turned his attention to Babylonia, where Nabonidus was unpopular because of his neglect of the worship of Marduk, having devoted his attention to Sin the moon-god. Belshazzar, son of Nabonidus, and regent in Babylon, was defeated and Babylon itself surrendered in October 539 B.C. to Gobyras (Gubaru, Ugbaru), Cyrus' general. From early 538 B.C., when he himself entered Babylon, Cyrus described himself as 'king of Babylon and king of the countries'; he claimed to have been welcomed by the people, and especially by the priests and nobles, as a liberator, chosen by Marduk to be his restorer. He also returned other gods to their homes and asks that they should intercede for him with Marduk (Bel) and Nabu. Subsequently he established a new capital at Pasargadae, north of Persepolis, and reigned until 529 B.C., when he was killed on campaign in the east, having appointed his son Cambyses as ruler in Babylon.

Cyrus is referred to as 'king of Persia' 2 Ch 36[22] = Ezr 1[1], Dn 10[1] and often; as 'the Persian' Dn 6[28]; 'king of Babylon' Ezr 5[13]. In Deutero-Isaiah, he is described as specially destined by Yahweh to redeem Israel, and to execute judgment upon Babylon, to set free the captives and restore Jerusalem and its Temple (by name 44[28] 45[1]). He had not known Yahweh before his call, but carried out his mission in Yahweh's name, and is styled 'the friend of Yahweh' and 'Yahweh's anointed.' According to Ezr 1[1-4], he granted permission to the Jews to return to Palestine and to rebuild the Temple; but the other copy of the decree in Ezr 6[2-5] does not mention permission to return, so that it may well be that only a commissioner and some leaders were sent. It may indeed be doubted whether Cyrus exercised more than nominal control of Syria and Palestine; only under Cambyses was the west visited by a Persian ruler.

The sources of information for his reign are various, notably the so-called Nabonidus Chronicle, and the Cyrus Cylinder which describes him as called by Marduk. A text from Ur attributes his victory to Sin, the moon-god. The Old Testament claims the honour for Yahweh. The career of Cyrus not unnaturally led to the gathering of legends about him, concerning his birth and upbringing, various versions of which may be found in classical literature. C. H. W. J.—**P. R. A.**

D

DABAREH, Jos 21[28] (AV).—See DABERATH.

DABBASHETH, Jos 19[11] (AV).—See DABBESHETH.

DABBESHETH (? 'hump').—A town of Zebulun, Jos 19[11] (AV **Dabbasheth**); perhaps modern *Tell esh-Shammām*.

DABERATH.—A city assigned to Zebulun, Jos 19[12], but said to be a Levitical city of Issachar, Jos 21[28] (AV **Dabareh**), 1 Ch 6[72]; perhaps on the border between the two tribes; probably modern *Dabûriyeh*, at the foot of Mount Tabor. Abel (*Géographie* ii, 61) reads Daberath for **Rabbith** (q.v.) in Jos 19[20].

DABRIA.—One of the five scribes who wrote to the dictation of Ezra (2 Es 14[24]).

DACOBI, 1 Es 5[28] (AV).—See AKKUB, **2.**

DACUBI, 1 Es 5[28] (RV).—See AKKUB, **2.**

DADDEUS, 1 Es 8[46] (AV).—See IDDO, **1.**

DAGGER.—See ARMOUR, ARMS, **1** (*c*).

DAGON.—A god whose worship was general among the Philistines (at Gaza, Jg 16[23]; at Ashdod, 1 S 5[2-7], 1 Mac 10[83f] 11[4]; perhaps at Beth-shan, 1 Ch 10[10], cf 1 S 31[10]; probably at the southern Beth-dagon (q.v.), which may at one time have been under Philistine rule). Dagon (earlier form, Dagan) was an old Semitic agricultural deity worshipped in Mesopotamia before 2400 B.C. From there he passed to Syria, having a temple in his honour at Ugarit (see RÂS SHAMRA), where he was considered the father of Baal (q.v.). Next his cult was found in northern Palestine (Jos 19^{27}), then in the south (Jos 15^{41}), whence it was probably taken over by the non-Semitic Philistines. The rare Hebrew word *dāghān*, meaning 'corn' ('grain') or 'bread,' is probably to be explained from the name and nature of the god. The name of this deity also appears on a Phoenician seal cylinder of the 7th cent. B.C. now in the Ashmolean Museum, Oxford, and again on the later Phoenician sarcophagus of Eshmunʿazar in connexion with the city of Joppa. It survives in the Palestinian place-name *Khirbet Dajūn* (and *Beit Dajān*) near Joppa (Abel, *Géog. de la Pal.*, ii, 269). There is also a *Beit Dajān* near Nâblus. The older explanation, connecting the name of the deity with the Hebrew word *dāgh*, 'fish,' and thus making Dagon a fish-god, seems no longer tenable (see Albright, *Archaeol. and the Rel. of Israel*, 74 f). N. K.—**W. F. S.**

DAISAN, 1 Es 5^{31} AV and RV=**Rezin,** Ezr 2^{48}, Neh 7^{50}. The form in 1 Esdras is due to confusion of Hebrew *r* and *l*; RSV **Rezin.** See REZIN, **2.**

DALAIAH, 1 Ch 3^{24} (AV).—See DELAIAH, **1.**

DALAN, 1 Es 5^{37} (RV).—See DELAIAH, **5.**

DALETH.—The fourth letter of Hebrew alphabet, and so used to introduce the fourth part of Ps 119, every verse of which begins with this letter.

DALMANUTHA.—The place to which Jesus sailed after the feeding of the four thousand (Mk 8^{10}). In Mt 15^{39} the name is **Magadan,** which Eusebius asserts is the right reading, and which some MSS also read in Mk 8^{10}. The Palestinian Syriac Gospel has *Magdal*, which probably is the correct form of the name. Dalmanutha is the product of a series of errors by copyists of NT MSS. E. G. K.

DALMATIA.—A mountainous district on the E. coast of the Adriatic Sea. More exactly used, it is the southern half of the Roman province Illyricum (q.v.). The writer of the Second Epistle to Timothy makes Titus journey there (2 Ti 4^{10}). The nearest Paul came to it in recorded travels is Beroea (Ac 17^{10}), still 90 miles away from Dalmatia. A. So.—**E. G. K.**

DALPHON.—Second son of Haman, put to death by the Jews, Est 9^{7}.

DAMARIS.—A convert at Athens (Ac 17^{34}). As women of the upper classes were kept more in the background there than in Macedonia or Asia Minor, she was probably not of noble birth (cf $17^{4,12}$). But Codex Laudianus (E) describes her as *timia*.

A. J. M.—**F. C. G.**

DAMASCUS.—1. Situation, etc.—The chief city of inland Syria and the modern political capital, it lies in a plain E. of the Anti-Lebanon famous for its beauty and fertility and watered by the Baradā River, biblical Abana (q.v.). It derives its modern importance from local manufactures (woodwork, furniture, artistic metal, and textile work), from its situation as the metropolis of the N. Arabian steppe and from its position as the capital of the state. Formerly it was the starting-point of the annual Syrian pilgrim caravan to Mecca. In Ottoman times it was connected by rail with Beirut, Haifa, Aleppo, and Medina, the last line now being discontinued at Maʿân.

The history of Damascus begins reputedly in remote antiquity, this being suggested by its favourable natural situation, though its actual origins are not certainly known. It certainly appears as the capital of a city-state in Egyptian inscriptions of the 15th cent. B.C.

2. OT references.—Reference is made to Damascus in defining the line of Abram's pursuit of the four kings (Gn 14^{15}). In Gn 15^{2} the name of Abram's steward is given in the MT as *Dammesek Eliezer* (so RV). It is explained in the Targum and Syriac version as 'Eliezer the Damascene' (cf RSV), though this does violence to Hebrew grammar. Probably *dammesheq* of the MT is an early Midrashic gloss such as the Qumrân 'commentaries' have made familiar to us. As a reprisal for assistance given to Hadadezer, king of Zobah, David garrisoned Damascus and reduced it to a tributary condition (2 S 8^{5f}, 1 Ch 18^{5}). Rezon, however, Hadadezer's general, succeeded in establishing himself as king in Damascus in the time of Solomon and made himself continuously a very troublesome neighbour (1 K 11^{23f}). In the wars between Asa and Baasha (1 K 15^{17ff}, 2 Ch 16^{2ff}) the king of Judah invoked the aid of Benhadad, king of Aram, whose royal city was Damascus, against his Israelite enemy, suborning him to break the existing truce with Israel, thus enabling Judah to fortify her N. frontier to within two miles of Bethel. Hostilities continued between Aram (Damascus) and Israel till the days of Ahab; Ahab's sparing of Benhadad after the battle of Aphek and his making a truce with him were the cause of a prophetic denunciation (1 K 20^{42}). This incident may be connected with an alliance of W. Asiatic states against Assyrian aggression culminating in the famous stand at the battle of Qarqar (853 B.C.). The relative significance of Damascus is indicated by the fact that in the inscription of Shalmaneser III. Ahab is recorded as having sent 2000 chariots and 10,000 footmen, while Damascus sent 1200 chariots and the same number of mounted cavalry, and 20,000 footmen. In the reign of Jehoram, the Syrian general Naaman came to be cleansed of leprosy and Elisha's directions led to his famous depreciating comparison of the muddy Jordan with his own Abana and Pharpar (2 K 5). The Chronicler reports a victorious invasion by Damascus on Judah in the days of Joash (2 Ch 24^{23}). During this time, however, Damascus bore the brunt of Assyrian attack and it was probably after one of her many reverses that Jeroboam II. took the city (2 K 14^{28}), though he apparently could not hold it, since it was again in open revolt against Assyria in the time of Ahaz under its king Rezin (2 K 16) in alliance with Pekah of Israel. Prophetic denunciations of Damascus are found in Is 17, Jer 49^{23}, Am 1^{3-5}, and Zec 9^{1}, the last referring to Damascus and Hamath as part of the Seleucid Empire in the 2nd cent. B.C. The state of which Damascus was the capital was liquidated by Assyria in 732 B.C. Damascus as a commercial centre was always of great importance and Ezekiel (27^{18}) alludes to trade in wine and wool. It is included in the imaginary restoration of the kingdom (Ezk 47^{17}).

3. NT references.—Damascus appears only with reference to St. Paul. His conversion is located here (Ac $9^{22,26}$), and his escape from Aretas (q.v.), the Nabataean ruler, by being lowered in a basket over the wall (Ac 9^{25}, 2 Co 11^{32f}), and here he returned after his Arabian retirement (Gal 1^{17}).

4. Later history.—After the Asiatic campaigns of Alexander the Great, Damascus became a centre of Hellenism, being occupied both by Ptolemies and Seleucids. As the metropolis of the N. Arabian steppe and an important land-port it was the object of Nabataean ambition and twice fell into their hands, once in the 1st cent. B.C. and again in the time of St. Paul. At other times in the same period it was one of the cities in the mercantile federation of the Decapolis. The great temple of the city, devoted to the cult of Baal-Hadad, was transformed into a church, dedicated to St. John, which was converted into the famous Umayyad mosque, the principal mosque in the city, which contains the tomb of Salāh ed-Dîn. Since A.D. 635 Damascus has been a Moslem city. It was the brilliant capital of the Umayyad Caliphs under whom the Empire of Islam reached the Pyrenees. It was conquered by the Seljuk Turks in 1075. In the Crusades it was the fatal mistake of the Crusaders to allow it to stand untaken as a vital link in the internal line of communication between Iraq and Egypt. The Umayyad mosque, a mediaeval castle, and part of the Byzantine walls are the principal relics of antiquity to be seen in the modern city. There are the usual traditional sites of historical events, such as the house of Ananias and the street called Straight, but these are not more trustworthy at Damascus than they are in Palestine, though, if, as

is probable, 'the street called Straight' referred to the main thoroughfare, *cardo maximus*, of the Graeco-Roman city, tradition here is more than usually reliable.
R. A. S. M.—**J. Gr.**

DAMNATION.—The words 'damn,' 'damnable,' and 'damnation' have, through their use in the literature of theology, come to express *condemnation to everlasting punishment*. But in the English Bible they mean no more than is now expressed by 'condemn' or 'condemnation.' RSV omits 'damnation' and cognates. In some places a better translation than 'condemnation' is 'judgment,' as in Jn 5[29] 'the resurrection of damnation' (Gr. *krisis*, RSV 'judgment'). See JUDGMENT.

DAN.—According to the popular tradition, Dan was the fifth son of Jacob, and full brother of Naphtali, by Bilhah, Rachel's handmaid (Gn 30[6, 8]). Rachel, who had no children, exclaimed *dānannî* ('God hath judged me'), and he was therefore called *Dan*. As in the case of so many names in the OT, this is clearly a 'popular etymology.' Probably Dan was the titular attribute of a tribal god whose name has dropped out (cf Assyr. *Ashur-dan*).

Of this eponymous ancestor of the tribe tradition has preserved no details, but some of the most interesting stories in the Book of Judges tell of the exploits of the Danite Samson in border wars against the Philistines. These are heroic rather than historical tales, yet they are suggestive of the conditions that prevailed when the tribes were settling Palestine.

P makes Dan a large tribe, giving the fighting strength of Dan in the Wilderness census as 62,700, more than that of any other except Judah (Nu 1[33]; cf 26[43], Moab census). All the other data point in the opposite direction. J (Jg 18[11]) speaks of Dan as a 'family' (Heb. *mishpāḥāh*), which is less than a tribe; elsewhere Dan is said to have had only one son, Hushim or Shuham (Gn 46[23], Nu 26[42]). The tribe at first occupied the hill-country in the SW. of Ephraim, and thence attempted to spread out into the Valleys of Aijalon and Sorek. That it ever reached the sea, either here or later in the N. is unlikely. The passage in Jg 5[17] ('And Dan—why did he abide in ships?'), if the text is correct, must refer to the location of the tribe by Lake Huleh. In the S. the Danites were severely pressed by the Amorites and the Philistines, and the major part were compelled to emigrate northward, where they found at the foot of Mt. Hermon an isolated Sidonian colony, Laish or Leshem, at the headwaters of one of the sources of the Jordan, adjoining the territory of Naphtali, with whom they had the closest affinity among the Hebrew tribes (Jos 19[47], Jg 18). This settlement the Danites ruthlessly destroyed. A new town was built, to which they gave the name of Dan, the Arab name of the site being *Tell el-Qâḍî* ('Mound of the Judge'). In this colony there were only 600 armed men and their families. On their way thither they induced the domestic priest of the Ephraimite Micah to accompany them with his sacred equipment, an ephod, a graven and molten image, and the teraphim, which were duly installed in a permanent sanctuary, in which the descendants of Moses are said to have ministered until the Exile (Jg 18[30]). 'From Dan to Beersheba' denoted the extent of the Israelite occupation, and at Dan Jeroboam I. established a rival shrine to Jerusalem, a feature of which was the use of the bull as a sacred symbol of the presence of Yahweh. Here Jeroboam possibly adapted the local Phoenician cult of Baal, whose cult-animal was the bull, to the worship of Yahweh. That the remnant of the Danites left in the S. was either destroyed by their enemies, or, more likely, absorbed by the neighbouring Hebrew tribes is made probable by Jg 1[35], which ascribes the victory over their enemies to the 'house of Joseph'; cf Jos 19[41-46], which assigns to Dan certain localities elsewhere assigned to Judah and Ephraim. Gn 49[17] says 'Dan shall be a serpent in the way, an adder in the path'; and Dt 33[22] 'Dan is a lion's whelp that leapeth forth from Bashan,' the latter passage alluding probably to Dan's northern habitat. The allusions may be to the harassing of caravans from the Hauran to Phoenicia, or to border warfare with Damascus. It would aptly refer to guerilla tactics in the Assyrian wars of the 8th cent., but the passage is probably much earlier than that. See also TRIBES.
J. A. C.—**J. Gr.**

DAN.—A city in northern Palestine, once called **Laish** (Jg 18[29]) or **Leshem** (Jos 19[47]), though the ancient record of the battle of four kings against five gives the later name (Gn 14[14]). It was a city remote from assistance, and therefore fell an easy prey to a band of marauding Danites, searching for a dwelling-place. It was in the north boundary of Palestine. The story of the Danites stealing the shrine of Micah is told to account for its sanctity, which Jeroboam I. recognized by setting up here one of his calf-shrines (1 K 12[29]). It was perhaps the same as **Dan-jaan,** 2 S 24[6] (AV, RV; RSV **Dan**), one of the borders of Joab's census district. It was captured by Ben-hadad (1 K 15[20]). It is identified with *Tell el-Qâḍî* on account of the similarity of meaning of the names, Arabic *qâḍî*=Hebrew *dān*='judge.' The site would well suit the geographical context of the narratives.
R. A. S. M.—**H. H. R.**

DANCING.—See GAMES.

DANIEL.—**1.** Two passages in the book of Ezekiel (14[14, 20] 28[3]) mention a Daniel who was famed for righteousness and wisdom, and named with Noah and Job. All three evidently belonged to the far-distant past, and Daniel, occupying the middle place, cannot be conceived of as the latest of them. He is not, therefore, to be identified with **2** below. We now have a long epic text from Râs Shamra about Danel and his son Aqhat, where the name is spelt as in Ezekiel. It is probable that he was the person referred to in the above passages. **2.** The hero of the book of Daniel, who was probably created by the author of the book, who used older materials and traditions, which he adapted for a practical purpose. See next article. Stories continued to grow round Daniel's name, and in Greek MSS some have been preserved. See APOCRYPHA, **10, 11, 12. 3.** A son of David and Abigail, 1 Ch 3[1]; called **Chileab** in 2 S 3[3]. **4.** A priest of the house of Ithamar who accompanied Ezra to Jerusalem, Ezr 8[2]; called **Gamael** in 1 Es 8[29]. **5.** One who sealed the covenant, Neh 10[6].
J. T.—**H. H. R.**

DANIEL, BOOK OF.—**1. Authorship and Date.**—The first six chapters of this book contain a series of narratives which tell of (*a*) the fidelity of Daniel and his friends to their religion, and (*b*) the incomparable superiority of their God to the deities of Babylon. The remaining six chapters relate four visions seen by Daniel and the interpretation of them. Chs. 1–6 speak of Daniel in the third person; ch. 7 begins in the third person but turns over to the first; chs. 8–12 are in the first person (but cf 10[1]). The traditional view has been that the whole is from the hand of Daniel who lived in Babylon in the 6th cent. B.C. Porphyry argued against this in the 3rd cent. A.D., and it is now generally abandoned, for such reasons as the following: (1) Neither the man nor the book is mentioned in the list of Sir 44–50 (*c* 200 B.C.): and Sir 49[15] seems to have been written by one who was not acquainted with the story. (2) There is no reason for believing that a collection of sacred writings, including Jeremiah, had been formed in the reign of Darius, as is implied Dn 9[2]. (3) The Hebrew of Daniel is of a later type than even that of Chronicles. The Aramaic (see below, **2**) can be dated with certainty later than the 5th cent. B.C., and with probability not earlier than the 3rd cent. B.C. (cf Rowley, *The Aramaic of the OT*, 1929). (4) More Persian words are employed than a Hebrew author would be familiar with at the close of the Babylonian empire, and the few Greek loan-words imply the Greek period as the setting. One of these, *symphonia* ('bagpipe,' Dn 3[5]), first occurs in Greek literature as the name of a musical instrument in the 2nd cent. B.C. (5) There are inaccuracies which a contemporary would have avoided. Nebuchadnezzar did not besiege Jerusalem in the 3rd year of Jehoiakim. The name 'Chaldaeans' as designating the learned class is a later usage (2[2]). Belshazzar was not 'the king' (5[1])—though for many years he administered the state while his father Nabonidus was in Tema—nor was Nebuchadnezzar his ancestor (5[2, 11]). Darius the Mede (5[31]) is an unhistorical character (cf Rowley, *Darius the Mede*[2], 1959). Xerxes did not follow Artaxerxes (11[2]) but preceded him. (6) The relations between Syria and Egypt, from the 4th to the 2nd cents. B.C., are described with a fulness of detail which differentiates Dn 7, 11 from all OT prophecy: see the precision with which the reign of Antiochus Epiphanes is related in ch. 11; the events from 323–175 B.C. occupy 16 verses; those from 175–164 B.C. take up 25; at v.[34] the lines become less definite, because this is the point at which the book was written; at v.[40] *prediction* begins, and the language no longer corresponds with the facts of history. There can be little doubt that Daniel appeared about 164 B.C. Its object was to encourage the faithful Jews to adhere to their religion, in the assurance that God would intervene. The unknown writer was intensely sure of the truths in which he believed: to him and to his readers the historical setting was but a framework. Not that he invented the stories. He worked with older stories which he adapted and attached to Daniel. One of the Dead Sea Scrolls tells a story of Nabonidus which may be the source of Dn 4, where the madness is transferred to Nebuchadnezzar. It is possible that Dn 4 was first about Nabonidus, and that a subsequent substitution of the name of Nebuchadnezzar here and in 5[2, 11, 18] gave rise to the historical error noted above.

2. Language, Unity, Theology.—(1) From 2[4] to 7[28] is in *Aramaic*. Five explanations have been offered: (*a*) This section was originally written in Aramaic, about 300 B.C., and incorporated, with additions, into the work of 166 B.C. (*b*) The corresponding portion of a Hebrew original was lost and its place filled by an already current Aramaic translation. (*c*) The author introduced the 'Chaldees' as speaking what he supposed was their language, and then continued to write it because it was more familiar than Hebrew to himself and his readers. (*d*) The entire book was Aramaic, but would not have found admission into the Canon if it had not been enclosed, so to speak, in a frame of Hebrew, the sacred language. (*e*) The stories were first created and circulated in Aramaic separately, and later the first vision was composed in Aramaic; but this was less suitable for popular narration, and subsequent visions, still less suitable for this, were written in Hebrew, which was still the literary language. When the stories were collected, ch. 1 was rewritten to make it the introduction to the whole book (*e.g.* Daniel's three friends were introduced), and was now written in Hebrew, the language of the later sections. The point of transition was determined by the amount that needed to be rewritten.

(2) The *unity of the book* has been increasingly impugned in recent years. There is no agreement amongst those who divide the book as to where it should be divided, and in particular to which part ch. 7 belongs. Those who attach it to the first part hold it to be glossed, while those who attach it to the second part do not. Similarly ch. 2 must be held to be glossed by those who make it older than the visions. In language ch. 7 is linked with the stories; in ideas with the visions. Ch. 2 is closely linked with ch. 7. The climax of the expectations of chs. 2, 7, 8–12 lies in the Maccabaean age, and particularly in the attack of Antiochus on the faith of the Jews. The phrase 'abomination of desolation,' found in varying forms in 8[13] 9[27] 11[31] 12[11], indicates the heathen image and altar set up in the Temple by Antiochus. Moreover all the stories would have point in that age. Hence it is preferable to hold to the unity of the book (cf Rowley, 'The Unity of the Book of Daniel,' *HUCA* xxiii, Part 1, 1951, 233 ff).

(3) The *pseudonymity of the book* is variously accounted for. Some have supposed that it was to gain a hearing. But the stories are not pseudonymous. Probably the creator of the stories, which became immediately popular and encouraged resistance to Antiochus, wrote the visions under the name of Daniel, not to conceal his identity, but to attach the prestige of the stories to the visions.

(4) The *theological features* are what might be expected in the 2nd cent. B.C. Eschatology is prominent. The visions and their interpretations all culminate in the final establishment of the Kingdom of God. And in this connexion it should be mentioned that Daniel is the earliest example of a fully developed *Apocalypse*. The doctrine of the Resurrection is also distinctly asserted: *individuals* are to rise again; not all men, or even all Israelites, but the martyrs and the apostates. At no earlier period is there such an angelology. Watchers and holy ones determine the destinies of an arrogant king. Two angels have proper names, Gabriel and Michael. To each nation a heavenly patron has been assigned, and its fortunes here depend on the struggle waged by its representative above. All of these features closely link the book with the apocalyptic works which began to appear in the 2nd cent. B.C. (cf Rowley, *The Relevance of Apocalyptic*[2], 1947).

3. Text.—The early Church set aside the LXX in favour of the less paraphrastic version of Theodotion. In both translations are found the Additions to Daniel (see APOCRYPHA, **10, 11, 12**). (1) Sixty-seven verses are inserted after 3[22], consisting of (*a*) the *Prayer of Azariah*, (*b*) details concerning *the heating of the furnace*, (*c*) the *Benedicite*. These teach the proper frame of mind for all confessors, and dilate on the miraculous element in the Divine deliverance. (2) *The History of Susanna*, which demonstrates God's protection of the unjustly accused and illustrates the sagacity in judgment of the youth who is rightly named *Daniel*, 'El is my judge.' (3) *Bel and the Dragon*, two tracts which expose the imbecility of idolatry, and bring out Daniel's cleverness and God's care for His servant in peril. Swete (*Introd. to OT in Greek*, p. 260) rightly remarks that internal evidence appears to show that (1) and (2) originally had a separate circulation. J. T.—H. H. R.

DAN-JAAN.—Joab and his officers in taking the census came 'to Dan-jaan and round about to Zidon,' 2 S 24[6] (RV, cf AV). No such place is mentioned anywhere else in OT, and it is generally assumed that the text is corrupt. The reference is probably to the city of Dan, and accordingly RSV reads 'to Dan, and from Dan they went around to Sidon.'

DANNAH.—A town of Judah mentioned next to Debir and Socoh, Jos 15[49]. Its site is unknown, but it was clearly in the mountains SW. of Hebron.

DAPHNE.—A place mentioned in 2 Mac 4[33] to which Onias withdrew for refuge, but from which he was decoyed by Andronicus and treacherously slain. It is the modern *Beit el-Mâ* ('House of Waters') about 5 miles from Antioch. Daphne was famous for its fountain, its temple in honour of Apollo and Diana, its oracle, and its right of asylum. See also ANTIOCH.

DARA.—See DARDA.

DARDA.—Mentioned with Ethan the Ezrahite, Heman, and Calcol as a son of Mahol, and a proverbial type of wisdom, but yet surpassed by Solomon (1 K 4[32]). In 1 Ch 2[6] apparently the same four (**Dara** is probably an error for *Darda*) are mentioned with Zimri as sons of Zerah, the son of Judah by Tamar (Gn 38[30]). See also MAHOL.

DARIC.—See MONEY, **3**.

DARIUS.—**1.** Darius I., the Great, son of Hystaspes, king of Persia 522–486 B.C., well-known from the Greek historian Herodotus, and from his inscriptions, especially the trilingual account at Behistun of how he gained the crown after considerable struggles. He is especially noted as organizer of the Persian empire (cf Dn 6[1]). When Haggai and Zechariah were encouraging the rebuilding of the Temple, and the authority for this was demanded by Tattenai, governor of 'Beyond the

River,' an inquiry was sent to Darius and the decree of Cyrus authorizing the work was found in Ecbatana. Darius confirmed this and ordered provision to be made for the building and for sacrifices. The Temple was completed in his sixth year (Ezr 5–6). **2.** Darius the Persian (Neh 12[22]). Possibly Darius III. Codomannus (336–330 B.C.), last king of Persia (cf 1 Mac 1[1]). **3.** 'Darius' (1 Mac 12[7] AV) is an error for the Spartan 'Arius' q.v. (so Old Lat., Josephus, RV, RSV. Cf v.[20]). **4.** 'Darius the Mede' (Dn 11[1]), son of Ahasuerus q.v. (9[1]) is said (5[31]) to have become king of Babylon at the age of sixty-two years after Belshazzar's death. Dn 6[1] indicates identification with No. **1**, But this account does not correspond to what we know of any king called Darius. Attempted identifications with Gobyras, Cyrus' general who actually entered Babylon, or with Cyrus, or some other historical character, are none of them satisfactory. It is easiest to believe that the author of Daniel confused the fall of Babylon in 538 B.C. with that in 520 B.C., and believed that a 'kingdom of the Medes' preceded the rule of Cyrus the Persian (cf Dn 6[28] and Is 13[17]). C. H. W. J.—**P. R. A.**

DARKNESS.—See LIGHT.

DARKON.—His sons were among those who returned with Zerubbabel, Ezr 2[56], Neh 7[58]; called in 1 Es 5[33] **Lozon.**

DARK SAYING.—See RIDDLE.

DARLING.—Ps 22[20] (AV, RV) 'Deliver my darling from the power of the dog'; 35[17] (AV, RV) 'rescue my soul from their destructions, my darling from the lions.' The Hebrew word (*yāḥîdh*) means an only son. In the Psalms it is used poetically of the psalmist's own life, as his unique and priceless possession. RSV renders 'my life.'

DART.—See ARMOUR, ARMS, **1** (b).

DATES.—See CHRONOLOGY.

DATHAN.—A Reubenite, who conspired with Abiram against Moses (Nu 16[1], Dt 11[6], Ps 106[17]). See KORAH.

DATHEMA (1 Mac 5[9]).—A fortress in Bashan. It may perhaps be the modern *Dāmeh* on the S. border of the Lejā district, N. of Ashteroth-karnaim.

DAUGHTER.—See FAMILY.

DAVID.—The second and greatest of the kings of Israel; the youngest of the eight sons of Jesse, the Bethlehemite; he belonged to the tribe of Judah. There is no sound basis for the old theory that the name means 'beloved,' and its derivation remains uncertain.

The details of David's life are gathered from 1 S 16[3]–1 K 2[11], 1 Ch 11[1]–29[30] (besides some scattered notices in the earlier chapters of 1 Chronicles), the Psalms which may bear on this period, and Book VII. of the *Antiquities* of Josephus, although the last two items add but little to our knowledge. It is necessary to bear in mind two points of importance in dealing with the records of the life of David: Firstly, the Hebrew text is in a number of cases very corrupt (notably in the books of Samuel), and in not a few passages the text of the LXX is to be preferred, as evidenced by the Qumrân Scrolls; secondly, our records have been gathered from a number of sources, and therefore do not present a connected whole, and for this reason they are sometimes at variance with one another.

1. Early years.—David was a shepherd by calling, and he continued this occupation until he had reached full manhood. There are altogether three different accounts of David's entry into public life:

(i) 1 S 16[1–13]. David is here represented as having been designated by Yahweh as Saul's successor; Samuel is sent to Bethlehem to anoint him; seven sons of Jesse pass before the prophet, but the Spirit does not move him to anoint any of these; in perplexity he asks the father if he has any more children, whereupon the youngest is produced, and Samuel anoints him.

(ii) 1 S 16[14–23]. In this second account the servants of Saul recommend that the king should send for someone who is a skilful player on the lyre (not harp), in order that by means of music the mental disorder from which Saul is suffering may be allayed. The son of Jesse is proposed, and forthwith sent for. When Saul is again attacked by the malady—said to be occasioned by 'an evil spirit from God'—David plays upon the lyre, and Saul 'is refreshed' in spirit.

(iii) 1 S 17. The Greek version omits a large part of this account (vv.[12–31, 55–58]), which seems itself to have been put together from different sources. According to it David's first appearance was on the eve of a battle between the Israelites and the Philistines. His father is in the habit of sending him to the Israelite camp with provisions for his oldest brothers, who are among the warriors in the Israelite army; on one such occasion he finds the camp in consternation on account of the defiance of a Philistine hero, the giant Goliath. This man offers to fight in single combat with any Israelite who will come out and face him, but in spite of the high reward offered by the king to anyone who will slay him—namely, great riches and the king's daughter in marriage—nobody comes forward to answer the challenge. David gathers these details from different people in the camp, and feeling sure of the help of Yahweh, he determines to fight the giant. He communicates his purpose to Saul, who at first discourages him, but on seeing his firmness and confidence he arms him and bids him go forth in the name of Yahweh. David, however, finds the armour too cumbersome and discards it, taking instead nothing but five smooth stones and a sling. After mutual defiance David slings one of the stones; the giant is hit and falls down dead; David rushes up, draws the sword of the dead warrior, and cuts off his head. Thereupon panic takes hold of the Philistine host, and they flee, pursued by the Israelites, who thus win a complete victory.

It is worthy of note that these three accounts connect with David just those three characteristics which subsequent ages loved to dwell on. The first presents him as the beloved of Yahweh, who was specially chosen, the man after God's own heart, the son of Jesse; the second presents him as the musician whose playing on the lyre had a soothing effect on Saul; while the third presents him as the warrior-hero. Of these three accounts some have thought that the third is nearest to actual history, but it is not at all certain that David was the slayer of Goliath, because 2 S 21[19] gives that honour to Elhanan (q.v.), but 1 Ch 20[5], apparently in an effort to harmonize the two accounts, says that the giant slain by Elhanan was Goliath's brother, Lahmi. In any case there is good reason to believe that David did win a victory over some Philistine giant, who was perhaps nameless at first, and only later had the name Goliath transferred to him. David's heroic deed called forth the admiration and later the love of the king's son, Jonathan; a covenant of friendship was made between the two, in token and in ratification of which Jonathan took off his robe and armour, and presented David with them. This friendship lasted until the death of Jonathan, and David's pathetic lamentation over him (2 S 1[22–27]) points to the reality of their love.

In recognition of David's victory over the Philistine giant Saul gave him an important command in his army, but as David's victories continued amid the acclaim of the people, it aroused Saul's envy, a not wholly unnatural feeling under the circumstances. The adage in 1 S 18[7]—assuredly one of the most ancient authentic fragments of the history of the time—

'Saul has slain his thousands,
And David his ten thousands'

was not flattering to one who in days gone by had been Israel's foremost warrior. For the present, however, Saul conceals his real feelings (1 S 18[10f] are evidently out of place, and do not appear in the Greek version), intending to rid himself of David in such a way that no blame would attach to himself. In fulfilment of his promise to the slayer of the Philistine he expresses his intention of giving his daughter Michal to David in marriage, but as David can offer no marriage-price, all he asks is a hundred Philistine foreskins, hoping that David would lose his life in attempting to procure these (1 S 18[25]). The scheme fails, and David receives Michal in marriage. A further attempt to get rid of David is frustrated by Jonathan (19[1-7]), and at last Saul himself tries to kill him by throwing a javelin at him while he was playing on his lyre; again he fails, for David nimbly avoids the javelin and escapes to his own house (19[9ff]). Thither Saul sends men to kill him, but with the help of his wife he again escapes and flees to Ramah to seek counsel from Samuel. On Samuel's advice, apparently, he goes to Jonathan by stealth to see if there is any possibility of reconciliation with the king; Jonathan does his best, but in vain (20[1-42]), and David realizes that his life will be in danger so long as he is anywhere within reach of Saul or his emissaries.

2. David as refugee.—As in the case of the earlier period of David's life, the records of this second period consist of a number of fragments from different sources, not very skilfully put together. We can do no more here than enumerate the various localities in which David sought refuge from Saul's vindictiveness, pointing out at the same time the more important episodes in his refugee life.

David flees first of all to *Nob*, the priestly city (1 S 21[1]). His stay here is short, for he is seen by Doeg, one of Saul's followers, and he takes refuge in the *cave of Adullam* (22[1]). Here his relatives come to him, and he gathers together a band of desperadoes, who make him their captain. Finding that this kind of life is not fitted for his parents, he takes them to *Mizpeh* and entrusts them to the care of the king of Moab (22[3]). On his return he is advised by the prophet Gad to leave the stronghold; he therefore takes refuge in the forest of *Hereth* (22[5]). While hiding here, news is brought to him that the Philistines are attacking Keilah; he hastens to succour the inhabitants by attacking the Philistines; these he overcomes with great slaughter, and thereupon he takes up his abode in *Keilah* (23[7]). In the meantime Saul's spies discover the whereabouts of the fugitive, and David, hearing that the men of Keilah will deliver him up to his enemy, escapes with his followers to the hill-country in the wilderness of *Ziph* (23[14]). A very vigorous pursuit is now undertaken by Saul, who seems determined to catch the elusive fugitive, and the chase is carried on among the wilds of *Ziph*, *Maon*, and *Engedi* (23[18-29]). It is during these wanderings that Saul falls into the power of David, but is magnanimously spared (chs. 24, 26). The episode of David's dealings with Nabal, and his marrying Abigail and Ahinoam, also falls within this period (ch. 25). At one time there seemed to be some hope of reconciliation between Saul and David (26[24f]), but evidently this was short-lived, for soon afterwards David escapes once more, and finally is driven to flee with six hundred followers to the court of Achish, king of Gath, who welcomes him as an ally and gives him the city of *Ziklag* (ch. 27). David stays there for a year and four months (27[7]), occupying the time by fighting against the enemies of his country, the Geshurites, Amalekites, etc. At the end of this time war again breaks out between the Israelites and the Philistines. The question arises whether David shall join the forces of Achish against the Israelites; David himself seems willing to fight on the side of the Philistines 29[8]), but the Philistines suspect treachery on his part, and at the request of Achish he returns to *Ziklag* (ch. 29). On his arrival here he finds that the place has been sacked by the Amalekites, and forthwith he sets out to take revenge. This is ample and complete; part of the spoil he sends as a present to the elders of Judah and to his friends (30[26-31]), a fact which shows that there was a party favourable to him in Judah. In the meantime the war between Israel and the Philistines ends disastrously for the former, and Saul and Jonathan are slain. David received news of this during his sojourn in Ziklag. With this ends the refugee life of David, for, leaving Ziklag, he comes to Hebron, where the men of Judah anoint him king over the house of Judah (2 S 2[4]), evidently with the approval of the Philistines. David must have ruled at Hebron under the suzerainty of the Philistines, because otherwise there surely would have been war with them, for they controlled Judah at this time, as they did practically all of Palestine.

3. David as king.—For seven years David ruled over Judah, with his capital at Hebron. In spite of his evident desire to make peace with the followers of Saul (2 S 9), it was but natural that a vigorous attempt should be made to uphold the dynasty of the late king, at all events in Israel, as distinct from Judah (see ISHBOSHETH). It is therefore just what we should expect when we read that 'there was a long war between the house of Saul and the house of David' (3[1]). The final victory lay with David, and in due time the elders of Israel came to him in Hebron, and he was anointed king over Israel (5[3]). That made him king over the whole land, and that meant defiance of the Philistines and immediate war with them (5[17ff]). He realized now that he needed a stronger and more central capital than Hebron; so he fixed on Jerusalem, a neutral city lying on the border between Israel and Judah. With his personal army he captured it from the Jebusites, and renamed it 'City of David' (5[7]). Thither he brought the Ark with great ceremony (6[1ff]), thus making his own City of David the religious, as well as the political and military, capital of his state. Yahwism was made the official religion of the united state, and to secure it in that place the priests were organized under Abiathar as chief priest, and he and Zadok, together with the leading priests, were made members of the royal court at Jerusalem (8[17]), and according to v.[18] David's sons were made priests.

David owes his greatness largely to his genuis in organization which he seems to have borrowed in large part from Egypt, either directly or through the Phoenicians, with whom he was on friendly terms (2 S 5[11], 1 Ch 14[1]), and who helped him build his palace in Jerusalem. We have two lists of his officials, 2 S 8[16-18] and 20[23-25], presumably from different times and differing only slightly. In both Jehoshaphat is listed as 'the recorder,' the exact equivalent of the Egyptian Royal Herald, the officer of public relations, who regulated the ceremonies in the palace, and was the intermediary between the king and the people. Another of David's officials was 'the scribe,' again corresponding to an official in Egypt. He functioned as the royal private secretary and the secretary of state. His name is given in a different form every time it is mentioned, but whatever it was, Shisha or the like, it is evidently Egyptian and not Hebrew. Two of his sons were scribes of Solomon, and one of these was named Elihoreph (1 K 4[3]), again manifestly an Egyptian name, at least in its second element. The taking of a census (2 S 24), despite popular prejudice against it, was another device on David's part to centralize the authority in himself and break down the old tribal system; and for the same reason he divided the land into districts, because it was apparently he who initiated the practice, although Solomon carried it out in more sweeping fashion.

Not only was the government reorganized, but the army as well. Early in his career David had gathered about himself his own band of professional soldiers, whose loyalties were to him alone, and around this solid core he built an army of peasants that was invincible, with Joab as commander of the whole, and Benaiah the commander of the mercenaries. In addition there was a special band of warriors of exceptional ability, known as the Thirty, and a still more exclusive group known as the Three (2 S 23[8ff]).

Despite all of David's attempts to unify the country and despite the esteem in which he himself was held the old rivalries between north and south continued, and there were revolts against him, the most serious of which was led by his own son Absalom. Of an ambitious nature, Absalom sought the succession, even at the expense of dethroning his father. After four (not 'forty' as in EV) years of ingratiating himself with the people (2 S 15^{1-7}) the rebellion broke out. At first Absalom was successful; he attacked Jerusalem, from which David had to flee. David withdraws across the Jordan and halts at Mahanaim; here he marshals his forces under the leadership of Joab. The decisive battle follows; Absalom is defeated, and fleeing, he is caught by his hair on the overhanging branch of a tree. While hanging thus, he is slain by Joab, despite David's strict command that he should not be harmed. The touching account of David's sorrow is given in 2 S 19^{1-4}. A second rebellion, of a much less serious character, was that of Sheba, who sought to draw the northern tribes away from their allegiance; it was, however, easily quelled by Joab (ch. 20). Another rebellion (if such it can be called) was that of Adonijah, which occurred at the very end of David's reign (see ADONIJAH).

One of the features of David's reign was its many foreign wars. It is, however, necessary to bear in mind that in the case of a newly established dynasty this is only to be expected. Also the spoils and tribute of successful war helped David to meet his many expenses. The following is, very briefly, a list of David's foreign wars; they are put in the order found in 2 Samuel, but this order is not strictly chronological; moreover, it seems probable that in one or two cases duplicate, but varying accounts appear: Philistines (5^{17-25}), Moabites (8^{2}), Zobah (8^{3f}), Aramaeans (8^{5-13}), Edomites (8^{13f}), Ammonites, Aramaeans (10^{1} 11^{1} 12^{26-31}), and Philistines (21^{15-22}). David was victorious over all these peoples, the result being a great extension of his kingdom, which reached, according to tradition, right up to the Euphrates (cf Ex 23^{31-33}, Dt 11^{23-25}).

While it is impossible to deny that the role of musician in which we are accustomed to picture David is largely the product of later ages, there can be no doubt that the role is based to some degree on fact (cf *e.g.* Am 6^{5}), and he must evidently be regarded as one of the sources of inspiration which guided the nation's musicians of successive generations (see article PSALMS).

The character of David offers an intensely interesting complex of good and bad, in which the former largely predominates. As a ruler, warrior, and organizer he stands pre-eminent among the heroes of Israel. His importance in the domain of the national religion lies mainly in his founding of the sanctuary of Zion, with all that this denotes. While his virtues of open-heartedness, generosity, and valour, besides those already noted, stand out as clear as the day, his faults are to a large degree due to the age in which he lived, and must be discounted accordingly.

W. O. E. O.—T. J. M.

DAVID, CITY OF.—See JERUSALEM.

DAY.—See TIME.

DAY OF ATONEMENT.—See ATONEMENT [DAY OF].

DAY OF THE LORD.—The day of Yahweh's decisive intervention in history, the day of his judgment upon his foes and the triumphant vindication of his kingly rule. The concept is fundamental to OT eschatology and informs many passages even where the term is not used (often 'in that day' etc.). It is first attested in the 8th cent. (Am 5^{18ff}) but, since it was even then an established popular belief, it was certainly much older. Its origins, however, are disputed. Possibly recollection through cultic recitation of the great days in the past on which Yahweh had intervened in behalf of His people, together with confidence in His promise for the future, had conspired to produce the expectation of a coming day of definitive intervention when the Divine purpose for Israel would be brought to fruition. Amos' hearers expected the Day of Yahweh in the near future and looked forward to it as a day of national triumph. Amos, however, denouncing their crimes against justice, declared that Yahweh would on that day judge Israel also. Succeeding prophets for the most part followed in the path of Amos, viewing the Day of Yahweh as the day of His judgment on the nations of the world (see the oracles against the nations in various prophetic books), and on sinful Israel as well (*e.g.* Is 2^{6-21}, Zeph 1–2). This judgment they expected in the form of historical calamity; the destruction of the nation by the Babylonians was widely regarded as the fulfilment of that judgment (cf Lamentations). But since the prophets did not surrender faith in the promises of Yahweh, the expectation grew that, beyond the judgment, Yahweh would establish a repentant and purified remnant of His people (*e.g.* Hos 2^{14ff}, Is 9^{1ff} 10^{20ff}, Zeph 3^{8ff}, Jer 31^{31ff}, Ezk 37).

In the exile and after, the Day of Yahweh was looked forward to as the great, final turning point in history when Yahweh would redeem His people and consummate His purposes for them. This hope is expressed in various ways: the overthrow of Babylon and the restoration of Israel (Is 13^{1}–14^{23}); the rejuvenation of creation after a terrible judgment (Is 34 f); a new Exodus deliverance and the establishment of Yahweh's rule in all the earth (Is 40–66, *passim*); the final battle between Yahweh and the enemies of His rule (Ezk 38 f, Zec 14); cosmic and earthly cataclysms, and the outpouring of Yahweh's spirit upon His people (Joel). Progressively the Day of Yahweh came to be viewed as a supra-historical day of judgment (*e.g.* Is 24–27, Daniel), when Yahweh's foes celestial and terrestrial would be destroyed and His universal rule would be established.

The NT transmutes the concept into the day of Christ's coming in glory: 'that day' (1 Th 5^{4}); 'the day' (1 Co 3^{13}), 'the day of the Lord Jesus' (2 Co 1^{14}), etc. It is the day of final judgment (Ro 2^{5-16}), and also of the establishment of Christ's rule forever. J. Br.

DAY STAR, Is 14^{12} (RV, RSV; AV 'Lucifer'), 2 P 1^{19} (AV, RV; RSV 'morning star').—See STARS.

DAY'S JOURNEY.—A 'day's journey' (Nu 11^{31}, 1 K 19^{4}, Jon 3^{4}, Lk 2^{44}; cf three days' journey, Gn 30^{36}, Ex 3^{18}, etc.; seven days, Gn 31^{23}) was not, like the 'sabbath day's journey' (see WEIGHTS AND MEASURES), a definite measure of length, but, like our 'stone's throw,' 'bow-shot,' etc., a popular and somewhat indefinite indication of distance. This would naturally vary with the urgency and *impedimenta* of the traveller or the caravan. Laban in hot pursuit of Jacob, and the Hebrew host in the wilderness, may be taken to represent the extremes in this matter of a 'day's journey' (see above), although it is scarcely possible to take literally the 'seven days' journey' of the former (Gn 31^{23})—from Haran to Gilead, *c* 350 miles in 7 days. From 20 to 30 miles is probably a fair estimate of an average day's journey with baggage animals.

A. R. S. K.

DAYSMAN.—A daysman is an arbiter. The compound arose from the use of the word 'day' in a technical sense, to signify a day for dispensing justice. The same use is found in Greek; thus 1 Co 4^{3} 'human court' is literally 'man's day.' The word occurs in Job 9^{33} 'Neither is there any daysman betwixt us' (AV, RV; RSV 'umpire,' with AVm, RVm). Tyndale translates Ex 21^{22}, 'he shall paye as the dayesmen appoynte him' (EV 'as the judges determine').

DAYSPRING.—An old English expression denoting the dawn ('the day sprynge or dawnynge of the daye gyveth a certeyne lyght before the rysinge of the sonne,' Eden, *Decades*, 1555, p. 264). It occurs in Job 38^{12} 'Hast thou . . . caused the dayspring to know its place?' (AV, RV; RSV 'the dawn'); Wis 16^{28} 'at the dayspring pray unto thee' (RV; RSV 'at the dawning of the light'). Virtually the same expression occurs in AV and RV in Jg 19^{25} and 1 S 9^{26}; cf also Ps 65^{8} (east and west called 'the outgoings of the morning and evening'). In Lk 1^{78} the expression 'dayspring from on high' (AV, RV; RSV 'the day shall dawn upon us from on high') probably goes back to a Hebrew original which was a well-understood personal designation of the Messiah (combining the ideas of 'light' and ' sprout ') ; it would then be a poetical equivalent for ' Messiah from heaven.' G. H. B.

DEACON.—The Greek word *diakonos*, as well as the corresponding verb and abstract noun, is of very frequent occurrence in the text of the NT, but in AV is always translated ' servant ' or ' minister ' except in Ph 1[1], 1 Ti 3[8-13], where it is rendered ' deacon,' these being the only two passages where it is evidently used in a technical sense.

In the Gospels the word has the general meaning of ' servant ' (cf Mt 20[26] ||, 23[11], Jn 2[5, 9]). St. Paul employs it constantly of one who is engaged in Christian service, the service of God or Christ or the Church (*e.g.* 2 Co 6[4] 11[23], Col 1[23-25]), but without any trace as yet of an official signification. Once in Romans we find him distinguishing *diakonia* (' service ') from prophecy and teaching and exhortation (12[6-8]) ; but it seems evident that he is speaking here of differences in function, not in office.

In Acts the word *diakonos* is never once employed, but 6[1-6], where we read of the appointment of the Seven, sheds a ray of light on its history, and probably serves to explain how from the general sense of one who renders Christian service it came to be applied to a special officer of the Church. The Seven are nowhere called deacons, nor is there any real justification in the NT for the traditional description of them by that title. The qualifications demanded of them (v[3]., cf v.[5]) are higher than those laid down in 1 Timothy for the office of the deacon ; and Stephen and Philip, the only two of their number of whom we know anything, exercise functions far above those of the later diaconate (6[8ff] 8[5-13, 26ff]). But the fact that the special duty to which they were appointed is called a *diakonia* or ministration (v.[1]) and that this ministration was a definite part of the work of the Church in Jerusalem, so that ' the *diakonia* ' came to be used as a specific term in this reference (cf Ac 11[29] 12[25], Ro 15[25, 31], 2 Co 8[4] 9[1, 12f]), makes it natural to find in their appointment the germ of the institution of the diaconate.

It is in the mission churches of the Gentile world that we first find the deacon as a regular official, called to office after probation (1 Ti 3[10]), and standing alongside the bishop in the ministry of the Church (Ph 1[1], 1 Ti 3[1-13]). As to his *functions* nothing is said precisely. We can infer that the *diakonia* of the deacons, like the *diakonia* of the Seven in Jerusalem, was in the first place a ministry to the poor, closely associated with the deacons' assistance in ' serving tables ' at the Church's Eucharist. In the Gentile as in the Jewish world it would naturally be a service of a responsible, delicate, and often private kind—an inference that is borne out by what is said in 1 Timothy as to the deacon's qualifications.

Comparing these *qualifications* with those of the bishop we observe that the difference is just what would be suggested by the names bishop or ' overseer ' and deacon or ' servant ' respectively. Bishops were to rule and take charge of the Church (1 Ti 3[5]) ; deacons were to ' serve well ' (v.[13]). Bishops must be ' apt to teach ' (v.[2]) ; deacons were only called to ' hold the mystery of the faith with a clear conscience ' (v.[9]). That the work of the deacon and his fellow-servant the deaconess (q.v.) was of a house-to-house kind is suggested by the warnings given against talebearing (v.[8]) and backbiting (v.[11]). That it had to do with the distribution of Church moneys, and so brought temptations to pilfering, is further suggested by the demand that the deacon should not be greedy of filthy lucre (v.[8]) and that his female counterpart should be ' faithful (*i.e.* trustworthy) in all things ' (v.[11]). J. C. L.—M. H. S.

DEACONESS.—The word occurs in RSV in Ro 16[1]. In this verse Phoebe is described as ' a *diakonos* of the church at Cenchreae.' AV and RV render ' servant,' RVm ' deaconess.' The term may describe a technical office in the Church, or may refer only to service in general.

In 1 Ti 3[11], however, although the word ' deaconess ' is not used, it may be that female deacons are referred to. AV makes it appear that the wives of deacons are spoken of ; RV corrects this by rendering ' Women in like manner must be grave, not slanderers, temperate, faithful in all things.' And when the whole passage (vv.[8-13]) is read, it seems possible that the women referred to in v.[11] are *diakonoi* ' in like manner ' as the men described both before and after. We know from Pliny, writing early in the 2nd cent., that by that time there were deaconesses in the Christian Churches of Bithynia (*Ep.* x. 96). And in the ancient world the need must have been early felt for a class of women who could perform some at least of the duties of the diaconate for their own sex in particular.
J. C. L.—M. H. S.

DEAD.—See DEATH.

DEAD SEA.—An inland lake 53 miles long and from 2¾ to 10 miles in breadth, which is fed by the Jordan. Its level is about 1290 feet below that of the Mediterranean, being the lowest body of water on the earth's surface. It has no outlet, and the water received by it is all carried off by evaporation. In consequence, the waters of the lake are impregnated with mineral substances to a remarkable degree ; they yield 25 per cent. salt, whereas the ocean yields but 4 to 6 per cent. Valuable as a source of salt in Biblical times (Ezk 47[11]), its mineral deposits are exploited commercially to-day.

The modern name is of late origin (first used apparently by Pausanias) and refers to the total absence of life in its waters—in contrast with the apocalyptic hope of Ezk 47[8-10]. Hebrew writers spoke of it as the ' Salt Sea ' (Gn 14[3], Nu 34[3], Jos 15[5], etc.), the ' sea of the Arabah ' (Dt 3[17], 4[49]) and the ' eastern sea ' (Ezk 47[18], Jl 2[20]). Greek writers called it ' Asphalt Lake,' because asphalt sometimes rises to the surface and floats ashore. In Arabic it is known as *Baḥr Lûṭ*, ' the sea of Lot,' a name probably due to the direct influence of the history as related in the Qur'ān. South of the lake was once the **Valley of Siddim** (Gn 14[10]) where stood the cities of **Sodom and Gomorrah**, which are believed to be entirely submerged by water. Earthquakes, accompanied by irruptions of ignited petroleum and gas, may have contributed to the sinking of the valley.

The Dead Sea owes its origin to a fracture produced in the surface of the region by earth-movements whereby the land of Palestine was raised above sea-level. This fault took place towards the end of the Eocene period ; it extends along the whole Jordan Valley from the Gulf of 'Aqaba to Hermon. Thus the general appearance of the lake has not radically altered during the whole period of human existence.

Round the border of the lake are numerous small springs, some bursting actually under its waters, others forming lagoons of comparatively brackish water. The springs of **En-Gedi** and *'Ain Feshkhah* on the western side made possible the cultivation of crops—the latter place by the Essene community of Khirbet Qumrân. In the lagoons small fish are to be found ; but in the main body of water life of any kind is impossible.

Modern observations show that the surface of the lake varies. An island that was a conspicuous feature at the north end disappeared under the surface in 1892, and became visible again in 1960.
R. A. S. M.—W. H. Br.

DEAD SEA SCROLLS.—On the west side of the Dead Sea, not far from its northern end, a rugged valley named Wâdī Qumrân descends from the Judaean plateau. A promontory on its northern edge bears a ruin called Khirbet Qumrân (Qumrân Ruin), which has been shown by excavation to be the remains of a Jewish monastic establishment of the last century B.C. and the first century of our era. The major occupation of the site was in two periods, separated by a gap of about thirty years corresponding roughly to the reign of Herod the Great, just before the beginning of the Christian era. Coins found in the excavation indicated that the first period began near the end of the 2nd cent. B.C., in or shortly before the reign of Alexander Jannaeus (103–76 B.C.). It was brought to an end by an earthquake in 31 B.C., and the buildings were not restored and reoccupied until some time in the reign of Archelaus (4 B.C.–A.D. 6). The second period of occupation then lasted until A.D. 68, when the settlement was violently destroyed, probably by the Romans.

The excavation of this site was a consequence of a previous discovery. At some time during the years 1945–47 an Arab goatherd accidentally found a cave, about half a mile north of Khirbet Qumrân, containing Hebrew and Aramaic manuscripts stored in clay jars. In 1947 these scrolls were brought to Jerusalem. Four of the seven documents contained in them were bought by the Syrian Orthodox Archbishop there and three by the Hebrew University, which later acquired the others also.

In 1949 the cave was scientifically excavated by the Department of Antiquities of Jordan and the French School of Archaeology at Jerusalem, and hundreds of fragments of manuscripts were unearthed. The excavation of Khirbet Qumrân followed in 1951–56; meanwhile and after the completion of the excavation ten more caves containing a few scrolls and thousands of fragments were found. The results of the excavations, combined with the palaeographical evidence of the manuscripts themselves, made it clear that all but the oldest of them had been made by the community at Khirbet Qumrân.

During the course of these discoveries another and quite unconnected collection of fragments was found in another valley some miles to the south, the Wâdī Murabba'ât. These came from the 2nd cent. A.D. and consisted of letters, contracts, and similar documents, as well as biblical manuscripts, from the period of the revolt of Bar Cochba (A.D. 132–35). A third body of material, coming from later Christian centuries, appeared in the excavation of Khirbet Mird, the ruins of a Byzantine monastery farther up in the hills. All three collections are included under the term Dead Sea Scrolls in its widest sense, and all have their own importance. Major interest, however, has naturally centred in the oldest and largest collection, the fragments and scrolls from the Wâdī Qumrân. Most of these are of leather, some of papyrus, and one of copper. With the exception of the seven documents found in the initial discovery, which are now in Israel, all the material is in Jordan at the Palestine Archaeological Museum of Jerusalem, where it is being studied and published by an international and interconfessional team of scholars.

The contents of the Qumrân texts exhibit an astonishing range and variety, though all are of a religious nature. Roughly a fourth of them are biblical manuscripts. All the books of the OT except Esther are represented, some of them in several copies. There are also selections of texts, paraphrases, and even commentaries on Genesis, Psalms, and several of the prophetic books. Several of the Apocrypha and Pseudepigrapha, including Tobit, Sirach, Enoch, and Jubilees, have been found also.

In addition to these there are many non-biblical works, both in Hebrew and in Aramaic. Most of them were previously quite unknown. Portions of the Damascus Document (Zadokite Fragments) were found in three of the caves. An almost complete copy of a composition resembling it, the Manual of Discipline or Rule of the Community, was found in the first cave; parts of eleven other copies appeared in another (Cave 4). The Rule of the Congregation is still another composition closely related to the Manual of Discipline and included in the same scroll with it in the copy from Cave 1. There are also collections of psalms, hymns, prayers, and blessings. Other scrolls contain directions for worship. Several texts have to do with the impending end of this world and with the world to come.

From all this emerges a vivid picture of a strict monastic order within Judaism, a community which regarded itself as the true Israel of the last days, deeply involved in the cosmic struggle between the sons of light and the sons of darkness, the 'lot' of God and the 'lot' of Belial. Many of the texts reflect a quiet group withdrawn from the world and devoted to worship and study. One scroll, however, gives detailed directions for the conduct of the war against the hosts of evil, with weapons and military tactics plainly copied from those of the Romans. The community's life at Qumrân was strictly regulated by rules of probation, admission, discipline, the sharing of property, eating together, and the continual, ardent searching of the Scriptures. The nature of their life and organization and the location of their settlement make it natural to identify them with the Essenes (q.v.), described by Josephus and Philo. They were at least a closely related sect, part of the same general movement.

The significance of the Dead Sea Scrolls for biblical studies is twofold. The biblical manuscripts provide a wealth of material for the textual criticism of the OT; the other texts acquaint us with a little known phase of Jewish history and by so doing fill in an important part of the background of the NT. For textual criticism the importance of these texts lies in the fact that they are a thousand years and more older than the oldest Hebrew manuscripts of the OT previously known. They carry us back to a stage in the history of the text before it had been standardized in the form preserved by all the later manuscripts. In the Wâdī Murabba'ât manuscripts of the 2nd cent. the standardization is complete; in the Qumrân fragments and scrolls the text is still much more fluid. In some books there is little difference from the traditional (Massoretic) text; in others there is a notably close relation with the text represented by the Septuagint. Many readings not found in any other form of the text are found, and occasionally they seem to be superior to the traditional readings. Fragmentary as the Qumrân texts are, they afford invaluable assistance for the correction of the text and still more for the reconstruction of its history.

For the study of the NT the literature of the Qumrân sect affords many striking parallels in language, thought, and practice. The sense of living in the last days was characteristic of both the sect and the early church. The sharp division between the realms of light and darkness recalls many passages in the NT, especially in the Johannine writings. The stress on the sinfulness of man and on salvation by the grace of God alone reveals a surprising affinity with the experience and doctrine of Paul. The life of the early apostolic church at Jerusalem resembled that of the Qumrân community at such points as the common meals and the sharing of property. Many scholars, impressed by these contacts, have inferred that the sect had some direct influence on the early church, through John the Baptist or through Jesus or through later connexions. If there was any such influence, which is possible but cannot be proved, there were also radical differences which were even more significant. In any case, the vocabulary, presuppositions, and ways of thinking inherited by the first Christians from Judaism are illuminated at many points by the Dead Sea Scrolls. M. B.

DEAFNESS.—See MEDICINE.

DEAL.—A deal is a part or share. It is still in use in the phrase 'a great deal' or 'a good deal.' In AV occurs 'tenth deal,' Ex 29[40], Lv 14[21] etc. (RV 'tenth part'; RSV 'tenth measure' or 'tenth'), the Hebrew *'iśśārôn* being a measure used in meal-offerings. See WEIGHTS AND MEASURES, II.

DEATH.—I. IN THE OT.—**1.** The Hebrew term *māweth* and our corresponding word 'death' alike spring from primitive roots belonging to the very beginnings of speech. One of man's first needs was a word to denote that stark fact of experience—the final cessation of life to which he and the whole animated creation, and the very trees and plants, were all subject. It is, of course, in this ordinary sense of the term as denoting a physical fact that the expressions 'death' and 'die' are mostly used in the Scriptures.

2. The Scriptures have nothing directly to say as to

the place of death in the economy of nature. St. Paul's words in Ro 5^{12ff} as to the connexion between sin and death must be explained in harmony with this fact; and, for that matter, in harmony also with his own words in Ro 6^{23}, where death, the 'wages of sin,' cannot be simply physical death. The Creation narratives are silent on this point, yet in Gn 2^{17} man is expected to know what it is to die. We are not to look for exact information on matters such as this from writings of this kind. If the belief enshrined in the story of the Fall in Gn 3 regarded death in the ordinary sense as the penalty of Adam and Eve's transgression, they at any rate did not die 'in the day' of their transgression; v.^{22} suggests that even then, could he but also eat of 'the tree of life,' man might escape mortality. All we can say is that in the dawn of human history man appears as one already familiar with the correlative mysteries of life and death.

3. From the contemplation of the act of dying it is an easy step to the thought of death as a state or condition. This is a distinct stage towards believing in existence of some kind beyond the grave. And to the vast mass of mankind to say 'he is dead' has never meant 'he is non-existent.'

4. Divergent beliefs as to what the state of death is show themselves in the OT.—(*a*) In some instances death is represented as *a condition of considerable activity and consciousness.* Certain dead are regarded as 'knowing ones,' able to impart information and counsel to the living. Such are indicated by the term translated 'wizards' in Lv 19^{31} 20^{6}, Is 8^{19} 19^{3}. These are departed spirits who are sought unto or inquired of 'on behalf of the living.' A vivid instance of this belief is furnished in the story of the medium at Endor (1 S 28), in which the departed Samuel 'coming up out of the earth' is called 'a god' ('*ᵉlōhîm*, v.^{13}). Also in Is 14^{9f} there is a graphic description of the commotion caused in Sheol by the arrival of the king of Babylon. Some scholars have held that in all this there is a relic of ancient Semitic ancestor worship. In any case, the frequency of strict OT prohibitions of necromancy and the cult of the dead (Ex 22^{18}, Lv $19^{26,\,31}$ $20^{6,\,27}$, Dt 18^{10f}) indicates the probable pagan origin of such beliefs and practices.

(*b*) In contrast to necromancy with its weird appeals to the dead for guidance and information, in the common OT view the state of death was *one of unconsciousness, forgetfulness, and silence* (Ps 88^{12} 94^{17} 115^{17}). The present world is emphatically 'the land of the living' (Ps 27^{13} 116^{9}). Death is simply 'being gathered to one's fathers' (Jg 2^{10}, 2 K 22^{20}) who are now departed souls in the underworld or Sheol. Death is man's common fate, even shared by the beasts (Ps $49^{10-12,\,18-20}$, Ec 3^{20}). It is regarded as tragic primarily when premature or violent, but for one who has lived out his days in righteousness the realm of death may be regarded as well-earned rest (Gn 15^{15} 25^{8}, Nu 23^{10}, 1 K 2^{6}, Ps 116^{15}, Jer 34^{4f}). Sheol also appears inviting to a soul in distress because it is a state of tranquility and sleep (Job $3^{13,\,17}$); and there is nothing to be known or to be done there (Ec 9^{10}). In a few instances death is described as non-existence or complete dissolution 'like water spilt on the ground' (2 S 14^{14}, cf Job 7^{21}, Ps 39^{13}). Usually, however, death is the state of being in a very weakened state, with vitality and strength lost, and the soul (*nephesh*) either emptied out or escaped from the body (Gn 35^{18}, 1 K 17^{21}, Is 14^{10} 53^{12}). Thus there continues only a dreary, meaningless existence cut off from 'the land of the living' with no hope of return (Job 10^{21f}), and, most distressing of all, cut off also from all communion with Yahweh (Is $38^{10f,\,18}$, Ps 6^{5} 115^{17}). Therefore death was often regarded as 'bitter,' a 'terror,' and a 'snare' (see below, **6**). These OT ideas concerning death show affinities, perhaps not primarily with those of Egypt, but certainly with Mesopotamian conceptions, as in the Epic of Gilgamesh.

(*c*) The inevitability and finality of death are taken for granted in most of the OT. However, since this limitation of human life was set by Yahweh, He could allow certain rare individuals to escape death: the patriarch Enoch (Gn 5^{24}) and the prophet Elijah (2 K 2^{1-12}). A peculiarly pious soul might hope to escape the customary snares of Sheol (Job 19^{25f}, Ps 16^{10f} 49^{15} 73^{23f}). God's power working through a prophet may restore a dead boy to life (1 K 17^{22}, 2 K 4^{32-35}). But normally death is completely victorious (Hos 13^{14}). Only in late apocalyptic passages (Is 26^{19}, Dn 12^{2}) does firm belief in the resurrection of the dead appear.

5. Death as standing in penal relation to man's sin and unrighteousness is frequently insisted on. This insight is most clearly expressed in Gn 3 (see above, **2**): 'You are dust, and to dust you shall return' (v.^{19}). This connexion between death and sin apparently arose from the realization that sin, like death, separates man from God. Thus both sin and death are alien to the Divine nature. While no account is given as to the origin of death, it seems evident that death was not regarded as part of God's original intention in creation. That death as penalty for sin may be something more than natural death, perhaps spiritual death, seems clear from such an antithesis as in Dt $30^{15,\,19}$ ('life and good: death and evil'), and this set in strict relation to conduct and faithfulness to Israel's covenant with Yahweh. Cf the burden of Ezk 18, 'the soul that sins shall die,' with the correlative promise of life; cf Pr 15^{10}. In this sense Yahweh takes 'no pleasure in the death of anyone' (Ezk 18^{32}).

6. OT poetical uses of references to death may be pointed out: 'bitterness of death,' 1 S 15^{32}, cf Ec 7^{26}; 'chambers of death,' Pr 7^{27}; 'gates of death,' Job 38^{17}, Ps 9^{13} 107^{18}, cf Is 38^{10} and Babylonian and Egyptian mythologies where death is a walled city with strong gates from which escape is impossible; 'dust of death,' Ps 22^{15}, cf Gn 3^{19}, Ec 12^{7}; death as 'the reaper,' Jer 9^{22}; 'the sleep of death,' Ps 13^{3}, cf Dn 12^{2}; 'snares of death,' 2 S 22^{6}, Ps 18^{5} 116^{3}, Pr 13^{14} 14^{27}, cf Pr 21^{6} RSV LXX and 'cords of death,' Ps 18^{4}, as though death were a monster setting traps; 'terrors of death,' Ps 55^{4}; the phrase 'vexed to death,' Jg 16^{16}, *i.e.* 'to an extreme degree'; 'waves of death,' 2 S 22^{5}. J. S. C.—**C. F. K.**

II. In the Apocrypha.—**1.** The chief advance in the conception of death found in the Apocrypha is the belief in the resurrection (q.v.), especially in 2 Mac (*e.g.* $7^{9,\,11,\,23}$), and the immortality of the soul, in the Wisdom of Solomon (especially chs. 1–5). (*a*) In Sirach, the longest book in the Apocrypha, there is no clear conception of either; the old, traditional view of *Sheōl* still prevails, and the dead are not to be mourned overmuch (38^{23}); death may come either as a relentless foe (40^{1-11}), whom all men fear (cf He 2^{15}), or as a friend bringing grateful release (41^{1-4}). 'Whether life is for ten or a hundred or a thousand years, there is no inquiry about it in Hades (=*Sheōl*).' (*b*) The wicked take a dismal view both of this life and the life to come: men are born by mere chance, and when life is extinguished the body turns to ashes, and the spirit 'dissolves like empty air' (Wis 2^{2f}). Yet God did not make death (1^{13}); indeed He intended men for incorruption (2^{23}), and the 'eat, drink, and be merry' ethics of the materialists, who are also persecutors of the righteous (1^{6-20}), is unfounded. 'The souls of the righteous are in the hand of God, and no torment will ever touch them' (3^{1}), but the ungodly will be punished 'as their reasoning deserves' (3^{10}). **2.** On a historical view, Sirach (*c* 185 B.C.; translated into Greek 132 B.C.) antedates the Book of Daniel (*c* 164 B.C.), where the first strong affirmation of belief in the resurrection is to be found (12^{2f}); this is followed by 2 Maccabees (*c* 65 B.C.) and Wisdom (*c* 50 B.C.). But the Book of Wisdom comes from Alexandria, and is Greek not only in language but in thought and ideology; the influence of popular Platonism is quite apparent in it, and the Palestinian conception of resurrection is not mentioned. **3.** As James Denney pointed out in his *Factors of Faith in Immortality*, the belief in resurrection was born of martyrdom: God, being just, will not permit those who have given their lives in His service (in the Maccabaean revolt) to lie down in the dust for ever, but will raise them to a glorious life in the age to come. On the other hand, the conception of immortality involves theories of the soul as a centre of force or vitality, superior to death, and perhaps pre-existent, and it views the separation of the soul from the body as an advantage. Both views contribute to the shaping of the Christian doctrine of the life to come, which retains the conception of resurrection but with strong emphasis on the transformation of the body (cf Paul's doctrine of the ' spiritual body ' in 1 Co 15^{35-54}, and his antipathy for mere bodiless survival in 2 Co 5^{1-5}). 2 Maccabees also represents the Maccabees as offering sacrifice for the departed, even for the disloyal (12^{39-45}), and is thus one more testimony to the religious variety found within Hellenistic Judaism. (2 Maccabees was an abridgement of the five-volume work on the Maccabaean War by Jason of Cyrene ; see 2^{23}.)

F. C. G.

III. In the NT.—**1. The Gospels.**—(*a*) Our Lord says nothing about death as a physical phenomenon. He makes no attempt to explain what death will be like nor to answer the questions that have always excited man's curiosity. Even in stories that concern the raising of the dead there are no references to these matters. In this respect the attitude of Jesus and the evangelists is in strong contrast with that found in Rabbinical writings. The conception of ' the angel of death,' so characteristic of the latter, is absent, though traceable perhaps in 1 Co 15^{26}, He 2^{14}, and Rev 20^{13f}.

(*b*) The current Jewish view that death was an evil persists in the Gospels but never becomes obtrusive. There are various stories of Jesus raising the dead, but they are not given particular prominence and there is no sign of preoccupation with this problem. If one searches, however, signs of the common view come to light. Those aspects of death that make the living and active shrink from it are evident. Jesus in Rabbinic phrase speaks of *tasting* death (Mk 9^{1}) and of *seeing* death (Jn 8^{51}), and the overtone of these expressions is the antithesis of that attaching to ' seeing life ' and ' seeing many days.' Death is to common human feeling an unwelcome, though inevitable, draught. When Jesus approached death Himself, He was ' greatly distressed and troubled ' (Mk 14^{33}), a mental state due not to fear of men or of pain but to revulsion from death itself. The cry of dereliction (Mk 15^{34}) and the other inarticulate cry that accompanied His last breath (Mk 15^{37}) bear witness to the fact that in His humanity Jesus experienced even the horror of death. For all this, the pessimism of parts of the OT never appears in the Gospels, Jesus does not often point to death as the solemn and inescapable end (Lk 12^{16-21} and Jn 9^{4} are two exceptions). His intense concern for this life, coupled with His promise that believers will never die (Jn 11^{26}), supplies the reason.

(*c*) Jesus speaks of death as a sleep (Jn 11^{11-13}, see also Mt 27^{52}) ; but the same euphemistic use is found in the OT and in extra-Biblical writers. It did not of itself lessen the terrors of death (Ps 13^{3}). In conjunction with the Christian doctrine of resurrection, however, this representation of death does mitigate its bitterness (1 Th 4^{13ff}). The figure of sleep only describes the relation of the dead to the activities and interests of this world. Death is a falling asleep after life's day—and ' we sleep to wake ' : but there is nothing here to shed light on the question of whether that sleep is a prolonged period of unconsciousness or not.

(*d*) More important than natural death is the much larger and more solemn conception found in the fourth Gospel where death is primarily the condition of man resulting from sin (5^{24} $6^{20, 50}$ 8^{51f}). The exemption and deliverance promised in Jn 11^{25f} relate to this spiritual death, and by that deliverance natural death is shorn of its real terrors. The process of life begins here and now and reaches its consummation hereafter. Physical death, for the believer, is simply a moment of transition. It derives its solemn significance from its frequent association with the tragedy of sin and unbelief. The Johannine point of view is summed up in 1 Jn 3^{14}, ' We know that we have passed out of death into life, because we love the brethren. He who does not love remains in death.' The conception, however, is not found exclusively in the Johannine writings. The saying in Lk 9^{60} has a bearing on this point. In Mt 7^{13f} ' destruction ' is the antithesis of ' life ' (see also Mt 5^{29f} Mk 8^{35}, cf Jn 3^{16}). Luke's reference to ' perishing ' ($13^{3, 5}$) conveys the same impression. Hardened impenitence means the loss of all that makes the man.

2. The rest of the NT.—(*a*) The Pauline doctrine that *natural* death was the consequence of the first sin (Ro 5^{12-17}, 1 Co 15^{21f}) was drawn from common Jewish belief (see, for example, 2 Bar 17^{3} 19^{8} 23^{4}). It finds no direct support in the Gospels.

(*b*) The notion that ' the sting of death is sin ' (1 Co 15^{56}) is found throughout the NT. It means that, had there been no sin, death would have been a simple and desirable form of transition. Sin and unbelief have transformed the situation so that what was a stepping-stone is now a snare.

(*c*) The use of the term ' death ' to denote a spiritual state in which men may live and still be destitute of all that is worth calling ' life ' is common (Eph $2^{1, 5}$ 5^{14}, Col 2^{13}, 1 Ti 5^{6}, Ja 1^{15}, Jd ^{12}, Rev 3^{1}).

(*d*) The universal horror of death, to Paul Satan's supreme achievement, is only a passing show. Death, the last enemy (1 Co 15^{26}), will be destroyed. It will be swallowed up in the great victory (1 Co 15^{54-57}). The answer to the death of Adam was the resurrection of Christ.

(*e*) Paul's longing for death (2 Co 5^{8}, Ph 1^{23}) was possible because he believed that God had overcome death for him (Ro 6^{8}, 2 Ti 1^{10}).

(*f*) The figure of death is used to describe the change, from the life of sin to the life of righteousness. The believer, the man spiritually alive, is ' dead to sin ' (Ro 6^{2}, 1 P 2^{24}) and ' dead with Christ ' (Ro 6^{8}, Col 2^{20}).

(*g*) The phrase ' the second death ' occurs in Revelation for the final doom of ' the cowardly, the faithless, the polluted,' etc. (21^{8}). It is equated with ' the lake of fire ' (20^{14}). The phrase is taken from current Jewish writings. Over the faithful who have conquered their tribulations and who are gathered up in the first resurrection the ' second death ' has no power (2^{11} 20^{6}).

J. S. C.—**W. D. S.**

DEBATE.—This word had formerly the meaning of ' strife,' as in the Geneva translation of Gn 13^{7}, ' there was debate betweene the heardmen of Abrams cattell, and the heardmen of Lots cattell.'

DEBIR.—**1.** A town first known as **Kiriath-sepher** (Jos 15^{15}, Jg 1^{11}) in the neighbourhood of Hebron, and inhabited by Anakim (Jos 11^{21}), conquered by Joshua (10^{38} 11^{21} 12^{13}), or more specifically by Othniel (15^{17}), assigned as a Levitical city (21^{15}, 1 Ch 6^{58}) in the tribe of Judah (Jos 15^{49}). An alternative name **Kiriath-sannah,** once recorded (15^{49}), is probably a corruption of Kiriath-sepher, due primarily to the similarity of *p* and *n* in the old Hebrew alphabet. It is identified with *Tell Beit Mirsim*, excavated by M. G. Kyle and W. F. Albright, who found remains of more than ten cities.

2. A place named in the northern boundary of Judah, near the valley of Achor (Jos 15^{7}) ; possibly modern *Throghet ed-Debr*.

3. A place, not identified, in the border of the trans-Jordanic territory of Gad (Jos 13^{26}). An alternative reading is **Lidebir** (see Lo-debar).

DEBIR.—The king of Eglon, who according to Jos 10^{3} joined other four kings against Joshua, but was defeated and put to death along with his allies at Makkedah.

DEBORAH (' bee ').—**1.** Rebekah's nurse, who accompanied her mistress to her new home when she married Isaac (Gn 24^{59}).

2. The fourth of the leaders or ' Judges ' of Israel ; called also a ' prophetess,' *i.e.* an inspired woman—one of four mentioned in the OT—of the tribe of Issachar

(Jg 5[12]), wife of Lappidoth (4[4]). Her home was between Bethel and Ramah in the hill-country of Ephraim; here the Israelites came to her for guidance. She was the deliverer of the Israelites when they had sunk into a state of impotence through the oppression of Jabin, king of Hazor. A personality of great power and outstanding character, she was looked up to as a 'mother in Israel' (5[7]).

Deborah's Song (Jg 5[2-31]), better called **Song to Deborah** (since the poem is addressed to her), is the most ancient and magnificent example of early Hebrew literature. It is probably to be dated *c* 1125 B.C., at which time Megiddo lay in ruins and hence not it, but Taanach, was used to indicate the location of the battle (Jg 5[19]). The poem has many parallels with Canaanite literature in language, imagery, and literary technique, particularly its ascending parallelism. In fact, like Ps 29, it may have been a Canaanite poem originally, made over later into a Yahweh hymn. Its great antiquity makes it difficult to translate, but the general sense is clear.

It is a song of victory, sung in honour of Israel's triumph under the leadership of Deborah and Barak over Sisera and the kings of Canaan. The vivid pictures which the poem brings up before the mind's eye make it certain that the writer lived at the time of the events described. The parallel and somewhat later prose account (Jg 4[4-24]) agrees in the main with the poem. The Song may be divided into four distinct sections:

Praise to Yahweh, and the terror of his approach, vv. 2–5.
Condition of Israel prior to Deborah's activity, vv. 6–11.
Gathering of the tribes of Israel, vv. 12–18.
Victory of Israel and death of Sisera, vv. 19–31.

The chief importance of the Song lies in its historical *data* and the light it throws on some of early Israel's conceptions of Yahweh. Of the former, the main points are: that at this time the Israelites had securely settled in the hill-country, but had not as yet obtained any hold on the fertile lands of the Plain; that unity had not yet been established among the tribes of Israel; and that the 'twelve tribes' of later times had not yet come into existence.

Of the latter, the main points are: that Yahweh has His dwelling-place in the mountains of the South; that therefore He has not yet come to dwell among His people; that He comes forth from His dwelling-place to lead His people in battle; and that His might is so great that the very elements are shaken at His approach.

3. The mother of Tobit's father; she seems to have taught her grandchild the duty of almsgiving (To 1[8]).

W. O. E. O.—**T. J. M.**

DEBT.—1. In OT.—Loans in the OT period were not of a commercial nature. They were not granted to enable a man to start or extend his business, but to meet the pressure of poverty. To the borrower they were a misfortune (Dt 28[12, 44]); to the lender a form of charity. Hence the tone of *legislation* on the subject.

Interest is forbidden in all three codes (Ex 22[25] [JE], Dt 23[19], Lv 25[36] [H]); it was making a profit out of a brother's distress. In Deuteronomy it may be taken from a foreigner. Pledges were allowed, but under strict limitations (Dt 24[10], Job 24[3]). In Dt 15 is a remarkable law providing for the 'letting drop' of loans every seventh year (see Driver, *ad loc.*). Its relation to the law of the Sabbatical year in Ex 23[10] (JE), Lv 25[1ff] (H) is not clear, but the cessation of agriculture would obviously lead to serious financial difficulties, and debtors might reasonably look for some relief. This consideration makes for the modern view, that the passage implies only the suspension for a year of the creditor's right to demand payment. It must be admitted, however, that apart from *a priori* considerations the obvious interpretation is a total remission of debts (so the older, and Jewish commentators). Foreigners do not come under the law. The other codes have no parallel, except where the debt may have led to the bondage of the debtor's person.

Historically the legislation seems to have been largely ignored. In 2 K 4[1-7] a small debt involves the bondage of a widow's two sons (cf Is 50[1], Mt 18[23]), and Elisha helps her, not by invoking the law, but by a miracle. In Neh 5 mortgaged lands and interest are restored under the pressure of an economic crisis. Nehemiah himself has been a creditor and taken interest. There is an apparent reference to Dt 15 in Neh 10[31]. In later times the strictness of the law was evaded by various legal fictions: Hillel introduced a system of 'contracting out.' That loans played a large part in social life is shown by frequent references in the Prophets, Psalms, and Proverbs (Is 24[2], Ps 15[5] 37[21], Pr 19[17] 28[8]). Jer 15[10] shows that the relation between debtor and creditor was proverbially an unpleasant one. In Ps 37[21] it is part of the misfortune of the wicked that he shall be unable to pay his debts; there is no reference to dishonesty. Pr 22[7], Sir 18[33] warn against borrowing, and Sir 29 has some delightful common sense advice on the whole subject.

2. In NT.—Loans are assumed by our Lord as a normal factor in social life (Mt 25[27], Lk 16[5] 19[23]). Lk 6[34f] suggests that the Christian will not always stand on his rights in this respect. *Debt* is used as a synonym for *sin* in Mt 6[12] (cf the two parables Mt 18[23], Lk 7[41]; and Col 2[14]). The context of these passages is a sufficient warning against the external and legalistic view of sin which might be suggested by the word itself. Christ does not imply that it is a debt which can be paid by any amount of good deeds or retributive suffering. The word is chosen to emphasize our duty of forgiveness, and it has a wide meaning, including all we owe to God. The metaphor of the money payment has ceased to be prominent, except where it is implied by the context.

C. W. E.—**J. W. W.**

DECALOGUE.—See TEN COMMANDMENTS.

DECAPOLIS.—Originally a league of ten cities, Greek in population and constitution, for mutual defence against the Semitic tribes around them. It must have come into existence about the beginning of the Christian era; perhaps in the time of Pompey (see GERASA and PERAEA). The original ten cities, as enumerated by Pliny, were Scythopolis, Pella, Dion, Gerasa, Philadelphia, Gadara, Raphana, Kanatha, Hippos, and Damascus. Other cities joined the league from time to time. The region of Decapolis (Mt 4[25], Mk 5[20] 7[31]) was the territory in which these cities were situated; that is (excluding Damascus), roughly speaking, the country E. and SE. of the Sea of Galilee. R. A. S. M.—**F. C. G.**

DECEASE.—The Greek word *exodos* ('exodus,' 'outgoing') is translated 'departure' in Lk 9[31] and 2 P 1[15], *i.e.* departure out of the world. In this sense the Greek word is used also in Wis 3[2] 7[6], Sir 38[23]. The opposite, *eisodos*, is used of the 'coming' of Christ. The only other occurrence of the Greek *exodos* in NT is in He 11[22], of the Exodus from Egypt (AV and RV 'departure' but RSV 'exodus').

DECENTLY.—1 Co 14[40], 'All things should be done decently and in order,' that is, in a proper or decorous manner; for that is the old meaning of 'decent,' and it is the meaning of the Greek word used.

DECISION.—Duly constituted and recognized authorities have the power of decision granted to them in all questions of right in the Bible. Moses (Ex 18[16]), the judges (1 S 7[16]), and the kings (1 K 3[16ff]) exercise this power upon occasion. Questions of right between Christian brethren are to be decided by Church courts—*i.e.* either by the Church assembled as a court, or by a judge or judges chosen by the Church—and not by civil authorities (Mt 18[17], 1 Co 6[1-8]). The only method of decision sanctioned in the NT is the exercise of godly judgment on the part of the individual to whom authority has been granted. The casting of lots by heathen soldiers (Mk 15[24]) and the sortilege of Ac 1[21-26] cannot be cited as examples for the Christian Church to follow. See MAGIC. D. A. H.

DECISION, VALLEY OF.—The phrase is found only in Jl 3[14] ' Multitudes, multitudes in the valley of decision; for the day of the Lord is near in the valley of decision.' This valley is evidently the valley of Jehoshaphat mentioned in the preceding context (vv.[2, 12]). The decision is that of Yahweh Himself, His final judgment upon the heathen assembled. The scene of this judgment has been fixed by Jews, Roman Catholics, and Mohammedans in the Valley of the Kidron. The valley of Jehoshaphat has been identified with the Valley of the Kidron since the time of Eusebius. Many scholars are of the opinion that the valley of this prophecy is purely a symbolic one, the valley of ' Yahweh's judgment,' as the Hebrew name *Jehoshaphat* (' Yahweh hath judged ') suggests. D. A. H.

DECREE.—What theologians speak of as the ' decrees of God,' and describe as one, immutable, eternal, all-embracing, free, etc., do not receive this designation in Scripture. The equivalents are to be sought for under such headings as ELECTION, PREDESTINATION, PROVIDENCE, REPROBATE. In the EV the term is frequently used in Esther, Ezra, Daniel, with different Hebrew and Aramaic words, for royal decrees (in Dn 6 RV and RSV ' interdict '; in 2[9] RV ' law ' [RSV ' sentence '], elsewhere ' decree '). In the NT also the Greek word *dogmata* is employed of decrees of Caesar (Lk 2[1], Ac 17[7]); in Ac 16[4] it is used of decisions of the Church; elsewhere (Eph 2[15], Col 2[20]) it is translated **' ordinances '** (RSV ' regulations ' in the latter). The nearest approach to the theological sense of the term is, in OT, in the Hebrew word *ḥôḳ*, ordinarily translated **' statute '** or ' decree ' (sometimes ' limit ' or ' bound '), which is used in various places of God's sovereign appointments in nature and providence (Job 28[26], Ps 148[6], Pr 8[29], Jer 5[22], Zeph 2[2] [but cf RSV in the last]). The Hebrews had not the modern conception of ' laws of nature,' but they had a good equivalent in the idea of the world as ordered and founded by God's decrees; as regulated by His ordinances (cf Ps 104[5, 9] 119[88-91], Jer 10[12ff]). The same word is used in Ps 2[7] of God's ' decree ' regarding His king; in Dn 4[17, 24] (Aramaic) we have ' decree ' of ' the watchers ' and ' the Most High.' J. O.

DEDAN.—A north Arabian people, according to Gn 10[7] descended from Cush, and according to 25[3] from Abraham through Keturah. The combination is not difficult to understand when we remember the Arabian affiliations of the Cushites (see CUSH). In Ezk 25[13] Dedan is placed almost within the Edomite territory, which it must have bordered in the south-east (cf Jer 25[23] 49[8]). The Dedanites were among the Arabian peoples who sent their native wares to the markets of Tyre (Ezk 27[20]). Dedan is probably the oasis of *el-ʿUlâ*. In Ezk 27[15] read ' Rodan '=**Rhodes** (so RSV) for ' Dedan.' J. F. McC.

DEDICATION.—See HOUSE, 3.

DEDICATION, FEAST OF THE (Heb. *Ḥanukkāh*).—An annual eight-day festival instituted by Judas Maccabaeus. Following his recapture of the Temple in the still beleaguered Jerusalem, he removed the heathen altar that had been set up three years earlier, during Antiochus Epiphanes' campaign of forceful hellenization of Judaea, and restored and rededicated (*ḥanukkāh*) the altar of the God of Israel with festivities and illuminations on 25th of Kislev, 165 B.C. (1 Mac 4[59]). The festivities lasted eight days. (According to 2 Mac 10[6-8], the number corresponded to the days of the Feast of Tabernacles, which had not been observed during the Syrian occupation.) The events which the festival commemorated are recorded in 1 and 2 Maccabees and in Josephus, and are referred to in *Megillath Taʿanith*, which includes the feast among the days on which no fasting was to take place. The scholium to this scroll includes the legend, which appears also in the Talmud (Sabbath 21b), concerning the small cruse of consecrated oil which the priests found as they entered the Temple, just enough to feed the *menôrāh* (lamp) one day, but which miraculously burned for eight days.

The 25th of Kislev roughly corresponds to the date of laying the cornerstone of the Second Temple (Hag 2[18]), and the number eight to the duration of the feast of the dedication of the Temple by Solomon (1 K 8[63-66]).

The letter of the senate of Jerusalem, recommending to the Jews of Alexandria the observance of Hanukkah, refers to it as ' the feast of fire ' because of the miraculous lighting of the altar fire at the time of the Temple dedication by Nehemiah (2 Mac 1[18f]).

The legend of the cruse of oil aims to account for the duration of the festival and for its character as a ' Feast of Lights,' by which name Josephus knew it. This name and its chief ceremonial, consisting of public kindling of lights in a progressive number during the evenings of the festival, seem to point to the earlier observance of a winter solstice festival, which was fused with the Maccabaean feast.

Psalm 30, introduced as ' a song at the dedication of the Temple,' came to form part of the liturgy of the festival. It is also marked by chanting the *Hallel* (Pss 113–118). The Pentateuchal readings for the eight days are taken from Numbers 7 (cf vv.[84-88]). The Prophetic lesson for the Sabbath of Hanukkah is from Zec 2[14]–4[7] (because of the symbolism of the menorah) If a second Sabbath occurs during the festival, the second Prophetic lesson is from 1 K 7[40-50]. Thus the festival is linked with the erection of the Tabernacle and of the First and Second Temples. S. S. C.

DEEP.—See ABYSS.

DEER.—See FALLOW-DEER, HART.

DEFENCED.—In AV and RV ' defenced ' means ' provided with fences,' ' protected,' ' fortified.' It is used of fortified cities (Is 25[2] 27[10], Jer 1[18]; ' fortified ' in RSV), and in AVm and RVm in Zec 11[2] of a forest (RSV ' thick ').

DEFILEMENT.—See CLEAN AND UNCLEAN.

DEGREES, SONGS OF.—See PSALMS.

DEHAITES.—In Ezr 4[9] (RV) the Dehaites (AV **Dehavites**) are mentioned among the peoples settled in Samaria by Osnappar (q.v.). But it is probable that the consonants should be differently vocalized, and the word understood to mean ' that is ' (so RSV).

DEHAVITES, Ezr 4[9] (AV).—See DEHAITES.

DEKAR, 1 K 4[9] (AV).—See BEN-DEKER.

DELAIAH.—**1.** One of the sons of Elioenai, 1 Ch 3[24] (AV **Dalaiah**). **2.** A priest and leader of the 23rd course of priests, 1 Ch 24[18]. **3.** The son of Shemaiah, Jer 36[12, 25]. **4.** The son of Mehetabel, and father of Shemaiah, Neh 6[10]. **5.** The head of a family that returned with Zerubbabel, Ezr 2[60], Neh 7[62], 1 Es 5[37] (AV **Ladan,** RV **Dalan**). **6.** Though he is not mentioned in the Bible, we know from the Elephantine Papyri that Sanballat, the adversary of Nehemiah, had a son named Delaiah.

DELILAH.—The Philistine woman who betrayed Samson into the hands of the Philistines. See SAMSON.

DELOS.—A small rocky island in the Aegean Sea, which has played an extraordinary part in history. It belongs to the Cyclades. It was the seat of a widespread worship of Apollo, who, with his sister Artemis, was said to have been born there. In 478 B.C. it was chosen as the meeting-place of the confederacy of Greek States united against their common enemy the Persians, and became a rival of Athens. In the 2nd and 1st cents. B.C. it became a great harbour, and was under Roman protection from 197 to 168 B.C. It flourished greatly after Corinth was destroyed (146 B.C.). It was later a portion of the Roman province Achaia. It is mentioned in the letter of the Romans in favour of the Jews (139–138 B.C., 1 Mac 15[16-23]). It was a great

DELUGE

exchange, where slaves and products from the E. were bought for the Italian market. It was the scene in 87 B.C. of a horrible massacre carried out by Mithridates, king of Pontus, who slaughtered 80,000 Italians of the province of Asia there and in neighbouring islands. Its mercantile position was damaged by the refounding of Corinth in 46 or 44 B.C. A. So.—E. G. K.

DELUGE.—1. The Biblical story, Gn 6^{5}–9^{17} [6^{1-4} is probably a separate tradition, unconnected with the Deluge (see Driver, *Genesis*, p. 82)]. The two narratives of J and P have been combined; the verses are assigned by Driver as follows: J 6^{5-8} $7^{1-5, 7-10, 12, 16b, 17b, 22, 23}$ $8^{2a-3b, 6-12, 13b, 20-22}$; P 6^{9-22} $7^{6, 11, 13-16a, 17a, 18-21, 24}$ $8^{1, 2a, 3b-5, 13a, 14-19}$ 9^{1-17}. J alone relates the sending out of the birds, and the sacrifice with which Y″ is so pleased that He determines never again to curse the ground. P alone gives the directions with regard to the size and construction of the Ark, the blessing of Noah, the commands against murder and the eating of blood, and the covenant with the sign of the rainbow. In the portions in which the two narratives overlap, they are at variance in the following points. (*a*) In P one pair of every kind of animal (6^{18-20}), in J one pair of the unclean and seven of the clean (7^{2f}), are to be taken into the Ark. (In 7^{9} a redactor has added the words 'two and two' to make J's representation conform to that of P). The reason for the difference is that, according to P, animals were not eaten at all till after the Deluge (9^{3}), so that there was no distinction required between clean and unclean. (*b*) In P the cause of the Deluge is not only rain but also the bursting forth of the subterranean abyss (6^{11}); J mentions rain only (v.^{12}). (*c*) In P the water begins to abate after 150 days (8^{3}), the mountain tops are visible after 8 months and 13 days (7^{11} 8^{5}), and the earth is dry after a year and 10 days (8^{14}); in J the Flood lasts only 40 days (7^{12} 8^{6}), and the water had begun to abate before that.

2. The Historicity of the story.—Efforts to establish the historicity of the Flood by archaeological discoveries are futile. Stories of the finding of remains of the Ark on Mount Ararat crop up every now and then, but even if the finds themselves can ever be authenticated, there is no evidence to connect them with Noah's Ark. Usually, indeed, the stories refute themselves by presupposing things archaeologically impossible. More respectable claims have been made for the thick layers of clay found in Babylonian excavations, particularly at Ur and Kish. That these were deposited by floods is unquestionable, but they were not deposited by the same flood, since they are demonstrably from different periods, and other sites in the region have no such deposits from any of these periods. The inundations in question were therefore evidently of a local nature. The modern study of geology and comparative mythology has made it impossible to see in the story of the Deluge the literal record of an historical event. The fact that marine fossils are found on the tops of hills cannot be used as an argument, for, though it proves that some spots which are now at the tops of hills were at one time submerged, that is not equivalent to asserting that a flood ever occurred which covered the whole planet—apart from the extreme improbability that the submergence of mountains was within the period of man's existence. All the water in the world, together with all the vapour if reduced to water, would not cover the whole earth to the height of Mount Ararat. The collection by Noah of a pair of every kind of animal, bird, and creeping thing, which would include species peculiar to different countries from the arctic regions to the tropics, is inconceivable. And no less so the housing of them all in a single chest, the feeding and care of them by eight persons, the arrangements to prevent their devouring one another, and the provision of the widely diverse conditions of life necessary for creatures from different countries and climates. From every point of view it is clear that the story is legendary, and similar in character to the legends which are found in folk-lore of all peoples.

3. Other Flood-stories.—Such stories are found principally in America, but also in India, Cashmir, Tibet, China, Kamschatka, Australia, some of the Polynesian Islands, Lithuania, and Greece. In the great majority of cases the flood is caused by some startling natural phenomenon, which often has a special connexion with the locality to which it belongs; *e.g.* the melting of the ice or snow, in the extreme N. of America; earthquakes, on the American coastlands where they frequently occur; the submergence or emergence of islands, in districts liable to volcanic eruptions; among inland peoples the cause is frequently the bursting of the banks of rivers which have been swollen by rains. Sometimes the stories have grown up to account for various facts of observation; *e.g.* the dispersion of peoples, and differences of language; the red colour, or the pale colour, of certain tribes; the discovery of marine fossils inland, and so on. In some cases these stories have been coloured by the Bible story, owing to the teaching of Christian missionaries in modern times, and often mixed up with other Bible stories, and reproduced with grotesque details by local adaptation. But there are very many which are quite unconnected with the story of Noah. (For a much fuller discussion of the various flood-stories see the valuable article 'Flood' in Hastings' *DB* ii.). It is reasonable, therefore, to treat the Hebrew story as one of these old-world legends, and to look for the cause of it in the natural features of the land which gave it birth. And we are fortunate in the possession of an earlier form of the legend, which belongs to Babylonia, and makes it probable that its origin is to be ascribed to the inundation of the large Babylonian plain by the bursting forth of one of the rivers by which it is intersected, and perhaps also, as some think, to the incursion of a tidal wave due to an earthquake somewhere in the South. This, among a people whose world was bounded by very narrow limits, would easily be magnified in oral tradition into a universal Deluge.

4. The Babylonian story.—(*a*) One form of the story has long been known from the fragments of Berosus, an Egyptian priest of the 3rd cent. B.C. It differs in certain details from the other form known to us; *e.g.* when the birds return the second time, clay is seen to be attaching to their legs (a point which finds parallels in some N. American flood-legends); and not only the hero of the story, Xisuthros, and his wife, but also his daughter and the pilot of the ship are carried away by the gods.

(*b*) The other and more important form is contained in Akkadian cuneiform tablets in the British Museum, first deciphered in 1872. It is part of an epic in 12 parts, each connected with a sign of the Zodiac; the Flood story is the 11th, and is connected with Aquarius, the 'water-bearer.' Gilgamesh of Uruk (Erech, Gn 10^{10}), the hero of the epic, contrived to visit his ancestor Ut-napishtim, who had received the gift of immortality. The latter is in one passage called Adra-ḫasis, which being inverted as Ḫasis-adra appears in Greek as Xisuthros. He relates to Gilgamesh how, for his piety, he had been preserved from a great flood. When Bel and three other gods determined to destroy Shurippak, a city 'lying on the Euphrates,' Ea warned him to build a ship. He built it 120 cubits in height and breadth with 6 decks, divided into 7 storeys, each with 9 compartments; it had a mast, and was smeared with bitumen. He took on board all his possessions, 'the seed of life of every kind that I possessed,' cattle and beasts of the field, his family, servants, and craftsmen. He entered the ship and shut the door. Then Ramman the storm-god thundered, and the spirits of heaven brought lightnings; the gods were terrified; they fled to heaven, and cowered in a heap like a dog in his kennel. On the 7th day the rain ceased, and all mankind were turned to clay. The ship grounded on Mount Nisir, E. of the Tigris, where it remained 6 days. Then Ut-napishtim sent forth a dove, a swallow, and a raven, and the last did not return.

He then sent the animals to the four winds, and offered sacrifice on an altar at the top of the mountain. The gods smelled the savour and gathered like flies. The great goddess Ishtar lighted up the rainbow. She reproached Bel for destroying all mankind instead of one city only. Bel, on the other hand, was angry at the escape of Ut-napishtim, and refused to come to the sacrifice. But he was pacified by Ea, and at length entered the ship, and made a covenant with Ut-napishtim, and translated him and his wife to 'the mouth of the rivers,' and made them immortal.

The similarities to the Hebrew story, and the differences from it, are alike obvious. It dates from at least 3000 B.C., and it would pass through a long course of oral repetition before it reached the Hebrew form. And herein is seen the religious value of the latter. The genius of the Hebrew race under Divine inspiration gradually stripped it of all its crude polytheism, and made it the vehicle of spiritual truth. It teaches the unity and omnipotence of Y″; His hatred of sin and His punishment of sinners; but at the same time His merciful kindness to them that obey Him, which is shown in rescuing them from destruction, and in entering into a covenant with them.

5. It is strange that, apart from Gn 9[28] 10[1, 32] 11[10], there are only two allusions in the OT to the Flood, Is 54[9] and Ps 29[10] (the latter uncertain; see commentaries). In the Apocrypha: 2 Es 3[9f], Wis 10[4], Sir 44[17f] (40[10] in LXX, but not in Hebrew). In the NT: Mt 24[38f], Lk 17[27], He 11[7], 1 P 3[20], 2 P 2[5].

A. H. McN.—**M. B.**

DELUS.—AV form of **Delos** (q.v.).

DEMAS (=Demetrius?).—A companion of St. Paul in an imprisonment (Col 4[14], Phn [24]). According to the Pastoral Epistles, he deserted the Apostle, 'being in love with this present world' (2 Ti 4[10]). It has been conjectured, on the basis of this same allusion, that he was a native of Thessalonica. A. J. M.—**J. K.**

DEMETRIUS.—**1.** *Soter*, the son of Seleucus *Philopator*. In his boyhood he was sent (175 B.C.) to Rome as a hostage, but made his escape after the death of his uncle, Antiochus Epiphanes. Landing at Tripolis, he was joined by large bodies of the people, and even by the bodyguard of his cousin, Antiochus Eupator. Eupator was soon defeated and put to death, and in 162 B.C., Demetrius was proclaimed king (1 Mac 7[1–4], 2 Mac 14[1f]; Jos. *Ant.* XII. x. 1 [389 f]). After seven years, Alexander Balas (q.v.) was set up as a claimant to the crown of Syria (153 B.C.); and he and Demetrius competed for the support of Jonathan (1 Mac 10[1–21]; Jos. *Ant.* XIII. ii. 1–3 [35 ff]). Balas prevailed in spite of the attempts of his rival to outbid him (1 Mac 10[25–45]). In 150 B.C. a decisive engagement took place, in which Demetrius was defeated and slain (1 Mac 10[48–50]; Jos. *Ant.* XIII. ii. 4 [58–60]).

2. *Nicator*, sent by his father, D. *Soter*, for safety to Cnidus after the success of Balas seemed probable. After several years of exile he landed (147 B.C.) with an army of Cretan mercenaries on the Cilician coast, and finally inflicted a fatal defeat upon Balas (145 B.C.) on the banks of the Oenoparas, from which event Demetrius derived his surname (1 Mac 11[14–19]; Jos. *Ant.* XIII. iv. 8 [116 f]). He bought off the opposition of Jonathan by the addition of three Samaritan provinces to Judaea, and the exemption from tribute of the country thus enlarged (1 Mac 11[20–37]; Jos. *Ant.* XIII. iv. 9 [124–128]). After varying fortunes in the war with Trypho (q.v.) Demetrius invaded the dominions of the king of Parthia, by whom, in 140 B.C., he was taken prisoner (1 Mac 14[1–3]). Upon regaining his liberty at the end of ten years, he undertook a war against Ptolemy *Physcon* of Egypt. Having been defeated by Zabinas at Damascus, he fled to Ptolemais, and thence to Tyre, where in 125 B.C. he was murdered (Jos. *Ant.* XIII. ix. 3 [268]), possibly at the instigation of his wife Cleopatra (Appian, *Syr.* 68; Livy, *Epit.* lx.).

3. *Eucaerus*, grandson of D. *Nicator*. On the death of his father he established himself in Coele-Syria, with Damascus as his capital (Jos. *Ant.* XIII. xiii 4 [370]). When civil war broke out between Alexander Jannaeus and his Pharisee subjects, the latter invited the assistance of Demetrius (Jos. *Ant.* XIII. xiii. 5 [372–376], *BJ* I. iv. 4 [92]), who defeated Jannaeus in a pitched battle near Shechem (Jos. *Ant.* XIII. xiv. 1 [377 f], *BJ* I. iv. 5 [93–95]). After a chequered career, Demetrius fell into the hands of the Parthians, by whom he was detained in captivity until his death (Jos. *Ant.* XIII. xiv. 3 [385 f]).

4. 5. Two persons of the name are mentioned in NT—the ringleader in the riot at Ephesus (Ac 19[24]), and a disciple commended in 3 Jn [12]. Probably the same name occurs in a contracted form as *Demas*.

S. M.—**F. C. G.**

DEMONS AND DEMONOLOGY.—In common with most ancient peoples, the Biblical writers believed in the existence of spiritual beings capable of exerting a malign influence on human affairs. **1. Terminology**—The most general term for a being of this kind is 'demon' (Gr. *daimōn*). The etymology of this word is uncertain. In the earliest Greek usage, it meant a divine being. Then the demons came to be understood as beings intermediate between the gods and men, often as the companions or guardians of particular men. Such demons might be either good or bad. The final stage in the development of the term was reached when all demons came to be recognized as evil. This stage had, of course, already been reached when the term was used in the NT. The word 'demon' does not occur in AV, where it is represented by 'devil.' In RV it is substituted for 'devil' in the margin of many passages and also occurs twice in the text (Dt 32[17], Ps 106[37]), representing a word denoting a species of genii or demi-gods who were conceived as invested with power for good or evil, and to whom even human sacrifices were offered. In RSV 'demon' is used in the text as the general term for a malevolent spiritual being, while 'devil' is reserved for Satan, and this procedure restores the diversity of terminology found in the NT.

The term 'devil' is also of Greek origin (=*diabolos*). Meaning the 'accuser,' it came to stand for the accuser and traducer of men, the supreme spirit of evil, and even the enemy of God. As noted above, the term takes the place of 'demon' in AV, but is primarily applied, as in RSV, to the chief or prince of the demons, who is known also by various proper names (see SATAN; BAALZEBUB).

We notice also the terms 'evil spirit,' 'lying spirit,' 'unclean spirit.' In the OT an evil spirit is represented as being sent by God. The treachery of the men of Shechem is so explained (Jg 9[23]), also Saul's moodiness (1 S 16[14]) and his raving against David (1 S 18[10] 19[9]). Micaiah speaks of a 'lying spirit' from God (1 K 22[21–23], 2 Ch 18[20–23]). These spirits, therefore, are represented as under the control of God, but in some of the writers this control is more direct and active, in others more permissive. But God's supreme control is recognized by all, and in using or permitting the activity of these spirits God is assumed or asserted to be punishing people for their sins. In that sense God has 'a company of destroying angels' (Ps 78[49]). As the understanding of God's nature and purpose developed, the activity of these spirits was conceived more and more in a permissive way. Thus, whereas David was incited to number Israel through the anger of the Lord against the people (2 S 24[1]), according to the Chronicler it was Satan who instigated David (1 Ch 21[1]). Jeremiah denies the inspiration of lying prophets, and makes them entirely responsible for their own words and influence (23[16, 21, 25f]). They are not used by God, and will be called to account. They speak out of their own heart, and are so far from executing God's justice or anger upon the wicked that He interposes to check them, and to protect men from being misled. Thus the idea of an 'evil spirit' moves gradually from the conception of an angel of God to that of a quasi-independent force working against God, though powerless to withdraw from God's ultimate control. This is the sense in the NT, where St. Luke uses the expression 'evil spirit' as a synonym for 'demon' (7[21] 8[2], Ac 19[12, 13, 15, 16]). Another common expression in the Synoptic Gospels is 'unclean spirit.' Since the demons are usually represented in the Synoptic Gospels as the cause of physical rather than moral evils, we may suppose that the adjective 'unclean' refers rather to the wretched state of the victim than to moral or ceremonial defilement.

2. History and Development.—Ancient Semitic demonology recognized a host of spirits, most of which were probably regarded as hostile. An important class of these were embodied in animals, especially in animals found in lonely places—in the desert, among tombs, in ruined houses. There are traces of these beliefs in the OT—the serpent in Gn 3[15], the satyrs (Lv 17[7], 2 Ch 11[15], Is 13[21] 34[14]), the night hag (Is 34[14], cf Ps 91[5]), Rahab (Is 51[9]), Behemoth (Job 40[15f]), Leviathan (Job 41[1f], Ps 74[14] 104[26], Is 27[1]), and the catalogue of animals in Is 34. The enigmatic figure of Azazel (Lv 16[8f]) may come into the same category. Very diverse activities were ascribed to these early demons, especially any 'unnatural' happening or mischance, and above all, sickness, madness, and death.

Further development took place under various foreign influences—Babylonian, Persian, Greek. In Judaism the range of demonic beings is increased to take in a host of invisible bodiless spirits, for Babylonian and Persian thought had made familiar the idea of a multitude of spiritual beings with graded powers. To these demons were attributed all ills, moral as well as physical. They came to be thought of as organized in their own kingdom, under the leadership of Satan, but it is important to notice that since Satan was conceived as a fallen angel, not as an independent spirit like the Persian Ahriman, we never arrive at a thoroughgoing dualism, for God is always supreme. Another important idea, which later became very prominent in the Early Church, was that the heathen gods are demons (Dt 32[17], Ps 106[37], cf Ps 96[5]).

It was against the background of this fully developed demonology that the NT was written, yet its references to demons are remarkably restrained and avoid the crudities which are so common in later Christian writings. As already noted, the Synoptic Gospels represent the demons primarily as producing physical evils (including madness). Yet they are under the rule of the prince of demons whose activities are more definitely in the moral sphere. It is he who tempts Christ (Mt 4[1f], Lk 4[2f]), and in the parables sows tares (Mt 13[39]) and snatches up the good seed (Lk 8[12]). He thus appears as the enemy of God's good purposes. In the Fourth Gospel, the subordinate demons tend to fall into the background, and demonic activity is concentrated in the person of the devil. It is he who prompts the treason of Judas (13[2]) and he is described as a liar and a murderer (8[44]). St. Paul refers to the belief that the pagan deities are demons (1 Co 10[20]). For him, the activities of demonic powers are primarily in the moral and spiritual sphere. But he speaks of these demonic powers as 'rulers of this age' (1 Co 2[6, 8]), 'principalities' (Ro 8[39], Col 2[15]) under the 'god of this world' (2 Co 4[4]). The language is that of dualism and some scholars assign to it a Gnostic origin, but we are also told that 'thrones,' 'dominions,' 'principalities,' 'authorities' are all created (Col 1[16]) and there is certainly no absolute dualism in St. Paul's thought. St. James (2[19]) speaks also of demons in a way which shows them as ultimately subject to God. The idea that the demons inhabit the air appears in Eph 2[2]. In this epistle, and also in 1 P (5[8]) and Rev (2[18] 12[9f] 20[10]) the tendency is, as in the Johannine literature, to emphasize the place of Satan so that the lesser demons are not so prominent. (See SATAN.)

3. Significance.—The final picture which emerges represents the superhuman evil of the world in terms of an organized realm of evil set over against God. The 'dominion of darkness' is contrasted with 'the kingdom of his [God's] beloved Son' (Col 1[13]), the devil is the 'ruler of this world' and Christ's kingdom is contrasted with it (Jn 12[31] 18[36]). Yet nowhere is there anything like an exact co-ordination of the two. The representation is not that of a dualism, but that of the revolt of a subordinate, though superhuman power. Even now, this power is broken (Jn 16[11], Col 2[15]) and its defeat will be final and complete (1 Co 15[24f]). See BAALZEBUB, and EVIL SPIRITS. See also EXORCISM; POSSESSION; SATAN.

J. Macq.

DEMOPHON (2 Mac 12[2]).—A Syrian commandant in Palestine under Antiochus *Eupator*.

DEN.—The six Hebrew or Aramaic words represented by 'den' signify respectively 'hollow place,' 'cave' (Is 32[14], Jer 7[11]; cf Mt 21[13] and ||s), 'thicket' (Ps 10[9] AV, RV; RSV 'covert'), 'place of ambush' (Job 37[8] AV; RV 'covert'; RSV 'lair'), 'hiding place' (Job 37[8] RV, RSV; AV 'places'), 'place of light' (Is 11[8]; but the text may be corrupt), 'pit' (Dn 6[7]).

DENARIUS.—See MONEY, **6, 7.**

DEPUTY.—**1.** AV of Est 8[9] 9[3] (RV, RSV 'governor') as translation of *peḥāh*. See GOVERNOR. **2.** RV of Jer 51[23, 28] (AV 'ruler'; RSV 'commander'), Dn 3[2f, 27] (AV 'governor'; RSV 'prefect' as translation of *sāgān* or its Aramaic equivalent. The term denotes in these passages a superior official or prefect of the Babylonian Empire. It is applied elsewhere (Ezr 9[2], Neh 2[16] 4[14, 19] etc.) to petty officials in Judah (RVm 'deputies'; AV, RV 'rulers'; RSV 'chief man' or 'officials'). **3.** AV, RV and RSV of 1 K 22[47] as translation of *niṣṣābh* (literally one set up *or* appointed), used of the vassal-king of Edom. **4.** AV of Ac 13[7f, 12] 18[12] 19[38] (RV, RSV 'proconsul') as translation of Greek *anthupatos*.

DERBE.—A city in the ethnic district Lycaonia and in the region Lycaonia-Galatica of the Roman province of Galatia. It lay on the road from the Cilician Gates to Lystra and Iconium. The city belonged for a while to Antipater, friend of Cicero, but was then annexed by Amyntas, king of Galatia in 27 B.C. and formed part of the province of Galatia as at first organized in 25 B.C. after the death of that ruler. Eventually, along with Laranda, it seems to have passed under the rule of Antiochus of Commagene. It was honoured with the prefix *Claudio-*. It was in that period that St. Paul visited it (Ac 14[6]), and then retraced his steps to Lystra (q.v.). On his second and third journeys he came to Derbe first, coming from Cilicia. Gaius of Derbe was one of Paul's helpers (Ac 20[4]). The Lycaonian tongue was still spoken at Derbe (Ac 14[11]). Second cent. coins of Derbe are known. The site of the city seems now to have been recovered through an inscription found in 1956 at *Kerti Hüyük*, 13 miles from *Karaman*. It thus lay NNE. of Laranda, and not as close to Lystra as had been supposed. The site is in a plain that was marshy until recently.

A. So.—E. G. K.

DESCENT INTO HELL.—In the OT 'hell' (Heb. *sheʾōl*, Gr. *Hadēs*) is the shadowy nether world which is the dwelling place of the dead. Initially it is morally neutral, but later it is identified at times with Gehenna, a place of torment for the wicked. Our Lord makes use of this connotation in the NT. In the parable, Dives is said to be in torment whereas Lazarus is represented as in the company of Abraham (Lk 16[19-31]). It should, however, be observed that it is not the point of the parable to describe the nature of hell. The promise to the penitent robber (Lk 23[43]) raises the problem implicit in the parable: how far and in what sense Jesus accepted or sanctioned the conventional doctrine of his day.

Ac 2[24-31] certainly suggests apostolic belief that Christ himself passed at his death into Hades. The descent of a redeemer into the underworld may be exemplified outside the Jewish sphere (*e.g.* the Babylonian Ishtar, the Greek mysteries, and Mandaism), but no direct connexion with non-Jewish sources has been established. In the passage cited, Peter alludes to Ps 16[10]: 'For thou wilt not abandon my soul to Hades.' This is taken as a prophecy of the Resurrection. Paul wrote in Ro 10^{7} to the effect that since Christ has risen from the dead there is no need to 'descend into the abyss' to bring Him up (cf Dt 30^{13}). Eph 4^{9} is more ambiguous ('In saying "He ascended" what does it mean but that he also descended into the lower parts of the earth?'): this has been taken by some to refer not to His descent into Hades but to His descent in the Incarnation (cf Gnostic parallels). But Ps 63^{9} has the phrase 'shall go down into the depths of the earth' meaning Hades, so the NT passage may also be understood in this sense. The implication would then be that through obedience even unto death Christ became Lord of the underworld also, His descent being an assertion of this Lordship. Cf Ph 2^{10} and Rev 1^{18}.

Rudolf Bultmann denies that the crucial passage 1 P 3$^{18-20}$ originally referred to a descent into hell; but it has traditionally been considered in this light. It runs: 'For Christ also died for sins once for all, the righteous for the unrighteous, that he might bring us to God, being put to death in the flesh but made alive in the spirit; *in which he went and preached to the spirits in prison,* who formerly did not obey, when God's patience waited in the days of Noah, during the building of the ark, in which a few, that is, eight persons, were saved through water.' (Bultmann alludes to a Gnostic myth in which the prison of the dead is in the *air*.)

There is evidence of a Jewish belief that a time of repentance would be allowed to the sinners who perished in the Flood; and until the time of Augustine Christian interpretations followed the line that Christ preached to their spirits. Augustine himself suggested that it was Christ *in Noah* who preached to these men of Noah's time.

Mention in *Enoch* of preaching punishment to the fallen angels has led a number of critics in more modern times to link this passage with that, particularly since 2 P 2^{4} and Jd ^{6} show the acquaintance of the early Christians with such apocryphal literature. But *Enoch* says nothing of preaching repentance or salvation to the souls of the departed, which is required by the context, and particularly by 1 P 4^{6}, 'For this is why the gospel was preached even to the dead, that though judged in the flesh like men, they might live in the spirit like God.'

The connexion with *Enoch* has led also to the notable conjecture of Rendel Harris (followed by James Moffatt and others) that in 3^{19} *en hō kai* should be followed by *Enōch*, omitted by haplography. But there is no MS evidence to back this up and traditional interpretations from Patristic times onwards may be placed against it. Moreover the Christian 'New Testament Apocrypha' develop the notion of the descent of Jesus Christ (M. R. James, *The Apocryphal New Testament*: index).

In the present state of scholarship it may fairly be said that the concept, known traditionally as the Harrowing of Hell, can be regarded as a product of apocalyptic thought-forms dominant in the Jewish-Christian world of apostolic times. Its validity for credal dogma and as the basis of conceptions such as limbo has to be examined—*e.g.* in the light of Bultmann's interpretation of such facets on the 'first century world-view' as myth which is existentially significant. Many would represent it (whatever categories they use) as a natural attempt to vindicate the love, power, and justice of God towards those who could not know Christ in the flesh. J. C. G. G.

DESERT.—See WILDERNESS.

DESSAU.—A village where an encounter took place between the Jews and Nicanor, 2 Mac 14^{16} (RV **Lessau**). The site is unknown, and the text is uncertain.

DESTROY (utterly).—See BAN.

DEUEL.—Father of Eliasaph, leader of Gad, Nu 1^{14} 7$^{42, 47}$ 10^{20}; also 2^{14} (AV, RV **Reuel**).

DEUTERONOMY.—1. Place in the Canon.—Deuteronomy is the fifth book of the Torah, the first division of the Hebrew canon. It is likely that at one time it formed the first part of the Deuteronomist history of Israel, which continued through Joshua, Judges, 1 and 2 Samuel, and 1 and 2 Kings (see article on JOSHUA, BOOK OF).

2. Contents.—The nucleus of the book is a code of laws, represented as having been promulgated by Moses in a speech delivered east of the Jordan just before his death. This begins with a reference to the covenant made at Horeb, rehearses the Decalogue given there, exhorts the people to obey its commands (ch. 5), and passes into a further exhortation to obey the laws about to be proclaimed (6^{1}–11^{25}). In this Moses affirms the unity of Yahweh (6^{4}) who is the God of the whole earth (10$^{14, 17}$) and who has taken Israel to be His people (7^{6} 10^{15}) and cared for them (8$^{2-4, 14b-16}$), not for any merit of theirs—for they are stubborn and rebellious (9^{6}–10$^{5, 10f}$)—but because of the promise He made to their forefathers to give the land to their descendants (6^{10} 7$^{7-9}$), a promise He is now about to fulfil (7$^{1f, 17-24}$ 8$^{7-10, 17f}$ 9$^{1-3}$). Israel's obligation is to serve Him only and to keep His commandments (6$^{5-9, 13, 16-18, 20-25}$ 8^{6} 10^{12f} 11$^{13, 18-20}$). If they do this it will be well with them (6^{18f} 7$^{11-15}$ 8^{1} 11$^{9-15, 21-25}$), but if they forget Him and serve other gods He will destroy them (6$^{12, 14f}$ 7$^{2-5, 16, 25f}$ 8$^{11-14, 19f}$ 11^{16f}). A command, pointing ahead to ch. 27 and Jos 8^{30ff}, to set a blessing on Mount Gerizim and a curse on Mount Ebal when they have crossed the Jordan to take possession of the land (11$^{26-32}$) is followed by the code (12^{1}–26^{15}), with a brief concluding exhortation (26$^{16-19}$).

The recurrence of the various themes in 6^{1}–11^{25} and the awkward way in which the story of the golden calf (9^{8}–10^{11}) is introduced into the exhortation suggest that the present form of the introductory speech is an expanded version of a more concise original, whether the expansion was by casual redactional addition from time to time or by conflation with a parallel introduction.

Preceding this speech is an historical sketch of events from Israel's departure from Horeb until their arrival in the valley by Beth-peor (1^{6}–3^{29}), cast in the form of another speech delivered by Moses beyond the Jordan (1$^{1-5}$). This is substantially a unity, and may have been written as an introduction to the deuteronomist history of Israel referred to above. At any rate it stands outside the immediate introduction to the code and it is presumably by another than the author of that part of chs. 5–11 from which 5^{3} (cf 11^{2ff}) is derived; for 5^{3} represents Moses as speaking to the men with whom Yahweh had made His covenant at Horeb whereas 1^{35ff} 2$^{14-16}$ state that all these men were dead with the exception of Caleb and Joshua. The sketch passes into an exhortation to the people to obey the statutes and ordinances about to be proclaimed (4$^{1-40}$), and this is followed by a notice of the setting apart of three cities of refuge E. of the Jordan (4$^{41-43}$), and two sentences introducing the code (4$^{44, 45-46a}$), which, however, are left hanging in the air for they lead up only to a summary of events (4^{46b-48}) already recounted at some length in 2^{26}–3^{8}.

What the relation of 4$^{1-40}$ is to chs. 5–11 it is difficult to say. Its argument is a summary of the argument of chs. 6–11, and indications are not wanting that it may not be a unity: *e.g.* 4^{23} (cf vv.$^{10, 33}$) refers to 'the covenant of the Lord your God which he made with you,' but 4^{31} speaks of 'the covenant with your fathers which he swore to them.' This may indeed be an allusion to Yahweh's promise to Abraham, Isaac, and Jacob (cf 6^{9} 7^{8}), but this promise is not referred to as a 'covenant' elsewhere in Deuteronomy. Furthermore, the implication of 4$^{10-14}$ is that the deuteronomic code was delivered to Moses by Yahweh at Horeb, and so that its authority was equal to that of the ten words which Yahweh had spoken at that time. The same claim is made in ch. 5, and this suggests that the chapters originally stood in different contexts. The meaning of 4^{3}, 'Behold, I have taught you statutes,' etc., is ambiguous, but if it refers to the code of Deuteronomy it

DEUTERONOMY

indicates that 4^{1-40}, in whole or in part, originally came not before but after the code. Certainly 4^{41-43} would better follow than precede 19^{1-13}.

Following the speech containing the code is an account of Moses commanding the people to erect an altar on Mount Ebal 'on the day you pass over the Jordan,' and in a solemn ceremony to lay a curse upon those who shall break the laws just promulgated (ch. 27). This charge passes into an enumeration of the blessings which Yahweh will pour out upon the nation if they keep the law (28^{1-14}), followed by a warning of the dire consequences of disobedience (vv.$^{15-68}$). Moses then summons all Israel again to remind them of what Yahweh has done for them in the past and to warn them of the fate awaiting them if they fail to keep the terms of the 'sworn covenant of the Lord your God which the Lord your God makes with you this day' (29^{2-29})—a covenant which supplements that made at Horeb (29^{1}). He then goes on to assure them that Yahweh will always be ready to forgive them if they turn back to Him in their distress (30^{1-14}), and puts before them the choice they must now make between 'life and death, blessing and curse' (30^{11-20}).

There can be no doubt that at one stage in the history of the material 28^{2} followed immediately on 26^{19}, the substance of which, 'the Lord will set you on high above all the nations of the earth,' is repeated in 28^{1}. That is to say, ch. 27 is derived from another tradition than 26^{16-19} $28^{2\text{ff}}$. The nucleus of vv.$^{1-8}$ appears to have been taken from the older (JE) history; the account of the fulfilment of the command it contains is now found in Jos $8^{30\text{ff}}$. Vv.$^{9\text{f}}$ connect vv.$^{1-8}$ with vv.$^{11-26}$ in which a liturgy of some kind is preserved. Similarly ch. 29 breaks the connexion between chs. 28 and 30. Its intent appears to be to make explicit the fact that the code, like the Decalogue in ch. 5, is the basis of a covenant (vv.$^{10-15}$), to insist upon the obligation of the individual Israelite to conform to it (vv.$^{18-21}$), and to interpret the exile as the consequence of the failure of the nation to fulfil its requirements (vv.$^{22\text{ff}}$). The fact that the material in these two chapters comes where it does can only be due to the exigencies of conflation.

Chs. 28 and 30 provide a conclusion to the speech in 5^{1}–26^{19}. The indications are that it is the result of expansion from time to time. The blessings in 28^{2-6} are balanced by the curses in vv.$^{15-19}$; but where the exposition of the blessings comprises only eight verses ($^{7-14}$) that of the curses runs through forty-nine verses ($^{20-68}$). There is furthermore considerable repetition in this latter section: diseases of the body are referred to in vv.$^{21-22a, 27, 35, 59-62}$; natural disaster affecting crops and animals in vv.$^{22b-24, 38-40, 42}$; enemy action in vv.$^{29b-34, 36\text{f}, 41, 47-57, 63-68}$; 30^{1-10} with its promise of restoration on repentance quite destroys the effect of the picture of hopeless misery presented in 28^{20-68}; and $30^{11\text{ff}}$ does not connect smoothly with vv.$^{1-10}$, which, indeed, are not presupposed by v.^{18}.

Chs. 31–33 are in the nature of a supplement. In addition to an account of Moses' last days (31, 32^{44-52}), they contain a song which he is represented as having composed and recited to the people (32^{1-43})—a didactic poem giving an interpretation of Israel's entire history and bearing traces of influence from the Wisdom Literature; and the blessing with which he blessed Israel (ch. 33), composed of oracles on the several tribes, with an introduction and a conclusion. Ch. 34 records Moses' death.

There can be no doubt that the framework to the code (1^{1}–11^{32} 26^{16}–34^{12}) has a somewhat complicated literary history the pattern of which it is difficult to recover. The code itself is also the result of elaboration, and it is reasonable to suppose that the pattern of this may throw some light upon the structure of the framework.

The first law in the code is the so-called law of the central sanctuary (12^{5-25}), which lays it down that sacrifice may legitimately be offered to Yahweh only in the place which He 'will choose out of all your tribes to put his name there.' One version of this is contained in vv.$^{5-7, 17-25}$, and a second in vv.$^{11-14, 26-28}$. The difficulty to which this law would give rise—that it would make it impossible for anyone to eat meat at home—is met by the permission to kill and eat animals apart from the context of sacrifice provided the blood is not eaten; this permission is also given twice (vv.$^{15\text{f}, 20-25}$).

Wherever sacrifice is mentioned in the laws which follow the requirement that it shall be offered in the place which the Lord shall choose is repeated (15^{20} $16^{2, 6, 10\text{f}, 15\text{f}}$ 26^{2}). But here there is a difficulty, for in three places it is explicitly laid down that the sacrifice shall be eaten by the offerer and his household (15^{19} $16^{11, 14}$); the household must accordingly be present at the sacrifice, an obvious impossibility if it was offered at the central sanctuary. These laws are, moreover, found, without mention of the central sanctuary, in Ex 34^{19-22}; they are thus earlier than Deuteronomy, and were adapted to their new setting by the compiler of the code.

The laws in the code seem to be arranged in no logical order. The law of the central sanctuary is followed not by the laws concerning the cult, as might have been expected, but by a number of laws prescribing death for anyone who tries to entice an Israelite to idolatry (12^{29}–13^{18}). Then comes a prohibition of certain mourning customs ($14^{1\text{f}}$); a series of dietary laws (vv.$^{3-21}$); laws of the tithe (vv.$^{22-29}$), of the year of release (15^{1-11}), of the manumission of Hebrew slaves (vv.$^{12-18}$), of firstlings (vv.$^{19-23}$), and of the annual festivals (16^{1-17}). These are followed by directions concerning the administration of justice (16^{18-20} 17^{2-13}), in the middle of which are three laws, completely unrelated to the context, prohibiting the planting of a tree, or the erection of a pillar, beside the the altar of Yahweh, and the offering of a blemished animal in sacrifice (16^{21}–17^{1}). Related to the laws on the administration of justice are the laws concerning official persons: the king (17^{14-20}), the Levitical priests (18^{1-8}), and the prophets (18^{15-22}). Again the series is interrupted by the prohibition of magic and soothsaying (18^{9-14}). Laws prescribing the setting apart of cities of refuge and dealing with the right of sanctuary (19^{1-13}) are followed by an isolated command not to remove a neighbour's landmark (v.^{14}). Then comes a law against false witness (vv.$^{15-21}$), which might have been expected after 17^{13}. Laws concerning warfare follow (20^{1-20} 21^{10-14}) in the middle of which is laid down the procedure for the expiation of an unknown murderer's crime (21^{1-9}). Two laws on family relations (21^{15-21}) are followed by a law requiring that the body of a criminal be buried on the day he is executed ($21^{22\text{f}}$). This in turn is followed by a law laying down what a man should do when he finds a straying animal belonging to another (22^{1-4}). Four laws concerning chastity ($22^{13-21, 22, 23-27, 28\text{f}}$) and one against incest (22^{30}) are followed by four laws excluding certain classes of people from 'the assembly of the Lord' (23^{1-8}), two of them for reasons having to do with sex; but the principle on which the laws which follow are arranged is not immediately apparent: two laws having to do with ritual cleanness in camp during warfare (23^{9-14}), which would have been expected after 21^{14}; laws concerning an escaped slave (vv.$^{15\text{f}}$), prohibiting cult prostitution, male or female (vv.$^{17\text{f}}$), prohibiting the taking of interest (vv.$^{19\text{f}}$), concerning vows (vv.$^{21-23}$), concerning gleaning (vv.$^{24\text{f}}$), prohibiting a man from again marrying his divorced wife (24^{1-4}), exempting a newly married man from military service for a year (v.^{5}), concerning a pledge for a loan (v.^{6}), which would fit better after 23^{20}; and seven miscellaneous laws (vv.$^{5-12}$): a woman is not to wear a man's clothing or a man a woman's (v.^{5}), young birds or eggs may be taken from a nest, but not the mother (vv.$^{6\text{f}}$), the roof of a house must have a parapet (v.^{8}), crops may not be sown in a vineyard (v.^{9}), ox and ass may not be yoked together (v.^{10}), clothing may not be of mingled stuff (v.^{11}), tassels are required on a cloak (v.^{12}). The laws in vv.$^{6-8}$ break the connexion between those in v.^{5} and vv.$^{9-11}$, which are obviously related to each other. These are followed by a law against abducting a man and selling him into slavery (v.^{7}), which would have come better after 15^{18} ; laws concerning leprosy (vv.^{8ff}), concerning pledges for a loan (vv.$^{10-13}$), related to that in 24^{6}, concerning the payment of a hired servant (vv.^{14f}), two more laws concerning the administration of justice (vv.$^{16-18}$), which would seem to belong with 16^{18ff} 17^{2ff} 19$^{15-21}$; on gleaning (vv.$^{19-22}$), related to that in 23^{24f}, and still another on the administration of justice (25$^{1-3}$). After a law against muzzling an ox when it treads out the grain (v.^{4}), completely unrelated to its context, comes the law concerning levirate marriage (vv.$^{5-10}$), a law concerning a woman who seizes a man fighting with her husband ' by the private parts ' (vv.^{11f}), a law concerning just weights and measures (vv.$^{13-16}$), and a command to 'blot out the remembrance of Amalek from under heaven ' (vv.$^{17-19}$). The code closes with a law concerning the offering of first-fruits and the disposition of the tithe (26$^{1-15}$).

It is difficult to determine to what extent this disorder is due to the addition of other laws to an original deuteronomic code, and to what extent it is due to the haphazard introduction of new laws from time to time into the earlier codes from which the compilers of the deuteronomic code presumably derived much of their material. A number of scholars who believe that it is for the most part due to additions to an original deuteroonmic code have endeavoured to reconstruct this by putting to one side laws which break the connexion between two related laws (*e.g.* 16^{21}–17^{1} between 16$^{18-20}$ and 17^{2ff}), and by taking account of the alternation of singular (thou/thee) and plural (you) in certain laws (*e.g.* 12$^{2-12, 16, 32}$, plural ; vv.$^{13-15, 17-31}$, singular ; 13$^{1-3a, 5a\gamma b}$, singular ; vv.$^{3b-5a\alpha\beta}$, plural). None of these attempts has met with general acceptance, nor has any satisfactory explanation been suggested as to why the scribes who added these ' secondary ' laws added them where they did.

Another possible solution is suggested by the duplication of the law of the central sanctuary and of the permission for non-sacrificial slaughter in ch. 12 : that the disorder is due, in part, to the conflation of two codes, regarded as of equal authority and to some extent overlapping, to each of which new laws had earlier been added at different times. The code is patient of analysis along these lines, and this solution has this in its favour, that it leaves fewer loose ends than the hypothesis of gradual and casual expansion of an original deuteronomic code. It also suggests that the duplications and repetitions in the framework may in part be due to the conflation of the introductory and concluding speeches of the respective codes—*in part*, for it is highly probable that additions have been made, subsequent to this conflation, both to the code and to the framework. But such a solution would have to stand the test of historical criticism. Each of the codes postulated would presumably represent the use and customs of a particular sanctuary. This in itself would create no difficulty, were it not that, *ex hypothesi*, each code contained the law of the central sanctuary, and this in each case would, it may be assumed, refer to the sanctuary to which the code in question belonged. This would seem to indicate that the law of the central sanctuary was in the first instance regional ; that in course of time a similar law was made for another region ; that eventually each of the two sanctuaries claimed to be the sole legitimate cult centre for the whole land ; and that the fusion of the uses and customs of both sanctuaries to form the present deuteronomic code was part of an attempt to reconcile their conflicting claims.

In favour of the validity of this theory is the fact that it suggests a solution to the problem raised by Dt 11$^{29-31}$ 27$^{2-8}$, Jos 8$^{30-34}$. These passages together point to a tradition that on the day the Israelites crossed the Jordan an altar was erected in the vicinity of Shechem and sacrifice offered thereon to Yahweh. A number of scholars have maintained that the fact that this tradition is preserved in Deuteronomy is evidence that the law of the central sanctuary in ch. 12 originally referred to Shechem. This reading of the evidence has been disputed on the ground that the account of the discovery of the deuteronomic code and the initial enforcement of the law of the central sanctuary (2 K 22 f) clearly indicates that Jerusalem was the sanctuary referred to ; and this is supported by the deuteronomic editing of the books of the Kings (*e.g.* 2 K 12^{2f} 14^{3f}). On the hypothesis that the present deuteronomic code is a conflation of two codes, each containing a law prescribing a central sanctuary, it might be argued that one of these codes originated in Shechem, and that the code upon which Josiah based his reforms was drawn up under the influence of this northern code, to claim for Jerusalem in the south the position claimed for Shechem in the north as the sole legitimate place of sacrifice.

The possibility thus stated assumes that the account of Josiah's reformation is a literary unity. This however has been called in question and the thesis advanced that the reformation was in fact limited to a purging of the Temple of Assyrian cult objects which had been placed there by Manasseh. The account of this, it is argued, is the nucleus of 2 K 23^{4ff}, and this was later elaborated to make it an account of the implementation of the deuteronomic code with its law of the central sanctuary, which, it was claimed, had just been ' discovered ' in the Temple. This article is not the place for an examination of this thesis, but this much may be noted, that even supposing the thesis is valid, the fact that an original account of Josiah's somewhat limited reforms was thus expanded suggests, if it does not indeed indicate, that those reforms were undertaken under the influence of the deuteronomic programme which had already been put into effect elsewhere—most likely at Shechem. And from this a further inference might reasonably be drawn : that the ' Shechem code ' was one of the first-fruits of the prophetic movement, and that it was drawn up as a ' constitution ' for the Yahwist community remaining in the north after the fall of the kingdom, when Samaria had become a province of the Assyrian empire—a community which was a ' church ' freed from the control of the State. And there is the further possibility, that during the half-century of the Babylonian exile it was Shechem with its deuteronomic code which was the real centre of Palestinian Yahwism. The community there may not have welcomed the re-establishment of Jerusalem at the restoration—the books of Ezra and Nehemiah indeed reflect their opposition—but the very existence of Deuteronomy in its present form and the fact of the Samaritan Pentateuch witness to the effort which was made to reconcile the traditions of the north and the south, even though it was ultimately unsuccessful and Shechem became the centre of the Samaritan schism.

Admittedly this discussion of the origin of the code is conjectural. It may nevertheless throw some light upon the question as to the purpose of the centralization of the cult in the first place. For this was a radical departure from the past in that it made illegal the sacrificial worship which had long been offered to Yahweh in every place where he caused His name to be remembered (cf Ex 20^{24}), that is in the village sanctuaries throughout the land. On the assumption that the new law originated as part of the programme of reform put into effect by Josiah, it has been maintained that it was simply a measure designed to ensure the purification of the cult by confining it to one centre where it could be supervised and controlled. Others have held that the compilers of the code had come to realize that the multiplicity of sanctuaries was a hindrance to faith in the unity of Yahweh (cf 6^{4}), for the reason that the old idea of baalism that each sanctuary had its own god still lingered on, even though the sanctuaries had long been Yahwist sanctuaries. They hoped that the restriction of the cult to one sanctuary would make for monotheism. If the code originated at Shechem after the fall of Samaria the compilers were more likely influenced by this latter consideration, for they could scarcely have been planning a programme of cult purification if there was no longer any king to enforce it. In this case, the 'central sanctuary' may at first have been central only to a very limited area; and the idea of one sanctuary for the whole land will have developed from this.

3. Main Principles.—However complex the history of the book may be, in its contents it is theologically and religiously consistent throughout. (*a*) Its fundamental principle is 'The Lord our God is one Lord' (6^{4}); He is the God of the whole earth (10^{14}), and ultimately the arbiter of history (9^{5} 32^{8}). This carries with it the consequence that idolatry is the supreme sin (6^{13} $17^{2\mathrm{ff}}$ etc.). It is to prevent even the possibility of this that Israel is commanded to destroy utterly the inhabitants of Palestine ($7^{1\mathrm{ff}}$ etc.), and older customs of worship are forbidden (16^{21} etc.). (*b*) As He is God of the whole earth, Yahweh's will is the moral law, and in connexion with its requirements He rewards and punishes (cf the teaching of Amos). Also as the God of Israel, the fundamental principles of His relation to His people are ethical. (*c*) He is a person, not merely a moral principle or a glorified code. He revealed Himself to Israel and chose them to be His people, and His love to them was shown before they could prove any desert ($9^{4\mathrm{f}}$ etc.). He gave them their land—a gift they must not imagine themselves to have merited ($8^{7\mathrm{ff}}$). Hence love is the supreme return for His love ($6^{4\mathrm{f}}$ etc., and cf Hosea). Hence also the necessity for worship and prayer. Their cult, an expression of their loving gratitude, is to be joyous in character, not like the darker superstitions to which national disaster and foreign rites were making them incline (12^{18} etc.). (*d*) A religion, the heart of which is loving gratitude, naturally expresses itself in humanity towards all with whom men live, even towards the lower animals ($22^{6\mathrm{f}}$ 25^{4}). A religion also with so strong a sense of the Divine personality brings with it respect for human personality ($24^{10\mathrm{ff}}$). (*e*) Because Yahweh made Himself known through events in history, the cult is to commemorate these events, and the national festivals which in their origin were harvest festivals are associated with them ($16^{3,12}$). Even the individual Israelite is to commemorate this past in his worship as he acknowledges that the fruits of the land come not from the baalim but from Yahweh ($26^{1\mathrm{ff}}$). (*f*) Such a religion with its strong sense of the historic unity of God's dealings with the nation and its conviction of the reasonableness of God's demands can and ought to be taught. Children are to have it explained to them ($6^{6\mathrm{f}}$ 11^{19}); and means are to be used to bring it into men's thoughts daily (6^{9} 11^{20}). The book thus represents a valiant attempt to relate the entire work and life of the people to Yahweh. Its great defect is that it shows no concern for the Gentiles as objects of Yahweh's love, and that its only vision for the future is a reconstruction of the past. C. A. Si.

DEVIL.—See Demons.

DEVOTED.—See Ban.

DEW.—The process whereby dew is formed is enhanced in Eastern countries like Palestine, where the surface of the ground and the air in contact therewith are highly heated during the daytime, but where at night, and particularly under a cloudless sky, the heat of the ground is radiated into space and the air becomes rapidly cooled down. The excess of moisture in the air then gently 'falls as dew on the tender herb,' and sometimes so copiously as to sustain the life of many plants which would otherwise perish during the rainless season; or even, as in the case of Gideon, to saturate a fleece of wool (Jg 6^{38}). Deprivation of dew, as well as of rain, becomes a terrible calamity in the East. On this account 'dew and rain' are associated in the imprecation called down by David on the mountains of Gilboa (2 S 1^{21}); and in the curse pronounced on Ahab and his kingdom by Elijah (1 K 17^{1}), as also by the prophet Haggai on the Jews after the Restoration (Hag 1^{10}) owing to their unwillingness to rebuild the Temple. In the Book of Job the formation of dew is pointed to as one of the mysteries of nature insoluble by man (Job 38^{28}); but in Proverbs it is ascribed to the omniscience and power of the Lord (Pr 3^{20}). Dew is a favourite emblem in Scripture: (*a*) *richness and fertility* (Gn 27^{28}, Dt 33^{13}); (*b*) *refreshing and vivifying effects* (Dt 32^{2}, Is 18^{4}); (*c*) *stealth* (2 S 17^{12}); (*d*) *inconstancy* (Hos 6^{4} 13^{3}); (*e*) *the young warriors of the Messianic king* (Ps 110^{3}).

DIADEM.—See Crown, and Dress, **5.**

DIAL (2 K 20^{11}, Is 38^{8}).—The Hebrew word commonly denotes 'steps' (see Ex 20^{26},1 K 10^{20}), and is so rendered elsewhere in this narrative (2 K 20^{9-11}, Is 38^{8}; AV 'degrees'). The 'steps' referred to doubtless formed part of some kind of sun-clock. According to Herod. ii. 109, the Babylonians were the inventors of the *polos* or concave dial, the *gnōmon*, and the division of the day into 12 hours. The introduction by Ahaz of a device for measuring the time may be regarded as a result of his intercourse with the Assyrians (2 K $16^{10\mathrm{ff}}$), but it is uncertain what kind of clock is intended. See also Time.

DIAMOND.—See Adamant, and Jewels and Precious Stones.

DIANA OF THE EPHESIANS.—See Artemis.

DIASPORA.—See Dispersion.

DIBLAH.—An unknown place mentioned by Ezekiel, 6^{14} (RV; AV **Diblath**). A variant reading, followed by RSV, is **Riblah** (q.v.).

DIBLAIM.—The father of Gomer, Hosea's wife, Hos 1^{3}; see Hosea.

DIBLATH, Ezk 6^{14} (AV).—See Diblah.

DIBON.—**1.** A city E. of the Dead Sea and N. of the Arnon, in the land which, before the coming of the Israelites, Sihon, the king of the Amorites, had taken from a former king of Moab (Nu $21^{26,30}$). The tradition in Jos ($13^{9,17}$) states that the Hebrews dispossessed Sihon, and the territory was assigned to Reuben. Dibon, however, is mentioned as among the places built (or rebuilt) by Gad (Nu $32^{3,34}$), hence the name **Dibon-gad** (Nu 33^{45}). It was taken by Moab under King Mesha, who was of a family of Dibon apparently, and is mentioned several times in his famous stele, which was actually discovered at *Dhîbān*, about 2 miles N. of *'Ar'â'ir* on the edge of the Arnon valley (*Wâdī el-Mûjib*). Dibon is noted in Is 15^{2} and Jer $48^{18,22}$ as a Moabite town. The large mound of *Dhîbān* has recently been excavated, but, though abundant Nabataean and Roman remains were found, little was found of the Iron Age except tombs from the 9th cent. onwards. Glueck's surface exploration, however, has discovered Early Iron Age potsherds NE. of the main area of excavation, and it is evident that Moabite Dibon was situated at the southern extremity of the fertile corn-land.

In Is 15^{9} AV and RV follow the Hebrew in reading **Dimon,** while RSV has Dibon. The form Dimon may have been used here for the word play with 'blood' (*dām*).

2. A town in Judah inhabited in Nehemiah's time by returned exiles (Neh 11^{25}). Its association with Kiriath-arba (Hebron) indicates its location, but since there is no mention of Dibon in the description of the territory of Judah and Caleb in Jos 15, we may suspect textual corruption of some other name, possibly Debir (Kiriath-sepher) or **Dimonah** (Jos 15^{22}). J. Gr.

DIBON-GAD.—See Dibon, **1.**

DIBRI.—A Danite, grandfather of the blasphemer who was stoned to death, Lv 24^{11}.

DICTIONARIES.—**1. Of the Bible.**—W. Smith, *Dict. of Bible* (3 vols., 1863); J. D. Davis, *Dict. of the Bible* (1898); rev. ed., by H. S. Gehman (1944); P. Schaff, *Religious Encyclopaedia*, based on Herzog's *PRE* (3 vols., 1883); M'Clintock-Strong, *Cyclopaedia of Biblical, Theological, and Eccles. Literature* (10 vols. and 2 vols.

suppl., 1871–87); J. J. Herzog, *Realencyclopädie f. protest. Theol. u. Kirche* (18 vols., 1877–88), new ed., by A. Hauck (22 vols. and 2 vols. suppl., 1896–1913); *The New Schaff-Herzog Encyclop. of Religious Knowledge*, based on the preceding, ed. by S. M. Jackson (12 vols., 1908–12); revised ed., with Index and 2 additional vols., ed. by L. A. Loetscher (15 vols., 1955); F. Vigouroux, *Dict. de la Bible* (5 vols., 1895–1912), *Supplément*, ed. by L. Pirot, A. Robert, and H. Cazelles (1928– , seventh vol. in progress); *Jewish Encyclopedia*, ed. by I. Singer (12 vols., 1901–06); *Encyclopaedia Biblica*, ed. by T. K. Cheyne and J. S. Black (4 vols., 1899–1903); J. Hastings, *Dictionary of the Bible* (4 vols. and extra vol., 1898–1904), also *Dictionary of Christ and the Gospels* (2 vols., 1906–08) and *Dictionary of the Apostolic Church* (2 vols., 1915–18); *Die Religion in Geschichte u. Gegenwart*, ed. by F. M. Schiele and L. Zscharnack (5 vols., 1909–13), 2nd ed. by H. Gunkel and L. Zscharnack (5 vols., 1927–31), 3rd ed. by K. Galling (1957– , sixth vol. in progress); A. Westphal, *Dict. encyclopédique de la Bible* (2 vols., 1932–35); E. Kalt, *Biblisches Reallexikon* (2 vols., 1938–39); *Bijbelsch Woordenboek*, ed. by A. van den Born (1941); H. Haag, *Bibel-Lexikon*, based on preceding but revised (1951); *Romen's Bijbels Woordenboek*, rev. ed. (1954–57), translated into French as *Dict. encyclopédique de la Bible* (1960); I. Engnell and A. Fridrichsen, *Svenskt Bibliskt Uppslagsverk* (2 vols., 1948–52); *Harper's Bible Dictionary*, by M. S. and J. L. Miller (1952); *Catholic Biblical Encyclopedia*, by J. E. Steinmueller and K. Sullivan (1955); *Calwer Bibel-Lexikon* (1959– , in progress); *Seventh-Day Adventist Bible Dict.*, by S. Horn (1960); F. Rienecker, *Lexikon zur Bibel* (1960). H. H. R.

2. Hebrew, Aramaic, Syriac.—(*a*) W. Gesenius (translation E. Robinson), *Thesaurus Philologicus Criticus Linguae Heb. et Chald. Veteris Testamenti* (1829–42); C. Siegfried and B. Stade, *Hebräisches Wörterbuch z. A. T. mit 2 Anhängen*: (i) *Lexicon z. d. aramäischen Stücken*, (ii) *Deutsch-hebräisches Wörterbuch* (1893); F. Brown, S. R. Driver, C. A. Briggs, *Hebrew and English Lexicon of the OT with an appendix containing the Biblical Aramaic* (1906); F. Buhl, *W. Gesenius' Hebr. u. Aram. Handwörterbuch über das AT*, 17th ed. (1921); E. König, *Hebr. u. Aram. Wörterbuch z. AT* (1931); L. Koehler and W. Baumgartner, *Lexicon in V.T. Libros* (1953) and *Supplementum* (1958); F. Zorell, *Lexicon Hebr. et Aram. Veteris Testamenti* (1946–). (*b*) J. Buxtorf and B. Fischer, *Lexicon Chaldäicum Talmudicum et Rabbinicum* (1869); J. Levy, *Chaldäisches Wörterbuch über die Targumim* (2 vols., 1867–68), and *Neuhebräisches u. Chaldäisches Wörterbuch über die Talmudim u. Midraschim* (4 vols., 1875–89); M. Jastrow, *Dictionary of the Targumim, Talmud Babli and Yerushalmi, and Midrashic Literature* (2 vols., 1903); G. H. Dalman, *Aramäisch-Neuhebräisches Handwörterbuch* (1938). (*c*) R. Payne Smith, *Thesaurus Syriacus* (2 vols., 1879–1901) and J. P. Margoliouth, *Supplement to the Thesaurus Syriacus* (1927); J. Payne Smith (Mrs. Margoliouth), *Compendious Syriac Dictionary* (1903); C. Brockelmann, *Lexicon Syriacum*, 2nd ed. (1928); F. Schultess, *Lexicon Syropalaestinum* (1903). G. R. D.

3. Greek (especially NT).—*A Greek-English Lexicon of the New Testament and Other Early Christian Literature*, by Wm. F. Arndt and F. Wilbur Gingrich (Cambridge and Chicago, 1957), now supersedes all earlier Greek NT lexicons. It is a translation and adaptation of Walter Bauer's German work (4th ed., 1952), and takes fuller account of British and American studies. *The Vocabulary of the Greek New Testament Illustrated from the Papyri and Other Non-Literary Sources*, by J. H. Moulton and G. Milligan (London, 1930), is a rich treasury of illustrative material. For classical Greek, the new edition of Liddell and Scott's *Greek-English Lexicon* by H. S. Jones and R. McKenzie (Oxford, 1940) is indispensable. The theological articles in R. Kittel, *Theologisches Wörterbuch zum Neuen Testament*, begun in 1933 and continued after Dr. Kittel's death by Gerhard Friedrich, takes the place of older works of this type. A number of the longer articles have been translated into English. For further titles, see Arndt and Gingrich, pp. xxxiii. ff. F. C. G.

DIDRACHMA.—In margin of older EV at Mt 17[24]; AV has 'tribute money,' RV correctly 'half-shekel,' RSV 'the half-shekel tax' (*i.e.* the temple tax as the tax *par excellence*). The corresponding Greek word, of which there is more than one form, is used in LXX to translate the Hebrew *shekel*, a rendering not infrequently corrected by Aquila to '*stater*.' See MONEY, **7.** H. St. J. H.

DIDYMUS.—See THOMAS.

DIET.—This word occurs only in Jer 52[34] (AV; RV, RSV more correctly 'allowance,' *i.e.* of food, as in AV, RV, RSV in the parallel 2 K 25[30]; the same word is rendered 'victuals' in AV, RV in Jer 40[5] and 'allowance' in RVm, RSV) and Sir 30[25] (AV, RV; RSV 'food').

DIKLAH.—The name of a son of Joktan (Gn 10[27], 1 Ch 1[21]), probably representing a nation or community. The names immediately preceding and following Diklah give no clue to its identification.

DILAN, Jos 15[38] (AV).—See DILEAN.

DILEAN.—A town of Judah, in the same group with Lachish and Eglon, Jos 15[38] (AV **Dilan**); possibly modern *Tell en-Nejileh*.

DILL.—See ANISE and FITCHES.

DIMNAH.—A Levitical city in Zebulun, Jos 21[35]. The name is possibly a copyist's error for **Rimmon,** Jos 19[13]. See RIMMON, **4.**

DIMON.—See DIBON, **1.**

DIMONAH.—See DIBON, **2.**

DINAH.—The daughter of Jacob by Leah, and sister of Simeon and Levi, according to Gn 30[21].

This verse appears to have been inserted by a late redactor, perhaps the one who added the section Gn 46[8–27] (cf v.[15]). Nothing is said in 29[31]–30[24] 35[16ff], where the birth stories of Jacob's children are given, of other daughters of Jacob; but 37[35] (J) and 46[7] (P) speak of 'all his daughters.' P, moreover, clearly distinguishes between his 'daughters' and his 'daughters-in-law.'

In Gn 34 we have a composite narrative of the seizure of Dinah by the Hivite prince, Shechem, the son of Hamor. The probable remnants of J's story make it appear that the tale, as it was first told, was a very simple one. Shechem took Dinah to his house and cohabited with her, and her father and brothers resented the defilement. Shechem, acting on his own behalf, proposed marriage, promising to accept any conditions of dower her father and brothers might impose. The marriage took place, and afterwards her full brothers, Simeon and Levi, slew Shechem and took Dinah out of his house. Jacob rebuked them for this, because of the vengeance it was liable to bring upon his house. Jacob thinks only of consequences here. If, as is generally supposed, Gn 49[5ff] refers to this act, the reprimand administered was based by him not upon the dread of consequences, but upon the turpitude of a cruel revenge.

The remaining verses of ch. 34 make Hamor spokesman for his son. He not only offered generously to make honourable amends for Shechem's misconduct, but also proposed a mutual covenant of general intercourse, including the *connubium*. Jacob and his sons see their opportunity for revenge, and refuse, except upon the one condition that all the males of the city be circumcised. When, as a result, the latter were unable to defend themselves, all the sons of Jacob fell upon them with the sword, sparing only the women and children, whom they took captive with the spoil of the city. The words 'two of' and 'Simeon and Levi, Dinah's brothers' in v.[25] are interpolated (cf v.[13]). This story is clearly an elaboration of the earlier form, despite its one or two more antique touches, and suggests, moreover, the spirit at work in Ezra's marriage reforms.

This story reflects a tradition that the tribes of Simeon and Levi overthrew Shechem, but did not inhabit it.

According to Gn 48^{22} it was given to the House of Joseph ('one mountain slope'; Hebrew *shᵉkhem,* 'shoulder'). The excuse for their action was an outrage on their sister, Dinah, who may here represent a smaller group of Jacob-peoples whom the Hivites overcame and incorporated by treaty, which, however, was violated by Simeon and Levi. Gn 34^{26} 'and went away' would then refer to their migration elsewhere (cf Gn 49^{7}), and to the disappearance of the Dinah-group as such.

J. A. C.—**R. A. B.**

DINAITES.—According to AV and RV of Ezr 4^{6}, a people settled in Samaria by Osnappar (q.v.). They have been variously identified, but no secure identity can be found. Many scholars think the Aramaic word should be differently vocalized to yield the meaning 'judges' (so RSV). Other words in this verse may be official titles rather than gentilics.

DINHABAH.—The capital city of king Bela in Edom, Gn 36^{32}, 1 Ch 1^{43}; its location is unknown.

DINNER.—See Meals, **2.**

DIONYSIA, a feast in honour of the Greek god Dionysus (q.v.), also known as Bacchus (2 Mac 6^{7}), the Italian god with whom he was identified. Dionysus was the god of tree life, but especially the life of the vine and its produce, wine. In time his cult acquired emotional features not associated with wine or its effects; these may be seen in the Athenian drama, in the international association of Dionysiac artists, and in the widespread and popular Hellenistic-Roman mystery cult. The primitive festival celebrated the revival of the life-giving vine and of nature as a whole after the deadness of winter. It was accompanied by orgiastic excesses (see Euripides, *Bacchae*), at once symbolic of and caused by this renewal. The most famous festivals of Dionysus, four in all, were held in Attica at various periods of the year, corresponding more or less to the stages in the life of the vine: the *Anthesteria* in the spring, the *Lenaea* in the winter, the *Lesser* or Rural, and the *Greater* or City *Dionysia.* The Rural Dionysia was a vintage festival held in the country in December; the City Dionysia was held at Athens in the spring, and it was in connexion with this festival that the tragedies and comedies were produced in the theatre of Dionysus. Attendance at these plays was an act of worship—at least of devotion. In 2 Mac 6^{7} we are told that Antiochus Epiphanes compelled Jews to attend a festival of Dionysus, walking in the procession in honour of the god and wearing wreaths of ivy, a plant sacred to him. See A. W. Pickard-Cambridge, *The Dramatic Festivals of Athens* (1953).

A. So.—**F. C. G.**

DIONYSIUS THE AREOPAGITE.—A member of the Court of the Areopagus (q.v.) at Athens, converted by Paul (Ac 17^{34}). Eusebius in his *Church History* (iii. iv. 10), naming Dionysius of Corinth (*fl* A.D. 171) as his authority, designated the Areopagite as the first bishop of Athens. Some three or four centuries later, a series of theological writings, pronouncedly Neoplatonic in character, were attributed to him (*On the Celestial Hierarchy* [of Angels], *On the Ecclesiastical Hierarchy, On the Divine Names,* and *The Mystical Theology*). Throughout the Middle Ages these works were widely read and influential. Another misleading tradition (in the 9th cent.) identified the Areopagite with St. Denys, martyr and patron saint of France.

H. R. W. and F. C. G.

DIONYSUS.—One of the various names applied to the god who is most commonly called Bacchus, because of the Hellenistic identification of Dionysus with the Italian god of the vine. It is probable that, to begin with, he was a god of vegetation in general, but as time went on he became identified exclusively with the vine. It is supposed that this specialization originated in Thrace. Still later the worship took on the form of mysteries, like those of Demeter. Mythology told of a triumphal journey taken by the god to India. His worship was widely disseminated in Greek lands, and it was assumed by enthusiastic Hellenizers that even Jews in the homeland could be induced or compelled to participate in Dionysian cultic acts (2 Mac 6^{7} 14^{33}). Ptolemy Philopator also attempted to force the worship of Dionysus, the god of his family, upon the Jews living in Egypt (3 Mac 2^{29}).

A. So.—**H. R. W.**

DIOSCORINTHIUS.—See Time.

DIOSCURI (RVm), or **The Twin Brothers** (RV, RSV), or **Castor and Pollux** (AV).—The sign or figurehead of the Alexandrian ship in which St. Paul sailed from Malta (Ac 28^{11}), perhaps one of those employed to bring grain to Rome. The Twins (*Gemini*) were the protectors of sailors; in mythology they were sons of Zeus and Leda, and were placed in the sky as a constellation for their brotherly love.

A. J. M.

DIOTREPHES.—A person, otherwise unknown, who is introduced in 3 John (vv.^{9f}) as ambitious, resisting the writer's authority, and standing in the way of the hospitable reception of brethren who visited the Church.

DIPHATH.—One of the sons of Gomer, 1 Ch 1^{6} (RV, RSV); probably a scribal error for **Riphath** (so AV), as in the parallel Gn 10^{3}.

DISALLOW.—1 P 2^{4} AV, 'a living stone, disallowed indeed of men, but chosen of God'; 2^{7}, 'the stone which the builders disallowed.' The English word means emphatically *disowned*, as in the AV heading to 1 S 29, 'David, marching with the Philistines, is disallowed by their princes.' RSV gives 'rejected,' as the same Greek verb is rendered in Mt 21^{42}, Mk 8^{31}, Lk 17^{25}. But in Nu $30^{5,8,11}$ 'disallow' means no more than *disapprove*, as in Barlowe's *Dialogue*, p. 83, 'ye can not fynde that they be dysalowed of God, but rather approved.'

DISCIPLES.—In the ancient world every teacher had his company of disciples or learners. The only use of the word in the OT, in Is 8^{16}, is not certain, for the text is ambiguous. The Greek philosophers and the Jewish Rabbis had theirs, and John the Baptist had his (Mk 2^{18} 'John's disciples and the disciples of the Pharisees'; cf Jn 1^{35}, Mt 14^{12}). In like manner Jesus had His disciples. The term had two applications, a wider and a narrower. It denoted (1) all who believed in Him, though they remained where He had found them, pursuing their former vocations, yet rendering no small service to His cause by confessing their allegiance and testifying to His grace (cf Lk 6^{13} 19^{37}, Jn 4^{1} $6^{60,66f}$). (2) The inner circle of the Twelve, also called 'Apostles,' and whom He required to forsake their old lives and follow Him whithersoever He went, not merely that they might strengthen Him by their sympathy (cf Lk 22^{28}), but that they might aid Him in His ministry (Mt 9^{37} $10^{1,5}$), and, above all, that they might be trained by daily intercourse and discipline to carry forward the work after He was gone. These were 'the disciples' *par excellence* (Mt 10^{1} $12^{1,49}$ $15^{23,32}$, Mk 8^{27}, Lk 8^{9}, Jn 11^{7} 12^{4} $16^{17,29}$). See also Apostles. D. S.—**J. H. Sc.**

DISCOVER.—In AV 'discover' is used in some obsolete meanings. **1.** To *uncover*, make to be seen, as Knox, *Hist.* p. 250, 'who rashly discovering himself in the Trenches, was shot in the head.' So Ps 29^{9}, 'The voice of the Lord . . . discovereth the forests,' and other passages. **2.** To *disclose*, as Shakespeare, *Merry Wives*, ii. ii. 190, 'I shall discover a thing to you,' So Pr 25^{9}, 'discover not a secret to another,' etc. **3.** To *descry*, get sight of, as Ac 21^{3}, 'When we had discovered Cyprus, we left it on the left hand'; 27^{39} 'they discovered a certain creek.'

DISCUS.—See Games.

DISEASE.—See Medicine.

DISH.—See Charger; House, **9**; Meals, **5**; and Tabernacle, **6** (*a*).

DISHAN ('ibex' or 'mountain goat').—A son of Seir (q.v.), Gn $36^{21,28,30}$, 1 Ch $1^{38,42}$; eponym of a Horite clan.

DISHON ('ibex' or 'mountain goat').—**1.** A son of Seir (q.v.), Gn 36^{21}, 1 Ch 1^{38}. **2.** A son of Anah and grandson of Seir, Gn $36^{25,30}$, 1 Ch 1^{41}. In Gn 36^{26}

Hebrew has Dishan, but Dishon should be read with AV, RV, RSV (cf 1 Ch 1^{41}). The name is the eponym of a Horite clan.

DISPERSION.—The name (Gr. *Diaspora*) given to the Jewish communities outside Palestine (2 Mac 1^{27}, Jn 7^{35}, Ja 1^{1}, 1 P 1^{1}). The word is derived from *diaspeirō*, to scatter, which is used in the LXX for the ultimate degree of God's punishment of disobedient Israel (*e.g.* Lv 26^{33}). It is not a merely geographical term, but means separation from the unity of the nation in the holy land, and suffering among the Gentiles. In Jewish eschatology the regathering of the people and their restoration to the country chosen for them by God was a constant feature (*e.g.* Is 11^{12} 56^{8}).

It is uncertain when the establishment of non-Palestinian Jewish communities began. It appears from 1 K 20^{34} that an Israelitish colony was established in Damascus in the reign of Ahab. In the 8th cent. Tiglath-pileser III. carried many Israelites captive to Assyria (2 K 15^{29}) and Sargon transported from Samaria 27,290 Hebrews (cf *KIB* ii, 55), and settled them in Mesopotamia and Media (2 K 17^{6}). Probably they were absorbed and thus lost to Israel.

The real Dispersion began with the Babylonian Exile. Nebuchadrezzar transplanted to Babylonia the choicest of the Judaean population (2 K 24^{12-16} 25^{11}, Jer 52^{15}). Probably 50,000 were transported, and Jewish communities were formed in Babylonia at many points, as at Tel-abib (Ezk 3^{15}) and Casiphia (Ezr 8^{17}). Here the Jewish religion was maintained, prophets like Ezekiel and priests like Ezra sprang up, the old laws were studied and worked over, the Pentateuch elaborated, and from this centre the Jews radiated to many parts of the East (Neh 1^{1ff}, To 1^{9-22}, Is 11^{11}). Thus the Jews reached Media, Persia, Cappadocia, Armenia, and the Black Sea. Only a few of these Babylonian Jews returned to Palestine. They maintained the Jewish communities in Babylonia till about A.D. 1000. Here, in the 5th cent. of the Christian era, the Babylonian Talmud was compiled.

In 608 B.C., Necho took king Jehoahaz and probably others to Egypt. In this general period colonies of Jews were living at Memphis, Migdol, Tahpanhes, and Pathros in Egypt (Jer 44^{1}). The Aswan Papyri prove the existence of a large Jewish colony and a Jewish temple at the First Cataract, in the 5th cent. B.C. Other Jews seem to have followed Alexander the Great to Egypt (Jos. *BJ* II. xviii. 8 [494 ff]; *c. Apion.* ii. 4 [33 f]). Many others migrated to Egypt under the Ptolemies (*Ant.* XII. i. 1 [7]; ii. 1 ff [11 ff]). Philo estimated the number of Jews in Egypt in the reign of Caligula (A.D. 38–41) at a million (*In Flac.* 6 [43]).

Josephus states that Seleucus I. (312–280 B.C.) gave the Jews rights in all the cities founded by him in Syria and Asia (*Ant.* XII. iii. 1 [119]). This has been doubted by some, who suppose that the spread of Jews over Syria occurred after the Maccabaean uprising (168–143 B.C.). At all events by the 1st cent. B.C. Jews were in all this region, as well as in Greece and Rome, in the most important centres about the Mediterranean, and had also penetrated to Arabia (Ac 2^{11}).

At Leontopolis in Egypt, Onias III., the legitimate Aaronic high priest, who had left Palestine because he hated Antiochus IV., founded a temple about 170 B.C., as a fulfilment of Is 19^{19}; this temple was destroyed in A.D. 73. It had little importance. With few exceptions the Dispersion was loyal to the religion of the home land. Far removed from the Temple, they developed in the synagogue a spiritual worship without sacrifice, which, after the destruction of Jerusalem in A.D. 70, kept Judaism alive. All Jews paid the annual half-shekel tax for the support of the Temple cultus, and at the great feasts they made pilgrimages to Jerusalem from all parts of the world (Ac 2^{10f}). They soon lost the use of Hebrew, and had the Greek translation—the Septuagint—made for their use. Contact with the world gave some of them a broader outlook than the Palestinian Jews, and they tried to express the fundamental ideas of their religion in forms appealing to adherents of Greek and Roman philosophy. Through the Diaspora, Judaism exerted a great influence upon its surroundings and paved the way for Christianity. On the other hand, it aroused hostile feelings among Gentiles, as may be seen in the writings of several classical authors (*e.g.* Tacitus); this antagonism sometimes exploded into pogroms, as in Alexandria in A.D. 36 and in Antioch at the beginning of the Jewish revolt in A.D. 67. On the whole, Roman legislation was favourably disposed toward the Jews. The scattering of the Jews after A.D. 70 was not spoken of as a 'dispersion'; instead, it was described as a new Exile. The term Diaspora was taken over by the Christians as an image of the Church (Ja 1^{1}, 1 P 1^{1}). G. A. B.—**W. C. v. U.**

DISTAFF.—See SPINNING AND WEAVING.

DIVES.—See LAZARUS.

DIVINATION.—See MAGIC, DIVINATION, AND SORCERY.

DIVINERS' OAK.—A place mentioned only in Jg 9^{37} (AV 'plain of **Meonenim**,' RV 'oak of **Meonenim**'). The word *m$^{e'}$ōn^{e}nîm*, of uncertain derivation, is frequently used in OT for 'diviners' or 'soothsayers,' and RSV rendering is to be preferred.

DIVORCE.—See MARRIAGE.

DIZAHAB.—A place in Moab, mentioned only Dt 1^{1}, standing 'over against Suph.' Its site is unknown. Probably the text is corrupt. In Nu 21^{14} we find Suphah (cf Dt 1^{1} Suph) in conjunction with **Waheb** (AVm, RV **Vaheb**), and *Waheb* is almost identical in writing with *Zahab*, which LXX read. There seems to be some relationship between the two passages, but neither has been satisfactorily explained. In Gn 36^{39}, 1 Ch 1^{50} we have **Mezahab** (='waters of gold'), which looks more like the name of a place than a person, and this may be the proper form of the name. J. T.—**H. H. R.**

DOCTOR.—In Lk 2^{46} AV, RV, it is said that the boy Jesus was found in the Temple, 'sitting in the midst of the doctors.' The English word, like the Greek (*didaskalos*), means simply 'teacher' (so RSV). In Lk 5^{17} and Ac 5^{34}, the Greek for 'teacher of the law' is one word (*nomodidaskalos*). Lord Bacon called St. Paul 'the Doctor of the Gentiles.'

DOCTRINE.—The OT word *leḳaḥ* which means instruction, or literally 'what is received,' is rendered 'doctrine' by the AV (Dt 32^{2}, Job 11^{4}, Pr 4^{2}, Is 29^{24}). RSV keeps 'doctrine' in Job 11^{4} but substitutes 'teaching' or 'instruction' in the others. In the NT, RSV agrees with AV in retaining 'doctrine' for *logos* in He 6^{1}. Otherwise 'doctrine' is used for *didachē* and *didaskalia*, of which the former denotes especially the act of teaching, the latter the collection of specific things taught. For *didaskalia* RSV sometimes retains the 'doctrine' of AV (1 Ti 1^{10}, Tit $2^{1,10}$) but sometimes uses 'teaching' (2 Ti 4^{3}). It is noteworthy that *didaskalia* is never used of the teaching of Jesus, always *didachē*. For *didachē* RSV sometimes changes AV's 'doctrine' to 'teaching' (Mk 1^{22}, Ro 6^{17}, Rev $2^{14f.24}$), but in 2 Jn ^{9f} RSV keeps 'doctrine.' *Didaskalia* is found chiefly in the Pastoral Epp., and outside of these, with two exceptions (Ro 12^{7} 15^{4}), it refers to worldly teachings opposed to the Gospel (Mt 15^{9}, Mk 7^{7}, Eph 4^{14}, Col 2^{22}). This is in keeping with a distinction between the use of *didachē* for the substance of the teaching appropriate to the communication of the Gospel, and *didaskalia* as meaning specific items of belief in a system of propositions.

This linguistic development reflects the transition from the earliest proclamation of the Gospel when the message of Jesus Christ was creating and shaping the first Christian communities, to a later period when the crystallization of doctrine and ecclesiastical interests led to the prescription of items of belief deemed essential for the preservation of Christian truth. D. D. W.

DODAI.—See DODO.

DODANIM.—Named in the MT of Gn 10 among the descendants of Javan, or Ionians. The LXX and Samaritan versions and the parallel passage 1 Ch 1[7] read **Rodanim,** *i.e.* Rhodians. Cf the true reading of Ezk 27[15] under DEDAN.

DODAVAH, 2 Ch 20[37] (AV).—See DODAVAHU.

DODAVAHU (? 'Y″ is my uncle').—Father of Eliezer of Mareshah, the prophet who censured Jehoshaphat for entering into alliance with Ahaziah, 2 Ch 20[37] (AV **Dodavah**).

DODO.—**1.** The father of Eleazar, the second of David's three mighty men, 2 S 23[9] (RV **Dodai,** with *kᵉthîbh*), 1 Ch 11[12] (where 'the Ahohite' stands instead of the erroneous 'son of Ahohi' of 2 S 23[9]); called **Dodai** in 1 Ch 27[4], where he is described as in charge of the division of the second month, but the words 'Eleazar the son of' appear to have been accidentally omitted. **2.** A Bethlehemite, father of El-hanan, one of 'the thirty,' 2 S 23[24], 1 Ch 11[26]. **3.** A man of Issachar, the forefather of Tola the judge, Jg 10[1].

DOE.—Named in Pr 5[19] (RV, RSV; AV 'roe'), Hebrew *yaʿalāh,* this is the *female ibex.* See 'Wild goat,' *s.v.* GOAT.

DOEG.—An Edomite, and chief of the herdmen [or some prefer 'runners,' reading *hā-rāṣîm* for *hā-rōʿîm*] of king Saul. When David fled to Nob to Ahimelech (or Ahijah) the priest, Doeg was there 'detained before the Lord.' Upon his report Saul ordered Ahimelech and his companions to be slain. The order was carried out by Doeg, when the rest of the king's guard shrank from obeying it (1 S 21[7] 22[9-19]). Doeg is mentioned in the title of Ps 52.

DOG.—Hebrew *kelebh,* Greek *kuōn.* The biblical references to dogs generally breathe the traditional oriental dislike of them as unclean animals; they are pariahs, living as scavengers, feeding on carrion and meat unfit for human consumption (Ex 22[31]) and even on human bodies thrown out unburied (1 K 14[11] 16[4] 21[24], Ps 68[23], Jer 15[3]), as happened in the case of Jezebel (2 K 9[36]). They are described as prowling about the streets at night and making sleep impossible with their noise (Ps 59[6f, 14f]). No wise man will meddle with them (Pr 26[17]). A man beset by foes may speak of himself as surrounded by such a snarling pack (Ps 22[16, 20]). They may attach themselves to an encampment for the food thrown to them, and will then become useful sentinels; but 'dumb dogs' that 'cannot bark' are useless watchmen (Is 56[10f]). Even under modern conditions packs of dogs may become a menace in the Near East if they are left uncontrolled; in the summer of 1957 Israel and Jordanian police had to collaborate in clearing the 'no man's land' between the two parts of Jerusalem of pariah dogs which had multiplied unchecked during the preceding years and some of which were suffering from rabies. In OT to call a man a dog is a grave insult; to call him a dead dog (2 S 16[9]) or a dog's head (2 S 3[8]) is even worse. But a man may use such terms of himself to express humility, as in 2 S 9[8], 2 K 8[13]; the idiom in the latter passage ('What is your servant, who is but a dog, that he should do this . . . ?') is paralleled in Lachish Letter 6. 'The price of a dog' (Dt 23[18]) refers probably to the hire of a *ḳādhēsh,* a male prostitute attached to a Canaanite fertility cult.

Sheepdogs (Job 30[1]) are dogs of a much superior quality; many of them are handsome beasts of a Kurdish breed and have the intelligent ways of the best sheepdogs in western lands.

The *saluqi,* a hound not unlike our greyhound, has been common in the Near and Middle East since the 4th millennium B.C., when it appears on seals from Tepe Gawra, NW. of Nineveh; it is used in hunting the gazelle. It is considered to be a different animal from the dog, is kept in the home and treated as a pet and companion. In Pr 30[31] 'greyhound' (AV, RV) is literally 'girt of loins'; RSV follows LXX in rendering it 'strutting cock'; the sense is quite uncertain.

Tobias's dog (To 5[16] 11[4]) is the first example in Hebrew literature of the dog as man's friend and fellow-traveller.

The general OT attitude to dogs persists in NT. The dogs that licked Lazarus's sores (Lk 16[21]) aggravated his misery; they were not expressing sympathy. Holy flesh must not be thrown out like carrion for dogs to eat (Mt 7[6]); this proverbial saying is extended to teach that sacred truths should not be exposed to the abuse of people unable to appreciate their sacredness (cf *Didache* 9[5]). In the story of the Syrophoenician woman the dogs which eat the children's crumbs (Mt 15[26f], Mk 7[27f]) are *kynaria,* 'pups.' It is doubtful if the diminutive was expressed in Aramaic (if that was the language spoken on this occasion); but in any case it was probably young dogs that were envisaged in association with children. Even pariah pups are attractive pets while they are small; cf M. Wheeler, *Walls of Jericho,* p. 8: 'She [Dr. Kathleen Kenyon] rules us all, but the stray pariah puppies who seek sanctuary in the camp rule her.'

The 'dogs' against whom Paul warns his converts in Ph 3[2] are Judaizing marauders, disturbing the peace of the church; the 'dogs' excluded from the New Jerusalem in Rev 22[15] are people of unclean lives.

E. W. G. M.—F. F. B.

DOK.—A fortress near Jericho, where Simon the Maccabee, along with two of his sons, was murdered by his son-in-law Ptolemy, 1 Mac 16[15]. The name survives in the modern *ʿAin Dûk,* 4 miles NW. of Jericho.

DOLEFUL CREATURE.—See JACKAL.

DOMINION.—Lordship, or the possession and exercise of the power to rule. In Col 1[16] the word is used in the plural, along with 'thrones,' 'principalities,' and 'authorities' (powers), to denote supernatural beings possessed of the power of lordship, and ranking as so many kings, princes, and potentates of the heavenly regions. The same word in the singular, and in essentially the same meaning, appears in Eph 1[21], where allusion is made to the exaltation of Christ 'far above all rule and authority and power and dominion, and above every name that is named, not only in this age, but also in that which is to come.' There is no necessary reference in either of these texts to evil angels, but a comparison of what is written in Eph 2[2] 6[12] shows that 'the spiritual hosts of wickedness in the heavenly places' need not be excluded. Similar indefiniteness is apparent in the other two passages, 2 P 2[10], Jd [8], where the same word is found. It is understood by some to refer here to the lordship of civil rulers, or to any concrete representative of such lordship. Others believe that the reference is to angels, either good or evil, as representing some form of supernatural power and dominion, and the reference in the context to Michael, the archangel, not bringing a railing judgment even against the devil, may be thought to favour this view. A third explanation is also possible, and is favoured by the mention in Jd [4] of 'our only Master and Lord, Jesus Christ.' Those ungodly men, who deny the Lord Jesus, would not hesitate to despise, set at nought, and rail at all manner of glorious lordships and dignities. See AUTHORITY, POWER. M. S. T.

DOMITIAN.—Titus Flavius Domitianus, younger son of Vespasian (q.v.), succeeded his brother Titus (q.v.) as emperor in A.D. 81. Under him the provinces were generally well administered and the frontiers soundly defended, with notable advances in Britain and Germany. But Domitian was increasingly disposed to press his claims as 'master and god' (*dominus et deus*), and suspicious of all possible rivals (hence perhaps the episode, recorded by church historians, of the arrest of obscure survivors of the family of Jesus, as descendants of David). Among the victims of his tyranny were his niece Domitilla and her husband, Domitian's cousin Flavius Clemens, accused of 'atheism,' probably meaning Jewish or Christian sympathies; the distresses of the Roman Church referred to at the beginning of the First Epistle of Clement (q.v.) may be connected with these events. Pressure in the province of Asia to take part in the imperial cult as a sign of loyalty is the background of the persecutions referred to in Revelation (1⁹ 2¹³), where the beast (ch. 13) is the line of emperors and the second beast the civic priesthood of the deified rulers. Domitian's behaviour finally turned his close associates against him, and led to his assassination on September 16, A.D. 96. E. R. H.

DOOR, DOORKEEPER, DOORPOST.—See HOUSE, **6.** For 'doorkeeper' in the Temple, see PRIESTS AND LEVITES.

DOPHKAH.—A station in the itinerary of the children of Israel, Nu 33^{12f}; possibly modern *Serābîṭ el-Khâdim.*

DOR.—One of the cities which joined Jabin against Joshua, and whose king was killed, Jos 11^2 12^{23} (RSV **Naphoth-dor** and **Naphath-dor**). It lay apparently on or near the border between Manasseh and Asher, so that its possession was ambiguous, 17^{11}. The aborigines were not driven out, Jg 1^{27}. It was administered by Ben-abinadab for Solomon, 1 K 4^{11} (RSV **Naphath-dor**). It is mentioned in 1 Mac $15^{11, 13, 25}$ (RV, RSV; AV **Dora**). Though Josephus refers to it as on the sea-coast, and it is generally identified with *el-Burj*, N. of *eṭ-Ṭanṭûrah*, N. of Caesarea, the reference to the 'heights of Dor' (*i.e. nāphôth dôr*) rather suggests that it was in some hilly district such as the slope of the range of Carmel. R. A. S. M.—**H. H. R.**

DORA, 1 Mac $15^{11, 13, 25}$ (AV).—See DOR.

DORCAS (Gr. form of Aram. *Tabitha*, literally 'gazelle,' Ac 9^{36ff}).—The name of a Christian woman at Joppa, 'full of good works and almsdeeds,' who, having died, was raised by St. Peter's prayer and the words 'Tabitha, rise.' The description recalls the 'Talitha cumi' spoken by Jesus in Jairus' house (Mk 5^{41}). A. J. M.

DORYMENES.—The father of Ptolemy Macron, who was a trusted friend of Antiochus Epiphanes (2 Mac 4^{45}), and was chosen by Lysias to command the Syrian army in Palestine in conjunction with Nicanor and Gorgias (1 Mac 3^{38}).

DOSITHEUS.—**1.** The priest who, according to a note in one of the Greek recensions of Esther, brought the book to Alexandria in the 4th year of Ptolemy Philometor (?) and Cleopatra, *c* 178 B.C. (Ad. Est 11^1). **2.** A soldier of Judas Maccabaeus, who made a vain attempt to take Gorgias prisoner (2 Mac 12^{35}). **3.** A renegade Jew who frustrated the plot of Theodotus to assassinate king Ptolemy Philopator (3 Mac 1^3). **4.** An officer of Judas Maccabaeus (2 Mac $12^{19, 24}$).

DOT.—See JOT AND TITTLE.

DOTAEA, Jth 3^9 (RV).—See DOTHAN.

DOTHAIM, Jth 4^6 $7^{3, 18}$ 8^3 (AV, RV).—See DOTHAN.

DOTHAN (Gn 37^{17}, 2 K 6^{13}, Jth 3^9 (RV **Dotaea,** AV **Judea**), 4^6 (AV, RV **Dothaim**)).—To-day *Tell Dôthā*, some 15 miles N. of Shechem, a strategic point at the entrance to the pass leading into the great Plain of Esdraelon. The *tell* to-day covers 10 acres, and the steeply sloping sides include several more acres. It is surrounded on three sides by hills (2 K 6^{17}), and must have been of great importance when the neighbouring highroad, still much used, was a main thoroughfare between Egypt and the countries to the east. Its pastures are even finer than those at Shechem, and several seasons of excavation on the site since 1953 show that the city was a flourishing one from very early times. T. J. M.

DOUBT (from Lat. *dubitare*, 'to hold two (opinions),' 'hesitate').—The AV used 'doubt' (verb and noun) to translate a variety of Greek words, such as *aporeō* Jn 13^{22} (RSV 'be uncertain') and *airō* Jn 10^{24} (RSV 'hold in suspense'). The word has increasingly become obsolete in these senses, and the RSV completes the tendency begun in the RV by using 'doubt' only eight times in the NT, apart from the fixed phrase 'no doubt' in Ac 28^4. In six of these eight occurrences it translates *diakrinō*, which means basically 'separate,' 'distinguish,' but which comes in the NT to signify 'be at odds with oneself,' 'doubt,' 'hesitate,' 'waver' (*e.g.* Mt 21^{21}, Ro 14^{23}; cf Ro 4^{20}). In the other two (Mt 14^{31} 28^{17}) it renders *distazō*, 'hesitate in choosing between two possibilities.' As used in these passages, 'doubt' has a religious signification, and stands in express or tacit antithesis to 'faith' (q.v.). It indicates a state of *qualified faith*, of faith mixed with misgiving, something between whole-hearted faith and decided unbelief. Thus wavering, faith is robbed of its power; hence such hesitation, in regard to Christ and the promises and commands of God, is strongly deprecated and reproved. In the above examples the doubt, affecting the mind of a believer, arises from contradictory circumstances or conscientious scruples; unless this be the case in Mt 28^{17} (cf Lk 24^{38}), it has none of the quality of rationalistic doubt or scepticism. G. G. F.—**F. W. G.**

DOVE.—The words translated 'dove' apply equally to doves and pigeons. In Palestine seven varieties of the *Columbae* are found. The most noticeable are: the wood pigeons or ring-doves (*Columba palumbus*), which fly in great flocks all over the land; the turtle-dove (*Turtur communis*), a harbinger of spring, arriving in the land of April (Jer 8^7, Ca 2^{12}); and the palm turtle-dove (*Turtur senegalensis*), which is common in a semi-domesticated state in the streets and courts of Jerusalem. 'Dove' is a favourite name of affection (Ca 1^{15} 4^1 $5^{2, 12}$ 6^9), and to-day it is one of the commonest names given to girls by Eastern Jewish parents. It is typical of harmlessness (Mt 10^{16}), helplessness (Ps 74^{19}), and innocence. The last quality doubtless makes it typical of the Holy Spirit (Mt 3^{16} etc.). Doves were used in sacrifice (Lv 5^7 12^6 etc.), and have been kept as pets for long ages. E. W. G. M.

DOVES' DUNG.—'A fourth of a kab' of this material was sold at a high price in Samaria during the siege (2 K 6^{25}). The words *ḥ^a^rê yônîm*, as they stand, are plain, and no suggested alternative has cleared up the difficulty. It is an example of the actual extremity of the siege comparable with the threats of the approaching siege of 2 K 18^{27}. Whether, as Josephus suggests, the dung was a source of salt, or was used as medicine or as food, it is impossible to say. E. W. G. M.

DOWRY.—See MARRIAGE.

DRACHM.—See DRAM; MONEY.

DRAGON.—Hebrew *tannîn* (*tannîm* in Ezk 29^3 32^2), Greek *drakōn*. The Hebrew word is used of 'sea monsters' (Gn 1^{21}, Job 7^{12}, Ps 148^7, Jer 51^{34}) and of the serpents into which the rods were turned in Moses and Aaron's trial of strength with the Egyptian magicians (Ex 7^{9ff}; cf Ps 91^{13}, AV 'dragon,' RV and RSV 'serpent'), but principally of the seven-headed chaos-monster Leviathan (Ugaritic *Lotan*) and his associates (Ps 74^{13}, Is 27^1, 51^9), historicized to denote the king of Egypt (Ezk 29^3 32^2, where the crocodile has influenced the details of the picture; cf Job 41^{1ff}). The seven-headed chaos-monster reappears as the great red dragon of Rev 12^{1ff}, where he is further identified with the serpent of Eden and with Satan.

In AV 'dragons' appears thirteen times where 'jackals' is the proper rendering (Job 30^{29}, Ps 44^{19}, Is 13^{22} 34^{13} 35^7 43^{20}, Jer 9^{11} 10^{22} 14^6 49^{33} 51^{37}, Mic 1^8, Mal 1^3); this is the sense also in La 4^3 (AV 'sea monsters'). See JACKAL. F. F. B.

DRAM, from the Greek *drachma*, is used in AV to render two words which RV, RSV render 'darics' (see more fully under MONEY, **4**). The 'ten silver coins' of Lk 15^{8f}, however, were real drachmas, for which see MONEY, **7.**

DRAUGHT (AV and RV in Mt 15^{17}, Mk 7^{19}) and **DRAUGHT HOUSE** (AV and RV in 2 K 10^{27}; RSV 'latrine') both signify a privy or closet, which in the Mishnah is 'water-house.' Jehu, according to the last-cited passage, turned the temple of Baal in Samaria into public latrines.

DREAMS.—Sleep impressed primitive man as a great

mystery, and a peculiar significance was accordingly attributed to the dreams of sleepers, as phenomena which they could not control by their will or explain by their reason. In lower stages of culture all dreams were regarded as objectively real experiences; a god or spirit actually visited the dreamer, the events dreamed actually occurred. Hence anyone subject to frequent dreaming was regarded as a special medium of divine energy, and many sought to produce the state by artificial means such as fasting or drugs. Later, dreams came to be treated rather as Divine warnings than as actual occurrences. Such admonitions could be deliberately sought, *e.g.* by sleeping in a sacred spot, such as the temples of Asklepios or Serapis or the cave of Trophonius; or they could come unsought, when the gods wished to make a revelation to someone, or even to deceive him (but Plato denies that the gods could ever wish to deceive men). Thus among the Hittites, the Babylonians, the Assyrians, the Egyptians, and the Arabs, a profound importance was attached to dreams. Typical is the account by the Hittite king Hattusilis III. (*c* 1290–1260 B.C.) of his accession to the throne by grace of Ishtar, his patron-goddess, who prepared the way for this by communications given in dreams both to his father and to himself. In these cultures there were professional interpreters of dreams (cf Gn $40^{5,8}$ 41^{1}, Dn 2^{5}), and manuals were compiled to aid in their elucidation (*e.g.* the *Oneirocritica* of Artemidorus of Ephesus). Wiser theorists might discriminate between dreams, but the popular tendency was to regard them all as omens, to be explained as far as possible in accordance with definite rules.

1. Among the Jews.—In both Testaments significance is attached to dreams; cf Gn $37^{6,9}$ 41^{25}, Jg 7^{13}, Dn 2^{1ff} 4^{5ff} 7^{1ff}, Mt 1^{20} $2^{13,20}$, Ac 23^{11} 27^{23}. We find hardly any traces, however, of dreams being regularly sought; Saul's expedition to Endor can scarcely be brought within this category, although he had previously been unable to obtain a divine response by dreams (1 S $28^{6,8ff}$). Jacob's dream at Bethel (Gn 28^{12ff}) and Solomon's at Gibeon (1 K 3^{5}) have been linked with the practice of 'incubation'—sleeping in a sacred place in order to receive a divine communication in sleep—but in neither case does the text suggest any such intention on the sleeper's part. The general trend of OT teaching is as follows: Dreams may be genuine communications from God (Job 4^{12ff} 33^{15}); in the 'E' narratives of Genesis they are his regular means of communicating with men, as compared with the theophanies of the 'J' narratives. But Nu 12^{6-8} treats dreams as an inferior medium of revelation, and in Jer 23^{28} Yahweh dismisses 'the prophet who has a dream' with short shrift by contrast with 'him who has my word.' For there are false dreams and lying dreamers, against whom precautions are necessary (Dt 13^{1ff}). Habitual dreaming is no sure sign of Divine inspiration (Jer 23^{25ff} 27^{9} 29^{8}; Zec 10^{2}, Ec 5^{7}). The interpretation of dreams belongs to God and is not a matter of human codification (Gn 40^{8}, Dn 2^{27f}).

2. General.—The consideration of dreams belongs chiefly to those branches of study which treat of the general relation of body and mind, in particular, psychology and parapsychology. Freud's attempt to account for all dreams in terms of wish-fulfilment or attempted wish-fulfilment is well known, and has proved in some ways remarkably fruitful. But as yet the interpretation of dream symbols is a matter of great uncertainty, as appears from the diverse interpretations given by the different schools of analytical psychology. It seems clear, however, that dreams are connected with physical states, and that their psychological origin lies mainly in the region beneath the threshold of consciousness. But if any dreams can be regarded as vehicles of divine or other communication, this can be only because of the character and content of the messages conveyed. It is a matter of experience that the power of intellectual and spiritual perception can occasionally be heightened in the dream-state, so that insights can be obtained or problems solved in a way that the waking consciousness had found impossible. A line of poetry necessary to complete a poem has taken shape in the dream state—more rarely, indeed, a complete poem, of which Coleridge's *Kubla Khan* is the best known example. Similarly Condorcet is said to have solved in a dream a mathematical problem which baffled his waking powers. But in any circumstances the interpretation of a dream 'belongs to God'; its religious significance (if any) must be settled by an appeal to the higher reason or the spiritual consciousness, which will reach a decision in line with what is already known of the Divine nature and will. The awakened intelligence, enlightened by the Word and Spirit of God, must criticize and appraise the deliverances received in dreams, and its verdict must determine how much attention should be paid to them. Dreams, in short, may be the source of suggestions, but not of authoritative directions. A. W. F. B.—**F. F. B.**

DRESS.—The numerous synonyms for 'dress' to be found in English versions—'apparel,' 'attire,' 'clothes,' 'raiment,' 'garments,' etc.—fairly reflect a similar wealth of terminology in the original Hebrew and Greek, more especially the former. As regards the particular articles of dress, the identification of these is in many cases rendered almost impossible for the English reader by the curious lack of consistency in the renderings of the translators, illustrations of which will be met with in this article. For this and other reasons it will be necessary to have recourse to transliteration as the only certain means of distinguishing garments to be discussed.

In seeking to describe the various garments worn in Biblical times, we must not assume that they were similar to the clothes of modern Palestinians, especially the Bedouin Arabs. A more trustworthy source of information is the representation of ancient Palestinians and Syrians on Near Eastern monuments of various kinds. No clothes of pre-Roman times have been discovered, but these representations may be considered fairly reliable if we remember that they were usually made by foreigners, that they often depict captives or tribute-bearers, and that they probably tend to be standardized. Many of these representations may be seen in *ANEP*, 1954. Of special importance are the Megiddo ivories (frontispiece and No. 125), the *Beni Hasan* tomb painting of the 19th cent. B.C. (No. 3), the Black Obelisk of Shalmaneser III., second register (Nos. 351–355), and the Assyrian sculptures depicting the fall of Lachish (Nos. 371–373).

1. Materials.—Scripture and anthropology are in agreement as to the great antiquity of the **skins of animals,** wild and domesticated, as dress material (Gn 3^{21} 'garments of skins'; cf for later times, He 11^{37}). The favourite materials in Palestine, however, were **wool** and **flax** (Pr 31^{13}). The finest quality of linen, byssus, was probably an importation from Egypt (see LINEN). **Goats' hair** and **camels' hair** supplied the materials for coarser fabrics. The first certain mention of **silk** is in Rev 18^{12}, for the meaning of the word so rendered in Ezk $16^{10,13}$ is doubtful, and the silk of Pr 31^{22} (AV) is really 'fine linen' as in RSV.

2. Under Garments.—(*a*) The oldest and most widely distributed of all the articles of human apparel is the **loin-cloth** or **waistcloth** (Heb. *'ēzōr*), originally a strip of skin or cloth wrapped round the loins and fastened with a knot. On Egyptian monuments of the Middle and Late Bronze Ages, Syrians and possibly Palestinians are frequently represented as wearing a waistcloth, which is either a wrap-around type of garment or a kilt (*ANEP*, Nos. 1–8). These are in many cases captives, and thus probably soldiers. On the Lachish scenes, the soldiers wear kilt-like waistcloths, over which are tunics. It appears that the waistcloth was the basic garment of Israelite soldiers and workers; it is possible that others wore it as an undergarment, but this is not certain.

In the OT, *'ēzōr* is usually rendered incorrectly by **girdle,'** a term which should be reserved for *ḥᵃghôrāh* (see below). RSV correctly renders it by 'waistcloth' in Is 5^{27}, Jer 13^{1ff}, and Job 12^{18}. Some of the prophets wore the wasitcloth, such as Elijah, who ‘ was girt about with an *'ēzōr* of leather on his loins ’ (2 K 1^{8}), and John the Baptist (Mt 3^{4}, Mk 1^{6}). Jeremiah on one occasion put on a waistcloth of linen in a symbolic action (Jer 13$^{1\text{ff}}$; this may have been a vision experience).

The noun and the cognate verb are frequently used in figurative senses, the point of which is lost unless it is remembered that the waistcloth was always worn next the skin, as *e.g.* Jer 13^{11}, Is 11^{5}, the figure in the latter case signifying that righteousness and faithfulness are essential and inseparable elements in the character of the Messianic ‘ Shoot.’

(*b*) The **aprons** (Gr. *simikinthia*) of Ac 19^{12} were the Roman *semicinctium*, a short waistcloth worn especially by slaves and workmen.

(*c*) In early times the priests wore a waistcloth of linen, which bore the special name of the **ephod** (1 S 2^{18}), and which the incident recorded in 2 S 6$^{14\text{ff}}$—David, as priest, dancing before the Ark—shows to have been of the nature of a short kilt. By the Priests' Code, however, the priests were required to wear the under garment described under BREECHES.

(*d*) In OT, the ordinary under garment for both sexes is the shirt or **tunic** (*kuttōneth* or *k^{e}tōneth*, a term which reappears in Greek as *chitōn*). English versions often translate this word as ‘ coat.’ RSV renders it by four different words : (*a*) ‘ garment,’ Gn 3^{21}, Ca 5^{3}, Ezr 2^{69}, Neh 7$^{70,\,72}$; (*b*) ‘ coat,’ Ex 28^{4}, 2 S 15^{32} etc. ; (*c*) ‘ robe,’ Gn 37, 2 S 13$^{18\text{f}}$, Is 22^{21} ; and (*d*) ‘ tunic ’ in Job 30^{18} only. In the NT, *chitōn* is rendered by RSV as ‘ tunic ’ in Mt 10^{10}, Lk 9^{3}, and Mk 6^{9} ; as ‘ coat ’ in Mt 5^{40}, Lk 3^{11} ; and as ‘ garment ’ in Jd ^{23}.

The Assyrian sculpture representing the siege and capture of Lachish by Sennacherib shows the Jewish captives, male and female alike, dressed in a moderately tight garment fitting close to the neck (cf Job 30^{18}) and reaching almost to the ankles. The soldiers have over the waistcloth, described above, a long shirt reaching below the waist ; or it may be a long tunic which is drawn up above the knees and fastened in place by the waistbands. On the Megiddo ivories of about the 12th cent. B.C., men and women wear a long tunic reaching to the ankles.

As regards **sleeves,** which are not expressly mentioned in OT—but see RSV at Gn 37^{3} (Joseph) and 2 S 13^{18} (Tamar)—three modes are found. The early Egyptian representation of a group of Semitic traders, from *Beni Hasan*, shows a highly coloured sleeveless tunic, which fastens on the left shoulder, leaving the right shoulder bare. The Lachish tunics, above mentioned, have short sleeves reaching almost to the elbows. This probably represents the prevailing type of tunic among the Hebrews of the earlier period at least, since a third variety, fitted with long and wider sleeves and reaching almost to the ground, was evidently restricted to the upper and wealthier classes. This is the ‘ tunic of (*i.e.* reaching to) palms and soles ’ (‘ long robe with sleeves,’ RSV) worn by Joseph and the royal princess Tamar (see above). It is more familiar as the **‘ coat of many** (or diverse) **colours,’** a rendering which represents a now generally abandoned tradition. In Josephus' day the long white linen tunic, which was the chief garment of the ordinary priesthood, had sleeves which for practical reasons were tied to the arms (Jos. *Ant.* III. vii. 2 [154]). By this time, also, it had become usual even among the lower ranks of the people to wear an under tunic or real shirt (*ib.* XVII. v. 7 [136]) ; Mishnah, *passim*, where this garment is named *ḥālûḳ*). In this case the upper tunic, the *kuttōneth* proper, would be taken off at night (Ca 5^{3}).

The ordinary tunic was made in at least three ways. (1) It might consist of two similar pieces of woollen or linen cloth cut from a larger web, which were sewed together along the sides and top. (2) The material for a single tunic might be woven on the loom, and afterwards put together without cutting, in the manner of the Egyptian tunics described and figured in Smith's *Dict. of Gr. and Rom. Antiq.*^{3} *s.v.* ‘ Tunica ’ (ii. 904). (3) As we known from the description of the *chitōn* worn by our Lord at the time of His Passion (Jn 19^{23}), and from other sources, a third variety was woven ‘ without seam ’ on a special loom (see SPINNING AND WEAVING) and required no further adjustment.

The garment intended by the ‘ coats ’ of Dn 3$^{21,\,27}$ (AV) is uncertain. Most recent authorities favour mantles (so RSV). For the ‘ coat of mail,’ see ARMOUR, **2** (*c*).

3. The Girdle.—Almost as indispensable as the tunic was the **girdle** (Heb. *ḥ^{a}ghôrāh* or *ḥ^{a}ghôr*). This is the usual rendering of English versions, including RSV, but the item of apparel is not that which is ordinarily called a ‘ girdle ’ to-day. It was a belt or waistband, and usually consisted of a long strip of cloth, folded several times and wound round the waist over the tunic, with or without the ends hanging down in front. The *ḥ^{a}ghôrāh* varied in material and workmanship from a simple rope (Is 3^{24}) to the rich and elaborate waistbelt of the priests, and the ‘ golden girdles ’ of Rev 1^{13} 15^{6}. When a person was working or travelling, the lower part of the tunic might be drawn up and tucked into the *ḥ^{a}ghôrāh*. Hence this operation of ‘ girding the loins ’ became a figure for energetic action. The waistband served also as a sword-belt (2 S 20^{8}) ; through it probably was stuck the writing-case (Ezk 9$^{3,\,11}$), while its folds served as a purse (Mt 10^{9}). The special priests' waistband, termed *'abnēṭ* (Ex 28^{4} and often) was a richly embroidered sash wound several times round the waist, according to Josephus (*Ant.* III. vii. 2 [154 f]), and tied in front, the ends falling to the ankles.

4. Upper Garments.—While the *kuttōneth* or tunic was the garment in which the work of the day was done (see Mt 24^{18}, Mk 13^{16}), men and women alike possessed a second garment, which served as a protection against inclement weather by day and as a covering by night (Ex 22$^{26\text{f}}$). The two are sharply distinguished in the familiar saying of Jesus : ‘ If any one would sue you and take your **coat** (*chitōn*), let him have your **cloak** (*himation*) as well ’ (Mt 5^{40}).

(*a*) This upper garment had several names ; we cannot now be certain of the differences in the various garments, if indeed the various names stood for different garments. In the OT, the commonest name is *śimlāh* or *śalmāh*, and in the NT *himation* ; these words sometimes signified, however, garments or clothing in general (Gn 41^{14} 44^{13}, Ex 19^{10}, Lk 8^{27} etc.).

The figures on the *Beni Hasan* tomb painting do not have any garment over the multi-coloured tunic. On Egyptian tomb paintings of the Late Bronze Age (15th–13th cents. B.C.), Syrians are often represented as wearing over the tunic a robe that is wound around the body and thrown over the shoulders as a cape (see *ANEP*, nos. 43, 47, 49, 52–54). The edges of the cloth usually have an embroidered hem. The Megiddo ivories show a robe over the tunic reaching to the knees or almost to the ground. On the Black Obelisk of Shalmaneser III. the Israelites have a fringed upper garment that is almost as long as the tunic. On the Assyrian sculptures of the Lachish surrender, the women have over the tunic a long shawl that covers the head and reaches to the ankle.

From these representations it is apparent that the *śimlāh*, or upper garment, varied in its appearance. Sometimes it was wrapped around the body. At other times, it was a fringed garment that was put on, like the tunic. In the Israelite period, the latter form may have predominated, and the *śimlāh* was obviously not unlike the *'abayeh* of the modern Palestinian Arab.

In the English versions, *śimlāh* (or *śalmāh*) is rendered in a variety of ways. RSV translates it as ‘ mantle(s) ’ in Ex 12^{34} 22^{27}, Is 3$^{6,\,7}$, and ‘ cloak ’ in Dt 24^{13}. Greek *himation* is rendered as ‘ mantle ’ in Mt 24^{18}, Mk 13^{16}, Lk 22^{36}, and ‘ robe ’ in Jn 19^{2}, Rev 19^{16}. Usually a colourless rendering such as ‘ garment,’ ‘ clothes,’ or ‘ clothing ’ is used, and frequently it is difficult to determine whether a specific garment is intended.

(*b*) Another variety of upper garment known as the *m$^{e\text{'}}$îl* is mentioned only in connexion with men of high social position or of the priestly order. It is the robe of Saul—the skirt (literally ‘ corner ’) of which was cut off by David (1 S 24^{4f})—of Jonathan (18^{4}), and of Ezra (Ezr $9^{3, 5}$), the little robe of the boy-priest Samuel (1 S 2^{19}) and his robe at a later stage (15^{27}). RSV usually has ' robe ' for *meʿîl*, sometimes ' mantle.' We do not know just how the *meʿîl* differed from the *śimlāh*. From its constant association with men of rank and of the priesthood, we may assume that it was more elaborate and ornate. The violet ' robe of the ephod ' prescribed for the High Priest (Ex 28^{31ff} 39^{22ff}) had ' in it an opening for the head, with a woven binding around the opening,' and was trimmed with an elaborate bell-and-pomegranate fringe. By the time of Josephus, the High Priest's *meʿîl* had become a sleeveless and seamless upper tunic of blue, held by a sash (*Ant*. III. vii. 4 [159]).

(*c*) A third variety of upper garment, the *'addereth*, appears to have been the distinctive garment of the prophets (see Zec 13^{4} RSV ' hairy mantle '). Elijah's **mantle**, in particular, is always so named (1 K $19^{13, 19}$, 2 K $2^{8, 13f}$). In 2 K 1^{8} Elijah is called a *baʿal śēʿār*; RSV renders, ' He wore a garment of haircloth.' In Gn 25^{25} the body of Esau at birth is said to have been ' like a hairy mantle.' John the Baptist wore a mantle of camel's hair (Mt 3^{4}, Mk 1^{6}). The *'addereth* may not always have been made of haircloth, for Achan coveted and stole ' a beautiful *'addereth* from Shinar ' (Jos $7^{21, 24}$), and in Jon 3^{6} the robe of the king of Nineveh is denoted by this word. See also RUG.

(*d*) Among the products of the domestic loom was a fourth garment, the *sādhîn* (Pr 31^{24}). From the Mishnah we learn that it was a plain **sheet** of fine linen, sometimes with tassels, which could be used as a light upper garment, as a curtain, and as a shroud. In this last respect it resembled the NT *sindōn*, the ' linen shroud ' of Mt 27^{59}, Mk 15^{46}. It is probably as an upper garment of fine white linen for gala use that the *sādhîn* is introduced in Jg 14^{12f} and Is 3^{23} (RSV ' linen garments ' in both passages).

(*e*) Mention must also be made of the ' scarlet robe ' (*chlamys*) in which Jesus was arrayed by the Roman soldiers (Mt $27^{28, 31}$). It is the *paludamentum* or military cloak worn over their armour by the superior officers of the Roman army. The **' cloak '** (*phailonēs*) which St. Paul left at Troas (2 Ti 4^{13}) was the Roman *paenula*, a circular travelling cape. For the brooch or buckle by which an upper garment was sometimes fastened, see ORNAMENTS, **5**.

5. Headdress.—(*a*) The Hebrews appear at first to have had no covering for the head, except on special occasions, such as war, when a leather **helmet** was worn (see ARMOUR, **2** (*b*)). On the Egyptian monuments of the Middle and Late Bronze Ages, Syrian men are represented as bare-headed or only with a rope or cord on the hair, serving as a fillet. The name for this may have been *peʾēr*, as in Is 3^{20} $61^{3, 10}$ (but see Ex 39^{28}, Ezk $24^{17, 23}$ 44^{18}, and cf 1 K 20^{31f}). In cases of prolonged exposure to the sun, it is probable that recourse would be had to a covering in the style of the modern *keffiyeh*, which protects not only the head but also the neck and shoulders. A clay figurine found at Gezer, probably from the Late Bronze Age, appears to be wearing a *keffiyeh* (Macalister, *Excavation of Gezer*, ii, p. 77, fig. 271). Jehu's tribute-carriers on the Black Obelisk are depicted in a ' stocking cap ' which resembles the familiar Phrygian cap. On the Assyrian sculptures of the Lachish siege, the men often have a turban on the head. This is the *ṣānîph*, from a root signifying to ' wind round.' It is the royal **' diadem '** of Is 62^{3}, the **' turban '** of Is 3^{23} (AV **' hood '**) and Zec 3^{5} (the last a priestly headgear; AV **' mitre '**). A kindred word, *miṣnepheth*, is used for the High Priest's turban in Ex 28^{4} etc. for which see MITRE. The **' hats '** (Aram. *karbelā'*) of Dn 3^{21} were probably a variety of the conical Babylonian headdress; it is incorrect to render as ' mantles.' Antiochus Epiphanes, it is recorded, induced the young Jewish nobles to wear the *petasus*, the low, broad-brimmed hat associated with Hermes (2 Mac 4^{12}, RSV ' the Greek hat '; RV **' cap '**).

In NT times, as may be learned from the Mishnah, many forms of headdress were in use. One was the *sûdhār*, a scarf wound about the head and hanging down over the neck. The name resembles Latin *sudarium*, a cloth for wiping off perspiration. The latter is Greek *soudarion*, translated as **' napkin '** in Lk 19^{20}, Jn 20^{7}, the **' cloth '** in which Lazarus' face was wrapped, Jn 11^{44}, and **' handkerchief '** in Ac 19^{12}.

(*b*) As regards the headdress of the female sex, Is 3^{23} indicates that women sometimes wore the turban, mentioned above. On the Egyptian monuments, Syrian women are often bare-headed or wear only a headband on the hair. The female captives from Lachish wear over their tunics an upper garment like a very long shawl, covering the hair and falling down over the shoulders as far as the ankles. Whether this is the garment intended by any of the words rendered **vail** in AV it is impossible to say: such as that of Ruth (3^{15} *miṭpaḥath* RSV ' mantle '), or the ' veils for the head ' (*mispāḥāh*) of Ezk 13^{18} RSV, or the word *redhidh*, ' veils ' in Is 3^{23} RSV, ' mantle ' in Ca 5^{7} RSV. The veil (*ṣāʿîph*) with which Rebekah and Tamar covered themselves (Gn 24^{65} 38^{14}), was more probably a large mantle with which the whole body could be wrapped. Indeed, it is impossible to draw a clear distinction in OT between the mantle and the veil. The only express mention of a face-veil is in the case of Moses (Ex 34^{33}).

6. Shoes and sandals.—Within doors the Hebrews went barefoot. On the monuments Hebrew or Syrian captives are usually thus represented (cf Is 20^{2}). Out of doors it was customary to wear sandals or shoes, mostly the former. The simplest form of **sandal** consisted of a plain sole of leather, bound to the feet by a leather thong, the **' sandal-thong '** of Gn 14^{23} and the **' thong '** (AV, RV **' latchet '**) of Mk 1^{7} etc. The Assyrians preferred a sandal fitted with a heel-cap, by which they are distinguished from Jehu's attendants on the Obelisk of Shalmaneser III., who wear shoes completely covering the feet and turned up at the toes, like the Hittite shoe. The laced **boot** of the soldier is apparently referred to in Is 9^{5}. The sandals were removed not only in cases of mourning (2 S 15^{30}) and of a visit to a friend, but also on entering a sacred precinct (Ex 3^{5}, Jos 5^{15}); the Jewish priests, accordingly, performed all their offices in the Temple barefoot.

7. It need hardly be said that the taste for ' purple and fine linen ' was not peculiar to the days of Dives, as may be seen from the remarkable list of finery and ornaments in Is 3^{18ff}. Richly embroidered garments are mentioned as early as the time of the Judges (Jg 5^{30} RSV). King Josiah had an official who bore the title of ' keeper of the wardrobe ' (2 K 22^{14}). The **' changes of raiment,'** however, several times mentioned in OT, were not so many complete outfits, but special gala robes, for which one's ordinary garments were ' changed '; RSV renders as ' festal garments ' (Gn 45^{22}, Jg 14^{12ff}, 2 K $5^{5, 22f}$). In the East, such robes have continued a favourite form of gift and expression of esteem from sovereigns and other persons of high rank to the present day.

For what may be termed accessories of dress, see ORNAMENTS, SEAL, STAFF.

8. A special interest must always attach to the question of the outward appearance of the Man of Nazareth, so far as it is associated with the dress He wore. This must have consisted of at least six separate articles. By the 1st cent. it had become usual to wear a linen shirt (*ḥālûḳ*) beneath the tunic (see **2** (*d*) above). In our Lord's case this seems required by the mention of the upper garments (*himatia*, *i.e.* mantle and tunic) which He laid aside before washing the disciples' feet (Jn 13^{4}). The tunic proper, we know, was ' woven without seam ' throughout, and therefore fitted closely at the neck, with the usual short sleeves as above described. Above the tunic was the linen girdle wound several times round the waist. On His feet were leather sandals (Mt 3^{11}). His upper garment, *himation*, was probably of white woollen cloth, as is suggested by the details of the Transfiguration narrative in Mk 9^{3}, with the four prescribed tassels at the corners. To the form of His headdress we have no clue, but it may be regarded as certain—the traditional artistic convention notwithstanding—that no Jewish teacher of that period would appear in public with head uncovered. Probably a white linen 'napkin' (*sûdhār*) was tied round the head as a simple turban, the ends falling down over the neck. A. R. S. K.—**J. P. H.**

DRINK.—See MEALS, **6**, WINE AND STRONG DRINK.

DRINK-OFFERING.—See SACRIFICE AND OFFERING.

DROMEDARY.—See CAMEL.

DROPSY.—See MEDICINE.

DROVE, 1 K 10[28], 2 Ch 1[16] (RV).—See KUE.

DRUNKENNESS.—See WINE AND STRONG DRINK.

DRUSILLA.—The wife of the procurator Felix (Ac 24[24]). She was the youngest daughter of Herod Agrippa I., born *c* A.D. 37, and is said to have been persuaded by a Jewish astrologer (perhaps Atomos of Cyprus; see Haenchen *ad. loc.*) to desert her first husband, Azizus king of Emesa, for Felix. She was sister to Agrippa II. and Bernice (25[13]). See Jos. *Ant.* XX. vii. 2 (141 ff). F. C. G.

DUALISM.—The belief in, or doctrine of, two ultimate conflicting principles, powers, or tendencies in the universe. Haeckel describes as dualism the distinction between God and the world, and between matter and mind, and opposes to it his monism, which identifies both (*Riddle of the Universe*, ch. 1, p. 8). In this sense of the word the Bible teaches dualism. It does distinguish God as Creator from the world as created (Gn 1[1], Is 40[26], Jn 1[3]), and describes God as Spirit in contrast with matter (Jn 4[24]). In man it distinguishes the body taken from the dust, and the spirit given by God (Gn 2[7], Ec 12[7]). This conclusion need not be proved further, as this view is implied in all the teaching of the Bible about God, world, man. But, setting aside this new sense of the term, we must consider whether the Bible gives evidence of dualism in the older sense, as opposing to God any antagonist or hindrance in His creating, preserving, and ruling the world. It is held that dualism in three forms can be traced in the Bible—(1) the mythical, (2) the metaphysical, (3) the ethical. Each must be separately examined.

1. Mythical dualism.—In the Babylonian cosmology, *Marduk*, the champion of the upper deities, wages war against *Tiamat*, who leads the lower deities; at last he slays her, divides her body, and makes part a covering for the heavens to hold back the upper waters. There is little doubt that the account of the Creation in Gn 1 reproduces some of the features of this myth, but it is transformed by the monotheism of the author. Tiamat appears under the name **Rahab** in several passages (Job 9[13] [RV] 26[12f] [see Davidson's *Job*, p. 54), Is 51[9], cf 27[1] 'leviathan the swift serpent,' 'leviathan the crooked serpent,' 'the dragon that is in the sea'). See Cheyne's notes on these passages in the *Prophecies of Isaiah*, i, 158, ii, 31. In illustration of Is 51[9] he quotes the address to *Ra* in the Egyptian Book of the Dead: 'Hail! thou who hast cut in pieces the Scorner and strangled the *Apophis*' [*i.e.* the evil serpent, Ps 89[10], cf Ps 74[13f] 'the dragons,' 'leviathan']. This name is used as a symbolic name of Egypt (Ps 87[4], Is 30[7]), probably on account of its position on the Nile, and its hostility to the people of God. The **sea** is regarded as God's foe (Dn 7[3] 'four great beasts came up from the sea'; Rev 13[1] 'a beast coming up out of the sea,' 21[1] 'the sea is no more,' that is, the power hostile to God has ceased), a conception in which the myth survives. The influence of the myth is seen only in the poetical language, but not in the religious beliefs of the Holy Scriptures.

2. Metaphysical dualism.—Greek thought was dualistic. Anaxagoras assumed *hylē*, 'matter,' as well as *nous*, 'mind,' as the ultimate principles. Plato does not harmonize the world of ideas and the world of sense. Aristotle begins with matter and form. Neo-Platonism seeks to fill up the gulf between God and the world by a series of emanations. In Gnosticism the *plērōma* and the *logos* mediate between the essential and the phenomenal existence. St. John (1[1, 14]) meets this Greek thought of his environment by asserting that Christ is the Word who is with God and is God, and who has become flesh. Against Gnostic heretics St. Paul in *Colossians* (1[19] 2[9]) asserts that the *plērōma*, the fulness of the Godhead, dwells bodily in Christ; to this dualism is opposed the union of Creator and creation, reason and matter in Christ.

From this metaphysical there resulted a practical dualism in Greek thought, between sense and reason. While Aristotle thought that reason might use sense as an artist his material, Neo-Platonism taught that only by an ascetic discipline could reason be emancipated from the bondage of sense; and Stoicism treated sense as a usurper in man's nature, to be crushed and cast out by reason. Holsten has tried to show that this dualism is involved in St. Paul's doctrine of the **flesh,** and Pfleiderer also holds this position. It is held that St. Paul, starting from the common Hebraic notion of flesh (*sarx*), 'according to which it signifies material substance, which is void indeed of the spirit, but not contrary to it, which is certainly weak and perishable, and so far unclean, but not positively evil,' advances to the conception of the flesh as 'an agency opposed to the spirit,' having 'an active tendency towards death.' 'From the opposition of physically different substances results the dualism of antagonistic moral principles' (Pfleiderer's *Paulinism*, i. 52 ff). This conclusion is, however, generally challenged with good reason, and cannot be regarded as proved. The question will be more fully discussed in article FLESH.

3. Ethical dualism.—In Persian thought there are opposed to one another, as in conflict with one another, *Ormuzd* and *Ahriman*, the personal principles of good and evil. While the OT recognizes the power of sin in the world, yet God's ultimate causality and sole supremacy are affirmed. In post-exilic Judaism, however, there was a twofold tendency so to assert the transcendence of God that angels must be recognized as mediating between Him and the world, and to preserve His moral perfection by assigning the evil in the world to the agency of evil spirits under the leadership of *Satan*, the adversary. While these tendencies may be regarded as inherent in the development of Hebrew monotheism, both were doubtless stimulated by the influence of Persian thought with its elaborate angelology and demonology. In the Apocalyptic literature the present world is represented as under Satan's dominion, and as wrested from him only by a supernatural manifestation of God's power to establish His Kingdom. This dualism pervades the Apocalypse. In the NT generally the doctrine of the *devil* current in Judaism is taken over, but the Divine supremacy is never denied, and the Divine victory over all evil is always confidently anticipated. (See articles PSEUDEPIGRAPHA, DEVIL, ESCHATOLOGY.)

While in the Bible there are these traces of the threefold dualism, it is never developed; and monotheism is throughout maintained, God's sole eternity, ultimate causality, and final victory being asserted, while God is distinguished from the world, and in the world a distinction between matter and mind is recognized.
A. E. G.

DUKE.—The title of 'duke' in the AV has a very general meaning. It is an inheritance from the English versions, in which (after Vulg. *dux* 'duke' meant any leader or chief. Latimer calls Gideon a duke, and Wycliffe uses this title of Christ, as in his *Works* (iii. 137), 'Jesus Christ, duke of oure batel.' The title of 'duke' is confined in AV to the chiefs of Edom (RV also has 'dukes,' but RSV 'chiefs'), with the exception of Jos 13[21] 'dukes of Sihon' (RV, RSV 'princes'), and 1 Mac 10[65] (applied to Jonathan Maccabaeus; RV 'captain,' RSV 'general').

DULCIMER.—This term, which denotes a *stringed* instrument (? the mediaeval 'psaltery'; see MUSIC, **4**

1) (*b*)), is given incorrectly by AV, RV in Dn $3^{5, 15}$ as translation of *sûmpônyāh* (Gr. loan-word), which probably=' bagpipe ' (so RSV) ; see MUSIC, **4** (2) (*d*).

DUMAH.—1. Cited in Gn 25^{14}, 1 Ch 1^{30} as among the twelve tribes of Ishmael. The region thus indicated is supposed to be the oasis formerly called by the Arabs *Dûmat el-Jendel* and now known as *el-Jôf*, about three-fourths of the way from Damascus to Medina. The same place may be referred to in the obscure oracle Is 21^{11}, but the LXX has ' Idumaea,' and it is possible that Edom is meant. **2.** The name of a town in the highlands of Judah (Jos 15^{52}). The reading is not certain. The LXX and Vulgate indicate *Rumah*, and not all editions of the Hebrew agree. If the received text is correct, an identification may be plausibly made with *ed-Dômeh* 10 miles SW. of Hebron. J. F. McC.

DUMBNESS.—See MEDICINE.

DUNG.—1. Used in the East as manure (Lk 13^{8}) and for fuel ; especially that of cattle, where wood and charcoal are scarce or unattainable. Directions for personal cleanliness are given in Dt 23^{13-14} ; and in the case of sacrifices the dung of the animals was burnt outside the camp (Ex 29^{14}, Lv $4^{11f.}$ 8^{17}, Nu 19^{5}). **2.** The word is used (*a*) to express contempt and abhorrence, as in the case of the carcase of Jezebel (2 K 9^{37}) ; and in that of the Jews (Jer 9^{22}, Zeph 1^{17}). (*b*) To spread dung upon the face was a sign of humiliation (Mal 2^{3}). (*c*) As representing worthlessness, Paul counted all things but dung that he might win Christ (Ph 3^{8}).

DUNG GATE.—See JERUSALEM, GATES OF.

DURA, PLAIN OF.—Mentioned Dn 3^{1}. The precise locality is uncertain, but it must have been in the vicinity of Babylon. Perhaps the name is derived from the Babylonian *dūru*=' wall,' which is frequently used as a town name. Oppert (*Exped. en Mésop.* I. 238) found a small river so named, falling into the Euphrates 6 or 7 miles SE. of Babylon, the neighbouring mounds being also named *Tulûl Dûra* (cf also Baumgartner, *ZAW* xliv, 40 n.). A curious Talmudic legend makes this plain the scene of Ezekiel's vision (37^{1-14}), which it regards as an actual event (*Sanh.* 92 *b*).

DWARF.—The rendering in EV in Lv 21^{20} of *daḳ*, a word denoting one of the physical disqualifications by which a priest was unfitted for service. The word means *thin, lean, small*. The conjecture that it here means a dwarf is plausible. But others regard it as meaning an unnaturally thin man—a consumptive, perhaps.

DYEING.—See ARTS AND CRAFTS, **6** ; COLOURS, **6.**

DYSENTERY.—See MEDICINE.

E

EAGLE.—The Hebrew *nesher*, whose name is an onomatopoeic term describing a bird that drops flashing through the air, is commonly taken as the eagle (LXX and Vulgate). It certainly is the ' imperial eagle ' (*aquila heliaca*), which is very common in Palestine, when described as flying towards heaven (Pr 23^{5}) ; for, having a peculiar membrane over the eyes, it can see against the sun, as the Ugaritic *nšr* can do (Aqhat I. ii. 56–57 ; cf Shakespeare 3 *Henry the Sixth* II. i. 91–92). In passages referring to its speed (2 S 1^{23}, Jer 4^{13}, La 4^{19}) the ' golden eagle ' (*aquila chrysaetus*), which can attain a speed of 3 or 4 miles in 10 minutes, may be meant ; and the female of this eagle has been seen, even though only on a few occasions, to catch her falling young and carry it off on her back (Ex 19^{4}, Dt 32^{11}). Contrariwise, when reference is made to its bald patch (Mic 1^{16}), the bird is the ' griffon-vulture ' (*gyps fulvus*) which has a white patch giving the effect of baldness on its head ; and the same bird is remarkable for the width of its wings (Ezk 17^{3}), which may reach 8 or 10 feet across. Further, this bird begins the consumption of its victims by attacking the eyes and other soft parts of the body ; and this habit explains the proverb about the unfilial son (Pr 3^{7}). Other features characteristic of vultures rather than eagles are nesting on cliffs (Jer 44^{16} ; cf Job 39^{27-30}), which vultures regularly and eagles (which also build on trees) only sometimes do, and gathering from distant places to devour the spoil (Dt 28^{49}, Hab 1^{8}) ; for, while eagles are mostly solitary, vultures often congregate in considerable numbers from invisible distances, for which their keen sight is invaluable (Jer 44^{22}), to devour dead or dying beasts. The description of the *nesher* as renewing its youth (Ps 103^{5} ; cf Is 40^{31}) is an allusion to the notion that moulting gives it fresh strength. The Hebrew *nesher*, then, like the Arabic *nisr*, designates eagles and vultures of every kind, and which of the 8 eagles and 4 vultures found in Palestine is meant will depend on the context. The Greek *aetos*, which also is an onomatopoeic term (cf Heb. *'ayiṭ* ' bird of prey ' from *'âṭ* ' screamed '), is used for both the eagle and the vulture, which is clearly intended in the NT (Mt 24^{28}, Lk 17^{37}) ; elsewhere identification is uncertain (Rev 4^{7} 12^{14}).

The Hebrew *rāḥām*(*āh*), variously mistranslated ' swan ' and ' peacock ' (LXX), ' coot,' or ' moorhen ' (Vulgate) is another raptor, since it is classed as unclean (Lv 11^{18}, Dt 14^{17}) ; it can hardly be the ' gier-eagle ' (AV) or ' vulture ' (RV, RSV ; in Dt 14^{17} RSV ' carrion vulture '), since these are otherwise named. The Arabic *raḥamu* ' white carrion-bird ' cannot override this fact ; but this word, as well as *'arḥamu* ' (horse) having a white back and black body ' and *ruḥâmu* ' soft white stone,' suggests the ' osprey ' (*pandion haliaetus*), an almost cosmopolitan bird found also in Palestine ; for it is a large brown bird whose head and nape are white with brown streaks and its lower parts white. If so, it appropriately heads the aquatic birds in the list of unclean birds. G. R. D.

EANES, 1 Es 9^{21} (AV).—See MAASEIAH, **2.**

EAR.—Both in OT and NT the spiritual disposition to attend, which issues in obedience, is thus designated (*e.g.* Is 6^{10}, Mt 11^{15}, Rev 2^{7}). Hence ' to uncover the ear ' (RVm, 1 S 9^{15} etc.)=to reveal ; the ' uncircumcised ear ' (Jer 6^{10} AV, RV ; RSV ' closed ')=the ear which remains unpurified and clogged and therefore unable to perceive ; hence ' thou hast given me an open ear ' (Ps 40^{6})=Thou hast enabled me to understand. The perforated ear was a sign of slavery or dependence, indicating the obligation to attend (Ex 21^{6}, Dt 15^{16f}). The tip of the priest's right ear was touched with blood in token that the sense of hearing was consecrated to God's service (Ex 29^{20}, Lv 8^{23}).

EARING.—Gn 45^{6} (AV), ' There shall be neither earing nor harvest.' ' Earing ' is the old expression for ' ploughing ' (RV, RSV ' plowing '). The verb ' to ear ' (connected with Lat. *arare*) also occurs, at Dt 21^{4} ' a rough valley, which is neither eared nor sown ' (RV, RSV ' plowed ').

EARNEST.—In 2 Co 1^{22} 5^{5}, Eph 1^{14} AV, St. Paul describes the Holy Spirit as the believer's ' earnest,' RSV ' guarantee.' The word means ' part-payment,' the deposit being the same in kind as what is to follow. Cf Tyndale's (1533) use of ' earnest-penny ' : ' that assured saving health and earnest-penny of everlasting life.' Rabbi Greenstone (*JE* v, 26) quotes *Kid.* 3*a* to the effect that the payment of a *peruṭah*, the smallest coin of Palestinian currency, on account of the purchase, was sufficient to bind the bargain. The Greek word was probably introduced by the Phoenicians. Deissmann (*Bible Studies*, pp. 108 f) shows that in 2 Co 1[21] the verb 'establishes' connotes a legal idea and stands in 'an essential relation' to 'earnest' in v.[22]. St. Paul represents the relation of God to believers under the image of 'a legally guaranteed security.' J. G. T.

EAR-RING.—See Ornaments, **2.**

EARTH in OT stands for one or other of the Hebrew words *'ereṣ* and *'ᵃdhāmāh*. In AV these are rendered indiscriminately 'earth' and **'ground,'** but RV distinguished them by using, to some extent, 'earth' for the former, and 'ground' for the latter. Both words have a wide range of meanings, some of which they possess in common, while others are peculiar to each. Thus *'ereṣ* denoted: (*a*) earth as opposed to heaven (Gn 1[1]), and (*b*) dry land as opposed to sea (1[20]). *'ᵃdhāmāh* is specially used: (*a*) for earth as a specific substance (Gn 2[7], 2 K 5[17]); and (*b*) for the surface of the ground, in such phrases as 'face of the earth.' Both words are employed to describe (*a*) the soil from which plants grow, *'ᵃdhāmāh* being the more common term in this sense; (*b*) the whole earth with its inhabitants, for which, however, *'ᵃdhāmāh* is but rarely used; and (*c*) a land or country, this also being usually expressed by *'ereṣ*. In one or two cases it is doubtful in which of the two last senses *'ereṣ* is to be taken, *e.g.* Jer 22[29] (AV, RV 'earth'; RVm, RSV 'land').

In NT the Greek words for 'earth' are *gē* and *oikoumenē*, the former having practically all the variety of meanings mentioned above, while the latter denoted specially the whole inhabited earth, and is once used (He 2[5]) in a still wider sense for the universe of the future. See World. J. Pk.

EARTHQUAKE.—The great Rift Valley, and the associated faulting on either side, show that Palestine must have suffered intense earthquake activity in geological history. This activity is not yet quite exhausted, earth tremors being not uncommon, and a major earthquake occurring about twice a century. Great damage and loss of life on both sides of the Jordan were caused by the last earthquake in 1927, and more recently slight tremors have shaken the structure of the Holy Sepulchre and the Dome of the Rock. A severe earthquake occurred in the reign of Uzziah and was long remembered (Am 1[1], Zec 14[5]). Josephus records another at the time of the battle of Actium, in the seventh year of the reign of Herod the Great (*Ant.* xv. v. 2 [121]), and the imagery of an earthquake is common in the OT.

Among the earthquakes which belong to the OT accounts of theophanies, or Divine manifestations of wrath, must be included such references as Ex 19[18], 1 K 19[11], Nu 16[31], Ps 18[7] 68[8] 104[4], Is 29[6] etc. In the NT an earthquake is recorded during St. Paul's imprisonment at Philippi (Ac 16[26]), and Matthew speaks of earthquakes at the Crucifixion and Resurrection (Mt 27[51, 54] 28[2]). Further, it is foretold that there shall be earthquakes at Christ's second coming (Mt 24[7], Mk 13[8], Lk 21[11]); their mention in Revelation is characteristic of apocalyptic literature. W. O. E. O.—**A. D. B.**

EAST GATE.—The name of a gate of Jerusalem, Neh 3[29]. In Jer 19[2], where AV has 'east gate' we should read **Potsherd Gate** (q.v.), with RVm, RSV.

EAST, PEOPLE OF THE.—A common designation of the inhabitants of the Syrian desert (AV, RV 'children of the east'), who were partly Aramaean and partly Arabian (Jg 6[3] 8[10], Ezk 25[4, 10], Is 11[14], Jer 49[28], Job 1[3]). Certain of them had obtained great renown for wisdom (1 K 4[30]).

EAST SEA, EASTERN SEA.—See Dead Sea.

EASTER (AV of Ac 12[4]; RV, RSV 'the Passover').—The anachronism of AV was inherited from older VSS which avoided, as far as possible, expressions which could not be understood by the people.

EBAL.—**1.** Name of a son of Joktan, 1 Ch 1[22]; called **Obal** in Gn 10[28]. The name probably represents a place of tribe in Arabia. **2.** A son of Shobal son of Seir, Gn 36[23], 1 Ch 1[40].

EBAL.—Now *Jebel Eslāmîyeh*, a mountain N. of *Nâblus* (Shechem), 1207 feet above the valley, 3077 feet above the sea. Ruins of a fortress and of a building called a 'little church' exist on its summit, as well as a Mohammedan shrine said to contain the skull of John the Baptist. The mountain commands an extensive view over almost the whole of Galilee, which includes points from Hermon to Jerusalem and from the sea to the Hauran. On this mountain Joshua built an altar and erected a monument bearing the law of Moses (Jos 8[30]); and the curses for breaches of the moral law were here proclaimed to the assembled Israelites on their formally taking possession of the Promised Land (Dt 11[29] 27[4, 13], Jos 8[33]). R. A. S. M.

EBED.—**1.** The father of Gaal, Jg 9[26ff]. **2.** One of those who returned from Babylon with Ezra, Ezr 8[6]; called **Obed** in 1 Es 8[32] (AV, RV **Obeth**).

EBED-MELECH.—An Ethiopian eunuch, by whom Jeremiah was released from the pit-prison (Jer 38[7ff] 39[15ff]). It is possible that the name *Ebed-melech*, which means 'servant of [the] king,' may have been an official title.

EBEN-EZER ('the stone of help' [LXX 'of the helper']).—**1.** The scene of a disastrous battle in which the Ark was lost, 1 S 4[1] 5[1]. **2.** The name of the stone erected to commemorate an equally glorious victory, 7[12]. The precise situation is uncertain, but if Jeshanah, 7[12] (RSV; AV, RV **Shen**) is modern *Burj el-Isâneh*, the locality is approximately defined. Samuel's explanatory words should be read thus: 'This is a witness that Yahweh has helped us.'

EBER.—**1.** The eponymous ancestor of the Hebrews (the first letter in both words being the same in the Hebrew), the great-grandson of Shem, and 'father' of Peleg and Joktan (Gn 10[21, 25] 11[14ff]). He is mentioned in Lk 3[35] in the genealogy of Jesus. The word *'ēbher* signifies 'the other side,' 'across'; and *'ibhri*, **'Hebrew,'** which is in form a gentilic name, denoting the inhabitant of a country or member of a tribe, is usually explained as denoting those who have come from *'ēbher han-nāhār* (see Jos 24[2, 3]), or '*the other side* of the River' (the Euphrates), *i.e.* from Haran (Gn 11[31]), in Aram-naharaim, the home of Abraham and Nahor (Gn 24[4, 7, 10]).

Many writers have connected the word Hebrew rather with the *Ḫabiru* (or *Ḫapiru*) mentioned in the Tell el-Amarna letters, or with the *'Apiru* of Egyptian texts. No simple equation can be made here, however, since the *Ḫabiru* were very widely spread in the early part of the 2nd millennium B.C. and included far more than the Israelites or Hebrews. In many texts the term has social rather than ethnic significance. See Habiru.

2. A Gadite, 1 Ch 5[13] (AV **Heber**). **3.** A Benjamite, 1 Ch 8[12]. **4.** Another Benjamite, 1 Ch 8[22] (AV **Heber**). **5.** Head of a priestly family, Neh 12[20]. **6.** Eber is mentioned with Asshur in Nu 24[24]; but the meaning here is quite uncertain. S. R. D.—**H. H. R.**

EBEZ.—A city of Issachar, Jos 19[20] (AV **Abez**). The site is unknown.

EBIASAPH ('father has increased').—See Abiasaph.

EBONY.—Hebrew *hobhnîm* (Ezk 27[15]) is the black heart-wood of the date-plum, *Diospyros ebenum*, imported from S. India and Ceylon. It was extensively imported by Phoenicians, Babylonians, and Egyptians for the manufacture of valuable vessels and of idols. In Am 4[15] for 'great houses' some editors read 'houses of ebony.' E. W. G. M.

EBRON.—A town of Asher, Jos 19[28] (AV **Hebron**), probably the same as **Abdon, 5** (q.v.).

ECBATANA.—The capital of Media (in Old Persian *Haghmatāna*), modern *Hamadân*. The Aramaic form of the name is **Achmetha** (AV, RV in Ezr 6[2]). It is mentioned but once in the canonical books as the place where the archives of the reign of Cyrus were deposited

Ezr 6^{2}), but it stands several times in the Apocrypha (2 Mac 9^{3}, To 3^{7} 6^{5} 7^{1} 14^{13f}, Jth $1^{1f, 14}$).

ECCLESIASTES.—1. Title and Canonicity.—The title has come to us through Jerome from the LXX, in which it was the translation of the Hebrew **Ḳōheleth,** which in form is a feminine singular participle, apparently a title used as a proper name after the order of *Sōphereth* (*Ezr* 2^{55}) and *Pōkhereth* (v.^{57}), but the exact meaning is quite unknown. That which accords best with the character of the book is 'one who assembles wise sayings for the purpose of teaching' (cf 12^{9ff}). The book belongs to the third group in the Hebrew Bible—the *K^{e}thûbhîm* or 'Writings'—which were the latest to receive recognition as canonical Scripture. After long controversy between the Palestinian school of Shammai and the less stringent Babylonian school of Hillel, it was finally accepted by A.D. 100. In Judaism it is read on the third day of the Feast of Booths (Tabernacles).

2. Author and Date.—The book contains the outpourings of the mind of a rich Jew, at the beginning of the 2nd cent. B.C. We may perhaps gather that he was in a high station of life, for otherwise his very unorthodox reflexions could hardly have escaped oblivion. He could provide himself with every luxury (2^{4-10}). But he had private sorrows and disappointments; 7^{26-28} seems to imply that his life had been saddened by a woman who was unworthy of him. He was apparently an old man, because his attempts to find the *summum bonum* of life in pleasure and in wisdom, which could hardly have been abandoned in a few years, were now bygone memories (1^{2}–2^{11}). And he lived in or near Jerusalem, for he was an eye-witness of events which occurred at the 'holy place' (8^{10}). That is all that he reveals about himself. But he paints a lurid picture of the state of his country. The king was 'a child' (10^{16a})—much too young for his responsible position, and his courtiers spent their days in drunken revelry (v.^{16b}); he was capricious in his favouritism (vv.$^{5-7}$), violent in temper (v.^{4}), and despotic ($8^{2a, 4}$). The result was that wickedness usurped the place of justice (3^{16}), and the upper classes crushed the poor with an oppression from which there was no escape (4^{1}); the country groaned under an irresponsible officialism, each official being unable to move a finger in the cause of justice, because he was under the thumb of a higher one, and the highest was a creature of the tyrannous king (5^{7}); and in such a realm of social rottenness espionage was rife (10^{20}). The only passage which distinctly alludes to contemporary history is 4^{13-16}, but no period has been found which suits all the facts. In 8^{10} an historical allusion is improbable, and 9^{13-15} is too vague to afford any indication of date.

In the superscription (1^{1}) *Ḳōheleth* is identified with Solomon, but the literary convention is dropped in 2^{12}. That Solomon could not have been the author of the book is clear from its language. From the time of the book of Kings changes began to appear in the Hebrew language. In Ezra, Nehemiah, and Malachi the changes are more marked, and still more evident in Chronicles, Esther, and Ecclesiastes, the last named, rather clearly, the latest of them all, but somewhat earlier than Jesus ben Sira (*c* 180 B.C.), who alludes to several passages in Ecclesiastes. It may thus be dated *c* 200 B.C. or slightly earlier. The language of the book is peculiar to itself. It is manifestly the work of a North Israelite who wrote in the northern dialect of Hebrew, influenced by the spoken language of his day, which was Aramaic, and by the language of the neighbouring Phoenicians. It is only thus that certain of its usages in grammar, syntax, and vocabulary can be explained.

3. Composition.—It used to be thought that the book is full of pious interpolations, intended to counterbalance the scepticism of the original writer, but the prevailing opinion to-day is that it is the work of a single author with very few interpolations, of which the clearest is 12^{9-14}, which was probably added by a pupil. *Ḳōheleth* lived in an age when there was much intermingling of cultures throughout the Near East, from west to east through the Greeks, and from east to west through the Phoenicians. It was the Phoenician Zeno who brought Stoicism to Greece, and it was the Greek Epicurus who developed a counter-philosophy that swept the world and aroused everywhere the thinking of man on the problem of life, and amongst those stimulated by the clashing currents of thought was the author of Ecclesiastes. Like Jesus ben Sira he was a member of the wisdom school, a professional teacher of wisdom, an honest thinker who bared his soul to the world, with all its perplexities and doubts. He wrote partly in prose and partly in poetry.

4. Ḳoheleth's reflections.—(*a*) *His view of life.*—After the exordium (1^{1}–2^{11}), in which, under the guise of Solomon, he explains that he made every possible attempt to discover the meaning and aim of life, the rest of his writing consists of a miscellaneous series of pictures, illustrating his recurrent thought that 'all is vanity and a striving after wind' (2^{17}), or better translated, 'everything is futile and fret of spirit.' And the conclusion at which he arrives is that man can aim at nothing, can guide himself by nothing. His only course is to fall back on present enjoyment and industry, and to this conclusion he incessantly returns whenever he finds life's mysteries insoluble: 2^{24f} $3^{12f, 22}$ 5^{17-19} 8^{15} 9^{7-10} 11^{1-10} 12^{1-7}.

(*b*) *His religious ideas.*—It is improbable that he read Greek or came into immediate contact with any of the Greek schools of thought, but Greek ideas were in the air, and they undoubtedly helped to mould his thought. His statements regarding chance and destiny seem tinged with Epicureanism, and likewise his idea that the enjoyment of life is man's highest good, and his belief that there is no future life (3^{19ff}). His idea of the cyclic recurrence of natural phenomena (1^{5ff}) is close to Stoicism, and closer still is his statement in 12^{7} that 'the dust returns to the earth as it was, and the spirit returns to God who gave it.' But there is little, if anything, that a thinking Jew of a philosophical turn of mind could not have arrived at independently. *Ḳoheleth* occupies what may be called debatable ground between Semitic and Greek thought. He has lost the vitality of belief in a personal God, which inspired the prophets, and he takes his stand on a somewhat colourless monotheism. He never uses the personal name 'Yahweh,' but always the descriptive title 'Elohim' (four times), 'God,' or 'the Elohim' (sixteen times), 'the Deity' who manifests Himself in the inscrutable and irresistible forces of Nature. At the same time he never commits himself to any definitely pantheistic statements. He has not quite lost his Semitic belief that God is more than Nature, for God's action shows evidence of design ($3^{11, 18, 22}$ 6^{12b} 7^{14} 8^{17} 11^{5}). Moreover, God's work—the course of Nature—appears in the form of an endless cycle. Events and phenomena are brought upon the stage of life and then banished into the past, only to be recalled and banished again (1^{4-11} 3^{15}). And this, for *Ḳōheleth*, paralyses all real effort; for no amount of labour can produce anything new or of real profit—no one can add to, or subtract from, the unswerving chain of facts (1^{15} $3^{1-9, 14a}$ 7^{13}); no one can contend with him who is mightier than he (6^{10}). *Ḳōheleth* gains no relief from the expectation of Messianic peace and perfection, which animated the orthodox Jew of his day. There are left only the shreds of the religious convictions of his fathers, with a species of 'natural religion' which has fatalism and altruism among its ingredients.

5. The value of the book for us lies largely in the light that it sheds on Jewish thinking in its time. Here was a man who dared to delve deep into the riddle of the universe, even though he had to end up with most of his problems unsolved, and for his candour and honesty he has been justly praised. As one of his own pupils says of him in 12^{10}, '*Ḳōheleth* tried to find pleasing words, but honestly to write down the truth,' and his courage in a day not so tolerant as our own must ever be a challenge to all his readers even to-day.

A. H. McN.—**T. J. M.**

ECCLESIASTICUS.—**See APOCRYPHA, 7.**

ECLIPSE.—See SUN.

ECSTASY.—No completely satisfactory psychological definition of the term *ecstasy* has ever been formulated. The common feature of all ecstasies is the increased activity of certain functions of the psyche. Consciousness, will, and sensory perception are often depressed or altogether suspended. The subject experiences a temporary access of extraordinary power or receptivity and may speak or act in a very abnormal manner. Greek literature employs the word in this sense and in several others. Philo, for example, distinguishes four kinds of ecstasy and describes the last as 'what happens to the man who is divinely possessed and inspired' (*Quis rerum divinarum heres*, 258). The human *nous*, withdrawing when the Spirit approaches, does not resume its place until the ecstasy is over. This extreme view has no real Biblical counterpart, despite a multitude of references to phenomena of a more or less ecstatic nature (Nu 11[25], Jg 14[19], 1 S 19[23f], 1 K 19[9ff], 2 K 3[15], Is 21[1-10], Jer 4[19-21], Mk 1[9ff], Ac 9[3ff] 22[17ff]). LXX *ekstasis* and *existēmi* translate a rich Hebrew vocabulary denoting partly the symptoms of fear (occasionally joy) and similar emotions and partly the states themselves. Much of this 'ecstasy' is the immediate result of God's action. NT usage has approximately the same range, with emphasis on amazement at God's wonders. Yet even in passages like Ac 10[9ff] 11[5ff] and—to cite an example of the experience without the name—2 Co 12[2ff] the NT is far removed from Philo's idea of ecstasy. All in all, the Biblical attitude towards 'ecstasy' is wholesomely and soundly critical. See also PROPHECY. W. C. K.

ED.—In the Hebrew (and also in the Greek) text of Jos 22[34] the name given by the two and a half tribes to the altar erected by them on the east bank of the Jordan has dropped out. Our English translators have filled the gap by inserting *Ed* (AV, RV) = *Witness* (RSV) as the name of the altar in question. For this they have the authority of a few MSS.

EDAR, Gn 35[21] (AV).—See EDER, **1.**

EDDIAS, 1 Es 9[26] (AV).—See IZZIAH.

EDDINUS.—One of the 'holy houses' at Josiah's passover (1 Es 1[15]). In the parallel passage 2 Ch 35[15] the corresponding name is **Jeduthun,** which is read also, contrary to MS authority, by AV in 1 Esdras. The text of the latter is probably corrupt.

EDEN.—2 Ch 29[12] 31[15], a Levite, or possibly two. It is not certain that *Eden* is the true form of the name: LXX has *Jodan* in the first, *Odom* in the second passage. When it transliterates Eden elsewhere it is usually in the form *Edem.*

EDEN.—Mentioned in 2 K 19[12], Is 37[12], where the 'people of Eden' are said to have been in **Telassar** (q.v.), and to have been conquered by the Assyrians. Eden was in trade relations with Tyre, Ezk 27[23] (see CANNEH). It is probably to be identified with the *Bît Adini* of the Assyrian inscriptions, situated S. of Haran. See BETH-EDEN.

EDEN, GARDEN OF.—The JE account of creation is a composite narrative consisting of two interwoven strands of different origin. The first has a Palestinian background and represents the scene of Yahweh's creative activities as a waterless steppe where nothing grows and no rain has fallen. The Yahwist has interwoven with this a myth of Mesopotamian origin which represents Yahweh, after forming man out of 'dust' from earth (*'ᵃdhāmāh*), as 'planting' a garden in Eden, in the east (*mikḳedhem*), where He placed the man whom He had formed. Much ingenuity has been expended on the question of the locality of Eden, but recent research has shown that the original source of the Eden myth is to be found in the Sumerian myth of Enki and Ninhursag. In this text (translated in *ANET*, pp. 37–41; explained by Jacobsen in *The Intellectual Adventure of Ancient Man*, pp. 157–160), the Sumerian paradise was located in the land of Dilmun, a land that was probably situated in SW. Persia. In this 'land of the living' there was neither sickness nor death, and the animals did not harm one another. It was watered by fresh water brought up from under the earth. Among other details the myth provides an explanation why Adam's rib was chosen as the material from which Eve was formed. There can be little doubt that this Sumerian myth, taken over by the Semitic invaders of Sumer and Akkad, is the ultimate source of the myth in the form in which it was known to the Yahwist. By him it was purged of its grossness and made the great symbolic picture of man's state before the act of disobedience which broke the relationship between God and man and 'brought death into the world and all our woe.' According to the myth Eden was the source whence the four great rivers of the world flowed, and while two of them, the Tigris and the Euphrates, are mentioned by their Hebrew names, the other two, Gihon and Pishon, cannot be identified, although many untenable suggestions have been put forward. Neither can the 'land of Havilah' be identified. It is clear that we are dealing with mythical cosmography, and not with any real geography. There are a number of references in the OT to the mythical garden, and the detailed description in Ezk 28[11-19] shows that there were other forms of the myth known to the Hebrew writers. In that great lamentation for the king of Tyre the garden is placed in the mountain of the gods and is the abode of 'the anointed cherub,' a semi-divine being, who falls from his high estate by reason of pride, 'thy heart was lifted up.' Other references to the garden occur in Gn 13[10], Is 51[3], Jl 2[3], Rev 2[7]. The word 'Paradise' which is used in the NT is the LXX form of the Hebrew word *pardēs*, a Persian loan-word, meaning an enclosed garden, or park (Neh 2[8], Ca 4[13], Ec 2[5]). The theme of the garden has been much expanded in later apocalyptic literature, and has coloured the description of the heavenly city in Rev 21. S. H. He.

EDEN, HOUSE OF, Am 1[5] (AV, RV).—See BETH-EDEN.

EDER.—**1.** Gn 35[21] 'And Israel journeyed, and spread his tent beyond the tower of Eder' (**AV Edar**). *'Edher* means 'a flock'; and the phrase **Migdal-eder** ('tower of the flock,' cf Mic 4[8]) would have been the appellation given to a tower occupied by shepherds for the protection of their flocks against robbers (cf 2 K 18[8], 2 Ch 26[10]). The tower here mentioned lay between Bethlehem and Hebron (cf vv.[19, 27]). Jerome mentions a Jewish tradition that this Eder was the site of the Temple, but himself prefers to think that it was the spot on which the shepherds received the angels' message. **2.** A town of Judah, in the south, near the Edomite frontier, Jos 15[21]; possibly identical with **Arad, 1** (q.v.). **3.** A Merarite Levite in the days of David, 1 Ch 23[23] 24[30]. **4.** A Benjamite, 1 Ch 8[15] (**AV Ader**).

EDES, 1 Es 9[35] (AV).—See IDDO, **3.**

EDNA.—Wife of Raguel of Ecbatana, and mother of Sarah, who became wife of Tobias (To 7[8] 10[12] 11[1]).

EDOM, EDOMITES.—The Edomites were a tribe or group of tribes residing in early Biblical times in Mount Seir (Gn 32[3], Jg 5[4]), but covering territory on both sides of it. At times their territory seems to have included the whole region from the Dead Sea to the Red Sea and Sinai (1 K 9[26], Jg 5[4]). The original population of this region were the Horites (Hurrians) whom the Edomites dispossessed at some early time in their history (Dt 2[12], Gn 14[6] 36[21f]). Edom or **Esau** was their reputed ancestor. The Israelites were conscious that the Edomites were their near kinsmen and an older nation, hence the tradition that Esau was the firstborn twin brother of Jacob (Gn 25[24f]). The story how Jacob tricked Esau out of his birthright (Gn 27), with the result that enmity arose between the brothers, is an actual reflection of the hostile relations of the Edomites and Israelites, for which the latter were to a considerable degree responsible.

Before the conquest of Canaan, Edom is said to have refused to let Israel pass through his territory. During the monarchy Saul fought the Edomites (1 S 14[47]) and

David conquered Edom and put garrisons in the country (2 S 8[13f]). Solomon exploited the rich copper and iron mines of Edom and built the metal-manufacturing city of Ezion-geber on the Gulf of ʿAqaba as N. Glueck's explorations have revealed (*AASOR*, xv [1935], 22 ff; *BASOR*, 71 [1938], 3–18; 72 [1938], 2–13; 75 [1939], 8–22; 79 [1940], 2–18). Ezion-geber also served as port of departure for Solomon's Ophir expeditions (1 K 9[26], 2 Ch 8[17]). These evidences show how important Edom had become in the economy of Solomon's empire. The country seems to have regained its independence shortly before Solomon's death (1 K 11[14–22]), but Jehoshaphat reconquered it a century later during his reign (cf 1 K 22[47f]), and Edomites helped him in his war with Moab (2 K 3). In the reign of Joram, his successor, the Edomites regained their independence after a bloody revolution (8[20–22]). At the beginning of the 8th cent. B.C. Amaziah reconquered them for a short time. He even captured Sela, their capital, slaughtering a large number of Edomites (2 K 14[7]). However, Edom quickly regained its independence from Judah, and took revenge on his former masters. Amos accuses Edom of pursuing his brother with the sword (Am 1[11f]).

In Assyrian records Edom appears for the first time under Adadnirari III., spelled *Udummu* (*ANET*, p. 281b). King Kaushmalaku of Edom paid tribute to Tiglath-pileser III. (*ANET*, p. 282a) and Aiarammu to Sennacherib (*ANET*, p. 287b), while Esarhaddon summoned to him Qaushgabri, King of Edom (*ANET*, p. 291a), who also paid tribute to Ashurbanipal (*ANET*, p. 294a).

In connexion with the wars of Nebuchadnezzar, which resulted in the destruction of Jerusalem in 586 B.C., many Jews migrated to Edom (Jer 40[11]); but the Edomites rejoiced in the overthrow of the Jews. This deepened the old-time enmity, and called forth bitter denunciations and predictions of vengeance from Israel's prophets (cf Ezk 25[12–14], Ob 1[ff]). A little later the **Nabataeans** overran Edom and pushed the Edomites into southern Judah. This invasion of Nabataeans is probably referred to in Mal 1[4ff], for by 312 B.C. they were in this region and Antigonus and Demetrius came in contact with them (cf Diodorus Siculus, x. 95, 96, 100).

From that time on the Edomites occupied the territory of Judah as far north as Beth-zur, which became the **Idumaea** of the NT period. Here Judas Maccabaeus fought with the Edomites (1 Mac 5[3, 65]), and John Hyrcanus shortly before the end of the 2nd cent. B.C. conquered them, and compelled them to be circumcised and to accept the Jewish religion (cf Jos. *Ant*. XIII. ix. 1 [257], XIV. i. 3 [8], and XV. vii. 9 [254]). This was the end of the Edomites as a nation, but they obtained a kind of revenge on the Jews by furnishing the Herodian dynasty to them. G. A. B.—**S. H. Hn.**

EDOS, 1 Es 9[35] (RV).—See IDDO, **3.**

EDREI.—1. A royal city of Og, king of Bashan (Dt 1[4] 3[10], Jos 12[4] 13[12]), the scene of the battle at which Og was defeated (Nu 21[33], Dt 3[1]); assigned to the eastern division of Manasseh (Jos 13[31]). It seems to be the modern *Derʿâ*, where are several important remains of antiquity, including a great subterranean catacomb. **2.** A town in Naphtali, Jos 19[37]. It was near Kedesh, possibly modern *Tell Khureibeh*.

EDUCATION.—In the importance which they attached to the education of the young, it may fairly be claimed that the Hebrews were *facile princeps* among the nations of antiquity. Indeed, if the ultimate aim of education be the formation of character, the Hebrew ideals and methods will bear comparison with the best even of modern times. In character Hebrew education was predominantly, one might almost say exclusively, religious and ethical. Its fundamental principle may be expressed in the familiar words: 'The fear of the Lord is the beginning of knowledge' (Pr 1[7]). Yet it recognized that conduct was the true test of character; in the words of Simeon, the son of Gamaliel, that 'not learning but doing is the chief thing.'

As to the educational attainments of the Hebrews before the conquest of Canaan, it is useless to speculate. On their settlement in Canaan, however, they were brought into contact with a civilization which for a thousand years or more had been under the influence of Babylonia, and in a less degree of Egypt. The language of Babylonia, with its complicated system of wedge-writing, had for long been a medium of communication not only between the rulers of the petty states of Canaan and the great powers outside its borders. The Canaanites themselves had developed an alphabetic system of writing, and an extensive literature This implies the existence of some provision for instruction in reading and writing. Although in this early period such accomplishments were probably confined to a limited number of high officials and professional scribes, the incident in Gideon's experience, Jg 8[14] (where we must render with RSV 'wrote down'), warns us against unduly restricting the number of those able to read and write in the somewhat later period of the Judges. The more stable political conditions under the monarchy, and in particular the development of the administration and the growth of commerce under Solomon, must undoubtedly have furthered the spread of education among all classes.

Of **schools** and schoolmasters, however, there is no evidence till after the Exile, for the expression 'schools of the prophets' has no Scripture warrant. Only once, indeed, is the word 'school' to be found even in NT (Ac 19[9]), and then only of the lecture-room of a Greek teacher in Ephesus. The explanation of this silence is found in the fact that the Hebrew child received his education in the home, with his parents as his only instructors. Although he grew up ignorant of much that 'every school-boy' knows to-day, he must not on that account be set down as uneducated. He had been instructed, first of all, in the truths of his ancestral religion (see Dt 6[20–25] and elsewhere); and in the ritual of the recurring festivals there were provided for him object-lessons in history and religion (Ex 12[26f] 13[8, 14]). In the traditions of his tribe and nation some of which are still preserved in the older parts of OT—he had a unique storehouse of the highest ideals of faith and conduct, and these after all are the things that matter.

Descending the stream of history, we reach an epoch-making event in the history of education, not less than of religion, among the Jews, in the assembly convened by Ezra and Nehemiah (Neh 8[1ff]), at which the people pledged themselves to accept 'the book of the law of Moses' as the norm of their life in all its relations. Henceforward the Jews were pre-eminently, in Mohammed's phrase, 'the people of the Book.' But if the Jewish community was henceforth to regulate its whole life, not according to the living word of priest and prophet, but according to the requirements of a written law, it was indispensable that provision should be made for the instruction of all classes in this law. To this practical necessity is due the origin of the **synagogue** (q.v.), which, from the Jewish point of view, was essentially a meeting-place for religious instruction, and, indeed, is expressly so named by Philo. In NT also the preacher or expounder in the synagogue is invariably said to 'teach' (Mt 4[23], Mk 1[21], and *passim*), and the education of youth continues to the last to be associated with the synagogue (see below). The situation created by this new zeal for the Law has been admirably described by Wellhausen: 'The Bible became the spelling-book, the community a school. . . . Piety and education were inseparable; whoever could not read was no true Jew. We may say that in this way were created the beginnings of popular education.'

This new educational movement was under the guidance of a body of students and teachers of the Law known as the *Sōpherîm* (literally 'book-men') or **scribes,** of whom Ezra is the typical example (Ezr 7[6]). Alongside these, if not identical with them, as many hold, we find an influential class of religious and moral teachers, known as the Sages or the Wise, whose activity culminates in the century preceding the fall of the Persian empire (430–330 B.C.). The arguments for the identity in all important respects of the early scribes and the sages are given in Hastings' *DB* i, 648; but even if the two classes were originally distinct, there can be no doubt that by the time of Jesus ben Sira, the author of Ecclesiasticus (*c* 180–170 B.C.), himself a scribe and the last of the sages, they had become merged in one.

To appreciate the religious and ethical teaching of the sages, we have only to open the Book of Proverbs. Here life is pictured as a discipline, the Hebrew word for which is found thirty times in this book. 'The whole of life,' it has been said, 'is here considered from the view-point of a paedagogic institution. God educates men, and men educate each other' (O. Holtzmann).

With the coming of the Greeks a new educational force in the shape of **Hellenistic culture** entered Palestine —a force which made itself felt in many directions in the pre-Maccabaean age. From a reference in Josephus (*Ant.* XII. iv. 6 [191]) it may be inferred that schools on the Greek model had been established in Jerusalem itself before 220 B.C. It was somewhere in this period, too, that the preacher could say: 'Of making many books there is no end; and much study is a weariness of the flesh' (Ec 12[12])—reflections which necessarily presuppose a wide-spread interest in intellectual pursuits. The edict of Antiochus Epiphanes at a later date (1 Mac 1[57]) equally implies a considerable circulation of the Torah among the people, with the ability to profit by its study.

Passing now, as this brief sketch requires, to the period of Jewish history that lies between the triumph of the Maccabees and the end of the Jewish State in A.D. 70, we find a tradition—there is no valid reason for rejecting it as untrustworthy—which illustrates the extent to which elementary education, at least, was fostered under the later Maccabaean princes. A famous scribe of the period (*c* 75 B.C.), Simon ben-Shetach, brother of Queen Alexandra, is said to have got a law passed ordaining that 'the children shall attend the elementary school.' This we understand on various grounds to mean, not that these schools were first instituted, but that attendance at them was henceforth to be compulsory. The elementary school, termed 'the house of the Book' (*i.e.* Scripture), in opposition to 'the house of study' or college of the scribes (see below), was always closely associated with the synagogue. In the smaller places, indeed, the same building served for both.

The elementary **teachers**, as we may call them, formed the lowest rank in the powerful guild of the scribes. They are 'the doctors (literally teachers) of the law,' who, in our Lord's day, were to be found in 'every village of Galilee and Judaea' (Lk 5[17] RV), and who figure so frequently in the Gospels. Attendance at the elementary school began at the age of six. Already the boy had learned to repeat the *Shema'* ('Hear, O Israel,' etc., Dt 6[4]), selected proverbs and verses from the Psalms. He now began to learn to read. His only textbooks were the rolls of the sacred Scriptures, especially the roll of the Law, the opening chapters of Leviticus being usually the first to be taken in hand. After the letters were mastered, the teacher copied a verse which the child had already learned by heart, and taught him to identify the individual words. The chief feature of the teaching was learning by rote, and that audibly, for the Jewish teachers were thorough believers in the Latin maxim, *repetitio mater studiorum*. The pupils sat on the floor at the teacher's feet, as did Saul at the feet of Gamaliel (Ac 22[3]).

The subjects taught were 'the three R's'—reading, writing, and arithmetic, the last in a very elementary form. The child's first attempts at writing were probably done, as in the Greek schools of the period, on sherds of pottery; from these he would be promoted to a wax tablet (Lk 1[63] RV), on which he wrote 'with a pointed style or metal instrument, very much as if one wrote on thickly buttered bread with a small stiletto.' Only after considerable progress had been made would he finally reach the dignity of papyrus.

For the mass of young Jews of the male sex, for whom alone public provision was made—the girls being still restricted to the tuition of the home—the teaching of the primary school sufficed. Those, however, who wished to be themselves teachers, or otherwise to devote themselves to the professional study of the Law, passed on to the higher schools or colleges above mentioned. At the beginning of our era the two most important of these colleges were taught by the famous 'doctors of the law,' Hillel and Shammai. It was a grandson of the former, Gamaliel I., who, thirty years later, numbered Saul of Tarsus among his students (Ac 22[3]). In the *Beth hammidrash* (house of study) the exclusive subjects of study were the interpretation of the OT, and the art of applying the regulations of the Torah, by means of certain exegetical canons, to the minutest details of the life of the time. See also SCHOOL.

A. R. S. K.—W. F. S.

EGG.—See FOOD, **7.**

EGLAH ('heifer').—One of the wives of David, and mother of Ithream, 2 S 3[5], 1 Ch 3[3].

EGLAIM.—A town of Moab, Is 15[8]; the site is unknown.

EGLATH-SHELISHIYAH.—A place mentioned in Is 15[5], Jer 48[34]. In both these passages RV and RSV take the word to be a proper name, RV giving in margin the alternative translation '[as] an heifer of three years old,' which is AV in Jer 48[34]. In Is 15[5] AV omits '[as].' It is uncertain whether the word is an appellative or a proper name, although the latter view has commended itself to the majority of modern scholars.

EGLON.—King of Moab, under whose leadership the Ammonites and Amalekites joined with the Moabites in fighting and defeating the Israelites. The latter 'served,' *i.e.* paid tribute to, Eglon for eighteen years. Towards the end of this period Ehud assassinated Eglon, and brought to an end the Moabite ascendancy over Israel (Jg 3[12ff]).

EGLON.—A town near Lachish, mentioned in connexion with the campaign of Joshua, Jos 10[3ff] 12[12]. Its king, Debir, joined the coalition against the Gibeonites (Jos 10[3]), and after the reduction of Lachish Joshua captured and destroyed it (10[34f]). It was later included in the territory of Judah, Jos 15[39]. It is probably to be identified with modern *Tell el-Ḥesī*.

EGYPT.—Modern Egypt lies at the NE. corner of Africa and has an area of about 400,000 square miles. The inhabitable and cultivable part of Egypt, excluding Sinai and the oases to the west of the Nile, only amounts to some 12,000 square miles, and was undoubtedly less in Pharaonic times. Egypt proper has always consisted only of that part of the Nile Valley between the Mediterranean Sea in the north and the 1st Cataract (Assuan) in the south that could be reached by the annual Nile flood and the fertile alluvium it deposited. The name Egypt is derived from the Greek *Aigyptos* from Egyptian *Hutkaptah*, a name of Memphis; the principal ancient names of the land were *To-meri* (Timuris) and *Kemet* 'The Black Land.'

Egypt is composed of two distinct portions: Lower Egypt comprising the broad, fan-shaped Delta and a small part of the valley to the S. of Memphis; and Upper Egypt, the narrow valley proper. In early times Upper Egypt appears to have been subdivided at Assiut, and even earlier the effective southern boundary seems to have been Jebel Silsileh, about 45 miles N. of Assuan. Each of the two main divisions was divided into a varying number of nomes or provinces, the standard numbers being 22 and 20 in Upper and Lower Egypt respectively.

Egypt has been formed by the action of the Nile, which in rainy periods roughly corresponding to the Ice Ages in Europe, gouged out a deep valley, and in the intervening inter-pluvials deposited deep layers of gravels and alluvium on the floor of the valley. The alluvium is about 30 feet in average depth and until very recently was accumulating by about 3 inches a century. The deposition of the alluvium thus began about 8000 B.C. and it was not until this process had continued for several thousand years that the valley floor could have been fit for occupation and exploitation by Man. Apart from the Mediterranean coast, rainfall is very slight—one or two inches per annum at Cairo, and practically nil S. of Cairo. Since the Nile receives no tributaries between Atbara (below the 5th Cataract) and the sea, the whole country is dependent on the river and wells for its water, the principal source being the annual inundation which brought both water and fertility to the soil. Egypt is equally deficient in other natural resources; its timber is useless for building, industrial or artistic purposes; it has no minerals except gold in the eastern desert and copper in Sinai. Its principal resources are the Nile mud, the basis of agriculture and an inexhaustible source of supply of mud-brick, and building stone from the cliffs—excellent limestone from Cairo to a point S. of Luxor, sandstone in the extreme south, and granite and other igneous rocks at the Cataracts.

The racial type of the Egyptians cannot be exactly defined. It is probable that the original population was composed of small groups and tribes attracted to the Nile valley by the gradual desiccation of the Sahara. The Ancient Egyptians were thus basically Hamitic in type, but essentially mixed. In modern Egypt there is a small Arab element in the population, and a rather greater negroid strain, especially in the south, but even the latter was not appreciable in Pharaonic times until after about 1500 B.C.

1. The History of Egypt.—*Chronology.*—The division of Egyptian history into thirty-one dynasties from the time of Menes, the founder of the 1st Dynasty, until the accession of Alexander the Great was the work of Manetho, an Egyptian priest who lived in the time of Ptolemy I. and II., who wrote in Greek a history of Egypt of which only a summary and the framework survive. The division into dynasties has proved to be approximately correct and has been adopted as a convenient tool, but Manetho's dates, especially those of the early dynasties, are less reliable. The Egyptians did not use era dates: in the earliest historical times each year was named after some important event, a system that was quickly succeeded by dating the events of each reign by the biennial cattle census. For the greater part of Egyptian history dating was by the regnal years of each king. By combining the evidence of Manetho, the surviving regnal years, the native king-lists and synchronisms with kings and events in neighbouring lands it is possible to draw up a loose chronological framework to part of which some precision can be given by astronomical data. The Egyptian civil year was of 365 days: it was supposed to commence on the first day of the annual rise of the Nile (19th July, Julian) on which day also occurred the heliacal rising of Sothis (Sirius). The discrepancy of a quarter of a day between the inaccurate civil year and the correct astronomical year produced a cycle of 1456 years, the Sothic Cycle. When native references to the rising of Sothis exist, events can be dated within a margin of error of four years. In this way it is possible to date the beginning of the 12th Dynasty to 1991 B.C. and by dead reckoning to assign the beginning of the 11th Dynasty to approximately 2133 B.C. Before this time there are no known Sothic dates and no absolute precision in dating is possible. Nevertheless, it is unlikely that the 1st Dynasty is to be put much earlier than 3000 B.C. and some modern authorities put it as low as 2850 B.C.

It is now customary to group the dynasties into a number of periods: the Proto-dynastic or Archaic Period (Dyns. 1 and 2, 3000–2780 B.C.); the Old Kingdom (Dyns. 3–6, 2780–2254 B.C.); the First Intermediate Period (Dyns. 8–11, 2254–1991 B.C.); the Middle Kingdom (Dyn. 12, 1991–1778 B.C.; the latter half of Dyn. 11, from 2040 B.C., would properly belong to this period); the Second Intermediate Period (Dyns. 13–17, 1778–1573 B.C.; in part contemporaneous and including the Hyksos 15th and 16th dynasties, approximately 1674–1567 B.C.); the New Kingdom (Dyns. 18–20, 1573–1085 B.C.); the Late Period (Dyns. 21–31, 1085–332 B.C., including the 25th (Ethiopian) Dynasty, 751–664 B.C., and the 26th (Saïte) Dynasty, 664–525 B.C.). Before the 1st Dynasty is the Predynastic Period, a long prehistoric period before the introduction of writing, for which no calendar dates can be presented, but it is highly unlikely that any predynastic cultures in the Nile Valley proper are to be dated much earlier than about 4500 B.C.

Historical Outline.—In Upper Egypt three *Predynastic* cultures have been found, *i.e.* people living on the valley floor or at its edges and subsequent to the prehistoric peoples of the Old Stone Age whose artefacts have been found on the river terraces. These three cultures are generally called Badarian, the earliest, Naqada I. (Amratian), and Naqada II. (Gerzean). They lived in settlements or villages, which in Naqada II. at the latest at times were genuine walled towns with mud-brick houses. Their dead were buried in cemeteries separate from the settlements. All had some knowledge of copper and practised agriculture. They made excellent hand-made pottery, some of which had painted decoration which in Naqada I. shows the influence of early Iran, and in Naqada II. that of Sumer. They clearly had a belief in some form of after-life, and their principal deity may have been the mother-goddess. These cultures are found in Upper Egypt only (and Naqada II. in Lower Nubia also). In the Fayum, at Merimde on the western edge of the Delta, and at El Omari slightly to the S. of Cairo, other predynastic sites have been found: these are entirely different from the Upper Egyptian series, they are much more primitive and do not know copper.

At the end of predynastic times a new, but not necessarily numerous, racial element entered Egypt, bringing with it influences from Sumer, notably the cylinder seal, the idea of writing, and certain architectural and artistic forms and techniques: these newcomers, however, were not Sumerians. Almost simultaneously the predynastic Upper Egyptian kingdom under Menes defeated Lower Egypt and thus united Egypt and founded the 1st Dynasty. Little detail is known of the political history of *Proto-dynastic* Egypt but it was clearly a time of very rapid development in the arts of civilization and most of the permanent features of Egyptian culture soon show themselves. Writing and written records develop slowly, the 365-day civil calendar was introduced, metal was exploited on a larger scale, magnificent stone vessels were produced, the first experiments were made in the use of stone for building, the royal tombs of the 1st Dynasty at Sakkara show a superb and exciting architecture, trading or exploring parties reached at least as far south as the 2nd Cataract, and timber was imported from Syria.

With the 3rd Dynasty we begin the *Old Kingdom.* The change is epitomized by the Step Pyramid at Sakkara, the tomb of Zoser first king of the 3rd Dynasty, and the first monumental building to be made of stone. There was rapid cultural and economic progress and a peak of power and prosperity is reached in the 4th Dynasty with its colossal pyramids, superb statuary and its very highly centralized and materialistic organization. The 5th Dynasty is marked by the triumph of the solar cult of Re of Heliopolis, but by a decline in the size and quality of pyramids: at the end of the dynasty first appear the Pyramid Texts. The 6th Dynasty saw the first systematic attempts to explore and trade in Africa, at least as far as the 3rd Cataract, but progressively declined as the power and position of the king deteriorated, as decentralization increased the powers of the monarchs and as economic distress provoked eventually some form of social upheaval; all these factors, combined with infiltration of Asiatics into the Delta, led to the complete collapse of the regime.

The story of the *First Intermediate Period* is very largely that of the struggle between the princes of Herakleopolis (Dyns. 9–10) with the princes of Thebes who ultimately formed the 11th Dynasty. The Delta was under Asiatic control. After a protracted civil war, the Thebans triumphed and Egypt was once more united (2040 B.C.). In spite of war and artistic decline, there was a high level of material prosperity and some of the most remarkable of all Egyptian literary works were written. Osiris finally triumphed as god of the dead and heaven, in a sense, was democratized.

The 11th Dynasty ended in civil war and confusion. The new ruling family was composed of remarkable and energetic kings who ruled for 200 years and raised Egypt to her second period of greatness, *the Middle Kingdom*. Nubia was conquered as far as the 2nd Cataract but the 12th Dynasty is essentially a peaceful era. Only one military expedition in Syria-Palestine is known, but Egyptian political and economic influence was paramount. Internally there was energetic exploitation of natural resources, vast and imaginative irrigation schemes were initiated towards the end of the dynasty, and the power of the provincial nobles was broken. This is the classical period of Egyptian language and literature; a very high standard was achieved in jewellery, royal statuary, and relief.

The *Second Intermediate Period* is very largely the story of the gradual decline from the prosperity of the Middle Kingdom, the obtaining of power by Semitic intruders known collectively as the Hyksos or Shepherd Kings, and Egyptian attempts to regain their independence. After the 12th Dynasty, the country split into two kingdoms, one in the Delta (Dyn. 14) of which little is known, and one over all Upper Egypt (Dyn. 13) which maintained its independence and a large measure of prosperity for about 100 years. The Hyksos infiltrated into the Delta as small groups of Semites. By 1720 they had occupied Avaris (the later Tanis) which became their capital, and by 1674, when their main (15th) dynasty was founded, they controlled all Egypt and Nubia. This wide domain was not long maintained; Nubia became independent, and the princes of Thebes (Dyn. 17) waged a long and eventually successful war of liberation. Several important innovations, including the horse, chariot, and composite bow, were introduced into Egypt in the later stages of the Hyksos Period.

The first years of Ahmose I., first king of the 18th Dynasty and founder of the *New Kingdom*, were occupied by the final stages of the expulsion of the Hyksos. After a brief interval to reorganize and regain control over Nubia, Egypt set out on a policy of expansion in Asia. This policy, after the peaceful interlude of the reign of Queen Hatshepsut, reached its peak in the seventeen successive Asiatic campaigns of Tuthmosis III. as a result of which Egyptian control extended from the Euphrates in the north to beyond the 4th Cataract in the south. But the political situation in Asia was changing; the growing power of Assyria and the Hittites forced Egypt and Mitanni to reverse their traditional policies and conclude an alliance. At this critical moment Egypt was ruled by supine kings and was disrupted by the attempts of Akhenaten to introduce a form of monotheism, the worship of the Aten or Sun's Disk. Ceaseless pressure and intrigues by the Hittites in Syria and infiltration by the *Ḫabiru* or *ʿAperu* from the east into Palestine eventually undermined the whole Egyptian position in Syria-Palestine with no noticeable Egyptian reaction. Akhenaten's religious reform failed; after his death the country reverted to the old ways, and the prime concern of the last king of the dynasty, Haremhab, was the restoration of internal law and order.

The new ruling family that formed the 19th Dynasty originated in the Delta, and it was to the eastern Delta that eventually they transferred their capital. A determined attempt was made to reassert Egyptian supremacy in Asia, but the drawn battle of Kadesh (1286 B.C.) between Ramesses II. and the Hittites led to a stalemate, and in 1270 B.C. a treaty of alliance was concluded. The Hittite alliance was dictated by the rise of Assyrian power and the growing menace of the Peoples of the Sea who, in the reign of Merenptah, made their first attack on Egypt, only repulsed after it had almost reached Memphis.

The 19th Dynasty collapsed after a brief period of weakness and confusion and Ramesses III. of the 20th Dynasty was almost immediately confronted with the necessity to deal with the final attacks of the Sea Peoples, who by now had destroyed the Hittite Empire. The Sea Peoples were eventually defeated after six years' struggle, but Egypt had exhausted herself in the process and the remainder of the dynasty is a sorry tale of increasing economic distress, weak kings, and growing priestly power and intrigues. Already a few years before the death of Ramesses XI., the 21st Dynasty was ruling independently in the Delta with capital at Tanis and eventually ruled over the whole land. The 21st Dynasty in turn was overthrown by the descendants of Libyan mercenaries who had been settled in the region of Herakleopolis and had acquired great power and authority. The outstanding figure of the 22nd Dynasty was its first king, Sheshonk I. (Shishak) who conducted a successful campaign in Palestine, but the latter years of the dynasty were times of civil war and the 22nd, 23rd, and 24th Dynasties were in part contemporary.

Egypt thus fell an easy prey to the Ethiopian king, Piankhi, who by 730 B.C had control of the Thebaid. At first the Ethiopians seem to have thought in terms of a protectorate rather than of direct rule but the intrigues and ambitions of local princes forced their hand, and Piankhi and his successor, Shabaka, were eventually forced to occupy and rule the whole land. The foreign policy of the 25th Dynasty was dominated by the threat from Assyria: the aim was clearly to establish some sort of buffer on the eastern frontier, but the kings were curiously parochial with little understanding of the international situation and all too often were in their Sudanese capital of Napata when most urgently needed in Egypt. The most active was Taharka (Tirhakah), but he was outmanoeuvred and defeated by Esarhaddon and forced to flee. When the Assyrians withdrew, Taharka returned, but was again surprised and defeated by Ashurbanipal (669 B.C.). Taharka's successor, Tanutamon, regained possession of Egypt but foolishly returned to Napata and was there when the final Assyrian attack developed, culminating in the sack of Thebes (664 B.C.).

The Assyrians left the control of Egypt in the hands of a group of princes of whom the leader, Psammetichus, gradually made himself independent of Assyria and founded the 26th Dynasty under whom Egypt for 140 years enjoyed a final period of relative power and prosperity. The power of the dynasty rested primarily on a picked body of Greek mercenaries, the encouragement of Greek traders, and the building of a powerful navy and mercantile marine. Internally, efforts were made to foster a nationalistic spirit by a conscious archaism, an interest in archaeology, and a deliberate emphasis on those things, such as animal worship, which were peculiarly Egyptian. The apparent inconsistency of the foreign policy of the dynasty, as reflected in the Bible narrative, is in reality the outcome of a deliberate policy of maintaining the balance of power and creating a buffer against the strongest power in Asia: it is this that explains why Egypt first supported Assyria against Babylon, and, after the fall of Assyria, Babylon against the Persians; Egyptian naval and economic power were the principal and potent weapons in the application of this policy. The only exception was Apries (Hophra) a young hot-head who, for no obvious reason except perhaps opportunism, challenged Babylonia but failed to prevent Nebuchadnezzar from capturing Jerusalem. Some of the Jews who escaped from the sack of Jerusalem fled to Egypt and formed colonies in various places, the best known being the Jewish military colony at Elephantine (*c* 586–399 B.C.). But Egypt could not withstand Persia indefinitely and in 525 B.C. Cambyses defeated Psammetichus III. and Egypt fell under direct Persian rule (Dyn. 27). At first Persian rule, especially under Darius I., a wise and moderate ruler, was mild, but the excessive harshness of the later kings provoked constant and unsuccessful native revolts until the successful rebellion of Amyrtaeus in 404 B.C. Thereafter for 63 years Egypt had a precarious and uneasy independence (Dyns. 28–30) until in 341 B.C. the Persians once more conquered the country (Dyn. 31). The second Persian dynasty came to an end with the victory of Alexander the Great at Issus (332 B.C.), when Egypt automatically became part of the Macedonian Empire.

After 332 B.C. the history of Egypt is that of the Hellenistic world. Under the Ptolemies Alexandria became the capital and the intellectual centre of the world. The country on the whole was prosperous, though prone to native revolts. The government and administration were Greek, but the native cults were encouraged as a matter of deliberate policy. Behind the façade of active temple building the old Egypt and the old gods were slowly dying, only the cults of Osiris, Isis, and later the mystery religions having any real life. The defeat of Cleopatra (30 B.C.) brought Egypt under Roman rule and for long she was very prosperous and the granary of the ancient world.

2. Egyptian Religion.—The ancient world was particularly impressed by the piety of the Egyptians, the multiplicity of their gods and their strange forms, and the mystery of their temples and priests: hence there was a tendency to read far more into the religion than really existed. Four points are characteristic: (*a*) conservatism—a belief, however primitive, was rarely completely abandoned, but was maintained no matter how contradictory it might appear when compared with other and later ideas; (*b*) parochialism—an emphasis on local cults; a man's loyalties were more to his local god than to the state god; this in part explains the great number of gods, the similarity of the attributes of many, and the ease with which syntheses and syncretisms were effected; (*c*) mildness—Egyptian religion is singularly lacking in fanaticism or excess of any sort; (*d*) the family—the human side of the god, the family organization of the principal gods in a temple, the domestic nature of the daily cult. There was no general dogma or system, no Sacred Book but plenty of religious books, no theological treatises and hence no heresy hunts. The basis of religion in Egypt was not belief but cult, and particularly the local cult; the essentials were ritual purity, and manual and oral perfection in the celebration of the ritual.

The earliest gods were probably nature gods, animals and birds, who were essentially localized and speedily partially or completely anthropomorphized: they were the natural outcome of primitive man's love, fear or reverence of forces or beings that were useful or good, that were powerful or harmful, or that were beyond his understanding. Also early were certain inanimate objects, whose origin is still uncertain but may have been due to purely local conditions. The cosmic gods, the forces of nature such as sun, moon, wind, and storm, were a somewhat later development; they were of a higher order, universal in character but speedily localized, and had either human or animal form. Animal gods always had a special place in Egypt, and in late times, possibly as a reaction to foreign domination, were particularly popular. Sometimes all of a species were worshipped in a locality: sometimes it was only one animal, distinguished by special markings, who was worshipped, tended, mummified, and buried; such for instance were the famous bulls, Apis of Heliopolis, Mnevis of Memphis, Buchis of Armant. Genii or familiar spirits were not infrequent, and from time to time, especially in the New Kingdom, foreign gods were introduced into the pantheon. A few human beings were sometimes deified, but their cult was usually short-lived and local; the two most notable exceptions were Imhotep, architect and chief minister of Zoser (Dyn. 3) who when deified was regarded as son of Ptah, and as a god of wisdom and medicine, later identified with Asklepios; and Amenophis son of Hapu, a famous minister and executive of Amenophis III. (Dyn. 18) who enjoyed a wide reputation as a god of wisdom. The special position of the king as a god is discussed below.

Three theological systems in particular must be mentioned. The first, Heliopolitan, postulated primeval chaos from which, self-engendered, emerged Atum, who produced from himself Shu (air) and Tefnut (moisture). The union of this couple produced Geb (earth) and Nut (sky), from whom were born Osiris, Seth, Isis, and Nephthys. These formed the Ennead. Later a Little Ennead, an artificial creation, was also formed. The Heliopolitan theology dominates Egyptian temple ritual from the 5th Dynasty onwards. The Hermopolitan system was the Ogdoad, or Company of Eight. From chaos emerged the primordial gods, created by the voice of Thoth as four frogs (male) and four snakes (female) who represented Night, Darkness, Mystery, and Eternity. They created at Hermopolis an egg from which appeared the Sun who conquered his enemies, created men, and organized the world. According to the Memphite system, Ptah was the supreme god who made eight other Ptahs who were all embodied in him; thus Atum was his thought, Horus his heart, Thoth his tongue. This system was probably formulated in the first half of the Old Kingdom to enhance the prestige of Memphis, the early dynastic capital, in order to combat the growing power of the solar cult. It is an intellectual system with little popular appeal; creation was an intellectual act, markedly different from the grosser concepts of the other cosmologies. Its essential feature is the Creative Word, an early formulation of the doctrine of the Logos. Although this system had no hold on the popular imagination, there is evidence to suggest that it always had an appeal to a small intellectual *élite* in the temples, and remarkable references to the idea of the creative word are to be found in the Graeco-Roman temples.

Entirely distinct is the Aten cult introduced by Akhenaten towards the end of the 18th Dynasty. It is differentiated above all by its intolerance and exclusiveness, in its abolition of all the old gods and the substitution for them of the worship of a single god, the Aten or Sun's Disk, and more particularly the life-giving power of the sun. It is a mistake to seek to detect foreign, still less Semitic, influences in Atenism: for all its revolutionary nature it is resolutely Egyptian and the seeds of such a cult already existed in Egypt. It is doubtful whether the movement was purely religious; it is far more likely that Akhenaten used religion for political ends—by abolishing the old gods and setting up a single new god with universalistic characteristics and with peculiarly close attachments to the king, he broke the menacing political power of the priesthood, created a new focus of loyalty to the throne by very closely linking the Aten with the person of the king, and simultaneously presented a single god that could be worshipped equally well by Egyptian, Syrian, and Nubian, all the peoples of the Egyptian Empire. The new religion necessitated a new type of temple with courts and sanctuary open to the sky and all rites celebrated in the open air. Unfortunately, Akhenaten failed to supply a teaching or an ethic; he swept away the old gods, he abolished the old funerary beliefs with their moral ideals and sanctions, and created nothing in their place. Atenism is frankly amoral; nobles profess veneration for Aten because it pleased the king who rewarded them. Because Atenism failed to fill the vacuum it had created and did not provide the people with a way of life, it did not take hold on the mass of the people, and failed.

Worship was of two kinds: the ordinary daily cult celebrated within the temples, and the great festivals which were mainly processional both inside and outside the temple. There were three daily services, at dawn, noon, and sunset. The morning service was the most elaborate and was essentially a religious dramatization of events of daily life: the god was awakened by a morning hymn, and then the officiant entered the sanctuary alone, disrobed the god, performed an elaborate toilet, and offered the god a meal. After the service and after the co-templar gods had been similarly awakened, dressed and fed, there was a reversion of the divine offerings within the temple to the royal ancestors, and then a second reversion outside the temple to the priests. There was no congregational worship ; the king alone, or his deputy, entered the sanctuary and performed the ritual by himself. Sacrifice bore no implication of atonement but symbolized the destruction of enemies or evil forces. The great calendar festivals were very numerous, varying in length from a single day to a whole month, and involved processions to other temples, either in the same town or in distant towns ; they were the occasions of great popular rejoicings and participation in free food and drink. Some festivals included dramatic performances somewhat like mystery plays.

The religious system described so far was the state religion, the only aspect that is sufficiently documented in the records. It is probable that this religion left the vast mass of the people largely untouched ; except at the popular festivals, the mass of the people had little direct contact with the state cult, though its ceremonies were conducted for their benefit. Nevertheless, special provision was made at the outer doors of the temple enclosure for private prayer, petition, devotion, and offering. The religion of the mass of the people was probably concentrated on much simpler, elemental, folk-type gods and genii ; thus the patroness of the necropolis workers at Thebes was the great peak that towers at the end of the Valley of the Kings and who was personified and worshipped as Ta-dehenet, 'The Peak.'

The cultus temple of the New Kingdom and later periods was shut off by massive walls which enclosed, in addition to the temple proper, a sacred lake, magazines, store-houses, abattoirs and administrative offices, and quarters for the priests on duty. The temple was in essence the house of the god, and the idea of house or home was always present, though naturally centuries of architectural development obscured this. The temple also to a very real extent was alive : at the dedication ceremony and at the annual renewal on New Year's Day the temple, all its reliefs and all statues underwent the ceremony of Opening the Mouth by virtue of which the temple and all in it was filled with permanent, latent life. The temple itself was a steady progress from the brilliant sunlight of the outer court, through the increasing gloom and mystery of one or more hypostyle halls (lit only by restricted clerestory lighting) to the pitch darkness of the sanctuary. The effect of mystery and darkness was enhanced by a slight but progressive raising of the floor level and a marked lowering of roof levels the nearer one approached the sanctuary.

In the Old Kingdom there was no professional priesthood : the King was in theory the sole officiant and the various cults were celebrated by duly delegated lay nomarchs and officials. Professionalism and the hereditary principle gradually grew through the need to ensure the continuity of the funerary cult. In the Middle Kingdom there was a considerable increase in professionalism, but a fully professional priesthood did not emerge until the New Kingdom. Many priests were pluralists ; all could engage in secular activities and many combined religious duties with the highest secular offices. The temple priesthood was divided into four companies or *phylae* (increased to five in Ptolemaic times) each of which served in rotation for a month at a time. There was a complicated organization : the senior grade was the prophet (Egyptian, 'servant of the god') divided into four classes ; the high priest was usually the first prophet, but in certain priesthoods bore a special title. Other important grades were 'father of the god' and 'lector' whose exceedingly important role was to ensure the literal accuracy of the recitation of the ritual. The ordinary priest was a *wâb*, 'pure one.' Priests could marry, engage in commerce and trade, and indulge in almost any secular activity. Payment was in kind, and appointment and installation in the higher grades at least was the direct act of the king. The strongest emphasis was laid on the ritual purity of the priests : the whole body, including the head, was shaved, circumcision may have been essential, and the normal dress was white linen. No priest of whatever grade could enter the temple or celebrate the ritual without first purifying himself either in the sacred lake or from some other source of purified water. There were also lay-priests, and from the New Kingdom onwards lay fraternities appear to have been linked with certain temples. The temples were great centres of learning and attached to the temple was the 'house of life,' a scriptorium for the copying of religious and learned works, astronomer priests who watched and recorded the hours, doctors, and scribes. Women normally acted as musician-priestesses, but in special circumstances could hold higher ranks. The strictly limited and very important office of 'God's Wife of Amun,' first introduced in the 18th Dynasty, was confined to certain ladies of blood royal and was in essence more political than religious.

The world has always been impressed by the importance laid by the Egyptians on their funerary beliefs and on preparations for death and the after life. This interest was not due to any morbid outlook but is explained by the paradox that the intense preoccupation of the Egyptians with preparations for death was due to their passionate desire to live. It was not physical death that the Egyptian feared, but the ultimate disaster of the 'second death,' *i.e.* the destruction of the last thing in which the soul (*Ba*) of the dead could find shelter, food and drink, for without these he would die. The soul was conceived as being able to leave the corpse and tomb by day, but needed to return at night for shelter and sustenance. The basis of funerary practice was therefore the overriding necessity to make that permanent provision for the soul on which survival depended. For this reason in Egypt the dead were far more afraid of the living than the living were of the dead, for it was the acts or omissions of the living that could most easily cause the second death.

From predynastic times onwards the provision for death was of the utmost importance, and almost at the same time survival and the preservation of the material body became ever more closely linked. The first attempts at mummification are attested at least as early as the 2nd Dynasty, but mummification was not in fairly general use until the Middle Kingdom. Mummification at its best consisted of the removal of the brain and the contents of the abdomen and thorax (the heart was left in the body) ; the corpse was then dehydrated by being surrounded with raw natron. At the end of this process the abdomen was packed with linen or other substances soaked in resin, and the body was wrapped in linen bandages in a long and complicated process ; sometimes amulets were inserted at appropriate points in the bandages. When mummification was complete, the mummy was stood upright on a heap of sand at the entrance to the tomb and the final rites were performed, including the Opening of the Mouth, which restored the vital functions to the body. The tomb of the private individual was normally decorated with scenes of daily life and with offering scenes ; since over these the Opening of the Mouth was probably performed, they were capable of serving the needs of the dead, but special provision was made for the endowment of mortuary priests and for the regular celebration of the funerary cult. The standard period of mummification was 70 days, 40 days for the dehydration, 30 days for bandaging.

In the Old Kingdom funerary practices were linked to the conception of a solar hereafter ; there was even a solar judgment of the dead. The triumph of the worship of Osiris in the First Intermediate Period entailed that thereafter it was the Osirian hereafter that prevailed. No man could hope to attain that hereafter without first passing a trial before Osiris and a court of forty-two assessors. The dead man had to make a Denial of Sin (the misnamed Negative Confession) to the gods, and his heart was weighed in the balances against a feather, the symbol of truth, justice ; if he failed to pass the test, he was devoured by a monster. In theory the judgment implied a very high ethical ideal; in practice the ideal was nullified because of the emphasis on the correct recital of the Denial of Sin, and the increasing use of magical practices which made it easy to escape the consequences of the most sinful life.

3. Social Organization and Institutions.—The Egyptian conception of the state and the cosmos was a static one. The world order was one instituted in all perfection at the moment that the first god-king brought kingship to the earth. It is significant that when Re, the first god-king, came to earth he brought with him his daughter Maat, goddess of truth and justice. This conception of truth and justice, brought to earth at the very foundation of the earth, is central to the whole Egyptian way of life. Gods, king, and men were all equally bound by the law and in theory could not break it. It is this central idea of truth, justice, that goes far to explain the essential mildness and humanity of the Egyptian social order. In Egypt there was no Utopian thought; in so far as the Egyptian thought of a better future, he considered that he lived in a world that had fallen short of a perfection instituted once and for all at the dawn of time, and thus he was constantly looking back over his shoulder, so to speak, hoping to return to a past Golden Age.

At the centre of Egyptian society stood the king, Pharaoh. He was in a very real sense a god, immensely elevated and remote from ordinary men, but a veritable good shepherd, as the texts repeatedly declare, and father of his people. He was the living Horus, the last of the divine kings. But Horus was the son of Osiris, who had avenged his murdered father, and whose claim to his father's throne had been upheld by a divine court of law. Thus every king on dying became Osiris, but in life he was the living Horus who had a legal title to the throne as a result of the verdict of the gods, as the dutiful son of his father, and by virtue of celebrating the cult of the royal ancestors. In theory the king was the source of all activity: he initiated legislation, he was the sole officiant in every temple, he led his people in all activities of peace and war. His health and prosperity automatically entailed the prosperity of Egypt and her people. In practice, of course, the king delegated most of his religious, military, and social duties, but he always remained the genuine mainspring.

In the Old Kingdom society was essentially amateur, any man could be delegated to perform any type of duty in temple, on field of battle, on expeditions to quarries or for trade, or in the administration. In the New Kingdom society was organized on a more rigidly professional basis but still one man could play many parts. The chief minister of the king was the vizier, who apart from daily audience with the king, was responsible for finance, taxation, the administration and execution of justice, and a host of other duties. Under him was a vast organization of governors, administrators, inspectors, and a very large and efficient civil service of scribes. The professional army was the creation of the New Kingdom: it was then organized, in the field, in four divisions, and was composed of chariotry (the *élite*), the infantry, and mercenaries. The Egyptian as a whole was not warlike and the native element was conscript. The mass of the people were simple, unlettered peasants working in the fields, with a smaller proportion engaged in minor industries, quarries, etc. A system of *corvée* entitled the state to call on every man, unless specially exempted by law, to perform any manner of duties in times of national emergency. Slavery as an institution is exceptionally difficult to define and isolate in Egypt: in the Old Kingdom slavery did not exist, every man was free, but economic distress at the end of the Old Kingdom certainly produced a kind of serfdom. In the New Kingdom most slaves were prisoners obtained in the wars of empire, but as power and prosperity declined the number of native slaves increased and so did the institution of voluntary servitude.

The position of women in Egypt was extraordinarily free and high. A woman was free and respected, there was no system of *purdah*, and she was not veiled. She could reign as sovereign, she could buy, sell, and inherit property, and engage in commerce on her own. Her rights in marriage and divorce, which was recognized, were strictly safeguarded; it is not known if there was any special marriage ceremony. Contrary to popular belief, brother-sister marriage, except in the royal family, was relatively rare.

4. Egypt in the Bible.—Egyptian records are conspiciously lacking in direct reference to events and persons familiar in the Bible narratives. Israel is mentioned once only in an inscription of the fifth year of Merenptah (*c* 1219 B.C.) in the words 'Israel is destroyed, its seed does not exist.' The visit of Abraham is probably to be assigned to the first hundred years of the 12th Dynasty (*c* 2000–1900 B.C.). It is known that parties of Semites were in Egypt at this time: a tomb in Middle Egypt depicts the visit of thirty-seven Semites in the reign of Amenemhet II.; a 13th Dynasty papyrus preserves the names of seventy-seven slaves of whom forty-eight are Asiatic, some of the Semitic names being directly related to those of the patriarchal family; the same papyrus throws much light on the prison system.

The story of Joseph, the Sojourn in Egypt and the Exodus raises serious problems of chronology for which no precise solution is yet possible. It is certain that the immediate background of the Biblical narrative is Ramesside Egypt to which all the local colour applies. A conservative appreciation of the facts suggests that the entry of Joseph into Egypt should be placed at an undefined point in the Hykos Period (probably after 1700 B.C.) and that the most probable date of the Exodus is in the latter half of the reign of Ramesses II. (1290–1223 B.C.).

Topographical details in the Bible indicate a familiarity with the eastern Delta; Upper Egypt is virtually unknown except for No (Thebes) and Syene (Elephantine Assuan). Many of the towns mentioned can be identified with reasonable certainty.

Many attempts have been made to identify a variety of linguistic influences and borrowings from Egypt in the OT, and it has been suggested, for reasons difficult to justify, that portions of Psalm 104 are influenced by Akhenaten's Hymn to the Aten. There is no reason to doubt that there may have been borrowings, but in all oriental languages there must have been many common expressions and ways of thinking, and it would be unwise to press them too far. Similarly, some stress has been laid on the supposed influence of Egyptian Messianic literature. It is true that there are 'Messianic' works of a kind, but the works in question were exclusively political in purpose: it is doubtful whether these works had any serious influence on the Hebrews.

The well-known Teaching of Amenemope (*c* Dyn. 20–21) has aroused much interest because of its remarkable resemblance to passages in the Book of Proverbs, especially Pr 22^{17}–24^{22}, and it has been suggested that these passages are a direct, and somewhat imperfect, translation from the Egyptian. The resemblances are striking, but there are very great difficulties in such a theory, principally because of the extreme difficulty of the text of Amenemope, its frequent use of non-Egyptian idioms and ideas, and its employment of an unusually large proportion of Semitic loan-words. A recent study has therefore suggested that the Teaching of Amenemope is itself a translation from an Aramaic original. This raises the problem of a proto-Proverbs and other difficulties, and the only wise course is to conclude that a satisfactory solution has not yet been found. H. W. F.

EGYPT, RIVER (RV, RSV 'brook,' better 'wady') **OF.**—The SW. boundary of Palestine (Nu 34^5, Is 27^{12} etc.; cf 'river [*nāhār*] of Egypt,' Gn 15^{18}, and simply 'the wady,' Ezk 47^{19} 48^{28} [RV, RSV add 'of Egypt']). It is the *Wâdī el-ʿArîsh*, still the boundary of Egypt, in the desert half-way between Pelusium and Gaza. Water is always to be found by digging in the bed of the wady, and after heavy rain the latter is filled with a rushing stream. *El-ʿArîsh*, where the wady reaches the Mediterranean, was an Egyptian frontier post to which malefactors were banished after having their noses cut off; hence its Greek name *Rhinocorura*. See also SHIHOR, SHUR. F. Ll. G.

EGYPTIAN, THE.—An unnamed leader of the 'Assassins' or 'Sicarii' for whom Claudius Lysias took St. Paul (Ac 21[38]). This man is also mentioned by Josephus as a leader defeated by Felix, but not as connected with the 'Assassins' (*Ant.* xx. viii. 6 [169–172]. See also *BJ* II. xiii. 3–6 [254–265], which points more directly toward Zealotism. In his *Ant.*, Josephus was playing down this revolutionary movement, for the benefit of his Graeco-Roman readers). The Egyptian escaped, and Lysias thought that he had secured him in St. Paul's person. The discrepancies between Josephus and St. Luke here make mutual borrowing improbable. See THEUDAS. A. J. M.—**F. C. G.**

EGYPTIAN VERSIONS.—See TEXT OF THE NEW TESTAMENT.

EHI.—See AHIRAM.

EHUD.—**1.** The deliverer of Israel from Eglon, king of Moab, Jg 3[12–30]. The story of how Ehud slew Eglon bears upon it the stamp of genuineness; according to it, Ehud was the bearer of a present from the children of Israel to their conqueror, the king of Moab. On being left alone with the king, Ehud plunges his sword into the body of Eglon, and makes good his escape into the hill-country of Ephraim. Israel is thus delivered from the Moabite supremacy. **2.** Son of Bilhan, a Benjamite, 1 Ch 7[10] 8[6].

EKER.—A Jerahmeelite, 1 Ch 2[27].

EKREBEL.—See ACRABA.

EKRON.—Most northerly of the five important cities of the Philistine plain. It was not conquered by Joshua (Jos 13[3]), but was theoretically a border city of Judah (15[11]) and Dan (19[43]); said, in a passage which is probably an interpolation, to have been smitten by Judah (Jg 1[18]). Hither the captured Ark was brought from Ashdod (1 S 5[10]), and on its restoration, the Philistine lords who had followed it to Beth-shemesh returned to Ekron (1 S 6[16]). Ekron was the border town of a territory that passed in the days of Samuel from the Philistines to Israel (1 S 7[14]), and it was the limit of the pursuit of the Philistines after the slaying of Goliath by David (17[52]). Its local *numen* was Baal-zebub, whose oracle Ahaziah consulted after his accident (2 K 1[2]). Like the other Philistine cities, it is made the subject of denunciation by Jeremiah, Amos, Zephaniah, and the anonymous prophet whose writing occupies Zec 9–11, but it does not appear in the OT as a place of great importance. This city is commonly identified with the modern *ʿÂqir*, a village on the Philistine plain between Gezer and the sea. Scripture references point to a site in this general area, but the identification with *ʿÂqir* is uncertain, depending largely on the coincidence of name, and Albright identifies with *Qaṭra*. No remains of antiquity have been found at *ʿÂqir*.
R. A. S. M.—**A. G. McL.**

EL.—See GOD.

ELA.—**1.** 1 Es 9[27] (AV, RV); see ELAM, **4. 2.** 1 K 4[18], father of Solomon's commissariat officer in Benjamin. See also SHAMMAH, 3.

ELAH.—**1.** A 'duke' of Edom, Gn 36[41], 1 Ch 1[52]. **2.** Son of Baasha, king of Israel. He had nominal possession of the throne two years or fractions of years, 1 K 16[8–14]. He gave himself to drunken dissipation, until Zimri, one of his generals, revolted and killed him. The usual extirpation of the defeated dynasty followed. **3.** Father of Hoshea, 2 K 15[30] 17[1] 18[1, 9]. **4.** Second son of Caleb, 1 Ch 4[15]. **5.** A Benjamite, 1 Ch 9[8].

ELAH ('terebinth').—A valley in the Shephelah, the scene of the battle between David and Goliath, 1 S 17, 21[9]. It is most likely the modern *Wâdī es-Sanṭ*, which, rising in the mountains about Jeba, about 11 miles due SW. of Jerusalem, runs westward, under various names, till it opens on the Maritime Plain at *Tell eṣ-Ṣâfī*. In the middle of the valley is a watercourse which runs in winter only; the bottom is full of small stones such as David might have selected for his sling.

ELAM.—**1.** A son of Shem (Gn 10[22], 1 Ch 1[17]), the eponymous ancestor of the Elamites (see following article). **2.** A Korahite, 1 Ch 26[3]. **3.** A Benjamite, 1 Ch 8[24]. **4.** The eponym of a family of which 1254 returned with Zerubbabel (Ezr 2[7], Neh 7[12], 1 Es 5[12]) and 70 with Ezra (Ezr 8[7], 1 Es 8[33]). It was one of the Bene-Elam that urged Ezra to take action against mixed marriages (Ezr 10[2]), and six of the same family are reported to have put away their foreign wives (Ezr 10[26], 1 Es 9[27] [AV, RV **Ela**]). Elam according to Neh 10[14] 'sealed the covenant.' **5.** In the parallel lists Ezr 2[31], Neh 7[34] 'the other Elam' has also 1254 descendants who return with Zerubbabel, but in 1 Es 5[22] (so RSV; AV, RV **Calamolalus,** q.v.) 725. **6.** A priest who took part in the dedication of the walls, Neh 12[42].

ELAM.—An important country of Western Asia, called *Elamtu* by the Babylonians and *Elymais* by the Greeks (also *Susiana*, from **Shushan** or **Susa** the capital). It corresponds nearly to the modern *Chuzistan*, lying to the east of the lower *Tigris*, but including also the mountains that skirt the plain. The portion south of Susa was known as Anshan (Anzan). In Gn 10[22] (1 Ch 1[17]) Elam is called a son of Shem, from the mistaken idea that the people were of the Semitic race. They belonged to the great family of barbarous or semi-barbarous tribes which occupied the highlands to the east and north of the Semites before the influx of the Aryans.

Historically Elam's most important place in the Bible is found in Gn 14[1ff], where it is mentioned as the suzerain of Babylonia and therewith of the whole western country including Palestine. The period there alluded to was that of Elam's greatest power, a little later than 1800 B.C. For many centuries previous, Elam had upon the whole been subordinate to the ruling power of Babylonia, no matter which of the great cities west of the Tigris happened to be supreme. Not many years later, Hammurabi of Babylon (formerly believed to be alluded to in Gn 14[1] under the name **Amraphel,** q.v.) threw off the yoke of Elam, which henceforth held an inferior place. Wars between the two countries were, however, very common, and Elam frequently had the advantage. The splendidly defensible position of the capital contributed greatly to its independence and recuperative power, and thus Susa became a repository of much valuable spoil secured from the Babylonian cities. This explains how it came about that the Code of Hammurabi was found in the ruins of Susa. A change in relations gradually took place after Assyria began to control Babylonia and thus encroach upon Elam, which was thenceforth, as a rule, in league with the patriotic Babylonians, especially with the Chaldaeans from the south-land. Interesting and tragic is the story of the combined efforts of the Chaldaeans and Elamites to repel the invaders. The last scene of the drama was the capture and sack of Susa (*c* 645 B.C.). The conqueror Ashurbanipal (Biblical Osnappar [q.v.]) completed the subjugation of Elam by deporting many of its inhabitants, among the exiles being a detachment sent to the province of Samaria (Ezr 4[9]). Shortly thereafter, when Assyria itself declined and fell, Elam was occupied by the rising Aryan tribes, the Medes from the north and the Persians from the south. Cyrus the Persian (born about 590 B.C.) was the fourth hereditary prince of Anshan.

Elam has a somewhat prominent place in the prophetic writings, in which Media + Elam = Persian empire. See especially Is 21[2ff], Jer 49[34ff], and cf Is 22[6], Jer 25[25], Ezk 32[24]. Particular interest attached to the part taken by the Elamites in the overthrow of Babylonia. An effect of this participation is perhaps shown in the fact that after the Exile, Elam was a fairly common name among the Jews themselves (Ezr 2[7, 31], Neh 7[12], 1 Ch 8[24] *et al.*). Jews from Elam were present at the first Pentecost, Ac 2[9]. J. F. McC.—**C. J. M. W.**

ELASA (1 Mac 9^{5}).—The scene of the defeat and death of Judas Maccabaeus (AV **Eleasa**). The site may be at the ruin *Il'asa*, near Beth-horon.

ELASAH (' God hath made ').—**1.** One of those who had married a foreign wife, Ezr 10^{22}, 1 Es 9^{22} (AV **Talsas,** RV **Saloas**). **2.** The son of Shaphan, who, along with Gemariah the son of Hilkiah, carried a message from king Zedekiah to Babylon, Jer 29^{3}.

ELATH (called also **Eloth,** Aram. ' trees ') is mentioned together with Ezion-geber as one of the places passed by the Israelites in their wanderings (Dt 2^{8}) and in connexion with Solomon's trading voyages down the Red Sea (1 K 9^{26}, 2 Ch 8^{17}). Hence it is to be located on the N. shore of the Gulf of ʿAqaba. Taken by the Israelites from the Edomites in the time of David, it remained in their hands apparently till the time of Joram, when it seems to have been lost in the Edomite revolt (2 K 8^{20}). It was recovered under Amaziah (2 K 14^{22}), its rebuilding being completed by Uzziah (2 Ch 26^{2}), but was finally lost in the time of Ahaz (2 K 16^{6}, where Aram is a scribal error for Edom and Rezin a gloss). Strategically important in its situation on the caravan route from Arabia to Gaza and Egypt, it flourished in Nabataean and Roman times, and in Byzantine, Arab, and Crusading times it was named *Aela*. These periods of occupation are attested by large deposits of potsherds at a site just over half a mile WNW. of *ʿAqaba*. There is no trace here of earlier occupation, and it is supposed that the Hebrew and Edomite towns were sanded up before the later occupation. W. O. E. O.—**J. Gr.**

EL-BERITH.—See Baal-Berith.

EL-BETHEL.—The name which Jacob is said to have given to the scene of his vision on his way back from Paddan-aram, Gn 35^{7}.

ELCIA, Jth 8^{1} (AV).—See Elkiah.

ELDAAH.—A son of Midian, Gn 25^{4}, 1 Ch 1^{33}.

ELDAD.—One of the seventy elders appointed to assist Moses in the government of the people. On one occasion he and another named **Medad** were not present with Moses and the rest of the elders at the door of the Tabernacle to hear God's message and receive His spirit. But the spirit of the Lord came upon them where they were, and they prophesied in the camp. Joshua regarded this as an irregularity, but Moses declined to interfere (Nu 11$^{26-29}$).

ELDER (in OT).—The rudimentary form of government which prevailed amongst the Hebrews in primitive times grew out of family life. As the father is head of the household, so the chiefs of the principal families ruled the clan and the tribe, their authority being ill-defined, and, like that of an Arab sheikh, depending on the consent of the governed. In our earliest documents the ' elders of Israel ' are the men of position and influence, who represent the community in both religious and civil affairs (Ex 3$^{16, 18}$ 12^{21} 17^{5f} 18^{12} 19^{7}, Nu 11^{16}, Dt 5^{23} 27^{1} 31^{28}) : the ' elders ' of Ex 24^{1} are the ' chief men ' of v.^{11}. Josephus sums up correctly when he makes Moses declare : ' Aristocracy . . . is the best constitution ' (*Ant.* iv. viii. 17 [223]). The system existed in other Semitic races (Nu 22^{4}, Jos 9^{11}, Ezk 27^{9}, Ps 105^{22}). After the settlement in Canaan the ' elders ' still possessed much weight (1 S 4^{3} 8^{4} 15^{30}, 2 S 3^{17} 5^{3} 17^{15f}, 1 K 8^{1}). And now we find ' elders of the city ' the governing body of the town (Ru 4$^{2, 9}$, 1 S 11^{3}, 1 K 21$^{8, 11}$, 2 K 10$^{1, 5}$) ; the little town of Succoth boasted no fewer than seventy-seven (Jg 8^{14}). Deuteronomy brings into prominence their judicial functions (Dt 16^{18} 19^{12} 21^{2ff} 22^{15ff} 25^{7ff}), which were doubtless infringed upon by the position of the king as supreme judge (1 S 8^{20}, 2 S 15^{4}, 1 K 3^{9}, 2 K 15^{5}, Is 11^{5}, Am 2^{3}), but could not be abolished (1 K 20^{7ff}, 2 K 10^{1ff} 23^{1}). During the Exile the ' elders ' are the centre of the people's life (Jer 29^{1}, Ezk 8^{1} 14^{1} 20^{1}, Ezr 5^{9ff} 6^{7ff} ; cf Sus ^{5}), and after the Return they continue active (Ezr 10$^{8, 14}$, Ps 107^{32}, Pr 31^{23}, Jl 1^{14} 2^{16}). It is not improbable that the later Sanhedrin is a development of this institution. J. T.

ELDER (in NT).—See Bishop ; Church Government.

ELEAD.—An Ephraimite, 1 Ch 7^{21}.

ELEADAH.—An Ephraimite, 1 Ch 7^{20}.

ELEALEH.—A town of the Moabite plateau, conquered by Gad and Reuben, and rebuilt by the latter tribe, Nu 32$^{3, 37}$, Is 15^{4} 16^{9}, Jer 48^{34}. It is now the ruined mound of *el-ʿÂl*, about a mile N. of Heshbon.

ELEASA, 1 Mac 9^{5} (AV).—See Elasa.

ELEASAH.—**1.** A Judahite, 1 Ch 2^{39f}. **2.** A descendant of Saul, 1 Ch 8^{37} 9^{43}.

ELEAZAR (' God hath helped ').—**1.** A son of Aaron. It was natural that priestly traditions should have much to say about him. But in earlier writings his name appears only twice, both probably from E : Dt 10^{6} (his succession to the priestly office at Aaron's death), Jos 24^{33} (his death and burial). In P he is the third son of Aaron by Elisheba, his brothers being Nadab, Abihu, and Ithamar (Ex 6^{23}, Nu 3^{2}). With them he was consecrated priest (Ex 28^{1}), and was chief over the Levites (Nu 3^{32}). Nadab and Abihu having died (Lv 10^{1f}), he succeeded Aaron as chief priest (Nu 20$^{25-28}$). He took part in the census in Moab (Nu 26$^{1, 63}$), and afterwards played a prominent part in the history of the settlement under Joshua (Jos 14^{1} 17^{4} 19^{51} 21^{1}). He married a daughter of Putiel, and she bore him Phinehas (Ex 6^{25}). When the Zadokite priests returned from Babylon, they traced their descent to Aaron through Eleazar, ignoring the house of Eli (1 Ch 6$^{3-8}$) ; in some cases, however, the claim was made through Ithamar (1 Ch 24^{5f}). **2.** Son of Abinadab (1 S 7^{1}). **3.** One of David's three heroes (1 Ch 11^{12f}) ; called **Shammah** in 2 S 23^{11}. See Shammah, 3. **4.** A Levite, 1 Ch 23^{21f}). **5.** One of the messengers to Iddo (1 Es 8^{43} AV, RV ; RSV **Eliezar**) ; called **Eliezer** in Ezr 8^{16}. **6.** A priest (Ezr 8^{33}, Neh 12^{42}, 1 Es 8^{63}). **7.** A priest who had married a foreign wife (1 Es 9^{19} AV, RV ; RSV **Eliezar**) ; called **Eliezer** in Ezr 8^{16}. **8.** One who took a non-Israelite wife (Ezr 10^{25}, 1 Es 9^{26}). **9.** A brother of Judas Maccabaeus (1 Mac 2^{5} 6$^{43-46}$, 2 Mac 8^{23}). **10.** A martyr under Antiochus Epiphanes (2 Mac 6$^{18-31}$). **11.** Father of Jason (1 Mac 8^{17}). **12.** Sirach Eleazar (Sir 50^{27} RV ; RSV ' Sirach, son of Eleazar ' ; AV ' Sirach of Jerusalem '). **13.** An ancestor of Jesus (Mt 1^{15}). A. H. McN.—**H. H. R.**

ELEAZURUS, 1 Es 9^{24} (AV).—See Eliashib, **2.**

ELECTION.—The idea of election, as expressive of God's method of accomplishing His purpose for the world in both providence and grace, though (as befits the character of the Bible as peculiarly ' the history of redemption ') especially in grace, goes to the heart of Scripture teaching. The word ' election ' itself occurs but a few times (Ac 9^{15} ' vessel of election,' Ro 9^{11} 11$^{5, 7, 28}$, 1 Th 1^{4}, 2 P 1^{10}) ; ' elect ' in NT much oftener (see below) ; but equivalent words in OT and NT, as ' choose,' ' chosen,' ' foreknow ' (in sense of ' fore-designate '), etc., considerably extend the range of usage. In the OT, as will be seen, the special object of the Divine election is Israel (*e.g.* Dt 4^{37} 7^{7} etc.) ; but within Israel are special elections, as of the tribe of Levi, the house of Aaron, Judah, David and his house, etc. ; while, in a broader sense, the idea, if not the expression, is present wherever individuals are raised up, or separated, for special service (thus of Cyrus, is 44^{28} 45$^{1-6}$). In the NT the term ' elect ' is frequently used, both by Christ and by the Apostles, for those who are heirs of salvation (*e.g.* Mt 24$^{22, 24, 31}$, Lk 18^{7}, Ro 8^{33}, Col 3^{12}, 2 Ti 2^{10}, Tit 1^{1}, 1 P 1^{2}), and the Church, as the new Israel, is described as ' an elect race ' (1 P 2^{9}). Jesus Himself is called, with reference to Is 42^{1}, God's ' chosen ' or ' elect ' One (Mt 12^{18}, Lk 9^{35} RV, 23^{35}) ; and mention is once made of ' elect ' angels (1 Ti 5^{21}). In St. Paul's Epistles the idea has great prominence (Ro 9, Eph 1^{4} etc.). It is now necessary to investigate the implications of this idea more carefully.

Election, etymologically, is **the choice of one, or of some, out of many.** In the usage we are investigating, election is always, and only, of God. It is the method by which in the exercise of His holy freedom, He carries out His purpose ('God's purpose of election,' Ro 9[11]). The **'call'** which brings the election to light in this world, as in the call of Abraham, Israel, believers, is in time, but the call rests on God's prior, eternal determination (Ro 8[28f]). Israel was chosen of God's free love (Dt 7[6ff]); believers are declared to be blessed in Christ, 'even as he chose' them 'in him'—the One in whom is the ground of all salvation—'before the foundation of the world' (Eph 1[4]). It is strongly insisted on, therefore, that the reason of election is not anything in the object itself (Ro 9[11, 16]); the ground of the election of believers is not in their holiness or good works, or even in *fides praevisa*, but solely in God's free grace and mercy (Eph 1[1-4]; holiness as result, not a cause). They are 'destined and appointed' 'according to the purpose of him who accomplishes all things according to the counsel of his will' (Eph 1[11f]); or, as in an earlier verse, 'according to the purpose of his will to the praise of his glorious grace' (v.[6]). It is nevertheless plain that there is no unrighteousness with God (Ro 9[14]); that His loving will embraces the whole world (Jn 3[16], 1 Ti 2[4]); that He can never, in even the slightest degree, act partially or capriciously (Ac 10[34], 2 Ti 2[13]); and that, as salvation in the case of none is compulsory, but is always in accordance with the saved person's own free choice, so none perishes but by his own fault or unbelief. It is obvious that difficult problems arise on this subject which can be solved only by close attention to all Scripture indications and in the continued and growing experience of the believer.

1. In the OT.—Valuable help is afforded, first, by observing how this idea shapes itself, and is developed, in the OT. From the first, then, we see that God's purpose advances by a method of election, but observe also that, while sovereign and free, the election is never an end in itself, but is subordinated as a means to a wider end. It is obvious also that it was only by an election—that is, by beginning with some individual or people, at some time, in some place—that such ends as God had in view in His Kingdom could be realized. Abraham, accordingly, is chosen, and God calls him, and makes His covenant with him, and with his seed; not, however, as a private, personal transaction, but that in him and in his seed all families of the earth should be blessed (Gn 12[2f] etc.). Further elections narrow down this line of promise—Isaac, not Ishmael; Jacob, not Esau (cf Ro 9[7-13])—till Israel is grown, and prepared for the national covenant at Sinai. Israel, again, is chosen from among the families of the earth (Ex 19[3-6], Dt 4[34], Am 3[2]); not, however, for its own sake, but that it may be a means of blessing to the Gentiles. This is the ideal calling of Israel which peculiarly comes out in the prophecies of the Deutero-Isaiah (Is 40–55)—a calling of which the nation as a whole so fatally fell short (Is 42[19f]). So far as these prophecies of the Servant point to Christ—the Elect One in the supreme sense, as both Augustine and Calvin emphasize—His mission also was one of salvation to the world.

Here, however, it will naturally be asked—Is there not, after all, a reason for these and similar elections in the greater congruity of the object with the purpose for which it was designed? If God chose Abraham, was it not because Abraham was the best fitted among existing men for such a vocation? Was Isaac not better fitted than Ishmael, and Jacob than Esau, to be the transmitters of the promise? This leads to a remark which carries us much deeper into the nature of election. We err grievously if we think of God's relation to the objects of His choice as that of a workman to a set of tools provided for him, from which he selects that most suited to his end. It is a shallow view of the Divine election which regards it as simply availing itself of happy varieties of character spontaneously presenting themselves in the course of natural development. Election goes deeper than grace—even into the sphere of nature. It presides, to use a happy phrase of Lange's, at the *making* of its object (Abraham, Moses, David, Paul, etc.), as well as uses it when made. The question is not simply how, a man of the gifts and qualifications of Abraham, or Moses, or Paul, being given, God should use him in the way He did, but rather how a man of this spiritual build, and these gifts and qualifications, came at that precise juncture to be there at all. The answer to that question can be found only in the Divine ordering; election working in the natural sphere prior to its being revealed in the spiritual. God does not simply find His instruments—He creates them: He has had them, in a true sense, in view, and has been preparing them from the foundation of things. Hence St. Paul's saying of himself that he was separated from his mother's womb (Gal 1[15]; cf of Jeremiah, Jer 1[5]; cf of Cyrus, Is 45[5] etc.).

Here comes in another consideration. Israel was the elect nation, but as a nation it miserably failed in its vocation (so sometimes with the outward Church). It would seem, then, as if, on the external side, election had failed of its result; but it did not do so really. This is the next step in the OT development—the realization of an election within the election, of a true and spiritual Israel within the natural, of individual election as distinct from national. This idea is seen shaping itself in the greater prophets in the doctrine of the remnant (cf Is 1[9] 6[13] 8[16-18] etc.); in the idea of a godly kernel in Israel in distinction from the unbelieving mass (involved in prophecies of the Servant); and is laid hold of, and effectively used, by St. Paul in his rebutting of the supposition that the word of God had failed (Ro 9[6] 'for they are not all Israel that are of Israel,' 11[5, 7] etc). This yields us the natural transition to the NT conception.

2. In the NT.—The difference in the NT standpoint in regard to election may perhaps now be thus defined. (1) Whereas the election in the OT is primarily national, and only gradually works round to the idea of an inner, spiritual election, the opposite is the case in the NT—election is there at first personal and individual, and the Church as an elect body is viewed as made up of these individual believers and all others professing faith in Christ (a distinction thus again arising between inward and outward). (2) Whereas the personal aspect of election in the OT is throughout subordinate to the idea of service, in the NT, on the other hand, stress is laid on the personal election to eternal salvation; and the aspect of election as a means to an end beyond itself falls into the background, without, however, being at all intended to be lost sight of. The believer, according to NT teaching, is called to nothing so much as to active service; he is to be a light of the world (Mt 5[13-16]), a worker together with God (1 Co 3[9]), a living epistle, known and read of all men (2 Co 3[2f]); the light has shined in his heart that he should give it forth to others (2 Co 4[6]); he is elected to the end that he may show forth the excellencies of Him who called him (1 P 2[9]), etc. St. Paul is a 'vessel of election' to the definite end that he should bear Christ's name to the Gentiles (Ac 9[15]). Believers are a kind of 'first-fruits' unto God (Ro 16[5], 1 Co 16[15], Ja 1[18], Rev 14[4]); there is a 'fulness' to be brought in (Ro 11[25]).

As carrying us, perhaps, most deeply into the comprehension of the NT doctrine of election, it is lastly to be observed that, apart from the inheritance of ideas from the OT, there is an experiential basis for this doctrine, from which, in the living consciousness of faith, it can never be divorced. In general it is to be remembered how God's providence is everywhere in Scripture represented as extending over all persons and events—nothing escaping His notice, or falling outside of His counsel (not even the great crime of the Crucifixion, Ac 4[28])—and how uniformly everything good and gracious is ascribed to His Spirit as its author (*e.g.* Ac 11[18], Eph 2[8], Ph 2[13], He 13[20f]). It cannot, therefore, be that in so great a matter as a soul's regeneration (see REGENERATION), and the translating of it out of the darkness of sin into the light and blessing of Christ's Kingdom (Ac 26[18], Col 1[12f], 1 P 2[9f]), the change should not be viewed as a supreme triumph of the grace of God in that soul, and should not be referred to an eternal act of God, choosing the individual, and in His love calling him in His own good time into this felicity. Thus also, in the experience of salvation, the soul, conscious of the part of God in bringing it to Himself, and hourly realizing its entire dependence on Him for everything good, will desire to regard it and will regard it; and will feel that in this thought of God's everlasting choice of it lies its true ground of security and comfort (Ro 8[28, 33, 38f]). It is not the soul that has chosen God, but God that has chosen it (cf Jn 15[16]), and all the comforting and assuring promises which Christ gives to those whom He describes as 'given' Him by the Father (Jn 6[37, 39] etc)—as His 'sheep' (Jn 10[3-5] etc)—are humbly appropriated by it for its consolation and encouragement (cf Jn 6[39] 10[27-29] etc).

On the experimental basis Calvinist and Arminian may be trusted to agree, though it leaves the speculative question still unsolved of how precisely God's grace and human freedom work together in the production of this great change. That is a question which meets us wherever God's purpose and man's free will touch and probably will be found to embrace unsolved elements till the end. Start from the Divine side, and the work of salvation is all of grace; start from the human side, there is responsibility and choice. The elect, on any showing, must always be those in whom grace is regarded as effecting its result; the will, on the other hand, must be freely won; but this winning of the will may be viewed as itself the last triumph of grace—God working in us to will and to do of His good pleasure (Ph 2[13], He 13[20f]). From this highest point of view the antinomy disappears; the believer is ready to acknowledge that it is not anything in self, not his willing and running, that has brought him into the Kingdom (Ro 9[16]), but only God's eternal mercy. See, further, PREDESTINATION, REGENERATION, REPROBATE.

J. O.—**N. H. S.**

ELECT LADY.—See JOHN [EPISTLES OF, II.].

EL-ELOHE-ISRAEL.—Upon the piece of land which he had bought at Shechem, Jacob built an altar and called it *El-elohe-Israel*, 'El, the god of Israel,' Gn 33[20] (E). This appears a strange name for an *altar*, and it is just possible that we should emend the text, so as to read with the LXX, 'he called upon the God of Israel.'

EL-ELYON.—See GOD, and MOST HIGH.

ELEMENT.—A component or constituent part of a complex body or a link in a series. 'Elements' can mean the first or fundamental principles. The ancient philosophers inquired after the essential constituent elements, principles, or substances of the physical universe; and many supposed them to consist of earth, air, fire, and water. But in later Greek language also the heavenly bodies, the stars, could be called 'elements.' As used in the NT the word always appears in the plural.

1. In 2 P 3[10, 12] the physical elements of the heavens and the earth are referred to as destined to destruction at the sudden coming of the Day of the Lord, 'because of which the heavens will be kindled and dissolved, and the elements will melt with fire.' In the same sense the Book of Wisdom (7[17]) employs the word, and speaks of 'the structure of the world and the activity of the elements.' But possibly the elements in 2 P 3[10, 12] are the heavenly bodies. It should be observed also that the later Jewish angelology conceived these different elements and all the heavenly bodies as animated by living spirits, so that there were angels of the waters, the winds, the clouds, the hail, the frost, and the various seasons of the year. Thus we read in the NT Apocalypse of the four angels of the four winds, the angel that has power over fire, the angel of the waters, the winds, and an angel standing in the sun. And so every element and every star had its controlling spirit or angel, and this concept of the animism of nature has been widespread among the nations (see ANGEL).

2. The exact meaning of the phrase 'elements of the world' in the four texts of Gal 4[3, 9] and Col 2[8, 20] has been found difficult to determine. (*a*) Not a few interpreters, both ancient and modern, understand the 'elements' mentioned in these passages to refer to the physical elements possessed and presided over by angels or demons. It is argued that the context in both these Epistles favours this opinion, and the express statement that the Galatians 'were in bondage to beings that by nature are no gods' (Gal 4[8]), and the admonition in Colossians against 'philosophy and empty deceit,' and 'worship of angels' (Col 2[8, 18]), show that the Apostle had in mind a current superstitious belief in cosmic spiritual beings, and a worship of them as princes of the powers of the air and world-rulers of darkness. RSV reads 'elemental spirits of the universe.' Such a low and superstitious bondage might well be pronounced both 'weak and beggarly.' (*b*) Other interpreters understand by these 'elements of the world' the ordinances and customs of Jewish legalism. But against this interpretation it must be said that the 'we' of Gal 4[3] includes both Jews and Gentiles. Therefore the 'elements' must be understood as the cosmic powers and especially as the rulers of the stars to which the Jews are subjected as well as the Gentiles. The 'elements of the world' are identical with the 'angels' of Gal 3[19], just as the 'elements of the world' in Col 2[8, 20] are identical with the 'angels' of Col 2[18]. The interesting point is that the Apostle treats alike the Jewish ritualism (especially the observing of 'days and months and seasons,' Gal 4[10]) and the heathen worship.

3. The word is found also with yet another meaning in He 5[12], where the persons addressed are said to need instruction in 'the first principles of God's word.' Here the term 'element' is used in the well-known sense of the first elements of Christian education or instruction as they are enumerated in He 6[1f]. M. S. T.—**R. B.**

ELEMENTAL SPIRITS.—See DEMONS, **2.**

ELEPH, Jos 18[28] (AV, RV).—See HA-ELEPH.

ELEPHANT.—Job 40[15] (AVm); see BEHEMOTH. The use of elephants in warfare is frequently noticed in the Books of Maccabees (*e.g.* 1 Mac 3[34] 6[30] 8[6] 11[56], 2 Mac 11[4] 13[15]). See also IVORY.

ELEPHANTINE PAPYRI.—Aramaic documents of the 5th cent. B.C. found on Elephantine Island opposite Assuan (see SEVENEH). The publication of a first group of these texts by A. H. Sayce and A. E. Cowley in 1906 was an event in OT and Semitic studies. The texts have a great importance for the period of Ezra and Nehemiah. They revealed the existence of a military colony containing many Jews and provided with a temple of the god Yahweh (written **Yhw,** and pronounced Yahu or Yaho). The texts were of a legal nature, but a Berlin Museum expedition under O. Rubensohn, which dug on the island, recovered other kinds of papyri. The publication of these finds by E. Sachau (in final and complete form in 1911) greatly enriched the picture of the life of the colony and above all shed light on the history of the Yahu temple. The prize piece was the letter of the Jews of Elephantine to **Bagoas,** governor of Judaea (**Yehud**), appealing for his aid in obtaining a restoration of the temple of Yahu which had been destroyed in 410 B.C. at the instigation of the priests of Khnum, ram-headed patron divinity of Elephantine. Mention is made of **Sanballat** (q.v.) and the high priest Johanan (Neh 12[22]). Brief but significant is the papyrus instructing the Jewish messenger to convey to Arsames, the satrap of Egypt, the recommendation of Bagoas and a son of Sanballat that the temple should be rebuilt. Other documents of prime importance were: a letter ordering the Jews in the name of Darius II. to celebrate the feast of Unleavened Bread in 419 B.C. and perhaps reflecting the first introduction of that festival among the Jews; a list of temple-contributors, showing that the treasurer not only handled funds for the god Yahu but also for the deities Eshem-bethel and Anathbethel (called Anathyahu in another text); part of an Aramaic version of the Behistun inscription of Darius I.; and portions of an Aramaic book of **Ahikar** (q.v.). After all these texts had been thoroughly discussed by scholars, A. E. Cowley published an invaluable handbook of them in 1923. Recently the Elephantine repertoire has been augmented by the surprising turning up of what must be regarded as the first find of all—a body of texts acquired in 1893 by the American Egyptologist Charles Edwin Wilbour. Indeed, it appears likely that Sayce got on the track of the 'Assuan Papyri' through Wilbour, who had shown him some fragments he had acquired. The new texts were published by the Brooklyn Museum. They are largely the family archive of a man who had some kind of a position at the Yahu temple, Ananiah bar Azariah, and contain some texts of significance for ancient law—notably with respect to slavery. A number of the texts date from the time of Artaxerxes II. The latter is in no way differentiated from Artaxerxes I. and this is of interest in connexion with the dating of Ezra (q.v.). The new papyri show that the Elephantine temple must have been restored, and further that Persian sovereignty was still recognized on the island as late as the end of 402 B.C. Pharaoh Amyrtaeus thus did not gain control until the spring of 401 B.C.—the time of the Anabasis of Cyrus the Younger. A document dated under Amyrtaeus was published by Sachau. One of the Brooklyn texts mentions the end of Amyrtaeus' reign and the accession of Nepherites I. (399–393 B.C.). This Pharaoh probably terminated the existence of the Jewish temple and of the Jewish element in the colony. The Elephantine papyri are supplemented by numerous ostraca, a corpus of which is to be published by A. Dupont-Sommer, and by the Aramaic Leather Documents acquired by L. Borchardt and published in 1954 by G. R. Driver. These are from the archives of Nehti-Hur, major domo of the satrap Arsames.

The Jewish temple, according to the Bagoas letter, existed already when Cambyses invaded Egypt (525 B.C.). The oldest dated papyrus is from 495 B.C. Some have argued that the Jews of Elephantine were sent down from Judah in the 7th cent., or were from Israelite territory. That the kings of Judah sent mercenaries down to Egypt is revealed by Dt 17[16]. But it seems more likely that the Elephantine colony was established under Pharaoh Amasis (569–526 B.C.).

See E. G. Kraeling, *The Brooklyn Museum Aramaic Papyri*, 1953, pp. 3–119. E. G. K.

ELEUTHERUS (1 Mac 11[7] 12[30]).—A river which separated Syria and Phoenicia, the modern *Nahr el-Kebîr* or 'Great River,' which divides the Lebanon in two north of Tripoli.

ELHANAN ('God is gracious').—**1.** The son of **Jair** according to 1 Ch 20[5], of **Jaare-oregim** according to 2 S 21[19]; in the former text he is represented as slaying **Lahmi** the brother of Goliath, in the latter as a Bethlehemite who slew Goliath himself. A comparison of the Hebrew of these two texts is instructive, because they offer one of the clearest and simplest examples of how easy it is for corruptions to creep into the OT text. It is difficult, without using Hebrew letters, to show how this is the case here; but the following points may be noticed. *Oregim* means 'weavers,' a word which occurs in the latter half of the verse in each case, and may easily have got displaced in the 2 Samuel passage; in both the texts the word which should be the equivalent of *Jair* is wrongly written; the words 'the Bethlehemite' (2 S) and 'Lahmi the brother of' (1 Ch) look almost identical when written in Hebrew. The original text, of which each of these two verses is a corruption, probably ran: 'And Elhanan the son of Jair, the Bethlehemite, slew Goliath the Gittite, the staff of whose spear was like a weaver's beam.' But if this is so, how are we to reconcile it with what we read of David's killing Goliath? Judging from what we know of the natural tendency there is to ascribe heroic deeds to great national warriors, realizing the very corrupt state of the Hebrew text of the Books of Samuel, and remembering the conflicting accounts given of David's first introduction to public life (see DAVID, **1**), the probability is that Elhanan slew Goliath and that this heroic deed was in later times ascribed to David.

2. In 2 S 23[24] and 1 Ch 11[26] Elhanan the son of Dodo of Bethlehem is numbered among David's 'mighty men.' Remembering that the word *Jair* above is wrongly written in each case, and that it thus shows signs of corruption, it is quite possible that this Elhanan and the one just referred to are one and the same. W. O. E. O.

ELI, ELI, LAMA SABACHTHANI.—See ELOI, ELOI, etc.

ELI.—A 'judge' and high priest in the important sanctuary at Shiloh, where the Ark was kept. He belonged to the house of Ithamar, the fourth son of Aaron. Excepting in the final scene of his life, every time he comes before us it is in connexion with others who occupy the position of greater interest. Thus in his interviews with Hannah, in the first one it is she in whom the chief interest centres (1 S 1[12ff]); in the second it is the child Samuel (1 S 1[24ff]). The next time he is mentioned it is only as the father of Hophni and Phinehas, the whole passage being occupied with an account of their evil doings (1 S 2[12ff]). Again, in 1 S 2[27ff], Eli is mentioned only as the listener to 'a man of God' who utters his prophecy of evil (a prophecy which is said to be fulfilled by the incident recorded in 1 K 2[27]). And lastly, in his dealings with the boy Samuel, the whole account (1 S 3) is really concerned with Samuel, while Eli plays a quite subsidiary part. All this seems to illustrate the personality of Eli as that of a humble-minded, good man of weak character; his lack of influence over his sons serves to emphasize this estimate. His death takes place when he learns that the Philistines have captured the Ark. W. O. E. O.—**E. R. R.**

ELIAB ('God is father').—**1.** The representative, or 'prince,' of the tribe of Zebulun, who assisted Moses and Aaron in numbering the children of Israel in the wilderness of Sinai, Nu 1[9]. **2.** The father of Dathan and Abiram, Nu 16[1]. **3.** The eldest brother of David, and thought by Samuel to have been destined for kingship in Israel on account of his beauty and stature, 1 S 16[6f]. He is mentioned as being a warrior in the Israelite camp on the occasion of Goliath's challenge to and defiance of the armies of Israel (17[13]); he rebukes his younger brother David for his presumption in mixing himself up with the affairs of the army (17[28]); his attitude towards David, after the victory of the latter over Goliath, is not mentioned. **4.** One of the musicians who were appointed by the Levites, at David's command, to accompany the procession which was formed on the occasion of bringing the Ark from the house of Obed-edom up to Jerusalem, 1 Ch 15[18]. **5.** One of the Gadites who joined David, during his outlaw life, in the hold in the wilderness, 1 Ch 12[9]. **6.** An ancestor of Samuel, 1 Ch 6[27] (see ELIHU, **1**); called **Eliel** (q.v.) in v.[34]. **7.** One of Judith's ancestors, Jth 8[1]. W. O. E. O.

ELIADA ('El knows').—**1.** A son of David, 2 S 5[16]; called **Beeliada** in 1 Ch 14[7]. **2.** Father of Rezon, an 'adversary' of Solomon, 1 K 11[23] (AV **Eliadah**). **3.** A Benjamite, one of Jehoshaphat's commanders, 2 Ch 17[17].

ELIADAH, 1 K 11[23] (AV).—See ELIADA, **2.**

ELIADAS 1 Es 9[28] (AV, RV).—See ELIOENAI, **5.**

ELIADUN, 1 Es 5[58] (AV).—See ILIADUN.

ELIAH.—**1.** 1 Ch 8[27] (AV); see ELIJAH, **2.** **2.** Ezr 10[26] (AV); see ELIJAH, **4.**

ELIAHBA.—One of David's 'Thirty,' 2 S 23[32], 1 Ch 11[33].

ELIAKIM ('God will establish').—**1.** The son of Hilkiah, he who was 'over the household' of king Hezekiah, and one of the three who represented the king during the interview with Sennacherib's emissaries, 2 K 18[18], Is 36[3]. In Is 22[20–24] (v.[25] seems to be out of place) he is contrasted favourably with his predecessor Shebna (who is still in office), and the prophet prophecies that Eliakim shall be a 'father' in the land. **2.** The name of king Josiah's son, who reigned after him; Pharaoh Neco changed his name to **Jehoiakim,** 2 K 23^{34}. **3.** In Neh 12^{41} a priest of this name is mentioned as one among those who assisted at the ceremony of the dedication of the wall. **4.** The son of Abiud (Mt 1^{13}). **5.** The son of Melea (Lk 3^{30}). The last two occur in the genealogies of our Lord. W. O. E. O.

ELIALI, 1 Es 9^{34} (AV, RV).—See ELIALIS.

ELIALIS.—This name, found in 1 Es 9^{34} (AV, RV **Eliali**), is unrepresented in Ezr 10^{38}.

ELIAM (' El is kinsman ').—**1.** Father of Bathsheba, whose first husband was Uriah the Hittite, 2 S 11^{3}; called **Ammiel** in 1 Ch 3^{5}; see AMMIEL, **4. 2.** Son of Ahithophel, of Gilo, and one of David's heroes, 2 S 23^{34}; possibly the same as the preceding.

ELIAONIAS, 1 Es 8^{31} (AV, RV).—See ELIEHOENAI, **2.**

ELIAS.—The AV form of **Elijah** (q.v.) in NT.

ELIASAPH.—**1.** Son of Deuel or Reuel, and prince of Gad at the first census, Nu 1^{14} 2^{14} $7^{42, 47}$ 10^{20}. **2.** Son of Lael, and prince of the Gershonites, Nu 3^{24}.

ELIASHIB.—**1.** The High Priest who was contemporary with Nehemiah. He was son of Jozadak, the contemporary of Zerubbabel (Neh 12^{10}, Ezr 3^{1}), and father of Joiada (Neh 12^{10} 13^{28}). He assisted in the rebuilding of the walls of Jerusalem during Nehemiah's governorship (Neh 3^{1}). He can have had no sympathy with the exclusive policy of Ezra and Nehemiah, for both he himself and members of his family allied themselves with the leading foreign opponents of Nehemiah. See JOIADA, **2,** TOBIAH, and SANBALLAT. **2.** A singer of the time of Ezra, who had married a foreign wife, Ezr 10^{24}, 1 Es 9^{24} (AV **Eleazurus,** RV **Eliasibus**). **3.** An Israelite of the family of Zattu, Ezr 10^{27}, 1 Es 9^{28} (AV **Elisimus,** RV **Eliasimus**); and **4.** another of the family of Bani, Ezr 10^{36}, 1 Es 9^{34} (AV, RV **Enasibus**), who had married foreign wives. **5.** A son of Elioenai, 1 Ch 3^{24}. **6.** The name of a priestly house, 1 Ch 24^{12}. **7.** Father of Jehohanan, to whose chamber in the Temple Ezra resorted, Ezr 10^{6}, 1 Es 9^{1} (AV, RV **Eliasib**); probably identical with **1.**

ELIASIB, 1 Es 9^{1} (AV, RV).—See ELIASHIB, **7.**

ELIASIBUS, 1 Es 9^{24} (RV).—See ELIASHIB, **2.**

ELIASIMUS, 1 Es 9^{28} (RV).—See ELIASHIB, **3.**

ELIASIS (1 Es 9^{34}).—This name corresponds to **Jaasu** of Ezr 10^{37}.

ELIATHAH.—A Hemanite, whose family formed the twentieth division of the Temple service, 1 Ch $25^{4, 27}$.

ELIDAD.—Son of Chislon, and Benjamin's representative for dividing the land, Nu 34^{21}; perhaps the same as **Eldad** (q.v.).

ELIEHOENAI.—**1.** A Korahite, 1 Ch 26^{3} (AV **Elioenai**). **2.** The head of a family of exiles that returned, Ezr 8^{4}, 1 Es 8^{31} (AV, RV **Eliaonias**).

ELIEL.—**1.** A Korahite, 1 Ch 6^{34}; called **Eliab** in v.^{27} and **Elihu** in 1 S 1^{1}. **2, 3, 4.** Mighty men in the service of David, 1 Ch 11^{46f} 12^{11}. **5.** A chief of eastern Manasseh, 1 Ch 5^{24}. **6, 7.** Two Benjamite chiefs, 1 Ch $8^{20, 22}$. **8.** A Levite mentioned in connexion with the removal of the Ark from the house of Obed-edom, 1 Ch $15^{9, 11}$. **9.** A Levite in time of Hezekiah, 2 Ch 31^{13}.

ELIENAI.—A Benjamite, 1 Ch 8^{20}.

ELIEZAR.—**1.** One of the messengers to Iddo, 1 Es 8^{43} (RSV; AV and RV **Eleazar**); called **Eliezer** in Ezr 8^{16}. **2.** A priest who had married a foreign wife, 1 Es 9^{19} (RSV; AV and RV **Eleazar**); called **Eliezer** in Ezr 10^{18}.

ELIEZER (cf ELEAZAR).—**1.** Abraham's chief servant, a Damascene (Gn 15^{2} AV, RVm, RSV. The construction here is difficult, but the words can hardly be rendered as a double proper name as RV, ' Dammesek Eliezer.' Whatever the exact construction, the words, unless there is a corruption in the text, must be intended to suggest that Eliezer was in some way connected with Damascus). This same Eliezer is probably the servant referred to in Gn 24. **2.** A son of Moses by Zipporah; so named to commemorate the deliverance of Moses from Pharaoh, Ex 18^{4}, 1 Ch $23^{15, 17}$. **3.** The son of Becher, a Benjamite, 1 Ch 7^{8}. **4.** The son of Zichri, chief officer of the tribe of Reuben in David's reign, 1 Ch 27^{16}. **5.** The son of Dodavahu of Mareshah, who prophesied the destruction of the fleet of ships which Jehoshaphat built in co-operation with Ahaziah, 2 Ch 20^{37}. **6.** One of the messengers Ezra sent to Casiphia, Ezr 8^{16}; called **Eliezar** (RSV; AV and RV **Eleazar**) in 1 Es 8^{43}. **7.** A priest who had married a foreign wife, Ezr 10^{18}; called **Eliezar** (RSV; AV and RV **Eleazar**) in 1 Es 9^{19}. **8.** A Levite who had married a foreign wife, Ezr 10^{31}; called **Jonah** (AV, RV **Jonas**) in 1 Es 9^{23}. **9.** A son of Harim who had married a foreign wife, Ezr 10^{23}; called **Elionas** in 1 Es 9^{32}. **10.** One of the priests appointed to blow with the trumpets before the Ark of God when David brought it from the house of Obed-edom to Jerusalem, 1 Ch 15^{24}. **11.** A Levite, 1 Ch 26^{25}. **12.** An ancestor of our Lord, Lk 3^{29}.

ELIHOREPH.—One of Solomon's secretaries, 1 K 4^{3}.

ELIHU.—**1.** An ancestor of Samuel, 1 S 1^{1}; called **Eliel** in 1 Ch 6^{34} and **Eliab** in v.^{27}. **2.** A brother of David, 1 Ch 27^{18}; possibly the same as **Eliab, 3. 3.** A Manassite who joined David at Ziklag, 1 Ch 12^{20}. **4.** A Korahite porter, 1 Ch 26^{7}. **5.** See JOB [BOOK OF]. **6.** An ancestor of Judith, Jth 8^{1} (RV; AV **Eliu**; RSV **Elijah**).

ELIJAH.—**1.** Elijah, probably the strangest figure among the prophets of Israel, steps across the threshold of history when Ahab is on the throne (*c* 869–850 B.C.), and is last seen in the reign of Ahaziah (*c* 850–849 B.C.), although posthumous activity is attributed to him in 2 Ch 21^{12-15}. A resident of Gilead (1 K 17^{1}), he appears on the scene unheralded; there is no hint of his birth and parentage. He is called a Tishbite, but the meaning of this term is uncertain (see TISHBITE). A rugged Bedouin-like figure in his haircloth mantle (2 K 1^{8}), Elijah appears as a representative of the nomadic stage of Hebrew civilization, a sort of reincarnation of an earlier and more austere period. His name (' Yahweh is God ') may be regarded as the motto of his life, and expresses the aim of his mission as a prophet.

A religious crisis had been brought on by the marriage of Ahab to Jezebel, a daughter of the Tyrian king Ethbaal, who had been a priest of Melkart, the Tyrian Baal. True to her early training and environment, Jezebel not only persuaded her husband to build a temple of Baal in Samaria (1 K 16^{31ff}), but became a zealous propagandist for her cult, and persecuted the followers of Y″. The very existence of Yahwism was thus threatened.

Such was the situation, when Elijah suddenly appears before Ahab as the champion of Y″. The apostate king and people are to be chastened by a drought (17^{1}), lasting three years (18^{1}). Providence first guides the stern prophet to ' the brook Cherith,' a small stream in a ravine opposite Samaria east of the Jordan ($17^{3, 5}$; not the *Wâdī Qelt* near Jericho as often asserted). Soon the little stream runs dry, and Elijah flees to Zarephath in the territory of Sidon, also suffering from drought (17^{14}; Jos. *Ant.* VIII. xiii. 2 [320]). As the guest of a poor widow, he brings blessings to her household (cf Lk 4^{25}, Ja 5^{17}) by miraculously increasing their meagre supply of food. Soon the widow's son dies, but Elijah brings joy to the bereaved mother by restoring the child to life (17^{23}; cf Lk 7^{11-15}).

During the long drought the hearts of Ahab's subjects have been mellowed, and many are ready to return to their old allegiance. It is time for action, and the prophet returns to confront the king (18^{1-16}). As the two meet, we have the first skirmish of the battle. ' Is it you, you troubler of Israel? ' is the monarch's greeting; but the prophet's reply puts the matter in a truer light: ' I have not troubled Israel; but you have, . . . because you have forsaken . . . the LORD and followed the Baals ' (18^{17f}). At Elijah's suggestion the prophets of Baal and the prophets of Asherah, the goddess consort of Baal, are summoned to Mount Carmel to a trial of power, to see which deity, Baal or Yahweh, will respond to an appeal by his followers to send down fire to consume an unkindled sacrifice. The scene that follows is too well known to bear repetition. Suffice it to say that the prophets of Baal rave, dance, and cut themselves (according to the crudely ecstatic practice of their cult) from morning till late afternoon in an effort to persuade their deity to ignite their sacrifice; but nothing happens. Then Elijah, to make the performance more impressive, or perhaps as a token of the coming rain, orders Y″'s altar to be drenched with water before his invocation. At the prayer of the prophet, fire falls from heaven, devouring the altar along with the sacrificial victim. The people are convinced and shout, 'The LORD, he is God; the LORD, he is God' (18^{39}). Immediately Elijah orders the people to seize the prophets of the foreign deities and slay them by the river Kishon, where Canaanite blood had flowed in the time of the Judges (18^{40}, cf Jg 5^{21}). The guilt of the land has been atoned for, and the long awaited rain arrives. Elijah, in spite of his dignified position, runs before the chariot of Ahab, indicating that he is willing to serve the king as well as lead Yahweh's people (18^{41-46}).

The implacable Jezebel now threatens the life of the prophet who has dared to order the death of her minions (19^{1f}). Yahweh's champion loses heart, and flees to Beer-sheba in the far south. Gaining new strength, he presses on to Horeb, the earlier dwelling-place of his God, deep in the desert. There, after experiencing a great wind, an earthquake, and a fire, he hears Y″'s new message in the form of 'a still small voice' (19^{12}), but the message is not a gentle or quieting one. There remains much to be done in the battle against Baalism. Y″ gives His faithful servant a threefold commission: Hazael is to be anointed king of Syria and Jehu anointed king of Israel, both changes requiring the assassination of the reigning kings, with much additional bloodshed; and Elisha is to be appointed his successor in the prophetic order. Only the last of these three commissions was executed by Elijah; the other two were carried out by Elisha (see ELISHA).

Elijah is also the champion of that social righteousness enjoined by law on his people. Naboth owns a vineyard desired by Ahab. The king offers to purchase the vineyard at a good price, but the owner refuses to sell on good legal grounds (cf Lv 25^{23}, Nu 36^{8}). Ahab sulks, feeling there is nothing more he can do. But Jezebel has other ideas. At her suggestion false witnesses are bribed to swear that Naboth had cursed God and the king. The citizens, thus deceived, stone their fellow-townsman to death. Ahab, on his way to take possession of his ill-gotten estate, meets his old antagonist, who pronounces the judgment of God upon him, including the imminent end of his dynasty (21^{15-24}). These predictions, although delayed for a time on account of the repentance of Ahab, were all fulfilled (21^{27ff} 22^{38}, 2 K $9^{25f,\ 30-37}$ 10^{7-14}).

Ahaziah is a true son of Ahab and Jezebel. Having suffered a serious accident, he sends messengers to Ekron to inquire concerning his recovery of Ekron's god Baal-zebub (more correctly Baal-zebul), a deity closely related to Jezebel's god, Baal-Melkart. Elijah intercepts the emissaries of the king, bidding them return to their master with this word from Y″: 'Is it because there is no god in Israel that you are sending to inquire of Baal-zebub, the god of Ekron? Therefore you shall not come down from the bed to which you have gone, but shall surely die.' Ahaziah recognizes the giver of this message, and sends soldiers to apprehend the prophet, who escapes twice, miraculously. Finally, at God's bidding, the prophet allows himself to be brought before the ailing king and reiterates the message of doom with impunity (2 K 1).

Like all the events of his life, the end of this powerful personality left a dramatic impression in the tradition. Accompanied by his faithful follower Elisha, he passes from Bethel to Jericho, then across the Jordan, after having parted the waters by striking them with his mantle. As the two of them go on their way conversing, there suddenly appears a chariot of fire with horses of fire; and Elijah goes up by a whirlwind to heaven (2^{1-12}).

In the history of prophecy Elijah holds a prominent position. Prophetism had two important duties to perform: (1) to extirpate the worship of heathen deities from Israel, and (2) to raise the religion of Yahweh to a higher ethical level. To the former of these two tasks Elijah addressed himself with zeal, though not with complete success (cf $10^{29,\ 31}$); the latter was left mainly to his successors in the following century. In his battle against Baal, he used inevitably some of the violent methods, the 'assassination technique,' of his enemies. It was a mighty struggle in an uncouth age; no quarter was given by either side. For example, Hazael was to be made king of Syria because he would afflict and punish Israel from without more than Ben-hadad had done; Jehu was chosen to attempt to kill every worshipper of Baal within Israel. Such drastic methods weakened the country without accomplishing their purpose. Hosea repudiated Jehu's acts of slaughter (Hos 1^{4}). All of the later prophets adopted a 'preaching technique,' so to speak: they warned of the judgment of God, even by the sword, but they did not themselves take the sword in hand. Prophecy had thus to be refined before it could give its greatest messages to the world. In the process the kingdom of Israel fell, never to rise again, while true prophecy lives for ever.

Elijah figures largely in later tradition: he is the harbinger of the Day of the Lord (Mal 4^{5}); in the NT he is looked upon as the herald of the Messiah, and the prediction of his coming is fulfilled in the advent of John the Baptist (Mt 11^{7-14}). On the Mount of Transfiguration he appears as the representative of OT prophecy (Mt 17^{3}, Mk 9^{4}, Lk 9^{30}). The prophet whose 'word burned like a torch' (Sir 48^{1}) was a favourite with the later Jews; a host of Rabbinical legends grew up around his name. Elijah was to precede the Messiah, to restore families to purity, to settle controversies, and perform miracles (cf *JE*, article 'Elijah' and Klausner, *Messianic Idea*, 451 ff). Origen (on Mt 27^{9}) mentions an apocryphal work, *The Apocalypse of Elijah*, and maintains that 1 Co 2^{9} is a quotation from it. Elijah is also found in the Qur'an (vi. 85, xxxvii. 123–130), and many legends concerning him are current in Arabic literature.

2. A Benjamite chief, 1 Ch 8^{27} (AV **Eliah**). **3.** A priest who had married a foreign wife, Ezr 10^{21}. **4.** A layman who had married a foreign wife, Ezr 10^{26} (AV **Eliah**), 1 Es 9^{27} (AV, RV **Aedias**). **5.** An ancestor of Judith, Jth 8^{1} (AV **Eliu**, RV **Elihu**). J. A. K.—**W. F. S.**

ELIKA.—One of David's 'Thirty,' 2 S 23^{25}.

ELIM.—One of the stations in the wanderings of the children of Israel, Ex 15^{27}, Nu 33^{9}; apparently the fourth station after the passage of the Red Sea, and the first place where the Israelites met with fresh water. It was also marked by an abundant growth of palm trees (cf Ex 15^{27}, twelve wells and seventy palms). If the traditional site of Mount Sinai be correct, the likeliest place for Elim is the *Wâdī Gharandel*, where there is a good deal of vegetation, especially stunted palms, and a number of water-holes in the sand.

ELIMELECH.—The husband of Naomi and father of Mahlon and Chilion, Ephrathites of Bethlehem in Judah, Ru 1^{2}. He migrated to Moab and there died, 1^{3}. He was a kinsman of Boaz ($2^{1,\ 3}$ 4^{3}), who bought some land in Bethlehem which still belonged to Elimelech and his family, 4^{9}.

ELIOENAI.—**1.** A Simeonite chief, 1 Ch 4^{36}. **2.** A Benjamite, 1 Ch 7^{8}. **3.** A descendant of David who lived after the Exile, 1 Ch 3^{23f}. **4.** A son of Pashhur who had married a foreign wife, Ezr 10^{22}, 1 Es 9^{22} (AV, RV **Elionas**). **5.** A son of Zattu who had committed the same offence, Ezr 10^{27}, 1 Es 9^{28} (AV, RV **Eliadas**). **6.** A priest, Neh 12^{41}. **7.** 1 Ch 26^{3} (AV); see ELIEHOENAI, **1.**

ELIONAS.—**1.** 1 Es 9^{22} (AV, RV); see Elioenai, **4.** **2.** One who had married a foreign wife, 1 Es 9^{32}; called **Eliezer** in Ezr 10^{31}.

ELIPHAL.—One of David's heroes, 1 Ch 11^{35}; perhaps the same as **Eliphelet, 2.**

ELIPHALAT.—**1.** 1 Es 8^{39} (RV); see Eliphelet, **4.** **2.** 1 Es 9^{23} (AV, RV); see Eliphelet, **5.**

ELIPHALET.—**1.** 2 S 5^{16}, 1 Ch 14^{7} (AV); see Eliphelet, **1.** **2.** 1 Es 8^{39} (AV); see Eliphelet, **4.**

ELIPHAZ.—**1.** Eliphaz appears in the Edomite genealogy of Gn 36 (and hence 1 Ch 1^{35f}) as son of Esau by Adah (vv.$^{4, 10}$), and father of Amalek by his Horite concubine Timna (v.^{12}). **2.** See Job [Book of].

ELIPHELEH, 1 Ch $15^{18, 21}$ (AV).—See Eliphelehu.

ELIPHELEHU.—A doorkeeper, 1 Ch $15^{18, 21}$ (AV **Elipheleh**).

ELIPHELET.—**1.** One of David's sons, 2 S 5^{16}, 1 Ch 14^{7} (both AV **Eliphalet**), 1 Ch $3^{6, 8}$; called **Elpelet** in 1 Ch 14^{5} (AV **Elpalet**). The double occurrence of the name in Chronicles ($14^{5, 7}$), as if David had had two sons named Eliphelet, is probably due to a scribal error. **2.** One of David's mighty men, 2 S 23^{34}; perhaps the same as **Eliphal** (q.v.). **3.** A descendant of Jonathan, 1 Ch 8^{39}. **4.** One of the sons of Adonikam who returned from exile, Ezr 8^{13}, 1 Es 8^{39} (AV **Eliphalet,** RV **Eliphalat**). **5.** A son of Hashum who had married a foreign wife, Ezr 10^{33}, 1 Es 9^{33} (AV, RV **Eliphalat**).

H. H. R.

ELISABETH, Lk 1^{5ff} (AV, RV).—See Elizabeth.

ELISEUS.—The AV form of **Elisha** (q.v.) in NT.

ELISHA.—Elisha was a native of Abel-meholah, situated, according to Jerome, in the Jordan valley 10 Roman miles S. of Scythopolis (OT Beth-shean or Beth-shan, modern *Beisān*). The exact location is uncertain, though it was certainly near Jabesh-gilead, E. of the Jordan. Elisha's father was a well-to-do farmer, and thus he represented the newer form of Hebrew society, in contrast to Elijah. On his return from Horeb, Elijah cast his mantle upon the younger man, as he was engaged in extensive ploughing operations on his father's estate. Elisha at once recognized the call from God. Following a hastily devised farewell feast, he left the parental abode (1 K 19^{19ff}), and ever after he was known as the man 'who poured water on the hands of Elijah' (2 K 3^{11}). His devotion to, and his admiration for, his master are apparent from the tradition of the closing scenes of the latter's life. A double portion of Elijah's spirit is the *summum bonum* which he craved (cf the right of the firstborn to a double portion of the patrimony). In order to receive this boon he must be a witness of the translation of the mighty hero of Yahweh; and as Elijah is whirled away in the chariot of fire, his mantle falls upon his disciple, who immediately makes use of it in parting the waters of the Jordan. After Elisha has recrossed the river, he is greeted by 'the sons of the prophets' (members of the prophetic order) as their leader (2 K 2^{9-15}).

It is impossible to reduce the incidents of Elisha's life to any chronological sequence. His ministry covered half a century (roughly 850–800 B.C.), and during this period four monarchs, Jehoram, Jehu, Jehoahaz, and Joash, sat on the throne of Israel (2 K 3^{1ff}, cf 13^{14ff}). The story of Elisha was taken by the author of the Book of Kings from some cycle of prophetic stories of the Northern Kingdom, and probably rearranged according to subject-matter. In our canonical Book of Kings, the larger part of Elisha's activities is placed within the reign of Jehoram (2 K 3^{1ff}, cf 9^{1ff}). He may have reached the zenith of his influence at the end of these few years with the making of a new king and dynasty, but all the recorded events of his life cannot be crowded into this short period.

His name, *Elisha* (= 'God is salvation'), like that of his master, tersely describes his character and expresses his mission. Elisha is a somewhat gentler and more gracious man than Elijah. He loves the haunts of men, and resides in cities like Dothan and Samaria. His miracles are often deeds of mercy. We find him at the headquarters of the prophetic order making his benign presence felt. He sweetens a spring of brackish water at Jericho (2 K 2^{19ff}); he renders a poisonous mess of pottage harmless for the members of the prophetic order (4^{38ff}); he multiplies the oil for the poor widow of a prophet (4^{1ff}); he multiplies a few loaves of bread to feed a great company (4^{42-44}, cf the NT miracle of the loaves and fishes, Mk 6^{34-44} and elsewhere). The sympathy of the prophet goes out in a practical way for the man who has lost his axe (6^{1-7}). One of the most beautiful stories in Scripture is that of the relationship of Elisha to the home of the Shunammite woman. Her hospitality and the prophet's gratitude form a charming picture. In the restoration of her son to life, Elisha performs one of his greatest miracles (4^{8-37} 8^{1-6}). In his treatment of the Syrian (Aramaean) troops which had been despatched to capture him he showed a most generous spirit (6^{11-23}). The familiar incident of the healing of the leprosy of Naaman not only gives an idea of the influence and power of the prophet, but the story is suggestive of the profoundest spiritual truths (5^{1-19}).

The contrast between the spirit of master and disciple must not be overemphasized. Elisha could be as stern as Elijah: on the way to Bethel he shows no mercy to the mocking children (2^{23f}), though this story seems out of harmony with the rest of the tradition; and no touch of pity can be detected in the sentence that falls on Gehazi (5^{27}). The estimate of Ben-Sira is in accord with the OT narrative: 'in all his days he did not tremble before any ruler, and no one brought him into subjection' (Sir 48^{12}). This severer side of the prophet's character appears mostly in his public rather than in his private life. In the campaign against Moab, the allied kings seek his counsel. His greeting to Jehoram of Israel, 'What have I to do with you? Go to the prophets of your father and the prophets of your mother,' indicates that Elisha had not forgotten the past and the conflicts of his master (3^{13}). Later, the relations between the reigning monarch and the prophet seem more cordial, for the man of God reveals the plans of the Syrians to Israel's king (6^{8ff}). This change of attitude on the part of the prophet may be due to the fact that Jehoram attempted to do away with Baal worship (3^{2}); but Elisha had not forgotten the doom pronounced on the house of Ahab by Elijah. While Jehu is commanding the forces besieging Ramoth-gilead, Elisha sends one of the members of the prophetic order to anoint the general as king, and thus he executes the commission which Elijah received from Yahweh at Horeb (1 K 19^{16}, 2 K 9^{1ff}).

Elisha's relations with the Syrians are exceedingly interesting. On one occasion he appears to be as much at home in Damascus as in Samaria. Benhadad, suffering from a severe ailment, hears of the prophet's presence in his capital, and sends Hazael to the man of God to inquire concerning the outcome of the illness. The prophet reads the mind of the messenger, and predicts both the king's recovery and his assassination by Hazael (2 K 8^{7-15}). Nothing is said of a formal anointing, but again Elisha seems to have carried out a commission received by Elijah (1 K $19^{15, 17}$). The severe siege of Samaria (2 K 6^{24}–7^{20}) probably falls in the reign of Jehoahaz. That the prophet is held by the king to be responsible for the plight of the city is an eloquent tribute to his political influence; and Elisha's prediction of deliverance is speedily fulfilled, though later the nation again falls to a low estate (13^{7}). Joash, the next king, weeps over the prophet as he lies on his deathbed: 'My father, my father! The chariots of Israel and its horsemen' (13^{14}). Directing the monarch to perform a symbolic act, the dying man of God gives the king assurance of victory (13^{15ff}). Even after his burial his bones were said to have had the power to give life miraculously (13^{20f}).

An incident in Elisha's life throws light on prophetic

psychology and practice. Before declaring the result of the campaign to the three kings, he asks for a minstrel to play a stringed instrument. The music induces an ecstatic state, in which the prophet gives his oracle (3^{15ff}). It was an age of ecstatic prophecy; but this gentler, more artistic, more urbane method of inducing the ecstatic state was in keeping with the character and personality of Elisha (cf 1 S 10^{5}). We are reminded of the use of this method to alleviate the emotional instability of Saul (1 S 16^{14-23}; see *Interpreter's Bible* iii, 200 f). J. A. K.—**W. F. S.**

ELISHAH.—The eldest 'son' of Javan (Gn 10^{4}, 1 Ch 1^{7}), whence the Tyrians obtained the purple dye (Ezk 27^{7}). The latter favours identification with South Italy and Sicily, or Carthage and N. African coast, both districts famous for the purple dye. Elissa, or Dido, the traditional foundress of Carthage, may indicate Elissa as an early name of Carthage, and Syncellus gives the gloss 'Elissa, whence the Sikeloi.' The Targum on Ezekiel gives 'the provinces of Italy.' The Tell el-Amarna tablets include letters to the king of Egypt from the king of *Alashia*, Egyptian *Alsa*, which has been identified with Cyprus; known to Sargon, king of Assyria, as the land of the Ionians, Javan. There are difficulties in all these identifications, possibly because the name itself denoted different districts at different epochs, and no certainty can yet be attained. Cf J. Simons, *Geographical and Topographical Texts of OT*, 1959, 28 f. C. H. W. J.—**H. H. R.**

ELISHAMA.—**1.** A prince of the tribe of Ephraim at the census in the wilderness, son of Ammihud and grandfather of Joshua, Nu 1^{10} 2^{18}, 1 Ch 7^{26}. **2.** One of David's sons, born in Jerusalem, 2 S 5^{16}, 1 Ch 3^{8} 14^{7}. **3.** In 1 Ch 3^{6} by mistake for **Elishua** of 2 S 5^{15}, 1 Ch 14^{5}. **4.** A descendant of Judah, father of Jekamiah, 1 Ch 2^{41}. **5.** The father of Nethaniah, and grandfather of Ishmael, of the royal family, who killed Gedaliah at the time of the Exile, 2 K 25^{25}, Jer 41^{1}. **6.** A secretary to Jehoiakim, Jer $36^{12, 20f}$. **7.** A priest sent by Jehoshaphat to teach the Law in the cities of Judah, 2 Ch 17^{8}.

ELISHAPHAT.—One of the captains who helped Jehoiada to install king Joash, 2 Ch 23^{1}.

ELISHEBA.—Daughter of Amminadab and wife of Aaron, Ex 6^{23}.

ELISHUA.—A son of David, 2 S 5^{15}, 1 Ch 14^{5}; called **Elishama** in 1 Ch 3^{6}.

ELISIMUS, 1 Es 9^{28} (AV).—See ELIASHIB, **3.**

ELIU, Jth 8^{1} (AV).—See ELIHU, **6.**

ELIUD.—An ancestor of Jesus (Mt 1^{15}).

ELIZABETH.—The wife of Zechariah (AV, RV Zacharias) and mother of John the Baptist, Lk 1^{5ff} (AV, RV **Elisabeth**). The Hebrew form of the name is *Elisheba* (Ex 6^{23}). Elizabeth was of a priestly family, 'the kinswoman' of Mary (Lk 1^{36}), whom she greeted as the mother of the Messiah (v.^{43}).

ELIZAPHAN.—**1.** A chief of the Kohathites, Nu 3^{30}, 1 Ch 15^{8}, 2 Ch 29^{13}; called **Elzaphan** in Ex 6^{22}, Lv 10^{4}. **2.** Zebulun's representative for dividing the land, Nu34^{25}.

ELIZUR ('God is a rock,' cf *Zuriel*).—Prince of Reuben at the first census, Nu 1^{5} 2^{10} $7^{30, 35}$ 10^{18}.

ELKANAH ('God hath acquired').—**1.** A son of Korah, Ex 6^{24}. **2.** An Ephraimite, husband of Peninnah and Hannah (1 S 1^{1f}); by the former he had several children, but Hannah was for many years childless. Her rival mocked her for this as they went up year by year with Elkanah to sacrifice in Shiloh (v.^{6}). Elkanah loved Hannah more than Peninnah, and sought, in vain, to comfort her in her distress (v.^{8}). At length Hannah conceived, and bore a son, Samuel (v.^{20}). Afterwards three sons and two daughters were born to them (see HANNAH, and SAMUEL). **3.** The son of Assir, 1 Ch 6^{23}. **4.** The father of Zophai (Zuph), a descendant of **3,** 1 Ch $6^{26, 35}$. **5.** A Levite who dwelt in a village of the Netophathites, 1 Ch 9^{16}. **6.** One of the mighty men who came to David to Ziklag, 1 Ch 12^{6}. **7.** A doorkeeper for the Ark, 1 Ch 15^{23}. **8.** A high official, 'next to the king,' at the court of Ahaz, 2 Ch 28^{7}.

ELKIAH.—An ancestor of Judith, Jth 8^{1} (AV **Elcia**).

ELKOSHITE.—See NAHUM.

ELLASAR.—Arioch king of Ellasar was allied with Chedorlaomer in the campaign against the kings of the plain, Gn 14^{1}. He has been identified with Rim-sin, king of Larsa, and consequently 'Ellasar' is thought to be for *al-Larsa*, 'the city of Larsa.' Larsa, modern *Senkereh* in Lower Babylonia on the east bank of the Euphrates, was celebrated for its temple and worship of the sun-god Shamash. Böhl proposed an alternative identification of Arioch with the Hurrian name *Arriwuk*, known from the Mari texts (*BiOr* ii, p. 66), in which case Ellasar may be *Ilanzura*. But this is doubtful (cf Noth, *VT* i, 136 ff).

ELM.—In Hos 4^{13} AV has this mistranslation for **terebinth** (q.v.), as in RV, RSV. See also PLANE TREE.

ELMADAM.—An ancestor of Jesus (Lk 3^{28}).

ELNAAM.—The father of two of David's mighty men, 1 Ch 11^{46}.

ELNATHAN.—**1.** The father of Nehushta, the mother of Jehoiachin, 2 K 24^{8}. **2.** The son of Achbor, the chief of those sent to Egypt to fetch Uriah, who had offended Jehoiakim by his prophecy (Jer 26^{22f}); and one of those who had entreated the king not to burn the roll (36^{25}). It is possible that he is identical with **1. 3.** The name occurs no fewer than three times in the list of those sent for by Ezra when he encamped near Ahava (Ezr 8^{16}). In 1 Es 8^{44} there are only two corresponding names (AV **Alnathan** and **Eunatan**; RV **Elnathan** and **Ennatan**).

ELOHIM.—See GOD.

ELOHIST.—See PENTATEUCH.

ELOI, ELOI, LAMA SABACHTHANI.—The words, both in Mk 15^{34} and Mt 27^{46}, are an attempt to transliterate an Aramaic rendering of the opening words of Ps 22. Under the physical distress of crucifixion Jesus began to recite this Psalm of an Israelite in distress, reciting it, however, not in Hebrew, but in His native Galilean Aramaic, *Elâhi, Elâhi, lᵉmā shᵉbaqtani*, 'My God, my God, why hast Thou abandoned me?' The Greek MSS, as might be expected in a case of transliteration, present variant spellings of all three words. The commonly accepted text in Matthew has *Eli*, which is the Hebrew form, but was also widely used in Aramaic. Either word might easily have been mistaken for *Eliyah*, the local name for Elijah. The scribe of Codex Bezae (D), followed by some Latin MSS, writes *Elei, Elei, lama zaphthanei*, which is an attempt to transliterate the original Hebrew of the phrase. A. J.

ELON ('terebinth').—**1.** Of the tribe of Zebulun, one of the minor judges, Jg 12^{11f}. All that is told of him is simply that he judged Israel for ten years, that he died, and was buried in Elon in Zebulun. **2.** A son of Zebulun, Gn 46^{14}, and Nu 26^{26} where the gentilic name **Elonites** occurs. **3.** A Hittite, the father-in-law of Esau, Gn 26^{34} 36^{2}.

ELON.—**1.** A town in the territory of Dan, now unknown, Jos 19^{43}. **2.** A place mentioned in 1 K 4^{9}; perhaps the same as **Aijalon.** EV combine with the following name to give **Elon-beth-hanan. 3.** In Jg 12^{12}, where EV have **Aijalon** as a site in Zebulun, LXX reads **Elon,** probably rightly. Its site is unknown.

ELON-BETH-HANAN.—See preceding article.

ELOTH.—See ELATH.

ELPAAL.—A Benjamite family, 1 Ch $8^{11f, 18}$.

ELPALET, 1 Ch 14^{5} (AV).—See ELPELET.

ELPARAN (Gn 14^{6}).—See PARAN.

ELPELET.—One of David's sons, 1 Ch 14^{5} (AV **Elpalet**); called **Eliphelet** in 2 S 5^{16}.

EL-SHADDAI.—See GOD.

ELTEKE.—See ELTEKEH.

ELTEKEH.—A town in Dan associated with Ekron and Gibbethon (Jos 19[44]), probably the *Altaqū* mentioned by Sennacherib as the locality of his defeat of the Philistines and Egyptians in the time of Hezekiah just before his capture of Ekron. It was a Levitical city, Jos 21[23] (RV, RSV **Elteke**). It is possibly modern *Kh. el-Muqanna'*.

ELTEKON.—A town of Judah, noticed with Maarath and Beth-anoth, Jos 15[59]; possibly modern *Kh. ed-Deir*.

ELTOLAD.—A town in the extreme south of Judah, Jos 15[30]. It was assigned to Simeon, 19[4]. It is called **Tolad** in 1 Ch 4[29]. The site is unknown.

ELUL (Neh 6[15], 1 Mac 14[27]).—See TIME.

ELUZAI.—One of the mighty men who joined David at Ziklag, 1 Ch 12[5].

ELYMAIS.—This name, which represents the OT **Elam**, was given to a district of Persia, lying along the southern spurs of Mt. Zagros, S. of Media and N. of Susiana. In 1 Mac 6[1], according to the common reading, which is adopted by the RSV, Elymais is named as a rich city in Persia. No such city, however, is mentioned elsewhere, except by Josephus, who is simply following 1 Mac. It may be, therefore, that we should correct the text and read with RV, ' in Elymais in Persia there was a city.' The variant readings appear to support this.

ELYMAS.—See BAR-JESUS.

ELZABAD.—**1.** A Gad chief who joined David, 1 Ch 12[12]. **2.** A Korahite doorkeeper, 1 Ch 26[7].

ELZAPHAN.—A chief of the Kohathites, Ex 6[22], Lv 10[4]; called **Elizaphan** in Nu 3[30], 1 Ch 15[8], 2 Ch 29[13].

EMADABUN (1 Es 5[58]).—One of the Levites who superintended the restoration of the Temple. The name does not occur in the parallel Ezr 3[9]: it is probably due to a repetition of the name which follows, *Iliadun*.

EMATHEIS, 1 Es 9[29] (RV).—See EMATHIS.

EMATHIS.—A Jew who had married a foreign wife, 1 Es 9[29] (AV **Amatheis,** RV **Ematheis**); called **Athlai** in Ezr 10[28].

EMBALMING.—This specifically Egyptian (non-Israelitish) method of treating dead bodies is mentioned in Scripture only in the cases of Jacob and Joseph (Gn 50[2f, 26]).

EMBROIDERY AND NEEDLEWORK.—Embroidery is the art of working patterns or figures on textile fabrics with woollen, linen, silk, or gold thread by means of a needle. The process was exactly described by the Romans as painting with a needle (*acu pingere*).

The Hebrew word for embroidery (*riḳmāh*) is rendered by AV in Jg 5[30] and Ps 45[14] by **' needlework,'** for which RV substitutes ' embroidery,' ' broidered work,' and in Ezk 16[10, 13, 18] 26[16] 27[7, 16, 24] by **' broidered** work ' or ' broidered garments,' which RV retains. RSV has ' embroidered work ' or ' embroidered cloth,' save in Ps 45[14], where it has ' many coloured robes.' Similarly in connexion with certain fabrics of the Tabernacle and the high priest's girdle, where a form from the same Hebrew root is used, for ' wrought with needlework ' RV has the more literal rendering ' the work of the **embroiderer** ' (Ex 26[36] 27[16] 28[39] etc. ; RSV ' embroidered with needlework '), whom AV and RSV also introduce in 35[35] 38[23]. (The word *riḳmāh* is used of variegated plumage in Ezk 17[3] and of varicoloured stones in 1 Ch 29[2].)

An entirely different root, *sh-b-ṣ*, is used for weaving in patterns or the woven settings of jewels on clothing. This also is rendered in AV by ' embroider ' (Ex 28[39]), for which RV and RSV have ' weave in **checker work** ' (for which see SPINNING AND WEAVING). So for a ' broidered coat ' (Ex 28[4]) RV and RSV have ' a coat of checker work.'

The art of embroidery was an invention of the Babylonians, from whom it passed, through the medium of the Phrygians, to the Greeks and the other nations of the West. Mummy cloths are still preserved showing that the art was also practised in Egypt. No actual specimens of Babylonian embroidery have survived, but the sculptures of Assyrian palaces, notably a sculptured figure of Ashurnazirpal, show the royal robes ornamented with borders of the most elaborate embroidery. The various designs are discussed, with illustrations, by Perrot and Chipiez, *Hist. of Art in Chaldaea and Assyria*, ii. 363 ff.

If, as is generally believed, the Priest's Code was compiled in Babylonia, we may trace the influence of the latter in the embroideries introduced into the Tabernacle screens and elsewhere (references above). In the passages in question the work of ' the embroiderer ' (*rōḳēm*) is distinguished from, and mentioned after, the work of the ' designer ' (*ḥōshēbh*), who appears to have woven his designs *into* the fabric after the manner of tapestry (see SPINNING AND WEAVING). The materials used by both artists were the same, linen thread dyed 'blue, purple, and scarlet,' and fine gold thread, the preparation of which is minutely described, Ex 39[3].

An illustration in colours of the sails which Tyre imported from Egypt, ' of fine embroidered linen ' (Ezk 27[7]), may be seen in the frontispiece to Wilkinson's *Ancient Egyptians*, vol. ii. A. R. S. K.

EMEK-KEZIZ.—A place mentioned among the towns of Benjamin, apparently near Jericho, Jos 18[21] (AV ' the valley of Keziz '). The site is unknown.

EMERALD.—See JEWELS AND PRECIOUS STONES.

EMERODS.—See MEDICINE.

EMIM.—Primitive inhabitants of Moab (AV ' Emims '), mentioned in Dt 2[10f] and Gn 14[5]; they were of gigantic stature and associated with the Rephaim (q.v.).

EMMANUEL.—See IMMANUEL.

EMMAUS.—The objective of Cleopas and his companion, said to be sixty stadia from Jerusalem (Lk 24[13]). Those who rely on the estimate of distance and considerations of time in the narrative seek it at el-Iqbēbeh, NW. of the city. But the name is a safer guide. The name comes from *Ḥammā*, ' warm well,' and there are none such at the place mentioned. Emmaus is clearly the *Ammaous* of Josephus, called Nicopolis in Eusebius' time and to-day *Amwās*. Here there are several warm-water wells. As it is twenty miles from Jerusalem, rather than seven as suggested by Luke, this causes perplexity for those who would press the details of the story. The *Codex Sinaiticus* reads ' 160 stadia ' instead of sixty. Emmaus was on the road to Jaffa. It was the scene of an engagement between Judas Maccabaeus and Gorgias (1 Mac 3[40, 57] 4[3-27]) and was fortified by Bacchides (1 Mac 9[50]). The supposed other *Ammaous* where Vespasian settled veterans (*BJ* VII. vi. 6 [217]) is probably miswritten from *Ammosa*—the Mozah of Jos 18[26]. E. G. K.

EMMER, 1 Es 9[21] (AV, RV).—See IMMER, **1.**

EMMERUTH (1 Es 5[24] RV).—A corruption of **Immer** in Ezr 2[37]. See AMARIAH, **7,** and IMMER, **1.**

EMPEROR WORSHIP.—The cult of the abstract goddess Roma and eventually of the Roman Emperors, living and dead, which arose spontaneously in western Asia Minor. It was at first a recognition of the order and stability which Roman intervention had brought to a land long accustomed to the greed and rapacity of boundary-jumping petty princes and of corrupt officials ; in time it developed into a definite State religion throughout the Roman Empire.

The earliest definite evidence of what was thus to become a State cult was the erection in Smyrna in 195 B.C. of a temple to *Roma*, in grateful appreciation of Rome's support against the inroads of the Seleucid King Antiochus the Great. The practice of hailing victorious Roman generals, and subsequently even proconsuls, as saviour deities was widespread in the newly constituted province of Asia ; so also was the creation of a new goddess, *Roma*, who personified the might and power of their conquerors and liberators.

EMPEROR WORSHIP

The East had long been accustomed to regard its rulers as divine. In Egypt the Pharaoh was king because he was a god. In Assyria, Babylonia, and Persia the practice of regarding and designating the sovereign a 'son of god' was long established. Alexander the Great, in consequence of his amazing and spectacular conquests, fell heir to this not unnatural practice and zealously cultivated it as an effective means of welding together into some sort of unity the varied and disparate regions which he had overrun and conquered. In Egypt he had been hailed a son of Zeus (or Amon Rē); at Susa he had sat on the throne of the 'king of kings.' Upon his death similar titles were bestowed upon or demanded by his successors. Thus in Egypt, Ptolemy I. was styled 'Saviour and God' (*sōtēr kai theos*) in an inscription (*c* 306 B.C.) found at Halicarnassus, while various of the Seleucids bore similar epithets, of which the one affected by Antiochus IV., *Epiphanēs* (*i.e.* God Manifest), is revealing.

With the triumph of Octavian at Actium (31 B.C.) and the subsequent rise of the Roman Empire, the worship of Rome and her emperors received fresh stimulus. The same reasons which had led to considering Alexander divine were effective for Octavian: after a century of chaos and confusion he had brought peace and security. Surely a divine power or *genius* was in him. Within two years of Actium, temples to *Roma* and to the deceased Julius Caesar had been erected in Ephesus and Nicaea; Roman citizens who resided in those areas were directed by the victor to worship at these shrines. At Pergamum in Asia and at Nicomedia in Bithynia, Augustus permitted temples to be erected for the joint worship of *Roma* and himself. For forty years this temple in Asia Pergamum was the sole seat of what can now be literally styled emperor worship. This proud privilege of the Asian metropolis explains the bitter epithet, 'Satan's seat,' which the author of Rev 2^{13} bestows upon this city. As the years passed other prominent cities of wealth and importance were granted the right to dedicate similar temples and thus make claim to the proud title *Neōkoros*.

In Rome, Augustus and his obedient Senate were rather more cautious. Well did Augustus remember the price which his uncle Julius had paid for his too great popularity. By the people at large the latter had been commonly regarded, even during his lifetime, as virtually divine. A statue with the inscription 'to the invincible god' had been set up on the Quirinal in his honour in 45 B.C.; a few months later he had had his own temple, with the title Jupiter Julius. Then had come his assassination, followed, to be sure, by his official apotheosis, which transformed him into a real god—had not a dazzling comet appeared in the midst of the rites, thus proving that he had been received among the immortals! (Pliny, *Nat. Hist.* II. 24).

Nevertheless, Julius had been assassinated. Augustus was properly wary lest his own amazing triumphs should lead to a similar fate. While he was well aware of the superlative political value of this spontaneous acclamation of himself as the living embodiment of the *genius* which the awed and grateful East recognized, as the bond of unity among peoples of widely diverse stocks and traditions, he had not the slightest intention of letting it get out of control. Actually it was this ability of ever seeming forced to accept, always with reluctance, one dignity or badge of authority after another which is Augustus' chief claim to genius. In the eastern provinces he permitted the erection of a few temples to himself, but only when they were to be dedicated jointly to himself and Rome, and only, in the case of the provincial cult, when the province itself made the overture. There seem to have been two distinct types of emperor worship: the municipal and the provincial. For the former, official permission from Rome was not necessary. The temple might be erected and the rites performed in honour of the various emperors, living and dead, on the initiative of the city itself and with little apparent control even by the provincial governor. A provincial cult, however, could be established only upon the direct authorization of the emperor, and regularly only in the provincial centre. The various cities of the province sent delegates to form a provincial assembly and elected the chief priest, styled variously Asiarch (q.v.), Galatarch, Bithyniarch. To be permitted to be the seat of this all-important worship was the source of great pride to the city so honoured. And Augustus was astute enough to see that the honour was not lessened by over-frequent bestowal. See AUGUSTUS.

But it should not be forgotten, despite the values which successive emperors saw in this very effective cult of patriotism, and despite their efforts to keep it such, that it was not imposed on the provincials by Rome herself; instead, it sprang from the voluntary desire of the provincials themselves. In addition, Augustus and the more astute of his successors—Tiberius, Claudius, Vespasian—were most cautious, even reluctant, in permitting even such honours for themselves while living. Caligula, Nero, and especially Domitian were less restrained, and at times encountered serious difficulties because of their too-ready acceptance of the proffered heady drink. Caligula's ill-starred attempt to set up a statue of himself in the Jewish temple in Jerusalem is only one conspicuous example of a danger Augustus and Tiberius had carefully avoided. (See GAIUS.)

In Rome, Augustus and his early successors were still more cautious, resolutely forbidding divine honours of too conspicuous a sort to be rendered them while still alive. The former did accept with proper reluctance the honorific title *Augustus*, welcomed the *Augustalia* (sacred rites and games), and permitted the month of August to be dedicated to him; but no temple in Rome was to be so dedicated. It was only after his death that the city might officially enshrine him among the immortals.

All this was no mere flattery or kowtowing. It was the expression of genuine gratitude for the definite reality of the *pax Romana*. The emperor had done what their local rulers had been unable to do. Tyranny, irresponsible and costly war, and banditry were over; highways were open and safe for trade and travel; earlier abuses by rapacious governors were effectively checked. It is not surprising that to people long accustomed to regard their rulers as of more than common clay this amazing betterment could be explained only in terms of a divine genius to whom glad tribute was only proper: 'The birthday of God has brought to the world glad tidings. . . . From his birthday a new era begins'—so reads the inscription in honour of Augustus found in Priene (Dittenberger, *Orientis Graeci Inscriptiones Selectae*, 458).

Nor was this attitude restricted to the East. In Italy, too, peace and prosperity had followed the awful years of bloodshed and confusion which attended the dying republic. The future loomed bright and propitious. This widespread attitude is clear in the so-called Messianic *Fourth Eclogue* of Virgil: the end of the age of iron has at last come; the age of gold is even now rising for the whole world.

As the emergence of emperor worship was the natural and spontaneous expression of real appreciation and also, in no small part, of genuine gratitude—not the invention of power-mad tyrants—so too the cult never regarded itself as a substitute for other religions. It neither sought to replace them nor to quarrel with them. For a man living in Asia or Bithynia to burn a bit of incense to the emperor was essentially the same thing as removing one's hat to the flag or rising for the national anthem is to a normal American or Briton. The appreciative recognition of a new goddess *Roma* in no wise interfered with obligations or loyalties to other deities. Actually, as the years went by and the earlier gratitude to Rome, whose blessings had then seemed so immediate, tended to lapse, it was not unnatural that more and more the visible embodiment of the now somewhat abstract *Roma*—that is, the living emperor—tended to come increasingly to the fore. But he too did not oust or even replace the other local deities. Rather he became associated with them. Thus in the 2nd cent. many inscriptions, notably on coins, reveal the virtual identification of the divine emperor with this or that local god: Artemis, Persephone, Zeus, Nemesis, Asklepios. The State cult did not owe its success to the decay or destruction of older religions; instead, it was its natural alliance with them that actually assured its triumph.

While not imposed from above, but a spontaneous outgrowth from below, refusal to perform the normal rites or, even more, open hostility to them, meant serious trouble. For the most part there seems to have been little such hostility. To be sure, Tacitus (*Annals*, IV. 36) recounts that the citizens of Cyzicus lost their privileges because they had let the ceremonies in honour of Augustus lapse; but this was most unusual, and his subsequent remark (*ib.*, IV. 56), 'Eleven cities rivalled each other, not in power or opulence, but with equal zeal contending for the preference [*i.e.* the authorization to build a temple to the reigning emperor],' is far more indicative of the normal attitude at home as well as abroad. Few people, save Jews and Christians, had any objection to divine humanity. For centuries, Greeks had been placidly making gods in their own image from heroes, alike living and dead. In the East, the apotheosis of dead rulers was not regarded as the way they became divine; rather, it was the natural consequence of their already possessed divinity.

To the Jew and the Christian alone it was an intolerable and blasphemous outrage. Occasionally the Jews had suffered for their refusal to join in the common acclaim, but this was rare. Caligula, the first of the emperors to demand the title *Dominus et Deus Noster*, had sought by a bloody persecution of Jews in Alexandria to force them to join in the common rites. The attempt signally failed, and Claudius promptly sent an edict to the Egyptian viceroy approving the Jews' refusal to regard the emperor as a god and empowering them to maintain their ancestral attitudes and practices unmolested. This edict, repeated throughout the Roman domain and in keeping with the toleration regularly granted them from the days of the grateful Julius, ensured them, as a *religio licita*, immunity from retribution for their unusual refusal. Rome had the sense to recognize that this refusal was no evidence of disloyalty, but simply a traditional inheritance far antedating the establishment of the State cult; and it was a mark of Roman genius for administration to be unwilling to permit local customs or *mores*, however crude or boorish they might seem to the cultivated Roman himself, to become a political menace by unwise or too costly prohibition.

For the Christians, however, the outcome was very different. Inheriting the Jews' unwillingness to worship any pagan deity, and especially to accord divine honours to any human being, whatever his worldly status, they speedily came into open conflict with the state. So long as they were regarded as merely an obscure sect within Judaism, they appear to have enjoyed immunity. But when the ways parted and the Christians became independent, their immunity ceased. It was not true that the new religion was only one more cult; instead, it was all too clear that it regarded itself as the only true religion and divinely directed to oppose all others. That spelled trouble. In addition, unlike Judaism, it had a central figure, Jesus Christ, who was the real and only king. Many of the titles such as saviour, lord, son of god, god, god manifest, which were commonly bestowed upon the Roman ruler, were in Christian eyes solely and uniquely Christ's. Thus to the Christian, regardless of his political feelings, emperor worship was blasphemy, and must always be refused and attacked. From the days of the Antonines, when the cult of the living emperor had become the universal practice, and when refusal to conform was regarded as deliberate rebellion and treason, Christians were constantly liable to arrest and even death. It is not surprising that the better the emperor, notably Marcus Aurelius, the more real the danger. But actually, while occasional reprisals took place, it was not until the middle of the 3rd cent. that any deliberate attempt was made by the Roman government to blot out the new religion. This reluctance, in view of the many deliberately provocative gestures and acts by zealous Christians, is really remarkable. Hitherto, it had been, so to speak, always an open season. A Christian head, whenever raised, was in danger; but it was not until Decius that a deliberate attempt to crush this upstart faith was seriously and methodically undertaken. During the earlier period, it is safe to say, it had not been the Roman emperors, nor even the Roman proconsuls or other administrative officials, but the priests of the several imperial cult centres who were most hostile and the leading instigators of local persecution. In a word, it was the Asiarch or the Bithyniarch, not the emperor, who was the real antagonist to be feared. And it may well be added that Jewish hostility to the new movement —which had arrogated to itself the claim to be the only true Judaism and the sole rightful heir and interpreter of the ancient scriptures—was one of the most constant aids and incentives to this zeal on the part of local priests of the imperial cult. But with the astutely convenient conversion of Constantine came the public and official recognition and endorsement of the Christian cult. It had now finally triumphed over all its rivals, not alone over Mithras but even over Caesar himself. Virgil's early line, *Deus nobis haec otia fecit* (Ecl. 1), which had been prompted by Octavian's first successes, was now seen to be fulfilled in the Lord Jesus Christ, who was the real and only king and emperor before whom every knee must bow. M. S. E.

ENAIM.—A place mentioned only in Gn $38^{14, 21}$ (AV 'an open place,' 'openly'). From the narrative we gather that it lay between Adullam and Timnah. Its site is unidentified. It is probably the same as **Enam.**

ENAM.—A town of Judah in the Shephelah, Jos 15^{34}; possibly the same as **Enaim** (q.v.).

ENAN.—Prince of Naphtali at the first census, Nu 1^{15} 2^{29} $7^{78, 83}$ 10^{27}.

ENASIBUS, 1 Es 9^{34} (AV, RV).—See ELIASHIB, **4.**

ENCAMPMENT BY THE SEA.—One of the stations in the itinerary of the children of Israel, where they encamped after leaving Elim, Nu 33^{10}. If the position of Elim be in the *Wâdī Gharandel*, then the camp by the sea is on the shore of the Gulf of Suez, somewhere south of the point where the *Wâdī eṭ-Ṭaiyibeh* opens to the coast. The curious return of the line of march to the seashore is a phenomenon that has always arrested the attention of travellers to Mt. Sinai: and if Mt. Sinai be really in the so-called Sinaitic peninsula, the camp can be located within a half-mile.

ENCHANTMENT.—See MAGIC, DIVINATION, AND SORCERY.

EN-DOR.—A town of Manasseh in the territory of Issachar, Jos 17^{11}; the home of a woman with a familiar spirit consulted by Saul on the eve of the battle of Gilboa, 1 S 28^{7ff}; and, according to a psalmist (83^{10}), the scene of the rout of Jabin and Sisera. It is probably modern *Endôr*, S. of Mount Tabor, where are several ancient caves.

EN-EGLAIM.—A locality on the Dead Sea, mentioned along with En-gedi, Ezk 47^{10}. It has not been identified, but is not improbably *ʿAin Feshkhah*, near *Qumrân*. Alternatively *ʿAin-el-Ḥajlah* has been suggested.

ENEMESSAR.—Name of a king of Assyria in Greek MSS and in AV and RV of To 1^2, where the Syriac and Latin give *Shalmaneser*, who is probably meant; so RSV. The corruption is best accounted for by the loss of *Sh* and *l* and the transposition of *m* and *n*; but naturally many explanations may be offered without conviction.

ENENEUS, 1 Es 5^8 (RV).—One of the twelve leaders of the return from Babylon under Zerubbabel (AV **Enenius**). The name is omitted in the parallel list in Ezr 2, which gives only eleven leaders; but answers to **Nahamani** or **Bigvai** of Neh 7^7 (RSV reads the latter).

ENENIUS, 1 Es 5^{8} (AV).—See ENENEUS.

EN-GANNIM ('spring of gardens').—**1.** A town of Judah, mentioned with Zanoah and Eshtaol, Jos 15^{34}; possibly modern *Beit Jemâl*. **2.** A Levitical city of Issachar, Jos 19^{21} 21^{29}. The parallel list in 1 Ch 6^{73} has **Anem** (q.v.). In NT times it was called **Ginaea** (Josephus, *BJ* III. iii. 4 [48]); modern *Jenîn*, which has a fine spring, gardens, and palms.

EN-GEDI ('spring of the kid').—A place in the wilderness in the tribe of Judah (Jos 15^{62}), where David maintained himself for a time when he fled from Saul (1 S 23^{29} 24^{1}). Here the Moabites and Ammonites came against Jehoshaphat (2 Ch 20^{2}). The Shulammite compares her beloved to henna flowers in En-gedi (Ca 1^{14}); and in Ezekiel's vision of the healing of the Dead Sea waters, he visualizes fishers spreading their nets here (Ezk 47^{10}). An alternative name **Hazazon-tamar** is given in 2 Ch 20^{2}, which is also mentioned in Gn 14^{7}. There is no doubt of the identification of En-gedi with *'Ain Jidi*, a spring of warm water that rises 330 feet above the level of the Dead Sea, about the middle of its W. side. The ancient settlement is to be particularly located at *Tell el-Jurn*, where the water of this spring was led by an aqueduct in the Roman period. The desert of En-gedi is mentioned by Pliny the Elder (*Hist. Nat.* v. xvii.) in connexion with Essene settlements, but the discovery of such settlements at *Khirbet Qumrân* and *'Ain Feshkha* make it uncertain whether Engedi itself was such a settlement. It is possible that the vision of Ezekiel determined the sectaries' choice of Engedi or its general vicinity as the site of their settlements.

R. A. S. M.—**J. Gr.**

ENGINE.—See FORTIFICATION, etc.

ENGLISH VERSIONS.—**1.** The history of the English Bible begins early in the history of the English people, though not quite at the beginning of it, and only slowly attains to any magnitude. The Bible which was brought into the country by the first missionaries, by Aidan in the north and Augustine in the south, was the Latin Bible; and for some considerable time after the first preaching of Christianity to the English no vernacular version would be required. Nor is there any trace of a vernacular Bible in the Celtic Church, which still existed in Wales and Ireland. The literary language of the educated minority was Latin; and the instruction of the newly converted English tribes was carried on by oral teaching and preaching. As time went on, however, and monasteries were founded, many of whose inmates were imperfectly acquainted with English or with Latin, a demand arose for English translations of the Scriptures. This took two forms. On the one hand, there was a call for word-for-word translations of the Latin, which might assist readers to a comprehension of the Latin Bible; and, on the other, for continuous versions or paraphrases, which might be read to, or by, those whose skill in reading Latin was small.

2. The earliest form, so far as is known, in which this demand was met was the poem of **Caedmon**, the work of a monk of Whitby in the third quarter of the 7th cent., which gives a metrical paraphrase of parts of both Testaments. The only extant MS of the poem (in the Bodleian) belongs to the end of the 10th cent., and it is doubtful how much of it really goes back to the time of Caedmon. In any case, the poem as it stands here does not appear to be later than the 8th cent. A tradition, originating with Bale, attributed an English version of the Psalms to Aldhelm, bishop of Sherborne († 707), but it appears to be quite baseless (see A. S. Cook, *Bibl. Quot. in Old Eng. Prose Writers*, 1878, pp. xiv–xviii). An Anglo-Saxon Psalter in an 11th cent. MS at Paris (partly in prose and partly in verse) has been identified, without any evidence, with this imaginary work. The well-known story of the death of **Bede** (in 735) shows him engaged on an English translation of St. John's Gospel [one early MS (at St. Gall) represents this as extending only to Jn 6^{9}; but so abrupt a conclusion seems inconsistent with the course of the narrative]; but of this all traces have disappeared. The scholarship of the monasteries of Wearmouth and Jarrow, which had an important influence on the textual history of the Latin Vulgate, did not concern itself with vernacular translations; and no further trace of an English Bible appears until the 9th cent. To that period is assigned a word-for-word translation of the Psalter, written between the lines of a Latin MS (Cotton MS Vespasian A.I., in the British Museum), which was the progenitor of several similar glosses between that date and the 12th cent.; and to it certainly belongs the attempt of **Alfred** to educate his people by English translations of the works which he thought most needful to them. He is said to have undertaken a version of the Psalms, of which no portion survives, unless the prose portion (Ps 1–50) of the above-mentioned Paris MS is a relic of it; but we still have the translation of the Decalogue, the summary of the Mosaic law, and the letter of the Council of Jerusalem (Ac 15^{23-29}), which he prefixed to his code of laws. To the 10th cent. belongs probably the verse portion of the Paris MS and the interlinear translation of the Gospels in Northumbrian dialect inserted by the priest Aldred in the **Lindisfarne Gospels** (British Museum), which is repeated in the Rushworth Gospels (Bodleian) of the same century, with the difference that the version of Matthew is there in the Mercian dialect. This is the earliest extant translation of the Gospels into English.

3. The earliest independent version of any of the books of the Bible has likewise generally been assigned to the 10th cent., but if this claim can be made good at all, it can apply only to the last years of that century. The version in question is a translation of the Gospels in the dialect of Wessex, of which six MSS (with a fragment of a seventh) are now extant. It was edited by W. Skeat, *The Holy Gospels in Anglo-Saxon* (1871–1877); two MSS are in the British Museum, two at Cambridge, and two (with a fragment of another) at Oxford. From the number of copies which still survive, it must be presumed to have had a certain circulation, at any rate in Wessex, and it continued to be copied for at least a century. The earliest MSS are assigned to the beginning of the 11th cent.; but it is observable that Aelfric the Grammarian, abbot of Eynsham, writing about 990, says that the English at that time 'had not the evangelical doctrines among their writings, . . . those books excepted which King Alfred wisely turned from Latin into English' (preface to Aelfric's *Homilies*, edited by B. Thorpe, London, 1843–46). In a subsequent treatise (*Treatise concerning the Old and New Testament*, ed. W. Lisle, London, 1623) also (the date of which is said to be about 1010, see Dietrich, *Zeitsch. f. hist. Theol.* 1856, quoted by Cook, *op. cit.*, p. lxiv) he speaks as if no English version of the Gospels were in existence, and refers his readers to his own homilies on the Gospels. Since Aelfric had been a monk at Winchester and abbot of Cerne, in Dorset, it is difficult to understand how he could have failed to know of the Wessex version of the Gospels, if it had been produced and circulated much before 1000; and it seems probable that it only came into existence early in the 11th cent. In this case it was contemporaneous with another work of translation, due to **Aelfric** himself. Aelfric, at the request of Aethelweard, son of his patron Aethelmaer, ealdorman of Devonshire and founder of Eynsham Abbey, produced a paraphrase of the Heptateuch, homilies containing epitomes of the Books of Kings and Job, and brief versions of Esther, Judith, and Maccabees. These have the interest of being the earliest extant English version of the narrative books of the OT. [The Heptateuch and Job were printed by E. Thwaites (Oxford, 1698). For the rest, see Cook, *op. cit.*]

4. The Norman Conquest checked for a time all the vernacular literature of England, including the translations of the Bible. One of the first signs of its revival was the production of the *Ormulum*, a poem which embodies metrical versions of the Gospels and Acts, written about the end of the 12th cent. The main

Biblical literature of this period, however, was French. For the benefit of the Norman settlers in England, translations of the greater part of both OT and NT were produced during the 12th and 13th cents. Especially notable among these was the version of the Apocalypse, because it was frequently accompanied by a series of illustrations, the best examples of which are the finest (and also the most quaint) artistic productions of the period in the sphere of book-illustration. Nearly 90 MSS of this version are known, ranging from the first half of the 12th cent. to the first half of the 15th [see S. Berger, *La Bible Française au moyen âge*, p. 78 ff; L. Delisle and P. Meyer, *L'Apocalypse en Français* (Paris, 1901); and *New Palaeographical Society*, part 2, plates 38, 39], some having been produced in England, and others in France; and in the 14th cent. it reappears in an English dress, having been translated apparently about that time. This English version (which at one time was attributed to Wycliffe) is known in no less than 16 MSS, which fall into at least two classes [see Miss A. C. Paues, *A Fourteenth Century English Biblical Version* (Cambridge, 1902), pp. 24–30]; and it is noteworthy that from the second of these was derived the version which appears in the revised Wycliffite Bible, to be mentioned presently.

5. The 14th cent., which saw the practical extinction of the general use of the French language in England, and the rise of a real native literature, saw also a great revival of vernacular Biblical literature, beginning apparently with the Book of Psalms. Two English versions of the Psalter were produced at this period, one of which enjoyed great popularity. This was the work of **Richard Rolle**, hermit of Hampole, in Yorkshire (d 1349). It contains the Latin text of the Psalter, followed verse by verse by an English translation and commentary. Originally written in the northern dialect, it soon spread over all England, and many MSS of it still exist in which the dialect has been altered to suit southern tastes. Towards the end of the century Rolle's work suffered further change, the commentary being re-written from a strongly Lollard point of view, and in this shape it continued to circulate far into the 16th cent. Another version of the Psalter was produced contemporaneously with Rolle's, somewhere in the West Midlands. The authorship of it was formerly attributed to William of Shoreham, vicar of Chart Sutton, in Kent, but for no other reason than that in one of the two MSS in which it is preserved (Brit. Mus. Add. MS 17376, the other being at Trinity College, Dublin) it is now bound up with his religious poems. The dialect, however, proves that this authorship is impossible, and the version must be put down as anonymous. As in the case of Rolle's translation, the Latin and English texts are intermixed, verse by verse; but there is no commentary. [See K. S. Bülbring, *The Earliest Complete English Prose Psalter* (Early English Text Society), 1891.]

6. The Psalter was not the only part of the Bible of which versions came into existence in the course of the 14th cent. At Magdalene College, Cambridge (Pepys MS 2498), is an English narrative of the Life of Christ, compiled out of a re-arrangement of the Gospels for Sundays and holy days throughout the year. Quite recently, too, a group of MSS, which (so far as they were known at all) had been regarded as belonging to the Wycliffite Bible, has been shown by Miss Anna C. Paues [*A Fourteenth Century English Biblical Version* (Cambridge, 1902)] to contain an independent translation of the NT. It is not complete, the Gospels being represented only by Mt 1^1–6^8, and the Apocalypse being altogether omitted. The original nucleus seems, indeed, to have consisted of the four larger Catholic Epistles and the Epistles of St. Paul, to which were subsequently added 2 and 3 John, Jude, Acts, and Mt 1^1–6^8. Four MSS of this version are at present known, the oldest being one at Selwyn College, Cambridge, which was written about 1400. The prologue narrates that the translation was made at the request of a monk and a nun by their superior, who defers to their earnest desire, although, as he says, it is at the risk of his life. This phrase seems to show that the work was produced after the rise of the great party controversy which is associated with the name of Wycliffe.

7. With **Wycliffe** (1320–1384) we reach a landmark in the history of the English Bible, in the production of the first complete version of both OT and NT. It belongs to the last period of Wycliffe's life, that in which he was engaged in open war with the Papacy and with most of the official chiefs of the English Church. It was connected with his institution of 'poor priests,' or mission preachers, and formed part of his scheme of appealing to the populace in general against the doctrines and supremacy of Rome. The NT seems to have been completed about 1380, the OT between 1382 and 1384. Exactly how much of it was done by Wycliffe's own hand is uncertain. The greater part of the OT (as far as Bar 3^{20}) is assigned in an Oxford MS to Nicholas Hereford, one of Wycliffe's principal supporters at that university; and it is certain that this part of the translation is in a different style (more stiff and pedantic) from the rest. The NT is generally attributed to Wycliffe himself, and he may also have completed the OT, which Hereford apparently had to abandon abruptly, perhaps when he was summoned to London and excommunicated in 1382. This part of the work is free and vigorous in style, though its interpretation of the original is often strange, and many sentences in it can have conveyed very little idea of their meaning to its readers. Such as it was, however, it was a complete English Bible, addressed to the whole English people, high and low, rich and poor. That this is the case is proved by the character of the copies which have survived (about 30 in number). Some are large folio volumes, handsomely written and illuminated in the best, or nearly the best, style of the period; such is the fine copy, in two volumes (now Brit. Mus. Egerton MSS 617, 618), which once belonged to Thomas, Duke of Gloucester, uncle of Richard II. Others are plain copies of ordinary size, intended for private persons or monastic libraries; for it is clear that, in spite of official disfavour and eventual prohibition, there were many places in England where Wycliffe and his Bible were welcomed. Wycliffe, indeed, enjoyed advantages from personal repute and influential support such as had been enjoyed by no English translator since Alfred. An Oxford scholar, at one time Master of Balliol, holder of livings successively from his college and the Crown, employed officially on behalf of his country in controversy with the Pope, the friend and protégé of John of Gaunt and other prominent nobles, and enjoying as a rule the strenuous support of the University of Oxford, Wycliffe was in all respects a person of weight and influence in the realm, who could not be silenced or isolated by the opposition of bishops such as Arundel. The work that he had done had struck its roots too deep to be destroyed, and though it was identified with Lollardism by its adversaries, its range was much wider than that of any one sect or party.

8. Wycliffe's translation, however, though too strong to be overthrown by its opponents, was capable of improvement by its friends. The difference of style between Hereford and his continuator or continuators, the stiff and unpopular character of the work of the former, and the imperfections inevitable in a first attempt on so large a scale, called aloud for revision; and a second Wycliffite Bible, the result of a very complete revision of its predecessor, saw the light not many years after the Reformer's death. The authorship of the second version is doubtful. It was assigned by Forshall and Madden, the editors of the Wycliffite Bible, to **John Purvey**, one of Wycliffe's most intimate followers; but the evidence is purely circumstantial, and rests mainly on verbal resemblances between the translator's preface and known works of Purvey, together with the fact that a copy of this preface is found attached to a copy of the earlier version which was once Purvey's property. What is certain is that the second version is

ENGLISH VERSIONS

based upon the first, and that the translator's preface is permeated with Wycliffite opinions. This version speedily superseded the other, and in spite of a decree passed, at Arundel's instigation, by the Council of Blackfriars in 1408, it must have circulated in large numbers. Over 140 copies are still in existence, many of them small pocket volumes such as must have been the personal property of private individuals for their own study. Others belonged to the greatest personages in the land, and copies are still in existence which formerly had for owners Henry VI., Henry VII., Edward VI., and Elizabeth.

9. At this point it seems necessary to say something of the theory which has been propounded by the well-known Roman Catholic historian, Abbot Gasquet, to the effect that the versions which pass under the name of 'Wycliffite' were not produced by Wycliffe or his followers at all, but were translations authorized and circulated by the heads of the Church of England, Wycliffe's particular enemies [*The Old English Bible*, 1897, pp. 102–178]. The strongest argument adduced in support of this view is the possession of copies of the versions in question both by kings and princes of England, and by religious houses and persons of unquestioned orthodoxy. This does, indeed, prove that the persecution of the English Bible and its possessors by the authorities of the Catholic Church was not so universal or continuous as it is sometimes represented to have been, but it does not go far towards disproving the Wycliffite authorship of versions which can be demonstratively connected, as these are, with the names of leading supporters of Wycliffe, such as Hereford and Purvey; the more so since the evidence of orthodox ownership of many of the copies in question dates from times long after the cessation of the Lollard persecution. Dr. Gasquet also denies that there is any real evidence connecting Wycliffe with the production of an English Bible at all; but in order to make good this assertion he has to ignore several passages in Wycliffe's own writings in which he refers to the importance of a vernacular version (to the existence of his own version he could not refer, since that was produced only at the end of his life), and to do violence alike to the proper translation and to the natural interpretation of passages written by Wycliffe's opponents (Arundel, Knyghton, and the Council of Oxford in 1408) in which Wycliffe's work is mentioned and condemned. Further, Dr. Gasquet denies that the Lollards made a special point of the circulation of the Scriptures in the vernacular, or were charged with so doing by the ecclesiastical authorities who prosecuted them; and in particular he draws a distinction between the versions now extant and the Bible on account of the heretical nature of which (among other charges) one Richard Hun was condemned by the Bishop of London in 1514. It has, however, been shown conclusively that the depositions of the witnesses against the Lollards (which cannot be regarded as wholly irrelevant to the charges brought against them) constantly make mention of the possession of vernacular Bibles; and that the charges against Richard Hun, based upon the prologue to the Bible in his possession, are taken verbatim from the prologue to the version which we now know as Purvey's. It is true that Dr. Gasquet makes the explicit statement that 'we shall look in vain in the edition of Wyclifite Scriptures published by Forshall and Madden for any trace of these errors' (*i.e.* the errors found by Hun's prosecutors in the prologue to his Bible); but a writer in the *Church Quarterly Review* (Jan. 1901, pp. 292 ff) has printed in parallel columns the charges against Hun and the corresponding passages in Purvey's prologue, which leave no possibility of doubt that Hun was condemned for possessing a copy of the version which is commonly known as Purvey's, or as the later Wycliffite version. The article in the *Church Quarterly Review* must be read by everyone who wishes to investigate Dr. Gasquet's theory fully; the evidence there adduced is decisive as to the unsoundness of Dr. Gasquet's historical position. It is impossible to attribute to the official heads of the English Church a translation the prologue to which (to quote but two phrases) speaks of 'the pardouns of the bisschopis of Rome, that ben opin leesingis,' and declares that 'to eschewe pride and speke onour of God and of his lawe, and repreue synne bi weie of charite, is matir and cause now whi prelatis and summe lordis sclaundren men, and clepen hem lollardis, eretikis, and riseris of debate and of treson agens the king.' In the face of this evidence it will be impossible in future to deny that the Wycliffite Bible is identical with that which we now possess, and that it was at times the cause of the persecution of its owners by the authorities of the Church. That this persecution was partial and temporary is likely enough. Much of it was due to the activity of individual bishops, such as Arundel; but not all the bishops shared Arundel's views. Wycliffe had powerful supporters, notably John of Gaunt and the University of Oxford, and under their protection copies of the vernacular Bible could be produced and circulated. It is, moreover, likely, not to say certain, that as time went on the Wycliffite origin of the version would often be forgotten. Apart from the preface to Purvey's edition, which appears only rarely in the extant MSS, there is nothing in the translation itself which would betray its Lollard origin; and it is quite probable that many persons in the 15th and early 16th cent. used it without any suspicion of its connexion with Wycliffe. Sir Thomas More, whose good faith there is no reason to question, appears to have done so; otherwise it can only be supposed that the orthodox English Bibles of which he speaks, and which he expressly distinguishes from the Bible which caused the condemnation of Richard Hun, have wholly disappeared, which is hardly likely. If this be admitted, the rest of More's evidence falls to the ground. The history of the Wycliffite Bible, and of its reception in England, would in some points bear re-statement; but the ingenious, and at first sight plausible, theory of Abbot Gasquet has failed to stand examination, and it is to be hoped that it may be allowed to lapse.

10. With the production of the second Wycliffite version the history of the manuscript English Bible comes to an end. Purvey's work was on the level of the best scholarship and textual knowledge of the age, and it satisfied the requirements of those who needed a vernacular Bible. That it did not reach modern standards in these respects goes without saying. In the first place, it was translated from the Latin Vulgate, not from the original Hebrew and Greek, with which there is no reason to suppose that Wycliffe or his assistants were familiar. Secondly, its exegesis is often deficient, and some passages in it must have been wholly unintelligible to its readers. This, however, may be said even of some parts of the AV, so that it is small reproach to Wycliffe and Purvey; and on the whole it is a straightforward and intelligible version of the Scriptures. A few examples of this, the first complete English Bible, and the first version in which the English approaches sufficiently near to its modern form to be generally intelligible, may be given here:

Jn 14^{1-7}. Be not youre herte affraied, ne drede it. Ye bileuen in god, and bileue ye in me. In the hous of my fadir ben many dwellyngis: if ony thing lasse I hadde seid to you, for I go to make redi to you a place. And if I go and make redi to you a place, eftsone I come and I schal take you to my silf, that where I am, ye be. And whidir I go ye witen: and ye witen the wey. Thomas seith to him, Lord, we witen not whidir thou goist, and hou moun we wite the weie. Ihesus seith to him, I am weye truthe and liif: no man cometh to the fadir, but bi me. If ye hadden knowe me, sothli ye hadden knowe also my fadir: and aftirwarde ye schuln knowe him, and ye han seen hym.

2 Co 1^{17-20}. But whanne I wolde this thing, whether I uside unstidfastnesse? ether tho thingis that I thenke, I thenke aftir the fleische, that at me be it is and it is not. But god is trewe, for oure word that was at you, is and is not, is not thereinne, but is in it. Forwhi ihesus crist the sone of god, which is prechid among you bi us, bi me

and siluan and tymothe, ther was not in hym is and is not, but is was in hym. Forwhi hou many euer ben biheestis of god, in thilke is ben fulfillid. And therfor and bi him we seien Amen to god, to oure glorie.

Eph 3^{14-21}. For grace of this thing I bowe my knees to the fadir of oure lord ihesus crist, of whom eche fadirheed in heuenes and in erthe is named, that he geue to you aftir the richessis of his glorie, vertu to be strengthid bi his spirit in the ynner man ; that criste dwelle bi feith in youre hertis ; that ye rootid and groundid in charite, moun comprehende with alle seyntis whiche is the breede and the lengthe and the highist and the depnesse ; also to wite the charite of crist more excellent thanne science, that ye be fillid in all the plente of god. And to hym that is myghti to do alle thingis more plenteuousli thanne we axen, or undirstande bi the vertu that worchith in us, to hym be glorie in the chirche and in crist ihesus in to alle the generaciouns of the worldis. Amen.

11. The English manuscript Bible was now complete, and no further translation was issued in this form. The Lollard controversy died down amid the strain of the French wars and the passions of the wars of the Roses ; and when, in the 16th cent., religious questions once more came to the front, the situation had been fundamentally changed through the invention of printing. The first book that issued from the press was the Latin Bible (popularly known as the Mazarin Bible), published by Fust and Gutenberg in 1456. For the Latin Bible (the form in which the Scriptures had hitherto been mainly known in Western Europe) there was indeed so great a demand, that no less than 124 editions of it are said to have been issued before the end of the 15th cent. ; but it was only slowly that scholars realized the importance of utilizing the printing press for the circulation of the Scriptures, either in their original tongues, or in the vernaculars of Europe. The Hebrew Psalter was printed in 1477, the complete OT in 1488. The Greek Bible, both OT and NT, was included in the great Complutensian Polyglot of Cardinal Ximenes, printed in 1514–1517, but not published till 1522. The Greek NT (edited by Erasmus) was first published by Froben in 1516, the OT by the Aldine press in 1518. In the way of vernacular versions, a French Bible was printed at Lyons about 1478, and another about 1487 ; a Spanish Pentateuch was printed (by Jews) in 1497 ; a German Bible was printed at Strassburg by Mentelin in 1466, and was followed by eighteen others (besides many Psalters and other separate books) between that date and 1522, when the first portion of Luther's translation appeared. In England, Caxton inserted the main part of the OT narrative in his translation of the *Golden Legend* (which in its original form already contained the Gospel story), published in 1483 ; but no regular English version of the Bible was printed until 1525, with which date a new chapter in the history of the English Bible begins.

12. It was not the fault of the translator that it did not appear at least as early as Luther's. **William Tyndale** (*c* 1490–1536) devoted himself early to Scripture studies, and by the time he had reached the age of about 30 he had taken for the work of his life the translation of the Bible into English. He was born in Gloucestershire, where his family seems to have used the name of Hutchins or Hychins, as well as that of Tyndale, so that he is himself sometimes described by both names ; and he became a member of Magdalen Hall (a dependency of Magdalen College) at Oxford, where he definitely associated himself with the Protestant party and became known as one of its leaders. He took his degree as B.A. in 1512, as M.A. in 1515, and at some uncertain date he is said (by Foxe) to have gone to Cambridge. If this was between 1511 and 1515, he would have found Erasmus there ; but in that case it could have been only an interlude in the middle of his Oxford course, and perhaps it is more probable that his visit belongs to some part of the years 1515 to 1520, as to which there is no definite information. About 1520 he became resident tutor in the house of Sir John Walsh, at Little Sodbury in Gloucestershire, to which period belongs his famous saying, in controversy with an opponent : 'If God spare my life, ere many years I will cause a boy that driveth the plough shall know more of the Scripture than thou doest.' With this object he came up to London in 1523, and sought a place in the service of Tunstall, bishop of London, a scholar and patron of scholars, of whom Erasmus had spoken favourably ; but here he received no encouragement. He was, however, taken in by Alderman Humphrey Monmouth, in whose house he lived as chaplain and studied for six months ; at the end of which time he was forced to the conclusion 'not only that there was no room in my lord of London's palace to translate the New Testament, but also that there was no place to do it in all England.'

13. About May 1524, therefore, Tyndale left England and settled in the free city of Hamburg, and in the course of the next twelve months the first stage of his great work was completed. Whether during this time he visited Luther at Wittenberg is quite uncertain ; what is certain, and more important, is that he was acquainted with Luther's writings. In 1525, the translation of the NT being finished, he went to Cologne to have it printed at the press of Peter Quentel. Three thousand copies of the first ten sheets of it, in quarto, had been printed off when rumours of the work came to the ears of John Cochlaeus, a bitter enemy of the Reformation. To obtain information he approached the printers (who were also engaged upon work for him), and having loosened their tongues with wine he learnt the full details of Tyndale's enterprise, and sent warning forthwith to England. Meanwhile Tyndale escaped with the printed sheets to Worms, in the Lutheran disposition of which place he was secure from interference, and proceeded with his work at the press of Peter Schoeffer. Since, however, a description of the Cologne edition had been sent to England, a change was made in the *format*. The text was set up again in octavo, and without the marginal notes of the quarto edition ; and in this form the first printed English NT was given to the world early in 1526. About the same time an edition in small quarto, with marginal notes, was also issued, and it is probable (though full proof is wanting) that this was the completion of the interrupted Cologne edition. Three thousand copies of each edition were struck off ; but so active were the enemies of the Reformation in their destruction, that they have nearly disappeared off the face of the earth. One copy of the octavo edition, complete but for the loss of its title-page, is at the Baptist College at Bristol, whither it found its way from the Harley Library, to which it once belonged ; and an imperfect copy is in the library of St. Paul's Cathedral. Of the quarto, all that survives is a fragment consisting of eight sheets (Mt 1^{1}–22^{12}) in the Grenville Library in the British Museum.

14. The hostility of the authorities in Church and State in England was indeed undisguised. Sir T. More attacked the translation as false and heretical, and as disregarding ecclesiastical terminology. Wolsey and the bishops, with Henry's assent, decreed that it should be burnt ; and burnt it was at Paul's Cross, after a sermon from Bishop Tunstall. Nevertheless, fresh supplies continued to pour into England, the money expended in buying up copies for destruction serving to pay for the production of fresh editions. Six editions are said to have been issued between 1526 and 1530 ; and the zeal of the authorities for its destruction was fairly matched by the zeal of the reforming party for its circulation. It was, in fact, evident that the appetite for an English Bible, once fairly excited, could not be wholly balked. In 1530 an assembly convoked by Archbishop Warham, while maintaining the previous condemnation of Tyndale, and asserting that it was not expedient at that time to divulge the Scripture in the English tongue, announced that the king would have the NT faithfully translated by learned men, and published 'as soon as he might see their manners and behaviour meet, apt, and convenient to receive the same.'

15. Tyndale's first NT was epoch-making in many ways. It was the first English printed NT; it laid the foundations, and much more than the foundations, of the AV of 1611; it set on foot the movement which went forward without a break until it culminated in the production of that AV; and it was the first English Bible that was translated directly from the original language. All the English manuscript Bibles were translations from the Vulgate; but Tyndale's NT was taken from the Greek, which he knew from the editions by Erasmus, published in 1516, 1519, and 1522. As subsidiary aids he employed the Latin version attached by Erasmus to his Greek text, Luther's German translation of 1522, and the Vulgate; but it has been made abundantly clear that he exercised independent judgment in his use of these materials, and was by no means a slavish copier of Luther. In the marginal notes attached to the quarto edition his debt to Luther was greater; for (so far as can be gathered from the extant fragment) more than half the notes were taken direct from the German Bible, the rest being independent. It is in this connexion with Luther, rather than in anything to be found in the work itself, that the secret of the official hostility to Tyndale's version is to be found. That the translation itself was not seriously to blame is shown by the extent to which it was incorporated in the AV, though no doubt to persons who knew the Scriptures only in the Latin Vulgate its divergence from accuracy may have appeared greater than was in fact the case. The octavo edition had no extraneous matter except a short preface, and therefore could not be obnoxious on controversial grounds; and the comments in the quarto edition are generally exegetical, and not polemical. Still, there could be no doubt that they were the work of an adherent of the Reformation, and as such the whole translation fell under the ban of the opponents of the Reformation.

16. Tyndale's work did not cease with the production of his NT. Early in 1530 a translation of the Pentateuch was printed for him by Hans Luft, at Marburg in Hesse. The colophon to Genesis is dated Jan. 17, 1530. In England, where the year began on March 25, this would have meant 1531 according to our modern reckoning; but in Germany the year generally began on Jan. 1, or at Christmas. The only perfect copy of this edition is in the British Museum. The different books must have been set up separately, since Genesis and Numbers are printed in black letter, Exodus, Leviticus, and Deuteronomy in Roman; but there is no evidence that they were issued separately. The translation was made (for the first time) from the Hebrew, with which language there is express evidence that Tyndale was acquainted. The book was provided with a prologue and with marginal notes, the latter being often controversial. In 1531 he published a translation of the Book of Jonah, of which a single copy (now in the British Museum) came to light in 1861. After this he seems to have reverted to the NT, of which he issued a revised edition in 1534. The immediate occasion of this was the appearance of an unauthorized revision of the translation of 1525, by one George Joye, in which many alterations were made of which Tyndale disapproved. Tyndale's new edition was printed by Martin Empereur of Antwerp, and published in Nov. 1534. One copy of it was printed on vellum, illuminated, and presented to Anne Boleyn, who had shown favour to one of the agents employed in distributing Tyndale's earlier work. It bears her name on the fore-edge, and is now in the British Museum. The volume is a small octavo, and embodies a careful revision of his previous work. Since it was intended for liturgical use, the church lections were marked in it, and in an appendix were added, 'The Epistles taken out of the Old Testament, which are read in the church after the use of Salisbury upon certain days of the year.' These consist of 42 short passages from the OT (8 being taken from the Apocrypha), and constitute an addition to Tyndale's work as a translator of the OT. The text of the NT is accompanied throughout by marginal notes, differing (so far as we are in a position to compare them) from those in the quarto of 1525, and very rarely polemical. Nearly all the books are preceded by prologues, which are for the most part derived from Luther (except that to Hebrews, in which Tyndale expressly combats Luther's rejection of its Apostolic authority).

17. The edition of 1534 did not finally satisfy Tyndale, and in the following year he put forth another edition 'yet once again corrected.' [The volume bears two dates, 1535 and 1534, but the former, which stands on the first title-page, must be taken to be that of the completion of the work.] It bears the monogram of the publisher, Godfried van der Haghen, and is sometimes known as the GH edition. It has no marginal notes. Another edition, which is stated on its title-page to have been finished in 1535, contains practically the same text, but is notable for its spelling, which appears to be due to a Flemish compositor, working by ear and not by sight. These editions of 1535, which embody several small changes from the text of 1534, represent Tyndale's work in its final form. Several editions were issued in 1536, but Tyndale was not then in a position to supervise them. In May 1535, through the treachery of one Phillips, he was seized by some officers of the emperor, and carried off from Antwerp (where he had lived for a year past) to the castle of Vilvorde. After some months' imprisonment he was brought to trial, condemned, and finally strangled and burnt at the stake on October 16, 1536, crying 'with a fervent, great, and a loud voice, "Lord, open the King of England's eyes."'

18. Coverdale's Bible (1535).—Tyndale never had the satisfaction of completing his gift of an English Bible to his country; but during his imprisonment he may have learnt that a complete translation, based largely upon his own, had actually been produced. The credit for this achievement, the first complete printed English Bible, is due to Miles Coverdale (1488–1569), afterwards bishop of Exeter (1551–1553). The details of its production are obscure. Coverdale met Tyndale abroad in 1529, and is said to have assisted him in the translation of the Pentateuch. His own work was done under the patronage of Cromwell, who was anxious for the publication of an English Bible; and it was no doubt forwarded by the action of Convocation, which, under Cranmer's leading, had petitioned in 1534 for the undertaking of such a work. It was probably printed by Froschover at Zürich; but this has never been absolutely demonstrated. It was published at the end of 1535, with a dedication to Henry VIII. By this time the conditions were more favourable to a Protestant Bible than they had been in 1525. Henry had finally broken with the Pope, and had committed himself to the principle of an English Bible. Coverdale's work was accordingly tolerated by authority, and when the second edition of it appeared in 1537 (printed by an English printer, Nycolson of Southwark), it bore on its title-page the words, 'Set forth with the Kinges moost gracious licence.' In thus licensing Coverdale's translation, Henry probably did not know how far he was sanctioning the work of Tyndale, which he had previously condemned. In the NT, in particular, Tyndale's version is the basis of Coverdale's, and to a somewhat less extent this is also the case in the Pentateuch and Jonah; but Coverdale revised the work of his predecessor with the help of the Zürich German Bible of Zwingli and others (1524–1529), a Latin version by Pagninus, the Vulgate, and Luther. In his preface he explicitly disclaims originality as a translator, and there is no sign that he made any noticeable use of the Greek and Hebrew; but he used the available Latin, German, and English versions with judgment. In the parts of the OT which Tyndale had not published he appears to have translated mainly from the Zürich Bible [Coverdale's Bible of 1535 was reprinted by Bagster (1838)].

19. In one respect Coverdale's Bible was epoch-making, namely, in the arrangement of the Books of the

OT. In the Vulgate, as is well known, the books which are now classed as Apocrypha are intermingled with the other books of the OT. This was also the case with the LXX, and in general it may be said that the Christian Church had adopted this view of the Canon. It is true that many of the greatest Christian Fathers had protested against it, and had preferred the Hebrew Canon, which rejects these books. The Canon of Athanasius places the Apocrypha in a class apart ; the Syriac Bible omitted them ; Eusebius and Gregory Nazianzen appear to have held similar views ; and Jerome refused to translate them for his Latin Bible. Nevertheless the Church at large, both East and West, retained them in its Bible, and the provincial Council of Carthage (A.D. 397), under the influence of Augustine, expressly included them in the Canon. In spite of Jerome, the Vulgate, as it circulated in Western Europe, regularly included the disputed books ; and Wycliffe's Bible, being a translation from the Vulgate, naturally has them too. On the other hand, Luther, though recognizing these books as profitable and good for reading, placed them in a class apart, as 'Apocrypha,' and in the same way he segregated Hebrews, James, Jude, and Revelation at the end of the NT, as of less value and authority than the rest. This arrangement appears in the table of contents of Tyndale's NT in 1525, and was adopted by Coverdale, Matthew, and Taverner. It is to Tyndale's example, no doubt, that the action of Coverdale is due. His Bible is divided into six parts—(1) Pentateuch ; (2) Joshua–Esther ; (3) Job–' Solomon's Balettes ' (*i.e.* Cant.) ; (4) Prophets ; (5) ' Apocripha, the bokes and treatises which amonge the fathers of olde are not rekened to be of like authorite with the other bokes of the byble, nether are they founde in the Canon of the Hebrue ' ; (6) NT. This represents the view generally taken by the Reformers, both in Germany and in England, and so far as concerns the English Bible, Coverdale's exampl was decisive. On the other hand, the Roman Church, at the Council of Trent (1546), adopted by a majority the opinion that all the books of the larger Canon should be received as of equal authority, and for the first time made this a dogma of the Church, enforced by an anathema. In 1538, Coverdale published a NT with Latin (Vulgate) and English in parallel columns, revising his English to bring it into conformity with the Latin ; but this (which went through three editions with various changes) may be passed over, as it had no influence on the general history of the English Bible.

20. Matthew's Bible (1537).—In the same year as the second edition of Coverdale's Bible another English Bible appeared, which likewise bore upon its title-page the statement that it was ' set forth with the Kinges most gracyous lycence.' It was completed not later than Aug. 4, 1537, on which day Cranmer sent a copy of it to Cromwell, commending the translation, and begging Cromwell to obtain for it the king's licence ; in which, as the title-page prominently shows, he was successful. The origin of this version is slightly obscure, and certainly was not realized by Henry when he sanctioned it. The Pentateuch and NT are taken direct from Tyndale with little variation (the latter from the final ' GH ' revision of 1535). The books of the OT from Ezra to Malachi (including Jonah) are taken from Coverdale, as also is the Apocrypha. But the historical books of the OT (Joshua–2 Chronicles) are a new translation, as to the origin of which no statement is made. It is, however, fairly certain, from a combination of evidence, that it was Tyndale's (see Westcott[3], pp. 169–179). The style agrees with that of Tyndale's other work ; the passages which Tyndale published as ' Epistles ' from the OT in his NT of 1534 agree in the main with the present version in these books, but not in those taken from Coverdale ; and it is expressly stated in Hall's *Chronicle* (completed and published by Grafton, one of the publishers of Matthew's Bible) that Tyndale, in addition to the NT, translated also ' the v bookes of Moses, Josua, Judicum, Ruth, the bookes of the Kynges and the bookes of Paralipomenon, Nehemias or the fyrst of Esdras, the prophet Jonas, and no more of ye holy scripture.' If we suppose the version of Ezra-Nehemiah to have been incomplete, or for some reason unavailable, this statement harmonizes perfectly with the data of the problem. Tyndale may have executed the translation during his imprisonment, at which time we know that he applied for the use of his Hebrew books. The book was printed abroad, at the expense of R. Grafton and E. Whitchurch, two citizens of London, who issued it in London. On the title-page is the statement that the translator was Thomas Matthew, and the same name stands at the foot of the dedication to Henry VIII. Nothing is known of any such person, but tradition identifies him with **John Rogers** (who in the register of his arrest in 1555 is described as ' John Rogers *alias* Matthew '), a friend and companion of Tyndale. It is therefore generally believed that this Bible is due to the editorial work of John Rogers, who had come into possession of Tyndale's unpublished translation of the historical books of the OT, and published them with the rest of his friend's work, completing the Bible with the help of Coverdale. It may be added that the initials I. R. (Rogers), W. T. (Tyndale), R. G. and E. W. (Grafton and Whitchurch), and H. R. (unidentified, ? Henricus Rex), are printed in large letters on various blank spaces throughout the OT. The arrangement of the book is in four sections : (1) Genesis–Canticles, (2) Prophets, (3) Apocrypha (including for the first time the Prayer of Manasses, translated from the French of Olivetan), (4) NT. There are copious annotations, of a decidedly Protestant tendency, and Tyndale's outspoken Prologue to the Romans is included in it. The whole work, therefore, was eminently calculated to extend the impulse given by Tyndale, and to perpetuate his work.

21. Taverner's Bible (1539).—Matthew's Bible formed the basis for yet another version, which deserves brief mention, though it had no influence on the general development of the English Bible. Richard Taverner, formerly a student of Cardinal College [Christ Church], Oxford, was invited by some London printers (' John Byddell for Thomas Barthlet ') to prepare at short notice a revision of the existing Bible. In the OT his alterations are verbal, and aim at the improvement of the style of the translation ; in the NT, being a good Greek scholar, he was able to revise it with reference to the original Greek. The NT was issued separately in two editions, in the same year (1539) as the complete Bible ; but the success of the official version next to be mentioned speedily extinguished such a personal venture as this. Taverner's Bible is sometimes said to have been the first English Bible completely printed in England ; but this honour appears to belong rather to Coverdale's second edition.

22. The Great Bible (1539–1541).—The fact that Taverner was invited to revise Matthew's Bible almost immediately after its publication shows that it was not universally regarded as successful ; but there were in addition other reasons why those who had promoted the circulation and authorization of Matthew's Bible should be anxious to see it superseded. As stated above, it was highly controversial in character, and bore plentiful evidence of its origin from Tyndale. Cromwell and Cranmer had, no doubt, been careful not to call Henry's attention to these circumstances ; but they might at any time be brought to his notice, when their own position would become highly precarious. It is, indeed, strange that they ever embarked on so risky an enterprise. However that may be, they lost little time in inviting Coverdale to undertake a complete revision of the whole, which was ready for the press early in 1538. The printing was begun by Regnault of Paris, where more sumptuous typography was possible than in England. In spite, however, of the assent of the French king having been obtained, the Inquisition intervened, stopped the printing, and seized the sheets. Some of the sheets, however, had previously been got away to England ; others were re-purchased from a tradesman to whom they had been sold ; and ultimately, under Cromwell's direction, printers and presses were transported from Paris to London, and the work completed there by Grafton and Whitchurch, whose imprint stands on the magnificent title-page (traditionally ascribed to Holbein) depicting the dissemination of the Scriptures from the hands of Henry, through the instrumentality of Cromwell and Cranmer, to the general mass of the loyal and rejoicing populace. [A special copy on vellum, with illuminations, was prepared for Cromwell himself, and is now in the library of St. John's College, Cambridge.]

23. The first edition of the Great Bible appeared in April 1539, and an injunction was issued by Cromwell that a copy of it should be set up in every parish church. It was consequently the first (and only) English Bible formally authorized for public use; and contemporary evidence proves that it was welcomed and read with avidity. No doubt, as at an earlier day (Ph 1^{15}), some read the gospel 'from envy and rivalry, but others from good will'; but in one way or another, for edification or for controversy, the reading of the Bible took a firm hold on the people of England, a hold which has never since been relaxed, and which had much to do with the stable foundation of the Protestant Church in Great Britain. Nor was the translation, though still falling short of the perfection reached three-quarters of a century later, unworthy of its position. It had many positive merits, and marked a distinct advance upon all its predecessors. Coverdale, though without the force and originality, or even the scholarship, of Tyndale, had some of the more valuable gifts of a translator, and was well qualified to make the best use of the labours of his predecessors. He had scholarship enough to choose and follow the best authorities, he had a happy gift of smooth and effective phraseology, and his whole heart was in his work. As the basis of his revision he had Tyndale's work and his own previous version; and these he revised with reference to the Hebrew, Greek, and Latin, with special assistance in the OT from the Latin translation by Sebastian Münster published in 1534–1535 (a work decidedly superior to the Zürich Bible, which had been his principal guide in 1534), while in the NT he made considerable use of Erasmus. With regard to the use of ecclesiastical terms he followed his own previous example, against Tyndale, in retaining the familiar Latin phrases; and he introduced a considerable number of words and sentences from the Vulgate, which do not appear in the Hebrew or Greek. The text is divided into five sections —(1) Pentateuch, (2) Joshua–Job, (3) Psalms–Malachi, (4) Apocrypha, here entitled 'Hagiographa,' though quite different from the books to which that term is applied in the Hebrew Bible, (5) NT, in which the traditional order of the books is restored in place of Luther's. Coverdale intended to add a commentary at the end, and with this view inserted various marks in the margins, the purpose of which he explains in the Prologue; but he was unable to obtain the sanction of the Privy Council for these, and after standing in the margin for three editions the sign-post marks were withdrawn.

24. The first edition was exhausted within twelve months, and in April 1540 a second edition appeared, this time with a prologue by Cranmer (from which fact the Great Bible is sometimes known as **Cranmer's Bible,** though he had no part in the translation). Two more editions followed in July and November, the latter (Cromwell having now been overthrown and executed) appearing under the nominal patronage of Bishops Tunstall and Heath. In 1541 three editions were issued. None of these editions was a simple reprint. The Prophets, in particular, were carefully revised with the help of Münster for the second edition. The fourth edition (Nov. 1540) and its successors revert in part to the first. These seven editions spread the knowledge of the Bible in a sound, though not perfect, version broad-cast through the land; and one portion of it has never lost its place in the liturgy. In the first Prayer Book of Edward VI. the Psalter (like the other Scripture passages) was taken from the Great Bible. In 1662, when the other passages were taken from the version of 1611, a special exception was made of the Psalter, on account of the familiarity which it had achieved, and consequently Coverdale's version has held its place in the Book of Common Prayer to this day, and it is in his words that the Psalms have become the familiar household treasures of the English-speaking peoples.

25. With the appearance of the Great Bible comes the first pause in the rapid sequence of vernacular versions set on foot by Tyndale. The English Bible was now fully authorized, and accessible to every Englishman in his parish church; and the translation, both in style and in scholarship, was fairly abreast of the attainments and requirements of the age. We hear no more, therefore, at present of further revisions of it. Another circumstance which may have contributed to the same result was the reaction of Henry in his latter years against Protestantism. There was talk in Convocation about a translation to be made by the bishops, which anticipated the plan of the Bible of 1568; and Cranmer prompted Henry to transfer the work to the universities, which anticipated a vital part of the plan of the Bible of 1611; but nothing came of either project. The only practical steps taken were in the direction of the destruction of the earlier versions. In 1543 a proclamation was issued against Tyndale's versions, and requiring the obliteration of all notes; in 1546 Coverdale's NT was likewise prohibited. The anti-Protestant reaction, however, was soon terminated by Henry's death (Jan. 1547); and during the reign of Edward VI., though no new translation (except a small part of the Gospels by Sir J. Cheke) was attempted, many new editions of Tyndale, Coverdale, Matthew, and the Great Bible issued from the press. The accession of Mary naturally put a stop to the printing and circulation of vernacular Bibles in England; and, during the attempt to put the clock back by force, Rogers and Cranmer followed Tyndale to the stake, while Coverdale was imprisoned, but was released, and took refuge at Geneva.

26. The Geneva Bible (1557–1560).—Geneva was the place at which the next link in the chain was to be forged. Already famous, through the work of Beza, as a centre of Biblical scholarship, it became the rallying place of the more advanced members of the Protestant party in exile, and under the strong rule of Calvin it was identified with Puritanism in its most rigid form. Puritanism, in fact, was here consolidated into a living and active principle, and demonstrated its strength as a motive power in the religious and social life of Europe. It was by a relative of Calvin, and under his own patronage, that the work of improving the English translation of the Bible was once more taken in hand. This was W. Whittingham, a Fellow of All Souls' College, Oxford, and subsequently dean of Durham, who in 1557 published the NT at Geneva in a small octavo volume, the handiest form in which the English Scriptures had yet been given to the world. In two other respects also this marked an epoch in the history of the English Bible. It was the first version to be printed in Roman type, and the first in which the division of the text into numbered verses (originally made by R. Stephanus for his Graeco-Latin Bible of 1551) was introduced. A preface was contributed by Calvin himself. The translator claims to have made constant use of the original Greek and of translations in other tongues, and he added a full marginal commentary. If the matter had ended there, as the work of a single scholar on one part of the Bible, it would probably have left little mark; but it was at once made the basis of a revised version of both Testaments by a group of Puritan scholars. The details of the work are not recorded, but the principal workers, apart from Whittingham himself, appear to have been Thomas Sampson, formerly dean of Chichester, and afterwards dean of Christ Church, and A. Gilby, of Christ's College, Cambridge. A version of the Psalter was issued in 1559 [four copies are known to exist, one (incomplete) formerly belonging to Mr. Aldis Wright and now in Trinity College Library, Cambridge, one formerly belonging to the Earl of Ellesmere and now in the Huntington Library, San

Marino, one in Aberdeen University Library, and one owned by the Massachusetts Historical Society, Boston], and in 1560 the complete Bible was given to the world, with the imprint of Rowland Hall, at Geneva. The Psalter in this was the same as that of 1559 ; but the NT had been largely revised since 1557. The book was a moderate-sized quarto, and contained a dedication to Elizabeth, an address to the brethren at home, the books of the OT (including Apocrypha) and NT in the same order as in the Great Bible and our modern Bibles, copious marginal notes (those to the NT taken from Whittingham with some additions), and an apparatus of maps and woodcuts. In type and verse-division it followed the example of Whittingham's NT.

27. The Genevan revisers took the Great Bible as their basis in the OT, and Matthew's Bible (*i.e.* Tyndale) in the NT. For the former they had the assistance of the Latin Bible of Leo Juda (1544), in addition to Pagninus (1527), and they were in consultation with the scholars (including Calvin and Beza) who were then engaged at Geneva in a similar work of revision of the French Bible. In the NT their principal guide was Beza, whose reputation stood highest among all the Biblical scholars of the age. The result was a version which completely outdistanced its predecessors in scholarship, while in style and vocabulary it worthily carried on the great tradition established by Tyndale. Its success was as decisive as it was well deserved ; and in one respect it met a want which none of its predecessors (except perhaps Tyndale's) had attempted to meet. Coverdale's, Matthew's, and the Great Bible were all large folios, suitable for use in church, but unsuited both in size and in price for private possession and domestic study. The Geneva Bible, on the contrary, was moderate in both respects, and achieved instant and long-enduring popularity as the Bible for personal use. For a full century it continued to be the Bible of the people, and it was upon this version, and not upon that of King James, that the Bible knowledge of the Puritans of the Civil War was built up. Its notes furnished them with a full commentary on the sacred text, predominantly hortatory or monitory in character, but Calvinistic in general tone, and occasionally definitely polemical. Over 160 editions of it are said to have been issued, but the only one which requires separate notice is a revision of the NT by Laurence Tomson in 1567, which carried still further the principle of deference to Beza ; this revised NT was successful, and was frequently bound up with the Genevan OT in place of the edition of 1560. [The Geneva Bible is frequently called (in booksellers' catalogues and elsewhere) the 'Breeches' Bible, on account of this word being used in the translation of Gn 3[7].]

28. The Bishops' Bible (1568).—Meanwhile there was one quarter in which the Geneva Bible could hardly be expected to find favour, namely, among the leaders of the Church in England. Elizabeth herself was not too well disposed towards the Puritans, and the bishops in general belonged to the less extreme party in the Church. On the other hand, the superiority of the Genevan to the Great Bible could not be contested. Under these circumstances the old project of a translation to be produced by the bishops was revived. The archbishop of Canterbury, Matthew Parker, was himself a scholar, and took up the task with interest. The basis of the new version was to be the authorized Great Bible. Portions of the text were assigned to various revisers, the majority of whom were bishops. The archbishop exercised a general supervision over the work, but there does not appear to have been any organized system of collaboration or revision, and the results were naturally unequal. In the OT the alterations are mainly verbal, and do not show much originality or genius. In the NT the scholarship shown is on a much higher level, and there is much more independence in style and judgment. In both, use is made of the Geneva Bible, as well as of other versions. The volume was equipped with notes, shorter than those of the Geneva Bible, and generally exegetical. It appeared in 1568, from the press of R. Jugge, in a large folio volume, slightly exceeding even the dimensions of the Great Bible. Parker applied through Cecil for the royal sanction, but it does not appear that he ever obtained it ; But Convocation in 1571 required a copy to be kept in every archbishop's and bishop's house and in every cathedral, and, as far as could conveniently be done, in all churches. The Bishop's Bible, in fact, superseded the Great Bible as the official version, and its predecessor ceased henceforth to be reprinted ; but it never attained the popularity and influence of the Geneva Bible. A second edition was issued in 1569, in which a considerable number of alterations were made, partly, it appears, as the result of the criticisms of Giles Laurence, professor of Greek at Oxford. In 1572 a third edition appeared, of importance chiefly in the NT, and in some cases reverting to the first edition of 1568. In this form the Bishops' Bible continued in official use until its supersession by the version of 1611, of which it formed the immediate basis.

29. The Rheims and Douai Bible (1582–1609).—The English exiles for religious causes were not all of one kind or of one faith. There were Roman Catholic refugees on the Continent as well as Puritan, and from the one, as from the other, there proceeded an English version of the Bible. The centre of the English Roman Catholics was the English College at Douai, the foundation (in 1568) of William Allen, formerly of Queen's College, Oxford, and subsequently cardinal ; and it was from this college that a new version of the Bible emanated which was intended to serve as a counterblast to the Protestant versions, with which England was now flooded. The first instalment of it appeared in 1582, during a temporary migration of the college to Rheims. This was the NT, the work mainly of Gregory Martin, formerly Fellow of St. John's College, Oxford, with the assistance of a small band of scholars from the same university. The OT is stated to have been ready at the same time, but for want of funds it could not be printed until 1609, after the college had returned to Douai, when it appeared just in time to be of some use to the preparers of King James' version. As was natural, the Roman scholars did not concern themselves with the Hebrew and Greek originals, which they definitely rejected as inferior, but translated from the Latin Vulgate, following it with a close fidelity which is not infrequently fatal, not merely to the style, but even to the sense in English. The following short passage (Eph 3[6-12]), taken almost at random, is a fair example of the Latinization of their style.

'The Gentils to be coheires and concorporat and comparticipant of his promis in Christ Jesus by the Gospel : whereof I am made a minister according to the gift of the grace of God, which is given me according to the operation of his power. To me the least of al the sainctes is given this grace, among the Gentils to evangelize the unsearchable riches of Christ, and to illuminate al men what is the dispensation of the sacrament hidden from worldes in God, who created al things ; that the manifold wisedom of God may be notified to the Princes and Potestats in the celestials by the Church, according to the prefinition of worldes, which he made in Christ Jesus our Lord. In whom we have affiance and accesse in confidence, by the faith of him.'

The translation, being prepared with a definite polemical purpose, was naturally equipped with notes of a controversial character, and with a preface in which the object and method of the work were explained. It had, however, as a whole, little success. The OT was reprinted only once in the course of a century, and the NT not much oftener. In England the greater part of its circulation was due to the action of a vehement adversary, W. Fulke, who, in order to expose its errors, printed the Rheims NT in parallel columns with the Bishops' version of 1572, and the Rheims annotations with his own refutations of them ; and this work had a considerable vogue. Regarded from the point of view of scholarship, the Rheims and Douai Bible is of no importance, marking retrogression rather than advance ; but it needs mention in a history of the English Bible, because it is one of the versions of which King James' translators made use. The AV is indeed distinguished by the strongly *English* (as distinct from Latin) character of its vocabulary; but of the Latin words used (and used effectively), many were derived from the Bible of Rheims and Douai.

30. The Authorized Version (1611).—The version which was destined to put the crown on nearly a century of labour, and, after extinguishing by its excellence all rivals, to print an indelible mark on English religion and English literature, came into being almost by accident. It arose out of the Hampton Court Conference, held by James I. in 1604, with the object of arriving at a settlement between the Puritan and Anglican elements in the Church; but it was not one of the prime or original subjects of the conference. In the course of discussion, Dr. Reynolds, president of Corpus Christi College, Oxford, the leader of the moderate Puritan party, referred to the imperfections and disagreements of the existing translations; and the suggestion of a new version, to be prepared by the best scholars in the country, was warmly taken up by the king. The conference, as a whole, was a failure; but James did not allow the idea of the revision to drop. He took an active part in the preparation of instructions for the work, and to him appears to be due the credit of two features which went far to secure its success. He suggested that the translation should be committed in the first instance to the universities (subject to subsequent review by the bishops and the Privy Council, which practically came to nothing), and thereby secured the services of the best scholars in the country, working in co-operation; and (on the suggestion of the bishop of London) he laid down that no marginal notes should be added, which preserved the new version from being the organ of any one party in the Church.

31. Ultimately it was arranged that six companies of translators should be formed, two at Westminster, two at Oxford, and two at Cambridge. The companies varied in strength from 7 to 10 members, the total (though there is some little doubt with regard to a few names) being 47. The Westminister companies undertook Genesis–2 Kings and the Epistles, the Oxford companies the Prophets and the Gospels, Acts, and Apocalypse, and the Cambridge companies 1 Chronicles–Ecclesiastes and the Apocrypha. A series of rules was drawn up for their guidance. The Bishops' Bible was to be taken as the basis. The old ecclesiastical terms were to be kept. No marginal notes were to be affixed, except for the explanation of Hebrew or Greek words. Marginal references, on the contrary, were to be supplied. As each company finished a book, it was to send it to the other companies for their consideration. Suggestions were to be invited from the clergy generally, and opinions requested on passages of special difficulty from any learned man in the land. 'These translations to be used when they agree better with the text than the Bishops' Bible, namely, Tyndale's, Matthew's, Coverdale's, Whitchurch's [*i.e.* the Great Bible], Geneva.' The translators claim further to have consulted all the available versions and commentaries in other languages, and to have repeatedly revised their own work, without grudging the time which it required. The time occupied by the whole work is stated by themselves as two years and three-quarters. The several companies appear to have begun their labours about the end of 1607, and to have taken two years in completing their several shares. A final revision, occupying nine months, was then made by a smaller body, consisting of two representatives from each company, after which it was seen through the press by Dr. Miles Smith and Bishop Bilson; and in 1611 the new version, printed by R. Barker, the king's printer, was given to the world in a large folio volume (the largest of all the series of English Bibles) of black letter type. The details of its issue are obscure. There were at least two issues in 1611, set up independently, known respectively as the 'He' and 'She' Bibles, from their divergence in the translation of the last words of Ru 3[15]; and bibliographers have differed as to their priority, though the general opinion is in favour of the former. Some copies have a wood-block, others an engraved title-page, with different designs. The title-page was followed by the dedication to King James, which still stands in our ordinary copies of the AV, and this by the translators' preface (believed to have been written by Dr. Miles Smith), which is habitually omitted. [It is printed in the present King's Printers' Variorum Bible, and is interesting and valuable both as an example of the learning of the age and for its description of the translators' labours.] For the rest, the contents and arrangement of the AV are too well known to every reader to need description.

32. Nor is it necessary to dwell at length on the characteristics of the translation. Not only was it superior to all its predecessors, but its excellence was so marked that no further revision was attempted for over 250 years. Its success must be attributed to the fact which differentiated it from its predecessors, namely, that it was not the work of a single scholar (like Tyndale's, Coverdale's, and Matthew's Bibles), or of a small group (like the Geneva and Douai Bibles), or of a larger number of men working independently with little supervision (like the Bishops' Bible), but was produced by the collaboration of a carefully selected band of scholars, working with ample time and with full and repeated revision. Nevertheless, it was not a new translation. It owed much to its predecessors. The translators themselves say, in their preface: 'We never thought from the beginning that we should need to make a new translation, nor yet to make of a bad one a good one, . . . but to make a good one better, or out of many good ones one principal good one, not justly to be excepted against; that hath been our endeavour, that our mark.' The description is very just. The foundations of the AV were laid by Tyndale, and a great part of his work continued through every revision. Each succeeding version added something to the original stock, Coverdale (in his own and the Great Bible) and the Genevan scholars contributing the largest share; and the crown was set upon the whole by the skilled labour of the Jacobean divines, making free use of the materials accumulated by others, and happily inspired by the gift of style which was the noblest literary achievement of the age in which they lived. A sense of the solemnity of their subject saved them from the extravagances and conceits which sometimes mar that style; and, as a result, they produced a work which, from the merely literary point of view, is the finest example of Jacobean prose, and has influenced incalculably the whole subsequent course of English literature. On the character and spiritual history of the nation it has left an even deeper mark, to which many writers have borne eloquent testimony; and if England has been, and is, a Bible-reading and Bible-loving country, it is in no small measure due to her possession of a version so nobly executed as the AV.

33. The history of the AV after 1611 can be briefly sketched. In spite of the name by which it is commonly known, and in spite of the statement on both title-pages of 1611 that it was 'appointed to be read in churches,' there is no evidence that it was ever officially authorized either by the Crown or by Convocation. Its authorization seems to have been tacit and gradual. The Bishops' Bible, hitherto the official version, ceased to be reprinted, and the AV no doubt gradually replaced it in churches as occasion arose. In domestic use its fortunes were for a time more doubtful, and for two generations it existed concurrently with the Geneva Bible; but before the century was out its predominance was assured. The first quarto and octavo editions were issued in 1612; and thenceforward editions were so numerous that it is useless to refer to any except a few of them. The early editions were not very correctly printed. In 1638 an attempt to secure a correct text was made by a small group of Cambridge scholars. In 1633 the first edition printed in Scotland was published. In 1701 Bishop Lloyd superintended the printing of an edition at Oxford, in which Archbishop Ussher's dates for Scripture chronology were printed in the margin, where they thenceforth remained. In 1717 a fine edition, printed by Baskett at Oxford, earned bibliographical notoriety as 'The Vinegar Bible' from a misprint in the headline over Lk 20. In 1762 a carefully revised edition was published at Cambridge under the editorship of Dr. T. Paris, and a similar edition, superintended by Dr. B. Blayney, appeared at Oxford in 1769. These two editions, in which the text was carefully revised, the spelling modernized, the punctuation corrected, and considerable alteration made in the marginal notes, formed the standard for subsequent reprints of the AV, which differ in a number of details, small in importance but fairly numerous in the aggregate, from the original text of 1611. One other detail remains to be mentioned. The Nonconformists took much objection to the Apocrypha, and in 1644 the Long Parliament forbade the reading of lessons from it in public; but the lectionary of the English Church always included lessons from it. It was omitted from many editions, however. The first edition printed in America (apart from a surreptitious edition of 1752), in 1782, is without it. In 1826 the British and Foreign Bible Society, which has been one of the principal agents in the circulation of the Scriptures throughout the world, decided never in future to print or circulate copies containing the Apocrypha; and this decision has been carried into effect ever since.

34. So far as concerned the translation of the Hebrew and Greek texts which lay before them, the work of the authors of the AV, as has been shown above, was done not merely well but excellently. There were, no doubt, occasional errors of interpretation; and in regard to the OT in particular the Hebrew scholarship of the age was not always equal to the demands made upon it. But such errors as were made were not of such magnitude or quantity as to have made any extensive revision necessary or desirable even now, after a lapse of three hundred and fifty years. There was, however, another defect, less important (and indeed necessarily invisible at the time), which the lapse of years ultimately forced into prominence, namely, in the text (and especially the Greek text) which they translated. Criticism of the Greek text of the NT had not yet begun. Scholars were content to take the text as it first came to hand, from the late MSS which were most readily accessible to them. The NT of Erasmus, which first made the Greek text generally available in Western Europe, was based upon a small group of relatively late MSS, which happened to be within his reach at Basle. The edition of Stephanus in 1550, which practically established the 'Received Text' which held the field till the 19th cent., rested upon a somewhat superficial examination of 15 MSS, mostly at Paris, of which only two were uncials, and these were but slightly used. None of the great MSS which now stand at the head of our list of authorities was known to the scholars of 1611. None of the ancient versions had been critically edited; and so far as King James' translators made use of them (as we know they did), it was as aids to interpretation, and not as evidence for the text, that they employed them. In saying this there is no imputation of blame. The materials for a critical study and restoration of the text were not then extant; and men were concerned only to translate the text which lay before them in the current Hebrew, Greek, and Latin Bibles. Nevertheless it was in this inevitable defectiveness of text that the weakness lay which ultimately undermined the authority of the AV.

35. The Revised Version (1881–1895).—It was not until the progress of criticism had revealed the defective state of the received Greek text of the NT that any serious movement was set on foot for the revision of the AV. About the year 1855 the question began to be mooted in magazine articles and motions in Convocation, and by way of bringing it to a head a small group of scholars [Dr. Ellicott, afterwards bishop of Gloucester, Dr. Moberly, head master of Winchester and afterwards bishop of Salisbury, Dr. Barron, principal of St. Edmund Hall, Oxford, the Rev. H. Alford, afterwards dean of Canterbury, and the Rev. W. G. Humphrey; with the Rev. E. Hawkins, secretary of the S.P.G., and afterwards canon of Westminster, as their secretary] undertook a revision of the AV of John, which was published in 1857. Six of the Epistles followed in 1861 and 1863, by which time the object of the work, in calling attention to the need and the possibility of a revision, had been accomplished. Meanwhile a great stimulus to the interest in textual criticism had been given by the discovery of the Codex Sinaiticus, and by the work of Tischendorf and Tregelles. In Feb. 1870 a motion for a committee to consider the desirability of a revision was adopted by both Houses of the Convocation of Canterbury; and definite motions in favour of such a revision were passed in the following May. The Convocation of York did not concur, and thenceforward the Southern Houses proceeded alone. A committee of both Houses drew up the lists of revisers, and framed the rules for their guidance. The OT company consisted of 25 (afterwards 27) members, the NT of 26. The rules prescribed the introduction of as few alterations in the AV as possible consistently with faithfulness; the text to be adopted for which the evidence is decidedly preponderating, and when it differs from that from which the AV was made, the alteration to be indicated in the margin (this rule was found impracticable); alterations to be made on the first revision by simple majorities, but to be retained only if passed by a two-thirds majority on the second revision. Both companies commenced work at Westminister on June 22, 1870. The NT company met on 407 days in the course of eleven years, the OT company on 792 days in 15 years. Early in the work the co-operation of American scholars was invited, and in consequence two companies of 15 and 16 members respectively were formed, which began work in 1872, considering the results of the English revision as each section of it was forwarded to them. The collaboration of the English and American companies was perfectly harmonious; and by agreement those recommendations of the American Revisers which were not adopted by the English companies, but to which the proposers nevertheless wished to adhere, were printed in an appendix to the published Bible. Publication took place, in the case of the NT, on May 17, 1881, and in the case of the canonical books of the OT almost exactly four years later. The revision of the Apocrypha was divided between the two English companies, and was taken up by each company on the completion of its main work. The NT company distributed Sirach, Tobit, Judith, Wisdom, 1 and 2 Maccabees among three groups of its members, and the OT company appointed a small committee to deal with the remaining books. The work dragged on over many years, involving some inequalities in revision, and ultimately the Apocrypha was published in 1895.

36. In dealing with the OT the Revisers were not greatly concerned with questions of text. The Massoretic Hebrew text available in 1870 was substantially the same as that which King James' translators had before them; and the criticism of the LXX version was not sufficiently advanced to enable them safely to make much use of it except in marginal notes. Their work consisted mainly in the correction of mistranslations which imperfect Hebrew scholarship had left in the AV. Their changes as a rule are slight, but tend very markedly to remove obscurities and to improve the intelligibility of the translation. The gain is greatest in the poetical and prophetical books (poetical passages are throughout printed as such, which in itself is a great improvement), and there cannot be much doubt that if the revision of the OT had stood by itself it would have been generally accepted without much opposition. With the new version of the NT the case was different. The changes were necessarily more numerous than in the OT, and the greater familiarity with the NT possessed by readers in general made the alterations more conspicuous. The NT Revisers had, in effect, to form a new Greek text before they could proceed to translate it. In this part of their work they were largely influenced by the presence of Drs. Westcott and Hort, who were keen and convinced champions of the type of text of which the best representative is the Codex Vaticanus. At the same time Dr. Scrivener, who took a less advanced view of the necessity of changes in the Received Text, was also a prominent member of the company, and it is probably true that not many new readings were adopted which had not the support of Tischendorf and Tregelles, and which would not be regarded by nearly all scholars acquainted with textual criticism as preferable to those of the AV. To Westcott and Hort may be assigned a large part of the credit for leading the Revisers definitely along the path of critical science; but the Revisers did not follow their leaders the whole way, and their text (edited by Archdeacon Palmer for the Oxford Press in 1881) represents a more conservative attitude than that of the two great Cambridge scholars. Nevertheless the amount of textual change was considerable, and to this was added a very large amount of verbal change, sometimes (especially in the Epistles) to secure greater intelligibility, but oftener (and this is more noticeable in the Gospels) to secure uniformity in the translation of Greek words which the AV deliberately rendered differently in different places (even in parallel narratives of the same event), and precision in the representation of moods and tenses. It was to the great number of changes of this kind, which by themselves appeared needless and pedantic, that most of the criticism bestowed upon the RV was due; but it must be remembered that where the words and phrases of a book are often strained to the uttermost in popular application, it is of great importance that those words and phrases should be as accurately rendered as possible. On the whole, it is certain that the RV marked a great advance on the AV in respect of accuracy, and the main criticisms to which it is justly open are that the principles of classical Greek were applied too rigidly to Greek which is not classical, and that the Revisers, in their careful attention to the Greek, were less happily inspired than their predecessors with the genius of the English language. It should be remembered, too, that renderings which appear in the margin not infrequently represent the views of more than half the Revisers, though they failed to obtain the necessary two-thirds majority. This is perhaps especially the case in the OT, where the RV shows a greater adherence to the AV than in the NT.

37. The American Standard Version (1901) and **The Revised Standard Version** (1946–1957).—Reference has already been made to the co-operation of two American companies in the production of the RV and to the agreement whereby such of their recommendations as did not commend themselves to the English companies were printed in an appendix. The agreement was for a term of fourteen years only, and when it expired the surviving members of the American companies published in 1901 what was in effect an ‘ inverted ’ RV. Those readings in the RV appendix which still seemed preferable to the Americans, together with some others subsequently agreed upon, were incorporated into the text and the readings so displaced were relegated to a new appendix. The resulting ‘ Standard ’ edition of the RV Bible attained a far greater popularity in America than the RV ever attained in England. In 1928 the copyright passed to the International Council of Religious Education (later included in the National Council of Churches), a body in which the educational boards of all the major Protestant churches of the United States and Canada were associated, and an American Standard Bible Committee, consisting entirely of scholars under the chairmanship of Luther A. Weigle of the Yale Divinity School, was appointed to have charge of the text and undertake any further revision that might seem desirable. For more than two years the Committee discussed their commission in all its aspects and eventually reported in favour of a thoroughgoing revision of the version of 1901. At first the work was hampered by lack of funds; but in 1937 the necessary budget was provided and the revision proceeded with the authority of a vote from the International Council that ‘ There is need for a version which embodies the best results of modern scholarship as to the meaning of the Scriptures, and expresses this meaning in English diction which is designed for use in public and private worship and preserves those qualities which have given to the King James version a supreme place in English literature. We, therefore, define the task of the American Standard Bible Committee to be that of revision of the present American Standard Bible in the light of the results of modern scholarship . . . and to be in the diction of the simple, classic English style of the King James Version.’ The Committee worked in two sections, one dealing with the OT and the other with the NT: altogether 31 members served at one time or another; and it is interesting to note that the regulations governing procedure laid down that all changes in the text were to be agreed upon by a two-thirds majority of the total membership of the Committee —a more conservative ruling tnan had governed procedure hitherto, which required only a two-thirds majority of those present at any particular meeting. The NT of the new ‘ Revised Standard Version ’ appeared in 1946, and the OT in 1952. After publication had been completed the Committee was asked by the General Convention of the Protestant Episcopal Church to prepare a revision of the Apocrypha, and a special Apocrypha section was constituted consisting of 5 members of the Committee with 4 additional members. The same general principles were followed, and the Apocrypha appeared in 1957.

38. The New English Bible (1961–   ).—In the same year that the NT portion of the RSV was published in America (1946) the General Assembly of the Church of Scotland circularized the other churches of the British Isles in favour of a completely new translation into contemporary English, on the ground that the archaic language of both the AV and the RV seriously hindered the churches' work. After discussion, the Church of Scotland's proposal was accepted. In 1947 representatives of all the churches met (other than Roman Catholic) and formed a Joint Committee of direction, which in turn appointed three panels of translators (one for the NT, one for the OT, and one for the Apocrypha) as well as a special panel of advisers on literary style. The general procedure adopted was that the various Biblical books were divided among the three translation panels and each member of a panel was asked to prepare a draft translation of a book or group of books. His draft, when ready, was sent to the other members of his panel, which then met and discussed it. When agreement was reached within the panel the result was forwarded to the literary panel, who, after expressing their views, returned it to the translators. The final form of the version accordingly represents agreement between the literary panel and the appropriate translation panel. So far, only the NT has been published (March 14, 1961); and it is obviously too soon to attempt anything more than a provisional assessment of the version's worth as a whole. One thing, however, is clear enough—that, whatever its merits as literature may be, not only its declared aim to be ‘ contemporary ’ in its English, but also its manifest concern to avoid at all costs any trace of literalism in its renderings, make it a far less satisfactory basis for serious study of the Bible than either the RV or the RSV.

39. Finally, a few words must be added about modern versions published by individuals. The most important are those of Ferrar Fenton (Romans, 1882; Epistles, 1884; NT, 1895; whole Bible, 1903), R. F. Weymouth (*The New Testament in Modern Speech*, 1902), and James Moffatt (NT, 1913; OT, 1924; revised edition of the whole Bible, 1935). In 1940 R. A. Knox was commissioned by the English Roman Catholic authorities to produce a new translation of the Vulgate which could be read by Catholics alongside the Rheims and Douai Bible of 1582–1609. The NT (' authorized by the Archbishops and Bishops of England and Wales ') was published in 1945 : the OT (' for private use only ') in 1949. Of the stylistic excellence and general readability of the Knox version there can be no doubt ; but it is very far from being an exact rendering of the Vulgate. F. G. K.—**H. F. D. S.**

EN-HADDAH.—A city of Issachar noticed with En-gannim and Remeth, Jos 19[21] ; it is perhaps modern *el-Hadetheh.*

EN-HAKKORE (' spring of the partridge ' ; cf 1 S 26[20], Jer 17[11] *ḳōrē'*).—The name of a fountain at Lehi, Jg 15[19]. The narrator of the story characteristically connects *haḳḳōrē'* with the word *yiḳrā'* (' he called ') of v.[18], and evidently interprets *'En-haḳḳōrē'* as ' the spring of him that called ' (cf AVm, RVm, RSVm). The whole narrative is rather obscure, and the translation in some instances doubtful. The situation of En-haḳḳore is also quite uncertain.

EN-HAZOR (' spring of Hazor ').—A town of Naphtali, Jos 19[37] ; perhaps modern, *Kh. Ḥaṣîreh*, near *Ḥazzûr*, on the W. slopes of the mountains of Upper Galilee, W. of Kedesh.

EN-MISHPAT (' spring of judgment ').—A name for Kadesh (Gn 14[7]), probably Kadesh-barnea. See Kadesh.

ENNATAN, 1 Es 8[44] (RV) —See Ẹlnathan, **3.**

ENOCH (Heb. *Ḥ^anôkh*) is the ' seventh from Adam ' (Jd [14]) in the Sethite genealogy of Gn 5 (see vv.[18-24]). In the Cainite genealogy of 4[17ff] he is the son of Cain, and therefore the third from Adam. The resemblances between the two lists seem to show that they rest on a common tradition, preserved in different forms by J (ch. 4) and P (ch. 5), though it is not possible to say which version is the more original.—The notice which invests the figure of Enoch with its peculiar significance is found in 5[24] ' Enoch walked with God ; and he was not, for God took him.' The idea here suggested—that because of his perfect fellowship with God this patriarch was ' translated ' to heaven without tasting death (cf **Sir** 44[16] 49[14], He 11[5])—appears to have exerted a certain influence on the OT doctrine of immortality (see Ps 49[15] 73[24]).—A much fuller tradition is presupposed by the remarkable development of the Enoch legend in the Apocalyptic literature, where Enoch appears as a preacher of repentance, a prophet of future events, and the recipient of supernatural knowledge of the secrets of heaven and earth, etc. The origin of this tradition has probably been discovered in a striking Babylonian parallel. The seventh name in the list of ten antediluvian kings given by Berosus is Evedoranchus, which (it seems certain) is a corruption of Enmeduranki, a king of Sippar who was received into the fellowship of Shamash (the sun-god) and Ramman, was initiated into the mysteries of heaven and earth, and became the founder of a guild of priestly diviners. When or how this myth became known to the Jews we cannot tell. A trace of an original connexion with the sun-god has been suspected in the 365 years of Enoch's life (the number of days in the solar year). At all events it is highly probable that the Babylonian legend contains the germ of the later conception of Enoch as embodied in the apocalyptic Book of Enoch (see Pseudepigrapha, **1** (*a*)), and the later Book of the Secrets of Enoch (see Pseudepigrapha, **1** (*b*)).—A citation from the Book of Enoch occurs in Jd [14f] (=En 1[9] 5[4], 27[2]). J. S.

ENOS.—See Enosh.

ENOSH.—The name is a poetical word, meaning ' man.' It was borne by the son of Seth, and grandson of Adam, Gn 4[26] 5[6ff]. As the time of Cain was marked by sin and violence, so that of Seth was marked by piety. In the days of Enosh men began to ' call with the name of Y″,' *i.e.* to use His name in invocations. The name Y″ having been known practically from the beginning of human life, the writer (J) always employs it in preference to the title ' Elohim.' In E (Ex 3[14]) and P (6[2f]) it is not used until after the revelation to Moses. The name stands in Lk 3[38] as **Enos.** A. H. McN.

EN-RIMMON (' spring of pomegranate ').—One of the settlements of the Judahites after the return from the Exile, Neh 11[29]. In Jos 15[32], 1 Ch 4[32], Ain and Rimmon appear as two towns, but we should read En-rimmon ; in Jos 19[7] RSV so reads, where AV, RV read as two towns ; modern *Khirbet Umm er-Ramāmîn,* NNE. of Beersheba.

EN-ROGEL (' spring of the fuller ').—In the border of the territory of Judah (Jos 15[7]) and Benjamin (18[16]). It was outside Jerusalem ; and David's spies, Jonathan and Ahimaaz, were here stationed in quest of news of the revolt of Absalom (2 S 17[17]). Here Adonijah made a feast ' by the stone of **Zoheleth**,' when he endeavoured to seize the kingdom (1 K 1[9]). The identification of this spring is usually made with *Bîr Ayyûb* (' Job's Well ') ; some have argued for the Virgin's Fountain. The strongest argument for the latter is its proximity to a cliff face called *Zaḥweileh,* in which an attempt has been made to recognize Zoheleth. This, however, is uncertain, as *Zaḥweileh* is a cliff, not an isolated stone. R. A. S. M.

ENSAMPLE.—' Ensample ' and ' example ' (both from Lat. *exemplum*) are both used in AV. Tyndale has ' ensample ' only, and so all the English versions until the Rheims appeared. That version used ' example ' probably as being nearer the Vulgate word *exemplum.* The AV frequently reveals the influence of the Rheims version.

EN-SHEMESH (' sun-spring ').—A spring E. of En-rogel, on the way to Jericho, Jos 15[7] 18[17]. It is believed to be modern *'Ain el-Ḥôḍ,* on the Jericho road, E. of Olivet.

ENSIGN.—See Banner.

ENSUE.—The verb ' ensue ' is used intransitively, meaning to *follow,* in Jth 9[5] (AV, RV) ; and transitively, with the full force of *pursue,* in 1 P 3[11] (AV).

EN-TAPPUAH.—A place on the boundary of Manasseh, Jos 17[7] ; probably the same as **Tappuah, 2** (q.v.).

ENTREAT.—See Intreat.

ENVOY.—See Ambassador.

ENVY.—Envy leads to strife, division, railing, hatred, and sometimes to murder. The Bible classes it with these things (Mt 27[18], Ro 1[29] 13[13], 1 Co 3[3], 2 Co 12[20], Gal 5[21], 1 Ti 6[4], Tit 3[3], Ja 3[14, 16]). So does the Litany : ' envy, hatred, and malice.' It is the antithesis of Christian love. Envy loves not, and love envies not (1 Co 13[4]). Bacon closes his essay on ' Envy ' with this sentence : ' Envy is the vilest affection and the most depraved ; for which cause it is the proper attribute of the Devil, who is called, The envious man, that soweth tares amongst the wheat by night (Mt 13[25, 39]) ; as it always cometh to pass, that Envy worketh subtilly and in the dark, and to the prejudice of good things, such as is the wheat.' Chrysostom said : ' As a moth gnaws a garment, so doth envy consume a man, to be a living anatomy, a skeleton, to be a lean and pale carcass, quickened with a fiend.' These are Scriptural estimates. Envy is devilish, and absolutely inconsistent with the highest life. Cf Wis 2[24] ' Through the devil's envy death entered the world.' Examples abound in the Bible, such as are suggested by the relations between Cain and Abel, Jacob and Esau, Rachel and Leah, Joseph and his brothers, Saul and David, Haman and Mordecai, the elder brother and the prodigal son, the rival evangelists of Ph 1[15] and the Apostle Paul, and many others. D. A. H.—**F. C. G.**

EPAENETUS.—A beloved friend of St. Paul, greeted in Ro 16[5] ; he was ' the first convert in Asia for Christ.'

EPAPHRAS.—Mentioned by Paul in Col 1[7] 4[12], Phn [23] ; and described by him as his ' fellow-servant,' and also as a ' servant ' and ' faithful minister ' of Christ. He was apparently a native or inhabitant of

Colossae (Col 4^{12}), and as Paul's representative (1^{7}) founded the Church there (1^{7}). The fact of his prayerful zeal for Laodicea and Hierapolis suggests his having brought the faith to these cities also (4^{13}). He brought news of the Colossian Church to the Apostle during an imprisonment of the latter, perhaps undertaking the journey to obtain Paul's advice as to the heresies that were there prevalent. He is spoken of as Paul's 'fellow-prisoner' (Phn ^{23}), a title probably meaning that his care of the Apostle entailed the *practical* sharing of his captivity. The Epistle to the Colossians was a result of this visit, and Epaphras brought it back with him to his flock. *Epaphras* is a shortened form of *Epaphroditus* (Ph 2^{25}), but, as the name was in common use, it is not probable that the two are to be identified.

C. T. P. G.—**J. K.**

EPAPHRODITUS.—Mentioned by Paul in Ph 2^{25-30} 4^{18}, and described by him as his 'brother, fellow-worker, and fellow-soldier' (2^{25}). He was the messenger by whom the Philippians sent the offerings which fully supplied the necessities of Paul during an imprisonment (2^{25} 4^{18}). While with Paul he laboured so zealously for the Church and for the Apostle as to 'risk' his life (2^{30}); indeed, he 'nearly died,' but God had mercy on him, and the Apostle was spared this 'sorrow upon sorrow' (v.^{27}). News of his illness reached Philippi, and the distress thus caused his friends made him long to return (v.^{26}). Paul was 'the more eager to send him,' thus to relieve their minds and at the same time lessen his own sorrow by his knowledge of their joy at receiving him back in health. Apparently the Epistle to the Philippians was sent by him.

C. T. P. G.—**J. K.**

EPHAH.—**1.** A son of Midian, descended from Abraham and Keturah (Gn 25^{4}, 1 Ch 1^{33}), the eponymous ancestor of an Arabian tribe whose identity is uncertain. This tribe appears in Is 60^{6} as engaged in the transport of gold and frankincense from Sheba. **2.** A concubine of Caleb, 1 Ch 2^{46}. **3.** A Judahite, 1 Ch 2^{47}.

EPHAH.—See WEIGHTS AND MEASURES.

EPHAI.—A Netophathite (see NETOPHAH), whose sons were amongst the 'captains of the forces' who joined Gedaliah at Mizpah, Jer 40^{8}; they were murdered by Ishmael, Jer 41^{3}.

EPHER.—**1.** The name of the second of the sons of Midian mentioned in Gn 25^{4}, 1 Ch 1^{33}, and recorded as one of the descendants of Abraham by his wife Keturah (Gn 25^{1}). **2.** The name of one of the sons of Ezrah, 1 Ch 4^{17}. **3.** The first of a group of five heads of fathers' houses belonging to the half tribe of Manasseh, 1 Ch 5^{24}.

EPHES-DAMMIM.—The place in Judah where the Philistines were encamped at the time when David slew Goliath, 1 S 17^{1}. The same name appears in 1 Ch 11^{13} (and probably originally in 2 S 23^{9}) as **Pas-dammim.** The site is not known.

EPHESIANS, EPISTLE TO.—This Epistle belongs to the group of Epistles of the Captivity, and if genuine, was written by Paul and sent by Tychicus at the same time as the Epistles to the Colossians and to Philemon (see COLOSSIANS).

1. Destination.—To whom was it addressed? That it was specifically written to the Ephesian Church is improbable, for two reasons—(1) The words 'at Ephesus' in 1^{1} are absent from two of the earliest MSS, and apparently from the Epistle as known to Marcion (A.D. 140), who refers to it as addressed to the Laodiceans. Origen also had access to a copy of the Epistle from which they were absent. (2) The Epistle is almost entirely devoid of the personal touches—references to St. Paul's long stay at Ephesus, greetings to friends, etc.—that we should expect to find in an Epistle to a Church with which the Apostle's relations had been as close as they had been with the Ephesian Church. On the other hand, early tradition, as shown in the title, associated the Epistle with Ephesus, and, except Marcion, no early writer associated it with any other Church. Moreover, personal touches are not wholly absent. St. Paul has heard of the faith and love of those to whom he writes (1^{15}); they had been saddened by news of his imprisonment (3^{13}), they apparently know Tychicus (6^{21f}). Many have concluded that the best explanation of all the facts is to be found in the suggestion made by Ussher, and adopted by Lightfoot (*Biblical Essays*), that the Epistle is really a circular-letter to the Churches of Asia (cf the First Epistle of St. Peter). Possibly the space where 'at Ephesus' now appears was left blank for Tychicus to fill in as he left copies of the letter at the various churches on his line of route. If this solution is the true one, this Epistle is most probably the letter referred to in Col 4^{16}.

It is more widely held, however, that the Epistle was a general letter addressed, not to any particular church or group of churches, but to Christians everywhere. In line with this understanding is the general character of the Epistle. Unlike most of Paul's letters, it does not appear to have been written with a view to any particular controversy or problem of Church life. Of all the Pauline Epistles it has most the character of a treatise or homily. Its keynote is the union of the Christian body, Jewish and Gentile, in Christ, in whom all things are being fulfilled.

2. Authenticity.—The authenticity of the Epistle is well attested by external testimony, but has been disputed during the last century on internal grounds. The chief of these are—(1) *Difference of style from the earlier Epistles.* This is very marked, as any reader will quickly see. (2) *Doctrinal differences.* The chief of these are: (*a*) the prominence given to the 'Catholic' idea of the Church; (*b*) the doctrine of the pre-existent Christ as the agent of creation; (*c*) the substitution of the idea of the gradual fulfilment of the Divine purpose for the earlier idea of an imminent return (*Parousia*) of Christ. (3) *The references to 'apostles and prophets'* in 3^{5} 4^{11}, which seem to suggest that the writer is looking back on the Apostolic age from the standpoint of the next generation. (4) *The writer of the Epistle seems to have been dependent upon the other letters of Paul, especially Colossians, in a way Paul himself would not naturally have been.* Those who defend the Pauline authorship of the Epistle acknowledge these difficulties but discount the third and fourth and appeal to possible developments in Paul's thought and literary style in countering the other two. They also emphasize the strength of the external evidence.

A mediating view, defended particularly by E. J. Goodspeed, sees Ephesians as the work of whoever collected the letters of Paul. This collection seems to have occurred near the end of the 1st cent. Since the letters had all been addressed to particular churches, whereas the collection itself was being presented as the message of Paul for the whole church, the collector and editor would have wished a general epistle as a kind of preface or 'covering letter.' This he, or some contemporary of his, composed for the purpose, using the nine genuine letters as sources and models. This helps to account for the genuinely Pauline features of the Epistle—its true authenticity—and since this introductory Epistle would have achieved a wide circulation as early as any of the church letters, the strength of the external evidence is also understandable.

3. Characteristics.—The following are among the distinctive lines of thought of the Epistle. (1) The stress laid on the idea of *the Church as the fulfilment of the eternal purpose of God*—the body of which Christ is the head (1^{23} 2^{16} 3^{6} $4^{12, 16}$), the building of which Christ is the corner-stone (2^{20-22}), the bride (5^{23-27}). (2) *The cosmic significance of the Atonement* ($1^{10, 14}$ 2^{7} 3^{10}). (3) The prominence given to *the work of the Holy Spirit* ($1^{13, 17}$ 2^{18} 3^{16} $4^{3, 30}$ 5^{9}). In this the Epistle differs from Colossians, and resembles 1 Corinthians. (4) Repeated exhortations to *unity*, and the graces that make for unity ($4^{1-7, 13, 25-32}$ 5^{2} etc.). (5) The conception of the Christian *household* (5^{22}–6^{9}) and of the Christian *warrior* (6^{10-18}).

4. Relation to other books.—The Epistle has lines of thought recalling 1 Corinthians. See, *e.g.* in 1 Corinthians the idea of the riches (1^{5}) and the mystery (2$^{7-10}$) of the gospel, the work of the Spirit (2^{10f} 12^{4}*J*), the building (3$^{9-11, 16}$), the one body (10^{17} 12$^{4-6, 12-16}$), all things subjected to Christ (15$^{24-28}$). The relation to Colossians is very close. 'The one is the general and systematic exposition of the same truths which appear in a special bearing in the other' (Lightfoot). Cf the relation of Galatians and Romans. Ephesians and Philippians have many thoughts in common. See, *e.g.* the Christian citizenship (Eph 2$^{12, 19}$, Ph 1^{27} 3^{20}), the exaltation of Christ (Eph 1^{20}, Ph 2^{9}), the true circumcision (Eph 2^{11}, Ph 3^{3}), unity and stability (Eph 2^{18}*J* 4^{3} 6^{13}, Ph 1^{27}). Cf also Eph 6^{18} with Ph 4^{6}, and Eph 5^{2} with Ph 4^{18}. In regard to Romans and Ephesians, 'the unity at which the former Epistle seems to arrive by slow and painful steps is assumed in the latter as a starting-point, with a vista of wondrous possibilities beyond' (Hort).

There is a close connexion between this Epistle and 1 Peter, not so much in details as in 'identities of thought and similarity in the structure of the two Epistles as wholes' (Hort). If there is any direct relation, it is probable that the author of 1 Peter used this Epistle, as he certainly used Romans. In some respects this Epistle shows an approximation of Pauline thought to the teaching of the Fourth Gospel. See, *e.g.* the teaching of both on grace, on the contrast of light and darkness, on the work of the pre-incarnate Logos; and compare Jn 17 with the whole Epistle. Cf also Rev 21$^{10, 14}$ with Eph 2^{20f}, Rev 19^{7} with Eph 5$^{25-27}$, and Rev 13^{8} with Eph 3^{11}. J. H. B. M.—**J. K.**

EPHESUS.—The capital of the Roman province Asia; a large and ancient city at the mouth of the river Cayster. The origin of the name, which is native and not Greek, is unknown. It stood at the entrance to one of the four clefts in the surrounding hills. It is along these valleys that the roads through the central plateau of Asia Minor pass. The chief of these was the route up the Maeander as far as the Lycus, its tributary, then along the Lycus towards Apamea. It was the most important avenue of civilization in Asia Minor under the Roman Empire. **Miletus** had been in earlier times a more important harbour than Ephesus, but the track across from the main road to Ephesus was much shorter than the road to Miletus, and was over a pass only 600 feet high. Consequently Ephesus replaced Miletus before and during the Roman Empire, especially as the Maeander had silted up so much as to spoil the harbour at the latter place. It became the great emporium for all the trade N. of Mount Taurus.

Ephesus was on the main route from Rome to the East, and many side roads and sea-routes converged at it (Ac 19^{21} 20$^{1, 17}$, 1 Ti 1^{3}, 2 Ti 4^{12}). The governors of the provinces in Asia Minor had always to land at Ephesus. It was an obvious centre for the work of St. Paul, as influences from there spread over the whole province (Ac 19^{10}). Corinth was the next great station on the way to Rome, and communication between the two places was constant. The ship in Ac 18^{19}, bound from Corinth for the Syrian coast, touched first at Ephesus.

Besides Paul, Tychicus (Eph 6^{21f}) and Timothy (according to 1 Ti 1^{3}, 2 Ti 4^{9}), John Mark (Col 4^{10}, 1 P 5^{13}), and the writer of the Apocalypse (1^{11} 2^{1}) were acquainted with Asia or Ephesus.

The harbour of Ephesus was kept large enough and deep enough only by constant attention. The alluvial deposits were (and are) so great that, when once the Roman Empire had ceased to hold sway, the harbour became gradually smaller and smaller, so that now Ephesus is four miles from the sea. Even in St. Paul's time there appear to have been difficulties about navigating the channel, and ships avoided Ephesus except when loading or unloading was necessary (cf Ac 20^{16}). The route by the high lands, from Ephesus to the East, was suitable for foot passengers and light traffic, and was used by St. Paul (Ac 19^{1}; probably also 16^{6}). The alternative was the main road through Colossae and Laodicea, neither of which St. Paul ever visited (Col 2^{1}).

In the open plain, about 5 miles from the sea, S. of the river, stands a little hill which has always been a religious centre. Below its SW. slope was the temple sacred to Artemis (q.v.). The Greek city Ephesus was built at a distance of 1–2 miles SW. of this hill. The history of the town turns very much on the opposition between the free Greek spirit of progress and the slavish submission of the Oriental population to the goddess. Croesus the Lydian represented the predominance of the latter over the former, but Lysimachus (295 B.C.) revived the Greek influence. Ephesus, however, was always proud of the position of 'Warden of the Temple of Artemis' (Ac 19^{35}). The festivals were thronged by crowds from the whole of the province of Asia. St. Paul, whose residence in Ephesus lasted 2 years and 3 months (Ac 19$^{8, 10}$), or, roughly expressed, 3 years (Ac 20^{31}), at first incurred no opposition from the devotees of the goddess; but when his teaching proved prejudicial to the money interests of the people who made a living out of the worship, he was at once bitterly attacked. Prior to this occurrence, his influence had caused many of the famous magicians of the place to burn their books (Ac 19$^{13-19}$). The riot of 19^{32} was no mere passing fury of a section of the populace. The references to Ephesus in the Epistles show that the opposition to Christianity there was as long-continued as it was virulent (1 Co 15^{32} 16^{9}, 2 Co 1$^{8-10}$).

The scene in Ac 19^{23ff} derives some illustration from an account of the topography and the government of the city. The ruins of the theatre are large, and it has been calculated that it could hold 24,000 people. It was on the western slope of Mount Pion, and overlooked the harbour. The Asiarchs (see ASIARCH), who were friendly to St. Paul, may have been present in Ephesus at that time on account of a meeting of their body (Ac 19^{31}). The town-clerk (q.v.) or secretary of the city appears as a person of importance, and this is exactly in accordance with what is known of municipal affairs in such cities. The Empire brought decay of the influence of popular assemblies, which tended more and more to come into the hands of the officials, though the assembly at Ephesus was really the highest municipal authority (Ac 19^{39}), and the Roman courts and the proconsuls (Ac 19^{38}) were the final judicial authority in processes against individuals. The meeting of the assembly described in Acts was not a legal meeting. Legal meetings could be summoned only by the *Roman* officials, who had the power to call together the people when they pleased. The secretary tried to act as intermediary between the people and these officials, and save the people from trouble at their hands. The temple of Artemis which existed in St. Paul's day was of enormous size. Apart from religious purposes, it was used as a treasure-house: as to the precise arrangements for the charge of this treasure we are in ignorance.

There is evidence outside the NT also for the presence of Jews in Ephesus. The twelve who had been baptized with the baptism of John (Ac 19^{3}) may have been persons who had emigrated to Ephesus before the mission of Jesus began. When St. Paul turned from the Jews to the population in general, he appeared, as earlier in Athens, as a lecturer in philosophy, and occupied the school of Tyrannus out of school hours. The earlier part of the day, beginning before dawn, he spent in manual labour. The actual foundation of Christianity in Ephesus may have been due to Priscilla and Aquila (Ac 18^{19}).

'Ephesian' occurs as a variant reading in the 'Western' text of Ac 20^{4} for the words 'of Asia,' as applied to Tychicus and Trophimus. Trophimus was an inhabitant of Ephesus (Ac 21^{29}), capital of Asia; but Tychicus was probably merely an inhabitant of the province Asia; hence they are coupled under the only adjective applicable to both.

The city of Ephesus was an object of exploration on

the part of J. T. Wood, who determined the location of the temple of Artemis in 1877, NE. of the city at the foot of the hill *Ayassoluk*, on which Justinian built the church dedicated to St. John the Divine. This temple, now deeply buried in the ground, was one of the seven wonders of the ancient world. An Austrian expedition did research and excavation at Ephesus (1906–1937). The reconstruction of the *Arkadiane*, the wide street leading from the theatre to the Harbour Gate, is one of its achievements. This street was flanked by colonnades and shops. Much archaeological work remains to be done at Ephesus. A. So.—**E. G. K.**

EPHLAL.—A descendant of Judah, 1 Ch 2[37].

EPHOD.—1. Father of Hanniel, Nu 34[23]. **2.** See DRESS, **2** (*c*), and PRIESTS AND LEVITES, **1** (*d*). **3.** The ' ephod ' of Jg 8[27] 17[15] 18[14, 17, 20] is probably an image.

EPHPHATHA (or with some MSS and Jerome, *ephphetha*) in Mk 7[34] is an attempt at transliterating an Aramaic word, the imperative of either the Ithpaʿal or the Ithpeʿel from the verb *pᵉthaḥ* ' to open.' In either case it means ' Be thou opened.' Since the imperative meant seems to be masculine singular, Jesus' command was doubtless addressed to the man who, being a deaf mute, had been closed and was now to be opened. It might, however, have been addressed either to the mouth or the ears, which in Aramaic are at times spoken of as being ' opened ' (cf Lk 1[64] and the Targum to Is 50[4]). A. J.

EPHRAIM.—Brother of Manasseh and second son of Joseph by Asenath, the daughter of Potiphera, priest of On (Gn 41[50ff]), and eponym of the tribe of Ephraim. Popular etymology connected his name with the Hebrew root ' to be fruitful ' (Gn 41[52]), reflecting the strength and prosperity of the tribe. It is clear from passages such as Jos 16[10], Jg 1[29] 8[1]–9[57], and the story about Shechem in Gn 34 that Ephraim was of mixed Canaanite-Hebrew blood and originally worshipped a deity called Baal-berith (Lord of the Covenant). In Gn 48[13ff] we have the story of the adoption of Ephraim and Manasseh by Jacob (Israel), and in the blessing that follows Jacob gives precedence to Ephraim as against the older but less powerful Manasseh. In the early period the three tribes, Ephraim, Manasseh, and Benjamin, constituted a single group under the title of ' Joseph ' or ' house of Joseph.' As late as 2 S 19[20] Benjamin apparently is still a member of the group, and by the time of the Blessing of Jacob (Gn 49) Joseph still comprised Ephraim and Manasseh, but Benjamin had become a separate tribe, and this is the situation also in the Blessing of Moses (Dt 33). In the Song of Deborah (Jg 5) Ephraim is mentioned along with Benjamin and Machir, the first-born of Manasseh (Jos 17[1], Gn 50[23]), but not Manasseh himself. Even as late as Solomon it was an Ephraimite, Jeroboam, who was answerable for the whole ' house of Joseph ' (1 K 11[28]). Exactly how and when Joseph broke up into its component parts we have no means at present of knowing. It was probably a loose organization that kept the group together, and they may have come in and out of the union more or less at will.

Ephraim occupied north-central Palestine (Jos 16[5–10]), but not a word is said in the records about the conquest of that region, manifestly because it was already in the hands of Hebrews or of people so friendly to them that they joined the invaders without a struggle. Joshua himself was an Ephraimite (Jos 19[50]). Shechem, the capital city, was the scene of the gathering of the tribes for the covenant ceremonies (Jos 8[30–35]), and again after the conquest was completed (Jos 24[1–22]). The early and important sanctuary of Shiloh was within its borders, and likewise the equally important sanctuary of Shechem, which city became the capital. Being rich and powerful, Ephraim was rather domineering throughout its history and jealous of its authority. It quarrelled with Gideon (Jg 8[1–3]) and with Jephthah (Jg 12[1–6]). After Saul's death Ephraim helped to set up Ishbosheth as king in opposition to David and the tribe of Judah (2 S 2[8ff]), and it was an Ephraimite, Jeroboam, who revolted against Solomon, and was eventually made king over all Israel (1 K 12[20]). As a result Ephraim, along with Israel, became the name of the northern kingdom, and its capital, originally Tirzah (1 K 14[17]) and later Samaria (1 K 16[24]), was situated in Ephraimite territory. Because Ephraim dominated the economic and political scene, there was a tendency, particularly among the prophets, to call the whole country Ephraim. See also TRIBES OF ISRAEL. T. J. M.

EPHRAIM.—A town in the vicinity of Baal-hazor (q.v.) mentioned in 2 S 13[23] as the scene of Absalom's plot against Amnon. It may be identical with the Ephraim named in the *Onomasticon*, although the distance of 20 Roman miles N. of Jerusalem is doubtless too great if its proximity to Baal-hazor is correct. It also designated a larger area in the region of Shechem where the descendants of Ephraim settled (Jos 16[4], Jg 5[14]). The name of the town probably gave its name in later times to the district of Samaria called *Aphairema* (1 Mac 11[34] [AV **Apherema**, RV **Aphaerema**] ; Jos. *Ant.* XIII. iv. 9 [127]). Most scholars identify the town with the Ephraim ' near the wilderness ' to which Jesus retired after the raising of Lazarus (Jn 11[54]). The *Onomasticon* mentions an ' Efraim ' 5 Roman miles E. of Bethel. The description of Vespasian's march against Jerusalem refers to his capture of ' Bethel and Ephraim, two small cities ' (Jos. *War* IV. ix. 9 [551]) as if they were close together. Two modern sites which have been proposed as Ephraim are *eṭ-Ṭaiyibeh*, about 4 miles NE. of *Beitîn* (ancient Bethel), and *Samieh*, in the same region but closer to the Jordan valley. Both give evidence of occupation in Biblical times. See also EPHRON.

The Forest of Ephraim (Heb. *yaʿar 'Ephrayim*) was probably not a forest in our sense of the term, but a stretch of rough country such as the Arabs still call *waʿr*, abounding in rocks and thickets of brushwood. The location is not known, but it must have been E. of the Jordan, in the neighbourhood of Mahanaim. It was the scene of Absalom's defeat and death (2 S 18[6ff] ; cf 17[22, 24, 26f]). The origin of the name is also uncertain, although it possibly preserves the memory of some association of the Ephraimites with the district (cf Jg 12[1ff]).

Mount Ephraim (Heb. *har 'Ephrayim*) is the name given to that part of the central range of Western Palestine occupied by Ephraim, corresponding in part to the modern *Jebel Nâblus*, the region near modern *Nâblus* and the site of ancient Shechem. Because the region so designated might better be described as hilly in character rather than a single mountain, the RV and RSV use the phrase ' the hill country of Ephraim ' instead of the ' mount Ephraim ' of the AV (cf Jos 17[15], Jg 3[27], 1 S 1[1] etc.). W. E.—**W. L. R.**

EPHRAIM GATE.—See JERUSALEM, GATES OF.

EPHRAIN, 2 Ch 13[19] (AV).—See EPHRON, **4.**

EPHRATH, EPHRATHAH.—See BETHLEHEM, and CALEB-EPHRATHAH.

EPHRATHITE.—1. A native of Bethlehem, Ru 1[2], 1 S 17[12]. **2.** An Ephraimite, Jg 12[4] (where EV render **Ephraimite**), 1 S 1[2], 1 K 11[26] (AV, RSV Ephraimite in both cases).

EPHRON.—1. The Hittite from whom Abraham purchased the field or plot of ground in which was the cave of Machpelah, Gn 23[8ff]. The purchase is described with great particularity ; and the transactions between Ephron and Abraham are conducted with an elaborate courtesy characteristic of Oriental proceedings. Ephron received 400 shekels' weight of silver (23[15]) : coined money did not exist at that time. If we compare the sale of the site with other instances (Gn 33[19], 1 K 16[24]), Ephron seems to have made a good bargain. **2.** A mountain district, containing cities, on the border of Judah, between Nephtoah and Kiriath-jearim, Jos 15[9]. It is probably modern *eṭ-Ṭaiyibeh*, SE. of the Sea of Galilee. **3.** A strong fortress in the W. part of Bashan between Ashteroth-karnaim and Bethshean (1 Mac 5[46ff], 2 Mac 12[27]). The site is unknown. **4.** A place mentioned in 2 Ch 13[19] (AV **Ephrain**); probably the same as **Ephraim, 2** (q.v.).

EPICUREANS.—St. Paul's visit to Athens (Ac 17[15-34]) led to an encounter with 'some of the Epicurean and Stoic philosophers,' representatives of the two leading schools of philosophy of that time.

Epicureanism took its name from its founder Epicurus, who was born in the island of Samos in the year 341 B.C. In 306 B.C. he settled in Athens, where he died in 270 B.C. A man of blameless life and of a most amiable character, Epicurus gathered around him, in the garden which he had purchased at Athens, a brotherhood of attached followers, who came to be known either as Epicureans or 'the philosophers of the Garden.' His aim was a practical one. He regarded 'pleasure'—really happiness, not sensual enjoyment—as the absolute good. He did not restrict it, as the earlier Cyrenaic school had done, to immediate bodily pleasures. Whatever may have been the practical outcome of the system, Epicurus and his more worthy followers must be acquitted of the charge of sensuality. What he advocated and aimed at was the happiness of a tranquil life as free from pain as possible, undisturbed by social conventions or political excitement or superstitious fears—such as the fear of capricious and malevolent gods or the terrors of the life to come.

To deliver men from 'the fear of the gods' was the chief endeavour and, according to his famous follower the Roman poet Lucretius, the crowning service of Epicurus. Thus it may be said that, at one point at least, the paths of the Christian Apostle and the Epicurean philosopher touched each other. Epicurus sought to achieve his end by showing that in the physical organization of the world there is no room for the interference of such beings as the gods of the popular theology. There is nothing which is not material, and the primal condition of matter is that of atoms which, falling in empty space with an inherent tendency to swerve slightly from the perpendicular, come into contact with each other, and form the world as it appears to the senses. All is material and mechanical. The gods—he does not deny the existence of gods—have no part or lot in the affairs of men. They are relegated to a realm of their own in the spaces between the worlds. Further, since the test of life is feeling, death, in which there is no feeling, cannot mean anything at all, and is not a thing to be feared either in prospect or in fact.

One of the most attractive summaries of Epicurean teaching is the fugitive *tetractys* found among the fragments of Epicurus's work *On Nature* recovered from the ruins of Herculaneum: *Nothing to fear in God–Nothing to feel in death–Good can be attained–Evil can be endured.* In a world of scepticism and superstition, such convictions were 'on the side of the angels' and helped prepare the way for the Christian gospel. Yet the total effect of Epicureanism was negative, especially in its later Roman form. Its wide-spread and powerful influence must be accounted for by the personal charm of its founder, and by the conditions of the age in which it appeared and flourished. It takes its place as one of the negative but widening influences, leading up to 'the fulness of time' which saw the birth of Christianity.

W. M. McD.—**F. C. G.**

EPIGRAPHY.—The study of **inscriptions** (q.v.). Like many another traditional term it is chiefly one of convenience and fails to satisfy. It arose at a time when surviving monumental inscriptions were found to give valuable supplementary information for the knowledge of classical antiquity. The discovery of ancient texts written in the same characters on papyrus, leather, parchment, and clay has made it rather impracticable to isolate the monumental inscriptions as a separate field of study. Nevertheless, when the word epigraphy is used it should be reserved for texts that were done by the stone cutter, the engraver, or the maker of casts, rather than by the scribe or wielder of the stylus. Assyriologists of a former generation often spoke of inscriptions, when meaning only clay tablets. The word epigraphy requires further definition by the language or group of languages with which one is concerned. Thus North Semitic Epigraphy (cf M. Lidzbarski, *Handbuch der nordsemitischen Epigraphik*, 1898) is used to cover inscriptions in the Canaanitic and Aramaic dialects. South Semitic Epigraphy applies especially to the South Arabian dialects. Greek and Latin Epigraphy (cf W. Larfeld, *Handbuch der griechischen Epigraphik*, 1907, R. Cagnat, *Cours élémentaire d'épigraphie Latine*, 3rd ed. 1898) are self-explanatory terms. A particular slant may be stressed, as when one speaks of Early Christian Epigraphy (cf C. M. Kaufmann, *Handbuch der altchristlichen Epigraphik*, 1917); in that case the language is generally Greek or Latin, but the subject matter looms so important it crowds out mention of the languages.

E. G. K.

EPILEPSY.—See MEDICINE.

EPIPHI (3 Mac 6[38]).—See TIME.

ER.—**1.** The eldest son of Judah by his Canaanitish wife, the daughter of Shua. For wickedness, the nature of which is not described, 'Y″ slew him,' Gn 38[3-7], Nu 26[19]. **2.** A son of Shelah the son of Judah, 1 Ch 4[21]. **3.** An ancestor of Jesus, Lk 3[28].

ERAN.—Grandson of Ephraim, Nu 26[36]. Patronymic, **Eranites,** *ib.*

ERASTUS.—The name occurs thrice in NT among the Pauline company. An Erastus sends greetings in Ro 16[23], and is called 'the treasurer (AV 'chamberlain') of the city' (Corinth). The Erastus who was sent by St. Paul from Ephesus to Macedonia (Ac 19[22]), and who later remained in Corinth (2 Ti 4[20]), is perhaps the same.

A. J. M.

ERECH.—An ancient city of Babylonia, called *Uruk* in Babylonian and Assyrian texts, mentioned in Gn 10[10] amongst Nimrod's cities; modern *Warka*, S. of Babylon. Some of the inhabitants were deported as colonists to Samaria by Ashurbanipal, and are mentioned in Ezr 4[9] (RSV 'men of Erech'; AV, RV '**Archevites**'). The deportation may indicate that Erech sided with Babylon in the revolt of Shamash-shum-ukin against the Assyrian king.

ERI.—Son of Gad, Gn 46[16], Nu 26[16]. Patronymic **Erites,** Nu 26[16].

ERUPTION.—See MEDICINE.

ESAIAS.—The familiar AV spelling of **Isaiah** in Apocrypha and NT; it is retained by RV only in 2 Es 2[18], but is not found in RSV.

ESARHADDON, son and successor of Sennacherib (2 K 19[37], Is 37[38]), reigned over Assyria 680–669 B.C. He practically re-founded Babylon, which Sennacherib had destroyed, and was a great restorer of temples. He was also a great conqueror, making three expeditions to Egypt, and finally conquered the whole North, garrisoning the chief cities and appointing vassal kings. He subdued all Syria, and received tribute from Manasseh, and Ezr 4[2] mentions his colonization of Samaria. He ruled over Babylonia as well as Assyria, which explains the statement of 2 Ch 33[1] that Manasseh was carried captive there.

ESAU.—**1.** The name is best explained as meaning 'hairy' (Gn 25[25], cf 27[11]); **Edom** or 'ruddy' was sometimes substituted for it (v.[30]), and Esau is represented as the progenitor of the Edomites (36[9, 43], Jer 49[7ff], Ob [8]). He displaced the Horites from the hilly land of Seir, and settled there with his followers (Gn 32[3] 36[8], Dt 2[12]). His career is sketched briefly but finely by weaving incidents collected from two sources (J and E; in the early part, chiefly the former), whilst the Priestly writer is supposed to have contributed a few particulars (Gn 26[34f] 28[9] 36). The standing feature of Esau's history is rivalry with Jacob, which is represented as even preceding the birth of the twins (Gn 25[22f], Hos 12[3]). The facts may be collected into four groups. The sale of the birthright (Gn 25[29ff]) carried with it the loss of precedence after the father's death (27[29]), and probably loss of the domestic priesthood (Nu 3[12f]), and of the double portion of the patrimony (Dt 21^{17}). For this act the NT calls Esau 'irreligious' (He 12^{16}; AV, RV 'profane'), thus revealing the secret of his character; the word (Gr. *bebēlos*) suggests the quality of a man to whom nothing is sacred, whose heart and thought range over only what is material and sensibly present. To propitiate his parents, Esau sought a wife of his own kin (Gn 28^{8f}), though already married to two Hittite women (26^{34f}). His father's proposed blessing was diverted by Jacob's artifice; and, doomed to live by war and the chase (27^{40}), Esau resolved to recover his lost honours by killing his brother. Twenty years later the brothers were reconciled (33^{4}); after which Esau made Seir his principal abode, and on the death of Isaac settled there permanently (35^{29} 36^{6}, Dt 2^{4f}, Jos 24^{4}).

By a few writers Esau has been regarded as a mythical personage, the personification of the roughness of Idumaea. It is at least as likely that a man of Esau's character and habits would himself choose to live in a country of such a kind (Mal 1^{3}); and mere legends about the brothers, as the early Targums are a witness, would not have made Esau the more attractive man, and the venerated Jacob, in comparison, timid, tricky, and full of deceits. Against the historicity of the record there is really no substantial evidence.

2. 1 Es 5^{29} (AV, RV); see Ziha. R. W. M.

ESCHATOLOGY is that department of theology which is concerned with the 'last things.' Though the term is not itself a Biblical one, it relates to such matters as the consummation of the Divine purpose in history, the final judgment, the estate of individuals after death, and the like, all of which occupy important places in the theology of the Bible.

1. The Beginnings of Eschatology in Pre-Exilic Israel.—Whether or not one describes the future hope of pre-exilic Israel as an eschatology is purely a question of definition. If by eschatology is meant a developed doctrine, or complex of ideas, relating to the end of the age and the estate of individuals after death, as in Judaism or Christianity, then it must be admitted that eschatology makes its appearance only late in the OT period. But this is probably too narrow a definition to be fully useful. Since Israel's faith from earliest times exhibited the profound conviction that Yahweh acted purposefully in history, guiding events toward the fulfilment of promise (beyond which there was no need to look), it can be said to have had an eschatological orientation from the beginning. In the future hope of old Israel the beginnings of a fully developed eschatology are to be found.

Though the origins of this future hope are disputed, it probably represents a development of a primitive feature in Israel's faith. It was scarcely essentially a borrowing from the pagan environment, since the ancient paganisms lacked any sense of history or of a divine purpose in history. Moreover, though Israel's future hope was given shape in the cult, and lent intensity by the frustration of national ambition, it hardly owed its origin to these things but to certain distinctive elements in Israel's faith itself. The belief that their God had promised them land and progeny seems, in fact, to have been an original feature in the religion of Israel's semi-nomadic ancestors. It is scarcely surprising, therefore, that a note of promise for the future should have distinguished Israel's faith from the beginning. Moreover, the covenant which made Israel a people, which was patterned on a suzerainty treaty between overlord and vassal, while it laid stringent demands on its recipients, implicitly carried the assurance that if the covenant stipulations were met the divine Overlord's favour would be endlessly continued. In any event, we may see in Israel's earliest literature (*e.g.* Gn 49, Nu 23–24, Dt 33, Jg 5, Ps 68) a robust confidence that she would be assured possession of her land, given material blessings by her God and made victorious over her foes.

The reign of David must have seemed to many Israelites virtually the fulfilment of promise. But its glories did not last. After they had slipped away (by the 8th cent., but almost certainly earlier) Israel's future hope began to assume certain definite forms. Important among these was the expectation of the Day of Yahweh, of which we hear for the first time in Amos (5^{18ff}), but which, since it was then an established popular belief, was certainly older. Though the origins of this belief are disputed, it entailed the expectation of a coming day when Yahweh would intervene definitively in behalf of His people and, judging His foes and theirs, make the promises actual. Certain features in the official cult of the Jerusalem Temple, which under David and Solomon had been made the national religious centre, likewise played an important part in shaping Israel's future hope. There the notion quite early entrenched itself that Yahweh had chosen Zion as His earthly seat and had promised to the Davidic dynasty an eternal rule. As certain Psalms indicate (*e.g.* Ps 2, 72, 89, 110, 132; cf 2 S 7^{4-17} 23^{1-7}), the promises to the dynasty and the dynastic ideal were reaffirmed in the cult. We may suppose that as this theology was cultically reiterated, especially as difficult times made it seem less of a present reality, the hope of a future improvement of the national fortunes and of the coming of a Davidide (perhaps the next one) under whom the promises to David would be realized.

This national hope was radically transmuted by the great prophets of the 8th and 7th cents. The first of these was Amos who, denouncing Israel's sin, declared that the Day of Yahweh would come as no glad day of national victory, but as the day of Divine judgment. Like Amos, the other pre-exilic prophets viewed the Day of Yahweh as the day of Yahweh's vengeance upon the nation for its sins; and they expected this to be accomplished through the historical agent of Yahweh's judgment, whether Assyria or Babylon. This meant, since these prophets did not surrender hope for the future, that hope was pushed ahead beyond the Day of Yahweh and, in the process, given various new forms. Particularly important in this connexion is Isaiah, who, building on the promises of the official theology, but stressing the note of chastisement for sin inherent in it, viewed Yahweh's judgment as a purge out of which He would bring forth a purified remnant of His people (1^{21-26} etc); his classic descriptions (9^{2-7} 11^{1-9}; cf Mic 5^{2ff}) of the coming ideal David laid the basis for Israel's hope of the Messiah. Equally important is Jeremiah, who, developing a note found already in Hosea, declared that the nation, having by its sins broken covenant with Yahweh, was doomed; hope, for him, lay in the farther future, in a new act of the Divine grace which would give to Israel a new covenant (31^{31-34}). Yet, in spite of the fact that the prophets pushed hope beyond calamity and beyond the existing order, as long as the nation endured the popular mind continued to envision the future in terms of a continuation and consummation of the national history.

2. Eschatology in Later OT Literature and in Judaism.—The Exile, here as elsewhere, marked a great watershed. The national hope could no longer be held in its old form. Instead, exiled Jews looked forward to a new and definitive act whereby Yahweh would redeem His people from bondage and restore them to their land. This took various forms: the expectation of the Day of Yahweh as the day when Babylon would be destroyed and the Jews released (*e.g.* Is 13^{1}–14^{23}); the hope of a national resurrection and a restored Davidic state (Ezk 37 etc.); the vision of a sacral community reconstituted about the restored Temple and its cult (Ezk 40–48), etc. Second Isaiah, in particular, hailed Cyrus as the agent of Yahweh's purpose and viewed the coming deliverance as a new Exodus experience which would mark a great turning point in history, leading to the triumphant establishment of Yahweh's rule in the earth and the turning of all nations to His worship; in the figure of the suffering Servant of Yahweh he described both Israel's mission and destiny and the pattern of the coming redemption.

The restoration of the Jewish community under the Persian kings gave these hopes at best only partial fulfilment. The result was a heightened stress on eschatological expectations, but with these thrust forward into a new future and divorced ever more completely from the existing order. In post-exilic literature some of the forms in which hope had previously expressed itself play little part. After the disappointment of the Messianic hopes attached to Zerubbabel by Haggai and Zechariah, the figure of the Davidic king is seldom mentioned, though expectation of the Messiah of course continued and was much to the fore in NT times. The Servant of Yahweh likewise plays little part, save apparently as a model of humble piety. As for the ideal of the new covenant, it is probable that most Jews (cf Ps 37^{31} 40^{8}) felt that it had been realized in the reconstituted law community. The dominant eschatological pattern in post-exilic literature is that of the Day of Yahweh. This is described in various forms (*e.g.* Ezk 38 f, Joel, Zec 14, Is 24–27), but always as Yahweh's catastrophic intervention to judge the world and the nations and to establish His triumphant rule over His people. Though eschatological expectations still have a this-worldly context, they are not conceived of in terms of a continuation, or even a radical improvement, of the existing order, but as the intrusion into it of a new and different order.

In the 2nd cent. B.C. and after Jewish eschatology began to express itself in a novel form known as apocalyptic. Though the Book of Daniel is the only true apocalypse in the OT, a profusion of similar works were produced which did not gain admittance to the canon. Apocalyptic draws many of its motifs from concepts originally at home in Iranian religion, or in ancient Oriental myth, as these had been developed in popular Jewish thought. Its theology, however, is essentially Jewish with its roots in the eschatology of Judaism as this had been developed through the post-exilic period. Apocalypse means 'revelation.' Normally making use of the device of pseudonymity, apocalyptic literature seeks to set forth in cryptic language the programme of the end events. It was believed that the present age was drawing to a close, and that current happenings indicated that the climactic struggle between God and evil, light and darkness was beginning. Definite dualistic tendencies are in evidence, with angelic and demonic powers arrayed against one another. Apocalyptic is characterized by the manipulation of numbers, the division of history into world periods, the description of world powers in the guise of beasts, the reinterpretation of the words of earlier prophets, and the like. It expects no longer a mere dramatic turning point in history, but a supra-historical consummation and the coming of a new age. In apocalyptic literature we encounter the figure of the Son of Man. Though in Dn 7^{13f} the Son of Man appears to be a corporate designation for the vindicated saints of the Most High, in later portions of 1 Enoch he is thought of as a pre-existent heavenly deliverer who comes to rule over the saints in the last days.

Jewish eschatological expectations in NT times were varied and unsystematized. Some Jews (especially more worldly minded Sadducees) were little concerned with eschatology at all; others were nationalists who hoped for the coming of a political Messiah; still others (the Pharisees), though they looked for the redemption of Israel, were chary both of apocalyptic speculations and nationalistic enthusiasm. Apocalyptic appears to have been developed particularly in sectarian circles, as is seen from the scrolls of Qumrân. Here we see a sect (probably the Essenes) which, with a peculiar interpretation of the law, a peculiar religious calendar and a quasi-monastic discipline, regarded itself as the people of the New Covenant. It awaited the imminent consummation of the age; it looked (cf also Test. XII. Pat.) for the Messiah of Israel who would stand beside, but yield pre-eminence to, the Messiah of Aaron (the anointed priest).

Note must be made here of eschatological beliefs as they concerned the individual. Early Israel, while it did not suppose that death meant extinction, had no belief either in a resurrection or in rewards and punishments after death. It was thought that the dead, good and bad alike, pursued a shadowy existence in Sheol and, in general, that good conduct and bad received a material reward in this life; what immortality the individual might be said to have had lay in his seed and in the nation. The post-exilic period, however, witnessed the beginnings of a belief in the resurrection of the dead and in rewards and punishments after death. This belief owed its development perhaps partly to concepts of Iranian origin, but perhaps even more than has been supposed to ancient native notions regarding the cult of the dead which normative Yahwism had suppressed. In particular, however, it arose from the necessity of harmonizing the divine justice with the facts of experience; whatever the orthodox teaching might be, it had become obvious to many that individuals did not always receive their just deserts in this life. Hints of belief in a future life in the OT are, however, few and ambiguous (Ps 49^{14f} 73^{23ff}, Is 26^{19}, etc., have been suggested). Only in Dn 12^{1f} is resurrection both of righteous and wicked explicit, and even here the resurrection is selective rather than universal. It is probable that the Maccabaean struggle, when many godly Jews lost their lives for the faith, cast the deciding vote and made belief in future awards imperative. In any event, as contemporary literature shows, belief in a resurrection and a final judgment had become well established by NT times, though some (the Sadducees) continued to deny it (*e.g.* Mk 12^{18-27}, Ac 23^{6-10}).

3. Eschatology in the NT.—Though many points regarding the eschatology of the NT are in dispute, particularly the relationship of the teachings of the Evangelists and other NT writers on the subject to Jesus' own understanding of Himself and His mission, there can be no doubt that the theology of the NT (and of Jesus Himself) is one in which eschatology is the controlling factor. The NT writers consistently affirm that all the hope of Israel had been given fulfilment in Christ, and that in Him the power of the age to come had intruded into this age. The primitive *kērygma* of the earliest church, which we see reflected in various passages (*e.g.* Ac 3^{12ff} 10^{36ff}, Ro 1^{1ff}, 1 Co 15^{3ff}) stresses this thought, while Jesus' own preaching seems to have been concerned to announce the imminent approach, indeed the actual presence, of the Kingdom of God in His person (Mk 1^{15} etc.). The Gospel writers understood Jesus' ministry, specifically His mighty works, as evidences of the power of the new age in conflict with the power of Satan (*e.g.* Mt 12^{28}, Lk 10^{18} 11^{20}). John, in particular, using categories borrowed from sectarian Judaism, described Jesus' ministry in terms of the eschatological conflict of light with darkness (Jn 1^{1ff} 8^{12} 12^{35ff}). The NT views the cross and resurrection as the decisive victory in that conflict and the defeat of the powers of evil—indeed as the event by which the whole course of human history since Adam has been reversed (Ro 5^{12ff}).

In announcing Jesus as the fulfilment of the hope of Israel, the various forms in which that hope had expressed itself were taken over and applied to Him; He is hailed as Messiah (Christ is the Greek equivalent of the Hebrew Messiah: 'the anointed one'), as Son of Man (*e.g.* Christ as the New Adam: 1 Co $15^{20ff,\ 45ff}$), and as Servant of the Lord (*e.g.* Ph 2^{5ff}). To what degree these identifications were made by Jesus Himself, to what degree by the early Church, is disputed; but this was certainly done both early and consistently. Indeed, it is not unreasonable to suppose that Jesus, though refusing to be the political Messiah whom the people expected, saw it as His mission to give the Messianic hope of Israel fulfilment and, moreover, suffusing this and other eschatological patterns with the concept of vicarious sacrifice, set out to do so in the form of the Suffering Servant (cf Lk 4^{17ff}) spoken of by the prophet.

Viewing its Lord as the bringer of the new age, the Church saw itself as living in the end time, as an eschatological community (*e.g.* Ac 2^{16ff}). It believed itself to be the true remnant of Israel spoken of by Isaiah (*e.g.* Ro 9^{6ff} $11^{5,\ 17ff}$, Gal 6^{16}, 1 P 2^{9f}), and the recipient of the new covenant spoken of by Jeremiah (cf the words at the Last Supper; also 2 Co 3^{4ff}, He 8^{6ff} etc.). The Christian believer already had eternal life (John, *passim*; Ro 5^{21} 6^{23} etc.), for he lived already in the age to come as one whose citizenship was in heaven (*e.g.* Gal 1^{4}, Ph 3^{20}, He 6^{5}). On his death he would partake of the resurrection (1 Co 15)—though it is not altogether clear whether it was believed that this would transpire immediately or (1 Th 4^{15ff}) at the Lord's return.

Yet in spite of the affirmation of the NT that the hope of Israel had been fulfilled in Christ, the Church could not view eschatology as something wholly 'realized,' for it was evident that the victory of Christ's kingdom lay still in the future. It therefore awaited, and prayed for (1 Co 16^{22} etc.), the return of the Lord in glory (*e.g.* Ac 1^{11}, 1 Th 4^{15ff}, Tit 2^{13}) and the final victory when all powers celestial and terrestrial would bow at His feet (*e.g.* Ac 3^{21}, 1 Co 15^{25}, Ph 1^{6}). This consummation, at least at first, was expected to come soon and suddenly (*e.g.* Ro 13^{11}, 1 Co 7^{29} 15^{51ff}, 1 Th 4^{17} 5^{1ff}), and its postponement evoked tension. The eschatological orientation of the gospel was, however, never lost; it finds classical expression in the final book of the canon, Revelation. This book is an apocalypse which utilizes various elements drawn from Jewish apocalyptic eschatology in the interests of the Christian faith, and which seeks to set forth in detail the programme of the last events. The conflict of the two ages, which is both celestial and terrestrial, is described; there is a resurrection of the saints, a period during which Satan is bound, a final conflict and the last judgment, followed by a picture of the new heaven and the new earth. The NT Church continued to live in tension between eschatology fulfilled and unfulfilled; and so, theologically speaking, the Church does, and must do, even yet. J. Br.

ESCHEW.—In the older English versions of the Bible 'eschew' is common. In AV it occurs only in Job $1^{1,8}$ 2^{3} of Job himself, as 1^{1} 'one that feared God, and eschewed evil,' and in 1 P 3^{11} 'Let him eschew evil, and do good.' The meaning is 'turn away from' (as RV at 1 P 3^{11} and RSV everywhere).

ESDRAELON.—The name of the great plain N. and E. of Mount Carmel. The word is a transliteration of the Greek name which is itself thought to be derived from the Hebrew **Jezreel** (q.v.). Although the name Esdraelon as such does not appear in the Hebrew of the OT or the Greek of the NT, and is found in the Apocrypha only in Jth 1^{8}, 3^{9} 4^{6} 7^{3}, it has come to be the best-known designation of the great plain. The Arabic name is *Merj Ibn ʿÂmir*; its territory was divided in 1948 between Israel and the Kingdom of the Jordan. It is probable that the name of the city Jezreel (q.v.) was applied to its adjacent plain (Jos 17^{16}, Jg 6^{33}, Hos 1^{5}), and then to the entire plain. Similarly, the name of the city Megiddo was applied to the plain (2 Ch 35^{22}, Zec 12^{11}), although in both cases it is difficult to determine whether the names apply to all or to a part of the great plain.

It is roughly triangular in shape covering an area of about 20 miles NW. to SE., and 14 miles NE. to SW. From the sea-coast to the Bay of ʿAkkā (and modern Haifa) it affords passage into the mountainous interior of Palestine. It is drained by the Kishon (q.v.) and is, over nearly all its area, remarkably fertile, although in the rainy seasons it has become marshy. Great cities such as Megiddo and Taanach (q.v.) lined its borders, and it served as a bread-basket for a much larger region.

Under the various names discussed above, the plain is frequently referred to as a battlefield. Here Deborah and Barak routed the armies of Jabin and Sisera (Jg 4), and here Gideon defeated the Midianites (7). Saul here fought his last battle with the Philistines (1 S 28–31). Josiah here attacked Pharaoh Neco on his way to Mesopotamia and was slain (2 K 23^{30}). It was the scene of the encampment of Holofernes (Jth 7^{3}), and of Saladin in 1186. Napoleon defeated an army of Arabs here in 1799, and General Allenby won a decisive victory over the Turks here in 1917. The plain was referred to by the Apocalyptic writer (Rev 16^{16}) as Armageddon (q.v.), the scene of the final battle between the cosmic forces of good and evil.

R. A. S. M.—**W. L. R.**

ESDRAS.—See Apocrypha, **1, 2,** and Pseudepigrapha, **7.**

ESDRIS.—Mentioned only in 2 Mac 12^{36}. The text is probably corrupt. AV has *Gorgias*, and this is likely enough to be correct.

ESEBRIAS, 1 Es 8^{54} (AV).—See Sherebiah.

ESEK ('contention').—A well dug by Isaac in the region near Rehoboth and Garar, Gn 26^{20}. The site is unknown.

ESEREBIAS, 1 Es 8^{54} (RV).—See Sherebiah.

ESHAN.—A town of Judah, in the Hebron mountains, noticed with Arab and Dumah, Jos 15^{52} (AV **Eshean**). The site is unknown.

ESHBAAL.—See Ishbosheth.

ESHBAN.—An Edomite chief, Gn 36^{26}, 1 Ch 1^{41}.

ESHCOL.—**1.** The brother of Mamre and Aner, the Amorite confederates of Abraham, who assisted the patriarch in his pursuit and defeat of Chedorlaomer's forces, Gn $14^{13,24}$). He lived in the neighbourhood of Hebron, Gn 13^{18}; and possibly gave his name to the valley of Eshcol, which lay a little to the N. of Hebron, Nu 13^{23}. **2.** A wady, with vineyards and pomegranates, apparently near Hebron, Nu 13^{23f} 32^{9}, Dt 1^{24}. *Eshcol* is usually rendered 'bunch of grapes.' The name has not been recovered.

ESHEAN, Jos 15^{52} (AV).—See Eshan.

ESHEK.—A descendant of Saul, 1 Ch 8^{39}.

ESHTAOL.—A lowland city of Judah (Jos 15^{33}) on the borders of Dan (19^{41}), near which Samson began to feel 'the spirit of the Lord' (Jg 13^{25}), and was buried (16^{31}); the home of some of the Danites who attacked Laish ($18^{2,11}$). It is possibly modern *Eshwāʿ*, near *ʿAin Shems*. The **Eshtaolites** are enumerated among the Calebites, 1 Ch 2^{53} (AV **Eshtaulites**).

ESHTEMOA.—A Levitical city in the district of Hebron (Jos 21^{14}, 1 Ch 6^{57}), to which David sent a share of the spoil of the Philistines (1 S 30^{28}); called **Eshtemoh** in Jos 15^{50}. It is treated as a person in 1 Ch $4^{17,19}$. It is probably modern *es-Semûʿ*, about 8 miles S. of Hebron.

ESHTEMOH.—A town of Judah 15^{50}; elsewhere called **Eshtemoa** (q.v.).

ESHTON.—A Judahite, 1 Ch 4^{11f}.

ESLI.—An ancestor of Jesus (Lk 3^{25}).

ESRIL, 1 Es 9^{34} (AV).—See Azarel, **4.**

ESSENES.—To the student of NT times the Essenes present a problem of extreme difficulty. The very existence of a monastic order within the pale of Judaism is an extraordinary phenomenon. Until the discovery of the Dead Sea Scrolls (q.v.) it was almost incredible. In India such things would have been a matter of course. But the deep racial consciousness and the tenacious national will of the Jews make it hard to account for. When, approaching the subject in this mood, the student straightway finds as features of the order the habit of worshipping towards the sun and the refusal to share in the public services of the Temple, he is tempted to explain Essenism by foreign influences. Yet the Essenes were Jews in good standing. They were inside, not outside, the pale of strictest Judaism. Hence they give the student a problem as interesting as it is difficult.

No small part of the difficulty is due to the character of our witness. Unless the sect of Qumrân, which produced the Dead Sea Scrolls is to be identified with the Essenes, we are dependent upon brief descriptions given by outsiders whose understanding was limited. Essenism was the first form of organized monasticism in the Mediterranean world. The Greeks who followed Alexander to India marvelled at the Ascetics or Gymnosophists. But not until Essenism took shape did the men of the Mediterranean world see monasticism at close quarters. Wonderment and the children of wonderment—fancy and legend—soon set to work on the facts, colouring and distorting them. One of our sources, Pliny (*HN* v. 17), is in part the product of the imagination. Another, Philo (*Quod omnis probus liber*, 12 f, and in Euseb. *Praep. Ev.* viii. ii. 1), writes in the mood of the preacher to whom facts have no value except as texts for sermons. And even Josephus (*Ant.* xiii. v. 9 [171 ff], xv. x. 4, 5 [371 ff], xviii. i. 2, 5 [11, 18 ff]; *Vita*, 2 [10 f]; *BJ* ii. viii. 2–13 [119 ff], our best source, is at times under suspicion. But a rough outline of the main facts is discernible.

The foundations of Essenism were laid in the half-century preceding the Maccabaean War. The high priesthood was disintegrating. In part this was due to the fact that the loose-jointed Persian Empire had been succeeded by the more coherent kingdom of the Seleucids. With this closer political order, which made Jewish autonomy more difficult of attainment, went the appealing and compelling forces of Hellenism, both as a mode of life and as a reasoned view of the world. The combined pressure of the political, the social, and the intellectual elements of the Greek over-lordship went far towards disorganizing and demoralizing the ruling class in Jerusalem.

But a deeper cause was at work, the genius of Judaism itself (see Pharisees). When the Hebrew monarchy fell, the political principle lost control. To popularize monotheism, to build up the OT Canon, organize and hold together the widely separated parts of the Jewish people—this work called for a new form of social order which mixed the ecclesiastical with the political. The man whom the times required in order to carry this work through was not the priest, but the Bible scholar. And he was necessarily an intense separatist. Taking Ezra's words, ' Separate yourselves from the people of the land ' (Ezr 10[11]) as the keynote of life, his aim was to free God's people from all taint of heathenism. In the critical period of fifty years preceding the War this class of men was coming more and more into prominence. They stood on the Torah as their platform; the Law of Moses was both their patrimony and their obligation. In them the genius of Judaism was beginning to sound the rally against both the good and the evil of Hellenism, against its illumining culture as well as against the corroding Graeco-Syrian morality. The priestly aristocracy of Palestine being in close touch with Hellenism, it naturally resulted that the high priesthood, and the Temple which was inseparable from the high priesthood, suffered a fall in religious value.

Into this situation came the life-and-death struggle against the attempt of Antiochus to Hellenize Judaism. In the life of a modern nation a great war has large results. Far greater were the effects of the Maccabaean War upon a small nation. It was a supreme point of precipitation wherein the genius of Judaism reached clear self-knowledge and definition. The Essenes appear as a party shortly after the war. It is not necessary to suppose that at the outset they were a monastic order. It is more likely that they at first took form as small groups or brotherhoods of men intent on holiness, according to the Jewish model. This meant a kind of holiness that put an immense emphasis on Levitical precision. To keep the Torah in its smallest details was part and parcel of the very essence of morality. The groups of men who devoted themselves to the realization of that ideal started with a bias against the Temple as a place made unclean by the heathenism of the priests. This bias was strengthened through the assumption of the high priesthood by the Hasmonaean house, an event which still further discounted the sacramental value of the Temple services. So these men, knit into closely coherent groups, mainly in Judaea, found the satisfactions of life in deepening fellowship, and an ever more intense devotion to the ideal of Levitical perfection. In course of time, as the logic of life carried them forward into positions of which they had not at first dreamed, the groups became more and more closely knit, and at the same time more fundamentally separatistic regarding the common life of the Jews. So we find, possibly late in the 1st cent. B.C., the main group of Essenes colonizing near the Dead Sea, and constituting a true monastic order.

The stricter Essenes abjured private property and marriage in order to secure entire attention to the Torah. The Levitical laws of holiness were observed with great zeal. An Essene of the higher class became unclean if a fellow-Essene of lower degree so much as touched his garment. They held the name of Moses next in honour to the name of God. And their Sabbatarianism went to such lengths that the bowels must not perform their wonted functions on the Seventh Day.

At the same time, there are reasons for thinking that foreign influences had a hand in their constitution. They worshipped towards the sun, not towards the Temple. This may have been due to the influence of Parsism. Their doctrine of immortality was Hellenic, not Pharisaic. Foreign influences in this period are quite possible, for it was not until the wars with Rome imposed on Judaism a hard-and-fast form that the doors were locked and bolted. Yet, when all is said, the foreign influence gave nothing more than small change to Essenism. Its innermost nature and its deepest motive were thoroughly Jewish.

It is possible that John the Baptist was affected by Essenism. It is possible that our Lord and the Apostolic Church may have been influenced to a certain extent. But influence of a primary sort is out of the question. The impassioned yet sane moral enthusiasm of early Christianity was too strong in its own kind to be deeply touched by a spirit so unlike its own. The Dead Sea Scrolls on the whole confirm these impressions. Whether the sect which produced them was identical with the Essenes or a distinct but closely related group, what has been said here applies to it as well as to the people described by Josephus, Philo, and Pliny. The Scrolls, however, give us an incomparably richer and more authentic picture of the sect. H. S. N.—**M. B.**

ESTATE.—' State ' and ' estate ' occur in AV almost an equal number of times, and with the same meaning. Cf Col 4[7] ' All my state shall Tychicus declare unto you,' with the next verse, ' that he might know your estate.' In Ac 22[5] ' all the estate of the elders ' (Gr. ' all the presbytery ') means all the members of the Sanhedrin. The plural occurs in the Preface to AV, and in Ezk 36[11] ' I will settle you after your old estates,' *i.e.* according to your former position in life. The heading of Ps 37 is ' David persuadeth to patience and confidence in God, by the different estate of the godly and the wicked.' It occurs nine times in RSV (OT and NT): twice meaning property, seven times condition or position.

ESTHER (' star ').—The Jewish name, of which this is the Persian (or Babylonian) form, is **Hadassah** (Est 2[7]), which means ' myrtle.' The form Esther may have some connexion with the name of the common Semitic goddess, *Ishtar*. She was the daughter of Abihail, of the tribe of Benjamin, and was brought up, an orphan, in the house of her cousin **Mordecai**, in Susa. When the Persian king, Xerxes, banned Vashti the queen from his presence he had the most beautiful girls of the kingdom found for him. Among them was Esther, who, owing to her beauty, became a favourite and eventually succeeded Vashti. The combined wisdom of Mordecai and courage of Esther became the means of doing a great service to the very large number of Jews living under Persian rule; for, owing to the craft and hatred of Haman, the chief court favourite, the Jews were in danger of being massacred *en bloc*; but Esther, instigated by Mordecai, revealed her Jewish nationality to the king, who realized thereby that she was in danger of losing her life, owing to the royal decree, obtained by Haman, to the effect that all those of Jewish nationality in the king's dominions were to be put to death. Esther's action brought about an entire reversal of the decree. Haman was put to death, and Mordecai was honoured by the king for saving him from a plot on his life (ch. 2). Esther's own position was strengthened and the Jews were permitted to take revenge on those who had sought their destruction. Mordecai and Esther sent out two decrees: first, that the 14th and 15th days of the month Adar were to be kept annually as 'days of feasting and gladness, and of sending portions one to another, and gifts to the poor' (Est 9^{22}); and, second, that a day of mourning and fasting should be observed in memory of the sorrow which the king's first decree had occasioned to the Jewish people (9^{29-32}, cf 4^{1-3}).

Attempts have been made to identify the chief characters with known historical persons, but, apart from the king Ahasuerus, they almost necessarily fail since the book is undoubtedly a historical novel (see the next article). W. O. E. O.—**L. H. B.**

ESTHER, BOOK OF.—1. Place in Canon.—In the Hebrew Canon the book is found among the 'Writings' and is one of the *Megilloth* or 'Rolls' (*i.e.* Canticles, Ruth, Lamentations, Ecclesiastes, Esther). It was not without much discussion that it was admitted into the Canon. As late as the 2nd cent. A.D. some Jewish scholars denied its canonicity and it was not recognized as Scripture by some early Christian scholars. Neither Athanasius († 373) nor Gregory of Nazianzus († 391) included it in lists of the canonical books made towards the end of the 4th cent. A.D. Luther said, 'I am so hostile to the book and to Esther that I wish they did not exist at all; for they Judaize too much and have much heathen perverseness' (*Tischreden*, Weimar ed. XXII. 2080). It is clear that Esther was not universally accepted as a book of the Bible until a late date.

2. Date and authorship.—The language of Esther points unmistakably to a late date. The Hebrew style is laboured as though it were the work of one who was trying to imitate a classical style. The author was clearly familiar with Aramaic and there are several words of Persian origin. Further, the Persian empire is spoken of as belonging to a period of history long since past (cf 'in those days,' 1^{2}); the words, 'There is a certain people scattered abroad and dispersed among the peoples in all the provinces of your kingdom' (3^{8}) show that the dispersion had already for long been an accomplished fact. Moreover, the spirit of the book points to a time when great bitterness and hatred had been engendered between Jew and Gentile. The probability, therefore, is that Esther belongs to the earlier half of the 2nd cent. B.C. Of its authorship we know nothing further than that the writer was a Jew who must have been in some way connected with Persia. His racial prejudice was much stronger than his religious fervour; the name of God nowhere occurs in the book, which was clearly one of the reasons for its tardy acceptance as canonical.

3. Contents.—The book, which may be described as a historical novel, offers an account of how the Jewish feast of *Purim* ('Lots') first originated. Xerxes, king of the Medes and Persians, gives a great feast to the nobles and princes of the 127 provinces over which he rules; the queen, Vashti, also gives a feast to her women. On the seventh day of the feast the king commands Vashti to appear before the princes in order that they may see her beauty. On her refusing to obey, the king, acting on advice from his courtiers, chooses the Jewess Esther to take her place. Esther is the adopted daughter of a Jew named **Mordecai** who had been the means of saving the king from the hands of assassins (2^{19-23}). But Mordecai falls out with the court favourite, **Haman,** on account of his refusing to bow down and do reverence to the latter. Haman resolves to avenge himself for this insult; he has lots cast in order to find out which is the most suitable day for presenting a petition to the king; the day being appointed, the petition is presented and granted, the promised payment of ten thousand talents of silver into the royal treasury (3^{9}) no doubt contributing towards this. The petition was that a royal decree should be put forth to the effect that all Jews were to be killed, and their belongings treated as spoil. On this becoming known, there is great grief among the Jews. Esther, instructed by Mordecai, undertakes to interpose for her people before the king. She invites both the king and Haman to a banquet, and repeats the invitation for the next day. Haman, believing himself to be in favour with the royal couple, determines to gratify his hatred for Mordecai in a special way, and prepares a gallows on which to hang him (5^{14}). In the night after the first banquet, Xerxes (Ahasuerus), being unable to sleep, commands that the book of memorable deeds be brought; in this he finds the account of Mordecai's former service (2^{19-23}) which has never been rewarded. Haman is sent for, and the king asks him what should be done to the man whom the king delights to honour; Haman, thinking that it is he himself who is uppermost in the king's mind, describes how such a man should be honoured. The king thereupon directs that all that Haman has said is to be done to Mordecai. Haman returns in grief to his house. While consulting his friends, the king's chamberlains come to escort him to the queen's second banquet (6^{1ff}). During this Esther makes her petition to the king on behalf of her people, as well as for her own life, which is threatened, for the royal decree is directed against all Jews and Jewesses within his domains; she also discloses Haman's plot against Mordecai. The king, as the result of this, orders Haman to be hanged on the gallows which he had prepared for Mordecai, the latter receiving the honours which had before belonged to Haman. Esther then has letters sent in all directions in order to avert the threatened destruction of her people; but the attempt is yet made by the enemies of the Jews to carry out Haman's intentions. The Jews defend themselves with success, and a great feast is held on the 14th of Adar, on which the Jews 'rested and made that a day of feasting and gladness.' Moreover, two days of feasting are appointed to be observed for all time; they are called *Purim*, because of the lot (*pûr*) which Haman cast for the destruction of the Jews (chs. 8, 9). The book concludes with a further reference to the power of Ahasuerus and the greatness of his favourite, Mordecai.

4. Historicity of the book.—There are several reasons for concluding that this a historical romance. The book is full of improbabilities: if Mordecai was carried into exile in 597 B.C. he would be well over 110 years of age in the reign of Xerxes (485–465 B.C.); it is improbable that a Persian king would choose a Jewess for his consort, although it should be added that the story of Nehemiah does not preclude the possibility of both Esther and Mordecai obtaining favoured positions at court. Again, a specific purpose of the book is to glorify the Jewish nation and to ridicule the Gentiles. Close reading of the narrative reveals many small inconsistencies that are more likely to occur in fiction than in history. Some scholars have seen similarities between proper names in the book and the names of deities—Haman = Human, Esther = Ishtar, Vashti = Mashti, Mordecai = Marduk—and have suggested that the story embodies a well-known myth and tried thereby to prove Babylonian origin for the book. The equations are not conclusive however; Esther may be a Persian name meaning 'star,' while Mordecai may either be an abbreviated theophorous name, or it may be another Persian name meaning 'kind.' All that can safely be said of the origin of the book is that the festival of Purim is almost certainly of pagan origin and that the book may have been written outside Israel in the land where Purim was first adopted by the Israelites. The fact that it is celebrated on the two days following Nicanor's day (1 Mac 7^{49}, 2 Mac 15^{36}) has led to its connexion with the Maccabaean wars.

5. Purim. The feast is said to derive its name from the word *pûr* (of which *pûrîm* is a plural form) meaning 'lot,' a word that appears to be Akkadian in origin. Nothing is said in the book that throws any light on the origin of the feast. The command to celebrate it with rejoicing and feasting was often taken very literally, so much so that a 'Babylonian authority of the fourth century, Raba, took it that a man should drink till he cannot distinguish between Cursed be Haman! and Blessed be Mordecai!' (Moore, *Judaism* ii, p. 53). The book of Esther was the proper reading for the festival, either in public or in private.

W. O. E. O.—L. H. B.

ESYELUS, 1 Es 1^{8} (RV).—See Jehiel, 6.

ETAM.—1. An altogether obscure place name, applied to a rock in a cleft of which Samson took refuge (Jg 15^{8}), and whence he was dislodged by the Judahites (vv.^{11ff}), and therefore presumably in Judahite territory. **2.** A town in Judah, mentioned in Jos 15^{59} (LXX, but not in Hebrew or EV); it was fortified by Rehoboam, 2 Ch 11^{6}. It is perhaps modern *Kh. el-Khôkh*, SW. of Bethlehem, near *ʿAin ʿAṭân*. **3.** A place included in the territory of Simeon, 1 Ch 4^{32}; its site is unknown. **4.** A descendant of Judah, 1 Ch 4^{3}.

ETERNAL LIFE.—See Immortality, and Life.

ETHAM.—The station to Succoth in the wanderings, Ex 13^{20}, Nu 33^{6ff}. It lay 'on the edge of the wilderness,' evidently at the E. end of the *Wâdī Ṭumilât*. The name is not known in Egyptian, and its location is uncertain. The 'wilderness of Ethan' (Nu 33^{8}) lay to the E. of Etham.

ETHAN.—1. 'The Ezrahite' of 1 K 4^{31} and Ps 89 (title). In the first of these passages he is mentioned along with other contemporaries (?) of Solomon, who were all surpassed in wisdom by the Jewish monarch. In 1 Ch 2^{6} he is said to have been a Judaean of the family of **Zerah**, which is probably another form of *Ezrah* (hence the patronymic *Ezrahite*). Instead of 'the Ezrahite' it has been proposed to render *'ezrāḥî* of 1 K 4^{31} 'the native,' *i.e.* the *Israelite*, in opposition to some of the other wise men named, who were *foreigners*. **2.** An ancestor of Asaph, 1 Ch 6^{42}. In v.^{21} he is apparently called **Joah**. **3.** The eponymous ancestor of a guild of Temple-singers, 1 Ch 6^{44} $15^{17, 19}$ etc.

ETHANIM.—The name of a month, 1 K 8^{2}; see Time.

ETHANUS.—One of the five scribes trained to write rapidly, who wrote at the dictation of Ezra (2 Es 14^{24}).

ETHBAAL ('with Baal,' *i.e.* enjoying his favour and protection).—King of the Sidonians, and father of Jezebel, wife of Ahab king of Israel (1 K 16^{31}).

ETHER.—1. A town of Judah, mentioned with Libnah, Jos 15^{42}; possibly modern *Khirbet el-ʿAter*. **2.** A town of Simeon, mentioned with En-rimmon, Jos 19^{7}; apparently S. of **1**, and perhaps modern *Khirbet ʿAttîr*. **Athach** (q.v.) may be the same place.

ETHICS.—The present article will be confined to Biblical Ethics. As there is no systematic presentation of the subject, all that can be done is to gather from the Jewish and Christian writings the moral conceptions that were formed by historians, prophets, poets, apostles. The old history culminates in the story of the perfect One, the Lord Jesus Christ, from whom there issued a life of higher order and ampler range.

1. OT Ethics.—As the dates of many of the books are uncertain, special difficulty attends any endeavour to trace with precision the stages of moral development amongst the Hebrews. The existence of a moral order of the world is assumed; human beings are credited with the freedom, the intelligence, etc., which make morality possible. The term 'conscience' does not appear till NT times, and perhaps it was then borrowed from the Stoics; but the thing itself is conspicuous enough in the records of God's ancient people. In Gn 3^{5} we have the two categories 'good' and 'evil'; the former seems to signify in 1^{31} 'answering to design' and in 2^{18} 'conducive to well-being.' These terms—applied sometimes to ends, sometimes to means—probably denote ultimates of consciousness, and so, like pain and pleasure, are not to be defined. Moral phenomena present themselves, of course, in the story of the patriarchs; men are described as mean or chivalrous, truthful or false, meritorious or blameworthy, long before legislation—Mosaic or other—takes shape.

1. In Hebrew literature the *religious aspects of life* are of vital moment, and therefore morals and worship are inextricably entangled. God is seen; there is desire to please Him; there is a shrinking from aught that would arouse His anger (Gn 20^{6} 39^{9}). Hence the immoral is sinful. Allegiance is due—not to an impersonal law, but to a Holy Person, and duty to man is duty also to God. Morality is under Divine protection: are not the tables of the Law in the Ark that occupies the most sacred place in Y″'s shrine (Ex 40^{20}, Dt 10^{5}, 1 K 8^{9}, He 9^{4})? The commandments, instead of being arbitrary, are the outflowings of the character of God. He who enjoins righteousness and mercy calls men to possess attributes which He Himself prizes as His own peculiar glory (Ex 33^{18f} 34^{6f}). Hosea represents the Divine love as longing for the response of human love, and Amos demands righteousness in the name of the Righteous One. Man's goodness is the same in kind as the goodness of God so that both may be characterized by the same terms; as appears from a comparison of Pss 111 and 112.

2. The OT outlook is *national* rather than individual. The elements of the community count for little, unless they contribute to the common good. A man is only a fractional part of an organism, and he may be slain with the group to which he belongs, if grievous sin can be brought home to any part of that group (Jos 7^{19-26}). It is Israel—the people as a whole—that is called God's son. Prayers, sacrifices, festivals, fasts, are national affairs. The highest form of excellence is willingness to perish if only Israel may be saved (Ex 32^{31f}, Jg 5^{15-18}). Frequently the laws are such as only a judge may administer: thus the claim of 'an eye for an eye, and a tooth for a tooth' (Dt 19^{21}), being a maxim of fairness to be observed by a magistrate who has to decide between contending parties, is too harsh for guidance outside a court of law (Mt 5^{38f}). When Israel sinned, it was punished; when it obeyed God, it prospered. It was not till Hebrew national life was destroyed that individual experiences excited questions as to the equity of Providence (Job, Pss 37, 73) and in regard to personal immortality. In the later prophets, even when the soul of each man is deemed to be of immense interest (Ezk 18), national ideals have the ascendency in thought. It is the nation that is to have a resurrection (Is 25^{8}, Ezk 37^{1-14}, Hos 13^{14}, Zec 8^{1-8}). This ardent devotion to corporate well-being—a noble protest against absorption in individual interests—is the golden thread on which the finest pearls of Hebrew history are strung.

3. The *Covenant* is always regarded as the *standard* by which conduct is to be judged. Deference to the Covenant is deference to God (Hos 6^{7} 8^{1}, Am 3^{1-3}). As God is always faithful, His people prosper so long as they observe the conditions to which their fathers gave solemn assent (Ex $24^{3, 7}$). The Decalogue, which is an outline of the demands made by the Covenant on Israel, requires in its early clauses faith, reverence, and service; then (Ex 20, Commandments 5 to 9) the duty of man to man is set forth as part of man's duty to Y″, for Moses and all the prophets declare that God is pleased or displeased by our behaviour to one another. The Tenth Commandment, penetrating as it does to the inward life, should be taken as a reminder that all commandments are to be read in the spirit and not in the letter alone (Lv 19^{17f}, Dt 6^{5f}, Ps 139, Ro 7^{14}). Human obligations—details of which are sometimes massed together as in Ex 20–23, Ps 15 and 24—include both moral and ceremonial requirements. Nothing is more common in the prophets than complaints of a disposition to neglect the former (Is 1^{11f}, Jer 6^{20} 7^{21f}, Hos 6^{6}, Am 5^{21f}). The requirements embrace a great number of particulars, and every department of experience is recognized. Stress is laid upon kindness to the *physically defective* (Lv 19^{14}), and to the *poor* and to *strangers* (Dt 10^{18f} 15^{7-11} 24^{17ff}, Job $31^{16ff, 32}$, Ps 41^{1},

Is 58[6ff], Jer 7[5ff.] 22[3], Zec 7[9f]). *Parents* and *aged* persons are to be reverenced (Ex 20[12], Dt 5[16], Lv 19[32]). The education of *children* is enjoined (Ex 12[26f] 13[8, 14], Dt 4[9] 6[7, 20–25] 11[19] 31[12f] 32[46], Ps 78[5f]). In Proverbs emphasis is laid upon *industry* (6[6–11]), *purity* (7[6] etc), *kindness* to the needy (14[21]), *truthfulness* (17[7] etc.), *forethought* (24[27]). The claims of *animals* are not omitted (Ex 23[11], Lv 25[7], Dt 22[4, 6] 25[4], Ps 104[11f] 148[10], Pr 12[10], Jon 4[11]). Occasionally there are charming pictures of special characters (the housewife, Pr 31 ; the king, 2 S 23[3f] ; the priest, Mal 2[5ff]). God's rule over man is parallel with His rule over the universe, and men should feel that God embraces all interests in His thought, for He is so great that He can attend equally to the stars and to human sorrows (Ps 19, 33, 147[3–6]).

4. The *sanctions* of conduct are chiefly temporal (harvests, droughts, victories over enemies, etc.), yet, as they are national, self-regard is not obtrusive. Moreover, it would be a mistake to suppose that no Hebrew minds felt the intrinsic value of morality. The legal spirit was not universal. The prophets were glad to think that God was not limiting Himself to the letter of the Covenant, the very existence of which implied that Y″, in the greatness of His love, had chosen Israel to be His peculiar treasure. By grace and not by bare justice Divine action was guided. God was the compassionate Redeemer (Dt 7[8], Hos 11[1] 14[4]). Even the people's disregard of the Law did not extinguish His forgiving love (Ps 25[6ff] 103[8ff], Is 63[9], Jer 3[12] 31[3] 33[7f], Mic 7[18f]). In response to this manifested generosity, an unmercenary spirit was begotten in Israel, so that God was loved for His own sake, and His smile was regarded as wealth and light when poverty and darkness had to be endured. 'Whom have I in heaven but thee?' 'Oh, how I love thy law!' are expressions the like of which abound in the devotional literature of Israel, and they evince a disinterested devotion to God Himself and a genuine delight in duty. To the same purport is the remarkable appreciation of the beauty and splendour of wisdom recorded in Pr 8.

II. NT Ethics.—While admitting many novel elements (Mt 11[11] 13[17, 35, 52], Mk 2[21f], Jn 13[34], Eph 2[15], He 10[20], Rev 2[17] 3[12] 5[9]), Christianity reaffirmed the best portions of OT teaching (Mt 5[17], Ro 3[31]). Whatsoever things were valuable, Christ conserved, unified, and developed. The old doctrine acquired wings, and sang a nobler, sweeter song (Jn 1[17]). But the glad and noble life which Jesus came to produce could come only from close attention to man's actual condition.

1. Accordingly, Christian Ethics takes full account of *sin*. The guilty state of human nature, together with the presence of temptations from within, without, and beneath, presents a problem far different from any that can be seen when it is assumed that men are good or only unmoral. Is our need met by lessons in the art of advancing from good to better? Is not the human will defective and rebellious? The moral ravages in the individual and in society call for Divine redemptive activities and for human penitence and faith. Though the sense of sin has been most conspicuous since Christ dwelt among men, the Hebrew consciousness had its moral anguish. The vocabulary of the ancient revelation calls attention to many of the aspects of moral disorder. Sin is a ravenous beast, crouching ready to spring (Gn 4[7]) ; a cause of wide-spreading misery (Gn 3[15–19] 9[25] 20[9], Ex 20[5]) ; is universal (Gn 6[5] 8[21], 1 K 8[46], Ps 130[3] 143[2]) ; is folly (Proverbs *passim*) ; a missing of the mark, violence, transgression, rebellion, pollution (Ps 51). This grave view is shared by the NT. The Lord and His Apostles labour to produce contrition. It is one of the functions of the Holy Spirit to convict the world of sin (Jn 16[8]). It is not supposed that a good life can be lived unless moral evil is renounced by a penitent heart. The fountains of conduct are considered to have need of cleansing. It is always assumed that great difficulties beset the soul in its upward movements, because of its past corrupt state and its exposure to fierce and subtle temptations.

2. In harmony with the doctrine of depravity is the distinctness with which *individuality* is recognized. Sin is possible only to a person. Ability to sin is a mark of that high rank in nature denoted by 'personality.' Christianity has respect to a man's separateness. It sees a nature ringed round with barriers that other beings cannot pass, capacities for great and varied wickednesses and excellencies, a world among other worlds, and not a mere wave upon the sea. A human being is in himself an end, and God loves us one by one. Jesus asserted the immense value of the individual. The Shepherd cares for the one lost sheep (Lk 15[4–7]), and has names for all the members of the flock (Jn 10[14]). The Physician, who (it is conceivable) could have healed crowds by some general word, lays His beneficent hands upon each sufferer (Lk 4[40]). Remove from the Gospels and the Acts the stories of private ministrations, and what gaps are made (Jn 13[5ff] 3, 4, Ac 8[26–39] 16 etc.). Taking the individual as the unit, and working from him as a centre, the NT Ethic declines to consider his deeds alone (Mt 6, Ro 2[28f]). Actions are looked at on their inner side (Mt 5[21f. 27f] 6[1, 4, 6, 18] 12[34f] 23[5, 27], Mk 7[2–8, 18–23], Lk 16[15] 18[10–14], Jn 4[23f]). This is a prolongation of ideas present to the best minds prior to the Advent (1 S 16[7], Ps 7[9] 24[3f] 51[17] 139[2f, 23], Jer 17[10] 31[33]).

3. The *social* aspects of experience are not overlooked. Everyone is to bear his own burden (Ro 14[4], Gal 6[5]), and must answer for himself to the Judge of all men (2 Co 5[10]) ; but he is not isolated. Regard for others is imperative ; for an unforgiving temper cannot find forgiveness (Mt 6[14f] 18[23–35]), worship without brotherliness is rejected (Mt 5[23f]), and Christian love is a sign of regeneration (1 Jn 5[1]). The mere absence of malevolent deeds cannot shield one from condemnation ; positive helpfulness is required (Mt 25[41–45], Lk 10[25–37] 16[19–31], Eph 4[28f]). This helpfulness is the new ritualism (He 13[16], Ja 1[27]). The family with its parents, children, and servants (Eph 5[22]–6[9], Col 3[18]–4[1]) ; the Church with its various orders of character and gifts (Ro 14, 15, Gal 6[1f], 1 Co 13, 14, 15) ; the State with its monarch and magistrates (Mk 12[14–17], Ro 13[1–7], 1 Ti 2[1f]), provide the spheres wherein the servant of Christ is to manifest his devotion to the Most High. 'Obedience, patience, benevolence, purity, humility, alienation from the world and the "flesh," are the chief novel or striking features which the Christian ideal of practice suggests' (Sidgwick), and they involve the conception that Christian Ethics is based on the recognition of sin, of individuality, of social demands, and of the need of heavenly assistance.

4. The Christian *standard* is *the character of the Lord Jesus Christ*, who lived perfectly for God and man. He overcame evil (Mt 4[1–11], Jn 16[33]), completed His life's task (Jn 17[4]), and sinned not (Jn 8[46], 2 Co 5[21], He 4[15], 1 P 2[22], 1 Jn 3[5]). His is the pattern life, inasmuch as it is completely (1) filial, and (2) fraternal. As to (1), we mark the upward look, His readiness to let the heat of His love burst into the flame of praise and prayer, His dutifulness and submissiveness : He lived 'in the bosom of the Father,' and wished to do only that which God desired. As to (2), His pity for men was unbounded, His sacrifice for human good knew no limits. 'Thou shalt love God' ; 'thou shalt love man.' Between these two poles the perfect life revolved. He and His teachings are one. It is because the moral law is alive in Him that He must needs claim lordship over man's thoughts, feelings, actions. He is preached 'as Lord' (2 Co 4[5]), and the homage which neither man (Ac 10[25f]) nor angel (Rev 22[8f]) can receive He deems it proper to accept (Jn 13[13]). Could it be otherwise? The moral law must be supreme, and He is it. Hence alienation from Him has the fatal place which idolatry had under the Old Covenant, and for a similar reason, seeing that idolatry was a renunciation of Him who is the righteous and gracious One. Since Jesus by virtue of His filial and fraternal perfectness is Lord, to stand apart from Him is ruinous (Lk 10[13–16], Jn 3[18] 8[24] 15[22–24] 16[8f], He 2[3] 6[4–8] 10[26]). Wife or child or life itself must not be preferred to the claims of truth and righteousness, and therefore must not be preferred to Christ, who is truth and righteousness in personal form (Mt 10[37-39], Lk 9[59f] 14[26f]). To call oneself the bond-servant of Jesus Christ (Ro 1[1], Ja 1[1], 2 P 1[1]) was to assert at once the strongest affection for the wise and gracious One, and the utmost loyalty to God's holy will as embodied in His Son. The will of God becomes one's own by affectionate deference to Jesus Christ, to suffer for whom may become a veritable bliss (Mt 5[10-12], Ac 5[41], 2 Co 4[11], Ph 1[29], 1 Th 2[14], He 10[32-34]).

5. Christian Ethics is marked quite as much by *promises of assistance* as by loftiness of standard. The kindliness of God, fully illustrated in the gift and sacrifice of His Son, is a great incentive to holiness. Men come into the sunshine of Divine favour. Heavenly sympathy is with them in their struggles. The virtues to be acquired (Mt 5[1-16], Gal 5[22f], Col 3[12-17], 2 P 1[5ff], Tit 2[12]) and the vices to be shunned (Mk 7[21f], Gal 5[19ff], Col 3[5-9]) are viewed in connexion with the assurance of efficient aid. There is a wonderful love upon which the aspirant may depend (Jn 3[16], Ro 5[7f], 2 Co 5[19f]). The hearty acceptance of that love is faith, ranked as a virtue and as the parent of virtues (2 P 1[5], Ro 5[1f], 1 Co 13, He 11). Faith, hope, love, transfigure and supplement the ancient virtues—temperance, courage, wisdom, justice—while around them grow many gentle excellences not recognized before Christ gave them their true rank; and yet it is not by its wealth of moral teaching so much as by its assurance of ability to resist temptation and to attain spiritual manhood that Christianity has gained pre-eminence. Christ's miracles are illustrations of His gospel of pardon, regeneration, and added faculties (Mt 9[5f]). The life set before man was lived by Jesus, who regenerates men by His Spirit, and takes them into union with Himself (Jn 3[3, 6] 8[36] 15[1-10], Ro 8[2, 9, 29], 1 Co 1[30], 2 Co 5[17], Gal 5[22f], Ph 2[5, 12f], Col 3[1-4], Ja 1[18], 1 P 2[21], 1 Jn 2[6]). The connexion between the Lord and the disciple is permanent (Mt 28[20], Jn 14[3, 19] 17[24], He 2[11-18], 1 Jn 3[1-3]), and hence the aspiration to become sober, righteous, godly (relation to *self*, *man*, and *God*, Tit 2[12-14]) receives ample support. Sanctity is not only within the reach of persons at one time despised as moral incapables (Mk 2[16f], Lk 7[47] 15, 19[8f] 23[42f], 1 Co 6[11], Eph 2[1-7]), but every Christian is supposed to be capable, sooner or later, of the most precious forms of goodness (Mt 5[1-10]), for there is no caste (Col 1[28]). Immortality is promised to the soul, and with it perpetual communion with the Saviour, whose image is to be repeated in every man He saves (Ro 8[37ff], 1 Co 15[49-58], 2 Co 5[8], Ph 3[8-14], 1 Th 4[17], 1 Jn 3[2f], Rev 22[4]).

The objections which have been made to Biblical Ethics cannot be ignored, though the subject can be merely touched in this article. Some passages in the OT have been stigmatized as immoral; some in the NT are said to contain impracticable precepts, and certain important spheres of duty are declared to receive very inadequate treatment.

(i) As to the OT, it is to be observed that we need not feel guilty of disrespect to inspiration when our moral sense is offended; for the Lord Jesus authorizes the belief that the Mosaic legislation was imperfect (Mt 5[21ff] Mk 10[2-9]), and both Jeremiah and Ezekiel comment adversely on doctrines which had been accepted on what seemed to be Divine authority (cf Ex 20[5] with Jer 31[29f] and Ezk 18[2f, 19f]). It is reasonable to admit that if men were to be improved at all there must have been some accommodation to circumstances and states of mind very unlike our own; yet some of the laws are shocking. While such institutions as polygamy and slavery, which could not be at once abolished, were restricted in their range and stripped of some of their worst evils (Ex 21[2ff], Lv 25[42-49], 1 Ch 2[35], Pr 17[2]), there remain many enactments and transactions which must have been always abhorrent to God though His sanction is claimed for them (Ex 22[18-20] 31[14f] 35[2f], Lv 20[27], Nu 15[32-36] 31, Dt 13[5, 16] 17[1-5] 18[20] 21[10-14], 2 S 21[1-9]). Had men always remembered these illustrations of the fact that passions and opinions utterly immoral may seem to be in harmony with God's will, the cruelties inflicted on heretics in the same name of God would not have disgraced the Church's history; and, indeed, these frightful mistakes of OT days may have been recorded to teach us to be cautious lest while doing wrong we imagine that God is served (Jn 16[2]). The limited area of the unworthy teaching would be noticed if care were taken to observe that (1) some of the wicked incidents are barely recorded, (2) some are reprobated in the context, (3) some are evidently left without comment because the historian assumes that they will be immediately condemned by the reader. In regard to the rest, it is certain that the Divine seal has been used contrary to the Divine will. It must be added that the very disapproval of the enormities has been made possible by the book which contains the objectionable passages, and that it is grossly unfair to overlook the high tone manifested generally throughout a great and noble literature, and the justice, mercy, and truth commended by Israel's poets, historians, and prophets, generation after generation.

(ii) As to the NT, it is alleged that, even if the Sermon on the Mount could be obeyed, obedience would be ruinous. This, however, is directly in the teeth of Christ's own comment (Mt 7[24-27]), and is due in part to a supposition that every law is for every man. The disciples, having a special task, might be under special orders, just as the Lord Himself gave up all His wealth (2 Co 8[9]) and carried out literally most of the precepts included in His discourse. The paradoxical forms employed should be a sufficient guard against a bald construction of many of the sayings, and should compel us to meditate upon principles that ought to guide all lives. It is the voice of love that we hear, not the voice of legality. The Christian Ethic is supposed to be careless of social institutions, and Christianity is blamed for not preaching at once against slavery, etc. Probably more harm than good would have resulted from political and economic discourses delivered by men who were ostracized. But it is improbable that the Christian mind was sufficiently instructed to advance any new doctrine for the State. Moreover, the supposition that the world was near its close must have diverted attention from social schemes. The alienation from the world was an alienation from wickedness, not indifference to human pain and sorrow. The poverty of believers, the scorn felt for them by the great, the impossibility of attending public functions without countenancing idolatry, the lack of toleration by the State, all tended to keep the Christian distinct from his fellows. Mob and State and cultured class, by their hatred or contempt, compelled Christianity to move on its own lines. At first it was saved from contamination by various kinds of persecution, and the isolation has proved to be a blessing to mankind; for the new life was able to gather its forces and to acquire knowledge of its own powers and mission. The new ideal was protected by its very unpopularity. Meanwhile there was the attempt to live a life of love to God and man, and to treasure Gospels and Epistles that kept securely for a more promising season many sacred seeds destined to grow into trees bearing many kinds of fruit. The doctrine of the Divine Fatherhood implicitly condemns every social and political wrong, while it begets endeavours directed to the promotion of peace among nations, and to the uplifting of the poor and ignorant and depraved of every land into realms of material, intellectual, and moral blessing. There is no kind of good which is absent from the prayers: 'Thy kingdom come'; 'Thy will be done on earth as it is in heaven. W. J. He.

ETHIOPIA is a translation of the Hebrew **Cush**, which is derived from *Kôsh*, the Egyptian name of Nubia (beginning at the First Cataract). The cultivable land in this region is very meagre. The scanty and barbarous population of the valley and the deserts on either side was divided in early times among different tribes, which were completely at the mercy of the Egyptians. Individually, however, the Sudanese were sturdy warriors, and were constantly employed by the Pharaohs as mercenary soldiers and police. In the time of the New Kingdom, Cush, S. to Napata, was a province of Egypt, dotted with Egyptian temples and governed by a viceroy.

With the weakening of the Egyptian power Cush grew into a separate kingdom, with Napata as its capital. Its rulers were perhaps of Egyptian descent; they are represented as being entirely subservient to Amon, *i.e.* to his priests, elected by him, acting only upon his oracles, and ready to abdicate or even to commit suicide at his command. We first hear of a king of Ethiopia about 725 B.C., when a certain Piankhi, reigning at Napata and already in possession of the Egyptian Thebaid, added most of Middle Egypt to his dominions and exacted homage from the princes of the Delta. A little later an Ethiopian dynasty (the 25th) sat on the throne of the Pharaohs for nearly fifty years (715–656 B.C.). The last of these, Tirhakah (q.v.), intrigued with the kinglets of Syria and Phoenicia against the Assyrians, but only to the ruin of himself and his dynasty. Tirhakah and his successor Tanutamon were driven into Ethiopia by the Assyrian invasions, and Egypt became independent under the powerful 26th Dynasty.

For the Persian period it is known that Ethiopia, or part of it, was included in one satrapy with Egypt under Darius. In the 3rd cent. B.C. king Ergamenes freed himself from the power of the priests of Amon by a great slaughter of them. From about this time forward Meroë, the southern residence, was the capital of Ethiopia. The worship of Amon, however, as the national god of 'Negroland,' as Ethiopia was then called, still continued. In 24 B.C. the Romans invaded Ethiopia in answer to an attack on Egypt by queen Candace, and destroyed Napata, but the kingdom continued to be independent. The Egyptian culture of Ethiopia had by that time fallen into a very barbarous state. Inscriptions exist written in a special script known as Meroitic and in the native language, as yet only partially deciphered; others are in a debased form of Egyptian hieroglyphic.

The name of Cush was familiar to the Hebrews through the part that its kings played in Egypt and Syria from 730–664 B.C., and the Aramaic papyri from Elephantine prove that there were Jewish settlements on the Ethiopian border at Syene by the 6th cent. B.C. See also CUSH. F. Ll. G.—**R. J. W.**

ETHIOPIAN EUNUCH.—Ac 8^{26-39} recounts how the deacon Philip met, near Gaza, an Ethiopian eunuch, treasurer to one of the CANDACE rulers of Meroë, who was on his way home from a visit to Jerusalem. Hearing him reading aloud in his carriage from a copy of Isaiah the passage 53^{7ff}, Philip preached to him the Christian gospel, converted him, and by the wayside baptized him. He may have been a Jew from Meroë, or a proselyte, but he may have been a pagan sent with a gift to the Jerusalem shrine. There would be nothing unusual in such a person studying a Greek scroll of Isaiah. V. ^{37}, though an interpolation, seems to be an early baptismal formula. A. J.

ETHIOPIAN WOMAN.—According to Nu 12^{1}, when the children of Israel were at Hazeroth, Miriam and Aaron 'spoke against' Moses on account of his marriage with an Ethiopian (RV, RSV 'Cushite') woman. As the 'Ethiopian woman' is mentioned nowhere else, and the death of Moses' wife Zipporah is not recorded, some of the early interpreters thought the two must be identical; and this view is favoured by the Jewish expositors. But it is more likely that a black slave-girl is meant, and that the fault found by Miriam and Aaron was with the indignity of such a union. It may perhaps be inferred from the context that the marriage was of recent occurrence.

ETHIOPIC VERSIONS OF OT.—See GREEK VERSIONS OF OT, **11.**

ETH-KAZIN.—A town on the E. frontier of Zebulun, whose site has not been identified, Jos 19^{13} (AV **Ittah-kazin**).

ETHMA, 1 Es 9^{35} (AV).—See NEBO, **3.**

ETHNAN.—A Judahite, 1 Ch 4^{7}.

ETHNARCH.—Governor of an ethnic unit, usually administered according to its own laws even though surrounded by or subject to, an alien people. Cf the *exilarch* of Babylonian Jewry. In 2 Co 11^{32} the term is used of the 'governor' of Damascus serving 'under King Aretas. Applied to Simon Maccabaeus it denoted wide administrative authority: he is said to have 'consented to fill the office of high-priest, and to be captain and governor'—1 Mac 14^{47} (cf 15^{1f}; Jos. *Ant.* XIII. vi. 6 [212]). Julius Caesar appointed Hyrcanus II. 'high-priest and ethnarch' (Jos. *Ant.* XIV. viii. 5 [143]), offices which he promised to him and his descendants 'for ever' (Jos. *Ant.* XIV. x. 2 [191 ff]). One who held these combined offices became official spokesman for Jews throughout the Roman Empire. Refusal of the diadem by Pompey to this Hyrcanus (Jos. *Ant.* XX. x. 4 [244]) and later by Augustus to Herod's son Archelaus (Jos. *Ant.* XVII. xi. 4 [317]); *BJ* II. vi. 3 [93]) would seem to have affected only prestige. Archelaus was also given the title 'ethnarch.' But the powers it conferred had to do with taxes and keeping the peace rather than administration of the Judaean Temple state; Josephus informs us that even during the time of Herod and Archelaus certain high-priests had served as 'political governors of the people' (Jos. *Ant.* XX. x. 5 [251]). After the removal of Herod by death and his son by banishment, the powers of the high-priesthood were still further extended: 'The government became an aristocracy, and the high-priests were entrusted with dominion over the nation' (*ibid.*).

In the relations between Caiaphas and Pilate, as earlier between Hyrcanus and Antipas, the ethnarch appears to have outranked the procurator in all matters that did not affect the safety of the state—a fact of no small importance for assessing the true nature of the crime attributed to Jesus. See PROCURATOR. J. S. K.

ETHNI.—An ancestor of Asaph, 1 Ch 6^{41}; called **Jeatherai** in v.^{21} (AV **Jeaterai**).

EUBULUS.—A leading member of the Christian community at Rome, who sends greeting to Timothy through St. Paul (2 Ti 4^{21}). His name is Greek, but nothing further is known of him.

EUCHARIST.—This is the earliest title for the sacrament of the body and blood of Christ. It is found in Ignatius and the *Didache*, and is based upon the *eucharistia* or giving of thanks with which our Lord set apart the bread and wine at the Last Supper as memorials of Himself (Mt 26^{27}, Lk $22^{17, 19}$, 1 Co 11^{24}). The name **Lord's Supper**, though legitimately derived from 1 Co 11^{20}, is not there applied to the sacrament itself, but to the Love-feast or *Agape*, a meal commemorating the Last Supper, and not yet separated from the Eucharist when St. Paul wrote. The irregularities rebuked by the Apostle ($11^{21, 29}$) are such as could only have accompanied the wider celebration, and doubtless contributed to the speedy separation of the essential rite from the unnecessary accessories. The title **Communion** (q.v.) comes from 1 Co 10^{16}, where, however, the word is a predicate not used technically (RSV, 'participation'). The breaking of (the) bread (Ac $2^{42, 46}$) probably refers to the Eucharist (cf 20^{7}, Lk 24^{35}?), but until modern times does not seem to have been adopted as a title.

1. The institution is recorded by each of the Synoptic Gospels, but not by St. John. A fourth account appears in 1 Corinthians.

Mk 14^{22-25}	Mt 26^{26-29}
And as they were eating, he took bread, and blessed, and broke it, and gave it to them, and said, 'Take; this is my body.' ^{23} And he took a cup, and when he had given thanks he gave it to them, and they all drank of it. ^{24} And he said to	Now as they were eating, Jesus took bread, and blessed, and broke it, and gave it to the disciples and said, 'Take, eat; this is my body.' ^{27} And he took a cup, and when he had given thanks he gave it to them, saying, 'Drink of it,

them, 'This is my blood of the covenant, which is poured out for many. [25] Truly, I say to you, I shall not drink again of the fruit of the vine until that day when I drink it new in the kingdom of God.'

all of you; [28] for this is my blood of the covenant, which is poured out for many for the forgiveness of sins. [29] I tell you I shall not drink again of this fruit of the vine until that day when I drink it new with you in my Father's kingdom.'

Lk 22[14-20]

And when the hour came, he sat at table, and the apostles with him. [15] And he said to them, 'I have earnestly desired to eat this passover with you before I suffer; [16] for I tell you I shall never eat it again until it is fulfilled in the kingdom of God.' [17] And he took a cup, and when he had given thanks he said, 'Take this, and divide it among yourselves; [18] for I tell you that from now on I shall not drink of the fruit of the vine until the kingdom of God comes.' [19] And he took bread, and when he had given thanks he broke it and gave it to them, saying, 'This is my body [*which is given for you. Do this in remembrance of me.*' [20] *And likewise the cup after supper, saying, 'This cup which is poured out for you is the new covenant in my blood.*']

1 Cor 11[23-25]

For I received from the Lord what I also delivered to you, that the Lord Jesus on the night when he was betrayed took bread, [24] and when he had given thanks, he broke it, and said, 'This is my body which is broken for you. Do this in remembrance of me.' [25] In the same way also the cup, after supper, saying, 'This cup is the new covenant in my blood. Do this, as often as you drink it, in remembrance of me.'

Lk 22[19b-20], italicized and bracketed above, is omitted by D it (Codex Bezae and some of the Old Latin MSS); the Old Syriac rearranges the text, Syr[c] reading it in the order 19, 17, 18, Syr[s] reading 19a+'after the dinner'+17+'This my blood is the new covenant'+18; the Peshitta omits 17–18; Old Latin *b e* reads 19a, 17, 18—all evidently in an effort to harmonize the 'longer' text with the parallels in Matthew, Mark, and 1 Corinthians (see Westcott and Hort's note). But the grounds for preferring the shorter text are not primarily these later changes, but the improbability that the longer text was written by Luke. *Prima facie*, vv.[19b-20] looks like harmonization, where it now stands in Luke. Equally important is the historical improbability. For it seems scarcely credible that at a supreme moment, like that in which a sacred rite was being established, our Lord should have created the possibility of confusion by solemnly delivering two of the Paschal cups, dividing between them the words which, according to the other Synoptics, belong, as it would seem appropriately, to one. Nor, if He were about to hallow a succeeding cup as Eucharistic, is it likely that He would have spoken of the fulfilment of the Paschal wine in relation to another (v.[17]). In spite, therefore, of the fact that the majority of MSS and Versions favour its inclusion, Westcott and Hort and other modern editors are probably right in regarding the passage inclosed in brackets above as an interpolation. With this omitted, the narrative is assimilated to the other Synoptics. The inversion of bread and cup, which now becomes apparent and which probably belongs not to Luke but to his source, is perhaps due to the fact that the writer, dwelling on the Lord's intention that the Passover should be fulfilled in a Messianic rite, records at the opening of his narrative a declaration similar to that which Matthew and Mark assign to a later stage, the delivery of the cup (Mt 26[29], Mk 14[25]). These words, though referring more particularly to the Eucharistic bread, yet, as extending to the whole meal ('this passover'), require no mention of the action that would accompany them; whereas the companion statement concerning the fruit of the vine (Lk 22[18]) necessitates the mention of the cup (v.[17]). The first half of v.[19] (the consecration of the bread), which, if the account were symmetrical, would appear before v.[15], is then added to complete the institution. A copyist, assuming a part of the narrative to be wanting, would then introduce, probably from a contemporary liturgical formula, the second half of v.[19] and v.[20], which bear a striking resemblance to the Pauline account, of which Luke is otherwise independent. A similar inversion is found in the *Didache* (ch. 9).

2. From the Synoptic record the following inferences may be drawn: (1) *The words of institution cannot themselves determine the meaning of the rite.* Luke (unless v.[20] be genuine) omits 'This is my blood of the covenant.' [Notice also that the other traditional form varies the phrase—'the new covenant in my blood' (1 Co 11[25])]. This may be due to the fact that Luke introduces the cup primarily in relation to our Lord's utterance concerning the fruit of the vine. But the sentence may be an interpretation of Christ's action, based on its correspondence with the hallowing of the bread. Moreover, the sentence, if original, would have lacked a verb: in Aramaic it would have been simply, 'This my body,' 'This my blood,' without any word corresponding to *is*. Matthew further amplifies by adding the words, 'for the forgiveness of sins' (Mt 26[28]). It is clear that although formulas were probably already in use, the language was not yet stereotyped. We cannot, therefore, be certain of the precise form of words that our Lord used.

(2) *The rite, like the gospel of which it is an ordinance, is Apostolic.* All of the Twelve, but no others, are present with Jesus (Mk 14[17]||). Judas had not yet gone out (Lk 22[21]). The significant relation of the Apostles to the congregation of the spiritual Israel, prominent from the first, is not only emphasized by their seclusion with Jesus in this supreme hour, but explicitly stated by Luke (22[24-34]). Although, therefore, there is nothing beyond the form of the record itself to indicate the permanent character of the institution, yet the place which from the first the rite assumed as the bond of Christian fellowship, and for which Christians like Ignatius in the sub-Apostolic age claimed the authority of the Apostles, accords with and interprets the Synoptic narrative. To go behind the Apostolic Eucharist is no more possible for historic Christianity than to separate the actual Christ from the Apostolic witness.

(3) *The origin of the rite.*—As presented in the Synoptic gospels, the Eucharist is Paschal in origin and idea. Yet it is unnecessary to determine whether the Last Supper was in fact a Passover meal, as the Synoptists assume, or anticipated the Jewish feast by one day, as the Fourth Gospel presupposes. Paul does not describe the scene as a Passover, though he may have assumed it. No mention is made of the lamb, in the four narratives, and the identification of Christ's body and blood with the bread and wine, rather than with the lamb, suggests that the lamb was absent. The bread is presumably ordinary *artos*, not the unleavened bread (*azyma*) required at the Passover meal. Moreover, the frequent observance of the Supper in the early Church, rather than once a year, suggests that in its origin the rite had an even broader basis, and must be sought in the ordinary and repeated meals of Jesus and His disciples, including the Feedings of the Multitude (which are narrated in eucharistic language in the gospels), and that only the *Last* Supper took its strongly sacrificial tone from the Passover meal with which it was associated in the early gospel tradition. Many modern scholars find the origin of the rite in the 'Kiddush' or 'Sanctification' of the day which was about to begin at sundown—ordinarily the sabbath, but in this case the Passover. In this observance, a group of men would gather in the afternoon to read and study the Bible, exchanging comments on it, and finally concluding with prayers and a simple meal of bread and

wine. Where evidence is so scanty or entirely lacking, no one can affirm positively that this hypothesis is correct; but it meets many of the conditions and solves most of the problems involved in the narratives of the Institution.

3. *St. Paul's account of the Institution* (see above) was written not later than A.D. 58, and is therefore older than the Synoptics. He claims to have received it as part of the inviolable deposit of the gospel (1 Co 11[23]), which he must hand on unimpaired to those to whom he ministers the word. The phrase 'from the Lord' can hardly imply, as some have maintained, that a direct revelation was given to himself, extending to the form of words; but only that the record is part of that original message of which the Apostles were the guardians rather than the interpreters (1 Co 15[3], Gal 1[6-9]). The form of tradition here produced brings out explicitly the fact that the Eucharist was regarded in the Apostolic Church as an ordinance to be observed in Christian congregations till the Lord's Coming ('as often as you drink,' with comment v.[26]). St. Paul is the only NT writer who introduces the command, 'Do this in remembrance of me' (v.[24]), an expression fruitful in controversy. It has been urged that the word rendered 'do' means 'offer,' and that the Eucharist is, therefore, by its terms sacrificial. Not only is this an uncommon use of the Greek, unsuspected by the Greek commentators themselves, but the word 'this' (Greek neuter) which follows can only be 'this action,' not 'this bread,' which would require the masculine form of the Greek pronoun. Clearly, however, the phrase refers to the whole Eucharistic action, not to the particular acts of eating and drinking, the latter of which is differentiated from it in v.[26]. It is further argued that the word used for 'remembrance' (*anamnēsis*, vv.[24f]) implies a ritual memorial before God. The word, however, almost invariably used in the LXX with this signification is different (*mnēmosynon*, Lv 2[2, 9, 16] 5[12], Nu 5[26]; *anamnēsis* is found in Lv 24[7] and Nu 10[10]). And, though the form of words in which, according to the traditional ritual, the house-father recalled the redemption from Egypt is probably present to the Apostle's mind, it is uncertain whether this recital of Divine deliverance was directed towards God. As now used it would seem to be intended to carry out the injunction of the Law given in Ex 12[26f] (see the *Haggadah for Passover*). The same uncertainty attaches to St. Paul's explanatory statement—'you proclaim the Lord's death'—though the natural interpretation of the Greek is in favour of the idea suggested by the RV, viz. announcement to men rather than commemoration before God (cf 1 Co 9[14]). The evidential value, not the mystical significance, of the rite is here asserted.

4. The *sacrificial character* of the Eucharist is implied in the declaration that the bread broken is a communion of the body, the cup of blessing a communion of the blood, of Christ (1 Co 10[16]). The table of the Lord is contrasted with the table of demons (v.[21]) through the medium of the sacrificial system of the OT, of which it is a fundamental principle that to eat of the offerings is to have communion with the altar (v.[18]). The words 'Lord's table' and 'altar' are found as synonyms in Malachi (1[7, 12]). The Levitical code includes many forms of oblation in which feeding on the sacrifice, if it ever existed, has disappeared; but provision is made for it in the case of the peace-offerings (Lv 7[15-21]). A closer study of the OT brings into greater prominence the connexion between sacrifice (q.v.) and feasting (Ex 32[6ff], Dt 12[5, 12] 26[10f], 1 S 1[3ff] 16[2, 11]). The end of sacrifice in Israel, as among other nations, is the union of the worshipper with the object of worship, through the covering which the priest supplies (W. R. Smith, *RS*[2] Lect. xi.). This is especially evident in the Passover, which is a sacrifice (Ex 12[27] 34[25], Nu 9[7, 13]), and, as including a repast, should rank among the peace-offerings. The Eucharist, therefore, is a sacrifice, not as the commemoration of the death of Christ, but as the means of participation in the Paschal Lamb slain for us (1 Co 5[7]), in the offering of the body of Christ once made on the Cross (He 10[10]; cf Jn 19[36], 1 Co 10[17]). The crucifixion of Christ's natural body resulted in the institution of the sacramental body, in respect of which the unworthy partaker is guilty (1 Co 11[27], but see below), and through which the faithful have fellowship with Christ in His mystical body (10[16f]). The transition from one application of the word 'body' to the others—'one bread, one body'—is very subtle, and they are no doubt so vitally connected in the mind of St. Paul as hardly to be capable of exact distinction. But it is unlikely that in a passage where the argument would have been satisfied by the use of one word—'body'—on the analogy of the common pagan identification of the god with the sacrifice, he should have used the longer phrase—'communion of the body'—if he had not felt that the single word would have failed to give the exact meaning. The sense of the whole passage depends upon the reality of the gift conveyed through the feast in which it is symbolically presented. St. Paul holds that there is a real communion in the sacrificial feasts of the heathen, though in this case with demons (v.[20]), whose presence is incompatible with that of Christ (v.[21]).

5. The crucial words of the second passage (11[17-34]) are 'without discerning the body.' 'Lord's' is an interpolation of the TR, which the RV and RSV properly reject (v.[29]). The RV also brings out the fact that the verb translated 'discern' (v.[29]) is again used in v.[31]—'if we judged ourselves truly'—thus showing that the word does not mean 'perceive' but 'discriminate.' 'Body' is left undefined, including, as it apparently does, the mystical body which the unworthy despise in the Church of God, the sacramental elements which they dishonour by profane use, and the sacrifice of Christ with which they reject communion, thereby becoming guilty in respect of each (vv.[21f, 26f]).

6. Both passages express what is implicit in the division of the sacrament into two kinds. It is the body and blood as separated in death through which communion is attained. In 1 Co 10[16], by placing the cup first, as in St. Luke's account of the institution, St. Paul emphasizes the sacrificial death of Christ as a necessary element in the Eucharistic feast. The Epistle to the Hebrews shows that access to the Holy Place is gained through the offered body and sprinkled blood (He 10[19-22]); St. John, that union with Christ is found in that Living Bread which implies death because it is flesh and blood (Jn 6[52-58]). There is nothing to warrant the inference that the phrase 'flesh and blood' is equivalent to 'personality,' and that therefore 'the whole Christ' is *sacramentally* present in the Eucharistic elements. But it does imply vital union with Him who became dead and is alive for evermore (Rev 1[18]), a Lamb 'as though it had been slain' (5[6]), a Priest upon His throne (Zec 6[13]; cf He 8[1]), who through the one offering of Himself has perfected for ever (10[14]) those who come to God through Him.

7. In conclusion, however, it must be frankly admitted that, while one view of the sacrament may seem on the whole to express more fully than others the general tenor of NT teaching on the subject, none of the explanations which have divided Christendom since the 16th cent., not even the theory of transubstantiation when precisely defined, can be regarded as wholly inconsistent with the language of Scripture. See LOVE FEAST.

J. G. S.—F. C. G.

EUERGETES (Prologue to Sirach).—See BENEFACTOR.

EUMENES II.—The king of Pergamum, to whom Rome gave a large slice of the territory of Antiochus III., king of Syria (190 B.C.), including, not 'India' (1 Mac 8[6-8]), but the greater part of Asia north of the Taurus (Liv. xxxvii. 44). J. T.

EUNATAN, 1 Es 8[44] (AV).—See ELNATHAN, 3.

EUNICE.—The Jewish mother of Timothy (2 Ti 1[5], Ac 16[1]), married to a Gentile husband, and dwelling at Lystra. She had given her son a careful religious training, but had not circumcised him. A. J. M.

EUNUCH.—In the proper sense of the word a eunuch is an emasculated human being (Dt 23[1]), but it is not absolutely certain that the Hebrew *sārîs* always has this signification, and the uncertainty is reflected in our English translation, where **'officer'** and **'chamberlain'** are frequently found. It is interesting to note that the group of scholars who rendered Jeremiah for the AV adhered to 'eunuch' throughout: unhappily the Revisers have spoiled the symmetry by conforming Jer 52[25] to 2 K 25[19]. The following reasons, none of which is decisive, have been advanced in favour of some such rendering of *sārîs* as 'officer' or 'chamberlain.' **1.** That Potiphar (Gn 37[36]) was married. But actual eunuchs were not precluded from this (see Ter. *Eun.* 4, 3, 24; Juv. vi. 366; Sir 20[4] 30[20] etc.). It may be that the words in Gn 39[1] which identify Joseph's first master with the husband of his temptress are an interpolation. **2.** That in 2 K 25[19] etc. 'eunuchs' hold military commands, whereas they are generally unwarlike (*imbelles*, Juv. *l.c.*). But there have been competent commanders amongst them. **3.** That the strict meaning cannot be insisted on at Gn 40[2, 7]. Yet even here it is admissible.

The kings of Israel and Judah imitated their powerful neighbours in employing eunuchs (1) as guardians of the harem (2 K 9[32], Jer 41[16]); Est 1[12] 4[4] are instances of Persian usage; (2) in military and other important posts (1 S 8[15], 1 K 22[9], 2 K 8[6] 23[11] 24[12, 15] 25[19], 1 Ch 28[1], 2 Ch 18[8], Jer 29[2] 34[19] 38[7]; cf Gn 37[36] 40[2, 7], Ac 8[27]. Dn 1[3] does not of necessity imply that the captives were made eunuchs). For the services rendered at court by persons of this class and the power which they often acquired, see Jos. *Ant.* XVI. viii. 1 (230). But their acquisitions could not remove the sense of degradation and loss (2 K 20[18], Is 39[7]). Dt 23[1] excluded them from public worship, partly because self-mutilation was often performed in honour of a heathen deity, and partly because a maimed creature was judged unfit for the service of Yahweh (Lv 21[20] 22[24]). The author of Is 56[4f] insists that holding fast to the ethical demands of the covenant cancels this ban. Eusebius (*HE* vi. 8) relates how Origen misunderstood the figurative language of Mt 19[12]; Origen's own comment on the passage shows that he afterwards regretted having taken it literally and acted on it. See also Ethiopian Eunuch.

J. T.—**N. H. S.**

EUODIA.—This is clearly the correct form of the name, not *Euodias* as AV (Ph 4[2f]), for a woman is intended. St. Paul beseeches her and **Syntyche** to be reconciled; perhaps they were deaconesses at Philippi.

EUPATOR.—See Antiochus V.

EUPHRATES, one of the rivers of Eden (Gn 2[14]), derives its name from the Assyrian *Purattu*, which became *Ufrâtu* in Persian, where the prosthetic vowel was supposed by the Greeks to be the word *eu*, 'good.' In the OT the Euphrates is generally known as 'the river.' It rises in the Armenian mountains from two sources, the northern branch being called the Frat or Kara-su, and the southern and larger branch the Murad-su (the *Arsanias* of ancient geography). The present length of the river is 1780 miles. The salt marshes through which it passed were called *nārMarratu* (**Merathaim** in Jer 50[21]), where the Aramaean Chaldaeans lived. The alluvial plain between the Euphrates and the Tigris constituted Babylonia, the water of the annual inundation (which took place in May, and was caused by the melting of the snows in Armenia) being regulated by means of canals and barrages. The Hittite city of Carchemish stood at the point where the Euphrates touched Northern Syria, and commanded one of the chief fords over the river; south of it came the Balikh and Khabur, the last affluents of the Euphrates. The promise made to the Israelites that their territory should extend to 'the great river' (Gn 15[18] etc.) was fulfilled through the conquests of David (2 S 8[3] 10[16–19], 1 K 4[24]). A. H. S.—**T. F.**

EURAQUILO (Ac 27[14] RV; RSV 'the northeaster').—There is some doubt as to the reading. The Greek MSS which are esteemed to be the best read *Eurakylon*; so do the Bohairic Version, which was made in Egypt in the 6th or 7th cent. from a MS very like these, and the Sahidic Version made in the 3rd cent.; the Vulgate Latin revision, made towards the close of the 4th cent., reads *Euroaquilo*, which points to a Greek original reading *Euroakylon*. Our later authorities, along with the Pesh. and Hark. Syriac, read *Euroclydon* (so AV). No doubt *Eur(o)akylon* is the correct name, and the other is an attempt to get a form capable of derivation. The word is, then, a sailor's word, and expresses an ENE. wind, by compounding two words, a Greek word (*euros*) meaning E. wind, and a Latin word (*aquilo*) meaning NE. wind. This is exactly the kind of wind which frequently arises in Cretan waters at the present day, swooping down from the mountains in strong gusts and squalls. The *euraquilo* which drove St. Paul's ship before it was the cause of the shipwreck. A. So.

EUROCLYDON, Ac 27[14] (AV) = **Euraquilo** (q.v.).

EUTYCHUS.—A young man who fell down from a third storey window while asleep during St. Paul's sermon at Troas, and was 'taken up dead' (Ac 20[9]). St. Paul bent over him and, embracing him, declared his life to be in him. It is not actually said that Eutychus was dead, but that seems at least to have been the general belief. The incident is described in parallel terms with the raising of Dorcas and of Jairus' daughter. A. J. M.

EVANGELIST ('one who proclaims good tidings' ['evangel,' 'gospel']).—The word occurs three times in NT (Ac 21[8] Eph 4[11], 2 Ti 4[5]), and in each case with reference to the proclamation of the *Christian* gospel.

Ac 21[8] gives what appears to be the primary Christian use of the word. Philip, one of the Seven (cf Ac 6[1–6]), is there called 'the evangelist,' presumably because after Stephen's martyrdom he left Jerusalem and 'preached the gospel' (literally *evangelized*) in Samaria, in the wilderness, and in all the cities of the coastland between Azotus and Caesarea (Ac 8[4f, 12, 35, 40]). In the first place, then, the evangelist was a travelling Christian missionary, one who preached the good news of Christ to those who had never heard it before.

In Eph 4[11] apostles, prophets, evangelists, pastors, and teachers (or, pastoral teachers) are all named as gifts bestowed on the Church by the ascended Christ. St. Paul in 1 Co 12[28] and Ro 12[7f] does not mention 'evangelists.' If Ephesians be sub-Pauline, a later disciple may have thought (because of Philip?) that evangelists should find a place in the list; and yet it seems unlikely that there was any distinctive function or office that could be described as that of an evangelist, even during the 2nd cent. St. Paul himself, while discharging the exceptional functions of the apostolate, was equally an evangelist and teacher. Some have concluded, therefore, that the evangelist as such was not an official but simply one who had a gift for proclaiming the gospel.

That 'evangelist' denotes the function of preaching the gospel and not a special office in a local congregation or in the Church at large may be confirmed by 2 Ti 4[5] ('do the work of an evangelist'). In his earlier life, Timothy, as St. Paul's travel-companion (Ac 16[1ff] 19[22] 20[4], Ro 16[21] etc.), had been an evangelist of the journeying type (cf Epaphras, Col 1[7] 4[12]). But in the Pastorals Timothy and Titus are rather the settled pastors and stated teachers, who watch over the morals of the flock and attend to their upbuilding in sound doctrine. It is significant, however, that the author of the letters includes the task of preaching the gospel to the unbelievers in the commission to Timothy as an apostolic delegate; and that the bishop-elders, who must be apt to teach, are not so commissioned. This marks a transition phase in the establishment of the Church at a time when heresy was a real danger within the community of faith. But Christianity never ceased to be a missionary religion.

The special use of 'evangelist' in the sense of an author of a *written* 'Gospel' or narrative of Christ's life, and specifically the author of one of the four canonical Gospels, is much later than the NT, no instance being found till the 3rd cent. J. C. L.—**G. J.**

EVE (Hebrew *Ḥawwāh*; the name probably denotes

'life'; other proposed explanations are 'life-giving,' 'living,' 'kinship,' and some would connect it with an Arabic word for 'serpent').—**1.** Eve is little more, in Genesis, than a personification of human life which is perpetuated by woman, Gn 3^{20} 4^{1}. See ADAM. **2.** In the NT Eve is mentioned in 2 Co 11^{3}, 1 Ti 2^{13-15}. The former is a reference to her deception by the serpent. The latter teaches that since 'Adam was formed first, then Eve,' women must live in quiet subordination to their husbands. And a second reason seems to be added, *i.e.* that Adam was 'not deceived,' in the fundamental manner that Eve was, for 'the woman was deceived and became a transgression.' Here St. Paul distinctly takes Eve to be a personification of all women. The personification continues in v.^{15}, which is obscure, and must be studied in the commentaries.

EVENING.—See TIME.

EVI.—One of the five kings of Midian slain, Nu 31^{8}, Jos 13^{21}.

EVIDENTLY.—Ac 10^{3} AV 'He saw in a vision evidently about the ninth hour of the day' (RSV 'clearly'); Gal 3^{1} 'before whose eyes Jesus Christ hath been evidently set forth' (RSV 'publicly'). Cf *Robinson Crusoe* (Golden Treasury ed. p. 250), 'He saw evidently what Stock of Corn and Rice I had laid up.'

EVIL.—This concept is not easily made precise in Biblical thought, for it is hard to distinguish between what we would call sin on one hand and what we would call disaster on the other. Knowledge of good and evil is a characteristic of judges and governors, 1 K 3^{9}, and of course of divine beings. This power of distinction was not innate in man but was assumed in disobedience to God and in the aspiration to be more like him; but the power now exists in man (Gn 2–3). One can hardly say the OT explains the origin of evil; but it connects it with the power to distinguish evil. Afterwards, however, evil and violence become characteristic of human life (Gn $6^{5, 11f.}$ 8^{21}). Evil in the OT is, however, a more comprehensive term than deliberate moral depravity. A man may be eaten by an evil beast; catastrophe may fall on a city, and this is evil, which God must have done (Am 3^{6}); God is indeed creator of evil or woe as well as of welfare, Is 45^{7}. There are spirits of evil, who are, however, under God's control (Jg 9^{23}, 1K 22^{22}, Job 1–2). The true Israelite, however, is one who turns away from evil and seeks God.

In the Qumrân texts we see the spirit of lies and evil become much more prominent, with the doctrine of the two spirits in man. The spirit of error leads men into all kinds of evil, and this evil has its seat in their flesh. The members of the community are conscious of the assault of evil against them, and of how nearly they have succumbed to it; but they are confident of cleansing from it. There is an epoch of evil now permitted at the end of which evil will be unmasked and purified away.

In the NT the evil spirits are also prominent, causing all kinds of sickness and destruction, and Jesus makes His attack on evil by casting them out and healing the sick. The 'Evil One' is the prince or controller of this world, which lies 'in the Evil One'; he is judged, condemned, and destroyed by Christ (1 Jn 5^{19}, Jn 16^{11}). For deliverance from evil or the Evil One the disciples pray, for evil attacks and tempts them continually. Words, thoughts, desires, the heart of unbelief, the conscience, may all be evil; but the Church should and must be cleansed by the work of Christ. Meanwhile pain and suffering, which in the OT would be included under 'evil,' continue in the fleshly existence of the Church's members, but are turned to good by God and made to show forth His goodness, as did also the evil of the Cross. The full destruction of evil and the evil powers awaits the consummation (Mt 25^{41}, 2 Th 2, Rev 20). For 'evil eye' see EYE. J. Ba.

EVIL-MERODACH, the *Amel-Marduk* of the Babylonians, son and successor of Nebuchadrezzar on the throne of Babylon (2 K 25^{27-30}, Jer 52^{31-34}), released Jehoiachin in the thirty-seventh year of his captivity. He reigned 561–560 B.C. Berosus describes him as reigning lawlessly and without restraint, and he was put to death by his brother-in-law Neriglissar, who succeeded him.

EVIL-SPEAKING in the Bible covers sins of untruthfulness as well as of malice. It includes abuse, thoughtless talebearing, imputing of bad motives, slander, and deliberate false witness. Warnings against it are frequent; it is forbidden in the legislation of the OT (Ninth Commandment; cf Dt 19^{16-19}) and of the NT (Mt 5^{22} 12^{32} 15^{19}). Christians must expect this form of persecution (Mt 5^{11}), but must be careful to give no handle to it (Ro 14^{16}, Ti 2^{8}, 1 P 2^{12} 3^{16}). C. W. E.

EVIL SPIRITS.—As a natural synonym for **demons** or devils, this phrase is used in the NT only by St. Luke (7^{21} 8^{2}, Ac $19^{12f, 15f}$), and presents no difficulty. But in the OT, especially the historical books, reference is made to an evil spirit as coming from or sent by God; and the context invests this spirit with personality. The treachery of the men of Shechem is so explained (Jg 9^{23}), though in this case the spirit may not be personal but merely a temper or purpose of ill-will. Elsewhere there is not the same ground for doubt: 'an evil spirit from the Lord' is the alleged cause of Saul's moodiness (1 S 16^{14}, where notice the antithetical 'the spirit of the Lord'), and of his raving against David (1 S 18^{10} 19^{9}). Similarly Micaiah speaks of 'a lying spirit' from God (1 K 22^{21-23}, 2 Ch 18^{20-23}). It has been suggested that in all these cases the reference is to God Himself as exerting power, and effecting good or evil in men according to the character of each. The nearest approach to this is perhaps in Ex $12^{13, 23}$, where Yahweh and the destroyer are apparently identified, though the language admits equally of the view that the destroyer is the agent of Yahweh's will (cf 2 S 24^{16}). But the theory is inconsistent with what is known to have been the current demonology of the day (see DEVIL), as well as with the natural suggestion of the phrases. These spirits are not represented as constituting the personal energy of God, but as under His control, which was direct and active according to some of the writers, but only permissive according to others. The fact of God's control is acknowledged by all, and is even a postulate of Scripture; and in using or permitting the activity of these spirits God is assumed or asserted to be punishing people for their sins. In this sense He has 'a company of destroying angels' (Ps 78^{49}), who may yet be called 'angels of the Lord' (2 K 19^{35}, Is 37^{36}), as carrying out His purposes. Micaiah evidently considered Zedekiah as used by God in order to entice Ahab to his merited doom. Ezekiel propounds a similar view (14^{9}), that a prophet may be deceived by God, and so made the means of his own destruction and of that of his dupes, much as David was moved to number Israel through the anger of the Lord against the people (2 S 24^{1}). As the conception of God developed and was purified, the permitted action of some evil spirit is substituted for the Divine activity, whether direct or through the agency of messengers, considered as themselves ethically good but capable of employment on any kind of service. Accordingly the Chronicler represents Satan as the instigator of David (1 Ch 21^{1}). Jeremiah denies the inspiration of lying prophets, and makes them entirely responsible for their own words and influence ($23^{16, 21, 25f}$); they are not used by God, and will be called to account. They speak out of their own heart, and are so far from executing God's justice or anger upon the wicked that He interposes to check them, and to protect men from being misled.

An evil spirit, therefore, wherever the phrase occurs in a personal sense in the earlier historical books of the OT, must be thought of simply as an angel or messenger of God, sent for the punishment of evil (cf 1 S 19^{9} RVm). His coming to a man was a sign that God's patience with him was approaching exhaustion, and a prelude of doom. Gradually the phrase was diverted from this use to denote a personal spirit, the 'demon' of the NT (RVm

and RSV), essentially evil and working against God, though powerless to withdraw entirely from His rule.
R. W. M.

EXCELLENCY, EXCELLENT. — These English words are used for a great variety of Hebrew and Greek expressions, a complete list of which will be found in Driver's *Daniel* (Cambridge Bible), pp. 32–34. The words (from Lat. *excello*, ' to rise up out of,' ' surpass ') formerly had the meaning of *pre-eminence* and *pre-eminent*, and were thus good equivalents for the Hebrew and Greek expressions. But since 1611 they have become greatly weakened; and, as Driver says, ' it is to be regretted that they have been retained in RV in passages in which the real meaning is something so very different.' The force of ' excellency ' may be clearly seen in AVm at Gn 4[7], where ' have the excellency ' is suggested for ' be accepted ' in the text; or the margin at Ec 2[13], where instead of ' wisdom excelleth folly ' is suggested ' there is an excellency in wisdom more than in folly.' In Dn 1[20] it is said that ' in all matters of wisdom and understanding, that the king inquired of them, he found them ten times better than all the magicians and astrologers that were in all his realm '; and this is summed up in the heading of the chapter in the words, ' their excellency in wisdom.' The force of Hamilton's *Catechism*, ' Of the pre-eminent and excellent dignitie of the Paternoster '; or from Sir John Mandeville, *Travels*, p. 1, ' the Holy Land, . . . passing all other lands, is the most worthy land, most excellent, and lady and sovereign of all other lands.' RSV occasionally retains the use of the word ' excellent ' in the sense of ' surpassing,' ' pre-eminent,' *e.g.* Dn 5[12, 14] 6[3].

EXCHANGER.—See MONEY-CHANGER.

EXCOMMUNICATION.—Israel as a covenanted community required penalties for breach of civil or religious law (Gn 12[14], Dt 27[15ff]). In the case of man the ancient Hebrew *ḥērem*, **curse** or **ban**, involved death, in the case of property devotion or destruction (Lv 27[29]). ' To be cut off from the people ' is the Priestly Code phrase (Ezr 10[8]; cf Ex12[15] 30[32f], Lv 17[9] 20[18f], Ps 109[13]). Conversely, proselytes and eunuchs faithful to the covenant are assured of acceptance (Is 56[3, 5]). The forms said to be in vogue in Jesus' day were: (1) *neẓîphāh*, a light punishment; (2) *niddûy* and *shammattā'*, exclusion from fellow-Jews other than immediate family, though not from the cult or synagogue worship. The initial period of thirty days could be extended to ninety; (3) *ḥērem*, which could mean death, the sentence to be executed by the Gentile rulers as in the case of Jesus (Mk 15, Gal 3[13]), but not Stephen (Ac 7[58ff]). Power to excommunicate was confined probably to the Sanhedrin, unless for minor synagogal discipline. Among the Essenes excommunication was a dreadful thing bound to lead to apostasy or death (Jos. *BJ* II. viii. 8 [143 f]). At Qumrân penalties ranged from 10 days to 2 years for dishonesty, revenge, slander against a brother, and voluntary withdrawal followed by return. For slander against the *Yaḥadh*, and for betrayal by a member of 10 years' standing the punishment was eternal exile (1 QS 6[23]–7[25], CD 9[1, 16ff]). The horror of the curse hangs over the OT (Mal 4[6], Zec 14[11]). *Anathema*, the LXX equivalent of *ḥērem* (*e.g.* in Dt 7[26], Jos 6[17], Nu 21[3]), appears in 1 Co 16[22] (which refers, as does also Gal 1[8], to a permanent exclusion from the Church and doubtless from the Kingdom of God) and in 1 Co 12[3] (with which cf the twelfth Jewish Benediction against the heretics or apostates, *Berak.* 20b). References in the NT to some form of Jewish procedure are: Lk 6[22], Jn 9[22] 12[42] 6[12].

Christian discipline was founded on Jewish precedents and on such a word of Jesus as Mk 3[29] (the sin against the Holy Spirit is unpardonable). Peter had authority to interpret, according to Mt 16[19]. Mt 18[15–17] (probably not authentic) reflects primitive Jewish Christian practice: private admonition, charges in the presence of two or three witnesses, and finally formal accusation before the Church (cf He 10[28], Tit 3[10]). Efforts to win back the offenders are mandatory (Ja 5[19f], 1 Jn 5[16a]). The curious story of Ananias and his wife (Ac 5[4ff]) suggests a special position for Peter and a virtual sentence of death rather than mere superstitious fear in the accused.

Remedial principles prevailed in the Pauline churches too. Paul sternly advises that Christian should not prosecute Christian in pagan courts (1 Co 6[1–6]). Reasons for discipline included idleness, disobedience to the Apostle, or rejection of his teaching (2 Th 3[6, 14f]); immorality, greed, idolatry, slander (as at Qumrân), drunkenness, and theft (1 Co 5[9–13]; cf He 13[4], Jd [22f], Rev 2[14f, 20] 22[15]). Paul's leading opponent at Corinth was dealt with at a meeting of the congregation (RSV ' majority ' may represent *rabbîm*, technical in Qumrân literature for the congregation), but details are lacking; presumably he was excommunicated for a limited time. Later the Church was admonished to forgive the offender, as Paul himself had done, ' to keep Satan from gaining the advantage over us ' (2 Co 2[6–11] 7[8–13]), *i.e.* lest the man or the congregation fall prey to ' worldly grief ' or even death, and thus be cut off from Christ in his Body. A quite different case is discussed in 1 Co 5[1–5], that of a Corinthian who ' has ' a wife of his father (cf Dt 22[30] 27[20]). It is uncertain whether the father was then alive, and also whether the wife was pagan or Christian. So serious, however, was the offence that it demanded, apparently, the death penalty: ' deliver this man to Satan for the destruction of the flesh, that his spirit may be saved in the day of the Lord Jesus,' *i.e.* at the *Parousia* (with 1 Co 5[13]; cf Dt 13[5] 17[7] 22[24]). The death penalty could be enforced either by terror (1 Co 11[30]), starvation caused by the excommunication, or by prosecution in a Gentile court since he had become an ' outsider.' This view is challenged by those who interpret ' flesh ' even here as meaning man's creaturely, sinful nature.

Excommunication for apostasy appears in He 6[4–6] 10[26–31]; it is permanent and leads to yet more awful divine judgment. 1 Jn 5[16b] may refer to this too, or to heresy (cf 2 Jn [10]). Diotrephes expelled the Elder's adherents (3 Jn [10]), perhaps as presiding presbyter of a local church. (1 Jn 2[19] implies excommunication of the orthodox in a schism.) ' Delivery to Satan ' (1 Ti 1[20]) recalls 1 Co 5[5] and certainly means excommunication, but there seems to be no implication of a death sentence. The cause was heresy (2 Ti 2[17]) or at least departure from the apostolic tradition in its Pauline form. The loss of social and spiritual fellowship was intended to lead, in such cases, to recantation of opinions, as in others to repentance for sin.
F. R. M. H.—**G. J.**

EXILE.—See ISRAEL, I., **22.**

EXODUS.—The book tells the story of the leadership of Moses and the exodus from Egypt, of the stay in the wilderness and the erection of the Tabernacle. There are four focal points in the narrative in its present form: (*a*) the revelation of Yahweh by name to Moses (chs. 3 and 6); (*b*) the Exodus and the institution of the Passover in commemoration of it; (*c*) the revelation of Yahweh to the people at Mount Sinai and the covenant then made which found expression ultimately in a code of laws of which three different collections are incorporated in the book [20[1–17] 21[1]–23[19] (this is capable of subdivision into two parts, (i) Judgments, 21[1]–22[17], and (ii) sundry laws relating to worship and festivals, moral and social evils, 22[18]–23[19]); 34[11–28] 35[1–3] hints at yet a fourth collection which has evidently been lost or placed elsewhere, except for a fragment in the law of the sabbath]; (*d*) the erection of a tabernacle and the manufacture of its equipment.

But the narrative is a composite one and shows many marks of editorial activity in the binding together of its component material. A clear result of an editor's work may be seen in the apparent intrusion of chs. 32–34 between the command to build a tabernacle and the description of its completion. We may note also the broken sequence between 10[29] and 11[8b], and the awkward transition from 19[25] to 20[1]. In the main it is the product of the fusion of three separate accounts, although the limits assigned to each, in particular those designated J and E, cannot be delineated with any great certainty.

1. The narrative of P, which can be most surely distinguished, is given first.

Beginning with a list of the sons of Israel (1^{1-5}), it briefly relates the oppression ($1^{7, 13f}$ 2^{23b-25}), and describes the call of Moses, which takes place in Egypt, the revelation of the name *Yahweh*, and the appointment of Aaron (6^2–7^{13}). The plagues ($7^{19, 20a, 21b, 22}$ $8^{5-7, 15b-19}$ 9^{8-12} 11^{9f}), which are wrought by Aaron, form a trial of strength with Pharaoh's magicians. The last plague introduces directions for the Passover, the feast of unleavened bread, the sanctification of the firstborn, and the annual Passover ($12^{1-20, 28, 40-51}$ 13^{1f}). Emphasis is laid, not on the blood-sprinkling, but on the eating, which was the perpetual feature.

The route to the Red Sea (which gives occasion to a statement about the length of the sojourn, 12^{40f}) is represented as deliberately chosen in order that Israel and Egypt may witness Yahweh's power over Pharaoh (12^{37} 13^{20} 14^{1-4}). When Moses stretches out his hand, the waters are miraculously divided and restored ($14^{8f, 15a, 16b-18, 21ac, 22f, 26, 27a, 28a}$ 15^{19}).

Between the Red Sea and Sinai the names of some halting-places are given (16^{1-3} 17^{1a} 19^{2a}). Ch. 16 is also largely (vv.$^{6-13a, 16-24, 31-36}$) from P. But the mention of the Testimony, *i.e.* the divine charge contained in the Ten Words, shows that the story belongs to a later date than Sinai at which, according to tradition, the Ten Words were revealed.

On the arrival at Sinai, Yahweh's glory appears in a fiery cloud on the mountain. As no priests have been consecrated, and the people must not draw near, Moses ascends alone to receive the tables of the testimony ($24^{15b-18a}$) written by Yahweh on both sides. He remains (probably for 40 days) to receive plans for a sanctuary, with Yahweh's promise to meet with Israel (in the Tent of Meeting) and to dwell with Israel (in the Tabernacle) (25^1–31^{18a} 32^{15}). He returns (34^{29-35}), deposits the testimony in an Ark he has caused to be prepared, and constructs the Tabernacle (35–40). The differing order in the plans as ordered and as executed, and the condition of the text in the LXX, prove that these sections underwent alterations before reaching their present form.

This account was evidently written to provide the background for the annual celebration of the Passover and to demonstrate the antiquity of the institution of the Sanctuary and its appurtenances.

2. The narrative of JE.—The rest of the book is substantially from JE (with an occasional inclusion of material from older traditions such as 4^{24-26} $24^{1f, 9-11}$, which seem to belong to neither J nor E), but it is extremely difficult to distinguish J from E. For (1) with the revelation of the name of Yahweh, one of our criteria, the avoidance of this name by E disappears ; (2) special care has been taken to weld the accounts of the law-giving together, and it is often difficult to decide how much is the work of the editor. We give the broad lines of the separation, but remark that in certain passages this must remain tentative.

A. *Israel in Egypt.*

According to J, the people are cattle-owners, living apart in Goshen, where they increase so rapidly as to alarm Pharaoh ($1^{6, 8-12}$). Moses, after receiving his revelation and commission in Midian (2^{11-22} $3^{2-4a, 5, 7f, 16-20}$ $4^{1-16, 19, 20a, 24-26a, 29-31}$) demands from Pharaoh liberty to depart three days' journey to sacrifice ($5^{3, 5-23}$). The specification of time suggests that a definite place was in mind, which might well have been Kadesh. On Pharaoh's refusal the plagues, which are natural calamities brought by Yahweh, and which are limited to Egypt, follow Moses' repeated announcement ($7^{14, 16, 17a, 18, 21a, 24f}$ $8^{1-4, 8-15a, 20}$–$9^{7, 13-35}$ $10^{1-11, 13b, 14b, 15a, 15c-19, 24-26, 28f}$ 11^{4-8}). In connexion with the Passover (12^{21-27}), blood-sprinkling, not eating, is insisted on. The escape is hurried ($^{29-34, 37-39}$), and so a historical meaning is attached to the use of unleavened bread (13^{3-16} [based on J]).

According to E, the people live among the Egyptians as royal pensioners and without cattle. Their numbers are so small that two midwives suffice for them ($1^{15-20a, 21f}$). Moses (2^{1-10}), whose father-in-law is Jethro (3^1), receives his revelation ($3^{6, 9b-15, 21f}$) and commission ($4^{17f, 20-23, 27f}$) on Horeb. Obeying, he demands that Israel be freed ($5^{1f, 4}$) in order to worship their God on this mountain—a greater distance than three days' journey. E's account of the plagues has survived merely in fragments, but from these it would appear that Moses speaks only once to Pharaoh, and that the plagues follow his mere gesture, while the miraculous element is heightened ($7^{15, 17b, 20b, 23}$ 9^{22-25} $10^{12, 13a, 14a, 15b, 20-23, 27}$). The Israelites, however, have no immunity except from the darkness. The Exodus is deliberate, since the people have time to borrow from their neighbours (11^{1-3} 12^{35f}).

B. *The Exodus.*

According to J, an unarmed host is guided by the pillar of fire and cloud (13^{21f}). Pharaoh pursues to recover his slaves (14^{5f}), and when the people are dismayed, Moses encourages them ($14^{10-14, 19b, 20b}$). An east wind drives back the water, so that the Israelites are able to cross during the night ($14^{21b, 24, 25b, 27b, 28f, 30f}$). but the water returns to overwhelm the Egyptians. Israel offers thanks in a hymn of praise (15^1) ; but soon in the wilderness tempts Yahweh by murmuring for water (vv.$^{22-25a, 27}$ $17^{3, 2b, 7}$).

According to E, an armed body march out in so leisurely a fashion that they are able to bring Joseph's bones. For fear of the Philistines they avoid the route of the isthmus (13^{17-19}). Pharaoh pursues ($14^{9a, 10b}$), but the people, protected by an angel, cross when Moses lifts his rod (vv.$^{15b, 16a, 19a, 20a, 25a, 29}$). The women celebrate the escape ($15^{2-18, 20f}$) ; and in the wilderness Yahweh tests Israel, whether they can live on a daily provision from Him ($16^{4, 15a, 19a, 16a, 19b-21, 35a}$). Water, for which they murmur, is brought by Moses striking the rock with his rod ($17^{1b, 2a, 4-6, 7b}$). Jethro visits and advises Moses (ch. 18 [in the main from E]). The condition of the account of the journey between the Red Sea and Sinai, and the fact that events of a later date have certainly come into P's account, make it likely that JE had very little on this stage, the account of which was amplified with material from the wilderness journey after Sinai.

C. *At Sinai* [here the accounts are exceptionally difficult to disentangle, and the results correspondingly tentative].

According to J, Yahweh descends on Sinai in fire ($19^{2b, 18}$), and commands the people to remain afar off, while the consecrated priests approach (vv.$^{11b, 12, 20-22, 24f}$). Aaron, Nadab, Abihu, and seventy elders ascend (24^{1f}) and celebrate a covenant feast (vv.$^{9-11}$). This is probably an older tradition of communion with God which has been incorporated here so as to include representatives of the people in the ratification of the covenant. Moses then goes up alone and stays forty days and forty nights during which he writes the words of the covenant, the ten commandments, on the tables of stone. This probably here refers to the so-called ritual decalogue found embedded in ch. 34. It is a traditional code appropriated by J but of unknown origin.

This code is the outcome of the earliest effort to embody the essential observances of the Yahweh religion. The feasts are agricultural festivals without the historical significance given them in Deuteronomy, and the observances are of a ceremonial character, for, according to J, it is the priests who are summoned to Sinai. Efforts have been frequently made (since Goethe suggested it) to prove that this is J's decalogue—a ceremonial decalogue. Any division into ten laws, however, has always an artificial character.

According to E, Yahweh descends in a cloud before the whole people (19^{3-11a}), whom Moses therefore sanctifies (vv.[14-17]). They hear Yahweh utter the Decalogue (v.[19] 20[1-17]), but, as they are afraid (20[18-21]), the further revelation with its covenant is delivered to Moses alone (20[22]–23[33] in part). The people, however, assent to its terms (24[3-8]). Moses ascends the Mount with Joshua to receive the stone tables, on which Yahweh has inscribed the Decalogue (24[12-15a]), and remains forty days (v.[18b]) to receive further commands. He returns with the tables (31[18b]), to discover and deal with the outbreak of idolatry (32[1-6, 16-24]). On his intercession he receives a promise of angelic guidance (vv.[30-35]). The account in Dt 10[1ff] of the events which followed Moses' intercession has given rise to the conjecture that Ex 33 originally had some reference to the making of the Ark and the Tent of Meeting and that the stripping off of ornaments (33[4, 6]) was for the purpose of adorning them.

E's account thus contains three of the four collections of laws found in Exodus, for 21–23 consists of two codes, a civil (21[1]–22[17]) and a ceremonial (22[18]–23[33] [roughly]). Probably the ceremonial section was originally E's counterpart to ch. 34 in J, while the civil section may have stood in connexion with ch. 18. As it now stands, E is the prophetic version of the law-giving. The basis of the Yahweh religion is the Decalogue with its clearly marked moral and spiritual character. (Cf article DEUTERONOMY.) This is delivered not to the priests (like ch. 34 in J), but to the whole people. When, however, the people shrink back, Moses, the prophetic intermediary, receives the further law from Yahweh. Yet the ceremonial and civil codes have a secondary place, and are parallel. The Decalogue, a common possession of the whole nation, with its appeal to the people's moral and religious sense, is fundamental. On it all the national institutions, whether civil or ceremonial, are based. Civil and ceremonial law have equal authority and equal value. As yet, however, the principles which inform the Decalogue are not brought into conscious connexion with the codes which control and guide the national life. The Book of Deuteronomy proves how at a later date the effort was made to penetrate the entire legislation with the spirit of the Decalogue, and to make this a means by which the national life was guided by the national faith. A. C. W.—L. H. B.

EXORCISM.—The word may be defined as denoting the action of expelling an evil spirit by the performance of certain rites, including almost always the invocation of a reputedly holy name. An anticipation of the later methods occurs in David's attempt to expel Saul's melancholia by means of music (1 S 16[16, 23]); and in the perception of the benefit of music may possibly be found the origin of the incantations that became a marked feature of the process. A more complicated method is prescribed by the angel Raphael (To 6[16f] 8[2]). In NT times the art had developed; professional exorcists had become numerous (Ac 19[13, 19]), whilst other persons were adepts, and practised as occasion needed (Mt 12[27], Lk 11[19]). An old division of the Babylonian religious literature (cf *Cuneif. Texts from Tablets in Brit. Mus.*, pts. xvi, xvii) contains many specimens of incantations; and the connexion of the Jews with that country, especially during the Exile, is an obvious explanation of the great extension both of the conception of the influence of demons and of the means adopted for their treatment. Exorcism was a recognized occupation and need in the Jewish life of the 1st cent., as it became afterwards in certain sections of the Christian Church.

In the procedure and formulae of exorcism, differences are traceable in the practice of the Jews, of Christ, and of His disciples. An illustration of the Jewish method may be found in Josephus (*Ant.* VIII. ii. 5 [45]), who claims Solomon for its author, and describes a case that he had himself witnessed. Other instances occur in the papyri (*e.g.* Dieterich, *Abraxas*, 138 ff), and in the Talmud (*e.g. Berakhoth*, 51*a*; *Pesachim*, 112*b*). The vital part of the procedure was the invocation of a name (or a series of names) of a deity or an angel, at the mention of which the evil spirit was supposed to recognize the presence of a superior power and to decline a combat, as though a spell had been put upon him. Christ, on the other hand, uses no spell, but in virtue of His own authority bids the evil spirits retire, and they render His slightest word unquestioning obedience. Sometimes He describes Himself as acting 'by the finger of God' (Lk 11[20]) or 'by the Spirit of God' (Mt 12[28]), and sometimes His will is indicated even without speech (Lk 13[13, 16]); but the general method is a stern or peremptory command (Mt 8[16], Mk 1[25] 9[25], Lk 8[29]). He does not require any previous preparation on the part of the sufferer, though occasionally (Mt 9[23f]) He uses the incident to excite faith on the part of the relatives. His own personality, His mere presence on the scene, are enough to alarm the evil spirits and to put an end to their mischief. In the case of His disciples, the power to exorcise was given both before and after the resurrection (Mt 10[1, 8], Mk 3[15] 16[17], Lk 9[1]), and was successfully exercised by them (Mk 6[13,] Lk 10[17], Ac 5[16] 8[7] 19[12]); but the authority was derived, and on that ground, if not by explicit command (cf 'In my name,' Mk 16[17]), the invocation of the name of Jesus was probably substituted for His direct command. That was clearly the course adopted by St. Paul (Ac 16[18] 19[13-16]), as by St. Peter and the Apostles generally in other miracles (Ac 3[6] 4[10], Ja 5[14]). The name of Jesus was not recited as a spell, but appealed to as the source of all spiritual power, as not only the badge of discipleship but the name of the ever-present Lord of spirits and Saviour of men (Mt 28[19f], Jn 14[13]). R. W. M.

EXPECT.—'From henceforth expecting' (He 10[13]) becomes 'then to wait' in RSV. In the Douai Version the comment on Sir 11[8] is: 'Expect the end of another man's speech before you begin to answer. Expect also if anie that is elder, or better able, will answer first.'

EXPERIENCE.—This word, which plays so large a part in modern philosophy and religion, occurs four times (including 'experiment') in AV. Of these instances only one survived in RV, viz., Ec 1[16], where 'hath had great experience of' = 'hath seen much of (wisdom),' etc. In Gn 30[27] 'I have learnt by experience' (= 'experiment') becomes 'I have divined,' the Hebrew verb being the same as in Gn 44[5, 15], Dt 18[10]. RSV uses the word five times, twice in OT (Jg 3[1], Ec 1[16]), thrice in NT (2 Co 1[6], Gal 3[4], 1 P 5[9]). The verb 'experienced' occurs four times. In Ro 5[4] (RV 'probation') 'experience,' and in 2 Co 9[13] (RV 'proving') 'experiment,' was the AV rendering of a Greek word borrowed from the assaying of metal, which signified the *testing*, or *test*, of personal worth; the same noun appears in AV as 'trial' (RV 'proof') in 2 Co 2[9] 8[2], and 'proof' in 2 Co 13[3] and Ph 2[22]. 'Christian experience,' in modern phraseology, covers what is spoken of in Scripture as the knowledge of God, of Christ, etc., and as 'the seal' or 'witness (testimony) of the Holy Spirit,' of our conscience,' etc., or as peace, assurance, salvation, and the like. Cf next article. G. G. F.—F. C. G.

EXPERIMENT.—In 2 Co 9[13] AV 'experiment' means *proof*: 'by the experiment of this ministration they glorify God.' Prefer RSV, 'under the test of this service.' It is proof arising out of experience, as in Hall, *Works*, iii. 467: 'We have known, indeed, some holy souls, which out of the general precepts of piety, and their own happy experiments of God's mercy, have, through the grace of God, grown to a great measure of perfection this way; which yet might have been much expedited and compleated, by those helps which the greater illumination and experience of others might have afforded them.' Cf preceding article.

EXPIATION.—1. Plan and Terminology.—The word 'expiation' appears in the RSV in certain important NT passages (Ro 3[25], 1 Jn 2[2] 4[10]) where AV had 'propitiation.' 'Expiation' seems better here, since it implies an action directed towards the removal of sin, while 'propitiation' suggests primarily the appeasement of an offended God (see PROPITIATION). The Greek words here translated have their background however in

EXPIATION

a Hebrew expression which is sometimes translated by RSV 'expiate' (*e.g.* 1 S 3[14]) or 'make expiation' (Dt 32[43]) but more commonly 'make atonement' as in AV (Lv 1[4] and frequently). Since the terms 'expiation' and 'atonement' go back to the same Hebrew terms and are not readily distinguishable, it seems best to deal with them together here. The scope of this article therefore will be the technical vocabulary for the removal of sin, including 'expiation' and 'atonement' as used in the RSV, along with other relevant terms. This material is not repeated in the article ATONEMENT, which deals with the more general and theological understanding of the problem.

2. The Expiatory Offerings.—Within the Levitical sacrificial system we find two offerings which have a special relation to the removal of sin and may be called 'expiatory' in a peculiar sense. These are the *ḥaṭṭā'th*, or 'sin offering,' and the *'āshām*, or guilt offering (AV 'trespass offering'). The basic codes for these offerings may be found in Lv 4[1]–6[7] 6[24]–7[7], and the two have a number of points of ritual in common in which they differ from other offerings (for details, see SACRIFICE AND OFFERING).

We further have to determine what was the extent of the sins expiated by these offerings. For the sin offering it is explicitly stated that it applies to sins committed 'in error' (RSV 'unwittingly') (Lv 4[2]) and that he who sins 'with a high hand' is cut off from the community (Nu 15[30]), and his iniquity is upon him, *i.e.* it is unexpiated and remains a burden upon him. It is clear that the sins expiated by the sin offering would in most cases be ritual and ceremonial offences rather than what we would call moral faults. It should be remembered, on the other hand, that the distinction of moral and ritual offences is foreign to the Levitical legislation; to regard the latter as insignificant compared to the former is to use a modern standard. It is also important that 'error' in this context hardly means simply 'accident,' a concept hardly known to the ancient Hebrews, but may go as far as the blind superhuman drive or 'infatuation'; for the same word is used for the infatuation of the lover, the uncontrolled words and deeds of the drunkard, of Saul's fanatical pursuit of David (1 S 26[21]). (Cf the interesting remarks of Quell, *ThWB* i, 274–5.)

Along with the sin offering we may usefully mention the use of the verb 'to sin' in its intensive form with a privative sense which we can perhaps render as 'to unsin' hence 'cleanse, purify.' It is used for one who has been defiled by contact with a corpse, Nu 19[19], and for the purifying of the altar with the blood of a sin offering, Lv 8[15]. The related noun, the same as used of a sin offering, is found for an expiatory or purificatory object or ritual which is not however an altar sacrifice like the sin offering. Such is the cleansing after contact with a corpse, Nu 19[19], or the ritual of the red cow by which is produced a water 'for the removal of sin,' Nu 19[1-10].

The guilt offering or *'āshām*, on the other hand, is prescribed in the Levitical system for cases involving restitution, *e.g.* when a man finds something lost and keeps it, refuses to return a deposit, or swears falsely in property questions (Lv 6[1-7] EV). In these cases restitution is made (with an addition of one fifth as compensation), and the restitution is accompanied by the guilt offering to Yahweh. We note also from a much earlier time the guilt offering of the Philistines when they make restitution of the Ark to Israel, in this case a gift of restitution rather than a sacrifice (1 S 6[1-9]). The occasion of the sacrifice may then reasonably be held to be restoration or reintegration to normality of life after an offence. In this case the offences are mostly what we would call moral offences, but the distinguishing of the moral nature of the offence is no more the point here than in the sin offering. The interpretation of the sacrifice as one of reintegration fits with such passages as Ezr 10[19] (for priests after putting away foreign wives), Nu 6[12] (for the Nazirite as he resumes his period of consecration after its interruption by contact with the dead), Lv 14 (restoration of the leper). In Lv 19[20-22] the offering is explicitly connected with cleansing or forgiveness of 'the sin which he has committed' (intercourse with a slave woman); such a formula is recurrent in Lv 4–5. In Lv 5[17-19] the guilt offering is related like the sin offering to unconscious sins.

We may conclude then that, with due reservation concerning the conception of 'sin' involved, which differs so much from our modern conception, the sacrificial system in its developed form contained a category of specially expiatory offerings, the sin and guilt offerings. On certain solemn occasions we have a combination of the expiatory with other categories of sacrifice, and then the expiatory type normally appears first, *e.g.* the order expiatory offering—burnt offering—peace offering in Lv 9.

3. The phrase 'to make expiation.'—The word intended here is the Hebrew *kippēr*, commonly translated 'to make expiation' or 'to make atonement' (see above, **1**). For a case where it is used of appeasement of one man by another, see PROPITIATION.

The derivation of this word has been much in dispute, and its original sense has been given as either 'cover' or 'wipe.' The sense 'wipe' is adopted here as the more probable, especially since it may well have meant both 'wipe on' and 'wipe off,' and the first of these could perhaps satisfy the cases where 'cover' is suggested. In any case it is doubtful if the original etymology can do much to determine the exact sense in Israelite usage, where in the overwhelming majority of cases it is a technical sacrificial term meaning 'to expiate.' It is followed by a preposition indicating the person or object or sin for which expiation is made, or by the direct object, or without any complement. The fact that the object of this verb, or the content of the prepositional phrase following it, is never God, seems decisive against the interpretation of it as propitiation or appeasement of God rather than expiation, although it is likely that the sense of appeasement has been more important in the earlier history of the word. In one early case, 2 S 21[3-4], expiation by money payment seems to be thought of, and in Ex 32[30] it is not clear by what means Moses hoped he might 'perhaps make expiation'—in these two passages the technical sacrificial sense is not yet quite dominant.

We have already mentioned the connexion of the expiatory sacrifices with forgiveness, and it is in fact in the codes for this group that a phrase with *kippēr* ('and he shall make expiation' or the like) is linked with forgiveness (Lv 4[20] etc.). This conjunction of expiation and forgiveness is not found in the codes for sacrifices of other types.

The great importance of the phrase 'to make expiation,' however, is that in the present form of the Levitical system it has been extended far beyond the specifically expiatory offerings to a large number of other rituals and actions. Typical examples are: 1. Burnt offerings, Lv 1[4], with the phrase 'it shall be accepted for him to make expiation for him.' 2. The ritual for cleansing a 'leprous' house with two birds, Lv 14[53]. 3. Such events in narrative as the incense offered by Aaron in the plague (Nu 16[46]), the execution of evildoers by Phinehas (Nu 25[13]), the presentation of the Midianite booty (Nu 31[50]). 4. Murder is expiated only by the blood of the murderer, Nu 35[33]. 5. The half-shekel tax or 'atonement money' of Ex 30[11-16] should perhaps be reckoned with 'ransom' rather than with expiation, and this might apply to the case of the Midianite booty as well. 6. All sacrificial blood is regarded as expiatory upon the altar, Lv 17[11]. This is of primary importance, and although He 9[22] accurately notes that almost all purification in the OT is by blood, and not absolutely all, it is equally right in seeing the central expiatory virtue in rituals which include the shedding of blood. This is not to say that all sacrificial killing is itself expiatory in purpose; but the life is in the blood, and the casting of the blood on the altar seems to be the returning of the life to its creator with expiatory effect. A distinguishing feature of the sin offering is the more elaborate blood ritual, including its application to the horns of the altar.

It will be noticed that in a number of the cases of 'expiate' in narrative contexts (Nu 16^{46} 25^{9-11}, Ex 30^{12}), mention is made of the impending anger of God or of the plague as its manifestation. It has seemed best, for reasons given at the beginning of this article, not to translate *kippēr* as 'propitiate,' since God never appears as object of this verb. But in a more general sense it is clear that there is an apotropaic sense in the cases mentioned, an awareness that the anger of God follows closely on the offence done and will not be turned away unless proper expiation is made. In such cases it may be that no absolute distinction can be made between expiation and propitiation as the general purpose of the action as a whole.

No full treatment will be given here of the great day of expiation on 10th Tishri (Lv 16; see ATONEMENT, DAY OF). Its importance was that it was the time of expiation and purification for the sanctuary and the priestly house, themselves the centres of expiation and purity for nation and individual. Even the most holy could not be left without expiation. A heavy emphasis is laid on the sin offerings and their complicated blood ritual, in this case including the taking of the blood not only to the altar but into the most holy place itself. The sending out of the so-called scapegoat is not, curiously enough, described as expiation or atonement, and indeed takes place after the high priest has finished the task of expiation for the sanctuary (Lv 16^{20}); but it is beyond doubt that it is a ritual for the removal of sin, and represents a culmination of the day's ceremonies, after which the burnt offerings can follow.

4. Other OT material.—Mention should here be made of the golden slab which was laid on top of the Ark in the Priestly accounts, and which was called *kappōreth*, from the same root as the word to expiate. The customary English translation is 'mercy-seat.' Its name may be taken from its place in the Day of Atonement ritual (Lv 16^{13f}), and it was at any rate so understood by the LXX, which translated it *hilastērion*, 'place of expiation,' from the verb *hilaskesthai*, with which it translated *kippēr*. Its importance includes its value for the interpretation of Ro 3^{25} where the word occurs again used of Jesus Christ.

Another word related to Hebrew *kippēr* is *kōpher*, 'price' with the sense of either 'ransom' or 'bribe.' This seems to have no close connexion in the OT with the terminology of expiation, although a certain degree of propinquity may be seen in the cases of the half-shekel and the Midianite booty mentioned above. No sacrificial act is called a 'ransom.' But in Job 33^{24} the ransom has the effect of averting Divine anger and catastrophe such as we have seen in some cases of expiation. In the NT the image of the 'ransom' reappears in description of the work of Christ (Mk 10^{45}).

The term *'āshām*, guilt offering, reappears in one quite isolated but very important passage, the Servant Song of Is 53 (in v.^{10}). The Servant makes himself, or may be made, a guilt offering (the text presents some difficulties). It is not easy to see precisely what is meant, especially since the term probably did not always carry the precise sense of the Levitical code. But the interpretation is helped by the mention of 'sin-bearing' in vv.^{11f}, and most probably it is meant that the suffering of the Servant is a vicarious expiation.

5. Christ as expiation.—In Ro 3^{25} Christ is described as the one whom God put forward or displayed as a *hilastērion* in His blood. The reference could be to the 'mercy-seat' or cover of the Ark, which is represented by this word in the LXX; or it could be in a more general way the 'place of propitiation,' which is the way LXX interprets the ledge of the altar, in Ezk $43^{14,17}$. But since Paul does not seem to be discussing the technicalities of sacrificial methods here, it is more likely that the word means generally 'of expiatory virtue, expiation.' Christ, then, is the expiation set forth by God, and as in most expiation the blood is of central importance.

In 1 Jn 2^2 4^{10} Christ is called the *hilasmos* for our sins. This is from the same root and again probably means 'expiation,' although it would be possible to relate it more precisely to one of the expiatory offerings (sin or guilt offering) for which it is sporadically used in the LXX. Again the general sense seems more probable, and all these three NT passages may then be regarded as reflecting the sense of Hebrew *kippēr*. It would be over-precision to say that the altar or place of expiation, or the sacrificial animal, or any particular expiatory ritual, is specially meant. The act of expiation, in which all these are involved, and the centre of expiation, are in Christ. The scope of the expiation is in the Johannine passages explicitly stated as 'our sins' and 1 Jn 2^2 adds 'not for our sins only, but also for the whole world.' The expiation is not a limited one for a certain area only. In none of these passages is it clear that the expiatory work is related to any single act or time in the mission of Jesus, except that the mention of blood in Ro 3^{25} will refer especially to the death of Christ; but if the tense of the verb in the Johannine passages may be pressed so far, it would seem that Christ 'is' and not only 'has been' an expiation for us. The continual availability of expiation through Christ seems to be indicated by the connexion of 1 Jn 2^{1-2}.

Some remarks may now be made about the 'guilt offering' of the Servant in Is 53. The LXX translated as 'for sin,' along with other changes in the structure of the sentence (the Isaiah LXX often misrepresented the text badly). 'For sin' is a common LXX rendering for the sin offering, and thus in Is 53 as in a number of places the distinction of sin and guilt offerings was not preserved precisely by LXX. The phraseology 'for sin' or 'for sins' in the sense of 'the sin offering' occurs in LXX quotations in the NT (*e.g.* He 10^6) and may have some effect on the more general phraseology of expiation or atonement 'for sin' (preposition *peri*), *e.g.* 1 P 3^{18}; but it seems excessively precise to translate these 'as a sin offering.'

The most thorough development of the theme of expiation in the NT is the letter to the Hebrews, where a comparison is made between the Levitical expiation which had to be repeated and the final and perfect expiation made by Christ. The centre of interest is the Day of Atonement and the entry of the High Priest into the most holy place. Christ is the High Priest, who is to make expiation for the sins of the people, He 2^{17}. The task of priesthood is understood as essentially expiatory, 5^1, and the existence in ancient Israel of sacrifices which were not predominantly expiatory in purpose, if at all, is overlooked or left aside for the present purpose. Blood is the centre of expiation, and occupies more attention than the killing of the victim. This is because the centre of attention is the entry of the High Priest to the holiest place with blood. Christ the priest goes in not with the blood of animals but with His own blood. The emphasis on the finality of the expiation by Christ carries with it a certain depreciation of the OT sacrifices on the grounds that their repeatedness indicates their impotence and that animal blood cannot make real expiation. The OT system does not lead to a finality where the consciousness of sins would remain no more, but rather brings sin to mind, 10^{2-3}. The OT expiation, like the OT worship as a whole, is a shadow of what is to come, 10^1. In 13^{11-14}, in a rather different connexion, mention is made of the victims of that class of sin offerings from which the blood was taken into the holiest place. These victims were not burned on the altar (except for certain parts) but were taken outside of the camp (Lv 4); so Christ suffered outside the city, and His followers must be ready to go outside with Him.

In 2 Co 5^{21}, 'he made him to be sin who knew no sin,' it is also possible to interpret as 'He made Him a sin offering on our behalf,' on the basis of passages like Lv 4^{24} LXX, where *hamartia* 'sin' is in fact the sin offering. This however is not certain. But in any case it is hardly in doubt that the content of the verse intends the expiation of sin.

This may suffice as a study of the terminology of expiation proper in the NT. Expiation is a real and essential element in the NT's understanding of the work of Christ, and is based on the OT sacrificial expiatory system. As so often in the NT, however, the lines of connexion with one section of the OT background are linked and crossed by lines from other aspects of that background, so that the full place which expiation takes in the work of Christ can be seen only when the field of study is made wider. For a study of these more general contexts of the removal of sin in the NT, see the article ATONEMENT. J. Ba.

EYE.—The eye was supposed to be the organ or window by which light had access to the whole body (Mt 6^{22}). For beauty of eyes cf 1 S 16^{12} (RSV), Ca 1^{15} 5^{12}, and the name Dorcas (=' gazelle,' so called because of its large bright eyes) in Ac 9^{36}; in Gn 29^{17} the reference seems to be to Leah's *weak* eyes (so RSV). The wanton or alluring eyes of women are referred to in Pr 6^{25}, Is 3^{16}. Their beauty was intensified by painting, **antimony** being used for darkening the eyelashes (2 K 9^{30}, Jer 4^{30}, Ezk 23^{40}). *Keren-happuch* (Job 42^{14}) means ' horn of eyepaint.' Pr 23^{29} speaks of the drunkard's redness of eye. In Dt 6^{8} 14^{1} ' between the eyes ' means ' on the forehead ' (so RSV in latter passage). Shaving the eyebrows was part of the purification of the leper (Lv 14^{9}).

' Eye ' is used in many *figurative phrases*: as the avenue of temptation (Gn 3^{6}, Job 31^{1}); of spiritual knowledge and blindness; as indicating feelings—pride (2 K 19^{22}), favour [especially God's providence (Ps 33^{18})], hostility (Ps 10^{8}). An *evil eye* implies envy (Mk 7^{22}, RSV ' envy '; cf 1 S 18^{9}, the only use of the verb in this sense in English) or niggardliness (Dt 15^{9}, Pr 28^{22} [literally ' he that hath an evil eye,' RSV ' a miserly man '], and probably Mt 6^{22}, where the ' sound ' eye may mean ' liberality '; cf Pr 22^{9}). In Rev 3^{18} **eye-salve** or collyrium is a Phrygian powder mentioned by Galen, for which the medical school at Laodicea seems to have been famous. (See Ramsay, *Seven Churches*, p. 419). The reference is to the restoring of spiritual vision.

C. W. E.

EZAR, 1 Ch 1^{38} (AV).—See EZER, 1.

EZBAI.—The father of Naarai, one of David's mighty men, 1 Ch 11^{37}.

EZBON.—**1.** Eponym of a Gadite family, Gn 46^{16}; called **Ozni** in Nu 26^{16}. **2.** A grandson of Benjamin, 1 Ch 7^{7}.

EZECHIAS, 1 Es 9^{14} (AV).—See JAHZEIAH.

EZECIAS, 1 Es 9^{43} (AV).—See HEZEKIAH, **4.**

EZEKIAS.—**1.** 1 Es 9^{14} (RV); see JAHZEIAH. **2.** 1 Es 9^{43} (RV); see HEZEKIAH, **4.**

EZEKIEL (=' El strengthens ').—I. THE MAN. Ezekiel, son of Buzi, was both priest (1^{3}) and prophet. He was a contemporary of Jeremiah and suffered exile in Babylon. The date of his birth is not known, but we have dated prophecies which show a prophetic activity extending over a period of twenty-two years, from the fifth year of the exile of king Jehoiachin until the twenty-seventh year, *i.e.* from 593 to 571 B.C. His priestly interests show clearly in chs. 40–48 where the reconstituted Temple, city and state are described. His prophetic activity is patent throughout the book and was clearly the stronger force in his life. The vision of a book roll, written on front and back with lamentations and mourning and woes (2^{8}–3^{3}), which he was told to eat, may be regarded as an inaugural vision for his prophetic ministry, especially that part of it which preceded the fall of Jerusalem, a ministry in which he felt called upon to denounce the sins of the people and impress upon them their personal and individual responsibility. The chariot vision (ch. 1) on the other hand, may also be regarded as an inaugural vision, but its main purpose was to show the prophet that whatever may have happened to His Temple and city in Palestine, Yahweh was still with His people even though they were exiled in Babylon. It may be felt that Ezekiel needed to have his call to prophecy confirmed in this way when it became clear that God was left without an abiding home in Jerusalem. Ezekiel's prophetic work before the fall of Jerusalem in 586 B.C. was mainly, if not entirely, directed towards the people in Judaea. His task was to convince them of their sin and to preach of the calamity that would befall them. After 586 B.C. he turned to the more distant future and felt himself called to be a watchman (3^{17ff}, 33^{7-9}) heralding the new age that would dawn for the next generation. Very little indeed is known of his personal life. We may imagine him to have been a well-known figure, partly on account of the acted prophecies which are one of the striking features of his ministry, and partly on account of a liability to suffer sudden seizures or fits which would temporarily deprive him of speech. Nine of his symbolic actions are recorded, $4^{1-3,\,7}$ 4^{4-8} $4^{10f,\,16f}$ $4^{9,\,12-15}$ 5^{1-17} $12^{1-16,\,17-20}$ 24^{15-24} 37^{15-17}; the last but one of these (24^{15-24}) shows him refraining from mourning the death of his wife as a symbol of the way the people will behave when Jerusalem and the Temple are reduced to ruins. This, though incidental, is the only reference to his wife. Another of the symbols, 4^{4-8}, may have been a utilization of his proneness to cataleptic fits, for he lay on his left side for 190 days (so LXX, Hebrew 390) and on his right side for forty days, symbolizing the exile of northern Israel and of Judah, a day for a year. The loss of speech from which he suffered (3^{25-27} 24^{25-27}) may also have been a symptom of his pathological condition which he was able to bring into service in his prophetic work. These things would in themselves compel an audience, if only out of curiosity, but he seems to have been gifted with a manner of speech that was in itself a pleasure to listen to (33^{32}: ' like one who sings love songs with a beautiful voice and plays well on an instrument '). During the exile he was a recognized leader in the community in Babylon and regularly held meetings of the elders in his own home (8^{1} 14^{1} 20^{1}).

II. THE BOOK.—**1. Contents and message.**—The book falls roughly into two parts separated by a collection of foreign oracles. The division coincides with the siege and fall of Jerusalem (ch. 24). Chs. 1–24 in the main contain denunciations of sin and predictions of judgment. Then follow eight chapters of oracles concerning foreign peoples, and then the second part (chs. 33–48) are occupied with hopes for the future. In the first part, after the introduction (1^{1}–3^{21}) there follows a series of prophecies in act and word (3^{22}–7^{27}), a strong denunciation of idolatrous practices in Jerusalem (8–11) and the remaining chapters (12–24) contain denunciations of sin, warnings of the consequences, and an appeal to each member of the community to accept his responsibility. The chapters against foreign peoples begin with a threat of punishment on the Ammonites, Moabites, Edomites, and Philistines for their malice towards Israel (25) then there are two chapters about Tyre, one of which (27) includes the poem depicting Tyre as a stately ship, a further chapter on the princes of Tyre and finally four chapters concerning Egypt (29–32). The second part (33–48) begins with the announcement of the fall of the city and the call to Ezekiel to become a watchman (the appointment as watchman was anticipated in 3^{17ff}, perhaps placed there by an editor). Then the shepherds who have misled the people are denounced and the people promised comfort, and a new shepherd of Davidic descent will be given them (34). Ch. 35 is a prophecy against Seir and in the next chapter the mountains of Israel are addressed with a promise of restoration. Ch. 37 predicts the resurrection of the nation, under the figure of a valley full of dry bones, and goes on to promise the re-union of Israel and Judah and the return of a Davidic prince. Chs. 38 and 39 telling of the invasion and defeat of Gog from the land of Magog foretell the final catastrophe and overthrow of the enemies of Israel. (The chapters break the sequence of the theme of restoration and may have been inserted here by a later editor. It is generally thought that they were written later; their apocalyptic nature suggests a later date.) Finally in chs. 40–48 there is a detailed plan for the new state, city, and Temple, with the priesthood as the most important body within it.

Ezekiel's verdict on the national history is of unmixed severity. From their starting-point in Egypt the people had behaved ill (cf 20^{5-13} with Jer 2^{2}). Jerusalem—to him almost synonymous with the nation—was pagan in origin and character (16). The root of their wickedness was an inveterate love of idolatry (5^{11} 7^{20} etc.). Even Ezekiel's own contemporaries longed to be heathens: their God could hold them back only by extreme violence (20^{32-38}). The exiles were somewhat less guilty than their brethren in Jerusalem (14^{22f}). But, on the whole, princes, priests, and people were an abandoned race. They loved the worship of the high places, which, according to Ezekiel, had always been idolatrous and illegitimate. They ate flesh with the blood in it, disregarded the Sabbath, polluted the Temple with ceremonial and moral defilements, committed adultery and other sexual abominations, were guilty of murder, oppression, the exaction of usury, harshness to debtors. The list can be paralleled from other prophetic writings, but the stress is here laid on offences against God. And this is in accordance with the strong light in which Ezekiel always sees God's claims. The vision with which the book opens points to God's transcendent majesty. The title 'son of man' by which the prophet is addressed nearly 100 times, marks the gulf between the creature and his maker. The most regrettable result of Israel's calamities is that they seem to suggest impotence on Yahweh's part to protect His own. The motive which has induced Him to spare them hitherto, and will, hereafter, ensure their restoration, is the desire to vindicate His own honour. In the ideal future the prince's palace shall be built at a proper distance from Yahweh's, and not even the prince shall ever pass through the gate which has been hallowed by the returning glory of the Lord. Hence it is natural that the reformation and restoration of Israel are God's work. He will sprinkle clean water on them, give them a new heart, produce in them humility and self-loathing. He will destroy their foes and bless their land with supernatural fertility. Yet the people have their part to play. Ezekiel protests against the traditional notion that the present generation were suffering for their ancestors' faults: to acquiesce in that is to deaden the sense of responsibility and destroy the springs of action. Here he joins hands with Jeremiah (Jer 31^{29f}), both alike coming to close quarters with the individual conscience. He pushes almost too far the truth that a change of conduct brings a change of fortune (33^{14-16}). But there is immense practical value in his insistence on appropriate action, his appeal to the individual, and the tenderness of the appeal ($18^{23, 31}$ 33^{11}). Nowhere is Yahweh's longing for the deliverance of His people more pathetically expressed. And, notwithstanding their continual wrongdoing, the bond of union is so close that He resents as a personal wrong the spitefulness of their neighbours (25–32, 35). The heathen, as such, have no future, although individual settlers will share common privileges (47^{22f}).

The concluding chapters, 40–48, are a carefully elaborated sketch of the polity of repatriated Israel—Israel, *i.e.* not as a nation, but as an ecclesiastical organization. In the foreground is the Temple and its services. Its position, surroundings, size, arrangements, are minutely detailed; even the place and number of the tables on which the victims must be slain are settled. The ordinances respecting the priesthood are precise; none but the Zadokites may officiate; priests who had ministered outside Jerusalem are reduced to the menial duties of the sanctuary (cf Dt 18^{6-8}). Adequate provision is made for the maintenance of the legitimate priests. Rules are laid down to ensure their ceremonial purity. The office of high priest is not recognized. And there is no real king. In ch. 37 the ruler, of David's line, seems to count for something; not so here. True, he is warned against oppressing his subjects (45^{9} 46^{16-18}), but he has no political role. A domain is set apart to provide him a revenue, and his chief function is to supply the sacrifices for the festivals. The country is divided into equal portions, one for each tribe, all of whom are brought back to Palestine. No land is to be permanently alienated from the family to which it was assigned. God's glory returns to the remodelled and rebuilt sanctuary, and Ezekiel's prophecy reaches its climax in the concluding words, 'The name of the city from that day shall be, Yahweh is there.' This picture of the ideal state had a profound effect on subsequent thought and practice. Some details, such as the equal division of the land, the arrangements respecting the position and revenue of the prince, the relation of the tribes to the city, were impracticable. But the limitation of the priesthood to a particular class, the introduction of a much more scrupulous avoidance of ceremonial defilement, the eradication of pagan elements of worship, the exclusion of all rival objects of worship, went a long way towards creating Judaism. And whilst this has been the practical result, the chapters in question, together with Ezekiel's vision of the chariot and the cherubim, have had no little influence in the symbolism and imaginative presentation of Jewish apocalyptic literature and Christian views of the unseen world.

2. Literary criticism of the book.—The plan of the book is so simple and straightforward that until the present century scholars were prepared to accept it as a product of Ezekiel's own hand, both in its contents and its arrangement, assigning only isolated fragments (apart from chs. 38 and 39) to subsequent editors. This view of the book is still accepted by some scholars. But there are some problems which have made other scholars hesitant to accept the traditional view. Despite the apparent care with which the book was compiled and equipped with a clear scheme of dating (1^{1f} 8^{1} 20^{1} 24^{1} 26^{1} $29^{1, 17}$ 30^{20} 31^{1} $32^{1, 17}$ 33^{21} 40^{1}) nearly all in chronological order, there are several difficulties that have emerged during more recent study of the book. Two things stand out clearly, first, there are many duplications and repetitions (cf 3^{16-21} and 33^{7-9}, 7^{2-4}, and 7^{5-9}, 43^{1-12} and 44^{1-8} etc.) which seem to be due to a later editor rather than to the prophet himself as editor; second, although the opening verses of the book imply that the prophet was in Babylon for the whole of his prophetic life, the prophecies in the first part of the book are addressed to the rebellious house of Israel and show first hand knowledge of the prevailing situation in Jerusalem and Judaea. The symbolic acts were necessarily performed before an audience; some of them indeed would lose their point if not performed in the presence of the very people concerned, notably the symbol of removal into exile. If one forgets the method of visionary transport (8^{3} $11^{1, 24}$) one forms the impression on reading the book that the prophet is actually in Jerusalem seeing the things he describes and denounces, and that as the time of the siege draws near he moves out of the city to a neighbouring town (12^{3}) whither they bring him news of the city's fall (24^{26} 33^{21}). Thereafter the prophetic work recorded in the book was undoubtedly carried out in Babylon. The first of these problems, the duplications and repetitions, is readily explained as due to the editorial work that was done on the book, whether by the prophet himself with only a few later additions, or by subsequent editors. How much of the material is to be ascribed to the editor or editors depends on the point of view from which the book is treated. One scholar (Hölscher) limited the work of the prophet himself to the poetical parts of the book; this is an extreme view but it does at least recognize that Ezekiel, like other prophets, expressed his message often in poetic language. Other scholars, whilst accepting the fact that Ezekiel may have been his own first editor and may himself have put in the dated sections which, with the exception of 26^{1} and 29^{17}, are in chronological sequence, think that there has been further editing;

varying amounts of secondary material are then laid to the editors' responsibility. As regards the prophet's place of residence, the book in its present form places him in Babylon from 597 B.C. onwards and enables him to have contact with Palestine through clairvoyance and through spiritual transport. Another possibility, however, and one that has commended itself to several scholars since it was first published (Bertholet, 1936) is to regard those passages that place him in Babylon before 586 B.C. as editorial. This means that the prophet had, in effect, two periods of ministry, the first from 593 to 586 B.C. when he lived and prophesied in Jerusalem and Judaea and the second in Babylon from 586 B.C. to the end of his active life (the last date given is 571 B.C.). On this view the Judaean ministry may be thought to have been inaugurated by the vision of a roll of a book (2^{8}–3^{5}) and the Babylonian by the chariot vision in ch. 1. That vision gains much in meaning if it is thought to take place *after* the fall of the Temple when Yahweh would no longer have a home in the sanctuary in Jerusalem; in a vision rich in symbolism He showed the prophet that, although His people were removed to Babylon in exile, He was still with them in all His power and majesty. (For a survey of other recent views on Ezekiel, see H. H. Rowley, *The Book of Ezekiel in Modern Study*, *BJRL* xxxvi (1953–1954), 146 ff.)

J. T.—**L. H. B.**

EZEL.—The spot where Jonathan arranged to meet David before the latter's final departure from the court of Saul, 1 S 20^{19} (AV, RV). The place is not mentioned elsewhere, and it is now generally admitted that the Hebrew text of this passage is corrupt. The true reading seems to have been preserved by the LXX, following which RSV reads in v.^{19} 'yonder stone heap,' and in v.^{41} 'from beside the stone heap.'

EZEM ('bone').—A town of Judah or Simeon, Jos 15^{29} 19^{3} (AV **Azem**), 1 Ch 4^{29}; possibly modern *Umm el-ʿAẓam*, SE. of Beersheba.

EZER.—**1.** A Horite 'duke,' Gn 36^{21}, 1 Ch 1^{38} (AV **Ezar**). **2.** An Ephraimite who, according to 1 Ch 7^{21} was slain by the men of Gath. **3.** A Judahite, 1 Ch 4^{4}. **4.** A Gadite chief who joined David, 1 Ch 12^{9}. **5.** A son of Jeshua who helped to repair the wall, Neh 3^{19} **6.** A priest who officiated at the dedication of the walls, Neh 12^{42}.

EZERIAS, 1 Es 8^{1} (AV).—See AZARIAH, **9.**

EZIAS, 1 Es 8^{2} (AV).—See UZZI, **1.**

EZION-GEBER, later called Elath, still later Berenice (Jos. *Ant.* VIII. vi. 4 [163]).—A port on the Red Sea (Gulf of ʿAqaba) used by Solomon for his commerce (1 K 9^{26}). A great copper refinery was uncovered here by Nelson Glueck (*The Other Side of the Jordan* [1940]), dating from the 10th–9th cents. B.C. It was rebuilt under the name of Elath by Uzziah, king of Judah, in the 8th cent. (2 K 14^{22}). According to tradition, the Israelites encamped here on the journey through the wilderness (Nu 33^{35}, Dt 2^{8}). It is the modern *Tell el-Kheleifeh*. A. J. M.—**D. N. F.**

EZNITE.—In 2 S 23^{8} AV and RV have 'Adino the Eznite.' The text is corrupt and in RSV it is restored from the parallel 1 Ch 11^{11}. Both 'Adino' and 'Eznite' thus disappear.

EZORA.—In 1 Es 9^{34} RV 'the sons of Ezora' (AV **Ozora**) appear to replace **Machnadebai** (q.v.) in the list of those who had married foreign wives; but RSV substitutes **Machnadebai** for RV **Mamnitanemus** (q.v.).

EZRA (perhaps an abbreviation of *Azariah*='Yahweh helps').—**1.** A Jewish exile in Babylon in the reign of Artaxerxes (which Artaxerxes is not stated), who is on record as having played a very notable part in the critical period of reform associated with the governorship of Nehemiah. Our sources of information regarding him are (1) the autobiographical narratives embodied in Ezr 7–10 and Neh 8–10; and (2) later tradition as embodied in the narrative of the compiler of Ezra-Nehemiah, and the accounts in the apocryphal books.

According to Ezr 7^{1-5}, Ezra was of priestly descent, and in fact a member of the high-priestly family (a 'Zadokite'). But his priestly descent has been called in question. His work and achievements rather suggest the character of the 'scribe' (*sōphēr*) *par excellence.* He is described as 'Ezra the priest, the scribe of the law of the God of heaven,' in Ezr 7^{11-21}; as 'Ezra the priest, the scribe,' in Neh 8^{9} 12^{26}; and as 'the priest' alone in Ezr $10^{10, 16}$, Neh 8^{2}.

In order to form a just estimate of Ezra's work and aims, we must picture him as a diligent student of the Law. He doubtless stood at the head—or, at any rate, was a leading figure—of a new order which had grown up in the Exile among the Jews of the 'Golah' or captivity in Babylonia. Among these exiles great literary activity apparently prevailed during the later years of the Exile and onwards. The so-called 'Priestly Code'—which must be regarded as the work of a whole school of writers—was formed, or at least the principal part of it, probably between the closing years of the Exile and the arrival of Ezra in Jerusalem, and was doubtless the 'law of God' which Ezra brought with him to Jerusalem. The centre of Jewish culture, wealth, and leisure was at this time—and for some time continued to be—Babylonia, where external circumstances had become (since the Persian supremacy) comparatively favourable for the Jews. In this respect the position of the Jerusalem community, during these years, afforded a painful contrast. The tiny community in Judah had to wage as a whole a long and sordid struggle against poverty and adverse surroundings. Its religious condition was much inferior to that of the 'Golah.' Moved by religious zeal, and also, it would seem, with the statesman-like view of making Jerusalem once more the real spiritual metropolis of Judaism, Ezra conceived the idea of infusing new life and new ideals into the Judaean community, by leading a fresh band of zealously religious exiles from Babylonia back to Judah on a mission of reform. With the aid, possibly, of Jews at court, he enlisted the good-will of Artaxerxes, and secured an Imperial firman investing him with all the authority necessary for his purpose. This edict is recorded in Ezr 7^{12-26}. All Jews who so wished could depart from Babylon; offerings were to be carried to the Temple in Jerusalem and the Law of God was to be enforced. While many scholars accept this edict as trustworthy, others criticize its obviously Jewish terminology, and refuse to believe that the Persian government of that day would ever have given such powers as are specified in the firman to one who was not a public official. In the seventh year of Artaxerxes Ezra collected a band of 1496 men (Ezr 8^{1-14}; in 1 Es 8^{28-41} the number is given as 1690), besides women and children, and started on his journey across the desert. In four months they reached their destination.

Here, after the sacred gifts had been offered in the Temple, Ezra soon learned of the lax state of affairs that prevailed in the holy city, and among the Judaean villages. The 'holy seed' (including even priests and Levites) had 'mingled themselves with the peoples of the lands,' and 'the hand of the princes and deputies' had 'been first in this trespass' (Ezr 9^{2}). Ezra's consequent prayer and confession, in the presence of a large assemblage of the people, lead to drastic measures of reform. A general congregation of the community authorizes the establishment of a divorce court, presided over by Ezra, which finishes its labours after three months' work, many innocent women and children being made to suffer in the process.

In the present form of the narrative Ezra is also said to have acted in association with Nehemiah, after the latter had arrived in Jerusalem and re-erected and dedicated the city walls. Thereafter it is stated that the Book of the Law was read by Ezra before the people in solemn assembly, and they pledged themselves to obey it. But Neh 8–10, within which this record is found, is undated; its authenticity has been seriously questioned and the view has been propounded that these chapters have as their purpose the greater honour of the Chronicler's hero Ezra (see NEHEMIAH, BOOK OF).

The sequence of events as described above is not without difficulties. How is the long interval between Ezra's arrival in Jerusalem (if 458 B.C.) and the promulgation of the Law (444 B.C.) to be explained? It may be, as Stade has suggested, that the compulsory divorce proceedings alienated a considerable body of the people, and that the opportune moment for introducing the code was in consequence postponed. But strong reasons have been advanced for placing Ezra's work in Jerusalem subsequent to Nehemiah's governorship. As has been mentioned above, the Artaxerxes named in the text is not precisely specified; if it was Artaxerxes I., Ezra's arrival in Jerusalem must have been in 458 B.C.; but, if it was Artaxerxes II., in 397 B.C. The following considerations have been adduced in support of the later date: Nehemiah in his day found the city of Jerusalem deserted (7[4]), while Ezra found the city wall (although the word used is not the common one for 'city wall') rebuilt and the city itself populous (Ezr 9[9] 10[1]); the measures adopted by Ezra against foreign wives (10[3-5, 10ff]) were much more stringent than those of Nehemiah (13[25]); Nehemiah was a contemporary of the high priest Eliashib (Neh 3[1, 20f] etc.), and Ezra of Eliashib's grandson Johanan (Ezr 10[6]), and there seems to be available supporting evidence for this argument from one of the Elephantine Papyri (cf A. Cowley, *Aramaic Papyri of the Fifth Century B.C.*, 108 ff; see further H. H. Rowley, *The Servant of the Lord and Other Essays on the Old Testament*, pp. 131–159).

By investing the Law with a sanctity and influence that it had never before possessed, and making it the possession of the entire community, Ezra endowed the Jewish people with a cohesive power which was proof against all attacks from without.

2. Eponym of a family which returned with Zerubbabel (Neh 12[1, 13, 33]).

3. 1 Ch 4[17] (AV); see EZRAH. G. H. B.—**J. Ma.**

EZRA, BOOK OF.—Our present Book of Ezra, which consists of ten chapters, is really part of a composite work, Ezra-Nehemiah, which, again, is the continuation of Chronicles. The entire work—Chronicles–Ezra–Nehemiah—is a compilation made by the Chronicler. See further, NEHEMIAH (BOOK OF), 1.

1. Analysis of the book.—The Book of Ezra falls into two main divisions: (*a*) chs. 1–6; (*b*) chs. 7–10.

(*a*) Chs. 1–6 give an account of the Return and the rebuilding of the Temple. Ch. 1 tells how Cyrus, after the capture of Babylon in 538 B.C., issued an edict permitting the exiles to return, and commanding his Babylonian subjects to contribute to the cost of the Temple—a most unlikely thing for the newly established king to do. It should be noted that 6[3-5] contains another form of the edict in Aramaic, giving instructions that the cost of rebuilding of the Temple is to be defrayed from the royal treasury. Since the issue of this decree was affirmed in the days of Darius (6[1ff]) it has sometimes been objected that the Jews would never have built so poor a Temple as Haggai mentions (Hag 2[3]) if such official help had been available to meet the cost of building; but the reluctance to build and the mediocrity of the finished structure may have been due to lack of religious faith and of moral strength rather than lack of funds. 40,000 of the exiles availed themselves of the opportunity to return to Judah under Joshua the high priest and Zerubbabel, a member of the royal Davidic family, who was appointed governor (*peḥāh*) by Cyrus 538–537 B.C. Ch. 2 contains a list of those who returned and of their offerings for the building of the Temple; it is a copy of Neh 7[6-73a], which is a register of the province of Judah in the 5th cent. Ch. 3 describes how in October 537 B.C. the altar of burnt-offering was re-erected on its ancient site, the foundation-stone of the Temple laid (May 536 B.C.), and the work of rebuilding begun. Ch. 4 tells that, owing to the unfriendly action of neighbouring populations, the building of the Temple was suspended during the rest of the reigns of Cyrus and Cambyses. It contains the correspondence between Rehum, Shimshai, and their companions, and king Artaxerxes. In 5[1-5] we are informed that, as a consequence of the earnest exhortations of the prophets Haggai and Zechariah, the building of the Temple was energetically resumed in the second year of Darius I. (520 B.C.). In chs. 4 and 5 there seems to be considerable confusion. 3[8] and 5[16] state that the foundation stone of the Temple was laid immediately after the return of the Jews from Babylon in terms of the edict of Cyrus; but 5[1f] says it took place in 520; possibly not unrelated to that apparent contradiction, 4[24] says that the work on the Temple was stopped until 520, but 5[5] seems to say that there was no such stoppage; 4[6-23] refers to the building of the city walls in the time of Artaxerxes, while 4[24], immediately following, makes mention of the interruption in the building until 520, and 5[3], by its use of the words 'to build this house and to finish this structure,' might refer to both Temple and walls. In 5[6]–6[12] we have the correspondence between the satrap Tattenai and Darius. We read in 6[13-22] of how the Temple was successfully completed on the 3rd March 515 B.C.

(*b*) Chs. 7–10 deal with Ezra's personal work (which is concluded in Neh 7[73b]–10[39]). In ch. 7 the silence of many years is broken, when Ezra, the *teacher of the Law*, at the head of a fresh band of exiles, leaves Babylonia bearing a commission from Artaxerxes to bring about a settlement in the religious condition of the Judaean community. Ch. 8 gives a list of the heads of families who journeyed with him, and tells of their arrival in Jerusalem. Ch. 9 describes the proceedings against the foreign wives, and contains Ezra's penitential prayer. In ch. 10 we read that an assembly of the whole people appointed a commission to deal with the mixed marriages. The narrative abruptly breaks off with an enumeration of *the men who had married strange women.*

2. Sources of the book.—In its present form the Book of Ezra-Nehemiah is, as has been pointed out, the work of the Chronicler. The compilation, however, embraces older material. The most important parts of this latter are undoubtedly the autobiographical sections, which have been taken partly from Ezra's, partly from Nehemiah's, personal memoirs.

(*a*) *Extracts from Ezra's memoirs embodied in the Book of Ezra.*—The long passage Ezr 7[27]–9[15] (except 8[35f]) is generally admitted to be an authentic extract from Ezra's memoirs. The abrupt break which takes place at 9[15] must be due to a compiler. [It is probable that an even larger excerpt from these memoirs is to be seen in Neh 9[6]–10[40].] But the association of Ezra and Nehemiah in 444 B.C., which is described in Neh 8–9, has been seriously questioned (see EZRA above).

It seems probable that these memoirs were not used by the Chronicler in their original form, but in a form adapted and arranged by a later hand, to which Ezr 10 is due. This latter narrative is of first-rate importance and rests upon extremely good information. It was probably written by the same hand that composed the main part of Neh 8–10 (see NEHEMIAH [BOOK OF], **2**).

(*b*) *Other sources of the book.*—The other most important source used by the Chronicler was an *Aramaic* one, written, perhaps, not long after 450 B.C., which contained a history of the building of the Temple, the city walls, etc., and cited original documents. From this authority come Ezr 4[8-22] 5[1]–6[16] 7[12-26].

The Chronicler, however, partly misunderstood his Aramaic source. He has misconceived 4[6], and assigned a false position to the document embodied in 4[7-23].

(*c*) *Passages written by the Chronicler.*—The following passages bear clear marks of being the actual composition of the Chronicler: Ezr 1, 3[2]–4[7] 4[24] 6[17]–7[11] 8[35f].

3. Separation of Ezra from Chronicles.—It would appear that after the great work of the Chronicler had been completed (1 and 2 Chronicles, Ezra-Nehemiah), the part which contained narratives of otherwise unrecorded events was first received into the Canon. Hence, in the Jewish Canon, Ezra-Nehemiah precedes the Book of Chronicles. In the process of separation certain verses are repeated (Ezr 1^{1-3a}=2 Ch 36^{22f}); v.^{23} seems to have been added in 2 Ch 36 to avoid a dismal ending (v.^{21}).

For the historical value of the book cf what is said under NEHEMIAH [BOOK OF], **3.** G. H. B.—**J. Ma.**

EZRAH.—A Judahite, 1 Ch 4^{17} (AV **Ezra**).

EZRAHITE.—A name given to Heman in the title of Ps 88, and to Ethan (q.v.) in Ps 89. It is used of Ethan also in 1 K 4^{31}.

EZRI.—David's superintendent of agriculture, 1 Ch 27^{26}.

EZRIL, 1 Es 9^{34} (RV).—See AZAREL, **4.**

F

FABLE.—Like parable, a didactic narrative, differing from the latter, however, in that its actors are not human but animals or plants that behave or talk like human beings. Both are distinct from allegory, which is concerned with the recorded events (actual or imaginative) not in themselves, but only as symbols of another level of meaning (cf Gal 4^{22-31}). Fables are mentioned in AV in 1 Ti 1^4 4^7, 2 Ti 4^4, Tit 1^4, 2 P 1^{16}; but RSV in each case correctly reads 'myths.' Reference is not at all to the true fable, but the writers have chosen a term expressive of contempt for some aspects of contemporary Jewish and Gentile thought that was making an appeal to certain Christians. Notwithstanding the large and famous bulk of parables in the Gospels, the NT contains little fable, and that little is not immediately apparent. Paul's postulated debate among the members of the human body (1 Co 12^{14-26}) echoes a fable known in an Egyptian source of approximately the 9th cent. B.C. and probably widely disseminated, with variations, through the orient. Since our text is a schoolboy's copy, it must have been already well known and was probably of considerable antiquity.

By contrast the word fable is absent from the OT—Biblical Hebrew has no specific equivalent, though *māshāl* (commonly rendered 'proverb,' but in Ezk 24^3 'allegory' in RSV) might cover the meaning, as perhaps it does in 1 K 4^{32}—but the reality is present in Jotham's speech to the men of Shechem (Jg 9^{7-15}) and Jehoash's retort to Amaziah (2 K 14^9). Further, the reference in 1 K 4^{33} is clearly an allusion to plant and animal fables which perhaps were a part of Solomon's 'three thousand proverbs' (v.^{32}) and expressive of his function as a 'wise man.' Yet this is not all; some of the illustrations employed by the prophets approach the status of fable, such as Isaiah's poem about a vineyard, which though not represented as speaking is almost endowed with a conscious will in antagonism to its owner (Is 5^{1-7}), and the poem about a lioness and her whelps in Ezk 19^{2-9}, and, less directly, that about a vine in vv.$^{10-14}$; farther away is the oracle about a great eagle in 17^{3-10}. The intimate relation of simile and metaphor, and of both in turn with fable is suggested by passages such as Job 8^{11-13} 12^{7-9}, Ps 1^{4-6}, Pr $30^{18f, 24-31}$, Ezk 15^{1-5}. They imply also the didactic purpose which was the objective of the fable—and of the teaching of the wise men.

Such pervasive consciousness, and use or near-use, of the fable is not at all surprising; approached from the direction of thought and literary expression in the wider Near East it is seen that Israel's familiarity with this teaching device is only one further aspect of the nation's normal place in its world and its dependence on the literature and thinking of its time. The similarities and differences of human and animal conduct had long attracted the interest of thoughtful persons; the fable was an obvious expression of this and at the same time a ready tool for the wise men's concern with the good life and modes of conduct conducing thereto.

We possess a considerable bulk of literary and artistic remains of this centuries-long activity. It is no novel idea that Aesop's fables are actually of oriental origin. In addition there exists the considerable collection known as Kalila wa-Dimna, or the Bidpai Fables. Much older than either and richly evidencing the widespread use of the fable in the ancient world are the numerous stories and literary vignettes in Egyptian, Sumerian, and Akkadian literatures. There exist also Egyptian graphic illustrations of satiric animal situations, such as a mouse in his chariot pursuing an army of cats, which may point to fables otherwise lost, and emphasize the currency of this form of teaching in the ancient world (see Ronald J. Williams, 'The Fable in the Ancient Near East' in *A Stubborn Faith* (1956), ed. Edward C. Hobbs). W. A. I.

FACE is used freely of animals, as well as of men; also of the surface of the wilderness (Ex 16^4), of the earth, of the waters or deep, of the sky. It is used of the front of a house (Ezk 41^{14}), of a porch (40^{15} 41^{25}), of a throne (Job 26^9). *Covering the face* in 2 S 19^4 is a sign of mourning (cf covering the head); it is also a mark of reverence (Ex 3^6, 1 K 19^{13}, Is 6^2). In Gn 24^{65} it indicates modesty. Otherwise it is used simply of blindfolding, literal (Mk 14^{65}), or metaphorical (Job 9^{24}). *To fall on the face* is the customary Eastern obeisance, whether to man or to God. *Spitting in the face* is the climax of contempt (Nu 12^{14}, Dt 25^9, Mt 26^{67}). The Oriental will say, 'I spit in your face,' while he actually spits on the ground. The face naturally expresses various emotions—fear, sorrow, shame, or joy. The 'fallen face' (Gn 4^5) is used of displeasure; 'hardening the face' of obstinate sin (Pr 21^{29}, Jer 5^3). The face was 'disfigured' in fasting (Mt 6^{16}). It may be the expression of favour, particularly of God to man (Nu 6^{25}, Ps 31^{16}), or conversely of man turning his face to God (Jer 2^{27} 32^{33}); or of disfavour, as in the phrase 'to set the face against' (Ps 34^{16}, Jer 21^{10}, and often in Ezekiel), or 'to hide the face.' [*N.B.* In Ps 51^9 the phrase is used differently, meaning to forget or ignore, cf Ps 90^8.] Closely related are the usages connected with 'beholding the face.' This meant to be admitted to the presence of a potentate, king, or god (Gn 33^{10} $43^{3,5}$, 2 K 25^{19}, Est 1^{14} $4^{11,16}$; cf 'angel(s) of the face or presence,' Is 63^9, To 12^{15}, Rev 8^2, and often in apocalyptic literature). So 'to look upon the face' is to accept (Ps 84^9), 'to turn away the face' is to reject (Ps 132^{10}, 1 K 2^{16} RVm). To 'behold the face' of God may be used either literally of appearing before His presence in the sanctuary or elsewhere (Gn 32^{30} [*Peniel* is 'the face of God'], Ex 33^{11}, Ps 42^2; the 'showbread' is 'the bread of the face or presence'), or with a more spiritual reference to the inward reality of communion which lies behind (Ps 17^{15}); so 'seeking the face' of God (Ps 24^6 27^8). There are instances, however, where *pānîm* (face) with a suffix is used as a periphrasis for the personal pronoun (1 S 17^{11}). Further, *pānîm* is also used (cf 'place,' 'heaven,' 'name') as a substitute for the Divine Name, in a specially personal way; *e.g.* 'the bread of the Presence' may mean 'Yahweh's personal bread,' placed on His very own table. On the other hand, in 2 K 14^8 'see face to face' is used in a sinister sense of meeting in battle.

The Hebrew word for 'face' is used very freely, both alone and in many prepositional phrases, as an idiomatic periphrasis, *e.g.* 'honour the face of the old man' (Lv 19^{32}), 'grind the face of the poor' (Is 3^{15}), or the common phrase 'before my face' (Dt 8[20], Mk 1[2]), or 'before the face of Israel' (Ex 14[25]). Many of these usages are disguised in our versions, not being in accordance with English idioms; the pronoun is substituted, or 'presence,' 'countenance' are used, 'face' being often indicated in AVm or RVm (Gn 1[20], 1 K 2[16]); so in the phrase 'respect persons' (Dt 1[17]). On the other hand, 'face' is wrongly given for 'eye' in AV of 1 K 20[38, 41], where 'ashes on face' should be 'head-band over eye'; in 2 K 9[30], Jer 4[30], the reference is to painting the eye; in Gn 24[47] RV substitutes 'nose,' in Ezk 38[18] 'nostrils.' On the use of 'face' as an expression of personality cf A. R. Johnson, *The Vitality of the Individual in the Thought of Ancient Israel*, 1949, pp. 42 ff. C. W. E.—**N. H. S.**

FAIR HAVENS.—A harbour on the south coast of Crete, near Lasea, where St. Paul's ship took shelter on the voyage to Rome (Ac 27[8]). It still retains its name.

FAITH.—**General.**—It is common in modern English usage to take faith in God to mean something more than belief in God, faith meaning a personal trust and commitment, belief only an intellectual or impersonal acceptance or credence, or a traditional dogmatic statement. In older English, however, 'belief' was used for trusting or confiding in a person or thing (so *OED*), and even in modern usage the verb 'believe' corresponds frequently to the noun 'faith,' although one may emphasize the personal relation by using 'trust.' In any case our task is not to define 'faith' abstractly or to demarcate it by definition from other terms such as 'belief,' but by investigating Biblical usage to give it its proper content as it stands within its Biblical context. The scope of this article is roughly the NT Greek word-group *pistis* 'faith,' *pisteuō* 'believe,' with related words, and the various Hebrew words which form the relevant OT background.

1. In OT.—In the NT the word-group 'faith' occupies a quite central and controlling position,as expressing the proper and characteristic relationship of man to God. We can hardly say that any one word takes so central a place in the OT. On the one hand a number of words exist which express that trust of God which is the inner life of the true worshipper. On the other hand this inner life is often expressed not only by terms for trust but by terms for fear. It might indeed be suggested that the terms for trust and those for fear might be taken together to give something in the OT which would roughly correspond to faith in the NT.

The central Hebrew term for 'believe' comes from the root *'āman*. The original sense of this is commonly taken to have been that of 'firmness,' but in usage the basic senses are of trust and constancy. One of its best-known forms is the familiar *Amen*, 'it is sure.' One form of the verb (the *hiph'il*) means 'put one's trust in' (*Hiph'il* for the entering into, and continuing in, a state, cf Gesenius-Kautzsch-Cowley, *Hebrew Grammar*, § 53e). The reflexive on the other hand means 'be reliable, constant, well-founded,' and appears as 'be established' in Is 7[9]. Thus God is reliable or trustworthy, Dt 7[9]; David will have a reliable or well-established or permanent house, 2 S 7[16]; a future priest will be reliable in the sense of personal trustworthiness, and his family will be constant or permanent in the priesthood, 1 S 2[35]. The same form may also mean a trust committed, *e.g.* to Moses, Nu 12[7], perhaps also to Samuel, 1 S 3[20]. The nouns from the same stem have a general sense between 'faithfulness' and 'truth,' *e.g.* Ps 19[9] 25[5, 10] 26[3]; the sense of 'honesty' appears in 2 K 22[7].

This then is the most important component of the OT background of the NT 'faith,' although as indicated above it is used on a rather narrower front. It is used mainly where the interest is not on an inward trust or feeling of safety but on a placing of confidence in the person, the words, the office of another. The usage is not necessarily religious: *e.g.* we have 'constant' or 'lasting' plagues and sicknesses in Dt 28[59]; or again, we hear that the Queen of Sheba 'did not believe' the stories of Solomon's court until she visited it.

The sense of inward trust and the feeling of security are expressed in the OT rather by the verb *bāṭaḥ*, 'be secure, feel secure, trust in.' In Jg 18[7] a city which has taken no defensive measures is described with this root as 'in security' and 'unsuspecting.' The noun means 'safety, security,' and is frequent with the verb 'dwell,' especially in the prophets, in whose time insecurity was so commonly the mark of Israel's life. The verb is frequent in the Psalms, *e.g.* 4[5] 9[10] 13[5]. It is realized, however, and especially by the prophets, that the sense of security may be falsely grounded, and many passages point out the futility of a sense of security based on human power, on military defence, on false gods (*e.g.* Jer 5[17] 7[4, 8, 14] 9[4] 17[5, 7], Is 42[17]).

Another relevant and fairly frequent word is *ḥāsāh*, 'seek or take refuge, shelter'; especially in the Psalms we hear of the worshipper as one whose refuge and shelter is God, *e.g.* 2[11] 5[11] 7[1] 46[1]. This word brings out strongly the position of dependence of the person, and is seldom used of false security. We must also mention the place of the various terms approximately meaning 'hope.' As in the NT, hope and trust are closely similar, and the aspect of hope appears where there is a reference to the future and a contrast with a present dark or unhappy situation; *e.g.* Ps 42[5, 11] 43[5], 2 K 6[33], Is 8[16–17] 40[27–31]. Finally, there is the important word *ḥesedh*. Although this hardly corresponds to 'faith' in its usual senses, and is part of the background rather for the NT word 'grace,' it frequently means 'loyalty' or 'faithfulness' and the actions expressive of these; and especially in a covenant relation between persons or families, particularly when the more powerful person shows loyalty by fulfilling the obligations involved; so David to the house of Saul, 1 S 20[15], 2 S 9[1] (RSV 'kindness'), and God to His servants, Ex 20[6] etc.

We may say then that one of the contributions which the OT makes to the Biblical notion of faith is the way in which its conception of trust is connected with the trustworthiness and reliability of what is trusted. Clearly the general thought is of trust rather than of faith as belief in true doctrine or the like. For what we would call belief of this kind they would use rather verbs like 'hearing and doing.'

We may now ask what was the importance of this trust in Yahweh within the wider structure of OT religion. We should not think here of 'faith' in an absolute sense as a 'source' of understanding of God and man's relation to him. The trust is rather the proper recognition of God as He is known in the tradition of Israel. Certain situations may be indicated which called forth this recognition. Clearly one was the attitude of worship, where the worshipper takes refuge in God, like one claiming hospitality-protection, or like one seeking asylum at the sanctuary. Inwardly he recognizes that his security lies in God. Another situation was that of warfare. In the sacral warfare of old Israel it was God who controlled and won the battles, and Israel had to trust in Him. Does trust then mean passivity? Not in old stories like Jg 5, where Israel had to 'come to the help of the Lord.' Even so victory is recognized in old traditions to depend not on heaping up the maximum human forces, but on following the Divine directions. Some late traditions increase the element of human passivity in order to enhance the effect of Divine power (*e.g.* 2 Ch 20[20–24]). When in the time of the prophets the attacks of foreign powers are understood as the instrument of God in chastising His people, there is a repeated challenge to faith with, in particular, a repudiation of military alliances as a means of defence (Is 30, especially v.[15] 31[1–5]). Another situation which called for trust was the giving of promises and visions of the future, and this occurs in the two important passages Gn 15[1–6], Hab 2[1–4].

Special mention must be given briefly to the special contribution made in this matter by Isaiah. The famous 7th chapter of that prophet begins with a challenge for trust in Divine protection; and it is when this way of trust is rejected that the sign of the coming birth is announced. Without trust there will be no stability for the house of David (7^{9}, using two different forms of the same verb, as described above). The stability or permanence here in question probably refers to the traditional promise of permanence to the Davidic house, 2 S 7^{16} etc. The question of trust during this difficult situation is a test of the destiny of the Messianic house.

In later Judaism, with the growing concentration upon the law, more attention is given to belief in the statutes and commands of God, an aspect which appears already *e.g.* in Ps 119^{66}. Sir 32^{24} places in parallel ' he that believes in the law ' and ' he that trusts in the Lord,' and 33^{3} speaks of the corresponding trustworthiness of the law. The faith of the Jews appears in their persecutions, *e.g.* 4 Mac 15^{24} 16^{22}, and non-Jews, becoming convinced of the greatness of the God of Israel, are said to ' come to believe in God,' *e.g.* Jth 14^{10}.

In the Qumrân texts the OT terms for trust and faith are rather less prominent than one might expect, considering the strong sense of dependence on God which we find in their thought. In particular the Qumrân hymns use these terms considerably less than the OT Psalms. There is, however, much mention of the truth, faithfulness, and steadfast love of God. But in general the typical term for the ideal members of the community is not so much ' those who believe or trust ' as ' those who hold fast to or stick to or walk in ' the true statutes of God. The Habakkuk commentary, however, says of the enemies of the sect that they did not ' believe the covenant of God ' and did not ' believe when they heard what was coming upon the last generation ' (ii. 4, 6) ; the important text Hab 2^{4} is interpreted of the pious whom God will deliver ' because of their toil and their faith in the teacher of righteousness ' (viii. 2–3) ; faith or belief in these cases seems most probably to be acceptance as truth of the teachings and interpretations mentioned.

J. Ba.

2. In NT.—The NT use of *pistis, pisteuō* is based on that of common Greek, where persuasion is the radical idea of the word. From this sprang two principal notions, meeting in the NT conception : (*a*) the ethical notion of confidence, trust in a person, his word, promise, etc., and then mutual trust, or the expression thereof in a pledge—a usage with only a casual religious application in non-Biblical Greek ; and (*b*) the intellectual notion of conviction, belief (in distinction from knowledge), covering all the shades of meaning from practical assurance down to conjecture, but always connoting sincerity, a belief held in good faith. The use of ' faith ' in Mt 23^{23} belongs to OT phraseology (cf Dt 32^{20}) ; also in Ro3^{3} and Gal 5^{22} *pistis* is understood to mean ' faithfulness,' as often in classical Greek. In sense (*b*) *pistis* came into the language of Greek theology, the gods being assigned (*e.g.* by Plutarch as a religious philosopher) to the province of faith, since they are beyond the reach of sense-perception and logical demonstration.

(1) In this way faith came to signify the religious faculty in the broadest sense—a generalization foreign to the OT. Philo Judaeus, the philosopher of Judaism, thus employs the term ; quoting Gn 15^{6}, he takes Abraham for the embodiment of faith so understood, viewing it as the crown of human character, ' the queen of the virtues ' ; for faith is, with Philo, a steady intuition of Divine things, transcending sense and logic. It is, in fact, the highest knowledge, the consummation of reason. This broad Hellenistic meaning is conspicuous in Hebrews (11^{1} 6^{27} etc.) and appears in St. Paul (2 Co 4^{18} and 5^{7} : ' We walk by faith, not by sight '). There is nothing distinctively Christian about faith understood in the bare significance of ' seeing the invisible '—since ' even the demons believe and shudder ' ; the belief that contains no more is the ' dead faith ' which condemns rather than justifies (Ja 2^{14-26}). Abraham, beyond the ' belief that God is,' recognized what God is and yielded Him a loyal trust, which carried the whole man with it and determined character and action. His faith included sense (*a*) of *pisteuō* (which is inherent in the Hebrew verb ' believe ') along with sense (*b*). In this combination lies the rich and powerful import of NT ' believing ' ; it is a spiritual apprehension joined with personal commitment—the recognition of truth and the placing of trust in the Unseen. In this twofold sense ' man believes with his heart and so is justified ' (Ro 10^{10}). Those familiar with the spirit of the OT could not use the word *pistis* in relation to God without attaching to it, besides the rational idea of supersensible apprehension, the warmer consciousness of moral trust and allegiance bound up with it already in human relationships.

(2) Contact with Jesus Christ gave to the word a greatly increased use and a heightened power. ' Believing ' meant to Christ's disciples something new and different since they had Him to believe in ; and ' believers ' became a common name for His followers (cf Ac 2^{44} 5^{14} 15^{5} 19^{18}, 1 Co 14^{22}, 1 Th 1^{7}, 1 Ti 4^{12}). Some members of the Church seem to have been given a special endowment of the capacity for this ' faith ' (cf 1 Co 12^{9}). Faith was Jesus' principal and constant demand from men ; He preached and did mighty works so as to elicit and direct it. That faith which was attracted initially by ' signs and wonders ' could be a stepping-stone to a much higher faith in the Person and teaching of God's Messiah. The miracles of Jesus were conditioned by one injunction : ' Only believe ! ' ' All things are possible to him who believes ' (Mk 9^{23}). There was a faith in Jesus, real so far as it went but not sufficient for true discipleship, since it attached itself to His miracle-working power and failed to recognize His character and spiritual aims (cf Jn 2^{23} 4^{48} 6^{14} 7^{31} 8^{30} 11^{45} 12^{11}) ; this Jesus rejected. Closely related to it, though more active, is the faith that calls him ' Lord ' and ' removes mountains ' in His name, but which Jesus disowns because it does not in love do the Father's will (Mt 7^{21ff}, 1 Co 13^{2}). Following the Baptist, Jesus begins His ministry with the summons : ' Repent, and believe in the Gospel,' *i.e.* the good news that ' the Kingdom of God is at hand ' (Mk 1^{15}). Like Moses, He expects Israel to recognize His mission as from God, showing ' signs ' which belief will see as proof (cf Jn 2^{11} 3^{2} 4^{54} 6^{14} etc. ; Ac 2^{22}, He 4^{2}). As Jesus' teaching unfolds, it becomes clear that He requires an unparalleled faith in Himself along with His message, that the Kingdom of God of which He speaks centres in His Person and that in fact He is Himself ' the word ' of God He brings, the light and life whose coming He announces, ' the bread from heaven ' that He has to give to a starving world (Jn 6^{33ff} 8^{12} 11^{25} 14^{6}). For those ' who received him,' who ' believed in his name ' in this complete sense, faith acquired an entirely new scope ; it signified the unique attachment which gathered around the Person of Jesus—a human trust, in its purity and intensity such as no other man had ever elicited, which grew up into and identified itself with its possessor's belief in God, transforming that belief in doing so, and which drew the whole being of the believer into the will and life of His Master. When Thomas hails Jesus as ' My Lord and my God ! ' (Jn 20^{28}), he has believed. The two faiths are now welded inseparably. The Son is known through the Father and the Father through the Son, and Thomas gives his full allegiance to both in one. As Jesus was exalted, God in the same degree became nearer to these men ; and their faith in God became richer in content and more firmly grasped. So sure and direct was the communion with the Father opened by Jesus to His disciples, that the word ' faith,' as commonly used, failed to express it. ' Henceforth you know him (the Father) and have seen him,' says Jesus (Jn 14^{7}). The Fourth Evangelist uses the verb ' believe ' more than any other NT writer (seventy-nine times), but the related noun ' faith ' is found only once in the Johannine Gospel and Epistles (1 Jn 5^{4}). To know God is the Christian's highest privilege. The departure of Jesus and the shock and trial of His death were needed in order to perfect the disciples' faith (Jn 16^{7}), removing its earthly supports and breaking its links with all materialistic Messianism. As Jesus ' goes to the Father,' they realize that He and the Father are

one. Their faith rests no longer, in any degree, on a Christ 'regarded from a human point of view' (2 Co 5^{16}). They are ready to receive and to be empowered by the Spirit whom Jesus sends to them 'from the Father.' Jesus is henceforth linked with the spiritual and eternal order. To the faith which thus acknowledges Him He gives the benediction: 'Blessed are those who have not seen and yet believe' (Jn 20^{29}; cf 1 P 1^{8}). To define this specific faith a new grammatical construction appears in NT Greek. One does not simply believe Jesus or believe on or in Him; one commits himself to Him or His name (which contains the import of His Person and office) as in Mt 18^{6}, regularly in John (1^{12} $2^{11, 23}$ $3^{16, 18, 36}$ 4^{39} $6^{29, 35}$) and also in Paul (Ro 10^{14}, Gal 2^{16}, Ph 1^{29}). The construction suggests a kind of belief that causes the disciple to come to Him, realizing what He is. That the mission of Jesus Christ was an appeal for faith, with His own Person as its chief ground and matter, is assumed in Jn 20^{21}: 'These (signs) are written that you may believe that Jesus is the Christ, the Son of God, and that believing you may have life in his name.' Christian faith is the decisive action of the whole inner man—understanding, feeling, and will; it is the trustful and self-surrendering acknowledgment of God in Christ. For Paul faith springs from the intimate relationship between the believer and the Lord Jesus Christ. It leads to perfect trust in God and so produces obedience to His commands. Faith 'justifies,' as the works of the Law could never do (Ro 1^{17}). In the Epistle to the Hebrews (11^{1}) faith is seen as firm knowledge of a reality which stands behind the evidence of the physical senses and which is supremely demonstrated in Jesus Christ.

(3) Further, Jesus called on the world to believe the good news of His mission of redemption. This role, suggested in OT prophecy and related to His birth (Lk 1^{68-79}) and baptism (Jn 1^{29}), Jesus connected with His death throughout His ministry (cf Mk 2^{19f} 8^{31} 9^{12} $10^{38, 45}$ 12^{1-12}, Lk 13^{32f} 18^{25}, Jn 2^{19-22} 3^{14f}). The words of Jesus at the Last Supper (Mk 14^{22-25}||Mt 26^{26-29}|| Lk 22^{15-20}; cf 1 Co 11^{23-25}) make it clear that He regarded His death as the culmination of His mission. He stands ready to offer His 'blood' to ratify 'the [new] covenant' under which 'forgiveness of sins' will be universally guaranteed (cf Jer 31^{31-34}). Having concentrated on Himself the faith of men, giving to it thereby a new meaning and power, He finally directed that faith to a consideration of His death. In the early Church it was seen that by His death Jesus had 'entered into his glory' and 'received from the Father the promise of the Spirit,' in the strength of which His followers are commissioned to 'preach to all nations repentance and forgiveness of sins' (Ac 2^{22-38}; cf Lk 24^{46-48}). The Apostles understood and proclaimed their Master's death as the pivotal point of the relations between God and man that centre in Christ. The cross was regarded as the means of deliverance from sin and the revelation of God's saving purpose toward the race (Ac 3^{18f} 20^{28}, 1 Co 1^{18-25}, 2 Co 5^{14-21}, 1 P 3^{18}, Rev 1^{5f}). Faith in the resurrection of Jesus was logically antecedent to faith in His sacrificial death, for His rising from the dead set His dying in its true perspective (Ac 4^{10-12}), as a full expiation for the sins of men (He 2^{9}; Ro 4^{25}). To 'confess with one's lips that Jesus is Lord and believe in one's heart that God raised him from the dead' was therefore to fulfil the essential conditions of Christian salvation (Ro 10^{9}), since the resurrection and exaltation of Jesus give assurance of the peace with God won by His perfect sacrifice (He 7^{25} 9^{11-14} $10^{19, 22}$). His rising from the dead is the vindication of His divine Sonship and verification of His claims on man's allegiance (Ro 1^{4}, Ac 2^{36}, 1 P 1^{21}). It is the guarantee of 'the redemption of our bodies' and the consummated salvation that is in Christ Jesus both for the individual and the Church (1 Co 15^{20-28}, Ro 8^{15-23}, Eph 1^{16-23}, Ac 17^{31}). The Christian faith is to 'believe that Jesus died and rose again' (1 Th 4^{14})—that in dying He atoned for human sin and in rising He abolished death. St. Paul was the chief exponent and defender of this 'word of the Cross' which is at the same time 'the word of faith' (Ro 10^{8}). Its various aspects and issues appear under the terms (q.v.) Justification, Atonement, Expiation, Grace, Law (in NT). The redeeming work of Jesus is also focused in the Cross in 1 Peter, I John, and Revelation. According to the whole purport of the NT, the forgiving grace of God there meets the sin of mankind. Faith is the hand reached out to accept God's gifts of mercy extended from the cross of Christ. The faculty of faith, understood in its fundamental meaning as the spiritual sense and consciousness of God, is in no wise narrowed or diverted when it fixes itself on 'Jesus Christ and him crucified,' for, as St. Paul insists, 'God shows his love for us in that Christ died for us,' and 'God was in Christ reconciling the world to himself.' The 'glory of God' shines in our hearts, His nature becomes for the first time fully revealed, and faith is complete and satisfied when God is beheld 'in the face of Christ' (Ro 5^{8}, 2 Co 4^{6} 5^{18-21}). G. G. F.—**H. M. S.**

FAITHLESS.—Wherever this word occurs in AV, it means, not untrustworthy, but unbelieving, just as in the *Merchant of Venice* Shylock is called 'a faithless Jew,' simply because he was an unbeliever in Christ.

FALCON.—RV and RSV translation of *'ayyāh* in Lv 11^{14} (AV 'kite'), Job 28^{7} (AV 'vulture'). In Dt 14^{13} RV has 'falcon,' while AV and RSV have 'kite.' See Kite.

FALL.—The story of the Fall in Gn 3 is the immediate sequel to the account of man's creation with which the Yahwistic document opens (see Creation). It tells how the first man and woman, living in childlike innocence and happiness in the Garden of Eden, were tempted by the subtle serpent to doubt the goodness of their Creator, and aim at the possession of forbidden knowledge by tasting the fruit of the one tree of which they had been expressly charged not to eat. Their transgression was speedily followed by detection and punishment; on the serpent was laid the curse of perpetual enmity between it and mankind; the woman was doomed to the pains of child-bearing; and the man to unremitting toil in the cultivation of the ground, which was cursed on account of his sin. Finally, lest the man should use his newly acquired insight to secure the boon of immortality by partaking of the tree of life, he was expelled from the garden, which appears to be conceived as still existing, though barred to human approach by the cherubim and the flaming sword.

It is right to point out that certain incongruities of representation suggest that one or more originally separate traditions have been combined in the source from which the passage is taken (J). The chief difficulty arises in connexion with the two trees on which the destiny of mankind is made to turn. In 2^{9} the tree of life and the tree of the knowledge of good and evil grow together in the midst of the garden; in 2^{17} the second alone is made the test of man's obedience. But ch. 3 (down to v.^{22}) knows of only one central tree, and that obviously (though it is never so named) the tree of knowledge. The tree of life plays no real part in the story except in $3^{22, 24}$; and its introduction there creates embarrassment; for if this tree also was forbidden, the writer's silence regarding the prohibition is inexplicable, and if it was not forbidden, can we suppose that the Divine prerogative of immortality was placed within man's reach during the period of his probation? While these incongruities may, as some think, indicate a two-fold recension of the Paradise story, they more probably arise for the most part out of the long history of oral transmission through which the material passed before reaching the hand of the Yahwist, in the course of which originally disparate traditions were combined without always being harmonized. We may suppose that the tree of knowledge and the tree of life represent traditions of different origin, the latter playing a relatively minor role in the narrative as the Yahwist has shaped it.

It is unnecessary to regard this profoundly suggestive narrative as a literal record of a historic occurrence. It is, rather, supra-historical: a theological explanation of creation and of man's predicament. It is probable that the Yahwist has made use of mythological traditions current among the ancient Semites and, purging them of mythological traits and shaping them for his own purposes, has made of them a vehicle for setting forth in terms appropriate to Israel's faith the purposes of God for man in Creation, and the manner in which man betrayed those purposes. It is true that no complete extra-Biblical parallel to these stories has yet been discovered; the utmost that can be claimed is that particular elements or motives of the Biblical story seem to be reflected in some of the Babylonian myths, and still more in the religious symbolism displayed on the monuments (tree of life, serpent, cherubim, etc.). Reminiscences of similar myths are to be seen elsewhere in the Bible (*e.g.* Is 14[4-21], Ezk 28[1-19]). These coincidences are sufficiently striking to suggest the inference that a mythical account of man's original condition and his fall existed in Babylonia, and had obtained wide currency in the East. It is a reasonable conjecture that such a myth, 'stripped of its primitive polytheism, and retaining only faint traces of what was probably its original mythological character, formed the material setting which was adapted by the [Biblical] narrative for the purpose of exhibiting, under a striking and vivid imaginative form, the deep spiritual truths which he was inspired to discern' (Driver). These spiritual truths, in which the real significance of the narrative lies, we must endeavour very briefly to indicate.

(1) The story offers, on the face of it, an explanation of the outstanding ills that flesh is heir to: the hard, toilsome lot of the husbandman, the travail of the woman and her subjection to man, the universal fate of death. These evils, it is taught, are inconsistent with the ideal of human life, and contrary to the intention of a good God. Man, as originally created, was exempt from them; and to the question, Whence came they? the answer is that they are the effect of a Divine curse to which the race is subject; though it is to be noted that no curse is pronounced on the first pair, but only on the *serpent* as the organ of temptation, and the *ground* which is cursed *for man's sake*.

(2) The consequences of the curse are the penalty of a single sin, by which man incurred the just anger of God. The author's conception of sin may be considered from two points of view. Formally, it is the transgression of a Divine commandment, involving distrust of the wisdom and goodness of the Almighty, and breaking the harmony which had subsisted between man and his Maker. The process by which these evil thoughts are insinuated into the mind of the woman is described with a masterly insight into the psychology of temptation which is unsurpassed in literature. A reason for the Divine injunction, and a reason for man's transgression of it, is clearly suggested in the story. To eat of the tree would make man like God, knowing good and evil; and God does not wish man to be like Himself. The essence of sin is therefore presumption, an overstepping of the limits of creaturehood, and an encroachment on the prerogatives of the Deity. Nevertheless, the Yahwist does not seem greatly interested in discussing these questions. As he tells the story, the fact that God gave the command is its sufficient reason; it is not to be argued with or discussed. As one scholar (von Rad) says, it was the serpent who first suggested that it was possible to discuss it. According to the narrative, then, the condition of life in Paradise is unquestioning obedience to the Divine command.

(3) What, then, is meant by the 'knowledge of good and evil,' which was acquired by eating of the tree? Does it mean simply an enlargement of experience such as the transition from childhood to maturity naturally brings with it, and of which the feeling of shame (3[7]) is the significant index? Or is it, as has generally been held, the experimental knowledge of moral distinctions, the awaking of the conscience, the faculty of discerning between right and wrong? While it is not easy to say which of these interpretations expresses the thought in the mind of the writer, it is in accordance with Hebrew idiom to hold that knowledge of good and evil is equivalent to knowledge in general. Though it is not entirely certain that that is the sense in which the phrase is here used, there is nothing to show that it refers to the moral sense; and the fact that neither of the ways in which the newly acquired faculty manifests itself (the perception of sex, and insight into the mystic virtue of the tree of life, v.[22]) is a distinctively ethical cognition, rather favours the opinion that the knowledge referred to is the power to discern the secret meanings of things and utilize them for human ends, regardless of the will and purpose of God —the knowledge, in short, which is the principle of a godless civilization. The idea may be that succinctly expressed by the writer of Ecclesiastes: 'God made man upright; but they have sought out many devices' (Ec 7[29]).

(4) One specific feature of the story remains to be considered, namely, the rôle assigned to the serpent, and his character. The identification of the serpent with the devil appears first in the Apocryphal literature (Wis 2[24]); in the narrative itself he is simply the most subtle of the creatures that God has made (3[1]), and there is not the slightest reason to suppose that he is there regarded as the mouthpiece of the evil spirit. At the same time it is impossible to escape the impression that the serpent is conceived as a malevolent being, designedly insinuating suspicion of God into the minds of our first parents, and inciting them to an act which will frustrate the Divine purpose regarding mankind. There is thus a certain ambiguity in the representation of the serpent, which may have its source in some more primitive phase of the story; but which also points the way, under the influence of a deeper apprehension of the nature of moral evil than had been attained in the time of the writer, to that identification of the serpent with the Evil One which we find in the NT (Ro 16[20], Rev 12[9] 20[2]). In the same way, and with the same justification, the reflection of later ages read into the curse on the serpent (v.[15]) the promise of ultimate redemption from the power of evil through the coming of Christ. Strictly interpreted, the words imply nothing more than a perpetual antagonism between the human race and the repulsive reptiles which excite its instinctive antipathy. It is only the general scope of the passage that can be thought to warrant the inference that the victory is to be on the side of humanity; and it is a still higher flight of religious inspiration to conceive of that victory as culminating in the triumph of Him whose mission it was to destroy the works of the devil. J. S.—**J. Br.**

FALLOW-DEER.—This word occurs in the AV among the clean animals (Dt 14[5]), and in the list of game furnished for Solomon's daily table (1 K 4[23]). In each list *'ayyāl*, *ṣᵉbhî*, and *yaḥmûr* occur in the same order. The first is correctly translated, in EV, 'hart' (see HART). The second is incorrectly translated in AV 'roebuck,' and correctly in RV and RSV 'gazelle' (see GAZELLE). The third is incorrectly translated in AV 'fallow-deer,' and correctly in RV and RSV 'roebuck' (see ROE, ROEBUCK).

FAMILIAR.—The expression 'familiar spirit' was taken into the AV from the Geneva Version, as the translation of Hebrew *'ôbh* (RSV 'medium'). See MAGIC, etc. The word is also used as a substitute in Jer 20[10], 'All my familiars watched for my halting' (RV, RSV 'familiar friends,' Hebrew 'men of my place').

FAMILY.—1. Character of the family in OT.—'Family' in the OT has a wider significance than that which we usually associate with the term. The word translated 'household' (Gn 7[1]) approaches most nearly to our word 'family': but a man's 'household' might consist of his mother; his wives and wives' children; his concubines and their children; sons-in-law and daughters-in-law, with their offspring; illegitimate sons (Jg 11^{1}); dependants and aliens; and slaves of both sexes. Polygamy was in part the cause of the large size of the Hebrew household; in part the cause of it may be found in the insecurity of early times, when safety lay in numbers, and consequently not only the married sons and daughters dwelt, for the sake of protection, with their father, but remote relatives and even foreigners ('the sojourners within your gates') would attach themselves, with a similar object, to a great household. The idea of the family sometimes had an even wider significance, extending to and including the nation, or even the whole race of mankind. Of this a familiar illustration is the figure of Abraham, who was regarded as being in a very real sense the father of the nation. So also the same feeling for the idea of the family is to be found in the careful assigning of a 'father' to every known nation and tribe (Gn 10). From this it is easily perceived that the family played an important part in Hebrew thought and affairs. It formed the base on which the social structure was built up; its indistinguishable merging into the wider sense of clan or tribe indicates how it affected the political life of the whole nation.

Polygamy and bigamy were recognized features of the family life. From the Oriental point of view there was nothing immoral in the practice of polygamy. It was the means of ensuring the survival of the family by providing male children. Concubinage with slave women had the same object. Female slaves were in every respect the property of their master, and became his concubines, except in certain cases, when they seem to have belonged exclusively to their mistress, and could not be appropriated by the man except by her suggestion or consent (Gn 16^{2f}). The slave-concubines were obtained as booty in time of war (Jg 5^{30}), or bought from poverty-stricken parents (Ex 21^{7}); or, possibly, in the ordinary slave traffic with foreign nations. In addition to his concubines a man might take several wives, and from familiar examples in the OT it seems that it was usual for wealthy and important personages to do so; Abraham, Jacob, David, Solomon, occur as instances. Elkanah, the husband of Hannah and Peninnah, is an interesting example of a man of no particular position who nevertheless had more than one wife; this may be an indication that bigamy, at least, if not polygamy, was not confined to the very wealthy and exalted. At all events, polygamy was an established and recognized institution from the earliest times. The gradual evolution in the OT of monogamy as the ideal is therefore of the highest interest. The earliest codes attempt in various ways to regulate the custom of polygamy. The Deuteronomic code in particular actually forbids kings to multiply wives (Dt 17^{17}); this is the fruit, apparently, of the experience of Solomon's reign. In the prophetic writings the note of protest is more clearly sounded. Not only Adam but also Noah, the second founder of the human race, represents monogamy, and on that account recommends it as God's ordinance. It is in the line of Cain that bigamy is first represented, as though to emphasize the consequences of the Fall. Reasons are given in explanation of the bigamy of Abraham (Gn 16) and of Jacob (29^{23}). Hosea and other prophets constantly dwell upon the thought of a monogamous marriage as being a symbol of the union between God and His people; and denounce idolatry as unfaithfulness to this spiritual marriage-tie.

2. Position of the wife.—Side by side with the growth of the recognition of monogamy as the ideal form of marriage, polygamy was practised even as late as NT times. The natural accompaniment of such a practice was the subordinate position of the wife. She was ordinarily regarded as a piece of property, as the wording of the Tenth Commandment testifies. Also her rights and privileges were necessarily shared with others. The relative positions of wives and concubines were determined mainly by the husband's favour. The children of the wife claimed the greater part, or the whole, of the inheritance; otherwise there does not seem to have been any inferiority in the position of the concubine as compared with that of the wife, nor was any idea of illegitimacy, in our sense of the word, connected with her children.

The husband had supreme authority over the wife. He was permitted by the Deuteronomy code to divorce her with apparently little reason. The various passages (Dt $22^{13, 19, 28f}$, Is 50^{1}, Jer 3^{8}, Mal 2^{16}) referring to and regulating divorce, indicate that it was of frequent occurrence. Yet wives, and even concubines who had been bought in the first place as slaves, might not be sold (Ex 21^{7-11}, Dt 21^{14}). Indeed, the Law throughout proves itself sympathetic towards the position of the wife, and desirous of improving her condition (Dt 21^{10-17}). This very attitude of the Law, however, indicates that there was need of improvement. The wife seems to have had no redress if wronged by the husband; she could not divorce him; and absolute faithfulness, though required of the wife, was not expected of the husband, so long as he did not injure the rights of any other man.

The wife, then, in theory was the mere chattel of her husband. A woman of character, however, could improve her situation and attain to a considerable degree of importance and influence as well as of personal freedom. Thus we read not only of Hagars, who were dealt hardly with and were obliged to submit themselves under the hands of their masters and rivals, but also of Sarahs and Rebekahs and Abigails, who could act independently and even against the wishes of their husbands in order to gain their own ends. And the Book of Proverbs testifies to the advantage accruing to a man in the possession of a good wife (19^{14} 31^{10ff}), and to the misery which it is in the power of a contentious woman to inflict (19^{13} etc.). The position the wife enjoyed depended in part on her own gifts, but also, no doubt, on the strength of her own family to see that she was not wronged.

3. Children.—In a household consisting of several families, the mother of each set of children would naturally have more to do with them than the father, and the maternal relationship would usually be more close and affectionate than between the father and his children. Although it was recognized to be disastrous for a household to be divided against itself, yet friction between the various families could hardly have been avoided. 'One whom his mother comforts' (Is 66^{13}) must have been a sight common enough—a mother consoling her injured son for the taunts and blows of her rivals' children. Thus the mother would have the early care and education of her children under her own control. The father, on the other hand, had complete power over the lives and fortunes of his children, and would represent to them the idea of authority rather than of tenderness. He it was who arranged the marriage of his sons (Gn 24^{4} 28^{2}, Jg 14^{2}), and he had the right to sell his daughters (Ex 21^{7}). The father seems even to have had powers of life and death over his children (Jg 11^{39}); and the Law provided that an unworthy son might be stoned to death upon the accusation of his parents (Dt 21^{18-21}). The Decalogue commands respect towards both parents, and death is the penalty laid down for striking (Ex 21^{15}) and for cursing (Ex 21^{17}, Lv 20^{9}) father or mother. See also CHILD.

4. Family duties.—The claims of the family upon the various members of it were strongly felt. Many laws provide for the vengeance and protection of the injured and defenceless by their next-of-kin, called the *gō'ēl*. Brothers were the guardians of their sisters (Gn 34). A childless widow could demand, though not enforce, re-marriage with her brother-in-law (Dt 25^{5-10}). Boaz, after a nearer relative had renounced his rights, performed the duty of a *gō'ēl* to Ruth. Lv 20^{21} prohibits a man from marrying his brother's wife, but this is to be regarded as the general rule to which Dt 25^{5ff} gives the exception, for levirate marriage seems to have been practised at the time of Christ (Mt 22^{23ff}). In the OT its purpose appears to be the preservation of the particular branch of the family rather than the advantage of the widow herself, though that end was also served. In any case it illustrates the strong sense of duty towards the family as a whole.

Children owed obedience and respect to their parents. Even a married man would consider himself still under the authority of his father, whether living with him or not; and his wife would be subject to her father-in-law even after her husband's death.

To an Israelite, 'family' conveyed the notions of unity, security, order, and discipline. These conceptions were nourished by the religious customs and observances in the home. In the patriarchal times, the head of each family offered sacrifice on his own altar. The Passover was celebrated as a family rite. Later it became the responsibility of the family to see that all its members were instructed in the Law of Y″ (Dt 6^{7}). Such observances, no doubt, helped to bind the members of the family in close religious and spiritual sympathies. The strong bonds of kinship and common concern tended to keep the family together, and contributed to the survival of the Jewish nation through centuries of political insignificance. E. G. R.—**A. G. McL.**

FAMINE.—In Palestine, famine is usually due to failure of the rainfall (Lv 26^{19}, Am 4^{6f}). Both crops and pasturage depend on the proper amount falling at the right time, the 'early rain' in October–November, the 'latter' in March–April. Its importance and uncertainty caused it to be regarded as the special gift of God (Dt $11^{11,14}$). Accordingly famine is almost always a direct judgment from Him (1 K 17^{1}, Ezk 5, and continually in the Prophets; Ja 5^{17}). Hence we find it amongst the terrors of the eschatological passages of NT (Mk 13^{8}, Rev 18^{8}). The idea is spiritualized in Am 8^{11} 'a famine of hearing the words of the Lord.' In Egypt, famine is due to the failure of the annual inundation of the Nile, which is ultimately traceable to lack of rain in the Abyssinian highlands of the interior.

Crops may be destroyed by other causes—hail and thunder-storms (Ex 9^{31}, 1 S 12^{17}); locusts and similar pests (Ex 10^{15}, Jl 1^{4}, Am 4^{9}). Further, famine is the usual accompaniment of war, the most horrible accounts of famines being connected with sieges (2 K 6^{25} 25^{3}, Jer 21^{9}, La 4^{10}).

These passages should be compared with the terrible description of Dt 28^{49-57}, and with Josephus' account of the last siege of Jerusalem (*BJ* v. x. 3 [429 ff]). So in Rev 6^{5} scarcity, connected with the black horse, follows on bloodshed and conquest; but a maximum price is fixed for wheat and barley, and oil and wine are untouched, so that the full horrors of famine are delayed. A natural result of famine is pestilence, due to improper and insufficient food, lack of water, and insanitary conditions. The two are frequently connected, especially in Ezekiel and Jeremiah (1 K 8^{37}, Jer 21^{9}, Lk 21^{11} [not Mt 24^{7}]).

Famines are recorded in connexion with Abraham (Gn 12^{10}) and Isaac (26^{1}). There is the famous seven years' famine of Gn 41 ff, which included Syria as well as Egypt. It apparently affected cereals rather than pasturage, beasts of transport being unharmed (cf *per contra* 1 K 18^{5}). The device by which Joseph warded off its worst effects is illustrated by Egyptian inscriptions. In one, Baba, who lived *about* the time of Joseph, says: 'I collected corn, as a friend of the harvest-god, and was watchful at the time of sowing. And when a famine arose, lasting many years, I distributed corn to the city each year of famine' (see Driver, *Genesis*, p. 346). Other famines, besides those already referred to, are mentioned in Ru 1^{1}, 2 S 21^{1}. The famine of Ac 11^{28} is usually identified with one mentioned by Josephus (*Ant.* xx. ii 5 [51–53], v. 2 [101], which is dated A.D. 45. But famines were characteristic of the reign of Claudius (Suetonius mentions 'assiduae sterilitates'), so that the exact reference remains uncertain. C. W. E.

FAN.—The fan of Scripture (Is 30^{24}, Mt 3^{12}, Lk 3^{17}) is the five- or six-pronged wooden **winnowing-fork** (so RSV) for which see AGRICULTURE, 3. The corresponding verb is rendered '**winnow**,' Is 30^{24}, Ru 3^{2}, but 'fan' elsewhere (RSV has 'winnow' throughout); the **fanners** of Jer 51^{2} (AV, RVm) are the 'winnowers' (RSV). Fanning or winnowing is a frequent figure for the Divine sifting and chastisement, Jer 4^{11} 15^{7} etc. A. R. S. K.

FANG.—See GRINDER.

FARTHING.—See MONEY, 7.

FASTING.—1. In the OT.—The discipline of fasting, in the sense of abstinence from food, was widespread throughout the religions of the world. The earliest motive was possibly the fear of demons, who were thought to exercise power over men in the process of eating. In the OT, fasting is sometimes a preparation for theophany, as in the case of Moses (Ex 34^{28}, Dt 9^{9}) and Daniel (9^{3} $10^{2f,12}$). But more generally, it is a sign of humility before God, as is clearly shown in the parallel expression 'to afflict the soul,' *i.e.* 'to humble oneself' in Lv $16^{29,31}$ $23^{27,32}$, Nu 29^{7} 30^{13}; cf Ps 35^{13}, Is $58^{3,5}$. It accompanied mourning (1 S 31^{13}; cf Zec 7^{3}), or repentance (1 K 21^{27}). In times of necessity or danger, it was appropriate for an individual or for the whole community to fast (2 S 12^{16ff}, Ps 35^{13} 69^{11}, Jg 20^{26}, 1 S 7^{6}, Jer $36^{6,9}$ etc.). Fasting, so to speak, reinforced urgent prayer. How seriously it might be taken up, to the extent that an earnest man of prayer might become weak and thin through lack of nourishment, is shown by Ps 109^{24}.

After the fall of Jerusalem in 586 B.C, fasting took on a new importance, and became one of the special notes of the religious life of the period that followed. It is probable that a form of public confession can be found within the prophecies that are collected under the name of Isaiah (ch. 59), while the previous chapter (58) deals with the question, 'Why have we fasted and thou seest not?' Evidently the fasts are those which commemorated the fall of Jerusalem, for which the five laments of the book of Lamentations had probably been composed, and of which there is plain evidence in Zec 7^{3-5} 8^{9}. But most important of all was the annual Day of Atonement (Lv 16^{29ff} 23^{27ff}, Nu 29^{7}, 'the Fast' of Ac 27^{9}), designed to cover the otherwise unexpiated sins of the whole people for the whole year (*i.e.*, of course, those sins for which atonement was possible). A prophetic protest was raised against the easy assumption that fasts were an *opus operatum* (Jer 14^{12}, Is 58^{12}, Zec 7^{5ff} 8^{19}, Jl 2^{13}).

In the Judaism of NT times and after, the Jews were noted, as a people, for their fasts. There is frequent mention of fasting in the intertestamental literature. Occasional voices insisted on the uselessness of fasting without a corresponding inner disposition (Sir 34^{26}), but the Pharisees made much of it (Ps Sol 3^{8}, Mk 2^{18}, Lk 18^{12}), and regarded fasting as a work of merit. It became the custom of the specially devout to fast on Mondays and Thursdays, though there is no evidence that this was binding on all. In addition to the fasts of the calendar, fasts might be appointed by authority in case of famine, plague or war. If a man undertook a fast, his fast took precedence of sacrificial offerings and was regarded as more efficacious than almsgiving. 'He who prays and gets no answer must fast.'

2. In the NT.—Jesus laid down no specific injunctions to fast. But while He denounced the ostentation of the Pharisees, He seems to have assumed that His disciples would fast (Mt 6^{16f}). He introduced a new note, emphasizing secrecy, as though to stress that fasting is not so much a meritorious work as a sign of a contrite heart. His own fasting in the wilderness was for a period of forty days, and took place not *before* revelation, as with Moses, but *after* His baptismal experience, as a preparation for His messianic office. It is not stated that He fasted during His public ministry, but His general conduct makes it likely that He observed the public fasts. His most striking teaching is given in relation to the fasting of the disciples of John the Baptist (Mk 2^{18f}).

There, it is made plain that while fasting is excluded in the presence of the bridegroom, yet between the breaking in of the Kingdom (in His own life and death) and the End (*i.e. between the times*), fasting will have its place.

There is no NT evidence that fasts were part of the *regular* life of the apostolic church. But St. Paul certainly undertook fasts (2 Co 6^{5} 11^{27}), which may have been private; and there was a tendency for the Church to practise spontaneous fasting at times of special importance, as when Barnabas and Saul were ordained for their missionary labours (Ac 13^{3}), and when elders were appointed (14^{23}). The absence of any *problem* of fasting in the letters of St. Paul suggests that it was not a prominent question in the hellenistic churches. It may well have been comprehended in the Apostle's general teaching on Christian askesis or training in 1 Co 9^{24}.

D. R. J.

FAT.—See Food, **10**, Sacrifice and Offering, **12.**

FAT.—The same word as **vat** (RSV), a large vessel for holding liquids, but in OT and NT only in connexion with the making of wine. See Wine and Strong Drink, **2.**

FATE.—The word ' fate ' is found a number of times in RSV, but an examination of the context shows that nowhere is a blind fatalism presented. Sometimes the reference is to the common lot of men, and sometimes to the doom which men bring on themselves or which is brought on the community. Cf Nu 16^{29} (AV, RV ' common death '), Ps 49^{13} (AV, RV ' way ') 81^{15} (AV, RV ' time '), Ec 2^{14} 9^{2f} (AV, RV ' event ') 3^{19} (AV, RV ' that which befalleth '), Jer 49^{20} 50^{15} (AV and RV quite different), La 3^{50} (AV, RV ' because of ').

FATHER.—See Family, Genealogy, **1.**

FATHERHOOD OF GOD.—See God, **12.**

FATHERLESS.—See Orphan.

FATHOM.—See Weights and Measures.

FAUCHION (Jth 13^{6} AV; RV **' scimitar '**; RSV **' sword '**).—The English word denoted originally ' a broad sword more or less curved on the convex side '; but in later use and in poetry it signified a sword of any kind.

FAVOUR.—The English word ' favour ' is used in AV in the modern sense of ' goodwill '; but in ' well-favoured ' and ' ill-favoured ' we see the older meaning of personal appearance. RSV substitutes ' lovely,' ' graceful,' ' handsome ' in references to persons, and ' sleek ' or ' gaunt ' for animals. In Jos 11^{20} the word seems to be used in the old sense of ' mercy ' (so RSV)—' that he might utterly destroy them, that they might have no favour ' (AV, RV)—as in Elyot, *The Governour*, ii. 298: ' And they, which by that lawe were condemned, were put to dethe without any fauour.' For the theology of the word see Grace.

FAWN.—See Roe, **3.**

FEAR.—In the Bible the word ' fear ' is, of course, often used to connote physical or moral fear in the usual sense of these terms, but it is the phrase ' the fear of the Lord ' which is particularly noteworthy. It may signify a self-regarding feeling or attitude on the part of a man who knows he has fallen short of God's requirements and fears the penalty. The more God's demands are made known, the more can a man become filled with the fear that he will never merit God's favour. So the sinner, under condemnation of the Law, is in ' bondage unto fear ' (Ro 8^{15}) and, inasmuch as ' the sting of death is sin ' (1 Co 15^{56}), he is also ' through fear of death . . . subject to lifelong bondage ' (He 2^{15}). But ' the fear of the Lord ' can have a more positive connotation, meaning reverence, religious faith, or piety. Thus Job is told by one of his friends that his ' fear ' in this sense ought to be his ground of assurance (4^{6}). The Law-giving at Sinai, where God revealed Himself in glory and majesty, implanted this fear in the hearts of the Israelites (Dt 4^{10}); it is the response of man the creature to God the Creator, who is also God of righteousness and of judgment, and the life of obedience and faithfulness which flows from that response and gives expression to it.

Only those who in some degree know God can experience this fear; the fool who says in his heart that there is no God (Ps 14^{1} 53^{1}) knows nothing of it. Not only did the early Christians walk in the fear of the Lord (Ac 9^{31}) but there is mentioned with them a class of ' God-fearers ' who were fundamentally religious, although they were not yet Christians (Ac 10^{2} etc). The law of love revealed in Jesus Christ delivers men from that bondage to fear (Ro 8^{5}) which was represented by the Law and gives them the adoption of sons (Jn 15^{15}, Ro 8^{15}, Gal 4^{5f}); perfect love casts out fear (1 Jn 4^{18}). So men can be delivered from the fear of judgment and from the fear caused by the hard-taskmaster conception of God (Mt 25^{24}, Lk 19^{22}), but not from that attitude of reverence and awe (q.v.) which is proper for the creature before the Creator. Those who know that fear and who know also the love of God in Jesus Christ are constrained by that love to persuade others to be reconciled to God (2 Co 5^{11ff}). J. G. T.—**J. Ma.**

FEARFULNESS.—The adjective ' fearful ' is often used in AV in the sense, not of causing fear, but of feeling it; and ' fearfulness ' always denoted the emotion of fear. Thus Mt 8^{26} ' Why are ye fearful (AV and RV; RSV ' afraid), O ye of little faith? '; Ps 55^{5} ' Fearfulness (AV and RV; RSV ' fear ') and trembling are come upon me.' In the RV of the NT the only meaning of ' fearful ' is full of fear, the Revisers, Westcott tells us, having purposely retained this use in order that ' fear,' ' fearful,' and ' fearfulness ' might all agree in meaning. They have accordingly changed ' fearful sights ' in Lk 21^{11} into ' terrors ' (so RSV). The Revisers of the OT, however, had no such thought, and they have left the word unchanged. RSV retains ' fearfulness ' in the sense of ' fear ' in Ezk 4^{16} 12^{18f}, and ' fearful ' in the sense of ' afraid ' in Dt 20^{8}, Jg 7^{3}, Is 35^{4}, Jer 51^{46}.

FEASTS.—*Introductory*.—The sacred festivals of the Jews were primarily occasions of rejoicing, treated as a part of religion. To ' rejoice before God ' was synonymous with ' to celebrate a festival.' In process of time this characteristic was modified, and a probably late institution, like the Day of Atonement, could be regarded as a feast, though its prevalent note was not one of joy. But the most primitive feasts were marked by religious merriment; they were accompanied with dances (Jg 21^{21}), and, as it seems, led to serious excesses in many cases (1 S 1^{13}, Am 2^{7}, 2 K 23^{7}, Dt 23^{18}). Most of the feasts were only local assemblies for acts and purposes of sacred worship; but the three great national festivals were the occasions for general assemblies of the people, at which all males were supposed to appear (Ex 23$^{14, 17}$ 34^{23}, Dt 16^{16}).

I. Feasts connected with the Sabbath.—These were calculated on the basis of the sacred number 7, which regulated all the great dates of the Jewish sacred year. Thus the 7th was the sacred month, the feasts of Unleavened Bread and Tabernacles each lasted for 7 days, Pentecost was 49 days after the Feast of Unleavened Bread, Passover and Tabernacles each began on the 14th day of their respective months, and there were 7 days of holy convocation in the year.

1. The Sabbath and the observances akin to it were lunar in character (cf Am 8^{5}, Hos 2^{11}, Is 1^{13}, 2 K 4^{23}). The sabbath ordinances are treated in Ex 20^{11} 31^{17} as designed to commemorate the completion of creation, but Dt 5^{14f} connects them with the redemption from Egypt, and Ex 23^{12} ascribes them to humanitarian motives. On this day work of all sorts was forbidden, and the daily morning and evening sacrifices were doubled. Sabbath-breaking was punishable with death (Nu 15$^{32-36}$, Ex 31^{14f}). No evidence of Sabbath observance is traced in the accounts of the patriarchal age, and very little in pre-exilic records (Is 56$^{2, 6}$ 58^{13}, Jer 17$^{20-24}$, Ezk 20$^{12f, 16, 20}$). But after the Captivity the rules were more strictly enforced (Neh 13$^{15, 22}$), and in later times the Rabbinical prohibitions multiplied to an inordinate extent. See SABBATH.

2. At the **New Moon** special sacrifices were offered (Nu 28[11-15]), and the silver trumpets were blown over them (Nu 10[10]). All trade and business were discontinued, as well as work in the fields (Am 8[5]). It appears also that this was the occasion of a common sacred meal and family sacrifices (cf 1 S 20[5f. 18, 24]), and it seems to have been a regular day on which to consult prophets (2 K 4[23]).

3. The Feast of Trumpets took place at the New Moon of the 7th month, Tishri (October). See TRUMPETS.

4. The Sabbatical year.—An extension of the Sabbath principle led to the rule that in every 7th year the land was to be allowed to lie fallow, and fields were to be neither tilled nor reaped. See SABBATICAL YEAR.

5. By a further extension, every 50th year was to be treated as a **year of Jubilee,** when Hebrew slaves were emancipated and mortgaged property reverted to its owners. See SABBATICAL YEAR.

II. GREAT NATIONAL FESTIVALS.—These were solar festivals and mostly connected with different stages of the harvest. The Jews also ascribed to them a commemorative significance and traditionally referred their inauguration to various events in their national history. They were :

1. The Passover followed immediately by the **Feast of Unleavened Bread** (*Maṣṣôth*). These two feasts were of different origin (Lv 23[5f], Nu 28[16f]) and Josephus distinguishes between them. *Pesaḥ* or Passover is a survival from Israel's nomadic days and *Maṣṣôth* or Unleavened Bread is a Canaanite feast of the barley harvest when unleavened cakes were eaten. For the characteristic features of these two festivals see PASSOVER.

2. The Feast of Weeks or **Pentecost** was a purely agricultural celebration. It fell in summer with the beginning of wheat harvest which followed (at least theoretically) seven weeks after cutting of first stalks of barley (see PENTECOST).

3. The Feast of Ingathering or **Tabernacles** (*Sukkôth*).—This feast eclipsed the others and was frequently referred to as 'the feast.' It would appear that in the Temple at Jerusalem where it was cut off from its close association with the vintage this autumn festival assumed the character of a New Year celebration and absorbed many Canaanite elements. At this feast the king appears to have played a leading rôle and through him and his proper discharge of the elaborate ritual God's blessing was assured to the people and the land for another year. Whatever be the precise nature of this feast 'at the turn of the year' it seems to have been marked by thanksgiving for the harvest safely ingathered and petition for continued blessing (see TABERNACLES).

III. MINOR HISTORICAL FESTIVALS.—**1. The Feast of Purim,** dating from the Persian period of Jewish history, commemorated the nation's deliverance from the intrigues of Haman (see PURIM).

2. The Feast of Dedication (*Ḥ^anukkāh*) recalled the purification of the Temple after its desecration by Antiochus Epiphanes (168 B.C.). See DEDICATION.

3. The Feast of the Wood Offering or of the Wood-carriers, on the 15th day of Abib (April) marked the last of the nine occasions on which offerings of wood were brought for the use of the Temple (Neh 10[34] 13[31]).

Besides these there were certain minor feasts, alluded to in Josephus and the Apocrypha, but these do not appear to have been generally observed or to have attained any religious importance. Such are : *The Feast of the Reading of the Law* (1 Es 9[50], cf Neh 8[9] ; *the Feast of Nicanor* on 13th day of Adar (March) (1 Mac 7[49] ; see PURIM) ; *the Feast of the Captured Fortress* (1 Mac 13[50-52]). A. W. F. B.—**J. Pn.**

FELIX, ANTONIUS.—The procurator who kept the Apostle Paul in prison for two years, either in hope of a bribe or as a favour to 'the Jews' (Ac 24[26f]). His commission originally to Samaria was extended in A.D. 52 to include the whole of Palestine less four Galilean cities assigned to Agrippa II. An ex-slave and presumably a Greek, he belonged to the new bureaucracy staffed mostly by freedmen whom the emperor Claudius found more dependable than the Roman knighthood for administering his affairs. To his brother Pallas, one of the three powerful freedmen who administered the government, he must have owed his appointment as he did later his reprieve (see FESTUS). The snobbish Tacitus found in the slave origin of Felix the source of his alleged cruelty and tyranny (*Hist.* v. 9 ; *Ann.* xii. 54). Felix was ruthless. But even to men of moderation ruthlessness must have appeared to be the only means by which to cope with the rising tide of Messianism. According to Josephus, 'Of the brigands [the standard term for Zealot patriots] whom he crucified, and of the common people who were convicted of complicity with them and punished by him, the number was incalculable' (*BJ* II. xiii. 2 [253]). Yet when numbers are specified they may even suggest moderation. Thus of the '30,000' who are said to have gathered at the instigation of an Egyptian prophet on the Mount of Olives for a miraculous assault on Jerusalem, the alleged casualties totalled only 400 killed and 200 captured. In his handling of the riots at Caesarea there was a needless slaughter and plunder of Jews, which but for the entreaty of his brother Pallas could have entailed his own serious punishment (*Ant.* xx. viii. 7, 9 [177, 182] ; cf *BJ* II. xiii. 7 [270]). But here too Felix knew when to check his soldiers and he left decisions with the Emperor. His endeavour to crush Messianism failed. Through treachery he caught and sent to Rome a patriotic leader named Eleazar ben Dinai who 'for twenty years' had terrorized the foes of independence ; but the more he attempted to repress such 'brigands,' the more their movement spread (*BJ* II. xii. 4 [235] ; xiii. 2 [253] ; *Ant.* xx. vi. 1 [121] ; viii. 5 [161]). Driven under cover, extremer nationalists, the *Sicarii* ('men of the dagger'), now had recourse to wholesale assassinations. Their chief foes were the pro-Roman aristocracy (*BJ* II. xiii. 3 f [254 ff] ; *Ant.* xx. viii. 6–9 [167 ff]). Their first victim was the high-priest Jonathan, whose recommendation had led to Felix's appointment as procurator of Judaea. That Felix himself instigated the murder is dubious : although Josephus asserts it in his *Antiquities,* he fails to make the charge in his earlier work. Nevertheless, some friction between the high-priest as governor and a procurator as ruthless as Felix was inevitable (see PROCURATOR). Thus it appears that the prosecuting attorney at the trial of the Apostle Paul could hardly have chosen more ironical words with which to address Felix than those imputed to him by the author of Acts, 'through you we enjoy much peace' (Ac 24[2]). He had failed to achieve even the Oriental sort of 'peace'—the levelling of opposition. His ineptitude appears further in selecting for his third marriage a certain Drusilla, mentioned in Ac 24[24]. She was a Jewess, the sister of Agrippa II. At the time when Felix seduced her she was the wife of Azizus, the Judaizing king of Emesa. Such conduct inevitably fed the spirit of revolt. J. S. K.

FELLOW.—This English word is used in AV with the meaning either (1) of companion, or (2) of person. Thus (1) Ps 45[7] 'God, thy God, hath anointed thee with the oil of gladness above thy fellows' (retained in RV, RSV) ; (2) Mt 26[71] 'This *fellow* was also with Jesus of Nazareth' (RV, RSV 'man' ; there is no word in the Greek). Cf Tyndale's translation of Gn 39[2] 'And the LORDE was with Joseph, and he was a luckie fellowe.' Although the word when used in AV for *person* may have a touch of disparagement, nowhere is it used to express strong contempt as now.

FELLOWSHIP (Gr. *koinōnia*).—*Koinōnia* occurs some twenty times in the NT. In RSV it is translated 'fellowship' in nine (AV, twelve ; RV, fifteen) of these occurrences. While 'fellowship' is frequently the most satisfactory of the alternative renderings which the English language offers, it is not always adequate (as the translators have recognized) to convey the rich meanings associated with *koinōnia*. It is desirable, therefore, to give individual attention to the more important usages of this word which is so pregnant with meaning both for early and for contemporary Christianity.

Koinōnia comes from an adjective which means 'common' and literally means a *common* participation or sharing in something. Similarly, in the NT the concrete noun *koinōnos* is used of a partner in the ownership of a fishing boat (Lk 5[10]); the verb *koinōnein* of sharing something with another, whether by way of giving (Ro 12[13], Gal 6[6]) or of receiving (Ro 15[27]); and the adjective *koinōnikos* (1 Ti 6[18]) is rendered 'generous' in RSV ('willing to communicate' in AV, RV).

1. *Koinōnia* meets us first in Ac 2[42]: 'They devoted themselves steadfastly to the apostles' teaching and (the) *fellowship*, to the breaking of bread and the prayers.' While the abstract idea of brotherly unity is clearly to be understood here, the presence of the definite article in Greek (omitted in AV, RV, RSV) may indicate that the word is here being used in a technical sense with reference to the particular socio-economic practice of the Jerusalem community of Christians. The reference probably is to that 'having all things in common' which is referred to immediately after (v.[44f]), and the nature and extent of which St. Luke explains more fully at a later stage (4[32]–5[4]). It is possible that the *koinōnia* was the regular expression for that 'community of goods' which was a marked feature of the Christianity of the first days, and which owed its origin not only to the unselfish enthusiasm of that Pentecostal period and the expectation of the Lord's imminent return, but to the actual needs of the poorer Christians in Jerusalem, cut off from the means of self-support by the social ostracism attendant on ex-communication from the synagogue (Jn 9[22, 34] 12[42] 16[2]).

2. The type of *koinōnia* described in Ac 2 seems to have disappeared very soon, but its place was taken by an organized *diakonia*, a daily 'distribution' to the poor (6[1, 2]). When the Church spread into a larger world free from the hostile influences of the synagogue, those social conditions were absent which in Jerusalem had seemed to make it necessary that Christ's followers should have all things in common. But it was a special feature of St. Paul's teaching that Christians everywhere were members one of another, sharers in each other's wealth whether material or spiritual. In particular he pressed upon the wealthier Gentile churches the duty of taking part in the *diakonia* carried on in Jerusalem in behalf of the poor saints. In this connexion we find him in 2 Co 8[4] using the striking expression 'the *koinōnia* of the *diakonia* ('the fellowship of the ministering,' AV) to the saints.' The Christians of Corinth might have fellowship with their brethren in Jerusalem by imparting to them out of their own abundance. Hence, by a natural process in the development of speech, *koinōnia*, from meaning a common participation and sharing, came to be applied to the gifts which enabled that participation to be realized. In Ro 15[26] and 2 Co 9[13], accordingly, the word is properly enough rendered 'contribution.' And yet in the Apostolic Church it could never be forgotten that a contribution for the poor brethren was a form of Christian fellowship.

3. From the first, however, *koinōnia* had a larger and deeper sense than those technical ones on which we have been dwelling. It was out of the consciousness of a common participation in certain great spiritual blessings that Christians were impelled to manifest their fellowship in these specific ways. According to St. Paul's teaching, those who believed in Christ enjoyed a common participation in Christ Himself which bound them to one another in a holy unity (1 Co 1[9]; cf v.[10ff]). In the great central rite of their faith this common participation in Christ, and above all in His death and its fruits, was visibly set forth: the cup of blessing was a 'participation' ('communion,' AV, RV, RSVm) in the blood of Christ; the broken bread a 'participation' in the body of Christ (1 Co 10[16]). Flowing again from this common participation in Christ, there was a common participation in the Holy Spirit, for it is from the love of God as manifested in the grace of Christ that there results that 'fellowship of the Holy Spirit' which is the strongest bond of unity and peace (2 Co 13[14], cf v.[11], Ph 2[1f]). Thus the fellowship of the Christian Church came to mean a fund of spiritual privilege which was common to all the members but also peculiar to them, so that the admission of a man to the fellowship or his exclusion from it was his admission to, or exclusion from, the Church of Christ itself. When the Jerusalem apostles gave 'the right hand of fellowship' to Paul and Barnabas (Gal 2[9]), that was a symbolic recognition on their part that these missionaries to the uncircumcision were true disciples and apostles of Christ, sharers with themselves in all the blessings of the Christian faith.

4. We have seen that in its root-meaning *koinōnia* is a partnership either in giving or in receiving. Hence it was applied to Christian duties and obligations as well as to Christian privileges. The right hand of fellowship given to Paul and Barnabas was not only a recognition of grace received in common, but mutual pledges of an Apostolic service to the circumcision on the one hand and the Gentiles on the other (Gal 2[9]). St. Paul thanks God for the 'partnership' of the Philippians in the furtherance of the gospel (Ph 1[5]), and prays on behalf of Philemon that the 'sharing' of his faith may become effectual (Phn 6), *i.e.* that the Christian sympathies and charities inspired by his faith may come into full operation. It is the same use of *koinōnia* that we find in He 13[16], where the rendering in RSV is: 'Do not neglect to do good and *to share what you have*.' Here also the *koinōnia* means the acts of charity that spring from Christian faith, with a special reference perhaps to the technical sense referred to above, as a sharing of one's material wealth with the poorer brethren.

5. In all the foregoing passages the *koinōnia* seems to denote a mutual sharing, whether in privilege or in duty, of Christians with one another. But there are some cases in which the 'fellowship' evidently denotes a more exalted partnership, the partnership of a Christian with Christ or with God. This is what meets us when St. Paul speaks in Ph 3[10] of the *koinōnia* of Christ's sufferings. He means a drinking of the cup of which Christ drank (cf Mt 20[22f]), a moral partnership with the Redeemer in His pains and tears (cf Ro 8[17]). But it is St. John who brings this higher *koinōnia* before us in the most absolute way when he writes, 'Our fellowship is with the Father and with his Son Jesus Christ' (1 Jn 1[3], cf v.[6]), and makes our fellowship one with another depend upon this previous fellowship with God (v.[7], cf v.[6]). Yet, though the *koinōnia* or fellowship is now raised to a higher power, it has still the same meaning as before. It is a mutual sharing, a reciprocal giving and receiving. And in his Gospel St. John sets the law of this fellowship clearly before us when he records the words of the Lord Himself, 'Abide in me, and I in you' (Jn 15[4]). The fellowship of the human and the Divine is a mutual activity, which may be summed up in the two words *grace* and *faith*. For grace is the spontaneous and unstinted Divine giving as revealed and mediated by Jesus Christ, while faith in its ideal form is the action of a soul which, receiving the Divine grace, surrenders itself without any reserve unto the Lord.

J. C. L.—**H. L. R.**

FENCE.—Ps 62[3] is the only occurrence of the substantive, and probably the word there has its modern meaning (Coverdale 'hedge'). But the participle **'fenced'** (used of a city; see also DEFENCED) always means 'fortified' (so RSV). See FORTIFICATION.

FERRET (*'anākāh*).—An unclean animal, Lv 11[30], RV, RSV **'gecko.'** Rabbinical writers suggest the hedgehog, but this is unlikely. See LIZARD.

FESTUS, PORCIUS.—Procurator of Judaea A.D. 60 to 62, after FELIX (q.v.). The date is important to NT studies as it fixes the time when the Apostle Paul was sent to Rome (Ac 25 f). An earlier date, such as the A.D. 56 of Eusebius, claims support from the acquittal of Felix through 'the importunate supplications of his brother Pallas' (Jos. *Ant.* xx. viii. 9 [182]); Pallas was dismissed as Claudius' financial secretary in A.D. 55. But the downgrading—by Seneca, not by Nero, who as yet took little interest in politics—does not seem to have affected the cordial relations with his imperial master for another six years. Felix bequeathed to Festus the prodigious task of curbing Messianism, which was to culminate in A.D. 66 in war with Rome. Even though historians have pictured Festus as less tyrannical in repressing civil disorders than his predecessor Felix, there appears to have been little difference in their methods. Josephus speaks of the arrest and execution of large numbers of Jewish patriots—' brigands,' he calls them—and the exterminating of ' a certain impostor along with his followers, who looked for God's miraculous deliverance in the desert ' (*BJ* II. xiv. 1 [271] ; *Ant.* xx. viii. 10 [188]). The friendship of Festus for Agrippa II., reflected in Ac 25^{13ff}, is confirmed by his siding with him against the Temple priesthood who had built a wall to prevent Agrippa from viewing Temple activities from a vantage point. Nero settled the controversy against Agrippa and Festus, ' in order to gratify Poppea, Nero's wife ' (*Ant.* xx. viii. 11 [195 f]). Josephus knew her personally. She had become the wife of Nero in A.D. 62.

J. S. K.

FETTER.—See CHAIN.

FEVER.—See MEDICINE.

FIERY SERPENT.—See SERPENT, SERAPHIM.

FIG (t^{e}'*ēnāh*).—The common fig, fruit of the *Ficus carica*, is cultivated from one end of Palestine to the other, especially in mountainous regions, occupying a place to-day as important as in Bible times. The failure of fig and grape harvest still brings distress (Jer 5^{17}, Hab 3^{17}). Although figs are all of one genus, the *fellahīn* distinguish many varieties according to quality and colour.

The summer foliage is thick, excelling other trees for its cool and grateful shade—particularly to the traveller at midday. In summer, owners of gardens may be seen sitting, like Nathanael, in the shadow of their fig trees. The references in Mic 4^{4}, Zec 3^{10} may be to this, or to the not uncommon custom of having fig trees overhang rural dwellings. But when erstwhile rural districts become urban the trees often fail to bear fruit. So too self-sown fig trees are usually barren and are known as wild or ' male.' Trees are of medium height, but some specimens reach to over 25 feet. The fruiting of the tree is interesting and peculiar and is naturally earlier in the plains. The trees, which during the winter months have lost all their leaves, begin putting forth the tender leaf buds about the end of March (Mk 13^{28f}, Mt 24^{32f}, Lk 21^{29ff}). At the junction of the old wood with these new leaves tiny figs may also appear, the branch being *hapalos* or full of sap. The little figs develop along with the leaves to about the size of a cherry ; but with every gust of wind the majority fall to the ground. These immature figs are known as *taksh*, and are eaten by the *fellahīn* and may even be on sale in the Jerusalem market. Unripe fruit of different kinds is not unwelcome to the Palestinian palate. These figs would be the *paggim* of Ca 2^{13} ; and perhaps the *olynthoi* of Rev 6^{13}. RSV calls these ' winter fruit,' which falls off because of the spring-time working of the sap. Van Dyck in his edition of the Arabic NT (1857) uses *suqat* (' droppings '), used also in respect of the unripe dates of palm trees. The AV ' untimely ' seems the most inclusive rendering. The *paggîm* which remain to reach ripeness in June are called *dafūr* (mentioned in Is 28^{4}, Jer 24^{2}, Hos 9^{10}, Mic 7^{1}, as *bikkûrāh*, a common Semitic root for anything ' early '). These, esteemed for their delicate flavour, may have the ripening process accelerated by the application of olive oil.

Already, however, the buds of the next crop begin to appear higher up the branches. These steadily develop and form the real harvest of the fig season, reaching its height in August. This Luke likens to the Kingdom of God. He knew the fig harvest in the eastern Mediterranean. In the much discussed ' miracle ' of our Lord (Mk $11^{12-14, 20f}$, Mt 21^{18ff}) there cannot have been the expectation of *dafūr*, or *olynthoi*—the latter would be untimely but not unripe. In April, however, the possibility of *taksh* is present (certainly in the Jerusalem area as has been noticed this century). The young leaves are on the fig trees. Any tree likely to bear fruit at all will have some *taksh*, though the proper season of figs ' is not yet.' Mark's Greek implies the possibility only. Such figs are not ripe, but would be reckoned edible by any Palestinian. They are a guarantee of the harvest to come. The tree in the gospel story had no promise of future usefulness. It was this condition that lent itself to the picture of the ' want of fruitfulness in the Jewish nation.' This tree was prejudged as ' barren.' It should be noted too that in May fig trees may be found round Jerusalem, which have dropped their green figs, so that none ripen as *dafūr*, and yet have no sign of the buds of the summer crop.

The fig is welcome as fruit and as medicine, not only fresh but dried. The fruit is threaded on to long strips for convenience. It is also pressed into a solid cake that can be cut in slices (Is 25^{18} 30^{12}, 1 Ch 12^{40}). A lump of such was used as a poultice for Hezekiah's boil (2 K 20^{7}, Is 28^{21}). Just as dates in this dried or ' lumpy ' condition are known as *'ajweh*, figs are called *quttain*. In many countries where figs are a staple diet when dried, they are packed as well as pressed for export. The generic Arabic word is *tīneh* (the Hebrew *'āleph* becoming a long vowel).

E. W. G. M.—E. F. F. B.

FILE.—Only 1 S 13^{21}, but the passage is very corrupt. The word probably means ' the act of filing,' ' sharpening,' and RSV renders ' the charge (sc for sharpening) was a pim.'

FILLET.—A technical term found in Ex 27^{10f} 36^{38} $38^{10-12, 17, 19, 28}$ for the silver rings which bound the pillars of the Tabernacle together.

FINE.—The verb ' to fine ' (modern ' refine ') is used in Job 28^{1} ' Surely there is a vein for silver, and a place for gold where they fine it ' (RV, RSV ' which they refine '). ' Fining pot ' occurs in Pr 17^{3} 27^{21} (AV, RV ; RSV ' crucible ') ; and ' finer ' in Pr 25^{4} (AV, RV ; RSV ' smith '). See REFINER.

FINES.—See CRIMES AND PUNISHMENTS, **8.**

FIR.—**1.** *b^{e}rôsh* is rendered ' fir tree ' in AV and RV (but *cypress* in RVm in many places), while RSV has normally ' **cypress** ' (q.v.), but ' fir ' in 2 S 6^{5} (RSVm), Ezk 27^{5} 31^{8}, Ps 104^{17}. The *b^{e}rôsh* was a tree of large growth (2 K 19^{23}, Ezk 31^{8}), evergreen (Hos 14^{8}), a chief element in the glory of Lebanon (Is 60^{13}), and associated with cedars (Ps 104^{16f}, Is 14^{8}, Zec 11^{2}). The timber of the *b^{e}rôsh* ranked with the cedar for house- and ship-building (1 K $5^{8, 10}$ etc.). Cypress is accepted by most modern authorities, but *b^{e}rôsh* may have included also several varieties of pine.

2. *'ōren* is rendered by ' fir ' in RV in Is 44^{14} (AV, RVm ' **ash** ' ; RSV reads *'erez* and renders ' cedar '). See also ASH.

E. W. G. M.—H. H. R.

FIRE.—See HOUSE, **7**, and next article.

FIREPAN.—**1.** A pan of bronze (Ex 27^{3} etc.), silver (Mishnah, *Yōma*, iv. 4), or gold (1 K 7^{50} etc.), for removing charcoal, and probably ashes also, from the altar of burnt-offering. According to the Mishnah (*loc. cit.*), the fire-pans or coal-pans were of various sizes, there given, and were each furnished with a long or a short handle. They seem, therefore, to have resembled ladles, or the now obsolete bed-warmers.

When used to hold live charcoal for the burning of incense the coal-pan becomes a **censer** (Lv 10^{1} 16^{12} etc.). Hence in Nu 4^{14}, 1 K 7^{50}, 2 Ch 4^{22} RV and RSV have ' firepans ' for AV ' censers,' there being no reference in these passages to incense. The same utensil was used for removing the burnt portions of the lamp-wicks of the golden ' candlestick ' or lamp-stand, although rendered snuff-dishes (AV, RV ; RSV ' trays '), for which Tyndale has rightly ' firepans.' See SNUFF DISHES.

2. In Zec 12^{6} RV there is mention of ' a pan (AV hearth) of fire ' ; in other words, a **brazier**. See COAL ; HOUSE, **7.** A. R. S. K.

FIRKIN.—See WEIGHTS AND MEASURES.

FIRMAMENT.—According to the Hebrew conception of the universe, the earth is surmounted by a rigid vault called the firmament, above which the waters of a heavenly ocean are spread. The Hebrew word for firmament, *rāḳîaʿ*, comes from a root meaning ' to beat out ' ; cf Ex 39^{3}, where it is used of beating out thin plates of gold. It was therefore thought of as a solid vault.

FIRSTBORN.—**1.** The **dedication of the firstborn** of men and beasts was probably a primitive nomadic custom, and therefore earlier than the offering of first-fruits, which could not arise until the Israelites had settled into agricultural life in Canaan. The origin of the belief that a peculiar value attached to the firstborn cannot be definitely traced ; but it would be a natural inference that what was valuable to the parent would be valuable to his God. And thus the word ' firstborn ' could be used figuratively of Israel as the firstborn of Y″ among the nations (Ex 4^{22}, cf Jer 31^{9}), and the seed of David among dynasties (Ps 89^{28}). The law of the dedication of the firstborn is found in JE (Ex 13^{11-16} $22^{29b, 30}$ 34^{19f}), D (Dt 15^{19-23}), P (Ex 13^{1f}, Nu $3^{11-13, 40-51}$ 18^{15-18}). It is not impossible that in very primitive times firstborn sons were sometimes actually sacrificed (cf 2 K 3^{27}, Mic 6^{7}), but the practice would soon grow up of ' redeeming ' them by money or payments in kind.

2. The firstborn (*bᵉkhōr*) enjoyed the **birthright** (*bᵉkhōrāh*). He succeeded his father as head of the family, and took the largest share of the property ; this was fixed in Dt 21^{17} as a ' double portion.' [In 2 Ch 21^{3} the principle of the birthright is extended to the succession to the throne. But this is a late passage, and it is not certain that the firstborn was necessarily the heir apparent]. If a man died without children, the heir was the firstborn of his widow by his brother or next-of-kin (Dt 25^{5-10}). The right of the firstborn, however, was often disturbed, owing to the jealousies and quarrels arising from the polygamy practised in Israel. The law in Dt 21^{15-17} is directed against the abuse. Reuben, although the son of Leah, the less favoured of Jacob's two wives, was considered the firstborn, and lost the right only because of his sin (Gn 49^{3f}, 1 Ch 5^{1}). But Ishmael was allowed no share at all in the father's property (Gn 21^{10}) ; and the superiority of Jacob over Esau (symbolizing the superiority of Israel over Edom) is described as having been foretold before their birth (25^{23}), and as brought about by Esau's voluntary surrender of the birthright (vv.$^{29-34}$). And other instances occur of the younger being preferred to the elder, *e.g.* Ephraim (48^{13-20}), Solomon (1 K 1), Shimri (1 Ch 26^{10}).

3. The **death of the firstborn** was the last of the punishments sent upon Egypt for Pharaoh's refusal to let the Israelites go. Moses gave him due warning (Ex 11^{4-8}), and on his continued refusal the stroke fell (12^{29f}). The event is referred to in Ps 78^{51} 105^{36} 135^{8} 136^{10}, He 11^{28}. It is probable (see PLAGUES OF EGYPT) that the stories of all the other plagues have been founded on historical occurrences, and that the Egyptians suffered from a series of ' natural ' catastrophes. If this is true of the first nine, it is reasonable to assume it for the last, and we may suppose that a pestilence raged which created great havoc, but did not spread to the Israelite quarter. The growth of the tradition into its present form must be explained by the ' aetiological ' interest of the Hebrew writer—the tendency to create idealized situations in a remote past for the purpose of explaining facts or institutions whose origin was forgotten. Thus the Feast of Booths was accounted for at a late date by the dwelling of the Israelites in booths after the Exodus (Lv 23^{43}), the Feast of Unleavened Cakes by the haste with which they departed from Egypt (Ex 12^{34} 13^{7f}), the Feast of the Passover by the passing over of the houses marked with blood at the destruction of the firstborn ($12^{12f, 23, 27}$). And similarly the singling out of the firstborn for destruction was itself connected with the ancient practice of offering to God annually in spring the firstlings of beasts. Moses demanded release in order to offer the sacrifice (10^{25f}), and because Pharaoh refused to allow them to offer their firstlings, Y″ took from the Egyptians their firstborn. This explanation, though not explicitly given, is implied in the close connexion of the dedication of the firstborn with the Passover (13^{11-13}, Dt 15^{19} 16^{1-8}). In a redactional passage (Ex 4^{22f}) a different explanation is offered. The death of the firstborn would be a punishment for refusal to release Israel, who was Y″'s firstborn.

4. In the NT the term ' firstborn ' (*prōtotokos*) is used of Christ (Ro 8^{29}, Col $1^{15, 18}$, He 1^{6}, Rev 1^{5}), and of Christians who have died (He 12^{23}) ; see the commentaries. A. H. McN.

FIRSTFRUITS.—See SACRIFICE AND OFFERING.

FISH would appear to have always been a favourite article of diet among the Hebrews (Nu 11^{5} and references in the Gospels), as it is to-day. Fish are found in enormous numbers in all the inland waters of Palestine, and especially in the Lake of Galilee, Lake Huleh, and the ' meadow lakes ' of Damascus. The extraordinary feature of these fish is the number of species peculiar to the Jordan valley. Out of a total of forty-three species found in the region, no fewer than fourteen are peculiar to this district. Many of these are quite small. The chief edible fish are members of the *Chromides* and of the *Cyprinidae* (carps). The cat-fish, *Clarias macracanthus*, not being a scaly fish, cannot be eaten by the Jews (Dt 14^{9}), though considered a delicacy by the Christians of Damascus. It is thought by some to be the ' bad fish ' of Mt 13^{47f}. In NT times fish-curing was extensively carried on at Taricheae on the Lake of Tiberias. Some of the native fish is still salted to-day. The ' *fish*-pools ' of Ca 7^{4} (AV ; RV, RSV ' pools ') and the ' ponds for *fish* ' in Is 19^{10} (AV ; RSV ' will be grieved,' cf RV) are both mistranslations. See also FOOD, **6.** E. W. G. M.

FISH GATE.—See JERUSALEM, GATES OF.

FITCHES.—**1.** *Ḳeṣaḥ* (Is $28^{25, 27}$), RVm **' black cummin '** (RSV **' dill '**), the seeds of the aromatic herb *Nigella sativa*, commonly used to-day in Palestine as a condiment, especially on the top of loaves of bread. The contrast between the staff for the ' fitches ' and the rod for the cummin is the more instructive when the great similarity of the two seeds is noticed. **2.** *kussemeth*, ' fitches ' in Ezk 4^{9} (AV ; AVm, RV, RSV ' spelt '), and ' rie ' in Ex 9^{32}, Is 28^{25} (AV ; RV and RSV ' spelt '). **Spelt** (*Triticum spelta*) is an inferior kind of wheat, the grains of which are peculiarly adherent to the sheath. E. W. G. M.

FLAG.—**1.** *'āḥû*, Job 8^{11}, is rendered ' flag ' in AV and RV (RSV ' reeds '). In Gn $41^{2, 18}$ the same word is rendered ' meadow ' in AV (RV, RSV ' reed grass '). It denotes marsh grasses or reeds. **2.** *sûph* is rendered by ' flags ' in AV and RV in Ex $2^{3, 5}$ (RSV ' reeds '), Is 19^{6} (RSV ' rushes '). In Jon 2^{5} it is rendered by ' weeds ' in AV, RV, and RSV, and *yam sûph*, or ' Reed Sea,' is the Hebrew name which is rendered ' Red Sea.' The word denotes sedgy plants.

FLAGON.—This word occurs five times in AV, but in only one of these instances is the translation retained by RV and RSV, namely, Is 22^{24}. Here it is a large earthenware storage jar. The same word is elsewhere rendered by AV and RV ' bottle ' and by RSV ' jar ' (*e.g.* Jer 48^{12}). On the other hand RV and RSV introduce ' flagons ' in two instances where AV has ' covers,' namely, Ex 25^{29} 37^{16}. To these RSV adds Nu 4^{7}, where RV has ' cups ' (AV ' covers ') for the same word. In the remaining four instances where AV has ' flagons ' (2 S 6^{19}, 1 Ch 16^{3}, Hos 3^{1}, Ca 2^{5}), the meaning of the Hebrew word is a ' pressed cake . . . composed of meal, oil, and *dibs* ' (W. R. Smith, *OTJC*[1] 434, n. 7). Hence RV and RSV render by ' cake of **raisins**,' or ' raisins ' in all these cases.

FLASK.—1. Hebrew *pakh*, 2 K $9^{1, 3}$ (AV **'box'**; RV **'vial'**). The same word is rendered 'vial' in 1 S 10^{1} in AV, RV, and RSV. **2.** *baḳbūḳ*, Jer $19^{1, 10}$ (AV, RV 'bottle'). The same word is rendered 'jar' in 1 K 14^{3} (AV, RV 'cruse'). **3.** Greek *angeion*, Mt 25^{4} (AV, RV 'vessel'). **4.** *alabastron*='alabaster flask,' Lk 7^{37} (so RVm; AV 'alabaster box'; RV 'alabaster cruse'). The same word is rendered 'alabaster jar' in Mt 26^{7}, Mk 14^{3} (AV and RV as in Lk 7^{37}).

FLAX (*pishtāh*).—The plant *Linum usitatissimum*, and the prepared fibres used for making linen. It was early cultivated in Palestine (Jos 2^{6}); the failure of the flax was one of God's judgments (Hos 2^{9}). The plant is about two to three feet high, with pretty blue flowers; the flax is said to be 'bolled' (RSV 'in bud'; Ex 9^{31}) when the seed vessels reach maturity and the plant is ready for gathering. The stalks were dried on the housetops (Jos 2^{6}), and then soaked in water and the fibre combed out (Is 19^{9} RV, RSV). The 'tow' of Is 43^{17} (AV; RV 'flax,' RSV 'wick') is teased-out flax. The oil of the seeds is the well-known linseed oil.
E. W. G. M.

FLEA (*parʿōsh*).—The common flea, *Pulex irritans*, is a universal pest in Palestine. It is mentioned in 1 S 24^{14} and in AV and RV in 26^{20} (RSV has 'my life'). Fleas are present in incredible numbers in the dust of caves to which goats resort. RVm has 'fleas' for 'lice' (AV, RV) in Ex 8^{16} (RSV 'gnats').

FLESH.—In the OT man is flesh, *bāśār*; animals also are flesh. What is not flesh is God or belongs to His celestial realm of 'spirit' (Is 31^{3}). The soul or *nephesh* of man is not independent of his flesh, nor is it a governing power active upon the flesh; rather it is the life of the flesh, the blood, the self of the fleshly person. Sometimes flesh and soul come very close together, and what happens to one happens to the other (Ps 84^{2} 16^{9f}); there is no soul without flesh, but they can be distinguished. The flesh is not individualized, but communities share their flesh; man and woman in marriage become one flesh; a family shares its flesh, 'all flesh' is all humanity, or indeed all living creation. The term 'body' is almost lacking in the OT (apart from a corpse, for which words exist), and we hear rather of the part of the man which is especially active, hand or ear or eye as it may be, or of the flesh of a group of men in common. There is no suggestion that human existence is sinful because it is fleshly; on the contrary, it could not exist except in flesh, and man and woman were flesh in the garden of Eden (Gn 2^{23f}). But at an early stage all flesh had corrupted its way (Gn 6^{12} etc.). All flesh then is living creation seen as other than God; upon all flesh He executes judgment, Is 66^{16}. But flesh as such is in no way incapable of finding communion with God, Ps 16^{9}. Flesh is weak and mortal compared with spirit, Gn 6^{3}, Job 34^{15}; but God pities man because he is flesh, Ps 78^{39}. God so acts that all flesh may see and know, Is 40^{5}, Ezk 21^{5}.

The word is of course very frequent for flesh as food, what we would call meat.

In Rabbinic Judaism 'flesh and blood' is a common designation for mankind; cf Sir 14^{18}. In the Qumrân texts man is often called 'flesh,' and in statements of the frailty of man and his weakness compared with God this is often associated with the term 'clay.' In the *Manual of Discipline*, xi. 9, 'I belong to mankind of evil, to the company of flesh of iniquity'; xi. 12 considers 'if I stumble in the iniquity of flesh.' Flesh is a realm not only of weakness in comparison with God but of proneness to sin against Him. The OT contrast of flesh and spirit is retained, but is complicated because there are two spirits of truth and error ruling in men. The member of the community, redeemed and secured, still feels his belonging to weak and sinful flesh. Evil meanwhile has a hidden seat in the flesh, but at the end of the period of evil God (*Manual*, iv. 20) 'will purify with his truth all the deeds of man and refine for himself the frame of each man, to consume all spirit of iniquity from the inward parts of his flesh.' By submission of soul to God's statutes 'his flesh will be cleansed, that he may be sprinkled with water for impurity' (iii. 8–9). It is impossible here to distinguish 'moral,' 'neutral,' and 'physical' senses of the word; the whole point is that these run into one another and belong together, though one aspect may be more prominent at any time.

In the NT we have 'flesh and blood' again for man as he is, with his own resources, in contrast to God (Mt 16^{17}, 1 Co 15^{50}). The being of mankind is flesh, and the incarnation is the word becoming flesh (Jn 1^{14}). The continuities and relationships of man are flesh, *e.g.* kinship (Ro 4^{1}). On the other hand, as in OT flesh can be contrasted with spirit and seen as the typically sinful continuum of human life, so that the mind or aspiration of the flesh is enmity against God, Ro 8^{7}. But this fleshly sinfulness does not simply mean bodily sins (sexual or greedy appetites) as we would call them, but mental attitudes, Gal 5^{19-21}. In Ephesians evil can have 'spiritual' elements, 6^{12}, so that there is no question of flesh as such being evil, just because it is not spirit (cf also 2 Co 7^{1}).

In Paul 'body' and 'flesh' are related but are not the same. We have 'body of sin' and 'flesh of sin,' Ro 6^{6} 8^{3}; flesh and body are alike involved in sin, 8^{13}; the body dies through sin, 8^{10}. But the resurrection is thought of as a renewal and transformation of the body rather than the flesh (1 Co 15), and the Church is the body and not the flesh of Christ; its knowledge of Christ is no longer 'according to flesh' as it once was, 2 Co 5^{16} (RSV 'from a human point of view').

Flesh is related to sin, to death, and to law (Ro 7^{5}). Christ in His passion submitted Himself to the power of these, in a likeness made of flesh of sin, literally, Ro 8^{3}, in His body of flesh, Col 1^{22}; thus He condemned sin in the flesh and defeated it, Ro 8^{3}. His fleshly coming and suffering thus overcomes the sin which is seated in the flesh. The risen Christ after His triumph is no ghost, but has flesh and bones, Lk 24^{39}; but the resurrection is more commonly understood through the term 'body.' Following Him, Christians have crucified the flesh and its lusts, Gal 5^{24}, and can no longer live for the flesh but for and by the Spirit. But the OT understanding of fleshly community and solidarity remains for the relation of man and wife, Christ and Church, Eph 5^{22-33}.
J. Ba.

FLESH-HOOK.—The flesh-hooks (RSV 'forks') of bronze and gold mentioned in connexion with the Tabernacle (Ex 27^{3} 38^{3}) and Temple (1 Ch 28^{17}, 2 Ch 4^{16}) were probably three-pronged forks, like that used by the priest's servant at Shiloh (1 S 2^{13}).

FLESHLY, FLESHY.—There is a distinction preserved in the AV between these words. 'Fleshly' is that which belongs to the flesh, *carnal*, as Col 2^{18} 'fleshly mind,' RSV 'sensuous,' as opposed to 'spiritually minded' (cf Ro 8^{6}). 'Fleshy' is that which is made of flesh, *tender*, as 2 Co 3^{3} 'written . . . not on tablets of stone but on tablets of human hearts' (RSV).

FLESHPOTS (Ex 16^{3}).—See House, **9.**

FLINT.—See Mining and Metals.

FLOAT, 1 K 5^{9} (AV), 2 Ch 2^{16} (RV).—See Ships and Boats.

FLOCK.—See Sheep.

FLOOD.—In addition to *mabbûl* (*i.e.* the flood in the time of Noah, see Deluge) several words for river and stream are translated by flood in AV, *e.g.* Is 44^{3} 'floods upon the dry ground' (RV and RSV 'streams'). In a few psalms and hymns RV (and less frequently RSV) has retained 'flood' or 'floods' (Ps 24^{2} 93^{3} 98^{8}, Ex 15^{8}, Ca 8^{7}, Jon 2^{3}), but mostly RV and RSV use 'river' or 'stream.'

Where it occurs in the AV it refers sometimes to the Euphrates, Jos $24^{2, 14f}$ (where RSV has 'Euphrates'), sometimes to the Nile, Jer 46^{7f}, Am 8^{8} 9^{5} (RSV 'Nile'), and perhaps also the Jordan in Ps 66[6]. In Ps 69[2] the word used is *shibbōleth* (which the Ephraimites pronounced *sibbōleth*); AV and RV have 'floods,' RSV 'flood.' L. H. B.

FLOOR.—Used in AV (*a*) in the primary sense of a house-floor, and (*b*) in the secondary sense of a threshing-floor, the Hebrew words for which are quite distinct. Under (*a*) we have the earthen floor of the Temple, 1 K 6[15] (see HOUSE, **4**). By 'from floor to floor,' 7[7] (RV), is meant 'from floor to ceiling,' a sense implied in the better reading 'from floor to rafters' (RSV); cf 6[15] (RSV). In Am 9[3] our EV have obscured the figure 'the floor of the sea.'

(*b*) Where 'floor' occurs in the sense of 'threshing-floor' (see AGRICULTURE, **3**), the latter has been substituted by RV except in three passages (Gn 50[11], Is 21[10], Jl 2[24]). In two of these (Gn 50[11], Jl 2[24]) RSV has 'threshing floor,' but in the third (Is 21[10]) it substitutes 'my winnowed one' for 'corn of my floor.' The same word (*gōren*) appears as **barnfloor** (2 K 6[27] AV; RV, RSV 'threshing floor') and **cornfloor** (Hos 9[1] AV, RV; RSV 'threshing floor'). A. R. S. K.

FLOTE, 2 Ch 2[16] (AV).—See SHIPS AND BOATS.

FLOUR.—See BREAD, FOOD, **2**, MILL.

FLOWERS.—**1.** *nēṣ*, Gn 40[10], used of vine blossom. **2.** *niṣṣāh*, Job 15[33], used of olive blossom. **3.** *niṣṣān*, Ca 2[12], used of flowers generally. **4.** *peraḥ*, Ex 25[33], Nu 17[8], 1 K 7[26], Is 5[24] 18[5], Nah 1[4], used of buds (including those of Aaron's rod) or of the flowers in the ornamentation of the Tabernacle or the Temple. **5.** *ṣiṣ*, Nu 17[8], Is 28[1, 4] 40[6], Job 14[2], used of the flowers on Aaron's rod or of flowers generally, usually with some reference to their ephemeral nature. All of these are general terms. For specific flowers see under their individual names. Flowers are one of the attractive features of Palestine; they come in the early spring (Ca 2[12]), but fade all too soon, the brilliant display being a matter of but a few short weeks. Hence they are an appropriate symbol of the evanescence of human life (Job 14[2], Ps 103[15] etc.). The 'lilies of the field' of Mt 6[28] may have been a comprehensive term for the brilliant and many-coloured anemones, the irises, the gladioli, etc., which lend such enchantment to the hillsides in March and April. E. W. G. M.

FLUTE.—See MUSIC AND MUSICAL INSTRUMENTS.

FLUX.—The expression 'a bloody flux' (1611 'bloody-flixe') is used in AV for Greek *dysenterion* (Ac 28[8]; RV and RSV 'dysentery'). This translation is first found in Wycliffe, who offers the alternative 'dissenterie, or flix.' See MEDICINE.

FLY.—**1.** *zᵉbhûbh*, Ec 10[1], Is 7[18]; also Baal-zebub (q.v.). **2.** *'ārōbh*, Ex 8[21ff], Ps 78[45] 105[31], the insects of one of the plagues of Egypt, thought by some to have been cockroaches. Flies of many kinds, mosquitoes, 'sand-flies,' etc., swarm in Palestine and Egypt. In summer any sweet preparation left uncovered is at once defiled by flies falling into it (Ec 10[1]). Flies carry ophthalmia and infect food with the micro-organisms of other diseases, *e.g.* cholera, enteric fever, etc. They frequently deposit their eggs in unclean wounds and discharging ears, and these eggs develop into maggots. Special flies, in Africa at any rate, carry the *trypanosoma*, which produce fatal disease in cattle and 'sleeping sickness' in man. Mosquitoes, which may have been included in the *'ārōbh* (the 'swarms of flies') in Egypt, are now known to be the carriers of the poison of malaria, the greatest scourge of parts of Palestine. E. W. G. M.

FODDER (*bᵉlîl*).—Job 6[5] (AV, RV, RSV) 24[6] (RSV; AV 'corn,' RV 'provender'), Jg 19[21] (RV; AV, RSV 'provender'). See PROVENDER.

FOLK.—This English word is used in the NT indefinitely for 'persons,' there being no word in the Greek (Mk 6[5], Jn 5[3], Ac 5[16]). But in the OT the word has the definite meaning of *nation* or *people*, even Pr 30[26] 'The conies are but a feeble folk,' having this meaning. The word is found in RSV only in Jer 6[11] ('old folk') 25[20] ('foreign folk'). In the metrical version of Ps 100[3], 'flock' should be 'folk,' corresponding to 'people' in the prose version. So the author wrote—

'The Lord ye know is God in dede
With out our aide, he did us make:
We are his folck, he doth us fede,
And for his shepe, he doth us take.'

FOLLOW.—This English verb means now no more than to come after, but in older English it was often equivalent to pursue. Now it states no more than the relative place of two persons, formerly it expressed purpose or determination. Tyndale translates Lv 26[17] 'ye shal flee when no man foloweth you,' and Dt 28[22] 'they [the diseases named] shall folowe the, intyll thou perishe.' In AV 'to follow' is sometimes 'to imitate,' as 2 Th 3[7] 'For yourselves know how ye ought to follow us' (RV, RSV 'imitate').

FOOD.—This article will deal only with foodstuffs, in other words with the principal articles of food among the Hebrews in Bible times, the preparation and serving of these being reserved for the complementary article MEALS.

1. The food of a typical Hebrew household in historical times was almost exclusively vegetarian. For all but the very rich the use of meat was confined to some special occasion—a family festival, the visit of an honoured guest, a sacrificial meal at the local sanctuary, and the like. According to the author of the Priest's Code, indeed, the food of men and beasts alike was exclusively herbaceous in the period before the Deluge (Gn 1[29f]), permission to eat the flesh of animals, under stipulation as to drawing off the blood, having been first accorded to Noah (9[3ff]). In Isaiah's vision of the future, when 'the lion shall eat straw like the ox' (11[7]), a return is contemplated to the idyllic conditions of the first age of all.

Some idea of the basic foods of the ancient Hebrew is afforded by the Gezer calendar, a small limestone plaque of *c* the 10th cent. B.C., upon which are listed, perhaps by a schoolboy, the chief crops and the months in which the farmer worked them. Aside from flax, all mentioned are food crops: olives, grapes, summer fruit (figs, pomegranates, etc.), barley, other grains (wheat, spelt, etc.), and 'late planting' (summer crops: millet, sesame, vegetables, etc.). These items supplied the staple diet of the average Israelite. The growth of luxury under the monarchy (cf Am 6[4ff] and similar passages) is well illustrated by a comparison of 2 S 17[28f] with 1 K 4[22f]. In the former there is brought for the entertainment of David and his followers 'wheat, barley, meal, parched grain, beans and lentils, honey and curds and sheep and cheese from the herd'; while, according to the latter passage, Solomon's daily provision was 'thirty measures of fine flour and sixty measures of meal, ten fat oxen, and twenty pasture-fed cattle, a hundred sheep, besides harts, gazelles, roebucks, and fatted fowl.'

2. The first place in the list of Hebrew foodstuffs must be given to the various cereals included under the general name of 'corn'—in RSV, ARV always 'grain'—the two most important of which were **wheat** and **barley. Millet** (Ezk 4[9]) and **spelt** (see FITCHES, RIE), are only casually mentioned. The most primitive method of using corn was to pluck the 'fresh ears' (Lv 23[14] ARV, RV, 2 K 4[42]) and remove the husk by rubbing in the hands (Dt 23[25], Mt 12[1] etc.). When bruised in a mortar, these ears yielded the 'crushed grain' of Lv 2[14, 16] RSV. A favourite practice in all periods down to the present day has been to roast the ears on an iron plate or otherwise. The result is the **parched grain** so frequently mentioned in OT. Parched corn and bread with a light sour wine furnished the midday meal of Boaz's reapers (Ru 2[14]). The chief use, however, to which wheat and barley were put was to supply the household with **bread** (q.v.). Wheaten and barley **'meal'** (RV) were prepared by rubbing the grain between two stones, frequently pieces of coarse black basalt. Excavations show that these simple rubbing stones survived the introduction of the quern or hand-mill (for references to illustrations of both, see MILL). The **'fine flour'** of our EV was obtained from the coarser variety by bolting the latter with a fine sieve. **Barley bread** (Jg 7[13], Jn 6[9, 13]) was the usual bread, indeed the principal food, of the poorer classes. (For details of break-making, see BREAD). The word rendered 'coarse meal' in Nu 15[20], Neh 10[37], Ezk 44[30] (RSV, RV, and ARVm) is obscure; some believe that it denoted flour mixed with water, *i.e.* 'dough' (so AV, RV) in the first stage of making.

3. Next in importance to wheat and barley as food-stuffs may be ranked the seeds of various members of the pulse family (**Leguminosae**), although only two leguminous plants (**lentils** and **beans**) are mentioned by name in OT. The **pulse** (AV, RV) of Dn 1[12, 16] denotes edible herbs generally (so RVm); RSV reads 'vegetables.' The 'parched (pulse)' of 2 S 17[28] (AV, RV), on the other hand, is due to a mistaken rendering of the word for 'parched grain' here repeated by a copyist's slip. Of red lentils Jacob made his fateful **pottage** (Gn 25[29ff]), probably a stew in which the lentils were flavoured with onions and other ingredients, as is done at the present day in Syria. Lentils and beans (the 'beans' of OT were actually coarse horse-beans) were occasionally ground to make bread (Ezk 4[9]).

Next to its fish, the Hebrews in the wilderness looked back wistfully on the 'cucumbers, melons, leeks, onions and garlic' of Egypt (Nu 11[5]), all of them subsequently cultivated by them in Palestine. It is to the agricultural treatises of the Mishnah, however, that the student must turn for fuller information regarding the rich supplies available either for a 'dinner of herbs' (Pr 15[17]) alone, or for supplementing a meat diet. At least four varieties of bean, for example, are named, also the chickpea (which the Vulgate substitutes for the 'parched pulse' above referred to), various species of chicory and endive —the **bitter herbs** of the Passover ritual (Ex 12[8])— mustard (Mt 13[31]), radish, and many others.

4. Passing now to the 'food-trees' (Lv 19[23]), we may follow the example of Jotham in his parable (Jg 9[8ff]), and begin with the **olive,** although as it happens, the olive 'berry' (Is 17[6]) is never expressly mentioned in Scripture as an article of diet. Apart, however, from their extensive use in furnishing **oil** (q.v.), itself an invaluable aid in the preparation of food, olives were not only eaten in the fresh state, but were at all times preserved for later use by being soaked in brine. Such pickled olives were, and still are, used as a relish with bread by rich and poor alike.

Next to the olive in rank, Jotham's parable places the fig tree, whose 'sweetness' and 'good fruit' it extols (Jg 9[11]). The great economic importance of the **fig** need not be emphasized. From Is 28[4], Jer 24[2] it appears that the 'first ripe fig,' *i.e.* the early fig which appears on last year's wood, was regarded as a special delicacy. The bulk of the year's fruit was dried for use out of the season, as was the case also among the Greeks and Romans, by whom dried figs were the most extensively used of all fruits. When pressed in a mould they formed **'cakes of figs'** (1 S 25[18], 1 Ch 12[40]). A fig cake, it will be remembered, was prescribed by Isaiah as a poultice (AV 'plaister,' RSV 'apply it') for Hezekiah's boil (Is 38[21] = 2 K 20[7] RV). In the Râs Shamra texts it is recommended as a medicine for horses!

With the fig Hebrew writers constantly associate the **grape,** the 'fruit of the vine' (Mt 26[29] ||). Like the former, grapes were not only enjoyed in their natural state, but also, by exposure to the sun after being gathered, dried into **raisins,** the 'dried grapes' of Nu 6[3]. In this form they were better suited for the use of travellers and soldiers (1 S 25[18], 1 Ch 12[40]). The word in 2 S 6[19], Is 16[7], Hos 3[1] rendered by AV 'flagon of wine' or) 'foundation'!) is best understood as denoting a 'raisin-cake' (so RV, RSV). By far the greater part of the produce of the vineyards was used for the manufacture of **wine** (q.v.). Probably 'honey' on occasion is actually a syrup of figs or grapes or other fruit; see HONEY.

Dates are only once mentioned in AV, and that without any justification, as the marginal alternative of 'honey,' 2 Ch 31[5]; yet the 'palm tree' is mentioned a number of times (*e.g.* Ps 92[12], Jl 1[12]), and from the Mishnah we learn that dates, like the fruits already discussed, were not only eaten as they came from the palm, but were dried in clusters and also pressed into cakes for convenience of transport.

For other less important fruits, such as the pomegranate, the *tappûaḥ*—the 'apple' of EV, according to others the *quince* (see APPLE)—the fruit of the sycamore or fig-mulberry, associated with Amos the prophet, and the **husks** (Lk 15[16]), or rather pods of the carob tree (RSV 'pods'), reference must be made to the separate articles. To these there fall to be added here **almonds** and **nuts** of more than one variety.

5. As compared with the wide range of foods supplied by the cereals, vegetables and fruits above mentioned, the supply of flesh-food was confined to such animals and birds as were technically described as 'clean.' For this important term, and the principles underlying the distinction between clean and unclean, see CLEAN AND UNCLEAN. The clean animals admitted to the table according to the 'official' lists in Lv 11[2-23], Dt 14[4-20] (conveniently arranged in parallel columns for purposes of comparison in Driver's *Deut. ad. loc.*), may be ranged under the two categories, **domestic animals,** which alone were admitted as sacrifice to the 'table of Yahweh' (Mal 1[7, 12]), and **game.** The former comprised the two classes of 'the flock,' *i.e.* sheep and goats, and 'the herd.'

The flesh of the **goat,** and especially of the 'kid of the goats,' was eaten by the ancient Hebrews as it is by the present inhabitants of Palestine, though the goat was more valued then, as to-day, for its milk. A kid, as less valuable than a well-fleeced lamb, was the most frequent and readiest victim, especially among the poor, a fact which gives point to the complaint of the Elder Son in the parable (Lk 15[29f]). The thrice-repeated injunction against boiling a kid in its mother's milk (Ex 23[19] ||) must be understood in the light of a reference in the Râs Shamra texts to cooking a kid in milk, as a prohibition of an otherwise unknown Canaanite sacrificial custom.

Regarding the **sheep** as food, it may be noted that in the case of the fat-tailed breed the tail was regarded as a great delicacy (cf 1 S 9[24], where the words 'upper portion' [RSV], 'that which was upon it' [AV, RV] should be translated 'the fat tail') and as such, according to the Priest's Code at least, had to be offered with certain other portions of the fat (see **10** below) upon the altar (Ex 29[22], Lv 3[9], both RV and RSV). Of the neat **cattle,** the flesh of females as well as of males was eaten, the Hebrews not having that repugnance to cow's flesh which distinguished the Egyptians of antiquity, as it does the Hindus of to-day. Calves, of course, supplied the daintiest food, and might be taken directly from the herd, as was done by Abraham (Gn 18[7], cf 1 K 4[23]), or specially fattened for the table. The 'fatted calf' of Lk 15[23] will be at once recalled, also the 'fatlings' and the 'stalled,' *i.e.* stall-fed (RSV 'fatted') ox (Pr 15[17]) of OT. 'One ox and six choice sheep' were Nehemiah's daily portion (Neh 5[18]); Solomon's has already been given (**1**). From the females of the herd and of the flock (Dt 32[14]), especially from the she-goat (Pr 27[27]), in nomadic society also from the milch-camel (Gn 32[15]), came the supply of **milk** and its preparations, butter, curds, and cheese, for which see MILK.

Of the seven species of game mentioned in Dt 14[15], it is evident from 12[15] that the **gazelle** and the **hart** were the typical animals of the chase hunted for the sake of their flesh. They are also named along with the **roebuck** in Solomon's list, 1 K 4[23]. One or more of these, doubtless, supplied the game (AV, RV 'venison') from which Esau was wont to make the 'savoury food' which his father loved (Gn 25[28] 27[5f]). Among the unclean animals which were taboo to the Hebrews the most interesting are the swine (Lv 11[7], Dt 14[8]; cf Mt 8[30ff]||), the camel, the hare, and the ass (but see 2 K 6[25]).

6. In the Deuteronomic list above cited, the permitted and forbidden quadrupeds are followed by this provision regarding **fish**: 'of all that are in the waters you may eat these: whatever has fins and scales you may eat, and whatever does not have fins and scales you shall not eat; it is unclean for you' (Dt 14[9f] RSV; cf Lv 11[9-12]). No particular species of fish is named in OT, either as food or otherwise, although no fewer than forty-three species are said to be found in the Jordan system alone. Yet we may be sure that the fish which the Hebrews enjoyed in Egypt 'for nothing' (Nu 11[5] RSV) had their successors in Canaan. Indeed, it is usual to find in the words of Dt 33[19], 'they suck the affluence of the seas,' a contemporary reference to the fisheries possessed by the tribes of Zebulun (cf Gn 49[13]) and Issachar. In the days of Nehemiah a considerable trade in cured fish was carried on by Tyrian, *i.e.* Phoenician, merchants with Jerusalem (Neh 13[16]), where a market must have been held at or near the Fish-gate (3[3] etc.). In still later times, as is so abundantly testified by the Gospels and Josephus, the Sea of Galilee was the centre of a great fishing industry. In addition to the demand for fresh fish, a thriving trade was done in the salting and curing of fish for sale throughout the country. The fish of our Lord's two miracles of feeding were almost certainly of this kind, fish cleaned, split open, salted, and finally dried in the sun, having been at all times a favourite form of provision for a journey.

7. Regarding the 'clean' **birds,** all of which were allowed as food (Dt 14[11]), no definite criterion is prescribed, but a list of prohibited species is given (Lv 11[13-19], Dt 14[11-18]), mostly birds of prey, including the bat. In the ritual of various sacrifices, however, **pigeons** and **turtle doves,** and these only, find a place, and are therefore to be reckoned as 'clean' for ordinary purposes as well. The early domestication of these birds is shown by the reference to the 'windows' of the dove-cotes in Is 60[8], while the Mishnah has much to say regarding various breeds of domestic pigeons, their 'towers,' feeding, etc. Domestic **poultry** and eggs did not become common until the Persian period (2 Es 1[30], Mt 23[37] 26[34]||), although a drawing of a rooster on a seal of *c* 600 B.C. found at *Tell en-Naṣbeh*, 8 m. N. of Jerusalem, shows that chickens were known earlier. Though it is not certain that the **fatted fowl** for Solomon's table (1 K 4[23]) were **geese** as some have supposed, geese together with poultry and house-pigeons are frequently named in the Mishnah. Roast goose was a favourite food of the Egyptians, and has, indeed, been called their national dish.

Among the edible game birds mention is made of the **partridge** and the **quail** (qq.v.). Most or all of these were probably included in the 'fowls' (literally birds) which appeared on Nehemiah's table (5[18]). The humble **sparrow** (Mt 10[29], Lk 12[6]) would have been beneath the dignity of a Persian governor. The **eggs** of all the clean birds were also important articles of food (Dt 22[6], Is 10[14], Lk 11[12]).

8. Under the head of animal food must also be reckoned the various edible insects enumerated, Lv 11[22f], apparently four species of the **locust** family (see LOCUST). Locusts were regarded as delicacies by the Assyrians, formed part of the food of John the Baptist (Mt 3[4], Mk 1[6]), and are still eaten by the Arabs. By the latter they are prepared in various ways, one of the commonest being to remove the head, legs, and wings, and to fry the body in *samn* or clarified butter. Locusts may also be preserved by salting. This is the place, further, to refer to the article HONEY for information regarding that important article of food.

9. Nothing has as yet been said on the subject of **condiments. Salt,** the chief of condiments, will be treated separately (see SALT). Of the others it has been said that, 'before pepper was discovered or came into general use, seeds like cummin, the coriander, etc., naturally played a more important role.' Of these the greyish-white seeds of the **coriander** are named in Ex 16[31], Nu 11[7]; these are still used in the East as a spice in bread-making and to flavour sweetmeats. Similarly the seeds of the **black cummin** (Is 28[25] RVm) are sprinkled on bread like caraway seeds among ourselves. For the other condiments, **mint, anise** (RSV 'dill'), **cummin,** and **rue,** see the separate articles; to these may be added **mustard** (Mt 13[31]). Pepper is first mentioned in the Mishnah. The **caper-berry** (Ec 12[5] RV, ARVm) was eaten before meals as an appetizer, rather than used as a condiment.

10. Reference has already been made to the restrictions laid upon Hebrews in the matter of animal food by the all-important distinction between 'clean' and 'unclean,' as applied not only to quadrupeds, but to fish, birds, and winged creatures generally. All creatures technically 'unclean' were taboo, to use the modern term (see ABOMINATION, CLEAN AND UNCLEAN). There were other food taboos, however, which require a brief mention here. The chief of these was the absolute prohibition of the **blood** even of 'clean' beasts and birds, which occupies a prominent place in all the stages of the Hebrew dietary legislation (Dt 12[16, 23, 25] 15[23], Lv 17[10ff] [H] 3[17] 7[26f] [P], etc.). Its antiquity is attested by the incident recorded 1 S 14[32ff]. According to P, indeed, it is coeval with the Divine permission to eat animal food (Gn 9[4]). All sacrificial animals had therefore to be drained of their blood before any part could be offered to God or man, and so with all animals slaughtered for domestic use only (Dt 12[15f]), and with all game of beast and bird taken in the chase (Lv 17[13]).

Closely associated with the above (cf Lv 3[17]) is the taboo imposed upon certain specified portions of the intestinal **fat** of the three sacrificial species, the ox, the sheep, and the goat (Lv 3[3ff] 7[22ff] etc.), to which, as we have seen, the fat tail of the sheep was added. There was forbidden, further, the flesh of every animal that had died a natural death (Dt 14[21], Lv 17[15]), or had been done to death by a beast of prey (Ex 22[31], Lv 17[15]); in short, all flesh was rigidly taboo except that of an animal which had been ritually slaughtered as above prescribed. For another curious taboo, see Gn 32[32]. The Jews of the present day eat only such meat as has been certified by their own authorities as *kosher*, *i.e.* as having been killed in the manner prescribed by Rabbinic law.

The intimate association in early times between flesh-food and sacrifice explains the abhorrence of the Hebrew for all food prepared by the heathen, as illustrated by Daniel (Dn 1[8]), Judas Maccabaeus (2 Mac 5[27]), Josephus (*Vita* 3 [14]), and their associates (cf also Ac 15[20, 29], 1 Co 8[1-10] 10[19, 28]).

11. A word finally as to the sources of the Hebrew food-supply. Under the simpler conditions of early times the exclusive source of supply was the householder's own herd (Gn 18[7]) or flock (27[9]), his vineyard and oliveyard or his 'vegetable garden' (1 K 21[2]). As the Hebrews became dwellers in cities their foodstuffs naturally became more and more articles of commerce. The bakers, for example, who gave their name to a street in Jerusalem (Jer 37[21]), not only fired the dough prepared in private houses, as at the present day, but, doubtless, baked and sold bread to the public, as did their successors in the 1st and 2nd cents. (see Mishnah, *passim*). An active trade in food is attested for Nehemiah's day (13[15f]), when we hear of the 'fish gate' (3[3]) and the 'sheep gate' (3[1]), so named doubtless, from their respective markets. The disciples were accustomed to buy provisions as they journeyed through the land (Jn 4[8]; cf 13[29]); and Corinth, we may be sure, was not the only city of the time that had a meat-market (1 Co 10[25]). In Jerusalem, again, cheese was to be bought in the Cheesemakers' Valley (Tyropoeon), and oil at the oil-merchants (Mt 25[9]), and so on. In the early morning especially, the streets near the city gates on the north and west, which led to the country, were doubtless then, as now, transformed into market-places, lined with men and women offering for sale the produce of their farms and gardens. Even the outer court of the Temple itself had in our Lord's day become a 'house of trade' (Jn 2^{16}). A. R. S. K.—**J. Br.**

FOOL.—The Hebrew language is rich in words which express various kinds of folly. **1.** The *k^esîl* is glib of tongue, 'his mouth is his ruin' (Pr 18^{7}; cf 9^{13} 14^{33}); in Ec 5^{1f} 'the sacrifice of fools' is offered by him who is rash with his mouth. But such an one is 'light-hearted, thoughtless and noisy rather than vicious.' **2.** The *sākhāl* manifests his folly not in speech, but in action; it was after David had numbered the people that he reproached himself for acting 'very foolishly' (2 S 24^{10}). Consequences prove that fools of this class have blundered in their calculations (Gn 31^{28}, 1 S 13^{13}, Is 44^{25}). **3.** The *'^ewîl* is stupid, impatient of reproof, often sullen and quarrelsome. He despises wisdom and instruction (Pr 1^{7}, cf 15^{5}), is soon angry (Pr 12^{16} 27^{3}), and may sometimes be described as sinful (Pr 5^{22f} 24^{9}). **4.** The folly of the *nābhāl* is never mere intellectual deficiency or stupidity; it is a moral fault, sometimes a crime, always a sin. 'To commit folly' is a euphemism for gross unchastity (Dt 22^{21}, Jer 29^{23}); the word is used also of sacrilege (Jos 7^{15}; RSV 'a shameful thing'), of blasphemy (Ps 74^{18}; RSV 'impious people'), as well as of impiety in general (Dt 32^{6}, Ps 14^{1}). These words are sometimes employed in a more general sense; to determine the shade of meaning applicable in any passage, a study of the context is essential. For further details see Kennedy, *Hebrew Synonyms*, pp. 29 ff.

In the NT the Greek words for 'fool' describe him as 'deficient in understanding' (Lk 24^{25}), 'unwise' (Eph 5^{15}), 'senseless' (Lk 12^{20}), 'unintelligent' (Ro 1^{21}). The Greek word which corresponds to the 'impious fool' of the OT is fod win Mt 5^{22}: *Raca* expresses 'contempt for a man's head=you stupid!' But 'fool' (*mōre*) expresses 'contempt for his heart and character=you scoundrel!' (Bruce, *EGT*, *in loc.*). If *mōre* were 'a Hebrew expression of condemnation' (RVm), it would 'enjoy the distinction of being the *only* pure Hebrew word in the Greek Testament' (Field, *Notes on the Translation of NT*, p. 3). A '*pure* Hebrew word' means a word not taken from the LXX and not Aramaic. J. G. T.

FOOT.—Is $3^{16,18}$ refers to the ornaments of women's feet. Most of the metaphorical or figurative usages are connected with the idea of the feet as the lowest part of the body, opposed to the head; hence falling at a man's feet, as the extreme of reverence or humility, kissing the feet (Lk 7^{38}), sitting at the feet, as the attitude of the pupil (Lk 10^{39}, Ac 22^{3}). The foot was literally placed on the neck of conquered foes (Jos 10^{24}), as may be seen in Egyptian monuments. Hence 'under foot' is used of subjection (Ps 8^{6}, 1 Co 15^{27}). In Dt 11^{10} the reference is to some system of irrigation in vogue in Egypt, either to the turning of a water-wheel by the foot, or to a method of distributing water from a canal 'by making or breaking down with the foot the small ridges which regulate its flow' (Driver, *ad loc.*). Other usages arise from the feet as stained or defiled in walking. The shaking of dust from the feet (Mt 10^{14}, Ac 13^{51}) was the sign of complete rejection; the land was as a heathen land, and its dust unclean. So the sandals were removed as a sign of reverence (Ex 3^{5}, Jos 5^{15}; cf covering the feet, Is 6^{2}). To remove the sandal was also the sign of the renunciation of a right (Dt 25^{9}, Ru 4^{8}). To *walk* barefoot was the symbol of mourning (2 S 15^{30}), or slavery (Is 20^{2}). Jer 2^{25} 'Keep your foot from going unshod,' *i.e.* do not wear the shoes off your feet in running after strange gods.

Washing the feet stained with the dust of the road was part of the regular duty of hospitality (Gn 18^{4}, Ex 30^{19}, 2 S 11^{8}, Ca 5^{3}, Lk 7^{44}). The use of ointment for this purpose was the sign of the penitent's lavish love (Lk 7^{38}, Jn 12^{3}). **The washing of the feet at the Last Supper** is primarily connected with this custom (Jn 13). Christ 'the Lord and Master' assumes the garb and does the work of a slave (13^{4}). The lesson is not merely one of humility (cf the dispute in Lk 22^{24}), but of ready and self-sacrificing service. An interesting Rabbinic parallel is quoted on Ezk 16^{9}: 'Among men the slave washes his master; but with God it is not so.' Edersheim further sees in the act a substitute for the washing of hands which was part of the Paschal ceremonial; and there may be a reference to the proverb, connected with the Greek mysteries, that a great undertaking must not be entered upon 'with unwashed feet.' The service of the Kingdom of heaven (or in particular the crisis of that night) is not to be approached in the spirit of unthinking pride shown in the dispute about precedence (see D. Smith, *The Days of His Flesh*, p. 440). Besides the lesson of humility, there is also the symbolism of purification. St. Peter, at first protesting, afterwards characteristically accepts this as literal. Christ's reply takes up the figure of one who has walked from the bath to his host's house, and needs only to have the dust of his journey removed. Broadly, they are clean by their consecration to Him, but they need continual cleansing from the defilements of daily life. 'It seems impossible not to see in the word "bathed" a foreshadowing of the idea of Christian baptism' (Westcott, *ad loc.*). The same or other commentaries should be consulted for later imitations of the ceremony (cf 1 Ti 5^{10}). C. W. E.

FOOTMAN.—This word is used in two different senses: **1.** *A foot-soldier*, always in plural 'footmen,' foot-soldiers, infantry. Footmen probably composed the whole of the Israelite forces (1 S 4^{10} 15^{4}) before the time of David. In RSV the word is retained only in 2 K 13^{7}. **2.** *A runner on foot*: 1 S 22^{17} (AV; AVm, RV, RSV 'guard'). '**Runners**' would be the literal, and at the same time the most appropriate rendering. The king had a body of runners about him, not so much to guard his person as to run his errands and do his bidding. They formed a recognized part of the royal state (1 S 8^{11}, 2 S 15^{1}); they served as executioners (1 S 22^{17}, 2 K 10^{25}); and, accompanying the king or his general into battle, they brought back official tidings of its progress or event (2 S 18^{19}). In Jer 12^{5} both the Hebrew and the English (footmen) seem to be used in the more general sense of racers *on foot* (so RSV).

FOOTSTOOL.—See House, **8.**

FORBEARANCE.—See Longsuffering.

FORD.—Of the numerous 'fords' or passages of the Jordan, two in ancient times were of chief importance; that opposite Jericho near Gilgal (Jos 2^{7}, Jg 3^{28}), and that at Bethany beyond Jordan (Jn 1^{28} RV, RSV; AV Bethabara, q.v.). Bridges are now used in crossing the Jordan. In 2 S 15^{28} 17^{16} the AV has 'plain' for 'fords' (RV, RSV), and in Jg 12^{5f} 'passages' (RV, RSV 'fords'). Other fords were those of the Jabbok (Gn 32^{22}) and the Arnon (Is 16^{2}). G. L. R.

FOREHEAD.—In Jer 3^{3} a harlot's forehead (RSV 'brow') is a type of shamelessness; in Ezk 3^{8f} the forehead stands for obstinacy. In 9^{4} the righteous receive a mark, probably the letter *Tāw*, on their forehead. Hence the symbolism in Rev 7^{3} etc., where the mark is the Divine signet. It is doubtful what is the mark of the beast (Rev 13^{16}); see Swete, *ad loc.* 17^{5} is a probable allusion to a custom of Roman harlots. Shaving the forehead in sign of mourning is forbidden (Dt 14^{1}). In Ezk 16^{12} read 'nose' with AVm, RV, RSV. See also Marks. C. W. E.

FOREIGNER.—See Nations, Stranger.

FOREKNOWLEDGE.—See Predestination.

FOREORDINATION.—See Predestination.

FORERUNNER.—The English word gives the exact sense of the Greek *prodromos*, which, in its classical usage, signifies 'one who goes before'; it may be as a scout to reconnoitre, or as a herald to announce the coming of the king and to make ready the way for the royal journey.

1. John the Baptist was our Lord's 'forerunner.' The word is never applied to him in the NT, but he was the 'messenger' sent 'before the face' of the Lord 'to prepare his way' (Mt 11^{10}, Mk 1^{2}, Lk 7^{27}; cf Mal 3^{1}), and to exhort others to 'make his paths straight' (Mk 1^{2}; cf Is 40^{3ff}).

2. Only in He 6[20] is the word 'forerunner' found in the EV (Wycliffe 'the bifor goer,' Rheims 'the precursor'). Instead of the AV 'whither the forerunner has for us entered, even Jesus,' the RSV rightly renders: 'where Jesus has gone as a forerunner on our behalf.' The change is important. To the readers of this Epistle it would be a startling announcement that Jesus had entered the Holy of Holies *as a forerunner*. Thither the Jewish High Priest, one day in the year, went alone (He 9[7]). He was the people's representative, but he was not their forerunner, for none might dare to follow him. The key-note of the Epistle is that all believers have access with boldness to the presence of the Most Holy God 'in the blood of Jesus'; they have the boldness because their High Priest has inaugurated for them a fresh and living way (10[19ff]). Already within the veil hope enters with assurance for Jesus has 'gone that we may follow too.' As the Forerunner of His redeemed He has inaugurated their entrance, He makes intercession for them, and He is preparing for them a place (Jn 14[2]).

J. G. T.—F. W. G.

FOREST.—1. *ya'ar* (root meaning a 'rugged' place), Dt 19[5], Jer 46[23], Mic 3[12] (RSV 'wooded height'), etc.; sometimes rendered 'wood'; *e.g.* 2 K 2[24]. **2.** *ḥōresh*, a 'wooded place,' 2 Ch 27[4] (RSV 'wooded hills'), etc.; translated 'wood' 1 S 23[15] (RSV **Horesh,** a proper name). **3.** *pardēs*, a Persian loan-word, meaning a 'park,' Neh 2[8] (AV, RV, RSV 'forest'; RVm 'park'). From the many references it is clear that Palestine had more extensive forests in ancient times than to-day—indeed, within living memory there has been a vast destruction of trees for fuel. Considerable patches of woodland still exist, *e.g.* on Tabor and Carmel, in parts of N. Galilee, around Bāniās, and specially in Gilead between *es-Salṭ* and the Jabbok.

E. W. G. M.

FORGETFULNESS.—Ps 88[12] 'Are thy wonders known in the darkness, or thy saving help in the land of forgetfulness?' The meaning is general, as Coverdale 'the londe where all thinges are forgotten,' but probably more passive than active, that the person is forgotten rather than that he forgets. So Wis 17[3]; but in Wis 14[26] 16[11] the word expresses the tendency to forget (so also Sir 11[25] AV, RV).

FORGIVENESS.—Like many other words employed to convey ideas connected with the relations of God and man, this covers a variety of thoughts. In both OT and NT we have evidences of a more elastic vocabulary than the EV would lead us to suppose. **1.** The OT has at least three different words all translated 'forgiveness' or 'pardon,' referring either to God's actions with regard to men (cf Ex 34[7], Ps 86[5], Neh 9[17]) or to forgiveness extended to men by each other (cf Gn 50[17], 1 S 25[28]). At a very early period of human, or at least of Jewish, history, some sense of the need of forgiveness by God seems to have been felt. This will be especially evident if the words of despairing complaint put into the mouth of Cain be translated literally (see Driver, *The Book of Genesis*, on 4[13], cf RVm). The power to forgive came to be looked on as inherent in God, who not only possessed the authority, but loved thus to exhibit His mercy (Dn 9[9], Neh 9[17], Jer 36[3]). In order, however, to obtain this gift, a corresponding condition of humiliation and repentance on man's part had to be fulfilled (2 Ch 7[14], Ps 86[5]), and without a conscious determination of the transgressor to amend and turn towards his God, no hope of pardon was held out (Jos 24[19], 2 K 24[4], Jer 5[1, 7]). On the other hand, as soon as men acknowledged their errors, and asked God to forgive, no limit was set to His love in this respect (1 K 8[36, 50], Ps 103[3]; cf Dt 30[1-10]). Nor could this condition be regarded as unreasonable, for holiness, the essential characteristic of the Divine nature, demanded an answering correspondence on the part of man made in God's image. Without this correspondence forgiveness was rendered impossible, and that, so to speak, automatically (cf Lv 19[2], Jos 24[19]; see Nu 14[18], Job 10[14], Nah 1[3]).

According to the Levitical code, when wrong was done between man and man, the first requisite in order to secure Divine pardon was restitution, which had to be followed up by a service of atonement (Lv 6[2-7]). Even in the case of sins of ignorance, repentance and its outward expression in sacrifice had to precede forgiveness (Lv 4[13ff], Nu 15[23ff] etc.). Here the educative influence of the Law must have been powerful, inculcating as it did at once the transcendent holiness of God and the need of a similar holiness on the part of His people (Lv 11[44]). Thus the Pauline saying, 'The law was our custodian until Christ came' (Gal 3[24]), is profoundly true, and the great priestly services of the Temple, with the solemn and ornate ritual, must have given glimpses of the approach by which men could feel their way and obtain the help indispensable for the needs adumbrated by the demands of the Mosaic institutions. The burden of the prophetic exhortations, 'Turn back, turn back . . . why will you die?' (Ezk 33[11]; cf Is 44[22], Jer 35[15] 18[11], Hos 14[1], Jl 2[13] etc.), would be meaningless if the power to obey were withheld, or the way kept hidden. Indeed, these preachers of moral righteousness did not hesitate to emphasize the converse side of this truth in dwelling on the 'repentance' of God and His returning to His afflicted but repentant people (Jon 3[9], Mal 3[7] etc.). The resultant effect of this mutual approach was the restoration to Divine favour of those who had been alienated, by the free act of forgiveness on the part of God (Ps 85[4], Is 55[7] 59[20], Jer 13[17, 24] etc.).

2. We are thus not surprised to learn that belief in the forgiveness of sins was a cardinal article of the Jewish faith in the time of Jesus (Mk 2[7] ‖ Lk 5[21], cf Is 43[25]). Nor was the teaching of Jesus in any instance out of line with the national belief, for, according to His words, the source of all pardon was His Father (Mk 11[25f], Mt 6[14f]; cf His appeal on the cross, 'Father, forgive them,' Lk 23[34]). It is true that 'the Son of Man has authority on earth to forgive sins' (Mk 2[10] ‖ Mt 9[6] ‖ Lk 5[24]), but the form of the expression shows that Jesus was laying claim to a delegated authority (cf Lk 7[48], where, as in the case of the palsied man, the words are declaratory rather than absolute; see Plummer, *ICC, in loc.*). This is more clearly seen by a reference to NT epistolary literature, where again and again forgiveness and restoration are spoken of as mediated 'in' or 'through' Christ (Eph 4[32], Col 2[12ff], 1 P 5[10]; cf Eph 1[7], Rev 1[5], 1 Jn 2[12] etc.). Here, as in OT, only more insistently dwelt on, the consciousness of guilt and of the need of personal holiness is the first step on the road to God's forgiveness (1 Jn 1[9], cf Ps 32[5] 51[3] etc.); and the open acknowledgment of these feelings is looked on as the natural outcome of their existence (Ac 19[18]; cf Ro 10[10], 1 Jn 1[9]). The hopelessness which at times seemed to have settled down on Jesus, when confronted by Pharisaic opposition, was the result of the moral and spiritual blindness of the religious teachers to their real position (Jn 9[40f]).

3. Again, following along the line we have traced in the OT, only more definitely and specifically emphasized, the NT writers affirm the necessity for a moral likeness between God and man (cf Mt 5[48]). It is in this region, perhaps, that the most striking development is to be seen. Without exhibiting, in their relations to each other, the Divine spirit of forgiveness, men need never hope to experience God's pardon for themselves. This, we are inclined to think, is the most striking feature in the ethical creations of Jesus' teaching. By almost every method of instruction, from incidental postulate (Mt 6[12] ‖ Lk 11[4], Mk 11[25]) to deliberate statement (Mt 18[21ff] 6[15], Mk 11[26], Lk 17[4]) and elaborate parable (Mt 18[23-35]), He sought to attune the minds of His hearers to this high and difficult note of the Christian spirit (cf Col 3[13], 1 Jn 4[11]). Once more, Jesus definitely asserts the limitation to which the pardon and mercy even of God are subjected. Whatever may be the precise meaning attaching to the words 'an eternal sin' (Mk 3[29]), it is plain that some definite border-line is referred to as the line of demarcation between those who may hope for this evidence of God's love and those who are outside its scope (Mt 12[32]). See article SIN, III. **1.**

4. We have lastly to consider the words, recorded only by St. John, of the risen Jesus to His assembled disciples (Jn 20[23]). It is remarkable that this is the only place in the Fourth Gospel where the word translated 'forgive' (RV) occurs, and we must not forget that the incident of conferring the power of absolution on the body of believers, as they were gathered together, is peculiar to this writer. At the same time, it is instructive to remember that nowhere is St. John much concerned with a simple narrative of events as such; he seems to be engaged rather in choosing those facts which he can subordinate to his teaching purposes. The choice, then, of this circumstance must have been intentional, as having a particular significance, and when the immediately preceding context is read, it is seen that the peculiar power transmitted is consequent upon the gift of the Holy Spirit. On two other occasions somewhat similar powers were promised, once personally to St. Peter as the great representative of that complete faith in the Incarnation of which the Church is the guardian in the world (Mt 16[19]), and once to the Church in its corporate capacity as the final judge of the terms of fellowship for each of its members (Mt 18[18]). In both these instances the words used by Jesus with regard to this spiritual power differ from those found in the narrative of the Fourth Gospel, and the latter is seen to be more definite, profound, and far-reaching in its scope than the former. The abiding presence of the living Spirit in the Church is the sure guarantee that her powers in judging spiritual things are inherent in her (cf 1 Co 2[12-15]) as the Body of Christ. Henceforth she carries in her bosom the authority so emphatically claimed by her Lord, to declare the wondrous fact of Divine forgiveness (Ac 13[38]) and to set forth the conditions upon which it ultimately rests (see Westcott, *Gospel of St. John, in loc.*). Closely connected with the exercise of this Divinely given authority is the rite of Baptism, conditioned by repentance and issuing in 'the forgiveness of sins' (Ac 2[38]). It is the initial act in virtue of which the Church claims to rule, guide, and upbuild the life of her members. It is symbolic, as was John's baptism, of a 'death unto sin and a new birth unto righteousness' (Mk 1[4]=Lk 3[3]; cf Ro 6[4], Col 2[12]). To some it is more than symbolic, for by it, as by visible channel, the living and active Spirit of God is conveyed to the soul, where the fruition of the promised forgiveness is seen in the fulness of the Christian life (Ac 2[38], cf 10[43, 47] 19[5f]).

5. On more than one occasion St. Paul speaks of the forgiveness of sins as constituting the redemption of the human race effected by the death of Christ ('through his blood' Eph 1[7], cf Col 1[14]); and the author of the Epistle to the Hebrews emphasizes this aspect of the atoning work of Jesus by showing its harmony with all with which previous revelation had made us familiar, for 'without the shedding of blood there is no forgiveness' (9[22]). The same writer, moreover, asserts that once this object has been accomplished, nothing further remains to be done, as 'there is no longer any offering for sin' (10[18]) than that which the 'blood of Jesus' (10[19]) has accomplished. The triumphant cry of the Crucified, 'It is finished' (Jn 19[30]), is for this writer the guarantee not only that 'the death of Christ is the objective ground on which the sins of men are remitted' (Dale, *The Atonement*, pp. 430 f); it is also the assurance that forgiveness of sin is the goal of the life and death of Him whose first words from the cross breathed a prayer for the forgiveness of His tormentors.

J. R. W.—N. H. S.

FORK.—See FAN and FLESH-HOOK.

FORM CRITICISM.—See CRITICISM [BIBLICAL], **4.**

FORMER RAIN.—See RAIN.

FORNICATION.—See CRIMES AND PUNISHMENTS, **3.**

FORTIFICATION AND SIEGECRAFT.—Except in so far as armies might be sent out to engage an invading enemy in open battle (1 K 20), defensive tactics of both Israelites and their predecessors seem to have been based on withdrawal to their walled cities (Heb. *'ārê mibhṣār*), where, until the Assyrians developed the art of siegecraft, the inhabitants were usually safe (2 S 5[6]), unless provisions or water gave out (2 K 6[24-29]), or there was a traitor within the gates (Jg 1[24f] and perhaps Jos 2[18]); however, the OT does record successful attacks on fortified buildings and cities even with very primitive methods (Jg 9[46-49], 2 S 12[26-28]—though 'city of waters' probably means the fort guarding the water supply, so that Rabbath Ammon was perhaps forced to capitulate owing to the loss of its water supply). Main reliance, after utilizing any natural advantages such as a rock outcrop or a sufficiently large mound, was put on encircling **walls,** frequently double (Gibeah), sometimes in several concentric rings (Samaria). The main wall was called *ḥômāh*; the outer **rampart** (or ditch?), *ḥêl*. At *Tell en-Naṣbeh* (Mizpah?) which Judah fortified against Israel *c* 900 B.C. it is estimated that the wall may have been well over 25 feet high; but no Canaanite or Israelite city wall has survived in its original height; many were realigned, strengthened, or destroyed at different stages of their history, so that their reconstruction for any given period is not always possible. We are told that the mound of Jericho contains traces of fourteen different walls or wall-components, even though almost everything later than 2000 B.C. (long before Joshua) has disappeared. Walls might be very differently built; thickness depending partly on material and ultimate height, partly on the site and on the labour available. Several Hyksos settlements show the use of earthen ramparts combined with a ditch. Extensive use of brick may show Egyptian influence, as in the 23-feet thick wall built around Sharuhen, possibly by Shishak himself (1 K 14[25]), and in the 20 feet thick summit wall of Lachish, fortified by Rehoboam (2 Ch 11[9]); though in the revetment lower down the mound stone as well as brick is used. Very often the upper courses of a stone wall were continued in brick, and might even be topped with wooden battlements, as appears to have been the case at Lachish. Stone walling might be megalithic or cyclopean, *i.e.*, using extraordinarily big blocks, as in Shechem, *Tell en-Naṣbeh* and Jericho [the wall of the temple enclosure at Jerusalem still contains stones over 30 feet by 8 feet by 3½ feet, weighing more than 80 tons]; but we find also the use of rough stone, occasionally plastered to hinder climbing, as at *Tell en-Naṣbeh*. As stone working technique and tools improved, or finances allowed, we find an extending use of ashlar, first merely for the more exposed parts such as corners (so in the 9th cent. fort of Hazor), but then to face complete walls, as in the massive Jebusite (?) wall of Jerusalem, which is still 27 feet thick at its highest surviving level, and maybe even 40 feet at its base. Particularly worthy of mention are the defences of Samaria, of which it has been said, 'the stone masonry is of such superb workmanship that nothing has ever been found in Palestine that surpasses it' (G. E. Wright, *Biblical Archaeology*, p. 153). A popular Israelite technique, possibly borrowed from Hittite examples, was the casemate system, in which the 'rooms' in a double wall with cross partitions were filled with packed rubble, as in the Solomonic wall of Hazor.

Attacks on the walls were met by building out **bastions** along their length, especially at the corners (2 Ch 26[15], Zeph 1[16] RVm), spaced not more widely than double bow or sling shot. Danger from calcination (Jg 9[49]) and ramming (Is 7[6]) was minimized by having a sloping revetment along the foot of the wall, as at Lachish. An important precaution, not always sufficiently observed, was to take the foundations down to bedrock, as in Samaria, or at least, well down into earlier strata of the *tell*.

The **gates** were an obvious point of weakness; in troubled times one, or at most, two is the usual number, but in Nehemiah's Jerusalem the names of nine gates are recorded (Neh 3^{1-32}). Even the simplest gates usually had bastions or **gate towers** on each side (2 Ch 26^{9}), and it was customary to have a gate on the outer and inner face of the wall, as at Mahanaim, where David is found sitting 'between the two gates' (2 S 18^{24}). Here we further learn that there was a stair leading up to an upper storey in the gate tower (v.[33]), the roof of which was apparently on a level with the top of the city wall (v.[24]). In *Tell Beit Mirsim* (Debir or Kiriath-sepher) the two 'entrances were so constructed that one approached with his left side to the city wall, passed in through one gate, and then turned at right angles to enter the city itself by a second gate, an indirect mode of ingress which is still to be seen in the Damascus and Jaffa gates in Jerusalem' (C. C. McCown, *The Ladder of Progress in Palestine*, p. 94). One of these gateways was sufficiently wide to admit a chariot, but the other was no more than 3 feet wide. Many city entrances had three sets of doors, with guardrooms opening off each bay, so giving a plan reminiscent of two E's opposed, 'E Ǝ' (*e.g.* the NW. gate of Shechem).

The gate itself, the 'door of the gate' (Neh 6^{1}), consisted ordinarily of two leaves (Is 45^{1}) of wood. For greater security against fire these were often overlaid with bronze (Ps 107^{16}, Is 45^{2}). The leaves were hung on pivots which turned in sockets in sill and lintel, and were kept closed by bolts let into the former. A strong bar, or bars, of wood, bronze (1 K 4^{13}), or iron (Ps 107^{16}, Is 45^{2}) secured the whole gate, passing transversely into sockets in the gate-posts, as we learn from Samson's exploit at Gaza (Jg 16^{1-3}), and proved by the discovery of the actual running slot in one gate-post and the receiver in the other at *Tell en-Naṣbeh*. 'To have charge of the gate' (2 K 7^{17}) was a military post of honour. In war-time, at least, a sentinel was posted on the roof of the gate-house or tower (2 S 18^{24}, 2 K 9^{17}). [Plans, etc., may be found in *ANEP*, figs. 711–721.]

It remains to deal briefly with the **siegecraft** of the Hebrews and their contemporaries. A fortified (RV 'fenced') place might be captured in three ways: (*a*) by assault or storm, (*b*) by a blockade, or (*c*) by a regular siege. (*a*) The first method was most likely to succeed in the case of places of moderate strength, or where treachery was at work (cf Jg 1^{23ff}). The assault was directed against the weakest point of the *enceinte*, particularly the gates (cf Is 28^{6}). Before the Hebrews learnéd the use of the battering-ram, entrance to an enemy's city or fortress was obtained by setting fire to the gates (Jg $9^{49, 52}$), and by scaling the walls by means of scaling-ladders, under cover of a shower of arrows and sling-stones. According to 1 Ch 11^{6}, Joab was the first to scale the walls of the Jebusite fortress of Zion, when David took it by assault. Although **scaling-ladders** are explicitly mentioned only in 1 Mac 5^{30}—a prior reference may be found in Pr 21^{22}—they are familiar objects in the Egyptian representations of sieges from an early date, as well as in the later Assyrian representations, and may be assumed to have been used by the Hebrews from the first. In early times, as is plain from the accounts of the capture of Ai (Jos 8^{10ff}) and Shechem (Jg 9^{42ff}), a favourite stratagem was to entice the defenders from the city by a pretended flight, and then a force placed in ambush would make a dash for the gate.

(*b*) The second method was to surround the city, and by preventing ingress and egress, to starve it into surrender. This was evidently the method adopted by Joab at the **blockade** of Rabbath-Ammon (see above).

(*c*) In conducting a regular **siege**, which of course included both blockade and assault, the first step was to 'cast up a **mound**' (2 S 20^{15}, 2 K 19^{32}, Is 37^{33}—AV '**bank**,' RV '**mount**'). This was of earth which was gradually advanced till it reached the walls, and was almost equal to them in height, and from which the besiegers could meet the besieged on more equal terms. The 'mound' is first met with in the account of Joab's siege of Abel of Beth-maacah (2 S 20^{15ff}). Joab is represented as 'battering' (RVm, 'undermining') the wall, but the text is here in some disorder. **Battering-rams** are first mentioned in Ezekiel, and are scarcely to be expected so early as the time of David. The Egyptians used a long pole, with a metal point shaped like a spear head, which was not swung but worked by hand, and could only be effective, therefore, against walls of crude brick (see illustration in Wilkinson, *Anc. Egypt*, i, 242).

The **battering rams** (Ezk 26^{9}; RV 'battering engines'; AV 'engines of war') of the Assyrians were called 'rams' by the Hebrews (Ezk 4^{2} 21^{22}), from their butting action, although they were without the familiar ram's head of the Roman *aries*. The Assyrian battering-ram ended either in a large spear-head, as with the Egyptians, or in a flat head shod with metal, and was worked under the shelter of large wooden towers mounted on four or six wheels, of which there are many representations in the Assyrian sculptures (illustrated in Toy's *Ezekiel*, 102). These towers were sometimes of several storeys, in which archers were stationed, and were moved forward against the walls on the mounds described above.

When Nebuchadnezzar laid siege to Jerusalem, his troops are said to have 'built **siegeworks** against it round about' (2 K 25^{1}, cf Ezk 4^{2}), but the original term is obscure, though probably to be understood in the sense of a siege-wall or *circumvallatio*—the 'bank' of Lk 19^{43}—for the purpose of making the blockade effective. On the other hand, the siegeworks of Dt 20^{20}, also Ec 9^{14}, which had to be made of wood other than 'trees for food,' properly denote wooden forts or other **siege works** (Is 29^{3}) built for the protection of the besiegers in their efforts to storm or undermine the walls.

The Assyrian sculptures give life-like pictures of the various operations of ancient siegecraft (see *ANEP*, Section IV). Here we see the massive battering rams detaching the stones or bricks from an angle of the wall, while the defenders, by means of a grappling chain, are attempting to drag the ram from its covering tower. There the archers are pouring a heavy fire on the men upon the wall, from behind large rectangular shields or **screens** of wood or wickerwork, standing on the ground, with a small projecting cover. These are intended by the 'shield' of 2 K 19^{32}, the 'roof of shields' of Ezk 26^{8}, and the '**mantelet**' of Nah 2^{5}, all named in connexion with siege works. In another place **miners** are busy undermining the wall with picks, protected by a curved screen of wickerwork supported by a pole (illustrations of both screens in Toy, *op. cit.*, 149; cf Wilkinson, *op. cit.* i, 243).

The monuments also show that the Assyrians had machines for casting large stones long before the *tormenta*, or siege-artillery, are said to have been invented in Sicily in 399 B.C. By the 'artillery' of 1 S 20^{40} AV is, of course, meant the ordinary bow and arrows; but Uzziah is credited by the Chronicler with having 'made **engines**, invented by skilful men, to be on the towers and the corners, to shoot arrows and great stones' (2 Ch 26^{15}). The Books of the Maccabees show that by the 2nd cent. at least, the Jews were not behind their neighbours in the use of the **artillery** (1 Mac 6^{51f} AV) of the period, 'engines of war, and instruments for casting fire and stones, and pieces to cast darts and slings.' (A detailed description, with illustrations, of these *catapultae* and *ballistae*, as the Romans termed them, will be found in the article 'Tormentum' in Smith's *Dict. of Gr. and Rom. Antiq.*). At the siege of Gezer (such is the best reading, 1 Mac 13^{43}) Simon is even said to have used effectively a piece of the most formidable siege-artillery then known, the *helepolis* (literally 'city-taker,' RV 'engine of siege'), which Titus also employed in the siege of Jerusalem (for description see 'Helepolis' in Smith, *op. cit.*). In this siege the Jews had 300 pieces for discharging arrows or rather bolts (*catapultae*), and 40 pieces for casting stones (*ballistae*), according to Josephus, who gives a graphic account of the working of these formidable 'engines of war' in his story of the siege of Jotapata (*BJ* III. vii. 23 [240 ff]).

The aim of the besieged was by every artifice in their power to counteract the efforts of the besiegers to scale or to make a breach in the walls (Am 4[3]), and in particular to destroy their siege works and artillery. The battering-rams were rendered ineffective by letting down bags of chaff and other fenders from the battlements, or were thrown out of action by grappling chains, or by having the head broken off by huge stones hurled from above. The mounds supporting the besiegers' towers were undermined, and the towers themselves and the other engines set on fire (1 Mac 6[13]; cf the 'flaming darts' or arrows of Eph 6[16]).

In addition to the efforts of the bowmen, slingers, and javelin-throwers, who manned the walls, boiling oil was poured on those attempting to place the scaling-ladders, or to pass the boarding bridges from the towers to the battlements. Of all these and many other expedients the *Jewish War* of Josephus is a familiar repertoire. There, too, will be found the fullest account of the dire distress to which a city might be reduced by a prolonged siege (cf 2 K 6[25ff]). See also Bulwark, Citadel.

A. R. S. K.—**D. R. Ap-T.**

FORTRESS.—See Citadel.

FORTUNATUS.—The name of a member of the household of Stephanas, and a Corinthian. With Stephanas and Achaicus he visited St. Paul at Ephesus (1 Co 16[17]); he had probably been baptized by the Apostle himself (1[16]).—The former view that he is identical with the Fortunatus mentioned in 1 Clem 65 has been abandoned: this other Fortunatus had always lived at Rome (63) and nothing suggests that this name belongs to a Corinthian. E. H.

FORTUNE.—See Gad (tribe and god).

FOUNDATION.—Great importance was attached to the laying of the foundation. It was accompanied by human sacrifice, as may be seen in the Babylonian records; a possible trace occurs in the story of Hiel (1 K 16[34]; but see *ICC*, *ad loc.*). Hence the stress on the size and splendour of the foundation, as in Solomon's Temple (7[9]). It is a natural metaphor for the ultimate basis on which a thing rests (Job 4[19], Ezk 13[14], Mt 7[25], Lk 6[48]). Righteousness and judgment are the foundation of God's throne (Ps 89[14] 97[2] RV and RSV). 'The city which has foundations' is the type of the real and eternal (He 11[10]). The Apostles themselves are the foundation of the New Jerusalem, formed of all manner of precious stones (Rev 21[14, 19]). 'The Apostolic Church is conditioned through the ages by the preaching and work of the Apostolate' (Swete, *ad loc.*; cf Is 28[16], Mt 16[18], Eph 2[20]). In 1 Co 3[10] the metaphor is slightly different, the preaching of Jesus Christ being the one foundation (cf Is 19[10] RVm, where the word is used of the chief men of the State [RV 'pillars'; RSV 'the pillars of the land']). In the frequent phrase 'from the foundation of the world,' the word is active, meaning 'founding.' 'Foundations' occurs similarly in a passive sense, the earth being more or less literally conceived of as a huge building resting on pillars, etc. (Ps 18[7, 15] 24[2], Is 24[18]). In Ps 11[3] 75[3] 82[5], Ezk 30[4], the idea is applied metaphorically to the 'fundamental' principles of law and justice on which the moral order rests. In 2 Ch 3[3], Is 6[4] 16[7], Jer 50[15], RV or RSV should be followed. In 2 Ch 23[5] the 'gate of the foundation' is obscure; possibly we should read 'the horse-gate.' See also House, 3. C. W. E.

FOUNDATION, GATE OF THE.—See Jerusalem, Gates of.

FOUNTAIN.—A word applied to living springs of water as contrasted with cisterns (Lv 11[36]; RSV 'spring'); specifically of Beer-lahai-roi (Gn 16[7]; RSV 'spring'), Elim (Nu 33[9]; RV, RSV 'spring'), Nephtoah (Jos 15[9]; RSV 'spring'), and Jezreel (1 S 29[1]; so RSV here). The porous chalky limestone of Palestine abounds in good springs of water, which, owing to their importance in a country rainless half the year, were eagerly coveted (Jg 1[15]). In many springs the flow of water has been directed and increased by enlarging tunnels the fissures through which the water trickled; many of these tunnels are of considerable length. Specimens exist at ʿUrtas, Bittîr, and other places near Jerusalem. R. A. S. M.

FOUNTAIN GATE.—See Jerusalem, Gates of.

FOWL.—The word 'fowl' is used in AV and RV for any kind of bird, *e.g.* Gn 1[20] (RSV 'birds'), where the Hebrew word is *ʿôph*. RSV retains 'fowl' for this word only at Lv 7[26]. Sometimes the two words 'bird' and 'fowl' are employed in AV simply for the sake of variety, or perhaps to distinguish two different words in the original. Thus Gn 15[10] 'the birds (Heb. *ṣippōr*) divided he not,' 15[11] 'when the fowls (Heb. *ʿayiṭ*) came down' (RV, RSV 'birds' and 'birds of prey'); Jer 12[9] 'the birds (Heb. *ʿayiṭ*) round about' (RV, RSV 'birds of prey'), Ps 8[8] 'the fowl (Heb. *ṣippōr*) of the air' (so RV; RSV 'birds'). In 1 K 4[23] RSV retains from AV and RV 'fatted fowl' for *barbūrîm*, which denotes some kind of table bird which cannot be certainly identified. See Bird.

FOWLER.—See Snares.

FOX.—**1.** *shûʿāl* is rendered 'fox' in AV and RV (but RVm 'jackal' except Ezk 13[4], Ca 2[15]), while RSV has 'fox' in Jg 15[4], Ezk 13[4], Ca 2[15], Neh 4[3], but 'jackal' in Ps 63[10], La 5[18]. See Jackal. **2.** *alōpēx* (Gr.), Mt 8[20], Lk 9[58] 13[32]. In the NT there is no doubt that the common fox and not the jackal is intended. It is noted in Rabbinical literature and in Palestinian folklore for its cunning and treachery. It burrows in the ground (Lk 9[58]). The small Egyptian fox (*Vulpes nilotica*) is common in S. Palestine, while the Tawny fox (*V. flavescens*), a larger animal of lighter colour, occurs farther north.

FRANKINCENSE (Heb. *lᵉbhônāh*; Gr. *libanos* Mt 2[11], Rev 18[13]).—Frankincense is in six passages (Is 43[23] 60[6] 66[3], Jer 6[20] 17[26] 41[5]) mistranslated in AV '**incense**' but correctly in RV (RSV retains 'incense' in the last of these). It is a sweet-smelling gum, obtained as a milky exudation from various species of *Boswellia*, the frankincense tree, an ally of the terebinth. The gum was imported from S. Arabia (Is 60[6], Jer 6[20]); it was a constituent of incense (Ex 30[34]); it is often associated with myrrh (Ca 3[6] 4[6], Mt 2[11]); it was offered with the showbread (Lv 24[7]). E. W. G. M.

FRAY.—This obsolete English verb is found in AV, Zec 1[21] and 1 Mac 14[12] ('every man sat under his vine and his fig tree, and there was none to fray them'); and 'fray away' occurs in Dt 28[26], Jer 7[33], Sir 22[20] ('whoso casteth a stone at the birds frayeth them away'). It is a shortened form of 'afray,' of which the past participle 'afraid' is still in use.

FREE.—In the use of this adjective in the English Bible notice 1 P 2[16] 'as free men, yet without using your freedom as a pretext for evil; but live as servants of God,' that is, free from the Law, yet servants (slaves) to the higher law of love to God. Ps 88[5] 'free among the dead,' is a difficult passage; the probable meaning of the Hebrew is 'forsaken among.' Ac 22[28] AV 'I was free born,' that is, as a Roman citizen. 2 Th 3[1] 'Pray for us, that the word of the Lord may have free course' (Greek literally 'may run,' as AVm and RV='speed on and triumph' (RSV). 'Free' means 'unhindered' as in Shakespeare's *Love's Labour's Lost*, v. ii. 738, 'For mine own part, I breathe free breath.' Ps 51[12] 'uphold me with thy free spirit' (RVm and ARV 'willing,' RSV 'a willing'): the word means generous, noble, and the reference is to the man's own spirit (RV 'with a free spirit').

FREEDMEN.—Ac 6[9] mentions a synagogue 'of the Freedmen (as it was called), and of the Cyrenians, and of the Alexandrians.' According to this text the 'Freedmen' (AV '**Libertines**') of Rome could have been descendants of those Jews of Jerusalem whom Pompey had carried away as slaves. But the Armenian text reads 'Libyans,' and this would tally with the two other African groups. E. H.

FREEDOM.—See Liberty.

FREELY.—The use to observe is when 'freely' means 'gratuitously,' as Nu 11[5] 'We remember the fish, which we did eat in Egypt freely' (RSV 'for nothing'; Vulgate *gratis*); Mt 10[8] 'freely ye received, freely give' (RSV 'without pay').

FREEWILL.—See PREDESTINATION.

FRESHET.—Found only in Job 6[15] RSV, where it renders *'ᵃphîḳ nᵉḥālîm*, a combination of two words elsewhere rendered 'stream' or 'brook'; see BROOK. AV has 'stream of brooks,' and RV 'channel of brooks.'

FRINGES.—In Nu 15[37ff] (AV) the Hebrews are commanded to 'make them fringes (Heb. *ṣîṣîth*) in the **borders** of their garments' (RSV '**tassels** on the corners of their garments'). A similar ordinance is found in Dt 22[12]: 'You shall make yourself tassels (RVm 'twisted threads,' Heb. *gᵉdhîlîm*) on the four corners of your cloak with which you cover yourself' (RSV). The 'cloak' (Heb. *kᵉsûth*, literally 'covering') here referred to is the upper garment of the Hebrews, as is evident from Ex 22[27], where the same word is defined as the *śimlāh* or 'mantle,' the upper garment in question, as described under DRESS, **4** (*a*).

The 'fringes' made for this garment, however, are not to be considered a continuous fringe (or row of tassels) all around, like those portrayed on Assyrian reliefs, but with RSV as tassels of twisted or plaited threads fastened to the four corners of the outer garment. It was further required 'to put upon the tassel of each corner a cord of blue' (Nu 15[38] RSV). The precise meaning of this injunction is uncertain. It is usually taken to mean that each tassel was to be attached by means of this cord of blue, actually blue-purple or violet (see COLOURS, **5**), to a corner of the garment.

That this ordinance was observed by the Jews of NT times is probably to be seen in the reference to the 'long fringes' of the Pharisees in Mt 23[5]. The references to the significance of the 'fringe' (AV '**hem**' or 'border'; RV '**border**') of our Lord's upper garment (Mt 9[20] 14[36], Mk 6[56], Lk 8[44]) may point up the continued observance of the ancient ordinance. In the passage of Numbers it is expressly said that the object of this ordinance was to furnish the Hebrews with a visible reminder of the obligation resting upon them as Yahweh's chosen people to walk in His law and to keep all His commandments. Since tasselled garments are known through representations on the walls of Egyptian tombs and elsewhere to have been used much earlier than the time of the Hebrews, it is altogether probable that the object of the Hebrew legislation was 'to make a deeply rooted custom serve a fitting religious purpose' (G. B. Gray, *Numbers*, ICC, 183 f).

These tassels are still worn by orthodox Jews, attached to the tallith or prayer-shawl, and to the smaller tallith, a kind of undergarment covering the chest and the upper part of the back. The addition of the blue thread is no longer necessary. (For details and illustrations, see Hastings' *DB* i, 627[a]; ii, 69[a]; *Jewish Ency*. xi, 677; *Universal Jewish Ency*. iv, 461.) A. R. S. K.—**W. F. S.**

FROCK.—In the Greek text of Sir 40[4] the poor man's dress is said to be of unbleached linen, paraphrased in AV as 'a linen' and in RV as 'a hempen frock,' RSV '**burlap.**' The Hebrew original has, 'he that wraps himself in a mantle of hair' (Smend) for which see DRESS, **4** (*c*).

FROG.—**1.** Heb. *ṣᵉphardēaʿ*, Ex 8[2-14], Ps 78[45] 105[30]—one of the plagues of Egypt. **2.** Greek *batrachos*, Rev 16[13f], a type of uncleanness. The edible frog and the little green tree-frog are both common all over the Holy Land.

FRONTLETS.—See ORNAMENTS, **2**; PHYLACTERIES.

FROWARD.—'Froward' is a dialectic form of 'fromward'; it is the opposite of 'toward,' as we say 'to and fro' for 'to and from.' Thus its meaning is *perverse*. The word is used chiefly in Proverbs, AV. In NT it occurs only once, 1 P 2[18] (RSV 'overbearing'), where the Greek means literally tortuous like the course of a river, and then is applied to conduct that is not straightforward. **Frowardly** is found in Is 57[17] 'and he went on frowardly (RSV 'backsliding') turning away,' as AVm. **Frowardness** occurs only in Proverbs (2[14] 6[14] 10[32]). Barlowe says 'Moyses the most faythfull seruaunte of God was partely by their frowardnes debarred fro the plesaunte lande of behest.'

FRUIT.—See FOOD, **4.**

FRYING PAN.—See HOUSE, **9.**

FUEL.—The principal 'fuel [literally 'food'] of fire' (Is 9[5, 19]) in use among the Hebrews was undoubtedly wood, either in its natural state or, among the wealthier classes, as charcoal (see COAL). The trees which furnished the main supply (cf Is 44[14ff]) probably differed little from those so employed in Syria at the present day, for which see *PEFSt.*, 1891, 118 ff. Among other sources of supply were shrubs and undergrowth of all kinds, including the broom (Ps 120[4] RVm, RSV; AV, RV 'juniper') and the buck-thorn (58[9]); also chaff and other refuse of the threshing-floor (Mt 3[12]); and withered herbage, the 'grass' of Mt 6[30]. The use of dried animal dung as fuel, which is universal in the modern East, was apparently not unknown to the Hebrews (cf Ezk 4[12-15]). See further, HOUSE, **7.**

FULFIL.—This verb is used in the Bible in several senses.

1. To denote the completion of a fixed time, as the time of pregnancy (Gn 25[24], Lk 2[6] [RV]), or of a period ordained by God (Ex 23[26], Mk 1[15], Lk 21[24]).

2. To express the satisfying of a request (Ps 20[5], Est 5[8]) or desire (Ps 145[19], Pr 13[19]).

3. To denote the execution of a vow (Lv 22[21], Nu 15[3]).

4. To express perfect obedience to the law of Moses (Ro 13[10]) or of Christ (Gal 5[13f] 6[2], Ja 2[8]), or to the demands of righteousness (Mt 3[15]).

5. To indicate the correspondence of events with the prior announcement or promise of God (1 S 3[12], 1 K 12[15], 2 Ch 36[21], Jer 29[10]). The NT frequently notes the fulfilment of the hope or promise of the OT in Christ (Mt 14[49], Lk 24[44], Jn 18[9] 19[24, 36], Ac 3[18] 13[27, 32f]), especially in Matthew (1[22] 2[15, 17, 23] 4[14] 8[17] 12[17] 13[14, 35] 21[4] 26[54, 56] 27[9]). The idea of the fulfilment of the hope or promise of the OT in Christ is often present when the term is not used (Lk 24[27, 32], Ac 17[2f] 28[23], 1 Co 15[3f]).

FULLER.—See ARTS AND CRAFTS, **6.**

FULLER'S FIELD.—An unidentified spot near Jerusalem. Beside the conduit in the highway leading to it Isaiah met Ahaz (Is 7[3]), and here the messengers of Sennacherib stood to demand the surrender of the city (2 K 18[17], Is 36[2]).

FULNESS.—See PLEROMA.

FURLONG.—See WEIGHTS AND MEASURES.

FURNACE.—EV translation of **1.** *kibhshān* in Gn 19[28] (also AV and RV in Ex 9[8] etc.; RSV 'kiln'); **2.** *ʿᵃlîl* in Ps 12[6]; **3.** *kûr* in Dt 4[20], 1 K 8[51] etc.; **4.** *'attûn* in Dn 3[6, 11] etc. These all stand for either a brick-kiln or a smelting furnace. **5.** *tannûr* in Is 31[9] (also AV and RV in Gn 15[17] [RSV 'firepot']; RV in Mal 4[1] [AV and RSV 'oven'] and Ps 21[9] [AV and RSV 'oven']). This is better rendered 'oven' (as in EV in Ex 8[3], Lv 2[4] etc., La 5[10], Hos 7[4, 6]). See BREAD.

At Ezion-geber (q.v.) Nelson Glueck uncovered the furnaces of a great copper refinery, probably dating from the time of Solomon.

FURNACES, TOWER OF THE.—See JERUSALEM [GATES OF].

FURNITURE.—In the AV 'furniture' is used in the general sense of furnishings, just as Bunyan speaks of 'soldiers and their furniture' (*Holy War*, p. 112). **1.** For the details of house furniture, see HOUSE, **8.** In this sense we read also of 'the furniture of the tabernacle' (Ex 31[7] AV and RV [RSV 'furnishings]', Nu 3[8] RV

[AV ' instruments,' RSV ' furnishings ']), and elsewhere. For the less appropriate ' furniture ' of the table of showbread and of ' the candlestick ' (Ex 31^{8f}), RV has ' vessels ' and RSV ' utensils.'

2. The ' camel's furniture ' of Gn 31^{34} AV and RV (RSV ' saddle ') was a ' camel-palankeen ' (*Oxf. Heb. Lex.*, p. 1124), ' a crated frame, with cushions and carpets inside, and protected by an awning above, fastened to the camel's saddle ' (Driver, *Genesis*, *in loc.*), still used by women travellers in the East. A. R. S. K.

G

GAAL, son of Ebed (Jg 9^{26ff}), organized the rising against Abimelech by the discontented in Shechem. Zebul, Abimelech's officer there, warned his master, who came with a strong force, and defeated the rebels under Gaal outside the city. Gaal and his brethren were driven out of Shechem, and terrible vengeance was taken upon the disaffected city. See Abimelech, **2.** W. E.

GAASH.—A mountain in Ephraim (Jos 24^{30}, Jg 2^{9}), near Timnath-serah (q.v.). The brooks of Gaash are mentioned in 2 S 23^{30}, 1 Ch 11^{32}.

GABA.—AV form of **Geba** (q.v.) in Jos 18^{24}, Ezr 2^{26}, Neh 7^{30}.

GABAEL.—**1.** A distant ancestor of Tobit (To 1^{1}). **2.** A friend and kinsman of Tobit, residing at Rages in Media. To him Tobit, when purveyor to the king of Assyria, once entrusted, as a deposit, ten talents of silver (To 1^{14}). When blindness and poverty came on Tobit in Nineveh, he recollected, after prayer, the long-forgotten treasure (To 4^{1}), and wished his son Tobias to fetch it (v.^{20}). Tobias found a guide, Raphael in disguise, who said he had lodged with Gabael (To 5^{6}). When Tobias married Sarah in Ecbatana, he sent Raphael for the deposit (9^{2}).

GABATHA.—One of two eunuchs whose plot against Artaxerxes (the Ahasuerus, *i.e.* Xerxes, of canonical Esther) was discovered and frustrated by Mordecai (AV, RV Mardocheus), Ad. Est 12^{1}. In Est 2^{21} he is called **Bigthan** and in 6^{2} **Bigthana.**

GABBAI.—A Benjamite (Neh 11^{8}, but text doubtful).

GABBATHA (Jn 19^{13}).—The meaning of this word is ' height ' or ' elevation.' It is the Aramaic word rendered by the Greek *lithostrōton* or **' pavement.'** Tradition has identified as Gabbatha an extensive sheet of Roman pavement excavated near the Ecce Homo Arch. It certainly covered a large area, and the blocks of stone composing it are massive, the average size being 4 ft. by 3 ft. 6 in. and nearly 2 ft. thick. The pavement is in parts roughened for the passage of animals and chariots, but over most of the area it is smooth. The paved area was on a lofty place, the ground rapidly falling to east and west, and was in close proximity to, if not actually included within, the Antonia, the Roman fortress north of the Temple. E. W. G. M.—E. G. K.

GABBE, 1 Es 5^{20} (RV).—See Geba, **1.**

GABDES, 1 Es 5^{20} (AV).—See Geba, **1.**

GABRIAS.—The *brother* of the Gabael to whom Tobit entrusted ten talents of silver (To 1^{14}; in 4^{20} AV, RV, and RSV following LXX have ' Gabael the *son* of Gabrias ').

GABRIEL (' man of God ' or perhaps ' God has shown himself mighty ').—Appears in the Bible four times. To Daniel he explains the vision of the ram and the he-goat, Dn 8$^{15-26}$, and relates the decree of the seventy weeks of years, Dn 9$^{21-27}$. In Lk 1$^{11-20}$, Gabriel announces to Zechariah the birth of a son John to Elizabeth, in 1$^{26-35}$ to Mary the birth to her of a son Jesus. Gabriel is regarded as one of the first seven angels on the basis of such passages as To 12^{15}, En 90^{21}, Rev 8^{2}. He is also named as one of the first four, En 9^{1} 40^{9} 54^{6}, and is probably included as one of the first three in En 90^{31}. He ranks next to Michael. According to the Bible he stands before God, Lk 1^{19}, and reveals His will and purpose to men. In the extra-biblical literature in addition he prays and intercedes for mankind, at the same time destroying the wicked, including Sodom and Sennacherib's host. He presides over ' all the powers,' particularly fire, thunder, and the ripening processes of nature. C. C. Ro.

GAD.—A god whose name appears in Gn 30^{11} (' by the help of Gad ' ; so in v.^{13} ' by the help of Asherah ') ; in the place-names Baal-gad (Jos 11^{17} 12^{7} 13^{5}) and Migdal-gad (Jos 15^{37}) ; and in the personal name Azgad (Ezr 2^{12}, Neh 7^{17} 10^{15}). In Is 65^{11} Gad (RV, RSV ' Fortune ') and Meni (RV, RSV ' Destiny ') are named as two demons with whom the Israelites held communion (see Meni). Gad was probably an appellative before it became a personal name for a divinity, and is of Aramaean, Arabian, and Syrian provenance, but not Babylonian. He was the god who gave good fortune (Gr. *Tyche*), and presided over a person, house, or mountain. W. F. C.

GAD.—' The seer ' (1 Ch 29^{29}), ' David's ' or ' the king's seer ' (2 S 24^{11}, 1 Ch 21^{9}, 2 Ch 29^{25}), or ' the prophet ' (1 S 22^{5}, 2 S 24^{11}), who acted as David's counsellor in peril during the period when David dwelt in ' the stronghold ' (1 S 22^{5}), and who announced the Divine condemnation on the royal census and advised the erection of an altar on Araunah's threshing-floor (2 S 24^{11ff}, 1 Ch 21^{9ff}). The Chronicler names him as having written an account of some part of his master's reign (1 Ch 29^{29}). A late conception associated him with the prophet Nathan in the task of planning some of the king's regulations with reference to the musical part of the service (2 Ch 29^{25}).

GAD.—The first son of Zilpah, Leah's maid, by Jacob, and full brother to Asher (Gn 30^{9ff} 35^{26}). According to 30^{11} the name, meaning ' Fortune,' was given to the child by Leah because his birth had brought her good fortune. It is, despite this popular etymology, most probably the name of a deity referred to in Is 65^{11}. Gn 49^{19} implies that the name means a raiding troop and connects it with the tribe's experience in border warfare. Similarly in Dt 33^{20} the tribe is compared to ' a lion that tears the arm and the crown of the head,' and in 1 Ch 12$^{8, 14}$ the Gadites who joined David are described as leonine in appearance and incomparable in combat: ' Their faces are as the faces of lions, the smallest is equal to a hundred and the greatest to a thousand ' (RV, a translation preferable to that of RSV).

Gad and Asher were respectively eponyms of an east-Jordan tribe and of a tribe bordering on Tyre in the north. It has been suggested that the reason for their association as the two sons of Zilpah was that, like Gad, Asher was the name of a deity. Present-day scholars are, however, inclined to question this ; and even if it were so, it would leave unexplained the figure of Zilpah, whose children were reckoned as children of Leah her mistress (cf Gn 30^{3}). Possibly some light is thrown upon the problem by Leah's words in Gn 30$^{11, 13}$, ' Good fortune ' and ' happy am I.' These curiously ignore the fact that she had already borne Jacob four sons ; and this may suggest that the author of the birth chronicle of Jacob's children at this point incorporated in his narrative an independent tradition of the births of Gad and Asher, in which their close association reflected some historical or legendary relationship, unconnected with Israelite history, and therefore simply ignored in the context of the Jacob legend. (Cf the article on SIMEON where it is suggested that the close association of Simeon and Levi reflected in Gn 34^{25ff} 49^{5ff} may possibly reflect the tradition of a relationship which ante-dated their inclusion among the sons of Jacob.) If this is the case it is not impossible that the Asher in this tradition was another figure than the eponym of the Israelite tribe with whom he was secondarily identified by the author of the birth chronicle. (Cf the article on CAIN where it is suggested that the Cain of Gn 4^{13-15} was originally another figure than the Cain of vv.^{3ff}.)

It appears that Gad, notwithstanding the genealogy, was a late tribe. In the Song of Deborah the two east-Jordan groups referred to are Reuben and Gilead ; Gad is not mentioned.

The families of Gad are given by P in Gn 46^{16} and Nu 26^{15ff}. 1 Ch 5^{11ff} repeats them with variations. In the Sinai census they had 46,650 men of war (Nu 1^{24f}) ; in the census in the plains of Moab they numbered 40,500 (26^{15ff}). In the lists of the tribes in Numbers, the position of Gad varies : 11th in 1^{14} ; 6th in 2^{14f} ; 3rd in 10^{20}.

The reason assigned by the tradition for the settlement of Gad and Reuben east of the Jordan is that they were pastoral tribes, with large herds and flocks, and that they found the land pre-eminently adapted to their needs. They therefore obtained from Moses permission to settle there on condition that they first helped the west-Jordan tribes in the work of the conquest (Nu 32^{1-33}, Dt 3^{18}, Jos 13^{8ff} 22^{1ff}). Nu 32^{34-38} lists eight towns lying within the territory of Gad. The most southerly, Aroer, lay upon the Arnon ; the most northerly, Jogbehah, not far from the Jabbok. Ataroth, another of these towns, is mentioned on the Moabite stone (see MESHA), and the 'men of Gad' are there said to have dwelt within it 'from of old.' Within this region six towns, clustering around Heshbon, are assigned to Reuben. But in Jos 13^{15ff} Reuben has all to the south of Heshbon, and Gad all to the north of it. The fact is there was no clearly marked boundary between the two tribes and Gad ultimately absorbed Reuben. The boundary between Gad and the half-tribe of Manasseh was similarly unstable.

In the time of the Judges, Gilead (including the territory of Gad) was threatened, if not occupied, by the Ammonites until Jephthah defeated them (Jg 11). According to 1 Ch $12^{1, 8-15}$, the Gadites supported David against Saul ; no mention is made of this in 1 Samuel, however, so that the Chronicler's statement should be received with the utmost caution. 1 K 12^{25} says that Jeroboam built (that is rebuilt) Penuel which was in the territory of Gad. Some have interpreted the passage as meaning that Jeroboam moved his capital to Penuel, but there is no suggestion of this elsewhere in 1 Kings. Possibly he withdrew there temporarily in the face of Shishak's invasion of Palestine (cf 1 K 14^{25}).

In 734 Tiglath-pileser III., intervening against Rezin of Syria and Pekah of Israel, following the appeal of Ahaz of Judah for help (2 K 16^{7ff}), seized the territory of Gad, and 'carried the people captive to Assyria' (2 K 15^{29}). While it is impossible to determine the actual extent of the deportation it is significant that Gad henceforth played no part in the history of Israel.

J. A. C.—**C. A. Si.**

GAD (VALLEY OF).—Mentioned only in 2 S 24^{5} (AVm, RV ; AV 'river of Gad'), and there the text should read 'in the midst of the valley *toward* Gad' (so RVm, RSV), the valley (*wady*) here being the Arnon (q.v.).

GADARA.—A town on the Yarmuk river about six miles SE. of the Lake of Galilee, which is visible from it. Its territory may have extended to the Lake. On some of its coins a ship is portrayed. The ancient name has clung to some caves among the ruins, but in general the place is called *Muqēs*. The site is a large one and has never received much exploration. The name indicates that it was a Semitic settlement. Its capture by Antiochus III. (218 B.C.) is the first mention of it in history. It was taken by the Jews under Alexander Jannaeus (103–76 B.C.), but liberated by Pompey in 63 B.C. It joined the federation of Greek cities called the Decapolis. Temporarily it lost that status when Augustus granted it to Herod the Great. It was famous for its hot springs at nearby Hammath Geder (*el-Ḥammeh*). The region belonging to Gadara is the scene of the healing of the man possessed by a demon (Mt 8^{28}). In the parallel texts (Mk 5^{1}, Lk 8^{26}) the best MSS read Gerasenes, others Gergesenes and some Gadarenes. The Gergesenes are a dubious entity—the linking of that name with a place called *Kurseh* on the eastern shore of the Lake of Galilee is unwarranted. The territory of Gerasa did not reach to the lake, while that of Gadara easily could have done so. The reading Gadarenes thus must be accounted as the most probable.

E. G. K.

GADARENES.—See GADARA.

GADDI (? 'my fortune').—**1.** The Manassite spy, Nu 13^{11}. **2.** The surname of Johanan or John, the eldest brother of Judas Maccabaeus, 1 Mac 2^{2} (AV **Caddis,** RV **Gaddis**).

GADDIS, 1 Mac 2^{2} (RV).—See GADDI, **2.**

GADDIEL.—The Zebulunite spy, Nu 13^{10}.

GADI.—Father of Menahem king of Israel, 2 K $15^{14, 17}$.

GADITES.—See GAD (tribe).

GAHAM.—A son of Nahor by his concubine Reumah, Gn 22^{24}.

GAHAR.—A family of Nethinim (q.v.) who returned with Zerubbabel, Ezr 2^{47}, Neh 7^{49}, 1 Es 5^{30} (AV, RV **Geddur**).

GAI.—Given as a proper name in RV of 1 S 17^{52} 'until thou comest to Gai,' where AV has 'until thou comest to the valley.' The LXX, as is noted in RVm, has *Gath* (and so RSV), and this would suit the context.

GAIUS.—This name is mentioned in five places of NT. One Gaius was St. Paul's host at Corinth, converted and baptized by him (Ro 16^{23}, 1 Co 1^{14}). He was perhaps the same as 'Gaius of Derbe' who accompanied the Apostle from Greece to Asia (Ac 20^{4}) ; if so, he would be a native of Derbe, but a dweller at Corinth. The Gaius of Macedonia, St. Paul's 'companion in travel' who was seized in the riot at Ephesus (Ac 19^{29}), and the Gaius addressed by St. John (3 Jn ^{1}), were probably different men.

A. J. M.

GAIUS. — As emperor Gaius Caesar Augustus Germanicus, born A.D. 12 (and nicknamed Caligula, 'Boots,' from the soldier's uniform made for him as a boy), the son of Tiberius' popular nephew Germanicus, succeeded his grand-uncle as emperor in A.D. 37, although without experience of public life. At first well-intentioned, he became arbitrary and despotic, and took with insane seriousness the formal ascription to him of divinity. Though friend and patron of Herod Agrippa (q.v.), he was increasingly hostile to the monotheistic Jews ; only his death on Jan. 24, A.D. 41 (at the hands of officers of the praetorian guard whom he had alienated) prevented execution of an order for the erection of his statue in the Temple at Jerusalem. This threatened profanation may well be the 'desolating sacrilege' (RSV ; AV 'abomination of desolation') referred to in Mk 13^{14}, paralleling the similar action of Antiochus Epiphanes (q.v. ; Dn 11^{31f}).

E. R. H.

GALAL.—The name of two Levites, 1 Ch 9^{15f}, Neh 11^{17}.

GALATIA is a Greek word, derived from *Galatae* the Greek name for the **Gauls** who invaded Asia Minor in the year 278–277 B.C. (Lat. *Gallograeci* [='Greek Gauls'], to distinguish them from their kindred who lived in France and Northern Italy). These Gauls had been ravaging the south-eastern parts of Europe, Greece,

Macedonia, and Thrace, and crossed into Asia Minor at the invitation of Nicomedes, king of Bithynia. Part of the same southward tendency appears in their movements in Italy and their conflicts with the Romans in the early centuries of the Republic. Those who entered Asia Minor came as a nation with wives and families, not as mercenary soldiers. After some fifty years' raiding and warring, they found a permanent settlement in north-eastern Phrygia, where the population was unwarlike. Their history down to the time of the Roman Empire may be studied in Wm. Ramsay's *Histor. Com. on Galatians*, pp. 45 ff. They continued throughout these two centuries to be the ruling caste of the district, greatly outnumbered by the native Phrygian population, who, though in many respects an inferior race, had a powerful influence on the religion, customs, and habits of the Gauls, as subject races often have over their conquerors. The earlier sense of the term *Galatia* is, then, the country occupied by the Gaulish immigrants, the former north-eastern part of Phrygia, and the term *Galatae* is used after the occupation to include the subject Phrygians as well as the *Galatae* strictly so called (*e.g.* 1 Mac 8[2], where RSV reads ' Gauls ').

About 160 B.C. the Gauls acquired a portion of Lycaonia on their southern frontier, taking in Iconium and Lystra. About the same time also they had taken in Pessinus in the NW. These and other expansions they ultimately owed to the support of Rome. From 64 B.C. Galatia was a client state of Rome. At the beginning of that period it was under three rulers ; from 44 B.C. it was under one only. Deiotarus, the greatest of the Galatian chiefs, received Armenia Minor from Pompey in 64 B.C. Mark Antony conferred the eastern part of Paphlagonia on Castor as sole Galatian king in 40 B.C., and at the same time gave Amyntas a kingdom comprising Pisidic Phrygia and Pisidia generally. In 36 B.C., Castor's Galatian dominions and Pamphylia were added to Amyntas' kingdom. He was also given Iconium and the old Lycaonian tetrarchy, which Antony had formerly given to Polemon. After the battle of Actium in 31 B.C., Octavian conferred on Amyntas the additional country of Cilicia Tracheia. He had thus to keep order for Rome on the south side of the plateau and on the Taurus mountains. He governed by Roman methods, and, when he died in 25 B.C., he left his kingdom in such a state that Augustus resolved to take the greater part of it into the Empire in the stricter sense of that term, and made it into a province which he called *Galatia*. This is the second sense in which the term Galatia is used in ancient documents, namely, the sphere of administrative responsibility which included the ethnic districts, Paphlagonia, Pontus Galaticus, Galatia (in the original narrower sense), Phrygia Galatica, and Lycaonia Galatica (with ' the Added Land,' part of the original Lycaonian tetrarchy). Galatia, as a province, means all these territories together, under one Roman governor, and the inhabitants of such a province, whatever their race, were, in conformity with invariable Roman custom, denominated by a name etymologically connected with the name of the province. Thus *Galatae* (' Galatians ') has a second sense, in conformity with the second sense of the term *Galatia* : it is used to include all the inhabitants of the province (see the first map in the above-mentioned work of Ramsay).

The word ' Galatia ' occurs three times in the NT (1 Co 16[1], Gal 1[2], and 1 P 1[1]). A possible fourth case (2 Ti 4[10]) must be left out of account, as the reading there is doubtful. There is an alternative ' Gallia,' which, even if it be not the original, suggests that the word ' Galatia ' there should be taken in the sense of ' Gallia ' (that is, France). It is beyond doubt that in the passage of 1 Peter the word must be taken in the sense of the province. The bearer of the letter evidently landed at some port on the Black Sea, perhaps Sinope, and visited the provinces in the order in which they appear in the address of the letter :—Pontus, Galatia, Cappadocia, Asia, and Bithynia, taking ship again at the Black Sea for Rome. The Taurus range of mountains was always conceived of as dividing the peninsula of Asia Minor into two parts, and St. Peter here appears as supervising or advising the whole body of Christians north of the Taurus range. (The effect of taking ' Galatia ' in the other sense would be to leave out certain Pauline churches, Derbe, Lystra, Iconium, and Pisidian Antioch, and perhaps these alone, in all that vast region : which is absurd). With regard to the two passages in St. Paul, the case is settled by his unvarying usage. It has been noted that, proud of his Roman citizenship, he invariably uses geographical terms in the *Roman* sense, and that he even does violence to the Greek language by forcing the Latin names for ' Philippians ' (Ph 4[15]) and ' Illyricum ' (Ro 15[19]) into Greek, and passes by the proper Greek term in each case. We are bound, therefore, to believe that he uses ' Galatia ' in the Roman sense, namely in the meaning of the Roman province as above defined. (This province had, as we have seen, ' Galatia ' in the narrower and earlier sense as one of its parts). It follows, therefore, that he uses ' Galatians ' (Gal 3[1]) also in the wider sense of all (Christian) inhabitants of the province, irrespective of their race, as far as they were known to him.

In order to discover what communities in this vast province are especially addressed by the Apostle in his Epistle, it is necessary to make a critical examination of the only two passages in Acts which afford us a clue (16[6] 18[23]). It is important to note that St. Luke never uses the term ' Galatia ' or the term ' Galatians,' but only the adjective ' Galatic ' (16[6] 18[23]). In 16[6] the rules of the Greek language require us to translate :—' the Phrygo-Galatic region ' or ' the region which is both Phrygian and Galatian ' ; that is, ' the region which according to one nomenclature is Phrygian, and according to another is Galatian.' This can be none other than that section of the province Galatia which was known as Phrygia Galatica, and which contained Pisidian Antioch and Iconium, exactly the places we should expect St. Paul and his companions to go to after Derbe and Lystra. In 18[23] the Greek may be translated either ' the Galatico-Phrygian region ' or ' the Galatian region and Phrygia,' preferably the latter, as it is difficult otherwise to account for the order in the Greek. ' The Galatian region,' then, will cover Derbe and Lystra ; ' Phrygia ' will include Iconium and Pisidian Antioch. We conclude then that, whether any other churches are comprised in the address of the Epistle to the Galatians or not—and a negative answer is probably correct—the churches of Derbe, Lystra, Iconium, and Pisidian Antioch are included. There is not a scrap of evidence that St. Paul had visited any other cities in that great province. A. So.

GALATIANS, EPISTLE TO THE.—1. Occasion of the Epistle.—From internal evidence we gather that St. Paul had, when he wrote, paid two visits to the Galatians. On the first visit, which was due to an illness (4[13]), he was welcomed in the most friendly way ; on the second he warned them against Judaizers (1[9] 5[3] ' again,' cf 4[13] ' the former time,' though this *may* be translated ' formerly '). After the second visit Judaizers came among the Galatians, and persuaded them that they must be circumcised, that St. Paul had changed his mind and was inconsistent, that he had refrained from preaching circumcision to *them* only from a desire to be ' all things to all men,' but that he had preached it (at any rate as the better way) to others. It is doubtful if the Judaizers upheld circumcision as necessary to salvation, or only as necessary to a complete Christianity—*i.e.* in order to be ' perfect,' those ' led by the Spirit ' must also keep the Mosaic Law, which is still the divinely ordained body of commandments ' whereby a man shall live and not die.' It depends on whether we fix the date before or after the Council of Ac 15, which of these views we adopt (see **4**). Further, the Judaizers disparaged St. Paul's authority as compared with that of the Twelve. On hearing this the Apostle hastily wrote the Epistle to check the evil, and (probably) soon followed up the Epistle with a personal visit.

2. To whom written. The North Galatian and South Galatian theories.—It is disputed whether the inhabitants of N. Galatia are addressed (Lightfoot, Salmon, the older commentators, Schmiedel in *Encyc. Bibl.*, Moffatt, *et al.*), or the inhabitants of Pisidian Antioch, Iconium, Lystra, and Derbe, which lay in the S. part of the Roman province Galatia (Ramsay, Sanday, Zahn, Renan, Pfleiderer, Burton, *et al.*). Those who hold the N. Galatian theory take Ac 16⁶ 18²³ as indicating that St. Paul visited Galatia proper, making a long detour. They press the argument that he would not have called men of the four cities by the name 'Galatians,' as these lay outside Galatia proper, and that 'Galatians' must mean men who are Gauls by blood and descent; also that 'by writers speaking familiarly of the scenes in which they had themselves taken part' popular usage rather than official is probable, and therefore to call the Christian communities in the four cities 'the churches of Galatia' would be unnatural. On the other hand, the N. Galatian theory creates Churches unheard of elsewhere in 1st cent. records; it is difficult on this hypothesis to understand the silence of Acts, which narrates all the critical points of St. Paul's work. But Acts does tell us very fully of the foundation of the Church in S. Galatia. Then, again, on the N. Galatian theory, St. Paul nowhere in his Epistles mentions the four cities (mentioned once by the Paulinist author of 2 Ti 3^{11})—a silence made more remarkable by the fact that in the collection of the alms he *does* mention 'the churches of Galatia' (1 Co 16^{1}). If the four cities are not here referred to, why were they omitted? The main argument of the N. Galatian theory, given above, is sufficiently answered by taking into account St. Paul's relation to the Roman Empire (see LUKE-ACTS; also PAUL, 7).

With regard to the nomenclature, we notice that St. Luke sometimes uses popular non-political names like 'Phrygia' or 'Mysia' (Ac 2^{10} 16^{8}); but St. Paul, as a Roman citizen, uses place-names in their Roman sense throughout, *e.g.* 'Achaia' (which in Greek popular usage had a much narrower meaning than the Roman province, and did not include Athens, while St. Paul contrasts it with Macedonia, the only other Roman province in Greece, and therefore clearly uses it in its Roman sense, Ro 15^{26}, 2 Co 9^{2} 11^{10}, 1 Th 1^{7f}; cf 1 Co 16^{5}), 'Macedonia,' 'Illyricum' (Ro 15^{19} only; the Greeks did not use this name popularly as a substantive, and none but a Roman could so denote the province; 'Syria and Cilicia' (one Roman province), and 'Asia' (the Roman province of that name, the W. part of Asia Minor, including Mysia). We may compare the nomenclature in 1 P 1^{1}, where the the author is so much influenced by Pauline ideas that he designates all Asia Minor north of the Taurus by enumerating the Roman provinces. St. Paul, then, calls all citizens of the province of Galatia by the honourable name 'Galatians.' To call the inhabitants of the four cities 'Phrygians' or 'Lycaonians' would be as discourteous as to call them 'slaves' or 'barbarians.' The Roman colonies like Pisidian Antioch were most jealous of their Roman connexion.

The S. Galatian theory reconciles the Epistle and Acts without the somewhat violent hypotheses of the rival theory. The crucial passages are Ac 16^{6} 18^{23}, which are appealed to on both sides. In 16^{6} St. Paul comes from Syro-Cilicia to Derbe and Lystra, no doubt by land, through the Cilician Gates [Derbe being mentioned first as being reached first, while in 14^{6} Lystra was reached first and mentioned first], and then 'they went through (*v.l.* going through) the region of Phrygia and Galatia,' literally 'the Phrygian and Galatic region' [so all the best MSS read these last words]. This 'region,' then probably a technical term for the subdivision of a province), was a single district to which the epithets 'Phrygian' and 'Galatic' could both be applied; that is, it was that district which was part of the old country of Phrygia, and also part of the Roman province of Galatia. But no part of the old Galatia overlapped Phrygia, and the only district satisfying the requirements is the region around Pisidian Antioch and Iconium; therefore in 16^{6} a detour to N. Galatia is excluded. Moreover, no route from N. Galatia to Bithynia could bring the travellers 'over against Mysia' (16^{7}). They would have had to return almost to the spot from which they started on their hypothetic journey to N. Galatia. Attempts to translate this passage, even as read by the best MSS, as if it were 'Phrygia and the Galatic region,' as the AV text (following inferior MSS) has it, have been made by a citation of Lk 3^{1}, but this appears to be a mistake; the word translated there 'Ituraea' is really an adjective 'Ituraean,' and the meaning probably is 'the Ituraean region which is also called Trachonitis.'

In the other passage, Ac 18^{23}, the grammar and therefore the meaning are different. St. Paul comes, probably, by the same land route as before, and to the same district; yet now Derbe and Lystra are not mentioned by name. St. Paul went in succession through 'the Galatic region' and through 'Phrygia' (or '[the] Phrygian [region]'). The grammar requires two different districts here. The first is the 'Galatic region' [of Lycaonia]—that part of old Lycaonia which was in the province Galatia, *i.e.* the region round Derbe and Lystra. The second is the 'Phrygian region' [of Galatia], *i.e.* what was in 16^{6} called the Phrygo-Galatic region, that around Antioch and Iconium. In using a different phrase St. Luke considers the travellers' point of view; for in the latter case they leave Syrian Antioch, and enter, by way of non-Roman Lycaonia, into Galatic Lycaonia ('the Galatic region'), while in the former case they start from Lystra and enter the Phrygo-Galatic region near Iconium.

All this is clear on the S. Galatian theory. But on the other theory it is very hard to reconcile the Epistle with Acts. The S. Galatian theory also fits in very well with incidental notices in the Epistle, such as the fact that the Galatians evidently knew Barnabas well, and were aware that he was the champion of the Gentiles (2^{13} '*even* Barnabas'); but Barnabas did not accompany Paul on the Second Missionary Journey, when, on the N. Galatian theory, the Galatians were first evangelized. Again, Gal 4^{13} fits in very well with Ac 13^{14} on the S. Galatian theory; for the very thing to do, if attacked by an illness in the low-lying lands of Pamphylia, would be to go to the high uplands of Pisidian Antioch. This seems to have been an unexpected change of plan (one which perhaps caused Mark's defection). On the other hand, if a visit to Galatia proper had been part of the plan in Ac 16 to visit Bithynia, Gal 4^{13} would have been unintelligible.

3. St. Paul's autobiography.—In chs. 1, 2 the Apostle vindicates his authority by saying that he received it direct from God, and not through the older Apostles, with whom the Judaizers compared him unfavourably. For this purpose he tells of his conversion, of his relations with the Twelve, and of his visits to Jerusalem; and shows that he did not receive his commission from men. Wm. Ramsay urged with much force that it was essential to Paul's argument that he should mention all visits paid by him to Jerusalem between his conversion and the time of his evangelizing the Galatians. In the Epistle we read of two visits (1^{18} 2^{1}), the former three years after his conversion (or after his return to Damascus), to visit Cephas, when of the Apostles he saw only James the Lord's brother besides, and the latter fourteen years after his conversion (or after his first visit), when he went 'by revelation' with Barnabas and Titus and privately laid before the Twelve (this probably is the meaning of 'them' in 2^{2}: James, Cephas, and John are mentioned) the gospel which he preached among the Gentiles. We have, then, to ask, To which, if any, of the visits recorded in Acts do these correspond? Most scholars agree that Gal 1^{18}=Ac 9^{26ff}, and that the word 'Apostles' in the latter place may mean Peter and James only. But there is much diversity of opinion concerning Gal 2^{1}. A majority of scholars identify this visit with that of Ac 15^{2} (the Jerusalem Council). A minority identify the visit with that of Ac 11^{30}, since otherwise St. Paul would be suppressing a point which would tell in favour of his opponents, it being essential to his argument to mention all his visits.

It should be noted that a solution of the major critical problems, *i.e.* whether the churches addressed by Paul were located in north or south Galatia and how the biographical data of Galatians are to be reconciled with Acts, is of relatively minor importance so far as the interpretation of the letter itself is concerned. On the south Galatian hypothesis, now held by most scholars, we may identify the churches addressed in Galatia with the cities named in Acts (see article GALATIA). Acts tells us so little about these churches, however, that little light is thrown upon the Epistle.

4. Date and place of writing.—Upholders of the N. Galatian theory, understanding Ac 16^6 18^{23} to represent the two visits to the Galatians implied in Gal 4^{13}, usually fix on Ephesus as the place of writing, and suppose that the Epistle dates from the long stay there recorded in Ac 19^{8ff}, probably early in the stay (cf Gal 1^6 'you are *so quickly* deserting'); but J. B. Lightfoot postponed the date for some two years, and thought that the Epistle was written from Macedonia (Ac 20^1), rather earlier than Romans and after 2 Corinthians. He gaves a comparison of these Epistles, showing the very close connexion between Romans and Galatians: the same use of OT, the same ideas and same arguments, founded on the same texts; in the doctrinal part of Galatians we can find a parallel for almost every thought and argument in Romans. It is generally agreed that the latter, a systematic treatise, is later than the former, a personal and fragmentary Epistle. (See also Hans Lietzmann.) The likeness is much less marked between Galatians and 1 and 2 Corinthians; but in 2 Corinthians the Apostle vindicates his authority much as in Galatians. The opposition to him evidently died away with the controversy about circumcision. Thus it is clear that these four Epistles hang together and are to be separated chronologically from the rest.

On the S. Galatian theory, the Epistle was written from Antioch. Ramsay puts it at the end of the Second Missionary Journey (Ac 18^{22}). Timothy, he thinks, had been sent to his home at Lystra from Corinth, and rejoined Paul at Syrian Antioch, bringing news of the Galatian defection. Paul wrote off hastily, dispatched Timothy back with the letter, and as soon as possible followed himself (Ac 18^{23}). On this supposition the two visits to the Galatians implied by the Epistle would be those of Ac 13 f and 16. The intended visit of Paul would be announced by Timothy, though it was not mentioned in the letter, which in any case was clearly written in great haste. It is certainly strange, on the Ephesus or Macedonia hypothesis, that Paul neither took any steps to visit the erring Galatians, nor, if he could not go to them, explained the reason of his inability. Ramsay's view, however, has the disadvantage that it separates Galatians and Romans by some years. Yet if St. Paul kept a copy of his letters, he might well have elaborated his hastily sketched argument in Galatians into the treatise in Romans, at some little interval of time. Ramsay gives A.D. 53 for Galatians, the other three Epistles following in A.D. 56 and 57.

Another view is that of V. Weber, who also holds that Syrian Antioch was the place of writing, but dates the Epistle *before* the Council (see Ac 14^{28}). He agrees with Ramsay as to the two visits to Jerusalem; but he thinks that the manner of the Judaizers' attack points to a time before the Apostolic decree. Gal 6^{12} ('compel') suggests that they insisted on circumcision as necessary *for salvation* (**1**). If so, their action could hardly have taken place after the Council. A strong argument on this side is that St. Paul makes no allusion to the decision of the Council. The chronological difficulty of the fourteen years (2^1) is met by placing the conversion of St. Paul in A.D. 32. Weber thinks that 5^2 could not have been written after the circumcision of Timothy; but this is doubtful. The two visits to the Galatians, on this view, would be those of Ac 13, on the outward and the homeward journey respectively. The strongest argument against Weber's date is that it necessitates such a long interval between Galatians and Romans.

5. Abstract of the Epistle.—Chs. 1, 2. Answer to the Judaizers' disparagement of Paul's office and message. Narrative of his life from his conversion onwards, showing that he did not receive his Apostleship and his gospel through the medium of other Apostles, but direct from God.

3^1–5^{12}. Doctrinal exposition of the freedom of the gospel, as against the legalism of the Judaizers. Abraham was justified by faith, not by the Law, and so are the children of Abraham. The Law was an inferior dispensation, though good for the time, and useful as educating the world for freedom; the Galatians are bent on returning to a state of tutelage, and their present attitude is retrogressive.

5^{13}–6^{10}. Hortatory. 'Hold fast by freedom, but do not mistake it for licence. Be forbearing and liberal.'

6^{11-18}. Conclusion. Summing up of the whole in Paul's own hand, written in large characters (6^{11} RV) to show the importance of the subject of the autograph.

6. Genuineness of the Epistle.—The genuineness of Galatians, together with Romans and 1 and 2 Corinthians, has seldom been questioned. As for the testimony, Clement of Rome explicitly mentions and quotes 1 Corinthians, and his date cannot be brought down later than A.D. 100. Our Epistle is probably alluded to or cited by Barnabas, Hermas, and Ignatius (five times); certainly by Polycarp (four times), the *Epistle to Diognetus*, Justin Martyr, Melito, Athenagoras, and the *Acts of Paul and Thecla*. It is found in the Old Latin and Syriac versions and in the Muratorian Fragment (*c* A.D. 180–200). It was used by 2nd cent. heretics, alluded to by adversaries like Celsus and the writer of the *Clementine Homilies*, and quoted by name and distinctly (as their fashion was) by Irenaeus, Clement of Alexandria, and Tertullian, at the end of the 2nd cent. But, apart from this external testimony, the spontaneous nature of the Epistle is decisive in favour of its genuineness. There is no possible motive for forgery. An anti-Jewish Gnostic would not have used expressions of deference to the Apostles of the Circumcision; an Ebionite would not have used the arguments of the Epistle against the Mosaic Law (thus the *Clementine Homilies*, an Ebionite work, clearly hits at the Epistle in several passages); an orthodox forger would avoid all appearance of conflict between Peter and Paul. After A.D. 70 there never was the least danger of the Gentile Christians being made to submit to the Law. A. J. M.—A. C. P.

GALBANUM (Heb. *ḥelbᵉnāh*).—One of the ingredients of the sacred incense (Ex 30^{34}). It is a brownish-yellow, pleasant-smelling resin from various species of *Ferula*; it is imported from Persia.

GALEED ('cairn of witness').—The name which, according to Gn 31^{47}, was given by Jacob to the cairn erected on the occasion of the compact between him and Laban. There is evidently a characteristic attempt also to account in this way for the name *Gilead*. The respective proceedings of Jacob and of Laban are uncertain, for the narrative is not only of composite origin, but has suffered through the introduction of glosses into the text. It is almost certain that we should read 'Laban' instead of 'Jacob' in v.^{45}. The LXX seeks unsuccessfully to reduce the narrative to order by means of transpositions.

GALILEE.—1. Position.—Galilee was the region of Palestine N. of Samaria. It was bounded southward by the Carmel range and the southern border of the plain of Esdraelon, whence it stretched eastward by Bethshean (Scythopolis, *Beisān*) to the Jordan. Eastward it was limited by the Jordan and the western bank of its expansions (the Sea of Galilee and Lake Semechonitis). Northward and to the north-west it was bounded by Syria and Phoenicia; it reached the sea only in the region round the bay of '*Akkā* and immediately north of it. Its maximum extent therefore was somewhere about 60 miles north to south, and 30 east to west.

2. Name.—The name *Galilee* is of Canaanitic or Hebrew origin, and signifies a 'ring' or 'circuit.' The name may be a contraction of a fuller expression, preserved by Is 9[1], namely, 'Galilee of the nations' though the possibility that the fuller expression is an expansion cannot be ruled out. It could originally have described a ring of cities lying about the hill country. The Hebrew form *gālîl* is found Aramaized as *Galila* in the Greek Zenon Papyri (259 B.C.); the form *Galilaia* is a gentilic derived from Galila.

3. History.—In the system of tribal allotments in the Book of Joshua the territory of Galilee was divided among Asher, Naphtali, Zebulun, and part of Issachar. In the OT history the tribal designations are generally used when subdivisions of the country are denoted; this is no doubt the reason why the name 'Galilee' occurs so rarely in the Hebrew Scriptures—though Is 9[1], as well as the references to Kedesh and other cities 'in Galilee' (Jos 20[7] 21[32], 1 K 9[11], 2 K 15[29], 1 Ch 6[76]), show that the name was familiar and employed upon occasion. Some of the most important of the historical events of the early Hebrew history took place within the borders of Galilee. The region was devastated by Benhadad I. of Damascus (1 K 15[20]), and again by Hazael (2 K 12[18]). It was recovered by Jeroboam II. (2 K 13[22]). From 2 K 15[29] and from the Assyrian inscriptions we learn that in 732 B.C. Tiglathpileser III. annexed Galilee and made it part of the Assyrian province of Megiddo. It seems improbable that the whole population was deported. The ancient rulers were interested in having agriculture continue and provide revenues. Much of Galilee seems to have become crown-land.

An expedition to rescue Jews of Galilee took place under Judas Maccabaeus, but apparently only the region near Acco and Mount Carmel is meant (1 Mac 5[21-23]). It was not till its conquest, by John Hyrcanus, that Galilee was included in Jewish territory. Under the pressure of Egyptian and Roman invaders the national patriotism developed rapidly, and it became as intensely Jewish as Jerusalem itself. Under the Roman domination Galilee was governed as a tetrarchate, held by members of the Herod family. Herod the Great was ruler of Galilee in 47 B.C., and was succeeded by his son Antipas, as tetrarch, in 4 B.C. In the 3rd cent. A.D., Galilee became the centre of Rabbinic life. Remains of Jewish synagogues of this era are to be seen among the ruins of Galilaean cities. But it is as the principal theatre of Jesus' life and work that Galilee commands its greatest interest. Almost the whole of His life was spent within its borders. The disciples no doubt were also natives of this area.

4. Physical Characteristics.—Owing to moisture derived from the Lebanon mountains, Galilee is the best watered district of Palestine, and abounds in streams and springs, though the actual rainfall is little greater than that of Judaea. The result of this enhanced water supply is seen in the fertility of the soil, which is far greater than anywhere in Southern Palestine. It was famous for oil, wheat, barley, and fruit, as well as cattle. The fisheries about the Sea of Galilee were also important. The formation of the country is limestone, broken by frequent dykes and outflows of trap and other volcanic rocks. Hot springs at Tiberias and elsewhere, and not infrequent earthquakes, indicate a continuance of volcanic and analogous energies.

5. Population.—Galilee in the time of Christ was inhabited by a mixed population. There was the Jewish element, grafted no doubt on a substratum of Israelites, Aramaeans, and Canaanites. Besides these there was the cultivated class—the inhabitants of the Greek cities and the military representatives of the dominant power of Rome. In Judaea the Galilaeans were looked down upon. 'Can any good thing come out of Nazareth?' (Jn 1[46]) was one proverb. 'Out of Galilee ariseth no prophet' (7[52]) was another. The Galilaeans spoke an Aramaic dialect differing from the dialects used in Samaria and Judaea. It betrayed Peter when he endeavoured to deny his discipleship (Mt 26[73]).

R. A. S. M.—**E. G. K.**

GALILEE, SEA OF.—1. Situation, etc.—The Sea of Galilee is an expansion of the Jordan, 13 miles long, about 8 miles in maximum breadth; its surface is 680 feet below that of the Mediterranean; its maximum depth is about 150 feet. In shape it is like a pear, the narrow end pointing southward. Like the Dead Sea, it is set deep among hills, which rise on the east side to a height of about 2000 feet. At the emergence of the Jordan, however, the Lake impinges on the plain of the Ghōr.

2. Names.—The original name of the Sea seems to have been **Chinnereth** or **Chinneroth.** It takes its name from an old Canaanite city (Jos 11[2] 19[35], 1 K 15[20]), which lay at *Tell el ʿOreimeh* above its north-western shore. By this name it is referred to in assigning the border of the Promised Land (Nu 34[11]), in stating the boundary of the trans-Jordanic tribes (Dt 3[12], Jos 13[27]), and in enumerating the kings conquered by Joshua (Jos 12[3]). The Lake is referred to also by the name *Gennesar* in Josephus (always), and in 1 Mac 11[67] (AV). That is really the name of the plain stretching along the west side of the lake S. of Chinnereth. In the Gospels it is referred to under a variety of names: besides such general terms as 'the lake' (Lk 8[22] etc.), or 'the sea' (Jn 6[16]), we find **Lake of Gennesaret** (only in Lk 5[1], the final *et* probably being an error), **Sea of Tiberias** (Jn 21[1], and also as an explanatory or alternative name in Jn 6[1]), but most frequently *Sea of Galilee.* The modern name is *Baḥr Ṭabarîyeh,* 'Lake of Tiberias.'

3. Importance in NT times.—The Sea in the time of Jesus was surrounded by a number of important cities. Such were Tiberias, Bethsaida, Capernaum, Chorazin, and Magdala. The fishing industry was important, and where now but a few small boats are to be seen, there evidently were formerly numerous fishing vessels. Owing to the great height of the mountains surrounding the Lake, differences of temperature are produced which give rise to sudden and violent storms. Two such storms are mentioned in the Gospels—one in Mt 8[23], Mk 4[36], Lk 8[22], the other in Mt 14[22], Mk 6[45], Jn 6[16].

R. A. S. M.—**E. G. K.**

GALL.—(1) *rōsh*, some very bitter plant, Dt 29[18] AV, RV; RSV 'poisonous fruit'), La 3[19]; 'water of gall' (AV, RV; RSV 'poisoned water'), Jer 8[14] 9[15]; translated 'hemlock,' Hos 10[4] (AV, RV; RSV 'poisonous weeds'), 'poison,' Job 20[16]. Hemlock (*Conium maculatum*), colocynth (*Citrullus colocynthis*), and the poppy (*Papaver somniferum*) have all been suggested. (2) *mᵉrērāh* (Job 16[13]) and *mᵉrōrāh* (Job 20[14, 25]) refer to the bile. The poison of serpents was supposed to lie in their bile (20[14]). The gall (Gr. *cholē*) of Mt 27[34] evidently refers to the LXX version of Ps 69[21], where *cholē* is a translation of *rōsh*. E. W. G. M.

GALLERY.—1. AV in Ca 7[5] reads 'The king is held in the galleries.' The Hebrew is *barᵉhāṭîm*, which, there is no reasonable doubt, means 'in the tresses' (so RV, RSV). The king is captivated, that is to say, by the tresses of this 'prince's daughter.' **2.** AV, RV, and RSV translation of *'attîḳ*, a word used in the description of Ezekiel's temple and whose etymology and meaning are both obscure, in Ezk 42[3, 5]; but in Ezk 41[15] RSV has 'walls' and in 41[16] 'recessed' (AV, RV both 'galleries').

GALLEY.—See SHIPS AND BOATS.

GALLIM ('heaps').—A place near Jerusalem (1 S 25[44]). It is personified, along with Anathoth and other towns, in Is 10[30]. It is generally placed to the N. of Jerusalem, and is perhaps *Kh. Kaʿkûl*, near Anathoth.

GALLIO.—The elder brother of the philosopher Seneca. According to an inscription found at Delphi, Gallio was proconsul of Achaia in A.D. 51–52 or A.D. 52–53. The earlier date is the more probable; Paul left Corinth in the early autumn of the year A.D. 51. The Jews of Corinth had brought him before Gallio, when Gallio reached Corinth, perhaps early in May. They did not yet know that the new governor was of an anti-Semitic family. He refused to accept the charge against Paul, and when the heathen mob beat the leader of the Jewish delegation, Gallio 'paid no attention to this' (Ac 18$^{12-17}$). E. H.

GALLOWS.—This word occurs nine times in RSV (eight in AV and RV) in the book of Esther only (5^{14} etc.) as the rendering of the ordinary Hebrew word for 'tree' (see margins). It is very doubtful if death by strangulation is intended—'tree' in all probability having here its frequent sense of 'pole,' on which, as was customary in Persia, the criminal was impaled (see CRIMES AND PUNISHMENTS, **10**). A. R. S. K.

GAMAD (MEN OF).—Mentioned only in Ezk 27^{11} (RSV; AV 'Gammadims,' RV 'Gammadim'). No place of this name is known, but a proper name is what the context seems to demand. RVm 'valorous men' has not commended itself to the majority of scholars.

GAMAEL (1 Es 8^{29}) = **Daniel, 4** (Ezr 8^{2}).

GAMALIEL.—**1.** The son of Pedahzur, and 'prince of the children of Manasseh' (Nu 1^{10} 2^{20} etc.). **2.** Gamaliel I., the grandson (or perhaps the son) of Hillel, was a Pharisee, and regarded as one of the most distinguished teachers of the Law in his age. He was a member of the Sanhedrin in the time of Jesus and Paul. To him have been ascribed views which were tolerant and large-hearted; he emphasized the human side of the Law, relaxing somewhat the rigour of Sabbatical observance, regulating the customs of divorce so as the more to protect helpless women, and inculcating kindness on the part of Jews towards surrounding heathen. In Ac 5$^{34-40}$ he urges the Sanhedrin to let the future disclose whether or not the Christian movement is blessed with God's favour. In 22^{3}, Paul is said to have sat at Gamaliel's feet. Historical scholars have questioned the reliability of both passages.

The *Clementine Recognitions* absurdly state that by the advice of the Apostles he remained among the Jews as a secret believer in Christ. A host of later legends even suppose that he became an open convert. The Mishnah deplores that 'with the death of Gamaliel I., reverence for the Divine Law ceased, and the observance of purity and piety became extinct.' C. T. P. G.—**S. S.**

GAMES.—I. AMONG THE ISRAELITES.—The Jews were essentially a serious people. What in other nations developed into play and games of various kinds, had with them a seriously practical and often a religious character. Their **dances** were a common form of religious exercise, which might indeed degenerate into disorderly or unseemly behaviour, but were only exceptionally a source of healthy social amusement (Ps 150^{4}, Ex 32$^{6, 19}$, 2 S 6^{14ff}, Jer 31^{4}, Ec 3^{4}). **Music,** again, was especially associated with sacred song. Its secular use was condemned by Isaiah as a sign of extravagant luxury (Is 5^{12}). **Lots** and the like were used as a means of ascertaining the Divine will, not for amusement or profit. Even what with children might be called games of 'make believe' became with some of the prophets vehicles of religious instruction. The symbolic object-lessons of Ezekiel were like the play of children, but at the same time adapted to a religious purpose (see especially ch. 4). Even this humour of the prophets, striking as it was, was intensely serious: witness the scathing ridicule of idolatry by Elijah and Deutero-Isaiah (1 K 18^{27}, Is 44$^{12-20}$ 46^{1f}).

It is a matter of some dispute whether manly sports had any place in the social life of the Israelites. There was undoubtedly some sort of training in the use of weapons, particularly the **sling** (among the Benjamites especially) and the **bow,** for the purposes of warfare and the chase. We have a definite reference to the custom of practising at a mark in 1 S 20$^{20, 35ff}$, and there are several metaphorical allusions to the same practice (Job 16^{12f}, La 3^{12}). Again, it has also been thought that we have in the heavy stone of Zec 12^{3} an allusion to a custom of **lifting a heavy stone** either as a test of strength or as a means of strengthening the muscles; but there is no actual proof that there was any sort of competitive contest in such exercises. It may be suggested, however, on the other hand, that the practice of determining combats by selected champions, one or more, from either side, which we read of in 1 S 17^{10}, 2 S 2$^{13-16}$, and the expression used in the latter case, 'let the young men . . . arise and play before us,' makes it likely that friendly **tournaments** were not unknown.

Riddle-guessing is the one form of competition of which we have any certain proof. In Jg 14$^{12-14}$ the propounding and guessing of riddles as a wager appears as part of the entertainment of a marriage feast. The questions put by the queen of Sheba to Solomon probably belong to the same category (1 K 10$^{1, 3}$). Indeed, the propounding of 'dark sayings,' or 'riddles,' was a common element in proverbial literature (Ps 78^{2}, Pr 1^{6}).

Children's Games.—Games of play are so invariable an element of child life among all peoples, that it hardly needs proof that the Israelites were no exception to the rule. The playing of the boys and girls in the streets of the glorified Jerusalem (Zec 8^{5}) might indeed mean nothing more than kitten play; but fortunately we have in Mt 11^{16f}||Lk 7^{31f} a most interesting allusion to the games (mock-weddings and mock-funerals) played in the market-place in our Lord's time, as they are played in Palestine at the present day.

We read in 2 Mac 4$^{9-17}$ how Jason the high priest and the head of the Hellenizing party, having bribed Antiochus Epiphanes with 150 talents of silver, set up 'a place of exercise' (gymnasium) for the training up of youths in Greek customs. The only game specifically mentioned is the **discus.** There is also mentioned in v.^{18} 'a game' that was held every fifth year at Tyre—evidently an imitation of the Olympic games. Later, Herod the Great appears from Josephus (*Ant.* xv. viii. 1 [268]) to have provoked a conspiracy of the Jews by building a **theatre** and an amphitheatre at Jerusalem for the spectacular combats of wild beasts, and to have initiated very splendid games every five years in honour of Caesar. These included wrestling and chariot races, and competitors were attracted from all countries by the very costly prizes.

II. GAMES OF GREECE AND ROME.—Athletic contests formed a very important feature in the social life of the Greeks. They originated in pre-historic times, and were closely associated with religious worship. Thus the Olympic games were held in honour of Olympian Zeus in connexion with the magnificent temple at Olympia in Elis; the Isthmian games on the Isthmus of Corinth in honour of Poseidon; the Pythian were associated with the worship of the Pythian Apollo at Delphi; the Nemean were celebrated at Nemea, a valley of Argolis, to commemorate the Nemean Zeus. These four games were great Pan-Hellenic festivals, to which crowds came from all parts, not only free-born Greeks, but also foreigners, although the latter, except the Romans in later times, were not allowed to compete. The most important of these games were the Olympic. They were held every four years, and so great was the occasion that from the year 264 B.C. events as far back as 776 were computed by them. The period between one celebration and another was called an Olympiad, and an event was said to have occurred in the 1st, 2nd, 3rd, or 4th year of such an Olympiad. The Isthmian games, which took place biennially in the first and third year of each Olympiad, seem to have been modelled on very much the same lines as the Olympic. To the Biblical student they have a more direct interest, as it is highly probable that the frequent allusions to such contests by St. Paul (see especially 1 Co 9$^{24-27}$) were due to his personal observation of these games, which may have taken place while he was at Corinth. As, however, our knowledge of the Olympic games, of which several ancient writers have left us particulars, is far more complete, it often happens that the language of St. Paul is more easily illustrated from them. It should be mentioned also in this connexion that besides these four great athletic contests, games of a local character, often in imitation of the Olympic, were held throughout Greece and her colonies in all towns of importance, which had both their stadium and their theatre. The most important of these, from the Biblical student's point of view, were the games of Ephesus. With these St. Paul was certainly familiar, and, as will be seen below, allusions to games are remarkably frequent in writings connected with Ephesus.

The contests at Olympia included running, boxing, wrestling, chariot races, and other competitions both for men and for youths. The judges, who seem also to have acted as a sort of managing committee, with many dependents, were chosen by lot, one for each division of Elis. They held at once a highly honoured and a very difficult post, and were required to spend ten months in learning the duties of their office. For the last thirty days of this period they were required personally to superintend the training of the athletes who were preparing to compete. In addition to this, the athletes were required to swear before competing that they had spent ten months previously in training. We thus realize the force of such allusions as that of 1 Ti 4^{7f}, where St. Paul insists on the greater importance of the training in godliness than that of the body. These facts also add point to the allusions in 2 Ti 2^{5}. An athlete is not crowned unless he contend 'according to the rules.' These regulations required the disqualification not only of the disfranchized and criminals, but of those who had not undergone the required training. It is the last to which the passage seems especially to point.

The **prize,** while it differed in different places, was always a crown of leaves. At Olympia it was made of wild olive; in the Isthmus, in St. Paul's time, of pine leaves; at Delphi, of 'laurel'; at Nemea, of parsley. In addition to this, at Olympia, Delphi, and probably elsewhere, the victor had handed to him a palm-branch, as a token of victory. It is almost impossible to exaggerate the honour attached to winning the prize in these contests. The victor entered his native city in triumphal procession; he had conferred upon him many privileges and immunities, and his victory was frequently celebrated in verse. His statue might be, and often was, placed in the sacred grove of Elis, and he was looked upon as a public benefactor. St. Paul in 1 Co 9^{24-27} makes use of the spirit of these contests to illustrate to the Corinthians, to whom it must have specially appealed, the self-denial, the strenuousness, and the glorious issue of the Christian conflict, drawing his metaphorical allusions partly from the foot-race and partly from the boxing and wrestling matches. 'They do it to receive a perishable wreath, but we an imperishable. Well, I do not run aimlessly, I do not box as one beating the air; but I pommel my body and subdue it . . .'

There is a very interesting allusion to the games of Ephesus in 2 Ti 4^{7} 'I have fought the good fight, I have finished the race . . . henceforth there is laid up for me the crown of righteousness,' etc. This stands in striking contrast to Ph 3^{12-16} 'Not that I have already obtained this, or am already perfect; but I press on . . . forgetting what lies behind, and straining forward to what lies ahead, I press on toward the goal for the prize of the upward call of God in Christ Jesus.' Here again it is the intense eagerness of the athlete that is specially in St. Paul's mind. We have many other allusions by St. Paul to the **foot-race,** as in Ro 9^{16}, Gal 2^{2} 5^{7}, Ph 2^{16}, Ac 20^{24}. These generally refer to the 'course' of life and conduct. The last passage, it should be remembered, is addressed to the elders at Ephesus. The full significance of Ro 9^{16} is missed unless we realize the intensity of effort required by the racer. The supreme effort of the will is worthless without the grace of God.

We have allusions to the **wrestling match** certainly in Eph 6^{12}, where St. Paul speaks of wrestling against spiritual forces, and probably to boxing in 4^{27}, where 'giving place' means giving vantage-ground to the spiritual foe. In connexion with Ephesus we may notice also the allusion in Ac 19^{31} to the Asiarchs—the officers who superintended the games. The reference to fighting 'with wild beasts at Ephesus' in 1 Co 15^{32} is probably a metaphorical allusion to such contests as were common afterwards in the Colosseum at Rome. After the capture of Jerusalem Titus gave at Caesarea Philippi shows, in which a number of Jewish captives were thrown to wild beasts (Jos. *BJ* VII. ii. 1[23]).

Outside St. Paul's writings there is an important reference to athletic contests in He 12^{1-2}. Here the two points emphasized are: (1) the 'cloud of witnesses' (Gr. *martyres*), whose past achievements are to encourage the Christian combatants for the faith; (2) the self-sacrifice and earnestness needed in running the Christian race. The Christian athlete must lay aside every 'weight' —every hindrance to his work, just as the runner divested himself of his garments, having previously by hard training got rid of all superfluous flesh—and look only to Christ. Again, in Rev 7^{9} we have in the palms in the hands of the great company of martyrs a very probable reference to the palms given to the successful competitors in the games. Here, again, it should be borne in mind that it was to Ephesus and the surrounding towns, the district of the great Ephesian games, that the author of the Apocalypse was writing. F. H. W.—H. S. G.

GAMMADIM.—See GAMAD.

GAMUL ('weaned').—A chief of the Levites, and head of the 22nd course of priests, 1 Ch 24^{17}.

GANGRENE.—In 2 Ti 2^{17} (AVm, RV, RSV) this renders Greek *gangraina*, a medical term for spreading ulcers. AV has 'canker.'

GAR, 1 Es 5^{34} (AV).—See GAS.

GARDEN (Heb. *gan* ['enclosure'], *gannāh*, which, like the Persian [modern Armenian] *pardēs* [Neh 2^{8}, EV 'forest'], and the Arabic *jannah* and *bustān*, may mean a garden of vegetables [Dt 11^{10}, 1 K 21^{2} etc.], a fruit orchard [Jer $29^{5, 28}$, Am 4^{9} etc.], or a park-like pleasure-ground [2 K 25^{4}, Est 1^{5} etc.]).—Flowers were cultivated (Ca 6^{2}), and doubtless, as in modern times, crops of grain or vegetables were grown in the spaces between the trees. In the long dry summer of Palestine the fruitfulness of the garden depends upon abundant water supply (Nu 24^{6}). Perennial fountains fleck the landscape with the luxuriant green and delicious shade of gardens, as *e.g.* at *Jenîn* (Ca 4^{15}). Great cisterns and reservoirs collect the water during the rains, and from these, by numerous conduits, it is led at evening to refresh all parts of the garden. Failure of water is soon evident in withered leaves and wilted plants (Is 58^{11}, cf 1^{30}). The orange and lemon groves of Jaffa and Sidon are famous; and the orchards around Damascus form one of the main attractions of that 'earthly paradise.' The cool shade of the trees, the music of the stream, and the delightful variety of fruits in their season, make the gardens a favourite place of resort (Est 7^{7}, Ca 4^{16} etc.), especially towards evening; and in the summer months many spend the night there. In the sweet air, under the sheltering boughs, in the gardens of Olivet, Jesus no doubt passed many of the dark hours (Mk 11^{19} RV, Lk 21^{37}). From His agony in a garden (Jn $18^{1, 26}$) He went to His doom.

The gardens, with their luxuriant foliage and soft obscurities, were greatly resorted to for purposes of idolatry (Is 65^{3}). There the Moslem may be seen to-day, spreading his cloth or garment under orange, fig, or mulberry, and performing his devotions. The garden furnishes the charms of his heaven (*el-jannah*, or *Firdaus*); see articles PARADISE, EDEN [GARDEN OF].

Tombs were often cut in the rock between the trees (2 K 21^{18} etc.): in such a tomb the body of Jesus was laid (Jn 19^{41}). W. E.

GARDEN HOUSE, 2 K 9^{27} (AV, RV).—See BETH-HAGGAN.

GAREB.—1. One of David's 'Thirty,' 2 S 23^{38}, 1 Ch 11^{40}. **2.** A hill near Jerusalem, Jer 31^{39}. Its situation is uncertain, being located by some to the SW., while others place it to the N. of the capital.

GARLAND.—The 'garlands' (Gr. *stemmata*) of Ac 14^{13} were probably intended to be put on the heads of the sacrificial victims. For the use of a garland (Gr.

stephanos) as a prize to the victor in the games, see article Crown, **2,** and cf Games.

GARLIC (Nu 11^{5}).—The familiar *Allium sativum*, still a very great favourite in Palestine, especially with the Jews. Originally a product of Central Asia, and once a delicacy of kings, it is only in the East that it retains its place in the affections of all classes.

GARMENT.—See Dress.

GARMITE.—A gentilic name applied in a totally obscure sense to Keilah in 1 Ch 4^{19}.

GARNER.—'Garner,' which is now archaic, and 'granary,' the form now in use, both come from Latin *granaria*, a storehouse for grain. RSV retains 'garner' in Ps 144^{13} (so AV, RV; Heb. *māzû*), but substitutes 'storehouses' in Jl 1^{17} for AV, RV 'garner, Hebrew *'ôṣār*. RV, RSV use the verb 'to garner' in Is 62^{9} for AV 'to gather' (Heb. *'āsaph*). In Mt 3^{12}, Lk 3^{17} RSV has 'granary' for AV, RV 'garner' (Gr. *apothēkē*; elsewhere rendered **barn** (q.v.) in AV, RV, RSV).

GARRISON.—**1.** Various words, all from the root *nṣb*, which means 'to stand,' are rendered 'garrison' in AV, RV, RSV in 1 S 13^{23} 14$^{1, 4, 6, 11, 15}$, 2 S 23^{14}; 1 S 14^{12}; 1 S 10^{5} 13^{3f}, 2 S 8$^{6, 14}$, 1 Ch 11^{16} 18^{13}, 2 Ch 17^{2}. From the same root comes *maṣṣēbhāh*, 'pillar,' which RV and RSV have in Ezk 26^{11}, where AV has 'garrisons' (RVm 'obelisks'). See Pillar, **2** (*c*). RVm has 'garrison' in Jg 9^{6} for 'pillar' (AV, RV, RSV), and in Zec 9^{8} (AV 'because of the army,' RV 'against the army'), where RSV takes the same view and renders 'as a guard.' **2.** In 2 Co 11^{32} AV renders the Greek *phrourein* by 'keep with a garrison,' where RV and RSV have simply 'guard.'

GAS (1 Es 5^{34}).—His sons were among the 'temple servants' (Ezra and Nehemiah omit). AV has **Gar.**

GASHMU, Neh 6^{6} (AV, RV).—See Geshem.

GATAM.—The son of Eliphaz (Gn 36^{11} = 1 Ch 1^{36}), and 'duke' of an Edomite clan (Gn 36^{16}) which has not been identified.

GATE.—See City, Fortification and Siegecraft, Jerusalem [Gates of], Temple.

GATH.—(Hebrew meaning, 'a wine-press.') A city of the Philistine Pentapolis. It is mentioned in Jos 11^{22} as a place where the Anakim took refuge; but Joshua is significantly silent about the apportioning of the city to any of the tribes. The Ark was brought here from Ashdod (1 S 5^{8}) and thence to Ekron (5^{10}). It was the home of Goliath (1 S 17^{4}, 2 S 21^{19}), and after the rout of the Philistines at Ephes-dammim, it was the limit of their pursuit (1 S 17^{52} [LXX]). David during his outlawry took refuge with its king, Achish (1 S 21^{10}). A bodyguard of Gittites was attached to David's person under the leadership of a certain Ittai; these remained faithful to the king after the revolt of Absalom (2 S 15^{18}). Shimei's slaves ran away to Gath, and he followed them there in disregard of Solomon's order not to leave Jerusalem (1 K 2^{40}). According to the Chronicler, Gath was captured by David (1 Ch 18^{1}), suggesting that he identified the unknown Methegh-ammah mentioned in 2 S 8^{1} with Gath. According to 2 Ch 11^{8}, the city was fortified by Rehoboam, was captured by Hazael of Syria (2 K 12^{17}) and later retaken from the Philistines by Uzziah (2 Ch 26^{6}). Amos, in a passage which is probably a later interpolation, refers to it in terms which imply that some great calamity has befallen it (6^{2}); the later prophets, though they mention other cities of the Pentapolis, are silent respecting Gath which dropped out of existence. Its final destruction was at the hands of Sargon the Assyrian invader who captured it along with other Philistine cities in 711 b.c. The original site of Gath has not yet been certainly identified. The topographical references in Scripture indicate a site in the Shephelah, near the borders of Hebrew territory, not far from Ekron in N. Philistia. Grollenberg proposes the modern *'Arâq el-Menshîyeh*, but others point to the great mound *Tell es-Ṣâfiyeh* as the most probable site for the identification of Gath. It stands at the mouth of the valley of Elah, and clearly represents a large and important town. Limited excavation has produced archaeological material going back to the early Canaanite period, but nothing definitely to identify the site with the ancient Gath. R. A. S. M.—**A. G. Mc.L**

GATH-HEPHER ('winepress of the well').—A place in Zebulun, Jos 19^{13} (AV wrongly *Gittah-hepher*, which is simply the form of the name with *He locale*). It was the home of the prophet Jonah, 2 K 14^{25}. It lay on the border of Zebulun, and is mentioned with Japhia and Rimmon—modern *Yâfā* and *Rummâneh*. It is now usually identified with *Kh. ez-Zurrâ'*.

GATH-RIMMON.—**1.** A city of Dan, near Jehud and Bene-berak, Jos 19^{45}. It was a Levitical city, assigned to the Kohathites (21^{24}), and reckoned to Ephraim, 1 Ch 6^{69}. Its site is possibly modern *Tell Jerîsheh*. **2.** A city of Manasseh, assigned as a Levitical city to the Kohathites, Jos 21^{25}. But the name may have come in by a scribal error from v.^{24}, and it should perhaps be replaced by **Bileam** = **Ibleam** (q.v.) which stands in the parallel 1 Ch 6^{7}. It is identified by some with modern *Rummâneh*.

GAULANITIS.—See Golan.

GAULS.—See Galatia.

GAUZE.—Found only in Is 3^{23} RSV; see Glass.

GAZA.—A city of the Philistine Pentapolis. It is referred to in Genesis (10^{19}) as a border city of the Canaanites, and in Jos 10^{41} as a limit of the south country conquered by Joshua; a refuge of the Anakim (Jos 11^{22}), theoretically assigned to Judah (15^{47}). Samson was here shut in by the Philistines, and escaped by carrying away the gates (Jg 16$^{1-3}$); he was, however, brought back here in captivity after being betrayed by Delilah, and here he destroyed himself and the Philistines by pulling down the temple (16$^{21-30}$). It formed the SW. boundary of Solomon's kingdom (1 K 4^{24}), but was never for long in Israelite hands. It was occupied by Pharaoh Neco (Jer 47^{1ff}), but withstood Alexander for two months in 332 b.c. (Jos. *Ant.* xi. viii. 4 [325]). In the 2nd cent. b.c. it was besieged and taken by Jonathan (1 Mac 11^{61f}). In 96 b.c. it was razed to the ground by Alexander Jannaeus after a year's siege (*Ant.* xiii. xiii. 3 [364]), but in 57 b.c. it was rebuilt by Gabinius on a new site (*Ant.* xiv. v. 3 [88]), the previous site being distinguished as 'Old' or 'Desert' Gaza (cf Ac 8^{26}). It was successively in Greek, Byzantine Christian (a.d. 402), Muslim (a.d. 635), and Crusader hands; it was finally lost by the Franks in 1244. A Crusaders' church remains in the town, now a mosque. It is now a city of about 16,000 inhabitants, and bears the name *Ghazzeh*. The gentilic is **Gazites,** Jos 13^{3} (RV; AV **Gazathites,** RSV 'men of Gaza'), Jg 16^{2}. For 1 Mac 13^{43ff} (AV) see Gezer.

R. A. S. M.—**H. H. R.**

GAZARA.—An important stronghold often mentioned during the Maccabaean struggle (1 Mac 4^{15} 7^{45} [AV **Gazera**] 9^{52} 13^{53} 14$^{7, 34}$ 15^{28} 16^{1}, 2 Mac 10^{32}). In *Ant.* xii. vii. 4 [308], xiv. v. 4 [91], *BJ* i. viii. 5 [170], it is called *Gadara*). It is the OT **Gezer** (q.v.).

GAZATHITES, Jos 13^{3} (AV).—See Gaza.

GAZELLE (Heb. *ṣ^{e}bhî*).—Mentioned in RV and RSV in 2 S 2^{18}, 1 Ch 12^{8} etc. (AV 'roe'), Dt 14^{5} (AV 'roebuck'). The gazelle (Arab. *ghazal*, also *ẓaby*) is one of the commonest of the larger animals of Palestine; it is one of the most beautiful and graceful of antelopes. It is fawn and white in colour; it is much hunted (Pr 6^{5}, Is 13^{14}); it is noted for its speed (2 S 2^{18}, 1 Ch 12^{8}); its flesh is considered, at least in towns, a delicacy.

Ghazaleh ('female gazelle') is a favourable name for a girl among the Yemen Jews, as *Dorcas* and *Tabitha*, with the same meaning, were in NT times (Ac 9$^{36, 40}$).

E. W. G. M.

GAZERA.—**1.** 1 Mac 4^{15} 7^{45} (AV); see Gazara. **2.** 1 Es 5^{31} (AV, RV); see Gazzam.

GAZEZ.—**1.** A son of Ephah, Caleb's concubine, 1 Ch 2[46]. **2.** In same verse a second Gazez is mentioned as a son of Haran, who was another of Ephah's sons.

GAZITES.—See GAZA.

GAZZAM.—A family of Nethinim (q.v.) who returned with Zerubbabel, Ezr 2[48], Neh 7[51], 1 Es 5[31] (RSV erroneously **Gazzan**; AR, RV **Gazera**).

GAZZAN.—See GAZZAM.

GEBA (Heb. *gebhaʿ*, 'a hill').—A city of Benjamin, on the NE. frontier (Jos 18[24]), assigned to the Levites (Jos 21[17], 1 Ch 6[60]). It stands for the northern limit of the kingdom of Judah (2 K 23[8] 'from Geba to Beersheba'). In 2 S 5[25] we should probably read 'Gibeon' (so LXX) as in 1 Ch 14[16]. The position of Geba is fixed in 1 S 14[5] S. of the great *Wâdī Ṣuweinīṭ*, over against Michmash, the modern *Mukhmâs*. This was the scene of Jonathan's famous exploit against the Philistines. Everything points to its identity with *Jebaʿ*, a village 6 miles N. of Jerusalem. It occupied an important position commanding the passage of the valley from the north. It was fortified by Asa (1 K 15[22]). It appears in Isaiah's picture of the approach of the Assyrian upon Jerusalem (10[28ff]). It is mentioned also as occupied after the Exile (Neh 11[31], Ezr 2[26], 1 Es 5[20] [AV **Gabdes, RV Gabbe**]). It seems to be confused with the neighbouring Gibeah in Jg 20[10] (Heb. *Geba*; EV *Gibeah*) [33] (Heb. *Geba*; so RSV; AV *Gibeah* with LXX, RV **Maareh-geba,** q.v.), 1 S 13[3] (EV Geba, following Hebrew; LXX *Gibeah*) [16] (see Driver, *Notes on . . . Samuel*[2], 1913, 101 f). **2.** A stronghold in Samaria, between which and Scythopolis Holofernes pitched his camp (Jth 3[10]). W. E.—**H. H. R.**

GEBAL.—**1.** A place apparently S. of the Dead Sea, whose inhabitants made a league with Edomites, Moabites, and the Bedouin of the Arabah against Israel, on some unknown occasion, Ps 83[7]. Its site is unknown. **2.** A Phoenician city, Ezk 27[9]. It was theoretically (never actually) within the borders of the Promised Land, Jos 13[5]; it provided builders for Solomon, 1 K 5[18] (AV 'stonesquarers'), and ships' caulkers for Tyre, Ezk 27[9]. The gentilic is **Gebalites,** Jos 13[5] (RV, RSV; AV **Giblites**). Its Greek name was Byblos, and it is the modern *Jebeil.* It has been excavated by Montet and Dunand and has yielded important finds, including the sarcophagus of Ahiram and inscriptions in pre-alphabetic script (cf M. Dunand, *Byblia grammata*, 1945).

GEBER.—**1.** 1 K 4[13] (AV); see BEN-GEBER. **2.** One of Solomon's twelve commissariat officers, 1 K 4[19], whose district lay E. of Jordan. At the end of the verse AV and RV read 'and he was the only officer which was in the land,' referring this clause to Geber. But the clause reads strangely. It has been suggested that we should render 'and one officer was over all the land,' *i.e.* there was one officer (*i.e.* Azariah; cf v.[5]) over all the other officers. Alternative suggestions are that a word has fallen out, and that we should read 'and there was one officer over the land of Gilead,' or 'of Gad,' or 'of Judah.' RSV adopts the last of these suggestions.

GEBIM.—A place N. of Jerusalem mentioned only in Is 10[31]. Its location is unknown.

GECKO.—See FERRET, LIZARD.

GEDALIAH.—**1.** Son of Ahikam (2 K 25[22ff]), who had protected Jeremiah from the anti-Chaldaean party (Jer 26[24]), and probably grandson of Shaphan, the pious scribe (2 K 22[3ff]). Gedaliah naturally shared the views of Jeremiah. This commended him to Nebuchadrezzar, who made him governor over the people who remained in the land (2 K 25[22]). His two months' rule and treacherous murder are detailed in Jer 40 f; cf 2 K 25[22–25]. The anniversary of Gedaliah's murder—the third day of the seventh month, Tishri (Zec 7[5] 8[19])—has ever since been observed as one of the four Jewish fasts. **2.** Eldest 'son' of Jeduthun, 1 Ch 25[3, 9]. **3.** A priest 'of the sons of Jeshua,' who had married a foreign wife, Ezr 10[18]; called **Jodan** in 1 Es 9[19] (AV, RV **Joadanus**). **4.** A priest of the sons of Pashhur who married a foreign wife, 1 Es 9[22] (RSV; AV, RV **Ocidelus**); called **Jozabad** in Ezr 10[22]. **5.** Son of Pashhur, a prince in the reign of Zedekiah, Jer 38[1]. **6.** Grandfather of the prophet Zephaniah, Zeph 1[1].

GEDDUR, 1 Es 5[30] (AV, RV).—See GAHAR.

GEDEON, He 11[32] (AV) = **Gideon** (q.v.).

GEDER.—A Canaanite town, whose king was amongst those conquered by Joshua, Jos 12[13]; possibly the same as **Beth-gader** (q.v.). The gentilic Gederite is used of Baal-hanan in 1 Ch 27[28].

GEDERAH.—A town of Judah, in the lowland, Jos 15[36]; probably modern *Kh. Jedîreh.* The same place is perhaps referred to in 1 Ch 4[23] (RV, RSV), where AV has 'those that dwelt among plants and hedges' for 'inhabitants of Netaim and Gederah.' The gentilic **Gederathite** occurs in 1 Ch 12[4] (RSV 'of Gederah').

GEDEROTH.—A town of Judah in the Shephelah, Jos 15[41]; captured by the Philistines in the time of Ahaz, 2 Ch 28[18]. Its location is unknown. Some have identified it with **Kedron** (q.v.); but cf J. Simons, *The Geographical and Topographical Texts of the OT*, 1959, p. 147).

GEDEROTHAIM occurs in Jos 15[36] as one of the fourteen cities of Judah that lay in the Shephelah. There are, however, fourteen cities without it, and it is probable that the name has arisen by dittography from the preceding **Gederah.** The subterfuge of the AVm 'Gederah *or* Gederothaim' is not permissible.

GEDOR.—**1.** A town of Judah, in the hill country, Jos 15[58], probably modern *Kh. Jedûr.* **2.** The district from which the Simeonites are said to have expelled the Hamite settlers, 1 Ch 4[39ff]. The LXX, however, reads **Gerar** (q.v.), and this well suits as to direction. **3.** A place in Judah ('son' of Penuel), mentioned in 1 Ch 4[4]. **4.** Another place in Judah ('son' of Jered), mentioned in 1 Ch 4[18]. Possibly either **3** or **4** should be identified with **1.** **5.** The town where the Benjamite Jeroham lived, 1 Ch 12[7]. Its site is unknown. **6.** A Benjamite, great-uncle of king Saul, 1 Ch 8[31] 9[37].

GE-HARASHIM ('valley of craftsmen').—Mentioned in 1 Ch 4[14] (AV 'valley of **Charashim**') and Neh 11[35] (EV 'the valley of craftsmen'). In the latter passage it occurs with Lod and Ono. Its location is unknown.

GEHAZI.—Of the antecedents of Gehazi we are told nothing. He is referred to by name as the 'servant' (*naʿar*; see SLAVE, **2**) of Elisha four times (2 K 4[12, 25] 5[20] 8[4]). If at 2 K 4[43] the reference is to Gehazi, it should be noted that a different Hebrew word is there translated 'servant' by RSV (AV 'servitor,' RVm 'minister'; the word as applied to Joshua is rendered by the RSV 'minister' at Nu 11[28], Jos 1[1], and 'servant' at Ex 24[13] 33[11]).

Gehazi appears in three narratives in 2 Kings. He is first introduced in the episode of the Shunammite woman (2 K 4[8–37]), where the prophet consults familiarly with him. Gehazi bears Elisha's message to her: 'See, you have taken all this trouble for us; what is to be done for you?' (2 K 4[13]). When she declines the suggested favours, Gehazi reminds his master that the woman is childless. Elisha promises that a son will be born to her 'at this season, when the time comes round' (v.[16]), and the prediction is fulfilled. Later, when the child dies and she comes in her grief to the prophet and clasps his feet, Gehazi would thrust her away, but instead he is bidden take the prophet's staff and go and lay it on the child's face. He does so and nothing happens, but where he fails his master succeeds (2 K 4[18–37]).

In the story of Naaman (q.v.) in 2 K 5 the prophet's refusal to receive any payment from the Syrian general for the cure which had been effected does not meet with the approval of Gehazi. He runs after Naaman, and, fabricating a message from his master, begs a talent of silver and two changes of raiment for two young men of the sons of the prophets, who are supposed to be on a visit to Elisha. The fraud is revealed to the prophet, who pronounces his servant's punishment: 'Therefore the leprosy of Naaman shall cleave to you, and to your descendants for ever.' So he went out from his presence a leper, as white as snow (2 K 5[27]).

The third narrative (2 K 8[1-6]), about the position of which there is some doubt, is an epilogue to the story of the Shunammite woman. Having had to leave her home and land to escape famine, she now returns and petitions the king for the restoration of her possessions just as Gehazi is relating to him how Elisha had brought the dead to life. Gehazi recognizes her: 'My lord, O king here is the woman, and here is her son whom Elisha restored to life,' and the king grants her request.

In later Jewish writings Gehazi is depicted as denying the resurrection of the dead, a judgment which must derive from his failure with the prophet's staff (2 K 4[31]). It is held too that the four lepers who entered the Syrian camp during the siege of Samaria and found it deserted (2 K 7) were Gehazi and his sons. There is a tradition that Elisha went to Gehazi at Damascus to persuade him to repent but was unsuccessful. Later Jewish thought considered that Elisha's treatment of his servant had been too severe. J. A. K.—**W. D. McH.**

GEHENNA.—A transcription of Hebrew *Gê-Hinnōm*, the name of the valley to the south of Jerusalem where the kings Ahaz and Manasseh are said to have offered their sons to the god Moloch (2 Ch 28[3] 33[6], Jer 32[35]). Polluted by Josiah in the course of his reform (2 K 23[10]), it is thought subsequently to have become the city's garbage dump, where dead animals were thrown and refuse burned. Its sinister associations and the smoke that continually ascended from it made it an appropriate symbol of woe and judgment, and as such it figures in various prophetic oracles (*e.g.* Jer 7[31] 19[6], Is 66[24]). In Jewish apocalyptic it became the place of the final punishment of the wicked, which was to take place in the sight of the righteous (1 En 27, 90[26f]).

In NT Gehenna (always translated 'hell') is the place of eternal punishment (Mt 5[29] 10[28]). It is not to be confused with **Hades** (also translated 'hell' in AV), which is the resting place of the dead pending the resurrection. Gehenna is a place of torment, of unquenchable fire and the consuming worm (Mt 18[8f], Mk 9[44ff] etc.); it is a furnace (Mt 13[42]), a lake of fire (Rev 20[14]), outer darkness (Mt 8[12] etc.). The word Gehenna occurs rarely (not even in all the passages just cited), and almost always on the lips of Jesus. But the concept of final punishment for those who reject Christ is common to all the NT and expressed in various ways: wrath (Ro 5[9]), destruction (Ro 9[22]), corruption (Gal 6[8]), death (Jn 8[21]), the second death (Rev 20[6, 14]), etc. In 2 P 2[4] the word rendered 'hell' is **Tartarus,** which to the Greeks was the place where the wicked are punished in the bowels of the earth far deeper than Hades. None of the NT writers delight to dwell on the miseries of the lost, or make any attempt to give exact descriptions of the place of punishment. While we need not literalize their descriptions of physical torment, we cannot explain the symbolism away and do justice to their teaching. NT speaks of Gehenna and perdition always with the purpose of warning and awakening responsibility.
J. Br.

GELILOTH ('stone circles').—Mentioned in Jos 18[17]; identical with the **Gilgal** of Jos 15[7], and possibly with the **Beth-gilgal** of Neh 12[29]. It was a place on the border of Benjamin and Judah near the Ascent of Adummim. This last was probably in the neighbourhood of *Tal'at ed-Damm*, a hill near the so-called 'Inn of the Good Samaritan' on the carriage road to Jericho. The word *g*[e]*lîlôth* occurs also in the Hebrew in Jos 13[2] 22[10f] and Jl 3[4], and is translated in AV either 'borders' or 'coasts,' RV and RSV 'regions.' E. W. G. M.

GEM.—See Jewels and Precious Stones.

GEMALLI.—Father of the Danite spy, Nu 13[12].

GEMARA.—See Talmud.

GEMARIAH.—1. A son of Shaphan the scribe; he vainly sought to deter king Jehoiakim from burning the roll, Jer 36[10ff, 25]. **2.** A son of Hilkiah who carried a letter from Jeremiah to the captives at Babylon, Jer 29[3].

GENEALOGY.—The genealogies of the OT fall into two classes, national and individual, though the two are sometimes combined, the genealogy of the individual passing into that of the nation.

1. National genealogies.—These belong to a well-recognized type, by which the relationship of nations, tribes, and families is explained as due to descent from a common ancestor, who is often an 'eponymous hero,' invented to account for the name of the nation. The principle was prevalent in Greece (see Grote, *Hist.* vol. i. ch. iv. etc. and p. 416); *e.g.* Hellen is the **'father'** of Dorus, Aeolus, and Xuthus, who is in turn the 'father' of Ion and Achaeus, the existence of the various branches of the Greek races being thus explained. M'Lennan (*Studies in Ancient History*, 2nd series, ix) gives further examples from Rome (genealogies traced to Numa), Scotland, India, Arabia, and Africa; the Berbers ('barbarians') of N. Africa invented an ancestor Berr and connected him with Noah. The Arabs derived all their subdivisions from Nebaioth or Joktan. The genealogies of Genesis are of the same type. The groundwork of the Priestly narrative (P) is a series of interconnected genealogies, each beginning with the formula, 'These are the generations (*tôl*[e]*dhôth*) of . . .' (2[4] 5[1] 6[9] etc.). The gap between Adam and Noah is filled by a genealogy of ten generations (Gn 5), and in Gn 10 the nations of the world, as known to the writer, are traced in a genealogical tree to Noah's three sons. We find in the list plural or dual names (*e.g.* Mizraim, Ludim, Anamim), names of places (Tarshish, Sidon, Ophir) or of nations (the Jebusite, Amorite, etc.). An 'Eber' appears as the eponymous ancestor of the Hebrews. Sometimes the names might in form represent either individuals or nations (Asshur, Moab, Edom), but there can in most cases be little doubt that the ancestor has been invented to account for the nation. In later chapters the same method is followed with regard to tribes more or less closely related to Israel; the connexion is explained by deriving them from an ancestor related to Abraham. In Gn 22[20] the twelve Aramaean tribes are derived from Nahor his brother; in 25[12] twelve N. Arabian tribes, nearer akin, are traced to Ishmael and Hagar; six others, a step farther removed, to Keturah, his second wife, or concubine (25[1]). The Edomites, as most nearly related, are derived from Esau (36). The frequent recurrence of the number 12 in these lists is a sign of artificiality. The same principle is applied to Israel itself. The existence of all the twelve sons of Jacob as individuals is on various grounds improbable; they represent tribes, and in many cases their 'descendants' are simply individual names coined to account for cities, clans, and subdivisions of the tribes (Gn 46[8], Nu 26). A good illustration is found in the case of Gilead. In Dt 3[15] we are told that Moses gave Gilead to Machir, son of Manasseh. In Nu 26[29] etc. Gilead has become the 'son' of Manasseh, and in Jg 11[1] 'begets' Jephthah. So among the 'sons' of Caleb we find cities of Judah (Hebron, Tappuah, Ziph, Gibea, etc., 1 Ch 2[42ff]), and Kiriath-jearim and Bethlehem are descendants of Hur (2[51]). It is indeed obvious that, whether consciously or not, terms of relationship are used in an artificial sense. **'Father'** often means founder of a city; in Gn 4[20] it stands for the originator of occupations and professions; members of a guild or clan are its 'sons.' The towns of a district are its 'daughters' (Jg 1[27] RVm).

With regard to the *historical value* of these genealogies, two remarks may be made: (*a*) The records, though in most cases worthless if regarded as referring to individuals, are of the highest importance as evidence of the movements and history of peoples and clans, and of the beliefs entertained about them. Gn 10 gives geographical and ethnographical information of great value. A good example is found in what we learn of Caleb and the Calebites. In the earliest tradition (Nu 32[12], Jos 14[6, 14]) he is descended from Kenaz, a tribe of Edom, and ' grandson ' of Esau (Gn 36[11, 42]) ; in 1 S 25[3] 30[14] the Calebite territory is still distinct from Judah. But in 1 Ch 2[4ff] Caleb has become a descendant of Judah. We gather that the Calebites (' dog-tribe ') were a related but alien clan, which entered into friendly relations with Judah at the time of the conquest of Canaan, and perhaps took the lead in the invasion. Ultimately they coalesced with Judah, and were regarded as pure Israelites. So generally, though no uniform interpretation of the genealogies is possible, a marriage will often point to the incorporation of new elements into the tribe, a birth to a fresh subdivision or migration, or an unfruitful marriage to the disappearance of a clan. Contradictory accounts of an individual in documents of different date may tell us of the history of a tribe at successive periods, as in the case of Calebites.

(*b*) Though the genealogical names usually represent nations, there is, no doubt, in certain cases a personal element as well. The patriarchs and more prominent figures, such as Ishmael and Esau and Caleb, were no doubt individuals, and their history is not entirely figurative. On this point see Driver, *Genesis*, pp. liv. ff ; also see ABRAHAM, and TRIBES. We should note that the distinctive feature of the Greek genealogies, which traced national descent from the gods, is absent from the OT. A trace remains in Gn 6[4] (cf Lk 3[38]).

2. Genealogies of individuals.—Whatever view be taken of the genealogies of our Lord (see next article), their incorporation in the Gospels proves the importance attached to descent in the NT period ; they also show that at that time records were kept which made the construction of such tables a possibility. St. Paul was conscious of his pure pedigree (Ph 3[5]), and in several cases in the NT the name of a person's tribe is preserved. The hope of being the ancestor of the Messiah, and the natural pride of royal descent probably caused the records of the house of David to be preserved with great care. In the same way Josephus, in the opening chapter of his *Life*, sets out his genealogy as vouched for by the public records, though only as far back as his grandfather Simon. In *c. Apion.* i. 7 (30 ff), he speaks of the careful preservation of the priestly genealogies ; and the story of Africanus (*ap.* Eus. *HE* i. 7, 13), that Herod the Great destroyed the genealogical records of the Jews in order to conceal his own origin, is at least an indication of the existence of such records and of the value attached to them. The Talmud speaks of professional genealogists, and in the present day many Jews, especially among the priests, treasure long and detailed family trees, showing their pure descent (cf, for an earlier period, 1 Mac 2[1], Bar 1[1], To 1[1]).

There can be no doubt that this careful recording of genealogies received its main impetus in the time of Ezra. It was then that the line between the Jews and other nations became sharply drawn, and stress was laid on purity of descent, whether real or fictitious. After the return from Babylon, it was more important to be able to trace descent from the exiles than to be a native of Judah (Ezr 9). Certain families were excluded from the priesthood for lack of the requisite genealogical records (2[61], Neh 7[63]). And in fact practically all the detailed genealogies of individuals as preserved in P, Chronicles, and kindred writings, date from this or a later period. No doubt the injunctions of Dt 23[3] and the arrangements for a census (2 S 24) imply that there was some sort of registration of families before this, and the stage of civilization reached under the monarchy makes it probable that records were kept of royal and important houses. But the genealogical notes which really date from the earlier period rarely go further back than two or three generations, and the later genealogies bear many traces of their artificiality. The names are in many cases late and post-exilic, and there is no evidence outside the genealogies that they were in use at an earlier period. Of the twenty-four courses of the sons of Aaron in 1 Ch 24[1ff], sixteen names are post-exilic. Names of places and clans appear as individuals (2[18-24] 7[30-40]). Gaps are filled up by the repetition of the same name in several generations (*e.g.* 6[4-14]). At a later time it was usual for a child to be named after his father or kinsman (Lk 1[59, 61]), but there are probably no cases where this is recorded for the pre-exilic period, except in the Chronicler's lists (see Gray, *HPN*). There are numerous discrepancies in the various lists, and there is a strongly marked tendency to ascribe a Levitical descent to all engaged in the service of the sanctuary, *e.g.* the guilds of singers and porters. So Samuel is made a Levite by the Chronicler (6[22, 33]), almost certainly wrongly, as his story shows. In the same way the position of clans, such as Caleb and Jerahmeel, which in the early history appear as alien, is legitimized by artificial genealogies (1 Ch 2). In 25[4] the names of the sons of Heman seem to be simply fragments of a hymn or psalm. In 6[4] there are, including Aaron, twenty-three priests from the Exodus to the Captivity—an evidently artificial reconstruction ; forty years is a generation, and $40 \times 12 = 480$ years to the building of the Temple (1 K 6[1]), the other eleven priests filling up the period till the Exile, which took place in the eleventh generation after Solomon. Such marks of artificiality, combined with lateness of date, forbid us to regard the lists as entirely historical. No doubt in certain cases the genealogist had family records to work upon, but the form in which our material has reached us makes it almost impossible to disentangle these with any degree of certainty. W. R. Smith (*Kinship and Marriage in Early Arabia*, p. 6) gives an interesting parallel to this development of genealogizing activity at a particular period. The Arabian genealogies all date from the reign of Caliph Omar, when circumstances made purity of descent of great importance. C. W. E.

GENEALOGY OF JESUS CHRIST.—1. The two genealogies.—Both the First and Third Evangelists (Mt 1[1-16], Lk 3[23-38]) give our Lord's ancestry, but they differ widely. Luke traces back the genealogy to Adam, Matthew to Abraham only. Both lists agree from Abraham to David, except that Aram or Ram in Mt 1[3] = Arni in Lk 3[33] (best text) ; but between David and Joseph the lists have only Shealtiel and Zerubbabel, and possibly two other names (see below), in common.

(*a*) *The Matthaean list* from Perez to David is taken almost verbatim from Ru 4[18b-22] LXX (inserting Rahab and Ruth, and calling David ' the king '), and agrees with 1 Ch 2[1-15] ; it then gives the names of the kings to Jechoniah, from 1 Ch 3[10-15], but inserts ' the [wife] of Uriah ' and omits kings Ahaziah, Joash, and Amaziah between Joram and Uzziah (=Azariah), and also Jehoiakim son of Josiah and father of Jechoniah (Coniah, Jer 22[24]) or Jehoiachin (2 Ch 36[8]). This last omission may be merely a mistake, for the list is made up of three artificial divisions of fourteen generations each, and Jechoniah appears both at the end of the second and at the beginning of the third division, being counted twice. Perhaps, then, originally Jehoiakim ended the second division, and Jehoiachin began the third, and they became confused owing to the similarity of spelling and were written alike (as in 1 Ch 3[15], Jer 52[31] LXX) ; then the synonym Jechoniah was substituted for both. In the third division, the names Shealtiel, Zerubbabel (both in Luke also) are from Ezr 3[2], 1 Ch 3[17, 19], but we notice that in Matthew and Ezra Zerubbabel is called son of Shealtiel, whereas in 1 Chronicles (except in some MSS of the LXX) he is his nephew. Both in Matthew and 1 Chronicles Shealtiel is called son of Jechoniah. Between Zerubbabel and Joseph the names are perhaps from some traditional list of the heirs of the kings, but some names here also have been omitted, for in Matthew ten generations are spread over nearly 500 years, while Luke gives nineteen generations for the same period. Matthew's genealogy ends with Matthan, Jacob, Joseph.

(*b*) *The Lucan list*, which inverts the order, beginning at Jesus and ending at Adam, takes the line from Adam to Abraham from Gn 5, 10$^{21-25}$ (to Peleg), 1 Ch 1$^{1-27}$, but inserts Cainan between Arphaxad and Shelah, as does the LXX in Genesis and 1 Chronicles; it practically agrees with Matthew (see above) from Abraham to David, but then gives the line to Shealtiel through David's son Nathan, making Shealtiel the son of Neri, not of king Jechoniah (see **2** below). The names between Nathan and Shealtiel are not derived from the OT, and those between Zerubbabel and Joseph are otherwise unknown to us, unless, as Plummer supposes (*ICC*, 'St. Luke,' p. 104), Joanan (Lk 3^{27} RSV) = Hananiah son of Zerubbabel (1 Ch 3^{19})—the name Rhesa being really a title ('Zerubbabel Rhesa' = 'Z. the prince'), misunderstood by some copyist before Luke—and Joda (Lk 3^{26} RSV) = Abiud (Mt 1^{13}) = Hodaviah (1 Ch 3^{24} RSV, a descendant of Zerubbabel, not son of Hananiah). Some think that Matthat (Lk 3^{24}) = Matthan (Mt 1^{15}).

2. Reason of the differences.—It is not enough merely to say that the four Gospels cannot be harmonized, and that (see GOSPELS, **3**) Matthew and Luke each wrote without knowing the other's work. The question is, why did two independent writers, both professing to give the genealogy of Jesus, produce such different lists of names. Jewish genealogies were frequently artificial; that of Matthew is obviously so. For example, its omissions were made, apparently, for the purpose of equalizing the three divisions (though actually there are only 13+14+12 generations). It is often assumed that Matthew compiled his genealogy for use in his Gospel. His fondness for triadic grouping is apparent elsewhere (see SERMON ON THE MOUNT, **3**) and supports this view. Moreover, the details about Tamar, Rahab, Ruth, Bathsheba, which would not be expected in a genealogy (see below), suited his purposes, and so did the artificial dividing points (David, the Exile). One of his objects may have been to refute an early 2nd-cent. slander that Jesus was born out of wedlock—a slander certainly known to Celsus (Origen, *c. Cels.* i. 28, etc.), though it may be argued, contrariwise, that this libel was only a perverse and garbled echo of the story in Matthew. Stylistic and lexical evidence shows that Mt 1–2 is by the author of the rest of the book, and cannot be a later addition. This view may, however, be subject to a slight modification on the hypothesis that Matthew's list was due to a Christian predecessor or to one of his sources, perhaps in the 'school' of Matthew which gave to the evangelic tradition its peculiarly formal and didactic character (*e.g.* the rhyming Beatitudes, in their Aramaic original, or the confusion of Jehoiakim and Jehoiachin: see above). Presumably the genealogy existed before it was adapted to the doctrine of the Virgin Birth (v.^{16}; cf the modification of Luke's genealogy in 3^{23}).

Despite ancient and modern arguments to the contrary, the word 'begat' (*egennēsen*; RSV 'was the father of') implies physical descent, not merely legal heirship (see vv.$^{18, 20}$; Luke's language would fit the 'legal' theory better than Matthew's). Nevertheless, Matthew clearly believed in the Virgin Birth, which he derives midrashically from the LXX of Is 7^{14}, and he locates the genealogy immediately before the assertion of it in vv.$^{18-25}$; if only physical descent was understood, the genealogy through Joseph would be meaningless. What Matthew is trying to prove is that Jesus was legally the descendant of David—and Abraham—as the true 'Son of David.' The list may therefore have been compiled with the purpose of showing the 'throne succession,' *i.e.* the list of legal heirs. Luke, on the other hand, may give Joseph's actual physical descent according to some list preserved in his family. On this view, Joseph was really the son of Heli (Lk 3^{23}) but the legal heir of Jacob (Mt 1^{16}). But the phrase, 'as was supposed' (Lk 3^{23}), scarcely applies to other names in the genealogies, and does not bear *prima facie* the meaning of either 'legal' or 'physical' descent as contrasted with the other. The best evidence for the theory is in the case of Shealtiel and Zerubbabel, who appear in both lists. Jechoniah was childless, or at least his heirs died out (Jer 22$^{24, 30}$), and Shealtiel, though called his 'son' in 1 Ch 3^{17}, was probably only his legal heir, being in reality son of Neri (Lk 3^{27}). But see JEHOIACHIN.

It is probably wiser not to try to combine or even to correlate the two genealogies. They represent two independent efforts to show (*a*) that the title 'Son of David' rightfully belonged to Jesus, (*b*) that he was a true Jew, descended from Abraham, and (*c*) in Luke, that he was descended from Adam the First Man, and therefore truly human, a Son of God in the lower sense as well as in the highest—perhaps as against incipient Gnostic theories of his Divine nature. Matthew's genealogy is obviously symbolical, like a Tree of Jesse window at the entrance of the Gospel; but Luke's is also symbolic, to a considerable degree.

The reason for Matthew's insertion of the names of four women is not wholly obvious. Two were foreigners (Gentiles), three were of ill repute (Tamar, guilty of incest, Gn 38$^{12-26}$; Rahab, a harlot, Jos 2$^{1-21}$; Ruth, a Moabitess, Ru 1^{4} 4$^{13-17}$; Bathsheba—unnamed—an adulteress, 2 S 11$^{2-5}$). Mary was unique, of purely Jewish origin and unsullied character. It may be that the compiler of the genealogy, or the author of the Gospel, intended to point out that all sorts and conditions of men—and women—including Gentiles as well as Jews, sinners as well as saints, made up the Messiah's ancestry. In the ancient synagogue the characters of Tamar and Ruth were exalted, as ancestresses of the royal line of Judah and of the coming Messiah, while Bathsheba was exonerated (the sin was David's), and Rahab was made the wife of Joshua (see also He 11^{31}). The moral significance of the male figures was quaintly pointed out by Thomas Fuller (*Scripture Observations*, 1645): 'Rehoboam begat Abiam: a bad father begat a bad son. Abiam begat Asa: a bad father a good son. Asa begat Jehoshaphat: a good father a good son. Jehoshaphat begat Joram: a good father a bad son. I see, Lord, from hence, that my father's piety cannot be entailed; that is bad news for me. But I see also that actual impiety is not always hereditary; that is good news for my son.'

3. Other solutions.—(*a*) Julius Africanus, perhaps the earliest writer to discuss Biblical questions in a critical manner (*c* A.D. 220), treats of these genealogies in his *Letter to Aristides* (Euseb. *HE* i. 7, vi. 31). He harmonizes them (expressly, however, not as a matter of tradition) on the theory of levirate marriages, supposing that two half-brothers, sons of different fathers, married the same woman, and that the issue of the second marriage was therefore legally accounted to the elder, but physically to the younger brother. It is a difficulty that two, or even three, such marriages must be supposed in the list; and this theory is almost universally rejected by moderns. Africanus had no doubt that both genealogies were Joseph's.

Africanus says that Herod the Great destroyed all the Jewish genealogies kept in the archives, so as to hide his own ignoble descent, but that not a few had private records of their own (Euseb. *HE* i. 7). Here clearly Africanus exaggerates. Josephus says that his own genealogy was given in the public records, and that the priests' pedigrees, even among Jews of the Dispersion, were carefully preserved (*Life*, 1 [1–6], *c. Ap.* i. 7 [30–36]). There is no reason why Luke should not have found a genealogy in Joseph's family. Africanus says that our Lord's relatives, called *desposyni*, prided themselves on preserving the memory of their noble descent.

(*b*) A more modern theory, first expounded by Annius of Viterbo (*c* 1490), is that Matthew gives Joseph's pedigree, Luke Mary's. This theory requires us to render Lk 3^{23} thus: 'being the son (as was supposed) of Joseph [but really the grandson] of Heli.' But this translation is incredible; it contradicts the clear statements of both Gospels, and a birthright derived through the mother would be incompatible with both Jewish and Gentile ideas of legal descent. Luke assumes that Jesus' ancestry was to be traced through Joseph, the phrase 'as was supposed' being supplied in order to conform the statement to the doctrine of the Virgin Birth; the phrase in 1[34] (' since I know not a man,' RSV ' since I have no husband ') may also have been inserted for the same reason.

It must, however, be added that Joseph and Mary may have been near relatives. We cannot, indeed, say with Eusebius (*HE* i. 7) that they must have been of the same tribe, ' inasmuch as intermarriage between different tribes was not permitted.' Eusebius was evidently referring to Nu 36[6f], but this relates only to heiresses, who, if they married out of their tribe, would forfeit their inheritance. Mary and Elizabeth were kinswomen, though the latter was descended from Aaron (Lk 1[5, 36]). But it was undoubtedly the belief of the early Christians that Jesus was descended, according to the flesh, from David, and was of the tribe of Judah (Ac 2[30] 13[23], Ro 1[3], 2 Ti 2[8], He 7[14], Rev 5[5] 22[16]; cf Mk 10[47] 11[10]). At the same time it is noteworthy that our Lord did not base any claims on his Davidic descent (cf Mk 12[35-37a]). A violent translation of Lk 1[27] would make Mary a descendant of David ; but the case is pointless—and the Virgin Birth was unknown in the NT outside Matthew and Luke. In the *Testaments of the Twelve Patriarchs* we read (Sim 7[2], cf Gad 8[1]), ' The Lord shall raise one from Levi as high priest and [one] from Judah as king.' This has been thought to be an inference from Lk 1[36], but it is more probably related to the eschatology of the Dead Sea Scrolls. See *Manual of Discipline*, ix. 10 f, where the coming of the prophet, the priest, and the king is envisaged (three eschatological figures) ; cf *Manual for the Congregation*, ii. 12–17, where the protocol to be observed by the Messianic king and the high priest (not two Messiahs !) is under consideration.

4. The Matthaean text.—In Mt 1[16] the reading of almost all Greek MSS, attested by Tertullian, is that of EV, ' Jacob begat Joseph the husband of Mary, of whom was born Jesus,' etc. The Sinaitic Syriac palimpsest (Syr[s]) reads, ' Jacob begat Joseph ; Joseph, to whom was betrothed Mary the Virgin, begat Jesus.' This self-contradictory reading (either ' virgin ' or ' begat ' is impossible !) was carefully discussed by F. C. Burkitt in his *Evangelion da-Mepharreshe*, ii, 262 ff ; he concluded that it was derived from a variant of tne ordinary text : ' Jacob begat Joseph, to whom being betrothed the Virgin Mary bare [literally *begat*, as often] Jesus.' It is to be noted that the reconstruction of the Greek underlying the Syriac is not above question : Nestle and Huck, *e.g.* disagree in their rendering of both the Sinaitic and the Curetonian Syriac. On the other hand, it has been suggested that the Sinaitic palimpsest retains the original reading of a source of Matthew, perhaps of the original genealogy, which did not contain or presuppose the Virgin Birth. A. J. M.—**F. C. G.**

GENERAL.—This adjective means in AV ' universal,' as Latimer, *Sermons*, 182, ' The promises of God our Saviour are general ; they pertain to all mankind.' So in He 12[23], ' the general assembly ' means the gathering of all without exception (RSV omits ' general '). **Generally** in like maner means ' universally,' 2 S 17[11] ' I counsel that all Israel be generally gathered unto thee ' (RSV omits). The substantive ' general ' is once (1 Ch 27[34] ; RSV ' commander ') used for Hebrew *śar*, of which the more usual rendering is ' captain ' (cf Army, **2**).

GENERATION.—' Generation ' is used in AV to translate **1.** Hebrew *dôr*, which is used (*a*) generally for a *period*, especially in the phrases *dôr wādhôr*, etc., of limitless duration ; past, Is 51[8] ; future, Ps 10[6] ; past and future, Ps 102[24] ; (*b*) of all men living at any given time (Gn 6[9]) ; (*c*) of a class of men with some special characteristic, Pr 30[11-14] (where RSV has ' there are those who ') of four **types** of bad men ; (*d*) in Is 38[12] (AV, RV ' mine age ' ; RVm ' my habitation ' ; RSV ' my dwelling ') and Ps 49[19] *dôr* is sometimes taken as ' dwelling-place.' **2.** Hebrew *tôlᵉdhôth* (from *yāladh*, ' beget ' or ' bear children '), which is used in the sense of (*a*) *genealogies* Gn 5[1], figuratively of the account of creation, Gn 2[4] ; also (*b*) *divisions of a tribe*, as based on genealogy ; *tôlᵉdhôth* occurs only in the Priestly Code, in Ru 4[18] (RSV ' descendants'), and in 1 Chronicles. **3.** Greek *genea* in same sense as **1** (*a*), Col 1[26] ; as **1** (*b*), Mt 24[34]. **4.** *genesis*=2 (*a*), Mt 1[1] (RSV ' genealogy '), an imitation of LXX use of *genesis* for *tôlᵉdhôth*. **5.** *Gennēma*, ' offspring '=**1** (*c*) : so Mt 3[7] ‖ (RV ' offspring ' ; RSV ' brood '). **6.** *genos*, ' race '=**1** (*c*) : so 1 P 2[9] (AV ' chosen generation ' ; RV ' elect race ' ; RSV ' a chosen race '). Where not otherwise noted, RSV retains ' generation ' in all the passages above cited.

GENESIS.—1. Name, Contents, and Plan.—The name ' Genesis,' as applied to the first book of the Bible, is derived from the LXX, in one or two MSS of which the book is entitled *Genesis kosmou* (' origin of the world '). A more appropriate designation, represented by the heading of one Greek MS, is ' The Book of Origins ' ; for Genesis is pre-eminently the Book of Hebrew Origins. It is a collection of the earliest traditions of the Israelites regarding the beginnings of things, and particularly of their national history ; these traditions being woven into a continuous narrative, commencing with the creation of the world and ending with the death of Joseph. The story is continued in the book of Exodus, and indeed forms the introduction to a historical work which may be said to terminate either with the conquest of Palestine (Hexateuch) or with the Babylonian captivity (2 Kings). The narrative comprised in Genesis falls naturally into two main divisions—(i) *The history of primeval mankind* (chs. 1–11), including the creation of the world, the origin of evil, the beginnings of civilization, the Flood, and the dispersion of peoples. (ii) *The history of the patriarchs* (chs. 12–50), which is again divided into three sections, corresponding to the lives of Abraham (12–**25**[18]), Isaac (25[19]–36), and Jacob (chs. 37–50) ; although in the last two periods the story is really occupied with the fortunes of Jacob and Joseph respectively. The transition from one period to another is marked by a series of genealogies, some of which (*e.g.* chs. 5, 11[10ff]) serve a chronological purpose and bridge over intervals of time with regard to which tradition was silent, while others (chs. 10, 36, etc.) exhibit the nearer or remoter relation to Israel of the various races and peoples of mankind. These genealogies constitute a sort of framework for the history, and at the same time reveal the plan on which the book is constructed. As the different branches of the human family are successively enumerated and dismissed, and the history converges more and more on the chosen line, we are meant to trace the unfolding of the Divine purpose by which Israel was separated from all the nations of the earth to be the people of the true God.

2. Literary sources.—The unity of plan which characterizes the Book of Genesis does not necessarily exclude the supposition that it is composed of separate documents ; and a careful study of the structure of the book proves beyond all doubt that this is actually the case. The clue to the analysis was obtained when (in 1753) attention was directed to the significant alternation of two names for God, *Yahweh* and *Elohim*. This at once suggested a compilation from *two* pre-existing sources ; although it is obvious that a preference for one or other Divine name might be common to many independent writers, and does not by itself establish the unity of all the passages in which it appears. It was speedily discovered, however, that this characteristic does not occur alone, but is associated with a number of other features, linguistic, literary, and religious, which were found to correspond in general with the division based on the use of the Divine names. Hence the conviction gradually gained ground that in Genesis we have to do not with an indefinite number of disconnected fragments, but with a few homogeneous compositions, each with a literary character of its own. The attempts to determine the relation of the several components to one another proved more or less abortive until it was finally established in 1853 that the use of *Elohim* is a peculiarity common to two quite dissimilar groups of passages; and that one of these has much closer affinities with the sections where *Yahweh* is used than with the other Elohistic sections. Since then, criticism has rapidly advanced to the positions now held by the great majority of OT scholars, which may be briefly summarized as follows:

(1) Practically the whole of Genesis is resolved into three originally separate documents, each containing a complete and consecutive narrative: (*a*) the *Yahwistic* (J), characterized by the use of 'Yahweh,' commencing with the Creation ($2^{4b\text{ff}}$) and continued to the end of the book; (*b*) the *Elohistic* (E), using 'Elohim,' beginning at ch. 20; (*c*) the *Priestly Code* (P), also using 'Elohim,' which opens with the first account of the Creation ($1\text{–}2^{4a}$). (2) In the compilation from these sources of our present Book of Genesis, two main stages are recognized: first, the fusion of J and E into a single work (JE); and second, the amalgamation of the combined work JE with P (an intermediate stage; the combination of JE with the book of Deuteronomy, is here passed over because it has no appreciable influence on the composition of Genesis). (3) The oldest documents are J and E, which represent slightly varying recensions of a common body of patriarchal tradition, to which J has prefixed traditions from the early history of mankind. Both belong to the best age of Hebrew writing, and must have been composed before the middle of the 8th cent. B.C. The composite work JE is the basis of the Genesis narrative; to it belong all the graphic, picturesque, and racy stories which give life and charm to the book. Differences of standpoint between the two components are clearly marked; but both bear the stamp of popular literature, full of local colour and human interest, yet deeply pervaded by the religious spirit. Their view of God and His converse with men is primitive and childlike; but the bold anthropomorphic representations which abound in J are strikingly absent from E, where the element of theological reflexion is somewhat more pronounced than in J. (4) The third source, P, reproduces the traditional scheme of history laid down in JE; but the writer's unequal treatment of the material at his disposal reveals a prevailing interest in the history of the sacred institutions which were to be the basis of the Sinaitic legislation. As a rule he enlarges only on those epochs of the history at which some new religious observance was introduced, viz., the Creation, when the Sabbath was instituted; the Flood, followed by the prohibition of eating the blood; and the Abrahamic Covenant, of which circumcision was the perpetual seal. For the rest, the narrative is mostly a meagre and colourless epitome, based on JE, and scarcely intelligible apart from it. While there is evidence that P used other sources than JE, it is significant that, with the exception of ch. 23, there is no single episode to which a parallel is not found in the older and fuller narrative. To P, however, we owe the chronological scheme, and the series of genealogies already referred to as constituting the framework of the book as a whole. The Code belongs to a comparatively late period of Hebrew literature, and is generally assigned by critics to the early post-exilic age.

It must be added, however, that, although the main lines of the Documentary hypothesis are likely to continue to be accepted by most scholars, yet it has been subjected to considerable criticism in detail from various quarters, and a formidable frontal attack has been launched against it from Scandinavia.

First of all the Elohist source has been attacked by Volz and Rudolph who have thrown doubt on its existence as an independent document, maintaining that if E existed at all, he was at best a redactor of the original J document. Then Mowinckel, without rejecting E as an independent document, revived Dillmann's theory that E was represented in the primeval history. In his study *Le Décalogue* he put forward the view that, underlying the combined JE narrative, lay the cult-legend of Sinai as it was recited by the priests at the autumn New Year festival. A further modification was suggested by Eissfeldt who found traces of a documentary source which he called the Lay-source (L), showing a secular interest as contrasted with the interest in ritual and ecclesiastical matters exhibited by P.

But the so-called Uppsala School have broken entirely with the Documentary hypothesis, and have put forward a new approach to which they have given the name of the Traditio-historical Method. Its characteristic feature is its emphasis on the part played by oral tradition in the transmission and shaping of the Pentateuchal material. The names of Engnell and Widengren are specially connected with this movement, but their work rests upon the foundation laid by such Scandinavian scholars as Nyberg, Mowinckel, and Pedersen.

Briefly stated Engnell's thesis is that the mass of the tradition-material in the OT falls into three divisions: (*a*) Genesis–Numbers, a collection of traditions which he calls the 'P-work,' or the Tetrateuch, though it should be noted that the symbol P does not bear for Engnell the meaning which it has in the Documentary Hypothesis; (*b*) Deuteronomy–**2** Kings, which he calls the Deuteronomistic history-work; and (*c*) 1 Chronicles–Nehemiah.

3. Nature of the material.—That the contents of Genesis are not *historical* in the technical sense, is implied in the fact that even the oldest of its written documents are far from being contemporary with the events related. They consist for the most part of traditions which for an indefinite period had circulated orally amongst the Israelites, and which (as divergences in the written records testify) had undergone modification in the course of transmission. No one denies that oral tradition may embody authentic recollection of actual occurrences; but the extent to which this is the case is uncertain, and will naturally vary in different parts of the narrative. Thus a broad distinction may be drawn between the primitive traditions of chs. 1–11 on the one hand, and those relating to the patriarchs on the other. The accounts of the Creation, the Fall, the Flood, and the Dispersion, all exhibit more or less clearly the influence of Babylonian mythology; and with regard to these the question is one not of trustworthy historical memory, but of the avenue through which certain mythical representations came to the knowledge of Israel. For the patriarchal period the conditions are different: here the tradition is ostensibly national; the presumed interval of oral transmission is perhaps not beyond the compass of the retentive Oriental memory; and it would be surprising if some real knowledge of its own antecedents had not persisted in the national recollection of Israel. These considerations may be held to justify the belief that a substratum of historic fact underlies the patriarchal narratives of Genesis; but it must be added that to distinguish that substratum from legendary accretions is hardly possible in the present state of our knowledge. The process by which the two elements came to be blended can, however, partly be explained. The patriarchs, for instance, are conceived as ancestors of tribes and nations; and it is certain that in some narratives the characteristics, the mutual relations, and even the history, of tribes are reflected in what is told as the personal biography of the ancestors. Again, the patriarchs are founders of sanctuaries; and it is natural to suppose that legends explanatory of customs observed at these sanctuaries are attached to the names of their reputed founders and go to enrich the traditional narrative. Once more, they are types of character; and in the inevitable simplification which accompanies popular narration the features of the type tended to be emphasized, and the figures of the patriarchs were gradually idealized as patterns of Hebrew piety and virtue. No greater mistake could be made than to think that these non-historical, legendary or imaginative, parts of the tradition are valueless for the ends of revelation. They are inseparably woven into that ideal background of history which bounded the horizon of ancient Israel, and was perhaps more influential in the moulding of national character than a knowledge of the naked reality would have been. The inspiration of the Biblical narrators is seen in the fashioning of the floating mass of legend and folklore and historical reminiscences into an expression of their Divinely given apprehension of religious truth, and so transforming what would otherwise have been a constant source of religious error and moral corruption as to make it a vehicle of instruction in the knowledge and fear of God. Once the principle is admitted that every genuine and worthy mode of literary expression is a suitable medium of God's word to men, it is impossible to suppose that the mythic faculty, which plays so important a part in the thinking of all early peoples, was alone ignored in the Divine education of Israel.

J. S.—**S. H. He.**

GENEVA BIBLE.—See English Versions, **26.**

GENIZAH.—Storage-place, for Shemoth, *i.e.* written or printed documents, either outworn or heretical, but containing *inter alia* the Name of God. Genizoth have been found in some old synagogues and cemeteries and caves. The most famous one is that of the synagogue of Fosṭaṭ near Cairo, emptied in the 19th cent. J. Bo.

GENNAEUS.—The father of Apollonius, a Syrian commander of a district in Palestine, 2 Mac 12^2 (AV **Genneus**).

GENNESARET, LAKE OF.—See Galilee [Sea of].

GENNESARET, LAND OF.—Mentioned only in AV of Mt 14^{34}, Mk 6^{53}. RSV reads 'came to land at Gennesaret' which was probably the low shore at the NW. corner of the Lake of Galilee.

GENNEUS, 2 Mac 12^2 (AV).—See Gennaeus.

GENTILES.—See Nations. For 'Court of the Gentiles,' see Temple.

GENTLENESS.—The word 'gentle' occurs five times in NT (AV). In 1 Th 2^7 and 2 Ti 2^{24} it corresponds to Greek *ēpios*; it is the character proper to a nurse among trying children, or a teacher with refractory pupils. In Tit 3^2, Ja 3^{17}, 1 P 2^{18} 'gentle' is the AV translation of *epieikēs*, which is uniformly so rendered in RV. The word occurs three times in OT, seven in NT (RSV). 'Gentleness' occurs seven times (NT only). The general idea of the Greek word is that which is suggested by equity as opposed to strict legal justice; it expresses the quality of considerateness, of readiness to look humanely and reasonably at the facts of a case. There is a good discussion of it in Trench, *Syn.* p. xliii; he thinks there are no words in English which answer exactly to it, the ideas of equity and fairness, which are essential to its import, usually getting less than justice in the proposed equivalents.

In 2 S 22^{36}=Ps 18^{35} ('Thy gentleness hath made me great') RV keeps 'gentleness' in the text, but gives 'condescension' in the margin; RSV reads 'help,' with 'gentleness' in margin. The key to the meaning is found in comparing such passages as Ps 113^{5f}, Is 57^{15}, Zec 9^9, Mt 11^{29}.

GENUBATH.—Son of Hadad, the fugitive Edomite prince, by the sister of queen Tahpenes, 1 K 11^{20}.

GEOGRAPHY OF PALESTINE.—See Palestine.

GEOLOGY OF PALESTINE.—I. Main Divisions.—Palestine is divided into four major north-south regions: (i) the *Coast Plain*, (ii) the *Cis-jordan Highlands*, (iii) the central *Rift Valley*, (iv) the *Trans-jordan Tableland.*

II. Geological Formations.—Palestine has always been a coastal region, with its shoreline fluctuating according to whether the sea of *Tethys* to the west encroached upon, or receded from, the Arabian tableland. Thus, terrestial sandstones are thicker in the east, and marine deposits in the west. The most important rocks are: (i) the crystalline *Archaean* rocks of the underlying Arabian platform, exposed only in southern Trans-jordan, (ii) the *Nubian Sandstone* (mid-Cambrian to early Cretaceous), east of the Dead Sea and Wâdī ʿArabāh. The cupriferous sandstone of Edom was important (Dt 8^9), and copper was mined at Punon, possibly the site of the raising of the brazen serpent (Nu 21^9). The Nabataean city of Petra was carved out of this rock. (iii) The *Cenomanian-Turonian Limestones*, the major rock of Cis-jordan, providing excellent building stone, and forming the steep, defensive cliffs and narrow valleys of Judah and Ephraim. (iv) The *Senonian Chalk*, soft and infertile, and useless for building (Is 27^9). Its gentle valleys provided most of the OT roads, including the three passes across Carmel, and the Valley of Ajalon. (v) The *Eocene Limestone* of the Shephelah, central Samaria, the central part of Carmel between Sharon and Esdraelon (probably the 'Shephelah of Israel' of Jos 11^{16}) and southern Galilee. Much of the flint desert of eastern Trans-jordan results from the Eocene transgression. (vi) *Post-Eocene deposits*, including the Lisân marls of the Jordan Valley and Dead Sea, the Mousterian Red Sand of Sharon, the thin line of Pleistocene limestone hillocks along the coast, and the alluvium of the Coast Plain and down-faulted basins.

III. Structure.—The most important time for earth-movements was the Miocene-Pliocene. Three types of movement took place concurrently: (i) *Warping* of the underlying platform produced the major highlands; (ii) *Folding* of the sedimentary rocks on top of the warped platform; (iii) *Faulting*, or the breaking of the platform, occurred when the strain became too great. This faulting was extremely complex and produced (*a*) the great NS. Rift Valley of the Ghôr, (*b*) the Acre-Beisân corridor, (*c*) NS. faults outlining the hill country of Cis-jordan, (*d*) several important EW. faults such as that dividing Upper from Lower Galilee, (*e*) hinge-faults cutting in obliquely on either side of the Ghôr. Such faults created the major canyons which divide the Trans-jordan table-land. There also occurred the great basalt outflows which formed the mountain of Bashan (Jebel Druze) and Trachonitis, and in Cis-jordan, the Hill of Moreh and the basalt dam which fills the Ghôr north of the Lake of Galilee.

IV. Regional.—Palestine is divided structurally, not only into the four NS. regions, but also into three EW. zones cutting across them. (i) The *Central Zone*, in the latitude of the Dead Sea, is one of relative structural simplicity. West of the Jordan the Judaean plateau is formed of a single upwarp of Cenomanian limestone. On either flank the Senonian Chalk forms an important protective area. On the drier eastern side is the desolate chalk Wilderness of Judaea, and on the west the narrow chalk moat dividing Judah from the Eocene Shephelah. East of the Jordan, in Moab, the strata are remarkably level and undisturbed, except where they have been pulled down into the Ghôr in a great plunging monocline. This zone is everywhere concluded on the north by hinge-faults, the Valley of Ajalon, the Valley of Achor north of Jericho, and the Plains of Moab north-east of the Dead Sea. (ii) The *Northern Zone* is more complex. Ephraim is a Cenomanian dome, but Manasseh north of it is a basin in which the Eocene limestone in the centre stands up as hills (*e.g.* Ebal and Gerizim). The Senonian here forms interior valleys, making entry to the region much simpler than in Judah. Galilee is much broken into up-faulted hills and down-faulted basins, the eastern side being obscured by basalt outflows. East of the Jordan is the great dome of Gilead in which the Jabbok canyon cuts through the Cenomanian to the Nubian sandstone. There is also the large fault basin of the Beqāʿ. (iii) The *Southern Zone*, south of the Dead Sea, is largely desert. In Cis-jordan the Negeb Uplands consist of a series of upwards which are nowhere very high, and have been broken open in three places to form great 'cauldrons' surrounded by steep cliffs, *e.g. Wâdī Ramân.* The Ghôr here rises to 650 feet *above* sea-level in the Cretaceous fold of *Jebel er-Rîsheh.* East of the Ghôr the plateau has been pushed up to its greatest height (5600 feet) in Edom. To the south of Edom the plateau ends abruptly, and is succeeded by the huge Archaean wedge of the Mountains of Midian, and the wild sandstone mountains of *Jebel Ṭubeiq.* A. D. B.

GEORGIAN VERSION OF OT.—See Greek Versions of OT, **11.**

GEPHYRUN.—A city captured by Judas Maccabaeus, 2 Mac 12[13] (RV). AV and RSV eliminate the name, the former reading ' He also went about to make a bridge to a certain strong city, which was fenced about with walls ' and the latter ' he also attacked a certain city, which was strongly fortified with earthworks and walls.' The text is probably corrupt. No city of this name is known.

GER.—See STRANGER.

GERA.—One of Benjamin's sons (Gn 46[21], omitted in Nu 26[38-40]). According to 1 Ch 8[3, 5, 7] he was a son of Bela and a grandson of Benjamin. Gera was evidently a well-known Benjamite clan, to which belonged Ehud (Jg 3[15]) and Shimei (2 S 16[5], 19[16, 18], 1 K 2[8]).

GERAH, the twentieth part of the shekel (Ex 30[13], Lv 27[25] etc.). See MONEY, **3** ; WEIGHTS AND MEASURES, III.

GERAR.—A place mentioned in Gn 10[19] in the description of the Canaanite territory. Here Abraham sojourned and came in contact with Abimelech, king of Gerar (20[1f]). A similar experience is recorded of Isaac (26[1ff]), and here Abimelech is said to have been a Philistine ; but the reference to Philistines in the age of the patriarchs is an anachronism. Gerar reappears in the description of the rout of the Ethiopians by Asa, when Gerar was the limit of the pursuit (2 Ch 14[13f]). In the LXX of 1 Ch 4[39] Gerar stands in place of Hebrew **Gedor** as the name of a place occupied by the Simeonites (see GEDOR, **1**). The site is unknown ; *Tell Jemmeh*, S. of Gaza, and *Tell Abū Hureirah* are among the sites proposed. See GERRHENIANS.

GERASA.—A city of the Decapolis (q.v.) in Transjordan, north of the middle stretch of the Jabbok. It may originally have been founded by Perdiccas, to whom its citizens still raised a statue centuries after his time. But Antiochus IV. Epiphanes may have refounded it, for it was called Antioch on the Chrysorrhoas, for a while, and had a temple of Zeus Olympios, such as that ruler also had built at Dura. The city was an inviolable sanctuary for the 2nd cent. B.C. Transjordanian tyrants. It was taken by Alexander Jannaeus *c* 78 B.C. It was liberated by Pompey in 63 B.C., at which time it became one of the federation called Decapolis. The Jews seem to have inflicted damage on it in the Jewish war (*BJ* II. xviii. 1 [458]), but the kindly attitude of the Gerasenes toward Jewish residents subsequently (*ib.* 5 [480]) shows that it cannot have been enough to cause rancour. The real flowering of Gerasa took place in the centuries under the Roman emperors. The ruins near the village bearing the name *Jerash* are among the most impressive of the Near East. A full record was made of them by a Yale University expedition, which also carried on some excavations.

Gerasa is not mentioned in the OT, though its Semitic name indicates pre-Hellenistic origin. Glueck was able to show that a Bronze Age city had existed about 200 metres away from the NE. wall of Roman Gerasa. Its history had ended in the 20th cent. B.C. Remains of an Iron Age city have not yet been located.

The people of Gerasa are mentioned in Mk 5[1], Lk 8[26] (RSV, but AV Gadarenes). But Gerasa was too far away, and the reading ' Gadarenes ' (Mt 8[28] RSV, but AV Gergesenes) is more plausible and has displaced ' Gerasenes ' in the received text of the other passages. The fame of Gerasa in the early centuries may have led to the seeking of its mention in the NT. E. G. K.

GERASENES, GERGESENES.—See GADARA and GERASA.

GERIZIM.—A mountain which with Ebal encloses the valley in which is built the town of *Nâblus* (Shechem). The Samaritan sect regard it as holy, it being to them what Jerusalem and Mount Zion are to the Jew. According to Samaritan tradition the sacrifice of Isaac took place there. From Gerizim were pronounced the blessings attached to observance of the Law (Jos 8[33]), when the Israelites formally took possession of the country. Here Jotham spoke his parable to the elders of Shechem (Jg 9[7]).

The acoustic properties of the valley are said to be remarkable, and experiment has shown that from some parts of the mountain it is possible with very little effort to make the voice carry over a very considerable area. A ledge of rock half-way up the hill is still often called ' Jotham's pulpit.' Gerizim probably had been a sacred mountain long before the time of the Samaritans (the emergence of whom as a separate sect must be post-exilic), or indeed before the entry of the Israelites.

On this mountain was erected, probably at the beginning of the 4th cent. B.C., a Samaritan Temple, which was destroyed in 126 B.C. by Hyrcanus. Its site is pointed out on a small level plateau, under the hill-top. The Passover is annually celebrated here. Three times a year, on the seventh day of Unleavened Bread, on Pentecost and at Tabernacles, the Samaritans perform a pilgrimage from their synagogue at the foot of Mount Gerizim to the top of the mountain to appear before the Lord. The pilgrims as they ascend, read selected paragraphs from Deuteronomy ; chs. 27 and 28 are, however, read in full. Is there some connexion here between the ceremony described in Joshua and the Samaritan pilgrimages? Do the Samaritan pilgrimages seek to commemorate the covenant made at Shechem and at the same time fulfil the command to appear thrice yearly before the Lord? Certainly the practice is important as a survival of an ancient Hebrew pilgrimage. After reaching the first of the many holy places on the mountain, visits are made to the various altars. It matters not that they be called the altars of Adam, Seth, Noah, Isaac, etc. ; the memory of the altars and the numerous *maṣṣēbhôth* testifies to the multiplication of altars and *maṣṣēbhôth* condemned by Hosea.

Other ruins of less interest are to be seen on the mountain top, such as the remains of a castle and a Byzantine Church. The summit of the mountain commands a view embracing nearly the whole of Palestine. Contrary to the statement of Josephus, it is not the highest of the mountains of Samaria, Ebal and *Jebel ʿAṣûr* being rather higher. R. A. S. M.—**J. Bo.**

GERON should possibly appear as a proper name in 2 Mac 6[1] (AV and RV ' an old man of Athens ' ; RVm ' Geron an Athenian ; RSV ' an Athenian senator ').

GERRHENIANS (2 Mac 13[24] AV).—The true reading and the people intended are both uncertain. The analogy of 1 Mac 11[59] suggests some place near the border of Egypt ; but *Gerrha*, between Pelusium and Rhinocolura, was in Egyptian territory. It has been suggested that the reference is to **Gerar** (so RSV), an ancient Philistine city SE. of Gaza. On the other hand, Syriac reads *Gazar*, *i.e.* Gezer or Gazara, not far from Lydda (cf 1 Mac 15[28, 35]). RV has **Gerrenians.**

GERSHOM.—**1.** The elder of the two sons borne to Moses by Zipporah (Ex 2[22] 18[2-6] ; the explanation of the name given in these two passages is folk-etymology). According to Ex 4[25f], the origin of circumcision among the Israelites was connected with that of Gershom ; the rite was performed by his mother ; this was contrary to later usage, according to which this was always done by a man. The son of Gershom, **Jonathan,** and his descendants were priests to the tribe of the Danites ; but the fact that these latter set up for themselves a graven image, and that therefore the descendants of Gershom were connected with worship of this kind, was regarded as a grave evil by later generations, for which reason the word ' Moses ' in Jg 18[30] (so RV, RSV) was read ' Manasseh ' (so AV) by the insertion of an *n* above the text ; it was thought derogatory to the memory of Moses that descendants of his should have been guilty of the worship of graven images. In Jg 17[7] there is a possible reference to Gershom, for the words ' and he sojourned there ' can also be read ' and he (was) Gershom ' (W. H. Bennett). In 1 Ch 23[16] 26[20] the sons of Gershom are mentioned, Shebuel (in 24[24]

Shubael) being their chief. **2.** A son of Levi, 1 Ch 6^{16}; see GERSHON. **3.** A descendant of Phinehas, one of the 'heads of houses' who went up with Ezra from Babylon in the reign of Artaxerxes, Ezr 8^{2}, 1 Es 8^{29} (AV, RV **Gerson**). W. O. E. O.

GERSHON, GERSHONITES.—The name Gershon is given to the eldest son of Levi, to whom a division of the Levites traced their descent (Gn 46^{11}, Ex 6^{16}, Nu 3^{17}, 1 Ch $6^{1, 16}$ [**Gershom**] 23^{6}). The title 'Gershonites' is found in Nu $3^{21, 23f}$ $4^{24, 27f}$ 26^{57}, Jos 21^{33}, 1 Ch 23^{7} 26^{21}, 2 Ch 29^{12}; and of an individual, 1 Ch 26^{21} 29^{8}; the 'sons of Gershon' (Ex 6^{17}, Nu $3^{18, 25}$ $4^{22, 38, 41}$ 7^{7} 10^{17}, Jos $21^{6, 27}$), or 'of Gershom' (1 Ch $6^{17, 62, 71}$ 15^{7}). They were subdivided into two groups, the **Libnites** and the **Shimeites** (Nu 3^{21} 26^{58}), each being traced to a 'son' of Gershon (Ex 6^{17}, Nu 3^{18}, 1 Ch $6^{17, 20}$ [42, Shimei is omitted from the genealogy]). 'Ladan' stands for Libni in 1 Ch 23^{7ff} 26^{21}. From these families fragments of genealogies remain (see 1 Ch 23^{8-11}). Comparatively little is related of the Gershonites after the Exile. Certain of them are mentioned in 1 Ch 9^{15} and Neh $11^{17a, 22}$ as dwelling in Jerusalem immediately after the Return. Of the 'sons of Asaph' (Gershonites), 128 (Ezr 2^{41}) or 148 (Neh 7^{44}) returned with Zerubbabel after the exile. Asaphites led the music at the foundation of the Temple (Ezr 3^{10}); and certain of them blew trumpets in the procession at the dedication of the city walls (Neh 12^{35}).

P and the Chronicler introduce the family into the earlier history. (1) During the desert wanderings the Gershonites were on the west side of the Tent (Nu 3^{23}); their duty was to carry all the hangings which composed the Tent proper, and the outer coverings and the hangings of the court, with their cords (3^{25f} 4^{24ff} 10^{17}), for which they were given two wagons and four oxen (7^{7}); and they were superintended by Ithamar, the youngest son of Aaron (4^{33} 7^{8}). (2) After the settlement in Palestine, thirteen cities were assigned to them (Jos $21^{6, 27-33}$ = 1 Ch $6^{62, 71-76}$). (3) In David's reign the Chronicler relates that the Temple music was managed partly by Asaph, a Gershonite, and his family (1 Ch 6^{39-43} $25^{1f, 6, 9a, 10, 12, 14}$; and see $15^{7, 17-19}$). David divided the Levites into courses 'according to the sons of Levi' (23^{6}; Gershonites, vv.$^{7-11}$); and particular offices of Gershonites are stated in 26^{21f}. (4) Jahaziel, an Asaphite, prophesied to Jehoshaphat before the battle of En-gedi (2 Ch 20^{14-17}). (5) They took part in the cleansing of the Temple under Hezekiah (29^{12f}). Cf also KOHATH.
A. H. McN.

GERSON, 1 Es 8^{29} (AV, RV).—See GERSHOM, **3.**

GERUTH-CHIMHAM.—A halting place on Johanan's flight to Egypt (Jer 41^{17}), near Bethlehem. The name, '*Khan*' (or perhaps 'cattle pen') of Chimham (AV 'habitation of Chimham'), probably derived its name from **Chimham** (q.v.).

GESHAM, 1 Ch 2^{47} (AV).—See GESHAN.

GESHAN.—A descendant of Caleb, 1 Ch 2^{47}. Modern editions of AV have **Gesham,** although the correct form of the name appears in edition of 1611.

GESHEM.—An Arabian who is named, along with Sanballat the Horonite and Tobiah the Ammonite, as an opponent of Nehemiah during the rebuilding of the walls of Jerusalem (Neh 2^{19} 6^{1f}). In Neh 6^{6} Hebrew has **Gashmu** (so AV, RV; RSV 'Geshem'). He may have belonged to an Arab community which, as we learn from the monuments, was settled by Sargon in Samaria, *c* 715 B.C.—this would explain his close connexion with the Samaritans; or he may have been the chief of an Arab tribe dwelling in the S. of Judah, in which case his presence would point to a coalition of all the neighbouring peoples against Jerusalem.

GESHUR, GESHURITES.—1. A small Aramaean tribe, whose territory, together with that of Maacah (q.v.), formed the W. border of Bashan (Dt 3^{14}, Jos 12^{5} 13^{11}). The Geshurites were not expelled by the half-tribe of Manasseh, to whom their land had been allotted (Jos 13^{13}), and were still ruled by an independent king in the reign of David, who married the daughter of Talmai, king of Geshur (2 S 3^{3}). After the murder of his half-brother Amnon, Absalom took refuge with his maternal grandfather in 'Geshur of Aram' (2 S 13^{37} 15^{8}). Geshur and Maacah were probably situated in the modern *Jōlân,* if they are not to be identified with it. In 1 Ch 2^{23} Geshur and Aram are said to have taken the villages of Jair from the Israelites. **2.** A people living in the neighbourhood of the Philistines, Jos 13^{2}, 1 S 27^{8}.

GESTURES.—The Oriental is a natural expert in appropriate and expressive gesture. To his impulsive and emotional temperament, attitude and action form a more apt vehicle for thought and feeling than even speech. Movement of feature, shrug of shoulder, turn of hand, express much, and suggest delicate shades of meaning which cannot be put in words. Conversation is accompanied by a sort of running commentary of gestures. Easterns conduct argument and altercation at the pitch of their voices: emphasis is supplied almost wholly by gestures. These are often so violent that an unskilled witness might naturally expect to see bloodshed follow.

The word does not occur in Scripture, but the thing, in various forms, is constantly appearing. *Bowing the head or body* marks reverence, homage, or worship (Gn 18^{2}, Ex 20^{5}, 1 Ch 21^{21}, Ps 95^{6}, Is 60^{14}). The same is true of *kneeling* (1 K 19^{18}, 2 K 1^{13}, Ps 95^{6}, Mk 1^{40}). Kneeling was a common attitude in prayer (1 K 8^{54}, Ezr 9^{5}, Dn 6^{10}, Lk 22^{41}, Eph 3^{14} etc.). *Prostration* (Gr. *proskynēsis*), was the gesture of homage paid to divine beings, or to kings. It consisted of bowing down with forehead to the ground, and is depicted on many ancient monuments. For a description of the gesture in the OT cf Is 49^{7}. This was the gesture which the devil sought from Jesus in the Temptation (Mt 4^{9}||). The *glance of the eye* may mean appeal, as the upward look in prayer (Job 22^{26}, Mk 6^{41} etc.), anger (Mk 3^{5}), or reproach (Lk 22^{61}). A *shake of the head* may express scorn or derision (2 K 19^{21}, Ps 109^{25}, Mk 15^{29} etc.). A *grimace of the lip* is a sign of contempt (Ps 22^{7}). *Shaking the dust off the feet*, or *shaking*, however gently, *one's raiment*, indicates complete severance (Mt 10^{14} etc.), denial of responsibility (Ac 18^{16}), and often now, total ignorance of any matter referred to. *Rending the garments* betokens consternation, real (Gn 37^{29}, Jos 7^{6}, Ac 14^{14} etc.) or assumed (2 Ch 23^{13}, Mt 26^{65}), and grief (Jg 11^{35}, 2 S 1^{11} etc.). Joy was expressed by *dancing* (Ex 15^{20}, 1 S 30^{16}, Jer 31^{4} etc.), and *clapping the hands* (Ps 47^{1}, Is 55^{12} etc.). *Spitting upon, or in the face*, indicated deep despite (Nu 12^{14}, Is 50^{6}, Mt 26^{67} etc.). See HAND, MOURNING CUSTOMS, SALUTATION.

Some gestures in common use are probably ancient. One who narrowly escapes danger, describing his experience, will crack his thumb nail off the edge of his front teeth, suggesting Job's 'with the skin of my teeth' (19^{20}). One charged with a fault will put his elbows to his sides, turn his palms outward, and shrug his shoulders, with a slight side inclination of the head, repudiating responsibility for an act which, in his judgment,was plainly inevitable. W. E.—**S. H. He.**

GETHER.—Named in Gn 10^{23}, along with Uz, Hul, and Mash, as one of the 'sons of Aram' (in 1 Ch 1^{17} simply 'sons of Shem'). The clan of which he is the eponymous founder has not been identified.

GETHSEMANE.—A place to which Jesus retired with His disciples (Mt 26^{36}, Mk 14^{32}), and where Judas betrayed Him. The name, usually taken to mean 'press of oils,' is uncertain. Jerome gives it as *Gesamani* and connects it with the phrase 'fat valley' of Is 28^{1} (*gê' shᵉmānîm*). There are two traditional sites, side by side, one under the Greeks, the other under the Latins. It may be admitted that they are somewhere near the proper site, on the W. slope of the Mount of Olives above the Kidron; but there is no justification for the exact localization of the site. The oldest tradition held the garden to lie on the ground now occupied by the tomb of the Virgin. R. A. S. M.—**E. G. K.**

GEUEL.—The Gadite spy, Nu 13[15].

GEZER.—An ancient city of the Shephelah, on the border of the Philistine plain (modern *Tell Jezer*). The site was excavated by R. A. S. Macalister for the Palestine Exploration Fund between 1902 and 1909. It was populated in Chalcolithic times (4th millennium B.C.) by inhabitants of Semito-Hamitic stock, and became a Canaanite city in the Bronze Age. To the Canaanite period belongs the famous 'high place,' excavated by Macalister—more precisely, an alignment of stone menhirs set up as a funerary shrine towards the end of the Early Bronze Age (21st cent. B.C.) and still used as such in the Late Bronze period (16th–13th cents. B.C.). Gezer was conquered and fortified by Thothmes III. of Egypt (*c* 1470 B.C.) but had regained its independence by the Amarna Age, a century later.

The Canaanite city covered some 22 acres. It was not taken by the Israelites in the early days of their settlement (Jos 16[10], Jg 1[29]). In David's time it was apparently held by the Philistines (1 Ch 20[4]). It was captured by an Egyptian king of the 21st Dynasty (*c* 970 B.C.) and given by him as a dowry to his daughter, Solomon's queen; Solomon thereupon rebuilt it as one of his fortified cities (1 K 9[15ff]). Traces of this rebuilding have been found in the form of characteristic Solomonic masonry. But there is an almost complete gap in the history of its occupation between the end of the Solomonic period (when it fell to Shishak's invading army) and the 5th cent. B.C.

In Hellenistic times it was refounded as a Greek city (**Gazara**; AV has **Gaza**), which was captured by Simon Maccabaeus in 142 B.C. Simon built himself a palace there (1 Mac 13[43ff]), the remains of which were uncovered during the excavation of Gezer. One of the stones had a line of Greek verse scratched on it (presumably by a prisoner-of-war employed on the construction): 'May fire burn up Simon's palace!'

Inscriptions have been found at Gezer from a much earlier date—early Semitic alphabetic inscriptions of date 1800–1500 B.C., comparable to those discovered at Lachish and Shechem, cuneiform tablets from the 15th and 14th cents. B.C., and the 'Gezer Calendar,' a rhythmical Hebrew summary of the successive operations of the agricultural year, copied on a piece of limestone as a schoolboy's exercise about the time of Solomon.

R. A. S. M.—**F. F. B.**

GHOST.—A ghost = German *Geist* (the *h* has crept into the word through what Earle calls an Italian affectation of spelling) is a spirit. The word is also used in Old English of the breath, the soul or spirit of a living person, and even a dead body. In AV it occurs only in the phrase 'give up *or* yield up the ghost' and in the name 'the Holy Ghost.' Wherever in AV *hagion* 'holy' occurs with *pneuma* 'spirit,' the translation is 'Holy Ghost'; but when *pneuma* occurs alone, it is always rendered 'Spirit' or 'spirit,' according as it is supposed to refer to God or to man. RSV has 'ghost' in Is 29[4] ('like the voice of a ghost'), Mt 14[26], Mk 6[49] (*phantasma*). See Holy Spirit and Spirit.

GIAH.—Named in the account of Joab's pursuit of Abner (2 S 2[24]). Its situation is quite unknown; the text is perhaps corrupt.

GIANT.—I. In the OT.—**1.** As translation of Hebrew *n^e^phîlîm*, 'fallen ones,' with no explicit reference to gigantic stature (Gn 6[4]). The context suggests that they were among the antediluvians destroyed by the Flood, and reflects the common tradition of vanished giant races. In Nu 13[33] the name is applied to Anakim with clear reference to giant height.

2. As translation of Hebrew *r^e^phā'îm*. This word, frequently left untranslated in EV, is used of several probably different aboriginal peoples of Palestine, probably thought of as giants. The **Rephaim** included the **Anakim** of the coastal plain and the hill-country of Judah about Hebron (Dt 2[11]); the **Emim**, 'Terrors,' the aborigines of Moab (Dt 2[10]); the **Zamzummim**, 'Howlers,' the aborigines of Ammon (Dt 2[20]), who are probably identical with the **Zuzim** of Gn 14[5], which may be a scribal error; and the ancient inhabitants of Bashan (Dt 3[11]). The statement that **Og**, whose gigantic bedstead (perhaps a sarcophagus; see S. R. Driver, *ad loc.*) was still to be seen at Rabbah, was one of the Rephaim appears to be confirmed by Gn 14[5], where the Rephaim are the first of the peoples smitten by the four kings on their journey south, these being followed by the Zuzim and Emim. Besides these references there is a reminiscence of the Rephaim in the plain of that name near Jerusalem (Jos 15[8f]) and apparently also in Ephraim (Jos 17[15]). This evidence suggests that the *r^e^phā'îm* denoted the aboriginal inhabitants of Palestine, though their association with the 'Terrors' and 'Howlers' suggests folklore rather than sober ethnology.

3. As translation of the singular word *rāphāh* or *rāphā'*. In 2 S 21[15-22], part of which recurs in 1 Ch 20[4-8], four mighty Philistines, including Goliath of Gath, are called 'sons of the giant,' though the word here is possibly the singular used collectively. Goliath is not explicitly termed a giant in the well-known story of his encounter with David in 1 S 17, though his height of 6 cubits and a span (between 7½ and 9½ feet) and the enormous weight of his weapons and armour, even allowing for the exaggeration of saga, certainly suggests more than common stature.

The tradition of giants in the Philistine country may originate from the fact that the Philistines may have been a taller race than the Israelites, as is suggested by Egyptian sculptures from the time of Rameses III., while belief in a giant race in Transjordan was probably suggested by the massive dolmens of Chalcolithic burial, which are a feature of that region. The Râs Shamra texts have been cited as evidence for the historicity of the Rephaim. These, however, are members of a guild associated with the king in certain fertility-rites; hence the translation 'Dispensers of Fertility.' In later Phoenician inscriptions the Rephaim are the shades of the dead, the only feasible philological interpretation of which is 'those joined together' (*i.e.* in the common lot of death).

4. As translation of Hebrew *gibbôr*, 'mighty man,' as in Job 16[14]; cf Ps 19[5] (cf Prayer Book version). This is not an accurate translation of the term.

II. In the Apocrypha.—We find here some interesting allusions: (1) to the supposed destruction of the *N^e^philîm* by the Flood (Wis 14[6], Sir 16[7], Bar 3[26-28]); see also Jth 16[7] 'tall giants' (= the sons of the Titans?); (2) to the slaughter of the 'giant' by David (Sir 47[4]). See also Titans.

F. H. W.—**J. Gr.**

GIBBAR.—A family which returned with Zerubbabel, Ezr 2[20]; called **Gibeon**, Neh 7[25].

GIBBETHON ('mound').—A town belonging to the tribe of Dan, and a Levitical city (Jos 19[44] 21[23]). Nadab, king of Israel, was besieging it when he was slain by Baasha (1 K 15[27]); and Omri was similarly engaged when he was made king by the army (1 K 16[15ff]). It is probably modern *Tell el-Melât*.

GIBEA.—A grandson of Caleb, 1 Ch 2[49]. The list of the descendants of Judah through Caleb given in 1 Ch 2[42ff] is geographical rather than genealogical, and comprises all the towns lying in the *Negeb* of Judah to the S. of Hebron. *Gibea* is probably only a variation in spelling of the more common *Gibeah*. See Gibeah, **1.**

GIBEAH.—**1.** This is one of three Hebrew variants, Gibe'ah, Geba', and Gibe'on, all meaning 'a hill,' the last being a diminutive. Owing to the proximity of Gibe'ah, Geba', and Gibe'on, all in Benjamin within a radius of two miles, there is apt to be confusion, which is especially noteworthy in the account of Saul's campaign about Michmash (1 S 13). The confusion of the text may be sorted out by local knowledge. Though so close together, Gibeah and Geba lay on different sides of the watershed. If the action at Michmash was visible, then the site was Geba. Gibeon was a famous sanctuary, hence Gibeah ('the Hill') of God (1 S 10[5] RVm; RSV Gibeath-elohim). Gibeah, on the other hand, is usually defined as Gibeah of Benjamin or Gibeah of Saul (1 S 11^{4}, Is 10^{29}), whose home it was (1 S 10^{26}). It is also noted as the scene of the outrage on the Levite's concubine and the collective vengeance of Israel upon the tribe of Benjamin (Jg 19^{12}). It had a Philistine garrison, against which Saul rose (1 S 13^{3}, after LXX and Targ.). It appears in Isaiah's description of the Assyrian advance on Jerusalem (10^{28-32}). The location of Gibeah indicated in Jg 20^{31-33} and Josephus, who places it 30 stadia N. of Jerusalem (*BJ* v. ii. 1 [51]), suggests the site *Tell el-Fûl.* Albright's excavations here have demonstrated settlement in the Early Iron Age *c* 1200 and destruction *c* 1150, possibly a trace of the civil war (Jg 19^{12ff}). It was rebuilt about a century later, with a considerable fortress with casemate walling. This is often represented as the palace of Saul, but it may have originally been the post of the Philistine garrison. There is little doubt, however, that it was used by Saul and possibly served as quarters for his professional soldiers, including David. Under the House of David Gibeah declined in importance, its fortress being reduced to the proportions of a watchtower, which was finally destroyed at the fall of Jerusalem. It continued as an insignificant village, and is mentioned as such by Josephus (*loc. cit.*). **2.** A village in Judah near Hebron (Jos 15^{57}), probably modern *el-Jibʿah*, *c* 10 miles NNW. of Hebron. **3.** The 'hill,' where the Ark remained in the house of Amminadab (1 S 7^{1}, 2 S 6^{3}) in the vicinity of Kiriath-jearim, is possibly to be regarded as another Gibeah, which the numerical list in Jos 18^{28} requires in association with Kiriath-jearim. This is possibly to be located at *Khirbet el-Jabʿah,* about 2 miles SW. of *Qiryat el-ʿInab* (Kiriath-jearim). W. E.—**J. Gr.**

GIBEATH (Heb. *gibhʿath*, construct state of *gibhʿāh*), 'hill of,' enters into the composition of place names and is occasionally retained untranslated by AVm, RVm, and RSV. Such instances are: (*a*) 'hill of the foreskins,' where the Israelites were circumcised, Jos 5^{3} (RSV **Gibeath-haaraloth**). (*b*) *Gibeath-Phinehas*, in Mount Ephraim, where Eleazar was buried, Jos 24^{33}; site unknown. (*c*) *Gibeath ham-Moreh*, Jg 7^{1} etc.; see Moreh, **2.** (*d*) 'the hill of God,' 1 S 10^{5} (RSV **Gibeath-elohim** = Gibeah, **2**). (*e*) *Gibeath ha-Hachilah*, 1 S 23^{19} etc.; see Hachilah. (*f*) *Gibeath Ammah*, 2 S 2^{24}; see Ammah. (*g*) *Gibeath Gareb*, Jer 31^{39}; see Gareb, **2.** W. E.

GIBEATH-ELOHIM.—See Gibeah, **2.**

GIBEATH-HAARALOTH.—See Gibeath (*a*).

GIBEON.—A prominent city of Benjamin N. of Jerusalem. The men of Gibeon, fearing an attack by Joshua, obtained through a ruse a covenant of peace with the Israelites (Jos 9). When the deception was discovered the Gibeonites were cursed and assigned a place of perpetual servitude. Gibeon is mentioned with Chephirah, Beeroth, and Kiriath-jearim (Jos 9^{17}) and its people are called Hivites in Jos 9^{7} and 11^{19}. The 'pool of Gibeon' is the scene of the contest between the forces of David under Joab and those of Saul's son Ishbosheth led by Abner (2 S 2^{12-18}). Twelve men from each side transfixed their opponents with swords at Hilkath-hazzurim, 'the field of sword-edges.' Amasa was slaughtered by Joab at 'the great stone which is in Gibeon' (2 S 20^{8-10}). Seven sons of Saul were hanged by the Gibeonites (2 S 21^{1-9}). Solomon offered sacrifices at the great high place of Gibeon (1 K 3^{4}) and it was the place where he had his famous dream (1 K 3^{5-15}). The false prophet Hananiah, who opposed Jeremiah, was from Gibeon (Jer 28^{1}). Jer 41^{12} mentions the 'great pool which is in Gibeon' in connexion with the flight of the remnant from Jerusalem after the attack and destruction by Nebuchadnezzar in 586 B.C. The men of Gibeon were among those who helped rebuild the wall of Jerusalem in the 5th cent. (Neh 3^{7}). The city is mentioned in a list of King Shishak (Sheshonk I.) of the 10th cent. According to Josephus, Cestius pitched his camp there in A.D. 66.

Although Gibeon has long been identified with *el-Jîb*, 6 miles N. of Jerusalem, the American excavations at the site in 1956 and 1957 have produced twenty-four jar handles inscribed with the name 'Gibeon' in the archaic Hebrew script of the 7th cent. The inscriptions on handles also contained the names Amariah, Azariah, Hananiah, Nera, Domla, and Shubel, apparently citizens of the town. A cylindrical pool or stair well cut from solid rock, 37 feet in diameter and equipped with a circular stairway of seventy-nine steps which led down to a spring 82 feet below the surface was a part of the extensive water system of the city. A second access to water was had through a stepped tunnel which extended for 167 feet from inside the wall to the spring which flowed from the base of the mound below. There are ninety-three steps cut into the rock floor of this passageway. These installations substantiate the reputation which Gibeon had in the Biblical passages for its water (2 S 2^{13}, Jer 41^{12}). J. B. P.

GIBEON.—A family which returned with Zerubbabel, Neh 7^{25}; called **Gibbar,** Ezr 2^{20}.

GIDDALTI ('I magnify [God]').—A son of Heman, 1 Ch $25^{4, 29}$.

GIDDEL ('very great').—**1.** The eponym of a family of Nethinim, Ezr 2^{47}, Neh 7^{49}; called in 1 Es 5^{30} **Cathua. 2.** The eponym of a family of 'Solomon's servants,' Ezr 2^{56}, Neh 7^{58}, 1 Es 5^{33} (AV, RV **Isdael**).

GIDEON.—A judge from the tribe of Manasseh, son of Joash the Abiezrite (Jg 6^{1}–8^{35}). The narrative is obviously composite, *e.g.* there are two accounts of his call to leadership (6^{7-24} and vv.$^{25-32}$), and note also the story of 7^{24}–8^{3} which interrupts the narrative.

The general outline of the history of Gideon, disregarding details, is as follows:

(*a*) *Introduction.* In accord with the general theme of the book of Judges the people had apostatized with the inevitable result that the land was subjected to the plundering raids of neighbouring tribes, in this case the Midianites and Amalekites. After a number of years the people realizing their apostasy called upon Yahweh their God who heard their cry and sent a prophet to rebuke them.

(*b*) *Gideon's call.* In the first version the Angel of Yahweh (see Angel of the Lord) appears to Gideon while he is surreptitiously engaged in threshing wheat, and bids him assume the charismatic role of deliverer of the people from the Midianites. He is given a Divine sign assuring him of the angel's identity and good intention, whereupon Gideon builds an altar.

In the second version Yahweh commanded Gideon to tear down the Baal altar in the city along with the Asherah (q.v.) beside it, build a legitimate altar to Yahweh in its place, and offer a holocaust. When the townsmen became aware of what had happened on the following morning, they were infuriated and wanted to kill Gideon. His father cleverly intervened by saying: *Jerubbaal, i.e.* 'Let Baal contend (for himself).' This word became another name by which Gideon was known (*e.g.* 7^{1}), which a later editor changed for religious reasons to Jerubbesheth in 2 S 11^{21} ('Let the shameful one contend').

(*c*) *Gideon's victory.* Baal having been deposed and Yahweh again recognized as the people's God, Gideon now becomes the charismatic hero, *i.e.* 'the Spirit of Yahweh took possession' of him. A volunteer army of Northern tribesmen is assembled and Gideon is again assured of Divine help by the sign of the miraculous dew on the fleece. At God's command Gideon's army is twice reduced from an original 32,000 to a mere 300. Once more Gideon receives assurance of victory through an overheard account of a Midianite soldier's dream.

For the actual onslaught each man was given an empty jar containing a flaming torch as well as a trumpet. In the dead of night they surrounded the camp of the Midianites and at a prearranged signal broke the jars, waved the torches, blew on the trumpets, and with a war cry fell on the sleeping camp. This threw the camp into complete panic and immediate flight. The pursuit, described in some detail, became a complete rout, with the princes and army commanders captured and killed. Of the original army all but 15,000 (out of 135,000) were killed according to the tradition at 8^{10}.

(*d*) *Gideon's refusal of kingship and his defection.* After the miraculous victory the men of Israel spontaneously requested Gideon to accept rule as king over Israel. Gideon refused the offer, asking instead for a leader's percentage of the spoils. With these he fashioned an ephod for his city which ' became a snare to Gideon and his family ' (8^{27}). According to v.^{33}, however, Israel's defection began after Gideon's death, which apparent discrepancy may well indicate two different literary sources.

The section 7^{24}–8^{3} is undoubtedly ancient; it tells of how the Ephraimites, at Gideon's command, cut off part of the fugitive Midianite host under two chieftains, Oreb and Zeeb, whom the Ephraimites slew. When the victorious band with Gideon join with them, they complain to Gideon of his failure to invite them to take part in the large-scale attack. Gideon satisfies them by shrewd flattery. This section appears to be a fragment of a source which presumably went on to detail what further action the Ephraimites took during the campaign.

W. O. E. O.—**J. W. W.**

GIDEONI.—Father of Abidan, prince of Benjamin, Nu 1^{11} 2^{22} 7$^{60, 65}$ 10^{24}.

GIDOM.—The limit of the pursuit of Benjamin by the other tribes, Jg 20^{45}. Possibly the word is not a proper name, but may be read as an infinitive, ' till they cut them off.' No place of the name of Gidom is mentioned elsewhere.

GIER EAGLE.—Two Hebrew words in the lists of unclean birds (Lv 11$^{13, 18}$, Dt 14$^{12, 17}$) are translated ' gier-eagle ' (cf German *Geier*, ' vulture,' suggesting ' vulture-eagle ') ; but the English name suggests nothing definite. These are the *peres* (RV ; but ' ossifrage ' in AV, ' ossifrage ' and ' vulture ' in RSV) and the *rāḥām* or *rāḥāmāh* (AV ; but ' vulture ' in RV, ' vulture ' and ' carrion vulture ' in RSV). I. As *pāras* ' broke (bones or bread) in pieces ' shows, the *peres* is the ' smasher ' and its position in the lists suggests a vulture, possibly ' Arrian's vulture,' which drops its victims from a great height on to a rock or stone, repeating the procedure until all the bones are shattered, when it consumes it. The Targum translates the word *'azyâ* or *'uzyâ*, ' goat-like (bird),' apparently alluding to the colouring of its back, which is predominately black. II. The name of the *rāḥām(āh)* comes from a root describing what is black and white, as the Arabic *'arḥamu* ' having a white head and black body ' and *raḥamu* ' vulture with a white neck and body but black wings, white carrion vulture ; sea-eagle ; pelican ' show. The position of the *rāḥām(āh)* in the list shows that no vulture can be meant ; the sea-eagle rarely visits Palestine, and the pelican is not likely to have been considered unclean (see PELICAN). Possibly the ' osprey ' is meant. This is a large brown bird having head and nape white with brown streaks and white underparts, and found in Palestine ; and its habits suggest an affinity on the one hand with the raptorial owls and on the other hand with the stork or heron and cormorant, which are fishers. G. R. D.

GIFT, GIVING.—I. In the OT.—1. In the East what is described as a ' gift ' is often hardly worthy of the name. ' Gift ' may be a courtesy title for much that is of the nature of barter or exchange, tribute or compulsory homage, or even of bribery. It is well understood that a gift accepted lays the recipient under the obligation of returning a *quid pro quo* in some form or other. The queen of Sheba's gifts to Solomon were a sort of royal commerce. The charming picture of Ephron's generosity to Abraham with regard to the cave of Machpelah (Gn 23) must be interpreted in the light of Oriental custom ; it is a mere piece of politeness, not intended to be accepted. An Arab will give anything to an intending buyer, and appeal to witnesses that he does so, but it is understood to be only a form, to help him to raise the price (see Driver, *Genesis*, *ad loc.*). Cf the transaction between David and Araunah (2 S 24^{22}). In other cases the return is of a less material character, consisting of the granting of a request or the restoring of favour. Hence Jacob's anxiety as to Esau's acceptance of his gifts (Gn 32^{20} 33^{10}) ; cf the present to Joseph (43^{11}) and 1 S 25^{27} 30^{26}. The principle is stated in Pr 18^{16} ' A man's gift maketh room for him, and bringeth him before great men ' (cf 19^{6}). It is obvious that a gift in this sense easily becomes a bribe ; hence the frequent commands to receive no bribe, ' for a bribe blinds the officials ' (Ex 23^{8}, Dt 16^{19} 27^{25}, Pr 17$^{8, 23}$, Ps 15^{5}, Is 1^{23} 5^{23} etc.). It should be noticed that in this connexion a special Hebrew word (*shōḥadh*) is used, meaning a ' bribe ' ; AV and RV often translate ' gift ' or ' reward ' ; RSV normally ' bribe.' In 1 K 15^{19}, 2 K 16^{8} it is used of a bribe from king to king. Even the Roman Felix expects a gift (Ac 24^{26}).

2. In a more legitimate sense we find gifts offered to kings, etc., by way of homage (1 S 10^{27}, Ps 45^{12}), or tribute (Jg 3^{15}, 2 S 8$^{2, 6}$, 1 K 4^{21}, Ps 72^{10}) ; the presents to Assyria, etc., are clearly not spontaneous, and the receiving of such homage from subject kings is a favourite subject of sculptures and paintings. 1 S 25 illustrates the ground on which such a gift was sometimes claimed ; it was a payment for protection. Gifts were expected in consulting a prophet or oracle (Nu 22, 1 S 9^{7}, 2 K 5^{5}, 2 K 8^{9}, Dn 5^{17}). Whether regulated or unregulated, they formed the chief support of priests and Levites, and were the necessary accompaniment of worship. ' None shall appear before me empty-handed ' (Ex 23^{15} 34^{20}). One side of sacrifice is giving to God. The spiritual religion realized that Y″'s favour did not depend on those things (Is 1, Ps 50), still more that He was not to be bribed. In Dt 10^{17} it is said that He is One who ' takes no bribe.' But there can be no doubt that in the popular view a gift to God was supposed to operate in precisely the same manner as a gift to a judge or earthly monarch (Mal 1^{8}). Its acceptance was the sign of favour and of the granting of the request (Jg 13^{23}, 2 Ch 7^{1}) ; its rejection, of disfavour (Gn 4^{4}, Mal 1^{10}). 1 S 26^{19} shows that a gift was regarded as propitiatory, and the machinery of the vow takes the same point of view. It should be noted that the word *minḥāh*, which is continually used of gifts and homage to men, is also specially used of offerings to God, and in P technically of the ' meal-offering.' For the meaning of ' gift ' or Corban in Mk 7^{11} etc., see article SACRIFICE AND OFFERING. Almsgiving became one of the three things by which merit was earned before God, the other two being prayer and fasting ; and magnificent gifts to the Temple were a means of personal display (Lk 21^{5}, Jos. *Ant.* xv. xi. 3 [402]).

3. Passing from cases where the gift is neither spontaneous nor disinterested, but is only a polite Oriental periphrasis for other things, we turn to instances where the word is used in a truer sense. If the king looked for ' gifts ' from his subjects, he was also expected to return them in the shape of largess, especially on festive occasions (Est 2^{18}). This often took the form of an allowance from the royal table (Gn 43^{34}, 2 S 11^{8}, Jer 40^{5}). We read more generally of gifts to the needy in Neh 8^{10}, Est 9^{22}, Ec 11^{2}, Ps 112^{9} (see ALMSGIVING). The gift of a robe, or other article from the person, was of special significance (1 S 18^{4}). Interchanges of gifts between equals are mentioned in Est 9^{19}, Rev 11^{10}. On the occasion of a wedding, presents are sent by friends to the bridegroom's house. Gifts, as distinct from the ' dowry,' were sometimes given by the bridegroom to the bride (Gn 24^{53} 34^{12}) ; sometimes by the bride's father (Jg 1^{14}, 1 K 9^{16}).

II. In the NT.—It is characteristic of the NT that many of its usages of the word ' gift ' are connected with God's gifts to men—His Son, life, the Holy Spirit, etc. ' Grace ' is the free gift of God. ' Gifts ' is specially used of the manifestations of the Spirit (see SPIRITUAL GIFTS). Eph 4^{8} illustrates well the change of attitude. St. Paul quotes from Ps 68^{19}, where the point is the homage which Y″ receives from vanquished foes, and applies the words to the gifts which the victorious Christ has won for His Church. It is more Divine, more characteristic of God, to give than to receive. This is, in fact, the teaching of the NT on the subject. As the Father and His Son freely give all things, so must the Christian. Almsgiving is restored to its proper place; the true gift is not given to win merit from God, or to gain the praise of men, but proceeds from love, hoping for nothing again (Mt 6^{1}, Lk 6^{32}; see ALMSGIVING). Our Lord Himself accepted gifts, and taught that it is our highest privilege to give to Him and His 'little ones' (Lk 5^{29} 7^{37} 8^{3}, Jn 12^{2}). And giving remains an integral part of Christian worship, as a willing homage to God, the wrong ideas of compulsion or persuasion being cast aside (1 Ch 29^{14}, Mt 2^{11} 5^{23}, 2 Co 9^{7ff}, Rev 21^{24}). The gifts to St. Paul from his converts (Ph 4^{16}), and from the Gentile Churches to Jerusalem (Ac 11^{29}, Ro 15^{26}, 1 Co 8, 9), play a very important part in the history of the early Church. C. W. E.

GIHON ('a bursting forth').—**1.** A spring near Jerusalem, evidently sacred and therefore selected as the scene of Solomon's coronation, 1 K 1$^{33, 38, 45}$. Hezekiah made an aqueduct from it, 2 Ch 32^{30}; and Manasseh built a wall of the city W. of it, 2 Ch 33^{14}. Undoubtedly modern *'Ain Sittī Maryam*, or 'Virgin's Fount.' See SILOAM. **2.** One of the four rivers of Paradise, Gn 2^{13}; cf Sir 24^{27}. See EDEN [GARDEN OF].

GILALAI.—A Levitical musician, Neh 12^{36}.

GILBOA.—A range of hills, now called *Jebel Fuqqû'ah*, on the E. boundary of the Plain of Esdraelon, where Saul and Jonathan died, 1 S 28^{4} 31$^{1-8}$, 1 Ch 10$^{1, 8}$; cf 2 S 1$^{6, 21}$ 21^{12}. They run from *Zer'în* (Jezreel) due SE., and from the eastern extremity a prolongation runs S. towards the hills of Samaria. They are most imposing from the Vale of Jezreel and Jordan Valley, but nowhere reach a height of more than 1700 feet above sea-level. The little village of *Jelbûn* on the slopes of *Jebel Fuqqû'ah* is thought to retain an echo of the name Gilboa. The slopes of these hills are steep, rugged, and bare. At the N. foot lies *'Ain Jālûd*, almost certainly the spring of Harod (q.v.). E. W. G. M.

GILEAD.—**1.** A son of Machir, son of Manasseh (Nu 26^{29}, 1 Ch 2^{21}), and grandfather of Zelophehad (Nu 27^{1}), and presumably the eponym of **2.** An Israelite tribe or clan (Jg 5^{17} 10^{3} 12^{7}) living S. of the Jabbok E. of the Jordan. **3.** The father of Jephthah (Jg 11^{1})—a late tradition and clearly dependent on **1** and **2.** **4.** A Gadite, son of Michael (1 Ch 5^{14}). **5.** A mountain mentioned in Jg 7^{3} (RSVm); this cannot be the trans-Jordanic Gilead and no other is known. The text is undoubtedly corrupt, but no proposed emendation has won general acceptance. **6.** The name first of a small area E. of the Jordan, S. of the Jabbok (cf **2**), which came to be used also of the territory northward to the Yarmuk and southward to the Arnon (cf Jos 22^{9ff}, Jg 20^{1}, 2 K 10^{33}), bounded on the E. by the desert. It is a lofty plateau, about 2000 feet above sea-level, wooded in places, with productive fields intersected by valleys and streams. Nu 32^{1} indicates that it was good pasture land; cf Ca 4^{1} 6^{5} referring to 'goats moving down the slopes of Gilead.' From Jer 8^{22} 46^{11} it may be inferred that it was famous for its medicinal balm; cf Gn 37^{25} which shows that the Ishmaelite traders to whom Joseph was sold were carrying gum, balm, and myrrh from Gilead to Egypt. It is mentioned first as the place where Jacob in his flight from Laban was overtaken by him and where they raised a heap of stones and a pillar as a witness to the covenant they made each with the other (Gn 31).

According to Nu 21^{20ff} the Israelites secured possession of Gilead when they defeated Sihon, king of the Amorites; his territory is defined as reaching from the Arnon to the Jabbok and Nu 32^{5ff} says it was divided between the tribes of Reuben and Gad (cf Jos 13$^{15-28}$). Nu 32^{39ff} says that Gilead, here the land between the Jabbok and the Yarmuk (cf 2 S 24^{6}), was taken from the Amorites by Machir and Jair (cf Jg 10^{2} where Jair is a Gileadite), sons of Manasseh; cf the reference to the half-tribe of Manasseh in Nu 32^{33} and Jos 13$^{29-31}$, which include Bashan in this Manassite territory.

Some of the Hebrews took refuge in Gilead from the Philistines (1 S 13^{7}). Gilead was part of the short-lived kingdom of Ish-bosheth (2 S 2^{9}). Hither David fled from Absalom (2 S 17^{22}), and was succoured by Barzillai the Gileadite (17^{27}) whose descendants are referred to in post-exilic records (Ezr 2^{61}=Neh 7^{63}). Gilead was administered by Ben-geber and Ahinadab (1 K 4^{13f}) for Solomon. It was the land of Elijah's origin. For cruelties to Gileadites, Damascus and Ammon are denounced by Amos (1$^{3, 13}$) while on the other hand Hosea (12^{11}) refers to the iniquity of Gilead, and (6^{8}) to Gilead as 'a city of evil doers, tracked with blood'; but there is no other mention of a city named Gilead so the reference here may be to the capital of the district, or to Ramoth-gilead, or Jabesh-gilead. Pekah's following of fifty Gileadites (2 K 15^{25}) possibly suggests some kind of revolutionary activity there and the incident referred to by Hosea may be connected with this. 2 K 15^{29} states that the inhabitants of Gilead were 'carried captive to Assyria'; what the actual extent of the deportation was it is impossible to say. 1 Ch 2^{21} seems to refer to a migration from Judah to Gilead N. of the Jabbok; this may have occurred at the end of the 8th cent., though it could be later. It was possibly at this time that the Ammonites moved in (cf Jer 49^{1}). Jer 50^{19}, Mi 7^{14} imply that Gilead is in foreign hands. R. A. S. M.—C. A. Si.

GILGAL.—**1.** A place on the E. border of Jericho (Jos 4^{19}), where the Israelites first encamped after crossing the Jordan, and which, according to Jos 14^{6}, remained the headquarters of the congregation till after the defeat of the northern kings at Merom. The stone circle from which it certainly took its name (cf the impossible etymology in Jos 5^{9}) was no doubt that to which the tradition embodied in Jos 4^{20} refers, and the same as the 'images' by Gilgal in the story of Ehud (Jg 3^{19} RVm; RSV 'sculptured stones'). The twelve stones are significant in view of the rôle of Gilgal as an amphictyonic shrine of the twelve-tribe confederacy of Israel. It was associated with the work of Samuel as a judge (1 S 7^{16}), and was the place where the kingship of Saul was formally consecrated (reading 'let us consecrate,' *n^{e}ḳaddēsh*, for 'let us renew,' *n^{e}ḥaddēsh*) after his succour of Jabesh-Gilead (1 S 11^{14}). It was the rallying-point for national resistance in Saul's Philistine wars (1 S 13$^{4-15}$), the scene of Samuel's breach with Saul (1 S 13$^{8-15}$), and of the hewing of the Amalekite king Agag in pieces before the Lord (1 S 15^{12f}). It was here that the men of Judah met David returning after Absalom's revolt (2 S 19^{5}), possibly to take a new oath of allegiance at the shrine, though that is not explicitly mentioned. The importance of the Gilgal sanctuary must have waned with the passing of the power from Benjamin to the House of David and the increased importance of Jerusalem as the seat of the Ark and a national shrine. It never quite lost its significance, however, and was probably always a centre of pilgrimage, a religious institution in favour among the Semites. It was certainly a place of pilgrimage in the middle of the 8th cent. and ranked with Bethel, the national shrine under royal patronage (Am 4^{4} 5^{5}, Hos 4^{15} 9^{15} 12^{11}). The significance of this shrine as a conservatory of the traditions of the Hebrew occupation has recently been emphasized by A. Alt, M. Noth, G. von Rad, H. J. Kraus, and K. Galling. It is suggested that the sacramental experience of the shrine of Gilgal has coloured the narrative of the conquest in Jos 1–9 and Jg 2$^{1-5}$.

Modern tradition has varied regarding the location of Gilgal at *Khirbet en-Nitla* just over 2 miles SE. of old Jericho and, on the other hand, at *Khirbet el-Mefjer*, the site of the winter palace of the Umayyad Caliph Hishām (A.D. 724–743). Excavations by Kelso and Muilenburg at *en-Nitla* show no traces of occupation before the Byzantine period. Excavations by Muilenburg, however, revealed Iron Age remains near *Khirbet el-Mefjer* and the identification would seem to be clinched by Josephus' location of Gilgal 10 stadia from Jericho and 50 stadia from the Jordan, *i.e.* from the ford of *el-Mukhdâs* (*Ant.* v. i. 4 [20]), directions which rule out *en-Nitla.* Pillars inscribed with the cross in the Umayyad palace at *el-Mefjer* are obviously from a Christian church, clearly associated with Gilgal and probably that noticed by mediaeval pilgrims N. (actually NE.) of Jericho.

2. A place of the same name near Dor mentioned in a list of conquered kings (Jos 12[23]), possibly *Jiljûlieh* about 4 miles N. of Antipatris (*Râs el-ʿAin*). **3.** A place in the hill-country of Ephraim (2 K 4[38]) somewhere near Bethel (2[1]), possibly *Jiljîlieh* 8 miles NW. of Bethel. **4.** Gilgal of Dt 11[30] is not certainly identified. The close connexion with Ebal and Gerizim suggests *Juleijil* 2½ miles SE. of *Nâblus.* **5.** A place on the border of Judah, near Adummim (q.v.), mentioned in Jos 15[7]; possibly the same as **1.**

The name is generally used in Hebrew with the definite article, which suggests that it is a common noun, 'stone-circle,' a relic of early local religion, hence its common usage as a place-name in Hebrew and Arabic.

R. A. S. M.—**J. Gr.**

GILGAL, HOUSE OF, Neh 12[29] (AV).—See Beth-gilgal.

GILOH.—A city in the southern hills of Judah, Jos 15[51] (**Gilo** in RSV in 2 S 23[34]); the birthplace of Ahithophel the **Gilonite,** the famous counsellor of David, 2 S 15[12] 23[34]. It is perhaps modern *Kh. Jâlā.*

GIMEL.—Third letter of Hebrew alphabet, and so used to introduce the third part of Ps 119, every verse of which begins with this letter.

GIMZO.—A town on the border of Philistia, 2 Ch 28[18]. It is the modern *Jimzū* near Aijalon.

GIN.—See Snares.

GINATH.—Father of Tibni, who unsuccessfully laid claim against Omri to the throne of Israel, 1 K 16[21f].

GINNETHOI.—A priest among the returned exiles, Neh 12[4]; called **Ginnethon** in 12[6] 10[6].

GINNETHON.—See Ginnethoi.

GIRDING THE LOINS, GIRDLE.—See Dress, **2, 3.**

GIRGASHITES (in Hebrew always singular 'the Girgashite,' and so rendered in RV).—Very little is known of this people, whose name, though occurring several times in OT in the list of Canaanite tribes (Gn 10[16] 15[21], Dt 7[1] [and 20[17] in Sam. and LXX], Jos 3[10] 24[11], 1 Ch 1[14], Neh 9[8]), affords no indication of their position, or to what branch of the Canaanites they belonged, except in two instances, namely, Gn 10[16], where the 'Girgashite' is given as the name of the fifth son of Canaan; and Jos 24[11], where the Girgashites would seem to have inhabited the tract on the W. of Jordan, the Israelites having been obliged to cross over that river in order to fight the men of Jericho, among whom were the Girgashites.

GIRZITES.—According to 1 S 27[8], David and his men, while living at the court of Achish king of Gath, 'made raids upon the Geshurites, the Girzites (RVm **Gizrites**), and the Amalekites; for these were the inhabitants of the land from of old, as far as Shur, to the land of Egypt.' The LXX (B) is probably correct in reading only one name 'Gizrites' for Geshurites and Girzites, viz. the Canaanite inhabitants of Gezer (q.v.), a town on the SW. border of Ephraim (Jos 10[33] 16[3, 10], Jg 1[29]).

GISHPA.—An overseer of the Nethinim, Neh 11[21]; but the text is probably corrupt.

GITTAIM ('the two wine-presses').—A town to which the Beerothites fled, 2 S 4[3]; mentioned with Hazor and Ramah, Neh 11[33]. The site is unknown.

GITTITES.—See Gath.

GITTITH.—See Psalms (titles).

GIZONITE.—A gentilic name which occurs in 1 Ch 11[34] in the collocation 'Hashem the Gizonite.' In all probability this should be corrected to 'Jashen (cf the parallel passage 2 S 23[32]) the Gunite.' See Jashen and Guni, **3.**

GIZRITES.—See Girzites.

GLASS, LOOKING-GLASS, MIRROR.—This indispensable article of a lady's toilet is first met with in Ex 38[8], where the 'laver of bronze' and its base are said to have been made of the 'mirrors (AV 'looking-glasses') of the ministering women who ministered at the door of the tent of meeting' (RSV; cf RV). This passage shows that the mirrors of the Hebrews, like those of the other peoples of antiquity, were made of polished bronze, as is 'molten mirror' (RV and RSV; AV 'looking-glass'). A different Hebrew word is rendered 'hand mirror' by RV (AV 'glasses'; RSV 'garments of gauze') in the list of toilet articles, Is 3[23]. The fact that this word denotes a writing 'tablet' in 8[1] (RV and RSV) perhaps indicates that in the former passage we have an oblong mirror in a wooden frame. The usual shape, however, of the Egyptian (see Wilkinson, *Anc. Egyp.* ii, 350 f. with illustration), as of the Greek, hand-mirrors was round or slightly oval. As a rule they were furnished with a tang, which fitted into a handle of wood or metal, often delicately carved. Specimens of circular mirrors of bronze, one 5 inches, the other 4½, in diameter, have been discovered in graves at Gezer (*PEFSt*, 1905, 321; 1907, 199 with illustrations).

In the Apocrypha there is a reference, Sir 12[11], to the rust that gathered on these metal mirrors, and in Wis 7[26] the Divine wisdom is described as 'a spotless mirror of the working of God' the only occurrence in AV of 'mirror,' which RV and RSV substitute for 'glass' throughout. The NT references, finally, are those by Paul (1 Co 13[12] [AV 'glass'; RV and RSV 'mirror'], 2 Co 3[18] [AV 'glass'; RV 'mirror'; RSV 'beholding the glory of God,' but RSVm 'reflecting'], Ja 1[23] [AV 'glass'; RV and RSV 'mirror']). For the 'sea of glass' (AV and RSV; RV 'glassy sea') of Rev 4[6] 15[2] see Sea of Glass. A. R. S. K.

GLEANING.—For the humanitarian provisions of the Pentateuchal codes, by which the gleanings of the cornfield, vineyard, and oliveyard were the perquisites of the poor, the fatherless, the widow, and the *gēr* or outlander see Lv 19[9f] 23[22] (both H), Dt 24[19-21]. See Agriculture, **3**; Poverty.

GLEDE.—See Buzzard and Kite.

GLORY (in OT).—The principal Hebrew word for glory is *kābhôdh*, and is derived from the verbal root *kābhēdh*, 'to be heavy' like the weight of Absalom's hair in 2 S 14[26], or the heavy rock in a weary land in Is 32[2], or the iniquities of Israel in Is 1[4] or Ps 38[4 (Heb. 5)]: 'for my iniquities . . . weigh like burdens too heavy for me.' It thus acquires other meanings such as *wealth* or *abundance* (Gn 13[2] of Abraham, 31[1] of Jacob), of *esteem, dignity, prestige,* and *honour* (Is 5[13], Nu 24[11]), which is frequently applied to God (Is 42[8] 43[7] 48[11]), and *splendour* (Gn 45[13], Hag 2[9]). Its associations are frequently with light and radiance and fire (Ex 24[16], Ezk 1[28]), and it is the term *par excellence* for the Divine self-manifestation. It is therefore frequently associated with holiness.

1. Secular usage includes such expressions as 'the glory (or splendour) of Lebanon' (Is 35[2]), *i.e.* the cedars; 'the glory of his house' (Ps 49[16 (Heb. 17)]), *i.e.* a man's material possessions; 'your splendid chariots' (Is 22[18]); 'the glory of Moab' (Is 16[14]) or 'the glory of Kedar' (Is 21[16]), *i.e.* the esteem or honour they possess. Note also the 'glory' of the forests of Assyria which Yahweh will destroy (Is 10[18]). It also denotes the noblest or distinctive part of a man as in Gn 49[6], Ps 16[9] 30[12 (Heb. 13)] 57[8 (Heb. 9)]). Yahweh crowns man with glory and honour, *kābhôdh wᵉhādhār* (Ps 8[5 (Heb. 6)]). Yahweh is Israel's 'glory,' its proudest possession (Jer 2[11]; cf also the Ark in 1 S 4[21])).

2. The glory of Yahweh is frequently employed in storm theophanies. In the psalm of the thunderstorm He is the God of glory (*'ēl kābhôdh* 29[3]). The best illustration, of course, is the great theophany of Ezk 1^{4-28a}, which is profuse in its imagery of storm, and culminates in the vision of the glory bright like a rainbow (1^{28}). In the P sections of the Pentateuch such manifestations are frequent (see Ex 24^{16-18}, Lv 9^{6} etc.). The visible and invisible motives in God's self-manifestation are combined in the story of Yahweh's theophany to Moses (Ex 33^{17-23} 34^{6f}). Here the visible glory, the brightness of Yahweh's face, may not be seen. The spiritual glory is revealed in the proclamation of the name of Yahweh, full of compassion and gracious.

3. The *glory* of Yahweh also has eschatological associations, as we should expect, for in the eschaton He will manifest Himself to all flesh (Is 40^{5}). The idea of Yahweh's glory filling the whole earth is present in Is 6^{3}, but it is more frequently an expectation of an event to be realized. The second book of the Psalter closes with the petition, 'May his glory fill the whole earth' (72^{19}; cf $57^{5, 11}$ (Heb. 6, 12)). As God manifests His glory at the beginning (cf Ex 24^{16f}) and at the end (cf Is 40^{5}), so He manifests it also in history and in His sovereignty over the nations (Nu 14^{22}, Ezk 39^{21}) and in nature (Ps 104^{31f}). W. J. M.—**J. Mu.**

GLORY (in Apocrypha and NT).—In the NT of the RSV, 'glory' as a noun is always the translation of Greek *doxa*. This word, coming from a root meaning 'to seem,' might signify outward appearance only, or, in a secondary sense, opinion. This use is not found in the Biblical writings, but the derived classical use—favourable opinion or reputation, and hence exalted honour—or, as applied to things, splendour, is very common (Wis 8^{10}, 2 Co 3^{7}, Bar 2^{17}, Sir 43^{1} 50^{7}). The special LXX use of 'glory' for the physical or ethical manifestation of the greatness of God is also frequent. In RSV of NT *doxa* is occasionally translated 'honour' (2 Co 6^{8}); in Apocrypha sometimes 'honour' (1 Es 8^{4} RSV 'favour'), and a few times 'pomp' (1 Mac 10^{86} 11^{6} etc.), or 'majesty' (Ad. Est 15^{7} RSV 'splendour'). As a verb, 'glory' in the sense of boast (Gr. *kauchaomai*) is frequently found (Sir 11^{4}, Gal 6^{13f}).

A few examples of the use of 'glory' to denote the brightness of goodness may be given. In Bar 5^{4} is the striking phrase 'the glory of godliness,' whilst wisdom is called 'a clear effluence of the glory of the Almighty' (Wis 7^{25}). In Jn 1^{14} the 'glory' of the Only-begotten consists in grace and truth (cf Jn 2^{11} $17^{5, 22}$). In Ro 3^{23} the 'glory' of God, of which men have fallen short, is His manifested excellence, revealed at first in man made in God's image (cf 1 Co 11^{7a}), lost through sin, but meant to be recovered as he is transfigured 'from one degree of glory to another' (2 Co 3^{18}). For 'glory' as used to express the visible brightness, cf To 12^{15}, where Raphael goes in before the glory of the Holy One (cf 2 Mac 3^{26}, of angels). In NT, cf Lk 2^{9} 'The glory of the Lord shone around them.' In 2 Co 3^{7-11} the double use of 'glory' (RSV 'splendour') is clearly seen: the fading brightness on the face of Moses is contrasted with the abiding spiritual glory of the New Covenant. Passages which combine both the ethical and the physical meanings are those which speak of the glory of the Son of Man (Mt 16^{27} etc.), and the glory, both of brightness and of purity, which gives light to the heavenly city (Rev 21^{23}). 'Glory,' as applied to the saints, culminates in a state where both body and spirit are fully changed into the likeness of the glorified Lord (Ph 3^{21}, Col 3^{4}). *Doxa* is rendered in the RSV by 'praise' in Jn 9^{24} and 'glorious one' in 2 P 2^{10}.

In Wis 18^{24} a special use appears, where 'the glories of the fathers' is a phrase for the names of the twelve tribes, written on the precious stones of the high-priestly breastplate. Doubtless this is suggested by the flashing gems. An interesting parallel is given in Murray, *Eng. Dict. s.v.*: 'They presented to his Electoral Highness . . . the Two Stars or Glories, and Two Pieces of Ribbon of the Order [of the Garter]'; cf Kalisch on Ex 28 'The jewels are the emblems of the stars, which they rival in splendour.' W. J. M.—**F. W. G.**

GLOSSOLALIA.—See TONGUES [GIFT OF], PROPHECY.

GNAT.—1. Hebrew *kēn*, plural *kinnim*, Ex 8^{16-18} (AV, RV **lice**; RVm **sand flies** or **fleas**), Ps 105^{31} (AV, RV **lice**), Is 51^{6} (AV, RV 'in like manner'; RVm 'like gnats'). **2.** Greek *kōnōps*, Mt 23^{24}.

Various members of the *Culicidae*, mosquitoes and true gnats, are found in Palestine; of the former, four species which are fever-bearing are known. These and such small insects are very apt to fall into food or liquid, and required to be 'strained out' (Mt 23^{24}), especially in connexion with Lv 11^{23f}. An Arab proverb well illustrates the ideas of Mt 23^{24}: 'He eats an elephant and is suffocated by a gnat.' On the OT passages see LICE. E. G. W. M.

GNOSTICISM.—The name gnosticism is a modern term used to classify a wide variety of religious sects in existence from the 1st cent. of our era until at least the 9th. What they had in common was the belief that the universe was made and controlled by hostile powers or angels, that the essence of true human nature was a divine element (spark, spirit) not created by these powers, and that a redeemer had descended from the highest heaven to awaken the divine element in those men who were capable of redemption; redemption was given in the reception of this knowledge (*gnōsis*). Redemption-revelation is thus on the one hand knowledge of the true self and on the other knowledge of the alien nature of the universe; the destiny of the spark or spirit is to escape from the universe to the supreme deity above.

Our knowledge of gnosticism is derived largely from the early church fathers (Justin, Irenaeus, Clement, Tertullian, Hippolytus, Epiphanius) who combatted it as a Christian heresy and often reproduced gnostic documents. More recently documents, chiefly in Coptic translations from Greek, have been found; the most important discoveries were made in 1945 at Nag-Hammadi (Chenoboskion) in Egypt, where a whole gnostic library was found, including such works as the *Gospel of Truth*, the *Gospel of Thomas*, and many other documents which illuminate the history of various gnostic sects.

According to some of the fathers, the first gnostic was SIMON MAGUS (q.v.), and other gnostics simply modified his teaching. This is probably a claim made in opposition to various gnostics' own assertions that their teaching came from the Christian apostles; Basilides said he was a successor of Peter, while Valentinus claimed to be a successor of Paul. Other gnostics used apocryphal documents containing revelations supposedly given by Jesus after his resurrection. Almost all of them provide stories of creation which are ultimately based on the book of Genesis, though severely modified by their dualistic world-view, especially in their treatment of Yahweh as an evil angel.

Gnosticism contains elements derived from various sources and of varying importance: dualism chiefly from Iran, probably via heterodox Judaism; the figure of a great Mother probably from Mesopotamia, though related to the Wisdom of the Jewish wisdom-literature; the picture of the redeemer probably from heterodox Jewish Christianity; and the allegorization of all kinds of religious texts from Hellenism, perhaps via Hellenistic Judaism. The matrix in which these elements existed before the rise of gnosticism as such seems to have been (1) heterodox Judaism (as represented, on the one hand, in the Dead Sea Scrolls and other apocalyptic literature and, on the other, in speculative allegorizers mentioned by Philo as going farther than he did), and (2) heterodox Jewish Christianity (as represented in various forms of Ebionism, in the heretics opposed by Ignatius, and in the doctrines reflected by many of the apostolic fathers).

The crystallization of these elements seems to be due historically to two main factors: (1) the rise of Christianity, and (2) the failure of the Jewish apocalyptic hope, first after the war of 66–70 but more significantly after the Messianic struggle of 132–135. It is after the first failure that we encounter the doctrines of Simon, Menander, Saturninus, and Basilides, and after the second that we meet the great Christian gnostics such as Marcion and Valentinus, both of whom taught at Rome and contended with more orthodox Jewish Christians there.

If this analysis is correct, it is possible that gnostic ideas were present among Paul's opponents at Corinth; they misinterpreted his gospel by treating the eschatology as fully 'realized.' If the essence of gnosticism is to be found in the further dualizing of apocalyptic thought, however, it can be said that some elements in Pauline and Johannine thought lie on the border-line between apocalyptic and gnostic thought, though neither Paul nor John was a gnostic, and at some points John is anti-gnostic. Examples of this 'border-line' type of expression can be found in Paul's allusion to Satan as 'the god of this age' (2 Co 4[4], 'world,' RSV) and in John's statement (8[44]) that the father of 'the Jews' is the devil.

The heresy combatted in Colossians is not necessarily gnostic, but doctrines like those of the later Cainites seem to be opposed in Jude, while the opponents envisaged in the Pastoral Epistles are probably gnostics (1 Ti 6[20]). Doctrines similar to those opposed in 1 John were taught by a Jewish-Christian gnostic named Cerinthus. The Apocalypse of John speaks of a 'prophetess' who apparently was teaching 'the deep things of Satan' (Rev 2[20, 24]); she may well have been a gnostic teacher.

Christians rejected gnosticism not only because of its 'myths and endless genealogies' (1 Ti 1[4]) but because of its rejection of the goodness of creation (4[4]), its denial that Jesus Christ came in the flesh (1 Jn 4[2]), and in some cases its advocacy of immorality (Jude, Rev 2[20]). The reaction against gnosticism led to the full formulation of credal statements, to the more precise definition of the NT canon (to exclude apocrypha used by gnostics and to include books rejected by them), and to a less fluid conception of church government. This process is most clearly reflected in the work of Irenaeus (*c* 180), who insists on the oneness of God and of Jesus Christ, on the oneness of OT and NT, and on the oneness of the Catholic Church. R. M. G.

GOAD.—See Agriculture, **1.**

GOAH.—An unknown locality near Jerusalem, Jer 31[39] (AV **Goath**).

GOAT.—(1) *'ēz*, used generically, both sexes, Gn 30[35], Ex 12[5], Ezr 6[17] etc. (2) *ṣāphîr* (root 'to leap'), 'he-goat,' 2 Ch 29[21], Ezr 8[35], Dn 8[5, 8]. (3) *śā'îr* (root 'hairy'), usually a he-goat, *e.g.* Dn 8[21] 'shaggy he-goat' RSVm; ('rough he-goat' RV); *śe'îrāh*, Lv 5[6] 'she-goat'; *śe'îrîm*, translated 'satyrs' Lv 17[7], 2 Ch 11[15], Is 13[21] 34[14]. See Satyr. (4) *'attûdh*, only in plural *'attûdhîm*, 'he-goats' Gn 31[10, 12], RSV 'leaders' Is 14[9] (RVm 'he-goats'). (5) *tayish* 'he-goat,' Pr 30[31] etc. In NT *eriphos*, *eriphion*, Mt 25[32f]; *tragos*, He 9[12f, 19] 10[4]. Goats are among the most valued possessions of the people of Palestine. Nabal had a thousand goats (1 S 25[2]; see also Gn 30[33, 35] 32[14] etc.). They are led to pasture with the sheep, but are from time to time separated from them for milking, herding, and even feeding (Mt 25[32]). Goats thrive on extraordinarily bare pasturage, but they do immeasurable destruction to young trees and shrubs, and are responsible for much of the barrenness of the hills. Goats supply most of the milk used in Palestine (Pr 27[27]); they are also killed for food, especially the young kids (Gn 27[9], Jg 6[19] 13[15] etc.). They are also required for a sin-offering, Nu 7[16, 22] etc. The Syrian goat (*Capra mambrica*) is black or grey, exceptionally white, and has shaggy hair and remarkably long ears. Goats' hair is extensively woven into cloaks and material for tents (Ex 26[7] 36[14]), and their skins are tanned entire to make water-bottles. See Bottle.

Wild goat.—(1) *yā'ēl* (cf proper name *Jael*), used in plural *ye'ēlîm*, 1 S 24[2], Ps 104[18], and Job 39[1]. (2) *'akkô*, Dt 14[5]. Probably both these terms refer to the wild goat or ibex, *Capra beden*, the *beden* or 'goats of Moses' of the Arabs. It is common on the inaccessible cliffs round the Dead Sea, some of which are known as *jebel el-beden*, the 'mountains of the wild goats' (cf 1 S 24[2]). The ibex is very shy, and difficult to shoot. Though about the size of an ordinary goat, its great curved horns, often 3 feet long, give it a much more imposing appearance. E. W. G. M.—**R. A. B.**

GOATH, Jer 31[39] (AV).—See Goah.

GOATSKIN.—Ex 25[5] 26[14] etc. (RSV); see Porpoise.

GOB ('cistern').—A place mentioned only in 2 S 21[18] as the scene of an exploit of one of David's warriors. In the parallel passage 1 Ch 20[4] Gob appears as *Gezer*; many texts read it as *Nob*. The Greek and Syriac versions have *Gath*. Nothing is known of Gob as a separate place.

GOD.—1. The English word.—The English word 'God' is not itself a product of the Jewish-Christian tradition, but existed in the Germanic family of languages in pre-Christian times. Its original sense is doubtful, and according to the Shorter OED the senses 'what is invoked' or 'what is worshipped by sacrifice' have been suggested as the primary meaning. With the adoption of the word by Christianity its pre-Christian inherited colouring was overlaid with the Jewish-Christian tradition and was to a great extent lost. Within that tradition therefore its significance corresponds fairly exactly to the content of the Hebrew and Greek words which it is used to translate. On the other hand it was a matter of general knowledge, and one which the Bible itself shares and does not attempt to conceal, that recognition and worship have often been extended to others than the Jewish-Christian God, and the term 'god' or 'gods' is used for them also, as are the respective Greek and Hebrew words. It is the custom to use a capital G for the God of the Jewish-Christian tradition, and a small letter for the others.

2. Method of this article.—This article is intended fundamentally to be a study of what is meant by 'God' within the Bible. It will show something of the history of its usage within the Bible and indicate some of the more important characteristics and problems of that usage. It will not discuss the concept of God in other religions, or possible purely philosophic concepts of God, except where such discussion is occasioned by Biblical data; and it will not try to describe in full the later theological formulations of the doctrine of God, although these may be kept in mind at certain points of comparison. The perspective will be historical, in that texts will be thought of in the circumstances of their time and place; but the sequence will not be strictly chronological, for various separate aspects will require attention in turn.

3. Pre-history of the idea of God.—From the later 19th cent. onwards it has been frequently maintained that the notion of 'gods' is the end of a long religious evolution, of which the most important earlier stage is the so-called 'animism' or belief in spirits dwelling within trees, stones, rivers, and the like, spirits not yet sufficiently independent and individualized to be classified as deities. This earlier stage in religion was often associated with sociological phenomena such as totemism or with the realm of magic and *tabu*.

On the other hand, in somewhat more recent times, another school of thought has argued that true deities or 'high gods' are to be found at an early stage of religious development, and that the simple evolutionistic picture of a development from animism up to polytheism is a false one. For the present we may say that although extreme opinions in favour of universal primitive 'high gods' or even of 'Primitive Monotheism' are not widely accepted, they have had sufficient force to break down the simple evolutionism with its over-emphasis on animism. Thus if we find within one set of traditions a river-spirit, for example, side by side with a real distinct god, we do not necessarily have to explain the former as a survival from an earlier stage, and we may have to take the two together as part of one given religious pattern.

To these questions about the pre-history of religion, however, the Biblical sources furnish few or no answers directly. Only a small proportion of them attained their present form much before 1000 B.C. As we go back before this time the tradition becomes gradually thinner and for the ancestors of Israel before 1750 or so it has become so lacking in detail and circumstantiality as to make the religious history before this time quite obscure. There is no sign in the OT of any consciousness of a pre-theistic stage, of a time when gods were not yet known, and the texts depict their God as having relations with man from the beginning of history. The question which they do discuss to some extent is not whether He was really a God, but by what name He was known.

In a number of stories and traditions it is possible to suspect or detect a pre-history of the story, which, relating earlier to an older Palestinian deity, has in the course of time been taken over and transferred to the God of the Israelite faith. This is a different matter, however, from a pre-history of the idea of God as such, and will be taken up later. In general, however, and as a point of method, it may be said here that in an article of this type the first purpose will be to explain the story in its Israelite form and not the story in another form which it may have had before; but the previous form will be specially relevant wherever it is needed to explain the peculiarities of the later—but for which peculiarities, it may be added, the existence of a previous form might not have been detectable.

4. Names of God in the OT.—For convenience we may here gather the more important Divine names of the Hebrew OT; some of the problems of their use must wait for treatment later.

(*a*) **El.**—This is fairly commonly taken to mean ' power ' or ' the strong one,' cf a Hebrew phrase ' it is in the power (*'ēl*) of my hand to . . .' (*e.g.* Gn 31[29]). But it is noticeable that this word and the following (viz. *'ᵉlōhîm*) are both closely similar to common Semitic deictic elements used in demonstratives and similar particles, so that they may go back to a sense like ' that one ' or ' that one there.' This would not necessarily exclude some connexion with *'ēl* ' power.'

In any case we find *'ēl* and its cognates as a general Semitic term for a god, and the plural *ilâni* ' the gods ' is frequent in Akkadian. On the other hand we find El as the name of a particular deity, and that on Canaanite soil in the Ugaritic literature, where El occupies a senior and venerable position among the gods, but is hardly the principal actor in the myths which we possess.

In the OT we may classify usage threefold: (1) *El* is used for ' God,' *i.e.* the God of Israel, and occasionally for some other god, *e.g.* Is 44[17], and the plural for ' the gods,' as Ex 15[11]. The word is generally poetical. (2) In the compound names or titles associated especially with the appearances to the patriarchs at holy places, *e.g.* El Shaddai, Gn 17[1] (RSV ' God Almighty '), El Roi, Gn 16[13] (RSV ' a God of seeing '). In these there is a fair probability that the original reference is to the particular deity *El* or to special local deities whose designations include his name, and that later the names were taken to refer to the God of Israel. (3) The use in proper names like Eliakim ' May *'ēl* raise up ' or Ezekiel ' May *'ēl* strengthen.' Though it is possible to argue here for an original reference to the proper name *El* (*e.g.* J. Gray, *Legacy of Canaan*, 1957, p. 120), it would seem better to think of a general reference, ' the god,' *i.e.* the god of this tribe or family, on the analogy of other theophoric elements such as ' the father ' or ' the brother.'

(*b*) **Elohim,** the ordinary Hebrew word for God. For derivation see above under *El*. The word has a plural form, and the singular form *'ᵉlōah* is found in Job frequently and occasionally elsewhere. In syntax the normal plural form is treated as singular for congruence with verbs and adjectives, with few exceptions, where the sense is ' God '; when used of other deities than the God of Israel, as in the phrase ' other gods ' it is commonly plural in sense and syntactically treated as such.

The plural form has always excited great curiosity. It should not be treated as a discernment of a plurality within the being of God, and has developed rather from the usage of emphasizing the importance of one god by seeming to concentrate within Him the being of all the gods. So we already find in Akkadian the plural *ilâni* ' gods ' in the Tell-Amarna letters with a singular verb, meaning ' the deity,' and in the same letters when a man writes to Pharaoh as ' my lord, my gods and the sun ' he is not seeing Pharaoh as a plurality but regarding him as comprehending all deity in himself. The usage does not imply a monotheism but a desire to generalize in the whole divine realm or to concentrate emphasis upon a particular god. But the widespread usage in Hebrew of this plural form (far exceeding the frequency in other Semitic languages) was almost certainly encouraged by the belief in the Israelite God as the only one of significance in Israel and therefore as the sum and total of deity.

There are a few places where we may have to think of *Elohim* as a realm or class of divine or superhuman beings; these beings are sometimes called ' sons of *'ᵉlōhîm* ' or ' sons of gods,' the word ' son ' indicating less physical paternity than membership of a group. In Ps 8[5], for example, man is made a little less than *'ᵉlōhîm*, and the comparison may be not with God but with the divine beings as a class. The Greek text recognized this by interpreting as ' a little less than the angels,' so He 2[7].

(*c*) **Yahweh,** usually translated into English as ' the LORD.' This is a personal proper name, a fact rather obscured by the usual translation. The Jews in later times ceased to pronounce the name, and used in its place substitutes, such as *Adonai* (' My Lord '), or ' The Name.' The sacred name is sometimes called the Tetragrammaton, consisting in the Hebrew consonantal script of the four letters YHWH. The pronunciation *Jehovah* has no authority at all and appeared only in late mediaeval times; it is an attempt to vocalize the Tetragrammaton using the vowels written under it by the scribes, which vowels however were never intended to be combined with the four consonants of this word. That the pronunciation in ancient times was Yahweh is concluded from transcriptions in the early Christian Fathers.

In personal names, however, we find at the end of the name *Yahu* or *Yah*, *e.g.* Azariah (*'ᵃzaryāhû* or *'ᵃzaryāh*, Yahweh has helped) and at the beginning of the name Yeho-, *e.g.* Jehoiakim (*yᵉhô-yāḳîm*, May Yahweh raise up). The form Yah (see JAH) occasionally occurs alone, and frequently in the phrase Hallelujah, ' Praise ye Yahweh.' Forms of the Yahu type are attested from Assyrian texts and from the Elephantine papyri of about 400 B.C.

The problem has been much discussed (*a*) what was the meaning of the name; (*b*) whether the earliest form was Yahweh or Yahu, the two questions being very much interdependent. Ex 3[14] gives what is intended as an interpretation of the name in the words ' I am who I am ' (RSV) or rather ' I will be as I will be '; in any case connecting the name with the verb ' to be.' The form Yahu could perhaps be explained as an abbreviation of Yahweh, but has often been taken to be a primitive cultic cry, *yā-hû* ' oh he.' It is not impossible that this latter explanation should be reconciled with the interpretation from the verb ' to be,' since it is possible to regard this verb (*hāwāh, hāyāh*) as a verbalized form related to the old Semitic deictic pronoun (*huwa*, Heb. *hū'*)—cf Rundgren, *Über Bildungen mit š- und n-t-Demonstrativen im Semitischen*, 1955, p. 154. The writer would prefer then to take it as connected with the verb ' to be ' in the sense ' he is, he shows himself to be ' and also with an old cultic cry in the sense ' oh he '—in English we should almost have to say ' oh thou.' It should be added that the interpretation of this name is very controversial among scholars, and numerous suggestions cannot be mentioned here. Of Albright's opinion that the word is causative and must mean 'he causes to be, brings into being,' something will be said later. In any case it is clear that usage over much of the OT period was determined by Ex 3[14] in the sense 'he is.'

The Greek translators represented the word usually by *kyrios* 'Lord.'

Questions about the history of the veneration of Yahweh in Israel will be treated below.

(*d*) **Shaddai,** in prose often in the compound El Shaddai, is usually translated 'the Almighty' in English. It has been plausibly connected with Akkadian *šadû* 'mountain' in the sense of 'he of the mountain,' but this remains uncertain. It occurs in poetry in Job and elsewhere, but its chief importance is the statement of Ex 6[3] that God appeared to the patriarchs not by His name Yahweh but as El Shaddai. This passage is usually taken to be from P, and in P passages in Genesis we find El Shaddai, *e.g.* 17[1], 35[11]. Its antiquity is probably confirmed by its use in the ancient list of names in Nu 1[5-15], *e.g.* Ammishaddai, 'My kinsman is Shaddai.'

(*e*) Of other Divine names **Elyon,** 'Most High,' should be mentioned. As a divine title this also is known on Canaanite soil, and it appears conspicuously as 'El Elyon' or 'God Most High' in Gn 14, probably connected with Jerusalem. Here it may well be a title of a pre-Israelite deity later assimilated with Yahweh. The word also occurs in poetry quite frequently, and is an epithet for, or an alternative expression for, Yahweh. It should be remembered that the parallelism of Hebrew poetry often required the use of two different words for the same thing, so that there was a certain demand which could well be filled by words which could represent God acceptably.

5. The Understanding of God before Moses.—The assessment of this depends to a large extent on the degree of accuracy we assign to the Genesis traditions as a picture of the religious situation before Moses. It may seem probable that the migratory groups who were the ancestors of the later Israelites came into Canaan with at the centre of their religious consciousness a veneration for a tribal deity, whose close integration with the tribe and its fortunes was expressed by the designations as 'the Father,' 'the Brother,' or 'the Kinsman,' (Heb. *'ābh, 'āh, 'am*), manifest in early names such as Abram, 'the Father is lofty,' Amram, 'the Kinsman is lofty.' We have suggested above that *El* in the same context is 'the god,' *i.e.* the one related to our group. This type of usage does not divulge the actual name of the deity. It does not necessarily mean, however, that the deity had no name, and the phrase 'the God of your fathers' was as much as could be said to designate Him. That the name was Shaddai is the belief of Ex 6[3]. In any case we discern in the 'God of the fathers' a strongly personal attachment; He goes with members of the family even in exile, and is tied to no particular sanctuary. It is interesting that we have no 'localization' of Shaddai as appearing at a particular place.

On the other hand we have several cases of Divine appearances to the patriarchs at holy places under *El*-names, such as El-Roi in Gn 16[13] at the holy well of Beer-Lahai-Roi. (See above under *El*.) It is reasonably probable that the place of the patriarch is in hallowing for Israelite tradition with a foundation-story a holy place existing from ancient times. The *El* of the holy place comes in any case to be identical with the personal God of the patriarchs, so that in Gn 35[1ff], for example, Jacob venerates at Bethel the *El* who was with him on his travels.

How far can the term 'monotheism' be used for the patriarchal religion? The problem of monotheism must be taken up later, but for the present we may say that the central place in the patriarchal period was taken by the personal family deity; and the veneration of the El at certain old shrines may have been understood as manifestation of this same deity, as it certainly came to be understood later. Other gods may have occupied other aspects of the patriarchal life which were unimportant for the main theme as it has been transmitted to us. To assert that the patriarchs were polytheists in any full sense, with a complete and varied pantheon of deities, including goddesses and chthonic and fertility deities, is quite without justification on the Biblical evidence, and implies that Genesis gave a very distorted picture of the time. There is no evidence in the early Hebrew nomenclature for a wide variety of deities of central importance. No word for 'goddess' exists in Biblical Hebrew.

Was the name Yahweh known in the patriarchal period? Although Ex 6[3] denies it, it is well known that other sources use Yahweh in Genesis and carry the name back to the earliest men (Gn 4[26]). This may rest on Kenite tradition (Gn 4 is the saga of the first generations of the Kenites), but one can hardly attribute all the old Yahwistic saga to the Kenites, and one may regard it as doubtful whether Genesis would have become so deeply penetrated by the name Yahweh if that name was totally unknown before Moses. It should therefore be considered possible that the name was already circulating in some group of the ancestors of the later Israel, and that it was associated with stories of the old saga brought on the migration from Mesopotamia (creation, deluge, tower of Babel).

Within the present framework the relations of the patriarchs with their God are very much a theme of promise and fulfilment: a small group later to be a great nation, a land visited but not yet possessed—all looking forward to the Exodus and the entry to Canaan.

6. Moses and Monotheism.—It is of general importance that the Israelites do not distinguish between absolute existence and existence with significance. Thus when the fool says in his heart 'There is no God' (Ps 14[1]), he is not stating an abstract atheism, the absolute non-existence of God, but is saying that God is not to be reckoned with. Israel's monotheism, one of her contributions to history for which she is most famed, was likewise not an absolute assertion of the non-existence of other gods, but a declaration that they are not to be reckoned with. It is usually said that with Deutero-Isaiah we move to a statement of absolute non-existence for other gods, but it is hard to see where his language goes beyond Ps 14[1], asserting their complete ineffectiveness and insignificance in the matters which He most has at heart, viz. creation, the fulfilment of a purpose announced from the beginning, and the emptiness of idolatry. The more abstract and absolute form of monotheism is reached not in but after Deutero-Isaiah, and the Chronicler can still say 'Our God is greater than all gods' (2 Ch 2[5]). The difference between 'henotheism'—where one God was worshipped but the existence of others not absolutely denied—and monotheism is thus irrelevant for OT thinking. The effective attention of Israel to one God only is there from a fairly early date, even though from time to time some oblique reference is made to the other gods and their domain elsewhere (Jg 11[24], 1 S 26[19]).

The question how far Moses was responsible for the concentration of Israel on the one jealous God is difficult, for it depends on a decision how much of the large tradition attributed to Moses in fact goes back to him. The claim that Moses was the author of Israelite monotheism has recently been supported by Albright, who (1) connects this with monotheistic and universalistic inclinations in Egyptian religion in the 18th Dynasty and after, (2) regards Moses as having inculcated the name Yahweh, understood as causative ('He who causes to be' or 'brings into being') and so indicating creation, which was a main interest in these Egyptian religious trends. Against this we may argue (1) the causative of this verb does not occur in Hebrew elsewhere, (2) there is a wide social, political, and intellectual gap between early Israel and imperial Egypt, (3) there is no evidence for a belief in creation as an important part of the Mosaic contribution to Israelite religion.

It would seem more likely that the concentration on one God has its origin not in the inculcation of 'monotheism' by Moses so much as in the events of the Exodus, with which of course Moses was, or came to be, associated. The deliverance there, and the covenant and lawgiving that followed, are attributed to Yahweh alone, and form the basis of Israel as a community. Henceforth numerous individual and group variations may appear, and the place of other gods in special connexions may be known, but the constituting of Israel and its fundamental cult belong to Yahweh. The trait of Yahweh as a jealous God probably belongs to the Mosaic time and to the picture of the Exodus as a conflict of gods and nations.

Mention should be made at this point of the important place in the Exodus-Sinai traditions of the Kenites and especially of the father-in-law of Moses, which has given rise to the 'Kenite hypothesis,' namely, that Moses learned of Yahweh while exiled in Midian with a Kenite group, and adopted their deity for his people. This theory may go too far, and it may be more probable that a very important part in the transmission of the Sinai traditions and of the Yahwistic faith was played by the Kenites, some of whom came to settle within Israel, and who were strongly conscious in their nomadic life of Yahweh as their protector (Gn 4[15f]).

Ex 3 is important for its interpretation of the name Yahweh. The central emphasis of the passage is not the historical information that Moses invented or adopted the name, or that it was first known to him, but its etymologizing interpretation from the verb *hāyāh* or *hāwāh* 'to be,' hence 'I am that I am' or better 'I will be as I will be.' Moses asks for the name because the people, hearing of the God of their fathers, will ask him the name. This is not because they have forgotten the name during their stay in Egypt, nor because the God of the Fathers never had a name, but because the literary design of the passage is to make Moses ask the name, just as Jacob before him and Manoah afterwards in their relations with deity. Moses' request is answered not with a mere handing over of the name Yahweh, but with an interpretation, the point of which is most probably the freedom of Yahweh to be, or show himself in action, as He will.

In personal nomenclature only one example of what might be a Yahweh-name appears before Moses, namely his mother Jochebed; but this isolated case might have another explanation. After Moses Yahweh-names appear only slowly and gradually; only a few cases exist from the time of the Judges; but after David they become the numerically dominant theophoric name-type in Israel.

In general, the dominant characterisics of Israel's God are traceable to this early period—the covenant with Israel, on which that sacral community is based; the existence of certain commands or legal sanctions which went with this covenant, although it is hard to know precisely which commands were then formulated; the character of Yahweh as jealous God, His conflict with and triumph over other powers, and the celebration of Him above all as one who had acted in a particular series of events for the redemption of His people. It is also probable that this early age saw some limitation on the iconic representation of God, such as is in a more developed form lodged in the Decalogue, and which in the end became a complete rejection of all idolatry and one of the most noted features of Judaism. Like the monotheism of the time, the early stages of the anti-iconic prohibition were probably not understood as absolute and binding in every connexion of life, and examples of the use of images continue to appear.

7. The God of Israel and Canaanite Religion.—The religion of the settled culture of Canaan is characterized by its functional directedness towards the fertility of flock and field and the sustenance of the ordered and harmonious social-economic world. Sex as the principle of fertility had its place in the world of the gods, reflected on earth by cultic prostitution at holy places and times. The mythology of dying and rising gods corresponds to the death and life of vegetation.

It is probable that the realm of fertility was not integrated into Yahweh's nature at the Israelite conquest, and there was a natural tendency, while honouring Yahweh's place in the historic foundation of the nation, to turn for the underpinning of the agricultural society to the deities long associated with the land. This would be thought of not as an abolition of Yahweh but as a natural adaptation, with more or less degree of coalescence between Yahweh and the Canaanite deity. Of these deities the most important is Baal; his name can be used in the plural of the 'lords' of different localities, but his name as a proper name of a great god is now well known from Ugarit.

Another form of integration with the older religious complex is the adoption of female divine symbols, and of goddesses, to correspond with Yahweh-Baal. The chief such symbol was the *Asherah* (plural *Asherim*, AV 'groves,' an inexact rendering). Asherah was a goddess well known from Ugarit; the *'ªshērāh* was a pole or trunk planted in the sanctuary, representing her. With the *'ªshērāh* the cultic prostitution appears (1 K 14[23-24] and elsewhere).

Such forms of Canaanite influence appear again and again from the Judges down to the end of the kingdom, and appear at times to have been dominant in popular religion and among kings and other leaders. On the other hand the extent of survival of older and purer Yahwism may have been greater than our sources indicate, because the Deuteronomic editors of Kings look on the religious history of the kingdom pessimistically from their own special point of interest. The chief part in the Yahwistic reaction against Canaanite syncretism is taken by the prophets from Elijah onwards. Elijah asserts the dominance of Yahweh over Baal in the latter's own proper sphere of rain and fertility (1 K 17–18), at a time when the effort to establish Baal in Israel is particularly strenuous. Elijah's action here determines the main line for Yahwistic prophecy afterwards. The prophetic message, however, drew its inspiration to a great extent from the ancient Israelite tradition of the Exodus, the jealous God, the covenant and commandments. Syncretism, idolatry, and social ethics are all measured by this ancient standard. What is real in the divine dominance of nature and fertility is firmly set under Yahweh, the God of the Israelite historical tradition. The sense of the historical tradition is reaffirmed by the announcement of new acts of Yahweh upon His people in relation to the other peoples. The functional sense of the mythological harmony is rejected in the prophets and accepted into Yahwism only on Yahwistic conditions and under the control of the older Yahwistic tradition.

In all this the prophets did not stand for mere reaction to an earlier way of life, as did some of their supporters like the Rechabites. Prophecy itself was very largely a phenomenon of life in Canaan. It does not merely reiterate the old traditions of Yahweh but gives them new life by drawing out their significance in a new situation.

On a more positive side, Yahweh settles down in Canaan during this same time and former Canaanite sanctuaries are devoted to Him. Of particular importance is Jerusalem and the act of David in bringing the Ark there, thus embodying old national religious traditions in the royal sanctuary. For the later development of Yahwism much importance attached to these sanctuaries and their priesthood, among certain circles of which the Deuteronomic school grew up, and many problems of the book of Deuteronomy concern relations between Yahweh and the land and place where He has chosen to dwell.

In the later Judaean monarchy, powerful blows are struck against Canaanite syncretism by reforming kings like Hezekiah and Josiah; but from Jeremiah we know that Canaanite influences in worship were still real at the end of the monarchy. But from the exile onwards the appeal and the temptation of Canaanite religion for Israel was for the most part over.

8. God in the likeness of man.—It is well known that in the OT anthropomorphic expressions are liberally used of God. We hear of His hand, His eyes, His ears; He rises early, walks in the garden of Eden, closes the door of Noah's Ark, even sometimes repents or changes His mind. These expressions clearly come quite naturally to the writers, and it is usually pointed out how well they fit in with the strongly active, personal, and living character of the OT God. Most of them are in fact intended as descriptions not of God but of His actions.

A more serious problem is set by those theophanies or appearances of God where He is seen in human form. Unlike the first type, these are a real attempt to say what was seen when God appeared. Theophany is a recognized and significant phenomenon in ancient religion. Distinct cases of a theophany being in human form wholly or partly are Gn 18^{1ff}, Ezk 1^{26}. On the other hand we have many appearances of God where no attempt is made to describe the manifestation, and the interest lies on what is said, *e.g.* Gn 12^{7}. The matter is complicated because in some cases the appearance of Yahweh seems to merge into the appearance of His angel (*e.g.* Gn 18–19), and we also have the statement that Yahweh does not let Himself be seen at all (Ex 33^{20}). Perhaps we may venture the statement at any rate that when God lets Himself be seen He shows Himself in human form; this is as it were His proper form, and might perhaps be connected with the statement that man is made in the image of God.

In general we may say that it is impossible to discern any direct progress from the more 'material' anthropomorphic expressions to a 'higher and more spiritual' conception. It is true that such forms of representation of God as His angel, His glory, His name, His face, have been commonly interpreted as attempts to soften down the traditional anthropomorphisms by presenting a less direct presence or action of God. But if this was their purpose it was singularly unsuccessful, for these representations are left in the texts alongside the crassest anthropomorphisms. The purpose of the introduction of angels and the like cannot be discussed here; all we can say here is that it was not normally the avoidance of anthropomorphism, although incidentally they may have softened its incidence in some places.

It is worth remarking that the reason why this problem is a difficult one lies in one of the main insights of the OT, namely the deep difference between God and man, between God and nature. Unlike the gods of so many mythologies, the God of Israel does not share a common origin with the world or with men (contrast the Babylonian Creation Story). The de-mythologizing of the relation between God and world and men is one of the chief achievements of the Israelite consciousness.

9. Conclusion.—In the later stages of the OT the main outlines of the understanding of God are now accepted, and the temptations and problems of earlier times are imperfectly remembered. Monotheism and the prohibition of idols are more absolute. Although some new designations appear, such as 'the God of Heaven' popular in the Persian period, they do not mean important changes in the conception of God.

10. Words for God in the NT.—In its general understanding of God the NT builds very much on the accepted positions of Judaism in the later period of the OT and after. The variety of Divine names known in earlier times is now replaced for the most part by the simple and general term *theos*, 'God.' The most characteristic Israelite name of all, the proper name Yahweh, was in the Septuagint translated by *kyrios*, 'Lord,' most commonly without the article, the omission of which is a trace of the old personal name. This usage continues in the NT, with or without the article (*e.g.* Lk 1^{6}), but side by side with it we have the common usage of *kyrios* of Jesus Christ. The question of the pronunciation or meaning of the old name Yahweh seems never to be raised in the NT.

It is well known that late Judaism often used substitutes for the Divine names out of reverence for them, and an example in the NT may be the use of 'Heaven' as in Lk 15^{18}, Mt 21^{25}. Matthew uses 'kingdom of heaven' corresponding to Mark's 'kingdom of God.' It is difficult however to explain this purely as a mere substitute term, since Matthew is in fact not shy of the word 'God' and uses it freely, and even occasionally the phrase 'kingdom of God.' It is perhaps more probable that the usage 'kingdom of heaven' in Matthew represents a change of emphasis, deliberately intending the idea of a heavenly kingdom.

As in OT usage, the word *theos* is used for other gods than the Jewish-Christian, 1 Co 8^{5} etc.

11. The development of OT thinking.—(*a*) **Monotheism.** Monotheism of a type familiar in later OT thought—is taken for granted in the NT, and no more than the OT does the NT precede its message about God with an attempt to prove His existence. This monotheism formed an accepted common ground with the Jews, and was not without important contact in the Gentile world also, for the message of the One God was a central part of the Jewish proselytizing appeal, and a part likely to meet with some response in Hellenic minds. Even so, in Paul's mind, as in the OT, the monotheism is not of the most absolute and theoretical kind. He can assume that 'there is no God but one' (1 Co 8^{4}) and can go on to talk rather imprecisely of the existence of so-called gods and lords; Gal 4^{8} can talk of a bondage to the gods who by nature are not; and 2 Co 4^{4} speaks of a god of this world who has blinded the unbelievers.

Considering how strongly conscious the Jews were of their monotheism, it is interesting to note that as far as the NT evidence goes the Jewish opposition did not charge the Christian movement with tritheism or polytheism, a common Jewish criticism later. The complaint was rather that the man Jesus assumed the place of God (Jn 10^{33}) and thus confused the distinction of God and man which the OT had insisted on, than that He intrcduced a plurality in the deity. In Mk 12^{28-34} Jesus, asked what is the first of the commandments, begins His answer with the *Shema'*, the classical declaration of the oneness of God from Dt 6^{4}; later, at Corinth, the same certainty is something that 'we know' (1 Co 8^{4}), being inherited from the OT without change. The problems of NT theology which were taken up in the later Trinitarianism existed not because the monotheistic basis of Judaism was departed from, but precisely because the oneness of God remained as a fixed certainty alongside of the Christological development.

(*b*) **The problem of anthropomorphism.**—In post-Biblical Judaism the anthropomorphic representation of God was no longer living and productive, but it is too much to say that it was repudiated. Rather the examples of it were guarded in exegesis, so as to protect the distance between God and Man. In spite of many statements to the contrary, it is not the case that anthropomorphisms were systematically expunged in the translation of the OT into Greek. They certainly do drop out in a number of cases, but many of these can be accounted for from other aspects of the translation technique. The 'repentance' of God disappears in Gn 6^{6} but remains in 1 S 15^{35}. The Targums in general go farther than the LXX in replacing anthropomorphic expressions, but compared with the LXX are much more interpretative paraphrases and much less simple translations. It was still later Judaism that in the middle ages moved to an absolute conception of the incorporeality of God.

The NT also can be said to give a much less anthropomorphic impression of God than the OT. This is however not because of a fading of anthropomorphic thinking, but because in its place there appears a much more complete and radical human representation of God in Jesus Christ, who fills the earthly foreground of the actions of God. This argument does not intend to assimilate Jesus to the OT anthropomorphisms, but only to indicate how His presence made an essential change to the possibility or validity of anthropomorphism. In Ph 2^{5-10} we hear of how He, originally in the form (*morphē*) of God, took the form of a slave and became in the likeness of man. The humanity and tangibility of Jesus do not make God more remote, but make it possible to preserve His separation from humanity without depriving Him of real and personal representation on earth. Assertions such as 'God is Spirit' (Jn 4^{24}) or 'God is love' now become possible; or where they are not new in the NT they fit within a new frame of significance. Angelic mediation or representation, which is important in many strands of the OT, in the Gospels is relegated to the periphery at the birth and Resurrection of Jesus for the most part.

12. The place of Christology. (Cf CHRISTOLOGY, JESUS CHRIST.) The relation between Jesus and God is not incidental to the picture of God in the NT, but is essential to it. Nevertheless only part of the Christological problem can be handled here.

In general, in His teaching Jesus does not describe Himself directly as 'God,' and speaks of God as another. So Mk 10^{18}, 'Why do you call me good? No one is good but God alone.' He speaks in the third person of God in such contexts as the creation of the world by God (Mk 13^{19} 10^{9}); in the word from the Cross He calls upon 'my God' (Mk 15^{34}), making His own the Psalmist's expression of human worship. In the Synoptic Gospels the expression 'Son of God,' really a Messianic designation, is rather used of Jesus than by Him of Himself. The important passage Mt 11^{25-27}, Lk 10^{21f} in the synoptic teaching describes the intimate and unique relationship of Father and Son; and the special naming of Jesus as the Son appears in the Baptism and Transfiguration narratives. In John on the other hand the relation of Son and Father is a frequently recurring theme, and we find such statements as that 'I and the Father are one' (Jn 10^{30}) and 'He who has seen me has seen the Father' (14^{9}). In the remaining literature of the NT the designation of Jesus as 'Son of God' is frequent also.

The chief reason for the peculiar manner of statement of these relations is that the NT does not conceive of the relation between God and Christ as a static one which could be once stated and would then be unchangeably valid and fitting in all situations. Rather, the relation is messianic and eschatological; by this we mean that it has its being only in, and not apart from, the mission of Jesus as Messiah and its movement through a series of events to the crucifixion, resurrection, and ascension, and beyond that to the *parousia*. Until the consummation the Synoptics indicate a certain reserving or withholding of an open statement such as is allowed by John's more deeply interpretative method. Outside the Gospels the standpoint is clearly post-ascension and the declaration of Jesus as Son of God is normal. Even there we see how the relation of Christ to God is messianological, as in Ro 1^{3f}, where we hear how the Son of God was descended from David according to the flesh and was designated Son of God in power by the resurrection. In the NT the relation of God to Christ cannot be extracted from the movement of Messianic mission and petrified as an independent formulation.

Mention should also be made of some cases where Jesus is spoken of as 'God,' of which the most notable are Jn 20^{28}, 'My Lord and my God,' spoken by Thomas, and Jn 1^{18}, accepting the well-attested reading 'the only-begotten God.' He 1^{8f} takes the word God in an OT passage to refer to the Son, and Tit 2^{13} speaks of Jesus Christ as 'Our great God and Saviour.' In Jn 1^{1} the Logos, later to become flesh in Jesus, is God. Ro 9^{5} can perhaps be taken this way; so AV. The usage is common in Ignatius soon after the NT period. It seems clear that the designation of Jesus Christ as 'God,' if hardly normal, is not felt to be objectionable, and indeed is quite proper on some occasions. None of the passages represent Jesus as the totality of God.

Some mention should be made of Jn 10^{34-36}, where Jesus, accused of making Himself God, quotes Ps 82^{6}, 'I said, you are gods.' If those to whom the word of God came could be so called, why is it impossible for Jesus to say He is Son of God? Neither the original nor the quotation is intending to attribute divinity to man in general. The original reference is clearly to gods, or to superhuman judges. If such beings can be addressed as 'gods,' then Jesus can be called 'Son of God.'

The messianological and eschatological approach taken to the relation of God and Christ is also relevant for the triple structure of Father, Son, and Spirit. The fatherhood of God is not a universal fact discerned and taught, but a relation to the messianic Son and through Him to His disciples; in the epistles men are adopted into sonship. The relation of Father and Son appears therefore as it is connected with the mission of Jesus. Similarly the Spirit follows and confirms that mission, and is present in the Church and joins it with its ascended Lord and the heavenly world, or in other words the coming Lord and the future world. In the NT these relations can still be seen under many aspects, as connected with different moments of the Divine action. We therefore have no systematic trinitarianism, and in particular no example of the 'three-in-one' type of formula which is a result of reflection linking the triadic presentation with the axiomatic monotheism. Triadic formulae do, however, occur fairly frequently, and with the elements in different orders, *e.g.* Mt 28^{19} (Father, Son, Spirit), 2 Co 13^{14} (Lord Jesus Christ, God, Spirit), 1 Co 12^{4-6} (Spirit, Lord, God). There is still much fluidity, and formulae with two elements are also common, *e.g.* 1 Ti 2^{5} (one God, one mediator), 1 Co 8^{6} (one God the Father, one Lord Jesus Christ). Varied formulae appear, like Eph 4^{4-6}, including beside the Divine elements the acts and institutions of salvation—one body, one Spirit, one hope, one Lord, one faith, one baptism, one God. Terms like 'Lord' and 'Paraclete' can vary in their application between Christ and the Spirit. J. Ba.

GOEL.—See AVENGER OF BLOOD, and KIN [NEXT OF].

GOG.—**1.** Name of a Reubenite (1 Ch 5^{4}), possibly meaning a valuable made of gold. **2.** The 'chief prince of Meshech and Tubal' (AV, RV 'prince of Rosh, Meshech and Tubal,' Ezk 38^{2} and often in chs. 38, 39) of the land of Magog (actually 'the Magog,' see MAGOG), pictured as leading a great host of nations from the north against the restored Israel, and as being ignominiously defeated by Yahweh's intervention upon the mountains of Canaan. The section (Ezk 38–39) is complex, and may well contain more than one tradition; nor is it certain that it is original to the book of Ezekiel. The idea of an enemy from the north may also be seen in Jl 2^{20} and Jer 1^{14}.

Various theories have been proposed to explain the origin of the name, of which the two most probable seem to be: (1) He is to be identified with Gyges of Lydia (Akk. *Gugu*, Gr. *Gyges*), the famous king described by Herodotus (i. 8 ff), and who is said by Ashurbanipal (669–*c* 632 B.C.) to have expelled the invading Gimirrâ (Cimmerians) with Assyrian help. Meshech and Tubal also suggest Asia Minor, and Gomer (=Cimmerians) is mentioned as one of Gog's allies, suggesting the possibility that a somewhat garbled account of tribal movements in the north has provided the basis for this strongly apocryphal picture. (2) He is to be connected with *Gaga* (Gagâ'a in the Amarna tablets), a corruption of Gašga, a wild district in the region of Armenia and Cappadocia. The people of this area having passed into oblivion, the name appears to have survived with the general meaning of 'barbarian.' Gog would thus retain a reminiscence of a barbaric people whose identity had long been forgotten. Other suggestions are *Gaga*, a Babylonian deity, and *Gagi*, a ruler of the city of Sabi mentioned by Ashurbanipal.

Upon the basis of Ezk 38, 39, Gog and Magog appear in later Jewish eschatology as leading the final, but abortive, assault of the powers of the world upon the kingdom of God. Rev 20⁷⁻⁹ depicts Satan gathering the nations of the whole earth, that is Gog and Magog, to bring them to disaster as they surround the saints and the beloved city (cf also Ps 2 for the idea). Cf also *Sib. Orac.* iii. 319–322, 512; LXX in Nu 24⁷ (for Agag) and Am 7¹; Rabbinic literature (cf J. Bonsirven, *Jud. Pal.* i (1934), 460 ff, S. Mowinckel, *He that cometh* (1956) (Index), and Arabic legend.

S. R. D.—**P. R. A.**

GOIIM is the Hebrew word which in EV is variously rendered 'Gentiles,' 'nations,' 'heathen' (see Preface to RV of OT). In the obscure expression in Gn 14¹, where AV has 'king of nations,' RV and RSV retain *Goiim* as a proper name, although RVm offers the alternative rendering 'nations.' The same difference in rendering between AV on the one hand and RV and RSV on the other is found also in Jos 12²³. Böhl identifies Tidal King of Goiim in Gn 14¹ with Tudḫalia, King of the Hittites (*ZAW*, N.F. i, 1924, 148 ff).

GOLAN.—A Levitical city and one of the three cities of refuge E. of the Jordan (Dt 4⁴³, Jos 20⁸), assigned to the sons of Gershon (Jos 21²⁷, 1 Ch 6⁷¹), in the territory belonging to the half-tribe of Manasseh in Bashan. Both the town, Golan, and a district, **Gaulanitis,** were known to Josephus (*Ant.* xiii. xv. 3 [393], xvii. viii. 1 [189]). The latter is called by the Arabs *Jōlân*. The exact site of the city is uncertain, but it is perhaps modern *Saḥem el-Jōlân*, 17 miles E. of the Sea of Galilee. G. L. R.

GOLD.—See Mining and Metals.

GOLGOTHA (Mt 27³³, Mk 15²², Jn 19¹⁷, from the Aramaic *Gulgultā'*. In Lk 23³³ 'the place called *Kranion*' (RSV 'the skull,' AV '**Calvary,**' based on the Vulgate's *locus calvariae*)).—The situation was evidently outside the city (He 13¹²), but near it (Jn 19²⁰); it was a site visible from a distance (Mk 15⁴⁰, Lk 23⁴⁹), and was probably near a high road (Mt 27³⁹).

Two reasons may be advanced for the name. (1) That it was a place where skulls were to be found, perhaps a place of public execution. (2) That the 'hill' was skull-shaped. This is a popular modern view. Against it may be urged that there is no evidence that Golgotha was a hill at all, for it is referred to merely as a 'place.'

Of the many proposed sites for Golgotha two have received the most attention: the traditional site and the *ez-Zāhira* hill or 'Gordon's Calvary,' strongly urged by General C. G. Gordon in 1883, following the theory of Thenius (1842). The traditional site included in the Church of the Sepulchre and in close proximity to the tomb itself has a continuous tradition attaching to it from the days of Constantine. In favour of this site it may be argued that it is unlikely that all tradition of a spot so important in the eyes of Christians should have been lost, even allowing all consideration for the vicissitudes that the city passed through between the Crucifixion and the days of Constantine. The topographical difficulties are dealt with in the discussion of the site of the second wall [see Jerusalem, 6], but it may safely be said that investigations have certainly tended in recent years to reduce them. With regard to the *ez-Zāhira* hill outside the Damascus gate, its claims are based upon the four presuppositions that Golgotha was shaped like a skull, that the present skull-shaped hill had such an appearance at the time of the Crucifixion, that the ancient road and wall ran as they do to-day, and that the Crucifixion was near the Jewish 'place of stoning' (which some modern Jews, without a basis in any tradition, have held to be situated here). All these hypotheses are extremely doubtful. E. W. G. M.—**E. G. K.**

GOLIATH.—A giant, said to have been a descendant of the early race of Anakim. He was slain, in single combat, by David (or, according to another tradition, 2 S 21¹⁹, by Elhanan) at Ephes-dammim, before an impending battle between the Philistines and the Israelites. That this 'duel' was of a religious character comes out clearly in 1 S 17⁴³⁻ ⁴⁵, where we are told that 'the Philistine cursed David by his gods,' while David replies, 'And I come to thee in the name of the Lord of hosts.' The fact that David brings the giant's sword as an offering into the sanctuary at Nob points in the same direction. Goliath is described as being 'six cubits and a span' in height, *i.e.* over nine feet, at the likeliest reckoning; his armour and weapons were proportionate to his great height. Human skeletons have been found of equal height, so that there is nothing improbable in the Biblical account of his stature. The flight of the Philistines on the death of their champion could be accounted for by their belief that the Israelite God had shown Himself superior to their god (but see 2 S 23⁹⁻¹², 1 Ch 11¹²ᶠᶠ); see, further, David, Elhanan.

W. O. E. O.

GOMER.—**1.** One of the sons of Japheth and the father of Ashkenaz, Riphath, and Togarmah (Gn 10²ᶠ, 1 Ch 1⁵ᶠ), who along with Togarmah is included by Ezekiel in the army of Gog (Ezk 38⁶). Gomer represents the people termed *Gimirrâ* by the Assyrians, and **Cimmerians** by the Greeks. Their original home appears to have been north of the Euxine, but by the 7th cent. B.C. they had completely conquered Cappadocia and settled there.

2. Daughter of Diblaim, wife of the prophet Hosea (q.v.). L. W. K.

GOMORRAH.—See Plain [Cities of the].

GOMORRHA.—AV form of **Gomorrah** (q.v.) in Apocrypha and NT.

GOODMAN.—The only occurrence of this English word in the OT is Pr 7¹⁹ (AV, RV; RSV 'my husband'). The Hebrew is simply 'the man'; but as the reference is to the woman's husband, 'goodman,' still used in Scotland for 'husband,' was in 1611 an accurate rendering. In the NT the word occurs (in AV and RV; but never in RSV) twelve times (always in the Synoptic Gospels) as the translation of *oikodespotēs*, 'master of the house.' The same Greek word is translated 'master of the house' or 'householder' in Mt 10²⁵ 13²⁷⁻ ⁵² 20¹ 21³³, Lk 13²⁵.

GOPHER WOOD (Gn 6¹⁴), of which the Ark was constructed, was by tradition cypress wood, and this, or else the cedar, may be inferred as probable.

E. W. G. M.

GORGIAS.—A general of Antiochus Epiphanes, who is described as one of the 'mighty men among the king's friends (1 Mac 3³⁸), and 'a general and a man of experience in military service' (2 Mac 8⁹). When Antiochus set out on his Parthian campaign 166 or 165 B.C., his chancellor, Lysias, who was charged with the suppression of the revolt in Palestine, dispatched a large army to Judaea, under the command of Ptolemy, Nicanor, and Gorgias. The fortunes of the war are described in 1 Mac 3⁴⁰–4²⁵ 5¹⁶ᶠᶠ⁻ ⁵⁵ᶠᶠ, 2 Mac 8¹²⁻²⁹ 10¹⁴ᶠᶠ 12³²ᶠᶠ; Jos. *Ant.* xii. vii. 4 [305–308], viii. 6 [351–353].

GORTYNA.—The most important city in Crete, after Cnossus, situated about midway between the two ends of the island. It is named (1 Mac 15²³) among the autonomous States and communes to which were sent copies of the decree of the Roman Senate in favour of the Jews.

GOSHEN.—**1.** An unknown city in Judah (Jos 15⁵¹). **2.** An unknown territory in S. Palestine, probably the environs of **1** (Jos 10⁴¹). **3.** A division of Egypt in which the children of Israel were settled between Jacob's entry into Egypt and the Exodus. It was a place of good pasture, on or near the frontier of Palestine, and plentiful in vegetables and fish (Nu 11⁵). It cannot be defined with exactness. Jth 1⁹ᶠ is probably wrong in incluoing the names of Tanis and Memphis in Goshen. The LXX reads 'Gesem of Arabia' in Gn 45¹⁰ 46³⁴, elsewhere 'Gesem.' Now Arabia is defined by Ptolemy, the geographer, as an Egyptian name on the East border of the Delta of the Nile, and this seems to be the locality most probably contemplated by the narrator. It runs eastwards from opposite the modern *Zagazig* (Bubastis) to the Bitter Lakes and includes the long shallow valley known as the *Wâdī Ṭumilât*. There seems to be no Egyptian origin for the name and it is most probably of Semitic origin, as is suggested by its occurrence outside Egyptian territory. R. A. S. M.—**T. W. T.**

GOSPEL.—This word (originally **god spel**, *i.e.* 'good tidings,' later understood as 'God-story') represents Greek *euangelion*, which reappears in one form or another in ecclesiastical Latin and in most modern languages. In classical Greek the word means the reward given to a bearer of good tidings (so 2 S 4[10] LXX in plural), but afterwards it came to mean the message itself. In 2 S 18[20, 22, 25] [LXX] a cognate word is used in this sense. In NT the word means 'good tidings' about the salvation of the world by the coming of Jesus Christ. It is not there used of the written record. A genitive case or a possessive pronoun accompanying it denotes: (*a*) the person or the thing preached (the Gospel of Christ, or of peace, or of salvation, or of the grace of God, or of God, or of the Kingdom, Mt 4[23] 9[35] 24[14], Mk 1[14], Ac 20[24], Ro 15[19], Eph 1[13] 6[15] etc.); or sometimes (*b*) the preacher (Mk 1[1] (?), Ro 2[16] 16[25], 2 Co 4[3] etc.); or rarely (*c*) the persons preached to (Gal 2[7]).

Difficulty is found in defining the meaning in a few of the passages where 'of God,' 'of Christ,' etc., follow the word (subjective or objective genitive ?). As God is author of the Gospel and His saving acts its matter, and as Christ both commissions the preacher and is the content of the message the emphasis may fall on one or other of these aspects (Mk 1[14] RSV, Ro 1[1] 15[16], 2 Co 11[7], 1 Th 2[2, 8f], 1 P 4[17]; Mk 1[1], Ro 1[9] 15[19] 1 Co 9[12], Gal 1[7], 1 Th 3[2] etc.). 'The gospel' is often used in NT absolutely, as in Mk 1[15] 8[35] 14[9] RSV, 16[15], Ac 15[7], Ro 11[28], 2 Co 8[18] (where the idea must not be entertained that the reference is to Luke as an *Evangelist*), and so 'this gospel,' Mt 26[13]; but English readers should bear in mind that usually (though not in Mk 16[15]) the EV phrase 'to preach the gospel' represents a simple verb of the Greek. The noun is not found in Luke or Hebrews, and only once in the Catholic Epistles and in the Johannine writings (1 P 4[17], Rev 14[6], 'an eternal gospel'—an angelic message). In Ro 10[16] 'the gospel' is used absolutely of the message of the OT prophets.

The written record was not called 'the Gospel' till a later age. By the earliest generation of Christians the oral teaching was the main thing regarded; men told what they had heard and seen, or what they had received from eye-witnesses. As these died out and the written record alone remained, the perspective altered. The earliest *certain* use of the word in this sense is in Justin Martyr (*c* A.D. 150: 'The Apostles in the Memoirs written by themselves, which are called Gospels,' *Apol.* i. 66; cf 'the Memoirs which were drawn up by His Apostles and those who followed them,' *Dial.* 103). In earlier writings (Ignatius, the *Didache*) 'the gospel' or 'His gospel' seems to refer to the body of tradition, written or oral, rather than to a single written Gospel. The earliest known titles of the Evangelic records (which however, we cannot assert to be contemporary with the records themselves) are simply 'According to Matthew,' etc. A. J. M.—**A. B.**

GOSPELS.—Under this heading we consider the four Gospels as a whole, and their relations to one another, leaving detailed questions of date and authorship to the separate articles.

1. General form and characteristics.—Each of the Gospels would originally be written on a roll of papyrus, though there is definite evidence that Christians in the early 2nd cent. used copies in the form of paged books (codices). Mt, Lk, and Jn would each fill a roll of normal length (about 30 feet), Mk one about two-thirds of that size. This raises the question whether the limitations of a papyrus roll have influenced the form of the narrative sections of the Gospels. The brevity of some sections of Mt and Lk may be partly so explained, but in general we must seek the explanation in the forms of the tradition received by the Evangelists and in their own interests and purposes. It may be confidently affirmed that all four Gospels were written in Greek. Behind them lies the earliest tradition in Aramaic, the language of Palestine in the time of Jesus; there are many indications, notably in the poetical form of much of Jesus' teaching, that at some stage Aramaic sources were translated into Greek; and some difficult expressions in our Gospels have been explained as mistranslations from Aramaic (Dalman, Burney, Black). But the theory of some scholars (as Torrey) that our Gospels are themselves translations has not won favour in view of the evidence that the Evangelists used and edited sources already existing in Greek.

All four Gospels give an account of the ministry, death, and resurrection of Jesus. The presence of four such accounts in NT is itself a fact of great significance. We must suppose that at first each Gospel had a local currency and favour. As others became known, differences would be obvious. The Fourth Gospel is distinct in substance and style from the first three (the Synoptics) and they by variation combined with close resemblance seem even more to be in competition. But the Church has followed neither of the 2nd cent. attempts to remove the seeming offence—Tatian's harmony, the *Diatessaron*, and Marcion's selection of Lk. The Church has been content with a plurality of Gospels. It has thus rejected a rigid literalism and has preferred a fourfold account enriched by its diversity. This satisfaction with variety is shown also in the history of the text. In the course of MS transmission before the invention of printing it was natural that there should be a tendency to assimilation of text (frequently retained in AV, removed in RV, RSV) in parallel passages of the Synoptic Gospels. But the surprising thing is that such assimilation was not thoroughly and deliberately done. Even the diversity between the two forms of the Lord's Prayer (Mt 6[9ff], Lk 11[2ff]) where liturgical use must have encouraged assimilation most strongly, was only partly removed (cf Lk 11[2ff] in AV and RSV).

2. The aims and interests of the Evangelists.—For a clear understanding of the Gospels we must subordinate the elaborations made by preachers, commentators, and artists through the centuries and even such early external evidence on the occasion and authorship of the Gospels as has reached us, and draw our inferences from a close study of the writings themselves. In two of the Gospels an explicit statement of purpose is given. Luke in his preface (1[1-4]) states that others had already written Gospel narratives, that he and they depended for their authority on eye-witnesses who were also 'ministers of the word,' and that his purpose was to write an orderly and reliable account of the events which were the basis of the Church's preaching and instruction. The Fourth Gospel (Jn 20[31]) was written to induce and confirm belief. These statements and the contents of all four Gospels lead us to negative and positive conclusions. (*a*) The Gospels are not like modern biographies, though many attempts have been made to expand the Gospels and construct Lives of Jesus. Biography seeks to relate all the principal events of the life described, whereas the Gospels are silent about many things which from a biographical interest we would wish to know, and they aim at producing faith by describing a few significant incidents taken out of a much larger whole. Penetrating psychological insight marks many passages of the Gospels, but we cannot say that psychological portraiture is a predominant interest in them as it is in modern biography. Similarly, the Gospels are not impartial histories written with scientific objectivity, though we must give full weight to their dependence on eye-witness testimony and to their closeness in time to the events recorded. Nor are they the product of literary ambitions on the part of the authors. (*b*) Positively, the Gospels record, with faithfulness to the authentic tradition combined with a certain freedom in the handling of it, events deemed to be of supreme religious significance. They are the product of faith based upon historical events, and in that sense theological works, and their form and content are adapted to the needs and mission of the 1st cent. Greek-speaking Christian communities.

3. The Synoptic Gospels.—(*a*) *The Marcan source.*—The first three Gospels are called Synoptic because they give the same general survey of the ministry of Jesus. They have (sometimes all three, sometimes two) a large number of passages in common, and when these are placed side by side and compared, it is seen that the correspondence goes beyond the sharing of topics to the use of the same or similar words, arrangement of sentences and passages, and treatment of detail. The likeness goes far beyond what might be expected from three writers independently relating the same series of facts. What, then, are their sources? The outstanding fact when comparison is made throughout the Gospels is that almost the whole substance of Mk is found also, often with a high degree of verbal correspondence, in Mt or Lk or both. Only some thirty of Mk's 661 verses have no parallel either in Mt or Lk, and these include some which are merely descriptive expansions of narrative. This fact, taken by itself, would admit of various explanations.

The order of Mk is also preserved in Mt or Lk or both. At no important point do they agree in this respect against Mk. Matthew's deviations from Mark's order, more numerous than Luke's, actually are a tribute to his use of Mk, as we can reasonably assign motives for the changes. After 4^{22} (=Mk 1^{20}) where Matthew has been following Mk closely, he meets in the next verse of Mk a reference to Jesus' teaching. Immediately he prepares the setting for the Sermon on the Mount, bringing up 1^{39} and $3^{7f, 10}$ from later points in Mk for this purpose. At the close of the Sermon he returns to the Marcan context exactly where he left it (7^{28f}, Mk 1^{22}). Mark here opens an account of Jesus' healing ministry characteristically with an exorcism. Matthew prefers to put at the head of the miracles the healing of a leper, brought up from Mk 1^{40ff}. To group representative miracles he further brings up from later in Mk the stilling of the storm, the cure of the Gadarene demoniac (two in Mt), the raising of Jairus' daughter, and the healing of a woman with issue of blood (Mt 8^{23-34} 9^{18-26}, Mk 4^{35-41} 5^{1-43}). Matthew has now used his source up to 2^{23}, where Mark relates the controversy about the disciples' plucking of grain on the Sabbath. Matthew seems to regard this as the appropriate point to relate the appointment of the Twelve and their mission (10^{1-25}, later in Mk, 3^{13-19} 6^{7-13} 13^{9-13}). The plucking of the grain is taken up at Mt 12^{1}, and thence to the end of the Gospel, except for bringing the cursing and the withering of the fig-tree together (21^{18-22}), Mt has no deviation from the Marcan order. Thus all Matthew's variations from Marcan order are seen to fit the hypothesis that Mk is prior to and a source of Mt. Lk has more omissions of Marcan material (especially Mk 6^{45}–8^{26}) but usually preserves Mark's order. A notable feature of Luke's method is the substitution in other contexts of alternatives to sections of Mk which he omits (*e.g.* Lk 4^{16-30} 5^{1-11} 7^{36-50} 10^{25-28}, cf Mk 6^{1-6} 1^{16-20} 14^{3-9} 12^{28-34}). Such facts prove a *literary* relationship between the Synoptic Gospels and point to Mk, substantially as we have it, as a source of the other two. They also point to the insufficiency of other views once held, such as the Oral Theory which supposed that a *continuous* Gospel narrative originating from the Apostles was transmitted orally and committed to writing by the Evangelists as an aid to memory, and the Theory of a Primitive Aramaic Gospel independently translated into Greek by Matthew, Mark, and Luke.

The full confirmation of Marcan priority comes from a study of detail. The literary relationship is shown by the occurrence of parentheses—not at all likely in oral transmission—(Mt 9^{6}=Mk 2^{10}=Lk 5^{24}; Mt 14^{3ff}, Mk 6^{17ff} contrast the position of Lk 3^{19f}; Mt 24^{15}, Mk 13^{14}) and the literary priority of Mk is shown by improvements of Mk's sometimes uncouth Greek or redundancies (*e.g.* 13^{19} 13^{2} 2^{25} and ||s). The preservation of the original Aramaic words of Jesus is another sign that Mk is primitive (5^{41} 7^{34} 15^{34}). Mt and Lk heighten expressions of reverence for Jesus (Mk 4^{38}, 'Teacher, do you not care if we perish?', Mt 8^{25}, 'Save, Lord; we are perishing,' Lk 8^{24}, 'Master, master, we are perishing'; Mk 6^{5f}, cf Mt 13^{58}). Mk has much vivid descriptive detail absent from the other Gospels but attractive to the modern mind. He is not an abbreviator of Mt (Augustine) nor of Lk. His is a shorter Gospel, but why, if working on Mt, should he omit half of it while expanding what he uses? Mk, probably because of the fuller record of Jesus' teaching in Mt and Lk, appears to have been rather neglected in early centuries. Its importance has been realized with the advance of modern literary and historical study.

(*b*) *Non-Marcan material common to Mt and Lk.*—Mt and Lk show agreement in passages, amounting to over 200 verses, which are not found in Mk. There are, however, instances of overlapping with Mk, parallel accounts and numerous duplicated sayings ('doublets,' distinguished as Marcan and non-Marcan by their context). Overlapping is seen in the Temptation narratives, the Beelzebul section, the parable of the Mustard Seed, etc.; parallel accounts in the Mission of the Twelve and of the Seventy, separate in Lk (9^{1ff} 10^{1ff}), combined in Mt (9^{35ff} 10^{1ff}); cf Mk 6^{6ff}. The degree of verbal correspondence varies in these non-Marcan passages; in some so slight (*e.g.* Mt 25^{14ff}, Lk 19^{11ff}) that they seem unlikely to come from the same source, but in others so close (*e.g.* Mt 3^{7-10}, Lk 3^{7-9}; Mt 6^{24-33}, Lk 16^{13} 12^{22-31}; Mt 23^{37-39}, Lk 13^{34f}) that it seems necessary to suppose a written Greek original. Most of this material consists of the teaching of Jesus. It is natural, therefore, to connect it with the statement of Papias (*c* A.D. 140, quoted by Eusebius *HE* iii. 39) that (the Apostle) 'Matthew composed the sayings (logia) in the Hebrew language, and each one translated (? interpreted) them as he could.' Accordingly, the non-Marcan source of Mt and Lk has been named the Logia or the Sayings-document; commonly it is denoted by the symbol Q (German *Quelle*, source). The latter is preferred because the material consists of narrative as well as sayings (*e.g.* Lk 4^{3ff} 7^{18ff} 10^{1ff} and ||s in Mt). The connexion of narrative and teaching (note how the healing of the centurion's servant follows closely on the Great Sermon in both Mt 8^{5ff} and Lk 7^{1ff}) points to a single source. Its order is more likely preserved in Lk than in Mt, as Matthew's method is to gather all his material at the appropriate places in the Marcan outline. But attempts to reconstruct Q (as by Harnack) or even to delimit its content must be tentative. As the Passion Narratives of Mt and Lk have nothing in common where they depart from Mk it is unlikely that Q was a complete Gospel. The teaching of Jesus preserved in the Great Sermon of Mt and Lk and in other Q passages contains some of the most treasured portions of the Gospel records.

(*c*) *Material found in one Synoptic Gospel only.*—Peculiar to Mk are a parable (4^{26ff}), two miraculous healings (7^{31ff} 8^{22ff}), one or two sayings of Jesus (9^{49f}), an incident at the arrest of Jesus (14^{51f}), also some brief remarks (3^{20f} 7^{3f} 11^{16}) and descriptive details.

The special material of Mt, apart from the Infancy narrative which is || to Luke's but independent of it, is easily analysed into two parts. On the one hand there are sayings of Jesus, such as those incorporated in the Sermon on the Mount, parables, denunciations of the scribes and Pharisees, additions to the Marcan eschatological passages. These show some of the interests prominent in this Gospel, such as the fulfilment of OT prophecy, Jesus' attitude to the Jewish law, and life within the Church community. Some scholars assign this sayings material to a written source (symbol M) circulating first in Jerusalem. The other part of Mt's special material consists mainly of a few short narratives which seem to be expansions of the earlier traditions (14^{28-31} 17^{24ff} $27^{3-10, 19, 24f, 51-53, 62ff}$ $28^{2-4, 11-15}$).

Luke in the greater part of his Gospel presents the Marcan material in blocks of some length (as 5^{12}–6^{19}

8^{4}–9^{50} 18$^{15-43}$ 19^{28}–22^{13}) alternating with blocks in which Q is combined with narrative and teaching peculiar to this Gospel (symbol L). L is extensive, amounting, if the Infancy narratives are included, to about half of the Gospel, and it contains many of the most familiar and most moving passages of the NT. The alternation of Q plus L with Marcan material up to 22^{13}, the considerable departure from Mk in the Passion narrative following, and other facts have led to the Proto-Luke theory adopted by some scholars. According to this, Luke or a predecessor had already combined Q and L into a Gospel covering the whole ministry of Jesus from His Baptism to the Resurrection; into this Luke inserted sections of Mk to form our third Gospel. The effect of this theory is to give L as a *written* source a somewhat earlier date than otherwise might be assigned to it. The theory is disputed, and the establishment of the earlier date for L is not vital for its authenticity.

Questions of date and origin will be found discussed in the separate articles, but it may be useful to state, in concluding this survey of Synoptic sources, one scholar's assignment of dates and places of origin: Mk, A.D. 60, Rome; Q, A.D. 50, Antioch; M, A.D. 65, Jerusalem; L, A.D. 60, Caesarea; Mt, A.D. 85, Antioch; Lk, A.D. 80, Corinth ? (B. H. Streeter). Many date Mk a few years later, and the other dates must be regarded as approximate.

4. Form history.—Behind the Gospels and their sources lies the period between the events of Jesus' life and the committal to writing of the traditions. How did the tradition develop in this period? The investigation of this question has led to the form-historical method which is applied to all the NT writings but bears specially on the Synoptic Gospels. It is assumed that at first there was no connected Gospel such as we possess (the Passion story would be the first to be given in continuity), that the tradition circulated in small units used in preaching, instruction, etc., and that the form of the tradition underwent development as it was adapted to the changing situation of the Church. Form-history attempts to analyse and as it were to disentangle the distinctive elements in the NT contributed by the earliest Palestinian Christian circle, by the Hellenistic Jewish and Gentile Christian communities before Paul, by Paul himself, and by post-Pauline Christians, and also by movements in the non-Christian Gentile world—gnosticism, the mystery religions and so on. The analysis is valuable. In the Gospels it distinguishes Pronouncement-stories, culminating in a saying of Jesus important to the early Christians (*e.g.* Mk 3$^{1-6}$ on Sabbath-healing, 10$^{1-9}$ on adultery, 12$^{13-17}$ on tribute to Caesar); Miracle-stories (*e.g.* Mk 1$^{40-45}$ 4$^{35-41}$); Stories about Jesus (Baptism, Temptation, Rejection at Nazareth, Transfiguration, Last Supper, Crucifixion; Groups of Sayings; Parables; and it is illuminating to connect each such form with the purpose for which it may have been useful in the early Church. Form-criticism, however, has tended to stress the creative activity of the Church in the shaping of the tradition, and to shift the centre of historical certainty from the events of Jesus' ministry to a later scene. It seems right that this tendency should be balanced by attention to the factor of testimony in the Gospel records. Not only is it probable that the testimony of the original eye-witnesses would be valued and preserved, but there are many positive indications that the fundamental principle of testimony—'At the mouth of two witnesses, or at the mouth of three witnesses, shall the matter be established' (Dt 19^{15} AV)—had a formative influence on the Gospel narrative. The incidents in which Peter figures along with one or more of the other disciples may rightly be considered in this connexion, and be viewed in the light of the belief of the 2nd cent. Church that Mark received his information from the preaching of Peter (*e.g.* Papias, see article MARK—GOSPEL ACCORDING TO). Though the Gospel message has been passed on as shaped by men of Christian faith, it can be maintained that the history in its essentials has been substantially preserved and that the historical scepticism to which some form-critics have been led is not justified. See CRITICISM, **4.**

5. Relation of the Fourth Gospel to the Synoptics.—Each of the Synoptic writers has made a specific contribution to the Gospel story (see the separate articles). Their common characteristics may be indicated in a comparison with the Fourth Gospel.

(*a*) *Literary.*—The Synoptics record a great number of varied events and short pregnant sayings of Jesus. John builds up his Gospel round a few incidents with which are associated dialogue and extended discourses. This different treatment makes it difficult to decide how far John was dependent on the earlier Gospels. Certainly there is considerable verbal correspondence with Mk in a few passages and striking agreement with Mk in some words and phrases (*e.g.* Jn 12^{3,5}, Mk 14^{3,5}; Jn 6^{7}, Mk 6^{37}; Jn 5^{8f}, Mk 2^{11f} RSV 'pallet') and some correspondence in substance with Lk (Martha and Mary, details of the Passion, Resurrection appearances). If a literary relation to the Synoptics is granted, John may have written to supplement and complete the Synoptic account (the view generally held till modern times), to interpret it by way of commentary, or to supersede it. It is not necessary to hold exclusively to one of these views in every place where Jn has a connexion with the Synoptics.

(*b*) *Chronology and Geography.*—The idea that Jesus' ministry lasted for three years is derived from John, who mentions Passovers and other feasts (2^{13} 5^{1} 6^{4} 7^{2} 10^{22} 12^{1}). In the Synoptics precise marks are wanting; there is a continuous series of actions which might even be crowded into one year, as some early Fathers believed, thus interpreting 'the acceptable year of the Lord' (Is 61^{2}, Lk 4^{19}). The cleansing of the Temple is placed by John at the beginning of the ministry (2^{13ff}), by the Synoptists at the end (Mk 11^{15ff}) where it brings hostility to Jesus to a head. The outstanding chronological difference is the date of the Crucifixion. All four Gospels agree that the Crucifixion took place on a Friday, but in Jn Jesus dies on the day of preparation for the Passover (14th of the month Nisan), in the Synoptics after the Passover Supper (15th Nisan). There are indications in the Synoptics of tradition agreeing with Jn (Mk 14^{2}, Mt 26^{5}) and of activity not likely to be permitted on 15th Nisan (Mk 15^{21,42f,46}); on the other hand symbolical appropriateness (Jesus dying at the hour when the Passover lambs were slain) may have influenced John's account. This difference has been noticed from the earliest times. Present opinion is divided on the historical point.

The Synoptists lay the scene of the ministry for the most part in Galilee, John in Judaea. In neither case, however, is interest confined to the one region. In the Synoptics the final journey to Jerusalem begins as early as Mk 10^{1}, Mt 19^{1}, Lk 9^{51}. The disciple Judas belongs to Kerioth, in Judaea. Jesus knows Joseph of Arimathaea (Lk 23^{51}), the household at Bethany (Mk 14^{3}), and places near and in Jerusalem (Mk 11^{1ff} 14^{12ff}). The lament over Jerusalem (Mt 23^{37}, Lk 13^{34}) implies previous visits during the ministry. On the other hand John records visits to Samaria and Galilee (2^{1ff} 4^{1ff} 6^{1}–7^{10}). It is therefore not difficult to reconcile the Synoptic and Johannine accounts here; but the interest in Judaea shown in the Fourth Gospel has a bearing on its authorship.

(*c*) *Miracles and discourses.*—The miracles in the Synoptics are numerous and varied, works of power prompted by compassion and expressive of Jesus' Messianic mission. In Jn there is a selection of a few which have been described as 'downright wonders of omnipotence.' They do not admit of psychological or other natural explanation. Cures of demoniacs, which others could work, are absent. Yet these miracles are not set before us as in themselves the ground of faith. They are 'signs,' pointing to the wine of a new dispensation, to the light of the world, to Him who is the Resurrection and the Life, and so on. So they lead to discourses, composed in a flowing style which contrasts strikingly with the short pithy sayings frequent in the Synoptics, and which in matter deal mostly with Christ Himself—His origin, His relation to the Father, His glory, and the gift of eternal life which He bestows. This teaching, and especially the claims made by John for Jesus and by Jesus Himself, are in the terms of a more advanced theology than that of the Synoptics, and a major historical question is raised by the fact that in Jn they are publicly proclaimed from the beginning of Jesus' ministry, whereas in the Synoptics it is not till Peter's confession at Caesarea Philippi (Mk 8[27ff] and ‖ s) that anything approaching the truth of the Master's vocation and Person is disclosed to the disciples. (The 'Messianic secret' is a dominant theme in Mk.) These differences are relative. There are sayings of the Fourth Gospel which resemble those of the Synoptics (*e.g.* 2[16] 12[8, 25] 13[16, 20]) and at least one instance in the Synoptic account (Mt 11[27], Lk 10[22]) where Jesus speaks in the manner of the Fourth Gospel. There are unique claims, invitations, challenges, assertions in the Synoptics as well as in Jn (Lord of the Sabbath, Mk 2[28]; restating the Law, Mt 5[17, 21f] etc.; the eschatological Son of Man, Mk 8[38] 14[62]; the future Judge, Mt 25[31ff]; His death a ransom for many, Mk 10[45] cf 14[22ff]). The historical differences, also, are less obtrusive if we bear in mind that there are different ways of writing history, even in the 20th cent.

The distinction in style and matter is, however, a real one. Parables of the Synoptic type are absent; instead we have allegorical pictures, the Shepherd (ch. 10), the Vine (ch. 15). There is less about the Kingdom of God, more about the Holy Spirit; less of detailed ethical guidance, more about the supreme principle of love; less of apocalyptic eschatology, more of the abiding presence of Christ and the Spirit. Clearly the earlier tradition has been reshaped by reflection; but Christians have always felt that John brings to light its deepest truth.

(*d*) *The portrait of Jesus.*—Clement of Alexandria (*c* A.D. 200) states that he learned from 'the ancient elders' that John, last of the Evangelists, seeing that the external (literally 'bodily') facts had already been sufficiently set forth in the other Gospels, composed, at the request of his disciples and with the inspiration of the Spirit, a 'spiritual' Gospel (quoted by Eusebius *HE* vi. 14). While this justly recognizes a distinction between the Synoptic and Johannine portraits it is misleading; it suggests that the Synoptics deal with the human Jesus, Jn with the Divine Christ—too sweeping a generalization. If in the Synoptics Jesus' Sonship is rather conceived as pertaining to His Messianic vocation than as an eternal relationship to the Father, yet the Synoptic Messiah clearly is endowed with supernatural powers. In Mt and Lk He has a miraculous birth. He teaches and forgives with authority. Sayings on His Sonship show Him in a special relation both to God and men (Mk 9[37] and ‖ s; Mt 10[40], Lk 10[16]; Mk 13[32], Mt 24[36]). Prominent in the Synoptics is the title 'Son of Man.' It has sometimes been understood to denote simply Jesus' humanity, His participation in human experience. But the Son of Man of apocalyptic prophecy is a resplendent supernatural being, and this self-designation of Jesus carries in the Synoptics a significance which bare 'humanity' does not convey. The title is found also in Jn, where it has special association with descending and ascending (including elevation on the Cross) and moves easily to and from the idea of the Son of God (1[51] 3[13-18] 5[25-27] 6[27, 53ff] 8[28] 12[23ff] 13[31]). But in the Synoptics it brings to a focus the whole intention of Jesus' Messianic vocation.

On the other hand the humanity of Jesus is stressed in Jn. The Word became flesh (1[14]). Jesus' mother and brethren are mentioned in a natural way. He has normal human friendships. He describes Himself as a man (8[40]). He suffers from weariness, thirst, grief (*e.g.* 4[6-9] 19[28] 11[35]). Even in relation to God He shares much with men, His followers; obedience, subordination to the Father's will is emphasized (4[34ff] 6[38] 8[28] 14[28] 15[10] 17[4]).

The diversity of the portraits, however, remains. There is a wider range of human experience and emotion in the Synoptic Gospels. Compassion is emphasized, wrath and astonishment are attributed to Jesus. He wrestles with temptation. In Jn too (against docetism) the full humanity of Christ is affirmed, but all is subordinated to the theme of the Divine origin, powers, and glory of the Son of God. Diversity is not contradiction. The Synoptics from three standpoints give a portrait diverse from that of the Fourth Gospel, but all are united in their tribute to the one historical person. At no other period could the Gospels have been produced. They are unique works centring upon a unique historical revelation.

6. Early use of the Gospels.—The accidental discovery of Christian papyrus fragments (Pap[52], Egerton Pap[2]) has shown that the Fourth Gospel circulated in Egypt early in the 2nd cent., and it is no longer necessary to counter the former arguments that the Gospels were works of 2nd cent. writers out of reach of the authentic history. In the extant Christian writings of the first half of that century we find that where there is occasion to refer to the events (and especially to the teaching) recorded in our Gospels the writers do not quote formally, naming authors, but in a way that suggests loose quotation from memory, or the survival of oral tradition alongside the written Gospels, or possibly the use of harmonies. Thus some of their allusions are difficult to identify; but allowing for this uncertainty we note the following indications of knowledge of the Gospels: (*a*) the period A.D. 90–120—Clement of Rome (96) Lk, ? Mt; Ignatius (*c* 115) Mt, ? Jn; Polycarp (*c* 115) Mt, ? Mk, 1 Jn, ? Jn; (*b*) of uncertain date, but may be placed in the period A.D. 120–150—*Didache*, Mt, ? Lk; Papias, Mk, also reference to a work by 'Matthew,' 1 Jn, ? Jn; Barnabas, ? Mt; *Shepherd* of Hermas, first quotation closely corresponding to Mk. (*c*) At mid-century Justin almost certainly means our four when he writes of 'memoirs which, I say, were composed by His Apostles and those who followed them' (*Dial.* 103), but he quotes inexactly, chiefly Mt, Lk. Tatian (*c* A.D. 170) makes of the four Gospels a harmony, the *Diatessaron*. (*d*) With Irenaeus (*c* A.D. 180) begins the period of definite and extensive quotation; for him there are only four canonical Gospels, and this in the nature of things. From the end of the century Clement of Alexandria, Tertullian, Origen, and their successors in all geographical regions quote from the undisputed four. A. J. M.—**A. B.**

GOSPELS, APOCRYPHAL.—See APOCRYPHAL NEW TESTAMENT.

GOTHIC VERSION OF OT.—See GREEK VERSIONS OF OT, **11.**

GOTHOLIAH.—Father of Jeshaiah, who returned with Ezra, 1 Es 8[33] (AV, RV **Gotholias**); called in Ezr 8[7] **Athaliah,** which was thus both a male and a female name (2 K 11[1]).

GOTHOLIAS, 1 Es 8[33] (AV, RV).—See GOTHOLIAH.

GOTHONIEL.—The father of Chabris, one of the rulers of Bethulia (Jth 6[15]).

GOURD (*ḳîḳāyôn*, Jon 4[6]; *paḳḳuʿôth*, 2 K 4[39]).—The Hebrew *ḳîḳāyôn*, translated 'colocynth' (LXX) or 'ivy' (Vulgate), is certainly a gourd of some kind. It is generally equated with the Egyptian *kꜣkꜣ*=Greek *kiki*, which is identified as *ricinus communis*; but the equation of the Egyptian *k* with the Hebrew *ḳ* is irregular, except perhaps in foreign loan-words. The Assyrian *kukkānîtum*, which is the name of an unknown plant, must be similarly ruled out of the discussion (Thompson, *Assyrian Botany*, 132, n. 2). The *ricinus communis* or *palma Christi*, if the identification is accepted (Arias *ap.* Celsus, *Hierobotanicon*, II. 273–83), is found in waste places, especially near water, in Palestine and the neighbouring countries and it grows very rapidly (Pliny, *NH* xv. 7 § 25) to a height of some 12 feet, putting forth huge leaves which afford some shade; but it is hardly suitable for training over a booth (Jon 4[6]). The plant meant, therefore, is

GOVERNMENT

rather the ' bottle-gourd ' (*cucurbita pepo* or *lagenaria*), which is very commonly trained over trellises and booths in the Middle East ; it grows very quickly and withers as quickly (Tristram, *Natural History of the Bible*[2], 449–50, and Moldenko, *Plants of the Bible*, 203–204).

The Hebrew *paḳḳu'ôth* denotes a plant whose fruit bursts (cf Heb. *pāḳa'*, ' split ') and is of a reddish-yellow colour (cf Arab. *faqa'a*, ' was deep yellow,' and *faqi'a*, ' was red ') ; and it is described as a vine whose fruit is toxic (2 K 4[40]). Accordingly it may be safely taken as ' (wild) colocynth ' (*citrullus colocynthus*), which is a true vine prostrate on the ground and climbing by means of tendrils and which produces fruit of the size and colour of an orange ; this bursts when trodden, has an intensely bitter taste and is highly toxic ; further, it grows profusely in Palestine and may easily be mistaken for a melon (Tristram, *op. cit.* 451–52, and Moldenko, *op. cit.* 78–9). The LXX's ' wild colcynth ' and the Vulgate's *colocynthides agri*, the cognate Assyrian *piqû*, ' wild cucumber, colocynth,' and the Syrian *paqû'â* ' colocynth ' (or the similar *cucumis prophetarum*), as well as experiments on dogs, which have shown that its poisonous effects can be counteracted by eating bread (Macht in the *Jewish Quarterly Review*, N.S. x [1917], 185–97), all confirm this identification. The ' knobs ' (Heb. *pᵉḳā'îm*) in Solomon's Temple (1 K 6[18] 7[27]) were ornaments carved in the shape of wild colocynths. See also KNOP, **2.**

G. R. D.

GOVERNMENT.—The purpose of this article will be to sketch in outline the forms of government among the Hebrews at successive periods of their history. The indications are in many cases vague, and it is impossible to reconstruct the complete system ; at no period was there a definitely conceived, still less a written, constitution in the modern sense. For fuller details reference should be made throughout to the separate articles on the officials, etc., mentioned.

We may at once set aside *Legislation*, one of the most important departments of government as now understood. In ancient communities, law rested on Divine command and immemorial custom, and could as a rule be altered only by ' fictions.' The idea of avowedly new legislation to meet fresh circumstances was foreign to early modes of thought. At no period do we find a legislative body in the Bible. Grote's dictum that ' The human king on earth is not a law-maker, but a judge,' applies to all the Biblical forms of government. The main functions of government were judicial, military, and at later periods financial, and to a limited extent administrative.

1. *During the nomadic or patriarchal age* the unit is the family or clan, and, for certain purposes, the tribe. The head of the house, owing to his position and experience, was the supreme ruler and judge, in fact the only permanent official. He had undisputed authority within his family group (Gn 22, 38[24], Dt 21[18], Jg 11[34]). Heads of families make agreements with one another and settle quarrels among their dependents (Gn 21[22] 31[45]) ; the only sanction to which they can appeal is the Divine justice which ' watches ' between them (31[49, 53] 49[7]). Their hold over the individual lay in the fact that to disobey was to become an outlaw ; and to be an outcast from the tribe was to be without protector or avenger. The heads of families combined to form, in a somewhat more advanced stage, the **' elders '** (Ex 3[16] 18[21], Nu 22[7]) ; and sometimes, particularly in time of war, there is a single chief for the whole tribe. Moses is an extreme instance of this, and we can see that his position was felt to be unusual (Ex 2[14] 4[1], Nu 16). It was undefined, and rested on his personal influence, backed by the Divine sanction, which, as his followers realized, had marked him out. This enables him to nominate Joshua as his successor.

2. *The period of the* **' Judges '** marks a higher stage ; at the same time, as a period of transition it appeared rightly to later generations as a time of lawlessness. The name ' Judges,' though including the notion of champion or deliverer, points to the fact that their chief function was judicial. The position was not hereditary, thus differing from that of king (Jg 9 ff Gideon and Abimelech), though Samuel is able to delegate his authority to his sons (1 S 8[1]). Their status was gained by personal exploits, implying Divine sanction, which was sometimes expressed in other ways ; *e.g.* gift of prophecy (Deborah, Samuel). Their power rested on the moral authority of the strong man, and, though sometimes extending over several tribes, was probably never national. During this period the nomadic tribe gives way to the local ; ties of place are more important than ties of birth. A town holds together its neighbouring villages (' daughters '), as able to give them protection (Nu 21[25, 32], Jos 17[11]). The **elders** become the ' elders of the city ' ; Jg 8[6, 14, 16] mentions officials (*śārîm*) and elders of Succoth, *i.e.* heads of the leading families, responsible for its government. In 11[5] the elders of Gilead have power in an emergency to appoint a leader from outside.

3. *The Monarchy* came into being mainly under the pressure of Philistine invasion. The **king** was a centre of unity, the leader of the nation in war, and a judge (1 S 8[20]). His power rested largely on a personal basis. As long as he was successful and strong, and retained the allegiance of his immediate followers, his will was absolute (David, Ahab, Jehu ; cf Jer 36, 37). At the same time there were elements which prevented the Jewish monarchy from developing the worst features of an Oriental despotism. At least at first the people had a voice in his election (David, Rehoboam). In Judah the hereditary principle prevailed (there were no rival tribes to cause jealousy, and David's line was the centre of the national hopes), but the people still had influence (2 K 14[21] 21[24]). In the Northern Kingdom the position of the reigning house was always insecure, and the ultimate penalty of misgovernment was the rise of a new dynasty. A more important check was found in the religious control, democratic in its best sense, exercised by the prophets (Samuel, Nathan, Elijah, Elisha, Jeremiah, etc.). The Jewish king had at least to hear the truth, and was never allowed to believe that he was indeed a god on earth. At the same time there is no constitutional check on misrule ; the ' law of the kingdom ' in Dt 17[14] deals rather with moral and religious requirements as no doubt did Jehoiada's covenant (2 K 11[17]). With the kingdom came the establishment of a standing army, David's ' mighty men ' quickly developing into the more organized forces of Solomon's and later times. The command of the forces was essential to the king's power ; cf the insurrection of Jehu ' the captain ' (2 K 9), and Jehoiada's care to get control of the army (11[4]). Side by side with the power of the sword came the growth of a court, with its harem and luxurious *entourage*, its palace and its throne. These were visible symbols of the royal power, impressing the popular mind. The lists of officers (2 S 8[16], 1 K 4) are significant ; they indicate the growth of the king's authority, and the development of relations with others States. The real power of government has passed into the hands of the king's *clientèle*. His servants hold office at his pleasure, and, provided they retain his favour, there is little to limit their power. They may at times show independence of spirit (1 S 22[17], Jer 36[25]), but are usually his ready tools (2 S 11[14] ; cf the old and the young counsellors of Rehoboam, 1 K 12[6ff]). The prophetic pictures of the court and its administration are not favourable (Am 3[9] 4[1] 6, Is 5 etc.). The methods of raising revenue were undefined, and being undefined were oppressive. We hear of gifts and tribute (1 S 10[27], 2 S 8[10], 1 K 4[7, 21-23] 10[11-25]), of tolls and royal monopolies (10[15, 28f]), of forced labour (5[13]) and of the ' king's mowings ' (Am 7[1]), of confiscation (1 K 21), and, in an emergency, of stripping the Temple (2 K 18[15]). In time of peace the main function of the king is the administration of justice (2 S 15[2], 2 K 15[5]) ; his subjects have the right of direct access (2 K 8[3]). This must have lessened the power of the local **elders,** who no doubt had also to yield to the central court officials. ' The elders of the city ' appear during this period as a local authority, sometimes respected and consulted (2 S 19^{11}, 1 K 20^{7}, 2 K 23^{1}), sometimes the obedient agents of the king's will (1 K $21^{8, 11}$, 2 K $10^{1, 5}$). 2 Ch 19^{5-11} describes a judicial system organized by Jehoshaphat, which agrees in its main features with that implied by Dt 16^{18} 17^{8-13}; there are local courts, with a central tribunal. In Deuteronomy the elders appear mainly as judicial authorities, but have the power of executing their decisions (19^{12} 21, 22^{15} etc.). The influence of the priesthood in this connexion should be noticed. The administration of justice always included a Divine element (Ex $18^{15, 19}$ 21^{6} 22^{8}; cf the word 'Torah'), and in the Deuteronomic code the priests appear side by side with the lay element in the central court (17^{9} 19^{17}; cf Is 28^{7}, Ezk 44^{24} etc.). But the government is not yet theocratic. Jehoiada relies on his personal influence, and acts in concert with the chiefs of the army (2 K 11, 12), and even after the Exile Joshua is only the fellow of Zerubbabel. The appointment of Levites as judges, ascribed to David in 1 Ch 23^{4} 26^{29}, is no doubt an anachronism. Cf also article JUSTICE (II.).

4. *Post-exilic period*.—Under the Persians Judaea was a subdistrict of the great province west of the Euphrates, and subject to its governor (Ezr 5^{3}). It had also its local governor (Neh 5^{14}), with a measure of local independence (Ezr 10^{14}); we read, too, of a special official 'at the king's hand in all matters concerning the people' (Neh 11^{24}). The **elders** are prominent during this period both in exile (Ezk 8^{1} 14^{1} 20^{1}) and in Judaea (Ezr 5^{9} 6^{7} 10^{8}, Neh 2^{16}). The chief feature of the subsequent period was the development of the priestly power, and the rise to importance of the office of the **high priest.** Under Greek rule (after 333 B.C.) the Jews were to a great extent allowed the privileges of self-government. The 'elders' develop into a *gerousia* or **senate**—an aristocracy comprising the secular nobility and the priesthood (1 Mac 12^{6} 14^{20}); it is not known when the name 'Sanhedrin' was first used. The High Priest became the head of the State, and its official representative, his political power receiving a great development under the Hasmonaeans. Owing to the growing importance of the office, the Seleucids always claimed the power of appointment. In 142 B.C., Simon is declared to be 'high priest, captain, and governor for ever' (1 Mac 14^{27-47}). The title 'ethnarch' (see GOVERNOR) is used of him and other high priests. Aristobulus becomes king (105 B.C.), and Alexander Jannaeus uses the title on coins (104–78 B.C.). Under Roman rule (63 B.C.) the situation becomes complicated by the rise to power of the Herodian dynasty. Palestine passed through the varying forms of government known to the Roman Imperial constitution. Herod the Great was its titular king, with considerable independence subject to good behaviour (*rex socius*). Archelaus forfeited his position (A.D. 6). Thenceforward Judaea was under the direct rule of a procurator (see next article), except from A.D. 41 to 44, when Agrippa I. was king. Antipas was 'tetrarch' of Galilee and Peraea; Mark's title of 'king' (6^{14}) is corrected by Matthew and Luke. The position was less honourable and less independent than that of king. The High Priest (now appointed by the Romans) and the Sanhedrin regained the power which they had lost under Herod; the government became once more an aristocracy (Jos. *Ant.* XX. x. [224 ff]). Except for the power of life and death, the Sanhedrin held the supreme judicial authority; there were also local courts connected with the Synagogue (Mt 5^{22}). Its moral authority extended to Jews outside Palestine. In the Diaspora, the Jews, tenacious of their national peculiarities, were in many cases allowed a large measure of self-government, particularly in judicial matters. In Alexandria, in particular, they had special privileges and an 'ethnarch' of their own (Jos. *Ant.* XIV. vii. 2 [117]). For the cities of Asia Minor, see Ramsay, *Letters to the Seven Churches*, chs. xi, xii.

For '**governments**' (1 Co 12^{28} AV, RV) see HELPS.

C. W. E.—**J. Pn.**

GOVERNOR.—This word represents various Hebrew and Greek words, technical and non-technical. In Gn 42^{6} (Joseph, cf 41^{40}) it is probably the *Ta-te*, the second after the king in the court of the palace; cf 1 K 18^{3}, Dn 2^{48} for similar offices. It frequently represents an Assyrian word, *peḥāh*, used of Persian satraps in general (Est 3^{12} 8^{9}), and of Assyrian generals (2 K 18^{24}, cf 1 K 20^{24}). It is applied particularly to Tattenai, the governor of the large Persian province of which Judaea was a sub-district (Ezr 5^{3} 6^{6} etc., cf Neh 2^{7}). It is also, like *tirshatha* (q.v.), applied to the subordinate governor of Judaea (Ezr 5^{14} [Sheshbazzar] 6^{7}, Hag $1^{1, 14}$ [Zerubbabel]). The first passage shows that the subordinate *peḥāh* was directly appointed by the king.

In the NT the word usually represents Greek *hēgemōn*, and is used of Pontius Pilate (Lk 3^{1} etc.), of Felix (Ac 23^{26}), and of Festus (26^{30}). The proper title of these governors was '**procurator**' (Tac. *Ann.* xv. 44), of which originally *eparchos* and then *epitropos* were the Greek equivalents. Josephus, however, uses *hēgemōn*, as well as these words, for the governor of Judaea, so that there is no inaccuracy in its employment by NT writers. But, being a general word, it does not help us to decide the nature of the 'governorship' of Quirinius (Lk 2^{2}). The procurator, originally a financial official, was appointed directly by the Emperor to govern provinces, such as Thrace, Cappadocia, and Judaea, which were in a transitional state, being no longer ruled by subject kings, but not yet fully Romanized, and requiring special treatment. The procurator was in a sense subordinate to the legate of the neighbouring 'province,' *e.g.* Cappadocia to Galatia, Judaea to Syria; but except in emergencies he had full authority, military, judicial, and financial. In 1 P 2^{14} the word is specially appropriate to any provincial governor, as 'sent' by the Emperor. In 2 Co 11^{32} it represents '**ethnarch**,' a word apparently used originally of the ruler of a nation (*ethnos*) living with laws of its own in a foreign community; but as applied to Aretas it may mean no more than petty king. In Gal 4^{2} it means '**trustee**' (RSV) or '**steward**' (RV), the 'guardian' (AV 'tutor') controlling the ward's person, the steward of his property (Lightfoot, *ad loc.*). In Ja 3^{4} RSV has 'pilot' (RV 'steersman'). The '**governor of the feast**' (Jn 2^{8} AV; RV 'ruler,' RSV 'steward') was probably a guest, not a servant, chosen to control and arrange for the feast; it is doubtful whether he is to be identified with the 'friend of the bridegroom' or best man. C. W. E.

GOZAN.—One of the places to which Israelites were deported by the king of Assyria on the capture of Samaria (2 K 17^{6} 18^{11}, 1 Ch 5^{26}; mentioned also in 2 K 19^{12}, Is 37^{12}). It is probably modern *Tell Ḥalâf* situated on the banks of the *Khābūr*.

GRACE, from Latin *gratia* (favour), a translation of *charis*, NT term for God's good-will and His empowering of His people. This specific use is common through NT, although there are other associated meanings (*e.g.* favour, pleasingness, thanks, and thankfulness).

The primary meaning of the OT passages in which the Hebrew original is employed seems to suggest 'finding' or 'securing' the 'favour' or 'good-will' of God (see Gn 6^{8}); likewise the 'favour' or 'good-will' of one's fellow men (Gn 39^{4}). This same usage is found in NT in several places, *e.g.* Lk 2^{52}. The associated OT sense of 'loving-kindness' or 'mercy' (as in Ps 77^{9}) is also reproduced in NT, with the difference that whereas the former tends to think of God's mercy towards His sinful and finite children, the latter consistently speaks of His gracious attitude.

One other usage should be noted before attention is given to the main NT view of grace. In several passages, the word appears to denote 'charm' or 'attractiveness,' as in Lk 4^{22} and Co 4^{6}. This also is a continuation of an OT meaning, as in Ps 45^{2}.

The principal meaning of grace in NT, however, has reference to the good-will (the Divine favour) of God to men; associated with this is God's empowering them, by His favour, to be pleasing to Him. It is chiefly in the

Pauline epistles that this set of ideas is expounded, although elsewhere, as in the Johannine prologue (Jn 1^{14-17}), the same teaching is found either directly or by implication. In the Pauline writings, the word 'grace' occurs twice as often as in all the rest of NT; it is plainly a favourite conception of the Apostle, who uses it to sum up God's attitude and action towards His children. For Paul, grace is given by God to men, apart from any merit on their part; there is no place in his writings for such a later theological refinement as, *e.g.* 'grace of congruity.' God, of His own will and because His nature essentially is love, acts towards men in grace, winning from them their response to His prevenient action—a response which itself is a gracious one in that it is of God's effecting as primary source. On the other hand, the Apostle does not imply that men need make no effort, moral or religious; his view is that such 'work' is consequent upon, and the manifestation of, the gift of grace from God. A modern writer has suggested that for Paul the basic meaning of grace is 'God's love in action towards men'; this definition rightly suggests that for Paul the concept is not simply that of 'favour,' but is a dynamic idea, including within it the sense of the Divine activity in empowering the men whom God regards with favour.

For the Apostle, the summation of God's grace towards men is seen in the life, death, and resurrection of Christ. For him, as for the Johannine writer, this means that God's gracious dealings are not according to law but are of a free and spontaneous character. A principal result of God's gracious work is the overcoming of sin, both in the fact of His giving His Son to men and also in God's continued activity in the lives of those who have been turned to Him through Christ.

It will be seen, then, that grace excludes all thought of 'merit' and is entirely in opposition to a legal conception of religion. Deliverance from such a legal or commercial idea was the consequence of Paul's conversion; therefore he could speak only of the freely given, unmerited, and extra-legal nature of God's dealing with sinners.

Because of the close identification which NT makes, especially in Paul and the Fourth Gospel, between the grace of God and the total fact of Christ, it is possible to speak (as Paul does, *e.g.* in 2 Co 8^9, and in the so-called 'grace of the Lord Jesus Christ," 13^{14}) of this grace as being Christ's as well as the Father's. There seems to be both identity and difference in Ro 5^{15}, where the grace of God and the grace of Christ are implied as distinct and yet at one. It is from such passages as these that the Church found material for developing a trinitarian conception, as well as from the basic facts of apostolic experience of the Father, Christ, and the Holy Spirit.

In some modern writing, there has been a tendency to identify the Holy Spirit and the grace of God. This view cannot properly be sustained on the basis of NT evidence, for the Holy Spirit is commonly God's immanent operation, while grace appears to be not so much *in* as *towards* men. A final reference may be made to the notion in Ephesians (Eph 4^7) of grace as including 'gifts' for ministering—*i.e.* a *charisma*; and to the idea in Romans (5^2) of a continuation 'in grace,' by which is meant living with God, through Christ, in a state of constant dependence upon the Divine favour and strengthening. W. N. P.

GRACIOUS.—This English adjective is now used only in an active sense = 'bestowing grace,' 'showing favour.' And this is its most frequent use in AV, as Ex 33^{19} 'And [I] will be gracious to whom I will be gracious.' But it was formerly used passively also = 'favoured,' 'accepted,' as 1 Es 8^{80} 'Yea, when we were in bondage, we were not forsaken of our Lord; but he made us gracious (RSV 'brought us into favour') before the kings of Persia, so that they gave us food.' And from this it came to signify 'attractive,' as Pr 11^{16} 'a gracious woman retaineth honour,' literally 'a woman of grace,' that is, of attractive appearance and manner; Lk 4^{22} 'the gracious words which proceeded out of his mouth,' literally, as RV, 'words of grace,' that is, says Plummer, 'winning words'; he adds, 'the very first meaning of *charis* is comeliness, winsomeness.'

GRAFF.—Obsolete form of 'graft' found in AV in Ro 11^{17ff}.

GRAFTING.—In the cultivation of the olive, which was common throughout the ancient Mediterranean world (see OIL, OIL TREE, and OLIVE), grafting of cultivated branches upon the stock of the wild olive was a universal practice. In Ro 11^{17-24} Paul reverses the process for the purpose of illustrating his point, the dependence of the Gentiles upon the Jews; but he says that the process he is describing is 'contrary to nature.' Much of the discussion in modern times of Paul's supposed ignorance of horticulture, and his assumed mistaking of the oleaster for the wild olive, and other absurdities, including a considerable amount of pseudo-science provided for the occasion, would have been impossible if commentators had paid attention to Paul's own statement. Ancient Jewish parables drawn from nature (see A. Feldman, *The Parables and Similes of the Rabbis: Agricultural and Pastoral*, Cambridge, 1927, especially ch. vi.) were not intended to teach scientific agriculture, and were often allegorical in method. Here it suits Paul's purpose to describe a process 'contrary to nature' in order to convey the important lesson that the Gentiles, including his Roman readers, owed their admission to the Church (the 'true Israel') to the failure of the Jews to respond to the Gospel; they are the 'wild' branches which are being grafted on to the cultivated tree in place of the 'natural' branches which have been broken off. This is clearly not a description of the procedure of olive-growers, but an *ad hoc* illustration of what has taken place—and is still taking place—in the religious world. That it is 'contrary to nature' is not to be stressed as an example of Divine or miraculous power (though some commentators so take it); it is only a passing admission that the case is not the normal procedure in an olive grove. We must recognize the distinction between parable (q.v.) and allegory; the one relates a natural process and uses it to illustrate one point in a spiritual or moral teaching; the other conforms the narrative to the requirements or presuppositions of the religious teaching, without regard to normal procedures or probabilities. F. C. G.

GRAPES.—See WINE AND STRONG DRINK.

GRASS.—(1) *ḥāṣîr*—equivalent of Arabic *khudra*, which includes green vegetables; many references, *e.g.* 1 K 18^5, 2 K 19^{26}; translated '**hay**' in AV and RV in Pr 27^{25} (RSV 'grass') and in AV in Is 15^6 (RV, RSV 'grass'), and 'leeks' in AV, RV, and RSV in Nu 11^5; refers to herbage in general. (2) *deshe'* (Aram. *dethe'*), Jer 14^5, Pr 27^{25} (RSV 'new growth'), Job 38^{27}, Is 66^{14} (AV 'an herb,' RV 'tender grass'), Dn $4^{15, 23}$ (EV 'tender grass'). (3) *yereḳ*, translated 'grass,' Nu 22^4; see HERB. (4) *'ēśebh*, Dt 11^{15} etc., but translated 'herb' in other places (so Dt 32^3 RV and RSV; AV 'grass'); see HERB. (5) *chortos*, Mt 6^{30}, Mk 6^{39} etc. Pasturage, as it occurs in Western lands, is unknown in Palestine. Such green herbage appears only for a few weeks, and when the rains cease soon perishes. Hence grass is in the OT a frequent symbol of the shortness of human life (Ps 90^{5f} 103^{15}, Is 40^6; cf 1 P 1^{24}). Even more brief is the existence of 'the grass upon the [mud-made] house-tops, which withers before it grows up' (Ps 129^6). E. W. G. M.

GRASSHOPPER.—See LOCUST.

GRATE, GRATING.—See TABERNACLE, **4** (*b*).

GRAVE.—See MOURNING CUSTOMS, TOMB.

GRAVEN IMAGE.—See IMAGES.

GRAY.—See COLOURS, **1.**

GREAT BIBLE.—See ENGLISH VERSIONS, **22.**

GREAT SEA.—See SEA.

GREAT SYNAGOGUE.—See SYNAGOGUE, **7.**

GREAVES.—See ARMOUR, **2** (*d*).

GREECE is the fringed and island-studded southern end of the Balkan peninsula, together with the great archipelago of the Peloponnesus with which it is joined by the Isthmus of Corinth. Although much of the land is mountainous, the soil is especially good for vines and olives, but not for cereal crops. Its central mountain ranges, though not high, divide the country into many small territories or cantons, populated in ancient times by a variety of clans descended from the three invading stocks of Aeolians, Ionians, and Dorians. These invasions began *c* 1900 B.C. and were completed by *c* 1000 B.C. The 8th cent. saw the rise of city states and the founding of overseas colonies, the result of over-population at home. By *c* 500 B.C. the old monarchical rule of the cities had given way to aristocratic local governments, and these in turn to 'tyrannies,' which were followed by oligarchies or—as at Athens—by a democracy. The great crisis of the early 5th cent., the Persian invasions of 490 and 480 B.C. which were repelled by the combined forces of most of the Greek states, was followed by the rise of the Athenian sea-empire, and this by the revolt of the subjects and allies and the prolonged Peloponnesian War which ended in 404 B.C. From the lasting effects of this catastrophic struggle, an ancient 'thirty years war,' Greece never recovered. Its era of greatest brilliance, the 5th cent., was over, and its chief contributions to literature and art—but not philosophy—had now been made. For the next thirty years Sparta ruled Greece with an iron hand, but the subject states again rebelled; Thebes was in the ascendant from 371 to 362 B.C.; but the disunity and rivalries of the Greeks only prepared for the Macedonian conquest under Philip II. in 338 B.C. His son Alexander (known as the Great) succeeded him in 336 B.C., and under the pretext of freeing the Ionian cities of western Asia Minor and also in order to avenge his father's assassination, he began the conquest of the Persian Empire, which ended with the invasion of Hither India in 327–325 B.C. Alexander died in 323 B.C., at the age of thirty-three, but his work was done. The Greek language had been carried to the borders of India, and with it Greek ideas, forms of Greek art and literature, and even certain Greek religious ideas.

The age that followed is known as the Alexandrine age, or the age of Hellenism, when Hellenistic culture spread over the whole known world, from the Rhone to the Indus. The dynasties founded by Alexander's generals, especially the Seleucids in Syria and the Ptolemies in Egypt, continued the work of cultural unification and penetration, so that when Rome began to interfere in the affairs of the East, about the beginning of the 2nd cent. B.C., Greek was already the common language of that part of the world. When, about three centuries after Alexander, practically all his former dominions had become Roman provinces, Greek was the one language which could be used throughout the Mediterranean world and the Near East. The Roman Empire had two official languages, Latin for Italy and the provinces north, west, and south-west of it; Greek for every region east and south-east of Italy. The Romans wisely made no effort to force Latin upon the eastern peoples and were content to permit Greek to remain in undisputed sway. All Roman officials understood, spoke, and wrote it. Inscriptions, like the great *Monumentum Ancyranum* at Ankara, which recounted the achievements of the Emperor Augustus, were in Greek, and so were the legislative and administrative enactments affecting the eastern provinces. Thus it came about that the Christian message was proclaimed in Greek, that the NT books were all written in Greek, and that the language of the church, according to all the available evidence, remained Greek until at least the middle of the 2nd cent. A.D. Even later, in Gaul (see Irenaeus's *Against Heresies*, *c* A.D. 185, and the Letter of the Churches of Lyons and Vienne, regarding the persecution there in A.D. 177) Greek was still in use; while in Rome itself such a work as Hippolytus's *Apostolic Tradition*, A.D. 217, and parts of the Roman liturgy to this day, are evidence of its continued use.

After 200 B.C., the history of Greece becomes more and more closely allied to that of Rome until, with the annexation of Macedonia in 148 B.C. and the destruction of Corinth in 146 B.C., Greece itself became a Roman province (Achaia, as in Ac 18[12]). Although the Greeks still continued to enjoy a measure of local autonomy, they were in reality a subject people, and found their freedom only in literature, art, and philosophy, not in political activity. A. So.—**F. C. G.**

GREEKS, GRECIANS.—Both these terms are used indifferently in AV of OT Apocrypha to designate persons of Greek extraction (1 Mac 1[10] 6[2] 8[9], 2 Mac 4[36] etc.); RSV uses 'Greeks.' In NT the linguistic usage of AV and RV make a distinction between the terms 'Greeks' and 'Grecians' (RSV does not use '*Grecians*'). '*Greeks*' uniformly represents the word *Hellēnes*, which may denote persons of Greek descent in the narrowest sense (Ac 16[1] 18[4], Ro 1[14]), or may be a general designation for all who are not of Jewish extraction (Jn 12[20], Ro 1[16] 10[12], Gal 3[28]). '*Grecians*,' on the other hand (Ac 6[1] 9[29]), is AV translation of *Hellēnistai*, which means Greek-speaking *Jews* (RV '*Grecian Jews*'; RSV correctly '*Hellenists*,' q.v.). See preceding article and DISPERSION. An interesting question is that of the correct reading of Ac 11[20]. Were those to whom the men of Cyprus and Cyrene preached Hellenists, *i.e.* Greek-speaking Jews, or Greeks? There is strong MS evidence for 'Hellenists,' but the context, and all that has gone before in Acts, from ch. 2 onwards, favours 'Greeks.' F. C. G.

GREEK VERSIONS OF OT.—I. The Septuagint (LXX).—**1.** The Septuagint, or Version of the Seventy, has special characteristics which differentiate it strongly from all other versions of the Scriptures; as the Greek OT of the Christian community from its earliest days, it has a special historical importance which no other version can claim, and only the Vulgate can approach. The LXX, moreover, is the only version of the OT which has a pre-Christian provenience.

2. There is no doubt that the LXX originated in Alexandria, in the time of the Macedonian dynasty in Egypt. Greeks had been sporadically present in Egypt even before the conquest of the country by Alexander, and under the Ptolemies they increased and multiplied greatly. Hundreds of documents discovered in Egypt within recent years testify to the presence of Greeks and the wide-spread knowledge of the Greek language from the days of Ptolemy Soter onwards. Among them, especially in Alexandria, were many Jews, to whom Greek became the language of daily life, while the knowledge of Aramaic, and still more of literary Hebrew, decayed among them. It was among such surroundings that the LXX came into existence. The principal authority on the classic view of its origin is the so-called *Letter of Aristeas* (edited by H. St. J. Thackeray in Swete's *Introduction to the OT in Greek* [1900], by P. Wendland in the Teubner series [1900], and by M. Hadas in the series *Jewish Apocryphal Lit.*, Dropsie College Edition [1951]). This document, which purports to be written by a Greek official of high rank in the court of Ptolemy II. (Philadelphus, 285–247 B.C.), narrates that it was Demetrius of Phalerum who suggested that the *Law* of the Jews should have a place in the royal library at Alexandria, and accordingly at Ptolemy's command preparations were made for carrying the plan into effect. An embassy was dispatched to Eleazar, the High Priest at Jerusalem, who sent six elders from each of the twelve tribes, or seventy-two men in all, to Alexandria to make the desired version. They brought with them de luxe manuscripts of the Pentateuch, and after they had been fêted by Ptolemy, the seventy-two translators were given quarters on the island of Pharos in the harbour of Alexandria, where they performed their labours in seventy-two days; the document ascribed to Aristeas adds: 'as if this coincidence had been the result of some design.' At any rate, this correspondence of numbers is a mere literary embellishment. It should be noted, however, that Aristeas makes room for editorial harmonization 'by mutual comparisons,' adding: 'The appropriate result of the harmonization was reduced to writing under the direction of Demetrius.' Even though this document is regarded as not contemporary and as spurious, at any rate it presents a plausible account of the editorial method of producing the Greek Pentateuch. On the contrary, Philo maintains that each of the translators independently arrived at the same phraseology by Divine inspiration, and this view of identical verbal agreement among the various interpreters was further elaborated by some of the Church Fathers. The date of Aristeas is uncertain. E. Bickermann makes 145 B.C. the upper limit; H. G. Meecham favours 100 B.C. M. Hadas prefers a date shortly after 132 B.C. as reasonable. The name Aristeas is a pseudonym, and the author, a Jew, was Hellenized in all but religion.

Originally the term Septuagint was applied to the Pentateuch and only later was extended to the entire Greek Old Testament; it may be more accurate to speak of the Old Greek, but so long as we limit the name LXX to the original translation to the exclusion of later recensions, we shall avoid confusion of terminology. On the basis of the account in Aristeas we might assume that seventy was merely a convenient approximation for the original number seventy-two. Josephus (*Ant.* XII. ii. 7 [57]) gives seventy as the number of translators, although immediately before he refers to the traditional number of six from each tribe. Another origin of the figure, however, has been suggested. Thus there were seventy elders of Israel with Moses, Aaron, and Abihu at Sinai (Ex 24[1, 9]; cf Nu 11[16]). There also were seventy members of the Sanhedrin. In Lk 10[1] Jesus appointed seventy other disciples, but here some MSS read seventy-two. In other words, the figure seventy was rather prominent in Jewish thought. If seventy be the original number of translators, then Aristeas chose the multiple of twelve nearest to seventy. The whole matter is uncertain and encrusted with legend, but the name LXX endures. It may, however, not be especially significant to know precisely how many interpreters were employed on the Pentateuch and exactly when the work was done. The important thing is that we have the LXX, that it is pre-Christian, that it represents a pre-Massoretic text, that it is of great value in OT textual and exegetical studies, and that it is indispensable in the study of NT language and theology.

P. E. Kahle (cf *The Cairo Geniza* [Schweich lectures, 1941]) maintains that there were earlier translations of the Pentateuch, of which a revision was made in the time of Ptolemy, which became the standard Torah. For the other books of the OT he also postulates independent Greek renderings. In other words, he does not believe that there was one original Old Greek version. This is in contrast to P. de Lagarde, who saw the problem involved and the methodology for recovering the text of the original LXX. He was followed by A. Rahlfs (*Septuaginta Studien*, 3. Heft, 1911), who is also the editor of a complete text of the LXX (Stuttgart, 1935). A thoroughgoing attempt at establishing the text of one LXX book on Lagardian principles was made by M. L. Margolis, *The Book of Joshua in Greek*, 1931. The methods initiated by Lagarde were successfully applied by J. A. Montgomery in his two commentaries in the *ICC*: *Daniel* (1912) and *Kings* (1951). In this connexion should be mentioned the editorial work of J. Ziegler in the Göttingen LXX; cf also H. M. Orlinsky, 'On the Present State of Proto-LXX Studies,' *JAOS* lxi (1941), 81–91, and *Max Leopold Margolis—Scholar and Teacher* (1952), pp. 35–44; P. Katz, 'Das Problem des Urtextes in der LXX,' *ThZ* v (1949), 1–24.

3. That the *Letter of Aristeas* is substantially right in assigning the original translation of the Law to the time of one of the early Ptolemies there is no reason to doubt; but the story has the air of having been considerably embellished, and it is impossible to say where history stops and fiction begins. Demetrius of Phalerum probably never was chief of the Alexandrian Library, but he was in favour with Ptolemy I. Upon the accession of Ptolemy Philadelphus in 285 B.C. he was banished and later died in exile; accordingly he can hardly have been the prime mover in bringing about the rendering of the Pentateuch into Greek. It will be observed that Aristeas speaks only of 'the Law,' *i.e.* the Pentateuch; and there is no reason to doubt that this was the first part of the OT to be translated, and that the other books followed at different times and from the hands of different translators. A lower limit for the completion of the work, or of the main part of it, is given in the prologue to Sirach (written probably in 132 B.C.), where the writer, in speaking of 'the law itself and the prophets and the rest of the books' (*sc.* the Hagiographa), implies that they had been already translated. It may therefore be taken as fairly certain that the LXX as a whole was produced between 285 and 150 B.C.

4. Its character cannot be described in a word. It is written in Greek, which in vocabulary and accidence is substantially that *koinē dialektos*, or Hellenistic Greek, which was in common use throughout the empire of Alexander, and of which our knowledge, in its non-literary form, has been greatly extended by the discoveries of Greek papyri in Egypt. In its syntax, however, it is strongly tinged with Hebraisms, which give it a distinct character of its own. The general tendency of the LXX translators was to be very literal, and they repeatedly followed Hebrew usage (notably in the use of pronouns, prepositions, and participial constructions) to an extent which runs entirely counter to the genius of the Greek language. [Cf H. St. J. Thackeray, *A Grammar of the OT in Greek* (1909) and the Introduction to *Selections from the Septuagint*, by F. C. Conybeare and St. George Stock (1905). For the Hebraic character of LXX Greek cf H. S. Gehman *V.T.* i (1951), 81–90; iii (1953), 141–148.] The quality of the translation varies in different books. It is at its best in the Pentateuch, which was probably the most deliberately prepared portion of the translation. It is at its worst in the Prophets, which presented the greatest difficulties in the way of interpretation. Sometimes it is necessary to refer to the Hebrew text in order to understand the Greek of the LXX; in some cases Greek words are used rather arbitrarily with a distinct Hebrew meaning. Something has been done to distinguish the work of different translators. [See H. St. J. Thackeray in *JThSt* iv, 245, 398, 578, viii, 262; also *The Septuagint and Jewish Worship* (Schweich Lectures, 1920).] It has been shown that Jeremiah is probably the work of two translators, who respectively translated chs. 1–28 and 29–51 (in the Greek order of the chapters), the latter, who was an inferior scholar, being responsible also for Baruch. Ezekiel likewise shows traces of two translators, one taking chs. 1–27 and 40–48, the other 28–39. The Minor Prophets form a single group, which has considerable affinities with the first translators of both Jeremiah and Ezekiel. Isaiah stands markedly apart from all of these, exhibiting a more classical style, but less fidelity to the Hebrew. 1 Kings (=1 Samuel) similarly stands apart from 2–4 Kings, the latter having features in common with Judges.

5. Some other features of the LXX must be mentioned, which show that each book, or group of books, requires separate study. In Judges the two principal MSS (Codd. A and B, see below, **10**) differ so extensively as to show that they represent different recensions. In some books (notably the latter chapters of Exodus, 3 K 4–11, Pr 24–29, Jer 25–51) the order of the LXX differs completely from that of the Hebrew, testifying to an arrangement of the text quite different from that of the Massoretes. Elsewhere the differences are not in arrangement but in contents. This is especially the case in the latter chapters of Jos., 1 Kings (=1 Samuel) 17–18, where the LXX omits (or the Hebrew adds) several verses; 3 K 8 and 12, where the LXX incorporates material from some other

GREEK VERSIONS OF OT

source; Ps 151, which is added in the LXX; Job, the original LXX text of which was much shorter than that of the Massoretic Hebrew; Esther, where the Greek has large additions, which now appear separately in our Apocrypha, but which are an integral part of the LXX; Jeremiah, where small omissions and additions are frequent; and Daniel, where the LXX includes the episodes of Susanna, Bel and the Dragon, and the Song of the Three Children, which have now been relegated (in obedience to Jerome's example) to the Apocrypha.

6. The mention of the Apocrypha suggests the largest and most striking difference between the LXX and the Hebrew OT, namely, in the books included in their respective canons; for the Apocrypha, as it stands to-day in our Bibles, consists (with the exception of 2 (4) Esdras and the Prayer of Manasseh) of books which form an integral part of the LXX canon, but were excluded from the Hebrew canon when that was finally determined about the end of the 1st cent. [see CANON OF OT]. Nor did these books stand apart from the others in the LXX as a separate group. The historical books (1 Esdras, Tobit, Judith, and sometimes Maccabees) have their place with Chronicles, Ezra, Nehemiah; the poetical books (Wisdom, Sirach) stand beside Proverbs, Ecclesiastes, and Canticles; and Baruch is attached to Jeremiah. The whole arrangement of the OT books differs, indeed, from the definite order of the Massoretic Text. The latter has its three fixed divisions—(i) the Law, *i.e.* the Pentateuch; (ii) the Prophets, consisting of the Former Prophets (Joshua, Judges, 1–4 Kings) and the Latter Prophets (Isaiah, Jeremiah, Ezekiel, and the Minor Prophets); (iii) the Hagiographa, including Psalms, Job, Proverbs, Ruth, Canticles, Ecclesiastes, Lamentations, Esther, Daniel, Ezra, Nehemiah, Chronicles. But the LXX attaches Ruth to Judges, Chronicles, and Ezra-Nehemiah to Kings, Baruch and Lamentations to Jeremiah, and Daniel to the three Major Prophets. Its principle of arrangement is, in fact, different. In place of divisions which substantially represent three different stages of canonization, it classifies the books in groups according to the character of their subject-matter—Law, History, Poetry, and Prophecy. The details of the order of the books differ in various MSS and authoritative lists, but substantially the principle is as here stated; and the divergence has had considerable historical importance. In spite of the dissent of several of the leading Fathers, such as Origen and Athanasius, the LXX canon was generally accepted by the early Christian Church. Through the medium of the Old Latin Version it passed into the West, and in spite of Jerome's adoption of the Hebrew canon in his Vulgate, the impugned books made their way back into all Latin Bibles, and have remained there from that day to this. [For an explanation of the curious misapprehension whereby 1 Esdras (on which see **17**) was excepted from this favourable reception in the Latin printed Bibles, and relegated to an appendix, see an article by Sir H. Howorth in *JThSt* vii (1906), 343]. Luther and the English translators followed Jerome in adopting the Hebrew canon, and relegated the remaining books to the Apocrypha. The authority attaching to the LXX and Massoretic canons respectively is a matter of controversy which cannot be settled offhand; but the fact of their divergence is certain and historically important.

7. If the LXX had come down to us in the state in which it was at the time when its canon was complete (say in the 1st cent. B.C.), it would still have presented to the critic problems more than enough, by reason of its differences from the Hebrew in contents and arrangement, and the doubt attaching to its fidelity as a translation; but these difficulties are multiplied tenfold by the modifications which it underwent between this time and the date to which our earliest MSS belong. It has been shown above that the LXX was the Bible of the Greek-speaking world at the time when Christianity spread over it. It was in that form that the Gentile Christians received the OT; and they were under no temptation to desert it for the Hebrew Bible (which was the property of their enemies, the Jews), even if they had been able to read it. The LXX consequently became the Bible of the early Christian Church, to which the books of the NT were added in course of time. But the more the Christians were attached to the LXX, the less willing became the Jews to admit its authority; and from the time of the activity of the Rabbinical school of Jamnia, about the end of the 1st cent. A.D., to which period the fixing of the Massoretic canon and text may be assigned with fair certainty, they definitely repudiated it. This repudiation did not, however, do away with the need which non-Palestinian Jews felt for a Greek OT; and the result was the production, in the course of the 2nd cent., of no less than three new translations. These translations, which are known under the names of Aquila, Theodotion, and Symmachus, are described below (**15–18**); here it is sufficient to say that they were all translated from a Hebrew text very close to the Massoretic OT, and represent it with different degrees of fidelity, from the pedantic verbal imitation of Aquila to the literary freedom of Symmachus. By the beginning of the 3rd cent. there were, therefore, four Greek versions of the OT in the field, besides portions of others which will be mentioned below.

8. Such was the state of things when Origen (A.D. 185–253), the greatest scholar produced by the early Church, entered the field of textual criticism. His labours therein had the most far-reaching effect on the fortunes of the LXX, and are the cause of a large part of our difficulties in respect of its text to-day. Struck by the discrepancies between the LXX and the Hebrew, he conceived the idea of a vast work which should set the facts plainly before the student. This was the **Hexapla,** or sixfold version of the OT, in which two Hebrew texts and four versions were set forth in six parallel columns. The six columns were as follows—(1) the Hebrew text; (2) the same transliterated in Greek characters; (3) the version of Aquila, which of all the versions was the nearest to the Hebrew; (4) the version of Symmachus; (5) his own edition of the LXX; (6) the version of Theodotion. In the case of the Psalms, no less than three additional Greek versions were included, of which very little is known; they are called simply *Quinta*, *Sexta*, and *Septima*. Elsewhere also there is occasional evidence of an additional version having been included; but these are unimportant. A separate copy of the four main Greek versions was also made, and was known as the Tetrapla; according to H. M. Orlinsky (*World Congress of Jewish Studies*, 1947 [1952]), however, the Tetrapla was no separate work, but was a loose term referring to the four Greek columns of the Hexapla. The principal extant fragment of a MS of the Hexapla (a 10th cent. palimpsest at Milan, containing about eleven Psalms) omits the Hebrew column, but makes up the total of six by a column containing various isolated readings. The only other fragment is a 7th cent. leaf discovered at Cairo in a *genizah* (room for damaged and disused synagogue MSS), and now at Cambridge. It contains Ps 22[15–18, 20–28], and has been edited by Dr. C. Taylor (*Cairo Genizah Palimpsests*, 1900). Origen's Hebrew text was substantially identical with the Massoretic; and Aquila, Symmachus, and Theodotion, as has been stated above, were translations from such an original; but the LXX, in view of its wide and frequent discrepancies, received special treatment. Passages present in the LXX, but wanting in the Hebrew, were marked with an obelus (— or ÷); passages wanting in the LXX, but present in the Hebrew, were supplied from Aquila or Theodotion, and marked with an asterisk (*); the close of the passage to which the signs applied being marked by a metobelus (: or ·/. or ⋌). In cases of divergences in arrangement, the order of the Hebrew was followed (except in Proverbs), and the text of the LXX was considerably corrected so as to bring it into better conformity with the Hebrew. The establishment of such a conformity was in fact Origen's main object, though his conscience as a scholar and his reverence for the LXX did not

GREEK VERSIONS OF OT

allow him altogether to cast out passages which occurred in it, even though they had no sanction in the Hebrew text as he knew it.

9. The great MSS of the Hexapla and Tetrapla were preserved for a long time in the library established by Origen's disciple, Pamphilus, at Caesarea, and references are made to them in the scholia and subscriptions of some of the extant MSS of the LXX (notably ℵ and Q). So long as they were in existence, with their apparatus of critical signs, the work of Origen in reconciling the Greek and Hebrew texts of the OT could always be undone, and the original text of the LXX substantially restored. But MSS so huge could not easily be copied, and the natural tendency was to excerpt the LXX column by itself, as representing a Greek text improved by restoration to more authentic form. Such an edition, containing Origen's fifth column, with its apparatus of critical signs, was produced early in the 4th cent. by Pamphilus, the founder of the library at Caesarea, and his disciple Eusebius; and almost simultaneously two fresh recensions of the LXX were published in the two principal provinces of Greek Christianity, by Hesychius at Alexandria, and by Lucian at Antioch (†311/312). The appearance of Lucianic readings preceding Lucian along with their occurrence in Old Latin texts has raised problems, and accordingly an Ur-Lucian or a pre-Lucianic version native to Antioch and Syria has been postulated. It is from these three recensions that the majority of the extant MSS of the LXX have descended; but the intricacies of the descent are indescribably great. In the case of Hexaplaric MSS, the inevitable tendency of scribes was to omit, more or less completely, the critical signs which distinguished the true LXX text from the passages imported from Aquila or Theodotion; the versions of Aquila, Theodotion, and Symmachus have disappeared, and exist now only in fragments, so that we cannot distinguish all such interpolations with certainty; Hexaplaric, Hesychian, and Lucianic MSS acted and reacted on one another, so that it is very difficult to identify MSS as containing one or other of these recensions; and although some MSS can be assigned to one or other of them with fair confidence, the majority contain mixed and undetermined texts.

10. The materials for its solution are, as in the NT, threefold—Manuscripts, Versions, Patristic Quotations; and these must be briefly described. The earliest MSS are fragments on papyrus, some of which go back to the 2nd and 3rd cents., and one even to the 1st or 2nd cent. B.C. The total number of papyrus fragments is now considerable. Those of substantial value are the following:

U. British Museum Papyrus 37. This, the first Biblical papyrus to be discovered, comes from Thebes and was acquired by the British Museum in 1836. It contains the greater part of Ps 10–34.

X. Freer Greek MS V, at Washington, D.C. (probably latter part of 3rd cent.), Am 1^{10} to end of Malachi.

905 Oxyrhynchus P. 656, Bodleian Library, early 3rd cent., parts of 4 leaves containing fragments of Genesis.

911 Berlin, Staatsbibliothek Gr. fol. 66 I, II, 32 leaves, probably 4th cent., a great part of Genesis as far as 35^{8}.

919 Heidelberg LXX P. 1, containing parts of Zec 4^{6}–Mal 4^{5}.

952 British Museum, P. 2486, early 4th cent., Song of Songs 5^{12}–6^{10}.

957 John Rylands Library, P. Gr. 458, 2nd cent. B.C., Dt 23^{24}–24^{3} 25^{1-3} $26^{12, 17-19}$ 28^{31-33}.

961 Chester Beatty P. IV, Gn 9^{1}–44^{22}.

962 Chester Beatty P. V, Gn 8^{13}–9^{1} 24^{13}–25^{21} 30^{24}–46^{33}. From papyri 911, 961, 962 we have evidence for the text of Genesis in Egypt about the end of the 3rd cent.

963 Chester Beatty P. VI, not later than the middle of 2nd cent. Portions of 50 leaves, of which 28 are substantially preserved, portions of Numbers and Deuteronomy. With the exception of 957 and Fouad 266 it is the earliest MS of the Greek Bible.

964 Chester Beatty P. XI, probably 4th cent., 2 leaves, one complete and one incomplete of Ecclestiasticus.

965 Chester Beatty P. VII, fragments of 33 leaves, first half of 3rd cent., portions of Isaiah.

966 Chester Beatty P. VIII, small portions of 2 leaves, end of 2nd cent., portions of Jeremiah.

967, 968 Chester Beatty P. IX, X, 29 imperfect leaves of a codex, Ezekiel, Daniel, Esther, first half of 3rd cent. or the borderline of 2nd and 3rd cents. Twenty-one leaves of this codex are known as the John H. Scheide Biblical Papyri, Ezk 19^{12}–39^{29} with gaps of 5 leaves. The Scheide Papyri have been deposited in the Library of Princeton University; they have been edited with commentary and various chapters by A. C. Johnson, H. S. Gehman, and E. H. Kase, Princeton University Press, 1938; cf also Gehman, *JBL*, lvii (1938), 281–287; *JAOS*, lviii (1938), 92–102; J. Ziegler, *ZAW*, lxi (1945–1948), 76–94.

2013 Leipzig P. 39, latter part of 4th cent., Ps 30–55.

2019 British Museum P. 230, end of 3rd cent., Ps 11 $(12)^{7}$–$14\,(15)^{14}$.

2055 P. Società Italiana 980, late 3rd or 4th cent., Ps 143 $(144)^{14}$–148^{3}.

P. Fouad 266, Cairo, 1st and 2nd cents. B.C., Dt 31^{28}–32^{7}. The divine name is written in Hebrew characters.

In 1950 C. H. Roberts published the first volume of a new series of papyrus fragments ranging from the 2nd to the 4th cents.

The principal vellum uncial MSS, which are of course the main foundation of our textual knowledge, are as follows (see also TEXT OF NT):

ℵ or S. *Codex Sinaiticus*, 4th cent., 43 leaves at Leipzig, 156 (besides the whole NT) in the British Museum, containing fragments of Genesis and Numbers, 1 Ch 9^{27}–19^{17}, 2 Es 9^{9} to end, Esther, Tobit, Judith, 1 and 4 Maccabees, Isaiah, Jeremiah, La 1^{1}–2^{20}, Joel, Obadiah, Jonah, Nahum–Malachi, and the poetical books. Its text is of a very mixed character. It has a strong element in common with B, and yet is often independent of it. In Tobit it has a quite different text from that of A and B. Its origin is probably composite, so that it is not possible to assign it to any one school. Its most important correctors are C^{a} and C^{b}, both of the end of the 6th or the beginning of the 7th cents., the former of whom states, in a note appended to Esdras and Esther, that he collated the MS with a very early copy, which itself had been corrected by the hand of Pamphilus.

A. *Codex Alexandrinus*, 5th cent., in the British Museum; complete except in Ps 49^{19}–79^{10} and smaller lacunae, chiefly in Genesis; 3 and 4 Maccabees are included. The Psalter is liturgical, and is preceded by the Epistle of Athanasius on the Psalter, and the *Hypotheseis* of Eusebius; a number of canticles, or chants are appended to it. The text is written by at least two scribes; the principal corrections are by the original scribes and a reviser of not much later date. It is almost certainly of Egyptian origin, and has sometimes been supposed to represent the edition of Hesychius, but this is by no means certain yet. In Judges it has a text wholly different from that of B, and in general the two MSS represent different types of text; the quotations from the LXX in the NT tend to support A rather than B.

B. *Codex Vaticanus*, 4th cent., in the Vatican; complete, except for the loss of Gn 1^{1}–46^{28}, 2 Kings (=2 Samuel) $2^{5-7, 10-13}$, Ps $105(106)^{27}$–$137(138)^{6}$, and the omission of 1–4 Maccabees. Its character appears to vary in different books, but in general Hort's description seems sound, that it is closely akin to the text which Origen had before him when he set about his Hexapla. It is probably of Egyptian origin, and is the oldest and generally the best extant copy of the Greek OT. Its quality varies in different books; in Deuteronomy, Isaiah, 1 Chronicles, and 1–2 Esdras it seems to be inferior to A, but elsewhere on the whole superior.

C. *Codex Ephraemi rescriptus*, 5th cent., at Paris; 64 leaves, palimpsest, containing parts of the poetical books.

GREEK VERSIONS OF OT

D. *The Cotton Genesis*, 5th cent., in the British Museum; an illustrated copy of Genesis, almost wholly destroyed by fire in 1731, but partially known from collations made previously.

E. *The Bodleian Genesis*, 10th cent., Oxford, lacks Gn 14^{7}–18^{24} 20^{14}–24^{54}.

F. *Codex Ambrosianus*, 5th cent., Milan, contains Gn 31^{15}–Jos 12^{12} with numerous losses and fragments of Isaiah and Malachi.

G. *Codex Sarravianus*, 5th cent., 130 leaves at Leiden, 22 at Paris, and one at Leningrad; contains portions of the Octateuch in a Hexaplaric text, with Origen's apparatus (incompletely reproduced, however) of asterisks and obeli.

H. *Codex Petropolitanus*, 6th cent., Leningrad, a palimpsest containing portions of Numbers.

I. *Bodleian MS of Psalms*, 9th cent. In the margin it gives many readings from Aquila, Theodotion, Symmachus, the Quinta, and the Septima.

K. *Codex Lipsiensis*, 7th cent., palimpsest of 22 leaves, fragments of Numbers, Deuteronomy, Joshua, Judges.

L. *The Vienna Genesis*, 5th or 6th cent., in silver letters on purple vellum, with illustrations; contains Genesis incomplete.

M. *Codex Coislinianus*, 7th cent., Paris, Gn–3 K (1 K) 8^{40} with some losses.

N–V. *Codex Basiliano-Venetus*, 8th or 9th cent., partly in the Vatican and partly at Venice; contains portions of the OT, from Lv 13^{59}–4 Mac. Of importance chiefly as having been used (in conjunction with B) for the Sistine edition of the LXX printed at Rome in 1587.

O. *Codex Dublinensis rescriptus*, 6th cent., Trinity College, Dublin; a palimpsest of 8 leaves written in Egypt, apparently representing the text of Hesychius.

Q. *Codex Marchalianus*, 6th cent., in the Vatican; contains the Prophets, complete. Written in Egypt; its text is believed to be Hesychian, and it contains a large number of Hexaplaric signs and readings from the Hexapla in its margins, which are of great importance.

R. *Codex Veronensis*, 6th cent., at Verona; contains Psalter, in Greek and Latin, with the addition of several canticles.

T. *Zürich Psalter*, 7th cent., written in silver letters, with gold initials, on purple vellum; the canticles are included.

Γ. Codex Cryptoferratensis, 8th or 9th cent., in Basilian Monastery of Grotta Ferrata. It consists partly of palimpsest leaves, which once belonged to a great codex of the Prophets.

Θ. Theta, Codex Washingtonianus I., of the 6th cent., found in Egypt, contains Deuteronomy and Joshua.

Of minuscule MSS over 300 are known, and some of them are of considerable importance in establishing the texts of the various recensions of the LXX. Most of them are known mainly from the collations of Holmes and Parsons, which are often imperfect; the Cambridge and Göttingen editions of the LXX, now in progress, give more exact information with regard to selected representatives of them. In the edition of Holmes and Parsons no less than 277 such MSS are described. The total number of minuscules may be about 1560.

11. The Versions of the LXX are of considerable importance for identifying the various local texts. The following are the most important.

(*a*) The *Bohairic* version of Lower Egypt, the latest of the Coptic versions, and the only one which is complete. The analysis of its character is still imperfect. It is natural to look to it for the Hesychian text, but it is doubtful how far this can be assumed, and in the case of the Minor Prophets it has been denied by Deissmann as the result of his examination of the Heidelberg papyrus. In the Psalms it agrees closely with B, in the Major Prophets rather with AQ, while in the Book of Daniel it is Hexaplaric with an Egyptian or Hesychian background.

(*b*) The *Sahidic* version of Upper Egypt; Job and Psalms are extant complete, and there are considerable fragments of other books. In Psalms the text agrees substantially with that of the papyrus Psalters, and is said to be pre-Origenian, but considerably corrupted. In Job also it is pre-Origenian, and its text is shorter by one-sixth than the received text. In the Book of Daniel it was translated from Theodotion with Hexaplaric influence on an Egyptian or Hesychian background [cf H. S. Gehman, *JBL* xlvi (1927), 279–330].

(*c*) The *Syriac* versions. The Old Syriac, so important for the NT, is not known to have existed for the OT. The Peshitta appears to have been made from the Hebrew, but to have been subsequently affected by the influence of the LXX, and consequently is not wholly trustworthy for either. The most important Syriac version of the OT is the translation made from the LXX column of the Hexapla by Paul of Tella in A.D. 616–617, in which Origen's critical signs were carefully preserved; an 8th cent. MS at Milan contains the Prophets and the poetical books, while Exodus and Ruth are extant complete in other MSS, with parts of Genesis, Numbers, Joshua, Judges, and 3 and 4 Kings. The other historical books were edited in the 16th cent. from a MS which has since disappeared. This is one of the most important sources of our knowledge of Origen's work; cf H. B. Swete, *Intro. to OT in Greek* (1914), pp. 112–114.

(*d*) The *Latin* versions. These were two in number, the *Old Latin* and the *Vulgate*. On the origin of the OL, see TEXT OF THE NT. The greater part of the Heptateuch (Gn 16^{9}–Jg 20^{31}, but with mutilations) is extant in a MS at Lyons of the 5th–6th cent. Portions of the Prophets and Daniel are extant in *Codd. Wirceburgensis* (5th cent.), *Constantiensis* (5th cent.), and *Sangallensis* (9th–10th cent.). The non-Massoretic books (our Apocrypha), except Judith and Tobit, were not translated by Jerome, and consequently were incorporated in the Vulgate from the OL; Ruth survives in one MS, the Psalms in two, and Esther in several; and considerable fragments of most of the other books are extant in palimpsests and other incomplete MSS. In addition we have the quotations of Cyprian and other early Latin Fathers; cf *Corpus Scriptorum Eccl. Lat.* (Vienna, 1866–); Sabatier, P., *Latinae Ver. Ant. seu Vetus Italica* (Rheims, 1739–1749; Paris, 1751). The importance of the OL lies in the fact that its origin goes back to the 2nd cent., and it is consequently pre-Hexaplaric. Also, since its affinities are rather with Antioch than with Alexandria, it preserves readings from a type of text prevalent in Syria, that, namely, on which Lucian subsequently based his recension. This type of text may not be superior to the Alexandrian, but at least it deserves consideration. On the OL, see Kennedy in Hastings' *DB*, Burkitt's *The Old Latin and the Itala* (1896), and Montgomery, *Daniel*, *ICC*, 29–32 (1927). On the Vulgate, see article *s.v.* Since it was, in the main, a re-translation from the Hebrew, it does not (except in the Psalter) come into consideration in connexion with the LXX.

The *Arabic* versions. The expansion of Islam beyond the confines of Arabia after the death of Mohammed (632) was followed by the translation of the Bible into Arabic. Probably partial translations were prepared in the 7th cent. for Christians in the Orient. It is recorded that in 724 a version was made in Spain by John, bishop of Seville, with the intentions of helping the Christians and the Moors. Psalms, Proverbs, and the Prophets seem to be based on a Greek text resembling that of A. In the case of the Book of Daniel the text of the Paris (1645) and the London (1657) Polyglots is vastly superior to that of A, and for this book it is the best representative of the Hexaplaric text that we possess [cf H. S. Gehman, *JBL* xlv (1925), 327–352].

The *Ethiopic* versions. According to tradition Christianity was brought to Ethiopia in the time of Constantine the Great (324–337). Frumentius, a Syrian, was consecrated bishop of Fthiopia before 370, *c* 330 by Athanasius, the patriarch of Alexandria. It is possible that Frumentius began the work of rendering the Scriptures from Greek into Ethiopic or had it done under his supervision. According to another tradition the Bible was translated into Ethiopic by the Nine

GREEK VERSIONS OF OT

Saints, who had fled after the Council of Chalcedon (451) from Syria to Egypt, whence they went to Abyssinia. Probably the translation was begun in the second half of the 4th cent. before the arrival of the Nine Saints, who may have revised the original rendering. In Kings the Ethiopic is based on a Greek text like that of B with a strong Lucianic influence. Probably these two strands may indicate the introduction of Christianity from Alexandria and from Syria. The Old Ethiopic has a decided value in LXX studies. Later the Ethiopic Bible was revised on the basis of Arabic translations [cf H. S. Gehman, *JBL* l (1931), 81–114].

The *Armenian* and *Georgian* versions. According to Moses of Chorene, an Armenian writer of the 5th cent., the first edition was translated from a Syriac text by Sahak (patriarch 390–428). It is said that by 411 Mesrop, with the aid of Rufinus, had translated the entire Bible from Greek, beginning with Proverbs; this may imply that the previous books had been rendered by unknown translators. After the Council of Ephesus (431) a Greek Bible from Constantinople was used by Sahak and Mesrop in making a revision. Subsequently Moses of Chorene and others were sent to Alexandria, and it seems that this visit had a decided influence upon the Armenian text. Generally the Armenian of the OT is based on the Hexaplaric recension. In the Book of Daniel it represents an Origenian-Constantinopolitan text, but it has agreements with the Hesychian group; an influence from Syriac is also apparent. The Armenian language is so well adapted to render the Greek literally that an Armenian codex has almost the same value for the critic as the Greek original on which it is based [cf H. S. Gehman, *ZAW*, Neue Folge vii (1930), 82–99; *Arm. Version of I and II Kings*, *JAOS* liv (1934), 53–59].

The Georgian Bible, aptly called the twin sister of the Armenian, was completed by the end of the 6th cent. The original rendering has an Armenian-Syriac foundation, but also shows some Greek influence.

The *Gothic* version was made from the Greek *c* 350 by Ulfilas, bishop of the Visigoths. The few fragments of the OT that remain show that it was rendered from the Lucianic recension.

12. The evidence of the Fathers has been less fully used for the LXX than for the NT, but its importance in distinguishing and localizing types of text is increasingly recognized.

Origen is of particular importance for his express statements on textual matters, though his declared acceptance of the Hebrew as the standard of truth has to be remembered in weighing his evidence. Much the same may be said of *Jerome*. Fathers who had no interest in textual criticism are often more valuable as witnesses to the type of text in use in their age and country. Thus *Cyril of Alexandria* gives us an Egyptian text, which may probably be that of Hesychius. *Theodoret* and *Chrysostom*, who belong to Antioch, represent the Syrian text, *i.e.* the recension of Lucian. *Cyprian* is a principal witness for the African Old Latin. The Apostolic Fathers, notably *Clement of Rome* and *Barnabas*, carry us farther back, and contribute some evidence towards a decision between the rival texts represented by A and B, their tendency on the whole being in favour of the former; and the same is the case with *Irenaeus, Justin*, and *Clement of Alexandria*, though their results are by no means uniform.

13. With these materials the critic has to approach the problem of the restoration of the text of the LXX. Ideally, what is desirable is that it should be possible to point out the three main recensions, those of Origen, Lucian, and Hesychius, and thence to go back to the text which lies behind them all, that of the LXX or Old Greek. Some progress has been made in this direction. Some MSS are generally recognized as being predominantly Lucianic; some readings are certainly known to be Hexaplaric; but we are still far from an agreement on all points. Especially is this the case with the recension of Hesychius. Some scholars have identified it (notably in the Prophets) with the text of A, which, however, seems certainly to have been modified by the influence of Origen. More recently the tendency has been to find it in B; but here it is still open to question whether B is not mainly both pre-Hesychian and pre-Origenian. It would be unjustifiable to pretend at present that certainty has been arrived at on these points. And with regard to the great bulk of MSS, it is clear that their texts are of a mixed character. In the Psalms it would appear that the recension of Lucian was, in the main, adopted at Constantinople, and so became the common text of the Church; but in regard to the other books, the common text, which appears in the bulk of the later MSS, cannot be identified with any of the three primary recensions. The influence of the Hebrew, especially after the example of Origen, was constantly a disturbing factor; it should be pointed out that there were also pre-recensional revisions in Greek MSS on the basis of a Hebrew text, as may be noted in the Scheide papyri of Ezekiel.

14. And when that is done, the question of the relation of the LXX to the Hebrew still remains. No other version differs so widely from its presumed original as the LXX does from the Massoretic Hebrew; but it is by no means easy to say how far this is due to the mistakes and liberties of the translators, and how far to the fact that the text before them differed from the Massoretic. That the latter was the case to some extent is certain. Readings in which the LXX is supported against the Massoretic by the Samaritan text must almost certainly represent a divergent Hebrew original; but unfortunately the Samaritan exists only for the Pentateuch, in which the variants are least. Elsewhere we have generally to depend on internal evidence; and the more the LXX is studied in detail, the less willing, as a rule, is the student to maintain its authority against the Hebrew, and the less certain that its variants really represent differences in the original text. In this respect the Dead Sea Scrolls will have great importance, and it appears that the Qumrân fragments were influenced by the Hebrew tradition that lies behind the LXX, but naturally they do not reproduce the same Hebrew text as lay before the translators. While the St. Mark's scroll of Isaiah, in the main, confirms the accuracy and antiquity of MT, it has a number of readings in agreement with the LXX. On this subject, cf F. M. Cross, *The Ancient Library of Qumran and Modern Biblical Studies* (1958); M. Burrows, *More Light on the Dead Sea Scrolls* (1958). There are also divergences arising, not from a different Hebrew text, but from supplying different vowel points to a text which originally had none. All these factors have to be taken into account before we can safely say that the Hebrew which lay before the LXX translators must have been different from the Massoretic text; and each passage must be judged on its own merits.

The literalisms in the LXX often imply that the interpreters had a high regard for the exact letter, and some of the crudities of the Greek may give such an origin. Yet often in the same verse or in adjacent verses are found both literalisms and extreme freedom of rendering. With such a style a certain balance of approach was maintained by the translators, and there should also be stressed the spirit of freedom in the LXX; this may be observed even in the naming and arrangement of various books. Sometimes it appears that a translator by playing with a root obtained the meaning he desired or achieved good sense. The freedom of the Septuagint is often to be observed in the realm of theology, as, *e.g.*, in its anti-anthropomorphisms or in passages which were changed or toned down to avoid offence. Yet the translators did not set out to rewrite the text, and due restraint was exercised in making changes for theological reasons. When all is considered, it appears that the LXX had a Hebrew original closer to MT than commentators have often assumed. In textual studies, however, it is also important to consult the Hebrew variants collated by Kennicott and de Rossi, for here are found some agreements with the Old Greek and the recensions [cf H. S. Gehman, 'Theological Approach of

Gr. Translator of Job 1–15,' *JBL*, lxviii (1949), 231–240; 'Exegetical Methods—Gr. Translator of 1 Sam.,' *JAOS*, lxx (1950), 292–296; C. T. Fritsch, *The Anti-Anthropomorphisms of the Gr. Pentateuch* (1943); D. H. Gard, *The Exeg. Method of the Gr. Translator—Job, JBL Monograph Series*, viii (1952)].

II. Aquila (Aq.).—15. Of the rival Greek versions which, as mentioned in **7**, came into being in the 2nd cent., the first usually cited is that of Aquila, a Gentile of Sinope, in Pontus, who was converted first to Christianity and then to Judaism. It is probable, however, that Theodotion should precede him chronologically. He is said to have been a pupil of Rabbi Akiba, and to have flourished in the reign of Hadrian (A.D. 117–138). His translation of the OT was made in the interests of Jewish orthodoxy. The text which subsequently received the name of Massoretic had practically been fixed by the Jewish scholars at the end of the 1st cent., and Aquila followed it with slavish fidelity. All thought for the genius and usage of the Greek language was thrown aside, and the Greek was forced to follow the idiosyncrasies of the Hebrew in defiance of sense and grammar. Aq. would consequently be an excellent witness to the Hebrew text of the 2nd cent., if only it existed intact; but we possess only small fragments of it. These consist for the most part (until recently, wholly) of fragments of Origen's third column preserved in the margins of Hexaplar MSS (such as Q); but they have been supplemented by modern discoveries. The Milan palimpsest of the Hexapla (see **8**), discovered by Mercati in 1896, contains the text of Aq. for eleven Psalms. The Cambridge fragment published by Dr. C. Taylor gives the text of Ps $22^{15-18, 20-28}$. In 1897 F. C. Burkitt discovered three palimpsest leaves of a MS of Aq. (5th–6th cent.) among a large quantity of tattered MSS brought, like the last-mentioned fragment, from Cairo; and these, which contain 3 K 20^{7-17} and 4 K 23^{11-27}, were published in 1897. Further fragments, from the same source and of the same date, published by Dr. C. Taylor (1900), contain Ps 90^{17}–92^{10} 96^{7}–97^{12} 98^{3} 102^{16}–103^{13}; and in 1900 Messrs. Grenfell and Hunt published Gn 1^{1-5} in the versions of the LXX and Aq. from a papyrus of the 4th cent. in the collection of Lord Amherst. These discoveries confirm our previous knowledge of the characteristics of Aq.; and it is noteworthy that in the Cambridge MSS of Aq. the Divine Tetragrammaton is written in the old Hebrew characters.

III. Theodotion (Theod.).—16. The origin of this version must be ascribed to a desire to have a Greek version of the OT which should correspond better than the LXX with the current Hebrew text. Theodotion, though sometimes described as a Jewish proselyte, appears rather to have been an Ebionitic Christian, who lived at Ephesus about the first third of the 2nd cent. This version follows in the main the authorized Hebrew, but is much more free than Aq., and agrees more with the LXX. Hence when Origen, in the execution of his plan for bringing the LXX into accord with the Hebrew, had to supply omissions in the LXX, he had recourse to Theod. for the purpose. Further, the LXX version of Daniel being regarded as unsatisfactory, the version of Theod. was taken into use instead, and so effectually that the LXX of this book has survived in but one single MS. (Chigi, or 87). It is probable, however, that Theod. was not wholly original in this book, for there are strong traces of Theodotionic readings in the NT (Hebrews and Apocalypse), Hermas, Clement, and Justin; whence it seems necessary to conclude that Theod. based his version on one which had been previously in existence side by side with the LXX; this is generally referred to as Ur-Theodotion, or pre-Theodotion.

17. Besides this complete book and the extracts from the Hexapla and the Milan palimpsest (the Theodotion column in the Cambridge MS is lost), there is some reason to believe that still more of Theod. has survived than was formerly supposed. It is well known that the book which appears in our Apocrypha as 1 Esdras, and in the Greek Bible as *Ἔσδρας Α'*, is simply a different recension of the canonical book of Ezra (with parts of 2 Chronicles and Nehemiah), which in the Greek Bible appears (with Nehemiah) as *Ἔσδρας Β'*. *Ἔσδρας Β'* faithfully represents the Massoretic Hebrew; *Ἔσδρας Α'* is freely paraphrastic, and contains some additional matter (1Es 3^{1}–5^{6}). Josephus, who knew the LXX, but not, of course, Theod., plainly follows *Ἔσδ. Α'*; and it has been argued by Whiston (in 1722) and Sir H. Howorth (*PSBA*, May 1901–Nov. 1902) that *Ἔσδ. Α'* is the original LXX version, and *Ἔσδ. Β'* the version of Theod., which, as in Daniel, has ousted its predecessor from general use.

IV. Symmachus (Symm.).—18. Of Symm. there is less to say. Like Theodotion, he has been called an Ebionite, and like both Theodotion and Aquila, he has been said to be a proselyte to Judaism; the former statement is probably true. His work was known to Origen by about 228, and was probably produced quite at the end of the 2nd cent. From the literary point of view, it was the best of all the Greek versions of the OT. It was based, like Aq. and Theod., on a text like the Massoretic Hebrew, but it aimed at rendering it into idiomatic Greek. Consequently, it neither had the reputation which Aq. acquired among the Jews, nor was it so well fitted as Theod. to make good the defects, real or supposed, of the LXX among the Christians; and its historical importance is therefore less than that of its rivals. The extant materials for its study are practically the same as in the case of Aq., namely, the two fragments of MSS of the Hexapla [the Cambridge fragment contains the Symm. column for Ps $22^{15-18, 20-24}$; the precise extent of the Milan MS is not known], and the copious extracts from the Hexapla in the margins of certain MSS and the quotations of the Fathers.

LITERATURE.—An indispensable handbook for LXX studies is H. B. Swete's *Introd. to the OT in Greek*, revised by R. R. Ottley (1914). See also Nestle's article in Hastings' *DB*, and his *Septuagintastudien* (1886–1907); cf H. S. Gehman 'Septuagint' in *Twentieth Century Encyclopedia of Religious Knowledge* (1955). A popular account with a description of all the uncial MSS is given in Kenyon's *Our Bible and the Ancient MSS* (revised by A. W. Adams, 1958). Important works are Rahlfs' *Septuaginta-Studien* (I., 1904), on the text of Kings; II., 1907, on Psalms) and R. L. Ottley's *Book of Isaiah according to the Septuagint* (2 vols., 1904–1906). The remains of the Hexapla are collected in F. Field's *Origenis Hexaplorum quae supersunt* (Oxford, 1875). Ceriani's study of the Codex Marchalianus and Deissmann's of the Heidelberg Prophets-papyrus make important contributions to the classification of the MSS. The English translation of the LXX by Charles Thomson was published in Philadelphia in 1808; in 1904 the same version with an editorial preface by S. F. Pells was reprinted in London. Finally, the Thomson translation, edited and revised by C. A. Muses, was published by the Falcon Press (Indian Hills, Colo., 1954). Another by L. C. L. Brenton was published in 1844.

Editions.—The LXX was first printed in the Complutensian Polyglot (1514–1517, published 1521), but first published by Aldus (1519). The standard edition is that issued at Rome by Pope Sixtus V. in 1587. This, by excellent fortune, was based mainly on the Codex Vaticanus (B), with the help of the Venice MS (V), and others, but it is not a critical edition in the modern sense. An edition based on the Codex Alexandrinus (A) was published at Oxford by Grabe in 1707–1720. The textual criticism of the LXX rests upon the great edition of R. Holmes and J. Parsons (Oxford, 1798–1827), who printed the Sixtine text with an apparatus drawn from 20 uncial and 277 minuscule MSS, besides versions. Unfortunately several of the collations made by their assistants were not up to modern standards of accuracy. Tischendorf published a revised text, with various readings from a few of the leading uncials (1850; 7th edition, 1887); but the foundation of recent textual study of the LXX was laid by the Cambridge manual edition (*The Old Testament in Greek*) in three volumes by Swete (1887–1894; revised 1895–1899). In this the text is printed from B, when available; otherwise from A or א, and the textual apparatus gives all the variants in the principal uncial MSS. A larger edition, giving the same text, but with the addition of the evidence of all the uncials, a considerable number of carefully selected and representative minuscules, and the principal versions and patristic quotations, was begun under the editorship of A. E. Brooke and N. Mclean. Vol. I: *The Octateuch* was published in four parts (1906–1917). The same scholars together with H. St. J. Thackeray edited Vol. II: *The Later Historical Books* (Samuel, Kings, Chronicles, 1 Esdras, 2 Esdras (Ezra–Nehemiah), which appeared in four parts (1927–1935); Vol. III, part 1 (Esther, Judith, Tobit) edited by the same three men, was published in 1940. Another important edition with an extensive critical apparatus is the *Septuaginta, V. T. Graecum* (Göttingen). The following have appeared to date: Vol. IX, 1: 1 *Maccabees*, edited W. Kappler (1931); Vol. IX, 2: 2 *Maccabees*, edited by R. Hanhart (1959); Vol. IX, 3: 3 *Maccabees*, edited by R. Hanhart 1960); Vol. X: *Psalms with the Odes*, edited A. Rahlfs (1931); Vol. XIII: *Twelve Minor Prophets* (1943); Vol. XIV: *Isaiah* (1939); Vol. XV: *Jeremiah, Baruch, Lamentations, Epistle of Jeremiah* (1957); Vol. XVI, 1: *Ezekiel* (1952); Vol. XVI, 2: *Susanna, Daniel, Bel and the Dragon* (1954). The last five publications have been edited by J. Ziegler. A good manual edition is that by A. Rahlfs, *Septuaginta, id est V. T. Graece iuxta LXX Interpretes*, Stuttgart, 1935. F. G. K.—H. S. G.

GREEN, GREENISH.—See Colours, **1.**

GREETING.—See Salutation.

GREYHOUND.—See Dog.

GRIDDLE.—Lv 2^{5} 6^{21} 7^{9} (RSV); see House, **9.**

GRINDER.—In Ec 12^{3} the 'grinders' are the teeth, as the context clearly indicates. In Job 29^{17}, where AVm has 'grinders' (AV, RV 'jaws'), RSV has 'fangs,' as also in Ps 58^{6} (AV, RV 'great teeth'), Jl 1^{6} (AV 'cheek teeth,' RV 'jaw teeth'), where the same word is used.

GRISLED.—See Colours, **1.**

GROUND.—See Earth.

GROVE.—Apart from Gn 21^{33}, to be presently mentioned, 'grove' is everywhere in AV a mistaken translation, which goes back through the Vulgate to the LXX, of the name of the Canaanite goddess *Asherah*. The 'groves,' so often said to have been, or to be deserving to be, 'cut down,' were the wooden poles set up as symbols of Asherah. See further the article Asherah.

In Gn 21^{33} the grove which AV makes Abraham plant in Beer-sheba was really 'a **tamarisk** tree' (so RV, RSV), a tree which also figures in the story of Saul, 1 S 22^{6} 31^{13} (both RV, RSV). A. R. S. K.

GRUDGE.—The word 'grudge' formerly stood for dissatisfaction expressed aloud, *i.e.* murmur, grumble; but by 1611 it was becoming confined to the feeling rather than the open expression, so that it occurs in AV less frequently than in the older versions. It has the older meaning in AV in Ps 59^{15} 'Let them wander up and down for meat, and grudge if they be not satisfied' (RSV 'growl,' RV 'tarry all night'). The older meaning is found also in AV in Wis 12^{27} (RV 'were indignant,' RSV 'became incensed'), Sir 10^{25} (RV 'murmur,' RSV 'grumble'), and Ja 5^{9} (RV 'murmur,' RSV 'grumble').

GUARANTEE.—See Earnest.

GUARD, BODY-GUARD.—The former is used in EV almost exclusively for the body-guard of royal and other high-placed personages, such as Nehemiah (Neh 4^{22f}) and Holofernes (Jth 12^{7}). 'Body-guard' occurs in RV only in 1 Es 3^{4} (so RSV) of the 'guard' (AV) of Darius, but it occurs several times else in RSV (1 S 22^{14} 28^{2}, **2** S 23^{23}, 2 K 25^{8}, 1 Ch 11^{25}, Jer 52^{12}) for a variety of expressions in AV and RV. The members of the body-guard of the Pharaoh of Gn 37^{36} and of Nebuchadnezzar (2 K 25^{8} etc.) are, in the original style, 'slaughterers (of animals for food),' not as RVm 'executioners.' Those composing the body-guard of the Hebrew kings, on the other hand, are styled '**runners**' (1 S 22^{17} RV and margin, 2 K 10^{25} 11^{4} etc.), one of their duties being to run in front of the royal state-chariot (cf 2 S 15^{1}, 1 K 1^{5}). In 1 K 14^{28} we hear of a guardroom. The office of 'the captain of the guard' was at all times one of great dignity and responsibility. David's body-guard consisted of foreign mercenaries, the Cherethites, and Pelethites (see Cherethites), commanded by Benaiah (2 S 20^{23} compared with 23^{23}). The famous **Praetorian guard** of the Roman emperors is mentioned in Ph 1^{13} RV and RSV; also Ac 28^{16} AV in a passage absent from the best texts (also RV and RSV). A. R. S. K.

GUARD, GATE OF THE.—A gate on the NE. side of Jerusalem, Neh 12^{39} (AV **the prison gate**). Its location is uncertain. Vincent thinks it is the same as the **Muster Gate** (q.v.).

GUDGODAH.—A station in the journeyings of the Israelites (Dt 10^{7}), when they proceeded to Jotbathah. There can be little doubt that **Hor-haggidgad** (AV **Hor-hagidgad**) in the itinerary of Nu 33^{32f} indicates the same place. It perhaps lay in the *Wâdī Khaḍākhid*.

GUEST, GUESTCHAMBER.—See Hospitality.

GUILT.—In a series of OT usages it is hardly possible to distinguish sin itself, guilt as the state of responsibility for sin committed, and punishment as the consequence. Such a case is in the story of Cain, Gn 4^{13}, using *ʿāwōn* 'iniquity,' where it would be equally possible to translate by Cain's iniquity, his punishment or his guilt. The sin is a reality which has to be 'carried,' and remains to display guilt and invoke punishment. So we have the phrase 'to bear his iniquity,' where the same triple connotation is found (Lv 5$^{1, 17}$ etc.). Only by the proper expiation is the sin removed, and with it the guilt and punishment, if these latter can be distinguished. Where there is no expiation, 'his iniquity shall be upon him' (Nu 15^{31}), *i.e.* it and its destructive effects are not wiped away (see Expiation).

'Guilt' is also an approximate rendering in many contexts of the Hebrew *'āshām*, the range of whose meaning might be given as damage done, responsibility for damage done, restitution of damage, and the offering of reintegration ('guilt offering') which accompanies the restitution. Joseph's brothers are responsible or guilty, because of their unmerciful treatment of him, and so distress comes upon them (Gn 42^{21}). Guilt may exist even where the person is unconscious of wrong done (Lv 5^{17}), and must be expiated. The sin of the anointed priest may be 'to the guilt of the people,' Lv 4^{3}. Here too punishment may be included in the range of meaning, *e.g.* Hos 13^{16}, where the verbal form of this root, 'shall be guilty' (RSV 'bear her guilt'), seems clearly to have the content of 'shall pay the penalty' of guilt. The emphasis is generally not on subjective feelings of guilt, but on an actual burden of sin; on the other hand the existence of this guilt is destructive to the integrity of the person.

In judicial use, however, it is most usual to use the terms *rāshāʿ* 'evildoer, person in the wrong' and *ṣaddiḳ* 'person in the right,' and the causative forms of the related verbs in a declarative sense as 'declare in the wrong, guilty' and 'declare in the right, vindicate.' Such are the terms of a judge's decision, Dt 25^{1}. God as judge does the same thing, and recompenses men for their conduct, 1 K 8^{32}. A general judicial sense appears in the NT in places like the trial of Jesus by Pilate, where Pilate finds no *aition*, no guilt deserving punishment, in the man Jesus (Lk 23$^{4, 14, 22}$).

We also have in the NT the term *enochos*, which is often connected syntactically not with the crime but with the punishment, and is therefore often rendered in English 'liable to.' In the LXX this term is sometimes used to translate the Hebrew phrases where 'blood' is a term for guilt or responsibility and also for the corresponding recompense or exaction of justice. In Jos 2^{19f} an oath includes particulars of the circumstances in which the parties shall be clean or guiltless and in which 'the blood shall be on their head,' or as LXX puts it, they shall be responsible or guilty. So LXX in Lv $20^{9, 11}$ etc. The prime cause of blood-guiltiness (Hebrew usually simply 'blood') is of course the killing of a man, and even where this is accidental, as we would call it, expiatory measures must be taken, and asylum is provided for the killer, on whom otherwise vengeance will properly be taken (Dt 19^{4-13} 21^{1-9}, Nu 35^{9-34}). For the guilt of intentional murder there is no expiation but by the blood of the guilty (Nu 35^{33}).

In the NT the term *enochos* then means guilty of or liable to fault or punishment. So in the straight legal sense Mt 26^{66} (RSV 'he deserves death'), and for Mt 5^{22} the sense has been suggested 'guilty enough to go into the hell of fire.' The sense 'guilty' is clear in Mk 3^{29} (of the blasphemy against the Holy Spirit), and in two passages the reference is to that which is violated or outraged: 1 Co 11^{27} (the body and blood of the Lord) and Ja 2^{10} (the whole of the law).

For the more general problems in which the concept of guilt is a part see Sin, Atonement, Justification, etc.

J. Ba.

GUILT-OFFERING.—See Sacrifice and Offering.

GULF.—The only instance of the use of this word in the Bible occurs in the parable of Dives and Lazarus (Lk 16^{26} AV; RSV 'chasm'; cf Nu 16^{30} where the word 'pit' is the translation of *Hades* or *Sheol*; RSV 'Sheol'). Some commentators have discovered in Jesus' employment of this term as well as in His assertion of the possibility of conversation, an approval in general terms of a current Jewish belief that the souls of the righteous and of the wicked exist after death in different compartments of the same under-world. It is not possible, however, to construct a theory of Jesus' teaching as to the intermediate state from evidence so scanty.

GUNI.—**1.** The eponym of a Naphtalite family, Gn 46^{24}, 1 Ch 7^{13} (cf Nu 26^{48} where the gentilic **Gunites** occurs). **2.** A Gadite chief, 1 Ch 5^{15}. **3.** Probably we should also read 'the Gunite' for '**Jonathan**' in 2 S 23^{32} (cf S. R. Driver, *Notes on . . . the Books of Samuel*², 1913, p. 371); and for 'the **Gizonite**' in 1 Ch 11^{34}.

GUR.—An 'ascent' by Ibleam and Beth-haggan, 2 K 9^{27}. The site is unknown. LXX read *Gai*='valley,' and it is possible that no place-name Gur existed (cf J. Simons, *The Geographical . . . Texts of the OT*, 1959, p. 363); but Albright identified Gur with Akkadian *Gurra* (*BASOR* 94, 1944, 21).

GUR-BAAL ('dwelling of Baal').—An unknown locality named in 2 Ch 26^{7}.

GUTTER.—See House, **5.**

H

HAAHASHTARI.—A descendant of Judah, 1 Ch 4^{6}.

HABAIAH ('Y" hath hidden').—The head of a priestly family which returned with Zerubbabel, but, being unable to trace their genealogy, were not allowed to serve, Ezr 2^{61}, Neh 7^{63} (AV; RV, RSV **Hobaiah**), 1 Es 5^{38} (AV, RV **Obdia**).

HABAKKUK.—The eighth of the Minor Prophets. Except for legends, *e.g.* in Bel and the Dragon (vv.$^{33-42}$), nothing is known of him outside of the book that bears his name.

1. The Book of Habakkuk, read as it now stands and assumed to be a unity, must be dated shortly after the appearance of the Chaldaeans on the stage of world-history, seeing that their descent on the nations is imminent. It must therefore be later than the fall of Nineveh to the combined forces of Babylon and the Medes in 612 B.C., and earlier than the first Judaean captivity in 597 B.C. If composed about the year 600 B.C., it falls in the reign of Jehoiakim, in the period of reaction that followed the defeat and death of Josiah at Megiddo (608 B.C.). That event, apparently falsifying the promises of the recently discovered law book, had led to a general neglect of its ethical claims, and to a recrudescence of the religious abuses of the time of Manasseh (cf 2 K 23^{37}, Jer 19^{4ff} 25, etc.). The book was the work of a Judaean prophet, who probably resided in Jerusalem. It may be divided into six sections. The first four contain two dialogues between Yahweh and the prophet, while the last contain confident declarations springing from and expanding the Divine reply.

(1) 1^{1-4}. Habakkuk, compelled to live in the midst of violent wrong-doing and contempt for the Law manifesting itself in the oppression of the righteous by the wicked, complains strongly of the silence and indifference of God.

(2) 1^{5-11}. He receives an answer that a new and startling display of the Divine justice is about to be made. The Chaldaeans, swift, bitter, and terrible, are to sweep down and overwhelm the whole world. No fortress can resist their onslaught.

(3) 1^{12-17}. Some time may now be supposed to elapse before the next prophecy is spoken. During this period the prophet watches the progress of the Chaldaeans, who have now (2^{17}) penetrated into Palestine. His observation raises a new and insoluble problem. This reckless, insolent, cruel, insatiable conqueror is worse than those he has been appointed to chastise. How can a holy God, so ready to punish the 'wicked' in Israel, permit one who deserves far more than the name 'wicked' to rage unchecked? Are wrong and violence to possess the earth for ever?

(4) 2^{1-4}. The prophet, retiring to his watch-tower (a place of spiritual meditation), scans with eager longing the incongruities of life, expectantly awaiting a Divine answer to his lament. He receives an oracle which he is bidden to write down on tablets for all to read. He is told that the purpose of God is hastening to its fulfilment, and is encouraged to wait for it. Then follows the famous sentence (RV), 'Behold, his soul is puffed up, it is not upright in him: but the just shall live by his faith'—better 'faithfulness' (so RSVm). Despite the obscurity of the text, the meaning seems to be that tyranny is self-destructive and carries with it the seeds of doom. But while the evil-doer passes away, the just man, steadfast in the face of all contradiction, shall live, and last out the storm of judgment.

(5) 2^{5-20}. Content with this message, the prophet utters, triumphantly, a five-fold series of woes against the pride, the greed, the cruel building enterprises, the sensuality, the idolatry of the heathen power.

(6) Ch. 3. Finally, in a magnificent lyric, the prophet laments the present turmoil, recalls God's awesome interventions in the past (especially the Exodus), and expresses confidence that God will appear once more and bring hopeless ruin upon the enemy.

So read, this short book is seen to be a prophetic autobiography of inner experience comparable to the meditations of Jeremiah. It marks the beginnings of Hebrew reflective thought as to the workings of Providence in history, afterwards so powerfully expressed in Job and in the later prophets.

2. The presence of such diverse elements has led many to question the unity of the book and to extract from it a nucleus of genuine material which has several times been supplemented and disarranged. Sometimes the divine-human encounter has been simplified by combining the laments (parts 1 and 3) and following them with the oracles (parts 2 and 4). On the side of this procedure is the use of the word 'wicked' in 1^{4} and 1^{13}, which, it is claimed, should refer to the same party. Yet 1^{1-4} best describes internal oppression, whereas 1^{12-17} depicts oppression by a foreign power.

The form-critical approach sees nothing strange in the present arrangement, the whole being organized as a liturgy for use in the Temple (or alternatively, for lectionary use in the synagogue). The alternation of lament and oracle is in this view perfectly in order. The second oracle of doom is naturally followed by the series of woes. These in turn end with a note of expectation that the Lord who resides in His holy Temple will appear to deliver His people (2^{20}; cf Zeph 1^{7}, Zec 2^{13}). The psalm (ch. 3) follows in natural sequence, not merely as an ode of faith, but by reason of the theophany which answers the expectation of 2^{20}. Habakkuk is therefore considered a cultic prophet attached to the Temple, who brilliantly conceived this liturgy and daringly carried it out in a service of public worship designed to criticize contemporary society, to invoke the judgment of God upon it, and to give assurance to the righteous of their ultimate triumph.

The arrangement of the materials may well be liturgically inspired, even if the prophet himself did not compose them all. Certainly the fifth woe (2^{18f}) reveals editorial activity; for its repudiation of idolatry is obviously unsuitable in the mouth of heathen nations (cf 2^{5f}). Ch. 3 has all the marks of having been lifted out of a song-book and inserted in this place. Its psalmlike superscription, its periodic insertion of **Selah,** and its musical subscription are found in no other prophet. The subscription is probably the heading of the hymn which followed this one in the song-book from which it was derived. This position is strengthened by the fact that the ancient commentary upon Habakkuk found in the first Qumrân Scroll Cave did not include ch. 3—despite the fact that the community which produced this scroll did write commentaries upon other Psalms.

Though some have sought to identify the 'vision' of 2^{2f} with 1^{5-11} or even ch. 3 (with consequent rearranging of the materials), the word probably means here simply 'revelation,' and is to be identified with $2^{4,\,5a}$. Only a brief text is suitable for placarding upon stone or wooden plaques (cf Is 8^{1} and 30^{8}), and certainly $2^{4,\,5a}$ is profoundly suitable as a concise summary of the prophet's message for public exhibition. With the help of the ancient versions and the newly found Habakkuk Commentary, the rather corrupt text may be restored somewhat as follows:

4a Behold, [the naughty] is haughty;
b his soul is not humble within him.
5a Be he ever so audacious and treacherous,
b the presumptuous man shall not survive;
4c but the righteous by his faithfulness shall live.

(Cf Brownlee, *The Text of Habakkuk in the Ancient Commentary from Qumrân*, *JBL* Monograph Series, vol. xi, pp. 44–48.)

Section 5, then, should begin with 5c: '*Assyria* enlarged his appetite as Sheol.' For 'Assyria' the traditional reading is 'who,' but the two words in the original consonantal text are spelled the same. The misreading of the word as 'who' required the removal of 4c from its original position in order to find a suitable antecedent. It is not at all surprising that Habakkuk should have composed a section of taunt songs concerning Assyria (cf Nahum), even though, as seems probable, the oppressor in 1^{6} is truly the Chaldaeans; for concurrent with the rise of Babylonia was the fall of Assyria. Section 5, therefore, may have been composed shortly after the fall of Nineveh (612 B.C.), or even after the Battle of Carchemish (605 B.C.) when the last vestige of the Assyrian kingdom was obliterated. The lesson concerning the fall of Assyria was placed here as an historical illustration of the principle enunciated in $2^{4,\,5a}$: 'tyranny is suicide, and may be expected to repeat itself in the case of the Chaldaeans.'

3. Considerable interest attaches to the Commentary of Hab found among the Dead Sea Scrolls. Portion by portion the text of the first two chapters is quoted and interpreted. The text is valuable, though sometimes shaped by sectarian interests. The interpretations are midrashic in character. They employ far-fetched verbal play and twisting in order to discover the hidden meanings of the prophet concerning the latter days. The 'Chaldaeans' are the 'Kittim,' itself a cryptic cypher (as some think) for the Seleucid rulers of Syria Palestine, or even more probably for the Romans who had but recently arrived as the new conquerors of the world. The 'wicked one' who circumvented the 'righteous' (1^{4}) is the Wicked Priest who persecuted the Teacher of Righteousness and his followers. The term Wicked Priest (*hak-kōhēn hā-rāshā'*) parodies the title Chief Priest (*hak-kōhēn hā-rō'sh*) and doubtless refers to some Hasmonaean (or pre-Hasmonaean) priest(s) who oppressed the Teacher and his community. The Wicked Priest is the understood object of the taunts of 2^{5-17} also.

The most significant interpretation is that of 2^{4}: 'The righteous shall live by his faithfulness.' The explanation is: 'Its meaning concerns the doers of the Law in the house of Judah, whom God will deliver from the house of damnation for the sake of their painful toil and their faith in the Teacher of Righteousness.' The equations of this exposition are clear: 'righteous' equals 'doers of the law,' 'faithfulness' (Heb. *'emûnāh*) means both 'painful toil' (therefore 'faithfulness') and 'faith.' 'To live' means to survive the persecution of the 'house of damnation' (the Hasmonaean party ?) and possibly also to escape the eschatological doom of that house. This prepares the way for Paul's application of the verse to faith in Jesus the Christ (Ro 1^{17}, Gal 3^{11}). The meaning of the OT was not static, but by constant reinterpretation was prepared to become an adequate witness to the Redeemer who fulfilled the highest hopes attached to the OT prophecies, and even surpassed them. In the present case, Paul's interpretation is salvation by faith alone (though naturally it will be completed by works) and even this is the condition rather than the meritorious ground for deliverance. The linking of 'painful toil and faith' in the Hab Commentary suggests that 'faith' is but another meritorious work. This becomes certain when one observes that the Teacher of the Scroll was in no way a redeemer, like the Christ, but only a revealer of God's eschatological will. The deliverances are also different, for salvation in Paul's understanding is no mere safeguard of the righteous, but it is the power of God whereby the wicked may become righteous and partake of eternal life.

W. J. M.—W. H. Br.

HABAZINIAH, Jer 35^{3} (AV).—See HABAZZINIAH.

HABAZZINIAH.—The grandfather of Jaazaniah, one of the Rechabites who were put to the proof by the prophet Jeremiah, Jer 35^{3} (AV **Habaziniah**).

HABERGEON.—An obsolete term replaced in RV by 'coat of mail' (Ex 28^{32} 39^{3}; but RSV 'garment'). In 2 Ch 26^{14}, Neh 4^{16} RV and RSV have 'coat of mail.' In Job 41^{26}, where a different word stands, RV has 'pointed shaft' and RSV 'javelin.' See also ARMOUR, ARMS, **2** (*c*).

HABIRU.—Akkadian *ḫa-*BI*-ru*, or ideograph SA.GAZ or GAZ; Egyptian *'pr.w*. The Habiru were heterogeneous, uprooted people who joined together to find a means of subsistence for themselves and their families by entering the service of individuals, cities, and states in various areas of the Near East during the 2nd millennium B.C. They are first mentioned in a Sumerian text from Ur in the 20th cent. In the 20th–18th cents.

the Habiru appear as state-supported soldiers in southern Mesopotamia, as dependent troops at Alishar in Asia Minor, and as royal forces and independent raiders in the areas of Harran and Mari. Texts from 15th cent. Alalakh in Syria mention Habiru who appear to be foreigners, some of them vagrants, who enjoyed limited civic rights. Contemporary texts from the Hurrian Nuzi in Assyria record the voluntary entry of Habiru into the service of an official, Tehiptilla. In the Tell el-Amarna letters the Habiru are depicted as lawless bands who sold their services to local chiefs in Syria and Palestine during the first half of the 14th cent. Their status was that of outcasts from society who engaged in acts of outlawry when paid or supported by leaders of more responsible groups (cf 1 S 22[2]). Records throughout the Empire Period of Egypt contain references to *'apr.w*. This servile element in the Egyptian population can be equated with the Habiru not only by a place of dependence in society but by the discovery of the equation *'prm*=SA. GAZ at Râs Shamra.

The identification of the Habiru with the Hebrews is subject to some difficulties. The root of Hebrew *'brî* does not coincide easily with *'apiru*, the West Semitic form of Habiru. The biblical *'ibhrî* is a gentilic for Israelites, while Habiru is a term denoting an inferior social status. Nor is it easy to resolve the chronological differences between the activity of the Habiru in Palestine during the first half of the 14th cent. and the generally accepted date of the 13th cent. for the conquest of Canaan by the Israelites. However it is probable that the earliest Hebrews were related in some way to the widely attested groups known as Habiru. J. B. P.

HABOR.—A river flowing through the district of **Gozan**, on the banks of which Israelites were settled when deported from Samaria (2 K 17[6] 18[11], 1 Ch 5[26]). It is a tributary of the Euphrates, the *Chaboras* of the Greeks, the modern *Khābûr*.

HACALIAH.—The father of Nehemiah, Neh 1[1] 10[1] (AV **Hachaliah**).

HACHALIAH, Neh 1[1] 10[1] (AV).—See HACALIAH.

HACHILAH.—A hill near the wilderness of Ziph in which David hid (1 S 23[19]), and on which, during his pursuit, Saul pitched his camp (26[1, 3]). Ziph is modern *Tell ez-Zîf*, to the S. of Hebron. Some authors suggest that Hachilah may be the hill *Ḍahret el-Kôlâ*, but this is perhaps rather far to the east.

HACHMONI, HACHMONITE.—Both represent one and the same Hebrew word, but in 1 Ch 27[32] the latter is translated as a proper name, 'Jehiel the son of Hachmoni,' whereas in 1 Ch 11[11] Jashobeam is called 'a Hachmonite.' We should probably render it in both cases as a gentilic name. In 2 S 23[8], which is parallel to 1 Ch 11[11], we have 'the **Tahchemonite**' (AV **Tachmonite**), which is probably a textual error (see ADINO, JOSHEB-BASSHEBETH).

HADAD.—**1.** Hadad (Akkadian Adad) was a god worshipped among the Amorites in Palestine, Syria, and Mesopotamia at least from the 19th cent. B.C. and named in Aramaean inscriptions from Syria in the 8th cent. (cf the theophoric name Benhadad or Barhadad borne by three kings of Damascus).

Hadad is known particularly from the Râs Shamra texts as the proper name of the Canaanite Baal, the Amorite storm-god manifest in thunder, lightning, and the rains of autumn and winter. The name probably means 'the Thunderer' (Arabic *hadda*[tun], 'thunder' from the verb *hadda*, 'to crash'), and the god is represented as a kilted, striding warrior armed with mace and thunderbolt, his helmet garnished with a bull's horns. He is also identified in the Râs Shamra mythology with the vegetation he stimulated and he is a dying and rising god, like Mesopotamian Tammuz. He is identical with Hadad-Rimmon (see RIMMON, another term for 'Thunderer'), for whom public mourning was made in the great central plain of Palestine by Megiddo (Zec 12[11]). This was probably a rite which had its mythical counterpart in the mourning for the dead Baal in the Râs Shamra texts by his sister, the goddess Anat.

2. The eighth son of Ishmael (1 Ch 1[30], and also Gn 25[15] according to RSV and the best readings). **3.** The fourth of the eight ancient kings of Edom (Gn 36[35]; cf 1 Ch 1[46]). **4.** The eighth of the kings of Edom in the same list as the above-named (1 Ch 1[50]; in Gn 36[39] miswritten **Hadar**). **5.** The son of a king of Edom in the 10th cent. (1 K 11[14ff]). He escaped the massacre of Edomites perpetrated by Joab, David's general, and fled (according to the received reading) to Egypt, whose king befriended him, and gave him his sister-in-law to wife. After the death of David he returned to Edom, and his efforts seem to have rescued Edom from the yoke of Solomon. In all those cases Hadad is probably the truncated form of a theophoric compound name.
J. F. McC.—**J. Gr.**

HADADEZER.—The name of a king of Zobah (q.v.) in the time of David, 2 S 8[3ff], 1 K 11[23], 1 Ch 18[3ff] (in the last passage AV and RV have the less correct **Hadarezer,** following Hebrew). He was at the head of the combination of the Aramaeans of Northern Palestine against David, was repeatedly defeated, and finally made tributary. The word means 'Adad is (my) helper' (cf Heb. *Eliezer*, *Ebenezer*, *Azariah*, etc.). It is found on the Black Obelisk of the Assyrian Shalmaneser III. under the more Aramaic form *Adadidri*, as the equivalent of *Benhadad* of Damascus, who led the great combination, including Ahab of Israel, against the Assyrians at Qarqar in 853 B.C. J. F. McC.

HADADRIMMON.—A proper name occurring in Zec 12[11] 'as the mourning for Hadadrimmon in the plain of Megiddo.' It was formerly supposed to be a place-name (cf AV, RV 'mourning of Hadadrimmon in the valley of Megiddon'). According to a notice by Jerome, it would be equivalent to **Megiddo** itself. The word, however, is a combination of the two names of a divinity (see HADAD), and it is probable that the weeping for Tammuz, referred to in Ezk 8[14], is here meant, and that the old Semitic deity Hadad-Rimmon had by now become identified with Tammuz. There is no ground for supposing an allusion to the mourning for king Josiah, which, of course, took place in Jerusalem, not in the valley of Megiddo. J. F. McC.

HADAR (Gn 36[39]).—See HADAD, **4.**

HADAREZER, 1 Ch 18[3ff] (AV, RV).—See HADADEZER.

HADASHAH.—A town in the lowland of Judah, near Gath, Jos 15[37]; the site is unknown.

HADASSAH ('myrtle').—The Jewish name of Esther (Est 2[7] only). See ESTHER.

HADATTAH, Jos 15[25] (AV).—See HAZOR-HADATTAH.

HADES.—The Greek term for the abode of departed spirits, equivalent of the Hebrew *Sheol*. It was conceived of as a great cavern or pit under the earth, in which the shades lived. Just what degree of activity the shades possessed seems to have been somewhat doubtful. According to the Greeks, they were engaged in the occupations in which they had been employed on earth. The Hebrews, however, seem rather to have thought of their condition as one of inactivity. (See SHEOL and GEHENNA.) The word, translated as 'hell' in AV, is consistently read 'Hades' in RSV, except in Mt 16[18] ('death'; but margin 'Hades'). S. M.—**J. Br.**

HADID.—A city named with Lod and Ono (Ezr 2[33], Neh 7[37]), peopled by Benjamites after the Captivity (Neh 11[34]), probably identical with **Adida** (1 Mac 12[38] 13[13]); modern *el-Ḥadîtheh*, about 3¼ miles NE. of Lydda.

HADLAI.—An Ephraimite, 2 Ch 28[12].

HADORAM.—**1.** The fifth son of Joktan, Gn 10[27], 1 Ch 1[21]. **2.** The son of Tou, king of Hamath, 1 Ch 18[10]. In the parallel passage (2 S 8[9f]) he wrongly appears as **Joram.** **3.** A form of the name **Adoram** (q.v.), found in 2 Ch 10[18].

HADRACH.—A place in Syria mentioned in Zec 9[1] as being, at the time of the writing of that passage, confederate with Damascus. Hadrach is undoubtedly identical with *Hatarikka* of the Assyrian inscriptions. It was the object of three expeditions by Assur-dan III., and Tiglath pileser III. refers to it in the account of his war with 'Azariah the Judaean.' W. M. N.

HA-ELEPH.—A town of Benjamin, Jos 18[28] (AV, RV **Eleph**); but perhaps this name should be joined to the preceding name, as in LXX, giving **Zela-ha-eleph**. See ZELA.

HAFT.—'Haft,' still used locally for 'handle,' occurs in Jg 3[22] (AV, RV) 'the haft (RSV 'hilt') also went in after the blade.'

HAG.—See NIGHT HAG.

HAGAB.—One whose descendants returned with Zerubbabel, Ezr 2[46], 1 Es 5[30] (AV **Agaba**, RV **Accaba**); unmentioned in the parallel list in Neh 7.

HAGABA.—The head of a family of Nethinim (q.v.) who returned with Zerubbabel, Neh 7[48]. See HAGABAH.

HAGABAH.—The slightly different form in which the last-mentioned name appears in Ezr 2[45], 1 Es 5[29] (AV, RV **Aggaba**). Perhaps the same person as the foregoing.

HAGAR (probably 'emigrant' or 'fugitive') was Sarah's Egyptian maid (Gn 16[1] 21[9]). Her story shows that Sarah renounced the hope of bearing children to Abraham, and gave him Hagar as concubine. Her exultation so irritated Sarah that the maid had to flee from the encampment, and took refuge in the wilderness of Shur (16[7] 25[18]), between Philistia and Egypt. Thence she was sent back by 'the angel of the Lord'; and soon after her return she gave birth to Ishmael. After the weaning of Isaac, the sight of Ishmael aroused Sarah's jealousy and fear (21[9]); and Abraham was reluctantly persuaded to send away Hagar and her son. Again 'the angel of God' cheered her; and she found her way southwards to the wilderness of Paran (21[21]), where her son settled.

Literary criticism has found the three main pentateuchal sources J, E, and P in the Hagar story. Gn 16 is largely J, but verses 1a, 3, 15, and 16 are regarded as P. Gn 21[8-21] is entirely E. There are thus two parallel accounts, and Gn 16[9f] may be an editorial addition inserted to account for the presence of the E tradition.

Light on Sarah's action in giving her maid to Abraham because she herself was childless (Gn 16[2]) is thrown by marriage contracts from Nuzu in NE. Mesopotamia. These contracts stipulate that a wife who fails to produce an heir shall provide for her husband a slave who may bear him a son. The purpose of marriage was procreation, and Sarah was conforming to a custom known among Abraham's neighbours. Further, the expulsion of the offspring of such a union was illegal according to the Nuzian code, and this, apart from any natural feelings, would explain Abraham's unwillingness to accede to Sarah's request (Gn 21[10f]) and the Divine dispensation which allows him to comply (Gn 21[12f]).

The story is an important part of the biography of Abraham, illustrating both the variety of trials by which his faith was perfected and the active concern of God in even the distracted conditions of a chosen household. Further interest attaches to the narrative as containing the earliest reference in Scripture to the angel of Yahweh (Gn 16[7]), and as being the first of a series (Tamar, Rahab, Ruth, Naaman) in which the regard of God is represented as singling out for blessing persons outside Israel, and thus as preparing for the universal mission of Christ. There is but one other important allusion to Hagar in the OT. She is mentioned in Gn 25[12] in a sketch of the family of Ishmael (so in Bar 3[23] the Arabians are said to be her sons); and she has been assumed with much improbability to have been the ancestress of the Hagrites or Hagarenes of 1 Ch 5[10] and Ps 83[6] (see HAGRITES). In Gal 4[22ff] Paul applies her story allegorically, with a view to show the superiority of the new covenant. He contrasts Hagar the bondwoman with Sarah, and Ishmael 'born according to the flesh' with Isaac 'born through promise'; thence freedom and grace appear as the characteristic qualities of Christianity. There is good MS authority for the omission of 'Hagar' in v.[25], as in RSVm; in which case the meaning is that **Sinai** is a mountain in Arabia, the land of bondmen and the country of Hagar's descendants. Even if the reading of the text stands, the meaning of the phrase will not be very different, 'This Hagar of the allegory is or represents Sinai, because Sinai is in Arabia, where Hagar and her descendants dwelt.' R. W. M.—**W. D. McH.**

HAGARENES, Ps 83[6] (AV, RV).—See HAGRITE(s).

HAGARITES, 1 Ch 5[5, 19f] (AV).—See HAGRITE(s).

HAGERITE, 1 Ch 27[31] (AV).—See HAGRITE(s).

HAGGADAH.—See TALMUD.

HAGGAI (Apocrypha AV **Aggeus**; RV **Aggaeus**).—A prophet whose book appears tenth in the Book of the Twelve (Minor Prophets).

1. The man and his work.—The sphere of Haggai's activity was the post-exilic community in Judah. The dates in the book cover only a few months in the second year of Darius I. Hystaspis (522–486 B.C.), but the prophet's activity was not necessarily confined to so short a period. Of his prophetic calling and experience, nothing is known; but 1[13] stresses that he is one commissioned by Yahweh, speaking with authority the message given to him. His name is perhaps a shortened form of Haggiah (1 Ch 6[30], cf Mattenai, Mattaniah, Ezr 10[33, 36]), and may mean 'feast of Yahweh' or 'festal' *i.e.* 'born on the feast day' (from *ḥagh*, cf Barzillai from *barzel*). The same or similar names are to be found on seals and in the Elephantine papyri. Later tradition describes him as born in Babylon, and it has usually been assumed that he came to Judah with Zerubbabel. He is associated by the Chronicler with Zechariah (Ezr 5[1] 6[14]), and there are certain similarities in the structure and content of this book and Zec 1–8 which render this association appropriate, quite apart from the contemporaneous activity of the two prophets. The names of the two are prefixed to certain psalms in the Versions 111 (112) (Vulgate), 125 and 126 (Peshitta), 137 (LXX), 145 (LXX, Vulgate, Peshitta), 146–148 (LXX, Peshitta).

His prophecies were evoked by the delay that attended the reconstruction of the Temple. If the narrative of the book of Ezra is followed (though this is not without historical difficulties), the Jews on returning to Palestine in the first year of Cyrus, at once set up the altar of the Lord (Ezr 3[3]), and in the following year laid the foundation of the Temple (3[8-10]). The work, however, was almost immediately suspended through the opposition of the 'people of the land,' the 'adversaries of Judah and Benjamin,' descendants of the Assyrian colonists (Ezr 4[1-5], cf 2 K 17[24-41]). These difficulties led to a cessation of the work for some fifteen years. Haggai found the people loath to rebuild in a time of economic distress (1[4]), but his exhortation, and that of Zechariah, resulted in the completion of the rebuilding by the sixth year of Darius I. (516 B.C., so Ezr 6[14f]).

2. The book.—The prophecies of Haggai are divided into four dated sections.

(1) 1[1-14], assigned to the first day of the sixth month (August–September), contains the prophet's exhortation to build, and his explanation of the present economic distress and bad harvests as due to the failure to restore the Temple. The people have been content to beautify their own dwellings, but have not recognized that material well-being is dependent upon a right assessment of values, and that the Temple, as symbol of the Divine presence, is the necessary pre-requisite of blessing. The response of the leaders, Zerubbabel and Joshua, and of the people is recorded, and the beginning of the work described. 1[15a] is probably an explanatory gloss, or a fragment of a date-heading.

(2) 1[15b]–2[9], assigned to the twenty-first day of the seventh month (September–October), provides an answer to the discouragement experienced when the glory of the

first Temple is contrasted with the meanness of the second (cf the elaboration of this in Ezr 3[12f]). The prophet exhorts leaders and people (described in 2[2] as the 'remnant') to work and not to fear. God's spirit is among them, and He will bring the treasures of the nations into the rebuilt Temple (cf Is 60), and will fill it with glory, *i.e.* His own royal presence (cf Ps 24[7-10]). Reference is made to a shaking of heavens and earth, and it may be that the prophet was alluding to the disturbances at the beginning of the reign of Darius, though it is not clear that he believed that political change would bring about renewed fortune for his people. His expectation is of Divine action.

(3) 2[10-19], assigned to the twenty-fourth day of the ninth month (November–December) emphasizes, by means of questions directed to the priests, that pollution is more contagious than holiness. The corruption at the centre (14) pollutes the whole life and activity of the people. The passage has been interpreted as a reference to the repudiation of offers of help from the 'adversaries' (Ezr 4[1-3]), *i.e.* Samaritans; but it is perhaps rather to be construed as indicating that the rebuilding of the Temple is not an immediate guarantee of prosperity. The second section (15–19) contrasts the distress of the past with the coming blessings (cf Zec 8[9-12]).

(4) 2[20-23], assigned to the same date, proclaims Zerubbabel 'my servant' to be the signet-ring of Yahweh (cf Jer 22[24]). An allusion to upheavals is made as in 2[6], but this again need not be understood in purely political terms.

The message of Haggai reflects the needs of his time, a period of depression and economic and political insecurity, in which the prophet sees the paramount need of rebuilding the Temple, the centre and focus of life for the community in Judah, returned exiles and others alike. The closest contacts of the book are with Zec 1–8, and also with Is 56–66 and Malachi. At first sight, the emphasis appears to be on the externals of religion, yet there is here the fundamental recognition that prosperity and life depend upon the presence and blessing of Yahweh.

The style of Haggai, as it may be discerned in the oracles, is plain, but not without its rhythm, and a sonorous effect is produced by repetition. The text is straightforward at most points, glossed in all probability in 2[5a, 17f], and subsequently further glossed in the LXX (2[9, 14]). G. W. W.—**P. R. A.**

HAGGEDOLIM.—Father of Zabdiel, Neh 11[14] (AV, RVm 'one of the great men').

HAGGERI, 1 Ch 11[38] (AV).—See Hagri.

HAGGI ('born on a festival').—Son of Gad, Gn 46[16], Nu 26[15]; patronymic, **Haggites,** Nu 26[15].

HAGGIAH ('feast of Y″').—A Levite descended from Merari, 1 Ch 6[30].

HAGGITES.—See Haggi.

HAGGITH ('festal').—The mother of Adonijah, 2 S 3[4], 1 K 1[5] 2[13].

HAGIA, 1 Es 5[34] (AV).—See Hattil.

HAGIOGRAPHA.—See Bible, **2.**

HAGRI.—Father of Mibhar, one of David's heroes, 1 Ch 11[38] (AV **Haggeri**); the parallel passage (2 S 23[36]) reads 'of Zobah, Bani the Gadite,' which is probably the correct text.

HAGRITE(S).—A tribe of Arabian or Aramaean origin inhabiting territory to the E. of Gilead. Twice they were the object of campaigns by the trans-Jordan Israelite tribes, by whom they were crushingly defeated and expelled from their land, 1 Ch 5[5, 19f] (AV **Hagarites**). They are referred to also in Ps 83[6] (AV, RV **Hagarenes**). Jaziz, a Hagrite, was 'over the flocks' of king David, 1 Ch 27[31] (AV **Hagerite**). Because the name appears only in late passages, some have conjectured that it was a late appellation for Bedouin. It has been connected with the name **Hagar** (q.v.) and thought to mean 'descendants of Hagar,' *i.e.* Ishmaelites. But this is unlikely, since the Hagrites are named along with other tribes which, according to this view, they included. The Hagrites are mentioned in an inscription of Tiglath-pileser iii. among a group of Aramaean tribes.
W. M. N.—**H. H. R.**

HAHIROTH.—See Pi-hahiroth.

HAIL.—See Plagues of Egypt.

HAIR.—The usual word in OT is *śēʿār*, in NT *thrix*. Black hair was greatly admired by the Hebrews (Ca 4[1] 5[11] 7[5]). Women have always worn the hair long, **baldness** or short hair being to them a disgrace (Is 3[24] Ezk 16[7], 1 Co 11[15], Rev 9[8]). Absalom's hair was cut once a year (2 S 14[26]; cf rules for priests, Ezk 44[20]), but men seem to have worn the hair longer than is seemly among us (Ca 5[2, 11]). In NT times it was a shame for a man to have long hair (1 Co 11[6ff]). This probably never applied to the Arabs, who still wear the hair in long plaits. The locks of the Nazirite were, of course, an exception (Jg 16[13] etc.). The Israelites were forbidden to cut the **corners** of their hair (Lv 19[27] 21[5]). In neighbouring nations the locks on the temples, in front of the ears, were allowed to grow in youth, and their removal was part of certain idolatrous rites connected with puberty and initiation to manhood. These peoples are referred to as those that 'cut the corners of the hair' (Jer 9[26]). The practice was probably followed by Israel in early times, and the prohibition was required to distinguish them from idolaters. One curious result of the precept is seen among the orthodox Jews of to-day, who religiously preserve the love-locks which, in the far past, their ancestors religiously cut.

The Assyrians wore the hair long (Herod. i. 195). In Egypt the women wore long hair. The men shaved both head and **beard** (Gn 41[14]), but they wore imposing wigs and false beards, the shape of the latter indicating the rank and dignity of the wearer (Herod. ii. 36, iii. 12; Wilkinson, *Anc. Egyp.* ii, 324, etc.). Josephus says that young gallants among the horsemen of Solomon sprinkled gold dust on their long hair, 'so that their heads sparkled with the reflection of the sunbeams from the gold' (*Ant.* viii. vii. 3 [185]). Jezebel dressed her hair (2 K 9[30]). Judith arranged her hair and put on a head-dress (Jth 10[3]). St. Paul deprecates too much attention to 'braided hair' (1 Ti 2[9], cf 1 P 3[3]). Artificial curls are mentioned in Is 3[24]. The fillet of twisted silk or other material by which the hair was held in position stands for the hair itself in Jer 7[29]. Combs are not mentioned in Scripture; but they were used in Egypt (Wilkinson, *op. cit.* ii, 349), and were doubtless well known in Palestine. The **barber** with his **razor** appears in Ezk 5[1] (cf *Shab.* i. 2, *Shebi.* viii. 5). Herod the Great dyed his hair black, to make himself look younger (Jos. *Ant.* xvi. viii. 1 [233]). We hear of false hair only once, and then it is used as a disguise (*ib.*, *Vit.* 11 [47]). Light ornaments of metal were worn on the hair (Is 3[18]); in modern times coins of silver and gold are commonly worn; often a tiny bell is hung at the end of the tress. It is a grievous insult to cut or pluck the hair of head or cheek (2 S 10[4ff], Is 7[20] 50[6], Jer 48[37]). Letting loose a woman's hair is a mark of abasement (Nu 5[18]); or it may indicate self-humiliation (Lk 7[38]). As a token of grief it was customary to cut the hair of both head and **beard** (Is 15[2], Jer 16[6] 41[5], Am 8[10]), to leave the beard untrimmed (2 S 19[24]), and even to pluck out the hair (Ezr 9[3]). Tearing the hair is still a common Oriental expression of sorrow. Arab women cut off their hair in mourning.

The hair of the lifelong **Nazirite** might never be cut (Jg 13[5], 1 S 1[11]). The Nazirite for a specified time cut his hair only when the vow was performed. If, after the period of separation had begun, he contracted defilement, his head was shaved and the period began anew (Nu 6[5ff]). An Arab who is under vow must neither cut, comb, nor cleanse his hair, until the vow is fulfilled and his offering made. Then cutting the hair marks his return from the consecrated to the common condition (Wellhausen, *Skizzen*, iii, 167). Offerings of hair were common among ancient peoples

(W. R. Smith, *RS*[2] 324 ff; Wellhausen, *op. cit.* 118 f). It was believed that some part of a man's life resided in the hair, and that possession of hair from his head maintained a certain connexion with him, even after his death. Before freeing a prisoner, the Arabs cut a portion of his hair, and retained it, as evidence that he had been in their power (Wellh. *op. cit.* 118). Chalid b. al-Walīd wore, in his military head-gear, hair from the head of Mohammed (ib. 146).

The colour of the hair was observed in the detection of leprosy (Lv 13[30ff] etc.). Thorough disinfection involved removal of the hair (14[8f]). The shaving of the head of the slave-girl to be married by her captor marked the change in her condition and prospects (Dt 21[12]; W. R. Smith, *Kinship*[2], 209). Swearing by the hair (Mt 5[36]) is now generally confined to the beard. The hoary head is held in honour (Pr 16[31], Wis 2[10] etc.), and white hair is associated with the appearance of Divine majesty (Dn 7[9], Rev 1[14]). W. E.

HAJEHUDIJAH occurs in RVm of 1 Ch 4[18] in an obscure genealogical list. It is probably not a proper name, but means 'the Jewess' (so AVm, RV, RSV). AV reads **Jehudijah.**

HAKKATAN (' the smallest ').—The head of a family of returning exiles, Ezr 8[12], 1 Es 8[38] (AV **Acatan**, RV **Akatan**).

HAKKOZ (? ' thorn ').—**1.** The eponym of a priestly family, 1 Ch 24[10], Ezr 2[61] (AV **Koz**), Neh 3[4, 21] 7[63] (AV all **Koz**), 1 Es 5[38] (AV **Accoz**, RV **Akkos**). They were unable to prove their pedigree. **2.** In 1 Ch 4[8] RV has Hakkoz, where AV has **Coz** and RSV **Koz** (q.v.).

HAKUPHA.—Eponym of a family of Nethinim (q.v.), who returned with Zerubbabel, Ezr 2[51], Neh 7[53], 1 Es 5[31] (AV **Acipha**, RV **Achipha**).

HALAH.—One of the places to which Israelites were deported by the king of Assyria on the capture of Samaria, 2 K 17[6] 18[11], 1 Ch 5[26], Ob [20] (RSV; AV, RV ' this host '). It was situated in the region of Gozan (q.v.), but it has not yet been satisfactorily identified.

HALAK (' smooth mountain ').—An eminence that formed the southern limit of Joshua's conquests, Jos 11[17] 12[7]; probably modern *Jebel Ḥalâq.*

HALAKHAH.—See Talmud.

HALHUL.—A city of Judah, Jos 15[58]. It is the modern *Ḥalhûl*, a large village 4 miles N. of Hebron.

HALI.—A city belonging to the tribe of Asher, Jos 19[25]. The site is unknown.

HALICARNASSUS was one of the six Dorian colonies on the coast of Caria. Though excluded from the Dorian confederacy (Hexapolis) on account of some ancient dispute (Herod. i. 144), it was a very important city in respect of politics, commerce, literature, and art. It was one of the States to which the Roman Senate sent letters in favour of the Jews in 139 B.C. (1 Mac 15[23]). It must therefore have been a free and self-governing city at that time. The decree of the city passed in the 1st cent. B.C., granting to the Jews religious liberty and the right to build their *proseuchai* beside the sea (Jos. *Ant.* XIV. x. 23 [256 ff]), attests the existence of an early Jewish colony in the city; and this was natural, as Halicarnassus was a considerable centre of trade owing to its favourable position on a bay opposite Cos, on the NW. side of the Ceramic Gulf. The city extended round the bay from promontory to promontory, and contained, among other buildings, a famous temple of Aphrodite.

The site of Halicarnassus is now called *Bodrum* (*i.e.* ' fortress '), from the Castle of St. Peter which was built by the Knights of St. John (whose headquarters were in Rhodes), under their Grand Master de Naillac, A.D. 1404.

HALL.—See Praetorium.

HALLEL.—The name given in Rabbinical writings to the Pss 113–118—called the ' Egyptian Hallel ' in distinction from the ' Great Hallel ' (Ps 136), and from Pss 146–148, which are also psalms of Hallel character. The Hallel proper (Pss 113–118) was always regarded as forming one whole. The word *Hallel* means ' Praise,' and the name was given on account of the oft-recurring word *Hallelujah* (' Praise ye the Lord ') in these psalms. The ' Hallel ' was sung at the great Jewish festivals—Passover, Tabernacles, Pentecost, and Hanukkah (' Dedication ' of the Temple).

HALLELUJAH.—A Hebrew expression, used liturgically in Hebrew worship as a short doxology, meaning ' praise ye Yah.' In the LXX it was transliterated, and from this came the Vulgate form and the AV **Alleluia** (To 13[18], Rev 19[1, 3f, 6]). In EV it is always translated ' praise the Lord ' in OT, where, with one exception (Ps 135[3]) it occurs only at the beginning or the end of psalms, or both: at the beginning only in Pss 111 f; at the beginning and end in Pss 106, 113, 135, 146–150; at the end only in Pss 104 f, 115–117. In the LXX, however, it occurs only at the *beginning* of psalms as a *heading*, and this would seem to be the more natural usage. The double occurrence in the Hebrew text may in some cases be explained as due to accidental displacement (the heading of the following psalm being attached to the conclusion of the previous one).

As a liturgical heading the term served to mark off certain well-defined groups of psalms which were probably intended in the first instance for synagogue use, and may once have existed as an independent collection. With the exception of Ps 135, these groups (in the Heb. text) are three in number, viz. 104–106; 111–113, 115–117; and 146–150. But in the LXX a larger number of psalms is so distinguished, and the consequent grouping is more coherent, viz. 105–107; 111–119 (135–136); 146–150. In the synagogue liturgy the last-mentioned group (146–150), together with 135–136, has a well-defined place in the daily morning service, forming an integral part of the great ' Benediction of Song ' (in certain parts of the early Church, also, it was customary to recite the ' Hallelujah ' psalms daily).

The ' Hallel ' (Pss 113–118), which forms a liturgical unit in the synagogue liturgy, is the most complete example of ' Hallelujah ' psalms in collected form. (In the LXX, notice all the individual psalms of the group are headed ' **Alleluia.**')

Like other Jewish liturgical terms (*e.g.* ' Amen '), ' Hallelujah ' passed from the OT to the NT (cf Rev 19[1–7]), from the Jewish to the Christian Church (cf especially the early liturgies), and so to modern hymnody. G.H.B.—**H.H.R.**

HALLOHESH.—An individual or a family mentioned in connexion with the repairing of the wall, Neh 3[12] (AV **Halohesh**); he was one who sealed the covenant, 10[24].

HALLOW.—To ' hallow ' is either ' to make holy ' or ' to regard as holy.' Both meanings are very old. Thus Wycliffe translates Jn 17[17] ' Halwe thou hem in treuthe,' and Dt 32[51] ' Ye halwide not me amonge the sones of Yreal ' (1388, ' Israel '). In the Lord's Prayer (Mt 6[9], Lk 11[2], the only places where ' hallow ' occurs in the NT) the meaning is ' regard as sacred.' All the English versions have ' hallowed ' in these verses except the Rhemish (Roman Catholic), which has ' sanctified '; but in the modern editions of this version the change has been made to ' hallowed.' Cf the ancient form of the Jewish Kaddish: ' May His great Name be magnified and hallowed in the world which He has created.'

HALOHESH, Neh 3[12] (AV).—See Hallohesh.

HALT.—This English word is used (1) literally, as a verb ' to be lame, to limp,' or as an adjective ' lame.' Cf Tyndale's translation of Mt 11[5] ' The blynd se, the halt goo, the lepers are clensed.' Or (2) figuratively ' to stumble, fail,' as Jer 20[10] ' All my familiars watched for my halting.' From this comes the meaning (3) ' to be undecided, waver,' 1 K 18[21] ' How long halt [literally ' limp,' as on unequal legs] ye between two opinions ? ' The Revisers have introduced (4) the modern meaning ' to stop,' Is 10[32] ' This very day he will halt at Nob.'

HAM.—According to Gn 10^{6} (P), the ancestor of the peoples linked geographically and politically with Egypt. In this verse his four sons are given as Cush (Nubia), Mizraim (Egypt), Put (? Libya), and Canaan. It has been suggested that Canaan is included because of its political and cultural dependence upon Egypt for many centuries. Cush may have been placed first either because the author listed the countries in their geographical position, starting with the south, or because Nubia was the predominant political power at the time when the list was composed. The genealogies of the nations in Gn 9, 10 contain several interwoven traditions. According to one tradition, Noah and his family being the sole survivors of the Flood, the whole earth was populated by their descendants (9^{18f}), and his three sons people the whole of the known world: the three sons were **Shem, Ham,** and **Japheth.** According to another tradition Shem, **Canaan,** and Japheth were the three sons of Noah. That Canaan was the son, and not Ham, is clear from the fact that it was he who was cursed (Gn 9$^{20-27}$). To combine the two traditions a redactor has added the words 'and Ham is the father of Canaan' in v.^{18} and 'Ham the father of' in v.^{22}. In the first mentioned tradition the three sons are represented as ancestors of large divisions of the world: in the second tradition they appear to be ancestors of much smaller units, perhaps within the limits of Syria-Palestine, but there is much dispute among scholars as to the peoples here intended. In Ps 78^{51} 105 $^{23, 27}$ 106^{22} Ham denotes Egypt, a usage which appears to be late and poetical. The name 'Ham' cannot be derived from any known Egyptian word for 'Egypt' or 'Nubia' and has, indeed, been connected with the West Semitic god Ḥammu. It seems probable that in the P tradition the peoples of the world were originally apportioned to the three sons of Noah on an entirely geographical basis—eastern (Shem), southern (Ham), and northern (Japheth). Because the southern group was under the political domination of the inhabitants of the Nile valley, Ham became synonymous with Egypt and the sphere of Egyptian influence. A. H. McN.—**T. W. T.**

HAM.—According to Gn 14^{5}, the district inhabited by the Zuzim, (q.v.). It is the modern *Hâm.*

HAM, LAND OF.—A poetical designation of Egypt used in the Psalms in reference to the sojourn there of the Children of Israel (Ps 105$^{23, 27}$ 106^{22}). So also 'the tabernacles (RV, RSV 'tents') of Ham' (Ps 78^{51}) stands for the dwellings of the Egyptians. The Egyptian etymologies that have been proposed for *Ḥām* are untenable, and the name must be connected with that of the son of Noah. F. Ll. G.

HAMAN.—The son of Hammedatha and enemy of the Jews in the Book of Esther. See Esther. In Ad. Est 12^{6} 16$^{10, 17}$ (AV, RV) his name appears as **Aman** (RSV Haman).

In later times, at the Feast of Purim, it seems to have been customary to hang an effigy of Haman; but as the gibbet was sometimes made in the form of a cross, riots between Jews and Christians were the result, and a warning against insults to the Christian faith was issued by the emperor Theodosius II. (Cod. Theod. XVI. viii. 18; cf 21).

HAMATH.—A city on the Orontes, the capital of the kingdom of Hamath, to the territory of which the border of Israel extended in the reign of Solomon (1 K 8^{65}), who is said to have built store-cities there (2 Ch 8^{4}). Jeroboam II., the son of Joash, restored the kingdom to this northern limit (2 K 14$^{25, 28}$), and it was regarded as the legitimate border of the land of Israel (Nu 34^{8}, Jos 13^{5}), and was employed as a geographical term (Nu 13^{21}, cf Jg 3^{3}). It is thought by some that the phrase rendered 'the entrance of Hamath' should be rendered as a proper name **Lebo-hamath.** The **Hamathite** is mentioned last of the sons of Canaan in the table of nations (Gn 10^{18}, 1 Ch 1^{16}). During the time of David, Toi was king of Hamath (2 S 8^{9}); the greatness of the city is referred to by the prophet Amos (Am 6^{2}), and it is classed by Zechariah with Damascus, Tyre, and Sidon (Zec 9^{1f}). The city was conquered by Tiglath-pileser III. and Sargon, and part of its inhabitants were deported and the land was largely colonized by Assyrians; its capture and subjugation are referred to in the prophetic literature (Is 10^{9}, Jer 49^{23}; cf also 2 K 18^{34}, Is 36^{19}, 2 K 19^{13}). Hamath is mentioned as one of the places to which Israelites were exiled (Is 11^{11}), and it was also one of the places whose inhabitants were deported to colonize Israelite territory on the capture of Samaria (2 K 17$^{24, 30}$). Jonathan advanced to Hamath against Demetrius (1 Mac 11^{25}). Its name was changed by Antiochus IV. to Epiphania, but the old name survives in the modern *Ḥamā*. It has been excavated by a Danish expedition. See Ashima. L. W. K.—**H. H. R.**

HAMATH-ZOBAH.—A city in the neighbourhood of Tadmor, conquered by Solomon, 2 Ch 8^{3}. Some have conjectured that it is identical with Hamath (q.v.), and that *Zobah* is used here in a broader sense than usual. On the other hand, it may be another Hamath situated in the territory of Zobah proper.

HAMMATH ('hot spring').—**1.** 'Father of the house of Rechab,' 1 Ch 2^{55} (AV **Hemath**). **2.** One of the fortified cities of Naphtali, Jos 19^{35}; probably the same as **Hammon** of 1 Ch 6^{76} and **Hammoth-dor** of Jos 21^{32}. It is doubtless the *Hamata* of the Talmud, the *Emmaus* or *Ammathus* of Josephus (*Ant.* XVIII. ii. 3 [36]), and the modern *Hammâm Tabarîyeh*, thirty-five minutes' walk S. of Tiberias, famous for its hot baths.

HAMMEAH, THE TOWER OF.—See Hundred, The Tower of.

HAMMEDATHA.—The father of Haman, the chief minister of Ahasuerus and enemy of the Jews (Est 3$^{1, 10}$ 8^{5} 9$^{10, 24}$). In Ad. Est 12^{6} 16$^{10, 17}$ (AV, RV) he is called **Amadathus.** The name is Persian, possibly from *mâh*, 'moon,' and *data* 'given'; or *hama*, 'equal,' and *dātā* 'giver' (so Gehman, *JBL* xliii, 326).

HAMMELECH occurs as a proper name in AV and RVm of Jer 36^{26} 38^{6}, but there is little doubt that the rendering ought to be 'the king,' as in AVm, RV, RSV.

HAMMER.—See Arts and Crafts, **1, 2, 3.**

HAMMIPHKAD, GATE OF, Neh 3^{31} (AV).—See Muster Gate.

HAMMOLECHETH ('the queen' ?).—The daughter of Machir and sister of Gilead, 1 Ch 7^{17f} (AV **Hammoleketh).**

HAMMOLEKETH, 1 Ch 7^{18} (AV).—See Hammolecheth.

HAMMON ('hot spring').—**1.** A Levitical city in Naphtali, 1 Ch 6^{76}; probably identical with **Hammath, 2** (q.v.). **2.** A town in Asher, Jos 19^{28}; possibly modern *Umm il-'Awāmîd.*

HAMMOTH-DOR.—A Levitical city in Naphtali, Jos 21^{32}; probably identical with **Hammath, 2** (q.v.).

HAMMUEL.—A Simeonite of the family of Shaul, 1 Ch 4^{26} (AV **Hamuel).**

HAMMURABI was the sixth king of the 1st Dynasty of Babylon. Other kings, in N. Syria, contemporary with Hammurabi bore the same name. Hence attempts to identify Amraphel (Gn 14^{1}) with Hammurabi of Babylon are arbitrary. The precise date of his accession is much disputed. Opinion ranges from *c* 1900 to 1728 B.C. The evidence makes plausible a choice between 1792–1750 B.C. and 1728–1686 B.C. as the dates of his long reign. His stock was Semitic. Amorites, westlanders, originally nomadic shepherds and caravaneers, founded the dynasty, with Babylon as royal capital. According to literary evidence from Babylonia and particularly from Mari, 375 miles from Babylon, on the Euphrates, the chief political centres were Isin and Larsa to the SE., Eshnunna to the NE., Mari to the NW., and Assur on upper Tigris, far N. of Babylon, which was a comparatively small power at the time of Hammurabi's accession. Between the sixth and thirty-third years of Hammurabi's reign he destroyed these by force of arms and became undisputed master of territories from the Persian Gulf to Assur, and from Elam to Syria. In forty-two years this ' king of Amurru ' became ' king of Sumer and Akkad, king of the four quarters ' (of the world).

Hammurabi's own letters to his officials within his kingdom, the forty-two date-formulae of his reign, his ' Code ' of laws, and many documents relating to legal and business transactions, are evidence of Hammurabi's successful drive towards centralized administration in every department of government under himself, through his officials, chiefly in Babylon, Sippar, and Larsa. The land, the canals which irrigated it, and the labourers who worked it, were objects of his special care, for all was, apparently, crown-land. Taxation, in kind or in silver, was universal, including even the temples. Trade was done on behalf of the government on a wide scale. Private wealth was rare. The state had its slaves, under an official, for duties on public works and in the palace.

Hammurabi seems to have ' secularized ' the state more than did any of his predecessors, but he made the gods, their temples, and their staffs a chief concern. He reformed nothing in traditional religion, but he furthered a tendency which led to the national supremacy of the local god Marduk. Already under the third king of this dynasty, Babylonians swore by Shamash and Marduk. Shamash was the sun god, source of light which laid bare all human conduct. Hence he was judge and avenger of evil. Hammurabi was his ' favourite,' and the names of his five successors include Shamash. But he was also the ' darling ' of Marduk whose name means ' young buffalo of the sun ' or ' young sun.' At the beginning of his ' Code,' Hammurabi declares : ' The sublime Anu, king of the Anunnaki, and Enlil, lord of heaven and earth, who fixes men's destinies, have bestowed on Marduk, the beloved son of Enki, the dignity of Enlil (*i.e.* supremacy) over all peoples and have raised him above the Igigi.' From this time, by degrees, Marduk, a local god, became the national god of whom were predicated all the rôles of other and older deities. His temple was Esagila in which Hammurabi's statue as ' King of Justice ' prayed without ceasing for the king. T. F.

HAMONAH (' multitude ').—The name of a city in the valley of **Hamon-gog** (q.v.), Ezk 39^{16}.

HAMON-GOG (' Gog's multitude ').—The name to be given to the valley (outside the Holy Land) where Gog and his multitude are to be buried, Ezk 39^{11,15}.

HAMOR (' he-ass ').—The ancestor of the **Shechemites.** In Jg 9^{28} the inhabitants of Shechem are called ' men of Hamor.' The Hamorites were in turn a branch of the Hivites (Gn 34^{2}). The term ' father of Shechem ' may simply mean founder of the city of Shechem (cf similar usage in 1 Ch 2$^{45, 49-51}$).

Gn 34 contains an early Shechem tradition of relations between the Simeon-Levi Israelite tribes and the Hamorites of Shechem. According to the personalized tale Shechem loved Dinah, the sister of Simeon and Levi and forces her. Hamor negotiates with her father and brothers for a marriage alliance between them. The alliance is agreed upon on condition that all male Hamorites undergo circumcision. While thus weakened they are treacherously attacked by Simeon and Levi and all the males are slain. For this unnatural breaking of tribal alliances these two are roundly condemned (Gn 49$^{5-7}$).

There is a curious fusion of traditions in Ac 7^{16}, where Jacob ' and our fathers ' are said to have been ' laid in the tomb that Abraham had bought for a sum of silver from the sons of Hamor in Shechem.' Abraham bought a tomb in Machpelah, not in Shechem (Gn 23^{17f}), and Jacob was buried there (50^{13}). Of the latter's sons Joseph alone is related in the OT as having been buried in the tomb bought from the sons of Hamor (Jos 24^{32}). A. H. McN.—**J. W. W.**

HAMRAN.—An Edomite, 1 Ch 1^{41} (AV **Amram**) ; called **Hemdan** in Gn 36^{26}.

HAMSTRING.—See Hock.

HAMUEL, 1 Ch 4^{26} (AV).—See Hammuel.

HAMUL (' spared ').—A son of Perez and grandson of Judah, Gn 46^{12}, Nu 26^{21}, 1 Ch 2^{5}. The gentilic **Hamulites** occurs in Nu 26^{21}.

HAMUTAL.—Mother of the kings Jehoahaz and Zedekiah, sons of Josiah, 2 K 23^{31} 24^{18}, Jer 52^{1}.

HANA.—Eponym of a family of Temple servants, 1 Es 5^{30} (RSV ; AV, RV **Anan**) ; called **Hanan** in Ezr 2^{46}, Neh 7^{49}.

HANAMEEL, Jer 32$^{7-9, 12}$ (AV).—See Hanamel.

HANAMEL.—Jeremiah's cousin, the son of his uncle Shallum, Jer 32$^{7-9, 12}$ (AV **Hanameel**).

HANAN (' gracious ').—**1.** One of David's mighty men, 1 Ch 11^{43}. **2.** A Benjamite chief, 1 Ch 8^{23}. **3.** The youngest son of Azel, a descendant of Saul, 1 Ch 8^{38} 9^{44}. **4.** The son of Igdaliah ; his sons had a chamber in the Temple, Jer 35^{4}. **5.** The head of a family of Nethinim (q.v.) who returned with Zerubbabel, Ezr 2^{46}, Neh 7^{49} ; called **Hana** in 1 Es 5^{30} (RSV ; AV, RV **Anan**) ; probably the same as the signatory to the covenant, Neh 10^{10}. **6.** One of the Levites who assisted Ezra in expounding the Law, Neh 8^{7}, 1 Es 9^{48} (AV, RV **Ananias**). **7.** The son of Zaccur and one of the four treasurers appointed by Nehemiah, Neh 13^{13}. **8, 9.** Two of those who sealed the covenant, Neh 10$^{22, 26}$.

HANANEEL.—See Hananel.

HANANEL (' El is gracious ').—The name of a tower on the wall of Jerusalem (AV **Hananeel**). It is mentioned in Neh 3^{1} in connexion with the repairing, and in 12^{39} in connexion with the dedication, of the walls, and in Jer 31^{38} and Zec 14^{10} as a boundary of the restored and glorified Jerusalem. In both the passages in Nehemiah it is coupled with the tower of the **Hundred** (q.v.).

HANANI (probably hypocoristic ' Y″ is gracious ').—**1.** A brother, or more probably near kinsman, of Nehemiah, who brought tidings to Susa of the distressed condition of the Jews in Palestine, Neh 1^{2}. Under Nehemiah he was made one of the governors of Jerusalem, 7^{2}. **2.** A son of Heman, 1 Ch 25$^{4, 25}$. **3.** The father of Jehu the seer, 1 K 16$^{1, 7}$, 2 Ch 19^{2} 20^{34}. Hanani reproved Asa for entering into alliance with Syria, and the angry king cast him into prison, 2 Ch 16^{7}. **4.** A priest of the sons of Immer who had married a foreign wife, Ezr 10^{20}, 1 Es 9^{21} (AV, RV **Ananias**). **5.** A chief musician mentioned in connexion with the dedication of the walls of Jerusalem, Neh 12^{36}.

HANANIAH (' Y″ has been gracious ').—**1.** One of the sons of Shashak, of the tribe of Benjamin, 1 Ch 8^{24f}. **2.** One of the sons of Heman (1 Ch 25^{4}), who could ' prophesy with lyres, with harps, and with cymbals ' (v.^{1} ; cf v.^{6}). **3.** One of king Uzziah's commanders, 2 Ch 26^{11}. **4.** The son of Azzur, a Gibeonite (Jer 28^{1}), who was condemned by Jeremiah, in the reign of Zedekiah, for prophesying falsely. The prophecy of Hananiah was to the effect that king Jeconiah and the captives in Babylon would all return in two years' time, bringing back with them the vessels of the Lord's house which Nebuchadnezzar had carried away (cf Dn 1^{1f}). He expressed this in symbolic fashion by taking the ' bar ' (cf Jer 27^{2}) from Jeremiah's neck and breaking it, with the words, ' Thus says the Lord : Even so will I break the yoke of Nebuchadnezzar King of Babylon from the neck of all the nations within two years ' (28^{11}). In reply Jeremiah declares this prophecy to be false, and that because Hananiah has made the people to trust in a lie, he will die within the year. The words of Jeremiah come to pass : Hananiah dies in the seventh month (v.^{17}). **5.** Father of Zedekiah, one of the princes of Judah, Jer 36^{12}. **6.** Grandfather of Irijah, who arrested Jeremiah, 37^{13}. **7.** A son of Zerubbabel, 1 Ch 3^{19}. **8.** A priest, head of the house of Jeremiah, who returned with Nehemiah from Babylon, Neh 12^{12}. **9.** Governor of ' the castle,' who, together with Hanani, was appointed by Nehemiah to the ' charge over

Jerusalem,' Neh 7^{2}. **10.** The friend of Daniel, who received the name *Shadrach* from the chief of the eunuchs, Dn 1$^{6f. 11}$. **11.** A Levite, whose 'sons' were contemporary with Ezra, 1 Es 8^{48} (AV **Channuneus,** RV **Chanuneus**); **Merari** stands in the parallel Ezr 8^{19}. Several others also bear this name, but they are not of importance (see Ezr 10^{28}, Neh 3$^{8, 30}$ 10^{23} 12^{41}; these are not necessarily *all* different people).

W. O. E. O.—H. H. R.

HAND is EV translation of Hebrew *yādh,* 'the open hand,' *kaph,* 'the closed hand,' and Greek *cheir,* 'hand.' Sometimes it is idiomatic, *e.g.* 'at hand' (Is 13^{6} etc., Heb. *ḳārôbh,* Mt 26^{18} etc., Gr. *engys,* literally 'near'). In determining the directions in the Orient, the face is turned to the east, not to the north as with us. So it comes that *yāmîn,* 'right hand,' and *śᵉmō'l,* 'left hand,' like the Arabiac *yamīn* and *shimāl,* denote respectively 'south' and 'north.'

Of the two hands, the 'right hand' was the more important. To be at someone's right hand was to be allocated a place of honour (1 K 2^{19}, Ps 110^{1}; cf also Lk 22^{69}, Ro 8^{34} etc., the Redeemer at the right hand of God). The protector and the accuser in the law court stood on the right hand (cf Ps 109^{31}, Zec 3^{1}). The left hand bears the shield in battle, thus leaving the right hand free to fight and attack. If a person is left-handed, this demands special mention (Jg 3$^{15, 21}$ 20^{16}—all references to the Benjamites, and this suggests that left-handedness was common among them).

When a person is set apart to the priesthood, the phrase used is 'to fill the hand' (cf RVm at Ex 28^{41} etc.). Again to pour water on another's hands was to be his servant (2 K 3^{11}). Washing of the hands was a declaration of innocence (Dt 21^{6}, Ps 26^{6}, Mt 27^{24}), and clean hands were a symbol of a righteous life (Job 22^{30}, Ps 18^{20} 24^{4} etc.). It also appears that certain marks or cuttings on the hands were evidence of what deity one served (Is 44^{5}; cf Gal 6^{17} and Rev 20^{4}, where the mark of the beast 'upon their hand' is probably an allusion to this custom).

But to acquire a correct understanding of a number of references to the hand in the OT, it has to be remembered that the Israelites regarded man as a psychophysical organism. Hence the hand is not merely an instrument of the self, but is thought of as revealing psychical properties, and its various postures and actions reveal the various moods, feelings, aspirations, and desires of the individual (see A. R. Johnson, *The Vitality of the Individual in the Thought of Ancient Israel*). The hand on the head indicates grief or shame (2 S 13^{19}, Jer 2^{37}). To raise or stretch the hand (especially towards God) is an expression of supplication (1 K 8^{22}, Ps 28^{2}). Anger is expressed by clapping the hands (Nu 24^{10} etc.). In the same way the action of the hands is an indication of the purpose of the self; this is evident from the oft occurring phrase 'to send forth the hand.' The purpose may be for good or evil, or can be aggressive, *e.g.* the hand laid upon one in judgment, to raise the hand against someone, and to act with a high hand is to act in a defiant manner. The action of the hand also ratifies or reinforces the spoken or the written word, *e.g.* to shake or clasp or strike the hands in ratifying an agreement, to place the hand under the thigh in making a vow or taking an oath. The hand is also associated with 'power,' and in certain passages it is correct to regard it as a synonym of power. The laying on of hands conveys this power (Gn 48^{14}). And 'the hand of the Lord' and 'mighty hand' stand for the power of God. So real is this use of hand as an extension of the personality that it can be equivalent to the personal pronoun, especially when accompanied by the possessive pronoun, cf Is 45^{12} 'I, even my hands,' to emphasize the personal pronoun.

Thrice (1 S 15^{12}, 2 S 18^{18}, Is 56^{5}) *yādh* clearly means 'monument' or 'memorial,' probably a stone block or pillar; a hand may have been carved upon it, but this is uncertain. W. E.—E. R. R.

HANDBAG.—See Bag.

HANDBREATH.—See Weights and Measures.

HANDKERCHIEFS, only Ac 19^{12}, *soudaria,* a loan-word from the Latin, elsewhere rendered '**napkin**' or '**cloth**'; see Dress, **5** (*a*).

HANDPIKES.—Only Ezk 39^{9} (AV, RV **handstaves**), either clubs or the equally primitive throw-sticks.

HANDSTAVES.—See Handpikes.

HANES is associated with Zoan in a difficult context, Is 30^{4}. Some would place it in Lower Egypt, with Anysis in Herodotus, and *Khininshi* in the annals of Ashurbanipal; but there can be little doubt that it is the Egyptian *Hnēs* (Heracleopolis Magna) on the west side of the Nile, just south of the Fayyum. Hnēs was apparently the home of the family from which the 22nd Dynasty arose, and the scanty documents of succeeding dynasties show it to have been of great importance: in the 25th and 26th Dynasties (*c* 715–600 B.C.) the standard silver of Egypt was specifically that of the treasury of Harshafe, the ram-headed god of Hnēs, and during the long reign of Psammetichus I. (*c* 660–610 B.C.) Hnēs was the centre of government for the whole of Upper Egypt. The LXX does not recognize the name of the city, and shows a wide divergence of reading, and appears to have read 'in vain' (*ḥinnām*) for Hanes (Ḥānēs). F. Ll. G.

HANGING.—See Crimes and Punishments, **10**; Gallows.

HANGING, HANGINGS.—**1.** The former is AV's term for the *portière* closing the entrance to the court of the Tent of Meeting (Ex 35^{17} etc.), for the similar curtain at the entrance to the Tent itself (26^{36f} etc.), and in Nu 3^{31} for the 'veil' or hanging separating the Holy of Holies from the rest of the Tabernacle. In the last passage we should probably read, as in 4^{5}, 'the veil of the screen' (so RV, RSV; AV 'the covering vail'), **screen** being the substitute for 'hanging' in RV and RSV throughout. RV and RSV retain 'hangings,' however, as the translation of a different Hebrew word denoting the curtains 'of fine twined linen' which surrounded the court (Ex 27^{9} etc.). See Tabernacle.

2. In a corrupt passage, 2 K 23^{7}, we read of 'hangings for the Asherah' (RV, RSV; AV 'hangings for the grove'), woven by the women of Jerusalem. The true text is probably Lucian's, which has 'tunics,' the reference being to robes for an image of the goddess Asherah (q.v.). In the religious literature of Babylonia there is frequent reference to gifts of sheepskins, wool, etc., as clothing 'for the god' (*ana lubushti ili*).

A. R. S. K.

HANIEL, 1 Ch 7^{39} (AV).—See Hanniel, **2.**

HANNAH ('grace').—The wife of Elkanah, and mother of Samuel, 1 S 1 f. She came year by year to the sanctuary at Shiloh praying that she might become a mother; on one occasion she made a vow that if God would hear her prayer and grant her a son, she would dedicate him 'to the Lord all the days of his life.' Eli, the high priest, mistakes the silent movement of her lips as she prays, and accuses her of drunkenness; but when he finds out the mistake he had made, he gives her his blessing, and prays that her petition may be granted. Hannah returns home in peace, and in faith. In due time she gives birth to Samuel; when she has weaned him she brings him to Shiloh and dedicates him to God. It is on this occasion that the 'song' contained in 1 S 2$^{1-10}$ is put into her mouth. Afterwards she comes to visit him once a year, bringing him each time a 'little robe.' Hannah bore her husband three sons and two daughters after the birth of Samuel, 1 S 2^{21}. See Elkanah, Samuel. W. O. E. O.

HANNATHON.—A place on the N. border of Zebulun, Jos 19^{14}; possibly modern *Tell el-Bedeiwîyeh.*

HANNIEL ('grace of El').—**1.** Son of Ephod, and Manasseh's representative for dividing the land, Nu 34^{23}. **2.** An Asherite, son of Ulla, 1 Ch 7^{39} (AV **Haniel**).

HANOCH.—**1.** A grandson of Abraham by Keturah, and third of the sons of Midian, Gn 25^{4}, 1 Ch 1^{33}.

2. The eldest son of Reuben, Gn 46[9], Ex 6[14], Nu 26[5], 1 Ch 5[3]. The gentilic **Hanochites** occurs in Nu 26[5].

HANUN ('favoured').—**1.** The son of Nahash, king of the Ammonites. Upon the death of the latter, David sent a message of condolence to Hanun, who, however, resented this action, and grossly insulted the messengers. The consequence was a war, which proved most disastrous to the Ammonites, 2 S 10[1ff], 1 Ch 19[1ff]. **2, 3.** The name occurs twice in the list of those who repaired the wall and the gates of Jerusalem, Neh 3[13, 30].

HAP, HAPLY.—The old word 'hap,' which means *chance*, is found in Ru 2[3] 'her hap was to light on a part of the field belonging to Boaz' (RV; RSV 'she happened to come'). The Hebrew is literally 'her chance chanced' (AVm 'her hap happened'). 'Haply' is 'by hap.' 'Happily' is the same word under a different spelling, and had formerly the same meaning, though it now means 'by *good* luck.' In AV the spelling is now always 'haply,' but in the first edition it was 'happily' in 2 Co 9[4] 'Lest happily if they of Macedonia come with mee, and find you unprepared, wee (that wee say not, you) should bee ashamed in this same confident boasting.' In RSV 'hapless' is found in Ps 10[8, 10, 14], where AV has 'poor' and RV 'helpless.'

HAPHARAIM.—A town in Issachar, Jos 19[19] (AV **Haphraim**). The *Onomasticon* places it 6 Roman miles N. of Legio. The site cannot be identified with any confidence; it is possibly modern *eṭ-Ṭaiyibeh.*

HAPPIZZEZ.—The head of the eighteenth course of priests, 1 Ch 24[15] (AV **Aphses**).

HARA.—Mentioned in 1 Ch 5[26] as one of the places to which Israelites were deported by the king of Assyria on the capture of Samaria. But in the corresponding accounts (2 K 17[6] 18[11]) Hara is not mentioned, and most probably the name 'Hara' in 1 Ch 5[26] is due to a corruption of the text. It is possible that the original text read *hārê Mādai*, 'mountains of Media,' corresponding to the cities of Media of the parallel passages (LXX 'the Median mountains'); and that *Mādai* dropped out of the text, and *hārê*, 'mountains of,' was changed to the proper name *Hara.* L. W. K.

HARADAH.—A station in the journeyings of the Israelites, mentioned only in Nu 33[24, 25]. It has not been identified, but was possibly in *Wâdî Lussân.*

HARAN.—**1.** Son of Terah, younger brother of Abram, and father of Lot, Gn 11[26], also father of Milcah and Iscah, v.[29]. **2.** A Gershonite Levite, 1 Ch 23[9].

HARAN.—A city in the NW. of Mesopotamia, marked by the modern village of *Ḥarrân*, situated on the *Balîkh*, a tributary of the Euphrates, and about nine hours' ride SE. of Edessa (*Urfa*). Terah and his son Abram and his family dwelt there on their way from Ur of the Chaldees to Canaan (Gn 11[31] 12[4, 5]; cf Ac 7[2]), and Terah died there (Gn 11[32]; cf Ac 7[4]). Nahor, Abram's brother, settled there; hence it is called 'the city of Nahor' in the story of Isaac and Jacob (cf Gn 24[10] 27[43]). Its position on one of the main trade-routes between Babylonia and the Mediterranean coast rendered it commercially of great importance (cf Ezk 27[23]). It was an important seat of the worship of Sin, the moon-god, and the frequent references to the city in the Assyrian inscriptions have to do mainly with the worship of this deity and the restoration of his temple. It is probable that Haran rebelled along with the city of Ashur in 763 B.C., and a reference to its subsequent capture and the suppression of the revolt may be seen in 2 K 19[12]; Sargon later on restored the ancient religious privileges of which the city had been then deprived. The worship of the moon-god at Haran appears to have long survived the introduction of Christianity. L. W. K.

HARARITE.—An epithet of doubtful meaning (possibly 'mountain-dweller,' but more probably 'native of [an unknown] Haran') applied to two of David's heroes. **1.** Shammah the son of Agee, 2 S 23[11, 33], 1 Ch 11[34] (where **Shagee** should probably be **Shammah**). **2.** Ahiam the son of Sharar, 2 S 23[33] (RV **Ararite**; AV, RSV **Hararite**), 1 Ch 11[35].

HARBONA.—The third of the seven eunuchs or chamberlains of King Ahasuerus, Est 1[10] 7[9] (in the latter AV, RV **Harbonah**). It was on his suggestion that Haman was hanged upon the gallows which he had prepared for Mordecai.

HARBONAH, Est 7[9] (AV, RV).—See HARBONA.

HARD.—Besides other meanings which are still in use, 'hard' sometimes means *close*: Jg 9[52] 'And Abimelech . . . went hard unto (RSV 'drew near to') the door of the tower to burn it with fire'; Ps 63[8] 'My soul followeth hard after (RSV 'clings to') thee'; Ac 18[7] 'Justus . . . whose house joined hard to (RSV 'was next door to') the synagogue.' Cf Job 17[1] in Coverdale, 'I am harde at deathes dore.'

Hardiness is used in AV in Jth 16[10] for courage: 'the Medes were daunted at her hardiness' (RV 'boldness,' RSV 'daring').

Hardly means either 'harshly,' as Gn 16[6] 'Sarai dealt hardly (RSV 'harshly') with her,' or 'with difficulty,' as Ex 13[15] 'Pharaoh would hardly let us (RSV 'stubbornly refused to let us') go'; Mt 19[23] (AV) 'a rich man shall hardly enter (RSV 'it will be hard for a rich man to enter'; cf RV) into the kingdom of heaven'; Lk 9[39] 'bruising him, hardly departeth from (RSV 'will hardly leave') him; Ac 27[8] 'And, hardly passing it (RSV 'coasting along it with difficulty'; cf RV), came unto a place which is called The fair havens.'

Hardness for modern 'hardship' occurs in 2 Ti 2[3] (AV) 'endure hardness (RSV 'take your share of suffering'; cf RV) as a good soldier.' Cf Shakespeare, *Cymb.* III. vi. 21—

'Hardness ever
Of hardiness is mother.'

HARDENING.—Both in the OT (1 S 6[6]) and in the NT (Ro 9[17f]) Pharaoh's hardening is regarded as typical. In Exodus, two explanations are given of his stubbornness: (1) 'Pharaoh hardened his heart' (8[15, 32]); (2) 'the Lord hardened the heart of Pharaoh' (9[12]). The former statement recognizes man's moral responsibility, and is in accord with the exhortation, 'Harden not your hearts' (Ps 95[8], He 3[8]). To the latter statement St. Paul confines his thought when he insists on the sovereignty of God as manifested in the election of grace (Ro 9[18]); but having vindicated the absolute freedom of the Divine action, the Apostle proceeds to show that the Divine choice is neither arbitrary nor unjust. The difficulty involved in combining the two statements is philosophical rather than theological. 'The attempt to understand the relation between the human will and the Divine seems to lead of necessity to an antinomy which thought has not as yet succeeded in transcending' (Denney, *EGT* ii. 663). The same Divine action softens the heart of him who repents and finds mercy, but hardens the heart of him who obstinately refuses to give heed to the Divine call. 'The sweet persuasion of His voice respects thy sanctity of will.' The RV rightly renders Mk 3[5] 'being grieved at the hardening of their heart'; grief is the permanent attitude of the Saviour towards all in whom there is any sign of this 'process of moral ossification which renders men insensible to spiritual truth' (Swete, *Com. in loc.*). J. G. T.

HARE (Lv 11[6], Dt 14[7]).—Four species of hare are known in Palestine, of which the commonest is the *Lepus syriacus.* The hare does not really 'chew the cud,' though, like the coney, it appears to do so; it was however, unclean because it did not 'divide the hoof.' Hares are to-day eaten by the Arabs.

HAREM.—Found in RSV in Est 2[3, 9, 11, 13f], where AV and RV have 'house of the women.'

HAREPH.—A Judahite chief, 1 Ch 2[51].

HARHAIAH.—Father of Uzziah, a goldsmith who repaired a portion of the wall of Jerusalem, Neh 3[8].

HARHAS.—Ancestor of Shallum, the husband of the prophetess Huldah, 2 K 22[14]; called **Hasrah** in 2 Ch 34[22].

HAR-HERES.—A mountain from which the Danites failed to expel the Amorites, Jg 1[34f] (AV, RV 'mount **Heres**'). It is probably connected with **Beth-shemesh** (1 K 4[9], 2 Ch 28[18]) or **Ir-shemesh** (Jos 19[41]) on the boundary between Judah and Dan. See BETH-SHEMESH, **1.**

HARHUR.—One whose sons returned among the Nethinim (q.v.) with Zerubbabel, Ezr 2[51], Neh 7[53]; called **Asur** in 1 Es 5[31] (AV **Assur**).

HARIM.—**1.** A lay family which appears in the list of the returning exiles, Ezr 2[32] = Neh 7[35]; of those who had married foreign wives, Ezr 10[31] (perhaps the **Annan** of 1 Es 9[32] [AV, RV **Annas**]); and of those who signed the covenant, Neh 10[27]. **2.** A priestly family in the same lists, Ezr 2[39] = Neh 7[42] = 1 Es 5[25] (AV **Carme,** RV **Charme**), Ezr 10[21], Neh 10[5]. The name is found among the heads of priestly families in the days of Joiakim, Neh 12[15], and as the third of the twenty-four courses, 1 Ch 24[8]. If the conjecture that **Rehum** in Neh 12[3] is a miswriting of Harim is correct, the name is found also among the priests and Levites who returned with Zerubbabel. To which family Malchijah the son of Harim, one of the builders of the wall (Neh 3[11]), belonged cannot be determined.

HARIPH.—The head of a family of which 112 members returned with Zerubbabel, Neh 7[24], and who signed the covenant, Neh 10[19]; called **Jorah** in Ezr 2[18], 1 Es 5[16] (AV **Azephurith,** RV **Arsiphurith**). In 1 Ch 12[5] one of David's companions is called a **Haruphite,** where the *Ḳ^erê* has **Hariphite.** If the latter reading is correct it connects with the same name, Hariph.

HARLOT (Heb. *zōnāh*, *'ishshāh nokrīyyāh* [literally 'strange woman'], *ḳ[e]dhēshāh*, Gr *pornē*) in EV denotes unchaste women, especially those devoted to immoral service in idol sanctuaries, or given to a dissolute life for gain. We find evidence of their existence in very early times (Gn 38). From the name 'strange woman' in Pr 6[24] 23[27] etc. (cf 1 K 11[1], Ezr 10[2] etc.), we may perhaps infer that in later times they were chiefly foreigners. By songs (Is 23[16]) and insinuating arts (Pr 6[24] etc.) they captivated the unwary. They acted also as decoys to the dens of robbery and murder (Pr 7[22, 27] etc.). Wealth was lavished upon them (Ezk 16[33, 39] 23[26] etc.; cf Lk 15[30]). Apart from breaches of the marriage vows, immoral relations between the sexes were deemed venial (Dt 22[28ff]). A man might not compel his daughter to sin (Lv 19[29]), but apparently she was free herself to take that way. Children of harlots were practical outlaws (Dt 23[2], Jg 11[1ff], Jn 8[41]), and in NT times the harlot lived under social ban (Mt 21[32] etc.).

The picture takes a darker hue when we remember that in ancient Syria the reproductive forces of nature were deified, and worshipped in grossly immoral rites. Both men and women prostituted themselves in the service of the gods. The Canaanite sanctuaries were practically gigantic brothels, legalized by the sanctions of religion. The appeal made to the baser passions of the Israelites was all too successful (Am 2[7], Hos 4[13ff] etc.), and it is grimly significant that the prophets designate apostasy and declension by 'whoredom.' There were therefore special reasons for the exceptional law regarding the priest's daughter (Lv 21[9]). Religious prostitution was prohibited in Israel (Dt 23[17]), and all gain from the unholy calling as Temple revenue was spurned (see Driver, *Deut.*, *in loc.*). The pure religion of Y″ was delivered from this peril only by the stern discipline of the Exile. A similar danger beset the early Church, *e.g.* in Greece and Asia Minor; hence such passages as Ro 1[24ff], 1 Co 6[9ff], Gal 5[19] etc., and the decree of the Apostolic Council (Ac 15[20, 29]). W. E.

HAR-MAGEDON, Rev 16[16] (RV).—See ARMAGEDDON.

HARMON.—Place to which the people of Samaria were to be exiled, Am 4[3] (AV 'the palace'). No place of this name is known.

HARMONIES OF THE GOSPELS.—This term is applied to two quite different types of works: (1) an interwoven, continuous narrative utilizing the four Gospels or at least the Synoptics; and (2) an arrangement in parallel columns of these three or four, showing correspondences and divergencies.

(1) The beginnings of the first kind go back to Tatian, who about A.D. 175 combined in his *Diatessaron* the four Gospels into one continuous narrative, probably first in Greek (a small fragment from Dura Europos was published in 1935).

(2) The first known example of the second type, an arrangement of the Gospels in parallel columns, is the work of Ammonius (3rd cent.), who is said to have taken Matthew and to have placed beside it (in full? or in references?) the corresponding passages from the other Gospels. The *Sections* and *Canons* of Eusebius (4th cent.) develop this still further, enabling one to discover at a glance the parallel passages. The following are the principal modern harmonies of the second type: A. Huck, *Synopse der drei ersten Evangelien*[10] [in Greek] (Tübingen: Mohr, 1950); E. D. Burton and E. J. Goodspeed, *A Harmony of the Synoptic Gospels in Greek* (University of Chicago, 1920); B. H. Throckmorton, *Gospel Parallels: A Synopsis of the First Three Gospels* [in the Revised Standard Version] (Nelson, 1949); and W. Bundy, *A Syllabus and Synopsis of the First Three Gospels* (Bobbs-Merrill, 1932). J. S. B.—**J. H. S.**

HARNEPHER.—An Asherite, 1 Ch 7[36].

HARNESS.—See, generally ARMOUR, which RV and RSV substitute in most places for AV 'harness.' Similarly 'harnessed' (Ex 13[18]) becomes 'armed' (RV) or 'equipped' (RSV), and the 'well harnessed' camp of 1 Mac 4[7] becomes 'fortified.' For 'the joints of the harness' of 1 K 22[34] RVm substitutes 'the lower armour and breastplate' and RSV 'the scale armour and the breastplate,' the former being probably 'the *tassets* or jointed appendages of the cuirass, covering the abdomen' (Skinner, *Cent. Bible, in loc.*). The only passage in AV where 'harness' as a verb has its modern signification is Jer 46[4] 'harness the horses' (so RV, RSV), the verb in the original being that used in Gn 46[29], Ex 14[6] etc. for yoking the horses to the chariots. In Mic 1[13] RSV has 'harness the steeds' where Hebrew employs a different verb (AV, RV 'bind'). A. R. S. K.

HAROD.—A spring, not a well as in AV, near the mountains of Gilboa (q.v.), where Gideon tested his men (Jg 7[1]), and which was probably the site of Saul's camp before his fatal battle with the Philistines (1 S 29[1]). It has been very generally identified with the copious *'Ain Jālûd* in the Vale of Jezreel, E. of *Zer'în*. The water rises in a natural cavern and spreads itself out into a considerable pool, partially artificial, before descending the valley. It is one of the most plentiful and beautiful fountains in Palestine, and one that must always have been taken into account in military movements in the neighbourhood. The place from which Shammah came (see next article) may or may not have been beside this spring. E. W. G. M.

HARODITE.—A gentilic from Harod (q.v.), applied in 2 S 23[25] to two of David's heroes, Shammah and Elika (so AV, RV; RSV 'of Harod'). The second is wanting in LXX and in the parallel 1 Ch 11[27]. In the latter passage, by a common scribal error 'Harodite' has become **Harorite** (so AV, RV; RSV 'of Harod').

HAROEH ('the seer').—A Judahite, 1 Ch 2[52]. Perhaps the name should be corrected to **Reaiah,** which stands in 1 Ch 4[2].

HARORITE.—See HARODITE.

HAROSHETH-HA-GOIIM.—A place mentioned only in the account of the fight with Sisera, Jg 4[2, 13, 16] (AV, RV 'Harosheth of the Gentiles'). From it Sisera advanced, and thither he fled. It may be modern *Tell 'Amr*, near *el-Ḥāriṭîyeh*. We do not know why the descriptive 'of the Gentiles' is added.

HARP.—See MUSIC AND MUSICAL INSTRUMENTS, **4 (1).**

HARPOON.—Found only in RSV in Job 41^{7}, where AV and RSV have ‘ barbed irons.’

HARROW.—In 2 S 12^{31}—a passage which had become corrupt before the date of 1 Ch 20^{3}—as rendered in AV and RV, David is represented as torturing the Ammonites ‘ under harrows of iron.’ The true text and rendering, however, have reference to various forms of forced labour (so RSV), and the ‘ harrows ’ become ‘ iron picks ’ or some similar implement.

The Hebrew verb translated ‘ harrow ’ in Job 39^{10} is elsewhere rendered ‘ break the clods ’; so Hos 10^{11}, Is 28^{24} (AV, RV; RSV ‘ harrow ’ in both passages). In Hastings’ *DB* ii, 306 several reasons were given for rejecting the universal modern rendering of the original by ‘ harrow.’ This conclusion has since been confirmed by the discovery of the original Hebrew of Sir 38^{26} where ‘ who setteth his mind to “ harrow ” in the furrows ’ would be an absurd rendering. There is no evidence that the Hebrews at any time made use of an implement corresponding to our harrow. Stiff soil was broken up by the plough or the mattock.

A. R. S. K.

HARSHA.—Eponym of a family of Nethinim (q.v.), Ezr 2^{52}, Neh 7^{54}, called **Charea** in 1 Es 5^{32}.

HARSITH, Jer 19^{2} (RV).—See POTSHERD GATE.

HART, HIND (*'ayyāl*, *'ayyālāh*, and *'ayyeleth*).—This is the fallow-deer, the *'iyyāl* of the Arabs, *Cervus dama.* It is not common in W. Palestine to-day, but evidently was so once, 1 K 4^{23}; it is mentioned as a clean animal in Dt 12$^{15, 22}$ etc. Its habits when pursued are referred to in Ps 42^{1} and La 1^{6}. The ‘ **fallow-deer** ’ of Dt 14^{5} and 1 K 4^{23} (AV; RV, RSV ‘ roebuck ’ in both passages) refers to the **roe** (q.v.). The hind is mentioned in Gn 49^{21}, Job 39^{1}, Ps 29^{9} (RSV ‘ oaks ’ in the last), etc. Its care of its young (Jer 14^{5}), the secrecy of its hiding-place when calving (Job 39^{1}), and its timidity at such times (Ps 29^{9}; but see above) are all noticed. In Gn 49^{21} Naphtali is compared to ‘ a hind let loose,’ although many prefer to render a ‘ slender terebinth.’

E. W. G. M.

HARUM.—A Judahite, 1 Ch 4^{8}.

HARUMAPH.—Father of Jedaiah, who assisted in repairing the walls of Jerusalem, Neh 3^{10}.

HARUPHITE.—See HARIPH.

HARUZ.—Father of Meshullemeth, mother of Amon king of Judah, 2 K 21^{19}.

HARVEST.—See AGRICULTURE.

HASADIAH (‘ Y″ is kind ’).—**1.** A son of Zerubbabel, 1 Ch 3^{20}. **2.** An ancestor of Baruch, Bar 1^{1} (AV, RV **Asadias**).

HASENUAH, 1 Ch 9^{7} (AV).—See HASSENUAH.

HASHABIAH (‘ Y″ has taken account ’).—**1, 2.** Two Levites of the family of Merari, 1 Ch 6^{45} 9^{14}, Neh 11^{15}. **3.** One of the sons of Jeduthun, 1 Ch 25$^{3, 19}$. **4.** A Hebronite, 1 Ch 26^{30}. **5.** The officer over the Levites, 1 Ch 27^{17}. **6.** A chief of the Levites in the time of Josiah, 2 Ch 35^{9}, 1 Es 1^{9} (AV **Assabias,** RV **Sabias**). **7.** One of the Levites who returned with Ezra, Ezr 8^{19}, 1 Es 8^{48} (AV **Asebia,** RV **Asebias**). **8.** One of the twelve priests entrusted with the holy vessels, Ezr 8^{24}, 1 Es 8^{54} (AV **Assanias,** RV **Assamias**). **9.** The ‘ ruler of half the district of Keilah,’ who helped to repair the wall (Neh 3^{17}), and sealed the covenant (Neh 10^{11} 12^{24}). **10.** A Levite, Neh 11^{22}. **11.** A priest, Neh 12^{21}. In all probability these eleven are not all distinct, but we have not sufficient data to enable us to make the necessary reduction of the list. In Ezr 10^{25} RSV substitutes Hashabiah for **Malchijah** (2°) to agree with 1 Es 9^{26} where Greek has **Asibias** (q.v.).

HASHABNAH.—One of those who sealed the covenant, Neh 10^{25}.

HASHABNEIAH.—**1.** Father of a builder of the wall, Neh 3^{10}. **2.** A Levite, Neh 9^{5}. It is possible that we ought to identify this name with **Hashabiah** of Ezr 8$^{19, 24}$, Neh 10^{11} 11^{22} 12^{24}.

HASHABNIAH.—AV spelling of **Hashabneiah** (q.v.).

HASHBADANA, Neh 8^{4} (AV).—See HASHBADDANAH.

HASHBADDANAH.—One of the men who stood on the left hand of Ezra at the reading of the Law, Neh 8^{4} (AV **Hashbadana**); called **Nabariah** in 1 Es 9^{44} (AV, RV **Nabarias**).

HASHEM.—See GIZONITE, JASHEN.

HASHMONAH.—A station in the journeyings of the Israelites, near Kadesh-barnea, Nu 33^{29f}: possibly modern *Wâdī el-Hashim.*

HASHUB, Neh 3$^{11, 23}$ 10^{23} 11^{15} (AV).—See HASSHUB.

HASHUBAH.—A son of Zerubbabel, 1 Ch 3^{20}.

HASHUM.—**1.** The eponym of a family of returning exiles, Ezr 2^{19} 10^{33}, Neh 7^{22} 10^{18}, 1 Es 9^{33} (AV, RV **Asom**). **2.** One of those who stood on Ezra’s left hand at the reading of the Law, Neh 8^{4}; called **Lothasubus** in 1 Es 9^{44}.

HASIDAEANS (AV **Assideans**; Heb. *ḥ^{a}sîdhîm* ‘ the pious ’). A religious group in Judaea in the early 2nd cent. B.C. (1 Mac 2^{42}), to be distinguished from the priestly party who had come under the influence of Hellenism. The Hasidaeans were devoted to the Law, and refused to compromise in any way with the Hellenizing policy enforced by Antiochus IV. They furnished the martyrs of the persecution under that monarch. Strictly speaking, they were not a political party, and probably lived in the smaller Jewish towns, as well as in Jerusalem. They joined with Mattathias in his revolt against the Syrians, but were not interested in the political outcome of the struggle, except as it gave them the right to worship God according to the Torah. After Judas had cleansed the Temple, they separated themselves from the Hasmonaean or Maccabaean party, and united with them only temporarily, when they found that under Alcimus the Temple worship was again threatened. Their defection from Judas was largely the cause of his downfall.

Their precise relation to the Scribal movement cannot be stated because of lack of data. The Hasidaeans may have included all the orthodox scribes and may have been devotees to the growing Oral Law. If so, they were thus the forerunners of the Pharisees and possibly of the Essenes. The latter party, although differing from them in rejecting animal sacrifice, is often regarded as preserving their name, for some suppose that ‘ Essene ’ is a variant of *ḥāsîdh.*

A similarly named group, usually called the Hasidim, originated in Eastern Europe in the 18th cent. No relationship exists between the two. The later movement has been popularized by Martin Buber.

S. M.—**S. S.**

HASMONAEANS.—See MACCABEES.

HASRAH.—**1.** Grandfather of Shallum, the husband of Huldah the prophetess, 2 Ch 34^{22}; called **Harhas** in 2 K 22^{14}. **2.** The head of a family of Nethinim (q.v.), which returned with Zerubbabel, 1 Es 5^{31} (RSV; AV **Azara,** RV **Asara**); omitted in the parallel lists in Ezra and Nehemiah.

HASSENAAH.—His sons built the Fish Gate, Neh 3^{3}. The name, which is probably the same as **Hassenuah** (q.v.), seems to be derived from some place *Senaah* (cf Ezr 2^{35}, Neh 7^{38}). See SENAAH.

HASSENUAH.—A family name found in two different connexions in the two lists of Benjamite inhabitants of Jerusalem, 1 Ch 9^{7} (AV **Hasenuah**), Neh 11^{9} (AV **Senuah**). Cf preceding article.

HASSHUB.—**1. 2.** Two builders of the wall, Neh 3$^{11, 23}$ (AV **Hashub**). **3.** One of those who signed the covenant, Neh 10^{23} (AV **Hashub**). **4.** A Levite of the sons of Merari, 1 Ch 9^{14}, Neh 11^{15} (AV **Hashub** in latter).

HASSOPHERETH.—A family of Nethinim, Ezr 2^{55} (AV **Sophereth**), 1 Es 5^{33} (AV **Azaphion,** RV **Assaphioth**): called **Sophereth** in Neh 7^{57}.

HASUPHA.—The head of a family of Nethinim (q.v.) who returned with Zerubbabel, Ezr 2[43], Neh 7[46], 1 Es 5[29] (AV, RV **Asipha**).

HAT.—See Dress, **5** (*a*).

HATACH, Est 4[5] etc. (AV).—See Hathach.

HATCHET.—Ps 74[6] (RV, RSV; AV **axe**).—See Arts and Crafts, **1.**

HATHACH.—A eunuch appointed by the king to attend on queen Esther. By his means Esther learned from Mordecai the details of Haman's plot against the Jews, Est 4[5, 6, 9, 10] (AV, **Hatach**).

HATHATH.—A son of Othniel, 1 Ch 4[13].

HATIPHA.—Eponym of a family of Nethinim (q.v.), who returned with Zerubbabel, Ezr 2[54], Neh 7[56], 1 Es 5[32] (AV, RV **Atipha**).

HATITA.—Eponym of a guild of porters, who returned with Zerubbabel, Ezr 2[42], Neh 7[45], 1 Es 5[28] (AV **Teta,** RV **Ateta**).

HATRED.—Personal hatred is permitted in the OT, but forbidden in the NT (Mt 5[43–45]). Love is to characterize the Christian life (Mt 22[37–40]). The only hatred it can express is hatred of evil (He 1[9], Jd [23], Rev 2[6] 17[16]). In Lk 14[26] and Jn 12[25] the use of the verb 'hate' by Jesus is usually explained as Oriental hyperbole. D. A. H.

HATTIL.—Eponym of a family of 'the sons of Solomon's servants,' Ezr 2[57], Neh 7[59], 1 Es 5[34] (AV **Hagia,** RV **Agia**).

HATTUSH.—**1.** A priestly family that returned with Zerubbabel (Neh 12[2]), and signed the covenant (Neh 10[4]). **2.** A descendant of David who returned with Ezra, Ezr 8[2] (where we should read 'Hattush, the son of Shecaniah'; cf 1 Es 8[29], where AV has **Lettus** and RV **Attus**), 1 Ch 3[22]. **3.** A builder of the wall of Jerusalem, Neh 3[10].

HAUNT.—In older English 'haunt' conveyed no reproach, but meant simply to spend time in or frequent a place. Thus Tyndale translates Jn 3[22] 'After these thinges cam Jesus and his disciples into the Jewes londe, and ther he haunted with them and baptized.' So 1 S 30[31], Ezk 26[17], and the substantive in 1 S 23[22] 'know and see the place where his haunt is.'

HAURAN.—The elevated district SE. from Mt. Hermon; in particular the fertile basin, about 50 miles square and 2000 feet above sea-level, between the *Jaulân* and *Lejâ*. Only in Ezk 47[16, 18] is the name mentioned, and there as the ideal border of Canaan on the east. The modern Arabs call essentially the same district *el-Ḥaurân* or *Jebel Ḥaurân*. However, the (Mount) Salmon of Ps 68[14] has sometimes been equated with the *Jebel Ḥaurân*. The name occurs also in the ancient inscriptions of Assyria. In Graeco-Roman times the same general region was known as *Auranitis*; it was bounded on the N. by Trachonitis, and on the NW. by Gaulanitis and Batanaea. All these districts belonged to Herod the Great. Upon his death they fell to Philip (Lk 3[1]). The eastern portion is now inhabited by Druzes. The entire territory is to-day practically treeless, and is noted for its production of wheat. G. L. R.—**E. G. K.**

HAURAN, 2 Mac 4[40] (RV).—See Auranus.

HAVILAH.—**1.** Son of Cush, Gn 10[7], 1 Ch 1[9]. **2.** Son of Joktan, Gn 10[29], 1 Ch 1[23]. **3.** The land of Havilah is said to have been compassed by the Pishon, one of the four rivers of the Garden of Eden, Gn 2[11] (see Eden, Garden of). It is said to have produced gold, bdellium, and onyx, v.[12]. **4.** The limits of Ishmaelite territory are described as 'from Havilah to Shur,' Gn 25[18]. It was in this area that Saul defeated the Amalekites, 1 S 25[7]. It seems likely that more than one region is indicated by these references, but it is impossible to identify them with any security, despite the many conjectures which have been made.

HAVOTH-JAIR.—The AV spelling of **Havvoth-jair** (q.v.).

HAVVOTH-JAIR.—The word Havvoth means 'tent villages.' In Nu 32[41] these villages are assigned to Gilead, but in Dt 3[14] and Jos 13[20] to Bashan. It is possible that the boundaries varied in different periods. According to Nu 32[41], Dt 3[14], and 1 K 4[13] they were named after Jair, the son of Manasseh, but according to Jg 10[4] after the minor Judge Jair. The Aramaean tribe of Geshur (q.v.) is said to have taken these villages, 1 Ch 2[23].

HAWK.—The Hebrew words for hawks, falcons, and kites, are not easily distinguished for lack of adequate information. The Hebrew *nēṣ* (cf Ugar. *nṣ*) from *nāṣaṣ* 'flashed' is apparently a generic term (cf Ezk 1[7]) for the hawk (LXX, Vulgate), of which some eighteen species exist in Palestine; its position in the list of unclean birds, which are given in diminishing order of size, suggests 'kestrel' (*falco tinnunculus*) and/or 'sparrow-hawk' (*accipiter nisus*) as meant in the OT. The kestrel, which is a resident, abounds almost everywhere, and the sparrow-hawk is almost equally common. The description of the *nēṣ* as spreading its wings to the south (Job 39[26]) refers to the habit of many small hawks of migrating, after breeding in the north, southwards to the basin of the Red Sea; and their raptorial habit of life explains why they are accounted unclean (Lv 11[16], Dt 14[15]). The translation of the Hebrew *taḥmās* as 'night-hawk' (EV) is a contradiction in terms, since the hawk is a diurnal hunter; the bird meant is perhaps the 'short-eared owl' (cf LXX, Vulgate), which too as a raptor is included with the unclean birds (Lv 11[16], Dt 14[15]). G. R. D.

HAY.—See Grass.

HAZAEL usurped the throne of Syria (*c* 843 B.C.) by murdering Ben-hadad (q.v.). An inscription on a basalt statue of Shalmaneser III. says: 'Hazael, son of a nobody, seized the throne.' According to 1 K 19[15] Elijah is commanded by Yahweh to anoint Hazael to be king of Syria. The next mention of him describes how Ben-hadad, who is ill, sends Hazael to Elisha to enquire whether he will recover. Elisha says to Hazael: 'Go, say to him, "You shall certainly recover"; but the Lord has shown me that he shall certainly die.' . . . 'The Lord has shown me that you are to be king over Syria' (2 K 8[10, 13]). Ben-hadad was murdered next day and Hazael succeeded him (2 K 8[15]). The similarities in those two stories have led some to regard them as two accounts from different sources of the same event.

Shalmaneser records on the famous Black Obelisk his expedition against Hazael in 841 B.C. He claims a great victory and says he ravaged the land, but Damascus did not fall. The next biblical mention of Hazael shows him fighting at Ramoth-gilead against the allied armies of Joram, king of Israel, and Ahaziah, king of Judah (2 K 8[28f] 9[14f]); the narrative here breaks off to deal with other matters, and does not say what the result of the fighting was, but from 2 K 10[32ff] it is clear not only that Hazael was victorious then, but that he continued to be so for a number of years (see, further, 2 K 12[17ff]); indeed, it was not until his death that the Israelites were once more able to assert themselves. The Syrian oppression is recorded by Amos (1[3–5]), and this prophet who inveighs against those who lie on beds inlaid with ivory (6[4]) might have connected Hazael with the same fault, for at Arslan Tash in northern Syria such a piece of ivory decoration has been found inscribed with Hazael's name. The date of Hazael's death is uncertain, but probably it was *c* 801 B.C. (see 2 K 13[22]). W. O. E. O.—**W. D. McH.**

HAZAIAH.—A descendant of Judah, Neh 11[5].

HAZAR-ADDAR.—A place on the southern border of Canaan, W. of Kadesh-barnea (Nu 34[4]); possibly modern *Khirbet el-Qudeirât*. See also Addar, Hezron, **3.**

HAZAR-ENAN.—A place mentioned in Nu 34[9f] as the northern boundary of Israel. In Ezk 48[1] (RSV **Hazar-enon**) it figures as one of the ideal boundaries.

In Ezk 47^{17} it is called **Hazar-enon** (so RV, RSV ; AV **Hazar-enan**), and this is added by RSV in v.^{18}, from which it seems to have dropped out. Its location is unknown, but it appears to have been in the neighbourhood of Damascus. See also Hazer-hatticon.

HAZAR-ENON.—See Hazar-enan.

HAZAR-GADDAH.—An unknown town in the extreme south of Judah, Jos 15^{27}.

HAZAR-HATTICON, Ezr 47^{16} (AV).—See Hazer-hatticon.

HAZARMAVETH.—The eponym of a Joktanite clan, Gn 10^{26}, 1 Ch 1^{20}, described as a 'son' of Joktan, fifth in order from Shem. Its identity with the modern *Ḥaḍramaut* is certain. It was celebrated for its traffic in frankincense.

HAZAR-SHUAL.—A place in S. Judah, Jos 15^{28}, 1 Ch 4^{28} or Simeon (Jos 19^{3}), repeopled by Jews after the Captivity (Neh 11^{27}). It is possibly *Kh. Waṭan*, E. of Beersheba.

HAZAR-SUSAH.—A city in Simeon, Jos 19^{5} ; called **Hazar-susim** in 1 Ch 4^{31}. It is possibly modern *Sbalat Abû Sûsein.*

HAZAR-SUSIM.—See Hazar-susah.

HAZAZON-TAMAR.—A city occupied by Amorites, Gn 14^{7} (AV **Hazezon-tamar**) ; in 2 Ch 20^{2} it is identified with **En-gedi.** It was probably near modern *'Ain el-'Arûs*. See also Atharim.

HAZEL, Gn 30^{37} (AV).—See Almond.

HAZELELPONI, 1 Ch 43 (AV).—See Hazzelelponi.

HAZER-HATTICON ('the middle Hazer').—A place named among the boundaries of ideal Israel, Ezk 47^{16} (AV **Hazar-hatticon**). It is described as 'by the border of Hauran.' It is perhaps to be identified with **Hazar-enan** (q.v.).

HAZERIM.—In AV a place occupied by the Avvim, Dt 2^{23} ; but RV and RSV replace by 'villages.'

HAZEROTH.—A station in the wilderness wanderings of Israel, Nu 11^{35} 12^{16} 33^{17f}, Dt 1^{1}. It is usually identified with *'Ain Khaḍrā*, about 30 miles NE. of *Jebel Mûsā*.

HAZEZON-TAMAR, Gn 14^{7} (AV).—See Hazazon-tamar.

HAZIEL.—A Gershonite Levite, 1 Ch 23^{9}.

HAZO.—The eponym of a Nahorite clan, Gn 22^{22}. It is no doubt identical with *Hazū*, which along with *Bazū* is mentioned in an inscription of Esarhaddon.

HAZOR.—**1.** The city of Jabin (Jos 11^{1} etc.), in Naphtali (Jos 19^{36}), S. of Kedesh (1 Mac $11^{63, 67}$ etc., called in To 1^{2} **Asher**), overlooking Lake Semechonitis = *el-Ḥûleh* (Jos. *Ant.* v. v. 1 [199]). It is identified with *el-Qedaḥ* (*Khirbet Waqqaṣ*) about 3 miles south-west of Thella on the lake. The archaeological history of the site has been determined by the James A. de Rothschild expedition, 1955–1958, directed by Y. Yadin (*Hazor I* [1958], II [1959], III, and IV in preparation ; preliminary reports in *BA* and *IEJ* [1956–1959]). It is described in Jos 11^{10} as 'the head of all those kingdoms.' Its pre-eminence dates from the 18th cent. B.C., as attested by the Mari archives ; it also figures as a major political and commercial centre in the Amarna age (14th cent.). By the time of Joshua its influence had begun to wane, though it still ranked at the head of the northern coalition. Its destruction by the Israelites toward the end of the 13th cent. has been confirmed by the excavations. Solomon fortified it (1 K 9^{15}). It was taken by Tiglath-pileser III. (2 K 15^{29}). **2.** A town in the Negeb of Judah (Jos 15^{23}), unidentified. **3.** A town also in the Negeb, identified with **Kerioth-hezron** (Jos 15^{25}) ; but the text is difficult (cf J. Simons, *The Geographical and Topographical Texts of the Old Testament* [1959], p. 143). **4.** A place in Benjamin, N. of Jerusalem (Neh 11^{33}), probably *Khirbet Ḥazzūr*, between *Beit Ḥanînah* and *Neby Samwîl*. **5.** The kingdoms of Hazor, named with Kedar (Jer 49^{28} etc.), an Arabian district, possibly on the border of the desert.

W. E.—**D. N. F.**

HAZOR-HADATTAH.—A town of Judah, in the Negeb, Jos 15^{25} (AV **Hazor, Hadattah**). The name means 'the new Hazor.' The site is unknown.

HAZOR-ITHNAN.—See Ithnan.

HAZZELELPONI.—A female name in the genealogy of Judah, 1 Ch 4^{3} (AV **Hazelelponi**).

HE.—Fifth letter of the Hebrew alphabet, and so used to introduce the fifth part of Ps 119, every verse of which begins with this letter.

HEAD.—The Hebrews did not regard the head as the seat of the intellect ; it was, however, the seat of life, and was naturally held in honour. Hence phrases such as 'keeper of my head' (1 S 28^{2} ; cf Ps 140^{7}), 'swearing by the head' (Mt 5^{36}), and the metaphorical use common to all languages, as equivalent to 'chief.' In Dt 28^{13}, Is 9^{14}, we find 'head and tail' as a proverbial expression. Christ is the head of the Church (Eph 4^{15}, Col 1^{18} 2^{19}), as man is of the woman (Eph 5^{23}). *To lift up the head* is to grant success (Ps 27^{6} 110^{7}, Gn 41^{13}, where there is an obvious ironical parallel in v.^{19}). *The hand on the head* was a sign of mourning (2 S 13^{19}, Jer 2^{37}) ; so dust or ashes (2 S 1^{2}, La 2^{10}) ; or *covering the head* (2 S 15^{30}, Jer 14^{3}). On the other hand, to *uncover the head, i.e.* to loose the turban and leave the hair in disorder, was also a sign of mourning (see AV and RVm, Lv 10^{6} 13^{45}, Ezk 24^{17}). Similarly *shaving the head*, a common practice in the East (Job 1^{20}, Is 15^{2} 22^{12}, Ezk 7^{18}, Am 8^{10}) ; it was forbidden to priests (Lv 21^{5}), and, in special forms, to all Israelites (19^{27}, Dt 14^{1}). It might also mark the close of a period of mourning (Dt 21^{12}), or of a Nazirite's vow (Nu 6^{9}, Ac 18^{18}), or of a Levite's purification (Nu 8^{7}). In Dt 32^{42} there is a reference to the warrior's long hair, RVm. *Laying hands on the head* was (*a*) part of the symbolism of sacrifice (Lv 16^{21}), (*b*) a sign of blessing (Gn 48^{14}), (*c*) a sign of consecration or ordination (Nu 27^{23}, Ac 6^{6}). In 2 K 2^{3} the reference seems to be to the pupil sitting at the feet of his master. 'Head' is also used, like 'face,' as a synonym for 'self' (Ps 7^{16} ; and probably Pr 25^{22}, Ro 12^{20}).

C. W. E.

HEADBAND.—**1.** In 1 K $20^{38, 41}$, where AV has **ashes,** RV has 'headband' (RSV 'bandage'). Beyond the fact that it covered the wearer's forehead its form is unknown. **2.** In Is 3^{20} AV has 'headbands,' where we should read, with RV and RSV **sashes.** The same word is used in Jer 2^{32} for the sash or girdle (EV 'attire') with which a bride 'girds' herself (cf Is 49^{18}, where the cognate verb is used). **3.** In Is 3^{18}, where AV and RV have **cauls** (q.v.), RSV has 'headbands.'

HEADSTONE, more correctly 'head stone,' Zec 4^{7} (RSV 'top stone') etc.—See Corner, Corner-stone.

HEADTIRE, TIRE.—The former is found in AV, as one word, only in 1 Es 3^{6} (so RV ; RSV **turban**), for the *kidaris*, the stiff upright headdress of the Persian kings. In RV **headtire** replaces AV's **bonnet** (q.v.) in Ex 28^{40} 29^{9} 39^{28} (RSV **cap**), Is 3^{20} (RSV **headdress**). In Ezk 44^{18} RV has **tire** (RSV **turban**) for AV **bonnet.** For AV's 'the tire of thine head,' Ezr 24^{17}, RV has 'thy headtire' (RSV **turban**). For AV's the 'round tires like the moon' of Is 3^{18}, RV and RSV have **crescents.** See Ornaments and Dress, **5** (*a*).

HEADY.—This form of the English word has been displaced by 'headstrong.' It occurs in 2 Ti 3^{4}, where the same Greek word is used as is translated 'rashly' (RV, RSV 'rash') in Ac 19^{36}. Bishop Hall (*Works*, ii, 109) says, 'We may offend as well in our heddye acceleration, as in our delay.' RSV reads 'reckless.'

HEALTH.—The word formerly covered (*a*) healing, (*b*) spiritual soundness, (*c*) general well-being. For (*a*) cf Pr 12^{18} 13^{17}, Jer 8^{15}, where it represents the word usually translated 'healing' (so RSV in all cases, and RV in Jer 8^{15}). (*b*) In Ps 42^{11} 43^{5} (RSV 'help') 67^{2} (RSV 'power'), and frequently in Prayer Book Version, it stands for the word otherwise translated 'salvation' or 'help.' In these usages it is active. (*c*) The wider passive use, including general well-being of body and soul, not merely the absence of disease, is illustrated by Ac 27^{34} (RSV 'strength'), 3 Jn^{2}. Cf *General Confession*, 'There is no health in us.' See MEDICINE.

C. W. E.

HEART.—1. Instances are not wanting in the OT of the employment of this word in a physiological sense, though they are not numerous. Jacob, for example, seems to have suffered in his old age from weakness of the heart; a sudden failure of its action occurred on receipt of the unexpected but joyful news of Joseph's great prosperity (Gn 45^{26}). A similar failure proved fatal in the case of Eli, also in extreme old age (1 S 4^{13-18}; cf the case of the exhausted king, 28^{20}). The effect of the rending of the pericardium is referred to by Hosea as well known (13^{8}); and although the proverb 'a tranquil mind (RV 'sound heart') is the life of the flesh' (Pr 14^{30}) is primarily intended as a psychological truth, the simile is evidently borrowed from a universally recognized physiological fact (cf 4^{23}). The aphorism attributed to 'the Preacher' (Ec 10^{2}) may be interpreted in the same way; the 'right hand' is the symbol of strength and firmness, and the left of weakness and indecision (cf 2^{14}). Nor does it appear that OT writers were ignorant of the vital functions which the heart is called on to discharge. This will be seen by their habit of using the word metaphorically as almost a synonym for the entire life (cf Ps 22^{26} 69^{32}, Is 1^{5}, where 'head' and 'heart' cover man's whole being).

2. The preponderating use of the word is, however, psychological; and it is in this way made to cover a large variety of thought. Thus it is employed to denote *the centre of man's personal activities*, the source whence the principles of his action derive their origin (see Gn 6^{5} 8^{21}, where men's evil deeds are attributed to corruption of the heart). We are, therefore, able to understand the significance of the Psalmist's penitential prayer, 'Create in me a clean heart' (Ps 51^{10}), and the meaning of the prophet's declaration, 'a new heart also I will give you' (Ezk 36^{26}; cf 11^{19}). The heart, moreover, was considered to be *the seat of the emotions and passions* (Dt 19^{6}, 1 K 8^{38}, Is 30^{29}; cf Ps 104^{15}, where the heart is said to be moved to gladness by the use of wine). It was a characteristic, too, of Hebraistic thought which made this organ *the seat of the various activities of the intellect*, such as understanding (Job $34^{10,\,34}$, 1 K 4^{29}), purpose or determination (Ex 14^{5}, 1 S 7^{3}, 1 K 8^{48}, Is 10^{7}), consciousness (Pr 14^{10}, where, if EV be an accurate translation of the original text, the heart is said to be conscious both of sorrow and of joy; cf 1 S 2^{1}), imagination (cf Lk 1^{51}, Gn 8^{21}), memory (Ps 31^{12}, 1 S 21^{12}; cf Lk $2^{19,\,51}$ 16^{6}). *The monitions of the conscience* are said to proceed from the heart (Job 27^{6}), and the counterpart of the NT expression 'branded in their own conscience as with a hot iron' (1 Ti 4^{2} RV) is found in the OT words 'I will harden his heart' (Ex 4^{21}; cf Dt 2^{30}, Jos 11^{20} etc.). Closely connected with the idea of conscience is that of moral character, and so we find 'a new heart' as the great desideratum of a people needing restoration to full and intimate relationship with God (Ezk 18^{31}; cf Dt 9^{5}, 1 K 11^{4}). It is, therefore, in those movements which characterize repentance, placed in antithesis to outward manifestations of sorrow for sin, 'Rend your hearts and not your garments' (Jl 2^{13}).

3. Moving along in the direction thus outlined and not forgetting the influence of the Apocryphal writings on later thought (cf *e.g.* Wis 8^{19} 17^{11}, Sir 42^{18} etc.), we shall be enabled to grasp the religious ideas enshrined in the teaching of the NT. In the recorded utterances of Jesus, so profoundly influenced by the ancient writings of the Jewish Church, the heart occupies a very central place. The beatific vision is reserved for those whose hearts are 'pure' (Mt 5^{8}; cf 2 Ti 2^{22}, 1 P 1^{22} RVm). The heart is compared to the soil on which seed is sown; it contains moral potentialities which spring into objective existence in the outward life of the receiver (Lk 8^{15}, cf, however, Mk 4^{15-20}, where no mention is made of this organ; see also Mt 13^{19}, in which the heart is referred to, as in Is 6^{10}, as the seat of the spiritual understanding). Hidden within the remote recesses of the heart are those principles and thoughts which will inevitably spring into active life, revealing its purity or its native corruption (Lk 6^{45}; cf Mt 12^{34f} 15^{18f}). It is thus that men's characters reveal themselves in naked reality (1 P 3^{4}). It is the infallible index of human character, but can be read only by Him who 'searches the hearts' (Ro 8^{27}; cf 1 S 16^{7}, Pr 21^{2}, Lk 16^{15}). Human judgment can proceed only according to the unerring evidence tendered by this resultant of inner forces, for 'you will know them by their fruits' (Mt 7^{20}). The more strictly Jewish of the NT writers show the influence of OT thought in their teaching. Where we should employ the word '**conscience**' St. John uses 'heart,' whose judgments in the moral sphere are final (1 Jn 3^{20f}). Nor is St. Paul free from the influence of this nomenclature. He seems, in fact, to regard conscience as a function of the heart rather than as an independent moral and spiritual organ (Ro 2^{15}, where both words occur; cf the quotation He 10^{16}). In spite of the fact that the last-named Apostle frequently employs the terms 'mind,' 'understanding,' 'reason,' 'thinkings,' etc., to express the elements of intellectual activity in man, we find him constantly reverting to the heart as discharging functions closely allied to these (cf 'the eyes of your hearts,' Eph 1^{18}; see also 2 Co 4^{6}). With St. Paul, too, the heart is the seat of the determination or will (cf 1 Co 7^{37}, where 'firmly established in heart' is equivalent to will-power). In all these and similar cases, however, it will be noticed that it is man's moral nature that he has in view; and the moral and spiritual life, having its roots struck deep in his being, is appropriately conceived of as springing ultimately from the most essentially vital organ of his personal life.

J. R. W.—N. H. S.

HEARTH.—See HOUSE, 7.

HEATH.—See TAMARISK.

HEATHEN.—See IDOLATRY, NATIONS.

HEAVEN.—In the cosmic theory of the ancient world, and of the Hebrews in particular, the earth was flat, lying between a great pit into which the shades of the dead departed, and the heavens above in which God and the angels dwelt, and to which it came to be thought the righteous went, after having been raised from the dead to live for ever. It was natural to think of the heavens as concave above the earth, and resting on some foundation, possibly of pillars, set at the extreme horizon (2 S 22^{8}, Pr 8^{27-29}).

The Hebrews, like other ancient peoples, believed in a plurality of heavens (Dt 10^{14}), and the literature of Judaism speaks of seven. In the highest, or *Aravoth*, was the throne of God. Although the descriptions of these heavens varied, it would seem that it was not unusual to regard the third heaven as Paradise. It was to this that St. Paul said he (*i.e.* 'a man in Christ,' probably himself) had been caught up (2 Co 12^{2}).

This series of superimposed heavens was regarded as filled by different sorts of superhuman beings. The second heaven in later Jewish thought was regarded as the abode of evil spirits and angels awaiting punishment. The NT, however, does not commit itself to these precise speculations, although in Eph 6^{12} it speaks of 'principalities . . . powers . . . the world rulers of this present darkness' (cf Eph 2^{2}). Presumably these were the 'elemental spirits of the universe' (Gal 4^{3}), which in the spherical cosmology of popular Hellenistic religion occupied the realm below the moon. See DEMONS; GNOSTICISM.

This conception of heaven as being above a flat earth underlies many religious expressions which are still current. There have been various attempts to locate heaven, as, for example, in Sirius as the central sun of our system. Similarly, there have been innumerable speculations endeavouring to set forth in sensuous form the sort of life which is to be lived in heaven. All such speculations, however, lie outside the region of positive knowledge, and rest ultimately on the cosmogony of pre-scientific times. They may be of value in cultivating religious emotion, but they belong to the region of speculation. The Biblical descriptions of heaven are not scientific, but symbolical. Practically all these are to be found in the Johannine Apocalypse. It was undoubtedly conceived of eschatologically by the NT writers, but they maintained a great reserve in all their descriptions of the life of the redeemed. It is, however, possible to state definitely that, while they conceived of the heavenly condition as involving social relations, they did not regard it as one in which the physical organism survived. The sensuous descriptions of heaven to be found in the ancient Jewish apocalypses and in Islam are altogether excluded by the sayings of Jesus relative to marriage in the new age (Mk 12^{25}||), and those of St. Paul relative to the 'spiritual body' (1 Co 15). The prevailing tendency at the present time among theologians, to regard heaven as a state of the soul rather than a place, belongs likewise to the region of opinion. The degree of its probability will be determined by one's general view as to the nature of immortality and eternal life.

S. M.—F. C. G.

HEAVE-OFFERING.—See Sacrifice and Offering.

HEAVINESS.—The English word 'heaviness' is used in AV in the sense of 'grief,' and in no other sense. Thus Pr 10^{1} 'A wise man maketh a glad father; but a foolish son is the heaviness (so RV; RSV 'sorrow') of his mother.' Compare Coverdale's translation of Ps 30^{5} 'hevynesse maye well endure for a night, but joye commeth in the mornynge,' whence the Prayer Book version 'heaviness may endure for a night.'

HEBER.—**1.** A man of Asher, Gn 46^{17}, Nu 26^{45}, 1 Ch 7^{31f}. The gentilic **Heberites** occurs in Nu 26^{45}. **2.** The Kenite, according to Jg 4^{17} 5^{24}, husband of Jael. He separated himself (Jg 4^{11}) from his Bedouin caste of Kenites or nomad smiths, whose wanderings were confined chiefly to the S. of Judah, and settled for a time near Kedesh on the plain to the W. of the Sea of Galilee. **3.** A man of Judah, 1 Ch 4^{18}. **4.** A Benjamite, 1 Ch 8^{17}. **5.** 1 Ch 5^{13} (AV); see Eber, **2.** **6.** 1 Ch 8^{22} (AV); see Eber, **4.**

HEBREW.—See Eber, **1**; Habiru; Text and Versions of OT.

HEBREW, except for certain small portions in Aramaic (q.v.), is the language of the OT, where it is used as an ethnic term, connected with Eber (*e.g.* Gn 10^{21}) and deriving from a root probably signifying 'nomad,' the language itself being described as 'the speech of Canaan' (Is 19^{18}). This accords with the mixed nature of its grammar and vocabulary and its closely knit relationship with other Semitic languages (*e.g.* Aramaic, Ugaritic, Akkadian, Arabic). Comparative study of these languages (aided by continuing discovery of epigraphs and texts) together with examination of the LXX and other ancient VSS is making possible a clearer understanding of the grammatical structure (*e.g.* tenses) and vocabulary (*e.g.* recovery of lost meanings) of Hebrew. Indications of the pronunciation of Hebrew in Biblical times, obscured through its standardization by the Mas(s)oretes (successors of the Scribes from *c* 5th cent. A.D.), have been augmented by MSS from the Dead Sea caves. Written originally in the Phoenician-Old Hebrew characters, Hebrew after the Exile came to be recorded in Aramaic square script as in the printed Bibles of to-day.

E. T. R.

HEBREWS, EPISTLE TO.—*Introductory.*—At first sight it is not easy to understand why this treatise has been designated an Epistle. The only direct references by the writer to the character of his work are found in 13^{22}, where he styles it a 'word of exhortation' (cf Ac 13^{15}, 4 Mac 1^{1}), and speaks of having written '(a letter) to you briefly.' The general salutation of 13^{24} is similar to what is found in most of the NT Epistles (cf Ro 16^{3ff}, 1 Co 16^{19ff}, 2 Co 13^{12f}, Ph 4^{21f}, Col 4^{10ff} etc.). At the same time, there are numerous personal references scattered throughout the writing (13^{7} 5^{11} 4^{1} 10^{19} 6^{9} etc.), and in most cases the author places himself on the same level with those to whom he is writing (3^{19} 8^{18ff} 11^{40} 10^{10} etc.). In spite of the formality which might characterize this writing as a theological essay, it is evident that the early instinct of the Church in regarding it as essentially an Epistle is substantially sound and correct (cf Deissmann, *Bible Studies*, pp. 49 f). Of course, the title 'The Epistle of Paul the Apostle to the Hebrews' (AV) is without early textual authority. The oldest MSS have merely the superscription 'to Hebrews,' just as they have in the case of other NT epistles ('to Romans,' etc.). The only other early description to which it is necessary to refer is that given to it by Tertullian, who expressly quotes it by the title of 'Barnabas to the Hebrews' (*de Pud.* 20). It seems to have been unanimously accepted from the very earliest period that the objective of the Epistle was correctly described by this title. Whether, however, this conclusion was based on sound traditional evidence or was merely arrived at from the internal character of the writing itself, must be left to conjecture; for we must not suppose that the words 'to Hebrews' form any part of the original document.

1. Authorship.—Notwithstanding the fact that this writing was known by the most ancient Christian writers, at all events by those belonging to the Church in Rome, it is noteworthy that all traces as to its authorship seem to have been lost very soon. The only information, with regard to this question, to be gleaned from the Roman Church is of the negative character that it was not written by St. Paul. Indeed, the Western Church as a whole seems to have allowed its presence in the Canon only by the beginning of the 5th cent., accepting it on the authority of the Eastern churches who remained confident of Pauline authorship.

The Muratorian Fragment does not include it in its catalogue, and implicity denies its Pauline authorship ('The blessed Apostle Paul himself, following the example of his predecessor John, wrote only to seven Churches by name,' etc., see Westcott, *Canon of the NT*, App. C.), as does also Gaius. Of more direct value are the testimonies of Hippolytus and Irenaeus, both of whom were acquainted with the Epistle, but denied that St. Paul wrote it (cf Eusebius, *HE* v. 26, vi. 20). The Churches of North Africa and Alexandria, on the contrary, have their respective positive traditions on this question. The former, as has been noted already, attributed the writing to Barnabas—a theory preserved by Tertullian and destined to fall into complete oblivion until quite recent times (cf *e.g.* Zahn, *Einleitung*, ii, pp. 116 f).

The Alexandrian belief in the authorship of St. Paul, indirectly at least, dates as far back as the closing years of the 2nd cent. Clement of Alexandria goes so far as to suggest that St. Paul wrote it originally in Hebrew, suppressing his name from motives of expediency, and that St. Luke translated it for the use of those who understood only Greek. Origen, who had his own doubts as to the reliability of the local tradition, nevertheless upheld St. Paul as the ultimate author; and his influence undoubtedly had powerful weight in overcoming the Western hesitation. At all events, by the 5th cent. it was almost universally held to be the product of St. Paul's literary activity; and this belief was not disturbed until the revival of learning in the 16th cent., when again a wide divergence of opinion displayed itself.

Erasmus, the first to express the latent feelings of uncertainty, conjectured in a characteristically modest fashion that Clement of Rome was possibly the author. Luther, with his usual boldness and independence, hazarded the unsupported guess that its author was Apollos. Calvin wavered between St. Luke and Clement, following, no doubt, some of the statements of Origen as to traditions current in his day (see Eusebius, *HE* vi. 25).

We have thus no resource but to appeal to the writing itself in order to arrive at a decision as to the *kind* of person likely to have penned such a document (cf article 'Hebrews' in Hastings' *DB*, vol. ii, 338*a*). The author seems to have a personal and an intimate knowledge of the character and history of those whom he addresses (cf 6^{9f} 10^{34} $13^{7,19}$). It is quite possible, of course, that this may have been gained through the medium of others, and that he is speaking of a reputation established and well known. When we consider, however, the numerous instances in which close ties of relationship betray themselves, we are forced to the conclusion that the writer and his readers were personally known to each other. Timothy was a mutual friend (13^{23}), although it is confessed that both the author and those addressed belong to the second generation of Christians (2^{3}). There is, moreover, a constant use of the first personal pronoun (1^{2} $2^{1ff.9}$ $3^{6.14}$ $4^{3.14}$ 6^{18ff} 8^{1} 9^{24} 10^{10} $^{19-25,30}$ 11^{3} 13^{10}), even in places where we should have expected that of the second person (*e.g.* $12^{1f.28}$ 13^{13ff}). To the present writer the words translated 'that I may be restored to you the sooner' (13^{19}) seem to convey the meaning that he had been amongst them once, although Westcott is inclined to see here but a suggestion of 'the idea of service which he had rendered and could render to his readers' (Comm., *in loc.* and Int., pp. lxxv f). If thus he were a close personal acquaintance, these reminiscences of their former endurance, and of the faithfulness of those through whose instrumentality they had embraced the Christian faith, gain force and point (cf 10^{32} 13^{7}). There is, moreover, a tone of authority throughout, as if the writer had no fear that his words would be resented or misinterpreted (12^{4f} 13^{9} $10^{25,35}$ 5^{11ff} 3^{12} etc.).

To these notes of authorship must be added the evidence of wide literary culture observable throughout the Epistle. This characteristic has been, and is, universally acknowledged. The author did not use the Hebrew OT, and in the single quotation where he varies from the LXX we gather, either that he was acquainted with the Epistle to the Romans, or that he gives a variant reading preserved and popularized by the Targum Onkelos (cf 10^{30} and Ro 12^{19}). There is no other NT writer who displays the same rhetorical skill in presenting the final truths of the Christian religion in their world-wide relations (cf 1^{1-4} 2^{14-18} 6^{17-20} 11^{1-40} etc.). His vocabulary is rich and varied, and in this respect stands closer to the writings of St. Luke than to any other of the NT books. 'The number of words found in the Epistle which have a peculiar Biblical sense is comparatively small' (Westcott, *ib.*, p. xlvi). For these and similar reasons it is generally believed that our author was a scholar of Hellenistic training and most probably an Alexandrian Jew of philosophic temperament and education (see Bacon, *Introd. to NT*, p. 141).

2. Destination, circumstances of readers, date.—When we ask ourselves the question, Who were the people addressed in this Epistle ?, we are again met with a confusing variety of opinion. The chief rival claimants to this honour are three : *Palestine*, which has the most ancient tradition in its favour, and which is countenanced by the superscription ; *Alexandria* ; and *Rome*, where the Epistle seems first to have been known and recognized. One conclusion may, at any rate, be accepted as certain : the addressees formed a definite homogeneous body of Christians. The writer has a local Church in view, founded at a specific period, and suffering persecution at a definite date (note the tense of the verbs, 'you were enlightened,' 'you endured,' 10^{32}). He addresses this Church independently of its recognized 'leaders' (13^{24}). In his exhortation to patience and endurance he reminds his readers of the speedy return of Jesus, as if they had already begun to despair of the fulfilment of that promise (10^{36ff} ; cf 2 P 3^{8ff}, Rev 3^{3}, 2 Th 2^{1ff}). He had been with them at some period prior to his writing, and he hoped once again to visit them with Timothy as his companion ($13^{19,23}$). Their spiritual growth was arrested just at the point where he had looked for vigour and force (5^{11ff} 6^{1ff}), and this resulted in moral decline (5^{11} 12^{5} 3^{12}), and in neglect of that ordinance which promotes social intercourse and Christian fellowship (10^{25}). As a Church, too, they were in a position to help their poorer brethren (6^{10}), and he expected them to continue that help in the future (6^{11})—a feature of early Christian activity which reminds us of the poverty of the Church in Judaea (cf Ac 11^{29} 24^{17}, Ro 15^{26}, 1 Co 16^{1ff} etc.). To many scholars, this allusion in itself presents a formidable, if not a fatal, objection to the theory that Palestine was the destination of our Epistle. This conclusion is strengthened by the elegant Greek in which the Epistle is written, and by the writer's use of the LXX instead of the Hebrew OT. On the other hand, the only direct internal evidence pointing to the readers' relations with Rome is found in the salutation, 'They of Italy salute you' (13^{24} RV ; 'Those who come from Italy send you greetings' RSV). It is true that this is sufficient to establish a connexion ; but it would be futile to deny that it is capable of a double explanation—that the Epistle was written either *from* or *to* Italy. The former seems at first sight the more natural interpretation of the words (cf Col 4^{16}), and we are not surprised to find such scholars as Theodoret and Primasius expressing their belief that our author here discloses the place from which he writes. Indeed, on the supposition that 'they of Italy' were the writer's companions who were absent with him from Rome, the words do not seem the most felicitous method of expressing their regards. It would be natural to mention some at least of their names in sending greetings from them to their brethren, with whom they must have been on terms of the most intimate fellowship (cf Ro 16^{21ff}, 1 Co 16^{19}). Besides, if he wrote from Rome we have a natural explanation, amounting to a *vera causa*, of the fact that our Epistle was known there from the very first ; for it must not be supposed that a writing like this was allowed to go forth without copies having been made beforehand (for a supposed instance of this kind in the case of St. Luke's writings, see Friedrich Blass, *Ev. sec. Lucam*, and *Acta Apostolorum*, especially the Praefatio and Prolegomena respectively, where that scholar contends that the remarkable textual variations in these writings can be explained only by the theory of a second edition of each).

Nor can the claim of Alexandria to be the destination of the Epistle be said to have much force. The argument on which this theory is mainly based has to do with the discrepancies between the writer's descriptions of Levitical worship and that which obtained in the Jewish Temple in accordance with the Mosaic code (cf *e.g.* 9^{3f} 7^{27} etc.). It has been supposed that he had in his mind the temple of Onias at Leontopolis in Egypt. This, however, is pure conjecture (cf Westcott, *ib.* Int. p. xxxix), and is contradicted by the historical evidence of the late date at which the Epistle seems to have been known in Alexandria, and by the fact that its authorship was completely hidden from the heads of the Church in that place. We are thus reduced to the balancing of probabilities in selecting an objective for our Epistle, and in so doing we have to ask ourselves the much canvassed question: What were the antecedents of the readers ? Were they Gentile or Jewish converts ? Until a comparatively recent date it was believed universally that the writer had Jewish Christians before his mind. A formidable array, however, of NT critics, both European and American, have advocated the theory that, in spite of appearances to the contrary, the original readers of our Epistle were Gentiles or mainly Gentiles (*e.g.* von Soden, Jülicher, Weizsäcker, Pfleiderer, Windisch, Michel, McGiffert, Bacon, etc.). Certainly among the Christians of the first two or three generations there must have been a large number of proselytes who were well acquainted with the Levitical ceremonial, and to whom the description of the furniture of the Tabernacle would have been perfectly intelligible (9^{2ff} ; cf vv.$^{13ff.19ff}$ 10^{11ff} etc.). That the addressees included Jews cannot be denied (see 6^{6f} 13^{9-16} etc.). At the same time, it would be futile to base an argument for the purely Jewish destination of the Epistle upon such passages as speak of OT prophetic revelations having been made to ' our fathers ' (1^{1}), or of ' the descendants of Abraham ' (2^{16}) as constituting the basis of Jesus' human nature. A similar identification is made by St. Paul in writing to the Church in Rome (Ro 4^{1-25}), where undoubtedly there was a large admixture of Gentile Christians. Moreover, Clement of Rome again and again refers to ' our fathers,' though he too is writing to a Church largely Gentile (see chs. 4, 31, 62, etc.). It is also well to remember that the Christian Churches, for a century at least after they had begun to take definite shape as organized bodies, were dependent, to a very large extent, upon the OT Scriptures for their spiritual nourishment and guidance. These were to them the chief, if not the only, authoritative record of God's revelation of Himself and His purposes to the world. It was perfectly natural, therefore, that St. Paul should presuppose a wide knowledge of OT history, and, indeed of the Jewish interpretations of that history (cf Ro 5^{12ff}, 1 Co 15^{22}, 2 Co 3^{7ff} 6^{16}, Gal 3^{29}), on the part of his Gentile readers, just as Clement of Rome does.

When we turn to our Epistle, we are struck at once by the fact that the writer is not moving in, or thinking of, a living practical Leviticalism. He is dealing with Mosaism in its ideal conditions. The ritualism about which he addresses his readers seems to be, not that which actually obtained in the later Temple services (cf *e.g.* 7^{27} 10^{11} 9^{21}), but that splendid theoretical ceremonial every detail of which was believed to be a type and a shadow ' of the good things that have come ' (9^{11} ; cf W. R. Smith's article ' Hebrews ' in *EBrit.*). Indeed, the typological and allegorizing elements in the Epistle claim for it almost peremptorily a non-Eastern objective ; and though we cannot see our way to accept Zahn's conclusion that the addressees formed a compact body of Jewish Christians within a large Gentile community of believers, we are ready to yield to his exhaustive study of the problem when he points to Rome as offering the fewest objections on the whole,, to be the destination of the writing (*Einleit. in das NT*, ii, pp. 146 ff).

Accepting this conclusion as at least a provisional, and it may be a temporary, solution of the difficult question arising out of the objective of our Epistle, we shall find several allusions to *the existing conditions of life in the Church addressed.* Nor shall we be left completely in the dark as to the probable *date* of its composition. Looking first for incidental remarks, independently of the *locale* of the readers, we find several hints pointing to a comparatively late period in the history of the early Church. Both writer and readers were separated by at least a generation from the first circle of believers (2^{3}). The readers, moreover, had been long enough under the influence of the Christian faith to give our author grounds for hope that they could occupy the position of teachers and of ' mature ' professors of their religion (5^{11ff} ; note the verb translated ' you have become,' which expresses the end of a lengthened process of decline). This hope was bitterly disappointed, although he is careful to recall a period when their love was warm and their Christian profession an active force in their lives (6^{9f}). Basing his appeal on this memory, he strives to encourage them to revert to their former earnestness (6^{11}) ; and, in order to prevent that dullness to which they had already given way from developing further, he urges them to take for a pattern those Christian teachers who had already spent their lives in the service of the faith (6^{12}). It is probable that their own leaders of the preceding generation had signalized their fidelity to Christ by enduring martyrdom for His sake (cf Westcott, Comm., *in loc.*). The first freshness of their enthusiasm for the gospel was wearing off, and some at least amongst them were in danger of a complete lapse from Church membership (10^{25}). The cause of this temptation is not far to seek. In an earlier period of their history they had ' endured a hard struggle with sufferings ' (10^{32ff}), and the writer hints at another and a similar experience, of which the beginnings were making themselves felt (cf 12^{3f} ; note the warning tone in 10^{36} exhorting to the cultivation of patience). Persecution on this occasion had not as yet burst with its full fury upon them (12^{4}). That he sees it fast coming is evident from the writer's continually appealing for an exhibition of fortitude and patient endurance (12^{1ff} 11 etc.). Indeed, he understands the dangers to which a Church, enjoying a period of freedom from the stress of active opposition, is exposed when brought face to face with a sudden storm of persecution and relentless hatred ($12^{5, 7f}$). He seems to fear apostasy as the result of moral relaxation (12^{12f}), and encourages his readers by telling them of the liberation of Timothy from his imprisonment for the faith (13^{23}). It is not impossible that one of his reasons for writing directly to the Church, instead of addressing it through their leaders (13^{24}), was that he feared a similar fate for the latter, or that, like himself, they were compulsorily separated from their brethren (13^{19}) by the persecuting authorities. Now, if we accept Rome as the destination of our Epistle, and see in 13^{7} an allusion to the martyrdom of St. Peter and St. Paul, and at the same time remember that we have the Epistle of Clement to the Corinthian Church as its *terminus ad quem,* we have reduced the limits of the date of its composition to the period between the Neronic and Domitianic persecutions. Rather we should say, following some of the allusions referred to above, that it was written at the beginning of the latter crisis ; in other words, the date would be within the closing years of the 8th and opening years of the 9th decade of the 1st cent. (Domitian reigned A.D. 81–96). The fact that Timothy was alive when our author wrote does not militate against this date, as he seems to have been a young man when converted through the instrumentality of St. Paul (cf 1 Co 16^{11}, 1 Ti 4^{12}, 2 Ti 2^{22}).

Besides the danger to the faith arising from physical sufferings and persecutions, another and a more deadly enemy seems to have been threatening to undermine the foundations of the Church at this period. After the destruction of the Jerusalem Temple, Judaism seems to have been endowed with a new and vigorous life. Hellenistic Judaism, with its syncretistic tendencies and its bitter proselytizing spirit, must have appealed very strongly to that class of Christians for whom an eclectic belief always has a subtle charm (cf the warning ' Do not be led away by diverse and strange teachings,' and the reference to the distinctions regarding ' foods ' in 13^{9}, which forcibly remind us of St. Paul's language in Col 2^{16}) ; for an exhaustive survey of the extent and number of proselytes to Judaism, and the eagerness with which this work was pursued (see Schürer, *HJP* II. ii, 291–327 ; and see article DISPERSION).

3. Purpose and contents.—In order to counteract this influence, the writer sets about proving the final and universalistic character of the Christian revelation. It is with this practical aim that he takes his pen in hand, and he himself gives its true designation to his literary effort when he styles it ' a word of exhortation ' (13^{22}). At the same time, it is evident that our author moves on a high plane both of thought and of language. No other NT writer seems to have grasped so fully the cosmological significance attaching to the earthly life and experiences of Jesus (5^{7f} 4^{15} $2^{9ff, 17f}$), or to have set forth so clearly His present activity on behalf of ' all who obey him ' (5^{9} 2^{18} 7^{25} $9^{15, 24}$, cf Ro 8^{34}). For him the Incarnation has bridged once and for all the hitherto impassable gulf separating God and man, and has made intelligible for man the exhortation ' Let us draw near ' to God, for a ' new and living way ' has been opened for us through His flesh (10^{20ff}, cf 7^{19}). It may be said, indeed, that the author regards Christianity as the final stage in the age-long process of religious development. The Levitical institutions, with their elaborate ceremonialism, constituted the preceding and preparatory step in the Divine plan of world-salvation. This too was good in its way, and necessary, but of course imperfect. It did its duty as a good servant, faithfully and well, but had to give way when the ' heir of all things ' (1^{2}) came to claim His inheritance (cf 3^{5f}).

In order to establish emphatically the pre-eminence of Christianity over all that went before, the Epistle opens with a series of comparisons between Christ and the great representatives of the former dispensation. (*a*) In the 'old time' the messages of God were delivered 'in many and various ways' through the prophets, but now 'in these last days' He has spoken His final word 'by a Son' (1^{1ff}). (*b*) The Law of Moses was revealed through the mediation of angels and was 'valid' (2^2); but angels were employed in service 'for the sake of those who are to obtain salvation' (1^{14}), whereas the revelation through the medium of the Son 'who for a little while was made lower than the angels' was correspondingly of a higher order than that which had these beings as intermediaries (1^{4-14} 2^{5-9}). (*c*) The great lawgiver Moses occupied but the position of servant, and therefore holds a subordinate place to that of the Son in the Divine scheme of redemption (3^{2-6}). (*d*) Finally, as Christ is personally superior to Aaron, so His office is essentially more profound and efficacious than that which typified it.

This last comparison is elaborated at much greater length than the others (8^1–10^{18}), and indeed in its argumentative treatment is developed into a contrast. The discussion here is simple but effective. Everyone recognizes that 'under the law almost everything is purified with blood, and without the shedding of blood there is no forgiveness of sins' (9^{22}), but Aaron and his successors went into the holy place 'with blood not their own' (9^{25}), the blood of bulls and of goats, which cannot possibly take away sins (10^4). Moreover, the first requisite to the high-priestly service of atonement is that a sin-offering had to be made for the officiating priest himself before he offered for the people (9^7 5^3). The temporary makeshift character of these ordinances was shown and acknowledged by the fact that they had to be constantly repeated ('once a year,' 9^7, cf 10^3). They had in themselves no moral uplifting force, cleansing the consciences of, and perfecting, 'those who draw near' (10^{1f}). On the other hand, Christ 'entered once for all into the Holy Place, taking not the blood of goats and calves but his own blood, thus securing an eternal redemption' (9^{12}), and, though He 'is able to sympathize with our weaknesses, since in every respect he has been tempted as we are, yet [it is] without sinning' (4^{15}). He needed not to offer on His own behalf, for temptation and suffering proved to Him but stages in the process of perfecting His Sonship (2^{10} 5^{2f} 7^{28}). In describing the personal character of the High Priest suited to our needs, the writer is at the same time describing the character of the sacrifice which Christ offered, for 'he offered up himself' (7^{26ff}). In order to obviate any objection likely to be made against the irregularity of a priesthood outside the Levitical order, he has already pointed to an OT case in point, and here he strengthens his plea by quoting from a Psalm universally recognized as Messianic. Melchizedek (q.v.) was a priest who had no genealogical affinity with the tribe of Levi, and yet he was greater than Aaron (7^{4-10}); and it was said by God of His own Son that He should be 'a priest for ever, after the order of Melchizedek' (5^6 7^{17}).

4. Christology.—We have said above that the central thought of our Epistle is the discovery by Christianity of a way, hitherto hidden from the eyes of man, of access to God (cf 4^{16} 10^{19} $7^{19, 25}$). Once this was accomplished, nothing further remained to be done (10^{18}) but to enter on that path which leads to the Sabbath-rest reserved for the people of God (4^9). We may now ask the question, What are the author's conceptions with regard to the Being and Personality of the High Priest upon whose functions he sets such value? In other words, *What are the chief features of the Christology of the Epistle*? We have not to proceed far in the study of our Epistle before we are brought face to face with a thought which dominates each discussion of the relative claims of Christ and the OT ministers of revelation and redemption. It is upon His Sonship that the superiority of Jesus is based. Neither the prophets nor the ministering angels, neither Moses nor Aaron, could lay claim to that relationship which is inherent in the Person of Jesus Christ. In consequence of the unique position occupied by 'the Son of God' (4^{14}; cf $1^{2, 6}$ 3^6 5^8 7^{28} 10^{29}), it follows that the dispensation ushered in by Him is above all that went before it. The latter was but the dim outline ('shadow'), not even the full representation ('the true form') 'of the good things to come' (10^1). Regarded as a means of revealing God to man, this superiority is self-evident, as the Son is above both prophets and angels. Looked on as a mediatorial scheme of redemption and of reconciliation, it stands immeasurably above that whose representatives were Moses the lawgiver and Aaron the priest.

It is evident from what has been said that this feature of the Personality of Jesus is transcendent and unique. It is also evident that sonship in a general sense is not unknown to the author (cf 2^{10} $12^{5, 7f}$). As if to preclude all misunderstanding of his meaning, he at the outset defines his belief when he represents the Son as 'the heir of all things' and the agent of God's creative activity (3^{3f}; cf Jn 1^3), the effulgence of His glory and the very image of His Person—'He reflects the glory of God and bears the very stamp of his nature' (RSV). Not only do we see in these words the definition of a faith which confesses Jesus as the great world-sustaining power (He 1^3); there is also implied, so far as a non-technical terminology can do so, belief in the eternity of His Being. It is true that the term 'first-born' (1^6) does not necessarily carry the idea of eternity with it, or even the statement that He is the Maker of the ages (1^2). On the other hand, we must remember that these are but supplemental to the grand Christological confession of v.2, which excludes the notion of the non-existence of the Son at any time in the ages of eternity. The shining of light is coeval with the light itself, and the impress of the seal on wax is the exact reproduction of the original engraving. It is true that we have here no systematic declaration of Christological belief. The time had not yet come for the constructive theologian. At the same time, it is difficult to see how the author could have framed a more emphatic expression of his belief that Jesus the Son of God is a Divine Person from eternity to eternity (cf 7^{28}). The grand and final scene in the Divine process of self-revelation is painted in words of magnificent solemnity, referred to incidentally, and repeated again and again. As the Son of God, Jesus had a Divine inheritance into which He entered, after His work of redemption was completed on earth, by sitting down at the right hand of the Majesty on High (1^3; cf 1^{13} 2^{9f} 4^{14} 6^{20} 7^{26}, Lk 22^{69}, Mk 16^{19}).

In his reference to the work of the Son in 'making purification for sins' (1^3) the author implies at once his belief in the humanity of the Son. Although he gives us no direct clue to the extent of his knowledge of the conditions under which the Incarnation was effected, he leaves us in no doubt not only that the manhood of the Son is a reality, but that for the work of redemption it was necessary that it should be so. The fact that his allusions to this doctrine are always indirect point to the conclusion that he expected his readers to be familiar with it as an indisputable article of the Christian faith. Besides, he reinforces his arguments by a running commentary upon those Psalms wherein he sees prophetic expressions of the humiliation of the Christ (cf $2^{7, 9, 14, 16, 18}$ 5^7). Incorporated with them we have numerous references to the earthly experiences of Jesus. The manner of His death (12^2, cf $2^{9, 14}$), His general temptations (2^{18} 4^{15}), and, in particular, that of Gethsemane (5^7, where the author boldly refers to Jesus' prayer to His Father in the face of an awful calamity, and the cause which occasioned that prayer), His work as preacher of salvation, and the delegation by Him of the work of proclamation to those who heard Him (1^2 2^3), His protracted struggle with implacable religious enemies (12^3)—all point to our author's minute acquaintance with the historical facts of Jesus' life.

No attempt is made by the writer to minimize the extent and character of Jesus' earthly sufferings and the limitations to which He was subjected. It seems as if, above all things, he is anxious to impress his readers with

HEBREWS, EPISTLE TO

their stern reality, and as if they, in their turn, were tempted to despise the salvation which was wrought out through such humiliation (2^{3}). For him this humiliation is filled with a moral and spiritual significance of the most vital importance. In His constant endurance and His ultimate triumph Jesus has left an abiding example to all who suffer temptation and persecution (12^{2f}; cf the expression 'we see Jesus,' etc., 2^{9}). The power of this example is the greater because of the oneness of Jesus and His people (cf 2^{11}), by which their endurance and witness become the embodiment and extension of His work in this respect (cf 5^{12} 13^{7} 12^{1}). The spiritual significance of the earthly life of Jesus is no less real and splendid. 'It was fitting' that Jesus should be perfected 'through suffering' ($2^{10, 17}$), not only because He thereby attained to the captaincy of salvation, becoming merciful and faithful (2^{17}) and sympathizing (4^{15}), but because the ability to help 'his brethren' (cf $2^{11, 17}$) springs from the double fact that He is one with them in His experiences, and at the same time victorious over sin ('without sinning,' 4^{15}, cf 7^{26} 9^{28}) as they are not. The profound synthesis of the humiliation and the glory of Jesus thus effected by our author is enhanced as it reaches its climax in the bold assertion that development in character was a necessary element in His earthly life (5^{8}, cf the words 'made perfect for ever,' 7^{28}).

In order that his readers may fully appreciate the character of the work accomplished by the life and death of Jesus, the writer proceeds to answer objections which may be raised against the propriety of His discharging the priestly functions of mediation and atonement. This he does by a twofold process of reasoning. First, reverting to the language of the great Messianic Psalm, he demonstrates the superiority in point of order, as in that of time, of the priesthood of Melchizedek to that of Aaron ($5^{6, 10}$ $7^{4ff, 17}$ &c.). Next he shows how the ideals dimly foreshadowed by the functions of the Aaronic priesthood have become fully and finally realized in the priesthood of Jesus (8^{4ff} $9^{8f, 14f}$). There are certain characteristics in the Melchizedekian order which, by an allegorical method of interpretation, are shown to be typical in the sublime sense of the priesthood of Christ. It was (*a*) royal, (*b*) righteous, (*c*) peaceful, (*d*) personal, (*e*) eternal (7^{2f}). A high priest having these ideal attributes realized in himself answers to man's fallen condition, and they all meet in the Person of the Son 'made perfect for ever' (cf 7^{26ff}). No mention is made of the sacrificial aspect of Melchizedek's work, but this is implied in the assertion that our high priest 'offered up himself once for all' (7^{27}). Indeed, it may be said that the latter characteristic is inseparable from the above-mentioned five, for the priesthood which realizes in itself the ethical ideals here outlined will inevitably crown itself by the act of self-sacrifice. The argument is then transferred from the Melchizedekian to the Levitical order, where the last-named function found detailed expression in the Mosaic ritual institutions. Here an answer is given to the question, 'What has this man to offer?' The Aaronic priests offered sacrifices continually, and in his description of the functions incidental to their position we seem to hear echoes of contrasts out of the very parallelisms instituted. The Levitical priest is not (*a*) royal; he 'is appointed' to fulfil certain obligations (8^{3}, cf 5^{1}); he is not (*b*) essentially righteous; he has, before he fulfils his mediatorial functions, first to offer for his own sins (8^{7}, cf 5^{3}); his work does not conduce to (*c*) peace, for 'consciousness of sin' is still, in spite of priestly activity, alive, and 'perfection' is not thereby attained (10^{1f}); his priesthood is not (*d*) personal; it is an inherited authority 'according to a legal requirement concerning bodily descent' (7^{16}), and the personal equation is shown to be eliminated by the fact that it is the blood of goats and calves that he offers (9^{12}); finally, it is not (*e*) eternal; its ordinances were temporary, 'imposed until the time of reformation' (9^{10}). In every instance 'the much more excellent ministry' (8^{6}) of Jesus is substantiated, while the repeated assertions of the sacrificial character of His priestly work, by the emphatic declarations that He is not only the Priest but the Sacrifice (7^{27} $9^{12, 26}$), show the difficulty the writer must have felt in sustaining a comparison which is summed up in an antithesis ('once a year' 9^{7}, and 'eternal' 9^{12}). The whole discussion may be regarded as an *a fortiori* argument on behalf of the superiority of the priesthood of Jesus. The ritual of the Day of Atonement is selected as the basis of his contention, and it was here that the Levitical ceremonial was at its noblest (9^{1-7}). Even here the above-mentioned antithesis is observable; the Levitical ministry was discharged in a Tabernacle which was but 'a copy and shadow of the heavenly sanctuary' (8^{5}), while that of Christ fulfils itself in 'the true tabernacle' (8^{2}), where alone are displayed the eternal realities of priestly sacrifice and mediation. The offering of Himself is not merely the material sacrifice of His body on the cross, though that is a necessary phase in His ministerial priesthood (cf $2^{8, 14}$); it is the transcendent spiritual act of One who is sinless ('through the eternal Spirit offered himself without blemish,' 9^{14} 7^{26} 4^{15}). This gives the offering its eternal validity ('once for all,' 7^{27} 9^{12} 10^{10}), and although 'the sacrifice of himself' was consummated 'at the end of the age,' its force and value reach back to 'the foundation of the world' (9^{26}, cf 9^{15}), and continue for all the time that is to come (7^{25} 9^{24}).

5. Salvation and Faith.—Two other interdependent ideas remain to be briefly considered. It has already been said that our author may be described as a theological evolutionist, and in no sphere of his thought is this more evident than in his ideas of salvation and of faith. Salvation is not so much the present realization of the redemptive value of Christ's atoning work as a movement commencing here and now towards that realization in all its fulness. It is true that faith is for him the power to bring the unseen realities into touch with the present life (11^{1ff}). At the same time, the dominant conception of salvation in the writer's mind is the fruition of hopes originated and vitalized by the teaching and experiences of Jesus. Future dominion in a new world ordered and inhabited in perfect moral harmony (see Westcott, *Ep. to Heb.* on 2^{5}) awaits those who neglect not 'such a great salvation' (2^{3}). The basis upon which this lordship rests is the actualized crowned Kingship of the Man Jesus, which is at once the guarantee and the *rationale* of the vision (2^{9ff}). Immediately following this view another conception arises dealing with the realization, in the future, of a dominion based upon conquest. Death and the author of death are the enemies which Jesus has 'destroyed'; and not only has He done this, but He delivers those who all their life were in bondage 'through fear.' The perfect humanity of Jesus is again the avenue along which this goal is reached. No other way is possible, and in Him all may find their servitude transmuted into freedom and dominion (cf 2^{14-18}). Once more, arguing from the imperfect realization by the Israelites, under Joshua, of their hopes, the author points out that what they looked for in vain is a type of a higher thing which is now actually awaiting 'the people of God.' Salvation consists in entering into that eternal Sabbath-rest where Jesus has gone before, and where the presence of God is (cf 4^{9ff}). The pivotal conception round which these ideas revolve is the unity of Christ and man, the likeness in all things, sin alone excepted, which was effected by the Incarnation.

Our author's habit of looking on faith as an active force in men's lives displays the same tendency to make the future rather than the present the field of his vision. At the same time, it would be a great mistake to imagine that the present is outside the scope of his thought. *Obedience*, however, is the word and thought preferred by him when he speaks of the present grounds of salvation (5^{8f}, cf 11^{8}). Faith is for him a force working towards ethical ideals, a power which enables men of every nation and class to live lives of noble self-denial for righteousness' sake, 'as seeing him who is invisible' (11^{27}; cf 11^{1-40} 4^{2} 6^{12} 10^{39}). Of this faith Jesus is 'the pioneer and perfecter' (12^{2}), and here, too, we get a glimpse of that quickening Divine humanity upon which the writer lays such constant stress, and which is the source of the effort demanded from his readers when he asks them to imitate their former leaders in a faith which issued in a glorious martyrdom. J. R. W.—H. C.

HEBRON.—1. The third son of Kohath, known to us only from P (Ex 6^{18}, Nu $3^{19, 27}$) and the Chronicler (1 Ch $6^{2, 18}$ 15^{9} $23^{12, 19}$ 24^{23}). The **Hebronites** are mentioned at the census taken in the wilderness of Sinai (Nu 3^{27}), and appear again at the later census in the plains of Moab (26^{58}); cf also 1 Ch $26^{23, 30f}$. **2.** A son of Mareshah and father of Korah, Tappuah, Rekem, and Shema, 1 Ch 2^{43f}.

HEBRON.—1. A very ancient city in Palestine, 20 miles SSW. from Jerusalem. It is in a basin on one of the highest points of the Judaean ridge, being about 3040 feet above sea-level. A note of its antiquity is given in Nu 13^{22}, which states that it was ' seven years older than Zoan in Egypt.' Zoan is probably to be identified with Avaris and later Rameses; its founding may be dated by the so-called 400 year stele of Rameses II. to the late 18th cent. B.C. Hebron's original name seems to have been **Kiriath-arba** (*i.e.* probably *Tetrapolis*, or ' Four Cities '), and it was a stronghold of the Anakim. In the time of Abraham, however (whose history is much bound up with this place), we read of Hittites here. From Ephron the Hittite he purchased the cave of Machpelah for the burial of Sarah his wife (Gn 23). This allusion has given rise to much controversy. At the time of the entry of the Israelites it was held by three chieftains of great stature, Sheshai, Ahiman, and Talmai (Nu 13^{22}). On the partition of the country it was allotted to the tribe of Judah, or rather to the Calebites (Jos 14^{12} 15^{14}), who captured it for the Israelite immigrants (Jg 1^{9f}). In Jos $10^{1-27, 36-39}$ a different account of the capture of Hebron is given (cf also Jos 11^{21}). According to this story, Hoham was king of Hebron at the time; he joined a coalition of five Amorite kings, headed by Adoni-zedek of Jerusalem against Gibeon, which was allied with the Israelites. Joshua defeated the coalition at Gibeon in the spectacular episode when the ' sun stood still,' and he slaughtered the kings at the cave of Makkedah. Following this, Hebron was destroyed and its inhabitants put to the sword. The relationship of the two accounts is not clear. The Alt-Noth school takes the Joshua story to be an etiology, and unhistorical (cf M. Noth, *Das Buch Josua*² [*HAT*; 1953]). Opposed is the view of the Baltimore School, which regards the stories as essentially historical, though the sequence and date of the events are not certain (cf W. F. Albright, *BASOR*, No. 74 [1939], 11–23; G. E. Wright, *JNES*, v [1946], 105–114). A third view is expressed by Y. Kaufmann in *The Biblical Account of the Conquest of Palestine* (Jerusalem, 1953), who holds that the account in Judges 1 is subsequent to that in Joshua; nonetheless the situation regarding Hebron remains complex. For a judicious evaluation of the evidence see J. Bright, *IB*, ii (1953), 541 ff. The city itself was allotted to the Kohathite Levites, and it was set apart as a city of refuge (Jos 20^{7}). Here David reigned seven and a half years over Judah (2 S 5^{5}), till his capture of Jerusalem from the Jebusites fixed there the capital of the country. It was here also that the rebellious Absalom established himself as king (2 S 15^{7ff}). It was fortified by Rehoboam (2 Ch 11^{10}). From the period of the monarchy in Judah (8th cent. on), come many large storage jars stamped with the royal seal, and bearing the name of one of four cities (among them Hebron) in which these jars were apparently produced. They were of fixed capacity, two baths (about 10 gallons), and were intended for use in commerce and the payment of taxes in kind (cf G. E. Wright, *Biblical Archaeology* [1957], pp. 193 f). After the Captivity it was for a time in the hands of the Edomites (though from Neh 11^{25} it would appear to have been temporarily colonized by the returned Jews), but was re-captured by Judas Maccabaeus (1 Mac 5^{65}). In the war under Vespasian it was burned. In 1167 it became the see of a Latin bishop; in 1187 it was captured for the Muslims by Saladin. **2.** Jos 19^{28} (AV), see EBRON.
R. A. S. M.—D. N. F.

HEDGE.—1. *m^e sûkhāh*, a thorn hedge (Is 5^{5}). **2.** *gādhēr* or *g^e dhērāh*—probably a stone wall (Ps 89^{40} etc.). **3.** *phragmos* (Greek), Mt 21^{33}, Mk 12^{1}, Lk 14^{23}—a ' partition ' of any kind.

HEDGEHOG, Is 34^{11} (RSV).—See BITTERN.

HEGAI.—A eunuch of Ahasuerus, and keeper of the women, to whom the maidens were entrusted before they were brought in to the king, Est 2^{3} (AV **Hege**) $^{8, 15}$.

HEGE, Est 2^{3} (AV).—See HEGAI.

HEGEMONIDES (2 Mac 13^{24}).—An officer left in command of the district from Ptolemais to Gerar, by Lysias when he was forced to return to Syria to oppose the chancellor Philip (162 B.C.). AV renders ' principal governor.'

HEGLAM.—A son of Ehud, 1 Ch 8^{7}. AV and RV treat the name as a verb and translate ' he removed them,' or ' he carried them away.'

HEIFER.—The heifer was used in agriculture (Jg 14^{18}, Jer 50^{11}, Hos 10^{11}), and in religious ritual (Gn 15^{9}, 1 S 16^{2}, Nu 19^{2f} etc.). Israel is compared to a heifer in Hos 4^{16}, and so is Egypt in Jer 46^{20}, and Chaldaea in Jer 50^{11}. See also OX, RED HEIFER.

HEIR.—See INHERITANCE.

HELAH.—One of the wives of Ashhur the ' father ' of Tekoa, 1 Ch $4^{5, 7}$.

HELAM.—A city in Transjordan mentioned in 2 S 10^{16f}, where Hadadezer met David and was defeated. It is also mentioned in LXX in Ezk 47^{16} 48^{1}, but not in Hebrew. Its location is uncertain, but possibly modern *Almā*, in the plain of Hauran. See also ALEMA.

HELBAH.—A town of Asher, Jg 1^{31}. Possibly a doublet of Ahlab in this verse, and then to be identified with **Mahalab** (q.v.).

HELBON.—A place celebrated in old times for the excellence of its wines, Ezk 27^{18}. It is identified with *Ḥalbûn*, about 12 miles N. of Damascus. Grapes are still grown extensively on the surrounding slopes.

HELCHIAH, 1 Es 8^{1} (AV).—See HILKIAH, 3.

HELDAI.—1. The captain of the military guard appointed for the twelfth monthly course of the Temple service, 1 Ch 27^{15}. He is probably to be identified with ' **Heleb** the son of Baanah the Netophathite,' one of David's thirty heroes, 2 S 23^{29}. In the parallel list (1 Ch 11^{30}) the name is more correctly given as **Heled.** The form *Heldai* is supported by Zec 6^{10}, and should probably be restored in the other two passages. **2.** According to Zec 6^{10}, one of a small band who brought gifts of gold and silver from Babylon to those of the exiles who had returned under Zerubbabel. From these gifts Zechariah was told to make a crown for Joshua the high priest, which was to be placed in the Temple as a memorial of Heldai and his companions. In v.^{14} **Helem** (AV, RV following Hebrew) is clearly an error for Heldai (so RSV).

HELEB.—See HELDAI, 1.

HELED.—See HELDAI, 1.

HELEK.—Son of Gilead the Manassite, Nu 26^{30}, Jos 17^{2}. Patronymic, **Helekites,** Nu 26^{30}.

HELEM.—1. A man of Asher, 1 Ch 7^{35} (RSV wrongly **Heler**). Many scholars read **Hotham** to agree with v.^{32}. **2.** Zec 6^{14} (AV, RV); see HELDAI, 2.

HELEPH.—A town on the border of Naphtali, Jos 19^{33}. Although mentioned in the Jerusalem Talmud (*Erubin* 20a, *Megillah* 70a) Heleph has not been identified: J. Simons (*Geographical and Topographical Texts of OT* 196) suggests *Kh. 'Arbâdah.*

HELER.—See HELEM, 1.

HELEZ.—1. One of David's thirty heroes, 2 S 23^{26}. He is described as a **Paltite,** *i.e.* a native of Beth-pelet (q.v.) in the Negeb of Judah. But in 1 Ch 11^{27} he is called, probably erroneously, a **Pelonite** (q.v.). **2.** David's officer for the seventh month, 1 Ch 27^{10}. He also is called a **Pelonite,** and is commonly identified with the preceding. But as he was an Ephraimite, he could not have been from Beth-pelet. Possibly he was from an unknown Palon. **3.** A Judahite, 1 Ch 2^{39}.

HELI.—**1.** The father of Joseph, in the genealogy of Jesus (Lk 3^{23}). **2.** An ancestor of Ezra (2 Es 1^{2}, RSV 'Eli'); omitted in parallel passages, 1 Es 8^{2}, Ezr 7^{2f}.

HELIODORUS.—The chancellor of Seleucus iv. Philopator. At the instigation of Apollonius he was sent by the king to plunder the private treasures kept in the Temple of Jerusalem; but was prevented from carrying out his design by an apparition (2 Mac 3). In 175 B.C., Heliodorus murdered Seleucus, and attempted to seize the Syrian crown; but he was driven out by Eumenes of Pergamum and his brother Attalus; and Antiochus Epiphanes, brother of Seleucus, ascended the throne. There is commonly supposed to be a reference to Heliodorus in Dn 11^{20}, but the interpretation of the passage is doubtful. Further, he is frequently reckoned as one of the *ten* or the *three* kings of Dn 7^{7f}. (But see R. H. Charles, Comm.)

HELIOPOLIS, in Egyptian *'Iwnw,* the On of the Bible (Gn $41^{45, 50}$ 46^{20}), capital of the 13th Lower Egyptian nome, lies some 7 miles NE. of Cairo, near the village of Matarieh. From at least the 5th Dynasty it was the principal centre of sun-worship and one of the most important cities and temples in Egypt. The principal god in historic times was the hawk-headed sun-god Rē, Rē-Harakhte, who replaced the older god Atum, whose sacred animal was the ichneumon. Other sacred animals were the phoenix, supposed to alight on the sacred *benben*-stone in the temple, and the Mnevis bull, the living manifestation of Rē-Atum. Only the enclosure wall of the temple and an obelisk of Sesostris i. (*c* 1942 B.C.) now survive. The primitive form of the temple of Atum was a high mound of sand surmounted by the *benben* on which Atum as phoenix alighted at sunrise. The ritual elaborated at Heliopolis, with emphasis on righteousness and purity, and lustration and toilet of the god, became the state ritual throughout Egypt. The priesthood was famed for its learning: tradition states that Plato and other Greek philosophers studied there, but by the time of Strabo the city was already in ruins. H. W. F.

HELKAI.—A priest who returned with Zerubbabel, Neh 12^{15}.

HELKATH.—A Levitical city belonging to the tribe of Asher, Jos 19^{25} 21^{31}. The site is uncertain; possibly *Tell el-Harbaj.* The same place, owing probably to a textual error, appears in 1 Ch 6^{75} as **Hukok.**

HELKATH-HAZZURIM.—The name given to the spot at Gibeon where the fatal combat took place between the twelve champions chosen on either side from the men of Abner and Joab, 2 S 2^{16}. The name means 'the field of flints' or 'of sword edges' (S. R. Driver). We should perhaps read **Helkath-hazzidim,** 'field of sides' (so Driver).

HELKIAS.—See Hilkiah, **3, 9, 10.**

HELL.—See Eschatology, Gehenna, Hades, Sheol.

HELLENISM.—See Education, Greece.

HELLENISTS (AV, Grecians), Greek-speaking Jews referred to in Ac 6^{1} 9^{29} and a variant reading at 11^{20}. In the account of the appointment of the Seven, they are contrasted with the 'Hebrews,' *i.e.* Jews who spoke Hebrew or, more probably, Aramaic. The tension between the two groups not only affected the administration of the daily provision of food but also presumably the attitudes later taken over the admission of Gentiles to the Church and the requirement of circumcision and observance of the Mosaic Law. Though not mentioned in Ac 15 or Gal 1–2, the language barrier and the divergent ideologies of the two groups were undoubtedly important. It is not difficult to imagine that the groups mentioned in Ac 2^{9ff} were designated as 'Hellenists' by their Palestinian co-religionists, since the former undoubtedly spoke or at least understood the Greek language—the *lingua franca* of the whole Near and Middle East in the 1st cent. It was the Hellenists in the early Church who bridged over the gulf between Jews and Gentiles, and the eventual triumph of the principle of admission of Gentiles without requiring observance of the Law was made possible by their existence and activity. The world-wide mission of Judaism (Mt 23^{15}), which had resulted in the class of God-fearers (Ac 17^{4} 18^{7}), thus prepared the way for the spread of the Gospel. Many of these Greek-speaking, more or less Greek-thinking, Jews were among the earliest converts to Christianity in the areas about the Mediterranean. See Greeks. F. C. G.

HELMET.—See Armour, **2** (*b*).

HELON.—Father of Eliab, the prince of Zebulun at the first census, Nu 1^{9} 2^{7} $7^{24, 29}$ 10^{16}.

HELPS.—Ac 27^{17} AV, 'they used helps, undergirding the ship.' The reference is probably to 'cables passed round the hull of the ship, and tightly secured on deck, to prevent the timbers from starting, especially amidships, where in ancient vessels with one large mast the strain was very great. The technical English word is *frapping*, but the process has only been rarely employed since the early part of the [19th] century, owing to improvements in shipbuilding' (Page's *Acts of the Apostles*; see Smith's *Voyage and Shipwreck of St. Paul*, p. 105). RSV reads, 'they took measures to undergird the ship.'

HELPS (RSV 'helpers').—In 1 Co 12^{28} St. Paul, in order to show the diversity in unity found in the Church as the body of Christ, gives a list of services performed by various members of the churchly body. In the course of his enumeration he uses two Greek nouns (*antilēmpseis* and *kybernēseis*) employed nowhere else in the NT, and rendered in AV 'helps,' 'governments.' 'Helps' may suggest a lowly kind of service, as of one who acts as assistant to a superior. The usage of the Greek word, however, both in the LXX and in the papyri, points to succour given to the needy by those who are stronger; and this is borne out for the NT when the same word in its verbal form occurs in St. Paul's exhortation to the elders of the Ephesian Church to 'help the weak' (Ac 20^{35} RSV). 'Helps' in this list of churchly gifts and services thus denotes such attentions to the poor and afflicted as were specially assigned at a later time to the office of the deacon; while '**governments**' (RVm 'wise counsels,' cf Pr 1^{5} 11^{14} 24^{6}, LXX) suggests that rule and guidance which afterwards fell to presbyters or bishops. (RSV reads 'administrators.')

We are not to think, however, that there is necessarily any reference in this passage to deacons and bishops as Church officials. The fact that abstract terms are used instead of concrete and personal ones as in the earlier part of the list, shows that it is functions, not offices, of which the Apostle is thinking throughout. 'Helps,' as Hort says (*Chr. Ecclesia*, p. 159) are 'anything that could be done for poor or weak or outcast brethren, either by rich or powerful or influential brethren, or by the devotion of those who stood on no such eminence.' 'Governments,' again, refers to 'men who by wise counsels did for the community what the steersman or pilot does for the ship.' J. C. L.—M. H. S.

HELVE.—Dt 19^{5} (AV, RV); a word nearly obsolete, equivalent to 'handle' (so RSV).

HEM.—See Fringes.

HEMAM, Gn 36^{22} (AV, RV).—See Heman, **1.**

HEMAN.—**1.** A Horite clan of Edom, Gn 36^{22}. Hebrew, followed by AV and RV, has **Hemam.** 1 Ch 1^{39} has **Homam,** but the LXX in both places has **Heman.** Many scholars follow LXX, and so RSV in Gn 36^{22}. **2.** A legendary wise man whose wisdom Solomon excelled, 1 K 4^{31}. **3.** A son (or clan) of Zerah of the tribe of Judah, 1 Ch 2^{6}; probably also alluded to in the title of Ps 88 as Heman the Ezrahite, Ezrah being another form of *Zerah.* **4.** A Korahite singer of the time of David, said to be the son of Joel the son of Samuel,

1 Ch 6^{33} (cf $15^{17, 19}$ 16^{41f} 25^{1-6}). As Chronicles in a number of cases confuses the genealogy of Judah with that of Levi, and as the wise men of 1 K 4^{31} are legendary, it is probable that **2, 3,** and **4** are the same legendary ancestor of a clan celebrated for its music and wisdom. This view finds some support in the fact that the title of Ps 88 makes Heman both an Ezrahite (Judahite) and a Korahite (Levite).

HEMATH, 1 Ch 2^{55} (AV).—See HAMMATH, **1.**

HEMDAN.—See HAMRAN.

HEMORRHAGE.—See MEDICINE.

HEMLOCK.—See GALL, WORMWOOD.

HEN.—In Zec 6^{14} 'Hen the son of Zephaniah' is mentioned amongst those whose memory was to be perpetuated by the crowns laid up in the Temple (so AV, RV). RSV substitutes for 'Hen' the name of Josiah, found in v.^{10}.

HEN.—See COCK.

HENA.—A city named with Ivvah (q.v.) in 2 K 18^{34} 19^{13}, Is 37^{13}, as conquered by the Assyrians; its site is unknown.

HENADAD.—A Levite, Ezr 3^{9}, Neh $3^{18, 24}$ 10^{9}.

HENNA (Heb. *kōpher*).—The henna plant (Ca 1^{14} 4^{13}; AV **camphire**) is a small shrub (*Lawsonia alba*) which may still be found at Engedi. It is a great favourite with the people of Palestine to-day, and a 'cluster' of the flowers is often put in the hair; the perfume is much admired. It is also extensively used for staining the hands (especially the nails), the feet, and the hair; it stains an ochre-red, but further treatment of the nails with a mixture of lime and ammonia turns the colour almost black. Old women frequently redden their hair, and Moslems their beards, by means of henna.

E. W. G. M.

HEPHER.—**1.** A son of Gilead, the Manassite, Nu 26^{32} 27^{1}, Jos 17^{2f}. Patronymic, **Hepherites,** Nu 26^{32}. **2.** A man of the tribe of Judah, 1 Ch 4^{6}. **3.** One of David's heroes, 1 Ch 11^{36} (but the text is uncertain). **4.** A Canaanite royal city, named immediately before Aphek (q.v.), Jos 12^{17}. **5.** A place in Solomon's 3rd district, 1 K 4^{10}, probably in Manasseh (cf **1** above). It is named together with Soco (q.v.), which is probably modern *Tell er-Râs,* WNW. of Samaria.

HEPHZI-BAH ('she in whom is my delight').—**1.** The mother of Manasseh, king of Judah, 2 K 21^{1}. **2.** Symbolic name of the Zion of Messianic times, Is 62^{4} (RSV translates 'My delight is in her').

HERALD.—The word occurs in AV only in Dn 3^{4} (so RV, RSV) as translation of Aramaic *kārôz* (probably —Greek *kēryx*). The herald is the mouthpiece of the king's commands (cf Gn 41^{42}, Est 6^{9}). The word 'herald' is found in RSV in Is 40^{9} 41^{27} of the prophet as herald of God, and in 2 P 2^{5} of Noah as a preacher of righteousness; in RVm it is found in 2 P 2^{5} and in 1 Ti 2^{7}, 2 Ti 1^{11} of St. Paul as the herald of God. The cognate Greek verb and noun are regularly used in NT of 'preaching.' In Sir 20^{15}, where AV and RV have 'crier,' RSV has 'herald.' There is no instance in the Bible of the employment of 'heralds' in war.

HERB.—**1.** *yārāḳ, yereḳ*; twice translated 'green thing,' Ex 10^{15}, Is 15^{6} (RSV 'verdure' in latter); *gan yereḳ*, 'garden of herbs,' Dt 11^{10} (RSV 'a garden of vegetables'), 1 K 21^{2} (RSV 'a vegetable garden'). RSV renders *yārāḳ* by 'herb' in Gn 2^{5}. **2.** *'ēsebh* (cf Arabic *'ushb*), herbage in general, Gn 1^{11} (RSV 'vegetation'). RSV renders *'ēsebh* by 'herb' in Dt 32^{2} and by 'herbage' in Is 42^{15}, Jer 14^{6}. A kindred word is rendered by 'herbage' in Pr 27^{25}. See GRASS. **3.** *deshe'* is translated 'herb' in AV six times, Dt 32^{2}, 2 K 19^{26}, Job 38^{27}, Ps 37^{2}, Is 37^{27} 66^{14} (RV 'green herb' in 2 K 19^{26}, Ps 37^{2}, Is 37^{27}; 'tender grass' in the others; RSV 'green herb' in Ps 37^{2}, 'tender grass' or 'grass' in the others). **4.** *'ôrôth*, 2 K 4^{39} 'herbs.' This is explained to be the plant colewort, but may have been any eatable herbs that survived the drought. The expressions 'dew of herbs' (Is 26^{19} AV, RV; RSV 'dew of light') and 'upon herbs' (Is 18^{4} AV; RV, RSV 'in sunshine') are obscure. In the NT we have the Greek terms *botanē* (He 6^{7} 'herbs' AV, RV; RSV 'vegetation') and *lachanon=yereḳ* (Mt 13^{32} 'herbs' AV, RV; RSV 'shrubs'). RSV renders *lachanon* by 'herbs' in Lk 11^{42}. See also BITTER HERBS.

E. W. G. M.—H. H. R.

HERCULES (Gr. **Heracles**) is mentioned by this name only in 2 Mac 4^{19f}, where Jason, the head of the Hellenizing party in Jerusalem (174 B.C.) sent 300 silver drachmas to Tyre as an offering in honour of Hercules, the tutelary deity of that city. Hercules was the most widely worshipped of all Greek heroes; at Tyre his worship dated from very early times, and his temple there was (according to Herodotus ii. 44) as old as the city itself. As Herodotus insists, he was worshipped both as hero and as god.

During Hellenistic and Roman times, Hercules or Heracles achieved pre-eminence as the typical and popular hero-divinity who, through toil and suffering for the benefit of mankind, won his way to immortality and a place among the Olympian gods. The classic Twelve Labours of Heracles were the best-known illustrative series of such beneficent and heroic accomplishments on behalf of needy and suffering men. Stoic and Cynic teachers found in Heracles their prime exemplar of strenuous activist excellence, most worthy of human emulation.

H. R. W.

HERD.—See CATTLE, OX, SHEEP.

HEREAFTER.—In Mt 26^{64} 'Hereafter you will see the Son of Man seated at the right hand of Power, and coming on the clouds of heaven,' the meaning of 'hereafter' is 'from this time' (RV 'henceforth'). So Mk 11^{14} ('no one ever again'), Lk 22^{69} ('from now on'). Elsewhere the meaning is 'at some time in the future,' as Jn 13^{7} AV, 'What I do thou knowest not now, but thou shalt know hereafter' (RSV 'afterward').

HEREDITY, which may be defined as 'the hereditary transmission of qualities, or even acquirements,' so far as it is a scientific theory, is not anticipated in Holy Scripture. That men are 'made from one' (Ac 17^{26}; AV 'of one blood') is a fact of experience, which, in common with all literature, the Bible assumes. The unsophisticated are content to argue from like to like, that is, by analogy. But the modern doctrine of heredity, rooted as it is in the science of biology, involves the recognition of a principle or law according to which characters are transmitted from parents to offspring. Of this there is no trace in the Bible. Theology is therefore not directly interested in the differences between Weismann and the older exponents of Evolution.

1. In the OT, which is the basis of the doctrine of the NT, there is no dogmatic purpose, and therefore no attempt to account for the fact that 'all flesh' has 'corrupted their way upon the earth' (Gn 6^{12}), and that 'there is none that does good' (Ps 14^{1}). A perfectly consistent point of view is not to be expected. Not a philosophical people, the Hebrews start from the obvious fact of the unity of the race in the possession of common flesh and blood (Job 14^{1} 15^{14}), the son being begotten after the image of the father (Gn 5^{3}; cf He 2^{14}). This is more especially emphasized in the unity of the race of Abraham, that 'Israel after the flesh' (1 Co 10^{18} AV and RV), whose were the fathers and the promises (Ro 9^{4f}). But the Bible never commits itself to a theory of the generation or procreation of the spirit, which is apparently given by God to each individual (Gn 2^{7} 7^{23}, Job 33^{4}), constitutes the personality ('life' 2 S 1^{9}, 'person' [RV 'soul'] Nu 5^{6}), and is withdrawn at death (Ec 12^{7}). This is the source of Ezekiel's emphasis on individual responsibility (18^{4}), a criticism of the proverb concerning sour grapes (v.^{2}), which was made to rest on an admitted principle of the Mosaic covenant, the visitation upon the children of the fathers' sins (Ex 20^{5}). This principle involves corporate guilt; which, though sometimes reduced to a pardonable weakness inseparable from flesh (Ps 78[39] 103[14], Job 10[9]), and therefore suggestive of heredity, yet, as involving Divine wrath and punishment, cannot be regarded as a palliation of transgression (Ex 34[7], Ps 71[1], Ro 1[18]). Sin in the OT is disobedience, a breach of personal relations, needing from God forgiveness (Ex 34[6f], Is 43[25]); and cannot therefore be explained on the principle of hereditary transmission. Moreover, the unity of Israel is as much one of external status as of physical nature, of the inheritance of the firstborn no less than of community in flesh and blood (Ex 4[22]; cf Gn 25[23] 27[35]). Similarly Adam is represented as degraded to a lower status by his sin, as cast out of the garden and begetting children in banishment from God's presence.

2. Such are the materials from which NT theology works out its doctrine of **original sin,** not a transmitted tendency or bias towards evil, but a submission to the power of the devil which may be predicated of the whole race. (See SIN.) J. G. S.

HERES.—1. Jg 1[35] (AV, RV); see HAR-HERES. **2.** In Jg 8[13] (RV, RSV) 'the ascent of Heres' (AV 'before the sun was up') is mentioned as the spot from which Gideon returned after the defeat of Zebah and Zalmunna. Both the topography and the text of the narrative are doubtful. See also IR-HA-HERES, TIMNATH-HERES, TIMNATH-SERAH.

HERESH.—A Levite, 1 Ch 9[15].

HERESY.—The word 'heresy' (Gr. *hairesis*) is not used in the NT in the sense which it acquired by the first quarter of the 2nd cent., as a doctrinal departure from the faith of the church which must lead to a disruption of its life. The usual NT meaning of *hairesis* is simply party, school, or sect, and sect is the word by which it is most frequently rendered. In Acts this is the invariable use. Thus it is applied to the 'parties' (RSV) of the Pharisees and Sadducees (Ac 5[17] 15[5] 26[5]), precisely as in Josephus (*Ant.* XIII. v. 9 [171]). Similarly it is used of the followers of Christ, though not by themselves (24[5, 14] 28[22]). In 24[14] Paul deliberately uses 'the Way' to designate what his accusers call a 'sect.' The reason may be that in his usage *hairesis*, while still bearing the general sense of 'party,' had come to convey a reproach as applied to Christians.

Paul's pleas for the unity of the church continually lead him to a condemnation of the spirit of factionalism or division. *Hairesis*, RSV 'party-spirit,' is one of the evils listed in Gal 5[20], and in 1 Cor 11[18f] he speaks with distress of divisions in the church. The individual who is 'factious' (RSV) is singled out for condemnation in Tit 3[10] (AV and RV have 'heretical.') In 1 Cor 11[18f] *hairesis* is divisiveness or schism, and schism is a rending or cleaving of the body of Christ (12[25]). It is not doctrinal aberrations but rather breaches of the spirit of brotherly unity appropriate to the followers of Christ which are in view here.

Outside of Acts and the Pauline Epistles, *hairesis* is used in the NT only in 2 P 2[1]. In this late NT writing we see a sharper identification of false teaching as the source of error and division. The 'damnable' (RSV 'destructive') heresies here spoken of are the false teachings of those who invade the Church from outside and introduce a denial of its very foundation. There has not yet developed the later ecclesiastical concept of heresy as the holding or teaching of erroneous doctrine by one who stands within the church and maintains allegiance to its faith, though his error would disrupt it from within. D. D. W.

HERETH.—A forest which was one of the hiding-places of David, 1 S 22[5] (AV **Hareth**). The reference may be to the wooded mountain E. of Adullam, where the village of *Khārās* now stands.

HERMAS.—A Christian at Rome, saluted in Ro 16[14]. The name is a common one, especially among slaves. Origen's identification of this Hermas as the author of the well-known *Shepherd of Hermas*, a book written at Rome probably in the thirties or forties of the 2nd cent., is very improbable. J. L.

HERMES.—One of those greeted in Ro 16[14]. The name is common. At first, like all the names of gods, it was used exclusively for slaves, but in imperial times (as a result of manumissions) it became a fairly common name for free men also. J. L.

HERMES (translated *Mercury* in AV, RV of Ac 14[12]), was the spokesman of the gods, and hence was regarded by the Greeks as the god of eloquence. Hence, when Paul and Barnabas healed the cripple at Lystra, the former was hailed as Hermes, 'because he was the chief speaker.' The identification of Hermes with Mercury was due to another attribute. As the messenger of the gods, Hermes was the god who brought good fortune to men. Mercury was the Roman god of commerce (cf *merx, mercari*), and success in commerce was attributed to him. Hence the mythology of the two was confused. In the words of Sir William Ramsay, 'The origin and real character of Hermes are perhaps more difficult to define than is the case with any other Greek deity.' In popular religion this ancient god had many more attributes and functions, especially as *psychopompos* or guide of souls to the other world, beyond death. The so-called Hermetic writings, which contain a quasi-gnostic system of thought, owe their connexion with Hermes solely to his identification with the Egyptian god Thoth (*Tat*) in the age of Hellenistic syncretism. In some areas he was thought to be the finder of lost or hidden things. A. E. H.—**F. C. G.**

HERMOGENES.—One of a group of Asiatics, formerly companions of St. Paul, who at some point deserted him (2 Ti 1[17]). J. L.

HERMON.—The highest mountain in Syria (9150 feet high), a spur of the Anti-Lebanon. Its name means 'apart' or 'sanctuary,' and refers to its ancient sanctity (cf Ps 89[12]; and the name 'Mount **Baal-hermon**,' Jg 3[3]). Meagre traces of ruins remain on its summit, probably connected, at least partly, with a former high place. According to Dt 3[9], it was called **Sirion** by the Sidonians and **Senir** (q.v.) by the Amorites. It may have been the scene of the Transfiguration, Mk 9[2]. The summit has three peaks, that on the SE. being the highest. Snow lies on the top throughout the year, except in the autumn of some years; but usually there is a certain amount in the ravines. The top is bare above the snow-line; below it is richly wooded and covered with vine-yards. The Syrian bear can sometimes be seen here; seldom, if ever, anywhere else. The modern name is *Jebel esh-Sheikh*, 'the mountain of the Chief.' R. A. S. M.

HERMONITES.—A mistaken translation in Ps 42[6] AV, corrected in RV to **Hermons** (RSV **Hermon**), and referring to the three peaks of the summit of Hermon (q.v.).

HEROD.—The main interest attaching to the Herods is not concerned with their character as individual rulers. They acquire dignity when they are viewed as parts of a supremely dramatic situation in universal history. The fundamental elements in the situation are two. First, the course of world-power in antiquity, and the relation between it and the political principle in the constitution of the Jewish people. Second, the religious genius of Judaism, and its relation to the political elements in the experience of the Jews.

A glance at the map shows that Palestine is an organic part of the Mediterranean world. When, under the successors of Alexander, the centre of political gravity shifted from Persia to the shores of the Mediterranean Sea, the door was finally closed against the possibility of political autonomy in Palestine. The kingdom of the Seleucids had a much larger stake in the internal affairs of the country than the Persian Empire had thought of claiming. For one thing, the political genius of the Greeks demanded a more closely knit State than the Persian. For another, the fact that Palestine was the frontier towards Egypt made its political assimilation to Northern Syria a military necessity. The Maccabaean

War give rise to the second Jewish State. But it was shortlived. Only during the disintegration of the house of Seleucus could it breathe freely. The moment Rome stretched out her hands to Syria its knell was rung.

The Hasmonaean house was obliged to face a hopeless foreign situation. World-politics made an independent career impossible. In addition, it had to face an irreconcilable element in the constitution of Judaism. The rise of the Pharisees and the development of the Essenes plainly showed that the fortune of the Jews was not to be made in the political field. In truth, Judaism was vexed by an insoluble contradiction. The soul of this people longed for universal dominion. But efficient political methods for the attainment of dominion were made impossible by their religion. The Hasmonaean house was caught—between the upper and the nether millstone.

The foundations of the Herodian house were laid by Antipater, an Idumaean, who had succeeded his father, also Antipater, as military governor of Idumaea in the days of Alexander Jannaeus and his doughty wife Alexandra (Jos. *Ant.* XIV. i. 3 [8–10]). Apparently the Idumaeans, converted by the sword, were never Jewish to the core. More than once the Pharisees flung the reproach 'half-Jew' in the teeth of Herod. Antipater was a man of undistinguished family, and fought his way up by strength and cunning. The decay of the Hasmonaean house favoured his career. Palestine needed a strong hand. The power of Syria and the power of Egypt were gone. Rome was passing through the decay of the senatorial régime. The Empire had not yet appeared, to gather up the loose ends of provincial government. Pompey's capture of Jerusalem had shattered what little was left of Hasmonaean prestige. Yet Rome was not ready to assume direct control of Palestine. It was in this situation that Antipater showed his astuteness. It was his policy to be the directing power behind the scenes. In the years of confusion and revolt which followed the death of Alexandra and during the early years of Roman control he proved himself a valuable and efficient tool of Rome, and thus established himself and his two sons as Rome's native agents.

1. Herod the Great.—Antipater's son, Herod, had shown himself before his father's death both masterful and merciless. His courage was high, his understanding capable of large conceptions, and his will able to adhere persistently to a distant end of action. His temperament was one of headlong passion; and when, in the later period of his life, the power and suspiciousness of the tyrant had sapped the real magnanimity of his nature, it converted him into a butcher, exercising his trade upon his own household as well as upon his opponents. His marriage with Mariamme, the heiress of the Hasmonaean house, and his league with Rome, indicate the story of his life. His marriage was one both of love and of policy. His league was a matter of clear insight into the situation. He was once driven out of Palestine by an alliance between the Hasmonaean house and the Parthians (Jos. *Ant.* XIV. xiii. 7 [352 f]). But, backed by Rome, he returned with irresistible force. Mutual interest made the alliance close. Herod served the Empire well. And Augustus and his successors showed their appreciation. They stood by Herod and his descendants even when the task was not wholly pleasing. They also conferred various privileges and exemptions upon the practice of Judaism outside Palestine.

Josephus calls Herod a man of extraordinary force and political discernment. He owed his good fortune largely to himself, manifesting powers which might have made him, in a less difficult field, fully deserving of his title 'the Great.' He enjoyed the life-long favour of Augustus and his minister Agrippa. He made life and property in Palestine safe from every foe but his own tyranny. And though he showed himself a brutal murderer of Mariamme and his own children, not to speak of the massacre of the Innocents—an incident unrecorded by Josephus and mentioned only in Mt 2—it must be remembered that Jerusalem was a hot-bed of intrigue. This does not justify him, but it explains his apparently insensate blood-lust.

His sympathy with Hellenism was a matter of honest conviction. The Empire was slowly closing in on Palestine. An independent Jewish power was impossible. The man who ruled the country was bound to work in the interest of Rome. Hellenism in the Holy Land was the political order of the day. So Herod built cities and gave them imperial names. He built amphitheatres, patronized the Greek games and, as far as his temperament and opportunities permitted, Greek literature. At the same time, while he was but 'half-Jew,' he sincerely desired to do large things for Judaism. He was a stout defender of the rights of the Jews in the Diaspora. He rebuilt the Temple with great splendour. But his supreme gift to the Jews, a gift which they were not capable of appreciating, was a native Palestinian power, which, whatever its methods, was by profession Jewish. When he died, after a long reign (37–4 B.C.), and the Jews petitioned the Emperor for direct Roman rule (Jos. *Ant.* XVII. xi. 2 [314]), they showed their incompetence to read the signs of the times. Roman rule was a very different thing from Persian rule or Ptolemaic. When it came, the iron entered into the soul of Judaism.

2. Archelaus.—After some delay Herod's third will was carried out substantially. His sons were set up in power,—Archelaus over Judaea, Samaria, and Idumaea, Antipas over Galilee and Peraea, Philip over Batanaea, Trachonitis, Ituraea, and Auranitis. To Archelaus had fallen the greatest prize, and at the same time the hardest task. After maintaining himself until the year A.D. 6, his misgovernment and weakness, combined with the impossible elements in Judaism, caused his downfall and exile. The Jews now had their own wish. Judaea came under direct Roman rule. A tax was levied. Judas of Gamala rose in rebellion. He was easily put down. But the significance of his little rebellion was immense. For now what Josephus calls 'the fourth philosophical sect' amongst the Jews (*Ant.* XVIII. i. 6 [23]) came into prominence, namely, a militant and thoroughgoing nationalistic or home-rule group. That this group originated at precisely this moment, as Josephus suggests, is perhaps improbable. It had been present from the earliest days of the Roman rule. Actually it was Herod's successful opposition to this movement, when sent by his father Antipater to be governor of Galilee (Jos. *Ant.* XIV. ix. 2–5 [158 ff]) which had apparently first brought him to Rome's favourable attention. From this militant group, always present and increasingly vocal as Rome's hand grew heavier, were eventually to come the Zealots, as Josephus styles the fanatical followers of John of Gischala, in the days of the great war against Rome (A.D. 66–73). That this movement had its first start in the days of Judas of Gamala, or that in his days it was already styled Zealot is constantly asserted but highly improbable. This faction dragged into the light the self-contradiction within Judaism. The Jews could not build a State themselves. Their principles made it impossible for them to keep the peace with their heathen overlord. Conflict was inevitable.

3. Herod Antipas, called 'the tetrarch' (Mt 14[1], Lk 3[19] 9[7], Ac 13[1]), had better fortune. Jesus is said to have described him as a 'fox' (Lk 13[32]). The name gives the clue to his nature. He was a man of craft rather than strength. But cunning served him well, and he kept his seat until the year A.D. 39. The corroding immorality of his line shows itself in his marriage with Herodias, his brother's wife (see JOHN THE BAPTIST). His lust proved his undoing. Herodias, an ambitious woman, spurred him out of his caution. In rivalry with Herod Agrippa I., he asked of Caligula the royal title. This exciting suspicion, his doings were looked into and he was banished.

4. Philip (Lk 3[1]) seems to have been the best among the sons of Herod. And it was his good fortune to rule over an outlying country where the questions always rife in Jerusalem were not pressed. His character and

GENEALOGICAL TABLE OF THE FAMILY OF HEROD

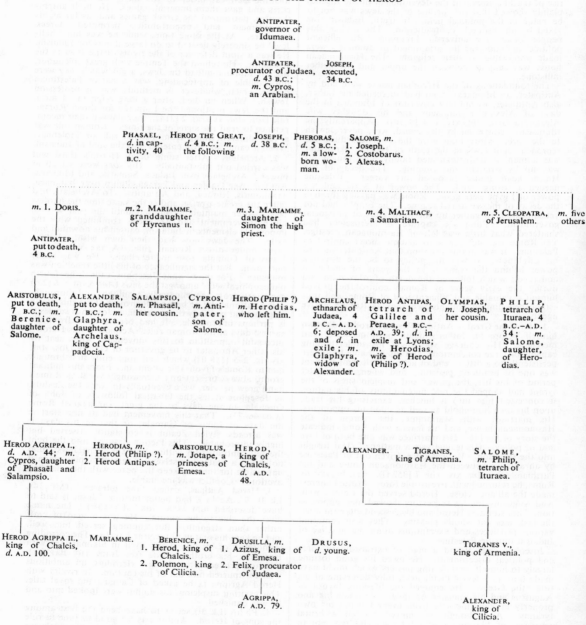

- **Antipater**, governor of Idumaea.
  - **Antipater**, procurator of Judaea, *d.* 43 B.C.; *m.* Cypros, an Arabian.
    - **Phasael**, *d.* in captivity, 40 B.C.
    - **Herod the Great**, *d.* 4 B.C.; *m.* the following
    - **Joseph**, *d.* 38 B.C.
    - **Pheroras**, *d.* 5 B.C.; *m.* a low-born woman.
    - **Salome**, *m.* 1. Joseph. 2. Costobarus. 3. Alexas.
  - **Joseph**, executed, 34 B.C.

Herod the Great *m.* the following:

- *m.* 1. **Doris.**
  - **Antipater**, put to death, 4 B.C.
- *m.* 2. **Mariamme**, granddaughter of Hyrcanus II.
  - **Aristobulus**, put to death, 7 B.C.; *m.* Berenice, daughter of Salome.
    - **Herod Agrippa I.**, *d.* A.D. 44; *m.* Cypros, daughter of Phasaël and Salampsio.
      - **Herod Agrippa II.**, king of Chalcis, *d.* A.D. 100.
      - **Mariamme.**
      - **Berenice**, *m.* 1. Herod, king of Chalcis. 2. Polemon, king of Cilicia.
      - **Drusilla**, *m.* 1. Azizus, king of Emesa. 2. Felix, procurator of Judaea.
        - **Agrippa**, *d.* A.D. 79.
      - **Drusus**, *d.* young.
    - **Herodias**, *m.* 1. Herod (Philip ?). 2. Herod Antipas.
    - **Aristobulus**, *m.* Jotape, a princess of Emesa.
    - **Herod**, king of Chalcis, *d.* A.D. 48.
  - **Alexander**, put to death, 7 B.C.; *m.* Glaphyra, daughter of Archelaus, king of Cappadocia.
    - **Alexander.**
    - **Tigranes**, king of Armenia.
      - **Tigranes V.**, king of Armenia.
        - **Alexander**, king of Cilicia.
  - **Salampsio**, *m.* Phasaël, her cousin.
  - **Cypros**, *m.* Antipater, son of Salome.
- *m.* 3. **Mariamme**, daughter of Simon the high priest.
  - **Herod (Philip ?)** *m.* Herodias, who left him.
    - **Salome**, *m.* Philip, tetrarch of Ituraea.
- *m.* 4. **Malthace**, a Samaritan.
  - **Archelaus**, ethnarch of Judaea, 4 B.C.–A.D. 6; deposed and *d.* in exile; *m.* Glaphyra, widow of Alexander.
  - **Herod Antipas**, tetrarch of Galilee and Peraea, 4 B.C.–A.D. 39; *d.* in exile at Lyons; *m.* Herodias, wife of Herod (Philip ?).
  - **Olympias**, *m.* Joseph, her cousin.
- *m.* 5. **Cleopatra**, of Jerusalem.
  - **Philip**, tetrarch of Ituraea, 4 B.C.–A.D. 34; *m.* Salome, daughter of Herodias.
- *m.* five others

his good fortune together gave him a long and peaceful rule († A.D. 34).

5. Another **Philip** (son of Herod the Great and Mariamme, daughter of Simon the high priest) is mentioned in Mt 14^{3}, Mk 6^{17} as the first husband of Herodias. Actually his name appears to have been Herod (Jos. *Ant.* XVIII. v. 1 [109]), and his mention as 'Philip' in the Gospel story would seem to be due to confusing him with Philip the tetrarch, who married Salome, the daughter of Herodias and her former husband Herod (*Ant.* XVIII. v. 4 [137]).

6. In **Herod Agrippa I.**, the Herodian house seemed at one time to have reached the high water-mark of power. He had served a long apprenticeship in the Imperial Court, where immorality, adaptability, and flattery were the price of position. That he was not altogether unmanned is proved by his attempting to dissuade Caligula from his proposal to set up a statue of himself in the Temple; for, in setting himself against the tyrant's whim, he staked life and fortune (Jos. *Ant.* XVIII. viii. 7 f [289 ff]). In high favour with Caligula, he was successively granted by him what had been the tetrarchies of Philip and Antipas. He continued in imperial favour, and his territory was expanded by Claudius to include the Roman province of Judaea (including Samaria). Thus for a brief period (A.D. 41–44) he reigned with the title king over a reunited Palestine. His reign was the Indian summer of Judaism. Even the Pharisees thought well of him. When in Rome he lived as one who knew Rome well. But in Jerusalem he wore his Judaism as a garment made to order. He was quite willing to gratify the Jews by putting leading Christians to death (Ac 12^{1f}). In high favour both at Jerusalem and at Rome, he seemed to be beyond attack. But the veto put on his proposal to rebuild the walls of his capital showed clearly his insecurity. And the pagan streak in him was sure, sooner or later, to come to light. The story of his death, wherein the Book of Acts (12^{20-23}) and Josephus (*Ant.* XIX. viii. 2 [343 ff]) substantially agree, brings this out. At Caesarea he paraded himself before a servile multitude as if he were a little Caesar, a god on earth. Smitten by a terrible disease, he died in great agony (A.D. 44). Jews and Christians alike looked on his end as a fitting punishment for his heathenism. The house of Herod was 'half-Jew' to the last.

7. Herod Agrippa II., son of the last named, before whom St. Paul delivered the discourse contained in Ac 26. As he was only seventeen years of age when his father died, the emperor Claudius would not make him king of Palestine; but in the year A.D. 50, when his uncle Herod king of Chalcis died, he was made ruler of this tiny kingdom in the Lebanons. He seems to have been non-resident, living in Rome; but in A.D. 53 he was given the territories formerly ruled by Philip the tetrarch, Lysanias, and the eparchy ruled by Varus. He tried to persuade the Palestinian Jews not to revolt, in A.D. 66, pointing out the impossibility of victory; but he failed to convince them (Jos. *War*, II. xvi. 4 [345 ff]. He ruled long and peacefully, and died in A.D. 100.

See the accompanying genealogical table.

H. S. N.—M. S. E.

HERODIANS.—The name of a political party among the Jews, which derived its name from the support it gave to the dynasty of Herod (cf Jos. *Ant.* XIV. xv. 10 [450]). Perhaps they hoped for the restoration of the national kingdom under one of the sons of Herod. The Herodians appear in the Gospels on two occasions (Mk 3^{6}, Mt 22^{16} ‖ Mk 12^{13}) as making common cause with the Pharisees against Jesus.

HERODIAS.—See HEROD, **3**, and JOHN THE BAPTIST.

HERODION.—A Christian mentioned in Ro 16^{11}, apparently a Jew, and perhaps a freedman of the Herods.

HERON (*'ᵃnāphāh*; Lv 11^{19}, Dt 14^{18}).—What bird is meant by *'ᵃnāphāh* is quite uncertain; and the Assyrian *anpatu*, which has been cited to explain it, is equally unidentified, being known only as a bird of ill omen and as having been brought home from across the Euphrates by an Assyrian king. No evidence that it is the 'heron' (AV, RV) has ever been produced (see STORK); and 'ibis' (RVm) is absurd, since this bird is not found in Palestine. It is rendered by the ancient versions 'thick-kneed plover' (LXX, Vulgate), 'black hawk' and 'white hawk' (Targum of Pseudo-Jonathan). The root of the name, if any guide, suggests a bird with a beak shaped like a nose (Heb. *'aph*=Aram. *'anpâ* 'nose'), and its position immediately after the osprey and the stork suggests one living on or by water. It may then be the 'cormorant,' a large blackish bird with a long neck and white cheeks and a hooked beak. Both the ordinary cormorant (*phalacrocorax carbo*) and the pygmy cormorant (*phalacrocorax pygmaeus*) are found in abundance on the coast and beside all the streams in Palestine. It covers an extensive piece of ground round its nest with its greenish white excrement, which is fatal to the vegetation in contact with it and emits a disgusting odour, mingled with that of decaying regurgitated fragments of fish, so that it is properly included for this reason as also as a *raptor* amongst unclean birds. G. R. D.

HESED, 1 K 4^{10} (AV).—See BEN-HESED.

HESHBON is the modern *Ḥesbân*, finely situated close to the edge of the great plateau of Eastern Palestine. The extensive ruins, mainly of Roman times, lie on two hills connected by a saddle. The site commands views, E. and S., of rolling country; N., of hills including *e.g.* that on which *el-'Âl* (Elealeh) lies; and W., in the distance, of the hills of Judah and nearer, through a gap in the near hills, of the Jordan valley, which lies some 4000 feet below, the river itself being barely 20 miles distant. Allotted to Reuben (Jos 13^{17}), Heshbon appears in the OT most frequently as being, or having been, the capital of Sihon (q.v.), king of the Amorites (Dt 2^{26} and often), or, like many other towns in this neighbourhood, in the actual possession of the Moabites (Is 15^{4} 16^{8f}, Jer $48^{2, 34f}$) to whom, according to Nu 21^{26}, it had belonged before Sihon captured it. Jer 49^{3}, which appears to make Heshbon an Ammonite city, is probably corrupt (cf Driver, *Book of the Prophet Jeremiah*). According to Josephus (*Ant.* XIII. xv. 4 [397]), it was in the hands of the Jews in the time of Alexander Jannaeus (104–78 B.C.). The **pools** in Heshbon, mentioned in Ca 7^{4}, were perhaps pools near the spring which rises 600 feet below the city, and in the neighbourhood of which are traces of ancient conduits.

G. B. G.

HESHMON.—An unknown town in the extreme S. of Judah, Jos 15^{27}.

HETH.—A 'son' of Canaan, Gn 10^{15}, 1 Ch 1^{13}. The wives of Esau are called in Gn 27^{46} 'daughters of Heth' (RSV 'Hittite women'); and in Gn 23^{3ff} 25^{10} 49^{32} 'children of Heth,' *i.e.* Hittites (so RSV), are located at Mamre. See, further, HITTITES.

ḤETH.—Eighth letter of Hebrew alphabet, and so used to introduce the eighth part of Ps 119, every verse of which begins with this letter.

HETHLON.—A place mentioned by Ezekiel (47^{15} 48^{1}) as situated on the ideal northern boundary of Israel. The site is unknown; possibly modern *Ḥeitelâ*, NE. of Tripolis.

HEXATEUCH.—See PENTATEUCH.

HEZEKIAH.—**1.** One of the most prominent kings of Judah. He came to the throne after his father Ahaz, about 715 B.C. The assertions that Samaria was captured in his sixth year and that Sennacherib's invasion came in his fourteenth year are inconsistent (2 K $18^{10, 13}$). The latter has probability on its side, and as we know that Sennacherib invaded Palestine in 701 B.C. the calculation is easily made.

Politically Hezekiah had a difficult task. His father had submitted to Assyria, but the vassalage was felt to be severe. The petty kingdoms of Palestine were restive under the yoke, and they were encouraged by the

Egyptians to make an effort for independence. There was always an Egyptian party at the court of Jerusalem, though at this time Egypt was suffering from internal dissensions. In the East the kingdom of Babylon, under Merodach-baladan, was also making trouble for the Assyrians. Hezekiah seems to have remained faithful to the suzerain for some years after his accession, but when, about the time of Sennacherib's accession (705 B.C.), a coalition was formed against the oppressor, he joined it. We may venture to suppose that about this time he received the embassy from Merodach-baladan (2 K 20^{12ff}, Is 39^{1ff}), which was intended to secure the co-operation of the Western States with Babylon in the effort then being made. Isaiah, as we know from his own discourses, was opposed to the Egyptian alliance, and apparently to the whole movement. The Philistines were for revolt; only Padi, king of Ekron, held out for his master the king of Assyria. For this reason Hezekiah invaded his territory and took him prisoner. If, as the Biblical account seems to intimate (2 K 18^{8}), he incorporated the conquered land in his own kingdom, the gain was not for a long time. In 701 B.C. Sennacherib appeared on the scene, and there was no possibility of serious resistance. The inscriptions tell us that the invaders captured forty-six walled towns, and carried 200,150 Judaeans into captivity. The Egyptian army made a show of coming to the help of its allies, but was met on the border and defeated. Hezekiah was compelled to release the captive Padi, who returned to his throne in triumph. Sennacherib was detained at Lachish by the stubborn resistance of that fortress, and sent a detachment of his troops to Jerusalem. With it went an embassy, the account of which can be read in 2 K 18, 19 and Is 36, 37. The laconic sentence, 'Hezekiah king of Judah sent to the king of Assyria at Lachish, saying, 'I have done wrong; withdraw from me; whatever you impose on me I will bear."' (2 K 18^{14}) shows that abject submission was made. The price of peace was a heavy one—thirty talents of gold and three hundred talents of silver (according to the Biblical account) or eight hundred talents of silver (according to the Assyrian record). To pay it, all the gold and silver that could be found was gathered together, even the Temple doors being stripped of their precious metal (v.^{16}).

In our accounts we read of a great destruction which came upon the Assyrian army (2 K 19^{35}, Is 37^{36}). Some scholars believe this occurred at the time of a *second* expedition of Sennacherib to the west, but the evidence for such an expedition is obscure. Other scholars believe that, as a result of Hezekiah's surrender of Jerusalem and the consequent sparing of the city, the legend grew up of a supernatural deliverance of the city, promised and foretold by the prophet Isaiah. The latter is more probable. At any rate the evidence is abundantly clear that the 'deliverance' of Jerusalem in 701 B.C. was the result of Hezekiah's surrender. Hezekiah's sickness is dated by the Biblical writer in the time of this invasion, which can hardly be correct if the king lived fifteen years after that experience.

The account of Hezekiah's religious reforms is more sweeping than seems probable for that date. There seems no reason to doubt, however, that he destroyed the brazen serpent, which had been an object of worship in the Temple (2 K 18^{4}). The cleansing of the country sanctuaries from idolatry, under the influence of Isaiah, may have been accomplished at the same time. The expansions of the Chronicler (2 Ch 29 ff) must be received with reserve.

Sometime during his reign Hezekiah had a tunnel dug to bring water from the Virgin's Spring (Gihon) to the Pool of Siloam within the city (2 K 20^{20}, 2 Ch 32^{30}; see SILOAM). The purpose was to attempt to ensure a water supply for Jerusalem in case of a siege.

2. An ancestor of the prophet Zephaniah (Zeph 1^{1}), possibly to be identified with the king of the same name. **3.** Head of a family of exiles who returned, Ezr 2^{16} = Neh 7^{21} (cf 10^{17}). **4.** A companion of Ezra at the reading of the Law, 1 Es 9^{43} (RSV; AV **Ezecias**, RV **Ezekias**); called **Hilkiah** in Neh 8^{4}. **5.** 1 Ch 3^{23} (AV); see HIZKIAH.

H. P. S.—**J. P. H.**

HEZION.—Father of Tabrimmon, and grandfather of Benhadad, the Syrian king, 1 K 15^{18}. It has been plausibly suggested that Hezion is identical with **Rezon** (q.v.) of 1 K 11^{23}, the founder of the kingdom of Damascus, and an adversary to Solomon.

HEZIR.—**1.** The 17th of the priestly courses, 1 Ch 24^{15}. **2.** A lay family, which signed the covenant, Neh 10^{20}.

HEZRAI, 2 S 23^{35} (AV, RV).—See HEZRO.

HEZRO.—One of David's thirty heroes, 2 S 23^{35} (RSV; AV, RV **Hezrai**), 1 Ch 11^{37}.

HEZRON.—**1.** The eponymous head of a Reubenite family, Gn 46^{9}, Ex 6^{14}, Nu 26^{6}, 1 Ch 5^{3}. **2.** The eponymous head of a Judahite family, Gn 46^{12}, Nu 26^{21}, Ru 4^{18f}, 1 Ch $2^{5, 9, 18, 21, 24f}$ 4^{1}. This Hezron appears also in NT in the genealogy of our Lord, Mt 1^{3}, Lk 3^{33}. The gentilic **Hezronites** occurs in Nu 26^{6} referring to the descendants of **1**, and in v.^{21} referring to those of **2** above. **3.** A town in the south of Judah, Jos 15^{3}, where probably Hezron and Addar together constitute **Hazar-addar** (q.v.) of Nu 34^{4}.

HIDDAI.—One of David's thirty heroes, 2 S 23^{30}; called **Hurai** in the parallel 1 Ch 11^{32}.

HIDDEKEL.—The river Tigris, mentioned as the third river of Paradise, Gn 2^{14}. By this river Daniel had his vision, Dn 10^{4} (RSV here **Tigris**, but Hiddekel in Gn 2^{14}). The Hebrew *Ḥiddeḳel* was taken from the Babylonian name for the Tigris, *Idiglat* or *Diglat*, which was in turn derived from its Sumerian name, *Idigna*.

HIEL.—The name of a certain Bethelite who in the days of Ahab fortified Jericho, and possibly sacrificed his two sons to appease the gods of the disturbed earth, 1 K 16^{34}. Some obscure event is here applied as a comment on the curse on Jericho pronounced by Joshua.

HIERAPOLIS ('holy city') is mentioned in the Bible only in Col 4^{13}, in association with the neighbouring towns Laodicea and Colossae. All three were situated in the valley of the Lycus, a tributary of the Maeander, in Phrygia, Hierapolis on the north side being about 6 miles from the former and 12 miles from the latter. It derived its title from the medicinal hot springs there, which revealed plainly to the ancient mind the presence of a divinity. The water is strongly impregnated with alum, and the calcareous deposit which it forms explains the name of the adjacent village *Pambuk-Kalessi* (Cotton Castle). Another sacred place nearby is a grotto called the Plutonium, with an opening the size of a man's body, from which noxious vapours issued: any animal entering it fell dead. Strabo (in the time of Augustus) himself made the experiment with some sparrows. The city owed all its importance in NT times to its religious character. It had not been visited by St. Paul, but derived its Christianity from his influence (cf Ac 19^{10} and Col). Traditions of the early centuries declare that the Apostles Philip and John preached there. The former allegedly was martyred there. The city remained important throughout the Empire, and was the birthplace of Epictetus, the Stoic. The patron goddess of the city was Leto, mother of Apollo and Artemis.

A. So.—**E. G. K.**

HIEREEL, 1 Es 9^{21} (AV, RV).—See JEHIEL, **10.**

HIEREMOTH, 1 Es $9^{27, 30}$ (AV, RV).—See JEREMOTH, **6, 8.**

HIERIELUS, 1 Es 9^{27} (AV).—See JEHIEL, **9.**

HIERMAS, 1 Es 9^{26} (AV, RV).—See RAMIAH.

HIERONYMUS.—A Syrian officer in command of a district of Palestine under Antiochus v. Eupator, who harassed the Jews after the withdrawal of Lysias in 165 B.C. (2 Mac 12^{2}).

HIGGAION.—See PSALMS, **2.**

HIGH PLACE, SANCTUARY.—The term 'sanctuary' is used by modern students of Semitic religion in two senses, a wider and a narrower. On the one hand, it may denote, as the etymology suggests, any 'holy place,' the sacredness of which is derived from its association with the presence of a deity. In the narrower sense 'sanctuary' is used of every recognized place of worship, provided with an altar and other apparatus of the cult, the special designation of which in OT is *bâmāh*, EV '**high place.**' In this latter sense 'sanctuary' and 'high place' are used synonymously in the older prophetic literature, as in Am 7[9] 'the high places of Isaac shall be made desolate, and the sanctuaries of Israel shall be laid waste.'

1. In the wider sense of 'sanctuary,' as above defined, any arbitrarily chosen spot may become a holy place, if tradition associates it with a theophany, or visible manifestation of a Divine being. Such, indeed, was the origin of the most famous of the world's sanctuaries (see 2 S 24[16ff]). On the other hand, certain objects of nature—springs and rivers, trees, rocks, and, in particular, mountains—have been regarded with special reverence by many primitive peoples as 'the homes or haunts of the gods.' Thus the belief in the peculiar sacredness of **springs** and **wells** of 'living water' is one that has survived to our own day, even among advanced races. It was to this belief that the ancient sanctuary of Beersheba (q.v.) owed its origin. A similar belief in sacred **trees** as the abode of superhuman spirits or *numina* has been scarcely less tenacious. The holy places which figure so conspicuously in the stories of the patriarchs are in many cases tree-sanctuaries of immemorial antiquity, such as 'the terebinth of Moreh,' at Shechem, under which Abram is said to have built his first altar in Canaan (Gn 12[6f]; cf 13[18]).

More sympathetic to the modern mind is the choice of **mountains** and hills as holy places. On mountain-tops, men, from remote ages, have felt themselves nearer to the Divine beings with whom they sought to hold converse (cf Ps 121[1]). From OT the names of Horeb (or Sinai), the 'mountain of God' (Ex 3[1]), of Ebal and Gerizim, of Carmel and Tabor (Hos 5[1]), at once suggest themselves as sanctuaries where the Hebrews worshipped their God.

2. From these natural sanctuaries, which are by no means peculiar to the Hebrews or even to the Semitic family, we may now pass to a fuller discussion of the local sanctuaries or 'high places,' which were the recognized places of worship in Israel until near the close of the 7th cent. B.C. Whatever may be the precise etymological significance of the term *bâmāh* (plural *bâmôth*), there can be no doubt that 'high place' is a sufficiently accurate rendering. Repeatedly in OT the worshippers are said to 'go up' to, and to 'come down' from, the high places. The normal situation of a high place relative to the city whose sanctuary it was is very clearly brought out in the account of the meeting of Samuel and Saul at Ramah (1 S 9[13-25]). It is important, however, to note that a local sanctuary, even when it bore the name *bâmāh*, might be, and presumably often was, *within* the city, and was not necessarily situated on a height. Thus Jeremiah speaks of 'high places' (*bâmôth*) in the valley of Topheth at Jerusalem (7[31] 19[6] RV and RSV; cf Ezk 6[3]), and the high place, as we must call it, of the city of Gezer, lay in a depression between the two hills on which the city was built.

With few exceptions the high places of OT are much older, as places of worship, than the Hebrew conquest. Of this the Hebrews in later times were well aware, as is shown by the endeavour on the part of the popular tradition to claim their own patriarchs as the founders of the more famous sanctuaries. Prominent among these was the 'king's sanctuary' (Am 7[13] RV and RSV) at Bethel, with its companion sanctuary at Dan; scarcely less important were those of Gilgal and Beersheba, and 'the great high place' at Gibeon (1 K 3[4]). In the period of the Judges the chief sanctuary in Ephraim was that consecrated by the presence of the Ark at Shiloh (Jg 21[19], 1 S 1[3] etc.), which was succeeded by the sanctuary at Nob (1 S 21[1]). But while these and others attracted worshippers from near and far at the time of the great festivals, it may safely be assumed that every village throughout the land had, like Ramah, its local *bâmāh*.

The problem of the *bâmāh*, its function and place in the life of Israel, have occupied scholars for several generations without notable progress towards a solution until very recently. In an important paper, VTS, iv (1957), 242–258, W. F. Albright has brought together an accumulation of data which places the whole subject on a new footing. A summary of his views, with a few comments, follows. The essential meaning of *bâmāh*, 'high place,' has always been recognized, but a precise etymology has been lacking. Albright derives the Hebrew variants *bâmāh* and *bômāh* from an original **bahmatu* (related to *beʰēmāh* 'beast' from **bahimatu*) meaning, 'back, torso, ridge.' We have the same root in Ugaritic *bmt* 'back, torso (of an animal)'; and Akkadian *bāntu* (from *bāmtu*, from **bāmatu*) 'trunk, torso (of an animal),' plural *bamāti* 'ridges, heights.' From biblical and archaeological data, the meaning of Hebrew *bâmāh* can be further extended to include, 'height, hill, mound, a projecting mass of rock, and a stone burial cairn.'

In support of this interpretation, several passages in the OT are analysed, *e.g.* Is 53[9], where for the puzzling *beʰmôthâw* of MT, 1QIs[a] reads *bômāthô* 'his burial cairn,' which is in parallel construction with *ḳibhrô* 'his grave.' Similarly in Ezk 43[7b] *pegher* (which here signifies the funerary stele rather than the corpse) is connected with *bômāh* (the burial place). The close association of the *maṣṣēbhāh*, 'burial monument or commemorative stele,' and the 'high place' is well known. However, the two need not be in physical proximity as the traditions concerning Absalom's death show (cf 2 S 18[17-18]). The burial cairn was located in the forests of Gilead, but the memorial stone had previously been erected by Absalom himself in the Valley of the Kings.

On the archaeological side, many new high places have been discovered and examined, in addition to those which were known in earlier years, *e.g.* Gezer, Sinai, Petra. Petrie's and Albright's explorations at *Serābîṭ el-Khâdim* in Sinai revealed three sets of funerary installations dating from the 4th–3rd millennium B.C. down to the 15th cent. B.C. The inscribed stelae in the vicinity of the sanctuary are characteristic of such installations. Similar constructions have been found in South Arabia and the Negeb. Mrs. R. Amiran has excavated a typical 'high place' near *Mālḥah* SW. of Jerusalem, dating from the period of the Judahite monarchy (7th cent.). Similar high places have been excavated at Megiddo by G. Loud (dating from the 3rd millennium to the 18th cent. B.C.) and at Nahariyah by M. Dothan (18th cent. B.C.). In both cases the burial cairns are in the vicinity of a sanctuary. Two recent explorations at Byblos and Hazor have turned up numerous funerary stelae located in the high place (cf M. Dunand, *Bulletin du Musee de Beyrouth*, i [1937], 102 ff, ii [1938], 113, and *Fouilles de Byblos*, ii [1954], Plates XXII–XXXII; Y. Yadin, *Hazor* I [1958], pp. 83 ff, and Plates XXVII–XXXI).

It appears that the cairn high place was brought in from the desert, and that its primary association was with funerary practice, whether the body was actually buried in the area, or only represented by an appropriate stele. The conclusion is that the high place in the Bible was primarily a mortuary shrine. It served, therefore, as the focal point of the cult of heroes, widespread in the ancient world (particularly in Hellenic and Hellenistic areas), and sporadically attested in the OT (*e.g.* with regard to Samuel, Elisha, and others). In addition to its funerary associations, the high place was the local centre for paganizing fertility rites under Canaanite influence. It was the latter which provoked the wrath of the prophets and ultimately resulted in the permanent destruction of the high places in the time of Josiah, though the upholders of Yahwism would have been equally aware of the dangers of the hero cult, which tended to elevate the departed to superhuman or semi-divine status.

In view of this analysis of the high place and its rôle in Israelite life, it is clear that a reconstruction of the history of biblical religion, other than that of the traditional Wellhausenists, is not only implied but required. Thus there was no essential conflict between the central sanctuary—which had existed from the days of Moses —and the local high places, with their sanctuaries, which served as sacred cemeteries or memorial groves. They catered to the religious concerns and needs of ordinary people in an area almost entirely ignored by Mosaic Yahwism, *e.g.* death and life after death. In time the cult of the dead might produce a series of semi-divine figures as the direct objects of popular veneration and supplication, and so offer a challenge to the austere monotheism of the prophetic tradition. The high place, at a later time, also supplied a form of worship, which was not merely ignored but rigidly repudiated by orthodox Yahwism: the Canaanite or Canaanizing fertility cult. Only then was the issue radically joined, and it spelled the ultimate doom of the high places. From the start the Tabernacle and then the Temple functioned as the central, national, sanctuary, though these local shrines served their lesser purposes. If the so-called Deuteronomic reform innovated at all, it was in adopting the prophetic denunciation of the high places as a definite programme for their eradication. With the suppression of the fertility rites went also the cult of the dead. But the problems with which the latter dealt remained as a legacy for post-Exilic Judaism; they were ultimately resolved in the renovation of the faith achieved by the Hasidim and their successors, which is reflected in the doctrines of resurrection and eternal life common both to Judaism and Christianity.

4. Combining the materials furnished by these recent discoveries with the OT data, we find that the first essential of a Hebrew high place was the **altar.** This might consist merely of a heap of earth or unhewn stones, as commanded by Ex 20^{25}; or, as shown by surviving examples (see ALTAR, **2**), it might be hewn out of the solid rock and approached by steps. Against this more elaborate type the legislation of Ex 20^{25f} was intended as a protest. Equally indispensable to the proper equipment of a high place (cf Dt 12^{3}, Hos 10^{1} RV etc.) were the stone **pillars** or *maṣṣēbhôth*, the symbols of the deity (see PILLAR), and the wooden tree-stumps or **poles,** known as *'ᵃshērim* (see ASHERAH). To these must be added a **laver** or other apparatus for the ceremonial ablutions of the worshippers. If the sanctuary possessed an image of the deity, such as the golden bulls at Dan and Bethel, or other sacred object—an ark, an ephod or the like—a building of some sort was required to shelter and protect it. Such was Micah's 'house of gods' (Jg 17^{5}), and the 'houses of high places' of 1 K 12^{31} (RV; cf RSV). The Ark was housed at Shiloh in a **temple** (1 S 1^{9} 3^{3}), and a similar building is presupposed at Nob ($21^{6, 9}$). Every sanctuary of importance presumably had a **dining-hall** (9^{22}), where the worshippers joined in the sacrificial feast (cf 1^{4ff}).

5. At these local sanctuaries, and at these alone, the early Hebrews worshipped Y″ their God. The new sanctuary established by David at the threshing-floor of Araunah, where afterwards the Temple of Solomon was erected, was at first but another added to the list of Hebrew high places. At these, from Dan to Beersheba, **sacrifices** were offered by individuals, by the family (1 S 1^{3}), and by the clan (20^{6}); there men ate and drank 'before the LORD' at the joyful sacrificial meal. Thither were brought the **tithes** and other thankofferings for the good gifts of God; thither men resorted to consult the priestly **oracle,** to inquire of the 'Lord' in cases of difficulty; and there justice was administered in the name of Y″. At the local sanctuary, when a campaign was impending, the soldiers were consecrated for 'the wars of Y″' (see WAR). There, too, the manslayer and certain others enjoyed the right of **asylum.** But there was a darker side to the picture. The feasts were not seldom accompanied by excess (Am 2^{8}, Is 28^{7}; cf 1 S 1^{13}), prostitution even was practised with religious sanction (Dt 23^{18}, 1 K 14^{24}).

6. 'The history of the high places is the history of the old religion of Israel' (Moore). As the Hebrews gradually became masters of Canaan, the high places at which Baal and Astarte had been worshipped in local forms became, as we have seen, the legitimate sanctuaries of Y″, in harmony with the universal experience of history as to the permanence of sacred sites through all the changes of race and religion. At these the most zealous champions of the religion of Y″ were content to worship. It was inevitable, however, that in the circumstances heathen elements should mingle with the purer ritual of Y″ worship. It is this contamination and **corruption of the cultus** at the local sanctuaries that the 8th-cent. prophets attack with such vehemence, not the high places themselves. In Hosea's day the higher aspects of the religion of Y″ were so completely lost sight of by the mass of the people, that this prophet could describe the religion of his contemporaries as unadulterated heathenism, and their worship as idolatry.

While this was the state of matters in the Northern Kingdom, the unique position which the sanctuary at Jerusalem had acquired in the south, and the comparative purity of the cultus as there practised, gradually led, under the Divine guidance, to the great thought that, as *Y″ Himself was one, the place of His worship should also be one*, and this place Jerusalem. The Book of Deuteronomy is the deposit of this epoch-making teaching (see especially 12^{4ff}). Whatever may have been the extent of Hezekiah's efforts in this direction, it was not until the eighteenth year of the reign of Josiah (622–621 B.C.) that effective measures were taken, under the immediate impulse of Deuteronomy, for the destruction of the high places and the suppression of the worship which for so many centuries had been offered at the local shrines (2 K 23^{5ff}). But the break with the ideas and customs of the past was too violent. With the early death of Josiah the local cults revived, and it needed the discipline of the Exile to secure the victory of the Deuteronomic demand for the centralization of the cultus.

7. To men inspired by the ideals of Deuteronomy we owe the compilation of the Books of Kings. For them, accordingly, the worship at the local sanctuaries became illegal from the date of the erection of Solomon's Temple —'The people were sacrificing at the high places, however, because no house had yet been built for the name of the Lord' (1 K 3^{2}). From this standpoint the editors of Kings pass judgment on the successive sovereigns, by whom 'the high places were not taken away' (1 K 15^{14}). This adverse judgment is now seen to be unhistorical and undeserved.

A. R. S. K.—**D. N. F.**

HIGH PRIEST.—See PRIESTS AND LEVITES.

HIGHWAY.—See ROADS AND TRAVEL.

HILEN.—See HOLON, 1.

HILEZ.—See HOLON, 1.

HILKIAH ('Y″ is my portion').—A favourite priestly name. **1.** Father of Eliakim, Hezekiah's chief of the household, 2 K 18^{18} etc., Is 22^{20ff} 36^{3} etc. **2.** A priest of Anathoth, probably of the line of Eli (see 1 K 2^{26f}), father of Jeremiah (Jer 1^{1}); he is not to be identified with the next. **3.** The high priest in 621 B.C., who 'found' during the repairs of the Temple and brought to Josiah's notice, through Shaphan, 'the book of the law' (2 K 22^{3-11}, 2 Ch 34^{8-19}), which occasioned the reformation of religion thereafter effected (2 K 23^{1-24}, 2 Ch 34^{29}–35^{19}). Hilkiah headed the deputation sent to consult Huldah on this discovery (2 K 14^{-20}, 2 Ch 34^{22-28}); and presided over the subsequent purification of the Temple (2 K 23^{4ff}). He was a chief actor in the whole movement. There is no reason to doubt that his find was the genuine discovery of a lost law-book; this book was unmistakably the code of Deuteronomy (q.v.). According to 2 Ch 35^{8}, 1 Es 1^{8} (AV, RV **Helkias**) he subscribed handsomely to Josiah's Passover. He is mentioned in Ezr 7[1], 1 Es 8[1] (AV **Helchiah, RV Helkias)** as the great-grandfather of Ezra, and in Bar 1[7] (AV **Chelcias,** RV **Helkias)** as the father of Jehoiakim, who was high priest in the reign of Zedekiah. **4.** Father of the Gemariah of Jer 29[3]. **5, 6.** Levites of the clan of Merari, 1 Ch 6[45] 26[11]. **7.** A 'chief of the priests' returning with Zerubbabel, Neh 12[7, 21]. **8.** A companion of Ezra at the public reading of the Law, Neh 8[4]; called **Hezekiah** in 1 Es 9[43] (AV **Ezecias,** RV **Ezekias**). **9.** A distant ancestor of Baruch, Bar 1[1] (AV **Chelcias,** RV **Helkias**). **10.** The father of Susanna, Sus [2, 29] (AV **Chelcias,** RV **Helkias**). G. G. F.

HILL, HILL COUNTRY.—These terms in RV represent Hebrew *gibhʿāh*, *har*, and Greek names for either an isolated eminence, or a table-land, or a mountain-range, or a mountainous district. *Gibhʿāh* denotes properly 'the large rounded hills, mostly bare or nearly so, so conspicuous in parts of Palestine, especially in Judah.' Cf 'Gibeah of Saul,' 'of Phinehas,' 'of the foreskins,' 'of Moreh,' 'of Hachilah,' 'of Ammah,' 'of Gareb,' and 'of Elohim.' *har* is to *gibhʿāh* as the genus is to the species, and includes not merely a single mound, but also a large range or a district. It is usually applied to Zion. It is especially the description of the central mountainous tract of Palestine reaching from the plain of Jezreel on the N. to the Negeb or dry country in the S.; the Shephelah or lowlands of the SW.; the *midhbār* or moorland, and the *ʿarābhāh* or steppes of the SE. The best-known *har-* or hill-country in Palestine is the 'hill-country of Ephraim,' but besides this we hear of the 'hill-country of Judah' (*e.g.* in Jos 11[21]), the 'hill-country of Naphtali' (20[7]), the 'hill-country of Ammon' (Dt 2[37]), and of Gilead (3[12]). Among the eminences of Palestine as distinct from hill districts are Zion, the hill of Samaria, the triple-peaked Hermon, Tabor, and Carmel.
W. F. C.

HILLEL.—Father of Abdon, Jg 12[13, 15].

HIN.—See Weights and Measures.

HIND.—See Hart.

HINGE.—See House, 6.

HINNOM, VALLEY OF (called also 'valley of the son [Jer 7[32]] *or* children [2 K 23[10]] of Hinnom,' and 'the valley' [2 Ch 26[9], Neh 2[13, 15] 3[13] in referring to the 'Valley Gate,' and perhaps Jer 2[23]]).—It was close to the walls of Jerusalem 'at the entry of the Potsherd Gate' (Jer 19[2] RSV, translated 'east gate' AV, and 'gate Harsith' RV, Hebrew *shaʿar haḥarsôth*). The location of the Potsherd Gate is unknown; the Targum calls it 'Dung Gate.' Jeremiah's name for it may have come from the fact that it opened toward the Valley of Hinnom where the potters' workshops were doubtless surrounded with broken pieces of pottery (Jer 18[1]). Another name for it may have been the Valley Gate which opened into the Valley of Hinnom. This valley formed part of the boundary between Judah and Benjamin (Jos 15[8] 18[16]). The place acquired an evil reputation on account of the idolatrous practices carried on there (2 K 23[10], 2 Ch 28[3] 33[6]), and on this account Jeremiah (7[32] 19[6]) announced that it was to receive the name 'valley of Slaughter.' Here perpetual fires are said to have been kept burning to consume the rubbish of the city. Such associations with the Valley led afterwards to *Ge-hinnom* (NT *Gehenna*) becoming the type of hell.

The situation of the Valley of Hinnom has been much disputed. Of the three valleys of Jerusalem—the Kidron on the E., the Tyropoeon in the centre, and the *Wâdī er-Rabâbi* on the W.—each has in turn been identified with it. In favour of the Kidron is the fact that the theological *Gehinnom* or Arabic *Jahannum* of Jewish, Christian, and early Moslem writers is located here; but this was probably a transference of name after the old geographical site was lost, for there are strong reasons (see below) against it. As the Tyropoeon was incorporated within the city walls before the days of Manasseh, it is practically impossible that it could have been the scene of the sacrifice of children, which must have been outside the city bounds (2 K 23[10] etc.). The chief data are found in Jos 15[8] 18[16], where the boundary of Judah and Benjamin is described. If *Bîr Ayyûb* is En-rogel, as certainly is most probable, then the *Wâdī er-Rabâbi*, known traditionally as Hinnom, is correctly so designated. Then this Valley of Hinnom is a *gai* or gorge, but the Valley of Kidron is always described as a *naḥal* ('wady'). It is, of course, possible that the Valley of Hinnom may have included part of the open land formed by the junction of the three valleys below Siloam; and **Topheth** may have lain there, as is suggested by some authorities, but there is no necessity to extend the name beyond the limits of the actual gorge. The *Wâdī er-Rabâbi* commences as a shallow open valley due W. of the modern Jaffa Gate; near this gate it turns due S. for about half a mile, and then gradually curves to the E. It is this lower part, with its bare rocky scarps, that presents the characteristics of a *gai* or gorge. Near the junction of the valley with the Kidron is the traditional site of Akeldama (q.v.). For further details concerning the location of Hinnom, see J. Simons, *Jerusalem in the Old Testament* (1952), pp. 10 ff, 52.
E. W. G. M.—**W. L. R.**

HIPPOPOTAMUS.—See Behemoth.

HIRAH.—The Adullamite with whom Judah, according to the story of Gn 38[1], appears to have entered into a kind of partnership in the matter of flocks. After Tamar had successfully carried out her stratagem, it was by the hand of his 'friend' Hirah that Judah sent the promised kid to the supposed *ḳᵉdhēshāh*, Gn 38[20ff].

HIRAM.—1. King of Tyre, son and successor of Abibaal who reigned, according to the Tyrian annals cited by Menander of Ephesus, 969–936 B.C. When David was firmly established on his throne, Hiram sent messengers to him, and, in order to show his goodwill, gave David materials for building his palace, sending at the same time workmen to assist in the building (2 S 5[11], 1 Ch 14[1]). This first mention of Hiram is somewhat abrupt, and leads to the supposition that there must have been some earlier intercourse between him and David, the details of which have not come down to us. A real friendship, however, undoubtedly existed between the two (1 K 5[1]), and this was extended to Solomon after the death of David. A regular alliance was made when Solomon came to the throne, Hiram supplying men and materials for the building of the house of the Lord, while Solomon, in return, sent corn and oil to Hiram. Another sign of friendliness was their joint enterprise in sending ships to Ophir to procure gold (1 K 9[26-28] 10[11], 2 Ch 8[17f] 9[10, 21]). A curious episode is recounted in 1 K 9[10, 14], according to which Solomon gave Hiram 'twenty cities in the land of Galilee.' Hiram was dissatisfied with the gift, though he gave Solomon 'one hundred and twenty talents of gold.' In the parallel account (2 Ch 8[1f]) it is Hiram who gives cities (the number is not specified) to Solomon.

There is altogether considerable confusion in the Biblical references to Hiram, as a study of the passages in question shows. When these are compared with extra-Biblical information which we possess in the writings of early historians, discrepancies are emphasized. While, therefore, the friendly intercourse between Hiram and Solomon (as well as with David) is unquestionably historical, it is not always possible to say the same of the details.

2. The name of an artificer from Tyre 'full of wisdom, understanding, and skill, for making any work in bronze' (see 1 K 7[13-47]); he is also spoken of as 'trained to work in gold, silver, bronze, iron, stone, and wood, and in purple, blue, and crimson fabrics and fine linen . . .' (2 Ch 2[14]). There is a discrepancy regarding his parentage: in 1 K 7[14] he is said to have been the son of a widow of the tribe of Naphtali, and his father a man of Tyre; according to 2 Ch 2[14] his mother belonged to the tribe of Dan, though here, too, his father was a Tyrian.

The form of the name is usually *Hiram* in the Books

of Samuel and Kings, but the Chronicler mostly uses the form **Huram,** while we find also **Hirom** in the Hebrew (see RVm) in 1 K 5[10, 18] 7[40] (EV **Hiram**).

W. O. E. O.—**W. D. McH.**

HIRE, HIRELING.—The former is used in EV alongside of its synonym 'wages,' by which it has been supplanted in modern English as in Gn 31[8] (cf 30[18, 32f] with 29[15] 30[28] etc.). A **hireling** is a person 'hired' to work for a stipulated wage, such as field-labourer (Mal 3[5]), shepherd (Jn 10[12f]), or mercenary soldier (Is 16[14], cf Jer 46[21]). No imputation of unfaithfulness or dishonesty is necessarily conveyed by the term, although these ideas have now become associated with it owing to our Lord's application of the word to an unfaithful shepherd in Jn 10[12f]. A. R. S. K.

HIROM.—See Hiram.

HITTITES.—The Hittites appear in OT (1) as an important nation which gave its name to the whole Syrian region, 'from the wilderness and this Lebanon as far as the great river, the river Euphrates, all the land of the Hittites to the Great Sea [Mediterranean] toward the going down of the sun' (Jos 1[4]); (2) as one of the ethnic groups living in Canaan from patriarchal times until after the Israelite settlement (Gn 15[20], Dt 7[1], Jg 3[5]), sometimes called 'the children of Heth' after Heth, their eponymous ancestor, a son of Canaan (Gn 10[15]).

1. The Hittite Empire was established *c* 1800 B.C. by an Indo-European people that settled in Asia Minor in city-states *c* 2000 B.C. The name 'Hittite' was transferred to them from the *Ḫatti,* the earlier inhabitants of those regions, nowadays sometimes distinguished as the 'Proto-Hittites.' As the Hittite Empire increased, the term 'Hittites' was extended to the lands over which it extended and the peoples which it dominated. One of the earlier Hittite kings, Tudhaliyas I. (*c* 1720 B.C.) has been identified with Tidal king of Goiim (Gn 14[1]). About 1600 B.C. Hattusilis I. extended his empire southward into N. Syria. His successor Mursilis I. moved the imperial capital to Hattusas (modern *Boghaz-köy*), east of the Halys. (The archives unearthed here since 1906 have contributed greatly to our knowledge of Hittite history and culture.) Mursilis I. captured Aleppo and later made a raid on Babylon (*c* 1560 B.C.) which precipitated the fall of the First Babylonian Dynasty.

The great age of the Hittite Empire dawned under Suppiluliumas I. (*c* 1380–1350 B.C.). It was in his realm, in the Anatolian territory of Kizzuwatna, that iron was first smelted on a significant scale in the Near East. After consolidating his power in Asia Minor, Suppiluliumas established his supremacy over Mitanni in Upper Mesopotamia and over Syria so far south as the Lebanon. This brought the Hittites into collision with the Egyptian Empire in Asia, and desultory hostilities continued between the two powers until the indecisive battle of Kadesh on the Orontes (1286 B.C.), which was followed seventeen years later by a non-aggression pact between Hattusilis III. and Rameses II., recognizing the common frontier of their two empires on the Orontes.

Around 1200 B.C. the Hittite Empire fell before attacks by enemies from the west. The Hittite power in Asia Minor disappeared, the twenty-four city-states of the Tabali thenceforth becoming heirs to the Hittite home territory on the Anatolian side of the Taurus range. But seven city-states in Syria which had belonged to the Hittite Empire survived for several centuries, and their rulers were called 'the kings of the Hittites.' Outstanding among these states were Hamath on the Orontes and Carchemish on the Euphrates. Hamath entered into close relationship with David (2 S 8[9ff]), whose kingdom bordered on 'Kadesh in the land of the Hittites' (2 S 24[6], so RSV for the meaningless MT *Taḥtim-ḥodhshi*). Solomon traded and intermarried with these 'kings of the Hittites' (1 K 10[28f] 11[1]); their military power in the 9th cent. B.C. was sufficient to strike terror into a Damascene army (2 K 7[6]). But these seven states were reduced one by one by the Assyrians in the 8th cent.; Hamath fell in 720 B.C. and Carchemish three years later (cf 2 K 18[34] 19[13], Is 10[9] etc.). The whole of Syria is called 'the land of the *Ḫatti*' in Assyrian records of this period; Sargon II. in 711 B.C. even refers to the people of Ashdod as 'the faithless *Ḫatti.*' In the Chaldaean chronicles Nebuchadrezzar similarly speaks of Palestine as 'the land of the *Ḫatti.*'

2. The Hittites of Canaan in patriarchal times present an unsolved problem. They appear as inhabiting the central ridge of Judah, particularly the Hebron district. In Gn 23 they are the native population of Hebron ('the people of the land') among whom Abraham lives as 'a stranger and a sojourner.' Esau grieved his parents by marrying two 'daughters of Heth . . . daughters of the land'—apparently in the Beersheba district (Gn 26[34f] 27[46]). Jerusalem, according to Ezk 16[3, 45], had a mixed Hittite and Amorite foundation. The name of Araunah the Jebusite (2 S 24[16ff]) has been connected with Hittite *arawanis* ('freeman,' 'noble'), and Uriah the Hittite (evidently a man of Jerusalem) was one of David's mighty men (2 S 23[39]).

But the Hittite Empire never extended so faı south as Judah. Sir Leonard Woolley has suggested that these Hittites were survivors of a wave of *Khirbet Kerak* people who left the southern Caucasus in the latter part of the 4th millennium B.C. and settled east of the Gulf of Alexandretta; the original producers of the *Khirbet Kerak* pottery being the ancestors both of the Anatolian Hittites and of the Canaanite Hittites. Another view is that the Canaanite Hittites were really Hurrians. More probably they were early migrants from some part of the Hittite Empire. The record of Abraham's purchase of the cave of Machpelah at Hebron from Ephron the Hittite is said to be 'permeated with intricate subtleties of Hittite laws and customs, correctly corresponding to the time of Abraham' (M. R. Lehmann).

3. The Hittite laws were codified by King Telepinus (*c* 1480 B.C.). There are some striking resemblances between the Hittite laws and the OT law-codes, although these resemblances appear more in matters of detail and arrangement than in general outlook. Whereas the OT codes, like other ancient law-codes of Western Asia known to us, exhibit the *lex talionis* as a basic principle, the Hittite code is dominated rather by the characteristically Indo-European concept of compensation (*Wergeld*).

4. The Hittite texts of the imperial age before 1200 B.C. are written in cuneiform; the language was first identified as Indo-European by B. Hrozny in 1917. The language of the later Hittite states, showing dialect differences from the earlier imperial language, is known from hieroglyphic texts, which have been deciphered more recently, notably by I. J. Gelb. Their decipherment was already far advanced when it was greatly facilitated by the discovery at Karatepe in Cilicia (1946–1947) of bilingual inscriptions in hieroglyphic Hittite and Phoenician. F. F. B.

HIVITES.—One of the peoples of Canaan which the Hebrews displaced (Ex 3[8, 17] 23[23] 33[2] etc.). Their original *habitat* seems to have been the plain between the Līṭânī and Ḥaṣbânī rivers in the Lebanon (Jos 11[3], Jg 3[3], see Maisler, *Untersuchungen zur alten Geschichte und Ethnographie Syriens und Palästinas*, i, 1930, p. 75). Many have read with Wellhausen Hittites for Hivites in these passages, but this suggestion has found no general acceptance. The Hivites were, furthermore, located in the hill country N. of Jerusalem. The cities Gibeon, Chephirah, Beeroth, Kiriath-jearim, and Shechem are said to have been inhabited by Hivites (Jos 9[17], Gn 34[2]). Fearing to meet the Israelites in battle, they made a covenant with them by a ruse (Jos 9[3-15]), and were later subjected to semi-servitude by the Israelites (Jos 9[27]). Many have identified these Palestinian Hivites with the Hurrians, since the LXX suggests this identification by reading 'Choraios' in Gn 34[2] and Jos 9[7]. R. de Vaux agrees with this view, the more so, since they were uncircumcised (Gn 34[2, 14]), hence were no Semites (*RB*, lv [1948], 325). However, nothing certain is known either of their racial affinities or of the etymology of their name. S. H. Hn.

HIZKI.—A Benjamite, 1 Ch 8[17].

HIZKIAH.—A son of Neariah, a descendant of David, 1 Ch 3[23] (AV **Hezekiah**).

HOBAB.—In E (Ex 3[1] 4[18] 18[1ff]) the father-in-law of Moses is uniformly named **Jethro.** But Nu 10[29] (J) speaks of 'Hobab the son of **Reuel** the Midianite Moses' father-in-law' (*ḥōthēn*). It is uncertain how this should be punctuated, and whether Hobab or Reuel was Moses' father-in-law. The former view is found in Jg 4[11] (cf 1[16]), the latter in Ex 2[18]. The RV in Jg 1[16] 4[11] attempts to harmonize the two by rendering *ḥōthēn* 'brother-in-law.' But this harmonization is doubtful, for (1) though it is true that in Aramaic and Arabic the cognate word can be used rather loosely to describe a wife's relations, there is no evidence that it is ever so used in Hebrew; and it would be strange to find the father and the brother of the same man's wife described by the same term; (2) Ex 2[16] appears to imply that the priest of Midian had no sons. It is probable that the name Reuel was added in v.[18] by one who misunderstood Nu 10[29]. The suggestion that 'Hobab the son of' has accidentally dropped out before Reuel is very improbable. Thus Jethro (E) and Hobab (J) are the names of Moses' father-in-law, and Reuel is Hobab's father. A Mohammedan tradition identifies Sho'aib (perhaps a corruption of Hobab), a prophet sent to the Midianites, with Moses' father-in-law. On his nationality, and the events connected with him, see KENITES, MIDIAN, JETHRO.
A. H. McN.

HOBAH.—The place to which, according to Gn 15[15], Abraham pursued the defeated army of Chedorlaomer. It is described as 'on the left hand (*i.e.* 'to the north') of Damascus.' The site cannot be identified with security.

HOBAIAH.—See HABAIAH.

HOCK.—The hock (older spelling 'hough' in AV, RV) of a quadruped is the joint between the knee and the fetlock in the hind leg; in man the back of the knee joint, called the ham. To 'hock' is to cut the tendon of the hock, to hamstring. The substantive occurs in 2 Es 15[36] 'the camel's hock' (AVm 'pastern *or* litter'). The verb is found in AV and RV (always replaced by 'hamstring' in RSV) in Jos 11[8f], 2 S 8[4], 1 Ch 18[4] of hocking horses. Tyndale translates Gn 49[6] 'in their selfe-will they houghed an oxe,' which is retained in AVm; and inserted into the text of RV (cf RSV) in place of AV 'they digged down a wall.'

HOD ('majesty').—An Asherite, 1 Ch 7[37].

HODAVIAH ('Y″ is majesty').—**1.** A Manassite clan, 1 Ch 5[24]. **2.** The name of a Benjamite family, 1 Ch 9[7]. **3.** A Levite, Ezr 2[40]; called **Hodevah** in Neh 7[43]; see JODA, **1.** **4.** A descendant of David, 1 Ch 3[24].

HODESH ('new moon').—One of the wives of Shaharaim, a Benjamite, 1 Ch 8[9].

HODEVAH ('Y″ is majesty').—See HODAVIAH, **3,** and JODA, **1.**

HODIAH.—**1.** A man of Judah, 1 Ch 4[19]. AV wrongly takes it as a woman's name. **2.** A Levite in the time of Ezra, Neh 8[7] 9[5] (AV **Hodijah**); cf 1 Es 9[48], where AV, RV have **Auteas**), who sealed the covenant, Neh 10[10] (AV **Hodijah**). **3.** Another Levite who signed the covenant, Neh 10[13] (AV **Hodijah**). **4.** A leader of the people who signed the covenant, Neh 10[18] (AV **Hodijah**).

HODIJAH.—The AV spelling of **Hodiah** (q.v.) in Neh 8[7] 9[5] 10[10, 13, 18].

HOE.—See MATTOCK.

HOGLAH ('partridge').—Daughter of Zelophehad, Nu 26[33] 27[1] 36[11], Jos 17[3].

HOHAM, king of Hebron, formed an alliance with other four kings against Gibeon, but was defeated by Joshua at Beth-horon, and put to death along with his allies at Makkedah, Jos 10[3ff].

HOLD.—See CITADEL.

HOLINESS.—I. IN OT.—The Hebrew words connected with the Semitic root *ḳdsh* (those connected with the root *ḥrm* may be left out of the inquiry: cf article BAN), namely, *ḳōdhesh* 'holiness,' *ḳādhôsh* 'holy,' *ḳiddēsh*, etc., 'sanctify,' the derived noun *miḳdāsh* 'sanctuary,' *ḳādhēsh, ḳ*^e^*dhēshāh* 'whore,' 'harlot'—occur in about 830 passages in OT, about 350 of which are in the Pentateuch. The Aramaic *ḳaddîsh* 'holy' is met with thirteen times in the Book of Daniel. *ḳādhēsh* and *ḳ*^e^*dhēshāh* have almost exclusively heathen associations, *ḳaddîsh* is used in a few passages of the gods, but otherwise the Biblical words from this root refer exclusively to Yahweh, and persons or things connected with Him. The primary meaning is debated, some making it to be that of 'separation' or 'cutting off,' others connecting with *ḥādhāsh* 'new,' and the east Semitic *quddushu* 'pure,' 'bright.' The term *quddushu* has also been held to refer originally to 'that which pertains to the gods.' On this view, the notion of 'separation' would be supported also by the east Semitic root. In actual use 'holiness' in OT is always a religious term, being, when applied to deity, almost equivalent to 'divine,' and meaning, when used of persons or things, 'set apart from common use to the divine purpose.' The positive connotations of such 'set-apartness' are more important than the negative ones; in OT, it is the use of holy persons and things in the purpose of Yahweh upon which stress is laid.

1. Holiness of God.—'I am God and not man, the Holy One in your midst . . .' This passage from the prophet Hosea (11[9]) contains the best summary of the meaning of the holiness of God to be found in OT. On the one hand, it lays stress upon the 'otherness' of God: His majesty and incomparability with any created thing. On the other hand, it affirms the nearness of God to man: His involvement in the affairs of His people, His persistent love and graciousness which will not be put off by human rebellion and apostasy. Holiness is a term for power. In 'primitive' religions, such power may be manifested in a variety of ways: through natural objects, through the phenomena of storm, the movement of the heavenly bodies, the processes of fertility, etc. In more 'advanced' religions, a vast pantheon may be conceived to be the agents of holy power. These manifestations of power are without specific moral content, yet in course of time the conduct of man is inseparably related to his understanding of how he is to deal with the Holy, with that revelation of power in his midst the reality of which is indubitable. For Israel, Yahweh was the God who had taken possession of holiness—of all effective powers within the universe. He had done so, not to reserve such power to Himself, although His glory (Heb. *kābhōdh*) consists in His sovereign and holy power, but rather to bring life and blessing to mankind through His people Israel (Gn 12[1-3] etc.). Thus the notion of 'separation' inherent in the term 'holiness' means, in reference to Yahweh, His set-apartness over against all other beings—divine, human, or demonic—for the sake of being Himself and of accomplishing His determined purpose among men. He is the 'Holy One of Israel' (Is 1[4] 5[19, 24] etc.), 'Yahweh of Hosts,' who uses the host of heaven for His purposes (Jg 5[20]). His holiness is equivalent to His very selfhood: when Yahweh swears by His holiness he swears by Himself (Am 4[2] 6[8]). The distinctive mark of the holiness of God in OT is its close connexion with the righteous purposes of Yahweh. The God who appears to Moses and commands him to lead the slaves from Egypt is one who has 'seen their afflictions' and 'heard their cry' (Ex 3[7]); this awe-inspiring deity of the burning bush is, from the first, concerned with righteousness. The 'Holy God shows Himself holy in righteousness' (Is 5[16]). Both the majesty of Yahweh and His righteousness are depicted in the Temple vision of Isaiah (ch. 6). The chant of the seraphim tells that 'the fulness of the whole earth is His glory,' and the prophet's response to the vision shows how the glory and the righteousness of Yahweh cohere: 'Woe is me! For I am lost; for I am a man of unclean lips, and I dwell in the midst of a people of unclean lips. . . .'

2. Holiness of Israel.—The holiness of Yahweh is to find reflection in the holiness of His people: 'You shall be holy, for I Yahweh your God am holy' (Lv 19^{2}). Israel is created to be a 'kingdom of priests and a holy nation' (Ex 19^{6}). Israel's holiness consisted fundamentally in her having been set apart to the specific purposes of Yahweh in the world. She was to be His people and He would be her God (Hos 2^{23}, Ezk 37^{27}). Israel's entire life was to be regulated by Yahweh's saving purpose in her midst. The requirements of the covenant law, the cultic regulations and the whole body of social and ethical legislation of the Pentateuch were designed to enable Israel to be God's holy people, showing forth His glory to the ends of the earth. It is not surprising, therefore, that ethical and ceremonial elements are intermingled in the so-called *Law of Holiness* (H, contained chiefly in Lv 17–26), a collection which, though completed about the time of Ezekiel, contains very ancient materials. The holiness which Yahweh requires and which reflects His own holiness includes not only honesty (Lv $19^{11, 36}$), truthfulness (v.^{11}), respect for parents (v.^{3}, 20^{9}), fair dealing with servants (19^{13}), kindness to strangers (v.^{34}), the weak and helpless (vv.$^{14, 32}$), and the poor (v.^{9f}), social purity ($20^{11ff, 18ff}$), and love of neighbours (19^{18}), but also abstinence from blood as an article of food (17^{10ff} 19^{26}), from mixtures of animals, seeds, and stuffs (19^{19}), and from the fruit of newly planted trees for the first four years (v.^{23ff}); and, for priests, compliance with special rules about mourning and marriage (21^{1-15}). The concern for the holiness of Israel expressed in this portion of the priestly tradition is the maintenance of the set-apartness of Yahweh's people to His purpose in the world. The people of the covenant must be discernible as Yahweh's people. While it is true that priestly concerns might well have overstressed the external aspects of holiness, it would be wrong sharply to contrast the priestly emphasis upon externals with the prophetic emphasis upon ethical considerations. A faith which is to find expression in the total life of a people must perforce have its ceremonial and ritual aspects.

3. Holy things.—For the same reason, objects set apart to the purpose of Yahweh are also holy. The land of the Promise is holy (Zec 2^{12}), the Temple was holy (Ps 11^{4} etc.), and the city of the Temple (Is 52^{1}, Neh 11^{1}). Every part of the Temple (or Tabernacle) was holy, and all its utensils and appurtenances (1 K 8^{4}); the altars of incense and burnt-offering (Ex 30^{27f}), the flesh of a sacrifice (Hag 2^{12}), the incense (Ex 30^{36}), the table (Ex 30^{27}), the show-bread (1 S 21^{6}), the candlestick (Ex 30^{27}), the Ark (v.^{26}, 2 Ch 35^{3}), and the anointing oil (Ex 30^{25}). Occasional references indicate that such holiness was an abiding characteristic of these objects (2 S 6^{6f}), but the basic Israelite understanding of holiness is not reflected in such popular notions. The contagion of uncleanness is not matched by a similar contagion of holiness (Hag 2^{12-14}). Holy objects are holy solely in virtue of their having been designated to the specific purposes of Yahweh. He, the 'Holy One of Israel,' determines what is holy and what is common or unclean. See Ban, Uncleanness.

II. In NT.—The word 'holiness' in RSV stands for *hosiotēs* (Lk 1^{75}, Eph 4^{24}), *hagiotēs* (2 Co 1^{12}, He 12^{10}), *hagiōsynē* (Ro 1^{4}, 2 Co 7^{1}, 1 Th 3^{13}), *hagiasmos* (1 Th $4^{4, 7}$, 1 Ti 2^{15}, He 12^{14}, but in the other five passages in which the word occurs we find 'sanctification'). The idea of holiness, however, is conveyed mainly by the adjective *hagios*, 'holy' (about 230 times), and the verb *hagiazō* (twenty-seven times, in fifteen of which it is rendered in RSV 'sanctify'), also by *hosios* (Ac 2^{27} 13^{34f}, 1 Ti 2^{8}, Tit 1^{8}, He 7^{26}, Rev 15^{4} 16^{5}) and *hieros* (1 Co 9^{13} RSV 'those who are employed in the temple service'; 2 Ti 3^{15} RSV 'sacred'). Of these words by far the most important is the group which has *hagios* for its centre, and which is the real equivalent of *ḳōdhesh*, *ḳādhōsh*, etc., *hieros* referring rather to external holiness and *hosios* (in reference to man) to reverence, piety. In OT quotations or allusions, *ho hosios* is the equivalent of *ḳ^edhōsh Yiśrā'ēl* 'the Holy One of Israel' which NT authors take to refer to Christ (Ac 2^{27} 13^{35}) or to God (Rev 16^{5}). *Hagios*, freely used in LXX, is quite rare in classical Greek apart from certain cultic texts. The term is widely used in the mystery religions but is seldom found in common Greek (apart from Christian texts). In NT it refers only occasionally to ceremonial or cultic purity (cf 1 Co 7^{14}, 2 P 1^{18}) except in quotations from OT or references to Jewish ritual (He $9^{2f, 8, 24}$ 10^{19}) and in current Jewish expressions, *e.g.* 'the holy city,' Mt 4^{5} etc. Otherwise it designates the new quality of life conferred by God's work of redemption in Christ and to the ethical and religious demands which issue from God's redemption.

Three uses demand special notice. (1) The term 'holy' is seldom applied directly to God (Lk 1^{49}, Jn 17^{11}, 1 P 1^{15f}, Rev 4^{8} 6^{10}), but is very often used of the Spirit of God ('the Holy Spirit' ninety-one times, fifty-four of which are in the writings of Luke: cf article Holy Spirit). (2) The epithet is used in ten passages of Christ ('the Holy One of God,' Mk 1^{24}, Lk 4^{34}, Jn 6^{69}; also Lk 1^{35}, Ac 3^{14} $4^{27, 30}$, He 7^{26}, 1 Jn 2^{20}, Rev 3^{7}). (3) It is very often used of Christians. They are called 'saints' or 'holy ones' (*hagioi*) sixty times, thirty-nine in the Pauline Epistles. The expression is no doubt of OT origin, and means 'set apart to the service and praise of God,' made holy by the saving work of God in Christ Jesus and summoned to live in righteousness and purity of life (cf 1 Co 1^{2} 'sanctified in Christ Jesus, called to be saints'). In this use the ethical element is generally in the foreground. So we find *hagios* associated with *amōmos*, 'blameless' or 'without blemish,' RSV Eph 1^{4} 5^{27}, Col 1^{22}; and with *dikaios*, 'righteous,' Mk 6^{20} RSV Ac 3^{14}. The three words *hagiotēs*, *hagiosynē*, and *hagiasmos* designate respectively the quality of holiness, the state of holiness, and the process or result. For the sphere and source of holiness, see Sanctification.

W. T. S.—W. J. Ha.

HOLM TREE.—See Cypress, 2.

HOLOFERNES.—According to the Book of Judith, Holofernes was the general entrusted by Nebuchadnezzar, 'king of Nineveh,' with the task of wreaking vengeance on 'the whole region' of the West (2^{1}); in 2^{4} he is described as 'lord of the whole earth.' Before his vast army, nation after nation submitted and acknowledged Nebuchadnezzar as a god. The Jews alone would not yield; and Holofernes accordingly blockaded their city of Bethulia. For the subsequent story and the death of Holofernes at the hands of Judith, see article Judith.

Holofernes has been variously identified with Ashurbanipal, Cambyses, Orophernes of Cappadocia (a friend of Demetrius Soter, the enemy of the Jews), Nicanor (the Syrian general conquered by Judas Maccabaeus), Scaurus (Pompey's lieutenant in Syria), and Severus (Hadrian's general). But the date and theme of the book point toward an early 2nd-cent. identification.

W. M. N.—F. C. G.

HOLON.—**1.** A Levitical city of Judah in the Hebron hills, Jos 15^{51} 21^{15}. In the parallel passage, 1 Ch 6^{58}, it is called **Hilen** (so some Hebrew MSS; others **Hilez**). It is perhaps modern *Khirbet 'Alîn*. **2.** A city of Moab, near Heshbon, Jer 28^{41}. The site is unknown.

HOLY OF HOLIES, HOLY PLACE.—See Tabernacle and Temple.

HOLY ONE OF ISRAEL.—A title of God that occurs more than thirty times in the OT, though obviously the concept is far more frequent and in its origins reaches back into primitive thinking where it is quite devoid of the notion of exalted righteousness, which it conveys for us. The use of the title seems to have originated with the prophet Isaiah, with whom it became so characteristic that the unconvinced populace made sport of it and him. He quotes them as saying, if one may paraphrase, 'Let your " Holy One of Israel " hurry up those plans of his ; we want to see them ' (5^{19}), and ' Away with your " Holy One of Israel " ' (30^{11}). The title aptly expresses the religious faith and vision that were basic in his entire ministry. For him God is supremely transcendent in righteousness and might ; it is not too much to say that the whole subsequent course of Israel's faith bears the imprint of his faith. And true to our deepest insights, it was attained through profound stress and need. When a period of tranquil security was ending, he saw the Lord, thrice holy, enthroned on high (6^{1ff}) ; as his people's fortunes steadily went from bad to worse under the encroachments of the invincible Assyrians, the more clear and insistent became his emphasis on faith in God as the one solution of the crisis (10^{5-15} ; cf 28^{16} 30^{15} 31^{1}).

W. A. I.

HOLY SEPULCHRE.—See Jerusalem, 7.

HOLY SPIRIT.—The mysterious creative power of God, possessing and inspiring men, manifested especially in ecstatic conditions, prophesying, and special gifts and abilities such as strength, leadership, wisdom, judgment, and skill ; sometimes conceived as a quasi-physical force impelling its recipient somewhat in the manner of the wind setting in motion the dust of the ground, but coming to be recognized as the personal activity of God Himself ; in the NT the Spirit of God ' anointing ' Jesus as the Messianic Son of God at His Baptism and ' resting ' upon Him ; then, as the consequence of the completion of His saving work in His resurrection and ascension, bestowed by the exalted Christ upon His disciples, to be the witness to Christ through the Church's mission, the inner principle of the new life ' in Christ ' of the Christian community and its individual members, the mode or medium by which the risen Christ is present in the Church and in the Christian, and, in Johannine theology, the ' paraclete ' who brings Christ's deeds and words to His people's remembrance and guides them into full personal knowledge of Him ; hence recognized as a fully personal mode of the Divine operation in creation and re-creation.

A. The Old Testament.—(i) *General.*—(ii) The activity of the Spirit : (*a*) inspiring heroes and mighty men ; (*b*) manifested in artistic genius, insight, and wisdom ; (*c*) active in the wisdom and judgment of rulers and lawgivers ; (*d*) especially manifested in prophecy ; (*e*) the future hope of a general outpouring on Israel ; (*f*) as the mode of God's activity in history ; (*g*) as the creative Spirit ; (*h*) as the living energy of a personal God.

B. The Extra-Canonical Writings.

C. The New Testament.—(i) The Synoptic Evangelists : (*a*) The Spirit and the preparation for the Christ ; (*b*) The Spirit and the mission of Jesus. (ii) The Spirit in the Acts of the Apostles. (iii) The Spirit in the Pauline Epistles. (iv) The Spirit in the Johannine teaching. (v) The Spirit in other NT writings : (*a*) The Pastoral Epistles ; (*b*) The Epistle to the Hebrews ; (*c*) 1 Peter ; (*d*) Jude ; (*e*) Revelation. (vi) The Spirit and the Scriptures.

A. The Old Testament.—(i) *General.*—The word *rûaḥ* (usually represented in LXX by *pneuma*, but sometimes by *anemos* [fifty-two times], *thymos* [five times], *pnoē* [four times], *psychē* [twice], belongs to a root *rûaḥ* signifying ' blow,' ' breathe,' used only in the Hiph'il, *hēriaḥ*, denoting ' smell ' (Gn 8^{21}). The meanings of *rûaḥ* in OT are (1) ' wind ' or ' breeze,' as in the expression *beruaḥ hayyôm* (LXX *to deilinon*, Aq. *en tō anemō tēs hēmeras*, Symm. *dia pneumatos hēmeras*), and as in Nu 11^{31}, Job 4^{15} 41^{16}, Jer 2^{24} 14^{6} ; (2) ' breath ' of man, and hence (3) the vital principle, both in the phrase *rûaḥ ḥayyîm*, ' breath of life ' (Gn 6^{17} $7^{15,22}$) and absolutely (Gn 45^{27}, 1 K 10^{5}, Job 12^{10} 34^{14}, Ps 104^{29}, Ec 3^{19}, (4) human emotion (Gn 41^{8}, where Pharaoh's ' spirit ' is troubled as a result of his dream, Nu 5^{14}, ' spirit of jealousy ' ; 2 S 21^{5}, Pr 25^{28}), (5) intellectual activity (Dt 34^{9}, ' spirit of wisdom ' ; Job 32^{8}, where the ' spirit ' in man, which ' makes him understand,' is ' the breath of the Almighty ' ; Jer 51^{11}, where the allusion is to purposive thought or intention) ; (6) the whole of man's personality, that is, man considered as a spiritual being possessing a relationship to God (Nu 27^{16}, Ps 31^{5}, ' into thy hand I commit my spirit '). As applied to God, the word may retain its primary sense : his wrath may be described as the blast (*rûaḥ*) of his nostrils ' (Ex 15^{8}), cf Job 4^{9}, Ps 18^{15}, and his creative power is the ' breath of his mouth ' (Ps 33^{6}). It may, on the other hand, denote the dynamic activity which is peculiarly characteristic of God, and so indicate the Divine nature itself, as when Isaiah sets in parallel contrast ' men ' over against ' God ' and ' flesh ' over against ' spirit ' (Is 31^{3}).

The term ' Spirit of God (the Lord) ' occurs very frequently in OT. There are a few cases where this, or a similar phrase, denotes the wind sent by God (Ex 15^{10}, Is 40^{7} 59^{19}, Hos 13^{15}), or the breath of man as infused into him by the Divine inbreathing (Job 27^{3}, ' as long as . . . the spirit of God is in my nostrils ' ; cf Gn 2^{7}). Usually, however, it signifies the Divine energy in its relation to creation and especially to man. This is manifested in supernatural endowments of many kinds, ranging from physical strength to the most profound ethical and spiritual understanding.

(ii) The Spirit as *a mysterious power* taking possession of man and manifesting its activity in special endowments and qualities : (*a*) Inspiring Israel's heroes and energizing them for the performance of feats of strength and the exercise of leadership in war. Thus the career of Samson begins when ' the Spirit of the Lord began to stir in him ' (Jg 13^{25}), and it is when ' the Spirit of the Lord came mightily upon him ' that he tore a lion asunder (Jg 14^{6}), slew thirty Philistines (14^{19}), and freed himself from bonds (15^{14}). Under the same inspiration or ' invasion ' of the mysterious power of the Spirit of the Lord Othniel took the leadership in Israel and won victory for the people (Jg 3^{10}) ; Gideon was possessed by the Spirit (literally ' the Spirit of the Lord clothed itself with Gideon,' so that the hero is made to be an embodiment of the Spirit) and was thus enabled to summon Israel to repel the Midianites (Jg 6^{34}). Jephthah and Saul are also represented as Spirit-possessed leaders who rouse the nation to drive back its enemies (Jg 11^{29} 1 S 11^{6}). So, too, the Spirit is associated with the gift of heroism in battle as well as with the ruler's gift of judgment (Is 28^{6}).

(*b*) The Spirit's operation is manifested in *artistic genius*, as in the case of Bezalel, who was ' filled with the Spirit of God, with ability and intelligence, with knowlege and all craftsmanship, to devise artistic designs ' (Ex 31^{3} 35^{31}), and in the possession by certain individuals of peculiar powers of *understanding and insight*, such as Joseph and Daniel displayed in the interpretation of dreams and other Divine revelations (Gn 41^{38}, Dn 5^{14}), and in the exercise of sagacity and discernment (Sus 45). Sir 39^{6} sums up the character of the pious and learned devotee of the Law as one who, if the Lord wills, will be filled with the Spirit of understanding. In the later Wisdom writings the idea that the wise man is one into whom the Spirit (RSV ' thoughts ') of Wisdom has been infused (Pr 1^{23}) is extended to the point where the Wisdom and the Spirit of God are virtually identified as modes of God's operation among men and in creation as a whole (Wis 1^{5} $7^{7,22}$ 9^{17}).

(*c*) The working of the Spirit is especially associated with the wisdom and judgment of *the ruler and lawgiver*. The inspiration of Moses is imparted to the seventy elders (Nu 11^{25}), and is here regarded as a combination of the spirit of the ruler with that of the prophet. Joshua receives the Spirit of Wisdom as the successor to Moses in the leadership of the people. It is imparted to him by the imposition of the hands of his predecessor, a sign of personal identification through which he becomes as it were a second Moses (Dt 34^{9}). Nu 27^{18} also describes Joshua as ' a man in whom is the Spirit,' and therefore as one fitted for command, but in this passage his possession of the Spirit appears to precede, and be independent of, his commissioning as the successor of Moses by the laying-on of his hand. The coming of the Spirit upon the ruler is directly associated in the case of David with his anointing by Samuel: 'Then Samuel took the horn of oil, and anointed him in the midst of his brothers; and the Spirit of the Lord came mightily upon David from that day forward' (1 S 16^{13}). The coming of the Spirit upon David coincides with the departure of the Spirit of the Lord from Saul, whom God, through the prophet, has rejected from the kingship (1 S 16^{14}, cf 1). The spirit of judgment, exercised by the wise ruler, is promised as a personal gift of God (Is 28^{6}), and all the endowments necessary for right government are portrayed in Isaiah's picture of the ideal king as operations of the Divine Spirit: 'There shall come forth a shoot from the stump of Jesse . . . and the Spirit of the LORD shall rest upon him, the spirit of wisdom and understanding, the spirit of counsel and might, the spirit of knowledge and the fear of the LORD' (Is 11^{2}).

This expectation of a ruler of Israel who shall be fully endowed with the Divine Spirit reappears in the inter-testamental literature in the messianic hope of the Psalms of Solomon which look for one anointed of the Lord who shall be strong in Holy Spirit (17^{42}) and so be endowed with wisdom and understanding, strength, and righteousness.

(*d*) The inspiration of the Spirit is supremely manifested in *prophecy*. The prophet is pre-eminently 'the man of the Spirit' (Hos 9^{7}), whether he is a primitive diviner such as Balaam, upon whom the Spirit of God came as he gazed upon the camp of Israel (Nu 24^{2}), one like Saul who was seized with infectious ecstasy as he encountered a band of wandering prophets with their music (1 S 10$^{6, 10}$), or an inspired man who is enabled by the Spirit to enter into communion with God and to understand and interpret His will and purpose, such as Micah who can say of himself, in contrast with the false prophets: 'But as for me, I am filled with power, with the Spirit of the Lord, and with justice and might, to declare to Jacob his transgression and to Israel his sin' (Mic 3^{8}). The prophetic Spirit may sometimes be thought of in terms of a quasi-physical force, driving or carrying the prophet from place to place (1 K 18^{12}, 2 K 2^{16}, Ezk 3^{14} 8^{3} 11^{1} 43^{5}); but it is also the inner working of God in the prophet's own being, enabling him to discern the mind and will of God. 'The Spirit of the Lord speaks by me,' says David in his last oracles, 'his word is upon my tongue. The God of Israel has spoken, the Rock of Israel has said to me' (2 S 23^{2f}). It is the Spirit of the Lord which speaks to the prophet when he utters his oracles (1 K 22^{24}), and when Elisha succeeds Elijah as the great prophet in Israel the Spirit which inspired Elijah is transferred to the new leader (2 K 2^{15}). When the Spirit enters into the prophet he is enabled to hear the voice of God (Ezk 2^{2} 11^{5}). In later times, when prophecy had ceased in Israel, it was to Elijah and Elisha that men looked back as the great examples of Spirit-inspired men (Sir 48$^{12, 24}$).

A particularly important instance of the operation of the Spirit, in which the prophetic aspect predominates but may be combined with the spirit of the ruler or leader, as in the case of Moses, is to be found in the description of the Servant of the Lord in the poems of the Second Isaiah. It is said of the Servant, 'I have put my spirit upon him, he will bring forth justice to the nations' (Is 42^{1}), and, at least in the NT interpretation of these prophecies, if not in pre-Christian exegesis, there was associated with the Servant poems the picture of the Spirit-possessed prophet of Is 61^{1}, of whom it is said: 'The Spirit of the Lord GOD is upon me, because the LORD has anointed me to bring good tidings to the afflicted.'

(*e*) Although the Spirit is manifested only in certain exceptional individuals, there is a hope expressed in the OT that *all Israel*, as the people of God, will be inspired by his Spirit. 'Would that all the Lord's people were prophets,' exclaims Moses, 'that the Lord would put his spirit upon them' (Nu 11^{29}), and the same expectation of a general outpouring of the Spirit of prophecy is expressed at length in Joel (2^{28f}). In a wider sense, the Spirit is associated with a renewal of Israel as the covenant people, and this expectation becomes an important element in the OT hope of the age of fulfilment. It is a part of the universal recreative work of God (Is 32^{15}), but it is especially connected with the cleansing and repentance of Israel which will enable her to be reconstituted as the true people of God: 'A new heart I will give you, and a new spirit I will put within you . . . and I will put my spirit within you, and cause you to walk in my statutes and be careful to observe my ordinances' (Ezk 36^{26f}). The vision of the dry bones points to the same promise of the re-creation of God's people through the inspiration of the Spirit: 'And I will put my Spirit within you and you shall live, and I will place you in your own land' (Ezk 37^{14}). The time of the outpouring of God's Spirit on Israel will come when the nation is gathered together once more out of the peoples among whom they have been dispersed (Ezk 39^{29}), and it is associated with their naming as the peculiar possession of God (Is 44^{3}). The presence of God's Spirit among His people is to be the sign and pledge of the fulfilment of the covenant promise (Is 59^{21}), and this is no less than the mode of the personal dwelling of God Himself in their midst (Hag 2^{5}). It must not be forgotten that if the Servant is intended to represent the faithful of Israel, his possession of the Spirit is another reminder of the strength of this hope of a general outpouring of the Spirit upon the covenant people and the frequency with which it is encountered in the Hebrew prophets. This promise of the presence of the Spirit in Israel is linked with God's judgment and forgiveness (Is 4^{4}) and the people's repentance (Zec 12^{10}).

(*f*) The Spirit is the mode of *God's activity in history*, especially in respect of His guidance of the destinies of his people. When Judah seeks an alliance with Egypt against the revealed will of God she acts against His Spirit (Is 30^{1}); it is by the Spirit that God intervenes in the events which follow the Return (Zec 4^{6} 6^{8}).

(*g*) From its manifestation in history the activity of the Spirit is traced back to *the beginning of creation*. The Spirit of God broods (RSV 'was moving') over the primeval deep (Gn 1^{2}). The LXX rendering, *epephereto*, suggests the movement of the wind over the face of the waters, but the Hebrew verb denotes rather the vitalizing energy of the divine Spirit, giving life to the creation that is about to be called into being by God's word. The same combination of the 'word' and the 'breath' or spirit of God in creation is found in Ps 33^{6}, and through the agency of the Divine Spirit the world of living creatures is maintained in being for so long as God wills (Job 33^{4}, cf Ps 104^{30}). The association, or virtual identification, of the Spirit with Wisdom (Wis 9^{17} etc.) serves to emphasize the creative aspect of the Spirit's operation.

(*h*) It will be clear from what has been said that in the developed thought of the OT the Spirit is *the living energy of a personal God*. It is not an independent hypostasis; it is God in one aspect of His activity towards His creation. As such, the Spirit is spoken of in personal terms, and in a number of passages is practically a synonym for 'God.' Thus the 'good Spirit' of God can be said to 'instruct' Israel (Neh 9^{20}); the phrase 'his Spirit' is parallel to 'the Lord God' in Is 48^{16}; the Spirit is identical with the Divine presence (Hag 2^{5}); and in this sense the Spirit can be said to have been 'grieved' by Israel's rebellion against God's protective care (Is 63$^{10-12}$). This last passage marks the climax of OT thought about the personal presence of the Spirit in the community of God's people, and it is one of the rare occasions on which the Spirit is described as 'his holy Spirit,' that is, the Spirit of the holy God. A similar realization that the Spirit's work is the work of God Himself is seen in Ps 51^{11}, where the thought is of God's presence in the life of the individual:

Cast me not away from thy presence, and take not thy holy Spirit from me.' With this we may compare Ps 139[7]: 'Whither shall I go from thy Spirit? Or whither shall I flee from thy presence?'

(B) Extra-Canonical Literature.—The literature of the inter-Testamental period adds comparatively little to the OT thought concerning the Spirit of God. The expectation of a Spirit-possessed messianic leader, as it appears in the Psalms of Solomon, has been mentioned already (A. (ii) (*c*) above). The language of Is 11[2] is echoed in the description of the resting of the Spirit upon the Elect One, the Son of Man, in Enoch (49[3]); the Spirit of righteousness is poured out upon him (1 En 62[2]). If the *Testaments of the XII Patriarchs* may be reckoned among the pre-Christian literature, they provide further evidence for the hope of a Spirit-possessed Messiah (Test. Jud. 24[2], Test. Lev. 18[7]) through whom the Spirit will be given to the people of God (Test. Lev. 18[11]). A cleansing by the Holy Spirit from all wickedness is part of the expectation of the Qumrân community (*Manual of Discipline* iv; cf also Jubilees 1[21-25]). In the Qumran scrolls, however, the concept of the Spirit is somewhat obscured by the prominent doctrine of the two created spirits, of light and darkness, which wage an incessant conflict in man. This teaching is in line with the general tendency of the later Jewish literature to devote much attention to the idea of a hierarchy of created spirits, angels, and demons. This, together with the decline of prophecy, may be the reason for the relative lack of interest during the inter-Testamental period in the Spirit as the personal activity of God. It should be noted that the Jewish avoidance of dualism, which involves the ascription of the creation of the evil spirit to God Himself, is anticipated in the OT with its references to evil spirits sent by or from God (Jg 9[23], 1 S 16[14] 18[10], 1 K 22[21ff]) or to 'an evil spirit of God (Is 19[9], cf LXX).

On the whole, during this period, the Spirit continues to be regarded as pre-eminently the Spirit of prophecy which inspired the great prophets of old (Sir 48[12, 24]; 1 En 91[1], cf Jos. *c. Ap.* i. 8), and hence as the inspirer of Scripture (cf 2 Es 14[22]). In the thought of Philo this conception of prophetic inspiration approximates closely to the Hellenistic idea of 'enthusiasm,' the prophets, and even the LXX translators, being possessed by the Divine Spirit in a manner which involves the suspension of the normal rational faculty (*De spec. legg.* 8; cf *Quis rer. div. her.* 53; *Vit. Mos.* ii. 7).

The chief exception to the general lack of progress in inter-Testamental thought about the Spirit is the teaching of the Wisdom of Solomon. Its identification of Wisdom with the Spirit has already been mentioned (A. (ii) (*b*) above). It also presents the Spirit as the Divine power sustaining, conserving, and pervading the universe (Wis 1[7] 12[1]), as the source of man's intellectual and spiritual endowments and of the knowledge of God (7[7] 9[17] 15[11]), and as the indwelling power of Wisdom (7[22f]). A similar interpretation of the Spirit's operation is found in Philo, who asserts that the Spirit of God is the Wisdom in which every wise man participates (*Gig.* 5).

C. The New Testament.—(i) *The Synoptic Evangelists.* (*a*) The Spirit and *the preparation for the Christ.* All the Synoptic Gospels concur in regarding John the Baptist as a prophet, like, but indeed greater than, the prophets of old; he is presented in Mark as Elijah *redivivus* (1[6] 9[13], cf Lk 1[17]); he is believed by the people to be a real prophet (Mk 11[32] and par.); and is said by Jesus to be greater than other prophets, being the messianic fore-runner (Mt 11[9], Lk 7[26], Mt 11[13], Lk 16[16]). Luke is especially concerned to show that the prophetic Spirit, long dormant in Israel, revived in a new outburst of prophesying as the age of fulfilment dawned. Thus John is described as an inspired prophet from his birth (Lk 1[15]; cf Jer 1[1]), whose 'call' is reminiscent of that of some of the OT prophets (Lk 3[2]; cf Hag 1[1], Zec 1[1]). His parents also were empowered by the Spirit to declare Divine messages (Lk 1[41, 67]). His baptism of repentance is intended to prepare a purified remnant of Israel for the coming of the 'stronger one' who is to execute judgment and to 'baptize' with Holy Spirit in accordance with the ancient expectation of the last times (Mk 1[8], Mt 3[11], Lk 3[16]; cf Ac 1[5], Jn 1[33]). Meanwhile, the birth of Jesus has taken place, in a setting, according to Luke, of the renewed outburst of the Spirit of prophecy (Lk 1[41] 2[25-27]; cf v.[36]), and as a result of a new creative act of the Spirit (Lk 1[35], Mt 1[18, 20]).

(*b*) The Spirit and *the mission of Jesus.* While the crowds were baptized by John as a penitent remnant awaiting the age of fulfilment, Jesus, when He joined the multitudes and received John's baptism, experienced the promised descent of the Spirit, and the association of water with the Spirit which had been made in the metaphorical language of the prophets (*e.g.* Ezk 36[25-27]) was translated into reality. The descent of the Spirit is likened to that of a dove (Mk 1[10], Mt 3[16], Lk 3[22]), the symbolism being perhaps intended to recall the brooding of the Spirit over the waters at Creation, and to indicate a new act of the creative Spirit in relation to man, but more probably to allude to the dove of Noah which was the harbinger of the first covenant between God and man. The theory that there may be an allusion to the interpretation of Gn 15[9], by which wisdom is symbolized as a dove (Philo, *Quis rer. div. her.* 126), is very improbable. In Philo's exegesis the *peristera* (the word used by the evangelists) signifies human, as opposed to divine, wisdom, and could not be identified with the Spirit. In any case, the symbolism denotes the completeness and perfection of the illapse of the Spirit on Jesus which is unparallelled in the case of any of the prophets of old. The descent of the Spirit is accompanied by the Divine assurance to Jesus of His messianic sonship, combined with an interpretation of that sonship in terms of the vocation of the Servant of the Lord (Mk 1[11], Mt 3[17], Lk 3[22], 'Alexandrian' text, the 'Western' reading signifying messianic sonship only; cf Ps 2[7], Is 42[1] 44[1]). In this consecration by the Spirit for His vocation as Servant-Messiah, Jesus received His anointing as the Christ: 'God anointed Jesus of Nazareth with the Holy Spirit and with power (Ac 10[38]; cf 4[27]).

The Spirit-possession of Jesus was a permanent condition, an aspect of His messianic sonship. The Spirit is manifested in His mighty works, His teaching, and His entire ministry. It is under the compulsion of the Spirit that Jesus goes from His baptism by John to wrestle with the temptations which were inseparable from His vocation as Servant-Messiah (Mk 1[12], Mt 4[1], Lk 4[1]). The direct opposition to the Divine power manifested in His mighty works which would ascribe them to the operation of the devil is blasphemy against the Holy Spirit, and is the ultimate sin (Mk 3[29], Mt 12[31f]). The fact that Jesus casts out demons by the Spirit of God is evidence enough that the Kingdom of God is already operative by anticipation in His ministry (Mt 12[28]). This ministry is recognized as the fulfilment of the vocation of the Servant, of whom God had said 'I will put my Spirit upon him' (Mt 12[18], citing Is 42[1-4]). The Synoptic Gospels record the promise of Jesus that His followers who acknowledge Him under persecution will be directly inspired by the Spirit to make their public confession of faith (Mk 13[11], Mt 10[20], Lk 12[12]), and Matthew ascribes to the risen Christ the command to baptize in the name of the Father and of the Son and of the Holy Spirit (Mt 28[19]), a passage which no doubt reads back later baptismal practice into the time of the resurrection appearances, but which, as a probably authentic part of Matthew, is evidence for a fully developed doctrine of the Spirit's divinity by the time that Matthew was written.

References to the Spirit in the Synoptic Gospels are relatively scanty. It is the common teaching of the NT as a whole that the age of the Spirit's operation properly begins when the saving work of Christ has been completed in His death, resurrection, and ascension, and that during His earthly ministry the Spirit was upon Him uniquely, yet manifested only to the eye of faith.

What is implied in the other evangelists is clarified in Luke, whose two-volume work is constructed to show how the Spirit, by whose operation Jesus was conceived, descended upon Him at His baptism, was the source and focus of His authority and power during His ministry in such a way that He fulfilled the expectation of the coming of a 'prophet like Moses' (Ac 3^{22} 7^{37}; cf Lk 24^{19}, Dt 18^{15-18}), and as a consequence of His exaltation through death was bestowed by Him upon His followers to operate in the community of the Church and reproduce in it the works of Jesus Himself. Thus Luke sets the birth of Jesus in the context of a revival of the prophetic Spirit (C. (i) (*a*) above); emphasizes the creative act of the Spirit in His conception, making Jesus more than the most completely inspired prophet; lays stress on the power of the Spirit as the motive of the departure of Jesus to face temptations in the desert (Lk 4^{1}) and of His return to begin the Galilaean ministry (4^{14}); and introduces, as a prelude to the story of Luke-Acts, the announcement by Jesus at Nazareth that His mission is the fulfilment of the prophecy of the Spirit-anointed prophet who was to come to proclaim good tidings to the oppressed (4^{18}, Is 61^{1}). It is in the Holy Spirit that Jesus rejoices after the return of the Seventy (10^{21}), and in the central section of Luke the teaching of Jesus is related to the post-Pentecostal Church's experience of the same Spirit which Jesus Himself possessed. Thus the gift of the Spirit is the supreme object of the Christian disciples' prayer (11^{13}; cf the variant reading, 'May thy Holy Spirit come upon us and cleanse us' in the Lord's Prayer, 11^{2}, which may conceivably be authentic) and the saying about blasphemy against the Spirit is set in juxta-position to the promise that the Spirit will inspire the faithful confessor, indicating that for Luke the sin against the Spirit is apostasy with the rejection of the promised inspiration (12^{10-12}). Finally, it is through the Holy Spirit that the risen Christ gives instruction to His disciples (Ac 1^{2}).

(ii) *The Spirit in the Acts of the Apostles.*—The risen Christ promised that through His exaltation the hope of a general outpouring of the Spirit would be fulfilled and that His followers would be 'clothed with power from on high' (Lk 24^{49}), 'baptized with the Holy Spirit' in accordance with the Baptist's prophecy (Ac 1^{5}; cf Lk 3^{16}), so as to receive power, 'when the Holy Spirit has come upon you' for the mission of witness to the end of the earth (Ac 1^{8}). This was fulfilled in the 'invasion' of the Spirit at Pentecost, when the original leaders of the Church's mission were empowered for their task by the gift of the Spirit of proclamation or 'tongues.' The symbolism of the Pentecostal sights and sounds is related to the fact that Pentecost was the commemoration or the giving of the Law; the general outpouring of the Spirit is the inauguration of the new covenant, an antitype of Sinai. The language of Luke may also indicate that he sees in this event a reversal of the confusion of speech at Babel (Gn 11^{1-9}). It is not possible to answer the question of what actually happened at Pentecost. The narrative is an attempt to give symbolical expression to the inexpressible, but it is clear that the disciples were seized with an overwhelming spiritual power, inspiring them to proclaim the gospel of the decisive event of Christ and to convey it to the crowd in Jerusalem, drawn from all the nations of the earth and foreshadowing or typifying the future hearers of the world-wide proclamation by the apostolic missionaries. The details of the symbolic narrative should not be pressed to the point of asking why the crowd was apparently unable to understand except in their individual languages, or what relation this apparent miracle bears to the phenomenon of 'speaking with tongues' mentioned elsewhere in Acts (10^{46} 19^{6}) and in 1 Co 12–14. It is probable, however, in view of the parallel drawn between the event of Pentecost and that of Ac 10^{46} (10^{47} 11^{15-17}), that Luke's symbolical picture is based on an occurrence, in overwhelming force and with infectious enthusiasm, of the ecstatic utterance which we encounter later in the history of the primitive Church. This tremendous experience of the Spirit was the fulfilment of the prophecy of Jl 2^{28-32}, and was the final proof of the exaltation of Jesus as Messiah: 'Being therefore exalted at the right hand of God, and having received from the Father the promise of the Holy Spirit, he has poured out this which you see and hear' (Ac 2^{33}).

Spirit-possession is now the distinctive mark of all the people of God. Through baptism 'in the name of Jesus Messiah' (Ac 2^{38}) the promise of the Spirit is fulfilled for every convert. At this point the account of the operation of the Spirit given in Acts becomes somewhat obscure. The reason for this is that Luke, being concerned with the story of the Church's progress rather than with doctrinal exposition, does not clearly differentiate between two aspects of the work of the Spirit which he treats together in his narrative. On the one hand, the Spirit is the inner principle of the life of the Christian community; it is manifested in the whole character of the society, its unity and brotherhood, expressed in the sharing of possessions (Ac 2^{42-47} 4^{32-37}), in its administration and charitable organization (6^{3}), and particularly in the joy (cf 13^{52}) which is associated with the activity of the Spirit in the NT as a whole and especially in the Lucan writings. A deliberate offence against the brotherhood is thus a sin against the Spirit (Ac $5^{3, 9}$). On the other hand, the Spirit is more often thought of in Acts as being pre-eminently the guide and inspirer of the mission to the world, the Spirit of the Christian *paraclēsis* or proclamation of the good news of the gospel (9^{31}; cf. 4^{36}), manifested chiefly in the missionary endowments of 'tongues,' prophesying, and the signs and wonders which accompanied the spread of the Church's witness. It thus inspires the preaching of Peter (4^{8}), giving to him and to John 'boldness' of speech before the Sanhedrin (cf 4^{13}), and boldness to the community as a whole to witness to Christ under persecution (4^{31}). The Spirit in the apostles testifies to the truth of the gospel (5^{32}), and it is manifested most strikingly in the preaching of Stephen (6^{10}) and in his martyrdom (7^{55}), when the promise is fulfilled that the faithful confessor would be directly inspired (Lk 12^{11f}). The Spirit guides the movements of the missionaries ($8^{29, 39}$ 16^{6f}), enables the leaders of the work to direct and control it (11^{22-24} 15^{28}), and inspires the appointment of missionaries to their tasks ($13^{2, 4}$) and the ordination of ministers for the congregations as they are established (20^{28}). Just as the Spirit directs and empowers the work of Peter and others in Jerusalem and its neighbourhood, so it is the guide and motive force in the Gentile mission of Paul, enabling him to confront Elymas (13^{9}), to plan the final journey to Jerusalem (19^{21}; cf the guidance of Paul and Silas to Troas in 16^{6f}), to prepare for suffering in Jerusalem (20^{22f}), and warning him of the difficulties ahead ($21^{4, 11}$).

At the important turning-point in the mission represented by the extension of the preaching to Samaria, visible manifestations of the Pentecostal Spirit, withheld (though apparently expected) when the Samaritan converts were baptized, were bestowed through the imposition of the hands of the leaders of the Jerusalem apostles, Peter and John, probably conferred as a sign of fellowship and solidarity transcending the ancient schism between Jew and Samaritan. The visible signs which so impressed Simon Magus were probably the phenomena of tongues and prophesying (8^{14-19}). Such signs are explicitly mentioned at the even greater crisis of the extension of the mission to Gentiles, when a repetition of Pentecost gives convincing proof that the household of Cornelius must be baptized into the Christian society (10^{44-48} 11^{15-17}). The whole of this most important episode took place, of course, under the Spirit's direction (10^{19} 11^{12}). A similar manifestation of the Spirit in tongues and prophesying occurs when Paul baptizes at Ephesus the disciples who had known only the baptism of John, and lays his hands upon them (19^{1-7}). This, again, may represent a renewal of the Pentecostal gift for the mission at an important moment in its development, the foundation of the Ephesian Church, the chief centre of the Pauline Gentile mission. In concentrating attention on these aspects of the Spirit's work, it is most unlikely that Luke intends either to ignore the function of the Spirit as the regular principle of the Christian life of the individual and the society, or to suggest that the peculiar phenomena associated with Pentecost, the conversions at Samaria, or the incorporation into the Church of the Ephesian disciples were ordinarily reproduced in the normal life and work of the community. It should be mentioned that although little is said in Acts about the nature, as opposed to the operation, of the Spirit, it is asserted both that the Spirit is received through the exalted Jesus (2^{33}) and that it is the Spirit which had been uniquely his own, 'the Spirit of Jesus' (16^{7}).

(iii) *The Spirit in the Pauline Epistles.*—Here the doctrine of the Spirit, while not different from that in the Gospels and Acts, is far more fully developed in a manner corresponding to the fact that Paul is not concerned with the pre-Resurrection situation but is writing to Christians for whom the manifest presence and operation of the Spirit are the central element in their corporate and individual life. The Spirit is now recognized as being both the Spirit of the Father, 'the Spirit of him who raised Jesus from the dead' (Ro 8^{11}), and the Spirit of Christ (Ro 8^{9}) or 'the Spirit of his Son' (Gal 4^{6}). The grace of Christ, the love of God, and the participation in (or fellowship of) the Holy Spirit can therefore be set in parallel as modes of the Christian experience (2 Co 13^{14}, a text which, with Mt 28^{19}, was rightly seen by the early Church to imply full Trinitarian belief). It would be untrue to suggest that Paul identifies the Spirit with the risen and ascended Christ. 'The Lord is the Spirit' (2 Co 3^{17}) bears no such meaning; Paul is here developing an allegorical exegesis of Ex 34^{34}, and is saying that just as when Moses went in before the Lord he took the veil off, so when Israel turns to the Lord the veil which lies upon their understanding of the scriptures will be removed; and for them the phrase, 'the Lord,' means 'the Spirit' which is given through Christ, as opposed to the old covenant of the Law. Yet it is true to say that terms such as 'in Christ' and 'in the Spirit' can be used interchangeably, for the Spirit indwelling the Church and the individual believer is the mode or medium by which the ascended Christ is present to His people and they are in communion with Him. The Spirit is the principle and power of life 'in Christ,' which is an anticipation in the present order of the resurrection life of the age to come. As the Spirit of the resurrection life it mediates Christ's indwelling presence; hence Paul can speak indifferently of life 'in the Spirit,' the indwelling of the Spirit of God, having the Spirit of Christ, Christ being 'in you,' and being led by the Spirit of God (Ro 8^{9-14}). The Spirit, as the principle of the new life, stands in total opposition to the principle of unredeemed human life, of man's condition in his sinful state of alienation from God. It is this latter which is denoted by the term 'flesh' as generally used by Paul. The Christian life is a life 'not according to the flesh but according to the Spirit' (Ro 8^{4}). 'To set the mind on the flesh is death, but to set the mind on the Spirit is life and peace' (Ro 8^{6}). 'You are not in the flesh but in the Spirit, if the Spirit of Christ really dwells in you' (Ro 8^{9}). This Spirit-possession means that the believer is already in a measure 'spiritual,' that is, open to the energy and direction of the Spirit; he is already in part 'spirit,' though still living in the 'flesh,' the natural condition of the present sinful order; and he may look forward to the completion of his redemption when the resurrection life will be imparted to the mortal body through the indwelling of the Spirit, and he will become wholly 'spiritual,' endowed with a 'spiritual' body, that is, a body fitted for fellowship with, and the service of, God (Ro 8^{11}; cf 8^{23}, 1 Co 15^{44ff}, Ph 3^{21}). For the present the indwelling Spirit contends against the 'flesh,' the principle of man's self-assertion against God (Gal 5^{16-18}, 1 Co 2^{14ff}), but it constitutes the 'first fruits' of the believer's final redemption (Ro 8^{23}); it is the 'first instalment' which guarantees the whole (2 Co 1^{22} 5^{5}), or, in another metaphor, the seal or mark of God's ownership by which He will recognize and claim His people in the day of total redemption (2 Co 1^{22}, Eph 1^{13-14} 4^{30}). The Spirit is to the Christian, as to Jesus at His baptism, the assurance of sonship. The proof of sonship is that God has sent the Spirit of His Son into our hearts, crying Abba, Father! (Gal 4^{6}, Ro 8^{14-21}). The Spirit dwelling in the believer conforms him to the likeness of Christ (2 Co 3^{18}; cf Ro 8^{29f} 12^{2}) in a progressive process of making him become, or enter into the meaning of, what he has been made by his justification, that is, a son of God. This Divine indwelling constitutes the members of the Church, collectively and individually, a temple in which the Spirit dwells (1 Co 3^{16} 6^{19}). It is the principle of the life of the Church as the body of Christ (1 Co 12^{13}, Eph 4^{4}), the source of its unity (Eph 4^{3}), the medium by which Jew and Gentile have come to attain access to God in the fellowship of the community (Eph 2^{18}), so as to constitute a single dwelling-place of God (Eph 2^{22}). The life of the Church consists in its participation in the Spirit (2 Co 13^{14}, Ph 2^{1}). It is, indeed, only through the inspiration of the Spirit that the Church member can make his initial confession of faith in Christ as Lord (1 Co 12^{3}).

The Spirit is the mode of man's communion with God, and as such is spoken of in terms which leave no doubt that Paul thinks of the Spirit as personal, at least in the sense of being the personal working of the personal God: 'it is the Spirit himself bearing witness with our spirit that we are children of God' (Ro 8^{16}); 'The Spirit helps us in our weakness; for we do not know how to pray as we ought, but the Spirit himself intercedes for us with sighs too deep for words. And he who searches the hearts of men knows what is the mind of the Spirit, because the Spirit intercedes for the saints according to the will of God' (Ro 8^{26f}). Thus the Spirit communicates God's revelation to man (1 Co 2^{10-13}). The dispensation of the Spirit stands in sharp contrast over against that of the Law, which could only effect man's condemnation: 'We serve not under the old written code but in the new life of the Spirit' (Ro 7^{6}); 'The written code kills, but the Spirit gives life' (2 Co 3^{6}.) The Christian who is led by the Spirit is not under the Law (Gal 5^{18}). The manifestations of the indwelling of the Spirit are many and varied. They include freedom, the confidence before God which is the essential characteristic of those who have received the status of sons of God (Gal 5, 2 Co 3^{17}); the power by which the gospel is attested (1 Th 1^{5}, 1 Co 2^{4}), joy (1 Th 1^{6}, Ro 14^{17}); zeal (Ro 12^{11}); consecration to membership of the holy people of God (1 Th 4^{8}, 2 Th 2^{13}). The charismata of prophecy and ecstatic utterance are valued by Paul (1 Th 5^{19}; cf 1 Co 14^{18}), but he insists, against the tendency of Corinthian Christians to take particular pride in such gifts, that the manifestations of the Spirit are manifold, all having their proper place in the life of the Body (1 Co 12^{4-11}), that prophecy, which is intelligible to all and therefore edifying, is preferable to 'inspired gibberish' of 'tongues' (1 Co 14), and that the greatest gifts of the Spirit are faith, hope, and love, with love as their crown (1 Co 13). Love is the supreme manifestation of the Spirit (cf Col 1^{8}), but all the specifically Christian qualities of life are its fruit (Gal 5^{22f}). It remains to add that the means by which the Spirit is received are, according to the Pauline teaching, the response of faith to the preaching of the gospel (Gal 3^{2-5}), and baptism (1 Co 12^{13}; cf Ro 6^{4} 8^{2ff}).

(iv) *The Spirit in the Johannine teaching.*—The Fourto Gospel, which does not narrate the baptism of Jesus, clearly explains its significance. As the one upon whom the Spirit descended and remained, He is marked cut as the Son of God, who will baptize with the Holy Spirit (Jn 1^{32-34}). He has received the Spirit in a fulness and completeness which differentiates Him from the prophets or the Baptist, as the one who utters the words of God (Jn 3^{34}). His teaching points to the rebirth through the Spirit, that is, entry upon a new state of life whose inner principle is the Spirit, as the only way of entering the Kingdom of God; and this is described in language which indicates the association of water and Spirit in Christian baptism (Jn 3^{5-8}; cf 1^{13}). This rebirth in the Spirit can take place only after the completion of the saving work of Christ in His death and exaltation (cf 3^{14ff}); hence the promise of the Spirit in Christ's teaching looks to the future: 'Now this he said about the Spirit, which those who believed in him were to receive; for as yet the Spirit had not been given [or, Spirit was not yet], because Jesus was not yet glorified' (7^{39}). The fullest teaching on the Spirit is to be found in the discourses which follow the Last Supper. Here the Spirit is called the *paraclete* (RSV 'Counsellor'), a term which properly denotes 'advocate' (cf 1 Jn 2^{1}, where it is applied to Christ) or 'intercessor,' but which in this context may rather mean the Spirit of *paraclēsis*, that is the proclamation of the comfort and encouragement of the gospel of the age of fulfilment. With this term, and the use of masculine rather than neuter pronouns, the concept of the Spirit becomes more fully personal than at any other point in Scripture. The Paraclete is to be sent by God the Father in response to the prayer of Christ (14^{16}), by Christ Himself (16^{7}), by the Father in Christ's name (14^{26}), or by Christ from the Father (15^{26}). He is to represent and mediate the glorified Christ to His followers; He is to be the medium through whom they will enter into a full understanding of the historic revelation in the incarnate Christ, teaching and instructing them and through them witnessing to the world concerning Christ and the salvation and judgment that He has brought. As the Spirit of Christ, who is Himself the truth (14^{6}), He is the Spirit of truth (14^{17} 15^{26} 16^{13}) guiding Christ's disciples into all the truth as he unfolds the meaning of the revelation of God in Christ's deeds and words. He will mediate Christ's presence to them (cf 14^{18}), bringing to their remembrance and instructing them in the full significance of the things which Jesus has said to them (14^{26}). He will bear witness to Jesus, declaring to the disciples the meaning of His words and acts (16^{12-15}) in a way which was impossible during the earthly ministry, and through their mission, especially under persecution, testifying to the hostile world (15^{26}–16^{4}). This mission of the Paraclete, like that of Jesus Himself, is two-sided; for to the world which has rejected Christ it brings judgment. He will convict the world in respect of the sin of its unbelief, in respect of the vindication of Jesus in His exaltation to the Father, and in respect of the condemnation of the devil through His death and glorification (16^{8-11}). This cannot take place until Jesus has been exalted (16^{7}), and it is after the resurrection (and probably the ascension) that Christ bestows the Spirit upon His disciples, extending to them the mission on which He had Himself been sent by the Father, and, in an act of new creation, empowering them to execute His own mission of forgiveness and judgment through their proclamation of the gospel (20^{21-23}). This is the Johannine interpretation of 'Pentecost,' and, as in Acts, it is through the Spirit imparted by the glorified Messiah that the Church is commissioned for its task.

1 John lays stress on the 'abiding' of Christ in His people through the agency of the Spirit which He has given to them (1 Jn 3^{24}), the Spirit being the assurance of the mutual indwelling of Christ and His followers (4^{13}). The Spirit is the Spirit of truth, testifying to Christ in the sacraments of the gospel (5^{6-8}), and the Spirit is the inward anointing of the messianic people, by which they are taught the truth of Christ (2^{20-27}).

(v) *The Spirit in other NT writings.*—The rest of the NT adds little to the doctrine of the Spirit. (*a*) *The Pastoral Epistles.* Apart from a use of 'spirit' to denote the Divine being of Christ (1 Ti 3^{16}; cf He 9^{14}, Ro 1^{3}, and of God, Jn 4^{24}), the Spirit appears in these books as the Spirit of prophecy (1 Ti 4^{1}), the inspiration of the ministers of the Church in their task of safeguarding the truth (2 Ti 1^{14}), and as the agent and principle of the new life entered into in baptism (Tit 3^{5}). (*b*) *The Epistle to the Hebrews.* The Christian gospel has been attested by the gifts of the Holy Spirit which have accompanied its reception (2^{4}), and baptized Christians have been made 'partakers of the Holy Spirit' (6^{4}). (*c*) 1 *Peter.* Christians are sanctified by the Spirit as the people of Christ (1^{2}). The message of the prophets, before the gospel events, and that of the apostolic missionaries after it, are alike inspired by the Spirit (1^{11f}). The Spirit is the principle of the resurrection life (4^{6}; cf 3^{18}, of Christ); and those who suffer persecution for Christ receive a special blessing of the 'Spirit of glory' (4^{14}). (*d*) *Jude.* The Christian life of faith and of prayer in the Holy Spirit is contrasted with the divisions set up by those worldly people who are devoid of the Spirit ($^{19-20}$). (*c*) *Revelation.* In this book the Spirit is primarily regarded as the Spirit of prophecy, in whose power the seer sees and declares his revelations (1^{10} 2^{7} etc.). The Spirit in the Christian prophet bears testimony to Jesus (19^{10}), and it is the Spirit in the Church which prays for the final consummation (22^{17}).

(vi) *The Spirit and the Scriptures.*—The NT as a whole testifies to the belief that the prophetic writers of the OT were inspired by the Spirit. Ps 110^{1} is cited with the introduction: 'David himself, in the Holy Spirit, declared' (Mk 12^{36}, Mt 22^{43}), and similar language is used in relation to other OT quotations (*e.g.* Ac 1^{16} 4^{25} 28^{25}). Ps 95^{7-11} is introduced in the Epistle to the Hebrews (3^{7}) with the words, 'Therefore, as the Holy Spirit says' (cf the way in which Jer 31^{33} is introduced at 10^{15}). Similarly, the typology of the Day of Atonement ritual is explained (9^{8}) as a means by which the Holy Spirit indicates certain truths. Hence the NT conception of the work of the Spirit in the scriptural writers can be summed up by 2 Peter in the dictum that 'no prophecy of scripture is a matter of one's own interpretation, because no prophecy ever came by the impulse of man, but men moved by the Holy Spirit spoke from God.' J. G. S.—**G. W. H. L.**

HOMAM.—See Hemam.

HOMER.—See Weights and Measures.

HOMICIDE.—See Crimes, **7**, Refuge [Cities of].

HOMOSEXUALITY.—The term 'homosexual' is found only in 1 Co 6^{9} RSV (AV, RV 'abusers of themselves with mankind' or 'with men'). The practice is condemned in Ro 1^{26f}. It is frequently referred to in OT, particularly in connexion with male prostitutes at shrines, and always stands under condemnation. See Crimes and Punishments, **3**.

HONEST, HONESTY.—In 2 Es 16^{49} 'honest' (AV, RV) has the meaning of 'chaste' (RSV 'respectable'). Elsewhere it means either 'honourable' or 'becoming.' For the meaning 'honourable' compare Ru 1^{22} Coverdale 'There was a kinsman also . . . whose name was Boos, which was an honest man'; and for 'becoming,' Is 52^{1} Coverdale 'Put on thine honest rayment, O Jerusalem, thou citie of the holy one.' In RSV 'honest' has its modern sense in a number of passages. 'Honesty' in 1 Ti 2^{2}, its only occurrence in AV, means 'seemliness' (RV 'gravity,' RSV 'respectful'). In RSV in Gn 30^{33} it has its modern sense (AV, RV 'righteousness').

HONEY.—The appreciation of honey by the Hebrews from the earliest times, and its abundance in Canaan, are evident from the oft-recurring description of that country as a 'land flowing with milk and honey' (Ex $3^{8,17}$ onwards). What is not so clear is precisely what is meant by 'honey.' Certainly sometimes bee-honey is meant, since it was found in hollow tree-trunks (1 S 14^{26}, but the Hebrew text here is uncertain), and in the dead body of an animal (Jg 14^{8ff}). There is no mention of bee-keeping in the OT, so it is probable that all bee-honey mentioned in OT is the honey of the wild bee (see Bee). In later times, as is evident from the Mishnah, bee-keeping was widely practised by the Jews,

The hives were of straw or wicker-work. Before removing the combs the bee-keepers stupefied the bees with fumes of charcoal and cow-dung, burnt in front of the hives.

The Arabic *dibs*, however, is date-honey, and this was known in Mishnaic times (see article 'Honey' in *EBi* col. 2105, where details of manufacture are described both from dates and grape-juice). It is plain that the Hebrew *d^ebhash* is used of both types of honey. The honey which formed part of the first fruits presented at the sanctuary probably included both types, since both were liable to fermentation. The combination of 'milk and honey' suggests the honey of the wild-bee, but where we find the combination 'oil (olive) and honey' the reference is probably to date-juice, boiled and reboiled till its colour was a dark golden brown like maple molasses. Sugar was unknown in Bible times, and so 'honey' was used in the making of 'bakemeats' and all sorts of sweet cakes (Ex 16^{31}). Honey for domestic use was kept in earthen jars (1 K 14^{3} EV 'cruse'), in which, doubtless, it was also put for transport (Gn 43^{11}) and export (Ezk 27^{17}).

In addition to the proverbial expression of fertility above quoted, honey, in virtue of its sweetness, is frequently employed in simile and metaphor in Hebrew literature; see Ps 19^{10} 119^{103}, Pr 16^{24} 24^{13f}, Ca 4^{11} 5^{1}, Sir 42^{20} 49^{1} etc. A. R. S. K.—**N. H. S.**

HONOUR.—Various words are rendered by 'honour,' including Hebrew *hādhār* (*e.g.* Ps 8^{5}), *hôdh* (*e.g.* Ps 96^{6}), *y^ekār* (*e.g.* Est 1^{20}), *kābhôdh* (*e.g.* Nu 24^{11}, Pr 26^{8}), and *tiph'ereth* (*e.g.* Dt 26^{19}), and Greek *doxa* (*e.g.* 2 Co 6^{8}) and *timē* (*e.g.* Jn 4^{44}, 1 Co 12^{23f}). Several of these words are elsewhere rendered 'glory,' while related verbs are translated 'glorify' or 'honour.'

1. In OT honour is said to belong to God (Ps 104^{1}) and to His work (Ps 111^{3}), and to be His due (Pr 3^{9}). It should also be given to parents (Ex 20^{12}) and to the aged (Lv 19^{32}). It may be earned from others by righteousness (Pr 21^{21}), but true honour comes from God (1 S 2^{30}), who gives it to those who honour Him (*ibid.*), but withholds it from those who do wrong (2 Ch 26^{18}). Nevertheless, in his very manhood man is crowned with honour by God (Ps 8^{5}). Honour is not fitting for a fool (Pr 26^{1}).

2. In the Apocrypha the human race is said to be worthy of honour and unworthy of honour, those who fear the Lord being worthy of the honour and those who transgress unworthy (Sir 10^{19-23}). The honour of him who fears the Lord exceeds that of the nobleman, the judge, or the ruler (Sir 10^{24}). Humility and knowledge bring higher honour than wealth (Sir $10^{28, 30}$), for a good name is more enduring than riches (Sir 41^{12f}), and death is preferable to dishonour (1 Mac 9^{10}). The fear of the Lord is the crown of wisdom (Sir 1^{18}), for God exalts them that hold her fast (Sir 1^{19}). The priest (Sir 7^{21}) and the physician (Sir 38^{1}) are to be held in honour, and wisdom deserves to be honoured by kings (Wis 6^{21}). The honour due to parents is stressed (Sir 3^{3ff}), and it is extended to parents-in-law (To 10^{12}).

3. In NT the honour due to parents is reaffirmed (Mt 15^{4} ||), and it is declared to be due to widows (1 Ti 5^{3}), to masters (1 Ti 6^{1}), and to the emperor (1 P 2^{17}). Marriage, too, is to be held in honour (He 13^{4}). Moreover, honour is due to Christ, and in honouring Him men honour God (Jn 5^{23}). As the Lamb that was slain He is worthy to receive honour (Rev 5^{12}), and is destined to receive it eternally (Rev 5^{13}). See also GLORY.

HOODS.—Only in Is 2^{23} AV, for which RV and RSV have rightly 'turbans.' See DRESS, **5** (*a*).

HOOK.—**1.** *wāw*, a hook or ring with a spike driven into wood, Ex 26^{32} etc. **2.** A hook for fishing or for dragging, Is 19^{8}, Job 41^{1}, Am 4^{2}, Mt 17^{27}. The hook used in fishing was of course attached to a line, but whether the latter was simply held in the hand or was attached to a rod cannot be decided.

HOOPOE (Lv 11^{19}, Dt 14^{18}).—The Hebrew *dûkhîphath* 'hoopoe' (RV, RSV with LXX and Vulgate), not 'lapwing' (AV), like the corresponding Coptic *koukoupat* and Latin *upupa* and other names, is an attempt to reproduce this bird's note, variously given as 'hoh-hoh' or 'pou-pou' or 'hoop-hoop' or the like. The hoopoe is a common visitor in spring to Palestine, where its striking plumage and tall crest and its odd movements make it conspicuous. Pleasing however as its appearance is, its habits are very different; and it was considered unclean because its nest is commonly foul, it picks up its food on dunghills, and its flesh, though tasty (being still eaten by peasants), is malodorous. E. W. G. M.—**G. R. D.**

HOPE.—A number of Hebrew words, ranging in meaning from 'trust' to 'expectation' are translated by 'hope' in EV, but the characteristic words are from the root *ḳwh* 'wait for, look eagerly for.' Some men hope for the wrong things and then their hope is 'stupidity' (*kesel*, Job 8^{13f}, RSV 'confidence'). True hope is in Yahweh (Ps 71^{5}) and in His word (Ps $119^{74, 81, 114}$); its justification is the known character of God (Ps 130^{7}). *Individuals* hope for deliverance from enemies (Ps 71^{14}), from illness (Ps $31^{14, 24}$ 39^{7}), from death (Ps 16^{9}, RSV 'dwells secure'), and for the forgiveness of sins (Ps 130^{5}), and in general for the reversal of their present unhappy circumstances (Ps 42^{5}). *Israel's* hope is that Yahweh will prove a saviour in time of trouble (Jer 14^{8}), even in the disaster of the Exile (Jer 29^{11} 31^{17}), and also will be found a refuge (AV 'hope') for His people in the day of eschatological judgment (Jl 3^{16}). But hope is not characteristically an eschatological word in OT. (The Hebrews did have eschatological expectations, and eagerly awaited their fulfilment—see DAY OF THE LORD, KINGDOM OF GOD, MESSIAH.)

When, however, we turn to NT we find the term 'hope' (Gr. *elpis*) is characteristically eschatological in content. It is significant that whereas in Greek thought *elpis* could denote an expectation of something good or bad and came increasingly to mean 'anxiety, fear,' in NT it always means a looking forward to something good and favourable. It is sometimes used in ordinary senses (*e.g.* Lk 6^{34}) but its distinctive sense is hope of salvation (1 Th 5^{8}). The ground of this hope is what God has done in Christ—in particular His overthrow of death by Christ's dying and rising again (1 P 1^{3}). Its content is that we too shall rise from death (Ac 23^{6}, Ro 8^{24}, Tit 1^{2} 3^{7}) and enter into the full inheritance of God's Kingdom (Eph 1^{18}, 1 Co 15^{50}). This is the 'hope of the gospel' (Col 1^{23}), *i.e.* the hope which the gospel brings to birth in us; and we may confidently entertain this hope because we already know the power of Christ working in us. Thus it is Christ in us who is Himself the author of our hope of glory (Col 1^{27}, 1 Ti 1^{1}). But this hope of salvation is not limited to the individual believer. His hope embraces the salvation of His fellow Christians (2 Co 1^{7}) and this implies a universal day of salvation, at the parousia of Christ (Tit 2^{13}). Thus our hope is for the re-creation of the whole universe and is cosmic in its scope (Ro 8^{22-24}).

To be a Christian means to possess this hope—non-Christians are characterized by the absence of it (Eph 2^{12}, 1 Th 4^{13}). Thus hope is one of the marks of a Christian and takes its place with faith and love as one of three distinctive Christian virtues (1 Co 13^{13}, 1 Th 1^{3}). It is a sure hope because we have an earnest of its fulfilment in that the love of God has been already poured into our hearts by the Holy Spirit (Ro 5^{5}). Indeed, it is a proleptic possession of the world to come, and anchors the soul firmly to that other world into which it has already entered (He 6^{19}). Paul recognizes that hope attained ceases to be hope (Ro 8^{24}) but in 1 Co 13^{13} he appears to say that while expository powers, glossolalia, earthly insights, will prove transient, hope like faith and love will always remain as characteristics of redeemed personality. Probably he meant that the Christian will never have fully attained all that God has to give and that there will always be something new and fresh to look forward to, expectantly and confidently. 'What no eye has seen, nor ear heard, nor the heart of

man conceived, what God has prepared for those who love him,' those are the riches of our inheritance in the saints, and we may expect never to exhaust them.
S. B. F.

HOPHNI AND PHINEHAS.—The two sons of Eli; they were priests in the sanctuary at Shiloh, where, in spite of the presence of their father, they carried on their evil practices. In consequence of their deeds a curse is twice pronounced upon the house of Eli, first by 'a man of God' (1 S 2^{27}) who is not named, and again by the mouth of Samuel (ch. 3). The curse was accomplished when Hophni and Phinehas were slain at the battle of Aphek, and the Ark of God was lost—an incident which was the cause of the death of Eli (ch. 4). The malpractices of these two consisted in their claiming and appropriating more than their due of the sacrifices ($2^{13, 17}$), and in their immoral actions in the Tabernacle (v.^{22}; cf Am 2^{7f}). W. O. E. O.

HOPHRA.—The Egyptian Wahebrē, Apries of Herodotus, fourth king of the 26th Dynasty (*c* 588–569 B.C.), and grandson of Neco, mentioned in Jer 44^{30}. He, or possibly his predecessor Psammetichus II., is also referred to as Pharaoh in Jer $37^{5, 7, 11}$, Ezk 29^{3} etc. Little is certainly known of his reign. He induced Zedekiah to join a coalition and to rebel against Babylon. Hophra must have been defeated by Nebuchadrezzar in Syria in attempting to resist the progress of the Babylonian army, and he received the fugitives from Palestine after the destruction of Jerusalem in 586 B.C. There is no evidence that Nebuchadrezzar plundered Egypt, as was anticipated by Ezekiel, though he seems to have attacked Hophra's successor Amasis in 568 B.C. with some success, and may have overrun some part of Lower Egypt. The Syrian and other mercenary soldiers stationed at Elephantine revolted in the reign of Hophra, but were brought again to submission. Another mutiny of the Egyptian soldiery, recorded by Herodotus, resulted in Amasis being put upon the throne as champion of the natives. Hophra relied on the Greek mercenaries, and maintained himself, perhaps in a forced co-regency, in Lower Egypt until the third year of Amasis, when he was defeated and slain. F. Ll. G.

HOPPER.—See LOCUST.

HOR.—**1.** A mountain 'on the edge of the land of Edom' (Nu 33^{37}), where Aaron died. Constant tradition, at least since Josephus, sees Mount Hor in *Jebel Hārûn*, 'the Mountain of Aaron,' above Petra. This is regarded by the Arabs as the mountain sacred to the great high priest, and his tomb is shewn and reverenced under a small dome on its summit. Some modern writers, especially H. C. Trumbull, have doubted the tradition and endeavoured to fix other sites, such as *Jebel Maḍeira*, NW. of *'Ain Qedeis*. *Jebel Hārûn* rises 4780 feet above the sea-level. Its western side is an unscalable precipice; it is ascended from the pass leading into Petra. A very wide view over the Arabian desert, down to the Red Sea and up to the Ghôr, is commanded from the summit. **2.** A mountain mentioned in Nu 34^{7f}, as in the northern boundary of the Promised Land. In all probability this is meant for *Hermon*. R. A. S. M.

HORAM.—A king of Gezer defeated and slain by Joshua, Jos 10^{53}.

HOREB.—See SINAI.

HOREM.—A city of Naphtali in the mountains, Jos 19^{38}; its location is unknown.

HORESH.—The word *hōresh* means 'wooded height' in Is 17^{9} (where, however, RVm and RSV follow LXX and read 'Hivites'), Ezk 31^{3}, 2 Ch 27^{4}, but in 1 S $23^{15f, 18}$ it is probably a proper name of a place where David took refuge (so RVm, RSV). It is perhaps modern *Kh. Khureisā*. See FOREST.

HOR-HAGGIDGAD.—A station in the journeyings of the Israelites, Nu 33^{32f}. Probably identical with **Gudgodah,** q.v. It perhaps lay in the *Wâdī Khaḍākhid*.

HOR-HAGIDGAD, Nu 33^{32f} (AV).—See HOR-HAGGIDGAD.

HORI.—**1.** A son of Seir, Gn 36^{22}, 1 Ch 1^{39}. **2.** The father of Shaphat the Simeonite spy, Nu 13^{5}.

HORIMS, Dt $2^{12, 22}$ (AV) = **Horites** (q.v.).

HORITES.—The pre-Edomite inhabitants of Seir or Edom according to Gn 14^{6} and Dt $2^{12, 22}$, who were governed by chieftains (Gn 36^{29f}). The name Horites was formerly taken to mean 'cave-dwellers,' being derived from Hebrew *ḥôr*. This popular etymology is no longer accepted since the discovery of the Hurrians as an ethnic element in the Near East. The Hurrians entered northern and north-eastern Mesopotamia about the beginning of the 2nd millennium B.C., and later spread over the whole of Syria and Palestine with the result that the Egyptians frequently called Palestine *Kharu*. The Kingdom of Mitanni on the upper Euphrates was Hurrian, though its rulers were Indo-Europeans. The patriarchal stories of the Bible reflect many Hurrian customs and legal rights (Gordon, *BA*, iii [1940], 1–12). The Hurrian language, still incompletely understood, became first known through one of the Amarna Letters. Later on texts in the same language were found at Boghazköy, Ugarit, and elsewhere. The chief god of the Hurrians was Teshub, the god of thunder. S. H. Hn.

HORMAH ('devoted' or 'accursed') was a city, apparently not far from Kadesh, where the Israelites were overthrown, when, after the death of the ten spies, they insisted on going forward, Nu 14^{45}, Dt 1^{44}. At a later time it was taken and destroyed by Israel (Nu 21^{3}, Jos 12^{14}), this feat being attributed in Jg 1^{17} to Judah and Simeon. There we learn that the former name was **Zephath.** Possibly the memory of the previous disaster here led to its being called 'Accursed.' It was one of 'the cities belonging to the tribe of the people of Judah in the extreme South, towards the boundary of Edom,' and is named between Chesil and Ziklag (Jos 15^{30}), also between Bethul (or Bethuel) and Ziklag (Jos 19^{4}, 1 Ch 4^{30}) in the territory occupied by Simeon. It was one of the towns to which David sent a share of the booty taken from the Amalekites who had raided Ziklag in his absence (1 S 30^{30}). It is probably to be identified with modern *Tell el Mishâsh*. W. E.—**H. H. R.**

HORN (Heb. *ḳeren*, Gr. *keras*).—Sometimes horns were wrought into vessels in which oil was stored (1 K 1^{39}) or carried (1 S 16^{1}). Probably with some dainty ornamentation, they were used to hold eye-paint (Job 42^{14}, *Keren-happuch*). Of rams' horns a kind of trumpet was made (Jos 6^{4}); see MUSIC, **4** (2) (*e*). 'Horns' in poetry symbolized strength (Dt 33^{17} etc.). 'Horn' in Ps 18^{2} = 2 S 22^{3} stands for offensive weapons, as 'shield' for defensive (Perowne). To 'exalt one's horn,' or 'cause it to bud' (grow), is to strengthen and prosper him, 1 S 2^{10} (cf RSV 'to exalt the power'), Ezk 29^{21} etc. For one to 'lift his horn' is to be arrogant, Ps 75^{4f}. To crush or weaken one is to 'break *or* cut off his horn,' Jer 48^{25}, La 2^{3} (RSV 'might'). In prophetic symbolism horns stand for kings and military powers, Dn 7^{8} 8^{21} etc. The altar horns (Ex 27^{2}), to which fugitives seeking asylum clung (1 K 1^{50} etc.), were projections at the four corners, and apparently peculiarly sacred (Ex 30^{10} etc.); but their significance and use are now unknown. W. E.

HORN, LITTLE.—See LITTLE HORN.

HORNED OWL.—See OWL.

HORNED SNAKE.—See SERPENT.

HORNET (Ex 23^{28}, Dt 7^{20}, Jos 24^{12}).—In all three references the hornet is mentioned as an instrument of the Lord to drive out the Canaanites. By most interpreters a literal interpretation is accepted, but a metaphorical use of the word is contended for by some. Sayce suggested that the reference may be to the armies of Rameses III., as the standard-bearers wore two devices like flies, and Garstang has adopted a similar view that the hornet is a symbol for Egypt. The most plentiful hornet in Palestine is the *Vespa orientalis*. Hornets attack only when interfered with.

HORONAIM.—A city of Moab, mentioned in Is 15[5], Jer 48[3, 5, 34], and also on the Moabite Stone (ll. 31, 32). Its site is unknown.

HORONITE.—A title given to Sanballat (q.v.), the opponent of Nehemiah, Neh 2[10, 19] 13[28]. The name may denote an inhabitant of Beth-horon (q.v.).

HORSE.—Horses were introduced into the Near East early in the 2nd millennium, having earlier been domesticated in central Asia, apparently by Indo-Iranian wandering groups. They were used extensively by the Mitanni, who bred and trained them for chariot warfare; and also by the Hittites and Kassites. The Hyksos brought them to Egypt, where they proved extremely popular. By the middle of the 2nd millennium the war-horse and chariot were standard equipment in the armies of the Near East. Israelites were thus familiar with horses from the earliest times, but were slow in adopting them for use. The mountainous regions of Palestine were unsuitable for chariot warfare; likewise social and economic conditions before the monarchy were not favourable for the creation of a knightly caste or military élite such as developed among the Canaanites, and the surrounding peoples. With the monarchy a gradual change took place. David continued the practice of crippling horses captured in warfare, but kept a few for his newly-acquired chariotry (2 S 8[4], 1 Ch 18[4]). Solomon greatly added to their numbers, maintaining 40,000 stalls of horses for his chariots and 12,000 charioteers (according to 1 K 4[26]). Well-appointed royal stables dating from the 10th cent. have been unearthed at Megiddo, Hazor, and Gezer; doubtless other installations were scattered about the country. Moreover, Solomon conducted a brisk trade in horses and chariots: 'And Solomon's import of horses was from Egypt and Kue (Cilicia), and the king's traders received them from Kue at a price. A chariot could be imported from Egypt for 600 shekels of silver, and a horse for 150; and so through the king's traders they were exported to all the kings of the Hittites and the kings of Syria' (1 K 10[28f], 2 Ch 1[16f]). While the text is not entirely clear, it appears that Solomon and his agents acted as middlemen between Egypt and the north, transferring horses from Cilicia (which was famous for its mettlesome steeds) to Egypt, while the chariots moved in the opposite direction. There is no need, however, to change Egypt (*Miṣrayim*) to a so-called northern *Muṣri*.

The kings of Israel were warned against multiplying horses (Dt 17[16]). Trust in horses is put in antithesis to trust in the Lord (Is 30[16], Ps 20[7] 33[17]). Before the reforms of Josiah, horses sacred to the sun were kept in the Temple (2 K 23[11]; cf 11[16]). The appearance of the war-horse seems to have made a deep impression (Job 39[19-25], Jer 47[3], Nah 3[2] etc.). After the Exile horses were much more common: the returning Jews brought 736 horses with them (Neh 7[68]). Horses were fed on barley and *tibn* (chopped straw) in Solomon's time as in Palestine to-day (1 K 4[28]). Although the breeding of horses has become so intimately associated with our ideas of the Arabs, it would seem that during the whole OT period horses were unknown, or at least scarce, in Arabia. The equipment of horses is mentioned in the Bible—the bit and bridle (Ps 32[9], Pr 26[3]), bells of the horses (Zec 14[20]), and 'saddlecloths for riding' (Ezk 27[20]). In OT times they were apparently unshod (Is 5[28]). E. W. G. M.—**D. N. F.**

HORSE GATE.—See JERUSALEM [GATES OF].

HORSELEACH, Pr 30[15] (AV, RV).—See LEECH.

HOSAH ('refuge').—**1.** A Levitical doorkeeper of the Temple, 1 Ch 16[38] 26[10f, 16]. **2.** A city of Asher, apparently S. of Tyre, Jos 19[29]. The site is unknown.

HOSAI.—See HOZAI.

HOSANNA.—An acclamation used by the people on Palm Sunday in greeting Jesus on His last entry into Jerusalem, and afterwards by the children in the Temple (Mt 21[9, 15]). It occurs six times in the Gospels (all in the connexion above noted).

(1) The most usual view of its origin is as follows. In Hebrew the expression was *hôshîʿāh-nnā'* (a strongly expressed imperative of the verb *to save*), used as an invocation of blessing, becoming *hosanna* when this popular cry was written in Greek. The same kind of thing has occurred with the Hebrew forms 'Amen' and 'Hallelujah.' When the word Hosanna passed into the early Church it was misunderstood as a shout of homage or greeting—'Hail' or 'Glory to.' The simplest form of the Palm Sunday greeting occurs in Mk 11[9] and Jn 12[13] 'Hosanna! Blessed be he who comes in the name of the Lord!' which really was the cry of the people. The additions that occur in the other passages ('Hosanna *to the Son of David*!' Mt 21[9, 15], and 'Hosanna in the highest!' Mt 21[9], Mk 11[10]) seem really to be later amplifications due to misunderstanding of the real meaning of Hosanna. The Hosanna cry (cf Ps 118[25f]) and the palm branches naturally suggest the Feast of Tabernacles, when the people used to raise the cry of 'Hosanna,' while marching in procession and waving branches of palm, myrtle, and willow. The great occasion for this was the seventh day of the Feast, when the Hosanna processions were most frequent. Hence this day was early designated 'Day of Hoshaʿna' [Hosanna], and the *lulab* branches then used also received the same name. Such processions were not peculiar to Tabernacles. They might be extemporized for other occasions of a joyous character (cf 1 Mac 13[51], 2 Mac 10[7]), and this was the case in the scene described in the Gospels. Hosanna passed early into liturgical use (cf *e.g. Didache* 10[6] 'Hosanna to the God of David'), as an interjection of praise and joy, and was developed on these lines. The early misunderstanding of its meaning was perpetuated.

(2) Over against that view is the possibility that the Aramaic word *'ûshᵉnā'* (*power*) lies behind it, and that it really means 'Praise!' This would save us from having to suppose that the tradition behind Mk 11[10], Mt 21[9, 15] and the *Didache* betrays ignorance of some Hebrew origin of the word on the part of the earliest Church. It gives the good sense: 'Praise to the Son of David!' and 'Praise to the highest!' in these passages. N. T.

HOSEA.—The name of the prophet is identical with that of Joshua ('Yahweh delivers') in its original form (Nu 13[8]) and that of Hoshea, the last king of Israel (2 K 15[30]). The name Jesus is the Greek form of the word whose root meaning is 'space' or 'room,' hence 'deliverance' or 'salvation.' In the case of Hosea it is a name well bestowed, for he is essentially an evangelist, the prophet of grace. 'Ben Beeri' is probably not a true patronymic but may indicate the sept or family from which he came.

The one fact the prophet tells us concerning himself is that he married Gomer bath-Diblaim who bore him three children and was guilty of marital infidelity. Whether Diblaim is her father's name or the name of her birthplace remains uncertain. We learn further from the prophet's story that he belonged to the northern kingdom (1[2] 7[15]) for which his favourite name is Ephraim (it occurs thirty-six times in the book). His obvious interest in the hill-towns of Benjamin (Gibeah, Ramah, and Bethel [5[8]]) would seem to support the theory of Guthe and Hölscher that his home was in that fertile mountain strip of Benjamin overlooking the Jordan valley between Bethel and Jerusalem. This, too, would account for the apparent familiarity of Jeremiah with Hosea and for the influence which the latter has exercised upon the man of Anathoth. In addition it may be noted that Hosea follows the Elohistic traditions of Ephraim rather than those of the Judaean Yahwistic writer (2[15] [Heb. 2[17]] 9[15] 11[8] 12[9] [Heb. 12[10]]).

Concerning the date of his birth we are not informed, but his period of prophetic activity must be placed somewhere between 750 B.C. and the fall of Samaria in 721 B.C. G. A. Smith would set the lower limit at 732 B.C. but Alt, Sellin, and Hölscher would allow the larger period. That he was called to be a prophet at some particular point of time is clearly indicated in the book though no precise date is given. Various opinions are held as to his occupation prior to his call. From the numerous references he makes to ovens and baking it has been thought that he was a baker. More probably, however, he was a small farmer living on the land. His speech smacks most frequently of the soil: he may have belonged to the solid yeoman class of Israel, a class which formed the backbone of the nation. Others have thought that he was member of the prophetic guilds (9^{8}): this might account for the note of asceticism in his prophecies, in which characteristic he resembles the Rechabites. Hosea does appear to accord a high place to the *N^ebhî'îm* ($12^{10, 13}$ [Heb. $12^{11, 14}$]) and he nowhere attacks the group in the manner of Amos. Sellin rightly calls him '*eine richtige Johannesnatur*.' Thus we can understand his impassioned style that oscillates between violent threats and tender promises and entreaties. Inasmuch as his prophecies are seldom provided with a definite location or with a particular audience some have thought of him as a wandering prophet after the style of Elijah and Elisha. It may be that many of his words were addressed to a small band of disciples.

Hosea may be said to differ from the other prophets in that the Divine revelation here is mediated through his tragic domestic experience. Here, as in the case of Jeremiah, who owes much to Hosea, human experience became the channel of the Divine revelation. 'He learned obedience by what he suffered.' And that this experience was profoundly real there can be no doubt. The attempt to interpret this life and blood story as an allegory finds little support: the general consensus of critical opinion is that we are here dealing with sordid solid facts. 'She was, therefore, no dream or fancy, this woman, but flesh and blood: the sorrow, the despair, the sphinx of the prophet's life, yet a sphinx who in the end yielded her riddle to love' (G. A. Smith). We may not doubt that Hosea's prophetic mission was most closely bound up with his tragic marital experience.

The story of that experience is told in ch. 1 and again in ch. 3: in the former instance we have a biographical account in the third person while in the latter the form is autobiographical. Much discussion has centred around the relation and interpretation of these two versions. Marti has maintained that (*a*) ch. 3 does not have reference to Gomer, (*b*) that, unlike ch. 1, ch. 3 is allegorical, (*c*) that ch. 3 formed no part of the original book of Hosea. Majority opinion, however, holds that both chapters deal with the same story: this seems the most satisfactory interpretation. A further suggestion has been made that Gomer was, before marriage, a temple prostitute, a hierodule in the service of heathen rites (T. H. Robinson). This suggestion has commended itself to many scholars, though it seems difficult to understand how the analogy which the prophet is setting up between Yahweh and Israel on the one hand and his own situation on the other hand can be properly maintained. Allwohn has suggested that Hosea was the victim of a strong sex obsession. Such has been found true in many cases, *e.g.* Augustine, Tertullian, but Allwohn does not make a good case here. It may be that one could say rather that in the case of the prophet, as contrasted with Gomer and the people Israel, the sex instinct was sublimated into love of God and of man for God's sake.

Both narratives indicate that Hosea received a command to marry a harlot (*'ēsheth z^enûnîm*). To modern minds such a command seems unworthy of God. This question raises difficulties. It may be that the prophet was so commanded: in view of the large amount of symbol and symbolic action in OT prophecy it is conceivable (Is 5, Jer 28, 32, Ezekiel *passim*). But it is also possible, and indeed more probable, that the prophet is here describing his experience from the viewpoint of later time when he had come to understand the meaning of his experience. He had discovered the gospel buried deep in, and built upon, his suffering. This was the Lord's doing and it was wonderful in his eyes. This seems natural when we recall the character of Hebrew thought and language. The Hebrew was so impressed with the idea of Divine sovereignty that he was constrained to describe as purpose that which we would call consequence or result (cf Is 6^{9f}, Jer 7^{10}, Ps 51^{4}). In these instances the writer seems to be looking back and interpreting experience: he is setting forth that which finally eventuated and declaring that to be the original purpose and plan of the Almighty. Thus we have the record as it is and we learn how in this instance the human experience of the prophet became the channel of the Divine revelation, and how that experience gave him insight into the Divine passion and the final intention of the Divine heart.

Thus Gomer may be regarded as pure and chaste before her marriage. But the prophet was to learn that all the time Gomer had within her latent potentialities which were later to become patent. There was within her the tendency to infidelity, the potentiality of becoming an *'ēsheth z^enûnîm*. That potentiality developed after her marriage and the sorrow of Hosea's life made plain to the prophet the sorrow of God over Israel, once His bride, but now become the vile strumpet of the Baalim. As to when Hosea perceived Gomer's infidelity we may not be certain. 1^{2} might seem to class all the children as *yal^edhê z^enûnîm*, but it seems more probable, from the names given, that Gomer revealed her real nature after the birth of her first child (Jezreel). It may be inferred that Gomer left Hosea and went further on the path of shame. But it is clear that Hosea did not cease to love her. So deep and strong was his love that it could not be quenched by all the folly and waywardness of Gomer. Through that strong love and his deep passion Hosea came to understand the passion of God, and through the vision of the Divine love he was moved to the act of redemption (ch. 3).

We need not exaggerate the apparent differences between Amos and Hosea. Each spoke a word in season. Amos spoke of righteousness and Hosea spoke of mercy, for he saw beyond the fact of judgment to the triumph of grace. Amos's eyes were in the ends of the earth: the world was his parish. Hosea's heart's desire is that Israel may be saved and that God's bride may return to her first love. Amos is extensive while Hosea is intensive: none enters further into 'the secret of the Lord' or has such sympathy with the Divine *pathos* (Heschel). Hosea does not merely teach; he incarnates the Divine love. Only in Jeremiah may we find such spiritual fervour or an equal weight of passion. To know God and to serve Him with undeviating loyalty—that is religion (cf Jn 17^{3}). In Hosea we find the most profound conception of sin, of repentance, and forgiveness. In him hope is moralized by the prophet's revelation of the longsuffering of God, while social ethics are purified and elevated, as righteousness is completed in love. The succession of regicides on the throne of Israel induces despair of the monarchy and Israel's only hope is seen to be in faithful allegiance to her God and prevailing goodwill among men. Egypt or Assyria cannot avail: her only hope is in Yahweh. It may be noted that no prophet is more frequently quoted in the NT: more than thirty, direct or indirect, quotations from his book are found there. It is not too much to say that Hosea is the *fons et origo* of the entire faith and theology of later Israel and that he is the forerunner who prepared the way of the Lord. J. Pn.

HOSEA, BOOK OF.—The Book of Hosea forms the first section of a collection of prophetic writings which was formed after the Exile, probably towards the end of the 3rd cent. B.C., and entitled 'The Twelve Prophets.' The greater part of the Book of Hosea consists of the writings of Hosea, the son of Beeri, who prophesied about the middle of the 8th cent. B.C. (see preceding article), but it also contains material added by later editors between the 8th and 3rd cents. B.C. It is not always possible to determine with certainty these additions and interpolations.

The Book of Hosea falls naturally into two unequal parts: (*a*) chs. 1–3, (*b*) chs. 4–14. In (*a*) the text is better preserved than in (*b*). In (*a*) we have a biographical (ch. 1) and autobiographical (ch. 3) account of Hosea's marriage, with a small collection of poems dealing with Yahweh's relation to Israel (ch. 2) as symbolized in chs. 1 and 3. At what date these chapters were committed to writing we may not be certain. Sellin and Eissfeldt would date them some five or seven years after Hosea's call to the prophetic office. These chapters may not have been actually written down by the prophet himself but were probably preserved at first in oral tradition. Oral tradition in the Near East may be regarded as strong and reliable as a written source: it was usually preserved in the memories and minds of disciple groups. The book as it now lies before us has come through the hands of Judaean editors, as is clear from the superscription in 1[1]. These editors adapted the book to the needs of their time and it may have undergone more than one redaction. Nevertheless there is no reason to doubt the general authenticity of these three chapters. Except for a few minor additions (1[10]–2[1] [Heb. 2[1–3]] 2[21–23] [Heb. 2[23–25]]) and the words 'and David their king' (3[5]) we seem to have the genuine words of Hosea.

In (*b*) we have a series of oracles dealing with the sorry state of Israel's religious, social, and political life. Here the prophet utters denunciations of people, priests, and kings. In 4[1]–9[9] it is frequently difficult to delimit precisely the bounds of these several brief speeches, but in 9[10]–14[8] [Heb. 14[9]] we have mainly a group of poems dealing with historical retrospect and concluding with an added solemn appeal to lay all these words to heart. These poems are marked by a spirit of reflection and differ from the usual prophetic style in that they are not directly addressed to any particular group. It may be, as Sellin suggests, that they were addressed to a small band of the prophet's disciples. No dates are attached to these speeches but it may be that 4[1]–5[7] should be assigned to the time of Jeroboam II., while 5[8]–6[6] might well belong to the period of the Syro-Ephraimitic war. 6[7]–7[2] with 7[3–7] may belong to the reign of Pekah, while 7[8f] is probably to be set in the reign of Hoshea. The prophecy of judgment in 13[15f] [Heb. 13[15] 14[1]] may be Hosea's last word of judgment in 725 B.C.

The text in 4[1]–14[9] is frequently corrupt but interpolations and additions are not as numerous as was once thought. It is no longer possible, with Marti, Nowack, Hölscher, and Volz, to reject all prophecies of *Heil* in pre-exilic prophecy on the ground that these prophets spoke only of *Unheil*. Such a theory is no longer tenable and is to be rejected. The prophecies of weal follow on the prophecies of woe and this accords with a principle abundantly illustrated in the OT. Nor may we delete the frequent references to Judah throughout the book, save in some obvious instances (1[7, 11] [Heb. 2[2]] 4[15] 5[5, 10, 12–14] 6[4, 11] 8[14] 11[12] 12[2] [Heb. 12[1, 3]]). Additions seem to be present in 4[3, 9] 7[10] 14[10] [Heb. 14[9]].

Apart from these slight additions and interpolations the text has suffered considerably in the course of its transmission. The LXX shows considerable divergence and would seem to point to a text earlier than the MT. A critical text as given by G. A. Smith (*Book of the Twelve Prophets*) or the RSV is essential for a proper understanding of the book. J. Pn.

HOSEN.—The plural of 'hose' (cf 'ox,' 'oxen'), found only in Dn 3[21] (AV and RV, but for different words), and now obsolete in the sense, here intended, of breeches or trousers. The articles of dress intended are uncertain. RV 'hosen' is rendered 'coats' in AV, and 'mantles' in AVm, RSV. AV 'hosen' is rendered 'tunics' by RV, RSV. According to an early tradition (LXX *tiara*), some form of headdress is intended (cf RVm 'turbans'), but modern opinion favours 'coats' or 'tunics' as in RV.

HOSHAIAH ('Y″ has saved').—**1.** A man who led half the princes of Judah in the procession at the dedication of the walls of Jerusalem, Neh 12[32]. **2.** The father of Jezaniah (Jer 42[1]; so Hebrew followed by AV, RV; RSV Azariah), or Azariah 43[2].

HOSHAMA.—A descendant of David, 1 Ch 3[18].

HOSHEA.—**1.** See JOSHUA. **2.** An Ephraimite (1 Ch 27[20]). **3.** One of those who sealed the covenant (Neh 10[23]). **4.** The last king of Israel. Two dates are given for the accession of the latter to the throne, but we know now from the Assyrian records that this occurred in 732 B.C. His immediate predecessor, Pekah (q.v.), with his ally Rezin, king of Aram, attacked Ahaz, king of Judah, who immediately appealed for help to Tiglath-pileser (q.v.) of Assyria, and this was promptly forthcoming (2 K 16[5–9]; Isa 7[1–9]). The Assyrian armies swept over Israel (2 K 15[29]), Pekah was deposed and slain, and Hoshea, the leader of the pro-Assyrian faction, was made king (2 K 15[30]), but under the suzerainty of Assyria, with heavy tribute to pay from year to year (2 K 17[3]). For a few years he remained loyal to Assyria, but presently he grew tired of the burden and defaulted in 724 B.C., relying on the very dubious offer of help from So (q.v.), so-called king of Egypt. The new king of Assyria (Shalmaneser v.) moved quickly; he captured and imprisoned Hoshea, and he laid seige to the capital, Samaria. It speaks well for the strength of Samaria and for the courage of its people that the city held out for more than two years, falling at last early in 721 B.C. The surrender was followed by the deportation of a considerable portion of the population and the planting of foreign colonists in their place (2 K 17[6, 24]). Sargon, who succeeded to the Assyrian throne just before the surrender, had no desire to experiment further with vassal kings, so he set an Assyrian governor over the wasted province. Thus ended the kingdom of Israel. H. P. S.—**T. J. M.**

HOSPITALITY.—In the life of the East there are no more attractive features than those that centre in the practice of hospitality. The virtue of hospitality ranked high in the ancient Orient, and the laws regulating its observance hold undisputed sway in the desert still. The pleasing picture of the magnanimous sheikh, bidding strangers welcome to his tent and to the best he owns (Gn 18), is often repeated to this hour in the Arabian wilderness. It was to Lot's credit and advantage that he had preserved this virtue amid the corruptions of Sodom (Gn 19[2ff]). To shirk an opportunity for its exercise was shameful (Jg 19[15, 18]). A man's worth was illustrated by his princely hospitality (Job 31[31f]). Jesus sent forth the Twelve (Mt 10[9f]), and the Seventy (Lk 10[4ff]), relying on the hospitality of the people. Its exercise secured His blessing; woe threatened such as refused it. The Samaritans' churlish denial of hospitality to Jesus excited the wrath of His disciples (Lk 9[53]). The guest had a right to expect certain attentions (Lk 7[44ff]). The practice of hospitality distinguished those on the right from those on the left hand (Mt 25[35]; cf 10[40], Jn 13[20]). It is commended by precept (Ro 12[13, 20], 1 Ti 3[2] etc.), and also by example (He 13[2]).

Hospitality was highly esteemed amongst other ancient peoples. In Egypt its practice was thought to favour the soul in the future life. By kindness to strangers the Greeks secured the approval of Zeus Xenios, their protector. For the Romans hospitality was a sacred obligation.

In its simplest aspect, hospitality is the reception of the wayfarer as an honoured guest, providing shelter and food. In the ancient, as indeed for the most part in the modern, Orient, men journey only under necessity. Travel for purposes of pleasure and education is practically unknown. Save in cities, therefore, and in trading centres along the great highways, there was little call for places of public entertainment. Villages probably always contained what is called the *medāfeh*—properly *madyafah*—a chamber reserved for guests, whose entertainment is a charge upon the whole community.

From personal experience the present writer knows how solicitous the humblest villagers are for the comfort and well-being of their guests. If the chief man in a village be well off, he greatly adds to his prestige by a liberal display of hospitality.

In the desert, every tent, however poor its owner, offers welcome to the traveller. In the master's absence the women receive the guests, and according to their means do the honours of the 'house of hair.' It is the master's pride to be known as a generous man; any lack of civility or of kindness to a guest meets severe reprobation. In the guest's presence he calls neither his tent, nor anything it contains, his own. During his sojourn the visitor is owner. The women bake bread; the master slays a 'sacrifice,' usually a lamb, kid, or sheep, which is forthwith dressed, cooked, and served with the bread. The proud son of the wilds has high ideas of his own dignity and honour; but he himself waits upon his guest, seeking to gratify with alacrity his every wish. If his visitors are of superior rank he stands by them (Gn 18[8]), and in any case sits down only if they invite him. The safety and comfort of the guests are the first consideration; many place them before even the honour of wife and daughter (Gn 19[8], Jg 19[24]; cf Lane, *Mod. Egyp.* 297). If a guest arrives after sunset h is entitled only to shelter, as the host might then be unable to prepare a meal creditable to himself. If food is offered, it is of the host's goodwill (Lk 11[5ff]). The guest, careful of the host's honour, will indicate that more than he requires has been provided by leaving a portion in the dish.

The open hand, as the token of a liberal heart, wins the respect and esteem of the Arabs. Leadership does not of necessity descend from father to son. Right to the position must be vindicated by wisdom, courage, dignity, and not least by generous hospitality. For the niggard in this regard there is nothing but contempt. It is a coveted distinction to be known as a 'coffee sheikh,' one who without stint supplies his visitors with the fragrant beverage.

The Arabs are sometimes charged with want of gratitude; justly, as it seems from our point of view. But what seems ingratitude to us may be due simply to the influence of immemorial custom, in a land where the necessities of life are never sold, but held as common good, of which the traveller may of right claim a share. The 'right of a guest' may be taken, if not freely offered. The man who refuses covers himself with perpetual shame. The guest enjoys only *his right*; therefore no thanks mingle with his farewell.

The right, however, is limited. 'Whoever,' says the Prophet, 'believes in God and the day of resurrection must respect his guest; and the time of being kind to him is one day and one night; and the period of entertaining him is three days; and if after that he does it longer, he benefits him more: but it is not right for the guest to stay in the house of his host so long as to incommode him' (Lane, *Arabian Society in the Middle Ages*, 143). After three days, or, some say, three days and four hours, the host may ask if he proposes to honour him by a longer stay. The guest may wish to reach some point under protection of the tribe. If so, he is welcome to stay; only, the host may give him work to do. To remain while refusing to do this is highly dishonourable. But the guest may go to another tent at the expiry of every third day, thus renewing his 'right,' and sojourn with the tribe as long as is necessary.

Hospitality involves protection as well as maintenance. 'It is a principle alike in old and new Arabia that the guest is inviolable' (W. R. Smith, *Kinship*[2], 48). That this provision applies to enemies as well as to friends shows the magnanimity of the desert law. Every stranger met in the open is assumed to be an enemy: he will owe his safety either to his own prowess or to fear that his tribe will exact vengeance if he is injured. But the stranger who enters the tent is *daif Ullah*, the guest whom God has sent, to be well entreated for His sake. In an enemy's country one's perils are over when he reaches a tent, and touches even a tent peg. A father's murderer may find sure asylum even in the tent of his victim's son. When he has eaten of the host's bread, the two are at once bound as brothers for mutual help and protection. It is said that 'there is **salt** between them.' Not that literal salt is required. This is a term covering milk, and indeed food of any kind. A draught of water taken by stealth, or even against his will, from a man's dish, serves the purpose. When protection is secured from one, the whole tribe is bound by it (W. R. Smith, *RS*[2] 76).

To understand this we must remember (1) that in Arabia all recognition of mutual rights and duties rests upon kinship. Those outside the kin may be dealt with according to each man's inclination and ability. (2) Kinship is not exclusively a matter of birth. It may be acquired. When men eat and drink together, they renew their blood from the one source, and to that extent are partakers in the same blood. The stranger eating with a clansman becomes 'kinsman' to all the members of the clan, as regards 'the fundamental rights and duties that turn on the sanctity of kindred blood' (Wellhausen *Reste Arab. Heid.* 119 f; W. R. Smith, *RS*[2] 273 n.) This sanctity may be traced to the ancient belief that the clan god shared its life, and when an animal was slain for food took part in the common meal. The clan's friends were therefore the god's friends, whom to injure was to outrage the deity. That the slaughter of the victim was a religious act involving the whole kin is borne out (*a*) by the fact that when an animal is slain all have an undisputed right to come to the feast; (*b*) by the name *dhabīhah*, 'sacrifice,' still applied to it. The present writer was once entertained in the camp of a rather wild and unkempt tribe. His attendants supped with the crowd. Fearing this might not be agreeable to a European, the chief's son, who presided in his father's absence, with innate Arab courtesy, asked him to sup with him in the sheikh's tent. Bringing in a portion of the flesh, the youth repeatedly remarked, as if for the stranger's reassurance, *edh-dhabīhah wāhideh*, 'the slaughtering—sacrifice—is one'; *i.e.* the tribesmen and he ate from the same victim.

The bond thus formed was temporary, holding good for 36 hours after parting. By frequent renewal, however, it might become permanent. 'There was a sworn alliance between the Lihyan and the Mostalic: they were wont to eat and drink together' (*RS*[2] 270 f). A man may declare himself the *dakhīl*—from *dakhala*, 'to enter,' *i.e.* to claim protection—of a powerful man, and thus pass under shelter of his name even before his tent is reached. Whoever should injure him then would have to reckon with the man whose name he had invoked. The rights of sanctuary associated with temples, and until recently with certain churches, originated in an appeal to the hospitality of the local deity. The refugee's safety depended on the respect paid to the god. Joab would have been safe had he not outlawed himself in this regard (1 K 2[31ff]). Jael's dastard deed could be approved only in the heat of patriotic fanaticism (Jg 4[17] 5[24]).

In OT times it can hardly be said that **inns** in the later sense existed. The ordinary traveller was provided for by the laws of hospitality. The *mālôn* of Gn 42[27] etc. was probably nothing more than a place where caravans were accustomed to halt and pass the night. A building of some kind may be intended by the 'lodge of wayfaring men' in the wilderness (Jer 9[2]). For *gērûth* (Jer 41[17]) we should probably read *gidrôth*, 'folds' (cf Jos. *Ant.* x. ix. 5 [175]). Great changes were wrought by Greek and Roman influence, and there can be no doubt that in NT times, especially in the larger centres of population, inns were numerous and well appointed. The name *pandocheion*=Arabic *funduq*, shows that the inn was a foreign importation. Those on the highways would in some respects resemble the *khāns* of modern times, and the buildings that stood for centuries on the great lines of caravan traffic, before the sea became the highway of commerce. These were places of strength, as well as of entertainment for man and beast. Such was probably the inn of the Good Samaritan (Lk 10^{34}), identified with *Khān Hadrūr*, on the road to Jericho. The inns would be frequented by men of all nationalities and of all characters. Rabbinical references show that their reputation was not high. It was natural that Christians should, for their own safety, avoid the inn, and practise hospitality among themselves (1 P 4^{9} etc.).

In Lk 2^{7} 'inn' (*kataluma*) probably means, as it does in Mk 14^{14} and Lk 22^{11}, the **guest-chamber** in a private house. Such guest-chambers were open freely to Jews visiting Jerusalem at the great feasts (*Aboth R. Nathan*, cap. 34). It is reasonable to suppose that they would be equally open on an occasion like the registration, requiring the presence of such numbers. If Joseph and Mary, arriving late, found the hoped-for guest-chamber already occupied, they might have no resort but the *khān*, where, in the animals' quarters, Jesus was born. W. E.

HOST.—See next article and ARMY.

HOST OF HEAVEN.—The phrase 'host (or army) of heaven' occurs in the OT in two apparently different senses—referring to (1) stars and (2) angels.

1. The 'host of heaven' is mentioned as *the object of idolatrous worship*; it is frequently coupled with 'sun and moon,' the stars being obviously meant; where 'sun and moon' are not specifically mentioned, the phrase may nevertheless include them. The worship of the astral bodies in Palestine from long before the Israelite occupation is indicated in the place-names Bethshemesh and Jericho, in theophoric names of local Amorite chiefs mentioned in the Egyptian Execration Texts from *c* 1850 B.C., and possibly in fragments of mural frescoes from the end of the 3rd millennium at *Teleilât el-Ghassûl*, E. of the mouth of the Jordan. Dt 4^{9} speaks of this worship as a special temptation to Israel; it has been appointed or allotted 'to all the peoples,' *i.e.* the heathen, and is absolutely inconsistent with the worship of Yahweh; the penalty is stoning (17^{3}). The references to it suggest that it became prominent in Israel in the 7th cent. B.C., when Manasseh introduced it to the Temple (2 K 21^{5}); its abolition was part of Josiah's reform ($23^{4f, 12}$). The mention, in the last verse, of 'the altars which were on the roof of the upper chamber of Ahaz' suggests that the worship was, in fact, older than the reign of Manasseh, and had been practised by Ahaz; it was carried on on the roofs of houses (Jer 19^{13}, Zeph 1^{5}), so that 2 K 23^{12} may well refer to it. The 'sun-pillars' which Isaiah (17^{8}) mentions as characteristic of the idolatry of Ahaz' reign, are now known to be incense-altars, with nothing essentially to do with sun-worship. 2 K 17^{16}, which speaks of the worship of the host of heaven as prevalent in the Northern Kingdom, is a 'Deuteronomic' passage, which can hardly be pressed historically. Whilst, then, there are early traces of this type of nature-worship, the systematized worship of the 'host of heaven' belongs to the period of special Assyrian and Babylonian influence, as the names *Sakkuth* (AV 'the tabernacle,' RV Siccuth) and *Kaiwan* (AV, RV Chiun) in Am 5^{26} show, these being well known as names of the Assyrian god Ninib, manifest in the planet Saturn.

The phrase is used in other contexts of the stars as *the armies of Yahweh*, innumerable, ordered, and obedient (Gn 2^{1}, Ps 33^{6}, Is 34^{4} 45^{12}, Jer 33^{22}), Is 40^{26} coming very near to personification. In Dn 8^{10} the assault of 'the little horn' on the 'host of heaven' and the stars, together with the passage in Rev 12^{4}, clearly refers to a myth, where the dragon or serpent of Chaos menaces the celestials, the stars being regarded as animate warriors of Yahweh their captain. The reference in Jg 5^{20} to the stars in their courses fighting against Sisera may be an allusion to the same mythology, though we think it more likely that the allusion is to a rain-storm, the Râs Shamra texts referring to the stars as the source of rain. The parallelism in Job 38^{7} between 'the morning stars' and 'the sons of God,' alludes to a creation myth, and is elucidated by one of the Râs Shamra texts, which describes the procreation of the Morning and Evening Star by the senior god El. D. Nielsen in his study of South Arabian religion (much later attested than the religion of Israel) has familiarized us with a well-developed astral religion and with the conception of creation as procreation. In the OT passages, such personifications, whatever their origins, are merely poetic figures. A striking instance of the poetic use of pagan mythology is Is 14^{12ff}, where Babylon is compared to 'the Bright One, Son of the Dawn' who had aspired to exalt his throne 'above the stars of God,' but had fallen to lowest Hell. This is now elucidated by the Râs Shamra text which describes the discomfiture of the god Athtar, well known from other Semitic sources as the Venus-star, in his attempt to fill the throne of Baal. Rev $9^{1, 11}$ apparently makes use of the same myth; cf also Lk 10^{18}.

2. Passages such as these lead to the consideration of others where 'host of heaven'=angels. The chief is 1 K 22^{19} (Micaiah's vision); cf Ps 103^{21}, Lk 2^{13}. Though this actual phrase is not often used, the attendant ministers of Yahweh are often spoken of as an organized army (Gn 32^{2}, Jos 5^{14}, 2 K 6^{17}, Job 25^{3}). Cf in this connexion the title 'Lord of hosts (Sabaoth),' which, though it may have been originally used of Yahweh as leader of the armies of Israel, admittedly came to be used of him as ruler of the celestial hosts (see LORD OF HOSTS). There are passages where the phrase 'host of heaven' is ambiguous, and may refer either to stars or angels (Dn 4^{35}, Neh 9^{6}, Ps 148^{2} [where it connects angels and sun, moon, and stars]).

3. Regarding the *connexion between the two uses of the phrase*, it has been supposed by some to be merely verbal, stars and angels being independently compared to an army; it has also been suggested that the stars were 'the visible image' of the host of angels. But a study of the passages cited above will probably lead to a conclusion that the connexion is closer. The idolaters evidently regard the stars as animate; the poets of Israel seem to do so too. This being so, the assimilation of the stars to the angels is natural. The question is as to the extent to which the Hebrew poets used the mythological matter figuratively. Wis 13^{2} protests against any idea that the heavenly bodies are animate, and it has been suggested that Ezekiel's avoidance of the phrase 'Lord of hosts' may be due to a fear of seeming to lend any countenance to star-worship. C. W. E.—**J. Gr.**

HOTHAM.—**1.** An Asherite, 1 Ch 7^{32}. Perhaps this name should be read in v.^{35} for **Helem** (see HELEM, **1**). **2.** Father of two of David's heroes, 1 Ch 11^{44} (AV **Hothan**).

HOTHAN, 1 Ch 11^{44} (AV).—See HOTHAM, **2.**

HOTHIR.—A son of Heman, 1 Ch $25^{4, 28}$.

HOUGH.—See HOCK.

HOUR.—See TIME.

HOUSE.—The history of human habitation in the Near East goes back to the Paleolithic (Old Stone) Age, at least 200,000 years ago (see G. Ernest Wright, *Biblical Archaeology*, 1957, 29–33). The excavations and discoveries, especially during the 1920's and 1930's, have introduced us to the pre-historic inhabitants who lived in caves near Bethlehem, in the Galilee region and near Mount Carmel (see D. A. E. Garrod and D. M. A. Bate, *The Stone Age of Mount Carmel*, 1937). Skeletal and other remains have also been discovered in Palestine that date from the Mesolithic and Neolithic periods. During the latter period, and at least as early as 6000 B.C., man had advanced sufficiently in such places as Jericho to build towns with well-constructed homes having plastered floors and being surrounded by a strong defensive wall of stone. Elsewhere in Palestine some communities still dwelt in the natural limestone caves in which Palestine abounds. In the historical period underground **Caves** (for descriptions and diagrams of some of the more celebrated, see Schumacher,

Across the Jordan, 135–270; Bliss and Macalister, *Excavations in Palestine*, 204–270; M. S. and J. L. Miller, *Encyclopedia of Bible Life*, 233 ff) were used by the Hebrews as places of refuge in times of national danger (Jg 6^{2}, 1 S 13^{6}) and religious persecution (2 Mac 6^{11}, He 11^{38}). But it is not with these, or with the **Tents** in which the patriarchs and their descendants lived before the conquest of Canaan, that this article has to deal, but with the houses of clay, stone, and wood which were built and occupied after that epoch.

1. Materials.—The most primitive of all the houses (apart from caves) for which man has been indebted to his own inventiveness is that formed of a few leafy boughs from the woods or forests, represented in Hebrew history to this day by the **booths** of OT (see BOOTH). Of more permanent habitations, the earliest of which traces have been discovered are probably the **mud huts,** whose foundations were found by Macalister in the lowest stratum at Gezer, and which were regarded by him as the work of the cave dwellers of the Late Stone Age (*PEFSt*, 1904, 110; cf various reports by John Garstang, and later by Kathleen Kenyon, on the Neolithic houses at Jericho). **Clay** in the form of bricks, either sun-dried or, less frequently, baked in a kiln (see BRICKS) and **Stone** (Lv $14^{40\text{ff}}$, Is 9^{10} etc.), have been in all ages the building materials of the successive inhabitants of Palestine. Even in districts where stone was available, as at the Moabite capital, Dibon, modern *Dhîbān*, the more tractable material was sometimes preferred. Houses built of crude brick are the 'houses of clay,' the unsubstantial nature of which is emphasized in Job $4^{19\text{f}}$, and whose walls a thief or another could easily dig through (Ezk 12^{5}, Mt $6^{19\text{f}}$).

Excavations at such places as Gezer, Taanach, Jericho, and Ezion-geber have shown that there is no uniformity in the size of bricks, which are both rectangular and square in shape, although bricks manufactured in one place at a particular time are quite similar. Bricks were found at Taanach measuring roughly 21 inches by $15\frac{3}{4}$ and $4\frac{3}{4}$ inches in thickness. At Gezer a common size was a square brick 15 inches in the side and 7 inches thick (*PEFSt*, 1902, 319). In the Neolithic levels at Jericho, cigar-shaped bricks were found that measured about 17 by 5 by 5 inches being marked by the two thumbs of the manufacturer forming a kind of herring-bone pattern (see *BASOR*, No. 127, 1952, p. 12) along the length of the brick. In the Mishnah the standard size is a square brick 9 inches each way (three hand-breadths), although the mention of a half-brick suggests a variation in size (*Erubin*, i. 3).

The stone used for house building varied from common field stones and larger, roughly shaped, quarry stones to the carefully dressed **wrought stone** (*gāzîth*, 1 K 5^{17} RV), 'dressed stones' RSV) or 'costly stones, hewn according to measure, sawed with saws, back and front,' (7^{9} RSV), such as was used by Solomon in his building operations. Similarly rubble, wrought stone, and brick are named in the Mishnah as the building materials of the time (*Baba bathra*, i. 1). For **mortar** clay was the usual material, although the use of **bitumen** (q.v.) was not unknown (Gn 11^{3} AV, 'slime,' RSV 'bitumen'). **Wood** as a building material was employed mainly for roofing, and to a less extent for internal decoration (see below). Mud brick walls were often built on stone foundations.

2. General plan of Hebrew houses.—Excavations at Gezer, and more recently at Jericho, Megiddo, Beth-shean, and Kiriath-sepher (*Tell beit Mirsim*) have shown that the simplest type of house in Palestine has scarcely altered in any respect for four thousand years. Indeed, its construction is so simple that the possibility of change is reduced to a minimum. In a Palestinian village of modern times the typical abode of the *fellah* consists of a walled enclosure, within which is a small court closed at the farther end by a house of a single room. This is frequently divided into two parts, one level with the entrance, assigned at night to the domestic animals, cows, ass, etc.; the other, about 18 inches higher, occupied by the owner and his family. A somewhat better class of house consisted of two or three rooms, of which the largest is the family living and sleeping room, a second was assigned to the cattle, while a third serves as general store-room (AV **closet**). Houses of both rectangular and rounded shapes have been found at Jericho, Megiddo, and Beth-shean, although a rectangular plan was most common. The arrangement of rooms and courtyards changed somewhat, probably under Mesopotamian, Hyksos, and Egyptian influence, during the course of the centuries (see Millar Burrows, *What Mean These Stones?*, 1941, 116–136), and in some periods and places houses of more than one storey were constructed. They were often crowded closely together as at Ezion-geber. It is thought that an impression of the external appearance of early houses can be secured by a study of the ossuaries (chests for the bones of the dead) that were fashioned in the shape of miniature houses.

The Canaanite houses, which the Hebrews inherited (Dt $6^{10\text{f}}$) and copied, are now known to have been arranged on similar lines (see the diagram of a typical Canaanite house in Gezer, restored by Macalister in his *Bible Sidelights from Gezer*, 1906, fig. 25, and Burrows, *op. cit.*, figs. 6, 8, 11). As in most Near Eastern domestic architecture, the rooms were built on one or more sides of an open **court** (2 S 17^{18}, Jer 32^{2} etc.). These rooms were of small dimensions, 12 to 15 feet square as a rule, with which may be compared the legal definition of 'large' and 'small' rooms in the late period of the Mishnah. The former was held to measure 15 feet by 12, with a height, following the model of the Temple (1 K $6^{2\text{ff}}$), equal to half the sum of the length and breadth, namely $13\frac{1}{2}$ feet; a 'small' room measured 12 feet by 9, with a height of $10\frac{1}{2}$ feet (*Baba bathra*, vi. 4). Ruined houses excavated by modern archaeologists seldom have the upper sections of the walls and the roofs standing, so there is uncertainty concerning the appearance of the upper parts of the dwellings.

Should occasion arise, through the marriage of a son, or some other need, to enlarge the house, this was done by building one or more rooms on another side of the court. In the case of a 'man of wealth' (1 S 9^{1} RSV), the house would consist of two or even more courts, in which case the rooms about the 'inner court' (Est 4^{11}) were appropriated to the women of the family, although in such cases the dwellings might better be designated 'palaces' than 'houses.' The court, further, often contained a **cistern** to catch and retain the precious supply of water that fell in the rainy seasons (2 S 17^{18}, RSV 'well'). For the question of an upper storey see **4.**

3. Foundation and dedication rites.—In building a house, the first step was to dig out the space required for the foundation (cf Mt $7^{24\text{ff}}$), although, as archaeology has demonstrated, simple houses were often built by levelling off the debris of a previous occupation and placing the stone or brick on the surface. After this came the ceremony of the laying of the **foundation stone,** the 'precious cornerstone, of a sure foundation' Is 28^{16} (cf CORNER-STONE). 'The day of the foundation' (2 Ch 8^{16}), as we learn from the poetic figure of Job $38^{6\text{ff}}$, was, as it is at the present day, one of great rejoicing (cf Ezr 3^{11}). The festivities at the beginning of a domestic dwelling were doubtless less impressive than those which accompanied the building of a palace or temple.

With the exception of a passage to be cited presently, the OT is silent regarding a foundation rite on which some light has been cast by excavations in modern Palestine. It is now probable that the Canaanites, and the Hebrews after them, did, on occasion, consecrate the foundation of a new building by a **human sacrifice.** The precise details of the rite are still uncertain, but there is some evidence to show that, down even to 'the latter half of the Hebrew monarchy' (*PEFSt*, 1903, 224), it was a frequent practice to bury infants, whether alive, after previous sacrifice, or when deceased from natural causes is still doubtful, in large jars 'generally under the ends of walls,—that is, at the corners of houses or chambers or just under the door jambs' (*ibid.* 306). At Megiddo the first excavators found the skeleton of a girl of about fifteen years, who had probably been built alive into the foundation of a fortress; at Taanach was found one of about ten years of age; and skeletons of adults and children have also been discovered in or near houses at Jericho, *Teleilât el-Ghassûl*, Byblos (Gebal), and other sites. Later excavators at Megiddo and other Palestinian sites also discovered infant burials in jars but held that these were not cases of infant sacrifice (see C. C. McCown, *The Ladder of Progress in Palestine*, 1943, 59, 176).

An interesting development of the rite of **foundation sacrifice** can be traced from the 15th cent. B.C. onwards. With the jar containing the body of the victim there were at first deposited other jars containing jugs, bowls, and a lamp, perhaps also food, as in ordinary burials. Gradually, it would seem, lamps and bowls came to be buried alone, as substitutes and symbols of the human victim, most frequently a lamp within a bowl, with another bowl as covering. Full details of this curious rite cannot be given here, but no other theory so plausible has yet been suggested to explain these 'lamp and bowl deposits' (see Macalister's reports in *PEFSt*, from 1903—especially pp. 306 ff with illustrations—onwards, also his *Bible Sidelights*, 165 ff; Vincent, *Canaan*, 50 f, 192, 198 ff). The only reference to a possible foundation sacrifice in OT is the case of Hiel the Bethelite, who rebuilt Jericho and 'laid its foundation at the cost of Abiram his first-born, and set up its gates at the cost of his youngest son Segub' (1 K 16[34] RSV). Although this may refer to foundation sacrifices, it is also possible that some accident befell the sons of Hiel which was attributed to the power of the curse of Joshua (Jos 6[26]).

A rite of formal **dedication** of a private house is attested by Dt 20[5], although the references in Hebrew literature to the actual ceremony are confined to sacred and public buildings (Lv 8[10ff], 1 K 8[1ff, 10ff], Ezr 6[16f], Neh 3[1] 12[27], 1 Mac 4[52ff]). It is not improbable that some of the human victims above alluded to may have been offered in connexion with the dedication or restoration of important buildings (cf 1 K 16[34] above). In the light of Gn 22[13] which reports Abraham's sacrifice of a ram instead of his son Isaac, and in view of the fact that the death of Hiel's sons may be open to different interpretations, it is probable that the Hebrews at an early date rejected the practice of human sacrifice and employed other ways of dedicating their homes and public buildings.

Judging from the ideas and practice of the Bedouin when a new tent or 'house of hair' is set up, we might seek the explanation of the rite of foundation sacrifice—a practice which obtains among many races widely separated in space and time—in the desire to propitiate the spirit whose abode is supposed to be disturbed by the new foundation (cf Trumbull, *Threshold Covenant*, 46 ff); it may also involve the wish to secure the spirit of the victim as the tutelary genius of the new building. An ancient custom still survives in the sacrifice of a sheep or other animal, which some would consider indispensable to the safe occupation of a new house in Moslem lands, and even to the successful inauguration of a public work, such as a railway or electric lighting installation. In the words of an Arab sheikh: 'Every house must have its death—man, woman, child, or animal' (Curtiss, *Primitive Semitic Religion To-day*). However, the OT descriptions of dedicatory rites suggest that the elements of thanksgiving to the Lord and community rejoicing came to have a prominent place.

4. Details of construction, walls, and floor.—The **walls** of Canaanite and Hebrew houses were for the most part, as we have seen, of crude brick or stone. At *Tell el-Ḥesī* (first incorrectly identified as Lachish), for example, the excavators found at one period house walls of 'dark-brown clay with little straw'; at another, walls of 'reddish-yellow clay, full of straw' (Bliss, *A Mound of Many Cities*, 44). At Gezer Macalister found a wall that was 'remarkable for being built in alternate courses of red and white bricks, the red course being four inches in height, the white five inches' (*PEFSt*, 1903, 216). At *Teleilât el-Ghassûl*, many mud-brick walls from before 3400 B.C., covered with fresco paintings in several colours were found by the excavators (see W. F. Albright, *The Archaeology of Palestine*, 1954, 66 ff). As a rule, however, house walls were unpainted; the Gezer house walls consisted 'of common field stones, among which dressed stones—even at corners and door posts—are of the rarest possible occurrence. The joints are wide and irregular, and filled with mud packed in the widest places with smaller stones' (*ibid.* 215). The explanation of this simple architecture is that in early times each family built its own house, expert **builders** (Ps 118[22]) or **masons** (see ARTS AND CRAFTS, **3**) being employed only on royal residences, city walls, and other buildings of importance. Hence squared and dressed stones are mentioned in OT only in connexion with such works (1 K 5[17], 7[9]) and the houses of the wealthy (Am 5[11], Is 9[10]). In the Gezer houses of the post-exilic period, however, 'the stones are well dressed and squared, often as well shaped as a modern brick' (*PEFSt*, 1904, 124, with photograph, 125). Between these two extremes are found walls of rubble, and quarry stones of various sizes, roughly trimmed with a hammer. Mud was used as **mortar**; it was not until Roman times that a more substantial bonding material was used. In the Early Iron period (1200–900 B.C.), Israelite houses were not as well constructed as they had been in the previous period, evidence that the newcomers had to learn a new art (see Burrows, *op. cit.* 124). Improvement in house construction continued until the Roman period when very substantial homes were erected. In early Israelite times when trees were more common than they are now in the region, some houses were built of wood (cf 2 Sam 7[2]).

In many houses the thickness of the outside walls varied from 18 to 24 inches; that of partition walls, on the other hand, did not exceed 9 to 12 inches. In NT times the thickness varied somewhat with the materials employed (see *Baba bathra*, i. 1). It is probable that the **corner stone** mentioned in Ps 118[22] and NT passages (see CORNER) has reference to the foundation stone at the corner of two walls, not to a stone in the topmost course of masonry.

The inside walls of stone houses received a '**plaster**' (RSV) of clay (Lv 14[41ff], AV 'dust,' RV 'mortar'), or, in the better houses, of lime or gypsum (Dn 5[5], 'plaster' RSV). The 'untempered mortar' of Ezk 13[11], 22[28] was some sort of **whitewash** applied to the outside walls, as is attested for NT times (Mt 23[27], Ac 23[3], 'you whitewashed wall!'). In the houses of the wealthy, as in the Temple, it was customary to line the walls with cypress (2 Ch 3[5], EV 'fir'), cedar, and other valuable woods (1 K 6[15, 18] 7[7]). The 'cieled houses' of AV and RV (Jer 22[14], Hag 1[4] etc.) are houses panelled with wood in this way (see CEILED). The acme of elegance was represented by cedar panels inlaid with ivory (see SAMARIA), such as earned for Ahab's pleasure palace the name of 'the ivory house' (1 K 22[39]), and incurred the denunciation of Amos (Am 3[15]). We also hear of the panelled ceilings of the successive Temples (1 K 6[15], 2 Mac 1[16], RSV).

The **floors** of the houses were in all periods made of hard beaten clay, the permanence of which to this day has proved to the excavators a precious indication of the successive occupation of the buried cities of Palestine. As early as the Neolithic period at Jericho excellent plastered floors were constructed. Public buildings have been found paved with slabs of stone. The better sort of private houses were no doubt, like the Temple (1 K 6[15]), floored with cypress and other woods which were subject to decay or plundering long before the appearance of archaeologists.

The presence of vaults or **cellars**, in the larger houses

at least, is shown by Lk 11[33] RSV. The excavations also show that when a wholly or partly ruined town was rebuilt, the houses of the older stratum were frequently retained as underground storerooms of the new houses on the higher level. The reference in 1 Ch 27[27f] to wine and oil ' cellars ' (RSV) is to ' stores ' of these commodities and does not indicate whether the places of storage were underground or simply in storerooms in the palace.

5. The roof.—The ancient houses of Canaan, like their modern representatives, had flat **roofs,** supported by stout wooden **beams** laid from wall to wall. Across these were laid smaller **rafters** (Ca 1[17]), then brushwood, reeds, and the like, above which was a layer of earth several inches thick, while on the top of all came a thick plaster of clay or of clay and lime. It was such a roofing (AV **tiling,** RSV **tiles,** Lk 5[19]) that the friends of the paralytic ' broke up ' in order to lower him into the room below (Mk 2[4]). The wood for the roof-beams was furnished mostly by the common sycamore, cypress (Ca 1[17]), and cedar (1 K 6[9]) being reserved for the homes of the wealthy. Hence the point of Isaiah's contrast between the humble houses of crude brick, roofed with sycamore and the stately edifices of hewn stone roofed with cedar (Is 9[10]). Although most houses had flat roofs, some were gabled, and others were approached by outside stairs (see Burrows, *op. cit.* 116, 130 ; K. Galling, *Biblisches Reallexikon,* 1937, 266–274), and doubtless consisted of two or three storeys.

It was, and is, difficult to keep a flat roof watertight in the rainy season, as Pr 27[15] shows. At *Tell beit Mirsim* and other excavated sites, **stone rollers** were found that doubtless were used to roll the roofs after they were repaired prior to the approach of the rainy seasons. In several houses at Gezer a primitive drain of jars was found for carrying the water from the leaking roof (Ec 10[18] RV) through the floor to the foundations beneath (*PEFSt,* 1904, 14, with illustration). In the Mishnah there is mention of at least two kinds of spout or **gutter** (2 S 5[8] AV, but the sense here is doubtful and may have reference to ' water shaft,' RSV) for conveying the rain water from the roof to the cistern. Evidence has accumulated in recent years showing that even in the smallest houses it was usual to have the beams of the roof supported by a row of wooden posts, generally three in number, resting on stone bases, ' from 1 foot 6 inches to 2 feet in diameter ' (*PEFSt,* 1904, 115, with photograph). The same method was adopted for the roofs of large public buildings (see Bliss, *A Mound of Many Cities,* 91 f, with plan) ; Macalister has ingeniously explained Samson's feat at the temple of Dagon, by supposing that he slid two of the massive wooden pillars (Jg 16[29f]) supporting the portico from their stone supports, thus causing its collapse (*Bible Sidelights,* 136 ff with illustration).

The roof was required by law to be surrounded by a **battlement,** or rather a **parapet,** as a protection against accident (Dt 22[8]). Access to the roof was apparently obtained, as at the present day, by an **outside stair** leading from the court. In 1 K 6[8] the AV mentions **winding stairs** as a part of the Temple ; RSV has ' stairs ' in view of the fact that winding stairs are unknown for the period of Solomon ; some sort of inner stair is required by the reference to the secret trap-door in 2 Mac 1[16], and seems to be implied in 1 K 6[8]. The roof or **housetop** was put to many uses, domestic (Jos 2[6]) and other. It was used, in particular, for recreation (2 S 11[2]) and for sleeping (1 S 9[25f]), also for prayer and meditation (Ac 10[9]), lamentation (Is 15[3], Jer 48[38]), and even for idolatrous worship (Jer 19[13], Zeph 1[5]). For these and other purposes a tent (2 S 16[22]) or a booth (Neh 8[16]) might be provided, or a permanent **roof-chamber** might be erected. Such were the ' roof chambers with walls ' (2 K 4[10], RSV) erected for Elisha, the ' summer **parlour** ' (Jg 3[20], literally as RSV, ' cool roof chamber ') of Eglon, and the ' **loft** ' (RSV ' upper chamber ') of 1 K 17[19].

Otherwise the houses of Palestine were, as a rule, of one storey. Exceptions were confined to the houses of the great, and to crowded cities like Jerusalem and Samaria. Ahaziah's upper chamber in the latter city (2 K 1[2]) may well have been a room in the second storey of the royal palace, where was evidently the lattice or window from which Jezebel was thrown (9[33]). The same may be said of the ' upper room ' in which the Last Supper was held (Mk 14[15] ; cf Ac 1[13]). It was a Greek city, however, in which Eutychus fell from a window in the ' **third story** ' (Ac 20[9] RSV).

6. The door and its parts.—The door consisted of four distinct parts : the **door** proper, the **threshold,** the **lintel** (Ex 12[7] RSV), and the two **doorposts.** The first of these was of wood, and was hung upon projecting pivots of wood, the **hinges** of Pr 26[14], which turned in corresponding sockets in the threshold and lintel respectively. Like the Egyptians and Babylonians, the Hebrews probably cased the pivots and sockets of heavy doors with bronze ; those of the Temple doors were sheathed in gold (1 K 7[50]). In the Hauran, doors of a single slab of stone with stone pivots are still found *in situ.* Many stone door sockets from houses of Biblical times have been found (see G. A. Barton, *Archaeology and the Bible,* 1933, 171 f). **Folding doors** are mentioned only in connexion with the Temple (1 K 6[34]).

The **threshold** (Jg 19[27], 1 K 14[17] etc.) or sill must have been invariably of stone. Among the Hebrews, as among so many other peoples of antiquity, a special sanctity attached to the threshold (see Trumbull, *The Threshold Covenant, passim*). The **doorposts** or jambs were square posts of wood (1 K 7[5], Ezk 41[21]) or of stone. The command of Dt 6[9], 11[20] gave rise to the practice, still observed in many Jewish houses, of enclosing a piece of parchment containing the words of Dt 6[4–9] 11[13–21] in a small case of metal or wood, which is nailed to the doorpost, hence its modern name *mezûzāh* (' doorpost ').

Doors were locked (Jg 3[23f]) by an arrangement similar to that still in use in Palestine (see the illustration in Hastings' *DB* ii. 836). This consists of a short upright piece of wood, fastened on the inside of the door, through which a square wooden **bolt** (Ca 5[5], Neh 3[3] RSV, for AV **lock**) passes at right angles into a socket in the jamb of the door. When the bolt is shot by the hand, three to six small iron pins drop from the upright into holes in the bolt, which is hollow at this part. The latter cannot now be drawn back without the proper **key.** This is a flat piece of wood—straight or bent as the case may be —into the upper surface of which pins have been fixed corresponding exactly in number and position to the holes in the bolt. The person wishing to enter the house puts ' his hand to the latch ' (Ca 5[4] RSV), and inserts the key into the hollow part of the bolt in such a way that the pins of the key will displace those in the holes of the bolt, which is then easily withdrawn from the socket and the door is open.

In the larger houses it was customary to have a man (Mk 13[34]) or a woman (2 S 4[6] RSV, Jn 18[17]) to act as a **doorkeeper** or **porter.** In the palaces of royalty this was a military duty (1 K 14[27]) and an office of distinction (Est 2[21] 6[2]).

7. Lighting and heating.—The ancient Hebrew houses must have been very imperfectly lighted. Indeed, it is almost certain that, in the poorer houses at least, the only light available was admitted through the doorway (cf Sir 42[11] [Hebrew text], ' Let there be no casement (lattice) where thy daughter dwells '). In any case, such windows as did exist were placed high up in the walls, at least six feet from the ground, according to the Mishnah. We have no certain monumental evidence as to the size and construction of the **windows** of Hebrew houses (but see for a probable stone window-frame, 20 inches high, Bliss and Macalister, *Excavs. in Palest.* 143 and pl. 73). They may, however, safely be assumed to have been much smaller than those to which we are accustomed, although the commonest variety, the *ḥallôn,* was large enough to allow a man to pass through going out (Jos 2[15], 1 S 19[12]) or in (Jl 2[9]). Another variety ('*ᵃrubbāh*) was evidently smaller, since it is used also to designate the holes of a dovecot (Is 60^{8} RSV 'windows'). These and other terms are rendered in our versions by 'window,' **lattice,** and **casement** (Pr 7^{6} AV, window and casement, RSV, window and lattice). None of these, of course, was filled with glass. Like the windows of Egyptian houses, they were doubtless closed with wood or lattice-work, which could be opened when necessary (2 K 13^{17}). An obscure expression in 1 K 6^{4} is rendered 'windows of narrow lights' (AV), 'windows of fixed lattice-work' (RV), 'windows with recessed frames' (RSV). The Hebrew is uncertain but may have reference to windows designed for defensive purposes with a large opening on the inside narrowing to a small slit on the outside through which arrows could be shot by the defender but not by the attacker. During the hours of darkness, light was supplied in the houses by the small oil lamp which was kept continually burning (see LAMP).

Most of the houses excavated show a depression of varying dimensions in the floor, either in the centre or in a corner, which, from the obvious traces of fire, was clearly the family **hearth** (Is 30^{14}). Wood was the chief **fuel** (see COAL), supplemented by withered vegetation of all sorts (Mt 6^{30}), and probably, as at the present day, by dried cow and camel dung (Ezk 4^{15}). The **oven** was a portable jar or terra cotta receptacle, which could be heated and in which bread was baked. The pungent smoke, which was trying to the eyes (Pr 10^{26}), escaped by the door or by the window; the **chimney** of Hos 13^{3} (AV) is properly 'window' (RSV) or 'casement' (*ᵃrubbāh*, see above). In the cold season the upper classes warmed their rooms by means of a **brazier** (Jer 36^{22f} RSV), or **fire-pan** (Zech 12^{6} RV, AV 'hearth of fire,' RSV 'blazing pot').

8. Furniture of the house.—In early times this included only a few simple items. Even at the present day the *fellahîn* sit and sleep mostly on **mats** and mattresses spread upon the floor. So the Hebrew will once have slept, wrapped in his *śimlāh* or cloak as 'his only covering' (Ex 22^{27}), while his household gear will have consisted mainly of the necessary utensils for the preparation of food, to which the following section is devoted. Under the monarchy, however, when a certain 'wealthy woman' of Shunem proposed to furnish 'a small roof chamber with walls' for Elisha, she named 'a bed, a table, a chair, and a lamp' (2 K 4^{10}, RSV), and we know otherwise that while the poor man slept on a simple mat of straw or rushes in the single room that served as living- and sleeping-room, the well-to-do had not only **beds** but **bedchambers** (2 S 4^{7}, 2 K 11^{2}, Jth 16^{19} etc.). The former consisted of a framework of wood, on which were laid **cushions** (Am 3^{12} RV, RSV noting uncertainty of Hebrew renders 'part' of a bed), and 'coverings, coloured spreads of Egyptian linen' (Pr 7^{16} RSV). We hear also of the 'bed's head' (Gn 47^{31}) or curved end, as figured by Wilkinson, *Anc. Egyp.* i, 416, fig. 191 (where note the steps for 'going up' to the bed; cf 1 K 1^{4}). Probably both because of its size and its iron framework, Hebrew tradition remembered the bedstead of iron which belonged to Og (Dt 3^{11}). **Bolsters** have rightly disappeared from RV and RSV, which render otherwise (see 1 S 19^{13} 26^{7} etc.); the **pillow** also from Gn 28$^{11, 18}$ and Mk 4^{38} (RSV here, 'cushion'), and where it is retained, as 1 S 19^{13}, the sense is doubtful. Reference may be made to the richly appointed bed of Holofernes, with its gorgeous **canopy** (Jth 10^{21} 13^{9} thought by some scholars to be a **mosquito curtain**).

The bed often served as a **couch** by day (Ezk 23^{41}, Am 3^{12} RSV—see also MEALS, 3), and it is sometimes uncertain which is the more suitable rendering. In Est 1^{6}, for example, RSV rightly substitutes 'couches' for 'beds' in the description of the magnificent divans of gold and silver in the palace of Ahasuerus (cf 7^{8}). The wealthy contemporaries of Amos had their beds and couches inlaid with ivory (Am 6^{4}), and furnished, according to RV, with 'silken cushions' (3^{12}, but see RSV).

As regards the stool above referred to, and the seats or chairs of the Hebrews generally, it must suffice to state that the seats of the contemporary Egyptians (for illustrations see Wilkinson, *op. cit.* i, 408 ff) and Assyrians were of two main varieties, namely, **stools** and **chairs.** The former were constructed either with a square frame or after the shape of our camp-stools; the latter with a straight or rounded back only, or with a back and arms. The Hebrew word for Elisha's stool is always applied elsewhere to the seats of persons of distinction and the thrones of kings; it must therefore have been a chair rather than a stool, although the latter is its usual meaning in the Mishnah (Krengel, *Das Hausgerät in der Mishnah*, 10 f—a mine of information regarding the furniture, native and foreign, to be found in Jewish houses in later times). **Footstools** were also in use (2 Ch 9^{18} and often, especially in metaphors).

The **tables** were chiefly of wood, and, like those of the Egyptians (Wilkinson, *op. cit.* i, 417 f with illustrations), were 'round, square, or oblong,' as the Mishnah attests. They were relatively much smaller and lower than ours (see, further, MEALS, **4**). A remarkable wooden table resembling a large, modern tray was found in one of the tombs near ancient Jericho (*Tell es-Sulṭân*).

The fourth article in Elisha's room was a **lampstand** (RSV) rather than a **candlestick** (AV), for which see LAMP. In OT the lampstand is named only in 2 K 4^{10} as being in a house; elsewhere it is part of the furnishing of a place of worship. It would extend this article beyond due limits to discuss even a selection from the many other articles of furniture, apart from those reserved for the closing section, which are named in Biblical and post-Biblical literature, or which have been brought to light in surprising abundance by recent excavations. Mention can be made only of articles of toilet, such as the 'molten **mirror**' of Job 37^{18} (AV **looking-glass,** actually a polished metal mirror), the cosmetic palette (2 K 9^{30}, a stone dish for antimony or colouring with which to paint the face), pins and needles, of which many specimens in bone, bronze, and silver have been found; of the distaff, spindle, and loom (see SPINNING AND WEAVING), for the manufacture of the family garments, and the chest for holding them, and finally, of the children's cradle (Krengel, *op. cit.* 26), and their toys of clay and bone.

9. Utensils connected with food.—Conspicuous among the 'earthen vessels' (2 S 17^{28}) of every household was the waterjar or **pitcher** (*kadh*)—the **barrel** of 1 K 18^{33} (AV), **jar** (RSV)—in which water was carried from the village well (Gn 24^{15}, Mk 14^{13}, and often). From this smaller jar, carried on head or shoulder, the water was emptied into the larger **waterpots** of Jn 2^{6}. Large jars were also required for the household provisions of wheat and barley—one variety in NT times was large enough to hold a man; equally large storage jars from the Early Bronze Age have been found. Other such jars held the store of olives and other fruits. The Dead Sea Scrolls were found in jars that were covered with ceramic lids (see *BASOR*, No. 125, 1952, 5–7); the kiln in which they were probably fired has been excavated at Qumrân in the vicinity of the caves. The **cruse** was a smaller jar with one or two handles, used for carrying water on a journey (1 S 26^{11f}, 1 K 19^{6}, 'cruse,' AV, 'jar,' RSV), also for holding oil (1 K 17^{12}, 'cruse,' AV, RSV). The potter's earthen **flask** (Jer 9$^{1, 10}$, RSV, 'earthen bottle,' AV) was a water decanter, the Hebrew name of which may have been derived from the gurgling sound made by the water when poured out. Pilgrim flasks, a kind of canteen, have also been found. (See, further, POTTERY, and the elaborate studies, with illustrations, of the thousands of 'potter's vessels' which the excavations have brought to light, as published in the various reports, and also Bliss and Macalister, *Excavations in Palestine*, 1898–1900, pp. 71–141, with plates 20–55; Vincent, *Canaan d'après l'exploration récente*, 1907, pp. 296–360, with the illustrations there and throughout the book; G. E. Wright, *The Pottery of Palestine from the Earliest Times to the end of the Early Bronze Age*, 1938.)

The **bucket** of Nu 24[7], Is 40[15] was a water-skin probably adapted, as at the present day, for drawing water by having two pieces of wood inserted crosswise at the mouth. The main use of skins among the Hebrews, however, was to hold the wine and other fermented liquors. The misleading rendering **bottle** of AV is retained by RSV only in Ps 33[7] 56[8] where the Hebrew is uncertain but might better be translated 'flask' or 'jar.' Elsewhere, 'bottles' of AV properly become **'wineskins'** in RSV as can be judged by context (Jos 9[4, 13], Mt 9[17]). For another use of skins see MILK. 'After the water-skins,' says Doughty, 'a pair of **millstones** is the most necessary husbandry in an Arabian household,' and so it was among the Hebrews, as may be seen in the article MILL.

No house was complete without a supply of **baskets** of various sizes and shapes for the bread (Ex 29[23]) and the fruit (Dt 26[2]), and even in early times for the serving of meat (Jg 6[19]). Among the 'vessels of wood' of Lv 15[12] was the indispensable wooden bowl, which served as a **kneading bowl** (Ex 12[34] RSV, **'kneading-trough'** AV), and various other **bowls,** such as the 'lordly bowl' of the nomad Jael (Jg 5[25]) and the bowl of Gideon (6[38]), although the bowls were mostly of earthenware (see BOWL).

As regards the actual preparation of food, apart from the **oven** (for which see BREAD), our attention is drawn chiefly to the various members of the pot family, so to say. Four of these are named together in 1 S 2[14], the *kiyyôr*, the *dûdh*, the *ḳallahath*, and the *pārûr*, rendered respectively the **pan**, the **kettle**, the **cauldron**, and the **pot.** Elsewhere these terms are rendered with small attempt at consistency; while a fifth, the most frequently named of all, the *sîr*, is the **fleshpot** of Ex 16[3], the 'great pot' of 2 K 4[38], and the 'pot' or 'cauldron' of Jer 1[13]. In what respect these differed it is impossible to say. The *sîr* was evidently of large size and made of bronze (1 K 7[45]), while the *pārûr* was small and of earthenware, hence ben-Sirach's question: 'What fellowship hath the (earthen) pot with the (bronze) cauldron?' (Sir 13[2], Hebrew text, RSV: 'How can the clay pot associate with the iron kettle?'). The *kiyyôr*, again, was wide and shallow, rather than narrow and deep. Numerous illustrations of cooking-pots from OT times may be seen in the works above referred to. See also James L. Kelso, *The Ceramic Vocabulary of the Old Testament*, *BASOR*, Sup. St. Nos. 5 and 6, 1948, 1–48. The only cooking utensils known to be of iron are the **griddle** (Lv 2[5] RSV, 'pan' AV, 'baking-pan' RV), probably a shallow iron plate (see Ezk 4[3]), and the **frying-pan** (Lv 2[7]). A **knife,** originally of flint (Jos 5[2]) and later of bronze, was required for cutting up the meat to be cooked (Gn 22[6, 10], Jg 19[29]), and a **fork** for lifting it from the pot (1 S 2[13], 'a fleshhook of three teeth' AV; 'a three-pronged fork' RSV). See FLESHHOOK.

In the collection of pottery figured in Bliss and Macalister's work, and in other publications of pottery from recent excavations in Palestine, one must seek the counterparts of the various dishes, mostly wide, deep bowls, in which we read of food being served, such as the **'dish'** from which the sluggard is too lazy to withdraw his hand (Pr 19[24] RSV), and the plates of Nu 7[13] (RSV, 'chargers' AV), although here they are of silver (see, further, MEALS, **5**). Excavators have found an almost endless variety of **cups,** some for drawing the 'cup of cold water' from the large water-jars, others for wine—**flagons,** jugs, and juglets. The material of all these will have ascended from the coarsest earthenware to bronze (Lv 6[28]), and from bronze to silver (Nu 7[13], Jth 12[1]), and gold (1 K 10[21], Est 1[7], the latter 'goblets' RSV), according to the rank and wealth of their owners, and the purposes for which they were designed. Mention should be made of the exquisite egg-shell, painted bowls of ceramic ware produced by the Nabataeans in the Roman period at Petra, Dibon, and elsewhere.

10. Objects of personal adornment.—In addition to the above, houses are often found by the excavators to contain objects of personal adornment such as sea shells, bracelets, finger rings, bead necklaces, earrings, armlets, and seals (Nu 31[50]). Wearing apparel has long since disappeared, but some impression of its appearance can be gained by a study of its representation in early Near Eastern art. See especially James B. Pritchard, *ANEP*, 1954, 1–70. A. R. S. K.—**W. L. R.**

HOZAI.—A personal name in RV of 2 Ch 33[19], where AV, RVm, and RSV have 'the Seers,' following LXX. AVm has **Hosai** and RSVm Hozai. A person of this name is not known otherwise.

HUKKOK.—A place near Tabor on the west of Naphtali, Jos 19[34]. It may be the present village *Yāqûq* near the edge of the plateau to the NW. of the Sea of Galilee.

HUKOK.—See HELKATH.

HUL.—The eponym of an Aramaean tribe, Gn 10[23] 1 Ch 1[17]; its location is quite uncertain.

HULDAH (?'weasel').—'The prophetess, wife of Shallum, keeper of the wardrobe,' living in a part of Jerusalem called the *Mishneh* (RV, RSV 'second quarter'; AV 'the college'), whose advice Josiah sought, by a deputation of his chief ministers, on the alarming discovery of the 'book of the law' in the Temple, in 621 B.C. (2 K 22[14ff], 2 Ch 34[22ff]). Her response was threatening for the nation, in the strain of Jeremiah, while promising exemption to the pious king. Huldah ranks with Deborah and Hannah among the rare women-prophets of the OT. G. G. F.

HUMILITY.—To the modern ear, the term 'humility' is apt to suggest self-effacement, the depreciation of oneself. This connotation has more in common with the thought of ancient Greece and Rome than with the Bible. The pagan world, despite its vaunted humanism, regarded the very conditions of finite existence as a stigma. From Homer to Marcus Aurelius, it was haunted by the refrain, 'Better never to have been born.' Humility therefore consisted in the acknowledgment of the wretchedness of the human condition. When the Delphic Oracle enjoins, 'Know thyself,' it does not mean, as popular interpretation would have it, 'Engage in critical introspection'; it means, 'Understand your insignificance as a human being.' The person who foolishly imagines himself to be of any ultimate importance becomes, like the hero of tragic drama, the unwitting agent of his own downfall.

In the Bible, too, 'the pride of men shall be humbled' (Is 2[11]), but the sense is quite different. Metaphysically considered, man is, as the pagan confessed, mere dust of the ground (Gn 3[19], Is 40[6f]). On the Hebraic view, however, the value of a thing did not derive from its constituent elements, but from the will of God. A thing or person had value if it found favour in the eyes of the Lord. Whether or not human existence was a blessing or a curse depended entirely upon God's attitude towards the human race. St. John's answer to this question speaks for the entire Bible, from Genesis to Revelation: 'God so loved the world that he gave his only Son, that whoever believes in him should not perish, but have eternal life' (Jn 3[16]).

Thanks to the unaccountable fact of God's favourable disposition towards mankind, human existence has value without limit. In the classic OT expression, man was made in the image of God (Gn 1[26] 9[6]). This exaltation of the human status reaches its climax in the NT, which declares that the character of God Himself can be fully known only in a particular human life. Small wonder that Jew and Christian appeared to the educated pagan as anything but humble! To him, the prophetic exhortation to 'walk humbly with your God' (Mic 6[8]) would be a contradiction in terms. The idea of walking with God at all would seem presumptuous in the extreme.

Within the Biblical frame of reference, humility is not primarily an attitude towards oneself at all, but towards God and towards other persons. Briefly, it means the willingness to let God be God; that is, to acknowledge one's dependence upon His creative power ; to rejoice in gratitude for His blessings ; to adopt the ways of the Lord as one's own ; to accept in contrition the judgment of God when one falls short ; to trust His power and willingness to forgive and to redeem. The 'broken spirit' (Ps 51[17]) commended by the psalmist makes no claim upon God, but acknowledges Him alone as the final arbiter of good and evil. When Adam and Eve ate of the tree of knowledge of good and evil, they usurped this prerogative (Gn 2[17] 3[5]). From the Biblical point of view, the pagan devaluation of human life is not humble at all, but arrogant. It presumes to contradict God's declaration that His creation is 'very good' (Gn 1[31]).

In relations between persons, humility is again not primarily an attitude towards oneself, but towards others. By no means is it a synonym for selflessness (a word which does not occur in the Bible) or for a divinely sanctioned inferiority complex. Far in advance of Friedrich Nietzsche, the prophets knew that an attitude of 'lowlier than thou' is but a covert form of 'holier than thou.' Biblical humility entails the recognition of others as invited guests at the Lord's own banquet table. The result is a regard for the will, the purposes, the feelings of others for which the pagan had no rationale. Since, according to him, his fellow men were of so little consequence, he had no compunction about 'lording it over them' (Mt 20[25]) wherever possible. By contrast, when Christ 'humbled himself' (Ph 2[8]), He used His power, not to domineer, but to serve. There is no suggestion of an appeasing or grovelling mentality. Because Biblical humility is not negative but positive, it can lead a man to do what the pagan could only regard as folly : 'to lay down his life for his friends' (Jn 15[13]).

The early Christian apologist, alert to discover points of contact with his prospective converts, fancied the virtue of humility, celebrated alike in Biblical and pagan thought, ideally suited to his purpose. St Augustine, for example, argues that while all agree on the need for humility, Christianity enables men to achieve what the pagans can only preach. Overlooking, in his missionary zeal, the disparity between Biblical and pagan meanings of the same word, he himself tended to slip into the pagan usage. The best known illustration is his ascribing to citizens of the heavenly city a 'love of God to the *contempt of self*.' Considering the great weight of St Augustine's authority, it should hardly be surprising if subsequent thought occasionally reflected his position, and forgot, as a modern Biblical scholar has said, that the greatest sin of man is to forget that he is, by the grace of God, a prince. E. L. C.

HUMTAH.—A city of Judah, Jos 15[54]. The site is unknown.

HUNCHBACK.—See MEDICINE.

HUNDRED, THE TOWER OF THE.—A tower on the walls of Jerusalem, near the tower of **Hananel** (q.v.), between the Sheep Gate on the east and the Fish Gate on the west, Neh 3[1] 12[39] (AV **the tower of Meah,** RV **the tower of Hammeah**). These two towers were probably situated near the NE. corner of the city (cf Jer 31[38], Zec 14[10]). The origin of the name is obscure. It has been suggested that the tower was 100 cubits high, or that it was approached by 100 steps, or that it required a garrison of 100 men.

HUNTING is not conspicuous in the literature of the Hebrews that remains for us. It was probably carried on more as a necessity than as a sport. Nimrod, the patron of hunters who is described as 'a mighty hunter before the Lord,' was considered a son of Cush (Gn 10[8-9]). Esau, skilful in the **chase,** is depicted as somewhat uncouth and simple (Gn 25[27] etc.). Assyrian and Egyptian kings are represented on the monuments as hunting from their chariots, particularly hunting lions with bow and arrow ; and Josephus describes Herod as an excellent hunter (*BJ* I. xxi. 13 [429]). Wild animals and birds were appreciated as food (Lv 17[13], 1 S 26[20] etc.) ; in a country like Palestine, abounding in beasts and birds of prey, some proficiency in the huntsman's art was necessary in order to secure the safety of the community and the protection of the flocks. Among these 'evil beasts' lions and bears were the most dangerous (Gn 37[33], 1 K 13[24], 2 K 2[24], Pr 28[15] etc.). Deeds of prowess in the slaughter of such animals—by Samson in self-defence (Jg 14[6]), David the shepherd to rescue his charges (1 S 17[34]), and Benaiah, who 'slew a lion in a pit on a day when snow had fallen' (2 S 23[20])—gained for these men abiding fame.

Among the animals hunted for food were the gazelle, the hart, the roebuck, and the wild goat (Dt 12[15, 22] 14[5] etc.). The first three are mentioned specially as furnishing the table of Solomon (1 K 4[23]). The partridge was perhaps the bird chiefly hunted in ancient times, as it is at the present day (1 S 26[20]). Neither beast nor bird might be eaten unless the blood had been 'poured out' (Lv 17[13], Dt 12[16] etc.)—a law still observed by the Moslems.

Little information is given in Scripture as to the methods followed by the huntsmen. The hunting dog is not mentioned, but is sometimes represented on non-Israelite monuments. The following implements were in use : the bow and arrow (Gn 27[3] etc.), the club (Job 41[29]), nets (Job 19[6], Ps 9[15], Is 51[20] etc.), pits, in which there might be a net, dug and concealed to entrap the larger animals (Ps 9[15], Ezk 19[8] etc.), the sling (1 S 17[40]), and the snare of the fowler (Ps 64[5] 91[3] 124[7]). The tame partridge in a cage was used as a decoy (Sir 11[30]).

Hunting scenes occur with frequency on the monuments of Near Eastern nations ; see J. B. Pritchard, *ANEP*, Nos. 182–190. In addition to animals named above these sometimes represent wild bulls, wild asses, and rabbits as being hunted ; some of these may have been hunted in Palestine. Of special interest is a gold plate from Râs Shamra (Syria) depicting a scene in which a man (a king?) hunts bulls and gazelles with bow and arrow from a chariot, with the aid of dogs (*ibid.* No 183).

See also NETS, SNARES, etc. W. E.—**J. P. H.**

HUPHAM.—A Benjamite, Nu 26[39] ; elsewhere called **Huppim** (q.v.). The gentilic **Huphamites** is found in Nu 26[39].

HUPPAH.—A priest of the 13th course, 1 Ch 24[13].

HUPPIM.—The head of a Benjamite family, Gn 46[21], 1 Ch 7[12, 15] ; called **Hupham** (q.v.) in Nu 26[39].

HUR.—A name of possibly Egyptian origin. **1.** An attendant on Moses who with Aaron held up Moses' hands, in order that by the continual upholding of the sacred staff Israel might prevail over Amalek, Ex 17[10, 12]. With Aaron he was left in charge of the people when Moses ascended the mountain, 24[14]. **2.** A Judahite, the grandfather of Bezalel, Ex 31[2] 35[30] 38[22]. According to the Chronicler, he was descended from Perez, through Hezron and Caleb, 1 Ch 2[19f] 4[1]. Josephus says he married Miriam and is identical with **1** (*Ant.* III. ii. 4 [54], vi. 1 [105]). **3.** One of the kings of Midian slain after the sin at Peor, Nu 31[8] ; described as a 'leader' of Midian and a 'prince' of Sihon, Jos 13[21]. **4.** 1 K 4[8] (AV) ; see BEN-HUR. **5.** The father of Rephaiah, who was a ruler of half Jerusalem, and who helped to repair the walls, Neh 3[9]. LXX omits the name Hur.

HURAI.—See HIDDAI.

HURAM.—**1.** A Benjamite, 1 Ch 8[5]. **2, 3.** See HIRAM, **1.** and **2.**

HURAM-ABI.—An artificer who helped in the erection of the Temple, 2 Ch 2[13] 4[16] (AV, RV 'Huram my [or his] father'). He is to be identified with Hiram, **2.**

HURI.—A Gadite, 1 Ch 5[14].

HURRIANS.—See HORITES.

HUSBAND.—See FAMILY.

HUSBANDMAN, HUSBANDRY.—In AV the former is, in most cases, synonymous with a 'tiller,' which RV and RSV have substituted for it in Zec 13[5]—in modern English, a farmer. The first farmer mentioned in OT, therefore, is not Noah, the 'husbandman' (Gn 9[20]), but Cain, the 'tiller of the ground' (4[2]).

RSV nowhere uses 'husbandman.' In Jn 15[1], however, this has the more limited sense of vinedresser (so RSV): 'I am the true vine and my Father is the vinedresser' (AV and RV 'husbandman'). So, too, in the parable of the Vineyard (Mt 21[33ff]; RSV 'tenants').

'Husbandry,' in the same way, is tillage, farming. Thus of king Uzziah it is said that 'he loved husbandry' (literally 'the land' [RSV 'the soil'] in the modern sense, 2 Ch 26[10]), that is, as the context shows, he loved and fostered agriculture, including viticulture. In 1 Co 3[9] 'husbandry' is used by metonymy of the land tilled (RSV 'field'; cf RVm). A. R. S. K.

HUSHAH.—Son of Ezer the son of Hur (see Hur, **2**), and therefore of the tribe of Judah, 1 Ch 4[4].

HUSHAI.—An Archite (2 S 15[32] 17[5, 14]), *i.e.* a native of 'the territory of the Archites' (Jos 16[2]) to the W. of Bethel. He is further described as 'David's friend' (2 S 15[37]), while in 16[16] the two titles are united. At the rebellion of Absalom he was induced by David to act as if he favoured the cause of the king's son. By so doing he was enabled both to defeat the plans of Ahithophel and to keep David informed (by means of Ahimaaz and Jonathan, the sons of Zadok and Abiathar the priests) of the progress of events in Jerusalem, 2 S 16[16]–17[23]. He is probably to be identified with the father of Baana, one of Solomon's twelve commissariat officers, 1 K 4[16].

HUSHAM.—A king of Edom, Gn 36[34f], 1 Ch 1[45f].

HUSHATHITE (probably = an inhabitant of Hushah). —This description is applied to **Sibbecai** (q.v.), one of David's thirty heroes, 2 S 21[18] 23[27], 1 Ch 11[29] 20[4] 27[11].

HUSHIM.—**1.** The eponym of a Danite family, Gn 46[23]; called **Shuham** in Nu 26[42]. **2.** A Benjamite, 1 Ch 7[12]. **3.** The wife of Shaharaim the Benjamite, 1 Ch 8[8, 11].

HUSKS.—See Pods.

HUZ, Gn 22[21] (AV).—See Uz, **2.**

HUZZAB.—A word occurring in Nah 2[7] (AV, RV). Gesenius derived it from a verb *ṣābhabh*, and read 'the palace is dissolved and *made to flow down*,' Many recent authorities regard it as from *nāṣabh*, and translated 'it is decreed.' RSV renders 'its mistress' and takes it to refer to the Assyrian queen.

HYACINTH.—See Jewels and Precious Stones (*sub* **Jacinth**).

HYDASPES.—A river mentioned in Jth 1[6] as on the Medo-Babylonian frontier. The name is probably the result of a confusion with the well-known Hydaspes in India (now the *Jalam*). In view of the fictitious character of the Book of Judith, speculation as to the identity of this river is likely to remain fruitless. However there may be a suggestion in the fact that the Syriac version reads **Ulai** (q.v.). W. M. N.

HYENA.—The hyena (Arabic *ḍabʿ*) is a very common Palestine animal, concerning which the *fellahīn* have countless tales. It is both hated and dreaded; it consumes dead bodies, and will even dig up corpses in the cemeteries; such rifling of graves has been known to take place on the Mount of Olives. It is nocturnal in its habits; in the day-time it hides in solitary caves, to which the *fellahīn* often follow it and attack it by various curious devices. In the gathering dusk and at night the hungry hyena frequently becomes very bold and will follow with relentless persistence a solitary pedestrian, who, if he cannot reach safety, will surely be killed. In spite of its habits it is eaten at times by the Bedouin. In OT it figures in The Valley of Zeboim (q.v.) = The Valley of Hyenas, and some find it in Jer 12[9] (see Speckled Bird), where a word from the same root as Zeboim, and cognate with Arabic *ḍabʿ*, is found. RSV renders a different word, which means 'howlers,' by 'hyenas' in Is 13[22] 34[14] (AV 'wild beasts,' RV 'wolves'), where some would render 'jackals.'
E. W. G. M.—**H. H. R.**

HYKSOS.—The early 18th cent. B.C. witnessed a series of ethnic migrations which led to the settlement of the Hittites in Asia Minor, the Hurrians (OT Horites) in Mitanni on the upper Euphrates, and somewhat later the Kassites (see Cossaeans) in Mesopotamia. The effect of these movements was to dislodge the native populations. A mixed horde of peoples from the N. and E., known as the Hyksos, consisting of Semites, Hurrians, and others, took advantage of the period of anarchy which followed the 12th Dynasty to invade and settle in the E. Delta of Egypt *c* 1720 B.C. Possessing a marked military superiority, they introduced into Egypt the horse and chariot, new types of bronze weapons and body armour, the composite bow, and extensive town fortifications.

They established their capital at Avaris (later Tanis, OT Zoan), where the cult of their Semitic god Baal was identified with that of the Egyptian Seth (Sutakh). In the late 17th cent. they occupied Palestine-Syria, and built towns in the hill-country. The Hyksos domination of Egypt coincided with the period of the Hebrew patriarchs, who probably made their way into Egypt during this time. Josephus mistakenly identifies the Hyksos with the Hebrews. He quotes Manetho's account (*c. Ap.* I. 14 [75–83]), who derives the name *hyksōs* (or *hykūssōs*) from a supposed Egyptian *ḥīqū-shōse*, 'shepherd kings.' The term actually represents the Egyptian expression (occurring as early as 12th Dynasty) *ḥīqū-ḫāsowe*, 'rulers of foreign lands,' used to designate the Asiatic tribal chieftains. The Hyksos were finally expelled *c* 1570 B.C. by Ahmose who established the 18th Dynasty. R. J. W.

HYMENAEUS.—A false teacher condemned in 1 Ti 1[19f] and 2 Ti 2[17f], associated with Alexander in the former and with Philetus in the latter passage. There is no reason to doubt that the same Hymenaeus is meant. His error consisted in the assertion that the resurrection had already taken place, *i.e.*, in a gnostic dualistic denial of a future bodily resurrection. A similar heresy is referred to in the *Acts of Paul and Thecla* 14, Justin *Apology* I. xxvi. 4 (of Menander), and Irenaeus, *Adv. Haer.* I. xxiii. 5. In 1 Ti 1[20] the offender is said to have been delivered by Paul to Satan (cf 1 Co 5[5]). In 1 Corinthians the death of the culprit is envisaged, here clearly not. The aim is reclamation after a chastisement probably thought of as illness. The sequence of the two passages has been invoked as an argument for the priority of 2 Timothy; very uncertainly. J. L.

HYMN (in NT; for OT, see Music, Poetry, Psalms). —The Greek word signified specifically a poem in praise of a god or hero, but it is used, less exactly, also for a religious poem, even one of petition. The use of hymns in the early Christian Church was to be anticipated from the very nature of worship, and from the close connexion between the worship of the disciples and that of the Jews of that and earlier centuries. It is proved by the numerous incidental references in the NT (cf Ac 16[25], 1 Co 14[26], Eph 5[19], Ja 5[13], and the passages cited below), and by the famous letter of Pliny to Trajan describing the customs of the Christians. We lack, however, any collection of hymns comparable to the Psalms of the OT. Doubtless the Psalms were largely used, in the tradition of the Synagogue, but giving them a Christian meaning. The mode of singing was that of the *psalmus responsorius*, a type of recitative chant with a constant refrain by the congregation to the verses of the cantor. In addition new songs would be written to express the intense emotions of the disciples, and even their spontaneous utterances in the gatherings of early Christians would almost inevitably take a rhythmical form, modelled more or less closely upon the Psalms. In some localities, perhaps, Greek hymns served as the models. St. Paul insists (1 Co 14[15], Col 3[16]) that the singing be with the spirit and the understanding, an intelligent expression of real religious feeling. These passages specify 'psalms, hymns, and spiritual songs.' While at first it seems as if three classes of composition are here distinguished, either as to source or character, it is probably not the case, especially as in Mt 26[30], Mk 14[26] the verb 'to hymn' is used of singing a psalm. Luke's Gospel contains several hymns, but does not mention their use by the disciples. They are the *Magnificat* (Lk 1[46-55]), the *Benedictus* (1[68-79]), the *Gloria in Excelsis* (2[14]), and the *Nunc Dimittis* (2[29-32]). Whether these were Jewish or Jewish-Christian in origin is disputed. The free introduction of hymns of praise in the Apocalypse, in description of the worship of the new Jerusalem, points to their use by the early Church. The poetical and liturgical character of some other NT passages is asserted with more or less reason by different scholars (*e.g.* Eph 5[14], 1 Ti 1[17] 3[16] 6[16], 2 Ti 4[18]). The earliest Christian hymn-book we possess is the *Odes of Solomon*, written in Greek around A.D. 150. See Hastings' *DCG*, article 'Hymn,' *ERE*, vii, 5–12, and *Interpreter's Dictionary of the Bible*. O. H. G.—**C. C. Ri.**

HYPOCRITE.—This word occurs in the NT only in the Synoptic Gospels (sixteen times, of which thirteen are in Matthew); 'hypocrisy' is used once by each synoptist. In the Epistles (Gal 2[13], 1 Ti 4[2], 1 P 2[1]) the RSV prefers 'insincerity'. The hypocrisy of the Gospels is the 'appearing before men what one ought to be, but is not, before God.' At times it is a deliberately played part (*e.g.* Mt 6[2, 5, 16] 22[18] etc.), at others it is a deception of which the actor himself is unconscious (*e.g.* Mk 7[6], Lk 6[42] 12[56] etc.). Thus all who play the part of religion, whether consciously or unconsciously, without being religious, are hypocrites; and so fall under the sternest denunciation (Mt 23, where it cannot be supposed that *all* scribes and Pharisees were meant). This use of the word has led some to give it the wider interpretation of 'godlessness' in some passages (*e.g.* Mt 24[51]; cf Lk 12[46]); but as there may always be seen in the word the idea of a religious cloak over the godlessness, the ordinary sense should stand.

In the AV of OT (*e.g.* Job 8[13], Is 9[17]) 'hypocrite' is a mistranslation of the Hebrew word *ḥānēph*. It passed into the AV from the Latin, which followed the Greek Versions. In RV, RSV it is rendered 'godless,' 'profane.' C. T. P. G.—**F. C. G.**

HYRCANUS.—**1.** The son of Tobias, who had money deposited at Jerusalem, in the Temple treasury, at the time of the visit of Heliodorus (2 Mac 3[11]). The name seems to be a local appellative. Its use among the Jews is perhaps to be explained from the fact that Artaxerxes Ochus transported a number of Jews to Hyrcania. **2.** See MACCABEES, **5.**

HYSSOP is mentioned several times in the Bible. It was used for sprinkling blood (Ex 12[22]), and in the ritual of the cleansing of lepers (Lv 14[4], Nu 19[6]); it was an insignificant plant growing out of the wall (1 K 4[33]); it could afford a branch strong enough to support a wet sponge (Jn 19[29]). It is possible that all these references are not to a single species. Among many suggested plants the most probable is either a species of marjoram, *e.g. Origanum maru*, or the common caper-plant (*Capparis spinosa*), which may be seen growing out of crevices in walls all over Palestine. See CAPER-BERRY. E. W. G. M.

I

IADINUS, 1 Es 9[48] (RV).—See JAMIN, **3.**

IBEX, Dt 14[5] (RSV).—See PYGARG.

IBHAR.—One of David's sons, born at Jerusalem, 2 S 5[15], 1 Ch 3[6] 14[5].

IBIS.—Mentioned only in Lv 11[17] (RSV; AV and RV 'great owl') and Lv 11[19] (RVm; AV, RV, RSV 'heron'); see HERON, and OWL.

IBLEAM.—A town in Asher assigned to West Manasseh, Jos 17[11]. The Manassites were not able to drive out the Canaanites, Jg 1[27]. It was a Levitical city, 1 Ch 6[7]—where it is called **Bileam.** It is mentioned in 2 K 9[27] in connexion with the death of King Ahaziah, which took place close by. Zechariah, king of Israel, was assassinated here, 2 K 15[10] (RSV; AV, RV have 'before the people' for 'in Ibleam'). It is identified with modern *Tell Belʿameh*, between Samaria and Jezreel.

IBNEIAH.—A Benjamite, 1 Ch 9[8].

IBNIJAH.—A Benjamite, 1 Ch 9[8].

IBRI.—A Merarite Levite, 1 Ch 24[27].

IBSAM.—A descendant of Issachar, 1 Ch 7[2] (AV **Jibsam**).

IBZAN.—One of the minor judges, following Jephthah, Jg 12[8-10]. He came from Bethlehem, probably the Bethlehem in Zebulun (Jos 19[15]; see BETHLEHEM, **2**), 7 miles NW. of Nazareth. He had thirty sons and thirty daughters—an evidence of his social importance—and arranged their marriages. He judged Israel seven years, and was buried at Bethlehem. According to Jewish tradition, Ibzan was the same as Boaz.

ICHABOD.—Son of Phinehas and grandson of Eli, 1 S 4[21]. The name means 'inglorious,' but probably should be 'Y" is glory,' from an original *Jochebed.* If this guess be well founded, then the turn given to the story in 1 S 4[21] is due to a desire to mould it on the story of the birth of Benjamin in Gn 25[18].

ICONIUM, now called *Konia*, is an ancient city of continuous importance from early times to the present day. Situated at the western edge of the vast central plain of Asia Minor, and well watered, it has always been a busy place. It is surrounded by beautiful orchards, which cover the meanness of its modern buildings. About the beginning of the Christian era it was on the border of the two ethnic districts, Lycaonia and Phrygia. It was in reality the easternmost city of Phrygia, and the inhabitants considered themselves Phrygians, but ancient writers commonly speak of it as a city of Lycaonia (q.v.), the fate of which it generally shared. In the 3rd cent. B.C. it was ruled by the Seleucids, and about 164 B.C., probably, it passed under the power of the Galatae (Asiatic Celts). It was the property of the Pontic kings from about 130 B.C., was set free during the Mithridatic wars, and in 39 B.C. was given by Mark Antony to Polemon, king of Cilicia Tracheia. In 36 B.C. Antony gave it to Amyntas, who was at that time made king of Galatia (q.v.). On his death in 25 B.C. the whole of his kingdom became the Roman province of Galatia. Iconium could thus be spoken of as Lycaonian, Phrygian, or Galatic, according to the speaker's point of view. In the time of the Emperor Claudius, it, along with Derbe, received the honorary prefix Claudio-, becoming *Claudiconium*, but it was not till Hadrian's time (A.D. 117–138) that it became a Roman colony (q.v.). It was 18 miles distant from Lystra, and a direct route passed between them.

The gospel was brought to Iconium by Paul and Barnabas, who visited it twice on the first missionary journey (Ac 13[51] 14[21]). The presence of Jews there is confirmed by the evidence of inscriptions. According to the 'south Galatian hypothesis,' now most widely held, it was within 'the Phrygo-Galatic region' of Ac 16[6] and the 'Galatic region and Phrygia' of Ac 18[23]. It was therefore visited four times in all by St. Paul, who addressed it among other cities in his Epistle to the Galatians. During the absence of Paul it had been visited by Judaizers, who pretended that Paul was a mere messenger of the earlier Apostles, and contended that the Jewish ceremonial law was binding on the Christian converts. Paul's Epistle appears to have been successful, and the Galatians afterwards contributed to the collection for the poor Christians of Jerusalem. The alternative view (the 'north Galatian hypothesis') is that Iconium is not really included in the Acts narrative after 16^{2ff}, and that the words quoted above from Ac 16^{6} and 18^{23} refer to the territory of Galatia proper, which lay far north of Iconium, and that the Epistle to the Galatians, being addressed to that northern district, had no connexion with Iconium. In any case, the (province) Galatia which is addressed in 1 P 1^{2} will by that time (late 1st cent.) have included Iconium. The large number of Christian inscriptions which have been found there reveal the existence of a vigorous Christian life in the 3rd and following centuries.

A. So.—**E. G. K.**

IDALAH.—A town of Zebulun, Jos 19^{15}. It is possibly modern *Kh. el-Ḥawārah*, about a mile SW. of Bethlehem, **2** (q.v.).

IDBASH.—One of the sons of the father of Etam, 1 Ch 4^{3}.

IDDO.—A name which represents several different names in Hebrew. **1.** The chief at Casiphia, who provided Ezra with Levites and Nethinim, Ezr 8^{17}, 1 Es 8^{45f} (AV **Saddeus** and **Daddeus**, RV **Loddeus**). **2.** A son of Zechariah, captain of half the tribe of Manasseh in Gilead, 1 Ch 27^{21}; perhaps = **4.** **3.** One of those who had married foreign wives, Ezr 10^{43} (AV **Jadau**), 1 Es 9^{35} (AV **Edes**, RV **Edos**). **4.** Father of Abinadab, who was Solomon's officer in Mahanaim, 1 K 4^{14} (see **2**). **5.** A Gershonite Levite, 1 Ch 6^{21}; called **Adaiah** v.^{41}. **6.** A seer and prophet cited by the Chronicler as an authority for the reigns of Solomon (2 Ch 9^{29}), Rehoboam (2 Ch 12^{15}), and Abijah (2 Ch 13^{22}). **7.** Grandfather (Zec $1^{1,7}$) or father (Ezr 5^{1} 6^{14}, 1 Es 6^{1} [AV, RV **Addo**]) of the prophet Zechariah. **8.** One of the priestly clans that went up with Zerubbabel, Neh $12^{4,16}$.

IDOLATRY.—Two forms of idolatry may be distinguished in the Bible, according as idolatry is considered a breach of the first commandment or of the second. In the former case, it is the worship of other gods than the God of Israel; in the latter, it is the cultic use of material representations of Yahweh and *a fortiori* of any other god. In either case idolatry was a capital offence. Strictly speaking, the latter definition is the proper one (cf Gr. *eidōlolatreia*, 'the worship of *eidōla*, images'); but in practice the term is used more widely and the two senses cannot be completely dissociated. The idol or image was regarded as something in which the god's personality resided, so that it was charged with his power.

1. The worship of other gods.—The ancestors of the Israelites are said to have worshipped 'other gods' when they lived in Mesopotamia (Jos 24^{2}), but from the call of Abraham onwards the patriarchs worshipped one God—the God (or Shield) of Abraham, the God (or Fear) of Isaac, and the God (or Mighty One) of Jacob —whom they knew as El Shaddai, and who in Moses' time revealed Himself to the Israelites by His name Yahweh (Ex 6^{2f}). Their worship of Him did not carry with it the belief that other gods had no existence, but it did carry with it the belief that other gods were weak and negligible. Yahweh's triumph at the Exodus confirmed Israel's faith in Him (Ex 15^{1ff}) and was viewed as the execution of His judgment against all the gods of Egypt (Ex 12^{12}). Hence the decalogue, the constituent charter given to Israel on the morrow of the Exodus, opens with the words: 'I am Yahweh your God, who brought you out of the land of Egypt, out of the house of bondage: you shall have no other gods before me' (Ex 20^{2f}, Dt 5^{6f}).

But the Israelites, who had largely ceased to worship the God of their fathers during their Egyptian servitude (Ezk $23^{3,8,27}$), were constantly prone to pay homage to other gods, even in the wilderness and much more so after their settlement in Canaan. During their wilderness wanderings occurred the incident of the golden calf—which may, however, have been intended as a representation or rather pedestal of Yahweh, for when it was set up Aaron proclaimed 'a feast to Yahweh' (Ex 32^{5})—and their worship of the Baal of Peor in Moab (Nu 25^{1-5}).

After the settlement in Canaan there was a strong temptation to conform to the local fertility-cults, in which Baal, the fructifying rain-god, and his consorts (Asherah, Ashtoreth, or Anath according to the part of the country) played leading rôles. The desire to ensure rainfall and good crops inclined them to imitate the ritual of their Canaanite neighbours, which was calculated to promote these ends, rather than to follow the way of Yahweh who had gone before them as guide and defender in the wilderness. This did not necessarily mean a conscious renunciation of Yahweh-worship in favour of Baalism; sometimes Yahweh was simply baalized (and there is adequate evidence that the title *baʿal*, 'lord,' was given to him by such devout Yahwists as Saul and David, as the names of some of their sons, such as Eshbaal and Baaliada, indicate). But if Yahweh was thoroughly baalized so that He came to be regarded as a fertility-deity and little more, the practical effect was as complete an abandonment of essential Yahwism as if there had been deliberate apostasy from Him. This conformity to Canaanite worship loosened the covenant-bond that bound the tribes of Israel to Yahweh and to one another, and weakened them before their enemies: 'when new gods were chosen, then war was in the gates' (Jg 5^{8}). Not surprisingly, then, a return to covenant-loyalty was regularly attended by liberation and victory, as under Deborah (Jg 4, 5), Gideon (Jg 6–8), and Samuel; *e.g.* Samuel's command to the people to 'put away the foreign gods and the Ashtaroth' and return in heart to Yahweh resulted in their offering a successful resistance to the Philistines (1 S 7^{3ff}).

David's winning of national independence and extension of his power over foreign peoples brought prestige to the name of Yahweh as lord over all nations (cf Ps 18^{49} 47). Solomon's installation of private shrines for his heathen wives is reprobated (1 K 11^{1ff}) especially for the bad example that it showed; he himself, moreover, is said to have been influenced by his wives to pay some tokens of respect to their gods, while he remained essentially a Yahwist.

The greatest apostasy in the northern kingdom was the landslide in favour of Baal-worship which followed Ahab's marriage to Jezebel; Jezebel's devotion to the Tyrian god Melkart encouraged a revival of Canaanite Baal-worship, which no doubt had close similarities to the cult of Melkart. Even the triumph of Yahwism on Mount Carmel did not completely undo this apostasy; it had to be washed out in the bloodshed of Jehu's revolt.

The Assyrian domination of the 8th and 7th cents. B.C. involved the recognition of the Assyrian gods, in both the northern and southern kingdoms. In the southern kingdom Ahaz and Manasseh receive special condemnation because they introduced into Jerusalem the elaborate apparatus of Assyrian worship, as faithful vassals of the Great King; the religious reformations under Hezekiah and Josiah included the removal of this apparatus (a political as well as a religious act). One prominent feature of Assyrian worship was the cult of the planets, 'the host of heaven' (2 K 17^{16})—although astrolatry was nothing new in the 8th cent. B.C.; it had figured prominently in the religion of the earliest Semitic nomads. Among the planets the sun, Venus and Saturn receive special mention. Josiah abolished the horses and chariots dedicated to the sun-god (2 K 23^{11}); the women of Judah a generation afterwards remembered Josiah's reformation because it was then that they left off presenting incense, cakes, and libations to 'the queen of heaven,' *i.e.* Astarte or Venus (Jer 44^{19}; cf Jer 7^{18}, where the practice obtaining before Josiah's reformation is described). And over a century before Josiah's time

Amos assured the people of the northern kingdom that when they went into exile 'beyond Damascus' they would carry there with them the images of 'Sakkuth your king . . . Kaiwan your star-god,' *i.e.* Saturn (Am 5[26]).

Some of the idolatrous features of the religion of Judah before Josiah's reformation are mentioned in Zeph 1[4ff]—cf the denunciation of those 'who bow down and swear to Yahweh and yet swear by Milcom' (1[5]), Milcom being identified in 1 K 11[5] as the god of the Ammonites.

There was evidently a wholesale reaction after Josiah's death; to judge by Ezekiel's description of idolatrous practices in the Jerusalem Temple (Ezk 8[3ff]) the situation in the decade before the Babylonian exile was no better than it had been before Josiah's reformation. Tammuz-worship by the women and sun-worship by the men are among the 'abominations' which Ezekiel relates.

It is probably the relics of such 'unreformed' Jewish worship that are to be recognized in the Elephantine papyri of the 5th cent. B.C., where compound names like Anathyahu, Anathbethel, Ḥerembethel, and Ishumbethel reflect, verbally at least, an earlier syncretism of Yahwism with Canaanite worship, although by this time they may have denoted little more than hypostatizations of Yahweh.

Tammuz (a name of Sumerian origin) was identical with the Syrian Adonis, whose worship is probably implied in the 'gardens which you have chosen' (Is 1[29]) and the 'sacrificing in gardens' (Is 65[3]). Other forms of false worship are mentioned in the latter context (vv.[4, 11]) where condemnation is pronounced on those 'who sit in tombs, and spend the night in secret places, who eat swine's flesh, and broth of abominable things is in their vessels . . . who set a table for Fortune (Gad) and fill cups of mixed wine for Destiny (Meni).' Even after the Exile idolatry was slow in being completely extirpated, especially (we may suppose) among those who had remained in Palestine.

The later Jewish horror of idolatry in any form finds expression in the transmission of the Biblical text, where 'Baal' (particularly when it appears as an element in compound proper names) is frequently changed to *bōsheth* or *besheth* ('shame') and a word like *shiḳḳûṣ* or *tô'ēbhāh* ('abomination') is used in the sense of 'false god' or 'idol.' Sometimes the consonants of a false god's name are retained, but the vowel-points accompanying them indicate that one of these substitute-words is to be pronounced in its place, since the taking of a false god's name upon one's lips was felt to be a defilement (cf Ps 16[4]). Thus Molech and Ashtoreth represent Melech and Ashtart with the vowels of *bōsheth*; Siccuth and Chiun (Am 5[26]) represent Sakkuth and Kaiwan with the vowels of *shiḳḳûṣ*.

The best known instance of the use of *shiḳḳûṣ* to denote a false god is in Dn 11[31] 12[11] (cf 1 Mac 1[54], Mk 13[14]), where 'the abomination that makes desolate' (*shiḳḳûṣ meshōmēm, shiḳḳûṣ shōmēm*) is a derogatory pun on *Ba'al Shāmēm*, the Syrian deity identified with Olympian Zeus, whose altar was set up in the Jerusalem Temple by order of Antiochus IV. in 167 B.C. While the intention may have been syncretistic (Yahweh being assimilated to Olympian Zeus as *Ba'al Shāmēm* was), the new cult was repudiated as a sacrilege by all pious Jews, and the ill-conceived experiment was brought to an end after three years.

2. The worship of images.—In the OT no practical distinction is made between an idol and the god whom it represents. Whatever the character and purpose of the golden calf in the wilderness may have been, Moses confesses with horror that the people have made 'gods of gold' (Ex 32[31]). In later attacks on idolatry (*e.g.* Ps 115[4ff], Is 40[19f] 41[6f] 44[9ff]) the heathen gods have no existence apart from their images; they themselves are nonentities. When the images of Babylonian gods are loaded on to pack-animals to be carried off by the conqueror, it is Bel and Nebo themselves who are pictured as going into exile (Is 46[1f]).

The prohibition in the decalogue of the making and worshipping of any 'graven image' (Ex 20[4], Dt 5[8]) is paralleled by the ban on the making of 'molten gods' in Ex 34[17] (in an ancient ritual, possibly Kenite, code); cf the prohibition of 'gods of silver' and 'gods of gold' in Ex 20[23]. The aniconic principle is thus imposed from the earliest days of Israel's history as a people. It is perhaps significant that no representation of Yahweh has been found from any stage of Israel's history; the S. Palestinian coin (*c* 400 B.C.) in the British Museum formerly thought to bear his image as a 'solar Zeus' is now known to bear the superscription YHD (Judah), not YHW (Yahweh). In addition, representations of any male deity are conspicuous by their absence from Israelite territory. As for female deities, no plaques or figurines of Ashtoreth have been discovered in Early Israelite levels of Central Palestine, their absence from these levels contrasting remarkably with their frequency in corresponding deposits of the Late Bronze Age (16th–13th cents.) and Iron II (9th cent. onwards). It was different on the periphery of the Israelite area of settlement, where Yahwism was weaker and there was closer contact with the Canaanites.

The golden bull-calves which Jeroboam set up in the shrines of Dan and Bethel were probably intended as pedestals for Yahweh's invisible throne. In the Jerusalem Temple Yahweh sat 'enthroned upon the cherubim' (Ps 80[1]). The calves, however, were too closely associated with Canaanite fertility worship to be acceptable; the cherubim on the other hand, had no such association, being purely symbolical forms, representing the storm-winds on which Yahweh rode through the heavens (cf Ps 18[10]). The invisible throne of Yahweh which they supported becomes visible in Ezekiel's vision of the chariot-throne (Ezk 1[4ff]).

The *teraphim* which Rachel took from her father's house (Gn 31[19, 30ff]), and which were probably buried with other 'foreign gods' at Jacob's command under the oak at Shechem (Gn 35[2ff]), were evidently ancestral images conveying certain rights of inheritance to those who possessed them. Elsewhere the word appears as a general term for images (cf 1 S 19[13, 16]); in 1 S 15[23] it is translated 'idolatry.' In Hos 3[4] the *teraphim* are conjoined with the *ephod*. While the ephod is normally a priestly vestment, it appears occasionally to have been an image of some sort. Gideon's golden ephod (Jg 8[27]) was no doubt installed in the sanctuary at Ophrah in honour of Yahweh, but it apparently became an object of idolatrous devotion, so that 'it became a snare to Gideon and to his family.' Ephod, teraphim, and a graven or molten image, such as Micah made for his shrine (Jg 17[4f]), may have been popularly regarded as the proper furniture for a wayside sanctuary where travellers might consult the divine will.

Various forms of idol-worship are attested under the monarchy, *e.g.* the queen-mother Maacah's 'abominable image for Asherah' (1 K 15[13]). Sacred poles of Asherah and pillars (*maṣṣēbhôth*) of Baal are mentioned in both northern and southern kingdoms (1 K 16[33], 2 K 3[2] 10[26] 11[18] 17[10, 16] 18[4] 21[3] 23[4ff]). These were put down, along with the Assyrian cult-apparatus, by Hezekiah and Josiah. Special interest attaches to Nehushtan, the bronze serpent, which Hezekiah destroyed (2 K 18[4]); it had been worshipped with incense from time immemorial, and its identification with the bronze *śārāph* ('fiery serpent') which Moses had made (Nu 21[8f]) suggests some association with the *seraphim* of Isaiah's inaugural vision (Is 6[2]).

Ezekiel's vision of the idolatry in Jerusalem in the closing years of the southern monarchy includes references to the 'slab of jealousy' (the figured slab or orthostate depicting cultic and mythological scenes, which provoked Yahweh to jealousy) and to representations of reptiles and other animals (belonging possibly to a cult of Egyptian origin).

3. In NT.—Idolatry in NT is usually mentioned as a feature of paganism; *e.g.* Paul's indignation was stirred when he saw Athens 'full of idols' (Ac 17[16]). But even Christians may be tainted with idolatry if they have fellowship in idol banquets, although they themselves know that ' an idol has no real existence ' (1 Co 8[4] 10[14]). A subtler form of idolatry than bowing down to wood and stone is implied in the injunction ' Little children, keep yourselves from idols ' (1 Jn 5[21]); here the term covers all false and unworthy ideals which men may set before themselves, and by which their communion may be broken with Him who is ' the true God and eternal life ' (v.[20]). F. F. B.

IDUEL (1 Es 8[43]) = Ezr 8[16] **Ariel.** The form is due to confusion of Hebrew *d* and *r*.

IDUMAEA.—The Greek equivalent (in NT only in Mk 3[8]) of the name **Edom,** originally the territory E. of the Jordan-Arabah valley and S. of the land of Moab. This country was inhabited, when we first catch a glimpse of it, by a primitive race known as Horites, of whom little but the name is known. The apparent meaning of the name (' cave-dwellers ') and comparison with the remains of what seems to have been an analogous race discovered in excavations elsewhere, show that this race was at a low stage of civilization. They were partly destroyed, partly absorbed, by the Bedouin tribes who claimed descent through Esau from Abraham, and who were acknowledged by the Israelites as late as the date of the Deuteronomic codes as brethren (Dt 23[7]). They were governed by sheikhs and by a non-hereditary monarchy whose records belonged to a period anterior to the time of Saul (Gn 36[31-39], 1 Ch 1[43-54]). See Edom.

After the fall of Babylon the pressure of the desert Arabs forced the Edomites across the Jordan-Arabah valley, and the people and name were extended westward. In 1 Mac 5[65] we find Hebron included in Idumaea. Josephus, with whom Jerome agrees, makes Idumaea extend from Beit Jibrîn to Petra; Jerome assigns the great caves at the former place to the troglodyte Horites. The Herod family was by origin Idumaean in this extended sense. In the 2nd cent. A.D. the geographer Ptolemy restricts Idumaea to the cis-Jordanic area, and includes the original trans-Jordanic Edom in Arabia. See Maps 10, 15. R. A. S. M.—**F. C. G.**

IEDDIAS, 1 Es 9[26] (RV).—See Izziah.

IEZER.—The form of the name **Abiezer** (q.v.) found in Nu 26[30] (AV **Jeezer**). The patronymic **Iezerites** (AV **Jeezerites**) stands in the same verse.

IGAL.—**1.** The spy representing the tribe of Issachar, Nu 13[7]. **2.** One of David's heroes, the son of Nathan of Zobah, 2 S 23[36]. In the parallel list (1 Ch 11[38]) the name is given as ' **Joel,** the brother of Nathan.' **3.** Son of Shemaiah of the royal house of David, 1 Ch 3[22] (AV **Igeal**).

IGDALIAH.—A ' man of God,' father of Haman, whose name is mentioned in connexion with Jeremiah's interview with the Rechabites, Jer 35[4].

IGEAL, 1 Ch 3[22] (AV).—See Igal, **3.**

IGNORANCE.—It appears to be in accordance with natural justice that ignorance should be regarded as modifying moral responsibility, and this is fully recognized in the Scriptures. In the OT, indeed, the knowledge of God is often spoken of as equivalent to true religion (see Knowledge), and therefore ignorance is regarded as its opposite (1 S 2[12], Hos 4[1] 6[6]). But the Levitical law recognizes sins of ignorance as needing some expiation, but with a minor degree of guilt (Lv 4, Nu 15[22-32]). So ' **ignorances** ' are spoken of in 1 Es 8[75] (RSV ' mistakes '), To 3[3], Sir 23[2f] as partly involuntary (cf He 5[2] 9[7]). The whole of the OT, however, is the history of a process of gradual moral and spiritual enlightenment, so that actions which are regarded as pardonable, or even praiseworthy, at one period, become inexcusable in a more advanced state of knowledge. In the NT the difference between the ' times of ignorance ' and the light of Christianity is recognized in Ac 17[30] (cf 1 Ti 1[13], 1 P 1[14]), and ignorance is spoken of as modifying responsibility in Ac 3[17], 1 Co 2[8], Lk 23[34]. This last passage, especially, suggests that sin is pardonable because it contains an element of ignorance, while Mk 3[29] appears to contemplate the possibility of an absolutely wilful choice of evil with full knowledge of what it is, which will be unpardonable (cf 1 Jn 5[16]). Immoral and guilty ignorance is also spoken of in Ro 1[18ff], Eph 4[18]. For the question whether Christ in His human nature could be ignorant, see Kenosis, Knowledge. J. H. Ma.

IIM.—A city of Judah, Jos 15[29]; site unknown. For Iim, Nu 33[45] (AV), see Iye-Abarim.

IJE-ABARIM, Nu 21[11] 33[44] (AV).—See Iye-Abarim.

IJON.—A town in the north part of the mountains of Naphtali, noticed in 1 K 15[20], 2 Ch 16[4], as taken by Benhadad. It was also captured and depopulated by Tiglath-pileser, 2 K 15[29]. It is probably modern *Tell Dibbîn,* on the plateau *Merj 'Ayûn,* which preserves the name.

IKKESH.—The father of Ira, one of David's heroes, 2 S 23[26], 1 Ch 11[28] 27[9].

ILAI.—One of David's heroes, 1 Ch 11[29]; called **Zalmon,** perhaps the more correct form, in 2 S 23[28].

ILIADUN (1 Es 5[58]).—Perhaps to be identified with **Henadad** of Ezr 3[9]. AV has **Eliadun.**

ILLYRICUM.—The only Scripture mention is Ro 15[19], where St. Paul points to the fact that he had fully preached the gospel from the outer edge of Jerusalem, so to speak, round about (through various countries) as far as the border of Illyricum. These provinces in order are Syria, Cilicia, Galatia, Asia, and Macedonia, and a journey through them in succession describes a segment of a rough circle. The provinces Macedonia and Illyricum are coterminous, and the nearest city in Macedonia in which we know St. Paul to have preached is **Beroea** (Ac 17[10ff]). *Illyricum* is a Latin word, and denotes the Roman province which extended along the Adriatic from Italy and Pannonia on the north to the province Macedonia on the south. A province Illyria had been formed in 167 B.C., and during the succeeding two centuries all accessions of territory in that quarter were incorporated in that province. In A.D. 10 Augustus separated Pannonia from Illyricum, and gave the latter a settled constitution. The government of this important province was difficult, and was entrusted to an ex-consul with the title *legatus Augusti pro praetore.* The northern half was called Liburnia and the southern Dalmatia (q.v.). The latter term gradually came to indicate the whole province of Illyricum. A. So.—**E. G. K.**

IMAGE.—In theological usage the term ' image ' occurs in two connexions: (1) as defining the nature of man (' God created man in his own image,' Gn 1[27]), and (2) as describing the relation of Christ as Son to God the Father (' who is the image of the invisible God,' Col 1[15]). These two senses are not unconnected. Because man was created in God's image, it was not inappropriate for God to be pictured under ' the likeness as it were of a human form ' (Ezk 1[26]), or for the Son of God in due course to become incarnate as man (' it was fitting,' He 2[10]); and as man is recreated in the image of God, obscured and defaced through sin (Col 3[10]; cf Eph 4[24]), it is the image of Christ which he bears in his renewed state (1 Co 15[49], 2 Co 3[18]). These Biblical uses of the term ' image ' claim further consideration.

1. As regards *man,* the fundamental text is Gn 1[26f]. Here man is called into being, not, like the other creatures, by a simple fiat, but as the result of a solemn and deliberate act of counsel on the Creator's part: ' Let us make man in our image, after our likeness. . . . So God created man in his own image, in the image of God he created him, male and female he created them.' Attempts have been made from Irenaeus onward to distinguish between ' image ' (*ṣelem*) and ' likeness ' (*d^emûth*), but it is now generally accepted that no difference of meaning is intended. The two words combine to emphasize the idea of resemblance to God. In Gn 1[27] (cf 9[6]) the single word ' image ' expresses the total idea, and in 5[1] the single word ' likeness.' The expression occurs repeatedly in NT; cf 1 Co 11[7], Col 3[10] (' image,' Gr. *eikōn*); Ja 3[9] (' likeness,' Gr. *homoiōsis*). The terminology in Genesis is indeed peculiar to the 'Priestly' narrative, but the *idea* underlies the view of man in the Yahwistic sections as well, for only as made in God's image is man capable of knowledge of God, fellowship with Him, covenant relationship to Him, and character conformable to God's own. To 'be like God'—a sham likeness in place of the reality—was the serpent's allurement to Eve (Gn 3^5).

Ps 8 echoes Gn 1^{26ff} without actually using the term 'image.' Man's status as 'little less than God' (Ps 8^5) is due to his being made in the Divine image; he does not possess equality with God (contrast Ph 2^6, where Christ possesses this equality but does not exploit it for His self-aggrandisement). But since man was made in God's image, no other image of God is necessary or indeed permissible.

In what, then, did this Divine image, this likeness to God, consist? Not in physical form, nor yet in some fancied analogy between man, viewed as a tripartite being, as spirit, soul, and body (1 Th 5^{23}), and the Holy Trinity. Since it was man, and not the lower animals, that God made in His image, the image of God in man has to do with those features which distinguish man from the lower creation: his dignity as God's representative, ruling over the rest of animate nature and over the earth in general; his endowment with the power of responsible moral choice; his capacity for communion with God. A good part of what is nowadays called 'personality' goes to make up the Divine image in man. In addition, there is the insight which finds expression in Wis 2^{23}: 'God created man for incorruption, and made him in the image of his own eternity'—carried even farther by Augustine at the beginning of his *Confessions*: 'Thou hast made us for thyself, and our heart is restless till it rests in thee.'

In the idea of the image, too, lies the germ of sonship: man responds freely to God's love by offering God his love, service, and obedience. To this must be added, in the light of such passages as Eph 4^{24} and Col 3^{10}, the conception of actual moral conformity, in knowledge, righteousness, and holiness, as pertaining to the perfection of the image. Sin has not destroyed the essential elements of God's image in man, but it has shattered the image in a moral respect; and grace renews it in Christ.

2. The presentation of *Christ*, the Son, as the image (*eikōn*) of God (*e.g.* 2 Co 4^4), is bound up with the Christian doctrine of the Godhead, and finds expression in various ways in NT, notably in He 1^3, where the Son 'reflects the glory of God and bears the very stamp of His nature' (cf Wis 7^{26}, where wisdom 'is a reflection of eternal light, a spotless mirror of the working of God'). This refers to a supra-temporal and essential relation between the Son and the Father; God, in His eternal being, reflects Himself, and beholds His infinite perfection and glory mirrored, in the Son (Jn 1^1 17^5). Accordingly the Son, as the Father's eternal Word or self-expression, becomes in incarnation His perfect revelation to the world (Jn $1^{14, 18}$ 14^9). And therefore those who bear Christ's image bear the image of God; being renewed in God's image, they are conformed to the image of His Son (Ro 8^{29}). J. O.—**F. F. B.**

IMAGES.—1. Representations of the deity or of the manifest power of the Holy are known from most ancient times among the peoples of the ancient Near East. Such representations were of various kinds: stone pillars (Heb. *maṣṣēbhôth*), wooden poles, plain or decorated (Heb. *'ᵃshērîm*); clay figures representing the mother goddess (perhaps the Heb. *tᵉrāphîm*); small bronze images of the deity in human form; and larger images in animal or human form venerated at the great temples. In OT, approximately twenty terms are used to refer to images, the most important of which are *pesel* ('graven image'), *ṣelem* ('image,' 'statue'), *massēkhāh* ('molten image') and *dᵉmûth* ('likeness').

2. In OT, sharp strictures against the making of any image of God appear in quite early texts, perhaps from time of Moses (Ex 20^4, Dt 27^{15} etc.; see DECALOGUE). In the centuries-long struggle with Canaanite worship and cultic practices, the Israelites often yielded to the natural pressures to represent the deity in human, animal, or other forms. Israelite cult objects such as the Ark, the ephod, the golden calf, and the serpent Nehushtan were no doubt popularly conceived by some Israelites to be actual representations of Yahweh (Nu 10^{35f} 21^{8f}, 1 S 21^9, 1 K 12^{28} etc.). Such cult objects are not properly understood to be images of the deity, however; Ark and golden calf were generally conceived to be the seat and the pedestal, respectively, upon which the invisible Yahweh was enthroned. The ephod refers to a variety of garments used in cultic practices, some of which were heavily ornamented with precious metals (Jg 8^{27}, 1 S 21^9; see Ex 28^{1-39}). The serpent Nehushtan was a cult object used in apotropaic medicine. The household gods (Heb. *tᵉrāphîm*), perhaps originally connected with ancestor worship, appear to have become identified with the representations of the mother goddess, employed by women as aids to fertility and child-bearing (Gn 31^{19}, 1 S 19^{13}).

3. The prohibitions in Israel against all forms of idolatry and image-making are one of the major distinguishing marks of OT religion. Yahweh could not be controlled nor His power manipulated by man. Even the anthropomorphic descriptions of the deity in OT are generally quite restrained (Ex 24^{9f} 33^{17-33}, 1 K 19^{11-13}, Is 6, Ezk 1). The imageless Yahweh cult of Israel conveyed the meaning of the deity's dealings with His people through representations of Yahweh's action in history: past, present, and future.

4. Nonetheless, image-making flourished at various times in Israelite history. The materials used in idol manufacture were clay (Wis 15^{13}, Bel ^{7}), wood (Is 44^{15}, Wis 13^{13}), silver and gold (Hos 8^4, Dn 3^1). They might be painted (Wis 13^{14} 15^4), dressed up (Jer 10^9, Ezk 16^{18}), crowned and armed (Bar $6^{9, 15}$). They were kept in shrines (Jg 17^5, Wis 13^{15} etc.), and secured from tumbling down (Is 41^7, Jer 10^4). Refreshments (Is 65^{11}, Jer 7^{18}) and kisses (Hos 13^2, 1 K 19^{18}) were offered to them, as well as sacrifice and incense. They figured in processions (cf ancient sculptures, and Is 46^7, Jer 10^5). See also IDOLATRY. H. F. B. C.—**W. J. Ha.**

IMAGINATION.—In the EV imagine always means 'contrive,' and imagination 'contrivance.' In the case of imagination a bad intention is always present (except in Is 26^3 AVm), as in Ro 1^{21} 'they . . . became vain in their imaginations' (RV 'reasonings'; RSV 'thinking'). 2 Co 10^5 'casting down imaginations and every high thing that exalteth itself' (RVm 'reasonings'; RSV 'arguments'). The Greek words have in these passages the same evil intent as the AV word. Coverdale translates Is 55^7 'Let the ungodly man forsake his wayes, and the unrightuous his ymaginacions, and turne agayne unto the Lorde.'

IMALCUE, 1 Mac 11^{39} (RV).—See IMALKUE.

IMALKUE.—An Arab prince to whom Alexander Balas entrusted his youthful son Antiochus, 1 Mac 11^{39} (AV **Simalcue,** RV **Imalcue**). After the death of Alexander, in 145 B.C., Imalkue reluctantly gave up the boy to Tryphon, who placed him on the throne of Syria as Antiochus VI. in opposition to Demetrius II.

IMLA, 2 Ch 18^{7f} (AV, RV).—See IMLAH.

IMLAH.—The father of Micaiah, a prophet of Y″ in the days of Ahab, 1 K 22^{8f}, 2 Ch 18^{7f} (AV, RV **Imla**).

IMMANUEL.—The symbolic name of the child whose birth is foretold by Isaiah (Is 7^{14} 8^8). The spelling **Emmanuel** (AV, RVm, RSV, Mt 1^{23}) is based on LXX. The meaning of the name is 'God is with us' and its interpretation involves discussion of Is 7, especially vv.$^{10-17}$.

1. *Grammatical difficulties.*—A literal translation of Is 7^{14} is 'Therefore the Lord himself will give you a sign. See, the young woman is pregnant and will bear a son, and will call his name Immanuel.' An equally correct translation could be 'will be pregnant' (cf RSV) but the close similarity to Gn 16^{11} favours the present tense. For 'young woman' RSVm has 'virgin,' probably in deference to tradition. For the meaning of the word (*'almāh*) see VIRGIN; it is not the ordinary word for virgin (*b^ethûlāh*), nor one which would be used if virginity was to be stressed. The definite article ('*the* young woman') may either indicate that the prophet had a particular woman in mind, or be generic, *i.e.* referring to a class, in which case the translation could be 'young women' in the sense of *any* young woman (RSV 'a young woman'). It has been argued that in 8^{8} the translation should be '. . . . of the land, for God is with us' (cf v.^{10}), but this would be nonsense in the context.

2. *Historical situation.*—In 734 B.C. Syria and Ephraim attacked Judah with the object of forcing her into an alliance against Assyria. Ahaz and his court were panic-striken (7^{2}) and thought of appealing to Assyria for protection. This would have been to surrender both political and religious (cf 2 K 16^{10-18}) independence. Isaiah offered Ahaz any miraculous sign he might ask from Yahweh as the assurance of Divine protection. The king declined to ask and cloaked his refusal in words of apparent piety (v.^{12}, cf Dt 6^{16}). Whereupon Isaiah, addressing the whole court, stated that 'the Lord himself' (some MSS, including Dead Sea Scroll *a*, have 'Yahweh') would give them a sign. The sign was to be the birth of Immanuel.

3. *Was the sign a promise or a threat*? This question is difficult to answer. Isaiah's pronouncement may have been enigmatical even to those to whom it was addressed. It may be that Is 7 was early expanded in attempts to interpret the sign, though there is little in it that is not in the vein of Isaiah, whose early pronouncements were mostly of impending judgment. Proposals to delete this or that verse have no text-critical support and have been dictated by the opinions of individual exegetes on how the question, promise or threat, should be answered. The only safe course is to take the text as it stands, except that 'the king of Assyria' (v.^{17}) hangs loosely where it stands and is widely regarded as a later addition. It is clear that Isaiah was indignant with Ahaz (v.^{13}). 'Therefore' (v.^{14}) may preface a threat (cf 1^{24} $5^{13,\,24}$) but it could introduce a promise (cf Jer 16^{14f}), and there is no exception to the rule that annunciations in the Bible are promises of good (Gn 16^{11} 17^{19}, Jg 13^{3}, Mt 1^{21}, Lk $1^{13f,\,31f}$). 'Curds and honey' (v.^{15}) were luxury foods (Gn 18^{8}, Dt 32^{14}, Jg 5^{25}, 2 S 17^{29}, Job 20^{17}; extra-biblical parallels could be quoted), though they do seem to indicate the breakdown of agricultural and a return to a pastoral economy (v.^{22}). Syria and Ephraim are to be deserted (v.^{16} 8^{4}), and, if 'the king of Assyria' is omitted, the rest of v.^{17} seems to anticipate prosperity unequalled since the disruption of Solomon's kingdom (cf Mic 5^{3}). Finally, the refrain 'Yahweh of hosts is with us' occurs in a psalm in which exultation triumphs over desolation (Ps $46^{7,\,11}$). We conclude that the sign was a promise but that Judah would suffer severe privation before what was good in it could be fully apparent (cf 8^{8}).

4. *Who is the child*?—(*a*) The traditional Christian interpretation is that the Immanuel pronouncement was nothing other or more than a prediction of the virgin-birth of Christ, and this seemed supported by the LXX rendering of *'almāh* by *parthenos*. But how could Ahaz be expected to act differently on a sign which was not to be fulfilled until seven centuries later? Besides, it is clearly stated that by the time the child is weaned, Syria and Ephraim will be deserted (vv.^{15f}). (That vv.^{15f} refer to the weaning of the child is apparent from 2 S 19^{35}, where RSV rightly renders Hebrew 'know between good and evil' by 'discern what is pleasant [*sc.* to eat] and what is not.') And Damascus was destroyed in 733–732 B.C. (*b*) The Jewish view was that the *'almāh* was the wife of Ahaz, and the child Hezekiah. The Christian retort was that a comparison of 2 K 16^{2} and 2 K 18^{2} showed that Hezekiah must already have been nine years old. The Jews do not seem to have observed that the same passages would make Ahaz only eleven years older than his son, and that the chronology must be wrong somewhere. (*c*) Instead, they identified the *'almāh* with either the wife of Isaiah or another wife of Ahaz. But Isaiah calls his wife 'the prophetess' (8^{3}) and it is unlikely that a woman who had already borne a child (Shear-jashub) would still be called *'almāh*. (*d*) Since the end of the 18th cent., Christians have largely abandoned the traditional interpretation. Many have taken the article with *'almāh* generically (see **1** above) and the import of the sign to be that by the time the children of women already pregnant have been born, the situation would be so improved that mothers would be calling their boys Immanuel. This makes Isaiah's solemn pronouncement little more than a note of time: 'before children shortly to be born grow up, certain things will have happened,' as if with the births of the Immanuel children all will be well; and that is not the overall impression which the pericope conveys. (*e*) Another version of this interpretation explains the *'almāh* as Zion personified, and 'Immanuel' as the coming generation. But the word for Zion and countries in such personifications is always *b^ethûlāh*, not *'almāh* (see VIRGIN). (*f*) There have never been wanting scholars who have insisted that the passage must have a messianic reference of the kind implied in 2 S 7^{12-16}. There must, it is said, to judge from Is 7^{14} (*the 'almāh*) and Mic 5^{3}, have been an expectation of the birth of a 'wonder-child' to the house of David, one who would restore the tarnished fortunes of the dynasty. This would relate Is 7^{14} once more to 9^{1-7} and 11^{1-9}. Babylonian and Egyptian parallels to such a wonder-child have been quoted. Whether we are impressed by them depends upon whether we are, or are not, convinced on general grounds that Israelite religion was influenced by Babylon and Egypt. Parallels from Greek religion are not very cogent, except insofar as they may indicate that certain ideas are common to nature religions everywhere; and Israelite religion is largely a protest against nature- (=Baal) worship. On the other hand, there is evidence enough in the OT that the Hebrews were influenced by their Canaanite neighbours and predecessors, especially in what concerned the kingship. And two passages from Râs Shamra texts have set the Immanuel problem in a new light. One is 'See! the *ģlmt* (=Heb. *'almāh*) will bear a son.' In the other, Danel cries 'for a son is born to me' (cf Is 9^{6}). In both contexts the parents are of divine or at least royal dignity. Further, at Râs Shamra *ģlmt* and *btlt* (Heb. *b^ethûlāh*) had a cultic rather than physiological signification. Of course, Is 7^{14} and 9^{6} cannot be direct quotations from tablets which had been buried for many centuries, but they do seem to indicate a survival of deeply-rooted expectations of an exceptional birth. While it is not certain, it is not impossible that the wife of king Ahaz, whose kingship had a sacral quality (see KING), could share something of his endowment, and be called 'the *'almāh*.' In that case the expected child might be Hezekiah, who, notwithstanding his faults, was a better king than his father (2 K 18^{1-8}). The chronological difficulties are not decisive against this view: see (*b*) above. Not that Hezekiah, any more than Jesus (Mt 1^{23f}), was actually named Immanuel. The name is symbolical and its meaning 'God is with us' (RSVm), not 'God-with-us.' How Isaiah could have known what, at the time, even Ahaz himself did not know, that the queen was pregnant and that her child would be a boy, it is perhaps vain to inquire; but there is every reason to believe that prophets were, on occasion, gifted with abnormal intuitive insight.

5. *Application to the Virgin-birth.*—The tentative conclusion that the proximate fulfilment of the Immanuel sign was the birth of Hezekiah does not rule out altogether the traditional interpretation of a longer range fulfilment in Christ, of which even Isaiah himself might have been quite unconscious. Christianity is the fulfilment not only of the higher religion of the OT but also of the twilight gropings of pagan nature religions.

When LXX translated *'almāh* by *parthenos* it was neither in ignorance nor with intent to deceive, but, as it now appears, because the translators were aware, whether fully or only vaguely, of the age-old tradition of a wonder-child. In that case they may have wished to make it clear that the *'almāh* was not any ordinary Hebrew wife and mother. In Mt 1[23] *parthenos* has come to mean *virgo intacta*. But there is no evidence that the LXX interpretation of Is 7[14] was sufficiently prominent or definite to give rise to the belief in the virgin-birth of Jesus. The text was quoted to illustrate the fact or the belief in the fact; the fact was not imagined to meet the requirements of the LXX reading. (Lk 1[26-38] can hardly be read otherwise than as pointing to a virgin-birth and in it Is 7[14] is not referred to.) Neither Is 7[14] nor the LXX translation of it is *proof* of the Virgin-birth. Whether the nativity stories in Matthew and Luke are historical or not is therefore a question which must be decided on its merits; it lies outside the scope of the present article (see MARY, **4**). C. R. N.

IMMER.—1. Eponym of a priestly family which returned to Jerusalem and sealed the covenant under Nehemiah, 1 Ch 24[14], Ezr 2[37] 10[20], Neh 3[29] 7[40] 11[13] (cf 1 Ch 9[12]), 1 Es 5[24] (AV **Meruth, RV Emmeruth**; cf Ezr 2[37]) 9[21] (AV, RV **Emmer**; cf Ezr 10[20]); probably the same as **Amariah,** Neh 10[3] 12[2, 13]. **2.** The father of a priest contemporary with Jeremiah, Jer 20[1]. **3.** Apparently the name of a place in Ezr 2[59], Neh 7[61]. The text is uncertain, however; cf 1 Es 5[36] in RSV (AV, RV are quite different).

IMMORALITY.—See CRIMES AND PUNISHMENTS, **3.**

IMMORTALITY.—The word 'immortality' is found five times in NT in AV and RSV, three rendering Greek *athanasia* (1 Co 15[53f], 1 Ti 6[16]; so RV in both), and two rendering Greek *aphtharsia* (Ro 2[7], 2 Ti 1[10]; RV 'incorruption' in both). The adjective 'immortal' is found in RSV in Ro 1[23] and 1 Ti 1[17] (AV, RV 'incorruptible' in both), where it renders Greek *aphthartos*, which is rendered 'imperishable' in 1 Co 15[52] and 1 P 1[23] (AV, RV 'incorruptible' in both). Immortality is ascribed to God (Ro 1[23], 1 Ti 1[17]; cf Dt 32[40], Sir 18[1]), to whom alone it belongs (1 Ti 6[16]); it is desired by the Christian (Ro 2[7]), brought to light through the gospel (2 Ti 1[10]), promised to the believer (1 Co 15[53f]), and attained through the resurrection by the Christian (1 Co 15[52f]), who is born anew of imperishable seed (1 P 1[23]).

In the book of Wisdom the idea of immortality or incorruptibility figures frequently. It is said to be the hope of the righteous (3[4]), and attained through wisdom (8[13, 17] 15[3]), and men are said to have been created for incorruptibility (2[23]), through which they are brought near to God (6[19], where RSV has 'immortality'). It is there also declared that the incorruptible (RSV 'immortal') spirit of God is in all things (12[1]).

See also LIFE and RESURRECTION.

IMNA.—An Asherite chief, 1 Ch 7[35].

IMNAH.—1. The eldest son of Asher, Nu 26[44] (AV **Jimna**), 1 Ch 7[30]. The gentilic **Imnites** stands in Nu 26[44] (AV **Jimnites**). **2.** A Levite in the time of Hezekiah, 2 Ch 31[14].

IMPORTUNITY.—The Greek word so translated in Lk 11[8] is literally 'shamelessness.' It is translated 'impudence' in Sir 25[22]. These are its only occurrences in the Bible. It is probable, however, that it had lost some of its original force, and that 'importunity' is a fair rendering. The English word signified originally 'difficulty of access' (*in-portus*), hence persistence. It is now practically obsolete, and 'persistence' might have been used.

IMPOTENT.—This word, now obsolescent in common speech—it is not used in RSV—means literally 'without strength.' It is used in AV as the translation of Greek words which mean 'without power' (Bar 6[28], Ac 14[8]) or 'without strength' (Jn 5[3, 7], Ac 4[9]). 'When religion is at the stake,' says Fuller (*Holy State*, ii. 19, p. 124), 'there must be no lookers on (except impotent people, who also help by their prayers), and every one is bound to lay his shoulders to the work.'

IMPRISONMENT.—See CRIMES AND PUNISHMENTS, **9.**

IMRAH.—An Asherite chief, 1 Ch 7[36].

IMRI.—1. A Judahite, 1 Ch 9[4]. **2.** Father of Zaccur, who helped to build the wall, Neh 3[2].

INCANTATIONS.—See MAGIC, DIVINATION, AND SORCERY.

INCARNATION.—The word is a non-biblical theological term to state the Christian conviction that in Jesus Christ God 'has visited and redeemed his people' (Lk 1[68]). Christianity consists in faith in the person, Jesus Christ, who in consequence of the significance which He has acquired in the life and experience of His followers is believed to be more than man; He is believed to be in some genuine sense Divine, so that He can be described as being 'as human as any man, as Divine as God himself.' This article will consider the Biblical material which bears upon the Christian assertion, with a brief reference in conclusion to the development of christological thought in the early history of the Church.

1. OT intimations.—At one time it was thought that the OT contained 'prophecies' clearly pointing to the appearance of God incarnate in history. In more recent years, a somewhat sophisticated use of typology has often approximated this view. A critical study of the documents, in the light of modern historical science, can build little on such a foundation, however valuable it may be in some metaphorical sense. On the other hand, the OT conception of man as made in 'the image of God' (Gn 1[26] 9[6]), however this be interpreted, and the general Jewish notion of man's sharing, to some extent at least, in the moral attributes of God, suggest that man is made for communion with his Creator by the exercise of his freedom in obedience to the Divine purpose. Furthermore, the OT plainly emphasizes the Divine revelation through historical events as well as by prophets to whom the Word of God comes. The Jewish belief that history is moving to some great consummation, in which God will fulfil His object in creation, is also significant at this point. In this consummation Messiah would have an important rôle, although the interpretation of this rôle varied greatly.

The tendency in Jewish thought to distinguish somewhat between God and His actions and His attributes came at length to what amounted almost to an hypostatization of the latter; especially was this true for 'Word' and 'Wisdom.' In Proverbs (8[22]) as well as in the Wisdom literature found among the apocryphal writings (*e.g.* Wis 7[23]), the references to the Wisdom of God seem almost to make clear a distinct mode of existence of a personal sort for God's activity in the affairs of men. Hellenistic Judaism, as represented by Philo, went far beyond this, especially with respect to the Word of God. Finally, the messianic concept, already noted in connexion with the consummation of God's purposes, pointed to some figure who as the agent of God would be both on the Divine side of the action and also in some sense an historical and human figure.

Along these different lines, we have intimations that the religious experience and faith of the OT require for their fulfilment some further action on God's part in which God and man would be brought into a close unity, to be shared in by those whom God would make His people.

2. The NT material.—It should be understood that the historical figure of Jesus does not, as such, compel the interpretation of Him as Divine; that He is the incarnation of God is a religious judgment made on the basis of the total impression of His person and the consequences of His life, teaching, mighty works, death, and resurrection. Thus we see, in the first place, that the NT is clear on the true humanity of Christ. He was truly born, although the traditional legends about His birth imply a miraculous departure from normal procreation. He developed gradually (Lk 2[52]), shared the ordinary experiences of hunger (Mt 4[2]), fatigue (Mk 4[38]), and limitations in knowledge (Mk 13[36]); he felt human emotion (Mk 14[33]), a sense of compassion (Mk 8[2]) and anger (Mk 8[12]). This list could be extended if the evidence of the Fourth Gospel were cited. Furthermore, he underwent real death on the Cross. Thus it is clear that the gospels cannot be interpreted as presenting a Jesus who is less than full man.

On the other hand, the NT testifies to the conviction that He is more than man. In the Pauline epistles Jesus is taken to be the Christ of God, who in the fully developed Pauline interpretation, as in Colossians (1[18]), is that one in whom ' all the fullness of God was pleased to dwell.' Even in earlier Pauline epistles (*e.g.* Galatians), there is no doubt of the unique relationship to God which Jesus is believed to have enjoyed, nor of His unique place in the effecting of God's purpose among men. The fact that He is the ' living Lord,' risen from the dead, is understood to mean that by God's mighty act His earthly ministry was vindicated and He was ' designated Son of God in power according to the Spirit of holiness by his resurrection from the dead ' (Ro 1[4]). In later Pauline thought He is the ' principle of concretion ' of the whole creation, through whom all things have come into being and in whom they hold together (Col 1[17]). The teaching of Hebrews and the Johannine literature (especially the prologue of the Fourth Gospel, Jn 1[1-18]) similarly exalts Jesus to a place which is, in effect, fully Divine. Thus we can say that the primitive Christian evaluation of Jesus, as found in the NT itself, is such that He is not only man in the fullest sense but also in some genuine fashion at one with God and even (as in Jn 1[1] and elsewhere in NT) Himself fully Divine.

An older reading of the gospels suggested that Jesus made such claims for Himself. It would appear impossible to maintain this to-day; but it can be said that He spoke ' with authority,' that His whole life appeared to those who knew Him to be so filled with creative goodness that a later interpretation could rightly say that He was ' without sin '; that He regarded Himself as integral to the accomplishment of the Divine purpose (either as the last of the Prophets or as Messiah Himself), that He demanded a kind of allegiance which no man before Him seems to have asked, and that His ' mighty works ' of healing and exorcism manifested His close relationship with the source of all health and divine power. The impression which He made, coupled with the compelling quality of His teaching and His obvious intimate communion with the Father, was such that His rising from the dead appeared to be, in one sense, the most natural thing in the world. As an early writer credits Peter with saying, one such as He could not be held by death (Ac 2[24]).

But whatever may be thought of the details of the gospels, the fact remains that the risen Lord was a present and effectual reality in the primitive Christian experience. He could not be contained within any set of ideas which made Him only the greatest of men; and the later NT literature shows that increasingly exalted claims were made for Him, until in the end He is acclaimed as ' the Word of God,' who ' became flesh and dwelt among us, full of grace and truth ' (Jn 1[14]). This is obviously a judgment of faith in the light of experience and the facts which were experienced; it contains, none the less, the unique differentia of Christianity from all other religions.

3. Purpose and results of the Incarnation.—These may be considered under four headings: (1) *The redemption of men.* This is the major emphasis in the Pauline teaching, in which Jesus Christ is affirmed to be the saviour from sin, who by an act of sacrifice reconciled men with God (see ATONEMENT). (2) *The supreme revelation of God.* Whatever may have been known of God otherwise—and the NT does not deny that there is such knowledge (cf Ac 14[17], Ro 1[20])—in Him God has been revealed as perfect love, as ' Christ-like '; and this revelation has not been by word only but by a life lived on this earth. (3) The bringing of men into *fellowship with God.* Christ not only offers a perfect example of what man is intended to be, in the Divine purpose, by reason of His obedience to His Father (Jn 8[29]); He makes it possible for His followers to share in His relationship with the Father. This occurs in Christ's Body the Church, about which Paul writes at length in Romans, 1 Corinthians, and Colossians (cf also Ephesians, where a Paulinist continues the theme). Thus the union of God and man achieved in Christ is one in which others may participate as they are made one body with the Lord. (4) *The consummation of the Divine plan,* both in humanity and in the cosmos. This conception, found in Colossians and Ephesians, suggests that Christ is the central fact of human history; he is also, in some sense, the embodiment of the Divine cosmic principle of unity by which all things are brought to their purposed fulfilment.

4. Later Christology.—It was on the basis of this NT material that the Church in later times worked out its doctrinal statement of the Incarnation. Through a period of controversy in which many suggested views were put forward and rejected as inadequate or misleading, the Church came finally to believe that the significance of the person of Jesus Christ is such that three things must be said concerning Him: (*a*) He is truly man, and man in the fullest sense; (*b*) He is truly Divine, although He is not *all* of God—He is, rather, the Word of God; or, more carefully stated, that in Him which is Divine is the second hypostasis of the triune God, the Son or Word; and (*c*) the humanity and the divinity are in Him united so closely that this union is appropriately called, not ' they ' but ' he.' Alexandrine thought tended to speak of this union in such a fashion that the divinity in a sense engulfed the humanity; Syrian (Antiochene) thought sought to preserve more carefully the distinction between humanity and divinity, while yet insisting on the intimate and abiding reality of the union of the two in Christ. The former has tended to think of Jesus *as* God; the latter has rather thought of Jesus as that One *in whom* God lived as man.

The Christian faith is in the Incarnate Lord Himself, as a person, in whom God is known, worshipped, served; the doctrine of the Incarnation is an attempt to state the significance of this faith in terms which will preserve its fullness. Provided the basic facts of this faith are preserved, the Church has felt at liberty to continue its task of discovering human language which will not inadequately state the place which Jesus Christ holds in relation to God and man; the classical definitions are not so much stop-signs as pointers to indicate the right direction for all such interpretations of His significance. See CHRISTOLOGY. W. N. P.

INCENSE.—(1) *l[e]bhônāh,* which should always be translated ' frankincense ' (q.v.). It was white in colour, hence the Hebrew name. It was burnt with the cereal offering (Lv 2[1, 2, 15f] 6[15] etc.), and offered with the showbread (Lv 24[7-9]). (2) *k[e]ṭôreth,* literally ' smoke.' In pre-exilic writings, the reference is to the smoke of the fire-offerings, but in post-exilic writings, it refers to incense: cf Is 1[13] and Lv 10[1], Ezk 8[11] etc. (3) The Greek *thymiama* (Lk 1[10], Rev 5[8] 8[3] 18[13]) is strictly a spice used for incense, fumigation, or embalming. In the NT it means ' incense ' generally. The holy incense (Ex 30[34]) was made from spices and frankincense in equal portions. The spices were resin, aromatic shell, and galban. These were mixed, salted, and ground into a fine powder. The incense of later times was more complicated and had thirteen constituents (*BJ* v. v. 5 [218]). It was offered daily (Jth 9[1], Lk 1[8-10]). N. H. S.

INCENSE, ALTAR OF.—See TABERNACLE, **6** (*c*), and TEMPLE, **9.**

INCEST.—See CRIMES AND PUNISHMENTS, **3.**

INDIA (Heb. *Hōddû*) is named as the E. boundary of the empire of Ahasuerus, Est 1[1] 8[9]. The Hebrew is contracted from *Hondu,* the name of the river Indus.

It indicated the country through which that river flows; not the great peninsula of Hindustan. So also in 1 Mac 8[8], Ad. Est 13[1] 16[1], 1 Es 3[2]. Possibly the drivers of the elephants (1 Mac 6[37]) were true Indians. If India proper is not named, there is little doubt that from ancient times Israel had relations with this country, by means of the caravan trade through Arabia. Many of the articles of commerce in the account given of this trade are of Indian origin; *e.g.* 'ivory and ebony,' 'cassia and calamus,' 'embroidered work,' and 'carpets of coloured stuff' (Ezk 27[15, 19, 24]). W. E.

INDITE.—This English verb is now somewhat old-fashioned. When it is used it means 'to write.' But formerly, and as found in AV, it meant to inspire or dictate to the writer. Thus St. Paul indited and Tertius wrote, Ro 16[22]. The word occurs in the Preface to the AV and in Ps 45[1] AV 'My heart is inditing a good matter.' In the Douai version (though this word is not used) there is a note: 'I have received by divine inspiration in my hart and cogitation a most high Mysterie.'

INFIDEL.—This word has more force now than formerly. In AV it signifies no more than 'unbeliever.' It occurs in 2 Co 6[15], 1 Ti 5[8] (RV and RSV 'unbeliever' in both). So 'infidelity' in 2 Es 7[44] is simply 'unbelief' (Lat. *incredulitas*).

INGATHERING.—See TABERNACLES (FEAST OF).

INHERITANCE.—It is a remarkable fact that the Hebrew language fails to discriminate between the inheritance of property and its possession or acquisition in any other manner. The two words most constantly used in this connexion denote the idea of settled possession, but are quite indeterminate as to the manner in which that possession has been acquired. As might easily be inferred, from the historical circumstances of Israel's evolution, the words became largely restricted to the holding of land, obviously the most important of all kinds of property among a pastoral or agricultural people.

I. INHERITANCE IN LAW AND CUSTOM.—**1. Property.**—While land was the most important part of an inheritance, the rules for succession show that it was regarded as belonging properly to the family or clan, and to the individual heir only as representing family or tribal rights. Cattle, household goods, and slaves would be more personal possessions, which a man could divide among his sons (Dt 21[16]). Originally wives, too, as part of the property of the deceased, would fall to the possession of the heir-in-chief (cf 2 S 16[20-23], 1 K 2[13ff]).

2. Heirs.—(*a*) The *firstborn son*, as the new head of the family, responsible for providing for the rest, inherited the land and had also his claim to a double portion of other kinds of wealth (Dt 21[17]). To be the son of a concubine or inferior wife was not a bar to heirship (Gn 21[10], 1 Ch 5[1]); though a jealous wife might prevail on her husband to deprive such a son of the right of succession (Gn 21[10]). That a father had power to transfer the birthright from the firstborn to another is implied in the cases of Ishmael and Isaac (Gn 21[10]), Esau and Jacob (27[37]), Reuben and Joseph (1 Ch 5[1]), Adonijah and Solomon (1 K 1[11ff]). But this was contrary to social usage, and is prohibited in Dt 21[15-17]. Moreover, the exceptions to the rule are presented as examples of a Divine election rather than a human preference (Isaac, Gn 21[12]; Jacob, Mal 1[2f], Ro 9[13]; Joseph, Gn 49[24ff]; Solomon, 1 Ch 22[9f]), and can hardly be adduced as survivals of the ancient custom of 'Junior Right.' (*b*) At first a *daughter* could not succeed (the inheritance of the daughters of Job [Job 42[15]] is noted as exceptional)—an arrangement that has been referred either to the influence of ancestor-worship, in which a male heir was necessary as priest of the family cult, or to the connexion between inheritance and the duty of blood revenge. For unmarried daughters, however, husbands would almost invariably be found. In the case of the daughters of Zelophehad (Nu 27[1-11]) we see the introduction of a change; but it is to be noted that this very case is associated with the provision (Nu 36[1-12]) that heiresses should marry only within their father's tribe, so that the inheritance might not be alienated from it. (*c*) For the *widow* no immediate place was found in the succession. So far from being eligible as an heir, she was strictly a part of the property belonging to the inheritance. According to the levirate law, however, when a man died leaving no son, his brother or other next-of-kin (*gō'ēl*) must marry the widow, and her firstborn son by this marriage became the heir of her previous husband (Dt 25[6]). (*d*) For the *order of succession* the rule is laid down in Nu 27[8-11] that if a man die without male issue the right of inheritance shall fall successively to his daughter, his brothers, his father's brothers, his next kinsman thereafter. The provision for the daughter was an innovation, as the context shows, but the rest of the rule is in harmony with the ancient laws of kinship.

II. NATIONAL AND RELIGIOUS INHERITANCE.—**1.** The possession of the land of Canaan was commonly regarded as the inheritance of the whole people. In this particular case the inheritance was won only as the result of conflict and effort; moreover, theoretically at any rate, it involved the annihilation of the previous inhabitants. Consequently the inheritance of Canaan was not entirely devoid of the idea of succession. But the extermination of the Canaanites was never effected; and although the conquest was achieved only by the most strenuous effort, yet the Israelites were so strongly impressed with a vivid sense of Yahweh's intervention on their behalf, that to subsequent generations it seemed as if they had entered into the labours of others, not in any sense whatever by their own power, but solely by Yahweh's grace. The inheritance of Canaan signified the secure possession of the land, as the gift of God to His people. 'The dominant Biblical sense of inheritance is the enjoyment by a rightful title of that which is not the fruit of personal exertion' (Westcott, *Heb.*, 168).

2. It is not surprising that the idea of inheritance soon acquired religious associations. The Hebrew mind invested all social and political institutions with a religious significance. As Israel became increasingly conscious of its mission *in*, and began dimly to apprehend its mission *to*, the world, the peaceful and secure possession of Canaan seemed an indispensable condition of that self-development which was itself the necessary prelude to a more universal mission. The threatening attitude of the great world powers in the eighth and subsequent centuries B.C. brought the question prominently to the front. Over and over again it seemed as if Jerusalem must succumb to the hordes of barbarian invaders, and as if the last remnant of Canaan must be irretrievably lost; but the prophets persistently declared that the land should not be lost; they realized the impossibility of Israel's ever realizing her true vocation, unless, at any rate for some centuries, she preserved her national independence; and the latter would, of course, be wholly unthinkable without territorial security. The career of Israel, as a nation, the influence, even the existence, of its religion, would be endangered by the dispossession of Canaan; moreover, it was recognized that as long as the people remained true to Yahweh, He on His part would remain true to them, and would not suffer them to be dispossessed, but would make them dwell securely in their own land, in order that they might establish on their side those conditions of righteousness and justice which represented the national obligations, if Yahweh's covenant with them was to be maintained.

3. The possession of the land, the inheritance of Canaan, symbolized the people's living in covenant with their God, and all those spiritual blessings which flowed from such a covenant. And inasmuch as the validity of the covenant implied the continuance of Divine favour, the inheritance of the Holy Land was viewed as the outward and visible sign of God's presence and power among His own. We know how the remorseless logic of history seemed to point to an opposite conclusion. The Exile spelt disinheritance; and disinheritance meant a great deal more than the loss of a little strip of territory; it meant the forfeiture of spiritual blessings as a consequence of national sin. The more ardent spirits of the nation refused, however, to believe that these high privileges were permanently abrogated; they were only temporarily withdrawn; and they looked forward to a new covenant whose spiritual efficacy should be guaranteed by national restoration. In the reconstituted theocracy, the Messiah figured as the mediator both of temporal and of spiritual blessings. The idea of a restored inheritance suggested at once the glorious anticipations of the Messianic age, when the people, not by works which they had done, but by Yahweh's grace, should recover that which they had lost; and renew the covenant that had been broken.

4. In this sense 'the inheritance' became almost equivalent to the Messianic salvation; and participation in this salvation is not a future privilege, but a present possession. In the OT the secure inheritance of the Holy Land was the outward symbol of these spiritual blessings; under the New Dispensation they are assured by membership in the Christian body.

5. As every Jew regarded himself as an inheritor of the land of Canaan, so also is each Christian an inheritor of the Kingdom of heaven. He is not the heir, in the sense of enjoying an honorary distinction, or of anticipating future privileges; but as one who is already in a position of assured privilege, conferred upon him with absolute validity. As Lightfoot remarks, 'Our Father never dies; the inheritance never passes away from Him; yet nevertheless we succeed to the full possession of it' (*Galatians*[8], 165).

6. Three particular usages remain to be noticed. (*a*) The Jews never lost the conviction that Yahweh was the supreme overlord of the land, and of the people that dwelt in it. Accordingly Canaan is the Holy Land, and Yahweh's own inheritance; and Messiah when incarnate 'came to His own country, and His own people received Him not.' (*b*) The Jews also recognized that the possession of Canaan had value only in so far as it assured them of the free exercise of their religion, and all other spiritual blessings. This they strove to express by boldly declaring that Yahweh was Himself the inheritance of His people. (*c*) The Messiah, through whom the disinheritance should be brought to a close, and the covenant should be renewed, was naturally regarded as the supreme 'inheritor' or 'heir' of all the promises and privileges implied in the covenant. As, moreover, the Messiah's unique relation to the Father became more clearly defined, the idea of His inheritance, connoting His unique primogeniture and universal supremacy, became enlarged and expanded. It was, moreover, through the humanity which He restored that the Son proved and realized His heirship of all things: and thus His actual position is the potential exaltation of redeemed mankind. J. C. L. and E. A. E.

INIQUITY.—See Sin.

INJURIOUS.—In the language of the AV 'injurious' is more than hurtful; it is also insulting. It 'adds insult to injury.' It occurs Sir 8[11], 1 Ti 1[13]; and the Greek word used in these places is in Ro 1[30] translated 'despiteful' (RSV 'insolent').

INK is mentioned once in OT, Jer 36[18]. Ex 32[33] and Nu 5[23] are adduced as evidence that the old Hebrew ink (derived from lamp black [?]) could be washed off. From the bright colours that still survive in some papyri, it is evident that the ink used by the Egyptians must have been of a superior kind. Moreover, in Israel metallic ink is known to have been used as early as the fall of Jerusalem in 586 B.C., since the ink used in the Lachish Letters contained iron (cf *Lachish I*, pp. 188 ff). On the other hand, the ink used for the Dead Sea Scrolls was made of carbon (cf H. J. Plenderleith, *JTVI* lxxxii, 146 f). The *Letter of Aristeas* (176) says that the copy of the Law sent to Ptolemy II. was inscribed in gold, but later practice forbade the writing of Biblical works in anything but black, effaceable ink (cf *JE* viii. 303b). The NT term for 'ink,' occurring three times (2 Co 3[3], 2 Jn [12], 3 Jn [13]) is *melan* (literally 'black'). See, further, under Writing.

INKHORN.—In one of Ezekiel's visions (Ezk 9[2f, 11]) a man appears with a scribe's inkhorn (RSV 'writing case') by his side (literally 'upon his loins'). The 'inkhorn' consisted of a case for the reed pens, with a cup or bulb for holding the ink, near the upper end of the case. It was carried in the girdle (hence the above expression).

INN.—See Hospitality.

INNER MAN.—The contrast implied by this expression is found in the Pauline correspondence and in the literature for the guidance of early churches. The author of 1 Peter points up the antithesis between the adorning of the visible body and 'the imperishable jewel of a gentle and quiet spirit,' 'the hidden person of the heart' (3[3ff]). Paul sharpens the ethical contrast between the 'inmost self,' which delights in the law of God, and the 'members,' in which the 'law of sin . . . dwells' (Ro 7[22f]). On one hand is the law which passion blindly follows, on the other is the informed conscience which yields a reasoned and delighted obedience.

Different from this is the contrast in 2 Co 4[16ff], where 'our outer nature,' decaying and dying, stands over against 'our inner nature,' which is in a constant state of renewal. Here is the antithesis of the 'transient' and the 'eternal' elements in man's complex personality. The author of Ephesians employs the phrase, 'the inner man,' to describe the entire basis of man's higher life, on which God's spirit works and in which Christ dwells (3[16ff]). Correct moral and intellectual apprehension of the work of Christ depend upon the rootage of this 'inner man' in the Divine love which surpasses knowledge (cf Jn 3[16]). J. R. W.—**H. H. H.**

INSCRIPTIONS.—Ancient texts executed by a craftsman. They are the concern of **Epigraphy** (q.v.). The inscriptions in question may then be specified by language, people, or region of origin, or some other distinguishing characteristic. The interest in collecting Latin and Greek inscriptions is of long standing. Those in Italy and Europe were naturally collected first. Travel and exploration and finally excavation vastly increased the number. One of the greatest of inscriptions is that of Darius I. at **Behistun,** first copied by Sir Henry Rawlinson. The greatest inscription of the classical period is the *Monumentum Ancyranum*—the account of the stewardship of Caesar Augustus, composed as he approached death in A.D.14. Mystifying, of course, were the inscriptions in unknown languages that travellers copied in the East. The short Persepolis inscriptions in wedge-shaped writing were successfully deciphered by Grotefend. (1802), but their Old Persian language only became more thoroughly understood by Rawlinson's decipherment of the Behistun text (1846 f). Since that text was trilingual it also gave the key to the Babylonian-Assyrian and the Elamitic languages, though progress with the former was so rapid only because of the syllabaries found in the excavations at Nineveh. The famous **Rosetta stone,** discovered in trench-digging by Napoleon's soldiery, and giving a hieroglyphic and demotic Egyptian text with a Greek translation, furnished Champollion the key to deciphering the hieroglyphs (from 1821 on) and thus opened the world of ancient Egypt. Much effort and ingenuity was expended on the hieroglyphic writing that first was observed on the 'Hamath Stones,' and that was identified as 'Hittite,' when the historical rôle of that people became known. Great progress was made in recent years, and Bossert's discovery of a bilingual Phoenician and hieroglyphic-Hittite inscription at **Karatepe** in Cilicia assures full success. The oldest alphabetic inscriptions are the **Sinaitic** ones found by Petrie at *Serābîṭ el-Khādem* and first deciphered by Gardiner (1917). The Phoenician inscriptions were first dealt with in satisfactory manner in 1837 by W.

Gesenius, the father of Hebrew grammar and lexicography of the modern era. **Hebrew** inscriptions, found on coins and seals (see SEAL, SIGNET), were obviously written in the same script, if less gracefully executed, as the Phoenician. Actual Hebrew inscriptions apart from the brief ones just mentioned seem to begin with the calendar inscription discovered at Gezer, now held to be of the 10th cent. B.C. To the last third of the 9th cent. belongs the stela of king **Mesha** (q.v.) of Moab, which showed that the Moabites spoke a language identical with Hebrew. The Siloam inscription of Hezekiah's time (*c* 700 B.C.) found in the Siloam tunnel in 1880, and the short inscription that was cut out from over a rock tomb near Siloam village, commemorating a 'steward of the house' such as Shebna (Is 22^{14f}), are the leading examples of real pre-exilic Judaean inscriptions. The Samarian ostraca of the time of Jeroboam II. and the Lachish ostraca of *c* 589 B.C. provide important texts in old Hebrew writing, but are outside the definition of inscriptions. In post-exilic times the related Aramaic style of writing, which first became known to scholars through inscriptions and papyri from Egypt, supplanted the old Hebrew style. The present Hebrew 'square' script is descended from it. The name of 'Tobiah,' carved over a rock tomb at *'Arâq el-Emîr* in Transjordan, probably in the 3rd cent. B.C., and commemorating a successor of the Tobiah of Neh 2^{19} etc., is in this Aramaic type of writing. There were, however, revivals or conservative continuations of the old Hebrew script, as shown by Jewish coins of *c* A.D. 70 and of the Bar-Cochba revolt (as well as by some Dead Sea scroll texts). Aramaic not only in script but in language are ossuary inscriptions, and above all the plaque mentioning king Uzziah of Judah (cf Is 6^{1}) discovered in a Jerusalem collection by Sukenik in 1931.

Greek inscriptions naturally have great interest and importance for the student of the NT and of the early Church. The inscription from the Jewish temple, of the time of Herod, found by Clermont-Ganneau, warning Gentiles from entry into the hedge and *peribolos* around the sacred precincts, deserves outstanding mention. Important, too, is the Theodotus inscription found by Weill in his 1913–1914 excavations. For it necessarily antedates the fall of Jerusalem and was apparently set up in honour of a freedman, and may even mark the site of the synagogue of the Libertines of Ac 6^{9}. The Greek ossuary inscriptions from Palestine are naturally also of considerable interest for their personal names. Most Greek inscriptions, notably in the Roman *Provincia Arabia* are of later vintage (from the 5th cent. on). Those at Gerasa, city of the Decapolis, are illustrative of the life of this period. The Roman mile-stone inscriptions (bilingual) mention the name of the emperor under whom a road was built or repaired, the provincial officials and the distance to the next place.

Of greater interest, however, to the student of the Bible are such inscriptions as the one on the altar of Demeter at **Pergamum,** which the torch-bearer Kapiton dedicated to 'unknown gods.' as it must have been such a one that Paul saw at Athens (Ac 17^{23}). Important, too, is the Gallio inscription from Delphi, which helps to fix the date of the proconsul in whose time Paul came to Corinth (Ac 18^{12f}). On the theological side a considerable interest attaches to such inscriptions as those from Priene and Halicarnassus, in which the natal day of the emperor Augustus is viewed as bringing on the golden age and in which he is celebrated as Sōtēr or saviour, much as Jesus is in the Pastoral epistles and in the Gospel of John. A recently discovered inscription has helped to fix the site of **Derbe** (q.v.). There are thus innumerable points of contact between study of inscriptions and that of the Bible.

Inscriptions may be either of a public or private character. To the former class belong those recording laws, decrees, treaties, etc. Those of a private nature are chiefly mortuary, memorial or dedicatory. The Latin inscriptions have been collected most fully in the CIL (*Corpus inscriptionum Latinarum,* 1863–1899), the Greek inscriptions in the CIG (*Corpus inscriptionum Graecarum,* 1825–1877), and its successor IG (*Inscriptiones Graecae,* 1902 ff). Selected Greek inscriptions are conveniently given in the works of W. Dittenberger, *Sylloge inscriptionum Graecarum,* ed. 1898–1901, and *Orientis Graecae inscriptiones selectae,* 1903–1905; Latin in H. Dessau, *Inscriptiones Latinae selectae,* 1892–1916. For the Semitic inscriptions (exclusive of the cuneiform) the CIS (*Corpus inscriptionum Semiticarum,* 1888 ff) provides a great collection. The Hebrew inscriptions on seals, etc., will be found in D. Diringer, *Le iscrizioni antico-ebraiche palestinesi,* 1934. (See also references under EPIGRAPHY.) E. G. K.

INSPIRE, INSPIRATION.—In English the verb 'inspire' can be used in a wide variety of contexts, and this variety is reflected to some extent in the RSV, where the word appears thirteen times (it is absent from the AV). Besides the purely human efforts to inspire terror (Is 47^{12}) or to inspire horror (Jer 49^{16}), the Bible refers to the Divine activity in inspiring craftsmen to teach others (Ex 35^{34}) or in inspiring diverse spiritual gifts in the early Church (1 Co 12^{11}). Christians at Thessalonica experienced joy inspired by the Holy Spirit (1 Th 1^{6}), and Paul referred to the energy which Christ mightily inspired within him (Col 1^{29}). It was especially through prophets that God's Spirit operated, not only in the Old Testament days (Nu 24^{2-4}) when men moved by the Holy Spirit spoke from God (2 P 1^{21}), but also in the new dispensation when Simeon was inspired by the Spirit to recognize the identity of the child Jesus (Lk 2^{27}) and when prophetic utterances of persons in the early Church (Ac 11^{27f}, 1 Co 12^{1-4}, Eph 4^{11}) inspired fidelity of Christian testimony (1 Ti 1^{18}) and directed that the first missionaries be sent out (Ac 13^{1f}).

The noun 'inspiration,' which is absent from the RSV, appears twice in the AV. One of these passages (Job 32^{8}) declares that it is by Divine inspiration that man receives the capacity to discern what is right. The other passage (2 Ti 3^{16}), which makes an important predication regarding Scripture, is translated variously: AV, 'All scripture is given by inspiration of God, and is profitable for doctrine, for reproof, for correction, for instruction in righteousness'; RV and ASV, 'Every scripture inspired of God is also profitable . . .'; RSV, 'All scripture is inspired by God and profitable for teaching . . .' Here Scripture (which in the context refers to the OT) is characterized as *theopneustic* (literally 'God-breathed'), that is, the product of the creative breath of God. The emphasis falls upon the first part of the Greek compound, '*God*-inspired,' calling attention to the Divine source of the authority of the OT. As God had breathed into man's nostrils the breath of life (Gn 2^{7}; cf Ps 33^{6}), so He breathed life-giving truth into the Jewish Scriptures. Nothing is said of *how* God inspired these writings; the author is concerned only to state that the fact of inspiration makes them profitable for religious purposes.

In accord with the implications of this classical passage, Jesus Christ and His apostles are consistently represented as recognizing the OT to be trustworthy history, true doctrine, and sure prophecy. Thus, Jesus acknowledges the authority of the prophets (Lk 24^{25}), states that the Holy Spirit had inspired David (Mk 12^{36}), and more than once bases arguments on the presupposition that Scripture cannot be broken (Mt 26^{54}, Lk 22^{37}, Jn 10^{35}). In a similar vein Peter (in Ac 1^{16}), James (Ja 4^{5}), Stephen (in Ac 7^{38}), and Paul (Ro 3^{2}) refer explicitly or implicitly to the OT as oracles of God which cannot be set aside. Even among the formulas with which NT authors introduce their quotations from the OT, several (*e.g.* 'It is written,' 'It says,' 'Scripture says,' and 'God [or He] says') indicate their high view of the authority of what is quoted. In fact, occasionally the last-mentioned formula is used to introduce words which are not ascribed to God in the OT passages, but are spoken of or even addressed to Him and can be considered God's words only because they are part of the Scripture text (*e.g.* Mt 19^{5}, Ac 4^{24f} 13^{35}, He 1^{6-9} 4^{4}).

The doctrine of the inspiration of the NT grows out of the promise of Christ to His disciples that the Holy Spirit, whom the Father would send in His name, would teach them all things, and bring to their remembrance all that He had said to them (Jn 14^{26}; cf 16^{13}). The inspiration of Christ's own words is implied in His claim to be alone in knowing and revealing the Father (Mt 11^{27}), and in His placing His own statements on a par with, or in some cases above, the revealed will of God in the OT (*e.g.* Mt 5^{31-44}). In performing their work of proclaiming the Gospel, the apostolic authors are confident that they do so through the Holy Spirit (1 P 1^{12}), to whom they attribute the content of their teaching (1 Co 2^{13}). Therefore as spokesmen for God (1 Co 7^{40}, 1 Th 2^{13}) they issue commands with the completest authority (1 Th $4^{2, 15}$, 2 Th $3^{6, 12}$), and even make it the test of whether one has the Spirit that he should acknowledge that what they write are commandments of God (1 Co 14^{37}). On the other hand, the fact that a NT writer occasionally quoted an OT passage out of its context (*e.g.* Mt 2^{15} quoting Hos 11^{1}) or altered its phrasing (*e.g.* He 10^{5-7} quoting Ps 40^{6-8}) shows that he did not consider himself bound by the literal form of the OT statement, but regarded his own interpretation to be a justifiable modification and/or application of the author's original meaning.

Throughout the history of the Church many theories of the nature and mode of inspiration have been elaborated. These have ranged from a theory of dictation which leaves no room for human effort and tends to overlook the stylistic idiosyncrasies of the several authors, making of them mere automata, to theories of varying degrees and kinds of inspiration, sometimes involving scarcely more than a general illumination and superintendence of God's Spirit. Amid all discussions of inspiration, it must not be overlooked that the primary question relates to the category of revelation—whether God has spoken. Only when it is acknowledged that God has disclosed His will is it meaningful to formulate a theory of how He has inspired the authors of Scripture. Whatever the formulation (verbal, plenary, dynamic, etc.), it is hard to conceive of an inspiration that does not pertain to the words of Scripture—for thought of necessity is expressed in words. That this, however, does not imply a mechanical, literalistic inspiration is evident from a consideration of the presence of divergent reports of sayings of Jesus in the Gospels. Not only in different Gospels (*e.g.* Mk 10^{17ff} and Mt 19^{16ff}, Mt 6^{9ff} and Lk 11^{2ff}) but even within the same Gospel (*e.g.* Jn 3^{3} and 3^{7}; 8^{51} and 8^{52}; 13^{10} and 13^{11}) Jesus' words are found to vary in phraseology, though the idea conveyed in these divergent forms is usually the same. Furthermore, theories of inspiration must take account of the presence of occasional imperfections in the Bible as regards both style and statement. (Fortunately the religious conviction that the Scriptures are the only infallible rule of faith and life does not depend upon their formal inerrancy, otherwise no translation could be satisfactory.) Nor is it permissible to declare *a priori* what forms of literature it is appropriate for God to inspire; *e.g.* that He could inspire history, poetry, epistles, and prophecy to reveal His redemptive purpose, but not folk-sagas, legends, or myths. Such matters are to be determined inductively from the Scriptures themselves, not deductively from dogmatic presuppositions. A satisfying theory of inspiration will recognize that in the Scriptures *omnia ex Deo, omnia ex hominibus* (' all things are from God; all things are from men '), and that in some respects the relation of the human and the Divine in the written Word is analogous to the Incarnation of the living Word in human flesh. The testimony of the Church universal has been that the Bible is inspired in a sense in which no other book is inspired; that, having been produced by the effectual guidance of the Holy Spirit, it perfectly embodies the Divine revelation of God's saving will and work. See REVELATION. B. M. M.

INSTANT.—' Instant ' and ' instantly ' are now used only of time. In AV they have their earlier meaning of ' urgent,' ' urgently,' as in Lk 23^{23} ' they were instant [RSV ' urgent '] with loud voices, requiring that he might be crucified '; Lk 7^{4} ' they besought him instantly ' (RSV ' earnestly '). Cf Erasmus, *Paraphrase*, i. 31, ' whoso knocketh at the doore instantly, to him it shal be opened.'

INSTRUMENT.—For musical instruments see MUSIC. The word is also frequently used in AV (though only twice in NT, both times in Ro 6^{13}) for any utensil, implement, or weapon; and in To 7^{14}, 1 Mac 13^{42} for a legal document or deed (RSV ' contract '). RSV uses it frequently in OT and four times in NT.

INTERCESSION.—See PRAYER.

INTEREST.—See USURY.

INTERMEDIATE STATE.—See PARADISE, 3.

INTERPRETATION.—In general, in the Bible this means the clarification of obscure, uncertain or incomplete communication. But there is a considerable variety of particular connexions in which it is used.

1. Dreams were in ancient Israel commonly taken to be Divine communication. In many cases their sense was obvious and no explicit interpretation was needed (*e.g.* Gn 37^{5-11}); but in others the meaning could not be known without interpretation. Such interpretation was recognized to be the province of the ' wise,' the class trained in the international polite learning, and of those skilled in magic. Dream interpretation is a central interest in the Joseph story, which has close connexions with the thought of Israelite ' wisdom ' (Gn 40–41). The story dissociates interpretative skill from magic. Interpretation comes from God, and even where no skilled practitioner can be found God makes known the meaning to His humble but exemplary servant (40^{8}). The wise of Egypt are seen to fail, while Joseph succeeds because the resource for interpretation is not his but God's ($41^{8, 15-16}$). The dreams in the Joseph story are prophetic of the future. The same features occur in the Daniel stories, which belong to the same tradition in some respects as the Joseph story (Dn 2, 4). In Dn 2 the difficulty is heightened in that the king will not or cannot relate the dream which has to be interpreted.

Apart from the particular reference to dreams, the interest in the understanding and interpretation of the obscure remains a feature of Israelite wisdom down into late times, Pr 1^{6}, 2 Ch 9^{1}, Sir 47^{17} (these two of Solomon), Ec 8^{1}, Wis 8^{8}.

2. Interpretation may also mean translation from one language to another. Such is the natural sense in Gn 42^{23}; an Egyptian official would normally have an interpreter when dealing with Asiatic nomads. In modern English we use ' interpret ' for this kind of immediate oral translation, but for written texts we tend to distinguish between ' translating ' as literal rendering and ' interpreting ' as a combination of exposition or commentary with translation. In the older English of the AV ' interpret ' is often simply ' translate,' *e.g.* Mt 1^{23}, Mk 5^{41}. But the boundaries between literal translation and interpretative rendering are not easily drawn. When the Jews came to translate their Scriptures from Hebrew, the results showed a wide range from literal accuracy to expository paraphrases; the LXX is quite literal in parts, while the Aramaic translation or Targum is often very free. It is probably the origin of this Targum that is narrated of Ezra in Neh 8^{8}. Mention may be made at this point of the early Church tradition about the origin of the Gospels: Papias relates that Mark had been ' Peter's interpreter ' and that Matthew ' put together the oracles in Hebrew, and each one interpreted (*i.e.* translated) them as he was able '; although there is considerable question how this latter statement is connected with the Gospels as we have them.

3. Once a recognized body of sacred tradition existed in Israel, a further kind of interpretation came to be needed and practised: the exposition of the tradition in the sense of explanation of difficult passages and examination of their relevance and meaning for newer times. Going back a little farther, the shaping of the sacred tradition by its later redactions, the work of selecting, omitting, annotating and juxtaposing, is itself a kind of interpretation of the individual elements of material adopted. But with the consolidation of the tradition a new stage is reached. Daniel, a book which is much concerned with the interpreting of dreams and other supernatural communications, takes up in ch. 9 the interpretation of a difficult passage in Jeremiah. Here the solution is given by an angel (as normally in Dn 7–12); cf Job 33^{23}. The problem exists for Daniel because he is trying to fit in the prophetic tradition with later history and the events of his own time, especially the desecration of the Temple under Antiochus.

Of great importance is the interpretative activity of the Qumrân community, which may reasonably be supposed to go back to before 100 B.C. Fragments have been found of numerous commentaries on prophetic and poetical passages, of which the most extensive is the Habakkuk commentary. The centre of the interpretative method is the attachment of the passages to the life of the Qumrân sect, so that the words of the prophet have their interpretation in incidents of its history, the work of its teacher, the machinations of its enemies, and features of its eschatological expectation. The Zadokite Document contains the same kind of interpretation. It is the conviction that the sect is living in the end of days and that the prophetic or obscure passages must now be in fulfilment which dominates the understanding of Scripture.

Jesus and the early Church likewise believed the eschatological promises to be coming to fulfilment in their time, and much of their sayings can be broadly stated to have dealt with scriptural interpretation. We do not, however, have from the NT period any verse-by-verse commentaries on the OT on the Qumrân pattern. But some broad surveys of Scripture appear, such as the Stephen speech (Ac 7). Curiously, however, the actual word 'interpretation' in this sense is hardly found, and much its most important occurrence is in Lk 24^{27}, where the risen Christ interprets to His disciples 'the things concerning himself in all the scriptures' (*i.e.* of the OT). For the Church with its entry into the Gentile world the problem of linguistic translation appears anew, but the story of the Day of Pentecost (Ac 2) sees in the making intelligible of the message to foreign ears the work of the Holy Spirit and a reversal of the baleful effects of the Tower of Babel incident.

4. From Corinth we hear of the activity in the Church of those who spoke with 'tongues,' unintelligible utterances (especially 1 Co 14). This is a good activity according to St. Paul and by no means to be prevented. But it is speaking to God and not to men; other members of the Church are not assisted by it, and therefore if some one speaks with tongues in the Church it should be interpreted (14$^{5, 27-28}$) by himself or another, so that it may be understood and serve to the upbuilding of the Church. Such interpretation is a charisma or spiritual gift just as speaking with tongues is; the speaker should pray for it, for in the interpretation of the utterances the mind is exercised and becomes mature (1 Co 12^{10} 14$^{13-15}$).

5. A rather special case is 2 P 1^{20}, which asserts that scriptural prophecy is not a matter 'of one's own private interpretation.' It is possible that the contrast is between such personal interpretation and the interpretation of the Church as a whole, or of spiritually qualified persons in it. But nothing else is said about interpretation as such, and the rest of the argument is from the reliability of prophecy because of its *source*. It is therefore perhaps also possible that the contrast is between one's own interpretation, which is not the basis of the prophetic truth, and the intention, not of man but of God, which is the real origin and basis of prophecy (cf the treatment of the promises of the end in ch. 3). J. Ba.

INTREAT.—Besides the modern sense of 'beseech,' intreat (spelled also 'entreat') means 'deal with,' 'handle,' modern 'treat,' always with an adverb 'well,' 'ill,' 'shamefully,' etc. Coverdale translates Is 40^{11} 'He shal gather the lambes together with his arme, and carie them in his bosome, and shal kindly intreate those that beare yonge.'

It is even more important to notice that when the meaning seems to be as now, viz. 'beseech,' the word is often in reality much stronger, 'prevail on by entreaty.' Thus Gn 25^{21} 'And Isaac intreated (RSV 'prayed to') the Lord for his wife, . . . and the Lord was intreated of him,' *i.e.* yielded to the entreaty (RSV 'granted his prayer'). Cf Grafton, *Chron.* ii, 768, 'Howbeit she could in no wise be intreated with her good wyll to delyver him.'

In Jer 15^{11} in AV and AVm the two meanings of the word and the two spellings are used as alternative renderings, 'I will cause the enemy to entreat thee well,' margin 'I will intreat the enemy for thee' (RV 'I will cause the enemy to make supplication unto thee'; cf RSV).

INWARDS, INWARD PARTS.—1. The former of these expressions is frequently found in AV and RV (Exodus and Leviticus), meaning the entrails (so RSV) or bowels of the animals to be sacrificed according to the Levitical institutions (Ex 29$^{13, 22}$, Lv 3$^{3, 9, 14}$ 4$^{8, 11}$ 7^{3} 8$^{16, 21}$ etc.). The same idea is found in Gn 41^{21}, where EV has 'had eaten them up,' and LXX renders 'came into their belly' (see AVm which gives the alternative 'had come to the inward parts of them'; cf also 1 K 17^{21} AVm). For the most part, however, the expression 'inward parts' (rare in RSV) is used in a metaphorical sense, to denote the contrast between the inward reality and the outward clothing of human character. Situated within the 'inward parts' is the capacity for wisdom (Job 38^{36}; but RVm, RSV 'clouds'), truth (Ps 51^{6}), ethical knowledge, and moral renovation (Jer 31^{33} where 'inward parts' [AV, RV] is almost synonymous with 'heart,' cf Pr 20^{30}). Here, too, lie hidden the springs of active wickedness (Ps 5^{9}), and deceitful language (Ps 62^{3} AVm). The power of deceiving as to character and motives comes from man's inherent ability to secrete, within the profound depths of the 'innermost parts,' his daily thoughts (Pr 18^{8}; cf Ps 64^{6}). At the same time, these hidden designs are as an open book, beneath the bright light of a lamp, to the Lord (Pr 20^{27}; cf for a similar thought Ps 26^{2} 7^{9}, Jer 11^{20}, Rev 2^{23} etc.).

2. In the NT the expression is used only to denote the power of the hypocrites to deceive their fellow-men (Lk 11^{39}; cf Mt 7^{15} 23^{28}). The curious phrase 'give for alms those things which are within' (Lk 11^{41}) may be taken as an incidental reference by Jesus to the necessity and the possibility of man's inmost life being renewed and restored to a right relationship with God and men (cf Is 58^{10}). At least it is permissible to take the word rendered 'the things which are within' as equivalent to 'the inward man,' or 'the inward parts' (see Plummer, *ICC, in loc.*; cf Mk 7^{18f}). It is not enough to give alms mechanically; the gift must be accompanied by the spontaneous bestowal of the giver's self, as it were, to the receiver. J. R. W.

IOB.—See Jashub, **1.**

IOTA.—See Jot and Tittle.

IPHDEIAH.—A Benjamite chief, 1 Ch 8^{25} (AV **Iphedeiah**).

IPHEDEIAH, 1 Ch 8^{25} (AV).—See Iphdeiah.

IPHTAH.—A town in the Shephēlah of Judah, Jos 15^{43} (AV **Jiphtah**); possibly modern *Taiqûmiya.*

IPHTAH-EL.—A ravine NW. of Hannathon, on the north border of Zebulun, Jos 19$^{14, 27}$ (AV **Jiphtah-el**); possibly modern *Sahl el-Baṭṭôf.*

IR.—A Benjamite, 1 Ch 7^{12}; called **Iri** in v.^{7}.

IRA.—1. The Jairite who was *kōhēn* or priest to David, 2 S 20^{26}. His name is omitted from the original (?) passage in 2 S 8^{18}, and from the passage in 1 Ch 18^{17}. 'The Jairite' denotes that he was of the Gileadite clan of the Jairites. The name probably means 'the watchful.' **2.** The Ithrite, one of David's heroes (2 S 23^{38}, where perhaps *Ithrite* should be *Jattirite*, from Jattir [q.v.]). **3.** The son of Ikkesh of Tekoa (2 S 23^{26}), another of David's heroes.

IRAD.—Son of Enoch and grandson of Cain, Gn 4^{18}.

IRAM.—A 'duke' of Edom, Gn 36^{43}, 1 Ch 1^{54}.

IR-HA-HERES.—In Is 19^{18} the name to be given in the ideal future to one of the 'five cities in the land of Egypt that speak the language of Canaan, and swear to Yahweh of hosts'; AV and RV 'one shall be called, The city of destruction'; RSV 'one of these will be called the City of the Sun.' The usually accepted explanation of the passage is that the name 'city of *heres*,' or 'destruction,'—or, more exactly, 'of tearing down' (the verb *hāras* being used of 'pulling' or 'tearing down' cities, altars, walls, etc., Jg 6^{25}, Is 14^{17}, Ezk 13^{14})—is chosen for the sake of a punning allusion to *ḥeres*, in Hebrew a rare word for 'sun' (Job 9^{7}), the 'city of *ḥeres*,' or 'the sun' being a designation which might have been given in Hebrew to On (q.v.), the Heliopolis of the Greeks, a city a few miles NE. of the modern Cairo, in ancient times the chief centre of sun-worship in Egypt, and full of obelisks dedicated to the sun-god Re. The meaning of the passage would then be that the place which has hitherto been a 'city of the sun' will in the future be called the 'city of destroying,' *i.e.* a city devoted to destroying the temples and emblems of the sun (cf Jer 43^{13}). [The LXX have *polis hasedek*, *i.e.* 'city of righteousness,' a reading which is open to the suspicion of being an alteration based on 1^{26}.]

To some scholars, however, this explanation appears artificial; and the question is further complicated by historical considerations. The high priest Onias III., after his deposition by Antiochus Epiphanes in 175 B.C. (2 Mac 4$^{7-9}$), despairing of better times in Judah, sought refuge in Egypt with Ptolemy Philometor. He (or, according to some scholars, his son Onias IV.) conceived the idea of building there a temple dedicated to Yahweh, in which the ancient rites of his people might be carried on without molestation, and which might form a religious centre for the Jews settled in Egypt. Ptolemy granted him a site at Leontopolis in the 'nome,' or district, of Heliopolis, and there Onias erected his temple (Jos. *BJ* I. i. 1 [33], *Ant.* XIII. iii. 1–3 [62 ff], and elsewhere; Ewald, *Hist.* v, 355 f), not improbably at *Tell el-Yehūdîyeh*, about 10 miles N. of Heliopolis, near which there are remains of a Jewish necropolis (Naville, *The Mound of the Jew and the City of Onias*, pp. 18–20). In support of his plan, Onias had pointed to Is 19^{18} and its context as a prediction that a temple to Yahweh was to be built in Egypt (Jos. *Ant.* XIII. iii. 1 [68]). These facts have indeed no bearing on Is 19^{18}, supposing the passage to be really Isaiah's; but many modern scholars are of opinion that Is 19$^{16\,(18)-25}$ are not Isaiah's, and even those who do not go so far as this would be ready to grant that 19^{18b} (from 'one shall be called') might be a later addition to the original text of Isaiah.

The following are the chief views taken by those who hold that this clause (with or without its context) is not Isaiah's. (1) Duhm and Marti render boldly 'shall be called Lion-city (*or* Leontopolis),' explaining *heres* from the Arabic *haris*, properly the 'bruiser,' 'crusher,' a poetical name for a lion. But that a very special and figurative application of an Arabic root, not occurring in Hebrew even in its usual Arabic sense, should be found in Hebrew is not probable. (2) Dillmann, while accepting the prophecy as a whole as Isaiah's, threw out the suggestion that v.^{18b} was added after the temple of Onias was built, *ḥeres*, 'sun' (so Symmachus, Vulgate, and some Hebrew MSS), being the original reading, which was altered afterwards by the Jews of Palestine into *heres*, 'destruction,' in order to obtain a condemnation of the Egyptian temple, and by the Jews of Egypt into *ṣedheḳ*, 'righteousness' (LXX), in order to make the prophecy more distinctly favourable to it. (3) Cheyne (*Introd. to Is.*, pp. 102–110) and Skinner, understanding v.^{18} ('there shall be five cities,' etc.), not (as is done upon the ordinary view) of the conversion of Egyptian cities to the worship of Yahweh, but of Jewish colonies in Egypt maintaining their national language and religion, suppose vv.$^{16-25}$ to have been written in the latter years of the 1st Ptolemy (Lagi), *c* 290 B.C., when there were undoubtedly many Jewish settlements in Egypt. The original reading, these scholars suppose with Dillmann, was 'city of the sun,' the meaning that one of these colonies, preserving loyally the faith of their fathers, should flourish even in Heliopolis, the city of the sun-god. The reading was altered afterwards, when the Jews of Palestine began to show hostility towards the Egyptian temple, by the Jews of Egypt into 'city of righteousness' (LXX), and then further, by the Jews of Palestine, as a counter-blow, into 'city of destruction' (Hebrew text). S. R. D.—**R. J. W.**

IRI.—**1.** See IR. **2.** 1 Es 8^{62} (AV); see URIAH, **4.**

IRIJAH.—A captain who arrested Jeremiah on the charge of intending to desert to the Chaldaeans, Jer 37^{13f}.

IR-NAHASH.—A city of Judah, 1 Ch 4^{12}; possibly modern *Deir Nakhkhâs.*

IRON.—**1.** Jos 19^{38} (AV, RV); see YIRON. **2.** See MINING AND METALS.

IRPEEL.—A city of Benjamin, Jos 18^{27}; possible *Rafât*, N. of Gibeon.

IRRIGATION.—Owing to the lack of a sufficient rainfall, Babylonia and Egypt have to be supplied with water from their respective rivers. This is conveyed over the country by canals. The water is conducted along these canals by various mechanical devices, and at a cost of great labour. In Palestine the need for artificial irrigation is not so great, as is indicated by the contrast with Egypt in Dt 11^{10}. As a rule the winter rainfall is sufficient for the ordinary cereal crops, and no special irrigation is necessary. The case is different, however, in vegetable and fruit gardens, which would be destroyed by the long summer droughts. They are always established near natural supplies of water, which is made to flow from the sources (either directly or raised when necessary, by a *sâkiyeh* or endless chain of buckets worked by a horse, ox, or donkey) into little channels ramifying through the garden. When the channels are, as often, simply dug in the earth, they can be stopped or diverted *with the foot*, as in the passage quoted. Artificial water-pools for gardens are referred to in Ec 2^{6}. A storage-pool is an almost universal feature in such gardens. R. A. S. M.

IR-SHEMESH.—See BETH-SHEMESH, **1.**

IRU.—The eldest son of Caleb, 1 Ch 4^{15}. The correct name is probably *Ir*, the -u being simply the conjunction 'and' coupling it with the following name Elah.

ISAAC.—Son of Abraham and Sarah. The meaning of the name is 'he laughs,' and several reasons for bestowing it are suggested (Gn 17^{17} 18^{12} 21^{6}). The narrative as it occurs in Scripture was derived from three principal sources, the hand of J being discernible in Gn 18$^{9-15}$ 21$^{1a,\,2a,\,7}$ 24 25$^{5,\,11b,\,21-26a,\,27-34}$ 26$^{1-33}$ 27$^{1-45}$, of E in 21^{6} 22$^{1-19}$, and of P in 17$^{15-21}$ 21$^{1b,\,2b-5}$ 25$^{11a,\,19f,\,26b}$ 26^{35} 27^{46}–28^{9} 35$^{27-29}$, although in some of these passages there are also indications of the JE redactor. Apparent discrepancies in the story, such as that Isaac, on his deathbed (27$^{1,\,41}$), blessed Jacob, and yet did not die until many years afterwards (35^{27}), are evidently due to original differences of tradition, which later editors were not careful to remove. Viewed as coming from independent witnesses, they present no serious difficulty, and do not destroy the verisimilitude of the story. In outline the narrative describes Isaac as circumcised when eight days old (21^{4}), and as spending his early youth with his father at Beersheba. Thence he was taken to 'the land of Moriah,' to be offered up as a burnt-offering at the bidding of God; and if Abraham's unquestioning faith is the primary lesson taught (22^{12} 26^{5}, He 11^{17ff}), Isaac's child-like confidence in his father is yet conspicuous, with the associated sense of security.

His mother died when he was thirty-six years of age; and Abraham sent a servant to fetch a wife for Isaac from amongst his kindred in Mesopotamia, according to Gn 24, where the religious spirit is as noticeable as the idyllic tone. For many years the couple were childless; but at length Isaac's prayers were heard, and Rebekah gave birth to the twins, Esau and Jacob. Famine and drought made it necessary for Isaac to shift his encampment to Gerar (26^{1}), where a story similar to that of Abraham's repudiation of Sarah is told of him (ch. 20, cf 12^{10-20}). The tradition was evidently a popular one, and may have found currency in several versions, though there is no actual impossibility in the imitation by the son of the father's device. Isaac's prosperity aroused the envy of the Philistine herdsmen (26^{20f}) amongst whom he dwelt, and eventually he withdrew again to Beersheba (26^{23}). He appears next as a decrepit and dying man ($27^{1,41}$), whose blessing, intended for Esau (25^{28} 27^{4}), was diverted by Rebekah upon Jacob. When the old man discovered the mistake, he was agitated at the deception practised upon him, but was unable to do more than predict for Esau a wild and independent career. To protect Jacob from his brother's resentment Isaac sent him away to obtain a wife from his mother's kindred in Paddan-aram (28^{2}), and repeated the benediction. The next record belongs to a period twenty-one years later, unless the paragraph (35^{27-29}) relates to a visit Jacob made to his home in the interval. It states that Isaac died at Hebron at the age of 180. He was buried by his sons in the cave of Machpelah (49^{31}).

Isaac is a less striking personality than his father. Deficient in the heroic qualities, he suffered in disposition from an excess of mildness and the love of quiet. His passion for 'savoury meat' (25^{28} 27^{4}) was probably a tribal failing. He was rather shifty and timid in his relations with Abimelech (26^{1-22}), too easily imposed upon, and not a good ruler of his household—a gracious and kindly but not a strong man. In 26^{5} he is subordinated to Abraham, and blessed for his sake; but the two are classed together along with Jacob (Ex 2^{24} 3^{6}, Mt 8^{11} 22^{32}, Ac 3^{13} *et al.*), as the three leading patriarchs of Israel, and in Am $7^{9,16}$ 'Isaac' is used as a synonym for Israel. If therefore the glory of Isaac was partly derived from the memory of his greater father, the impression made upon posterity by his almost instinctive trust in God (Gn 22^{7f}) and by the prevailing strength of his devotion (25^{21}) was deep and abiding. Jacob considered piety and reverent awe as specially characteristic of his father ($31^{42,53}$, where 'the Fear of Isaac' means the God tremblingly adored by him). The submission of Isaac plays a part, although a less important one than the faith of Abraham, in the NT references (He 11^{17f}, Ja 2^{21}). It is, however, alluded to in the Messianic Hymn of Levi 18^{1-14} (Test. 12 Pat.), where v.^{6} appears to refer to Gn 22^{8}; and the sacrificial obedience of Isaac is related in early Christian thought as a type fulfilled in that of the cross (*e.g.* Ep. Bar 7), and in medieval Judaism is representative of the submission of the whole race of Israel to God. R. W. M.—E. T. R.

ISAIAH.—It is not until relatively late in the history of Israel that a major prophet appears upon the scene in the southern kingdom of Judah. The prophets of the 9th cent.—Elijah, Elisha, and Micaiah—come from the north, as did the greatest of their successors, Hosea ben-Beeri. Amos, an earlier contemporary of Hosea, was born and reared in Judah, but his message is directed exclusively to Israel. Isaiah is the first of the great literary prophets to come from Jerusalem, to pursue his prophetic calling there, and to address himself primarily to the south. His name is associated more intimately with Jerusalem and the royal house of David than any of the other prophets, even more than Jeremiah, who remained throughout his life a loyal son of the tribe of Benjamin, and Ezekiel, who prophesied in exile. His life and prophetic activity are identified with the history of Judah and its capital in an extraordinary degree.

Like all the prophets of ancient Israel, Isaiah was acutely sensitive to the political and international events of his time. His prophecies must therefore be read against the background of the history of the Near East in the latter half of the 8th cent. B.C. The determining factor in this history is the military aggression of Assyria. Tiglath-pileser III. (744–727 B.C.) was the first of a succession of Assyrian monarchs to hold the lands of Western Asia under their sway for more than a century. He was followed by Shalmaneser V. (726–722 B.C.) and Sargon II. (721–705 B.C.), who pursued the same policy of military expansion. It was during their reigns that Samaria, the capital of the northern kingdom, was besieged and captured and its inhabitants carried into exile. They in turn were succeeded by Sennacherib (704–681 B.C.), who invaded Judah, destroyed its towns, and laid siege to Jerusalem. It was a stormy and turbulent time, and the little buffer state of Judah, between the Mesopotamian power and Egypt, the mistress of the Nile, lived in a constant state of nervous tension as campaign followed campaign. The little states of Western Asia strove in vain to stem the Assyrian tide, yet deluded themselves into thinking with the accession of each new monarch that the hour of liberation had arrived and the time for revolt was ripe.

It is impossible to construct a biography of the prophet Isaiah. The sources at our disposal have relatively little to say about his life. Moreover, his prophecies have not come down to us in chronological order, and many are without any clear indication of the date at which they were delivered. Nevertheless the essential facts of his life are known. He was born in Jerusalem presumably, and his father's name was Amoz, not to be confused with the prophet Amos. He was married and had two children, who bore symbolic names: Shear-jashub, 'A Remnant shall return,' and Maher-shalal-hash-baz, 'Speed spoil, haste prey.' The former name has been interpreted optimistically, but it is uncertain whether this was its primary intent. It may be a sentence of judgment, which is a major theme of Isaiah's message. The period of his ministry covers four decades, from the year of Uzziah's death *c* 738 B.C. until after Sennacherib's military campaign against Jerusalem in 701 B.C. Tradition has it that during the reign of Manasseh he was sawn in sunder (cf He 11^{37}).

Isaiah's ministry may be conveniently divided into the following periods: his call in *c* 738 B.C. (ch. 6), the Syro-Ephraimitic war in 734–733 B.C. (7^{1}–8^{18} 17^{1-6}), the siege and fall of Samaria in 724–722 B.C. (9^{8}–10^{4} 5^{24-30}), the siege of Ashdod in 711 B.C. (ch. 20), and the invasion of Sennacherib in 701 B.C. (cf chs. 36–39). The last-mentioned narratives belong, however, to quite another tradition from Isaiah's own oracles and must be assessed independently. Isaiah's call left a profound impress upon his whole life and work. In the year of the death of Uzziah (Azariah) he beheld in the Temple a vision of Yahweh enthroned as king. He listens to the thundering trisagion of the seraphs, and is overwhelmed by his sense of unworthiness. But his lips are touched with a glowing stone from the altar, and his guilt is atoned. He hears a call to proclaim the terrible message of doom. The last clause of the chapter is absent from the LXX, but this is probably due to homoioteleuton. The causes of this judgment Isaiah found in the prevalent social and moral disorder of the time (see *e.g.* 2^{6}–4^{1} 5^{8-24} for the kind of offences denounced), in the rebellion of the people against Yahweh (1^{3} 5^{1-7}), and in their failure to understand that the practices of the cult—sacrifice, festivals, prayer, etc.—were only instruments of profound corruption when they did not express inward contrition and repentance and moral transformation ($1^{10-17,21-23}$). But even more central is Isaiah's message of the holiness of God; Yahweh is the Holy One of Israel, *Ḳᵉdhôsh Yiśrā'ēl.* He is exalted in justice, and manifests His holiness in righteousness (5^{16}); His holiness is an active personal power which destroys all those forces in civilization and culture, all the instruments of pride and self-sufficiency, which men substitute for trust in Him. Like Amos, Isaiah sees that Yahweh's Day is darkness and not light (2^{6-22} ; cf Am 5^{18-20}). The holy God is Israel's King, the One who sits enthroned on the Ark, the Lord of the covenant bond. The motif of Yahweh's sovereignty runs like a silver cord through all the prophecies of Isaiah. He is the prophet of the Divine majesty, the effluence of whose radiant glory fills the earth. Over a long period of years he confronted changing political conditions in Judah and international crises evoked by Assyria's aggression in the Near East, but ever and again he urged his people to place their faith and trust in Yahweh, not in political alliances, whether with Assyria, Egypt, or Ethiopia (cf *e.g.* 7^{4-9} 20, and later in *c* 701 B.C. $30^{1-5, 15}$ 31^{1-3}). When his appeal to the royal house was rejected in 734–733 B.C. and the people refused ' the waters of Shiloah that flow gently,' he gathered about him a band of disciples who would ' wait for Yahweh, who is hiding his face from the house of Jacob ' and place their hope on Him ($8^{5-8, 16}$).

Although the imminence of judgment was the fundamental note of Isaiah's prophetic message, there was another note that marked it from the outset : a remnant would survive. While this message cannot with confidence be based upon the name of Isaiah's son, *Shear-jashub*, the closing line of the vision does contain this hope. Beyond judgment, he looked forward to a restored Jerusalem, ' the city of righteousness, the faithful city ' (1^{26}). How much further was Isaiah's view of the future developed? While many scholars have rejected the authenticity of the so-called messianic oracles (2^{2-4} 9^{1-6} [He 8^{23}–9^{5}] 11^{1-9} $32^{1-8, 15-20}$), there has been a greater proclivity in recent years to accept them in whole or in part as the work of the prophet. Some have relegated them to the closing years of his ministry, but with our increased knowledge of Near Eastern royal ideology and terminology the likelihood has grown that at least some of them form an integral part of his prophetic message. After all, there is an interior consistency between Isaiah's deep concern for the Davidic royal house from the beginning to the end of his career and the hope in the coming of a king from the stump of Jesse. It is true that later passages of promise have in some instances been added to earlier prophecies of judgment—indeed, the alternation of doom and felicity is a major feature of the composition of chs. 1–35 ; but the doctrine of the remnant provides some basis for such an expectation and the language of the relevant texts cannot be said to be late in view of the parallels to the Ugaritic rituals. Nor do these poems of the coming king contradict the prophecies of judgment ; they may be said indeed to confirm them, for in contrast to the present they look forward to a time when the sacral king of Judah will fulfil the obligations and functions that were expected of him as the Lord's ' messiah.'

We think of Isaiah as one of the great prophets of Israel, but he was also a poet of stature. Perhaps there is no one among the writers of ancient Israel to whom the adjective *classical* applies more appropriately. Despite the vigour and passion of his speech, he maintains an elevation, indeed a grandeur and prophetic eloquence, a restraint and rhythmic control, a kind of loftiness and elegance of speech, seldom if ever surpassed. He resorts to every manner of rhetorical device, yet never in a studied or awkward fashion. His refrains are perhaps the most powerful in the OT (cf 2^{6-22} 9^{8}–10^{4} $5^{24\text{ff}}$), his examples of paronomasia are not overdrawn (5^{7} $7^{9\text{b}}$), his climaxes are sure, *i.e.* they seem inevitable. His imagery moves over a vast area, his descriptions are superb ($1^{7\text{f}}$ $2^{10, 13, 19}$ $5^{1-6, 8, 10, 17, 24, 29}$ 6^{11-13} 7^{4} 8^{5-8} 9^{3-5} $28^{1-4, 7-8, 9-10, 20, 27-29}$). His literary forms and types are almost as varied as his images ; invectives and threats are most common, but songs, dirges, laments, mocking songs, and hymns are also present. Like the prophets before and after him, Isaiah places all this extraordinary wealth of literary composition at the service of prophecy. His language impressed itself upon the ancient community at Qumrân, upon the writers of the NT, and, later, upon the synagogue and the Church. G. B. G.—**J. Mu.**

ISAIAH, ASCENSION OF.—See PSEUDEPIGRAPHA, **6.**

ISAIAH, BOOK OF.—The Book of Isaiah is one of the four great collections of Hebrew prophecies. Like the book of ' The Twelve Prophets '—another of these great collections—it was formed by the compilation of a number of smaller collections, and contains prophecies of other prophets living at different periods ; with the exception of Isaiah's own work, the prophecies contained in the collection are anonymous, the term Deutero-Isaiah ' applied to chs. 40–55 (or 40–66) being nothing more than a modern symbol for one of the anonymous writers.

1. Composition and literary history of the present book.—The Book of Isaiah, substantially as we now have it, probably dates, like the ' Book of the Twelve Prophets,' from the post-exilic period. But the external evidence is scanty and some of it ambiguous ; and the internal evidence of certain sections is differently interpreted. The earlier view held by Duhm, Marti, and others that certain sections of the book, like chs. 33 and 34 f, were written about the middle of the 2nd cent. B.C., and chs. 24–27 not until 128 B.C., is no longer held by scholars. Among the Dead Sea Scrolls discovered in the spring of 1947 is a complete manuscript of the Book of Isaiah dating from the close of the 2nd cent. B.C., and it is exceedingly probable that it had long been extant in this form.

The most important piece of external evidence is contained in Sir 48^{23-24}. In this passage the author, writing about 180 B.C., refers to Isaiah as one of the godly men of Israel, worthy of praise, and, as afterwards (49^{6-8}) in the case of Ezekiel and of Jeremiah, he cites, or alludes to, certain sections which now stand in the book that bears the prophet's name (48^{22-25}). He refers to the narrative of Is 38 (=2 K 20), and is familiar with the recurrent arguments from prophecy in Is 44–48 (see *e.g.* 41^{21-24} 43^{9} 46^{9} $48^{4\text{ff}}$), while v.$^{24\text{b}}$ is clearly reminiscent of the phraseology of 40^{1} $61^{2\text{f}}$. The most probable inference is that, by the beginning of the 2nd cent. B.C., some (if not all) of the prophecies of chs. 1–35 had already been brought into a book, and that to these had been appended, not necessarily at the same time, (*a*) chs. 36–39, (*b*) chs. 40–66, and that the whole book at this time was attributed to Isaiah. This is now substantiated not only by the presence of a number of actual manuscripts of Isaiah among the Dead Sea Scrolls but also by the frequency with which the prophecy is quoted in the extra-biblical texts and by several commentaries. It is of course frequently cited in the NT also : 1^{9} is cited in Ro 9^{29} ; $6^{9\text{f}}$ in Mt $13^{14\text{f}}$, Jn 12^{40}, Ac $28^{25\text{f}}$; $9^{1\text{f}}$ in Mt $4^{14\text{ff}}$; 10^{22} in Ro $9^{27\text{f}}$; 11^{10} in Ro 15^{12} ; 20^{13} in Mk $7^{6\text{f}}$; 40^{3-5} in Mk 1^{3}, Mt 3^{3} ; 42^{1-4} in Mt 12^{17-21} ; $53^{1, 4, 7\text{f}}$ in Ro 10^{16}, Mt 8^{17}, Ac $8^{30, 32\text{f}}$; $61^{1\text{f}}$ in Lk 4^{17-19} ; $65^{1\text{f}}$ in Ro $10^{20\text{f}}$. The general considerations which, taken in conjunction with the proof offered in Sir 48^{17-25} that chs. 40–66 ranked as Isaiah's as early as 180 B.C., make it probable that by about that time the book was substantially of the same extent as at present are (*a*) the history of the formation of the Canon (see CANON OF OT), and (*b*) the probability, created by the allusions in the prologue to Sirach (132 B.C.) to translations of the prophetic canon, that our present Greek version dates from before 132 B.C.

Turning then to the internal evidence, we note first the structure of the book : (*a*) chs. 1–35—prophecies, some of which are attributed to Isaiah (1^{1} 2^{1} etc.), interspersed with narratives by or about Isaiah (chs 6, 7, 8, 20) ; (*b*) chs. 36–39—historical narratives of the life and times of Isaiah, identical in the main with 2 K 18–20 ; (*c*) chs. 40–66—anonymous prophecies. Comparison with the Book of Jeremiah, which concludes with a chapter (52) about the times of Jeremiah derived from 2 K $24^{18\text{ff}}$, suggests that our present book has resulted from the union of a prophetic volume, consisting (in the main) of prophecies by or attributed to Isaiah, with an historical appendix and a book of anonymous prophecies. This union, as we have seen above, took place before 180 B.C.

But, apart from internal evidence pointing to the different periods in which different sections originated, certain indications of the complexity of the literary process do exist, particularly in the case of chs 1–39; these we may consider. (1) The matter is not arranged chronologically: the call (cf Ezk 1, Jer 1) of Isaiah, which naturally preceded any of his prophecies, is recorded not in ch. 1, but in ch. 6. Similarly, in the Koran the record of Mohammed's call does not occur till *Sura* 96; in this case the reason is that the editors of the Koran followed the rather mechanical principle of arranging the *suras* according to their size. The cause of the order in the case of the Book of Isaiah may in part be found in the fact that (2) the occurrence of several titles and indications of different principles of editorial arrangement points to the fact that chs. 1–35 (39) is a collection of material, some of which had previously acquired a fixed arrangement; in other words, chs. 1–35 is a book formed not entirely, or perhaps even mainly, by the collection and free re-arrangement of prophetic pieces, but rather by the incorporation of whole earlier and smaller books. Following these clues, we may first divide these chapters thus: (1) ch. 1 with title (v.^{1}), probably intended to cover the larger collection; (2) chs. 2–12 with title 2^{1}; (3) chs. 13–23 with title 13^{1} naming Isaiah, and corresponding sub-titles not mentioning Isaiah, in 15^{1} 17^{1} 19^{1} $21^{1, 11, 13}$; 22^{1} 23^{1} (cf elsewhere 30^{6}); (4) chs. 24–27, distinguished from the preceding sections by the absence of titles, and from the following by the absence of the opening interjection; (5) chs. 28–31 (33)—a group of woes; see 28^{1} 29^{1} (RV 'Ho' represents the same Hebrew word that is translated 'Woe' in 28^{1} etc.) 30^{1} 31^{1} 33^{1}; (6) chs. 34, 35, which, like chs. 24–27, are without title. Some even of these sections seem to have arisen from the union of still smaller and earlier booklets. Thus it is reasonable to suppose that ch. 6 once formed the commencement of a booklet; again, chs. 2–4 are prophecies of judgment enclosed between 'messianic' prophecies 2^{2-7} and 4^{2-6}; ch. 5 contains a brief group of 'Woes' (vv.$^{8, 11, 18, 20, 21, 22}$).

It is more important to appreciate the general fact, which is clear, that the Book of Isaiah is the result of a long and complex literary history, than to be ready to subscribe to any particular theory of this history. But two points may be briefly touched on. (1) Much of the literary process just referred to lies after the Exile. As will be shown below, chs. 40–55 were not written till the last years of the Exile; chs. 56–66 are certainly of no earlier, and probably of later, origin. The union of chs. 1–39 and 40–66 cannot therefore fall before the close of the Exile, and, as shown above, it need not, so far as the external evidence is concerned, fall much before 180 B.C. But even 1–39 was not a volume of pre-exilic origin; for the appendix 36–39 is derived from Kings, which was not completed till, at the earliest, 561 B.C. (cf 2 K 25^{27}), or even in what may be regarded as its first edition (cf Driver, *LOT*^{9}, 198) before about 600 B.C. On this ground alone, then, the completion of chs. 1–39 by the inclusion of the appendix 36–39, cannot be placed earlier than the Exile, and should probably be placed later. It must indeed be placed later, unless we regard all the sections in chs. 1–35 which are of post-exilic origin (see below) as interpolations rather than as what, in many cases at least, they probably are, original parts of the booklets incorporated in chs. 1–39. Thus chs. 2–12 and 13–23 (apart from subsequent interpolations or amplifications), as they lay before the editor who united them, probably owed their form to post-exilic editors. (2) The earliest stage of this long literary process was not uniform. In chs 6 and 8^{1-8} we have what there is no reason to question are pieces of Isaiah's autobiography; Isaiah here speaks of himself in the first person. Chs. 7 and 20 may have the same origin, the fact that Isaiah is here referred to in the third person being perhaps in that case due to an editor; or these chapters may be drawn from early biographies of the prophet by a disciple. Thus chs 1, 2–12, 13–23, and 28–33 consist in large part of prophetic poems or sayings of Isaiah; many of them were (presumably) written as well as spoken by Isaiah himself, others we not improbably owe to the memory of his disciples. There is no reason for believing that the present arrangement of this matter, even within the several booklets goes back to Isaiah himself; the division into chapters and verses is of course of very much later origin, and in several cases does violence to the original connexion, either by uniting, as in ch. 5, originally quite distinct pieces, or dividing, as in the case of 9^{8}–10^{4}, what formed an undivided whole. Justice can be done to the prophetic literature only when the brevity of the several pieces is recognized, instead of being obscured by treating several distinct pieces as a single discourse. The analogy of the diverse treatment of the same sayings in the different Gospels may well warn us that sayings which lie side by side (as *e.g.* in 5^{8-24}) in the Book of Isaiah were not necessarily spoken in immediate succession.

But how far, if not in the order in which he spoke or wrote them, have the words of Isaiah reached us substantially as he spoke them? The question is not altogether easy to answer, particularly in one respect. Isaiah was pre-eminently a prophet of judgment; but intermingled with his warnings are many passages of promise: see *e.g.* 2^{2-4} and 4^{2-6}, enclosing 2^{7}–4^{1}, 9^{1-6} concluding the warnings of ch. 8, and the constant interchange of warning and promise in chs. 28–31. Are these passages of promise Isaiah's, or the work of some later writers with which later editors sought to comfort as well as to exhort their readers?

2. Structure and contents of the Book of Isaiah.—The following outline of the contents of the book and of the periods in which its several parts appear to have been written must be used in the light of the foregoing account of the origin of the book. The captions are designed to call attention to the major themes to which the prophet addresses himself; in many cases, however, the materials are so diverse in character and form that no single topic can adequately describe the contents of the literary units subsumed under it. For detailed discussion of the critical questions involved—date, occasion, provenance, literary type, etc.—the commentaries or critical introductions should be consulted.

Superscription.—An editor or compiler here provides the essential information for the understanding of the book: the name of the prophet, the people addressed, and the period of his prophetic activity.

I. *Oracles of judgment and promises of felicity:* chs. 1–12.

A. *Rebellion, judgment, and assurances of a happy future:* 1^{2-31}.—The chapter contains four or five separate literary units which come from different times in Isaiah's ministry. We should expect his call (ch. 6) to open the book, as in Jeremiah (1^{4-10}) and Ezekiel (1^{1}–2^{10}), but the impressive opening verses (vv.$^{2-4}$) were possibly considered an appropriate introduction to the oracles of judgment which follow. The view once championed by Ewald that the chapter constitutes a single discourse, 'The Great Arraignment,' is now generally rejected.

(1) *A sinful nation:* 1^{2-9}.—It is possible that vv.$^{10-17}$ belong with this section. The references to Sodom and Gomorrah (vv.$^{9-10}$) in any event connect the two passages. The invective has four strophes and a conclusion (v.^{9}). The date is to be determined by the description in vv.$^{7-8}$, which suggests the time after Sennacherib's invasion in 705 or 701 B.C.

(2) *Not sacrifice, but obedience:* 1^{10-17}.—Three strophes of invective are followed by an exhortation. The date is probably the same as that of vv.$^{2-9}$.

(3) *The alternatives: obedience or rebellion:* 1^{18-20}.—Conceivably these lines belong with vv.$^{2-17}$. The assurance in v.^{18} is by no means unconditioned, so there is no contradiction involved. The language is determined by the terminology and form of the covenant demands in Ex 19^{5-6}.

(4) *The faithless city:* 1^{21-26}.—Invective and threat. The conclusion repeats the motifs of the introduction.

(5) *Judgment by fire:* 1^{27-31}.—No certain date can be assigned to the last two literary units.

B. *The day of Yahweh and a series of woes:* 2^{1}–5^{30}.—Superscription: 2^{1}.

(1) *Universal peace:* 2^{2-4} [5 ?].—The words are paralleled in Mic 4^{1-5}. It is difficult to determine to whom they belong. The literary form and structure of Micah is superior to that of Isaiah, but it is possible that both are derived from another source.

(2) *The day of Yahweh:* 2^{6-22}.—The text is mutilated and disturbed. The refrains are not in place, and the original opening is lost. It is nevertheless one of the most powerful and awesome of the prophet's poems. For the theme of the day, compare Am 5^{18-20}.

(3) *Misleading leaders:* 3^{1-15}.—A poetic invective describing the imminent social disintegration of Jerusalem. It contains three substantial strophes (vv.$^{1-5, 6-8, 9-12}$) and a judicial encounter of Yahweh with His people vv.$^{13-15}$). It belongs to the early period of Isaiah's ministry.

(4) *The humiliation of the patrician ladies:* 3^{16}–4^{1}.—An oracle of invective and threat. The prose section of vv.$^{18-22}$ is generally considered late, but it may well be original. Literary form was employed with the greatest freedom and versatility by the Hebrew writers. The elaboration of female finery is not out of place here.

(5) *Zion, the covenant city:* 4^{2-6}.—Post-exilic.

(6) *Parable of the vineyard:* 5^{1-7}.—The folksong of four strophes with invective-threat motifs belongs to the prophet's early period.

(7) *Woes:* 5^{8-24}.—The original series of perhaps seven invectives and threats, certainly very early, have been thrown into disarray in the course of their transmission. Vv.$^{25-30}$ belong with 9^{8}–10^{4}.

C. *Biographical episodes:* 6^{1}–9^{7} (He 6^{1}–9^{6}).

(1) *The call of Isaiah:* 6^{1-13}.—Isaiah's own account of his call in the year of Uzziah's death (738 B.C.), written perhaps some years later.

(2) *The Syro-Ephraimitic war:* 7^{1}–8^{21}.—(*a*) Isaiah's interview with Ahaz: vv.$^{1-17}$. Traditionist expansion: vv.$^{18-24}$. (*b*) Maher-shalal-hash-baz: 8^{1-4}. (*c*) Waters of Shiloah: vv.$^{5-8}$. Traditionist expansion: vv.$^{9-10}$. (*d*) Yahweh is Israel's fear and dread: vv.$^{11-15}$. (*e*) Signs and portents in Israel: vv.$^{16-18}$. The obscure lines about necromancy are later expansion (vv.$^{19-21}$), though their origin is Isaianic.

(3) *The birth and righteous rule of the coming king:* 8^{22}–9^{7} (Heb. 8^{22}–9^{6}).—The passage forms the conclusion to the biographical section. Its genuineness is disputed, but it may well be original, belonging to the ideology of the sacral king of David's dynasty.

D. *Invectives against Judah, Israel, and Assyria and promises of a happy future:* 9^{8}–12^{6}.

(1) *The outstretched hand of judgment:* 9^{8}–10^{4} 5^{25-30}.—A carefully constructed poem of five strophes, each ending in a refrain ($9^{12, 17, 21}$ 10^{4} 5^{25}). It belongs to Isaiah's early period, and deals with the collapse of the northern kingdom before the Assyrians, who are vividly described in 5^{28-30}. Compare Amos 4^{6-11} for form and content.

(2) *Assyria, rod of Yahweh's anger:* 10^{5-34}.—Assyria will be punished for its pride and refusal to recognize that it is the instrument of Yahweh's purpose. Vv.$^{16-23}$, while Isaiah's, seem to be an insertion here. It is one of the greatest of the prophet's poetic compositions, but belongs to a later period of his career, perhaps between 715 and 701 B.C.

(3) *The ideal reign of peace:* 11^{1-16}.—(*a*) The king of David's lineage: vv.$^{1-9}$. A superbly constructed poem of three strophes, belonging to the same world of thought as 9^{1-7} (Heb. 8^{23}–9^{6}) and performing the same literary purpose at the close of a series of judgments. (*b*) The ensign to the peoples: vv.$^{10-16}$. Probably late, but belonging to the same sphere of thinking as Isaiah's.

(4) *A song of thanksgiving:* 12^{1-6}.—Probably not the work of Isaiah; it has many affinities with the Psalms.

II. *Oracles against the nations:* chs. 13–23.—The untitled sections, $14^{24-26\ (28-32)}$ 17^{12-14} 18 20, which deal with Judah, as contrasted with most of the oracles, which are against the foreign nations, perhaps formed no part of the original book.

A. *The 'Burden' of Babylon:* 13^{1}–14^{23}.—The section contains two poems (13^{2-22} and 14^{4b-21}) in lamentation meter; between the poems and at the close of the second are short prose passages ($14^{1-4a, 22f}$). The section throughout presupposes conditions of a much later time, after 586 B.C. To the Assyrians, who play so large a rôle in Isaiah's prophecies, there is no allusion; with the fall of Nineveh in 612 B.C. they ceased to exist, and Babylon, which in Isaiah's time was subject to Assyria, here figures as possessed of world dominion. Restoration from exile is referred to in 14^{1f}.

(1) *The fall of Babylon:* 13^{2-22}.—A deeply moving poem in the manner of the day of Yahweh oracles of Zephaniah, Ezekiel, and Joel. The date is probably after 538 B.C. (cf 13^{17}).

(2) *A taunt song against the king of Babylon:* 14^{4b-21}.—The poem itself does not name the king or his land; some have therefore upheld the substantial authenticity of the passage, identifying the ruling monarch with the king of Assyria.

B. *Yahweh's plan and purpose:* 14^{24-27}.—A pregnant oracle, perhaps of the year 701 B.C., predicting the overthrow of the Assyrian invader.

C. *A warning to Philistia:* vv.$^{28-32}$.—According to the title in the Hebrew text, the oracle was delivered in the year of the death of Ahaz (715 B.C.), but the original text may have simply referred to the death of the king, whom some have identified with Sargon II. in 705 B.C.

D. *The fate of Moab:* chs. 15–16.—The epilogue of 16^{13f} explains that the foregoing predictions will be fulfilled in three years. Much of the material of the poems appears to be a re-casting and revision of an older original. Compare the imitation of the poem in Jer $48^{5, 29-38}$. Both poems (15^{1-9} 16^{1-11}) are laments.

E. *The fall of Damascus, Syria, and Ephraim:* 17^{1-11}.—The poem belongs with the Syro-Ephraimitic prophecies of 7^{1}–8^{12} and is to be dated before 732 B.C.

F. *The uproar of the peoples:* 17^{12-14}.—The thunder of hostile nations (presumably in the Assyrian army) who are to be dispersed. It belongs to Isaiah, but the date is not certain.

G. *The Ethiopian avenger:* ch. 18.—A poem of highly poetic style, certainly original, to be dated after 715 B.C., the beginning of the 25th Dynasty.

H. *Oracle on Egypt:* 19^{1-15}.—Yahweh's judgment on Egypt, which will take the form of civil discord (v.^{2}), foreign domination (v.^{4}), and social distress. In vv.$^{16-25}$ we have a remarkable account of the conversion of Egypt, which, together with Assyria, will worship Yahweh. The date of the chapter is much disputed. Vv. $^{16-24}$ are probably not from Isaiah.

I. *Isaiah, a sign and symbol:* ch. 20.—Naked and barefoot, in the guise of a captive, Isaiah symbolizes the Assyrian conquest of Egypt and Ethiopia.

J. *Three 'burdens':* 21^{1-16}.

(1) *The wilderness of the sea:* 21^{1-10}.—Babylon is conquered by the Medes and Elamites. It is a remarkable revelation of the interior of the prophetic mind. The date is probably near to 538 B.C. when Babylon fell before Cyrus II. of Persia.

(2) *Oracles on Edom* (21^{11f}) *and the caravans* (21^{13-15}).

K. *Oracle concerning the valley of vision:* 22^{1-14}.—A vivid poem, in the manner of the invective and threat, employing the motifs of the day of Yahweh (cf 2^{6-22}), to be assigned either to *c* 711 B.C., when Sargon's troops were at Ashdod (ch. 20) or to the time of revelry following Sennacherib's withdrawal from Jerusalem in 701 B.C.

L. *Oracle to Shebna:* 22^{15-22}.—Singular among Isaiah's prophecies in that it is addressed to an individual, the steward of the palace, who is threatened with disgrace. An invective and threat composed before 701 B.C. since at that time he had already been demoted (cf 36^{22} 37^{2}).

M. *Oracle concerning Tyre:* vv.$^{1-14\ (15-18)}$.—It is possible that an original oracle against Sidon (vv.$^{1-4,\ 12-14}$) has been united with an oracle against Tyre (vv.$^{5-11}$). The date of the former is uncertain. Some refer the latter (or the whole oracle) to the siege of Tyre by Shalmaneser V. between 727 and 723 B.C., others to the destruction of Tyre by Artaxerxes III. Ochus in 348 B.C. The redactor of vv.$^{15-18}$ evidently has the destruction of the city by Alexander the Great in 332 B.C. in mind and of its later revival in 274 B.C. under Ptolemy II. (so Eissfeldt).

III. *Apocalyptic oracles, songs, and hymns:* chs. 24–27.—The section is generally recognized as a special collection of the Book of Isaiah, containing, however, a variety of literary materials: eschatological predictions (24$^{1-3,\ 13,\ 17-23}$ 25$^{6-8}$ 27$^{1,\ 12-13}$) and hymns (24$^{4-6,\ 7-9,\ 10-12,\ 14-16}$ 25$^{1-5}$; cf 25$^{9-12}$ 26$^{1-6}$). A prayer of lamentation is given in 26$^{7-19}$: vv.^{20f} are the Divine answer. A vineyard song is placed in the mouth of Yahweh in 27$^{2-5}$ (cf 5$^{1-7}$). The following verses (27$^{7-11}$) describe the destruction of the apostate cult objects and the expiation of Israel's guilt. The work as a whole is post-exilic as the many later ideas suggest: cf *e.g.* resurrection from the dead (26^{19}; see also 25^{8}) and patron angels.

IV. *Prophecies of woe and promises of felicity:* chs. 28–33.—The prophecies have been compiled by an editor on account of the similar opening of the sections with 'Woe' (see 28^{1} 29^{1} 29^{15} 30^{1} 31^{1}; cf 32^{1}). It is probable that these invectives circulated independently at one time. In this section there is, however, a remarkable alternation between menace and denunciation of Judah, on the one hand, and of consolation, on the other. The booklet falls into the following sections (references to oracles of promise are given in parentheses): 28$^{1-4}$ (28$^{5-6}$) 28$^{7-22\ (23-29)}$ 29$^{1-6\ (7)}$ (29^{8} and possibly parts of 29$^{1-7}$, according to the interpretation), 29$^{9-16}$ (29$^{17-24}$) 30$^{1-17}$ (30$^{18-33}$) 31$^{1-4}$ (31$^{5-9}$) 32$^{1-8}$ (32$^{9-14}$); 32$^{15-20\ (33)}$.

A. *Threat and invective against Samaria:* 28$^{1-22}$.—Certainly the work of Isaiah, the early verses (vv.$^{1-4}$ or ^{6} ?) during the last years of the northern kingdom, the rest somewhat later, the precise date being unclear.

B. *A prophetic 'instruction':* 28$^{23-29}$.

C. *Ariel, Ariel!:* 29$^{1-8}$.

D. *Three invectives and threats:* 29 $^{9-12,\ 13-14,\ 15}$.—The foregoing sections have sufficient claim to be original; 29^{16ff} is probably late.

E. *Egypt, a false support:* 30$^{1-5\ (7)}$.

F. *Invectives and threats:* 30$^{8-14,\ 15-17}$.

G. *The future felicity of Jerusalem:* 30$^{18-26}$.—The passage is generally recognized as late.

H. *Threat against Assyria:* 30$^{27-33}$.

I. *Invective against Egypt:* 31$^{1-9}$.

J. *The righteous king to come:* 32$^{1-5\ (8)}$.—The sacral king will reign in a transformed land and over a wise and godly people.

K. *Oracle to the complacent ladies:* 32$^{9-14\ (20)}$.—Compare 3^{16}–4^{1}.

L. *A prophetic liturgy:* ch. 33.—Since the time of Gunkel, this passage, which does not fall within the compass of the foregoing oracles, has been generally considered a liturgy: introductory invective (v.^{1}), popular lament (v.^{2}), prophetic word (vv.$^{3-6}$), popular lament (vv.$^{7-9}$), prophetic oracle (vv.$^{10-13}$), prophetic word (v.^{14a}), torah liturgy (vv.$^{14b-16}$), prophetic word (vv.$^{17-24}$). It is generally denied Isaiah.

V. *Eschatological prophecies:* chs. 34–35.—These chapters may have at one time formed the conclusion to the compilation of chs. 1–15. While they cannot claim the authorship of Isaiah, they form a great finale to his work and do justice to the major motifs of doom and felicity which are present throughout the preceding chapter. C. C. Torrey believes they belong with chs. 40–66 and form the introduction to that literary sequence.

A. *The day of Yahweh's vengeance on Edom:* 34$^{1-17}$.

B. *The redemption of Zion:* 35$^{1-10}$.

VI. *The Eschatological poems of Second Isaiah:* chs. 40–55.—Since the pioneering work of B. Duhm in his commentary of 1892, this section has been generally considered to constitute an independent literary unity. The historical situation; the literary style, vocabulary, and literary forms; and the theology of the poet separate them from the foregoing chapters. The poet and those whom he addresses are living in Babylonian exile. Cyrus II. is twice mentioned by name (44^{28} 45^{1}) and is quite clearly present in other contexts. He is pressing his military campaigns, and Babylon is at the eve of its downfall. The hill of Zion lies waste, but is about to be rebuilt (44^{28} 49$^{14-21}$ 51$^{3,\ 17-23}$ 52$^{7-12}$ 54). It is clearly within the range of the middle of the 6th cent. B.C. that the poet is moving, though his vision surveys the election-covenant faith of Israel from its earliest beginnings to the glorious finale in which the people of God are to be redeemed and the nations will witness that it is in Yahweh alone that they are to be saved. A note of exulting triumph rings throughout the poems. Again and again the poet breaks out into ecstatic singing (42$^{10-13}$ 44^{23} 45^{8} 49^{13}). He is the greatest poetic craftsman of ancient Israel. His theology profoundly influenced the NT as it did the holy men living at Qumrân before the dawn of the Christian era. See also *Servant of the Lord*.

VII. *Admonitions and promises:* 56^{1}–66^{24}.—While there are not a few similarities of a very striking nature between chs. 40–45 and chs. 56–66, especially in chs. 60–62, the differences between the two sections are so great that it is difficult to attribute them to the same writer. C. C. Torrey supports the literary integrity of the whole of chs. 34–35, 40–66, and others too have defended the unity of chs. 40–66. The character of the literary types, such as the Torah liturgy of 56$^{1-8}$ or the liturgical composition of 56^{9}–57^{21}, the tendency to quote lines from chs. 40–55, and the imitative style in certain contexts all suggest that we have to do with followers of Second Isaiah. While some scholars have sought to assign the composition to the 5th cent., during the time of Nehemiah and Ezra, it is more likely, in view of the numerous affinities with chs. 40–55 and the very similar style of some of the poems, that we are dealing with the disciples of the great poet. A date towards the close of the 6th cent. would therefore seem more appropriate. Such a view is confirmed by the historical situation reflected in the poems of chs. 56–66. The emphasis upon the Temple and its cultic observances implies that it has been rebuilt. The writer is also much more interested in the Torah, in the keeping of the Sabbath, the observance of the fasts, etc., than Second Isaiah. His contrast between the character and destiny of the apostates and the true Israelites, his condemnation of the idolatrous cults, and his description of strange pagan rites—all this is alien to his great predecessor.

It is fortunate that recent translations such as the RSV have done justice to the poetic character of much of Is 1–39 and nearly all of 40–55 and 56–66 by a proper arrangement of the poetic and parallel lines. It is a great aid for our literary appreciation of the prophets, but more than that, it not infrequently helps to overcome the obscurity of the text when it is produced as prose. The Book of Isaiah is a compilation from different times and situations. The proper delineation of the literary units is therefore a matter of the first importance for their interpretation. G. B. G.—**J. Mu.**

ISCAH.—A daughter of Haran and sister of Milcah, Gn 11^{29}.

ISCARIOT.—See JUDAS ISCARIOT.

ISDAEL, 1 Es 5^{33} (AV, RV).—See GIDDEL, **2.**

ISHBAH.—A Judahite, 1 Ch 4^{17}.

ISHBAK.—A son of Abraham by Keturah, Gn 25^{2}, 1 Ch 1^{32}. The tribe of which he is the eponym is somewhat uncertain.

ISHBI-BENOB.—One of the four Philistines of the giant stock who were slain by the mighty men of David, 2 S 21^{16f}.

ISHBOSHETH (' Man of Shame,' *i.e.* ' of Baal ').—**1.** The fourth son of Saul ; at the death of his father and three brothers on Mount Gilboa he appears to have been young and inexperienced (both numbers in the chronological comment in 2 S 2^{10} appear to be unreliable), so that Abner acts as regent for him as successor to Saul's kingdom [minus the tribe of Judah who elect to follow David]. Ishbosheth's capital was at Mahanaim in Transjordan, perhaps to escape Philistine pressure. Skirmishing between the rival kings continued for up to seven years, but eventually Abner deserted to David, and Ishbosheth was murdered without issue, bringing the whole kingdom to David (2 S 5^{1}). His name is given its more original form **Eshbaal** (for Ishbaal), ' Man of Baal,' *i.e.* ' Yahweh,' in 1 Ch 8^{33} 9^{39}, either because Chronicles was so little read by those who refused even to enunciate the hated word Baal that it was not thought necessary to change it here to Ish-bosheth ; or because, by the time of composition of Chronicles, Baalism was so dead that it was no longer dangerous (cf the similar cases of Mephibosheth/Meribbaal ; Jerubbesheth/Jerubbaal ; Beeliada/Eliada). The alternative form of his name **Ishvi** for Ishiah, ' Man of Yahweh ' (1 S 14^{49}), shows that at the commencement of the monarchy Yahweh was freely equated with Baal even by convinced Yahwists.

2. Ishbosheth or Ishbaal is probably the true reading for **Jashobeam** (1 Ch 11^{11}), which is further corrupted to **Josheb-basshebeth** (2 S 23^{8}). W. F. C.—**D. R. Ap-T.**

ISHHOD.—A Manassite, 1 Ch 7^{18} (AV **Ishod**).

ISHI.—**1.** A Jerahmeelite, 1 Ch 2^{31}. **2.** A Judahite chief, 1 Ch 4^{20}. **3.** A chief of East Manasseh, 1 Ch 5^{24}. **4.** One of the captains of the 500 men of the tribe of Simeon who smote the Amalekites at Mt. Seir, 1 Ch 4^{42}.

ISHI (' my husband ').—The name which Hosea (2^{16} ; RSV translates ' my husband ') recommends Israel to apply to Y″ instead of *Baali* (' my lord ').

ISHIAH, 1 Ch 7^{3} (AV).—See ISSHIAH, **1.**

ISHMA.—One of the sons of Etam, 1 Ch 4^{3}.

ISHMAEL.—**1.** The son of Abraham by Hagar. His name (' May God hear ') was decided upon before his birth (Gn 16^{11}). As in the history of his mother, three sources are used by the narrator. J supplied Gn 16^{4-14}, E 21^{6-21}, P adding such links as 16^{15f} 17^{18-27} $25^{7-10, 12-17}$. For the story of his life up to his settlement in the wilderness of Paran, the northern part of the Sinai peninsula, see HAGAR. At the age of thirteen he was circumcised on the same day as his father (Gn 17^{25f}). In Paran he married an Egyptian wife, and became famous as an archer (21^{20f}). No other incident is recorded, except that he was associated with his half-brother in the burial of Abraham (25^{9}) and himself died at the age of 137 (25^{17}). In view of the manifest association of Ishmael with folk-elements in North Sinai and Edom akin to the Hebrews, whose characteristics and habits he exhibited, it is difficult to accept the narratives of Ishmael as biography. It must, however, be admitted that there is much verisimilitude in these narratives. His birth, for instance, after Abraham's concubinage with Hagar by consent of Sarah, and his supersession by Isaac as Abraham's heir is known to be in accordance with regular social practice in Mesopotamia in the middle of the 2nd millennium B.C.

Ishmael is represented as the father of twelve sons (Gn 25^{12-16}, 1 Ch 1^{29-31}), and the phrase ' twelve princes according to their nations ' (cf Gn 17^{20}) suggests an attempt on the part of the writer at an exhibition of his view of racial origins. It is not possible to say whether at any time a religious confederacy of twelve tribes was formed under the name of Ishmael. The twelve-tribe amphictyony of Israel has analogies elsewhere, as has been pointed out by M. Noth, the number being possibly suggested by the twelve months of the year, so that it is quite possible that there was also a twelve-tribe amphictyony of Ishmael. On the other hand this may be an artificial schematization suggested to the author of P by the organization of Israel. Israel's racial affinity with these folk-elements is freely admitted, a significant fact in view of the hostile relation of the two in historical times. The Egyptian affinities of Ishmael through his mother and his wife probably reflect the political relationships of the North Sinai tribes with Egypt under the New Empire, when towns such as *Tell el-Ajjûl*, *Tell-Jemmeh*, and *Tell el-Fâr'ah* were fortified as frontier-posts along the line of the *Wâdī Ghazzeh* and the tribesmen of North Sinai were admitted in times of drought to water and grazing in the east of the Delta ' after the manner of their fathers from the beginning,' according to an inscription of Horemheb. Egyptian influence in language is still a feature of Arabic in that area.

There appears to be a certain confusion between **Midianites** and **Ishmaelites** (Gn 37^{28f}, Jg $8^{24, 26}$), though the two are distinguished in the genealogies of Gn $25^{1, 4, 13}$ (J). Midianites is clearly the geographic term and Ishmaelites the ethnic one. The Ishmaelites soon disappear from Scriptural history. A few individuals are described as of that nationality (1 Ch 2^{17} 27^{30}) ; but in later times the word could be used metaphorically of any hostile people (Ps 83^{6}).

2. A son of Azel, a descendant of Saul through Jonathan (1 Ch 8^{38} 9^{44}). **3.** Ancestor of the Zebadiah who was one of Jehoshaphat's judicial officers (2 Ch 19^{11}). **4.** A military officer associated with Jehoiada in the revolution in favour of Joash (2 Ch 23^{1}). **5.** A member of the royal house of David who took the principal part in the murder of Gedaliah (Jer $41^{1, 2}$). The story is told in Jer 40^{7}–41^{15}, with a summary in 2 K 25^{23-26}. It is probable that Ishmael resented Nebuchadrezzar's appointment of Gedaliah as governor of Judaea (Jer 40^{5}) instead of some member of the ruling family, and considered him as unpatriotic in consenting to represent an alien power. Further instigation was supplied by Baalis, king of Ammon (Jer 40^{14}), who was seeking either revenge or an opportunity to extend his dominions. Gedaliah and his retinue were killed after an entertainment given to Ishmael, who gained possession of Mizaph, the seat of government. Shortly afterwards he set out with his captives to join Baalis, but was overtaken by a body of Gedaliah's soldiers at the pool of Gibeon (Jer 41^{12}), and defeated. He made good his escape (41^{15}) with the majority of his associates ; but of his subsequent life nothing is known. The conspiracy may have been prompted by motives that were in part well considered, if on the whole mistaken ; but it is significant that Jeremiah supported Gedaliah (40^{6}), in memory of whose murder an annual fast was observed for some years in the month Tishri (Zec 7^{5} 8^{19}). **6.** One of the priests persuaded by Ezra to put away their foreign wives, Ezr 10^{22}, 1 Es 9^{22} (AV, RV **Ismael**). R. W. M.—**J. Gr.**

ISHMAIAH.—**1.** The ' ruler ' of the tribe of Zebulun, 1 Ch 27^{19}. **2.** One of David's thirty heroes, 1 Ch 12^{4} (AV **Ismaiah**).

ISHMERAI.—A Benjamite chief, 1 Ch 8^{18}.

ISHOD, 1 Ch 7^{18} (AV).—See ISHHOD.

ISHPAH.—The eponym of a Benjamite family, 1 Ch 8^{16} (AV **Ispah**).

ISHPAN.—A Benjamite chief, 1 Ch 8^{22}.

ISH-SECHEL.—In Ezr 8^{18} it is said : ' And by the good hand of our God upon us they brought us a man of discretion, of the sons of Mahli,' where RVm gives for ' man of discretion ' the proper name ' Ish-sechel.' That a proper name is required is certain, but whether Ish-sechel is that name is not so certain. *Issachar* has been suggested. W. F. C.

ISH-TOB, 2 S 10^{6ff} (AV).—See TOB.

ISHUAH, Gn 46^{17} (AV).—See ISHVAH.

ISHUAI, 1 Ch 7^{30} (AV).—See ISHVI.

ISHUI, 1 S 14^{49} (AV).—See ISHVI.

ISHVAH.—Second son of Asher, Gn 46^{17} (AV **Ishuah**), 1 Ch 7^{30} (AV **Isuah**).

ISHVI.—1. Third son of Asher, Gn 46^{17} (AV **Isui**), Nu 26^{44} (AV **Jesui**), 1 Ch 7^{30} (AV **Ishuai**); patronymic **Ishvites,** Nu 26^{44} (AV **Jesuites**). **2.** Second son of Saul by Abinoam, 1 S 14^{49} (AV **Ishui**); called **Eshbaal** in 1 Ch 8^{33} 9^{39}, and **Ishbosheth** (q.v.) in 2 S 2^{10} etc.

ISLAND, ISLE.—The Hebrew word *'î* means primarily 'coastlands' (so usually in RSV), but sometimes lands in general, and in one passage (Is 42^{15}) 'dry land' as opposed to water. In Is 20^{6} Palestine is called 'this isle' (AV; but RV and RSV 'coastland'). The islands of the Gentiles or heathen (Gn 10^{5}, Zeph 2^{11} AV; cf RV) are apparently the coasts of the W. Mediterranean; the 'isles of the sea' (Est 10^{1}, Ezk 26^{18} etc. AV and RV) are also the Mediterranean coasts; 'the isles' (Ps 72^{10} etc., Is 42^{10} etc.) means the West generally as contrasted with the East. Tyre is mentioned as an isle in Is 23^{2} (but RSV 'coast'), and here perhaps the term may be taken literally, as Tyre was actually at that time an island. The isle (RSV 'coasts') of Kittim (Jer 2^{10}, Ezk 27^{6}) is probably Cyprus, and the isle (RSV 'coastland') of Caphtor, Crete. In the NT five islands are mentioned: Cyprus (Ac 4^{36} 11^{19f} 13^{4} 15^{39} $21^{3,16}$ 27^{4}), Crete ($27^{7,12f,21}$), Cauda (v.^{16}), Malta (28^{1}), and Patmos (Rev 1^{9}).
E. W. G. M.

ISMACHIAH.—A Levite in the time of Hezekiah, 2 Ch 31^{13}. See SEMACHIAH.

ISMAEL, 1 Es 9^{22} (AV, RV).—See ISHMAEL, **6.**

ISMAERUS, 1 Es 9^{34} (RV).—See AMRAM, **2.**

ISMAIAH, 1 Ch 12^{4} (AV).—See ISHMAIAH, **2.**

ISPAH, 1 Ch 8^{16} (AV).—See ISHPAH.

ISRAEL.—The name Israel designates in the Bible (*a*) the patriarch Jacob (Gn 32^{29}); (*b*) several ethnic groups of heterogeneous origins which settled in the land of Canaan during the 13th cent. B.C.; (*c*) the northern kingdom which, under Jeroboam's leadership, seceded from the monarchic rule of Rehoboam soon after Solomon's death (922 B.C.) and was destroyed by the Assyrians (722 B.C.); (*d*) occasionally the southern kingdom of Judah (Is 5^{7}, Mic 3^{1}); (*e*) the eschatological remnant; and (*f*) the religious and political community of the Judaeans' descendants commonly known as the Jews, from the fall of Jerusalem under the Babylonians (586 B.C.) to the fall of Jerusalem under the Romans (A.D. 70; see G. A. Danell, *Studies in the Name Israel in the Old Testament*, 1946).

I. HISTORY.—**1. Sources.**—Documentation for Israel's history during the Biblical period has been traditionally found in (*a*) the canonical books and the Apocrypha of the OT; (*b*) the Jewish Pseudepigrapha and other writings of the Greco-Roman times, especially those of Flavius Josephus; (*d*) the works of the Greek and Roman historians; (*e*) the Mishnah and Talmud. Information obtained from these sources was generally accepted at its face value, particularly that which was offered by the OT, and contradictions found therein were either artificially resolved or ignored. In modern times, however, three major developments have radically transformed the task of Israel's historians: (*a*) the rise of Biblical criticism; (*b*) the growth of near-eastern archaeology; (*c*) the emergence of anthropology, sociology, and comparative religion.

(*a*) *The Rise of Biblical Criticism.*—Ever since the middle of the 17th cent., scholars have inquired into the composition, date, authorship, and historical reliability of the Biblical books (see especially PENTATEUCH, PROPHETS, PSALMS, WISDOM LITERATURE). At the beginning of the 20th cent., a majority of students accepted the results of the Graf-Wellhausen school, according to which narratives and legal material now found in the Pentateuch were edited in about 400 B.C. from four previously written documents: (i) the Yahwistic source (J), composed in Judah in about 800 B.C.; (ii) the Elohistic source (E), written in Northern Israel in about 750 B.C.; (iii) the Deuteronomic code and sermons (D), redacted between 650 and 560 B.C.; and (iv) the Priestly source (P), compiled in about 450 B.C. and including the slightly earlier Holiness Code (H). Such a view of the composition and date of the Pentateuch, which became known as the Documentary Hypothesis, led the historians of Israel to exercise extreme caution not only toward those sources to which a late date was ascribed but also toward the earlier documents, since a considerable period of time—in fact, several centuries—separated the writing of all the documents from the events which they purported to relate. A similarly negative attitude prevailed on most of the data preserved in the book of Joshua, the composition of which was associated with the final stage of Pentateuchal editing (see PENTATEUCH, JOSHUA). With Judges, Samuel, and Kings, the case was considered to be different. Although the framework of Judges was assigned to Deuteronomic editorship, literary analysis of the book revealed the presence of poems and narratives, such as the Song of Deborah (Jg 5), the antiquity of which constituted a strong argument in favour of their historical reliability. The court memoirs which were utilized in a large section of Samuel and the manifold uses of royal and Temple archives which are manifest in Kings were deemed to offer a relatively valid kind of information, although the presence of legendary material, such as the Elisha cycle of stories, and the chronological difficulties produced by the synchronisms which tie together the reigns of the Judaean and Israelite kings, revealed the constant need for critical evaluation. The work of the Chronicler (see CHRONICLES, EZRA, NEHEMIAH) was considered to be late (around 300 B.C.) and generally unreliable, as it chiefly retold the stories of Samuel and Kings from a Levitical bias.

Since the beginning of the 20th cent., successors of Wellhausen have accepted the major results of the Documentary Hypothesis, with three important modifications: (i) literary analysis of the various documents no longer extends to the minute dissecting of phrases and words with the degree of confidence which was at first granted to it; (ii) dates of the documents tend to be pushed back in time (*i.e.* 950 or perhaps 1000 B.C. for J); (iii) the documents themselves are held to represent faithfully a large number of early traditions, orally preserved, which bring the historians much closer to the events than it was hitherto suspected.

Already in 1908, Eerdmans showed that the ancient Hebrews were not as 'primitive' as generally supposed. At the same time, the oral traditions which lay behind the documents were analysed by Gunkel for Genesis (1901) and Gressmann for Exodus (1910). Patterns and forms of 'literary' although 'unwritten' traditions were ascertained (see A. Lods, 'Le rôle de la tradition orale dans la formation des récits de l'Ancien Testament,' *RHR*, lxxxviii [1923], 51–64; E. Nielsen, *Oral Tradition*, 1954). Oestreicher in 1923 and Welch in 1924 pointed out that many laws of Deuteronomy reflected the situation of Israel during the conquest and the early monarchy rather than that of Judah under Manasseh. Eissfeldt in 1934 demonstrated that much of the priestly legislation, late as it may have been in its finally edited form, rested on pre-exilic practices. Kaufmann maintained in 1930 and 1937 the priority of P over D; Volz in 1933 and Rudolph in 1938 questioned the existence of E. Nevertheless, the general validity of the Documentary Hypothesis has survived these attacks (see R. H. Pfeiffer, *Introduction to the Old Testament*, 1941; A Lods, *Histoire de la littérature hébraïque et juive*, 1945; C. R. North, 'Pentateuchal Criticism,' in H. H. Rowley, ed., *The Old Testament and Modern Study*, 1951, pp. 48–83; O. Eissfeldt, *Einleitung in das Alte Testament*, 1956; A. Weiser, *Einleitung in das Alte Testament*, 1957). Meanwhile,the narratives of Judges were investigated by Wiese in 1926, the traditions concerning Israel's election by Galling in 1928, the origin and growth of the twelve-tribe system by Noth in 1930, the Saul-David material by Rost in 1926 and von Rad in 1944. Cultic and civil-criminal laws were replaced in their respective 'life-situations' by Jirku in 1927, Alt in 1934, Begrich in 1936. The links of historiography to cultus were recognized and investigated (see G. von Rad, *Das formgeschichtliche Problem des Hexateuchs*, 1938; *Das erste Buch Mose*, 1949–1953; M. Noth, *Ueberlieferungsgeschichtliche Studien*, I, 1943; E. Jacob, *La tradition historique en Israël*, 1946; cf G. E. Wright, 'Recent European Study in the Pentateuch,' *JBR*, xviii [1950], 216–220). Literary criticism of other books of the OT and of the Apocrypha has likewise provided Israel's historians with a largely re-evaluated documentation. Moreover, the testimony of the written sources has been considerably complemented and in some cases corrected or confirmed by the results of near-eastern archaeology.

(*b*) *The Growth of Near-Eastern Archaeology.*—Inaugurated by Bonaparte's scientific and artistic expedition which accompanied the military invasion of Egypt in 1799, archaeology of the ancient Near East has considerably increased the knowledge of Israel's historians. Data furnished by archaeological investigations include: (i) the identification of Biblical sites, ways of communication, topographic and hydrographic features of the soil which in turn provide valuable information on the geography, the climate and the economic resources with their political and cultural consequences (see G. E. Wright and F. V. Filson, eds., *The Westminister Historical Atlas to the Bible*, 1956; L. H. Grollenberg, *Atlas of the Bible*, 1956; E. G. Kraeling, *Bible Atlas*, 1956; D. Baly, *The Geography of the Bible*, 1957; N. Glueck, *Rivers in the Desert*, 1959); (ii) the recovery of architectural and technological remains, with all artifacts, including weapons, tools, and instruments, ornaments and jewels, statuary and cultic objects; of especial importance is the excavation of Biblical sites, with the stratification of ashes and of datable pottery, which offers chronological clues of relative accuracy (see I. Benzinger, *Hebräische Archäologie*, 1927; C. Watzinger, *Denkmäler Palästinas*, 1933–1935; A. G. Barrois, *Manuel d'archéologie biblique*, 1939, 1953; G. Contenau, *Manuel d'archéologie orientale*, 1927–1947; W. F. Albright, *The Archaeology of Palestine*, 1949; 'The Old Testament and the Archaeology of Palestine,' and 'The Old Testament and the Archaeology of the Ancient Near East,' in H. H. Rowley, ed., *The Old Testament and Modern Study*, 1951, 1–47; J. Vandier, *Manuel d'archéologie égyptienne*, 1952–1958; J. B. Pritchard, *The Ancient Near East in Pictures*, 1954; *Archaeology and the Old Testament*, 1958; G. E. Wright, *Biblical Archaeology*, 1957); (iii) the unearthing, publication, translation, and interpretation of monumental inscriptions and literary texts, which have been relatively scarce in Palestine proper (even when cognizance is taken of the Dead Sea Scrolls), but quite numerous in Egypt, Iraq, Iran, Syria, Lebanon, and Turkey. These documents have been of considerable value for the reconstruction of the life and history of the world in which Israel lived (see H. Gressmann, *Altorientalische Texte und Bilder zum Alten Testament*, 1926–1927; G. A. Barton, *Archaeology and the Bible*, 1937; J. B. Pritchard, ed., *Ancient Near Eastern Texts Relating to the Old Testament*, 1955).

(*c*) *The Emergence of Anthropology, Sociology, and Comparative Religion.*—Studies on primitive man and society, the international folklore and magical rites offer no direct sources of information for the recovery of Israel's past. Nevertheless, these sciences have provided many clues for the interpretation of the Biblical material and the evaluation of the archaeological data. Actually, some scholars ascribe to them an exaggerated importance by postulating the identity of psychological, sociological, cultural, and especially religious processes, in Israel and in all primitive societies of mankind, thereby ignoring the distinctiveness of Israel's history. For example, many features of the Scandinavian thesis on Hebrew communal rites have been derived from Norse mythology rather than from the OT record. However, a knowledge of anthropology, sociology, and especially of Semitic comparative religion is indispensable to the historian of Israel, since the Hebrews were heavily dependent upon the cultures of the Ancient Near East.

The study of the pre-Islamic Arabs as well as of modern Bedouin tribes received an impulse from Wellhausen in 1883 and Musil in 1908 (see M. F. von Oppenheim, *Die Beduinen*, 1939–1952). Robertson Smith in 1889 and Lagrange in 1905 attempted to recapture, each in his own way, the religion of the ancient Semites. Frazer's monumental study of magic and religion (1890–1915) and folklore (1918) on the one hand and Winckler and Zimmern's publication of Babylonian texts (1893–1906) on the other hand have paved the way for highly conjectural reinterpretations of Israel's religious and political history by Mowinckel (1922–1926) and Hooke (1927, 1938, 1956, 1958) in the light of the Babylonian New Year Festival. Pedersen's emphasis on corporateness in his studies of Israel's popular culture (1926–1940) was paralleled by stresses which sociologists like Weber (1921) laid on economic factors or historians like Causse (1937) on the conflict between nomadic and agrarian modes of living, while Baron (1937) recognized not only the part played by social forces but also the decisive influence of Israel's élite. In the middle of the 20th cent., historians tended to maintain the moderate position occupied by Kittel and by Sellin in 1921. They were aware of elements of continuity and discontinuity in Israel's cultural affinities with the other nations of the ancient Near East.

2. The Early Traditions.—The majority of scholars, while making allowance for legendary and mythical elements, are confident that important outlines of tribal history are revealed in the early books of the Bible. The tenth chapter of Genesis contains a genealogical table in which nations are personified as men. Thus the sons of Ham were Cush (Nubia), Mizraim (Egypt), Put (East Africa ?), and Canaan. The sons of Shem were Elam, Assyria, Mesopotamia, Lud (a land of disputed situation, not Lydia), and Aram (the Aramaeans). If countries and peoples are here personified as men, the same may be the case elsewhere; in Abraham, Isaac, Jacob, Esau, and the twelve sons of Jacob, we may be dealing not with individuals but with tribes. The marriages of individuals may represent the alliances or union of tribes. Viewed in this way, these narratives disclose to us the formation of the Israelite nation.

The traditions may be classified in two ways: (*a*) as to origin, and (*b*) as to content.

(*a*) (i) Some traditions, such as those concerning kinship with non-Palestinian tribes, the deliverance from Egypt, and those concerning Moses, were brought into Palestine from the desert. (ii) Others, such as the traditions of Abraham's connexion with various shrines, and the stories of Jacob and his sons, were developed in the land of Canaan. (iii) Still others were received from the Canaanites. Thus we learn from an inscription of Thuthmose III. (1490–1435 B.C.), that *Jacob-el* was a place name in Palestine, Genesis (48^{9ff}) tells how Joseph was divided into two tribes, Ephraim and Manasseh. Probably the latter are Israelite, and are so called because they settled in the Joseph country. Lot or Luten (Egyptian *Ruten*) is an old name of Palestine or of a part of it. In Genesis, Moab and Ammon are said to be the children of Lot, probably because they settled in the country of Luten. In most cases where a tradition has blended two elements, one of these was learned from the Canaanites. (iv) Finally, a fourth set of traditions were derived from Babylonia. This is clearly the case with the Creation and Deluge narratives, parallels to which have been found in Mesopotamian literature. It is probable, however, that even these traditions were received through the Canaanites.

(*b*) Classified according to their content, the narratives are: (i) ancestral sagas which embody the history and movements of tribes; (ii) cultic legends which grew around the various shrines, like Bethel, Shechem, Hebron, and Beersheba; (iii) aetiological legends and myths, intended to explain the origin of some custom or the cause of some physical phenomenon. Thus Gn 18, 19—the destruction of Sodom and the other cities of the plain—is a story which grew up to account for the Dead

ISRAEL

Sea, with its asphalt and bitumen deposits and its desolate shore. Similarly Gn 22 is a story which was preserved in order to justify the principle of animal substitution in the firstborn sacrifices. (iv) Other narratives are devoted to cosmogony and primeval anthropology. Many scholars regard the patriarchal narratives as relating largely to tribes rather than individuals. Parts of the account of Abraham are local traditions of shrines, but the story of Abraham's migration is the narrative of the westward movement of a tribe or group of tribes from which the Hebrews were descended. Isaac is a shadowy figure confined mostly to the south, which possibly represents a south Palestinian clan afterwards absorbed by the Israelites. Jacob-Israel represents the nation itself. Israel is called an Aramaean (Dt 26^{5}), and the account of the marriage of Jacob (Gn 29–31) shows that Israel was kindred to the Aramaeans.

3. The Patriarchal Age.—While the Genesis traditions link Abraham with ' Ur of the Chaldaeans ' (Gn 11^{31}) in Lower Mesopotamia, they also relate that Terah, his father, had moved northward to Haran and that it was from there that Abraham emigrated to Canaan (Gn 11^{31} 12^{1-9}). Archaeological excavations have brought to light no external evidence on the historical accuracy of these traditions but they have enabled us to picture the Mesopotamian and Syro-Palestinian background of the patriarchal age with remarkable vividness and precision (see F. M. T. Böhl, ' Das Zeitalter Abrahams,' *Der alte Orient*, xxix [1930], 1 ; E. Dhorme, ' Abraham dans le cadre de l'histoire,' *RB* xxxvii [1928], 367–385, 481–511 ; xl [1931], 364–374, 503–518 ; R. de Vaux, ' Les patriarches hébreux et les découvertes modernes,' *RB* liii [1946], 321–348 ; lv [1948], 321–347 ; lvi [1949], 5–36 ; H. H. Rowley, ' Recent Discoveries and the Patriarchal Age,' in *The Servant of the Lord and Other Essays on the Old Testament*, 1952, pp. 271–305). The Sumerians had established in Lower Mesopotamia during the 3rd millennium B.C. a flourishing civilization. After suffering defeat under the Akkadians of Sargon I. (24th cent. B.C.), they finally succumbed to the onslaught of Elamitic hordes from the north-east. Amorite semi-nomads moved in Lower Mesopotamia from the desert of north-central Arabia and created the First Amorite Dynasty of Babylon. Through the impulse of their most dynamic monarch, Hammurabi (1728–1686 B.C.), the Amorites extended their domination of the Tigris and Euphrates valley northward and pushed westward their control of the Fertile Crescent (S. Moscati, *The Semites in Ancient History*, 1959).

The migration of Terah and Abraham are considered by many scholars to be a part of the Amorite expansion. Names of Amorite towns like Peleg, Serug, Nahor, Terah, and Haran are found in the Biblical narratives as personal names ascribed to ancestors or relatives of Abraham (Gn 10^{25} $11^{20, 25}$). Names of Amorite individuals include ' Benjamin,' ' Jacob-el,' and ' Abamram ' (Abram ?). The date of the Hebrews' march to the West remains uncertain. Some scholars have identified the Amraphel, king of Shinar, mentioned in Gn 14, with Hammurabi of Babylon, thereby situating Abraham in the 18th–17th cents. B.C. This identification remains hypothetical, however, since more than one individual appears to have borne the name of Hammurabi and the tradition of Abraham's military activities, although ancient, conflicts sharply with the pictures of a peaceful semi-nomad which emerges elsewhere in the patriarchal traditions.

Legal and other customs of the Hebrews during this period, far from reflecting the mores of Israel after the conquest, as Wellhausen maintained (*Prolegomena to the History of Israel*, 1885, pp. 318–319), are similar to those of the contemporary Hurrians (reflected in the Nuzu and Mari Tablets ; see I. J. Gelb, *Hurrians and Subarians*, 1944), an ethnic group which migrated southward from the Caucasian mountains and formed in the 15th and 14th cents. B.C. the Mittani empire. Thus several Hebrew customs on adoption, marriage, and property (Gn 15^{4} 16^{2} 21^{10} 25^{29-34} 29^{2ff} $30^{3, 9, 25ff}$ 31^{19ff}) were strikingly similar to those of the 2nd millennium Hurrians, while they had become obsolete when the early traditions came to be written down. Many Hurrians (the Horites of Gn 14^{6} ; cf 36^{20}) went to the land of Canaan (the Hurru of the Egyptian documents during the 18th Dynasty). The Hebrews' travels through Palestine in the patriarchal age may well have been a part of the Hurrian infiltrations.

In Canaan, the patriarchal Hebrews entered into close contacts with the local inhabitants (see, for example, Gn 34). The Phoenician-Canaanite culture has become in modern times quite well-known, not only through the excavation of Palestinian and Phoenician sites but also by the Tell el-Amarna tablets and the Râs Shamra (Ugarit) texts (see W. F. Albright, *The Rôle of the Canaanites in the History of Civilization*, 1942 ; B. Maisler, ' Canaan and the Canaanites,' *BASOR*, No. 102, April 1946, 7–12). The Hebrews also had economic and cultural relations with the Hittites (Gn 23^{9} 25^{9} 26^{34} etc.) who had expanded eastward and southward from their Asia Minor empire (see F. Sommer, *Hethiter und Hethitisch*, 1948 ; E. Cavaignac, *Les Hittites*, 1950 ; O. R. Gurney, *The Hittites*, 1952 ; R. Dussaud, *Prélydiens, Hittites et Achéens*, 1953). Archaeological evidence supports the view of many Biblical writers according to which Israel's ancestors consorted with foreign nations (for example, Ex 3^{17} ; cf Ezk 16^{3}).

Many documents of the 2nd millennium B.C., scattered on a wide area from Mesopotamia to Egypt, refer to the Habiru or Hapiru, semi-nomadic groups which moved about the Fertile Crescent between the 20th and the 12th cents. B.C. The assumption that the ' Hebrews ' were an ethnic community identical with the ' Habiru ' has not been demonstrated (see H. H. Rowley, ' Râs Shamra and the Habiru Question,' *PEQ*, lxxii [1940], 90–94 ; J. W. Jack, ' New Light on the Habiru-Hebrew Question,' *ibid.*, 95–115 ; G. Posener et J. Bottéro, *Le problème des Ḫabiru . . .*, 1954 ; M. Greenberg, *The Ḫab/piru*, 1955).

4. The Origins of Israel.—In all probability, the Hebrews of the patriarchal age formed a number of distinct clans, as shown by the traditions concerning Abraham's descendants and their relatives (Gn 19, 22^{20-24} $25^{1-4, 12-18}$ 36) and especially the sons of Jacob (Gn 29^{14}–30^{36} 35^{16-20}). The patrilineal surname ' Israel ' for Jacob (Gn 32^{28}, cf Hos 12^{12-13}, Is 41^{8} etc.) clearly suggests that the tribes designated by the names of his sons felt among themselves a degree and a quality of close kinship while they were aware of a more distant affinity with the other ' descendants ' of Abraham and Isaac. Some historians maintain that the twelve-tribe scheme (Gn 49, Dt 33, etc.) dates from the conquest rather than from an earlier age (see M. Noth, *Geschichte Israels*, 1956, pp. 54–104), but internal evidence requires a more confident appraisal of the traditions (see J. Bright, *Early Israel in Recent History Writing*, 1956 ; *A History of Israel*, 1959, pp. 60–127).

The sons of Jacob are divided into four groups. Six—Reuben, Simeon, Levi, Judah, Issachar, and Zebulun—are said to be the sons of Leah, a name which probably means ' wild cow.' Apparently these tribes were near of kin, and possessed as a common symbol the ' wild cow ' or ' bovine antelope.' The tribes of Manasseh, Ephraim, and Benjamin traced their descent from Rachel, a name which means ' ewe.' These tribes, though kindred to the other six, probably traced their origin to a different ethnic and cultic stock, symbolized by the ewe. Judah was, in the period before the conquest, a far smaller tribe than afterwards, for it seems that many Palestinian clans were absorbed into Judah. Benjamin is said to have been the youngest son of Jacob, born in Palestine a long time after the others. The name means ' son of the south ' or ' southerner ' and historians used to think that it applied to the geographical location of the tribe of Benjamin, S. of Ephraim. Recent discoveries make this view doubtful (J. Muilenburg, ' The Birth of Benjamin,' *JBL*, lxxv [1956], 194–201). Four sons of Jacob—

Dan, Naphtali, Gad, and Asher—are said to be the sons of concubines. This less honourable birth possibly meant that they joined the confederacy later than the others. The original Israel probably consisted of the eight tribes —Reuben, Simeon, Levi, Judah, Issachar, Zebulun, Manasseh, and Ephraim—though perhaps the Rachel tribes did not join the confederacy until they had escaped from Egypt. These tribes, along with the other Abrahamidae—the Edomites, and Moabites—moved westward from the Euphrates along the eastern borders of Palestine. The Ammonites, Moabites, and Edomites gained a foothold in the territories afterwards occupied by them. The Israelites appear to have been compelled to move on to the less fertile steppe to the south, between Beersheba and Egypt, roaming at times as far as Sinai.

The end of the patriarchal age is of uncertain date. Some time during the 2nd millennium, perhaps during the Hyksos invasion of Egypt (*c* 1710 B.C.; see R. M. Engberg, *The Hyksos Reconsidered*, 1944), perhaps later, a few of the Jacob tribes entered the Nile Delta while others remained in the Fertile Crescent.

5. The Egyptian Slavery.—The firm and constant tradition of Hebrew enslavement in Egypt, running as it does through all of the Pentateuchal documents and forming the background of all Israel's religious and prophetic consciousness, must have some historical content. We know from the Egyptian monuments that at different times Bedouin from Asia entered the country on account of its fertility. The famous Hyksos kings and their people found access to the land of the Nile in this way. Probability strengthens the tradition that the Hebrews so entered Egypt. Ex 1[11] states that they were compelled to aid in building the cities of Pithom and Raamses. Excavations have shown that these cities were either founded or rebuilt by Rameses II. (1292–1224 B.C.), although his father, Seti I. (1308–1292 B.C.) had already begun architectural renovations at Avaris (Tanis). It is known that both monarchs pressed into labour the semi-nomadic Asiatics who were living in that area, a fact which fits the stories of Ex 1 (see P. Montet, *Le drame d'Avaris: essai sur la pénétration des Sémites en Egypte*, 1940). The date of the Exodus presents a number of extremely complex problems because the data are quite contradictory (see H. H. Rowley, *From Joseph to Joshua*, 1950). Since Merenptah (1224–1216 B.C.) mentioned 'Israel' as a people (but not as a country) whom he crushed in Canaan in about 1220 B.C., it is probable that the bulk of Israel had only infiltrated the land at that date. This conclusion is confirmed by some of the archaeological evidence. Bethel, Eglon, Kiriath-sepher (Debir), and Lachish were violently destroyed during the 13th cent. B.C.; in the case of Lachish, the date may be more accurately determined as between 1240 and 1230 B.C. (cf Jos 10[31ff]). Excavations at Jericho and Ai offer inconclusive results. Moreover, the memory of a forty-year wandering in the Sinai and Kadesh wilderness, at least for the Joseph tribes and the Levi elements led by Moses and Aaron, is so firmly established that the date of the Exodus would seem to be the first half of the 13th cent. (*c* 1275 B.C.).

6. The Exodus.—The J, E, and P documents agree in their main picture of the Exodus, although J differs from the other two in holding that the worship of Yahweh was known at an earlier time. Moses, they tell us, fled from Egypt and took refuge in Midian with Jethro, a Kenite priest (cf Jg 1[16]). Here, according to E and P, at Horeb or Sinai, Yahweh's holy mount, Moses first learned to worship Yahweh, who, he believed, sent him to deliver from Egypt his oppressed brothers. After various plagues (J gives them as seven, E, five, and P, six) Moses led them out, and by Divine aid they escaped across the Red Sea. J presents this escape as the result of Yahweh's control of natural means (Ex 14[21]). Moses then led them to Sinai, where, according to both J and E, they entered into a solemn covenant with Yahweh, to serve Him as their God. According to E (Ex 18[12ff]), it was Jethro, the Kenite or Midianite priest, who initiated the covenant. After this the Rachel tribes probably allied themselves more closely to the Leah tribes, and, through the aid of Moses, gradually led them to adopt the worship of Yahweh.

The story of Moses is encumbered with folkloric details (*i.e.* Ex 2), but their legendary origin does not detract from the historical character of the Levi hero. His tribal ancestry called for valour (Gn 49[6–7]). He and several of his companions had been exposed to Egyptian culture, as shown by their names (Moses, Aaron, Hophni, Merari, Miriam, Phinehas, Puti-el), and his leadership extended to non-Hebrew elements (Ex 12[38], Nu 14[4]).

The route followed by the fugitives is a matter of controversy. There is evidence that Lake Timsah was during the 2nd millennium B.C. a shallow part of the Gulf of Suez (see C. Bourdon, 'La route de l'Exode ...,' *RB*, xli [1932], 370–392, 539–549; cf H. Cazelles, 'Les localisations de l'Exode et la critique littéraire,' *RB*, lxii [1955], 321–364). The *yam sûph* of Ex 15[4] is not 'the Red Sea' (LXX) but 'the sea of papyrus reeds,' and it may well have been in the Lake Timsah vicinity. The memory of a Divine deliverance at a time of utmost crisis became central to the faith of Israel and remained determinative, to a large extent, of her later history and religion. The antiquity of the victory song attributed to Miriam, the sister of Moses, offers strong literary support to the validity of the tradition (see F. M. Cross, jun., and D. N. Freedman, 'The Song of Miriam,' *JNES*, xiv [1955], 237–250.

7. The Wilderness Wandering.—For some time the *habitat* of Israel, as thus constituted, was the region between Sinai on the south and Kadesh—a spring some fifty miles S. of Beersheba—on the north. At Kadesh the fountain was sacred, and at Sinai there was a sacred mountain. Moses became during this period the sheikh of the united tribes. Because of his pre-eminence in the knowledge of Yahweh he acquired this paramount influence in all their counsels. In the traditions this period is called the Wandering in the Wilderness, and it is said to have continued forty years. The expression 'forty years' is, however, used by D and his followers in a vague way for an indefinite period of time. Nevertheless, the people remembered that all those who had left Egypt as adults died in the desert (Nu 14[26–35] 26[63–65]).

The region in which Israel now roamed was anything but fertile, and the people naturally turned their eyes to more promising pasture lands. This they did with the more confidence, because Yahweh, their God, had just delivered their fathers from Egypt in an extraordinary manner. Naturally they desired the most fertile land in the region, Canaan. Finding themselves unable, for some reason, to move directly upon it from the south (Nu 13, 14), perhaps because the hostile Amalekites interposed, they made a circuit to the eastward. According to the traditions, their detour extended around the territories of Edom and Moab, so that they came upon the territory N. of the Arnon, where an Amorite kingdom had previously been established, over which, in the city of Heshbon, Sihon ruled.

8. The Trans-Jordanic Conquest.—The account of the conquest of the kingdom of Sihon is given by E with a few additions from J in Nu 21. No details are included, but it appears that in the battles Israel was victorious. We learn from the P document in Nu 32 that the conquered cities of this region were divided between the tribes of Reuben and Gad. Perhaps it was at this moment that the tribe of Gad came into the confederacy. At least they appear in concrete history here for the first time. It is usually supposed that the territory of Reuben lay to the south of that of Gad, extending from the Arnon to Elealeh, N. of Heshbon; in fact, their territory interpenetrated (Nu 32[34]). Thus the Gadites had Dibon, Ataroth, and Aroer to the south, Jazer N. of Heshbon, and Beth-nimrah and Beth-haran in the Jordan valley; while the Reubenites had Baal-meon, Nebo, Heshbon, and Elealeh, which lay between these. Probably the country to the north was not conquered until later. To be sure, D claims that Og, the king of Bashan, was conquered at this time, but it is possible that the conquest of Bashan by a part of the tribe of Manasseh was a backward movement from the west after the conquest of Palestine was accomplished. During this period Moses died, and Joshua became the leader of the nation.

9. Crossing of the Jordan.—The conquests achieved by the tribe of Gad brought the Hebrews into the Jordan valley, but the swiftly flowing river with its banks of clay formed an insuperable obstacle. The Arabic historian Nuwairi tells of a land-slide of one of the clay hills that border the Jordan, which afforded an opportunity for the Arabs to complete a military bridge. A similar event may well have taken place at the time of Israel's military expedition westward. The stories which describe the crossing of the Jordan (Jos 3–5) explained the origin of a circle of sacred stones called *Gilgal*, which lay on the west of the river (see H. J. Kraus, 'Gilgal: ein Beitrag zur Kultusgeschichte Israels,' *VT*, i [1951], 181–199; J. Mauchline, 'Gilead and Gilgal: Some Reflections on the Israelite Occupation of Palestine,' *VT*, vi [1956], 19–33).

10. The Conquest of Canaan.—The first point of attack after crossing the Jordan was Jericho (Jos 6). As to the subsequent course of the conquest, the sources differ widely. The D and P strata of the book of Joshua, which form the main portion of it, represent Joshua as gaining possession of the country in two great battles, and as dividing it up among the tribes by lot. The J account of the conquest, however, which has been preserved in Jg 1 and Jos 8–10, $13^{1, 7a, 13}$ $15^{14-19, 63}$ $16^{1-3, 10}$ 17^{11-18} 19^{47}, while it represents Joshua as the leader of the Rachel tribes and as winning a decisive victory near Gibeon, declares that the tribes went up to win their territory singly, and that in the end their conquest was only partial. This representation is much older than the other, and is much more in accord with the subsequent course of events and with historical probability. (See W. F. Albright, 'The Israelite Conquest of Canaan,' *BASOR*, No. 74 [April, 1939], 11–23; G. E. Wright, 'The Literary and Historical Problem of Joshua 10 and Judges 1,' *JNES*, v [1946], 105–114; N. H. Snaith, 'The Historical Books,' in H. H. Rowley, ed., *The Old Testament and Modern Study*, 1951, pp. 84–95; M. Noth, *Das Buch Josua*, 1953; H. W. Hertzberg, *Die Bücher Josua, Richter, Ruth* . . ., 1953; Y. Kaufmann, *The Biblical Account of the Conquest of Palestine*, 1953.)

According to J, there seem to have been at least three lines of attack: (*a*) that which Joshua led up the valley from Jericho to Ai and Bethel, from which the territories afterwards occupied by Ephraim and Benjamin were secured; (*b*) a movement on the part of the tribe of Judah followed by the Simeonites, south-westward from Jericho into the hill-country about Bethlehem and Hebron; (*c*) lastly, there was the movement of the northern tribes into the hill-country which borders the plain of Jezreel. J in Jos $11^{1, 4-9}$ tells us that in a battle by the Waters of Merom Joshua won for the Israelites a victory over four petty kings of the north, which gave the Israelites a foothold there. In the course of these struggles a disaster befell the tribes of Simeon and Levi. They attempted to take Shechem, but the Shechemites practically annihilated Levi, and greatly weakened Simeon (cf Gn 34). This disaster was thought to be a Divine punishment for reprehensible conduct (Gn 49^{5-7}). J distinctly states (Jg 1) that the conquest was not complete, but that two lines of fortresses, remaining in the possession of the Canaanites, cut the Israelite territory into three sections. One of these consisted of Dor, Megiddo, Taanach, Ibleam, and Beth-shean, and gave the Canaanites control of the great plain of Jezreel, while, holding as they did Jerusalem, Aijalon, Har-heres (Beth-shemesh), and Gezer, they cut the tribe of Judah off from their northern kinsfolk. J further tells us distinctly that not all the Canaanites were driven out, but that the Canaanites and the Hebrews lived together. Later, the tradition says, Israel made slaves of the Canaanites. Although this latter statement is perhaps true for those Canaanites who held out in these fortresses, the are reasons for believing that by intermarriage a gradual fusion between Canaanites and Israelites took place.

The first event of major importance in the history of Israel as a nation took place at Shechem, where Joshua renewed the covenant (Jos 24; see E. Nielsen, *Shechem, A Traditio-historical Investigation*, 1955) and revived the memory of a common ancestry. He may have also created a tribal organization which some scholars have likened to the Greek amphictyony. It is possible that the Shechem covenant helped to seal a religious and political bond between those tribal elements which had settled in Canaan and Transjordania for several centuries and others which had sojourned in Egypt and the wilderness of Sinai. At what time the tribes of Naphtali and Dan joined the Hebrew federation we have no means of knowing. J tells us (Jg 1^{34f}) that the Danites struggled for a foothold in the Shephelah, where they obtained but an insecure footing. As they afterwards migrated from here (Jg 17, 18), and as a place in this region was called the 'Camp of Dan' (Jg 13^{25} 18^{12}), probably their hold was insecure. We learn from Jg 15 that they possessed the town of Zorah, where Samson was afterwards born (see H. H. Rowley, 'The Danite Migration to Laish,' *ET*, li [1939–1940], 465–471).

11. The Time of the Judges (*c* 1200–1020 B.C.).—For the first century of her occupation of the land, Israel learned agriculture and industrial technology from the Canaanites who lived there (see C. A. Simpson, *Composition of the Book of Judges*, 1957; W. F. Albright, *From the Stone Age to Christianity*, 1957; E. Taubler, *Biblische Studien: I. Die Epoche der Richter*, 1958). The chronology suggested by the Book of Judges is probably too long. The Deuteronomic editor, who is responsible for this chronology, may have reckoned forty years as the equivalent of a generation, and 1 K 6^{1} gives us the key to his scheme. He made the time from the Exodus to the founding of the Temple twelve generations. The so-called 'Minor Judges'—Tola, Jair, Ibzan, Elon, and Abdon (Jg 10^{1-5} 12^{8-15})—were not included in the editors' chronology. The statements concerning them were added by a later hand. As three of their names appear elsewhere as clan names (cf Gn 46^{13f}, Nu $26^{23, 26}$, Dt 3^{14}), and as another is a city (Jos 21^{30}), scholars are agreed that these were not real judges, but that they owe their existence to the evolution of the traditions. Some doubt attaches also to Othniel, who is elsewhere a younger brother of a Caleb. The Calebites were a branch of the Edomite clan of the Kenaz (cf Jg 1^{13} with Gn $36^{11, 13, 42}$) which had settled in Southern Judah. This doubt is increased by the fact that the whole of the narrative of the invasion of Cushan-rishathaim, king of Mesoptamia, is the work of the editor, and also by the fact that no king of Mesopotamia who could have made such an invasion is known to have existed at this time. Furthermore, had such a king invaded Israel, his power would have been felt in the north and not in Judah. If there is any historical kernel in this narrative, probably it was the Edomites who were the perpetrators of the invasion, and their name has become corrupted. It is difficult, then, to see how Othniel should have been a deliverer, as he seems to have belonged to a kindred clan, but the whole matter may have been confused by oral transmission. Perhaps the narrative is a distorted reminiscence of the settlement in Southern Judah of the Edomitic clans of Caleb and Othniel (see A. Malamat, 'Cushan Rishathaim and the Decline of the Near East around 1200 B.C.' *JNES*, xiii [1954], 231–242).

The major judges were Ehud, Deborah, Gideon, Jephthah, Eli, and Samuel. Samson was a kind of giant-hero, but he always fought single-handed; he was no leader and organizer of men, and it is difficult to see how he can justly be called a judge. The age was a period of great tribal restlessness. Others were trying to do what the Israelites had done, and gain a foothold in the relatively fertile land of Canaan. Each invader, coming from a different direction, affected a different part of the territory, and in the region thus concerned a patriot would arouse the Hebrews of the vicinity and expel the invader. The influence he acquired from his exploit and the position which the wealth derived from the spoil of war gave him, made such a hero the sheikh of his district for a few years. Thus the judges were in reality great tribal chieftains. They owed their office to personal prowess.

Deborah and Barak delivered Israel, not from invaders, but from Canaanites, who still controlled, with the help of ' iron chariots,' the lowlands of Palestine, especially the plain of Jezreel (Jg 4–5). At the battle of Megiddo (*c* 1125 B.C.), Sisera's army was routed and the Hebrew elements which had settled on the Galilean hills were no longer separated from the bulk of the tribes which occupied the central mountain range.

The conquest of Canaan by the Hebrews was made possible by a conjunction of events rather unusual in the ancient Near East. Toward the end of the 13th cent. B.C., Egypt lost her grip upon Western Asia, and except during the reign of Rameses III. (*c* 1175–1144 B.C.) remained politically weak for several generations. At the same time, Assyria did not yet constitute an imperialistic threat. During the age of the Judges, the Israelites were able to survive and to overcome Canaanite resistance without risking interference from the larger powers of the world. At the same time, they were able to pass from a nomadic and pastoral mode of existence to a sedentary and agrarian civilization.

There were, however, four serious invasions from the outside: (*a*) that of the Moabites, which called Ehud into prominence; (*b*) that of the Midianites, which gave Gideon his opportunity; (*c*) that of the Ammonites, from whom Jephthah delivered Gilead; and (*d*) that of the Philistines, against whom Samson, Eli, Samuel, and Saul struggled, and who were not overcome until the time of David.

The first of these invasions affected the territories of Reuben and Gad on the east of the Jordan, and of Benjamin on the west. It probably occurred early in the period of the Judges. The second invasion affected the country of Ephraim and Manasseh, and probably occurred about the middle of the period. Gideon's son Abimelech endeavoured to establish in Shechem a petty kingdom (*c* 1100 B.C.) but the attempt at kingship was premature (Jg 9; see especially Jotham's fable, vv.$^{5-7}$; C. F. Whitley, 'The Sources of the Gideon Stories,' *VT*, vii [1957], 157–164). The Ammonite invasion affected only Gilead, while the Philistine invasion, at a later time, threatened the life of the entire territory, and constituted the most important factor in the establishment of a hereditary monarchy.

The struggles with these invaders increased the national solidarity. At the end of the 12th cent. B.C., as the song of Deborah shows, a sense of kinship existed ' in Israel ' (Jg 5^{7f}). Although several tribes refused to join the coalition against Sisera (Jg 5^{16-18}) and the tribe of Judah is not even mentioned, the very fact that some tribes are blamed for their neutrality attests the reality of a consciousness of super-tribal solidarity. The existence of a twelve-tribe system is implied by the ritual act of the man from Ephraim (Jg 19^{29}) and by a similar gesture performed by Saul when he responded to a call of Jabesh-gilead at the time of a second Ammonite invasion (1 S 11^{7}). Some scholars maintain that throughout the period of the Judges, in spite of political anarchy, the idea of the nation ' Israel,' inherited from the Mosaic covenant, and renewed by Joshua at the Shechem shrine (Jos 24), was kept alive by yearly pilgrimages to the Ark at the central sanctuary of Shiloh (1 S $1^{3, 7, 21}$). According to this view, military threats did not create national unity. It should be conceded, however, that they accelerated the trend toward political solidarity and governmental centralization.

During these years the process of amalgamation between the Israelites and the Canaanites went steadily forward. The tribe of Judah probably absorbed not only the Kenizzites and Calebites but also the Shuaites and the Tamarites (cf Gn 38). The Kenites also united with Judah (Jg 1^{16}), as did also the Jerahmeelites (cf 1 S 30^{29} with 1 Ch 2^{9}). What went on in Judah occurred to some extent in all the tribes, though probably Judah excelled in this political and ethnic proliferation. Perhaps it was a larger admixture of foreign blood that gave Judah its sense of aloofness from the rest of Israel. Certain it is, however, that the great increase in strength which Israel experienced between the time of Deborah and the time of David cannot be accounted for on the basis of population growth alone. There were elements in the religion of the Israelites which, notwithstanding the absorption of culture from the Canaanites, enabled Israel to absorb in turn the Canaanites themselves.

The age of the Judges ended with the fall of Shiloh under the onslaught of the Philistine invasions (*c* 1050–1020 B.C.). The Philistines belonged to the waves of immigrants from the isles of Greece and the coasts of Asia Minor whom the Egyptians called ' the Peoples of the Sea.' Rameses III. (1175–1144 B.C.) succeeded in restraining their efforts to conquer Egypt. As a result, they settled on the coastal plain of Canaan where they established a confederation of city-states. From there, they attempted to seize the whole of the mountain range and they nearly succeeded. Indeed, their own name has been thereafter used to designate the whole land of ' Palestine.'

At the request of the elders of Israel, the Ark was moved from the temple of Shiloh to lead the Hebrew armies against the Philistine invaders, but it fell into the hands of the enemy. After the defeat of Eben-ezer, most of the Hebrew cities, including the sanctuary of Shiloh, were destroyed—an event which has been confirmed by archaeological excavations. The nation was saved from extinction by the activity of the priestly prophet Samuel, of the shrine of Shiloh, who discerned that, in the face of foreign occupation, the hierocratic form of government (Eli and his sons, Samuel and his sons) was incapable of opposing effective resistance. He was instrumental in instituting a hereditary monarchy.

12. The Reign of Saul (*c* 1020–1000 B.C.).—There are two accounts of Saul's accession to kingship. The older of these (1 S 9^{1}–$10^{16, 27b}$ 11^{1-15}) tells how Saul was led to Samuel in seeking some lost asses, how Samuel anointed him to be king, and how about a month later the men of Jabesh-gilead, whom the Ammonites were besieging, sent out messengers earnestly imploring aid. Saul made a ritual declaration of national emergency. The various tribes of Israel raised an army which, under Saul's leadership, delivered the besieged city. He was then recognized as king at Gilgal. The other account (which is found chiefly in 1 S 7^{3}–8^{22} 10^{17-27a} 12) presents a different picture. In this tradition, Samuel is not a local seer but a judge with legal and military responsibilities (7^{5-17}) whose activity centres in the sanctuaries of Bethel, Gilgal, and Mizpah. Saul is elected king at Mizpah, in spite of Samuel's reluctance. Although this anti-royalist view may have been edited at a later date, there is valid reason to believe that it depends upon an ancient tradition (see I. Mendelsohn, ' Samuel's Denunciation of Kingship in the Light of the Akkadian Documents from Ugarit,' *BASOR*, No. 143 [October, 1956], 17–22).

While details of Saul's elevation as reported in both sources may not be reconciled in a satisfactory way, it is probable that Samuel, who represented the theocratic party, yielded to popular demands for a new regime on account of the Philistine emergency.

The Philistines, upon hearing that Israel had a king, naturally endeavoured to crush him. They penetrated as far as Michmash, within ten miles of Gibeah, Saul's fortress. Their camp was separated from that of Israel by the deep gorge of Michmash. Owing to the daring and valour of Jonathan, the king's son, a victory was gained for Israel which gave Saul for a time freedom from these enemies (1 S 13, 14). Soon, however, he was compelled to take up arms once more against the Philistines, whom he fought with varying fortunes until they slew him in battle on Mount Gilboa. During the later years of his life, fits of insanity came upon him with increasing frequency. The tradition explained his disease as the evidence that Yahweh had abandoned him. There may be a kernel of historical accuracy in the story of Samuel's decision to repudiate Saul for a new leader, the young David of Judah (1 S 15–16), thereby insuring to the new dynasty the stamp of theocratic legitimacy.

Saul was the symbol of transition between the nomadic ways of the wilderness and the agrarian, industrial, and mercantile civilization of the Iron Age. The older source called him not 'a king' but 'a prince' (1 S 9^{16}) and described him as a charismatic leader sensitive to prophetic inspiration (10$^{1-8}$). His monarchy was of the constitutional kind, as indicated by the statement that Samuel wrote in a book the rights and duties of the kingship (1 S 10^{25}). Even after Samuel's death, the authority of the prophet remained for the king the source of his political and military decisions (1 S 28). With the ascent of David upon the throne, the concept of kingship evolved into the direction of absolute rule, which led, in due course, to Solomon's tyranny.

13. The Reign of David (*c* 1000–962 B.C.).—Before Saul's death, David, who had been expelled from the court, attached the men of Judah firmly to himself, and exhibited exceptional qualities of leadership. When Saul fell at Gilboa, David declared himself king of Judah at Hebron (2 S 2^{4}). As Jonathan, Saul's heir, had fallen in battle, Abner, Saul's faithful general, made Ish-baal, Saul's other son, king over Israel at Mahanaim in Transjordania. For seven and a half years civil war dragged itself along. Then Joab, David's general, removed Abner through treacherous murder, assassins disposed of the weak Ish-baal, and Israel and Judah were soon reunited under the rule of a single monarch, David. The statements of 2 S 5 show that the elders of Israel were hostile to him, but that they finally rallied to his leadership. David devoted his skill and energy to the consolidation of his kingdom. Just at the northern edge of the tribe of Judah, commanding the highway from north to south, stood the ancient fortress of Jerusalem. It had never been in the possession of the Israelites. The Jebusites, who had held it since Israel's entrance into Canaan, fondly believed that its position rendered it impregnable. This city David captured, and with the insight of genius made it his capital (2 S 5^{4ff}). This choice was a wise one in every way. Had he continued to dwell in Hebron, both Benjamin—which had been recently the royal tribe—and Ephraim—which never easily yielded precedence to any other group—would have regarded him as a Judaean rather than a national leader. Jerusalem was to the Israelites a new city. It not only had no associations with the tribal differences of the past, but, lying as it did on the borderland of two tribes, was neutral ground. Moreover, the natural facilities of its situation lent it a strategic and tactical significance. David rebuilt the Jebusite stronghold and took up his residence in it, and thus it became known as the city of David.

The Philistines, ever jealous of the rising power of Israel, soon attacked David in his new capital, but he gained such a victory over them (2 S 5^{18ff}) that he thereafter sought them out, city by city, and subdued them at his leisure (2 S 8^{1ff}). Having swept the Philistines out of the high land, he turned his attention to the Transjordanian territory. He attacked Moab, and after his victory treated the conquered with the greatest barbarity (2 S 8^{2}). Edom was also subdued (8^{13f}). Ammon needlessly provoked a war with Israel, and after a long siege their capital Rabbah, on the distant border of the desert, succumbed (12^{29}). The Aramaean state of Zobah was compelled to pay tribute (8^{3ff}). Damascus, whose inhabitants, as kinsfolk of the people of Zobah, tried to aid the latter, was finally made a tributary state also (8^{5ff}). Within a few years, David built up a considerable empire. This territory he did not attempt to organize in a political way, but according to the Oriental custom of the time he ruled it through submissive native princes. Toi, king of Hamath, and Hiram, king of Tyre, sent embassies to welcome David as a commercial partner. Thus Israel became a recognized power, for the first time in history, among the nations of the world.

This political success was made possible by the continuation of a state of weakness both in Mesopotamia and in the valley of the Nile. After Tiglath-pileser I. (*c* 1113–1075 B.C.), the Assyrians passed through a period of difficulties, from which they did not emerge until the middle of the 9th cent. B.C. Likewise, the 21st Egyptian Dynasty, divided by domestic intrigue, was unable to intervene in the affairs of the Fertile Crescent.

Upon his removal to Jerusalem, David organized his court on a scale hitherto unknown in Israel. Following Oriental mores, he married several wives. His fondness for his son Absalom and his paternal weakness produced dire political consequences. Absalom led a rebellion which drove the king from Jerusalem and nearly cost him the throne. David on this occasion, like Ish-baal before him, took refuge at Mahanaim, the east Jordanian stronghold. David's conduct towards the rebellious son was such that, without Joab's disregard of the royal command, the defeated Absalom would not have been put to death and might have triumphed in the end. The last days of David were further troubled by the attempt of his other son, Adonijah, to seize the crown (1 K 1). Having, however, fixed the succession upon Solomon, the son of Bathsheba, David probably left to him as an inheritance not only the kingdom but also the duty of taking vengeance upon Joab and Shimei (1 K 2^{1ff}). To the reign of David subsequent generations looked as the golden age of Israel. Never again did the boundaries of a united kingdom extend so far. These boundaries, magnified a little by fond imagination, became the ideal limits of the Promised Land. David himself, idealized by later ages, became the prototype of the Messiah.

14. The Reign of Solomon (962–922 B.C.).—Probably upon the accession of Solomon, certainly during his reign, two of the tributary states Edom and Damascus, gained their independence (1 K 11$^{14-25}$). The remainder of the empire of David was held by Solomon almost until his own death. While David had risen from the people, a simple shepherd who, not unlike Saul, had maintained fairly simple modes of living, Solomon imitated the conduct of the petty kings of the ancient Near East. He consummated a marriage with the daughter of the Pharaoh, probably one of the rulers of the Tanite branch of the 21st Dynasty. This marriage brought him in touch with the culture of Egypt. He developed a foreign service, with ambassadors who learned the methods of the international wise men, and probably on this account received at a later age a reputation for wisdom (1 K 3$^{16-23}$ 4$^{29-34}$ 10$^{1-10}$; see R. B. Y. Scott, 'Solomon and the beginnings of wisdom in Israel,' *Wisdom in Israel and in the Ancient Near East*, ed. by M. Noth and D. Winton Thomas [1955], pp. 262–279).

In order to equip his capital with public buildings suitable to the estate of an international monarch, Solomon hired Phoenician architects, and constructed a palace for himself, one for the Egyptian princess, and a royal chapel according to the design of Phoenician temples. This religious innovation was looked upon with disfavour by many of his contemporaries (1 K 12^{28b}), and his buildings, although the boast of a later age, were regarded with mingled feelings by those who were compelled to pay the taxes by which their erection was made possible. His expenditures forced him to cede to the king of Tyre a part of the Galilean territory.

Not only through his architectural projects but also in his whole establishment did Solomon depart from the simple ways of his father. He not only married the daughters of many of the petty kings who were his tributaries, but he also filled his harem with numerous beauties besides. Probably the statement that he had 700 wives and 300 concubines (1 K 11^{3}) is the exaggeration of popular legend, but, allowing for this, his harem

ISRAEL

must have been quite extensive and constituted a drain on the public treasury. His method of living was, of course, in accord with the magnificent palaces which he had erected.

To support this splendour, the old system of taxation was inadequate, and a new method had to be devised. The whole country was divided into twelve districts, each of which was placed under the charge of a tax-gatherer, in order to furnish for the king's house the provision for one month in each year (1 K 4^{7-18}). It is noteworthy that in this division economic conditions rather than tribal territories were followed. Not only were the tribes unequal in numbers, but the territory of certain sections was much more productive than that of others, and it appears that Judah received a favoured treatment. Solomon is also said to have departed from the simple ways of his father by introducing horses and chariots for his army and for his personal use. To house his chariotry, he built stables at Megiddo and elsewhere. The stables of Megiddo, which have been excavated, could accommodate almost 500 horses. The royal wealth was increased by trade with South Arabia and possibly the east coast of Africa and the west coast of India. Solomon established a fleet of trading vessels on the Red Sea and perhaps on the Indian Ocean as well, manned with Phoenician sailors (1 K 9^{26ff}). In order to shelter goods in transit, he built a number of warehouses in fortified centres which were also of use for the storing of taxed goods. He traded horses on an international basis (1 K 10^{28-29}). Excavations at the site of the ancient port of Ezion-geber, on the gulf of 'Aqaba, have brought to light large installations, including furnaces for the smelting and refining of copper and iron ore which was mined in the vicinity and in the Sinai peninsula.

Towards the close of Solomon's reign the tribe of Ephraim, which in the time of the Judges could hardly bear to allow another tribe to take precedence of it, became restless. Economic and political resentment against Solomon found support among the prophetic circles which represented the old Yahwism of the desert and condemned the king's alliances with foreign nations as well as the idolatrous worship practised in Jerusalem by his wives. The prophet Ahijah supported Jeroboam, a young Ephraimitic officer to whom Solomon had entrusted the administration of the Joseph tribes (1 K 11^{28}). Jeroboam's plans for rebelling involved the fortifying of his native city of Zeredah, which called Solomon's attention to his plot. Forced to flee the country, he found refuge in Egypt. The 21st Dynasty, with which Solomon was allied by marriage, had been terminated by Shishak (Sheshonk), who founded the 22nd Dynasty, reunited Egypt under one sceptre and entertained ambitions to renew Egypt's colonization of the Fertile Crescent. Shishak accordingly welcomed Jeroboam and offered him asylum.

15. The Division of the Kingdom (922 B.C.).—Upon the death of Solomon, his son Rehoboam was proclaimed king in Judah without opposition, but as some doubt concerning the loyalty of the other tribes seems to have existed, Rehoboam went to Shechem to be anointed king at the traditional shrine of Ephraim (1 K 12^{1ff}). Having been informed of the development in his Egyptian retreat, Jeroboam returned to Shechem at once and prompted the elders of the tribes assembled there to exact from Rehoboam a promise that in case they accepted him as monarch he would relieve them of the heavy taxation which his father had imposed upon them. After considering the matter for three days, Rehoboam replied, 'My little finger shall be thicker than my father's loins.' All the tribes except Judah and a portion of Benjamin refused to acknowledge the descendant of David, and they made Jeroboam their king. Judah remained faithful to the heir of their old hero, and, because Jerusalem was on the border of Benjamin, the Judaean kings were able to retain a strip of the land of that tribe from four to eight miles in width. All else was lost to the Davidic dynasty.

The chief forces which produced this disruption were economic and ethnic. Israel proper was aware of the divergence of racial elements which separated her from Judah. Religious conservatism also did its share. Solomon had in many ways contravened the religious customs of his nation. Jeroboam was aware of this antagonism when he used as a rallying slogan, 'Behold thy gods, O Israel, which brought thee up out of the land of Egypt!' Since the history of the schism has been preserved only through the Deuteronomic editor of the book of Kings, who was a propagandist of the Jerusalem cultus in a later era, modern scholars are careful to view the attitude of Jeroboam with impartiality. He was not a religious and political innovator but rather a conservative.

When the kingdom was divided, the tributary states of course gained their independence, and Israel's empire came to an end. The time of her political glory had been less than a century, and her empire disappeared never to return. The nation, being divided and its parts often warring with one another, could not easily become again a power of importance (see S. Yeivin, 'Social, Religious and Cultural Trends in Jerusalem under the Davidic Dynasty,' *VT*, iii [1953], 163 ff).

16. From Jeroboam to Ahab (922–850 B.C.).—The kingdom of Judah remained loyal to the Davidic dynasty for three and a half centuries, but in Israel military *coups d'état* imposed frequent and violent interruptions of dynastic succession. Only one family furnished more than four monarchs, some only two, while several failed to transmit the throne at all. The kings during the first period after the schism were:

ISRAEL		JUDAH	
Jeroboam I.	922–901	Rehoboam	922–915
Nadab	901–900	Abijam	915–913
Baasha	900–877	Asa	913–873
Elah	877–876	Jehoshaphat	873–849
Zimri	876		
Omri	876–869		
Ahab	869–850		

Jeroboam I. fortified Shechem (1 K 12^{25}), but Tirzah became the capital of his kingdom (1 K 14^{17}). He extended his patronage to two sanctuaries, Dan and Bethel, the one at the northern and the other at the southern extremity of his territory. There were, of course, hostile relations between him and Rehoboam as long as he lived. One might think that he was instrumental in bringing Shishak of Egypt to invade Judah (1 K 14^{25}). If so, his diplomatic intrigue turned against him as well as against the son of Solomon. For Shishak not only compelled Rehoboam to pay a tribute which stripped the Temple of much of its gold treasure and ornamentation but also marched northward as far as the sea of Galilee, captured the towns of Megiddo, Taanach, and Shunem in the plain of Jezreel, the town of Bethshean at the junction of Jezreel with the Jordan valley, and Transjordania as far as Mahanaim. How deep the enmity between Israel and Judah may have become is to be inferred from the fact that this attack of the Egyptian monarch did not effect between them a reconciliation.

Shishak's campaign seems to have been a mere plundering raid. It established no permanent Asiatic empire for Egypt. After this attack, Rehoboam strengthened the fortifications of his kingdom (2 Ch 11^{5-11}). His territory extended to Mareshah and Gath in the Shephelah, and southward as far as Hebron. No mention is made of any town N. of Jerusalem or in the Jordan valley.

The hostile relations between the two kingdoms were perpetuated after the death of Rehoboam, during the short reign of Abijam. In the early part of the reign of Asa, while Nadab was on the throne of Israel, active hostilities ceased sufficiently to allow the king of Israel to besiege the Palestine city of Gibbethon, a town in the northern part of the coastal plain. The Israelite monarch felt strong enough to endeavour to extend his dominions by compelling these ancient enemies of Israel to submit once more. During the siege of this town, Baasha, an ambitious man of the tribe of Issachar, assassinated Nadab and had himself proclaimed king in his stead (1 K 15[27-29]). Thus the dynasty of Jeroboam came to an end in the second generation.

Baasha upon his accession determined to push more vigorously the war with Judah. Entering into an alliance with Benhadad I. of Damascus, he proceeded to fortify Ramah, 5 miles N. of Jerusalem, as a base of operations against Judah. Asa in this crisis collected all the treasure that he could, sent it to Benhadad, and bought him off, persuading him to break his alliance with Israel and to enter into one with Judah. Benhadad thereupon attacked some of the towns in north-eastern Galilee, and Baasha was obliged to desist from his Judaean campaign and to defend his own borders. Asa took this opportunity to fortify Geba, about 8 miles NE. of Jerusalem, and Mizpah, 5 miles to the NW. of it (1 K 15[16-22]). The only other important event in Asa's reign known to us consisted of the erection by Asa's mother of an *asherah* —a cultic object used in Canaanite worship—which so shocked the sense of the time that Asa was compelled to remove it (15[13]).

During the reign of Elah of Israel, an attempt was made once more to capture Gibbethon. The siege was being prosecuted by an able general named Omri, while the weak king was enjoying himself at Tirzah, which had been the royal residence since the days of Jeroboam. Zimri, the commander of his chariots, killed the king in a drunken brawl, and was then proclaimed king. Omri, however, upon hearing of this, hastened from Gibbethon to Tirzah, overthrew and slew Zimri, and himself became king. Thus, once more did the dynasty change. Omri proved to be one of the ablest rulers of the Northern Kingdom. His fame spread to Assyria, where even after his dynasty had been overthrown Israel was still called 'the land of Omri.' Perceiving the splendid military possibilities and political advantages of the hill of Samaria, he chose it for his capital, fortified it, and made it one of his residences, thus introducing to history a name destined to play in succeeding generations an important part (see E. L. Sukenik, *The Buildings at Samaria*, 1942). He appears to have made a peaceful alliance with Damascus, so that war between the two kingdoms ceased. He also formed an alliance with the king of Tyre, taking Jezebel, the daughter of the Tyrian king Ethbaal, as a wife for his son Ahab. The Moabite Stone shows that Omri conquered Moab, compelling the Moabites to pay tribute. Of the nature of the relations between Israel and Judah during his reign, nothing is known. Peace probably prevailed since the next two kings of these kingdoms were allies.

With the reign of Ahab, peace at last was sealed between Jerusalem and Samaria, when Jehoram, the son of Jehoshaphat of Judah, married Athaliah, the daughter of Ahab and Jezebel (1 K 22[44], 2 K 8[26]). Ahab rebuilt and fortified Jericho (1 K 16[34]). The first part of his reign seems to have been prosperous, although the Moabites soon gained their independence. In 853 B.C. Ahab joined a confederacy of twelve kings who were headed by Benhadad II. of Damascus, and who fought Shalmaneser III. of Assyria at Qarqar on the Orontes. Although Shalmaneser claimed victory, it is clear that the western coalition practically defeated him, for he made no further inroads southward. In the following year, Benhadad invaded Israelite territory in Transjordania and he seized Ramoth-gilead. Trying to regain it with the assistance of his ally, Jehoshaphat of Judah, Ahab was wounded in battle and lost his life.

Meanwhile in Judah Jehoshaphat had a prosperous and long reign. He made Edom tributary to him (1 K 22[47]) and rebuilt the fleet on the Red Sea (22[48]).

17. From Ahaziah to Jeroboam II. (849–746 B.C.).—The monarchs of the two kingdoms were the following:

ISRAEL

Israel		Judah	
Ahaziah	850–849	Jehoram	849–842
Jehoram	849–842	Ahaziah	842
		Athaliah	842–837
Jehu	842–815	Jehoash	837–800
Jehoahaz	815–801	Amaziah	800–783
Jehoash	801–786	Azariah (Uzziah)	783–750
Jeroboam II.	786–746		

Of the short reign of Ahaziah of Israel, son of Ahab, nothing is known. His brother, Jehoram of Israel, another son of Ahab, became king in his place and attempted to resubjugate the Moabites (2 K 3). He besieged the king of Moab who, in his distress, offered his eldest son in sacrifice to Chemosh, the god of the Moabites. The siege was raised and the conquest of Moab abandoned.

Jehoram of Judah, the son of Jehoshaphat, lost control over Edom (2 K 8[20ff]). Ahaziah of Judah, Jehoram's son, who was also the son of Athaliah, and therefore the nephew of Jehoram of Israel, went to the help of his uncle in the siege of Ramoth-gilead, which was still in the possession of the Aramaeans of Damascus. Jehoram of Israel was wounded in battle, and the two monarchs returned to the royal residence at Jezreel while the wound was healing. The prophetic circles, opposed to syncretistic worship, determined to overthrow the house of Ahab. Elisha encouraged Jehu, a military officer employed in the siege of Ramoth-gilead, to return to Jezreel and to slay the king of Israel. This he did, and for good measure, he slew also the king of Judah, the queen-mother of Israel, Jezebel, and all the offspring of the royal family. Jehu then started for Samaria, called a solemn feast in honour of Baal, and when the worshippers were assembled, massacred them all (2 K 9, 10).

In the year that Jehu thus gained the throne (842 B.C.), Shalmaneser III. of Assyria marched into the West. This time, no powerful alliance was formed against him. Damascus and Israel, at war with each other, could not resist the Assyrian advance. Jehu hastened to pay tribute, an event which is recorded on the black obelisk of Shalmaneser. Jehu is there portrayed in the act of kissing the foot of the Assyrian monarch.

In Judah, Ahaziah's widow, Athaliah, who was also the daughter of Jezebel, seized the reins of government, put to death all the royal seed, and sat on the throne of David. One prince, however, had been rescued by the priest Jehoiada, and kept hidden in the Temple of Jerusalem for six years. Still a child, Jehoash was proclaimed king by the Temple hierarchy and the half-Phoenician queen was put to death (2 K 11).

In Israel, the young Jehoahaz succeeded his father Jehu. At first unable to gain victory against the Aramaeans, the new king finally imposed peace upon the new ruler of Damascus, Hazael, and a new era of prosperity began for the kingdom. Jehoash of Judah was not as successful and paid tribute to Hazael. Perhaps as a consequence of this national humiliation, a conspiracy rose against him. He was assassinated and his son Amaziah succeeded him.

Jehoahaz of Israel maintained the dynasty of Jehu on the throne of Samaria and his son Jehoash of Israel continued warfare with the Aramaeans and regained from them all the Transjordanian territory which had been previously snatched away from Israel (2 K 13[25]). In Judah, Amaziah executed the assassins of his father, reoccupied a part of Edom, but in a clash with Jehoash at Beth-shemesh lost the battle. Jerusalem itself was taken by the Israelites and part of its wall was dismantled. Amaziah, who had fled to Lachish, was slain there by conspirators. His son Azariah (Uzziah) became king of Judah in his place.

During the reigns of Jeroboam II. in Israel and of Uzziah in Judah, the ancient world passed through a new period of stability. While Adadnirari III. had made an incursion westward in 806 B.C. and had boasted receiving tribute not only from Tyre and Sidon but also from the 'land of Omri,' no more menace was arising from Nineveh. The Aramaeans had lost their power. Egypt remained weak. Between them, Jeroboam II. and Uzziah restored the territory almost to the limits of the Davidic empire. Israel ruled as far as Hamath and Damascus (2 K 14[28]) while Judah returned to the shore of the Red Sea (2 Ch 26) and imposed a tribute over the Philistine cities in the south-west. A vigorous and profitable trade sprang up. Freed from the necessity of continual warfare, the nation enriched itself, but wealth was not evenly distributed. Palaces were built for the ruling class, but the conditions of the poor husbandmen did hardly improve. Some were sold into slavery. It was social injustice which led a man like Amos to condemn the policies of Jeroboam (750 B.C.) and to announce the end of the kingdom.

18. The Fall of Samaria (746–722 B.C.).—In a few years, events rushed one behind the other. The kings of the two countries were then the following:

Israel		Judah	
Zechariah .	746–745	Jotham (regent)	750–742
Shallum . .	745	Jotham (king) .	742–735
Menahem .	745–738	Ahaz . . .	735–715
Pekahiah . .	738–737		
Pekah . .	737–732		
Hoshea . .	732–724		

After Jeroboam II. died (746 B.C.), his son, Zechariah reigned for six months, but a conspiracy removed him and placed Shallum on the throne. With Zechariah, the dynasty came to an end. Another revolution in Samaria soon removed Shallum, and Menahem became king of Israel (745 B.C.).

Tiglath-pileser III. had just seized power in Assyria. He proved himself to be a successful administrator and a brilliant general, and he soon pursued the ancient policy of westward expansion. He was, however, occupied until the year 742 B.C. in reducing the East to his sceptre. When he turned his attention to the West, the siege of Arpad detained him for two years. Uzziah of Judah, who in his old age had become a leper, and had associated his son Jotham with him as regent, appears to have taken a leading part in the organization of a coalition of nineteen states, including Hamath, Carchemish, and Damascus, to oppose the progress of the Assyrians. Tiglath-pileser marched southward along the Coastal Plain as though to attack Uzziah himself. Upon his approach Menahem deserted the confederacy and hastened to pay his tribute to Assyria.

Menahem died in about 735 B.C. His son Pekahiah was soon removed by a revolution, and Pekah became king in Samaria (2 K 15[22-27]). In Judah, Jotham was succeeded in the same year by his youthful son Ahaz. Pekah of Israel and Rezin, the new king of Damascus, tried to form a new confederacy in order to throw off the yoke of Assyria. Into this coalition they attempted to draw Ahaz, and when he declined to engage in the hopeless enterprise they threatened to make war jointly on Judah, depose Ahaz, and place a certain Tabeel on the throne of David. Upon the receipt of this news, consternation reigned in Jerusalem, and it was at this juncture that the prophet Isaiah asked the young king Ahaz to have faith in Yahweh (7[9]). Soon, Tiglath-pileser returned to the West (734 B.C.), took Damascus after a long and difficult siege (a city which his predecessors had at various times for more than a hundred years tried in vain to capture), made it an Assyrian colony, put Pekah of Israel to death, carried captive to Assyria the principal inhabitants of the Galilean hills (2 K 15[29ff]), made Hoshea king over a truncated Israel, and imposed upon him a heavy war tax.

At the approach of Tiglath-pileser, Ahaz of Judah had renewed his allegiance to his Assyrian overlord. After the capture of Damascus, he went thither to do obeisance in person to the Assyrian emperor. In effect, the two kingdoms of Israel and Judah, while remaining nominally independent, passed under the control of Nineveh.

Soon after the death of Tiglath-pileser (727 B.C.), Hoshea refused to continue payment of the national taxes to Assyria, and the new emperor, Shalmaneser V. (727–722 B.C.), sent an expeditionary force which overran the Israelite territory, cut off Hoshea's lines of supplies, and isolated him in his fortified capital, Samaria. The military genius of Omri had selected the site wisely: it is a marvel of defensive warfare that the city, in the midst of a country occupied by the enemy, could resist a siege of three years (725–722 B.C.). Shalmaneser V. died and was succeeded by Sargon II. (722–705 B.C.). The Assyrian commanders who were prosecuting the siege of Samaria probably did not know of the regnal change until after the city had fallen. At any rate, Sargon boasted of the fall of the Israelite capital as one of the achievements of his first year. He deported to the eastern borders of the empire 27,290 inhabitants of Samaria and other cities of the Northern Kingdom, including no doubt the élite of the population. (See H. G. May, 'The Deportation of Israel,' and 'The Israelites in Exile,' *BA*, vi [1943], 57–60). He thereupon resettled the territory with ethnic groups from Cuthah and Sippar in Babylonia and from Hamath in Syria. These new settlers intermingled with the peasant classes of Israel that had been left upon the land (2 K 17[24]). Sargon's demographic policy was partly responsible for the origin of the Samaritans. The new-comers were, of course, polytheists. When they were attacked by lions, however, they petitioned to have a priest of Yahweh teach them how to worship the God of the land. Sargon granted their request and sent back to them a a captive priest. In the course of time, the foreign settlers intermarried with the Israelites who had managed to remain in the mountains and their descendants became known as 'the Samaritans.'

19. Hezekiah (715–687 B.C.) **and the Siege of Jerusalem** (701 B.C.).—The kingdom of Judah escaped destruction when Samaria fell, no doubt because Ahaz maintained toward Assyria the submissive attitude which he had manifested toward Tiglath-pileser in 735 B.C. On the western borders of Judah, however, the city-states of Philistia were always plotting to throw off the Assyrian yoke, and endeavouring to secure the co-operation of the son of Ahaz, Hezekiah (715–685 B.C.). Such co-operation, the prophet Isaiah steadily opposed. In the year 711 B.C., the city of Ashdod succeeded in heading a coalition which she hoped would gain her freedom, but Sargon II. sent an army which soon brought her to terms (Is 20[1]). During those turbulent years, Hezekiah prepared for an eventual siege of Jerusalem by attempting to insure the water-supply of the city (709 B.C.; see G. E. Wright, *Biblical Archaeology* [1957], 164–172). His workmen dug a tunnel under the old city in order to by-pass the hitherto open-air and exposed canal which brought water to the sheltered Siloam pool, from the spring of Gihon (see SILOAM). It was perhaps on account of this feat of technology that the city survived the Assyrian onslaught which was to come within the next decade.

After the death of Sargon II. in 705 B.C., many subject states of the Fertile Crescent attempted to regain their independence before the new monarch could consolidate his power. Hezekiah yielded to the diplomatic entreaties of Merodach-baladan (Marduk-apal-iddin), the Babylonian prince whom Sargon II. had early in his reign driven from Babylon, and who now sought the opportunity to return to the throne (2 K 20[12ff], Is 39[1ff]). In this new coalition the Egyptians also, now under the stronger control of the 25th Dynasty, had a part. Although Isaiah still consistently opposed the move, Hezekiah accepted to join in the general revolt. Padi, king of Ekron, who remained faithful to the Assyrian overlord, was placed under arrest in Jerusalem. Sennacherib, the new king of Assyria (705–681 B.C.), had to avenge this insult. Military problems in the East delayed him for a while, but in 701 B.C. he led an army westward, defeated the allies at Eltekeh, besieged and took Ekron, impaled many of the rebellious inhabitants, and invaded Judah. Forty-six of the smaller towns were captured, and Jerusalem itself was invested. Its inhabitants were panic stricken, but Isaiah came forward, declaring Zion to be inviolable in the eyes of Yahweh (Is 31[4]). In the meantime, Hezekiah sent to Sennacherib's headquarters in Lachish and offered to pay a war indemnity. The sequence of events is not clear, and many scholars believe that the story of Sennacherib's invasion in 2 K 19 represents a combination of a least two different campaigns into a single expedition (W. F. Albright, 'New Light from Egypt on the Chronology and History of Israel and Judah,' *BASOR*, No. 130 [April 1953], 8–11; 'Further Light on Synchronisms between Egypt and Asia in the Period 935–685 B.C.,' *BASOR*, No. 141 [February 1956], 23–26). The traditions gathered at a later age by Herodotus in Egypt (ii. 141) confirm the Biblical account of a plague which decimated the Assyrian forces (2 K 19[35]). In any case, it appears from the totality of the documentation that the siege of Jerusalem was lifted and that the city was saved from destruction. The memory of this unexpected deliverance played in the subsequent centuries a major part in giving to the Temple of Jerusalem or its site the pre-eminence of sanctity it has maintained in Judaism, Christianity and Islam.

According to 2 K 18[4], Hezekiah attempted to abolish the country shrines and to purify the worship of Yahweh in the temple of Solomon (H. H. Rowley, 'Zadok and Nehushtan,' *JBL*, lviii [1939], 113 ff). Some historians have doubted the historicity of this reform, but others have thought that it is confirmed by an older document quoted in 2 K 18[22]. The king may have been prompted by Isaiah in initiating some kind of cultic purification. He thereby demonstrated his political independence from the Assyrian yoke to which his father Ahaz had submitted.

20. Manasseh (687–642 B.C.), **Amon** (642–640 B.C.), **and Josiah** (640 B.C.).—The editors of Kings have pictured Manasseh as the most criminal monarch who ever sat on the throne of David. Pagan practices which had been eradicated by Hezekiah were restored throughout the kingdom as well as in the Temple of Jerusalem (2 K 23[7]). At the same time, prophetic opposition to the royal policies was ruthlessly repressed (2 K 21[16]). It is probable, however, that the king had little choice, for the Assyrian emperors, although in the grip of domestic upheavals, were slowly consolidating their power over the entire Near East. Manasseh apparently became a vassal of Sennacherib and during his entire reign remained the subject of Nineveh. The worship of Assyrian deities was a necessary concomitant of Judah's political subservience to Assyria.

Sennacherib was murdered in 681 B.C. and Esarhaddon (681–669 B.C.), having secured the throne from his competitors, led Assyria to the conquest of Egypt and seized Memphis in 671 B.C. His son, Ashurbanipal (669–633 [?] B.C.), advanced to Upper Egypt and destroyed Thebes (663 B.C.). For a short while, Assyria ruled over the largest territory ever conquered up to that time in that part of the world. Political rivalries in Babylonia, however, threatened the security of Ashurbanipal at home (652 B.C.). The new Pharaoh, Psammetichus I. (650–609 B.C.), founder of the 26th Dynasty, soon declared the independence of Egypt (650 B.C.). While the Assyrian armies marched up and down the coast of Philistia, Judah escaped direct invasion, no doubt on account of Manasseh's acceptance of vassalage. According to one tradition (2 Ch 33[10-13]), he was once brought in chains before the Assyrian emperor, presumably on charges of political insubordination, but eventually was allowed to resume his reign.

The Assyrian empire had reached its apogee. The loss of Egypt was followed by threats of invasion in northern and eastern Mesopotamia. The Scythians and the Cimmerians were pushing across the Caucasus and the Medes exerted a similar pressure from the Iranian plateau.

While Amon (642–640 B.C.) continued the policy of acquiescence, the young king Josiah (640–609 B.C.) soon hailed the death of Ashurbanipal (633 B.C.?) and witnessed the fall of the Assyrian power. In the eighteenth year of Josiah's reign (622 B.C.), when the king was only twenty-six years old, a copy of the law was found in the Temple of Jerusalem. Upon hearing its contents, the king was profoundly disturbed. He consulted the prophetess Huldah who confirmed its authority (2 K 22), and he therefore set himself to adjust to its standards the worship and the institutions of the kingdom. Josiah's reform swept away all local shrines except the Jerusalem sanctuary, all cultic pillars and statuary, and attempted to wipe out the practices of a pagan character (2 K 23). Modern criticism has shown that the core of the law which was found at that time has been subsequently edited and incorporated in what is now called 'Deuteronomy.' The reform of Josiah, no doubt inspired chiefly by religious considerations, was also motivated by political concern. The king saw his opportunity to claim back from Assyrian control the whole territory of the ancient kingdom of Northern Israel (see F. M. Cross, jun., and D. N. Freedman, 'Josiah's Revolt Against Assyria,' [*JNES*, xii [1953], 56–58).

Nineveh was tottering to its fall (612 B.C.). Babylon had regained its independence soon after the death of Ashurbanipal and was rapidly growing in power. Egypt, which under the 26th Dynasty possessed once more a line of native kings, was led on the path of renascence by Neco II., an able administrator and general, who discerned that the fall of Nineveh and the revival of Babylon necessitated the establishment of a new balance of power. He marched an army into Asia and in 609 B.C. proceeded northward along the coastal plain of Palestine. Josiah, probably because he determined to claim sovereignty over all the territory formerly occupied by Northern Israel, marched northward with an army, fought Neco at the ancient battlefield of Megiddo, and met with death (2 K 23[29ff]; see M. B. Rowton, 'Jeremiah and the Death of Josiah,' *JNES*, x [1951], 128–130). A greater calamity could scarcely have befallen the party of Yahwistic rigorism. Not only was their king killed ignominiously, but also their hope of a prosperous Judaean kingdom, faithful to Yahweh's law, was annihilated.

21. The End of Judah (609–586 B.C.).—When the news of the Megiddo defeat reached Jerusalem, the leaders of the people placed Jehoahaz, a son of Josiah, on the throne. Neco meantime moved northward, taking possession of the whole country, and established his headquarters at Riblah in the territory of Hamath. Thither he summoned Jehoahaz, threw him into bonds, sent him to Egypt as a prisoner, and made his brother Eliakim king of Judah, imposing a heavy tribute upon the country (2 K 23[31ff]). Upon his accession, Eliakim took the name of Jehoiakim (597–509 B.C.; 2 K 23[34]) and became a vassal of the Pharaoh.

The renewed Babylonian power was pushing westward to secure as much of the Fertile Crescent as possible. At the same time, Neco was ambitious to follow up his previous success and to check the Babylonian army at a strategically sound point, and far away from Egypt. In 605–604 B.C. he was met in battle at Carchemish by the Babylonian crown prince, Nebuchadnezzar, and was defeated. The Egyptian dream of a new Asiatic empire was crushed, and Judah soon thereafter passed into vassalage to Babylon. Nebuchadnezzar, on the border of Egypt, ready to invade and conquer it, was informed of the death of his father, Nabopolassar, in Babylon, and hastened home to secure his crown. The new ruler appears to have encountered difficulties in several parts of Western Asia. He established his headquarters at Riblah, and for a few years sent out bands of soldiers whither they were needed. Jehoiakim, thinking to take advantage of this unsettled situation, withheld his tribute, and some of these bands, composed largely of men from the neighbouring states, were sent against Jerusalem (2 K 24[1ff]). Jehoiakim continued obstinate, however, and Nebuchadnezzar finally, in 597 B.C., sent a large army. Before it arrived, the Judaean king died, and his young son, Jehoiachin, was occupying the throne. Nebuchadnezzar laid siege to Jerusalem, which after three months was compelled to capitulate, whereupon the Babylonian king took ten thousand of the prominent men, princes, warriors, priests, and craftsmen, and transported them to Babylonia. Another son of Josiah, who now took the name of Zedekiah, was placed upon the throne, subject of course to a heavy Babylonian tribute. Jehoiachin, a youth of twenty, was taken prisoner to Babylon, to languish in prison for many years (J. P. Hyatt, ' New Light on Nebuchadrezzar and Judean History,' *JBL*, lxxv [1956], 277–284; D. J. Wiseman, *Chronicles of Chaldaean Kings*, 1956).

It was now to be seen whether Judah would repeat the history of the Northern Kingdom or whether her king would have the wisdom to remain faithful to Babylon. Jeremiah, as he had done for years, steadily proclaimed that Judah's sole safety lay in obedience to the Babylonian emperor; such was the will of Yahweh. There was in Jerusalem, however, a strong party who advocated an alliance with Egypt as a means of securing freedom from Babylon. The king himself was weak and unwise. Finally, in 588 B.C., when Hophra, filled with ambitions for an Asiatic empire, ascended the Egyptian throne, he made such promises of aid to Judah that the standard of revolt was raised. Jeremiah did not, as Isaiah had done a century before, proclaim Jerusalem inviolate. In 587 B.C., the Babylonian army appeared and the final siege of Jerusalem began. Early in 586 B.C., Hophra marched an army into Palestine, and Nebuchadnezzar was obliged to raise the siege to send his full force against the Pharaoh. Jerusalem was then wild with joy, thinking deliverance had come. Jeremiah and his party were laughed to scorn. But Hophra was soon defeated, the siege of Jerusalem renewed, and pressed to its bitter end. In August 586 B.C., the city surrendered, its walls were broken down, its Temple was destroyed, another large body of captives transported to Babylonia, and Zedekiah, after being blinded, was taken there too (2 K 25). Thus Jerusalem suffered the fate of Samaria. Before its fall, however, the word of its prophets had so taken root, and such reforms had been instituted, that the Judaean exiles did not disintegrate sociologically and culturally as the Israelites of the Northern Kingdom had apparently done a century previously. Those who were deported in 586 B.C. were again the more prominent citizens among those who had been left behind in 597 B.C. Some of the poorer people and the peasantry were allowed to remain in the land. Gedaliah was made governor of the territory of Judah. Since Jerusalem was desolate, Mizpah, five miles to the north-west, was made the administrative seat of the province. Gedaliah had been in office only two months when he was assassinated (2 K 25[25ff]).

22. The Babylonian Exile (586–538 B.C.).—Perhaps fifty thousand Judaeans, including women and children, had been transported to Babylonia in two deportations of Nebuchadnezzar. These, with the exception of a few political leaders, were settled in colonies, in which they were permitted to have houses of their own, to visit one another freely, and to engage in business (Jer 29[5ff]). Ezekiel gives the picture of one of these colonies at Tell-abib (Ezk 3[15] 8[1] 20[1ff] 24[18] etc.), by the river Chebar (a canal near Nippur), in which the Palestinian organization of ' elders ' was perpetuated. Thus, the Judaeans settled down in Babylonia. Many followed so thoroughly Jeremiah's advice (Jer 29) that they soon acquired economic security and social stability in a hitherto totally alien environment. From then on, they and their descendants may be called ' the Jews.'

The Judaean peasants who remained in Palestine kept up as best they could the old religion, in an ignorant and often superstitious way (cf Jer 41[5ff]), while the priests and the more intelligent of the religious devotees who had been transported to Babylon cherished the laws of the past, and fondly framed codes and programmes for a future which they were confident would come. Such an one was Ezekiel, who lived and wrote among the captives till about 570 B.C. After the destruction of the city of Jerusalem, he elaborated a new religious polity for the nation, hoping it would form the basis of Israel's organization when the time for the reconstruction of the state came. He prepared even an architect's ' blue-print ' for the rebuilding of the Temple which was so precise that several scholars have constructed from it realistic models (Ezk 40–48).

Some years later another writer of the Priestly School collated and published a body of cultic laws which have been preserved in Leviticus and are now designated as the Code of Holiness. Other priests were soon at work on a larger project: a history of the world from the time of its creation, together with a priestly version of the origins of Israel, destined to replace the earlier traditions, with a view to prepare the establishment of a priestly state in Jerusalem. This document became later the basis and the frame of the Pentateuch.

After the death of Nebuchadnezzar (562 B.C.), his son Amel-Marduk ascended the throne of Babylon. Two years later, Amel-Marduk was murdered by his brother-in-law, Neriglissar (560–555 B.C.) whose own son, Labashi-Marduk, was in turn put out of the way by Nabonidus (555–538 B.C.). Compelled to face invasions from the Arabs, Nabonidus left the administration of Babylon to his son Belshazzar and settled more or less permanently at the oasis of Tema, in Arabia. Babylonian society was soon demoralized and in no way could resist a new threat of unprecedented dimensions which was coming from the East.

Cyrus, a petty prince of Anshan, a small district of Elam, had rebelled against Astyages, his overlord, and became king of the Medes (550 B.C.). A few years later, Cyrus marched into Asia Minor and conquered Croesus, the fabulously wealthy king of Lydia (546 B.C.). It was probably at this juncture that one of the world's great poets and prophets appeared among the Jewish captives in Babylonia and taught them in most eloquent and poetic strain that Cyrus was the instrument of Yahweh (*māshîaḥ*, anointed one) and that he was conquering the world for the sake of Yahweh's people so that they would return and rebuild Jerusalem. The name of this prophet is lost, but his poems now form chs. 40–55 of the Book of Isaiah and he is referred to as ' Deutero-Isaiah.'

The hope of this prophet in Cyrus was justified, for in 538 B.C., the king of the Medes and Persians captured Babylon without waging a battle, overturned the Babylonian Empire and reversed the policy of mass deportations which Assyrians and Babylonians alike had pursued from the time of Tiglath-pileser III. Cyrus himself tells in his inscription that he permitted captive peoples to return to their lands and to rebuild their temples. This gave the Jews the opportunity for which Deutero-Isaiah had hoped. However, it was years before any considerable number of captives made use of their newly acquired liberty. They were interested in their religion, to be sure, but they had learned to practise it outside of Palestine without sacrificial ritual, and the opportunities in Mesopotamia and elsewhere for trade and the acquisition of riches were too good to be abandoned for the sterile soil of the land of their fathers. The Murashu tablets found at Nippur in Mesopotamia and the papyri discovered at Elephantine in Upper Egypt show the wide-spread character of the Jewish dispersion in the century following the Babylonian exile. In Mesopotamia, the Jews continued to live for fifteen hundred years. They frequently sent money contributions to those of their number who had returned to Jerusalem. Occasionally, a few of them joined the first ' Zionists.' Most of them, however, settled permanently and willingly in the land of their exile. After a time, they chose Exiliarchs, or 'Princes of the Captivity.' Schools of Jewish learning developed in their midst. In due course, the Babylonian Talmud was compiled in these schools, and the Babylonian Massorah (tradition) came to be written down and constitutes an important witness of the Biblical text.

These communities survived the vicissitudes of Persian, Macedonian, Parthian, Sassanian, and Arabian rule, continuing to have their Exiliarchs till the 11th cent. A.D., when the oppressions to which they were subjected led them gradually to migrate to other parts of the world.

23. The Jerusalem Restoration (538–333 B.C.).—The book of Ezra tells that a large number of exiles returned to Jerusalem as soon as Cyrus issued his permission to all captives to return to their home lands. It is probable that the 'Zionist' movement was at first very slow. Zerubbabel, a grandson of the unfortunate king Jehoiachin, became governor of Jerusalem, and a high priest named Joshua was the head of the hierarchy. The altar of Yahweh had been rebuilt on the old site and the Temple was still in ruins. The tolerance of the Persian administration is shown in allowing the Jews a governor of the Davidic blood. He, with a small retinue, had no doubt returned from Babylonia, but we have no evidence that the bulk of the population had also come back.

The Jewish peasantry which had remained in Palestine during the Babylonian exile, equally with those Jews who had returned from Babylonia, expected at some time the reconstruction of the Jewish institutions. A prolonged famine led Haggai in the second year of Darius I. (522–486 B.C.), to persuade the people that Yahweh had withheld rain because he was displeased that the Temple had not yet been rebuilt. Another prophet, Zechariah, took up the same burden, and under their leadership and inspiration the Temple was reconstructed on a smaller scale and with cheap materials, but on the ancient site (516 B.C.). Contributions to aid this enterprise had been received from the Jews of Babylonia.

The first six years of the reign of Darius I. were troublous times. It became necessary for him to reconquer his empire, as many of the subject nations took the opportunity to rebel. Zerubbabel probably took part in this rebellious movement. Zechariah regarded him as the Messiah and expected him to be crowned and to reign jointly with the high priest Joshua (Zec 3).

Since Zerubbabel disappeared abruptly from the historical scene, it is probable that the Persian overlords quickly put an end to the Jewish attempt at political independence. During the latter years of the reign of Darius I. and the entire reign of Xerxes (486–465 B.C.), little is known of the history of the Jews, either in the communities which were scattered throughout the Persian empire or in the still struggling congregation which had returned to the ruined city of Jerusalem. Some information may be gleaned from the anthology now contained in Is 56–66, large parts of which appear to come from this period, as well as from some poems of Joel and Malachi, which may also have emerged in the early part of the 5th cent. B.C. (although several scholars now favour an earlier date). It seems that the Jerusalem Jews were in a semi-anarchic state, with a decadent élite and depressed labourers. Zerubbabel was probably succeeded by a foreign governor (Mal 1[8]) who must have had little sympathy for the Jewish way of life. Moreover, pressure from the eastern and southern borders of Judah threatened the security of the tiny enclave. The Nabataeans had pushed the Edomites out of their old territory, S. of the Dead Sea, to Beersheba and Hebron, in southern Judah. The Samaritans, who had apparently spread to the valley of Aijalon, W. of Jerusalem, held many approaches to the city. The Jewish colony occupied but a small territory about Jerusalem, and some of the inhabitants in their distress, as their ancestors had done in the days of Manasseh, were seeking relief in the revival of Canaanite-Phoenician rites (Is 65[11]). Early in the reign of Artaxerxes I. (465–424 B.C.), an attempt was made to rebuild the walls of the city (Ezr 4[7–24]), and the Samaritans intervened at the Persian court. The reconstruction was abruptly interrupted, no doubt by imperial order.

Such a state of affairs profoundly moved Nehemiah, a young Jewish official at the court of Artaxerxes I. Having heard in 445 B.C. bad news from Jerusalem (Neh 1[4]), he at once secured an appointment to the governorship of Judah and the permission to rebuild the walls of its capital (see H. H. Rowley, 'Nehemiah's Mission and Its Backgound,' *Bulletin of the John Rylands Library*, xxxvii [1954–1955], 528–561). The energy with which Nehemiah devoted himself to this task, the opposition which he encountered from the surrounding settlers or invaders, especially from the Samaritans (see H. H. Rowley, 'Sanballat and the Samaritan Temple,' *Bulletin of the John Rylands Library*, xxxviii [1955–1956], 166–198), and the success which attended his labours, are forcibly depicted in his memoirs, now partly incorporated by the Chronicler in the book of Nehemiah (chs. 1–7). After a return to Persia, Nehemiah filled a second term as governor of Jerusalem (*c* 428 B.C.). Through the zeal and thoroughness of his administration, the Jewish community was reorganized as distinct from the Samaritans (Neh 13[28ff]) and mixed marriages were forbidden.

It is possible although not probable that Nehemiah was in Jerusalem at the same time as the scribe Ezra. According to that part of the work of the Chronicler which came to be known as the books of Ezra and Nehemiah, Ezra arrived in Jerusalem before Nehemiah in the seventh year of Artaxerxes I., namely in 458 B.C. (Ezra 7–8), but many scholars agree that his visit followed rather than preceded those of Nehemiah. Accordingly, the Persian king mentioned in Ezra 7[7–8] is probably Artaxerxes II. (404–358 B.C.) and Ezra came to Jerusalem in 398 B.C. (see H. H. Rowley, 'The Chronological Order of Ezra and Nehemiah,' in *The Servant of the Lord* [1952], pp. 129–159). Facing a situation of political corruption and of religious assimilation to the surrounding cultures, Ezra pursued with vigour the reforming spirit inaugurated by Nehemiah. He not only applied the ban on mixed marriages but he also succeeded in imposing divorces for the sake of maintaining the purity of the faith (Ezr 10[2–5]). Ezra's activity was more religious than political but it has its place in a general history of Israel for he became in effect the founder of legal Judaism (see H. Cazelles, 'La mission d'Esdras,' *VT*, iv [1954], 113–140). His ceremonial reading of the Pentateuch as the Law of Moses (Neh 8) and his part in the renewal of the covenant (Neh 9–10) exercised a major influence upon the development of Judaism in the subsequent centuries.

Information concerning the Jewish community during the last days of the Persian empire is almost entirely lacking. The Jewish historian Flavius Josephus tells (*Ant.* XI. vii. 1 [297]) that the Persian general Bagoas (whom he calls Bagoses) entered the Temple and oppressed the Jews for seven years, because the high priest John murdered his brother Joshua, a friend of Bagoas, for whom the latter had promised to obtain the high priesthood. Perhaps there was more underlying this than appears on the surface. Many have supposed, at least, that the action of Bagoas was the result of an attempt on the part of the Jews to regain their independence.

After the reign of Artaxerxes III. (358–338 B.C.) and that of Arses (338–336 B.C.), the Persian empire soon came to an end. Darius III. (336–331 B.C.) witnessed the meteoric rise of Alexander of Macedonia (336–323 B.C.).

24. The Hellenistic Rule (333–168 B.C.).—According to Flavius Josephus (*Ant.* XI. viii. 3 [318]), the high priest Jaddua was loyal to Darius III. During the siege of Tyre, Alexander in vain requested Jewish help. After the surrender of Gaza, he marched personally to Jerusalem to take vengeance. At his approach, the high priest, the priests, and the Levites, clad in ceremonial dress, walked in solemn procession toward Mount Scopus in order to welcome the world conqueror.

Alexander was so impressed that he forgot his wrath and refused to desecrate the Temple. This story is probably a legend. Arrian, for example, declares that the rest of Palestine had submitted before the siege of Gaza. Jerusalem was to Alexander simply one Syrian town among the others. It stood out of his route and probably was never visited by him. The chief element of truth reflected by this tradition, however, is that the high priest was then the head of the Jerusalem community. Another significance of the legend may lie in the fact that the Jews were soon to assimilate Hellenistic culture.

During the wars which followed the death of Alexander (323 B.C.), Judah endured her share of international disorder. The armies of Antigonus and Demetrius were at various times in the region. In 312 B.C., a great battle was fought near Gaza, and the political unrest which followed must have produced economic hardship for the Jews. For more than a century, Palestine remained under the rule of the Hellenico-Egyptian Ptolemies. The Seleucids, however, never gave up their claim upon it. Antiochus III, the Great (223–187 B.C.) briefly snatched the territory from Ptolemy IV. Philopator (221–203 B.C.) but failed to impose his presence for long. Twenty years later, however, after the battle of Paneion, the Jews passed under the Seleucid jurisdiction.

The chief connexion with the suzerain power during the Ptolemaic and the early years of the Seleucid rules was the payment of taxes. At one time, a Ptolemaic king became dissatisfied with the high priest's management of the finances, and he committed them to the care of one Joseph, son of Tobias, who with his sons led a life of spectacular adventures (*Ant.* XII. iv. 2 ff [160 ff]).

From the beginning of its existence, the metropolis of Alexandria seems to have included a prosperous Jewish community. Greek language became a convenient and even fashionable mode of exchange. Many Jews adopted not only the Greek tongue but also Greek ways which slowly were introduced in Jerusalem itself. Under the Seleucids, certain high priests even adopted Greek names. To court the favours of the kings at Antioch, they cultivated Greek habits. A Syrian garrison was stationed in Jerusalem. Gymnasia were popular. Some went so far as to attempt to remove artificially the signs of circumcision.

One curious aspect of this era of Hellenistic assimilation appears in the fact that one high priest, Onias III., deposed by the Seleucid authorites, went to Egypt and established at Leontopolis in the name of Heliopolis a dissident temple to Yahweh, which existed there for a hundred years.

The country towns of Palestine were more conservative than the capital, but even there Hellenistic culture would have found its way had not Antiochus IV. Epiphanes (175–163 B.C.) determined to impose by force upon all Jews not only Greek fashions and mores but also Greek religion.

25. The Maccabaean Revolt (168–135 B.C.).—Antiochus commanded in 168 B.C. that altars to Zeus be erected throughout the land, and especially in the Temple at Jerusalem. He also directed that swine flesh be offered in sacrifice upon them. The fear of the Syrian army secured wide-spread obedience to this decree. In the little town of Modin, however, an old priest, Mattathias, struck down the officiating traitor and raised the standard of revolt. The faithful soon rallied to his standard, and he made his son Judas captain over them. Unexpected victories speedily followed, and the successful Judas was surnamed *Makkab*, 'the hammer.' He has remained known as Judas Maccabaeus.

Mattathias died before the end of the first year of the revolt, but the struggle was continued by his sons. In the course of three years, the Syrian forces had been driven from the Temple, though they still held the fortress which overlooked it. Accordingly, in December, 165 B.C., a great feast was held for the purification and the rededication of the sanctuary—the Hanukkah. Up to this time, Judas had been aided by the Hasidim, or the pious, a set of religious devotees whose ideal was ceremonial puritanism. This party would have been satisfied to rest in what had already been achieved, but Judas and his brothers aimed at political independence. Although it estranged the Hasidim, Judas, with varying fortunes, maintained the struggle till 161 B.C. Antiochus IV. had died (163 B.C.), the forces of the young Antiochus V. (163–162 B.C.) were defeated, a great victory was won over Nicanor, whom Demetrius I. (162–150 B.C.) sent to Judah. This victory was long celebrated in a yearly festival, the day of Nicanor. Judas himself fell before the end of the year 161 B.C. in a battle with the forces which Demetrius had sent to avenge the death of Nicanor.

The leadership of the Jewish nation then passed on to Jonathan, one of the brothers of Judas, who for nearly twenty years maintained the struggle in heroic and desperate conditions (161–143 B.C.). At first Jonathan thought of taking refuge with the Nabataeans, but he was treacherously treated and his brother John was slain. After many unsuccessful attempts to capture him, the Syrians finally entered into a treaty with him whereby he was permitted to live at Michmash as a kind of licensed free-booter (153 B.C.). Not unlike David in his outlaw years, Jonathan ruled over such as came to him.

A little later Alexander Balas appeared in the field as a contestant for the Syrian crown. This proved a great help to the Maccabaean cause, as both parties were willing to bid high for the support of Jonathan. Demetrius was killed and Alexander secured the reins of government. Demetrius II., courting Jewish favour, recognized Jonathan as high priest and exempted the Jews from various taxes. The supporters of Alexander lured Jonathan to Ptolemais for a conference and treacherously put him to death (143 B.C.).

Another Maccabaean brother, Simon, assumed the leadership (143–135 B.C.). The star of Alexander Balas had set and Demetrius II. made with the Jews a treaty which once again recognized their independence. The event created the wildest joy. Never since the days of Josiah in the 7th cent. B.C. had the inhabitants of Jerusalem been politically free. It seemed like a new birth of the nation, and it stimulated the national genius in all directions. The whole civil and religious polity was reorganized. Simon was made both political head of the state and high priest, and it was ordained that these offices should continue in his house for ever, or until a faithful prophet should arise (1 Mac 14^{41ff}). Simon spent his energies in organizing his government and in consolidating his territory. He was successful in taking possession of Gezer, where he built a large castle, also Joppa, which he made his port, and on the other side of the mountain range, Jericho. At the latter place he was assassinated in 135 B.C. by his son-in-law, Ptolemy, who hoped to seize the government. Simon's son, John Hyrcanus, escaped, and maintained the Maccabaean family at the head of the nation. The dynasty became known as 'Hasmonaean' from the name of Mattathias' grandfather, Hashmoni.

26. The Hasmonaean Dynasty (135–63 B.C.).—During the early years of John Hyrcanus I. (135–105 B.C.), the vigorous Antiochus VII. Sidetes, who had gained the Syrian crown, pressed him so hard that the struggle for independence not only had to be renewed, but seemed for a time to end in failure. Weaker hands, however, soon came into possession of the Syrian sceptre, and Hyrcanus, his independence secure, set about consolidating the power of Judaea. He conquered the Edomites, who had centuries before been pushed up into southern Judah, and compelled them to accept Judaism. Later he conquered Samaria and lower Galilee, treating the latter country as he had treated Idumaea (*Ant.* XIII. x. 2 f [275 ff]). During the reign of John Hyrcanus I. (135–105 B.C.), the Pharisees and Sadducees began to emerge into well-defined and opposing parties. The former were developed out of the Hasidim of the earlier time. They desired separation from foreigners in order that they might devote themselves to the keeping of the Law. The Sadducees consisted largely of the old priestly families, whose wealth and position prevented them from either the narrowness or the devotion of the Pharisees. Other sects also appeared at that time, among them the Essenes, with whom the sectarians of the Qumrân community, near the Dead Sea, have been tentatively identified.

Aristobulus I. (105–104 B.C.), upon his accession to power, assumed the title of king (*Ant.* XIII. xi. 1 [301]—a step which still further estranged the Pharisees. He conquered and Judaized in the one year of his reign the region of upper Galilee. His widow, Alexandra was released from prison and married her brother-in-law, Alexander Jannaeus (104–79 B.C.) who conquered and Judaized Transjordan. By conquest and forcible conversion, the opposition of the Pharisees became extremely bitter. It was probably during his reign that the mysterious 'Teacher of Righteousness' of the Qumrân community met with a violent end. At last, Alexander committed the government to Alexandra, advising her to make peace with the Pharisees (*Ant.* XIII. xv. 5 [401]. Alexandra ruled for ten years (79–69 B.C.) and made her son, John Hyrcanus II., the high priest, but left civil authority to Aristobulus II., the younger of her two sons. Civil war between the rivals dragged itself on for several years.

An extraordinary man from Idumaea, Antipater, attached himself to Hyrcanus and persuaded him to flee to Aretas, king of the Nabataeans, in order to secure arms. When Pompey appeared in 64–63 B.C., both brothers appealed to him. Aristobulus, however, shut himself up in Jerusalem. After a siege of three months, Pompey entered the city (63 B.C.), restored Hyrcanus as high priest but reduced considerably the territory of his jurisdiction. The dream of a Jewish state was ended.

27. The Roman Rule (63 B.C.–A.D. 66).—Hyrcanus II. came more and more under the influence of Antipater, the Idumaean. After the death of Pompey in 48 B.C., Hyrcanus and Antipater were able to render Julius Caesar material aid at Alexandria, thus winning his favour. Antipater, as a reward, received Roman citizenship and the procuratorship of Judaea. Many privileges of which Pompey had deprived the Jews were returned to them. The old powers of the Sanhedrin, or council, were revived. Religious customs of the Jews were guaranteed, not only in Judaea, but also in Alexandria and elsewhere, and their taxes were remitted in the Sabbatical years (*Ant.* XIV. x. 45 [201]).

Antipater proceeded to build up the fortunes of his family, making his son Phasaelus governor of Jerusalem, and Herod governor of Galilee. Herod proved an able administrator but narrowly escaped condemnation by the Sanhedrin for presuming to exercise the power of life and death without its consent.

After Antipater was murdered, Hyrcanus passed under the influence of Herod and Phasaelus. When Cassius and Brutus were defeated at Philippi (42 B.C.), Antony moved eastward to secure Syria. Although many Jews complained bitterly of the sons of Antipater, Antony made them tetrarchs with full political power, leaving to Hyrcanus only the high priesthood.

While Antony was in Egypt, Antigonus, a son of Aristobulus II., gained the aid of the Parthians, who sent a force which captured Jerusalem (40 B.C.), and made Antigonus both king and high priest. Herod journeyed to Rome where he besought Augustus and Antony to make Aristobulus, a grandson of Hyrcanus II., king of Judaea. The Roman government, however, made Herod king and sent him back to conquer his kingdom, which he did after Antony could spare some of his troops which were then engaged against the Parthians.

Herod became in fact king of the Jews in 37 B.C. But he had to contend with the whims of Antony and the caprices of Cleopatra. After the battle of Actium (31 B.C.), Herod convinced Augustus of his loyalty to the new ruler of the world and his throne became secure.

Herod had a passion for building, and he knew how to extract money for his purposes. He therefore founded or rebuilt many cities, adorning them with the beauty of Hellenistic architecture. His enlarging and embellishing the Temple of Jerusalem is perhaps the best known of these undertakings, but it is only one of many. The taxes necessary for his various enterprises fell heavily upon his subjects. His domestic life was tragic as he executed many of his relatives, for fear of their political aspirations. During his reign, Hellenistic culture made new inroads in Judaea. At the same time, sectarian opposition to foreign influence found great success among the masses, and Pharisaism influenced the schools of Hillel and Shammai.

When Herod died in 4 B.C., Augustus divided his dominions among his sons. Archelaus received Judaea and Samaria; Antipas, Galilee and Peraea; and Philip, Ituraea and Trachonitis. Herod Antipas held his territory until A.D. 39, and was the tetrarch of Galilee during the public life of Jesus. Archelaus proved such a bad ruler that Augustus removed him in A.D. 6 and banished him to Gaul (Josephus, *Jewish Wars*, II. vii. 3 [111]). Judaea was then placed under Roman procurators as a part of the province of Syria. The fifth of these procurators was Pontius Pilate.

Once more, the dominions of Herod the Great were united under one of his grandsons, Herod Agrippa I. (A.D. 41–44), who was a protégé of Caligula. After his death, the country returned to the administrative rule of Roman procurators.

Many Jews had never submitted to Rome, either through the Idumaean kings or the procurators. The Zealots expected that military Messianism would soon expel the invaders, and their nationalistic fervour gradually gained influence. In A.D. 66, the political passions took shape in open rebellion. The Roman general Vespasian was sent to quell the uprising. He had reduced Galilee and the outlying cities of Galilee when he heard of the death of Nero and withdrew to Egypt. During the year A.D. 69, Vespasian was fighting for the control of the empire, which he finally won. In the meantime, the Jews were consuming one another in civil war.

In A.D. 70, Titus appeared before Jerusalem, and after the most terrible siege in the history of the site, the city was destroyed, the Temple was ruined, and its sacred objects taken to Rome (*BJ* VII. v. 5 [148 ff]). The tenth Roman legion was left in charge. A small garrison of Jewish soldiers who had captured the fortress of Masada, on the shore of the Dead Sea, held out for three years, but was finally captured.

The surviving Sanhedrin moved to Jamnia, a town in the Philistine plain, S. of Joppa, where at the end of the 1st cent. A.D. its sessions became famous for the discussions concerning the authority of the Holy Writings, or Hagiographa.

Under the reign of Trajan, in A.D. 116, Jews in Cyprus and Asia Minor revolted in vain. In A.D. 132, a new Jewish leader, called Bar Cochba, 'Son of the Star,' led a new and heroic movement against Rome and some of his followers held out in the desert until A.D. 133. Hadrian determined to erase the name of Jerusalem from the map. A Roman colony, called Aelia Capitolina, was accordingly founded on the site of the ancient capital. Jews were banished from it, and a temple to Jupiter was erected on the site of the Temple of Yahweh.

II. RELIGION.—**1. The religion of the ancient Hebrews.**—In a sense, the religion of Israel is the history of the religion of Yahweh. The ancient Hebrews, however, preserved in their national traditions the memory of an event, at a definite time, when the God worshipped by their fathers revealed His name to Moses as Yahweh (Ex 3^{13ff}; but see Gn 4^{26}). Before Moses, the religion of Israel's ancestors may not have been substantially different from that of the proto-Phoenicians and Canaanites. The Ugaritic literature shows that *El* was the supreme god. Likewise, the Genesis traditions concerning Abram and his family mention *El Elyon*, or 'God Most High' (Gn 14^{18-20}), *El Shaddai*, or 'God

Almighty' (Gn 17[1]), *El Olam*, or 'God of Eternity' (Gn 21[33]), *El Roi* (Gn 16[13]). The stories of the conquest call the god of Shechem *El Berith*, or 'God of the Covenant' (Jg 9[4]; see H. G. May, 'The Patriarchal Idea of God,' *JBL* lx [1941], 113–128). Many features of the Canaanite religion have survived in the popular cult of Israel, and some of them are common to all the ancient Semites. There is little doubt that the Hebrews inherited them from their distant ancestors.

(1) Totemism. Traces of a belief associating ancestors with certain animals have been discerned by a number of historians in the names of Leah, 'wild cow,' Rachel, 'ewe,' Simeon, 'wolf' (?), Caleb, 'dog,' etc., but there is no evidence that the Hebrews during the patriarchal age worshipped animals.

(2) Fertility. A conception common to the peoples of the Ancient Near East was that the divine reality manifested itself especially in the process of reproduction. Thus, the organs of generation were the object of religious significance. Such a belief survived in Israel in the patriarchal practice, during the making of an oath, of putting one's hand under the thigh (Gn 24[2]).

(3) The *maṣṣēbhāh*. A cultic object appeared again and again in the worship of Israel and Judah until the reform of Josiah (621 B.C.). The *maṣṣēbhāh* was a pillar or phallic symbol which in pre-Mosaic times may have represented the deity (Gn 28[22], Hos 3[4], Dt 7[5], 2 K 23[14]).

(4) The *'ᵃshērāh*. There is no general agreement as to the nature and meaning of this object. It may have been a representation of a deity, corresponding to the Ugaritic Ashirat of the Sea. Such a symbol stood by the altar of Yahweh in the Jerusalem Temple at the time of the Reform of Josiah (2 K 23[6]).

(5) Circumcision is an institution which the Hebrews inherited from their Semitic ancestry, since it was not peculiar to Israel but a practice which was common among many peoples of the ancient Near East. Like many other religious customs, circumcision underwent different interpretations at different periods; but its origin is clearly connected with the sacredness of the reproductive organs.

(6) From the pre-Mosaic period came also the idea that spirits dwelt in certain objects of the natural world, such as trees, stones, and springs. Sacred trees existed in many parts of Palestine. There was Abraham's oak at Mamre near Hebron (Gn 13[18] 18[1]); at Shechem stood another (Jos 24[26]) and still another at Ophrah (Jg 6[11, 19]). The fountain at Kadesh was called En-mishpat (Gn 14[7]) or 'the spring of judgment,' probably because oracular decisions were obtained there. The well of Lahai-roi (Gn 16[14]) had a story to account for its sacredness, as had also the wells of Beersheba (Gn 21[29]). En-rogel (to-day known as 'Job's well') was a spring in the vicinity of Jerusalem near which Adonijah offered a sacrifice (1 K 1[9ff]). Solomon was anointed at Gihon (now called 'Virgin's fountain' on account of Is 7[14]). A sacred circle of stones called Gilgal existed on the W. of the Jordan (Jos 4[19ff]). Stones played a part in the lives of the patriarchs, especially Jacob (Gn 28[18]). The high places or *bāmôth* had stone altars dating from prehistoric times, including the foundation rock of the altar near the Jerusalem Temple.

(7) Sacrifice. In the historical period of Israel's religion, sacrifice was regarded mainly as a gift of food to the deity (cf Ps 50) and probably in earlier times this idea was already present. Sacrifice in the Semitic religions, however, was primarily a commensal feast, in which the god and the worshipper partook of the same food, and their kinship was consequently renewed. Whether this was the sole feature of sacrifice among the ancient Hebrews or not is an open question (see Ex 24[11]). Human sacrifice was widely practised by the Canaanites (*e.g.*, excavations at Gezer), and Israel resorted to the practice in times of crisis (Ahaz, Manasseh, *et al.*). It is not impossible that human sacrifice originated in the ritual of impersonating the dying deity in the seasonal cycle of nature celebration (Jephthah's daughter, Jg 11[40]). The story of Isaac's sacrifice (Gn 22) points to the Hebrew memory of a change from human to animal sacrifice.

(8) The *ḥērem*, or 'ban.' Even before a battle, all the population of the enemy country and their property could be devoted to destruction as a solemn obligation to the deity (Nu 21[2], Jos 6[17], 1 S 15[3ff]). It seems to have been the custom of the Moabites, for Mesha says, 'I killed all the people of the city—a pleasing spectacle to Chemosh' (Moabite Stone, 11 ff).

(9) Blood revenge. It was a religious duty, when one was injured, to inflict a like injury, and if the blood of one's kinsman was shed, to shed the blood of those who had committed the deed (Code of Hammurabi, 18th cent. B.C., 127, 195–197, etc.). Many references to this practice are found in the OT (Gn 4[14ff, 23ff] etc.).

(10) The Passover (*pesaḥ*), or spring festival. One of the survivals of the early Semitic worship appears in the tradition that the celebration of a spring feast was anterior to the time of Moses (Ex 5[1] etc.). It was probably related to the fertility god (The Song of Songs is still chanted in Judaism at the passover celebration). The festival underwent a radical transformation under the historical event of the Exodus (Ex 12), but its vernal origin has not been forgotten by a later age (Ps 114).

(11) It is probable that an autumn festival, combined with a new year festival, was borrowed by the Hebrews from ancient Semitic paganism and was later transformed in the ritual of the Day of the Atonement and in the feast of Tabernacles.

(12) While the ancient Hebrews were not exactly polytheistic like their Canaanite neighbours and mentors, there is evidence that their henotheism was strongly corrupted by the worship of ancestral or tribal deities. The god of the tribe of Gad has survived with a specialized function (Is 65[11]). The Shield of Abraham (Gn 15[1]), the Fear or Kinsman of Isaac (Gn 31[42, 53]), and the Mighty One of Jacob (Gn 49[24]) were in all probability clan gods, perhaps not unrelated to the *tᵉrāphîm* or household gods of the Laban family (Gn 31[19]; see A. Alt, *Der Gott der Väter*, 1929). The nature of the documents concerning the religion of the patriarchs does not allow a high degree of certainty concerning the historicity of the promise made to Abram (Gn 12[1ff] etc.). Nevertheless, there seems to be a core of memories which point to the consciousness of an election for a special purpose in the history of mankind.

2. The Mosaic Covenant.—The originality of Israel's religion lies primarily in the event of its origin, the deliverance from Egypt after many years of bondage, under the leadership of Moses who acted in the name of Yahweh.

(1) It is probable that Yahweh was the god of the Kenites before He became the God of Israel. The reasons for this conjecture are as follows: (*a*) Of the three documents which narrate the Exodus, E and P tell of the introduction of the name Yahweh as a new name. In early religion a new name usually means a new deity. E, on which P is dependent in this part of the narrative, was preserved in northern Israel and based on traditions of the Joseph tribes. (*b*) The account of the institution of the covenant (Ex 18[12ff]) makes it clear that Jethro, the Kenite priest, offers the sacrifice. He really initiates the Hebrews in the worship of Yahweh. This is confirmed by the underlying thought of all the documents that Moses first learned of Yahweh among the Midianites (of whom the Kenites formed a clan). (*c*) Centuries later than Exodus, Sinai was regarded as the place where Yahweh manifested His presence. From there He marched north to help His people in time of crisis (Jg 5[4ff], Dt 33[2]; see Hab 3[1], Ps 68[4]). Elijah made a pilgrimage to Horeb in order to seek Yahweh (1 K 19). (*d*) The Kenites during several succeeding centuries were the champions of the pure worship of Yahweh. Jael killed Sisera (Jg 5[24ff]). The Rechabites, who from Jehu to Jeremiah (2 K 10[15], Jer 35) championed Yahweh, were Kenites (1 Ch 2[55]). (*e*) Some of the Kenites joined Israel in her migration (Nu 10[29ff]), mingling with Israel both in the north (Jg 5[24]) and in the south (Jg 1[16]):

some of them remained on the southern border of Judah, where they maintained a separate existence till the time of Saul (1 S 15[6]) and were finally, in the days of David, incorporated into the tribe of Judah (1 S 30[26ff, 29ff]). (*f*) It is this absorption of the Kenites by Judah which, if Yahweh were a Kenite deity, explains why the J document, written in Judah, regards the knowledge of Yahweh as immemorial (Gn 4[26]). The perpetual separateness of Judah from the other tribes tended to perpetuate this in spite of contrary currents from other quarters. It is therefore reasonable to maintain that Yahweh was originally the god of the Kenites, that some of the Hebrew tribes entangled in Egypt were ready to abandon their old gods for one that would deliver them, and that He became their god at the passage of the Sea of Reed (Ex 15).

(2) It is possible to define in broad outline the conception which the Hebrews had of their God at the time of Moses. Quite clearly, they conceived Him to be a God of war. The needs of the oppressed tribes demanded a warrior deity. The people are said to have sung after Miriam, Moses' sister, 'Yahweh is a man of war' (Ex 15[3]). A book of old epic poems was called 'the Book of the Wars of Yahweh' (Nu 21[14]), and the expression 'Yahweh of Hosts' (Lord Sabaoth) was afterwards one of His most constant names. There can be little doubt that this conception of Yahweh as a war-god had developed among the Kenites, and that it had a large influence in drawing the Hebrews into His worship.

There is reason also to believe that, as Yahweh had long been worshipped around Mount Sinai, where severe thunderstorms occur, He had come to be regarded as a God who manifested Himself especially in the phenomena of storms. He is usually represented in cultic poetry as coming in a thunderstorm (Ps 18, Ezk 1, Hab 3, Is 19[1], Job 38[1]) and the regular name for thunder was 'the voice of Yahweh' (Ps 29[3ff], Job 37[4]). He is also said to have led His people under the appearance of a cloud (Ex 13, 14), and to have manifested His presence on Mount Sinai and later in the Temple of Jerusalem in a thick cloud or thick darkness (Ex 19, 1 K 8[10f]); the cloud is furthermore used about forty times in the Pentateuch as a symbol of Yahweh's presence. Probably, then, the Israelites received Him from the Kenites as a god of war who manifested Himself in the storm-cloud and uttered His voice in thunder. At the same time, the importance of the thunder and lightning motif in the Ugaritic mythology should not prevent us from considering the proto-Phoenician or Canaanite influence upon this aspect of Hebrew theology.

These conceptions, however, did not exhaust the Hebrew thought of God. The Israelites were Semites, and they conceived Yahweh chiefly as a god of life. Had this not been so, circumcision would not have been his sign, the pillar and asherah would not have been symbolic instruments of His worship, the first born would not have been offered to Him in sacrifice, and the organs of generation would not have been the object of numinous attention.

(3) The name Yahweh, explained in Ex 3[14] as 'I cause to be whatever I cause to be' (the reading 'I am that I am' represents a late rabbinical interpretation, probably influenced by ontological speculations of Hellenistic philosophy), confirms the vitalizing and energizing quality of the God mediated to the people by Moses. Yahweh is the creator God, already in Mosaic theology, and the creator God is also the ruler of history. He can make a world and He can create a nation out of an amorphous gathering of uncouth slaves. Other theories explain the name Yahweh differently. Some think of the Arabic root *hawā*, 'to love passionately,' used in some forms especially of sexual desire. If this meaning were understood by the Hebrews at the time of Moses, it was lost as soon as the Israelites began to react against the magical aspect of Canaanite fertility cult.

(4) It is probable that the covenant between Yahweh and Israel involved at the time no more than that they would become His worshippers in return for deliverance, victory and continuing protection. In becoming His worshippers, however, it was necessary for them to gain knowledge of His ritual. Our oldest document seems to have been the lapidary form of the E decalogue (Ex 20, Dt 5), *i.e.*, the ten words without the elaboration which now accompanies a number of them. It is most remarkable that this primitive code is less concerned with ritual than with inward dedication and behaviour. The so-called J decalogue (Ex 34) represents not a nomadic and pastoral environment but a sedentary and agrarian situation. It reflects either the later period of the conquest, when Israel came in contact with its farming teachers, the Canaanites, or the patriarchal period, when the Hebrew fathers lived in a Palestinian milieu.

(5) The symbol of Yahweh's cultic presence in the time of Moses was the Ark. As the Egyptians, the Mesopotamians, and the pre-islamic Arabs possessed similar structures for carrying their gods, it is probable that the Ark was a kind of movable sanctuary for a nomadic people. A later tradition (1 K 8[9, 21]) says that it contained the ten words written on stone. At any rate, when the Ark was carried into the camp of the Philistines it was thought that Yahweh himself had come into the camp (1 S 8[4]).

In the J document the Ark plays a small part while it is prominent in the E document. J apparently thought much more of Sinai as the place of Divine self-disclosure. This peculiarity of the southern tradition may have come about from the fact that after the settlement in the land of Canaan the Ark was in the possession of the Joseph tribes and became their shrine.

(7) According to the oldest sources, there seems to have been no priesthood at the time of Moses, except that of Moses himself. J tells that when the covenant was ratified, Moses, Aaron, Nadab, Abihu, and seventy elders of Israel went up toward Yahweh's mountain, but only Moses was permitted to come before Him (Ex 24[1f, 9-11]), while E tells of a 'tent of meeting' which Moses used to pitch at a distance from the camp, and to which he would go to consult Yahweh (Ex 33[7-11]), and then return. In this tent, Joshua, Moses' minister, abode all the time (Ex 33[11]). It is clear that neither of these cultic story tellers had any conception of the choice of the tribe of Levi for the priesthood. Indeed, E makes no mention of the tribe of Levi anywhere. Moses was in this view apparently one of the Joseph tribes, and we do not know how the term 'Levite' for priest originated. One document tells of a Levite who belonged to the tribe of Judah (Jg 17[7]), so that here 'Levite' cannot have a tribal signification. J also tells of a tribe of Levi to which a calamity happened (Gn 34; see 49[5-7]). Another revealing incident is that of the men who in a crisis 'attached themselves' to Moses for the preservation of the religion of Yahweh, and were perhaps, accordingly, called *l^ewîyîm* [*lāwāh*='join'], 'Levites' (Ex 32[26-28]). Many scholars think that the later priesthood was developed out of this band, and that its identification with the unfortunate clan of Levi is due to a later confusion of names.

(8) The covenant form, as it appears for instance in the asseveration which opens the E Decalogue (Ex 20[2]), may have been borrowed from legal treatises, like those of the Hittites, in the 2nd millennium B.C. (G. E. Mendenhall, *Law and Covenant in Israel and in the Ancient Near East*, 1955). In these and other parallels, a king addresses his vassals and reminds them of his acts, makes stipulations which binds their allegiance to him and which they solemnly promise to accept (Ex 19). The Hebrew amphictyony appears to have found its origin in the religious contract which was accepted by the people at the foot of Mount Sinai (see Jos 24, Jg 5). Such a covenant was not a legal document enacted between equals, but on the contrary a kind of sacramental marriage between a sovereign and the people. The birth of the nation appears therefore primarily as a religious event, with a religious structure and a religious hope.

The promise is made dependent upon the fulfilment of obedience to the Divine words. Israel is not just a nation but a holy people (*'am ḳādhôsh*) with a priestly mission. In the covenant mediated by Moses lies the seed of the whole theology of the OT (literally, 'old covenant'). The prophets' critique and eschatology, in a later age, are based upon the centrality of the covenant theme in the consciousness of Israel (Am 3^{1ff}, Hos 2, Is 1, Jer 31^{31} etc.). The covenant is the source of Hebrew solidarity, Hebrew law, and Hebrew standards of morality.

(9) Yahweh alone is God. He alone created the world (Gn 2^{4bff}), and He alone must be worshipped (Ex 20^{5}).

3. The religion of Israel before the great prophets.—(1) The conquest of Canaan strengthened the faith of the Israelite tribes in Yahweh as the lord of history as well as the sovereign of nature. A Semitic people upon entering a new land always felt it necessary to propitiate the god of the land. As this was the case as late as the 8th cent. (2 K 17^{24-34}), it would be all the more true at the end of the 13th. At first, therefore, the Israelites mingled the worship of Yahweh with the worship of the *baalim* or owners and lords of the soil. When under David Israel emerged victorious, Yahweh was more than ever the lord of history as well as the lord of the land. Little by little the cult of Yahweh which took place in the ancient Canaanite shrines was corrupted by Canaanite ritual and beliefs. By the time of Gideon the term 'baal' was applied to Yahweh, as Jerub-baal, Gideon's real name, seems to indicate. Ish-baal and Meri-baal, sons of Saul, and Beeliada, a son of David, bear names which suggest the same syncretistic trend.

(2) During this period it was not thought wrong to make images of Yahweh. Gideon made an ephod-idol at Ophrah (Jg 8^{27}), Micah made an image to Yahweh (Jg 17^{3ff}). Sometimes images were in the form of bulls, as were those which Jeroboam I. set up at Bethel and Dan after the schism of Israel from Judah. These symbolized Yahweh as the giver of life and the god of pastoral wealth.

(3) In the whole of this period, it was thought that Yahweh might appear and talk with a human being, undistinguishable from a human form until the moment of His departure (Gn 18^{2ff}, Jg 6^{11ff} 13^{3ff}). Sometimes, it was the angel of Yahweh that appeared but the difference between Yahweh and the messenger of Yahweh was not always clear.

(4) The people were deeply religious, but the religion existed as a help to secular life. It consisted largely of inherited customs, while the main interest of all was centred in physical prosperity. Certain practices were considered to be wrong, as offences against Yahweh (*e.g.* the crime of Jg 19 and David's murder and adultery (in 2 S 11), but the ethical content of the religion was of a very rudimentary character. Stealing (Jg 18) and treachery could be at times glorified (Jg 3^{15ff} $5^{24, 27}$). The religion of Moses was maintained only through a minority, while the masses appear to have compromised in large measure with the rites, beliefs, and *mores* of the Canaanites.

(5) In every village was an open-air 'high place' marked by a rock altar, pillars, and other cultic objects, and connected with caves and underground structures. In some of these, as at Gezer and in Jerusalem, serpent worship was practised. Soon, some of the sacred places like Shiloh had their sanctuary (1 S 1–3) built with solid blocks of stone and containing rooms with doors. Solomon erected in Jerusalem an elaborate structure in the style of a Phoenician temple, departing in many ways from the cultic habits of the ancient Hebrews. Jeroboam I. likewise built temples at Bethel and at Dan (1 K 12^{31}, Am 7^{13}). A wealthy citizen might possess a private chapel in connexion with his residence (Jg 17).

(6) The priesthood in this period was not confined to any tribe. There seems to have been the thought that it was better to have a Levite for priest (whatever the term may have meant; cf Jg 17^{10}), but Micah, an Ephraimite, made his son a priest (Jg 17^{5}); Samuel, a member of one of the Joseph tribes, acted as priest (1 S 9^{12ff}); and David made his sons priests (2 S 8^{18}). Jonathan, a grandson of Moses according to tradition, started life as an impecunious resident of Bethlehem in Judah; in seeking his fortune he became a priest in the shrine of Micah, the Ephraimite; then at the instigation of the Danites he robbed that shrine and fled with them to the north, becoming the founder of a line of priests in the temple of Dan. Even if his descent from Moses is not to be credited, the story gives evidence of the kind of irregularity in the priesthood at the time of the Judges. So far as Jerusalem was concerned, David improved this chaotic condition by regulating the priestly corps.

(7) The festivals of that period were of a simple and joyous character (1 S 1, 2). The priests killed the sacrificial animal, pouring out the blood no doubt to Yahweh, and then the flesh was cooked. While it was cooking, the priest obtained his portion by a kind of chance (1 S 2^{13ff}), after which the victim was consumed by the worshippers in a festive banquet. It is probable that considerable licence accompanied such social and religious gatherings. The feast described here occurred annually, but there were lesser celebrations at the time of the new moons and other occasions (1 S 20^{5ff}).

(8) A glimpse into the household worship of the time is obtained from the *teraphim* (Jg 18^{26}, Hos 3^{4}). These objects seem to represent household deities, similar to those found in Babylon (Ezk 21^{21}) and among the Aramaeans (Gn 31^{19}). Some of them were apparently large enough to be mistaken for a man (1 S 19^{13ff}). They may have played a part in family divination (Zec 10^{2}), but it is not possible to state whether they had taken the place of Yahweh worship at a public shrine.

(9) During the centuries of the settlement, a class of religious professionals appeared called seers or prophets. They were related to the diviners and fortune tellers of the ancient Near East. In the time of Saul, there were ecstatic prophets who lived in groups and used music and dancing in their techniques for collective inspiration. Their frenzy possessed an epidemic quality (1 S 10^{9-13} 19^{23f}). In all probability these prophets were of Canaanite origin. The Egyptian Wen-Amon while reporting in about 1100 B.C. about his experiences in Byblos, on the coast of Phoenicia, tells of a youth who was thrown into a trance and uttered prophecies which moved the king of Byblos to conclude a business transaction. It appears that this Phoenician ecstatic was not part of a group but acted as an individual. In Israel, likewise, Samuel appears in one tradition at least to have been a solitary seer, different from the prophets of the guilds which he later supervised (1 S 9, 19^{20f}). Such men were held in high regard and obtained their living by telling people what they wished to know. Their oracles were mostly about the future, but often no doubt they told a man whether this or that action was in accord with the will of Yahweh. The Phoenician Baal as well as Yahweh had prophets (1 K 18^{19}). Such men became necessary adjuncts of the government. In the 9th cent., Ahab kept 400 of them about him (1 K 22^{6}). David and Solomon had probably done the same in their own time. Both in Israel and in Judah, powerful individual prophets, not unlike Samuel, intervened in the affairs of state. Some were public officials. Gad advised David and organized sacred music as well as wrote a history of the reign (1 S 22^{5}, 2 S 24^{11-14}, 1 Ch 29^{29}) Nathan rebuked David and served him and Solomon as well (2 S 7^{2ff} 12^{1-15}, 1 K 1^{22ff}, 1 Ch 29^{29}, 2 Ch 9^{29}). Other prophets appear to have been 'laymen' or private individuals who suddenly appeared from time to time in order to make a special pronouncement of public interest. Ahijah (1 K 11^{29ff}) and Micaiah, the son of Imlah (1 K 22^{8ff}), seemed to belong to this type. Elijah was probably the most influential of them, a true forerunner of the Great Prophets of the eighth and later centuries. His significance lies in the fact that in his opposition to

Phoenician syncretism, he revived the Yahwism of the Mosaic times, and upheld sharply the ethical standards of the nomadic covenant (1 K 17–19). At the same time, he understood that it was not possible to return to the old ways of the wilderness, and that the work of Yahweh could be best accomplished in history less through thaumaturgical manifestations than in the quiet and direct transformation of individuals. His theology allowed him to consider a foreigner like the king of Damascus as the instrument of Yahweh's will. He also appears to have initiated the idea of a religious society, within the political nation, which later influenced the growth of the idea of a remnant and of a spiritual congregation (1 K 19).

Elisha hardly deserves to be reckoned in this great succession. Although the heir of Elijah, he was the head of professional prophets. When absent from the band of his associates, he found it necessary to call a minstrel to work up his ecstasy before he could prophesy (2 K 3^{15}). It was he, however, who prompted Jehu to undertake the purification of Israel from the taint of Phoenician worship, and this religious reformation was of extreme significance for the survival of Yahwism, although it was accomplished at the price of ruthless massacres.

4. The religion of Israel during the great prophets.— With the exception of Nahum and Obadiah, whose preserved utterances present a rather violent kind of religious nationalism, the great prophets, from Amos to Second Isaiah formed a remarkable succession of men, whose impact upon the religion of later centuries cannot be overestimated. They were different from the ' sons of the prophets ' or prophetic guilds, for they were individuals with a compulsive sense of mission who spoke often against their own will in a way which endangered their own security. Their oracles, sermons, threats, and promises offer an interpretation of history which is unique in the ancient world. They did not represent the interests of a class or dynasty, or a nation. They hailed the sovereignty of the creator of the universe, even at the price of national extermination.

(1) Amos, the first of the great prophets, like Elijah, preached the universalism of Yahweh's jurisdiction. He traced the existence of all mankind to Yahweh's activity. Such a faith was certainly present in the Yahwist publisher of the patriarchal and covenantal traditions, but Amos applies it to concrete cases. Yahweh not only brought the Israelites out of Egypt, but also the Philistines from Caphtor and the Aramaeans from Kir (Am 9^{7}). More extraordinary still, even the distant Ethiopians are the object of His concern. Ethics, not ritual, was the basis of the covenant in the wilderness (Am 5$^{21-25}$). Covenant solidarity or righteousness must roll down as perennial waters, and religion must embrace the totality of life. Amos championed the cause of the poor, and rebuked the social impurities connected with the cult. Ritual cannot save Israel from her appointed doom.

(2) Hosea was a disciple of Amos and the burden of his message is likewise one of threat based on the highest sense of Divine justice. At the same time, Hosea developed the theology of Divine love, not the sexuality of the ancient Semitic religionists, by which man achieves communion with the Divine forces, thereby enlisting them for the fertility of nature and of mankind, but the self-sacrificing compassion of an anxious father or devoted husband, who would suffer in order to reclaim the fallen. Not less stern than Amos in his ethical standards, Hosea is less occupied with denouncing social oppression. He sees in the coming catastrophe not the extermination of Israel but a judgment of chastening and of purification ' in the wilderness.' While Amos concentrated on ethical corruption, Hosea understood that the root of social irresponsibility was to be found in idolatry.

(3) Isaiah continued in Judah the work initiated by Amos and Hosea in Northern Israel. He proclaimed the Holy God, whose holiness fills the earth. For forty years, in many crises and under varying figures, Isaiah set forth his interpretation of Yahweh's will for His people. Man is in the hand of God as clay in the hand of a potter. The powerful Assyrian is but the rod by which the ruler of history is chastising Israel : when God's will is accomplished, the rod shall be broken and discarded (Is 10^{5ff}). Isaiah was credited by his disciples as the initiator of Davidic messianism, looking forward to a new economy of history when a shoot of the house of Jesse would establish a kingdom described in terms of a reconciled humanity, living in a new paradise (Is 9, 11). Even if these poems were not to be credited to him, it seems clear that he believed in the raising of a remnant which would be converted by faith in Yahweh. His attitude toward the perenniality of Zion is not altogether clear, for he may have altered his views in the course of his long life. The sudden deliverance from the siege in 701 B.C. may have caused him to believe that Jerusalem would never be destroyed.

(4) Micah of Moresheth, Isaiah's contemporary, maintained the stern theology of doom proclaimed by Amos. He was profoundly concerned by the oppression of the poor and he announced irrevocably the destruction of the Temple in Zion (Mic 3^{12}). One of his disciples summarized the teaching of the three great prophets of the 8th cent. in a formula on the demands of Yahweh which has become symbolic of the whole theology of prophetism, ' nothing but to do [covenantal] righteousness, to love mercy and to walk humbly [in communion] with [one's] God ' (Mic 6^{8}).

(5) The Deuteronomists attempted to incorporate the high level of the 8th-cent. prophets in a body of laws for civil, criminal, and religious reformation. They saw that ritual should be retained. But the high places were to be eliminated and the cult was to be purified and centralized in Jerusalem, the chosen place of Yahweh's real presence. The ancient Covenant Code (Ex 20^{21ff}) which had been adapted through the centuries to changing conditions was completely revised, with new emphasis laid both on humanitarian morality and cultic fidelity. The preachers of Josiah's reform reflected on the theology of the covenant, insisted on the gracious character of the election, and preached inward and total devotion to the giver of life (Dt 6, 7).

(6) Jeremiah, the true heir of Hosea and Micah, discerned the dangers of a new formalism in the Deuteronomic reformation. He saw clearly that Yahweh was independent of a temple, even that of Jerusalem (Jer 7, 26). He understood that the covenant had been annulled and looked forward to a new covenant, when the law will be written no longer in a book but at the very core of man's intellect and will (Jer 31^{31ff}). By composing his intimate confessions, he gave impulse to religious introspection and profoundly influenced the literature of spirituality, from the psalms of lament and Job to the meditations of later Jewish and Christian saints. More specifically, he enabled the Judaeans exiled in Babylon to maintain their faith and their corporate identity (Jer 29), and must therefore be credited with having engendered Diaspora Judaism and indirectly the Christian Church.

(7) Habakkuk meditated on the problem of evil in history and developed the Isaianic concept of faith as a principle for living (Hab 2^{4}). His concept of joy at all cost, without any hope of material reward (3$^{17-18}$), announced the ' pure religion ' of Job and the Psalmists (especially Ps 73).

(8) Ezekiel occupies a peculiar position in the prophetic development. He stood, on one side, as a true disciple of Jeremiah, and on the other, being the son of a Jerusalem priestly family, prepared the restoration of ritual and legal Judaism. As a pastor in time of despair, he broke down the concept of collective guilt and proclaimed the dogma of individual responsibility (Ezk 18). He thought of the Messiah as primarily a shepherd, one whose chief function would be to save individuals. As a successor of the Deuteronomists, he endeavoured to adapt prophetic concepts to priestly institutions. He

accepted Isaiah's theme of Zion as the seat of Yahweh's real presence, and was instrumental in preparing a blueprint for the construction of a new Temple with an elaborate system of worship sharply distinguishing between the sacred and the profane and between clergy and laity (Ezk 40–48). His disciples composed the Code of Holiness (Lv 17–26) which revised ancient laws and adapted them to a new era.

(9) Second Isaiah (40–55) was the last of the great prophets. The anonymous poet of the exile proclaimed with a unique display of poetic and theological skill the certainty that Yahweh was the creator of the Universe, the ruler of the world, and the maker of history. Cyrus was hailed as the agent of deliverance. Israel is to be forever the servant of Yahweh, whose election is related to a universalistic mission. That mission was nothing less than to bring all the nations of the world to Yahweh. The path of this service was one of suffering and death. It is probable that Second Isaiah, on account of the Hebrew concept of collective personality, thought also of a lonely sufferer, the incarnation of Israel, whose death would be interpreted as an atoning sacrifice (Is 53).

The prophets have developed in the course of three centuries a unique interpretation of God, the world, man, and history. The Mosaic covenant, through their intervention, assumed a new meaning, which prevented the Judaean exiles from disintegrating and which created spiritual as well as ritual Judaism.

5. The religion of postexilic Judaism.—The rehabilitation of the Jewish community in Palestine during the Persian period was wholly due to a theology of cultic presence in Zion. If there were prophets, such as Haggai and Zechariah, Malachi and Joel, they uttered their visions to persuade the people to restore and maintain the sacred ceremonies. Nevertheless, the spirit of the great prophets had left a perennial trace.

(1) The Priestly Document became the cornerstone of restored Judaism and the framework of the written Pentateuch. From the prophets, the priests received and developed the lofty monotheism of Judaism. While the ritual which they proposed had been inherited largely from Semitic paganism, they transformed it to a remarkable degree in an attempt to inspire and transform the whole life of their community. They rewrote the history of the people, beginning with the myth of creation (Gn 1[1ff]), in order to justify their sacramental experience of communion with the maker of heaven and earth. They related the ritual laws, such as sabbath and circumcision, to the whole scheme of universal existence and of Israel's peculiar mission in history. This latter consideration, however, led them at the same time to accelerate the trend toward separatism from the world. For example, the menial tasks in the sanctuary were no longer to be performed by foreigners. The Levites, or descendants of the provincial priests who have been centralized in Jerusalem at the time of Josiah's reformation, became the attendants of the Temple. Sacrificial theology, through the experiences of the exile and the widespread awareness of national sin, changed its character, from a joyous communion meal to a ritual of atonement. The effects of the priestly ritual, however, were not as deadening as one might suppose. Various factors prevented it from stifling the religious vitality of the congregation. The teachings of the prophets were cherished and taught to children. During the exile, the Jews had learned to live a life of intense spirituality without the benefits or the shackles of ritual.

(2) The Psalter testifies to the extraordinary complexity of religion in the postexilic period. There is little doubt that in its present form, the Psalter was the hymnal of the Second Temple, but it represented the growth of all the centuries of the religious history of Israel from the time of Moses and David. Ancient hymns, some of which were borrowed from Canaanite liturgies, were adapted to covenantal faith and the historical theme now completely transformed the ancient naturistic ceremonies of the festivals. The hard lessons from history were presented lyrically or epically in the light of the prophetic interpretation of history. The joy of Divine presence, the burden of sin-consciousness either on the national or on the individual level, together with the delight of deliverance were sung in a great variety of style and imagery. Paradoxically, the Psalms composed chiefly for cultic celebration, and edited by Temple musicians for Temple ceremonies, adopt a rather lofty attitude of detachment toward sacrificial duties and may reflect levitical bias against priestly privileges and arrogance. Above all, the Psalter is penetrated with eschatological fever, insisting that Yahweh will triumph at the end of history since in the context of the cultic act, He is king for ever and ever.

(3) Ritual and legal exclusivism was represented by the priests and reformers of the type of Nehemiah and Ezra, who advocated divorce of foreign wives for the sake of racial and ritual purity. However, other voices were raised by powerful nonconformists who used literature as a vehicle of protest. Jonah and Ruth, with their concerns for the Ninevites and the Moabites respectively, together with the universalism of some parts of Joel and Malachi, reveal that Judaism after the Exile was not a monolithic monument of ritual observance but included within its ranks dynamic elements which continued in their own way the work of the pre-exilic giants of prophecy.

(4) There was also a class of men who lived apart from the ceremonies of the Temple, seemingly untouched by the concerns of the priests. They were the successors of the ancient sages, public servants who from the time of Solomon had worked in the diplomatic corps of the nation and had been in close contact with the intelligentsia of foreign courts. They treated religious and ethical problems of living from that practical commonsense point of view which the Hebrews called *ḥokhmāh*, Wisdom. The books produced by this class exercised a profound religious influence on later generations. The oldest of these, the Poem of Job, discusses in some of the noblest poetry ever written, the problem of existence in the light of undeserved suffering. The poet appears to have borrowed an ancient folktale as a setting for a discussion in which he treats his theme with complete freedom of thought, untrammelled by priestly or legal concerns. In his conclusion, he is more than a wise man and proves to be a prophet. Job does not find satisfaction till he receives an immediate vision of God, and becomes willing, through contemplative participation in the mystery of creation, to trust the Divine person, although his intellectual problem remains unsolved.

The Book of Proverbs contains the sayings of the sages of the practical, every-day sort. Wisdom is good because it rewards, and the fear of Yahweh (awesome reverence without the extreme of cultic practices) is the beginning of wisdom. Ecclesiastes (Ḳoheleth) is the work of a wise man who has not lost his faith although his outlook on life's mystery is both blasé and serene. The fact that his book was preserved indicates the extent of the influence exercised by intellectual classes in the midst of Judaism.

(5) During the postexilic period, the religious life of the scattered communities was centred in the synagogues. These 'houses of prayer' became the most potent factor in the preservation and development of Jewish faith in an alien culture. The education of the young together with sabbath worship were thus insured and the heritage of the past was transmitted to future generations. As often as they could, the Jews of the dispersion made pilgrimages to the Temple in Jerusalem and took part, especially at the time of the great festivals, in the ritual worship of the priestly community. Contact with pagan culture, however, broadened the vision and the piety of the Jews of the Diaspora. They saw that many heathen were actually decent individuals. At the same time, they began to make proselytes. The translation into Greek of their sacred Law, and later of the books of the prophets, which began in the 3rd cent. B.C., was demanded not only for the use of the Greek-

speaking Jews, but also as an instrument in the hands of those who would fulfil the missionary conception of Second Isaiah and win the world to Yahweh. Towards the end of this period, a missionary literature began to be written. One portion of this, the Sibylline Oracles, the oldest part of which dates perhaps from the Maccabaean age, represented the Sibyl, who was popular in the Hellenistic world, as recounting in Greek hexameters the history of the chosen people.

6. The triumph of Legalism.—With the beginning of the Hasmonaean dynasty, the creative period of Biblical Judaism began to wane, and the leaders, gathering up the heritage of the past, were crystallizing it into permanent form. This did not come about all at once, and its beginnings went back to the early postexilic times. The writers of the priestly law were the real intellectual and spiritual ancestors of the Hasidim, or enthusiasts for the Law, out of whom the Maccabaean heroes emerged. Until after the Maccabaean struggle, however, the religious life was too varied, and the nation too creative, for the priestly conceptions to impose themselves in a sort of cultural conformism. The struggle of the Maccabees for the life of the faith greatly strengthened the Hasidim, who early in the Hasmonaean rule developed into the Pharisees. More numerous than the Sadducees, and possessing among the country people a much greater reputation for piety, they soon became the dominant party in Palestine. Some might split off from them, and the Essenes, either at Qumrân or elsewhere, would develop a full-fledged sect, within and apart from, the larger community of Judaism. The Pharisees' aim was to apply the Law to all the details of the daily life. Some of its provisions were disturbing. It called on the Jews not to work on the sabbath, but some work was necessary, if man would live. The Pharisees endeavoured, therefore, to define what was and was not work within the meaning of the Pentateuch. Similarly they dealt with other laws. These definitions were not, for some centuries, committed to writing. Thus there grew up an Oral Law side by side with the Written Law, and in due time the Pharisees regarded this as of special authority. There was development and growth, of course, but this was accomplished, not by creating the new, but by interpreting the old. In the rabbinic schools, which were developed in the Roman period, this system fully unfolded itself, and formed in due course Talmudic Judaism.

Beginning with the Maccabaean struggles, a new class of literature, the Apocalyptic, was called into existence. The eschatological fever which had inspired the prophets and many of the psalmists was now transformed, under the impact of national suffering and persecution, into a furious attempt to discover the date of the end of the world and of the advent of the reign of God. The Apocalypse of Daniel (165–164 B.C.) became the pattern of a vast body of documents in which visions of the last throes were elaborately described. No fewer than seven of these works were attributed to Enoch, and six to Baruch; one was ascribed to Moses, one to Isaiah, while each of the twelve sons of Jacob had his 'testament,' and Solomon his 'psalms.'

In this literature, the consciousness of Judaism, in conflict first with Syria and then with Rome, finds its expression. The apocalyptic hopes were quite consistent with the Law; they pointed forward to that time when the faithful should have ability to serve God completely, and when the tribulations of the present economy of existence would at last be ended. They enabled men to endure and to stand, in spite of trials and oppression. It was in the midst of this passionate expectation for the deliverance of Israel that the Gospel of Jesus of Nazareth was born. G. A. B.—**S. L. T.**

ISRAELITE (Jn 1^{47}).—This is the only instance of the use of the word 'Israelite' in the gospels. It has the particular significance, suggested by the story of Jacob in Gn 32^{28} 35^{10}, of one belonging to the Jewish people, with special reference to the privileges conferred by God on His people, to whom 'belong the sonship, the glory, the covenants, the giving of the law, the worship, and the promises, . . .' (Ro 9^{4}). Its use (as distinct from 'Jew' and 'Hebrew') became closely associated with belief in the messianic hope (cf Jn 1^{45}), and the expression 'Israelite indeed,' addressed to Nathanael, breathes that sense of tragedy so apparent in the Fourth Gospel, inasmuch as those who were specially 'his own' received Him not. One may compare the attitude of 'the Jews' in ch. 6, who are pictured as blindly claiming religious privileges, and yet were enemies of Christ, with Nathanael, who overcame the very same prejudice (stated in both cases as objection to the commonplace origin of Jesus), and readily responded to Philip's invitation, 'come and see' (cf Jn 1^{46} with 6^{42}). It is in this sense that Nathanael is one 'in whom is no guile.' He does not allow his devout sense of privilege to destroy openness of heart toward the claim of Jesus of Nazareth. His action shows that he is sincere, frank, and without sinister aim. From the viewpoint of the writer of the Fourth Gospel, therefore, Nathanael is an object of surprise.

R. H. S.—**H. H. H.**

ISSACHAR.—The fifth son of Jacob by Leah, born after Gad and Asher, the sons of Zilpah, and the ninth of Jacob's sons (Gn 30^{18}, E; cf $35^{22b\text{ff}}$, P). The name (Heb. *yiśśākhār*) is peculiar in form and of quite uncertain significance. J and E both connect the name with the root *śākhar*, 'to hire': J because Leah 'hired' Jacob from Rachel with Reuben's mandrakes; E because she gave Zilpah to Jacob. The difference shows that the traditions are of little value as linguistic guides. Gn $49^{14\text{f}}$ also appears to play upon the root *śākhar* in its description of Issachar as a 'servant under task-work,' though the reference to Issachar as 'a bony ass' and the obvious allusion to the riches of the sea indicates that the services of Issachar were hired as caravaneers rather than forcibly conscripted. The affinities of Issachar with the surrounding Hebrew tribes would guarantee the security of this traffic.

P's census at Sinai gives the tribe 54,000 (Nu 1^{29}), and at Moab 64,300 (26^{25}); cf 1 Ch 7^{5}. For the clans see Gn 46^{13} and 1 Ch $7^{1\text{ff}}$.

The original seat of the tribe appears to have been S. of Naphtali and SE. of Zebulun. On the NW. it touched upon Mount Tabor, on the S. upon Mount Gilboa. P's lot (Jos 19^{17-23}) assigns to the tribe sixteen cities and their villages, scattered throughout the eastern end of the Plain of Esdraelon and the Valley of Jezreel. The tribe participated in the war against Sisera (Jg 5^{15}), and Deborah may have belonged to it. The 'with' before Deborah might be read 'people of'; but the verse is evidently corrupt. Baasha, the son of Ahijah, who succeeded Nadab, was 'of the house of Issachar' (1 K 15^{27}); and possibly also Omri, whose family property was probably at Jezreel. The Blessing of Jacob (Gn $49^{14\text{f}}$) refers to the geographical situation of Issachar at the bottleneck between the ridge of Gilboa and the hills of Lower Galilee, 'a bony ass crouching between converging fold-walls,' but indicates that by the early monarchy Issachar had lost its martial spirit. The Blessing of Moses (Dt $33^{18\text{f}}$), which refers to Issachar's share in commercial prosperity through the trade from the coast which passed through her district, associates Issachar with Zebulun in the cult at a mountain sanctuary. This is doubtless Tabor (cf Hos 5^{1}), which may have served as an amphictyonic shrine for the older, or Leah, tribes in the north, which may be the 'Israel' mentioned in connexion with localities in this neighbourhood on Merneptah's stele (1223 B.C.). One of the minor Judges, Tola, the grandson of Dodo, perhaps a hereditary law-giver and interpreter, was a man of Issachar (Jg 10^{1}). According to the Talmud, the Sanhedrin drew from Issachar its most prominent intellectuals. See also TRIBES OF ISRAEL.

J. A. C.—**J. Gr.**

ISSHIAH.—**1.** One of the heads of the tribe of Issachar, 1 Ch 7^{3} (AV **Ishiah**). **2.** A Korahite who joined David at Ziklag, 1 Ch 12^{6} (AV **Jesiah**). **3.** The son of Uzziel, 1 Ch 23^{20} (AV **Jesiah**), 24^{25}. **4.** A Levite, 1 Ch 24^{21}.

ISSHIJAH.—One of those who agreed to put away his foreign wife, Ezr 10^{31}; perhaps the **Asaias** of 1 Es 9^{32} (AV, RV **Aseas**).

ISSUE.—See MEDICINE.

ISTALCURUS.—See ZAKKUR.

ISUAH, 1 Ch 7^{30} (AV).—See ISHVAH.

ISUI, Gn 46^{17} (AV).—See ISHVI.

ITALIAN COHORT (AV, RV **band**).—See BAND.

ITALY.—This word varied in sense from time to time. It first signified only the Southern (the Greek) part of the peninsula; when Rome rose to power it appropriated the name to cover also its own territory up to the Rubicon; and finally, before the time of Christ, it had come to bear the meaning which it has now. Its central position in the Mediterranean, the conformation of its coast, and the capabilities of its soil under proper cultivation, fitted it to be the home and centre of a numerous and powerful people. In the 1st cent. A.D. there was constant communication between the capital Rome and every part of the Empire, by well-recognized routes. Among the routes to the E., which mainly concern the NT student, was that from Rome along the W. coast of Italy to Campania, where it crossed the country and eventually reached Brundisium. From the harbour there the traveller either sailed across the Adriatic to Dyrrhachium, and went by the Egnatian road to Thessalonica and beyond, or sailed across to the Gulf of Corinth, trans-shipped from Lechaeum to Cenchreae (q.v.), and from there sailed to Ephesus or Antioch or Alexandria, as he desired. A good account of the opposite journey is in Ac 27–28. The Jews poured into Italy, especially to Rome, and had been familiar to the people of Italy as far north as Rome long before Christianity arrived. A. So.—**E. G. K.**

ITCH.—See MEDICINE.

ITHAI.—See ITTAI, **2.**

ITHAMAR.—The fourth and youngest son of Aaron and Elisheba (Ex 6^{23} etc.); consecrated priest (Ex 28^{1ff}); forbidden to mourn for Nadab and Abihu (Lv 10^{6}), or to leave the Tent of Meeting (v.^{7}); afterwards entrusted by Moses with priestly duties (Lv 10^{12ff}) and rebuked by him for neglect (v.^{16ff}); set over the Gershonites and the Merarites in connexion with the service of the Tent of Meeting (Nu 4$^{21-33}$ 7^{7f}; cf also Ex 38^{21}); ancestor of Eli (cf 1 K 2^{27} with 1 Ch 24^{3}; Jos. *Ant.* VIII. i. 3 [11]). The family in David's time was only half the size of Eleazar's (1 Ch 24^{4}). It was represented among the returned exiles (Ezr 8^{2}).

W. T. S.

ITHIEL.—**1.** A Benjamite, Neh 11^{7}. **2.** One of two persons to whom Agur addressed his oracular sayings, the other being **Ucal,** Pr 30^{1}. Neither LXX nor Vulgate recognizes proper names here, and most modern commentators point differently and translate 'I have wearied myself, O God, I have wearied myself, O God, and am consumed.' So RVm.

ITHLAH.—A town of Dan, near Aijalon, Jos 19^{42} (AV **Jethlah**). The site is unknown.

ITHMAH.—A Moabite, one of David's heroes, 1 Ch 11^{46}.

ITHNAN.—A city in the Negeb of Judah, Jos 15^{23}. The LXX combines with the preceding name, **Hazor-ithnan.** The site is uncertain.

ITHRA.—The father of Amasa, and husband of Abigail (so 1 Ch 2^{16f}; Abigal in 2 S 17^{25} RV, RSV), David's sister; called **Jether** in 1 K 2$^{5, 32}$, 1 Ch 2^{17}. He is described as an Israelite in 2 S 17^{25} (AV, RV), but an Ishmaelite in 1 Ch 2^{17}, 2 S 17^{25} (RSV).

ITHRAN.—**1.** Eponym of a Horite clan, Gn 36^{26}, 1 Ch 1^{41}. **2.** A man of Asher, 1 Ch 7^{37}; called **Jether** in v.^{38}.

ITHREAM.—The sixth son of David, born to him at Hebron, 2 S 3^{5}, 1 Ch 3^{3}.

ITHRITE, THE.—A gentilic adjective applied to the descendants of a family of Kiriath-jearim (1 Ch 2^{53}), amongst whom were two of David's guard (1 S 23^{38}, 1 Ch 11^{40} Ira and Gareb). Possibly, however, the text of 2 S 23 and 1 Ch 11 should be pointed 'the **Jattirite,**' *i.e.* an inhabitant of Jattir (mentioned in 1 S 30^{27} as one of David's haunts) in the hill-country of Judah (Jos 15^{48} 21^{14}). See JATTIR.

ITS.—It is well known that this word occurs but once in AV, Lv 25^{5}, and that even there it is due to subsequent printers, the word in 1611 being 'it'—'that which groweth of it owne accord.' The use of 'it' for 'its' is well seen in Shakespeare's *King John*, II. i. 160,

> 'Go to it grandam, child:
> Give grandam kingdom, and it grandam will
> Give it a plum, a cherry, and a fig.'

The form 'its' was only beginning to come into use about 1611. The usual substitutes in AV are 'his' and 'thereof.' Thus Mt 6^{33} 'But seek ye first the kingdom of God, and his righteousness,' where Tyndale has 'the rightwisnes thereof' (RV and RSV take the pronoun to be masculine, referring to God, not kingdom, and retains 'his').

ITTAH-KAZIN, Jos 19^{13} (AV).—See ETH-KAZIN.

ITTAI.—**1.** A Gittite leader who, with a following of 600 Philistines, attached himself to David at the outbreak of Absalom's rebellion. In spite of being urged by David to return to his home, he determined to follow the king in his misfortune, affirming his faithfulness in the beautiful words 'As the Lord lives, and as my lord the king lives, wherever my lord the king shall be, whether for death or for life, there also will your servant be' (2 S 15^{21}). He therefore remained in the service of David, and soon rose to a position of great trust, being placed in command of a third part of the people (2 S 18^{2}). **2.** A Benjamite, son of Ribai, who was one of David's mighty men (2 S 23^{29}, 1 Ch 11^{31} [in the latter **Ithai**]).

W. O. E. O.

ITURAEA.—This region, with Trachonitis, constituted the tetrarchy of Philip (Lk 3^{1}). But whether 'Ituraea' is employed by the Evangelist as a noun or an adjective is a disputed point. Epiphanius and Eusebius seem to have been the first writers to use the word as the name of a country. The Ituraeans as a people were well known to classical writers. According to Cicero (*Philipp.* ii. 112), they were a 'predatory people'; according to Caesar (*Bell. Afr.* 20), they were 'skilful archers'; according to Strabo (XVI. ii. 10 etc.), they were 'lawless.' They seem to have migrated originally from the desert to the vicinity of Southern Lebanon and Coele-Syria. Both Strabo and Josephus (*Ant.* XIII. xi. 3 [318]) locate them in these parts. The Romans probably caused them to retreat toward the desert again shortly before the Christian era. Lysanias the son of Ptolemy is called by Dio Cassius (xlix. 32) 'king of the Ituraeans.' He was put to death by Mark Antony in 34 B.C. Zenodorus his successor died in 20 B.C., whereupon a part of his territory fell into the hands of Herod the Great; and when Herod's kingdom was divided, it became the possession of Philip (Jos. *Ant.* XVII. xi. 4 [319]). Whether Ituraea and Trachonitis overlapped, or were two distinct districts, is uncertain. The passage in Luke seems to favour a distinct and definite district, which was probably somewhere NE. of the Sea of Galilee.

G. L. R.—**F. C. G.**

IVAH.—The AV spelling of **Ivvah** (q.v.) in 2 K 18^{34} 19^{13}, Is 37^{13}.

IVORY (*shēn*, literally 'tooth'; and *shenhabbîm*, 'elephants' teeth,' 1 K 10^{22}, 2 Ch 9^{21}).—Ivory has been valued from the earliest times, witness the well-designed ointment-boxes of ivory found at Ugarit. Solomon imported it by sea (1 K 10^{22}), probably from Ophir; it was used in the decorations of palaces (22^{39}), as also in ships (Ezk 27^6) decks of pine were 'inlaid with ivory.' Archaeological finds at Samaria include ivory carvings, which were inlaid in the woodwork of the palace or its furniture. The 'ivory tower' (Ca 7^4) may also have been a building decorated with ivory. Solomon had a throne of ivory (1 K 10^{18-20}). 'Beds of ivory,' such as are mentioned in Am 6^4, were, according to a cuneiform inscription, included in the tribute paid by Hezekiah to Sennacherib. E. W. G. M.—**R. A. B.**

IVVAH.—A city named in 2 K 18^{34} 19^{13}, Is 37^{13} (AV all **Ivah**), along with Sepharvaim and Hena, as conquered by the Assyrians; probably to be identified with **Avva** (q.v.). It is probably modern *Tell Kefr ʿAyā*, on the Orontes.

IVY.—This plant (*Hedera helix*) grows wild in Palestine and Syria. It is mentioned in 2 Mac 6^7. See DIONYSIA.

IYE-ABARIM.—The station mentioned in Nu 21^{11} as 'in the wilderness which is opposite Moab toward the sunrise,' and in Nu 33^{44} as 'in the territory of Moab'; possibly modern *Maḥaiy* (AV **Ije-abarim** in both). In Nu 33^{45} it is called **Iyim** (AV **Iim**). This place is to be distingusihed from **Iim** (q.v.) of Jos 15^{29}.

IYIM ('ruins').—See IYE-ABARIM.

IYYAR.—See TIME.

IZEHAR, Nu 3^{19} (AV).—See IZHAR.

IZHAR ('he is tawny').—**1.** Son of Kohath the son of Levi, Ex $6^{18, 21}$, Nu 3^{19} (AV **Izehar**) 16^1, 1 Ch $6^{2, 18, 38}$ $23^{12, 18}$; patronymic **Izharites,** Nu 3^{27} (AV Izeharites), 1 Ch 24^{22} $26^{23, 29}$. **2.** A Judahite, 1 Ch 4^7 (RV, RSV); AV **Jezoar**). See ZOHAR, **3.**

IZLIAH.—A Benjamite chief, 1 Ch 8^{18} (AV **Jezliah**).

IZRAHIAH.—A chief of Issachar, 1 Ch 7^3. The same name is rendered **Jezrahiah** in Neh 12^{42}.

IZRAHITES.—Gentilic name in 1 Ch 27^8, possibly another form of **Zerahites,** vv.$^{11, 13}$ (AV **Zarhites**). See ZERAH.

IZRI.—Chief of one of the Levitical choirs, 1 Ch 25^{11}; called **Zeri** in v.^{3}.

IZZIAH.—One of those who had married a foreign wife, Ezr 10^{25} (AV **Jeziah**), 1 Es 9^{26} (AV **Eddias, RV Ieddias**).

J

JAAKAN.—A descendant of Esau, 1 Ch 1^{42} (AV **Jakan**); in Gn 36^{27} called **Akan.** See also BEEROTH-BENE-JAAKAN.

JAAKOBAH.—A Simeonite prince, 1 Ch 4^{36}.

JAALA.—See JAALAH.

JAALAH.—The name of a family of 'sons of Solomon's servants' who returned with Zerubbabel, Ezr 2^{56}, 1 Es 5^{33} (AV, RV **Jeeli**); called **Jaala** in Neh 7^{58}.

JAALAM.—The AV form of **Jalam** (q.v.).

JAANAI, 1 Ch 5^{12} (AV).—See JANAI.

JAAR.—A Hebrew word meaning 'wood,' 'forest,' 'thicket,' occurring about fifty times in the OT. It occurs once as a proper name, Ps 132^6 (so RVm, RSV; AV, RV 'the wood'). Here it is probably a shortened form of **Kiriath-jearim,** whence the Ark was brought to Jerusalem (cf 1 Ch 2^{50} where Kiriath-jearim is connected with Ephrathah, as here).

JAARE-OREGIM.—According to 2 S 21^{19}, the father of Elhanan, but according to 1 Ch 20^5 his name was **Jair.** See ELHANAN.

JAARESHIAH.—A Benjamite chief, 1 Ch 8^{27} (AV **Jaresiah**).

JAASAI, Ezr 10^{37} (RVm).—See JAASU.

JAASAU, Ezr 10^{37} (AV).—See JAASU.

JAASIEL.—The leader of Benjamin, 1 Ch 27^{21}, probably identical with the **Mezobaite** of 11^{47}.

JAASU.—One of those who had married foreign wives, Ezr 10^{37} (AV **Jaasau**; RVm **Jaasai,** following *Ḳ^{e}rê*); called **Eliasis** in 1 Es 9^{34}.

JAAZANIAH ('Yahweh hears').—**1.** A Maacathite military commander, contemporary with Gedaliah (2 K 25^{23} = **Jezaniah** Jer 40^8). **2.** A faithful Rechabite chieftain (Jer 35^3). **3.** An elder, the son of Shaphan, an idolater (Ezk 8^{11}). **4.** A prince of the people, son of Azzur, opposed by Ezekiel (Ezk 11^{1ff}). The name appears on a number of seals, and later, in Aramaic form, in the Elephantine papyri. It has been suggested that the Jaazaniah of a seal from *Tell en-Naṣbeh* is identical with **1** above. P. R. A.

JAAZER, Nu 21^{32} 32^{35} (AV).—See JAZER.

JAAZIAH.—A son of Merari, 1 Ch 24^{26f}.

JAAZIEL.—A Levite skilled in the use of the harp, 1 Ch 15^{18}; his name is abbreviated to **Aziel** in v.^{20}.

JABAL.—Son of Lamech by Adah, and originator of the nomadic way of life, Gn 4^{20}.

JABBOK.—A river now called *Nahr ez-Zerqā* ('the Blue River,' and it has been suggested that it was given this name because its water, from a distance, appears to be grey-blue in colour). It is one of the main streams which flow from the east into the Jordan. Its source is near *ʿAmmân*, the ancient Rabbath-ammon, and after running first NE., then N., NW., W., finally bends SW. to enter the Jordan at a point about 25–30 miles N. of the Dead Sea. On almost the whole of its curved course of 60 miles it runs through a deep valley, and forms a natural boundary. On its curved upper reaches it may be said practically to bound the desert, while the deep gorge of its lower, straighter course divides the land of Gilead into two halves. The first reference, and probably the most famous, is Gn 32^{22ff}, the incident of Jacob's wrestling with the Angel, where there is an attempt at an assonance between the Hebrew word for 'to wrestle' and the name of this river. Elsewhere, Nu 21^{24}, Dt 2^{37} 3^{16}, Jg $11^{13, 22}$, it is mentioned as a boundary or frontier. E. W. G. M.—**E. R. R.**

JABESH.—Father of Shallum, who usurped the kingdom of Israel by the assassination of king Zechariah, 2 K $15^{10, 13f}$.

JABESH, JABESH-GILEAD.—A town which appears in Jg 21^{1-14}, 1 S 11, 31^{11-13}, 2 S 2^{4-7} 21^{12} and 1 Ch 10^{11f}. According to Eusebius, *Onomasticon*, it was a village on high ground 6 miles from Pella. It lies in the Jabesh (modern *Yabis*) valley which runs into the Jordan valley from the east. It is chiefly, if not solely, associated with the story of Saul. It was rescued by him from the Ammonites and thereby spared the disgraceful terms which Nahash their king would have imposed on its inhabitants (1 S 11). In gratitude the men of Jabesh-gilead rescued Saul's body from the Philistines (1 S 31^{11-13} 2 S 21^{12}, 1 Ch 10^{11f}), an act which earned the commendation of David (2 S 2^4).

Jg 21^{1-14} tells of an attack on Jabesh-gilead by the Israelites to provide wives for the Benjamites. It is thought to be a late story and to have included Jabesh-gilead because of the town's strong links with Saul. R. A. S. M.—**L. H. B.**

JABEZ.—**1.** A city in Judah occupied by scribes, the descendants of Caleb, 1 Ch 2^{55}. The site is unknown.

2. A man of the family of Judah noted for his 'honourable' character, 1 Ch 4[9f]; called *Yaʿbēṣ*, which is connected by a word play *ʿōṣebh*, 'pain.' In his vow (v.[10]) there is again a play upon his name.

JABIN ('[God] perceives').—A Canaanite king who reigned in Hazor, a place near the Waters of Merom, not far from Kedesh. In the account in Jg 4, of the defeat of the two tribes of Zebulun and Naphtali of Jabin's host under Sisera, the former takes up quite a subordinate position. In another account (Jos 11[1-9]) of this episode the victory of the two tribes is represented as a conquest of the whole of northern Canaan by Joshua. Both accounts, Jos 11[1-9], Jg 4, are fragments taken from an earlier, and more elaborate source; the Jabin in each passage is therefore one and the same person.

W. O. E. O.

JABNEEL.—1. A town on the N. border of Judah, near Mt. Baalah, and close to the sea (Jos 15[11]). In 2 Ch 26[6] it is mentioned under the name **Jabneh,** along with Gath and Ashdod, as one of the cities captured from the Philistines by Uzziah. Although these are the only OT references, it is frequently mentioned (under the name **Jamnia**) in the Books of Maccabees (1 Mac 4[15] 5[58] 10[69] 15[40], 2 Mac 12[8, 9, 40]) and in Josephus. Judas is said to have burned its harbour; it was captured by Simon from the Syrians. It is mentioned in Jth 2[28] (AV, RV **Jemnaan**). After various vicissitudes it was captured in the war of the Jews by Vespasian. After the destruction of Jerusalem, Jamnia became the home of the Sanhedrin. At the time of the Crusades the castle *Ibelin* stood on the site. To-day the village of *Yebnā* stands on the ruined remains of these ancient occupations. It stands 170 feet above the sea on a prominent hill S. of the *Wâdī Rubin.* The ancient *Majumas* or harbour of Jamnia lies to the west. 'The port would seem to be naturally better than any along the coast of Palestine S. of Caesarea' (Warren). **2.** A site on the N. boundary of Naphtali, Jos 19[33]; possibly modern *Kh. Yemmā.*

E. W. G. M.

JABNEH.—See JABNEEL, **1.**

JACAN.—A Gadite chief, 1 Ch 5[13] (AV **Jachan**).

JACHAN, 1 Ch 5[13] (AV).—See JACAN.

JACHIN.—1. Fourth son of Simeon, Gn 46[10], Ex 6[15], Nu 26[12]; called **Jarib** in 1 Ch 4[24]. The patronymic **Jachinites** occurs in Nu 26[12]. **2.** Eponym of a priestly family, 1 Ch 9[10], Neh 11[10].

JACHIN AND BOAZ.—These are the names borne by two brazen, or more probably bronze, pillars belonging to Solomon's Temple. They evidently represented the highest artistic achievement of their author, Hiram of Tyre, 'the half-Tyrian copper-worker, whom Solomon fetched from Tyre to do foundry work for him,' whose name, however, was more probably Huram-abi (2 Ch 2[13], RSV). The description of them now found in 1 K 7[15-22] is exceedingly confused and corrupt, but with the help of the better preserved Greek text, and of other OT references (viz. 7[41f], 2 Ch 3[15-17] 4[12f], and Jer 52[21-23] =2 K 25[17]), scholars have restored the text of the primary passage somewhat as follows :—

'And he cast the two pillars of bronze for the porch of the temple; 18 cubits was the height of the one pillar, and a line of 12 cubits could compass it about, and its thickness was 4 finger-breadths (for it was) hollow [with this cf Jer 52[21]]. And the second pillar was similar. And he made two chapiters [*i.e.* capitals] of cast bronze for the tops of the pillars, etc. [as in RV]. And he made two sets of network to cover the chapiters which were upon the tops of the pillars, a network for the one chapiter and a network for the second chapiter. And he made the pomegranates; and two rows of pomegranates in bronze were upon the one network, and the pomegranates were 200, round about upon the one chapiter, and so he did for the second chapiter. And he set up the pillars at the porch of the temple,' etc. [as in v.[21] RV].

The original description apparently consisted of three parts: the pillars, their capitals, and the ornamentation of the latter. The pillars themselves were hollow, with a thickness of metal equal to 3 inches of our measure; their height, on the basis of the larger cubit of 20½ inches (see Hastings' *DB* iv. 907[a]), was about 31 feet, while their diameter works out at about 6½ feet. The capitals appear from 1 K 7[41] to have been globular or spheroidal in form, each about 8½ feet in height, giving a total height for the complete pillars of roughly 40 feet. The ornamentation of the capitals was twofold: first they were covered with a specially cast **network** of bronze. Over this were hung festoon-wise two wreaths of bronze pomegranates, each row containing 100 pomegranates, of which it is probable that four were fixed to the network, while the remaining 96 hung free (see Jer 52[23]).

As regards their position relative to the Temple, it may be regarded as certain that they were structurally independent of the Temple porch, and stood free in front of it—probably on plinths or bases—Jachin on the south and Boaz on the north (1 K 7[21]), one on either side of the steps leading up to the entrance to the porch (cf Ezk 40[49]). Such free-standing pillars were a common feature of temples in Syria, Phoenicia, and Cyprus, and beyond these areas east to Assyria, and west to the Phoenician colonies in the Mediterranean. The statements of classical authorities on this point have been confirmed by representations on Phoenician, Punic, and Etruscan seals, coins, and monuments.

Many proposals have been made concerning the original significance and purpose of the pillars. W. F. Albright has assembled a mass of evidence to support W. Robertson Smith's suggestion that the pillars were huge cressets or fire-altars, in which the 'suet of the sacrifices' was burned. Cf his *RS* (1894), pp. 487–490; Albright, *ARI*, pp. 144 ff. As to the names 'Jachin' and 'Boaz,' R. B. Y. Scott has offered a convincing explanation of their meaning, in *JBL*, lviii (1939), 143–149. He interprets the names as the first words of dynastic oracles inscribed in whole or part on the pillars, thus linking the Temple with the widely attested royal cult in Jerusalem. We may note the many passages in the historical and poetical books (including Prophets and Psalms) dealing with the special relationship between David and his house and Yahweh; moreover the Temple functioned both as national cult centre and more particularly as the royal chapel (cf the description of the Temple at Bethel in Am 7[13]). Scott suggests the following wording for the oracles: Jachin—'Yahweh will establish (*yākhîn*) the throne of David and his kingdom to his seed forever' (*op. cit.*, p. 148); while Albright reads, 'Yahweh will establish thy throne for ever' (*ARI*, p. 139); Boaz—'In the strength (*bᵃʿaz*) of Yahweh shall the king rejoice (Scott, *op. cit.*, p. 149; likewise Albright, *ARI*, p. 139).

A. R. S. K.—**D. N. F.**

JACINTH.—See JEWELS AND PRECIOUS STONES.

JACKAL.—The Bedouin of Palestine, though aware of the differences between jackals and foxes, habitually confused them in speech; and the Hebrew and Arabic names were apparently used indiscriminately. **1.** The Arabic *thaʿala* 'was numerous, formed a numerous party; had an excess of teats, teeth' might apply to either beast; for the jackal normally hunts in packs, while the vixen has six pairs of teats against from three to five in the female jackal. Contrariwise the Arabic *thaʿalala* 'was cowardly; turned quickly away to right or to left' is especially applicable to the fox (cf Lat. *vulpinari* 'to follow a tortuous course'). Both the jackal (*canis aureus*) and the fox (*vulpes flavescens* in the north and *vulpes niloticus* in the south) are common in Palestine. The Hebrew *shûʿāl*=Arabic *thuʿâlu* 'fox' (cf Pers. *šaġâl* 'jackal') is generally translated in the EV '**fox,**' but also occasionally 'jackal' (RVm at Jg 15[4], Neh 4[3], Ps 63[10], La 5[18] and RSV at Ps 63[10], La 5[18]) and ought probably always to be rendered '**jackal,**' which alone suits all passages. Both animals feed on grapes and other fruit (Ca 2[15]), occupy burrows (**Mt**

8[20]), haunt ruins and waste places (La 5[18]), make their way through holes into walled cities (Neh 4[3]; cf Tristram *Natural History of the Bible*[2], 110–111), and are proverbially cunning and sly (Ezk 13[4], Lk 13[32]); but only the jackal hunts in packs (Jg 15[4]) and preys on dead bodies (Ps 63[11]), so that Bedouin still talk of throwing an enemy's dead body to the jackals as a final insult.

2. An obvious onomatopoeic root for howling (Egyptian ꜣw 'lamented' and ꜣwꜣw 'wailed'; Arabic *'awā* 'moaned') underlies the Hebrew *'îy* '**jackal**' (Egyptian ꜣw and ꜣwꜣw, kind of dog; Arabic *ibn 'âwā* 'son of howling' and *wâwî* 'howler'='jackal'), so that the meaning is philologically well established; and the secondary Arabic *'awā* I 'resorted' (whence the Heb. *'îy* 'coast-land; island' is derived) and VI 'congregated together' confirms the identification, since jackals hunt in packs. The ancient translators did not understand the word, and modern translators offer various renderings, *e.g.* 'wild beasts of the island(s)' (AV), 'wolves' (RV) or 'howling creatures' (RVm); all are as unsatisfactory as a recent attempt to revive the LXX's 'demons' (Is 34[14]) and translate it 'goblins' as the *jinn* populating unknown coasts and islands (Torrey, *Second Isaiah*, 290–291) is unconvincing, if the accompanying beasts are taken as real, not mythical, creatures. The habits of the *'îy*, too, are those of the jackal; it haunts desolate Edom (Is 34[14]) and the ruins of Babylon (Is 13[22], Jer 50[39]), just as packs of jackals still haunt the desolate ravines of the Dead Sea and howl all night in the ruins of Baʿalbek (Tristram *op. cit.* 109). RSV renders by 'jackal' in Jer 50[39] and '**hyena**' in Is 13[22] 34[14].

3. The root *tnn* 'to coil, be spiral' seems to lie behind the Hebrew *tannîn* '(poisonous) serpent; (mythical) dragon, sea-monster; water-spout'; but what the Hebrew *tan*, which must be carefully distinguished from *tannîn* (though often confused with it in the MT), means is hard to say. The Greek translators had no tradition, having 'siren,' 'dragon,' 'bird,' 'ostrich,' and once 'lion' (Theodotion at Mic 1[8]); Jerome has 'goblins' (La 4[3], *lamiae*), 'sirens,' and 'dragons,' while the Peshitta and Targum almost always have *yārôrâ*, of which the meaning is uncertain. The AV has 'dragons,' for which the RV and RSV generally substitute 'jackals.' The *tan* haunts desolate places (Is 34[13] 35[7] 43[20], Jer 9[10] 10[22] 49[33] 51[37]), of which it is a symbolical denizen (Ps 44[20], Job 30[29]), and mourns or wails like the desert owl (Mic 1[8]). If the Arabic *tînânu* 'wolf' could be compared, this might be accepted as the meaning of the Hebrew word (Pococke); but the comparison is philologically inadmissible (Torrey, *op. cit.* 288–289). If the basic sense of the root *tnn* is pressed, either the jackal or fox from its tortuous course or the owl from its wavy flight may be meant; but the fact that only the plural form of the word occurs is against a solitary creature like the fox. Further, both it and the jackal have other names (*v. supra*). If however the Arabic *tinnu* 'companion' is any guide, the Hebrew *tannîm* 'companions' may designate '**wolves**'; these in search of prey *procedunt gemini ceu foedere iuncto hiberna sub nocte lupi* (Statius, *Achilleis* i. 704–705). This habit is recorded also of the large Syrian wolf (Tristram, *Natural History of the Bible*[2], 153–154; cf *Fauna and Flora of Palestine*, 20–21) and tells at the same time against the jackal, which hunts not in pairs but in packs of 200 or 300 beasts. The wolf by day lurks amongst rocks in desolate plains and wild ravines and by night comes out to prowl round the sheepfolds; and it howls in characteristic fashion. That 'the jackals give the breast' (La 4[3], RV and RSV) is absurd, and *tannîm* must be an error for *tannînîm* 'sea-monsters' (AV), *i.e.* whales or porpoises, whose two teats are hidden in a subcutaneous pouch from which, when swollen with milk, they are extruded and uncovered, so that the young can suck them (Aharoni).

4. Clearly the Hebrew *'ōaḥ* '**doleful creature**' (AV, RV) is an onomatopoeic term denoting some creature which makes a coughing, raucous, or rustling sound (cf Heb. *'āḥ* 'ah!,' Arab. *'aḥāḥa* 'cried alas!', and *'aḥḥa* 'coughed'; also *'aḥîḥu* 'rustling noise made by water-fowl passing through parted reeds). It is mentioned only once in connexion with ruined Babylon (Is 13[21]), but its meaning has long been lost; the versions have 'echoes' or 'cries' (LXX, Theodotion, Aquila) or 'dragons' (Vulgate) or 'wild beasts' (Peshitta; cf Targum), which throw no light on it. Also 'owl' possibly 'eagle-owl' has been suggested; but enough names for owls are already known (see Owl), and the name does not seem to indicate anything that hoots. It equally does not suggest 'jackal, wolf' (Delitzsch, *Hebrew Language*, 33–34) or '(laughing) hyaena' (Houghton in *TSBA* v, 328), which howl; and an Assyrian *aḫû* 'wolf, jackal, hyaena' cited in support of them rests on a misunderstanding. If coughing is pressed, the proverb that 'the cough of the fox leads to the grave' (Bochart & Rosenmüller, *Hierozoicon*, ii, 190–191) springs to the mind; but this alone is hardly enough to support the identification. The 'leopard,' too, coughs as it springs on the prey; but it like the fox does not haunt ruins, and 'their houses are full of foxes' or 'leopards' is an unlikely figure of speech. Further, several other words for both fox (see Fox) and leopard (see Leopard) occur. Alternatively, the '**porcupine**' may be meant; for this may have got its name from its habit of rustling or rattling its quills and vibrating its tail *rauco fragore* (Claudian, *de hystrice*, 25–26). It emerges from its hole only at night and shuns man, so that it will easily have become a symbol of desolation; also, as the prophet says that 'Babylon . . . shall be as when God overthrew Sodom and Gomorrah' (Is 13[19]), it is singularly suitable in the picture, inasmuch as it abounds round the Dead Sea, being one of the few mammals which do not require water (Tristram, *Natural History of the Bible*[2], 125–126). The only other possibility is that the word describes not a living creature but 'weird noises' as some versions suggest (Zorell).

5. The Hebrew *ṣîyîm*, if connected with *ṣîyāh* 'parched land,' may *a priori* denote 'inhabitants of the wilderness' or the like (AV, RV, RSV); but a particular rather than a general term is required for a creature regarded as a symbol of desolation (Is 13[21] 23[13] 34[14], Jer 50[39]). The VSS have various unsatisfactory renderings, including 'sirens' (LXX at Jer 50[39]) and 'demons' (LXX at Is 23[13]), which though equally unsuitable has recently been revived (Torrey, *op. cit.* 289); clearly the ancient translators had no tradition of its meaning. Bochart's 'wild cat' (cf Arabic *ḍaiwanu*, 'wild cat') is philologically impossible, although this is common enough in Palestine. Possible roots for the Hebrew word may be found in the Arabic *ṣawā* 'squeaked' (cf Aramaic *ṣawwe* and Arab. *ḍauḍā* 'shrieked') and *ṣawiya* 'was strong,' *ḍawâ* 'came by night' and *ḍawiya* 'was slender.' Ewald's 'jackal,' as a beast that howls, is unlikely, since it already has other names. Possibly the '**marmot**' (*spermophilus xanthoprimnus*) may be meant; this when alarmed emits a loud shrill whistling sound or shriek and is exceedingly abundant in the stony uplands of Gilead and Moab, burrowing often in the neighbourhood of ruins (Tristram, *Fauna and Flora of Palestine*, 15; cf Jerome *ap.* Migne, *Patrologia Latina* xxii, 861–862). Whether the Assyrian *ṣîtu*, the name of a creature which injures crops and fruit, is the same word is not clear.

In Ps 74[14] *ṣîyîm* is rendered by 'people inhabiting the wilderness' in AV and RV, but the statement that Leviathan was given 'to be meat to the people inhabiting the wilderness,' which is a grammatically impossible translation, may be corrected to read 'to the monsters of the sea,' *i.e.* the sharks (Löw, *DLZ* [N.F.] xxii, 1055, reading *lᵉʿamlᵉṣê yām* for *lᵉʿam lᵉṣîyîm*). In Ps 72[9] *ṣîyîm* again is not 'they that inhabit the wilderness' (RV, RSVm), but 'Ethiopians' (so LXX, Vulgate), the 'tallest and most beautiful' of men (Herodotus, *Hist.* iii. 20; cf Is 18[2, 7]), as the Arabic verb quoted above (**5**) suggests. G. R. D.

JACOB.—1. Son of Isaac and Rebekah. His name is probably an elliptical form of an original *Jakobʾel*,

'God follows' (*i.e.* 'rewards'), which has been found both on Babylonian tablets and on the pylons of the temple of Karnak. By the time of Jacob this earlier history of the word was overlooked or forgotten, and the name was understood as meaning 'one who takes by the heel, and thus tries to trip up or supplant' (Gn 25^{26} 27^{36}, Hos 12^{3}). His history is recounted in Gn 25^{21}–50^{13}, the materials being unequally contributed from three sources. P supplies but a brief outline; J and E are closely interwoven, though a degree of original independence is shown by an occasional divergence in tradition, which adds to the credibility of the joint narrative.

Jacob was born in answer to prayer (25^{21}), near Beersheba; and the later rivalry between Israel and Edom was thought of as prefigured in the strife of the twins in the womb (25^{22f}, 2 Es 3^{16} 6$^{8-10}$, Ro 9$^{11-13}$). The differences between the two brothers, each contrasting with the other in character and habit, were marked from the beginning. Jacob grew up a 'quiet man' (Gn 25^{27}), a shepherd and herdsman. Whilst still at home, he succeeded in overreaching Esau in two ways. He took advantage of Esau's hunger and heedlessness to secure the birthright, which gave him precedence even during the father's lifetime (43^{33}), and afterwards a double portion of the patrimony (Dt 21^{17}), with probably the domestic priesthood. At a later time, after careful consideration (Gn 27^{11ff}), he adopted the device suggested by his mother, and, allaying with ingenious falsehoods (27^{20}) his father's suspicion, intercepted also his blessing. Isaac was dismayed, but instead of revoking the blessing confirmed it (27$^{33-37}$), and was not able to remove Esau's bitterness. In both blessings later political and geographical conditions are reflected. To Jacob is promised Canaan, a well-watered land of fields and vineyards (Dt 11^{14} 33^{28}), with sovereignty over its peoples, even those who were 'brethren' or descended from the same ancestry as Israel (Gn 19^{37f}, 2 S 8$^{12, 14}$). Esau is consigned to the dry and rocky districts of Idumaea, with a life of war and plunder; but his subjection to Jacob is limited in duration (2 K 8^{22}), if not also in completeness (Gn 27^{40f}, which points to the restlessness of Edom).

Of this successful craft on Jacob's part the natural result on Esau's was hatred and resentment, to avoid which Jacob left his home to spend a few days (27^{44}) with his uncle in Haran. Two different motives are assigned. JE represents Rebekah as pleading with her son his danger from Esau; but P represents her as suggesting to Isaac the danger that Jacob might marry a Hittite wife (27^{46}). The traditions appear on literary grounds to have come from different sources; but there is no real difficulty in the narrative as it stands. Not only are man's motives often complex; but a woman would be likely to use different pleas to a husband and to a son, and if a mother can counsel her son to yield to his fear, a father would be more alive to the possibility of an outbreak of folly. On his way to Haran, Jacob passed a night at Bethel (cf 13^{3f}), and his sleep was, not unnaturally, disturbed by dreams; the cromlechs and stone terraces of the district seemed to arrange themselves into a ladder reaching from earth to heaven, with angels ascending and descending, whilst Yahweh Himself bent over him (28^{13} RSVm) with loving assurances. Reminded thus of the watchful providence of God, Jacob's alarms were transmuted into religious awe. He marked the sanctity of the spot by setting up as a sacred pillar the boulder on which his head had rested, and undertook to dedicate a tithe of all his gains. Thenceforward Bethel became a famous sanctuary, and Jacob himself visited it again (35^{1}; cf Hos 12^{4}).

Arrived at Haran, Jacob met in his uncle his superior for a time in the art of overreaching. By a ruse Laban secured fourteen years' service (29^{27}, Hos 12^{12}, Jth 8^{26}), to which six years more were added, under an ingenious arrangement in which the exacting uncle was at last outwitted (30^{31ff}). At the end of the term Jacob was the head of a household conspicuous even in those days for its magnitude and prosperity. Quarrels with Laban and his sons ensued, but God is represented as intervening to turn their arbitrary actions (31^{7ff}) to Jacob's advantage. At length he took flight whilst Laban was engaged in sheep-shearing, and, re-crossing the Euphrates on his way home, reached Gilead. There he was overtaken by Laban, whose exasperation was increased by the fact that his *teraphim*, or household gods, had been taken away by the fugitives, Rachel's hope in stealing them being to make Jacob the heir of her father. The dispute that followed was closed by an alliance of friendship, the double covenant being sealed by setting up in commemoration a cairn with a solitary boulder by its side (31$^{45f, 52}$), and by sharing a sacrificial meal. Jacob promised to treat Laban's daughters with special kindness, and both Jacob and Laban undertook to respect the boundary they had agreed upon between the territories of Israel and of the Syrians. Thereupon Laban returned home; and Jacob continued his journey to Canaan, and was met by the angels of God (32^{1}), as if to congratulate and welcome him as he approached the Land of Promise.

Jacob's next problem was to conciliate his brother, who was reported to be advancing against him with a large body of men (32^{6}). Three measures were adopted. When a submissive message elicited no response, Jacob in dismay turned to God, though without any expression of regret for the deceit by which he had wronged his brother, and proceeded to divide his party into two companies, in the hope that one at least would escape, and to try to appease Esau with a great gift. The next night came the turning-point in Jacob's life. Hitherto he had been ambitious, steady of purpose, subject to genuine religious feeling, but given up almost wholly to the use of crooked methods. Now the higher elements in his nature gain the ascendancy; and henceforth, though he is no less resourceful and politic, his fear of God ceases to be spoilt by intervening passions or a competing self-confidence. Alone on the banks of the Jabbok (*Wâdī Zerkā*), full of doubt as to the fate that would overtake him, he recognizes at last that his real antagonist is not Esau but God. All his fraud and deceit had been pre-eminently sin against God; and what he needed supremely was not reconciliation with his brother, but the blessing of God. So vivid was the impression, that the entire night seemed to be spent in actual wrestling with a living man. His thigh was sprained in the contest; but since his will was so fixed that he simply would not be refused, the blessing came with the daybreak (32^{28}). His name was changed to *Israel*, which means etymologically 'God perseveres,' but was applied to Jacob in the sense of Perseverer with God' (Hos 12^{3f}). And as a name was to a Hebrew a symbol of nature (Is 1^{26} 61^{3}), its change was a symbol of a changed character; and the supplanter became the one who persevered in putting forth his strength in communion with God, and therefore prevailed. His brother received him cordially (33^{4}), and offered to escort him during the rest of the journey. The offer was courteously declined, ostensibly because of the difference of pace between the two companies, but probably also with a view to incur no obligation and to risk no rupture. Esau returned to Seir; and Jacob moved on to a suitable site for an encampment, which received the name of Succoth, from the booths that were erected on it (33^{17}). It was east of the Jordan, and probably not far from the junction with the Jabbok. The valley was suitable for the recuperation of the flocks and herds after so long a journey; and it is probable, from the character of the buildings erected, as well as from the fact that opportunity must be given for Dinah, one of the youngest of the children (30^{21}), to reach a marriageable age (34^{2ff}), that Jacob stayed there for several years.

After a residence of uncertain length at Succoth, Jacob crossed the Jordan and advanced to **Shechem**, where he purchased a plot of ground which became afterwards of special interest. Joshua seems to have regarded it as the limit of his expedition, and there the Law was promulgated and Joseph's bones were buried (Jos 24$^{25, 32}$; cf Ac 7^{16}); and for a time it was the centre of the confederation of the northern tribes (1 K 12[1], 2 Ch 10[1]). Again Jacob's stay must not be measured by days; for he erected an altar (33[20]) and dug a well (Jn 4[6, 12]), and was detained by domestic troubles, if not of his own original intention. The troubles began with the seduction or outrage of Dinah; but the narrative that follows is evidently compacted of two traditions. According to the one, the transaction was personal, and involved a fulfilment by Shechem of a certain unspecified condition; according to the other, the entire clan was involved on either side, and the story is that of the danger of the absorption of Israel by the local Canaanites and its avoidance through the interposition of Simeon and Levi. But most of the difficulties disappear on the assumption that Shechem's marriage was, as was natural, expedited, a delight to himself and generally approved amongst his kindred (34[19]). That pressing matter being settled, the question of an alliance between the two clans, with the sinister motives that prevailed on either side, would be gradually, perhaps slowly, brought to an issue. There would be time to persuade the Shechemites to consent to be circumcised, and to arrange for the treacherous reprisal. Jacob's part in the proceedings was confined chiefly to a timid reproach of his sons for entangling his household in peril, to which they replied with the plea that the honour of the family was the first consideration.

The state of feeling aroused by the vengeance executed on Shechem made it desirable for Jacob to continue his journey. He was directed by God to proceed some twenty miles southwards to Bethel. Before starting, due preparations were made for a visit to so sacred a spot. The amulets and images of foreign gods in the possession of his retainers were collected and buried under a terebinth (35[4]; cf Jos 24[26], Jg 9[6]). The people through whom he passed were smitten with such a panic by the news of what had happened at Shechem as not to interfere with him. Arrived at Bethel, he added an altar (35[7]) to the monolith he had erected on his previous visit, and received in a theophany, for which in mood he was well prepared, a renewal of the promise of regal prosperity. The additional pillar he set up (35[14]) was probably a sepulchral stele to the memory of Deborah (cf 35[20]), dedicated with appropriate religious services; unless the verse is out of place in the narrative, and is really J's version of what E relates in 28[18]. From Bethel Jacob led his caravan to Ephrath, a few miles from which place Rachel died in childbirth. This Ephrath was evidently not far from Bethel, and well to the north of Jerusalem (1 S 10[2f], Jer 31[15]); and therefore the gloss 'the same is Bethlehem' must be due to a confusion with the other Ephrath (Ru 4[11], Mic 5[2]), which was S. of Jerusalem. The next stopping-place was the tower of Eder (35[21]) or 'the flock'—a generic name for the watch-towers erected to aid in the protection of the flocks from robbers and wild beasts. Mic 4[8] applies a similar term to the fortified southern spur of Zion. But it cannot be proved that the two allusions coalesce; and actually nothing is known of the site of Jacob's encampment, except that it was between Ephrath and Hebron. His journey was ended when he reached the last-named place (35[27]), the home of his fathers, where he met Esau again, and apparently for the last time, at the funeral of Isaac.

From the time of his return to Hebron, Jacob ceases to be the central figure of the Biblical narrative, which thenceforward revolves round Joseph. Among the leading incidents are Joseph's mission to inquire after his brethren's welfare, the inconsolable sorrow of the old man on the receipt of what seemed conclusive evidence of Joseph's death, the despatch of his surviving sons except Benjamin to buy corn in Egypt (cf Ac 7[12ff]), the bitterness of the reproach with which he greeted them on their return, and his belated and despairing consent to another expedition as the only alternative to death from famine. The story turns next to Jacob's delight at the news that Joseph is alive, and to his own journey to Egypt through Beersheba, his early home, where he was encouraged by God in visions of the night (46[1-7]). In Egypt he was met by Joseph, and, after an interview with the Pharaoh, settled in the pastoral district of Goshen (47[6]), afterwards known as 'the land of Rameses' (from Rameses II. of the 19th Dynasty), in the eastern part of the Delta (47[11]). This migration of Jacob to Egypt was an event of the first magnitude in the history of Israel (Dt 26[5f], Ac 7[14f]), as a stage in the great providential preparation for Redemption. Jacob lived in Egypt seventeen years (47[28]), at the close of which, feeling death to be nigh, he extracted a pledge from Joseph to bury him in Canaan, and adopted his two grandsons, placing the younger first in anticipation of the pre-eminence of the tribe that would descend from him (48[19], He 11[21]). To Joseph himself was promised, as a token of special affection, the conquered districts of Shechem on the lower slopes of Gerizim (48[22], Jn 4[5]). Finally, the old man gathered his sons about him, and pronounced upon each in turn a blessing, afterwards wrought up into the elaborate poetical form of 49[2-27]. The tribes are reviewed in order, and the character of each is sketched in a description of that of its founder. The atmosphere of the poem in regard alike to geography and to history is that of the period of the judges and early kings, when, therefore, the genuine tradition must have taken the form in which it has been preserved. After blessing his sons, Jacob gave them together the directions concerning his funeral which he had given previously to Joseph, and died (49[33]). His body was embalmed, convoyed to Canaan by a great procession according to the Egyptian custom, and buried in the cave of Machpelah near Hebron (50[13]).

Opinion is divided as to the degree to which Jacob has been idealized in the Biblical story. If it be remembered that the narrative is based upon popular oral tradition, and did not receive its present form until long after the time to which it relates, and that an interest in national origins is both natural and distinctly manifested in parts of Genesis, some idealization may readily be conceded. It may be sought in three directions—in the attempt to find explanations of existing institutions, in the anticipation of religious conceptions and sentiments that belonged to the narrator's times, and in the investment of the reputed ancestor with the characteristics of the tribe descended from him. All the conditions are best met by the view that Jacob was a real person, and that the incidents recorded of him are substantially historical. His character, as depicted, is a mixture of evil and good; and his career shows how, by discipline and grace, the better elements came to prevail, and God was enabled to use a faulty man for a great purpose.

2. Father of Joseph, the husband of Mary (Mt 1[15f]).

R. W. M.

JACOB'S WELL.—See SYCHAR.

JACUBUS, 1 Es 9[48] (AV, RV).—See AKKUB, **4**.

JADA.—A Jerahmeelite, 1 Ch 2[28, 32].

JADAU, Ezr 10[43] (AV).—See IDDO, **3**.

JADDUA.—**1.** One of those who sealed the covenant, Neh 10[21]. **2.** A high priest, Neh 12[11, 22]. He is doubtless the Jaddua who is named by Josephus in connexion with Alexander the Great (Jos. *Ant.* XI. viii. 4 [326]).

JADDUS.—A priest whose descendants were unable to trace their genealogy at the return under Zerubbabel, and were removed from office, 1 Es 5[38] (AV **Addus**). He is said to have married Agia (AV, RV Augia), a daughter of Barzillai (AV Berzelus, RV Zorzelleus). In Ezr 2[61], Neh 7[63] he is called **Barzillai.**

JADON.—A Meronothite (q.v.), who took part in rebuilding the wall of Jerusalem, Neh 3[7]. According to Josephus (*Ant.* VIII. viii. 5 [231], ix. 1 [241]), Jadon was the name of the man of God sent from Judah to Jeroboam (1 K 13). Rabbinic tradition identifies the prophet from Judah with Iddo, **6** (cf 2 Ch 9[29]).

JAEL.—The wife of Heber, the Kenite (Jg 4[11, 17] 5[24]), is celebrated both in prose (Jg 4[17-22]) and in poetry (Jg 5[24-27]) as the heroine who disposed of Sisera, the commander of Jabin's Canaanite forces, when he fled after his army was defeated by the Israelites under Barak at the R. Kishon.

The prose version gives details lacking in the poem where there is no mention of Sisera's going inside Jael's tent (Jg 4^{18ff}), nor of his murder taking place while he is asleep (4^{21}), nor of Barak arriving and being asked inside to see the result of Jael's action.

The poetical version (part of the ' Song of Deborah,' and so probably contemporary) concentrates on the two main actions, viz. the giving of special hospitality, and Jael's adroit seizing of the tent-peg and mallet to give the blow that brings Sisera to his knees to meet his death, as she shattered his head, ' pierced, spilled out his brains ' (so C. A. Simpson for the RSV ' and pierced his temple,' v.^{26b}). The fall of Sisera was complete at Jael's feet (literally ' between her feet ').

The question of whether the scene of the murder was inside the tent or outside ; or whether Sisera is lying asleep or standing drinking, as the poem seems to suggest, is not readily solved. In the poem (v.^{24}) Jael is described as ' of tent-dwelling women ' (literally ' from women in the tent ' ; RV ' above women in the tent '), and it may be that this phrase ' in the tent ' has determined the later prose writer's account.

The ascription of Jg 5^{24} ' most blessed of women be Jael ' is in keeping with the tense emotional enthusiasm of victory evident in the rest of the poem, that Israel was released from ' being oppressed cruelly ' by Jabin (Jg 4^{3}).

In Jg 5^{6} the words ' in the days of Jael ' are clearly a gloss intended to act as a preface to the later verses about Jael whose tent was possibly some 5 or 6 miles from the scene of the battle, cf Jg 4^{11}. The Kenites had been traditionally friendly to the Israelites, cf Jg 1^{16}.

R. A. B.

JAGUR.—A town in the extreme south of Judah, Jos 15^{21}. The site is unknown.

JAH.—Short form of Yahweh (see God, **4** [*c*]), found in Ps 68^{4} (AV, RV) 89^{8} (RV), and Ex 15^{2}, Is 12^{2} 26^{4} (all RVm).

JAHATH.—**1.** A grandson of Judah, 1 Ch 4^{2}. **2.** A great-grandson of Levi, 1 Ch $6^{20, 43}$. **3.** A son of Shimei, 1 Ch 23^{10}. **4.** One of the ' sons ' of Shelomoth, 1 Ch 24^{22}. **5.** A Merarite Levite in the time of Josiah, 2 Ch 34^{12}.

JAHAZ.—A town at which Sihon was defeated by Israel, Nu 21^{23}, Dt 2^{32}, Jg 11^{20}. After crossing the Arnon, messengers were sent to Sihon from ' the wilderness of Kedemoth,' Dt 2^{26}, and he ' went out against Israel to the wilderness and came to Jahaz,' Nu 21^{23}. Jahaz is mentioned in connexion with Kedemoth, Jos 13^{18} (AV **Jahaza**) 21^{36f} (AV **Jahazah**). These passages indicate a position for Jahaz in the SE. portion of Sihon's territory. Jahaz was one of the Levitical cities of Reuben belonging to the children of Merari, Jos 13^{18} 21^{36} (see note in RVm), 1 Ch 6^{78} (here called **Jahzah**). According to the Moabite Stone (ll. 18–20), the king of Israel dwelt at Jahaz while at war with king Mesha, but was driven out, and the town was taken and added to Moabite territory. It was later in the possession of Moab, Is 15^{4}, Jer 48^{21} (AV **Jahazah** ; RV, RSV **Jahzah**),^{34}. Various identifications have been proposed, but the location is uncertain.

JAHAZA.—Jos 13^{18} (AV).—See Jahaz.

JAHAZAH.—Jos 21^{36}, Jer 48^{21} (AV).—See Jahaz.

JAHAZIEL.—**1.** A Benjamite who joined David at Ziklag, 1 Ch 12^{4}. **2.** One of the two priests who blew trumpets before the Ark when it was brought by David to Jerusalem, 1 Ch 16^{6}. **3.** A Kohathite Levite, 1 Ch 23^{19} 24^{23}. **4.** An Asaphite Levite who encouraged Jehoshaphat and his army against an invading host, 2 Ch 20^{14}. **5.** The ancestor of a family of exiles who returned, Ezr 8^{5}, 1 Es 8^{32} (AV, RV **Jezelus**).

JAHDAI.—A Calebite, 1 Ch 2^{47}.

JAHDIEL.—A Manassite chief, 1 Ch 5^{24}.

JAHDO.—A Gadite, 1 Ch 5^{14}.

JAHLEEL.—Third son of Zebulun, Gn 46^{14}, Nu 26^{26} ; patronymic, **Jahleelites,** Nu 26^{26}.

JAHMAI.—A man of Issachar, 1 Ch 7^{2}.

JAHZAH.—See Jahaz.

JAHZEEL.—Naphtali's firstborn, Gn 46^{24}, Nu 26^{48} ; called **Jahziel** in 1 Ch 7^{13} ; patronymic, **Jahzeelites,** Nu 26^{48}.

JAHZEIAH.—One of four men who are mentioned as opposing (so RV, RSV) Ezra in the matter of the foreign wives, Ezr 10^{15}. The AV regarded Jahzeiah and his companions as supporters of Ezra, rendering ' were employed about this matter.' This view is supported by LXX, 1 Es 9^{14} (RSV ; AV **Ezechias,** RV **Ezekias**) ; but the Hebrew phrase here found elsewhere (cf 1 Ch 21^{1}, 2 Ch 20^{23}, Dn 11^{14}) expresses *opposition.*

JAHZERAH.—A priest, 1 Ch 9^{12} ; called **Ahzai,** Neh 11^{13} (AV **Ahasai**).

JAHZIEL.—See Jahzeel.

JAIR.—**1.** Eponym of a clan of Manasseh who lived on the E. of Jordan, Nu 32^{41}, Du 3^{14}, Jos 13^{30}, 1 K 4^{13}. The settlement of this clan marks a subsequent conquest to that of the W. of the Jordan. The gentilic **Jairite** is used for Ira, 2 S 20^{26}. **2.** One of the minor Judges, Jg 10^{3ff}. The ' villages of Jair ' (see Havvoth-jair), which are said to have been taken by **1,** were occupied by his sons, who equalled them in number. It is possible that there is some confusion between **1** and **2.** **3.** The father of Mordecai, Est 2^{5}. **4.** The father of Elhanan, 1 Ch 20^{5}. See Elhanan, Jaare-oregim.

JAIRUS (=**Jair**).—This Greek form of the name is used in the Apocrypha (Ad. Est 11^{2}) for Mordecai's father **Jair** (Est 2^{5}) ; and in 1 Es 5^{31} (RV ; AV **Airus,** RSV **Reaiah** ; see Reaiah, 3) for the head of a family of Temple servants. In NT it is the name of the ruler of the synagogue whose daughter Jesus raised from the dead (Mk 5^{22}, Lk 8^{41}). In ‖ Mt (9^{18}) he is not named.

A. J. M.

JAKAN, 1 Ch 1^{42} (AV).—See Jaakan.

JAKEH.—Father of Agur, the author of the proverbs contained in Pr 30.

JAKIM.—**1.** A Benjamite, 1 Ch 8^{19}. **2.** A priest, head of the 12th course, 1 Ch 24^{12}.

JALAM.—A ' son ' of Esau, Gn $36^{5, 14, 18}$, 1 Ch 1^{35} (AV **Jaalam** in all places).

JALON.—A Calebite, 1 Ch 4^{17}.

JAMBRES.—See Jannes and Jambres.

JAMBRI.—The name of an Arab group near Medeba who slew John the Maccabee and took as booty the cattle he was leading for safety into Nabataean territory, an outrage which was avenged by Simon and Jonathan, who slaughtered these ' sons of Jambri ' (probably *Banu Amri*) as they were returning from a wedding celebration (1 Mac 9^{35-42}). A. J.

JAMES.—**1. James, the son of Zebedee,** one of the Twelve, the elder brother of John. Their father was a Galilaean fisherman, evidently in a thriving way, since he employed ' hired servants ' (Mk 1^{20}). Their mother was Salome, and, since she was apparently a sister of the Virgin Mary (cf Mt 27^{56}=Mk 15^{40} with Jn 19^{25}), they were cousins of Jesus after the flesh. Like his brother, James worked with Zebedee in partnership with Simon and Andrew (Lk 5^{10}), and he was busy with boat and nets when Jesus called him to leave all and follow Him (Mt 4^{21f}=Mk 1^{19f}). His name is coupled with John's in the lists of the Apostles (Mt 10^{2}= Mk 3^{17}=Lk 6^{14}), which means that, when the Twelve were sent out two by two to preach the Kingdom of God (Mk 6^{7}), they went in company. And they seem to have been men of like spirit. They got from Jesus the same appellation, ' the Sons of Thunder ' (see Boanerges), and they stood, with Simon Peter, on terms of special intimacy with Him. James attained less distinction than his brother, but the reason is not that he had less devotion or aptitude, but that his life came to an untimely end. He was martyred by Herod Agrippa (Ac 12^{2}).

2. James, the son of Alphaeus (sometimes identified with **Clopas** of Jn 19^{25}), styled 'the Little' or 'the Younger' (not 'the Less'), probably on account of the shortness of his stature, to distinguish him from the other Apostle James, the son of Zebedee. He had a brother Joses, who was apparently a believer. See Mk 15^{40}, Jn 19^{25}, Mk 16^{1}.

3. James, the Lord's brother (see BRETHREN OF THE LORD). Like the rest of the Lord's brethren, James did not believe in Him while He lived, but acknowledged His claims after the Resurrection. He was won to faith by a special manifestation of the risen Lord (1 Co 15^{7}). Thereafter he rose to high eminence. He was the head of the Church at Jerusalem, and figures in that capacity on three occasions. (1) Three years after his conversion Paul went up to Jerusalem to interview Peter, and, though he stayed for fifteen days with him, he saw no one else except James (Gal 1^{18f}). So soon did James's authority rival Peter's. (2) After an interval of fourteen years Paul went up again to Jerusalem (Gal 2^{1-10}). This was the occasion of the historic conference regarding the terms on which the Gentiles should be admitted into the Christian Church; and James acted as president, his decision being unanimously accepted (Ac 15^{4-34}). (3) James was the acknowledged head of the Church at Jerusalem, and when Paul returned from his third missionary journey he waited on him and made a report to him in presence of the elders (Ac 21^{18-19}).

According to extra-canonical tradition, James was surnamed 'the Just'; he was a Nazirite from his mother's womb, abstaining from strong drink and animal food, and wearing linen; he was always kneeling in intercession for the people, so that his knees were callous like a camel's; he was cruelly martyred by the Scribes and Pharisees; they cast him down from the pinnacle of the Temple (cf Mt 4^{5}, Lk 4^{9}), and as the fall did not kill him they stoned him, and he was finally despatched with a fuller's club.

4. James, the father of the Apostle Judas (Lk 6^{16} RSV), otherwise unknown. The AV 'Judas the *brother* of James' is an impossible identification of the Apostle Judas with the author of the Epistle (Jd ^{1}).

D. S.—O. J. F. S.

JAMES, THE EPISTLE OF.—1. The author is described as 'James, a servant of God and of the Lord Jesus Christ' (1^{1}). Since the name (in Gr. *Jakōbos*) was common among Jews, appearing twice in lists of the Twelve (Mt 10^{2f}, Mk 3^{17f}, Lk 6^{14f}, Ac 1^{13}), and 'servant of God' is capable of general application, this description suffers from ambiguity which the Epistle fails to relieve. However, since the 3rd cent., ecclesiastical tradition has tended to assign it to the Lord's brother (see JAMES, 3). Origen (*c* 185–254), the earliest writer to quote it by name, according to the Latin version of his *Homilies* referred to its author as both Apostle and brother of the Lord. In spite of such attributions the Epistle was still disputed in the 4th cent. (Eusebius, *HE* ii. 23. 25, iii. 25. 3). According to Jerome it had at one time been asserted that the Epistle was published by some one else in the name of James (*de viris illustribus*, ii). In support of the traditional authorship it has been argued that if the Epistle had been pseudonymous, the writer would have defined the position of the James whose authority he wished to claim, and that the same objection holds good against any theory of interpolation. Again, it has been urged that if it had been written by a later James under his own name, he would have distinguished himself from his better known namesakes.

Quite different conclusions have been drawn from the address 'To the twelve tribes in the dispersion.' Since Christ is mentioned only twice by name (here and 2^{1}), the suggestion was made by F. Spitta (1896) that we have really a Jewish document which has been adapted by a Christian writer, as happened, *e.g.* with 2 Esdras and the *Didache*. To this it is objected that no editor would have been satisfied with so slight a revision. Arnold Meyer (1930) sought to solve what he termed 'the riddle' of this Epistle by positing a basic document addressed 'Jacob to the twelve patriarchs,' similar in character to the *Testaments of the Twelve Patriarchs*, a moralistic work composed near the end of the 2nd cent. B.C. In it the dictum of our author in 4^{7} 'the devil . . . will flee from you' is repeated at least four times with variations; other similarities to the thought of this Epistle are recognized. There seems to be nothing against the view that our author was familiar with the *Testaments* and freely appropriated some of their leading ideas. Indeed affinities between the Epistle and such works as 1 Clement and the Shepherd of Hermas may be accounted for by their authors' independent use of the same sources (see **4**). The 'scripture' cited in 4^{5} may have been one of the lost apocrypha, but the quotation in the next verse from Pr 3^{34} conforms to the LXX against the Hebrew (cf 1 P 5^{5}), as does the quotation from Gn 15^{6} in 2^{23} (cf Ro 4^{3}, Gal 3^{6}). Such dependence on the Greek version, together with the idiomatic rhetorical style, which is that of the Hellenistic diatribe, tends to exclude any theory of translation from Aramaic and to cast doubt on the traditional authorship. To this its defender may reply that we really know very little of the scope of Jewish education and that there was every opportunity for contact with Greeks in Galilee. Attention is also called to the remarkable coincidence in language between this Epistle and the speech of James in Ac 15.

On the other hand, it is no less remarkable that the Epistle contains no reference whatever to the central issues raised in Ac 15, viz. a demand for the circumcision of Gentile converts and a counter-proposal by James that they abstain from 'blood,' defined in most MSS as 'things strangled' (cf Lv 17^{10}). Paul, too, indicates that James was more conservative than Peter in this controversy (Gal 2^{12}), reminding his readers that if they accept circumcision they become obligated to keep the whole law with all its ritual observances (*ib.* 5^{3}). But when our author says that 'the whole law' must be kept, he refers only to ethical demands of the Decalogue (2^{10-12}), as if the debate over ceremonial and dietary regulations were long forgotten. [See further, **2** (*a*).]

2. Date.—The only indications of date are derived from indirect, internal evidence, the interpretation of which depends on the view taken of the main problems raised by the Epistle. It is variously put, either as one of the earliest of NT writings, or among the very latest. At one time it could be reported that an early date was given by 'most English writers,' limiting late dating to 'the general German opinion.' But among the authors of leading NT introductions and commentaries published in England and the U.S. during the past fifty years, such scholars as J. Moffatt, J. H. Ropes, and other commentators support a comparatively late date (A.D. 75–125), against J. B. Mayor, for example, who argued for the decade A.D. 40–50, or prior to the controversy of Ac 15. B. S. Easton, who adopted in modified form the views of Arnold Meyer (see above, **1**), placed the date of the Christian edition of James somewhere between A.D. 80 and 100 (*IB* xii, 14 ff). The chief problem is *the relationship to other writings of the NT*. The Epistle has striking resemblances to several books of the NT, and these resemblances have received various explanations.

(*a*) Most important is its *relation to St. Paul*. It has points of contact with Romans: 1^{22} 4^{11} and Ro 2^{13} (hearers and doers of the law); 1^{2-4} and Ro 5^{3-5} (the gradual work of temptation or tribulation); 4^{11} and Ro 2^{1} 14^{4} (the critic self-condemned); 1^{21} 4^{1} and Ro 7^{23} 13^{12}; and the contrast between 2^{21} and Ro 4^{1} (the faith of Abraham). Sanday and Headlam (*Romans*, p. lxxix) see 'no resemblances in style sufficient to prove literary connexion'; Mayor, on the other hand, supposes that St. Paul is working up hints received from James. But, as Montgomery notes (Hastings, *DAC*, i, p. 630) our author's exegetical *tour de force* in appealing to Gn 15^{6}, which is more favourable to Paul's argument than to his own, is not the procedure of a writer choosing his illustrations freely. This suggests that the priority belongs to Paul rather than to this Epistle.

The main question turns upon the apparent opposition between James and Paul with regard to '*faith and works.*' The chief passages are ch. 2, especially vv.$^{17, 21ff}$, and Ro 3^{28} 4, Gal 2^{16}. Both writers quote Gn 15^{6}, and deal with the case of Abraham as typical, but they draw from it apparently opposite conclusions—St. James that a man is justified, as Abraham was, by works and not by faith alone; St. Paul that justification is not by works but by faith. It is generally recognized that there is no real contradiction between the two. The writers mean different things by 'faith.' W. H. P. Hatch points out that while for Paul 'faith' is at once belief, trust, and loyalty, it is particularly the means whereby the believer comes into mystical union with Christ and receives the gift of the Spirit (see *The Pauline Idea of Faith in Its Relation to Jewish and Hellenistic Religion*, 1917). For the writer of this Epistle, 'faith' means primarily intellectual acceptance of the proposition that 'God is one,' shared even by demons (2^{19}), and, in contrast to doubt, the necessary condition for receiving any request from God (1$^{6-7}$). Similarly, for Paul the term 'works' is applicable only to human activity for which 'wages' are due, in contrast to the divine gift of grace; more specifically Paul speaks of 'works of the law,' including such ritual requirements as circumcision (Ro 3^{21}–4^{12}). For our author 'works' appear as the natural accompaniment of a vital faith, in contrast to one which he pronounces 'barren' or 'dead' (2$^{20, 26}$). Careful reading of the whole argument in 2$^{8-26}$ suggests that the Epistle was written, not only after Paul's views on 'justification by faith' had been put forward, but to correct misunderstandings of his teaching, which no doubt easily arose (2 P 3^{16}).

(*b*) The *points of contact with* 1 *Peter* (1^{10} 5^{20} with 1 P 1^{24} 4^{8}) and *Hebrews* (2^{25} with He 11^{31}), though striking, are inconclusive as to date. If direct literary dependence is to be considered, comparison of the crisp aphorism of 4^{7} with the more diffuse sentiment of 1 P 5^{8f} suggests that priority should be assigned to the former. However, the theory advanced by P. Carrington (in *The Primitive Christian Catechism*, 1940), that a common pattern of catechetical instruction may account for this and numerous other parallels in 1 Peter and James, as well as Colossians and Ephesians, has much to commend it.

(*c*) It will be convenient to treat here *the relation to the Gospels and particularly to the Sermon on the Mount*, though this too is not decisive as to date. While the variations are too strong to allow us to suppose direct literary reference to the written text, familiarity with teaching epitomized in *Matthew* is evident. Among the chief parallels are the condemnation of 'hearers only' (1$^{22, 25}$, Mt 7^{26}), of critics (4^{11}, Mt 7$^{1-5}$), of worldliness (1^{10} 2$^{5-6}$, Mt 6$^{19, 24}$); the teaching about prayer (1^{5}, Mt 7^{7}), concern for 'tomorrow' (4^{13}, Mt 6^{34}), references to 'moth and rust' (5$^{2-3}$, Mt 6^{19}), humility (4^{10}, Mt 23^{12}), the tree and its fruit (3^{12}, Mt 7^{16}). In relation to the injunction against swearing, it is pointed out that 5^{12} has a remarkable agreement with Justin (*Ap.* i. 16), as against Mt 5^{37}. But Ropes rejects the theory that James and Justin here show traces of oral tradition independent of *Matthew* as 'unlikely and unnecessary.' M. H. Shepherd, likewise, attributes the parallels to our author's familiarity with the Gospel and suggests a Syrian provenance for the Epistle (*JBL*, lxxv, 1956, pp. 40–51). In any case, such familiarity as its author shows with the teaching of Jesus can hardly be said to lend weight to his traditional identification as the Lord's brother.

3. The type of Christianity implied in the Epistle.—Opinions on this point are closely related to the foregoing questions, and vary accordingly. Upholders of the traditional authorship emphasize that the general tone of the Epistle is Judaic. The type of organization implied is said to be primitive, described mainly in Jewish phraseology: synagogue (2^{2} RV), elders of the church (5^{14}), anointing with oil and the connexion of sin and sickness (*ib*). Abraham is 'our father' (2^{21}), and God bears the OT title 'Lord of Sabaoth' (5^{4}) [here only in NT]. To this it may be replied that the term 'synagogue' was still applied to a Christian assembly for worship by 2nd cent. writers like Ignatius (*ad Polyc.* 4^{2}) and Hermas (*Mand.* xi. 9, 13–14). Hermas too speaks of presiding elders of the church (*Vis.* ii. 4. 2). Abraham is called 'our father' in 1 Clem 31^{2} and 'father of Gentiles who believe' in *Ep. Barn.* 13^{7} (cf Ro 4^{11f}). Even the title 'Lord of Sabaoth' occurs in 1 Clem 34^{6} citing Is 6^{3}. None of these expressions, therefore, furnishes compelling evidence either of Jewish Christian origin or of early date.

On the other hand, many critics see in the conditions with which the Epistle deals the description of a later age, when Christianity had had time to become formal and secularized, and moral degeneracy was disguised by intellectual orthodoxy. We may indeed believe that the Epistle has not yet yielded its full secret. It cannot be denied that it omits much that we should expect to find in a Christian document, and that its close is very abrupt. It is scarcely surprising that its epistolary address (1^{1}) has been suspected as a later addition to a homily originally intended for oral delivery.

4. Early quotations and canonicity.—Classifying James among the 'disputed' books of the NT, Eusebius observed 'not many of the ancients have mentioned it' (*HE* ii. 23. 25). Among the 'ancients' who were formerly thought to have shown familiarity with the Epistle are Clement of Rome and Hermas. A leading example is the use of the Greek term *dipsychos*, 'double-minded' (1^{8} 4^{8}), which our author was supposed to have coined (Moulton and Milligan, *Vocab. of the Greek Testament*, p. 166). However, this term occurs in a quotation from an unnamed apocryphal 'scripture' in 1 Clem 23^{3}, 2 Clem 11^{2}, apparently alluded to also by Hermas in *Mand.* ix. 5. Evidence suggests that James derived the term from the same source (*JBL* lxiii, 1944, pp. 131–140; lxvi, 1947, pp. 211–219). A rival view is that James shows indebtedness to 1 Clement (*JBL* lxvii, 1948, pp. 339–345). In the Muratorian fragment, James, along with Hebrews, 1 and 2 Peter, and at least one of the Johannine epistles, failed to receive any mention among the canonical books. Other evidence also indicates that it was acknowledged earlier in the East than in the West. The scarcity of early quotations from it has suggested that others before Luther may have found it 'an epistle of straw.' Yet when the author's purpose is understood, such a verdict must appear manifestly unfair.

5. Style and teaching.—While much of the thought of the Epistle can be illustrated from the OT and documents of late Judaism, the author's vocabulary and literary style, as indicated above (**1**), is Hellenistic. As in Hebrew wisdom literature, its subject-matter consists of a rather miscellaneous collection of moral maxims and exhortations loosely strung together, one idea suggesting another often by the mere association of a single word. Many of these ideas, *e.g.* endurance under trial, or humiliation; wisdom as a gift to be sought from God; the need for faith and avoidance of a divided heart in approaching God; God's mercy toward those who love Him, etc., are found in similarly close association in Ecclesiasticus (chs. 1–2). It is probable, therefore, that our author was well-acquainted with the Wisdom of Jesus the son of Sirach in its Greek version. Evidence of his familiarity with the Wisdom of Solomon is less extensive. The concept of double-mindedness, or as the Hebrew puts it literally 'a heart and a heart,' *i.e.* a double heart, has been detected in some of the recently discovered Dead Sea Scrolls (*ATR* xxxviii, 1956, pp. 166–175). But there is no sufficient reason to assume direct influence of any of these documents on our author's teaching, since the expression is found in 1 Ch 12^{33}, Ps 12^{2}. Later rabbinic exegesis developed the idea more fully in connexion with the two impulses of man's heart, tending toward good or evil. Our author's analysis of the origin of sin and temptation (1^{14}) is similar to the Jewish notion of the evil impulse, but he expresses it in characteristically Hellenistic phraseology, for which parallels can be found in 2 P 2^{18} and in Philo (*Quod omn. prob. liber* 22). Throughout the Epistle,

the author displays a fondness for pithy proverbs, rhetorical questions, and picturesque metaphors and similes. His main purpose was to encourage endurance under trials, together with consistency of life; and his leading ideas are the dangers of careless speech, of riches, of envious strife, and of worldliness, contrasted with the value of true faith, prayer, wisdom, and humility. The Epistle is essentially 'pragmatic': *i.e.* it insists that the test of belief lies in its 'value for conduct.' The writer's main interest lies in ethics, and he presents with sharp emphasis a side of Christianity which is always in danger of being forgotten. The practical mind will always feel the force of his message.
C. W. E.—**O. J. F. S.**

JAMES, PROTEVANGELIUM OF.—See Apocryphal New Testament, B **1.**

JAMIN.—1. A son of Simeon, Gn 46^{10}, Ex 6^{15}, Nu 26^{12}, 1 Ch 4^{24}. The gentilic name **Jaminites** occurs in Nu 26^{12}. **2.** A Judahite, 1 Ch 2^{27}. **3.** A priest (? or Levite) who took part in the promulgating of the Law, Neh 8^7, 1 Es 9^{48} (AV **Adinus,** RV **Iadinus**).

JAMLECH.—A Simeonite chief, 1 Ch 4^{34}.

JAMNIA (1 Mac 4^{15} 5^{58} 10^{69} 15^{40}, 2 Mac $12^{8f, 40}$).—The later name of **Jabneel** (q.v.). It is also known as **Jabneh** (2 Ch 26^6). Here was held the famous council of Jewish rabbis which settled the OT Canon (q.v.). For its location, near the coast, see Map 10 or 15. The gentilic name **Jamnites** occurs in 2 Mac 12^9 (AV, RV).

JANAI.—A Gadite chief, 1 Ch 5^{12} (AV **Jaanai**).

JANGLING.—'Jangling,' says Chaucer in the *Parson's Tale*, 'is whan man speketh to moche before folk, and clappeth as a mille, and taketh no kepe what he seith.' The word is used in AV in 1 Ti 1^6 'vain jangling' (RV 'vain talking,' RSV 'vain discussion'); and in the heading of 1 Ti 6 'to avoid profane janglings,' where it stands for 'babblings' in text (1 Ti 6^{20}); RSV has 'godless chatter.'

JANIM.—A town in the mountains of Hebron, near Beth-tappuah, Jos 15^{53} AV **Janum**); possibly modern *Benī Na'īm.*

JANNA, Lk 3^{24} (AV).—See Jannai.

JANNAI.—An ancestor of Jesus, Lk 3^{24} (AV **Janna**).

JANNES AND JAMBRES (or MAMBRES).—These names appear in 2 Ti 3^8 as those of two of the Egyptian magicians who opposed Moses, and so were symbolic of all who resisted and opposed the truth. In the Exodus story ($7^{11f. 22}$ $8^{7, 18f}$ 9^{11}) no names are mentioned, but these two names appear in various forms in the Talmud, Targums, and Rabbinic writings. Attempts to explain the names have so far remained guesses, and the probability is that they are meant to represent Egyptian names. Since in this letter to Timothy and in the literature of the Qumrân community they are referred to as familiarly known, it would seem that some Jewish apocryphon concerned with their story was in circulation in the 1st cent. B.C. This, or a Christian version of it, was known in the early Christian centuries. Theodoret (iii, 689, ed. Schultze) knew it as an oral tradition, but the references in Origen (*C. Celsum*, iv, 51; *Comment. in Matt.* xxvii, 8), in Ps.-Ambrose's commentary on 2 Timothy (*PL* xvii, 521), and the Ps.-Gelasian *Decretum de libris recipiendis et non recipiendis* (ed. von Dobschütz, p. 303) seem to be to a written work. The story was known to such pagan writers as Pliny, *Nat. Hist.* xxx, 11, Apuleius, *Apologia*, 90 and Numenius *Fragm.* 18, but is not mentioned by either Philo or Josephus in their accounts of Moses. Rabbinic tradition regarded them as sons and assistants of Balaam, famous for their power of flying through the air, who came to Egypt to be Pharaoh's magicians, opposed Moses in Egypt and at the Red Sea crossing, and distressed the Israelites during their desert wandering, where they were responsible for the incident of the golden calf. One tradition, which Muhammad later adopted into the Qur'an, told how the power of Moses and Aaron induced them to become proselytes. Christian tradition, both eastern and western, is largely dependent on 2 Timothy, and has used them as figures symbolic of Satanic arts and opposition to the truth. By the 5th cent. what were supposed to be their tombs were being visited by the curious.
A. J.

JANOAH.—1. A town in the northern mountains of Naphtali, near Kedesh, 2 K 15^{29}, possibly modern *Yānûḥ.* **2.** A place on the border of Ephraim, Jos 16^6 (AV **Janohah**); situated where the present *Kh. Yānûn* now stands, with the supposed tomb of Nun.

JANOHAH, Jos 16^{6f} (AV).—See Janoah, **2.**

JANUM, Jos 15^{53} (AV).—See Janim.

JAPHETH (Heb. *Yepheth*).—**1.** One of the sons of Noah. The meaning of the name is quite uncertain. Japheth and Shem acted modestly on the occasion of their father's drunkenness, and were in consequence blessed by Noah, $9^{23, 27}$. In Gn 9^{27} there is a play on the name—'God enlarge (*yapht*) Japheth [*i.e.* make room for him] and let him dwell in the tents of Shem.' The peoples connected with Japheth (10^{2-4}) occupy the northern portion of the known world, and include the Madai (Medes) on the E. of Assyria, Javan (Ionians, *i.e.* Greeks) on the W. coast and islands of Asia Minor, and Tarshish (? Tartessus) on the W. coast of Spain. On the two traditions respecting the sons of Noah see Ham. **2.** An unknown locality mentioned in Jth 2^{25}.
A. H. McN.

JAPHIA.—1. King of Lachish, defeated and slain by Joshua, Jos 10^{3ff}. **2.** One of David's sons born at Jerusalem, 2 S 5^{15}, 1 Ch 3^7 14^6. **3.** A town on the south border of Zebulun, Jos 19^{12}; probably the modern *Yâfā*, near the foot of the Nazareth hills.

JAPHLET.—An Asherite family, 1 Ch 7^{32f}.

JAPHLETI, Jos 16^3 (AV).—See Japhletites.

JAPHLETITES.—The name of an unidentified tribe mentioned in stating the boundaries of the children of Joseph, Jos 16^3 (AV **Japhleti**).

JAR.—See House, **9.**

JARAH.—A descendant of Saul, 1 Ch 9^{42}; called **Jehoaddah** in 8^{36} (AV **Jehoadah**).

JAREB.—The name of a King, according to AV and RV, Hos 5^{13} 10^6. It is not safe to pronounce dogmatically on the text and meaning. But our choice lies between two alternatives. If we adhere to the current text, we must regard **Jareb** (or *Jarib*) as a sobriquet coined by Hosea to indicate the love of conflict which characterized the Assyrian king. Thus 'King Jarib' = 'King Warrior,' 'King Striver,' 'King Combat,' or the like; and the events referred to are those of 738 B.C. (see 2 K 15^{19}). Most of the ancient versions support this, as, *e.g.* LXX 'King Jareim'; Symmachus and Vulgate 'King Avenger.' If we divide the Hebrew consonants differently we get 'the great king,' (so RSV) corresponding to the Assyrian *sharru rabbu* (cf 2 K $18^{19, 28}$, Is 36^4). It has even been thought that this signification may be accepted without any textual change. In any case linguistic and historical evidence is against the idea that Jareb is the proper name of an Assyrian or an Egyptian monarch. Other, less probable, emendations are 'king of Arabia,' king of Jathrib *or* of Aribi' (both in North Arabia).
J. T.

JARED.—The father of Enoch, Gn $5^{15f, 18-20}$, 1 Ch 1^2 (AV **Jered**), Lk 3^{37}.

JARESIAH, 1 Ch 8^{27} (AV).—See Jaareshiah.

JARHA.—An Egyptian slave who married the daughter of his master Sheshan, 1 Ch 2^{34f}.

JARIB, 1 Mac 14^{29} (AV).—See Jehoiarib.

JARIB.—1. The eponym of a Simeonite family, 1 Ch 4^{24}; called **Jachin** in Gn 46^{10}, Ex 6^{15}, Nu 26^{12}. **2.** One of the leading men who were sent by Ezra to Casiphia in search of Levites, Ezr 8^{16}, 1 Es 8^{44} (AV **Joribas,** RV **Joribus**). **3.** A priest who had married a foreign wife, Ezr 10^{18}, 1 Es 9^{19} (AV, RV **Joribus**).

JARIMOTH, 1 Es 9^{28} (AV, RV).—See JEREMOTH, **7.**

JARMUTH.—1. A royal city of the Canaanites, Jos 10^{3} etc., in the Shephēlah, assigned to Judah, Jos 15^{35}. It is probably identical with 'Jermucha' of the *Onomasticon* 10 Roman miles from Eleutheropolis, on the Jerusalem road. This is now *Khirbet Yarmûk*, about 8 miles N. of *Beit Jibrîn*. **2.** A city in Issachar, allotted to the Gershonite Levites, Jos 21^{29} (LXX^{B} *Remmath*). It corresponds to **Ramoth** in 1 Ch 6^{73}, and **Remeth** appears in Jos 19^{21} among the cities of Issachar. Albright suggests *Kôkab el-Hawâ*, but the site remains uncertain. W. E.—**H. H. R.**

JAROAH.—A Gadite chief (1 Ch 5^{14}).

JASAEL, 1 Es 9^{30} (AV).—See SHEAL.

JASAELUS, 1 Es 9^{30} (RV).—See SHEAL.

JASHAR, BOOK OF (*sēpher hay-yāshār*, 'Book of the Righteous One').—An ancient book of national songs, which most likely contained both religious and secular songs describing great events in the history of the nation. In the OT there are two quotations from this book—(*a*) Jos 10^{12f}; the original form must have been a poetical description of the battle of Gibeon, in which would have been included the old-world account of Yahweh casting down great stones from heaven upon Israel's enemies. (*b*) 2 S 1^{19-27}; in this case the quotation is a much longer one, consisting of David's lamentation over Saul and Jonathan. In each case the Book of Jashar is referred to as well known; one might expect therefore, that other quotations from it would be found in the OT, and perhaps this is actually the case with, *e.g.* the Song of Deborah (Jg 5) and some other ancient pieces, which originally may have had a reference to their sources in the title (*e.g.* 1 K 8^{12f}). W. O. E. O.

JASHEN.—The sons of Jashen are mentioned in the list of David's heroes given in 2 S 23^{32}. In the parallel list (1 Ch 11^{34}) they appear as the sons of **Hashem,** who is further described as the **Gizonite** (q.v.).

JASHOBEAM.—One of David's mighty men, 1 Ch 11^{11} 12^{6} 27^{2}. There is reason to believe that his real name was **Ishbosheth** (q.v.), *i.e.* Eshbaal ('man of Baal'). Cf JOSHEB-BASSHEBETH.

JASHUB.—1. Issachar's fourth son, Nu 26^{24}, 1 Ch 7^{1}; called **Iob** in Gn 46^{13} (AV **Job**); patronymic **Jashubites,** Nu 26^{24}. **2.** A returned exile who married a foreigner, Ezr 10^{29}, 1 Es 9^{30} (AV, RV **Jasubus**).

JASHUBI-LEHEM.—The eponym of a Judahite family, 1 Ch 4^{22} (AV, RV). The text is manifestly corrupt, and RSV renders 'and returned to Lehem.'

JASON.—This Greek name was adopted by many Jews whose Hebrew designation was Joshua (Jesus). **1.** The son of Eleazar deputed to make a treaty with the Romans, and father of Antipater who was later sent on a similar errand unless two different persons are meant (1 Mac 8^{17} 12^{16} 14^{22}). **2.** Jason of Cyrene, an author, of whose history 2 Maccabees (see $2^{23,26}$) is an epitome (written after 160 B.C.). **3.** Joshua the high priest, who ousted his brother Onias III. from the office in 174 B.C. (2 Mac 4^{7ff}), but was himself driven out three years later, and died among the Lacedaemonians at Sparta (2 Mac 5^{9f}). **4.** In Ac 17^{6ff} a Jason was St. Paul's host at Thessalonica, from whom the politarchs (RSV 'city authorities') took bail for his good behaviour, thus (as it seems) preventing St. Paul's return to Macedonia for a long time (see article PAUL THE APOSTLE). The Jason who sends greetings from Corinth in Ro 16^{21}, a 'kinsman' of St. Paul (*i.e.* a Jew), is probably the same man. A. J. M.

JASPER.—See JEWELS AND PRECIOUS STONES.

JASUBUS, 1 Es 9^{30} (AV, RV).—See JASHUB, **2.**

JATAL, 1 Es 5^{28} (AV).—See ATER, **1.**

JATHAN.—Son of Shemaiah 'the great,' and brother of Ananias the pretended father of Raphael, To 5^{15} (AV **Jonathas**).

JATHNIEL.—A Levitical family, 1 Ch 26^{2}.

JATTIR.—A Levitical city of Judah, in the southern mountains, Jos 15^{48} 21^{14}, 1 Ch 6^{57}. It was one of the cities to whose elders David sent of the spoil from Ziklag, 1 S 30^{27}. Its site is *Kh. 'Attîr*, NE. of Beersheba, on a hill spur close to the southern desert.

JAVAN, the Hebrew rendering of the Greek Iaōn, 'Ionian,' is a general term in the Bible for Ionians or Greeks; very similar forms of the name occur in the Assyrian and Egyptian inscriptions. In the genealogical table in Gn $10^{2,4}$ and 1 Ch $1^{5,7}$ Javan is described as a son of Japheth and the father of Elishah, Tarshish, Kittim, and Dodanim (or better, Rodanim, *i.e.* Rhodes); from the reference to **Kittim** (Kition) as his son, it is possible that the passage refers particularly to Cyprus. In Is 66^{19} Javan is included among the distant countries that will hear of Yahweh's glory. In Jl 3^{6} the sons of the Javanites (Greeks) are referred to as trading in Jewish captives with the Phoenicians and Philistines; in Ezk 27^{13} Javan, with Tubal and Meshech, is described as trading with Tyre in slaves and vessels of brass. In all three passages the references are to the Ionian colonies on the coast of Asia Minor. In Ezk 27^{19} (AV, RV) Javan appears a second time among the nations that traded with Tyre; clearly the Ionians are not intended, and, unless the text is corrupt (as is very probable; RSV renders 'wine'), the reference may be to an Arab tribe, or perhaps to a Greek colony in Arabia. See UZAL, **2.** In Dn 8^{21} 10^{20} 11^{2}, where 'the king,' 'the prince,' and 'the kingdom' of Javan (Greece) are mentioned, the passages have reference to the Graeco-Macedonian empire. L. W. K.

JAVELIN.—See ARMOUR, ARMS, **1** (*b*).

JAZAR, 1 Mac 5^{8} (AV).—See JAZER.

JAZER (Nu 21^{32}; AV **Jaazer**).—An Amorite town N. of Heshbon, taken by Israel, Nu 21^{32}; allotted to Gad (Jos 13^{25} etc.), and made a Levitical city (Jos 21^{39}, 1 Ch 6^{81}). It was fortified by Gad, Nu 32^{35} (AV **Jaazer**). It lay on the Ammonite border (Nu 21^{24}, where RSV reads 'Jazer was the boundary of the Ammonites' for AV, RV 'the boundary of the Ammonites was strong'), and was in a district rich in vines, Is 16^{8} etc., Jer 48^{32}. Judas Maccabaeus took the city which was then in the hands of the Ammonites, 1 Mac 5^{8} (AV **Jazar**), Jos. *Ant.* XII. viii. 1 [329]). It is probably modern *Kh. Jazzir*, near *es-Salt*. W. E.—**H. H. R.**

JAZIZ.—A Hagrite who was 'over the flocks' of king David, 1 Ch 27^{31}.

JEALOUSY.—Hebrew root *ḳ-n-'* (become dark-red, *i.e.* with emotion) is normally translated by LXX *zēloō* and derivatives. Both words indicate an intensity of emotion which may be directed towards a right or wrong exclusiveness. They are therefore sometimes translated in AV, RV by 'envy' (Ac 7^{9}) or 'zeal' (2 S 21^{2}) instead of 'jealousy.' In Biblical English 'jealous' retains a good sense as well as the bad sense which has largely dominated in modern English (but cf 'jealous for his country's honour'). Thus Elijah is 'jealous' for Yahweh (1 K 19^{10}) and Yahweh Himself is 'jealous' (Ex 20^{5}), and Paul has a 'divine jealousy' for the Corinthian Christians (2 Co 11^{2}); yet he himself can also say that love is not 'jealous' (RSV, 1 Co 13^{4}; AV 'envieth not'). Yahweh's own 'jealousy' is a strong emotion for what is right, especially with regard to the exclusive convenant-relationship of Israel with Himself alone (Ezk 8^{3}). He cannot brook any rivals in Israel's affections, and must punish Israel's defections from the covenant-relationship, and also those who seek to destroy that relationship from without (Nah 1^{2}). Thus 'jealousy' is often linked with marriage-bond metaphors (Nu 5^{11f}, Ezk 16^{38}, 2 Co 11^{2}).

The '**water of bitterness**' in Nu 5 was used in an instance of trial by ordeal, to determine whether a husband's jealous suspicions were rightly grounded or not. No doubt its efficacy lay in the state of the accused wife's mind, whether she knew herself to be guilty or innocent. The water itself, though decidedly unhygienic, was otherwise harmless, but a consciousness of guilt often produces somatic symptoms, and would do so more readily when the accused believed in the potency of the means enjoined. S. B. F.

JEARIM, MOUNT.—Mentioned only in Jos 15^{10}, where it is identified with **Chesalon** (q.v.).

JEATERAI, 1 Ch 6^{21} (AV).—See JEATHERAI.

JEATHERAI.—An ancestor of Asaph, 1 Ch 6^{21} (AV **Jeaterai**); called **Ethni** in v.^{41}.

JEBERECHIAH.—The father of Zechariah, a friend of Isaiah, Is 8^{2}.

JEBUS, JEBUSITES.—The Jebusites occur in numerous lists as one of the (mostly six) pre-Israelitish nations of Palestine (Ex $3^{8, 17}$ 23^{23} 33^{2}, Dt 7^{1}, Jos 3^{10} etc.). Repeatedly they are mentioned as the population of Jerusalem (Jos 15^{63}, Jg 1^{21}) for which reason Jerusalem occasionally is called 'Jebus' (Jos 18^{28}, Jg 19^{10}) or 'city of the Jebusites' (Jg 19^{11}). From the Egyptian execration texts (19th–18th cent. B.C.) and the Amarna Letters (14th cent. B.C.) it is evident that the official name of the city before the Hebrew conquest was Jerusalem (*Urusalim*). Hence, Jebus was used either merely as a popular name or officially only between the Amarna Age and the conquest of the city by David (Simons, *Jerusalem*, 1952, p. 247, n. 1). The Table of Nations declares the Jebusites to be descendants of Ham (Gn 10^{16}), but their ethnical origin is uncertain. The Jebusite Araunah (2 S 24^{16}) has a Hurrian name, while other pre-Hebrew kings of Jerusalem have either Amorite (Melchizedek = *Malki-ṣaduqa*, Gn 14^{18}; Adoni-zedek = *Aduna-ṣaduqa*, Jos 10^{1}) or Hittite names (*Abdu-Ḫeba* of the Amarna Letters). Ezekiel's claim that Jerusalem's aboriginal population had consisted of Amorites and Hittites ($16^{3, 45}$) is of interest in this connexion, indicating perhaps that the Jebusites had drawn their stock from these nations. Jebusites, like Araunah, remained in Jerusalem after David's conquest and were probably absorbed by the Israelites in the course of time. They are then lost from view.
S. H. Hn.

JECAMIAH, 1 Ch 3^{18} (AV).—See JEKAMIAH, **2.**

JECHILIAH, 2 Ch 26^{3} (RV).—See JECOLIAH.

JECHOLIAH, 2 K 15^{2} (AV).—See JECOLIAH.

JECHONIAH.—See JEHOIACHIN.

JECHONIAS.—**1.** The Greek form of the name of the king **Jeconiah** or **Jehoiachin** (q.v.). **2.** 1 Es 8^{92} (AV, RV); see SHECANIAH, **5.**

JECOLIAH.—The mother of King Uzziah, 2 K 15^{2} (AV **Jecholiah**), 2 Ch 26^{3} (RV **Jechiliah**).

JECONIAH.—**1.** See JEHOIACHIN. **2.** A Levite, 1 Es 1^{9} (RSV; AV, RV **Jeconias**); called **Conaniah** in 2 Ch 35^{9}. **3.** 1 Es 1^{34} (RSV; RVm **Jeconias**; AV, RV **Joachaz**); see JEHOAHAZ, **2.**

JECONIAS.—**1.** 1 Es 1^{9} (AV, RV); see JECONIAH, **2.** **2.** 1 Es 1^{34} (RVm); see JECONIAH, **3.**

JEDAIAH.—**1.** A priestly family, 1 Ch 9^{10} 24^{7}, Ezr 2^{36}, 1 Es 5^{24} (AV, RV **Jeddu**), Neh 7^{39} 11^{10} $12^{6f, 19, 21}$. **2.** One of the exiles sent with gifts of gold and silver for the sanctuary at Jerusalem, Zec $6^{10, 14}$. **3.** A Simeonite chief, 1 Ch 4^{37}. **4.** One of those who repaired the wall of Jerusalem, Neh 3^{10}.

JEDDU, 1 Es 5^{24} (V, ARV).—See JEDAIAH, **1.**

JEDEUS, 1 Es 9^{30} (AV, RV).—See ADAIAH, **6.**

JEDIAEL.—**1.** The eponym of a Benjamite family, 1 Ch $7^{6, 10f}$. **2.** One of David's heroes, 1 Ch 11^{45}; probably identical with the Manassite of 12^{20}. **3.** The eponym of a family of Korahite porters, 1 Ch 26^{2}.

JEDIDAH.—Mother of Josiah, 2 K 22^{1}.

JEDIDIAH ('beloved of Y″').—The name given to Solomon by the prophet Nathan (2 S 12^{25}) 'because of the Lord.' See SOLOMON.

JEDUTHUN.—An unintelligible name having to do with the music or the musicians of the Temple. According to 1 Ch 25^{1} etc., it was the name of one of the three musical guilds. *Jeduthun* occurs in the headings Pss 39, 62, 77, and appears to refer to an instrument or to a tune. But in our ignorance of Hebrew music it is impossible to do more than guess what Jeduthun really meant. See PSALMS, **2.**

JEELI, 1 Es 5^{33} (AV, RV).—See JAALAH.

JEELUS, 1 Es 8^{92} (AV, RV).—See JEHIEL, **8.**

JEEZER, Nu 26^{30} (AV).—See IEZER.

JEGAR-SAHADUTHA ('cairn of witness').—The name said to have been given by Laban to the cairn erected on the occasion of the compact between him and Jacob, Gn 31^{47}. It is the Aramaic equivalent of **Galeed** (q.v.).

JEHALELEEL, 1 Ch 4^{16} (AV).—See JEHALLELEL, **1.**

JEHALELEL, 2 Ch 29^{12} (AV).—See JEHALLELEL, **2.**

JEHALLELEL.—**1.** A Judahite, 1 Ch 4^{16} (AV **Jehaleleel**). **2.** A Levite, 2 Ch 29^{12} (AV **Jehalelel**).

JEHDEIAH.—**1.** The eponym of a Levitical family, 1 Ch 24^{20}. **2.** A Meronothite (q.v.), who was one of David's officers, 1 Ch 27^{30}.

JEHEZEKEL, 1 Ch 24^{16} (AV).—See JEHEZKEL.

JEHEZKEL ('God strengtheneth,' the same name as Ezekiel).—A priest, the head of the twentieth course, 1 Ch 24^{16} (AV **Jehezekel**).

JEHIAH.—The name of a Levitical family, 1 Ch 15^{24}.

JEHIEL.—**1.** One of David's chief musicians, 1 Ch $15^{18, 20}$ 16^{5}. **2.** A chief of the Levites, 1 Ch 23^{8} 29^{8}. **3.** One who 'attended the King's sons,' 1 Ch 27^{32}. **4.** One of Jehoshaphat's sons, 2 Ch 21^{2}. **5.** One of Hezekiah's 'overseers,' 2 Ch 31^{13}. **6.** A chief officer of the house of God in Josiah's reign, 2 Ch 35^{8}, 1 Es 1^{8} (AV **Syelus**, RV **Esyelus**). **7.** The father of Obadiah, a returned exile, Ezr 8^{9}, 1 Es 8^{35} (AV, RV **Jezelus**). **8.** Father of Shecaniah, Ezr 10^{2}, 1 Es 8^{92} (AV, RV **Jeelus**). **9.** One of those who had married foreign wives, Ezr 10^{26}, 1 Es 9^{27} (AV **Hierielus**, RV **Jezrielus**). **10.** A priest of the sons of Harim who had married a foreign wife, Ezr 10^{21}, 1 Es 9^{21} (AV, RV **Hiereel**). **11.** 2 Ch 29^{14} (AV); see JEHUEL.

JEHIELI.—A patronymic from **Jehiel, 2** (q.v.), 1 Ch 26^{21f}.

JEHIZKIAH.—An Ephraimite who supported the prophet Oded in opposing the bringing of Judaean captives to Samaria, 2 Ch 28^{12ff}.

JEHOADAH, 1 Ch 8^{36} (AV).—See JEHOADDAH.

JEHOADDAH.—A descendant of Saul, 1 Ch 8^{36} (AV **Jehoadah**); called **Jarah** in 9^{42}.

JEHOADDAN.—Mother of Amaziah, king of Judah, 2 K 14^{2} (AV; RV, RSV **Jehoaddin,** with *K^{e}thîbh*), 2 Ch 25^{1}.

JEHOADDIN.—See JEHOADDAN.

JEHOAHAZ.—**1. Johoahaz of Israel** (**Joahaz** in 2 K 14^{1}) succeeded his father Jehu. Our records tell us nothing of him except the length of his reign, which is given as seventeen years (2 K 13^{1}), and the low estate of his kingdom, owing to the aggressions of Syria. A turn for the better seems to have come before his death, because the forces of Assyria pressing on the N. of Damascus turned the attention of that country away from Israel (vv.$^{3-5}$).

2. Jehoahaz of Judah (**Joahaz** in 2 Ch $36^{2, 4}$ in RV, following Hebrew; **Joachaz** in 1 Es 1^{34} [AV and RV] and **Jeconiah** in 1 Es 1^{34} [RSV; cf RVm]) was the popular choice for the throne after the death of Josiah (2 K 23^{30}). But Pharaoh Neco, who had obtained possession of all Syria, regarded his coronation as an act of assumption, deposed him in favour of his brother Jehoiakim, and carried him away to Egypt, where he died (v.^{34}). Jeremiah, who calls him **Shallum,** finds his fate sadder than that of his father who fell in battle (Jer 22^{10-12}).

3. 2 Ch 21^{17} = **Ahaziah, 2.** He is called **Jehoahaz** also in 2 Ch 25^{23} in AV and RV, following Hebrew, but RSV substitutes **Ahaziah.** H. P. S.

JEHOASH, in the shorter form **JOASH,** is the name of a king in each of the two lines, Israel and Judah.

1. Jehoash of Judah was the son of Ahaziah. When an infant his brothers and cousins were massacred, some of them by Jehu and some by Athaliah. After being kept in concealment until he was seven years old, he was crowned by the bodyguard under the active leadership of Jehoiada, the chief priest. At his accession, he was invested with a sacred diadem and the testimony, the latter referring, apparently, to a document containing the Davidic Covenant (cf 2 S 23^{1-7}, Ps 132^{12}). In his earlier years he was under the influence of the man to whom he owed the throne, but later he manifested his independence. Besides an arrangement which he made with the priests about certain moneys which came into their hands, the record tells us only that an invasion of the Syrians compelled him to pay a heavy tribute. This was drawn from the Temple treasury. Jehoash was assassinated by some of his officers (2 K 11 f).

2. Jehoash of Israel was the third king of the line of Jehu. The turn of the tide in the affairs of Israel came about the time of his accession. The way in which the Biblical author indicates this is characteristic. He tells us that when Elisha was about to die Jehoash came to visit him, and wept over him as a great power about to be lost to Israel. Elisha bade him take bow and arrows and shoot the arrow of victory towards Damascus, then to strike the ground with the arrows. The three blows which he struck represent the three victories obtained by Jehoash, and the blame expressed by Elisha indicates that his contemporaries thought the king slack in following up his advantage. Jehoash also obtained a signal victory over Judah in a war wantonly provoked, it would seem, by Amaziah, king of Judah (2 K 13^{10ff}). H. P. S.—**A. S. H.**

JEHOHANAN.—**1.** A Korahite doorkeeper, 1 Ch 26^{3}. **2.** One of Jehoshaphat's five commanders, 2 Ch 17^{15}. **3.** A high priest, Ezr 10^{6}, 1 Es 9^{1} (AV **Joanan,** RV **Jonas**); called **Johanan** in Neh 12^{22f} and **Jonathan** in Neh 12^{11}. He is called son of Eliashib in Ezr 10^{6}, Neh 12^{23}, but was probably his grandson, Joiada being his father, Neh $12^{11,22}$. Josephus relates how Jehohanan slew his brother, to whom Bagoas had promised the high priesthood, in the Temple precincts (*Ant.* XI. vii. 1 [298 f]). **4.** One of those who had married foreign wives, Ezr 10^{28}, 1 Es 9^{29} (AV **Johannes,** RV **Joannes**). **5.** Son of Tobiah the Ammonite, Neh 6^{18}. **6.** A priest in the days of Joiakim, Neh 12^{13}. **7.** A priest present at the dedication of the walls, Neh 12^{42}.

JEHOIACHIN, king of Judah, ascended the throne when Nebuchadrezzar was on the march to punish the rebellion of Jehoiakim. On the approach of the Chaldaean army, the young king surrendered and was taken captive to Babylon (2 K 24^{8ff}). This is confirmed by fragments of 'The Babylonian Chronicle,' which state that Nebuchadrezzar 'in the seventh year mustered his troops and marched into the land of Hatti (*i.e.* Syria and Palestine), besieged the city of Judah, and on the second day of the month of Adar (*i.e.* mid March 597 B.C.) captured the city and took the king prisoner.' His reign had lasted only three months, but his confinement in Babylon extended for thirty-seven years, until the death of Nebuchadrezzar. At the accession of Evil-merodach he was freed from prison, and received a daily allowance from the palace (2 K 25^{27f}). This also has been confirmed by the discovery of a number of tablets on the site of the palace in ancient Babylon. His name and rank as the king of Judah are inscribed on these, and they indicate the supplies of oil which are to be provided to him and his five sons by the royal stewards. Jeremiah gives his name in 24^{1} 27^{20} 28^{4} 29^{2} as **Jeconiah,** and in $22^{24,28}$ 37^{1} as **Coniah.** He is mentioned in 1 Es 1^{43} (AV **Joacim,** RV **Joakim**), Ad. Est 11^{4} (AV, RV **Jechonias**; RSV **Jeconiah**), Bar $1^{3,9}$ (AV, RV **Jechonias**; RSV **Jeconiah**) and Mt 1^{11f} (AV **Jechonias**; RV, RSV **Jechoniah**). H. P. S.—**E. R. R.**

JEHOIADA.—**1.** Father of Benaiah, the successor of Joab, 2 S 8^{18} 20^{23} etc. It is probably the same man that is referred to in 1 Ch 12^{27} 27^{34}, where we should probably read 'Benaiah the son of Jehoiada.' **2.** The chief priest of the Temple at the time of Ahaziah's death (2 K 11^{4} etc.). The Book of Chronicles makes him the husband of the princess **Jehosheba** (or Jehoshabeath, 2 Ch 22^{11}), by whose presence of mind the infant prince Jehoash escaped the massacre by which Athaliah secured the throne for herself. Jehoiada must have been privy to the concealment of the prince, and it was he who arranged the *coup d'état* which placed the rightful heir on the throne. In this he may have been moved by a desire to save Judah from vassalage to Israel, as much as by zeal for the legitimate worship **3.** Neh 3^{6} (AV); see JOIADA, **1.** **4.** Neh 13^{28}; see JOIADA, **2.**

JEHOIAKIM.—**1.** Son of Josiah, originally named **Eliakim,** who was placed upon the throne of Judah by Pharaoh Neco, who deposed the more popular Jehoahaz. His reign of eleven years is not well spoken of by Jeremiah. The religious abuses which had been abolished by Josiah seem to have returned with greater strength than ever. At a time when the kingdom was impoverished by war and by the exactions of Egypt, Jehoiakim occupied himself in extravagant schemes of building to be carried out by forced labour (2 K 23^{24}–24^{7}). Things were so bad that in the fourth year of his reign Jeremiah dictated to Baruch a summary of all his earlier discourses, and bade him read it in public as though to indicate that there was no longer any hope. The king showed his contempt for the prophetic word by burning the roll. Active persecution of the prophetic party followed, in which one man at least was put to death. Jeremiah's escape was due to powerful friends at court (Jer 22^{13-19} 36^{1-26} 26^{20-24}). It was about the time of the burning of the Book of Jeremiah that the Egyptian supremacy was ended by the decisive battle of Carchemish. The evacuation of Palestine followed, and Jehoiakim was obliged to submit to the Babylonians. His heart, however, was with the Pharaoh, to whom he owed his elevation. After three years he revolted from the Babylonian rule. Nebuchadrezzar thought to bring him into subjection by sending guerilla bands to harry the country, but as this did not succeed, he invaded Judah with an army of regulars. Before he reached Jerusalem, Jehoiakim died, and the surrender which was inevitable was made by his son. Whether Jeremiah's prediction that the corpse of the king should be denied decent burial was fulfilled is not certain. **2.** A priest, son of Hilkiah, to whom the captives are said to have sent money for the purchase of offerings and incense, Bar 1^{7} (AV **Joachim,** RV **Joakim**).
H. P. S.

JEHOIARIB.—One of the twenty-four courses of priests, 1 Ch 9^{10} 24^{7}; called **Joiarib** in Neh 11^{10} $12^{6,19}$; called **Joarib** in 1 Mac 2^{1} 14^{29} (AV **Jarib**). It was the first in David's time (1 Ch 24^{7}), but seventeenth in the time of Zerubbabel, Neh 12^{6}, and of the high priest Joiakim, 12^{19}. The name is omitted, probably by accident, in the list of the priests that 'sealed the covenant,' Neh 10. The clan is mentioned among those that dwelt in Jerusalem in the time of Nehemiah, 11^{10}.

JEHONADAB.—See JONADAB, **2.**

JEHONATHAN.—A more exact rendering of the name usually represented in English as **Jonathan.** In RV and RSV this form occurs twice. **1.** 2 Ch 17^{8}, one of the Levites sent out by Jehoshaphat with the Book of the Law to teach the people in the cities of Judah. **2.** Neh 12^{18}, the head of the priestly family of Shemaiah in the days of Joiakim the son of Jeshua. In AV it is found also in **3.** 1 Ch 27^{25}, an overseer of David's treasuries (RV, RSV **Jonathan**). See JONATHAN, **12.**

JEHORAM, with a shorter form **Joram,** is the name of two kings in the OT.

1. Jehoram of Israel was the son of Ahab (2 K 3^{1}), and came to the throne after the brief reign of his brother Ahaziah, who had no sons to succeed him

(2 K 1^{17}). Early in his reign Moab rebelled, and Jehoram appealed for help to Jehoshaphat, king of Judah, but it does not appear that they were successful in their efforts to suppress the rebellion. At the crisis of the conflict the king of Moab sacrificed his son to his god Chemosh. The invading army was discouraged, and the allies retreated without having accomplished their purpose (2 K 3^{4ff}). The success of Moab was commemorated by Mesha the king by the erection of the **Moabite Stone** (see MOAB), which was discovered in Dibon, the Moabite capital, in 1868. The prophet Elisha was active during the reign of Jehoram, and it is probable that the siege of Samaria, of which we have so graphic an account in 2 K 6 and 7, also belongs to this period. Jehoram engaged in the siege of Ramoth-gilead, and was wounded there (2 Ch 22^{5ff}). His reign ended with the revolt of Jehu, by whom he was killed. See JEHU.

2. Jehoram of Judah, son of Jehoshaphat (1 K 22^{50}), came to the throne during the reign of the other Jehoram in Israel. He was married to Athaliah, daughter of Ahab and Jezebel (2 K 8^{18}). He was thirty-two when he became king, and reigned eight years (2 K 8^{17}, 2 Ch 21^{5}). One of his first acts was to kill all his brothers and some of the princes in Judah (2 Ch 21^{4}). During his reign Edom revolted successfully from Judah. In endeavouring to subdue this revolt Jehoram was in great danger, but with a few of his men he cut his way through the troops that surrounded him (2 K 8^{21}). He is described as one who walked in the ways of the kings of Israel, and at his death, it is stated that he was not buried in the tombs of the kings (2 Ch 21^{20}).

3. A priest sent by Jehoshaphat to teach the Law (2 Ch 17^{8}). H. P. S.—**E. R. R.**

JEHOSHABEATH.—See JEHOSHEBA.

JEHOSHAPHAT ('Y″ judges').—**1.** The 'recorder' in the reigns of David and Solomon (2 S 8^{16} etc., 1 K 4^{3}); see ASAPH, **1.** **2.** One of Solomon's commissariat officers (1 K 4^{17}). **3.** Father of king Jehu (2 K $9^{2, 14}$). **4.** The son of Asa king of Judah. He receives a good name from the compiler of the Book of Kings (1 K 22^{43}). This is clearly because he carried out the religious reforms of his father. The important thing in his reign was the alliance of Judah with Israel (v.^{44}), which put an end to their long hostility. Some suppose the smaller kingdom to have been tributary to the larger, but on this point our sources are silent. The alliance was cemented by the marriage of the crown prince Jehoram to Ahab's daughter Athaliah (2 K 8^{18}). Jehoshaphat appears as the ally of Ahab against Syria, and himself went into the battle of Ramoth-gilead (1 K 22). He also assisted Ahab's son against the Moabites (2 K 3). He seems to have had trouble with his own vassals in Edom, and his attempt to renew Solomon's commercial ventures on the Red Sea was unsuccessful (1 K 22^{48}). **5.** 1 Ch 15^{24} (AV); see JOSHAPHAT, **2.** H. P. S.

JEHOSHAPHAT, VALLEY OF (Jl $3^{2, 12}$).—The deep valley to the E. of Jerusalem, between the city and the Mount of Olives, has since the 4th cent. A.D. been identified by an unbroken Christian tradition with the Valley of Jehoshaphat. Moslems and Jews have also for centuries looked upon this valley as the scene of the Last Judgment. The Jews especially consider this of all places on earth the most suitable for burial, as it is taught that all bodies buried elsewhere must find their way thither at the last day. The valley was the ordinary place for graves in pre-exilic times (2 K 23^{6} etc.). In spite, however, of these traditions, it is quite probable that the name of this valley was at one time *Wâdī Sha'fât*, from the neighbouring village of *Sha'fât*, and that this suggested to early Christian pilgrims, in search of sites, the Biblical name *Jehoshaphat*. The so-called 'Tomb of Jehoshaphat,' which lies near the traditional 'Tomb of Absalom,' is an impossible site, for in 1 K 22^{50} and 2 Ch 21^{1} it is stated that he was buried in the city of David. The valley, moreover, does not suit the conditions, in that it is a *naḥal* (wady)—the *naḥal* Kidron (q.v.)—whereas the Valley of Jehoshaphat was in Hebrew an *'ēmeḳ* (a wide, open valley). It has been suggested that the valley (*'ēmeḳ*) of Beracah, where Jehoshaphat returned thanks after his great victory (2 Ch 20^{26}), may be the place referred to by Joel. It is, however, at least as probable that the prophet did not refer to any special locality and gave the name *Jehoshaphat, i.e.* 'Jehovah judges,' to an ideal spot. In this connexion it has been observed by A. S. Kapelrud, *Joel Studies*, 1948, 147, who points to an ancient valley-tradition with possible cultic affiliations (*e.g.* Jer 7^{30-34}, Is $22^{1-8, 12-14}$, Ezk 39^{11-29}, Zec 14^{1-15}), that this valley 'cannot be located on any map . . . belongs to the sphere of mythology. And yet, it was perhaps conceived as a valley in the vicinity of Jerusalem, for it was out from Zion and Jerusalem that Yahweh was to thunder,' Jl 3^{16f} (Heb. 4^{16f}). The name 'simply means . . . "Yahweh's valley of judgment."' E. W. G. M.—**E. T. R.**

JEHOSHEBA.—Daughter of Jehoram of Judah, 2 K 11^{2}; called **Jehoshabeath** in 2 Ch 22^{11}. On the death of her half-brother Ahaziah, she was instrumental in preserving the Davidic stock, by concealing the infant Jehoash in a bedroom of the Temple. According to the Chronicler, she was wife of Jehoiada.

JEHOVAH.—See GOD, **4** (*c*).

JEHOVAH-JIREH.—The name given by Abraham (Gn 22^{14} AV, RV) to the spot where he offered a ram in place of his son. The name means 'Y″ sees,' and probably also (with reference to Gn 22^{8}) 'Y″ provides' (cf RSV 'The Lord will provide'). The proverb connected in v.^{14} with the name clearly relates to the Temple hill, 'the mount of Y″.' But it is not easy to see the exact connexion between the name and the proverb. The most obvious translation is 'in the mount of Y″ one appears' (referring to the festal pilgrimages to Jerusalem), but in that case the connexion can be only verbal. Other possible translations are: (1) 'In the mount of Y″ it is seen,' *i.e.* provided; this is a possible translation in the context; but it appears to be suggested that the proverb had an existence independently of the tradition of Abraham's sacrifice; in which case the meaning assigned to the verb is not a natural or obvious one. (2) 'In the mount of Y″, Y″ is seen.' The significance of the phrase would then be that, as Y″ sees the needs of those who come to worship Him, so as a practical result He is seen by them as a helper. Other translations have been suggested which do not, however, alter the general sense. Driver decides that, unless the connexion be regarded as purely verbal, the last suggestion quoted above seems the most satisfactory. In any case, the point lies in the relation between the name which Abraham gave to the place of his sacrifice and some popular proverb dealing with the Temple at Jerusalem. A. W. F. B.

JEHOVAH-NISSI ('Y″ is my banner').—The name given by Moses to the altar he erected after the defeat of Amalek, Ex 17^{15} (AV, RV; RSV 'The Lord is my banner'). God is considered the centre or rallying-point of the army of Israel, and the name of God as their battle-cry (cf Ps 20^{7f}). The interpretation of v.^{16} is somewhat doubtful. Literally it means 'A hand upon the throne (*kēs*) of Yah' (which AV and RV interpret 'the Lord hath sworn'). But *kēs* (for *kissē'*) is found nowhere else, and many scholars read *nēs*, 'banner' (so RSV). The meaning is probably that Moses took an oath of war against Amalek, in token of which he laid his hand on the banner.

JEHOVAH-SHALOM.—The name given by Gideon to the altar he erected in Ophrah, Jg 6^{24} (AV, RV). The name means 'Y″ is peace' (*i.e.* well-disposed) and is translated in RSV 'The Lord is peace,' in allusion to Y″'s words in v.^{23} 'Peace be to you.'

JEHOVAH-SHAMMAH ('Y″ is there').—The name to be given to the restored and glorified Jerusalem, Ezk 48^{35} (AVm, RVm; but translated 'The Lord is there' in AV, RV, and RSV; cf Is 60^{14-22} 62^{2}, Rev 21^{2f}).

The prophet beheld the Lord forsake His Temple (ch. 11), and he beheld Him again enter it (ch. 43); now He abides in it among His people for ever.

JEHOVAH-TSIDKENU ('Y″ is our righteousness,' or 'Y″ our righteousness').—The title of the Branch, the perfectly righteous King, who is to rule over the people on their return from captivity, Jer 23^{6} 33^{16} (AVm; but translated in AV, RV, and RSV).

JEHOZABAD ('Y″ has bestowed').—**1.** One of the servants of king Joash, who conspired against his master and joined in his assassination, 2 K 12^{21}, 2 Ch 24^{26}. **2.** A Benjamite chief, 2 Ch 17^{18}. **3.** A Levitical family, 1 Ch 26^{4}. A shortened form of the name is **Jozabad** (q.v.).

JEHOZADAK.—Father of Joshua the high priest, 1 Ch 6^{14f}, Hag $1^{1,12,14}$ $2^{2,4}$, Zec 6^{11} (AV in Haggai and Zechariah **Josedech**). The name is shortened to **Jozadak** in Ezr $3^{2,8}$ 5^{2} 10^{18}, Neh 12^{26}, 1 Es $5^{5,48,56}$ 6^{2} 9^{19}, Sir 49^{12} (AV **Josedec** and RV **Josedek** in 1 Esdras and Sirach).

JEHU.—**1.** A prophet, the son of Hanani (1 K 16^{1} etc.). **2.** A Judahite (1 Ch 2^{38}). **3.** A Simeonite (1 Ch 4^{35}). **4.** One of David's heroes (1 Ch 12^{3}). **5.** A king of Israel. Like the other founders of dynasties in that country, he obtained the throne by the murder of his monarch. It is evident that a considerable party in Israel had long been dissatisfied with the house of Ahab. This was partly on account of its religious policy, but perhaps even more for its oppression of its subjects—so emphatically illustrated by the story of Naboth. The leader of the opposition was Elijah, and after him Elisha. Jehu, when in attendance upon Ahab, had heard Elijah's denunciation of the murder of Naboth (2 K 9^{25f}). Later he was general of the army, and commanded in the operations at Ramoth-gilead in the absence of king Jehoram. The latter had gone to Jezreel on account of wounds he had received. Elisha saw this to be the favourable moment to start the long-planned revolt. His disciple anointed the general, and the assent of the army was easily obtained. The vivid narrative of Jehu's prompt action is familiar to every reader of the OT. The king was taken completely by surprise, and he and his mother were slain at once (2 K 9, 10).

The extermination of Ahab's house was a foregone conclusion. The skill of Jehu is seen in his making the chief men in the kingdom partners in the crime. The extermination of the royal house in Judah seems uncalled for, but was perhaps excused by the times on account of the close relationship with the family of Ahab. It has been suggested that Jehu purposed to put an end to the independence of Judah, and to incorporate it fully with his own kingdom. But we have no direct evidence on this head. Hosea saw that the blood of Jezreel rested upon the house of Jehu, and that it would be avenged (Hos 1^{4}).

Elisha's activity extended through the reign of Jehu, but the narrative of the prophet's life tells us little of the king. From another source—the Assyrian inscriptions—we learn that Jehu paid tribute to Shalmaneser in the year 842 B.C., which must have been the year of his accession. He probably hoped to secure the great king's protection against Damascus. But he was disappointed in this, for after a single expedition to the West in 839 B.C. the Assyrians were occupied in the East. The latter portion of Jehu's reign was therefore a time of misfortune for Israel. H. P. S.

JEHUBBAH.—An Asherite, 1 Ch 7^{34}.

JEHUCAL.—A courtier sent by king Zedekiah to entreat for the prayers of Jeremiah, Jer 37^{3}; called **Jucal** in 38^{1}.

JEHUD.—A town of Dan, named between Baalath and Bene-berak, Jos 19^{45}. It is probably the modern *el-Yehûdîyeh*, 8 miles E. of Joppa.

JEHUDI ('a Jew').—An officer of Jehoiakim, at whose summons Baruch read to the princes of Judah the roll of Jeremiah's prophecies, and who was afterwards himself employed to read the roll to the king, Jer $36^{14,21,23}$.

JEHUDIJAH, 1 Ch 4^{18} (AV).—See HAJEHUDIJAH.

JEHUEL.—A Hemanite in Hezekiah's reign, 2 Ch 29^{14} (AV **Jehiel**).

JEHUSH, 1 Ch 8^{39} (AV).—See JEUSH, **3.**

JEIEL.—**1.** A Reubenite, 1 Ch 5^{7}. **2.** An ancestor of Saul (1 Ch 8^{29}, supplied in RV and RSV from 9^{35}). **3.** One of David's heroes, 1 Ch 11^{44}. **4. 5.** The name of two Levite families: (*a*) 1 Ch $15^{18,21}$ 16^{5}, 2 Ch 20^{14}; (*b*) 2 Ch 35^{9}; called **Ochiel** in 1 Es 1^{9} (RV **Ochielus**). **6.** A scribe in the reign of Uzziah, 2 Ch 26^{11}. **7.** One of those who had married foreign wives, Ezr 10^{43}. **8.** 2 Ch 29^{13} (AV); see JEUEL, **2.** **9.** Ezr 8^{13} (AV); see JEUEL, **3.** In **2, 3, 6, 7,** *Kᵉthîbh* has JEUEL.

JEKABZEEL.—See KABZEEL.

JEKAMEAM.—A Levite, 1 Ch 23^{19} 24^{23}.

JEKAMIAH.—**1.** A Judahite, 1 Ch 2^{41}. **2.** A son of king Jeconiah, 1 Ch 3^{18} (AV **Jecamiah**).

JEKUTHIEL.—A man of Judah, 1 Ch 4^{18}.

JEMIMA, Job 42^{14} (AV).—See JEMIMAH.

JEMIMAH.—The eldest of Job's daughters born to him after his restoration to prosperity, Job 42^{14} (AV **Jemima**).

JEMNAAN, Jth 2^{28} (AV, RV).—See JABNEEL, **1.**

JEMUEL.—A son of Simeon, Gn 46^{10}, Ex 6^{15}; called **Nemuel** in Nu 26^{12}, 1 Ch 4^{24}.

JEPHTHAE, He 11^{32} (AV) = **Jephthah** (q.v.).

JEPHTHAH.—The story of this 'judge' is given in Jg 11 f, to which Jg 10^{17f} is the introduction. He was a Gileadite, *i.e.* he belonged to the trans-Jordanic Israelites, was well known for his military skill, and was the 'son of a harlot.' The latter phrase may indicate no more than that he was, unlike his half-brothers, not of pure Israelite stock, cf Abimelech Jg 8^{31}. He was therefore excluded from the family inheritance and became a freebooter in the land of Tob, an Aramaean state to the N. of Gilead. But the Gileadite clan was threatened by the Ammonites, and the elders of the clan appealed to him to lead them against the attackers. He agreed on condition that he became the permanent head of the clan, a condition which the elders accepted.

The section which follows (11^{4-11}) presents difficulties, since while it is addressed to the Ammonite king, it appears to relate to the Moabites, and refers specifically to Chemosh, the Moabite god. It is possible that we have here a similar story of strife between Israelites and Moabites which has been assimilated to the Jephthah story.

Jephthah is then possessed by superhuman energy (the spirit of the Lord) and attacks the Ammonites. He makes a vow that on his return with victory from the battle, he will offer as a burnt-offering to God whoever first comes from his house to welcome him; that is one in whom the *nephesh* of Jephthah is, thus representing Jephthah himself. He is victorious in the battle and on his return home is met by his daughter, an only child. Distressed and grieved though he is, neither he nor his daughter contemplate any evasion of the vow. She asks for two months' delay in order to 'bewail her virginity,' after which she returns for the fulfilment of the vow. Then follows, 12^{1-6}, an incident which recalls 8^{1-3}, in which the Ephraimites again show their resentment to any challenge to their leadership in the tribal confederacy. The dispute leads to a battle in which the Ephraimites are defeated. It is in this instance that the dialect difference in pronunciation of Shibboleth/Sibboleth is noted as a means of distinguishing between Gileadite and Ephraimite. Jephthah's leadership lasted six years, but the tradition did not preserve the name of his place of burial.

The precise significance of the sacrifice of Jephthah's daughter is obscure, and is perhaps deliberately so in the interests of true Yahweh worship which appears to have been from an early period opposed to human sacrifice and intolerant of rites associated with pagan deities. In general the features of the story are: (1) The vow which, having once been uttered, has a concrete existence and must be carried into effect (Nu 30^{2ff}, Ps 66^{13ff}, Pr 20^{25}). (2) The sacrifice was a burnt offering, that is a gift whereby relationship is maintained; and the suggestion that it was expected to be a member of Jephthah's household may mean that it was thought of as a self-offering, since the 'soul' of the head of the house extends to all its members. (3) Jephthah's daughter led the company of maidens who came to meet the victor with a song of triumph, cf Ex 15^{20}, 1 S 18^{6}, Ps 68^{25}. (4) The mourning of her virginity which, as the story is presented, is a matter for lamentation that she died unmarried and childless. (5) The story lies at the heart of some religious custom of lamentation which was celebrated annually by Israelite women for four days. Nothing further is known of this custom in the OT. Since not even the time of the year is given, we can only regard as possible the attempt to relate this to the 'weeping for Tammuz' (Ezk 8^{14}) or some local Canaanite fertility rite. A. S. H.

JEPHUNNEH.—1. The father of Caleb, Nu 13^{6} etc. **2.** A son of Jether an Asherite, 1 Ch 7^{38}.

JERAH.—Mentioned in the genealogies of Gn 10^{26} and 1 Ch 1^{20} as a son of Joktan. Probably, in analogy with other names in this connexion, Jerah is to be taken as the designation of an Arabian tribe. The Arabic geographers refer to places named *Warâkh*, *Yurâkh*, *Yarâh*, with any one of which it might be identified. On the other hand, in Hebrew the word signifies 'new moon'; it may therefore be the translation of a totemic clan-name. In fact, Bochart pointed out that 'sons of the moon' is a patronymic still found in Arabia. W. M. N.

JERAHMEEL ('May El have compassion!').—**1.** A non-Israelite clan in the extreme S. of Palestine, with which David cultivated friendly relations during his exile (1 S 27^{10} 30^{29} **Jerahmeelites**). After Saul's death the Jerahmeelites formed part of the little principality over which he reigned in Hebron. How indistinct the recollection of them was appears from the various forms assumed by their name in MSS of the LXX: **Jesmega, Isramelei, Aermon, Israel, Jeramelei.** Subsequently they were considered to have been a Judahite clan (1 Ch 2$^{9, 25ff. 35-42}$: here Jerahmeel is Caleb's elder brother; the list of his descendants in vv.$^{35-42}$ is of later origin than vv.$^{9, 25-27}$ and brings them down to the Chronicler's day). We have no historical or other records connected with these names, save that Molid is a town mentioned by the name Moladah elsewhere (Jos 19^{2}, Neh 11^{26}). **2.** LXX and Old Latin read 'Jerahmeel' at 1 S 1^{1} as the name of Samuel's grandfather. In all probability the **Jeroham** of MT is an abbreviated form, like *Jacob* for *Jacob-el*, or the *Yarkhamu* found in a Babylonian list of Hammurabi's time. **3.** One of the three men ordered by Jehoiakim to arrest Jeremiah and Baruch, Jer 36^{26}. AV follows Vulgate (*filio Amelech*), calling him 'son of Hammelech'; RV and RSV, with LXX, 'the king's son.' He was a scion of the royal house, but not necessarily a child of Jehoiakim. **4.** In a list of Levites, 1 Ch 24$^{20-31}$, drawn up considerably later than that in 23^{6ff}, Jerahmeel's name is added (v.^{29}) as a son of Kish. There must at the time have been a division of Levites called after him, and not, as previously, after Kish. J. T.

JERECHU, 1 Es 5^{22} (RV) = **Jericho** (RSV; cf Ezr 2^{34}, Neh 7^{36}).

JERECHUS, 1 Es 5^{22} (AV).—See JERECHU.

JERED.—1. 1 Ch 1^{2} (AV); see JARED. **2.** A Judahite, 1 Ch 4^{18}.

JEREMAI.—A Jew of the family of Hashum who had married a foreign wife, Ezr 10^{33}, 1 Es 9^{34} (AV, RV **Jeremias**).

JEREMIAH.—1. A warrior of the tribe of Gad, fifth in reputation, 1 Ch 12^{10}. **2.** The tenth in reputation, 1 Ch 12^{13}, of the same Gadite band. **3.** A bowman and slinger of the tribe of Benjamin, 1 Ch 12^{4}. **4.** The head of a family in E. Manasseh, 1 Ch 5^{24}. **5.** A man of Libnah, whose daughter Hamutal was one of the wives of Josiah, and mother of Jehoahaz, 2 K 23^{31}, and Zedekiah, 2 K 24^{18}, Jer 53^{1}. **6.** The son of Habazziniah and father of Jaazaniah, the head of the Rechabites, Jer 35^{3}, in the time of the prophet Jeremiah. **7.** A priest who returned with Zerubbabel, Neh 12^{1}. His name was given to one of the twenty-two courses of priests (Neh 12^{12}). **8.** A priest who sealed the covenant, Neh 10^{2}, and took part in the dedication of the wall of Jerusalem, 12^{34}. **9.** The prophet. See next article.

JEREMIAH.—1. The times.—Jeremiah was born during the closing years of Manasseh's long reign (687–642 B.C.). In the thirteenth year of Josiah (640–609 B.C.) he was called to be 'a prophet to the nations' (1^{5}). His prophetic career extends from 627/626 B.C. to the fall of Jerusalem in 586 B.C. (1^{2f}) and for some time after this until he vanishes from sight among his fugitive fellow countrymen in Egypt (chs. 40–44). These four decades are among the most fateful in the history of the ancient Near East. A great Semitic empire came to a disastrous end, and another rose from its ashes. It was a turbulent and revolutionary time in which new vitalities asserted themselves, of rising empires and reviving nationalisms, of a new awakening—and yet of nostalgia for the past, of cultural change and literary activity.

(*a*) THE NEAR EAST.—Assyria had long ruled the East. From the time of the military campaigns of Ashur-nasir-pal II. (884–858 B.C.) and of his successor, Shalmaneser III. (858–824 B.C.), until its decline during the reign of Ashur-bani-pal (668–633 B.C.) it had been the dominant power in Western Asia, particularly since the accession to the imperial throne of the usurper Tiglath-pileser III. (744–727 B.C.). The zenith of its prestige was attained under Esarhaddon (680–669 B.C.) and the early years of Ashur-bani-pal, but it then entered a period of rapid decline. The latter's victory over Egypt at the Battle of Thebes in 663 B.C. was the turning point of Assyrian power (cf Nah 3^{8}). Invasion from without and intrigue from within, the rise of revolutionary movements throughout the empire, and seething resentment of Assyrian tyranny brought about widespread disintegration and finally collapse. Ashur-bani-pal consoled himself by collecting the literary monuments of the past in his great library at Nineveh. Egypt revived under Psammetichus I. (663–609 B.C.), the able monarch of the 26th Saïtic dynasty. Hordes of Cimmerians and Scythians from the north, probably the Umman-manda of the inscriptions, threatened the security of the empire (Herodotus, *History*, Book I, 103–106), and the Bedouin tribes along its fringes grew increasingly restive and revolutionary. While the foe from the north referred to in Jer 4^{5}–6^{30} and elsewhere cannot be simply identified with these invaders, it is probable that the international situation reflected in these movements lies behind them.

Ashur-bani-pal died in 631 B.C., and by 626 B.C. Nabopolassar, the Chaldaean governor, was in full revolt. The long period of conflict which followed is illuminated for us in the Babylonian Chronicle for the years 626–623 and 616–594 B.C. (see D. J. Wiseman, *Chronicles of the Chaldaean Kings*, 1956). In 616 B.C. Nabopolassar was campaigning in Assyria; shortly thereafter the Medes intervened under Cyaxares. In 614 B.C. the city of Ashur was besieged and captured. Finally, in 612 B.C., under the combined assault of the Chaldaean and Median armies with the aid of the Umman-manda, the city of Nineveh fell. The event is memorialized in the exultant poem of the prophet Nahum (ch. 3). Two years later the remnants of the Assyrian armies were defeated at Harran. The next year Pharaoh Neco (609–593 B.C.) on his way to come to the aid of the remnants of the Assyrian army stopped at Megiddo where he was met by Josiah, king of Judah, whom he forthwith put to death. The details of the episode are far from clear. Whether there was an actual military encounter or not, is uncertain. It may well be that Josiah sought to hinder the advance of the Egyptian army and so prevent the resuscitation of Assyria. In 605 B.C. the Egyptian garrison troops were routed at Carchemish by the Chaldaean army under Nebuchadrezzar, son of Nabopolassar. The Chaldaean Chronicle observes laconically, 'Nebuchadrezzar conquered the whole of Hatti.' The history of the Near East for the next half century lay in the hands of the Chaldaeans. Jeremiah seems to have been well aware of the significance of the event for the future of Western Asia.

(*b*) JUDAH.—Manasseh's subservience to Assyria brought about a long period of syncretism with the astral cults and a revival of Canaanite fertility worship on the high places. But already during his reign revolutionary forces were at work in Judah. With the end of Josiah's minority these came to a head. We are informed by 2 Chronicles (34^{3}) that already in his youth Josiah began to seek the God of David, 'and in the twelfth year began to purge Judah and Jerusalem.' This may well preserve an authentic reminiscence. If so, we may regard the Reformation of 621 B.C. as the culminating achievement of prophetic and priestly groups within the kingdom of Judah. It found expression not only in many humanitarian and religious reforms but also in nationalistic action. The king sought to re-establish the kingdom of David, and to bring it to something of its ancient prestige. Albrecht Alt (*PJB* XXI, 1925, 100 ff) and Martin Noth (*History of Israel*, pp. 271–274) believe that the boundaries given in Jos 15^{21-62} and 18^{21-28} reflect the limits of Josiah's kingdom. But more significant for the future was the religious Reformation. In protest against the plethora of nature cults of Assyria and Canaan, Josiah instituted a vast programme of reform. It was a time when Israel needed to be called back to her true origins in the Mosaic age. Although he was king of Judah, Josiah undid many of the practices of the royal cult, and called Israel back to its ancient heritage as a chosen, holy, and responsible people, bound by covenantal ties to Yahweh, the Lord of history. The reforms described in 2 K 23^{4-25}, probably an extract from the royal annals (so Noth), were designed to return Israel to the cultic life and ethical requirements of the old twelve-tribe amphictyony whose centre once lay at Shechem and later at Shiloh. The Book of the Covenant found by Hilkiah in the Temple (2 K 23^{2f}) is incorporated into our present Book of Deuteronomy, and it is now generally held that it had its provenance in the northern kingdom, as is suggested *inter alia* by its affinities with the Elohist and with Hosea and Jeremiah. The nature cults must be exterminated root and branch, the syncretistic rites and celebrations at the high places must cease, and the Temple at Jerusalem be recognized as the national centre for true worship. Israel is a holy people consecrated to the service of Yahweh. What this service implied is elaborated in great detail. The Reformation of 621 B.C. is the greatest event in the history of Israel's religion since the Mosaic age, and it was destined to exert a profound influence on its subsequent development. But it must be remembered that it was a *reformation*, a return to the election-covenant faith of Israel's beginnings and that even the style and language of the Book of the Covenant has its sources in ancient recital, rituals, and legal requirements.

The period from 621 B.C. to the death of Josiah at Megiddo in 609 B.C. is to all intents and purposes a blank in the prophetic career of Jeremiah, but, as we have seen, it is well documented so far as the history of the Near East is concerned. The tragic end to Josiah's prosperous and peaceful reign (Jer 22^{15b-16}) was a grievous blow to the reforming movement. Jehoahaz was anointed king over his older brother Eliakim, but was ordered by Neco to Riblah (22^{10-12}), and Eliakim was appointed by the latter as his successor and given the regnal name of Jehoiakim. Three years later, at the Battle of Carchemish, Nebuchadrezzar triumphed over his Egyptian foe (Jer 46^{1-12}; cf 25^{1} 36^{1} 45^{1}). In 603–602 B.C. Jehoiakim withheld tribute from his Chaldaean overlord. Bands of marauding Chaldaeans, Syrians, Moabites, and Ammonites invaded the land (2 K 24^{2}). A few years later, in 598 B.C., Jehoiakim again refused tribute. Jerusalem was subjected to siege. Many of its foremost citizens and skilled artisans were taken into captivity. Jehoiachin, was taken to Babylon with his family, where, according to inscriptions published by E. F. Weidner, he was given the preferential treatment of a captive monarch ('Jojachin, König von Juda, in Babylonischen Keilinschriften,' *Mélanges Syriens*, 1939, ii, 923–927). The following years were confused and troubled. Jerusalem was split between pro-Egyptian and pro-Chaldaean factions; the young king Zedekiah was too immature to assume leadership, and the prophets were at odds. The biographical narratives of the Book of Jeremiah give us a vivid account of the prophet's activity during these years. Zedekiah (597–586 B.C.), uncle of the lamented Jehoiachin, was under suspicion as the appointee of Nebuchadrezzar. He was insecure and timid, and proved unable to stem the tide of perfervid nationalism. He failed more through weakness than through evil intent; he sought Jeremiah's advice, but lacked decision to follow it. Early in his reign a conspiracy was on foot in Palestine against the Chaldaeans, which he was tempted to join (Jer $27^{1-11, 12-15}$. In v.[1] read *Zedekiah*; MT *Jehoiakim*; cf 28^{1}). The leaders in Judah, instead of being cowed by the disastrous siege and conquest of Jerusalem in 598–597 B.C., were eager for revolt. Both in the city (chs. 27–28) and among the exiles (ch. 29) the popular prophets were urging them on by their optimistic assurances. At last Zedekiah yielded to the tide, breaking his oaths of allegiance to Nebuchadrezzar—conduct sternly condemned by Ezekiel (17^{11-21}) as well as by Jeremiah, and Judah was launched on a struggle which was to end not only in national disaster, the destruction of the Temple, and the termination of the Davidic dynasty which had continued unbroken for more than four hundred years, but also in a profound modification of Israelite faith and understanding of history. The siege of Jerusalem was prolonged for a year and a half (587–586 B.C.). The Egyptians, under the new and ambitious Pharaoh Hophra (Apries, 588–569 B.C.), effected a diversion of the Chaldaean troops (Jer 37^{5-10}, Ezk 17^{15}), but as so often before Pharaoh proved 'a broken reed to those who trusted in him.' Reduced by famine, Jerusalem was stormed, Zedekiah was captured in his attempt to escape, his sons were slain before his eyes, he was blinded and then taken as a captive to Babylon (2 K 25^{1-7}). This time Nebuchadrezzar showed little mercy, having learned his lesson from his liberal treatment of the city in 597 B.C. The city was razed, the Temple destroyed, and the survivors of the siege and the executions that followed were carried into exile. Judah was made a province of the empire with its capital at Mizpah. Gedaliah, a member of the old family of Shaphan, was appointed its governor. The little remnant suffered more reverses. Gedaliah was slain as were many of his compatriots. In despair the survivors went to Egypt. Jeremiah, who had in vain resisted this migration, was carried with them; he had the distress of seeing his companions relapse into open idolatry, protesting that they had fared better when worshipping 'the queen of heaven' than under Yahweh. Jewish tradition relates that he died at the hands of his incensed fellow-exiles.

2. The life of Jeremiah.—The four decades of Jeremiah's prophetic ministry, from the Chaldaean declaration of independence in 626 B.C. to the fall of Jerusalem in 586 B.C., must be counted among the great international periods of human history. Not since the New Empire had the Near East suffered such profound political convulsion and ferment. The literature from Mesopotamia is richer in astrological omen texts from this period than from any other time of which we have knowledge.

JEREMIAH

In Israel it was pre-eminently an age of prophecy. Just as the history and daily life of the other peoples of the Near East are abundantly documented with annals and incantation texts, so the OT is richer in its documentation for this period than for any other equivalent time in Israel's history. For not only do we have such prophetic books as Zephaniah, Nahum, Habakkuk, Jeremiah, and Ezekiel, but also the substantial Deuteronomic literature whose true origin must be discerned primarily in the recrudescence of the prophetic movement. Moreover, both Jeremiah and Ezekiel refer to many other prophets who were active in their time. In all this literature the prophet Jeremiah occupies a position of central importance. He more than any other of the men of Israel was called to speak to his age, and his own life was a profoundly interior response to the Word of God as it was addressed to the men of Judah in the closing decades of the southern kingdom. Of no other prophet do we have so full and detailed and varied a record. His poetry, of which we have a substantial deposit, is unrivalled in the records of Semitic antiquity in the intensity of its lyricism, its dramatic power, its abundance of memorable images, its sensuousness and passionateness, its immediacy of response to every mood of nature and every nuance of the soul of man. His intimate self-disclosures in the so-called 'confessions' expose to us the very depths of his soul; only in Job and the Apostle Paul and Augustine and Luther and Kierkegaard do we encounter anything similar. Yet, in striking contrast to Jeremiah's own words, we are in possession of a number of biographical narratives from a writer of quite a different temper and spirit. Thus we are permitted to see the man not only through his own eyes but through the eyes of one who could record his observations in straightforward and circumstantial prose. In addition we have a third source where the style is strongly reminiscent of the so-called Deuteronomic school of writers. It is not too much to say that we know more about Jeremiah as a person than about any figure in the Bible, with the possible exception of the Apostle Paul. Of David too we have an ample record, but not of the kind we possess for Jeremiah. Here we are permitted to view a portrait in all its light and dark shadows.

It is clear that in Jeremiah we are looking into the face of a poet of extraordinary sensitivity, a man with a seeing eye and a hearing ear, quickly responsive to all that went on about him, with a rare ability to express in moving language all that he observed and felt and suffered, all that he had heard from Yahweh, even though it might offend his proclivities toward self-centredness and hostility. Yet, despite all his self-preoccupation, he was a man of the out-of-doors; he is a *Hebrew* Wordsworth in his feeling for the hidden mystery within the world of created things, but profoundly different from the English poet in his apprehension of the historical revelation which centred in the election-covenant events in Egypt and at Sinai (cf 2^{2b-13}), which for him was always prior to every manifestation in the world of nature. While he could observe the blossoming almond in early spring (1^{11-12}), the hot air of the sirocco (4^{11}), the migratory impulse within the stork and the times of the turtledove, swallow, and crane (8^{4}), the inchoate drive of the young camel and the sexual urge of the wild ass (2^{23-24}), and even the *pathos* of the heavens and the earth (2^{13} $4^{23-26, 28}$), they were but sign and symbol of Yahweh's active sovereignty. He needed the sustaining comfort and joys of family life, but they were denied him (16^{1-2}). He was consoled and strengthened by the awareness of Yahweh's presence, but he knew the spiritual torment of His absence ($1^{8, 19}$ 15^{20} 14^{8-9}); he could sense Yahweh's contending in his behalf like a dread warrior (20^{11}), live by faith in the power of His Word (1^{9} $15^{16, 19}$), though he could reel like a drunken man, utterly shaken and convulsed by its holy drive (23^{9}) and be consumed by its holy fire (20^{8f}). He was destined to be a separated man, separated from every area of normal human life it would seem, but worse, he was afflicted by a sense of alienation from God (14^{7-9} 15^{18} 17^{17} 20^{7}). This sensitive and passionate man was called to be a prophet to the nations (1^{5}), an intercessor for the people, yet denied this rôle when he deemed it most necessary (7^{16} 11^{14} 14^{11-12}), Yahweh's itinerant through the streets (5^{1-6}), a gleaner of the vines (6^{9}), a tester and refiner (6^{27-30}), a living parable (13^{1-11} 18^{1-3} $19^{1-2, 10-11}$), a 'fortified city, an iron pillar, and bronze walls against the whole land' (1^{18} 15^{20}). Ridiculed, rejected, persecuted, and denounced, he nevertheless gave expression to a faith which made it possible for Israel to transcend the collapse of the nation, the destruction of the Temple, and the end of the Davidic dynasty. Little wonder that the features of his portrait can be recognized in Second Isaiah's description of the Servant of the Lord (*e.g.* Is 49^{1-6} 50^{4-9} 53^{1-12}).

Jeremiah was born in the little village of Anathoth, modern *Râs el-Kharrûbeh*, about two and a half miles NE. of Jerusalem, a son of Hilkiah the priest whose lineage may be traced to Abiathar, whom Solomon expelled to Anathoth upon his accession to the throne (1 K 2^{26}). The town lay in Benjamin, for which Jeremiah seems to have had an enduring affection (6^{1} 11^{18-23} 32^{15}). Of his early years we know nothing, but it is clear that he was reared in the faith and traditions of his fathers. Already his earliest oracles reveal a firm grasp of his election-covenant heritage (2^{2b-3}) and an intimate familiarity with his prophetic predecessors, above all with Hosea, and perhaps with the reforming movement which was to eventuate in the great Reformation of 621 B.C. His call came in 626 B.C. Before his birth Yahweh had ordained that he should be His prophet and be set apart for His service. Like Moses, Jeremiah shrinks from the task that is laid upon him, but finally he yields to the power of Yahweh's Word. He is then commissioned 'over nations and over kingdoms, to pluck up and break down, to build and to plant' (1^{9b-10}). Two visions follow, one of an almond rod (*shāḳēdh*) a sign that Yahweh will watch over (*shōḳēdh*) His Word to bring it to realization; the other of a boiling pot or cauldron 'facing away from the north,' a portent of the imminent invasion.

Jeremiah's prophetic career may be ordered as follows:

A. From the call in 626 B.C. to the Reformation of 621 B.C.
B. From the Reformation to Josiah's death in 609 B.C.
C. From 609 B.C. to the Battle of Carchemish in 605 B.C.
D. From Carchemish to the first deportation in 597 B.C.
E. From 597 B.C. to the destruction of Jerusalem in 586 B.C.

A. FROM 626–621 B.C.—The prophet's activity during this period is addressed to two major themes: (1) Judah's syncretism with the nature cults and (2) the imminent coming of the foe from the north. He opens his oracles with a succinct summary of Israel's covenant life with Yahweh in the days of her origins (2^{2b-3}), and then contrasts with them existing conditions. Rulers, priests, prophets, and people have all abandoned their God and have gone after Canaanite Baal. 'Where are the gods you have made for yourself?' In a long oracle he calls upon his people to return to their God (3^{1}–4^{4}*; * indicates that the passage is composite). The following section is devoted mainly to the northern foe (4^{5}–6^{30}). Here the prophet rises to the heights of lyrical feeling. The foe has been identified with the Scythians, the Babylonians, and the Medes; some believe that the poems were first addressed to the Scythians, but upon their failure to appear were altered to suit the Chaldaeans. While a definitive solution has not been reached, it is probable that Jeremiah had no one power in mind, but was motivated by a deep presentiment of imminent disaster. Ch. 5 reflects the shocking impression made by his journey through the streets of Jerusalem. Later experience (ch. 6) eloquently confirmed his conviction that the people were one and all destined for judgment.

B. FROM 621–609 B.C.—Jeremiah's attitude towards Josiah's reformation is the enigma of his prophetic career. In 11^{1-8} we receive the impression that he first responded favourably to the words of the covenant. Although the language is Deuteronomic, it may well preserve an authentic reminiscence. Surely there was much in the Reformation to which he could give hearty assent, for it was based upon the election-covenant faith which was the heart of his own message. Moreover, the stress upon Israel's uniqueness as a holy people, upon Yahweh's abiding love for His people and a responding love on their part, upon the destruction of the high places, and upon moral reforms—all this surely had his approval. Yet the period after 621–609 B.C. is, so far as Jeremiah is concerned, one of silence. The Reformation may have been so successful during these years that Jeremiah did not feel it incumbent upon him to prophesy, or the experience of rejection and failure during his early ministry so acute that he was prompted to withdraw from prophetic activity, though there is no evidence for such a supposition. Be that as it may, the death of Josiah at Megiddo awakened the nation to its perilous state. When Jehoahaz was carried off to Riblah by Neco three months later Jeremiah lamented for him (22^{10}).

C. FROM 609–605 B.C.—Judah was in despair. At the beginning of Jehoiakim's reign, on the occasion of a national gathering at the Temple, perhaps the festival of the New Year associated with the coronation of Jehoiakim, Jeremiah preached a sermon denouncing the false reliance upon the Temple as a place of refuge, calling the people to amend their conduct, and reminding them of the evil fate that had befallen Shiloh, the centre of the twelve-tribe amphictyony in the days of the Judges (Jg 21, 1 S 1). The speech in 7^{1-15} is paralleled by the account of ch. 26, which describes the outrage of the priests and princes, how Jeremiah almost lost his life, the prophet's eloquent defence, and the verdict of the people. A false religion had entrenched itself within the forms of the Covenant, armed with the weapons of institutionalism and power. Jehoiakim proved to be a tyrannical and oppressive king, and the reforming movement suffered a sharp reversal during his reign ($7^{17-19,\,30f}$ 11^{9-13}). Jeremiah's activities in support of the Reformation were deeply resented, even by his own townsmen and relatives at Anathoth, who now sought to dispose of him (11^{18-23}). Moreover, Judah compensated for her faithlessness to the covenant bond and her disobedience to its demands by sacrificial offerings and cultic acts, which Jeremiah attacked with great rigour (7^{21-24} 11^{15f} 17^{1}). Insistently he warned the people of their peril, exhorted them to obedience ($7^{23-26,\,27-29}$ 22^{1-5}), and demanded a change of mind and heart (8^{4-7} 9^{5}), even though he had come to believe that they were incapable of true repentance. He launched a bitter invective against Jehoiakim and reminded him of the good deeds of his father Josiah (22^{13-19}). In the year of the Battle of Carchemish (605 B.C.) he was commanded to dictate all his words up to that time to Baruch, his amanuensis (36^{1-3}). The words were read on the occasion of a national fast (36^{9}) in the hearing of the people. The indictment was so serious that it was called to Jehoiakim's attention, and when the scroll was read aloud to him, he proceeded to cut off the columns and throw them into the fire. Jeremiah was forced into hiding and his fellow-prophet, Uriah, lost his life. Ch. 46 preserves a poem on the Battle of Carchemish, which may be the prophet's own composition. About this time, too, after he had again proclaimed the imminent doom of Jerusalem, Pashhur the priest put him in stocks for the night. When he returned to release Jeremiah, the prophet delivered a bitter denunciation of the priest and accompanied it with his original words (19^{14}–20^{6}).

D. FROM 605–597 B.C.—It is perhaps to this period we are to assign most of Jeremiah's 'confessions' (11^{18}–12^{6}* 15^{10-21}* 17^{12-18} 18^{18-23} 20^{7-18}). Such experiences as the furor aroused by his Temple address and the Pashhur episode doubtless exacted a heavy toll. In the confessional laments we hear him bewailing his birth, grieving that it is his fate always to stand in opposition, 'a man of strife and contention against the whole land' (15^{10}). He recalls times when God's Word was a delight (15^{16}), but he is afflicted by his sense of alienation: 'I sat alone because thy hand was upon me' (15^{17}). He even approaches blasphemy in accusing Yahweh of deceiving him (20^{7}; cf 14^{8}), and cries out in the bitterness of inward agony (15^{18}). But what is remarkable in these cries is that Jeremiah is able to hear YahEeh cancelling his protestations and calling upon him to return. In this same period Jeremiah brings the Rechabites to the Temple as an example of obedience to their vows (ch. 35). When Jehoiachin was taken to Babylon in 597 B.C. he gave no hope of his return.

E. FROM 597–586 B.C.—Nebuchadrezzar had dealt liberally with Judah. He permitted her to retain her own king, another son of Josiah and an uncle of the lamented Jehoiachin, whose regnal name was Zedekiah. But he was equipped neither by temperament nor by ability to direct the nation along a stable course. The fires of nationalism continued to blaze even after that terrible siege and the exile of many of the leaders and artisans, and the priests and prophets added fuel to the flames by encouraging the people to believe that Chaldaea would be defeated and that the exiles would soon return. From the beginning of his ministry Jeremiah had opposed their apostasy, but now the issue was crucial, and he did not hesitate to denounce their ungodliness and their slippery counsels (23^{9-12}). He urged the people not to listen to their optimistic predictions; their 'visions' were but fabrications of their own minds. None of them had stood in Yahweh's council or had heard His Word. When the representatives of the smaller nations gathered in Jerusalem, doubtless for the purpose of creating a common front against Chaldaea, he appeared before them as they were leaving the council chamber, with thongs and yoke-bars on his neck (27^{1ff}). He proclaimed Yahweh's sovereignty over the whole earth and asserted that it was He who determined the fate of nations. To Nebuchadrezzar His servant He had given all the lands; resistance was therefore futile. The prophets, diviners, soothsayers, and sorcerers were lying. Some time later, in the presence of a crowd of priests, prophets, and people gathered in the Temple, Hananiah, a prophet from Gibeon, proclaimed the imminent return of the exiles and of Jehoiachin. Jeremiah shared Hananiah's wish, but reminded him that the prophets 'of ancient times' prophesied only of doom and that the prophet who proclaimed 'peace' would be justified only by the event. Thereupon Hananiah took the yoke-bars from Jeremiah's neck and broke them, declaring that even so Yahweh would break the yoke of Nebuchadrezzar from the necks of the nations. Jeremiah departed, but later returned with bars of iron and told Hananiah that he had been sent by Yahweh and that within a year he would die (chs. 27–28). Perhaps it was about this time that Jeremiah wrote a letter to the exiles admonishing them not to be deceived by the dreams of the diviners and prophets. The exile would be long, and he urged them to seek the welfare of their captors, 'for in its welfare you will find your welfare' (29^{1-14}).

The demand for resistance grew more and more insistent, and Zedekiah was no longer able to withstand its pressure. Jeremiah had sought to uphold the hands of the young and unstable monarch by counselling him in season and out not to be deterred by all the pro-war propaganda, for to yield was only to invite destruction. But his efforts were unavailing. Nebuchadrezzar came with his army and besieged Jerusalem for a year and a half. The city was surrounded and the towns of Judah systematically destroyed. The Lachish ostraca which come from this time show a number of interesting affinities with the Book of Jeremiah (see J. B. Pritchard,

ANET, 321–322). During the siege Jeremiah went to the king to tell him that Yahweh had given the city to Nebuchadrezzar and that he would be carried off to Babylon (34^{1-6}). As the siege continued Zedekiah made a covenant with the people that they should emancipate their slaves ; at first the people held to their agreement, but in a short time took them back again. Jeremiah rebuked them severely for this breach of faith (34^{8-22}). The siege was lifted some time later at the approach of the Egyptian army. Zedekiah asked the prophet to pray for the city, but the Word of the Lord which came to him was that the city would certainly be destroyed (37^{1-10}). Jeremiah sought to take advantage of the temporary relief by going to his home at Anathoth, but was met at the Benjamin gate of the city by a sentry who forthwith arrested him. He was accused of desertion to the enemy which he heatedly denied. He was then taken to the princes, who were enraged. He was beaten and imprisoned. After he had languished there for some time Zedekiah sent for him to inquire whether there was any word from Yahweh. Jeremiah replied there was : 'You shall be delivered into the hand of the king of Babylon.' He then implored the king not to return him to prison ; his request was granted, and he was committed to the court of the guard (37^{16-21}). While here he received a word from Yahweh that he should purchase a field from his cousin Hanamel since the right of redemption was his. He interpreted the word as a sign that normal commercial actions would be resumed in the city (32^{1-15}). Jeremiah continued to urge capitulation to the Chaldaeans, even by individual citizens : it was a choice between life or death. His words evidently had some effect, for he was accused of weakening the morale of the troops. The princes demanded his death, and Zedekiah admitted that he could no longer resist their demands. So Jeremiah was confined to a cistern of the court of the guard. He was later rescued by Ebed-melech (38^{1-13}). Zedekiah received him at the entrance to the Temple, and a poignant interview followed. The king was desperate, and begged Jeremiah to withhold nothing from him. Jeremiah urged him to surrender, the only alternative being the destruction of the city. Zedekiah, however, feared the revenge of those who had already deserted. He then besought the prophet not to disclose the contents of the interview, even to deny what had taken place, and Jeremiah acceded to his request (38^{14-28}).

The Chaldaeans entered the city on the ninth of Ab, (39^{1-2}, 2 K 25^{8-21}). Nebuchadrezzar was evidently informed as to Jeremiah's activities and instructed the captain of the guard to show him special consideration. He was released from prison and went to Mizpah to join Gedaliah, the governor of the newly created Babylonian province appointed by the Chaldaean king. The little remnant suffered great reverses. Gedaliah and his attendants were slain. The leaders who were left turned to Jeremiah for counsel. After ten days he came with the Word of the Lord. They should remain in Palestine, entrust themselves to the Chaldaeans, and forget all plans of leaving the land. The leaders were incensed, and accused him of being instigated by Baruch. Then they set out for Egypt, taking Jeremiah and his amanuensis with them. While there Jeremiah performed a symbolic act, designed to show that Nebuchadrezzar would devastate Egypt. It may have been in Egypt that Baruch compiled Jeremiah's prophecies with his own prose narratives. It included a special collection known as 'The Little Book of Comfort' (chs. 30–31), much of which has the style and manner of the prophet's early poems. But more important was the prophecy of the new covenant (31^{31-34}), based upon forgiveness of all of Judah's transgressions, a covenant in which the Torah would be engraved on men's hearts, so that all men might know him, from the least to the greatest. It was a fit finale to the prophet's long and tortuous career, which had opened with his account of Yahweh's memories of Israel's days of faithfulness to the covenant at Sinai.

3. The book.—The book of Jeremiah is a fabric woven out of several strands. It is a compilation of compilations, containing a great variety of literary forms. While there are many indications of systematic ordering, especially within the collections, it is just as clear that the book as a whole has passed through an involved literary process, that intrusive elements disturb the literary and historical sequence, and that the final edition of the book was prepared long after Jeremiah's death. It is probable that the first edition of the book was the work of Baruch. In the year 604 B.C. Jeremiah dictated to Baruch 'all the words' he had spoken from the beginning of his prophetic ministry in 626 B.C., and later after the burning of the scroll by Jehoiakim (ch. 36) he added many other similar words. Many attempts have been made to reconstruct this scroll. It is probable that it is contained within 1^{5}–25^{13}, though much of this material cannot with propriety be assigned to it, *e.g.* the prophet's personal disclosures and some of the prose accounts. Yet it is in this section that we have by far the greatest amount of authentic Jeremianic prophecy. The second division of the book (chs. 26–45) is composed almost entirely of prose narratives, presumably from Baruch (chs. 30–31 are intrusive). The prophecies against the foreign nations (chs. 46–51) appear to have a different literary history from the rest of the book. Whether any of it stems from Jeremiah it is difficult to say. The vivid oracle on the Battle of Carchemish in 46^{3ff} may be his, and it is possible that his hand may be traced elsewhere. The final chapter of the book is derived from 2 K 24^{18}–$25^{21, 27-30}$, but fortunately includes the important record of the numbers carried into captivity in 597, 586, and 581 B.C. (52^{28-30}).

The most influential study of the composition of the book is the monograph by Sigmund Mowinckel, *Zur Komposition des Buches Jeremia* (1914). In this work Mowinckel recognized three major sources or strands : (A) the prophet's *ipsissima verba*, which are to be found exclusively within the compass of chs. 1–25 ; (B) the work of the author of the book as a whole, a personal-historical composition, present for the most part in chs. 26–45, but containing also $19^{1-2, 10-11a, 14}$ 20^{6} ; (C) a third source, already recognized by B. Duhm, of Deuteronomic style, with the characteristic introduction, 'The Word which came to Jeremiah from Yahweh.' Mowinckel denied that Baruch had any hand in the composition of the book, and assigned Source B to the period between 580–480 B.C. It is doubtful whether this position can be sustained, however, since much of this material has strong claim to be historical, and it may well have been composed during Jeremiah's own lifetime, probably during the years of exile in Egypt. Yet Mowinckel has properly discerned the major strata of the book, and his study forms a good foundation for the critical understanding of its composition.

The first major division of the book is devoted in the main to prophecies against Judah and Jerusalem (chs. 1–25). The superscription is the work of the compiler (1^{1-3}), presumably Baruch. Three episodes are associated with the call ($1^{4-10, 11-12, 13-19}$), the third a possible duplicate of the first, which certainly preserves an authentic record stemming from Jeremiah. The early oracles are genuine, though 3^{6-12a} and $^{15-18}$ are intrusive. In ch. 4, vv.$^{9-10}$ and $^{11-12}$ belong to Jeremiah though they disturb the sequence. The poems on the foe from the north (4^{5}–6^{30}) are authentic. 7^{1}–8^{3} is in prose, but its historicity cannot be questioned. The same applies to 11^{1}–12^{6}. The confessional laments (11^{18}–12^{6*} 15^{10-21*} 17^{12-18} 18^{18-23} 20^{7-18}) are generally recognized as Jeremiah's. The invectives against the kings in 21^{11}–23^{8*} and against the popular prophets in 23^{9-40} are also original. In its present form ch. 24 does not belong to Jeremiah, but it is based upon an authentic report. 25^{1-13} is Deuteronomic in style, but it witnesses to a crucial stage in the prophet's career.

The biographical narratives of chs. 36–45 (omitting late elements such as 33^{14-26}) give us Baruch's memoir of Jeremiah's activity and trials from the beginning of

Jehoiakim's reign (cf 26^{1}) to his exile in Egypt. The account of the uproar following the Temple speech is a duplicate of 7^{1-15}. The poems in chs. 30–31 do not belong in their present context. They contain both early and late elements. The following passages in all probability belong to Jeremiah: $30^{5-7, 12-17, 23-24}$ $31^{2-6, 7-9, 15-22}$. Some original material may have been reworked in other parts, but in the main the rest is late, bearing the stamp of later writers like Second Isaiah. The oracles against the foreign nations (chs. 46–51) have another history than the foregoing sections. Hans Bardtke ('Jeremia der Fremdvölkerprophet,' *ZAW* liii, 1935, 209–239; liv, 1936, 240–262) has argued for the authenticity of most of these poems. While there is much that is attractive in his view, it is doubtful whether his position can be sustained as he has stated it. Yet the possibility of Jeremianic elements in the prophecies cannot be summarily dismissed.

The Greek translation (LXX) of *Jeremiah* departs from the Massoretic text in two main respects. (1) The oracles against the foreign nations (chs. 46–51) are inserted after 25^{13} and appear in an entirely different order:

MT: Egypt (ch. 46), Philistines (ch. 47), Moab (ch. 48), Ammonites (49^{1-6}), Edom (49^{7-22}), Damascus (49^{23-27}), Kedar and Hazor (49^{28-33}), Elam (49^{34-39}), Babylon (50^{51-58}).

LXX: Elam, Egypt, Babylon, Philistines, Edom, Ammonites, Kedar, Damascus, Moab.

(2) The LXX also differs from MT in its length, being about one-eighth shorter. The subtracted matter usually represents individual verses or parts of verses. At least two omissions may be explained by homoioteleuton (39^{4-13} and $51^{44b-49a}$). Others are probably intentional, since they represent doublets in the Hebrew text (8^{10-12} 30^{10f} 48^{10f}). Still others may be plausibly explained by their omission from the Hebrew *Vorlage* employed by the translators, as in 33^{14-26}. Stylistic and cultic interests may also have played a rôle in some of the omissions. In assessing the value of one text over the other, it must be said that the LXX should be used with circumspection and that each case of divergence should be considered independently.

Outline of the Book

I. Prophecies Against Judah and Jerusalem: chs. 1–25
- A. Superscription: 1^{1-3}.
- B. The call: $1^{4-10, 11-12, 13-19}$.
- C. Oracles and poems of the early ministry: 2^{1}–6^{30}.
  1. Against the prevailing syncretism with alien cults: 2^{2}–4^{4}.
  2. Poems on the foe from the north: 4^{5}–6^{30}.
- D. Oracles against cultic practices: 7^{1}–8^{3}.
  1. The Temple sermon: 7^{1-15}.
  2. The queen of heaven: 7^{16-20}.
  3. Against sacrifice: 7^{21-28}.
  4. The rites in the valley of Hinnon: 7^{29}–8^{3}.
- E. Invectives, threats, exhortations, and laments: 8^{4}–10^{25}.
- F. Jeremiah's support of the covenant reforms: 11^{1}–12^{6}.
- G. Parables, laments, and warnings: 12^{7}–13^{27}.
- H. Liturgy of the great drought: 14^{1}–15^{9}.
- I. Confessions and judgments: 15^{10}–20^{18}.
- J. Invectives against kings and prophets: 21^{1}–23^{40}.
- K. Vision of the baskets of figs: 24^{1-10}.
- L. Summary and conclusion: 25^{1-13}.
- M. The cup of wrath for the nations: 25^{15-38}.

II. Biographical Narratives: the memoirs of Baruch: chs. 26–45.
- A. Conflicts with priests and prophets: 26^{1}–29^{32}.
  1. The Temple address and the ensuing crisis: 26^{1-24}.
  2. The international conclave: 27^{1-22}.
  3. Hananiah and Jeremiah: 28^{1-17}.
  4. Letters to the exiles: 29^{1-32}.
- B. The Little Book of Comfort: 30^{1}–31^{40} (a later insertion).
- C. The purchase of a field from Hanamel: 32^{1-35}.
- D. The restoration of Jerusalem: 32^{36}–33^{26}.
- E. Prophetic activity under Jehoiakim and Zedekiah: 34^{1}–36^{32}.
  1. Warning: 34^{1-7}.
  2. The broken covenant of emancipation: 34^{8-22}.
  3. The exemplary conduct of the Rechabites: 35^{1-19}.
  4. The scroll of judgment burned and rewritten: 36^{1-32}.
- F. Prophetic activity during the siege: 37^{1}–40^{6}.
  1. Imprisonment: 37^{1-21}.
  2. Ebed-melech's rescue: 38^{1-27}.
  3. The fall of Jerusalem: 39^{1-14}.
  4. Oracle concerning Ebed-melech: 39^{15-18}.
  5. Jeremiah's release: 40^{1-6}.
- G. Jeremiah at Mizpah and the flight to Egypt: 40^{7}–43^{7}.
- H. The last years: 43^{8}–44^{30}.
- I. Oracle to Baruch: 45^{1-5}.

III. Oracles Against the Foreign Nations: 46^{1}–51^{64}.

IV. Historical Appendix: 52^{1-34}.

G. G. F.—**J. Mu.**

JEREMIAH, LETTER (EPISTLE) OF.—See Apocrypha, **9.**

JEREMIAS, 1 Es 9^{34} (AV, RV).—See Jeremai.

JEREMIEL.—The archangel who in 2 Es 4^{36} answers the questions of the righteous dead. AV has *Uriel*, the angel sent to instruct Esdras (2 Es 4^{1} 5^{20} 10^{28}).

JEREMOTH.—**1. 2.** Two Benjamites, 1 Ch 7^{8} (AV **Jerimoth**) 8^{14}. **3. 4.** Two Levites, 1 Ch 23^{23} 25^{22}; the former called **Jerimoth** in 24^{30}. **5.** A Naphtalite, 1 Ch 27^{19} (AV **Jerimoth**). **6. 7. 8.** Three of those who had married foreign wives, Ezr 10^{26}, 1 Es 9^{27} (AV, RV **Hieremoth**); Ezr 10^{27}, 1 Es 9^{28} (AV, RV **Jarimoth**); Ezr 10^{29} (AV 'and Ramoth' following *Ḳᵉrê*), 1 Es 9^{30} (AV, RV **Hieremoth**).

JEREMY.—The form in which the name of the prophet *Jeremiah* appears in both AV and RV of 1 Es $1^{28, 32, 47, 57}$ 2^{1}, 2 Es 2^{18}, as well as in AV of 2 Mac $2^{1, 5, 7}$, Mt 2^{17} 27^{9}. In the last three passages RV has *Jeremiah*. The form *Jeremy* is used also in both AV and RV in the title of the Epistle ascribed to the prophet in Bar 6^{1}. RSV consistently uses Jeremiah. See Apocrypha, **9.**

JERIAH.—The chief of one of the Levitical courses, 1 Ch 23^{19} 24^{23}; called **Jerijah** in 26^{31}.

JERIBAI.—One of David's heroes, 1 Ch 11^{46}.

JERICHO.—A city situated in the Jordan Valley about 5 miles from the north end of the Dead Sea. It is chiefly famous in the Bible as the first city conquered by the Israelites after their passage of the Jordan (Jos 1–7). During the period covered by the OT, it does not thereafter appear as an important town, but is mentioned on a number of occasions during the periods of the United and Divided Kingdoms. The final defeat of Zedekiah, the last king of Judah, by the Babylonians took place at Jericho (2 K 25^{5}, Jer 39^{5} 52^{8}). Josephus records events here in the Maccabaean and early Roman periods. In the Gospels, Jericho figures in the stories of Bartimaeus (Mt 20^{29}, Mk 10^{46}, Lk 18^{35}), Zacchaeus (Lk 19^{1}), and the Good Samaritan (Lk 10^{30}).

Three major archaeological expeditions have investigated *Tell es-Sulṭân*, usually accepted as the site of OT Jericho, which lies at the source of *'Ain es-Sulṭân* or Elisha's spring. The most recent excavations, sponsored by the British School of Archaeology in Jerusalem, have shown that the settlement is the oldest yet found in Palestine, and indeed anywhere in the Near East. The first evidence is provided by a structure which is probably a sanctuary established near the stream by Mesolithic hunters, *c* 7800 B.C. The descendants of these hunters settled down beside the stream, living at first in a small settlement, in flimsy huts. Eventually they started to build solid houses, still round in plan like the huts, and these houses spread over an area of nearly ten acres. A population of this size indicates that an efficient agriculture had been evolved, and probably a system of irrigation. By about 7000 B.C. the settlement was defended by a massive stone wall, attached to which was at least one great stone tower. After a period of occupation which produced a large number of house levels one on top of another, this settlement, which can be claimed to be the earliest known town in the world, was destroyed, and the site was occupied by newcomers with a different equipment, still not including pottery. Their houses also were different and were of a more advanced rectilinear plan, with characteristically plastered floors. About 5800 B.C. this settlement also was surrounded by a wall.

The second Neolithic town was in turn destroyed, and the site was occupied by newcomers who brought the use of pottery with them but who had none of the attributes of town dwellers. A second wave of similarly backward people can be equated with a stage which represents the first beginnings of village life so far traced in the East or the Near East, *c* 4500 B.C.

It was not until the beginning of the Early Bronze Age, *c* 2900 B.C., that Jericho again became a town. Numerous rebuilds of the town walls during this period indicate the dangers to Jericho from its position on the route into the fertile Mediterranean countries for invading nomads from the semi-desert to the east, *c* 2300 B.C. Nomads finally overcame the civilization of the Palestinian Early Bronze Age, destroying Jericho and many other towns. These nomads can with great probability be identified with the Amorites, and evidence of their tribal character was found at Jericho. A fresh civilizing wave entered the country *c* 1900 B.C., coming from the Phoenician coastal area, and representing the Canaanites as found by the Patriarchs. The Jericho of this time was defended by a great bank, revetted at the foot with stone, the slope faced with plaster, and crowned by a wall. Small portions of the town with close-built houses flanking cobbled streets have been found, and also remarkable examples of the wooden furniture with which the houses were equipped.

About 1580 B.C. the town was destroyed, probably by the Egyptians, and there was a period of abandonment until *c* 1400 B.C. Of the succeeding town, which must be that of the period of the entry of the Israelites into Palestine, almost nothing has survived the erosion by weather to which this ancient mound has been subjected. The identification of town walls as those of the period of Joshua by the 1930–1936 expedition has been shown to be erroneous. What little evidence there is points to a date in the second half of the 14th cent. for the destruction of the town of this period.

Archaeology confirms the Biblical evidence of the abandonment of the site after this period. It does not however confirm a reoccupation by Hiel the Bethelite as early as the time of Omri (1 K 16^{34}). There is a considerable Iron Age occupation, but probably not earlier than the 7th cent., and ending at the time of the Second Exile.

From this time, *Tell es-Sulṭân* ceases to represent the site of the town of Jericho. Little evidence has been found concerning the settlement in the Hellenistic or Maccabaean period, but it may have been on the site of the Herodian town, which was centred on the waters of the *Wâdī Qelt* and not those of *'Ain es-Sulṭân.* There parts of a grandiose building, with a great terrace-facade in Roman style *opus reticulatum,* have been excavated, which may be Herod's palace. Traces of Roman occupation are spread over a wide area of the valley round about.

Arab remains often succeed the traces of Roman and Byzantine buildings in the area, and the Arab ruler Hisham (A.D. 724–743) built a magnificent palace about a mile N. of *Tell es-Sulṭân.* But during the Arab and Turkish rule, cultivation and irrigation decayed, until at the beginning of this century the site was only represented by the miserable village of *er-Riḥa.* Since 1948, however, great progress has been made, and *er-Riḥa* is now a thriving municipality, and the centre of a growing area of cultivation. R. A. S. M.—**K. M. K.**

JERIEL.—A chief of Issachar, 1 Ch 7^{2}.

JERIJAH.—See JERIAH.

JERIMOTH.—**1. 2.** Two Benjamites, 1 Ch 7^{7} 12^{5}. **3. 4. 5.** Three Levites, 1 Ch 24^{30} (called **Jeremoth** in 23^{23}), 25^{4}, 2 Ch 31^{13}. **6.** A son of David and father of Rehoboam's wife, 2 Ch 11^{18}. **7.** 1 Ch 7^{8} (AV ;) see JEREMOTH, **1.** **8.** 1 Ch 27^{19} (AV) ; see JEREMOTH, **5.**

JERIOTH.—One of Caleb's wives, 1 Ch 2^{18} ; but almost certainly the MT is corrupt.

JEROBOAM is the name of two kings of Israel.

1. Jeroboam I. was the first king of the northern tribes after the division. His first appearance in history is as head of the forced labourers levied by Solomon. This was perhaps because he was hereditary chief in Ephraim, but we must also suppose that he attracted the attention of Solomon by his ability and energy. At the same time he resented the tyranny of the prince whom he served, and plotted to overthrow it. The design came to the knowledge of Solomon, and Jeroboam fled to Egypt. On the king's death he returned, and although he did not appear on the scene when the northern tribes made their demand of Rehoboam, he was probably actively enlisted in the movement. When the refusal of Rehoboam threw the tribes into revolt, Jeroboam appeared as leader, and was made king (1 K 11^{26ff} 12^{1}–14^{20}). Jeroboam was a warlike prince, and hostilities with Judah continued throughout his reign. His country was plundered by the Egyptians at the time of their invasion of Judah. It is not clearly made out whether his fortification of Shechem and Penuel was suggested by the experiences of this campaign or not. His religious measures have received the reprobation of the Biblical writers, but they were intended by Jeroboam to please the God of Israel. He embellished the ancestral sanctuaries of Bethel and Dan with golden bulls, in continuance of early Israelite custom. It is fair to assume also that he had precedent for celebrating the autumn festival in the eighth instead of the seventh month.

2. Jeroboam II. was the grandson of Jehu. In his time Israel was able to assert its ancient vigour against its hereditary enemy Syria, and recover its lost territory. This was due to the attacks of the Assyrians upon the northern border of Damascus (2 K 14^{23-29}). The temporary prosperity of Israel was accompanied by social and moral degeneracy, as is set forth distinctly by Amos and Hosea. H. P. S.

JEROHAM.—**1.** The father of Elkanah and grandfather of Samuel, 1 S 1^{1}, 1 Ch $6^{27, 34}$; see JERAHMEEL, **2.** **2.** A Benjamite family name, 1 Ch 8^{27} 9^{8}. **3.** A priestly family, 1 Ch 9^{12}, Neh 11^{12}. **4.** 'Sons of Jeroham' were amongst David's heroes, 1 Ch 12^{7}. **5.** A Danite chief, 1 Ch 27^{22}. **6.** The father of Azariah, who helped Jehoiada in the overthrow of Athaliah, 2 Ch 23^{1}.

JERUBBAAL.—A name given to Gideon, Jg 6^{32} 7^{1} $8^{29, 35}$ $9^{1f, 5, 16, 19, 24, 28, 57}$, 1 S 12^{11}. It means 'Baal strives,' Baal being a name for Y″, as in *Ishbaal, Meribbaal* ; it cannot mean 'one who strives with Baal,' as Jg 6^{32} would suggest. This name was altered to **Jerubbesheth** (*besheth* = 'shame') when Baal could no longer be used of Y″ without offence (2 S 11^{21}) ; cf *Ishbosheth, Mephibosheth.*

JERUBBESHETH.—See JERUBBAAL.

JERUEL.—The part of the wilderness of Judaea that faces the west shore of the Dead Sea below En-gedi. It was here that Jehoshaphat encountered a great host of the children of Moab, Ammon, and other trans-Jordanic tribes, 2 Ch 20^{16}.

JERUSALEM.—I. SITUATION.—Jerusalem is the principal city of Palestine, situated in 31° 46′ 45″ N.

latitude and 35° 13′ 25″ E. longitude. It owes its importance to the command that its situation gives it of the central mountain ridge, forming the natural north-south highway.

1. The old city is built on two ridges which run south from an eastward spur of the central ridge. The southern ends of these spurs form steep promontories. On the east, the Valley of **Kidron,** or **Jehoshaphat,** has at its south end a slope of almost one in two, and the eastern spur, of which the southern end is known as **Ophel,** is flanked on its western side by the **Tyropoeon** Valley, of which the slope was originally almost equally steep; both these valleys originate well to the north of the city, and enclose a narrow spur which was the site of what was probably the oldest settlement and of the extension occupied by the Temple. The western spur is broader, and is bounded on the west by the **Valley of Hinnom,** with a slope of about one in four, originating some 600 metres south of the other two valleys, at a point where a lateral valley running down into the Tyropoeon nearly isolates the southern end of the western spur. The eastern spur is also cut into by a lateral valley running down into the Kidron, at a point slightly north of the last mentioned valley. Both spurs, therefore, have great natural advantages as defensive sites.

2. The chief drawback to the site is that it is not well provided with water. The only natural source is the spring **Gihon,** or the Virgin's Fountain, on the west slopes of Ophel, from which the waters naturally flow down the Kidron Valley. At all ages down to to-day, the city has largely depended upon cisterns storing the winter rains, but **conduits** of many ages have been engineered to bring in water from springs in the mountains to the west. An aqueduct traditionally ascribed to Solomon brought water from reservoirs beyond Bethlehem; others are of Roman date, and in the days of the Mandate the springs at *Râs el-ʿAin* were tapped.

II. History.—**1. Sources.**—For the history of the site before the 14th cent. B.C., we are entirely dependent upon archaeology. In the early 14th cent. the city enters the written record in the Amarna letters, and soon afterwards appears in the Biblical record. But it is not until *c* 1000 B.C., after its capture by David, that the Bible gives many details about Jerusalem. From then on, as the capital, first of the United Monarchy, and then of Judah, its history is of supreme importance, but for the translation of this history in territorial terms, the aid of archaeology is most necessary. The Biblical account after the 6th cent. return from the Babylonian exile is again most full, but once more cannot be fully interpreted without archaeological evidence. For the succeeding period, the written account becomes increasingly sparse, and it is only when the periods dealt with by Josephus are reached, culminating in the destruction of the city by Titus in A.D. 70, that we have a full account, with the aid of which the topography can be studied. For the next six hundred years, and again at the time of the Crusades, there are at intervals literary sources to provide a key to the topographical and structural history of the site.

But for all these periods, the literary account requires the confirmation of archaeology in the identification of the lines of the city walls, and indeed of the actual area occupied by the city. For this reason, the site has attracted the attention of archaeologists from the very beginnings of the attempts to reconstruct history by the examination of the surviving material remains. The results have been tantalizingly inconclusive. The earlier excavations, particularly those carried out for the Palestine Exploration Fund by Captain (later Sir Charles) Warren between 1864 and 1867, and by Messrs. Bliss and Dickie between 1894 and 1897, were models for their period. But though in both cases the records are so ample and exact that much can be deduced from them, the excavators of the period had not at their service the detailed knowledge of pottery chronology on which all archaeology must be based, which only became reliable in the decades between 1920 and 1940, nor of the stratigraphical technique which must be associated with it. It was only when excavations at various points on the city walls began to be carried out by the staff of the Department of Antiquities of the Mandate, notably by Mr. C. N. Johns at the Citadel and Mr. R. W. Hamilton against the existing north wall, that any exact criteria were established for dating masonry styles by stratigraphical association with pottery and coins. In 1961 the British School of Archaeology and the École Biblique began a new series of excavations, which produced important results.

2. The earliest periods.—It is now generally agreed that the nucleus of the first settlement was on Ophel, the southern extremity of the eastern ridge. This is the site most strongly defended by nature. Even to-day, its eastern slopes are so steep as to render the site almost inaccessible, and the Tyropoeon valley to the west was originally also as steep. It is the only part of the site, moreover, adjacent to a good natural spring, Gihon. The earliest objects found come from rock-cut tombs on the eastern slopes. They consist of the pottery of the period best described as Proto-Urban, for it is the period in which were laid the foundations of the growth of the towns of the Early Bronze Age, brought into Palestine by newcomers round about 3300 B.C. It is very probable that the site developed into a town, as so many places did, in the ensuing Early Bronze Age, covering much of the 2nd millennium. Excavators of the site have in fact claimed to identify evidence of this period, but the published details are not conclusive. In 1961 the first traces were found of the town wall of the Middle Bronze Age.

3. The town of the Jebusites.—Jerusalem first appears in written history in the Amarna letters of the first third of the 14th cent. B.C., when its ruler Abdi-Khiba was one of the princelings in correspondence with Egypt. Various fragments of rough walling have been ascribed to the town of the period. The 1961 excavations, however, disproved the identification of a tumbled mass of masonry on the crest of Ophel as a bastion of the Jebusite defences. Further work is required to discover what existing remains there are of this period, for stylistic grounds are inadequate when such rough masonry is involved; similar masonry may appear over a period of some two thousand years.

It is as a town of the Jebusites, a Canaanite clan, that Jerusalem first appears in the Biblical record. In the theoretical and obviously anticipatory division of Palestine among the Israelite tribes, it was assigned to Benjamin (Jos 18^{28}), and in Jg 1^{8} it is claimed that it was captured by Judah immediately after the death of Joshua. There is, however, no doubt that this is an interpolation. All archaeological evidence goes to show that the Israelite ascendancy was only very gradually achieved, as an infiltration rather than a mass immigration and over-running. The Biblical record is in fact explicit that Jerusalem was not captured, and that it remained a Jebusite stronghold (Jg 1^{21} 19^{11}). Its capture was the culminating point of David's campaign, which on the shortest chronology must be more than two hundred years later, and the importance of its position is emphasized by the fact that it was only by its capture that the north and the south could be united; the division that this Canaanite enclave had enforced on the growing Israelite nation was to have its permanent effect when the two halves once more fell apart after the death of Solomon.

The strength of the site is vividly illustrated by the account of David's attack. The Jebusites within the walls jeered at the Israelites assembled against it (2 S 5^{6}). David promised that whoever 'getteth up the gutter' (2 S 5^{8}) should become the captain of his armies, and apparently Joab succeeded in accomplishing this feat. 'The gutter' has been with great probability identified by Père L.-H. Vincent as the water-shaft which gave access to the spring Gihon from within the city. The whole complex of shafts and tunnels connected with this spring, the one source of water in Jerusalem, was revealed by the Parker excavations in 1911, and Père Vincent demonstrated that a shaft, part vertical and part oblique, was at least pre-Israelite, and as such could provide a means of penetrating the city and taking the defenders of the wall in the rear.

4. Jerusalem as capital under the United Monarchy and of the kingdom of Judah.—Having captured Jerusalem, David proceeded to fortify it. It is nowadays presumed that the site which he fortified was that of the preceding Jebusite stronghold on the eastern ridge. Archaeological evidence of this began to emerge in the 1961 excavations. The key point in his defences was **Millo,** from which he built round about and inward (2 S 5[9]). Millo was probably a tower, perhaps, from the probable Hebrew meaning of a filling, one built on a solid infilling of stone, but for its situation many suggestions have been made, and no archaeological evidence has been recovered. One of the difficulties is that there is no certain evidence of the position of the northern boundary of the original settlement. A ditch and fragments of a wall some 100 metres S. of the present city wall have been suggested as part of the line of the Jebusite defences, but they do not carry conviction.

Jerusalem was established as David's capital, and his plan was to make it a religious centre by providing a permanent home for the Ark of the Covenant (2 S 6). The actual construction of the **Temple** was, however, only carried out by his successor Solomon. The site of the Temple, with the adjoining royal palace, was on the northern portion of the eastern ridge, bounded on the north by the lateral valley mentioned in **1, 2.** It is probable that the site lay outside the original city wall, for the Biblical account describes it as the threshing-floor of Araunah the Jebusite (2 S 24[16]). The Biblical account shows that Solomon built the Temple and his palace with much magnificence. Excavations at Samaria, Megiddo, and Hazor have shown something of the sophisticated masonry and lavish decoration that the Israelites employed when for a short period they used the services of craftsmen from adjacent Phoenician lands. But though a few fragments beneath the subsequent Herodian Temple have been claimed as Solomonic work, there are no certain remains. On Ophel itself, there is nothing in this style surviving.

The summit of **Ophel** is exiguous in the extreme. A line of walls, exhibiting a number of building periods, has been traced along the southern crest, and parts of this have been ascribed to the period of David and Solomon. The 1961 excavations, however, showed that the so-called Davidic tower is in fact Maccabaean, and that great sub-structures to level up the ground, dating from the period of the Monarchy, extend far down the slope in front of it. The position of the town wall has not yet with certainty been identified, but it is at least 160 feet E. of the position hitherto suggested. The date at which occupation spread to the western ridge is uncertain. The literary evidence (2 K 14[13]) that Jehoash of Israel destroyed a length of 400 cubits (about 200 metres) suggests a north wall extending across the Tyropoeon Valley, for the defences of the narrow ridge of Ophel would not be of this length. Pottery of the 7th cent. B.C. has been found at the Citadel, probably the NW. corner of the expanded city, and at Bishop Gobert's School near the SE. angle of the western ridge.

The line traditionally ascribed to the north wall of the expanded city runs from the Citadel at the head of the Valley of Hinnom along a line just south of the present David Street, to meet the wall of the Temple enclosure about three-fifths of the way along its presumed contemporary length; the Temple would thus have formed a marked salient in the line of the city boundary. Along this line, suggestive fragments of wall have been found, though without dating evidence. The identification of this northern wall is however probable; that of the southern wall of the extended Israelite city is much less satisfactory. A wall crosses the Tyropoeon Valley between the points of the two spurs, but, as will be seen, the surviving remains belong to a much later period. Evidence of very considerable weight came from the excavations carried out in 1927 (*APEF* v.) that at a point 450 metres north of this wall there was no occupation in the bed of the Tyropoeon until the Maccabaean period. Moreover, in the 1961 excavations a number of soundings were made along the eastern slopes of the western ridge, in which no traces were found of occupation earlier than the 1st cent. A.D. Worth considering as the line of the southern wall (though it is only a hypothesis beside those proposed by many other writers) is a massive scarp with external fosse, and a wall in a style which is probably pre-Maccabaean, which runs down the western side of the western spur and turns north-eastward to follow the contours of the eastern side of the spur, onto which the Maccabaean wall crossing the valley was added. It need not necessarily render the line unworthy of consideration that further to the north-east its probable continuation was followed by a very much later, probably post-Crusader, wall, for the physical configuration of the site results time and time again in the return by later builders to the lines of their predecessors. The town-plan of Jerusalem in the time of the Divided Monarchy may thus have had a two-pronged outline to the south, following the contours of the two ridges.

That the history of the town when the United Monarchy fell apart after the death of Solomon in 935 B.C., and it became the capital of Judah, was eventful is shown only too clearly by the Biblical record. It fell to Shishak of Egypt *c* 925 B.C. in the reign of Rehoboam, to a coalition of Philistines and Arabs in the reign of Jehoram (*c* 850 B.C.), to Jehoash of Israel (796–781 B.C.), and was attacked by the kings of Syria and Israel in the reign of Ahaz of Judah (734–720 B.C.). The rebuildings and strengthenings of the walls of Jerusalem during these times were therefore innumerable, but archaeologically unidentifiable amongst the complex of rough walls revealed on the sides of Ophel. A still greater threat developed in the reign of Hezekiah (720–685 B.C.). The struggles between Judah, Israel, Syria, the Philistines, Edom, and Moab were struggles between petty powers of not unequal calibre. To all of them the revival of the great Mesopotamian empire under the Assyrians threatened annihilation. In 730 B.C. Megiddo and Hazor fell, and in 720 B.C. Samaria was destroyed by Sargon II., and the kingdom of Israel obliterated. Hezekiah realized that the next wave of advance was liable to engulf Judah. It is to his preparations to withstand the Assyrians that one of the few fragments of material evidence can be ascribed. In the Biblical account, Hezekiah stopped the waters ('that were without the city' (2 Ch 32[3-4]), so as to deprive the enemy of access to them. This was done by the remarkable engineering feat of blocking external access to Gihon, on the east slope of Ophel, and carrying the water in a tunnel right through the spur to the pool of Siloam, within the walls of Ophel towards the south-western extremity. The course of this famous **Siloam tunnel** is curiously winding, and it has been suggested that its line was designed to avoid some tombs, unfortunately robbed, which it is suggested were the Tombs of the Kings of Israel, and its level required some adjustment after it was pierced, but it was nevertheless a triumphant achievement, well celebrated by the inscription recording the meeting of the gangs working from each end. The epigraphy of the inscription and the surviving archaeological evidence would fit a dating of *c* 700 B.C., and the Biblical historical evidence confirms the probability of ascribing the operation to Hezekiah. Hezekiah also repaired the walls and added 'another wall without' (2 Ch 32[5]), perhaps to enclose the *mishneh* or 'redoublement' of the town which had grown up. This may be the much debated 'second wall' (see **6**). In the event, Jerusalem was saved by a mysterious calamity that befell the Assyrian army (2 K 19[35]).

Astute diplomacy enabled the kingdom of Judah to survive for another century, aided by the fact that Assyria was menaced at home, and eventually fell to

Babylon. The expansionist policies of Assyria were however inherited by Babylonia, and Judah's efforts to play off Egypt against Babylonia were of little avail. Jerusalem first fell to Nebuchadnezzar in 597 B.C. For a short time she was allowed to remain in existence, but intrigues with Egypt brought down Nebuchadnezzar's wrath on her again in 586 B.C. This time Jerusalem was utterly destroyed and all the people except the 'poor of the land' (2 K 25¹²) were taken away into captivity.

5. From the Return from Exile to the end of the Maccabaean period.—The destruction of Jerusalem was undoubtedly severe; though one need not suppose that it was razed to the gound. The walls were broken down, though probably breached in numerous places rather than completely levelled, and the Temple, the palace, the houses and specifically, all the houses of the great men were burnt (2 K 25⁶⁻⁷). Roofs and doors would thus be destroyed, but probably much of the stone-built walls remained standing. Still more disastrous would be the removal of all the inhabitants.

Jerusalem remained substantially in this state for fifty years. It is probable, however, that a faithful remnant carried on services of prayer and lamentation amidst the ruins of the Temple, for on the evidence of the Apocryphal Book of Baruch, the exiles in Babylon sent them vessels from the Temple that had been carried away as loot, and the wherewithal to perform sacrifices (Bar 1⁶⁻¹⁴). Similarly, no doubt, some reoccupation of the ruins took place.

But the revival of Jerusalem did not come till 537 B.C. The liberal policy towards subject peoples inaugurated by Cyrus when Babylonia fell to Persia in 538 B.C. enabled a group of the exiles to return with the specific purpose of rebuilding the Temple, which was accomplished by 516 B.C. Simultaneously, no doubt, they rebuilt their own houses. The great difference of this new Jerusalem from the old is that the Temple was the only focal point; no longer was it rivalled by an adjacent royal palace. It was now a holy city with the High Priest as the first citizen. The struggles between the priesthood and emergent temporal rulers forms the theme of much of the history for the next five hundred years.

The original royal edict allowed the re-establishment of the religious centre, but Jerusalem remained an unwalled city, a dangerous condition with jealous enemies no further away than Samaria and Ammon. There were, however, still Jews at the Persian court, and one of them, Nehemiah, persuaded King Artaxerxes to appoint him governor for the period, probably of 445–433 B.C., with the express purpose of rebuilding the walls.

The rebuilding was undertaken with much energy, various groups being allocated a set section, and accomplished in the remarkably short time of fifty-two days (Neh 6¹⁵). The course is described in much detail by Nehemiah (Neh 3, 12), but unfortunately there are too few fixed points in those parts of the circuit which are in doubt to establish what line was followed. This short period and the description of each gang that 'repaired' (Neh 3) its section, suggests that much of the work consisted of repairing breaches and gates, not of building a new wall. Much of Nehemiah's wall thus probably followed the course of the wall destroyed 150 years earlier. But the 1961 excavations on Ophel showed that this was not the case there. The destroyed buildings on the steep slope had been reduced to a tumble of stones by the winter rains. No attempt was made to restore them, and the town here shrank to the narrow summit of the ridge. The actual wall built by Nehemiah has not yet been identified, but it was probably approximately on the line of the Maccabaean wall. No evidence as to how this line ran to the south has so far been found, but it certainly did not cross the valley to the tip of the western ridge, as has hitherto been believed.

The next century was for Jerusalem a peaceful period under Persian rule; the governor appointed by the Persians was often a Jew, and real power was in the hands of the High Priest. The effect on the town of the struggles of the successor states of Alexander the Great's Empire is not certainly known, though Ptolemy Soter captured the town in 320 B.C., and the High Priest Simon the Just refortified both town and Temple about 300 B.C. (Sir 1¹⁻⁴). But a major effect on the life of the Jews was the spread of Hellenization amongst them, bitterly opposed by the orthodox. This reached a climax in 168 B.C., and Antiochus IV. Epiphanes took the opportunity to intervene and to sack Jerusalem with a great massacre. He then established a fortress '**Acra** of the Syrians' which for thirty years dominated the town and the Temple; the site is usually considered to be that subsequently occupied by **Antonia** to the north of the Temple.

It is at this stage that the Hasmonaean family of the Maccabees emerge as the champions of Jewish nationalism. The story of their rise, with the intrigues between their party and the Hellenizing one, and of the playing off of the Seleucid and Ptolemaic kingdoms one against another is not a pretty one, but brought success. In 142 B.C. Simon was granted autonomy, and at last succeeded in capturing the Acra. His successor John Hyrcanus survived an attack in 135 B.C. by Antiochus Sidetes, in which the walls were breached, being subsequently repaired, and thereafter had a long and successful reign until 107 B.C. The Hasmonaean dynasty had come to power as high priests, but the ideal of a theocratic state was dying, and John's sons Aristobulus (107–105 B.C.) and Alexander Jannaeus (105–79 B.C.) assumed the title of king. The final tragedy of the Hasmonaean dynasty came with the struggles of the latter's sons for power, which brought the Romans on the scene. In 63 B.C. Pompey besieged and captured the city. He respected the Temple, but according to Strabo (xvi) he entirely demolished the city walls.

During these two and a half centuries of struggles between the Hellenistic kingdoms, and then of the emergent nationalistic Jewish power, Jerusalem was the scene of many bitter battles. It is unlikely that archaeology will ever be able to trace minutely the history of building, destruction, and rebuilding of the city walls that the historical record suggests, for it is seldom that dating evidence is exact enough to distinguish between a succession of events within a few decades.

This is the period, however, within which we have for the first time reliable evidence for dating some part of the fortifications. In excavations extending between 1934 and 1948, Mr. C. N. Johns carried out an extensive examination of the present Citadel (*QDAP* xiv). The Citadel lies approximately in the centre of the west side of the present walled city, at the point at which the original wall turned east to join the western ridge to the eastern (**4**). He found here a line of wall curling round towards the east-west line, with on it three towers. In the structures three distinct building styles could be recognized, in chronological succession a style of roughly squared blocks, a style of stones with rough bosses and margins either comb-picked or chisel-dressed and thirdly a style with beautifully-squared stones with much slighter bosses and comb-picked margins. This third style is undoubtedly Herodian, and was found in the tower recognized as being Phasael, which Josephus says that Herod built as one of three at the north-west angle of the town. The other two styles were dated stratigraphically by the associated deposits. The second belongs to the period of Alexander Jannaeus, at the climax of the Hasmonaean rule. The first style could be dated less closely, but was certainly not earlier than the early Hellenistic or early Hasmonaean period.

These three styles can, as Johns showed, be recognized, from existing remains and from the admirable record, in the earlier of the two walls traced by Bliss and Dickie across the Tyropoeon Valley at the S. end of the western ridge. It was, however, probably not prolonged across to join the eastern ridge, as has hitherto been suggested, for the 1961 excavations found no trace of occupation of this period in the area concerned. Confirmation that the base of the Tyropoeon Valley was still not enclosed in the Maccabaean period is provided by the excavation of J. W. Crowfoot and G. M. Fitzgerald in 1927 (*APEF* v), in which a massively-built gateway, almost certainly part of a town wall, was found on the western side of Ophel at a distance of some 350 metres north of the point of the ridge, which was certainly in use down to the Maccabaean period. On the eastern side of the eastern ridge, the 1961 excavations confirmed work on the defences in the early Maccabaean period, for the town previously ascribed to the period of David can now be dated to *c* 150 B.C.

6. From the Herodian period to the destruction by Titus.—The Romans exercised considerable clemency after their victory. The Hasmonaean dynasty was allowed to retain sacerdotal power, and in 47 B.C. Caesar permitted the reconstruction of the city walls. This state of affairs was brought to an end by the characteristic internecine struggles of the members of the Hasmonaean dynasty, and eventually the Idumaean Herod, who had married into the Hasmonaean family, established himself in power and in 37 B.C. captured Jerusalem with Roman aid.

The Herodian period rivals the Solomonic in the external glories it conferred on Jerusalem. As in the Solomonic period, the artistic style was foreign. Herod was firmly Romanophil, and his buildings were in the Graeco-Roman tradition. Typical buildings, bitterly disliked by orthodox Jews, were a theatre and amphitheatre; the site of these is unknown. As far as is known he did not add to the circuit of the city, but he strengthened its fortifications by a great fortress, to which he gave the name Antonia, at the north-west angle of the Temple enclosure, and which he made his first abode, and by three great towers, Phasael, Hippicus, and Mariamne, at the north-west corner, beneath the present Citadel, in which the base of Phasael survives to a considerable height. On the archaeological evidence described in the last section, he also repaired and strengthened the southern circuit. By about 25 B.C. he had built himself a magnificent palace in the north-west corner of the city. But he was throughout distrusted and disliked by the Jews as a foreigner and as an introducer of atheistic Hellenistic innovations. It was in part as an attempt to combat this antipathy that he undertook his most grandiose construction, the complete rebuilding of the Temple. The description of this, involving massive new terrace walls, survives in Josephus' account, and portions of his foundation walls are still visible beneath the Ḥaram esh-Sherîf.

Herod died in 4 B.C. Complaints against the iniquities of his successor Archelaus brought in Roman intervention, and from A.D. 6 Judaea was annexed to the Roman province of Syria. The earlier years of direct Roman rule were peaceful, but when Pontius Pilate was appointed procurator in A.D. 26, he caused much offence to orthodox Jews. Under the Emperor Claudius comes the last period of relative Jewish autonomy. Herod Agrippa I., a grandson of Herod, was made king of Judaea, and his reign represents almost a golden age for Jerusalem. The expansion of the city was so great that he built a new wall to enclose the new northern quarter, the 'Third Wall' to be discussed below. The 1961 excavations showed that he also built a wall right across the Tyropoeon Valley to join the eastern and western ridges. After his death in A.D. 44, Judaea was ruled by Roman procurators.

This is the beginning of one of the darkest periods in Jewish history. The cruelties and excesses of the Roman procurators, unfortunately ill-selected, stimulated the fervent nationalism and messianic expectations of the Jews. This nationalistic fervour was fatally marred by bitter factional struggles amongst the Jews themselves; up to the very eve of the Roman retaliation for the revolt they were slaughtering one another.

The final attack by the Romans on Jerusalem came in A.D. 70, led by Titus after his father Vespasian had become Emperor. The events of the terrible siege and ensuing destruction are vividly described by Josephus. One by one the defences of the city fell, and finally the Temple was devastated.

It is with the description of the city by Josephus that the archaeological evidence is mainly concerned. Titus' attack was from the north, and Josephus describes three successive lines of wall, in addition to the defences of the Temple, which he had to storm. The Third Wall was built by Herod Agrippa. The First Wall, the old wall, which Josephus believed to have been built by David and Solomon, is probably that running east from the Citadel, just south of David Street, built, as has been shown in **4**, in the 8th or 7th cent. B.C. It is the line of the Second Wall which is of supreme importance to students of the Bible, for this is the wall which would have been the city wall at the time of the Crucifixion. The site of the Church of the **Holy Sepulchre**, identified as such some three hundred years later by Queen Helena, and of the adjacent rock of Calvary, lies on a knoll of rock on the north side of the lateral valley that cuts into the western ridge (**1, 2**). Any wall including a northern quarter of the city, and linking with the north-west corner of the Temple area, would have had to make a curious re-entrant angle to exclude this site. Portions of walling, on a scale which would agree with that of a town wall, have however been found following this line. Military experts have declared the line to be impossible strategically, and suggested a line curving considerably further to the north and enclosing the site of the Church (*e.g. PEQ* 1944), but no convincing archaeological proof of their theories has been adduced; on the opposing side, military reasons have been produced (*PEQ* 1946) to show that the artillery of the period mounted on the strong points undoubtedly built by Herod at Antonia and the three towers beneath the present Citadel could dominate the north-south and east-west stretches of the angular wall, and the high ground from which any attack on the blind ground of the re-entrant angle must be mounted, but would be largely useless if that high ground were within the city. But it must be admitted that there is absolutely no archaeological proof.

The position of the Third Wall is almost equally vehemently debated. For long it was accepted that this was on the line of the present north wall of the city. In support of this theory, it was shown in the excavations carried out by Mr. R. W. Hamilton (*QDAP* x) in 1937–1938 that there had been a Herodian-style tower on the site of the Damascus Gate, and other possible traces further east; these might belong either to the Second or Third Wall. On the other hand, remains of an exceedingly massive wall, including stones in a generally Herodian style, were traced in 1925–1927 by Professor E. L. Sukenik and Dr. L. A. Mayer at a distance of about 400 metres to the north of the present walls. The wall is imposing, and would agree with an expansion in the time of Herod Agrippa, but no archaeological evidence was provided to prove the dating.

A regrettable summary must be that archaeological evidence cannot yet prove the line of any of the north walls of Jerusalem.

7. Roman, Byzantine, and Islamic Jerusalem.—Jerusalem was devasted by Titus, and a garrison of Legion X Fretensis established on the western hill, to protect which the Herodian towers and a portion of the western wall were left standing. A fragment of a building of the legionary fortress was discovered in the excavations of 1934–1948 (*QDAP* xiv). There is reasonable evidence to suggest that the Jews soon filtered back into portions of the ruined city, and probably carried on trade with the Roman soldiers (*Jérusalem de l'Ancien Testament*, pp. 756–758). The complete obliteration of Jewish Jerusalem only came some forty years later. Irreconcilable Jewish nationalism brought about a series of disturbances, culminating in the Second Revolt, which was crushed by Hadrian in A.D. 135. Jewish Jerusalem was then abolished, and **Aelia Capitolina** took its place, a forbidden ground for Jews. It is usually considered that the lines of Aelia are approximately those of the present city walls. Hamilton (*QDAP* x) showed that it was very probable that the original building of the **Damascus Gate** belongs to this period, and the columned street running south from it, shown on the Madeba Map, may have originated at this period ; beneath it was a great sewer of Roman date which remains in use to-day. A rebuilding of the walls belonged to *c* A.D. 300.

In the Byzantine period, with the official acceptance of Christianity, a great period of prosperity began, with religious buildings such as the Church of the **Holy Sepulchre** springing up. The excavations of 1927 showed that the town was then once more expanding along Ophel. It is probable however that this area was not walled again until the time of the Empress Eudocia in the 6th cent. The church built by the Empress over the Pool of Siloam was explored by Bliss in 1897.

In the 7th cent., Jerusalem fell to the infidel. After an occupation by the Persians from A.D. 614–628, it fell to the invading Moslems in A.D. 637. Hamilton has shown (*QDAP* x) that the lower course of the present north wall for the most part belongs to an early Islamic building, and it is very probable, from the description of style, that the later wall found by Bliss and Dickie at the furthest south extent of the city between the tips of the two ridges belongs to this period. The supreme example of the early Arab work is the great sanctuary of the Dome of the Rock, on the site of the Jewish Temple.

The ephemeral Crusader occupation left many relics in Jerusalem, mainly in the churches, such as that of the Holy Sepulchre, but also at the Citadel, where the tower Phasael, the ‘ Tower of David ’, was transformed into both citadel and royal residence. Of the period when Jerusalem fell once more to the Moslems, there are few relics, but fragments of a wall found by Bliss and Dickie on the east slope of the western ridge suggest that parts of the southern ridges were included at this time. The present walls, bounding the Old City of Jerusalem, and excluding the southern spurs, were constructed by Suleiman the Magnificent after the Turkish conquest in A.D. 1517.

8. Modern Jerusalem—The city bounded by the wall built by Suleiman the Magnificent remained the essential Jerusalem down to the time of the British Mandate. Though a Moslem city, dominated by the great sanctuary of the Dome of the Rock, a remarkable tolerance enabled aliens to live there, and the Old City had its Christian, Armenian, and Jewish quarters. With the establishment of the British Mandate in 1919, Jerusalem became the headquarters of the Mandatory Power. A considerable expansion took place, and a New City grew up outside the walls, mainly to the west and north-west. When the division of Palestine between Arabs and Jews took place after the end of the Mandate in 1948, Jerusalem became the frontier point at the end of a Jewish salient into the hill-country. The western and half the northern walls of the Old City form to-day the boundary between the two. The New City is now entirely Jewish, and has expanded enormously. A new Arab city is rapidly growing up to the north of the old walls.

K. M. K.

JERUSALEM (GATES OF).—The following gates of Jerusalem are mentioned in the Bible : **1. Ephraim Gate** 2 K 14[13], 2 Ch 25[23], Neh 8[16] 12[39]. **2. Corner Gate,** 2 K 14[13], 2 Ch 25[23] 26[29], Jer 31[38], Zec 14[10]. **3. Gate between the two walls,** 2 K 25[4], Jer 39[4] 52[7]. **4. Gate of the Foundation,** 2 Ch 23[5]. **5. Horse Gate,** 2 Ch 23[15], Neh 3[28], Jer 31[40]. **6. Valley Gate,** 2 Ch 26[9], Neh 2[13, 15] 3[13]. **7. Fish Gate,** 2 Ch 33[14], Neh 3[3] 12[39], Zeph 1[10]. **8. Dung Gate,** Neh 2[13] 3[13f] 12[31]. **9. Fountain Gate,** Neh 2[14] 3[15] 12[37]. **10. Sheep Gate,** Neh 3[1, 32] 12[39]. **11. Old Gate,** Neh 3[6] 12[39]. **12. Water Gate,** Neh 3[26] 8[1, 3, 16] 12[37]. **13. Muster Gate,** Neh 3[31] (AV ‘ gate **Miphkad** ’ ; RV ‘ gate **Hammiphkad** ’). **14. Benjamin Gate,** Jer 17[19] (so RSV) 20[2] 37[13] 38[7] Zec 14[10]. **15. Potsherd Gate,** Jer 19[2] (AV ‘ east gate ’ ; RV ‘ gate **Harsith** ’).

Other features of the walls of Jerusalem mentioned are : **1. Broad Wall,** Neh 12[38]. **2. Tower of Hananel** (AV **Hananeel**), Neh 3[1] 12[39], Jer 31[38], Zec 14[10]. **3. Tower of the Hundred** (AV ‘ tower of **Meah** ’ ; RV ‘ tower of **Hammeah** ’). **4. Tower of the Furnaces,** Neh 3[11] (RSV **ovens**) 12[38].

It will be seen that many of these gates and other features of the walls figure mainly, if not exclusively, in the account of Nehemiah's rebuilding of the walls. The determination of the situation of all these gates is complex and difficult, and scholars who have examined the question on the ground of biblical and archaeological evidence are not agreed. The fullest examination of the question in recent years has been undertaken by H. Vincent, *Jérusalem de l'Ancien Testament*, 1954–1956, and J. Simons, *Jerusalem in the Old Testament*, 1952. In Map 13 the reconstruction of Vincent has been followed.

In addition certain gates of the Temple are named : **1. Gate Sur,** 2 K 11[6]. **2. Gate of the Guard,** 2 K 11[19], Neh 12[39] (AV ‘ prison gate ’). **3. Gate of Shallecheth,** 1 Ch 26[16]. **4. East Gate,** 2 Ch 31[14], Neh 3[29], Ezk 11[1]. **5. New Gate,** Jer 36[10]. **6. Beautiful Gate,** Ac 3[10].

JERUSHA.—Mother of Jotham king of Judah, 2 K 15[33] ; called **Jerushah** in 2 Ch 27[1].

JERUSHAH.—See JERUSHA.

JESAIAH.—**1.** 1 Ch 3[21] (AV) ; see JESHAIAH, **1.** **2.** Neh 11[7] (AV) ; see JESHAIAH, **6.**

JESHAIAH.—**1.** A grandson of Zerubbabel, 1 Ch 3[21] (AV **Jesaiah**). **2.** One of the sons of Jeduthun, 1 Ch 25[3, 15]. **3.** A Levite, 1 Ch 26[25]. **4.** The chief of the sons of Elam who returned, Ezr 8[7], 1 Es 8[33] (AV **Josias,** RV **Jesias**). **5.** Chief of the Merarites, Ezr 8[19], 1 Es 8[48] (AV, RV **Osaias**). **6.** A Benjamite, Neh 11[7] (AV **Jesaiah**).

JESHANAH.—A town taken from Jeroboam by Abijah, 2 Ch 13[19] ; mentioned also with Mizpah in 1 S 7[12] (RSV ; AV, RV **Shen**). It is usually identified with *Burj el-Isâneh*, N. of Jerusalem, or alternatively with *'Ain Sinyā*, N. of Bethel.

JESHARELAH.—An Asaphite, 1 Ch 25[14] ; called **Asharelah** in v.[2] (AV **Asarelah**).

JESHEBEAB.—A Levite, the head of the fourteenth course, 1 Ch 24[13].

JESHER.—A son of Caleb, 1 Ch 2[18].

JESHIMON.—This word, derived from a Hebrew root meaning ‘ to be waste *or* desolate,’ is used either as a common noun (=‘ desert,’ ‘ wilderness ’) or (with the article ‘ *the* Jeshimon ’) as a proper name, Nu 21[20] 23[28], 1 S 23[19, 24] 26[1, 3] (RSV translates in Nu 21[20] 23[28], and RV in all these cases).

JESHISHAI.—A Gadite family, 1 Ch 5[14].

JESHOHAIAH.—A Simeonite family, 1 Ch 4[36].

JESHUA (another form of **Joshua,** ‘ Yahweh is salvation ’).—**1.** Joshua the son of Nun (Neh 8[17]) **2.** The head of the ninth course of priests (1 Ch 24[11]). **3.** A Levite in the time of Hezekiah (2 Ch 31[15]). **4.** A man of the house of Pahath-moab (=‘ governor of Moab ’), whose descendants returned from exile, Ezr 2[6] =Neh 7[11]=1 Es 5[11] (RV **Jesus**). **5.** The high priest, son of Jehozadak (Jozadak). In Ezra and Nehemiah he is called **Jeshua** ; in Haggai and Zechariah **Joshua.** He took a leading part in the erection of the altar of burnt-offering and the laying of the foundations of the Temple (Ezr 3[2ff]). In Haggai and Zechariah, he is associated with Zerubbabel in the undertaking of building operations (cf Ezr 5[2]), and appears in two important symbolic actions in Zec 3 and 6 (Hag 1[1, 12, 14] 2[2, 4], Zec 3[1ff] 6[11]). His family is mentioned in Ezr 10[18], Neh 12[1, 7, 10, 26] and he is eulogized in Sir 49[12] (AV, RV **Jesus**). **6.** A priestly family, Ezr 2[36]=Neh 7[39]=1 Es 5[24] (AV, RV **Jesus**). **7.** The head of a Levitical family mentioned in connexion with the building of the Temple, Ezr 3[9], cf 2[40]=Neh 7[43]=1 Es 5[26] (AV **Jessue,** RV **Jesus**).

8. A Levite, mentioned in connexion with Ezra's reading of the Law (Neh 8^{7}), and the sealing of the covenant (Neh 9^{4f} 10^{9}), and in lists (Neh 12$^{8, 24}$), probably of the same family as **7.** **9.** A Levite, whose son was concerned with the receiving of gold and silver brought from the exiles by Ezra, Ezr 8^{33}=1 Es 8^{63} (AV **Jesu,** RV **Jesus**), possibly connected with **7** and **8.** **10.** The ruler of Mizpah, father of one of builders of the wall under Nehemiah (Neh 3^{19}). **11.** A town in South Judah (Neh 11^{26}), possibly *Tell es-Saʿwī*, E. of Beersheba.

JESHURUN.—A poetic or a pet-name for Israel which occurs four times in the OT, Dt 32^{15} 33$^{5, 26}$, Is 44^{2}. It is found in the later writings, and represents a patriotic feeling that Israel was=*yᵉshar-'El*, 'the upright of God.' If this be so then we may accept the rendering of *Jeshurun* as 'the righteous little people.' In Balaam's elegy, 'Let me die the death of the righteous' (Nu 23^{10}) seems to refer to the Israel of the preceding clause, and in Ps 73^{1} the thought which underlies *Jeshurun* appears, if we adopt the tempting reading: 'Truly God is good to the upright.' W. F. C.

JESIAH, 1 Ch 12^{16} 23^{20} (AV).—See ISSHIAH, **2, 3.**

JESIAS, 1 Es 8^{33} (RV).—See JESHAIAH, **4.**

JESIMIEL.—A Simeonite family, 1 Ch 4^{36}.

JESSE (more correctly *Jishai*, cf as regards formation, *Ittai*; perhaps an abbreviated form; the meaning of the name is quite uncertain).—A Bethlehemite, best known as the father of David. The earliest historical mention of him (1 S 17^{12}; see DAVID, **1**) represents him as already an old man. On this occasion he sends David to the Israelite camp with provisions for his brothers; this was destined to be a long separation between Jesse and his son, for after David's victory over the Philistine giant he entered definitely into Saul's service. There are two other accounts, each of which purports to mention Jesse for the first time: 1 S 16^{1ff}, in which Samuel is sent to Bethlehem to anoint David; and 1 S 16^{18}, in which Jesse's son is sent for to play the harp before Saul. Nothing further is heard of Jesse until we read of him and his 'house' coming to David in the 'cave' of Adullam; David then brings his father and mother to Mizpeh of Moab, and entrusts them to the care of the king of Moab (1 S 22^{3f}). This is the last we hear of him. In Is 11^{1} the 'stock of Jesse' is mentioned as that from which the Messiah is to issue; the thought probably being that of the humble descent of the Messiah as contrasted with His glorious Kingdom which is to be. W. O. E. O.

JESSUE, 1 Es 5^{26} (AV).—See JESHUA, **7.**

JESU, 1 Es 8^{63} (AV).—See JESHUA, **9.**

JESUI, Nu 26^{44} (AV).—See ISHVI.

JESUS, the Greek form of the name Joshua or Jeshua.—**1.** In AV in 1 Mac 2^{55}, 2 Es 7^{37}, Sir 46^{1}, Ac 7^{45}, He 4^{8}=**Joshua** (so RV, RSV), the son of Nun. **2.** 1 Es 5^{11} (RV); see JESHUA, **4.** **3.** 1 Es 5^{24} (AV, RV); see JESHUA, **6.** **4.** In AV and RV in 1 Es 5$^{5, 8, 48, 56, 68, 70}$ 6^{2} 9^{19}, Sir 49^{12}; see JESHUA, **5.** **5.** 1 Es 5^{26}(RV)^{58} (AV, RV) 8^{63} (RV) 9^{48} (AV, RV); see JESHUA, **7.** **6.** 1 Es 8^{63} (RV); see JESHUA, **9.** **7.** An ancestor of our Lord, Lk 3^{29} (AV **Jose**). **8.** Jesus, son of Sirach. See APOCRYPHA, **7.** **9.** Jesus, called **Justus,** a Jewish Christian residing in Rome, saluted by St. Paul in Col 4^{11}. **10.** In 2 Es 7^{28}, where AV and RV have 'my son Jesus,' following the Latin, RSV has 'my son the Messiah,' following the Syriac. **11.** See next article.

JESUS CHRIST.—The influence of Jesus Christ ranks with Greek culture and Roman law as one of the three most significant elements in the heritage of Western civilization, and no historical task could be more important than to set forth the life and teaching of the Lord of the Church. At the same time, this superlative undertaking has its peculiar difficulties. We are virtually limited to the NT for source material, and within the NT in the main to the Gospels. The Gospels were composed in the first instance to assist in converting unbelievers and in confirming the faithful, and therefore leave us in the dark about many matters of capital interest to the biographer. Interpreters tend to impose their own beliefs and practices, or those of the branch of the Church to which they belong, on the Jesus of history and His religion, and we need to be warned against the peril of finding in the NT records what we set out to discover. On the other hand, the techniques of historical, textual, and literary research in modern times enable us to undertake the task in the confidence that we can learn more of the mission and message of Jesus than could have been recovered by any other generation since the Apostolic Age.

1. Sources.—(A) CANONICAL: (1) *The Gospels.*—It is now generally recognized that the Gospel according to Mark is the earliest of the four that ultimately found a place in the NT canon. It opens with a brief account of John the Baptist and of Jesus' baptism, and then goes on to give a sketch of Jesus' own ministry, culminating in His arrest, trial, crucifixion, and burial in Jerusalem. It ends in ch. 16^{8} with the story of the discovery by some faithful women of the empty tomb. (At various times in the early centuries attempts were made to provide Mark with a more appropriate conclusion, and there has been much speculation in recent years about a so-called 'lost ending' of the Gospel. All this appears to be beside the point. The Gospel ends abruptly, but no more abruptly than it begins or when it makes a transition from one block of tradition to another.) While this Gospel is the source of most of our knowledge of the life of Jesus, its purpose was not historical nor biographical. It was a record of the tradition of the Church that missionaries had found useful in proclaiming God's saving purposes for mankind in Christ Jesus and was intended to be read aloud in gatherings for worship. The central section on 'the way of the Cross' (8^{27}–10^{45}) and the climactic Passion narrative (14–15), in particular, were also calculated to encourage a community enduring persecution and threatened with martyrdom.

The Gospel according to Matthew is best described as a revised and enlarged edition of Mark. It incorporates more than 90 per cent of the earlier Gospel and expands it with new material, mostly didactic, by more than 40 per cent. To the whole the editor prefixed a genealogy of Jesus and a number of birth and infancy narratives (1^{1}–2^{23}) and appended a cycle of resurrection stories and the missionary commission of the Risen Christ (28^{8b-20}). The new edition of Mark was intended to serve as a catechism for Christian faith and practice and as a demonstration that the Christ of the Church was the fulfilment of messianic predictions in the OT. (A feature of the Gospel is its frequent citation of OT passages taken from some early Christian collection of *testimonia*, possibly Matthew's *logia*, to which Papias refers [Euseb. *HE* iii. 39]). Matthew is frequently described as the Gospel of the Jewish Christians, but this description is based on inferences drawn, not from the Gospel as a whole, which is clearly the work of a Hellenist and a universalist, but from some of the special matter incorporated by the editor, which may have been collected and preserved in the first instance by Christian Jews in Jerusalem (the M source).

The Gospel according to Luke is completely independent of Matthew, but, like Matthew, is also dependent on Mark for the general framework of the gospel story. (The 'Proto-Luke' hypothesis, first suggested by B. H. Streeter and then worked out in detail by Vincent Taylor, has been widely accepted in recent times but falls short of demonstration at crucial points.) It supplements Mark with about two hundred and fifty verses, mostly didactic matter, drawn from a source known also to Matthew (the Q source), and also with a wealth of preaching, teaching, narrative, and parabolic tradition, approximating two hundred and eighty verses in all, derived from some special source or sources (L). Luke's story begins, as does Matthew's, with a cycle of birth and infancy narratives, although these are quite different from their counterparts in our First Gospel, and it ends with a variant and independent resurrection cycle. Luke approached his task in a more consciously historical spirit than his predecessors (see 1^{1-4}) and recognized an obligation to supply dates and to sketch in the political background of some events (2^2 $3^{1, 23}$). But for him also the main concern of an Evangelist was to emphasize the religious significance of his story, especially by exhibiting Jesus as the friend of outcasts and sinners and as the Saviour of the world. He is especially interested in incidents and sayings that illustrate the graciousness and the universality of the gospel. Prominence is given to the rejection of Jesus by Nazareth and Jerusalem (4^{16-30} 19^{41-44}) and to His discovery among the Gentiles of the faith for which He sought (17^{18f}). It is also characteristic of the author of the Third Gospel that he gives a full account of the missionary activity of the Church (10^{1-21}). These and other interests, notably a concern to demonstrate that Christianity is not a religion that should be condemned by the Roman state as subversive, are even more apparent in the Book of Acts, the second and concluding volume of Luke's account of the early Church.

The author of the Fourth Gospel appears to have been familiar with Mark. He may also have known Luke, but there is no indication that he had any acquaintance with Matthew. While Mark would have us believe that Galilee was the exclusive scene of Jesus' ministry until shortly before the end, John declares that Jesus began His work in Judaea and Jerusalem and made at least three journeys from Galilee to Jerusalem (2^{13} 5^1 7^{10}) prior to His final visit (the only one that Mark records). According to Mark, Jesus cleansed the Temple at the very end of His ministry; according to John, at the very beginning. According to Mark, Jesus was crucified on the Passover day; according to John, on the day before the Passover (13^1 18^{28} $19^{14, 31, 42}$). Although neither Mark nor John was primarily concerned with chronology, the divergencies in their accounts are real, and the historian, at least in the second and third of the instances cited, must choose between his authorities. To decline to do so on the ground that 'theology' has completely sublimated 'history' in all early Christian tradition is an irresponsible aberration on the part of some NT scholars in recent times. There is theology in the Synoptic Gospels as well as history; there is history as well as theology in the Gospel according to John, and the historian cannot evade the duty of attempting to distinguish fact from interpretation in the two accounts. There is a marked difference, however, in the degree of theological interest as between John and the Synoptists. John has reworked the historical stuff of his tradition more thoroughly, and his presentation of the gospel, as he himself declares, was written primarily to induce the belief that 'Jesus is the Christ, the Son of God' and to enable believers to have 'life in his name' (20^{30-31}).

(2) *Paul's Epistles.*—While Paul's letters are earlier than the Gospels, and earlier than most of the literary sources of the Gospels that we can distinguish, they serve only to confirm a few salient facts of the gospel tradition. The Risen Christ filled Paul's thought to the virtual exclusion of the Galilaean Jesus. Nevertheless, the few scattered notices that are found in his letters make it certain that the apostle's Christ was no purely mythological figure. Jesus Christ was an Israelite by race (Ro 9^5); descended from David according to the flesh (1^3); and born of a woman and subject to the law (Gal 4^4). He had several brothers (1 Co 9^5), one of whom was called James (Gal 1^{19}). His ministry had been among Jews (Ro 15^8); He had a circle of disciples known as 'the twelve' (1 Co 15^5); and He was betrayed on the night that He instituted the Lord's Supper (1 Co 11^{23-26}). He was crucified (2 Co 13^4) and the Jews were responsible for His death (1 Thes 2^{14-15}). He was buried and then, on the third day, was raised from the dead (1 Co 15^4). Furthermore, on two occasions Paul appears to cite sayings of Jesus recorded in the Gospels (1 Co 7^{10}=Mk 10^9; 1 Co 9^{14}=Lk 10^7), and a few other passages, possibly a dozen, may reasonably be held to be echoes of additional sayings familiar to us from the Synoptics.

(3) *Other NT Writings.*—There is an allusion to the Agony in He 5^7 and to the Transfiguration in 2 P 1^{17}. He 13^{12} locates the site of the Crucifixion "outside the gate" (*i.e.* of Jerusalem). Rev 5^5 and 22^{16} reflect the early Christian tradition of Jesus' Davidic descent. Ja 5^{12} may be a more primitive form of the words of Jesus than that in Mt 5^{37}, and Ac 20^{35} preserves an otherwise unrecorded saying.

(B) Extra-Canonical Sources: (1) *Christian*; (*a*) *Patristic and other references.*—The Fathers make only trifling additions to our knowledge of the facts of the life of Jesus. There is nothing more important than Eusebius' statement (derived from Hegesippus) that grandsons of Jude, a brother of Jesus, were members of the Christian community (presumably at Rome) during the reign of Domitian (*HE* iii. 19–20). More valuable are the so-called *Agrapha* (q.v.), non-canonical sayings purporting to come from Jesus that are found in some NT MSS, in the Early Fathers, and in papyri discovered in Egypt, especially at Oxyrhynchus. According to J. Jeremias (*Unknown Sayings of Jesus*, 1957), twenty-one of these have some claim to authenticity. Among the more interesting are the following:

(i) 'On the same day, seeing a man working on the Sabbath, Jesus said to him: "Man, if thou knowest what thou doest, blessed art thou; but if thou knowest not, thou art accursed and a transgressor of the law"' (added to Lk 6^5 in Codex Bezae).

(ii) 'He that is near me is near the fire, but he that is far from me is far from the kingdom' (Origen, *Hom. in Jer.* xx. 3).

(iii) 'Show yourselves tried money changers' (Clem. Alex. *Strom.* i. 28, *et al.*).

(iv) 'Ask for the big things, and the little shall be added unto you. Ask for the heavenly things, and the earthly shall be added unto you' (Origen, *de Orat.* 2).

(v) 'Raise the stone, and thou shalt find me. Cleave the wood, and there I am' (*Oxyr. Pap.* i. 4).

(*b*) *Non-canonical Writings.*—Fragments of the Gospels according to the *Hebrews*, the *Egyptians*, and *Peter* have been preserved in quotation, and numerous apocryphal Gospels and Acts have survived (see M. R. James, *The Apocryphal New Testament*, 1924). The former reflect early gnostic and docetic influences and appear to depend on our canonical Gospels for any history they contain. The latter fall into three groups according as they deal with the history of Joseph and Mary (*e.g. Protevangelium of James*), the Infancy (*e.g. Gospel of Thomas*), and Pilate (*e.g. Acts of Pilate*). Their fancies are frequently grotesque and repulsive and are of no value.

In 1946 Egyptian *fellahin* at Nag-Hamadi, a village in Upper Egypt, happened upon a cache of twelve volumes of Coptic Gnostic scriptures, including a document entitled *The Secret Words Which Jesus the Living Spoke and* (*Which*) *Didymus Judas Thomas Wrote* (R. M. Grant, D. N. Freedman, W. R. Schoedel, *The Secret Sayings of Jesus*, 1960). Of the 114 sayings credited to Jesus in this *Gospel of Thomas*, about one-half consists of variants of (or combinations of) logia familiar to us from the canonical Gospels; many are *agrapha* already known to us from other sources (the Oxyrhynchus papyri fragments referred to above appear to have been part of an earlier Greek version of this Coptic Gospel); and the remainder is made up of sayings hitherto unknown (most of them characteristically Gnostic in content and with little or no claim to authenticity).

(2) *Jewish sources.*—Although Josephus does refer to the martyrdom of James the brother of Jesus (*Ant.* xx. ix. 1 [200]), there is general agreement that the famous passage that discusses Jesus himself (xviii. iii. 3 [63 f]) is a Christian interpolation. According to Joseph Klausner, of the Hebrew University in Jerusalem, the few reliable

statements about Jesus in the Talmud are modified reflections of Christian tradition, and their only historical value is to confirm the fact that Jesus was a historical figure and that the general character of His works and His words is adequately depicted in the Gospels (*Jesus of Nazareth*, 1925).

(3) *Classical sources.*—There is evidence in classical authors for the historical existence, approximate date, and death of Jesus, but little else (Tac. *Ann.* xv. 44 ; Suetonius, *Life of Claudius*, xxv. 4, and *Life of Nero*, xvi. 2 ; Pliny the Younger, *Epp.* x. 96 ; cf J. Stevenson, *A New Eusebius*, 1957, pp. 1–4, 13–15).

2. Presuppositions.—Complete objectivity in the study of anything outside the field of the exact sciences is unattainable. Perhaps it is also undesirable, for absence of what some call ' bias ' or ' prejudice ' usually means either ignorance or indifference. The contributor of this article writes as a Christian. At the same time he makes an honest attempt, with the tools of historical research at his disposal, to differentiate history from interpretation in his source material, and he is particularly concerned to practice historical exegesis in sensitive areas where his conclusions may run counter to *a priori* assumptions on the part of some of his readers. (For a history of the study of the life of Jesus, see C. C. McCown, *The Search for the Real Jesus*, 1940, and J. M. Robinson, *A New Quest of the Historical Jesus*, 1959.)

3. Conditions in Palestine.—(1) *The political situation.*—From the age of the Exile, the Jews in Palestine were subject to one alien power after another—Persian, Greek, Egyptian, and Syrian. Following upon a century of independence under the Maccabees, the country was incorporated in the Roman Empire as a division of the province of Syria. In certain circumstances the Romans recognized a feudatory king, and it was with this status that Herod the Great ruled over Palestine. At his death in 4 B.C., his dominion was divided among three of his sons ; but on the deposition of Archelaus in A.D. 6, Judaea and Samaria were placed under a Roman procurator. Herod Antipas and Philip continued to govern as vassal princes, with the title of tetrarchs, over Galilee and Ituraea (and other contiguous areas) respectively. The pressure of Roman rule was felt in the stern measures which were taken to suppress any dangerous expressions of national feeling, and also in the exactions of the publicans to whom the taxes were farmed. Internal administration in Judaea was largely an affair of the Sanhedrin. To a high-spirited people like the Jews, with memories of former freedom, the loss of national independence was galling ; and their restlessness under the foreign yoke, combined as it was with the messianic hopes that formed a vital element of their religion, was a source of anxiety not only to the Roman authorities but also to their own leaders.

(2) *The religious situation.*—Judaism survived the debacle of A.D. 66–70 (the war of the Jews against Rome) because the real focus of its life had already become the Torah and the Synagogue. In Jesus' day, however, the religion of the people still appeared to centre about the Temple and the sacerdotal cult. Herod the Great had begun the construction of the Second Temple *c* 19 B.C., and the complex of Temple buildings and courts, while not actually completed until *c* A.D. 64—only to be destroyed by Titus and his legions after the capture of Jerusalem in A.D. 70—had long been a source of much pride to Jewry. Pilgrimages brought loyal Jews to Jerusalem at the time of the great festivals from the far corners of the earth. Tithes, taxes, and innumerable sacrificial offerings, both public and private, enriched the Temple treasury, and the priestly hierarchy enjoyed wealth, authority, and prestige. The Sadducees (q.v.) were the party of the priests, the great landowners, and the aristocracy. They controlled the Sanhedrin, the highest court of appeal in Judaism, and were entrusted with considerable political responsibility by the Roman state. Profiting from the political and economic stability maintained by Rome, they were opposed to all revolutionary movements and tendencies. They acknowledged the authority of the Torah, but not of the other parts of what we call the OT nor of the oral tradition of the Scribes. As a consequence they refused to accept doctrines, such as that of the resurrection (Mk 12[18], Ac 23[9]), that were not to be discovered in the Pentateuch. The Pharisees (q.v.) were a smaller but more popular and influential party and were more receptive to new ideas. They undertook to be familiar with both the written and the oral law and to govern their lives in accordance with this legislation. There were, to be sure, differences between various schools. The followers of Shammai, for example, were often severe in their interpretation of the Jewish laws, while those of Hillel were usually lenient. But disagreement in matters of detail was overshadowed by a broad measure of agreement in theology and in practice. The Scribes (q.v.) belonged in the main to the party of the Pharisees. They were the learned doctors of the law whose recognized task it was to relate the Torah to new situations as they emerged and to transmit to their students the oral tradition that had accumulated since the time of Ezra. Philo, Pliny the Elder, and Josephus all speak of a monastic order known as Essenes (q.v.). The Covenanters of Qumrân, whose monastery and library (the ' Dead Sea Scrolls,' q.v.) were discovered in 1947, appear to have been a related sect. Their peculiar tenets and practices may have been familiar to Jesus, although no reference is made to them or to the Essenes in the Gospels. The Zealots (q.v.) were the party of extremists who fomented the revolution against Rome in A.D. 66. While there were, no doubt, many in Jesus' day who hoped for the overthrow of Rome by violence, it is not clear that they were known as ' Zealots ' before the time of Herod Agrippa I. Most of the Jews in Palestine stood outside all such organized or semi-organized groups and are referred to in Rabbinic literature as ' the people of the land.' They appear to have held the Pharisees in high regard and to have attempted to fulfil the regulations of Pharisaic legalism as far as they were familiar with them and as the exigencies of earning a livelihood made their observance practicable. The larger towns in Palestine, with the single exception of Jerusalem, were predominantly non-Jewish, and Jesus, like most Palestinian Jews of His day, must have had some knowledge of Koine Greek and must have been exposed to some influence from the dominant Hellenistic culture of the Mediterranean world.

4. Date of Jesus' Birth (see CHRONOLOGY).—Since the Evangelists were not concerned with such matters as the date of Jesus' birth, modern biographers, depending on the Gospel narrative, which they have taken as a point of departure, have been able to reach at least four different conclusions. (1) According to Lk 3[1-3], John the Baptist began to preach in the fifteenth year of Tiberius Caesar—*i.e.* A.D. 28–29. If we were to allow a year or so for John's ministry before Jesus' baptism, this would place the latter event *c* A.D. 30. Luke says (3[23]) that Jesus at that time was ' about thirty years of age,' from which it can be concluded, with Dionysius Exiguus in the 6th cent., that He was born *c* A.D. 1. (2) In 2[1-7] Luke dates Jesus' birth at a time when Quirinius was governor of Syria and when Caesar Augustus ordered an imperial census. There is no evidence that Quirinius was governor before A.D. 6 nor that there was any earlier census than the one we know to have been taken in that year. According to this point of departure, Jesus was born in A.D. 6. (3) In Jn 8[57] certain Jews are said to have referred to Jesus in the course of His ministry as ' not yet fifty years old.' If Jesus were in His early thirties at the time, it would seem that, even speaking in round numbers, they would have said ' not yet forty years old.' It may be that the author of the Fourth Gospel thought of Jesus during the period of His ministry as between forty and fifty years of age and as having been born as early as 20–15 B.C. (4) In the birth and infancy narratives of the Gospel of Matthew, Jesus is said to have been born towards the end of the reign of Herod the Great. Since

Herod died in 4 B.C., it would appear from the Matthaean tradition that Jesus could not have been born much earlier or much later than 9–6 B.C. This dating is the one that has been commonly accepted by the Church. It may be said also to have some Lucan support, for Luke implies in 1^{5} that John the Baptist was born during Herod's reign and in 1^{26-38} that Jesus was conceived before John's birth.

5. Birth and Infancy.—(1) *The birth narratives.*—Mark's Gospel opens with an account of Jesus' baptism, but both Matthew and Luke begin with a cycle of birth and infancy narratives. The sharp divergence of the two post-Markan Gospels at this point is frequently overlooked because the reader has in mind a composite narrative. Matthew's story is told in 2^{1-23}. Joseph and Mary were residents of Bethlehem in Judaea, and Jesus was born there, presumably in His parents' home. Wise men from the East were led by a star to the place where the child was, and there offered Him gifts. Joseph was warned in a dream to flee to Egypt to avoid Herod's intended act of violence, and in another vision he was persuaded after Herod's death to settle with his family in Nazareth of Galilee rather than to resume residence in Bethlehem. Luke's story is told in 2^{1-39}. Joseph and Mary were residents of Nazareth rather than of Bethlehem and were brought to the city of David at the time of Jesus' birth by the exigencies of the census. Jesus was born in a manger because there was no room for His parents in the inn. Then follow the stories of the angelic chorus, the visit of the shepherds, Jesus' presentation in the Temple in Jerusalem, and the return of Joseph and Mary with their newborn son in due course to Nazareth. So far as form is concerned, Matthew's narratives are legends, but Luke's are more properly classified as poetry. Since the two Evangelists differ so greatly on all other points, the fact that they agree in stating that Jesus was born in Bethlehem leads many to believe that this is an historical datum. More probably the stories in Matthew and Luke are independent attempts at harmonizing two traditions: that Jesus was known to have been associated from infancy with Nazareth in Galilee; and that as Davidic Messiah He must have been born in Bethlehem.

(2) *The tradition of Jesus' Davidic descent.*—It was a commonly accepted element of Jewish expectation that the Messiah would be a descendant of the house of David, and both Matthew and Luke include genealogies to prove that Jesus fulfilled the Messianic hope. This belief was a matter of apologetic concern for the early Church, but soon lost importance once Christianity became predominantly a Gentile religion. Paul knew of the tradition that Jesus 'was descended from David according to the flesh' (Ro 1^{3}), but he never developed it, for it had little or no bearing on his Christology. The only other references in the NT outside the Gospels to Jesus' Davidic descent are in Rev 5^{5} and 22^{16}, where they are stereotyped phrases inherited from the past rather than items of any consequence to the author of the Apocalypse. Even in the Gospels there is one passage (Mk 12^{35-37} ||) in which Jesus Himself is said to have broached the question and (it would appear) to have disclaimed Davidic lineage. The presence of the genealogies in Mt 1^{1-16} and Lk 3^{23-38} must be due to the respect the Evangelists had for earlier beliefs, for they themselves hold that Jesus was conceived by the Virgin Mary of the Holy Spirit, and they resort to awkward apologies (Mt 1^{16}, Lk 3^{23}) for a doctrine they no longer find tenable. The two 'proofs' of Jesus' Davidic descent are mutually independent and incompatible. Matthew's traces Jesus' descent from Abraham (the father of the Jewish people) through Solomon to Jacob and Joseph, while Luke's reconstructs a line of descent from Adam (the father of mankind) through Nathan to Heli and Joseph. These and related differences defy the most ingenious attempts at harmonization. See GENEALOGY OF JESUS CHRIST.

(3) *The Virgin Birth.*—The doctrine of the Virgin Birth was not part of the primitive kerygma as we know it from references in Paul's letters and the early sermons in the book of Acts. There is no hint of the doctrine in Mark's Gospel nor in the tradition common to Matthew and Luke (Q). It has no place in the birth and infancy narratives in Lk 2^{1-52}, which assume throughout that Joseph was one of Jesus' parents ($2^{27, 33, 41, 43, 48}$). It must have been known to the Fourth Evangelist, but he makes no appeal to it. For him, Jesus Christ had appeared in time but did not have a beginning in time. As the Divine Word He had been with God from all eternity (1^{1}). The doctrine is implied in the parenthesis with which Luke introduces his version of the genealogy (3^{23}), but it is explicit in his Gospel only in 1^{34f}. If these verses were omitted, no one would suspect that the doctrine of the Virgin Birth lay behind the narrative in 1^{26-38}. Some scholars have held that evidence based on one Old Latin MS supports the hypothesis that vvs.$^{34-35}$ are an interpolation. More probably they were added by Luke himself to the source he was employing at this point. In the NT it is only in Matthew's birth narratives that the doctrine is basic to the proclamation of Jesus Christ, and even Matthew recognizes that it is at variance with the earlier belief that Jesus was descended from David (cf the awkward gloss in 1^{16}). In his account Matthew supports belief in the Virgin Birth by declaring that Jesus' supernatural conception fulfills the prediction of Is 7^{14}, a proof text taken from a narrative that had no messianic connotations for Isaiah and that loses all relevance when it is observed that the Greek word for 'virgin,' which Matthew took over from the LXX text, is a mistranslation of a Hebrew noun meaning nothing more specific than 'young woman.' The belief in the Virgin Birth among Christians of Matthew's time had a theological or apologetic rather than a historical origin. It was one means of articulating for non-Jews—the doctrine would have been utterly repugnant to Jews—the faith of the Church from the beginning, and the faith that is still the faith of the Church, that in Jesus Christ God had come into human life for our salvation.

6. Years of Preparation.—Of the Evangelists only Luke records an incident out of Jesus' boyhood (2^{40-52}), a visit that Jesus paid with His parents, when He was twelve years of age, to the Temple in Jerusalem. The point of the story is that even as a boy Jesus thought of God as Father and of God's house as His true sphere of work. Luke's narrative was originally independent of the Virgin Birth cycle, for it speaks of Joseph and Mary as Jesus' parents. It is in sharp contrast to the revolting tales of Jesus the boy wonder and magician that fill the later so-called 'Infancy Gospels,' and its very naturalness vouches for its authenticity. The child is represented as listening and asking questions rather than 'teaching.'

Since Nazareth was only a few short miles from Sepphoris, the second largest centre of population in Palestine (after Jerusalem) and a predominantly Gentile city, it is probable that the rural and pastoral setting of Jesus' early years has been overstressed in many 'lives of Jesus' and in some hymns. From Mk 6^{3} we learn that Jesus' family at the time He began His public ministry included His mother, four brothers, and at least two sisters. The fact that Joseph is not mentioned in this passage or in Mk 3^{31-35} lends some support to the conjecture that Jesus' father had died before the point at which the Gospel narrative of Jesus' ministry begins. One of Jesus' brothers, James, was among the first to be convinced, after the Crucifixion, that Jesus had risen from the dead (1 Co 15^{7}); soon thereafter he became the recognized leader of the church in Jerusalem (Gal 2^{12}, Ac 12^{17}). In our sources he is commonly referred to as 'the Lord's brother.' His character as delineated by references both in the NT and in Josephus (*Ant.* xx. ix. 1 [200]) throws some light on the nature of the home in which Jesus also was reared—a home devoted to orthodox Jewish piety. Jesus, furthermore, was no 'unlettered Galilaean peasant.' In His home and in the synagogue school He would have been thoroughly grounded in the Jewish Scriptures, and His recorded sayings show that He had caught not only the literary charm of the OT but also an understanding of its highest religion. In addition, as His parables reveal, He had acquired an intimate and sympathetic knowledge of nature and of rural and village life in Palestine: the fisherman with his boat and nets; the sower scattering his seed on his field; the shepherd herding his flock; the father caring for his children; the housewife baking bread or sweeping a one-roomed house; boys and girls playing in the market place; the lightning flashing from the sky; a cloud in the West or a wind from the South portending a change in the weather; the flowers of the field, the birds of the air; the growing grain; a crop ready for the harvest—and much else of a like character. To the discipline of the home, of the school, and of the world of man and of nature was added the discipline of work. In His early years Jesus learned the trade of a carpenter—apparently also His father's trade—and appears to have practised it until He reached the threshold of middle age (Mk 6^3).

7. Jesus and John the Baptist.—The accounts of John the Baptizer in our various Gospels can be supplemented with information derived from Josephus' *Ant.* XVIII. v. 2 [116 ff], a source that serves at several points (viz. the purpose of John's baptism, the cause of his arrest and execution, the place of his imprisonment) to correct the Markan tradition. Much speculation in recent years about John's possible connexion at one time with the Covenanter sect at Qumrân goes far beyond any actual evidence. According to all the Synoptic Gospels, John dressed and acted the rôle of a prophet and proclaimed (in conventional apocalyptic imagery) the near advent of the Messiah; according to Matthew, he anticipated Jesus' message of the kingdom of God (3^2) and may have implied that Jesus was the Messiah (3^{14}); according to the Fourth Gospel, he explicitly referred his disciples to Jesus as the Messiah ($1^{29, 35-36}$). The passage in Mt 11^2 (Lk 7^{18-19}), however, appears to indicate that John heard of Jesus only after his own ministry had been terminated by arrest and imprisonment, and therefore also appears to suggest that Jesus when He was baptized was but one among the many who had presented themselves to him at the Jordan river. The fact that Jesus was baptized by John caused the later Church some embarrassment. How could the sinless Son of God have submitted to a baptism for the remission of sins? The Gospel of John omits any direct account of the incident, and even Matthew appears to have been aware of the theological difficulty involved (3^{14-15}). Mark's account (1^{9-11}) is clearly the source of Matthew's and Luke's, and the earliest Evangelist reports the baptismal experience as one personal to Jesus Himself. (In Matthew the baptism becomes a public attestation of Jesus' Messiahship, and in Luke the descent of the dove is objectified as a physical miracle.) While the precise nature of Jesus' experience at the time is no longer recoverable, it is clear that contact with the Baptist's ministry was instrumental in bringing Him face to face with His prophet's task and that His baptism had for Him the character of a prophetic call or commission.

8. The Temptation.—According to the Synoptic Gospels the sequel to Jesus' baptismal experience was a period of withdrawal during which Jesus' new-found consciousness of Divine mission was put to test. Mark says only that 'he was in the wilderness forty days, tempted by Satan; and he was with the wild beasts; and the angels ministered to him' (1^{13}). Matthew and Luke supplement Mark's narrative at this point with an account taken from their common non-Markan source. Matthew's version (4^{1-11}) differs from Luke's (4^{1-13}) only in the order in which the three temptations are introduced, and many feel that the former arrangement works up to a more effective climax. Jesus is tempted to demonstrate His messianic dignity by ushering in an era of material abundance; by thrusting Himself into peril and compelling God to intervene by miracle on His behalf; and by assuming sovereignty over all the kingdoms of the world; tempted, that is to say, to assume the messianic rôles which popular thought of the time would have acclaimed. In each instance He is represented as putting the temptation aside. As we have them, the narratives are a commentary by the later Church, couched in mythological imagery, on the entire course of Jesus' ministry as believers recalled it. The story puts at the beginning of His public mission, in vivid and imaginative form, the temptations with which Jesus must often have had to contend. (John, for instance, reports that on one occasion certain of Jesus' followers wished to 'take him by force to make him king' [6^{15}] and that He would have none of it.) The OT tradition of Israel's forty years of testing in the wilderness, particularly as it is related in Dt 6 and 8 (from which all Jesus' answers to Satan are taken), has influenced the construction of the Q account. But it does not follow from this that the temptation stories are wholly mythological. The fact that the tradition of a sojourn in the wilderness and of a period of trial is preserved in two independent narratives—Mark and Q—makes it probable that these incidents have some basis in fact. However that may be, it is clear that the details of the narratives as we have them in Matthew and in Luke have been filled in and worked over by the piety of early churchmen.

9. Duration of the Ministry (see CHRONOLOGY).—According to all our sources Jesus was crucified by order of the Procurator Pontius Pilate, who (as we know from Josephus) held office in Judaea from A.D. 26–36. According to all our Gospels the Crucifixion took place on a Friday during a Passover season. According to the Synoptics this Friday was the Passover day itself, while according to John it was the day before the Passover day. If John's dating be accepted—reasons for doing so are adduced in **15** (6)—astronomical reckoning enables us to fix the date of Jesus' death on April 7, A.D. 30, or on April 3, A.D. 33. Since Luke, who was concerned with the relation of the Christian story to secular history, dates the emergence of John the Baptist as a prophet in the fifteenth year of the reign of Tiberius Caesar (3^1)—*i.e.* A.D. 28–29—we can scarcely assume that Jesus began His public ministry much earlier than A.D. 30. It is therefore probable that it covered a span of three years, from A.D. 30–33. It has been maintained that such a period may also be inferred from John's references to three Passovers during the course of Jesus' public mission (2^{13} 6^4 11^{55}); but it may properly be objected to this that the Fourth Evangelist speaks of Passover feasts for symbolical and typological rather than historical reasons. The Synoptic tradition was preserved and transmitted in Christian circles that had no interest whatsoever in chronology. To argue that the incident of plucking heads of wheat (Mk 2^{33}) points to the spring of one year, as the Passover of the Crucifixion does to that of another, and to conclude from this that Mark and the other Synoptists assume that Jesus' ministry lasted for a period of from twelve to eighteen months, is (in the judgment of this writer) an unwarranted deduction from the Synoptic source material.

10. Course of the Ministry.—According to Mark, Jesus began His ministry in Galilee after John the Baptist's arrest (1^{14}) and spent the early (and apparently much the greater) part of it exclusively in that northwestern province (1^{14}–7^{23}). Then, for what the reader gathers was a briefer stay, He went to the Phoenician area about Tyre and Sidon and, by a circuitous route that avoided Galilee, to the Decapolis and to those areas ruled over by the tetrarch Philip (7^{24}–9^{50}). (This extra-Galilean period in Jesus' ministry was interrupted, according to Mark, by an almost clandestine visit by boat to 'the district of Dalmanutha' [$8^{10, 13}$]—presumably in Galilee—and ended with a return to Capernaum.) The third division in the structure of the earliest Gospel is concerned with the journey to Jerusalem (10^{1-52}), and the final section (11^1–16^8) with Jesus' last week in the capital city.

According to John, Jesus' ministry began in Peraea with the choice of His first disciples (1^{40-42}) and then alternated between Galilee and Judaea (1^{43}–12^{11}), with several visits at the time of great festivals (2^{13} 5^{1} 7^{10}) to Jerusalem and with interludes in Samaria (4$^{4-42}$), the tetrarchy of Philip (6$^{1-21}$), and Peraea (10^{40}–11^{16}). The latter part of the Gospel (12^{12}–20^{13}, the point at which the Gospel appears originally to have ended) is the Fourth Evangelist's account of Jesus' last visit to His nation's capital, beginning with the entry and ending with the Passion and Resurrection.

There are indications in Mark's Gospel that Jesus was no stranger to Jerusalem when He went there for the visit that ended with His arrest and crucifixion. He had friends in Bethany, for instance, who extended Him hospitality during His stay. It may well be, then, that John's tradition of a ministry at various times in Judaea and of several visits to Jerusalem prior to the only one Mark records serves to correct the Markan outline. But typological and symbolical interests rather than historical concern seem to have determined John's discussion of the years during which the Word that became flesh dwelt among men, and the biographer is compelled in the main to depend on the account in Mark.

In recent times there have been many who have denied that Mark's chronology is of any value. They have pointed out that our earliest Evangelist employs a number of stereotyped references to place and time: in a synagogue; by the Sea of Galilee; in a boat anchored offshore; in a house; on a mountain; on a highway; in the morning; when evening had come; on that day; in those days; after some days. It is maintained that Mark, when he set out to compose a Gospel, had at his disposal a number of pericopes—units of tradition—that had circulated with little or no chronological or geographical reference. The Evangelist provided them with settings and arranged them in an arbitrary sequence, much as a maid might string a handful of pearls. The student of the Gospels may grant that there is much to be said for this contention, without therewith abandoning the general framework of Mark's Gospel as historically valueless. The Evangelist need not have been completely ignorant of, or utterly indifferent to, the course of Jesus' ministry. In broad outline his account carries conviction. Jesus' choice of disciples, for instance, was obviously made towards the beginning of His ministry, and the Passion and Resurrection mark its end. No historian is likely to insist that any given intervening event necessarily occurred in the particular setting and sequence that Mark has given it, but this admission does not justify an attitude toward our sources of unrelieved scepticism. We can reconstruct with a measure of confidence at least an outline of the ministry of the Church's Lord.

11. The Galilaean Ministry.—Because of the special concerns that characterize the portrayal of Jesus Christ in the Gospel of John, the extent to which Jesus may have carried on His ministry in Judaea prior to His last visit to Jerusalem can no longer be determined. But the Johannine account agrees with that of Mark in regarding Galilee as at least a major centre of Jesus' initial activity.

(1) *The opening of the ministry.*—Whatever may have been the nature of His experience in the wilderness, it persuaded Jesus to undertake a public mission. He detached Himself from His home and His former interests and devoted Himself to the new work to which God had called Him. According to the temptation narratives, His retirement in the wilderness had lasted for forty days. No doubt the figure of forty was suggested to the early narrators by OT analogy, but the period must have been of some duration—perhaps even longer than forty days—for it allowed for an event of the utmost consequence to Jesus and His ministry, the arrest and imprisonment of John the Baptist by Herod Antipas. According to Mk 6$^{17-18}$, the reason for this was a personal one: Herod was angry at John for denouncing his adulterous marriage. Josephus, on the other hand, tells us that John's arrest was due to Herod's political apprehensions. Galilee was in a state of turmoil, and the tetrarch was afraid that the excitement aroused by John's ministry might lead to armed insurrection (*Ant.* XVIII. v. 2 [118]). At any rate, when Jesus returned from the wilderness it was to find that John had been imprisoned and that the field was open for a new kind of ministry. At the same time it must have been made evident to Him that His mission would be fraught with danger. He could gather from the fate that had overtaken John a warning of what lay in store for Himself.

Mark tells us that when Jesus came into Galilee He began His ministry with the proclamation, 'The time is fulfilled, and the kingdom of God is at hand; repent and believe in the gospel' (1^{15}). According to Mt 3^{2}, this had also been the burden of John's message. But Jesus' manner of preaching was quite different from John's. The Baptist had modelled himself on OT prophets as to dress, habits, and figures of speech. He had lived in the wasteland and had required the people to go there to hear him. Jesus, on the contrary, went to the people, travelling from village to village. He affected no prophetic pose, but ate and drank and dressed as other people did, worked with ideas familiar to the people of His time, and employed ordinary forms of speech.

We gather from Mark's account that Jesus carried on His work for some little time without attracting much attention. Luke was disturbed by the absence in Mark of an impressive opening to Jesus' ministry. At the time he was composing his Gospel, Christianity was bidding fair to turn the world upside down (Ac 17^{6}). Surely its programme must have been inaugurated in some dramatic fashion! So Luke took an incident that in Mark's order had occurred late in the Galilaean ministry (6$^{1-6}$)—the story of Jesus' rejection by His fellow townsmen at Nazareth—and transposed it to the beginning (Lk 4$^{16-30}$). By elaborating the narrative he made it prefigure the later Gentile mission of the Church (cf Ac 28$^{25-28}$) and serve as a vivid frontispiece to the whole story in Luke–Acts.

All our accounts agree that Simon and Andrew were the first to join Jesus as disciples. John locates their call in Peraea (1$^{35-42}$), while Mark declares that it, as well as that of James and John the sons of Zebedee (who are not mentioned in the Fourth Gospel), was issued at the Sea of Galilee (1$^{16-20}$). Mark narrates the call as though nothing had preceded it. The Evangelist was not concerned with how Jesus came to be by the Sea of Galilee or with how His first followers had come to be impressed by His person and mission. It may be taken for granted that facts which the early gospel story ignored had prepared the way for these two pairs of brothers to throw in their lot with Jesus.

Mark's Gospel implies that Capernaum, the modern *Tell Ḥûm*, was Jesus' headquarters throughout His Galilaean ministry. Its choice may have been due to the fact that Simon had a house there (1^{29}) and put it at his Master's disposal. But quite apart from this, Capernaum was admirably situated as a base of operation, for it was a centre from which a network of Roman roads radiated to all parts of the province and from which ready access could be had by water to other parts of Palestine.

(2) *The disciples.*—Simon, Andrew, James, and John formed the nucleus of a group of intimate followers. As we learn from Mark's story of the man who rejected Jesus' call to discipleship (10$^{17-22}$||), not all who received an invitation to join this circle were willing to accept it. The NT tradition that this group came to number twelve has been called in question by some scholars in modern times. The argument against its historicity is as follows: After the Resurrection the Church came to think of itself as the true Israel. Just as Moses had proclaimed the old law to the twelve tribes, so Jesus as the new Moses must have given the new law to twelve representatives of the new Israel. It was known that Jesus had three or four intimate followers and a wider circle (Luke says it included certain faithful women) that fluctuated in size. Simon and Andrew, James and John

were declared to have been the initial members of a closed group, and the blank spaces in the list were filled out (so to speak) with names that remain mere shadows. This is an attractive hypothesis, but one that runs into serious difficulties. Paul's use of the name 'the twelve' in 1 Co 15[5], itself based on tradition the apostle had received from the Church before him, shows that the title was current at a very early date. Furthermore, if 'the twelve' were an invention of the early Church, would Judas have been included in the list? Jesus' selection of a disciple who proved unworthy of His choice later posed a problem that the Church would scarcely have created for itself. It seems to this writer that the number twelve could have been both historical and symbolical; that it was Jesus Himself who intended the intimate group of His followers to symbolize the purified Israel that would enter the new age of God's rule. In Luke 10[1-12] the Third Evangelist tells us that Jesus, in addition to the inner circle of twelve, also appointed a larger group of seventy, but this Lukan story appears to be literary rather than historical in origin. Both Mark and Q had accounts of the sending out of the Twelve. Matthew used the Q narrative to supplement Mark's in his version, but Luke used it as the basis of a separate account. In the OT 'seventy' is a round number used with reference to Gentile nations, and possibly Luke intended the story of the mission of the seventy to prefigure the later Christian mission to non-Jews.

Greek teachers in Jesus' time had their circles of students, and in Palestine each noted Rabbi had his band of disciples. (It has been estimated that in some rabbinical schools 'disciples' were expected to remember as many as 30,000 oral rules in addition to the precepts of the written Torah [by Talmudic enumeration, 365 prohibitions and 248 commands, totalling 613 rules in all]). But Jesus was neither a Greek philosopher with a body of formal instruction to convey, nor a professional Jewish Rabbi with a deposit of tradition to impart, and such analogies are not exact. Probably we cannot improve on Mark's observation (3[14]) that Jesus appointed twelve (1) 'to be with him' (for companionship); (2) 'to be sent out to preach' (as on the one occasion recorded in the Synoptic tradition); and (3) to 'have authority to cast out demons' (to participate in their Master's ministry of exorcism).

Mark's list of disciples (3[16-19]) appears to be that employed by the other Synoptists (including the enumeration which Luke gives in Ac 1[13], where Judas Iscariot, of course, is omitted). In all the listings Simon comes first and Judas Iscariot last. Mark arranges the names in four groups of three each, apparently in order of their importance. (1) Simon was the earliest convert and enjoyed a special relationship with Jesus. The significance of the nickname he was given, *Cephas* in Aramaic and *Petros* (Peter) in Greek, remains a puzzle. Mark speaks of him as Simon to the point of his enumeration in the list of the Twelve (3[16]), and as Peter throughout the rest of the Gospel. According to Matthew, Simon received the surname 'Peter' as a reward for his perspicacity in confessing Jesus as Messiah at Caesarea Philippi (16[18]). According to Jn 1[42], Jesus gave him the name on the occasion of their very first meeting. The only conclusion to be drawn from this is that the early Church was not certain why or when Simon got the name 'Peter.' The disciple's nature does not appear to have been so resolute and unbending as to warrant comparison to a 'rock.' The traditional Protestant interpretation of Mt 16[18], that 'the rock' on which Jesus said He would build His Church was Peter's faith, seems to this writer to depend on violent exegesis. Probably the Matthaean passage dates from a time when the Church at Antioch, which regarded Peter as its leader, asserted its precedence over the Church at Jerusalem headed by James the Lord's brother. It is possible that Jesus gave Simon the name Cephas (Peter) because, as His first convert and disciple, he could be regarded as the foundation stone of the new community. It is also possible that the name comes from the early days of the Church, when Simon Bar-Jona was known to have been the first to be convinced of the Resurrection (1 Co 15[5], Lk 24[33-34]). (2, 3) Mark says that Jesus gave the sons of Zebedee the surname 'Boanerges,' which he translates as 'sons of thunder.' This nickname, like that of Simon, remains enigmatical. It has been suggested that it is explained by the incident in Lk 9[54], where James and John wish Jesus to bid fire come down from heaven on the heads of inhospitable Samaritans. Since Luke does not refer to the nickname—or Matthew, for that matter—this explanation must be deemed improbable. James suffered martyrdom during the latter part of the reign of Herod Agrippa (*i.e.* A.D. 43–44; cf Ac 12[1-2]). The last we hear of John in the NT is in Gal 2, where we learn that in the controversy preceding the Apostolic Council he had thrown in his lot with the Jewish wing of the early Church. (For the tradition that John was the author of the Johannine cycle of literature, and for the conflicting tradition that he, like James, suffered early martyrdom [cf Mk 10[35-40], especially v.[39]], see JOHN, GOSPEL OF.) (4, 5) Andrew and Philip are pure Greek names, and this fact prompts several questions: Did they speak Greek? Could Jesus speak Greek? In what language did Jesus converse with the centurion from Capernaum? the Syrophoenician woman? Pontius Pilate? Andrew is elsewhere identified as Simon's brother. Philip the disciple is not to be confused with Philip the Evangelist, who (according to the early chapters of the book of Acts) played a significant rôle in the life of the later Church. (6) Bartholomew (Son of Ptolemy), (7) Matthew (Gift of God), and (8) Thomas (Twin) are all names from Aramaic roots. In the Gospel of Matthew the disciple Matthew has been confused with Levi the son of Alphaeus (cf Mt 9[9] and Mk 2[14]), a disciple who was not one of the Twelve. (9) James, who *is* listed as one of the Twelve, is identified as another 'son of Alphaeus.' (10) 'Thaddaeus' is the name of the tenth disciple in all texts of Mark and in the 'Neutral' texts of Matthew, while 'Lebbaeus' appears in the 'Western' texts of Matthew, and 'Judas the son [brother?] of James' in the texts of Luke and Acts. (11) 'Simon the Cananaean' in Mark and Matthew is 'Simon who was called the Zealot' in Luke and Acts. It is generally supposed that *kananaios* is the transliteration and *zēlōtēs* the translation of the Aramaic *ḳan'ānâ*, a noun derived from a verb which means 'to be zealous.' If this is the case, Mark's and Matthew's 'Cananaean' means the same as Luke's 'Zealot.' Zealots (q.v.) were the revolutionary extremists among the Jews during the period preceding the outbreak of the war against Rome, but it is doubtful that the party was known by this name as early as the time of Jesus' ministry. Probably Simon's nickname denoted only a distinctive trait in his character. (12) Judas Iscariot is mentioned last in all the lists. 'Iscariot' is usually interpreted as 'man of Kerioth,' *i.e.* a native of a town in Judaea near the Idumaean border. Others believe it is derived from 'sicarius' (assassin); and still others from an Aramaic word meaning 'false.' By the 2nd cent. the fact that Jesus had chosen Judas as a disciple raised several thorny problems for theologians. How could a man have lived under the influence of Jesus and have acted as Judas did? Was Jesus' foreknowledge at fault? The Fourth Evangelist seems to have had the latter question in mind, for he represents Jesus as aware from the beginning that Judas would betray Him (Jn 6[70]). In much modern literature, following a suggestion made early in the 19th cent. by Thomas De Quincey, Judas is pictured as a passionate, impulsive, high-minded individual who, distressed at the slow progress made by Jesus, betrayed his Lord in order that, by compelling Him to declare Himself as Messiah, he might hasten the coming of the Kingdom. There is not a shred of evidence for this conjecture. The Evangelists indicate that Judas acted simply out of motives of greed. Matthew, however, made an attempt to mitigate the enormity of Judas' crime. He declares that Judas repented of his treachery and committed suicide in remorse (27^{3-5}). But Luke knew of an entirely contradictory sequel. Judas, far from repenting, ' bought a field with the reward of his wickedness,' only to be visited with a punitive miracle. ' Falling headlong [or *swelling up*, RSVm] he burst open in the middle and all his bowels gushed out ' (Ac 1^{18}).

In the Gospel of John we are told that two of Jesus' disciples had formerly been followers of John the Baptist (1^{35-37} [Andrew is identified as one of the two in v.^{40}]). No doubt Jesus' preaching made a special appeal to men who had already been aroused by John's message, but there is no indication in the Synoptics that any of Jesus' followers had previously been disciples of John in any special sense.

(3) *The mighty works*.—Every stratum of the Synoptic tradition, Mark, Q, L, and M, contains narratives of the mighty works of Jesus, and sooner or later the student of the NT must reflect on the historical and theological problems they raise. In this connexion several facts should be kept in mind : (*a*) In the Gospel of John the miracles are referred to as ' signs.' It is asserted that Jesus performed them in order to demonstrate that He was the Son of God. But there is little of this apologetic in the first three Gospels. From their records we gather that Jesus healed the sick as an outflow of His great compassion for suffering people. The one exception to this is the indication in the Synoptics that Jesus thought of His powers over demons as evidence that the new age of God's rule had already broken in upon history. Lk 10^{18} appears to be Jesus' reflection on some visionary experience : ' I saw Satan fall like lightning from heaven.' The prince of demons had been dethroned ! In similar vein Matthew (12^{28}) quotes Jesus' words in the Beelzebul controversy : ' If it is by the Spirit of God that I cast out demons, then the kingdom of God has come upon you.' (*b*) According to the Biblical world-view, what we call a ' miracle ' was just something out of the ordinary. All things took place as acts of God, and normally they followed a familiar pattern. But there was no reason why God should not choose to have things happen in unfamiliar and abnormal ways. When an individual stepped into a lake, his feet sank at once to the bottom. But there was no reason why God should not empower him to walk on its surface. It was all a matter of God's volition. No intellectual problem—no problem of ' natural law '—was involved. (*c*) Disease, whether somatic or psychic, was believed to be caused by demon possession. A mild illness was due to the inhabitation of a victim by one demon. The more severe the malady, the more the demons who had taken control. Mary Magdalene had been possessed by seven, and the Gadarene demoniac, a case of violent lunacy, by a legion. (*d*) In the Gospels as in other traditions, both sacred and secular, once belief in the extraordinary or supernatural had been established, there was a tendency at later levels to heighten the miraculous element for purposes of effect. The simplest form of the miracle narratives in the Gospels is usually to be found in Mark. The accounts are ordinarily more elaborate and embellished in Matthew and in Luke. They are incapable of any natural explanation in John, and they become a tissue of impossibilities in the apocryphal gospels. (*e*) Occasionally it can be demonstrated that the ' miraculous ' element in a later version of a gospel story did not belong to it at the beginning. According to Mark's narrative of Jesus' baptism, as we have seen, it was Jesus alone who ' saw the heavens opened and the Spirit descending upon him like a dove ' (1^{10}). In Matthew what had been an experience personal to Jesus (in Mark) became a public attestation of the Messiah (3^{16-17}). In Luke ' the Holy Spirit descended . . . *in bodily* form, as a dove ' (3^{22}). In Mark's account of Jesus' arrest we are told only that ' one of those who stood by drew his sword, and struck the slave of the high priest and cut off his ear ' (14^{47}). In Luke the event became a miracle : ' But Jesus said, " No more of this ! " And he touched his ear and healed him ' (22^{51}).

Students of the patterns into which miracle stories were cast during the oral stage of their transmission point out that they usually begin with comments on the nature and severity of the malady, include a description of the methods of exorcism employed, reach a climax in some striking utterance of Jesus, and end with a reference to the effect of the miracle on bystanders. No classification of the miracle stories in the Gospels will appeal to every reader as a happy one—and it must be admitted that forms tend to be ' mixed '—but the following may be of assistance to some :

(*a*) *Miracles of healing in the realm of mental and nervous disease*.—Various neurotic and psychotic disturbances were at least as common in the ancient world as they are to-day and, because their victims were not confined to hospitals or other institutions, were much more in evidence. Most of the healings ascribed in the Synoptic Gospels to Jesus fall into this category, and they are also the mighty works for which there is best attestation in our sources. Modern progress in the science of psychology and its related disciplines enables us better to understand the conditions under which these healings were performed, even if we disclaim any ability to ' explain ' them. (*b*) *Miracles of bodily healing*.—Stories in the Gospels about the healing of the blind, the deaf, the dumb, the epileptic, the paralytic, etc., are perhaps the most difficult for the historian to evaluate. That they have often undergone legendary embellishment is clear. That many had a basis in fact is just as indubitable. Advances in the art of psychosomatic therapy in modern times again are of some assistance to the student as he reflects on this strand of the tradition. (*c*) *Nature miracles*.—Stories in the Gospels of miracles in the realm of nature—the walking on the water, the stilling of the storm, and so forth—do not constitute a large group. There is reason to believe that some became attached to the Christian tradition from Jewish or pagan sources. Others may conceivably have arisen from the heightening in narration of an originally purely natural event. (*d*) *Miracles that may have developed out of parables*.—It is probable that occasionally, perhaps very occasionally, there has been a confusion between what Jesus said and what He did. It is at least possible that the difficult miracle story of the fig tree that withered at Jesus' curse (Mk 11^{12-14}||) goes back to the parable of the fig tree that we have in Lk 13^{6-9}. (*e*) *Symbolic miracles*.—The Johannine ' signs ' are to be included in this category. One of the most illuminating is the story in Jn 21 of the miraculous catch of fish, with its apparent moral that men without Christ can do nothing. It is probable also that at least some of the miracle stories in the Synoptics were told in the first instance for their symbolic value—one thinks, for example, of the story of the feeding of the multitude, with the impression that the reader gets from it that in some sense it prefigures or anticipates the Eucharist.

(4) *Early opposition to Jesus*.—Opposition to Jesus arose early in His Galilaean ministry. From the beginning the Pharisees (q.v.) appear to have been antagonized by His preaching and practice. As guardians of the Torah they had ' built a hedge ' of exact interpretation about it, and they feared with some reason that He was impairing its authority. His disregard of the oral *halachah*, His impatience with the letter of regulations governing food, fasting, and sabbath observance, all undermined the legalistic basis of what they stood for in Judaism. In Mk 3^{6} we are told that almost at the outset of Jesus' ministry they entered into some sort of conspiracy against Him with the ' Herodians,' and there is a later reference to this alliance in Mk 12^{13}. Herodians appear to have been Jews who were political supporters of Herod Antipas, possibly royalists who wished to re-establish the Herodian monarchy. No doubt such secularist Jews would be indifferent to any religious consequences of Jesus' ministry but would be fearful of possible political repercussions.

On at least one occasion Jesus' opponents—identified by Mark as ' scribes who came down from Jerusalem '—tried to discredit Him with His public by insinuating that

He was ‘ possessed ’—*i.e.* that He was in league with Satan (Mk 3^{22}). This was an insidious and dangerous charge in a superstitious age, and the report that Jesus was a demoniac appears to have come to the ears of members of His family. Mk 3^{21} declares that they became apprehensive for His safety and even came to Capernaum in an abortive attempt to break off His public ministry. ‘ And when his friends [relatives] heard it, they went out to seize him, for they said [*i.e.* for people were saying], “ He is beside himself.” ’

(5) *Jesus' rejection at Nazareth.*—Towards the close of His Galilaean ministry Jesus paid a visit to His home village of Nazareth and taught in its synagogue (Mk 6^{1-6}). Luke's account (4^{16-30}), as we have already noted (see above (1)), is put at the beginning of Jesus' Galilaean activity and is much more detailed and dramatic than Mark's, but the latter appeared to be the source the Third Evangelist is using, and the special emphases in Mark's story are probably due to his artistic and apologetic concerns. There is no suggestion in Mark of any attempt on the part of Jesus' fellow townsmen to destroy Him or of any miraculous escape of Jesus from their toils (as in Lk 4^{28-30}), but the earlier account also admits that the mission was a failure. Those who had known Jesus and other members of His family had no pride in the man whose wisdom and whose mighty works had been bruited abroad. Mark adds the comment that Jesus ‘ could do no mighty work there . . . because of their unbelief (vv.$^{5-6}$). Faith, the Evangelist implies, was an indispensable condition for the exercise of Jesus' healing powers. Matthew, loath to admit that anything could limit Jesus' ability to work miracles, alters Mark to read, ‘ And he did not do many mighty works there ’ [13^{58}]).

(6) *The mission of the Twelve.*—According to Mk 3^{14}, one of the purposes that Jesus had in mind when He chose His twelve disciples was that they should ‘ be sent out to preach,’ but there is only one account in the Gospels of an independent mission in which His followers engaged (Mk 6^{7-13} ||). It must be kept in mind, however, that Jesus' ministry was prematurely interrupted, and He may have intended to use the Twelve more extensively in the proclamation of the gospel of the Kingdom than events permitted. According to Mark, Jesus sent out His disciples in six companies of two each to traverse the province. While Matthew used a parallel narrative in Q to supplement the account in Mark, Luke reserved the bulk of the material in that source for his account of the sending out of the Seventy (Lk 10^{1-11}; see above (2)). According to the Q narrative, the use of a staff and sandals was forbidden, but Mark's version (perhaps with the rigours of the Hellenistic mission in mind) permits it. The missioners were not to accept hospitality from more than one host in any one centre and were not to waste time on any who would not receive their message. (The urgency of Jesus' charge is to be understood, of course, against the eschatological background of His message.) In 10^{17-22} Matthew enlarges Mark with material taken in part from Mk 13^{9-13} (itself a late deposit in the earliest Gospel) and reflecting the persecution that was the experience of the later apostolic Church. It is clear that even Mark's narrative has been affected at points by the experience of early Christian evangelists, but there is no reason to doubt the historicity of the mission or of the general character of Jesus' instructions as they have been preserved.

12. Period of Withdrawal from Galilee.—According to Mk 7^{24}–9^{29}, Jesus interrupted His Galilaean ministry and withdrew for a period from the territories ruled over by Herod Antipas, travelling north to sparsely settled areas in Phoenicia and then, by a circuitous route, to parts of Palestine to the east and the north-east of the Galilaean lake. Matthew adheres to Mark's outline. Jn 6^{1-21} also preserves the tradition of a brief ministry in the tetrarchy of Philip. By omitting Mk 6^{45}–8^{26}, Luke gives the impression that Jesus went directly from Galilee to the district in Philip's tetrarchy about Caesarea Philippi.

Some scholars believe that most of this section in Mark was originally absent from the Gospel. They point to the confused and hazy geographical setting of the material and to the fact that much of it raises questions of critical concern. Several paragraphs in this Markan section look like doublets, like parallel versions of incidents already narrated. (1) The story of the feeding of four thousand in 8^{1-9} looks like a repetition of the earlier account of the feeding of five thousand in 6^{31-43}. (2) Both stories of the miraculous multiplication of loaves and fishes are followed by accounts of a voyage across the Sea of Galilee in which the failure of the disciples to understand the significance of the miracle is stressed (6^{52} 8^{17}). (3) The story of the cure of a blind man by means of spittle (8^{22-26}) looks like a doublet of the earlier narrative of the cure of a deaf-mute by similar means (7^{32-37}). (These two miracle stories are the only ones in the gospel tradition to assert that Jesus ever employed physical means in effecting His works of healing.)

It is one thing to suspect that in this section of his Gospel Mark has woven together two parallel versions of a period in Jesus' ministry in which He withdrew to the north and the north-east, and quite another to argue that the particular part of Mark missing from Luke at this point is an interpolation. Various other hypotheses could account even better for the lacuna in Luke. The Third Evangelist could have used a mutilated copy of Mark. More probably the explanation is that He deliberately omitted the material, partly because some of it (*e.g.* the story of the Syrophoenician woman) gave uncertain support to his interest in emphasizing the universal implications of Jesus' message, and partly in order to conserve manuscript space for the large amount of new matter that he wished to work into Mark's framework.

(1) *Reason for the withdrawal.*—If the tradition be accepted that Jesus for a period left Galilee for territories outside the jurisdiction of Herod Antipas (Mark refers to one brief re-entry [8^{10-13}]), the biographer looks for a reason to account for the withdrawal. Again it must be admitted that our sources give no unequivocal answer. It is improbable that Jesus went outside Galilee merely to extend the scope of His mission. Mark suggests that He wished to remain incognito. ‘ And he entered a house, and would not have any one know it ; yet he could not be hid ’ (7^{24}).

The most plausible hypothesis (in the judgment of this writer) is that Jesus left Galilee in order to avoid arrest and incarceration by Herod—in order to avoid the fate that had overtaken John the Baptist. In 3^{6} Mark mentions an alliance of Herodians and Pharisees against Jesus. In 6^{14-16} he tells his readers that Herod had heard of Jesus and His work and suspected that He might be John the Baptist risen from the dead. In 8^{15} Jesus is quoted as warning His disciples against ‘ the leaven of the Pharisees and the leaven of Herod.’ There may have been some crisis in Jesus' relations with the political authorities in Galilee, of which we learn nothing from Mark, that accounts for His departure ‘ to the region of Tyre and Sidon ’ (Mk 7^{24}).

Luke has preserved an interesting little passage (13^{31-33}) that lends this hypothesis some support. Certain friendly Pharisees warned Jesus : ‘ Get away from here, for Herod wants to kill you.’ The pericope is included in a long section in Luke (9^{51}–18^{14}) into which the Evangelist put undated material derived from various non-Markan sources. It may well be that the passage in question belongs to the Galilaean period of Jesus' ministry.

(2) *The confession at Caesarea Philippi.*—The most striking incident of this extra-Galilaean period in Jesus' ministry, an incident that serves as a virtual prelude to Mark's passion narrative, was the confession by the disciples, through Peter as their spokesman, of Jesus' Messiahship (8^{27-30} ||). The scene is located by Mark (or his source) in the neighbourhood of Caesarea Philippi, a new city that had formerly been known as

Paneas and that had been rebuilt by Herod Philip and renamed in honour of the emperor. To the question, 'Who do men say that I am ?' the disciples answered, '"John the Baptist"; and others, "Elijah"; and others, "One of the prophets."' To the question, 'But who do you say that I am ?' Peter replied, 'You are the Christ.' The whole matter of Jesus' interpretation of His mission is the subject of discussion at a later point in this article (see **21**). Suffice it for the time being to say that this narrative rests, in the judgment of the present writer, on a sound historical recollection.

(3) *The Transfiguration.*—The sequel to Peter's confession of Jesus' Messiahship, according to Mark, was Jesus' declaration that 'the Son of man must suffer many things' (8^{31}). Then follows the story of the Transfiguration (9^{2-8} ||). Some scholars believe that there is a core of historical reminiscence to this puzzling pericope. Others hold that it originally belonged to a resurrection cycle of tradition and has been moved forward by the Evangelist into his account of Jesus' earthly ministry. However that may be, what Mark means the story to indicate is clear. The Evangelist wishes to say: Jesus had tacitly admitted that He was Messiah but had coupled that admission with the prophecy that as Messiah He would have to suffer and die. To His three most intimate followers it was revealed that, despite the sufferings He would have to endure, He was nevertheless God's beloved Son. What all believers knew after the Resurrection had already become their secret before the Crucifixion.

13. The Journey to Jerusalem.—The direct route from Capernaum to Jerusalem led through Samaria, but it was often avoided by Jewish travellers because of Samaritan hostility. The longer route involved crossing the Jordan below the Sea of Galilee, journeying through the Decapolis and Peraea, and recrossing the river into Judaea at fords near Jericho. It would appear from Mk 10^{1} that Jesus chose this latter route for His last journey to the capital city. (It is often inferred from Luke's story of Jesus' rebuff at a Samaritan village after He had begun His journey [9^{51-56}] that the Third Evangelist followed at this point a tradition at variance with Mark's, but the fact that Luke also agrees that Jesus and His company arrived in the end at Jericho [18^{35}] seems to demonstrate that his Markan source was still his main reliance.) The Third Evangelist gives the impression that Jesus did more teaching during the course of this journey than during any previous period, but this is due entirely to the author's method of composition. (Lk 9^{51}–18^{14} is a block of non-Markan didactic matter inserted into the framework of Mk 10.) However, we gather also from Mark that 'the Way of the Cross' was a leisurely one, and Jesus may have found an unusually receptive and responsive audience in the territory in which John the Baptist had preached and baptized. It is clear that Jesus intended His arrival at Jerusalem to coincide with the ensuing Passover season. He must have been aware that the growing opposition to Him would come to a head in the Jewish capital, and both Mk 10^{32} and Lk 9^{51} emphasize the seriousness with which He and His disciples viewed the venture on which He had embarked.

14. The Week of the Passion.—Mark's chronology of the Passion week is as follows:—

Sunday: The triumphal entry into Jerusalem (11^{1-11}).

Monday: The cleansing of the Temple (11^{12-19}).

Tuesday: Debates with chief priests and scribes and some teaching (11^{20}–13^{37}).

Wednesday: The anointing at Bethany; Judas' agreement with the chief priests to betray his Lord (14^{1-11}).

Thursday: Preparation for the Passover; the Last Supper; the Agony; the betrayal and arrest; the trial before the Sanhedrin; Peter's denial (14^{12-72}).

Friday: A second meeting of the Sanhedrin; the trial before Pilate; the Barabbas interlude; Jesus' condemnation, crucifixion, and burial (15^{1-47}).

Those who discount the value of Mark's chronology regard it here also as arbitrary and artificial, and even more cautious scholars believe that the events of the Passion Story, the earliest and most important 'sermon' of the early Church, have been telescoped in narration. Jesus' protest at the time of His arrest, 'Day after day I was with you in the temple teaching, and you did not seize me' (Mk 14^{49}), points to a longer period than the two or three days that Mark's Gospel would allow. There is also some Talmudic evidence that money changers had to be out of the Temple by Nisan 1, and if this were the case the incident of the cleansing of the Temple must have taken place at least two or three weeks before the Crucifixion.

15. Events Preceding the Passion.—(1) *The entry into Jerusalem.*—The road from Jericho to Jerusalem rises 1300 feet by a long and sometimes precipitous ascent of 17 miles. (It was on this road that Jesus in His parable of the Good Samaritan put the man who 'fell among robbers,' Lk 10^{30}.) Following this route Jesus and the caravan with which He was travelling (including many who were not His immediate followers) in due course reached the outskirts of Jerusalem. Entrance to the city was made by way of Bethphage (according to Mt 21^{1}), a suburb that appears to have been located on the southern slope of the Mount of Olives. According to Mark the people who had travelled with Jesus hailed Him on His entry as the herald who had proclaimed 'the kingdom of our father David that is coming' (10^{10}). Matthew and Luke reinterpreted the tradition as an acclamation of Jesus as Messiah, and Matthew emphasized the fact that the entry was in literal fulfilment of the messianic prophecy in Zec 9^{9} (Matthew misunderstood the poetic parallelism of his OT proof text and consequently gave his readers an absurd picture of Jesus mounted on 'an ass, *and* a colt, the foal of an ass,' 21^{5}). In 12^{12} John represents the welcomers as pilgrims who had already been in the city for some time; in v.^{13} he substitutes 'branches of palm trees' for Mark's 'leafy branches' as the carpet of homage; and in v.^{15} he agrees with Mark and Luke that the event was a messianic welcome and with Matthew that it was a fulfilment of Zec 9^{9}.

(2) *The cleansing of the Temple.*—According to Mk 11^{11} the procession of which Jesus was a part went directly to the Temple on its arrival in the city. Jesus 'looked round at everything' and then, because of the lateness of the hour, proceeded to Bethany with the twelve, postponing any action until the following day. Matthew and Luke omit any reference to this preliminary reconnaissance. In their Gospels the purification of the Temple follows immediately upon the triumphal entry. John transposes the whole incident to the beginning of Jesus' ministry (2^{13-17}), presumably in order to portray the Lord of the Church as asserting His Divine authority from the very first.

In Jesus' day the Temple had become grossly commercialized. Provision had been made within the Temple precincts (the outer 'court of the Gentiles') for the purchase and slaughter of sacrificial victims. Mark makes specific mention only of 'pigeons,' but John adds 'sheep' and 'cattle,' and doubtless they also were for sale. Facilities had also to be provided for the payment of the annual Temple tax. Jews came from all parts of the Dispersion with Roman coins. Since these were stamped with the head of Tiberius or the deified Augustus, they could not be accepted by the Temple treasury (because of the Jewish law against 'images'), and money-changers were permitted in the Temple grounds for the purpose of converting pagan coinage, for a fee, into Jewish currency.

The priests had encouraged the commercialization of the Temple courts as one means of maintaining the sacerdotal system, and even Jewish scholars admit that there may have been 'occasions on which indignation such as that of Jesus would have been justified' (C. G. Montefiore). It is interesting to note that it is only in the Fourth Gospel that Jesus is expressly said to have used violence to achieve His ends. The implication in

JESUS CHRIST

Mark is that He relied on His moral authority. His prestige would be great, and in all probability He had the support of public sentiment. The Temple authorities (the Sanhedrin) would regard His interference as a direct challenge to their vested interests. Mark (v.^{18}) says that His action accentuated their opposition to Him. If not the immediate cause of the Crucifixion, this clash with the Sanhedrin was at least a contributing factor.

(3) *Opposition to Jesus in Jerusalem.*—The Pharisees may have been the real power behind the opposition to Jesus in Jerusalem, as they had been in Galilee, but the Romans had delegated official authority in Judaea only to the Sanhedrin, the High Court of Jewry, and it was the Sadducees, the party of the priests and the landed aristocracy, who controlled that body. In Jesus' day the Sadducees (q.v.) were staunch supporters of the Roman regime. It can hardly be doubted that they had been observing Jesus and His activities for some time. In Galilee He was under the jurisdiction of Herod Antipas, and they could only take official action against Him when He entered Judaea and Jerusalem. No doubt their opposition to Him was mainly political and ecclesiastical. As a teacher He would appear to them to be of little consequence. As one whose ministry might lead to a political disturbance or become a threat to their exploitation of the Temple, however, He would become to them an object of suspicion and distrust.

The ultimate authority with which Jesus came into conflict, of course, was the Roman government, represented in Judaea by the procurator, Pontius Pilate. There is a tendency in the Gospels to throw as much blame as possible for the Crucifixion on the Jews and to absolve the Romans of responsibility. Some scholars have concluded from this that Rome had much more to do with Jesus' death than any of the Evangelists admit, but there is no reason to doubt the Gospel evidence that Rome intervened only at the end. It was Roman policy not to interfere in matters of purely religious concern and to give free rein to national and local authorities until there was some open act of violence or disorder.

(4) *Controversies with opponents.*—Much of the matter in Mk 11^{20}–13^{37} (||) has to do with attempts by Jesus' opponents to involve Him in an incriminating utterance. In 11^{27-33} (||) we are told that members of the Sanhedrin challenged Jesus in the Temple with the question, 'By what authority are you doing these things, or who gave you this authority to do them?' This challenge may well belong to the moment immediately after the cleansing of the Temple, although Mark in his chronology locates it on the following day. Perhaps, as Mark seems to imply, Jesus wished to evade His opponents' plot by involving them in a dilemma with His counter-question: 'Was the baptism of John from heaven or from men? Answer me' (v.^{30}). More probably He intended by His question to suggest that there was a real connexion between John's ministry and His own.

Mk 12^{13-17} (||) relates that a deputation of Pharisees and Herodians endeavoured 'to entrap [Jesus] in his talk.' 'Is it lawful to pay taxes to Caesar, or not?' (v.^{14}). The question was a crafty and clever one. If Jesus were to answer 'No,' He would gain favour with nationalist extremists among His countrymen but would at the same time lay Himself open to a charge of treason. Jesus' famous reply, 'Render to Caesar the things that are Caesar's, and to God the things that are God's' (v.^{18}) has frequently been interpreted as evasive and non-committal. This can hardly be correct. Jesus declares that the tax is to be paid, but insists that obedience to the state is subordinate to man's higher loyalty to God.

(5) *The anointing of Jesus.*—According to Mark and Matthew, Jesus withdrew each evening from Jerusalem to Bethany, presumably to the home of friends in that village. Lk 21^{37} preserves a different tradition (to which Jn 18^{1-2} lends some support): 'And every day he was teaching in the temple, but at night he went and lodged on the mount called Olivet.'

Mk 14^{3-9} records a beautiful little incident that took place in Bethany at the home of one 'Simon the leper.' An unnamed woman brought an alabaster jar of costly ointment, broke it, and poured the 'pure nard' on Jesus' head. According to one improbable hypothesis, the whole occasion was prearranged as a formal anointing of Jesus as Messiah, and it was the fact of this messianic anointing that Judas later betrayed to the authorities. There is no support for this interpretation of the incident in any of our sources. Mark represents the woman's action as a spontaneous, generous, impulsive gesture of love and faith. The Lukan parallel to Mark's story has a Galilaean rather than a Judaean setting, and we are told that the incident occurred early in Jesus' ministry in the home of a Pharisee called Simon (7^{36-50}). The woman who showed Jesus honour is described as a sinner, and it is said that she anointed His feet (rather than His head) and wiped them with her tresses. In the Fourth Gospel (12^{1-8}) the scene of the incident, as in Mark, is in Bethany in Judaea, but it takes place in the home of Lazarus and his two sisters and belongs to the days before Jesus' triumphal entry into Jerusalem. The woman who anointed Jesus is identified as Mary, and we are told (as in Luke) that she anointed Jesus' feet. (Lazarus is not mentioned in the Synoptic tradition, and according to Lk 10^{28-42} Martha and Mary were Galilaeans, not Judaeans.)

(6) *The Last Supper.*—Various attempts have been made to account for the Christian rite of the Lord's Supper as a sacramental meal borrowed by the Church after the Resurrection from the practice of Oriental mystery cults, many of which celebrated stated sacred meals. Such a hypothesis, however, is untenable. It may well be that the Lord's Supper came to be interpreted as a sacrament under the influence of ideas associated with pagan cultic meals, but it is certain that it was celebrated in the early Church as a re-enactment of the Last Supper, and the Last Supper is one of the best attested incidents in the life of Jesus. We have St. Paul's account of it in 1 Co 11^{23-26}, a report that comes from a time not much more than twenty years after the event and that Paul declares he himself had 'received.' (This declaration may mean that the apostle's account came to him by direct revelation from the risen Lord, but more probably that it was transmitted to him from Christ through the medium of Church tradition.) And in the Synoptic Gospels we have two apparently independent narratives, that in Mk 14^{22-25} (closely followed by Mt 26^{26-29}), and that in Lk 22^{15-19a}. (Lk 22^{19b-20}, in the AV but omitted by the RSV, is an addition to the earliest Greek texts under the influence of 1 Co 11^{24b-25}.) See EUCHARIST.

The Synoptic Gospels put the Crucifixion on the day of the Jewish Passover festival. The Gospel of John, however, declares that Jesus was crucified during the last few hours before the Passover began. In other words, the Friday on which Jesus died, according to the Fourth Evangelist, was Nisan 14 rather than Nisan 15; the Day of Preparation rather than the Passover itself. While there is still much disagreement over the issue among NT scholars, it appears to this writer that in this instance the Johannine rather than the Synoptic tradition must be accepted. The Passover was one of the most sacred days in the Jewish calendar and was hedged about with the strictest regulations. It seems inconceivable that Jesus would have been arrested, tried, condemned, crucified, and buried on such a day. Even Mark reports that the Sanhedrin wished to encompass Jesus' destruction before the festival began, and we need not doubt that they were successful in their plans. 'It was now two days before the Passover. . . . And the chief priests and the scribes were seeking how to arrest him by stealth, and kill him; for they said, "Not during the feast, lest there be a tumult of the people"' (Mk 14^{1-2}).

If John rather than Mark is correct, viz. that Jesus died a few hours before the beginning of the Passover celebration, Jesus' last meal with His disciples could not have been the Passover meal that the Synoptists describe and should not be interpreted in the light of Passover symbolism. It would have been an ordinary meal eaten twenty-four hours before Jews ate their unleavened bread, bitter herbs, and paschal lamb ; and the memory of those who shared the meal with Jesus would go back to the occasion itself and the impression it made on them rather than to the meal as their last paschal observance with their Master.

While Paul's account differs in some details from the one in Mark–Matthew, it is apparent that both represent fundamentally the same tradition. Jesus took a loaf of bread, blessed it [Paul : 'when he had given thanks'], broke it, and said, 'This is my body' [Paul : 'which is broken for you']. Then Jesus gave His disciples a cup of wine [Mark–Matthew : 'when he had given thanks'] with the words : 'This [Paul : 'cup'] is my blood of the [Paul : 'new'] covenant.' Paul omits 'and gave it to them' in connexion with both the bread and the cup ; 'which is poured out for many' [Matthew adds : 'for the forgiveness of sins'] in connexion with the cup ; and also Jesus' prediction in Mk 14^{25} (Mt 26^{29}) : 'I shall not drink again of the fruit of the vine until that day when I drink it new in the kingdom of God.' Paul's most significant additions to the account in Mark–Matthew are the clause 'which is broken for you,' appended to the statement 'This is my body,' and the command that the Supper should be repeated (1 Co 11^{25b-26}).

In Luke's account (22^{15-19a} [the short or 'Western' text]), (1) the cup comes before the bread ; (2) the cup is not associated with the establishment of a new covenant ; and (3) the main emphasis is on the Supper as an eschatological feast that anticipated God's triumph in the new age of His rule (vv.$^{17-18}$). Luke's representation of the Last Supper is supported by the account in the Didache (9^{1-3}) of the celebration of the Lord's Supper in at least parts of the Church in the early 2nd cent. ; and it is also of importance to note that a passage in Acts that appears to refer to early Christian celebration of the Lord's Supper (2^{46} ; cf $20^{7,11}$) speaks of the celebrants as partaking of food 'with glad and generous hearts'—*i.e.* as a feast of joyous anticipation.

The place occupied in the Synoptics by the words of the institution of the Lord's Supper is taken in John by an account of Jesus' institution of the rite of footwashing (13^{2-11}). Apparently the Fourth Evangelist wished to associate the Church's sacrament of the Eucharist with Christ's life-giving power (cf the great 'Eucharistic chapter' in Jn 6) rather than with His death.

16. The Passion.—(1) *The Agony.*—Mark tells us (14^{26}) that Jesus and His disciples after partaking of the Supper departed to the Mount of Olives. If Luke's assertion is correct, that Jesus and His followers regularly spent the night on Olivet (21^{37} ; we learn from Josephus that pilgrims to Jerusalem at the time of the great festivals often camped on the Mount of Olives due to overcrowded conditions in the city), then Judas, who did not accompany Jesus' party, would be familiar with their rendezvous. (According to Jn 18^{1-2}, Jesus 'often met there with His disciples.')

According to the Passion Story, Jesus now left the main body of His followers and went with Peter and James and John into Gethsemane (Mk 14^{32-33}||), a word that means 'oil press' and that John (who, like Luke, omits the Aramaic name) tells us was a garden or orchard (18^{1}).

The account of Jesus in Gethsemane is one of the most exquisite and moving of the incidents in the gospel story. Even a Jewish scholar could write of it : 'The whole story bears the hall-mark of human truth. . . . The sorrows and sufferings of the solitary Son of Man, profound as they are, leave on every sympathetic heart, be it the heart of the believer or unbeliever, such an impression as may never be wiped out' (Joseph Klausner). The Synoptic account, which is supported by another in He 5^{7-9}, must be based on some historical reminiscence. The Church would scarcely have invented the story that Jesus, at the very end of His ministry, was still uncertain about its course and had to wrestle in prayer with doubts and fears. It is significant that the Fourth Evangelist omits any reference to the ordeal. It was not in accordance with his idea of the way the Son of God would have behaved. At the same time, the differentiation of the inner circle of three from the larger group of Jesus' followers appears to have been imposed on an earlier form of the story, and the account as we now have it reads like an acted parable or narrative version of the Lord's Prayer.

(2) *The arrest.*—Mark and the other Synoptists represent those who apprehended Jesus as an unorganized rabble that had come from the Sanhedrin. The Fourth Evangelist has an interesting variant, viz. that the arrest was effected by Roman soldiers (18^{3}), but this can hardly have been the case. Roman soldiers would have taken Jesus directly to Pilate rather than to the Jewish authorities. Probably Mark used the term 'crowd' loosely (or even incorrectly) for Temple police who had been commissioned by the Sanhedrin to bring Jesus before them. Judas had prearranged with his employers that he would identify their victim by a kiss, the ordinary form of friendly salute, for some such signal was necessary in the semi-darkness of a moonlit night. (While some critics regard the whole story of Judas and his betrayal as a dramatic but unhistorical embellishment of the Passion Narrative, it seems incredible to this writer that the early Church would have created in Judas a problem that it later found so difficult to solve [see above, **11** (2)].)

Mark mentions an unnamed disciple who drew a sword, attacked one of the arresting party, and cut off his ear (14^{47}). In Luke this incident is the prelude to a miracle. 'Jesus said, "No more of this !" And he touched his ear and healed him' (22^{51}). In John the disciple becomes Simon Peter (18^{10}). Jesus Himself offered no resistance, uttering only a dignified protest against the clandestine character of the whole affair (Mk 14^{48-49}||), but His disciples were not cast in any heroic mould. 'They all forsook him and fled' (Mk 14^{50}).

(3) *The trials.*—(i) The examination before Annas.—The Gospel of John says that Jesus was taken immediately after His arrest to the house of Annas for a preliminary examination (18^{13}). Annas had been High Priest for a period some twenty years before the gospel story. According to Jewish practice he would have remained High Priest for life, but the Romans, who disliked to contemplate such great power in the hands of one man for any length of time, had insisted on a limited tenure of office. Nevertheless, the High Priesthood remained in Annas' family for decades, and Annas' son-in-law, Caiaphas, was in office at the time of Jesus' arrest. Some scholars believe it to be probable that Annas still exercised chief power in the Sanhedrin in all but name, that nothing would be done without consulting him, and that John is correct in saying that Jesus was taken to him before being tried by the Sanhedrin. But Annas is not mentioned in Mark or Matthew, and only incidentally and in another connexion in Luke (3^{12}), and John's added detail would put still another event into the already crowded sequence of Thursday evening.

(ii) The hearing before the Sanhedrin.—Brought before the Sanhedrin, the highest Jewish court, Jesus was charged by witnesses with having threatened to destroy the Temple (Mk 14^{58}). The evidence not being consistent (v.^{59}), the High Priest appealed directly to Jesus to say if He claimed to be the Christ (v.^{61}). When He answered 'I am,' the claim was forthwith declared to be blasphemy and 'all condemned him as deserving death' (v.^{64}).

By appealing to the Talmud scholars have pointed out numerous irregularities in the trial procedure, notably that capital trials might be begun only in the daytime, that the Sanhedrin was a judging, not a prosecuting, body, and that confession did not warrant conviction unless what had been admitted had also been attested by at least two witnesses. As a consequence various conclusions have been drawn : (1) Jesus had a fair and legal trial, but our records are so confused that we can no longer get an adequate picture of it from them ;

(2) the trial was illegal from beginning to end but is reported with fair accuracy in the Gospels; (3) the proceedings before the Sanhedrin were not a formal trial, but a preliminary investigation held in order to frame a charge against Jesus to be laid before Pilate—a hearing comparable to grand jury procedure in American jurisprudence.

(iii) The trial before Pilate.—The hearing before the Sanhedrin ended late Thursday evening. Mk 15^1 tells us that the Council called a second meeting early the following morning to make arrangements to bring Jesus before Pilate. Luke knows of only one meeting, that on Friday morning (22^{66-71}).

Pontius Pilate (q.v.) had been appointed Procurator of Judaea by Tiberius Caesar in A.D. 26 and held office until A.D. 36. Philo describes him as corrupt, obstinate, and merciless, but the fact that he was left in office for ten years—much longer than any of his predecessors or successors—is an indication that his superiors were satisfied with his administration. A volume of legendary 'Acts of Pilate' literature came into being in later centuries, but it is historically worthless. We know nothing of Pilate's earlier or later career.

According to Jn 18^{28}, the trial before Pilate took place in the portico outside the praetorium, the official residence of the procurator in Jerusalem and probably the former palace of Herod the Great. Pilate gathered from the charges that Jesus in some way had claimed to be a king. He turned to the prisoner and asked Him, 'Are you the King of the Jews?' (Mk 15^2). Jesus answered, 'You have said so.' Some interpreters believe that these words were a recognized formula of affirmation. More probably, in Aramaic or Greek as in English, they were meant to be non-committal.

The story of Pilate's attempt to relieve himself of responsibility for the case by sending Jesus to Herod Antipas (23^{6-16}) is a Lukan addition to the basic Markan account. Herod may well have been in the city for the festival. Pilate may well have thought him more competent than himself to deal with a Galilaean. But it is more probable that Luke's embellishment is unhistorical, for in Ac 4^{26-27} the Evangelist represents the trial before Herod as well as that before Pilate as necessary for the fulfilment of Ps. 2^2.

Matthew's additions to Mark at this point are plainly legendary: $27^{19,\,24f}$ were added to intensify the guilt of the Jews in the condemnation of Jesus; and the story in 27^{3-10} was believed to mitigate the enormity of Judas' crime (see above, **11** (2)).

The story that Pilate wished to release Jesus but that the Jews demanded instead the freeing of a notorious criminal was taken over by Matthew and Luke from Mk 15^{6-15}. The record in the Gospels is our only authority for the fact that it was customary at the time for the Roman procurator to celebrate a Jewish festival by an act of clemency. The story serves the interest of the Evangelists in emphasizing Pilate's unwillingness to order Jesus' crucifixion (see above, **15** (3)), but that in itself is not enough to compel us to doubt its historicity. In the Sinaitic-Syriac text of Mt 27^{17} we are told that Pilate's question was, 'Whom do you wish me to release to you? *Jesus* Barabbas, or *Jesus* whom men call the Christ?' and there are some scholars who believe that this reading of Matthew preserves the original form of the gospel tradition.

Mark says that Pilate finally delivered Jesus to be crucified because he wished 'to satisfy the crowd' (15^{15}). The Fourth Evangelist adds that the Jewish mob intimidated the procurator with threats (19^{12}).

(4) *The Crucifixion.*—After Pilate had condemned Jesus he handed Him over to a guard of Roman soldiers to be crucified. According to Mk 15^{17-20} the soldiers then subjected their prisoner to a species of crude abuse and mockery. Luke omits the incident because he had already used the Markan details in a similar scene before Herod Antipas (23^{11}). Mark's tradition is that Jesus was crucified at a place called Golgotha, an Aramaic word meaning 'skull.' (In the AV the Greek 'skull' of Lk 23^{33} is translated by the Latin 'Calvary,' a word made familiar in Christian usage by the Vulgate.) Presumably the site of the Crucifixion was a skull-shaped mound or hill. According to He 13^{12} it lay 'outside the gate'—*i.e.* outside the city limits as defined by its wall. It was customary for the condemned criminal to carry his cross to the place of execution. According to the Synoptic record, Jesus was unequal to the task and a passer-by, identified as Simon of Cyrene and presumably a Diaspora Jew in Jerusalem for the festival, was pressed into service. (He may later have become a convert to Christianity, for his sons were evidently well known to the community for which Mark was written [cf 15^{21}]). The Fourth Evangelist deliberately corrected the Synoptic account at this point. Jesus, he says, 'went out, bearing his own cross' (19^{17}). Apparently some form of the later gnostic myth that Simon of Cyrene had been crucified in Jesus' stead was already current in the circles for which John was writing.

Crucifixion, a form of execution by torture that had been borrowed by the Romans from Carthaginian practice, was reserved for slaves and rebels and combined the height of ignominy with the extremity of suffering. Mark declares that Jesus was crucified at the third hour and remained on the cross to the ninth hour ($15^{25,\,34}$)—*i.e.* from 9 a.m. to 3 p.m. John says that Jesus was crucified about the sixth hour (19^{14})—*i.e.* about 12 noon—but does not say when He died. (The Church custom of a three-hour vigil on Good Friday is a result of combining data from John and Mark. Perhaps John chose the sixth hour for the time of Jesus' crucifixion for symbolic reasons, to correlate it with the hour when the paschal lambs were slain.) Jesus' ordeal, we are to assume, was mercifully brief, for victims of crucifixion usually died from exhaustion and the tortures of thirst rather than from the loss of blood and could often linger alive on a cross for days.

Some details of the crucifixion story may have been suggested to early narrators by OT prophecy: that Jesus was crucified together with two thieves may have been derived from Is 53^{12}; the mockery of Jesus on the Cross from Ps 22^{7-8}; the scene of the soldiers casting lots for Jesus' garments from Ps 22^{16-18}; and the incident in Mk 15^{35-36} (Mt 27^{47-48}) from Ps 69^{19-21}. The deviations of Matthew and Luke from Mark's account do not appear to rest on any independent tradition. In particular Luke's story of the repentant thief (23^{39-43}) was probably due only to the Evangelist's dramatic instinct.

According to Mk 15^{23}, Jesus on the Cross refused a proffered opiate, but according to Jn 19^{29-30} He accepted it. According to Mk 15^{26}, the executioners inscribed the words 'The King of the Jews' over the Cross as the charge on which Jesus had been condemned. According to Jn 19^{19-22}, the Jews interpreted the inscription as an insult, and the Fourth Evangelist mentions that it was written in 'Hebrew, in Latin, and in Greek' in order to symbolize the universal Lordship of the crucified Christ.

Of the Seven Words on the Cross, three are recorded by John only ($19^{26-27,\,28,\,30}$), three by Luke only ($23^{34,\,43,\,46}$), and only one is quoted by Mark and Matthew. The saying in Lk 23^{34}, 'Father, forgive them; for they know not what they do,' is textually insecure, for it is missing in all the earliest Greek MSS. Lk 23^{46}, 'Father, into thy hands I commit my spirit!' is a quotation from Ps 31^5 and is substituted by the Third Evangelist for the bitter cry recorded in Mark.

What of the one saying of Jesus on the Cross that is in Mark and Matthew? Mark says that darkness came over the land from the sixth to the ninth hour (15^{33}). (Luke is more explicit. He says that there was an eclipse—'the sun's light failed' [23^{45}]—an interpretation that is astronomically impossible at the time of the full moon.) At the ninth hour Jesus uttered a loud cry, a cry which Mark reproduces in Aramaic and Matthew in Hebrew before translating, and which is a quotation from Ps 22^1: 'My God, my God, why hast thou forsaken

JESUS CHRIST

me?' Some interpreters believe that this quotation became part of the Passion Story only after the Church had adopted a messianic interpretation of Ps 22 and point out that, according to Mark, none of Jesus' followers could have heard His words. All, except certain faithful women who stood 'looking on from afar' (15^{40}), had forsaken Him and fled (14^{50}). (The Fourth Evangelist, disturbed by the fact that Mark did not mention Mary the mother of Jesus among the women at the Cross, corrects the omission and adds that the enigmatic 'disciple whom [Jesus] loved' was also standing near [19^{25-27}].) Others, who cannot believe that the later Church would have ascribed such a cry of despair to its Lord on the Cross, are convinced that the words must have been uttered by Jesus. One popular hypothesis, but one that does not seem to this writer to be tenable, is that Jesus intended to quote the entire psalm—a psalm that opens to be sure, with a prayer of desperation, but that ends on a note of triumph (vv.$^{27-28}$).

Mk 15^{38} cites a symbolic miracle that accompanied the death of Jesus Christ: 'The curtain of the temple was torn in two, from top to bottom.' Much as the author of the Letter to the Hebrews was later to maintain, Mark wishes to say that Christ's death broke down barriers that heretofore had separated man from God. In 27^{51b-53} Matthew heaps miracle upon miracle. Mk 15^{39} records that a Roman officer who had witnessed Christ's death declared: 'Truly this man was a son of God'—*i.e.* a divine hero. Luke, in the interest of his thesis that Rome should not regard Christianity as a subversive religion, changes the centurion's words to read: 'Certainly this man was innocent' (23^{47}).

(5) *The burial.*—The Christian tradition is that the body of Jesus was given honourable burial by a certain Joseph of Arimathea. 'Arimathea' is probably a corruption of 'Ramathaim,' a village in Judaea near the Samaritan border. Mark says that Joseph was 'a respected member' of the Sanhedrin (15^{43}). If this were the case, what part had he taken in the proceedings against Jesus? Both John and Luke appear to have been aware of a difficulty at this point. According to Jn 19^{38}, Joseph kept his devotion to Jesus a secret for fear of the Jews. According to Lk 23^{51}, he had not consented to the Sanhedrin's purpose and deed.

Joseph obtained permission from Pilate to bury Jesus' body in a rock-hewn tomb. Matthew says that the tomb was Joseph's own (27^{60}); Luke that it was one in which 'no one had ever yet been laid' (23^{53}). The only witnesses of the burial were two women who Mark implies were well known in the early Christian community, 'Mary Magdalene and Mary the mother of Joses' (15^{47}). Because of the near approach of the sabbath, there was no time for the customary embalming of the body. It was simply wrapped in a linen shroud and left in Joseph's tomb.

17. The Resurrection.—Nothing is more certain than that the disciples of Jesus believed that, after being crucified, dead, and buried, He rose again from the dead on the third day, and that at intervals thereafter and in different places He appeared to them and made Himself known to them. The proof that they believed this is the existence of the Christian Church. It is inconceivable that the scattered and disheartened remnant of Jesus' former following could have found a rallying-point and a gospel in the memory of one who had been put to death as a criminal, if they had not believed that God had owned Him and had accredited His mission in raising Him from the dead. There are many difficulties connected with the subject, and the narratives, which are disappointingly meagre, also contain certain irreconcilable discrepancies; but the historian who follows the most exacting rules imposed by his scientific discipline finds the testimony sufficient to assure the fact.

(1) *The earliest testimony to the faith in the Resurrection.*—Much the earliest account of why the Church believed that Jesus Christ had risen from the dead is Paul's reminder to the Corinthian Christians of the gospel he had preached when first he had visited that turbulent community at the Achaean crossroads (1 Co 15^{1-11}). This gospel, the apostle declared, was delivered to them 'as of first importance,' was what he himself had also 'received' [from the Church before him?], and was the burden of the gospel that the other apostles also preached. It was the good news that Christ, who had died for our sins in accordance with the scriptures and who had been buried, had been raised on the third day and had appeared to Cephas, to the twelve, to more than five hundred brethren at one time, to James, to all the apostles, and last of all, to Paul himself.

It is apparent from this basic testimony to the apostolic preaching that the early Christian faith in the Resurrection was grounded, not in any negative argument that a tomb was found empty, but on the positive proof of appearances of the Risen Christ. There is no indication in Paul's letters that the apostle had any familiarity with the doctrine of the empty tomb. Furthermore, even if he had known it, it is improbable that he would have accepted it, for it is clear from the argument in 1 Co 15 that he believed that the resurrection body was not the body of this flesh. In this chapter the apostle asserts (*a*) that Christ rose from the dead (vv.$^{3-11}$); (*b*) that Christ's resurrection is the assurance that those who belong to Him will also be raised from the dead at His second coming (vv.$^{12-34}$); and (*c*) that the resurrection body will not be the physical body that is laid in the grave, but a spiritual body that differs from it as the plant differs from the seed that is sown in the ground (vv.$^{35-50}$). (In 2 Co 5^{1-5} Paul describes this spiritual body as 'a building from God, a house not made with hands, eternal in the heavens.')

Paul's witness that Cephas was the first to become convinced of Christ's resurrection may account for the early designation of Simon as the 'rock' apostle (see above **11** (2)) and is supported by the very early tradition to which Luke refers in 24^{33-34}. It is also reasonable to assume from 1 Co 15^{8} that Paul regarded the appearance of the Risen Christ to himself as of the same sort and of the same validity as that to his predecessors in the faith. Since we know at least something of the nature of Paul's experience of the Risen Christ from references in his own letters to his conversion (Gal 1^{15-16}, 1 Co 9^{1} 15^{8}, 2 Co 4^{6}) as well as from the accounts of it in the book of Acts (9^{3-6} 22^{6-10} 26^{13-19})—to the extent that the latter may be accepted as historical source material—we may also assume that the apperception of the Risen Christ by early believers rested in the first instance on the authority of ecstatic and visionary evidence.

While there are those who dismiss the resurrection faith as the product of individual and mass hallucination, more serious students of the beginnings of Christianity cannot believe that the Church, the NT, and almost two millennia of Christian history can be accounted for on such an hypothesis. They are grateful for the insights that psychological reflection on the origins of the Christian faith affords, but they also agree that description of some of the conditions under which the faith arose falls far short of its explanation, and that any explanation in the end becomes an article of faith.

The Matthaean tradition is that the first resurrection appearances were vouchsafed to erstwhile disciples after they had returned to Galilee, and this also appears to be the implication of at least one verse in Mark's Gospel (16^{7}). There is support for the Galilaean locale of the resurrection appearances also in the appendix to the Gospel of John (21), and it may reasonably be assumed that Paul had Galilee in mind when he spoke of the appearances of the Risen Christ to 'more than five hundred brethren at one time' (1 Co 15^{6}). The Gospel of Luke, on the other hand, locates all the resurrection appearances of Christ in or about the city of Jerusalem and in this respect it is followed by the tradition in Jn 20.

(2) *The doctrine of the empty tomb.*—If it be granted that the doctrine of the empty tomb is a secondary

argument for faith in the Resurrection and was apologetic rather than historical in origin, it must also be admitted that it had virtually displaced the primary argument in the areas and at the times in which the Gospels were written. The simplest form of the doctrine is in Mk 16^{1-8}. (It is not improbable that the statement in Mk 16^{8} that the women said nothing to any one about their discovery of the empty tomb 'for they were afraid' is the Evangelist's attempt to account for the late appearance of the doctrine in the life of the Church.) In 27^{62}–28^{20} Matthew elaborated Mark's account in a variety of ways. In order to combat an argument that had arisen that Christians had perpetrated a gigantic fraud by stealing away the body of Jesus, the First Evangelist prefixed 27^{62-6} to the Markan story: the Jews had thrown a guard about the tomb in addition to the stone that had been rolled in front of its entrance. Mt 28^{2-4} is a characteristic Matthaean embroidery on Mark's story; the 'young man . . . dressed in a white robe' of Mk 16^{5} becomes an angel (28^{5}); the women report to the disciples at once (v.^{8b}); the Risen Christ appears to the women (vv.$^{9-10}$); the Sanhedrin circulates the story that the disciples had stolen the body of Jesus while the soldiers slept on duty (vv.$^{11-15}$); and a rather vague account of an appearance of the Risen Christ to the eleven in Galilee and His missionary commission to them brings Matthew's Gospel to a close (vv.$^{16-20}$). Mark's story appears also to be basic to Luke's account (24). In 24^{4} we are told that there were 'two men [in the tomb] . . . in dazzling apparel' when the women arrived; in 24^{6b-7} the tradition in Mk 16^{7} is corrected; in 24^{7} we are told that the women reported their experiences to the eleven; in 24^{13-35} the Third Evangelist incorporates the story of the revelation of the Risen Christ to a certain Cleopas and his unnamed companion as they broke bread at Emmaus with an apparent stranger; and the first volume of Luke–Acts ends with an account of an appearance of Christ to the eleven and others in a room in Jerusalem (24^{36-49}) and of His parting from them at Bethany (vv.$^{50-53}$). The Fourth Evangelist records His special tradition in ch. 20, and an appearance of the Risen Christ to disciples by the Sea of Tiberias is recounted (in what appears to be an appendix to the Gospel) in ch. 21.

18. The Character of Jesus' Message.—The Greek verb 'to preach' is related to the Greek noun for 'herald,' and the early Church thought of Jesus' message as a proclamation rather than as a body of teaching. Jesus sought to summon His hearers to decision rather than to persuade or convince them of abstract truth. He appealed to their will rather than to their intellect.

Jesus began His public ministry in an inconspicuous fashion. His advent as the herald of good news had no dramatic prelude or frontispiece. He attempted no prophetic pose; on the contrary, He avoided even its suggestion. He did not dwell in the wasteland; He lived among the people. He did not clothe Himself in bizarre attire; He dressed as did ordinary men. He did not subsist on locusts and wild honey; He ate and drank as did the folk of His time. (On one occasion ill-wishers even accused Him of being a glutton and a drunkard, Mt 11^{19}=Lk 7^{34}.)

During the initial period of His ministry, Jesus gathered His circle of disciples, preached the good news of God's sovereignty, and exercised His gracious gift of healing. In the course of time it was inevitable that men should begin to ask questions about Him and His mission. Some appear to have hinted that He was in league with Beelzebul and that He performed His mighty works in collusion with the prince of demons. The Gospels tell us that this ugly and dangerous insinuation came to the ears of members of Jesus' immediate family and that they tried to compel Him to desist from His public ministry (Mk 3^{21}; see above, **11** (4)).

While some attributed Jesus' mission and message to demon possession, more serious folk tried to classify Him according to a familiar pattern. One of the first to suggest itself was the category of prophet. The great expositors of the will of God among the Israelites in early centuries had been the prophets. With the passage of time, however, the order had virtually died out. For almost three hundred years before the coming of Jesus Christ, no one had appeared in Judaea who seemed to the people to rank with the great of the past. There were some who thought that John the Baptist, when he preached and baptized in the barren wasteland E. of the Jordan, was standing in the prophetic succession. John's work, however, was soon interrupted by his arrest and imprisonment. Nevertheless, his ministry had quickened the life of many who had heard him, and it was natural that Jesus, when He undertook His mission and declared His message, should have been closely linked with His great predecessor. When Jesus is reported to have asked His disciples, 'Who do men say that I am?' their reply was, '"John the Baptist"; and others, "Elijah"; and others, "One of the prophets"' (Mk 8^{28}||). Matthew is our authority for the statement that Jesus, when He entered Jerusalem on His last visit to the capital city, was greeted by the crowds with the exclamation: 'This is the prophet Jesus from Nazareth of Galilee' (Mt 21^{11}).

In retrospect it is evident that 'prophet' was not an entirely inadequate description of Jesus. A study of His message soon demonstrates that much of it was a reiteration of the great insights of Amos, Hosea, Isaiah, Jeremiah, and the Prophet of the Exile. The God whom Jesus proclaimed—the God of absolute righteousness, of infinite patience, and of tender mercy—was the God whom the prophets had known and of whom they had spoken to the people of their times. The goal of history for Jesus was the realization of God's will upon earth as it is already realized in heaven. Jesus called this underlying purpose of God's holy design 'the kingdom of God.' The phrase was new or almost new but the idea was an ancient one and had been the burden of Isaiah's message as well as of Amos' and Micah's. There were fresh elements in Jesus' gospel, to be sure, and new emphases. The fatherhood of God, the joys of fellowship with God, the radical demands of the new righteousness—all this takes on a new urgency in the Gospels. Nevertheless, the gospel had its anticipation in the Hebrew prophetic tradition, and Jesus' spiritual ancestry was the great succession of men of God who had spoken to their people from the days of Moses and Elijah to those of the authors of the books of Ruth and Jonah.

Although Jesus is seldom called a 'teacher' in the Gospels, many of His sayings call to mind the words of the great 'Wisdom' teachers of Israel. As a rule Jesus did not deliver long discourses. He spoke tersely, vividly, and concretely. His utterances were illuminated, illustrated, and made memorable by figurative and poetic imagery—parables, proverbs, hyperboles, similes, and metaphors of every description. Both in form and content, His most familiar teachings leave us with impressions not unlike those conveyed by the finest passages in the books of Proverbs, Ecclesiasticus, the Wisdom of Solomon, and the Testaments of the Twelve Patriarchs.

For several hundred years before the Christian era, apocalyptic ideas had enjoyed wide popularity among the Jews. Their distant origins have been traced to Babylonian and Iranian mythology, but in post-exilic times they were naturalized within Judaism and served to comfort and encourage those who had lost faith in a God who would accomplish His purposes through the processes of history. The present age, dominated by Satan and his hosts, was about to be superseded by the new age of God's rule; the signs of the end were already in evidence; and God's intervention would come with dramatic and catastrophic suddenness.

Although Jesus' message had much in common with that of His apocalyptic contemporaries, He did not share their deep pessimism about the present, their absorbing interest in the signs of the end, or their avid curiosity concerning the nature of the new heaven and the new earth. It is noteworthy, furthermore, that the one discourse in the Gospels that is modelled on the familiar apocalyptic pattern—Mark 13 and ||—gives every indication of being based on a Jewish prototype. The early Church was much more interested than Jesus had been in the spectacular paraphernalia of apocalypticism !

A word may be added in conclusion about Jesus' use of parables. From their employment in the OT and in Rabbinical literature, it is apparent that their purpose was to make truth clear and memorable. In light of this the extraordinary interpretation of the purpose of parables that is given in Mk 4^{10-12} || must be adjudged incredible. Furthermore, as distinguished from allegory, the parable had but one point. Since it is not a body of doctrine in code but an illustration of one transparent truth, the details have no significance other than to give vividness and verisimilitude to the story. Where allegory now seems to be inherent in a parable, as is frequently the case in the gospel tradition, we may suspect the influence on its present form of later Church interpretation.

19. The Content of Jesus' Gospel.—(1) *The Heavenly Father and His children.*—The God in whom Jesus believed and whose will He proclaimed is the God whom we know from His religious inheritance—the OT and the thought of ancient Judaism as it is reflected in the literature of the intertestamental period. As for the pre-exilic prophets, God for Jesus is a God of radical goodness. Our Lord argues from the goodness that is partial and incomplete in man to the perfect goodness that is manifest in God. 'If you then, who are evil, know how to give good gifts to your children, how much more will your Father who is in heaven give good things to those who ask him?' (Mt 7^{11}=Lk 11^{13}).

Because God is a God of uncompromising righteousness, He cannot tolerate iniquity. Speaking in vivid hyperbole, Jesus declared that it were better that a man should pluck out an offending eye or cut off an offending hand or foot than that 'the whole body be thrown into hell' (Mt 18^{8-9} ||). Employing a metaphor that was common in His day, He spoke of the two ways: 'Enter by the narrow gate; for the gate is wide and the way is easy, that leads to destruction, and those who enter it are many. For the gate is narrow and the way is hard, that leads to life, and those who find it are few' (Mt 7^{13-14}=Lk 13^{24}).

But the just and righteous God of Amos, Micah, and Isaiah is also, in Jesus' thought, the God of infinite love and tender mercy, the God whom He knew from the teaching of Hosea, Jeremiah, Second Isaiah, and the author of the little book of Jonah, as well as from many of the greatest psalmists of His people. God is like the shepherd who searches for a lost sheep until he finds it and then calls together his friends and neighbours to rejoice with him (Mt 18^{12-14}=Lk 15^{4-7}). God is like the housewife who has lost a silver coin, sweeps her house till she finds it, and then calls in her friends and neighbours to rejoice with her over its recovery (Lk 15^{8-10}). God is like the father who waits for the return of a prodigal son, goes out to meet and embrace him as he returns, and celebrates the restoration of the family circle with a feast and merrymaking (Lk 15^{11-32}).

The righteousness and the loving-kindness of God are summed up by Jesus in the name 'Father.' This title is frequently employed in the OT as a means of describing God's relationship to His people and occasionally in intertestamental literature as a way of suggesting His relationship also to the individual believer (Sir $23^{1, 4}$, Wis 2^{16}); but it is only in the Gospels that its use becomes characteristic and distinctive of religious vocabulary. And from Jesus' usage the name passed over into the thought and everyday language of the early Church. It was Jesus who first taught men how to pray to God as Father, to think of Him as their Heavenly Father, and to regard themselves as His children. 'Blessed are the pure in heart, for they shall see God,' He said. 'Blessed are the peacemakers, for they shall be called sons of God' (Mt 5^{8-9}). 'When you pray, say: "Father"' (Lk 11^2).

(2) *The rule of God.*—At the beginning of his Gospel, Mark summarizes the burden of our Lord's proclamation with the words: 'The time is fulfilled, and the kingdom of God is at hand; repent, and believe in the gospel' (1^{15}). The Semitic phrase that lies back of the Greek for 'kingdom of God' could better be rendered in English as 'the rule of God,' and the best commentary on what Jesus meant by it is the addition that Matthew makes (6^{10}) to the form of the Lord's Prayer as it stands in Lk 11^2: 'Thy kingdom come, *Thy will be done, On earth as it is in heaven.*'

The more numerous and important 'kingdom' passages in the Synoptic Gospels (cf Mk 1^{14-15} 9^1 14^{25}, Mt 5^{3-10} 6^{10}) picture the kingdom of God as an *eschaton*, as an age that is to replace the present one at some point in the future. They indicate that Jesus believed its consummation would be sudden, catastrophic, and dramatic (cf Mt 24^{40-41}, Lk 12^{35-40}). Over against these are others that make it equally clear that Jesus thought of the kingdom of God as already in being. John the Baptist marked the end of the old age. Since John's time the kingdom has been a fact of present experience, manifesting itself in particular in Jesus' own ministry (Mt $11^{11, 12-13}$ 12^{28}, Lk $10^{10-11, 23-24}$). It is already working itself out in history as a mysterious process not evident to the ordinary understanding (Mk $4^{26-29, 30-32}$, Mt 13^{33}=Lk 13^{20-21}).

Any true understanding of the kingdom of God in Jesus' thought and preaching must reckon with the fact that Jesus took over the categories of contemporary apocalyptic thought, but that He also introduced some radically new elements and emphases. When our Lord spoke of the kingdom of God, He meant by it what His hearers would inevitably understand Him to mean. He was not speaking in riddles or attempting to mystify those who listened to Him. The kingdom of God was the new age of God's rule which was shortly to supersede the present. In common with the thought of His day, Jesus looked for the coming of the kingdom 'with power' in the very near future, during the lifetime of those to whom He spoke. But, while the full and dramatic realization of the new age awaited the fulfilment of God's mysterious purposes, Jesus taught also that it had already begun. It was already breaking in upon the world. This was the 'new' that Jesus taught. The coming of the kingdom with power belonged to the future and would be effected in the future, but the kingdom was already among men. John the Baptist marked the dividing-point. Since John's day the kingdom of God had been a fact of present experience, evidenced particularly in Jesus' ministry. In Rudolf Otto's words: 'He does not bring the kingdom, but he himself, according to the most certain of his utterances, is in his actions the personal manifestation of the inbreaking divine power' (*The Kingdom of God and the Son of Man* [1938], p. 104). The kingdom had brought Jesus with it; He was the instrument of its *dynamis*. God had begun to reign as King upon earth as He is King in heaven. The full manifestation of His reign belonged to the future. Jesus believed, in common with His contemporaries, that it would be the very near future. But the significant fact that confronted men was that the reign of God had already begun; men were faced with the reality, not simply the hope. They were confronted with an immediate, not simply a future, crisis.

The other seeming paradox in our source material concerning Jesus' message of the kingdom must be resolved in similar fashion. The kingdom of God 'with power' will be realized suddenly and catastrophically. It will be manifested in its fullness according to the familiar apocalyptic scheme. But the rule of God is already in effect in our midst, if men will but recognize it and associate themselves with it. It is like a seed growing by itself which will, in due course, bear its abundant fruit. Men may, indeed must, associate themselves with it here and now. Here and now they are to identify their wills and purposes with the will and purpose of God. 'The kingdom of God is at hand,' but also 'the kingdom of God has come upon you.' The new age will have its apocalypse, but it has already begun, in germ at least. God has already projected Himself and His purposes into history.

(3) *The ethic of radical obedience.*—The ethic of Jesus, like that of the Law and the Prophets, is a religious ethic. God is the only frame of reference Jesus considers. We are to love our enemies, not because that will turn them into friends, but because God showers His favours on the unjust as well as on the just. We are to refrain from resistance to evil, not because that is a clever and successful strategy, but because God demands it. We are to forgive a brother 'seventy times seven,' not because forgiveness will have any necessary effect on his attitude, but because God forgives us our trespasses. We are to give to everyone who begs from us, not because Jesus has considered the social consequences of such action, but because God has given us the injunction. We are to be merciful if we expect to obtain mercy from God. We are to be pure in heart if we wish to see God. We are to be peacemakers if we hope to be called sons of God.

Jesus gives His ethic its most radical phrasing as 'the imitation of God.' There is no special merit in conventional morality. Even Gentiles salute their brethren. It is God who sets us the supreme example to imitate. Just as He recognizes no limits to His bestowal of all that is good, so He requires us to be all-including in our good will. Just as He is whole and undivided in all His relationships with men, so we must be upright and sincere. 'You, therefore, must be perfect, as your heavenly Father is perfect' (Mt 5^{48}).

The ethic of Jesus is therefore an ethic of radical obedience to God. While man has no claims on God, God claims the whole loyalty of man, without question or qualification. Radical devotion to God tolerates no vacillation; no half-measures; no divided allegiance. It means to serve God without ceasing; to serve Him with one's whole being; and to serve Him alone. The obedience that God demands is complete and absolute. It requires freedom from all selfishness, from all desire for revenge, from all sensuality and covetousness. It forbids the very attitude of anger as well as the angry deed and the scurrilous word. It prohibits the lustful passion of which the adulterous act is but one evil consequence. It requires absolute truthfulness rather than the mere avoidance of perjury. It forbids retaliation in any form for injustice. It demands a purge of all selfish calculation from the whole of one's life, complete detachment from earthly treasures and anxieties, and unreserved commitment of one's whole self to the kingdom of God and His righteousness. It requires an attitude of love that includes God, one's neighbour, and one's enemy.

At a later time Paul was to take an 'either-or' attitude toward the Law of Moses: either attempt (in vain!) to fulfil its articulation of the will of God, or be 'justified' entirely apart from the Law by that response to the grace of God that the apostle called 'faith.' Jesus, on the other hand, was able to distinguish between the demands of the Law that were conditional and evanescent and those that were unconditional and permanent. He reverenced the Law of Moses as 'the commandment of God,' but challenged the validity of the scribal tradition (Mk 7^{1-13}). He confirmed the authority of the moral law (Mk 12^{29-31}), but questioned the sanctions of ceremonial legislation (Mt 23^{23}, Mk 12^{11-12} 2^{27}). He emphasized motive and attitude rather than precept and prescription—a set of the will rather than conformity to a pattern (Mt 5^{21-30}). He even described some commandments in the Law as faulty. He appealed from Moses' permission of divorce to a doctrine of the inviolability of the marriage bond implicit in the story of Creation (Mk 10^{2-9}). He declared that the law of 'an eye for an eye and a tooth for a tooth' was superseded by a higher principle of non-resistance to evil (Mt 5^{38-42}). He held that His own admonition to 'love your enemies' was just as mandatory as the Levitical counsel to 'love your neighbour' (Mt 5^{43-44}). And He went far beyond the strictest injunctions in the Law against false witness by forbidding the use of oaths for any purpose whatever (Mt 5^{27}).

In its scope, its emphasis, and its urgency, the new righteousness of the kingdom as Jesus proclaimed it exceeded anything demanded by the scribes or exemplified by the Pharisees. Nevertheless, in His ethics as in His theology, our Lord was deeply indebted to His Jewish heritage. Nowhere is this more evident than in His stress on sincerity, fidelity, humility, and the readiness to forgive, the qualities that fit a man for the kingdom of God. (i) *Sincerity.*—Jesus often emphasized the great importance of sincerity. He attacked evidences of externalism, pedantry, ostentation, and hypocrisy among His religious contemporaries. Those who will see God are the pure in heart. Men are to be so utterly truthful that their word will be their bond: 'Let what you say be simply "Yes" or "No"; anything more than this comes from evil' (Mt 5^{27}; cf Ja 5^{12}). (ii) *Fidelity.*—Jesus ranked fidelity high among the personal virtues. Again and again we are told that faithfulness is a prerequisite for discipleship: the parable of the door-keeper on guard for his master's return (Mk 13^{34}); the parable of the watchful householder (Mt 24^{43}; cf Lk 12^{39}); the parable of the faithful and unfaithful servants (Lk 12^{41-48}; cf Mt 24^{45-51}); and the parable of the wise and the foolish maidens, five of them ready for the bridegroom, and five of them caught unprepared by his arrival (Mt 25^{1-13}). 'No one,' said Jesus on one occasion, 'who puts his hand to the plough and looks back is fit for the kingdom of God' (Lk 9^{62}). (iii) *Humility.*—Jesus frequently singled out the virtue of humility for special emphasis. He Himself, He said, was among His disciples as 'one who serves' (Lk 22^{27}). 'For even the Son of man came not to be ministered unto, but to minister, and to give his life a ransom for many' (Mk 10^{45} AV). When His disciples rebuked those who brought children to Him for His blessing, Jesus turned to them and said indignantly, 'Truly, I say to you, whoever does not receive the kingdom of God like a child shall not enter it' (Mk 10^{15}). When His disciples disputed among themselves as to who was the greatest, our Lord, according to Matthew's version of the incident, took a child and put him among them and said, 'Whoever humbles himself like this child, he is the greatest in the kingdom of heaven' (Mt 18^{4}). In Mark's more primitive account we are told that Jesus drove home the lesson of His acted parable with the words, 'If any man would be first, he must be last of all and servant of all' (Mk 9^{35}). This last must have been one of Jesus' most characteristic sayings, for the Gospels reproduce it on no less than five occasions (Mk 10^{43-44}, Lk 22^{26}, Mt 20^{26-27} 23^{11}). (iv) *The readiness to forgive.*—Jesus' teaching that a man should always be willing to forgive was also a virtue occasionally stressed and highly praised in the OT (Pr 25^{21-22}; cf Ro 12^{20}). Nevertheless, the emphasis on the forgiving spirit is distinctive of Jesus' message, as it was not of the teachings of the prophets, the psalmists, and the wise men. A man, Jesus said, cannot profit from participation in the Temple ritual if, through his own fault, he is on bad terms with any of his fellow men (Mt 5^{23-24}). A forgiving spirit toward his fellows on the part of a petitioner in prayer is a necessary condition of God's response to his plea (Mk 11^{25}; cf Mt 5^{14-15}). We are to expect God's forgiveness for our trespasses only to the extent that we ourselves are ready to forgive those who have done us ill (Mt 6^{12} || Lk 11^{4}). And there is to be no limit to our readiness to forgive (Lk 17^{3-4} || Mt 18^{21-22}).

(4) *The practice of piety.*—In Judaism almsgiving, prayer, and fasting had come to be recognized as typical expressions of piety. According to Matthew, Jesus did not question their importance, but He did insist that such righteous acts must be done without ostentation if they are to have any value in the sight of God. 'When you give alms, do not let your left hand know what your

right hand is doing, so that your alms may be in secret; and your Father who sees [that which is] in secret will reward you' (Mt 6^{3-4}). 'When you pray, go into your room and shut your door and pray to your Father who is in secret; and your Father who sees [that which is] in secret will reward you' (v.^{6}). 'When you fast, anoint your head and wash your face, that your fasting may not be seen by men but by your Father who is in secret; and your Father who sees [that which is] in secret will reward you' (vv.$^{17-18}$).

All the Evangelists have much to say about Jesus' preaching and practice of prayer, but it is Luke who laid most stress on this aspect of the gospel tradition. According to the Third Evangelist, Jesus engaged in prayer at every significant crisis in His ministry: at the time of His baptism (3^{21}); after healing a man afflicted with leprosy (5^{16}); before choosing the Twelve (6^{12}); before He asked His disciples the question, 'Who do the people say that I am?' (9^{18}); at the time of His transfiguration (9^{28-29}); before He taught His disciples what we call the Lord's Prayer (11^{1}); on the Mount of Olives at the time of the Agony (22^{41}); and as He died on the cross (24^{46}).

It is to Luke, moreover, that we owe the preservation of the three parables in the gospel tradition that deal with the proper practice of prayer. The parable of the Pharisee and the Tax Collector (18^{9-14}) teaches that prayer has value only as it is directed to God. There is no place in it for pride or pretension. The twin parables of the Friend at Midnight (11^{5-8}) and the Unjust Judge (18^{1-5}) teach the importance of persistence in prayer. If perseverance achieves its ends in everyday human relationships, how much more in our relationships with God! (At this point it might be well to remind the reader of what has been pointed out above **[18]**, viz. that a parable, as distinguished from an allegory, has only one point. In the parables under discussion, the only moral is the importance of persistence in prayer. God is not compared to a reluctant friend or to an unjust judge!)

While emphasizing the importance of persistence in prayer, Jesus also warned against verbose and elaborate patterns (Mt 6^{7}). Prayer is not a flight in rhetoric. God is not compelled to listen by the petitioner's verbosity. He is aware of our needs before we can formulate them.

Most of Jesus' explicit teachings about prayer have to do with petitionary prayer, and He uses an analogical argument to support His faith that God will hear and answer us. No human father would give his son a stone when he asks for a loaf, or a serpent when he asks for a fish. 'If you then, who are evil, know how to give good gifts to your children, how much more will your Father who is in heaven give good things to those who ask him?' (Mt 7^{11} || Lk 11^{13}).

In the Sermon on the Mount, Jesus assumes that every prayer will be answered. 'Ask, and it will be given you; seek, and you will find; knock, and it will be opened to you' (Mt 7^{7-8} || Lk 11^{9-10}). The only hint of a qualification is in the phrases, 'good gifts' and 'good things.' If one has come by reflection, or as the result of bitter experience, to the conclusion that faith in the power of petitionary prayer requires some reservation, he cannot find much support for such a reservation in the Sermon on the Mount. But he can do so if he turns to the Synoptic account of Jesus at prayer in Gethsemane. The petitioner must acquiesce in the overriding purposes of God. 'Not what I will, but what thou wilt.' True petitionary prayer seeks to discover God's will and to submit to it. It is an act of exploration and an act of commitment.

20. The Relevance of Jesus' Ethic.—In discussing the relevance of Jesus' ethic, a careful distinction must be drawn between the functions of 'historical' and of 'theological' exegesis. The task of the former is to determine the original meaning of a text to the rigid exclusion of the interpreter's personal, apologetic, or polemical interests. Its related discipline is the history of Biblical religion. The task of the latter, on the other hand, is to relate the original content of a Biblical passage, as careful historical exegesis has determined it, to the religious needs of our time in the light of the faith, the history, and the experience of the Church. Its related discipline is Biblical theology.

Both historical and theological exegesis are legitimate and complementary activities, but too frequently their separate functions are confused. Occasionally the historian regards everything but his own findings with suspicion. Biblical studies are held to be an exercise in archaeology. Occasionally the theologian reinterprets and recasts his source material so as to force it into the service of the theological or philosophical position he represents.

Did Jesus substitute principle for precept in ethical behaviour? Did He teach attitude rather than proclaim legislation? Did He stress 'ethos' rather than 'ethics,' a 'set of the will' rather than a 'new commandment'? Such claims have been confidently put forward by a generation of handbooks, comforting the reader with the thought that Jesus anticipated the conclusions of modern liberal theology.

It is true that there are general principles enunciated in the Sermon on the Mount. Two striking instances are Mt 5^{48}: 'You, therefore, must be perfect, as your heavenly Father is perfect,' and 7^{12}: 'Whatever you wish that men would do to you, do so to them.' There are similar inclusive principles also in the Pentateuch, notably the *Shema'*. But most of the Sermon is made up of individual and specific precepts. The antitheses in the fifth chapter are frequently cited as typical of Jesus' emphasis on principle rather than on precept. Jesus goes back of the act to the attitude. The real sin is not the actual murder of a man but the spirit of anger that prompts it. The real sin is not the act of adultery but the lustful desires that occasion it. This insight is a true one, but it stops short of recognizing that Jesus substitutes new commandments for what had been 'said to the men of old.' His teaching continues to move in the sphere of legislation. Anger and insulting language and lustful looks are prohibited. The new law is more rigorous and far-reaching than the old. Modern ethical idealists deny that you can legislate for attitudes and thoughts and desires, but this is a nice distinction that never occurred to Jesus.

Orthodoxy is often ready to admit that Jesus meant what He said, but it is even more insistent than liberalism in asserting that Jesus' ethics are impossible for any individual or order of civilization. They lay bare man's ethical bankruptcy and postulate the Cross as his only way of salvation. They demonstrate that man needs a mediator and a saviour. This is good Paulinism and good Reformation theology, but there is little evidence that it has anything to do with the gospel Jesus preached. The Christology of the Sermon on the Mount represents Jesus as legislator, wisdom teacher, prophet, and messianic emissary with Divine authority, but not as Mediator or Saviour. In this sense it is distinctly pre-Pauline, and only violent *eisegesis* can equate its message with that, say, of the first chapter of the Epistle to the Colossians.

Much of Jesus' ethical teaching may seem impossible to us, but that does not justify the conclusion that Jesus intended it to be regarded in that light. All its radicalisms can be paralleled in some part of Hebrew-Jewish literature. And, while Jesus assumes that most men will find it impossible to do His words, He postulates a minority that will enter in by the narrow gate and that can be compared to a wise man who built his house upon the rock.

If it is modernization of Jesus to make His teaching approximate Kantian ethics or to regard it as prolegomena to Pauline soteriology, how can true theological exegesis proceed? The perfectionists have certainly the most consistent position, and to criticize them as utopian and fanatical is to criticize Jesus also. If we cannot follow Tolstoy and like-minded Christians, we must be prepared to recognize that we take factors into

JESUS CHRIST

account that Jesus did not, and make qualifications and applications and combinations of His sayings that never occurred either to Him or to the Evangelists.

(1) In the first place, theological exegesis will emphasize the fact that much of Jesus' ethical teaching is purified 'wisdom,' distilled and transparent truth that is not dependent for its validation on any theology or eschatology. Even a religious humanism can find some points of contact with it. (2) In the second place, theological exegesis can legitimately employ the ethical teaching of Jesus in conjunction with other parts of Scripture, both in the OT and in the New. Revelation has a wider base than Mt 5–7. It speaks to us in the OT with respect to issues that Jesus in His particular setting never considered or had occasion to consider, and it enables us to see Jesus' teaching in the perspective of the Cross and the resurrection faith. (3) In the third place, theological exegesis can supplement the imperatives of Jesus' ethic with faith in the Divine help that is given through the gracious inworking of the Holy Spirit, and with confident trust in the mercy and the forgiveness of God. Christian faith knows that the God who requires perfection and who passes judgment on every imperfection, is also the God who is ever ready to renew that fellowship with Himself that is broken by our sin. Theological exegesis will point out that the God of the Sermon on the Mount is also the God of the parables of the lost sheep and the lost son. And it will make its own that petition that in several Greek manuscripts is substituted for the second petition of Luke's version of the Lord's Prayer: 'May Thy holy spirit come upon us and cleanse us!' (4) In the fourth place, theological exegesis will not try to maintain that dogmatical and philosophical positions require Gospel validation at every point before they call themselves 'Christian.' Orthodoxy may be justified in its emphasis on the redemptive significance of Christ's death, even if in the light of historical exegesis it cannot claim that this found any place in Jesus' own message. The ethical idealist may be justified in maintaining the primacy of principle and attitude in Christian ethics, even if he must honestly admit that this is a modern insight for which there is no more than a suggestion in Jesus' teaching.

At a time when historical studies are often pressed uncritically into the service of dogma, and when some theologians are anxious to undergird their understanding of the Christian faith with Scripture, even if this has to be done at the expense of scientific objectivity, it is important to bear in mind that theological exegesis, while an imperative function of Biblical scholarship, must build upon the foundation laid by careful historical studies and be subject at all times to their criticism and correction.

21. Jesus' Interpretation of His Mission.—The various categories of thought employed by the early Church in its attempt to interpret the meaning of Jesus' mission in the light of God's purpose for mankind are discussed in another article in this dictionary (see CHRISTOLOGY): Suffering Servant, Davidic Messiah, Son of man, Son of God, Lord, Heavenly High Priest, Divine Logos, and still others. Since our sources for a study of the life and teaching of Jesus belong to strata of tradition deriving from the very earliest to almost the latest periods in the times covered by the NT, they reflect almost every form of primitive Christology, from the apparent 'adoptianist' thinking of Peter's speech at Pentecost (Ac 2^{22-36}) to the quasi-philosophical points of view in the Epistle to the Hebrews and in the prologue to the Gospel of John. And in this respect the honest interpreter must admit that it is virtually impossible to penetrate at many points beyond the interpretation of the preachers of the gospel to the original self-consciousness of our Lord.

As long as Christianity remained primarily a sect of Judaism, it was inevitable that it should draw upon the messianic concept to account for the fact that believers had found in Him who had lived and suffered and died and risen again from the dead, the revelation of God's redemptive purposes in human history. The hope of a messiah had emerged after the death of David among those who looked back on the glorious days that had gone and who longed for their return under the leadership of some descendant of the great king, 'a shoot from the stump of Jesse' whom God would 'anoint' as the instrument of their restoration. Several of the Hebrew prophets, notably Isaiah, purged the popular hope of its more materialistic and nationalistic elements and restated it in terms of the religious, ethical, and spiritual qualities of leadership the messiah would manifest. In post-exilic times the idea of the coming age came increasingly to take on the form of a theocracy in which God Himself would reign as King, but there still were sporadic revivals of the earlier prophetic expectation—Zechariah chs. 9–14 from the early Maccabaean period, the Testament of Levi from shortly before 106 B.C., and the 17th and 18th Psalms of Solomon from about the middle of the 1st cent. B.C. (The pre-Christian Qumrân sect seems to have anticipated *two* messiahs, one priestly and one royal.)

There are many who hold that the doctrine that Jesus was the Messiah did not arise until after the Resurrection. Early in the present century Wilhelm Wrede pointed out that Mark, the earliest Evangelist, makes much of the idea of a 'messianic secret.' Jesus was recognized as Messiah during His lifetime by the demons whom He had driven out of 'possessed' men and women (1^{24-25} 3^{11-12} etc.) and ultimately by the circle of the Twelve (8^{27-30}), but all this had not become common knowledge because Jesus had enjoined the strictest secrecy on both 'evil spirits' and disciples. By reading a secret claim into the records, Mark sought to account for the fact that Jesus was known to have made no public messianic declaration (the confession before the high priest, Mk 14^{61-62} ||, is subject to serious critical objections) and yet was proclaimed by the Church of the Evangelist's day as the Christ.

More conservative critics, including the writer of this article, are hesitant to conclude that the belief of the early Church that Jesus was the Messiah arose wholly without warrant in His own words. The incident at Caesarea Philippi (Mk 8^{27-30} ||) and the story of the inscription over the cross (15^{26} ||) appear to belong to the bedrock of early Christian tradition, and it is difficult to understand why Jesus was put to death by the Roman procurator if He had not been charged with revolutionary intent as a messianic claimant, and how such a charge could have been substantiated without some basis in His own words and deeds. (The Gospel accounts of the entry into Jerusalem and of the cleansing of the Temple certainly have messianic overtones, although these need not have been inherent in the incidents themselves.)

Nevertheless, the fact must be stressed that, if Jesus employed the messianic idea to interpret His understanding of the rôle He knew Himself called of God to fulfil, He must have revised the popular notion of what was involved in the Messiah's mission. One of the characteristic and distinctive ideas that Jesus emphasized was that true greatness consists in selfless service. 'And Jesus called them to him and said to them, "You know that those who are supposed to rule over the Gentiles lord it over them, and their great men exercise authority over them. But it shall not be so among you; but whoever would be great among you must be your servant, and whoever would be first among you must be slave of all"' (Mk 10^{42-44} ||; cf Mk 9^{35}, Mt 23^{11}, Lk 9^{48}). 'For which is the greater, one who sits at table, or one who serves? Is it not the one who sits at table? But I am among you as one who serves' (Lk 22^{27}). 'For the Son of man also came not to be served but to serve' (Mk 10^{45} || Mt 20^{28}). 'For every one who exalts himself will be humbled, and he who humbles himself will be exalted' (Lk 14^{11} || Mt 23^{12}; cf Lk 18^{14}).

It is clear that the Church at an early date saw the life and passion of Jesus Christ illuminated by the 'Servant of the Lord' poems in Second Isaiah. Paul appears to have been referring to the prophecy in Isaiah ch. 53

when he reminded his Corinthian readers that the gospel he had preached to them at the first and that he himself had 'received' was that 'Christ died for our sins in accordance with the scriptures' (1 Co 15^{1-3}). In Ac 8^{26-35} we are told that the evangelist Philip, when he had encountered the Ethiopian eunuch on the road from Jerusalem to Gaza, preached Christ to him from a text in Is 53^{7-8}. When Luke elaborated the story of Jesus' rejection at Nazareth to serve as a dramatic frontispiece to his account in Luke–Acts of the rise and expansion of Christianity (4^{16-30}), he made Jesus comment on the purpose of His mission from a text in Is 61^{1-2}.

Whether Jesus Himself had anticipated this association cannot any longer be determined. The only direct quotation from Isaiah ch. 53 that is attributed in the Gospels to Jesus is a passage in Luke 22^{37}, and the likelihood that this quotation goes back to our Lord is remote. Nevertheless, there is an echo of the Isaianic chapter in Mk 10^{45}: 'For the Son of man also came not to be served but to serve, and *to give his life as a ransom for many*,' and the possibility that Jesus had reflected on the OT passages about the Servant of the Lord as He sought to understand the mission He Himself had undertaken, while it cannot be demonstrated, ought not by the same token to be ruled out of consideration.

Jesus knew Himself summoned to proclaim the new age of God's rule, and He believed that, in some measure, the kingdom of God was being effected in and through His ministry. Perhaps that is all we know. 'What person knows a man's thoughts,' St. Paul once asked his Corinthian converts, 'except the spirit of man which is in him?' When the man in question is He whom God has highly exalted and on whom He has bestowed the name that is above every name, it is absurd to think that we can plumb the depth in Him of the riches and wisdom and knowledge of God. And perhaps Jesus as the herald and the vehicle of the kingdom is all that we need to know, for the response of the Christian to Jesus Christ is not a historical judgment about Him but an act of faith and awe. Together with all who are in heaven and on earth and under the earth, we bow the knee and confess the inscrutable mystery 'that Jesus Christ is Lord, to the glory of God the Father.'

22. A brief bibliography.—M. Black, *The Scrolls and Christian Origins* (1961). G. Bornkamm, *Jesus of Nazareth* (1960). B. H. Branscomb, *Jesus and the Law of Moses* (1930); *The Teachings of Jesus* (1956). R. Bultmann, *Jesus and the Word* (1934); *Primitive Christianity* (1956); *Theology of the NT* (1955). M. Dibelius, *Jesus* (1949); *The Sermon on the Mount* (1940). C. H. Dodd, *The Parables of the Kingdom* (1961). G. S. Duncan, *Jesus, Son of Man* (1947). M. Enslin, *The Prophet from Nazareth* (1961). S. M. Gilmour, *The Gospel Jesus Preached* (1957). M. Goguel, *The Life of Jesus* (1933). M. Goldstein, *Jesus in the Jewish Tradition* (1950). F. C. Grant, *The Gospel of the Kingdom* (1940); *An Introduction to NT Thought* (1950); *Ancient Judaism and the NT* (1959). C. Guignebert, *Jesus* (1935). M. R. James, *The Apocryphal NT* (1924). J. Jeremias, *The Parables of Jesus* (1955). S. E. Johnson, *Jesus in His Homeland* (1957). J. Knox, *Christ the Lord* (1945); *The Death of Christ* (1958); *The Man Christ Jesus* (1942). J. Klausner, *Jesus of Nazareth* (1925); *The Messianic Idea in Israel* (1955). C. H. Kraeling, *John the Baptist* (1951). W. G. Kümmel, *Promise and Fulfilment* (1957). K. Lake, *The Resurrection of Jesus Christ* (n.d.). T. W. Manson, *The Sayings of Jesus* (1949); *The Teaching of Jesus* (1935). L. H. Marshall, *The Challenge of NT Ethics* (1947). S. V. McCasland, *The Resurrection of Jesus* (1932). R. Otto, *The Kingdom of God and the Son of Man* (1943). A. M. Ramsey, *The Resurrection of Christ* (1950). A. Richardson, *The Miracle Stories in the Gospels* (1941). A. Schweitzer, *The Mystery of the Kingdom of God* (1925); *The Quest of the Historical Jesus* (1926). E. F. Scott, *The Ethical Teaching of Jesus* (1924); *The Kingdom and the Messiah* (1911). K. Stendahl (ed.), *The Scrolls and the NT* (1957). V. Taylor, *The Life and Ministry of Jesus* (1955). A. N. Wilder, *Eschatology and Ethics in the Teaching of Jesus* (1950). H. Windisch, *The Meaning of the Sermon on the Mount* (1951). W. P. P.—**S. M. G.**

JETHER.—1. Father-in-law of Moses, Ex 4^{18} (AVm, RVm, following Hebrew), an error for **Jethro** (q.v.). **2.** Eldest son of Gideon, Jg 8^{20}. **3.** An Ishmaelite, father of Amasa, 1 K $2^{5, 32}$, 1 Ch 2^{17}; called **Ithra** (q.v.) in 2 S 17^{25}. **4, 5.** Two men of Judah, 1 Ch 2^{32} 4^{17}. **6.** A man of Asher, 1 Ch 7^{38}; called in v.^{37} **Ithran,** the name of an Edomite clan (Gn 36^{26}).

JETHETH.—An Edomite clan, Gn 36^{40}, 1 Ch 1^{51}.

JETHLAH, Jos 19^{42} (AV).—See ITHLAH.

JETHRO (once, Ex 4^{18} [MT, followed by AVm, RVm] **Jether**).—An Arab sheikh and priest of the Sinaitic Peninsula, the father-in-law of Moses; referred to by this name in Ex 3^{1} 4^{18} and 18^{1ff} (E), as **Reuel** in the present text of Ex 2^{18} (J), and as **Hobab** in Nu 10^{29} (also J). He welcomed Moses and received him into his family (Ex 2^{21}), and many years later visited him at Sinai (Ex 18^{1ff}), heard with wonder and delight of the doings of Yahweh on behalf of Israel (v.^{9ff}), and gave advice about administration (vv.$^{17-26}$). Later still he probably acted as guide to the Israelites (Nu 10^{29ff}; cf the AV of Jg 1^{16} and 4^{11}). As to the two or three names, it may be noted that Arabic inscriptions (Minaean) repeatedly give a priest two names. The name *Jethro* may mean 'pre-eminence.' See HOBAB. W. T. S.

JETUR.—A son of Ishmael, Gn 25^{15}, 1 Ch 1^{31} 5^{19}. See ITURAEA (which is perhaps derived from Jetur).

JEUEL.—1. A Judahite, 1 Ch 9^{6}. **2.** A Levitical family name, 2 Ch 29^{13} (AV **Jeiel**). **3.** A contemporary of Ezra, Ezr 8^{13} (AV **Jeiel**).

JEUSH.—1. A son of Esau by Oholibamah; also the eponym of a Horite clan, Gn $36^{5, 14, 18}$, 1 Ch 1^{35}. **2.** A Benjamite chief, 7^{10}. **3.** A descendant of Saul, 8^{39} (AV **Jehush**). **4.** The name of a Levitical family, 23^{10f}. **5.** A son of Rehoboam, 2 Ch 11^{19}.

JEUZ.—The eponym of a Benjamite family, 1 Ch 8^{10}.

JEW.—The name by which the descendants of Israel have been known for many centuries. It is corrupted from *Judah*. After the division of the kingdom in 937 B.C., the southern portion was called by the name of the powerful tribe of Judah, which composed most of its inhabitants. It was in this kingdom that the Deuteronomic reform occurred, which was the first step in the creation of an organized religion sharply differentiated from the other religions of the world. This religion, developed during the Exile, bore the name of the kingdom of Judah. All Israelites who maintained their identity were its adherents, hence the name 'Jew' has absorbed the name 'Israel.' For history, see ISRAEL (I. **21–27**), DISPERSION; for religion, see ISRAEL (II. **5, 6**). G. A. B.

JEWELRY.—Gn 24^{53} 'the servant brought forth jewelry (AV, RV 'jewels') of silver and of gold.' They were not jewels set in silver and in gold. Ornaments made of gold or silver were in older English called jewels. Now the word is confined to precious stones.

JEWELS AND PRECIOUS STONES.—Most of the precious stones in the Bible occur in three lists which may be tabulated at the outset. These are: (A) the stones in the high priest's breastplate (Ex 28^{17-20} 39^{10-13}); (B) those in the 'covering' of the king of Tyre (Ezk 28^{13}); (C) those in the foundation of the New Jerusalem (Rev 21^{19-20}). The three lists are to some extent mutually connected: A contains twelve stones, B has nine, all taken from A, with traces of A's order in their arrangement; in the LXX the two lists are identical, and possibly the Hebrew text of B is corrupt; and C also has twelve stones and is evidently partly dependent on the LXX of A and B.

Reference to these tables will simplify the use of the following notes, which include other precious stones of the Bible besides those mentioned above. In endeavouring to identify the stones in List A, three things have to be kept in view. From the dimensions of the breastplate —a span (8 or 9 inches) each way (Ex 28^{16})—the twelve stones which composed it must, even after allowing

 JEWELS AND PRECIOUS STONES

space for their settings, have been of considerable size, and therefore of only moderate rarity. Further, as they were engraved with the names of the tribes, they can have been of only moderate hardness. Lastly, preference should be given to the stones which archaeology shows to have been actually used for ornamental work in early Biblical times (see Flinders Petrie in Hastings' *DB* iv, 619–621) and Quiring in *Sudhoff's Archiv*, xxxviii, 193–213; cf Lucas' *Ancient Egyptian Materials and Industries*^{2}, 335–354, and Thompson's *Dictionary of Assyrian Chemistry and Geology*, 123–193).

A. The High Priest's Breastplate (Ex 28$^{17-20}$ 39$^{10-13}$, P)

Hebrew Name	Translation in (i) LXX (ii) Vulgate	Translation in (i) AV (ii) RV (with margins)	Identification here proposed
1. *'ōdhem*	(i) *sardion* (ii) *sardius*	sardius (ruby)	brown sard
2. *piṭ^{e}dhāh*	(i) *topazion* (ii) *topazius*	topaz	greenish-yellow chrysolite
3. *bāreḳeth*	(i) *smaragdos* (ii) *smaragdus*	(i) carbuncle (ii) carbuncle (emerald)	green feldspar amazonite
4. *nōphekh*	(i) *anthrax* (ii) *carbunculus*	(i) emerald (ii) emerald (carbuncle)	purple garnet, almandine
5. *sappîr*	(i) *sappheiros* (ii) *sapphirus*	sapphire	lapis lazuli
6. *yah^{a}lōm*	*iaspis*	(i) diamond (ii) diamond, sardonyx	nephrite, jade
7. *leshem*	(i) *ligurion* (ii) *ligurius*	(i) ligure (ii) jacinth (amber)	blue feldspar or turquoise
8. *sh^{e}bhô*	*achates*	agate	agate, onyx
9. *'aḥlāmāh*	(i) *amethustos* (ii) *amethystus*	amethyst	red or brown jasper
10. *tarshîsh*	(i) *chrusolithos* (ii) *chrysolithus*	(i) beryl (ii) beryl (chalcedony)	Spanish topaz
11. *shōham*	(i) *bērullion* (ii) *onychinus*	(i) onyx (ii) onyx (beryl)	red carnelian
12. *yāsh^{e}phēh*	(i) *onuchion* (ii) *beryllus*	jasper	green jasper

(RSV agrees with RV, but without margins)

B. The covering of the King of Tyre (Ezk 28^{13})

The Hebrew text has only nine of the twelve stones in the high priest's breastplate, which the Versions translate similarly except where a different translation is here given in brackets: they are in the Hebrew (which differs from the Greek and Latin) order: 1. *'ōdhem*, 2. *piṭ^{e}dhāh*, 3. *yah^{a}lōm* (LXX *smaragdos*), 4. *tarshîsh*, 5. *shōham* (LXX *sappheiros*), 6. *yāsh^{e}phēh* (LXX *iaspis*), 7. *sappîr* (LXX *ligurion*), 8. *nōphekh* (LXX *achates*), 9. *bāreḳath* (LXX *amethustos*). In the LXX 10. *chrusolithos*, 11. *bērullion*, 12. *onuchion* are added. Clearly the Hebrew text has fallen into disorder and the three missing stones must once have found a place in it.

Too much weight must not be attached to the ancient translations of technical terms, which are often very loosely used in popular speech; and all such words tend to change their meanings with the passing of the centuries. That many of the words, too, must have been foreign loan-words will have increased the confusion in the use of them. The Hebrews had no scientific sense and probably attached only a very vague meaning to the names of most precious stones, in which they were probably influenced as much by colour and hardness as by any other qualities. Lastly, the Greek and Latin translations, where they are not purely conjectural, are probably as much traditional as scientific and can be accepted only if they can be otherwise confirmed.

Adamant (Ezk 3^{9}, Zec 7^{12}): see **Diamond.**

Agate (A 8). The Assyrian (*aban)šubû*, corresponding to the Hebrew *sh^{e}bhô*, designates the base of all the vitriols (white, yellow, green, blue, red), and the corresponding stone in the foundation of the New Jerusalem, being beryl (C 11), suggests a green stone also in the high priest's breast-plate. Both LXX and Vulgate have 'agate,' of which one variety known as moss-agate has a green or greenish hue; and ancient agate (cf Pliny *NH* xxxvii. 54 [139–142]) probably included such opaque varieties. The modern agate is a form of silica occurring in nodules which, when cut across, show concentric bands of varying transparency and colour. The parallelism of colour, however, can hardly be pressed; and onyx, which differs from agate only in the width of the bands of colour and was regarded by the ancients as a form of agate, may be meant (Quiring).

C. The Foundations of the New Jerusalem (Rev 21^{19f})

Greek Word	Vulgate Translation	Translation in (i) AV (ii) RV (with margins)	Identification here proposed
1. *iaspis*	*iaspis*	jasper	jasper
2. *sappheiros*	*sapphirus*	(i) sapphire (ii) sapphire (lapis lazuli)	lapis lazuli
3. *chalkēdon*	*carcedonius*	chalcedony	green dioptase
4. *smaragdos*	*zmaragdus*	emerald	emerald or beryl or green feldspar, amazonite
5. *sardonux*	*sardonix*	sardonyx	sardonyx
6. *sardion*	*sardinus*	sardius	sard, carnelian
7. *chrusolithos*	*crysolithus*	(i) chrysolyte (ii) chrysolite	(Spanish) topaz
8. *bērullos*	*beryllus*	beryl	beryl or aquamarine
9. *topazion*	*topazius*	topaz	greenish-yellow chrysolite
10. *chrusoprasos*	*crysoprassus*	(i) chrysoprasus (ii) chrysoprase	golden-tinted green chalcedony
11. *huakinthos*	*iacinthus*	(i) jacinth (ii) jacinth (sapphire)	turquoise or dark amethyst
12. *amethustos*	*amethystus*	amethyst	amethyst

(RSV agrees with RV, but without margins, save for 3. agate, 5. onyx, 6. carnelian.)

Amethyst (A 9, C 12).—The LXX and Vulgate's 'amethyst' has caused the Hebrew *'aḥlāmāh* to be identified with that stone, though without philological support. The Hebrew word is probably identical with the Egyptian *ḥmn.t* designating a precious stone of a red colour obtained from Nubia and much used for scarabs and amulets, possibly red or brown jasper, of which a yellowish-brown variety is said to be found on the banks of the Nile in Egypt.

Beryl (A 10, B 4, C 8; also Ca 5^{14}, Ezk 1^{16} 10^{9} Dn 10^{4}).—The Hebrew *tarshîsh* is commonly rendered 'beryl' (AV, RV) or 'chrysolite' (RVm). The Targum's 'beryl' (Ex 28^{20} 39^{13}) cannot stand if the name means the 'stone of Tarshish' and Tarshish is Tartessus in Spain, since the beryl is not found there. The other versions have 'carbuncle' (LXX), 'chrysolite' (LXX, Quinta and Sexta, Aquila, Vulgate) and 'jacinth'

(Symmachus, Vulgate); of these Spain produces only 'chrysolith' (Pliny, *NH* xxxvii. 43 [127]), which may be accepted as the meaning of the Hebrew word (Quiring). The ancient 'chrysolith' or 'chrysolite' was 'Spanish' or 'false topaz,' a yellow rock-crystal or citrine quartz, not the modern chrysolite or topaz which comes from Brazil. The corresponding stone (C 10) is 'chrysoprase,' a golden-tinted variety of the leek-green chalcedony, which tends to support this identification.

The Assyrian (*aban*)*burallu* (a name uncertainly connected with the Sanskrit *vaidūrya-*, *vaidūrya-* 'cat's eye' or 'beryl' = Pahlavi *veluriya-* 'lapis lazuli' = Prakrit *veluria-* or usually *verulia-* 'jewel') was probably beryl, and the cylinder-seals of a bluish beryl are known (Thompson). The Greek *bērullos*, *bērullion* included ordinary beryl, deep green emerald and pale-bluish aquamarine, as well as other varieties known as 'precious beryls'; its colour might be sea-blue or sea-green, brown or rarely pink, golden, yellow, or whitish (Pliny, *NH* xxxvii. 20 [76]). Whether it is the same stone as that 'called *belus*, found at Arbela; this is about the size of a walnut and looks like glass' (Democritus *ap.* Pliny, *NH* xxxvii. 55 (149); Thompson) cannot be said. Egypt, the hills to the NW. of Assyria, and India, were the ancient sources of beryl.

Carbuncle (A 3, B 9).—The Assyrian (*aban*)*barraqtu* and *barraqtu* = Hebrew *bāreḳeth*, *bār^{e}ḳath* 'sparkler' is a foreign word perhaps connected with the late Sanskrit *marakata* = Prakrit *maragda* = Greek (*s*)*maragdos* but assimilated to the native *birḳu*, *bārāḳ* 'lightning' (which Symmachus' *keraunios* 'jasper' reflects). The classical *smaragdus* denoted a green stone, including emerald and beryl (which hardly differ except in hardness and depth of green colour) and also jasper, pseudo-smaragdus or malachite and prase. Since however emerald has a low refractive power and when cut little brilliancy or fire, it is unlikely to have been called 'sparkler'; and the rainbow cannot have been compared to such a stone (Rev 4[3]) but only to some more or less colourless rock-crystal producing all the prismatic colours (Flinders Petrie). Further, Nero's eye-glass was a *smaragdus* (Pliny, *NH* xxxvii. 16 [64]), which could not have been an emerald. The 'shining *smaragdos*,' too, of which a *stele* is said to have been made (Herodotus, *Hist.* ii. 44 [2]); cf Theophrastus, *de lapid.* iv. 25), cannot have been a true emerald, since this is not found in columnar form, although large impure splinters are known; and true emerald is equally unsuitable for buildings (To 13[16], Rev 21[19]), for which also its rarity and costliness is prohibitive. Finally, all the supposed emeralds and beryls of pre-Ptolemaic age from Egypt have been proved to be green feldspar (amazonite), also called 'mother of emerald' (although it has no connexion with emerald), or olivine (Lucas); some form, then, of feldspar (green, pink, gray, or white) seems to suit all the passages here cited.

Clearly *bērullos* and *smaragdos* were not always distinguished or identified by the ancients; both must therefore be translated according to the context.

The Hebrew *'eḳdāḥ*, of which the gates of the restored Zion would be made (Is 54[12]), is also translated 'carbuncle' (AV, RV, RSV). The versions vary, having 'crystal' (LXX, Peshitta) and 'carbuncle' (Targum); the corresponding Arabic *qadâḥatu* means 'fire-stone,' *i.e.* stone from which fire is obtained by striking it. What is apparently meant is the precious garnet which may be colourless, yellow, green, brown, or black, but of which the typical variety has a deep red colour without any trace of violet in it and is called pyrope; in sunlight, and also in artificial light when it takes on a yellowish hue, it resembles a glowing coal (Theophrastus, *de lapid*, iii. 18–19 and Pliny, *NH* xxxvii. 25· [94]; cf Hebrew *ḳādaḥ* 'was kindled' and *ḳaddaḥath* 'jaundice'). Assyrian beads and rings of garnet are known, while rough garnets were apparently used by the Assyrians for thresholds and pavements (Thompson); translucent reddish brown and deep red garnets from Aswan and western Sinai were made into beads by the Egyptians (Lucas); and the Greeks had them in rings (Theophrastus).

Chalcedony (C 3).—The modern stone of this name is semi-opaque or milky silica, but the ancient one was probably the green 'dioptase' (silicate of copper). This at least seems to have been the *smaragdos* found in the copper-mines of Chalcedon (Pliny *NH* xxxvii. 18 [72–73]). There was some confusion, however, between the 'stone of Chalcedon' and the *carchedonia* (stone of Carthage), which was fiery red (Pliny, *ib.* xxxvii. 25 [92, 95–98] and 30 [104]); so *carchedon* occurs as a various reading for *chalcedon* in Rev 21[19].

Chrysolite (C 7).—In modern mineralogy this is the 'peridot' or 'peridote' (see **Topaz** below); but the ancient gem was some other golden-coloured stone, possibly yellow corundum or yellow quartz or topaz (Flinders Petrie) or Spanish topaz (Quiring).

Chrysoprase (RV, RSV; AV 'chrysoprasus') (C 10).—The *prasius* of Pliny (*NH* xxxvii. 34 [113–114]) was a leek-green 'chalcedony' (cf Gr. *prason* 'leek') of which there was a golden-tinted variety. The latter may be the chrysoprase of the NT. The modern chrysoprase is a slightly translucent silica, coloured a beautiful apple-green by oxide of nickel.

Coral (Job 28[18], Ezk 27[16]).—The Hebrew *râmôth* is vocalized as though meaning 'high things,' as several translators interpreted it (Theodotion, Symmachus, Vulgate); but it ought to be read *r^{e}'āmôth* as shown by Ugaritic *r'emt*, which designates a jewel worn by the goddess 'Anat (Baal V. iii. 19). If it is rightly taken as 'coral' (cf Arab. *ra'ama* 'twisted'), it must be black coral (Gesenius), which comes from the Indian Ocean and is more valuable than red coral; for there is another word for red coral (see **Ruby** below). Both *râmôth* and *r'emt*, however, have been taken as the same as the Arabic *ra'matu* 'sea-shell,' which has suggested that it may originally have had this sense and, as including the 'oyster,' may have been extended to mean also 'pearls' (Hölscher), which are obtained from the Persian Gulf and Ceylon; but pearls do not seem to have been used before the Ptolemaic period (Lucas) or to be mentioned by Greek and Roman writers before the 1st cent. A.D. (Liddell and Scott). Mother of pearl, too, which perhaps cannot be entirely ruled out (unless this was *dar*), was used in Egypt from pre-dynastic times (Lucas).

Crystal (Job 28[17]).—The Hebrew *z^{e}khôkhîth* 'clear stuff' is translated 'transparent rock-crystal' (colourless transparent quartz) by a Greek scholiast and 'glass' by Theodotion and in the other Greek versions; probably a vitreous paste (Koehler) or 'glass,' which was highly prized in antiquity, is meant. Babylonian prescriptions for making glass (Assyrian *aban zukāki* 'stone of clear stuff' and *zukû*, Neo-Babylonian *zakittu* 'clear stuff, glass') have been found and deciphered (Thompson).

The Hebrew *'elgābhîsh* is another word for 'crystal,' being almost certainly identical with the Egyptian *irqbś* 'rock-crystal'; it occurs only metaphorically in the phrase translated 'great hail-stones' (Ezk 13[11, 13] 38[22]; AV, RV, RSV), which therefore means literally 'stones of (*i.e.* hard as) crystal.' The ancient translators had lost the meaning of the word, rendering the phrase by 'sling-stones' (LXX), 'very great' or 'immense stones' (Vulgate) or 'stones of hardness' (Peshitta). Whether the Assyrian (*aban*)*algamišu* 'corundum, emery; amethyst' is connected with the Egyptian and Hebrew words is uncertain; all appear to be of non-Semitic origin.

The Hebrew *gābhîsh* 'gypsum' (Job 28[18]), which all the ancient translators misunderstood and for which the English translators have 'pearls' (AV) and 'crystal' (RV), seems to be a shortened form of the same word, with which the Arabic *jibsu* 'crystal' and *jibsînu* 'gypsum' are evidently connected.

Diamond (A 6, B 3; also Ezk 28[13]).—The Hebrew *yah^{a}lōm*, of which the true meaning is quite uncertain, is rendered in the ancient versions *iaspis* and *smaragdos* (LXX) or *iaspis* (Vulgate) and translated in the English Bible 'diamond' (Luther; AV, RV, RSV) or 'sardonyx'

JEWELS AND PRECIOUS STONES

RVm); it has also been identified as 'onyx' (Flinders Petrie) or 'moonstone' (Quiring). The diamond is out of the question; it first appears as an eye in a Greek work of art *c* 480 B.C. and is not known to have been cut before Roman times (Pliny, *NH* xxxvii. 15 [59–60]), being too hard for ancient tools. The word seems to be derived from the root of the Ugaritic *hlm*=Hebrew *hālam* 'hammered,' which suggests nephrite (true jade) or jadeite. These, though of a totally different mineral composition, cannot certainly be distinguished except chemically or through the microscope; both have a green clouded colour and when polished acquire a brilliant lustre. Jadeite was used for hammers and axes also for vases, while nephrite served for axe-heads and signet-rings (Lucas); and the Ugaritic verb was used of crushing the skull with a mace (Baal III* A 11–26).

The Hebrew *shāmîr* is also translated 'diamond' (cf Arabic *sâmûr, šammûr* 'diamond,' which the divergent *s* and *š* prove to be loan-words); it is mentioned as material for the point of a graving pen (Jer 17¹) and as a symbol of hardness of heart (Ezk 3⁹, Zec 7¹²). It cannot be diamond, for the reason given above, but is almost certainly 'corundum' or 'emery,' a very hard mineral substance (aluminium oxide), as the Assyrian (*aban*) AŠ. MUR and perhaps also the Egyptian *yšmr, šmr* (if this is the same word or denotes the same substance)= Greek *smiris, smuris* 'emery' shows. The Greek translators' *adamantinos* (Jer 17¹) means 'steely,' since *adamas* 'steel' in the sense of 'diamond' is late (Theophrastus, *d. lapid*, iii. 19). The Hebrew *shāmîr* means also some kind of thorn-bush, possibly because of the hard sharp point of the thorn.

Emerald (A 4, B 8; also Sir 32⁶).—The Hebrew *nōphekh* cannot mean 'emerald,' which is a green stone, since *nōphekh* 'of purple' is mentioned as a valuable article of trade (Ezk 27¹⁶; cf Targum *ad locum*); the colour therefore rules out any comparison also with the Egyptian *mfkȝ.t, mfkȝ.t* 'green turquoise.' The LXX's *anthrax* 'carbuncle, garnet' and Vulgate's *carbunculus* must give approximately the right sense; it will then be the beautiful violet-coloured or amethystine garnet called 'almandine.' So the best garnets in Roman eyes were those described as *carbunculi vero amethystizontes* (Pliny, *NH* xxxvii. 25 [93]).

Jacinth (C 11; also Rev 9¹⁷).—The breastplates of the visionary horsemen are compared to 'jacinth' (AV) or 'hyacinth' (RV; RSV 'sapphire'); but what stone is meant is not certain. It has been identified with aquamarine (Liddell and Scott), a bluish-green variety of beryl which, as compared with pure green beryl or emerald, has little value but which is a gem popular for its beauty (see **Ligure** below), and with dark amethyst (Pliny, *NH* xxxvii. 41 [125–126]), and also with purple corundum (Lewis and Short). The Assyrian (*aban*)*uqnû* as well as the Greek *kuanos* are perhaps the same word; the former is certainly lapis lazuli and probably also turquoise (which ranges from a sky-blue to a blue or bluish-green or green colour), ultramarine and azurite (Thompson), while the latter is lapis lazuli, dark-blue enamel and blue copper carbonate (Liddell and Scott), both thus supporting a blue or purplish-blue rather than a green stone. The modern 'jacinth' is quite different, being a rock which includes the yellow, orange-coloured, red and brown, zircons; these are found in parts of Europe, the Ural mountains, and Ceylon.

Jasper (A 12, B 6, C 3; also Ezk 28¹³).—The Assyrian (*i*)*ašpû, ašpû*, and the Hebrew *yāshᵉphēh* have long been equated. The Babylonians had red or rose-coloured jasper, as shown by extant seals; but the usual jasper of antiquity was green and often transparent, while the Persian jasper was sky-blue (Pliny, *NH* xxxvii. 37 [115]). It was the first hard stone worked by the Babylonians, who called it the 'stone of royalty,' using it for amulets and seals, for the decoration of gates and for tablets in foundations (cf Rev 21¹⁹). Further, the jasper of the NT was 'clear as crystal' and 'like unto clear glass' (Rev 21¹¹); the Biblical jasper, then, was the translucent green kind, which excludes jade or nephrite (Hess *ap.* Koehler; see **Diamond** above).

The Hebrew *kadhkōdh* 'agate' (AV, RSV) or 'ruby' (RV), of which the battlements of the restored Zion would be made (Is 54¹²), was a red stone (cf Arabic *kadkadatu* 'bright redness'). Three of the versions take it to be 'jasper' (LXX, Vulgate, Peshitta), one thinks of 'carchedon' (Symmachus), the 'stone of Carthage' which too was red (Pliny, *NH* xxxvii. 25 [92–98] and 30 [104]), and Sa'adya suggests the same stone. Certainly then a red stone, and most probably red jasper, which the Assyrians too used in building work, is meant.

Ligure (A 7).—The Hebrew *leshem* is translated *ligurius* (LXX, Vulgate), an obscure term supposed to be the same word as *lyngcurion*, a yellow stone popularly thought to be the congealed urine of a lynx (Pliny, *NH* xxxvii. 13 [52]), possibly the modern 'jacinth' (RV, RSV) or 'amber' (RVm; cf Pliny, *NH* xxxvii. 11 [33–34]); the former is yellow 'jargoon' (silicate of zircon), the latter is so called because it was obtained from Liguria. Another suggestion is yellow agate (Flinders Petrie). Most probably, however, the Hebrew word ought to be equated with the Egyptian *nšm.t* 'opal' (Hommel) or 'white-blue feldspar' (Müller) or bluish feldspar (Harris) or 'greenish blue turquoise' (Quiring).

The Hebrew *ḥashmal* (Ezk 1⁴·²⁷ 8²) is another word translated 'amber' (AV and RV, which has 'electrum' in the margin; RSV 'bronze'); but it almost certainly means 'brass' (see BRASS).

Onyx (A 11, B 5; also Gn 2¹², Ex 25⁷ 28⁹ 35⁹·²⁷ 39⁶, 1 Ch 29², Job 28¹⁶).—The Hebrew *shōham* is variously rendered in the ancient versions *sardius* (LXX), *onyx* (LXX, Aquila, Symmachus, Theodotion, Vulgate) or *sardonyx* (Vulgate), 'green stone' (LXX) or 'beryl' (LXX, Targum) or 'emerald' (LXX). The idea of a green stone is based on an absurd derivation from *shûm* 'garlic, leek' and has no independent value. The *sardius* was a transparent red stone (cf Peshitta at La 4⁷), which *shōham* seems to have been, if its Hebrew name and the Assyrian (*aban*)*sântu, sându* (< *sâmtu*) 'red stone' (Assyrian *sâmu* 'red') may be identified (in spite of the equation of *sh* with *s*; cf Assyrian *siba*= Hebrew *shebhaʿ* 'seven'). This was red carnelian, which was used for ornaments and seals from the bronze age onwards; its principal sources in antiquity are named as the *māt Meluḫḫa* and the 'land of Havilah' (Gn 2¹²), which have been hesitatingly identified, and in modern times Arabia and India.

Ruby (Job 28¹⁸, Pr 3¹⁵ 8¹¹ 20¹⁵ 31¹⁰, La 4⁷).—The Hebrew *pᵉnînîm* is translated 'rubies' (AV, RV) with the alternative 'coral' or 'red coral' or 'pearls' (RVm). RSV has 'pearls' in Job, 'jewels' or 'costly stones' in Proverbs, and 'corals' in Lamentations. Pearls are impossible, although once supported by an ancient version (Targum at Job 28¹⁸), because they do not seem to have been used at so early a date and because something red is required (La 4⁷); and ruby is not only not supported by philology but has also hardly ever been recovered in excavations. The Arabic *fananu* 'branch' shows that the Hebrew *pᵉnînîm* 'branches' must describe something branched, and this can only be coral, for the most part presumably red coral. Coral is the calcareous 'skeleton' which certain actinozoa secrete; in the living state the branching calcareous framework is covered by the coenosarc or common tissue of the organism, from which the individual polyps protrudes; in the coral of commerce the living tissue has disappeared, and only the solid 'skeleton' remains. Red coral (*corallium rubrum*) is found in the Mediterranean Sea, though now in diminishing quantities, and in the Indian Ocean.

Sardius (A 1, B 1, C 6; also Ezk 28¹³, Rev 4³).—No passage throws any light on the nature of the Hebrew *'ōdhem* (cf Ugaritic [*ủ*]*dm*), which, however, must denote a red stone (cf *'ādhōm* 'red,' describing blood, a nomad's skin, a horse or cow, grape-juice and earth); and accordingly it is translated in the ancient versions of the OT *sardius* (LXX, Vulgate, Peshitta) or 'ruby' (Saʿadya) or simply 'red stone' (Peshitta, Targum). The *sardius* was a reddish stone (cf Peshitta at La 4^7, where a man's ruddy skin is compared to a *sardôn*-stone), not red jasper (Flinders Petrie) but rather the transparent brown sard or sardine stone (Liddell and Scott), which probably is the stone meant in both OT and NT (Quiring).

Sapphire (A 6, C 5; also Ezk 1^{26}, La 4^7, Job 28^{16}).—The Hebrew *sappîr*, which is translated 'sapphire' in most versions (LXX, Vulgate, Peshitta, Targum Pseudo-Jonathan), is a blue stone, since the sky beneath God's throne is compared to a pavement of it (Ex 24^{10}); but it cannot be the precious stone called sapphire, which could not be found in blocks large enough for a foundation or pavement (Is 54^{11}) and had no 'dust of gold' in it (Job 28^6). It can only be *lapis lazuli* or 'Russian *lapis*,' a silicate of calcium, aluminium, and sodium, bright blue in colour but speckled with yellow iron pyrites, *i.e.* sulphide of iron (Theophrastus, *d. lapid.* iv. 23, and Pliny, *NH* xxxvii. 38 [119]). The Targum thinks of pieces of it large enough for the Tables of the Law (Pseudo-Jonathan at Ex 31^{18}, Dt 4^{13}), and a dedicatory stele of this substance has been found (Brit. Mus. 91013), and it was used, ground into paste, in mural decorations by the Babylonians (Koldewey, *Das wiedererstehende Babylon* [1925], 156, 166); and it was one of the most valued of ornamental gems in the 4th–2nd millennium B.C. The largest known piece is a carved globe of the world in the church of *il Gesù* at Rome. The name appears to be derived from the Sanskrit *śanipriya* 'slowly moving Saturn; sapphire,' whence it has passed into many languages as Assyrian *(aban)sipru*, *ṣipru*, and Aramaic *sampîrînâ*, *sampîrînôn*; cf Georgian *saperi* 'sky-blue'); the incorrect equation of *ṣ* with *s* is due to its being a foreign loan-word.

Topaz (A 12, B 2; also Job 28^{19}).—The Hebrew *piṭᵉdhah* is translated *topazius* in the earliest ancient versions (LXX, Vulgate); this is not the modern 'topaz' (silicate of aluminium, in which some of the oxygen is replaced by fluorine), usually honey-yellow but also sometimes pink or red (Epiphanius, *de xii lapidibus* 2) or grey or green in colour, but the 'peridot' or 'peridote' (transparent yellowish-green silicate of magnesium), which is the gem-form of olivine. Other ancient translators suggest a pink (Peshitta) or yellow-green (Targum) stone, while Saʿadya has 'emerald.' The Hebrew term seems to be an Indian loan-word meaning 'yellow' (cf Sanskrit *pīta-* 'yellow,' which is combined with *aśman-* 'stone' to yield *pītâsman-* 'topaz'); what is meant is maybe the saffron-yellow Indian topaz (Quiring) or perhaps the greenish-yellow transparent chrysolith or chrysolite, from which topaz is distinguished as a distinct stone (C 7, 9); this was obtained from the *Jazîrat Zabarjad* (Pliny's *Topazius insula*, now St. John's Island) in the Red Sea (Koehler), which was treated by ancient writers as a soft form of true topaz (Bolman). Hence it is inexactly described as coming from Cush (Job 28^{19}), the southern valley of the Nile.

If the stones above mentioned are classified according to their composition, it will appear that, in spite of the bewildering variety of names, the principal groups are comparatively few.

The largest number of stones come under *silica*, the crystallized form of which is distinguished as quartz; a second group is formed by the silicates (*silica* in combination with metallic oxides); and a third group consists of aluminium oxide (*alumina*).

The palace at Shushan is said to have been paved with four different stones (Est 1^6). The first (*bahaṭ*) has been identified with the Egyptian *ibhty*, *bht* an unknown stone from Nubia (from which the Arabic *bahtu* 'eagle-stone' may be a loan-word); the LXX translate it 'emerald-coloured stone,' possibly malachite or serpentine, while the Targum has 'crystal.' The second (*shēsh*) is almost certainly 'marble' which all the versions have (cf Syriac *šîšâ* 'marble; glass'). The third (*dar*) may be 'pearls,' which the Assyrians used to make a 'bed' in which they put foundation documents (Andrae, *Das wiedererstandene Assur* [1938], 144, 147, 150), or possibly 'mother-of-pearl' (LXX, followed by RSV in Est 1^6; cf Arabic *durru* 'pearls'), which was used with incrustations of marble to decorate the walls of churches (Van der Meer and Mohrmann, *Atlas of the Early Christian World*, 97), or perhaps 'shell-limestone, shell-marble,' a dark-brown stone with orange-coloured shells in it, found in Astrakhan (Harper). The fourth (*sōḥereth*), which the quite uncertain Assyrian *(aban)siḫru* has been invoked to explain (Meissner), may be red marble (cf Pahlavi *suḫr* 'red' and Persian *surḫ* 'red, purple') or perhaps **porphyry** (cf Pliny, *NH* xxxvi. 11 [57], where red porphyrites is mentioned).

Lastly, while the modern **alabaster** is calcium sulphate (gypsum), the ancient or Oriental alabaster like the Hebrew *shayish* was calcium carbonate; but Egyptian alabaster was geologically calcite (sometimes wrongly called aragonite), which is of the same composition but of different crystalline form and specific gravity. This was largely used for vases, being thought to be specially adapted for preserving unguents (Pliny, *NH* xiii. 3 [19]; cf Mt 26^7, Mk 14^3, Lk 7^{37}, where 'alabaster' means a 'box of alabaster'). J. Pk.—**G. R. D.**

JEWRY.—This old form occurs frequently in the older versions, but rarely in AV. In Dn 5^{13} it stands for *Judah*; in Lk 23^5, Jn 7^1 and occasionally in the Apocrypha, *e.g.* 1 Es 1^{32} 4^{49}, Bel ^{33}, 2 Mac 10^{24}, for *Judaea*.

JEZANIAH, a shortened form of **JAAZANIAH.**—A Maacathite military commander, contemporary with Gedaliah (Jer 40^8=**Jaazaniah** 2 K 25^{23}); called **Azariah** in Jer 42^1 (so RSV, with LXX; AV and RV 'Jezaniah') 43^2. Cf AZARIAH, **27.**

JEZEBEL (meaning uncertain; perhaps 'unexalted,' 'unhusbanded').—Daughter of Ethbaal, king of the Sidonians and previously priest of Astarte; wife of Ahab, king of Israel, of the dynasty of Omri (1 K 16^{31}). Jezebel's evil influence in the land of Israel, especially in combating the religion of Yahweh in the interests of Baal-worship, was exercised not only during the twenty-two years of Ahab's reign, but also during the thirteen years of the rule of her two sons, Ahaziah and Joram; moreover, this influence extended, though in a less degree, to the Southern Kingdom of Judah, where Athaliah, the daughter of Jezebel, seems to have followed in the footsteps of her mother (2 K 8^{18}). In her ruthlessness of character, her lust for power, her unshrinking and resolute activity, her remorseless brushing aside of anything and everything that interfered with the carrying out of her designs, she was the veritable prototype of Catherine de Medici.

In the OT the figure of Jezebel is presented in connexion with some dramatic episodes which are probably recorded as illustrations, rather than as exceptionally flagrant examples, of her normal mode of procedure. These are: the account of the trial of strength between the prophets of Baal and Elijah (1 K 18^{19}–19^3), the narrative about Naboth and his vineyard (1 K 21$^{1-16}$), and, as illustrating her obstinate, unbending character to the very end—note especially her words to Jehu in 2 K 9^{31}—the story of her death (2 K 9$^{30-37}$).

In Rev 2^{20} the name of Jezebel is applied to a woman of Thyatira, who called herself a prophetess, and tempted men to wickedness. In this connexion the name probably is symbolic and was given because of a resemblance between her and the wife of Ahab. W. O. E. O.—**H. S. G.**

JEZELUS.—1. 1 Es 8^{32} (AV, RV); see JAHAZIEL, **5. 2.** 1 Es 8^{35} (AV, RV); see JEHIEL, 7.

JEZER.—The head of the **Jezerites,** Nu 26^{49}, 1 Ch 7^{13}.

JEZIAH, Ezr 10^{25} (AV).—See IZZIAH.

JEZIEL.—A Benjamite, 1 Ch 12^3.

JEZLIAH, 1 Ch 8^{18} (AV).—See IZLIAH.

JEZOAR, 1 Ch 4^7 (AV).—See ZOHAR, 3.

JEZRAHIAH.—The leader of the singers at the dedication of the walls of Jerusalem, Neh 12^{42}. The same name is rendered **Izrahiah** in 1 Ch 7^{3bis}.

JEZREEL.—The name (' God sows ') refers to fertile land and is applied to two localities.

1. The Plain of Jezreel (whence the Greek **Esdraelon**) is so called from the town of Jezreel, which stood at the foot of the NW. spur of the Gilboa ridge, near the scene of Gideon's exploit against the Midianites and Saul's encampment ' by the fountain of Jezreel,' possibly *'Ain Jālûd*, before the disaster of Gilboa (1 S 29^1). In the district of Issachar (Jos 19^{18}), it is named as part of the land which remained loyal to the House of Saul after his death (2 S 2^9). Under Solomon it was in the administrative district of Baana (1 K 4^{12}). Commanding access from Bethshan to the main part of the Plain of Esdraelon it was occupied by Ahab, no doubt as a base of operations against Aram about Ramoth-gilead. It may also have served as a winter resort for the king (1 K 18^{45} 21^1), for whose amenity the vineyard of Naboth was confiscated (1 K 21). Jezreel may have been the home of the family of Omri, the father of Ahab. Here Joram, the son of Ahab, was slain by Jehu, with Jezebel and all the house of Ahab, on his withdrawal from Ramoth-gilead (2 K 8^{29} 9, 10). Jezreel thereafter sank into insignificance. The place survives in the Arab village of *Zer'în*, an unimportant hamlet. No trace of its former significance remains, but potsherds indicate occupation in the Late Bronze Age (*c* 1500–1200 B.C.), the Iron Age, and the Roman period.

2. Another Jezreel, of which nothing is known, was in Judah, probably E. or SE. of Hebron (Jos 15^{56}), and was the home of Abinoam, one of David's wives (1 S 25^{43}). **3.** A Judahite, or perhaps a family of Judah (1 Ch 4^3). **4.** Jezreel was the name given symbolically to one of his children by Hosea (1^4), who condemned the bloody opportunism of the House of Jehu, who had effected his *coup d'état* at Jezreel. **5.** EV Jezreel in Hos 2^{22} should possibly be translated literally ' God sows,' and treated as an exclamation.

R. A. S. M.—**J. Gr.**

JEZRIELUS, 1 Es 9^{27} (RV).—See JEHIEL, **9.**

JIBSAM, 1 Ch 7^2 (AV).—See IBSAM.

JIDLAPH.—A son of Nahor, Gn 22^{22}.

JIMNA, Nu 26^{44} (AV).—See IMNAH.

JIPHTAH, Jos 15^{43} (AV).—See IPHTAH.

JIPHTAH-EL, Jos $19^{14, 27}$ (AV).—See IPHTAH-EL.

JOAB (' Yahweh is Father ').—**1.** One of the sons of Zeruiah—the eldest according to 2 S 2^{18}, the second according to 1 Ch 2^{16}—and thus the nephew of David. It is perhaps not too much to say that, humanly speaking, the Davidic dynasty would not have been established had it not been for the military genius and the loyalty of Joab. So consistently loyal was Joab to the royal house (see ADONIJAH), that one is tempted to question whether the passage 1 K 2^{5f}, which describes David's ingratitude, is genuine; Joab, however, though loyal, was a rugged conservative and individualist who could never forgive a past enmity, as witness the fate of Abner and Amasa. He could never have acquiesced in Solomon's kingship after siding with Adonijah; he was no cosmopolite, his virtues as well as his vices were those of the blood-feuding Bedouin.

Above all, Joab was a *skilled general*; this is seen by the number of victories he gained, namely, over the army of Ishbosheth under the leadership of Abner (2 S 2^{12-32}); over the Jebusites (1 Ch 11^{6-9}); over the Syrians and Ammonites (2 S 10^{1-19} 11^1 12^{26-29}); over Absalom (18^{5-17}); over Sheba (20^{4-22}). These are specifically mentioned, but there must have been very many more, for those which are spoken of generally as David's victories were in all probability due to Joab, who is repeatedly spoken of as David's commander-in-chief (*e.g.* 2 S 8^{16} 20^{22} etc.).

Secondly, *his loyalty to the house of David* is illustrated by his whole life of devoted service, and especially by such conspicuous instances as his desire to make his victory over the Ammonites appear to have been gained by David (2 S 12^{26ff}); his slaying of Abner [though other motives, *e.g.* the blood-feud, undoubtedly played a part in this act, it is certain that Joab regarded Abner as a real danger to the State (3^{24f})]; the reconciliation which he brought about between David and Absalom (14^{1ff}); his slaying of Absalom when he realized his treachery to David (18^{14ff} 19^6); and lastly, his words to David in 2 S 19^{5-7}. How close was the tie between David and Joab may be seen, further, in the blind obedience of the latter, who was willing to be partaker in David's sin (2 S 11^{6-26}).

The darker side of Joab's character is to be seen in *his vindictiveness and ruthless cruelty*; for although it is only fair to plead the spirit of the age, the exigencies of the State's weal, and the demand of blood-revenge, yet the treacherous and blood-thirsty acts of which Joab was guilty constitute a dark blot upon his character (see 2 S 3^{22-27}, 1 K 11^{16}; cf 2 S 18^{14} 20^{9f}).

2. Son of Seraiah (1 Ch 4^{14}; cf Neh 11^{35}). **3.** A family which returned with Zerubbabel (Ezr 2^6=Neh 7^{11}=1 Es 5^{11}; cf Ezr 8^9=1 Es 8^{35}).

W. O. E. O.—**D. R. Ap-T.**

JOACHAZ, 1 Es 1^{34} (AV, RV).—See JEHOAHAZ, **2.**

JOACHIM.—**1.** Bar 1^3 (AV); see JEHOIAKIM, **1.** **2.** Bar 1^7 (AV); see JEHOIAKIM, **2.**

JOACIM.—**1.** 1 Es 1^{37-42} (AV); see JEHOIAKIM, **1.** **2.** 1 Es 1^{43} (AV); see JEHOIACHIN. **3.** Jth $4^{6, 14}$ (AV); see JOAKIM, **4.** **4.** 1 Es 5^5 (AV); see JOAKIM, **5.** **5.** Sus $^{1, 4, 63}$ (AV); see JOAKIM, **6.**

JOADANUS, 1 Es 9^{19} (AV, RV).—See JODAN.

JOAH.—**1.** Son of Asaph, and ' recorder ' at Hezekiah's court, 2 K $18^{18, 26, 37}$, Is $36^{3, 11, 22}$. **2.** A Levitical family name, 1 Ch 6^{21}, 2 Ch 29^{12}; apparently called **Ethan** in 1 Ch 6^{42}. **3.** A Levite, 1 Ch 26^4. **4.** Son of Joahaz, and ' recorder ' at Josiah's court, 2 Ch 34^8.

JOAHAZ.—**1.** Father of Joah the ' recorder,' 2 Ch 34^8. **2.** See JEHOAHAZ, **1.** **3.** See JEHOAHAZ, **2.**

JOAKIM.—**1.** 1 Es 1^{37-42}, Bar 1^3 (RV); see JEHOIAKIM, **1.** **2.** 1 Es 1^{43} (RV); see JEHOIACHIN. **3.** Bar 1^7 (RV); see JEHOIAKIM, **2.** **4.** A high priest in the days of Holofernes and Judith, Jth $4^{6, 14}$ (AV **Joacim**). **5.** A son of Zerubbabel, 1 Es 5^5 (AV **Joacim**). **6.** The husband of Susanna, Sus $^{1, 4, 63}$ (AV **Joacim**).

JOANAN, 1 Es 9^1 (AV).—See JEHOHANAN, **3.**

JOANNA.—The wife of Chuza, the steward of Herod Antipas, one of certain ' women who had been healed of evil spirits and infirmities.' She ministered to Jesus out of her means, and after the crucifixion helped to anoint His body (Lk 8^3 24^{10}).

JOANNES.—**1.** 1 Es 8^{38} (RV); see JOHANAN, **7.** **2.** 1 Es 9^{29} (RV); see JEHOHANAN, **4.**

JOARIB.—The head of the priestly family from which the Maccabees were descended (1 Mac 2^1 14^{29}). According to 1 Ch 24^7 this family, there called that of **Jehoiarib**, was the first of the twenty-four courses of priests.

JOASH.—**1.** See JEHOASH. **2.** The father of Gideon (Jg 6^{11} etc.). **3.** A son of Ahab (1 K 22^{26}). **4.** A son of Shelah (1 Ch 4^{22}). **5.** A Benjamite (1 Ch 12^3). **6.** A son of Becher (1 Ch 7^8). **7.** A servant of David (1 Ch 27^{28}).

JOAZABDUS, 1 Es 9^{48} (AV).—See JOZABAD, **8.**

JOB, Gn 46^{13} (AV).—See JASHUB, **1.**

JOB, the centre of interest in the book bearing his name, is referred to also in Ezk 14^{12-20} where he appears as a conspicuous example of righteousness; in Sir 49^9 (Hebrew text); in To 2^{12} (in Vulgate); and in Ja 5^{11}, the last two passages alluding to his patience. Nothing is known of him beyond these sources. Another Job is mentioned in Gn 46^{13} (AV), but since the Hebrew spelling is quite different RV, RSV give more correctly **Iob.** The account in the Book of Job builds up a quasi-patriarchal environment, apparently implying that he was a figure of the remote past; it makes him a sort of rich sheikh living where the fertile lands of Palestine-Syria stretch out toward the desert. More definitely he is located in the land of Uz (1^1), and among 'the people of the east' (1^3) (better, the tribesmen of Kedem) seeming to indicate an area east of the Lebanons. Whether he was an Israelite is not made clear, though it is incredible that a Gentile would be represented as arguing such exalted conceptions of God. The name is known from the 14th cent. B.C. to its somewhat wide occurrence in Moslem lands in recent times. But obviously none of these individuals bears any relation to the Biblical Job. The Hebrew form of the name (*'iyyôbh*) resembles the verb 'to be an enemy'; but one must be very cautious of drawing any conclusion from this; the name is probably foreign and very old. On the other hand, the literature of the ancient East provides us with several references to, or accounts of, a righteous sufferer. In these and in other famous writings we have, it is clear, the background of our Book of Job; he is the Hebraic 'righteous sufferer.' Clearly the author found inspiration here for his immortal tragedy in the way familiar to us from the work of Shakespeare, for example.

The book divides on the basis of its contents into five distinct sections; 1. The Prologue, chs. 1–2, that tells of Job's ideal circumstances then of the succession of disasters which befell him, as a result of the argument in Heaven between Y″ and the Satan; he stripped him of property and children as well as his wife's sympathy; he afflicted him with a distressing disease; his three friends came to console him but were overcome with sadness for his condition. 2. The Dialogue, chs. 3–31, in which Job and the friends each in turn speak about Job's condition and religious attitude; this continues into a third cycle of speeches which, however, is for some reason incomplete, but the section is rounded out with a long speech, ostensibly Job's (29–31), and a poem about the source of wisdom (28). 3. The Speeches of Elihu, chs. 32–37, introducing a hitherto unmentioned character who says he is impelled to rebuke Job, which supposedly goes on through four successive speeches. 4. The Speeches of Y″ with brief rejoinders by Job, 38^1–42^6, which, in a superb survey of the wonders of nature, inanimate and animate, apparently reduce Job to a sense of his rashness and insignificance. 5. The Epilogue, 42^{7-17}, sketching Job's restoration and the happy sequel.

Whether these sections were all written by one author has for long been a matter of inquiry and disagreement among students of the book. Certainly the action, if we may call it such, moves on in ostensible continuity; the book is a unit, whether or not of united authorship. However, most scholars are agreed that the Elihu Speeches and ch. 28 were not in the original work. Some hold the same view of the Epilogue; there is more diversity of opinion as to the Speeches of Y″, some holding that the book originally concluded with the first speech (chs. 38–39). Actually doubts are expressed by a few as to the originality of the Prologue, indispensible as it may seem for the dramatic action.

Be this as it may, no one can dispute that the heart of the book is the Dialogue. In the interchanges between Job and the friends the author presented what he had to say about his theme; although it is logically possible to contend that this view, whatever it was, found some sort of amplification or qualification in the Speeches of Y″ and the Epilogue. Indeed it is *a priori* plausible, since these finish the book, and so presumably give its conclusion. But close study reveals subtle and cogent lines of thought, leading the Dialogue onward toward a notable culmination, which, however, are lacking from the subsequent sections, and indeed are in conflict with them.

Who the author or authors of any or all these sections may have been we have no means of knowing apart from what the book itself provides; and there the author, great artist that he was, has effectively concealed himself. The locale of the story out on the margin of the desert, apparently away from, or at most on the fringe of, the land of Israel, along with the very unusual Hebrew of the book and its considerable number of strange, possibly foreign, words have engendered theories that it is not really Hebraic at all, but Edomite (Eliphaz, the foremost of the friends, was from Teman in Edom), or even Arabic. Rebuttal of such views necessarily depends on evidence as inconclusive as theirs; but it is cogent to claim that in all the ancient East no one except a Hebrew could possibly have composed a work of such elevation. Yet his date is likewise indefinite, and guesses have been advanced from the Mosaic age to Persian times. The book contains no certain historic allusions; however, Job's curse on his day of birth (3^{3-10}) is so similar to one of Jeremiah's 'confessions' (Jer 20^{14-17}) as to indicate some relationship; we can afford to dismiss possible explanations other than that Jeremiah's words are original. Affinities between Job and Second Isaiah have also been pointed out, but here the direction of influence is more difficult to decide. Otherwise we are dependent, in ascribing a date, upon what we may deduce from the content and quality of the thought in the book, always a precarious venture though not devoid of worth. The book's exalted concepts of God and of human duty can have arisen only when Judaism had attained the stature by which it was to be known through the centuries. Vague as the result is, we shall probably not be far wrong if we assign a date a little after 400 B.C.

It will surprise no one possessing even a slight knowledge of the transmission of the OT to learn that with an uncertain origin such as this, the Book has many passages where the Hebrew text is quite doubtful and apparently corrupted beyond recovery, numerous others where the original poem has almost certainly been expanded by someone other than the author. It has also a high proportion of rare, perhaps foreign, words, and its full quota of passages that reveal the difficulty of interpretation which sometimes attaches to profound literature—and all this in addition to the tantalizing, fragmentary termination of the Dialogue just at the point where one comes to believe he can almost lay his hand on a great concept which the author was in process of delineating.

The theme of the book, it is usual to assert, is the suffering of the righteous: in a world created and ruled by a God of goodness and justice, why do ethical and religious character and conduct bear such a slight correspondence with what commonly passes for well-being? The wicked 'have more than heart can wish,' while the righteous endure all sorts of disadvantages.

This interpretation is not to be ignored, for certainly the problem finds emphatic expression (*e.g.* chs. 18, 20–22). Nonetheless, closer study shows this to be only a subsidiary theme; the real intent of the Dialogue goes much deeper. We shall make a fruitful approach to the book only when we realize that it deals with human suffering as a whole: not why do the righteous suffer, but why is suffering an inescapable part of our human estate? Pain, loss, bereavement, frustration, sorrow, injustice, and eventually, for every one of us, death—that is what it is to be human! But why, if God is good, or, in more modern terms, if the universe is rational? The book thus takes its place in the great succession of tragic literature which from the time of the author of the Egyptian Song of the Harper, at latest, down to the best writing of our own days, has engaged the thought and art of the most profound minds. Side by side with the works of Aeschylus, Euripides, and Sophocles, the Book of Job must come into consideration in the total of the tragic literature of the ancient world. Whether or not it was influenced by the remarkable brilliance of the brief period of Greek tragedy has not been adequately investigated (cf Kallen: *The Book of Job as a Greek Tragedy*, 1918) although the time suggested above for its composition leaves this entirely possible. If such influence was actual, it merely discloses further the independence and stature of the Hebrew poet; for certainly his work, while more penetrating (as it is hoped will presently appear) than the best Greek tragic thought, yet in form and structure is very different. It seems to observe the three classic unities of form, it is true, but this is incidental and perhaps accidental; but there is little if any action, that is, *drama* in the etymological sense; and in every aspect, the poem goes strictly its own way. It is the Hebraic tragedy, of which, alas, we have no other example; probably none ever existed.

It is relevant to the question of the original unity of our book, that some scholars ascribe a different theme to the Prologue; they claim it deals with the question of disinterested piety. That may be so; certainly if we are to hold that it is concerned with the high problem apparent in the Dialogue, its answer is negligible. It would in that case merely fall back on the shallow solution provided by polytheisms, of denying that God is responsible for human woe. But it would then be necessary to point out that the writer had made out a poor case, for it was by Y″'s permission that the Satan was able to afflict Job. Similarly slight is the answer provided by the Epilogue; it seems to say that if the sufferer will only endure patiently, all will come out right in the end, a claim that is patently false to the facts of life. The Speeches of Y″, it is usual to assert, teach that God's justice is beyond the grasp of the human mind, and we must have faith where we cannot understand. Valuable as such insight is for the religious life, it remains very doubtful that the chapters really say anything of the sort. On the contrary the panorama of physical wonders presented, frequently with magnificent literary power, as the works of God, with their almost complete indifference to His ethical attributes and His love and concern for man, implies rather that the author, whoever he may have been, was only saying that the might and transcendence of God are so far beyond man that there is no right or recourse other than to submit, whatever may happen. It is an answer of despair, perhaps of fatalism, but not of faith.

We turn to the Dialogue. Understanding the high theme and purpose of the great poet, we recognize immediately the literary skill of a master, such as will become more and more apparent as one accompanies him. For setting out to pursue 'things unattempted yet in prose or rhyme,' he introduces us, not to a ponderous theological dissertation, but to a very sick man and his querulous complaining. Job curses the day of his birth. Why must one live when life means only bitterness? For this thing that has overtaken him is completely irrational; he was not even guilty of too great happiness, 'I was not at ease . . . but trouble came' (3^{26}). And that is all! Who might dream such to be the opening of a high theological quest? Yet as one's study advances, he realizes that already hints and themes have been introduced, with the delicacy that characterizes this author, which are to provide the foci around which Job's pilgrimage of faith revolves.

Apparently **Eliphaz** of Teman is presented as the eldest, hence the dominating one of the friends. He sets out (4^{2ff}) evidently to encourage Job, but soon it becomes apparent that his 'comfort' is first of all a rebuke of unconfessed sin, which for the orient lacks nothing of directness by virtue of being presented in mere allusions or innuendo. God is exalted far beyond man's furthest possibilities; Job has been guilty, *inter alia*, of vexation (5^{2}), surely a reference to the dull feeling of injustice with which his complaint had closed; he should 'seek God' (5^{8})—apparently confess the sins he will not admit, and accept patiently the Divine chastening. If so, there is a prospect of restoration and great happiness for him. **Bildad** and **Zophar** follow in turn, after intervening replies by Job. But while they are sketched as diverse individuals—Bildad blustering but kind, Zophar somewhat scholarly yet cutting—and although they add their differing emphases—Bildad the justice of God, Zophar His inscrutability—yet they contribute little beyond Eliphaz's views to the advance of the thought. In the second and third cycles of their speeches they provide mainly vociferous reaffirmation of their position and increasing abuse of Job through charges which have no validation elsewhere. It becomes evident that they function primarily as a foil and provocation for Job's thinking. Interest shifts to his speeches and to the groping evolution of a solution towards which the author with magnificent skill leads him onward. It is this progress of Job's thought which constitutes the core and meaning of the book. The plan of the writer early reveals itself. The friends are the voice of orthodoxy; the best thinking of the time relevant to the human predicament is cogently argued by them in turn. Against it Job is in open revolt; not at first, for he is too numbed by suffering to have any clear view, and presumably such attitude as he entertains is essentially theirs. But under the sting and disappointment of the friends' misunderstanding and their unfeeling application of their dogmas, he moves into a sense of the enormity of the issue and of its irrationality. He charges that the friends substitute pietistic phrases for honest thought, and that such is not piety at all (13^{7-12}). Yet we now are not ready to dismiss them so cursorily; there is much of high value in their emphases, in Eliphaz's belief in the transcendence of God, in Bildad's certainty of divine justice and of God's care of the just. Zophar's sense of the mystery of the transcendent divine wisdom, also, is well presented in the words of AV, even if they are a wrong translation, 'Canst thou by searching find out God' (11^{7}).

Nor is it clear that the author would entirely disparage the current orthodoxy, which he has the friends present. Rather he criticizes it for its inadequacy. Its great emphasis is that God is great and exalted—would any thoughtful individual of that time or the present question it? But if that is all, then the human tragedy has no answer beyond what the friends quite consistently reiterate: submit! A genuine religious faith and life can scarcely be built on such stern compulsion. We must know, in some way, that God is good and that He is touched with the feeling of our infirmities (He 4^{15}). Such is the quest on which the author launches the sick and groping Job—can one hold a faith of this sort? For equally it is apparent that the obverse of his plan is to use Job to voice his own convictions and have him work on through his dull suffering and sense of wrong to the answer which it is the poet's purpose to offer for this deepest of human questionings.

His literary artistry is a joy to witness—much of it unfortunately lost in translation, as is inevitable: the truth with which he handles the sick and hopeless Job, leading him on to steadily enlarging apprehensions of the problem which at first is only a personal obsession but presently is recognized as a typical bit of human woe; the deep understanding of human experience and human nature, perhaps most notably presented in the complaints of the despairing Job in words that to this day seem the instinctive voice of those most sick in body and mind; the charming vignettes of ancient life; the delicacy of allusion and innuendo; the heat of debate carried forward in what seems on casual reading not debate at all but a series of unrelated dissertations, but on closer study becomes a close-knit fabric of expostulation and reply; the light touch that has the sufferer stumble on a new apprehension only to drop it suddenly through the inability of his fevered mind to follow any consistent course of thought except obsession with its own misery; the thought, however, is not lost, but becomes, after vague gropings, the ground of a fresh advance, so that step by step from one moment's insight to a next somewhat higher, Job moves onward into faith and hope. Yet one further feature of the poet's skill becomes apparent only through close and informed study. Like every great writer, then or now, he is fully conversant with contemporary literature, not least the already classic treatments of the theme with which he is engrossed. A light touch and apt allusion—meaningful for the informed—weaves it into his enlarging tapestry of Job's pilgrimage.

In his reply to Eliphaz Job voiced first his pained incredulity that his friends had so grossly failed to understand and help. Perhaps this too is an important phase of the author's presentation; perhaps he is saying that orthodoxy is so engrossed in its impersonal postulates that it loses sight of the realities of personal need. Reiteration of his suffering brings Job then to the realization of its universal quality, and so to the full force of the problem; for how and why can God endure —how can He seemingly enjoy the pain of creatures so much less than Himself, which indeed He had called into being? This line of thought leads him very naturally, in his reply to Bildad, to an idea that is to be basic throughout the entirety of his further utterances, the wish for a cosmic hearing in which he could argue the injustice of the pains he suffers. The gradual development of this defiance into a very different mood is one of the subtle motifs of the Dialogue. But equally naturally he seizes upon another thought that is to be of far-reaching implication. What would be the use of such a meeting? God is immensely bigger than he, and 'there is no umpire between us who might lay his hand on us both' (9^{33})—the mysterious figure of the intermediary; he comes in twice more under different names and in quite different function, in 16^{19}, and in the famous passage, 19^{25}. Who is he? And just what is his function in this high quest? It is a most alluring, and yet baffling problem. But before we attempt it there is much that must be sketched as preliminary.

It is in his near blasphemous expostulations against God's unfeeling treatment of His finite creature that Job stumbles, almost to his surprise, it would seem, upon an admission that proves to be a turning point in his despair. Listing what God has done for a creature He now persecutes, Job tells in the quaint imagery of the ancient world, of God's shaping his prenatal development, then as though through an inadvertence he continues: 'Thou hast granted me life and steadfast love; and thy care has preserved my spirit' (10^{12}).

It is all so simply introduced that one can easily overlook its crucial importance in the poem. For the fact is that in his next speech Job has left behind his bitterness and set forth toward faith and hope which though only incipient, yet are the thread to guide his faltering steps toward recovery.

Still it is a transformation handled with the rare skill and insight of the author. Job falls back again and again into his despairing gloom, but his lucid moments become more pronounced and his wistful hope more certain. Every reader knows the preoccupation of ch. 14 with thoughts of death and the hereafter: 'Man that is born of woman is of few days and full of trouble. . . . Oh, that thou wouldst hide me in Sheol. . . . If a man die (and) live again . . .' and so on. But this is the thought that had obsessed Job in his very first speech; more than that, it had recurred in varying expression, in every one of them. Clearly there is here some vital thread in the author's evolving thought. Our long tradition of a faith in life beyond death naturally prompts the question whether he means this; and while the Hebraic concept of Sheol is very different from anything we hold, yet it becomes certain that such solution is part of his answer. The words of 19^{26}, beyond a doubt correctly translated in RSV, render this indisputable, notwithstanding the seemingly final denial in ch. 14, which, however, is but an expression of the author's methods in leading Job on from despair to dawning hope and ultimate certainty. However, the reiterated theme of death and the underworld has still more profound significance in the working out of the author's design.

Pervasive through the ancient world for millennia was a myth and liturgy of the god who died and rose again. Famous bodies of literature dealt with this phase of ancient faith, and still others carried greater or less allusions to it. In its simplest origins it was merely a personification of the annual fluctuations of the life process. In the springtime life bursts throbbing and triumphant; its zest slowly moderates into the maturity of early summer; soon blighting heat sears the landscape into long months of life's arrest, until once more the miracle of the new year again calls for life and hope and increase. Yet the religious implications, and resultant faith, went far beyond such crass cult of nature. In Egypt, for example, Osiris became the symbol and ground of belief in a glorious life beyond death. In Mesopotamia Tammuz was a healing god; Ishtar, his spouse, may be described, though none too accurately, as deified motherhood; an illuminating glimpse of the function of Nergal, one of the terrifying gods of the underworld, is given in a personal name, Nergal-mitu-uballit (Nergal makes the dead live). However, a striking feature of the myth was that the restoration of the dead god did not come about spontaneously through natural force, but a messenger from the high gods descended into the gloomy reaches of the underworld and by persuasion secured his release.

Allusions to this aspect of the thought of his contemporary world pervade the work of the author of the Dialogue. It is doubtful that all have been identified, for like any good poet his touch is frequently very light.

In some way the poet's answer to the riddle of human suffering is clearly interwoven with all this aspect of the thinking of his time. That he was too great a thinker merely to have adopted these pagan ideas needs no argument; he is employing them to lead Job onward from his black despair and rebellion, and doubtless at the same time is sketching their service in his own progress toward a faith and hope that can transform our woe into a thing of brightness and promise. We have noted that he reaches for a certainty of persistence beyond death; but clearly this is no more than part of his conclusion. The mysterious figure of Job's intermediary plays some vital rôle in his progress. This is attested by 33^{23}, which, though no part of the Dialogue, must be regarded as a use of it by some one who gave us this testimony to its conclusion subsequently lost. The three appearances of the intermediary in the Dialogue leave his function very uncertain except that he is a 'witness in the heavens' (16^{19}) and a 'redeemer' who will ensure that Job will see God as one not estranged from Him (19^{25ff}). We are led to see him as parallel to the messenger from the gods, in the pagan literature. And although the immediate sequel of his work is Job's grasp of what we may not inaccurately describe as a redeeming faith (23^{6-10}), yet the work of the intermediary in creating this is not clarified. There are many very important questions we would like to ask the poet. However, it is probable in the light of all we can adduce, that his meaning is approximately of this sort. As death and revival are an inextricable part of the natural world, we must see suffering as rooted in the nature of things. Probably we shall not exaggerate his thought if we say that it reaches right up to God Himself; He too suffers. Our human woe, then, is not an infliction by an arbitrary and indifferent Ruler of All; it is rather a part of being. To be is to suffer. Yet this does not lead to a doctrine of Nirvana, of escape through not-being. The poet is too great an optimist for this. He had the beginning of Job's recovery coincide with his startled realization that life is not entirely a vale of woe; its pain is balanced by 'steadfast love and care' that preserves one's spirit (10^{12}). Yet this, even along with his belief in some sort of survival of death, is not a final answer for the poet; neither would it be for us. He seems to say, as Paul did centuries later, that 'the whole creation has been groaning in travail until now' (Ro 8^{22}), and that it is our painful privilege to share in that universal agony. We all shrink from suffering; that is natural, it is its biological function. But if we can rise to a higher level, we may seize some, more or less adequate, understanding of its working in things of the spirit: its discipline, its refining fire, and its fellowship in the creative and redemptive pain that is universal up to God Himself.

Doubtless if the Dialogue were preserved complete, the precise formulation of the thought would be clearer than it is now; but its movement and the culmination at which our defective copy arrives, indicate that this sketch, even if dependent in some part on aspects of our Christian thinking, is yet not false to the answer the poet evolved with such superb skill. Its depth and height beyond other answers is apparent, and its remoteness from the superficiality which unfortunately afflicts most of the popular writers of our time who confidently elect themselves arbiters of the most difficult question which has engrossed and baffled all the ages.

Very little study will reveal that the rest of the Book of Job (except ch. 33, which gives a résumé of the Dialogue) is oblivious of the movement of thought that is the essential element of the Dialogue; likewise they lack the distinctive themes which it employs. They are not without value, some of it very high, but they contribute nothing to the insights which it has been the great worth of the Dialogue to open before us. The magnificent flights of poetic imagination found in the Speeches of Y″ have always constituted an attractive feature of the book. The stress in some of the Elihu speeches upon the disciplinary worth of suffering also merits mention. But attention will inevitably revert to the Dialogue as that part which most of all has created the enduring greatness of the book of Job. W. A. I.

JOBAB.—**1.** A son of Joktan in the genealogies, Gn 10^{29}, 1 Ch 1^{23}, and therefore probably an Arabian geographical name. Glaser identifies Jobab with YHYBB (probably *Yuhaybab*), a tribe mentioned in the Sabaean inscriptions. Sprenger through the LXX form *Iobor* relates it to *Wabār*, a considerable region in S. Arabia. **2.** A king of Edom, Gn 36^{33f}, 1 Ch 1^{44f}, confused, in the apocryphal appendix to the LXX version of Job, with Job (q.v.). **3.** A king of Madon, ally of Jabin of Hazor against Joshua, Jos 11^{1}. **4. 5.** Name of two Benjamites, 1 Ch $8^{9,18}$. W. M. N.

JOCHEBED.—A daughter of Levi, born after the descent into Egypt (Nu 26^{59}), and sister of Kohath, who married her nephew Amram and became the mother of Aaron and Moses (Ex 6^{20}) and Miriam (Nu 26^{59}). Her name is not mentioned in Ex 2^{1}, which records the birth of Moses. The name Jochebed appears to be compounded with the divine name Yahweh, but Noth (*Die israelitischen Personennamen*, 1928, 111) says this is uncertain, and the name may be of foreign origin.

JOD or **YODH.**—Tenth letter of Hebrew alphabet, and so used to introduce the tenth part of Ps 119, every verse of which begins with this letter.

JODA.—**1.** A Levite, 1 Es 5^{58}; called **Judah** (q.v.) in Ezr 3^{9}, **Hodaviah** in Ezr 2^{40}, **Hodevah** in Neh 7^{43}, and **Sudias** in 1 Es 5^{26}. **2.** An ancestor of Jesus, Lk 3^{26}.

JODAN.—One of the sons of Jeshua, the son of Jozadak, 1 Es 9^{19} (AV, RV **Joadanus**), called **Gedaliah** in Ezr 10^{18}.

JOED.—A Benjamite, Neh 11^{7}.

JOEL.—**1.** The prophet (see next article). Regarding his personal history we know nothing. **2.** A son of Samuel, 1 S 8^{2}, 1 Ch 6^{28} (RV, RSV; AV, following Hebrew, omits) ^{33}. **3.** An ancestor of Samuel, 1 Ch 6^{36}; called **Shaul** in v.^{24}. **4.** A Simeonite prince, 1 Ch 4^{35}. **5.** A Reubenite, 1 Ch $5^{4,8}$. **6.** A Gadite chief, 1 Ch 5^{12}. **7.** A chief of Issachar, 1 Ch 7^{3}. **8.** One of David's heroes, 1 Ch 11^{38}; see IGAL, **2.** **9. 10. 11.** Levites, 1 Ch $15^{7,11,17}$; 23^{8} 26^{22}; 2 Ch 29^{12}. **12.** A Manassite chief, 1 Ch 27^{20}. **13.** One of those who married a foreign wife, Ezr 10^{43}, 1 Es 9^{35} (AV, RV **Juel**). **14.** A Benjamite overseer after the Exile, Neh 11^{9}. **15.** One of those who married a foreign wife, 1 Es 9^{35} (AV, RV **Juel**); called **Uel** in Ezr 10^{34}.

JOEL, BOOK OF.—**1. Analysis.**—The Book of Joel clearly falls into two parts: (1) a call to repentance in view of present judgment and the approaching Day of Yahweh, with a prayer for deliverance, and the Divine answer promising relief (1–2^{27}); (2) the spiritual blessing, judgment on the Gentile world, and material prosperity for Judah and Jerusalem (2^{28}–3^{21} [Heb. 3^{1}–4^{21}]).

(1) The immediate occasion of the call to repentance is a plague of locusts of exceptional severity (1^{2f}), extending over several years (2^{25}), and followed by drought and famine so severe as to necessitate the discontinuance of the meal- and drink-offering (1^{9}), *i.e.* probably the daily sacrifice (cf Ex 29^{41}, where the same Hebrew words are used of the daily meal-offering and drink-offering). This fearful calamity, which is distinctly represented as present ('before our eyes' 1^{16}), heralds 'the great and very terrible day of Yahweh' (2^{11}), which will be ushered in by yet more fearful distress of the same kind (2^{1-11}). The reason of all this suffering actual and prospective is national sin, which, however, is not specified. Yahweh's people have turned away from Him (implied in 2^{12}). Let them turn back, giving expression to their penitent sorrow in tears, mourning garb, general fasting, and prayer offered by priests in the Temple (2^{12-17}).

'Then the Lord became jealous for his land and had pity on his people' (2^{18}). It seems to be implied that the people had repented and fasted, and that the priests had prayed on their behalf. This Divine pity, proceeds the prophet, speaking in Yahweh's name, will express itself in the removal of the locusts (2^{20}), and in the cessation of the drought, which will restore to the land its normal fertility, and so replace famine by plenty (2^{22-27}).

(2) Higher blessings yet are in store for the people of Yahweh. His Spirit shall afterwards be poured out on all, inclusive even of slaves (2^{28f} [Heb. 3^{1f}]). And when the Day of Yahweh comes in all its terror, it will be terrible only to the Gentile world which has oppressed Israel. The gathered hosts of the former, among whom Phoenicians and Philistines are singled out for special condemnation (3 [Heb. 4] $^{4-8}$), shall be destroyed by Yahweh and His angels in the Valley of Jehoshaphat (3 [Heb. 4] ^{11b}), and then Jerusalem shall be a holy city, no longer haunted by unclean aliens (3 [Heb. 4] ^{17}), and Judah, unlike Egypt and Edom, will be a happy nation dwelling in a happy, because well-watered, land, and Yahweh will ever abide in its midst (3 [Heb. 4] $^{18-21}$).

2. Integrity.—Eissfeldt states the problem of Joel to be whether the first section, defined above, is prophecy or narrative description of past or present events. If it is prophecy, the book is a unity; but if it is narrative, its unity is open to question. The common view to-day is that it is narrative, although the reference to the Day of the Lord must have future reference. Most scholars affirm the unity of the two sections, but some (*e.g.* Oesterley and Robinson, *Introduction to the Books of the Old Testament*) argue for a later date for the apocalyptic sections than for the rest, and in consequence do not regard the book as a unity.

3. Date.—There is no external evidence. The place of the book in the Canon is not conclusive, for the Book of Jonah, which was manifestly written after the fall of Nineveh, is also found in the former part of the collection of the Twelve, and comes before Micah, the earliest portions of which are beyond doubt much older. Hence the question can be answered, in so far as an answer is possible, only from the book itself.

The facts bearing upon it may be briefly stated as follows: (1) The people addressed are the inhabitants of Judah (3 [Heb. 4] ^{1,6,8,18ff}), and Jerusalem (2^{32} [Heb. 3^{5}] 3 [Heb. 4] ^{6,16f,20}). Zion is mentioned in $2^{1,15,23,32}$ [Heb. 3^{5}] 3 [Heb. 4] ^{16,17,21}. There is no trace of the kingdom of Samaria. The name 'Israel' is indeed used (2^{27} 3 [Heb. 4] ^{2,16}), but, as the first and last of these passages clearly show, it is not the kingdom of Israel that is meant, but the people of God, dwelling mainly about Jerusalem. (2) There is no mention of royalty or aristocracy. (3) The Temple is repeatedly referred to ($1^{9,13f,16}$ 2^{17} 3 [Heb. 4] ^{5}), and by implication in the phrase 'my holy mountain' (2^{1} 3 [Heb. 4] ^{17}: its ritual is regarded as of high importance ($1^{9,13}$ 2^{14}), and its ministers stand between the people and their God, giving expression to their penitence and prayer ($1^{9,13}$ 2^{17}). (4) The people are called on to repent of sin (2^{12f}), but in general terms. No mention is made of idolatry or formalism, or sensuality, or oppression—the sins so sternly denounced by Amos and Isaiah. (5) The foreign nations denounced as hostile to Israel are the Phoenicians (3 [Heb. 4] ^{4}), the Philistines (ib.), Egypt and Edom (3 [Heb. 4] ^{19}). Reference is also made to the Grecians (' sons of the Ionians,' 3 [Heb. 4] ^{6}), and the Sabaeans or S. Arabians (3 [Heb. 4] ^{8}) as slave-dealers. Assyria, Babylonia, and Aram are neither named nor alluded to. (6) The history of Judah and Jerusalem includes a national catastrophe when the people of Yahweh were scattered among the nations and the land of Yahweh was divided amongst new settlers (3 [Heb. 4] ^{2}). (7) This book of seventy-three verses contains twenty-seven expressions or clauses to which parallels, more or less close, can be adduced from other OT writings, mainly prophetic. In twelve passages there is verbal or almost verbal correspondence: cf 1^{15b} and Ezk 30^{2f}; 1^{15c} and Is 13^{6}; 2^{2} and Zeph 1^{15}; 2^{6} and Nah 2^{10} [Heb. 11]; 2^{13} and Ex 34^{6}; 2^{14} and 2 S 12^{22}; 2^{27b} and Ezk 36^{11} etc.; 2^{27c} and Is $45^{5f,\,18}$; 2^{31b} [Heb. 3^{4}] and Mal 4^{5} [Heb. 3^{23}]; 2^{32} [Heb. 3^{5}] and Ob ^{17}; 3 [Heb. 4] ^{16} and Am 1^{2}; 3 [Heb. 4] ^{1} and Jer 33^{15} etc. In two other places there is contrast as well as parallelism, 2^{28} [Heb. 3^{1}] answers to Ezk 39^{29}, but the latter has ' on the house of Israel,' the former ' on all flesh,' and 3 [Heb. 4] ^{10} is the reverse of Is 2^{4} and Mic 4^{3}. The last clause of 2^{13} is found also in Jon 4^{2} in the same connexion, and nowhere else. (8) The Hebrew exhibits some features which are more common in late than in the earlier literature. There are a few Aramaisms: *'ālāh* ' lament ' (1^{8}); *sōph* ' hinder part ' (2^{20}) for *qēṣ*: the Hiph'il of *nāḥath* (3 [Heb. 4] ^{11}), and *rōmaḥ* (3 [Heb. 4] ^{10}—a word of Aramaic affinities; and several expressions often met with in late writers. Still, it is not advisable to lay much stress on this point.

With these facts before them critics have concluded that the book must either be very early or late. Many, led by Credner, found evidence of pre-exilic date, and most of these, after him, selected the minority of Joash of Judah (*c* 737 B.C.). König prefers the latter part of the reign of Josiah (640–609 B.C.). Recent critics, with a few exceptions (Orelli, Kirkpatrick, Volck, and to some extent Baudissin) regard the book as post-exilic: *c* 500 B.C. (so Driver, but not without hesitation); after the reforms of Ezra and Nehemiah (E. Kautzsch, W. R. Smith, G. A. Smith on the whole, Marti, the school of Kuenen, Nowack, Cornill, and Horton). Several points seem to favour strongly post-exilic origin: the religious atmosphere, the political situation in so far as it can be discerned, reference to the Greeks, and the literary parallelisms, most of which are more intelligible on the assumption of borrowing by Joel than vice versa. While most scholars maintain the unity of the Book of Joel, some as mentioned above, separate the apocalyptic sections (especially 3^{1-21}) and attribute these to a later date (*c* 200 B.C.) than the rest (*c* 350 B.C.).

4. Interpretation.—The ancient Jews, as represented by the Targum, and the Fathers, who have been followed by Pusey, Hengstenberg, and others, to some extent even by Merx, regarded the locusts of the Book of Joel as not literal but symbolic. That view, however, is now generally abandoned. The seemingly extravagant descriptions of the locust-swarms, and the havoc wrought by them, have been confirmed in almost every point by modern observers. What is said about their number (1^{6}), the darkness they cause (2^{10}), their resemblance to horses (2^{4}), the noise they make in flight and when feeding (2^{5}), their irresistible advance (2^{7ff}), their amazing destructiveness ($1^{7,\,10ff}$ 2^{3}), and the burnt appearance of a region which they have ravaged (2^{3ab})—can hardly be pronounced exaggerated in view of the evidence collected by Pusey, Driver, G. A. Smith, and other commentators. The description of the locusts as ' the northern *army* ' (2^{20}) is indeed still unexplained, but is insufficient of itself to overthrow the literal interpretation. On the apocalyptic character of the latter portion of the book there is general agreement. Kapelrud (*Joel Studies*) has given a liturgical interpretation of the book and relates it on the one hand to Yahweh's enthronement festival and on the other brings it into close association with the ancient Canaanite fertility cult.

5. Doctrine.—As compared with some of the other prophetic writings, say with Deutero-Isaiah and Jonah, the Book of Joel as a whole is particularistic. The writer's hopes of a glorious future seem limited to Judah and Jerusalem, and perhaps the Dispersion (2^{32} [Heb 3^{5}]). On the other hand, it is remarkable that the outpouring of the Spirit is promised to ' all flesh,' not merely to ' the house of Israel '—a general way of stating the promise which made the NT application possible (Ac 2^{16ff}). So the book may be said to contain a germ of universalism. Its other most striking characteristic, from the doctrinal standpoint, is the importance attached to ritual and the priesthood, and the comparatively slight stress laid on conduct. Still, it is here that we find the caustic words: ' Rend your heart and not your garments ' (2^{13}).

6. Style.—In style the Book of Joel takes a very high place in Hebrew literature. It is throughout clearly, elegantly, and forcefully written. Skilful use is made of parallelism—note the five short clauses in 1^{10}; of Oriental hyperbole (2^{30f} [Heb. 3^{3f}]) and of word-play, *e.g. shuddadh śādheh* ' the field is wasted ' (1^{10}), *yābhēshû . . . hōbhîsh* ' are withered . . . is ashamed ' (1^{12}), *shōdh mish-shaddai* ' destruction from the Almighty ' (1^{15}), and the play on the verb *shāphaṭ* and the name Jehoshaphat in 3 [Heb. 4] $^{2,\,12}$. W. T. S.—**J. Ma.**

JOELAH.—A warrior who joined David at Ziklag, 1 Ch 12^{6}.

JOEZER.—One of David's followers at Ziklag, 1 Ch 12^{6}.

JOGBEHAH.—A town of Gad in Gilead, Nu 32^{35}, mentioned in connexion with Gideon's pursuit of the Midianites, Jg 8^{11}. It is the modern *Kh. Jubeihât* (or *Ajbeihât*), NW. of *'Ammân.*

JOGLI.—Father of the Danite chief who took part in the division of the land, Nu 34^{22}.

JOHA.—**1.** A Benjamite, 1 Ch 8^{16}. **2.** One of David's heroes, 1 Ch 11^{45}.

JOHANAN.—**1.** Son of Kareah, one of the military captains who, after the fall of Jerusalem, joined Gedaliah at Mizpah, 2 K 25^{23}, Jer 40^{8}–43^{7}. After the murder of Gedaliah he pursued Ishmael and the other conspirators, recovered the captives, and, in spite of the protest of Jeremiah, carried them to Egypt. **2.** A son of Josiah, 1 Ch 3^{15}. **3.** A post-exilic descendant of the line of David, 1 Ch 3^{24}. **4.** A high priest, 1 Ch 6^{9f}. **5. 6.** Two warriors who came to David to Ziklag, a Benjamite and a Gadite respectively, 1 Ch $12^{4,\,12}$. **7.** One of those who returned with Ezra, Ezr 8^{12}, 1 Es 8^{38} (AV **Johannes,** RV **Joannes**). **8.** An Ephraimite, 2 Ch 28^{12}. **9.** See JONATHAN, **7** and JEHOHANAN, **3.**

JOHANNES.—1 Es 9^{29} (AV); see JEHOHANAN, **4. 2.** 1 Es 8^{38} (AV); see JOHANAN, **7.**

JOHN.—**1.** The father of Mattathias, and grandfather of the five Maccabaean brothers (1 Mac 2^{1}). **2.** The eldest son of Mattathias (1 Mac 2^{2}). In 161 B.C. he was slain by the ' sons of Jambri ' (1 Mac 9^{35-42}). In 2 Mac 8^{22}, and perhaps again 10^{19}, he is by mistake called **Joseph.** **3.** The father of Eupolemus (1 Mac 8^{17}, 2 Mac 4^{11}), who was sent by Judas Maccabaeus as an ambassador to Rome. **4.** An envoy sent by the Jews to treat with Lysias (2 Mac 11^{17}). **5.** One of the sons of Simon the Maccabee (1 Mac 16^{2}), commonly known as John Hyrcanus, and described as a grown man in (1 Mac 13^{53}). See MACCABEES, **5.** **6.** The father of Simon Peter (Jn 1^{42} 21^{15-17} RV, RSV; AV **Jonas**), who is called in Mt 16^{17} **Bar-Jonah** (AV **Bar-Jona**). In the latter passage the form *Jōnās* may be a contraction for *Jōanēs*, or possibly Peter's father had two names, as in the case of *Saul—Paul.* **7.** One of the high-priestly family (Ac 4^{6}). **8.** John Mark (see MARK). **9. 10.** For the Baptist and the Apostle see the following two articles.

JOHN THE APOSTLE

JOHN THE APOSTLE.—The material for a life of St. John may be divided into three parts: (1) The specific information given in the canonical Scriptures; (2) early tradition; (3) later legends, which cannot be accepted as history but possess an interest and significance of their own. But when all the evidence is gathered, it is impossible to give more than fragmentary details of the life of one of the most important figures in the apostolic age.

1. The Scripture data.—John was a son of Zebedee, a fisherman in one of the towns on the Lake of Galilee, possibly Bethsaida. It is probable that his mother was Salome, one of the women who 'ministered' to Jesus in Galilee (Mk 15^{41}), a sister of Mary the mother of Jesus. This may be inferred from a comparison of Mt 27^{56} and Mk 15^{40f} 16^{1} with Jn 19^{25}. His family was in a position to engage hired help (Mk 1^{20}), and to support Jesus' work (Lk 8^{1-3}).

The passage in John is best understood as naming *four* women who stood by the Cross of Jesus—His mother, His mother's sister Salome, Mary wife of Clopas who was also mother of James and Joses, and Mary Magdalene. The interpretation which would find only three persons in the list, and identify Mary 'of Clopas' with the sister of Jesus' mother, is open to the objection that two sisters would have the same name, and it involves other serious difficulties. (See MARY.)

In Jn 1^{40} two disciples are mentioned as having heard the testimony of John the Baptist to Jesus and having accompanied the new Teacher to His home. One of these was Andrew, and it has been surmised that the other was John himself. If this was so, the incident must be understood as constituting the very beginning of John's discipleship.

In Mt 4^{18-22}, Mk 1^{16-20} an account is given in almost the same words of the call of four fishermen to follow Jesus. Two of these were John and his elder brother James, who were with their father in a boat on the Lake of Galilee, mending their nets. In Lk 5^{1-11} a different account of the call is given. Nothing is said of Andrew; Peter is the principal figure in the scene of the miraculous draught of fishes, while James and John are mentioned only incidentally as 'partners with Simon.' Presumably Luke has omitted the Marcan account in favour of his own (possibly derived from his special source, L), but has added to it the details which identify the other disciples who were called at the same time. His narrative has by some scholars been identified with the nucleus of the tradition in Jn 21^{1-14}. Directly or indirectly, however, we are told that to John, whilst engaged in his craft, the summons was given to leave his occupation and become a 'fisher of men.' The call was immediately obeyed, and constitutes an intermediate link between the initial stage of discipleship and the appointment to be one of twelve 'apostles.' In the lists of the Twelve (Mt 10^{2}, Mk 3^{14}, Lk 6^{13}, Ac 1^{13}), John is always named as one of the first four, and in the course of Christ's ministry he was one of an inner circle of three, who were honoured with special marks of confidence. These alone were permitted to be present on three occasions—the raising of Jairus' daughter, narrated in Mk 5^{37}, Lk 8^{51}; the Transfiguration, described in three accounts (Mt 17^{1}, Mk 9^{2}, Lk 9^{28}); and the Agony in the Garden of Gethsemane (Mt 26^{37}, Mk 14^{33}, Lk 22^{24}). On one or perhaps two occasions Andrew was associated with these three—possibly at the healing of Peter's wife's mother (Mk 1^{29}), and certainly at the interview described in Mk 13^{3}, when Jesus sat on the Mount of Olives and was 'asked privately' concerning His prediction of the overthrow of the Temple.

On two notable occasions the brothers James and John were associated together. They appear to have been alike in natural temperament. It is in this light that the statement of Mk 3^{17} is generally understood—'whom he surnamed **Boanerges,** that is, sons of thunder.' Some uncertainty attaches to the derivation of the word, and the note added by the Evangelist is not perfectly clear. But no better explanation has been given than that the title alluded to the zeal and vehemence of character which both the Apostles exhibited on the occasions when they appear together. In Lk 9^{54} they wish to call down fire from heaven and consume the Samaritan village which had refused hospitality to their Master. In Mk 10^{35} they come to Him with an eager request that to them might be allotted the two highest places in His Kingdom, and they profess their complete readiness to share with Him whatever suffering He may be called to pass through. According to Mt 20^{20}, their mother accompanied them and made the request, but v.^{24} shows that indignation was roused 'at the two brothers,' and that the petition was really their own. Once in the Gospels John is described as associated with Peter, the two being sent by Jesus to make ready the Passover (Lk 22^{8}). Once he figures by himself alone, as making inquiry concerning a man who cast out demons in the name of Jesus, though he did not belong to the company of the disciples (Mk 9^{38}, Lk 9^{49}). As an indication of character this is to be understood as evincing zealous, if mistaken, loyalty. Jesus' reply was, 'Do not forbid him'; evidently John was disposed to manifest on this occasion the fiery intolerant zeal which he and his brother together displayed in Samaria. Though the words 'You do not know what manner of spirit you are of' do not form part of the best attested text in Lk 9^{55}, they doubtless describe the kind of rebuke with which on both occasions the Master found it necessary to check the eagerness of a disciple who loved his Master well, but not wisely.

In the early part of the Acts, John is associated by name with Peter on three occasions. One was the healing of the lame man by the Temple gate (3^{4}). The next was their appearance before the Sanhedrin in ch. 4, when they were found to be men untrained in scribal teaching, 'uneducated, common men' (v.^{13}), and were also recognized by some present as having been personal followers of Jesus, and seen in His immediate company. In 8^{14ff} we read that the two were sent by their brother-Apostles to Samaria, after Philip had exercised his evangelistic ministry there. Many of the Samaritans had been baptized, and the two 'prayed for them that they might receive the Holy Spirit,' and laid their hands on them. These typical instances show that at the outset of the history of the Church Peter and John acted jointly as leaders, though they were very different in personal character, and Peter appears always to have been the spokesman. This note of personal leadership is confirmed by the incidental reference of Paul in Gal 2^{9}, where James (not the son of Zebedee), Cephas, and John are 'reputed to be pillars' in the Church at Jerusalem.

Our knowledge of John's life and character is largely increased, and the interest in his personality is greatly deepened, if he is identified with '*the disciple whom Jesus loved*,' the author of the Fourth Gospel, and the John of the Apocalypse. All three of these identifications are strongly contested in modern times. In Jn 13^{23} the disciple whom Jesus loved 'was lying close to the breast of Jesus' at the Last Supper. The phrase implies that on the chief couch at the meal, holding three persons, Jesus was in the middle and John on His right hand, thus being brought more directly face to face with the Master than Peter, who occupied the left-hand place. This explains the action in v.^{25} as well as Peter's 'beckoning' mentioned in v.^{24}. John has been also identified with the 'other disciple' mentioned in Jn 18^{15f} as known to the high priest and having a right of entrance into the court which was denied to Peter. Again, the disciple whom Jesus loved is described in Jn 19^{26} as standing by the cross of Jesus with His mother, as receiving the sacred charge implied by the words, 'Woman, behold your son!' and 'Behold your mother!' and as thenceforth providing a home for her—who was probably already one of his near kindred as well as the mother of his Lord. In 20^{3} he accompanies Peter to the tomb of Jesus; and while he reached the sepulchre first, Peter was the first to enter in, but John was apparently the first to 'believe' (v.[8]). In ch. 21 the two sons of Zebedee are among the group of seven disciples to whom our Lord appeared at the Sea of Tiberias, and again the disciple whom Jesus loved and Peter are distinguished; the one as the first to discern the risen Lord upon the shore, the other as the first to plunge into the water to go to Him. The Gospel closes with an account of Peter's inquiry concerning the future of his friend and companion on so many occasions; and in 19[35] as well as in 21[24] it is noted that the disciple 'who has written these things' bore witness of that which he himself had seen, and that his witness is true. But among scholars the probability has steadily grown, during the past fifty years, that the beloved disciple is an idealized figure, not a merely historical one. John is taken to represent the ideal Christian disciple, who responds to Jesus' teaching and signs, and attests the reality of the Incarnation as against the current Docetism and Gnosticism. (See JOHN, GOSPEL OF.)

It is only necessary to add that the John mentioned in Rev 1[4, 9] as writing to the Seven Churches in Asia from the island of Patmos was identified by early tradition with the son of Zebedee. If this be correct, much additional light is cast upon the later life of the Apostle John (see REVELATION, BOOK OF). But again the probability is that the Apocalypse of John is a pseudonymous work, like the Apocalypse of Peter and many other apocalypses in circulation in the early church.

2. Early tradition.—Outside the NT only vague tradition enables us to fill up the gap left by Christ's answer to Peter's question, 'Lord, what about this man?' It has been inferred that he spent several years in Jerusalem. After an indefinite interval he is understood to have settled in Ephesus. Eusebius states (*HE* iii. 18, 20) that during the persecution of Domitian 'the apostle and evangelist John' was banished to Patmos, and that on the accession of Nerva (A.D. 96) he returned from the island and took up his abode in Ephesus, according to 'an ancient Christian tradition' (literally 'the word of the ancients among us'). Tertullian mentions a miraculous deliverance from a cauldron of boiling oil to which John had been condemned during a persecution in Rome, presumably under Domitian. Eusebius further states that John was living in Asia and governing the churches there as late as the reign of Trajan. He bases this assertion upon the evidence of Irenaeus and Clement of Alexandria. The former says that 'all the elders associated with John the disciple of the Lord in Asia bear witness,' and that he remained in Ephesus until the time of Trajan. Clement recites at length the well-known touching incident concerning St. John and the young disciple who fell into evil ways and became the chief of a band of robbers, as having occurred when 'after the tyrant's death he returned from the isle of Patmos to Ephesus.' Tertullian confirms the tradition of a residence in Ephesus by quoting the evidence of the Church of Smyrna that their bishop Polycarp was appointed by John (*de Pr. Haer.* 32). Polycrates, bishop of Ephesus towards the end of the 2nd cent., in a letter to Victor, bishop of Rome, speaks of one among the 'great lights' in Asia—'John, who was both a witness and a teacher, who reclined upon the bosom of the Lord, and, being a priest, wore the sacerdotal plate,' as having fallen asleep at Ephesus. The Muratorian Fragment, which dates about A.D. 180, records an account of the origin of the Fourth Gospel, to the effect that John wrote it in obedience to a special revelation made to himself and Andrew. This story is not elsewhere confirmed, but it shows the early prevalence of the belief in the Apostolic origin of the Gospel. Irenaeus states that the Gospel was written specially to confute unbelievers like the Gnostic Cerinthus, and tells, on the authority of those who had heard it from Polycarp, the familiar story that St. John refused to remain under the same roof with the arch-heretic, lest the building should fall down upon him. Ephesus is said to have been the scene of this incident. All traditions agree that he lived to a great age, and it is Jerome (*in Gal.* vi. 10) who tells of his being carried into the church when unable to walk or preach, and simply repeating the words, 'Little children, love one another'—the language and theme of 1 John. Christ's enigmatical answer to Peter, 'If it is my will that he remain until I come, what is that to you?' led, as Jn 21[23] indicates, to the belief that John would not die, but would be translated.

Still, in spite of the record, the legend lingered for a long time (it is mentioned by Augustine), that though apparently dead, the beloved Apostle was only asleep, and that the dust upon his tomb rose and fell with his breathing. The poet Browning, in his *Death in the Desert*, adopts the ancient tradition concerning the Apostle's great age and lingering death and imagines him recalled from a deep trance and the very borderland of the grave to deliver a last inspired message.

But the belief of the early Church that St. John maintained a prolonged ministry in Ephesus has been widely challenged in modern times. The chief argument against it is the silence of writers who might well be expected to make some reference to it. Polycarp in his letter to the Philippians, and Ignatius in writing to the Ephesians, refer to Paul and his writings, but not to John or his ministry. Clement of Rome, writing about A.D. 96–98 concerning the Apostles and their successors, makes no reference to John as an eminent survivor, but speaks of the Apostolic age as if completely past. If John worked in the province of Asia for a generation, and was still living in the reign of Trajan, it is not unnatural to expect that fuller reference to the fact would be found in the writings of the sub-Apostolic Fathers. This is of course an argument from silence, and the Christian documentary evidence for the later years of the first and the early years of the 2nd cent. is extremely scanty.

Nevertheless, it may be said that the tradition has strong positive attestation. Irenaeus, in a letter to Florinus preserved for us by Eusebius, describes how as a boy he had listened to 'the blessed Polycarp,' and had heard 'the accounts which he gave of his intercourse with John and with the others who had seen the Lord.' And lest his memory should be discredited, he tells his correspondent that he remembers the events of that early time more clearly than those of recent years; 'for what boys learn, growing with their mind, becomes joined with it.' It is incredible that a writer brought so near to the very person of John, and having heard his words through only one intermediary, should have been entirely in error concerning his ministry in Asia. Polycrates, again, a bishop of the city in which St. John had long resided and laboured, wrote of his ministry there after an interval of only two or three generations (to *c* A.D. 190). His testimony obviously is not that of himself alone, but must represent that of the whole Ephesian Church; and what Irenaeus remembered as a boy others of the same generation must have remembered according to their opportunities of knowledge. The explicit testimony of three writers like Polycrates, Irenaeus, and Clement of Alexandria carries with it the implicit testimony of a whole generation of Christians extending over a very wide geographical area. The silence of others notwithstanding, it is hardly credible that these should have been mistaken on a matter of so much importance. It must be noted however that this evidence does not carry with it the Johannine authorship of the Fourth Gospel, the three epistles, or the Apocalypse. The once-popular theory that confusion had arisen between John the Apostle and a certain 'John the Elder' was sufficiently refuted in 1901 by Theodor Zahn in his famous article in the *Realencyklopädie für Protestantische Theologie und Kirche*, ix, especially pp. 282–284.

3. Later traditions.—It is only, however, as regards the main facts of history that the testimony of the 2nd cent. may be thus confidently relied on. Stories of doubtful authenticity would gather round an honoured name in a far shorter period than seventy or eighty years. Some of these legends may well be true, others

JOHN THE BAPTIST

probably contain an element of truth, whilst others are the result of mistake or the product of pious imagination. They are valuable chiefly as showing the directions in which tradition travelled and we need not draw on any of the interesting tales of later days in order to form a judgment on the person and character of John the Apostle.

The paucity of historical and biographical information about the Apostle John is not greater than that about many another religious leader in the ancient world and in the early church. In fact, the data for the life of John are far more numerous than for most of the other apostles. It was characteristic of early Christianity that it was not a literary, political, or philosophical movement, and, in view of its strong eschatological expectation, made little effort to preserve the records of its earliest leaders. But enough information survives to enable us to characterize John as an ardent, devoted disciple, rash and excitable in youth but becoming more calm and firm in later years and a constant preacher of that gospel of love which he had learned from Jesus.

W. T. D.—F. C. G.

JOHN THE BAPTIST.—The narrative of John's birth and circumcision (Lk 1) probably originated in the circle of his followers, independently of the narratives of the birth of Jesus in relation to which it now stands. Like Isaac, he was born to aged parents (v.^{7}) as the child of promise (v.^{13}). His name, John (' the Lord is gracious '), and his designation as a charismatic (vv.$^{15-17}$), comparable to Nazirites such as Samson and Samuel in early Israel, show that the redeeming action of God for which faithful Israelites longed was felt to have begun in him. He was of priestly stock (v.^{5}), and while apparently still a boy, he went into the Judaean wilderness facing the Dead Sea (v.^{80}), the *ʿᵃrābhāh* of Is 40^{3}. As a preacher of repentance he came out of the desert wearing a camel's hair mantle with ' leather girdle ' and eating ' locusts and wild honey ' (Mk 1^{6}). As an Elijah-like prophet he practised the simplicities of the desert (Lk 1^{17}) perhaps as signs of his separation and of his message.

The publication and interpretation of the Dead Sea Scrolls (q.v.) and the excavation of the sites at Qumrân have resulted in a growing consensus that there were close relationships between the sect of the Scrolls, probably Essenes, and John the Baptist. The affinities of the sect were with the Temple cultus and the priesthood. Its members dwelt apart in the Judaean wilderness, considering Israel under the Jerusalem priesthood as the realm of Belial; and in such epithets as ' sea serpents ' and ' dust crawlers ' (1 *QH* v. 27) matched John's description of the multitude as the ' brood of vipers ' (Lk 3^{7}). The community at Qumrân was a community of preparation, and, like John, defined the will of God in ethical terms. However, the Baptist's ministry of repentance was for the preparation of all Israel, and there is no evidence that he lived in a community. Ritual ablutions with water, symbolizing moral cleansing, were on the increase in the Temple at the beginning of the Christian era; the evidence indicates that this tendency was even farther advanced at Qumrân. But aside from these reported washings there may also have been a baptism for initiants which was, like John's, a once-for-all rite of admission (1 *QS* v. 13 f). The Dead Sea group practised the ' adoption ' of youths for instruction, and the closeness of the similarities has led some scholars to believe that John was one of these, and that he may have spent his youth as a novice of the community, later separating from it. But this is of course only a hypothesis.

In the wilderness ' the word of God came to John ' (Lk 3^{2}). John was the last of the prophets; he prepared the way for the final coming of God. In the Synoptics one can perceive a tendency to equate him with the expected Elijah (Mt 11^{14} 17$^{10-12}$, Lk 1^{17}). In the Fourth Gospel (1$^{19-22}$) he is simply the ' voice ' of Is 40^{3} and denies identity with either Elijah or the Messiah.

John's preaching was prophetic in its pronouncement of judgment against the Jewish community because of its moral delinquency. The Synoptic Gospels (Mt 3$^{1-12}$, Mk 1$^{1-8}$, Lk 3$^{1-20}$) tell of the stirring effects of his preaching in ever-widening circles (Mt 3^{15}), and give a summary of his message. It is probable that, in the course of his successful six months' ministry, John moved northwards along the then more thickly populated valley of the Jordan, proclaiming the coming of the Kingdom to the crowds that flocked to hear him from ' all the region about the Jordan ' (Lk 3^{3}); once at least (Jn 10^{40}) he crossed the river (cf G. Dalman, *Sacred Sites and Ways* (1935), pp. 87–93; and see BETHANY, SALIM). Like the great prophets, John insisted that sincere repentance was the only adequate preparation for the imminent advent. Descent from Abraham by itself was meaningless (Lk 3^{8}). Responsibility for the poor, honesty, and humaneness (Lk 3$^{10-14}$) were among the ways in which sincerity of repentance might be expressed. The axe was already ' laid to the root of the trees ' (Lk 3^{9}); but those bringing forth the fruits of repentance would be spared. Whereas the ' trees of the forest ' are often a simile for the Gentiles, fruit trees, as here, refer to the children of Israel; the imminent judgment will separate the complacent from the penitent. The ' threshing floor ' (Lk 3^{17}) scene, with its separation of wheat from chaff, which has a long history of development as a metaphor for the last judgment (Is 41^{15}, Jer 51^{33}, 2 Es 4$^{30, 38-39}$), is also employed of a Divine sifting in the house of Israel. The burning of the chaff, not an agricultural practice in the holy land, further strikes the eschatological note (Lk 3$^{15-18}$) in the Baptist's message.

The baptism of John, administered to all who responded to his preaching, was ' a baptism of repentance for the forgiveness of sins ' (Mk 1^{4}). It was the initiation rite of a gathering messianic community awaiting the baptism ' with the Holy Spirit ' (Lk 3^{16}). The antecedents for John's baptism can all be found in Jewish religious practice. Like the ' proselyte baptism ' for converts to Judaism, it admitted its recipients to a new community, a fellowship of repentance announcing and awaiting the coming of God. Like the rites of the scapegoat and the sprinkling of blood on the Jewish Day of Atonement (Lv 16; cf the Tractate *Yoma* in the Mishnah), its purpose was the forgiveness of sins. However, as in the rites of Atonement, this forgiveness is conditional upon true repentance, and, for John, would be made effective by the messianic advent. It was neither a rite of individual regeneration of the type found among the later Mandaeans or other Gnostic sects (cf C. H. Kraeling, *John the Baptist*, pp. 106 ff), nor one that simply marked a certain degree of individual moral and ethical achievement in those who received it, as Josephus implies (*Ant.* XVIII. v. 2 [117]). John's baptism, like his preaching, was preparatory. It was communal rather than individual and its context was eschatological. In the OT the metaphor of washing with water was symbolic both of man's repentance and reformation and of the divine cleansing in forgiveness (Is 1^{15f}, Ezk 36^{25}, Jer 2^{22} 4^{14}, Zec 13^{1}).

Jesus also was baptized by John (Mt 3^{13ff}, Mk 1^{9ff}, Lk 3^{21f}), though He did not come confessing sin as did all other men (Mt 3^{6}). The Baptist intimates that, as a sign of repentance, His baptism was superfluous for Jesus (Lk 3^{14}); but in insisting upon it Jesus endorses the ministry and community of John as the true form of eschatological preparation. The act marked Jesus' consecration to His messianic work and His identification of Himself with sinners. At His baptism Jesus received the Holy Spirit as a sign that in Him the community of realization suspended John's community of preparation. Jesus was the one ' mightier ' (Mk 1^{7}) who would baptize with the Holy Spirit and with fire (Lk 3^{16}). Whereas John's baptism was a sign of moral cleansing, the waters of Christ's baptism would be a vivifying flood bearing God's redemption (cf Is 44^{3}, Ezk 47^{7ff}).

The Synoptic narrative of the imprisonment and murder of John yields incidental evidence of his greatness as a prophet. There were some who accounted for the mighty works of Jesus by saying, 'John the baptizer has been raised from the dead' (Mk 6^{14}).

Josephus (*Ant. loc. cit.*) makes the preaching of John the cause of his execution and says nothing of his reproof of **Antipas** for his adultery with his brother's wife (Mk 6^{18}). But he may well have deleted the matter for prudential reasons, just as he seeks to avoid adding to the reputation of the Jews for tumultuousness by presenting the Baptist as a preacher of ethical reform rather than of eschatological preparation. While Herod's fear of political trouble was a real factor in his imprisonment of John, as Josephus intimates, it is not at all unlikely that, as the evangelists report, the Baptist had incurred the personal resentment of Herod and, especially, of **Herodias,** his brother Philip's wife.

The last mention of John in the Gospels (Mt 21^{26}, Mk 11^{32}, Lk 20^{6}) shows that Herod had good cause to fear the popular temper. John's influence must have been permanent as well as widespread when the chief priests were afraid of being stoned if they slighted him. After the transfiguration our Lord alluded to the sufferings of John, as He endeavoured to teach His disciples the lesson of His cross: 'I tell you that Elijah has come, and they did to him whatever they pleased' (Mk 9^{13}).

J. C. R.

JOHN, EPISTLES OF.—The three Epistles known by this name have usually, and certainly from the 2nd cent., been attributed to the Apostle John, and were recognized as canonical in the 3rd cent. Their obvious similarity in style and diction indicates a close relation between them, but their internal character and the external evidence in their favour are so different that it will be better to deal with them separately.

I. FIRST EPISTLE.—**1. Authorship.**—The Epistle ranked from the first among the *Homologoumena,* and the testimony in favour of its authenticity is early, varied, and explicit. Its great similarity to the Fourth Gospel in phraseology and general characteristics made it natural to attribute the two documents to the same author; and few questions, or none, were raised upon the subject in the early Church.

(1) So far as *external evidence* is concerned, Polycarp, writing about A.D. 115 to the Philippians, quotes the words, 'For whosoever does not confess that Jesus Christ is come in the flesh is antichrist,' with evident allusion to 1 Jn 4^{3}, though the author is not named. Polycarp was a disciple of John, as his own disciple Irenaeus informs us. Eusebius several times refers to this Epistle, saying (*HE* v. 20) that Papias used it and (v. 8) that Irenaeus made free use of it. The passages 1 Jn 2^{18} and 5^{1} are expressly attributed by Irenaeus to the Apostle. According to the Muratorian Canon (lines 26–34), Epistle and Gospel were closely associated: 'What wonder that John makes so many references to the Fourth Gospel in his Epistle, saying of himself'—and then follows a quotation of 1 Jn 1^{1}. Clement of Alexandria at the close of the 2nd cent. quotes 5^{16} as the words of 'John in his larger Epistle.' Tertullian quotes the language of 1^{1} as that of the Apostle John, and Origen definitely refers the words of 3^{8} to 'John in his catholic Epistle.' All the ancient versions include the Epistle among those canonically recognized, including the Peshitta and the Old Latin. The only exceptions to this practically universal recognition of its genuineness and authenticity are the group in Asia Minor, *c* A.D. 170, vaguely called *Alogi,* because they rejected the doctrine of the Logos, and Marcion, who accepted no books of NT except the Gospel of Luke, drastically revised, and the Epistles of Paul.

(2) The *similarity of diction and ideas* between Gospel and Epistle is so close that it cannot be accidental, and it cannot escape the notice of the most superficial reader.

(*a*) The repeated use, in a characteristic way, of such cardinal words as Life, Love, Truth, Light, and Darkness; the recurrence of phrases which in both documents figure as watchwords—'to be of the truth,' 'of the devil,' 'of the world'; 'the only begotten Son,' 'the Word,' 'knowing God,' 'walking in the light,' 'overcoming the world,' and the special use of the word 'believe,' speak for themselves. The use of literary parallels always requires care; but in this case the similarity is so close as incontestably to establish a connexion between the two documents, whilst the handling of the same vocabulary is so free as irresistibly to suggest, not that the writer of the Gospel borrowed from the Epistle, or vice versa, but that the two writings proceed from the same hand or circle, though which came first is uncertain.

(*b*) Moreover, the theological ideas are much the same, with only slight shades of difference, for example the eternal relation subsisting between the Father and the Son, the sending of the Son into the world by the Father, and His Incarnation and complete identification with human nature ('flesh'); the symbolic or mystical significance of the Water and the Blood (of Christ); Christ the Revealer of God and of Himself as the Son of God, one with the Father, not only Divine but 'God,' the Saviour of the world; also the Spirit of Truth, the Paraclete, the Counsellor or Helper; the great triad of concepts, viewed almost as hypostases, viz. Life, Light, and Love; the sharp, almost dualistic, distinction between God and the world, and the quasi-gnostic view of the latter; the judgment upon the world; the overcoming of the world; the conflict between God and the devil, 'the evil one'; the further dualism—or at least strong contrast—between love and hate, light and darkness, life and death, truth and lies (contrasts often emphasized in ancient religious literature); the devil portrayed as a liar and a murderer.

Turning from these theological and cosmological conceptions there are the more purely religious: believers are *born of God,* or are *from God,* or from or of *the Truth*; they dwell or abide or remain in God, either the Father or the Son; at the same time God dwells in them, *i.e. in us*; they (*i.e.* we) possess the knowledge of God—a point of great importance in view of the growing Gnostic crisis with its newly advanced view of salvation by supernatural knowledge in lieu of either simple obedience to the will of God or by means of divine grace, as in the earlier *kērygma*; the conception of 'doing' the truth; the new commandment which is at the same time the old and original one, 'from the beginning'; the idea of keeping or obeying the commandments or 'walking' in the truth, *i.e.* following the example of Christ. Still other common ideas could be listed; these are enough to show the vast area of agreement.

At the same time there are differences. The style of the Epistle is heavier, more repetitive, less varied, and as a rule more authoritative and dogmatic than that of the Gospel. Moreover, the Epistle contains a number of ideas that are lacking in the Gospel: that of *koinōnia,* fellowship, the close relation between love for God and love for the brethren, and the connexion of knowledge of God with obedience to God; the stronger emphasis on moral conduct; the stress upon expiation and purification through Christ or His blood; the forgiveness of sins, and the limitation set on forgiveness; the attitude of Christians to sins, and the spirit of boldness; the concepts of the Parousia and the Antichrist, and the firm opposition to false teachers. These may be accounted for by the practical aim of the Epistle; the actual milieu may be the same as that in which the Gospel was written or appeared.

At the same time there are ideas fundamental to the Gospel which are lacking in the Epistle: the idea of the Logos (though see 1^{1}); the Resurrection (in the full sense of the *Anastasis*); and the Glory (Doxa) of a heavenly being or a heavenly existence. Moreover, there are certain words common to the gospel tradition which do not appear in the Johannine epistles: be raised, rise again, Kingdom (of God), destroy, save, judge, Judgment, minister, Son of Man—words and concepts which are characteristic of the evangelic style and of the traditional *kērygma* of the Christian faith. Equally striking is the absence from the epistles of any

JOHN, EPISTLES OF

quotation from the OT—though there are echoes (*e.g.* the extraordinary one in 2^{14} from Pr 20^{29}).

The opening words of the First Epistle inescapably remind the reader of the opening of the Gospel with its 'hymn' celebrating the Logos. One may view it as likewise poetry, interpolated or supplemented with comments :

'That which was from the beginning,
Which we have heard,
Which we have seen with our eyes,
Which we have looked upon—

and [even] touched with our hands !—[it is] concerning the Word of Life [that we are writing you, for] the life was made manifest, and we saw it, and testify to it, and proclaim to you the eternal life which was with the Father and was made manifest to us—that which we have seen and heard we proclaim also to you, so that you may have fellowship with us ; and our fellowship is with the Father and His Son Jesus Christ' (1^{1-3}). This is more than an echo of Jn 1^{1-14} ; it is coin of the same mintage and standard.

As in the case of the Gospel, much of the exegesis and interpretation since the 18th cent. has been devoted to argumentation over questions of date, locality, and authorship. But the most important questions have to do with the character and purpose of the Epistle. The author's handling of Gnosticism, Docetism, and his identification of the heretics with Antichrist (2^{18}) make it very unlikely that John the son of Zebedee could have been the author. His self-designation as 'the elder' in Epistles 2 and 3 seems to many modern scholars wholly incompatible with apostleship.

The chief ground of the objections raised against the Johannine authorship of the First Epistle has been the alleged references to heretical modes of thought which belong to a later age. Docetism, Gnosticism, and even Montanism are, it is said, directly or indirectly rebuked, and these forms of error do not belong to the Apostolic period. The reply was threefold. (*a*) Those who ascribe the Epistle to John the Apostle do not date it before the last decade of the 1st cent., when the Apostolic age was passing into the sub-Apostolic. (*b*) No references to full-grown Gnosticism and other errors as they were known in the middle of the 2nd cent. can here be found. But (*c*) it can be shown from other sources that the germs of these heresies, the general tendencies which resulted afterwards in fully developed systems, existed in the Church for at least a generation before the period in question, and at the time named were both rife and mischievous.

The main points at issue are : the doctrine of the Logos ; the form of the rebuke given to the antichrists ; the references to 'knowledge' and 'anointing' ; the insistence upon the coming of Christ in the flesh, in condemnation of Docetic error ; the distinction between mortal and venial sins ; and some minor objections. But none of these is definite or explicit enough to require a date very much later than A.D. 100. The Epistle is indeed indirectly polemic in its character. While constructive in thought, the passing references made in it to opponents of the truth are strong enough to make it clear that the opposition was active and dangerous. But there is nothing to show that any of those condemned as enemies of Christ had more fully developed tendencies than, for example, Cerinthus is known to have manifested in his Christology at the end of the 1st cent. Jewish or at least Judaizing Gnosticism had appeared much earlier than this, as is evidenced by the Epistles to the Colossians and the Pastoral Epistles. In fact the Jewish origin of Gnosticism is now stressed by interpreters—as it was by the Church Fathers. The use of the words 'Paraclete' (2^{1}) and 'expiation' (2^{2}), and the way in which the coming of Christ is mentioned in 2^{28}, have also been brought forward as proofs of divergence from the teaching of the Gospel, on very slender and unconvincing grounds.

2. Place and Date.—Whilst very little evidence is forthcoming to enable us to fix exactly either of these, the general consensus of ancient testimony points very decidedly to Ephesus during the last few years of the 1st cent. Irenaeus (*adv. Haer.* iii. 1) testifies to the production of the Gospel by St. John during his residence in Asia ; presumably the author of the Epistles, even if he was not identical with the author of the Gospel, lived there also. But we have no positive evidence as to the place of writing. Some scholars now suspect that the Gospel and the Epistles were all written in Egypt (see JOHN, GOSPEL OF).

3. Form and Destination.—This document has some of the characteristics of a letter, and in some respects it is more like a theological treatise or homiletical essay. It may perhaps best be described as an Encyclical or Pastoral Epistle. It was addressed to a circle of readers, as is shown by the words, 'I am writing to you,' 'beloved,' and 'little children,' but it was not restricted to any particular church, nor does it contain any specific personal messages. The term 'catholic epistle' was used from very early times to indicate this form of composition, but in all probability the author had specific churches in mind. A reference in Augustine to 3^{2} as taken from John's 'Epistle to the Parthians' has given rise to much conjecture, but the title has seldom been taken seriously in its literal meaning. It is quite possible that there is some mistake in the text of the passage (*Quaest. Evang.* ii. 39).

4. Outline and Contents.—Whether Gospel or Epistle was written first, the relation between the two is perfectly clear. The author of the Gospel aims to show that the foundations of Christian faith and doctrine have a historical foundation, in the life of Jesus ; the author of the First Epistle traces the consequences of Christian belief in Christian practice. In both writings the same great central truths are exhibited, in the same form and almost in the same words ; but in the Gospel they are traced to their fount and origin ; in the Epistle they are followed out to their necessary results in the spirit and conduct of Christians in the world. 'The substance of the Gospel is a commentary on the Epistle ; the Epistle is (so to speak) the condensed moral and practical application of the Gospel' (Bp. Westcott).

The style is simple, but baffling in its very simpilcity. The sentences are easy for a child to read, their meaning is difficult for a wise man fully to analyse. So with the sequence of thought. Each statement follows very naturally upon the preceding, but when the relation of paragraphs is to be explained, and the plan or structure of the whole composition is to be described, systematization becomes difficult, if not impossible. Logical analysis is not, however, always the best mode of exposition, and if the writer has not consciously mapped out into exact subdivisions the ground he covers, he follows out to their issues two or three leading thoughts which he keeps consistently in view throughout. The theme is fellowship with the Father and the Son, realised in love of the brethren.

The Epistle may be outlined as follows :—

Theme and purpose of the Epistle (1^{1-4}).

I. The true faith contrasted with the false (1^{5}–2^{27}).

(*a*) The true Christian faith and its evidences (1^{5}–2^{17}). First criterion : the state of forgiveness (1^{5}–2^{2}). Second criterion : obedience (2^{3-6}). Third criterion : love (2^{7-11}).

A rhapsody on forgiveness (2^{12-14}).

'Love not the world'—which is passing away (2^{15-17}).

(*b*) The false teaching which threatens the church (2^{18-27}). The prediction of the Antichrist is being fulfilled (2^{18-20}). The Truth versus the Lie (2^{21-27}).

II. The life of the Church during the interval before the Judgment (2^{28}–4^{21}). Loyalty to Christ, who is about to appear (2^{28}–3^{3}).

(*a*) The test of true righteousness, and the safeguard against sin (3^{4-12}). The Christian brotherhood in a malevolent world (3^{13-18}). Christian certainty in evil times (3^{19-24}).

(*b*) The test of true inspiration (4^{1-6}).
(*c*) The test of brotherly love (4^{7-21}).

III. The assurance of victory (5^{1-21}). The mutual support of faith and love (5^{1-13}). The assurance of answer to prayer (5^{14-17}). The ultimate basis of certainty (5^{18-21}).

The writer does not, as has been asserted, 'ramble without method,' nor is the Epistle a 'shapeless mass.' The Epistle—or homily—is not rigidly analytical in arrangement, nor does it move forward: as in many sermons, including the discourses in the Fourth Gospel, the principle of arrangement is that of 'concentric circles' or rather a continuous spiral, returning upon itself and repeatedly echoing, reconsidering, or re-emphasizing the same truths. The author is no dreamer; more practical instruction is not to be found anywhere in the NT. But his exhortations are not detailed: he is concerned with principles of conduct, the minute application of which he leaves to the individual conscience. The enunciation of principles, however, is uncompromising and very searching. His standpoint is that of the ideal Christian life, not of the effort to attain it. One who is born of God 'cannot sin'; the 'love of God is perfected' in the believer, and perfect love casts out fear. The assured tone of the Epistle allows no room for doubt or hesitation or conflict; one who is guided by its teaching has no need to pray, 'Help thou my unbelief.' The spirit of truth and the spirit of error are in sharp antagonism, and the touchstone which distinguishes them must be resolutely applied. The 'world,' the 'evil one,' and 'antichrist' are to be repelled absolutely and to the uttermost: the writer and those whom he represents can say, 'We know that we are of God, and the whole world in the power of the evil one' (5^{19}). Bright light casts deep shadows, and the true Christian of the Epistle walks in the blaze of gospel day. One who knows the true God and has eternal life cannot but 'guard himself from idols.' This is the key to his 'perfectionism.'

The writer of such an Epistle is appropriately called the Apostle of love. Yet the title taken by itself is misleading. He is the Apostle equally of righteousness and of faith. He 'loved well because he hated—hated the wickedness which hinders loving.' There is a stern ring, implying however no harshness, about the very exhortations to love, which shows how indissolubly it is to be identified with immutable and inviolable righteousness. If to this Epistle we owe the great utterance, 'God is Love'—here twice repeated ($4^{8, 16}$), but found nowhere else in Scripture—to it we owe also the sublime declaration, 'God is Light and in him is no darkness at all' (1^{5}). The Epistle, like the Gospel, makes it abundantly clear that the spring of Christian love and the secret of Christian victory over evil are alike to be found in 'believing': in the immovable and ineradicable faith that Jesus Christ, the Son of God, has come in the flesh, and that in Him the love of God to man is so manifested and assured that those who trust Him already possess eternal life, together with all that it implies of strength and joy, and all that flows from it of obedience and loving service.

Textual questions can hardly be touched upon in this article. But it is perhaps worth pointing out that whilst the corrected text restores the latter half of 2^{23}, which in AV is printed in italics as doubtful, there can now be no question that the passage (5^{7f}) referring to the three witnesses in heaven, as read in AV, does not form part of the Epistle. The words are wanting in all Greek MSS except a few of exceedingly late date; nor are they found in the majority of the Greek Fathers, or in any ancient version except the Latin. They undoubtedly form a gloss which found its way into the text from Latin sources, presumably introduced by 4th cent. Spanish Priscillianists; and the insertion really breaks the connexion of thought in the paragraph.

II. The Second Epistle.—The Second and Third Epistles of St. John are distinguished from the First by their brevity, the absence of dogmatic teaching, and their private and personal character. They are found among the *Antilegomena* of the early Church in their relation to the Canon; apparently not because they were unknown, or because their authorship was questioned, but because their nature made them unsuitable for use in the public worship of the Church. The Muratorian Canon (A.D. 180) refers to two Epistles of John as received in the Catholic Church, and Irenaeus about the same date specifically quotes 2 Jn ^{10f} as coming from 'John the disciple of the Lord.' He also quotes v.^{7} apparently as occurring in the First Epistle. Clement of Alexandria by a mention of John's 'larger Epistle' shows that he was acquainted with at least one other shorter letter. Origen states that the two shorter letters were not accepted by all as genuine, but he adds that 'both together do not contain a hundred lines.' Dionysius of Alexandria appeals to them, adding that John's name was not affixed to them, but that they were signed 'the presbyter.' They are omitted from the Peshitta Version, and Eusebius describes them as disputed by some, but in the later 4th cent. they were fully acknowledged and received into the Canon. The Second Epistle, therefore, though not universally accepted from the first came in time to be widely recognized as apostolic in date and—presumably—in origin. The similarity in style to the First Epistle is very marked. Jerome among the Fathers, Erasmus at the time of the Reformation, and many modern critics, have ascribed the Epistle to 'John the Presbyter' of Ephesus, but there is no early reference to such a person except the statement of Papias quoted by Eusebius and referred to in a previous article (see John, Gospel of).

Much discussion has arisen concerning the person addressed. The two leading opinions are (1) that the words 'elect lady and her children' are to be understood literally of a Christian matron in Ephesus and her family; and (2) that a church personified, with its constituent members, was intended. Jerome in ancient times took the latter view, and in modern times it has been supported by most scholars. The exhortations given are more suited to a community; 'the children of your elect sister' can be understood only of a sister church; this mode of describing a church personified is not unusual (cf 1 P 5^{13}). On the other hand, it is urged that this mystical interpretation destroys the simplicity and natural meaning of the letter (see especially vv.$^{5, 10}$), that the church being constituted of members, the distinction between the 'lady' and her 'children' would disappear, and that if the lady be a private person of influence the parallel with the form of salutation to another private person in the Third Epistle is complete. This hypothesis still leaves difficulty in the exact interpretation of the words *Eklektē Kyria*. Some would take both these as the proper names of the person addressed; others take the former as her name, so that she would be 'the lady Eklektē,' others would render 'to the elect Kyria,' whilst the majority accept, in spite of its indefiniteness, the translation of AV, RV, and RSV. On the whole, this course is to be preferred, though the view that a church is intended not only is tenable but has much in its favour. The fact that the early churches so often gathered in a house, and that there was so strong a personal and individual element in their community-life, makes the analogy between a primitive church and a large and influential family to be very close (*e.g.* the household of Domitilla at Rome).

It remains only to say that, as in style, so in spirit, the similarity to 1 John is very noticeable. The same emphasis is laid on love, on obedience, on fellowship with the Father and the Son, and the inestimable importance of maintaining and abiding in the truth. The same strong resentment is manifested against deceivers and the Antichrist, and the same intensity of feeling against unbelievers or false teachers (the Docetists, v.^{7}), who are not to be received into the house of a believer, or to have any kindly greeting accorded them. Whether the Epistle was actually addressed to a private person or to a Christian community, it furnishes a most interesting picture of the life, the faith, and the dangers and temptations of the primitive Christians (presumably in Asia Minor), and it contains wholesome and uncompromising, not harsh and intolerant, exhortation, such as Christian Churches in all ages may well lay to heart.

III. Third Epistle.—The two shorter Epistles of St. John were called by Jerome 'twin sisters.' They appear to have been recognized together at least from the time of Dionysius of Alexandria, and they are mentioned together by Eusebius (*HE* iii. 25), who refers to the Epistles 'called the second and third of John, whether they belong to the Evangelist or to another person of the same name.' They are found together in the Old Latin Version, are both omitted from the Peshitta, and were included together in the lists of canonical books at the end of the 4th cent. by the Council of Laodicea and the Third Council of Carthage. References to the Third Epistle and quotations from it are naturally very few. It is short, it was written to a private person, it does not discuss doctrine, and its counsels and messages are almost entirely personal. But its close relationship to the Second Epistle is very obvious, and the two form companion pictures of value from the point of view of history; and St. John's Third Epistle, like St. Paul's personal letter to Philemon, is not without use for general edification.

The person to whom it is addressed is quite unknown. The name **Gaius** (Lat. *Caius*) is very common, and three other persons so called are mentioned in NT, viz. Gaius of Corinth (1 Co 1[14]; cf Ro 16[23]); Gaius of Derbe (Ac 20[4]); and Gaius of Macedonia (Ac 19[29]) (see Gaius). A bishop of Pergamum, appointed by the Apostle John and mentioned in the *Apostolic Consitutions*, was also called Gaius, and some critics have identified him with the elder's correspondent. This is, however, a mere conjecture, and the letter is addressed, not to a church official, but to a private layman, apparently of some wealth and influence. It is written in a free and natural style, and deals with the case of some of those travelling evangelists who figured so prominently in the primitive Church, and to whom reference is made in the *Didache* and elsewhere. Some of these, perhaps commissioned by the author himself, had visited the church to which Gaius belonged, had been hospitably entertained by him, and helped forward on their journey, probably with material assistance. But **Diotrephes** (q.v.)—an official of the church, perhaps its bishop or a leading elder—who loved power, asserted himself arrogantly, and was disposed to resist the author's authority—perhaps the authority behind the two other epistles. He declined to receive these worthy men who at their own charges were preaching the gospel in the district. He also stirred up feeling against them, and at least threatened to excommunicate any members of the church who entertained them. The evil example of Diotrephes is held up for condemnation, whilst in contrast to him, a certain **Demetrius** (q.v.) is praised, whose reputation in the Church was excellent, who had won the confidence of the elder, and—higher commendation still—had 'testimony from the truth itself' (v.[12]; cf the language of Jn 21[24]). Tried by the strictest and most searching test of all, the sterling metal of Demetrius' character rang true. Full information is not given us as to all the circumstances of the case. Perhaps Diotrephes was not wholly to be blamed. It was quite necessary, as the *Didache* shows us, to inquire carefully into the character of these itinerant preachers. Some of them were mercenary in their aims, and the conflict of opinion in this instance may have had some connexion with the current controversies between Jewish and Gentile Christians or between Gnostics or Docetists and the simple Christian believers. But it is the spirit of Diotrephes that is blameworthy, and the little picture here drawn of primitive ecclesiastical communities with their flaws and their excellences, their worthy members and ambitious officers, their generous hosts and kindly helpers, and the absent elder who bears the care of all the churches and is about to pay to this one a visit of fatherly and friendly inspection, is full of interest and instruction. W. T. D.—F. C. G.

JOHN, GOSPEL OF.—*Introductory*.—The Fourth Gospel is unique among the books of the NT. In its combination of minute historical detail with lofty spiritual teaching, in its testimony to the Person and work of the Lord Jesus Christ, and in the preparation it makes for the foundation of Christian doctrine, it stands alone. Its influence upon the thought and life of the Christian Church has been proportionately deep and far-reaching. It is no disparagement of other inspired Scriptures to say that no other book of the Bible has left such a mark at the same time upon the profoundest Christian thinkers, and upon simple-minded believers at large. At the same time we must recognize that we are not dependent on the Fourth Gospel for the basic historical facts upon which Christianity rests, or for the fundamental doctrines of the Person and work of Christ. The Synoptic Gospels and the Epistles of Paul are more than sufficient to establish the basis of the Christian faith, which on any hypothesis must have spread over a large part of the Roman Empire before this book was written. On any theory of authorship, the document in question is of great significance and value in the history of the Church. Those who do not accept it as historical have still to reckon with the fact of its composition, and to take account of its presence in and influence upon the Church of the 2nd cent.

Hence it is a matter of the very first importance to determine its character and purpose, and the historicity of its underlying traditions. It is rarely maintained, by scholars to-day, that it was the work of an eye-witness, belonging to the innermost circle of Jesus' disciples, who after a long interval wrote a trustworthy record—indeed the most trustworthy record—of what he had heard and seen, superior to the record of any other evangelist, and interpreted through the mellowing medium of half a century of Christian experience and service; nor, on the other hand, is it now viewed as a treatise in speculative theology, cast in the form of an imaginative biography of Jesus, dating from the second or third decade of the 2nd cent., and testifying only to the form which the new religion was then taking under the widely altered circumstances of the developing Church. Instead, it is now more commonly held that although John is the latest of the Gospels, probably coming from a date very late in the 1st or early in the 2nd cent., its value and importance are not to be determined by considerations of date and authorship, but by its total character. There are passages in this Gospel which read like the recollections of an eye-witness, and others which seem impossible to accept as historically credible, 'both because of their inherent improbability, and because they bear the marks of long reflection and meditation upon the earlier tradition' (C. K. Barrett). The only safe affirmations about the Gospel are those made on 'the objective but impersonal ground of its contents.'

Too much of the criticism and exegesis of the Fourth Gospel in the past has been limited to the defence of an early date, or the Johannine authorship, or the 'authenticity' of its historical tradition. Modern criticism now centres in the exposition of the character of the book, its place in ancient religious literature and specifically in early Christian literature, the central purpose of its author, and the type of religious mind or thought which he represents, whether mystical or theological or poetic—and whoever he was, wherever he lived.

According to the generally accepted tradition, extending from the third quarter of the 2nd cent. to the beginning of the 19th, John the Apostle, the son of Zebedee, was held to be the author of the Gospel, the three Epistles that went by his name, and the Apocalypse. This tradition, so far as the Gospel was concerned, was unbroken and almost unchallenged, the one exception being formed by an obscure and doubtful sect, or class of unbelievers, called Alogi by Epiphanius, who attributed the Gospel and the Apocalypse to Cerinthus ! From the beginning of the 19th cent., however, and especially after the publication of Bretschneider's *Probabilia* in 1820, the traditional belief has often been given up in favour of various hypotheses, *e.g.* that which attributes the Gospel to an Ephesian elder or an Alexandrian Christian philosopher belonging to the first half of the 2nd cent. F. C. Baur of Tübingen, in whose theories of doctrinal development this document held an important place, fixed its date about A.D. 170, but this view has long been given up as untenable. Theodore Keim, who argued strongly against the Johannine authorship, at first adopted the date A.D. 100–115, but afterwards regarded A.D. 130 as more probable.

Since about 1910 the view has steadily gained ground in English-speaking countries that the Gospel belongs not only to a later date than the generation of the Apostles, but to a later milieu. Its whole outlook, and the problems with which it deals, are those of the late 1st or 2nd cent., chiefly the struggle with Docetic Gnosticism. Moreover, its range of thought is far wider than that of the Synoptics, and its affinities are found not only in Judaism but also in Hellenism, in Philo and the Hermetica, in Gnosticism, and even in Mandaism, whose documents are far later in date but contain very old religious language and ideas. Finally, the very structure of the Gospel reflects the thought, discussion, and debate of the Church in a new and different environment (see the Outline, below under **3**). For a long time it was held that John supplemented, corrected, or to some extent even supplanted the Synoptic tradition, with which he was of course familiar. But it now appears that his knowledge of the Synoptics was either very slight or unimportant. As P. Gardner-Smith demonstrated in *St John and the Synoptic Gospels* (1938), the author's use of the earlier Gospels was usually confined to incidental or peripheral terms—those which would be used in any telling of the story; while the thought of the Gospel, *i.e.* its interpretation of the narratives, is wholly different.

1. External Evidence.—It is not questioned that considerably before the close of the 2nd cent. the four Gospels, substantially as we have them, were accepted as authoritative in the Christian Church. This is proved by the testimony of Irenaeus, bishop of Lyons, in Gaul, writing about A.D. 180; Theophilus, bishop of Antioch, about A.D. 170; Clement, head of the catechetical school in Alexandria, about A.D. 190; and Tertullian, the eloquent African Father, who wrote at the end of the century, and who quotes freely from all the Gospels by name. The full and explicit evidence of the Muratorian Canon may also be dated about A.D. 180. Irenaeus assumes the Johannine authorship of the Fourth Gospel as generally accepted and unquestioned. He expressly states that after the publication of the other three Gospels, 'John the disciple of the Lord, who also leaned upon His breast, himself also published the Gospel, while he was dwelling at Ephesus in Asia.' He tells us that he himself when a boy had heard from the lips of Polycarp his reminiscences of 'his familiar intercourse with John and the rest of those that had seen the Lord.' He dwells in mystical fashion upon the significance of the number four, and characterizes the Fourth Gospel as corresponding to the 'flying eagle' among the living creatures of Ezk 1^{10} and 10^{14}. (The order of these identifications, it may be noted, is that of the writing of the Gospels, as many now hold, viz. Mark, Luke, Matthew, John. John was always recognized as the latest of the four.) Theophilus of Antioch quotes it as follows: 'John says, In the beginning was the Word, and the Word was with God' (*Aut.* 22). The Muratorian Fragment, which gives a list of the canonical books recognized in the Western Church of the period, ascribes the Fourth Gospel to 'John, one of the disciples,' and whilst recognizing that 'in the single books of the Gospels different principles are taught,' the writer adds that they all alike confirm the faith of believers by their agreement in their teaching about Christ's birth, passion, death, resurrection, and twofold advent. Clement of Alexandria, in handing down 'the tradition of the Elders from the first,' says that 'John, last of all, having observed that the bodily things had been exhibited in the Gospels, exhorted by his friends and inspired by the Spirit, produced a spiritual [=allegorical?] Gospel' (Euseb. *HE* vi. 14). Tertullian, among other testimonies, shows his opinion of the authorship and his discrimination of the character of the Gospels by saying, 'Among the Apostles, John and Matthew form the faith within us; among the companions of the Apostles, Luke and Mark renovate it' (*adv. Marc.* iv. 2). These views cannot be taken as the considered judgment of later critics and historians; they represent only the popular homiletical and apologetic use of current Church tradition—as tradition, its value is not inconsiderable. And for some reason, obviously, the Gospel and three Epistles were attributed to the Apostle John, from an early date.

But was this clearly expressed and widespread belief of the Church well based? First of all it must be said that the personal link supplied by Irenaeus is of itself so important as to be almost conclusive, unless very strong counter-reasons can be alleged. It was impossible that he should be mistaken as to the general drift of Polycarp's teaching, and Polycarp had learned directly from John himself. On the broad issue of John's ministry in Asia and his composition of a Gospel, this testimony is of the first importance. (See the article JOHN THE APOSTLE.) The suggestion that confusion had arisen in his mind between the Apostle and a certain 'Presbyter John' of Asia is exceedingly unlikely. As Theodor Zahn held, it is only a modern hypothesis for escaping attribution of the Gospel to the Apostle John. At the same time, it cannot be said that Irenaeus's views are infallible. The NT has nothing to say of John's residence in Asia, and the very earliest evidence, in the *Acts of John*, *c* A.D. 150–160, is Gnostic. Evidently the Gnostics were not slow to claim John as one of themselves. The earliest commentary on the Gospel was by Heracleon, a Gnostic.

It is quite true that in the first half of the 2nd cent. the references to the Gospel are neither so direct nor so abundant as might have been expected. The question whether Justin Martyr knew, and recognized, our Gospels as such has been much debated. His references to the Gospel narrative are very numerous, and the coincidences between the form of the records which he quotes and our Gospels are often close and striking, but he mentions no authors' names. In his first *Apol.* ch. 61 (A.D. 155), however, we read, 'For Christ also said, Unless you are born again, you will not enter the kingdom of heaven,' which would appear to imply, though it does not prove, an acquaintance with the Fourth Gospel. Other references to Christ as 'only begotten Son' and the 'Word' are suggestive. The modern recovery of Tatian's *Diatessaron* (*c* A.D. 170) makes it certain that that 'harmony' of the Gospels began with the words, 'In the beginning was the Word,' and that the whole of the Fourth Gospel was interwoven into its substance. The Epistle of Polycarp to the Philippians (before A.D. 120) apparently quotes 1 John in the words, 'For every one who does not acknowledge that Jesus Christ has come in the flesh is antichrist,' but no express citation is made. The Epistles of Ignatius (*c* A.D. 110) apparently show traces of the Fourth Gospel in their references to 'living water,' 'children of light,' Christ as 'the Word' and as 'the door,' but these are not conclusive. Papias may have known and used this Gospel, as Irenaeus seems to imply (*adv. Haer.* 36); and Eusebius distinctly says that he 'used testimonies from the First Epistle of John' (*HE* iii. 39).

Some of the most noteworthy testimonies to the use of the Gospel in the former part of the 2nd cent. are drawn from heretical writings. It is certain that Heracleon of the Valentinian school of Gnostics knew and quoted the Gospel as a recognized authority, and it would even appear that he wrote an elaborate commentary on the whole Gospel. Origen quotes him as misapprehending the text, 'No one has seen God at any time.' Hippolytus in his *Refutation of all Heresies* (vi. 30) proves that Valentinus (*c* A.D. 140) quoted Jn 10[8], 'The Saviour says, All who came before me are thieves and robbers,' and that Basilides a little earlier made distinct reference to Jn 1[9]: 'As it is said in the Gospels, The true light that enlightens every man was coming into the world.' Slighter and more doubtful references are found in the *Clementine Homilies* and other heretical writings, and these go at least some way to show that the peculiar phraseology of the Fourth Gospel was known and appealed to as authoritative in the middle of the 2nd cent. Thus it is clear that between A.D. 150–180 four Gospels were recognized in the Church as inspired writings, read in the assemblies, and generally accepted as authoritative. Also that the fourth of these was with practical unanimity—so far as our evidence permits us to say—ascribed to St. John, as written by him in Asia at the very end of the 1st cent. This acceptance included districts as far apart as Syria and Gaul, Alexandria, Carthage, and Rome. The *prima facie* external evidence is undubitably in favour of Johannine authorship.

But does this carry us all the way back to John the Apostle? And by whom was the claim of Johannine authorship asserted? The silence of the rest of the NT, and the vagueness of the attestation at the end of the Appendix (21[24]), greatly weaken the force of the early patristic testimony. Too many religious books have been written *ad mentem* some revered religious leader or teacher, confident that were he still living this would be what he would say, for us to close our eyes to the possibility of such pseudonymous authorship—which is nevertheless not really pseudonymous, since the author never plainly states that he is John. It is not a case of 'conscious fraud,' as polemical writers used to say. It was a perfectly legitimate and in ancient times a widely practised art of pseudepigraphy—or of anonymity—especially in religious circles; the Bible itself, from the Book of Deuteronomy onward, supplies many examples.

2. Internal Evidence.—There can be no doubt that the Gospel itself claims to have the authority of an eye-witness for many of its statements, and for its general presentation, at least in narrative. The phrase 'We have beheld his glory' (1[14]) is not decisive, though, taken in connexion with 1 Jn 1[1-4], it appears to appeal to first-hand knowledge. There can be no question concerning the general meaning of 19[35], though its detailed exegesis presents difficulties. Surely the author is not claiming himself to have been present, but to be quoting the testimony of one who had been present, at the crucifixion of Jesus. In 21[34] further assurance is given of the accuracy of the disciple who had been an eye-witness of the events. Depending upon the authorship of this verse, either John was the disciple intended, or this was the interpretation placed upon the reference from an early date, presumably from a date almost as early as the Gospel itself. It appears to have been added to the Gospel by others. '*We* know that his witness is true' is probably intended as an endorsement on the part of certain church leaders or others, while the 'I suppose' of v.[25] may indicate still another hand. In addition to these more or less explicit testimonies, notes are freely introduced throughout the Gospel which come, presumably, from a member of the inner circle of Jesus' disciples, though the writer never mentions his own name—or that of his authority. Instead, he alludes to 'the disciple whom Jesus loved' in such a way that by a process of elimination it may be inferred (from chs. 20–21) that John was intended. It is often assumed that the writer thus delicately but unmistakably claims to be that disciple himself. An ordinary pseudonymous writer does not, as a rule, proceed in this fashion. The authority of an honoured name is sometimes claimed by an unknown author, as in the *Ascension of Isaiah* and the *Apocalypse of Baruch*, not fraudulently but as a literary device to give character to his theme. In this case, however, the indirect suggestion either indicates that the Apostle was the authority upon whom the author of the book relied, or else it points to a claim made by some later writer, who threw his own ideas into the form of a (largely imaginary) narrative. This later writer is supposed, by some interpreters, to have been one of the Apostle's own disciples. Thus viewed, there were three stages in the composition of the Gospel: the oral tradition of the Witness, the writing down of this tradition by the author, the identification of the Witness (or, later, of the author) with the Apostle John.

But even this modified view is difficult to maintain. The character of the work, its divergence from the Synoptic tradition and from that presupposed by St. Paul and other apostolic writers, and the problem of fitting such a representation of Christ's life and teaching into the course of development of early Christian thought, make it almost impossible to maintain to-day. There is no question that the book displays a minute knowledge of details which it would seem must have come from an eye-witness who was intimately acquainted, not only with the places and scenes, but with the persons concerned, their characters and motives. No artistic imagination could have enabled a Christian of the 2nd cent. either to insert the minute topographical and other touches which bespeak the eye-witness, or to invent incidents like those recorded in chs. 4 and 9. On the other hand, there is so much in the Gospel which implies a point of view entirely different from that of Christ's immediate contemporaries, and there are so many divergences from the Synoptics in the description of our Lord's ministry—as regards time, place, the manner of Christ's teaching, and particular incidents recorded—as to make it impossible to ascribe it to the son of Zebedee without a full explanation of serious difficulties and discrepancies. But for these two diverse aspects of the same document, there would be no 'Johannine problem.'

It has been usual, following Bishop Westcott, to arrange the evidence in narrowing circles; to show that the author must have been a Jew, a Palestinian, an eye-witness, one of the Twelve, and lastly the Apostle John. It is impossible, however, to array here all the proofs available. It must suffice to say that a close familiarity with Jewish customs and observances, such as could scarcely have been possessed by anyone in A.D. 120, is shown in the account of the Feast of Tabernacles (ch. 7), the Dedication (10[22]), the Jews and Samaritans (4[19f]), conversation with women in public (4[27]), ceremonial pollution (18[28]), and other minute touches, each slight in itself, but taken together of great weight. The numerous references to the Messianic hope in chs. 1, 4, 7, 8, and indeed throughout the Gospel, indicate one who was thoroughly acquainted with Jewish views and expectations from within (but cf Justin Martyr, *c* A.D. 150). Familiarity with the Jewish Scriptures and a free but reverent use of them are apparent throughout. The places mentioned are not such as a stranger would or could have introduced into an imaginary narrative. As examples we may mention Bethany beyond Jordan (1[28]), Aenon (3[23]), Ephraim (11[54]), the treasury (8[20]), the pool of Siloam (9[7]), Solomon's porch (10[23]), the Kidron (18[1]). It is true that difficulties have been raised with regard to some of these, *e.g.* Sychar (4[5]); but modern exploration has in several instances confirmed the writer's accuracy. Still further verisimilitude is now lent by the contacts in the Dead Sea Scrolls (q.v.) which were discovered in 1947. Again, the habit of the writer is to specify details of time, place, and number which must either indicate exceptional first-hand knowledge, or have been gratuitously inserted by one who wished to convey an impression of 'local colour.' The very hour of the day at which events happened is noted in 1[39] 4[6, 52] 19[14]; or 'the early morning' is mentioned, as in 18[28] 20[1] 21[4]; or the night, as in 3[2] 13[30]. The exact specification of six water-pots (2[6]), five husbands (4[18]), five and twenty furlongs (6[19]), two hundred cubits

JOHN, GOSPEL OF

(21^{8}), and the hundred and fifty-three fishes (21^{11}), has been claimed as a further illustration either of an old man's exact reminiscences of events long past or of a later writer's pretended acquaintance with precise details. But, once more, these figures are probably all allegorical, as the commentators have pointed out.

The portraiture of persons and incidents characteristic of the Gospel is noteworthy. The picture is so graphic and the effect is produced by so few strokes, often unexpected, that it must be ascribed either to an eye-witness or to a writer of altogether exceptional genius. The conversations recorded, the scene of the feet-washing, the representation of the Samaritan woman, of the man born blind, the portraiture of Peter, of Pilate, of the priests and the multitude, the questionings of the disciples, the revelation of secret motives and fears, the interpretations of Christ's hidden meanings and difficult sayings—*may*, as an abstract possibility, have been invented. But, again, these are examples of the great literary skill of the writer, who shows Jesus moving about in a world filled with various 'types' of human beings, in fact with 'all sorts and conditions of men'—from the urgent and importunate king's officer to the sceptical Nicodemus, and from the incredulous Pharisees to the cowardly Roman governor. We do not need to inquire, how could the writer have known all these persons. For as in a drama these are the *kinds* of persons of which the world—his world—was full, and who are still with us, everywhere. This fact explains the universalism of John and its undying religious appeal, especially to literary minds. Many writers, *e.g.* Barrett Wendell, have declared John to be their favourite gospel; and so have multitudes of ordinary, non-literary Christians. The author's genius lay in the realm of interpretation; his Christ is the exalted Christ of the Church's faith and worship, not the Galilean prophet of the third decade of the 1st cent. This is what distinguishes the Gospel of John from all apocryphal gospels, ancient and modern, and from all apocryphal additions to the canonical Gospels, whose character is purely fanciful, pedestrian, and unreal.

This characteristic of the author of John is especially evident in his profoundly and sensitively spiritual understanding of the Church's Divine Lord, here pictured as 'walking in Galilee.' His portrayal of Christ might well fill a volume—has in fact filled many volumes, some of them written by mystics and saints. Even the superficial reader will not fail to notice the remarkable combination of lowliness with sublimity, of superhuman dignity with human infirmities and limitations, which characterizes the Fourth Gospel. It is in it that we read of the Saviour's weariness by the well and His thirst upon the Cross, of the personal affection of Jesus for the family at Bethany, and His tender care of His mother in the very hour of His last agony. But it is in the same record that the characteristic 'glory' of His miracles is most fully brought out; in it the loftiest claims are made not only for the Master by a disciple, but by the Lord for Himself—as the Light of the World, the Bread from Heaven, the only true Shepherd of men, Himself the Resurrection and the Life. He is saluted not only by Mary as Rabboni, but by Thomas as 'my Lord and my God.' The writer claims an exceptional and intimate knowledge of Christ. He tells us what He felt, as in 11^{33} and 13^{21}; the reasons for His actions, as in 6^{6}; and he is bold to describe the Lord's secret thoughts and purposes ($6^{61, 64}$ 18^{4} 19^{28}). More than this, in the Prologue to a Gospel which describes the humanity of the Son of Man, He is set forth as the 'only' Son of God, the Word made flesh, the Word who in the beginning was with God and was God, Creator and Sustainer of all that is. This marked characteristic of the Gospel has indeed been made a ground of objection to it. We cannot conceive, it is said, that one who had moved in the circle of the immediate companions of Jesus of Nazareth could have spoken of Him in this fashion. The reply is obvious. What kind of a portrait is actually presented? If it be an entirely incredible picture, an extravagant attempt to portray a moral and spiritual prodigy or monstrosity, an impossible combination of the human and the Divine, then we may well suppose that only a clever imagination has been at work. But if a uniquely impressive Image is set forth in these pages, which has commanded the homage of saints and scholars for centuries, and won the hearts of millions of those simple souls to whom the highest spiritual truths are so often revealed, then it must be recognized that, since 'spiritual things are spiritually discerned,' this author was one who lived so close to the living Lord of the Church that he did not hesitate to project backward upon the screen of past history the grace and power familiar to him from his daily walk with Christ. As B. H. Streeter insisted, the 'I am' sayings probably ought to be reformulated, as the Church's testimony, to read, 'He is . . .', *i.e.* the Bread of Life, the Door of the Sheepfold, the Good Shepherd, the Son who is eternally one with the Father. The author of our Gospel was not a historian, but more a dramatist; and more than a religious dramatist a mystic, who saw no necessity for distinguishing between the actual historical utterances of Jesus of Nazareth and the eternal truths about His Divine person, His revelation of the Father, His voluntary and self-chosen death 'for his own,' and His resurrection and return to heavenly glory.

3. Scope of the Gospel and its Relation to the Synoptics.—It cannot be denied that there are grave difficulties confronting every one of the alternative views which have been described above, including the last. Some of these difficulties were felt as early as the 2nd and 3rd cents., when the simple identification of the author of John with the Apostle, the son of Zebedee, was probably held by all but a very small minority of readers, and they have always been more or less present to the minds of Christians. Others have been more clearly brought out by the debates over the Gospel during the past two centuries. In this section it will be convenient to try to answer the questions, How does this Gospel, if written by the Apostle John, stand related to the other three?, how can the obvious discrepancies be reconciled?, and how far do the writer's object and method and point of view account for the unique character of the narrative he has presented?

It is clear, to begin with, that the plan of the Fourth Gospel differs essentially from that of the Synoptics. This seems to be recognized in the Gospel itself: the author did not undertake to write a biography of Christ, even in the limited sense in which that may be said of Matthew, Mark, and Luke; he selected certain significant parts and aspects of Christ's work, for the purpose of winning or conserving faith in Him, presumably under special difficulties or dangers. We are therefore prepared for a difference in the very framework and structure of the book, and this we assuredly find.

The Fourth Gospel opens with an introduction to which there is no parallel in the NT. The circumstances of Christ's birth and childhood, His baptism and temptation, are entirely passed by. His relation to John the Baptist is dealt with from a later, doctrinal point of view, rather than from that of the chronicler describing events in their historical development. Only typical incidents from the ministry are selected, and only such aspects of these as lend themselves to didactic treatment. It will be convenient here to give a brief outline of the plan and contents of the Gospel.

OUTLINE OF THE GOSPEL OF JOHN

PROLOGUE: The Incarnation of the Word, 1^{1-18}.

I. Jesus, the Heavenly Messenger: His work in the world, 1^{19}–12^{50}.

A. The testimony of John, the Forerunner, 1^{19-34}.

B. The call of the first disciples, 1^{35-51}.

C. The Book of the Seven Signs, chs. 2–12.

Sign I. The marriage feast at Cana, 2^{1-12}.

The cleansing of the Temple, 2^{13-22}.

JOHN, GOSPEL OF

The visit of Nicodemus, 2^{23}–3^{21}.
Jesus and the Baptist, 3^{22-36}.
Jesus and the Samaritans, 4^{1-42}.
Sign II. Healing the nobleman's son, 4^{43-54}.
Sign III. The healing at the Pool of Bethzatha, 5^{1-16}.
The Christological Discourse, 5^{17-47}.
Sign IV. The feeding of the five thousand, 6^{1-13}.
Sign V. Jesus walks on the water, 6^{14-21}.
The Discourse on the Bread of Life, 6^{22-71}.
Jesus at the Feast of Tabernacles, 7^{1}–8^{59}.
Sign VI. Jesus restores a man born blind, 9^{1-41}.
The Shepherd Discourse, 10^{1-21}.
Jesus at the Feast of Dedication, 10^{22-42}.
Sign VII. The raising of Lazarus, 11^{1-46}.
The authorities decide to put Jesus to death, 11^{47-57}.
The anointing at Bethany, 12^{1-11}.
The triumphal entry, 12^{12-19}.
Jesus and the Gentiles, 12^{20-36}.
Conclusion of the Book of the Seven Signs, 12^{37-50}.

II. Jesus, the Heavenly Messenger: His return to the Father, 13^{1}–20^{29}.
A. The Last Supper, 13^{1-30}.
B. Farewell Discourse I, 13^{31}–14^{31}.
Farewell Discourse II, 15^{1}–16^{33}.
The High Priestly Prayer, 17^{1-26}.
C. The death of Jesus, 18^{1}–19^{42}.
D. The resurrection of Jesus, 20^{1-29}.
Conclusion of the Gospel, 20^{30f}.
An appendix, 21^{1-25}.

The following are some detailed differences of importance. The exact duration of Christ's ministry cannot be determined either by the Synoptic narratives or by St. John's; but it would appear that in the former it might be compressed within the compass of one year, whilst the latter in its mention of Passovers and Festivals would require more than three—though, as Charles Hedrick pointed out, the three Passovers turn out to be a timeless symbol, and are really one. Again, the Synoptic Gospels describe a ministry exercised almost entirely in Galilee up to the closing scenes in Jerusalem; St. John has little to say of Galilee, but he does mention an important visit to Samaria, and narrates at length events and controversies in Jerusalem of which the other Evangelists say nothing. On these points it has been argued that none of the Gospels professes to be complete; that an exact chronological outline can with difficulty be constructed from any of them; and that each gives passing hints of events of which the writer had cognisance, though it does not come within his purpose to describe them. But this is not a satisfactory solution. The whole purpose and ethos of Jesus' ministry is different in John. For example in John He proclaims Himself, and advances the claims made for Him by the early Church; but in the Synoptics His message is the coming Reign of God, and the necessary preparation men must make if they are to enter it.

Minute difficulties of detail cannot be discussed here. But the difference between the Synoptists and St. John with regard to the date of the Last Supper and Christ's death has a special importance of its own. The first three Gospels represent Jesus as partaking of the regular Passover with His disciples, and as being crucified on the 15th of Nisan; St. John describes the Last Supper as on the day of 'preparation,' and the crucifixion as taking place on the 14th Nisan, the great day of the Passover. Various modes of reconciliation have been proposed, turning upon the meaning of the phrase 'eating the Passover' and on the Jewish mode of reckoning days from sunset to sunset. It has been further suggested that the term 'Passover' was applied to the eating of the sacrifice called Chagigah, which was offered on the first Paschal day immediately after the morning service. Others have found a divergent chronology in the Torah, in some of the apocryphal and pseudepigraphical books, and in later traditions; or in the Galilean and Judaean calendars. The explanations offered of the discrepancy are ingenious, and one or other of them may be correct. But it can hardly be said that any has commanded general acceptance among critics, and meanwhile the difference remains. It must not be supposed, however, that this necessarily implies an error on the part of the Fourth Gospel. Many critics contend earnestly that St. John gives the more consistent and intelligible account of the Last Supper, the trial and the death of Jesus in relation to the Jewish festival, and that the phraseology of the Synoptists may be more easily and satisfactorily explained in terms of St. John's narrative than vice versa. One secular historian, A. T. Olmstead, unhesitatingly preferred the whole Johannine Passion Narrative to that in the Synoptics (*i.e.* the Marcan, which is its basis). The objection that the writer of the Fourth Gospel had a dogmatic reason for changing the day and representing Christ as the true Passover Sacrifice offered for the sins of the world, is not borne out by facts. The writer nowhere speaks of Christ as the Paschal Lamb, not even in 19^{36}, 'not a bone of him shall be broken'; and his allusion to the date is too slight and casual to warrant the supposition that he wishes to press home the teaching of 1 Co 5^{7}. Further, if the Synoptic tradition of the date had already been established, it is most unlikely that the writer would have set himself in opposition to it. The dating must therefore have been still open, and not decided in the general tradition, when John was written. It may be said in passing that the argument drawn from the Quartodeciman controversy—whether Christians ought to keep the Passover (*i.e.* Easter) at the same time as the Jews, *i.e.* always on 14th Nisan, whatever day of the week it might be, or always on Sunday as the first day of the week, on whatever day of the month it might fall—cannot legitimately be made to tell against the historicity of the Fourth Gospel. The controversy concerned the relation between Christians and Jews as such, rather than the exact date of Christ's death and its meaning as a Passover sacrifice. But it shows the indecisive state of the tradition even in the middle of the 2nd cent.

We reach the centre of difficulty, however, when we try to understand the marked difference between the body of the Synoptic narrative on the one hand and St. John's on the other. St. John's omissions are striking. He never refers to the miraculous birth of Christ; he gives no account of the Transfiguration, the institution of the Eucharist, or the Agony in the Garden; a large number of miracles are not described, nor is their occurrence hinted at; no parables are recorded, though the Synoptics make them a chief feature of Christ's teaching, and the very word for 'parable' in its strict sense does not occur in the book. On the other hand, his additions are notable. How is it that the Synoptists have nothing to say of the changing of Water into Wine, of the Feet-washing, and especially of the Raising of Lazarus? Is it conceivable that if such a miracle was actually worked it could have had no place in any of the great traditional accounts of His ministry? Certainly if it had led to Jesus' crucifixion ($11^{53, 57}$), it could not have been omitted by the Synoptics! Are we to understand that the Synoptists are correct when they place the Cleansing of the Temple at the end of Christ's ministry, or St. John when he describes it at the beginning? Other apparent discrepancies are of less importance. They concern the Anointing of Jn 12 as compared with the narratives of Mt 26, Mk 14, and Lk 7; the accounts of the trial of Jesus given in the Synoptics in their relation to that of John; and the appearances of the Lord after His Resurrection as recorded by St. John in the 20th and 21st chapters.

Further, even the superficial reader must be struck by the different representations of Christ's ministry in its main features. The Synoptic Gospels do not contain the long discourses which are reported in St. John,

JOHN, GOSPEL OF

always couched in a peculiar and characteristic diction, nor do they mention the frequent controversies with **'the Jews,'** who are represented in the Fourth Gospel as frequently interrupting Christ's addresses with questions and objections to which the Synoptists present no parallel. The very mention of 'the Jews,' so often and so unfavourably referred to, is, it is said, a sign of a later hand. The writer of the Fourth Gospel uses the same somewhat peculiar style, whether he is reporting Christ's words or adding his own comments, and it is sometimes difficult to distinguish between the two. In doctrine also, it is contended, there are irreconcilable differences between the first three Evangelists and the Fourth. Judgment is viewed by the Synoptists as a great eschatological event in the future, but by St. John as a present spiritual fact accomplished even whilst Christ was on earth. It is said, further, that Gnostic and other heresies of various kinds belonging to the 2nd cent. are alluded to in the Gospel, and that the Johannine authorship is therefore untenable. Last, but by no means least, the use of the word *Logos* to describe the Eternal Word, and the doctrines associated with the name that are found in the Prologue, point, it is said, conclusively to an Alexandrian origin, and are practically irreconcilable with the authorship of the son of Zebedee.

4. Purpose and Structure of the Gospel.—It is now much more generally recognized than in 1909 (the date of the first edition of this *Dictionary*) that these difficulties cannot be solved by comparing John and the Synoptics in detail and then by a forced 'harmonization' of the one with the other. John clearly was not revising the Synoptic narrative, nor even the Synoptic tradition, as a whole (some parts overlapped). Instead of the miracles, the 'mighty works' (*dynameis*) described in the earlier gospels, by which Jesus had rolled back the powers of darkness and opened the way for the coming of God's Reign (Lk 11^{20}), John describes the 'signs' of heavenly power and glory which shone through the veil of His human career—chiefly the seven great signs noted in the Outline above. John was not interested in history, or in biography, save as it symbolized, exemplified, or foreshadowed the invisible realities which are eternal. Christ not only healed—He heals. He not only revealed the Father—He reveals Him. He not only reconciled men to God—He reconciles. It is this constant and unending realization and fulfilment of the Incarnation that interests John far more than the events in Galilee and Jerusalem. The inner meaning of Christ's life completely dominates the narrative. This is a spiritual interpretation—or reinterpretation—of earlier tradition. Those for whom spiritual realities are as real as external events, or even 'more' real (as they say), will understand this; the rest of us are merely puzzled.

One theory which has recurred, in one form or another, for several generations, is that John is a composite work, and may be divided into two or three 'strands.' But the style, vocabulary, thought, and point of view are uniform throughout. Another and more promising distinction has been made between the discourses and the narratives. Rudolf Bultmann, in his *Meyer* Commentary (1941), distinguished the 'discourse source' (*Redequelle*, RQ), to which he attributed a Semitic (Aramaic or Syriac) and quasi-Gnostic origin. This source he did not undertake to reconstruct; but B. S. Easton worked it out, on the basis of the Commentary, in the *Journal of Biblical Literature*, lxv (1946), pp. 143–156. It begins with the Prologue ($1^{1-5, 9-12, 14, 16}$) and reaches its climax in the great passages in chs. 17, 15, 16, 14. But the view sometimes advanced, viz. that the narrative element in John was 'early,' and therefore came first, and that into this the discourses were inserted, is not supported by the phenomena of style, grammar, and vocabulary. One might argue—indeed Bultmann suggests—that the discourse material (RQ) came first, and the narrative was (or the narratives were) adapted to support it.

There is a continuity of theme (or themes) in the discourse material which goes quite beyond the limits of the several episodes, a fact which strongly supports the unity of the discourse material, whether or not one accepts Bultmann's view of it. The Prologue (omitting the narrative interpolations in vv.$^{6-8, 15}$) stands by itself, yet its thought is integral to the whole Gospel; it is no afterthought, as some late 19th cent. scholars supposed. Then begins the series of great themes, here given in the order of the Gospel (Bultmann rearranges the order): The Heavenly Witness (3^{11-12}), Redemption and Judgment (3^{16-21}), with a characteristic return to the former theme in 3^{31-36}); the Christological Discourse (5^{19-47}), where the Resurrection and Judgment theme (vv.$^{19-30}$) harks back to 3^{13-21}; the Witness *to* Christ of John the Baptist, Jesus' own works, and Moses (5^{31-47}, attaching to 3^{31-36}); the Bread of Life (6^{26-59})—three themes in one: Christ *gives* the Bread of Life, He *is* the Bread of Life, His *flesh* is the Bread of Life; He is also the Water of Life (6^{27-39}); the Witness theme again (7^{15-24} 8^{12-20}); the Shepherd discourse ($10^{1-18, 26-29}$); the final dialogue in 12^{20-36a}. Still more striking is the thematic arrangement—announcement followed by elaboration—in chs. 13–17, which follow the 'Book of the Seven Signs.' The Table Talk in 13^{31-35} introduces both of the Last Discourses in chs. 14–16 and also the great prayer in ch. 17.

Discourse I (ch. 14) elaborates the theme of 13^{33}.

Discourse II (chs. 15–16) elaborates (*a*) the idea of the *wine* (which is derived from the true *vine*) at the supper, especially 15^{1-8}, and (*b*) 13^{34-35}, especially 15^{9}–16^{33}.

The High Priestly Prayer (ch. 17) elaborates the theme of 13^{31b-32}. On this analysis, Bacon's theory that Discourses I and II were alternates cannot be maintained. Both were anticipated in the programmatic announcement of 13^{31-35}. In view of the closely knit structure of the discourse material, it is impossible to ignore the hypothesis that this really existed independently of the Gospel, either as a *Redequelle* or at least as a series of discourses —*i.e.* homilies, as Bacon thought, appropriate to the great festivals of the Christian Jewish religious year: Passover, Pentecost, Tabernacles, Rosh ha-Shanah and Yom Kippur, Hanukkah, Passover again. Until this question is settled, viz. the probable origin and the nature of this material, there is little likelihood of solving the riddle of the Fourth Gospel—the 'keystone,' as C. H. Dodd described it in his Inaugural at Cambridge (1938), to the whole arch of the literature and theology of the N.T.

The greatest advance in Johannine research during the past fifty years is probably in the area of the purpose and presuppositions of the author, whoever he was, wherever he lived, and whenever. His deepest aim was to set forth, in the language of his own and his readers' deepest spiritual needs and aspirations, the meaning which Christ had for His disciples, for the Church, and for the world. Christ was the Logos, the Divine Word, the eternal Reason, Power, Wisdom, and Voice of God the Creator of the Universe, who had become incarnate, lived on earth, was rejected by His own people, but gave to all who believed in Him the grace and power to become 'the children of God.' This is set forth in the Prologue (ch. 1).

1. In the beginning was the Word,
   And the Word was with God,
   And the Word was God.
2. He was in the beginning with God.
3. All things were made through Him,
   And without Him was not anything made
   [the rest of this line is a textual gloss].
4. In Him was life,
   And the life was the light of men.
5. The light shines in the darkness,
   And the darkness has not overcome it.
9. The true light that enlightens every man
   Was coming into the world.

10. He was in the world,
And the world was made through Him,
Yet the world knew Him not.
11. He came to His own [people],
And His own [people] received Him not.
12. But to all who received Him
[*i.e.* who believed in His name],
He gave power to become children of God,
13. Who were born, not of blood
Nor of the will of the flesh
Nor of the will of man,
But of God.
14. And the Word became flesh
And dwelt among us, full of grace and truth.
We have beheld His glory,
Glory as of the Only Son from the Father.
16. And from His fullness have we all received,
And grace upon grace.
17. For the Law was given through Moses,
But grace and truth came through Jesus Christ.
18. No one has ever seen God;
The Only Son, who is in the bosom of the Father,
He has made Him known.

This poem, sometimes inaccurately called a 'Hymn to the Logos,' sounds quasi-Gnostic, but if so it is Gnosticism with a difference. *Gnōsis* was not yet a Christian heresy, though it bore within itself the seeds of the later Gnostic sects. Its Jewish origin, affirmed by the Church fathers, is fairly clear—as the great opening tractate of the Hermetic *corpus*, the Poimandres, which sets forth the pagan parallel to the Gnostic writings, makes abundantly clear; its references to Gn 1 in the LXX are unmistakable. There were doubtless different types of nascent Gnosticism in the late 1st and early 2nd cents., but they doubtless shared a more or less common point of view. This was a fundamental dualism, at least a dualism *pro tempore*, until the affairs of the cosmos are finally terminated; matter and spirit are in total opposition, and as in Orphism the *sōma* (body) is viewed as the *sēma* (tomb) of the soul. As in the Hymn of the Soul (*Acts of Thomas*, 108–113) and other Gnostic writings, the soul, drugged and drowsy and lying in the dark dungeon at the bottom of the material universe, must be roused and wakened by some messenger, witness, or redeemer. (It is doubtful if the 'Gnostic Redeemer' appears anywhere outside Christian Gnosticism.) At last the soul may bestir itself and say, 'I will arise and go to my Father.' Elements of the world-wide popular astrology of the time were included, with its iron mechanism of inevitable fate; the malign or perverse reign of the 'governors,' the wicked archons who rule the heavenly spheres, and are in revolt against the one supreme God (cf 1 Jn 5[19b]); the passion of wicked spirits, aeons, *stoicheia* (the 'elemental spirits of the universe,' cf Gal 4[9]) for the lower levels of existence, especially for sexual gratification; the consequent evil of 'generation' or birth into the physical world—these are among the characteristic features of various schools of Gnostic thought, against which the author of John and the First Epistle of John firmly set his face. Salvation is by knowledge, *i.e.* by the acquisition of secret information about the origin and structure of the universe, the nature and destiny of the soul—this is the 'knowledge' which the vaunted teachers of this alien metaphysic set in opposition to, or offered in lieu of, the Christian tradition of the life, death, and resurrection of Christ and His ethical and religious teaching. The Grace and Truth which 'came through Jesus Christ' (1[17]) are not the Law of Moses, but something superior to that ancient code; they are also superior to the new would-be revelation contained in the secret lore of metaphysical doctrine which, had it prevailed, would have completely stifled and destroyed the Christian gospel with its fundamental emphasis upon history, upon the reality and significance of man's life in this physical world, and upon the meaning of Christ's victory over sin and death, which was achieved as man, in man, and for man. The Christian salvation was something very different from that offered by *Gnōsis*. Among NT writers, no one saw this more clearly than John. And the purpose of his Gospel and of the cognate First Epistle, perhaps also his writing, is quite clear. It was to declare and proclaim the Christian message of salvation, and the new life in Christ, as something very different from both Judaism and Gnosticism.

The finished Gospel, as we have it—not begging the question of its finality, since many hold that it was never finished—presents a number of inconsistencies, such as the statement in 6[1], where Jesus crosses the Lake of Galilee from Jerusalem (5[1]); or 14[31] ('Rise, let us go hence'), after which He continues speaking for three chapters (to 18[1]); or 5[18], which implies a prior claim to equality with God, as in 10[30a]. Various theories have been advanced to account for these discrepancies. Several of them presuppose a disarrangement of the text when a brittle papyrus codex fell apart and was put together again in the wrong order; the disarranged sections being of equal length, and even, on one theory, corresponding closely to the printed pages of Westcott and Hort's Greek Testament! Other theories assume that an older document was used by John (either a *Grundschrift* of the whole Gospel or a *Redequelle* underlying the discourses) and was rearranged to suit his conception of the topography, or the sequence of Jesus' ministry, or the seasons in the Christian Jewish calendar. Others, with more probability, assume that the Gospel was never finished, and its tentative drafts of various sections were edited by a person or persons (the 'we' and the 'I' of 21[24f]) who were unfamiliar with the geography of Palestine, and who did not venture to smooth out other inconsistencies. But it is a question if such inconsistencies troubled—or would have troubled—the author of John. His very style of writing is the intuitive, non-logical style of the mystic and devotee. Parallels may be found not only in ancient works like the *Odes of Solomon* or the *Ginza Rabbah* or the *Corpus Hermeticum*, but in more modern works like the *Imitation of Christ* or the older Dutch manual of devotion of the Brethren of the Common Life upon which it is based. The writer's thought moves in a circle, not a straight line; or in a spiral, returning to reconsider thoughts, truths, principles, expressions already used or stated, but now from a slightly different angle or point of view, or in the light of intervening conversations or events. What is true on the smaller scale of the discourses (*e.g.* the Bread of Life in ch. 6) is writ large in the composition of the Gospel as a whole. Consequently the rearrangement of chapters (*e.g.* of ch. 6 to precede ch. 5, or 15–16 to precede 14) or of sections or verses or parts of verses (as in Bultmann's RQ) still leaves unresolved problems, *aporien*, which call for further solution. It is probably better to leave the text as it stands, noting the difficulties but not attempting to solve them by any process of rearrangement. For it may well be that the author himself could not have solved them—except by omission. But his was a type of mind for which such difficulties were unimportant, and he preferred to leave his work without revision.

W. T. D.—F. C. G.

JOHN, THEOLOGY OF.—It is the object of this article to give a brief account of St. John's teaching as contained in his Gospel and Epistles. When we speak of the 'theology' of John we are using the word in a special sense—as also when we speak of the 'theology' of Paul, or the Synoptics, or Hebrews—or even of the NT as a whole. No fully articulated theological system is either set forth or presupposed in the Fourth Gospel, but a consistent body of intense and firmly held religious thought, with certain basic presuppositions, a characteristic vocabulary, and a vital, living contact with the convictions, hopes, and practices of the early church.

1. Some general characteristics of the teaching of St. John.—(1) It was appropriate that the later church fathers described John as the 'theologian' or the 'divine'; even some of the NT MSS so refer to him. For it was the evangelist's habit to consider every event in history and the religious teaching of Jesus *sub specie aeternitatis* and from the point of view of God. Not only is God to him the most real of all beings—that should be true of every religious man—but all the details of his very practical teaching are traced up to their origin in the nature and will of God. The opening of the Gospel is characteristic. History is viewed from the standpoint of eternity, the life of Jesus is to be narrated not from the point of view of mere human observation, but as a temporal manifestation of eternal realities.

(2) But *it must not for a moment be understood that the treatment of human affairs is vague, abstract, unreal.* John has a firm hold upon the concrete, and his insight into the actual life and needs of men is penetrating and profound. He is not analytical as Paul is, nor does he deal with individual virtues and vices as does James; nor does he deal with the history of salvation, the end of the ancient Levitical system, or the Atonement in Christ's blood, as the author of Hebrews does. But in the unity and simplicity of a few great principles he reaches to the very heart of things. His method is often described as intuitive, contemplative, mystical. The use of these epithets may be justified, but it would be misleading to suppose that a teacher who views life from so high a vantage ground sees less than others. The higher you climb up the mountain the farther you can see. Those who contrast the spiritual with the practical create a false antithesis. The spiritual teacher, and he alone, can perceive and deal with human nature, not according to its superficial appearances, but as it really is at its very core.

(3) Only it must not be forgotten that *the view thus taken of nature and conduct is ideal, absolute, uncompromising.* The moral dualism which is characteristic of John is in accordance with the sentence from the great Judgment-seat. Light and darkness—good and evil—truth and falsehood—life and death—these are brought into sharp and relentless contrast. Half-tones, delicate distinctions, the subtle and gradual fining down of principles in the complex working of motives in human life, disappear in the blaze of light which John causes to stream in from another world. 'No one born of God commits sin; for God's nature abides in him, and he cannot sin because he is born of God' (1 Jn 3^{9}); 'No one who denies the Son has the Father. He who confesses the Son has the Father also' (2^{23}); 'We know that we are of God, and the whole world is in the power of the evil one' (5^{19}). Such a mode of regarding life is not unreal, if only its point of view be borne in mind. In the drama of human society the sudden introduction of these absolute and irreconcilable principles of judgment would be destructive of distinctions which have an importance of their own, but the forces, as John describes them, are actually at work, and one day their fundamental and inalienable character will be made plain.

(4) Another feature of John's style and method which arrests attention at once is *his characteristic use of certain words and phrases*—'witness,' 'truth,' 'signs,' 'world,' 'eternal life,' 'know,' 'believe,' 'glory,' 'judgment,' are but specimens of many. They indicate a unity of thought in the writer which finds no precise parallel elsewhere in Scripture, the nearest approach, perhaps, being in the characteristic phraseology of Deuteronomy in the OT. John is not systematic in the sense of presenting his readers with carefully ordered reasoning—a progressive argument compacted by links of logical demonstration. He sees life whole, and presents it as a whole. But all that belongs to human life falls within categories which, from the outset, are very clear and definite to his own mind. The Gospel is carefully constructed as an artistic whole, the First Epistle is not. (See the OUTLINES OF CONTENTS in these articles.) But all the thoughts in both are presented in a setting prepared by the definite ideas of the writer. The molten metal of Christian thought and feeling has taken shape in the mould of a strikingly individual mind: the crystallization of the ideas is his work, and there is consequently a unity and system about his presentation of them which may be described as distinctly Johannine.

2. The doctrine of God which underlies these books is as sublime in its lofty monotheism as it is distinctively 'Christian' in its manifestation and unfolding. No writer of Scripture insists more strongly upon the unity and absoluteness of the only God (Jn 5^{41}), 'the only true God' (17^{3}), whom 'no one has ever seen (1^{18}); yet no one more completely recognizes the eternal Sonship of the Son, the fulness of the Godhead seen in Christ, the personality and Divine offices of the Holy Spirit. It is to John that we owe the three great utterances, 'God is Spirit' (Jn 4^{24}), 'God is Light' (1 Jn 1^{5}), 'God is Love' (1 Jn $4^{8, 16}$).

The inferences drawn from the doctrine of the spirituality of God show the importance of its practical aspects. God as Spirit is not remote from men, but this conception of His essence brings Him, though invisible, nearer to men than ever. God as Light exhibits Himself to us as truth, holiness, and righteousness. Some interpreters understand the phrase as designating the metaphysical being of God, others His self-revelation and self-impartation. The context, however, points rather to the ineffable purity of His nature and the need of holiness in those who profess to hold fellowship with Him. That God is loving to every man, or at least to Israel, was no new doctrine when John taught; but up to that time no one had ever pronounced the words in their profound simplicity—'God is Love.' Love is not so much an attribute of God as a name for Him in the intimate and changeless essence of His being. That there is the slightest inconsistency between the Divine love and the Divine righteousness is incredible; but if God is love, no manifestation of God's justice can ever contradict this quintessential principle of His inmost nature. Again, the words that follow the statement show that in the Apostle's mind the practical aspects of the doctrine were prominent. Contemplation with him does not mean speculation. Abstract *a priori* deductions from a theological conception are not in St. John's thought: his conclusions are 'He who does not love does not know God' (1 Jn 4^{8}), 'We also ought to love one another' (v.^{11}). Nor does this high teaching exclude careful discrimination. The love of the Father for the Son, His love of the world as the basis of all salvation, the closer sympathy and fellowship which He grants to believers as His own children, are not confused with one another. But the statement that God is love goes behind all these and teaches that the principle of self-impartation is essential, energetic, and ever operating in the Divine nature, and that it is in itself the source of all life, all purifying energy, and all that love which constitutes at the same time the binding and the motive power of the whole universe.

3. The Logos.—The object for which the Gospel was written, we are told, was that men might believe that Jesus was not only the Christ, but also the Son of God (20^{31}). The former belief would not necessarily change their views of the Godhead; the latter, if intelligently held and interpreted in the light of Thomas' confession (v.^{28}), would undoubtedly affect in some direction the intense monotheism of one who was born and bred a Jew. Was it possible to believe that in Jesus God Himself was incarnate, and at the same time to believe completely and ardently in the unity of God? The answer of the writer is given substantially in the Prologue, in the doctrine of the Eternal Word. It is unnecessary to discuss in detail whence John derived the word *Logos*: the doctrine was practically his own. The derivation of the term from ancient philosophy, *e.g.* Stoicism, throws little light upon its meaning for John: in fact it is the Gospel of John which throws light on the Logos doctrine, as held by the Early Church, rather than the reverse. There can be little question that the *Memra* of the Targums, based on the usage of such

JOHN, THEOLOGY OF

passages as Ps 33^{6} 147^{15}, and Is 55^{11}, had some connexion with the Johannine usage—though the written Targums are much later. Philo's conception of the Logos is very different from that of John. Hence it is most unlikely that John derived his conception from either the Aramaic paraphrasts or the Alexandrian Jewish philosopher. The sense is far closer, as Rudolf Bultmann has maintained, to the popular idea of a Mediator found in various Near Eastern religious cults and philosophies than it is to Philo, the Stoics, or Heraclitus. Taking a word which his hearers and readers obviously understood, he put his own stamp upon it. Philo and John both drew from Hebrew sources (*e.g.* Pr 8^{22-36}, Wis 7^{25f} 9^{9} etc.), where we find the doctrine of the divine Wisdom, the Agent of God in the creation of the universe. But Philo employed an expression which suited his philosophy because of its meaning 'reason,' and it was employed by him mainly in a metaphysical sense. By contrast, John availed himself of another meaning of the Greek word *Logos*, and he emphasizes the Divine 'utterance,' which reveals the mind and will of God Himself, giving a personal and historical interpretation to the phrase. The Word, according to the teaching of the Prologue, is Eternal, Divine, the Mediator of creation, the Light of mankind throughout its history; in the latter days the Word made flesh, tabernacling among men, is the Only-begotten from the Father full of grace and truth. This cardinal doctrine once laid down, there is no further reference to it in the Gospel, and in the only other places in NT where a similar expression is used (1 Jn 1^{1} and Rev 19^{13}) it is employed with a difference. Even in the Prologue the conception of the Word is not abstract and philosophical, but when the introduction to the Gospel is finished, the idea never appears again; the narrative of the only Son, revealing for the first time the Father in all His fulness, proceeds as if no account of the Logos had been given. (See JOHN, GOSPEL OF.) The Christology of John would be quite incomplete without his doctrine of the Logos, but it is not dependent on this. Christ's unique Personality as Son of God may be fully known from His life on earth, but the Prologue gives to the narrative of His ministry in the flesh a background of history and of eternity. In all ages the Logos was the medium of Divine revelation, as He had been of creation itself, and of the Godhead before the world was. Pre-temporal existence and pre-incarnate operation having been described with sublime brevity, the Evangelist proceeds calmly with the story to which this forms an august introduction. See also article LOGOS.

4. The Fatherhood of God, and the doctrine of the Holy Spirit.—It is unnecessary to point out how influential the Prologue has been in the history of Christian thought, but it is well to remember also that to the author of John more than to any other writer we owe the development of the Christian doctrine of the Godhead, as modified by the above cardinal conceptions. The doctrines of the Fatherhood of God and of the Holy Spirit as a Divine Person do not indeed depend upon the witness of John. The Synoptists and Paul, not to speak of other NT writers, would furnish a perfectly adequate basis for these vital truths of Christian faith. But neither would have influenced Christian thought so profoundly, and neither would have been so clearly understood, without John's teaching and the words of the Incarnate Lord as reported by him. The meaning of the term 'Son of God' as applied to Jesus is brought to light by the Fourth Gospel. Without it we might well have failed to gain an adequate conception of Fatherhood and Sonship as eternal elements in the Divine nature, and the unique relationship between the Father and the Son Incarnate is brought out in the fifth and other chapters of the Gospel as nowhere else. So with the Christian doctrine of the Holy Spirit. The whole of Scripture bears its testimony. Even in the OT more is said of the Spirit of God than is often recognized, and the teaching of Paul and Luke is full of instruction. But without the farewell discourses of Christ to His Apostles as recorded in Jn 14–16, our ideas of His Person and office would be comparatively meagre. The very term 'Paraclete,' not found outside the Gospel and the 1st Epistle, is itself a revelation. The personality of the Spirit and His distinctness from the Father and the Son, while Himself one with them, are elucidated with great clearness in these chapters. On the other hand, in his Epistle, John has much less to say than Paul of the Spirit in relation to the life of the believer.

5. On the subjects of **sin and salvation,** John's teaching harmonizes fully with that of the NT generally, while he maintains an individual note of his own, and brings out certain aspects of Christ's teaching as none of the Synoptists does. The language is that of the Church, but the thought goes back to Jesus. To John we owe the definition, 'sin is lawlessness' (1 Jn 3^{4}). He describes sin in the singular as a principle, rather than actual sins in the concrete. No dark lists enumerating the protean forms of sin, such as are found in Paul, occur in John, but he emphasizes with tremendous power the contrast between flesh and spirit, between light and darkness. The perennial conflict between these is hinted in the Prologue, and it is terribly manifest alike in the ministry of the Saviour and in the life of the Christian in the world. To John's writings chiefly we owe the idea of 'the world as a dark and dire enemy,' vague and shadowy in outline, but most formidable in its opposition to the love of the Father and the light of the life of sonship. The shades of meaning in which 'world' is employed vary (see 8^{23} 12^{31} $17^{14, 25}$ 18^{36} and 1 Jn 2^{15f}). The existence of evil spirits and their connexion with the sin of man are dwelt on by John in his own way. He does not dwell on the phenomena of demonic possession, but he has much to say of 'the devil' or 'the evil one' as a personal embodiment of the principle and power of evil. For his conception of Antichrist and of 'mortal sin,' see the articles ANTICHRIST and SIN, and the commentaries.

Potent as are the forces of evil, perfect conquest over them may be gained. The victory has already been virtually won by Christ as the all-sufficient Saviour, who as Son of God was manifested that He might undo or annul the works of the devil (1 Jn 3^{8}). His object was not to condemn the world, but to save it (3^{17}). That the Cross of Christ was the centre of His work, and His death the means through which eternal life was obtained for men, is made abundantly clear from several different points of view. John the Baptist points to the Lamb of God, who 'takes away the sin of the world' (1^{29}). The Son of Man is to be 'lifted up' like the serpent in the wilderness (3^{14}), and will draw all men to Himself (12^{32}). He gives His flesh for the life of the world (6^{51}). Only those who 'eat his flesh' and 'drink his blood' have eternal life (6^{53-56}). He is the expiation for the sins of the world (1 Jn 2^{2} 4^{10}), and it is His blood that cleanses from all sin those who walk in the light and have fellowship with the Father and the Son (1 Jn 1^{7}). John dwells but little on the legal aspects of sin and atonement; his doctrine on these matters is characteristic, confirming, whilst it supplements, the doctrines of Paul concerning justification and sanctification. What Paul describes as entire sanctification John eulogizes as perfect love—two names for the same full salvation, two paths to the same consummate goal.

It is most instructive to compare Paul and John in their references to faith and love. No student of these two great brethren in Christ could decide which of them deserves to be called the Apostle of faith, or which the Apostle of love. John uses the word 'faith' only once (1 Jn 5^{4}), but the verb 'believe' occurs nearly 200 times in his writings, and his usage of it is more plastic and versatile than that of Paul or the writer of Hebrews. Again, if the word 'love' occurs much more frequently in John, he has composed no such hymn in its honour as is found in 1 Co 13. The light he exhibits as a simple white ray Paul disperses into all the colours of the rainbow. The shades of meaning in John's use of the word 'believe' and his use of the two Greek words for 'love' deserve careful study.

6. The true believer in Christ enters upon **a new life.** The nature of this life is fully unfolded in John's writings, in terms which show an essential agreement with other parts of NT, but which are at the same time distinctly his own. The doctrine of the New Birth is one example of this. The Gospel gives a full statement of this in the discourse of Christ with Nicodemus (ch. 3), but both Gospel and Epistle contain many of the Apostle's own statements, which show no slavish imitation on his part either of the words of the Master or of Paul, but present his own views as a Christian teacher consistently worked out. In the Prologue the contrast between natural birth 'of blood, of the will of the flesh, of the will of man,' and the being spiritually 'born of God,' is very marked. Those whose life has been thus renewed are described as 'having the power [or right] to become children of God,' and the condition is the 'receiving' or 'believing in the name' of Him who, as Word of God, had come into the world. The phrase used for the most part in Jn 3 and in 1 Jn is 'born again' or 'anew' or 'from above.' The word 'born,' not employed thus by other NT writers, lays stress on the primary origin of the new life, not so much on its changed character. Two participles are employed in Greek, one of which emphasizes the initial act, the other the resulting state. But all the passages, including especially 1 Jn 2^{29} 3^{9} $5^{1, 18}$, draw a very sharp contrast between the new life which the believer in Christ enjoys and the natural life of the ordinary man. He to whom the new life has been imparted is a new being. He 'does righteousness,' he 'does not commit sin,' he 'cannot sin,' because he has been born of God and 'his seed abideth in him' (AV). Love and knowledge are marks of this new birth, and the new life is given to 'everyone who believes that Jesus is the Christ.' Some difficulty attaches to the interpretation of one clause in 1 Jn 5^{18}, but it is clear from that verse that he who enjoys the new life 'does not sin,' and that 'the evil one does not touch him.' The change is mysterious, but very real, and the term used by John to indicate this relation—'children,' instead of 'sons' as is usual with Paul—lays stress upon the close and intimate personal bond thus created, rather than upon the status and privileges of sonship. John, as we might expect, emphasizes the vital, not the legal element; believers are not merely *called* children, but 'so we are' (1 Jn 3^{1f}) and cannot be otherwise. When new life has actually been infused, it must manifest its characteristic qualities.

The nature of the Christian's vital union with God in Christ is illustrated from different points of view. The allegory—not a parable—of the Vine and the Branches (Jn 15^{1-11}) is full of instruction, but no analogy drawn from vegetable life suffices adequately to describe the fellowship between Christ and His disciples; this is rather to be moulded after the pattern of the spiritual fellowship between the Father and the Son (Jn 15^{9} 17^{21-23}); and the terms 'communion' and 'abiding' are strongly characteristic of the First Epistle (1^{3} $2^{6, 27f}$ 3^{24} 4^{12} etc.). The strong phrases of Jn 6 'eating the flesh' and 'drinking the blood' of Christ, are employed, partly to express the extreme closeness of the appropriation of Christ Himself by the believer, partly to emphasize the benefits of His sacrificial work, as the faithful receive in the Lord's Supper the symbols of His broken body and blood poured out for men. The description of this teaching as 'sacramental' depends upon the significance attached to that term.

Lest, however, what might be called the mystical element in John's theology should be exaggerated, it is well to note that the balance is redressed by the stress laid upon *love* in its most practical forms. Love of the world—that is, the bestowal of supreme regard upon the passing attractions of things outward and visible—is absolutely inconsistent with real love to the Father and real life in Christ (1 Jn 2^{15-17}). Similarly strong language is used as regards social relationships and the love of others; for the word 'brother' must not be narrowed down to mean exclusively those who belong to the Christian communion. No man whose life in relation to men is not actuated by love can be said to walk in the light (1 Jn 2^{9f}); hatred is murder ($3^{12, 15}$); willingness to help another in need is a test of true love, nominal and professed affection will not suffice (3^{17f}); a man who professes to love God and does not manifest a spirit of loving helpfulness adds falsehood to his other sins—'he is a liar' (4^{20}). The frequent repetition of some of these phrases and their interchange with others, such as 'doing righteousness,' 'walking in the truth,' 'being in the light,' 'abiding in him,' 'God abiding in us,' and the like, show that John is dealing with the very central core of spiritual life, and that for him as for Paul, it is true that 'he who loves his neighbour has fulfilled the law . . . for love is the fulfilling of the law' (cf Ro 13^{10}).

No more comprehensive phrase, however, to describe in brief the blessings of the gospel is to be found in St. John's theology than **'eternal life.'** It occurs seventeen times in the Gospel and six times in the First Epistle, while 'life' with substantially the same meaning is found much more frequently. 'Life' means for John that fulness of possession and enjoyment which alone realizes the great ends for which existence has been given to men, and it is to be realized only in the fulfilment of the highest human ideals through union with God in Christ. 'Eternal life' means this rich existence in perpetuity; sometimes it includes immortality, sometimes it distinctly refers to that which may be enjoyed here and now. In the latter case it is not unlike what is called in 1 Ti 6^{19} 'the life which is life indeed.' It is defined in Jn 17^{3} as consisting in the knowledge of God and Christ, where knowledge must certainly imply not a mere intellectual acquaintance, like the theoretical or speculative *gnōsis* of the false teachers, but a practical attainment in experience, including a state of heart and will as well as of mind, which makes God in Christ a true possession of the soul—that fellowship with God which constitutes the supreme possession for man upon the earth. But a contrast is drawn, *e.g.* in 3^{16} and 10^{28}, between 'eternal life' and 'perishing' or 'moral ruin'; and in one of John's sharp and startling contrasts, the choice open to man is described as including only these two solemn alternatives—'He who believes in the Son has eternal life; but he who does not obey the Son shall not see life, but the wrath of God rests on him' (3^{36}). The idea thus broached carries on beyond the boundaries of earthly existence; according to Christ's teaching, whoever keeps His word 'will never taste death' (8^{52}), and 'though he die, yet shall he live' (11^{25}). Knowledge of God and union with Christ impart to the believer a type of being which is not subject to the changes and chances of temporal existence, but is in itself unending, imperishable, so that in comparison with it no other kind of life deserves the name.

7. This opens up naturally the question of **John's Eschatology.** Some critics have found an inherent contradiction between John's view of judgment and that set forth by the Synoptists, and it may be pointed out in reply that he recognizes 'judgment' not merely as taking place here and now in history, but as still to be anticipated in its final form in the life beyond the grave. Similar statements have been made in reference to Christ's 'coming' and the 'resurrection.' That each of these three events is recognized as still in the future, to be anticipated as coming to pass at the end of the world, or at 'the last day,' is clear from such passages as the following: 'judgment' in Jn 12^{48} and 1 Jn 4^{17}; 'coming' in Jn 14^{3} and 1 Jn $2^{18, 28}$; 'resurrection' in Jn 5^{28f} 6^{39f} 11^{24} etc. But it cannot be questioned that John, much more than Paul or the Synoptists, uses these words in a spiritual sense to indicate a spiritual visitation which may be called a 'coming' of Christ (Jn $14^{18, 23, 28}$), as well as a judgment which was virtually pronounced in Christ's lifetime (12^{31} etc.). Similarly, in 5^{21} it is said that 'the Son gives life to whom he will,' where the reference cannot be to life beyond the grave—a view which is confirmed by vv.^{22f}, where we are told that he who hears Christ's word has passed from death to life, does not come into judgment, and that 'the hour now is' in which the dead shall hear His voice and live (v.^{25}). There is nothing in these descriptions of present spiritual blessing to interfere with the explicit statement that after death there shall be a resurrection of life and a resurrection of judgment (5^{29}), any more than the Saviour intended to deny Martha's statement concerning the resurrection at the last day, when He said to her, 'I am the resurrection and the life' (11^{25}).

It may perhaps be fairly said that John in the Gospel and Epistles lays emphasis upon the present spiritual blessings of salvation rather than upon future eschatological events described by means of the sensuous and material symbolism characteristic of apocalyptic. But the two ideas, so far from being inconsistent, confirm one another. The man who believes in the present moral government of God in the world is assured that there must be a great day of consummation hereafter; while he who is assured that God will vindicate Himself by some Great Assize in the future life cannot surely imagine that meantime He has left the history of the world in moral confusion. The spiritual man knows that the future lies hid in the hints and suggestions of the present; he is certain also that such hints and suggestions must find their perfect realization and issues in a consummation yet to come. No Christian teacher has understood the deep-lying unity between the material and the spiritual, the present and the future, the temporal and the eternal, more completely than John 'the divine.'

To sum up, we may say that the 'theology' of John is worked out in a milieu very different from that of Paul, the Synoptists, or the author of Hebrews. The *Gnōsis* which had appeared upon the horizon of Paul's later epistles has now become more fully developed, though it is a question if it yet deserves the name (which is really modern) of 'Gnosticism.' Clearly it was not the specific Gnosticism of Basilides, Valentinus, and others, but only the world-wide theory of the degradation of the soul through its contact with matter, salvation as release from the prison-house of the flesh, 'salvation by knowledge,' the ethics of ascetical renunciation—in a word 'Hellenistic spirituality,' or what Paul Wendland called 'the theology of Syncretism.'

The eschatological emphasis of the early kerygma is still apparent; in fact, as in Rudolf Bultmann's definition, for John faith is 'eschatological existence.' For Paul, faith had been a means to an end, Justification; for John, it is the new life itself (*Theology of the NT*, § 50). This does not really involve a dualistic world-view, since the world, which is now in the power of evil, is soon to pass away. 'The world passes away, and the lust of it; but he who does the will of God abides for ever' (1 Jn 2^{17}). This great text combines OT prophecy (cf Is 40^{8}) with evangelical teaching (cf Mt 7^{21}), in the spirit of both Christian cosmology and Christian eschatology. Here lies the great contrast with Gnosticism: salvation indeed consists in 'knowledge,' but this is not some esoteric metaphysic; it is a moral and religious life in obedience to the commands of God, not merely hearing or holding the truth, but 'doing' it.

There has been an effort to make John dependent upon a kind of esoteric Judaism, *e.g.* the doctrines of the sect at Qumrân, as some scholars have interpreted their documents; but the whole orientation and emphasis of the Fourth Evangelist is in another direction. Nor is his teaching compatible with that of Philo (q.v.), for whom the Logos is only one of the many 'Powers' of God, albeit the first and highest; for John, the Logos is the one and only 'Son of God,' whom to know is eternal life (17^{3}). Qumrân, Philo, the Gnostics, the Hermetists, the later Mandaeans and Manichees, even the later Jewish Cabbalists (theosophical rabbis) have some light to cast upon John's thought, but not much. In its fully orbed splendour it has light enough of its own, and to spare; not derived, but original; and shedding light upon both Jewish and Hellenistic types of spirituality, both of which really led, for their full satisfaction, nowhere else than to the One who came as Light into the world, that men might see and live. See two preceding articles. W. T. D.—**F. C. G.**

JOIADA.—1. One of the two who repaired the 'old gate,' Neh 3^{6} (AV **Jehoiada**). **2.** High priest, son of Eliashib, Neh $12^{10f, 22}$. One of his sons married the daughter of Sanballat the Horonite, Neh 13^{28} (RV, AV RSV **Jehoiada**).

JOIAKIM.—A high priest, son of Jeshua, Neh $12^{10, 12, 26}$.

JOIARIB.—1. One of the two teachers sent by Ezra to Iddo to ask for ministers for the Temple, Ezr 8^{16}. **2.** One of 'the chiefs of the province who lived in Jerusalem,' Neh 11^{5}. **3.** See JEHOIARIB.

JOKDEAM.—A city of Judah, Jos 15^{56}; called **Jorkeam** (q.v.) in 1 Ch 2^{44}. It is possibly *Kh. Raqa'*, S. of Hebron.

JOKIM.—A Judahite, 1 Ch 4^{22}.

JOKMEAM.—1. A town in Ephraim given to the Levites, near Beth-horon, 1 Ch 6^{68}; called **Kibzaim** in Jos 21^{22}. The site is unknown. **2.** A town in Solomon's fifth district, 1 K 4^{12} (AV **Jokneam**); probably to be equated with **Jokneam** (q.v.).

JOKNEAM.—A royal Canaanite city 'in Carmel,' Jos 12^{22}; on the boundary of Zebulun, 19^{11}, 'the brook' before it being the Kishon. It was assigned to the Merarite Levites, Jos 21^{34}. It is probably identical with **Cyamon** of Jth 7^{3}. The *Onomasticon* places 'Cimona' six Roman miles N. of Legio, on the road to Ptolemais. This points definitely to *Tell Qeimûn*, a striking mound SE. of Mount Carmel, with remains of ancient buildings. W. E.

JOKSHAN.—Son of Abraham and Keturah, and father of Sheba (Saba) and Dedan, Gn 25^{2}, 1 Ch 1^{32}. The name seems quite unknown, and the suggestion that it is identical with **Joktan** (q.v.) seems the most plausible.

JOKTAN, according to the genealogical tables in Genesis and 1 Chronicles, was one of the two sons of Eber, and the father of thirteen sons or races, Gn 10^{25-30}, 1 Ch 1^{19-23}; in the first table it is added that his descendants dwelt from Mesha to Sephar. Though the names of the majority of his sons have not been satisfactorily identified, it is clear that he is represented as the ancestor of the older Arabian tribes. The list of his sons is probably not to be taken as a scientific or geographical classification of the tribes or districts of Arabia, but rather as an attempt on the part of the writer to incorporate in the tables such names of Arabian races as were familiar to him and to his readers. It will be noted that Seba and Havilah occur also as the sons of Cush, Gn 10^{7}, the peculiar interest attaching to them having doubtless given rise to a variety of traditions with regard to their origin and racial affinities. The name of Joktan himself, like the names of many of his sons, has not yet been identified or explained. Its identification by the native Arab genealogists with *Kahtân*, the name of an Arabian tribe or district, is without foundation; there appears to have been no real connexion between the names, their slight similarity in sound having probably suggested their identification. The supposition that Joktan was a purely artificial name devised for the younger son of Eber, in order to serve as a link between the Hebrew and the Arab stocks, amounts to little more than a confession that the origin of the name is unknown. L. W. K.

JOKTHEEL.—1. A town of Judah in the lowland, Jos 15^{38}. Its site is unknown. **2.** The name given to Sela, the ancient capital of the Edomites, after its capture by Amaziah, king of Judah, 2 K 14^{7}.

JONADAB.—1. Son of Shimeah, David's brother, and the friend of Ammon the son of David. He is described as 'a very crafty man.' He aided Ammon to carry out his intrigue against his half-sister Tamar,

3 S 13[3ff], and after the assassination of Ammon was the first to grasp the true state of affairs, and to allay the king's distress by his prompt report of the safety of the royal princes, 2 S 13[30ff]. **2.** Son of Rechab, of the clan of the Kenites, 1 Ch 2[55], and formulator of the rules imposed upon descendants, the Rechabites (Jer 35; see RECHABITES). He is called **Jehonadab** in 2 K 10[15, 23], where we learn that he was thoroughly in sympathy with the measures adopted by Jehu for the vindication of the religion of Y″.

JONAH.—1. The man Jonah.—*Jonah* ('dove') is found in the Bible as the name of only one person, the Israelite prophet of 2 K 14[25] and of the Book of Jonah According to both, he was the son of Amittai (LXX and Vulgate *Amathi*), and the former connects him with Gath-hepher, a place named in Jos 19[13], in the territory of Zebulun, now probably represented by *Khirbet ez-Zurrâʿ*, not far from Kefr Kenna and Nazareth, in the neighbourhood of which is a grave of *Nebi Yûnus* or *Yûnis*. If this identification is right, Jonah was not only Israelite in the narrower sense, but Galilaean. His one prediction, recorded in Kings, of the extension of the kingdom of Samaria from Lebo-hamath (RSV 'the entrance of Hamath') as far as the Sea of the Arabah or Dead Sea, is said to have been fulfilled in the reign of Jeroboam II. (787/786–747/746 B.C.), and though it has generally been inferred that the prediction was also uttered in that reign it may have been delivered earlier. There is no mention in Kings of any connexion of Jonah with Assyria, and although it is possible that the memory of a visit to Nineveh was preserved by tradition or in some lost historical work no trace of such a story now exists, nor need its existence be postulated.

2. Book of Jonah.—(1) *Analysis.*—Jonah, the son of Amittai, is commanded by Yahweh to go to Nineveh and announce there impending judgment (1[1f]). For a reason not mentioned until near the end of the book (4[2f])—the fear that Yahweh will repent of His purpose, and spare the Ninevites—he refuses to obey, and in order to escape from Yahweh's immediate jurisdiction goes down to Joppa, and books himself a passage in a ship manned by heathen, almost certainly Phoenicians, and bound for Tarshish (1[3f]). (This used to be identified with Tartessus in Spain, near the mouth of the River Guadalquivir, and Jonah was represented as going as far west as he could; but on linguistic grounds the identification is doubtful, and as the root meaning of the word is connected with smelting or refining the place is probably some Phoenician colony where metal was worked, but whether this was in Sardinia or Tunis or even Spain cannot be decided.) When a violent storm comes on, and the prayers of the mariners to their gods of no avail, they conclude that there is someone on board who has offended some deity, and cast lots to discover the culprit. The lot falls on Jonah (1[4-7]),who acknowledges his guilt and advises them to cast him overboard (1[8-12]). After making futile efforts to bring the vessel to land (1[13]), the sailors reluctantly cast him into the sea, with the result that the storm at once subsides and the wondering heathen adore the God of the Hebrews (1[14-16]). Jonah is swallowed by a fish appointed for the purpose by Yahweh, and remains in its belly three days and three nights (1[17]), during which time he prays (2[1]). His prayer, which fills the greater part of the chapter, is rather a psalm of praise (2[2-9]). He is then cast by the fish on the land at a place not specified (2[10]), is commanded to discharge the neglected duty, goes to Nineveh and delivers his message over a third of the city (3[1-4]). King and people repent, and show their repentance in a public fast (which includes even the domestic animals), and pray (3[5-9]). Their penitence and prayer are accepted, to the prophet's disgust (3[10]–4[4]). As he sulks in a booth outside the city, waiting to see the issue, a remarkable series of experiences is arranged for his instruction (4[5-8]): the shooting up of a plant (RSVm: probably the castor oil plant; AV **gourd**; RVm **Palma Christi**) appointed by Yahweh, which delights him by its welcome shade; the killing of the plant by a worm, also appointed by Yahweh; and the springing up of a hot wind which also blows by Divine appointment, so that the now unshaded prophet is so tormented by the heat, that, like Elijah (1 K 19[4]), he longs for death. When he still sulks, it is pointed out to him that if he, a man, cares for the plant which sprang up and perished so quickly, and which was in no way the product of his toil, how much more must God care for the great city, which has in it so many thousands of little children and much cattle (4[9-11]).

(2) *Integrity.*—Although theories of composite authorship, interpolation, and transposition have been adduced to account for the difficulties in the way of accepting the unity of the book, most scholars now ascribe 1, 2[1, 10] 3 and 4, with the exception of a few glosses, to one writer. About the hymn or psalm in 2[2-9] there are three main views: (*a*) that it is by the writer of the rest of the book; (*b*) that it was used by him but not written by him; (*c*) that it was inserted by an editor who read that Jonah prayed to God and thought that the text of the prayer should be given. The last view is the likeliest. The poetic figures are drawn from the experience of sailors and the psalm fits in with the experience of a shipwrecked mariner who has reached the shore, rather than with the situation ascribed to Jonah (2[3-6]). How far it is from being a description of Jonah's plight may be gathered from v.[5]: 'weeds were wrapped about my head.' As Wellhausen remarked: 'Weeds do not grow in a whale's belly.' Further the psalm consists of quotations from or echoes of the Psalter, passages from Ps 3, 18, 30, 31, 42, 50, 116, 120, 142, which implies that the writer had a considerable part of our present Psalter before him, and so points to the study rather than the belly of a fish. Luther says: 'He was not so comfortably placed as to be able to indite so fine a poem.'

(3) *Date and Authorship.*—There is no claim in the book that it was composed by Jonah and there is no means of knowing the identity of the author. Since Nineveh is clearly referred to as no longer standing: 'Now Nineveh *was* an exceedingly great city' (3[3]), the *terminus a quo* cannot be placed earlier than about 600 B.C. (fall of Nineveh, 612 B.C.). The *terminus ad quem* is fixed by the mention of the Twelve Prophets in Sirach (49[10]), *c* 180 B.C. The anonymous reference to the Assyrian king and the description of him as 'king of Nineveh' (3[6]), a title not otherwise found applied to Assyrian monarchs, suggest a considerable interval between Assyrian times and the composition of the book. This is confirmed by the grossly exaggerated dimensions of Nineveh, which is described as so large that it would take three days to traverse (3[3]), whereas its area was less than three square miles, and by the related and also inflated estimate of its population (4[11]). If the writer was acquainted with the Book of Joel (compare 3[5] with Jl 1[13f], 3[9] with Jl 2[14], 4[2] with Jl 2[13]), which is probably to be referred to the latter half of the 5th cent. B.C., then Jonah would have to be placed in the 4th cent. In agreement with this is the linguistic evidence, words and forms showing Aramaic influence or found only in later Hebrew: *sᵉphînāh* 'ship,' *hithʿashshēth* in the sense of 'think,' *ṭaʿam* 'decree,' *minnāh* 'prepare' are examples. This evidence is supported by the thought and teaching of the book and makes probable a date between 400 and 200 B.C.

(4) *Interpretation.*—The ancient Jews seem to have regarded the book as historical (3 Mac 6[8], To 14[4, 8]; Jos. *Ant.* IX. x. 2 [208 ff]), and were followed by Christian interpreters, and, though this view has had defenders in more modern times, it is now largely given up. Some treat the book as an allegory of the fortunes of the people. Jonah, 'the dove,' represents Israel which was to prophesy amongst the nations. Because it shirked this task, it was swallowed by Babylon, represented by the great fish; during the Exile it turned to Yahweh and was restored to freedom. The plausibility of this view is increased if it is considered alongside Jer 51[34, 44];

it decreases the more consistency is sought in the interpretation of details. Cheyne, accepting this view, pointed out the mythical element in the story, the fish being the destroying dragon of the original myth and the link between the Jonah story and the myth being Jer 51[34, 44]. But it may be noted that in a 21st cent. B.C. cuneiform text Nineveh is represented ideogrammatically by a fish, the emblem of the goddess Nina, in the middle of a city. The book of Jonah has also been regarded as a Midrash on 2 K 14[25], but probably it fits best into the category of parable. Though the author may have drawn on historical incidents, myth and folklore, it is essentially the author's creation, a tale, fiction, but a story with a moral and it aims at instruction.

(5) *Teaching*.—The prominence given by Christian expositors to the incident of the fish has tended to obscure the chief aim of the writing—to protest against the narrowness of thought and sympathy which prevailed among the Jews of the time, and was daily growing in intensity. Whoever the author was, he had higher thoughts about God than most of his contemporaries, perhaps it may even be said than any other of the writers of the OT, and entertained more charitable feelings towards the Gentile world than most of his people. The God of Israel, he believed, cared for all men. Penitent Gentiles—and many in Gentile circles were ready to repent if only they were taught—could obtain pardon as readily as penitent Jews. Nay, Yahweh sought their repentance. Nowhere in pre-Christian literature can be found a broader, purer, loftier, tenderer conception of God than in this little anonymous Hebrew tract. Cornill describes it as 'one of the deepest and grandest things ever written.' 'I should like,' he adds, 'to exclaim to any one who approaches it: "Put thy shoes from off thy feet, for the place whereon thou standest is holy ground."' How high the teaching of the book rose above later Judaism, say the Judaism of the time of Christ, and the following generation, is strikingly shown by the way in which it is summarized by Josephus (*loc. cit.*). There is not a word there about the penitence of the Ninevites, or God's remonstrance with Jonah. The main lesson of the book is absolutely ignored by the proud Pharisaic priest. Another leading thought of the book is the duty of Israel to make its God known to the Gentiles.

(6) *The book in the Synagogue and the Church*.—It is said in the Mishnah (*Ta'anith*, ii. 1) that the ritual of a public fast in time of drought included reference by the leader of the congregation to the Book of Jonah, and it has been used from ancient times to the present day in the ceremonial of the Day of Atonement. Christians were early attracted to it by the remarkable allusions in the Gospels: Mt 12[39ff] 16[4], Lk 11[29f, 32]. The reference to the entombment in the fish is in Matthew only. The allusion to the repentance of the Ninevites is in both Matthew and Luke. The significance of the former has been much debated, and some have regarded it as a proof of the historicity of the OT narrative. That in no way follows. Our Lord found the story in the Scriptures, and appealed to it as something generally known to His hearers. His use of it fastened on the imagination of the early Christians, and led them to take great interest in the whole Book of Jonah. The remains of early Christian art in catacomb paintings, on sarcophagi, lamps, glasses, etc., include a very large number of pictures which have some part of the story of Jonah for their theme.

(7) *Parallels to Jonah*.—The fish episode, so far from being a unique and unparalleled adventure, is actually part of the mythological background not only of Palestine but of many parts of the world. Attention has often been called to the classical myths of Andromeda and Hesione, the scene of the former of which is laid in the neighbourhood of Joppa. From India there is a tale of a certain Mittavindaka who went to sea in defiance of his mother's objection. While the ship was on the sea it was seized by an unknown power and could not proceed until the offender was three times selected by lot and then cast overboard. From Egypt comes an account of a shipwrecked traveller being swallowed by a serpent and thus carried to land. That was the kind of story which was to be found in many parts of the ancient world, and the author of Jonah may have called one such story into use. But whatever mythical element there was in the original tale—and some see in the swallowing and disgorging of Jonah a reference to the disappearance and subsequent reappearance of the sun during an eclipse—this element has disappeared from our book, and the fish is used merely as a means of transport for the prophet, a way of getting Jonah back to land. What has been used as a test of orthodoxy is seen to be no more than a literary convention.

W. T. S.—**W. D. McH.**

JONAH (1 Es 9[23]).—See ELIEZER, **8.**

JONAM.—An ancestor of Jesus (Lk 3[30]).

JONAS.—**1.** 1 Es 9[1] (RV); see JEHOHANAN, **3.** **2.** 1 Es 9[23] (AV, RV); see ELIEZER, **8.** **3.** 2 Es 1[39] AV the prophet Jonah. **4.** See JOHN, **6.**

JONATHAN ('Y" hath given').—**1.** A Levite, the 'son' of Gershom (q.v.); according to Jg 18[30] he and his sons were priests to the tribe of Dan up to the Captivity. Jonathan was taken into the service of Micah as 'father and priest' (Jg 17[10]); but, not long after he had taken up his abode there, six hundred Danites came that way and induced Jonathan to leave Micah and join them as their priest (18[11-31]). **2.** The eldest son of Saul; he appears, in the first instance, as a brave and successful leader in battle. 1 S 13, 14 contain a graphic account of the way in which the Israelites threw off the Philistine yoke; in this campaign Jonathan took a leading part. He first of all, at the head of a thousand men, smote the Philistine garrison in Geba; this was the signal for the outbreak of war. The Philistine army gathered together and encamped in Michmash. Jonathan, accompanied only by his armour-bearer, at great risk surprised an advanced post of the Philistines, and slew about twenty men; the suddenness and success of this *coup* so terrified the Philistines that the whole host of them fled in panic. The popularity of Jonathan is well illustrated by the fact that the people prevented Saul from carrying out a vow which would have cost Jonathan his life (1 S 14[24-46]). The implicit trust which Saul placed in Jonathan is seen in the words of the latter in 1 S 20[2]: 'Behold, my father does nothing either great or small without disclosing it to me.' The faithfulness and trustworthiness of Jonathan as here shown gives an insight into what must have been that friendship for David which has become proverbial. All the characteristics of truest friendship are seen in Jonathan in their full beauty—love (1 S 18[1]), faithfulness (20[2ff]), disinterestedness (20[42]), and self-sacrifice (20[24-34]). The last we hear of Jonathan is his death upon the battlefield, fighting the foes of his country. In David's lament the spirit of the departed hero speaks in unison with his friend: 'Your love to me was wonderful, passing the love of women' (2 S 1[26]).

3. The son of the priest Mattathias; the youngest of the four Maccabaean brothers (2 Mac 8[22]), who played an important part during the Maccabaean revolt (see MACCABEES, **3**). **4.** A nephew of David (2 S 21[21]; called his 'uncle' in 1 Ch 27[32]). **5.** A son of Abiathar the priest (2 S 15[27ff] 17[17, 20], 1 K 1[42]). **6.** A scribe in whose house Jeremiah was imprisoned (Jer 37[15, 20] 38[26]). **7.** A high priest (Neh 12[11]); called **Johanan** in v.[22f] and **Jehohanan** in Ezr 10[6]. **8.** One of David's heroes (2 S 23[32], 1 Ch 11[34]). **9.** A Levite (Neh 12[35]). **10.** Son of Kareah (Jer 40[8]). His name is omitted in RSV, with some Hebrew MSS, LXX; it does not stand in 2 K 25[23]. **11.** The father of Peleth and Zaza (1 Ch 2[32f]). **12.** One of David's treasurers (1 Ch 27[25]). **13.** Father of Ebed (Ezr 8[6]). **14.** One of those who opposed (RV, RSV) or assisted (AV) Ezra in the matter of the foreign marriages (Ezr 10[15]). **15.** A priest (Neh 12[14]). **16.** Son of Absalom, in the time of Simon the Maccabee

(1 Mac 13^{11}). **17.** A priest who led the prayer at the first sacrifice after the Return in the time of Nehemiah (2 Mac 1^{23}). W. O. E. O.—**H. H. R.**

JONATHAS, To 5^{13} (AV).—See JATHAN.

JONATH ELEM RECHOKIM, Ps 56 (AV).—See PSALMS, **2.**

JONATH ELEM REHOKIM.—See PSALMS, **2.**

JOPPA.—The principal seaport of S. Palestine: a place of high antiquity, being mentioned in the tribute lists of Thothmes III., but never before the Exile in Israelite hands, being in Philistine territory. It was theoretically assigned to the tribe of Dan (Jos 19^{46}), and is spoken of as a seaport in 2 Ch 2^{16} and Ezr 3^{7} (where read with RSV 'to the sea, to Joppa' [cf RV], in place of AV 'to the sea of Joppa'): these, and its well-known connexion with the story of Jonah (1^{3}) are the only reference to the city to be found in the OT. The Maccabees wrested it more than once from the hands of their Syrian oppressors (1 Mac 10^{75} 12^{33} 13^{11}); it was restored to the latter by Pompey (Jos. *Ant.* XIV. iv. 4 [76]), but again given back to the Jews (*ib.* XIV. x. 6 [205]) some years later. Here St. Peter for a while lodged, restored Tabitha to life, and had his famous vision of the sheet (Ac 9^{36}–10^{48}). The traditional sites of Tabitha's tomb and Simon the tanner's house are shown to tourists and to pilgrims, but are of course without authority. The city was destroyed by Vespasian (A.D. 68). In the Crusader period the city passed from the Saracens to the Franks and back more than once: it was captured first in 1126, retaken by Saladin 1187, again conquered by Richard Coeur de Lion in 1191, and lost finally in 1196. In more recent times it is remarkable for Napoleon's successful storming of its walls in 1799. Its modern name is *Jaffa*, and it is now a flourishing seaport. A railway connects it with Jerusalem. It is also one of the chief centres of the fruit-growing industry in Palestine, and its orange gardens are world-famed. Tradition places here the story of Andromeda and the sea-monster. R. A. S. M.

JORAH.—The head of a family of which one hundred and twelve members returned with Zerubbabel, Ezr 2^{18}, 1 Es 5^{16} (AV **Azephurith**, RV **Arsiphurith**); called **Hariph** in Neh 7^{24}.

JORAI.—A Gadite chief, 1 Ch 5^{13}.

JORAM.—**1. 2.** See JEHORAM, **1** and **2.** **3.** Son of Tou, who was sent to congratulate David on his victory over Hadadezer, 2 S 8^{10}; called **Hadoram** in 1 Ch 18^{10}. **4.** A Levite, 1 Ch 26^{25}. **5.** A captain in the time of Josiah, 1 Es 1^{9}; called **Jozabad** in 2 Ch 35^{9}.

JORDAN.—The longest and most important river in Palestine. **1. Name.**—The name 'Jordan' is best derived from Hebrew *yāradh* 'to descend,' the noun *Yardēn* formed from it signifying 'the descender'; it is used almost invariably with the article. In Arabic the name is *esh-Sherî'ah*, or 'the watering-place,' though Arabic writers before the Crusades called it *el-Urdun.* Quite fanciful is Jerome's derivation of the name from *Jor* and *Dan*, the two main sources of the river, as no source by the name of Jor is known.

2. Geology.—The geology of the Jordan is unique. Rising high up among the foothills of Mount Hermon, it flows almost due south by a most tortuous course, through the two lakes of Huleh and Galilee, following the bottom of a rapidly descending and most remarkable geological fissure, and finally emptying itself into the Dead Sea, which is 1292 feet below the level of the Mediterranean. In its short course of a little more than 100 miles it falls about 3000 feet, and for the greater portion of the journey runs below the level of the ocean. No other part of the earth's surface, uncovered by water, sinks to a depth of even 300 feet below sea-level, except the great Sahara. Professor Hull, the eminent Irish geologist, accounts for this great natural cleft by supposing that towards the end of the Eocene period a great 'fault' or fracture was caused by the contraction from east to west of the limestone crust of the earth. Later, during the Pliocene period, the whole Jordan valley probably formed an inland lake more than 200 miles long, but at the close of the Glacial period the waters decreased until they reached their present state. Traces of water, at heights 1180 feet above the Dead Sea's present level, are found on the lateral slopes of the Jordan valley.

3. Sources.—The principal sources of the Jordan are three: (1) the river *Ḥaṣbānī*, which rises in a large fountain on the western slopes of Mount Hermon, near *Ḥāṣbeiyah*, at an altitude of 1700 feet; (2) the *Leddan*, which gushes forth from the celebrated fountain under *Tell el-Qâḍī*, or Dan, at an altitude of 500 feet—the most copious source of the Jordan; and (3) the river *Bâniyâs*, which issues from an immense cavern below *Bâniyâs* or Caesarea Philippi, having an altitude of 1200 feet. These last two meet about five miles below their fountain-heads at an altitude of 148 feet, and are joined about a half-mile farther on by the Ḥaṣbānī. Their commingled waters flow on across a dismal marsh of papyrus, and, after seven miles, empty into Lake Huleh, which is identified by some with 'the waters of Merom' (Jos $11^{5, 7}$). The lake is four miles long, its surface being but 7 feet above sea-level.

4. The **Upper Jordan** is a convenient designation for that portion of the river between Lake Huleh and the Sea of Galilee. Emerging from Lake Huleh, the river flows placidly for a space of two miles, and then dashes down over a rocky and tortuous bed until it enters the Sea of Galilee, whose altitude is 682 feet below the level of the Mediterranean. It falls, in this short stretch of 10½ miles, 689 feet. At certain seasons its turbid waters can be traced for quite a considerable distance into the sea, which is 12½ miles long.

5. The **Lower Jordan** is an appropriate designation for that portion of the river between the Sea of Galilee and the Dead Sea. The distance in a straight line between these two seas is but 65 miles, yet it is estimated that the river's actual course covers not less than 200, due to its sinuosity. In this stretch it falls 610 feet, the rate at first being 40 feet per mile. Its width varies from 90 to 200 feet. Along its banks grow thickets of tamarisks, poplars, oleanders, and bushes of different varieties, which are described by the prophets of the OT as 'the **pride** [RSV '**jungle**'] **of Jordan**' (Jer 12^{5} 49^{19} 50^{44}, Zec 11^{3}). Numerous rapids, whirlpools and islets characterize this portion of the Jordan. The river's entire length from *Bâniyâs* to the Dead Sea is 104 miles, measured in a straight line.

6. Tributaries.—Its most important tributaries flow into the Lower Jordan and from the East. The largest is the *Yarmuk* of the Rabbis, the *Hieromax* of the Greeks, and the *Sherî'at el-Menâḍireh* of the Arabs, which drains Gilead and Bashan in part. It enters the Jordan 5 miles south of the Sea of Galilee. The Bible never mentions it. The only other tributary of considerable importance is the Jabbok of the OT, called by the natives *Nahr ez-Zerkā* or *Wâdī el-'Arab.* It rises near *'Ammân* (Philadelphia), describes a semicircle, and flows into the Jordan at a point about equidistant from the two seas. On the west are the *Nahr el-Jālûd*, which rises in the spring of Harod at the base of Mount Gilboa and drains the valley of Jezreel; *Wâdī Fār'ah*, which rises near Mount Ebal and drains the district east of Shechem; and the *Wâdī el-Qelt*, by Jericho, which is sometimes identified with the brook Cherith.

7. Fords.—The fords of the Jordan are numerous. The most celebrated is that opposite Jericho known as *Makhāḍet el-Ḥajlah*, where modern pilgrims are accustomed to bathe. There is another called *el-Ghôrāniyeh* near the mouth of *Wâdī Nimrīn.* North of the Jabbok there are at least a score. In ancient times the Jordan seems to have been crossed almost exclusively by fords (1 S 13^{7}, 2 S 10^{17}); but David and his household were possibly conveyed across in a 'ferry-boat' (2 S 19^{18} RV; the rendering is doubtful, cf RSV 'ford').

8. Bridges are not mentioned in the Bible. Those which once spanned the Jordan were built by the Romans, or by their successors. The ruins of one, with a single arch, may be seen at *Jisr ed-Dâmiyeh*, about seven miles south of the Sea of Galilee. Another, built of black basalt and having three arches, is known as the *Jisr Benāt-Ya'qûb*, or 'bridge of the daughters of Jacob,' situated about two miles south of Lake Huleh on the direct caravan route from Acre to Damascus. The river is now crossed by bridges at *Jisr ed-Dâmiyeh*, by the Hussein (formerly Allenby) bridge, on the main road from Jericho via es-Salṭ to *'Ammân*, and by a bridge a little north of the Dead Sea, on the new road from *'Ammân* to Jerusalem opened in 1958.

9. The Jordan valley.—The broad and ever-descending valley through which the Jordan flows is called by the Arabs the *Ghôr* or 'bottom'; to the Hebrews it was known as the *'Arābhāh*. It is a long plain, sloping uniformly at the rate of 9 feet to the mile, being at the northern end 3, and at the southern end 12 miles broad. For the most part the valley is fertile, especially in the vicinity of *Beisân*, where the grass and grain grow freely. Near the Dead Sea, however, the soil is saline and barren. The ruins of ancient acqueducts here and there all over the plain give evidence of its having been at one time highly cultivated. To-day new aqueducts and the boring of wells is bringing large areas, particularly in the neighbourhood of Jericho, once more under cultivation. Grain crops and a large variety of excellent vegetables are grown. Cultivation is also carried out in the comparatively narrow floor bed of the river, known as the *Zôr*, varying from a quarter to two miles in width, and from 20 to 200 feet in depth below the *Ghôr* proper. This is the area which was overflowed every year 'all the time of harvest' (Jos 3[15]). It has been formed, doubtless, by the changing of the river bed from one side of the valley to the other.

10. The **climate** of the Jordan valley is hot. The Lower Jordan in particular, being shut in by two great walls of mountain, the one in the east, and the other on the west, is decidedly tropical. Between October and March, the days are often pleasantly warm, with occasional cold and rainy spells; the nights are however usually cool or cold. In summer both days and nights are torrid, especially at Jericho, where the thermometer has been known to register 130° Fahr. by day, and 100° after sunset. In spite of this, there was a considerable population in the Lower Jordan valley in ancient times. To-day this population is once more growing.

11. Flora and fauna.—The trees and shrubs of the Jordan valley are both numerous and varied. The *retem* or broom plant, thorns, oleanders, flowering bamboos, castor-oil plants, tamarisks, poplars, acacias, Dead Sea 'apples of Sodom,' and many other species of bush, all grow in the valley. The papyrus is especially luxuriant about Lake Huleh.

The only wild animals found in the valley to-day are the jackal, hyaena, and fox. The leopard, boar, and ibex were still found at the beginning of the 20th cent., but the lion disappeared during the 19th cent. The river abounds in fish of numerous species, many of them resembling those found in the Nile, and the lakes of tropical Africa. Of the thirty-five species, however, known to exist, sixteen are peculiar to the Jordan.

12. The Jordan as a boundary.—In view of what has been said, it is obvious that the Jordan forms a natural boundary to Palestine proper. In the earlier books of the OT we frequently meet with the expression 'on this side of the Jordan,' and 'on the other side of the Jordan,' which suggest that the Jordan was a dividing line and a natural boundary. In Nu 34[12], indeed, it is treated as the original eastern boundary of the Promised Land (cf Jos 22[35]). Yet, as Lucien Gautier suggests (article 'Jordan' in Hastings' *DCG*), it was not so much the Jordan that constituted the boundary as the depressed *Ghôr* valley as a whole.

During the British Mandate, the river formed the boundary between Palestine and Transjordan. It ceased to serve this function when the Hashemite Kindom of the Jordan was established.

13. Scripture references.—The Jordan is frequently mentioned in both the OT and the NT. Lot, for example, is said to have chosen 'all the circle of the Jordan' because 'it was well watered everywhere' (Gn 13[10]); Joshua and all Israel crossed over the Jordan on dry ground (Jos 3[17]); Ehud seized the fords of the Jordan against the Moabites, cutting off their retreat (Jg 3[28]); Gideon, Jephthah, David, Elijah, and Elisha were all well acquainted with the Jordan; Naaman the Syrian was directed to go and wash in the Jordan seven times, that his leprosy might depart from him (2 K 5[10]). And it was at the Jordan that John the Baptist preached and baptized, our Lord being among those who were here sacramentally consecrated (Mt 3 and parallels). To-day thousands of pilgrims from all parts of the civilized world visit the Jordan; so that, as G. A. Smith (*HGHL*, p. 496) reminds us, 'what was never a great Jewish river has become a very great Christian one.'

G. L. R.—**K. M. K.**

JORIBAS, 1 Es 8[44] (AV).—See Jarib, **2.**

JORIBUS.—**1.** 1 Es 8[44] (RV); see Jarib, **2. 2.** 1 Es 9[19] (AV, RV); see Jarib, **3.**

JORIM.—An ancestor of Jesus (Lk 3[29]).

JORKEAM.—A Judahite, 1 Ch 2[44]. But probably it represents a place name, and is to be identified with **Jokdeam** (q.v.).

JOSABAD.—**1.** 1 Ch 12[4] (AV); see Jozabad, **1. 2.** 1 Es 8[63] (AV); see Jozabad, **7. 3.** 1 Es 9[29] (AV); see Zabbai, **1.**

JOSABDUS, 1 Es 8[63] (RV).—See Jozabad, **7.**

JOSAPHIAS, 1 Es 8[36] (AV, RV).—See Josiphiah.

JOSE, Lk 3[29] (AV).—See Jesus, **6.**

JOSECH (AV **Joseph**).—An ancestor of Jesus (Lk 3[26]).

JOSEDEC.—AV form of **Jehozadak** (q.v.) in Apocrypha.

JOSEDECH.—AV form of **Jehozadak** (q.v.) in Haggai and Zechariah.

JOSEDEK.—RV form of **Jehozadak** (q.v.) in Apocrypha.

JOSEPH (in OT and Apocrypha).—**1.** The patriarch. See next article. **2.** A man of Issachar (Nu 13[7]). **3.** A son of Asaph (1 Ch 25[2, 9]). **4.** One of the sons of Bani who had married a foreign wife, Ezr 10[42], 1 Es 9[14] (AV, RV **Josephus**). **5.** A priest (Neh 12[14]). **6.** An ancestor of Judith (Jth 8[1]). **7.** An officer of Judas Maccabaeus (1 Mac 5[18, 56, 60]). **8.** In 2 Mac 8[22], and probably also 10[19], Joseph is read by mistake for **John,** one of the brothers of Judas Maccabaeus.

JOSEPH.—Jacob's eleventh son, the older of the two sons of Rachel; born in Haran. According to Gn 30[24] the name means 'may he (God) add,' but 30[23] apparently connects it with the root 'to take away' (the reproach of barrenness). Joseph is the hero of the stories in Gn 37–50. The occasional differences in the stories are evidence of original independence, and their imperfect harmonization favours their substantial historicity. In contrast with the earlier patriarchal stories they have less to do with Joseph, the tribe, and more with Joseph, the man.

The date of Joseph cannot be fixed with absolute certainty, but there are a number of considerations that point to the time of the Hyksos, who ruled Egypt *c* 1720–1550 B.C. The Pharaoh of the oppression is now generally taken to be Rameses II. of the 19th Dynasty (*c* 1290–1224 B.C.); and if this is correct, the addition of the years of residence in Egypt (430 years according to Ex 12[40f], or in round numbers, 400 years according to Gn 15[13]) would bring Joseph's term of office into the time of the later Hyksos kings. One of these bore the name of Jacob-har, indicating that Jacob was a good Hyksos name, and suggesting, too, that the Hebrews participated in the Hyksos regime, as does the Joseph story in general. Both the Hebrews and the Hyksos were predominately Semitic, and the Jewish historian, Josephus, definitely connects the two. The references in the OT account to horses and chariots indicate a period not earlier than the Hyksos when these were first introduced into Egypt, and the change in land tenure from a landed nobility before the Hyksos to a bureaucracy of governmental officials after the Hyksos seems to be reflected in Gn 47[19-26]. The OT locates the land of Goshen (probably the *Wâdī Ṭumilât*) in the eastern Delta in close proximity to the Egyptian capital, and the Hyksos period, when Zoan (*i.e.* Tanis or Avaris) was the capital, fits that situation as no other period does. The only other time when distant Thebes was not the capital was after 1300 B.C., but that is much too late for Joseph. It is also significant that in Ps 78[12] the region where the Hebrews lived in Egypt is called 'the fields of Zoan.' Finally, the note in Nu 13[22], stating that Hebron was built seven years before Zoan in Egypt, can only refer to the founding of the Hyksos capital there (*c* 1720 B.C.), and it suggests that Hebrews must have been connected with the Hyksos, and used that date as a reference point for calculating other dates. It is true that the Egyptian names which appear in the story, Potiphar (Gn 37[36]), Potiphera, Joseph's father-in-law, Asenath, his Egyptian wife, and his own Egyptian name, Zaphenath-paneah (41[45]), are not known in Egypt before 1000 B.C., but that simply shows that our story came to us from the late period, and the Egyptian names were made to agree with those current at the time. With the return of Jacob to Hebron (Gn 35[27]) he ceases to be the central figure in the story of the Hebrews, and Joseph takes his place. Of his life to the age of seventeen (Gn 37[2]) we are told simply that he was his father's favourite, and rather too free in carrying tales about his brothers and recounting his boyish dreams. Sent to Shechem, he found that his brothers had taken their flocks northward to Dothan. As soon as he came within sight, they planned to get rid of him and his dreams, but the traditions differ as to how this was accomplished. According to Gn 37[27f] he was sold to a passing caravan of Ishmaelites, but according to 40[15] he was kidnapped, apparently by a band of Midianites (37[28]). In any case he was carried off to Egypt, and the brothers manufactured the evidence of the blood-stained cloak to account for his disappearance (37[31ff]).

In Egypt Joseph was bought by Potiphar, a court official, and the alertness and trustworthiness of the slave led quickly to his appointment as *major domo*. Everything prospered under Joseph's management, but his comeliness and courtesy attracted the notice of his master's wife, whose advances, being repelled, were transformed into a resentment that knew no scruples. By means of an entirely false charge she secured the removal of Joseph to the state prison, which was in charge of Potiphar (40[3]), and where again he was soon raised to the position of overseer. In due course there came under his charge two of Pharaoh's officers, the chief butler and the chief baker, who had offended their lord. Both were perplexed with dreams, which Joseph interpreted for them. Two years later the Pharaoh himself had a dream of fat and lean cows and in another form, of plump and thin ears of grain; and so much significance was attached in Egypt to dreams that the king was distressed by his inability to find an interpreter. Thereupon the chief butler recalled Joseph's skill and mentioned him to the Pharaoh, who sent for him, and was so impressed by his sagacity that he made him Prime Minister or Vizier, with a degree of authority second only to that of the throne. The Egyptian name of **Zaphenath-paneah** was conferred on him, and he married **Asenath,** daughter of one of the most important dignitaries of the realm, the priest of the great national temple of the sun at On or Heliopolis, seven miles NE. of modern Cairo.

As Vizier Joseph's policy was to store the surplus grain during the years of plenty, and afterwards so to dispose of it as to change the system of land tenure. Famine in ancient Egypt, before the Nile was controlled, was due to failure or deficiency in the annual inundation, and several famines have been recorded in the inscriptions. One, written in the 2nd or early 1st cent. B.C., actually preserves the tradition of a famine of seven years in the reign of Djoser of the 3rd Dynasty (*c* 2700 B.C.). Joseph's procedure was to sell grain first for money (bars of gold whose weight was certified by special officials), and when all this was exhausted, grain was given in exchange for live stock, and finally for the land.

The peculiarity of the famine was that it extended over the neighbouring countries (41[56f]), and amongst others to Canaan, and the narrative in consequence resumes contact with Joseph's family there. The severity of the famine in Canaan led Jacob to send all his sons except Benjamin (42[4]) to buy grain in Egypt. On their arrival they secure an interview with Joseph (42[6]); but in the grown man, with his shaven face and Egyptian dress, they entirely failed to recognize their long-lost brother. The rough accusation that they were spies aroused their fears, and they defended themselves by giving a full account of their family, from which Joseph learned that their youngest brother, Benjamin, had not accompanied them. After further adding to the apprehension of his brothers, Joseph retains one as a hostage for the delivery of Benjamin, and he sends the rest home. On their return home, according to 42[35], or at the first camping-place, according to 42[27], the discovery by the brothers of their money in their sacks increased their anxiety. For a time their father positively refused to consent to further dealings with Egypt, but at length his resolution broke down under the pressure of the famine (43[11ff]), and the brothers went again to Egypt for food, accompanied this time by their brother Benjamin. In Egypt they were invited to a feast in Joseph's house, where they were seated according to age, much to their surprise (43[33]), and Benjamin was singled out for a special portion (43[34]). They set out for home in high spirits, unaware that Joseph had directed that each man's money should be placed in his sack and his own divining-cup in the sack of Benjamin (44[12]). Overtaken by Joseph's messenger, they were charged with theft, and returned in a body to Joseph's house. His reproaches elicited a frank and pathetic speech from Judah, after which Joseph could no longer maintain his *incognito*. He allayed the fears of his conscience-stricken brothers by the assurance that they had been the agents of Providence 'to preserve life' (45[5]; cf Ps 105[17ff]); and in the name of the Pharaoh he invited them with their father and households to settle in Egypt, with the promise of support during the five years of famine that remained.

Goshen, a pastoral district in the eastern Delta, was selected as the new home of Jacob and his family (46[34]), and here they settled and prospered (47[27f]). Before Jacob died, he blessed Joseph's two sons, Ephraim and Manasseh, giving preference to the younger in view of the greatness of the tribe to be derived from him, and leaving Joseph himself one portion above his brothers, viz. Shechem (48[22] RVm). After Jacob's death his body was embalmed according to Egyptian custom, he was mourned for the royal period of seventy days (50[3]) and buried with great pomp in the cave of Machpelah. Presently Joseph himself died at the age of 110 (50[22]), which in Egypt was considered the length of a prosperous life. The body was embalmed and placed in a coffin to await its transfer to Canaan. In due course it was taken over by Moses (Ex 13[19]) and eventually buried at Shechem (Jos 24[32]).

Of the general historicity of the story of Joseph there need be no doubt, but all the details are not necessarily correct. There are such striking likenesses between the Egyptian Tale of the Two Brothers and the story of Potiphar's wife (39[7-20]) that there must be some borrowing here. Allowance must also be made for the play of imagination in the long period that elapsed before the traditions were reduced to writing in their present form, and for the tendency to project the characteristics of a tribe backwards on some legendary hero. But the incidents as a whole are too natural and too closely related to be entirely a product of fiction. The Egyptian background is remarkably true to fact. The titles of the various officials are such as are found in Egyptian inscriptions. The embalming of Jacob and Joseph (Gn $50^{2, 26}$) was common Egyptian practice in the case of a personage of importance. The birthday of the Pharaoh is known to have been an occasion for feasting (cf 40^{20}). The Pharaoh's gifts to Joseph upon the latter's induction into the office of Vizier and the special robe of office (41^{42}) are quite in keeping with Egyptian customs as we know them. Also shepherds were an abomination to the Egyptians (46^{34}; cf 43^{32}) because they were foreigners from the desert.

The story of Joseph is remarkably well told. Its plot is unexcelled, and the interest is maintained to the very end. Joseph's own character as depicted is singularly attractive. Dutifulness (1 Mac 2^{53}) is perhaps its keynote, manifested alike in the resistance of temptation, in uncomplaining patience amid misfortune, and in the modesty with which he bore his elevation to rank and power. Instead of using that power for resentment he forgives his brothers and showers gifts upon them. On the other hand, there are blemishes which surprisingly are duly recorded. In his youth there was a degree of vanity that made him unpleasant. When invested with authority he treated the people in a way that would now be pronounced tyrannical, enriching and strengthening the throne at the expense of a people in distress. On the whole, however, he must be considered one of the great men of Israel, and in strength of right purpose he was second to none. R. W. M.—**T. J. M.**

JOSEPH (in NT).—**1. 2.** Two ancestors of our Lord, Lk $3^{24, 30}$.

3. The husband of Mary and 'father' of Jesus.—Every Jew kept a record of his lineage, and was proud if he could claim royal or priestly descent; Joseph was 'a son of David' (Mt 1^{20}, Lk 2^{4}). His family belonged to Bethlehem, David's city, but he had migrated to Nazareth (Lk 2^{4}), where he followed the trade of carpenter (Mt 13^{55}). To him was betrothed Mary, a maiden of Nazareth. It is usually assumed that he was much her senior, though the tradition of the apocryphal *History of Joseph* that he was in his ninety-third year and she in her fifteenth is a mere fable. The tradition that he was a widower and had children by his former wife probably arose in the interest of the dogma of Mary's perpetual virginity. The Evangelists tell us little about him, but what they do tell redounds to his credit. (1) He was a pious Israelite, faithful in his observance of the Jewish ordinances (Lk 2^{21-24}) and feasts (Lk $2^{41\text{f}}$). (2) He was a kindly man (Mt 1^{19}). When he discovered the condition of his betrothed, he drew the natural inference and decided to disown her, but he would do it as quietly as possible, and, so far as he might, spare her disgrace. And, when he was apprised of the truth, he was very kind to Mary. On being summoned to Bethlehem by the requirements of the census, he would not leave her at home to suffer the slanders of misjudging neighbours, but took her with him and treated her very gently in her time of need (Lk 2^{1-7}). (3) He exhibited this disposition also in the nurture of the Child so wondrously entrusted to his care, taking Him to his heart and well deserving to be called His 'father' (Lk $2^{33, 41, 48}$, Mt 13^{55}, Jn 1^{45} 6^{42}). Joseph never appears in the Gospel story after the visit to Jerusalem when Jesus had attained the age of twelve years and become 'a son of the Law' (Lk 2^{41-51}); and since Mary always appears alone in the narratives of the public ministry, it is a reasonable inference that he had died during the interval. Legend says that he died at the age of one hundred and eleven years, when Jesus was eighteen; but this belongs with the 'fable' described above.

4. One of the brothers of Jesus, Mt 13^{55}, where AV reads **Joses,** the Greek form of the name. Cf Mk 6^{3}.

5. Joseph of Arimathaea.—A wealthy and devout Israelite and a member of the Sanhedrin. He was a disciple of Jesus, but, dreading the hostility of his colleagues, he kept his faith secret. He took no part in the condemnation of Jesus, but neither did he protest against it; and the likelihood is that he prudently absented himself from the meeting. When all was over, he realized how cowardly a part he had played, and, stricken with shame and remorse, plucked up courage and 'went to Pilate, and asked for the body of Jesus' (Mk 15^{43}). It was common for friends of the crucified to purchase their bodies, which would else have been cast out as refuse, a prey to carrion birds and beasts, and give them decent burial; and Joseph would offer Pilate his price; in any case he obtained the body (Mk 15^{45}). Joseph had a garden close to Calvary, where he had hewn a sepulchre in the rock for his own last resting-place; and there aided by Nicodemus, he laid the body swathed in clean linen (Mt 27^{57-61} = Mk 15^{42-47} = Lk 23^{50-56} = Jn 19^{38-42}).

6. Joseph Barsabbas, the disciple who was nominated against Matthias as successor to Judas in the Apostolate. He was surnamed, like James the Lord's brother, ***Justus*** (Ac 1^{23}). Tradition says that he was one of the Seventy (Lk 10^{1}). **7.** See BARNABAS. **8.** Lk 3^{26} (AV); see JOSECH. D. S.—**F. C. G.**

JOSEPHUS, 1 Es 9^{34} (AV, RV).—See JOSEPH (in OT), **4.**

JOSEPHUS, FLAVIUS.—Jewish historian and general, born about A.D. 37 or 38, and died in the first years of the 2nd cent.

1. Life.—According to his *Life*, Josephus was descended from a Maccabaean house, and was thus of both royal and priestly lineage. He states that he showed great precocity, and that the learned men of his race used to consult him when he was fourteen years of age. At the age of sixteen he decided to investigate the teachings and practices of the Pharisees, Sadducees, and Essenes. His purpose was to choose the best sect after a thorough acquaintance with all three. These initial investigations, undertaken in Jerusalem, lasted only a few months and were inconclusive. They were followed by a three-year period of study and discipline as a disciple of a certain Banus who lived a very austere and pure life in the wilderness of Judaea. At the age of nineteen, having completed his investigations, he returned to Jerusalem and joined the Pharisees. At the age of twenty-six he went to Rome to bring about the acquittal of certain priests who had been arrested and sent to Rome for trial by Felix. In this he was successful, and even gained the favour of the Empress Poppaea.

Not long after his return from Rome the revolution of A.D. 66 broke out, and he was at once swept into its current. Of the events which follow he has given us two accounts, the earlier in the *Jewish War* [*BJ*], the later in his *Life*, written shortly before his death. These accounts are not always consistent, the latter showing more subservience to the Romans. In particular, he attempts to justify himself, and the Pharisees with whom he was associated, for participation in the revolt, by declaring that they judged it better for moderate men than for radicals to direct the course of events. The *BJ*, however, does not suggest this questionable proceeding on the part of the Jewish authorities.

The course of the war in Galilee, and particularly his own relations therewith, are minutely narrated by Josephus. His position was one of great difficulty. The Galilaeans were grouped in various parties, ranging from those who opposed war with Rome to radicals like those who followed John of Gischala. The plans of Josephus and his fellow-commissioners from Jerusalem were further complicated by jealousies between the various cities, particularly Sepphoris, Tiberias, and Tarichaeae. None the less, Josephus seems to have gone about the work of organizing the revolution energetically. He fortified the cities as well as he could, and attempted to introduce Roman military methods among the troops he was gathering. Whether he was, as he claims, too strict in the matter of booty, or, as his enemies claimed, too lukewarm in the cause of the revolution, complaints were lodged against him at Jerusalem, and an investigating committee was sent into Galilee. Various adventures then followed, but in the end Josephus seems to have been acquitted and to have gained a complete ascendancy over his local enemies. John of Gischala, however, subsequently went to Jerusalem, and proved a persistent enemy, while the Zealot party as a whole seems never to have been satisfied with the attitude of Josephus.

The approach of Vespasian from the north at once showed how half-hearted had been the revolutionary sympathies of many of the Galilaean cities. Several of them surrendered without serious fighting, and Vespasian, after one or two desperate battles, was soon in possession of all Galilee excepting Jotapata in the central section of Galilee, where Josephus and his surviving troops were entrenched. Reinforcements the Sanhedrin could not send, and for forty-seven days the Romans besieged the city. During that time Josephus, if his own account is to be believed, performed marvellous deeds of strategy and valour. But all to no purpose. The city fell, and was razed to the ground. Josephus was taken prisoner, after having by a trick escaped being killed by his own soldiers. On being brought to Vespasian he claimed prophetic ability, and saluted the general as Emperor. For this and other reasons he won favour with Vespasian, was given his freedom, and took his benefactor's family name, *Flavius*.

When Titus undertook the siege of Jerusalem, Josephus accompanied him as interpreter or herald. By this time, however, he had become hateful to the Jews, and could accomplish nothing in the way of inducing them to make terms with the Romans. When the city was captured, he was able to render some service to the unfortunate Jews because of the favour in which he stood with Titus. He was subsequently given estates in Judaea, and was thus enabled to live during the remainder of his long life as a gentleman of leisure, devoted to the pursuit of literature. He enjoyed the friendship of Titus and of king Agrippa II. He was several times married, and left several children.

2. Writings.—The chief importance of Josephus lies not in his career as a leader of the Jewish revolution, but in the works which have come down to us. Generally speaking, his writings are intended to disabuse his Greek and Roman contemporaries of some of the misconceptions that then existed concerning the Jews. To that end he does not hesitate to employ various ingenious interpretations of historical events, as well as legends, and even to hint that the Jewish records which he quotes have certain allegorical meanings to be disclosed in a subsequent work, which, however, he never wrote.

(1) The earliest of these writings is that *Concerning the Jewish War*, a work in seven books. It covers briefly the period from the time of Antiochus Epiphanes to the outbreak of the war of A.D. 66–70, and then narrates the events of the war in detail. It was originally written in Aramaic, but was rewritten by Josephus in Greek. It was probably issued before A.D. 79, as it was presented to Vespasian. Because of the reference to the Temple of Peace as finished (*BJ* VII. v. 7 [158]), it must have been written after A.D. 75. The work is basically an apology for the Romans. However, it is also an apology for the Jews, in that it pictures the extremist elements which favoured war with Rome as misguided, selfish, and cruel men who were in no way motivated by traditional Jewish religion. Allowing for this *Tendenz* the work is of inestimable value so far as its record of facts is concerned, and particularly for the light it throws on the state of society in the midst of which Jesus laboured. The book found favour with Vespasian and Titus and Agrippa II.

(2) *The Antiquities of the Jews.*—This great work in twenty books is one of the most important monuments which have come down to us from antiquity. It was published in the year A.D. 93. It covers the history of the Jews from the earliest Biblical times to the outbreak of the revolution of A.D. 66. It is particularly interesting as an illustration of the method by which the facts of Hebrew history could be rewritten for the edification of the Greeks and Romans. It abounds in legends and curious interpretations. Josephus was by no means dependent upon the OT exclusively. He constantly refers to non-Biblical writers, mentioning by name most of the Greek and Roman historians. He used constantly the works of Alexander Polyhistor, Nicolaus of Damascus, and Strabo. He probably also used Herodotus. The work abounds in collections of decrees and inscriptions which make it of great value to secular as well as to Biblical historians. The later books give very full accounts of the life of Herod I., for which Josephus is largely dependent upon Nicolaus of Damascus, the historiographer of Herod. In his treatment of the Maccabees he is largely dependent upon First Maccabees. His account of the successors of Herod is hardly more than a sketch, but that of the events leading up to the revolution is more complete.

(3) The *Life.*—This work was written in reply to Justus of Tiberias, in which Josephus was accused of causing the revolt. In his *Life* Josephus represents himself as a friend of the Romans, but many statements are disproved by his earlier work, the *BJ*. This *Life* appeared after the death of Agrippa II., that is, in the beginning of the 2nd cent.

(4) *Against Apion.*—This is a defence of the Jewish people against the attacks of their enemies and calumniators, chief among whom was Apion, a grammarian of Alexandria, who wrote during the first half of the 1st. cent. A.D. It was written probably about the same time as the *Life*, and is particularly valuable as a narrative of the charges brought against the Jewish religion by the Greeks. It also serves as an exposition of the customs and views of the Jews of the 1st cent., not only in Judaea but throughout the Dispersion.

3. The importance of Josephus to the Biblical student.—As a contemporary of the NT writers, Josephus describes the Jewish background of Christian history as does no other writer of antiquity. The Book of Acts is particularly illuminated by his writings, while the chronology of the Apostolic period is given its fixed dates by his references to Jewish and Roman rulers. Josephus, it is true, does not add to our knowledge of the life of Christ. While his reference to John the Baptist is possibly authentic, and while it is not impossible that he mentions Jesus, the entire passage (*Ant.* XVIII. iii. 3 [63 f]) can hardly have come from Josephus in its present form. At the same time, his narrative of the events of the Gospel period and his description of the character of the various rulers of Judaea serve to corroborate the accuracy of both the Gospels and Acts. As furnishing data for our knowledge of Jewish legends, parties, practices, and literature, his importance is exceptional. Even if we did not have the Mishnah, it would be possible from his passages to reconstruct a satisfactory picture of the Jewish life of NT times. His few references to the current Messianic expectations of his day are particularly valuable. On the other hand, his comments upon and explanations of the OT are of comparatively small value. S. M.—**W. R. F.**

JOSES.—**1.** One of the 'brethren of the Lord' (Mk 6^{3} $15^{40,47}$, Mt 27^{56}). In Mt 13^{55} AV has **Joses**, but RV, RSV correctly **Joseph. 2.** The natal name (Ac 4^{36}AV) of **Barnabas**; RV, RSV correctly **Joseph.**

JOSHAH.—A Simeonite chief, 1 Ch 4^{34}.

JOSHAPHAT.—**1.** One of David's heroes, 1 Ch 11^{43}. **2.** A priest in David's time, 1 Ch 15^{24} (AV **Jehoshaphat**).

JOSHAVIAH.—One of David's heroes, 1 Ch 11^{46}.

JOSHBEKASHAH.—A son of Heman, 1 Ch $25^{4,24}$. There is reason to believe that this and five of the names associated with it are really a fragment of a hymn or prayer.

JOSHEB-BASSHEBETH.—Name found in 2 S 23^{8} (RV, RSV) in place of the meaningless 'that sat in the seat' of AV. The text is corrupt, and the name **Jashobeam** should be restored from the parallel 2 Ch 11^{11}, though this in turn is probably a corruption of **Ishbaal.** Cf JASHOBEAM.

JOSHIBIAH.—A Simeonite chief, 1 Ch 4^{35} (AV **Josibiah**).

JOSHUA (on forms and meaning of the name see next article).—**1.** The successor of Moses. See next article. **2.** The Bethshemite in whose field was the stone on which the Ark was set, on its return from the land of the Philistines, 1 S $6^{14, 18}$. **3.** The governor of Jerusalem in the time of Josiah, 2 K 23^{8}. **4.** The high priest who along with Zerubbabel directed affairs at Jerusalem after the restoration, Hag $1^{1, 12, 14}$ etc., Zec $3^{1, 3, 6}$ etc. In the books of Haggai and Zechariah he is called **Joshua,** in Ezra and Nehemiah **Jeshua** (q.v.). See also JESUS, **4.**

JOSHUA (cf JESUS, **1**).—The son of Nun, and divinely appointed successor to Moses as leader of Israel (Nu 27^{18ff}, Dt 34^{9}, Jos 1^{1ff}). He is called **Hoshea** in Nu 13^{8}, and in 13^{16} this is represented as his original name, the name Joshua (*Yᵉhôshūaʿ*) having been given him by Moses. The intent of this would seem to be to account for the fact that one already grown up before the Divine name Yahweh was revealed (Ex 6^{2}) nevertheless bore a name of which Yeho (=Yahweh) was a component. Hoshea appears again in Dt 32^{44}, probably by a scribal error ; Samaritan and the versions read Joshua. The most likely rendering of the name is ‘ Yahweh is salvation.’

He commanded the army in the battle with Amalek (Ex 17^{8-16}), attended on Moses at the Mount of God (24^{13} 32^{17}) and at the Tent of Meeting (33^{11}, Nu 11^{28}) ; all these passages are from the northern tradition, E. He was one of the twelve spies (Nu $13^{8, 16}$ 14^{6}, P), and he and Caleb were the only adults who were not involved in the revolt against Moses following the mission of the spies and alone were spared to enter Palestine ($14^{30, 38}$, P). He was the leader in the conquest of Palestine, and the division of the land among the tribes was carried through under his auspices (see following article). He was buried in Timnath-serah (Jos 19^{50} 24^{30}=Timnath-heres, Jg 2^{9}) in the hill country of Ephraim. This explicit mention of his burying-place may be taken as an indication that there was when the story was written a grave at Timnath-serah known as the grave of Joshua, and this in turn points to Joshua's historical reality as a person, and tells against the view that he is simply a personification of a clan in Ephraim, and that his leadership in Israel represents, and puts back into the period of the conquest, the commanding position which that tribe had come to hold in the Israelite confederation. Nevertheless the question as to what part he actually played in Israel's history is a difficult one. The designation of him as an Ephraimite in Nu 13^{8} is supported by the location of his grave in the territory of that tribe. This being the case, he will have been the successor of Moses only if Ephraim or some of its clans were among those which escaped from Egypt. If, however, as has been argued by a number of scholars, the experience of the Exodus was limited to certain southern clans, which alone came under the influence of Moses, Joshua can scarcely have been his attendant or his successor, but will have been an independent figure who came to be associated with Moses when the traditions of the north and the south were unified. Again, the tradition makes Joshua a military leader. It might have been expected that it would tell of his conquest of the territory historically possessed by his own tribe ; yet, except for Hazor in the north (Jos 11^{1-9}) and Makkedah in the south (10^{16ff}), all the exploits recounted in Jos 1–12 occurred within the territory of Benjamin. And here there is a further difficulty : the taking of Jericho and the destruction of Ai cannot have been accomplished by the same man. There is as yet no agreement among archaeologists as to the date of the fall of Jericho, but on any reckoning it must have occurred more than 500 years after the destruction of Ai in 2000 B.C. There are, moreover, indications in the OT itself that the Israelite settlement in Palestine was not by conquest but by a slow process of infiltration. Thus the fighting described in the book of Joshua must have occurred not when the Israelites were coming in from the desert, but years later when they were gradually extending their control over the land. But this fighting in course of time may well have given rise to the tradition of a conquest rather than of infiltration, and have led to the fitting together of various legends of diverse origin to make a continuous narrative, of which the Ephraimite Joshua was made the hero, possibly because he was historically a military leader. On the other hand, his rôle may actually have been that of an administrator or statesman, such as Jos 12–14 represents him to have been. However that may be, the subsequent growth of the legend concerning him can scarcely have occurred if he had not in fact played an important part in the history of the northern tribes.

A. C. W.—**C. A. Si.**

JOSHUA, BOOK OF.—**1. Place in the Canon.**—The book was placed by the Jews among the Early Prophets, *i.e.* Joshua, Judges, Samuel, Kings. It might have been expected that since Genesis, which recounts the origins of the nation to which the Torah was delivered, was included in the Torah—the first division of the Canon—Joshua, which relates the conquest of the land in which the Torah was to be practised, would also be included. But this assumes that Deuteronomy was already regarded as the fifth book of the Torah when Joshua assumed its present form. The literary evidence, however, suggests that the book of Deuteronomy, as distinguished from the code, once formed part of a history of Israel which continued through Joshua, Judges, Samuel, and Kings. Later it was separated from this and made part of the Torah, both because of its legal content and because the growth of the legend of Moses had made him a key figure, not only in the tradition of the tribes of the Exodus, but in the national tradition as a whole, so that his death was held to mark the end of an era.

Modern criticism has at times tended to reverse this judgment and to connect Joshua more closely with the Pentateuch, on the ground that, since all the pentateuchal documents look forward to the fulfilment of Yahweh's promise of Palestine, Joshua, which relates the conquest, is a necessary sequel. It must be remembered, however, that the earlier histories upon which the pentateuchal narrative is based did not end with the conquest ; they continued the story to the disruption of the kingdom. Furthermore, Deuteronomy looks forward beyond the conquest to the establishment of a national sanctuary, for which Joshua provides the foundation. The connexion of Joshua with the Pentateuch is no closer than its connexion with Judges, Samuel, and Kings.

2. Structure and contents.—The book falls into three parts : (*a*) the conquest, chs. 1–12 ; (*b*) the division of the land, chs. 13–21 ; (*c*) a conclusion, chs. 22–24. It is convenient to discuss these separately.

(*a*) The foundation of chs. 1–12 is a narrative which is clearly a conflation of two accounts of the conquest, one of which is derived from the so-called J tradition, the other from that of E, whether or not they were compiled by the same authors as the corresponding material in the Pentateuch. It relates the mission of the spies to Jericho ($2^{1-9, 12-23}$), and the consequent passage of Jordan ($3^{1-6, 8b, 13-16}$ $4^{4a, 5, 8, 10f, 18}$). It recounts the circumcision at Gilgal, which it views as a novelty (‘ the second time ’ of 5^{2} is absent from the LXX), since by this means the reproach of the circumcised Egyptians is removed from the people ($5^{2f, 8f}$). The story of the capture of Jericho and of Ai follows, with the trespass of Achan (5^{13}–8^{29}). Joshua then makes a compact with the Gibeonites ($9^{3-9a, 11-15a, 16, 22f, 26, 27a}$), and advances to the victory at Beth-horon ($10^{1-7, 9-14}$), to the execution at Makkedah ($10^{15-24, 26f}$), and to the victory at the Waters of Merom (11^{1-9}).

All the incidents in this narrative, with the exception of the Makkedah episode (10^{15ff}) and the campaign against Hazor (11^{1-9}), occurred within a very limited area, practically co-terminous with the territory of Benjamin. This suggests that the author who first undertook to write an account of the conquest of central Palestine built it up round various local traditions of diverse origin—those of Gilgal, Jericho, Ai, Achan, and Gibeon—which, it has been cogently argued, had been preserved at the sanctuary of Gilgal. These he put together into a connected story, supplementing them with the Makkedah legend (to which that of Hazor was later added), and attaching them to the name of the Ephraimite hero Joshua (see preceding article). The conquest of the south had already been described by an earlier author, who utilized the traditions of the tribes concerned, together with a legend of the capture of Bethel (Jg 1^{3-26}). This the author of the earliest Joshua story left substantially intact, placing the events after the death of Joshua (Jg 1^{1f}). He said nothing, however, of the conquest of the land north of Benjamin, presumably because there was no tradition about this available to him. He must have closed his account with some statement to the effect that Joshua subdued the whole land (cf 11^{23a}), before passing on to his description of its division among the several tribes in section (*b*); see below. The second document underlying the present story in chs. 1–12 included the Hazor campaign (11^{1-9}) and the Shechem legend (8^{30ff} 24^{1-28}, in part; see below). But even when this material was conflated with the earlier work the resultant narrative still lacked any reference to a conquest of Ephraim and Manasseh.

This account has been thoroughly revised by an editor who is closely akin in spirit and language to the author of the framework of Deuteronomy. He added an introduction into which he has fused earlier material (ch. 1). He emphasized the activity of Yahweh in the events narrated (2^{24} 3^{9-11} $4^{1-3, 6f, 20-24}$ 9^{9b-10} $10^{8, 25}$), His exaltation of Joshua (3^{7} 4^{14}) and the fear inspired in the Canaanites (2^{10f} 5^{1} 9^{24f}); and further embellished the story with some minor details (3^{17} $4^{9, 12}$ $7^{7, 12}$ 9^{1f} 11^{10-15}). But it was the addition of the lists in 10^{28ff} 11^{16ff} and ch. 12 which completely changed the pattern of the narrative; for they not only extend the range of Joshua's conquests in the north (11^{16b} 12^{16b-24}) but also represent him as the conqueror of the south (10^{28-43} $11^{16a, 21f}$ $12^{8, 11-16b}$), thus rejecting Jg 1^{3-20} (cf Jos 14^{12} 15^{15ff}). Obviously the concern of this author was to reaffirm in concrete terms the faith of Israel that Yahweh had given them the land, and he did this by ascribing to one representative figure, and assigning to a relatively brief period, operations which had covered a considerable time and engaged many leaders. It was, it may reasonably be assumed, this editor who omitted Jg 1^{1}–2^{5} from the Joshua-Judges narrative (to which it was later restored), and inserted such parts of it as were not covered by Jos 10^{28-43} at the appropriate points in chs. 13–19: 15^{13-19} (=Jg $1^{10, 20, 11-15}$), 15^{63} (=Jg 1^{21}), 16^{10} (=Jg 1^{29}), 17^{11-13} (=Jg 1^{27f}). He may also be responsible for the present position of 17^{1b} and 13^{13}, derived from an earlier account of the conquest of Gilead by Machir (cf Nu $32^{39, 41f}$); and for 19^{47}, which was added when the story of the migration of the Danites (Jg 17 f) was omitted.

This deuteronomic narrative was subsequently edited by a redactor of the P school, who added $4^{13, 19}$ $5^{4-7, 10-12}$ $9^{15b, 17-21}$. Whether or not he was dependent upon a P account of the conquest, it is impossible to say.

(*b*) Chs. 13–21, more complex in structure than chs. 1–12, are a conflation of two accounts of the division of the land. The first, that of JE, told how Joshua first assigned their territory to Judah and the Joseph tribes (13^{1-8} 14^{6-15} 17^{14-18}), and then sent a commission through the country to divide the rest of the land into seven portions to be assigned to the remaining tribes by lot (18^{2-10}), Reuben and Gad having already received their territory, while Levi was to have no tribal possession. This was followed by an account of the actual assignment, each portion being described in terms of the cities it contained. It has been argued with considerable cogency that the lists of the cities of Judah (15^{21-62}), Benjamin (18^{21-28a}), Simeon (19^{2-8a}), and Dan (19^{41b-45}), were taken from an official record of the kingdom of Judah, prepared in the reign of Josiah, which had later been incorporated into the J document. The names of the cities in the territory of the other tribes ($19^{15, 18b-22a, 25b-28a, 29b \text{ in part}, 30a, 33 \text{ in part}, 35-38a}$) may have been derived from similar lists; with them belong the several references to 'the cities with their villages' in 19^{16ff}. 19^{49b-50} closes the account. It is impossible to determine the extent to which this JE material has been revised by the Deuteronomic editor; $13^{9-12, 14}$ certainly comes from his hand, as does 21^{43-45}.

The second account, with which the first is now conflated, gives the boundaries of the territory assigned to each of the tribes. This appears to be dependent upon an already existing document which, according to some scholars, was drawn up before the foundation of the State, and described not only the land actually possessed by the several tribes at that time, but also the land to which they laid claim. The fact that this material is in most cases here introduced by formulae in the style of P suggests that its inclusion is due to the activity of a redactor of the P school; and the further fact that it places the proceedings at Shiloh (18^{1}), not at Gilgal as is implied by 18^{5b} (JE), may point to some dependence upon the tradition of the pre-monarchical inter-tribal federation. The beginning of this account is now contained in 18^{1}, its present position being due to the exigencies of conflation. To it belong 13^{15}–14^{5} 5^{1-12a} 16^{1-9} 17^{1-10} $18^{11-20, 28b}$ $19^{1, 8b-9, 10-14, 16-18a, 22a\beta, 23-25a, 28b-29, 31-34, 39-41a, 46, 48a, 49a, 51}$. From the same priestly redactor come $20^{1-3, 6a, 7-9}$, the law and list of the cities of refuge (to which vv.$^{4f, 6b}$, missing from LXX, were later added), and 21^{1-42}, the list of Levitical cities.

(*c*) Underlying 22^{9-34} is the JE account of the return of the two and a half east-Jordan tribes to their own territory, for which the Deuteronomic editor provided an introduction, vv.$^{1-8}$. The original story has been heavily edited by the priestly redactor in the light of the tradition of the pre-monarchical federation. 24^{1-28} is the JE account of the renewal of the covenant at Shechem, to which the deuteronomic author of the book has made a number of minor additions (*e.g.* vv.$^{8b, 10a, 11b, 13, 16-18a}$). More important than these, however, is his substitution of vv.$^{22-24, 25b, 26a}$ for the account of the erection of the altar commanded in Dt 27^{5ff}. This he placed in its present position in ch. 8^{30-35} changing the original Gerizim in v.^{30} to Ebal, and by implication locating it near Gilgal (cf Dt 11^{30}) so as to counter the Samaritan claim that the sanctuary of Gerizim near Shechem was the central sanctuary referred to in Dt 12. To the account thus revised he prefixed Joshua's final counsels (ch. 23). The account of the death and burial of Joshua, the burial of Joseph's bones, the death and burial of Eleazar, he derived from JE, adding v.^{31} looking forward to the continuation of the story in Judges.

A. C. W.—C. A. Si.

JOSIAH.—1. King of Judah, who succeeded his father Amon when only eight years old (2 K 22^{1}). The religious condition of the people, which was bad under Amon, continued without essential improvement, so far as we know, until the eighteenth year of Josiah. The sudden change then made resulted from the finding of the Book of the Law in the Temple (v.^{8ff}); but it is possible that the minds of king and people were prepared for it by the Scythian invasion. The demand of the book for a thorough reformation powerfully affected the king and his officers. The book was read publicly, and king and people entered into a solemn covenant to act according to its injunctions. Its central demand was the removal of all altars in the country except the one at Jerusalem. This was henceforth to be the only sanctuary in Judah. The carrying out of this programme is related in detail, and we learn that the conclusion of the work was marked by the celebration of the Passover in a new manner and with unusual solemnity (23^{21ff}).

Josiah's reign was characterized by justice, as we learn from Jeremiah, but we know no more of it until the end of the king's life. The Assyrian empire was tottering to its fall, and Pharaoh Neco (see NECO), who marched to the aid of Assyria, thought to seize the provinces nearest him and attach them to Egypt. Josiah was ill-advised enough to attempt to resist him. In the battle which ensued he was slain (23^{29}). His motive in undertaking this expedition has been much discussed. Probably he hoped to restore the real independence of Judah. That he was beloved by his people is indicated by their deep and long-continued mourning. **2.** Son of Zephaniah (Zec 6^{10}). H. P. S.

JOSIAS.—**1.** AV and RV spelling of **Josiah,** King of Judah, in 1 Es $1^{1, 7, 18, 21-23, 25, 28f, 32-34}$, Bar 1^{8}. **2.** 1 Es 8^{33} (AV). See JESHAIAH, **4.**

JOSIBIAH, 1 Ch 4^{35} (AV).—See JOSHIBIAH.

JOSIPHIAH.—The father of one of Ezra's companions, Ezr 8^{10}, 1 Es 8^{36} (AV, RV **Josaphias**).

JOT AND TITTLE.—In Mt 5^{18} AV Jesus says, ' Till heaven and earth pass, one jot or one tittle shall in no wise pass from the law, till all be fulfilled ' (|| Lk 16^{17}). The Greek words *iōta* and *keraia* (WH *kerea*) were translated by Tyndale ' iott ' and ' tytle,' and these forms were retained in all the versions. The 1611 edition of AV has ' iote ' (one syllable) and ' title,' but modern printers have turned ' iote ' into ' jot,' and ' title ' into ' tittle.' The *iota* is the smallest letter of the Greek alphabet, as is the *yod* in the later Hebrew. The *keraia* (literally ' little horn ') is any small mark distinguishing one letter from another, like the stroke of a *t*. RSV reads, ' not an iota, not a dot.'

JOTBAH.—Home of the mother of King Amon, 2 K 21^{19}, possibly *Kh. Jefât* in Galilee, known as Jotapata in Roman times.

JOTBATH, Dt 10^{7} (AV).—See JOTBATHAH.

JOTBATHAH.—A station in the journeyings of the Israelites, Nu 33^{33f}, Dt 10^{7} (AV **Jotbath**). It is described as ' a land with brooks of water.' It is possibly modern *'Ain Ṭābah*, N. of the Gulf of 'Aqaba.

JOTHAM.—The youngest son of Jerubbaal, who, by hiding himself, escaped the massacre of his brethren by **Abimelech,** Jg 9^{5}. When Abimelech had been proclaimed king by the Shechemites, Jotham appeared, close to where they were assembled, on Mt. Gerizim, and addressed to them the ' Parable of the Trees ' (9^{8-20}). The parable, which is somewhat incongruous in parts, is intended as an appeal to the conscience of the Shechemites ; in case the appeal should turn out to be fruitless (which indeed proved to be the case), Jotham utters a curse (v.^{20}) against both Abimelech and the Shechemites. This curse is shortly afterwards fulfilled. After his address, Jotham flies to Beer (v.^{21}), and we hear of him no more. W. O. E. O.

JOTHAM.—**1.** A king of Judah in the time of Isaiah. His father was afflicted with leprosy, and Jotham had some sort of regency before becoming sole ruler, 2 K 15^{5}. We know nothing of him except that he rebuilt or ornamented one of the gates of the Temple (v.^{35}), and that the hostilities which later culminated in the invasion of Judah began before his death (vv.^{37f}). **2.** A Calebite, 1 Ch 2^{47}. H. P. S.

JOY.—Verbs and nouns expressive of joy are characteristic of Biblical religion, and are a notable feature of the cultus in the OT. There are, of course, the normal human occasions for rejoicing, as at a bountiful harvest or a military victory (Is 9^{3}), a happy marriage (Pr 5^{18}), the pleasures of food and comfort (Ec 8^{15}, Pr 27^{9}) and of health and strength (Ec 11^{9}). In general, it may be said that joy is the product of a healthy relationship between God and man, a fact that is expressed in the first psalm (' Blessed ' in v.^{1} means ' O the happiness of '). Yahweh Himself rejoices in His creative work (Ps 104^{31}) in the maintenance of His people's life (Dt 30^{9}), or at the restoration of His people from distress (Is 62^{5}). In Zeph 3^{17}, the whole vocabulary of joy is used of God in His saving work for His people. This thought is reflected in Lk $15^{7, 10}$ in relation to the repentance and salvation of the sinner, and is expressed in the Fourth Gospel at the heart of the Passion (Jo 15^{11} 17^{13} ; cf He 12^{2}). The Nativity is therefore a word of great joy (Lk 2^{10}).

The OT terminology expresses the emotion of joy (*śimḥāh, māśôś*), or joy as an aspect of ritual activity (*gîl, rinnāh*), though these are not sharply distinguished. The fullness of life experienced by the people of God produces joy, cf Ps 36^{5-9} 63^{1-7} ; it is known to those who live by God's constant love, faithfulness, righteousness, and salvation. It is not, however, merely an emotion ; it leads to the fulfilment of God's will in moral and ritual activity (Dt $12^{7, 10-12}$, Ps 19^{7-10} 27^{6} 119). It is a notable feature of the deuteronomic legislation and of the Psalter. The cultic terms for joy suggest that in origin the religious joy was of an uninhibited and ecstatic character, and even in the post-exilic religion the sound of rejoicing could be considerable (Neh 12^{43}).

The expectation of the fulfilment of the Divine sovereignty in the Day of the Lord is associated with the joy of His people (Is 12^{1-3} 65^{17-19}). So the expressions of gladness and mirth at the festivals of coronation come to full expression when the whole world of men rejoices that Yahweh is King (Ps 96^{7-13}) ; for the complete manifestation of His sovereignty is the fulfilment of the created order (cf also Is 35^{3-10} 49^{13} 55^{12f}, Zec 9^{9} etc.).

It is in these terms that the announcement of the birth of Jesus is associated with joy, and whatever be the origin of the hymns in Luke, it is appropriate that the Magnificat should be uttered by His Mother. Those who hear and recognize the proclamation of Jesus are described as supremely happy (Mt 13^{16}), as is Peter at the moment of revelation (Mt 16^{17}). The deep joy of Jesus as the signs of the New Age are manifested in the work of His disciples, is described in Lk 10^{21f}. This quality characterized the life of the early Church (Ac 2^{46}), and is especially apparent as the Gospel is effectively proclaimed among Samaritans (8^{8}) and Gentiles ($13^{48, 52}$ 15^{3} 16^{34}). One of the notable features of the Pauline epistles is the note of rejoicing. It is part of the harvest of the Spirit (Gal 5^{22} ; cf Ro 14^{17}), and is most manifest in adversity (Ph $1^{4, 18}$ 4^{4}) ; the Christian is to ' rejoice always ' (1 Th 5^{16}). Not only are the afflictions that beset the faithful servant of Christ unable to quench his joy, they may even be the occasion for rejoicing (Ro 5^{3-11}, Col 1^{24} ; cf 1 P 1^{6-12}), since they are evidence that the fulfilment of all things is at hand. It is in these terms that the persecuted Church is called to rejoice (Rev 19^{7}), and it is noteworthy that the Apocalypse has preserved, more than any other part of the NT, the hymns of the early Church (Rev 5^{9f} 12^{13} 7^{12} 15^{3f} etc.). A. S. H.

JOZABAD (' Y″ has bestowed ').—**1. 2. 3.** Three of David's heroes, 1 Ch 12^{4} (AV **Josabad**) $^{20, 20}$. **4.** A Levite in the time of Hezekiah, 2 Ch 31^{13}. **5.** A Levite in the time of Josiah, 2 Ch 35^{9} ; called **Joram** in 1 Es 1^{9}. **6.** A priest who had married a foreign wife, Ezr 10^{22} ; in 1 Es 9^{22} called **Gedaliah** (AV, RV **Ocidelus**). **7.** A Levite, Ezr 8^{33} 10^{23}, 1 Es 8^{63} (AV **Josabad,** RV **Josabdus**), 9^{23} (RV **Jozabdus**). **8.** A Levite who expounded the Law, Neh 8^{7}, 1 Es 9^{48} (AV **Joazabdus,** RV **Jozabdus**). **9.** A Levite of Jerusalem, Neh 11^{16}. Possibly **7, 8, 9,** are the same man. See also JEHOZABAD.

JOZABDUS.—**1.** 1 Es 9^{23} (RV) ; see JOZABAD, **7.** **2.** 1 Es 9^{29} (RV) ; see ZABBAI, **1.** **3.** 1 Es 9^{48} (RV) ; see JOZABAD, **8.**

JOZACAR.—In 2 K 12^{21} it is said that Jozacar (AV **Jozachar**) the son of Shimeath and Jehozabad the son of Shomer murdered Joash. In 2 Ch 24^{26} he is called **Zabad.** See SHIMEATH.

JOZACHAR, 2 K 12^{21} (AV).—See JOZACAR.

JOZADAK.—See JEHOZADAK.

JUBAL.—A son of Lamech by Adah, and inventor of musical instruments, Gn 4^{21}. The name probably contains an allusion to *yōbhēl*, ' ram's horn.'

JUBILEE.—See SABBATICAL YEAR.

JUBILEES, BOOK OF.—See PSEUDEPIGRAPHA, **2.**

JUCAL.—See JEHUCAL.

JUDAEA.—The Graeco-Latin name of Judah, but derived from the Aramaic gentilic *y*^{e}*hûdhā'î*. In Persian times it was called *Y*^{e}*hûdh* (so on coins), and the term was restricted to the district round Jerusalem. The oldest instance of the form Judaea is found in a fragment of *c* 320 B.C. (Jos., *c. Ap.* i. 22 [179]). It is regularly used in 2 Maccabees, but in 1 Maccabees both Judah and Judaea are employed. In the latter work the concept does not include the northern districts that were acquired under Jonathan in 147 B.C. (1 Mac $11^{28, 34}$). In the NT it can include these districts. Idumaea, which began south of Beth-zur (q.v.), was sometimes considered separate (Mk 3^{7}), though Josephus makes it one of the eleven districts of Judaea (*BJ* III. iii. 5 [55]). Samaria and Galilee were separate geographical concepts. However, the expansion of Judaea under the Maccabees, until the kingdom embraced all Palestine (except some Hellenistic cities), and the realm of Herod, which was governed from Jerusalem, gave the term Judaea a more comprehensive use, alongside of the narrower one. This can be seen in numerous passages of Josephus. In the NT we also find it employed broadly (cf Lk 1^{5} 4^{44} 7^{17} 23^{5}, Ac 10^{37} $11^{1, 29}$ 26^{20}). It can even be used of Transjordan (Mt 19^{1}). Its mention in the enumeration of Acts 2^{9} is uncertain as to dependability or application. The broad use once established continued even after Augustus ousted Archelaus (A.D. 6) and took Judaea proper as well as Samaria under Roman administration, with the governor residing at Caesarea, while Galilee and Peraea were left to the tetrarch Herod Antipas. A temporary restoration of Herodian Judaea took place under the kingship of Herod Agrippa (A.D. 41–44), but thereafter Roman governors held sway until the Jewish revolt broke out in A.D. 66.

A part of Judaea proper is the *wilderness of Judaea* (in the OT the wilderness of Judah, Jg 1^{16}, Ps 63^{1}), the bad-lands country of rocky gorges descending from the high plateau to the Jordan and the Dead Sea. John the Baptist was in the wilderness until he began his ministry (Lk 1^{80}). This suggests—as many believe—that he may have been a member of the Essene community at Qumrân, the Dead Sea Scrolls community made famous by modern discoveries. His preaching in the wilderness (Mk 1^{4} etc.) may, however, be an echo of prophecy (Is 40^{3}). Actually he preached at the Jordan fords. E. G. K.

JUDAH.—Popular etymologies regard the name as a semi-Aramaic Hophʿal imperfect of *yādhāh* ' to praise ' (Gn 29^{35} 49^{8}). He is represented as the fourth son of Leah by Jacob (Gn 29^{35} [J] 35^{23} [P]), and in the Judaean tradition (J) he is given precedence over Reuben, the first-born, who is favoured by the northern Ephraimite tradition (E). According to J, it was Judah who proposed to sell Joseph in order to avert the danger which threatened him at the hands of his brethren (Gn 37^{26ff}). Similarly, when they return to Joseph's house with the silver cup, J gives the pre-eminence to Judah, and makes him spokesman for all in his pathetic appeal to Joseph (44^{14-34}). The Blessing of Jacob (Gn 49) makes Judah the ruler, with Reuben displaced because of his lust towards Bilhah and his general instability (Gn 49^{4}), whilst the next two sons of Leah are scattered because of their barbarous conduct towards Shechem (Gn 34) and fall into disfavour with their brethren. Gn 49 probably reflects the situations of the tribes in the time of David. On the other hand the Blessing of Moses (Dt 33) reflects the time of the two monarchies with the northern kingdom much more powerful than Judah, the southern kingdom.

A tradition is preserved in Gn 38 which is generally supposed to be of great value as bearing upon the early development of the tribe. Judah is there said to have withdrawn himself from his brethren and to have gone down to meet a certain Adullamite whose name was Hirah. There he met with Bath-shua, a Canaanitess, whom he took to wife. She bore him three sons, Er, Onan, and Shelah. Er and Onan were slain by Yahweh for their wickedness. Er's widow, Tamar, a Canaanitess also it seems, posing by the wayside as a hierodule, enticed Judah to intercourse with her, and of her the twin sons Perez and Zerah were born to Judah. This story is usually held to be based upon facts of tribal history, and to show that, though we have here a personal narrative, Judah is certainly the eponymous head of the tribe. The story points to the settlement of Judah in the region of Adullam and equally clearly to the tribe's union with foreign stock. Hirah is a Canaanite clan ; Shelah, Perez, and Zerah continued as elements in Judah. Besides these, in the time of David the Calebites and the Jerahmeelites, mentioned in 1 Ch 2 as descendants of Perez, were incorporated into the tribe of Judah. In 1 S 27^{10} 30^{14} they still appear to be independent, though the Chronicler makes both of them to be descendants of Judah through Perez and Hezron, to whom also he traces David. In Nu 13 (P) Caleb belongs to Judah ; but in Nu 32^{12}, Jos $14^{6, 14}$, Jg 3 etc., he is a Kenizzite, the son of Kenaz. From the last passage we see that Othniel, whose chief centre was Kiriath-sepher (Debir), was another closely related tribe, and both appear from Gn $36^{16, 42}$ to have been Edomites. Kenites, commonly supposed to be of Midianite origin, we are told in Jg 1^{16}, also went up from Jericho with Judah into the southern Wilderness of Judah.

Of all these foreign elements by which the tribe of Judah was increased, the Calebite was the most important. It was the Calebite capital, Hebron, that under David became the capital of Judah in the days before David captured Jebus (Jerusalem). After this time the history of the tribe becomes the history of the Southern Kingdom. The territory of the tribe is described in Jos 15^{1ff} (P), but this is late and an ideal apportionment.

The 10th-cent. tribe of Judah was the creation of David, and was composed of the original Hebrew nucleus with the addition of all ' his friends ' mentioned in 1 S 30^{26-31}, those with whom he shared the spoil of his freebooting days. All the places here mentioned were S. of Hebron. See also TRIBES OF ISRAEL.

There were four men named Judah in Ezra's time : a Levite (Ezr 10^{23}), an overseer (Ne 11^{9}), a musician (Neh 12^{8}) and a priest (Neh 12^{36}). N. H. S.

JUDAH.—**1.** See preceding article. **2.** A Levite mentioned Ezr 3^{9} (cf Neh 12^{8}) ; called **Joda** (q.v.) in 1 Es 5^{58}. **3.** A Levite, Ezr 10^{23}, 1 Es 9^{23} (AV, RV **Judas**). **4.** An overseer, Neh 11^{9}. **5.** A priest's son, Neh 12^{36}. **6.** Lk 1^{39} ; see JUTTAH. **7.** See next article.

JUDAH.—According to Jos 19^{34} a town of Naphtali. The site is unknown, and the text is generally believed to be corrupt.

JUDAISM (Gr. *Judaismos*), a term coined by the Greek-speaking Jews to designate their religious way of life in contrast to that of their neighbours, known as Hellenism (2 Mac 2^{21} 8^{1} 14^{38}, 4 Mac 4^{26}). Paul similarly uses it in the sense of the Jewish religion and contrasts it with his new religion of Christianity (Gal 1^{13f}). Its Hebrew equivalent *Yah*^{a}*dhûth*, appearing neither in the Bible nor in the Talmud, dates from the Middle Ages (Rashi to Yebamot 23b. Esther Rabba 7 uses *Yah*^{a}*dhûth*).

While the name is late, the phenomenon to which it refers goes back to the beginnings of Jewish spiritual life, and represents the historical religious experience of the Jewish people. The distinction often made between the religion of Israel and Judaism, identifying the first with pre-exilic and the latter with post-exilic development, is purely artificial. The basic elements of post-exilic Judaism—ethical monotheism, the consciousness of Israel's mission as the servant of God, living under the divine law, angelology, and eschatology—have their roots in the earlier period.

The Babylonian exile broke up the geographic unity of the Jewish people and initiated their ever-widening diaspora. The Davidic dynasty disappeared only to grow into an object of Messianic hope. (See MESSIAH.) What was left of political independence took the form of a theocracy, headed by a high priest of the line of Zadok. The actual sovereignty passed into the power of the Persians, then of the Greeks and later of the Romans. The spiritual life centred in the Second Temple and to a lesser degree in the new democratic institution of the Synagogue (q.v.), which was nourished by the Reformation of Ezra and Nehemiah and by the adoption of the Torah (Pentateuch) as the supreme source of authority in Judaism. The post-exilic period was marked by the development of the three-fold canon (q.v.) of Scripture, by the growth of the extra-canonical books (see APOCRYPHA) and by the beginnings of the Oral Law. It witnessed the Samaritan (q.v.) secession, the resistance by the pietists or *Ḥasidim* of the tidal wave of Hellenism, the rise of the Essenes (q.v.) and of the Pharisees (q.v.) in opposition to the Zadokite priesthood (see SADDUCEES) as the leading force in Judaism, and the emergence of the new world religion of Christianity.

With the fall of the State and the destruction of the Temple (A.D. 70), Palestine came completely into foreign control and the Jews were driven into *Gālûth*, exile, as homeless wanderers among the nations, carrying with them the Written and the Oral Torah as their imperishable, spiritual fatherland. The synagogue now replaced the Temple as the centre of Jewish life. The sacrificial worship gave way to the service of prayer, study of Torah, and practice of charity. The leadership of the priests passed into the hands of the rabbis (q.v.), whose main function consisted in interpreting Scripture in the light of the ever new conditions that emerged. Out of their efforts grew the *Halachah* (law) and the *Haggadah* (lore), which are embodied in the *Mishnah* (3rd cent.) and in its interpretations, the Palestinian (4th cent.) and Babylonian (end of 5th cent.) *Gemaras* (see TALMUD) and in the *Midrashim*.

The growth of rabbinic Judaism roused the Karaitic opposition (8th cent.) which called for a return to Scripture. The rabbinic response to this challenge translated itself into a renewed study of the text of Scripture (see TEXT OF THE **OT, Massorah)**, in the cultivation of Hebrew grammar, philology and exegesis, the systematization of the Halachah, and the development of theology, philosophy, and *Cabbalah*. The undying Messianic hope, while offering anodyne to suffering Jewry, at times degenerated into vulgar imposture on the part of pseudo-messiahs, as in the case of Sabbetai Zevi and Jacob Frank (17th and 18th cent.). Its tragic aberrations were relieved by the deeply spiritual popular movement of *Hasidism* in 18th-cent. Poland. Its emotional mysticism evoked the opposition of rabbinic Judaism.

The modern era began with the Enlightenment movement in Germany, whence it spread to other lands, and was followed by the struggle for political emancipation and religious reform. In reaction to mounting anti-semitism, Jewish nationalism came to renewed life in the form of Zionism, which reached its climax in the restoration of the State of Israel in 1947. Contemporary Judaism contains variations from strictest Orthodoxy to Conservatism and Reform. S. S. C.

JUDAS (in Apocrypha), the Greek equivalent of the Hebrew name *Judah*. **1.** The third son of Mattathias, called Maccabaeus (1 Mac 2^{4} etc.). See MACCABEES, **2. 2.** One of two captains who stood by Jonathan at Hazor (1 Mac 11^{70}). **3.** A Jew holding some important position at Jerusalem; he is named in the title of a letter sent from the Jews of Jerusalem and Judaea and the Jewish Senate to their brethren in Egypt, and to a certain Aristobulus (2 Mac 1^{10}). **4.** A son, probably the eldest, of Simon the Maccabee (1 Mac 16^{2}). In 135 B.C., he, with his father and another brother named Mattathias, was murdered at Dok by Ptolemy, the son of Abubus (16^{11-17}). **5.** 1 Es 9^{23} (AV, RV); see JUDAH, **3.**

JUDAS (in NT).—**1. Judas Iscariot.**—See following article.

2. Judas, the son of James (see JAMES, **4**), one of the twelve Apostles (Lk 6^{16}, Ac 1^{13}), perhaps identical with the Thaddaeus (q.v.) named by Mark (3^{18}) and Matthew (10^{3}); some MSS read Lebbaeus (q.v.). The only thing recorded of him is that, when Jesus promised in the Upper Room to manifest Himself to the one who loved Him, he asked, ' Lord, how is it that you will manifest yourself to us, and not to the world? ' (Jn 14^{22}) —showing that he did not understand that Jesus' Kingdom is not of this world and therefore cannot be manifested to the world. Judas evidently still thought in terms of a visible and material messianic Kingdom.

3. Judas, the Lord's brother (Mt 13^{55} = Mk 6^{3}).—See BRETHREN OF THE LORD. He was presumably the author of the short Epistle of Jude (*i.e.* Judas), where he styles himself ' a servant of Jesus Christ and brother of James ' (v.^{1}), and, like James, exhibits a stern zeal for morality.

4. Judas, the Galilaean.—He is so called both in the NT (Ac 5^{37}) and in Josephus, though he belonged to Gamala in Gaulanitis on the eastern side of the Lake of Galilee; perhaps because Galilee was the scene of his patriotic enterprise. At the enrolment or census under Quirinius in A.D. 7, Judas raised an insurrection. He perished, and his followers were scattered, but their spirit did not die. They banded themselves into a religious and patriotic society under the significant name of the **Zealots,** pledged to undying hostility against the Roman tyranny and ever eager for an opportunity to throw off its yoke. Their motto was ' No king but God.' Their activity was one of the chief causes which led to the outbreak of the Jewish War against Rome in A.D. 66.

5. Judas, a Jew of Damascus (Ac 9^{11}).—His house was in the Straight Street, and Saul of Tarsus lodged there after his conversion.

6. Judas Barsabbas, one of two deputies—Silas being the other—who were chosen by the rulers of the Church at Jerusalem to accompany Paul and Barnabas to Antioch, and report to the believers there the Council's decision on the question on what terms the Gentiles should be admitted into the Christian Church (Ac 15^{22-33}). Judas and Silas are described as ' leading men among the brethren ' (v.^{22}) and ' prophets ' (v.^{32}). Since they bore the same patronymic, Judas may have been a brother of Joseph Barsabbas (Ac 1^{23}). **7.** An ancestor of Jesus (Lk 3^{30}). D. S.—**W. F.**

JUDAS ISCARIOT.—One of the twelve disciples, son of Simon Iscariot (Jn 6^{71} 13^{26}), the betrayer of Jesus. Little is known about Judas outside of his being the betrayer of Jesus and his being listed as one of the Twelve (Mk 3^{19} $14^{10, 43-46}$, Mt 10^{4} $26^{14-25, 47-49}$ 27^{3-10}, Lk 6^{16} $22^{3-6, 47-48}$, Jn 6^{70-71} 12^{1-6} $13^{2, 21-30}$ 14^{22}, Ac $1^{16-20, 25}$). He is the only Judaean disciple, and it is inferred that he was a person of promising leadership, perhaps with the rather common hope of sharing a place of importance in the coming kingdom. Though Judas seems to be an important member of the Twelve, as indicated by his being treasurer of the group (Jn 12^{6} 13^{29}) and the possibility of his reclining by Jesus at the Last Supper (Jn 13^{21-26}), his name in the NT is always placed last in the list of the disciples. This listing was due to his betrayal of Jesus, though in some lists of the Eastern Church Judas' name appears as third or sixth. Because of Judas' betrayal of Jesus the early Christians in penitence fasted on Wednesdays.

Judas is the Greek form of Judah, a name honoured by one of the twelve tribes of Israel and by the stalwart warrior of the Maccabees. Some have inferred that Judas was a brother of Lazarus, Mary, and Martha (Jn 12^{4-6}). The term Iscariot has had diverse interpretations. It has been translated as ' the man of Issachar,' ' the man from Sychar ' (which would make Judas a Samaritan), the carrier of the *scortea* (leather bag of the treasurer?). Codex Sinaiticus (in Jn 6^{71}) dissects the term into *ish Kariot* (' man from Kerioth '). The location of Kerioth (q.v.) is uncertain (Jos 15^{25}, Am 2^{2}, Jer 4^{24}), though it has been associated with modern Qaryaten in southern Palestine. The name may be derived from the early Aramaic root of ' liar ' or ' hypocrite,' a term applied by the Aramaic-speaking Christians to Judas the betrayer. Iscariot may also be a Semitic transliteration of the Latin term *sicarius*, meaning a dagger-man [Codex

Bezae and the Itala infer the term *skarioth* to have this meaning]. As a *sicarius* or dagger-man of the Zealots, and as one who is paired with Simon the Zealot, the interpretation of Judas' betrayal of the non-Zealotic Jesus is more clearly understood.

After Jesus openly accepts anointment (as Messiah?) at Bethany, Judas leaves to betray Him (Mk 14$^{3-11}$). Though it is not clear as to what Judas betrayed, it is assumed that Jesus believed Himself to be Messiah. Our gospel narrators do not make it clear that, after Judas left the scene of the anointing, he partook of the Last Supper before his betrayal of Jesus in the garden of Gethsemane. The writer of the Gospel of John alone mentions Judas' departure from the Last Supper, and since this Gospel does not record the institution of the supper, it is open to question as to whether Judas went out before or after the institution. From Lk 22$^{17-21}$ it is argued that he was present, but Luke's arrangement is different from that of Mark and Matthew, who place the institution after the announcement of the betrayal (Mt 26$^{21-29}$, Mk 14$^{18-25}$). According to the Gospel of John, Judas seems to have gone out immediately after the announcement (13^{30}), the institution then following, and ch. 14 being the address at the Last Supper.

Various motives have been suggested for Judas' betrayal of Jesus: (1) An early Gnostic sect, known as the Cainites, believed that Judas had attained a higher degree of spiritual insight than his fellows, and had hastened the death of Jesus because he knew that it would break the power of the evil spirits, the rulers of this world. (2) Judas as a greedy person, who desired thirty pieces of silver (Mt 26^{15}; cf Zec 11^{12}), had assumed that Jesus through His power or the help of His friends would escape His enemies. When Judas realized the awfulness of his error of faith, he cast the money into the Temple, and in remorse hanged himself. (3) Judas felt that Jesus was procrastinating in bringing in the kingdom through His leadership, and by His betrayal he hoped to force Jesus into bringing the kingdom to fruition in Jerusalem, where the masses would follow Jesus in their victory over His enemies. Through the conquest of His antagonists, Jesus' kingdom would result. (4) Judas' faith in Jesus' Messiahship was wavering. So Judas betrayed Him to test Jesus' real leadership. If Jesus were the Messiah, He would escape harm. If He were not the Messiah, He would perish. (5) God predestined Satan to enter the person of Judas, in order that His gospel of salvation might take its true course in Jesus' death and resurrection (Jn 13^{27}).

All of these theories about Judas' betrayal of Jesus seem unsatisfactory. The early Church interpreters were uncertain in their understanding of Judas, as evidenced by the diverse NT reports; and we are not certain to-day. But a realistic interpretation of Judas' betrayal as related to the historical scene at the time seems to get closer to an understanding. The atmosphere of the time called for a Messianic leader who would have Zealot tendencies, and with such abilities he would use the God-empowered sword in a holy war against Rome; in such a way God's kingdom would come into history. Zealots by the names of Judas of Gamala and Theudas, almost contemporaries of Jesus, had led bloody revolutions against Rome (Jos. *Ant.* XVIII. i. 1 [4 ff], XX. v. 2 ff [102 ff]; *BJ* II. viii. 1 [118], xvii. 8 [433 ff], VII. viii. 1 [253 ff]). Gamaliel lists Jesus with these Zealot leaders in the account in Acts (5$^{34-39}$); the Roman tribune associates Paul as a follower of a Zealot movement (Ac 21^{38}; cf Jos. *Ant.* XX. vii. 6 [169 ff]; *BJ* II. xiii. 5 [261 ff]). That Christianity was a Zealot movement by reputation was the result of some of Jesus' disciples being associated with the Zealots: James and John, the sons of Zebedee, were called *Boanerges* (Aramaic, 'sons of thunder'), and wished as Zealots to sit at the right and left hand of Jesus when He should be enthroned as the king of the world (Mk 10^{37}). Simon the Zealot (*kananaios*, better translated as 'Zealot' than 'Canaanite,' as is done in Lk 6^{15} and Ac 1^{13}), shows him to have been a member of the Zealots. Simon bar Jonah, according to G. Dalman, has been better understood by some as *barjonah*, an Akkadian word meaning 'terrorist,' a label for a member of the Zealot party. To accord with this, the Gospel of John (18^{10f}) indicates that Peter carried a sword; which indicates that he might have been a *sicarius* (dagger-man) of the Zealots. Judas as a *sicarius* or dagger-man of this group thus shared the initial hopes of this group that Jesus would use forceful, revolutionary means against Rome. In the later days at Jerusalem, when Judas came to realize that Jesus would not use these means against Rome, and that He even recommended paying taxes to Rome (Mk 12^{17} and parallels), Judas betrayed Jesus to the Jewish opposition.

The gospel accounts make it clear that Judas did not realize his betrayal of Jesus would result in Jesus' death. After the verdict of the Sanhedrin condemning Jesus to death, Judas cried out, 'I have sinned in betraying innocent blood' (Mt 27^{14}), threw the pieces of silver into the Temple, and hanged himself. Luke's account of Judas' death in Acts (1^{18f}) preserves the early Church legend that Judas bought a field with the money, whereupon he fell headlong with his bowels bursting open, giving the name of *Akeldama* (Field of Blood) to the field. These stories of Judas' death are similar to the deaths of other sinful men, such as the LXX account of Ahithophel (2 S 17^{23}); of Nadan (in the Story of Ahikar) whose bowels burst open; of Antiochus Epiphanes (2 Mac 9$^{5-13}$). Tradition has located the 'Field of Blood' where the valleys of Kidron, Tyropoeon, and Hinnom meet, though historians do not know the locality. Similarly much of the material about Judas rests on the interpretation of the early Church. He remains one of the most enigmatic figures of the NT.

T. S. K.

JUDE, EPISTLE OF.—This short epistle is addressed to a Church or a circle of churches, which have become exposed to a mischievous attack of false teachers. It rebukes in vigorous terms the immoral behaviour of these opponents and briefly admonishes the reader to hold fast to the received faith.

1. Contents.—(1) *Text.*—For its length Jude offers an unusual number of textual problems, the two most important being those in v.^{5} and vv.^{22f}. Though the RV is probably right in translating 'the Lord' in v.^{5} (despite the fact that the Greek has no article), several ancient authorities, including B, A, Vulgate, and Origen, read 'Jesus'; others read 'God'; the RSV has 'he.' Also, the position of 'once' is doubtful, some manuscripts and authorities placing it in the following clause. In vv.^{22f} editors differ as to whether there are two clauses or three. But there is much to be said for a two-clause sentence beginning with either 'have mercy' or 'refute.'

(2) *Outline of the letter.*—(*a*) In vv.$^{1-2}$ 'Jude, brother of James,' begins with a greeting in good Semitic style: 'Mercy, peace and love [*i.e.* from God] be multiplied upon you.' The place to which the letter is sent is not indicated. The readers are simply addressed as 'those who are called, beloved in God the Father and kept for Jesus Christ.'

(*b*) The occasion for the epistle is presented in vv.^{3f}: the Christian community has been secretly invested by those who 'pervert the grace of our God into licentiousness,' thereby denying in practice the Lordship of Jesus Christ. Hence Jude wishes to admonish his readers to 'contend for the faith which was once for all delivered to the saints.'

(*c*) Warnings from the history of the OT are cited in vv.$^{5-7}$. The examples of the Israelites in the wilderness, the angels of Gn 6^{1ff}, and Sodom and Gomorrah should warn the readers against the teaching and the way of life of these false teachers and arm them to resist their approaches.

(*d*) These intruders are described in vv.$^{8-16}$. (i) They claim to receive visions, they abandon themselves to sensuality, they infringe upon Divine sovereignty and blaspheme the 'powers' of the supernatural world, a thing which even Michael dared not do when he contended with the devil. But these persons do not hesitate to do this, acting as if they knew something about the matter, when in reality they know only the lusts of the senses and are bound for perdition (vv.$^{8-10}$). (ii) They are sinners like Cain, they are avaricious like Balaam and seize holy offices like Korah. They fearlessly partake of the love-feast of the community but are like clouds which bring no rain, like trees which in autumn are without fruit and like the fallen angels of the heavenly bodies who await the judgment (vv.$^{11-13}$). (iii) Enoch long ago prophesied their condemnation. They complain of their lot, they boast loudly and they flatter people for their own advantage (vv.$^{14-16}$).

(*e*) The readers are exhorted, in vv.$^{17-23}$, to remember how the apostles foretold that scoffers would appear in the last days. These are the intruders who, though they do not have the Spirit, assert that they do. The readers, however, are to edify themselves with their most holy faith, pray in the Holy Spirit, keep themselves in the love of God and await the mercy of Jesus Christ. They are to have compassion on their opponents who may perhaps be snatched from the fire at the last moment. For others, however, they are to feel fear as well as compassion and hence must hold themselves aloof from them.

(*f*) Vv.$^{24-25}$ contain the doxology: God alone can protect the readers; to Him be glory forever and ever through Jesus Christ.

2. The Heretics.—The heretics in Jude remind one in many ways of the movement with which Paul dealt in his letters to Corinth. Its most significant characteristic is its sexual libertinism (vv.^{7f}: they defile the flesh, vv.^{10,16}; cf 1 Co 5^{1ff} 6^{12ff} 10^{8}, 2 Co 12^{21}). In addition, however, these people have visions (v.^{8}: dreamers), a thing boasted of also by the opponents of Paul in Corinth (2 Co 12^{1ff}). They take money for their revelations like Balaam who according to the rabbis did the same (vv.^{11,16}); so also Paul's opponents claimed that they were justified in accepting the support of the congregation and reproached Paul for refusing it (1 Co 9, 2 Co 12^{13-16}). Their insolent language (v.^{16}) finds its parallel in the 'boasting' against which Paul also directs his attack (1 Co 4^{7}, 2 Co 5^{12} 10^{13} $11^{12,18}$). They claim to be 'spiritual' as may be deduced from the polemic in Jd ^{19} (cf 1 Co 7^{40b}, 2 Co 11^{4}); therefore they separate themselves (v.^{19}), *i.e.* they consider themselves to be Christians of a superior kind just as Paul's opponents exalted themselves above him. Fear is missing in their way of life (v.^{12}), as was also the case in Corinth, judging from what Paul tells us (1 Co 10^{22}). Therefore they regard the love-feasts as opportunities for carousing (v.^{12}) as did some of the Corinthians (1 Co 11^{20ff}). In short they pervert the grace of God into licentiousness (v.^{4}). Such men have worked their way into the congregations and have brought in new teachings (v.^{4f}) as did Paul's opponents in Corinth (2 Co 11^{4}). In face of this danger the readers are exhorted to hold firmly to the faith that was delivered once and for all (v.^{3}).

Now the significance of the first verses with which Jude exhorts his readers (vv.$^{5-7}$) can be seen: Jude refers to precisely the same example of the generation which wandered in the wilderness as did Paul in 1 Co 10^{1ff}. In both cases the point is made that the deliverance from Egypt, like the miracles which accompanied the Exodus, did not give a charter to the children of Israel for indulging in sin, but rather that their disobedience in the wilderness led to their destruction. This is directed against the idea of those opposed by both Paul and Jude that nothing can any longer harm them once they have become 'spiritual' men. The fallen angels are to remind the readers of Jude that even such exalted beings are not safe from condemnation brought on by disobedience. Thus the first Biblical examples in Jude deal with the basic issue. The reference to Korah's rebellious band (v.^{11}) contains the further condemnation of the heretics for usurping a position in the Church which does not belong to them. Apparently they claimed to be the prophetic leaders of the congregation.

But the intruders described in Jude show certain characteristics that we do not meet in the Corinthian correspondence: they 'revile the glorious ones' (v.^{8}). By that is meant the exalted beings of the created world which Paul calls powers, authorities, etc. Moreover, the opponents in Jude are called malcontents (v.^{16}), literally, those who complain of fate. Both concepts belong together, for the 'glorious ones' are the astral beings who determine fate. Later Gnosticism saw in them the embodiment of the power of the world hostile to God. The attitude taken up towards them is described by Jude in the verb 'to revile,' *i.e.* to quarrel with fate. Though no full-blown Gnostic system can be detected in Jude, these intruders (like Paul's opponents in Corinth) have taken a big step in that direction. Perhaps the puzzling expression 'to reject authority' (literally 'lordship') in v.^{8} already refers to contempt for the God of creation.

In addition to appealing to the OT and describing the heretics' sinful way of life, Jude opposes their activity in several other ways. (*a*) He reminds his readers of the faith handed on once and for all (vv.^{3,20}); the heretics are newcomers. (*b*) He urges the faithful to pray in the Holy Spirit; the heretics have visions and do not need to pray. (*c*) He exhorts his readers to remain in the love of God; the heretics need no such exhortation since they have no fear of losing the love of God. (*d*) He encourages them to wait for the mercy of Jesus Christ; such advice is not given to the heretics since they think that there is nothing that they may not do. (*e*) He reminds them that God can protect them (vv.$^{17-21}$). Hereby we are introduced, quite briefly to be sure, to the most important points which enable us to understand the situation. Jude urges his readers to feel compassion for their opponents, but a compassion mixed with fear. More exact information cannot be drawn from the difficult verses 22 and 23.

3. Author, destination, date, and place of composition.—These four problems cannot be dealt with separately. The author claims to be the brother of James. That this is the James mentioned in Mk 6^{3} is certain, since no other James was so well known that Jude could without a word of explanation introduce himself as his brother. The date is determined by the fact that v.^{17} can make reference to the words of the apostles of our Lord Jesus Christ. These words are known to the readers and they remind us of Mt 24^{11f}, 2 Th 2^{3}, 1 Ti 4^{1}, 2 Ti 3^{1f} 4^{3} in our NT. In any event that points to the time after the fall of Jerusalem and after the death of the majority of the apostles. In the preceding section we have seen that the heresy has gone a step beyond what it was at the time of Paul. Jude is peculiar because of the explicit quotation from the book of Enoch (v.^{14f} = 1 En 1^{9}) and because of its use of apocryphal tradition in v.^{9} which, according to the Church fathers, stems from the Ascension of Moses. Note too that the reference to Balaam's greed in v.^{11} goes beyond the OT and rests upon Jewish tradition. Thus one must at least consider the author a Jewish Christian.

The determination of the letter's date and destination is dependent on the question as to whether it could have been written by Jude the brother of James and of the Lord. If so, then one will have to look for the readers of the letter also among Jewish Christians, as a matter of fact, among those who lived in Palestine or Syria. It cannot be disputed that the influence of libertinism could have spread among Jewish Christians too. The use of extra-biblical Jewish tradition also speaks for such a circle of readers. The genuiness of the letter is supported by the fact that it is difficult to understand how a forger would have hit upon the idea of passing off the little known figure of Jude as the author, and further by the fact that Jude speaks of himself with a complete lack of undue emphasis. Chronologically there is no difficulty; he could have lived to see the destruction of Jerusalem and written the letter between say A.D. 70 and 80. What makes the situation puzzling is the indefiniteness of the salutation and the lack of any concrete remark that would bind the author and his readers together. The external witness to the letter does not help us: the Muratorian Canon mentions it, it is commented upon by Clement of Alexandria, and it is accepted by Origen and Tertullian. Eusebius places it among the 'disputed' books, saying that it had little early recognition. It is absent from the Peshitta version.

In any event one must reckon seriously with the possibility of the letter's genuineness. Absolute certainty cannot be reached. W. F.

JUDGES.—The Hebrew word for 'judge' is used in two senses in the OT: it denotes (1) those who administered the law in the courts, and (2) certain heroes under whose leadership the Israelites successfully resisted external aggression. This latter use of the word is confined to the book of Judges, and it is significant that it never occurs in the tribal legends which form the literary foundation of the book, but only in the Deuteronomic framework to those legends. The word is used in Judges in its other sense as well, in the lists of the so-called minor judges (10$^{1-5}$ 12$^{7-15}$). It may safely be assumed that these minor judges were officials of the pre-monarchical federation of the tribes of Israel. It is because the hero, Jephthah, was historically one of the 'judges' of Israel (Jg 12^{7}) that the title 'judge' was given by the Deuteronomists to the heroes of the other legends despite the fact that, so far as the extant evidence goes, none of them, with the possible exception of Jerubbaal, secondarily identified with Gideon, and Abimelech, who however is not called a 'judge,' ever functioned as 'judges' in the primary sense of the word.

Ex 18 tells of the appointment of judges by Moses on the advice of his Midianite father-in-law. Whatever its historicity in detail, the story throws considerable light upon the origins of the judiciary. In effect it affirms that the tribal administration of justice went back to Israel's nomad days and that the courts were ultimately of Midianite, that is of lay, origin. Further, it claims that this system was authenticated and regularized by Moses, whose decisions in the cases which came before him formed the basis of the law administered in the courts. The authority of the judges was a final authority derived from Moses; it was however of another order than that of Moses which was unique because of the uniqueness of his relationship to Yahweh (cf Ex 33^{11}, Nu 12^{7ff}). The story would seem to reflect the conflict between the priesthood, the custodians of the sacred oracle, who traced their authority to Moses, the priest and judge *par excellence*, and the secular judiciary (both the judges of the several tribes and those of the federation) as that had developed among the tribes which had not shared in the experience of the exodus. In claiming Mosaic authority for the judiciary it resolves the conflict in their favour without abrogating the judicial functions of the priesthood.

With the rise of the monarchy the king came to be regarded as the person in whom the fulness of judicial authority was vested. Furthermore, he himself acted as judge (cf 2 S 15$^{1-6}$, 1 K 3^{9}, 2 K 15^{5}, Ps 72; also Hos 7^{7}, Ps 2^{10} reflecting the close relationship between kings and judges). We need not suppose that the king actually appointed the judges throughout the country; but their authority will nevertheless have been a delegated authority in which the king was involved. The administrative system of Deuteronomy ignores the king except for 17^{14ff}. It does however represent the judiciary as independent of the priesthood, 16^{18ff}, thus reaffirming the pre-monarchical theory. The confusion in 17^{8ff} is in all probability due to a conflation of two laws, one defining certain powers of the priests and the other certain duties of the judges; if so, the section implicitly confirms the independent origin of the judiciary.

C. A. Si.

JUDGES (BOOK OF).—**1. Place in the Canon.**—The book belongs to the first section of the second division of the Hebrew canon, being reckoned among the 'Former Prophets' (Joshua, Judges, 1 and 2 Samuel, 1 and 2 Kings). Some MSS of the LXX include the Book of Ruth in Judges, while others treat the Pentateuch and Joshua, Judges, Ruth as one whole.

2. Text.—Generally speaking, the Hebrew text has come down to us in a good state, better preserved than any other of the historical books. A number of errors there certainly are, but these can in many cases be rectified by means of the versions and especially of the LXX. Only in the Song of Deborah (ch. 5) are there serious textual defects, and here there are some passages in which the original cannot with certainty be recovered.

3. Title.—The Hebrew title *Shōphᵉṭîm* ('Judges') is parallel to *Mᵉlākhîm* ('Kings'). Just as the title 'Kings' denotes that the book contains an account of the doings of various kings who ruled over Israel and Judah, so the title 'Judges' is given to the book because it describes the exploits of a number of champions during the period between the entry of Israel into Canaan and the rise of the monarchy. Five of these were judges of all Israel (10$^{1-5}$ 12$^{8-15}$), while the others, though also represented as national leaders, were in fact tribal chieftains. These latter figures are by implication referred to as 'judges' in 2^{16ff}, and Samson is explicitly so designated in 15^{20} 16^{31b}, despite the fact that of none of them is it recorded that he functioned in an administrative capacity, with the exception of Jephthah. It appears, however, from 12^{7} that the tribal chieftain Jephthah, whose exploits are recounted in 11^{1}–12^{6}, was included in the list of 'judges' of Israel from which 10$^{1-5}$ 12$^{8-15}$ were taken; and this is doubtless the reason for the designation of the other regional heroes as judges of all Israel (see JUDGES).

4. Contents.—The book opens with an account of the conquest of the south by the tribes of Judah and Simeon (1$^{1-21}$), Caleb, the conqueror of Hebron (v.^{20}), and Othniel, who later defeated Cushan-rishathaim (3$^{7-11}$), appearing as leaders of the former tribe. The capture of Bethel by the house of Joseph is then recorded (vv.$^{22-26}$), and this is followed by an enumeration of the districts which the northern tribes were unable to conquer (vv.$^{27-36}$). The reason for this is revealed by the angel of Yahweh: they had not obeyed the command of Yahweh but had made covenants with the inhabitants of the land and had refrained from breaking down their altars. The people hearing this wept (whence the name of the place *Bochim*), and sacrificed to Yahweh (2$^{1-5}$).

At this point the narrative is interrupted by an introductory outline of the period to be dealt with in chs. 3 ff. It begins with the notice of Joshua's death and of the passing of the generation to which he belonged (2$^{6-10}$; on the relation of this to Jos 24$^{29-31}$ see below). Up till that time Israel remained faithful to Yahweh, but then they forsook Him and worshipped the Baals and the Ashtaroth; as a consequence they were oppressed by the surrounding nations, until they cried to Yahweh, who raised up a judge to deliver them. But as soon as the judge was dead they again lapsed into idolatry, and the process of oppression, etc., was repeated (2$^{11-19}$). This highly schematized summary of events still to be presented in detail passes somewhat awkwardly into an account of Yahweh's decision not to drive out the nations left unconquered by Joshua but to use them to test Israel, leading up to a list of the nations so left (2$^{20-36}$).

Of the twelve Judges dealt with in 3^{7}–16^{31}, seven are given little more than a bare mention: Othniel (3$^{7-11}$; cf 1^{13}), Shamgar (3^{31}), and the five 'judges of Israel' referred to above, Tola (10^{1f}), Jair (10$^{3-5}$), Ibzan (12$^{8-10}$), Elon (12^{11f}), and Abdon (12$^{13-15}$). The accounts of the other five Judges are in the best manner of Hebrew storytelling: (1) 3$^{12-30}$, the story of Ehud, the left-handed warrior, who killed Eglon, king of Moab, and delivered his people from Moabite domination. This is a conflation of two slightly variant traditions of the same event. (2) The story of Barak (chs. 4–5), on the other hand, is a conflation of traditions of two different events: (*a*) The defeat of the forces of Jabin, king of Hazor, by Barak, leader of the tribes of Zebulun and Naphtali; and (*b*) the defeat of Sisera of Harosheth-ha-goiim by Barak commanding the armies of six tribes which had been summoned by the prophetess Deborah (5[12–15a, 18]). In addition to the name of the hero these traditions had this in common, that the enemy leader in each case was disposed of by a woman—Jabin by the wife of Heber the Kenite, and Sisera by Jael. To unify the traditions the conflator represented Sisera as the commander of Jabin's army (4[2]), and identified Jael with the wife of Heber the Kenite (4[17] 5[24]). The poem in ch. 5, possibly the most ancient piece of Hebrew literature which has come down to us, celebrates the victory over Sisera, and is generally held to have been composed immediately after the event.

(3) The story of Gideon (6[1]–8[29, 35]) begins with an account of the Midianite oppression of Israel (6[1–6]) because of their apostasy (6[7–10]). The call of Gideon is described in vv.[11–24]. This is followed by a satirical cult narrative (vv.[25–32]) telling how a certain sanctuary at which the Baal had been worshipped had been taken over by Yahwism. The purpose of the tale in its present context, breaking the connexion between v.[24] and v.[33], is to identify Gideon with Jerubbaal, the father of Abimelech. The invasion of the Midianites and Gideon's preparations to resist them are recounted in vv.[33–35]. The sign of the fleece (vv.[36–40]) may be an independent legend which was later incorporated into the Gideon cycle; at any rate it breaks the connexion between vv.[33–35] and the detailed account of the battle in which Gideon defeated the Midianites (7[1–24]). The execution of 'the two princes of Midian, Oreb and Zeeb' is recorded in 7[25], and in 8[1–3] Gideon's skilful handling of the Ephraimites' complaint that he had slighted them in not summoning them to help him. 8[4–21] tells of Gideon's pursuit, capture, and execution of 'the two kings of Midian, Zebah, and Zalmunna' (v.[12]), E. of the Jordan. Following his victory he was offered the rule over Israel for himself and his descendants, which he refused (8[22f]); but he asked for the golden earrings which had been taken as spoil, and of them he made an ephod which he placed in his city Ophrah (vv.[24–27]). The fact that there are two accounts of the execution of the Midianite leaders, together with other duplications in the narrative, indicates that it is a conflation of two slightly variant traditions. Both of these were of gradual growth. The Jerubbaal story and the story of the fleece (6[25–32, 36–40]) illustrate the way in which the second tradition was expanded from time to time, in accordance with the usual pattern. The development of the first tradition is more significant. The nucleus of this is contained in 8[4–21], and the clear implication of vv.[18–21] is that Gideon's purpose in pursuing the Midianite chieftains was a personal one—to avenge, as was his duty, the death of his brothers who had been killed by a marauding band of Midianites in a raid on Tabor. At one stage in the growth of the cycle, 8[4–21] must have been preceded by an account of this raid. This incident may have been the beginning of Gideon's career as a warrior; but he was also known as the military leader who by a clever ruse had defeated the Midianite attempt to settle in Palestine. The account of this (6[33–35] 7[16–23], in part) was in course of time prefixed to the earlier narrative (6[33ff] displacing the original story of the raid), together with the story of his call, giving expression to Israel's faith in Yahweh and His saving activity on their behalf. Other details such as that in 7[4–7] were also added.

(4) The story of Jephthah (11[1]–12[6]) tells how he was driven from Gilead by his brothers and became the leader of a gang of freebooters in the land of Tob (11[1–3]). When Ammon made war on Israel the elders of Gilead persuaded him to return home as leader of the army (11[4–11]). There follows an account of his protest to the king of Ammon who was laying claim to the land between the Arnon and the Jabbok which Jephthah maintained belonged to Israel for the reason that it had been given to them by Yahweh when he dispossessed the former inhabitants (11[12–27]). The king of Ammon rejected this protest; Jephthah therefore moved against him and defeated him, having first vowed that he would sacrifice to Yahweh 'whoever comes forth from the door of my house to meet me, when I return victorious from the Ammonites' (11[28–33]). On his return it was his only daughter who met him, and his fulfilment of his vow is described in a moving passage (11[34–40]). He was then attacked by the Ephraimites because he had not called on them for assistance (cf 8[1–3]). He defeated them also, and the fugitives from the battle were massacred as they tried to re-cross the Jordan, being detected because of their inability to say 'shibboleth' (12[1–6]). The god of the Ammonites was Milcom, while Chemosh was the god of Moab (1 K 11[33], 2 K 23[13]); the reference to the latter as 'your god' in 11[34] therefore indicates that the original context of some part of the material in 11[12–28] was a dispute not with Ammon but with Moab, and so that the Jephthah story, like those preceding, is a conflation of two traditions, one of which represented Moab as the enemy. The Ammonite tradition is the earlier. It has furthermore been pointed out that the grave oath made by Jephthah demands as its setting a personal feud rather than an ordinary war between Israel and a neighbouring nation, as is further suggested by v.[36b], 'now that the Lord has avenged you on your enemies'—'on the Ammonites' being an addition. It would thus seem that the development of the Jephthah story is similar to that of the story of Gideon.

(5) The history of Samson and his doings is recorded in chs. 13–16. Ch. 13 tells how an angel foretold his birth, and commanded that he should be a life-long Nazirite. Ch. 14 gives an account of his marriage with a Philistine woman, who played him false during the wedding festivities by extracting from him the answer to a riddle he had set and passing it on to the guests. Samson went back to his home in a rage, and his wife was given to his best man. Ch. 15 tells how he discovered this when he returned to Timnah to see his wife. In revenge he set fire to the standing grain of the Philistines and they retaliated by burning his wife and her father. He in return killed a large number of them and withdrew to Judah. The Philistines compelled the Judahites to hand him over to them, but he slew a thousand of them with the jaw-bone of an ass, and escaped. Ch. 16 tells how he carried off the gates of Gaza, and then describes his relationship with Delilah, who, having found out that his strength was in his hair, had his head shaved while he was asleep, and handed him over to the lords of the Philistines. They gouged out his eyes and put him in prison, where his strength returned as his hair grew again. On the occasion of a festival he was brought to the temple of Dagon to provide entertainment for the crowd. There he took hold of the two pillars by which he was standing and pulled the building down, killing himself and all who were in it. There are no signs of conflation in the Samson story; any inconsistencies there may be in the narrative are due to the gradual growth of the legend.

Between the stories of Gideon and Jephthah comes the story of Abimelech, son of Jerubbaal (ch. 9), who became king of Shechem after slaying all his brothers, seventy in number, except Jotham (vv.[1–6]), who fled after predicting in a parable Abimelech's downfall (vv.[7–21]). Trouble broke out between Abimelech and the Shechemites which one Gaal fanned into open revolt. Abimelech, however, defeated him, razed the city to the ground and destroyed the survivors who had taken refuge in the Tower (vv.[22–49]). He met his death when he was attacking the city of Thebez (vv.[50–57]). This narrative is a conflation of two recensions of the story of Abimelech, the first of which treated him as a hero who subdued Shechem and died bravely in an attack on Thebez. The second represented him as a ruthless adventurer who eventually met his just deserts. The conflator of the two recensions adopted the latter representation. In its present context the story is intended as an illustration of the kind of thing that happened during the periods of apostasy referred to in 2[19] 3[12a], etc., when 'every man did what was right in his own eyes' (17[6]).

This is also the reason for the inclusion of the stories in chs. 17 f and 19–21. The former tells of one Micah, an Ephraimite, who made for himself an image and put it in a shrine (literally god-house), along with an ephod and teraphim, and employed as his priest a Levite who happened to turn up on the scene. All went well until the tribe of Dan passed through the village on their migration northward, and persuaded the Levite to take Micah's image, with its paraphernalia, and come with them as their priest. Having captured the city of Laish, they renamed it Dan and set up the image there, with the Levite, now identified as a grandson of Moses, as priest of the new sanctuary. This narrative is a conflation of two stories of the origin of the famous sanctuary of Dan. The earlier of these was quite objective. It knew nothing of an image; the cult object was an ephod, and the Levite was a reputable character in no way to be blamed for going with the Danites as their priest. The second recension treated the affair with contemptuous scorn. Not only was the chief cult object an image, forbidden by the law (cf Ex 20$^{4, 23}$ 34^{17}), but an image of most dubious origin (Jg 17$^{2-4}$); and the priest a self-seeking adventurer. This scorn has been somewhat softened by the conflator of the two recensions, but the general impression remains that the less said about the founding of the sanctuary of Dan the better.

Chs. 19–21 offer another instance of the moral chaos which, the implication is, characterized the periods of apostasy. They tell the story of how the concubine of a certain Levite left him and returned to her father. The Levite went after her to bring her back. On their way home they stopped for the night in Gibeah, a city of Benjamin. The men of the city attempting an indecent assault on him, the Levite turned his concubine over to them and they so maltreated her that she died on the threshold of the house in which her master was staying. There he found her in the morning, brought her dead body home, cut it in pieces and sent them throughout all the territory of Israel as a call to avenge the outrage. The Israelites assembled and demanded that Benjamin hand over 'the base fellows in Gibeah' that they might be put to death. The Benjamites refused, and in the war that followed were annihilated except for six hundred men. But since the other Israelites had sworn that they would not allow their daughters to marry into Benjamin, the end of the tribe appeared to be inevitable. This disaster was averted, however, when it was found that there had been no one from Jabesh-gilead present when the oath was taken. So four hundred maidens were procured from there, and the remaining two hundred by abduction from those dancing in the vineyards at the annual festival at Shiloh.

It may be taken for granted that the stories of the heroes took their rise among the tribes to which they respectively belonged. That of Abimelech is of a slightly different character, containing less popular legendary material; in its primary form it may have been preserved in the archives of Shechem, and the primary form of the story in chs. 17 f in Dan. The story of the outrage at Gibeah is more difficult to place. It reflects some kind of an alliance between Gibeah and Jabesh-gilead even before the time of Saul; and it has been suggested that in its representation that the people of Jabesh-gilead took no part in the reprisals on Gibeah and subsequently provided wives for the surviving Benjamites the tale is a subtle piece of polemic against the memory of Saul, implying that it was this morally questionable relationship between the two cities which prompted his intervention on behalf of Jabesh-gilead (1 S 11). If this suggestion has any validity the story may have been preserved at the centre of the anti-Saul propaganda—possibly Bethlehem where David was born, which it represents as the home of the Levite's concubine.

Eventually a collection was made of these stories either by the author of the J narrative in the Pentateuch, or as a supplement to that narrative, to carry the history of Israel down to the time of the monarchy. This reduction of the stories to writing did not, however, prevent their further development and adaptation in the continued process of oral transmission. In the course of time another collection was made of them in their new form, and these two recensions were ultimately conflated to produce a unified history of the period.

The fact that both the phraseology of 2$^{6-22}$ and the basic thesis of the passage, that disaster is the sign of Divine displeasure, are characteristic of the author(s) of the framework to the code of Deuteronomy indicates that in the course of its literary history the collection of hero-stories was worked over and schematized by an editor or editors of the deuteronomic school. From their hand come also the several introductions and concluding notices to the stories in chs. 3–12, which impose upon them the pattern of apostasy, oppression, repentance, deliverance through a judge raised up by Yahweh, and, after an interval, apostasy again (cf 3$^{12-15a, 30}$ 4$^{1-4}$ 5^{31b} 6$^{1, 6b}$ 8^{28} 10^{6ff}). The work of these editors was, however, more extensive than this. The facts that the notice of the death of Joshua (Jg 2$^{6-10}$) occurs also in Jos 24$^{29-31}$, and that much of the material in Jg 1 is now found at different points in Joshua suggest that at one stage in the history of the book Jg 1^{1}–2^{5} was omitted, such information as the redactor desired to preserve being placed at appropriate points in Joshua (cf Jos 15$^{13-19, 63}$ 16^{10} 17$^{11-13, 16}$; see JOSHUA, BOOK OF); and the notice of Joshua's death (Jg 2$^{6-10}$) was placed after Jos 24^{32f}. The conjecture is not unreasonable that this operation was the work of the author of the deuteronomist history of Israel (running through Deuteronomy, Joshua, Judges, 1 and 2 Samuel, 1 and 2 Kings; see DEUTERONOMY and JOSHUA, BOOK OF) in its original form. From his hand comes also the basic material in Jg 2$^{11-12}$ (limited possibly to vv.$^{12a, 14a, 20b-21}$), catching up the pre-deuteronomic narrative in 2^{23}–3^{5} to which he added 3^{6} and continued with 3^{12b}, 'and the Lord strengthened the hand of Eglon the king of Moab against Israel,' the implication being that the Moabite oppression was the divinely ordained punishment for the apostasy noted in 3^{6}. The story of Ehud was then told, the deuteronomist historian being careful to state explicitly that he was the deliverer whom the Lord raised up (3^{15a}). We thus have the first instance of the characteristic deuteronomist pattern of apostasy, oppression, and deliverance. This editor provided a similar framework for the stories of Deborah and Barak and of Gideon (4^{1}–8$^{29, 33}$). The stylistic affinities of the introduction (8$^{30-32}$) to the story of Abimelech are with P rather than with the deuteronomist, indicating that the story was not included in the original deuteronomist history. Deuteronomist phraseology and ideas again appear in 10$^{6-18}$, a passage generally recognized as coming from more than one hand. The statement in v.^{7} that the Lord 'sold them into the hand of the Philistines' has, with its continuation, 'and into the hand of the Ammonites,' been taken by some as a combined introduction to the stories of Samson and Jephthah. Against this it has been pointed out that the Jephthah story comes before that of Samson; that the Samson story has its own deuteronomist introduction in 13^{1}; and that Samson is nowhere represented as a deliverer of Israel from oppression and no attempt is made to fit him into the deuteronomist pattern. But if the mention of Philistine oppression in 10^{7} does not point ahead to the Samson story it can only refer to the Philistine domination recorded in the opening chapters of 1 Samuel. This suggests the possibility that in its primary form the deuteronomist history of Israel passed from the story of Gideon to that of Eli. (The statement in 1 S 4^{18} that Eli had judged Israel for forty years indicates that at some stage he was included among the Judges.) If the first deuteronomist editor did indeed omit the stories in chs. 9–21 his reason is not far to seek. From his point of view those concerning Dan and Gibeah (chs. 17–21) were singularly unedifying; so too was that of Jephthah because it represented human sacrifice as permissible; and the figures of Abimelech and Samson could not be fitted into his scheme.

Subsequent deuteronomist editors restored Jg 1^{1}–2^{5}, without however disturbing the fragments therefrom which had been inserted in Joshua. The opening words of 1^{1}, 'after the death of Joshua,' required the replacement of the notice of Joshua's death in Jos 24^{29-31}, but Jg 2^{6-10} was retained as the necessary introduction to the schematic material following, which was gradually expanded into its present form. The story of Othniel (3^{7-11}) was added, presumably to supply a 'judge' from Judah. The story of Jephthah was restored, and the basic material in 10^{6ff} adapted as an introduction to it. The fact that it is twice recorded that Samson judged Israel for twenty years (15^{20}, 16^{31b}) suggests that the tales in chs. 13–15 were first restored to the narrative and ch. 16, with its explicit representation that Samson's strength was in his hair (contrast $14^{5, 19}$ 15^{14} where it is a manifestation of the power of the Spirit of Yahweh), only later.

There is no trace of deuteronomist editing in chs. 9 and 17–21. This suggests that these stories were restored by a later redactor who provided 8^{30-32} as an introduction to the Abimelech story. He also added the lists of judges in 10^{1-5} and 12^{8-15}, to which 12^{7}, naming Jephthah, belongs (see above). Of each of them we are told where he lived, for how many years he 'judged Israel,' where he was buried, and in three cases the number of his children, never less than thirty. The fact that Jerubbaal (secondarily identified with Gideon, cf 6^{25-32} 7^{1} 8^{29-35}) had seventy sons (8^{30}) suggests that his name may have been included in the record from which these lists were derived. Abimelech may also have been of their number, for if the implication of the phraseology of 10^{1} is that he was one of the deliverers of Israel it points to a tradition other than the story in ch. 9 which treats him as a ruthless and unprincipled oppressor. It has been argued by some scholars that both the names of these Judges and one of the component narratives of the story in chs. 19–21 have been derived from the tradition of the pre-monarchical federation of the tribes of Israel. If this view is sound, then the inclusion of this material in the book alongside the stories of the tribal heroes points to a survival of this tradition through the centuries of the monarchy into the post-exilic period. With the addition of the lists in 10^{1-5} 12^{8-15} the number of Judges, including Eli, was brought to twelve. When the story of Eli was separated from the others and placed in 1 Samuel, the name of Shamgar (3^{31}) was added, to prevent Abimelech being reckoned as a Judge.

5. Historical value.—1^{1}–2^{5} is, as a whole, a valuable source of information concerning the conquest and settlement of some of the Israelite tribes west of the Jordan; for the period of which it treats it is one of the most valuable records we possess.

2^{6}–3^{6}, which forms the introduction to the hero-stories is, with the exception of isolated notes such as 2^{9} 3^{5}, of little historical value. The statement that each oppression is due to Israel's apostasy from Yahweh is altogether out of harmony with the spirit of the book as a whole; nor can the theory on which it is based have been evolved until long after the period of the Judges.

3^{7-11} is nothing more than an illustration of the deuteronomist theory of apostasy, oppression, deliverance. Whether or not Othniel was an historical person, the passage cannot be regarded as an authentic record of events. In general, the other hero-stories reflect the crisis character of the religion of Yahweh in the period of the Judges and the energizing experience of seizure by His Spirit. The story of Ehud may well preserve a genuine memory of successful resistance to an attempt of the Moabites to establish themselves in Benjamin. The poem in ch. 5, commemorating Barak's defeat of Sisera, is one of the most important sources we have for the early history of Israel in Palestine. The prose narrative in ch. 4, being a conflation of two distinct stories, is of less value, though both the traditions preserved in it may have an historical foundation.

In the story of Gideon (6^{1}–8^{27}) the account of his capture and execution of the two raiding Midianite chiefs is a folk-tale based upon an authentic event; similarly the representation of him as a military leader may well be historical, whether or not the details of the ruse he adopted to defeat his enemies are anything more than popular legend. The accounts of his call, of his destruction of the Baal altar and of the sign of the fleece bear marks of their legendary character. The story of Abimelech (ch. 9) certainly contains historical information, though it is impossible to say whether Abimelech was a hero or a ruffian. The names of the Judges in 10^{1-5} and 12^{8-15} may be authentic even though there is some exaggeration in the number of children ascribed to them.

10^{6-18} is of the same character as 2^{6}–3^{6}. The representation of Jephthah (11^{1}–12^{7}) as the leader of a gang of freebooters who offered his daughter in sacrifice in payment of a vow is probably historical, as is the annual lamentation in Gilead, though it is unlikely that this had in origin anything to do with Jephthah's daughter. The shibboleth incident may also have an historical kernel. If there is any factual basis to the adventures of Samson (chs. 13–16) it is very slight; and it has been so overlaid with legend, some of it dependent upon the sun-god myth, as to be quite irrecoverable. Ch. 13 represents an attempt to give religious meaning to the tales which follow.

The trek of the Danites in chs. 17–18 is authentic, and the Levitical origin of the priesthood at Dan is scarcely an invention, though the details of the story are at least open to question. The representation of Micah first making his son his priest and then putting a Levite in his place is doubtless true to life. The story of the outrage at Gibeah (chs. 19–21) may be based on fact. Whether or not it was actually the reason for a war between the other tribes and Benjamin, which may itself be historical, the representation that this kind of thing was the concern of the inter-tribal federation is significant.

Finally, from the literary history of the material we can trace the process by which local traditions were given a wider significance and related to each other; we can detect the rivalries which threatened the underlying unity of the tribes; we can discern the emergence of new ideas as to the meaning of history, first in the exclusion from the record of anything deemed unedifying, and then in the reversal of this policy to produce a book which reflects the life of the period in all its aspects. C. A. Si.

JUDGING (Ethical).—In both OT and NT, 'ethical' judging is understood as judging in terms of God's righteousness, since God's will and not human excellence is the standard of judgment. **1. In the OT,** ethical judgment as a reflection of God's righteousness is seen especially in the prophets (*e.g.* Is 10^{1-4}, Jer 5^{1-5}), who also believe that a man may be called to pronounce God's judgments (Jer 19^{f}). The wisdom literature holds that common-sense knowledge of right and wrong reflects God's justice and can serve as the basis for ethical judgment of one's fellow men (*e.g.* Pr 26^{-15}).

2. The NT writers are concerned principally with ethical judgments made by Christians. The redeeming presence of God made known in Christ and the expectation of God's final judgment have two different results for the Christian's ethical judgments. (1) As a believer, his obligation and his power to make such judgments are intensified. The Spirit gives him a freedom in which he 'judges all things' (1 Co 2^{15}), and his human discernment is also involved when he must 'test everything' (1 Th 5^{21}, cf 1 Co 11^{13}). His guide in judgment is the 'mind of Christ' (1 Co 2^{16}), or the 'law of Christ' (Gal 6^{2}). The privilege and responsibility of making judgments which reflect God's judgment are most clearly shown in the faith that Christians will take part in the last Judgment; they will 'sit on thrones judging the twelve tribes of Israel' (Lk 22^{30} ||, cf 1 Co 6^{2f}). (2) On the other hand, the goodness of God as known in Christ and the expectation of the last Judgment lead also to a withholding of ethical judgment ('Judge not . . .', Mt 7^{1}). Withholding of judgment rests on several bases. (*a*) A keen sense of each man's responsibility to God requires concentration on one's own task rather than judgment of another's. 'Who are you to pass judgment on the servant of another? It is before his own master that he stands or falls' (Ro 14[4], cf 14[1-23]). (*b*) Men are warned not to undertake a task of judgment that is God's (Ja 4[11f]). The obscurity and difficulty of human judgments, made in so much ignorance, are contrasted with God's knowledge. 'Therefore do not pronounce judgment before the time, before the Lord comes, who will bring to light the things now hidden in darkness' (1 Co 4[5]). (*c*) The self-destructive effect of censorious judgment is seen; it results in self-deception ('hypocrisy') about one's own failings. 'Why do you see the speck that is in your brother's eye, but do not notice the log that is in your own eye?' (Mt 7[3], cf Ro 2[1]). (*d*) Many NT passages commanding the withholding of judgment stress the freedom and variety of belief and practice which Christians should accord to one another in things not central to the faith. 'Therefore let no one pass judgment on you in questions of food and drink or with regard to a festival or a new moon or a sabbath. These are only a shadow of what is to come' (Col 2[16f]; cf Ro 14). The need for respecting the views of 'weak' or immature believers is emphasized (Ro 14[13], 1 Co 10[28f]), as well as the importance of not insisting on one's own way (1 Co 6[7], cf 1 Co 13[5]). (*e*) Most important of all, the overwhelming sense of God's goodness in overruling a just judgment against the believer demands that he forgive other sinners (Mt 6[14f] 18[21-35], Eph 4[32]). Thus Jesus' warning: 'Judge not, that you be not judged' (Mt 7[1]) is not only a warning against harsh judgments of others. It finds its setting in a faith in the immeasurable love of God which seeks the lost (Lk 15, cf Ro 5[1-11]), and challenges men to rise above the standard of measured justice. Jesus' saying in Mt 7[1] finds an illustration in the story about the woman taken in adultery which has been added to the Gospel of John (Jn 8[1-11]).

3. Interpreters of the NT have not found it easy to unite the spiritual freedom to judge all things with the admonition to 'judge not.' Some have made a distinction between *actions and qualities*, which are to be judged, and *persons*, who are not. While this distinction rightly points toward forgiveness and acceptance of the sinner, it is not a distinction made in the NT itself, which understands actions and qualities as inseparably bound to persons. The tension between Christian faith as making possible truer judgments, and Christian faith as requiring one not to judge, springs from the fact that through faith Christians find themselves closer to God, and therefore better able to judge as He judges, and yet at the same time because close to God, humble and thankful before His majesty and goodness. Thus withholding of judgment does not mean withholding a just ethical decision, but holding the way open for a higher righteousness than that of retaliatory justice. In this sense the NT does not forbid judgment of others. It forbids judgments that are narrow, prejudiced, and censorious (Mt 7[1ff], Ja 4[11f]); and requires that a man judge himself first (Mt 7[3ff]), and not judge by appearances (Jn 7[24], cf 8[15]), respect the freedom of another's conscience (Ro 14, 1 Co 10[28f]), recognize the limitations of his knowledge, and not put himself in the place of the final Judge (Ro 14[10], 1 Co 4[5]), and above all, show himself ready to accept into fellowship and forgiveness one who does wrong (Mt 18[21f], Gal 6[1]). W. A. B.

JUDGMENT.—Biblical eschatology centres in the Divine Last Judgment of all mankind at the end of the present 'age.' In most NT books it is viewed as the beginning of the New or Messianic Age and will therefore take place at a specific time in the future, the 'day' of Judgment. Even St. Paul, though he denies any righteousness of man before God, does not weaken the thought of man's responsibility and Divine judgment upon human sin. As in late Jewish conceptions (1 En 61[8ff]), the early Christians looked forward to the Judgment to be conducted by the Son of Man as God's representative, assisted by the angels (Mt 13[41-43, 49f] 25[31-46]). Nevertheless it continues to be thought of as the Judgment of God (Mt 10[32f], Ro 2[16], He 12[23]). St. John points out that the Judgment begins on earth, since either to accept or to reject Christ is to determine one's eternal state (Jn 5[23] 9[39]). Those who accept Christ as their Lord need no longer fear the Judgment; hence by way of anticipation it may be said that they 'will not come into judgment' (Jn 5[24]; cf 3[18]). In Lk 22[30], 1 Co 6[2] Christians are also said to be judges. But in ancient oriental society there was a close connexion between the functions of ruling and judging (cf Lk 22[30], Mt 19[28]): *teste* the early 'judges' of Israel. Hence judging is a part of reigning with Christ (1 Co 4[8]).

The idea of the Judgment may be traced back to the conception of the Day of Yahweh held by the early Hebrews. But in the NT it is used in a strictly eschatological sense: it is the last and total Judgment of God upon His fallen creatures. Weeping and gnashing of teeth are mentioned (*e.g.* Mt 8[12]; cf Ps 111[10]). But the heart and substance of all the penalties inflicted is to be denied by Christ, to suffer 'everlasting destruction' away from the presence of the Lord and from the glory of His power (Mt 10[32], 2 Th 1[9]). Still more reserved are the statements about the destiny of the blessed: they shall 'see face to face,' they shall 'see Him as He is' (1 Co 13[12], 1 Jn 3[2]). See Abyss, Day of the Lord, Book of Life, Gehenna. For 'judgment' in the sense of justice, see Justice. H. G.

JUDGMENT HALL.—See Praetorium.

JUDGMENT-SEAT.—Of the two terms employed in NT, *bēma* denoted the raised dais from which a judge passed judgment (Mt 27[19], Jn 19[13], Ac 18[12, 16f] 25[6, 10, 17], Ro 14[10], 2 Co 5[10]) and *kritērion* the court (Ja 2[6]) or the judgment itself (1 Co 6[2, 4]). See Gabbatha. J. S. K.

JUDITH.—**1.** A wife of Esau, daughter of Beeri the Hittite (Gn 26[34]; cf 36[2]). **2.** Daughter of Merari, of the tribe of Simeon (Jth 8[1] [cf Nu 1[6]] 9[2]); widow of Manasseh of the same tribe. For the book of which she is the heroine see article Apocrypha, **4.**

JUEL.—1. 1 Es 9[34] (AV, RV); see Joel, **15.** **2.** 1 Es 9[35] (AV, RV); see Joel, **13.**

JULIA.—A Christian greeted by St. Paul in Ro 16[15], perhaps the wife or sister of Philologus. If Ro 16 was originally a letter to the Ephesian community, Julia must have lived at Ephesus. E. H.

JULIUS.—For the voyage to Rome St. Paul was committed with other prisoners to the charge of a centurion named Julius of the *cohors Augusta*. Sir W. Ramsay suggested that the ship was a government vessel, of which Julius had supreme command. But although Ac 27[11] can be interpreted in this way, the suggestion must be abandoned: inscriptions have proved that v.[11] speaks of the skipper and the owner of the ship. It was a private vessel, and Julius had the status of a passenger and not of a commander. The story of the voyage and shipwreck of St. Paul has lost its original form. Probably Paul was accused of the crime of sedition (Ac 24[5]) and was being held as a highly suspicious character. E. H.

JUNIA, Ro 16[7] (AV, RVm).—See Junias.

JUNIAS.—A Christian greeted by St. Paul in Ro 16[7]. The Greek form of the name could be the female name Junia too, but the context is against this interpretation. Papyrus 46 reads Julia; cf v.[15]. Andronicus (q.v.) and Junias were Jews and 'of note among the apostles,' *i.e.* missionaries like Paul himself. But they had become Christians before him. E. H.

JUNGLE.—See Jordan, **5.**

JUNIPER.—See Broom.

JUPITER.—See Zeus.

JUSHAB-HESED.—A son of Zerubbabel, 1 Ch 3[20].

JUSTICE (I.).—Time after time it is said in the OT that God is righteous. That cannot mean that God is blameless before the law, because God, being God, cannot be said to be subject to a law; otherwise the law would be made greater than God Himself. It does mean that He acts at all times consistently with His own nature and His own good and gracious purposes, so that there is in Him no variation or shadow due to change (Ja 1[17]). God's justice is that side of the Divine righteousness which reveals it as absolute fairness. This is what finds expression, for instance, in Abraham's question (Gn 18[25]) :' Shall not the Judge of all the earth do right?' It is then for man to be righteous and just in all his ways that he may be accepted of God (Is 1[17, 26], Am 5[24], Ps 146[8] etc.); it is by his righteousness that a man shall live (Ezk 18[9] 33[13] etc.); and it is by the practice of righteousness and justice that the human community is established. Thus it is said: ' Behold, I am laying in Zion for a foundation a stone, a tested stone . . . and I will make justice the line and righteousness the plummet' (Is 28[16f]). Man can be righteous and just as he is guided and empowered by the Spirit of God. Thus Yahweh is the source of Israelite law; it was He who gave it to Moses on Sinai (Ex 20[1ff] etc.); and every later codification of that law and every later decision in any particular case was made under the guidance of the self-same Spirit, that the will of Yahweh might be the more fully known and done and that His community of Israel might be maintained in a way acceptable to Him. It is for this reason that the Hebrew word *mishpāṭ* means not only judgment but justice, and in many passages it is the latter word that should be used in translation (*e.g.* Dt 32[4], Is 30[18] 42[1], Am 5[24] etc.). Indeed, *mishpāṭ* must even be translated ordinance in some contexts, *i.e.* the ordinance or law of God (*e.g.* Is 42[4] 51[4], Jer 8[7], Ezr 7[10] etc.) J. Ma.

JUSTICE (II.).—**Its Administration.**—**1. In early Israel.**—(*a*) The earliest form of the administration of justice was that exercised by the head of the family. He was not only the final authority to whom the members of a family appealed when questions of right and wrong had to be decided, and to whose sentence they had to submit, but he also had the power of pronouncing even the death penalty (cf Gn 38[24]). On the other hand, the maintenance of family strength and solidarity was of paramount importance; therefore, the rights of each member of the family were jealously guarded by all the rest. If injury was done to any member by a member of any other family, the relatives of the injured man made common cause to see that proper amends were made; if the injury resulted in death, a state of blood feud ensued between the two families, until vengeance was exacted by the injured family by their slaying a member of the murderer's family, preferably, but not necessarily, the murderer himself.

(*b*) The next stage was that in which a number of families, united by ties of kinship, became a clan or tribe, which was commonly a unity as closely knit together as the family itself. In this stage of the organization of society the procedure in deciding questions of right and wrong was doubtless much the same as that which obtains even up to the present day among Bedouin Arabs. Any matter in dispute which cannot be settled amicably by the disputants themselves but has to be referred to arbitration comes before the sheikh for decision. He hears both parties and, in coming to his decision, seeks at once an equitable decision for the sake of the disputants and one that will be for the good of the clan as a whole, since the interests of the individual must be kept subject to the welfare of the whole. Even if such a decision by a sheikh has not formal binding force, the consensus of the clan and the moral pressure that can be exerted towards the acceptance of the judgment that is given effectively give it such force. In Ex 18[13-27] it is recorded how Moses took measures for the administration of justice in Israel by the elders of clans, thus supplying the system we have just described to the larger community which was knit together at Sinai and which had now to be organized as a social unity. Moses himself continued to act as a **court of appeal.** Closely allied with the clan or tribal administration of justice was the system which was operative in the cities, with their daughter villages, in which the Israelites settled after their entry into Palestine. The elders sat in the city gate and all occasions of dispute were referred to them there. Dt 21[18-21] tells of the father of a rebellious son, who, finding his authority set at nought, appeals to the elders of the city; in the case of the son's being found guilty, the death sentence is pronounced against him and the sentence is carried out by representatives of the community. This seems to illustrate a case in which, in an earlier form of social organization, the father himself would have carried out the sentence after giving judgment; now he must bring the matter before the elders. It is to be noted in addition that, in the period of Israel's history which is described in the Book of Judges, the leader who emerges in a crisis is judge, priest, and leader in battle; that is to say, the life of the community is unified under him and, during the emergency at least, he has the obedience of the whole people.

It seems justifiable to assume that the elders and the judges in the gate dealt with all civil cases and with criminal ones in which the aid of precedents was available. But in particularly difficult cases, in which no precedent was available or the circumstantial evidence was not clear and statements had to be taken from the material **witnesses** on oath, a further procedure had to be followed. In Ex 22[8f] it is described as ' coming before God,' which probably means that the contending parties had to appear at a sanctuary that under solemn oath they might give their testimony and that the priests thereafter might seek God's guidance towards a decision. See also in this connexion Dt 21[1-9].

(*c*) *The king.*—The possibility that the unified pattern of community rule which is exemplified in the Book of Judges might be disturbed was laid open when there arose in Israel the demand for a king (1 S 8[4ff]). But a king was appointed in Israel and the practice developed that appeal might be made from the local judges to him (cf 1 S 8[20], 2 S 14[4ff] 15[2-6], 1 K 3[9], 2 K 15[5]). According to 1 K 7[7] Solomon had a throne room where he sat in judgment; it was very close to the royal palace. The king was supreme judge in the land; but it must very soon have become impossible for him to try personally all the cases which were referred to him, so that representatives must have been appointed to administer justice in his name. Now the local judges who gave judgment in the city gate knew the people of the community which they served and they were aware of the solidarity of the local social group. The king's representatives who administered justice in his name often had no personal knowledge of the litigants who came before them and the cases were decided out of their social context. That might result in an administration of justice which was uninfluenced by personal considerations whose relevance and fairness might be called in question, and was based on purely objective considerations; but it also opened the way to perversions of justice on the part of judges who were not subject to effective social controls and the power of public opinion. There is abundant evidence to show that the administration of justice was done more for the purpose of private gain than in the interests of equity. It is an ever-recurring theme in the prophetical books that justice is thwarted through **bribery**: ' Every one loves a bribe and runs after a gift' (Is 1[23]; cf 5[7, 20, 23], Mic 3[11] 7[3], Ezk 18[8] 22[12], etc.).

(*d*) *The priesthood.*—The greater the place which the priesthood came to hold in the community and the more socially developed Israel became, the greater must have become the rôle which the priests played in the administration of justice; and the Temple located beside the royal palace must have added to priestly prestige. This is illustrated very pointedly in Dt 19[15-21], where the outlines of a regular, formulated, judicial system seem to be referred to, in which the final authority is vested in the priesthood. What contributed to this development more than anything else must have been the old-established practice whereby the elders in the city gate, when they were confronted by a case which defied a satisfactory solution in the light of the available evidence, referred to the priests at a sanctuary. The priests sought an answer from God and announced that answer to those who came for judgment (cf Ex 22[8f] and Dt 33[8ff]). But the prophetical books tell how the priests themselves corrupted their office and acted falsely (cf Is 24[2] 28[7], Jer 6[13] 23[11], Hos 4[9]); they ought to have been teachers of the people, but they led them astray. The prophets also, who were associated with them at the sanctuaries, played false and prophesied for personal gain, proclaiming peace where there was no peace (cf Jer 5[13, 31] 14[13f] 23[21ff] 29[8], Mic 3[11]).

2. Post-exilic period.—In the time of Ezra we find that the administration of justice by the elders of the city, which had continued throughout the period of the monarchy, is still in vogue (cf Ezr 7[25] 10[14]); they presided over the **local courts** in the smaller provincial towns. These smaller courts consisted of seven members; in the larger towns the corresponding courts consisted of twenty-three members. In the event of these lower courts not being able to come to a decision regarding any matter brought before them, the case was carried to the superior court at Jerusalem, the Sanhedrin (q.v.). The procedure in these courts was of the simplest character; the injured person brought his complaint before the judges, previous notice having been given, and publicly gave his version of the matter. The accused in turn defended himself; if we may judge from Job 31[35], a written statement was sometimes read out. The testimony of **two witnesses** at least was required to substantiate an accusation; according to the Talmud, these witnesses had to be males and of age, but the testimony of a slave was not regarded as valid. Before witnesses gave their testimony they were adjured to speak the truth, and the *whole* truth. False witnesses—and these were evidently not unknown—had to suffer the same punishment as the victim of their false testimony would have had to undergo, or had undergone. If no witnesses were forthcoming, the truth of a matter had, as far as possible, to be obtained by the cross-questioning and acumen of the judges.

3. In the NT.—In NT times in Palestine the domestic administration of justice remained as it had been before the land became part of the Roman Empire. The elders functioned as usual, and when Jesus Christ was haled before the Sanhedrin we are informed that the scribes and the elders were there (Mt 26[57ff], Mk 14[53ff], Lk 22[54ff], Jn 18). The fact that the Sanhedrin had not the power to carry out the death sentence on their own authority is shown by the fact that the sentence upon Jesus Christ had to be confirmed by Pilate, the Roman governor (Mt 27[1f] etc.). Likewise the case of the high priest Ananias against St. Paul had to be referred to the Roman governor Felix (Ac 23[1f] 25[5]). The legal procedure which was adopted against St. Paul gives a clear indication of the course of the administration of justice, especially in the case of a Roman citizen. According to Roman law, when a Roman citizen was accused of anything, the magistrate could fix any time that suited him for the trial; however long the trial might be postponed, the accused was nevertheless imprisoned for the whole time. But there were different kinds of imprisonment recognized by Roman law, and it lay within the magistrate's power to decide which kind should be applied in any particular case. These different grades of custody were: the public gaol where the prisoner was bound in chains (Ac 12[6] 21[33]); in the custody of a soldier, who was responsible for the prisoner, and to whom the prisoner was chained; and an altogether milder form, according to which the accused was in custody only so far that he was under the supervision of a magistrate, who stood surety for him; it was only those of high rank to whom this indulgence was accorded. In the case of St. Paul it was the second of these which was put into force on the journey to Rome (Ac 27[1]) and during his time in Rome itself (Ac 28[16]).

With regard to **appeals** to the Emperor (Ac 25[11f]), the following conditions applied when one claimed this right. In the Roman provinces the supreme criminal jurisdiction was exercised by the governor of the province, whether proconsul, propraetor, or procurator; no appeal was permitted to provincials from a governor's judgment. But Roman citizens had the right of appealing to the tribunes, who had the power of ordering the case to be transferred to the ordinary tribunals at Rome. But from the time of Augustus the power of the tribunes was centred in the person of the Emperor; and with him alone, therefore, lay the power of hearing appeals. The form of such an appeal was the simple pronunciation of the word 'Appello'; there was no need to make a written appeal, the mere utterance of the word in court suspended all further proceedings there. Cf GOVERNMENT, ROMAN PUBLIC LAW. W. O. E. O.—**J. Ma.**

JUSTIFICATION, JUSTIFY.—Justification has been an important word in Christian theology primarily because of St. Paul's use of it. It was he who gave it what has become its characteristic meaning. It is found also, however, in the OT, and there are occasional uses of it in the Gospels and in the Epistle of St. James.

1. In the Biblical languages the word is derived from the same verbal root as 'righteousness.' The Greek for 'justify' is *dikaioō*, for 'justification' *dikaiōsis*, and for 'righteousness' *dikaiosynē*. The study of 'justification' in the Bible, therefore, must be supplemented by reference to the word 'righteousness' (q.v.).

The Vulgate translated the Greek word *dikaioō* by the Latin 'justificare,' which by derivation means 'to make righteous.' This was probably largely responsible for the mistaken belief that this is the meaning of 'justify' in the Bible. This, however, is a serious error. In the Bible it means 'to declare righteous,' 'pronounce innocent,' or 'treat as righteous,' but not 'to make righteous.' It describes a personal relationship rather than an ethical quality of character. It is a word said to be drawn from the vocabulary of the law courts, where a judge 'justified' an accused prisoner when he declared him innocent and acquitted him. It had come, however, to have a currency far wider than the law courts.

2. In the *Old Testament* occasionally it is God who is said to be 'justified.' This means that His actions and judgments are proved by events to be just, though men had felt doubt about their fairness (Ps 51[4], Lk 7[29]). It is Job's sin, in the eyes of Elihu, that he seeks to 'justify himself rather than God' (Job 32[2]). More usually, however, God is the subject rather than the object of 'justify.'

The word is applied also to men. For instance, it is the mark of an honourable man that he 'justifies' only those who are in fact 'just'; and it is a sign of gross wickedness in a judge if he 'justifies' one who is in fact guilty, especially if he does it in return for a bribe (Is 5[23]). In a less official way this is true of all men (Pr 17[15]). God too passes His judgment on human lives. Since He, as opposed to corrupt man, is perfectly righteous, His verdicts are always scrupulously just. Man's judgments may be unjust, whether through wickedness or ignorance, but God can be relied on never to 'justify the wicked' (Ex 23[7]). The upright man, therefore, though he may be wrongfully condemned by his fellows or even by unjust judges, can find comfort in the knowledge that God by His final verdict will at the last 'justify' him (Is 50[8]).

God's verdict can be trusted always to be fair. But this may be a cause of misgiving rather than comfort to a man of sensitive conscience, who knows that even his best is far short of God's perfect will for him. For 'how can a man be righteous (AV '**justified**') before God'? (Job 25[4]). 'In thy sight shall no living man be justified' (Ps 143[2] RV). It is true that He will never condemn unfairly, but how can He who knows the innermost secrets of every heart pronounce any man wholly innocent and guiltless? A man must hold a very superficial view of sin who can find complete comfort in the thought that God's dealings with him will be based on strict justice (Ps 130²).

There remains an unresolved dilemma in the OT. Some passages such as Ps 15 declare unequivocally that the only way for a man to be justified before God is for him to be actually innocent. Other passages, however, humbly recognize that mortal man is never truly innocent in the light of God's perfect holiness. A beginning of a solution is made by the recognition that in certain circumstances there is forgiveness with God, and that He is willing to accept a 'broken and a contrite heart,' when man has no actual righteousness to offer (Ps 51¹⁷); thus God provides 'justification' even when man himself has failed to provide justice. In Is 53¹¹ there is also mention of one, God's Servant, who will gain justification for those who cannot claim it on their own account: 'My righteous servant shall justify many' (RV).

3. In the *Gospels* the word 'justify' is infrequent. God (or the Wisdom of God) is said to be justified by His actions (Mt 11¹⁹, Lk 7²⁹, ³⁵). Men are spoken of as 'justifying themselves,' *i.e.* representing their conduct as free from blame (Lk 10²⁹ 16¹⁵). The importance of what we say, as well as what we do, for our justification (right standing) with God is stressed in Mt 12³⁷. The utter inadequacy in this connexion of a complacent fulfilment of external duties is clearly shown in the parable of the Pharisee and the Publican. The Publican, who has nothing to commend him but his penitence and his plea for mercy, is 'justified' rather than the Pharisee who has been punctilious in observing all the requirements of his religion (Lk 18¹⁴). This same emphasis is prominent elsewhere in our Lord's teaching, especially in the parables of the Prodigal Son and the Workers of the Vineyard, even though the word 'justify' is not used. In these three parables we find clearly presented the same truth which Paul later was to express in terms of 'justification' by grace through faith.

In *Acts* the only use of the word occurs in an account of an address by Paul (13³⁹, where RSV has 'freed'), and this faithfully reflects the teaching we find in his letters.

4. It is in the *Pauline Epistles* that the word is found most frequently. It is not, however, evenly distributed among them, but is largely confined to the two letters usually associated with the Judaistic controversy, Romans and Galatians. Of the twenty-nine uses of the word (and its derivatives) in Paul's letters, twenty-five occur in these two. For this reason it has been argued that the word is not one that Paul chose spontaneously as a metaphor suitable in itself for declaring the message of the Christian Gospel, but rather one which was forced upon him by his opponents in the controversy. The Judaizers sincerely believed that Paul was undermining the very foundations of morality and justice when he spoke of God's free forgiveness and acceptance of sinful men on the basis merely of their faith in Christ. They insisted that the only man who can be justified by God is one who has proved himself in his conduct to be a right-living man. Had not God explicitly said, 'I will not justify the wicked'? (Ex 23⁷).

In Romans 7 Paul reveals how keenly he had realized the hopelessness of sinful man if these stern words contained the whole truth about God's dealings with men. If man's acceptance by Him was dependent on his own poor attempts at goodness, then he must be for ever excluded from God's presence. Paul, however, had had made known to him another way by which he might find acceptance with God. It was through Christ. When a man committed his whole life in trust and obedience to Christ, he found himself forgiven by God, accepted by Him, and delivered from the weight of guilt. Through faith in Christ he was justified, without having to wait until he had made himself a righteous man.

Judaism, besides insisting that a man was justified only by his actual obedience to the commands of God, usually thought of God's verdict being declared at the end of life in the final judgment. Man's justification was therefore a matter of pious hope for the future, not of confident assurance in the present. 'The doers of the law *will* be justified,' was the way Paul represented the teaching of Judaism (Ro 2¹³).

Paul's Gospel was quite contrary to this. Through what God had done in Christ, man's justification did not depend any longer on his own moral achievements, but on his *faith* in Christ. It was not granted by God as a reward which man could earn by his good deeds, but was an act of God's *grace*, His free unmerited mercy, offered to man in his need as a free gift. Nor was it merely a hope for the future, but rather a *present* privilege.

It was a *present* privilege. Paul often used of it the present tense. All who believe in Christ 'are justified by his grace as a gift' (Ro 3²⁴). 'A man is justified by faith apart from works of law' (Ro 3²⁸). The matter is made even clearer by the use of past tenses in some cases. 'Now that we *have been* justified' is the literal translation of the tense in Ro 5¹ and 5⁹.

It is an act of *grace*, God's free unmerited gift. 'We are justified by grace as a gift' (Ro 3²⁴). Twice in Romans (5¹⁶, ¹⁸) justification is described as 'a free gift.' Since, however, the grace of God is nowhere so fully and vividly present as in the self-giving of Christ on the Cross, justification is often related to His death. It is mediated 'by his blood' (Ro 5⁹ 3²⁵). It is not, however, derived exclusively from the death of Christ, since Paul also declares: 'He was raised for our justification' (Ro 4²⁵).

The response in man which appropriates this gift of God, made available to him in Christ, is called *faith* (Ro 3²⁸ 5¹). Paul, however, gives his own fullness of meaning to this word. It is nothing less than the full acceptance of Christ into our lives, as the One on whom we depend, and whom we are pledged to obey. We take Him and all He has done for us, and put our lives at His disposal for whatever He sees we need, whether chastisement, rebuke, cleansing, healing, or command. That is faith. It is man's acceptance of God as He draws near in Christ.

The consequence in human life of this readjusted relationship with God is 'peace' (Ro 5¹).

In this way Paul helped to resolve the dilemma of OT writers. No man can make himself righteous before the holiness of God, yet he is required to be righteous if he is to be justified. There is, however, forgiveness with God. Paul combined these truths in his Gospel. Christ was the 'righteous servant' who would 'justify many' (Is 53¹¹). Through Christ God declared to be righteous those who had faith in Him. What the Law could not do, Christ had done.

While it is true that hopes expressed in the OT thus find their fulfilment in Paul's Gospel, it is also true that Paul's words ran counter to other OT affirmations. It is stated unmistakably in Pr 17¹⁵ that 'he who justifies the wicked is an abomination to the Lord'; yet Paul declared that God Himself 'justifies the ungodly' (Ro 4³). This must have sounded like sheer blasphemy to those who claimed to be loyal Jews, even though they were also Christians. It was by such startling words that Paul sought to make clear beyond any doubt the astonishing newness of the Gospel of Christ. He refused to allow it to be imprisoned in the strait-jacket of Judaism. For this reason justification by grace through faith has rightly come to represent the very core of the Gospel.

Sometimes the attempt is made to distinguish sharply what Paul meant by justification from such other great words as reconciliation, redemption, adoption, and salvation. All of them are brave attempts to find metaphors to declare what God has done for man through Christ. The word describing the remedy varies with the word describing the illness. If man's ailment is his estrangement from God, then reconciliation is the blessing which Christ brings; if it is bondage to evil, then Christ has brought redemption; if it is that religion seemed like a weary task laid on a reluctant slave, Christ was declared to have brought the privilege of sonship (adoption); if man was thought of as lost and doomed,

Christ's work for him was salvation. Similarly, if man's plight was that he was a guilty wrongdoer, worthy to be condemned to dreadful punishment, his forgiveness and release can be described as justification. It is not so much that these great words are sharply different from each other. Rather it is that taken all together they serve to describe the fullness of the benefits which God bestows through Christ.

5. The teaching of *St. James* on justification seems on the surface to be in plain contradiction to St. Paul. He writes: 'Abraham was justified by works,' not by faith (2^{21}), and 'By works a man is justified and not by faith alone' (2^{24}). It may be that James represented a form of Christianity which was sympathetic to the Jewish emphasis on good works as a prerequisite to acceptance with God, and felt uneasy about Paul's almost imprudent emphasis on the free grace of God in Christ. It is, however, not necessary to take this point of view. The contradiction may well be more apparent than real. It is, for instance, quite clear that the word 'faith' in this epistle bears a very different significance from that which Paul gave to it. For James it is merely an intellectual assent to certain articles of belief, which a demon knows to be true no less than an angel, but his life is unaffected by it (2^{19}). For Paul, on the other hand, it meant the total commitment of life, in trust and obedience, to Christ. Paul himself would have denounced as vehemently as James any false confidence in such a travesty of true faith. The faith he recognized and pleaded for was the 'faith which works through love' (Gal 5^{6}), and James too is pleading for the kind of faith which expresses itself in love. It is possible also that by justification James was thinking of God's final verdict on human life, which undoubtedly takes into account conduct as well as professed belief, as the parable of the Sheep and Goats makes clear (Mt 25^{31-46}). Paul, however, uses justification to describe, not the final verdict, but God's acceptance of man here and now. He, too, no less than James, assumes that at the Last Judgment, 'God will render to every man according to his works' (Ro 2^{6}). Probably, too, Paul primarily meant by 'works' a somewhat soulless observance of prescribed regulations, with the selfish motive of imposing on God an obligation to dispense the appropriate reward, whereas James meant humble love towards one's neighbour, as God commanded, and practised in the common ways of life. It is unlikely that James was contradicting Paul in what he wrote, though he may have been protesting against some distortion of Paul's teaching by people who found in it an excuse for avoiding the humble duties of Christian love.

Paul's exposition of this doctrine is of the very essence of the Gospel of Jesus Christ. Justification by grace through faith does not, however, make the humble duty of obedience to God unnecessary. Rather it is a gift from God to man's need, bestowed in order that from the healed relationship with God which it creates, man may find new power to obey God and also new joy in that obedience (Ro 8^{4}). C. L. M.

JUSTUS.—This surname is given to three persons in NT. **1. Joseph Barsabbas** (Ac 1^{23}). **2. Titus** or Titius, host of St. Paul at Corinth (Ac 18^{7} RV; the MSS vary between these two forms, and some omit the first name altogether; RSV, **Titius**), apparently a Roman citizen who was a 'God-fearer,' converted to Christianity by the Apostle. **3.** A Jew named **Jesus** or Joshua, who apparently was with St. Paul during his imprisonment (Col 4^{11}). A. J. M.—**F. C. G.**

JUTAH, Jos 15^{55} (RV).—See JUTTAH.

JUTTAH.—A town of Judah, Jos 15^{55} (RV **Jutah**); given to the priests as a city of refuge for the manslayer, Jos 21^{16}. It is omitted from the list of cities of refuge in 1 Ch 6^{59}. It has been suggested that Juttah was the residence of Zechariah and Elizabeth, and the birthplace of John the Baptist (Lk 1^{39} 'a city of Judah'). Juttah is probably modern *Yaṭṭā*, standing high on a ridge 16 miles from *Beit Jibrîn* (Eleutheropolis).

K

KAB.—See WEIGHTS AND MEASURES.

KABUL, Jos 19^{27} (RSV).—See CABUL.

KABZEEL.—A town in the extreme S. of Judah, on the border of Edom, Jos 15^{21}, 2 S 23^{20}, 1 Ch 11^{22}; called **Jekabzeel** in Neh 11^{25}. It is possibly modern *Kh. Hōrah*.

KADESH or **KADESH-BARNEA.**—This was an important oasis in the North Sinai desert. It is mentioned incidentally in Gn 14^{7} 16^{7}, and played a significant rôle in the desert wandering of the Israelites, being the scene of the striking of the rock by Moses (Nu 20^{2}). For long it was the centre of the tribes (Nu 20^{1}, Dt 1^{46}), the scene of Korah's rebellion (Nu 16) and of the death of Miriam (Nu 20^{1}). The spies were sent hence into Palestine (Nu 32^{8}, Dt 1^{20ff}), and returned hither (Nu 13^{26}), and from here a delegation was dispatched to the king of Edom (Nu 20^{14ff}, Jg 11^{16}).

Kadesh-barnea lay on the south boundary of the Amorite highlands (Dt 1^{19}) and on the confines of Edom (Nu 20^{6}). The conquest of Joshua is depicted as reaching thus far (Jos 10^{41}). Thus a location is visualized on a line, running from the Ascent of Akrabbim on the east to the Brook of Egypt on the west, which conventionally marked the southern boundary of Canaan (Nu 34^{4}, Jos 15^{3}). In Gn 20^{1} it is placed E. of Gerar but, as the latter place was located WNW. of Beersheba, the direction is only vague. In Ezk 47^{19} 48^{28} it is located between Tamar and the Brook of Egypt, again a rather vague location. These notices, however, do not exclude H. Clay Trumbull's location at a group of springs in the tribal territory of the *'Azāzimîn* Arabs, about fifty miles S. of Beersheba. One of these springs, *'Ain Qedeis*, probably preserves the Biblical name, but the most important settlement has been located at *'Ain Qedeirāt*, where the remains of an ancient fort were recognized by Woolley and Lawrence and later dated by Glueck to the early Hebrew monarchy. It is plausibly argued by Mowinckel that this place, a shrine three days' journey from Egypt, was the immediate objective of the Israelites at the Exodus, and that the desert wandering was rather a gravitation about this centre. He suggests further that as an important entrepôt of caravan trade it was the cause of the war between Amalek and Israel (Ex 17^{8ff}). The locality is still a much frequented oasis, and *'Ain Qedeirāt* has been successfully developed to the limit of its possibilities as an experimental farm by the Egyptian Government.

Tribal disputes and trials by ordeal were doubtless conducted here, as suggested by the names **En Mishpat,** 'Well of Judgment' (Gn 14^{7}), Waters of Meribah, 'Suit at Law,' Massah, 'Trial' (Ex 17^{1-7}), and Kadesh, 'Holy,' itself. The well as the abode of a *numen* is a common conception in ancient Semitic animism and modern Arab superstition. W. E.—**J. Gr.**

KADMIEL.—The name of a Levitical family which returned with Zerubbabel, Ezr 2^{40}, Neh 7^{43}, 1 Es 5^{26} (AV **Cadmiel**). In Ezr 3^{9} (cf 1 Es 5^{58} [AV **Cadmiel**]), in connexion with the laying of the foundation of the

Temple, as well as in Neh 9[4f] (the day of humiliation) and 10[9] (the sealing of the covenant), Kadmiel appears to be an individual. The name occurs further in Neh 12[8, 24].

KADMONITES.—One of the nations whose land was promised to Abram's seed, Gn 15[19]. Their *habitat* was probably in the region of the Dead Sea. The fact that *Kedemah* is said to be a son of Ishmael (Gn 25[15], 1 Ch 1[31]) renders it likely that they were Ishmaelite Arabs. Ewald, however, regarded *Ḳadhmōnî* as equivalent to *Bᵉnê Ḳedhem.*

KAIN.—1. A city in the uplands of Judah, Jos 15[57] AV **Cain**); probably to be identified with the modern *Kh. Yaqîn,* on a hill SW. of Hebron, with tombs, cisterns, and other traces of an ancient town. A neighbouring sanctuary is pointed out as the tomb of Cain. **2.** A clan name = the **Kenites** (q.v.), Nu 24[22] (RV, RSV; AV 'the Kenite'), Jg 4[11] (RVm; AV, RV, RSV 'the Kenites').

KAIWAN.—The name of a star-god, Am 5[26] (AV, RV **Chiun**); commonly identified with Akkadian *Kaiwānu,* the planet Saturn (= Ninib, war-god), whose temple, Bit Ninib, in the province of Jerusalem is mentioned by the Egyptian governors of this city as early as 1450 B.C. The vowels in MT were probably substituted from the word *shiḳḳuṣ* ('abomination'). But see STARS; also REPHAN, SAKKUTH. N. K.

KALLAI.—The head of a priestly family, Neh 12[20].

KAMON.—The burial-place of Jair, Jg 10[5] (AV **Camon**). The site is uncertain; possibly modern *Qamm,* SE. of the Sea of Galilee.

KANAH.—1. A 'brook' or *wady* in the borders of Ephraim, Jos 16[8] 17[9]. It is commonly identified with *Wâdī Qânah* near Shechem. **2.** A town in the northern boundary of Asher, Jos 19[28], probably to be identified with the modern *Qânah,* a short distance SE. of Tyre.

KAPH.—See CAPH.

KAREAH ('bald').—Father of Johanan, **1.**

KAREM.—A city of Judah, in the lowland, mentioned in Jos 15[59] in LXX, but not in the Hebrew; probably modern *ʿAin Karîm.*

KARIATHIARIUS, 1 Es 5[19] (RV).—See KIRIATH-ARIM.

KARKA.—An unknown place in the S. of Judah, Jos 15[3] (AV **Karkaa**).

KARKAA, Jos 15[3] (AV).—See KARKA.

KARKOR.—A place apparently in Gilead, Jg 8[10]. The site is unknown.

KARNAIM.—A city mentioned in Am 6[13] (RSV; AV, RV 'horns'); probably the same as **Ashteroth-Karnaim** (q.v.).

KARTAH.—A city of Zebulun, Jos 21[34]; not mentioned in the parallel passage, 1 Ch 6[77]. The site is unknown.

KARTAN.—A city of Naphtali, Jos 21[32]. The parallel passage, 1 Ch 6[76], has **Kiriathaim.** It is perhaps *Kh. el-Qureiyeh.*

KATTATH.—A city of Zebulun, Jos 19[15]; possibly modern *Kh. Quṭeineh.* It is perhaps to be identified with **Kitron.**

KEDAR.—The name of a nomadic people living to the E. of Palestine, whom P (Gn 25[13]) regards as a division of the Ishmaelites. Jeremiah (49[28]) counts them among the 'sons of the East,' and in 2[10] refers to them as symbolic of the East, as he does to Citium in Cyprus as symbolic of the West. In Isaiah (21[7]) they are said to produce skilful archers, to live in villages (42[11]), and (60[7]) to be devoted to sheepbreeding. The last passage associates them also with the **Nebaioth** (possibly Nabataeans). Jeremiah alludes also to their nomadic life, their sheep, camels, and tents (49[29]). Ezekiel (27[21]) couples them with 'Arab,' and speaks of their trade with Tyre in sheep and goats. In Ps 120[5] Kedar denotes the type of barbarous unfeeling people and in Ca 1[5] their tents are as a symbol of blackness. The Assyrian king Ashurbanipal (668–626 B.C.) in his account of his Arabian campaign mentions the Kedarites in connexion with the *Aribi* (Arabs) and the Nebaioth, mentioning asses, camels, and sheep as booty. More recently Kedar is mentioned in Aramaic inscriptions on two silver bowls from a shrine at *Tell el-Maskhûṭah* (possibly Succoth) east of the Nile Delta, which were given by 'Qaynu (Cain) the son of Gashmu, King of Kedar' in the Persian period. Gashmu is no doubt the adversary of Nehemiah, in which case Kedar could coincide with the Persian province of 'Arabia' in the south of Palestine to the Egyptian border. This region had been occupied after the Exile by Edomites and Arabs from E. of the *Wâdī ʿArabah,* so that, in agreement with earlier Assyrian inscriptions Kedar of Qaynu's inscriptions may refer to land here as well as the Persian province of Arabia west of the Arabah. G. A. B.—**J. Gr.**

KEDEMAH.—A son of Ishmael, Gn 25[15], 1 Ch 1[31]. The clan of which he is the eponymous head has not been identified. See also KADMONITES.

KEDEMOTH.—A place apparently on the upper course of the Arnon, assigned to Reuben, Jos 13[18]; a Levitical city, 21[37], 1 Ch 6[79]. From 'the wilderness of Kedemoth' messengers were sent by Moses to Sihon, Dt 2[26]. It is possibly modern *Qaṣr ez-Zaʿferân.*

KEDESH.—1. A city in the south of Judah, Jos 15[23]. See KADESH. **2.** A Levitical city of Issachar, 1 Ch 6[72]; called **Kishion** in the parallel list in Jos 21[28] (AV **Kishon**). It is perhaps *Tell Abū Qedeis.* **3.** See KEDESH IN NAPHTALI.

KEDESH IN GALILEE.—See KEDESH IN NAPHTALI.

KEDESH IN NAPHTALI.—A city of Naphtali, Jg 4[6] (AV, RV **Kadesh-naphtali**); called **Kedesh** in Jos 12[22] 19[37], Jg 4[9-11], 2 K 15[29], and **Kedesh in Galilee** in Jos 20[7] 21[32], 1 Ch 6[76]. Evidently, from the name ('holy'), a sacred site from ancient times. A Canaanite royal city, Jos 12[22]; and later a city of refuge (20[7]) and a Levitical city (21[32]). It was the home of Barak, Jg 4[6]. In the reign of Pekah it was captured by Tiglath-pileser, 2 K 15[29].

The site is modern *Tell Qades,* one of the most picturesque spots in Galilee; to the E. of the village the ground is strewn with ancient remains. There are several fine sarcophagi and the ruins of a large building, possibly once a Roman temple. E. W. G. M.

KEDESH-NAPHTALI, Jg 4[6] (AV, RV).—See KEDESH IN NAPHTALI.

KEDRON.—A place fortified by Cendebeus (1 Mac 15[39, 41] RSV; AV **Cedron,** RV **Kidron**), and the point to which he was pursued after his defeat by the sons of Simon the Maccabee (16[9]). It may be the modern *Qaṭra* near *Yebnā,* and is possibly identical with Gederoth of Jos 15[41], 2 Ch 28[18] (but cf J. Simons, *The Geographical and Topographical Texts of the OT,* p. 147).

KEHELATHAH.—One of the stopping places in the wanderings, Nu 33[22f]. The site is unknown.

KEILAH.—A city of Judah in the lowland, named with Nezib and Achzib, Jos 15[44]. David delivered it from the marauding Philistines, and it became his residence for a time. Becoming aware of the treachery of its inhabitants, he left it, 1 S 23[1ff]. It was reoccupied after the Exile, Neh 3[17f]. In 1 Ch 4[19] it has the epithet 'Garmite' (q.v.). It is commonly identified with *Kh. Qîlā,* about seven miles E. of *Beit Jibrîn.* It lies very high, however, for a city in the Shephelah, being over 1,500 feet above the level of the sea. W. E.

KELAIAH.—A Levite who had married a foreign wife, Ezr 10[23], 1 Es 9[23] (AV, RV **Colius**). He was also called **Kelita** (in AV, RV in 1 Es 9[23] **Calitas**). Kelita appears in Neh 8[7], 1 Es 9[48] (AV, RV **Calitas**) as one of the Levites who assisted Ezra in expounding the Law, and his name occurs amongst the signatories to the covenant, Neh 10[10]. It does not follow, however, that because Kelaiah was also called Kelita he is to be identified with *this* Kelita.

KELITA.—See Kelaiah.

KEMUEL.—1. The son of Nahor and father of Aram, Gn 22[31] (contrast 10[22], where Aram is son of Shem). **2.** Son of Shiphtan and prince of the tribe of Ephraim, one of the twelve commissioners for the dividing of the land, Nu 34[24]. **3.** The father of Hashabiah, the ruler of the Levites, 1 Ch 27[17].

KENAN.—Son of Enoch and father of Mahalelel, Gn 5[9, 12] (AV **Cainan**), 1 Ch 1[2]. The name is a variant of *Cain*.

KENATH.—A city to the E. of the Jordan, taken by **Nobah,** whose name for a time it bore, Nu 32[42]. Geshur and Aram reconquered it, 1 Ch 2[23]. It was later called *Kanata*, one of the towns of the Decapolis. It is usually identified with *Qanawât*, fully 16 miles N. of Bozrah. It occupies a commanding position on either bank of the *Wâdī Qanawât*, which here forms a picturesque waterfall. There are tall, graceful columns, and massive walls, together with other impressive remains of buildings from Graeco-Roman times. The modern village, lower down the slope, is now occupied by Druzes. W. E.

KENAZ.—See Kenizzites.

KENEZITE, Nu 32[12], Jos 14[6, 14] (AV).—See Kenizzites.

KENITES.—A nomadic people, closely connected with the Amalekites (q.v.), but having friendly relations with Israel, and ultimately, it seems, at least in the main, absorbed in Judah. **Hobab,** Moses' father-in-law (Jg 1[16] 4[11] RSV), who had been invited by Moses—and had doubtless accepted the invitation—to be a guide to Israel in the wilderness (Nu 10[29-32]), was a Kenite ; and his descendants came up from Jericho with the tribe of Judah into the S. part of their territory (Arad is mentioned here, about 17 miles S. of Hebron), though afterwards, true to their nomad instincts, they roamed beyond the border and are found among the Amalekites in N. Sinai (Jg 1[16] ; read here with MSS of LXX ' the Amalekite ' for ' the people '—the last three letters having dropped out in the Hebrew). When Saul, many years later, attacked the Amalekites, he gave the Kenites timely warning on the grounds of ancient friendship (1 S 15[6], alluding doubtless to Hobab's guidance, Nu 10[29-32]). In Jg 4[11] Heber the Kenite is mentioned as having separated himself from the main body of his people, and wandered northwards as far as the neighbourhood of Kedesh in Galilee (*Tell Abū Qedeis*, SW. of the Sea of Galilee), where his wife Jael dispatched Sisera after his defeat by Barak (Jg 4[17f]). From 1 S 27[10] 30[29] we learn that in the time of David there was a district in the S. of Judah inhabited by Kenites ; it is possible that **Kinah** in the Negeb of Judah (Jos 15[22]) and **Kain** in the hill-country (v.[57]) were Kenite settlements. The **Rechabites,** with whom the nomadic life had become a religious institution (Jer 35), were said to be Kenites (1 Ch 2[55]). In Gn 15[9] (J) the Kenites are mentioned among the ten nations whose land was to be taken possession of by the Israelites, a reference, no doubt, to the absorption of the Kenites in Judah. The folk-oracle in Nu 24[21f] plays on the resemblance of the name to the Hebrew *ḳēn*, ' nest,' and declares that though their ' nest ' is among the rocky crags (namely in the S. of Judah), they would in the end be carried away captive by the Assyrians (**' Kain '** in v.[22] is the proper name of the people of which ' Kenite ' is the gentilic adjective ; cf Jg 4[11] RVm. Note that the oracle on the Kenites follows closely upon that on the Amalekites).

The word *ḳain* means in Hebrew ' spear ' (2 S 21[16]), and in Arabic *qayyān* means an ' iron-smith ' ; the Aramaic cognate also denotes a metal-worker ; hence it has been conjectured (Sayce) that the Kenites were a nomad tribe of smiths. This is supported by their association with Midian (Ex 3[1]) and the Negeb in the vicinity of the copper mines of the Arabah. The condemnation of Cain to perpetual wandering and the prohibition of any violence to him (Gn 4[12-15]) probably reflects the nomad habits of the itinerant smith-caste, the Kenites, and the immunity which they enjoyed. It is also feasibly suggested that Yahweh was originally the god of the Kenites, though in what character is quite uncertain.
S. R. D.—**J. Gr.**

KENIZZITES.—A clan named from an eponymous ancestor, **Kenaz.** According to Jos 15[17], Jg 1[13], **Caleb** and **Othniel** were descended from him. (The inference sometimes made, that Kenaz was a brother of Caleb, arose from a misunderstanding of these passages.) In Jos 14[6, 14] Caleb is called a Kenizzite (AV **Kenezite**), and so in Nu 32[12] (AV **Kenezite**). In Gn 15[19-21] the Kenizzites are counted among the pre-Israelitish inhabitants of Palestine. P in Gn 36[42] enrols Kenaz among the ' dukes ' of Edom, while in vv.[11, 15] he is counted both as a ' duke ' and as a grandson of Esau. The Chronicler names Kenaz as a grandson of Esau (1 Ch 1[36]), and also as a descendant of Judah (1 Ch 4[13-15]). The probable meaning of all these passages is that the Kenizzites overspread a part of Edom and southern Judah before the Israelite conquest and continued to abide there, a part of them being absorbed by the Edomites, and a part by the tribe of Judah. This latter portion embraced the clans of Caleb and Othniel.
G. A. B.

KENOSIS.—The word means ' emptying.' As a noun, it is not found in NT, but the correlative verb occurs in Ph 2[7], ' emptied himself,' in which it is said that Christ ' though he was in the form of God, did not count equality with God a thing to be grasped, but emptied himself, taking the form of a servant, being born in the likeness of men.' In the context in which this occurs, Paul is urging the Philippians to emulate their Lord in His humility and concern for others ; the Apostle does not appear to be making a theological point so much as an ethical one.

However, this passage, along with such others as 2 Co 8[9], has been used by theologians in the last two centuries to suggest a view of the Incarnation in which the Eternal Word ' emptied himself,' giving up or leaving behind His metaphysical attributes, when He became man. The notion of *kenōsis*, so employed, has had special reference to the limitations both in knowledge and in action which attached to the Lord as He is portrayed fcr ɩs in the Gospels ; *kenōsis*, therefore, has been a NT concept upon which such theologians have sought to hang a doctrinal affirmation.

However, it appears that despite the use which Paul has made elsewhere of notions of a pre-existent Redeemer or Saviour who ' gave up ' His heavenly place to enter history for man's salvation, this passage has its primary intention for the Apostle in its insistence that the ' mind ' of Christ is to be reproduced in the life of the believer. The incidental references which may be made to a redeemer-god in terms of which the life of Jesus is explained are not central to the passage. On the other hand, the writer plainly wishes to assert that it was by the humility and obedience of the Lord that He was given the exalted place noted in Ph 2[9] and won the privilege of being called ' Lord.' W. N. P.

KERAS, 1 Es 5[29] (RV).—See Keros.

KERCHIEFS (from the French *couvrechef*, a covering for the head) are mentioned only in Ezr 13[18, 21] (AV, RV ; RSV **veils**), a somewhat obscure passage having reference to certain forms of divination or sorcery, which required the head to be covered. They evidently varied in length with the height of the wearer (v.[18]), and perhaps resembled the long veils worn by the female captives from Lachish represented on an Assyrian sculpture ; see Dress, **5** (*b*). A. R. S. K.

KERÊ or **QERÊ.**—See Text of OT.

KEREN-HAPPUCH (literally ' horn of antimony ').—The youngest daughter born to Job in his second estate of prosperity, Job 42[14]. The name is indicative of beautiful eyes, from the dye made of antimony, used to paint the edges of the eyelids, 2 K 9[30], Jer 4[30].

KERIOTH.—1. A city of Moab, named in Jer 48[24, 41], Am 2[2] (AV **Kirioth**), and in line 13 of the Moabite Stone (see MESHA). Some have suggested the identification with Ar, the capital of Moab, but this is doubtful. Equally doubtful is the identification with **Kir-heres** (q.v.). The site is unknown. **2.** Jos 15^{25} (AV); for 'Kerioth and Hezron' read **Kerioth-hezron** (q.v.).

KERIOTH-HEZRON.—A town in the Negeb, Jos 15^{25}, identical with **Hazor, 3** (q.v.).

KEROS.—Name of a family of Nethinim (q.v.) who returned with Zerubbabel, Ezr 2^{44}, Neh 7^{47}, 1 Es 5^{29} (AV **Ceras**, RV **Keras**).

KESITAH.—See QESITA.

KESTREL.—See HAWK.

KETAB (1 Es 5^{30}).—Head of a family of Temple servants who returned with Zerubbabel (AV **Cetab**). There is no corresponding name in the lists of Ezra and Nehemiah.

KETHÎBH.—See TEXT OF OT.

KETTLE.—In AV and RV in 1 S 2^{14} only. In RSV also in Mic 3^{3} (AV, RV 'pot'). See HOUSE, **9.**

KETURAH.—Abraham's wife (Gn 25$^{1-4}$), or concubine (1 Ch 1^{32f}; cf Gn 25^{6}) after the death of Sarah; named only by J and the Chronicler in the passages referred to; said to be the ancestress of sixteen tribes, several of which are distinctly Arabian—Midian, Sheba, Dedan. Some Arabic writers mention an Arabian tribe near Mecca called *Qaṭûrā*. The ancient Israelites evidently regarded some Arabs as distant relatives (see ABRAHAM, ESAU, HAGAR). The name *Ḳᵉṭûrāh* = 'incense,' is a perfume-name like *Ḳᵉṣîʿāh* (Job 42^{14}; see KEZIAH). W. T. S.

KEY.—See HOUSE, **6.** Of the passages where this word is used in a figurative sense the most important are Is 22^{22} (cf Rev 3^{7}), where the key is the symbol of authority and rule; Lk 11^{52} 'the key of knowledge'; and the *crux interpretum*, Mt 16^{19}, for which see next article. A. R. S. K.

KEYS, POWER OF THE.—In ecclesiastical history the phrase is associated primarily with the so-called 'Privilege of Peter,' upon which the dogma of papal supremacy has been built, but also with the delegated authority of an official priesthood to pronounce sentence of the absolution or the retention of sins.

1. The fundamental passage is Mt 16^{18f}. When St. Peter at Caesarea Philippi had made his great confession of Jesus as the Christ, Jesus blessed him and announced that upon this rock (*i.e.* either Peter or the Divine revelation he had received) He would build His Church. Then He added, 'I will give you the **keys of the kingdom of heaven**: and whatever you bind on earth shall be bound in heaven; and whatever you loose on earth shall be loosed in heaven.' That this double promise, like the one in the preceding verse, was made to St. Peter personally can hardly be doubted. The question is as to what it means. Evidently Jesus is carrying out the figure He has already used of a building founded upon **a rock**—the rock, viz., of believing confession, based upon a divine revelation (v.^{17}); and He now declares that as the reward of this confession he should have the privilege of wielding the keys of the Kingdom of heaven. There are some who think that by this gift of the keys St. Peter was appointed to the position of a steward in charge of his Lord's treasures, entrusted with the duty of feeding the household (Lk 12^{42}, cf Mt 13^{52}). But from the use of the word 'key' by Jesus Himself in Lk 11^{52}, and from the analogy of Is 22^{22}, Rev 3^{7}, it is probable that the keys are those not of the storehouse but of the mansion itself, and that the gift of them points to the privilege of admitting others into the Kingdom. The promise was fulfilled, accordingly, on the day of Pentecost, when St. Peter opened the doors of the Christian Church to the Jewish world (Ac 2^{41}); and again at Caesarea, when he, first of the Apostles, opened that same door to the Gentiles (Ac 10$^{34-38}$ 15^{7}). But, as the two incidents show, there was nothing arbitrary, official, or mysterious about St. Peter's exercise of the power of the keys on these occasions. It was his believing confession of Christ that had gained him the privilege, and both in Jerusalem and at Caesarea it was by a renewed confession of Christ, accompanied by a testimony to the truth regarding Him as that had been made known in the experience of faith (Ac 2$^{32-36}$ 10$^{36-43}$), that he opened the doors of the Kingdom alike to Jews and to Gentiles.

With regard to the second part of the verse, 'Whatever you bind on earth shall be bound in heaven; and whatever you loose on earth shall be loosed in heaven,' some scholars have regarded it as merely explaining what is meant by the keys of the Kingdom, while others hold that it confers an additional privilege. The latter view is the more probable. In Rabbinic language to **'bind'** and to **'loose'** were the regular terms for forbidding and permitting. Hence these words confer upon the Apostle a power of legislation in the Christian Church—*i.e.* of interpreting the Christian *halachah* and deciding questions of Christian duty—a power which we see him exercising by and by, along with the other Apostles and the elders, at the Jerusalem Conference (Ac 15$^{6-11, 22-29}$).

But now comes the question, Was this twofold promise, which was given to St. Peter personally, given him in any exclusive sense? As regards the second part of it, clearly not; for on a later occasion in this same Gospel we find Jesus bestowing precisely the same privilege on His disciples generally (18^{18}; cf v.^{1} and also vv.^{19f}). Moreover, the later NT history shows that St. Peter had no supreme position as a legislator in the Church (see Ac 15$^{13, 19}$, Gal 2^{11ff}). And if the power of binding and loosing was not given to him exclusively, the presumption is that the same thing holds of the parallel power of the keys. As a matter of fact, we find it to be so. Though St. Peter had the privilege of first opening the doors of the Kingdom to both Jews and Gentiles, the same privilege was soon exercised by others (Ac 8^{4} 11^{19ff} 13^{2ff}). By and by Peter falls into the background, and we find Paul and Barnabas rehearsing to the Church how God through their preaching had 'opened a door of faith to the Gentiles' (14^{27}). But this does not mean that the privilege was withdrawn from St. Peter; it means only that it was extended to others on their fulfilment of those same conditions of faith and testimony on which Peter had first received it.

2. In Mt 18^{18} there appears to be no reference whatever to the remission and retention of sins. As in 16^{18}, 'whatever' not 'whomever' is the word employed, and here as there the binding and loosing must be taken to refer to the enactment of ordinances for regulating the affairs of the Church, not to the discharge of such a purely spiritual function as the forgiveness of sins. In any case, the promise is made not to the Apostles, much less to an official priesthood deriving authority from them by an Apostolic succession, but to 'the Church' (v.^{17}).

3. In Jn 20^{23} we find the assurance definitely given of **a power to remit or retain sins.** But the gift is bestowed upon the whole company present (cf Lk 24^{33}) as representing the Christian society generally. That society, through its possession of the Holy Spirit (v.^{22}), is thus empowered to declare the forgiveness or the retention of sins (cf 1 Jn 2^{20}, Gal 6^{1}). As a matter of fact, this is the way penitential discipline and restoration were administered in the early church.

J. C. L.—**F. C. G.**

KEZIA, Job 42^{14} (AV).—See KEZIAH.

KEZIAH ('cassia').—The name of the second daughter born to Job after his restoration to prosperity, Job 42^{14} (AV **Kezia**).

KEZIZ, Jos 18^{21} (AV).—See EMEK-KEZIZ.

KIBROTH-HATTAAVAH ('graves of lust').—A station in the wanderings, Nu 11^{34f} 33^{16f}, Dt 9^{22}. The march from Taberah (Nu 11^{3}) is not mentioned in Nu 33, but Kibroth-hattaavah was one day's journey from the wilderness of Sinai. It is perhaps to be located at *el-Ebeirig*, NE of Sinai.

KIBZAIM.—See JOKMEAM, **1.**

KID.—See GOAT and (for Ex 23^{19}) MAGIC.

KIDNAPPING.—See CRIMES, etc., **7.**

KIDNEYS.—**1. Literal.**—(1) The choice portions of animals sacrificed to Y" included the kidneys (Ex $29^{13, 22}$, Lv $3^{4, 10, 15}$ 4^{9} 7^{4} $8^{16, 25}$ $9^{10, 19}$; cf Is 34^{6}). The term is even transferred to wheat (Dt 32^{14} AV, RV; RSV 'the finest of the wheat'). (2) Limited to poetry is the use of this term in regard to human beings, and the rendering in AV and RV is always 'reins' (see below). They are formed by Y" (Ps 139^{13}; RSV 'inward parts'), and are, metaphorically, wounded by Y"'s arrows (Job 16^{13}; RSV 'kidneys,' cf La 3^{13}, where RSV has 'heart'). They may be 'consumed' (Job 19^{27}; RSV 'my heart faints'). (3) AVm of Lv 15^{2} 22^{4} ('running of the reins') is incorrect; there is no mention of 'reins.'

2. Figurative.—Here the AV and RV rendering is always **'reins'** Latin *renes*, plural (the Greek equivalent being *nephroi*, whence 'nephritis,' etc.). The avoidance of the word 'kidneys' is desirable, because we do not regard them as the seat of emotion. But the Biblical writers did so regard them. It was as natural for them to say 'This gladdens my reins' as it is natural—and incorrect—for us to say 'This gladdens my heart.' And, in fact, in the passages now cited the terms 'reins' and 'heart' are often parallel: Ps 7^{9} 16^{7} 26^{2} 73^{21}, Pr 23^{16}, Jer 11^{20} 12^{2} 17^{10} 20^{12}, Wis 1^{6}, 1 Mac 2^{24}, Rev 2^{23} (RSV 'heart' in all these passages except Pr 23^{16} ['soul'], Wis 1^{6} ['inmost feelings'], Rev 2^{23} ['mind']). H. F. B. C.—**H. H. R.**

KIDRON, 1 Mac $15^{39, 41}$ (AV).—See KEDRON.

KIDRON, THE BROOK.—The name of a valley (*naḥal*, 'torrent valley,' 'wady,' 2 S 15^{23}, 1 K 2^{37}, 2 Ch 30^{14}, Neh 2^{15} etc.; Greek *cheimarrous*, Jn 18^{1}, where AV has **Cedron**), nearly 3 miles in length, which bounds the plateau of Jerusalem on the E. It is always dry except during and immediately after heavy rain; it is the same valley that is referred to as the **Valley of Jehoshaphat** (q.v.). It commences about $1\frac{1}{4}$ miles N. of the NW. corner of the city walls, as a wide, open, shallow valley. At first it runs SE., receiving tributaries from the W. and N., but where it is now crossed by the modern carriage road to the Mt. of Olives, it turns S. Near this spot (as well as higher up) there are a number of ancient tombs; among them on the W. side of the valley are the so-called 'Tombs of the Kings,' and on the E. the reputed tomb of 'Simon the Just,' much venerated by the Jews. The whole of this first open section of the valley is to-day known as *Wâdī el-Jawz* ('Valley of the Nuts'); it is full of fertile soil, and in a great part of its extent is sown with corn or planted with olives or almonds. As the valley approaches the E. wall of the city it rapidly deepens, and rocky scarps appear on each side; it now receives the name *Wâdī Sitti Maryam, i.e.* 'Valley of the Lady Mary.' Opposite the Temple area the bottom of the valley, now 40 feet below the present surface, is about 400 feet below the Temple platform. S. of this it continues to narrow and deepen, running between the village of *Silwân* (see SILOAM) on the E. and the hill Ophel on the W. Here lies the 'Virgin's Fount,' ancient **Gihon** (q.v.), whose waters to-day rise deep under the surface, though once they ran down the valley itself. A little farther on the valley again expands into a considerable open area, where vegetables are now cultivated, and which perhaps was once the **'King's Garden'** (q.v.). The Tyropoeon Valley, known now as *el-Wâd*, joins the Kidron Valley from the N., and farther on the *Wâdī er-Rabâbi*, traditionally **Hinnom** (q.v.), runs in from the W. The area again narrows at *Bîr Ayyûb*, the ancient **En-rogel** (q.v.), and the valley continues a long winding course under the name of *Wâdī en-Nâr* ('Valley of Fire') till it reaches the Dead Sea.

There is no doubt whatever that this is the Kidron of the OT and NT. It is interesting that the custom of burying Israelites there, which continued to modern times (see JEHOSHAPHAT [VALLEY OF]), is referred to in 2 K $23^{4, 6, 12}$ and 2 Ch 34^{5}. It is probable that the place of the 'graves of the common people' (Jer 26^{23}) was also here, and it has been suggested, from a comparison with Jer 31^{40}, with less plausibility, that this may have been the scene of Ezekiel's vision of the dry bones (Ezk 37). The 'fields of Kidron' (2 K 23^{4}), though generally identified with the open part of the valley when it is joined by the Tyropoeon Valley, are more likely to have been the upper reaches of the valley referred to above as *Wâdī el-Jawz*, which were on the way to Bethel.

The Valley of the Kidron is mentioned first and last in the Bible at two momentous historical crises—when David crossed it (2 S 15^{23}) amid the lamentations of his people as he fled before Absalom, and when Jesus 'went forth with His disciples over the brook Kidron' (Jn 18^{1}) for His great and terrible agony before His crucifixion. E. W. G. M.—**P. W.-M.**

KILAN.—Sixty-seven sons of Kilan and Azetas who returned with Zerubbabel, 1 Es 5^{15} (AV **Ceilan**); in the lists of Ezr 2 and Neh 7 the names are omitted.

KILN.—See FURNACE.

KIN (NEXT OF), KINSMAN, AVENGER OF BLOOD, GO'EL.—**1.** 'Next of kin' is the nearest equivalent in modern jurisprudence of the Hebrew *gō'ēl*, itself the participle of a verb originally signifying 'to claim' (*vindicare*), then 'to buy back,' or, according to A. R. Johnson, 'to cover.' The duties devolving on the *gō'ēl* belonged to the domain both of civil and of criminal law. If a Hebrew, for example, were reduced to selling a part, or the whole, of his property, it was the duty of his next of kin to purchase the property, if it was in his power to do so. The classical instance of the exercise of this 'right of redemption' is the case of the prophet Jeremiah, who purchased the property of his cousin Hanamel in Anathoth, on being asked to do so in virtue of his relationship (Jer 32^{8ff}). Similarly, should a sale have actually taken place, the right of redemption fell to the next of kin (Lv 25^{25}). The case of Naomi and the 'parcel of land' belonging to her deceased husband was complicated by the presence of Ruth, who went with the property. Ru 4^{5} reads, 'The day you buy the field from the hand of Naomi, you are also buying Ruth the Moabitess, the widow of the dead.' The true *gō'ēl* accordingly transferred his rights to Boaz, who came next to him in the degree of relationship. In all these cases the underlying idea is that the land is the inalienable property of the clan or 'family' (Ru 2^{1}) in the wider sense.

Boaz acted the part of the *gō'ēl* in keeping the land in the family; he also fulfilled another duty of the next of kin in raising an heir to the dead by marrying Ruth. In the duty of marrying a widow left childless, ideally the next of kin was the brother of the deceased husband (Dt 25^{5-10}), but in early days, as Gn 38 and the Book of Ruth show, he could be any kinsman. See MARRIAGE, **4.**

The duties of the *gō'ēl*, however, extended not merely to property and to the childless widow, but also to the person of a relative. Should the latter have been compelled by misfortune to sell himself as a slave, it fell to his next of kin to redeem him (Lv 25^{47ff}). Hence arose an extensive use of the verb and its participle in a figurative sense, by which Y" is represented as a *gō'ēl* (RSV **redeemer**), and Israel as His redeemed (so especially in Is 41^{14} 43^{14} and often).

2. The most serious of all the duties incumbent on the *gō'ēl*, in earlier times more particularly, was that of avenging the murder of a relative. In this capacity he was known as the **avenger of blood** (*gō'ēl had-dām*). The practice of blood-revenge is one of the most widely spread customs of human society, and is by no means confined to the Semitic races, although it is still found in full vigour among the modern Arabs. By the Bedouin of the Sinaitic peninsula, for instance, the hereditary vendetta is kept up to the fifth generation (see interesting details given in Lord Cromer's *Report* on Egypt, 1906, 13 ff, and W. H. Storm, *Whither Arabia*? 1938, 17 ff).

In primitive times, therefore, if a Hebrew was slain, it was the sacred duty of his next of kin to avenge his blood by procuring the death of his slayer. This, it must be emphasized, was in no sense a matter of private vengeance. It was the affair of the whole clan, and even tribe, of the murdered man (2 S 14[7]), the former, as it were, delegating its rights to the nearest relatives. OT legislation sought to limit the application, and generally to regulate the exercise, of this principle of a life for a life. Thus the Book of the Covenant removes from its application the case of the accidental homicide (Ex 21[13]; Dt 19[1-7], Nu 35[9-34]), the legislation of Deuteronomy further restricts the sphere of the vendetta to the actual criminal (Dt 24[16]), while in Dt 19[6, 12] and Nu 35[19, 24] references to 'the avenger of blood' suggest that one person only is thought of as having the duty of blood-revenge, he being the next of kin. In the older legislation the local high places appear as **asylums** for the man-slayer, until his case should be proved to be one of wilful murder, when he was handed over to the relatives of the man he had slain (Ex 21[13, 14]). With the abolition of the local sanctuaries by the reforms of Josiah it was necessary to appoint certain special sanctuaries, which are known as cities of refuge (Dt 19[1-7]) (see REFUGE [Cities of]).

An interesting feature of the regulations concerning blood-revenge among the Hebrews is the almost total absence of any legal provision for compounding with the relatives of the murdered man by means of a money payment (Nu 35[31], but see Ex 21[30]). Blood-revenge *must* be taken, for murder is not merely an offence against man, which the avenger of blood might be willing to settle with a fine: it is an offence against God which demands retaliation. See also AVENGER OF BLOOD.

A. R. S. K.—**A. G. McL.**

KINAH.—A town in the extreme south of Judah, Jos 15[22]. The site is unknown. Cf KENITES.

KINDNESS.—The pattern of all kindness is set before us in the Bible in the attitude of God to men. He gives the sunshine and the rain, and fruitful seasons and glad hearts, food and all the good they have to the just and the unjust alike (Mt 5[45] 7[11], Ac 14[17]). But the exceeding wealth of His grace is shown to us in kindness towards us in Christ Jesus (Eph 2[7]). God's glory no man can look upon and live. It is a light that no man can approach. It is inconceivably great, incomprehensibly grand, unimaginably exalted above the grasp of man's mind. But the kindness of God is God's glory stooping to man's need. It is God's power brought within man's reach. It is God's mercy and love and grace, as broad as the race, as deep as man's need, as enduring as man's immortality. The Bible reveals it. Jesus manifested it. In His life the kindness of God found its supreme manifestation (Tit 3[4-7]). All the children of God are to be like the Father in this regard (Mt 5[48], Ro 12[10], Col 3[12-14]). The philanthropy of God (Tit 3[4]) is to be reproduced in the philanthropy of men (2 P 1[7]). D. A. H.

KING (IN THE OT).—1. Etymology and use of the Hebrew term.—The Hebrew word for 'king' (*melekh*) is derived from a root which in Assyrian and Aramaic implies the giving of counsel or advice, so that in origin it appears to have signified 'counsellor' and so 'ruler.' In the patriarchal narratives and in the stories of the Hebrew conquest, for example, the title is applied to the rulers of small city-states in Canaan and its neighbourhood; but the term is also used of rulers over wider territories such as those of Egypt, Moab, Syria, and, in later times, Assyria, Babylonia, and Persia. The root also supplies the motif for the names of several Semitic deities, *e.g. Milcom*, the god of the Ammonites (1 K 11[5], 2 K 23[13]), and the Phoenician *Melkart*. For its use with reference to Yahweh, see KINGDOM OF GOD (OR HEAVEN), **2**, and PSALMS, **3** (A), **6** (1).

2. The office of king in Israel.—(1) *Institution.* The settlement of the people of Israel in Canaan, and the change from a nomadic to an agricultural life, laid the incomers open to ever fresh attacks from new adventurers. Thus in the time of the Judges we find Israel ever liable to hostile invasion. In order to preserve the nation from extermination, it became necessary that a closer connexion and a more intimate bond of union should exist between the different tribes. The Judges in the period subsequent to the settlement seem, with the possible exception of Gideon (Jg 8[22]), to have been little more than local or tribal heroes, carrying on guerilla warfare against their neighbours. The successes of the warlike Philistines made it clear to patriotic minds that the tribes must be more closely connected, and that a permanent leader in war was a necessity. Accordingly Saul the Benjamite was anointed by Samuel (1 S 10[1]), and appointed by popular acclamation (10[24] 11[14]). The exploits of Saul and his sons against the Ammonites (11[11ff]), against the Amalekites (15[7]), and against the Philistines (14[1ff]) showed the value of the kingly office; and when Saul and his sons fell on Mount Gilboa, it was not long till David the outlaw chief of Judah was invited to fill his place (2 S 2[1ff] 5[1ff]).

(2) *The duties of the king.* These are partly indicated by the history of the rise of the kingship. The king was (*a*) leader in war. He acted as general, and sometimes led the troops to battle in person (cf Saul on Mount Gilboa, 1 S 31[2]; Ahab at Ramoth-gilead, 1 K 22[29ff]). Under Solomon the standing army was developed, and fortifications were built at strategic points throughout the country (1 K 9[15ff] 10[26ff]). (*b*) Besides being leader of the army in war, the king was the supreme judge, to whom final appeal might be made from the findings of the local elders or professional judges (cf 2 S 14[1-20] 15[1-6], 1 K 3[16-28], 2 K 8[1-6], 2 Ch 19[5-11]). (*c*) Further, the king was also the chief person from a cultic point of view. Thus David and Solomon, like Saul before them (1 S 14[31ff]; cf 13[8ff]), offer sacrifice (2 S 6[13, 17] 24[25], 1 K 3[4]), and each blesses the people (2 S 6[18], 1 K 8[14]). Jeroboam sacrifices in person before the altar in Bethel (1 K 12[32f]), and Ahaz orders a special altar to be made, and offers in person on it (2 K 16[10ff]). In fact throughout the period of the monarchy the king takes the lead in organizing the nation's worship (cf 2 S 6, 1 K 5–8 12[26-32] 15[12-15], 2 K 12[4-16] 16[10-18] 22[3]–23[23], 1 Ch 22[2-19] 25).

(3) *The king as Yahweh's vicegerent.* The foregoing duties of the king should be seen in the light of what is now known as sacral kingship; for he held office as Yahweh's 'Anointed' (see MESSIAH), *i.e.* one who had been set aside by Yahweh for this purpose, and therefore should be regarded as sacrosanct (cf 1 S 24[10] 26[9], 2 S 1[14, 16]). So far as the House of David was concerned, the king's authority rested upon a special covenant between Yahweh and the founder of the dynasty (2 S 23[5], Ps 89[19ff] 132[11f]; cf 2 K 11[12]); and, in association with this, there was preserved in the worship of the Temple, which from the first was a royal sanctuary, an ideal of kingship which gave rise to the hope that from this line would issue a ruler whose loyalty to the obligations of the Davidic covenant would bring him world-wide dominion as the true 'Son' of Yahweh. (See PSALMS, **3** (F), **4** (*ad init.*), **5** (*ad fin.*), **6** (3).)

(4) *The kingship hereditary.* As is indicated in the preceding paragraph, it was a fixed idea in ancient Israel that the office of the kingship passed from father to son, as the judgeship passed from Gideon to his sons (Jg 9[2]), or from Samuel to his sons (1 S 8[1]). Although Saul was chosen by the people and David invited by the elders of Judah to be king, yet Saul himself regarded it as the natural thing that Jonathan should succeed him (1 S 20[30ff]). Adonijah assumed that, as David's son, he had a right to the throne (1 K 2[15]), and even the succession of his younger half-brother Solomon was secured without any popular election. The succession in Judah remained all along in the house of David, and in the kingdom of the Ten Tribes father always succeeded son, unless violence and revolution destroyed the royal house and brought a new adventurer to the throne.

(5) *Power of the king.* While the monarchy in Israel differed considerably from other Oriental despotisms, it could not be called a limited monarchy in our sense

of the term. The king's power was limited by the fact that, to begin with, the royal house differed little from other chief houses of the nation. Saul, even after his election, resided on his ancestral estate, and came forth only as necessity called him (cf 1 S 11^{4ff}). On the one hand, law and ancient custom exercised considerable restraint on the kings; while, on the other hand, acts of despotic violence were allowed to pass unquestioned. A powerful ruler like David or Solomon was able to do much that would have been impossible for a weakling like Rehoboam. Solomon was practically an Oriental despot, who ground down the people by taxation and forced labour. David had the power to compass the death of Uriah and take his wife, but public opinion, as expressed by the prophets, exerted a considerable influence on the kings (cf Nathan and David, Elijah and Ahab). The idea was never lost sight of that the office was instituted for the good of the nation, and that it ought to be a help, not a burden, to the people at large. Law and ancient custom were, in the people's minds, placed before the kingly authority. Naboth can refuse to sell his vineyard to Ahab, and the king is unable to compel him, or to appropriate it till Naboth has been regularly condemned before a judicial tribunal (1 K 21^{1ff}). Thus the king himself was under law (cf Dt 17^{14-20}), and he does not seem to have had the power to promulgate new enactments. Josiah bases his reform not on a new law, but on the newly found Book of the Law (2 K 23^{1-3}), to which he and the elders swear allegiance.

(6) *Royal income*. The early kings, Saul and David, do not seem to have subjected the people to heavy taxation. Saul's primitive court would be supported by his ancestral estate and by the booty taken from the enemy, perhaps along with presents, more or less compulsory, from his friends or subjects (1 S 10^{27} 16^{20}). The census taken by David (2 S 24^{1}) was probably intended as a basis for taxation, as was also Solomon's division of the land into twelve districts (1 K 4^{7}). Ezekiel (45^{7f} 48^{21}) speaks of crown lands, and such seem to have been held by David (1 Ch 27^{25ff}). The kings in the days of Amos laid claim to the first cutting of grass for the royal horses (Am 7^{1}). Caravans passing from Egypt to Damascus paid toll (1 K 10^{15}), and in the days of Solomon foreign trade by sea seems to have been a royal monopoly (1 K 10^{15}). It is not quite certain whether anything of the nature of a land tax or property tax existed, though something of this kind may be referred to in the reward promised by Saul to the slayer of Goliath (1 S 17^{25}); and it may have been the tenth mentioned in 1 S $8^{15, 17}$. Special taxes seem to have been imposed to meet special emergencies (cf 2 K 23^{35}), and the kings of Judah made free use of the Temple treasures.

(7) *Royal officials*. In Hebrew these have the general title *śārîm* (*e.g.* 1 K 4^{2}: AV, RV 'princes'; RSV 'high officials'); and of the following list the first three appear to have been the leading administrative figures throughout the monarchy. (*a*) The official who is described as 'governor of the palace' (literally 'over the household') enjoyed wide powers, and was evidently the chief officer of state, *i.e.* the vizier or prime-minister (*e.g.* 1 K 4^{6} 18^{3}, 2 K $18^{18, 37}$; cf Is 22^{15-25}). (*b*) The 'scribe' (RSV 'secretary') apparently acted both as private secretary to the king and as secretary of state (*e.g.* 2 S 8^{17} 20^{25}, 2 K 12^{10} 18^{18} 22^{3}, Jer 36^{12}). His office was clearly inferior to that of 'governor of the palace' (cf Is 22^{15-22} 36^{22}). (*c*) The 'recorder' (EV) or better, perhaps, 'herald' (literally 'one who calls to remembrance') is to be found grouped with both the foregoing. He seems to have been the king's personal agent or intermediary (*e.g.* 2 S 8^{16} 20^{24}, 2 K $18^{18, 37}$). (*d*) Other officials to whom reference is made are the commander-in-chief, who in the absence of the king led the royal forces (2 S 8^{16} 20^{23}; cf 12^{26ff}), the commander of the royal bodyguard (in David's time the Cherethites and Pelethites, 2 S 8^{18} 20^{23}), the officials in charge of forced labour (2 S 20^{24} RSV), and the commissariat (1 K $4^{5, 7ff}$), the 'king's servant' (2 K 22^{12}), the 'king's friend' (1 K 4^{5}; cf 1 Ch 27^{33}), the 'king's counsellor' (1 Ch 27^{33}), the 'keeper of the wardrobe' (2 K 22^{14}), and the 'governor of the city' (1 K 22^{26}).

W. F. B.—A. R. J.

KINGDOM OF GOD (or HEAVEN).—1. Title.—The exact phrase does not, strangely enough, appear in either the OT or in apocalyptic literature before the time of Jesus. In St. Matthew's Gospel 'Kingdom of Heaven' occurs thirty-two times, 'Kingdom of God' only four times. In the other Gospels and the rest of the NT 'Kingdom of God' is frequent, while 'Kingdom of Heaven' never occurs. Jewish reverence for the name of God led to the substitution of other words for the word 'God'; of these 'heaven' was the commonest (cf Lk 15^{18}, 'I have sinned against heaven and before you'). No difference of meaning is therefore to be sought in the two phrases 'Kingdom of God' and 'Kingdom of Heaven'; and Jesus no doubt used both—perhaps the latter more frequently, since it was presumably more often used by ordinary Jewish people. 'St. Matthew' is the Gospel of Jewish Christianity, and its writer would naturally prefer the Jewish paraphrase; most of the other authors of the NT were writing for Gentiles, and would not be inclined to use it.

2. In the Old Testament.—The thought of the OT is theocratic in the general sense that the Jews looked to Yahweh as both God and King; but this kind of thought was associated with a considerable variety of ideas as time went on. The Jewish equivalent of the NT 'Kingdom of God' or 'Kingdom of Heaven' means the 'sovereignty' or 'kingly rule' of God; it is abstract rather than concrete, pointing to the status of God Himself rather than to the people ruled or the place they inhabit. Cf 'The Lord will reign for ever and ever' (Ex 15^{18}), 'The Lord has established his throne in the heavens, and his kingdom rules over all' (Ps 103^{19}), 'His dominion is an everlasting dominion, and his kingdom endures from generation to generation' (Dn 4^{34}).

The first stage is the expectation of the 'Day of the Lord'—the day, that is, when God will vindicate Himself against His enemies and bring triumph to His own people. In the earliest period, down to about the 8th cent. B.C., the future was thought of as a time of material prosperity achieved through the overthrow of Israel's enemies—a conception which proceeded naturally enough from the very limited view of Yahweh as Israel's national God and no more. It is non-ethical; the coming of the Day of the Lord depends on due performance of ritual and sacrifice rather than on national morality. There is not here any idea of a Messiah; expectation centres on the rule of Yahweh Himself.

The great prophets of the 8th cent., Amos, Hosea, Isaiah, and Micah, with their idea of Yahweh as a moral ruler, gave the Day of the Lord a new meaning. It is to be a day of judgment, for Israel as well as for other nations—and for Israel with special severity in virtue of her privileged position. 'You only have I known of all the families of the earth; therefore I will punish you for all your iniquities' (Am 3^{2}). At this stage other nations are to be judged only in relation to Yahweh's own people—not, so to speak, in their own right. In Zephaniah (7th cent.) monotheism has gone further and the judgment seems to be universal; Yahweh challenges all nations Himself. 'Yea, at that time I will change the speech of the peoples to a pure speech, that all of them may call on the name of the Lord and serve him with one accord' (Zeph 3^{9}). There is still no mention of a Messianic king.

During and after the Exile thought changes considerably. Jeremiah and Ezekiel, as was natural when the Jewish state had practically ceased to exist, made the judgment individual rather than national. The Day of the Lord will mete out individual retribution, and as a result a new and better Israel will emerge—the kingdom of the Messiah. 'Behold, the days are coming, says the Lord, when I will raise up for David a righteous Branch, and he shall reign as king and deal wisely, and shall execute justice and righteousness in the land. In his days Judah will be saved, and Israel will dwell securely. And this is the name by which he will be called; "The Lord is our righteousness"' (Jer 23$^{5-6}$). 'This is the covenant which I will make with the house of Israel after those days, says the Lord; I will put my law within them, and I will write it in their hearts; and I will be their God, and they shall be my people. And no longer shall each man teach his neighbour and each his brother, saying "Know the Lord," for they shall all know me, from the least of them to the greatest, says the Lord; for I will forgive their iniquity, and I will remember their sin no more' (Jer 31$^{33-34}$). In Jeremiah the other nations will be converted and enter the kingdom; in Ezekiel they are doomed.

Two types of thought run side by side after the Exile, one in line with Jeremiah, the other with Ezekiel. In the 'Servant Songs' which are found among the writings of the Second Isaiah (42$^{1-4}$ 49$^{1-6}$ 50$^{4-9}$ 52^{13}–53^{12}), if, as is probable, the 'Servant of Yahweh' is the righteous remnant of Israel, the writer thinks of the nation's duty as essentially a missionary one. Yahweh has laid a special commission on His people, to bring all men to worship in His Kingdom. This shall be the fruit of the nation's suffering through the Exile. The same thought appears in many of the Psalms (*e.g.* Ps 87, with its picture of Jerusalem as the mother city of many nations); and in the remarkable prophecy of Is 19$^{18-25}$ (probably 3rd cent. B.C.), which pictures Egypt and Assyria as no less Yahweh's own people than Israel herself. In most of the later prophets, however, such as Haggai and Zechariah, the Day of the Lord will bring a Messianic kingdom for Israel alone, with the Gentiles either vassals or destroyed. The Jews were hard put to it to maintain themselves in Palestine; the rebuilding of the Temple was but sluggishly undertaken and spasmodically carried on, and Judaism became rigid and exclusive in its efforts to avoid contamination and hand on its system to posterity.

3. Between the Testaments.—The book of Daniel (168–167 B.C.) forms the link between OT ideas and apocalyptic thought. Apocalyptic is the fruit of pessimism; and its chief difference from OT thought on the subject we are considering is that in it a sudden intervention by God, and not the moral reformation of the nation, will bring the Kingdom into being. 'Prophecy still believes that this world is God's world,' says Dr. Charles, 'and that in this world His goodness and truth will yet be justified. The apocalyptic writer, on the other hand, almost wholly despairs of the present; his main interests are supermundane' (*Eschatology*, 1st ed., p. 174). Apocalyptic does not, like prophecy, see the future as arising naturally from the present; there is to be a complete break—in fact it is only after the darkest hour that the dawn will come. Subject as she had been for centuries to the sway of one or other of the great world-powers, the present world had no hope for Israel; God alone could save by breaking into history and bringing the world order to an end. At the same time the doctrine of personal immortality, almost wholly absent from pre-exilic writings, begins to appear. So the writer of Daniel looks forward to the sudden coming of the Kingdom at the moment when evil in the world has reached its climax. The throne of judgment will be set up, the world powers overthrown, the faithful will receive the Kingdom and the righteous dead will rise to share it with them.

In the numerous apocalyptic writings of the 2nd and 1st cents. B.C. the Kingdom on earth is at first regarded as temporary, and later on as to be established on a transformed, a 'new,' earth. The Messiah is to be the chief figure in the Kingdom, but two different ideas of him are found. Some writers picture him as a supernatural being, applying to him such titles as 'the Righteous One,' 'He in whom wisdom dwells,' 'the Elect One,' 'the Anointed' (=Christ), and, especially, 'the Son of Man.' Others speak of him as a Davidic king, who will destroy the ungodly nations, and 'rule a mighty people and a holy.'

4. In the Synoptic Gospels.—In Jesus' time both these ideas of Messiah were current, and with them different ideas of the Kingdom itself. In the popular mind national and political hopes were no doubt prominent, hopes based on belief in the restoration of national independence under a Davidic prince, and fed by hatred of Rome. After the fall of Jerusalem and the destruction of the Temple in A.D. 70 such hopes became dominant—the restoration of Jerusalem and of worship in its Temple, and the liberation of the Jews from a foreign yoke through the complete destruction of the empire of Rome. Before A.D. 70, however, what the Jewish rabbis believed and taught was much more spiritual than this; they bade men look forward to the universal reign of God, when His sovereignty would be acknowledged by all men, and a new era of righteousness and peace begin. The way to bring the Kingdom nearer, they taught, was not rebellion, but greater righteousness according to God's will as revealed in the Law.

Much injustice may be, and indeed often has been, done to Jewish thought by identifying the whole of belief and hope about the Kingdom at Jesus' time with the narrowly political ideas of it current after Jerusalem had fallen; or by suggesting that since Jesus' idea of the Kingdom had a strongly spiritual element in it, it was therefore quite un-Jewish. As in other matters, no doubt here also Jesus rejected some and accepted other elements in the thought of His people, and added something of His own. In His teaching about the Kingdom the spiritual element no doubt predominated to a greater degree than was the case in contemporary thought; but this is not to say that contemporary thought on the subject was wholly unspiritual, or that because it was wholly unspiritual Jesus would have nothing to do with it. Jesus cannot have believed, for example, that when the Kingdom came, it would be a Roman one. He would not encourage Jewish desire for rebellion against Rome; yet He must have expected that Rome's overthrow would come to pass when God established His Kingdom. Jesus did not feel the dominion of Rome to be as burdensome as the yoke of priests and scribes and Pharisees; yet the coming of the Kingdom would certainly put an end to both.

In the Synoptic Gospels some passages about the Kingdom regard it as future, others as present already, if incomplete; and others seem to identify it with the Christian Church. Here is a selection of each kind:

(1) 'The kingdom of God is at hand; repent and believe in the Gospel' (Mk 1^{15}). 'Truly, I say to you, there are some standing here who will not taste death before they see the kingdom of God come with power' (Mk 9^{1}). 'Truly, I say to you, I shall not drink again of the fruit of the vine until that day when I drink it new in the kingdom of God' (Mk 14^{25}). 'Not everyone who says to me "Lord, Lord," shall enter the kingdom of heaven, but he who does the will of my Father who is in heaven. On that day many will say to me . . .' (Mt 7$^{21-22}$), 'I tell you, many will come from east and west and sit at table with Abraham, Isaac and Jacob in the kingdom of heaven' (Mt 8^{11}). 'Command that these two sons of mine may sit one at your right hand and one at your left, in your kingdom' (Mt 20^{21}). Something over half of the passages in the Synoptic Gospels in which the Kingdom is mentioned appear to regard it as future.

(2) 'To you has been given the secret of the kingdom of God' (Mk 4^{11}). 'With what can we compare the kingdom of God, or what parable shall we use for it? It is like a grain of mustard seed, which, when sown upon the ground, is the smallest of all the seeds on earth; yet when it is sown it grows up and becomes the greatest of all shrubs' (Mk 4$^{30-32}$). 'Let the children come to me, do not hinder them; for to such belongs the kingdom of God. Truly, I say to you, whoever does not receive the kingdom of God like a child shall not enter it' (Mk 10$^{14-15}$). 'You are not far from the kingdom of God' (Mk 12^{34}). 'But seek first his kingdom and his righteousness, and all these things

shall be yours as well' (Mt 6[33]). 'But if it is by the Spirit of God that I cast out demons, then the kingdom of God has come upon you' (Mt 12[28]). 'The kingdom of heaven is like treasure hidden in a field, which a man found and covered up; then in his joy he goes and sells all that he has and buys that field. Again, the kingdom of heaven is like a merchant in search of fine pearls, who, on finding one pearl of great value, went and sold all that he had and bought it' (Mt 13[44-45]).

(3) 'Truly, I say to you, among those born of women there has risen no one greater than John the Baptist; yet he who is least in the kingdom of heaven is greater than he' (Mt 11[11]). 'The kingdom of heaven may be compared to a man who sowed good seed in his field; but while men were sleeping his enemy came and sowed weeds among the wheat' (Mt 13[24-25]). 'The kingdom of heaven is like leaven which a woman took and hid in three measures of meal, till it was all leavened' (Mt 13[33]). 'The kingdom of heaven is like a net which was thrown into the sea and gathered fish of every kind; when it was full, men drew it ashore and sat down and sorted the good into vessels but threw away the bad. So it will be at the close of the age' (Mt 13[47-49]). 'Therefore every scribe who has been trained for the kingdom of heaven is like a householder who brings out of his treasure what is new and what is old' (Mt 13[52]). 'I will give you the keys of the kingdom of heaven' (Mt 16[19]). It will be noticed that all these come from St. Matthew, which is the most 'ecclesiastical' of the Gospels. (It is the only Gospel in which the word 'church' occurs.) It represents Jewish Christianity, and one of its main themes is that Christianity is the new Law and the Christian Church the true Israel. So its writer naturally thinks of the Church as the Kingdom of Heaven. Some of the sayings quoted above may have been spoken by Jesus without this identification; others are no doubt the product of later Christian thought in a community such as that in which the author of the First Gospel wrote.

The implications of the first two groups above seem contradictory, and some critics have tried to eliminate one of them. It has been suggested either that Jesus always spoke of the kingdom as future, and the idea that He had also spoken of it as present was the product of developing Christian thought; or that He always spoke of it as present and spiritual, and the idea that He had also spoken of it as future and material was taken over by Christians from Jewish apocalyptic thought. Such attempts are not likely to be successful, since although a good many individual sayings and parables can be pressed towards either conception, the implications of the two groups as a whole are sufficiently decisive to compel the conclusion that both are genuine elements in Jesus' teaching about the kingdom.

An interesting example of a passage which can be interpreted in either sense is Lk 17[20-21]; 'Being asked by the Pharisees when the kingdom of God was coming he answered them, "The kingdom of God is not coming with signs to be observed; nor will they say, 'Lo here it is!' or 'There!' for behold, the kingdom of God is in the midst of you (marginal reading 'within you')."' The natural meaning of the Greek is 'within you,' and the sense will then be that the Kingdom is a spiritual one, which grows unseen in men's hearts. There are no outward signs of its coming. But the Greek may mean 'among you,' in which case two interpretations of the sentence are possible:—(*a*) 'The kingdom is present among you, growing already though you cannot see it.' The Kingdom is already beginning to be realized in Jesus' presence and work among men. This is similar to the thought of Mt 12[28] quoted in group (2) above—'If it is by the Spirit of God that I cast out demons, then the kingdom of God has come upon you.' (*b*) 'You cannot see the kingdom coming; it is there, among you, in a flash'—*i.e.* when it comes, it will come suddenly, without any warning. This refers to the Kingdom simply as future, and is similar to the thought of a later verse in the same chapter, 'For as the lightning flashes and lights up the sky from one side to the other, so will the Son of Man be in his day' (Lk 17[24]). The use of the Greek word with the meaning 'among' is uncommon; and if the sentence represents an Aramaic saying of Jesus, it seems doubtful whether this word would have been used to translate an Aramaic 'among' when the saying was turned into Greek. If that view is accepted, the passage should be included in group (2) above.

It may seem ironical that so much uncertainty should attach to the teaching of Jesus on a subject which must have been so prominent in His message, and is so often mentioned in the Gospels. The fact that this is so suggests that His teaching about the Kingdom was varied in conception and emphasis; and this is indeed what we should expect in view of the variety of Jewish ideas on the subject. It was entirely natural that Jesus should urge men to recognize God's sovereignty as a present reality, to be acknowledged by a spiritual response; and at the same time lead them to hope for a new age in which human hardness of heart should no longer prevent His sovereignty from being universal and complete.

It need not surprise us, moreover, that Jesus should have believed that the Kingdom would be set up by a sudden intervention of God in the future; in this He was a child of His age, His vision limited by the horizons of His time. The ideas which lay behind this belief were indeed fundamental in Jesus' own religious and moral outlook—faith in God in spite of appearances, and the inevitability of judgment by the standards which God Himself had set; what more natural than that He should accept without question the belief that when once the chosen people showed themselves spiritually prepared, God would declare the victory of goodness by such a judgment? This is not to say, of course, that Jesus accepted all the other ideas of the apocalyptic writers. There is much that He must have rejected in their views of God's character, as well as in their pictures of heaven and hell and the destiny of mankind.

5. In the rest of the New Testament.—The writer of the Fourth Gospel, at the end of the 1st cent. A.D. or later, finds the equivalent of the Kingdom in the gift of 'eternal life,' the coming of the 'Comforter,' and the life of the Christian community to which he belongs. The only two verses in which he uses the phrase 'Kingdom of God' regard it as present and spiritual; 'Truly, truly, I say to you, unless one is born anew, he cannot see the kingdom of God' (3[3]), and 'Truly, truly, I say to you, unless one is born of water and the Spirit, he cannot enter the kingdom of God' (3[5]). In the Acts and in St. Paul's earlier letters, as also in Revelation, the coming of the Kingdom is regarded as imminent. This belief led to the 'voluntary communism' of the early Church (Ac 4[32f]); and its vividness can be seen from St. Paul's first letter to the Thessalonians, written in A.D. 51, in which he tries to allay their fear that their friends who have died will be deprived of their share in the glory of the Kingdom (1 Th 4[13f]). As time goes on, St. Paul's ideas on this subject change in emphasis; in his later letters the imminence of the Kingdom has receded, and his thoughts dwell more on its moral and spiritual demands, and on God's plan for all mankind through the Church. H. K. L.

KINGS, BOOKS OF.—1. Title.—This is the name of two well-known narrative books of the OT. In Hebrew MSS and early printed editions they appear as one book, and the Massoretic note appears only at the end of the second book. In the Hebrew canon the Book of Kings constitutes the fourth book of the Former Prophets. Logically it is a continuation of the Book of Samuel without clearly marked literary distinction. The Books of Samuel and Kings are about of the same length, and for convenience the Greek scribes divided each of these books into two parts and numbered them consecutively as four books. Accordingly in the LXX there are four books of 'The Kingdoms' (or 'The Reigns'). This division into four books was followed by all the ancient

KINGS, BOOKS OF

versions of the OT ; in the Latin Bible these divisions are known as the four books of ' Kings.'

2. Method and sources.—What has just been said does not imply that the Books of Kings are exactly like the other historical books. They differ in their methods, and in the way in which the narrative is presented. The most striking feature is the attempt to date the events recorded, and to keep two parallel lines of history before the reader. The period of time they cover is something over 400 years, and when it is remembered that these books give us almost the only knowledge we have of events in Israel for this period, their historical value will be evident. At the same time, the light they throw on the method by which the Biblical authors worked is almost equally great. To estimate the historical value, it will be necessary to look at the literary method. The phenomenon which first strikes the reader's attention is the unevenness of the narrative. In some cases there is an extended and detailed story ; in others a long period of time is dismissed in a few words. The reign of Solomon occupies almost eleven chapters—about a fourth part of the work ; while the longer reign of Manasseh is disposed of in sixteen verses.

Still closer examination shows that there are well-marked characteristics of style in certain sections which are replaced by equally marked but totally different ones in other sections. Moreover, there are seemingly contradictory assertions which can hardly have come from the same pen, though they might have occurred in different documents. Thus the account of Solomon's levy of forced labour ' out of all Israel ' seems inconsistent with the other declaration that Solomon made no bond-servants of Israel (1 K 5^{13ff} ; cf 11^{28} and 9$^{20-22}$). In this connexion cf 2 Ch 2$^{17-18}$, where only aliens were drafted. The motive in this presentation was to free native Israelites from the stigma of serf-like labour. One passage (1 K 14^{30}) says without qualification that there was war between Rehoboam and Jeroboam all their days, and this is presumably true history, even though it may be a literary deduction from 1 K 15^{16}. Another (1 K 12$^{21-24}$) tells how Rehoboam gathered an army, but dismissed it at the word of a prophet without making war, thus saving national pride.

The editor of the Books of Kings acknowledges in many cases the sources from which he derived his information. A unique development of Hebrew history lies in the transition from annals and the purely archival form to the historical story with an interpretation of events. Official records were kept in the archives at the capital. In David's court were a scribe (secretary) and a recorder (2 S 8^{16f} 20^{24f}), while in the case of Solomon mention is made of two scribes and a recorder (1 K 4^{3}). The same offices also existed in the Southern Kingdom (2 K 18$^{18, 37}$, 2 Ch 34^{8}), and in accordance with the custom of the times it may be inferred that similar appointments were made in the Northern Kingdom. It was the recorder's duty to keep the current records of the reign in official journals or chronicles. From such archival material were derived the facts used in compiling two well-known sources which were used by the editors of Kings : ' the book of the chronicles of the kings of Israel ' (1 K 14^{19}) and ' the book of the chronicles of the kings of Judah ' (1 K 14^{29}). These works must not be confused with the two Books of Chronicles in the OT. It is not known in what form these royal ' chronicles ' were when they came into the hands of the editors of the Books of Kings. The original records of the North probably were destroyed in the Assyrian conquest, but scribes apparently had made copies, at least in abbreviated edition, which were in circulation. It was doubtless such a work that preserved the Northern chronicles for the Judaean editor of Kings. For the reign of Solomon (1 K 3–11) the editor quotes a source (1 K 11^{41}), ' the book of the acts of Solomon ' ; this, too, must have been based on official documents.

Beginning with Rehoboam and Jeroboam there is a fixed formula or framework for the commencement and end of each reign. For the Southern kings this includes an introductory synchronism with the Northern reign, the age of the king, length of reign, place of rule (in Jerusalem), the name of the mother. In conclusion there is a reference to the source, the burial of the king, and the name of the successor ; cf 1 K 14$^{21, 29-31}$ 15$^{1, 7f, 23f}$ 22$^{41f, 45}$, 2 K 12$^{1, 19, 21}$ 14$^{1f, 17f}$ 15$^{1f, 32f, 36}$ 16$^{1f, 19f}$ 18^{1f} 22^{1f}. In the Northern Kingdom similar formulas, including synchronisms, are given, but with fewer particulars ; cf 1 K 14^{19f} 15$^{25, 31}$ 16$^{8, 14f, 20, 23}$ (in Tirzah), 1 K 16$^{27-29}$ (in Samaria), 2 K 10$^{34-36}$ (in Samaria) 14$^{23, 28f}$ (in Samaria). To the historian the information of greatest importance is the chronology, which contains a double system of dates : the synchronisms and the regnal periods. There are difficulties involved in the dates, but in spite of certain inaccuracies the chronology is not artificial, but is based on archival sources.

Much of the archival material contains interesting personal notes and brief references which arouse in the reader a desire to know more of the details ; cf 1 K 15^{23} 16^{27} 22$^{45, 47-50}$, 2 K 10^{34} 13^{7f} 14$^{21, 28}$ 21^{17}. It is apparent that much historical material was abbreviated in the regal period.

Notice should also be taken of the direct citation of archival material ; cf 1 K 9^{25} ' So he finished the house ' ; 22^{48} ' Jehoshaphat made ships of Tarshish ' ; 2 K 1^{1} ' And Moab rebelled against Israel ' ; 2 K 15^{19} ' Pul the king of Assyria came.' Exact dates may be given : cf 1 K 6^{37f} 14^{25}. In 2 K 24–25 are a number of exact datings by year, month, and day, which suggest that the writer is a contemporary of the events.

Sometimes there is used the adverb ' then ' (1 K 9^{24}, 2 K 16^{5}), or parallel expressions of time, as ' in that day ' [the same day] (1 K 8^{64}), ' in those days ' (2 K 10^{32}), ' in his days ' (1 K 16^{34}), ' at that time ' (2 K 16^{6}). Such expressions have parallels in Akkadian annals, and accordingly they are of archival origin.

The plan of the Temple and the accounts of its furnishing and its dedication (1 K 6, 7, 8$^{1-13, 62-64}$) may properly be assigned to a Temple source. The construction of the Temple was entirely a royal undertaking, and the narrative does not reflect any priestly composition. While the Hebrews were not skilled in recording architectural details, the plan of the Temple may represent the architect's specifications, and the document may well have been deposited in the Temple. The account of the uprising against Athaliah (2 K 11) has no specific priestly tinge ; in fact, according to 2 K 12^{5ff} the priests had been guilty of mismanagement of sacred funds. In 2 K 16^{10ff} a priest is implicated in copying a foreign altar. In 2 K 22–23 King Josiah is the reformer, and the priests are his servants ; in ch. 22 the high priest Hilkiah has recourse to a prophetess to interpret the Book of the Law found in the Temple. It is noteworthy that the Books of Kings do not have priestly literary sources.

The Books of Kings also contain political narratives. 1 K 1–2 continues the history of the reign of David recorded in 2 Samuel with all the intrigues of the court. The story, apparently written by a member of the court who shared in the popular enthusiasm for David, is by no means a royal encomium. It is not known who the author of these chapters is, but some have conjectured that he was Abiathar. At any rate, it is objective history written in classical style. The account of the negotiations with Hiram of Tyre (1 K 5) is founded upon authentic details. The narratives of the revolt of the North under Jeroboam (1 K 11^{26}–12^{24}), the revolt against Athaliah (2 K 11), and the reformation under Josiah (2 K 22–23) bear the earmarks of contemporary history. 2 K 18^{13}–20 has a duplicate in Is 36–39, and is derived from contemporary memoirs.

Reference should also be made to stories of the prophets. The longest example of this literary development is found in the Elijah cycle (1 K 17–19, 21, 2 K 2) ; that of Elisha, entwined with that of Elijah, begins at 1 K 19^{19} and continues to 2 K 9 : there is also a postscript (2 K 13$^{14-21}$). Within these sagas are inserted two narratives : the rout of Ben-hadad (1 K 20) and the dramatic career of the lone prophet Micaiah (1 K 22).

Thus there is a continuous series of prophetical documents (1 K 17–2 K 10) interrupted only by annalistic items ; interspersed within these chapters are also stories which may be called *midrash* (for the word cf Hebrew text, 2 Ch 13^{22} 24^{27}) : 1 K 11^{29-39}, 1 K 13 and 2 K 23^{15-20}, 1 K $16^{1-4, 7, 12}$.

While the longer quotations from his sources usually show the compiler's religious intent, yet he often presents us with brief notices for which he is probably indebted to ' the books of the Chronicles,' but which have no very direct bearing on his main object. Thus in the case of Jehoshaphat he inserts in his framework a brief notice to the effect that this king made peace with Israel (1 K 22^{44}). In the three-membered contest between Zimri, Tibni, and Omri (1 K 16^{15-22}) he compresses the story of a prolonged civil war into a few lines. In the case of Omri we find a brief notice to the effect that this king built the city of Samaria, having bought the land from a man named Shemer (1 K 16^{24}). Such a notice probably compresses a detailed account in which Omri was glorified as the founder of the capital.

From such a variety of sources the Books of Kings were compiled. The work falls into three divisions : (1) a continuation of the story of David (1 K 1–2) ; (2) the history of Solomon ; (3) the history of the Divided Kingdoms (1 K 12–2 K 17) and of the surviving Southern Kingdom (2 K 18–25).

3. Purpose.—In this connexion it should be noted that the OT has given us the first presentation of a philosophy of history. In the Books of Kings we do not find annals or a mere recital of events as in a chronicle, but the facts of history with their interpretation. Such a work constitutes genuine history. In these two books history is written under a religious theory and with a practical aim to show how God directs the affairs of His people and of other nations and how He achieves His purposes in history. Moreover in these narratives one finds honest self-judgment. The schism of Israel from the God-ordained Davidic kingdom had its origin in Solomon's sin, and the fall of the North was due to the continual defiance of the true religion. On the other hand, the destruction of Jerusalem and the collapse of the Southern Kingdom was a fate deserved by Manasseh's sin. In this we see that the editor of the books belonged to the school of the Deuteronomists.

It has been noted above that a fixed formula is employed to denote the beginning and end of each reign with a synchronism of the kings of the North and of the South. In this connexion it is important to observe the judgment that is passed upon various kings. The standard expression used in condemning a king of the North contains, with a slight variation of phraseology, a reference to ' the way of Jeroboam, the son of Nebat, and the sin which he made Israel to sin.' Cf 1 K $15^{26, 34}$ 16^{25f} 22^{52}, 2 K 3^{3} 10^{29-31} $13^{2, 11}$ 14^{24} $15^{9, 18, 24, 28}$. A judgment with a mitigating comparison, however, may be passed on a king : 2 K 3^{2} 17^{2}. The worship of the golden calves at Bethel and Dan, in the mind of the author, was distinct rebellion against God, whose legitimate sanctuary was at Jerusalem. Judgment is also passed on southern kings for idolatry ; in the case of Rehoboam, the kingdom of Judah is condemned (1 K 14^{22-24}). The following passages also show that heathenism was the reason for condemning certain Judaean kings : 1 K 15^{3}, 2 K $8^{18, 27}$ 16^{2-4} $21^{2-9, 20-22}$ $23^{32, 37}$ 24^{9}. On the other hand, the praise of some good kings is restrained, because the high places were not removed : Asa (1 K 15^{11-14}), Jehoshaphat (1 K 22^{43}), Jehoash (2 K 12^{2f}), Amaziah (2 K 14^{3f}), Azariah or Uzziah (2 K 15^{3f}), and Jotham (2 K 15^{34f}). The high places were regarded as illegitimate places of worship, and accordingly the foregoing good kings did not receive unqualified commendation. David, the ideal monarch, received high praise (1 K 11^{32-38}), but a notable reservation is made (1 K 15^{3-5}). Two kings in their zeal for righteousness and religious reform are put in the same class with David : Hezekiah (2 K 18^{3-7}) and Josiah (2 K 22^{2} 23^{25}). According to the Book of Deuteronomy there was to be only one centre of worship, and the author who writes history with this religious conviction is called the Deuteronomist. The judgment passed on various kings and the evaluation of their influence plainly reflect the point of view of Deuteronomy. If various hands worked on the books or if later additions were made, the writers all belonged to the Deuteronomistic school. The attitude taken toward the high places is distinctly Deuteronomistic, for the demand that these sanctuaries should be abolished was first formulated by Deuteronomy. Josiah's reforms were the direct result of finding this book in the Temple. Hence the strong commendation of this king.

Moreover, it was laid down by Deuteronomy that obedience to the law will be followed by temporal well-being, and that disobedience will be punished by calamity. Now, one object of the writer or compiler of the Books of Kings is to show how this had proved true in the past. He is less thorough in the application of this theory than the author of the Books of Chronicles, but that he has it at heart will be evident on examination. The Northern Kingdom had perished because kings and people had from the first been disobedient to Yahweh, revolting from His legitimate sanctuary at Jerusalem, and provoking His wrath by the bulls of Bethel. In Judah the same lesson is taught. David, who laid the foundations of the kingdom, was of unusual piety, and was favoured by unusual prosperity. Solomon was the builder of the Temple, and to this extent an example of piety ; his prosperity was in proportion. But there were shadows in the picture of Solomon which our author was too honest to ignore. It had not been forgotten that this king built altars to foreign gods. History also told that he had suffered by the revolt of Edom and Damascus (1 K 11). It was easy to see in this the punishment for the king's sins. The size of Solomon's harem, which seems to be exaggerated, was accepted by the editor to explain the king's defection from God. Both the defection and the revolt are dated late in the king's reign, at a time when senile weakness would excuse the wise man for yielding to his wives.

The most distinct instance in which the author teaches his lesson is the prayer of Solomon at the dedication of the Temple (1 K 8^{14-61}). It was the custom with ancient historians to compose speeches for their heroes which tell us what ought to have been said rather than what was actually said. Our author makes use of this perfectly legitimate literary device. A reading of the prayer shows that it is Deuteronomistic in word and thought throughout. More than one hand has been concerned in it, but the tone is that of the Deuteronomistic school. It confirms what has been said about the purpose of the book. It follows that the historical value of the work must be estimated with due allowance for this main purpose.

4. Date.—The date of the Books of Kings in their present form cannot be earlier than the Babylonian exile. The latest event which it mentions is the release of king Jehoiachin from confinement, which took place in the year 561 B.C. ; and as the author speaks of the allowance made to the king all his life (2 K 25^{30}), we conclude that he wrote after his death. It will not be far out of the way, therefore, to say that the work was completed about 550 B.C. Some minor insertions may have been made later. While this is so, there are some things which point to an earlier date for the greater part of the work. The purpose of the author to keep his people from the mistakes of the past is intelligible only at a time when the avoidance of the mistakes was still possible—that is, before the fall of Jerusalem. We find also some phrases which seem to indicate that the final catastrophe had not yet come. The recurrence of the phrase ' to this day ' (1 K 8^{8} ; cf 9^{21} 12^{19}, 2 K 2^{22} 8^{22} 16^{6}) is one of these indications. On the other hand, the expression ' to this day ' (2 K 17^{34-41}) appears to have been inserted after the Samaritan schism had been completed. It is now generally held that the substance of the book was compiled about 600 B.C., by a writer who was anxious to enforce the lesson of Deuteronomic reform while there was yet hope. This first edition may have extended to 2 K 23[28], but this is uncertain. About fifty years later an editor living in the Exile, and who sympathized with the main purpose of the book, probably completed it in substantially its present form.

5. Text.—Against the commonly held assumption of a fixed *textus receptus* there have been preserved a number of Hebrew variants in the text, as can be seen in the lists collated by Kennicott (1776–1780) and de Rossi (1784–1788); in addition to the Kittel text of *Biblia Hebraica*[3] (1929–1937) there may be consulted the editions of Baer (1895) and Ginsburg (1894, 1926). The LXX does not always agree with the Massoretic text; there is a good deal of rearrangement in 1 K 5–7. There are also Greek supplements (1 K 2[35a–35a, 46a–46l]; 1 K 12[24a–24z]). In the Old Greek 1 K 9[15–25] and 1 K 14[1–20] are missing, but they were added in the Hexapla of Origen. In some cases obviously the Old Greek is based on a text which differs from the present Massoretic text. The meaning of the books, however, is not essentially affected. For a discussion of textual matters reference should be made to J. A. Montgomery, *A Critical and Exegetical Commentary on the Books of Kings, I.C.C.* (1951).

H. P. S.—**H. S. G.**

KING'S DALE.—See King's Valley.

KING'S GARDEN.—Mentioned in 2 K 25[4], Jer 39[4] 52[7], Neh 3[15]. This garden was clearly near the 'gate of the two walls' which was near the Pool of Siloam, and it was in all probability just outside the walls, being irrigated by over-flow water from the Siloam tunnel and pool, just as the land in this situation is treated to-day. Indeed, the garden may have covered much the same area as is now cultivated as irrigated vegetable garden by the women of *Silwân*. See Kidron [The Brook], Siloam.

E. W. G. M.

KING'S POOL.—Neh 2[14], probably identical with the Pool of Siloam. See Siloam.

KING'S VALLEY.—Gn 14[17] (AV **King's dale**, RV **King's vale**), 2 S 18[18] (AV, RV **King's dale**). See Shaveh, Valley of.

KIR.—An unidentified place, subject in the 8th and 7th cents. to Assyria. Amos predicted that the Aramaeans would be carried captive to Kir, 1[5]. In 9[7] he declares that Yahweh brought them from Kir. It is said in 2 K 16[9] that Tiglath-pileser carried the people of Damascus captive to Kir, while in Is 22[6] Kir is mentioned in connexion with Elam as furnishing soldiers to the Assyrian army which fought against Israel. Many conjectures as to its identification have been made, but in reality nothing certain is known of its location.

KIRAMA, 1 Es 5[20] (RV).—See Ramah, 3.

KIR-HARASETH, 2 K 3[25] (AV).—See Kir-hareseth.

KIR-HARESETH.—A place of great strength and importance in Moab, 2 K 3[25] (AV **Kir-haraseth**), Is 16[7]; called **Kir-heres** in Is 16[11] (AV **Kir-haresh**), Jer 48[31–36], and **Kir** in Is 15[1]. See Kerioth, Kir of Moab.

KIR-HARESH, Is 16[11] (AV).—See Kir-hareseth.

KIR-HERES.—See Kir-hareseth.

KIRIATH, Jos 18[28] (AV **Kirjath**) is the construct state of *Kiriah*, the complement of which, *-jearim*, seems to have fallen out, from its resemblance to the word for 'cities' which follows. Therefore we ought probably to read *Kiriath-jearim* (so RSV), a reading supported by the LXX.

KIRIATHAIM.—**1.** A town E. of the Jordan, in the disputed territory between Moab and Reuben, Nu 32[37], Jos 13[19] (AV **Kirjathaim**); later it became Moabite, Jer 48[1, 23], Ezr 25[9]. It is mentioned on the Moabite Stone. See Mesha. The *Onomasticon* locates it 10 Roman miles W. of Madeba. It is perhaps *Kh. el-Qureiyât*. See Shaveh-kiriathaim. **2.** A town in Naphtali, 1 Ch 6[76] (AV **Kirjathaim**); called **Kartan** (q.v.) in Jos 21[32].

KIRIATH-ARBA is used as a name for **Hebron** (q.v.) in Gn 23[2] etc. (AV **Kirjath-arba [city of Arba** in Jos 15[13] 21[11]]). Only in Gn 35[27] (AV **city of Arbah**) and Neh 11[25] is *Arbaʿ* written with the article. The city may have been so called as the seat of a confederacy between four men or tribes, or the name may be = *Tetrapolis*, 'the city of four quarters.' The Hebrew text explains it as 'the city of Arba,' 'the greatest man among the Anakim' (Jos 14[15] RV), or 'the father of Anak' (15[13] 21[11]). In the first passage LXX reads 'the city Argob, the metropolis of the Anakim': in the second 'the city Arbok, metropolis,' etc. Perhaps in the last two, therefore, we should read *'ēm*, 'mother,' *i.e.* 'mother-city,' instead of *'ᵃbhî*.

W. E.

KIRIATH-ARIM.—The form of the name **Kiriath-jearim** (q.v.) found in Ezr 2[25], 1 Es 5[19] (AV **Kiriathiarius.** RV **Kariathiarius**).

KIRIATH-BAAL.—The older name of **Kiriath-jearim** (q.v.), Jos 15[60].

KIRIATH-HUZOTH.—An unidentified spot apparently between Ar-moab and Bamoth-baal, Nu 22[39] (AV **Kirjath-huzoth**); cf vv.[36–41].

KIRIATHIARIUS, 1 Es 5[19] (AV).—See Kiriath-arim.

KIRIATH-JEARIM ('town of woods').—One of the towns of the Gibeonites (Jos 9[17]), occupied by the Danites (Jg 18[12]), on the border between Judah and Benjamin (Jos 15[9] 18[14]), but reckoned in the territory of Judah (Jos 15[60]). From there David brought up the Ark (2 S 6[2], 1 Ch 13[5], 2 Ch 1[4]). Its older names were **Kiriath-baal** (Jos 15[60]) and **Baalah** (Jos 15[9f], 1 Ch 13[6]). It is also mentioned as **Baale-judah** (2 S 6[2]), and through a textual error as **Kiriath-arim** (Ezr 2[25]; cf Neh 7[29]). It was probably, like Kedesh, Gezer, etc., an old Canaanite 'high place.' In Jer 26[20] it is mentioned as the home of Uriah the prophet, the son of Shemaiah. Other residents of the town are also referred to in 1 Ch 2[50, 53] and 1 Es 5[19], the latter naming the place **Kiriath-arim** (AV **Kiriathiarius**, RV **Kariathiarius**).

An early attempt to locate the town suggested *Khirbet ʿErma*, on the S. of the valley of Sorek, where the narrow valley opens into the plain. The supposed similarity of *ʿārîm* (Ezr 2[25]) and *ʿerma*, and the nearness of the site to Zorah and Eshtaol seemed to recommend it. However, its distance from the other Gibeonite towns (Jos 9[17]) raised some doubt. Later scholarship has identified Kiriath-jearim with *Deir el-Azhar*, a hill located W. of *Qaryet el-ʿEnab* (also called *Abū Ghôsh*), about nine miles from Jerusalem on the Jaffa-Jerusalem road. Although the excavators found chiefly medieval Arabic and Crusader remains at *Abū Ghôsh*, the pottery on the slopes of *Deir el-Azhar* indicated that it was occupied in OT times (cf F. T. Cooke, 'The Site of Kirjath-jearim,' *AASOR*, v (1925), 105–120; R. de Vaux and A. M. Steve, *Fouilles à Qaryet El-ʿEnab, Abū Gôsh* [1950], 10–14).

E. W. G. M.—**W. L. R.**

KIRIATH-SANNAH, KIRIATH-SEPHER.—See Debir, 1.

KIRIOTH, Am 2[2] (AV).—See Kerioth.

KIRJATH.—The AV form of names beginning with **Kiriath-** (q.v.). In Jos 18[28] AV has **Kirjath** as a complete name, and RV **Kiriath**, but RSV reads **Kiriath-jearim.**

KIRJATHAIM.—See Kiriathaim.

KIRJATH-ARBA.—AV form of **Kiriath-arba** (q.v.).

KIRJATH-HUZOTH, Nu 22[39] (AV).—See Kiriath huzoth.

KIR OF MOAB.—Coupled with **Ar** of Moab, Is 15[1], possibly identical with it. Following the Targum, Kir of Moab has long been identified with the modern *el-Kerak* a place of great importance in the times of the Crusades. Kerak is situated on a lofty spur about 4000 feet above the Dead Sea level. The hills behind rise much higher, so that it is commanded on every side by higher ground, which explains 2 K 3[25–27]. It was surrounded by a wall of great thickness, and there are remains of ancient rock-hewn cisterns. The gates were to be reached only through long tunnels in the solid rock. C. H. W. J.

KISEUS, Ad. Est 11^{2} (RV).—See Kish, **4.**

KISH.—1. The father of Saul the first king of Israel, 1 S 9^{1} 10^{21} 14^{51}, Ac 13^{21} (AV **Cis**). His home was at Gilbeah (rendered 'the hill of God' in both AV and RV of 1 S 10^{5} [RSV **Gibeath-elohim**] and 'the hill' in 10^{10} RSV [**Gibeah**]). **2.** The uncle of the foregoing, 1 Ch 8^{30} 9^{36}. **3.** The eponym of a family of Merarite Levites, 1 Ch 23^{21f} 24^{29}, 2 Ch 29^{12}. **4.** A Benjamite ancestor of Mordecai, Est 2^{5}, Ad. Est 11^{2} (AV **Cisai,** RV **Kiseus**).

KISHI.—A Merarite Levite, ancestor of Ethan, 1 Ch 6^{44}; called **Kushaiah** in 15^{17}. The latter is probably the correct form.

KISHION.—A town allotted to Issachar, Jos 19^{20}; assigned to the Levites, 21^{28} (AV **Kishon**); called **Kedesh** in 1 Ch 6^{72}. See Kedesh, **2.**

KISHON, Jos 21^{28} (AV).—See Kishion.

KISHON (Jg 4^{7} 5^{21}, 1 K 18^{40}, Ps 83^{9}).—The ancient name of the stream now called *Nahr el-Mukaṭṭaʿ*, which drains almost the whole area of the great Plain of Esdraelon. The main channel may be considered as rising near the W. foot of Mount Tabor, and running W. through the centre of the plain until it enters the narrow valley between the S. extension of the Galilaean hills and the E. end of Carmel. After emerging from this it enters the Plain of *ʿAkkā*, running a little N. of the whole length of Carmel, and enters the sea about a mile E. of Haifa. The total length is about twenty-three miles. In the first part of its course it is in winter a sluggish stream with a bottom of deep mud, and in summer but a chain of small marshes; from just below where the channel is crossed by the Nazareth road near Carmel it usually has a certain amount of water all the year round, and in parts the water, which is brackish, is 10 or 12 feet deep. At its mouth, however, it is almost always fordable. Numerous small water-courses from the Galilaean hills on the N. and more important tributaries from 'Little Hermon,' the Mountains of Gilboa and the whole southern range of Samaria and Carmel on the E. and S., contribute their waters to the main stream. The greater number of these channels, in places 10 or 15 feet deep with precipitous sides, are perfectly dry two-thirds of the year, but during the winter's rains are filled with raging torrents. A number of copious springs arise along the edge of the hills to the S. of the plain. At *Jenîn* there are plentiful fountains, but they are, during the summer, entirely used up in irrigation; at *Taʿannak*, at *Lejjūn*, near *Tell el-Kasîs*, at the E. end of Carmel, and at the *ʿAyūn el-Saʿdi*, perennial fountains pour their water into the main stream. Those who have seen the stream only in late spring or summer can hardly picture how treacherous and dangerous it may become when the winter's rain fills every channel with a tumultuous flood of chocolate-brown water over a bottom of sticky mud often itself several feet deep. Both animals and baggage have not infrequently been lost at such times. Under such conditions the Kishon, with its steep, uncertain banks, its extremely crooked course, and its treacherous fords, must have been very dangerous to a flying army of horses and chariots (Jg 5^{21f}). Of all parts the section of the river from Megiddo (q.v.) to 'Harosheth of the Gentiles' (now *el-Ḥārithiyeh*), where the fiercest part of the battle against Sisera was fought (cf Jg 5^{19} and 4^{16}), must have been the most dangerous. The other OT incident connected with the river is the slaughter there of the prophets of Baal after Elijah's vindication of Yahweh on the heights of Carmel (1 K 18^{40}). E. W. G. M.

KISON.—This form is found once in AV (Ps 83^{9}) for **Kishon** (q.v.).

KISS (Heb. *neshîḳāh*, Gr. *philēma*).—Kissing is a mark of affection between parents and children (Gn 27^{26f}, Ru 1^{9}, 1 K 19^{20} etc.), members of a family, or near connexions (Gn 29^{13} 45^{15}), and equals in rank (2 S 20^{9}, Ac 20^{37}). Guests are received with a kiss (Lk 7^{45}). A kiss from a superior marks condescension (2 S 15^{5} 19^{39}). These kisses may be on the lips, but are usually on the cheek or neck. The kiss was a token of love (Ca 1^{2} 8^{1}), of homage and submission (Job 31^{27}, Ps 2^{12}), and was also an act of idolatrous worship (1 K 19^{18}, Hos 13^{2}). The Moslems kiss the black stone at Mecca. Juniors and inferiors kiss the hands of seniors and superiors. A wife kisses the hand or beard of her husband. The hand, garments, even the feet of one appealed to may be kissed. Probably Judas presumed to salute with the kiss of an equal (Mt 26^{49} etc.). A kiss on the hand would have been natural. The 'holy kiss,' or 'kiss of love' (1 Co 16^{20}, 1 P 5^{14}), marked the tie that united Christians in a holy brotherhood. W. E.

KITCHEN.—Mentioned only in Ezk 46^{24} RSV, where AV has 'places of them that boil,' and RV 'boiling places.'

KITE.—Two words are translated 'kite'; these are *'ayyāh* (AV 'kite' and 'vulture,' RV 'falcon,' RSV 'falcon' and 'kite') and *dayyāh* (or *dā'āh*) (AV 'vulture,' RV 'kite,' RSV 'buzzard' and 'kite'). I. The Hebrew *'ayyāh* and the Arabic *yu'ya'u* have long been identified; but the identity of the Arabic bird is quite uncertain, being variously translated 'buzzard,' 'falcon,' and 'sparrow-hawk.' The words are clearly onomatopoeic and may represent the cry of any of these birds. Its position in the list of unclean birds (Lv 11^{14}, Dt 14^{13}) shows that it is a *raptor* between the vulture and raven in size (thus excluding the sparrow-hawk, which is too small). The buzzard, by reason of its great size naturally follows eagles and vultures, while harriers and some falcons do not fall far short: three kinds of buzzards (the red, large as a small eagle, the common, and the long-legged) are all well known in Palestine, as are several harriers (especially the marsh-harrier). There are also three falcons, of which the lanner is the commonest; it frequents the rocky gorges of the Dead Sea and the Jordan, is a permanent resident and finds no place too desolate. The reference to the *'ayyāh's* keen sight (Job 28^{7}) favours the '**falcon**' (so RV, RSV; AV 'vulture'), whose acuity of vision is well known; but the term may include the 'buzzard' and the 'harrier,' which are not distinguished by the Arabs. II. The *dayyāh* or *dā'āh* is also a *raptor*, put between the vulture and the falcon in the list of unclean birds (Lv 11^{14} [AV '**vulture,**' RV and RSV '**kite**'], Dt 14^{13} [AV and RV '**glede,**' RSV '**buzzard**']; and the Ugaritic *dey*, which is obviously the same word, denotes a bird mentioned beside the *nṣ* (Hebrew *nēṣ*) 'hawk.' Further *dā'āh* 'swooped,' which is a verb derived from the same root, is commonly applied to the vulture (Dt 28^{49}, Jer 48^{10} 49^{22}) and so suggests a bird of similar habits; this may be the 'kite.' The black kite is probably meant; for the red kite is only a visitor to Palestine and, flying at a great height, is not easily seen and therefore is not likely to have had a special name. Both birds will therefore have been designated by the same term. The black kite nests in trees or on ledges of buildings in cities and does not specifically haunt ruins; but it feeds on carrion and will therefore be present as a scavenger feeding on corpses and carcases when Edom is destroyed (Is 34^{15} [AV '**vulture,**' RV and RSV '**kite**']). G. R. D.

KITHLISH, Jos 15^{40} (AV).—See Chitlish.

KITRON.—A Canaanite town in the territory of Zebulun, Jg 1^{30}. Unless it is to be identified with **Kattath,** it cannot be located.

KITTIM.—This name designates properly the island of Cyprus, and is to be so understood in the geographical list of the descendants of **Javan** (q.v.), that is, the Ionians, in Gn 10^{4}. The name is based on that of the settlement on the south-east of the island, called Kition by the Greeks, the modern *Larnaka*. This was the first trading post of the Phoenicians on the Mediterranean, hence it is vaguely used in Ezk 27^{6} (AV **Chittim,** RSV **Cyprus**) as the mother-city of all the maritime settlements westward. The connexion with the Ionians or Greeks is not quite clear, since these were not the first settlers on the island. There were, however, undoubtedly Greek colonists there in the 8th cent. B.C., as we learn from the inscription of the Assyrian Sargon of 720 B.C., pointing to a settlement of Ionian Cyprians in Ashdod. A use of the word, still more vague, is found in Dn 11^{30} (AV **Chittim**), where it refers to the Romans, while in Nu 24^{24} (AV **Chittim**) it is applied apparently to the Macedonians; similarly in 1 Mac 1^{1} (AV **Chettiim,** RV **Chittim**), 8^{5} (AV **Citims,** RV **Chittim,** RSV **Macedonians**). The word also occurs in the Dead Sea Scrolls (q.v.), but whether it is applied there to the Romans or the Greeks (or to both) is a question on which scholars are not agreed. J. F. McC.—**P. W.-M.**

KNEADING-TROUGH.—In AV and RV in Ex 8^{3} 12^{34} (RSV ' kneading bowls ') and in RV and RSV in Dt $28^{5,17}$ (AV ' store '). See BREAD, HOUSE, **9.**

KNEE, KNEEL.—The knees are often referred to in Scripture as the place where weakness of the body, from whatever cause, readily manifests itself; *e.g.* from terror (Job 4^{4}, Dn 5^{6}), or fasting (Ps 109^{24}). The reference in Dt 28^{35} seems to be to ' joint leprosy,' in which, after the toes and fingers, the joints of the larger limbs are attacked (Driver, *Deut. in loc.*). The laying of children on the knees of father or grandfather seems to have involved recognition of them as legitimate members of the family (Gn 30^{3} 50^{23}). In many passages of Scripture kneeling is spoken of as the attitude assumed in prayer (1 K 8^{54}, Ps 95^{6}, Dn 6^{10}, Ac 20^{36} etc.). To ' bow the knee ' is equivalent to ' worship ' (Is 45^{23}, Ro 14^{11} etc.; in 1 K 19^{18} ' bow the knee to Baal ' may be a reference to a ritual dance with bent knees). To fall upon the knees before a superior is an act at once of reverence and entreaty (2 K 1^{13}, Mt 17^{14}, Lk 5^{8} etc.). W. E.

KNIFE.—Of the various sorts of knives noticed in the OT mention may be made of the flint knives used for the rite of circumcision (Jos 5^{2f}; cf Ex 4^{25})—an instance of conservatism in ritual, to which parallels may be found in all religions. The knives for ordinary purposes under the monarchy were mostly of bronze, of which, as of the earlier flint knives, excavations have furnished many varieties. We also read of sacrificial knives (Gn $22^{6,10}$; in Ezr 1^{9} RSV has ' censers ' for the word of uncertain meaning rendered ' knives ' in AV, RV). See also PENKNIFE, RAZOR. A. R. S. K.

KNOP.—Another form of ' knob,' is used to render two different words in EV. **1.** The knops of the stem arms of the golden candlestick, or rather lampstand, of the Tabernacle, Ex 25^{31} (AV, RV; RSV **capitals**) were the spheroidal ornaments still recognizable in the representation on the Arch of Titus. **2.** Knops also denote certain ornaments, probably egg- or gourd-shaped, carved on the cedar lining of the walls of Solomon's Temple (K 6^{18} AV, RV; RVm, RSV **gourds**), and similar ornaments on the ' brazen sea ' (7^{24}; RSV **gourds**). See GOURD. A. R. S. K.

KNOWLEDGE.—I. HUMAN KNOWLEDGE.—**1. In the OT.**—Knowledge, so far as it has a theological use, is moral rather than intellectual. It is assumed that a knowledge of God is possible, but this is the result of a revelation of Himself by God, and not a speculative knowledge achieved by man. So knowledge becomes practically equivalent to religion (Ps 25^{14}, Is 11^{2}), and ignorance to irreligion (1 S 2^{12}, Hos 4^{1} 6^{6}). The Messianic age is to bring knowledge, but this will be taught of God (Is 54^{13}). This knowledge of God is therefore quite consistent with speculative ignorance about the universe (Job 38, 39). Perhaps some expressions in the NT which seem to refer to Gnostic ideas may be explained by this view of knowledge.

2. In the NT.—(*a*) *In the Gospels* knowledge is spoken of in the same sense as in the OT. Christ alone possesses the knowledge of God (Mt 11^{25-27}). This knowledge gives a new relation to God, and without it man is still in darkness (Mt 5^{8}, Jn 7^{17} 17^{3}). (*b*) *In St. Paul's Epistles.*—In the earlier Epistles knowledge is spoken of as a gift of the Spirit (1 Co 1^{30} 2, 12^{8}), although God can to a certain extent be known through nature (Ac 14^{7}, Ro $1^{19,20}$). 1 Corinthians especially urges the subordination of knowledge to love. In Col 2 and 1 Ti 6^{20} a wrong kind of knowledge is spoken of—perhaps an early form of Gnosticism. True knowledge, however, centres in Christ, who is the mystery of God (Col 2^{2}). In Him all questions find their answer, and this knowledge is not, like Gnosticism, the property of a few, but is intended for all men (Col 1^{28}). In the Pastoral Epistles knowledge is spoken of with reference to a definite body of accepted teaching, which is repeatedly alluded to; it is, however, not merely intellectual but moral (Tit 1^{1}). (*c*) *In the other NT books* knowledge is not prominent, except in 2 Peter, where, however, there is nothing specially characteristic. In Hebrews the ordinary word for ' knowledge ' does not occur at all, but the main object of the Epistle is to create and confirm a certain kind of Christian knowledge. Although knowledge in both OT and NT is almost always moral, there is no trace of the Socratic doctrine that virtue is knowledge.

II. DIVINE KNOWLEDGE.—It is not necessary to show that perfect knowledge is ascribed to God throughout the Scriptures. In some OT books—Job and some Psalms—the ignorance of man is emphasized in order to bring God's omniscience into relief (cf also the personification of the Divine Wisdom in the Books of Proverbs and Wisdom).

III. DIVINE AND HUMAN KNOWLEDGE IN CHRIST.—The question has been much debated how Divine and human knowledge could coexist in Christ, and whether in His human nature He was capable of **ignorance.** It is a question that has often been argued on *a priori* grounds, but it should rather be considered with reference to the evidence in the records of His life. The Gospels certainly attribute to Christ an extraordinary and apparently a supernatural knowledge. But even supernatural illumination is not necessarily Divine consciousness, and the Gospel records also seem to attribute to our Lord such limitations of knowledge as may be supposed to make possible a really human experience. **1.** There are direct indications of ordinary limitations. He advanced in wisdom (Lk 2^{52}); He asked for information (Mk 6^{38} 8^{5} 9^{21}, Lk 8^{30}, Jn 11^{34}); He expressed surprise (Mk 6^{38} 8^{5} 9^{21}, Jn 11^{34}). His use of prayer, and especially the prayer in the garden (Mt 26^{39}) and the words upon the cross (Mk 15^{34}), point in the same direction. **2.** With regard to one point our Lord expressly disclaimed Divine knowledge (Mk 13^{32}). **3.** In the Fourth Gospel, while claiming unity with the Father, He speaks of His teaching as derived from the Father under the limitations of a human state (Jn 3^{34} 5^{19f} 8^{28} 12^{49f}). **4.** While speaking with authority, and in a way which precludes the possibility of fallibility in the deliverance of the Divine message, He never enlarged our store of natural knowledge, physical or historical. If it be true that Christ lived under limitations in respect of the use of His Divine omniscience, this is a part of the self-emptying which He undertook for us men and for our salvation (see KENOSIS). J. H. M.

KOA.—A people associated with Pekod and Shoa (Ezk 23^{23}), probably, therefore, a by-form of *Kutū* (also *Gutium*), often mentioned in Assyrian inscriptions in the same company. Their seat lay NE. of Babylonia, in the mountains between the upper *'Adhem* and the *Diyâlā.*

KOHATH, KOHATHITES.—The name *Kohath* is found nowhere except in P and Chronicles. The three main divisions of Levites bore the names of Gershon. Kohath, and Merari, and these are accordingly given as the names of the ' sons ' of Levi (Gn 46^{11}, Ex 6^{16}, Nu 3^{17}, 1 Ch $6^{1,16}$ 23^{6}). The second division is described either as ' the Kohathites ' (Nu $3^{27,30}$ $4^{18,34,37}$ 10^{21} 26^{57}, Jos $21^{4,11}$, 1 Ch $6^{33,54}$ 9^{32}, 2 Ch 20^{19} 29^{12}) or **' the sons of Kohath '** (Ex 6^{18}, Nu $3^{19,29}$ $4^{2,4,15}$ 7^{9}, Jos $21^{5,20,26}$, 1 Ch $6^{2,18,22,61,66,70}$ 15^{5} 23^{12}). These were subdivided into four groups, the Amramites, the Izharites, the Hebronites, and the Uzzielites (Nu 3^{27}), each being traced to a son of Kohath (Ex 6^{18}, Nu 3^{19}, 1 Ch $6^{2, 18}$ 23^{12}). From these families fragments of genealogies remain. Amram is of peculiar importance, because his children were Aaron and Moses (Ex 6^{20}, 1 Ch 23^{13-17}); and Korah, a son of Izhar, was notorious in priestly tradition (Nu 16). See KORAH, DATHAN, ABIRAM.

After the Exile every member of the Levitical or 'priestly' caste traced his descent through one line or another to Levi, and these genealogies were of the utmost importance. All the Levites occupied minor positions in the Second Temple, except those Kohathites who could trace their descent from Aaron. Some Kohathites are named as appointed to humble offices (1 Ch $9^{19, 31f}$, Ezr 2^{42}, Neh 12^{25}). But the tendency of the period to idealize ancient history led the Priestly writers, including the Chronicler, to construct narratives in which the eponymous ancestors of the Levitical families played a prominent part; see 1 Ch 9^{19}. (1) During the desert wanderings the Kohathites were on the south side of the Tent (Nu 3^{30}), and they carried the screen of the sanctuary and its furniture, after it had been prepared for travel by the greatest of all the descendants of Kohath—Aaron and his sons (3^{31} 4^{4-15} 10^{21}); they were privileged to carry their burdens upon their shoulders (7^{9}), instead of in wagons, as the Gershonites and Merarites; they were superintended by Eleazar, Aaron's son (4^{16}). (2) After the settlement in Palestine, twenty-three cities were assigned to them (Jos $21^{4f, 13-26}$ = 1 Ch $6^{57-61, 67-70}$). (3) In David's reign the Chronicler relates that the Temple music was managed partly by Heman, a Kohathite, and his family (1 Ch 6^{31-38} 16^{41f} $25^{1, 4-6, 13, 16, 18, 20, 22f, 25-31}$; and see $15^{5, 8-10, 17, 19}$). David divided the Levites into courses 'according to the sons of Levi' (23^{6}; Kohathites vv.$^{12-20}$ 24^{20-25}); and particular offices of Kohathites are stated in $26^{1-9, 12-13, 17-19, 23-31}$. (4) Under Jehoshaphat they led the song of praise at the battle of En-gedi (2 Ch 20^{19}). (5) Under Hezekiah they took part in the cleansing of the Temple ($29^{12, 14}$). A. H. McN.—**N. H. S.**

KOHELETH.—See ECCLESIASTES.

KOLA.—An unknown locality mentioned in Jth 15^{4} (AV **Cola,** RV **Chola**).

KOLAIAH.—**1.** The father of the false prophet Ahab, Jer 29^{21}. **2.** The name of a Benjamite family which settled in Jerusalem after the Captivity, Neh 11^{7}.

KONA (Jth 4^{4}).—An unknown town of Palestine (AV, following a different reading, 'the villages'; RV **Konae**).

KONAE, Jth 4^{4} (RV).—See KONA.

KOPH.—Nineteenth letter of Hebrew alphabet, and so used to introduce the nineteenth part of Ps 119, every verse of which begins with this letter.

KORAH, KORAHITES.—**1.** Korah is the name of one of the 'dukes' of Edom, a son of Esau and Oholibamah, Gn $36^{5, 14, 18}$. **2.** There was also a Korah

who was a 'son' of Hebron and was descended from Caleb the Kenizzite, 1 Ch 2^{43}. **3.** Korah son of Izhar, a Kohathite Levite, led a revolt against Moses (Nu 16) and perished 'with all his company.' The descendants of this Korah were probably at one time a guild of Temple singers: Ps 42–49 and 84 f, 87 f bear the superscription '. . . of the Sons of Korah.' Possibly these Korahites were of Edomite extraction and were reckoned as Levites in the post-exilic days when all the Temple personnel had to be able to prove their descent from Levi. Later they were down-graded and became 'doorkeepers of the thresholds of the tent' (1 Ch 9^{19}). See also next article. N. H. S.

KORAH, DATHAN, ABIRAM.—The story of the rebellion of Korah, as contained in Nu 16, 17, is now combined with what was originally an entirely different narrative—that of the resistance of **Dathan** and **Abiram,** who were *laymen*, to the *civil* authority of Moses. Refusing to obey Moses' summons to appear before him, Dathan and Abiram, along with their households, were swallowed up by the earth (Nu $16^{1b, 2a, 12-15, 25f, 27b-34}$ [JE]). The story of Korah proper contains two strata, the work of Priestly writers of different ages. The first of these (Nu $16^{1a, 2b-7a, 18-24, 27a, 32b, 35, 41-50}$ ch. 17) describes a revolt of Korah, at the head of 250 princes of the congregation, against Moses *and Aaron*, in the interests of *the people at large* as against *the tribe of Levi*. The matter is decided by the test of the censers, the rebels being consumed by fire from the Lord. The sequel is found in ch. 17—the blossoming of Aaron's rod. The latest narrative (Nu $16^{7b-11, 16f, 36-40}$) represents Korah at the head of 250 *Levites*, opposing, in the interests of the tribe of Levi, the monopoly of the *priesthood* claimed by Aaron. These last two narratives are memorials of the struggles that took place, and the various stages that were passed through, before the prerogatives of Levi were admitted by the other tribes, and those of the house of Aaron by the other Levitical families.

KORE.—**1.** The eponym of a Korahite guild of doorkeepers, 1 Ch 9^{19} 26^{1} (also 26^{19} AV; RV, RSV 'Korahites'). **2.** Son of Imnah, a Levite in the time of Hezekiah, 2 Ch 31^{14}.

KOZ (? 'thorn').—**1.** A Judahite, 1 Ch 4^{8} (AV **Coz,** RV **Hakkoz**). **2.** In Ezr 2^{61}, Neh $3^{4, 21}$ 7^{63} AV has **Koz,** where RV, RSV have **Hakkoz.** See HAKKOZ, **1.**

KUE.—The ancient name of a country in the eastern part of Cilicia, famed for its export of horses. It is found in Assyrian texts as *Ḳu-e*, and in an 8th-cent. Aramaic inscription of Zakir, king of Hamath. It is mentioned in 1 K 10^{28}, 2 Ch 1^{16} (so RSV; AV 'linen yarn,' RV 'droves'). The spelling differs slightly in the two passages, and that in 1 K 10^{28} agrees with the spelling of the Zakir inscription, RSV rendering follows Vulgate (*de Coa*), and has other ancient support.

KUSHAIAH.—See KISHI.

L

LAADAH.—A Judahite, father of Mareshah, 1 Ch 4^{21}.

LAADAN.—See LADAN, **1, 2.**

LABAN.—**1.** Son of Bethuel (Gn 25^{19} 28^{5}), and grandson of Nahor (Gn 29^{5}, where 'son of' is to be understood as 'grandson of'). He was the brother of Rebekah (Gn 24^{29}), father of Leah and Rachel (Gn 29). Though they are not named, it is stated that he had sons also (Gn 30^{35} 31^{1}). He was father-in-law and uncle of Jacob. He appears first in Scripture as engaged in betrothing his sister Rebekah to Isaac (Gn 24^{29-60}). We meet him next at Haran entertaining Jacob (Gn 29^{13f}), who had escaped from his brother Esau. The details of the transactions between Laban and Jacob for the fourteen years while the nephew served his uncle for his two daughters are described in Gn 29–31. At the end of this period Jacob was not only husband to Leah and Rachel and father of eleven sons, but also the owner of very many flocks and herds. As Laban was reluctant to part with Jacob, the departure took place secretly, while Laban was absent shearing his sheep. Jacob removed his property across the Euphrates, while Rachel took with her the *t^erāphîm* or household gods of the family. Laban pursued them and overtook them at Mount Gilead (Gn 31[32]).

The Nuzi Tablets have helped in the correct understanding of these stories in Gn 29–31, and the practice of 'adoption' which is mentioned in these tablets, has thrown a great deal of light on the relationship between Laban and Jacob. When Jacob came to Laban, it would appear that Laban had no son, and so he adopted Jacob, and thus he became the rightful heir to the inheritance of Laban his father-in-law. But according to the Nuzi Tablets, should a son be born to the adopter, then the son was to share in the inheritance, and in addition was to have possession of the *t^erāphîm*, the household gods. It is to be assumed that a son was born to Laban, and Jacob now conscious of the new situation and of his own wealth and strength, decided to leave and go back to the land of Canaan. Before the flight we read that his wife Rachel stole the *t^erāphîm*, and obviously her main intention was to put forward her husband's claim to the family inheritance. Now we can understand Laban's concern about the 'gods,' and his indignation that they had been stolen (Gn 31[30]).

Laban's home was Haran, which was in Paddan-aram, a district from which we are told that the patriarchs migrated to the land of Canaan, and these stories are important in that they demonstrate the contact which still existed between the Hebrew patriarchs and their ancestors in the land between the rivers.

2. A place name, apparently one of the stopping places on the route of the Exodus, mentioned in Dt 1[1], but site still unknown. T. A. M.—**E. R. R.**

LABANA, 1 Es 5[29] (AV, RV).—See LEBANA.

LABOUR.—See WORK.

LACCUNUS, 1 Es 9[31] (AV **Lacunus**) = Ezr 10[30] **Chelal** (q.v.).

LACE.—The English word 'lace' comes from Latin *laqueus*, a 'snare,' and is used in that sense in Old English. It is then employed for any cord or band, and that is its meaning in Ex 28[28, 37] 39[21, 31]. In Sir 6[30] for AV 'lace,' RV has 'riband' and RSV 'cord.'

LACEDAEMONIANS.—In 2 Mac 5[9] we read that Jason fled for refuge to the Lacedaemonians 'because of their kinship.' This claim is further set forth in 1 Mac 12[2ff]; cf 14[16, 20f] 15[23], where we read of **Sparta** (q.v.) and an alliance with the **Spartans**. It was, of course, entirely fanciful, the Hellenes and the Jews belonging respectively to the Indo-European and Semitic branches of the human race. A. E. H.

LACHISH.—A town in the south country of Judah referred to several times in the Tell el-Amarna tablets. In the Biblical records it first appears as joining the coalition headed by the king of Jerusalem against the Gibeonites (Jos 10[3]), and as being in consequence reduced by Joshua (v.[31]) in spite of the assistance given to it by the king of Gezer (v.[33]). It is enumerated among the cities of the tribe of Judah, 15[39]. Rehoboam fortified it, 2 Ch 11[9]. Hither Amaziah, king of Judah, fled from conspirators, and here he was murdered, 2 K 14[19], 2 Ch 25[27]. In the reign of Hezekiah, Sennacherib took Lachish, and while he was quartered there Hezekiah sent messengers to him to make terms (18[13–17]). Sennacherib's Lachish campaign is commemorated by a sculpture from Nineveh, now in the British Museum. Lachish and Azekah were the last cities to stand against the king of Babylon (Jer 34[7]). Lachish was one of the towns settled by the children of Judah after the Exile (Neh 11[30]). Micah's denunciation of Lachish as 'the beginning of sin to the daughter of Zion' (1[13]) doubtless refers to incidents of which we are quite ignorant.

Lachish is modern *Tell ed-Duweir*, which has been excavated and which has yielded important finds, including the Lachish ostraca, which date from shortly before the fall of Jerusalem to Nebuchadrezzar, from the time when only Lachish and Azekah held out, besides Jerusalem. These ostraca bear the text of letters exchanged between the military commanders.

R. A. S. M.

LACUNUS, 1 Es 9[31] (AV).—See LACCUNUS.

LADAN.—**1.** A name occurring in the genealogy of Joshua, 1 Ch 7[26] (AV **Laadan**). **2.** A Gershonite family name, 1 Ch 23[7–9] 26[21] (all AV **Laadan**); elsewhere called **Libni** (q.v.). **3.** 1 Es 5[37] (AV); see DELAIAH, **5.**

LADANUM.—See MYRRH.

LADDER.—In ancient times ladders were used chiefly for scaling the walls of a besieged city, as frequently shown on the Egyptian and Assyrian monuments (Wilkinson, *Anc. Egyp.* i, 243; Layard, *Nineveh*, ii, 372). Although this use of them is probably implied in Pr 21[22], scaling-ladders are first expressly mentioned in the time of the Maccabees (1 Mac 5[30]). See FORTIFICATION.

Jacob's 'ladder' (Gn 28[12], Heb. *sullām*, only here) seems to have been rather a 'flight of stone steps, rising up to heaven' (S. R. Driver, *The Book of Genesis*, 1904, 264, cf KB), and *inter alia* may have reference to the physical features of the locality, but cf J. Skinner, *Genesis*, 1910, 376 ff). A. R. S. K.—**E. T. R.**

LADY.—This renders three different words in AV. **1.** Hebrew *g^ebhereth*, Is 47[5, 7] (so RV; RSV 'mistress'). **2.** Hebrew *śārāh*, literally 'princess,' Jg 5[29] (so RV, RSV), Est 1[18] (so RSV; RV 'princess'). **3.** Greek *kyria*, 2 Jn [1, 5] (so RV, RSV). For 'elect lady' see JOHN [EPISTLES OF], II.

LAEL.—A Gershonite Levite, Nu 3[24].

LAHAD.—A Judahite family name, 1 Ch 4[2].

LAHAI-ROI.—See BEER-LAHAI-ROI.

LAHMAM.—A town of Judah, Jos 15[40] (RVm **Lahmas**); possibly modern *Kh. el-Laḥm*, near *Beit Jibrîn.*

LAHMAS, Jos 15[40] (RVm).—See LAHMAM.

LAHMI.—The brother of Goliath, according to 1 Ch 20[5], but in the parallel 2 S 21[19] his name is replaced by 'the Bethlehemite' as a description of Elhanan (q.v.).

LAIR.—In RSV 'lair' replaces AV 'den,' RV 'dwelling place' in Jer 9[11] 10[22]; AV and RV 'place' in Zeph 2[15]; and AV 'den,' RV 'covert' in Job 37[8].

LAISH.—**1.** The original name of the town of Dan, Jg 18[7, 14, 27, 29]. The variation **Leshem** occurs in Jos 19[47bis]. See DAN. The father of Palti or Paltiel, to whom Michal, David's wife, was given by Saul, 1 S 25[44], 2 S 3[15]. **3.** Is 10[30] (AV); see LAISHAH.

LAISHAH.—A place connected with Gallim, and mentioned along with other localities in Benjamin and Judah, Is 10[30] (AV **Laish**). It is possibly modern *el-Isāwîyeh*, NE. of Jerusalem.

LAKKUM.—A town of Naphtali, Jos 19[33] (AV **Lakum**). It is possibly *Kh. el-Manṣûrah.*

LAKUM, Jos 19[33] (AV).—See LAKKUM.

LAMA.—See ELOI, ELOI, LAMA SABACHTHANI.

LAMB.—See SHEEP, and next article.

LAMB OF GOD.—The lamb was the most common victim in the Jewish sacrifices, and the most familiar type to a Jew of an offering to God. The title 'the lamb of God' (*i.e.* the lamb given or provided by God; cf Gn 22[8]) is applied by John the Baptist to Jesus in Jn 1[29, 36]. The symbolism intended can be inferred from the symbolic allusions to the lamb in the OT. Thus in Jer 11[19] the prophet compares himself to a lamb, as the type of guilelessness and innocence. Again in Is 53[7] (cf Ac 8[32]) the lamb is used as the type of vicarious suffering, but the sense in John is clearly the *removal* of sin, not the mere 'bearing' of a penalty. It is also possible to see in the phrase a reference to the lamb which formed part of the daily sacrifice in the Temple, cf 1 P 1[19]; and also, perhaps, an allusion to the Paschal lamb which would soon be offered at the approaching Passover (Jn 2[13]), and which was the symbol of God's deliverance—though the sacrificial value of the Paschal lamb is not entirely certain. In Jn 19[36] the identification with the Paschal lamb seems to be implied.

The lamb is used twenty-seven times in the Apocalypse as the symbol of Christ, and on the first introduction of the term in Rev 5[6] the writer speaks specifically of 'a lamb as though it had been slain.' The term used in the Apocalypse (*arnion*) is not the same as that found in the Gospel (*amnos*), and the connotations are probably different. In Revelation the term is a mystic, apocalyptic designation (or title) of the glorified Christ, enthroned with God and destined to be victorious over all the opposing forces in the universe, both human and demonic. It may be that the term had been specially chosen (in the Province of Asia) to designate the One who 'through weakness was made strong'—since *arnion* was traditionally the symbol of innocence and weakness (cf Lk 10[3]; *Iliad* xxii. 263; Kaibel, *Epigrammata Graeca*, 1038, 38). The meaning of this for the persecuted churches of Asia was obvious—to them, but not to their persecutors. It does not seem to have been a Jewish messianic title. *Arnion* may even have been a cryptogram for Christ's coming victory; see RSV Commentary.
A. W. F. B.—F. C. G.

LAME, LAMENESS.—See MEDICINE.

LAMECH.—The name appears in Gn 4[18-24] (J) as the son of Methusael a descendant of Cain; and in Gn 5[25-31] (P) as the son of Methuselah, a descendant of Seth, and the father of Noah. It is this second tradition that is followed in 1 Ch 1[3] and Lk 3[36]. An examination of the genealogies would suggest that they are variants of the same tradition. It is evident that Lamech played a prominent part in popular tradition, although little use is made of that in the Bible. We are given the names of his two wives (Adah and Zillah), three sons (Jabal, Jubal, and Tubalcain) and a daughter (Naamah). The taunt song associated with him is the only fact recorded of him, and may have been originally intended to demonstrate the antiquity of the custom of blood-feud, deriving from the nomadic life. It is possible that the context of the song (Lamech in descent from Cain) may suggest a growing repugnance of the early worshippers of Yahweh to this custom. Jesus appears to be alluding to this passage in Mt 18[22], replacing unlimited revenge with unlimited forgiveness.

It may be noted that the *Genesis Apocryphon* discovered at Qumrân preserves an account of the conception and birth of Noah to Lamech and his wife Bath-enosh.
A. S. H.

LAMENTATIONS, BOOK OF.—1. Names.—The Hebrew name of Lamentations is *'Êkhāh* ('How!'), the first word of the book. It is also called *Ḳînôth* or 'Laments.' The LXX *Threnoi* (*Ieremiou*) and the Vulgate *Threni, id est lamentationes Jeremiae prophetae* have given rise to the English title 'The Lamentations of Jeremiah.'

2. Position in the Canon.—In the Hebrew Bible Lamentations is placed in the third division of the OT canon. Its place is generally in the middle of the five *Megilloth*, between Ruth and Ecclesiastes. The Jews recite the book on the Ninth of Ab—the anniversary of the destruction of Jerusalem. In the Greek OT and the other versions Lamentations is attached to the prophecies of Jeremiah, in accordance with the then current belief that he was the author.

3. Occasion.—The immediate background of the book is the capture and destruction of Jerusalem in 586 B.C. by Nebuchadnezzar. The more distant background is the continued Palestinian 'exile' with its political and spiritual despair. The precise occasion of the compositions was doubtless the annual fast days in recollection of the fall of Jerusalem (cf Jer 41[4-5], Zec 7[1-5]). A liturgical origin best accounts for several features of the poems: the acrostic form, the transfer of individual lament imagery to the nation, and the stark juxtaposition of grief and despair on the one side, and faith and hope on the other. It also accounts for the repetitious character of the successive poems which, composed separately, were eventually compiled as a lectionary.

4. Date.—The five poems belong to the Palestinian 'exile,' 586–538 B.C. They are not the work of a rabbinic versifier after Nehemiah's time. It is unnecessary to explain the greater vividness of the second and fourth poems by attributing them to eye-witnesses while the other three poems are credited to later generations or centuries. The abrupt fusion of literary types, especially in the third poem, is no proof of post-exilic origin. The duress of exile and the liturgical origin of the poems easily account for their literary unevenness.

5. Form.—Of the five poems, the first four are acrostics. The twenty-two strophes of chs. 1, 2, and 4 are introduced by the twenty-two letters of the Hebrew alphabet. Chs. 2–4 place the letter *Pê* before the letter *'Ayin*. The acrostic of ch. 3 is intensified with three lines beginning aaa, bbb, etc. The acrostic form was both an aid to memory and an expression of the totality of grief and hope, 'from "a" to "z."' The last poem is alphabetic in that it contains as many lines as there are letters in the Hebrew alphabet. The dominant metric pattern in Lamentations is 3 : 2 (the so-called *ḳînāh* or lament meter) but there are plentiful exceptions in the form of 2 : 2, 2 : 3, and 3 : 3 patterns. The fifth poem is basically 3 : 3.

The literary typology of the poems is complicated, but thoroughly understandable in terms of the historical crisis. Chs. 1, 2, and 4 are built on funeral song motifs (cf *e.g.* 2 S 1[17-21], Am 5[1-2]). Ch. 3 is technically an individual lament and ch. 5 a collective lament. In point of fact the first four poems are examples of individualistic imagery and vocabulary transferred to national catastrophe. The highly individualized conception of ch. 3 is analogous in some ways to the Suffering Servant of Deutero-Isaiah.

6. Authorship.—No author is named or implied in Lamentations itself. The tradition of Jeremianic authorship which appears in the versions is probably due to a misunderstanding of 2 Ch 35[25] which claims the prophet as the writer of lamentations over Josiah.

The evidence against Jeremianic authorship is cumulative and convincing. He would hardly have identified himself so closely with the superficial confidence of the people in king and foreign alliances (4[16, 19]). Since he remained in Palestine only a short time after Jerusalem's fall, the despair due to a long period of foreign occupation apparent in the fifth poem cannot be attributed to Jeremiah. There are no acrostic poems in the book of Jeremiah. Linguistic and ideological affinities with the book of Jeremiah are best explained as springing from general prophetic religion or as evidence that the poet has modelled the national suffering in part after the experience of Jeremiah, especially in the third poem.

The first four poems are probably the work of a single poet, although the fifth may have been added by the anthologist. The high regard for king and nobility (1[6] 4[19]) suggests that a courtier may have written the poems, possibly someone from the family of Shaphan which had been cordial to the Deuteronomic Reformation and to Jeremiah.

7. Theology.—The nub of the book is the crisis of faith precipitated by the discrepancy between the historical promises of Yahweh and the collapse of political and institutional Yahwism. The bitterly realistic descriptions of death and destruction, especially of the emaciated and dying children, are directed not only to the people but also to God in the hope that he might spare them further suffering.

The 'priestly' elements of intercession and complaint are matched by equally emphatic 'prophetic' elements. The fall of the city is deserved punishment. Yahweh has not deserted His people but remains with them in all their experiences. Syncretism and polytheism are resisted. God's covenant love portends a future return of good fortune. Suffering contains a creative and disciplinary possibility. Lamentations bridges the pre-exilic and post-exilic religious life of Israel and anticipates many of the insights more fully developed in Deutero-Isaiah and Job.
N. K. G.

LAMPS.—1. The archaeological evidence of methods of illumination other than lamps does not survive. Resinous wood may have been used as **torches** (*e.g.* in Gideon's adventures, Jg 7[16, 20]), but no material evidence of such use can be expected to survive. In RV, RSV the translation of **lamp** for the Hebrew *nēr* is substituted for the AV **candles**. There is abundant archaeological evidence for the use of lamps both in OT and NT times, and the use of pottery vessels for this purpose can be traced back to the late 4th millennium B.C. The vessels would have held oil, and a wick probably of twisted flax (Is 42[3] RVm, RSV) would have projected from the edge of the vessel.

2. The earliest evidence so far found comes from the Late Chalcolithic or Proto-Urban period, in the last centuries of the 4th millennium. In tombs of this period such as those found at *Tell el-Fâr'āh*, near *Nâblus* (*RB* lvi, 58), and at Jericho (*PEQ*, 1953), shallow round-based bowls seem, from marks of burning on the rims, to have been used as lamps. Similar round-based bowls continued in use for this purpose in the beginning of the Early Bronze Age (*c* 2900–2600 B.C.). In Early Bronze III, their place was taken by flat-based saucers with splaying sides. Neither the round-based bowls nor the flat-based saucers were necessarily made especially for this purpose, for only a proportion of the vessels are smoke-marked.

3. The first vessels especially made for the purpose were introduced in the Intermediate Early Bronze—Middle Bronze period, by the Amorite tribesmen who destroyed the Early Bronze civilization. These lamps are invariably four-spouted; some have a flat base and some a round base. In many tombs of the period, for instance at Jericho, a niche was cut in the wall of the tomb and the lamp placed lighted in it (*PEQ*, 1953, p. 93).

4. With the beginning of the Middle Bronze Age, *c* 1900 B.C., a new type of lamp was introduced, a small round-based bowl with the lip slightly pinched at one point for the wick. The development of the form from now on to the type used in the Iron Age is continuous. During the Middle Bronze Age, the pinching of the spout is usually slight, but with the beginning of the Late Bronze Age in the 16th cent., the wall of the vessel at the spout begins to be increasingly folded over. The base of the vessel is usually round, though some of the Middle Bronze Age lamps may have flat bases. In the Iron Age a flat rim round the area of the vessel develops, and the later Iron Age lamps are very shallow and have a flat or dish base.

5. Throughout the Bronze Age and the Iron Age up to post-exilic times, the lamp is an open vessel, though with the lip increasingly folded in. The known examples are in pottery. There were also no doubt metal lamps, for instance the silver lamps mentioned in Jth 10[22], and the gold lamps of the Tabernacle and Temple, but no examples have survived.

6. The increasing fold of the lip would make a transition to a closed body quite simple, but the transition apparently took place not in Palestine but Greece. Closed lamps, often black glazed, with central filling hole and a long projecting nozzle, were introduced in the Hellenistic period. In the Roman period, the Roman variant, with a round body and slightly projecting nozzle, often with a pictorial moulded decoration on the disk, was introduced. From this type a more oval form developed, with a moulded pattern, usually non-pictorial. This type continued throughout the Byzantine and Early Arab period. With the spread of Christianity in the 4th cent., the lamps often bear Christian symbols. K. M. K.

LAMPSACUS, 1 Mac 15[23] (AVm, RVm).—See SAMPSAMES.

LAMPSTAND.—See HOUSE, **8**.

LANCE, LANCET.—The former is found in AV only, Jer 50[42] (RV, RSV **spear**). The Hebrew is *Kîdhôn*, which is probably a *scimitar*. It is found in RV and RSV in 1 K 18[28] for Hebrew *rōmaḥ*, where AV has **lancet.** See ARMOUR AND ARMS, **1**.

LAND CROCODILE.—See CHAMELEON and LIZARD.

LANDMARK.—The word (*g^ebhûl*) so rendered must not be identified off-hand, as is usually done, with the *kudurru* or boundary-stone of the Babylonians, for the fundamental passage, Dt 19[14], 'Thou shalt not remove thy neighbour's landmark, which they of old time have set,' should rather be rendered: 'Thou shalt not remove (or 'set back') thy neighbour's *boundary*, which they . . . have drawn.' Under the old Hebrew system of the cultivation in common of the village land, the boundaries of the plots may have been indicated as at the present day by 'a furrow double in width to the ordinary one,' at each end of which a stone is set up, called the 'boundary-stone' (*PEFSt*, 1894, pp. 195 f). The form of land-grabbing by setting back a neighbour's boundary-line must have been common in OT times, to judge by the frequent references to, and condemnations of, the practice (Dt 19[14] 27[17], Hos 5[10], Pr 22[28] 23[10], Job 24[2]).
A. R. S. K.

LANGUAGE OF CHRIST.—Four languages were in use in Palestine in the first century of our era, Latin, Greek, Hebrew, and Aramaic, and it is at least not impossible that Jesus was acquainted to some degree with all of them; each of them, moreover, has been put forward at one time or another as the language in which Jesus *habitually* spoke and taught. It will suffice merely to mention, as a curiosity of criticism, the theory of the Jesuit Hardouin (1741) that Latin was the most widely used language in Palestine in the days of our Lord and was generally used by Him, and, further, that it was the original language of most of the books of the NT. In reality Latin seems to have been of importance principally to the Roman military establishment (Jos. *BJ*, III. v. 4 [92]); thus it is the language of the inscriptions on the milestones of the Palestinian military roads. Latin doubtless also served the purposes of Roman law, as magistrates were obliged to use it in all their work (Valerius Maximus, II. ii. 2), and it may have served in some measure as the language of commerce, to judge from Latin borrowings in Aramaic.

A few scholars (A. Roberts, 1862; T. K. Abbott, 1891) have maintained that Greek was the language normally used by Jesus. In support of this contention it is urged that Greek was the common language of all the lands formerly comprised in the empires of Alexander and his successors. It is ingeniously suggested that the retention of the Aramaic phrases *talitha cumi* (Mk 5[41]) and *ephphatha* (Mk 7[34]) may be best understood if Jesus habitually spoke Greek and in these instances used Aramaic because it was the only language known to the persons addressed. Apart from being the usual medium of commercial intercourse between the Jews and foreigners, however, Greek was the normal speech only of the hellenized upper classes and of the representatives of the Roman government. There were Greek-speaking Jews in Jerusalem who had their own synagogues (Ac 6[1, 9]), but these appear to have formed special communities; doubtless most of them were Jews returned from the Diaspora. It is true that Greek was widely understood throughout Palestine, especially, perhaps, in 'Galilee of the Gentiles,' but this understanding was far from universal: we learn from Eusebius that even in the 3rd cent. A.D., in the hellenized town of Scythopolis, it was necessary to render Greek sermons, lessons, and liturgical passages into Aramaic for the benefit of some of the peasants who attended the church (*Mart. Pal.*, Syriac version, ed. Cureton, p. 4). Thus the evidence hardly warrants the conclusion that Jesus habitually spoke Greek, but the number of Greek-speaking persons in Palestine, Jews and Gentiles, and the fact that some intercourse with Roman administrative officials was unavoidable are surely reason enough for supposing that Jesus had a knowledge of the language. In particular, it may be that he used Greek in speaking with the Syrophoenician woman (Mk 7[26]), the centurion (Mt 8[5-13], Lk 7[1-10]), and Pilate (Mk 15[2]). Of Jesus' disciples Matthew surely knew Greek, as he had been in the government's employ.

Recently it has been suggested (by H. Birkeland, 1954) that Hebrew never actually ceased to be a living language of the people of Palestine but persisted in isolated rural areas (much as Gaelic has persisted in the Scottish highlands) and was the language usually spoken by Jesus and, moreover, the language of the sources underlying our written Gospels. The Aramaic phrases referred to above are held to support this view also: they represent exceptional departures made by Jesus in exceptional cases, *i.e.* in speaking to persons who knew only Aramaic, and were left unaltered when the Gospel sources were translated into Greek, much as we might leave French phrases unchanged if they occurred in a German work we were rendering into English. The persistence of isolated pockets of 'popular' Hebrew is not impossible, but there is no real evidence at all for Jesus' use of such a dialect. However, if Jesus was a Galilean Rabbi or had any kind of formal Rabbinical training, it is not unlikely that He did use Hebrew as well as Aramaic, especially in His disputations with the Pharisees and on solemn occasions such as the Last Supper. But if Jesus did use Hebrew it was no hypothetical 'popular' dialect, but the scholastic language of the earliest Midrashim and, later, of the Mishnah. Jesus' use of the Hebrew Scriptures proves that His knowledge of them was extensive, so that it is reasonable to infer that he understood the Classical Hebrew in which they were written and that he was familiar with the Rabbinical idiom in which they were discussed. A number of scholars hold that a Hebrew, but not an Aramaic, source underlies the first two chapters of the third Gospel, but even if this is the case it can hardly have any bearing on the language used by Jesus.

The evidence for the view that Aramaic was the language normally used by our Lord is regarded by the majority of scholars as conclusive. In the first place it is clear that Aramaic had begun to replace Hebrew as the language of Palestine as early as the reign of Hezekiah. In Nehemiah's day the Law required explanation when read at public services (Neh 8^{7f}), and later a full translation into Aramaic was found to be necessary. Aramaic had become the language of the 'people of the land' and was, hence, the mother-tongue of our Lord: this is certified by the presence of Aramaisms in the sayings of Jesus in the Gospels (investigated by J. Wellhausen, C. C. Torrey, C. F. Burney, and most recently by M. Black). More obvious traces of Aramaic are to be seen in the name Cephas (Aram. *kêphā*) given to Simon, and in the occurrence of religious terms like *pascha* (Aram. *pasḥa*, not Heb. *pesaḥ*), *abba*, and *marana tha* which prove that the earliest church grew up in an Aramaic-speaking community. As for the Aramaic phrases in Mk 5^{41} 7^{34}, their retention is explained by some scholars as due to the desire of the evangelist to reproduce exactly the 'words of power' used by our Lord; but it is simpler to think of Mark's Gospel not as a translation at all, but as an original composition in Greek by a writer accustomed to think in Aramaic. Thus he occasionally gives us, as by inadvertence, the actual words of Jesus, and then adds an explanation in Greek.

On *a priori* grounds it would seem more probable that Jesus spoke a dialect more closely related to that of the Palestinian Pentateuch Targum than to that of the Targums of Onkelos and Jonathan, which has been assimilated to the dialect of the Babylonian Jews in addition to being rather artificially bound to the Hebrew original. There is some evidence to support this presupposition: the Gospel *rabbouní, rabbouneí* (Mk 10^{51}; Jn 20^{16}) occurs several times in the fragments of the Palestinian Pentateuch Targum which were found in the Cairo Genizah in 1930, and in Fragment D (Gn 44^{18}) it is twice found fully vocalized as *rabbūnî*, as against the Onkelos vocalization *ribbōnî, ribbōnanā'*. Quite recently a wealth of new material has come to light which will be of great value for the recovery of the language spoken by our Lord. In 1956 the Codex Neofiti I., in the Vatican Library, was identified as a copy of the complete Jerusalem Targum previously known only in fragments; this manuscript is dated to the 15th cent., but reflects, naturally, much earlier material. In the same year an Aramaic scroll came to light at Qumrân which has been called the *Genesis Apocryphon*, but which is actually part of a very ancient Targum to Genesis, dating probably from the 1st cent. B.C. E. G.

LANGUAGE OF THE NT.—The object of this article is to give a general non-technical account of the Greek in which the NT is written. It should be stated at the outset that the standpoint of scholarship in regard to this subject has materially altered since *c* 1900. We shall therefore briefly state the nature of the change in view, and then describe the NT Greek as we now regard it, without further reference to older theories.

1. The old view.—In every age of NT study, scholars have been struck by the fact that its Greek to a large extent stands alone. It differs immensely from the language of the great classics of the period which was closed some four centuries earlier, and not much less from that of post-classical writers of its own time, even when those writers were Palestinian Jews, as was Josephus. During the 17th cent. the 'Purist' school sought to minimize these differences, holding that deviation from the 'purity' of classic standards was a flaw in the perfection of the inspired Book, which must at all costs be cleared away. But, except for such eccentricities of learning, the efforts of scholars in general were steadily directed towards the establishment of some rationale for this isolation of what Rothe called the 'language of the Holy Ghost.' Two excellent reasons were found for the peculiarities of NT Greek. (1) NT writers were steeped in the language of the Greek OT, a translation which largely followed the Hebrew original with slavish literalness. A special religious phraseology was thus created, which not only contributed a large number of forms for direct quotation, but also supplied models for the general style of religious writing, much as the style of modern sermons or devotional books is modelled upon the English of the Bible. (2) The writers were mostly Jews who used Aramaic (a language closely related to Hebrew) in their daily life. When, therefore, they thought and wrote in Greek, they were prone to translate literally from their native tongue; and 'Aramaisms' thus infected the Greek, side by side with the 'Hebraisms' which came from the LXX. The degree to which either of these classes of Semitism was admitted to affect particular words or grammatical constructions in the Greek NT naturally differed in the judgment of different writers; but even J. H. Thayer, who wrote in *DB* iii. after the new lights had already begun to appear, showed no readiness to abandon the general thesis that the NT Greek lies outside the stream of progress in the development of the Greek language, and must be judged by principles of its own.

2. Newer views.—The credit of initiating a most far-reaching change of view, the full consequences of which are only beginning to be realized, belongs to a brilliant German theologian, Adolf Deissmann. His attention having been accidentally called to a volume of transcripts from the Egyptian papyri recently added to the Berlin Museum, he was immediately struck by their frequent points of contact with the vocabulary of NT Greek. He read through several collections of papyri, and of contemporary Greek inscriptions, and in 1895 and 1897 published the two volumes of his *Bible Studies* (English translation in one volume, 1901). Mainly on the ground of vocabulary, but not without reference to grammar and style, he showed that the isolation of NT Greek could no longer be maintained. Further study of the papyri he used, and of the immense masses of similar documents which have been published since, especially by the explorers of Oxford and Berlin, confirms his thesis and extends it to the whole field of grammar. To put the new views into two statements—(1) The NT is written in *the spoken Greek of daily life*, which can be proved from inscriptions to have differed but little, as found in nearly every corner of the Roman Empire in the 1st cent. (2) What is peculiar in 'Biblical Greek' lies in the presence of boldly literal translations from Hebrew OT or Aramaic 'sources': even this, however, seldom goes beyond clumsy and unidiomatic, but perfectly possible, Greek, and is generally restricted to the inordinate use of correct locutions which were rare in the ordinary spoken dialect. The Egyptian non-literary papyri of the three centuries before and after Christ, with the inscriptions of Asia Minor, the Aegean islands and Greece during the same period—though these must be used with caution because of the literary element which often invades them—supply us therefore with the long desiderated parallel for the language of the NT, by which we must continually test an exegesis too much dominated hitherto by the thought of classical Greek or Semitic idiom.

3. History and diffusion of the Greek language.—At this point, then, we should give a history of the world-Greek of NT times. A sister-language of Sanskrit, Latin, Slavonic, German, and English, and most other dialects of modern Europe, Greek comes before us earliest in the Homeric poems, the oldest parts of which may go back to the 10th cent. B.C. Small though the country was, the language of Greece was divided into more dialects, and dialects perhaps more widely differing, than English in the reign of Alfred. Few of these dialects gave birth to any literature; and the intellectual primacy of Athens by the end of the classical period (4th cent. B.C.) was so far above dispute that its dialect, the Attic, became for all future time the only permitted model for literary prose. When Attic as a spoken language was dead, it was enforced by rigid grammarians as the only 'correct' speech for educated people. Post-classical prose accordingly, while varying in the extent to which colloquial elements invade the purity of its artificial idiom, is always more or less dominated by the effort to avoid the Greek of daily life; while in the NT, on the contrary, it is only two or three writers who admit to a small extent a style differing from that used in common speech. Meanwhile the history of Greece, with its endless political independence and variation of dialect between neighbouring towns, had entered a new phase. The strong hand of Philip of Macedon brought Hellas under one rule; his son, the great Alexander, carried victorious Hellenism far out into the world beyond. Unification of speech was a natural result, when Greeks from different cities became fellow-soldiers in Alexander's army, or fellow-colonists in his new towns. Within about one generation we suddenly find that a compromise dialect, which was based mainly on Attic, but contained elements from all the old dialects, came to be established as the language of the new Greek world. This 'Common' Greek, or Hellenistic, once brought into being, remained for centuries a remarkably homogeneous and slowly changing speech over the larger part of the Roman Empire. In Rome itself it was so widely spoken and read that St. Paul's letter needed no translating, and a Latin Bible was first demanded far away from Latium. In Palestine and in Lycaonia the Book of *Acts* gives us clear evidence of bilingual conditions. The Jerusalem mob (Ac 21^{40} 22^{2}) expected St. Paul to address them in Greek; that at Lystra (14^{11}) similarly reverted with pleasure to their local patois, but had been following without difficulty addresses delivered in Greek. It was the one period in the history of the Empire when the gospel could be preached throughout the Roman world by the same missionary without interpreter or the need of learning foreign tongues. The conditions of Palestine demand a few more words. It seems fairly clear that Greek was understood and used there much as English is in Wales to-day. Jesus and the Apostles would use Aramaic among themselves, and in addressing the people in Judaea or Galilee, but Greek would often be needed in conversation with strangers. The Procurator would certainly use Greek (rarely Latin) in his official dealings with the Jews. There is no reason to believe that any NT writer who ever lived in Palestine learned Greek only as a foreign language when he went abroad. The degree of culture in grammar and idiom would vary, but the language itself was always entirely at command.

4. NT Greek.—We find, as we might expect, that 'NT Greek' is a general term covering a large range of individual divergence. The author of *Hebrews* writes on a level which we might best characterize by comparing the pulpit style of a cultured extempore preacher in this country—a spoken style, free from artificiality and archaisms, but free from anything really colloquial. The two *Lukan* books show similar culture in their author, who uses some distinctively literary idioms. But St. Luke's faithful reproduction of his various sources makes his work uneven in this respect. *St. Paul* handles Greek with the freedom and mastery of one who probably used it regularly all his life, except during actual residence in Jerusalem. He seems absolutely uninfluenced by literary style, and applies the Greek of common intercourse to his high themes, without stopping a moment to polish a diction the eloquence of which is wholly unstudied. Modern attempts to trace formal rhetoric and laws of rhythm in his writings have had little success. At the other end of the scale, as judged by Greek culture, stands the author of *the Apocalypse*, whose grammar is very incorrect, despite his copious vocabulary and rugged vigour of style. Nearly as unschooled is *St. Mark*, who often gives us very literal translations of the Aramaic in which his story was first wont to be told: there seems some reason to suspect that in the oldest form of his text this occurred more frequently still. The other main Gospel 'source,' the '*Sayings of Jesus*,' shows likewise the traces of processes of translation. Space forbids any attempt to distinguish the position of all the NT writers, but we may note that the papyri supply parallels in degrees of culture to compare with them in turn, except so far as sheer translation comes in.

5. Help derived from Modern Greek, and from reconstructed Aramaic originals.—We must now return to the development-history of Greek to observe that its later stages, even up to the present day, are full of important contributions to our study of the NT. The 'Common' or Hellenistic Greek, described above, is the direct ancestor of the vernacular of modern Greece and Greek-speaking districts elsewhere. We are daily learning more of the immense significance of this despised patois for interpreting the sacred language. Here the student must carefully eliminate the artificial 'Modern Greek' of Athenian newspapers and books, which is untrustworthy for this purpose, just as is the Greek of Plutarch or Josephus. The genuine vernacular—with its dialects, based on inconsiderable local variations in Hellenistic Greek—may be placed by the side of modern folk-ballads and mediaeval popular stories and saint-legends, to take us back to the papyri and inscriptions, as our latest-found tools for NT study. The literature, classical and post-classical, will of course retain the place it has always held, when modern methods have taught us how to check its testimony. And Comparative Philology, with lights on the meaning of cases and tenses and moods, may be added to the equipment with which purely linguistic science may now help forward the interpretation of Scripture. All this is on the side of the student of Greek itself. But the other side of NT language must naturally not be forgotten. Contributions of great value have recently been made to our knowledge of the Aramaic, in which nearly all the sayings of Christ must have been uttered, and in which Papias (as usually understood) shows they were first written down. The possibility of reconstructing to some extent the original of our Greek Gospel sources is drawing nearer, and the co-operation of Greek and Semitic scholars promises marked advances in our knowledge of the very kernel of the NT.

6. Characteristics of NT Greek.—A few concluding words may be given to the general characteristics of the language which had so providentially become the language of the civilized world just at the time when the gospel began its advance. It used to be frequently contrasted unfavourably with the classical Attic, which is undeniably the most perfect language the world has ever seen, for the clearness, subtlety, and beauty with which it can express thought. In Hellenistic Greek the subtlety, the sense of rhythm, and the literary delicacy have largely disappeared. But the old clearness is only enhanced by a greater simplicity; and the boundless resourcefulness of the language impresses us powerfully when in the NT for the first and (practically) last time the colloquial dialect of the people was enshrined in literature, the authors of which were nearly always unconscious that they were creating literature at all. The presentation of Christianity to the Western world as a system of thought could never have been accomplished in Hebrew, even if that language had attained universal currency. In Greek we are always conscious of a wealth of suggestiveness which no translation can convey, an accuracy and precision of thought which repay the utmost exactness of study. This is in no sense lost even when the simpler grammar of the later language becomes the tool of men who had no inheritance of Greek culture. A comparatively elementary knowledge of the simpler Greek, which can be attained without touching the complex structure of the classical language, will constantly reveal important elements in the writer's meaning that are beyond the reach of our language to convey directly. In our own time at last this language is being studied for its own sake; and even classical scholars are beginning to allow that the renewed youth of Greek, under conditions which make it largely a new language, produced a literature which the philologist, and not merely the theologian, can admire. J. H. Mo.—**F. C. G.**

LANGUAGES OF THE OT AND APOCRYPHA.—See Hebrew, Aramaic, Text and Versions of OT.

LANTERN.—Only Jn 18³, where some form of 'torch' is more probably intended. The Greek is *phanos*, a word not found elsewhere in Biblical Greek.

LAODICEA, to-day Eski Hissar, was situated in the valley of the Lycus, a tributary of the Maeander in Asia Minor. It was founded by Antiochus II. about the middle of the 3rd cent. B.C. It was planted in the lower Lycus glen, Colossae being situated in the upper. The Lycus glen was the most frequented path of trade from the interior of the country to the west, and the great road passed right through Laodicea. The city was nearly square, and strongly fortified, but dependent for its water supply on an aquedict 6 miles long. It played a comparatively small part in the dissemination of Greek culture. Its prosperity advanced greatly under the Romans, especially after Diocletian. It was an important manufacturing centre for a soft glossy black wool, which was made into garments of various kinds (cf Rev 3¹⁸). In connexion with the temple of the Phrygian god Men Karou (13 miles W. of Laodicea), there grew up a celebrated school of medicine. Its most famous medicines were an ointment made from spice nard, which strengthened the ears, and Phrygian powder, obtained by crushing Phrygian stone, which was used for the eyes (Rev 3¹⁸). There were many Jewish inhabitants of Laodicea, and the population as a whole was of very mixed race. The church there was not founded by St. Paul, but probably by one of his assistants, perhaps Epaphras (cf Col 4¹³). Paul wrote the Laodiceans a letter which they were to share with the Colossians, and directed the latter to share his letter to them with the Laodiceans (Col 4¹⁶). A Latin writer later tried to supply an Epistle to the Laodiceans. The author of the Apocalypse included Laodicea among the seven churches to which he sent letters (3¹⁴⁻²²), and reprimanded it severely. Laodicea was badly destroyed by an earthquake in A.D. 60–61. It was visited by Hadrian A.D. 123–124. A. So.—**E. G. K.**

LAP.—This renders five different words in RSV. **1.** Hebrew *beghedh*, literally 'garment,' 2 K 4³⁹ (so AV, RV). **2.** Hebrew *birkayim*, literally 'knees,' 2 K 4²⁰ (AV, RV 'knees'). **3.** Hebrew *ḥêḳ*, literally 'bosom,' Pr 16³³ (so AV, RV). **4.** Hebrew *ḥōṣen*, literally 'bosom,' Neh 5¹³ (so AV, RV). The closely related word *ḥēṣen*, where the meaning is the same, is rendered 'bosom' in EV in Ps 129⁷. **5.** Greek *kolpos*, literally 'bosom,' Lk 6³⁸ (AV, RV 'bosom'). In each case, except **2**, the reference is to a fold in the garment.

LAPIDOTH, Jg 4⁴ (AV).—See Lappidoth.

LAPPIDOTH ('torches' or 'lightning flashes').—The husband of Deborah the prophetess, Jg 4⁴ (AV **Lapidoth**). Some commentarors take the term to be descriptive of the character of Deborah, 'a woman of lightning flashes.' In favour of this they urge the feminine termination *-oth*, but the same termination is found elsewhere in men's names, *e.g. Meremoth.* T. A. M.

LAPWING.—See Hoopoe.

LASCIVIOUSNESS.—The Greek word so translated by AV in Mk 7²² etc., is translated '**wantonness**' in Ro 13¹³. This is the translation in the versions before AV in nearly all the passages where AV has 'lascivousness.' The idea of the Greek word is shameless conduct of any kind. RSV has 'licentiousness.'

LASEA (Lasaea) in Crete is mentioned by Luke (Ac 27⁸), but by no other ancient author. It was the nearest town to Fair Havens, but it was 5 miles away, and this, in addition to the inconvenience of the roadstead, would explain the reluctance of the captain of St. Paul's ship to winter there. The ruins of Lasea were rediscovered in 1856. The site still bears the ancient name. A. E. H.—**E. G. K.**

LASHA.—A place which marked the SE. boundary of the land of the Canaanites, Gn 10¹⁹. Jerome identified it with the hot springs of Callirrhoë, in the *Wâdī Zerqā Mā'în*. Wellhausen would identify it with **Laish, 1** (q.v.), on the N. frontier. There is nothing to support this but the resemblance in the name. Against it is the order in which the names occur. It cannot now be identified. W. E.

LASHARON.—A town taken by Joshua, Jos 12¹⁸ (RV **Lassharon**). LXX^B reads here 'the king of Aphek in Sharon,' and this is probably right. See Aphek, **1.**

LASSHARON, Jos 12¹⁸ (RV).—See Lasharon.

LAST SUPPER.—See Eucharist.

LAST THINGS.—See Eschatology.

LASTHENES.—An officer of high rank, 'kinsman' (1 Mac 11³¹) and 'father' (v.³²) of Demetrius II. He raised a body of Cretan mercenaries, and enabled Demetrius to land in Cilicia, and wrest the throne of Syria from Alexander Balas (Jos. *Ant.* XIII. iv. 3 [86]; cf 1 Mac 10⁶⁷). When Demetrius was endeavouring to make terms with Jonathan the Maccabaean, he wrote to Lasthenes in favour of the Jews, and forwarded a copy of his letter to the Jewish prince (1 Mac 11²⁹⁻³⁷).

LATCHET.—Found in AV and RV, but replaced by **thong** in RSV. See Dress, **6.**

LATIN.—In such provinces as Judaea the Latin language alone had place in official acts and Roman courts. Where Greek was allowed in court pleadings, it was, so to speak, an act of grace on the judge's part, and there can be little doubt that, *e.g.*, the speech of Tertullus in Ac 24 was in Latin. The Latin words used in a Greek form in the NT are mainly administrative, legal, or military (*e.g. census, custodia, praetorium, colonia, libertinus, centurio, legio*), or names of Roman coins (*denarius, quadrans*), but the total number of such Latin words occurring is only about twenty-five. The Gentile names adopted by Jews were generally of Greek form (*e.g. Philip*)—a Latin form like the name of St. Paul was an exception (to be expected perhaps with one so proud of Roman citizenship). Throughout Palestine, while Latin was the language of the administration, Greek was the main language of commerce, and Aramaic the language of common intercourse among Jews. Hence we find all three languages used for the superscription on the cross (Jn 19²⁰). **A. E. H.**

LATIN VERSIONS.—See TEXT (of OT and NT), GREEK VERSIONS OF OT, **11,** VULGATE.

LATRINE.—See DRAUGHT HOUSE.

LATTER RAIN.—See RAIN.

LATTICE.—See CASEMENT and HOUSE, **7.**

LAUD.—In Ro 15^{11} the AV has ' Praise the Lord, all ye Gentiles ; and laud him, all ye people.' The Greek verbs being different, two different English verbs are used. But RV and RSV turn ' laud ' into ' praise.' In the OT, however, ' laud ' and ' praise ' are both used in RV in order to distinguish two Hebrew verbs, as in Ps 117^{1} (RSV ' extol ' ; AV has ' praise ' twice) 145^{4} (so RSV ; AV ' praise '), though not quite consistently. In Ps 147^{12} the difference between the verbs is ignored in AV, RV, and RSV.

LAUGHTER.—Laughter is used in the Bible in three ways. (1) It is opposed to weeping, as Ec 3^{4} 7^{3}, Job 8^{21}, Ps 126^{2}, Lk 6^{21}. (2) It expresses incredulity, as Gn 17^{17} 18^{12}. (3) It signifies derision, as Ps 2^{14}, Bel ^{19}.

LAVER.—See TABERNACLE, **4,** TEMPLE, **6** (*d*).

LAW (IN OT).—1. That ' the law was given through Moses ' (Jn 1^{17}) represents a belief held by Jews and taken over by the early Christians. Moses was their first as well as their greatest lawgiver ; and in this matter religious tradition is supported by historical probability. The Exodus and subsequent wanderings constitute the formative epoch of Israel's career. This was the period of combination and adjustment between at least some of the tribes looking towards national unity. Such periods necessitate social experiments to develop a strong sense of corporate responsibility based on religious sanctions.

It therefore devolved upon Moses to establish a central authority for the administration of justice, which should be easily accessible and generally recognized throughout the group of tribes. There was only one method by which any such general recognition could be attained. That was by placing the legal and judicial system upon the basis of an appeal to that religion which had already been successful in rousing the people to a sense of unity and an effort towards freedom.

2. We can perhaps see the beginning of these legislative functions in Ex 18^{15}, where Moses explains how ' the people come to me to inquire of God ; when they have a dispute, they come to me and I decide between a man and his neighbour, and I make them know the statutes of God and his decisions (*tôrôth*).' Originally *tôrāh* (the usual word in the OT for ' law ') meant oral instruction or direction, as in this passage. This kind of *tôrāh* survived for long in Israel and Judah. It was practical and in conformity with the needs of primitive nations. Cases of exceptional difficulty were brought to the sanctuary, and the decisions rendered there were accepted as emanating from God (Ex 21^{6} 22^{8} RSV). The cases thus brought ' to God ' may be divided into three classes : (1) matters of moral obligation, (2) civil suits, (3) ritual difficulties. We read that Moses found it necessary to delegate some of this judicial work to various trustworthy men, who could handle the ordinary cases, leaving only the most difficult for the leader (Ex 18$^{13-26}$). Afterwards, local leaders, and finally the kings, assumed these judicial functions ; see JUDGES and JUSTICE (II.).

Here, then, we can trace the character of Hebrew legislation in its earliest stages. Law (*tôrāh*) means oral direction, gradually crystallizing into consuetudinary law, which finally assumes the form of a written code. Laws, oral or written, could also be taken over from other peoples, such as the Canaanites, with whom there was cultural contact. When all this legal material was classified and reduced to writing (cf Hos 8^{12}), *tôrāh* came to signify such a collection ; and eventually the same word was used as a comprehensive term for the Pentateuch, in which the most important legal collections were included. In later Jewish usage it came to mean sometimes the entire OT or even all religious literature. Other OT terms for various kinds of laws are : *d^{e}bhārîm*, ' words,' as in the Ten Words (or Commandments), also called the Decalogue (Ex 20^{1}, Dt 5^{22}) ; *miṣwôth*, ' commands ' or ' commandments ' ; *ḥukḳîm*, ' statutes ' ; and *mishpāṭîm*, ' judgments ' or ' ordinances ' (Dt 5^{31}). It is not safe to make fine distinctions between these terms, or to call the first ' sacred ' law and the other three ' secular ' law. The Hebrews and other ancient peoples did not make this distinction as moderns do. All of life was sacred, and all law required Divine sanction.

Knowledge of the contributions of foreign legislation to the development of Hebrew law has been revolutionized in recent years by archaeological discoveries. Most strikingly helpful of the discovered material are the Laws of Eshnunna (Old Akkadian), the Lipit-Ishtar Code (New Sumerian), the Code of Hammurabi (Old Babylonian or Amorite), the Middle Assyrian Laws, the Hittite Laws, and the Neo-Babylonian Laws (see *ANET* for translations). These codes, in various languages and dialects, all come from Mesopotamia or Asia Minor, and date from the 20th to the 7th cents. B.C. All are phrased in the hypothetical manner (' If a man . . .,' etc.) as are most of the Book of the Covenant (cf Ex 22^{1}), and parts of Deuteronomy and Leviticus in the OT (see below). This type of legislation is now sometimes called ' casuistic ' or case law, with the implication that it arises from actual court decisions. It seems fairly obvious that practically every established community in the Ancient Near East had this type of legislation, and that the Hebrews, as they developed into a homogeneous community in Palestine, followed the same pattern, probably borrowing certain codes from the Canaanites and modifying these to suit their own needs.

Another set of laws important for our purpose is that from Nuzi or Nuzu of the 15th cent. B.C. Nuzi was in the kingdom of the Mitanni or Hurrians (OT Horites) in Upper Mesopotamia. These laws throw a flood of light on certain patriarchal incidents in Genesis, such as the childless Abram's adoption of Eliezer as an heir, and then having a son of his own (Gn 15^{2ff}) ; and Rachel's theft of the household gods (Gn 31$^{19, 30-35}$), possession of which is now known to have served as a guarantee of inheriting the ancestral property. Here again we see legal aspects of the OT drawn from the larger background.

Let us now examine the main formal divisions of legal material in the OT.

3. The Ten Commandments and Other Decalogues.—The Ten Words or Ten Commandments, also sometimes called the Ethical Decalogue, occur in two recensions, Ex 20 and Dt 5. The former is sometimes called the E-Decalogue because it now stands in a section of the E-Document (see PENTATEUCH) ; the latter then receives the corresponding name, D-Decalogue. The only real difference is the reason given for the observance of the Sabbath (see SABBATH), the Deuteronomy version making the institution a commemoration of the escape from Egyptian bondage, while the Exodus version considers it an original part of the plan of Creation, seemingly presupposing Gn 1^{1}–2^{3}. For this reason, some scholars now class the present form of the Exodus version with the P-Document, thus making it later rather than earlier than the Deuteronomy version (see Pfeiffer, *IOT*, 228 ff).

Many scholars of all shades of opinion attribute this Decalogue, or a simplified form thereof, to Moses (see TEN COMMANDMENTS). Certainly the tradition resulting in this remarkable formulation stems from Moses, or at least was transmitted by him. For some of it is much older than Moses : from the earliest stages of human society there were laws against murder, adultery, perjury, theft, and the like, else there would have been no human society. On the other hand, such matters as the ownership of houses and livestock, having slaves or servants, and employing resident aliens belong to the era of settled national life in Palestine. The dates of the origin of the Sabbath and of the prohibition of idols are controversial. Perhaps the surest contribution of Moses is the insistence on complete loyalty to the One God,

Yahweh, and the inclusion of strong ethical demands in His worship. Surely this kind of contribution was highly original and absolutely fundamental to the life of our religious tradition.

In contrast to the casuistic or case-law type of specific legal formulation, this enunciation of general principles, presumably by a religious authority, is sometimes referred to as the 'apodictic' or 'categorical' type. Whereas the form and even much of the content of the casuistic type comes from outside sources, the apodictic type of legal declaration is more specifically Hebraic or Israelite in form ('You shall not . . .,' etc.) as well as in content. Thus there are no really good parallels from other ancient cultures to our Ethical Decalogue. However, the best that can be cited are: the Negative Confession or Protestation of Guiltlessness from the Egyptian 'Book of the Dead,' a long list of the sins and crimes that the deceased has not committed (*ANET*, 34 ff); and the series of Babylonian incantation texts known as *Shurpu* ('ritual burnings'), in which the worshippers seek to ward off evil by purifying themselves from various sins, which are listed, thus giving us a pattern of the moral standards of the worshippers' culture (Price, *Monuments and the OT*, 1958 ed., 174 f; *Archiv f. Orientforsch.*, Beiheft 11).

The use of ten or twelve convenient words or phrases to set forth a set of rules that should be remembered was not confined to our Ethical Decalogue. Another notable example is the so-called Ritual or Cultic Decalogue, usually mentioned as being found in Ex 34^{18-26}, but present also, though in disarranged form, in Ex $22^{29, 30}$ 23^{12-19}. The version in Ex 34 is sometimes called the J-Decalogue, because it is surrounded by J material. However, all these early legal sections should be considered on their own merits apart from the documents. Much of this ceremonial procedure came from the Canaanites. It is significant that the law of the sacrifice of the first-born in Ex 22^{29} requires the giving of the first-born son along with the first-born of the animals, whereas Ex 34^{20} provides for the redemption of the son by substituting an animal, as is done in Gn 22^{13}. Human sacrifice was common among the Canaanites; it sometimes appeared among the Hebrews, but their superior ethical sense caused their legislators and prophets to see the wrong of it.

The other early collection often cited in this connexion is Dt 27^{15-26}, really a dodecalogue consisting of twelve curses, the strongest form of prohibition. Since the arrangement is in the form of a litany, with the people answering 'Amen' after each curse, this collection must have once been a part of a primitive ritualistic service. Yet this is not a 'ritual dodecalogue' in the sense of the preceding paragraph, for the demands are ethical, and of a high order; hence, this litany was probably not borrowed, but developed within the worshipping Israelite community itself.

4. The Book of the Covenant or Covenant Code (roughly Ex 20^{22}–23^{19}) is a fragment of Hebrew case law, with revisions and insertions of other material. As pointed out above, it is that part of OT law most intimately connected with the recently discovered Mesopotamian codes. A good example is 21^{35}, dealing with the division of costs and compensation between the owners of two oxen that engage in combat leading to the death of one animal. The Laws of Eshnunna, a thousand years earlier than the present form of the Hebrew code, contain an exact parallel (No. 53). This example shows how certain laws could pass from country to country and remain constant over a long period of time, while others needed to be changed completely or abolished to suit local conditions.

The most famous parallel corpus is, of course, the Code of Hammurabi, now known for more than half a century (dated at *c* 1700 B.C.). So striking is the similarity that at first statements were made to the effect that the Covenant Code was taken or borrowed from Hammurabi's laws. Now it is understood that both codes stem from a common background of widespread legislation. Though the Hebrew code is later in date, it is in some ways simpler and more primitive in character than that of Hammurabi, since Babylonia was more advanced in material culture at an early date. A specific difference concerns boat traffic on the Euphrates river, which had no parallel in Palestine.

As noted above, other kinds of legal material have been inserted into or joined with the case laws. Already mentioned is the disarranged version of the Ritual Decalogue standing at the end of the Covenant Code. Another addition is the so-called Participial Code, each law beginning with a participle in Hebrew (but 'whoever' in RSV), and requiring the death penalty. There are seven of these ($21^{12, 15ff}$ 22^{19f} 31^{15b}, the last in another context). These laws are of the apodictic type; they are harsh, and were probably brought in by the Israelites from the desert. Finally, there is the *lex talionis* of 21^{23-25}, obviously interpolated somewhat awkwardly and yet necessarily included on principle. Christian love in human relations repudiates the 'eye for an eye' principle (Mt 5^{38}), but the legal need of making the punishment commensurate with the crime continued (cf Dt 19^{21}, Lv 24^{17-21}) and continues to-day. The substitution of a monetary compensation or fine instead of literal retaliation was already used in ancient times (cf Ex 21^{28-36} with Hammurabi 250–252).

5. The Law or Code of Deuteronomy is the legal core of Deuteronomy (chs. 12–26) usually connected by scholars with the law book found during the reform of Josiah about 621 B.C. (2 K 22–23; see DEUTERONOMY and PENTATEUCH). It is obviously a revision of some of the material already discussed here, with additions to bring it into line with 7th-cent. conditions. There is no attempt at logical arrangement, civil, cultic, and ethical laws appearing indiscriminately. Though a product of the Southern Kingdom, this code shows distinct northern influences. Apparently not all the literature of Israel was destroyed when that nation fell, but some was brought to Judah and became a part of the religious tradition there. Josiah's reform followed a period of apostasy, and this code attempts both to eliminate foreign religious practices and to purify the worship of Y". Both priests and prophets seem to have had a hand in the compilation, with perhaps the emphasis on the priestly element. The penalty against apostasy is extraordinarily severe—death, in fact (13^{6-11}). On the other hand, a new humanitarianism blossoms in the code, mitigating the institution of slavery (15^{12-18}, cf Ex 21^{2-11}), making it easier to borrow money (23^{19f}), and lightening military service (20^{1-9}); but the doctrine of the holy war against foreigners is maintained, because of the danger of apostasy (20^{10-18}). The most characteristic law and innovation is that of the centralization of all religious worship in the Temple in Jerusalem to put an end to the foreign and syncretistic practices of the outlying districts (12^{13-27}). Permission to slaughter food animals in the villages without ritual was granted for the first time as a corollary, since formerly slaughter involved sacrifice. Connexion with the central sanctuary had to be maintained by pilgrimages (16^{1-17}).

6. The Holiness Code (Lv 17–26), really a part of the Priestly Code, and imbedded therein, is in a way a parallel to the code of Deuteronomy. Some regard it as a kind of unsuccessful rival to Deuteronomy, others consider it a post-exilic composition drawing on earlier sources. It shows remarkable affinity with the prophetic book of Ezekiel, leading to the conclusion that Ezekiel and H draw from a common source. Both make much of the holiness of God and man that gives H its name.

At the very beginning private and nonritualistic slaughter is forbidden (17^{1-9}), in contrast to D. Apparently H gives the older law that became obsolete after promulgation of D. Some of the other more characteristic rules are: blood is not to be eaten, all forms of incest are forbidden, grain must be left in the corners of the fields for the poor to glean (cf Ru $2^{2f\ 8, 17}$), you must love your (Hebrew) neighbour and the resident alien as yourself ($19^{18, 34}$, cf Lk 10^{25-37}), human sacrifice is forbidden, the sabbatical and jubilee years are to be observed (see SABBATICAL YEAR), slaves are to be taken only from foreign nations, no interest is to be charged fellow-countrymen, priests must be without physical defect and live an especially consecrated life, the practice of magic must be punished by death. Thus it can be seen that H, like D, represents a 'mixed' type of legislative collection.

7. The Priestly Code, as distinct from the Priestly Document as a whole (see PENTATEUCH), comprises the latter part of Exodus (25^{1}–31^{17} 35–40), all of Leviticus (unless H be excepted), and most of Numbers (1^{1}–10^{10} 15, 17–19, 28–36). In contrast to some of the mixed material previously considered, particularly D and H, P lays special stress on ceremonial institutions in a most elaborate and detailed manner. The priesthood claims particular attention, hence the name now assigned. Only the descendants of Aaron could be priests (Ex 28^{1}, Nu 18^{7}), and the Levites were to be their servants (Nu 3^{5-9}); formerly all Levites were eligible to be priests (Dt $17^{9,18}$ 18^{1f}). The title 'high priest' (*kōhēn gādhôl*) had not yet come into use (see PRIESTS AND LEVITES), though the office is in effect under such names as 'anointed priest' (Lv 4^{3}), 'the priest who is chief among his brethren' (21^{10}), or simply 'the priest' (Nu $27^{19,21f}$).

The P-Code is the charter of post-exilic Judaism, completed by *c* 450 B.C. We must not conclude, however, that all the content is late. Much is of high antiquity; it is the elaboration that is characteristic of P. As a matter of fact, P does not profess to supplant all other laws. The author has simply collected the details of ceremonial legislation, and the rubrics of Temple worship for a special purpose, namely to preserve the corporate life of the Jewish community as a holy nation, or rather, church, under God. It was only by emphasizing their special *religious* peculiarities that this struggling group could survive. Ezekiel's ideal city was named 'The Lord is there' (48^{35}). P seeks to realize this ideal. All the laws, all the ceremonies, are intended to stamp indelibly upon the imagination of the people that Y″ is supreme. Therefore the sense of sin must be deepened, that sin may be removed; the need for purification must be constantly proclaimed, that the corrupting and disintegrating influences of surrounding heathenism may not prevail; the ideal of national holiness must be sacramentally symbolized, and, through the symbol, actually attained. (For parallel legislation from other cultures on the exact details of ritual, see Pritchard, *ANET*^{2}, 325 ff, 502 f; Gordon, *Ugaritic Manual*, 191 ff, *idem*, *Ugaritic Literature*, 111 ff).

8. It must be plain that such stress on ritual enactments inevitably facilitated the growth of formalism and even hypocrisy. Not always, however, was this the case. We must remember that glad and devout attitude manifested in Ps 1^{1ff} 19^{7-10} 119, Sir 35^{1-11}, and elsewhere. To this day the Jews have a phrase, 'joy in the law' (*śimḥath tôrāh*), which expresses very well a relation to the law that is not formalistic or burdensome. We must also remember that Judaism has preserved through the OT another tradition, the prophetic, of which a few words should be said in conclusion.

The *tôrāh* of the prophets had a moral, rather than a ceremonial, emphasis. The priests, by their official duties much engaged in ritual actions, nevertheless had opportunities for giving the worshippers true direction (*tôrāh*) on the principles underlying their religious observances. It is for their neglect of such opportunities, and not, as is sometimes maintained, on account of any inherent antagonism between priestly and prophetic ideals, that the prophets so frequently rebuke the priests (see PROPHECY). The priests claimed Divine sanction for their worship, and tradition ascribed the beginning of all Hebrew priestly institutions to Moses (or Aaron). This the prophets do not deny; but they do deny that the distinctive feature of the Mosaic tradition lay in anything but its moral excellence. In this connexion the words of Jeremiah cannot be quoted too often: 'For in the day that I brought them out of the land of Egypt, I did not speak to your fathers or command them concerning burnt offerings and sacrifices. But this command I gave them, "Obey my voice . . . and walk in all the way that I command you"' (Jer 7^{22f}). The correct interpretation of Am 5^{21-26} corroborates Jeremiah's position. It is probably unwarranted to say that the prophets condemned the sacrificial system as such, or denied its worth and Divine sanction. On the other hand, 'the law of the Lord' meant to the prophets something different from the punctilious observance of traditional ceremonies. What is more, they appeal without fear of contradiction to the Mosaic tradition as confirming their conviction that it is in the sphere of morality, rather than in the correct organizing of ritual, that the essence of Y″'s law is to be found. With this antithesis in mind, we are ready to consider the NT phase of the subject. (For post-Biblical Jewish law, see TALMUD.) E. A. E.—**W. F. S.**

LAW (IN NT).—This subject will be treated as follows: (1) the relation of Jesus Christ to the OT Law; (2) the doctrine of law in St. Paul's Epistles; (3) the complementary teaching of Hebrews; (4) the attitude of St. James representing primitive Jewish Christianity.

1. Our Lord stated His position in the saying of Mt 5^{17}: 'I did not come to destroy the law or the prophets, but to fulfil.' The expression covers the whole contents of Divine Scripture except the Hagiographa (sometimes for brevity, spoken of simply as 'the law'; see Jn 10^{34} 12^{34} 15^{25}), which He does not mean to invalidate in the least (Mt 5^{18}), as the novelty of His teaching led some to suppose (see 7^{28f}), but will vindicate and complete. But His 'fulfilment' was that of the Master, who knows the inner mind and real intent of the Scripture He expounds. It was not the fulfilment of one who rehearses a prescribed lesson or tracks out a path marked for him by predecessors, but the crowning of an edifice already founded, the carrying forward to their issue of the lines projected in Israelite revelation, the fulfilment of the blade and ear in 'the full corn.' Jesus penetrated the shell to reach the kernel of OT representations; and He regarded *Himself*—His Person, sacrifice, salvation, Kingdom—as the focus of manifold previous revelations (see Lk 4^{17-21} 16^{16} 24^{27}, Jn 1^{17} 6^{45}). The warning of Mt 5^{17-20} was aimed at the Jewish legalists, who dissolved the authority of the law, while jealously guarding its letter, by casuistical comments and smothering **traditions,** who put light and grave on a like footing, and blunted the sharpness of God's commands in favour of man's corrupt inclinations. The Corban formula, exposed in Mk 7^{7-13}, was a notorious instance of the Rabbinical quibbling that our Lord denounced. It is a severer not a laxer ethics that Jesus introduces, a searching in place of a superficial discipline; 'Your righteousness,' He says, 'must *exceed* that of the scribes and Pharisees.'

Our Lord's fulfilment of 'the law'—*i.e.* in the stricter sense, the body of Mosaic statutes regulating Israelite life and worship—included (*a*) *the personal and free submission* to it, due to His birth and circumcision as a son of Israel (Gal 4^{4}; cf Mt 3^{15} 8^{4} 15^{24} 17^{27}, Lk 2^{21ff}).

His fulfilment included (*b*) *the development of its unrecognized or partially disclosed principles.* Thus Jesus asserted, in accordance with views already advanced among the scribes, that 'the whole law and the prophets hang on the two commandments' of love to God and to our neighbour (Mt 22^{34-40}, Lk 10^{25-37})—the parable of the Good Samaritan gives to the second command an unprecedented scope. His distinction between 'the weightier matters' of 'justice, mercy, fidelity,' and the lighter of tithes and washings, was calculated to revolutionize current Judaism.

(*c*) A large part of the Sermon on the Mount (Mt 5^{21-48}) is devoted to *clearing the law from erroneous glosses and false applications*: on each point Jesus sets His 'I say to you' against what 'was said to the ancients'—mere antiquity goes for nothing; nor does He here distinguish between the text of the written law and the traditional modifications. With each correction the law in His hands grows more stringent; its observance is made a matter of inner disposition, of intrinsic loyalty, not of formal conduct; the criterion applied to all law-keeping is that it shall 'proceed out of the heart.'

(*d*) Further, our Lord's fulfilment of the law necessitated the *abrogation of temporary and defective statutes*. In such instances the letter of the old precept stood only till it should be translated into a worthier form and raised to a higher potency (Mt 5^{18}), by the sweeping away of limiting exceptions (as with the compromise in the matter of wedlock allowed to 'the hardness of heart' of Israelites, Mt 19$^{3-9}$), or by the translation of the symbolic into the spiritual, as when cleansing of hands and vessels is displaced by inner purification (Mk 7$^{14-23}$, Lk 11$^{37-41}$; cf Col 2^{16f}, He 9^{9f}). Our Lord's reformation of the marriage law is also a case for (*b*) above: He rectifies the law by the aid of the law; in man's creation He finds a principle which nullifies the provisions that facilitated divorce. He also states a difference between a commandment made by God Himself and one given by Moses, the first being far superior. The abolition of the distinction of 'foods' (Mk 7^{19}), making a rift in Jewish daily habits and in the whole Levitical scheme of life, is the one instance in which Jesus laid down what seemed to be a new principle of ethics. The maxim that 'what enters into the man from without cannot defile,' but only 'the things that issue out of the man,' was of far-reaching application, and supplied afterwards the charter of Gentile Christianity. Its underlying principle was, however, implicit in OT teaching, and belonged to the essence of the doctrine of Jesus. He could not consistently vindicate heart-religion without combating Judaism in the matter of its ablutions and food-regulations and Sabbath-keeping.

(*e*) Over the last question Jesus came into the severest conflict with Jewish orthodoxy; and in this struggle He revealed the consciousness, latent throughout His dealings with OT legislation, of being the sovereign, and not a subject like others, in this realm. Our Lord 'fulfilled the law' by *sealing it with His own final authority*. His 'I say to you,' spoken in a tone never assumed by Moses or the prophets, implied so much and was so understood by His Apostles (1 Co 7^{10}, Gal 6^{2}, 1 Jn 2^{3f} etc.). Christ arrogates the rôle of 'a son over his house,' whereas Moses was 'a servant in the house' (He 3^{5f}). Assuming to be 'greater than Solomon,' 'than Abraham,' 'than the temple' (Mt 12$^{6, 42}$, Jn 8^{53}), He acted as one greater than Moses! The Sabbath-law was the chosen battle-ground between Him and the established masters in Israel (Mk 2$^{23-28}$ 3^{2ff}, Lk 13$^{10-17}$, Jn 5$^{9-16}$). In the public Sabbath assemblies Jesus was oftenest confronted with cases of disease and demoniacal possession; He must do His work as God's 'sent' physician. The Sabbath-rules were clear and familiar; His infraction of them in acts of healing was flagrant, repeated, defiant; popular reverence for the day made accusations on this count particularly dangerous. Men were placed in a dilemma: the Sabbath-breaker is *ipso facto* 'a sinner'; on the other hand, 'how can a *sinner* do such signs?' (Jn 9$^{16, 24ff}$). Jesus argues the matter on legal grounds, showing from recognized practice that the 4th Commandment must be construed with common sense, and that 'it is lawful to do good on the Sabbath day' and to work in the service of God (Mt 12$^{5, 11f}$). He goes behind those examples to the governing principle (see (*b*) above), that 'the Sabbath was made for man, and not man for the Sabbath' (Mk 2^{27f}): the institution is designed for human benefit, and its usages should be determined by its object. But He is not content with saying this: the war against Him was driven on the Sabbath-question *à outrance*; Jesus draws the sword of His reserved authority. He claims, as sovereign in human affairs, to decide what is right in the matter—'The Son of Man is lord of the Sabbath'; more than this, He professes to have wrought His Sabbath works as God the Father does, to whom all days are alike in His beneficence, and through the insight of a Son watching the Father at His labour (Jn 5$^{17-20}$)—a pretension to Jewish ears, of blasphemous arrogance: 'He makes himself equal with God!' On this ground Jesus was condemned by the Sanhedrin (cf Jn 19^{7}), because He set Himself above the Sabbath, on the strength of being one with God. Thus the law of Moses put Jesus Christ to death; it was too small to hold Him; its administrators thought themselves bound to inflict the capital sentence on One who was understood to have said, 'I am the Son of the Blessed' (Mk 14^{61ff}).

(*f*) At the same time, Caiaphas, the official head of the system, gave another explanation, far deeper than he guessed, of the execution: 'That Jesus should die for the nation, and not for the nation only' (Jn 11^{49ff}). Virtually, He was offering Himself for 'the lamb' of the Paschal Feast, ready to be slain in sacrifice, that He might 'take away the sin of the world.' This mysterious relation of the death of Jesus to Divine law He had hinted at here and there (Mt 20^{28} 26^{28}, Lk 22^{37}, Jn 3^{14} 6^{51} 12^{24}); its exposition was reserved for His Apostles speaking in the light of this grandest of all fulfilments. Jesus *made good the implicit promise of the sacrificial institutions of Israel*.

2. The word 'law' occurs one hundred and eighteen times in St. Paul's Epistles—one hundred and three times in Romans and Galatians alone. It is manifest how absorbing an interest the subject had for this Apostle, and where that interest mainly lay. Gal 2^{19} puts us at the centre of St. Paul's position: 'I through law died to law, that I might live to God.' From legalism, as from a house of bondage, he had escaped into the freedom of the sons of God. Sometimes the Apostle, like Stephen (Ac 7^{53}), and as in the Epistle to Hebrews (2^{2}), emphasizes the fact that the Law was given by God not directly but through angels—which shows its inferiority to the Christian revelation. (*a*) Paul 'died to the law,' as he had understood and served it when a Pharisee, regarding obedience to its precepts as the sole ground of acceptance with God. He had sought there 'a righteousness of' his 'own, based on the law' (Ph 3^{9}), to be gained by 'works,' by which he strove to merit salvation as a 'debt' due from God for service rendered—a righteousness such as its possessor could 'boast of' as 'his own' (Ro 4$^{1-5}$ 9^{31}–10^{3}). Pursuing this path, 'Israel' had failed to win 'the righteousness of God,' such as is valid 'before God'; the method was impracticable—justification on the terms of 'the law of Moses' is unattainable (Ac 13^{38f}, Ro 8^{3}). Instead of destroying sin, the law arouses it to new vigour, 'multiplying' where it aimed at suppressing 'the trespass' (Ro 5^{20} 7$^{7-13}$, 1 Co 15^{56}). Not the 'law' in itself, but the 'carnal' sin-bound nature of the man, is to blame for this; arrayed against 'the law of God,' to which 'reason' bows, is 'another law' successfully oppugning it, that 'of sin' which occupies 'my members' (Ro 7$^{12-23}$), and which is, in effect, a 'law of death' (8^{2}).

(*b*) But St. Paul's Judaistic experience had a positive as well as a negative result: if he 'died to law,' it was '*through* law'; 'the law has proved our *paedagogus* for [leading us to] Christ' (Gal 3^{24}). Law awakened conscience and disciplined the moral faculties; the Jewish people were like 'an heir' placed 'under guardians and stewards until the appointed time,' and trained in bond-service with a view to their 'adoption' (Gal 4$^{1-5}$). Even the aggravations of sin caused by the law had their benefit, as they brought the disease to a head and reduced the patient to a state in which he was ready to accept the proffered remedy (Ro 7^{24}). 'The Scripture' had in this way 'shut up all things under sin,' blocking every door of escape and blighting every hope of a self-earned righteousness (Gal 3^{21f}), that the sinner might accept unconditionally the 'righteousness which is through faith in Christ' (Ph 3^{9}).

(*c*) Contact with Gentile life had widened St. Paul's conception of moral law; it was touched by the influences of Greek philosophy and Roman government. He discerned a law established 'by nature,' and 'inscribed in the hearts' of men ignorant of the Mosaic Code and counting with Jews as 'lawless.' This Divine *jus* (and *fas*) *gentium* served, in a less distinct but very real sense, the purpose of the written law in Israel; it impressed on the heathen moral responsibility and the consciousness of sin (Ro 2^{6-16}). The rule of right and wrong Paul regards as *a universal human institute*, operating so as to 'bring the whole world under judgment before God' (Ro 3^{9-19}); its action is manifested by the universal incidence of death: in this sense, and in the light of 2^{12-15}, should be read the obscure parenthesis of Ro 5^{13f}, as stating that 'law' is concomitant with 'sin'; the existence of sin, followed by death, in the generations between Adam and Moses proves that law was there all along, whether in a less or a more explicit form; the connexion of sin and death in humanity is, in fact, a fundamental legal principle (Ro 8^{2}).

(*d*) Having 'died to law' by renouncing the futile salvation it appeared to offer, the Apostle had learned to live to it again in a better way and under a nobler form, since he had begun to 'live to God' in Christ. St. Paul is at the farthest remove from Antinomianism; the charge made against him on this score was wholly mistaken. While no longer '*under* law,' he is 'not lawless toward God, but *in law* toward Christ' (Ro 6^{14f}, 1 Co 9^{21}). The old *ego*, 'the flesh with its passions and lusts,' has been 'crucified with Christ' (Gal 2^{20} 5^{16-24}). God's law ceases to press on him as an external power counteracted by 'the law of sin in the members'; the latter has been expelled by 'the Spirit of God's Son,' which 'forms Christ' in him; the new, Christian man is 'in law' as he is 'in Christ'—he sees the law now from the inside, in its unity and charm, and it constrains him with the inward force of 'the law of the Spirit of life in Christ Jesus' possessing his nature. He 'serves' indeed, but it is 'in the new' life wrought 'of the Spirit, and not in the old' servitude to 'the letter' (Ro 7^{6}, 2 Co 3^{6}). Constituting now 'one new man,' believers of every race and rank 'through love serve one another,' as the hand serves the eye or the head the feet; for them 'the whole law is fulfilled in one word, Thou shalt love thy neighbour as thyself' (Ro 13^{8-10}, 1 Co $12^{13,25f}$, Gal 5^{13f}, Eph 2^{15-18}). The Christian 'fulfils *the law of Christ*,' as the limb the law of the head. Thus St. Paul's doctrine of the Law joins hands with that of Jesus (see **1** above). Thus also, in his system of thought, the law of God revealed in the OT, when received from Christ revised and spiritualized, and planted by 'faith' along with Him in the believer's heart (cf Jer 31^{31-34}), becomes for the first time really valid and effective: 'Do we nullify law through faith? God forbid; nay,' he cries, 'we establish law!' (Ro 3^{31}).

(*e*) Neither Jesus nor Paul makes a formal distinction between the moral and the ceremonial law (see, however, Ro 9^{4}). St. Paul's teaching bears mainly on the former: as a Pharisee he had no ritualistic bent, and his ambition was for ethical perfection. 'Circumcision' has lost in his eyes all religious value, and remains a mere national custom, now that it ceases to be the covenant-sign and is replaced in this sense by baptism (1 Co 7^{18ff}, Gal 6^{15}, Col 2^{11ff}). It becomes a snare to Gentiles when imposed on them as necessary to salvation, or even to advancement in the favour of God; for it binds them 'to keep the whole law' of Moses, and leads into the fatal path of 'justification by law' (Gal 2^{2-5} 3^{2ff} 5^{3-6}). St. Paul's contention with the legalists of Jerusalem on this question was a life and death struggle, touching the very truth of the gospel' and 'the freedom' of the Church (Ac 15^{1-11}, Gal 2^{1-10} 5^{1}). The same interests were threatened, more insidiously, by the subsequent attempt, countenanced by Peter and Barnabas at Antioch, to separate Jewish from Gentile Christians at table through the reassertion of the Mosaic distinction of 'foods' which had been expressly discarded by Jesus. The assumption of a privileged legal status within the Church meant the surrender of the whole principle of salvation by faith and of Christian saintship (Gal 2^{11-21}, Ro 14^{17f}, 1 Co 8^{8}; cf Mk 7^{14-23}). In some Churches Paul had to deal with the inculcation of Jewish ritual from another point of view. At Colossae the dietary rules and sacred seasons of Mosaism were imposed on grounds of ascetic discipline, and of reverence towards angelic (*scil.* astral) powers; he pronounces them valueless in the former respect, and in the latter treasonous toward Christ, who supplies 'the body' of which those prescriptions were but a 'shadow' (Col 2^{16-23}).

3. Col 2^{17} forms a link between the doctrine of St. Paul on the Law and *the complementary teaching of the writer of Hebrews*—a Jew of very different temperament and antecedents from Saul of Tarsus. This author emphasizes the ceremonial, as Paul the moral, factors of the OT; the Temple, not the synagogue, was for him the centre of Judaism. 'The first covenant,' he says, 'had ordinances of divine service,' providing for and guarding man's approach to God in worship (He 9^{1} etc.); for St. Paul, it consisted chiefly of 'commandments expressed in ordinances' (Eph 2^{15}), which prescribe the path of righteousness in daily life. 'The law' means for this great Christian thinker the institutions of the Israelite priesthood, sanctuary, sacrifices—all consummated in Christ and His 'one offering,' by which 'he has perfected for ever them that are sanctified' (He 9^{1}–10^{14}). In his view, the law is superseded as the imperfect, provisional and ineffective, by the perfect, permanent and satisfying, as the shadowy outline by the full image of things Divine (7^{18f} 8^{1-4} 10^{1-4}); 'the sanctuary of this world' gives place to 'heaven itself,' revealed as the temple where the 'great high priest'—Divine-human in person, sinless in nature, perfected in experience, and immeasurably superior to the Aaronic order (4^{14ff} 7^{26ff})—'appears before the face of God for us,' 'having entered through the virtue of his own blood' as our 'surety' and 'the mediator of' our 'covenant,' who has won for mankind 'an eternal redemption' (2^{9} 7^{22} 8^{6} 9^{24-28}). Jesus thus 'inaugurated a new and living way into the holy place' (in contrast with the old and dead way of the law); as experience proves, He has 'cleansed the conscience from dead works to serve the living God,' while the law with its repeated animal sacrifices served to remind men of their sins rather than to remove them (7^{25} 9^{14} 10^{1-4}). Equally with St. Paul, the *auctor ad Hebraeos* regards 'remission of sins' as the initial blessing of the Christian state, which had been unattainable 'under law,' and 'the blood of Christ' as the means of procuring this immense boon. In Paul's interpretation, this offering 'justifies' the unrighteous 'before God' and restores them to the forfeited status of sonship; in the interpretation of Hebrews, it 'cleanses' worshippers and brings them 'nigh to God' within His sanctuary; on either view, the sacrifice of Calvary removes the barriers set up, by man's sin 'under the law,' between humanity and God.

4. For St. James also the OT law was transformed. He conceives the change in a less radical fashion than Paul or the writer of Hebrews; James stands sturdily on the platform of the Sermon on the Mount. Re-cast by 'the Lord of glory' and charged with 'the wisdom that comes from above,' the law is new and glorified in his eyes; like Paul, he knows it as 'the law of Christ.' All the disciples of Jesus were one in the place they gave to that which James calls 'the sovereign law, Thou shalt love thy neighbour as thyself' (2^{8-13}; cf 1 Co 13); deeds of pure brotherly love prove 'faith' alive and genuine; they make it 'perfect,' and guarantee the believer's 'justification' (ch. 2). When he describes this law as 'a perfect law, the law of liberty,' James' idea is substantially that of Paul in 1 Co 9^{21} and Ro $8^{2,4}$, viz. that the law of God is no yoke compelling the Christian man from without, but a life actuating him from within; the believer 'bends over it' in contemplation, till he grows one with it (1^{24}; cf 2 Co 3^{18}). 'The tongue' is the index of the heart, and St. James regards its control as a sure sign of perfection in law-keeping (3^{1-12}). James treats of the law, not, like Paul, as it affects the sinner's standing before God—nor, like the author of Hebrews, as it regulates his approach in worship—but as it governs the walk before God of the professed believer. His Epistle is, in effect, a comment on the last clause of Ro 8^4, ' that the righteousness of the law may be fulfilled in us.'

5. The word ' law ' is entirely wanting in the Epistles of St. Peter and of St. John. 1 P $1^{18, 19}$ 2^{24} 3^{18} manifest the influence of Paul's doctrine of salvation on the writer ; while 1 Jn $1^{7, 9}$ indicates a leaning to the mode of representation characteristic of Hebrews, and 1 Jn 2^2 and 4^{10} virtually sustain the doctrine of St. Paul on law, sin, and sacrifice.

6. On Roman law in NT see ROMAN PUBLIC LAW.

G. G. F.—**J. He.**

LAWGIVER.—The word is found six times in the AV of the OT (Gn 49^{10}, Nu 21^{18}, Dt 33^{21}, Ps 60^7 108^8, Is 33^{22}). The Hebrew *m^ehōḳēḳ*, which it translates, is from a root meaning to ' cut ' or ' engrave,' and hence to ' enact ' a law, afterwards to be engraved on the public archives. The Hebrew word appears to have two meanings : (1) ' ruler ' ; so in Dt 33^{21}, where RSV has ' commander ' (RV ' lawgiver ' ; RVm ' ruler '), and Is 33^{22} (RV ' lawgiver ' ; RSV ' ruler '), where the parallelism shows the meaning. (2) ' Ruler's staff ' ; so in Gn 49^{10}, where the word is parallel to ' sceptre ' (RV, RSV ' ruler's staff '), and in Ps 60^7 108^8 (RV, RSV ' sceptre '). In Nu 21^{18}, where AV has ' by the direction of the lawgiver,' RV and RSV have ' with the sceptre.'

In the NT the word ' lawgiver ' (Gr. *nomothetēs*) is found once only (Ja 4^{12}, AV, RV, and RSV) ; there it is applied to God as the ' one lawgiver and judge,' who is regarded as the Supreme Source of all law. Other passages (He 7^{11}, Ro 9^4) where kindred Greek words are used, have a reference to the law of Moses, or, to be more exact, the law of Israel. T. A. M.

LAWYER.—This term in Scripture does not belong so much to the legal as to the religious sphere. It occurs three times in the NT (RSV), Mt 22^{35}, Lk 10^{25}, Tit 3^{13} ; only the last refers, perhaps, to a secular jurisconsult. In Israel, the ' lawyers ' busied themselves with the study and exposition of the Written and the Oral Law of Israel, and were practically identical with the scribes (q.v.).

LAYING ON OF HANDS.—This ceremony, of frequent occurrence in both OT and NT, is a piece of natural symbolism with the central idea that through physical contact the person performing it identifies himself with the other in the presence of God. In OT this is done with a view to the transference (*a*) of a Divine blessing (Gn 48^{14ff} ; cf Nu $27^{18, 23}$, Dt 34^9) ; (*b*) of a burden of guilt (Lv 1^4 $4^{3f. 24}$ 16^{21f} etc.). In NT, while it is variously employed, the general idea is always that of blessing.

1. The simplest case is when Jesus lays hands of *blessing* on the little children (Mt $19^{13, 15}$ ||). The fact that the mothers desired Him to do so shows that this was a custom of the time and people. The narrative in Matthew shows further that, as used by Jesus, it was no magical form, but the symbolic expression of what was essentially an act of prayer (19^{13}).

2. In His deeds of *healing* Jesus constantly made use of this symbol (Mk 6^5 8^{23}, Lk 4^{40} 13^{13} ; cf Mt 9^{18} ||, Mk 7^{32})—an example which was followed by the Apostolic Church (Ac $9^{12, 17}$ 28^8). In these cases, however, besides its religious symbolism, the act may further have expressed the healer's sympathy (cf the hand laid even on the leper, Mk 1^{41}, Lk 5^{13}), or have been designed to bring a reinforcement to faith.

3. In the early Church the imposition of hands was used, sometimes in close association with the act of *baptism* (Ac 9^{17f} 19^{5f} ; cf He 6^2, which, however, may include all the various kinds of laying on of hands), but sometimes quite apart from it (Ac $8^{17, 19}$), as an *accompaniment of prayer* that believers might receive a special endowment of the Holy Spirit in charismatic forms. That this endowment does not mean the essential gift of spiritual life, but some kind of ' manifestation ' (1 Co 12^7), is proved when Ac 9^{17} (' filled with the Holy Spirit ') is compared with Ac 2^4, and when $8^{15, 17}$ is read in the light of the request of Simon Magus (v.^{18ff}), and 19^2 in the light of 19^6. The case of Ananias and Saul (9^{17}) suggests that the laying on of hands for this purpose was not a peculiar Apostolic prerogative.

4. In four passages the laying on of hands is referred to in connexion with an act that corresponds to **ordination.** The Seven, after being chosen by the multitude, were appointed to office by the Apostles, with prayer and the laying on of hands (Ac 6^6). The ' prophets and teachers ' of the Church at Antioch ' set apart ' Barnabas and Saul for their missionary work by laying their hands on them with fasting and prayer (13^3). Timothy received the gracious ' gift ' which was in him with the laying on of the hands of a body of elders (see article PRESBYTERY), with which St. Paul himself was associated (cf 1 Ti 4^{14} with 2 Ti 1^6).

5. Of the *manner* in which deacons, elders, and bishops were set apart to office no information is given in NT. The injunction ' Do not be hasty in the laying on of hands ' (1 Ti 5^{22}), has often been supposed to refer to the act of ordination ; but the fact that the whole passage (vv.$^{19-25}$) deals with offenders points rather to the imposition of hands in the restoration of the penitent (cf 2 Co 2^{6f}, Gal 6^1), a custom that certainly prevailed in the early Church at a later time. The fact, however, that Jewish Rabbis, soon after A.D. 70, employed this rite when a disciple was authorized to teach, favours the view that it was commonly practised in the Apostolic Church, as it was almost universally in the post-Apostolic in consecration to ministerial office. See, further, BISHOP. J. C. L.—**M. H. S.**

LAZARUS.—A common Jewish name, the Greek form of an abbreviation of Eleazar.

1. The brother of Martha and Mary, the friend of Jesus (Jn $11^{3, 11, 36}$, where ' love ' and ' friend ' represent the same root in Greek). The family, according to John, lived at Bethany in Judaea, probably to be identified with *El-ʿAzarîyeh* about two miles SE. of the Mount of Olives, and to be distinguished from the Bethany in Peraea where Jesus was when word came to Him of Lazarus' death (cf 10^{40} 12^8). Lazarus is the subject of the greatest miracle which Jesus performs in John, and the last of His signs (Jn 11^{1-44}). Jesus had retired to Bethany beyond the Jordan when He learned that Lazarus was ' ill ' (11^3). Jesus then stayed two more days in Peraea, probably to indicate that His return to Judaea, where He would be crucified, was not simply by force of the circumstance that Lazarus had died, but entirely by His own will. All His actions, from Cana (cf especially 2^4) to Bethany and Jerusalem, were done not under compulsion but in freedom.

Jesus finally left for Judaea. His disciples reminded Him that He was going to His death (11^8 ; cf v.^{16}) ; but He knew this. His raising of Lazarus could not be done independently of His own death ; in fact the former hinged on the latter. Christ is Himself both the life-giver and the Conqueror of death ; this is the significance of the sign of the raising of Lazarus, and this truth was revealed to those who could ' behold His glory ' during His historical ministry. The life which Christ gives is victory over death, and this victory is validated by His own exaltation and is pointed to by this sign. Jesus goes to Judaea to raise Lazarus and to die. Life is given through death (cf 10^{10f}).

When Jesus arrived in Bethany, Lazarus had been in the tomb four days. From the Jewish point of view this length of time (more than three days) indicated the absolute dissolution of life. By this time the face would not even be recognizable with certainty ; and the soul, which was believed to hover for three days over the body, would have departed. Martha reflects orthodox Pharisaism when she states her faith that Lazarus will be raised ' at the last day ' (v.^{24}) ; but Jesus declares that He is [even now] the resurrection and the life and that believers in Him shall not die (v.^{25}). He is indignant (vv.[33, 38]; RSV 'deeply moved') at the lack of faith in Him expressed by the general weeping; and, having prayed that it might be revealed that He was sent by the Father and could do nothing on His own authority (cf 5[30]), He commands Lazarus to come out. And 'the dead man came out' (v.[44]). The chief priests and Pharisees then considered what they should do with Jesus; and the high priest, Caiaphas, spoke more truth than he knew when he said that it was expedient 'that one man should die for the people' (v.[50]), and he 'prophesied' that Jesus would die 'to gather into one the children of God who are scattered abroad' (v.[52]). Thus the recreation of life seals the death of the life-giver, without which death the new life which is victory over death cannot be offered.

As for the historicity of this sign or miracle, it must be said that the event is not recorded in the Synoptics. It is found only in John. It may be, therefore, that John was using his own tradition which at this point is not reflected in the Synoptics; or that the narrative is related to Lk 16[19-31], and that a miracle story has developed from a parable (cf Mk 11[12-14, 20-23], where such a development may also be reflected). In any case John has edited whatever he had before him in his own theological interests.

Lazarus appears for the last time in ch. 12 where it is said that his presence, alive, led to increased numbers of Jews believing in Jesus; therefore the chief priests planned to have Lazarus executed (12[9-11]).

2. The beggar in our Lord's parable (Lk 16[19-31]).—This parable may be divided into two parts, (1) the first dealing with the respective fortunes of a rich man and a beggar in this life, and their reversal in Hades (vv.[19-26]), (2) the second being a petition from Hades that a sign be given to the living (vv.[27-31]). The first part of the parable is perhaps based on an old Egyptian folk-tale, probably well known in Palestine in the days of Jesus, which ended with the words: 'He who has been good on earth will be blessed in the kingdom of the dead, and he who has been evil on earth will suffer in the kingdom of the dead.' The rich man in Jesus' parable was evil in that he feasted sumptuously while the poor man at his gate went hungry; and although Jesus says nothing about the goodness of the poor man, in the story to which he alludes the poor man is humble and pious. When they die, both go to Hades (q.v.)—a name which describes an intermediate stage to which all go immediately after death. Gehenna, on the other hand, concerns the final state of men. In the intermediate state of Hades, the good and the evil are able to see each other in their very different conditions. The rich man sees Lazarus in Abraham's bosom—at the place of honour; and Lazarus sees the rich man 'in anguish' (v.[25]). Moreover, between them a 'great chasm has been fixed,' in order that there may be no passing from one place to the other.

The second part of the parable, sometimes called an 'epilogue,' contains Jesus' main point. He uses the folk-tale as a device for his message, that no sign shall be given on earth (cf Mk 8[12]). The rich man begs Abraham to send Lazarus to his father's house to warn his family lest they, too, suffer torment in Hades. But Abraham answers that they should listen to 'Moses and the prophets'—they should heed the revelation which has already been given them. So long as they ignore this revelation they will not receive any other. It is claimed by the rich man that if a resurrection should take place his evil family on earth would repent; but Abraham answers that not even a resurrection from the dead would lead Jews to repent who did not listen to Moses and the prophets. Jesus' point is that faithless Jews would not be convinced by any sign, even by a resurrection from the dead. One who will not hear the Word of God will not be converted by a miracle; hence no sign will be given.

It is interesting to compare Jn 11 where Lazarus *is* raised from the dead, but the Jews are only led to plot the death of both Jesus (vv.[45ff]) and Lazarus (12[10]). And the resurrection of the Lord Himself remained unconvincing. B. H. T.

LEAD.—See Mining and Metals.

LEAH.—The elder daughter of Laban, married to Jacob by stratagem, Gn 29[21ff]. Jacob's love for her was less than for Rachel (v.[30]); sometimes she is said to be hated (vv.[31, 33]), but by Hebrew idiom this means 'loved less.' She was the mother of Reuben, Simeon, Levi, Judah, Issachar, Zebulun, and a daughter Dinah (29[31-35] 30[18, 20f]). She was buried in the cave of Machpelah before Jacob went to Egypt (49[31]). She is mentioned in Ru 4[11]. By most her name is connected with an Arabic word, meaning 'wild cow.'

LEASING.—A 'leasing' is a lie, in archaic English. Wycliffe uses the word often. Thus Jn 8[44] 'Whanne he spekith a lesinge, he spekith of his owne thingis; for he is a lyiere, and fadir of it.' The word occurs in AV in Ps 4[2] 5[6] and 2 Es 14[18]. RV retains in 2 Es 14[18], but RSV nowhere uses it, substituting for it 'lies' or 'falsehood.'

LEATHER.—See Arts and Crafts, **5.** On Ezk 16[10] (RSV), see Porpoise.

LEAVEN.—The leaven both of OT and of NT may be assumed to have always consisted of a piece of fermented dough from a previous baking. There is no clear trace, even in the Mishnah, of other sorts of leaven, such as the lees of wine or those enumerated by Pliny (*NH* xviii. 26). In ordinary cases, in the preparation of the household bread, the lump of dough, above referred to, was either broken down into the water in the kneading-trough (see Bread) before the fresh flour was added, or it might be 'hid' in the latter and kneaded along with it, as in the parable, Mt 13[33]. The bread made from dough thus prepared was 'leavened bread' (Ex 12[15] and often); cakes made from flour without the addition of leaven received the special name **mazzoth,** 'unleavened cakes,' which gave their name to 'the feast of unleavened cakes' (Ex 23[15] etc., EV 'unleavened bread').

The prohibition of leavened bread during the continuance of this Feast, including the Passover, is probably another illustration of conservatism in ritual, the nomadic ancestors of the Hebrews, like the Bedouin of the present day, having made their bread without leaven. The further exclusion of leaven from the offerings placed upon the altar of Y″—although admitted when the bread was to be eaten by the priests (Lv 7[13] 23[17])—is to be explained, like the similar exclusion of honey, from the standpoint that fermentation implied a process of corruption in the dough. The antiquity of this prohibition is attested by its occurrence in the earliest legislation (Ex 34[25] 23[18]). It does not seem to have been observed, however, in Amos' day in the Northern Kingdom (see the Comm. on Am 4[5]).

This antique view of leaven as (in Plutarch's words) 'itself the offspring of corruption, and corrupting the mass of dough with which it has been mixed,' is reflected in the figurative use of 'leaven' in such passages as Mt 16[6] ||, and especially in the proverbial saying twice quoted by St. Paul, 'a little leaven ferments the whole lump' (1 Co 5[6], Gal 5[9]; cf 1 Co 5[7f]). In Mt 13[33], however, it is the silent but all-pervading action of leaven in the mass of the dough that is the point of comparison. A. R. S. K.

LEBANA.—The head of a family of returning exiles, Neh 7[48]; called **Lebanah** in Ezr 2[45], 1 Es 5[29] (AV, RV **Labana**).

LEBANAH.—See Lebana.

LEBANON, now *Jebel Libnân*, is mentioned more than sixty times in the OT. The name, from the same root as *lābhān* ('white'), was probably given on account of the mountain's covering of snow. The snow of Lebanon is mentioned in Jer 18[14]. Many passages refer to its beauty, particularly in relation to its cedars and other trees (see Ps 72[16], Ca 4[11], Hos 14[5, 7]). From Lebanon was obtained wood for building the first (2 Ch 2[8]) and the second

(Ezr 3[7]) Temple. Lebanon was famous for its fruitfulness (Ps 72[16]) and its wine (Hos 14[7]).

The term 'Lebanon' may be considered in most places as referring to the whole mountain mass, more correctly distinguished as Lebanon and Anti-Lebanon (**Libanus** and **Antilibanus** of Jth 1[7] [AV, RV]). The two ranges traverse N. Syria, running roughly parallel, from SW. to NE., and are separated by a deep valley—the *biḳʿāh* of Jos 11[17] 12[7]—known to-day as *el-Buqaʿ*. The western range, Lebanon proper, is nearly 100 miles long, but the eastern, if Hermon is deducted as a separate entity, is only 65 miles long. The former range is divided from the mountains of Galilee by the deep chasm made by the *Līṭânī* river in its passage seawards. In the N. a somewhat similar gorge formed by the *Nahr el-Kebîr*, the ancient Eleutherus, divides it from the *Jebel Nusairîyeh*. The summits of the range rise in height from south to north. In the S. a few points attain to almost 7000 feet; in the centre, E. of Beirut, *Jebel Kuneiseh* is 6960 feet, and *Jebel Sannīn* 8554 feet; further N., to the SE. of Tripoli, is a great semicircular group of mountains, sometimes known as the 'Cedar group,' on account of the famous group of these trees in their midst, where the highest point, *Jebel Mukhmal*, reaches 10,207 feet, and several other points are almost as lofty. Geologically the Lebanon is built of three main groups of strata. Lowest comes a thick layer of hard limestone, named—after its most characteristic fossil (*Cidaris glandaria*)—Glandaria limestone; above this are strata of Nubian sandstone, yellow and red in colour, and in places 1500 feet thick, overlaid and interlaced with strata of limestone containing fossil echinoderms and ammonites; and thirdly, above this group, and forming the bulk of the highest peaks, is another layer, many thousand feet thick in places, of a limestone containing countless fossils known as hippurites, radiolites, and such like. The sandstone strata are most important, for where they come to the surface is the richest soil and the most plentiful water, and here flourish most luxuriantly the pines which are such a characteristic feature of W. Lebanon scenery. A great contrast exists between the W. and E. slopes. The former are fertile and picturesque, while down their innumerable valleys course numberless mountain streams to feed the many rivers flowing seawards. The E. slopes are comparatively barren, and, except at one point, near *Zahleh*, there is no stream of importance. Of the Lebanon rivers besides the *Nahr Līṭânī* (Leontes) and the *Nahr el-Kebîr* (Eleutherus), the following may be enumerated from S. to N. as the more important: *Nahr ez-Zaharânī*, *Nahr el-ʿAuwâlī* (Bostrenus), *Nahr Beirūt* (Magoras), *Nahr el-Kelb* (Lycus), *Nahr Ibrahīm* (Adonis), and the *Nahr Qadîsha* or 'holy river,' near Tripoli.

The Lebanon is still fairly well wooded in a few places, though very scantily compared with ancient times, when Hiram, king of Tyre, supplied Solomon with 'cedar trees, fir trees, and algum trees out of Lebanon' (1 K 5[6], 2 Ch 2[8]). In regard to cultivation there has been a very great improvement in recent years, and the terraced lower slopes of the mountain are now covered with mulberry, walnut, and olive trees as well as vines. Many of the views in the Lebanon are of most romantic beauty, and the climate of many parts is superb. Wild animals are certainly scarcer than in olden days. Jackals, gazelles, hyaenas, wolves, bears, and panthers (in order of commonness) are found and, inland from Sidon, the coney (*Hyrax*) abounds.

Between the Lebanon and Anti-Lebanon is the great hollow known to the Greeks as **Coele-Syria**, and to-day called *Buqaʿ el-ʿAzîz*. Considered geologically, this wide valley is a product of the same great 'fault' as produced the deep Jordan valley. It is now a great, fertile, but little cultivated, plain, from 3 to 6 miles wide, and in it rise, not far from Baʿalbek, two famous rivers, the *Līṭânī* (Leontes), which flows S., and the *Nahr el-ʿĀṣī* (Orontes), which flows N., and enters the sea near Antioch. This hollow plain, besides being crossed transversely by the Damascus railway and road, is traversed over more than half its length by the line past Baʿalbek, Homs, and Hamath to Aleppo. Some part of this plain, 'the valley of the Lebanon,' would appear to have been conquered by the Israelites (Jos 11[17]).

The **Anti-Lebanon** is to-day known as *Jebel esh-Sherqi* or 'the east mountain,' the equivalent of 'Lebanon towards the sun-rising' of Jos 13[5]. In Ca 7[4] it is referred to as 'the tower of Lebanon that looketh towards Damascus.' In Dt 1[7] 3[25] 11[24], Jos 1[4] 9[1], the Hebrew 'Lebanon' is in the LXX translated 'Anti-Lebanon.' Anti-Lebanon is somewhat arbitrarily divided from Hermon, which is structurally its S. extremity, by a pass (along which the road runs), and especially by the *Wâdī Baradā*. In the N. it terminates in the plain around Homs. Its highest point is *Tālaʿat Mūsa* (8755 feet), but several other peaks are almost as lofty. A valley, like the *Buqaʿ* in miniature, traverses the S. part of the range from N. to S., and in this rises the *Nahr Yafûfeh*, which empties its water down the *Wâdī Yafûfeh* to join the *Līṭânī*; and the *Nahr Baradā*, which, after rising in a beautiful pool at the SW. extremity of this plain, runs down the *Wâdī Baradā* to Damascus. The N. part of this range is very bare.

Liberated from Turkish rule in World War I, Lebanon, like its neighbour Syria, became an area under French mandate 1920–1941. Foreign troops were withdrawn in 1946 and it is now a republic and member of the United Nations. It has a population of about 1,353,000 (1953 U.N. estimate). Beirut is the chief sea-port. The country is primarily agricultural, producing fruit, tobacco, olive oil, silk, and cotton.

E. W. G. M.—**E. G. K.**

LEBAOTH.—See Beth-lebaoth.

LEBBAEUS.—See Thaddaeus.

LEB-KAMAI.—Found in Jer 51[1] (RV); AV translates 'in the midst of them that run up against me' (so RVm). The expression is recognized as being an example of the Kabbalistic rule of hermeneutics whereby a cipher word was obtained by taking the letters of the alphabet in the reverse order, the last for the first, the last but one for the second, and so on. By this process (known as Atbash), *leb-ḳamai* gives us *Kasdim*='the Chaldaeans' (RSV 'Chaldaea').

LEBO-HAMATH.—See Hamath.

LEBONAH.—A place near Shiloh on the way to Shechem, Jg 21[19]. It is probably modern *Lubbân*. about three miles WNW. of *Seilûn* (Shiloh).

LECAH.—The 'son' of Er, 1 Ch 4[21].

LEECH (*ʿalûḳāh*, cf Arab. *ʿalaqeh*).—The horse-leech (*haemopis sanguisuga*) and the medicinal leech (*Hirudo medicinalis*) are very common in Palestine, and are the cause of much trouble, even sickness and death, to man and beast. They abound in many springs, streams, and pools, and lodge themselves, while still small, in the mouths of those drinking. Thence they not infrequently find their way to the pharynx, and even larynx, where they live and grow for many months. They cause frequent haemorrhages and, if not removed, lead to progressive anaemia and death. Their voracious appetite for blood, possibly referred to in Pr 30[15] (RSV 'leech'; AV and RV '**horseleach**'), is well illustrated by their habits as internal parasites. It is probable, however, that the reference here is not to the leech of common life, but to the mythological **vampire** (cf RVm) the *ghûl* of the Arabs. E. W. G. M.

LEEKS.—The Hebrew word *ḥāṣîr*, which is elsewhere translated 'grass' or 'herb,' is rendered 'leeks' in Nu 11[5], and in this passage, owing to the association with onions and garlic, the translation is probably correct, leeks being *the* herb *par excellence*. The leek (*Allium porrum*) is much grown in Palestine, where it is a general favourite. E. W. G. M.

LEES.—The sediment which settled at the bottom of the wine-jars, composed of morsels of husks, stalks, etc.; in OT only in figures. See Wine and Strong Drink, 3.

LEG.—**1.** Hebrew *kᵉrāʿayim*, a feminine dual, in which form alone it appears (Ex 12[9] etc.). It denotes the legs from knee to ankle. **2.** Hebrew *reghel* (1 S 17[6]), literally 'foot.' **3.** Hebrew *shôḳ*, the leg, apparently including the thigh, for which it stands in Ex 29[22, 27], Lv 7[32ff] 8[25f] 9[21] 10[14f], Nu 6[20] 18[18], 1 S 9[24], in all of which AV has 'shoulder,' but RV and RSV, correctly, **thigh** (save 1 S 9[24], where RSV has 'leg'). In Ps 147[10] 'the legs of a man' may possibly mean 'foot soldiers.' The proverbial phrase 'hip and thigh' is literally 'thigh upon hip' (Jg 15[8]), descriptive of the confusion of severed limbs. **4.** Hebrew *shōbhel* (Is 47[2]; AV 'make bare the leg') means 'the flowing skirt' (RV 'strip off the train,' RSV 'strip off your robe'). **5.** Greek *skelos* (Jn 19[31ff]). To hasten the death of the crucified, it was customary to break their legs.

LEGION.—This term, which means literally 'a gathering,' looks back to the early days of the Roman citizen army. In the time of the Empire it indicated a force of about 6000 infantry, together with complements of other arms. In NT times the Roman Empire maintained twenty-five legions, four of which were stationed in Syria. Provincials supplemented their ranks, as auxiliaries. The infantry proper were divided into ten **cohorts** (the word is translated '**band**' [q.v.] in Mt 27[27], Mk 15[16], Jn 18[3, 12], Ac 10[1] 21[31] 27[1], in AV and RV, but variously in RSV), each containing about 600 men, and each commanded on occasion by a military tribune. Of these tribunes there were six to a legion. A cohort was itself subdivided into six centuries, each commanded by a **centurion**. It is not necessary to remember all these facts in studying the NT use of the word 'legion' (Mt 26[53], Mk 5[9, 15], Lk 8[30]). What chiefly impressed Semites was apparently the size of the legion, and 'legion' appears to have become a proverb among them for a large number of persons in orderly combination. A. So.—**J. C. B.**

LEHABIM.—Occurs only Gn 10[13], 1 Ch 1[11] amongst the 'descendants' of Egypt (Mizraim). They are commonly identified with the *Lubim* or **Libyans** (q.v.), whether the word is an alternative traditional pronunciation of the name of this people, or whether, as is more probable, the form here given is due to textual corruption. The fact that *Lubim* or **Libyans** is a fairly common word, and that it is not found in the ethnological list of Gn 10, where it would naturally appear in the place of Lehabim, adds something to the evidence of identity. Some have thought *Ludim* in the same verse is another variant; but this is improbable. See Lud, Ludim, **2.** J. F. McC.—**H. H. R.**

LEHEM.—See Jashubi-lehem.

LEHI ('jawbone').—The scene of Samson's well-known adventure with the jawbone of an ass, Jg 15[9, 14, 19] (cf 2 S 23[11]). The site is unknown.

LEMUEL.—The name of a king, otherwise unknown, to whom Pr 31[1-9] is addressed by his mother. His identity has been much discussed; he has been identified by the Rabbinical commentators with Solomon, and by Grotius with Hezekiah. Cf also **Massa.** It is possible that the name is a fanciful title to represent any virtuous king, invented for the purpose of conveying certain maxims. T. A. M.

LENDING.—See Debt.

LENTILS.—Hebrew *ʿᵃdhāshîm*, Gn 25[34], 2 S 17[28] 23[11], Ezk 4[9]. These are without doubt the Arabic *ʿadas*—a kind of small reddish bean, the product of *Ervum lens*, a small leguminous plant 6 or 8 inches high, much cultivated in Palestine, and ripening in June or July. It is the bean from which the well-known *revalenta*, a food for invalids, is made. In Palestine a kind of 'pottage' known as *mujedderah*, universally popular, is made from it. It is of a reddish-brown colour, and is certainly the original '**red pottage**' of Esau (Gn 25[30]). E. W. G. M.

LEOPARD (*nāmēr*).—This animal (*Felis pardus*, Arab. *nimr*) is still found at times in the wilder parts of Palestine. Its beautiful spotted skin (Jer 13[23]) is from time to time brought into the towns for sale. Some dervishes clothe themselves in a leopard's skin. Its fierceness (Hos 13[7]), its agility (Hab 1[8]) and untameableness (Is 11[6]) are all mentioned. The name *Nimr* is a favourite one with the Arabs, who admire these qualities. In the names 'waters of *Nimrîm*' ('leopards,' Is 15[6], Jer 48[34]) and 'Beth-*nimrāh*' (female leopard, Nu 32[32, 36]) references to the leopard also occur; cf the 'mountains of *nᵉmērîm*' (*i.e.* 'the leopards' Ca 4[8]). The cheetah (*Felix jubata*) is found also in Galilee, and it too may have been included under the Hebrew word *nᵉmērîm*. E. W. G. M.

LEPROSY.—The Hebrew *ṣirʿāh* and *ṣāraʿath* 'prostration' are general terms for any prostrating experience or disabling disease (cf Arab. *ṣaraʿa* 'prostrated,' *ṣaruʿa* 'was prostrated by epilepsy' and *dariʿa* 'submitted oneself; was feeble, weak').

I. The former, incorrectly translated 'hornet' (LXX, Vulgate), which cannot be philologically justified, means rather 'demoralization' (Koehler; cf Saʿadya and 'Abu-Saʿîd), such as seems to have broken down Canaanite resistance before (cf Job 41[14]) the advancing Hebrews (Ex 23[28], Dt 7[20], Jos 24[12]); so the Assyrian writer of a letter to king Ashurbanipal says that the gods 'have caused fear to enter like a plague before the troops of my lord, king of kings' (Harper, *Assyrian and Babylonian Letters*, V. 460, O. 8–10).

II. The latter, commonly but incorrectly translated 'leprosy,' is the name given to several affections of the skin, the *leichēnes kai leprai kai leukai*, of which Greek physicians considered the last to be the most deadly (Hippocrates, *Prorrhesis* ii. 43); but it cannot be definitely identified.

A. The rules describing the various affections of the skin subsumed under *ṣāraʿath* are by no means clear; for the ancient priest had no scientific knowledge and no vocabulary adequate to describe what he was diagnosing. This difficulty long persisted, and subsequent laws added that a skilled layman should assist the priest in his examination, although the priest made the actual declaration of cleanness or uncleanness (Mishnah, *Negaim* ii. 5, iii. 1; cf *Zadokite Documents* xv. 7). Even when the lazar-houses in England and France were suppressed, as leprosy was dying out, many persons suffering from non-leprous diseases were found in them. The relative incidence of diseases, too, changes over the years; what in one period or in one society is trivial may be serious, even fatal, at another time or in another society. The clinical pattern of a specific disease may also vary considerably, depending on such factors as the virulence of the causal factor, the natural (racial or individual) immunity of the patient, and so on.

B. In the first group of affections discussed under *ṣāraʿath* the terms used are *śᵉʾēth* 'discoloured blotch, scar' [not 'swelling'] (LXX 'scar' and Vulgate *diversus color*; cognate Arab. *šiʾatu, šiyatu* 'colour, mark'), and *sappaḥath* 'scab' (LXX 'mark, scab,' Vulgate *pustula, erumpentes papulae*; Ass. *sapāḫu* 'to strew, sprinkle' perhaps cognate with the Hebrew term) and *bahereth* 'bright patch' (LXX 'conspicuous whiteness,' Symmachus 'efflorescence,' Vulgate 'shining patch, whiteness; scar'; cognate Heb. *bāhar* 'gleamed').

If a man develops any of these symptoms on his skin 'and it will become a lesion of *ṣāraʿath*,' *i.e.* if it looks like becoming *ṣāraʿath*; he must show it to the priest. If the lesion is subcutaneous and the hairs in it have turned white, it is a 'lesion of *ṣāraʿath*' and the patient is unclean. If it is a white 'bright patch' and the lesion appears to be superficial and the hairs are not affected, the patient is confined for seven days and, if necessary, another seven days for observation. By then, if the lesion has remained localized and is fading, it is simple 'scabbing' (*mispaḥath*); the patient must wash his clothes and is declared clean. If however the scabbing spreads, it is *ṣāraʿath* and the man is pronounced unclean (Lv 13[2-8]).

Any lesion in the skin, if it is deep-seated and tends to spread and the hairs turn white, is *ṣāraʿath* and therefore unclean; if it is superficial, remains localized and does not affect the hairs, and it starts to fade within fourteen days, it is not unclean. These seem to be general rules by which the diagnosis of unclean and clean lesions may be made; no specific diagnosis is possible here on the evidence.

1. If the priest examining the sufferer who has a 'lesion of *ṣāraʿath*' finds a 'white blotch' in which the hairs have turned white and 'raw flesh,' *i.e.* ulceration, appears, the condition is 'chronic *ṣāraʿath*' and does not call for diagnostic confinement (13^{9-11}); he is *ipso facto* unclean. This shows that *ṣāraʿath* with ulceration is a long-standing condition.

If the *ṣāraʿath* spreads all over the patient's body and the lesion has 'all turned white,' he is clean. If, however, 'raw flesh' appears, it is *ṣāraʿath* and unclean; but, if the 'raw flesh' heals and the rash becomes white, it is again regarded as clean (13^{12-17}).

That 'the lesion has all turned white' seems to imply healing by desquamation, in which the diseased superficial layer of skin flakes off, revealing fresh white skin underneath. If then a generalized eruption heals by desquamation, it is considered clean; but if, instead of healing, a secondary infection with ulceration occurs, it is unclean and remains so until the skin again becomes clear. For example, generalized *eczema* may heal by desquamation, leaving a clear white skin; but secondary infection may prevent healing and produce ulceration, which, too, may eventually heal by desquamation.

2. (*a*) If a healed ulcer (*shᵉḥîn*) develops a white 'blotch' or a reddish-white 'bright patch,' and the examining priest discovers a 'low,' *i.e.* deep-seated (*shāphāl*) lesion with whitened hairs, it is a lesion of *ṣāraʿath* and unclean. If he finds no white hairs and the lesion seems superficial and fading, the patient is put into diagnostic confinement for seven days; if the lesion spreads, it is a 'lesion of [*ṣāraʿath*]' (as read by the LXX and one Hebrew MS) and unclean; but, if it remains localized, it is merely the scar of the ulcer and clean (13^{18-23}).

Discoloration at the site of a healing ulcer may be associated locally with induration and atrophy of the hair or it may tend to spread; such a condition is regarded as unclean. If, however, the discoloration is superficial and after seven days it is still localized and fading, it is clean. The reference apparently is to an open lesion, an ulcer or a sore, of the skin; if there is a local inflammatory reaction causing induration at the base of the ulcer or one spreading in the skin (*cellulitis*), it is unclean; if there is no obvious inflammation and a tendency to heal, it is clean.

(*b*) When the same discolorations occur at the site of a burn and examination reveals a subcutaneous lesion in which the hairs have turned white, it is a 'lesion of *ṣāraʿath*' and unclean. If there are no white hairs and the lesion is superficial and fading, the patient is confined for seven days for examination; if it has spread, it is *ṣāraʿath* and unclean; if it has remained localized and continues to fade, it is simply the scar of the burn and clean (13^{24-28}).

If in a case of discoloration round a burn there is local induration with atrophy of the hair or if the discoloration tends to spread in the skin, it is unclean; but, if it is superficial and fading and after seven days is still localized and fading, it is clean. The inflammatory changes in view are presumably due to an infection at the site of the burn.

3. If white 'bright patches' which are dull or fading appear on the skin of a man or woman, this is *bōhaḳ* and clean (13^{38}).

This disease is *vitilligo* (*alba*) for which *alphos* 'dull white leprosy' (Liddell and Scott) is used by the LXX, and which (like *leucoderma*) is still called *bahaqu* by the Arabs. It is very common in tropical and subtropical countries. It begins insidiously as a small depigmentated spot without raw flesh; these spots spread and coalesce and the hair may go white. No other symptoms appear, and the sufferer's health is unimpaired, but recovery, except from a single patch at an early stage, is very unlikely; and it is not contagious. The introduction of *bōhaḳ* between two sections dealing with baldness (13^{29-37} and 13^{40-44}) suggest a displaced note from a different set of rules.

4. (*a*) If a man or woman develops a lesion in the scalp or under the beard which is subcutaneous and in which thin 'yellow' (*ṣāhôbh*) hairs appear, it is 'scurf' (*netheḳ*), classified as *ṣāraʿath* and therefore unclean.

If the lesion is superficial and 'yellowish' (LXX, 'Abū Saʿîd; Hebrew 'black') hairs appear, the patient is kept for seven days in diagnostic confinement. Then, if the affection has not spread and it shows no 'yellow' hairs and remains superficial, the hair round the affected area should be shaved off and the patient confined for another seven days. If the scurf is then still localized and superficial, he is pronounced clean and must wash his clothes; if the scurf subsequently spreads, it is unclean but, if it remains localized and black hairs appear in it, it is healed and declared clean (13^{29-37}).

A lesion of the hairy skin, if it is deep-seated and causes the hair to become thin and faded or tends to spread, is unclean; if it is superficial and does not injure the hair and does not spread during fourteen days of close observation, aided by shaving the surrounding hair, it is clean; when fresh hair grows again, it is regarded as healed.

No specific disease seems to be described, although many attack the hairy skin; the commonest are fungal (such as *tinea barbae*), others bacterial (such as *impetigo* and *sycosis barbae*) infections. The fungal infections usually produce superficial and circumscribed patches of scaly skin, in which the hairs are relatively light in colour and brittle and break off short; the condition may spread locally and, if complicated by acute inflammation, develop deep-seated lesions full of pus. The bacterial infections are superficial (*impetigo*) or deep-seated (*sycosis barbae*); they have little effect on the hair but have a great tendency to spread and suppurate (*i.e.* to ulcerate and produce pus).

Other disorders are *psoriasis* and *dermatitis seborrhoeica*. The former is an indolent condition characterized by patches of white scales; it does not affect the hair but sometimes spreads widely. The latter consists in a greasy scalp producing white powdery scales (*seborrhoea*, dandruff); for unknown reasons it may flare up, when the scalp becomes red and swollen and oozes serum which forms crusts and mats the hair.

In their simplest form these conditions are classified as 'scurf' (*netheḳ*; cf Heb. *nāthaḳ* 'pulled off, tore away' and Arab. *nataqa* 'pulled skin from the body'), *i.e.* desquamation of the skin, to which the *exuviae* of the hair-follicles are added; in complicated forms they may suppurate and injure the hair or spread, when they are classified as *ṣāraʿath* and unclean. These disorders may persist as simple lesions for long periods of time, they are liable to become complicated and are therefore potentially unclean.

The reference to hair turning yellow raises a difficulty; for no known pathological process can be equated with it, and the LXX's 'black' ought to be accepted for MT's 'yellow.' Diseased hair usually fades and becomes grey; but reddish hair may appear in malnutrition.

(*b*) When the hair falls out of a man's temples or head and no other symptoms appear, the condition is clean; but, if the baldness is accompanied by reddish-white 'discoloration' like that in *ṣāraʿath* elsewhere on the body, it is *ṣāraʿath* and unclean (13^{40-44}).

The text does not show whether the 'reddish-white lesion' is supposed to appear on an already bald scalp or if it is associated with the development of baldness. In the former case, it may be identified with the unclean eruptions of *ṣāraʿath* elsewhere on the body. In the latter several diagnoses are possible; the most probable diseases are fungal infections such as *syphilis*, seborrhoeic *dermatitis*, chronic *lupus erythematosus* and so on.

Leprosy only very seldom, and *psoriasis* never, produces baldness of the scalp.

C. Clearly *ṣāraʿath* has no specific aetiological or morphological meaning in relation to human disease, but its general import is clear. It is applied to a number of eruptions, single or multiple, on the hairy and the hairless skin. The eruptions in the Bible fall into two classes according as they are regarded by the Hebrew writer as benign or malignant. The former, in which the lesion is local, superficial and fading or faint, are not called *ṣāraʿath*; the latter, which are subcutaneous or deep-seated, spreading or chronic, and in which ulceration may occur and the hair lose its colour, are *ṣāraʿath* and unclean. The purpose of the lawgiver is simply to lay down sufficient rules regarding *ṣāraʿath* 'to teach when it is unclean and when it is clean' (Lv 14[57]), *i.e.* to guide the priest in the important practical problem of separating unclean from clean diseases of the skin, the benign from the malignant or potentially dangerous. Regarded in this way the rules make good sense; but, if they are regarded as a guide to precise diagnoses of specific dermatological conditions, they are totally inadequate on modern medical standards.

III. (*a*) True leprosy, not mentioned in these rules, is described in an Egyptian text *c* 1500 B.C. and is therefore likely to have been known to the Jews; it is sometimes called the 'Phoenician disease' (Hippocrates *l.c.*; cf Kuhn, *Medicorum Graecorum Opera*, xix, 152, when Galen so explains this term), and it is reported to be still common amongst Eastern Jews and some Moslems. It is of two kinds, lepromatous and non-lepromatous. The latter may heal itself. The characteristic lesion of the former is an ill-defined nodule infiltrating deep into the skin; these nodules commonly occur on the face or ears, fingers or buttocks. When they develop on the face (especially the forehead), the hair and eye-brows are lost, the skin becomes thickened (hence called *elephantiasis*) and the face acquires a 'cobble-stoned' or 'leonine' appearance (hence called *leontiasis*). If untreated, they tend to ulcerate, certain nerves become involved, sensation is lost, and the patient may injure himself; this ulceration may reach the bone, which then dies and sloughs off, so that the fingers become shortened, giving the appearance of having dropped off. Also, when nerves supplying the muscles are attacked, paralysis causing contractures may ensue. Lips, tongue, and throat may be so ulcerated that the sufferer dies of malnutrition and exhaustion. In maculo-anaesthetic and tuberculoid leprosy, in which the tissues have the upper hand, the patches are much more clearly defined. The surface of the skin is dry and scaly, and anaesthesia is an early sign, showing that the nerves are involved; these become rigid and thick, and the limbs which they supply are insensitive or paralysed, becoming wasted and susceptible to injury; in such cases proper treatment must be promptly applied if deformity is to be prevented, arrested or alleviated. Otherwise the long-continued effects of this wasting produce the grotesquely deformed extremities which are characteristic of the last stages of severe leprosy. The distinction between all these forms of leprosy is clear; but intermediate forms occur where both lepromatory and tuberculoid elements appear. As in tuberculosis, so in leprosy there is a great tendency to spontaneous healing in the less severe forms of the disease; but, once the more severe lepromatous form develops, it goes on its relentless course if untreated, however slowly, and sufferers may live for many years. Modern treatment, however, is highly successful in staying the ravages of this disease.

The descriptions of the two leprosies show that *ṣāraʿath* 'prostration,' may once have designated or included these diseases; for the normal termination of both may be emaciation and exhaustion, often accompanied by complications. The term will then have been extended to other affections of the skin which resemble true leprosy or which may accompany it. Several such affections begin with depigmentation or discoloration of the skin; their lesions are subcutaneous; the conditions are more or less persistent and incurable; some are mildly contagious; most, if not all, follow or are caused by emotional disturbance. Thus the true leprosies and the other affections classified as *ṣāraʿath* have so many similar symptoms that they may easily have been confused at certain stages by a priest without modern knowledge. In any case, if the lesser disorders brought under the heading of *ṣāraʿath* could have been confused by such a priest and condemned as unclean, the greater disease (namely true leprosy) would also have been unclean in his eyes.

(*b*) Whether true leprosy can be found in the Bible is a difficult question, although 'leprosy' appears in the translations at several places.

Moses on God's instruction put his hand into his bosom and, when he withdrew it, it was 'leprous (*m*ᵉ*ṣōraʿath*) white as snow' and when, after putting it back, he again withdrew it, it became like the rest of his flesh (Ex 4[6–7]). This evanescent attack was no ordinary case but a miracle and cannot be otherwise explained. When Miriam was punished by being made 'leprous white as snow,' Aaron prayed that she might not be 'as one dead, of whom the flesh is half-consumed when he cometh out of his mother's womb'; then, when Moses interceded with God, he was ordered to confine her for seven days, after which she was re-admitted to the camp, apparently cured (Nu 12[10–15]). This case too is miraculous but can be roughly explained. At first sight *eczema* is suggested by the acute onset of an apparently generalized eruption; but *eczema* with its red lesions is ruled out by the description of those in the story as 'white as snow,' and a related condition, *dermatitis exfoliativa*, may be meant. In mild forms of this disorder the superficial layers of the skin may flake or peel off; secondary infection may turn it into a dangerous disease which may destroy the skin (gross destruction of tissue). Aaron might then have hoped that Miriam would not become like a macerated foetus (*i.e.* one which had been dead in the womb for some time before delivery). His fear precludes true leprosy, which cannot be inherited or contracted by an unborn child in the womb. The case of Naaman is interesting because it describes a strong and healthy man as 'leprous' (*ṣārûaʿ*). On consulting Elisha he was bidden to bathe himself seven times in the Jordan, whereupon 'he turned and went away in a rage'; he did, however, on the persuasion of his attendants, return, whereupon 'his flesh came again like the flesh of a little child and he was clean' (2 K 5[1–14]). Here the disorder is one of those not accompanied by any systemic upset of which *psoriasis* is the commonest. This, or *leucoderma*, is suggested also by the whitening of the skin, which is never found in true leprosy. King Azariah or Uzziah went into the sanctuary to offer incense in spite of the protests of the priests and while he was angrily arguing with them *ṣāraʿath* broke out on his forehead; the priests immediately shunned him and he was forced to live 'in his own house, relieved of duties,' and the disorder afflicted him for the rest of his life (2 K 15[5] = 2 Ch 26[19–21]). Not improbably the king already had *ṣāraʿath* when he entered the sanctuary; but when he flew into a rage, his forehead became congested and the disease became obvious. That it started on the forehead suggests true leprosy; but this is by no means specific for that condition. Alternatively *lupus erythematosus*, which may start on the forehead, must be considered. Job's malady, which is nowhere called *ṣāraʿath* and of which the symptoms are variously described (Job 2[7–8]; cf 2[12] 3[25] 6[4] 7[5, 14f] 19[17] 30[17, 30]), has been identified with leprosy (Dillmann), possibly tuberculoid leprosy (Duhm); but this is most unlikely, as leprosy is not accompanied by itching. Only an intractable scabies, such as 'Norwegian scabies,' in an advanced or chronic state fits the description of Job's disease; in this the scratching is so intense that the skin is broken down, secondary infection sets in, and severe *dermatitis* with ulcers and scabs complicates the condition. Such ulcers, if large enough, would be infected with maggots, pains and terrors at night with feelings of strangulation would accompany the disease, and the ceaseless throbbing of the veins would refer to the sufferer's general condition produced by the constant irritation of an advanced scabitic condition. The *ṣāraʿath* afflicting the four lepers at the gate of Samaria (2 K 7[3-10]) and the malady of the 'lepers' mentioned in several passages of the NT (Mt 8[2], Mk 1[4]3, Lk 17[12]) are not described and therefore cannot be identified; but the 'lepers' of the NT cannot have had true leprosy, as the Greek word does not designate that disease.

(*c*) Many of the disorders of the skin here described (notably *dermatitis, eczema, leucoderma, psoriasis, vitilligo, lepra nervorum*) are caused by nerve-impulses and are due to or accompany emotional disturbances; and people who suffer from them are said commonly to have intelligence above the average. This connexion explains the stories of the sudden infliction of 'leprosy' as a divine punishment (Miriam; cf Herodotus, *Histories* i. 138) and as accompanied by outbursts of rage when caused (Azariah) or cured (Naaman), as also of its equally sudden cure (Miriam) and its response to faith-healing methods (Naaman; cf Mt 8[2-4], Lk 17[12-19]).

(*d*) The lawgiver does not refer in detail to true leprosy, being concerned with the recognition of certain states resembling or portending this disease. The seven days' confinement, therefore, is not a period of isolation or quarantine to check contagion, although the Babylonians understood the principle of isolation (Finet, in the *Annuaire de l'Institut de Philologie et d'Histoire Orientales et Slaves* xiv, 127–129), but a postponement to enable the priest to watch its progress, even if far too short, since leprosy may take from five to fifteen years to declare itself. The period, however, can be repeated (13[5]), presumably as often as necessary if the diagnosis is uncertain; even so, its shortness effectively precludes true leprosy. Only when the disease is clearly identified is the sufferer banished from human society (13[45-46]). The reason for this exclusion is certainly not fear of contagion; for the text says nothing of such a risk, the disease is treated as non-infectious in the Talmud, and it is in fact contagious only in certain circumstances, while many authorities consider that children are more susceptible to it than adults. The real reason is undoubtedly religious or ceremonial, as the expulsion of all 'lepers' from the holy camp in the wilderness is joined with that of others suffering from sexual pollution and contact with a corpse shows (Nu 5[2-4]). Nothing unseemly or impure may approach what is holy. So the Hebrews normally spoke of cleansing 'lepers' as though ceremonially or morally unclean, and the cure of 'leprosy' is described as healing only twice in the Bible (Lv 14[3], Lk 17[15]); it was thought as often as not to be a punishment for sin and so needed to be cleansed, and it was considered incurable except by Divine intervention (2 K 5[7]; cf Mt 8[2-4], Lk 17[12-19]).

IV. The scaly nature of many affections of the skin explains what is meant by *ṣāraʿath* in garments of linen or wool, on stone or in wood. The former is probably a fungus, mildew or mould, such as is likely to grow on garments worn for a long time in a hot climate unwashed, as they often are in the East, whether due to a specific parasite or not. If after a week's seclusion the spot spreads, the garment must be destroyed. If it has not spread, the garment must be washed and then secluded for another week; it must then be burnt if the spot is unchanged but must be washed and then may be used again if the spot, which must be torn out and burnt, is fading (Lv 13[47-59]). When reddish or greenish depressed patches appear on an inner wall, the house must be emptied and shut up for seven days. If the patches spread, the stone must be taken out and cast in an unclean place and the plaster scraped; if they do not return, the house may be reused but, if they do return, it must be destroyed (Lv 14[34-48]). What is meant is 'the formation of a flocculent mass of calcium nitrate, such as often takes place when the gases set free from decaying animal matter act on the lime of plaster and is sometimes called mural salt. This, with an accompaniment of mould or other hypomycetous fungus, produces an appearance like that described' (Macalister). The fungus, too, of dry rot eats into the woodwork, and sheets of felt-like texture with a greenish-yellow or red surface, half an inch or so thick, are formed between the lath and the plaster, especially in damp structures shut off from the circulation of the air (Creighton). So the Assyrian *sâmānu* 'redness' denotes both a disease of the head, apparently 'ringworm,' and *sal murale* which was prescribed as a drug for itch (Thompson, *Dictionary of Assyrian Chemistry and Geology*, 6–12) and the Arabic *bahaqu* 'leucoderma' means also 'lichen.'

G. R. D. with the help of R. G. C. and H. Go.

LESHEM.—A form, occurring only in Jos 19[47bis], of the name **Laish** (see DAN).

LESSAU, 2 Mac 14[16] (RV).—See DESSAU.

LET.—In Anglo-Saxon *laetan* meant 'to permit' and *lettan* 'to hinder.' In course of time both words were spelled 'let.' Consequently, in AV, besides its modern meaning of 'permit' the verb 'let' sometimes has the opposite meaning of 'hinder.' So in 2 Th 2[7] (RV, RSV 'restrain'). The other places are Ex 5[4] (RV 'loose,' RSV 'take away'), Nu 22[16] (AVm; RV, RSV 'hinder'), Is 43[13] (RV 'let,' RVm 'reverse,' RSV 'hinder'), Wis 7[22] (RV 'unhindered,' RSV 'invulnerable'), Ro 1[13] (RV 'hinder,' RSV 'prevent').

LETHECH, LETHEK.—See WEIGHTS AND MEASURES.

LETTER.—See WRITING.

LETTUS, 1 Es 8[29] (AV).—See HATTUSH, **2.**

LETUSHIM.—One of the Dedanite tribes in N. Arabia (Gn 25[3]), the others being **Leummim** and **Asshurim** (q.v.). In this verse LXX adds two other tribes; but in the parallel passage, 1 Ch 1[32], the sons of Dedan are omitted altogether both in MT and in most MSS of LXX. None of the three tribes has been identified.

J. F. McC.

LEUMMIM.—A tribe of Dedanites, Gn 25[3]. See LETUSHIM.

LEVI.—**1.** The third son of Jacob (Gn 29[34]). The meaning and origin of the name are unknown. The form is a gentilic noun, and in the story of Levi's birth a popular etymology connected it with the root *lwh*, 'to be joined.' A similar play upon this root occurs in the Priestly account in Nu 18[2, 4]: 'Bring your brethren also, the tribe of Levi . . . that they may *join* you. . . .'

2. The eponymous ancestor of one of the tribes of Israel. According to the Blessing of Jacob (Gn 49[5-7]): 'Simeon and Levi are brothers; Weapons of violence are their swords. . . .' This is a reflection of the story in Gn 34 in which Simeon and Levi took revenge on Shechem son of Hamor for the seduction of their sister. The story is probably a personalized account of ancient tribal history in which these two secular tribes had violated an alliance with the Shechemites in a particularly violent manner. The Blessing of Jacob reflects the lack of sympathy of the other tribes for their kinsmen's unnatural act.

3. An Israelite tribe (Dt 18[1] etc.), priestly in character. How the ancient secular tribe became a priestly one is completely unknown. As a priestly tribe they had no separate territory but were scattered throughout Israel. This may have been concerned in the episode related under **2** above (cf Gn 49[7]). For Levi as a priestly tribe see PRIESTS AND LEVITES and TRIBES OF ISRAEL.

4. Another name for the apostle **Matthew** (q.v.).

5. Two ancestors of Jesus, one the son of Melchi (Lk 3[24]), and the other the son of Symeon (vv.[29f]).

6. 1 Es 9[14]; see LEVIS. J. A. C.—**J. W. W.**

LEVIATHAN.—The Hebrew *liwyāthān*, variously translated in the oldest versions *drakōn* (LXX, Theodotion) and *mega kētos* (LXX), when not transliterated, or *draco* and *leviathan* (Vulgate), comes from the $\sqrt{}$*LWY* 'coiled, twisted, wreathed' (cf Akkadian *lawû* 'to surround,' *limîtu* 'circuit' and *la'ûtānu* 'escort,' Hebrew *liwyāh* 'chaplet,' Arabic *talawwa* 'coiled itself up' and *liyatu* 'snake'); and this root determines its meaning. I. When it is described as 'a slippery serpent, a writhing serpent' (Is 27[1]), and as having many heads (Ps 74[14]), as it also is in a text from Ugarit (see Râs Shamra), where its heads are said to be seven (B I* i. 1–3, 28–30), only a serpent, albeit a mythical one like the Lernaean hydra of Greek mythology, can be meant. II. Leviathan 'which thou didst form to sport in it,' *sc.* the sea, or as it has been (by Eissfeldt) rendered, 'whom Thou hast made to joust with him,' *sc.* the sea-monster (Ps 104[25–26]) is probably not a serpent but a dolphin or whale; for the whale, as the name suggests, lives in the sea, is notably gregarious and continues to accompany its young even when grown up. It is also probably the dolphin or whale in the famous poem (Job 41[1–8]) in which God asks Job whether he can catch him with a hook in his nose or barbs in his skin, play with him as a bird, whether it begs itself off when captured with an almost human voice or enters the service of man (as the dolphin does according to Pliny) or whether fishermen take shares in him (as the tunny-fishers do in the tunnies which they take). Lastly, the most potent binders of spells are those who can call up Leviathan, *i.e.* the whale, or other sea-monster (as the word must be read) to do their bidding (Job 3[8]; AV 'their mourning,' instead of Leviathan, goes back to the Targum through rabbinical sources). The Apocalyptic and Rabbinic writers gave full scope to their imagination in describing this and other mythical or semi-mythical monsters (see Behemoth): Leviathan was created with Behemoth on the fifth day, and the depths of the sea were assigned to him as his abode; God plays with him during the last quarter of each day; the Jordan empties itself into his mouth; his flesh will be food for the righteous at the Messianic banquet; part of his skin will be made into a tent for them and the rest will be spread on the walls of Jerusalem while its brightness will be visible to the ends of the earth (1 En 60[7–9], 2 Es 6[49], Apoc. Bar 29[4]; B. Talmud, *Aboda Zara*, 3b, and *Baba Bathra*, 74b–75b; Targum on Ca 8[2] and Est 2[37]). J. T.—**G. R. D.**

LEVIS (AV, RV; RSV '**Levi**').—This is taken in 1 Es 9[14] as a proper name; in Ezr 10[15] 'Shabbethai the Levite' stands in place of 'Levis and Sabbateus.'

LEVITES.—See Levi, and Priests and Levites.

LEVITICAL CITIES.—See Priests and Levites.

LEVITICUS.—The third book of the *Torah*, the first division of the Hebrew canon. Its title is derived from the name 'the Levitical book,' which was prefixed to it in the LXX, despite the fact that it nowhere refers to the special functions of the Levites. The title given to it in the Talmud, 'Law of the priests,' better indicates its scope, for it consists almost entirely of legislation; and the purpose of such narrative as it contains (8[1]–10[7]) is less to describe what once happened than to prescribe what is to be done in the future. Moreover, the legislation, except for that in chs. 18–20, 22 f, 25, has to do with the priesthood, the one living institution which persisted in Israel from its formation as a nation until the destruction of the Temple. It persisted because the praxis which regulated its services received the constant modification it required to meet the nation's changing circumstances. The unification of the diverse customs of different sanctuaries to form the code of the post-exilic Temple in Jerusalem—the process which is reflected in Leviticus—was an important aspect of this modification.

To discern the structure of the book one must begin with ch. 8. This describes the **consecration of Aaron** and his sons, and so records the fulfilment of the instructions given in Ex 29[1–35] 40[12–15]. It is thus part of the expansion of Ex 25–29 which is now contained in Ex 35–40. To this also belongs ch. 9, recounting the sacrifices offered at the inauguration of the sacrificial system. 10[1–7], the story of Nadab and Abihu offering 'unholy fire' before the Lord—quite unrelated to its context—seems to be an appendix to this narrative. It may represent an attempt to provide theological justification for the exclusion from the service of the Temple of certain priesthoods claiming descent from Nadab and Abihu, despite the statement in Nu 3[4] that they had no children. On 10[18–20] see below.

It is probable that the law of the **Day of Atonement** (16[2ff]) once followed immediately upon the story of Nadab and Abihu in ch. 10. When it was separated from this by the insertion of the material in chs. 11–15, v.[1] was prefixed to it to resume the connexion. The chapter gives rise to a number of problems. The ritual prescribed, especially in vv.[7–10, 15–28], is undoubtedly ancient, and yet in the surviving pre-exilic codes there is no reference to the observance, though there may be an echo of it in Ezk 46[18–20]. Furthermore, in the account of the promulgation of Ezra's code (Neh 8) it is completely ignored: the feast of Tabernacles (which, according to Lv 23[33] was to be kept on the fifteenth day of the seventh month) follows immediately on New Year's Day, on the second day of the seventh month. If Ezra's law book was, as seems likely, based upon the customs of the Jerusalem Temple for which authentication was claimed by the representation that they had been divinely prescribed to Moses at Sinai, the inference to be drawn is that the Day of Atonement was a feature in the observance of some other sanctuary than Jerusalem (possibly on New Year's Day; see below, on 25[9]), and that it was not given a place in the Jerusalem calendar until some time after the promulgation of Ezra's code—and indeed later than the writing of the account of its promulgation now contained in Neh 8. If so, its acceptance in Jerusalem was one of the concessions which had to be made to secure recognition of the Temple as the sole cult centre of Yahwism. It was prescribed for the tenth day of the seventh month (16[29])—ten days after New Year's Day—and Tabernacles was moved to the fifteenth day. If this reconstruction is valid, then it is likely that 16[2ff] was added to the narrative of the erection of the Tabernacle, the consecration of Aaron and his sons and the inauguration of the sacrificial system, immediately after ch. 9, from which it was separated, first, by the intrusion of the story of Nadab and Abihu, and then by the laws in chs. 11–15. It is to be noted that in the account of the inauguration of the sacrificial system in ch. 9 nothing is said of Aaron going into the most holy place within the veil; nor is there any indication in the material in Ex 25–31, 35–40 as to when or in what manner the most holy place was to be entered. It is accordingly not unlikely that underlying ch. 16 is a set of directions for the consecration of the most holy place—which may well have followed upon Ex 29[37]—and possibly an account of the fulfilment of these directions, and that this material was fused with the regulations for the Day of Atonement when these were added to the narrative.

It is probable that ch. 24 was also part of the framework. Vv.[1–4], commanding the provision of oil for the ever-burning light in the sanctuary, and vv.[5–9], giving directions regarding the **bread of the Presence,** are clearly out of context. The former law is found also in Ex 27[20f], where it is again out of place, for in its mention of Aaron and his sons as the ministers of the light it anticipates their designation as the priests of Yahweh in Ex 28[1]. On the other hand, Ex 39[37] assumes that oil for the light had already been prepared, and so that any directions for its preparation had been given previously. Ex 39[37], however, is part of the supplement (chs. 35–40) to Ex 25–29. The inference to be drawn from all this is that neither in Ex 25–29 nor in the supplement (Ex 35–40, Lv 8–9) were there originally any directions for the preparation of the oil, and so that Lv 24[1–4] is later than the supplement, and that it was added to it at the end of ch. 9, from which it was subsequently separated by the intrusion of chs. 10 and 16. The directions regarding the bread of the Presence (vv.[5–9])—referred to without explanation in Ex 25[30]—are, it may be assumed, from the same hand as vv.[1–4] (Ex 27[10f] will thus be an addition by some scribe who noticed that the directions were required by 39[37], but who did not remove them from Lv 24. He seems, however, to have overlooked the mention of the bread of the Presence in

Ex 39^{36} 40^{23}). If 24$^{1-9}$ belongs to the framework of the book, then it may be assumed that the following narrative, telling of the execution of a man who committed blasphemy (vv.$^{10-13, 23}$), is also part of it. Into it has been inserted a group of laws (vv.$^{15-22}$) against blasphemy and against injury to men and cattle.

The two dominant themes of Ex 25–29, 35–40, Lv 8–9 are the Tabernacle and the Aaronite priesthood. This material, together with 10$^{1-7}$ and chs. 16 and 24, is the framework into which have been fitted the other laws in the book : (*a*) Chs. 1–7. These laws were placed between the account of the Tabernacle being set up (Ex 40) and that of the consecration of the priests (Lv 8), presumably because it was thought suitable that the laws which regulated the sacrifices to be offered by the priests should precede ch. 9 which recounts the inauguration of the sacrificial system. Ch. 1 lays down the ritual precedure to be followed when a man ' brings a burnt offering from the herd ' (vv.$^{3-9}$), or ' from the flock ' (vv.$^{10-13}$), or ' of birds ' (vv.$^{14-17}$). The original continuation of this is to be found in ch. 3 (as is indicated by a comparison of 1^{2f} with 3^{1}, which reads in Hebrew ' if his offering . . .'), which deals with peace offerings, ' from the herd ' (vv.$^{1-5}$) and ' from the flock ' (vv.$^{6-17}$). In these chapters the references to the sons of Aaron are obviously secondary, a fact which indicates that the laws are earlier than those regarding the Aaronite priesthood in their present framework. A further fact to be noted is that the sanctuary is referred to throughout not as the Tabernacle but as the tent of meeting. This is the designation, in the earlier (JE) history, of the tent pitched outside the camp at which the people ' sought the Lord ' (=consulted the oracle), and where ' the Lord used to speak to Moses face to face ' (Ex 33$^{7-11}$; cf Nu 11$^{16, 24ff}$ 12^{4}). There is no suggestion in JE that it was the centre of an organized cult. In Ex 25–29, 35–40, on the other hand, ' tent of meeting ' designates the tent-like structure within the court of the Tabernacle, and in particular that part of it without the veil (*e.g.* 28^{43} 29$^{4, 42}$ 40^{26}) The usage however is not consistent, and this possibly suggests that underlying Ex 25–29, 35–40 there may be an earlier account of the cult in the wilderness which represented the older, simpler ' tent of meeting ' as the place of sacrifice, and that the detailed description of the sanctuary in Ex 25–29 is an elaboration of this. If this is the case, then the use of the ' tent of meeting ' in chs. 1 and 3 may indicate that the code from which they were taken had already been worked over to give it a desert provenance before the material was placed in its present context by the compiler of Leviticus, who is, it may be taken for granted, responsible for the insertion of the references to the sons of Aaron.

The intrusive position of ch. 2 between chs. 1 and 3, and the difference in the introductory formulae (' when ' in ch. 2, ' if ' in chs. 1 and 3) indicate that the laws regulating cereal offerings have been derived from another code than those of the burnt offerings and the peace offerings. Furthermore, the fact that in 2$^{1-3}$ the third person is used and vv.^{4ff} the second person suggests that the laws in the collection are of different dates. A comparison of v.^{2} with v.^{8} indicates that in v.^{2} the reference to ' Aaron's sons the priests ' is secondary, and this suggests either that vv.$^{3, 10}$ are an addition, or that ' Aaron and his sons ' is a substitution for ' the priest.'

Ch. 4 lays down the ritual procedure in connexion with sin-offerings. In the first two sections, dealing with the sin-offering of the anointed priest and of the whole congregation of Israel, the reference is to the ' tent of meeting ' (vv.$^{4, 7, 14, 18}$), a fact which suggests that they are related to if not derived from the same code as chs. 1 and 3 ; but in the sections dealing with the ruler and with ' any one of the common people ' neither tent of meeting nor Tabernacle is mentioned, indicating that the material in vv.$^{22-32}$ is from another date, if not indeed from another code, than that in vv.$^{3-21}$. Furthermore, a comparison of the laws in the first two sections with similar laws elsewhere reveals certain significant differences. Thus the sin offering for the congregation is a young bull here (v.^{14}) but a goat in 9^{15} (cf Nu 15^{24}) ; and the sin-offering of the anointed priest (vv.$^{3-12}$) is more elaborate than that of the high priest in 9$^{8-11}$ (cf Ex 29$^{10-14}$). The inference to be drawn is that the older law has been modified by the authors of its present frame-work (to which ch. 9 belongs) to meet changing circumstances.

Ch. 5^{1} mentions a sin which could not be called unintentional ; vv.$^{2-4}$, on the other hand, refer to unintentional sins for which a ' guilt-offering ' of a lamb or a goat is required (vv.^{5f}). V.^{1} would thus seem to be from another hand than vv.$^{2-6}$, and the fact that the term ' guilt-offering ' is used in vv.^{5f} instead of ' sin-offering ' as in ch. 4 suggests that the respective laws come from different dates or from different codes. Vv.$^{7-13}$ permit those who cannot afford an animal to offer a less expensive sacrifice ; in these verses ($^{7, 9, 11, 12}$) the term ' sin-offering ' is used, and ritual directions, lacking in vv.$^{2-6}$, are given. The section would thus seem to be from another code than vv.$^{2-6}$, and it is possible that in its original context it prescribed two birds as the normal sin-offering for all, not as a substitute for those who could not afford an animal. Vv.$^{14-19}$ mention further unintentional sins for which a ' guilt-offering ' is required ; they do not seem to belong with vv.$^{2-6}$, however, for (*a*) the offering prescribed is a ram (not a lamb or a goat) ; (*b*) the value of the ram is mentioned (vv.$^{15, 18}$) ; and (*c*) restitution is demanded (v.^{16a}) in addition to the sacrifice. These features rather suggest that the section is derived from the same code as 6$^{1-7}$, prescribing the guilt-offering of a ram for robbery and fraud.

Chs. 6$^{8-13, 24-30}$ 7$^{1-18}$ deal with matters ancillary to the sacrifices, and are especially concerned with dues for the priests. Each of the regulations is introduced by the formula ' this is the law of ' (6$^{9, 24}$ 7$^{1, 11}$). In this material the ' tent of meeting ' is referred to only three times (6$^{16, 26, 30}$) ; and a comparison of vv.^{16} and ^{26} with 7^{6} suggests that these two references may be secondary ; while v.^{30} seems to be harmonization with ch. 4. These laws would thus seem to be derived from another code than those in chs. 1 and 3. The formula ' this is the law of ' appears again in the subscription (7^{37f}), which ignores the laws in vv.$^{22-36}$. These are accordingly an addition to the basic material in the section ; vv.$^{22-27}$ forbid the eating of the fat and the blood, already prohibited, though in less detail in 3^{17}. The similarity of the concluding formula (v.^{27}) to that in v.^{21} suggests that vv.$^{19-21}$ and $^{22-27}$ are derived from the same source ; the law in vv.$^{19-21}$ was inserted here as a supplement to the law of the sacrifice of peace-offerings (vv.^{11ff}), and with it vv.$^{22-27}$. Vv.$^{28-34}$ give the wave breast and the right thigh of the peace-offering to the priest. The subscription to this (vv.^{35f}) would suggest that it is taken from a collection listing the dues assigned to the Aaronite priesthood, and that it was placed here by the compiler of the book. Ch. 6$^{19-23}$, prescribing the cereal offering to be made by Aaron and his successors on the day of their anointing, separates the law of the cereal offering from that of the sin-offering which are listed together in 7^{37}. Its mention here, whatever its origin, is also due in all probability to the compiler of the book, who then added ' of the consecration ' to the subscription in 7^{37}—though in the wrong place. Ch. 10$^{12-15}$ is a law requiring that the portion of the cereal offering reserved for the priests as their due shall be eaten by them in the sanctuary (cf 6^{16}), but permitting them to eat the wave breast and the right thigh of the peace offering, referred to in 7^{21ff}, ' in any clean place.' This is at variance with the command in 6^{26} 7^{6} that the priests shall eat their part of the sin offering and the guilt offering in the sanctuary ; it may reflect the practice of the sanctuary from which the law of peace offerings (7^{29ff}) was derived. If so, the compiler of the book reconciled the two customs by attaching this to the story of Nadab and Abihu and implicitly representing it as a modification of the previous commands. Ch. 10$^{16-20}$ may likewise reflect the similar custom of eating the sin offering outside the sanctuary (cf 6^{26} 7^{6}). Ch. 10$^{8-11}$ may well be from the same code.

(*b*) Chs. 11–15. The priests, however, had other functions in the life of the people besides those immediately connected with sacrifice. It was their business to determine on all questions connected with **uncleanness.** Therefore, following the account of the consecration of the priests and the inauguration of the sacrificial system, and preceding the regulations regarding the Day of Atonement (ch. 16), obviously regarded as the culminating duty of the priesthood, there comes a series of regulations bearing on this side of the priestly duties. The rules in ch. 11 on clean and unclean animals (vv.$^{2-23, 41-45}$) appear in a more primitive form in Dt 14$^{4-20}$. The subscription in vv.^{46f} is similar to 7^{37} in that it begins ' this is the law of.' This may be due to imitation on the part of the compiler ; on the other hand it may indicate that the material is derived from the same code as the law of the burnt offering, etc., in chs. 6 f. However that may be, the fact that the subscription ignores the law of defilement from touching unclean animals and all carcases (vv.$^{24-40}$) suggests that this is from another source than vv.$^{2-20, 41-45}$.

Chs. 12 and 15 prescribe the forms for the purification of a woman after childbirth and of any one who ' has a discharge from his body ' (15^{2}). In their basis these rules are very old, but the careful detail of derivative uncleanness (cf especially 15$^{1-12, 19-27}$) shows where a slow elaboration has been at work. To be noted is the fact that the ceremony of cleansing is in each case to be performed ' at the door of the tent of meeting ' (12^{6} 15$^{14, 29}$), which suggests that the material has the same immediate background as the code from which chs. 1 and 3 are derived ; in 15^{31}, however, the Tabernacle is referred to—indicating that this verse is from the hand of the writer who placed the material in its present framework. Chs. 13 and 14 contain a series of directions for the diagnosis of leprosy (q.v.) in human beings, clothing, leather and houses, and for the method of purification. The primitive character of the prescribed purification (14$^{2-8, 49-53}$), along with the fact that the cleansing of a man is carried out away from the sanctuary, indicates the early origin of the rules. The sacrifices to be offered following the cleansing are prescribed in 14$^{10-32}$, and here again the mention of the ' tent of meeting ' (vv.$^{11, 23}$) is to be noted as an indication of the history of the material.

(*c*) Chs. 17–23, 25–26. These chapters have come to be known as the **Holiness Code** or the Law of Holiness because of the frequent references they contain to (ritual) holiness, both of persons and of things. That they are derived from a collection other than the codes upon which chs. 1–3, 11–15 depend is suggested by the facts that the laws have a much wider scope than those in the preceding chapters, and that they refer in places to matters which have already been dealt with (cf *e.g.* 19$^{6-8}$ with 7$^{15-18}$; 20^{25} with ch. 11 ; and 23$^{26-32}$ with ch. 16). It should be noted, however, that in ch. 17 there is no reference to ' holiness ' ; nor does the proclamation ' I am the Lord (your God),' found repeatedly in chs. 18 ff, occur in it. Moreover, ch. 18 opens with a formal introduction (vv.$^{1-5}$) in which ' I am the Lord ' occurs three times, whereas ch. 17 begins simply with ' This is the thing which the Lord has commanded.' The question may accordingly be raised whether in fact ch. 17 is not from another source than chs. 18 ff.

Ch. 17 prescribes that all animals suitable for sacrifice must be slain at the sanctuary (vv.$^{1-6}$), and that such animals when sacrificed must be offered to Yahweh alone (vv.$^{7-9}$). These regulations, presupposing the existence of local sanctuaries throughout the land—for otherwise the killing of an animal for food would have been practically illegal—have been adapted to their present context by the substitution of ' the tent of meeting ' for some more general term. Vv.$^{10-14}$, forbidding the eating of blood, are a repetition at greater length of the prohibition in 7^{26f}. Vv.^{15f}, forbidding the eating of the carcase of ' what dies of itself or what is torn of beasts,' repeats Ex 22^{31}.

Ch. 18 is a series of laws on incest (vv.$^{6-18}$) and other sexual offences (vv.$^{19f, 22f}$), with an admonitory introduction (vv.$^{1-5}$) and a conclusion (vv.$^{24-30}$). In the middle of it is a prohibition of Molech worship (v.^{21}), placed here in all probability under the influence of ch. 20 which prescribes the penalty for its infraction together with the penalties for the other offences listed in ch. 18. Ch. 19 contains a group of miscellaneous laws—also with introduction and conclusion—which seems to be arranged in no kind of order. That in vv.$^{6-8}$ repeats 7$^{15-18}$; vv.^{9ff} are found again in 23^{22} and in Dt 24$^{19, 21}$. Vv.$^{11-18}$ contain a series of prohibitions of dishonesty and oppression in their various forms, ending with the command ' you shall love your neighbour as yourself.' V.^{19} prohibits cross-breeding of animals, sowing two kinds of seed in one field, and wearing a garment made of two kinds of stuff (cf Dt 22$^{9-11}$). Vv.$^{20-22}$ prescribe the sacrifice to be offered by a man who seduces a betrothed slave. Vv.$^{23-25}$ forbid the eating of the first four years' yield of a fruit tree. Vv.$^{26-28}$ prohibit the eating of blood (cf 3^{17} etc.), the practice of augury and witchcraft (cf Dt 18^{10}), and certain mourning customs (cf 21^{5}, Dt 14^{1}). Vv.$^{29-36}$ forbid a man to make his daughter a harlot, command the keeping of the sabbath, prohibit consultation of mediums and wizards, demand respect for the aged, justice for the sojourner, and just weights and measures. Ch. 20 prescribes the penalties for offences specified in the preceding chapters : vv.$^{2-5}$ for Molech worship (18^{21}) ; v.^{6} for resorting to mediums and wizards (19^{31}) ; v.^{9} for cursing one's parents (not previously mentioned in Leviticus, but cf Ex 21^{17}, Dt 27^{16}) ; vv.$^{10-21}$ for incest and other sexual offences (18$^{6-23}$). Vv.^{25f} refer to clean and unclean animals, etc., and perhaps suggest that laws like those in ch. 11 once stood in this place in the code. V.^{27} prescribes death for mediums and wizards. Chs. 21–22 deal with priests and offerings. Ch. 21$^{1-8}$ states the ceremonial restraints required of the priests in their daily life. V.^{9} prescribes death by burning for any priest's daughter who becomes a harlot. Vv.$^{10-15}$ duplicate vv.$^{1-8}$—v.^{11} going further than v.^{2} however in that it forbids a priest to touch the dead body of his father or his mother. Ch. 21$^{16-24}$ demands bodily perfection in every officiating priest. Ch 22$^{1-16}$ ordains that sacrificial food may be eaten only by those who are ceremonially clean and who can claim membership in the priestly family. Ch. 22$^{17-25}$ requires sacrificial animals to be perfect. Three minor regulations as to sacrifices (vv.$^{26-30}$) are followed by another exhortation (vv.$^{31-33}$). The laws in these chapters are presumably based on ancient custom but the original prescriptions have undoubtedly been added to and adapted to meet changing circumstances ; *e.g.* the list of possible disabilities in 21$^{18-20}$ bears the marks of such elaboration, as does 21^{4b-8}.

Ch. 23 is a calendar of the appointed **feasts** of the Lord. A comparison of v.^{2} with v.^{4}, and the wording of v.^{38} suggest that vv.^{2f}, commanding the observance of the sabbath, have been added to the original list. Vv.$^{5-8}$ command the observance of the Passover on the fourteenth day of the first month, and the Feast of Unleavened Bread for seven days beginning with the fifteenth day of the first month. The structure of the law and a comparison of it with Ex 23^{15} 34^{18}, in neither of which is there any reference to Passover (contrast Dt 16^{1ff}), suggests that the mention of it here is secondary. Vv.$^{9-14}$ contain the regulations for the offering of firstfruits, no date being prescribed (cf Dt 26$^{1-11}$) ; in the present context the implication is that this is part of the observance of Passover-Unleavened Bread. Vv.$^{15-20}$ deal with the offerings to be made seven weeks after the offering of the firstfruits, on what is referred to in Ex 34^{22}, Dt 16^{9f} as the Feast of Weeks. (Ex 23^{16} is ambiguous ; it refers to the firstfruits, and so is associated with Unleavened Bread, but at the same time it seems to be referring to another feast.) The material in vv.$^{10-20}$

may have been derived from another source than vv.[4, 6–8], and have displaced the explicit mention of the Feast of Weeks in that source, to which v.[21] also belongs. V.[22] (cf 19[9f], Dt 24[21]) appears to have been attracted here by the reference to (the implied seven weeks of) harvest in vv.[10, 15f]. Vv.[24–36] prescribe the observance of the three feasts of the seventh month (the first month of the ecclesiastical year): on the first day, the Feast of Trumpets (all that was left, apparently, of the great New Year's Day festival in pre-exilic Jerusalem); on the tenth, the Day of Atonement (cf ch. 16); and, beginning on the fifteenth day and lasting for seven days thereafter, the Feast of Booths (cf Ex 23[16b], Dt 16[13ff]). Vv.[37f] form the conclusion of the calendar. Vv.[39–43] contain further instructions regarding the Feast of Booths and may be derived from another code than vv.[24–36].

Reasons have already been advanced for holding that the material in ch. 24 once followed immediately on ch. 16, being part of the framework of the book. When he inserted the 'holiness' material (chs. 17, 18–23, 25 f) the compiler broke its continuity by placing chs. 25 f after the conclusion of the framework, for the reason, it may be assumed, that the laws regarding the sabbatical year and the year of jubilee were to be applicable only after the people had settled in the land (25[2]). The basic material on the sabbatical year would seem to be vv.[3–7], with vv.[19–22] as a supplement; that on the year of jubilee, vv.[8–13, 23], vv.[14–17] and [24–25] being supplementary, probably from a number of different hands. Vv.[19–22] were separated from vv.[3–7] in order to make the regulations contained in them apply to the year of jubilee as well as to the sabbatical year. This at once raises the question whether the sabbatical year and the jubilee were not ultimately derived from different codes. To be noted in this connexion is the fact that according to v.[9] the year of jubilee began on the tenth day of the seventh month—that is, the Day of Atonement by 23[16] (16[29]). This suggests the possibility that at one time the Day of Atonement may have coincided with New Year's Day. Vv.[25–27] contain a law regarding the right of redemption of alienated land, which is related to the jubilee legislation by v.[28]. Vv.[29, 30a] deal with the right of redemption of a house in a walled city, which, unlike houses in unwalled villages (v.[31]), does not come under the jubilee provisions (v.[30b]), except the houses of the Levites in their cities (vv.[32–34]). Vv.[35–38] forbid the exaction of interest. Vv.[39–46] extend the jubilee provisions from land to persons by ordering that an Israelite—but not a sojourner—who had sold himself into slavery should serve only 'until the year of the jubilee.' It is impossible to decide what the relation of this provision is to that in Dt 15[12–18], ordering that a Hebrew slave should be released at the end of seven years' service; it may be a modification of it because the latter had proved impracticable, or it may be an earlier custom which Deuteronomy was trying to liberalize, whether successfully or unsuccessfully. Vv.[47–55] demand that an Israelite who has sold himself to a sojourner shall have the same rights of redemption as he would have from an Israelite master.

Ch. 26, apart from two fragments, of which v.[1] is parallel to 19[4] and v.[2] identical with 19[30], contains the hortatory conclusion (vv.[3–45]) which the compiler of chs. 18–23, 25 appended to his collection. It closes with the subscription (v.[46]) which the editor of Leviticus added when he inserted the collection in its present position.

While the incidence of the characteristic formula 'I am the Lord (your God)' in chs. 18–23, 35 is lacking in regularity, there is nevertheless a pattern in its occurrence which would seem to warrant the assumption that (allowing for occasional additions) the material was derived from a single existing code. For although the formula does not occur in the detailed laws against incest and other sexual offences (18[7–12, 22f]), nor in the register of penalties for their infraction (20[6–20]), nor in the calendar of appointed feasts (ch. 23; v.[22] is an isolated intrusion), in each case it is found in a subscription (18[24–30] 20[22–26] 23[43]), and this would seem to indicate that even if, as seems likely, the material was earlier derived from another collection of laws, it was a part of the Holiness code as that lay before the compiler of Leviticus. It is evident, however, that chs. 18–23, 25 did not comprise the whole of the code; they contain a selection from it—those laws which the compiler decided must be included, both because of their intrinsic worth and because without them his code would not be accepted by the priesthood from which the Holiness code derived. And it may be assumed that the same principle governed the selection of the other laws in the book—and in the book of Numbers. It has been suggested by some scholars that other laws in the Pentateuch have been derived from the same collection as those in chs. 18–23, 35: *e.g.* Ex 31[13, 14a], Lv 11[1–23, 41–47], Nu 15[37–41]. This may be the case, for the compiler of Leviticus was in all probability responsible for the final form of the post-exilic material in Exodus and Numbers, and he may well have felt that these laws would fit better in their present contexts than in Leviticus. Nevertheless, undue significance must not be attributed to the appearance of the formulae 'I am the Lord,' 'I am the Lord who sanctify you,' since once some laws had been thus countersigned, there would be a natural tendency to attach the formulae to others.

Ch. 27 contains a number of rules on the commutation of **vows and tithes**. Following 26[46], it is clearly a supplement.

Compiled as it is from a number of earlier codes, the book of Leviticus reflects the process by which the uses, customs, and laws of the various sanctuaries throughout the land were gradually adapted and fused into one system, to be the law of the Jerusalem Temple in post-exilic times. And it shows, particularly in the Holiness code, that the interest of the priests was not limited to matters connected with the cult; they were concerned with human relationships, complex and varied even within the comparatively simple structure of an agricultural society, and saw that the holiness of God demands that 'you shall love your neighbour as yourself' (19[18])—and 'neighbour' included the sojourner (19[34]). C. A. Si.

LEVY.—See SOLOMON, **6.**

LEWD.—In the AV 'lewd' does not always mean 'lustful,' as it does now. That meaning, indeed, is not found in the Apocrypha or NT. There the meaning is simply 'wicked,' as Ac 17[5] 'certain lewd fellows of the baser sort'; RSV, 'some wicked fellows of the rabble.' So 'lewdness' is usually simply 'wickedness.'

LIBANUS.—The Greek form of the Hebrew name **Lebanon** (q.v.), 1 Es 4[48] 5[55], 2 Es 15[20], Jth 1[7], Sir 24[13] 50[12].

LIBATION.—See SACRIFICE, **11.**

LIBERTINES.—See FREEDMEN.

LIBERTY.—Although the Bible does not engage directly in the historic debate on the freedom of the will, a clear, consistent, and even sophisticated position may be detected between its lines. Its tacit assumption, from Adam's fall to Judas' betrayal, is the freedom of human beings as responsible, purposive agents, capable of decision and choice: 'Choose this day whom you will serve' (Jos 24[15]; cf 1 K 18[21]). Most of the parables of Jesus dramatize the Deuteronomic exhortation, 'Therefore choose life' (Dt 30[19]). Indeed, most of the Bible's key words are verbs which become meaningless the moment free will is denied: love, repent, forgive, judge, thank, rejoice, betray, obey.

Some interpreters, in the interest of theological doctrines like predestination, original sin, or irresistible grace, have feared that to grant human freedom would contravene the sovereignty of God. These interpreters appeal to passages in which God actually overrides human freedom, as when he hardens Pharaoh's heart (Ex 9[12] 10[20, 27] 11[10]), or puts a lying spirit in the mouth of the false prophets (1 K 22[23]). These citations, however, instead of contradicting the belief in human freedom, support it. Pharaoh and the false prophets were deprived of their *normal* capacity for free choice, presumably for having overtaxed God's patience. Before God intervened, Pharaoh had already hardened his own heart three times (Ex $8^{15, 32}$ 9^{34}). The principal significance of these passages is to establish that the same God who gave men the gift of freedom can also, under sufficient provocation, revoke it (cf Is 6^{9f}, Ro 1^{24}).

In the Bible, human freedom is contrasted, not with necessity, but with bondage. Only beings who are by nature free can suffer bondage. Animals cannot become slaves. Possessing the innate capacity for freedom, man may fall into physical serfdom, or, more subtly, into spiritual servitude. The latter, or 'bondage unto sin' (cf Jn 8^{34}, Ro 6^{17} 7^{14-25} 8^{15}, Gal 4^{9}), occurs whenever men try to order their lives without reference to God. They transfer their trust to some false god, which, having demanded their freedom as collateral, promptly forecloses. Whatever potential freedom they retain is like that of a man in prison. It only increases their frustration. 'Formerly, when you did not know God, you were in bondage to beings that by nature are no gods' (Gal 4^{8}). Victims of these false gods become in turn a part of the conspiracy against human freedom. They are likened to hucksters who 'promise . . . freedom, but are themselves slaves of corruption' (2 P 2^{19}).

Where false gods enslave men, the mark of the true God is to liberate (Is 61^{1}). The Lord delivered his people 'out of the house of bondage,' not only physically, but spiritually as well, by inviting Israel to 'walk in his ways.' The 'ways of the Lord' are the 'law of liberty' (Ja 1^{25}; cf Ps 119^{45}). The NT word 'ransom' (Mt 22^{28}, 1 Ti 2^{6}) likewise suggests the price paid to free a bond-servant. The Christian is set free from bondage to dumb idols (Hab 2^{18}, 1 Co 12^{2}), and incorporated into the 'glorious liberty of the children of God' (Ro 8^{21}; cf Jn 8^{32-36}, Gal 5^{1}). This liberty, however, differs significantly from the ordinary definition. It is customary to correlate freedom with independence, so that the maximum of freedom requires the maximum of self-sufficiency. For the Bible, however, the reverse is true. The way to preserve and enhance human freedom is to love and be loved. Men do not achieve this kind of liberation simply by taking thought. Rather, their deliverance is the work of God Himself who, through His Holy Spirit, knits them into a redemptive community (cf Ro 5^{5}). This experience, contradicting the definition of freedom as splendid isolation, leads the Christian to exclaim: 'Where the Spirit of the Lord is, there is freedom' (2 Co 3^{17}). E. L. C.

LIBNAH.—1. An unidentified station in the desert wanderings, Nu 33^{20f}. **2.** A Canaanite city taken by Joshua after Makkedah and before Lachish (Jos 10^{23} etc.), named between Arad and Adullam (13^{15}), and between Makkedah and Ether in the lowland (15^{42}). It was given to the Levites (21^{13}, 1 Ch 6^{57}). Taking advantage of an Edomite revolt, it rose against Judah under Joram, 2 K 8^{22}, 2 Ch 21^{10}. It was besieged by Sennacherib, 2 K 19^{8}, Is 37^{8}. Hamutal, mother of Jehoahaz and Zedekiah, was a native of Libnah, 2 K 23^{31} 24^{18}, Jer 52^{1}. It is possibly modern *Tell eṣ-Ṣâfī*.

LIBNI.—The eldest son of Gershon, that is to say, the eponym of a principal family of Gershonite Levites, Ex 6^{17}, Nu 3^{18}, 1 Ch $6^{17, 20}$. In 1 Ch 6^{29}, perhaps owing to some dislocation of the text, the name appears as that of the eponym of a family of Merarites. The patronymic **Libnites** occurs in Nu 3^{21} 26^{58}. Libni is called **Ladan** (AV **Laadan**) in 1 Ch 23^{7ff} 26^{21}; see LADAN, **2.**

LIBRARY.—See WRITING, **5.**

LIBYA, LIBYANS.—The name of a people mentioned in Nah 3^{9}, 2 Ch 12^{3} 16^{8} (in all of which AV, RV have **Lubim**), Dn 11^{43}. The place, Libya, is mentioned in RSV in Ezk 30^{5} (following LXX, where RV, following MT, has **Cub** [AV **Chub**]), Ac 2^{10}. AV 'Libya' in Ezk 30^{5} is an error for Put (RV, RSV). The Libyans were a very ancient people living W. of Egypt, who were subdued by the Egyptians at an early date and long furnished mercenary soldiers to their armies. At length they invaded Egypt, subdued it in the 10th cent. B.C., and established a powerful dynasty, of which the Biblical Shishak was the founder. Perhaps *Lubim* should be read for **Ludim** (q.v.) in certain passages. Cf LEHABIM.
J. F. McC.—**H. H. R.**

LICE.—Hebrew *kinnîm* is rendered **lice** in AV and RV in Ex 8^{16-18}, Ps 105^{31} (RVm **sandflies** or **fleas** at Ex 8^{16}). All the insects named are only too common in Palestine and Egypt. The three well-known varieties of *pediculi* or lice are perpetually prevalent among the dirty, and a plague of them would certainly be much more terrible than one of the harmless, though irritating, 'sandfly' (*Simulium*), and far more disgusting than one of the flea (*Pulex*). RSV in all these passages has **gnat** (q.v.). See also PLAGUES OF EGYPT. In Is 51^{6} *kēn* is rendered in AV, RV 'in like manner,' but in RVm, RSV 'like gnats.'

LICENTIOUSNESS.—See LASCIVIOUSNESS.

LICTOR.—See POLICE.

LIDEBIR.—Jos 13^{26} (RVm, RSVm), taken by EV to mean 'belonging to Debir' (see DEBIR, **3**); but we should read **Lo-debar** (q.v.).

LIE, LYING.—1. In the OT.—The simple lie, which is a deliberate suppression of the truth in conversation, was condemned by the Levitical code as contrary to the character of holiness demanded by, and becoming to, the people of Israel's holy God (Lv 19^{11f}, cf 6^{2f}). Perjury, as an aggravation of the ordinary sin, was emphatically condemned, and stringently punished in the legislative enactments of Israel (Ex 23^{1}, Dt 19^{16-20}). There can be no doubt that the moral consciousness of the Hebrews was alive to the sinfulness of deceit (Pr 19^{22} 21^{28} 24^{28} 25^{18} $30^{6, 8}$; cf Is 58^{11} AVm). The lying selfishness of Cain, and the reprehensible deception practised by Abraham, are recorded by the historian in a tone which reveals his attitude towards such acts (Gn 4^{9} 20^{2-16} 12^{11-20}; cf 2 K 5^{20-27} where Gehazi's punishment is the reward of his thoughtless levity at a time of national gloom, as well as of his deceitful conduct and words). The moral reprobation of falsehood reaches its climax in the utterances of the prophets. According to these teachers, it is at the foundation of all human depravity (Hos 7^{13} 12^{1}, Mic 6^{11f}). **Truth** can be arrived at and spoken only by those who are in personal touch with the sacred Fountain of truth (cf Is 65^{-8}). Indeed, some of the most emphatic declarations as to the moral attributes of Yahweh are based on the belief that He is above all else the God of truth (Nu 23^{19}, 1 S 15^{29}; cf Ps 89^{35}, Ezk 24^{14}, Mal 3^{5f}; see 2 Ti 2^{13}, Tit 1^{2}). Hence the enormity of the guilt of those teachers who had not Yahweh as the source of their inspiration, though they might speak in His name, who pandered to the prevailing moral degeneracy (Jer 5^{31} 6^{13} 29^{9}, Ezk 13^{6}; cf Wis 14^{28ff} etc.), or who encouraged their hearers in idolatry with its debasing ritual (Jer 16^{19}, Jon 2^{8}; cf Ps 31^{6}).

A curious phenomenon in the OT is the bold speculation which sought to explain the authorship of the lying instruction by which Yahweh's enemies were seduced to their own destruction. The fatuity of Ahab's conduct, and its fatal consequences, are detailed in the light of this conception (1 K 22), while a still more unequivocal directness, Samuel is said to have been counselled by God to deceive Saul (1 S 16^{1f}). In both instances the historian is evidently interpreting events by the ideas current in his day.

2. In the NT—Falsehood is here traced back to its source in the principle of evil. Jesus attributes its origin to Satan (Jn 8^{44}; cf Ac 5^{3}, Rev 12^{9}). Membership in the Christian body postulated a new creation 'in true righteousness and holiness' (Eph 4^{24f}), and forbade one member to lie to another (Col 3^{9}).

The denial of the Messiahship of Jesus is characterized by the Johannine author as a lie (1 Jn 2^{22}), while the same writer makes self-deceit the cause of that Pharisaic complacency which he so unsparingly condemns (1 Jn 1^{8ff}). The Pauline representation of paganism bases its degrading moral influence on the fact that it is founded essentially on a lie (Ro 1[22]).

The awful fate which awaits 'all liars' (Rev 21[8]) is the outcome and direct development of the OT judgment of this sin, for it fundamentally estranges the guilty from Him whose 'word is truth' (Jn 17[17]; cf Rev 21[27] 22[15], and see Ps 51[6] 24[4] 119[160]). Cf also TRUTH.

J. R. W.

LIEUTENANT.—See SATRAP.

LIFE.—1. In the OT.—This word is used to translate two main Hebrew expressions: (1) *ḥayyîm*, 'life,' with the related verb 'live' and adjective 'living'; its opposite is death; (2) *nephesh*, the word which is traditionally rendered 'soul.' There is not space for a discussion of this word here (see SOUL), but it might be roughly described as life as a formative and directive force active within and activating the *bāśār*, 'flesh,' of a man or a group. This soul which activates the flesh does not exist alone as a disembodied ghost; the living being, or the centre of life in the living being, is the *nephesh*. It is well translated as 'life' in many passages, *e.g.* Lv 17[14]: 'The life (*nephesh*) of all flesh (RSV every creature) is the blood of it'; or Ex 21[23], 'life (*nephesh*) for life, eye for eye . . .' But there are many places where *nephesh* can hardly be translated by 'life,' while the latter answers almost constantly to Hebrew *ḥayyîm*. Sometimes the two words are brought together in *nephesh ḥayyāh*, 'living *nephesh*.' Adam was made of dust, but when God gave him breath he became living *nephesh*, living being. This is not peculiar to man however, for the animal world is characteristically 'living *nephesh*,' living creature, also (Gn 2[7] 1[24]).

We may begin our survey with the concept of the living God and of life as the sphere of God in the OT. This may safely be reckoned to the early foundations of Yahwism (against L. Koehler, *Old Testament Theology*, 1957, pp. 53–54) and 'As Yahweh lives' is perhaps the commonest oath formula in Israel. The active God, intervening in history, is the living God, Jos 3[10], and no other god has life as He has, Dt 32[39ff]. The close attachment of life to Yahweh may be illustrated by contrast by remarking how the realm of death is from early times seen as apart from Yahweh (Ps 88[4-5] etc.) and all necromancy is abhorrent in Yahwism. Unlike some other Oriental deities who promote fertility and life, Yahweh does not pass through the cycle of death and life. But the living God is the source of life. The breath by which men and animals live, the cessation of which means death, is breathed into their nostrils by God, so that their life depends at each moment on Him (Ps 104[29]). In the cult the presence of the living God is a source of wonder and awe (Ps 42[2] 84[2]).

In the OT life is positively valued. To prefer death to life is abnormal, or is the result of experience which seems to contradict the Israelite understanding of life; that Job should prefer death is the measure of his desperation as a man tormented by God, and Ecclesiastes' sense of the futility of life is at least partly prompted by his knowledge that life is limited by death. But even he knows the typical Israelite belief; 'a living dog is better than a dead lion,' 9[4]. The pious Israelite will be one who 'desires life and covets many days,' Ps 34[12]. It is good for a man to die 'old and full of days' like Isaac (Gn 35[29]) and be gathered to his kindred. Suicide is very rare in the OT. Death correspondingly is lacking in positive content; its realm is shadowy, futile, vain, forgotten; there is no death-romanticism in the OT. But equally man is known to be mortal, and the longing for immortality is not part of Israelite thinking; a man wishes length of days, and content of blessing in them, but not to live for ever. He is excluded from the tree of life which is access to immortality (Gn 3[22-24]). But unless a man's life is vain and accursed he leaves behind him his name and remembrance in his children and property.

The life of man may be threatened or weakened, and he comes under the influence and dominion of death (frequent in Psalms, *e.g.* 18[4-6]). We see that 'life' and 'death' are not mere statements of physical fact; life is power or vitality, and may be augmented or diminished. Illness diminishes it, and the man who is healed 'lives' or 'comes to life,' 'revives' as we would say (*e.g.* Jos 5[8] where 'till they were healed' (RSV) is literally 'till they came alive'). Prayers for life and for delivery from death form an important part of the Psalter. Nevertheless man has a choice to exercise here, for in the covenant ceremonies God asks Israel to choose; He sets before them life and death, good and evil, blessing and curse (Dt 30[15-20]); to love Yahweh and serve Him means life and length of days.

If Yahweh is the source of life, life also belongs to Him and is not unreservedly at the disposal of men. We have already seen that the blood is, or can be regarded as, the life. Men are permitted to kill animals for food by the Noachic covenant (Gn 9[1-7]) but the life, *i.e.* the blood, is not consumed by man; it is meant, in all probability, that the life reverts to God. In the sacrificial system this is seen, for there the blood is applied to the altar or other holy places where God is specially present; and the application of blood or life to the altar has a powerful expiating effect (Lv 17[11]). The shedding of human blood, however, in the Noachic law is subject to Divine inquisition and human retribution, for man is in the image of God. For the taking of human life, therefore, as for certain other offences specially abhorrent to Yahweh, the offender is deprived of life (*e.g.* Nu 35[33]).

From what has been said it should be evident that a picture of a 'future life' or 'life after death' is not a normal element of the classical Israelite understanding of man. One should not, however, mistake this for a secularism where death is a physical extinction which cannot be challenged and which leaves no trace. Certainly Yahwism by its emphasis on life is hostile to all cult of the dead, and all necromancy, and shows none of the widespread interest in life after death such as we know from Egyptian religion. But several elements exist in Israelite tradition which show that death is not a factual extinction which sets a limit to Yahweh's interest in life. We may mention: old stories of the translation to Yahweh's presence of persons like Enoch and Elijah (Gn 5[24], 2 K 2[11]); miraculous healings or restorations to life by prophets and men of God (*e.g.* 2 K 4[32-37]); the influence of the constant prayers in the cult for life and delivery from death; and the problem of retribution and reward where either the retribution is concealed (as in the common question of the wicked who flourish) or the evildoing itself is concealed and its extent not yet manifested (*e.g.* Is 26[21]). Sheol, the shadowy abode of the dead, is not something accepted and recognized in the OT, even in quite early sources (note its absence from all creation stories) but something resisted or deplored at the least. How can the worshipper of Yahweh accept willingly a destiny where he is unremembered and unknown? (cf Ps 16[9-11]).

Accordingly, in certain mainly rather late passages we have assertions of restoration of life, and of these the most important are the Isaiah Apocalypse (a 4th cent. text?—Is 25[8] 26[19-21]) and Dn 12[2-3]; cf also Is 53[10], Hos 13[14], Ezk 37. Not all these texts go the same length, and none of them is very precise, certainly not so precise as to mean a universal resurrection of the dead; but they all seem to mean some restoration of life in the face of the power of death. Since life cannot be thought of as disembodied, the restoration is seen as rising of dead bodies, reclothing of dead bones with flesh, and so on. In Dn 12[2] we have the first and only occurrence of 'everlasting life.' This is not a timeless existence; it is 'life of *'ôlām*,' and *'ôlām* is the remotest time, the time of the first beginnings or the distant future. The contrast here is between continuing life and continuing corruption and abhorrence (cf Is 66[24]). Daniel's conception is shared with some other works of late Judaism, *e.g.* 1 En 58[3] 'the elect shall be in the light of eternal life, and the days of their life shall be unending.

2 Mac $7^{9, 14, 36}$ all refer to resurrection to eternal life. We cannot however at this point follow the problem of resurrection as such in later Judaism except in so far as it is needed for the understanding of the term 'life' (see RESURRECTION).

For the more general understanding of 'life' Wis 1–5 has some interesting contributions. God is the author of life, not of death, and does not rejoice at the destruction of sinners; men should not bring destruction on themselves by a misguided life (1^{11-15}). The view that life is short and painful, and that there is no healing in the face of death, is a mistaken one, and leads to a reckless life in which the poor and righteous are oppressed; it forgets that man is made for incorruption (ch. 2). The more sceptical view of life as less attractive than death still appears occasionally, following Ecclesiastes (Sir 30^{17}).

The Qumrân community also used the term 'life,' and appears to have followed OT usage fairly closely. It is still being discussed how far ideas of resurrection are important for them, but the term 'eternal life' occurs, in wording different from, but probably dependent on, Dn 12^{2}—*Zadokite Document*, iii. 20, 'they that hold fast to it (the sure house of the new covenant) are for eternal life.' In the *Manual of Discipline* iv. 6–8 we read how the counsels of the community are 'for healing and abundance of peace in length of days, and fruitfulness of seed, with all blessings of eternity and everlasting joy in eternal life.' This may seem to refer mainly to a future life, and is paralleled by a visitation of punishment on the wicked by fire, darkness, and corruption. We may wonder, however, whether something of this 'eternal life' does not already exist for the community, just as the covenant of its constitution is a 'covenant of eternal community' iii. 11. In the *Hymns* we find 'life' used rather as in the OT Psalms; the worshipper has been threatened by 'the Pit' or 'Sheol,' but his life is delivered by God; he can thank God that he has been put among trees of life. It is reasonable to suppose that something of the life in store is already tasted by the men who know such deliverance.

In Rabbinic Judaism the commonest phrase is 'The life of the world to come,' which can be contrasted with the life of this world.

2. In the NT.—'Life' here translates mainly three words: (1) *zōē*, which corresponds roughly to Hebrew *ḥayyîm*, and is the opposite of death; (2) *bios*, which is not very frequent in NT, and refers mainly to the conduct of everyday life (*e.g.* 2 Ti 2^{4}, contrasted with a soldier's proper calling), its ambitions and pleasures (Lk 8^{14}), property and the means of subsistence (Mk 12^{44}); (3) *psychē*, 'soul, life,' corresponding in its ambivalence to Hebrew *nephesh*, and certainly to be translated 'life' in places like Mk 10^{45} ('to give his life—or himself—as a ransom') or Mt 2^{20} ('to seek the life of' a person). For the NT conception of life the term *zōē* is by far the most important.

A great deal of what the NT says about life is shared with the OT. As in the latter, life is positively valued, and death is the enemy of life; so that when a little girl lies sick and dying, this is not accepted as an easy translation to a better sphere, but the question is how she may be saved and live (Mk 5^{23}). On the other hand the only security of life is in God, and it is vain to safeguard life by the accumulation of goods or by worrying about one's needs (Ja 4^{13}, Lk 12^{13-30}); property and anxiety only draw attention away from life itself. Life, then, is the most precious possession; but to seek to hedge one's life or self (*psychē*) with security is to lose it, while to lose it for Christ's sake is to gain (Mk 8^{34-38}). This conception of the giving up of precious life is drawn from OT sacrificial conceptions, from the sanctification of the first-born for the increase of holiness and life by depriving them of life, and from the Suffering Servant of Is 53, who 'poured out his soul to death.' Thus a line of thought about life which agrees with the OT is characteristically modified by its fusion with another line of OT thinking.

But the most important influence on NT thinking about life is the resurrection of Christ, and it is this new element which prevents the idea of giving up of life from leading to a life-denying form of thought. God has life in Himself, and has granted the Son to have that same life in Him (Jn 5^{26}); and He has come that men should have life. But His mission leads Him to a death which is a struggle with death; and the resurrection shows it to have been a victorious struggle. By it death, which operated through the barriers of sin and law dividing man from God, is defeated and will in the end be destroyed (1 Co $15^{20-26, 51-57}$). Because Christ is risen in the body, it is possible to see that this new life is one of incorruptibility and immortality, and yet a real life and not a shadowy existence beyond.

Meanwhile there exists for those who are in Christ a double time connexion; for they are incorporated in Him who has already passed from death into the resurrection life, and yet they remain in this present life and await the resurrection. But although an expectation of the future remains, it is already possible to live 'in newness of life' (Ro 6^{4}) *because* (and not although) they will share the resurrection. It is in the Johannine literature that this idea of possessing now the true or eternal life is most frequent. 'We have passed out of death into life' (1 Jn 3^{14}); Jesus is the resurrection and the life, and immortal life belongs to those who trust in Him (Jn 11^{25-26}). Or, in Pauline thought, the real life of the Christians is with the ascended Christ in heaven; it is hidden with Him, and the manifesting of Christ is also the manifestation of their life (Col 3^{3-4}). In the Church as ministering, the putting to death of Christ is active, in order that the life of Christ should be made manifest; in the Church as ministered to, this life is active (2 Co 4^{10-12}). The Spirit, who is active in the Church, is the Spirit of Life and gives life (Ro 8^{2}, 2 Co 3^{6}); witnessing of Christ in His life below and ascended, He is the Church's contact with Him and the guarantee of the life that is already hers in Him and that is also still to come. J. Ba.

LIGAMENTS.—This word is found only in Col 2^{19} in RSV (AV, RV 'bands'). The word means 'the things which bind [the body] together,' *i.e.* the sinews or ligaments.

LIGHT.—In Gn 1^{3} light is the first emergence of the creative act; God dwells in it (Ex 24^{10}) and is clothed with it (Ps 104^{2}). He is the light of Israel (Is 10^{17}), and the house of Jacob is called to walk in His light (Is 2^{5}). Apocalyptically, the advent of salvation brings light (Is 9^{2}) and the Servant of the Lord is a light to the Gentiles (Is 42^{6} 49^{6}). In later apocalyptic writings, and especially in the Qumrân Scrolls, the good are the sons of Light, the wicked the sons of Darkness (cf The Warfare Scroll particularly). The same duality underlies the NT, especially by the application of OT typology. Jesus is 'the light of the world' (Jn $1^{4f, 9}$ 8^{12}). His followers are also 'the light of the world' (Mt $5^{14, 16}$). On the contrary, a godless life is **darkness** (Jn 3^{19} 8^{12} 12^{46}, 1 Jn 2^{11}). Apart from this religious usage 'light' is also used in the OT with the physical meaning of morning light (Jg 16^{2}), broad daylight (sunshine) (Am 8^{9}). But in the NT the only physical light is that of a lamp (AV **candle**) (Mt 5^{15}). B. J. R.

LIGHTNING.—The colloquial use of 'fire' for 'lightning' had its counterpart in Hebrew, *e.g.* in such a phrase as 'fire (*'ēsh*) and hail' (Ex 9^{23} etc.; cf Gn 19^{24}, 1 K 18^{38} etc.). The Hebrew *'ôr* (Job 37^{3}) is literally 'light'; *bāzāḳ* (Ezk 1^{14}) should probably read *bārāḳ*; *lappîdh*, literally 'torch,' is used in the plural for 'lightnings' (Ex 20^{18}); a word of uncertain meaning, *ḥᵃzîz* (Job 28^{26} 38^{35}, Zec 10^{1} [AV here 'bright clouds, RSV 'storm clouds']), is evidently related to **thunder,** and should probably in each case be translated 'thunder-cloud.' The usual Hebrew word is *bārāḳ*, Greek *astrapē* (2 S 22^{15} etc., Mt 24^{27} etc.). It is used figuratively for the glitter of bright metal (Dt 32^{41}, literally 'the lightning of my sword'; cf Ezk 21^{10}, Nah 3^{3}, Hab 3^{11}), and for the glittering weapon itself (Job 20^{25}). It is suggested, either by the flash of polished metal, or by the speed of the chariot (Nah 2[4]). Lightning is associated with the appearance of God (Ex 19[16] etc.), and He alone can control it (Job 38[35], Ps 18[14]). With lightnings as with arrows, God scatters His enemies (Ps 144[6] etc.). A radiant face (Dn 10[6]), and gleaming garments (Mt 28[3]), are like lightning. There is vivid suggestiveness in the comparison of Satan's overthrow with the descent of lightning (Lk 10[18]). Cf the name *Barak* (Jg 4[6]) with the Carthaginian *Barka*. W. E.

LIGN-ALOES, Nu 24[6] (AV, RV).—See ALOES.

LIGURE.—See JEWELS AND PRECIOUS STONES.

LIKHI.—The eponym of a Manassite family, 1 Ch 7[19].

LIKING.—In older English ' liking ' was used for the outward appearance, qualified by good or ill. So Job 39[4] ' Their young ones are in good liking ' (AV, RV ; RSV ' become strong ').

LILITH.—Is 34[14] (AV ' screech owl,' RV ' night monster,' RSV ' night hag ') ; see OWL. The *Lilith* is mentioned in connexion with the desolation which would haunt Edom. Strange stories are told about *Lilith* by the Rabbis. It was a nocturnal spectre who assumed the form of a beautiful woman in order to beguile and destroy young children. In the Talmud she is associated with the legends of Adam, whose wife she was before Eve was created, and so became the mother of the demons. T. A. M.—**H. H. R.**

LILY.—The Hebrew word *shûshan* (1 K 7[19]), *shôshannāh* (2 Ch 4[5], Ca 2[1], Hos 14[5]), is probably a loan-word from the Egyptian for the ' lotus.' In Arabic it is *sûsan,* which includes a great number of allied flowers—lilies, irises, gladioli, etc. No doubt the Hebrew word was equally comprehensive. Flowers of this group are very plentiful in Palestine, the irises being pre-eminent for their handsome appearance. The **' lily work '** (1 K 7[19, 22, 26]) is likely to have been modelled after the lotus (*Nymphaea lotus*) itself : lotus-like flowers appear on some Jewish coins. The Greek *krinon* of Mt 6[28], Lk 12[27] probably had as wide a significance as *shûsan,* and included much more than actual lilies. E. W. M. G.

LIME (*śîdh,* LXX *konia*) is mentioned by name in EV only in Is 33[12], Am 2[1]. Is 33[12] ' the peoples shall be as the burnings of lime,' *i.e.* they shall be so utterly consumed as to be comparable to the heap of quicklime that is left after limestone has been burned in a furnace. In Am 2[1] the prophet denounces Moab because they ' burned the bones of the king of Edom into lime '—phosphate of lime being the chief ingredient of the ash of well-burned bones. In Dt 27[2, 4] *śîdh* occurs both as verb and noun, but is rendered **plaster** (AV, RV **plaister**). For Is 27[9] see CHALK-STONES. The **' whited sepulchres '** of Mt 23[27] (AV, RV ; RSV ' whitewashed tombs ') and the **' whited** (RSV ' whitewashed ') **wall** of Ac 23[3] are allusions to the whitewashing of tombs with diluted quicklime so as to render them conspicuous, and of walls for purposes of embellishment. J. C. L.

LIMP.—The Hebrew verb *pāsaḥ* is rendered ' to limp ' in RSV in 1 K 18[26] (AV, RV ' leaped '), where it denotes a ritual dance with bent, or contorted, body (see H. H. Rowley, *BJRL* xliii [1960–1961], 204 f). The same verb is similarly rendered in RSV in v.[21] (AV, RV ' halt '), where there may be some allusion to this. In 2 S 4[4] it is used of the gait of Mephibosheth, who was dropped by his nurse in his infancy, and who thereafter became ' crippled ' (RSV ; AV, RV ' lame ').

LINE.—**1.** *Ḳaw,* which is of most frequent occurrence, is properly a measuring line (*e.g.* Jer 31[39], Ezk 47[3], Zec 1[16]). Figuratively it denotes a rule of life (cf ' precept upon precept, line upon line ' of Isaiah's teaching, Is 28[10]). In Ps 19[4] ' their line (RSV ' voice ') is gone out through all the earth ' has been variously interpreted. The LXX, taking the line to be a resonant cord, rendered by *phthongos*—' a musical sound,' and St. Paul quotes that version Ro 10[18] (AV, RV ' sound ' ; RSV ' voice '). More probably, however, the idea is still that of a measuring line. Cf Perowne (*Psalms, in loc.*), who gives ' line or boundary, '—as the heavens seems to measure and mark out the earth (whence the term horizon or boundary).' **2.** *hebhel,* a rope or cord, especially a measuring cord used in measuring and dividing land (cf Ps 78[55], Am 7[17], Zec 2[1]). ' The lines have fallen for me in pleasant places ' (Ps 16[6]) alludes to the marking out of plots of land with a measuring cord. **3.** *tiḳwāh* (from the same root as *ḳaw*) is used of the cord of scarlet thread that Rahab bound in the window (Jos 2[18, 21]). **4.** *ḥûṭ,* properly a sewing-thread, only in 1 K 7[15]. **5.** *pāthîl,* a string or cord, only in Ezk 40[8]. **6.** *śeredh* in Is 44[13] is misrendered ' line ' for which RV and RSV give **' pencil,'** RVm ' red ochre.' **7.** In NT ' line ' occurs only in AV of 2 Co 10[16]. The Greek word is *kanōn,* a measuring rod (AVm ' rule,' RV ' province,' RVm ' limit,' RSV ' field '), and so, figuratively, a rule. Probably the Apostle's idea is that of a measuring line, as defining the boundary between his own province and another's. J. C. L.

LINEN is cloth made from the prepared fibre of **flax.** In ancient Egypt great proficiency was attained in its manufacture (Pliny, *HN* vii. 56 ; Strabo, xvii. 41 ; Herod. ii. 182), and a flourishing trade was carried on (Pr 7[16], Ezk 27[7]). As material of wearing apparel it has always been esteemed in the East. In a hot climate it tends to greater freshness and cleanliness than cotton or wool. The Egyptian priests were obliged to wear linen (Herod. ii. 37 ; Wilkinson, *Anc. Egyp.* iii, 117). The ' cotton garments ' mentioned on the Rosetta stone were probably worn over the linen, and left outside when the priests entered a temple. The embalmed bodies of men and animals were wrapped in strips of linen. No other material was used for this purpose (Wilkinson, *ib.* iii, 115, 116, 484). Perhaps we may trace Egyptian influence in the place given to linen in the hangings, etc., of the Tabernacle, and in the garments of the priests (Ex 25[4] 26[1] etc., 28[15] etc.). It formed part of the usual clothing of royalty, and of the wealthy classes Gn 41[42], Est 8[15], Lk 16[19]). It is the dress worn by persons engaged in religious service. The priests are those who ' wear a linen ephod ' (1 S 22[18]). The child Samuel in Shiloh (1 S 2[18]), and David, bringing back the Ark (2 S 6[14] etc.), also wear the linen ephod ; cf Ezk 9[2] 10[2], Dn 10[5]. It formed the garment of the Levite singers (2 Ch 5[12]). It was the fitting raiment of the Lamb's wife, ' the righteousness of the saints ' (Rev 19[8]) ; presumptuously assumed by ' the great city Babylon ' (18[16]) ; in it are also arrayed ' the armies that are in heaven ' (19[14]).

No clear and uniform distinction can be drawn between several Hebrew words translated ' linen.' *badh* appears to be always used of garments (Gn 41[42] etc.), while *shēsh* may perhaps mean the thread, as in the phrase ' *badh* of fine twined *shēsh* ' (Ex 39[28]), the cloth made from it (Ex 25[4] 26[1], Ezk 27[7] etc.), and also garments (Ex 28[5] etc.). We cannot, indeed, be certain that ' linen ' is always intended (Guthe, *Bib. Wörterbuch, s.v.*). The modern Arabic *shash* means ' cotton gauze.' *bûṣ* is a word of Aramaean origin, occurring only in later books (Ezk 27[16], 1 Ch 4[21], Est 1[6]), whence comes the Greek *byssos,* which covered both *badh* and *shēsh* (Jos. *Ant.* III. vi. 1 f [103, 110]). By later writers it was taken to represent cotton (Liddell and Scott[8], *s.v.*). *pishtîm* is a general term, denoting the flax, or anything made from it (Jos 2[6], Jg 15[14], Jer 13[1] etc.). *Sādhîn* was a sheet in which the whole body might be wrapped (Jg 14[12f], Pr 31[24] etc.). It probably corresponded to the *sindōn* **' linen cloth '** of Mk 14[51], and the **shroud** of Mt 27[59] etc. *'ēṭûn* (Pr 7[16]) is probably fine Egyptian thread, with which cloths and hangings were ornamented. *Othonē* (Ac 10[11]) is a large sheet : *othonia* (Jn 19[40] etc.) are strips for bandages. *Ōmolinon* (Sir 40[4]) was cloth of unbleached flax. *Sha'atnēz* (Lv 19[19]) was probably cloth composed of linen and cotton.

Linen yarn (1 K 10[28], 2 Ch 1[16] [AV], Hebrew *miḳweh*) should almost certainly be rendered with RSV **' from Kue '** (q.v.). W. E.

LINTEL.—See House, **6.**

LINUS.—One of the Christians at Rome, and presumably a prominent one, from whom St. Paul sends greetings at the end of Second Timothy (4^{21}). The Church tradition identifies him as the first bishop of Rome (after Peter and Paul). The earliest form of the tradition is in Irenaeus (*adv. Haer.* iii. 3. 2, 3): 'The blessed Apostles then, having founded and built up the Church, entrusted the office of bishop to Linus,' and it is repeated in Eusebius and the early Roman episcopal lists, in which the episcopate of Linus is said to have lasted twelve years. The name occurs elsewhere (in Martial and a group of inscriptions), but is not very common, and the tradition may be correct in the sense that Linus was a recognized leader of the Roman Church; but it is an open question whether anything like a monarchical episcopate was established in Rome at so early a date. The chronology is entirely uncertain.
J. L.

LION.—The Hebrew *'aryēh*, *'ᵃrî*, words cognate to which are general terms for any wild beast in the sister languages, is the ordinary word for the 'male lion,' while *lābhî'* is that for a 'lioness' (Is 5^{29}, Ezk 19^2 etc.); a 'young lion' is *kᵉphîr* (Ezk 19^3 etc.). Other words are *layish* (used also as a proper name) and as usually explained *shaḥal.* The former is the same word as the Akkadian *nêšu* 'male lion' and the Arabic *laithu* 'lion,' which is perhaps only a descriptive term meaning 'strong' (Arab. *laiyîthu* 'strong'); it is translated 'lion-cub' in most of the ancient versions (LXX and Peshitta at Is 30^6, Pr 30^{30}; Targum at Is 30^6) occasionally *leo* and even *tigris* (Vulgate at Job 4^{11}). The latter is generally translated 'lion' or 'lioness' (LXX, Vulgate), 'lion' (for which six or seven other names occur) and 'young lion' (Peshitta, Targum), but twice 'panther' (LXX at Hos 5^{14} 13^7). The Arabic *saḥḥalatu* '(newly born) lamb, kid; leveret above the age at which the mother leaves it' (cf *saḥala* 'drove away') perhaps justifies taking the Hebrew *shaḥal* as denoting a young beast, *e.g.* a lion-cub; but the context nowhere requires a cub. The word is perhaps rather in origin onomatopoeic (cf Akk. *šaḫālu* 'to emit a sound, to shout' and the Arabic *saḥala* 'made a rolling sound, brayed'), being then a general term for any of the large cats, whether lion (cf Aram. *shaḥlâ* at Ps 17^{12}, Targum), panther (large leopard), or leopard. This last crouches in tall grass or reeds beside a stream with its belly almost touching the ground and its head held down but its eyes kept just above the level of the grass, ready to spring on man or beast who comes to drink. Possibly Job refers to this habit when he says (if the MT's impossible *yigh'eh kashshaḥal* may be corrected to *kᵉshaḥal yigh'eh*) 'like a panther which rises to spring Thou dost hunt me' (Job 10^{16}; cf LXX). Indeed, the root of this verb may have originally been coined to represent the spasmodic raucous sounds emitted by some beasts before springing on the prey (cf Arab. *ja'ja'a* 'cried *ji' ji'*' when driving camels to water and 'breasted the waves'). The Greek *panthēr* includes several spotted cats beside the leopard, which has a different name (see Leopard). The leopard (*felis pardus*) is still met, though in small numbers, round the Dead Sea, in Gilead and Bashan, often lurking near watering places ready to pounce on any unwary cattle. The hunting leopard or cheetah (*felis jubata*) was still found in the 19th cent. round Tabor, in the hills of Galilee and in Gilead (Tristram). Two other *felidae*, the spotted lynx (*felis pardina*) and the red lynx (*felis caracal*), are found in Palestine; but whether these are subsumed under one or other of the terms for 'leopard' cannot be said.

Further, the meaning of 'Beersheba' may have been 'lion's well,' if a Hebrew**shebha'*=Arabic *sab'u* 'wild beast, lion' may be postulated; if so, this will be another place-name indicating Arab settlements in S. Palestine. The suggestion has also been made that the Arabic *'asadu* 'lion' in the sense of 'warrior' may lie behind the mysterious *'ēsh dāth* 'fire of law! (in)' *mîmîmô* (*'ēd shāth* corrected to) *'ᵃshādhôth lāmô* 'he has (warriors brave as) lions at his right hand' (Dt 33^2, Beeston). Finally *bᵉnê shaḥaṣ* 'sons of pride' (Job 28^8 41^{26}) is merely a poetic expression for 'lions' (cf Aram. *šaḥṣâ* 'lion') or other beasts of prey.

Lions, though extinct since the Crusades, must once have been common in Palestine, especially in the thickets of the Jordan (Jer 49^{19} 50^{44}, Zec 11^3); they were a source of danger to men (1 K 13^{24-25} 20^{36}, 2 K 17^{25}) and to flocks (1 S 17^{37}, Is 31^4, Am 3^{12}, Mic 5^8). Their roar was terrifying (Pr 19^{12} 20^2 etc.) and was compared to the voice of God (Am 3^8; cf Jer 25^{10}, Jl 3^{16}). In the OT Judah (Gn 49^9; cf Rev 5^5) and Israel (Nu 23^{24} 24^9) as well as Dan (Dt 33^{22}) are compared to lions; in the NT the lion is typical of Satan (1 P 5^8). G. R. D.

LIP.—**1.** Hebrew *śāphāh*, the usual OT word, and of very frequent occurrence. Only rarely are the lips referred to from the point of view of description of physical beauty and charm (Ca $4^{3, 11}$ 5^{13}). Once they are associated with kissing (Pr 24^{26}), once with drinking (Ca 7^9, with which cf Ps 45^2), once anthropomorphically (of Y″) as the source from which the breath issues (Is 11^4); once the protrusion of the lips occurs as a gesture of mocking contempt (Ps 22^7, AV, RV 'shoot out the lip'; RSV 'make mouths'). Twice (2 K 19^{28}, Is 37^{29}) we have an allusion to the cruel Assyrian custom of passing a ring through the lips (AV, RV 'my bridle in thy lips'; RSV 'my bit in your mouth') of captives and leading them about with a rope or thong. But in the great majority of cases the lips are referred to as organs of speech (Job 27^4, Ps 119^{171}, Pr 15^7 24^2). Hence, according to the kind of words they utter and the quality of the heart from which the words come, they are described figuratively as uncircumcised (Ex $6^{12, 30}$), flattering (Ps 12^{2f}), feigned (17^1), lying (31^{18}), joyful (63^5), crooked (Pr 4^{24}), righteous (16^{13}), wicked (17^4), burning (26^{23} AV; RV 'fervent,' RSV 'smooth'), unclean (Is 6^5). By an intensification or extension of this figurative use, swords are said to be in the lips (Ps 59^7 AV, RV; RSV 'snarling with their lips'), the poison of vipers to be under them (140^3) or in them a scorching fire (Pr 16^{27}). In Is 57^{18} 'the fruit of the lips'=praise. For Hos 14^2 see Calves of the Lips. **2.** Hebrew *śāphām* (Ezk $24^{17, 22}$, Mic 3^7, only in the phrase 'cover the lips'), whose equivalent is 'moustache,' it being the Eastern custom to cover this as a sign of stricken sorrow. **3.** Greek *cheilos* occurs six times in NT, always in quotations from LXX: Mt 15^8 and Mk 7^6=Is 29^{13}; Ro 3^{13}=Ps 140^3 [139^4]; 1 Co 14^{21}= Is 28^{11}; He 13^{15}=Hos 14^2; 1 P 3^{10}=Ps 33^{13} [33^{14}].
J. C. L.

LIST.—The Old English verb 'to list' occurs in Mt 17^{12}, Mk 9^{13}, Jn 3^8, Ja 3^4. It means 'to desire *or* choose.' RSV avoids the word, in this sense.

LITTLE HORN.—In Dn $7^{8ff, 20f}$ 8^{9ff} the expression 'Little Horn' refers to Antiochus Epiphanes (see Antiochus, **4**, and Daniel, **2**), whose persecution of the Jews and whose desecration of the Temple and suspension of the rightful sacrifices led to the Maccabaean rising. For a full discussion of this question (with the examination of other proposed identifications) and of the identification of the other horns of Dn 7, see H. H. Rowley, *Darius the Mede and the Four World Empires in the Book of Daniel*, 2nd ed., 1959, pp. 98 ff, where the identification of the three uprooted horns is particularly discussed.

LITTLE OWL.—See Owl.

LIVELY.—In AV 'lively' sometimes means 'living.' Thus in 1 P 2^5 Christians are 'lively stones,' while in the previous verse Christ is a 'living stone,' though the Greek word is the same in both verses. The other passages are Ac 7^{38} 'lively oracles' and 1 P 1^3 'lively hope.' RSV does not use the word.

LIVER (*kābhēdh*).—**1.** In the great majority of cases where the liver is mentioned, it is in connexion with the law of sacrifice as prescribed in P (Ex $29^{13, 22}$, Lv $3^{4, 10, 15}$ etc.), and always in association with the appendage of the liver (AV, RV **caul**; Hebrew *yōthereth*). The

LXX, followed by Josephus (*Ant.* III. ix. 2 [228]), takes *yōthereth* to be a lobe of the liver; but it is now agreed that it denotes the fatty mass at the opening of that organ. According to Semitic ideas, a peculiar holiness belonged to the liver and kidneys (q.v.), together with the fat attached to them; the reason being that they were regarded as the special seats not only of emotion but of life itself. Because of its sacredness the liver with its fat was not to be eaten, but was to be offered in sacrifice to Y″. **2.** Pr 7[23] 'till an arrow pierces its entrails' (*kābhēdh*), La 2[11] 'my heart (literally liver) is poured out in grief' (cf Job 16[13] 'he pours out my gall on the ground') are further illustrations of the physiological ideas referred to above. Either they are strong expressions for a deadly disease, or they denote sorrowful emotion of the most poignant kind. **3.** In Ezk 21[21] the king of Babylon, at the parting of the way, 'looks at the liver' as one of the three forms of divination he employed. **4.** In To 6[4-16] 8[2] the liver of a fish is used for the purpose of exorcism. See; further, MAGIC, DIVINATION AND SORCERY. J. C. L.

LIVING CREATURES.—See BEAST, **2.**

LIZARD.—(1) *leṭā'āh*, a generic name for lizard (so AV, RV, RSV).

(2) *ṣābh* (cf Arab. *ḍabb*) translated AV **tortoise,** RV and RSV **great lizard.**

(3) *'anāḳāh*, translated AV **ferret,** RV and RSV **gecko.**

(4) *kōaḥ*, translated AV **chameleon,** RV and RSV **land crocodile.**

(5) *ḥōmeṭ*, translated AV **snail,** RV and RSV **sand lizard.**

(6) *tinshemeth*, translated AV **mole,** RV and RSV **chameleon** (q.v.). All of these names occur only in Lv 11[27f] as 'unclean' animals; most of them are uncertain.

(7) *śemāmîth*, Pr 30[28], translated AV **spider,** RV and RSV **lizard.** Lizards are ubiquitous and exceedingly plentiful in Palestine, over forty species have been identified. The most common is the green lizard (*Lacerta viridis*). The Palestinian **gecko** (*Ptyodactylus Hasselquistii*) is common in all native houses; it is able to walk up the walls and along the ceilings by means of the disc-like suckers at the ends of its toes. If *śemāmîth* was, as many scholars claim, a lizard, then probably the gecko is the special species indicated. The *ḍabb* is a large lizard (*Uromastix spinipes*), with a long spiny tail. The **sand lizards** or skinks are common on soft, sandy soil; seven species are found in Palestine. The '**land crocodile,**' known to the Arabs as the *warrel*, is a large lizard, sometimes 5 feet long; two species have been found in the Jordan valley—the *Psammosaurus scineus* and the *Monitor niloticus.* The **chameleon** is dealt with in a separate article. E. W. G. M.

LOAF.—See BREAD.

LO-AMMI.—A symbolical name given to Hosea's son (Hos 1[9]), signifying 'not my people' (so RSV), as **Lo-ruhamah,** the name of his daughter, signifies 'not-pitied.' Opinions are divided as to whether these names are of actual persons used symbolically, or are purely allegorical. See HOSEA.

LOAN.—See DEBT.

LOCK.—See HOUSE, **6.**

LOCUST.—The insect is mentioned frequently in the Bible and was designated by various Hebrew and Greek words:

(1) *'arbeh* (root 'to multiply') occurs more than twenty times; in Jg 6[5] 7[12], Job 39[20], Jer 46[23] it was translated in AV as **grasshoppers** (q.v.); RSV regularly translates as 'locust.'

(2) *ḥāgābh* (translated AV, RV, RSV 'locust' in 2 Ch 7[13], elsewhere 'grasshopper'), possibly a small locust or any locust allowed for food: see Lv 11[22], Nu 13[33], Ec 12[5], Is 40[22].

(3) *gēbhîm* (plural, 'swarm'), Am 7[1], AV 'grasshoppers,' RV, RSV 'locusts,' AVm 'green worms'; *gōbhay*, Nah 3 [17],AV 'grasshoppers,' RV 'swarms of grasshoppers,' RSV 'locusts'; cf *gēbhîm*, Is 33[4], AV, RSV, 'locusts.'

The remaining Hebrew words are very uncertain. (4) *gāzām*, AV '**palmer worm**' (*i.e.* caterpillar), RSV 'cutting locust' and 'locust.' (5) *yeleḳ*, AV 'canker-worm,' RSV 'hopping locust.' (6) *ḥāsîl*, AV '**caterpillar,**' RSV 'destroying locust.' These three (Jl 1[4] 2[25] etc.), as the different translations above indicate, may all be stages in the development of the locust, or they may, less probably, be some varieties of grasshoppers. The greater size and ability of the locust to destroy foliage makes it probable that the locust rather than the grasshopper is involved in references to catastrophic events. (7) *ḥargōl*, Lv 11[22] (mistranslated in AV '**beetle**'; RV, RSV '**cricket**'), and (8) *sol'ām*, Lv 11[22] (translated AV, RV, RSV '**bald locust**') are also some varieties or stages of locust or grasshopper (it is impossible to be certain of the varieties specified). (9) *ṣelāṣal*, Dt 28[42]; the root is uncertain and may imply the strident noise of the *cicada* or cricket, or the shadow or darkness cast by the swarm of locusts; AV, RSV 'locust.'

Various words are used in the LXX to translate the Hebrew; the most common one is *akris* (Jg 6[5] 7[12], Am 7[1], Nah 3[17] etc.), which is also the NT word for 'locust' (Mt 3[4], Mk 1[6], Rev 9[3, 7]).

Locusts and grasshoppers are included in the family *Acrididae.* They are always plentiful in the Near East, but the locusts fortunately do not appear in swarms, except at intervals of years. The most destructive kinds are *Acridium peregrinum* and *Oedipoda migratoria*; they are to be distinguished from the *Cicada septendecim* (the seventeen-year locust or cricket) which is often called 'locust' in the United States. Some characteristics of the locust in the ancient Near East can be recognized by a study of the OT references to them. When they arrive in their countless millions, they darken the sky (Ex 10[15]). The poetical description in Jl 2[1-11] is full of faithful touches; particularly the extraordinary noise they make (v.[5]) when they are all feeding together. Their voracious onslaught is referred to in Is 33[4], and their sudden disappearance when they rise in clouds to seek new fields for destruction is mentioned in Nah 3[17]. They eat the foliage and fruit of every green thing in their path (Ex 10[15]). No more suitable figure can be conceived for an invading army (Jg 6[5] 7[12], Jer 46[23]). In modern times when the Anezi tribe of Bedouin Arabs from E. of the Jordan 'swarmed' or encamped on the Plain of Esdraelon, an eyewitness described the Plain as being stripped utterly bare, 'just as if the locusts had been over it.' When locusts are blown seaward, they fall into the water in vast numbers (Ex 10[19]). In recent years, travellers along the N. shore of the Dead Sea have reported seeing on occasions a continuous ridge of dead locusts washed up. The smell of such piles of rotting locusts is described as intolerable. The feebleness and insignificance of these insects, as viewed individually, are referred to in Nu 13[33], Ps 109[23], Is 40[22], although in such passages the translation is usually 'grasshopper' to distinguish the insect from the more formidable locust. Locusts are still eaten (cf Mt 3[4]). See FOOD, **8.**

Great strides have been made in the control of the locust, although control measures are difficult because of the extensive breeding grounds involved. During the 1930s several international locust control conferences were held, and in 1932 the Anti-Locust Research centre in London was established. Since the 19th cent., attempts have been made in such places as Cyprus to destroy the eggs and to kill the mature locust by the use of various types of traps and poison baits. A warning system has been established to announce the outbreak of a locust plague, and during World War II., ambitious programmes of control were undertaken. The use of the aeroplane to dust with insecticides the swarms and breeding grounds in Africa and Asia has become common. Such protection for Palestine has been provided with considerable success against the locust swarms originating in the Arabian desert. E. W. G. M.—**W. L. R.**

LOD, LYDDA.—A town in the territory of Benjamin, not apparently of pre-Israelite origin, but built (1 Ch 8[12]), along with Ono, by the Benjamite Shemed (but *Luthen* and *Auanau* occur side by side in the lists of Thothmes III.). Elsewhere it is mentioned only in the post-Captivity lists (Ezr 2[33], Neh 7[37] 11[35]); and in connexion with the healing of Aeneas at this place (Ac 9[32]). Its inhabitants were enslaved by Cassius, and freed by Anthony (Jos. *Ant.* XIV. xi. 2 [275], xii. 2 [304]). Cestius Gallus burned it, and it afterwards surrendered to Vespasian (*BJ* II. xix. 1 [516], IV. vii. 1 [144]). In the Middle Ages it was the seat of a bishopric. It is a centre of the cultus of that strange being called by the Christians St. George (to whom the church is dedicated), and by the Muslims *el-Khudr*—probably an ancient spirit of vegetation. It was known as *Diopholis* in the Byzantine period, but the old name *Ludd* is still attached to the site. R. A. S. M.

LODDEUS, 1 Es 8[45f] (RV).—See IDDO, **1.**

LO-DEBAR.—A place in Gilead, near to, and apparently E. from, Mahanaim. It was the retreat of Mephibosheth till he was summoned to court by David (2 S 9[4f]). It is mentioned also upon the occasion of David's flight to the E. of the Jordan (17[27]), and again in Am 6[13] (RSV; AV, RV translate the name, 'a thing of nought'). It is perhaps the same as **Lidebir** (q.v.). Its site is uncertain; possibly modern *Umm ed-Dabar*, S. of *Wâdī el-ʿArab*.

LODGE.—See CUCUMBERS.

LOFT.—See HOUSE, **5.**

LOG.—See WEIGHTS AND MEASURES.

LOGIA.—See GOSPELS.

LOGOS.—In classical Greek *logos* signifies both 'word' and 'reason,' but in the LXX and the NT it is used, with few exceptions, in the former sense only. When it is God's word that is spoken of, it denotes the declaration or revelation of the Divine will, and specifically the Christian gospel as the utterance of the Divine plan of salvation (*e.g.* Mt 13[19-23]||, Ph 1[14]). But in the Prologue to the Fourth Gospel (1[1] [three times] [14], with which cf 1 Jn 1[1] [5[7] of AV is spurious; see RSV] and Rev 19[13]) 'Logos' (EV **Word**) is applied to Jesus Christ, and is used to set forth His peculiar glory as the only-begotten Son of God, who is also the Life and Light of men. It is with this Johannine Logos that we have now to deal, and in doing so it seems necessary to consider (1) the content of John's Logos doctrine; (2) its sources; (3) its place in the Fourth Gospel; (4) its theological significance.

1. Content.—Three stages appear in the exposition of the Logos doctrine given in the Prologue. (*a*) First (vv.[1-5]), the nature and functions of the Logos are set forth in His relations to God, the world, and man. He was with *God* in the beginning, *i.e.* He eternally held a relation of communion with Him as a separate personality—a personality itself Divine, for 'the Word was God.' As to the *world*, it was made by Him (v.[3], cf v.[10]), perhaps with the further suggestion that from Him it draws continually the life by which it is sustained (v.[4]). But from Him there flows also the higher life of *man* as a spiritual being possessed of reason and conscience, for His life becomes the universal light of human souls (v.[5], cf v.[9]). (*b*) The second stage of the exposition (vv.[6-13]) is a contrast of the Logos with the word of God that came by John the Baptist. John was not the Light; he came only to bear witness to it. The Logos is the true Light, and the mediator of Divine life to all who believe in His name. (*c*) Finally (vv.[14-18]), the author describes the incarnation of the Logos in the flesh, and declares His identity with the historical Jesus Christ, the bringer of grace and truth. In v.[18] the whole Prologue is summed up. Here the writer returns to the point from which he set out (cf v.[1]), but his readers now understand that the eternal Logos is one with Jesus Christ, the Son of God.

2. Sources.—(1) For these some have been content to refer to *the OT and the post-canonical Jewish writings.* And it is true that a connexion is clearly to be traced. We can hardly mistake a reference in the Prologue (vv.[1, 3f, 10]) to the creative word of God in Gn 1. In the Psalms and Prophets, again, a personification of the word of the Lord is common (*e.g.* Ps 33[6], Is 55[11]). And in the Wisdom literature, both canonical and apocryphal, this personifying tendency is carried still further (Pr 8[22-31], Sir 24), though it is God's Wisdom, not His Word, that becomes His representative, and a full personification of the Word does not meet us till we have reached a point in Jewish history where Greek influences have begun to make themselves felt (Wis 9[1] 16[12]). All this, however, is very far from explaining the Johannine Logos doctrine. The most that can be said is that the doctrine of the Prologue reflects a tendency of Jewish thought, finding its roots in the OT, to conceive of the Divine self-revelation as mediated by the personified Wisdom or Word of the Lord.

(2) Some have held that John's Logos doctrine was derived entirely from *the Judaeo-Alexandrian philosophy*, and specifically from the teaching of **Philo** (q.v.). From early times there had grown up among the Greeks a conception of the Logos as the Divine Reason manifested in the universe, and explaining how God comes into relation with it. To this Logos philosophy Plato's doctrine of ideas had contributed, and afterwards the Stoic view of the Logos as the rational principle of the universe. In his efforts to blend Judaism with Hellenism, Philo adopted the term as one familiar alike to Jews and to Greeks, and sought to show by means of allegorical interpretations that the true philosophy of God and the world was revealed in the OT. And St. John, it is supposed, simply appropriated this teaching, and by means of an idealizing treatment of Christ's life constructed in his Gospel a philosophical treatise on the doctrine of Philo. The theory breaks down on any examination. To Philo the Logos was the principle of Reason; to St. John He was the Divine revealing Word. Philo's Logos is not really personal; St. John's certainly is. Philo does not identify the Logos with the Messiah; to St. John He is no other than the Christ, the Saviour of the world. Philo sees in the flesh a principle opposed to the Godhead; St. John glories in the fact of the Incarnation. With Philo the antithesis between God and the world is a metaphysical one; with St. John it is ethical and religious. St. John cannot, then, have derived his doctrine of the Logos from Philo. But he undoubtedly used the term because Philo and others had made it familiar to Graeco-Jewish thought as a means of expressing the idea of a mediation between God and the universe, and also perhaps because he himself had received certain formal influences from the Philonic philosophy (see *e.g.* the value he assigns to knowledge; his crystallization of the gospel into such general terms as 'light,' 'truth,' 'life'; his constant antithesis of light and darkness—though these were ancient religious symbols). Apart, however, from such formal influences and the convenience of a familiar and suggestive term, the real source of the Johannine Logos doctrine is still to seek.

(3) That source is assuredly to be found in *the actual historical personality of Jesus Himself* as we find it set forth in the rest of this Gospel. More and more it becomes impossible for the careful student of this book to treat it as a philosophical romance in which a purely idealizing treatment is given to the figure of Jesus; more and more the substantial historical truth of the presentation becomes evident. And, assuming the substantial truth of the narrative, it seems clear that St. John uses his Logos conception, not 'to manufacture the Light of the World out of the Messiah of Israel,' but to set forth, in a way that would appeal to readers of his own place and time, Christ's real relations to God and the universe as these had been attested by His words and deeds, by His dying and rising from the dead, and by all the facts of His self-revelation. We must bear in mind, moreover, that while the term 'Logos' was a new one to be applied to Christ, the place of dignity and power assigned to Him by John was by no means new. Both

St Paul and the author of Hebrews had taught the doctrine of Christ's eternal Sonship, and of His functions as the creator of the universe and the revealer of the Father (Ph 2^{5-11}, Col 1^{13-20} 2^{9}, He 1^{1-4}), and the teaching of both, already familiar and widely accepted in the Church, is subsumed in the Johannine doctrine of the Logos.

3. Place in the Fourth Gospel.—The attempt has been made to distinguish between the Logos doctrine in the Prologue as Hellenic, and the Gospel itself as Palestinian ; and it has been maintained that the influence of the Logos idea does not extend beyond the Prologue, and that it was merely intended to introduce to Greek readers the story of the Jewish Messiah with a view to making it more attractive and intelligible. We may remind ourselves, however, of Strauss's comparison of this Gospel to the seamless robe of Jesus, a judgment which has been verified by nearly every critical student of whatever school. It is true that when we pass beyond the Prologue the word ' Logos ' is not repeated. The author nowhere puts it into the mouth of Jesus—one evidence surely of his historical fidelity. But, all the same, the doctrine of the Prologue manifestly works right through the narrative from beginning to end (see such passages as 3^{13-21} 6^{53-58} 7^{28f} $8^{12, 14, 16}$ 10^{29ff} 12^{44-50} 14^{6-11} $17^{5, 8, 24}$ etc.). It is very noticeable that in 20^{31}, where, before laying down his pen, the writer reveals the motive of his work, he really sums up the great ideas of the Prologue as he declares that Jesus is the Christ, the Son of God, and that believing we may have life through His name. The Logos, then, is not a mere catchword, put forth in order to seize the eye and arouse the interest of the Greek reader. The Logos idea underlies the whole Gospel, and has much to do with the author's selection of his materials. In the Prologue, as in any other well-written introduction, the plan of the work is set out, and the Logos doctrine is stated there because it supplies the key to a right understanding of the history that follows.

4. Theological significance.—From the time of Justin and ever since, the Logos doctrine of St. John's Prologue has served as the material of many a Christian metaphysic. It is no doubt inevitable that this should be the case ; but we must be careful not to make St. John responsible for the theological constructions that have been woven out of his words. If an injustice is done him when his doctrine of the Logos is supposed to be nothing more than the fruitage of his study of Philo, another injustice is committed when it is assumed that he is setting forth here either a metaphysic of the Divine nature or a philosophy of the Incarnation. It is plain, on the contrary, that in all that he says it is the religious and ethical interests that are paramount. He uses the Logos conception for two great purposes—to set forth Jesus (1) as *the Revealer of God*, and (2) as *the Saviour of men*. The first of these ideas, as has been said, is one that we find already in the Pauline Epistles and in Hebrews ; but by his emphasis on the relations of Fatherhood and Sonship St. John imparts a peculiarly moral meaning to the essential nature of the God who is revealed in Christ. But it is above all for a soteriological purpose that he seems to employ the Logos idea. The Logos, who is identified with Jesus Christ, comes forth from the bosom of the Father, bringing life and light to men. He comes with a gospel that supersedes the Law of Moses, for it is a gospel of grace as well as of truth. Himself the Son of God, He offers to all who will believe in His name the right (or power) to become the children of God. And so, while the Logos is undoubtedly the agent of God's creative will, He is still more distinctively the mediator of God's redeeming purpose. It is therefore as a religious power, not as a metaphysical magnitude, that St. John brings Him before us. The Evangelist shows, it is true, that the absoluteness of Christ's historical mission and His exclusive mediation of the Divine saving grace are garuanteed by the fact that the roots of His personal life reach back into the eternal life of God. His Logos doctrine thus wards off every Christology that would see in Jesus no more than a prophetic personality of the highest originality. But, while the Logos idea ' illuminates the history with the light of eternity, it can reveal eternity to us only in the light of history, not in its own supernatural light ' (*PRE*[3] xi, 605). J. C. L.—**H. C.**

LOIS.—The grandmother of Timothy (2 Ti 1^{5}), and probably the mother of Eunice, Timothy's mother. The name is Greek. The family lived at Lystra (Ac 16^{1}), where St. Paul first made their acquaintance. Lois was a devout Jewess by conviction, who instructed her family diligently in the Holy Scripture. M. St.

LONGSUFFERING.—This word, regularly used in the AV (and sometimes retained by the RV) to translate *makrothymia* and its corresponding verb, is not found in the RSV, either OT or NT. In the NT it has been replaced by some form of ' patient ' except for Lk 18^{7} (' delay long '), 2 P 3^{9} (' be forbearing '), and 2 P 3^{15} (' forbearance ').

The Greek word means ' a long holding out of the mind before it gives room to action or passion—generally to passion ' (Trench, *Synonyms of NT*, liii) ; it implies the opposite of short temper ; cf Old English ' longanimity.' In the NT the patience of God is regarded as a proof of His ' goodness ' (Ro 2^{4} ; here and elsewhere ' patience,' || **' forbearance '** [*anochē*]) and of His faithfulness (2 P $3^{9, 15}$) ; it is manifested in the gracious restraint which characterizes His attitude towards those who deserve His wrath (Ro 9^{22}, 1 P 3^{20}). The Divine patience is perfectly exemplified in Christ's dealings with sinners (1 Ti 1^{16}). Patience is, therefore, a conspicuous grace in the ideal Christian character (2 Co 6^{6}, Eph 4^{2}, Col 3^{12}, 1 Th 5^{14}, 2 Ti 3^{10} 4^{2}) ; it is viewed as an evidence of Divine strengthening (Col 1^{11}), as a manifestation of love (1 Co 13^{4}), and as a fruit of the Spirit (Gal 5^{22}). J. G. T.—**F. W. G.**

LOOKING-GLASS.—See GLASS.

LOOM.—See SPINNING AND WEAVING.

LOOPS.—See TABERNACLE, **5** (*a*).

LORD.—The Hebrew, OT has three leading names for God : (1) ' the name of four letters ' (*tetragrammaton*) YHWH (familiar to us in the incorrect form ' Jehovah ' ; the real vocalization is almost certainly ' Yahweh ' [see GOD]) ; (2) *'Adhōnay* ; (3) *'Elohîm*. By the Greek period the Jews shrank from uttering the first of these (the LXX of Lv 24^{16} expressly forbids it), and added to its four consonants, in their reading of the OT, the *vowels* of either *'Adhōnay* or *'Elohîm*. When the vowels of the former were added, the AV, RV, and RSV generally translate the word by ' LORD,' when those of the latter, by ' GOD ' ; using small capitals in each case (ARV reads ' Jehovah ' in both cases). If, however, *'Adhōnay* is originally in the text, all versions represent it by ' Lord,' using an initial capital only. Thus in the OT (except in ARV) ' LORD ' represents *Yahweh* when it was read as *'Adhōnay* ; and ' Lord ' represents *'Adhōnay* when it stands in the original text. This distinctive printing is not observed in the NT. There are several other Hebrew words in the OT expressing the general idea of lordship, which are rendered by ' lord ' (Gn 45^{8}, Jg 3^{3}, Is 16^{8} etc.).

In the NT, AV uses ' Lord ' once (Mk 10^{51}) as translation of *Rabboni* (but RSV **' Master '**), and five times of *despotēs* (Lk 2^{29}, Ac 4^{24}, 2 P 2^{1}, Jd ^{4}, Rev 6^{10}). In the latter cases, however, RSV reads ' Lord,' ' Sovereign Lord,' or **' Master '** while RV and ARV have **' Master '** in text or margin. Elsewhere ' Lord ' represents *kyrios*, applying the title (1) to God (Mt 1^{20}, Ac 5^{19} etc.) ; (2) to Christ (Lk 6^{46}, Jn 20^{28} etc.). Indeed, as applied to Christ, it is the highest confession of His Person (1 Co 12^{3}, Ro 10^{9}, Rev 19^{16}). The form ' lord ' in NT indicates mere possession of authority (*e.g.* Mt 18^{25}), but in such cases RSV usually renders ' master ' or the like. C. T. P. G.—**J. Br.**

LORD OF HOSTS.—By NT times *Sabaoth* had become a Greek title (cf Ro 9^{29}, Ja 5^{4}, AV, RV, but not RSV), and the LXX likewise renders it, though by no means consistently, in transliteration. Where the rendering is interpretative, the meaning attached to the word is 'all-powerful,' 'sovereign,' 'lord of all creation.' This, probably, is also the meaning given to it by Christians to-day when they pronounce the word in public worship.

It might be argued that by adopting this now traditional Christian interpretation the Church merely uses a Hellenistic paraphrase and avoids anthropomorphism by introducing metaphysical theology, with the consequent loss of Hebraic realism. But a survey of the OT usage will show that a closer definition is well-nigh impossible. The title occurs nearly three hundred times in all, nearly two hundred and fifty of them in the prophetical books, and obviously its popularity betokens a long tradition, and a fundamental significance for Hebrew religion. Nevertheless, it is not used in the Pentateuch, and it first occurs historically in the military contexts of Samuel. In 1 S 17^{45} we have a definition, 'the Lord of Hosts, the God of the armies of Israel,' and it is sometimes thought that originally the form of the title was God of Hosts, in apposition to Yahweh, and the abbreviated Yahweh of Hosts came later. In Am 4^{13} 5^{27} the formula reads 'The Lord whose name is the God of hosts.' In 2 S 6^{2} the Ark 'is called by the name of the Lord of hosts,' and it lies to hand to suggest that the title was connected with military exploits, especially where the Ark accompanied the army. But in the Elijah story in 1 K 19^{14}, although a conflict is presupposed, the Lord of Hosts is opposed to natural and cosmic forces, and there is no hint that a change of connotation has taken place. Other passages from the same literary period show that the title was used in purely cultic, non-militaristic contexts, such as 1 S $1^{3,11}$ where it applies to the shrine at Shiloh, and 2 S 6^{18} where a cultic act is centred on the Ark in Jerusalem. The prevalence of the title in Royal Psalms likewise postulates a cultic use, which glorifies not only Yahweh's championship in battle but also over the forces of Nature. When we turn to the prophets' use of the title it becomes obvious that any recollection of Yahweh as military leader of Israel's forces has gone. The Lord of Hosts is here the cosmic Judge, who can abolish the false altars of Bethel (Am 3^{13f}), mediums and wizards (Is 8^{18}), and the false prophets (Jer 5^{14}), 'who touches the earth and it melts' (Am 9^{5}).

The most recent full treatment of the term, by Wambacq (*L'Épithète Divine Jahvé S^{e}ba'ôt*, 1947) traces a gradual growth of the idea from an original association with the military forces of Israel to the cosmic title of the prophets, but the reaction against such an evolutionary explanation is well expressed by G. von Rad (*Theologie des A.T.*, 1957), who says that the use of the title by the prophets can include everything except the nationalistic ideas of the Samuel passages. It is probably pessimistic, however, to follow von Rad further, and admit that such an ancient epithet, with obvious cultic associations, cannot be supplied with a rational explanation to accommodate all its uses. The clue to the discrepancy between the prophetic use and Samuel might be that the latter is secondary to the former, and is the result of applying incidentally a conception with a much wider connotation in the history of Hebrew religion.

A totally different explanation of the title has been offered by O. Eissfeldt, 'Jahwe Zebaoth,' *Miscellanea Academica Berolinensia II* 2 (1950). He regards the plural of the noun as an expression of abstract or intensive noun-form—by no means an isolated grammatical convention—and the title thus denotes 'power' or, adjectivally, 'the powerful one.' The point is a complicated one, but there is a growing tendency to accept the idea. So perhaps after all the Hellenists were nearer the mark than they have been credited with being! B. J. R.

LORD'S DAY.—1. Name and origin.—The title used in the Apocalypse (Rev 1^{10}), probably to describe the day upon which the Christian Church in Apostolic days assembled for worship. The Acts of the Apostles shows us the disciples of Christ immediately after Pentecost as a closely united body, 'of one heart and soul,' supported by daily meetings and the Eucharist (4^{32} $2^{42,46}$). Their new faith did not at first lead them to cut themselves off from their old Jewish worship, for their belief in Jesus as Messiah seemed to them to add to and fulfil, rather than to abolish, the religion of their childhood. This worship of Christians with their Jewish fellow-countrymen secured the continuation of the Church of God from one dispensation to another; while their exclusively Christian Eucharists consolidated the Church and enabled it to discover itself.

The *daily* worship of the Christian Church would no doubt soon prove impracticable, and a weekly gathering become customary. For this weekly gathering the **Sabbath** (q.v.) was unsuitable, as being then observed in a spirit radically different from the joy and liberty of the new faith; doubtless also the restrictions as to length of a Sabbath day's journey would prove a bar to the gathering together of the little body. Of the other six days none so naturally suggested itself as the first. To it our Lord had granted a certain approval; for on it He rose from the dead and appeared to His disciples, and on the following Sunday repeated His visitation (Jn $20^{1,26}$); while, if Pentecost that year fell on the first day of the week (which it did if the chronology of St. John be followed), it received a final seal as the special day of grace.

That this day was actually chosen is seen in the NT (Ac 20^{7}, 1 Co 16^{2}). And mention of it is found in the literature immediately following the Apostolic writings.

Not the least interesting evidence is found in a report to the Emperor Trajan written by Pliny, Governor of Bithynia in A.D. 112, which mentions that the custom of the Christians was to meet together early in the morning on a certain 'fixed day,' and sing hymns to Christ as a god, and bind themselves by a *sacramentum* to commit no crime. Ignatius, the earliest of post-Apostolic Christian writers, also speaks of it, telling the Magnesians to lead a life conformable to 'the Lord's Day' (9^{1}).

And from then to now a continuous stream of evidence shows that the Church has faithfully observed the custom ever since.

The *title* by which early Christian writers usually called the festival was 'the Lord's Day'; but before long the Church felt no difficulty in adopting the heathen title of '**Sunday**,' realizing that as on that day light was created, and the Sun of Righteousness arose on it, there was to them a peculiar fitness in the name.

The most valuable evidence as to the method by which the early Church observed the day is found in Justin Martyr's *Apology* (i. 67, A.D. 155), where we read that on the day called Sunday the Christians met together, out of both city and country, and held a religious service at which first the writings of Apostles and Prophets were read; then the president preached; after which common prayers were said; and when these were ended, bread and wine were brought to the president, who uttered prayers and thanksgivings, to which the people said, 'Amen'; all present then participated in the Eucharist, the deacons carrying it to the absent. Thus it is clear that the early Church continued the Apostolic custom (Ac 20^{7}) of celebrating the Lord's Supper every Lord's Day—a custom so widespread as to enable Chrysostom to call Sunday *dies panis*, or 'the day of bread.'

2. Relation to the Sabbath.—The Sabbath was originally instituted as a provision for deep physical and spiritual needs of human nature, providing by religious sanction for the definite setting apart of the seventh day as a time for rest from labour and for communion with God. Our Lord found the original institution almost hidden beneath a mass of traditional regulations. Thus His action towards the Sabbath as He found it, was to bring men back to its first ideal. This He did by showing that their tradition told how David broke the letter of its regulation and yet was guiltless (Lk 6^{3}); how charity and common sense led men to break their own rules (13^{15}); how the Sabbath was given to man as a blessing and not laid on him as a burden (Mk 2^{27});

and how He as Son of Man, fulfilling ideal manhood, was its Lord (2^{28}); but while our Lord thus purified the Sabbath, there is no proof that He abolished it.

We can best see God's will regarding the Sabbath and the Lord's Day in what actually happened in Apostolic times. The Acts shows us that the Christians who were originally Jews observed *both* the Sabbath and the Christian Lord's Day (Ac 21^{20f}); and this double observance lasted among them at least until the destruction of the Temple. The Jewish members of the Church were soon outnumbered by the Gentile, and these latter would feel in no way drawn to continuing the observance of the Jewish Sabbath as well as their own Lord's Day; and this the more so that they had received the gospel under the wider teaching of St. Paul, who had emphasized the danger of an undue observance of days, and had spoken of the Sabbath as 'a shadow of the things to come' (*i.e.* the Christian dispensation; cf Col 2^{16f}, Gal 4^{9-11}, Ro 14^{5f}). But if the Gentile Christian did not observe the Jewish Sabbath, yet he could not be ignorant of its deeper meaning, for he saw the Sabbath observed by his Jewish neighbours, and read in the OT of its institution and uses; and thus imperceptibly the essential principle of the Sabbath would pass into the Christian day of worship. But whereas the old Sabbath commemorated God's rest from His old creation, the Lord's Day became a celebration of God's new creation begun in the resurrection of Christ from the dead. C. T. P. G.—**M. H. S.**

LORD'S PRAYER—The Lord's Prayer is found in the Gospels of St. Matthew and St. Luke, but in different contexts and with considerable variations. In Mt 6^{9-13}, which is part of the Sermon on the Mount, it follows the warning 'When you pray, you must not be like the hypocrites . . .' It has eight clauses introduced by the words, 'Pray then like this:

v.^{9} (1) Our Father who art in heaven,
(2) Hallowed be thy name.
v.^{10} (3) Thy kingdom come,
(4) Thy will be done on earth as it is in heaven.
v.^{11} (5) Give us this day our daily bread;
v.^{12} (6) And forgive us our debts, as we also have forgiven our debtors.
v.^{13} (7) And lead us not into temptation.
(8) But deliver us from evil.'

Later MSS add a doxology 'For thine is the kingdom and the power and the glory for ever,' but few critics regard this as part of the true text.

In Lk 11^{1-4} the Prayer is introduced as given in answer to the request of a disciple: 'And he said to them, When ye pray, say,

v.^{2} (1) Father,
(2) Hallowed be thy name.
(3) Thy kingdom come.
v.^{3} (5) Give us each day our daily bread;
v.^{4} (6) And forgive us our sins, for we ourselves forgive everyone who is indebted to us.
(7) And lead us not into temptation.'

The Prayer in Luke is thus considerably shorter than in Matthew. Except in inferior texts the Third Gospel has nothing to correspond to Matthew's 'Our' or 'in heaven' in clause (1), and it omits clauses (4) and (8). This shorter version is probably nearer to the original than Matthew's, for while it is easy to imagine clauses being added in the Church's use, it is difficult to think that words or petitions would have been omitted. Matthew's additions are not difficult to account for:

(1) The words 'in heaven' are frequent in the First Gospel and may be compared with a Jewish use common in the 1st cent. A.D.; but they are seldom used when God is addressed directly, and for that reason they are probably not original in the Prayer.

(4) 'Thy will be done on earth as it is in heaven' may have been derived from Christ's own prayer in the garden (Mt 26^{42}); but a more probable suggestion is that the clause originated as an explanation of the preceding words 'Thy kingdom come' at a time when the Church's apocalyptic hopes were growing dim.

Similarly clause (8) may be an expansion of the petition 'Lead us not into temptation.' The word translated 'temptation' may mean any kind of trial or severe testing, and clause (7) is a prayer that God's providence may not bring upon the suppliant trials, physical or moral, greater than he can bear. Then clause (8) develops the thought—may God rather deliver His servant from every kind of evil. Jewish parallels may be quoted: C. Taylor, *Sayings of the Jewish Fathers*, p. 128, compares the rabbinic prayer, 'May it be thy will to deliver us from evil man, from evil hap, from evil disposition, from evil companion, from evil neighbour, and from Satan the destroyer' (B. T. D. Smith, *St. Matthew*).

The Greek word translated 'evil' in clause (8) might be masculine and refer to Satan, 'the evil one'; but it seems better to take it as neuter, *i.e.* evil in the wider sense. The suggestion that the reference is to the exceptional trials which Jewish thought associated with the coming of the kingdom (cf Mt 24^{6-22}) is possible but unnecessary, unless Schweitzer's contention that the whole Prayer is eschatological be accepted.

It is probable, then, that Luke's version is the more primitive. Taking the clauses in order:

(1) 'Father' translates the Aramaic 'Abba' which Mark records as having been Jesus' own address in prayer (Mk 14^{36}) and which St. Paul twice mentions as used in the early Church (Ro 8^{15}, Gal 4^{6}). That neither Matthew nor Luke quotes the Aramaic word in the Lord's Prayer is one of the indications that both evangelists were familiar with the Prayer as it had long been translated into Greek.

(2) 'Hallowed be thy Name' may be compared with similar clauses in many Jewish prayers, which were always primarily acts of worship. Ultimately the petition reflects Ezk 36^{25} 'I will sanctify my great name which has been profaned among the nations,' and it is a prayer for God's action rather than men's. Thus it looks forward to

(3) 'Thy Kingdom come' which expresses the eschatological hope of Israel adopted and transmuted by the Christian Church. W. O. E. Oesterley, *Jewish Background of the Christian Liturgy*, p. 73, quotes an ancient Jewish prayer, the 'Half-Kaddish,' "May he establish His kingdom in your lifetime and in your days." This may be said to have become the characteristic petition of the Christian Church (cf *Didache*, x).

(5) 'Give us each day our daily bread' is less easy to interpret owing to the use by both Matthew and Luke of a Greek word (*epiousion*) of which the translation is quite uncertain. Origen, writing early in the 3rd cent., was puzzled by it and could only suggest that it had been coined by the evangelists. It would seem to mean 'coming upon' or 'succeeding,' and then the petition would be 'Give us each day our bread for the coming, or next, day.' But no certainty can be claimed, and the various translations of the versions are evidence that the early Church could only guess the meaning. That the word occurs in both the Gospels is evidence that it represents a very early (and perhaps unfortunate) translation of some Aramaic word. The familiar English rendering 'daily' which is founded on the Vulgate's '*quotidianus*' may not be far wrong. The clause is a prayer that God will supply the daily needs of His people, and Schweitzer's attempt to connect it with the thought of the 'coming' kingdom is unconvincing.

(6) 'Forgive us our sins, for we ourselves forgive everyone who is indebted to us' may be paralleled in part from the sixth of the Jewish *Eighteen Benedictions*: 'Forgive us, our Father, for we have sinned: pardon us, our King, for we have transgressed'; and the reference to man's forgiveness of his neighbour may be compared with Sir 28^{2} 'Forgive thy neighbour the hurt that he has done thee, and then thy sins shall be pardoned when thou prayest.' For Matthew's 'debts' Luke substitutes 'sins'; but he has 'for we ourselves forgive every one who is indebted to us,' which suggests that Matthew's version is here nearer to the original. A slight difference

in meaning can be detected in the two versions of this clause. Matthew uses the perfect tense; we *have forgiven* our debtors, and can therefore ask for the same indulgence (cf Mt 18^{35}). Luke's ' Forgive us our sins, for we ourselves forgive' describes the consistent Christian attitude. Here again many commentators consider Matthew to be the more primitive.

(7) ' And lead us not into temptation.' As noted above, the word translated ' temptation ' is ambiguous. It may mean ' temptation to sin,' and is so used in some passages in the NT. Possibly some in the Early Church took this clause as implying that God's providence may deliberately confront men with temptation to do evil, and the author of the Epistle of James wished to correct that idea when he wrote (1^{13}), ' Let no one say, when he is tempted, " I am tempted by God " ; for God cannot be tempted with evil and he himself tempts no one.' But, as already noted, the Greek word may have a wider meaning, ' severe trial ' or ' testing ' (Gal 4^{14}, Rev 3^{10}), and this is more probable here. Then the petition is a prayer to be delivered from life's ills; but since suffering sometimes brings with it temptation to sin (as in the case of Job) the former meaning is not altogether excluded.

It is remarkable that there is no quotation from the Lord's Prayer in the rest of the NT Scriptures—unless 2 Ti 4^{18} is an echo of the final clauses in Matthew. It must have been used liturgically at an early date, and such use in the local churches provides the best explanation of the variations in the Gospels of Matthew and Luke; a clause might be added in one church and not in another, and slight differences in wording would creep in. At a later date the process was reversed and harmonization was inevitable. In late MSS, such as underlie the AV, the Prayer in Luke differs little from that in Matthew.

Taken as a whole, the Lord's Prayer in its earliest form is a simple act of worship, the elements of which can readily be paralleled from Jewish sources (I. Abrahams, *Studies*, 2nd series, p. xii). Yet the whole is more than a sum of its parts, and few will deny that the Lord's Prayer provides the perfect pattern of Christian devotion. Throughout the centuries the Church has used it in all its worship and has made it the type of more extended supplications. P. G.-S.

LORD'S SUPPER.—See EUCHARIST.

LORDS OF THE PHILISTINES.—The chieftains or ' tyrants ' of the five Philistine cities, Gaza, Ashkelon, Ashdod, Ekron, and Gath. Wherever they are mentioned (Jos 13^{3}, Jg 3^{3} 16$^{5, 8, 18, 27, 30}$, 1 S 5$^{8, 11}$ 6$^{4, 12, 16, 18}$ 7^{7} 29$^{2, 6f}$, 1 Ch 12^{19}) the word translated ' lord ' is a peculiar one, being identified with the Hebrew word for ' axle.' Once (1 S 18^{30}) the Hebrew word for ' princes ' is applied to them. Probably the peculiar word is a native Philistine title. Their functions, so far as can be gathered from the OT, were the same as those of petty kings. G. A. B.

LO-RUHAMAH.—See HOSEA, LO-AMMI.

LOT.—The son of Haran and nephew of Abraham. His name seems to be derived from a root meaning *to wrap closely*. The account of his life is contained in Gn 11^{27}–14^{16} 19. He was born in Ur, and went with Abraham to Haran, and thence to Canaan. He accompanied Abraham in much of his wandering. The separation (ch. 13) was due to a quarrel between their herdsmen, each having great possessions of live stock. As a result, Lot dwelt in the cities of the plain, making his home in Sodom. During the expedition of Chedorlaomer (ch. 14) he was carried away captive, but was eventually rescued by Abraham. In ch. 19 is narrated the escape of Lot and his daughters from Sodom, with the subsequent incidents. The city of **Zoar,** where they lived for a time, was near the southern end of the Dead Sea, in the Valley of Siddim (14^{3}), but the site is now unquestionably covered by the water of the Dead Sea, which has slowly risen. The mountain to which Lot finally went is doubtless the mountainous region later known as Moab. The story of the daughters of Lot (19$^{30-38}$) is now considered to be, not history, but a traditional account of the origin of the two nations, Moab and Ammon. The basis of the story is the popular etymology of the two names, and it was prompted also by national rivalry and hostility. Lot himself is supposed by modern scholars to personify the characteristics, migrations, and alliances of certain tribes, perhaps Aramaean, of which he was the supposed ancestor.

Lot's wife.—The story of Lot's wife and her transformation into **a pillar of salt** probably arose from the peculiarities of the cliffs in the vicinity of the Dead Sea. At its SW. extremity is a great salt mass stretching in a north-south direction, some 5 miles long, 3 miles wide, and 600 feet high, now called *Jebel Usdūm,* ' the mountain of Sodom.' It consists of crystallized rock salt, covered with chalky limestone and gypsum, and curiously furrowed and worn, so as sometimes to resemble a human figure. G. R. B.—**T. J. M.**

LOTAN.—A Horite clan, Gn 36$^{20, 22, 29}$, 1 Ch 1^{38f}.

LOTHASUBUS.—One of those who stood on Ezra's left hand at the reading of the Law, 1 Es 9^{44}; a corruption of **Hashum,** Neh 8^{4}.

LOTS.—See MAGIC, URIM AND THUMMIM, PURIM.

LOTUS.—This is the correct rendering of *ṣe'elîm* in Job 40^{21f} (RV ' lotus trees,' RSV ' lotus plants '; AV ' shady trees '), where it describes the haunt of Behemoth (q.v.). The tree is probably = the Arab *dâl*, the ' *dom*-tree,' and must not be confused with the Egyptian water-lilies. It is a prickly shrub found in N. Africa and S. Europe. See also LILY. W. E.

LOVE.—1. In the OT.—' Love ' (noun and verb) represent Hebrew words which ranged, like the English term, from (1) *sensuous*, and often evil, *desire* or passionate love between man and woman (as in Gn 25^{28}, 2 S 13^{4}, Jer 2^{33}), through (2) *family affection* and *natural friendship* (Gn 22^{2}, Ex 21^{5}, 1 S 18^{16}, 2 S 1^{26}), up to (3) *the highest spiritual passion*. Under (3) come the theological meanings: (*a*) *Y"'s love to* Israel, to the righteous, etc., as chosen by Him; this love is spontaneous, directed to the nation rather than to individuals (except perhaps in the Psalms); it condemns and judges sin, making moral demands (Dt 4^{37} 7^{6f}, Hos 3^{1} 9^{15} 11^{4} 14^{4}, Am 3^{2}, Jer 2^{2}, Is 43^{4} 48^{14} 63^{9}, Mal 1^{2}, Ps 11^{7} 47^{4} 78^{68} 87^{2} 146^{8}, Pr 3^{12} 8^{17}); at times it is not confined to one nation Israel (Am 9^{7}, Is 19^{19ff} 42^{1ff} 49^{6}); and (*b*) *Israel's love to Y"*, His name, word, house, salvation, law, etc. (*e.g.* Ex 20^{6}, Dt 6^{5} etc., Neh 1^{5}, 1 K 3^{3}—same verb as in 11^{1}, Ps 5^{11} 31^{23} 116^{1} 119^{97} etc., Mic 6^{8}); and (*c*) *dutiful love to one's neighbour* should perhaps be included here, for it is commanded even towards one's enemies (*e.g.* Ex 23^{4f}). Passages coming under (*b*) are relatively numerous, and date from the redemption of the Exodus. None of the instances under (*a*) is certainly earlier than Hosea, who first represented the covenant of Y" as a *spousal* contract. The books of Ruth and Jonah very strongly suggest that His love is shared by other nations. It is a love which induces repentance (Jer 31^{33}).

The unique place which love holds in the Israelite, as compared with other religions, is due to its insistence on a *reciprocal affection of God and people*. Abraham is the friend of God, and love to God is even demanded by Him. Moreover, the very word which expresses this love is drawn from a sphere which involves reciprocity, namely marriage relations and intimate friendship (as between David and Jonathan). But man's love to God is not primarily spontaneous; Y" loved man first and provoked his response. Y" chose Israel, not because of any merit or love on Israel's part (Dt 9^{4ff}, Ezk 16$^{3-14}$).

The character of Y", ' the Holy One of Israel,' gives to His love its qualities—purity, intensity, selflessness, fidelity; reciprocal love calls forth like qualities in His people (see the relevant expressions of love to Y" in the Psalms).

2. In the LXX.—All these varieties of love, human and Divine, may in the LXX be expressed by the verb *agapaō* and noun *agapē*. In the story of Samson and Delilah *agapaō* describes sexual relationship (Jg 16$^{4, 15}$), not to mention Solomon's legalized lust (3 K 11^{2}), besides expressing love in its higher reaches. *Phileō* is a much rarer word in the LXX, but it is not by any means confined to spontaneous or unreasoning love, for it does duty on occasion for the tenderness of parental love (Gn 37^{4}) and for the deliberate, reverential love of Wisdom (Pr 8^{17} 29^{3}). In the Greek Bible, in the form in which it must have been known to the NT writers, *agapaō* does duty for every shade and variety of love, from divine pity and preference for Israel right down to erotic passion. It is true that *agapaō* is not the only verb to express erotic love in the LXX, for there are also *pro-aireomai* and *enthumeomai* (Heb. *ḥshḳ* and *ethelō* (*ḥpṣ*); but it is very commonly used to render Hebrew *'hb* when the context makes plain that this very type of love or passion is intended. Nor has *agapaō* the monopoly for rendering what may be described as reasoning attachment: thus the more usual verbs for divine pity are *eleeō* and *oikteirō*. The noun *agapē* is usually connected with sex, or at least with love of women; or, it is a passion comparable in intensity with hatred; it is not at all a higher love than *philia*. Indeed, in the LXX *agapēsis* may be said to be a higher type of love than *agapē* (cf especially Hos 11^{4}, Zeph 3^{17}, Jer 38 $(31)^{3}$).

3. In the NT.—The Greek words used for 'love' are the verbs *agapaō* and *phileō* and the noun *agapē*. We have seen something of the history of these words in the Greek Bible, but naturally they are clothed in the NT with that new meaning of 'love' which is necessarily involved in the Christian gospel: love of and for Christ, and love of and for the Christian brethren. It is a mistake to suppose that *agapaō* and *agapē* are the sole means of expressing this, or that *phileō* involves a different kind of love. In the Synoptic Gospels the latter sometimes means 'to kiss,' but not always. In the Fourth Gospel it is quite indistinguishable from *agapaō*, and that is not surprising in view of what we have seen in the LXX. Apparently no other significance than a desire for variety in vocabulary may be read into such passages as Jn 21^{15ff}, where the Lord questions Peter three times and changes are rung on these two verbs; nor must 'the other disciple, the one whom Jesus loved' (20^{2}) be distinguished from 'that disciple whom Jesus loved' (21^{7}) on the ground that the two verbs are different. Some of the older commentators believed that in the NT there was a difference in meaning between the two verbs, *phileō* being the stronger, more spontaneous love, and *agapaō* the reasoning attachment which is based on deliberate choice of an object, involving the respect and reverence which are not essential to the other verb. So men can be, and in the NT are, commanded to love God with the verb *agapaō*, but not with *phileō*. Strictly speaking that may be so, but the fourth evangelist clearly did not maintain the distinction: he describes God's love for man as *agapaō* when God deliberately sets His love upon the world (3^{16}) and when He chooses to love him who loves Jesus ($14^{21, 23}$), but it is *phileō* when God chooses to love the disciples for the very same reason, that they love Jesus (16^{27}); the Father loves the Son (*agapaō* in 3^{35} 10^{17} 15^{9} $17^{23f, 26}$; but *phileō* in 5^{20}); the disciples may conceivably have loved their Master in two distinct ways (*agapaō* in $14^{15, 21, 23, 28}$; *phileō* in 16^{27}), but there is nothing in the immediate context or in the Gospel as a whole to suggest such a distinction. This evangelist is fond of ringing the changes on synonyms for no other apparent reason than love of variety (cf *send*, *ask*, *man*, and many other words).

If we leave aside the ordinary uses of 'love' in the NT (*e.g.* to love to do something, love of relatives, of fellowmen, of friends, or one's life, of praise, of gain from wrongdoing, of falsehood, salutations, and the best seats), we are left with certain qualities of a new Christian love, of which we have seen something already in the Fourth Gospel. It is God the Father's spontaneous love for the human race, inspiring a plan of redemption in which He loves the Son, and resulting in a family of disciples who share the Father's and the Son's mutual love, and who love all other members of the same brotherhood. In the Pauline Epistles, except where there is reference to marital affection (Ephesians, Colossians), 'love' is always used in this specialized sense, and is usually *agapē* and *agapaō*: it is God's and to God, and of Christians for one another (Romans); to God and Christ, of Paul for his converts, and Christian love in general (1 and 2 Corinthians; cf 1 Co 16^{22} where *phileō* is used interchangeably); it is Christ's love for us and ours for Him and His (Ephesians); it is the Christian's for the brethren (Philippians); it is God's and Christian love (Colossians); it is God's and Christ's, and of Christians for one another (1 and 2 Thessalonians); it is personal affection for Paul (Philemon); in the Pastoral Epistles it is the love of Christians for one another (*phileō* once) and love of Christ's appearing. In the remaining books, it is God's love (James), Christian love (Hebrews, 2 Peter), our love for Christ and one another (1 Peter), God's love for us and Christian love of God and one another (Johannine Epistles), God's and Christian love (Jude), Christ's and Christian love (Revelation, where *phileō* is used interchangeably of Christ's love).

Analysis of the above references to Divine and Christian love will reveal three main varieties. There is:

(*a*) *The love of God*, which is completed when Christians love one another; it unites them to the Father and to Christ and dwells in their hearts. This love is revealed by Christ, and shared by Himself, but it was already manifested in the creation of the world, in Divine providence, and God's dealings with man in general. Paul seems to be referring to this when he speaks so often of 'grace' (q.v.). For this Divine love in its various aspects, see 1 Jn 2^{5} 3^{24} $4^{11f\,16-21}$; Jn 17^{21-26}; Jn 3^{16f}; Ro 5^{5-8}; Ja 1^{17f}, 1 P 4^{19}; Ro 2^{4} 9^{22}, 1 Ti 1^{16}, 1 P 3^{20}; Ro $8^{35, 39}$, 2 Co 5^{14}, Ga 2^{20}, Eph 3^{19}.

(*b*) *The love of Christians towards God and Christ*, which is not so much a spontaneous response to the above, though it is caused by it (1 Jn 4^{19}), but it is implanted in the heart by God the Spirit Himself (Ro 5^{5}, Gal 5^{22}, Eph 3^{16-17}). It displaces the old loves in the Christian's life (of money, the world, self, and pleasure (1 Jn 2^{15ff}, Ja 4^{4}, 2 Ti 3^{2-5}, Lk 16^{13f}, Jn 15^{19-24}). Unbelief, the reverse of faith, is inconsistent with love for God and leads to persecution of Christians (Ro $8^{7, 38f}$, Gal 4^{29}, 1 Jn 3^{12f}).

(*c*) *Christians' love for all men, especially fellow Christians*; this is the most common use of 'love' in the NT. This too is not spontaneous but is rather a duty and a commandment and a proof of the Christian's love for God. 1 Co 13^{4-7} is the best description of the love required of Christians, in all its detail: the reverse of jealousy, boastfulness, arrogance, and rudeness; it is patient and kind, gives way to others without resentment or irritability; sympathetic, encouraging, optimistic, and unselfish. It was this quality which Paul was ever placing before the minds of his converts as the goal which may be achieved with the help of the Spirit, and without which all spiritual gifts and accomplishments appear very small. It is an expansion of the second half of Jesus' summary of the Law. It is also the means by which God's own love may reach the world.

G. G. F.—N. T.

LOVE FEAST (AGAPE).—The common meal of the early Christians, which took its name from a specialized meaning of the word for love (*agapē*). The custom dates from apostolic days, and was connected with the observance of the **Eucharist** (q.v.). The 'breaking of bread in their homes' (Ac 2^{46}) probably included both under the title 'the Lord's Supper' (1 Co 11^{20}). In Ac 20^{7} we are told that a religious observance connected with the Agape continued until dawn—though this may have been an exceptional case, Paul's farewell visit at Troas. The scandalous behaviour which Paul rebuked in 1 Co 11^{17-34} shows that not all who attended the observance were fit to communicate; again, this case was probably unusual. More serious evils were introduced by the false teachers described in Jd ^{12}: 'These are blemishes [margin, *or* reefs] on your love feasts, as they boldly carouse together, looking after themselves.' The writer is dependent upon 2 P 2^{13}: 'They count it pleasure to revel in the daytime. They are blots and blemishes, revelling in their dissipation (margin, *other ancient authorities read* love feasts), carousing with you.' But the criticism is so extravagant one cannot help recalling parallels from later ecclesiastical controversy and polemics which went beyond the facts in the case.

In spite of the disorders, which marred the religious value of these social club feasts and led eventually to their suppression, they lasted for a considerable time. Ignatius of Antioch wrote to the Church in Smyrna *c* 110 (*Smyrn.* 8): 'See that you follow the bishop. . . . It is not lawful either to baptize or to hold a love feast apart from the bishop, but whatever he approves is also pleasing to God; so that whatever you do may be safe and secure [or binding].' The context of this passage implies that this included the Eucharist. Tertullian (*Apol.* xxxix. 17 f) gives a vivid description of the feast explained by its own name. 'Before reclining at table, the banqueters first taste [the food] of prayer to God. Only so much is eaten as will satisfy hunger; only so much is drunk as will meet the needs of the modest. They satisfy themselves as those will who recall that even during the night they must worship God. Their conversation is that of those who know the Lord is listening. After the water is brought for the ablutions of the hands [after dinner], the lights are brought in, and each is asked to stand forth before the others and sing the praise of God, either from his own heart or from the Holy Scriptures. This also is evidence of how little we drink. Then the banquet ends, as it began, with prayer.'

The food apparently consisted of bread, fish, vegetables, and wine—the diet of the poor. The pictures of Love Feasts found in the murals in the catacombs give a prominent place to fish (*Ichthus*, 'fish,' was a common symbol or password among the Christians; it was the abbreviation of *Iēsous Christos Huios Theou Sōtēr*: Jesus Christ Son of God Saviour). Interesting examples of the prayers used are found in the *Didache*. The direction to give thanks 'after you are satisfied [with food]' clearly associates the prayer in ch. 10 with the Love Feast rather than the Eucharist: 'We give thee thanks, Holy Father, for thy Holy Name which thou hast made to tabernacle in our hearts, and for the knowledge and faith and immortality, which thou hast made known to us through thy Servant Jesus. To thee be the glory for ever and ever. Thou, Almighty Master, didst create all things for thy Name's sake, and didst give food and drink to men for enjoyment, that they might render thanks to thee; but didst bestow upon us spiritual food and drink and eternal life through thy Servant. Above all we give thanks to thee that thou art mighty. To thee be glory for ever! Remember, O Lord, thy Church, to deliver it from all evil and to make it perfect in thy love, and to gather it together, in its sanctification, from the four winds into thy Kingdom which thou hast prepared for it; for thine is the power and the glory for ever. Let grace come and let this world pass away! Hosanna to the God of David! If any man is holy, let him come. If any man is not, let him repent. *Marana tha*! Amen. (But permit the prophets to hold Eucharist as they will.)' This final sentence (or rubric) has led some modern scholars to doubt if the two chapters (9 and 10) are sharply to be distinguished, as referring first (ch. 9) to the Eucharist and then (ch. 10) to the Love Feast. Both begin alike: (ch. 9) 'Concerning the Eucharist, *give thanks as follows*: First concerning the Cup. . . . And concerning the Broken Bread. . . .' (Ch. 10) 'After you are satisfied, *give thanks as follows*. . . .' (Both prayers are eucharistic.) Moreover, the date of the *Didache* is still debated, many dating it *c* A.D. 135 or later, others *c* A.D. 98 (as if to anchor it securely within the 1st cent. !). In any event, the term 'Love Feast' does not appear in the *Didache*; the preferred term is Eucharist.

The term Love Feast was popular in the 19th cent. among groups which emphasized the social and religious fellowship (*koinōnia*) of the communion rite, and they sometimes used it to cover the whole observance of the Supper. But the usage of the NT does not support this one-sided interpretation. The separation of the Love Feast from the Eucharist seems to have been due largely to the attitude of the Roman government, which was always suspicious of secret societies, especially those claiming to be religious. Pliny's letter to Trajan (x. 96, *c* A.D. 110) speaks of the celebration of the Eucharist in the early morning as followed by a simple meal, which had been omitted since the edict forbidding clubs. On the other hand, fear of calumnies regarding any more or less secret feasts, and experience of such disorders as were found in Corinth and reflected in 2 Peter and Jude, provided motives which must have hindered the practice in certain places and eventually extinguished it.

A. E. B.—**F. C. G.**

LOVELY.—In 2 S 1^{23} the word means lovable. Elsewhere it is used of something which is agreeable and pleasing (as Esther seemed to the king in Est 5^{1}, where the Greek word is used in the LXX); the same Greek word with the same meaning is found in the NT at Ph 4^{8}, but in Sir 4^{7} 20^{13} this word has the rather different sense of popularity with respectable men ('beloved' RSV). N. T.

LOVER.—In the OT it is used with the less worthy sense of erotic love, as a *paramour*, especially in Jeremiah, Ezekiel, and Hosea; but also with the idea of ordinary friendship in Ps 38^{11} 88^{18}. In the NT, there are lovers of pleasure, who are contrasted with lovers of God (2 Ti 3^{4}), lovers of goodness (Ti 1^{8}), of self and of money (2 Ti 3^{2}). These are parts of a Greek compound word, compounded with *phil-* (see the article on LOVE). N. T.

LOVINGKINDNESS.—Two ideas are blended in this expressive word; it denotes *kindness* which springs from the loyalty of *love*. It is the frequent translation (30 times in the AV, 42 times in the RV) of the Hebrew word *ḥesedh* (which occurs nearly 250 times altogether), which G. A. Smith renders 'leal love' (*Book of the Twelve Prophets*, rev. ed., i. 255). N. H. Snaith renders 'covenant love' (*Distinctive Ideas of the OT*, pp. 94 ff.), and A. R. Johnson 'devotion' (*Interpretationes ad VT pertinentes S. Mowinckel missae*, pp. 100 ff.). AV and RV most frequently translate *ḥesedh* '**mercy**' and not seldom '**kindness,**' while RSV has '**steadfast love**' 177 times. The American RV has 'lovingkindness' uniformly when the reference is to God's love to man. The adoption of this suggestion would bring out the connexion between 'lovingkindness' as a fundamental attribute of the Divine nature (Ex 34^{6f} etc.), its poetic personification (Ps 42^{8} 57^{3} 89^{14}), and the appeal to God to be true to Himself—to save and redeem 'for His lovingkindness' sake' (Ps 6^{4} 44^{26} 115^{1}). For the combination of 'lovingkindness' with 'faithfulness' see Ps 89, where each word occurs seven times, and cf La 3^{22f}, Is 55^{3}. Cf also LOVE.

J. G. T.—**H. H. R.**

LOWLAND.—See PLAIN (5).

LOZON.—One whose sons returned with Zerubbabel, 1 Es 5^{33}; called **Darkon** in Ezr 2^{56}, Neh 7^{58}.

LUBIM.—See LIBYA, LIBYANS.

LUCAS, Phn ^{24} (AV), for **Luke.**

LUCIFER, Is 14^{12} (AV).—See STARS.

LUCIUS.—**1.** A 'consul of the Romans' (1 Mac 15^{16ff}), who transmitted the decree of the Senate in favour of the Jews. Probably the reference is to Lucius Calpurnius Piso, consul in 139 B.C. **2.** Of Cyrene, one of certain prophets and teachers at Antioch in Syria, mentioned in Ac 13^{1}, to whom it was revealed that Paul and Barnabas should be separated for the work to which they had been called. The suggestion that he was the same person as St. Luke, the Evangelist, has nothing to support it. **3.** Mentioned in Ro 16^{21}, as sending greetings to the brethren at Rome. Possibly the same person as **2**, but of this there is no certain proof. M. St.

LUCRE.—The English word 'lucre' is in AV always qualified by the adjective 'filthy,' because the word itself had not then the offensive meaning it has now. Erasmus speaks of God turning men's wickedness 'into the lucre and encreace of godlynesse.' It simply meant gain. Filthy lucre means sordid gain. RSV does not use the word.

LUD, LUDIM.—**1.** In Gn 10^{22}, 1 Ch 1^{17} *Lud* is named as one of the sons of Shem, along with the well-known Elam, Asshur, and Aram, and the uncertain Arpachsad. In this list the Elamites at least are not Semitic, but are regarded as such by reason of association with the Babylonians. In a similar way the Lydians, who are usually identified with the people of **Lydia** (q.v.), may be associated here with the Semitic Assyrians, whose rule once extended to the borders of the Lydian empire.

2. In Gn 10^{13}, 1 Ch 1^{11} *Ludim* is the name given to one of the descendants of Egypt (Mizraim) in a list of peoples all undoubtedly African. Here there can be no question of Asiatic Lydians. Either an unknown African people is referred to, or we should read *Lubim* = **Libyans** (q.v.). This reading would suit Jer 46^{9}, and *Lub* has been suggested for *Lud* in Ezk 27^{10} 30^{5}, Is 66^{19}. But it is improbable that the same error has invaded so many passages. J. F. McC.—**H. H. R.**

LUHITH.—The ascent of 'Luhith' (Is 15^{5}) is probably the path called the 'descent *or* going down of Horonaim,' the latter lying, probably, higher than Luhith (cf Jer 48^{5}). The *Onomasticon* places Luhith between Areopolis and Zoar, but the site cannot be identified.

LUKE (EVANGELIST).—Luke, a companion of St. Paul, is mentioned in Col 4^{14}, Phn ^{24}, 2 Ti 4^{11}, in all three places in connexion with Mark. He is generally believed to be the author of the Third Gospel and Acts, and therefore a frequent fellow-traveller with the Apostle of the Gentiles. (See the following article.) He has been identified, but without probability, with **Lucius of Cyrene** (Ac 13^{1}). He may have been converted by St. Paul as some have conjectured, possibly at Tarsus, where he could have studied medicine. (But the theory that Luke-Acts shows evidence of special knowledge of medicine has been greatly weakened by modern research, especially by H. J. Cadbury's demonstration that Luke's 'medical knowledge' was not greater than that of Lucian, who was not a physician.) Tertullian calls St. Paul his 'illuminator' and 'master' (*adv. Marc.* iv. 2), which perhaps has this meaning; but it may be a mere conjecture. Luke joined St. Paul on his Second Missionary Journey, apparently for the first time, at Troas. He was not an eye-witness of the gospel events (Lk 1^{2}), but had ample means of getting information from those who had been. He was a Gentile (cf Col 4^{10f} and v.^{14}); thus he could not have been of the Seventy, or the companion of Cleopas (Lk $24^{13, 18}$), as some have thought. He was a doctor (Col 4^{14}), and perhaps had attended St. Paul in his illnesses. A tradition, perhaps of the 6th cent., makes him a painter, who had made a picture of the Virgin. He was possibly of servile origin; his name, which seems to be an abbreviation of Lucanus, Lucius, Lucilius, or Lucianus, may well have been a slave's name; and physicians were often slaves. Chrysostom and Jerome take him for 'the brother who is famous among all the churches for his preaching of the gospel' (2 Co 8^{18} RSV; see GOSPEL). Other traditions connect him with Achaia, Bithynia or, Alexandria; some assign to him a martyr's crown.

The great difficulty in the identification of Luke, the companion of Paul, with the author of the Third Gospel and the Acts of the Apostles is that Paul himself, especially in 1 and 2 Corinthians, took a far more authoritative position relatively to his own converts and their churches than is represented or assumed in Acts; the author sees Paul in the light of a later period, according to which he and the original Twelve in Jerusalem were on the best of terms, Paul readily submitting to their authority. From Paul's own letters it is clear that in reality a wide gulf separated them, which Paul did his best to close, especially by his 'collection' for the poor among the 'saints' in the mother church. The relations between Christianity and Judaism are also differently described in Acts than in the Pauline letters. Accordingly, many modern scholars hesitate to identify Luke with the author of the Gospel), though admitting the possibility that he was the author of the 'we-sections' in the latter part of Acts. See next article, 3.

A. J. M.—**F. C. G.**

LUKE (GOSPEL ACCORDING TO) AND ACTS OF THE APOSTLES.—**1. Unity of authorship.**—That the two books are from the same hand is practically indisputable. Both are addressed to a certain Theophilus (Lk 1^{3}, Ac 1^{1}), who is otherwise quite unknown; and in the opening words of Acts the author refers to 'the first book,' in which he has 'dealt with all that Jesus began to do and teach, until the day when he was taken up, after he had given commandment through the Holy Spirit to the apostles whom he had chosen.' The reference here is manifestly to the Gospel; and we are clearly intended to conclude that Acts is a continuation of the Gospel, and, consequently, the work of the same author. This was, in fact, the conclusion universally drawn in antiquity; and it is the conclusion which holds the field to-day. It is, of course, open to an objector to point out that the direct evidence is drawn entirely from a comparison of the prefaces of the two books, and to maintain that a different author, writing Acts, may well have wished to represent it as a continuation of the Gospel and composed a preface accordingly. Such a supposition, however, in itself improbable, is made very much more improbable by closer inspection of the books themselves. From this it appears that there are a number of words which are either very rare or do not occur at all elsewhere in the NT, but which are fairly frequent in Luke–Acts—*e.g.* the adverb *parachrēma* (='immediately') occurs ten times in Luke, seven times in Acts, but elsewhere in the NT only twice (Mt 21^{19f}). Again, characteristic phrases that are found in the Gospel are found also in Acts—thus, the phrase 'as his custom was' is found only at Lk 4^{16} and Ac 17^{2}, and in each case it is connected with entry into a synagogue on the Sabbath. The same authors' interests, too, are discernible in both books (see **6**). Hence, if the author of both books is not the same, the later writer must so successfully have studied, absorbed, and imitated his predecessor's style, characteristics, and interests, as to make it impossible to tell the difference. That anyone should have been capable of doing this (even assuming that anyone would have wished to do it) is incredible.

2. Contents.—The two books taken together give the story of the origins of Christianity from its beginnings in remote Judaea 'in the days of Herod' (*i.e.* Herod the Great, 37–4 B.C.) until its firm establishment in Rome, the capital of the Empire, in the seventh decade of the 1st cent. A.D.

The Gospel opens with a Preface (the only one of its kind in the NT) setting forth the author's purpose in writing, his qualifications for writing, and the circumstances in which he wrote (1^{1-4}). This is followed by a collection of 'Birth and Childhood' narratives (1^{5}–2^{52}), which are noteworthy as giving an account of the birth and childhood of John the Baptist as well as of Jesus: all these narratives are peculiar to Luke. With the date at 3^{1f} (obviously designed to set the events he is about to record firmly within their historical context) the evangelist introduces us to the Ministry of Jesus, which in turn is introduced by the Ministry of John the Baptist. From this point until the close of the Galilean ministry (9^{50}) the material included is very roughly the same as that found in the earlier parts of Matthew and Mark: for the most part it appears in very much the same order, and not infrequently in very much the same words—typical exceptions are the Rejection in the Synagogue at Nazareth (4^{16-30}, which may reasonably be held to 'replace' the similar incident recorded at

LUKE (GOSPEL) AND ACTS

Mt 13$^{53-58}$ and Mk 6$^{1-6}$ as having happened later on, but in the strict sense cannot be regarded as ' parallel '), the Call of the First Disciples (5$^{1-11}$, which has points of contact both with the narratives recording the call of the same four disciples at Mt 4$^{18-22}$ and Mk 1$^{16-20}$, and also with the story of the Miraculous Draught of Fishes at Jn 21$^{1-14}$), and the Raising of the Widow's Son at Nain (7$^{11-17}$, peculiar to Luke). At 9^{51} a new section begins—the Journey to Jerusalem (9^{51}–19^{28}): it is impossible here to follow the route of the journey in anything except the broadest outline, and it looks rather as if the evangelist had used this section of his Gospel to gather together material which had no very obvious setting elsewhere: to this section belong several well-known incidents peculiar to Luke (*e.g.* the Mission of the Seventy, 10$^{1-16}$; the Healing of the Ten Lepers, 17$^{11-19}$; the Story of Zacchaeus, 19$^{1-10}$), as also a striking series of peculiarly Lukan parables (the Good Samaritan, 10$^{29-37}$; the Importunate Friend, 11$^{5-8}$; the Rich Fool, 12$^{16-21}$; the Barren Fig Tree, 13$^{6-9}$; the Prodigal Son, 15$^{11-32}$; the Unjust Steward, 16$^{1-13}$; the Rich Man and Lazarus, 16$^{19-31}$; the Unjust Judge, 18$^{1-8}$; the Pharisee and the Publican, 18$^{9-14}$). The account of the ministry in Jerusalem (19^{29}–21^{37}) follows similar lines to the corresponding accounts in Matthew and Mark. With the account of the Passion and Resurrection (22^{1}–24^{53}), however, it is otherwise; there are a number of incidents and sayings not found elsewhere (*e.g.* the account of Jesus before Herod, 23$^{6-16}$; the Lament over the Daughters of Jerusalem, 23$^{28-31}$; the story of the Two Disciples at Emmaus, 24$^{13-35}$); when the same incidents or sayings do occur elsewhere the Lukan version almost always has a distinctive ' slant '; while a comparison of the Lukan language in such cases with the language used in the other Gospels suggests the minimum of connexion.

Acts takes up the story where the Gospel left off. ' You shall be my witnesses in Jerusalem and in all Judaea and Samaria and to the end of the earth ' the Risen Lord is reported as saying to his disciples at the Ascension (1^{8}); and these words may be taken as the programme of the book. It falls naturally into two parts. The first part (1^{1}–12^{25}) deals with the activity ' in Jerusalem and in all Judaea and Samaria '; the gospel-message spreads outward from Jerusalem and as far northward as Antioch in Syria (11^{19}); at Caesarea the Gentile, Cornelius, is admitted to the Church (10$^{1-48}$); and at Antioch preaching to Gentiles is undertaken of set purpose (11^{20}). Throughout these events Peter is the leading figure. But in the second part of the book, which extends the horizon ' to the end of the earth ' (13^{1}–28^{31}), the reader's attention is fixed on the converted Pharisee, Saul. At 13^{9} his name is changed to Paul. By now he has already become a leader, in fact the outstanding leader, of the whole world-wide Christian mission. And we follow him on his travels, from Antioch (13^{3}) back to Antioch (14^{27}), again through Asia Minor (15^{36}–16^{10}) and on to the mainland of Europe (16^{11}–18^{17}), back again to Antioch (18^{22}), once more through Asia Minor and the European mainland (18^{23}–20^{12}), on his last journey to Jerusalem (20^{13}–21^{16}), and then finally to Rome (27^{1}–28^{16}). The Church has now expanded, and the gospel-message has been carried from the religious capital of Jewry to the capital of the civilized world.

3. Author.—Ecclesiastical tradition, from the days of Irenaeus (*c* A.D. 180) onwards, is unanimous that the author was Luke. With this tradition there is no need to quarrel. Luke is mentioned only three times in the Pauline Epistles (Col 4^{14}, 2 Ti 4^{11}, Phn ^{24}), and nowhere else in early Christian literature. His obscurity is accordingly the best possible argument for the soundness of the ecclesiastical tradition. The tradition, moreover, is to some extent supported by the internal evidence of Acts. From Acts it would appear that the author was a companion of Paul; he joins Paul at Troas on his Second Journey (Ac 16^{10}); and frequently thereafter he betrays his presence as a fellow-traveller by using the pronoun ' we ' (*e.g.* Ac 20^{13} 28^{11}). If these so-called ' we-passages ' are due to genuine reminiscence (and there is no sound reason for supposing they are not), and we take the names of Paul's companions given in the Epistles, we find that all but four must be excluded, either as having joined Paul after his arrival in Rome (the author certainly made the journey with him, Ac 27^{1}), or as being mentioned in a manner inconsistent with authorship. The four exceptions are Crescens, Jesus Justus, Titus, and Luke. Neither Crescens (2 Ti 4^{10}) nor Jesus Justus (Col 4^{11}), so far as we know, had either long or specially intimate connexions with Paul. The effective choice, therefore, is between Titus and Luke; and tradition favours Luke. According to Col 4$^{10-14}$ Luke was a Gentile and a physician; and even if it is possible to overestimate the importance of the allegedly ' medical ' language and interests of the author of Luke–Acts (*e.g.* Lk 4^{38} ' a *high* fever '; Ac 28$^{7-10}$), there can be no doubt about his interest in Gentiles and the Gentile mission (see **6**)—indeed, such a phrase as ' in their language ' with reference to Aramaic (Ac 1^{13}) betrays that he was a Gentile himself. The tradition, therefore, is amply confirmed by the contents of both the Gospel and Acts.

The Anti-Marcionite *Prologue to Luke* (either late 2nd cent. or early 3rd cent.) describes Luke as ' by nation a Syrian of Antioch '; Eusebius (*HE* III. iv. 7) says he was ' by birth of those from Antioch '; and this account of his origin is repeated by later Fathers. However, its accuracy is doubted because of ' the cold way ' in which the Syrian Antioch is referred to in Acts. Some conjecture that Pisidian Antioch is meant, and the description of the scenes in that neighbourhood is so vivid that it might well be by an eye-witness. But against this it is to be noted that the ' we-passages ' in Acts have not yet begun, and this seems decisive against the writer having been present. Others believe the author to have been a Macedonian of Philippi, since he took so great an interest in the claims of that colony (Ac 16^{12}). On the other hand, he appears to have had no home there but went to lodge with Lydia (Ac 16^{15}), and only ' supposed ' that there was a Jewish place of prayer by the riverside (Ac 16^{13}). His interest in Philippi may best be accounted for by his having been left in charge of the church there (Ac 17^{1}–20^{6}; in the interval between Paul's departure from Philippi on his Second Journey and his return on the Third the pronoun ' they ' is used instead of ' we '). Yet he may well have been a Macedonian of a Greek family once settled at Antioch. At any rate, he was certainly a Gentile, not without some contempt for the Jews; there is no evidence for his having been a Roman citizen, as was Paul; and his essentially Greek outlook shows itself in his calling the inhabitants of Melita ' barbarians ' (Ac 28^{2}), and in many other ways.

4. Style and Characteristics.—The author of Luke-Acts is the most accomplished stylist in the NT. The Preface at the head of the Gospel reminds us at once of similar prefaces in contemporary pagan writers, and its Greek is so much more idiomatic and literary than anything found elsewhere in the NT (or indeed in the rest of his own work) that it seems as if Luke was making a deliberate attempt to catch the eye of the world of letters. After this Preface, however, the change is abrupt. At Lk 1^{5} we are introduced to a simple, ' old world ' narrative such as might have come straight out of the pages of the OT, and which is marked by a very high concentration of Semitisms (*i.e.* expressions which though odd or inexplicable in Greek are readily explicable as literal translations of a Hebrew or Aramaic original). This concentration is highest in Lk 1 and 2, but Semitisms are found regularly (even if less frequently) throughout the rest of the Gospel and also throughout Acts (though again less frequently towards the end): as examples may be quoted ' And he sent yet a third ' (literally ' And he *added to send* a third ' Lk 20^{11}) with which may be compared ' He proceeded to arrest Peter also ' (literally ' He *added to arrest* Peter also ' Ac 12^{3}), and ' all who dwell upon *the face of* the whole earth ' (Lk 21^{35})

with which may be compared 'every nation of men to live on all *the face of* the earth' (Ac 17^{26}). A possible explanation of these Semitisms is that Luke derived them from Semitic or Semitizing sources. To some extent this may be true (see **5**). But the more probable explanation of the majority of them, in the light of a close study of their nature and distribution, is that they are due to conscious imitation of the Septuagint. They should, therefore, be termed 'Septuagintalisms' rather than 'Semitisms'; and we should think of Luke having deliberately employed them to emphasize the 'Biblical' character of his theme. That he could write good literary Greek is proved by the Preface to the Gospel. He chose, in Lk 1 and 2, to exchange this for a patently OT style because he was writing of the period before the birth of Christ. The Ministry took place in Palestine among Semitic-speaking people; the narrative of the Ministry accordingly has a suitable Semitic flavour. The same is true of the early chapters of Acts, which record the growth of the Church in Palestine; and it is only when the Church expands beyond Palestine that the Semitisms are reduced to the minimum. The style of Luke-Acts is thus seen to be an essential part of the plan of the work as a whole. The language, as it were, sets the scene.

According to the Preface to the Gospel the author was not an eye-witness of the events he describes; yet he has a keen sense of effective composition, as can be seen from the way in which he narrates his incidents (*e.g.* that of the sinful woman, Lk 7^{36-50}). The same sense is to be remarked in Acts, and the fact that no difference is discernible in this respect between the 'we-passages' and the rest of Acts makes it plain that Luke's powers of description were not dependent upon his having witnessed an incident himself. Despite the elaborate dating at Lk 3^{1f}, he is, on the whole, indifferent to chronology, and also (in the Gospel at least) to geography; time and again we meet vague phrases like 'on one of those days' (Lk 5^{17}), or 'in a certain place' (Lk 11^{1}), or 'on the way to Jerusalem he was passing along between Samaria and Galilee' (literally 'through the midst of Samaria and Galilee,' Lk 17^{11}). And at times this vagueness and indifference to detail result in obscurity and incoherence, even if not in contradiction. Thus, at Lk 1^{62} Zechariah is represented as deaf, although the angel had only threatened him with dumbness (Lk 1^{20}); at Lk 9^{10} Jesus withdraws 'apart to a city called Bethsaida'; and at Lk 19^{13} the nobleman in the parable calls '*ten* of his servants' yet only *three* appear in the sequel (Lk $19^{16, 18, 20}$). Similarly in Acts the author seized on the (to him) significant features and ignores the insignificant: so he tells us practically nothing of the missionary journey through Cyprus (Ac 13^{6}), though much work must have been done among the Jews on that occasion, while considerable space is devoted to the interview with the proconsul, Sergius Paulus. He leaves always a good deal to be understood; he states facts, and expects the reader to deduce the causes or inferences; he reports directions or instructions, and leaves it be inferred that they were carried into effect (*e.g.* at Ac 13^{13f} the reason for Mark's departure is not stated, neither is any reason given for Paul and Barnabas going to Pisidian Antioch; at Ac 17^{15} it is not recorded that the injunction was obeyed, but from 1 Th 3^{1} it is clear that Timothy had rejoined Paul at Athens and had been sent away again to Macedonia, whence he came to Corinth at Ac 18^{5}).

5. Sources.—The Preface to the Gospel states explicitly that the information contained in the Gospel was not first-hand; the evangelist knew of written 'narratives,' and he implies that he also had access to eye-witnesses, although he himself was not an eye-witness (Lk 1^{1f}). The question, therefore, arises as to how much of the Gospel depends on written sources and how much on oral testimony. There is general agreement that the primary written source was Mark. There is also fairly general agreement that Luke, like the author of Matthew, drew largely from the hypothetical document, or documents, known as Q. Whether he used any other written sources besides these is debated, It is often maintained that the more important narrative sections peculiar to the Gospel (such as the birth-stories Lk 1^{5}–2^{52}) were drawn from written sources; and many would say the same of the peculiarly Lukan parables (such as the Good Samaritan, Lk 10^{30-37}). But the Preface suggests that the author made careful inquiries and collected a fair proportion of his material by word of mouth. As a companion of Paul he was in an excellent position to do this. The two years at Caesarea would provide a first-rate opportunity. Mary, the mother of Jesus, may easily have been alive at the time (*c* A.D. 58), and Luke may have met, if not her, at least several of the women best known to her. In any case, he is bound to have come across many who had seen the Lord Himself in the flesh and companied with Him during His Ministry (including, perhaps, some of the Twelve), and it is to them that he presumably refers when he speaks in the Preface of the 'eye-witnesses and ministers of the word,' who 'delivered to us' an account 'of the things which have been accomplished among us.' If so, there is no need to conjecture additional written sources beyond Mark and Q. The considerable quantity of matter which is found in Luke alone is just as easily, and probably far more satisfactorily, accounted for as the evangelist's writing up of the results of his own inquiries.

The situation with regard to Acts is rather different. For the last part of Acts Luke was either his own informant or else could rely on information supplied by Paul or other members of the Pauline circle. For the earlier part (*i.e.* the part describing the growth of the Church in Palestine) he was in exactly the same position as he was in the Gospel; here he was necessarily limited either to the personal reminiscences of those he met in Palestine (*e.g.* Philip the Evangelist, who may have been the source of much of the material in Ac 6–8) or to written documents. Since he used at least two written sources in the Gospel there might seem at first sight to be a decided balance in favour of his having used written sources also in the first part of Acts. On investigation, however, the analogy breaks down. By the time Luke wrote, the term 'Gospel' had a very generally recognized content in Christian circles and there was plenty of written material available—Luke himself tells us that as a Gospel-writer he had 'many' predecessors (Lk 1^{1}). But there is nothing whatever to suggest that anyone else before him had ever thought of writing 'Acts.' This means that through sheer force of circumstances there would be for Acts no written material available, irrespective of whether the author would have made use of it or not. And study of the actual text yields an equally negative result. Many have spent much time in trying to distinguish written sources in Acts; but there is no general agreement. If we are not prepared to leave the question open, we must admit quite candidly that so far as the evidence goes it is very definitely against written sources and in favour of Luke's having been indebted partly to the stories told in the churches that he visited with Paul, partly to the first-hand accounts given him by the many Christians that he came across (including Paul), and partly to his own personal recollections.

6. Author's Interests.—Luke gives us a greater insight into his personal interests and outlook than most NT writers. Quite apart from his possible use of 'medical' language, he has a very evident interest in cures of all kinds (see **3**), which is consonant with his having been a physician; it may even be that the interest in sorcery apparent in Acts is due to his having regarded sorcery as a rival to medicine (*e.g.* Ac 8^{9-24} 13^{6-12} 19^{13-20}). In the Gospel several domestic scenes are described with understanding (*e.g.* Lk 2^{41-51} 10^{38-42} 11^{5-8}), and the author's sympathy with, and interest in, women has often been remarked in both the Gospel and Acts (*e.g.* Lk 7^{11-17} 8^{2f} 23^{27-31}, Ac 1^{14} 11^{36-43} $21^{5, 9}$). Of other 'minor' interests may be mentioned navigation (the voyages by sea and the various harbours are described minutely and vividly, while the land journeys are passed over summarily, *e.g.* Ac 20^{13-15} 21^{1-3} 27^{1}–28^{13}) and the frequent references to angels as agents of God in His dealings with men (*e.g.* Lk $1^{11, 26}$ $2^{9, 13}$ 22^{43} 24^{4}, Ac 1^{10} 8^{26} 12^{7-11} 27^{23}).

Of far greater importance, however, is the way in which certain major theological interests (perhaps we should rather call them 'themes') dominate the two books throughout. In Acts the task entrusted to the disciples at the Ascension was to be 'witnesses in Jerusalem and in all Judaea and Samaria and to the end of the earth' (Ac 1^{8}). The rest of the book shows how this task was carried out, attention being specially concentrated on the three missionary journeys of Paul, who preached always 'to the Jew first and also to the Greek' (Ro 1^{16} 2^{9}; cf Ac 13^{44-49} 18^{5f}). Yet it was the latter aspect of this double mission that appealed especially to Luke, himself a Gentile; and in the Gospel his interest in the Gentile mission is reflected in almost every page. The aged Simeon in the Temple, with the infant Jesus in his arms, sings of the 'salvation' which God has 'prepared in the presence of all peoples, a light for revelation to the Gentiles' (Lk 2^{30-32}). The quotation from Isaiah at Mk 1^{3} is of one verse only, but at Lk 3^{4-6} it is extended by two extra verses in order to end with the words 'and all flesh shall see the salvation of God.' The Seventy are sent out to preach (Lk 10^{1-16})—proleptically, it seems—to the seventy nations of the world. Again, when Luke comes to rewrite Mark's End-time discourse (Mk 13) in ch. 21, he speaks of the destruction of Jerusalem as decreed by God 'until the times of the Gentiles are fulfilled' (Lk 21^{23f}), and we are reminded of Paul's argument in Ro 9–11, and of his formula 'a hardening has come upon part of Israel, until the full number of the Gentiles come in' (Ro 11^{25}). And it is in conformity with this guiding principle that the Ministry of Jesus is presented. Historically that Ministry was limited to Palestine and for the most part confined to Jews. But Luke never tires of stressing the interest taken by Jesus in the outcasts from official Judaism ('tax collectors,' 'sinners,' 'Samaritans') and the encomiums pronounced upon them (*e.g.* Lk 7^{36-50} 10^{30-37} 19^{1-10}). The Mission of Jesus, Luke is saying, was universal from the start; it was only circumstance that might make it appear that it was not.

In other ways, too, the Gospel reflects the author's theological interests as fully worked out in Acts, and often anticipates, as it were, the later situation in the Church. At Ac 19^{1-7} an occasion at Ephesus is described when some 'disciples,' who had been baptized only 'into John's baptism,' had hands laid upon them by Paul, and at once received the Holy Spirit and 'spoke with tongues and prophesied' (*i.e.* they were received into the Church and showed immediate signs of having been legitimately received). In other words, it was axiomatic in the Church, and therefore for Luke, that John's ministry and baptism were merely preparatory. Accordingly, in his Gospel he emphasizes this aspect of the Baptist. John is appointed to 'go before' Jesus 'in the spirit and power of Elijah' (Lk 1^{17}); but he is *not* Elijah, and the section in Mk (9^{9-13}), which identifies him with Elijah, is designedly omitted. At Lk 3^{15-17} Luke has rewritten his Markan source in order to include a categorical denial from John himself that he was 'the Christ' as many were imagining. And the account of the imprisonment of John by Herod at Mk 6^{14-18} is transposed to Lk 3^{18-20} so that John may be removed effectively from the scene before the Ministry of Jesus begins.

No less than sixteen times in Luke Jesus is referred to in narrative as 'the Lord' (*e.g.* Lk 7^{13} 10^{1}). Since this usage is characteristic of Luke, being found in neither Mark nor Matthew, it is not fanciful to see here the influence of the ecclesiastical phraseology with which the author was familiar. For Gentile Christians the central figure of the story, whatever he may have been on earth in Palestine, was the exalted object of their worship, whom they had been enabled by the Spirit to confess as 'Lord' at their conversion (1 Co 8^{5f} 12^{3}), and whom they referred to habitually as 'the Lord' in daily life (*e.g.* 1 Co 9^{1f} 10^{21}). Luke, in consequence, slips naturally into the title to which he was accustomed.

Similarly, with the Twelve. In Acts they are 'the Apostles' and function, at least in the earlier stages, as the supreme governing body of the Church at Jerusalem (*e.g.* Ac 8^{1} 15^{6}). But in the Gospel too they are called 'apostles' (Lk 9^{10} 17^{5} 22^{14} 24^{10}). The name is said (by Luke only) to have been given to them when they were chosen (Lk 6^{13}). Passages in Mark in which they appear in a discreditable light are either omitted (*e.g.* Mk 8^{32f} 10^{35-45}), or else palliated by the addition of an excuse—as when 'Peter and those who were with him' are said to have been 'heavy with sleep' on the Mount of Transfiguration and therefore not responsible for what they said (Lk 9^{32}), or when, in the Garden of Gethsemane, they are represented as sleeping 'for sorrow' (Lk 22^{45}). Here Luke's natural reverence for the Twelve obtrudes itself. For by the time he wrote his Gospel they were looked back upon, and up to, as the pillars of the Church.

Sometimes, again, we see him answering a problem that was pressing on his contemporaries. The angels at the Ascension had promised that 'This Jesus, who was taken up from you into heaven, will come in the same way as you saw him go into heaven' (Ac 1^{11}). The speedy return of Jesus in glory 'on the clouds of heaven' was thus, not unnaturally, expected. But the years went by and he did not return. The result was the despair of many. In this situation Luke has a message for the Church. The faint-hearted can fortify themselves from the very words of Jesus. When asked on one occasion by the Pharisees 'when the kingdom of God was coming' Jesus Himself had warned them that 'the kingdom of God is not coming with signs to be observed' (Lk 17^{20f}). The Parable of the Pounds, moreover, which speaks of 'a nobleman' going 'into a far country to receive kingly power and then return,' had been uttered precisely because there were some with Jesus at that moment who erroneously 'supposed that the kingdom of God was to appear immediately' (Lk 19^{11ff}). The anxious must therefore be patient and wait on God's good time. They need have no anxiety. 'Fear not, little flock,' Jesus had said, 'for it is your Father's good pleasure to give you the kingdom' (Lk 12^{32}). In all this Luke is clearly addressing himself to the situation and needs of the Church as he knew them. His interests, to a far greater extent than is often recognized, were the interests of the Church of his day.

7. Author's Purpose.—An indication of purpose has already been given in the preceding section. Luke was a Gentile. It is clear also that he was writing for Gentiles. Thus, he omits the Aramaic *talitha cumi* when he comes to reproduce Mk 5^{41} at Lk 8^{54}: he regularly substitutes Greek names and titles for Semitic (*e.g.* 'Zelotes' for 'Cananaean' at Lk 6^{15} and Ac 1^{13}, 'the Skull' for 'Golgotha' at Lk 23^{33}, and 'Master' for 'Rabbi' at Lk 9^{33}); he explains Jewish customs (Lk 22^{1}), and adopts generally a 'western' point of view—as when he uses 'Judaea' for the whole of Palestine (*e.g.* Lk 7^{17}, Ac 10^{37}) and alters Mark's description of the breaking up of the mud roof through which the paralytic was let down (Mk 2^{4}) and speaks instead of the man being let down 'through the tiles' (Lk 5^{19}). Since, then, the Gentile Mission is a dominant, if not *the* dominant, theme in both the Gospel and Acts (see **6**), it is hardly fanciful to suppose that the provision of an account of the origin of that mission was the main purpose Luke had in mind in writing. In part this supposition is borne out by his own words. 'It seemed good to me also,' he states in his Preface to the Gospel, 'having followed all things closely for some time past, to write an orderly account for you, most excellent Theophilus, that you may know the truth concerning the things of which you have been informed.' The implication here, however, is that Luke is addressing, not a group or class of people (whether Christian or pagan), but an individual,

LUKE (GOSPEL) AND ACTS

and that that individual was not merely a Gentile, but also an instructed Gentile Christian. Unfortunately the name Theophilus by itself tells us little. The natural interpretation of the passage is that Theophilus was the real name of a converted pagan, probably of good social standing (the epithet ' most excellent ' may mean that he was a Roman official—cf Ac 23^{25} 24^{3} 26^{25}, where it is applied to Felix and Festus), who had commissioned the work ; in that case Theophilus will have been Luke's patron as Maecenas was the patron of Virgil. Some think it a pseudonym employed by Luke to conceal his patron's identity at a time when the profession of Christianity by those in high places might involve penalties. Others hold it to be a generic name for any Christian (since it means ' beloved of God '), and that Luke meant no more by it than ' Christian reader ' ; in which case the address is to the general Christian public, and the seemingly individual application is purely a literary device. But be this as it may, both the style and content of the Preface make us aware at the very beginning that ' the things which have been accomplished among us ' are being presented, not to any narrow circle of half-educated Jews or Jewish-Christians, but to a wider and more cultivated Gentile audience, familiar with the conventions established by the writers of Greece and Rome.

At all events, throughout both books Luke manifestly has his eye on this wider public and is concerned to relate the history of Christianity to Roman history and to present it in the most favourable possible light from the point of view of the Roman authorities. The elaborate date at Lk 3^{1f} starts with a reference to ' the fifteenth year of Tiberius Caesar, Pontius Pilate being governor of Judaea.' In the narrative of the Passion the responsibility for the death of Jesus is unequivocally fixed on the Jews ; at Lk 23^{2} they bring him to Pilate protesting ' We found this man perverting our nation, and forbidding us to give tribute to Caesar, and saying that he himself is Christ a king ' ; Pilate affirms categorically, no less than three times (Lk $23^{4,\,14-16,\,22}$), that he finds no justification for the charge ; and it is only when he can do nothing to persuade them that he yields, unwillingly, to their demand that Jesus should be crucified. And similarly in Acts. Paul is justly proud of his Roman citizenship (Ac 16^{37} 22^{25-28}) ; and the generally sympathetic attitude towards him on the part of the responsible Roman magistrates contrasts strikingly with the persistent opposition and persecution of him by the Jews. In Cyprus the proconsul, Sergius Paulus, heard ' the word of God ' and ' believed ' (Ac $13^{7,\,12}$) : at Corinth, when the Jews made ' a united attack ' on Paul and accused him in open court, another proconsul, Gallio, ' paid no attention ' and ' drove them from the tribunal ' (Ac 18^{12-17}) ; at Caesarea the slanders of the Jerusalem Jews carried no weight either with the procurator Felix (Ac 24^{22f}), or with his successor Festus (Ac 25^{14-21}) ; and after Paul had appealed to Caesar, and had made the journey to Rome, we are left with a picture of him living there ' two whole years . . . welcoming all who came to him, preaching . . . and teaching . . . quite openly and unhindered ' (Ac 28^{30f}). It is clear that Luke intends to point out that there was nothing criminal in either Jesus or Paul, nor was there anything treasonable in what they taught. From Christianity the Empire had nothing to fear ; and the best proof of the truth of this was a statement of facts from the very first. Looked at from this angle Luke-Acts takes on the character of an ' apology for Christianity ' in two parts, and it may legitimately be held to anticipate, though in a rather different way, the Apologies of the 2nd cent.

8. Date and Place of Writing.—These very largely depend upon what we think was the author's main purpose in writing. Two dates are commonly suggested, an earlier date *c* A.D. 63, and a later one *c* A.D. 80–90. In favour of the earlier date it is argued that the second half of Acts gives a fairly detailed account of Paul's movements and activities, particularly in the later chapters. We are told how he was arrested in Jerusalem, imprisoned at Caesarea, ' appealed to Caesar,' and made the journey to Rome. And then, after the excitement of the journey, Acts ends with the picture of Paul living ' two whole years ' in Rome ' preaching . . . and teaching . . . unhindered.' The reader wants to know what happened to Paul after all. Did he appear before Caesar? If he did, was he condemned or acquitted? Or if not, what did happen? The book clearly lacks a climax, and we feel instinctively that Luke owes us an answer to these questions. The fact that he gives no answer is said accordingly to be the best proof there possibly could be that at the time he was writing there was no answer to give, because Paul's fate was still undecided—*i.e.* Acts carries the narrative right down to the time of writing, and it was, therefore, finished two years after Paul's arrival in Rome, in A.D. 63, when the author himself was with him (Ac 28^{16}). Since at the beginning of Acts (the argument continues) Luke plainly refers to the Gospel as ' the first book,' in which he has ' dealt with all that Jesus began to do and teach, until the day when he was taken up ' (Ac 1^{1f}), the Gospel must have been written previously. How long previously we cannot precisely say ; but most probably also during the two-year period at Rome, or perhaps (if we may suppose that it survived the shipwreck !) during the three years that Paul was imprisoned at Caesarea (*c* A.D. 57–60).

In favour of the later date it is argued that Luke's knowledge of, and use of, Mark in the Gospel is decisive ; Mark is usually dated *c* A.D. 65–67 ; we must allow time for its having been sufficiently widely known and respected to have been used by Luke as a main source ; Luke, therefore, must have been written after A.D. 70, and Acts later still. Furthermore, there are indications that Luke was aware of the details of the Fall of Jerusalem which took place in A.D. 70 (Lk 19^{43f} 21^{20-24} 23^{27-32}). And if we add to this such considerations as have been mentioned in **6** (*e.g.* his attitude to the Twelve and his manifest concern to deal with the problem posed by the deferment of the return of Jesus) it appears that the claim that both Luke and Acts ' breathe the atmosphere of a later age ' has substance ; and a date *c* A.D. 80–90 seems more likely. It is possible, of course, to counter the arguments on either side ; to point out, for example, against the later date that Luke's use of Mark is not nearly so decisive as is maintained, since the date of Mark is far from certain and it may easily have been written in the 40's or 50's, which would allow time for Luke to have used it in A.D. 61–63, or even in A.D. 57–60 ; or again, against the earlier date, that we can legitimately argue little from the end of Acts, since Luke himself refers to the Gospel as his ' first (not ' former ') book,' and he may have intended to write a third in which the trial and death of Paul were described in detail—indeed, he may actually have written it, and it has been lost. But the issue really turns on the view we take of Luke as an author and of what he was trying to do. If we regard him merely as a historian, writing ' straight history,' then we shall probably incline to the earlier date. However, the more his interests, motives, and literary methods have been studied in recent years, the more obvious has it become that he was concerned far more to select and order his material to promote the causes he had at heart than simply to record ' what happened ' for its own sake. If he was primarily an apologist for Christianity, and the origin and progress of the Gentile Mission his main theme, then the details of Paul's death were as irrelevant as the details of the great Apostle's birth and his life as a Jew. Moreover, after taking considerable pains to show that throughout Paul's career as a Christian he had been consistently vindicated by every properly constituted civil court before which he had been brought, to conclude with an account of his execution in Rome must have seemed to Luke a stultification of his purpose. So the end of Acts falls naturally into place ; at the end of the Gospel the Church was securely rooted in Jerusalem, at the end of Acts in Rome. And it is for such reasons as these that most moderns prefer the later date. As we have seen, if the earlier date be preferred, probably both books were written in Rome. They may also have been written in Rome if we prefer the later date, but not necessarily—the Anti-Marcionite *Prologue to Luke* (see **3**), for instance, says that the Gospel was written 'in the regions of Achaea' (*i.e.* Greece).

9. Accuracy.—In the 19th cent., when it was the fashion among the more radical critics to date Luke–Acts in the 2nd cent., considerable play was made of the alleged inaccuracy of the author on certain points, with the result that his general trustworthiness as a historian was impugned. Particular points adduced were: (1) the description of the 'enrolment' in Lk 2^{1ff}, which was said to involve difficulties of all kinds, especially the statement that the enrolment took place 'when Quirinius was governor of Syria'—Quirinius did not become governor of Syria until A.D. 6, and his census in Judaea is to be dated in either A.D. 6 or 7, that is to say at least ten years *after* the death of Herod the Great (4 B.C.), in whose reign Luke implies that Jesus was born; (2) the reference at Ac 5^{36f}, in the speech of Gamaliel, to the rebellion of Theudas (A.D. 45) several years before it happened, and the placing of it *before* the rebellion of Judas (A.D. 7)—some explained this curious inaccuracy as due to a misconstruction on the author's part of a passage in Josephus's *Antiquities*, published *c* A.D. 93; and (3) the difficulty of reconciling the account of the Jerusalem Council in Ac 15 with the (presumably unimpeachable) statements in the Pauline Epistles, especially in Gal 1 and 2. Replies were made to these points, notably by Sir William Ramsay, who dedicated himself to a systematic defence of Luke as a reliable historian. It would have been impossible, Ramsay argued, for a 2nd-cent. writer to have avoided a number of pitfalls when describing situations involving Roman officials a century earlier. Yet these pitfalls the author of Luke–Acts avoids. Thus, the governor of Cyprus is correctly termed a 'pro-consul' and his name given as Sergius Paulus at Ac 13—Cyprus had only been under the rule of the Senate for a short time when Paul went there, and soon afterwards ceased to be so governed; much the same may be said about Gallio as 'pro-consul' of Achaia' (Ac 18^{12}); and, similarly, the right titles are given to 'the leading men' at Pisidian Antioch (Ac 13^{50}), 'the city authorities' (literally 'politarchs') at Thessalonica (Ac 17^{6}), and 'the Asiarchs' at Ephesus (Ac 19^{31}). The inference is that the author had moved in the world he is describing, and that he must be assigned, therefore, to the 1st, and not the 2nd, cent. There can be no doubt that, so far as the arguments drawn from the second half of Acts are concerned, Ramsay made out his case; and the controversy as he found it is now dead. On the other hand, it must be emphasized that in spite of his attempts to remove them, or palliate them, many of the difficulties still remain—in particular the 'enrolment' under Quirinius, Gamaliel's reference to the rebellion of Theudas, and the reconciliation of Ac 15 with Paul's own statements in Gal 1 and 2. In other words, Ramsay succeeded in proving only that Luke described accurately the world that he knew and had travelled in the company of Paul—*i.e.* the Graeco-Roman world in the period *c* A.D. 45–65. To go on from this and maintain that this shows him in general to be 'a trustworthy historian,' and that what he has to tell us about events in Palestine up to fifty years previously must therefore be accurate, in spite of evidence to the contrary, is unjustified. For the material in his Gospel Luke explicitly says in the Preface to the Gospel that he was dependent on information received; and we may reasonably assume that the same is true about the material in the first part of Acts. In consequence, it is not a simple matter of 'accurate' or 'inaccurate,' or of 'trustworthy' or 'untrustworthy,' throughout. There are in Luke–Acts varying degrees of 'accuracy' and different levels of 'trustworthiness'; for we have to take into account, not only the sources on which Luke was dependent, but also his interests, such motives as may have led him to select from his sources and on occasion to modify them, as well as his total purpose in writing. And the truth seems to be that he is most reliable when recording what he had seen and taken part in himself.

10. Luke–Acts in the Early Church.—Of 2nd-cent. writers the following can without doubt be said to have known the Gospel or to imply its previous composition: Justin Martyr (*c* A.D. 150), who gives particulars found in Luke only; Tatian, Justin's pupil, who included it in his Harmony (the *Diatessaron*); Marcion (*c* A.D. 150), who produced an adulterated version of it; and Celsus (*c* A.D. 180), who referred to the genealogy of Jesus from Adam. The first writers who name Luke in connexion with the Gospel are the author of the Muratorian Canon (*c* A.D. 170) and Irenaeus (*c* A.D. 180). There are probable references to Acts in Clement of Rome (*c* A.D. 95), in Ignatius (*c* A.D. 110), and in Polycarp (*c* A.D. 112): probably also in the Martyrdom of Polycarp (*c* A.D. 155). Full quotations are found towards the end of the century in Irenaeus and Tertullian (*c* A.D. 200), both of whom ascribe the book to Luke, as does also the Muratorian Canon. Moreover, the Apocryphal Acts of the 2nd cent. are built on the canonical Acts, which implies that their authors knew it and highly regarded it. H. F. D. S.

LUNATIC.—See MOON, POSSESSION.

LUST.—The English word 'lust,' which is now restricted to sexual desire, formerly expressed strong desire of any kind. And so, as Thomas Adams says, there can be a lusting of the Spirit, for the Spirit lusteth against the flesh (Gal 5^{17}).

LUTE.—See MUSIC AND MUSICAL INSTRUMENTS, **4** (1) (*b*).

LUZ.—**1.** A town mentioned in Gn 28^{19} 35^{6} 48^{3}, Jos 16^{2} 18^{13}, Jg $1^{23, 26}$. The exact locality is uncertain, and a comparison of the above passages will show that it is also uncertain whether Luz and **Bethel** were one or two sites. In Gn 28^{19} it is stated that Jacob changed the name of the place of his vision from Luz to Bethel (cf also Gn 35^{6}, Jg 1^{23}). The two passages in Joshua, however, seem to contradict this; both of them speak of Luz and Bethel as two distinct places. A possible solution is that Luz was the name of the old Canaanite city, and Bethel the pillar and altar of Jacob outside the city. **2.** Luz is also the name of a city built on Hittite territory after the destruction of the original Canaanite city, Jg 1^{26}. The site is unknown. T. A. M.

LYCAONIA meant originally the country inhabited by the Lycaones, a central tribe of Asia Minor. It is for the most part a level plain, which is merged on the north and east in the plains of Galatia and Cappadocia, and is bounded on the west and south by hills. It was and is an excellent country for pasturage. Its exact boundaries varied at different times. At some uncertain date a part of Lycaonia, containing fourteen cities, of which Iconium was one, was transferred to Galatia. (See ICONIUM.) Lycaonia was part of the Seleucid Empire until 190 B.C. Later the whole or part of it belonged successively to the Pergamenian kings, the Galatians, Cappadocia, and Pontus. At the settlement of 64 B.C. by Pompey, the north part was added to Galatia, the south-east to Cappadocia, and the west was added to the Roman Empire, to be administered by the governor of the Roman province Cilicia. The eastern part was independent under Antipater of Derbe. In 39 B.C. Mark Antony gave the western part (including Lystra and Iconium) to Polemon, but in 36 B.C. it was transferred to Amyntas, king of Pisidia, along with Galatia proper. (See GALATIA.) Amyntas conquered Derbe and Laranda, which were incorporated in the Roman Empire when Amyntas' kingdom was made into the province Galatia in 25 B.C. In A.D. 37 Eastern Lycaonia was placed under Antiochus of Commagene, along with most of Cilicia Tracheia, and got the name Lycaonia Antiochiana.

Under Claudius and Nero, when St. Paul visited the churches of South Galatia, Lycaonia included the two parts, the Roman and Antiochian. The former part included Lystra and Derbe and a number of smaller places, and it is correctly described in Ac 14[6]. The Apostles, when persecuted at Iconium in Phrygia (or the Phrygian district of the vast province Galatia), crossed into Lycaonia (another district of the same province). In Ac 16[1-4] this territory is not explicitly named, but its two cities are mentioned by name. In Ac 18[23] the same cities are included in the expression used.

Both parts of Lycaonia were comprised in the united province of Galatia-Cappadocia under Vespasian and his sons (A.D. 70 onwards). They were again divided by Trajan in A.D. 106. About A.D. 137 'the triple eparchy' was formed, consisting of Cilicia, Lycaonia, and Isauria.

The name of the Lycaonians is not mentioned in the Bible, but their language is in Ac 14[11]: it was no doubt prevalent in the villages and smaller towns.

A collection of Christian inscriptions (of 3rd cent. A.D. and later) has been discovered in Lycaonia, which for numbers cannot be matched in any other Eastern province. They show the wide diffusion of Christianty in this district evangelized by St. Paul.

A. So.—**E. G. K.**

LYCIA was a mountainous country in the SW. of Asia Minor, which played very little part in the early history of Christianity. In it were situated many great cities such as **Patara** (Ac 21[1]) and **Myra** (Ac 27[5], cf 21[1]). The former was a celebrated seat of the worship of Apollo, the latter an important harbour, between which and Alexandria there was constant traffic in ancient times. Lycia was ruled by the Persians, and conquered by Alexander the Great. After his death it belonged to the Seleucid Empire, was then taken from Antiochus by the Romans in 188 B.C., and given to Rhodes at first, but afterwards freed in 168 B.C. It was one of the self-governing states, to which the Romans allegedly sent letters in favour of the Jews among the population in 138–137 B.C. (1 Mac 15[23]); see CARIA, DELOS. Lycia was made a Roman province by Claudius in A.D. 43 on account of dissensions between its cities, and in A.D. 74 was formed into a double province along with Pamphylia. A. So.—**E. G. K.**

LYDDA.—See LOD.

LYDIA was the name for the central part of the coastland on the west of Asia Minor in ancient times, having been so called from the race which inhabited it, the Lydians. It was a prosperous kingdom with its capital at Sardis and the name of the last king, Croesus, has become proverbial for wealth. The Persians seized the kingdom from him in 546 B.C. ('Lydia' in Ezk 30[5] AV is corrected to '**Lud**' in RV and RSV). Alexander the Great conquered it in 334 B.C. The possession of it was disputed by the Pergamenians and Seleucids till 190 B.C., in which year it became definitely Pergamenian (cf 1 Mac 8[8]). In 133 B.C. it passed by will with the rest of the Pergamenian kingdom into the Roman Empire, and the whole kingdom was henceforth known as the province Asia, by which name alone it is indicated in the NT (see ASIA). After the formation of the province, the term 'Lydia' had only an ethnological significance. The chief interest of Lydia for us is that it contained several very ancient and important great cities (of the Ionian branch of Greek language and culture), Smyrna, Ephesus, Sardis, Colophon, etc., some of which were among the 'churches of Asia.' The evangelization of the country is connected with St. Paul's long residence in Ephesus (Ac 19[1ff]). Sardis has been the scene of important American excavations. A. So.—**E. G. K.**

LYDIA.—A woman of Thyatira in the district of Lydia, the west-central portion of the province Asia, a district famed for its purple dyes. She supported herself at Philippi by selling purple-dyed garments. Apparently she was wealthy, perhaps a widow. Lydia was not her proper name, but she was known as 'the Lydian' at Philippi. She is not mentioned by that name in Paul's Epistle to the Philippians, though her house was the first centre of the Christian community at Philippi (Ac 16[15, 40]). Zahn (*Apg.* 582) has supposed that the name was either Euodia (not Euodias!) or Syntyche (Ph 4[2]). The incident in Ac 16 illustrates the comparatively independent position of women in Asia Minor and Macedonia. A. J. M.—**E. H.**

LYE.—See NITRE and SOAP.

LYRE.—See MUSIC AND MUSICAL INSTRUMENTS, **4** (1) (*a*).

LYSANIAS.—This tetrarch is mentioned only in Lk 3[1]. His tetrarchy was the mountainous territory about Abila, at the S. end of the Anti-Lebanon range, about 18 miles NW. of Damascus. (See ABILENE.) There was a well-known Lysanias, son of the dynast Ptolemy of Chalcis in Coele-Syria (Dio Cassius, XLIX. xxxii. 5), who reigned 40–36 B.C. and was executed by Mark Antony. Some writers, assuming that Luke referred to this ruler, have accused Luke of an error in chronology at this point. But the reference was doubtless to a younger Lysanias who ruled in the 1st cent. and died some time between A.D. 28–37. Josephus refers to him (*Ant.* XIX. v. 1 [275]) and he is also known to us from inscriptions (*CIG* 4521, 4523; *OGIS* 606). F. C. G.

LYSIAS.—**1.** A general of Antiochus Epiphanes, charged with a war of extermination against the Jews (1 Mac 3[32ff], cf 2 Mac 10[11] 11[1ff]); defeated at Bethsura (1 Mac 4[34ff]); after the death of Epiphanes he championed the cause of Eupator, and finally suffered death along with the latter at the hands of Demetrius (6[14ff, 63] 7[2-4], 2 Mac 14[2]). Cf MACCABEES, **2.**

2. See next article.

LYSIAS, CLAUDIUS.—A Roman officer in command of the garrison in the fortress ('Castle') of Antonia, which adjoined the Temple in Jerusalem. He is said to have rescued Paul from a lynching mob. The title given him in Ac 21[31] is *chiliarchos*, 'commander of a thousand,' although the actual force in his charge may not have exceeded half or a third that number. Thus 'battalion major' would seem to approximate his rank. He was a Greek, as appears from his family name. According to Ac 22[28] he had purchased Roman citizenship 'for a large sum'; his first name indicates that he had been adopted into the Claudian gens. Beyond the further fact that he rescued Paul and sent him secretly to Caesarea with an accompanying letter to his superior in command, the procurator Felix (Ac 23[23ff]), we know nothing about him. J. S. K.

LYSIMACHUS.—**1.** The translator of the 'Letter of Purim' (=Esther) into Greek (Ad. Est 11[1]) in 114 B.C. **2.** The brother of the high priest Menelaus. He excited the hatred of the populace by his systematic plundering of the Temple treasures, and was finally killed in a riot (2 Mac 4[29, 39-42]).

LYSTRA (near modern *Khatyn Serai*).—A city situated about 18 miles SSW. of Iconium in the south of the Roman province Galatia and in the Lycaonian part of that province, connected with Pisidian Antioch by the direct military 'Imperial road,' which did not pass through Iconium. Both Pisidian Antioch and Lystra were 'colonies' (see COLONY) established by the Emperor Augustus in A.D. 6 to make the Roman occupation more effective. The site of Lystra was identified in 1885 by means of an inscription found there by the Wolfe expedition. Hardly any remains of the city exist above ground. No trace of the temple of Zeus-before-the-City (Ac 14[13]) has been found. The sacrifice to Barnabas and Paul as Zeus and Hermes (or the national Lycaonian gods corresponding to these) took place at the entrance to it. The town appears not to have been much Hellenized, and the uncultivated populace expressed themselves in Lycaonian. There were Jews in Lystra (Ac 16[1]), but there is no mention of a synagogue. Timothy was a native of Lystra, which was visited by St. Paul four times in all (Ac 14[6, 21] 16[1] 18[23]), and addressed by him in the Epistle to the Galatians. A. So.—**E. G. K.**

M

MAACAH.—1. A son of Nahor, Gn 22^{24} (AV **Maachah**). **2.** The daughter of Talmai, wife of David, and mother of Absalom, 2 S 3^{3} etc. **3.** The father of Achish, king of Gath, 1 K 2^{39} (AV **Maachah**), possibly the same as **Maoch**, 1 S 27^{2}. **4.** Wife of Rehoboam, and mother of Abijah, 2 Ch 11^{20} (AV **Maachah**). When she is called ' daughter ' of Absalom (1 K $15^{2,\,10}$, 2 Ch 11^{20f}), ' granddaughter ' may be intended, as Absalom had but one daughter, **Tamar**, who may have married Uriel of Gibeah, 2 Ch 13^{2}, where the name is given as **Micaiah** (AV **Michaiah** ; cf Jos. *Ant.* VIII. x. 1 [249]). Maacah fell under the spell of loathsome idolatry, for which Asa deposed her from the position of queen-mother, which she appears to have held till then (1 K 15^{13}, 2 Ch 15^{16}). **5.** A concubine of Caleb, 1 Ch 2^{48} (AV **Maachah**). **6.** Wife of Machir, 1 Ch 7^{15f} (AV **Maachah**). **7.** Wife of Jehiel, the father of Gibeon, 1 Ch 8^{29} 9^{35} (AV **Maachah**). **8.** One of David's warriors, father of Hanan, 1 Ch 11^{43} (AV **Maachah**). **9.** The father of Shephatiah, the captain of the Simeonites, 1 Ch 27^{16} (AV **Maachah**).

MAACAH.—A small Aramaean kingdom, whose people aided the Ammonites against David, and shared in their overthrow, 2 S 10^{6ff}, 1 Ch 19^{6ff}. In 1 Ch 19^{6} it is called **Aram-maacah** (AV **Syria-maachah**). The gentilic is **Maacathite**, Jos $13^{11,\,13}$, 2 S 23^{34} (RSV ' of Maacah '). The Israelites were not able to drive out its inhabitants, Jos 13^{13} (RV, RSV **Maacath** ; AV **Maachathites**). See GESHUR.

MAACATH.—See MAACAH.

MAACHAH.—AV spelling of **Maacah** (q.v.) in most of its occurrences.

MAADAI.—One of the sons of Bani, who had married a foreign wife, Ezr 10^{34}, 1 Es 9^{34} (AV, RV **Momdis**).

MAADIAH.—A priestly family which returned with Zerubbabel, Neh 12^{5} ; called **Moadiah** in v.^{17}.

MAAI.—One of the sons of Asaph who took part in the dedication of the walls, Neh 12^{36}.

MAALEH-ACRABBIM, Jos 15^{3} (AV).—See AKRABBIM, ASCENT OF.

MAANI.—1. 1 Es 9^{34} (AV) ; see BANI, **9. 2.** 1 Es 5^{31} (RV) ; see MEUNIM.

MAARATH.—A town of Judah, Jos 15^{59}, possibly modern *Beit Ummâr*. Some think it may be the same as **Maroth** (q.v.).

MAAREH-GEBA.—The place from which the men placed in ambush rushed forth to attack the Benjamites, Jg 20^{33} (RV ; AV ' the meadows of Gibeah ' ; RVm ' the meadow of Geba '). There can be little doubt that we should emend MT to ' *west* of Geba ' (so RSV), or better ' west of *Gibeah*.'

MAASAI.—The name of a priestly family, 1 Ch 9^{12} (AV **Maasiai**).

MAASEAS, Bar 1^{1} (RV).—See MAHSEIAH.

MAASEIAH.—1. A priest, of the sons of Jeshua, who had married a foreign wife, Ezr 10^{18}, 1 Es 9^{19} (AV **Matthelas, RV Mathelas**). **2.** A priest, of the sons of Harim, who had committed the same offence, Ezr 10^{21}, 1 Es 9^{21} (AV **Eanes, RV Manes**). Foreign wives had been taken also by **3.** and **4.**—a priest, of the sons of Pashhur (Ezr 10^{22}, 1 Es 9^{22} [AV, RV **Massias**]), and a layman, of the sons of Pahath-moab, Ezr 10^{30} (perhaps called **Moossias** [AV **Moosias**] in 1 Es 9^{31}). **5.** A wall-builder, Neh 3^{23}. **6.** One of those who stood upon the right hand of Ezra at the reading of the Law, Neh 8^{4} ; called **Baalsamus** in 1 Es 9^{43} (AV **Balasamus**). **7.** One of those who expounded the Law to the people, Neh 8^{7}, 1 Es 9^{48} (AV **Maianeas, RV Maiannas**). He is perhaps the same as the preceding. **8.** One of those who sealed the covenant, Neh 10^{25}. **9.** A Judahite, Neh 11^{5} ; probably the same as **Asaiah** in 1 Ch 9^{5}. **10.** A Benjamite, Neh 11^{7}. **11. 12.** Two priests, Neh 12^{41f}. **13.** A priest in the time of Zedekiah, Jer 21^{1} 29^{25} 35^{4} 37^{3}. **14.** The father of the false prophet Zedekiah, Jer 29^{21}. **15.** A Levitical singer, 1 Ch $15^{18,\,20}$. **16.** One of the captains who assisted Jehoiada in the overthrow of Athaliah, 2 Ch 23^{1}. **17.** An officer of Uzziah, 2 Ch 26^{11}. **18.** A son of Ahaz slain by Zichri the Ephraimite, 2 Ch 28^{7}. **19.** Governor of Jerusalem under Josiah, 2 Ch 34^{8}. **20.** In 1 Ch 6^{40} **Baaseiah** appears to be a textual error for **Maaseiah. 21.** Jer 32^{12} 51^{59} (AV) ; see MAHSEIAH.

MAASIAI, 1 Ch 9^{12} (AV).—See MAASAI.

MAASIAS, Bar 1^{1} (AV).—See MAHSEIAH.

MAASMAS.—Apparently a corrupt duplicate of Shemaiah in 1 Es 8^{43} (cf v.^{44}), where AV has **Masman** ; cf the corresponding list in Ezr 8^{16}.

MAATH.—An ancestor of Jesus (Lk 3^{26}).

MAAZ.—A Jerahmeelite, 1 Ch 2^{27}.

MAAZIAH.—A priestly family which constituted the 24th course, 1 Ch 24^{18}, Neh 10^{8}.

MABDAI, 1 Es 9^{34} (AV).—See BENAIAH, **3.**

MACALON, 1 Es 5^{21} (AV, RV).—See MICHMAS.

MACCABEES.—The name commonly given to the Jewish family otherwise known as **Hasmonaeans,** who led the revolt against Syria under Antiochus IV., and furnished the dynasty of leaders and rulers in the State thus formed. The family is said to have derived its name from a more or less mythical ancestor *Hasmonaeus*. The chief members of the house were :

1. Mattathias (166 B.C.), a citizen of Modin, and of priestly descent. When, in accordance with the policy of Antiochus IV., the royal officer attempted to establish heathen sacrifices in that town, Mattathias refused to conform, killed the officer and a Jew about to offer sacrifice, levelled the heathen altar to the ground, and fled with his five sons to the mountains. There he was joined by a number of other patriots and by ' the Pious ' (see HASIDAEANS). After a few months of vigorous fighting in behalf of the Torah, Mattathias died, leaving the conduct of the revolt to his five sons. Of these, Eleazar and John were killed in the succeeding struggle without having attained official standing. The other three were his successors (1 Mac 2).

2. Judas (165–160 B.C.), called *Maccabee*, or ' the Hammerer,' from which surname the entire family came to be known. Judas was essentially a warrior, whose plans involved not only the re-establishment of the Torah, but also, in all probability, the re-establishment of the Jewish State in at least a semi-independent position. He defeated successively the Syrian generals Apollonius and Seron. Antiochus IV. then sent **Lysias,** the imperial chancellor, to put down the revolt, and he in turn sent a large body of troops against Judas, under three generals —Ptolemy, Nicanor, and Gorgias. Judas called the fighting men of Galilee together at Mizpah, organized them, and at Emmaus surprised and utterly defeated the forces of **Gorgias** (165–164). In the autumn of 164 B.C., **Lysias** himself came against Judas at the head of a great army, but was defeated at Bethzur. Thereupon, in December 164 B.C., Judas cleansed the Temple of the Syrian pollutions and inaugurated the re-established worship with a great feast. For a year and a half he waged war on his enemies on the east of the Jordan, while his brother Simon brought the Jews scattered throughout Galilee back to Judaea for safety. Lysias returned with a great army, and at Beth-zacharias completely defeated Judas. He then laid siege to Jerusalem, where the citadel was still in Syrian hands. Jerusalem surrendered, but Lysias did not attempt again to disestablish the Jewish faith. He appointed Alcimus as high priest. Judas and his party remained in revolt, and when Lysias returned to Syria, undertook war against Alcimus himself. Demetrius I., who had succeeded Antiochus IV., sent **Nicanor** to put an end to the rebellion. He was defeated by Judas at Capharsalama, and retreated to Jerusalem, where he threatened to burn the Temple if Judas were not delivered up. This once more brought ' the Pious ' to the support of Judas, who decisively defeated the Syrians at Adasa, Nicanor himself being killed. Josephus states that at this time Alcimus died and Judas was made high priest. Although this is probably an error, Judas was now at the head of the State. He sent ambassadors to Rome asking for assistance, which was granted to the extent that the Senate sent word to Demetrius I. to desist from fighting the Jews, the allies of the Romans. Before the message of the Senate could reach Demetrius, Judas had been defeated by the Syrian general **Bacchides,** at Elasa, and killed (1 Mac 3–9[22]).

There is no sound basis for the notion that ' the Pious ' (Hasidaeans) were interested only in religious reform and not in national independence. There was an occasion in the early years of the revolt when certain scribes of 'the Pious ' sued for peace. During the parley their negotiators were perfidiously seized and killed (1 Mac 7[12–16]). The folly of trusting the enemy was thus made clear, and the main body of ' the Pious ' presumably continued to support Judas Maccabaeus (cf 2 Mac 14[6]). After the war, during the struggle for power in the newly established revolutionary state, party conflict seems to have developed between ' the Pious ' and the Maccabees (Hasmonaeans) over the questions of the legitimacy of the Maccabean claims to the high priesthood. This conflict can be dated as early as the composition of 1 Maccabees. Since its author, a court historian of the later Maccabees, disparages the legal interpretations of the scribes of ' the Pious ' of his day by drawing attention to the rueful mistake of those scribes of ' the Pious ' who during the revolution had misplaced their trust in a priestly family which, though from their point of view was legitimate, had turned out to be neither trustworthy nor just (1 Mac 7[12–18]).

3. Jonathan (160–142 B.C.) undertook the leadership of the revolt, only to suffer serious defeat E. of the Jordan, where he had gone to avenge the killing of his brother John by the ' sons of Jambri.' For a time it looked as if Syria would again establish its complete control over the country. The high priest Alcimus died, and Bacchides, believing the subjection of Judaea complete, returned to Syria (159 B.C.). The land, however, was not at peace, and in the interests of order Bacchides gave Jonathan the right to maintain an armed force at Michmash. The fortunes of the Maccabaean house now rose steadily. As a sort of licensed revolutionist, Jonathan was sought as an ally by the two rivals for the Syrian throne, Alexander Balas and Demetrius I. Each made him extravagant offers, but Jonathan preferred Alexander Balas ; and when the latter defeated his rival, Jonathan found himself a high priest, a prince of Syria, and military and civil governor of Judaea (152 B.C.). When Alexander Balas was conquered by Demetrius II., Jonathan laid siege to the citadel of Jerusalem, which was still in the hands of the Syrians. Demetrius did not find himself strong enough to punish the Jews, but apparently bought off the siege by adding to Judaea three sections of Samaria, and granting remission of tribute. Jonathan thereupon became a supporter of Demetrius II., and furnished him auxiliary troops at critical times. Thanks to the disturbance in the Syrian Empire, Jonathan conquered various cities in the Maritime Plain and to the south of Judaea, re-established treaties with Rome and Sparta, and strengthened the fortifications of Jerusalem, cutting off the Syrian garrison with a high wall. Joppa was garrisoned and various strategic points throughout Judaea fortified. This steady advance towards independence was checked, however, by the treacherous seizure of Jonathan by Trypho, the guardian and commanding general of the young Antiochus V., by whom he was subsequently (142 B.C.) executed (1 Mac 9[23]–12).

4. Simon (142–134 B.C.), another son of Mattathias, succeeded Jonathan when the affairs of the State were in a critical position. A man of extraordinary ability, he was so successful in diplomacy as seldom to be compelled to carry on war. It was greatly to his advantage that the Syrian State was torn by the struggles between the aspirants to the throne. Simon's first step was to make the recognition of the independence of Judaea a condition of an alliance with Demetrius II. The need of that monarch was too great to warrant his refusal of Simon's hard terms, and the political independence of Judaea was achieved. In May 141 Simon was able to seize the citadel, and in September 140, at a great assembly of priests and people, and princes of the people, and elders of the land, he was elected to be high priest and military commander and civil governor of the Jews, ' for ever, until a trustworthy prophet should arise.' That is to say, the high-priestly office became hereditary in Simon's family. Following the policy of his house, Simon re-established the treaty with Rome, although he became involved in a strenuous struggle with Syria, in which the Syrian general was defeated by his son, John Hyrcanus. Like his brothers, however, Simon met a violent death, being killed by his son-in-law at a banquet (1 Mac 13–16[16]).

5. John Hyrcanus (134–104 B.C.). Under this son of Simon, the Jewish State reached its greatest prosperity. Josephus describes him as high priest, king, and prophet, but strangely enough the records of his reign are scanty. At the opening of his reign, John's position, like that of his father and uncle, was critical. Antiochus VII. (Sidetes), the last energetic king of Syria, for a short time threatened to reduce Judaea again to political dependence. He besieged Jerusalem and starved it into surrender. For some reason, however, probably because of the interference of the Romans, he did not destroy the city, but, exacting severe terms, left it under the control of Hyrcanus. Antiochus was presently killed in a campaign against the Parthians, and was succeeded by the weak Demetrius II., who had been released from imprisonment by the same nation. John Hyrcanus from this time onwards paid small attention to Syrian power, and began a career of conquest of the territory on both sides of the Jordan and in Samaria. The affairs of Syria growing ever more desperate under the succession of feeble kings, John ceased payment of the tribute which had been exacted by Antiochus, and established a brilliant court, issuing coins as high priest and head of the Congregation of the Jews. He did not, however, take the title of ' king.' His long reign was marked by a break with the Pharisees, who, as successors of ' the Pious,' had been the traditional party of the government, and the establishment of friendship with the Sadducees, thereby fixing the high priesthood as one of the perquisites of that party. John died in peace, bequeathing to his family a well-rounded-out territory and an independent government (Jos. *Ant.* XIII. viii.–x [230–300] ; *BJ* I. ii. 3–8 [54–69]).

6. Aristobulus I. (Judas) (104–103 B.C.). According to the will of John Hyrcanus, the government was placed in his widow's hands, while the high priesthood was given to the oldest of his five sons, Aristobulus. The latter, however, put his mother in prison, where she starved to death, established his brother Antigonus as joint-ruler, and threw his other three brothers into prison. In a short time, urged on by suspicion, he had his brother Antigonus killed, and he himself took the title of ' king.' Of his short reign we know little except that he was regarded as a friend of the Greeks, and conquered and circumcised the Ituraeans, who probably lived in Galilee. At this time the final Judaizing of Galilee began (Jos. *Ant.* XIII. xi. [301–323] ; *BJ* I. iii. [70–84]).

7. Alexander Jannaeus (Jonathan) (103–76). After the death of Aristobulus, his widow Alexandra (Salome) released his three brothers from prison, and married the oldest of them, Alexander Jannaeus (or Jonathan), making him king and high priest. Alexander carried on still more vigorously the monarchical policy of Aristobulus, and undertook the extension of Judaea by the conquest of the surrounding cities, including those of Upper Galilee. He was essentially a warrior, but in his early campaigns was defeated by the Egyptians. Judaea might then have become a province of Egypt had not the Jewish counsellors of Cleopatra advised against the subjection of the land. The Egyptian army was withdrawn, and Alexander Jannaeus was left in control of the country. His monarchical ambitions, however, aroused the hostility of the Pharisees, and Judaea was rent by civil war. For six years the war raged, and it is said that 50,000 Jews perished. The Pharisees asked aid from Demetrius III., and succeeded in defeating Alexander. Thereupon, however, feeling that they were in danger of falling again into subjection to Syria, many of the Jews went over to Alexander and assisted him in putting down the rebellion. The consequent success of Alexander was marked by a series of terrible punishments inflicted upon those who had rebelled against him. During the latter part of his reign he was engaged in struggles with the Greek cities of Palestine, in the siege of one of which he died, bequeathing his kingdom to his wife Alexandra, with the advice that she should make friends with the Pharisees (Jos. *Ant.* XIII. xii–xv. [320–404] ; *BJ* I. iv. [85–106]).

8. Alexandra (Salome) (76–67 B.C.) was a woman of extraordinary ability, and her reign was one of great prosperity, according to the Pharisees, whose leaders were her chief advisers. She maintained the general foreign policy of her house, defending her kingdom against various foreign enemies, but particularly devoted herself, under the guidance of her brother Simon ben-Shetach, to the inner development of Judaea along lines of Pharisaic policy. The Sadducean leaders were to some extent persecuted, but seem to have been able to bring about their appointment to the charge of various frontier fortresses. The death of Alexandra alone prevented her being involved in a civil war (Jos. *Ant.* XIII. xvi. [405–432] ; *BJ* I. v. [107–119]).

9. Aristobulus II. (67–63 B.C.). After the death of Alexandra, civil war broke out. According to the queen's provision, her eldest son, Hyrcanus II., who was already high priest, was to have been her successor. In fact, he did undertake to administer the State, but his younger and more energetic brother Aristobulus organized the rebellion, defeated Hyrcanus, and compelled him to surrender. By the agreement that followed, Hyrcanus was reduced to private life in the enjoyment of a large revenue. It was at this time that **Antipater**, the father of Herod I., appeared on the scene. He was an Idumaean of boundless ambition and much experience. He undertook to replace Hyrcanus on the throne. With the assistance of Aretas, king of Arabia, he organized an army and besieged Aristobulus in the Temple Mount. As the war was proceeding, Pompey sent Scaurus to Syria (65 B.C.). Scaurus proceeded towards Judaea to take advantage of the struggle between the two brothers. Before he reached Judaea, however, both Aristobulus and Hyrcanus referred their quarrel to him. Scaurus favoured Aristobulus, and ordered Aretas to return to Arabia. This decision, however, did not end the controversy between the brothers, and they appealed to Pompey himself, who meantime had arrived at Damascus. The two brothers pleaded their cause, as did also an embassy of the Jewish people, which asked that the monarchy be abolished, and the government by the high priest be re-established. Pompey deferred his decision, and ordered the two brothers to maintain peace. Aristobulus, however, undertook to continue the revolt, fleeing to Alexandrium, a fortress on the Samaritan hills, above the Jordan Valley. At the command of Pompey he surrendered the fortress, but fled to Jerusalem, where he prepared to stand a siege. Pompey followed him, and Aristobulus promised to surrender. When, however, Gabinius, the Roman general, went to take possession of the city, he found the gates closed against him. Thereupon Pompey proceeded to beseige the city. The various divisions of Jerusalem surrendered to him except the Temple Mount. This was captured after a long siege, and at terrible cost (63 B.C.). Pompey went into the Holy of Holies, but did not touch the Temple treasures. He did, however, make Judaea tributary to Rome and greatly reduced its territory. Aristobulus was taken prisoner, and Hyrcanus was re-established as high priest, but without the title of ' king.' Great numbers of Jews were taken by Pompey to Rome at this time, together with Aristobulus, and became the nucleus of the Jewish community in the capital. With this conquest of Pompey's, the Maccabaean State really came to and end ; and Judaea became tributary to Rome (Jos. *Ant.* XIV. i.–iv. [1–79] ; *BJ* I. vi. f [120–158]).

10. Hyrcanus II. (Jonathan) was a weak man, but had for his adviser and *major domo* Antipater, an exceedingly able man. The State, as re-organized by Gabinius, was attached to Syria, and Hyrcanus exercised the function of high priest (63–40). During this time Judaea was swept more completely into the current of Roman history, because of the assistance rendered by Antipater and Hyrcanus to Caesar in his struggle with the party of Pompey in Egypt. In gratitude Caesar gave many rights and privileges to the Jews throughout the Roman world. Hyrcanus was, however, not appointed king, but ' ethnarch,' and Antipater was made procurator. The walls of Jerusalem, which had been broken down by Pompey, were now rebuilt, and various cities taken away by Pompey were restored to the Judaean territory. Hyrcanus, completely under the control of Antipater, supported Cassius in the struggle which followed the death of Caesar, but in the disturbances following the death of Brutus and Cassius espoused the cause of Antony. At this critical juncture Antipater was killed, and his two sons, Phasael and Herod, were appointed by Antony tetrarchs of the country of the Jews. Antigonus, however, the second son of Aristobulus, with the assistance of the Parthians, captured Phasael, compelled Herod to flee, and seized the State. Hyrcanus was carried away prisoner by the Parthians, and his ears were cut off, so that he could no longer act as high priest.

After Herod had been made king, Hyrcanus was brought back to Judaea, and became a centre of one of the various intrigues against Herod, who had married Hyrcanus' grand-daughter Mariamme. As a result, Herod had him executed (30 B.C.), on the charge of conspiracy with the king of Arabia (Jos. *Ant.* XIV. v.–xiii. [80–369] ; *BJ* I. viii.–xiii. [159–273]).

11. Alexander, the elder son of Aristobulus II., who escaped from Pompey on the journey to Rome, collected an army and headed an insurrection in Judaea (57 B.C.). He was finally defeated, and later during the civil wars was beheaded by order of Pompey as a friend of Caesar.

12. Antigonus (Mattathias) with his father Aristobulus, escaped from the Romans, and in 56 B.C. headed a revolt in Judaea. Aristobulus retreated to Machaerus, but after two years' siege was compelled to surrender, and went again as prisoner to Rome, where he was poisoned (49 B.C.), just as he was setting out to the East to assist Caesar. Antigonus in 47 B.C. attempted unsuccessfully to induce Caesar to establish him as king of Judaea in place of Hyrcanus and Antipater. After the death of Caesar and during the second triumvirate, Antigonus attempted to gain the throne of Judaea with the assistance of the Parthians, and in 40–37 maintained himself with the title of ' king and high priest.' At the end of that period, however, Herod I., who had been appointed king by the Romans, conquered Antigonus with the assistance of Rome. Antigonus was beheaded (37 B.C.) by Antony at the request of Herod (Jos. *Ant.* XIV. xiv.–xvi. [370–491] ; *BJ* I. xiv. 1–xviii. 3 [274–357]).

13. Alexandra, daughter of Hyrcanus II., married her cousin Alexander, son of Aristobulus II. She was a

MACCABEES

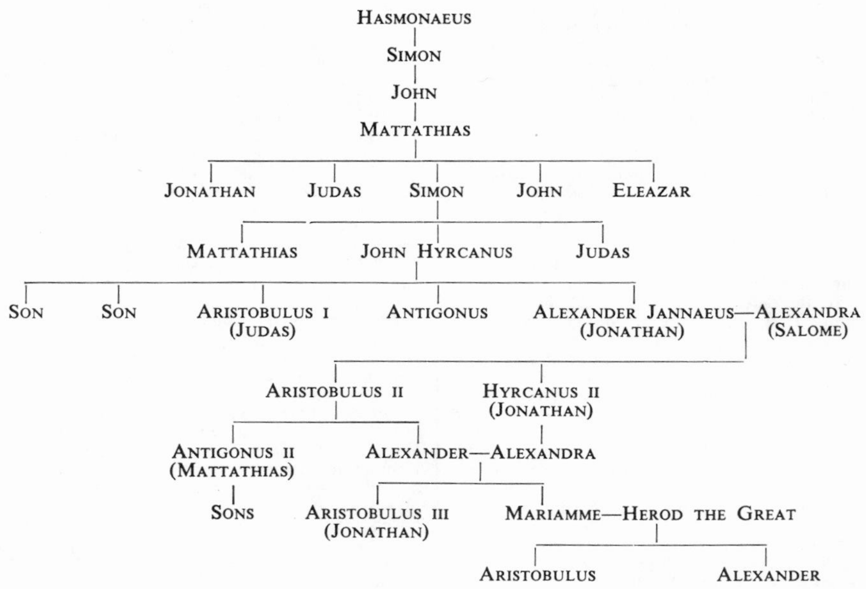

woman of great ability, and as the mother of Mariamme, wife of Herod i., was an object of bitter hatred on the part of Herod's sister Salome. She was executed by Herod in 28 B.C.

14. Aristobulus III. (Jonathan), son of Alexander and Alexandra, became a member of the household of Herod after the latter's marriage with Mariamme. He was possessed of great beauty, and like all Hasmonaeans he was a favourite with the people. At the request of his sister he was made high priest by Herod (35 B.C.). On account of his popularity, Herod had him drowned while he was bathing at Jericho, in the same year, when he had reached the age of seventeen.

15. Mariamme, daughter of Alexander and Alexandra, was reputed to be one of the most beautiful women of the time. She became the wife of Herod, who loved her jealously. Driven to madness, however, by the scandalous reports of his sister Salome, Herod had her executed in 29 B.C.

Although the direct line of Hasmonaeans was thus wiped out by Herod, the family was perpetuated in the sons of Herod himself by Mariamme—Alexander and Aristobulus. Both these sons, indeed, Herod caused to be executed because of alleged conspiracies against him, but the Maccabaean line still lived in the persons of Herod of Chalcis and Agrippa i. and ii. (see Herod).

S. M.—**W. R. F.**

MACCABEES, BOOKS OF.—See Apocrypha, **14, 15.**

MACEDONIA.—The Macedonians were a part of the Hellenic race who settled early in history in the region round the river Axius at the NW. corner of the Aegean. When they first came into Greek politics they had dominion from the mountains N. of Thessaly to the river Strymon, except where the Greek colonies of the peninsula of Chalcidice kept them back. Their race was probably much mixed with Illyrian and Thracian elements; they did not advance in culture with Southern Greece, but kept their primitive government under a king, and were regarded by the Greeks as aliens. Down to the time of Philip (359 B.C.) they played a minor part as allies of various Greek cities having interests in the N. Aegean. Under Philip, through his organization of an army and his diplomatic skill, they became masters of Greece, and under his son Alexander conquered the East. The dynasties which they established in Syria and Egypt were Macedonian, but in the subsequent Hellenization of the East they took no larger part than other Greek tribes. In their original dominions they remained a hardy and vigorous race. In the battle of Pydna (168 B.C.) the last king of the Macedonians was overcome by a Roman army under L. Aemilius Paullus. Macedonia was then divided into four separate districts with republican government, but it received the regular organization of a province in 146 B.C. The capital of the Macedonian kings was Pella, 23½ miles NW. of Thessalonica.

Macedonia was the scene of St. Paul's first work in Europe. See Paul, Philippi, Thessalonica, Beroea. The province at that time included Thessaly, and stretched across to the Adriatic; but Philippi was a colony, not subject to the governor of the province, and Thessalonica was also a 'free city,' with the right of appointing its own magistrates. The Via Egnatia ran across the province from Dyrrhachium to Neapolis, and St. Paul's journey was along this from Neapolis through Philippi, Amphipolis, Apollonia, to Thessalonica. A further visit is recorded in Ac 20^{3-6}, and the Pastoral Epistles imply another after his first imprisonment (1 Ti 1^{3}).

A. E. H.—**E. G. K.**

MACEDONIANS, 1 Mac 8^{5}.—See Kittim.

MACHAERUS.—A place E. of the Dead Sea, fortified by Alexander Jannaeus, and greatly enlarged and strengthened by Herod the Great (Jos. *BJ* vii. vi. 1 [163–170]). According to Josephus, the wife of Herod Antipas retired to this place when she got wind of her husband's intention to rid himself of her and wed Herodias. From there she escaped to her father Aretas, king of the Nabataeans. Josephus describes Machaerus as 'in the borders of the dominions of Aretas and Herod,' and then 'subject to her father' (*Ant.* xviii. v. 1 [111 f]). He goes on to say that here John was imprisoned and beheaded (Mk 6^{14-29} etc.). If it was then subject to Aretas, this is at least curious. The fortress was one of the last taken by the Romans in the war of independence

(*BJ* II. xviii. 6 [485 f], VII. vi. 1–5 [163–209]). It is identified with the ruin of *Mekāwer*, on the height about halfway between *Wâdī Zerkā Ma'în* and *Wâdī el-Môjib*. No thorough archaeological exploration has as yet been carried out here. W. E.—**E. G. K.**

MACHBANNAI.—A Gadite who joined David at Ziklag, 1 Ch 12^{13}.

MACHBENA, 1 Ch 2^{49} (RV).—See MACHBENAH.

MACHBENAH.—Named in the genealogical list of Judah, 1 Ch 2^{49} (RV **Machbena**). It is perhaps the name of a place, to be identified with **Cabbon** (q.v.).

MACHI.—The father of Geuel, the Gadite spy, Nu 13^{15}.

MACHIR.—**1.** The eldest ' son ' of Manasseh, Jos 17^{1}; in Nu 26^{29} the only son. Machir was also the ' father of Gilead.' These names are ethnographic, and their use suggests that the **Machirites** were either coterminous with the tribe of **Manasseh** (q.v.) or were its most warlike part. Settled on the W. of Jordan, they invaded N. Gilead some time after the days of Deborah, and so became the ' father of Gilead.' **2.** Son of Ammiel of Lo-debar on the E. of Jordan. He clung to the house of Saul as long as possible, and afterwards victualled David's men when that king was fleeing from Absalom, 2 S 9^{5} 17^{27}. W. F. C.

MACHNADEBAI.—One of the sons of Bani, who had married a foreign wife, Ezr 10^{40}; RSV substitutes this name in 1 Es 9^{34} for RV **Mamnitanemus** (q.v.; AV **Mamnitanaimus**).

MACHPELAH.—The name of a locality in which, according to P, were situated a field and a cave bought by Abraham from Ephron the Hittite as a burial-place for himself and his family (Gn 23^{17-18}). Here Sarah, and subsequently Abraham, Isaac, Rebekah, Leah, and Jacob were buried (Gn 49^{31}). The word is used with the definite article, which suggests that it is a common noun, perhaps surviving in its Ethiopic cognate, which means ' portion, lot.' The place is described as being ' before Mamre ' (Gn 25^{9}), Mamre (q.v.) being in the vicinity of Hebron (Gn 23^{19}), which lies on the sides of a narrow valley, the main portion of it lying on the face of the E. slope. The traditional site of the cave of Machpelah is on the E. hill also.

Above the supposed site of the cave there is now a rectangular precinct (Arab. *ḥarām*) measuring 181 feet by 93 feet internally (the longer axis running from NW. to SE.), and surrounded by massive walls 40 feet high dating from the time of Herod the Great. At the SE. end of the quadrangle is a mosque, once a Christian church, 70 feet by 93 feet, parts of which are attributed to the 12th cent. Within the mosque are cenotaphs of Isaac and Rebekah; in a porch on the NW. side are those of Abraham and Sarah; and at the opposite end of the enclosure are those of Jacob and Leah. The cave, which is reputed to be the real resting-place of the patriarchs and their wives, is below the floor of the mosque, and is thought to be double, in accordance with a tradition which is perhaps derived from the LXX rendering of *Machpelah* as ' double cave.' The entrances to it, of which there are said to be three, are in the flagged flooring of the building. G. W. W.—**J. Gr.**

MACRON.—Surname of Ptolemy (1 Mac 3^{38}, 2 Mac 4^{45}), who was governor of Cyprus (2 Mac 10^{12f}) and subsequently of Coele-Syria and Phoenicia (2 Mac 8^{8}).

MADAI.—Gn 10^{2}, 1 Ch 1^{5}; see MEDES.

MADMANNAH.—A town in the Negeb of Judah, named with Hormah and Ziklag, Jos 15^{31} (cf 1 Ch 2^{49}). Its place is taken in Jos 19^{5} etc. by **Beth-marcaboth** (q.v.). It is probably modern *Umm Deimneh*.

MADMEN.—A place in Moab, which, if the MT be correct, has not been identified. The name occurs only in Jer 48^{2} where there is a characteristic word-play: *gam Madhmēn tiddōmmî*, ' also, O Madmen, thou shalt be brought to silence ' (LXX *kai pausin pausetai*). It is a very natural suggestion that the initial *m* of *Madmen* has arisen by dittography from the final *m* of the preceding word, and that for *Madmen* we should read *Dimon* (q.v.); cf Is 15^{9}. See DIBON.

MADMENAH.—A place apparently N. of Jerusalem, named only in the ideal description of the Assyrian invasion, Is 10^{31}. The site is unknown.

MADON.—A royal city of the Canaanites in the north, Jos 11^{1} 12^{19}. It is probably modern *Qarn Ḥaṭṭîn*.

MAELUS, 1 Es 9^{26} (AV, RV).—See MIJAMIN, **1.**

MAGADAN.—See DALMANUTHA.

MAGBISH.—A family of returning exiles, Ezr 2^{30}, 1 Es 5^{21} (AV **Nephis**, RV **Niphis**), omitted from the parallel passage, Neh 7^{33}. Possibly Magbish is a Benjamite town, but if so it is unknown.

MAGDALA, MAGDALENE.—See MARY.

MAGDIEL.—A ' duke ' of Edom, Gn 36^{43}, 1 Ch 1^{54}.

MAGGOT.—See WORM.

MAGI, the plural of *magus*, is used in Mt 2^{1-12} for the ' wise men ' who came from the East to do obeisance to the newly born Christ-child at Bethlehem, having found indication of His birth in the appearance of a star. From v.^{12} it is evident that they were known to be men who received guidance not only from observation of celestial phenomena, but also through dreams. The word comes from the name of a priestly class in ancient Media, which appears in the Old Persian inscriptions in the form *magush*. Herodotus is aware that they were not only sacrificial priests (I. 101), but men who interpreted the significance for human affairs of celestial phenomena (VII. 37), and the meaning of dreams (I. 107, 108, 120, 128; VII. 19). Their reputation as men who had access to supernatural knowledge was widespread among the Greeks. One of them from Syria was known to have predicted the death of Socrates (Diogenes Laertius, II. v. 24). Perhaps because these priests continued to serve the old *daevas* who, after the success of Zoroaster's religious reformation, had been degraded to the status of demons, the word *magos* came to have a pejorative sense, and from as early as the 5th cent. B.C. is used in Greek to mean ' sorcerer ' or ' thaumaturge.' It has this sense in Ac $13^{6, 8}$, and in the name Magus given to the Simon of Ac 8^{9-24}. It is from this sense that we have our words ' magic ' and ' magician.'

Both the LXX and Theodotion use the word in Dn 2^{2} for the ' enchanters ' of the Chaldaeans, and the writer of the story in Matthew was doubtless thinking of wise men from Mesopotamia where, since the days of Nebuchadrezzar, there had been an interest in Palestinian affairs. Alerted by the rising of a star they had come to see the future king born in Bethlehem, bringing gold, frankincense, and myrrh, precious things brought to Mesopotamia by caravans from fabulous South Arabia, and hence appropriate for presentation as gifts. The form of their query: ' Where is he who is born king of the Jews?' suffices to show that they were thought of as non-Jews.

The story does not say how many they were. Oriental tradition has favoured the number twelve, but in the West, apparently on the ground of the threefold gift, they have generally been reckoned as but three. Later tradition knows their names, tells whence each one came and whither he went on his return, and has various fanciful interpretations of the significance of their gifts. Their remains were said to have been found in the East in the 4th cent. and brought to Constantinople, where they were placed in the church Hagia Sophia, only to be removed by Eustorgius to Milan and then in 1162 by Frederic Barbarossa to Cologne. As early as the 4th cent. the festival of the Epiphany seems to have celebrated the manifestation of the Christ to the Magi. See also STAR OF THE MAGI. A. J.

MAGIC, DIVINATION, AND SORCERY.—Magic, divination, sorcery, and witchcraft are all connected with belief in superhuman powers, and are methods whereby men endeavour to obtain from these powers knowledge of the future, or assistance in the affairs of life. Belief in magic and divination is most prevalent in the lower

MAGIC, DIVINATION, AND SORCERY

stages of civilization and religion. The arts of the magician and the diviner were founded upon the same logical processes as have issued in the development of modern science; but the limits within which deduction would be valid were disregarded, and the data were frequently imperfect. Accidental coincidence was often confused with causal sequence (see Hastings' *DB*, article 'Divination'). Magic and divination were derived from attempts at reasoning which were very often erroneous; but from such crude beginnings science has slowly grown.

In their beginning these arts were associated with religion; and diviners and magicians were those thought to be most intimately connected with the Deity, and, owing to their superior knowledge of Him and His ways, best able to learn His secrets or secure His aid. Among the Arabs the priest was originally also the **soothsayer**; the Hebrew *kōhēn*, 'priest,' is cognate with the Arabic *kāhin*, 'soothsayer'; the primitive priest had charge of the shrine of the god, and both offered sacrifices and gave responses. In this manner classes of professional diviners and magicians arose, as in Egypt (Gn 41[8], Ex 7[11]), in Babylon (Dn 2[2]), in connexion with Baal (1 K 18[19]), and even among the Israelites in the rank of professional prophets. Such officials were set apart for their office by some rite specially connecting them with the god, as the eating of a particular food, or the wearing of a sacred dress (cf 2 K 1[8], Zec 13[4]). The animism, in which magical arts had their root, soon passed beyond the simple belief that Nature was peopled with spirits, and began to distinguish between good and evil spirits. When that distinction had been attained, the art of the magician and diviner also became subject to moral distinctions, according to the character of the spirit whose aid was sought and the purpose in view. This diversity in the moral characteristics of magic and divination is illustrated in the history of Israel; for divination is akin to some of the institutions sanctioned by God, such as the Urim and Thummim (Ex 28[30], Lv 8[8]), and it includes, at the other extreme, such necromancy as that of the witch of Endor. Among Semitic races and by the Egyptians, magic and divination were associated with the worship of various gods and the belief in the existence of a vast number of demons. With the gradual rise of religion in Israel under the teaching of God, early modes of prying into the future, and magical methods of seeking superhuman help, were slowly abandoned, and, as revelation became clearer, they were forbidden. The teaching of the inspired prophets of Yahweh was very different from that of the professional prophets and from the religion of the common people. Throughout pre-exilic times there was a struggle in Israel between the pure worship of Y″ alone as inculcated by the great prophets, and the worship of 'other gods,' such as the local Canaanitish Baalim and idols in the homes of the people. In process of time magic and divination became closely linked with these illicit cults, and were consequently denounced by the great prophets; but at the same time the desire of the human heart to learn the future and to secure Divine help (which lies at the root of magic and divination) was met by God, purified, elevated, and satisfied by the revelation of His will through the prophets. God's revelation was suited to the stage of spiritual development to which the people had attained, hence His prophets sometimes employed methods similar to those of divination; consequently some forms of divination are allowed to pass without censure in many passages of the Bible, but these were gradually put aside as the people were educated to a more spiritual conception of religion. On the other hand, as men sought to prognosticate the future by illicit commerce with false gods and spirits, magic and divination became generally degraded and divorced from all that is right and good. This explains the increasing severity with which magic and divination are regarded in the Scripture; nevertheless we find it recorded, without any adverse comment, that Daniel was made head of the 'wise men' of Babylon—although these included magicians, enchanters, sorcerers, and 'Chaldaeans'—(Dn 2[2, 48]); and that the wise men (Mt 2[1]) were *magi* (see MAGI). In explanation it may be said that reliance upon divination is a moral evil in proportion to the religious light vouchsafed to the individuals concerned; and God accommodated the methods of His teaching to the condition of those to whom He revealed Himself.

General course of the history of magic and divination in Israel.—Several sources can be traced from which the Israelites derived their magical arts, and different periods are apparent at which these influences were felt. (*a*) *From patriarchal times up to Israel's contact with Assyria*, most of their occult arts were the outcome of the beliefs common to Semitic peoples. Although their sojourn in Egypt brought them into contact with a civilized nation which greatly practised divination and sorcery, we cannot trace any sign that they borrowed many magical arts from the Egyptians at that time. In this early period of Israelitish history we find divination by *teraphim*, the interpretation of dreams and necromancy, besides the authorized means of inquiry of God. The Book of the Covenant legislates against sorcery (Ex 22[18] E); and we read that Saul 'put the mediums and the wizards out of the land' (1 S 28[3]).

(*b*) *Under the influence of the Assyrian advance southward*, the small States of Palestine were driven into closer relations with one another, owing to the necessity of united opposition to the common foe. This was prejudicial to religion, through its rendering Israel more tolerant towards the gods of their allies (*e.g.* the worship of the Phoenician Baal, fostered by Ahab), and by its favouring the introduction of methods of magic and divination in use among their neighbours (cf Is 2[6]). This evil tendency was encouraged by Manasseh (2 K 21[6]), but in the reformation of Josiah, idolatry, witchcraft, and the use of *teraphim* were suppressed (2 K 23[24]) in accordance with Dt 18[10–12] (D).

(*c*) *The Captivity* brought Israel into contact with a much more fully developed system of magic and divination than they had known before. In Babylon, not only were illicit magical practices widely indulged in, but the use of such arts was recognized by their being entrusted to a privileged class (Dn 2[2]). The officials are here denominated **'magicians'** (*ḥarṭummîm*, scribes who were acquainted with occult arts), **'enchanters'** (*'ashshāphîm*, probably a Babylonian word meaning 'those who used conjurations,' but its derivation is uncertain), **'sorcerers'** (*m*[e]*khashsh*[e]*phîm*, in its root meaning perhaps indicating those who mixed ingredients for magical purposes [LXX *pharmakoi*], but this is not certain), and **'Chaldaeans'** (*kasdîm*, a name which, from being a national designation, had come to mean those who were skilled in the occult lore of Babylonia and could interpret dreams). In Babylonian religion and medicine, magic had a recognized, legitimate place. The Babylonians believed in a vast number of demons and evil spirits, which could be exorcised by appropriate means; they practised astrology (Is 47[12f]), augury from the inspection of the liver of victims (Ezk 21[21]), the use of amulets and talismans, etc. (see G. Contenau, *La Magie chez les Assyriens et les Babyloniens*, Paris, 1947).

(*d*) *Egyptian influences* were strongly felt in the century before, and the one following, the Christian era. The Mishnah shows the presence of a very strong tendency to occult sciences, and in the NT we find examples of Jews who practised them in Simon Magus (Ac 8[9]) and Elymas (13[8]). Among the Alexandrian Jews, and later by the Alexandrian Gnostics, magic was much used, and the name of Y″ in various forms entered into their spells and the inscriptions upon their amulets. Books of incantations, reputed to have been the work of Solomon, were extant, and the Babylonian Talmud is full of superstition (Schürer, *HJP* II. iii, 152). Such books and charms were burnt at Ephesus when their owners became Christians (Ac 19[19]). So celebrated was Ephesus for its magic, that 'Ephesian letters' was a common name for amulets made of leather, wood, or metal on which a magic spell was written (Farrar, *St. Paul*, ii, 26).

A. Distinguishing *divination*, in which prominence is

MAGIC, DIVINATION, AND SORCERY

given to the desire to know the future, from *magic*, which has for its object power to do something by supernatural aid, we have now to inquire into the modes of divination and magic which appear in the Scriptures.

Forms of divination mentioned in the Bible.—(*a*) *The casting of lots.*—The casting of lots was founded on the belief that God would so direct the result as to indicate His will (Pr 16^{33}). It was employed: (1) *In crises in national history and in individual lives.* The phrase ‘enquire of God’ sometimes referred to the drawing of lots, perhaps with the use of **Urim and Thummim**. This occurs in the arrangements for the conquest of Canaan (Jg 1^{1}), in the campaign against the Benjamites (20^{27}), in David's uncertainty after the death of Saul (2 S 2^{1}), and in war (5$^{19, 23}$). The Phoenicians cast lots to discover the cause of the tempest (Jon 1^{7}). (2) *In criminal investigation.* It was employed to discover the wrongdoer in the cases of Achan (Jos 7^{14}) and Jonathan (1 S 14^{41f}). (3) *In ritual.* Lots were cast in reference to the scapegoat (Lv 16^{8}). Two goats were brought, and lots were cast; one goat was offered as a sin-offering, and the other was sent away into the wilderness. (4) *In dividing the land of Canaan* (Nu 26^{55} 33^{54} 34^{13}, Jos 21$^{4, 6, 8}$). (5) *In selecting men for special duties*: the election of Saul (1 S 10^{20}), the choice of the men to attack Gibeah (Jg 20^{9}), the division of duties among the priests (1 Ch 24^{5}).

In most cases the method of casting the lot is not stated. Several ways were in use among the Israelites, some of which were directly sanctioned by God as a means of Divine guidance suited to the degree of religious knowledge attained by the people at the time. The following methods can be distinguished:

(i) *By Urim and Thummim.* Although not certain, it is believed by most scholars that the **Urim and Thummim** were two stones which were carried in a pouch under the breastplate of the priest, and which were drawn out as lots (see Hastings' *DB* s.v. ‘Urim and Thummim’). In connexion with this the **ephod** is mentioned. The employment of the Urim and Thummim for consulting God disappeared before the clearer guidance received through the inspired prophets. Apparently it had ceased by the time of Israel's return from the Captivity (Ezr 2^{63}). Inquiry respecting the future was also made of heathen deities (2 K 1^{2f}), and their responses were probably given by the drawing of lots.

(ii) *By belomancy and in other ways.* The word *ḳāsam* (which is specially applied to the drawing of lots as with headless arrows) is used of divination generally and frequently translated ‘to divine.’ It is generally referred to unfavourably (except Pr 16^{10}). **Arrows** are once specified as the means by which the lot was cast (Ezk 21^{21f}) This practice is found among the Arabs, and was also used in Babylonia. Arrows with the alternatives written upon them were shaken in a quiver at a sanctuary, and the first to fall out was taken as conveying the decision of the god. Nebuchadnezzar is represented as deciding in this manner his line of march (Ezk 21^{21}), and, as the result of casting the lot, holding in his hand ‘the divination Jerusalem,’ *i.e.* the arrow with ‘Jerusalem’ written upon it (see Driver, *Deut.* p. 224).

Without any indication of the method of divination, operations denoted by the word *ḳesem* appear among the Moabites (Balaam, Nu 23^{23}, payment being made for the service, 22^{7}), among the Philistines (1 S 6^{2}), and among the Babylonians (Is 44^{25}). It also appears as a method of the lower rank of prophets in Israel (Mic 3$^{6-11}$, Ezk 13$^{6, 9}$ 22^{28}). Prophets are named in connexion with diviners *ḳōsᵉmîm* (Jer 27^{9} 29^{8}). The word is used in relation to necromancy and the consultation of *tᵉrāphîm* (1 S 15^{23} 28^{8}, 2 K 17^{17}, Zec 10^{2}). The practice is forbidden in Dt 18^{10}.

(iii) *By rhabdomancy.* This is alluded to in Hos 4^{12}. Probably pieces of stick were used for drawing lots, as in the case of divination by arrows.

(*b*) *Dreams and visions.*—Numerous instances occur in which Divine intimations were communicated to men by **dreams** and visions. (1) In so far as these were spontaneous and unsought, they do not properly belong to the domain of divination. Such occur in Gn 20^{3} 28^{12} 31$^{10, 24}$ 37^{5}, 1 K 3^{5}, Mt 1^{20} 2^{12} 27^{19}. Dreams are spoken of as a legitimate channel for God's communications to His prophets and others (Nu 12^{6}, 1 S 28^{6}, Job 33^{15}, Jl 2^{28}). (2) But the belief in Divine warnings through dreams came very near to divination when interpreters were sought to make clear their meaning, as in Egypt (Gn 40^{5ff} 41^{8}; Pharaoh calls the *ḥarṭummîm*—a word used only in the sense of scribes possessed of occult knowledge), among the Midianites (Jg 7^{13}), and in Babylon (Dn 2^{2}). (3) Dreams were sought by the prophets of a lower order in Israel, and it is known that among the Egyptians and other ancient nations special means, such as fasting or drugs, were used to induce them, from the belief that they were Divine communications. In Egypt it was a common practice for worshippers to sleep within the precincts of the temples in order to obtain intimations by dreams, and some devotees lived by the rewards received by them for recounting the dreams which had come to them in the temple. References to misleading divination by dreams occur in Dt 13$^{1-5}$ (prophets were to be judged by the character of their teaching and to be put to death if they favoured idolatry), Jer 23$^{25-28}$ 27^{9} 29^{8}, Zec 10^{2}.

Vision (*ḥāzôn*, with its cognate words) has a similarly wide application, extending from the God-given experiences of the higher prophets to the misleading predictions of false prophets. Instances of its highest signification occur in Is 1^{1} 2^{1}, Am 1^{1}, Mic 1^{1}. The word is used respecting the deception practised by lower prophets, as in Nu 24$^{4, 16}$, where reference is apparently made to the seer receiving the intimation in a trance, but the interpretation is not quite certain (see Gray, *Numbers*, p. 361); other physical phenomena appear in connexion with prophesying (1 S 10^{10} 19$^{18-24}$). The word also appears in connexion with false prophets (Is 28^{7} 30^{10}, La 2^{14}, Ezk 12^{24} 13$^{6, 16, 23}$ 21^{29} 22^{28}, Zec 10^{2}).

(*c*) *Observation of omens* (**augury**).—*nāḥash*, translated ‘to divine’ or ‘to use enchantments,’ the agent being called ‘an enchanter’ (Dt 18^{10}), means ‘to learn by means of **omens**.’ Very probably the expression is derived from *nāḥāsh*, ‘a serpent,’ with the underlying idea that the intimation was obtained by the worshipper through the assistance of the serpent-god; another, but less likely, derivation is from the ‘hissing’ or ‘whispering’ tones of the diviner. The word is frequently used with a bad sense attaching to it.

Words were sometimes taken as omens of the future (1 K 20^{33}, RVm ‘took it as an omen’; also 1 S 14^{10}). The movements of animals also constituted omens. It was considered by the Arabs that some animals, under the influence of a higher power, could see what was invisible to men, and consequently their action became an omen. It would be quite in accordance with this that Balaam's ass should see what was hidden from her master (Nu 22^{27}); a similar belief in the significance of the movements of animals is shown in the lords of the Philistines watching the way the kine took with the Ark of God (1 S 6^{12}).

The methods of divination by omens are often unexpressed, as Gn 30^{27}, Lv 19^{26}, 2 K 17^{17} 21^{6}, 2 Ch 33^{6}. The following practices in divination by omens appear: (i) *By hydromancy* (Gn 44^{5}). In Egypt it was common to attempt to divine the future by the appearance of the liquid in a goblet or dish. (ii) *By the observation of the clouds.* The clouds were carefully studied by diviners among the Chaldaeans, and the word *ʿōnēn* seems to indicate this practice as existing among the Hebrews and Philistines (Is 2^{6}). Driver, however, leaves the kind of divination undecided, and suggests a derivation from an Arabic root meaning ‘to murmur’ or ‘whisper,’ the reference being to the mutterings of the soothsayer (*Deut.* p. 224). This form of augury was forbidden (Lv 19^{26}, Dt 18^{10}), and those practising it were denounced (Mic 5^{12}, Jer 27^{9}). Manasseh fostered it (2 K 21^{6}, 2 Ch 33^{6}). (iii) *By astrology.* The **stars** were very early believed to have an influence on the fortunes of men (Jg 5^{20}, Job 38^{33}). Professional **astrologers** were prominent among the Assyrians and Babylonians. Babylonian astrology, with its announcement of coming events and notification of favourable and unpropitious days (such as are now extant on Babylonian clay tablets), is mentioned in Is 47[13]; but astrology does not seem to have been practised by Israel in early times; Jer 10[2] speaks of it as 'the way of the nations,' and warns the people against it (the passage is probably late, from about the time of Second Isaiah). In later times astrology was regarded by the Jews in a less unfavourable light: *e.g.* Dn 2[48], where Daniel is made chief of the wise men who included astrologers (cf Mt 2, where the wise men, who appear to have been astrologers were met by God in their darkness, and led to the infant Saviour). (iv) *By inspecting victims.* Forecasting the future from the appearance of the livers of victims is mentioned in Ezk 21[21]. This was common in Babylon (Diod. Sic. ii. 29) and also among the Romans (Cic. *de Divin.* ii. 12). It does not appear to have been in use among the Israelites; the sacrifices of Balaam (Nu 23[1, 14]) were not for this purpose, but to propitiate the deity consulted.

Connected with the use of omens is the appointment of **'signs'** by prophets to assist their consulters in believing what they predicted. Signs were given by God and His prophets as well as by false prophets; these were exhibitions of Divine power in smaller matters by which men might be enabled to trust God in things of greater moment (Jg 6[36]); or they were instances of truth in small predictions, to awaken confidence in greater promises or threatenings (Ex 4[8] 10[2], Is 7[11]); or they were simply the attachment of particular meaning to ordinary facts to remind men of God's promises or threats (Gn 9[12] 17[11], Is 8[18], Ezk 12[11], Zec 3[8]). In the time of Christ such signs were demanded by the Jews (Mt 12[38] 16[1], Lk 11[16], Jn 4[48], 1 Co 1[22]). Cf SIGN.

(*d*) *Necromancy and* **familiar spirits.**—Of these there were two kinds: (1) A spirit (primarily a subterranean spirit, *'ôbh*) was conceived as dwelling in a human being (Lv 20[27]), most commonly in a woman. Those thus possessed were sometimes called *'ôbhôth* (Is 8[19]), or the woman was denominated *ba'ᵃlath 'ôbh* (1 S 28[7]). Another explanation (H. P. Smith, *Samuel*, p. 239) makes the *'ôbh* a sort of idol, on the ground that Manasseh 'made' an *'ôbh* (2 K 21[6]) and that it is classed with *tᵉrāphîm* (2 K 23[24]). These **necromancers** professed to have the power of calling up the dead (1 S 28[11], Is 8[19]). Of their method of procedure we know nothing. In the interview with the **witch of Endor,** it appears that Saul was told by the witch what she saw, but the king himself entered into the conversation. Necromancers seem to have deceived their inquirers by speaking in a thin weak voice to make it appear that it was the spirit speaking through them (Is 8[19] 29[4]). The LXX generally represents them as ventriloquists, *engastrimythoi* (cf *goētes*, 2 Ti 3[13]). A similar belief that a spirit might dwell in a human being and give responses appears in Ac 16[16]; this opinion was common in heathendom. The Jews had similar views respecting the indwelling of demons in cases of demoniacal possession.

(2) Other diviners represented themselves as having fellowship with a spirit from whom they could receive intimations. These spirits were called *yiddᵉ'ōnîm*, the meaning being either that the spirits were wise and acquainted with the future, or that they were known to the **wizards** and had become **'familiar spirits'** to them. The word occurs only in conjunction with *'ôbh*, as in Lv 19[31] 20[6], Dt 18[11].

(*e*) *Divination by teraphim.*—The **teraphim** were images in human form (cf Michal's stratagem, 1 S 19[13]), and they were worshipped as gods (Gn 31[19, 30], Jg 18[24]), but in later times they seem to have been degraded to magical uses.

Some suppose them to have been the remains of a primitive ancestor-worship, and connect the word with *rᵉphā'îm*, which means 'ghosts' (root *rāphāh*, 'to sink down,' 'to relax'). Some Jewish commentators (cf Moore, *Judges*, p. 382) have suggested that they were originally the mummied heads of human beings, and that images of wood or metal were substituted for these in later times.

Teraphim were apparently used for divination in later times. Nebuchadnezzar is represented as consulting them (Ezk 21[21]). Josiah abolished *teraphim* as well as other methods of illicit divination (2 K 23[24]), but they subsequently reappeared (Zec 10[2]). The use of the *teraphim* in divination is not stated, but it was probably somewhat similar to the consulting of familiar spirits, namely, the diviner gave the response which he represented himself to have received from the *teraphim*.

B. Magic, like divination, had both legitimate and illicit branches. The moral character of the attempt to obtain supernatural aid was determined by the purpose in view and the means used to attain it. **Witchcraft,** which sought to injure others by magical arts, has always been regarded as evil and worthy of punishment among all nations. Invocation of aid from false gods (who were still regarded as having real existence and power) and from evil spirits has been generally denounced. But there was also a magic, which has been denominated 'white magic,' having for its object the defeat of hostile witchcraft and the protection of individuals from evil influences.

1. Magic employed to counteract the work of evil spirits or the arts of malicious magicians.—This kind of magic was extensively practised among the Assyrians and Babylonians, and was the kind professed by the wise men who were under the patronage of Nebuchadnezzar (Dn 2[2]). It also appears in the ceremony of **exorcism.** In Babylonia illness was traced to possession by evil spirits, and exorcism was employed to expel them. Exorcism was practised by the later Jews (Ac 19[13], Mt 12[27]).

The method of a Jewish exorcist, Eleazar, in the time of Vespasian is described by Josephus (*Ant.* VIII. ii. 5 [47–49]). He placed a ring containing a magical root in the nostril of the demoniac; the man fell down immediately, and the exorcist, using incantations, said to have been composed by Solomon, adjured the demon to return no more.

This kind of magic is also exemplified in the use of **amulets** and **charms,** intended to defend the wearer from evil influences. These derived their power from the **spells** which had been pronounced over them (thus *lāḥash*, which began with the meaning of serpent-charming, came to mean the muttering of a spell, and from that it passed to the meaning of an amulet which had received its power through the spell pronounced over it), or from the words which were inscribed upon them, or the symbolic character of their form. They were used by all ancient peoples, and were opposed by the prophets only when they involved trust in other gods than Y″. Probably the earrings of Gn 35[4] and Hos 2[13] were amulets; so also were the moon-shaped ornaments of Jg 8[21, 26] and Is 3[18]; their shape was that of the crescent moon which symbolized to the Arabs growing good fortune, and formed a protection against the evil eye. Written words were often employed to keep away evil. The later Jew, understanding Dt 6[8f] in a literal sense, used **phylacteries** (Mt 23[5]), to which the virtue of amulets was attributed, although their origin apparently was mistaken exegesis rather than magic. The use of such charms was very prevalent in the early centuries of the Christian era among the Alexandrian Jews and the Gnostics. Phylacteries have been found among the Qumrân discoveries.

2. Magic in forms generally denounced by the great prophets.—(*a*) *Magic which was apparently dependent upon the occult virtues attributed to plants and other substances.*—The Hebrew term for this was *kesheph*. The root *kāshaph* means 'to cut,' and has been explained as denoting the cutting which the worshipper inflicted upon himself (as 1 K 18[28]), or (by W. Robertson Smith) as the cutting up of herbs shredded into the magic brew; the latter meaning is supported by the LXX translation of *kesheph* by *pharmaka*, and also by Mic 5[12], where *kᵉshāphîm* appear to be material things; such a decoction is perhaps referred to in Is 65[4]. A wider signification is, however, possible, as in 2 K 9[22], where *kᵉshāphîm* has the meaning of corrupting influences (RSV **'sorceries'**). Some derive *kāshaph* from an Assyrian root meaning **'to bewitch'** (see Hastings' *DB*, article MAGIC).

Hebrew magic came to a considerable extent from Assyria and Babylonia, where the art was practised by a class of men specially set apart for it (Dn 2[2]; cf also Is 47[9, 12], Nah 3[4]). Egyptian sorcerers are also noticed (Ex 7[11]), but Egyptian influence in the art was most strongly felt by the Jews in post-exilic times. The belief in the virtue of **mandrakes** as love-philtres appears in Gn 30[14] and Ca 7[13] (*dûdhā'im*, from the root *dûdh*, 'to fondle'). **Sorcerers** are frequently denounced in the Bible (Ex 22[18], Dt 18[10], 2 K 9[22], 2 Ch 33[6], Jer 27[9], Gal 5[20], Rev 9[21] 21[8]).

(*b*) *Magic by spells or the tying of knots.*—The tying of knots in a rope, accompanied by the whispered repetition of a **spell,** was common in Babylonia (cf Is 47[9, 12]) and in Arabia. This practice may lie behind the word *ḥābhar*, Dt 18[11], or the word may refer to the spell only as a binding together of words. *Ḥābhar* is also used with the special meaning of serpent-charming (Ps 58[5]). This art, as now found in India and Egypt, was also denominated by the word *lāḥash* (Ps 58[5], Ec 10[11], Jer 8[17]); from the muttering of the charm, the word gained the meaning of whispering (2 S 12[19], Ps 41[7]), and it is used of a whispered prayer (Is 26[16], or, as some understand it in this passage, 'compulsion by magic'). Magical power was also held to be present in the reiteration of spells or prayers as in the case of the priests of Baal (1 K 18[26]), and this repetition of the same words is rebuked by our Lord (Mt 6[7]).

In close connexion with the power of spells is the belief in the efficacy of **cursing and blessing** when these were uttered by specially endowed persons (Nu 22[6], Jg 5[23]).

An authorized ceremony closely approaching the methods of magicians is found in the ritual for the trial by **ordeal** of a wife charged with unfaithfulness (Nu 5[12–31]); the woman brought the prescribed offerings and the priest prepared a potion of water in which was put dust from the Tabernacle floor; the curse, which the woman acquiesced in as her due if guilty, was written and washed off with the water of the potion, the idea being that the curse was by this means put into the water, and the potion was afterwards drunk by the woman.

(*c*) *Symbolic magic.*—Magicians often made, in clay or other material, figures of those whom they desired to injure, and, to the accompaniment of fitting spells, inflicted upon these models the injuries they imprecated. They believed that in this way they sympathetically affected the persons represented. A trace of this symbolism is to be found in the placing of **golden mice and tumours** beside the Ark by the Philistines when they sent it back to Israel (1 S 6[5]); by this means they believed that they would rid themselves of the troubles which the Ark had brought to them. F. E. R.—**J. P. H.**

MAGISTRATE.—This word is used in the AV to represent either 'judge' or 'ruler'—'authority' in the most general sense. In Jg 18[7], where AV has 'there was no magistrate in the land' (cf RV), RSV has 'lacking nothing that is in the earth,' which rests on an amended text. In Ezr 7[25] (so also RV, RSV) it represents *shāphᵉṭīn*, the Aramaic form of the common Hebrew word rendered 'judges.' RSV employs the word in Dn 3[2f] for a word of uncertain meaning (AV, RV 'sheriffs'). In Lk 12[11, 58], Tit 3[1] it stands in AV for derivatives of the general word *archō*, 'to rule,' but in the passages from Luke with special reference to judges (RV and RSV 'magistrate' in Lk 11[58], 'rulers' in 12[11], Tit 3[1]). In Ac 16[20–38] (RV and RSV 'magistrates') the word is used to translate the Greek *stratēgoi*. This is often used as the equivalent of the Latin *praetores*, and in the older Roman colonies the two supreme magistrates were often known by this name. Here it appears to be no more than a courtesy title for the more precise *duoviri*. A. E. H.

MAGNIFICAL.—Obsolete for 'magnificent'; retained in AV and RV (RSV 'magnificent') in 1 Ch 22[5] from the Geneva version—'the house . . . must be exceeding magnifical.' The adverb occurs in Rhem. NT, Lk 16[19] 'He fared every day magnifically.'

MAGNIFICAT, BENEDICTUS, AND NUNC DIMITTIS.—The hymn *Magnificat* (Lk 1[46–55]) has been well described as 'something more than a psalm, and something less than a complete Christian hymn' (Liddon). The same characterization may apply to the *Benedictus* (Lk 1[68–79]). They are the poems of those who felt nearer to the fulfilment of the promises than any writer of the OT. But no Evangelist of the NT, writing after the Death and Resurrection of Christ, could have failed to speak of the event of salvation as having already occurred. Both hymns stand on the brink of the fulfilment, but the fulfilment has not yet been accomplished.

It is therefore widely believed to-day that both hymns emanate from circles associated with John the Baptist, which were still looking for the Coming One. Also, both hymns are detachable from their context. V.[56] follows directly upon v.[45], the 'her' of v.[56] then referring unambiguously to the speaker of v.[45]; similarly v.[80] follows naturally upon v.[66], since both speak of the growth of John the Baptist, while the whole hymn (1[68–79]) hangs somewhat in mid-air, and would come more appropriately after v.[64]. Thus it would seem that the Evangelist, or his source, has interpolated two liturgical compositions of a John the Baptist community into an already existing narrative.

This suggests a solution to the much discussed problem of the true reading in v.[46]. In the TR the hymn is ascribed to Mary, but there is a variant reading 'Elisabeth.' 'Mary' is the reading of all the Greek MSS, of the great majority of Latin MSS, and of many Early Fathers as far back as Tertullian (2nd cent.). On the other hand, three old Latin MSS (*a*, *b*, *l*) have 'Elisabeth.' (The frequent reference to Origen is a mistake.) Niceta of Remesiana (*fl*. *c* 400) quoted it in his treatise 'On the good of Psalmody,' ch. 11, and it occurs in two MSS of the Latin translation of Irenaeus *Adv. Haer.* IV. 12 (3rd cent.). There is much to be said for the view that the original text was simply 'and she said,' so that both 'Mary' and 'Elizabeth' should be regarded as glosses.

On the question which is the right gloss, opinions have been divided. As a Christian evangelist, however, proclaiming God's decisive act of redemption in Christ, Luke must surely have understood the *Magnificat* as a prophecy not of the redemptive act conceived merely as a future hope, but as a hope which had been fulfilled precisely in the Christ-event. It would therefore seem plausible to suppose that while the *Magnificat* was originally a hymn of a John the Baptist sect, it has been taken over to Christian usage, either by Luke himself, or by the Church before him, and transferred from Elisabeth to Mary, the Mother of the Christ, by the addition of v.[48b], which, as has frequently been pointed out, is more appropriate on the lips of Mary than of Elisabeth.

The *Magnificat* has four strophes. In strophe i (vv.[46–47]) Mary praises God with all the powers of soul and spirit. In ii (vv.[48–49]) she speaks of living in the memory of men, not as something deserved but because it is the will of the holy Lord. In iii (vv.[50–53]) she rises to a large view of the working out of God's purposes in human history, in the humbling of proud dynasties, and the triumph of the meek. In iv (vv.[54–55]) she comes back to the fulfilment of the promises in the Messianic time, beginning with the birth of the Christ, which is the crowning act of God's mercy and love.

The *Benedictus* falls into two parts. Part i (vv.[68–75]) praises God because his Messianic promises are now on the brink of fulfilment. The past tenses, 'has visited' etc. are 'prophetic'; so certain is the fulfilment, and so close at hand, that it can already be spoken of as having occurred. Part ii (vv.[76–79]) is a prophecy of John the Baptist's role as the forerunner of the Coming One, spoken of as the Star (RSVm 'dayspring') who will accomplish the redemptive act of God. In the John the Baptist community the advent of the Coming One still lay in the future. But in the perspective of the Evangelist he has already come in Jesus.

The *Nunc Dimittis* (2$^{29-32}$) is similarly detachable from its context, for it duplicates the prophecy in vv.$^{34b-35}$. Like the other canticles, it is probably a pre-Lucan liturgical hymn, but unlike them a Christian one. The Messianic salvation has already occurred (v.^{30}), and is not, as in the John the Baptist hymns, merely on the brink of fulfilment. Also, the salvation is defined in universalistic terms (v.^{32}; contrast 1^{55f} and $^{69, 73f}$). This hymn consists of three couplets: v.^{29}, in which the speaker recognizes that he may depart from this life 'in peace'; vv. $^{30-31}$, which state the reason for this, that the long-awaited Messianic salvation has now begun; v.^{32} a succinct definition of the content and scope of the salvation. A. E. B.—**R. H. F.**

MAGOG.—The name of a people, enumerated in Gn 10^{2} 1 Ch 1^{5} among the sons of Japheth, between Gomer (the Cimmerians) and Madai (the Medes). It appears also in Ezk 38^{2} (with the definite article) and 39^{6}, apparently as indicating the land under the rule of **Gog** 'chief prince of *Meshech* and *Tubal*' who is to lead a great expedition against the restored Israel, from 'the uttermost parts of the north,' and who has as his allies *Gomer* and (Beth)-*Togarmah*. The names italicised are also mentioned in Gn 10^{2f} as closely connected with Magog. From these notices it would seem that Magog was a people (or land) to the far north of Palestine, not far from Meshech and Tubal, whose home is shown by Assyrian records to have been NE. of Cilicia. Josephus (*Ant.* I. vi. 1 [123]) connected Magog with the Scythians, a people whom Herodotus designated as belonging N. of the Crimea (iv. 17–20, 47–58), and whose predatory incursions into Asia and elsewhere are known over a long period. If Gog is connected with Gyges of Lydia (see Gog), this seems unlikely; and neither this nor the interpretation of Gog as reminiscent of Gagâ'a (Gaga, Gašga)—barbarians, explains the name Magog, unless it is to be regarded either as an artificial form, simply denoting the home of Gog (a sort of rhyming couplet), or as a corruption of Assyrian *mat-Gugi*—land of Gyges. The suggestion has been made that Magog in Gn 10^{2} is simply an erroneous copying of Gomer (written with its consonants in the wrong order as *mgr*). In Ezk 38^{2} it has also been thought to be a marginal note, an abbreviation of the Hebrew equivalent (*hammagēdōn*) of Greek '*Ho Makedōn*' *i.e.* the Macedonian (Alexander the Great). It certainly needs to be explained why Magog appears here with the definite article (literally 'the land of the Magog'), and the reference in 39^{6} could equally be personal.

In Rev 20^{8} Gog and Magog represent the nations of the whole earth, gathered by Satan to be brought to disaster as they engage in a final assault on the saints and the holy city (see, further, Gog).

S. R. D.—**P. R. A.**

MAGOR-MISSABIB.—A nickname given (Jer 20^{3} AV, RV; RSV 'Terror on every side') by Jeremiah to Pashhur, chief officer in the Temple, who had caused Jeremiah to be beaten and put in the stocks as a false prophet. The name is an etymological play on the word *Pashhur*, and denoted 'fear-round-about'; but whether Pashhur (q.v.) was to be that to his surroundings, or *vice versa*, does not appear. W. F. C.

MAGPIASH.—One who sealed the covenant, Neh 10^{20}.

MAGUS.—See Bar-Jesus, Magi, Magic, Simon Magus.

MAHALAB.—A town of Asher, Jos 19^{29} (so RSV; Hebrew has *meḥebhel*, which AV renders 'from the coast,' and RV 'by the region of,' with margin 'from Hebel to'). **Ahlab** and **Helbah** (Jg 1^{31}) are probably both to be identified with this place, which figures in Sennacherib's inscription as *Maḥalliba*; modern *Khirbet el-Maḥâlib*.

MAHALAH, 1 Ch 7^{18} (AV).—See Mahlah, **2.**

MAHALALEEL.—See Mahalalel.

MAHALALEL.—**1.** Son of Kenan and great-grandson of Seth (Gn 5$^{12f, 15-17}$, 1 Ch 1^{2} [AV all **Mahalaleel**], Lk 3^{37} [AV, RV, RSV **Mahalaleel**]); called **Mehujael** in Gn 4^{18}. **2.** The son of Perez, who dwelt at Jerusalem after the Captivity, Neh 11^{4} (AV **Mahaleleel**).

MAHALATH.—**1.** Daughter of Ishmael and sister of Nebaioth, who became Esau's wife, Gn 28^{9}; called **Basemath** (q.v.) in Gn 36^{3}. **2.** Wife of Rehoboam, 2 Ch 11^{18}. **3.** See Psalms, **2.**

MAHALATH LEANNOTH.—See Psalms, **2.**

MAHANAIM ('two camps' or 'two hosts' [if the Hebrew word is really a dual, which is very doubtful]).—An important city E. of Jordan on the frontier of Gad and Manasseh (Jos 13$^{26, 30}$); it was a Levitical city within the territory of Gad (Jos 21^{38}). It was clearly N. of the Jabbok, as Jacob travelling S. reached it first (Gn 32$^{2, 22}$). Here Abner made Ish-bosheth, son of Saul, king (2 S 2^{8}), and here David took refuge from his rebel son Absalom (2 S 17$^{24-27}$ 19^{32}). Solomon put Abinadab in authority in this city (1 K 4^{14}). There is apparently a reference to Mahanaim in Ca 6^{13} (RV, AVm, RSVm). The site of Mahanaim is quite uncertain, and various identifications have been proposed; those recently maintained include *Kh. Maḥneh, Tell el-Ḥajjāj,* and *Tulūl eḏ-Ḏahab*. Of these the first is most favoured.

MAHANEH-DAN.—A town situated between Zorah and Eshtaol, W. of Kiriath-jearim, Jg 13^{25} (AV translates 'the camp of Dan') 18^{12}. The site is unknown.

MAHARAI.—One of David's thirty heroes, 2 S 23^{28}, 1 Ch 11^{30}; according to 1 Ch 27^{13}, of the family of Zerah, and captain of the Temple guard for the tenth monthly course.

MAHATH.—**1.** The eponym of a Kohathite family, 1 Ch 6^{35}, 2 Ch 29^{12}; perhaps to be identified with **Ahimoth** of 1 Ch 2^{65}. **2.** A Levite in the time of Hezekiah, 2 Ch 31^{13}.

MAHAVITE, THE.—The EV designation in 1 Ch 11^{46} of Eliel, one of David's heroes. The MT should perhaps be emended to read 'the Mahanaimite.'

MAHAZIOTH.—The Hemanite chief of the 23rd course of singers, 1 Ch 25$^{4, 30}$.

MAHER-SHALAL-HASH-BAZ ('spoil speeds, prey hastes').—A symbolical name given to one of Isaiah's sons to signify the speedy destruction of the power of the allied kings Rezin and Pekah by the king of Assyria, Is 8^{1f}.

MAHLAH.—**1.** One of the daughters of Zelophehad (q.v.), Nu 26^{33} 27^{1} 36^{11}, Jos 17^{3}. **2.** One of the sons of Hammolecheth, 1 Ch 7^{18} (AV **Mahalah**).

MAHLI.—In Ex 6^{19}, Nu 3^{30}, 1 Ch 24$^{26, 28}$, it is the name of a son of Merari, Levi's youngest son. In 1 Ch 23^{23} 24^{30} a son of Mushi, Mahli's brother, bears the same name. Ezr 8^{18}, 1 Es 8^{47} speak of a man of discretion (see Ish-Sechel) of the sons of Mahli (1 Es 8^{47}, AV **Moli**; RV **Mooli**) namely Sherebiah (in Ezr 8^{18}, AV and RV have 'and Sherebiah'). In Nu 3^{33} 26^{58} Mahli's descendants are called 'the family of the **Mahlites.**' According to 1 Ch 23^{22}, these Mahlites were descended from the daughters of Eleazar, the elder son of the Mahli mentioned in Ex 6^{19}. Eleazar left no male offspring. Their cousins, the sons of Kish, therefore took them in marriage, and prevented the extinction of their father's name.

MAHLON ('sickness').—Son of Elimelech and Naomi (Ru 1^{2}), who married Ruth (4^{10}), a Moabitess, and after a sojourn of ten years in Moabite territory died there. His widow subsequently married Boaz (q.v.).

MAHOL.—The father of Ethan the Ezrahite, Heman, Chalcol, and Darda (1 K 4^{31}), who are mentioned as famous for their wisdom, though surpassed in this respect by Solomon. But in 1 Ch 2^{6} the same four, with Zimri, are mentioned as sons of Zerah. The word *māḥôl* is elsewhere found amongst instruments of music (*e.g.* Ps 149^{3} 150^{4}, where EV have 'dance'), so that the four wise men mentioned above may really be described as ' sons of music, ' in which case their wisdom may have consisted chiefly in their skill in the composition of hymns. T. A. M.

MAHSEIAH.—Grandfather of Baruch and Seraiah, Jer 32^{12} 51^{59} (AV **Maaseiah**), Bar 1^{1} (AV **Maasias, RV Maaseas**).

MAIANEAS, 1 Es 9^{48} (AV).—See MAASEIAH, **7.**

MAIANNAS, 1 Es 9^{48} (RV).—See MAASEIAH, **7.**

MAIL.—See ARMOUR, **2** (*c*).

MAINSAIL.—See SHIPS AND BOATS.

MAJESTY.—A variety of words are used to express the idea of majesty, which is often ascribed to God (*e.g.* Ex 15$^{7, 11}$, Dt 33^{26}, 1 Ch 16^{27} 29^{11}, Job 13^{11} 31^{23} 37$^{4, 22}$, Ps 8$^{1, 9}$ 29^{4} 68^{34} 76^{4} 93^{1}, Is 2^{10} 30^{30}, Mic 5^{4}, 2 P 1^{17}, Jd ^{25}), or to Christ (2 P 1^{16}), but also to Zion (Is 60^{15}, La 1^{6}) or to kings (1 Ch 29^{25}, Ps 45^{3f}, Est 1^{4}, Dn 4$^{30, 36}$), or to mountains (Ps 76^{4}, Is 35^{2}) and trees (Is 10^{34} [AV, RV ' by a mighty one ']), or to animals (Dt 33^{17}, Job 39^{20}). In several of these cases the older EV render by ' excellency ' or ' glory.' See also GLORY.

MAKAZ.—A town on the W. slopes of Judah, 1 K 4^{9}. The LXX reading, *Michmash*, is impossible. It is possibly modern *Kh. el-Mukheizin.*

MAKE.—In Jg 18^{3} AV ' to make ' means ' to do '— ' What makest thou in this place? ' In Jn 8^{53} AV and RV ' Whom makest thou thyself? ', and in Jn 19^{7} AV, RV, and RSV ' He made Himself the Son of God,' ' make ' means ' pretend to be ' ; cf Jos 8^{15} AV and RV ' Joshua and all Israel made as if they were beaten.' This is the meaning also in 2 S 13^{5} AV, ' Lay thee down on thy bed, and make thyself sick.' In Ezk 17^{17} AV and RV ' Neither shall Pharaoh with his mighty army and great company make for him in the war,' ' make for ' means ' assist.'

MAKED.—A ' strong and great ' city in Gilead (1 Mac 5$^{26, 36}$). The site is unknown.

MAKHELOTH.—One of the twelve ' stations ' of the children of Israel, Nu 33^{25f} ; the site is unknown.

MAKKEDAH.—A Canaanite royal city in the ' lowland ' (Shephelah) of Judah (Jos 12^{16} 15^{41}), tentatively identified with modern *Khirbet el-Kheishûm*, 14½ miles W. of Bethlehem, about midway between Azekah and Beth-shemesh. Here Joshua encamped after the battle of Gibeon, and here he captured and killed the five kings whom he had defeated in that battle. At the same time he stormed Makkedah and massacred its inhabitants together with their king (Jos 10$^{10-29}$). F. F. B.

MAKTESH.—The name of a locality mentioned only in Zeph 1^{11} (AV, RV) as a commercial quarter of Jerusalem. The word denotes a mortar (hence RSV ' the **Mortar** '), and presumably was given to the place because it was basin-shaped. If so, a part of the Tyropoeon valley has as good a claim as any other locality to be regarded as what is referred to.

MALACHI.—This is not the personal name of the author of the book, to whose identity we have no clue, but rather a substitute for his name, derived from his allusion to the predicted ' messenger ' of 3^{1}. There may have been those who believed that this prophet himself was the messenger. However, his own meaning was that an angel of the Lord would come.

The position of the book at the end of the Minor Prophets suggests that it is post-exilic. The contents show that this is indeed the case. It is generally put between Haggai-Zechariah (520 B.C.) and Nehemiah (*c* 445 B.C.). It looks back on the recent destruction of Edom (*c* 460 B.C.). The Jews are ruled by a governor (1^{8})—presumably the one in Samaria, for it was only with Nehemiah's coming that Judaea became a separate province. In considering Edom's downfall as final the prophet was fully vindicated. The explorations of Glueck have shown that when Edom was again resettled it was by a new people, the Nabataeans.

The book of Malachi is unique in that the author has a question and answer method in getting into his topics. Fortunately there are no serious literary-critical difficulties. The only later addition seems to be the conclusion 3$^{22-24}$. There are six discourses or disputations.

(1) Proof that Yahweh loves Israel ; Esau is the rejected one (1$^{2-5}$).

(2) The priests are criticized for sacrificing blemished animals and the laity blamed for paying its vows with such. The former are threatened with punishment by the Lord (1^{6}–2^{10}).

(3) Jewish men are upbraided for divorcing their wives and marrying foreigners (2$^{10-16}$).

(4) Doubters are warned that the day of wrath will surely come (2^{17}–3^{5}).

(5) Hard times are blamed on the failure to pay tithes. Recovery is promised if this is done (3$^{6-12}$).

(6) Those sceptical of God's justice are assured that He will reward the godly and punish the evildoers (3$^{13-21}$).

The conclusion (3$^{22-24}$) is composed of two additions to the book. The first (v.^{22}) is an admonition to obey the Law, and the second (vv.^{23f}) provides a fresh interpretation of the ' messenger ' of 3^{1}. He is here identified with the prophet Elijah, who is to return to earth and act as restorer. He is virtually a substitute figure for a Messiah. In Sir 48$^{10-11}$ (written *c* 190 B.C.) the Malachi passage is referred to and augmented with allusion to Is 42^{6}. By the time of Jesus the returning Elijah had become a forerunner or attendant of the Messiah.

The original prophecy is a significant witness to the situation prevailing in Judaea before the introduction of the Law. It was a rather discouraged and demoralized life that was lived there. The community was urgently in need of new impulses.

Malachi has some very advanced ideas (see 1^{11} 2$^{10, 16}$), but on the OT level it was not possible to follow them through to their fullest extent. He shows the need for a new and higher order. E. G. K.

MALACHY.—2 Es 1^{40} (AV and RV) for **Malachi.**

MALCAM.—**1.** One of the heads of the fathers of Benjamin, and the son of Shaharaim and Hodesh, 1 Ch 8^{9} (AV **Malcham**). **2.** In Zeph 1^{5} *Malcam* (RV ; AV **Malcham**) is apparently the name of an idol, and might be rendered literally ' their king,' as in the margin of AV and RV. Quite possibly, however, there is an error in the pointing of the Hebrew word, and it should be rendered, as in RSV, **Milcom** (q.v.), the ' abomination ' of the children of Ammon, and identical with Molech. In Jer 49$^{1, 3}$ RV again has *Malcam* (AV ' their king ' ; AVm **Melcom**) where RSV has **Milcom.** See MOLECH.

MALCHAM.—AV form of **Malcam** (q.v.).

MALCHIAH.—**1.** A priest, the father of Pashhur Jer 21^{1} 38^{1} ; the same as **Malchijah, 2. 2.** A member of the royal family, to whom belonged the cistern-prison into which Jeremiah was let down, Jer 38^{6}.

MALCHIEL.—The eponym of an Asherite family, Gn 46^{17}, Nu 26^{45}, 1 Ch 7^{31}. The Gentilic name **Malchielites** occurs in Nu 26^{45}.

MALCHIJAH.—**1.** A descendant of Gershom, 1 Ch 6$^{40\,(\text{Heb. }25)}$. **2.** A priest, the father of Pashhur, 1 Ch 9^{12}, Neh 11^{12} ; the same as **Malchiah, 1. 3.** Head of the 5th course of priests, 1 Ch 24^{9} ; possibly the same as the preceding. **4.** A son of Parosh who had married a foreign wife, Ezr 10^{25}, 1 Es 9^{26} (AV, RV v.^{25} **Melchias**). **5.** A second son of Parosh who did the same according to the Hebrew of Ezr 10^{25} (so AV, RV), but RSV substitutes the name **Hashabiah,** on the basis of 1 Es 9^{26}, where Greek has **Asibias. 6.** One of the sons of Harim who had married a foreign wife, Ezr 10^{31} ; he took part in repairing the wall, Neh 3^{11} ; in 1 Es 9^{32} he is called **Melchias. 7.** The son of Rechab who repaired the Dung Gate, Neh 3^{14}. **8.** One of the guild of the goldsmiths who helped to repair the wall, Neh 3^{31}. **9.** One of those who stood at Ezra's left hand at the reading of the Law, Neh 8^{4}, 1 Es 9^{44} (AV, RV **Melchias**). **10.** One of those who sealed the covenant, Neh 10^{3} ; probably the same as **9. 11.** A priest who took part in the ceremony of dedicating the wall, Neh 12^{42}.

MALCHIRAM.—Son of Jeconiah, 1 Ch 3^{18}.

MALCHISHUA.—The third son of Saul, 1 S 14^{49} (AV **Melchishua**), slain by the Philistines at Mt. Gilboa, 1 S 31^{2} (AV **Melchishua**), 1 Ch 10^{2}.

MALCHUS.—The name of the high priest's slave whose ear Peter cut off in the Garden of Gethsemane at the arrest of our Lord. Only the Fourth Gospel mentions his name (Jn 18^{10}), a fact perhaps related to its source of information in the high priest's household (Jn 18^{15}). The incident is related in the other three Gospels (Mt 26^{51}, Mk 14^{47}, Lk 22^{50}), but without naming the slave. M. St.—**F. C. G.**

MALICE.—The word was not used by AV or RV in the OT, but does occur in Prayer-Book Psalter, in AV Apocrypha, and in NT in AV and RV. In these three versions, however, malice is generally to be understood in 17th cent. sense of ' wickedness ' in general (=Gr. *kakia*) ; and in the case of Apocrypha, RV substituted ' wickedness ' where AV had ' malice,' this having become a more accurate translation in view of the change of meaning of the English word. There are two passages in OT where the modern meaning of ' malice ' is the right translation (Ezk $25^{6, 15}$=*she'āṭ*) and two more (Ps 41^{5} 73^{8}) where the context shows it to be the right translation of *ra'* = ' evil ' (cf RSV). In NT there is no word other than *kakia* for malice, but it is understood from the context as having the special meaning of malice in Ro 1^{29}, 1 Co 5^{8}, Eph 4^{31}, Col 3^{8}, Tit 3^{3}, 1 P 2^{1}. *Ponēria* is similarly translated in Mt 22^{18}. Malice means ' a desire to hurt or harm ' and as such is quite contrary to the principle of love. S. B. F.

MALLOTHI.—A son of Heman, 1 Ch $25^{4, 26}$.

MALLOW.—Hebrew, *mallûaḥ*, connected with *melaḥ*, ' salt.' This word is found in Job 30^{4} (AV, RSV ; RV **salt-wort**). Almost certainly the sea orache (*Atriplex halimus*), a perennial shrub with leaves somewhat like the olive, common on saltish marshes, especially near the Dead Sea, where it is associated with the *retem* (See Broom). The sour-tasting leaves can be eaten, but only in dire necessity. In Job 24^{24} RSV restores ' mallow ' from the LXX.

MALLUCH.—**1.** A Merarite, ancestor of Ethan, 1 Ch 6^{44}. **2.** One of the sons of Bani who had married a foreign wife, Ezr 10^{29}, 1 Es 9^{30} (AV, RV **Mamuchus**). **3.** One of the sons of Harim who had married a foreign wife, Ezr 10^{32}. **4. 5.** Two of those who sealed the covenant, Neh $10^{4, 37}$. No **4.** is probably identical with **Malluchi** (q.v.).

MALLUCHI.—The eponym of a priestly family who returned with Zerubbabel, Neh 12^{14} (AV, RVm **Melicu**).

MALLUS.—A city of Cilicia which joined Tarsus in a rebellion against Antiochus Epiphanes about 171 B.C. (2 Mac 4^{30}). Tradition said that it was founded at the time of the Trojan War. Its coinage shows that it was an important town. Its site is doubtful, but ancient statements locate it near the river Pyramus, near the sea, and also on a hill. Sir Wm. Ramsay identified it with *Kara-Tash*, on a coast line of hills E. of Magarsa, which served as its port. The W. branch of the Pyramus has become almost completely dried up. A. E. H.

MALOBATHRON.—The name of a spice-yielding plant, named in RVm of Ca 2^{17}, where AV, RV have **Bether** (q.v.) and RSV has ' rugged (mountains).' Against RVm it is argued that the malobathron plant (*Laurus malabathrum*) did not grow wild on any of the mountains of Palestine.

MALTA.—An island about sixty miles S. of Sicily, with an area of about ninety-five square miles. Its excellent position as a commercial station led to its early colonization by Phoenicians and Greeks. It became subject to Carthage, but was conquered by the Romans in 218 B.C., and became part of the province of Sicily. But the Carthaginian and Libyan element predominated. hence Luke's use of the phrase ' the natives ' (Ac 28^{2}). There can be no doubt that this *Melitē* was the scene of St. Paul's shipwreck. The use of the name Adria (Ac 27^{27}) led to an attempt to identify it with Melita in the Adriatic, but the term ' Adria ' (q.v.) was freely applied to the sea E. and SE. of Sicily, and the wind ' Euraquilo ' (q.v. ; Ac 27^{14}) would drive them from Crete to Malta if the captain, realizing that his chief danger was the Syrtis quicksands (27^{17}), took the natural precaution of bearing up into the wind as much as the weather permitted. The description is precise. On the fourteenth night of their drifting, by sounding they found they were getting into shallower water, and cast out anchors ; but when day dawned they saw before them a bay with a shelving beach, on which they determined to run the vessel. Therefore they hastily cast off the anchors, unfastened the rudders, which had been lashed during their drifting, and with the aid of these and the foresail tried to steer the ship onto the beach. But before they reached it they ran on a shoal ' where two seas met,' and reached the shore only by swimming or floating on spars. Every detail of the narrative is satisfied by assuming that they landed on the W. side of St. Paul's Bay, eight miles from Valetta, five miles from the old capital Città-Vecchia. St. Luke relates only two incidents from St. Paul's three-months' stay. As they made a fire for the shipwrecked men, a viper, aroused from the wood by the heat, fastened on St. Paul's hand, and, to the surprise of the onlookers, did him no harm. The word ' venomous ' (28^{4} AV, RV) is not properly in the text, and Luke does not state that it was a miraculous deliverance. But the natives thought it was, and therefore there probably were venomous snakes in Malta then. There are none now, but in an island with 2000 inhabitants to the square mile they would be likely to become extinct. The other incident was the curing of dysentery of the father of Publius (q.v.). Naturally there are local traditions of St. Paul's residence, and the earliest map of Malta, a Venetian one of 1530, has a Church of St. Paul near the bay, but on its E. side. The first known bishop of Malta was at the Council of Chalcedon in 451.

Malta has had a varied history since. Vandals, Normans, Turks all left their mark on it. In 1530, Charles v. gave it to the knights of St. John, who defended it three times against the desperate attacks of the Turks. In 1798, Napoleon seized it, but the British took it from him in 1800, and it remained in British hands until 1960, when the island became independent. But the population remains very mixed. The native language, Maltese, is a descendant of the Phoenician. A. E. H.—**E. G. K.**

MALTANNEUS, 1 Es 9^{33} (RV).—See Mattenai, **2.**

MAMAIAS, 1 Es 8^{44} (AV).—See Shemaiah, **15.**

MAMBRES.—See Jannes.

MAMDAI (1 Es 9^{34}).—See Benaiah, **3.**

MAMMON, represents the Aramaic word *māmōn* ' riches ' or ' wealth,' (the English double *m* derives from late Greek MSS). Its derivation is disputed, but the probabilities are that it is from the common Semitic root *'mn* ' to be firm, reliable ' (the same root from which we have *Amen*) ; so that *māmōn* is something secure, that on which one may rely. In the NT it occurs only in the words of Jesus about serving God and Mammon (Mt 6^{24}=Lk 16^{13}) and in the parable of the unjust steward (Lk $16^{9, 11}$), but it is not uncommon in the Targums and Talmud, and is used in the Qumrân documents, in the Hebrew of Sirach (31^{8}), and in Mandaean. Augustine (*De serm. Dom. in monte*, ii, 47) says that in the Punic language of his day it was used with the meaning ' riches,' and was doubtless so common a word in Levantine Aramaic that the evangelist could use it without translation. Since in Mt 6^{24} and Lk 16^{13} it seems to be personified there was a notion, found as early as Gregory of Nyssa, that it was the name of a Canaanitish god or demon of riches, a Semitic Ploutos, but there is no satisfactory basis for such an idea. A. J.

MAMNITANAIMUS, 1 Es 9^{34} (AV).—See MAMNITANEMUS.

MAMNITANEMUS, 1 Es 9^{34} (RV).—This name appears to correspond to **Mattaniah, Mattenai** in Ezr 10^{37}, and to be a corruption of them; but RSV substitutes **Machnadebai** of Ezr 10^{40}, which seems rather to be replaced by 'the sons of **Ezora**' in 1 Es 9^{34} (RV).

MAMRE.—A name found several times in connexion with the history of Abraham. It occurs (*a*) in the expression **'terebinths of Mamre'** in Gn 13^{18} 18^{1} (both J), and 14^{13} (from an independent source) with the addition of 'the Amorite'; (*b*) in the expression 'which is before Mamre,' in descriptions of the cave of Machpelah, or of the field in which it was (Gn $23^{17, 19}$ 25^{9} 49^{30} 50^{13}), and in 35^{27}, where Mamre is mentioned as the place of Isaac's death; (*c*) in Gn 14^{24} as the name of one of Abraham's allies, in his expedition for the recovery of Lot. In (*b*) Mamre is an old name, either of **Hebron** or of a part of Hebron (cf 23^{19} 35^{27}); in Gn 14^{13} it is the name of a local sheikh or chief (cf v.^{24}), the owner of the terebinths called after him; in Gn 13^{18} 18^{1} it is not clear whether it is the name of a person or of a place. The 'terebinths of Mamre' are the spot at which Abraham pitched his tent in Hebron. The site is uncertain, though, if the present mosque, on the NE. edge of Hebron, is really built over the cave of Machpelah, and if 'before' has its usual topographical sense of 'east of,' it will have been to the W. of this, and at no great distance from it (for the terebinths are described as being 'in' Hebron, Gn 13^{18}). From Josephus' time (*BJ* IV. ix. 7 [533]) to the present day, terebinths or oaks called by name of the Abraham have been shown at different spots near Hebron; but none has any real claim to mark the authentic site of the ancient 'Mamre.' The oak mentioned by Josephus was 6 stadia from the city; but he does not indicate in which direction it lay. Sozomen (*HE* ii. 4), in speaking of the 'Abraham's Oak' of Constantine's day (2 miles N. of Hebron), states that it was regarded as sacred, and that an annual fair and feast was held beside it, at which sacrifices were offered, and libations and other offerings cast into a well close by. It is perhaps to be identified with *Râmet el-Khalîl* near Hebron. S. R. D.—**A. S. H.**

MAMUCHUS, 1 Es 9^{30} (AV, RV).—See MALLUCH, **2**

MAN.—The Bible is concerned with man only from the religious standpoint, with his relation to God. This article will deal only with the religious estimate of man, as other matters which might have been included will be found in other articles (CREATION, ESCHATOLOGY, FALL, SIN, PSYCHOLOGY). Man's dignity, as made by special resolve and distinct act of God in God's image and likeness (synonymous terms), with dominion over the other creatures, and for communion with God, as asserted in the double account of his Creation in Gn 1 and 2, and man's degradation by his own choice of evil, as presented figuratively in the story of his Fall in Gn 3, are the two aspects of man that are everywhere met with. The first is explicitly affirmed in Ps 8, an echo of Gn 1; the second, without any explicit reference to the story in Gn 3, is taken for granted in the OT (see especially Ps 51), and is still more emphasized in the NT, with distinct allusion to the Fall and its consequences (see especially Ro 5^{12-21} and 7^{7-25}). While the OT recognizes man's relation to the world around him, his materiality and frailty as 'flesh' (q.v.), and describes him as 'dust and ashes' in comparison with God (Gn 2^{7} 3^{19} 18^{27}), yet as made in God's image it endows him with reason, conscience, affection, free will. Adam is capable of recognizing the qualities of, and so of naming, the living creatures (2^{19}), cannot find a help meet among them (v.^{20}), is innocent (v.^{25}), and capable of moral obedience (v.^{16f}) and religious communion (3^{9f}). The Spirit of God is in man not only as life, but also as wisdom and understanding, counsel and might, skill and courage (see INSPIRATION). The Divine immanence in man as the Divine providence for man is affirmed (Pr 20^{27}).

In the NT man's dignity is represented as Divine sonship. In St. Luke's Gospel Adam is described as 'son of God' (3^{38}). St. Paul speaks of man as 'the image and glory of God' (1 Co 11^{7}), approves the poet's words, 'we also are his offspring,' asserts the unity of the race, and God's guidance in its history (Ac 17^{26-28}). In his argument in Romans regarding universal sinfulness, he assumes that even the Gentiles have the law of God written in their hearts, and thus can exercise moral judgment on themselves and others (2^{15}). Jesus' testimony to the Fatherhood of God, including the care and bounty in Providence as well as the grace in Redemption, has as its counterpart His estimate of the absolute worth of the human soul (see Mt 10^{30} 16^{26}, Lk 10^{20} 15). While God's care and bounty are unlimited, yet Jesus does not seem to limit the title 'child *or* son of God' to those who have religious fellowship and seek moral kinship with God (see Mt $5^{9, 45}$; cf Jn 1^{12}). St. Paul's doctrine of man's adoption by faith in God's grace does not contradict the teaching of Jesus. The writer of Hebrews sees the promise of man's dominion in Ps 8 fulfilled only in Christ (2^{8f}). Man's history, according to the Fourth Evangelist, is consummated in the Incarnation (Jn 1^{14}).

The Bible estimate of man's value is shown in its anticipation of his destiny—not merely continued existence, but a future life of weal or woe according to the moral quality, the relation to God, of the present life (see ESCHATOLOGY). The Biblical analysis of the nature of man is discussed in detail in article PSYCHOLOGY.

A. E. G.

MAN OF SIN (or **LAWLESSNESS**).—Probably the equivalent, in 2 Th 2^{3-10}, of the Jewish figure of **Antichrist** (q.v.). According to the Pauline view, the Parousia would be preceded by an apostasy of believers ('the rebellion') and the appearance of the 'man of lawlessness' (or sin) 'who opposes and exalts himself against every so-called god or object of worship, so that he takes his seat in the temple of God, proclaiming himself to be God' (v.^{3f}). The appearance of this evil one and his oppression of the believers were prevented by some force or person: 'You know what is restraining him now.' In the course of time, however, this restraint will be removed. The wicked one will then exercise his power until Christ comes and destroys him (vv.$^{6-8}$).

The precise meaning of the references contained in this statement is now lost beyond recovery. St. Paul may have had in mind some definite historical person or force. But the 'man of sin' may have been expected without any prior knowledge or theory as to his identity. In any case, he is not Satan, but his representative (v.^{9}), as the opposite of Jesus the representative of God. On the other hand, 'the one who restrains' must have been clearly recognizable, since 'you know him' (v.^{6}). We can only speculate as to the identity of this person or power. Was it the Roman Emperor? or the Roman State? or the still unfinished preaching of the Gospel in all the world (cf Mt 24^{14})? However, it is clear that the 'lawless one' was even now engaged in his mysterious activity (v.^{7}), that his lawlessness would continue and would rise to the highest pitch (v.^{9}; cf Mt 24^{12}). But at the Parousia of Christ this final opposition to God's work of salvation would be swept away (Mt 7^{23} 13^{41}).

H. G.

MANAEN.—**1.** One of the Greek forms used in the Septuagint for the Hebrew name Menahem (2 K 15^{14-23}). **2.** One of the Christian prophets and teachers at Antioch mentioned in Ac 13^{1}. In the same passage he is called 'a member of the court of Herod the Tetrarch' (RSV). Another possible meaning of this expression is '(one) who had been brought up with Herod' (Goodspeed). If the latter meaning is the correct one, he may have been related in some way with Manaen the Essene, who according to Josephus had predicted to Herod the Great, when a child, that he would become king of the Jews. But the former meaning is more likely in the light of the Hellenistic parallels first adduced by Deissmann.

W. R. S.

MANAHATH.—**1.** Mentioned only in 1 Ch 8^{6} as the place to which certain Benjamite clans were carried captive. The town is probably identical with that implied in **Manahathites** (q.v.), with the *Manochō* of the Greek text of Jos 15[59], and if the text in Judges is correct, with the **Menuhah** of Jg 20[43] RVm (but see NOHAH, **1**). It is probably modern *Mâlḥā*, SW. of Jerusalem. **2.** Eponymous ancestor of an Edomite clan, Gn 36[43], 1 Ch 1[40].

MANAHATHITES.—A gentilic found in 1 Ch 2[52] (AV **Manahethites**), and probably originally in v.[54] (RV, RSV **Menuhoth**; AV **Manahethites**). See MANAHATH, **1.**

MANAHETHITES, 1 Ch 2[52, 54] (AV).—See MANAHATHITES.

MANASSEAS.—See MANASSEH, **2.**

MANASSEH.—In MT and AV of Jg 18[30] *Manasseh* (cf RVm, RSVm) is a scribal change for dogmatic purposes, the original being *Moses* (so RV, RSV); see GERSHOM, **1. 2.** A son of Pahath-moab, Ezr 10[30], called **Manasseas** in 1 Es 9[31]. **3.** Son of Hashum, Ezr 10[33], 1 Es 9[33] (AV, RV **Manasses**). **4.** Judith's husband, Jth 8[2] (AV, RV **Manasses**). **5. 6.** See next two articles. **7.** For ' Prayer of Manasseh ' see APOCRYPHA, **13.**

MANASSEH.—The firstborn son of Joseph, and brother of Ephraim (Gn 41[51f]), by Asenath, the daughter of Poti-phera, priest of On. In form the name is a *Piʿēl* participle of the verb *nāshāh* and could bear the meaning ' one who makes to forget,' *i.e.* an earlier misfortune. He was the eponymous ancestor of the tribe that bears the name Manasseh. The two tribes, Ephraim and Manasseh, together form the ' tribe of Joseph ' (Jos 17[14]) and the ' house of Joseph ' (17[17] 18[5], Jg 1[22f, 35]). One lot is assigned to them in Jos 16[1-3]. Manasseh's son Machir is given Gilead and Bashan in Jos 17[1]. The names of the rest of the sons (or descendants) of Manasseh, Abiezer, Helek, Asriel, Shechem, Hepher, Shemida, as well as the five daughters of Zelophehad, the great-grandson of Machir, are probably all place-names, as some of them certainly are, and not personal names.

Uncertainty of interpretation rests on nearly everything that is recorded in connexion with the tribe of Manasseh. Four different lists of his descendants have been incorporated in the OT. (i) Jos 17[1f] (J), where he is the father of all the clans associated with the tribe of Manasseh and is the grandfather of Gilead. (ii) Nu 26[28-34] (P), where he is the father of Machir and grandfather of Gilead from whom the other Manassite clans are said to be descended. (iii) 1 Ch 7[14-19], which is noteworthy for its mention of an Aramaean concubine suggesting a consciousness of connexion between Manasseh and the Aramaeans. (iv) 1 Ch 2[21-23], whose interest lies in the connexion of a member of Judah with an east-Jordan tribe. In the Song of Deborah, the oldest source for the history of the tribal settlement, Ephraim is mentioned by name but Manasseh is clearly meant by **Machir** (v.[14]); in other traditions Machir is associated with east-Jordan and not west as in the song. The most likely theory is that, contrary to the assumption that Moses allotted territory E. of Jordan to half-Manasseh on condition of military help in the ' conquest,' Manasseh (Machir) first occupied territory W. of Jordan, but, finding the situation too cramped (Jos 17[14-18], Nu 32[39]) moved E. and occupied Gilead while kindred clans, Jair and Nobah, occupied neighbouring territory (Nu 32[41f]). The consequent readjustment of tribes and territory possibly led to the father-son relationship between Manasseh, Machir, and Gilead, although the latter was almost certainly a place-name in origin. Jair was also taken up into the genealogy (1 Ch 2[22]). The delineation of territory assigned to Ephraim and Manasseh is also a source of difficulty (Jos 16, 17) which emerges most clearly at 16[9] ' the towns which were set apart for the Ephraimites within the inheritance of Manasseh ' and at 17[11] ' Also in Issachar and in Asher Manasseh had Beth-shean and its villages, and Ibleam and its villages, etc.' Why should Ephraim hold cities within the land occupied by Manasseh? and why should the territory of Manasseh intrude within that of Issachar and Asher? The answer may well be that the actual historical situation was an ever changing one; that the tribe of Manasseh sprang to birth out of the tribe of Ephraim due to an expansion of that tribe northwards in the direction of the territory held by Canaanites, the plain of Esdraelon, and by Issachar and Asher, N. of the plain, and that parts of this northern element crossed the Jordan and settled in Gilead alongside the native inhabitants and other settlers (Jair and Nobah). Some such sequence of events may further be reflected in the fact that at one time Ephraim is given precedence over Manasseh (Gn 48[5]) as indicated in the way in which Jacob crossed his hands in giving his blessing (Gn 48[14]; cf also Dt 33[17]), but that Manasseh is otherwise regarded as the firstborn (Gn 41[51f]).

The tribe, owing to its situation, had much to endure during the Syrian wars (Am 1[3], 2 K 10[33]), and, according to 1 Ch 5[26], the eastern half was deported in 743 B.C. by Tiglath-pileser III. L. H. B.

MANASSEH, son of Hezekiah, reigned longer than any king of his line—fifty-five years, according to our sources (2 K 21[1]). His reign was remarkable for the religious reaction against the reforms which had been made by Hezekiah. The record (vv.[2-9]) is that he built again the altars which Hezekiah had destroyed, and erected altars for Baal, and made an *'ᵃshērāh*, as Ahab king of Israel had done, and that he worshipped the host of heaven and served them. In restoring the old altars he doubtless thought he was returning to the early worship of the nation, and the Baal whom he worshipped was probably identified in the minds of the people with the national God Yahweh. The *'ᵃshērāh* was a well-known accompaniment of altars in Israel down to the time of Hezekiah. The worship of the host of heaven was probably an obligation of his subjection to Assyrian domination. Both Esarhaddon and his successor Ashurbanipal list ' Manasseh king of Judah ' among their twenty-two vassal kings. The sacrifice of his son and the practice of witchcraft and magic were not unheard of practices in ancient Israel. The reaction was accompanied by active persecution of the prophetic party. It is no wonder that the record of *Kings* is couched in terms of strong condemnation. A different picture is given by the Chronicler, however. 2 Ch 33[11-13, 18, 19] tells of the captivity of Manasseh in Babylon, of his conversion and submission to God, and of his restoration to his own throne. The captivity may well be a true tradition for it is known that Ashurbanipal had several royal captives at his court. The Chronicler has probably embellished it in the interests of accounting for the longest reign enjoyed by the worst king. H. P. S.—L. H. B.

MANASSES.—**1.** 1 Es 9[33] (AV, RV); see MANASSEH, **3. 2.** Jth 8[2] (AV, RV); see MANASSEH, **4. 3.** To 14[10] (AV, RV); RSV reads **Ahikar** (q.v.). **4.** For ' Prayer of Manasses ' see APOCRYPHA, **13.**

MANDRAKE (*dûdhā'îm*, Gn 30[14-16] [RVm ' love apples ']; cf *dôdhîm* ' love,' Ca 7[13]).—Although other plants have been suggested, the mandrake (*Mandragora officinarum*), of the *Salanaceae* or Potato order, is most probable. It is a common plant in all parts of S. Palestine. Its long and branched root is very deeply imbedded in the earth, and an old superstition survives to-day that he who digs it up will be childless—but at the same time the effort of pulling it up will cure a bad lumbago. The ancients believed that this root gave a demoniacal scream as it was pulled up. Occasionally the root resembles a human figure, but most of those exhibited have been ' doctored ' to heighten the resemblance. The leaves are dark green, arranged in a rosette, and the flowers dark purple. The fruit, which ripens about May, about the time of the wheat harvest, is somewhat like a small tomato, and orange or reddish in colour; it is called by the natives *baiḍ el-jinn*, ' the eggs of the *jinn*.' It has a heavy narcotic smell and sweetish taste. It is still used medicinally, but is known to be poisonous, especially the seeds. The mandrake was known to the ancients as an aphrodisaic (see MAGIC, B, **2** (*a*)). E. W. G. M.

MANEH.—See Weights and Measures, iii.

MANES, 1 Es 9^{21} (RV).—See Maaseiah, **2.**

MANGER (Lk 2$^{7, 12, 16}$ 13^{15} RVm).—EV translation of *phatnē*, the LXX equivalent of Hebrew *'ēbhûs*, Job 39^{3} (EV **crib**). It also represents *'ūrāwôth* (MT *'ᵃwērôth*), 2 Ch 32^{28} (EV **stalls**), and *repheth* in Hab 3^{17} (EV **stalls**). In Job 39^{9} *'ēbhûs* may mean the stall or shelter ; in Is 1^{3} it is probably the **crib** (so EV) in which the food was placed. A like ambiguity attached to *'ūryāh* in 2 Ch 32^{28}. The Hebrew *repheth* in Hab 3^{17} clearly means ' stall.' The further Hebrew word *marbēḳ* (EV ' stall,' Am 6^{4}, Mal 4^{2}) is the place where the cattle are ' tied up.'

If *kataluma* (Lk 2^{7}) means ' guest chamber ' (see Hospitality, *ad fin.*) Joseph and Mary may have moved into the side of the house occupied by the cattle, from which the living-room is distinguished by a higher floor, with a little hollow in the edge, out of which the cattle eat. The present writer has seen a child laid in such a ' manger.' Or, in the crowded *khān*, only the animals' quarters may have afforded shelter. We do not now know. Ancient tradition places Jesus' birth in a cave near Bethlehem. Caves under the houses are extensively used in Palestine as stables. The *midhwad*, ' manger ' cut in the side, is an excellent ' crib ' for a baby. W. E.

MANI, 1 Es 9^{30} (AV, RV).—See Bani, **8.**

MANIUS.—According to 2 Mac 11^{34}, **Titus Manius** was one of two Roman legates who, being on their way to Antioch after the campaign of Lysias against Judaea in the year 164 B.C., sent a letter to the Jews confirming the concessions of Lysias, and offering to undertake the charge of their interests at Antioch in concert with their own envoy. This action would be in accord with the policy the Romans were following towards the Syrian kingdom, and is probable enough. But we have no knowledge from any other source of the presence in the East of any legate called Titus Manius. A. E. H.

MANNA.—A food of the Israelites during the wilderness wanderings (Ex 16^{35}, Nu 11^{6ff}, Jos 5^{12}).

1. The origin of the word is uncertain. In Ex 16^{15} the exclamation might be rendered, ' It is *mān* ! ' (note RVm). If so, the Israelites were reminded (but only vaguely, see v.^{15}) of some known substance. The similar Arabic word means ' gift.' More probably the words are a question—' What is it ? ' (So RSV).

2. The manna was flaky, small, and white (Ex 16$^{14, 31}$). It resembled the ' seed ' (better ' fruit ') of the coriander plant (Ex 16^{31}, Nu 11^{7}), and suggested bdellium (Nu 11^{7} [see 3]). It could be ground, and was stewed or baked (Ex 16^{23}, Nu 11^{8}). The taste is compared to that of honey-wafers (Ex 16^{31}), or oil (Nu 11^{8}). It was gathered fresh every morning early (but see **4**), for, if exposed to the sun, it melted (Ex 16^{21} ; cf Wis 19^{2}) ; if kept overnight (see **4**), it went bad (Ex 16^{19f}). Each person was entitled to a measured *'omer* of manna (Ex 16^{18}).

3. Manna has been explained as an edible lichen or as the sweet globules produced by the lichen *Lecanora esculenta*, though this plant is not now found in the Sinai region. Others have identified it with a sweet juice exuded in June by a shrub or tree, *Tamarix gallica mannifera*. Note that manna is likened (see **2**) to bdellium, which is a resinous exudation. One theory was that the manna oozed from holes made by an insect, but now it is generally held that manna is excreted by the insect which sucks large quantities of sap and gives out the excess carbohydrates as a liquid which in the air becomes the drops of sticky honeydew, characteristic of many plant lice and scale insects. The Biblical description of manna supports this identification. The appearance, season and geographical limits of natural manna agree with the Biblical account.

4. Manna would thus come under the category of ' special providences,' not ' miracles.' It was, however, regarded by the Biblical writers (Ex 16, Dt 8$^{3, 16}$, Neh 9$^{15, 20}$, Ps 78$^{23-25}$ 105^{40} ; Nu 11$^{7-9}$ may be an exception) as, like the quails, miraculously provided. (*a*) There is enough for a host of ' 600,000 footmen.' (*b*) The quantity gathered proves exactly suited to the consumer's appetite (Ex 16^{18}). (*c*) The Sabbath supply (gathered the previous day) retains its freshness (Ex 16^{23f}). (*d*) An *'omer* of it is kept as a sacred object near (Ex 16^{33f}) but not *within* (1 K 8^{9} ; cf He 9^{4}, Rev 2^{17}) the Ark. (*e*) Allusions to it suggest the supernatural (Neh 9^{20}, Ps 78^{24f} 105^{40}, 2 Es 1^{19}, Wis 16^{20} 19^{21}).

5. Philo allegorized the story of manna (*Legum Allegoria* iii. 169–176). For the rabbis manna was the food of the age to come. See *Eccles. R.*, 1^{28}, 2 Bar 29^{8}. In the NT Christ as the living bread is typified by manna (Jn 6^{31ff}, 1 Co 10^{3} ; cf ^{4}) ; and secret spiritual sustenance is the reward for ' him who conquers ' (Rev 2^{17}).

H. F. B. C.—**W. D. McH.**

MANOAH.—The father of Samson, of the town of Zorah, and of the family of the Danites, Jg 13^{2ff} 16^{31}. We learn but little of his character and occupation from the Bible narrative. He was a worshipper of Yahweh, and a man of reverent piety ; he was hospitable, like his ancestor Abraham ; he shared the dislike of his people for the alien surrounding tribes, and strongly deprecated an alliance between his son and the Philistines. His wife was barren, but she was warned by a Divine messenger that she was destined to bear a son who was to be a Nazirite and dedicated to Yahweh. The messenger appeared again when Manoah also was present, and repeated his prophecy. We hear of Manoah on four more occasions ; we find him remonstrating with his son about the proposed Philistine marriage (14^{2f}) ; he accompanied his son on the preliminary visit to Timnah (vv.^{5f}), and again to the marriage itself (vv.^{9f}). He did not survive his son, who was buried by his side (16^{31}). Cf Samson.

These scanty details are somewhat amplified by Josephus (*Ant.* v. viii. 2 f [276–284]), who was apparently following some ancient Jewish tradition. T. A. M.

MANSION.—The English word occurs in Scripture only in Jn 14^{2}, ' In my Father's house are many mansions ' (RVm ' Or, *abiding places* ' ; RSV ' rooms '). Its retention is an archaism, for the modern connotation of a house of some dignity is quite lacking from the word as used by Tyndale (1525), apparently from the Vulgate *mansiones*, ' abiding places.' The Greek word (*monē*), like the Latin, means (1) the act of abiding, (2) a place of abode. In the NT it occurs also in Jn 14^{23}, where ' make our home ' is Greek idiom for ' abide.' Hence the thought in Jn 14^{2} is simply that there is ample room for the disciples in the Father's house. In the LXX the Greek word occurs only once, viz. 1 Mac 7^{38}, ' give them no abiding place ' (RSV ' let them live no longer ').

MANSLAYER.—See Kin [Next of] and Refuge [Cities of].

MAN-STEALING.—See ' Kidnapping ' in article Crimes, **7.**

MANTELET.—See Fortification.

MANTLE.—See Dress, **4** (*c*).

MANUSCRIPTS.—See Text and Writing.

MAOCH.—The father of Achish, king of Gath, 1 S 27^{2}. See Maacah, **3.**

MAON.—A town in the hill-country of Judah, Jos 15^{55}. It was in the wilderness of Maon that Nabal dwelt (1 S 25^{2}), and in this district David sojourned on two occasions during the period of his outlaw life (23^{24ff} 25^{2ff}). It is the modern *Tell Ma'în.*

MAONITES.—In Jg 10^{12} the Maonites are mentioned together with the Sidonians and Amalekites as having oppressed Israel. They dwelt in Mt. Seir, S. of the Dead Sea. According to 1 Ch 4^{41f}, the Maonites (called **Meunim** [so RV, RSV ; AV ' habitations '] in this passage) were, in the reign of Hezekiah, driven out of their pasture land by the Simeonites. The passage is interesting as showing how long the original Canaanites held their own in the land after the Israelite invasion. In 2 Ch 26^{7} (RSV **Meunites,** AV **Mehunims,** RV **Meunim)** they are mentioned as having been overcome by Uzziah (cf 2 Ch 20[1]), where ' Ammonites ' should probably be **Meunites** [so RSV ; cf RVm]).

MARA.—The name which Naomi claimed for herself : ' Do not call me Naomi (' pleasant '), call me Mara (' bitter '), for the Almighty has dealt very bitterly with me,' Ru 1[20].

MARAH.—The first ' station ' of the Israelites after crossing the sea, Ex 15[23], Nu 33[8f]. It is possibly modern *'Ain Ḥawârah*.

MARALAH, Jos 19[11] (AV, RV).—See MAREAL.

MARANATHA is really two words, *māranā thā* (less likely *māran ethā*, and still less likely *māran athā*), an Aramaic expression meaning : ' O our Lord, come ! ' In the NT it occurs only in 1 Cor 16[22], but in form it is closely parallel to the ' Amen ! come Lord Jesus ' of Rev 22[20], and is actually used with *Amen* in *Didache* x. 6. It would seem, then, to have been an early Christian ejaculatory prayer in expectation of the early consummation of the Parousia, the glorious return of the Lord Jesus. Only if it were one of those phrases in common use, perhaps in liturgical use, such as *Amen*, *Hosannah*, can we understand the Apostle using an Aramaic phrase in a letter to the Greek-speaking community at Corinth. The fact that it is used immediately after the word *anathema*, soon led, in circles unacquainted with Aramaic, to the assumption that it was a Semitic word of imprecation, so that in this quite mistaken sense it appears in numerous documents from the 4th cent. onwards. A. J.

MARBLE.—See MINING AND METALS.

MARCHESVAN.—See TIME.

MARCUS.—AV of Col 4[10], Phn[24], 1 P 5[13] = **Mark.**

MARDOCHEUS.—See MORDECAI, **1, 2.**

MAREAL.—A place on the W. border of Zebulun, Jos 19[11] (AV, RV **Maralah**). It is possibly modern *Tell Ghaltah*.

MARESHAH.—**1.** The ' father ' of Hebron (1 Ch 2[42]). [On Mareshah (1°) in this verse, cf MESHA, **2.**] **2.** A Judahite, or family of Judah (1 Ch 4[21]). These genealogical data are connected with : **3.** An important city in the Shephelah of Judah (Jos 15[44]), fortified by Rehoboam (2 Ch 11[8] ; see also 2 Ch 14[9f] 20[37], Mic 1[15]). Later, under the name *Marissa*, Josephus describes its chequered history (*Ant.* XII. viii. 6 [353] etc.). The site of Marissa is *Tell es-Sandaḥannah*, just over a mile SSE. of *Beit Jibrîn* (now *Beth Gubrîn*), excavated by Bliss, who found under the Hellenistic town Jewish pottery and inscribed jar-handles, which carry the occupation back to *c* 800 B.C. The place was of strategic importance as a base for Seleucid operations against Judas Maccabaeus and his family (1 Mac 5[66], 2 Mac 12[32]), but with the extension of Jewish power to the S. it lost its significance and declined. After a brief revival in the Roman period it was finally destroyed by the Parthians in 40 B.C. The name is preserved in *Khirbet Mar'ash*, a small Roman site about half a mile to the NW. In the vicinity there are a number of striking cave-tombs with paintings and epitaphs which indicate a colony of Sidonians and Idumaeans in the 3rd cent. B.C. It is doubtful if this is Moresheth-Gath, which the mosaic map of Madaba places to the NNE. of Eleutheropolis (*Beit Jibrîn*). This suggests *Tell el-Judeideh*, which Bliss excavated and found evidence of occupation towards the end of the Hebrew monarchy. See MARISA.

E. W. G. M.—**J. Gr.**

MARI.—The identification of *Tell el-Ḥarîri* as the probable site of ancient Mari was made by W. F. Albright in 1932. This identification was confirmed almost immediately when excavations were undertaken by André Parrot and a number of associates at the site, which is about 11 km. NNE. of *Abû Kemal* on the Iraqi border, and not far from the Euphrates (which in ancient times flowed right past the city). Thus far there have been ten seasons of digging at Mari, the last campaign being conducted in 1954–1955. Numerous publications have appeared, though much more is yet to come : A. Parrot, *Studia Mariana* (1950) ; and his official *Mission Archéologique de Mari* : I. *Le temple d'Ishtar* (1956) ; II. *Le Palais* (in two parts ; 1958). In addition the vast hoard of tablets is gradually being edited and published by a number of scholars : *Archives Royales de Mari*, i–ix and xv (1950–1960).

While excavations have not yet reached the lowest levels, it is already clear that Mari had a long history of occupation. A Sumerian city flourished at the beginning of the 3rd millennium. Mari was captured by Sargon of Akkad (24th cent. B.C.), following which there is a break in occupation until the 3rd Dynasty of Ur (*c* 2000), when it was rebuilt by Ur-nammu. The Amorites moved in during the 19th cent., and established a dynasty which held the city, with one interruption, until its final destruction. The last king was Zimri-Lim, a contemporary of the great Hammurabi of Babylon, Rim-Sin of Larsa, and Shamshi-Adad of Assyria. Mari was taken and destroyed by Hammurabi in his 32nd year, *c* 1697 B.C. (according to the low chronology ; otherwise *c* 1750). The two spectacular discoveries at Mari are the royal palace, which covered 6 acres and contained over 250 rooms, and the royal archives which include over 20,000 tablets. Both are monuments to the reign and glory of Zimri-Lim.

According to Biblical tradition the Patriarchs came from Haran in northern Mesopotamia, and for a long time maintained contacts with their kinsmen in that region. With the discovery and publication of the Mari tablets our knowledge of these Northwest-Semitic nomads (the Amorites) who infiltrated and took possession of many of the city-states along the inside rim of the fertile crescent, has been greatly enriched. While no direct links with the Patriarchs have been established, the general background, orientation, and customs of the Patriarchs have been clarified to a considerable extent. The practice of sacrificing an ass to solemnize a contract finds an echo in the Biblical narrative of the Bene Ḥamor (*i.e.*, ' ass ') of Shechem (Gn 33[19f]), whose god was the ' Lord of the Covenant ' (Jg 9[4]). The use of fire signals for rapid communication is likewise echoed in the Lachish Letters of 1,000 years later. A group of troublesome nomads, whose name is semantically equivalent to the Biblical Benjamites is repeatedly referred to in the Mari correspondence. The 'Apiru are another frequently mentioned group in the Mari archives. While scholarly opinion is divided on the question of the relationship of the 'Apiru to the Biblical Hebrews (*'Ibhrîm*), some connexion is quite probable. The use of the term in the OT to characterize the Patriarchs and their descendants as foreigners (*i.e.*, stateless people) in relation to the settled population of Canaan and Egypt, corresponds to the description of the 'Apiru in various sources including the Mari letters (cf on the question of the 'Apiru, J. Bottéro, *Le Problème des Ḫabiru à la 4e rencontre assyriologique internationale* [1954] ; M. Greenberg, *The Hab/piru* [1955] ; for a comprehensive discussion of the relevant data, see H. H. Rowley, *From Joseph to Joshua* [1950], ch. i). Another point of contact with Biblical tradition concerns the phenomenon of prophecy. Quite apart from the usual techniques and procedures of divination, there was a class of religious functionaries at Mari, who received messages from the god under direct inspiration, and delivered them accordingly. These messengers, called *apilu*, spoke to the king and other officials in the name of their god, much as the later prophets of Israel, though the content and scope of the messages were quite different. It is possible that we have here more than a parallel, though less than a direct source. On the significance of the Mari excavations for Biblical studies, see G. E. Mendenhall, BA, xi (1948), 1–19 ; Albright, *Interpreter's Bible*, i (1952), 261–264 ; G. E. Wright, *Biblical Archaeology*, pp. 96–97.

D. N. F.

MARIMOTH, 2 Es 1[2] (AV, RV).—See MERAIOTH, **2.**

MARISA.—The Greek form of the name **Mareshah**. It occurs only in 2 Mac 12[35], but should be read also in 1 Mac 5[66] (so RVm, RSV), where all Greek MSS wrongly have ' Samaria ' (so AV, RV).

MARK (JOHN).—There are three groups of NT passages where the name Mark occurs.

(1) *John Mark* was a Jew and son of Mary, who was a leading Christian woman at Jerusalem. At her house the faithful assembled for prayer, and thither Peter went on his release from imprisonment, having perhaps previously lodged there (Ac 12^{12ff}). An improbable conjecture makes Mark the son of the 'good-man of the house' in Mk 14^{14}, and another identifies Mark himself with the 'young man' of Mk 14^{51}; but the Muratorian Canon (late 2nd cent.) apparently denied that Mark had ever seen our Lord. Probably Mary was a widow. 'Mark' would be an added name such as the Jews often took, in Roman fashion; it was a Roman *praenomen*, much used among Greek-speaking people, but not common among the Jews. John Mark was chosen as companion of Barnabas and Saul when they left Jerusalem for Antioch (Ac 12^{25}—the reading of RSVm is hardly possible), and taken by them on their first missionary journey (13^{5}), not as chosen expressly by the Holy Spirit (cf v.^{2}), and not as an equal; 'they had also John as their attendant (AV minister, RSV to assist them).' It has been suggested that Mark was a Levite (see below), and that the designation here used means 'a synagogue minister,' as in Lk 4^{20}. But this would make the words 'they had' intolerably harsh. Probably Mark's work was to arrange the Apostles' journeys, perhaps also to baptize—a work not usually performed by St. Paul himself (1 Co 1^{14}). Mark remained with the Apostles on their journey through Cyprus, but left them at Perga in Pamphylia (Ac 13^{13}) either from cowardice, or, more probably, because the journey to Pisidian Antioch and beyond, involving work among distant Gentiles, was a change of plan which he did not approve (Ramsay). He had not yet grasped the idea of a world-wide Christianity, as St. Paul had. His departure to Jerusalem led later to the estrangement of Paul and Barnabas; the latter wished to take Mark with them on the Second Journey (15^{37ff}), but Paul refused, and separated from Barnabas, who then took Mark to Cyprus.

(2) *The Mark of the Pauline Epistles* was cousin of Barnabas (Col 4^{10} RSV), probably of the Jewish colony of Cyprus, and a Levite (Ac 4^{36}). It is therefore generally agreed that he was the same as John Mark. If so, he became reconciled to St. Paul, and was his 'fellow-worker' and a 'comfort' to him (Col 4^{11}, Phn ^{24}), and 'very useful in serving' him (2 Ti 4^{11})—this was Mark's special office, not to be an original organizer but a useful assistant. We learn that Mark was contemplating a visit to Colossae, and perhaps that the Colossians had hesitated to receive him (Col 4^{10}).

(3) *The Petrine Mark.*—St. Peter speaks of a Mark as his 'son' (1 P 5^{13}), and as being with him at 'Babylon' when he wrote the First Epistle. It is usually held that 'Babylon' means Rome (cf Rev 14^{8ff} 17^{1ff} 18^{1ff}), as there seems not to have been a Jewish colony in the real Babylon at the time, and as all ecclesiastical tradition connects St. Peter's work with Rome. If this be so, we may safely identify all the three Marks as one person. The identification is made more likely by the fact that John Mark is connected with both Peter and Paul in Acts; and if 1 P 5^{13} refers to Rome, there is no reason why this double connexion should not have continued as long as both Apostles lived. And if, as is not impossible, St. Peter survived St. Paul for some time, we can well understand that Mark devoted himself exclusively to the former after the death of the latter, and that in this way the ecclesiastical tradition (see next article), which almost unanimously attaches him to Peter, grew up. By that tradition Mark's activity is associated both with Rome and with Alexandria; and the Egyptian Church assigns its principal liturgy to his name. But the early Alexandrian Fathers, Clement and Origen, are silent as to Mark's residence in Egypt. The *Acts of Mark* (5th cent.?) makes him a martyr.

A. J. M.—A. B.

MARK, GOSPEL ACCORDING TO.—**1. Position in Canon.**—The order of the four approved Gospels is not invariable in early MSS and lists. The early Western order, represented by a few Greek MSS and some versions, gives Mt and Jn precedence because of their accepted Apostolic authorship, with Mk occupying third or fourth place. Our order, which is that of nearly all the Greek MSS and soon prevailed throughout the Church, recognizes that Mt Mk Lk form a group (the Synoptics) in distinction from Jn; Mk occupies the second place in virtue of its resemblance to, and supposed dependence upon, Mt.

2. General characteristics.—All four Gospels are narratives dealing with the ministry, death and resurrection of Jesus. In Jn the events related are few, and the sections (usually an incident with accompanying teaching) into which the Gospel may be conveniently divided are comparatively lengthy (*e.g.*, 4$^{1-42}$ 9$^{1-41}$ 11$^{1-54}$ 14^{1}–16^{33}) In Mk, as in Mt–Lk, the units are numerous and generally brief, seldom exceeding twenty of our modern verse-divisions and frequently very condensed (*e.g.*, in Mk: Baptism of Jesus, three verses, Cleansing of the Temple, five verses, Last Supper, nine verses). Many of these sections, though embedded in a continuous narrative, have an internal unity and completeness apart from their present context, and may have circulated as independent stories, groups of sayings, etc., before Mk was compiled (see **4** (*b*)). The general plan of Mk is as follows. After a short introduction dealing with John the Baptist, the baptism of Jesus and His temptations, in which Jesus is declared Messiah and Son of God (1$^{1-13}$), Mark describes the opening of Jesus' ministry in Galilee. He comes preaching that the Kingdom of God is at hand, calls the first disciples, heals many possessed by demons and afflicted with various diseases, and by word and action asserts His authority (1^{14}–3^{6}). Already He has aroused the opposition of the Pharisees (especially by His attitude to the Sabbath) but His fame and popularity are widespread. He appoints the Twelve, teaches multitudes at the lake-side by means of parables, performs further miracles and sends out the Twelve on a preaching and healing mission (3^{7}–6^{13}). The next division includes a cycle of stories connected with the Lake—the feeding of five thousand, crossing the sea, discussion on defilement, and two miracles—followed by a somewhat similar cycle introduced by the feeding of four thousand (6^{14}–8^{26}). These activities have already taken Jesus beyond Galilee, to the other side of the Lake and to the region of Tyre. Now at Caesarea Philippi He hears Peter's confession of Him as the Christ, foretells His passion and calls for the full self-sacrifice of His followers. The Transfiguration is closely bound to that crisis in the ministry, and the shadow of the Cross falls again and again upon the narrative as Jesus journeys through Galilee, Peraea and Jericho to Jerusalem (8^{27}–10^{52}). The humble Messianic entry there is followed by the cleansing of the Temple, and action and teaching much of which is charged with judgment, including the apocalyptic discourse of ch. 13 (11^{1}–13^{37}). The Last Supper and the arrest in Gethsemane lead on to an account of the trial and crucifixion of Jesus, and the burial of His body (14^{1}–15^{47}). An incomplete account of resurrection appearances (16$^{1-8}$, see **7**) forms the conclusion of the Gospel. Mark must have received some parts of his story (especially the Passion Narrative) in a form in which a number of sections were already combined, but generally we must attribute the arrangement of the Gospel to him (assuming Mk to be the earliest of the Gospels, see **3**). It is written in a style that is unpolished from a literary point of view, but effective in its very simplicity (note the recurrent 'and . . . and' in sentence construction) and often vivid in its descriptive touches.

3. Relation to the other Gospels.—In this article we assume that Mk, substantially as we have it, was a source of Mt and Lk. (There is less interest now than formerly in the hypothesis of an Ur-Markus, an earlier form of the Gospel used by Matthew or Luke or both. For example, W. Bussmann argued for a first stage of Mk used by Luke, a second expanded with Galilean material and used by Matthew, and a third, our Mk, containing details not found in Mt or Lk. One of the aims of such hypotheses has been to explain the absence of parts of our Mk from Mt and Lk. In so far as it is assumed that Matthew and Luke must have made exhaustive use of their sources, Ur-Markus theories are on precarious ground, especially in the case of Luke who writes with great freedom.) The reasons that have led most scholars to accept the priority of Mk are given at some length in article GOSPELS, 3. Here they may be briefly summarized. (*a*) Nearly all of the material of Mk is found, with varying degrees of verbal correspondence, in Mt or Lk or both. (*b*) The order of Mk's sections is always preserved either in Mt or in Lk. (*c*) Where Mt and Lk differ in detail from Mk in || passages, the wording of Mt and Lk is frequently an evident revision or improvement of Mk. It follows, if Mk's priority is accepted, that the work of Mark in the compilation and ordering of his material is formative also in the other Synoptics. It follows also that a comparative study of details on the basis of the priority of Mk will illumine the distinctive interests of the three Evangelists and also show up tendencies of development of the traditions in the early Church. The relation of the Fourth Gospel to Mk is more difficult to assess. Where there is common ground with the Synoptics, there are some striking phrases not in Mt or Lk but common to Mk and Jn, *e.g.* 'loaves costing 200 denarii' Jn 6^{7}, Mk 6^{37}, 'pistic (RSV **pure**) nard' Jn 12^{3}, Mk 14^{3}, 'pallet' Jn 5^{8}, Mk 2^{11}. Jn is indebted to at least part of the Markan tradition, and probably to Mk as a whole.

4. The Sources of the Gospel.—Knowledge of the sources of Mk can be attained by a study of the contents of the Gospel (*a*) in conjunction with early external testimony (*b*) in relation to the life and interests of the early Church.

(*a*) *The Petrine tradition.*—Papias of Hierapolis (*c* A.D. 140, quoted by Eusebius *HE* iii. 39) gives the earliest statement connecting the Gospel with Peter's preaching, as follows:

'And the elder said this also: Mark, having become the interpreter of Peter, wrote down accurately all that he remembered of the things said or done by the Lord, but not, however, in order. For neither did he hear the Lord, nor did he follow Him, but afterwards, as I said, (attended) Peter, who adapted his teachings to the needs (of his hearers), but not as though he were drawing up a connected account of the Lord's oracles. So then Mark made no mistake in thus writing down some things just as he remembered them; for he made it his one care to omit nothing that he had heard and to make no false statement therein.'

Probably the words of the elder who was Papias' informant do not extend beyond the first sentence, the rest being Papias' comment. The statement has to be given due weight. It can hardly be doubted that it is our Mk that Papias and his informant have in mind. Evidently there is no dispute about its authorship; the writer is Mark (identified with the John called Mark associated with both Peter and Paul in Ac) a subordinate figure whom no one was likely to have connected with the Gospel unless he was known to have actually had a part in writing it. There may be a note of depreciation of the order of Mark's account (in comparison with Mt or Jn), but Apostolic authority for the contents of the Gospel outweighs any defect in presentation. It is not claimed that Mark himself was an eyewitness; he was dependent on Peter whom he served as an interpreter (? translating his Aramaic). Later writers locate Peter's preaching and Mark's writing in Rome (already 1 P 5^{13} is evidence of their association there, 'Babylon' = Rome) and Mark's writing is dated either before (Clement of Alexandria) or after (Irenaeus) the death of Peter.

Up to a point the contents of Mk are favourable to the tradition of Papias. At very many of the events related the presence of Peter is either expressly noted (the names Simon and Peter occur twenty-six times) or can be justly inferred. These are the very sections (mostly stories about Jesus Himself or His miracles) in which notes of place and time, gestures and emotions, and descriptive details (often omitted in the ||s in Mt and Lk) give the impression of eyewitness testimony. Examples of such vivid details peculiar to Mk are: (from chs. 1, 2) 1^{20} 'with the hired servants,' 1^{33} 'the whole city was gathered together about the door,' 1^{41} 'moved with pity,' 1^{43} 'sternly charged,' 2^{3} 'carried by four men,' 2^{4} 'removed the roof'; (from later chs.) 3^{34} 'looking around on those who sat about him,' 4^{38} 'in the stern, asleep on the cushion,' 6^{39} 'by companies upon the green grass,' 10^{21} 'looking upon him loved him.' In a few places Peter, James, and John are named as accompanying Jesus on specific occasions (5^{37} raising of Jairus' daughter, 9^{2} Transfiguration, 13^{3} prophetic teaching on the Mount of Olives, 14^{33} Gethesemane). It may be, as is usually supposed, that these formed an inner circle of disciples, but the chief interest in James and John here may be as corroborators of Peter's testimony. In any case it is remarkable that we hear so little of the rest of the Twelve. Legendary interest, which in the future will spin apocryphal tales round names like Andrew and Thomas, has not yet come to the front. Yet the rest of the Twelve must have had their own special experiences in contact with Jesus, and the fact that such are not recorded by Mark is a sign that he did not invent where he had no information, and a guarantee that what he records around the name of Peter has a historical basis. It should be noted that circumstantial detail is not found uniformly throughout Mk. It is less striking in the sections which Mark may be supposed to have incorporated from the general Church tradition or from fragmentary information. The vivid description should therefore not be attributed to Mark's imaginative invention but to his Petrine source.

(*b*) *Non-Petrine sources.*—The Gospels have been thoroughly analysed by the methods of Form-criticism, which seeks to classify the sections and relate the form of each to the activities and practical needs of the early Church. Thus some insight is gained into the period of oral tradition before the need of written Gospels came to be felt. Among the forms so distinguished the Pronouncement-stories are easily identified. Each of these culminates in a saying of Jesus treasured by the Church as important for guidance in its life (*e.g.* Mk 2^{18-20} on fasting, 10^{1-9} on divorce, 10^{13-16} on children, 12^{13-17} on tribute to Caesar). It is believed that such passages received their present form not at the hands of the Evangelists but by an earlier process of adaptation for purposes of preaching and instruction. It is putting unnecessary strain on the statement of Papias' elder to attribute to Peter's testimony all these stories, all the miracle and other narrative sections, and all the groups of sayings and parables found in Mk. And Papias' statement itself leads to the view that the planning and arrangement of the material to form a continuous Gospel was the work of Mark himself. Within the Gospel some sections are united in groups by occasion or by topic (*e.g.* 1^{21-38} a day in Capernaum, 2^{1}–3^{6} stories of controversy, 6^{30}–8^{26} lake-cycles, 14^{1}–16^{8} passion and resurrection narrative). Some of these groups may have been compiled by Mark himself, but others were probably connected in his sources.

5. The Theology of the Gospel.—In Mk we can distinguish (*a*) the theology of Jesus Himself, expressed in His teaching and actions, and preserved in Mark's sources, (*b*) the faith of the early Church reflecting upon and modifying the traditions, (*c*) the theological emphases of Mark himself. Our special interest here is in (*c*). Mark's work, however, is mainly a presentation of (*a*) and (*b*), much of it is taken over by Matthew and Luke, and much is confirmed in these Gospels by material derived from non-Markan sources. Jesus comes into Galilee after His baptism proclaiming the nearness of the Kingdom of God (primarily God's Kingly Rule), $1^{14f.}$ This is an eschatological message, challenging men to repentance and decision in face of the final fruition of God's purposes for the world. The Kingdom is future and imminent (1^{15} 9^{1} 14^{25}). But as its coming is closely associated with

MARK, GOSPEL ACCORDING TO

Jesus' own mission, the Kingdom in a sense is already present, and men may ' receive ' or ' enter ' it ($10^{15, 23ff}$). His works fulfil the promise of a Messianic age. Here Mark shows a special interest in Jesus' authority over demons or ' unclean spirits,' supernatural powers supposed to be responsible for various perversions of human personality. His first recorded miracle is an exorcism (1^{21ff}). Other cases of demon-possession follow (5^{1ff} 7^{25ff} 9^{14ff}). Summaries of Jesus' activities, and also of His disciples,' give it prominence ($1^{32ff, 39}$ $3^{11, 15}$ $6^{7, 13}$), and the opposition to Jesus, roused first by His authoritative attitude to the Law, takes the form of an accusation that He casts out demons by Beelzebul, prince of the demons (3^{22}). The effect is to give the Gospel the character of a supernatural drama, in which Jesus' conflict with the powers of evil brings Him to the Cross but in the end to the victory of the Resurrection.

In 1^{1}, ' Jesus Christ (Messiah) Son of God,' we see the main features of the presentation of Christ's Person and Work which is to follow. The personal name Jesus, which occurs eighty-one times in Mk, indicates the objective historical interest of the Gospel. The true humanity of Jesus is expressed in a simple and natural way. He is addressed frequently as ' Rabbi ' or ' Teacher' (for which Mt and Lk usually have the more reverential ' Lord ' or ' Master '). Reference is made to His eating and drinking and sleeping (2^{15} 14^{3} 4^{38}), to His compassion (1^{41} 6^{34}), to an impulse of love (10^{21}), to emotions such as anger, surprise, grief (1^{43} 3^{5} 10^{14} 14^{33f}). Questions are asked for information (5^{30} 8^{5} 9^{16}). And limitations of power and knowledge are indicated (6^{5} 13^{32}). Such expressions are peculiar to Mk in many cases. Jesus is referred to as the Son of God in $1^{1, 11}$ 3^{11} 5^{7} 9^{7} 14^{61}. The title in Mk does not evidently bear all (*e.g.*, pre-existence) that is expressed in the Christology of John and other NT writers, but it means much more than ' a son of God ' (Mk 15^{39} RSVm). It belongs to Jesus as a unique person in virtue of His unique vocation. The title Messiah, however, does not in itself have the same content, as it does not necessarily indicate, as Son of God does, a supernatural person.

The Messiahship of Jesus is a dominant theme of Mk. The word Christ is not frequent in the Gospel (1^{1} 8^{29} 9^{41} 12^{35} 13^{21} 14^{61} 15^{32}) and is not used by Jesus directly of Himself. The title, Son of David, occurs at 10^{47f}. This infrequency, especially in the earlier chapters of the Gospel, itself reflects Mark's interest in Jesus' Messiahship. Realizing the diversity of Jewish Messianic hopes and the originality of Jesus' purpose, Mark pictures Jesus as silencing the demons who recognize Him ($1^{24f, 34}$ 3^{11f}), checking publicity after miracles and exceptional experiences of the disciples (*e.g.*, 1^{44} 5^{43} 7^{36} $8^{26, 30}$ 9^{9}), and instructing the disciples in ' mysteries ' which it is given only to them to understand (4^{10ff}). Accordingly, the confession of Peter (8^{29}) and Jesus' admission before the high priest (14^{62}) are very dramatic and significant points in the narrative. Jesus' reserve in Mark's portrait led to Wrede's theory of the ' Messianic Secret ' (1901). It postulates that what we find in Mk is the product of (*a*) the fact that Jesus did not claim to be Messiah and (*b*) the disciples' belief after their Resurrection experiences that He was Messiah. To this theory, which makes Mark's picture an artificial construction, there are strong objections. It has no sufficient answer to the historical question how the disciples ever came to regard Jesus as Messiah, it overlooks the Messianic factors in the pre-Markan tradition and in the actual events culminating in the Crucifixion, and it makes Mark a more subtle writer than he is. On the other hand, the Messianic Secret regarded as historical, points to Jesus' originality in His conception of the Messiah's vocation. It is doubtful whether the designation Son of Man, used in the Gospels only by Jesus and always of Himself, was regarded as a Messianic title and whether suffering was ever attributed to the Messiah before Jesus. Jesus effectively brought together in thought and action, Messiahship, the Son of Man ideal, and the suffering of God's chosen Servant (cf Is 53). In Mk the term Son of Man at $2^{10, 28}$ may not have Messianic significance, but Peter's confession of Jesus as Christ (8^{29}) leads immediately to the first prophecy of the suffering, death and resurrection of the Son of Man. Similar forecasts of betrayal, passion and resurrection are found at $9^{9, 12, 31}$ 10^{33f} $14^{21, 41}$. In other passages the Son of Man whose Parousia in glory is prophesied is the supernatural figure of apocalyptic, developed from the symbolic ' one like a son of man ' of Dn 7 (8^{38} 13^{26} 14^{62}). 10^{45} tells of the redemptive mission of the Son of Man.

It has sometimes been argued that Mark's theology is derived from Paul. Certainly the Death and Resurrection of Christ, central in Paul's thinking, are in view early in Mark's Gospel, so that the Galilean ministry seems like an introduction to the Passion. And in other matters, as the stubborn resistance of the Jews to the Gospel, Mark and Paul have affinities. But the Evangelist and the writer of the Epistles have different approaches to the historical traditions, and what they have in common is most probably derived from the stock of early Christian ideas. Some characteristic doctrines of Paul do not appear in Mk.

6. Historical value.—The establishment in the 19th cent. of the priority and primitive character of Mk led to the production of elaborate Lives of Jesus in which the Markan sequence of events was relied on as the basis for biographical and psychological studies. Among the influences which have led to a reaction is Form-criticism (**4** (*b*)) which has shown the part played by the early Church in moulding and ordering the historical traditions. It has even been suggested that the order of Mk follows a liturgical sequence (Archbishop Carrington). Studies of the life and teaching of Jesus have become less sweeping in scope. Yet the outstanding landmarks of the ministry of Jesus, as set up in Mark's narrative, remain. And throughout his Gospel there are many indications of reliance on authentic memories of the events. There is the internal evidence, as well as the Church tradition (**4** (*a*)) of dependence upon Peter. There are names of places and persons which appear to have been brought down from the earliest tradition ; the geographical references are very numerous, those to persons include some peculiar to Mk (2^{14} 10^{46} 15^{21}—? the sons of Simon of Cyrene known to Mark and his readers). Among the signs that the Gospel rests ultimately on Aramaic sources are some words of Jesus preserved in the original Aramaic and explained to Mark's readers (3^{17} 5^{41} $7^{11, 34}$ 14^{36}). The importance of Mk as a historical source is beyond doubt ; whether we regard the Gospel itself as a historical work depends on what we expect from historians. Mk is not an impartial work, viewing the life of Jesus critically from a position of detachment. It is a product of faith, but of faith elicited by and centering upon historical events. Whether faith has given some of these events, *e.g.*, certain miracles, a form different from that which would have been noticed by a detached observer is a matter for discussion. But it is certain that the challenge of Jesus demands a response at a deeper level than cold impartiality if its historical significance is to be revealed.

7. The non-Markan conclusion.—The last twelve verses (16^{9-20}) are contained in nearly all the MSS, but are absent from two of the most reliable Greek MSS (the Vatican and the Sinaitic), the Sinaitic MS of the old Syriac, and MSS of the Armenian, Georgian and Ethiopic versions, and Greek MSS known to Eusebius. They are contained in an expanded form in the Washington Greek MS. A shorter conclusion is found in a few Greek MSS in addition to the usual ending, and in a MS of the old Latin version standing alone. It is as follows : ' But they reported briefly to Peter and those with him all that they had been told, And after this, Jesus himself sent out by means of them, from east to west, the sacred and imperishable proclamation of eternal salvation ' (RSV).

This also points to the absence in earlier MSS of 16^{9-20}. 16^{9} does not continue from v.^{8} but at the position of v.^{1} and vv.$^{9-20}$ seem to summarize material from the other

Gospels. As such they have their value, but not as part of the original Mk; RSV appends them to the Gospel. Is the original ending of Mk lost? 16^8 concludes with 'for they were afraid,' which may not even be the end of a sentence. While some scholars have felt that Mark has fulfilled his aim at 16^8, most feel that 'for they were afraid' is intolerably abrupt. There is also the consideration that to a 1st cent. reader 'they said nothing to anyone' would evoke the question where the Evangelist got his information and would suggest that 16^{1-8} arose from guesswork or imagination. The loss of the end of a papyrus roll or the last leaf of a codex is a not improbable accident; but it must have happened to the original writing, or if to a copy, the whole line of textual transmission must go back to it.

8. Authorship, place of writing, date, use in Church.—Doubtless the name of the writer was Mark, and though Marcus was a common name it is reasonable to accept the early testimony which identifies the writer with the Mark ('John whose other name was Mark,' Ac $12^{12, 25}$ 15^{37} RSV) associated elsewhere in NT both with Peter and Paul (see previous article). Rome is most probably the place of writing. Already in 1 P 5^{13} we find Mark in the company of Peter there. The anti-Marcionite Prologue to Mk (2nd cent.) states that Mark after the death of Peter wrote the Gospel 'in the regions of Italy.' Irenaeus (late 2nd cent.) has a similar statement specifying Rome as the place of writing (*Adv. Haer.* iii. 1, 2). Clement of Alexandria (*c* A.D. 200) also locates the origin of the Gospel in Rome, but within the lifetime of Peter (Eusebius *HE* vi. 14, 6f). In later writings it is stated that Mark became first bishop of Alexandria and wrote his Gospel there. The silence of the Alexandrians, Clement and Origen, is unfavourable to the first part of this statement and their mention of Rome (or 'Babylon') highly adverse to the second. Subsidiary evidence for Rome is found in a number of Graecised Latin words, some used in ||s in Mt and Lk, but a few peculiar to Mk (*e.g.*, 15^{39} 'centurion,' 6^{27} 'speculator' [AV 'executioner,' RSV 'soldier of the guard']). The date, if judgment is based on the external evidence, would be somewhat before (Clement) or somewhat after (Irenaeus) the death of Peter in Nero's persecution (A.D. 64). More probably the latter as the former tradition may be motivated by desire to emphasize the Apostolic authority of the Gospel. The internal testimony points approximately to the same period. The details of the apocalyptic discourse of chapter 13 and especially a comparison of 13^{14} with Lk 21^{20}, where the investment of Jerusalem by the Romans is definitely alluded to, has led many scholars to the conclusion that Mk was written before the culmination in A.D. 70 of the Jewish War. On the other hand, a much earlier date will not seem likely if allowance is made for the period of oral tradition preceding the need for written Gospels. A date between A.D. 65 and 70 is generally favoured.

There is reason to believe that after the publication of Mt and Lk with their fuller teaching content Mk was comparatively neglected in the Church. Victor of Antioch (? 5th cent.) did not know of a commentary on Mk earlier than his own. In Christian writings (Apostolic Fathers) down to *c* A.D. 150 there is very occasional use in apparent allusions to the Gospels of wording closer to Mk than to the other Synoptists; but even there loose oral tradition is possible. Such doubtful traces of knowledge of Mk are found in Polycarp, 1 Clement, Hermas, Barnabas. The earliest versions, however (Latin, Syriac, Coptic), contained Mk. Justin Martyr (*c* A.D. 150) refers to Peter's 'Memoirs' (*Dial.* 106) and mentions the name Boanerges, applied to the sons of Zebedee, which occurs only in Mk 3^{17}. That Mk by this time had a secure place among the Gospels is shown by Tatian's inclusion of Mk in his *Diatessaron* or Harmony of the Four. By the end of the 2nd cent., with Irenaeus, Tertullian, Clement of Alexandria, and others, representing all geographical regions, the period of frequent quotation has arrived. But it is only with the advance of literary and historical study in the 19th and 20th cents. that the special value of Mk has come to light. A. B.

MARKET, MARKET PLACE.—The former is found in OT in Ezk $27^{13, 17}$ etc., as the rendering of a collective noun signifying 'articles of exchange,' hence RV and RSV throughout **'merchandise,'** this last in v.^{15} being AV rendering of another word for which RV gives **'mart'** and RSV **'market.'** In NT 'market' has disappeared from RV in favour of the uniform 'market-place' (Gr. *agora*); so also RSV, save in 1 Co 10^{25}, where RSV has 'meat market' for AV and RV 'shambles.' Here we must distinguish between the 'market places' of Jerusalem (Mt 11^{16}, Mk 7^4 etc.), which were simply streets of shops—the 'bazaars' of a modern Eastern city—and the 'market place' (RV) of a Greek city (Ac 16^{19} 17^{17}). The latter was the centre of the public life of the city, and was a large open space adorned with colonnades and statues, and surrounded by temples and other public buildings. A. R. S. K.

MARKS.—1. The mark of circumcision.—This is an instance (among many) of the taking-over of a pre-existing rite, and adapting it to Yahweh-worship; whatever it may have meant in its origin—and opinions differ very widely on this point—it became among the Israelites the mark *par excellence* of a Yahweh-worshipper (cf Gn 17^{14}), the symbol of the covenant between Him and His people (see, further, CIRCUMCISION).

2. The mark of Cain.—In Gn 4^{15} we are told that 'the Lord put a mark on Cain, lest any who came upon him should kill him.' The Hebrew word for 'mark' here is *'ôth*, usually rendered 'sign.' The purpose of the sign was protective, but, in the setting which the Yahwist has given to the story of Cain and Abel, there was no other person on earth from whom the slayer would need protection. Hence it is clear that the story does not belong to its present context, and has passed through several stages of transmission, undergoing changes of meaning in the process. The intention of the Yahwist in using the ancient story was to show the rapid and tragic break-up of human relationships resulting from the first act of disobedience which broke the original relationship between man and God. But it is probable that in an early stage of its transmission, the story was a tradition of a ritual killing intended to remove the cause of a failure of the crops. The killer was a priest or ritual person who was rendered ritually unclean and had to flee from the community until he was cleansed. But he bore a mark indicating that his person was sacrosanct. The suggestion of Gunkel and Robertson Smith that the mark was a tribal mark is not satisfactory, as the mark would be common to all the members of the tribe. A parallel case is to be found in the Athenian ritual of Bouphonia, where the two men who slew the sacrificial bull were obliged to flee the community (Harrison, *Themis*, 142). The slayer was no common murderer but a priest or sacred person who had performed an act for the benefit of the community, an act involving temporary banishment of the slayer until he was purged from his ritual defilement. Hence the mark was probably a tattoo mark or other indication that the fugitive belonged to a sacred class. See article CAIN.

3. The mark of the prophet.—In 1 K 20^{35-43} there is the account of how one of the prophets 'disguised himself with a headband over his eyes'; the king does not recognize the man as a prophet until the latter takes away this covering from his face, whereupon the king 'discovered him as one of the prophets.' Clearly there must have been some distinguishing mark on the forehead of the man whereby he was recognized as belonging to the prophetic order. This conclusion is strengthened by several other considerations. (1) It is a fact that among other races the class of men corresponding to the prophetic order of the Israelites are distinguished by incisions made on their persons. (2) There is the analogy of circumcision; just as among the Israelites this was the distinguishing mark of the people of Yahweh, so those who, like the prophets, were more especially His close followers also had a special mark, a distinctive sign, which differentiated them from other men. (3) The custom of putting a mark upon cattle to denote ownership, and for the purpose of differentiating from other herds, was evidently well known in early Israel. When one remembers how rife anthropomorphisms were among the Israelites, it is perhaps not fanciful to see here an analogy: just as the owners of herds marked their own property, so Yahweh marked His own people; and as the prophets were differentiated from the ordinary people, so they would have their special mark. (4) There is the passage Zec 13[4–6]. These considerations point distinctly to marks of some kind or other which, either on the forehead or on the hand—possibly on both—were distinctive characteristics of a prophet among the Israelites.

4. Marks connected with Yahweh-worship.—It is possible that the 'sign' upon the hand and the 'memorial' between the eyes prescribed in Ex 13[9] were originally cuttings in the flesh, intended to mark the Israelites as the people of Yahweh. But in Nu 15[39] the 'sign' has become a 'tassel' attached to the corners of the garment, the Jewish 'tallith'; and in Dt 6[8] 11[18] the sign has become what is now called the 'phylactery,' whose very name indicates its protective purpose. There may be a reference to the early custom in Job 31[35], where Job says, 'Lo, here is my mark (RVm), let the Almighty answer me'; but the word for mark here is not *'ôth* ('sign'), but *tâw* (the letter Tau), the word which is also used in Ezk 9[4] for the protective mark placed on the foreheads of those who were to be preserved from the destruction of the idolatrous Israelites. Reference may also be made to the passage in Is 44[5] where it is said that a man will 'write on his hand, To the Lord.'

5. Cuttings for the dead.—The Canaanite practice of gashing the face and shaving the head and beard after a death, was evidently taken over by the Israelites after their settlement in Canaan, as may be seen from the prohibitions in Lv 19[28] 21[5], Dt 14[1]. It has been shown that such practices had their origin in the fear of the spirits of the dead, and were intended to prevent the spirits from recognizing their surviving relatives and harming them. But the practice may in later times have come to be signs of sorrow and of respect for the dead. The reason assigned in Dt 14[1] for the prohibition is to distinguish Israel as being specially Yahweh's people, separated out 'from all the peoples that are upon the face of the earth.' W. O. E. O.—S. H. He.

6. The Marks of Jesus.—The phrase occurs only in Gal 6[17], 'Henceforth let no man trouble me; for I bear on my body the marks (Gr. *stigmata*) of Jesus.' The reference is to scars and other evidences of hardships and scourgings suffered on missionary service (see 2 Co 11[23–27]). The remark has special point if Lystra, where Paul was stoned (Ac 14[19]), was one of the destinations of this letter. The figure suggests first that Paul's scars bore some physical resemblance to the wounds Jesus received from His scourging and crucifixion. For the apostle this implied a share in Christ's sufferings (Ph 3[10]) and a closer fellowship with Him (2 Co 4[10f]). For this reason Paul did not shrink from afflictions but embraced them (Col 1[24]). Secondly, the phrase refers to the practice of marking slaves with the sign of their owner. Paul saw himself scored with the proof-marks of his Master's service as a slave was branded with his master's name. Thirdly, and most appositely, religious devotees and the slaves attached to a temple were often branded with the name of the deity. Herodotus tells (ii. 113) of a temple of Heracles where, 'if any man's slave take refuge and have the sacred marks (*stigmata* as here) set upon him, *giving himself over to the god*, it is not lawful to lay hands upon him.' 'The marks of Jesus' were a sign that Paul had made a similar surrender.

Paul thus warns his Galatian converts that further animosity would be both unseemly and ineffective.

7. The Mark of the Beast.—The sign (Gr. *charagma*, 'engraving') set upon 'worshippers of the beast and its image' in the book of Revelation. The second beast of ch. 13 caused all those who worshipped the first beast to receive a mark on the forehead or the hand (13[16] 19[20]), without which, it appears, buying and selling in the common markets was impossible (13[17]). The mark would prove a curse, bringing plague on earth (16[2]) and wrath hereafter (14[9–11]). Those who steadfastly refused it would be sealed with the name of the Father on their foreheads (3[12] 7[3] 14[1] 22[4]) and would reign with Christ (20[4]). There are various explanations. V.[17] is the chief difficulty. *Charagma* was the technical name for the official seal of commercial documents. It was inscribed with details of the reigning emperor and it is possible that it was either denied to Christians or rejected by them. To possess it would thus be a sign of surrender and compliance. On the other hand, branding was not uncommon. Cattle, slaves, even soldiers were branded. Ptolemy Philopator branded Jews with the ivy leaf of Dionysus (3 Mac 2[29]), and devout Jews may have marked themselves with a sign of loyalty to Yahweh (see Is 44[5] and Zec 13[5f]). Whatever the explanation, 'the mark of the beast' is a reference to the inescapable and indelible stain of apostasy. W. D. S.

MARMOT.—See JACKAL, 5.

MARMOTH, 1 Es 8[62] (AV, RV).—See MEREMOTH, 1.

MAROTH ('bitterness').—A town mentioned only in Mic 1[12], where there is a play on the name. See MAARATH.

MARRIAGE.—1. Forms of Marriage.—There are two forms of marriage among primitive races: (1) where the husband becomes part of his wife's tribe, (2) where the wife becomes part of her husband's tribe.

(1) W. R. Smith (*Kinship and Marriage in Early Arabia*) gives to this form the name *ṣadīca*, from the *ṣadāc* or 'gift' given to the wife. (*a*) The union may be confined to an occasional visit to the wife in her home (*mota* marriage). This is distinguished from mere prostitution, in that no disgrace is attached, and the children are recognized by the tribe; cf Samson's marriage. (*b*) The husband may be definitely incorporated into his wife's tribe (*beena* marriage). The wife meets her husband on equal terms; children belong to her tribe, and descent is reckoned on the mother's side. Women could inherit in Arabia under this system (*op. cit.* p. 94). Possible traces in OT are the marriages of Jacob (Laban claims wives and children as his own, Gn 31[31, 43]), Moses (Ex 2[21] 4[18]), Samson (Jg 14, 15, 16[4]; there is no hint that he meant to take his wife home; his kid seems to be the *ṣadāc* or customary present). So the Shechemites must be circumcised (Gn 34[15]); Joseph's sons born in Egypt are *adopted* by Jacob (48[5]); Abimelech, the son of Gideon's Shechemite concubine (Jg 8[31]), is a Shechemite (9[1–5]). The words of Gn 2[24] may have originally referred to this custom, though they are evidently not intended to do so by the narrator, since *beena* marriages were already out of date when they were written. Many of the instances quoted can be explained as due to special circumstances, but the admitted existence of such marriages in Arabia makes it probable that we should find traces of them among the Semites in general. They make it easier to understand the existence of the primitive custom of the '*matriarchate*,' or reckoning of descent through females. In addition to the cases already quoted, we may add the closeness of maternal as compared with paternal relationships, evidenced in bars of marriage (see below, 3), and the special responsibility of the maternal uncle or brother (Gn 24[29] 34[25], 2 S 13[22]). It is evident that the influence of polygamy would be in the same direction, subdividing the family into smaller groups connected with each wife.

(2) The normal type is where the wife becomes the property of her husband, who is her 'Baal' or possessor (Hos 2[16]), she herself being 'Beulah' (Is 62[4]). She and her children belong to his tribe, and he alone has right of divorce. (*a*) In unsettled times the wife will be acquired by *war* (Jg 5[30]). She is not merely a temporary means of pleasure, or even a future mother, but a slave and an addition to a man's wealth. Dt 21[10–14] regulates the procedure in cases of capture; in Jg 19–21 we have an instance of the custom. Traces may remain

in later marriage procedure, *e.g.*, in the band of the bridegroom's friends escorting, *i.e.*, 'capturing,' the bride, and in her feigned resistance, as among the Bedouin (W. R. Smith, *op. cit.* p. 81). (*b*) Capture gives place to *purchase* and ultimately to *contract*. The daughter is valuable to the clan as a possible mother of warriors, and cannot be parted with except for a consideration. Hence the 'dowry' (see below, **5**) paid to the bride's parents.

2. Polygamy among the Hebrews was confined to a plurality of wives (polygyny). There is no certain trace in OT of a plurality of husbands (polyandry), though the Levirate marriage is sometimes supposed to be a survival. The chief causes of polygyny were—(*a*) the desire for a numerous offspring, or the barrenness of the first wife (Abraham's case is directly ascribed to this, and among many peoples it is permitted on this ground alone); (*b*) the position and importance offered by numerous alliances (*e.g.*, Solomon); (*c*) the existence of slavery, which almost implies it. It can obviously be prevalent only where there is a disproportionate number of females, and, except in a state of war, is possible only to those wealthy enough to provide the necessary 'dowry.' A further limitation is implied in the fact that in more advanced stages, when the harem is established, the wife when secured is a source, not of wealth, but of expense.

Polygamy meets us as a fact: *e.g.* Abraham, Jacob, the Judges, David, Solomon; 1 Ch 7^{4} is evidence of its prevalence in Issachar; Elkanah (1 S 1^{1f}) is significant as belonging to the middle class; Jehoiada (2 Ch 24^{3}) as a priest. But it is always treated with suspicion; it is incompatible with the ideal of Gn 2^{24}, and its origin is ascribed to Lamech, the Cainite (4^{19}). In Dt 17^{17} the king is warned not to multiply wives; later regulations fixed the number at eighteen for a king and four for an ordinary man. The quarrels and jealousies of such a narrative as Gn 29^{31}–30 are clearly intended to illustrate its evils, and it is in part the cause of the troubles of the reigns of David and Solomon. Legislation (see below, **6**) safeguarded the rights of various wives, slave or free; and according to the Rabbinic interpretation of Lv 21^{13} the high priest was not allowed to be a bigamist. Noah, Isaac, and Joseph had only one wife, and domestic happiness in the Bible is always connected with monogamy (2 K 4, Ps 128, P 31, Sir $25^{1,8}$ $26^{1,13}$). The marriage figure applied to the union of God and Israel (**10**) implied monogamy as the ideal state. Polygamy is, in fact, always an unnatural development from the point of view both of religion and of anthropology; 'monogamy is by far the most common form of human marriage; it was so also amongst the ancient peoples of whom we have any direct knowledge' (Westermarck, *Hum. Marr.*, p. 459). Being, however, apparently legalized, and having the advantage of precedent, it was long before polygamy was formally forbidden in Hebrew society, though practically it fell into disuse; the feeling of the Rabbis was strongly against it. Herod had nine wives at once (Jos. *Ant.* XVII. i. 3 [19]). Its possibility is implied by the technical continuance of the Levirate law, and is proved by the early interpretation of 1 Ti 3^{2}, whether correct or not (**8**). Justin (*Dial.* 134, 141) reproaches the Jews of his day with having 'four or even five wives,' and marrying 'as they wish, or as many as they wish.' The evidence of the Talmud shows that in this case at least the reproach had some foundation. Polygamy was not definitely forbidden among the Jews till the time of R. Gershom (*c* A.D. 1000), and then at first only for France and Germany. In Spain, Italy, and the East it persisted for some time longer, as it does still among the Jews in Mohammedan countries.

3. Bars to Marriage.—(1) *Prohibited degrees.*—Their range varies extraordinarily among different peoples, but on the whole it is wider among uncivilized than among civilized races (Westermarck, *op. cit.* p. 297), often embracing the whole tribe. The instinctive impulse was not against marriage with a near relative *qua* relative, but against marriage where there was early familiarity. 'Whatever is the origin of bars to marriage, they are certainly early associated with the feeling that it is indecent of housemates to intermarry' (W. R. Smith, *op. cit.* p. 170). The origin of the instinct is natural selection, consanguineous marriages being on the whole unfavourable to the species, in man as among animals. This, of course, was not consciously realized; the instinct took the form of a repulsion to union with those among whom one had lived; as these would usually be blood relations, that which we recognize as horror of incest was naturally developed (Westermarck, p. 352). We find in OT no trace of dislike to marriage within the tribe (*i.e.* endogamy), though, judging by Arab analogies, it may have originally existed; on the contrary, the Hebrews were strongly endogamous, marrying within the nation. The objection, however, to incestuous marriages was strong, though in early times there was laxity with regard to intermarriage with relatives on the *father's* side, a natural result of the 'matriarchate' and of polygamy, where each wife with her family formed a separate group in her own tent. Abram married his half-sister (Gn 20^{13}); 2 S 13^{13}, Ezk 22^{11} imply the continuance of the practice. Nahor married his niece (Gn 11^{29}), and Amram his paternal aunt (Ex 6^{20}). On marriage with a stepmother see below, **6.** Jacob married two sisters (cf Jg 15^{2}). Legislation is found in Lv 18^{7-17} 20^{11} (cf Dt $27^{20,22f}$); for details see the commentaries. We note the omission of prohibition of marriage with a niece, and with the widow of a maternal uncle. Lv 18^{18} forbids marriage not with a deceased but with a living wife's sister, *i.e.* a special form of polygamy. The 'bastard' of Dt 23^{2} is probably the offspring of an incestuous marriage. An heiress was not allowed to marry outside her tribe (Nu 36^{6}; cf 27^{4}, To 6^{12} 7^{12}). For restrictions on priests see Lv $21^{7,14}$. There were no caste restrictions, though difference in rank would naturally be an objection (1 S $18^{18,23}$). Outside the prohibited degrees consanguineous marriages were common (Gn 24^{4}, To 4^{12}); in Jg 14^{3} the best marriage is 'from thy brethren.' Jubilees 4 maintains that all the patriarchs from Adam to Noah married near relatives. Cousin marriages among the Jews are said to occur now three times more often than among other civilized peoples (Westermarck, p. 401).

Recent discoveries at Qumrân and the vicinity would seem to indicate that there was a certain laxity in later Judaism with regard to the forbidden degrees.' The Zadokite Document (iv. 21, v. 6) re-emphasizes the ancient regulations without which 'only a rickety wall may be built.' Monogamy is the original divine demand and in infraction of the 'forbidden degrees' the woman is held equally responsible with the man. 'The laws of forbidden degrees are written, to be sure, with reference to males, but they hold good equally for females' (v. 9). The Zadokite Covenanters were more stringent in enforcement of these laws.

(2) *Racial bars* arose from religious and historical causes. Gn 24, 28, 34, Nu 12^{1}, Jg 14^{3} illustrate the objection to foreign marriages; Esau's Hittite wives are a grief to his parents (Gn 26^{34} 27^{46}); cf Lv 24^{10}. The marriage of Joseph (Gn 41^{45}) is due to stress of circumstances, but David (2 S 3^{3}) and Solomon (1 K 3^{1} 11^{1}) set a deliberate example which was readily imitated (16^{31}). Among the common people there must have been other cases similar to Naomi's (Ru 1^{4}): Bathsheba (2 S 11^{3}), Hiram (1 K 7^{14}), Amasa (1 Ch 2^{17}), Jehozabad (2 Ch 24^{26}) are the children of mixed marriages. They are forbidden with the inhabitants of Canaan (Ex 34^{16}, Dt 7^{3}), but tolerated with Edomites and Egyptians (23^{7}). Their prevalence was a trouble to Ezra (9, 10) and to Nehemiah (10^{30} 13^{23}). To 4^{12} 6^{15}, 1 Mac 1^{15} renew the protest against them. In the Diaspora they were permitted on condition of proselytism, but Jubilees 30 forbids them absolutely; they are 'fornication.' Jewish strictness in this respect was notorious (Tacitus, *Hist.* v. **5**; cf Ac 10^{28}). The case of Timothy's parents (Ac 16^{1-3}) is an example of the greater laxity which prevailed in central Asia Minor. It is said that now the proportion of mixed

to pure marriages among the Jews is about 1 to 500 (Westermarck, p. 375), though it varies greatly in different countries. 1 Co 7[39] probably discourages marriage with a heathen (cf v.12ff 9[5]), but the general teaching of the Epistles would remove any religious bar to intermarriage between Christians of different race, though it does not touch the social or physiological advisability.

4. Levirate Marriage (Lat. *lēvir*, 'a brother-in-law').—In Dt 25[5-10] (no ‖ in other codes of OT) it is enacted that if a man die leaving no son ('child' LXX, Josephus, Mt 22[24]), his brother, if he lives on the same estate, is to take his widow, and the eldest child is to succeed to the name and inheritance of the deceased (cf Gn 38[9]). If the survivor refuses, a formal declaration is to be made before the elders of the city, and the widow is to express her contempt by loosing his sandal and spitting in his face. The law is a codification, possibly a restriction, of an existing custom. (*a*) It is presupposed for the patriarchal age in Gn 38, the object of this narrative being to insist on the duty of the survivor; (*b*) Hebrew has a special word = 'to perform the duty of a husband's brother'; (*c*) the custom is found with variations in different parts of the world—India, Tibet, Madagascar, etc. In India it is confined to the case where there is no child, and lasts only till an heir is born; sometimes it is only permissive. In other cases it operates without restriction, and may be connected with the form of polyandry where the wife is the common property of all the brothers. But it does not necessarily imply polyandry, of which indeed there is no trace in OT. Among the Indians, Persians, and Afghans it is connected with ancestor worship, the object being to ensure that there shall be some one to perform the sacrificial rites; the supposed indications of this among the Hebrews are very doubtful. In OT it is more probably connected with the desire to preserve the family name (a man lived through his children), and to prevent a division or alienation of property. On the other hand, the story of Ru 4 seems to belong to the circle of ideas according to which the wife is inherited as part of a man's property. Boaz marries Ruth as *gō'ēl*, not as *levir*, and the marriage is legally only a subordinate element in the redemption of the property. There is no stigma attached to the refusal of the nearer kinsman, and the son ranks as belonging to Boaz. The prohibited degrees in Lv 18 (P) make no exception in favour of the Levirate marriage, whether repealing or presupposing it is uncertain. In later times we have **the Sadducees' question** in Mk 12[19] ‖. It does not imply the continuance of the practice. It had fallen into disuse, and the Mishnah invents many limitations to avoid the necessity of compliance. It was agreed that the woman must have no child (Deuteronomy 'son'), and the school both of Shammai and of the Sadducees apparently confined the law to the case of a betrothed, not a wedded, wife. If so, the difficulty was twofold, striking at the Levirate custom as well as at the belief in the Resurrection (Edersheim, *LT* ii. 400).

5. Marriage Customs.—(1) *The arranging of a marriage* was normally in the hands of the parents (Gn 21[21] 24[3] 28[1] 34[4], Jg 14[2], 2 Es 9[47]); there are, in fact, few nations or periods where the children have a free choice. But (*a*) infant or child marriages were unknown; (*b*) the consent of the parties was, sometimes at least, sought (Gn 24[8]); (*c*) the rule was not absolute; it might be broken wilfully (26[34]), or under stress of circumstances (Ex 2[21]); (*d*) natural feeling will always make itself felt in spite of the restrictions of custom; the sexes met freely, and romantic attachments were not unknown (Gn 29[10] 34[3], Jg 14[1], 1 S 18[20]); in these cases the initiative was taken by the parties. One view of Canticles is that it is a drama celebrating the victory of a village maiden's faithfulness to her shepherd lover, in face of the attractions of a royal rival. It was a disgrace if a daughter remained unmarried (Sir 42[9]); this fact is the key to 1 Co 7[25ff]. (2) The **betrothal** was of a more formal and binding nature than our 'engagement'; among the Arabs it is the only legal ceremony connected with a marriage. Gn 24[58, 60] may preserve an ancient formula and blessing. Its central feature was the **dowry** (*mōhar*) paid to the parents or representatives of the bride, the daughter being a valuable possession. Dt 22[29] (cf Ex 22[16]) orders its payment in a case of seduction, and 50 shekels is named as the average. In Gn 34[12] Hamor offers 'never so much dowry'; cf the presents of ch. 24. It might take the form of service (Gn 29, Jacob; 1 S 18[25], David). Dowry, in our sense of provision for the wife, arose in two ways. (*a*) The parents provided for her, perhaps originally giving her a portion of the purchase money (Gn 24[61] 29[24]). Caleb gives his daughter a field (Jos 15[19] =Jg 1[15]); Solomon's princess brings a dowry of a city (1 K 9[16]); Raguel gives his daughter half his goods (To 8[21] 10[10]). This dowry was retained by the wife if divorced, except in case of adultery. (*b*) The husband naturally signified his generosity and affection by gifts to his bride (Gn 24[53] 34[12] [where gift is distinct from 'dowry'], Est 2[9]). According to the Mishnah, the later ceremony of betrothal consisted in payment of a piece of money, or a gift, or the conveyance of a writing, in presence of two witnesses. A third method (by co-habitation) was strongly discountenanced. *After betrothal* the parties were legally in the position of a married couple. Unfaithfulness was adultery (Dt 22[23], Mt 1[19]). The bridegroom was exempt from military service (Dt 20[7]). Non-fulfilment of the marriage was a serious slight (1 S 18[19], Jg 14[19]), but conceivable under certain circumstances (Gn 29[27]).

Archaeological discoveries have now revealed the presence of a hitherto unknown people—the Hurrians—in N. Mesopotamia, the home of Abraham's kinsfolk. They occupied this area from the late 3rd millennium B.C. to near the close of the 2nd millennium. The identity of this non-Indo-European, Armenoid, people was formerly concealed under the erroneous biblical translation 'Horites': these were commonly assumed to be Palestinian cave-dwellers or listed among the aboriginal giants. Their great civilization and high degree of culture has been made known to us through a vast collection of tablets discovered at Nuzi (modern Kirkuk), as also through the discoveries at Râs Shamra where the Hurrians constituted the second largest element in the population. In these Hurrian documents we find a customary law, in regard to marriage and family, that corresponds closely with that observed by the patriarchs, but is not common in later Hebrew practice. Much light is here shed upon adoption customs (Gn 24[2]) and it is clear that to those people the production of children was the main end of marriage. If a woman failed here her lot might be hard enough, but she could alleviate her lot by procuring children through surrender of her handmaid to her husband. Thus 'she could be built up' (Gn 30[3] 16[2]) for the children so born were accounted hers by adoption. The story of Jacob and Laban and their intromissions are not easily understood on a purely Hebrew basis, but the matter becomes clear in the light of the Nuzi tablets. There it was customary for a man to adopt a son, as Laban did, giving Leah and Rachel as wives. Jacob was heir unless Laban should beget sons—which he did—and the eldest became heir, and was entitled to receive the *t^erāphîm* (household gods). If no son was born to Laban Jacob would receive the *t^erāphîm*, and with these went the title to the property. As possessor of the *t^erāphîm* Jacob had the right to inheritance. Thus we can well understand the indignant cry of Laban, 'Wherefore hast thou stolen my gods?' (Gn 31[30]).

(2) *Wedding ceremonies.*—Great uncertainty attaches to the proceedings in Biblical times. We have to construct our picture from passing notices, combined with what we know of Arabic and later Jewish customs. In some cases there seems to have been nothing beyond the betrothal (Gn 24[63-67]); or the wedding festivities followed it at once; but in later times there was a distinct interval, not exceeding a year in case of a virgin. Tobit (7[14]) mentions a 'contract' (cf Mal 2[14]), which became a universal feature. The first ceremony was the *wedding procession* (Ps 45[15], 1 Mac 9[37]), which may be a relic of

'marriage by capture,' the bridegroom's friends (Mt 9^{15}, Jn 3^{29}; cf '60 mighty men' of Ca 3^{7}) going, often by night, to fetch the **bride** and her attendants; in Jg 14$^{11, 15, 20}$ Samson's comrades are necessarily taken from the bride's people. The rejoicings are evidenced by the proverbial 'voice of the **bridegroom**,' etc. (Jer 7^{34} etc., Rev 18^{23}). Gn 24^{53}, Ps 45$^{13-15}$, Jer 2^{32}, Rev 19^{8} 21^{2} speak of the magnificence of the bridal attire; Is 61^{10}, of the garland of the bridegroom and jewels of the bride (cf 49^{18}); the veil is mentioned in Gn 24^{65} 29^{23}; the supposed allusions to the lustral bath of the Greeks (Ru 3^{3}, Ezk 23^{40}, Eph 5^{26}) are very doubtful. The situation in Mt 25^{1} is not clear. Are the 'virgins' friends of the bridegroom waiting for his return with his bride, or friends of the bride waiting with her for him? All that it is possible to say is that the general conception is that of the wedding procession by night in which lights and torches have always played a large part. Another feature was the scattering of flowers and nuts; all who met the procession were expected to join in it or to salute it.

The marriage supper followed, usually in the home of the bridegroom (2 Es 9^{47}); Gn 29^{22}, Jg 14^{10}, To 8^{19} are easily explained exceptions. Hospitality was a sacred duty; 'he who does not invite me to his marriage will not have me to his funeral.' To refuse the invitation was a grave insult (Mt 22). Nothing is known of the custom, apparently implied in this passage, of providing a wedding garment for guests. Jn 2 gives us a picture of the feast in a middle-class home, where the resources are strained to the uttermost. It is doubtful whether the 'ruler of the feast' (cf Sir 32^{1f}) is 'the best man' (3^{29}, Jg 14^{20}), the office being unusual in the simple life of Galilee (Edersheim, *LT* i, 355). There is nowhere any hint of a *religious ceremony*, though marriage was regarded with great reverence as symbolizing the union of God with Israel (*ib.* 353). The feast was no doubt *quasi*-sacramental (cf the Latin 'confarreatio'), and the marriage was consummated by the entry into the 'chamber' (*ḥuppāh*). W. R. Smith (*op. cit.* p. 168) finds in this a relic of 'beena' marriage (see above, **1**), the *ḥuppāh* or canopy (Jl 2^{16}) being originally the wife's tent (Gn 24^{67}, Jg 4^{17}); cf the tent pitched for Absalom (2 S 16^{22}). In Arabic, Syriac, and Hebrew the bridegroom is said to 'go in' to the bride. Ps 19^{5} speaks of his exultant 'coming forth' on the following morning; 'the chamber' can hardly refer there to the 'canopy' under which in modern weddings the pair stand *during* the ceremony, though this has no doubt been evolved from the old tent.

The wedding festivities were not confined to the 'supper' of the first night, at any rate in OT times. As now in Syria, the feast lasted for 7 days (Gn 29^{27}, To 11^{19} 8^{19} [a fortnight]). The best picture is in Jg 14, with its eating and drinking and not very refined merriment. Canticles is generally supposed to contain songs sung during these festivities; those now sung in Syria show a remarkable similarity. 7$^{1-7}$ in particular would seem to be the chorus in praise of the bride's beauty, such as is now chanted, while she herself in a sword dance displays the charms of her person by the flashing firelight. During the week the pair are 'king and queen' enthroned on the threshing-board of the village. It is suggested that 'Solomon' (3^{7}) had become the nickname for this village king. Dt 24^{5} exempts the bridegroom from military service for a year (cf 20^{7}).

6. Position of the wife.—The practically universal form of marriage was the 'Baal' type, where the wife passed under the dominion of her 'lord' (Gn 3^{16}, Tenth Com.). Side by side with this was the ideal principle, according to which she was a 'help meet for him' (Gn 2^{18}), and the legal theory was always modified in practice by the affection of the husband or the strong personality of the wife; cf the position of the patriarchs' wives, of women in Judges or in Proverbs (especially 31); cf 1 S 25^{18}, 2 K 4^{8}. But her value was largely that of a mother of children, and the position of a childless wife was unpleasant (Gn 16^{4} 30$^{1-4}$, 1 S 1^{6}, 2 Es 9^{43}). Polygamy led to favouritism; the fellow-wife is a 'rival' (1 S 1^{6})—a technical term. Dt 21^{15ff} safeguards the right of the firstborn of a 'hated' wife; Ex 21^{10} provides for the rendering of the duties of marriage to a first wife, even if a purchased concubine; if they are withheld she is to go free (cf Dt 21^{14} of a captive). The difference between a wife and a **concubine** depended on the wife's higher position and birth, usually backed by relatives ready to defend her. She might claim the inheritance for her children (Gn 21^{10}); her slave could not be taken as concubine without her consent (16^{2}). As part of a man's chattels his wives were in certain cases *inherited by his heir*, with the limitation that a man could not take his own mother. The custom lasted in Arabia till forbidden by the Koran (ch. iv). In OT there is the case of Reuben and Bilhah (Gn 35^{22} 49^{4}), perhaps implying the continuance of the custom in the tribe of Reuben, after it had been proscribed elsewhere (Driver, *ad loc.*). It is presupposed in 2 S 3^{7}, where Ishbosheth reproaches Abner for encroaching on his birthright, and in 16^{22}, where Absalom thus publishes his claim to the kingdom. In 1 K 2^{22} Adonijah, in asking for Abishag, is claiming the eldest brother's inheritance. Ezk 22^{10} finds it still necessary to condemn the practice; cf Dt 22^{30}, Lv 18^{8}. Ru 4 shows how the wife is regarded as part of the inheritance. A **widow** normally remained unmarried. If poor, her position was bad; cf the injunctions in Deuteronomy, the prophets, and the Pastoral Epistles. In royal houses her influence might be greater than that of the wife; *e.g.* the difference in the attitude of Bathsheba in 1 K 1^{16} and in 2^{19}, and the power of the queen-mother (1 K 15^{13}, 2 K 11). There was a strong prejudice in later times against her re-marrying (Lk 2^{36}; Jos. *Ant.* xvii. xiii. 4 [349ff], xviii. vi. 6 [180]). There is no instance of a corresponding dislike to the marriage of a widower, but the wife was regarded as a man's property even after his death. St. Paul, however, permits re-marriage (1 Co 7^{39}), and even enjoins it for younger widows (1 Ti 5^{14}).

7. Adultery.—If a bride was found not to be a virgin, she was to be stoned (Dt 22$^{13-21}$). A man who violated an unmarried girl was compelled to marry her with payment of 'dowry' (v.^{29}, cf Ex 22^{16}). A priest's daughter playing the harlot was to be burnt (Lv 21^{9}). Adultery holds a prominent place among social sins (Seventh and Tenth Com., Ezk 18^{11}). If committed with a married or betrothed woman, the penalty was stoning for both parties, a betrothed damsel being spared if forced (Dt 22$^{22-27}$, Lv 20^{10}, Ezk 16^{40} 23^{45}). The earlier penalty was burning, as in Egypt (Gn 38^{24}; Tamar is virtually betrothed). In Nu 5$^{11-31}$ the fact of adultery is to be established by ordeal, a custom found in many nations. It is to be noted that the test is not poison, but holy water; *i.e.* the chances are in favour of the accused. The general point of view is that adultery with a married woman is an offence against a neighbour's property; the adultery of a wife is an offence against her husband, but she has no concern with his fidelity. It is not probable that the extreme penalty was ever carried out (2 S 11, Hos 3). The frequent denunciations in the prophets and Proverbs (2^{18} 5^{8} 6^{26}) show the prevalence of the crime; the usual penalty was divorce with loss of dowry (cf Mt 5^{31}). In the 'pericope' of Jn 8, part of the test is whether Christ will set Himself against Moses by sanctioning the abrogation of the Law; it is not implied that the punishment was ever actually inflicted; in fact, no instance of it is known. The answer (v.^{11}) pardons the sinner but by no means condones the sin: 'damnavit, sed peccatum non hominem' (Augustus); cf the treatment of 'the woman who was a sinner' (Lk 7^{47}). The NT is uncompromising in its attitude towards this sin, including in its view all acts of **unchastity** as offences against God and the true self, as sanctified by His indwelling, no less than against one's neighbour (Mt 5^{27}, Ac 15^{29}, 1 Co 5^{11} 6$^{9, 13-20}$, Gal 5^{19}, 1 Th 4^{3}). The blessing on the 'virgins' of Rev 14^{4} probably refers to chastity, not celibacy; cf 'the bed undefiled' of He 13^{4}. The laxity of the age made it necessary to insist on purity as a primary Christian virtue (see Swete, *ad loc.*).

8. Divorce is taken for granted in OT (Lv 21[7, 14] 22[13], Nu 30[9]), it being the traditional right of the husband, as in Arabia, to 'put away his wife' (Gn 21[14]). The story of Hosea probably embodies the older procedure, which is regulated by the law of Dt 24[1]. There must be a **bill of divorcement** (Is 50[1], Jer 3[8]), prepared on a definite charge, and therefore presumably before some public official, and formally given to the woman. (But cf Mt 1[19], where possibility of private divorce is contemplated [or repudiation of betrothal?]). The time and expense thus involved would act as a check. Further, if the *divorcée* re-marries, she may not return to her former husband—a deterrent on hasty divorce, also on re-marriage—if there is any prospect of reconciliation. The right of divorce is withheld in two cases (Dt 22[19, 29]). There was great divergence of opinion as regards *the ground* 'if she find no favour in his eyes, because he hath found in her the nakedness of a thing.' The school of Hillel emphasized the first clause, and interpreted it of the most trivial things, practically 'for any cause' (Mt 19[3]); that of Shammai laid stress rightly on the second clause, and confined it to **unchastity**. But the vague nature of the expression (cf Dt 23[14]), and the fact that 22[22] enacts death for unchastity, show that something wider must be meant, probably 'immodest or indecent behaviour' (Driver, *ad loc.*). In spite of the prohibition of Mal 2[13-16] and the stern attitude of many Rabbis, divorce continued to be frequent; Ezr 9, 10 encouraged it. The Mishnah allows it for violation of the Law or of Jewish customs, *e.g.* breaking a vow, appearing in public with dishevelled hair, or conversing indiscriminately with men. Practically the freedom was almost unlimited; the question was not what was lawful, but on what grounds a man ought to exercise the right the Law gave him. It was, of course, confined *to the husband* (1 S 25[44] is simply an outrage on the part of Saul). Women of rank such as Salome (Jos. *Ant.* xv. vii. 10 [259]) or Herodias (xviii. v. 4 [136]) might arrogate it, but it is condemned as a breach of Jewish law. Christ contemplates its possibility in Mk 10[12], perhaps having in view the Greek and Roman world, where it was legal. But the words caused a difficulty to the early versions, which substitute desertion for divorce, and may be a later insertion, added for the sake of completeness. In a later period the Talmud allowed a wife to claim a divorce in certain cases, *e.g.* if her husband had a loathsome disease.

In the NT divorce seems to be forbidden absolutely (Mk 10[11], Lk 16[8], 1 Co 7[10, 39]). Our Lord teaches that the OT permission was a concession to a low moral standard, and was opposed to the ideal of marriage as an inseparable union of body and soul (Gn 2[23]). But in Mt 5[32] 19[9] He seems to allow it for 'unchastity,' an exception which finds no place in the parallels (cf 1 Co 7[15], which allows re-marriage where a Christian partner is deserted by a heathen). (*a*) Fornication cannot here be sin before marriage; the sense of the passage demands that the word shall be taken in its wider sense (cf Hos 2[5], Am 7[17], 1 Co 5[1]); it defines the 'uncleanness' of Dt 24[1] as illicit sexual intercourse. (*b*) Divorce cannot be limited to separation 'from bed and board,' as by R.C. commentators (1 Co 7 uses quite different words). To a Jew it always carried with it the right of re-marriage, and the words 'makes her an adulteress' (Mt 5[32]) show that our Lord assumed that the *divorcée* would marry again. Hence if He allowed divorce under certain conditions, He allowed re-marriage. (*c*) It follows that Mt 19[9], as it stands, gives to an injured husband the right of divorce, and therefore of re-marriage, even if it be supposed that the words 'except for unchastity' qualify only the first clause, or if 'shall marry another' be omitted with B. A right given to an injured husband must on Christian principles be allowed to an injured wife. Further, re-marriage, if permitted to either party, is logically permitted both to innocent and to guilty, so far as the dissolution of the marriage bond is concerned, though it may well be forbidden to the latter as a matter of discipline and penalty. Mt 5[32] apparently allows the re-marriage of the justifiably divorced, *i.e.* guilty wife, though the interpretation of this verse is more doubtful than that of 19[9]. (*d*) The view implied by the exception is that adultery *ipso facto* dissolves the union, and so opens the way to re-marriage. But re-marriage also closes the door to reconciliation, which on Christian principles ought always to be possible; cf the teaching of Hosea and Jer 3; Hermas (*Mand.* iv. 1) allows no re-marriage, and lays great stress on the taking back of a repentant wife. (*e*) Hence much is to be said for the view which is steadily gaining ground, that the exception in Matthew is an editorial addition from the Judaic standpoint, or under the pressure of practical necessity, the absolute rule being found too hard. (For the authorities, see Hastings' *DB*, Ext. Vol. p. 27[b], and add Wright's *Synopsis* and Allen's *St. Matt.*). It is true that though the textual variations in both passages of Matthew are numerous, there is no MS authority for the entire omission of the words. But there is no hint of the exception in Mark, Luke, or 1 Corinthians; Mt 19[3] alters the question of Mk 10[2], adding the qualification 'for every cause,' which thus prepares the way for the qualified answer of v.[9]. This answer really admits the validity of the law of Dt 24[1], with its stricter interpretation (see above), whilst the language of v.[8] leads us to expect its abrogation. The introduction of the exception upsets the argument, which in Mark is clear and logical. Again, is it not contrary to Christ's method that He should legislate in detail? He rather lays down universal principles, the practical application of which He left to His Church (see below, **11**).

(*f*) The requirement in 1 Ti 3[2, 12], Tit 1[6], that the 'bishop' and 'deacon' shall be 'married only once,' is probably to be understood as a prohibition of divorce and other sins against the chastity of marriage (cf He 13[4]), made necessary by the low standard of the age. Of course, no greater laxity is allowed to the layman, any more than he is allowed to be 'a drunkard or violent'; but sins of this type are mentioned as peculiarly inconsistent with the ministry. Other views of the passage are that it forbids polygamy (a prohibition which could hardly be necessary in Christian circles) or a second marriage. But there was no feeling against the re-marriage of *men* (see above, **6**), and St. Paul himself saw in a second marriage nothing *per se* inconsistent with the Christian ideal (1 Ti 5[14]), so that it is hard to see on what grounds the supposed prohibition could rest.

9. The Teaching of NT.—(1) *Marriage and celibacy.* The prevalent Jewish conception was that marriage was the proper and honourable estate for all men. 'Any Jew who has not a wife is no man' (Talmud). The Essene, on the other hand, avoided it as unclean and a degradation. Of this view there is no sign in NT (1 Ti 4[3]). Christ does, however, emphasize the propriety of the unmarried state in certain circumstances (Mt 19[12] [? Rev 14[4]]). The views of St. Paul undoubtedly changed. In 1 Th 4[4] he regards marriage merely as a safeguard against immorality. The subject is prominent in 1 Corinthians. In 7[1, 7f, 38] he prefers the unmarried state, allowing marriage for the same reason as in 1 Thessalonians (1 Co 7[2, 9, 36]). He gives three reasons for his attitude, the one purely temporary, the others valid under certain conditions. (*a*) It is connected with the view he afterwards abandoned, of the nearness of the Parousia (v.[31]); there would be no need to provide for the continuance of the race. (*b*) It was a time of 'distress,' *i.e.* hardship and persecution (v.[26]). (*c*) Marriage brings distractions and cares (v.[32]). The one-sidedness of this view may be corrected by his later teaching as to (2) *the sanctity of the marriage state.* The keynote is struck by our Lord's action. The significance of the Cana miracle can hardly be exaggerated (Jn 2). It corresponds with His teaching that marriage is a Divine institution (Mt 19[9]). So Eph 5[22], Col 3[18], and the Pastoral Epistles assume the married state as normal in the Christian Church. It is raised to the highest pinnacle as the type of 'the union betwixt

Christ and His Church.' This conception emphasizes both the honourableness of the estate and the heinousness of all sins against it; husband and wife are one flesh (Eph 5; cf He 13[4]). (3) As regards *relations between husband and wife*, it cannot be said that St. Paul has entirely shaken himself free from the influences of his Jewish training (**6**). The duty of the husband is love (Eph 5[28]), of the wife obedience and fear, or reverence (v.[22, 33], Col 3[18]), the husband being the head of the wife (v.[23], 1 Co 11[3, 7-11]); she is saved 'through her childbearing' (1 Ti 2[11-15]). The view of 1 P 3[1-7] is similar. It adds the idea that each must help the other as 'joint heirs of the grace of life,' their common prayers being hindered by any misunderstanding. Whether the subordination of the wife can be maintained as ultimate may be questioned in view of such passages as Gal 3[28].

10. Spiritual applications of the Marriage Figure.—*In OT* the god was regarded as *baal*, 'husband' or 'owner,' of his land, which was the 'mother' of its inhabitants. Hence 'it lay very near to think of the god as the husband of the worshipping nationality, or mother land' (W. R. Smith, *Prophets*, 171); the idea was probably not peculiar to Israel. Its most striking development is found in Hosea. Led, as it seems, by the experience of his own married life, he emphasizes the following points. (1) Israel's idolatry is whoredom, adultery, the following of strange lovers (note the connexion of idolatry with literal fornication). (2) Y″ still loves her, as Hosea has loved his erring wife, and redeems her from slavery. (3) Hosea's own unquenchable love is but a faint shadow of Y″'s. A similar idea is found in Is 54[4]; in spite of her unfaithfulness, Israel has not been irrevocably divorced (50[1]). Cf Jer 3, 31[32], Ezk 16, Mal 2[11]. The direct spiritual or mystical application of Canticles is now generally abandoned.

In NT, Christ is the **bridegroom** (Mk 2[19], Jn 3[29]), the Church His **bride**. His love is emphasized, as in OT (Eph 5[25]), and His bride too must be holy and without blemish (v.[27], 2 Co 11[2]). In OT the stress is laid on the ingratitude and misery of sin as 'adultery,' in NT on the need of positive holiness and purity. Rev 19[7] develops the figure, the dazzling white of the bride's array being contrasted with the harlot's scarlet. In 21[2, 9] she is further identified with the New Jerusalem, two OT figures being combined, as in 2 Es 7[26]. For the coming of her Bridegroom she is now waiting (Rev 22[17], cf Mt 25[1]), and the final joy is represented under the symbol of the marriage feast (22[2], Rev 19[9]).

11. A general survey of the marriage laws and customs of the Jews shows that they cannot be regarded as a peculiar creation, apart from those of other nations. As already appears, they possess a remarkable affinity to those of other branches of the Semitic race; we may add the striking parallels found in the Code of Hammurabi, *e.g.* with regard to betrothal, dowry, and divorce. Anthropological researches have disclosed a wide general resemblance to the customs of more distant races. They have also emphasized the *relative* purity of OT sexual morality; in this, as in other respects, the Jews had their message for the world. But, of course, we shall not expect to find there the Christian standard. 'In the beginning' represents not the historical fact, but the ideal purpose. Gn 2 is an allegory of what marriage was intended to be, and of what it was understood to be in the best thought of the nation. This ideal was, however, seldom realized. Hence we cannot apply the letter of the Bible, or go to it for detailed rules. Where its rules are not obviously unsuited to modern conditions, or below the Christian level, a strange uncertainty obscures their exact interpretation, *e.g.* with regard to the prohibited degrees, divorce, or 'the husband of one wife'; there is even no direct condemnation of polygamy. On the other hand, the principle as expanded in NT is clear. It is the duty of the Christian to keep it steadily before him as the ideal of his own life. How far that ideal can be embodied in legislation and applied to the community as a whole must depend upon social conditions, and the general moral environment. C. W. E.—**J. Pn.**

MARSENA.—One of the seven princes who had the right of access to the royal presence, Est 1[14].

MARS' HILL.—See AREOPAGUS.

MARSHAL.—**1.** RV and RSV of Jg 5[14] have 'marshal.' It was the duty of this officer to muster the men available for a campaign. In later times he kept a register of their names (2 K 25[19], Jer 52[25], 2 Ch 26[11], where the same Heb. word is used; see also 1 Mac 5[42]). The staff (not 'pen') in his hand was an emblem of authority (Jg 5[14]; cf Nu 21[18]). **2.** The Hebrew *ṭiphsār* is identified with the Assyrian *dupsarru*, 'tablet-writer,' 'scribe.' In Jer 51[27] (RV, RSV 'marshal,' AV 'captain') and Nah 3[17] (RV, RSVm 'marshal'; AV 'captain,' RV 'scribe') it denotes a military official of high rank.

MART.—See MARKET.

MARTHA is mentioned in Lk 10[38-42] and in Jn 11[1-40] 12[2]. She lived with her sister Mary and, according to John, her brother Lazarus. Where they lived is not known. Luke simply says 'in a certain village' (10[38]). John identifies the village as Bethany near Jerusalem (11[18]); but Luke cannot be understood to locate them there, as Jesus is nowhere near Jerusalem at this point in his narrative. In Luke, Martha is contrasted with Mary (see MARY, **2**). She invited Jesus to her home and then was 'distracted with much serving' (10[40]), while Mary 'sat at the Lord's feet and listened to his teaching' (10[39]). It is to be noted that it was Martha, not Mary, who invited the Lord to her home; but when He came the Lord told her that while she was anxious about many things, she had need of only one thing—namely, of what Mary had chosen. It was more important for her at that moment that she cease her work for the Lord and listen to Him than that she serve Him.

In the Fourth Gospel when Jesus goes to Bethany to raise Lazarus from the dead, it is Martha who goes out to meet Him while Mary stays at home (11[20]); and it is Martha who makes the confession of faith in 11[27]. Martha is referred to for the last time in the NT as serving a meal to Jesus while Mary anointed His feet and wiped them with her hair (Jn 12[2f]). It is probable that John here reflects knowledge of some form of the story recorded in Lk 10[38ff]. B. H. T.

MARTYR.—See WITNESS.

MARY.—The Greek form of Hebrew Miriam.

1. Mary, mother of James and Joses, was one of the company of women who followed Jesus from Galilee, ministering to him, and who saw the crucifixion from afar (Mt 27[55f]). She is spoken of as 'the other Mary' (Mt 27[61] 28[1]), as 'the mother of James the younger and of Joses' (Mk 15[40]), as 'Mary the mother of Joses' (Mk 15[47]), and as 'Mary the mother of James' (Mk 16[1], Lk 24[10]). There is a question as to whether this Mary is the same as the one referred to in Jn 19[25] as 'Mary the wife of Clopas.' It is possible that 'James the son of Alphaeus' (Mk 3[18], etc.) is the James who is the son of the above Mary; in which case Alphaeus would have been the husband of this Mary. It is likewise possible that Clopas (in Jn 19[25]) is Alphaeus, the same Aramaic possibily underlying both names. (See Lightfoot, *Galatians*, p. 256; and *per contra* Schmiedel, *EBi*, article 'Clopas.')

2. Mary, the sister of Martha, is mentioned twice in the Gospels—(1) as sitting at the feet of Jesus listening to His teaching while her sister served (Lk 10[38-42]); and (2) as falling at His feet on His arrival to raise Lazarus from the grave (Jn 11[32]. See also 11[1, 19, 20, 28, 31, 33, 45]). Mary fulfils St. Paul's ideal in her 'undivided devotion to the Lord' (1 Co 7[35]). She knows what the 'good portion' is—that 'man shall not live by bread alone, but by every word that proceeds from the mouth of God' (Mt 4[4]). The Fourth Gospel identifies this Mary with the elsewhere unnamed woman who anointed Jesus (Mk 14[3-9], Mt 26[6-13], Lk 7[36-50]); but this identification is probably the work of John. Nowhere in the Synoptics is it even implied that the name of the woman was Mary.

3. Mary Magdalene, probably so called as coming

from Magdala, also known as Tarichaea, on the western side of the Sea of Galilee. She is first mentioned in Lk 8[2] as one of the women who, having been 'healed of evil spirits and infirmities . . . provided for them out of their means.' Seven demons had been cast out of her (cf Mk 16[9]), indicating, perhaps, that her affliction had been particularly serious (cf Mt 12[45], Mk 5[9]).

A questionable tradition identifies her with the unnamed sinful woman who anointed our Lord (Lk 7[37ff]); and she has thus been regarded as the typical reformed 'fallen woman.' But St. Luke, though he placed them consecutively in his narrative, did not identify them; and possession did not necessarily presuppose moral failing in the victim's character.

With the other women she accompanied Jesus on His last journey to Jerusalem; with them she beheld the crucifixion, at first 'from afar,' but afterwards standing by the Cross itself (Mt 27[55f], Jn 19[25]); she followed the body to the burial (Mk 15[47]), and then returned to prepare spices, resting on the Sabbath. On the first day of the week, while it was yet dark, she visited the sepulchre (Jn 20[1ff]). Finding the grave empty, she assumed that the body had been removed, and that she was thus deprived of the opportunity of paying her last tribute of love. She ran at once to Peter and John and said, 'They have taken the Lord out of the tomb, and we do not know where they have laid him.' They all three returned to the tomb, she remaining after the men had left. Weeping, she looked into the sepulchre, and saw two angels guarding the spot where Jesus had lain. To their question, 'Why are you weeping?' she repeated the words she had said to Peter and John. Apparently feeling that someone was standing behind her, she turned, and saw Jesus, but mistook Him for the gardener. The utterance of her name from His lips awoke her to the truth. She cried, 'Rabboni' ('my Master')—and would have clasped His feet. But Jesus forbade her, saying, 'Do not hold me; for I have not yet ascended to the Father.' She must no longer regard Him from a human point of view (2 Co 5[16]), but possess Him as a Divine being in spiritual communion. This first appearance of our Lord after His Resurrection (Mk 16[9]) conferred a special honour on one whose life of loving ministry had proved the reality and depth of her devotion.

4. Mary, the mother of Jesus.—(1) *Scripture data.*—The NT gives but little information regarding her. In the Gospels, aside from the references to her in the Infancy Narratives, she is mentioned directly only three times (Jn 2[1–12], Mk 3[31ff] and parallels in Matthew and Luke, Jn 19[25ff]), and indirectly thrice (Mk 6[3] and parallel in Matthew, Lk 11[27], Jn 6[42]). Outside the Gospels she is mentioned only once (Ac 1[14]). Thus the references to Mary are scant indeed. In Jn 19[25ff] Mary is said to have been one of four women (improbably three) who stood by the cross of Jesus; and it is here that Jesus commends Mary to the 'disciple whom he loved.' She plays in this scene only a passive rôle. In the references in Jn 2[1–12] Jesus declares His independence of His mother; and in Mk 3[31] and parallels He does the same, declaring that whoever does the will of God is His mother and brother and sister.

It is, therefore, only in the birth narratives of Matthew and Luke that Mary plays an important role in the NT. Neither Mark nor John records Jesus' birth. In Matthew the Lord's birth of a **virgin** is clearly stated, and it is said that the event took place in order that the prophecy might be fulfilled: 'Behold, a virgin shall conceive and bear a son, and his name shall be called Emmanuel' (Mt 1[23]). The reference here to birth of a virgin is based on the Greek translation of the Hebrew OT. This translation, which Matthew quotes, refers to a virgin; but the Hebrew text speaks of a 'young woman' (Is 7[14]). Elsewhere in his Gospel, however, Matthew assumes that Joseph was Jesus' father—as, for example, in his tracing of Jesus' genealogy (q.v.) back through Joseph (1[16]), and in the reference to Jesus as the 'carpenter's son' (13[55]).

Luke has only two references to Jesus as born of a virgin, one of which appears to be a gloss. The latter is found in 3[23], being the words 'as was supposed.' The insertion of these words makes the ensuing genealogy irrelevant and meaningless. The other Lucan reference to the Virgin Birth is in the question Mary addresses to the angel, 'How can this be, since I have no husband?' And the angel answers that the Holy Spirit will come upon her (1[34f]). Elsewhere, however, Luke speaks of Jesus' 'parents' (2[27]) and of Jesus' 'father' (2[33]). He also traced Jesus' genealogy back through Joseph (3[23]).

The significance of Jesus' birth of a virgin lies in its uniqueness and its predestined character. The understanding of Jesus as a pre-existent being (cf Ph 2[6]) points in the same direction, the end of which is to be seen in the Logos Christology of the Prologue to the Fourth Gospel. The doctrine of the Virgin Birth is not a proved miracle; it is understandable only by faith.

(2) *Place of the Virgin in the Christian Church.*—As early as the 4th cent., Epiphanius (*c* A.D. 374–377) rebuked heretics, called Collyridians, who worshipped the Virgin; soon thereafter the error found a welcome in the Church, and was heightened at the time of the Nestorian controversy (A.D. 431). In repudiating the views of Nestorius the Church insisted that our Lord had only one personality, and *that* Divine; it therefore emphasized the fact that He who was born of the Virgin was very God. It thus became the custom to give Mary the title *Theotokos* (bearer of God). The emphasis was on the divinity of Christ and not on the nature of Mary. The Church did not at this time call her 'mother of God.' Later the title was applied to her, as her worship increased.

With the worship of Mary arose a belief in her sinlessness. Finally, in the last century, her freedom from all taint of sin, whether original or actual, was officially declared an article of faith in the Roman Church by the dogma of the Immaculate Conception decreed by Pius IX in 1854. In 1950 Pius XII proclaimed the doctrine of the Assumption of Mary—viz. that after Mary's death her body was taken into heaven.

(3) *The perpetual Virginity of Mary* is an essential dogma of the Roman Catholic and Greek Churches. The main arguments in favour of the dogma are doctrinal. Militating against Mary's perpetual virginity are the references in the Gospels (*e.g.* Mk 3[32]) to Jesus' brothers (see BRETHREN, *of the Lord*). Epiphanius' view, held by many in the early church, was that these 'brothers' were children of Joseph by a former marriage. Jerome's view was that they were cousins. But the Greek language had a word for 'cousin' (cf Col 4[10]), and these brothers in the Gospels are associated with Jesus' mother. A further objection to the dogma is the implication of such passages as 'He knew her not *until* she had borne a son' (Mt 1[25]) and 'She gave birth to her *first*-born son' (Lk 2[7]). Such expressions as these would hardly have been used by writers who assumed Mary's perpetual virginity.

5. Mary, the mother of John Mark (Ac 12[12]).

6. Mary, saluted by St. Paul (Ro 16[6]). B. H. T.

MASCHIL.—AV and RV form of **Maskil.** See PSALMS, **2.**

MASH.—One of the sons of Aram, Gn 10[23]. The parallel passage, 1 Ch 1[17], gives **Meshech** (q.v.), as also does LXX in both passages. But this is wrong, as Meshech was Japhetic. Either Mons Massius is meant, or a region and people in the Syro-Arabian desert corresponding to the 'desert of Mash' of the Assyrian inscriptions. J. F. McC.

MASHAL.—See MISHAL.

MASIAH.—One of Solomon's servants, 1 Es 5[34] (AV, RV **Masias**); the name is missing from the parallel list in Ezra.

MASIAS, 1 Es 5[34] (AV, RV).—See MASIAH.

MASKIL.—See PSALMS, **2.**

MASMAN, 1 Es 8[43] (AV).—See MAASMAS.

MASON.—See ARTS AND CRAFTS, **3.**

MASPHA, 1 Mac 3[46] (AV).—See MIZPAH, **6.**

MASREKAH.—Mentioned as the home of an Edomite king, Samlah, Gn 36[36], 1 Ch 1[47]. The locality has not been identified.

MASSA.—A son of Ishmael, representing a N. Arabian tribe, Gn 25[14], 1 Ch 1[30]. Its exact location is unknown, but it seems to be mentioned in an inscription containing a report to king Ashurbanipal of Assyria (668–626 B.C.) of an attack made by the Massorites upon the people of **Nebaioth** (q.v.). The tribe of Massa would therefore seem to have lived not very far E. of Palestine. This view is confirmed by the fact that Pr 30 is ascribed to Agur, king of Massa (RVm, RSV), and Pr 31[1–10] to Lemuel, king of Massa (RVm, RSV), since Pr 30 and 31 belong to the borderland wisdom of Israel. J. F. McC.

MASSAH AND MERIBAH.—Ex 17[1–7] tells of a miraculous gift of water at a spot near Horeb, which was called *Massah* and *Meribah* (' testing ' and ' contention ') because the people tested Yahweh by doubting His providence and contended with Moses. 19[1] states this occurred within three months of the Exodus. Nu 20[1–13] tells a similar story, but puts the event some forty years later and locates it at Kadesh, which receives the name *Meribah* from the contention of Israel with Yahweh; it also tells of the sin of Moses and Aaron because of which they were not allowed to enter the Promised Land. There are references to the first passage in Dt 6[18] 9[22], Ps 81[7] 95[8]; and to the second in Nu 27[14], Dt 32[51], Ps 106[32]. The two stories are variants of a tradition associated with Kadesh (cf Meribath-kadesh Dt 32[51], Ezk 47[19] 48[28]), in the vicinity of which is a spring (*'Ain Qudeirāt*) bursting from a rock. Another, older, variant is echoed in Dt 33[8]: Yahweh proved (tested) Levi (=the priesthood) at *Massah* and strove with him at *Meribah*, giving him the sacred oracle, the Urim and Thummim. This suggests that *Meribah* originally meant the place of judgment (cf En-mishpat= Kadesh, Gn 14[7]), where Moses, priest and judge, delivered his oracular sentences and forged the tribes of the Exodus into a strong unity.

Massah stands alone in Dt 6[16] 9[22]; and it has been cogently argued that the reference in the tradition fragmentarily preserved in Ex 15[25b] was originally to *Massah* (not Marah) as the place where Yahweh proved Israel. These three passages suggest that the *Massah* legend may once have existed independently of that of *Meribah*. J. T.—**C. A. Si.**

MASSIAS, 1 Es 9[22] (AV, RV).—See MAASEIAH, **3.**

MASSORAH.—See TEXT OF OT.

MAST.—See SHIPS AND BOATS.

MASTER.—The Greek word for teacher is translated in AV as ' master ' in 2 Mac 1[10], Ja 3[1], and in all its occurrences in the Gospels except Lk 2[46], where it is ' doctor,' and Jn 3[2] ' teacher.' RSV prefers ' teacher.'

MASTIC.—Hebrew *ṣ^erî*, Gn 37[25] EV ' balm ' (q.v.), RVm ' mastic '; Greek *schinos*, Sus [54] (RSV ' mastic'; AV, RV ' mastick '). A dioecious shrub (the *pistacia lentiscus* L.) found in thickets on the Mediterranean seaboard. The gum obtained through cuttings in the bark is chewed as a dentifrice, and also for its pleasant taste and perfume. It is sometimes used as a flavouring by confectioners. W. E.

MATHANIAS, 1 Es 9[31] (AV).—See MATTANIAH, **6.**

MATHELAS, 1 Es 9[19] (RV).—See MAASEIAH, **1.**

MATHUSALA, Lk 3[37] (AV).—See METHUSELAH.

MATRED.—The mother-in-law (?) of Hadar (Genesis) or Hadad (Chronicles), one of the kings of Edom, Gn 36[39], 1 Ch 1[50]. In Genesis the LXX and Peshitta make Matred the *son* not the *daughter* of Me-zahab (q.v.).

MATRI, 1 S 10[21] (AV).—See MATRITES.

MATRITES.—A family of the tribe of Benjamin to which Saul belonged, 1 S 10[21] (AV **Matri**).

MATTAN.—**1.** Priest of Baal, 2 K 11[18], 2 Ch 23[17]. **2.** Father of Shephatiah, a contemporary of Jeremiah, Jer 38[1].

MATTANAH.—A stopping-place on the wanderings, Nu 21[18f]. The site is unknown.

MATTANIAH.—**1.** The original name of king Zedekiah, 2 K 24[17]. **2.** An Asaphite, 1 Ch 9[15]. He was the leader of the Temple choir, Neh 11[17, 22] 12[8], also a door-keeper, 12[25, 35]. **3.** Mattaniah in 2 Ch 20[14] should probably be identified with the preceding. **4. 5. 6. 7.** Four of those who had married foreign wives, Ezr 10[26], 1 Es 9[27] (AV **Matthanias**); Ezr 10[27] (called **Othoniah** in 1 Es 9[28] [AV, RV **Othonias**]); Ezr 10[30] (called **Bescaspasmys** in 1 Es 9[31] [AV **Mathanias**, RV **Matthanias**]); Ezr 10[57] (combined in 1 Es 9[34] with the following Mattenai into **Mamnitanemus** so RV; RSV **Machnadebai**, q.v.). **8.** A Levite who had charge of the offerings, Neh 13[13]. **9.** A Hemanite, 1 Ch 25[4, 16]. **10.** An Asaphite, 2 Ch 29[13].

MATTATHA.—An ancestor of Jesus, Lk 3[31].

MATTATHIAH.—See MATTITHIAH, **5.**

MATTATHIAS.—**1.** 1 Es 9[43] (AV, RV); see MATTITHIAH, **5. 2.** 1 Es 9[23] (RV); see MATTATTAH. **3.** The father of the five Maccabaean brothers, 1 Mac 2[1, 14, 16f, 19, 24, 27, 39, 45, 49] 14[29]; see MACCABEES, **1. 4.** A captain in the army of Jonathan the Maccabaean, 1 Mac 11[70]. **5.** A son of Simon the high priest, who was murdered, together with his father and brother Judas, at a banquet at Dok, by Ptolemy the son of Abubus, 1 Mac 16[14–16]. **6.** One of three envoys sent by Nicanor to treat with Judas Maccabaeus, 2 Mac 14[19]. **7. 8.** Two ancestors of Jesus, Lk 3[25f].

MATTATTAH.—A Jew who had married a foreign wife, Ezr 10[33], 1 Es 9[33] (AV **Matthias**, RV **Mattathias**).

MATTHAN.—Grandfather of Joseph (Mt 1[15]); perhaps to be identified with *Matthat*, who occupies the same place in Lk 3[24].

MATTHANIAS.—**1.** 1 Es 9[27] (AV, RV); see MATTANIAH, **4. 2.** 1 Es 9[31] (RV); see MATTANIAH, **6.**

MATTHAT.—**1.** See MATTHAN. **2.** Another ancestor of Jesus (Lk 3[29]).

MATTENAI.—**1. 2.** Two of those who had married foreign wives, Ezr 10[33], 1 Es 9[33] (AV **Altaneus**, RV **Maltanneus**) [37] (combined in 1 Es 9[34] with the preceding Mattaniah to form **Mamnitanemus**, q.v.). **3.** Representative of the priestly house of Joiarib in the days of Joiakim, Neh 12[19].

MATTHELAS, 1 Es 9[19] (AV).—See MAASEIAH, **1.**

MATTHEW (APOSTLE).—Two sets of parallel passages, probably from a Petrine tradition, tell us of this chosen companion of our Lord. The first (Mt 9[9], Mk 2[14], Lk 5[27]) narrates his call. He was named both ' Matthew ' (Mt) and **' Levi '** (Mk [where some Western MSS read ' James '] and Lk), and was the son of Alphaeus (Mk). He was a publican (Lk), and was ' sitting at the tax office ' (Mt, Mk, Lk) near Capernaum, which lay on the road from Damascus to the Mediterranean; here he collected dues for Herod the tetrarch. No doubt he was only an agent, not one of the wealthy farmers of the taxes. Nevertheless he must have been fairly rich, and had much to give up in following Jesus. The call is followed by a meal (Mt, Mk), a great feast given to Jesus by Matthew himself (Lk), which roused the anger of the ' scribes of the Pharisees.' The name ' Matthew ' probably means ' Gift of Yahweh ' (cf ' Theodore '), and is another form of ' Matthias '; though some take it as meaning ' strong,' ' manly.' It was doubtless given to Levi as an additional name, perhaps (like ' Peter ') by Jesus Himself.

The second set of passages gives the list of the Twelve (Mt 10[3], Mk 3[18], Lk 6[15], Ac 1[13]). In all these the surname ' Matthew ' is given, not ' Levi,' just as ' Bartholomew ' and ' Thomas ' are surnames; and in all four Bartholomew, Matthew, Thomas, and James the (son) of Alphaeus are mentioned together, though not always in the same order. In two lists (Mt, Ac) Matthew comes next to James (though they are not joined together as a pair); in the other two, next but one. If then we take the

MATTHEW, GOSPEL ACCORDING TO

view that this James is neither the brother of our Lord, nor yet the same as James the Little (Mk 15[40]), and if we negative the idea that 'Alphaeus' (Aram. *Ḥalphai*) and 'Clopas' are one name, there is perhaps something to be said for the opinion that Matthew and James were brothers. But they are not mentioned together elsewhere. Only in the Mt list is the designation 'the publican' added. For Matthew's connexion with the First Gospel, see the next article. We have no trustworthy information as to his later career. He is probably mentioned under the name Mattai in the Babylonian Talmud, *Sanhedrin* 43a. A. J. M.—**W. D. D.**

MATTHEW, GOSPEL ACCORDING TO.—1. The First Gospel in the Early Church.—Papias (*c* A.D. 140 or earlier), as quoted by Eusebius (*HE* iii. 39), says: 'Matthew, however, composed the *logia* in the Hebrew dialect, but each one interpreted them as he was able.' This remark occurs in his work *The Exposition of the Lord's Logia*, and is practically all the external information that we have about the Matthaean Gospel, except that Irenaeus says: 'Matthew among the Hebrews published a Gospel in their own dialect, when Peter and Paul were preaching in Rome and founding the Church' (*Haer.* iii. 1). Irenaeus is probably quoting from Papias. In the 4th cent. Eusebius tells a story of Pantaenus finding in the 2nd cent. the original Aramaic Matthew in India, but the story is very uncertain; Epiphanius says that the Aramaic Gospel of Matthew existed in his day in the possession of an Ebionite sect (distinguished in modern times as Elkasites) and describes it; and Jerome describes what he alleges to be the original of Matthew as in use among the Nazarenes, and says that he translated it into Greek. We have, therefore, first to interpret Papias and then to relate what he says to the later testimonies.

(*a*) *What does Papias mean by the logia?*—Two views have been held. First, that the term means 'oracles' and that it refers to OT prophecies of the Coming One, a collection of which was embedded in Matthew. Papias would not have confused *logia* (oracles) with *logoi* (sayings). The inclusion of this collection by Matthew in the Gospel explains the ascription of the latter to Matthew. This is the view favoured by F. C. Grant (in *The Gospels, Their Origins and Their Growth*, 1957) who claims for it the support of Eusebius §14 where the *logia Kyriaka*, the subject of Papias' exegesis (§1), are described as the oracles of the Lord, precisely as in the OT prophets. Secondly, by the term *logia* it is claimed that Papias here simply means our canonical Matthew. Two explanations of this are given. According to some (Westcott, Lightfoot, Donovan) *logia* is an early word for the Gospels so that Papias would naturally use it in this sense. Bacon, who regards Papias' references as pure guess-work, explained the choice of the term *logia* as an attempt to describe the Gospel in terms of its important contents, *i.e.* of the five great discourses incorporated in it. T. W. Manson rejects this, on the ground that Eusebius would hardly have troubled to quote Papias, of whose intelligence he had a low opinion, had he not thought that he was transmitting a tradition of value. He insists, therefore, that while Papias himself in using the term *logia* was thinking of the canonical Gospel, this was due to a confusion on his part. In the tradition that he had received, the term *logia*, referring to a work written by the Apostle Matthew, had reference not to the canonical Gospel but to an element which came to be incorporated in it, namely, Q, mainly a collection of the teaching of Jesus. T. W. Manson thus renewed a view urged earlier by Schleiermacher and Meyer. The term *logia*, as Grant has urged, is best translated by 'oracles,' but here refers to oracles of Jesus; and all that Papias notes concerning the *logia* fits what we know of Q, while it does not suit our canonical Matthew. Thus the latter cannot have originally been written in Hebrew because it incorporated a Greek document, Mark, and used the LXX. And only by a *tour de force* can the Gospel as a whole be characterized as *logia*. Though it contains *logia*, this does not constitute it as *the logia*, and its dependence on Mark makes it very improbable that it is the work of the Apostle Matthew. On the other hand, Q is a collection of *logia* probably written in Aramaic, Matthew and Luke having used different versions of it. There is no reason against its ascription to Matthew.

The view is tempting, therefore, that Papias had a tradition about a work by Matthew in Aramaic which he wrongly took to be the Gospel. This mistake of Papias may be the ground for other statements to the effect that there was an original Matthew in Hebrew and it was itself made plausible by the existence in Palestine, in that period, of information about a document or documents actually existing in a Semitic tongue and bearing a more or less close resemblance to our Matthew (Irenaeus, *Haer.* I. xxii, ed. by Harvey, i, p. 213); Eusebius, *HE* iii. 27. This view of Manson's is shared by Sherman Johnson.

Kilpatrick, on the other hand, rejects attempts to account for the ascription of the Gospel to Matthew in terms of its incorporation of Q, composed by Matthew or of Testimonia by him. The hypothesis of a translation of the original Matthew he thinks is due to the desire to meet objections to the apostolic authorship of the Gospel as it stood. These may have been due to knowledge that existed as to how the Gospel actually came into being. But this fails to exploit possibilities suggested by the existence of translations of the canonical Matthew. The views of Grant and Manson would seem best to meet the facts of the case and we are inclined, on the whole, to the position of the latter (so too S. E. Johnson, Wikenhauser) Grant's position demands the assumption that Papias did not know of the existence of a Gospel according to St. Matthew in the 2nd cent., though he knew of a testimony book of that title; but the probability is that the tradition of Matthaean authorship arose at least by *c* A.D. 125. Quotations from Matthew are found in the Epistle of 'Barnabas' (*c* A.D. 100?), one with the formula 'as it is written.'

There was a 'Gospel of the Hebrews' also current in the 2nd cent., known to Hegesippus, probably to the writer of the *Clementine Homilies*, perhaps to Ignatius. Jerome knew of it and gives extracts from it; and Epiphanius knew of a derived or kindred Gospel, used by the sect of the Nazarenes and containing several episodes different from our canonical narrative, *e.g.* in connexion with our Lord's baptism, and His appearance to James after the Resurrection (cf 1 Cor 15[7]). In this Gospel the Holy Spirit is called the 'Mother' of Christ, the word 'Spirit' being feminine in Aramaic. Most critics agree that this Gospel is later than our canonical four, and there are good reasons for deriving it directly from our canonical Matthew. Bacon regarded it as a targum of the latter. We have seen that the presence of such targums or translations of the canonical Matthew would help to explain the references in Papias.

2. Sources and characteristics of the Gospel.—The sources upon which Matthew drew for his work are the following. First, he takes over almost the whole of Mark. This is surprising because the point of view of Mark on crucial terms, *e.g.* the Law, is not that of Matthew (compare Mk 7[1-23] and Mt 15[1-20]). The way in which he uses Mark, conflating it freely with material he uses from other sources (see the alternation of Q and Markan material in ch. 12) shows that Matthew had long been familiar with Mark so that he could use it from memory. Grant suggests a familiarity of twenty years or so. There was free intercourse between Rome and Palestine or Syria where Matthew probably is to be located, and Mark was evidently regarded with profound respect because Matthew not only uses his material but also largely follows his order. Secondly, as we saw in Mt 12, Matthew has combined Markan material with Q, a collection of the teaching of Jesus with which he was probably familiar in his Church. Thirdly, he has drawn upon material which is peculiar to him. This material was possibly a document because it reveals a definite structure. Perry has shown that if we remove the Q material from the Sermon on the Mount the remainder gives (1) seven beatitudes 5[3-10]; (2) three contrasts between the Law and the new ethic of Jesus 5[17-20, 21-24, 27-30, 33-37]; (3)

three contrasts between ostentation and the new piety, introduced $6^{1-4, 5-8, 16-18}$. In addition, Matthew has drawn upon tradition probably from a Northern Palestinian or Syrian Church. F. C. Grant has isolated the following elements in this: (1) Christian Midrashic Haggadah (Mt 1–2, 14^{28-31} 16^{17-19} 17^{24-27} 27^{3-10}); (2) Christian exegesis and homiletics (*e.g.* $3^{14, 15}$ 12^{5-7} 13^{36-43}); (3) Material of a codal kind (cf the *Didache*; see the Sermon on the Mount, 10^{41} 18^{18} 19^{10-12} $23^{2f, 8-10}$); (4) early liturgical material probably underlies 6^{7-13} 11^{25-30} 18^{19-20} 28^{18-20}; (5) Apocalyptic material (*e.g.* 13^{24-30} 20^{1-16} 22^{1-14} 25 *passim*); (6) Apocryphal material $27^{19, 24f, 51b-53, 62-66}$ $28^{2-5, 11-15}$; (7) it is also possible that Matthew had a collection of OT passages or testimonia: the OT is adduced to explain certain events, and had influenced the tradition itself. (See especially the Birth and Passion Narratives.) How much of the above material Matthew found already in *written* form and how much of it he himself first put into writing must remain doubtful; but two factors are clear, first, that liturgical elements have strongly entered Matthew (though it cannot be regarded as a lectionary) and, secondly, that a Christian tradition of exegesis lies behind Matthew. Stendahl in his work *The School of Matthew* (1954) has indeed argued that Matthew is the product of a school of exegesis very similar to that revealed in the Dead Sea Scrolls: he does this on the basis of the so-called formula-quotations in Matthew. Not all, however, have been convinced that these reveal a use of Scripture either essentially like that of Qumrân or essentially peculiar to Matthew in the NT.

The characteristics of Matthew are chiefly, first, to use a loose term, its Jewishness. Even while Matthew presents attacks against Judaism (23), it also upholds the tradition of Judaism (5^{18} $23^{1f, 23}$); the themes that interest Matthew are the law, the Messiah, fulfilment of prophecy. But though this would suggest that Matthew stands over against Paul, some having found in 5^{19} a cryptic attack on that Apostle, this is probably not the case. (2) Coexisting with the 'Jewishness' of Matthew is its universalism: and it has been possible to claim that 'the assurance that the gentiles have displaced the Jews is the basic message and the gentile bias of Matthew' (K. W. Clark, *JBL* lxvi, 1947, p. 172). (See 8^{12} 12^{21} 21^{43} 28^{16-20}; see also $21^{28, 32, 33-43}$ 25^{1-13}). While this is to go too far, the ambiguity of Matthew must be fully recognized. (3) Matthew is the 'ecclesiastical gospel.' The Church is the 'new Israel' within the larger body of Jewry, but destined also to include the Gentiles. Expected to maintain the Law and go beyond its demands as they have been fulfilled in Christ, it has developed a discipline (Mt 18^{13ff}). The ecclesiastical interests of Matthew emerge in 9^{35}–10^{42} 16^{17-19} 17^{24}–18^{35}. (4) The interest of Matthew in the true interpretation of the will of God, *i.e.* in ethics, appears not only in the Sermon on the Mount, but elsewhere in his attempts at the application of the teaching of Jesus to life. While Matthew does not transform the gospel into a code of rules he does represent a casuistic interest. (5) Along with this we find a thoroughly apocalyptic–eschatological emphasis ($24^{12, 23f}$), which has led some to connect it specifically with the period at the beginning of the 2nd cent. when, culminating in the Bar Cochba revolt there was a heightened apocalyptic messianism (*e.g.* F. C. Grant).

3. The Purpose of the Gospel.—This has been variously understood. Matthew's catechetical traits have led some to regard it as a catechism for the use of members who had joined the Church; others have seen in it a Christian Manual of Discipline. Still others emphasize it as designed for liturgical purposes in the Church. But although there are catechetical, liturgical, and 'disciplinary' motifs in Matthew these are secondary. Are we to find in the Gospel primarily an appeal to the Jewish nation either after the disaster of A.D. 70 or before that of A.D. 135? This would explain the emphasis on 'peace,' but is hardly enough to illumine the whole purpose of Matthew. The same is true of the view, despite the element of truth that it contains, that Matthew's basic message is that the Gentiles have displaced the Jews as the chosen people. Matthew's central concern lies elsewhere. Jesus is for Matthew the Messiah and the Son of Man, but He has also become for him the Lord of the Church, His people. He has fulfilled the purpose of Judaism and become the living Lord of the New Israel, the worshipping Church. It is the illumination of Jesus as Lord of His community that Matthew has in mind, in their relation to the Law, Jesus being the new Moses of the new Sinai, and in relation to the world, His mission being henceforth to the Gentiles. Matthew is a gospel from a Church to a Church which asserts that in Jesus of Nazareth, Messiah, Son of Man, God is with us (1^{23} 28^{20}). But Jesus is all this as the Suffering Servant, who Himself was obedient and calls the Church to the same obedience. To expound all this to the Church is the purpose of Matthew.

4. Date and Place of Origin.—Attempts at dating Matthew, in Protestant scholarship, have been governed by the assumption that Matthew utilized Mark and is therefore to be dated after that Gospel. Since Mark is seldom dated before A.D. 65 (sometimes 70) Matthew has to be placed at least after this. The first piece of secure external evidence for the use of the Gospel occurs in Ignatius, so that Matthew can fall somewhere between A.D. 65 and 115. The following are the main arguments variously expressed which have been usually used to fix the Gospel in the last decade of the century.

(1) Mt 22^{7} points to a date after the Fall of Jerusalem in A.D. 70: 11^{12} 27^{8} 28^{15} also suggest some lapse of time since the days of Jesus.

(2) The conditions of Church life reflected in Matthew, namely, world persecution (24^{9}), dissension (24^{16}), the presence of false prophets (24^{11}), the lovelessness of Christians (24^{12}), a developed Church order and interest in the same, see 16^{19} 18^{17f}, and the increased reverence paid to the apostles 8^{26} 13^{16} 14^{33} 16^{9} $17^{4, 9, 23}$ (cf their Markan parallels), and the simultaneous rise of false Christian prophets $7^{15, 22}$. These conditions, it is claimed, point to a time not far removed from that which produced the book of Revelation, Clement, and the Pastorals.

(3) The external conditions—persecution 10^{22} 24^{9ff}—where Matthew is at pains to emphasize that hatred will be shown by all the Gentiles. But there is even more emphasis on false teaching than on persecution; this, according to Bacon, points to the later period of the reign of Domitian; documents from its earlier period reflect more preoccupation with persecution than with false teaching.

(4) The renewed emphasis on eschatology so widely noticed in Matthew suggests a time when the first expectations of the immediate return of the Son of Man had languished and had consequently to be revived: apocalyptic fervour to convince the faithful that though He tarried He would yet come is the mark of a late date. See 24^{37-51} 25^{1-12} 26^{13}. F. C. Grant emphasizes this reason for an early 2nd cent. date.

G. D. Kilpatrick—in this he was anticipated by von Dobschütz—shows anxiety to relate Matthew to Jamnia, and, apparently in this interest, insists that Mark reflects Palestinian conditions before A.D. 70, Matthew those after (*The Origins of the Gospel according to St. Matthew*, 1946). The Pharisees in Matthew have emerged as the significant group in Judaism, the Sadducees and other parties are overshadowed; the discussion of legal questions recalls those in the Mishnah; the niceties of the schools are introduced into them, *e.g.* the discussions of divorce and of the Sabbath; and it is significant that circumcision is a dead issue to Matthew. The use of 'their' in certain contexts in Matthew points to the exclusion of Christians from Jewish synagogues and Kilpatrick traces the impact on the Gospel of the *Birkath ham-Minim* in the Shemoneh Esreh. All in all he finds reflected in Matthew the late 1st cent. when Judaism and Christianity were consciously going their separate ways. Kilpatrick has thus added to the more general considerations advanced by Bacon and others for a date in the last decade of the 1st cent. and more specific considerations connecting Matthew with that decade through Jamnia.

Nevertheless not all have thought such a late date necessary. Allen found it impossible to date it much after A.D. 70. He takes 24^{29} to refer to events which are to follow immediately upon the Fall of Jerusalem: Paul's arrival at Rome was the fulfilment for Matthew of the ' preaching in all the world ' as a testimony to all nations. And this points to a period before A.D. 75. The ecclesiasticism of Matthew does not, he thinks, demand any later date. Nor does he seem to be in error here. Those passages which are cited as revealing a developed and therefore late ecclesiasticism would seem to be derived from regulations which were apparently commonly utilized among sectarian movements in Judaism: here the evidence of the Dead Sea Scrolls may be decisive. The points raised by Kilpatrick, used it would seem in anxiety to pin down the Gospel to the Rabbinical activity of the last decade, are all questionable. Thus his claim that the Sadduccees have ceased to be a party when Matthew was written is surely mistaken; discussions of divorce such as are recorded in Matthew took place before the Fall of Jerusalem and need not be taken to reflect Jamnia. T. W. Manson accordingly prefers a date between A.D. 70–80; so too Michaelis. Streeter (*The Four Gospels*, 1924) placed Matthew at about A.D. 85, and it is probable that such a date is to be accepted. Roman Catholic scholars have persisted in regarding Matthew as the first of the Gospels: this claim has been forcibly reiterated by Butler, in *The Originality of St. Matthew*.

Efforts to find the place where Matthew originated have been equally indecisive. Attempts to pin it down to Alexandria are to be dismissed outright because they flaunt all historical probability. The choice would appear to be somewhere in Palestine or Syria. Michaelis favoured Palestine and so too Schlatter, Allen, Schniewind. R. Bultmann, although he does not directly discuss the origin of Matthew, would seem to favour a Palestinian Jewish Christian milieu. The reasons which have led to this position can be broadly summarized thus: (1) The Gospel is concerned with carrying on an *Auseinandersetzung* with Judaism and thus suggests a Palestinian milieu; (2) the Greek of the Gospel points to a strong Semitic influence; (3) the audience addressed seems to be composed of Palestinian Jews; thus Jewish customs are referred to without explanation (15^{2} 23^{27}); so, too, Jewish dress (9^{20} 23^{5}); and a Jewish Christian religious practice and piety are presupposed (5^{20} 10^{5} 15^{24} 23^{3} 24^{20}). Moreover, the external evidence connects the Gospel with an eastern Jewish milieu. Papias, who is our earliest certain external attestation for Matthew, took Matthew to have been written in Hebrew or Aramaic (Eusebius, *HE* iii. 39).

On the other hand, there are elements in Matthew which have been claimed to point to Syria. Arguing that the Gospel was originally compiled for the use of a Great Church, Streeter in particular chose Antioch (Rome and Ephesus are ruled out by the external evidence) as its place of origin. This would explain the extraordinary interest shown by the author in Peter; because Antioch had followed Peter in adopting a *via media* between the Christianity of James and that of Paul. In addition it might well be the home of such haggadic expansions of Mark as we find in Matthew, and of its intermingling of Jewish and Gentile Christianity. An interesting detail seems to confirm all this, namely, that the *statēr* equalled two didrachmas only in Antioch and Damascus, according to Streeter; see Mt 17$^{24-27}$. Moreover, the external evidence points to Antioch. Ignatius Bishop of Antioch (*c* A.D. 115), shows most familiarity with Matthew, and so too does the *Didache* which Streeter dated about A.D. 100, and located in Syria. B. W. Bacon (*Studies in Matthew*, 1930) equally, like A. H. McNeile, admitted that the author of Matthew was remote from Palestine: he found indications of this in 7^{29} 9^{35} 11^{1} 13^{54}, where the use of ' their ' in referring to Jewish scribes, synagogues, and cities in these places is significant; so too the use of ' that ' in 9$^{26, 31}$ 14^{35}. The use of the term Canaanite in 15^{22} points to Syria, and the way in which reference is made in 27^{8} to the field bought for thirty pieces of silver points to an extra-Palestinian origin, as do the references to the Jews in 28^{15} and the vagueness of geographical references in 5^{1} 8^{28} 14^{35} 15$^{29, 39}$ 28^{16}. But Bacon further rejected Streeter's reasons for tying Matthew specifically to Antioch. This was the place of its dissemination, not of its composition. According to Bacon, Matthew came to Antioch from some eastern locality of mixed Aramaic and Greek speech, possibly Edessa. Streeter maintained that the authorship was ascribed to Matthew probably because the author of the Gospel knew that one of his sources was the work of the Apostle Matthew; the incorporation of a document written by Matthew would account for the ascription of the whole Gospel to Matthew. Bacon, on the other hand, regarded the title as given to distinguish this Gospel from other Gospels which were circulating in Antioch. Later on it was ' sponsored ' not only by Antioch but by Churches in Phrygia, Asia, and Rome: it was not the Gospel of the Antiochian Church in any peculiar sense. The evidence of Ignatius is not as clear as Streeter made out; his quotations from Matthew are very few and chiefly from 1^{18}–2^{12}. Ignatius has legendary material alien to Matthew; and in his discussion of the resurrection of the flesh, to which Matthew lends itself, he ignores Matthew. So, too, the *Didache* is later than Streeter allows, so that he cannot allow earlier testimony to Matthew than Ignatius. Bacon urges that we are to connect Luke–Acts with Antioch rather than Matthew. At the same time by making Antioch the second stage in the history of Matthew he preserves the advantages of Streeter's theory and avoids its difficulties.

The attack on Antioch as the place of origin has been carried still further by Kilpatrick (*The Origins of the Gospel according to St. Matthew*, 1946). However, he first of all allows full weight to the claims of Antioch as they are advanced by Streeter and others and indeed he introduces new factors in its favour—Antioch was near enough to the centre of Judaism to feel the effect of measures taken against Christianity, which Kilpatrick finds echoed in Matthew; the absence of parallels to Philo in Matthew, such as are found in John, may be due to the independence of thought which was always characteristic of Antioch. But there is a debit side. If Ignatius was Bishop of Antioch when Matthew was written, he shows no trace of the strong Jewish influence which is so prominent in Matthew. The importance of Peter in Antioch does not indicate that he need not also have been important in other areas, such for example as the Syrian ports. Indeed Ac 11$^{19-26}$ is against ascribing too much importance to Peter at Antioch: Peter was called, according to Gal 2^{8}, to be minister of the circumcision, whereas Antioch was the centre of the Gentile mission. This would, according to Kilpatrick, bring Peter and Matthew together and separate them both from Antioch. Kilpatrick is particularly concerned with gaining recognition for the fact that Matthew ' originated in a community in close contact with the Judaism of Jamnia,' and because this would be more true of a city like Tyre than of Antioch he prefers to place the origin of Matthew in the former or in some such Phoenician city; but the arguments by which he supports this view are not always convincing. It would seem that, on the whole, we can only pin Matthew to somewhere in Syria. Thus Kilpatrick holds that Matthew reserves the term *thalassa* for the Mediterranean, a fact which would suggest the Phoenician seaboard. But it is doubtful if his thesis can be maintained. W. D. D.

MATTHEW'S BIBLE.—See English Versions, 20.

MATTHIAS.—1. The disciple chosen by Lot (Ac 1$^{24-26}$) to take the place of the traitor Judas. The name, a shortened form of Mattathias, means ' gift of Yahweh.' Apart from the fact that he was one of the original group of disciples during Jesus' ministry, there is no reliable tradition about him. Clement of Alexandria identifies him with Zacchaeus, the Clementine Recognitions with Barnabas, and legend makes him an apostle to the Ethiopians and a compiler of 'Traditions' (a Gospel?). From this work Clement quotes the interesting saying, 'If an elect man's neighbour sin, the elect man has sinned.'

Modern criticism of the method of selection (by lot) is beside the point. Resort to the lot was an established Hebrew custom. **2.** 1 Es 9[33] (AV); see MATTATTAH.

J. L.

MATTITHIAH.—**1.** One of the sons of Nebo who had married a foreign wife, Ezr 10[43], 1 Es 9[35] (AV, RV **Mazitias**). **2.** A Korahite Levite, 1 Ch 9[31]. **3.** A Levite of the guild of Jeduthun, 1 Ch 15[18, 21] 25[3, 21]. **4.** An Asaphite Levite, 1 Ch 16[5]. **5.** One who stood at the right hand of Ezra during the reading of the Law, Neh 8[4]; called **Mattathiah** in 1 Es 9[43] (AV RV **Mattathias**).

MATTOCK.—The mattock of Is 7[25] (AV, RV) is rather the **hoe** (so RSV) with which land inaccessible to the plough was hoed—noun and verb being the same here, 5[6] RV and RSV 'hoed' for AV 'digged.' For descriptions and illustrations of the triangular hoe and the mattock, or pick, of modern Palestine, see *PEFSt*, 1901, p. 110f, and Hastings' *DB* iii, 306. The passage 1 S 13[20f] is very corrupt, and in v.[20] at least 'mattock' (AV, RV) should probably be 'goad' (but RSV 'sickle'). 2 Ch 34[6], where AV has 'mattocks' and AVm 'mauls,' is also corrupt, and RV and RSV read 'ruins.'

A. R. S. K.

MAUL.—See CLUB, **2**, and ARMOUR AND ARMS, **1** (*f*).

MAUZZIM.—The Hebrew phrase *'elōah mā'uzzîm* in Dn 11[38] (AVm 'God of Mauzzim') has been variously understood. RV and RSV translate 'god of fortresses,' and 'fortresses' for *mā'uzzîm* again in v.[39]. It is not so easy to decide which god is intended. Antiochus Epiphanes is the king referred to. He had begun to build a temple to Jupiter Capitolinus in Antioch (Livy, xli. 20). It has therefore been held that he is the god meant. But Antiochus also sent 'an old man from Athens' to 'pollute the temple in Jerusalem and call it the temple of Olympian Zeus' (2 Mac 6[2]). It is accordingly more probable that Jupiter Olympius is referred to.

MAW.—This old English word for the stomach is used by AV and RV in Dt 18[3] (RSV 'stomach') and by RV in Jer 51[34] (AV and RV 'belly'). Coverdale translates, 1 K 22[34], 'A certayne man bended his bowe harde and shott the kynge of Israel betwene the mawe and the longes.'

MAZITIAS, 1 Es 9[35] (AV, RV).—See MATTITHIAH, **1.**

MAZZALOTH.—See STARS.

MAZZEBAH (*maṣṣēbhāh*).—See PILLAR.

MAZZOTH (*maṣṣôth*).—See LEAVEN, PASSOVER.

MEADOW.—This word disappears from RV and RSV in the only two places where it is found in AV (Gn 41[2, 18], Jg 20[33]). In the former passages the Hebrew reads *āḥû*, an Egyptian word which probably means 'reed grass' (RV, RSV), and may possibly cover the natural pasture lands of old Egypt. It occurs again in Job 8[11] (AV, RV 'rush'; RVm, RSV 'papyrus'). In Jg 20[33] (AV 'the meadows of Gibeah') RV transliterates **Maareh-geba**; but it is practically certain that we should read *ma'arabh* and translate 'west of Geba' (so RSV). In RV 'meadows' stands for *'ārôth* in Is 19[7] (AV **paper reeds**), where RSV renders 'bare places.' RSV has 'meadows' in two places: Ps 65[13] (AV, RV 'pastures') for Hebrew *kārîm*; and Zeph 2[6] (AV 'cottages,' RV 'folds'), where MT has *newōth kerôth*, which is probably corrupt.

MEAH.—See HUNDRED, TOWER OF.

MEAL.—See FOOD, **2.**

MEAL-OFFERING.—See SACRIFICE, **11.**

MEALS.—In the article FOOD attention was confined to the various articles of diet supplied by the vegetable and animal kingdoms. It now remains to study the methods by which these were prepared for the table, the times at which, and the manner in which, they were served.

1. *Preparation of food.*—The preparation of the food of the household was the task of women from the days of Sarah (Gn 18[6]) to those of Martha (Lk 10[40]). Only the houses of royalty and the great nobles had apartments specially adapted for use as kitchens, with professional **cooks**, male (1 S 9[23]) and female (8[13]). At the chief sanctuaries, also, there must have been some provision for the cooking of the sacrificial meals (1 S 2[13ff]), although Ezekiel (46[24] RV; RSV **'kitchens'**) is the first to mention **'boiling-houses'** in this connexion (cf Ex 29[31], Lv 8[31]).

The usual method of cooking and serving meat can have differed but little from that most commonly observed at the present day in Syria. The meat is cut into larger or smaller pieces (1 S 2[13], Ezk 24[3ff]; cf Micah's telling metaphor 3[3]), and put into the cooking-pot with water. It is then left to stew, vegetables and rice being added. Such a stew—with perhaps crushed wheat in place of rice—was the 'savoury meat' which Rebekah prepared for her husband from 'two kids of the goats' (Gn 27[9]). When meat was boiled in a larger quantity of water than was required for the more usual stew, the result was the **broth** of Jg 6[19f], from which we learn that the meat and the broth might be served separately. The cooking-pots were of earthenware and bronze (Lv 6[28]). For an account of cooking utensils generally, with references to illustrations, see HOUSE, **9**.

In addition to boiling, or, as in AV, RV more frequently **seething** ('sod,' 'sodden,' Gn 25[29], Ex 12[9] etc.; but RSV has 'boil' throughout), **roasting** was much in vogue, and is, indeed, the oldest of all methods of preparing meat. Originally the meat was simply laid upon hot stones from which the embers had been removed, as in the parallel case of the 'cake baked on hot stones' (1 K 19[6] RSV). The **fish** of which the disciples partook by the Sea of Galilee was cooked on the charcoal itself. A more refined mode of roasting was by means of a spit of iron or wood. In NT times the Passover lamb had always to be roasted in an oven, suspended by a spit of pomegranate laid across the mouth.

Eggs (Job 6[6], Lk 11[12]), we read in the Mishnah, might be cooked by being boiled in the shell, or broken and fried, or mixed with oil and fried in a saucepan.

As regards the important group of the **cereals**, wheat and barley ears were roasted on an iron plate or in a pan, producing the **'parched corn'** (RSV 'parched grain') of OT. A porridge of coarse wheat or barley meal has also been referred to under FOOD, **2.** The seeds of the leguminous plants were mostly boiled (Gn 25[29]; cf 2 K 4[38]). A 'pleasing odour' (1 Es 1[12]) was imparted to the stew by the addition of other vegetables of a more pungent character, such as onions. In short, it may be affirmed that the Hebrew housewives were in no way behind their modern kinsfolk of the desert, of whom Doughty testifies that 'the Arab housewives make savoury messes of any grain, seething it and putting thereto only a little salt and *samn* [clarified butter].'

The direction in which Hebrew, like most Eastern, cooking diverged most widely from that of our northern climate was in the more extensive use of **olive oil,** which served many of the purposes of butter and fat among ourselves. Not only was oil mixed with vegetables, but it was largely used in cooking fish and eggs (as we have just seen), and in the finer sorts of baking. The poor widow of Zarephath's 'little oil' was not intended for her lamps, but to bake her 'handful of meal' (1 K 17[12]). The flour was first mixed with oil, then shaped into cakes and afterwards baked in the oven (Lv 2[4]); or a species of thin flat cake might first be baked in the usual way and then smeared with oil. The latter are the 'wafers spread with oil' of Ex 29[2] etc. **Honey** and oil were also used together in the baking of sweet cakes (Ezk 16[13, 19]). In this connexion it is interesting to note that while Ex 16[31] compares the taste of manna to that of 'wafers made with honey,' the parallel passage,

Nu 11[8], compares it to 'the taste of cakes baked with oil' (RSV).

2. *The two chief meals.*—Among the Hebrews, as among their contemporaries in classical lands, it was usual to have but two meals, properly so called, in the day. Before beginning the work of the day the farmer in the country and the artisan in the city might 'break their fast' (Jn 21[12, 15] RV) by eating a morsel of bread —the 'morning morsel' as it is called in the Talmud— with some simple relish, such as a few olives; but this was in no sense a meal. Indeed, to 'eat [a full meal] in the morning' was a matter for grave reproach (Ec 10[16]).

The first **meal-time** (Ru 2[14]), speaking generally, was at an hour when the climate demanded a rest from strenuous exertion, namely, about noon; the second and more important meal of the two was taken a little before or after sunset, when the labourers had 'come in from the field' (Lk 17[7]). This was the '**supper** time' of Lk 14[17]. The former, the *ariston* of the Greeks—in EV rendered **dinner**, Mt 22[4], also Lk 11[38] but RVm here **breakfast**—was in most cases a very simple meal. 'A servant plowing or keeping sheep' or harvesting would make his midday meal of bread soaked in light wine with a handful of parched corn (Ru 2[14]), or of 'pottage and bread broken into a bowl' (Bel [33]), or of bread and boiled fish (Jn 21[13]). All the evidence, including that of Josephus, goes to show that the second or evening meal was the principal meal of the day.

3. *Position at meals.*—Within the period covered by OT the posture of the Hebrews at meals, in so far as the men were concerned, was changed from **sitting** to **reclining.** In the earliest period of all, the Hebrews took their meals sitting, or more probably, squatting on the ground (Gn 37[25] etc.), like the Bedouin and fellahin of the present day, among whom squatting 'with both knees downwards, and with the legs gathered tailor-fashion, alone is the approved fashion when at table' (*PEFSt*, 1905, 124). The food was served in a large wooden bowl placed upon a mat of leather or plaited grass, round which the company gathered. The first advance on this primitive practice was to present the food on a wooden or other tray, set upon a low stand raised but a few inches from the ground. The next step was the introduction of seats, which would naturally follow upon the change from nomadic to agricultural life after the conquest of Canaan. Saul and his mess-mates sat upon 'seats' (1 S 20[25]), the precise form of which is not specified, as did Solomon and the high officials of his court (1 K 10[5], where the queen of Sheba admires the 'sitting,' *i.e.* the seated company of his servants; cf 13[20] etc.).

With the growth of wealth and luxury under the monarchy, the Syrian custom of reclining at meals gradually gained ground. In Amos's time it was still looked upon as an innovation peculiar to the wealthy nobles (Am 3[12] 6[4]). Two centuries later, Ezekiel is familiar with 'a stately bed' or couch (as Est 1[6]) with 'a table prepared before it' (Ezk 23[41]). In the post-exilic period the custom must have taken firm root, for by the end of the 3rd cent. B.C. it was probably universal save among the very poor (Jth 12[15], To 2[1]). In NT, accordingly, whenever '**sitting at table**' (AV, RV 'at meat') is mentioned, we are to understand 'reclining,' as the margin of RV everywhere reminds us. At table, that is to say, the men—for women and children still *sat*—reclined on **couches** (see House, **8**) with wooden frames, upholstered with mattresses and provided with cushions, on which they leaned the left elbow (see Sir 41[19]), using only the right hand to eat with (see **5** below).

4. From the Mishnah we learn that in NT times the **tables** (see House, **8**) were chiefly of wood, and furnished with three or four feet. They were lower and smaller than with us. The couches or divans were as a rule capable of accommodating several people. In the houses of the great each guest at a banquet might have a couch and table for himself. The Greek custom was to assign two, the Roman three, guests to each couch. As each guest reclined on his left elbow, *the person next on his right on the same couch* could be said to 'recline in the bosom' of his fellow-guest. Such were the relative positions of John and Jesus at the Last Supper (Jn 13[23]).

5. *Procedure at meals,* etc. In our Lord's day, as we learn from the Gospels, great importance was attached by the Jewish authorities to the '**washing of hands**' before meals. This consisted of pouring water (which had been kept from possible defilement in large closed jars, the 'stone jars' of Jn 2[6]) over the hands and allowing it to run to the wrist (cf Mk 7[3] RVm and commentaries).

This washing over, the food was brought in by the women of the household (Mk 1[31], Lk 10[40]); in wealthy families by male slaves, the 'servants' of 1 K 10[5], Jn 2[5, 9], 'attendants' of Jth 13[1]. At this stage **grace** was said. The date of the introduction of this custom is unknown, for 1 S 9[13] is not a case in point. In NT the blessing before a meal has the repeated sanction of our Lord's example (Mt 15[36] 26[26] etc.; cf Ac 27[35] for Paul).

As to what may be termed, with the Mishnah, 'the vessels for the service' of the table, these naturally varied with the social position of the household, and more or less with the progress of the centuries. In early times earthenware vessels would be used, for which, as civilization advanced, bronze would be substituted, and even in special cases, silver and gold (see House, **9**). Bread, we know, was usually served in shallow wicker **baskets** (Ex 29[23]). The main part of the meal in the homes of the people will have been served in one or more large **bowls** or **basins,** of earthenware or bronze, according to circumstances. Such was the '**dish**' into which our Lord dipped the 'sop' (Mt 26[23], Mk 14[20]). A shallower dish is that rendered '**platter**' in Mt 14[8, 11], and '**dish,**' Lk 11[39].

In the case of a typical dish of meat and vegetables, prepared as described above, those partaking of the meal helped themselves with the fingers of the right hand (Pr 19[24]=26[15], Mt 26[23])—knives and forks being, of course, unknown at table—while the more liquid parts were secured, as at the present day, by using pieces of thin wafer-like bread as improvised spoons, or simply by dipping a morsel of bread, the **sop** of Jn 13[26] (AV, RV), into the dish. It was customary, as this passage shows, for the head of the family to hand pieces of food to various members; these are the **portions** of 1 S 1[4].

6. In the event of a Jew of some position resolving to entertain his friends to dinner, it was usual to send the invitations by his servants (Mt 22[3]), and later to send them again with a reminder on the appointed day (v.[4], Lk 14[17]). Arrived at his host's residence, the guest is received with a kiss (Lk 7[45]), his feet are washed (v.[44]), and his head is anointed with perfumed oil (v.[38]; cf Ps 23[5]). He himself is dressed in white gala costume (Ec 9[8]; see Dress, **7**), for to come to such a feast in one's everyday garments would be an insult to one's host (cf Mt 22[11f]). After the '**places of honour**' (Mt 23[6]; AV 'uppermost rooms,' RV 'chief places') on the various couches had been assigned to the principal guests, the hands duly washed, and the blessing said, the meal began. This would consist of several courses, beginning with light appetizing dishes, such as salted fish, pickled olives, etc. During the course of the dinner those whom the host wished to single out for special distinction would receive, as a mark of favour, some dainty portion, such as Samuel had reserved for Saul (1 S 9[23]). These were the **portions** (AV, RV '**messes**') sent by Joseph to his brethren (Gn 43[34]—for a list of the parts of an animal in order of merit, so to say, used for this purpose at a fellahin banquet to-day, see *PEFSt*, 1905, 123).

At the close of the dinner the hands were again washed, the attendants bringing round the wherewithal, and tables with all sorts of fruit were brought in, over which a second blessing was said. Although wine was served in the first part of the **banquet** as well, it was at this second stage that the 'fruit of the vine' was chiefly enjoyed. The wine-cups were filled from the large mixing bowls (Jer 35[5]) in which the wine had been diluted with water and perfumed with aromatic herbs. It was usual, also, to appoint a '**steward of the feast**' (Jn 2[8]; cf Sir 32[1]) to regulate the manner and the quantity of the drinking, and to enforce penalties in the case of any breach of etiquette. 'Music and dancing' (Lk 15[25]) and other forms of entertainment, such as the guessing of riddles (Jg 14[12ff]), were features of this part of the banquet. For instruction in the 'minor morals' of the dinner-table, Jesus ben-Sira has provided the classical passages, Sir 31[12–18] 32[3–12], expanding the wise counsel of the canonical author of Pr 23[1f]. A. R. S. K.—**W. A. I.**

MEANI, 1 Es 5[31] (AV).—See Meunim.

MEARAH.—Mentioned amongst the districts of Palestine that had yet to be possessed, Jos 13[4]. We should perhaps read *mē-ʿārāh* 'from Arah.' Arah may be modern *Kh. ʿArah.*

MEASURES.—See Weights and Measures.

MEASURING LINE.—See Arts and Crafts, **1, 3.**

MEAT.—This word is used in AV for food in general, as it is in Scotland still. Thus 2 Es 12[51] AV 'I had my meat of the herbs'; cf Hall, *Works* i, 806, 'There was never any meat, except the forbidden fruit, so deare bought as this broth of Jacob.'

MEAT-OFFERING.—See Sacrifice, **11.**

MEBUNNAI.—The name of one of David's thirty heroes, 2 S 23[27]; elsewhere called **Sibbecai** (q.v.).

MECHERATHITE.—1 Ch 11[36], probably for **Maacathite.** See Maacah.

MECONAH.—A town inhabited after the exile, Neh 11[28] (RV and RSV needlessly alter AV **Mekonah**). The site is unknown.

MEDABA, 1 Mac 9[36] (AV and RV) = **Medeba** (q.v.).

MEDAD.—See Eldad.

MEDAN.—One of the sons of Abraham and Keturah, Gn 25[2], 1 Ch 1[32]. The existence of such a tribe, however, is very doubtful. In Gn 37[36] 'Medanites' (see RVm) is miswritten for **Midianites** (so EV), and there is every likelihood that in the former passage 'Medan' is a doublet of 'Midian,' the next word in the verse. Medan is unknown elsewhere in the Bible, nor is it represented by the name of any people in any extra-Biblical document. To connect it with the name of an Arabian god *Madân*, or with the similar name of a wady in NW. Arabia, is very hazardous, both because the associations are remote, and because the word-form is common in Semitic, and is liable to occur in various relations. J. F. McC.

MEDEBA (Nu 21[30], Jos 13[9, 16], 1 Ch 19[7], Is 15[2]).—A city in the fertile plain or tableland (Heb. *Mîshôr*), E. of the N. end of the Dead Sea, about 25 miles S. of ʿAmman (ancient Philadelphia) and 6 miles S. of Heshbon on the Roman road to Kerak. It appears to have been taken from the king of Moab by the Amorite Sihon and then conquered by Israel (Nu 21[24–26]; Hebrew mentions 'Medeba' in v.[30] where Greek has 'Moab' and Syriac reads 'wilderness,' but other geographical references in this passage indicate that the territory conquered could have included Medeba). It was assigned to Reuben (Jos 13[9]). In the time of David the Syrians who came to assist Ammon (1 Ch 19[6–15]) may have encamped at Medeba, which was apparently then Ammonite (cf v.[7] where Medeba is mentioned; because the parallel in 2 S 10[6–7] does not name the city, it is possible that another Ammonite city rather than the Moabite Medeba, figured in the campaign). When Moab was defeated by David it is probable that Medeba fell into Israelite hands (2 S 8[2]). According to the famous Moabite stone (see Moab), Medeba (l. 8) had been among the possessions held by Omri and his son (Ahab) for forty years until Mesha rebuilt it (l. 30) with other Moabite cities. Joram and Jehoshaphat made an unsuccessful attempt to retake the land of Moab (2 K 3), and in later Israelite times, the fortunes of Medeba must have paralleled those of Moab (cf Is 15[2] which implies that the city was held by the Moabites but was in a state of ruin).

In Maccabaean times it was the stronghold of a robber clan, Jambri, which killed John, eldest son of Mattathias. Jonathan avenged this (1 Mac 9[36–42]; Jos. *Ant.* xiii. i. 2, 4 [11, 18 ff]). John Hyrcanus besieged Medeba (Jos. *Ant.* xiii. ix. 1 [254]). Alexander Jannaeus took it from the Arabians, and Hyrcanus ii. promised to restore it to Aretas (*ib.* xiii. xv. 4 [397], xiv. i. 4 [18]). During the Byzantine period Medeba was a flourishing Christian centre, the seat of bishopric, and represented at the Council of Chalcedon. About 1880 a colony of Roman Catholics from Kerak settled there. Although no large-scale excavations are possible because it is one of the thriving cities of Jordan, now called Madeba, many ancient remains have come to light. These include a large reservoir with solid walls, remains of gates and towers, Moabite tombs, four churches, and some fine mosaics, especially the famous coloured mosaic map of Palestine and Egypt constructed in the 6th cent. A.D. and now in the floor of the Greek Orthodox church.
C. H. W. J.—**W. L. R.**

MEDES, MEDIA.—A people and country called by the same word **Madai** in Hebrew and Assyrian. The Medes were an Aryan (Iranian) people, the first known reference to whom (as Amadai) occurs in 836 B.C. as paying tribute to the Assyrian conqueror Shalmaneser ii. They occupied the mountainous country S. and SE. of the Caspian Sea, their chief city being Ecbatana (Achmetha in Ezr 6[2] AV, RV), modern *Hamadān.* Later Assyrian rulers campaigned against them, and Sargon in 715 and 713 received tribute from a substantial number of chieftains; 2 K 17[6] 18[11] records that Israelites from Samaria were deported to 'the cities of the Medes.' The Medes remained subject to Assyria until the second half of the 7th cent., when they regained their independence and became a dangerous rival. A dynasty was established claiming to derive from one Deioces, who is said to have founded Ecbatana and unified the country. Phraortes, his son, subjugated the **Persians** (q.v.) who had probably settled to the E. of the Persian Gulf at about the same time that the Medes settled farther N., being another branch of the same people. Phraortes was succeeded by Cyaxares i., who in alliance with Nabopolassar of Babylon succeeded in destroying Assyria, taking Nineveh in 612 B.C. While the Babylonians took control of the lowlands, the Medes ruled in the highlands, as far W. as Cappadocia. The power of the Medes was such that the exiled Jews expected the overthrow of Babylon at their hands (Is 13[17] 21[2], Jer 25[25] 51[11, 28]). But with the rebellion of **Cyrus** of Anshan (q.v.) Astyages, king of the Medes, was defeated in *c* 549 B.C., and although the Medes retained an important place in the new Persian empire, they did not again become independent. A Mede, Phraortes, claiming to be of the family of Cyaxares, was one of the rebels defeated by Darius i. at his accession. But their prominence as principal part of the Iranian population results in the name Medes being more frequently mentioned than that of the Persians, except in the later books of the OT. Madai is mentioned in Gn 10[2] among the sons of Japheth, with no allusion to the Persians. Persia and Media are mentioned together in Esther (1[3, 14, 18] 10[2]), while a belief in the unalterability of their law is expressed in 1[19] as also in Dn 6[8, 12, 15]. Dn 5[28] 9[1] 11[1] (cf 8[20]) erroneously inserts an empire of the Medes between that of Babylon and that of Persia, perhaps because of the prophecies of a Median conquest of Babylon. The Persians took over the Median culture, its religion, military and political organization, weapons, clothing and customs. In Ac 9[2] the Medes are mentioned, the reference being to Jews or proselytes living in Media and using the language of the country.

Media was occupied by Alexander the Great, and its southern part came under the Seleucid rulers and was intensively Hellenized. Later it fell to the Parthians, as did also the northern area which had enjoyed a period of independence. The varied traditions concerning Zoroaster associate his origin with Media, probably in the 7th or 6th cent.; he may have belonged to the old school of Median Magi, but it was in eastern Iran that the new faith first gained a firm foothold. J. F. McC.—**P. R. A.**

MEDIATOR, MEDIATION.—The word ' mediator ' (Gr. *mesitēs*) occurs in the NT, once of Moses as the mediator of the Law (Gal 3:19f), in the other instances of Christ as the ' one mediator between God and men ' (1 Ti 2:5), and the mediator of a ' better ' (He 8:6), or ' new ' (9:15 12:24, in latter passage ' new ' in sense of ' recent ') covenant. The verbal form occurs in He 6:17 [RSV ' interposed (Gr. mediated) with an oath ']. The LXX has the term once in Job 9:33 (AV and RV **'daysman,'** RSV ' umpire '). But the idea of mediation, that is, of God dealing with man, or man with God, not directly but through the interposition of another, has a leading place throughout Scripture. Different aspects of mediation, however, need to be distinguished. As regards the fundamental relation of man to God, Jesus, in the NT, is the one and sole Mediator.

1. The most general form of mediation is *intercessory prayer*. This is the privilege of all (cf Ja 5:16). Well-known Scripture examples are the intercession of Abraham for Sodom (Gn 18:23-33), of Moses for Israel (Ex 32:30-34), of Samuel for Israel (1 S 7:8-12). Jeremiah (15:1) singles out Moses and Samuel as the chief representatives of this form of prayer. Probably an element of intercession enters into all effective mediation. St. John (ch. 17) preserves the great intercessory prayer of Jesus after the Last Supper, and intercession is declared to be a chief exercise of Christ's mediatorial function in heaven (Ro 8:34, He 7:25, 1 Jn 1:1). Intercessory prayer is a duty of the Christian (1 Ti 2:1f), but always and only in the name of Christ, who in the same context is declared to be the ' one mediator ' (v.5).

2. Mediation has a peculiar place in *the formation of the great covenants*. It is the singular fact in connexion with the covenant with Abraham, of which St. Paul and the Epistle to the Hebrews in different ways take notice, that it involved no mediator (Gn 12:1-3 15, 17). It was a covenant of promise absolutely (Gal 3:15-18). This seems to be the force of St. Paul's peculiar saying, ' Now an intermediary implies more than one ; but God is one ' (Gal 3:20 ; there were not, as in the covenant through Moses, two contracting parties ; the covenant proceeded solely from God, and was unconditional). In He 6:13-18 this is carried further. God Himself took the place of Mediator in this covenant, and, because He could swear by no higher than Himself, ' interposed (mediated) with an oath ' in ratification of His promise (cf Gn 22:15-18). It is different in the covenant with Israel at Sinai, where Moses is throughout (by God's appointment and the people's own desire, Ex 19:10-25 20:18-21) the mediator between God and the people (Gal 3:19, point of contrast between law and promise). Finally, mediation is the law in the ' new ' and ' better ' covenant, as the passages in Hebrews declare. The reason is that this perfect and eternal covenant, procuring forgiveness of sins, and removing all barriers to access to God, could be formed only on the basis of a reconciling sacrifice ; and this Jesus alone, the Son of God, had the qualification to offer. It is noticeable, therefore, that all the passages that speak of Jesus as ' Mediator ' do it in direct connexion with His sacrificial death : 1 Ti 2:5 ' one mediator between God and men, the man Christ Jesus ' connects with v.6 ' who gave himself as a ransom for all ' ; He 9:15 declares : ' Therefore he is the mediator of a new covenant, so that those who are called may receive the promised eternal inheritance, since a death has occurred which redeems them from the transgressions under the first covenant ' (cf Ro 3:25) ; 12:24, where to come ' to Jesus the mediator of a new covenant ' is to come ' to the sprinkled blood that speaks more graciously than the blood of Abel ' ; so also 8:6 (cf the context, v.3). It is this fact, that Jesus has made the perfect sacrifice for sin, coupled with His unique dignity, as Son of God, which constitutes Him the Mediator *sui generis*.

3. Here, accordingly, is brought to consummation the last great aspect of mediation in the OT—the mediation of *a sacrificing priesthood*. Prophets also might be called mediators, as commissioned revealers of the will of God to the people ; but mediation is peculiarly connected with the functions of the priest. In earlier times the head of the family was the priest ; an interesting example of patriarchal mediation is given in the Book of Job (1:5 for his sons ; cf 42:7-9 for his friends). Under the Law the people could approach God only through the Aaronic priesthood ; but the mediatorial function was peculiarly vested in, and exemplified by, the high priest. To him it pertained, on the one hand, to represent the people before God (cf the ephod and breastplate, with their precious stones graven with the names of the twelve tribes of Israel, Ex 39:6-14), and to offer sacrifices for their sins (He 2:17 8:3 ; he alone had the right of entry into the Holy of Holies on the great annual Day of Atonement, He 9:7) ; and, on the other, to represent God to the people, in declaring His will by the Urim and Thummim, and blessing in His name (cf Dt 10:8 33:8, prerogatives of the high priest). This twofold aspect of the high-priestly function, as the Epistle to the Hebrews seeks to show, is in a perfect and abiding way realized in Christ, who is thus the one true Mediator, our ' great high priest who has passed through the heavens ' (4:14). See ATONEMENT, PROPITIATION, RECONCILIATION. J. O.

MEDICINE.—It is difficult to compare general health to-day with that of Bible times. If a number of diseases of Bible times have tended to recede, others have come to the fore. Infant mortality, as archaeological excavations show, was heavy ; the general expectation of life was shorter, and people attained maturity earlier.

1. The idea of a causal connexion between **health** and virtue finds frequent expression in OT : ' If you will diligently hearken to the voice of Yahweh your God . . . I will put none of the diseases upon you which I put upon the Egyptians ; for I am Yahweh your healer ' (Ex 15:26). **Disease** was popularly regarded as a penalty for wrong-doing (Jn 9:2) and as sent by God, either directly (Ex 4:11, Dt 32:39) or permissively by means of others (Job 2:7). It might also be caused by human envy (Job 5:2) or by physical excess (Sir 37:30f) ; but even so it was viewed as being ultimately authorized by God.

In these circumstances **healing** was treated as a token of Divine forgiveness (Ex 15:26). The connexion of priest with **physician** was correspondingly close. On the whole, medical knowledge was very defective, nor are there any traces of medical education in Palestine. Apart from Joseph's servants the physicians who embalmed Jacob (Gn 50:2), we have no Biblical record of physicians until the time of the monarchy, although Ex 21:19 may imply their existence in Israel. Jer 8:22 suggests that Gilead was the home of skilled healers. It has been inferred from 2 Ch 16:12 that the Chronicler thought it sinful to consult physicians ; if Asa suffered from senile gangrene in his feet, such ministration as physicians of his day would provide might well have aggravated the disease. A more modern attitude is expressed in Sir 38:2. The prayer of Sir 38:15 that the sinner may fall into the hands of a physician may simply mean ' may he fall sick ' ; in any case, the Hebrew text reads : ' He who sins against his Maker will behave arrogantly towards his physician.' Medical duties were frequently performed by priests (as in early Egypt) ; priests certainly had the supervision in the case of leprosy (Lv 13:2ff), and prophets also were applied to for medical advice (cf 1 K 14:2 17:18, 2 K 4:22 20:7). Even in Sir 38:14 physicians are regarded as intercessors, at least to the extent that they ' will pray to the Lord that he should grant them success in diagnosis and in healing, for the sake of preserving life.' The invalid is exhorted to pray, repent, and offer a sacrifice before visiting the physician (vv.9ff). In the NT Luke is called a physician (Col 4:14), a statement which finds some corroboration from certain features of Luke and Acts.

The medical knowledge of the priests, in whose charge the healing art remained for long, would be mainly traditional and empirical. The sacrificial ritual gave them some knowledge of animal morphology, but human anatomy can scarcely have existed as a science at all, in view of the ceremonial objections to touching the dead, not to speak of dissecting them. Biblical references to facts of anatomy and physiology are very few. The ban on eating blood (Gn 9^{4}, Lv 17^{11}) was an important sanitary precaution. A rudimentary embryology can be traced in Job 10^{10}, Ps 139^{15f} (cf Ec 11^{5}). But most of the physiological theories mentioned in the Bible are expressed in language of poetry and metaphor. The Jews (like other ancient peoples) evidently regarded the **heart** as the seat of mental and moral activity (Pr 2^{2} 4^{23} etc.), the **kidneys** (AV ' reins ') of impulse and conscience (Jer 11^{20} 12^{2}, Ps 7^{9}), and the **bowels** of sympathy (Ps 40^{8}, Job 30^{27}). (In Dn 2^{28} 4^{5} 7^{1} dreams are located in the **head.**) Proverbs about physicians are echoed in Sir 38^{1}, Mk 2^{17}, Lk 4^{23}. Visitation of the sick is a pious act (cf 2 K 13^{14} 20^{1}) ; it was enforced by Christ (Mt 25^{36}).

2. *General terms for disease.*—The words **' disease,' ' illness,' ' infirmity,' ' sickness,'** used in EV, usually represent Hebrew *ḥ^{o}lî* or one of its cognates or derivatives in OT and either Greek *astheneia* or *nosos* in NT. **' Pestilence '** and **' plague '** represent a variety of Hebrew and Greek words, many of which have the root sense of ' blow,' ' scourge,' or ' stroke.'

Some diseases, *e.g.* leprosy (q.v.), were regarded as unclean, and those suffering from them were excluded from cities and other centres of human habitation. But in general the sick were treated at home. We know very little about the treatment which they received. In later times the Jews followed the universal practice of bleeding : whether it was resorted to in earlier times we cannot say. The wording of Pr 30^{15} is too uncertain for us to draw any inference about the medicinal use of **leeches.**

3. *Specific diseases.*—Bible references to specific diseases are usually general and vague ; even where concrete mention of particular ailments is found it is not always easy to determine their exact nature. Occasionally symptoms are given, but sometimes very indefinitely.

In Dt 28^{22} there is a list of diseases which resemble one another in that they are sudden, severe, epidemic, and fatal. The first is **' consumption '** (*shaḥepheth*), which may include any wasting disease such as pulmonary tuberculosis ; the same word is used in Lv 26^{16}. The **' fever '** which is mentioned next (*ḳaddaḥath*) would usually be malaria, specially prevalent in the Jordan valley, but might include any other febrile illness such as typhoid. In Lv 26^{16} AV renders it **' burning ague.'** The **' inflammation '** (*dalleḳeth*) of Dt 28^{22} is rendered *rhigos,* ' ague,' in LXX ; it may be tertian malaria. Then comes **' fiery heat '** (*ḥarḥûr*), either some unspecified kind of irritating disease, or **erysipelas** (but this latter disease is not of frequent occurrence in Palestine).

The descriptions of disease given in Ps 38^{5} 39^{11}, Lv 26^{39}, Ezk 24^{23} 33^{10}, Zec 14^{12} suggest an attack of confluent **smallpox,** with its disfiguring and repulsive effects ; if in some of these places the language is figurative, the imagery may even so be borrowed from this ailment.

Allusions to **pestilence** or **plague** are very common in the OT. At least four outbreaks are recorded among the Israelites during their wilderness wanderings, viz. Nu 11^{33} (it has been suggested that the quails mentioned here came from a plague-stricken region) 14^{37} 16^{46} 25^{9} (in this last case it may have been communicated by the Moabites). For other references to plague, cf 2 S 24^{15}, 2 Ch 21^{14}, Ps 91$^{3, 6}$, Jer 21^{9} 42^{17}. Am 6$^{8-10}$ reminds one of the house-to-house searching for the dead recorded of the London plague of 1665. **Bubonic plague** was the periodic scourge of Bible lands ; it was probably this that destroyed Sennacherib's army (2 K 19^{35}). The mortality which broke out among the Philistines when the Ark was in their midst (1 S 5^{9ff}) appears to have been due to this plague (cf the death of the seventy men of Bethshemesh, 1 S 6^{19}). The **' tumours '** of 1 S 5$^{6, 9, 12}$ (AV **' emerods '**) were evidently the buboes of the plague. Pestilence was looked upon as a visitation from God, being one of His three sore judgments (cf 2 S 24^{12f}, Jer 24^{10} 32$^{24, 36}$).

Of **diseases in the digestive organs** the case of Jehoram in 2 Ch 21^{19} was one of chronic **dysentery** in its worst form, leading to a massive rectal prolapse. Dysentery such as accompanied the fever from which the father of Publius was healed (Ac 28^{8}, AV **' bloody flux '**) was very prevalent in Malta. The results of over-indulgence in alcohol are described in Pr 23^{29ff}, Is 19^{14} 28^{7f}.

Liver. Hebrew physicians regarded many disorders as due to an alteration in the bile (cf Job 16^{13}, La 2^{11}). Timothy's ailments (1 Ti 5^{23}) may have been some form of dyspepsia, possibly causing a diminution of energy (cf 1 Ti 4$^{12-16}$) ; the taking of alcohol would give temporary relief. Dryness of throat is mentioned in Ps 69^{3} as a result of acute emotional disturbance ; the flatulent distension of the colon mentioned in Is 16^{11}, Jer 4^{19} is due to the same cause.

Heart. There are few references to heart-disease. Cases of syncope have been (doubtfully) diagnosed in Gn 45^{26}, 1 S 4^{18} 28^{20}, Dn 8^{27}. The allusions to a ' broken heart ' are always metaphorical (cf Ps 69^{20}). Stroud's once popular theory that our Lord's death was due to rupture of the heart is now regarded as quite unacceptable.

Paralysis (AV, RV **palsy**). This is a disease of the central nervous system, which comes on rapidly as a rule, and disappears slowly, if at all. The paralytic of Mk 2^{3} and parallels evidently had paralysis of the legs, perhaps due to a spinal cord lesion, though severe infantile paralysis is not to be excluded. The centurion's servant (Mt 8^{6}) may have been suffering from tetanus ; this is suggested by his being in great pain and at the point of death. The **' withered hand '** of Mk 3^{1} and parallels was probably caused by a complete atrophy of the bones and muscles. The man born lame in Ac 3^{2} may have suffered from a severe degree of congenital club foot, or *spina bifida.* The man at the pool of Bethesda (Jn 5^{7}) may have suffered from withered limbs ; *locomotor ataxia* is less probable in view of the duration of his ailment (38 years). The sudden **' drying up '** of Jeroboam's hand (1 K 13^{4}) was probably due to sudden haemorrhage affecting part of the brain, which in certain circumstances may be only temporary.

Apoplexy. A typical seizure is recorded in Nabal's case (1 S 25^{37}), due to cerebral haemorrhage produced by excitement, supervening (in this instance) on a drinking bout. Apoplexy has also been diagnosed in the case of Uzzah (2 S 6^{7}), and of Ananias and Sapphira (Ac 5$^{5, 10}$).

Mental illness. Saul's ailment (1 S 16^{14}) would be diagnosed to-day as a case of manic-depressive insanity, with periods of black melancholy, flashes of homicidal violence, and deeply rooted delusions that David and others were plotting against him. Nebuchadnezzar's **madness** (Dn 4) was paranoia in the form of a fixed delusion that he was an ox (compare **lycanthropy,** in which the patient believes that he has been changed into a wolf). A Qumrân text (*The Prayer of Nabonidus*) may preserve a variant account in which the king is Nabonidus and the ailment some form of ' inflammation.' In the NT various nervous affections are probably included among the instances of **demon-possession** ; see POSSESSION.

Deafness and Dumbness. Cases of temporary aphasia arising from sudden emotion or the like are recorded of Ezekiel (Ezk 24^{72} 33^{22}), Daniel (Dn 10^{15}), Zechariah (Lk 1^{22}) and Paul (Ac 9^{7}). But Zechariah's dumbness was evidently attended by deafness (v.^{62}) ; such functional deafness is very uncommon. Some cases of dumbness in the NT are put down to possession (*e.g.* Mt 9^{32}, Mk 9^{25}). In Mk 7^{32} stammering is joined to deafness. Patience with the deaf is enjoined in Lv 19^{14}.

Epilepsy. The case of the boy in Mk 9^{18} and parallels is shown by the graphically described symptoms to have been one of epileptic fits, to which (like many epileptics) he had been subject from childhood. The word used in Mt 17^{15} to describe this trouble means literally ' to be moon-struck ' ; cf Mt 4^{24}, Ps 121^{6}. It was a very general belief that epilepsy was somehow connected with the phases of the moon ; such a theory was put forward as late as 1577 by the English court-physician Vicary.

Sunstroke. Sunstroke or heat-stroke (cf Ps 121^{6}, Is 49^{10}, Rev 7^{16}) probably caused the death of Judith's husband (Jth 8^{2f}) ; it has also been diagnosed in the case of the Shunammite's son (2 K 4[18ff]), although cerebral malaria is another possibility; his restoration was plainly miraculous. Jonah's plight when the sheltering plant withered (Jon 4[8]) may have been a case of heat syncope; he fainted from the heat, and on recovery was conscious of a severe headache and a feeling of intense prostration.

Dropsy. This disease was common in Jerusalem; a cure is recorded in Lk 14[2ff].

Gout. This disease is very uncommon in Palestine and is not, as a rule, fatal. The disease in his feet from which Asa suffered (1 K 15[23], 2 Ch 16[12]) was probably not gout but senile gangrene. The perfumed spices which the Chronicler mentions in connexion with his funeral may have been intended to counteract the stench inseparable from this disease.

The **spirit of infirmity** (Lk 13[11]) from which Jesus cured a woman in an unspecified synagogue appears to have been a case of severe spinal curvature due to bony fusion of the vertebrae (*spondylitis deformans*), either tuberculous or osteoarthritic. Such a condition disqualified a man from becoming a priest (Lv 21[20]). The evidence of mummies suggests that it was fairly common in Egypt.

Fracture of the skull. A case is recorded in Jg 9[53] (Abimelech), where insensibility did not immediately supervene, showing the absence of compression of the brain. In Ac 20[9] fatal compression and probably a broken neck were caused by the accident. Ahaziah's fall in 2 K 1[2] was also fatal.

Lameness. Mephibosheth's lameness was ascribed to an accident in childhood (2 S 4[4]); he may have sustained a fracture of both legs with gross displacement. Considering, however, the tendency of children's bone to grow straight again, we may wonder whether the lameness was not due to anterior poliomyelitis, although everyone blamed the fall. Lameness was a disqualification for the priesthood (Lv 21[18]). Jacob's lameness has been diagnosed as due to ruptured and prolapsed intervertebral disc producing severe and intractable sciatica from pressure on the nerve roots; that his hip joint was actually dislocated, as most versions indicate, is highly improbable (Gn 32[25]). The **hunchback** (AV, RV '**crookbackt**') was also disqualified for the priesthood (Lv 21[20]).

Congenital malformations. The possession of superfluous parts (cf the six fingers and toes of the giant in 2 S 21[20], 1 Ch 20[6]) disqualified a man for the priesthood (Lv 21[18]), as did various other congenital malformations. The term rendered 'flat nose' in Lv 21[18] (RSV 'mutilated face') might denote a hare-lip.

Of **skin diseases** the most important was leprosy (see under LEPROSY). But many minor skin affections receive mention in the Bible.

Baldness was not regarded as causing ceremonial uncleanness (Lv 13[40-43]). In Is 3[24], Ezk 29[18] it is the result of carrying burdens on the head.

Itch or **scabies** (Dt 28[27]) is caused by the spider-like *Sarcoptes scabiei*, which burrows under the skin, especially between the fingers and toes, but sometimes all over the body. It is very infectious. It was a disqualification for the priesthood (Lv 21[20]).

Scab or **scurvy** (Lv 21[20], Dt 28[27]) has nothing to do with the disease which we call scurvy, which is due to lack of fresh fruit and vegetables. The Hebrew words (*gārābh*, *yallepheth*) may cover a wide variety of skin diseases, including psoriasis and eczema; they disqualified a man for the priesthood (Lv 21[20]). The terms rendered '**scall**' or 'itch' (Lv 13[30]) and '**tetter**' (Lv 13[39] RV and RSV; AV '**freckled spot**') may denote leucodermia or psoriasis.

The **boils of Egypt** (Dt 28[27, 35] [AV '**botch**']; cf Job 2[7], Ex 9[9], 2 K 20[7], Is 38[21]) were accompanied by **blains**, *i.e.* pustules (Ex 9[10]). To us a boil is a swelling due to infection of a hair follicle; the Hebrew word (*sh*^e^*ḥin*) may have a wider connotation. In Dt 28[35] the knees and legs are particularly affected. Many of the features of **Job's disease** suggest smallpox, but the rare *dermatitis herpetiformis* has claims to be considered. The boils of Egypt may have been the papular stage of smallpox, followed by the pustules. Hezekiah's boil may have been a carbuncle (2 K 20[7]). Two further words, *sappaḥath* and *mispaḥath*, from the same root, found in Lv 13[2] 14[56] and Lv 13[6-8], are rendered '**scab**' in AV and RV, but '**eruption**' in RSV. On these see LEPROSY, II. (*a*).

More general terms for skin diseases are '**blemish**' (Lv 21[17] [AV, RV, RSV], Dt 32[5] [RV, RSV; AV '**spot**'], Job 11[15] [RSV; AV, RV 'spot']), Dn 1[4] [AV, RV, RSV]), '**flaw**' (Ca 4[7] [RSV; AV, RV 'spot']). For an animal suppurating sore AV and RV have '**wen**' in Lv 22[22], where RSV has '**discharge.**'

Our Lord's **sweat . . . like great drops of blood** (Lk 22[44]) has been discussed inconclusively. The simile may denote the size of the drops of perspiration, not their colour. A few old examples of blood-tinged sweat have been quoted, but they lack adequate authentication.

Poisonous serpents are mentioned in several places. In Nu 21[6] their bite is miraculously cured by the erection of a bronze model of a serpent on a pole in the middle of the camp (the use of this figure as a symbol of Asklepios, the Greek god of healing, is perhaps a coincidence). The reference in Mk 16[18] is probably to Paul's experience in Ac 28[3] (where it is disputed whether the creature was actually a viper, or *Coronella leopardinus*). Scorpion bites can be fatal, especially to children.

Worms, mentioned in connexion with the death of Herod Agrippa I. (Ac 12[23]), suggest (together with the more detailed account given by Josephus in *Ant.* XIX. viii. 2 [346–59]) that he was suddenly stricken with acute intestinal obstruction, possibly resulting from a strangulated hernia, for which to-day an operation would be performed. The worms which appeared subsequently would be regarded as the cause of his death. A similar description is given in 2 Mac 9[5-9] of the last illness of Antiochus Epiphanes, which may have been due to rectal cancer.

The third plague of Egypt (Ex 8[16]) is called one of **lice** (AV, RV) or **gnats** (RSV); but RVm suggests **sand-flies** or **fleas.** Possibly they were mosquitoes or sand-fleas, the latter of which breed in the dust.

Discharges or **issues** of various kinds caused ceremonial impurity (Lv 15[2ff]). Some of these were natural (Dt 23[10]), others would be due to gonorrhoea, and therefore infectious. In the absence of any means of distinguishing between them, it was safest to impose precautions in the case of all. It is uncertain how much the Hebrews and their neighbours knew of venereal diseases.

Blindness was exceedingly common in Palestine and the adjoining lands. The words denoting this affliction occur frequently in the Bible, in senses both literal and metaphorical. Two main forms of blindness appear to be recognized: (1) trachoma, a highly contagious form of conjunctivitis, due to a virus transmitted through the bodies of lice, still the cause of much blindness in the Near and Middle East, and (2) optic atrophy, found in old people like Isaac (Gn 27[1]), Eli (1 S 3[2]) and Ahijah (1 K 14[4]). Blindness was regarded as a visitation from God (Ex 4[11]), it disqualified a man for the priesthood (Lv 21[18]), but compassion for the blind was enjoined (Lv 19[14]) and offences against them were accursed (Dt 27[18]). Leah probably suffered from some minor form of ophthalmia (Gn 29[17]). In Lv 26[16] ophthalmia accompanies malarial fever. The blinding of Elymas in Ac 13[11] may have been hypnotic, as also possibly the blinding of the Syrian soldiers in 2 K 6[18]. The cases of blindness cured by our Lord are usually mentioned without specific characterization; the two of most interest are that of the man born blind (Jn 9[1]) and that of the man whose recovery was gradual (Mk 8[22]). In both cases the use of saliva (cf Mk 7[33]) may have been intended in part to strengthen their faith; a belief in the efficacy of saliva as a remedy for blindness and other troubles was widespread (cf Tacitus, *Hist.* iv. 8; Pliny, *Nat. Hist.* xxviii. 7). In the latter case we do not know whether the blindness was congenital or not; if it was, the intermediate stage of his recovery, in which he saw men 'like trees, walking,' would be one in which he was still unable properly to interpret and understand what he saw. Paul's blindness (Ac 9[8]) was possibly a temporary *amaurosis*, such as may be caused by looking at the sun, in which case the 'scales' which fell from his eyes would not have been material; others, however, would compare them with the 'white films' which 'scaled off from the corners' of Tobit's eyes (To 11^{13}). The remedy adopted for Tobit's blindness (fish gall) has a parallel in Pliny (*Nat. Hist.* xxxii. 24). Although the **eye-salve** of Rev 3^{18} is metaphorical, it is noteworthy that Laodicea was not only the home of a medical school but also a centre for the manufacture of collyrium, which was used as a medicine for various eye troubles in antiquity. The chemical-bearing mud of the thermal springs in the vicinity may have provided its basis. Paul's **thorn in the flesh** (2 Co 12^{7}) has sometimes been identified as trachoma or a similar disease of the eyes (although other suggestions have been made, *e.g.* malaria, epilepsy).

Senility. Here should be mentioned the famous passage in Ec 12, with its poetic description of the failing powers of old age.

Child-birth. The pain of childbearing is mentioned in Gn 3^{16} as the penalty for Eve's transgression. Two twin-births are described in some detail: that of Esau and Jacob (Gn 25^{22}) and that of Perez and Zerah (Gn $38^{29\text{ff}}$). The latter has been described as an account of the delivery of locked twins with (in one case) a transverse presentation. Rachel's case (Gn 35^{18}) was one of fatal *dystocia*. Phinehas's wife was taken in premature labour brought on by shock and proving fatal (1 S 4^{19}). Sarah (Gn 21^{2}), Manoah's wife (Jg 13^{24}), Hannah (1 S 1^{20}), the Shunammite woman (2 K 4^{17}) and Elizabeth (Lk 1^{57}) all bore their firstborn at a late period. Barrenness was regarded as a Divine judgment (Gn 20^{18} 30^{2}); fertility was correspondingly looked upon as a token of Divine favour (1 S 2^{5}, Ps 113^{9} $127^{3\text{ff}}$ 128^{3}). Miscarriage is invoked as a token of Divine displeasure in Hos 9^{14}. The attendants at birth were women (Gn 35^{17}), the **midwives** of Gn 38^{28}, Ex 1^{15}. The mother was seated (as is still done among Egyptian fellahin) on the double seat called the birthstool (Ex 1^{16}), or else on someone's knees (Gn 30^{3} 50^{23}, Job 3^{12}). After childbirth the mother was ceremonially unclean for seven days if the child was a boy, for fourteen if the child was a female. After this she continued in a state of modified 'uncleanness' for thirty-three or sixty-six days, as the case might be, during which period she was not allowed to visit the Temple. (The *lochia* was supposed to last longer in the case of a female child.) Nursing continued for two or three years (Gn 21^{8}, 1 S $1^{23\text{f}}$, 2 Mac 7^{27}). In 1 K 11^{20} a child is taken by a relative to wean. Ezk 16^{4} describes an infant with undivided umbilical cord, neither washed nor dressed. The skin of newborn infants was rubbed with salt to make it firm.

The legislation for the **menstrual period** and more irregular discharges of the same order is given in Lv $15^{19\text{ff}}$. A rigid purification was prescribed, including everything touched by the woman, and everyone who touched her or any of those things (see CLEAN AND UNCLEAN). The woman of Mk 5^{26} and parallels, who had suffered from twelve years' persistent **haemorrhage** (AV, RV **'issue of blood'**) had probably an uterine fibroid. The statement—watered down by Luke!—that she 'had suffered much under many physicians, and had spent all that she had' suggests that practitioners charged considerable fees and used drastic methods of treatment.

Infantile diseases appear to have been very severe in Palestine in Biblical days as in more recent times. We read of sick children in 2 S 12^{15}, 1 K 17^{17} and elsewhere. Christ healed many children.

Among cases of **unspecified diseases** may be mentioned those of Abijah (1 K 14^{1}), Benhadad (2 K 8^{7}), Elisha (2 K 13^{14}), Joash (2 Ch 24^{25}), Lazarus (Jn 11^{1}), Dorcas (Ac 9^{37}), Epaphroditus (Ph 2^{27}), Trophimus (2 Ti 4^{20}).

4. *Methods of Treatment.*—The Bible provides little information on this point. We read of washing (2 K 5^{10}), anointing with oil (Ja 5^{14}), the application of soothing ointment to wounds before binding them (Is 1^{6}), the use of oil and wine for wounds (Lk 10^{34}), a fig poultice for a boil or carbuncle (Is 38^{21}), the stimulation of bodily heat by contact (1 K 1^{2} 17^{21}, 2 K 4^{34}). The use of a roller bandage in the treatment of a fracture is mentioned in Ezk 30^{21}. **Balm** (particularly **balm of Gilead**) is mentioned in Gn 37^{25} 43^{11}, Jer 8^{22} 46^{11} 51^{8}, Ezk 27^{17}. This balm may have been of the nature of frankincense or some similar aromatic juice containing benzoin, pleasant in odour and antiseptic in effect. (See BALM.)

There are few examples in the Bible of the taking of medicine by mouth. That it was so taken is implied by such a proverb as 'A cheerful heart is a good medicine' (Pr 17^{22}). The manufacture and use of healing drugs are commended in Sir $38^{4\text{ff}}$. The **'wine mingled with myrrh'** offered to Jesus on the cross (Mk 15^{23}) was apparently intended as an alleviation of pain; myrrh is slightly sedative. Paul's advice to Timothy to take wine for his stomach (1 Ti 5^{23}) has been mentioned already. **Mandrakes** (*Mandragora officinarum*) were regarded as a stimulant to conception (Gn 30^{16}); the fruit was used as a drug. **Mint** (*Mentha silvestris*), **anise** (*Anethum graveolens*), and **cummin** (*Cuminum sativum*) were used as carminatives (Mt 23^{23}). The **caper-berry** (*Capparis spinosa*) was regarded as an aphrodisiac (Ec 12^{5}). Most of the remedies were dietary in the Jewish as in the Egyptian pharmacopoeia, *e.g.* meal, milk, vinegar, wine, water, almonds, figs, raisins, pomegranates, honey. The **apothecary's** art is mentioned in Ex $30^{22\text{ff}}$ 37^{29}, Ec 10^{1}, 2 Ch 16^{14}, Neh 3^{8}, Sir 49^{1}, but in all these passages the reference is really to the perfumer (cf RSV); Sir 38^{8}, however, speaks of the **pharmacist's** art. **Amulets** are mentioned in Is 3^{20}, Ezk $13^{18\text{ff}}$.

Hygienic enactments dealing with food, sanitation, and infectious diseases are particularly common in the Levitical code. Herbivorous ruminant animals were permitted for food, and all true fishes; but carnivorous birds were forbidden, and all invertebrates except locusts. The pig, which was forbidden, is an unclean feeder and harbours the trichina worm and a tapeworm which could be passed on to man. The flesh of animals dying of natural causes was prohibited (Dt 14^{21}); animals slaughtered for food must be inspected. Fat and blood were forbidden as food. The purity of water supplies were safeguarded. Frequent washing of the body and of clothing was prescribed. The prohibition of garments of mixed linen and woollen materials (Lv 19^{19}, Dt 22^{11}) was helpful in this regard, for such garments cannot be so easily or thoroughly cleansed as those of one material. The sanitary disposal of excreta and sewage (cf Dt 23^{12-14}) was a most important hygienic requirement. Isolation was enjoined in the case of infectious diseases. The periodic destruction of leaven (Ex 12^{19} 13^{7}, Dt 16^{3}) must have been of service for the maintenance of pure breadstuffs. Whatever may have been the original principle underlying some of these enactments, there is no doubt that their general effect was a remarkably high standard of social hygiene.

5. *Surgery.*—An **awl** for boring the ear is mentioned in Ex 21^{6}. The most important surgical operation was **circumcision,** which was originally performed with a flint-knife, even as late as the end of the Bronze Age (Ex 4^{25}, Jos $5^{2\text{f}}$). In Israel it was performed on male infants of eight days old; among some of their neighbours at puberty (cf Ishmael, Gn 17^{25}). Its original purpose may have been the imposition of a tribal mark; later it was regarded not only as a sign of membership in the Abrahamic covenant-community but also of purification (hence the metaphorical use of the term, as in Lv 26^{41}, Dt 10^{16}, Jer 4^{4} 6^{10} 9^{26}, Ezk 44^{7}). **Eunuchs** were originally excluded from the service of God (Dt 23^{1}), perhaps because of the fear of importing heathen rites into Israel; in Is $56^{3\text{ff}}$ the repeal of this exclusion is announced. Eunuchs were important court functionaries under the monarchy, as in Oriental courts generally (1 K 22^{9}, 2 K 8^{6} 9^{32} 24^{15}, Jer 29^{2} 34^{19} 38^{7} 41^{16}); later there were eunuchs at the court of the Herods, as elsewhere (Ac 8^{27}).

The healing ministry of Jesus was accepted as a heritage by the apostles, as well as His teaching; and the care of the sick continued to be regarded as a primary duty by the Church of the first Christian centuries, as by the Church of later days. A. W. F. B.—F. F. B.

MEEDA, 1 Es 5³² (AV).—See Mehida.

MEEDDA, 1 Es 5³² (RV).—See Mehida.

MEEKNESS.—Two related Hebrew words (*ʿānî* and *ʿānāw*) lie behind the occurrences of ' meek ' and ' meekness ' in the Bible. Their meaning is not ' meek ' in the modern English sense of ' mild and self-effacing ' but ' abased,' and so ' afflicted,' ' distressed,' ' lowly,' ' poor ' (cf the description in Job 24, which well illustrates the historical situation from which, in part, the words took their meaning). Since Yahweh is proclaimed as the champion of the afflicted and the poor they are promised special blessings (Ps 34⁴ᶠᶠ 37¹¹, quoted in Mt 5⁵, Is 26⁶, etc.) ; these blessings spring not only from their situation (the primary meaning of *ʿānî*), but from the humble, trustful attitude of mind which so often accompanies it (the characteristic meaning of *ʿānāw*). Thus to be meek is to submit to God's will at all times, rather than to exhibit a particular virtue (cf Nu 12³, Sir 45⁴, Ja 1²¹ where meekness in the modern sense is not intended). This line of OT thought is well summed up in the Magnificat (Lk 1⁴⁶ᶠᶠ), and it took concrete form in the godly remnant in Israel who, often despised by the rulers, lived devout lives nourishing their faith on the Scriptures and ' waiting for the consolation of Israel ' (Lk 2²⁵). In the OT ' meekness ' is never used of Yahweh ; but it did characterize the Messiah even in his kingly rôle (Zec 9⁹), and so, according to Mt 11²⁵⁻³⁰, Jesus claimed this status and character for Himself : a claim which He was enabled to make because of the poverty and the humble trust in God which characterized His earthly life (cf Mt 21⁵), and a claim made subsequently for Him by St. Paul, since the incarnation itself was the supreme example of humility and self-effacement (Ph 2¹⁻¹¹, cf 2 Co 10¹). Finally, the risen Christ gives this humility as a gift of the Spirit to His people, along with faith and love and other gifts (1 Co 4²¹, Gal 5²³ 6¹, Eph 4², Col 3¹²), so that by sharing His meekness in their relations with one another they may also share His glory. Here the non-biblical sense of the Greek word *praüs* (' meek ' in the sense of ' tamed and under control ') has fused with the Biblical (' humbly obedient to God's will ') to produce a description of character which is not a moral excellence so much as a gift of the Spirit ; but in this fusion the Biblical element remains dominant. R. S. B.

MEGIDDO (once **Megiddon,** Zec 12¹¹ AV and RV).—One of the most important of the fortress cities of ancient Canaan. It was captured by Thut-mose iii. about 1470 B.C., the spoils being magnificent ; it is mentioned several times in the Tell el-Amarna correspondence. Although the king of Megiddo among others was defeated by Joshua (Jos 12²¹) and the city was listed among the possessions of Manasseh (Jos 17¹¹, 1 Ch 7²⁹), it is clear that the Hebrews were not strong enough to drive out the inhabitants until some time after the Conquest (Jg 1²⁷). Near the ' waters of Megiddo ' the Canaanites under Sisera were defeated by Barak and Deborah (Jg 5¹⁹). In the time of Solomon the city served as the headquarters for the governor of one of the twelve administrative districts (1 K 4¹²), and by the use of forced labour the king built Megiddo as one of his strong chariot cities (1 K 9¹⁵⁻¹⁹). Here king Ahaziah died after being wounded by Jehu (2 K 9²⁷). Also at Megiddo king Josiah met and was killed by Pharaoh Neco who was en route to join the king of Assyria (2 K 23²⁹ᶠ, 2 Ch 35²²). Although Josiah is not mentioned by name in Zec 12¹¹, an ancient tradition holds that the verse alludes to the mourning for this good king ' in the plain of Megiddo.' Not all scholars agree but it is widely held that Armageddon (RV **Har-Magedon,** ' mount Megiddo ' ; AV, RSV **Armageddon**) in Rev 16¹⁶ is a designation of the region of the final struggle between the forces of good and evil at Megiddo because the place had so often been the scene of historic battles.

The site of Megiddo may now be considered as proved to be *Tell el-Mutesellim* (' Hill of the Governor '), a great mound overlooking the fertile plain of Esdraelon (q.v.) and the pass where the historic route through the Mount Carmel range leads from the seacoast to northern Palestine and Phoenicia. The armies of Thut-mose iii., Napoleon and General Allenby made use of the pass at Megiddo ; the city is near the border of Jordan and Israel, located in and defended by the latter.

Extensive excavations have been conducted at Megiddo, from 1903–1905 by the Deutsche Orient Gesellschaft and from 1925–1939 by the Oriental Institute of the University of Chicago. The summit of the mound covered about fifteen acres, and the slopes about thirty-five more. Proximity to fertile fields and a good water supply, plus its strategic location, made this a desirable city site for many generations, as demonstrated by deposits of more than seventy feet in some places and the remains of twenty super-imposed cities. Excavations have disclosed that the site was first occupied by settlers as early as 4000 B.C., although it was not until about a millennium later that public buildings were constructed. By the beginning of the Early Bronze Period (*c* 3000 B.C.) temples and city walls were constructed, and other archaeological evidence suggests that at Megiddo, as at other Near Eastern cities of the period, a high degree of civilization had been reached involving world trade with the regions of Egypt, Mesopotamia and Syria. While there is not complete agreement as to the dating of all the levels which follow, it is clear that city remains from the periods of the Canaanites, David, Solomon, Omri and Ahab have been found. The city appears to have been abandoned about 350 B.C. South of the mound is an abundant stream, and in Roman times a fortified post, the *Legio* of Eusebius, the modern *el-Lejjûn*, was established there.

Among the famous discoveries at Megiddo are an impressive water shaft, about 165 feet long, exquisite ivories, Solomon's stables large enough to have housed about 500 horses, an elaborate city gate, a fragment of an Egyptian stela bearing the name of Shishak, a seal containing the name of ' Shemaʿ, the servant of Jeroboam,' and a proto-Ionic capital (*c* 10th cent. B.C.). For technical reports of the excavations, consult the publications of the Deutsche Orient Gesellschaft, and of the Oriental Institute of the University of Chicago. For excellent popular surveys, see articles in *BA*, iii, No. 4 (Dec. 1940), iv, No. 1 (Feb. 1941) and xiii, No. 2 (May, 1950).

MEGILLOTH.—See Canon of OT, **8.**

MEHETABEL.—**1.** The grandfather of Shemaiah, Neh 6¹⁰. **2.** The wife of Hadar or Hadad, king of Edom, Gn 36³⁹, 1 Ch 1⁵⁰.

MEHIDA.—The eponym of a family of Nethinim (q.v.) who returned with Zerubbabel, Ezr 2⁵², Neh 7⁵⁴, 1 Es 5³² (AV **Meeda,** RV **Meedda**).

MEHIR.—A Judahite, 1 Ch 4¹¹.

MEHOLATHITE.—Gentilic found in 1 S 18¹⁹, 2 S 21⁸ ; probably an inhabitant of **Abel-meholah** (q.v.).

MEHUJAEL.—See Mahalael, **1.**

MEHUMAN.—One of the seven eunuchs in attendance upon king Ahasuerus, Est 1¹⁰.

MEHUNIM, Ezr 2⁵⁰ (AV).—See Meunim.

MEHUNIMS, 2 Ch 26⁷ (AV).—See Maonites.

ME-JARKON.—A city in Dan, Jos 19⁴⁶ ; but the site is not yet recovered. It is possibly *Tell Qasîleh.*

MEKONAH, Neh 11²⁸ (AV).—See Meconah.

MELATIAH.—A Gibeonite, Neh 3⁷.

MELCHI.—**1. 2.** Two ancestors of Jesus (Lk 3²⁴· ²⁸).

MELCHIAS.—**1.** 1 Es 9²⁶ (AV, RV) ; see Malchijah, **4. 2.** 1 Es 9³² ; see Malchijah, **6. 3.** 1 Es 9⁴⁴ (AV, RV) ; see Malchijah, **9.**

MELCHIEL.—The father of Charmis (Jth 6¹⁵).

MELCHISHUA, 1 S 14⁴⁹ 31² (AV).—See Malchishua.

MELCHIZEDEK.—Described as king of Salem and priest of God Most High (*'El 'Elyōn*), who met Abraham on his return from the slaughter of Chedorlaomer and his allies, refreshed him and his servants with bread and wine, blessed him, and received from him a tenth of the spoil he had taken (Gn 14[18-20]). **Salem** (q.v.) has been variously identified: (1) with the *Shalem* of Gn 33[18] (AV and RVm), a place a little to the E. of Mt. Gerizim and not far from Shechem; (2) with the *Salim* of Jn 3[23] in the Jordan Valley S. of Scythopolis; and (3) with *Jerusalem* which is called *Salem* in Ps 76[2]. the last identification is much the most probable; for though it is implied in Jos 15[8, 63], Jg 19[10] that Jerusalem was called *Jebus* so long as it was inhabited by the Jebusites (*i.e.* up to the time of David), the name *Jerusalem* really goes back to the 14th cent. B.C., since it appears in the Tell el-Amarna tablets as *Uru-salim*. This view has the support of Josephus (*Ant.* I. x. 2 [180]), and further obtains some slight confirmation from the resemblance of the name of Melchizedek to that of Adonizedek, who was king of Jerusalem in the time of Joshua (Jos 10[3]), the element *zedek* in each name being probably that of a Canaanite deity.

The historical character of the narrative in which Melchizedek is mentioned has been questioned on the ground of certain improbabilities which it contains; but though the events related have received no corroboration from other sources, the topography is reasonably satisfactory, and some of the names can be paralleled. The theory identifying Amraphel with Hammurabi, however, must be abandoned. For the name and personality of Melchizedek no independent confirmatory evidence has yet been obtained.

In Ps 110[4], a psalm probably composed for use at the enthronement of David himself and/or that of his successors, the king is promised an endless priesthood 'after the order of Melchizedek.' The reference to Melchizedek, like the story in Genesis 14, points to a piece of syncretism whereby the pre-Davidic kingship of Jerusalem and the worship of a supreme god under the title of 'El 'Elyōn were linked with Yahwism and the founding of the Davidic dynasty to foster the emergence of Jerusalem as Israel's cultic centre. (See also PSALMS.)

The writer of the Epistle to the Hebrews, identifying Jesus with the Messiah, and asserting His high priesthood, cites the words of Ps 110, and declares that He was 'designated by God a high priest after the order of Melchizedek' (He 5[10]). He then proceeds to show the superiority of Christ's priesthood over that of the Jewish priests, the descendants of Aaron, and seeks to illustrate it by the superiority of Melchizedek over Abraham, as he gathers it from Gn 14. He explains Melchizedek's name to mean 'king of righteousness,' and his title of 'king of Salem' to mean 'king of peace'; and then, arguing from the silence of the record respecting his parentage, birth, and death, describes him as 'without father or mother or genealogy,' and with 'neither beginning of days nor end of life, but resembling the Son of God,' and affirms him to have been greater than Abraham, since he blessed him ('for it is beyond dispute that the inferior is blessed by the superior') and received from him (and through him from his unborn descendants the Levitical priests) a tithe of his spoils (He 7[1-10]). In this passage much of the writer's argument is fanciful, the narrative in Genesis being handled in allegorical fashion, and the parallel drawn between our Lord and Melchizedek being largely based on the mere omission, in the OT record, of certain particulars about the latter, which, for the historian's purpose, were obviously irrelevant. But in antiquity such arguments were highly effective. See also PRIEST (IN NT). G. W. W.—**H. C.**

MELCOM.—See MALCAM.

MELEA.—An ancestor of Jesus (Lk 3[31]).

MELECH.—**1.** A great-grandson of Jonathan, 1 Ch 8[35] 9[41]. **2.** See MOLECH.

MELICU, Neh 12[14] (AV, RVm).—See MALLUCHI.

MELITA.—AV and RV for **Malta** (q.v.).

MELONS.—*'abaṭṭiḥîm* (the same word as the Arabic *baṭṭîkh*), Nu 11[5]. Here the water-melon is specially referred to, as it was common in Egypt in ancient times. No fruit is more appreciated in the arid wilderness. Melons flourish in Palestine, especially on the sands S. of Jaffa, and are eaten all over the land. E. W. G. M.

MELZAR.—A proper name (AV), or official title (RV, RSV 'steward') in Dn 1[11, 16]—in both cases with the article. It is generally agreed that the word is a loan-word from the Assyrian *maṣṣāru*, 'guardian,' and stands for one who was teacher and warden of the royal wards.

MEM.—Thirteenth letter of Hebrew alphabet, and so used to introduce the thirteenth part of Ps 119, every verse of which begins with this letter.

MEMEROTH, 1 Es 8[2] (RV).—See MERAIOTH, **1.**

MEMMIUS, QUINTUS.—Named along with Titus Manius (q.v.) as a Roman legate (2 Mac 11[34]).

MEMORY.—See REMEMBRANCE.

MEMPHIS.—The famous ancient capital of Egypt, during the Old Kingdom, a few miles S. of Cairo. According to tradition, Memphis was built by Menes, who first united the two kingdoms of Upper and Lower Egypt *c* 3000 B.C. Kings and dynasties might make their principal residences in the cities from which they sprang, but until Alexandria was founded as the capital of the Greek dynasty, no Egyptian city, except Thebes, under the New Kingdom equalled Memphis in size and importance. The palaces of most of the early kings (3rd–12th Dynasties) were at or near Memphis, their positions being now marked by the pyramids in which the same kings were buried. The pyramid-field extends on the edge of the desert about 20 miles, from *Dahshûr* on the S. to *Abū Rôsh* on the N., the great pyramids of Gizeh lying 12 miles N. of the central ruins of Memphis.

The Egyptian name *Menfi* (in Hebrew **Noph,** Is 19[13], Jer 2[16] 44[1] 46[14, 19], Ezk 30[13, 16]; once **Moph,** Hos 9[6]), was apparently taken from that of the palace and pyramid of Pepy I. of the 6th Dynasty, which were built close to the city.

According to Jer 44[1] some Jews fled to Memphis after the murder of Gedaliah in 586 B.C. At a later period, Tirhakah ruled at Memphis; Neco, Hophra, and the other kings of the 26th Dynasty were buried at their ancestral city Saïs, although their government was centred in Memphis. After the foundation of Alexandria the old capital fell to the second place, but it held a vast population till after the Arab conquest, when it rapidly declined. The growth of Fosṭaṭ and Cairo was accompanied by the destruction of all the stone buildings in Memphis for the sake of the materials, but the necropolis still bears witness to its former magnificence. The bull Apis (Egyp. *Ḥapi*), whose name is read in LXX at Jer 46[15] ('Why did Apis [so RSV; AV, RV follow MT] flee from thee?'), was worshipped at Memphis as sacred to Ptah (Hephaestus), the principal god of the city.

F. Ll. G.—**R. J. W.**

MEMUCAN.—One of the seven princes of Persia who had access to the royal presence, Est 1[14, 16, 21].

MENAHEM, one of the latest kings of Israel, was a usurper, like so many other monarchs in this period. He and **Shallum** (q.v.) planned to seize the throne about the same time (2 K 15[13f]), Shallum having possession of Samaria, while Menahem commanded the ancient fortress and former capital, Tirzah. War raged for a brief time with unusual ferocity, resulting in the defeat of Shallum. Menahem seems not to have felt secure on the throne, and to have purchased the help of Assyria, by paying a heavy tribute to Tiglath-pileser (called Pul in 2 K 15[19]). Or we may suppose the Assyrians to have invaded the country because it was so weakened by civil war that it could no longer make effective resistance. The tribute was a thousand talents of silver, and it was raised by a direct tax on the holders of landed property. The assessment of sixty shekels each shows that there were sixty thousand proprietors in Israel at this time.

From the Assyrian sources we learn that this tribute was paid in the year 738 B.C.

It is interesting to note that in the literature of Judaism *Menahem* (=' Comforter ') is a title of the Messiah. H. P. S.

MENE MENE TEKEL AND PARSIN (AV, RV **Upharsin**—the ' U ' being simply the conjunction).—The words of the handwriting on the wall, which, according to Dn 5[5, 25] appeared mysteriously at Belshazzar's feast, and was successfully read and interpreted by Daniel alone (vv.[25–28]). In v.[25] the words of the inscription (' the writing . . . *inscribed* ' RSV, RV [AV **written**]) are given as above, but in the explanation (vv.[26–28]) they are quoted in a divergent form, and no account is taken of the repetition of the first word. The discrepancy can best be accounted for by assuming that the words of the inscription as given in v.[25] already lay in their present form before the author and are not the product of his free invention. It is less satisfactory to emend the text (cf LXX, etc.), by omitting the first ' *mene* ' and altering ' *parsin* ' to ' *peres*,' for assimilation of text to interpretation is easier to understand than the present divergence. The freedom in the interpretation may be paralleled, *e.g.* in the Habakkuk Commentary of the Dead Sea Scrolls, and represents the author's application of the words, independently of their original meaning, to the situation in the narrative.

It appears most probable that the words are really the names of weights. *Mene* is the Aramaic equivalent of the Hebrew *māneh* (1 K 10[17], Ezr 2[69], Neh 7[71f], Ezk 45[12]) and = mina, equivalent to fifty shekels; *tekel* = shekel; and *parsin* is a plural, or better, dual form ' two parts, halves,' *i.e.* probably ' half-shekels ' rather than the half-mina which is often suggested (*peres*, literally = division). Thus the four words read consecutively: ' A mina, a mina, a shekel, and two half-shekels.' An alternative which has been suggested is to treat the first *mene* as meaning ' counted ' (cf v.[26]) and to regard the whole phrase as originally an expression of the counting-house: ' Counted: mina, shekel, half-shekel(s).' This might be a familiar, almost proverbial expression, or might represent an actually existing inscription utilized by the narrator of the story.

The inability of the wise men of Babylon to read the inscription (v.[8]) may be rationalized as due to its being in an unfamiliar script; but such rationalization is inappropriate to the atmosphere of the story. The theme of writing on a wall, or of mysterious writing as such, is not unfamiliar in folk-tales; and the emphasis must lie on the inability of all but the hero to read and interpret the words. Here, properly enough, it is Daniel, who elsewhere attributes his skill in interpretation to the power of God (2[20–23, 28]), who is enabled to read and interpret.

Each of the mysterious words is given a meaning suggested by philological affinity. The term for ' mina ' is linked to a root meaning ' to number,' and is taken to be a passive participle: ' numbered.' The meaning is elaborated to ' God has numbered the days of your kingdom and brought it to an end.' ' Tekel ' (shekel) is linked to a root meaning ' to weigh,' and hence ' you have been weighed in the balance and found wanting ' (an idea familiar from Egyptian thought about the dead). ' Peres ' (half-shekel) suggests a double play upon words, first connected with a root meaning ' to divide ' and second with the name ' Persians ' (*Pāras*), and so ' Your kingdom is divided, and given to the Medes and Persians,' which fits in with the author's belief that there were two separate empires following on the Babylonian (cf MEDES, PERSIA). As in the ' prophetic pun ' (cf Jer 1[11f], Am 8[1f]) the similarity or identity of sound is seen as meaningful; popular etymology works on the same principle of the identification of like words. Attempts at relating the words to particular rulers (*e.g.* Nebuchadnezzar, Evil-merodach [or Nabonidus], and Belshazzar) are ingenious, but there is no clear basis for such exegesis in the text. G. H. B.—**P. R. A.**

MENELAUS.—Brother of Simon the Benjamite (2 Mac 3[4]), or, according to Josephus (*Ant.* XII. v. 1 [238 f]), a younger brother of Jason and Onias. He purchased the office of high priest from Antiochus Epiphanes for the sum of 660 talents (*c* 172 B.C.), thereby causing the deposition of Jason, who had obtained the office by similar corrupt means. Being unable, through lack of funds, to pay the required sum, he was cited to appear before the king, but, finding the latter absent on warfare, he plundered the Temple of sacred vessels and thereby found means to silence his enemies. Having secured the death of Onias III., who threatened to divulge the sacrilege (2 Mac 4[27–34]), he became so unpopular that Jason marched against him to recover the office he had lost (5[5–10]). After this attempt of Jason, which ended in failure, Menelaus is lost to sight for some years, but finally suffered death at the hands of Antiochus Eupator (*c* 163 B.C.). T. A. M.

MENESTHEUS.—The father of Apollonius (2 Mac 4[21]).

MENI.—A deity named with **Gad** in Is 65[11]: ' Ye that . . . prepare a table for Gad (RV, RSV ' Fortune ') and that fill up mingled wine for Meni (RV, RSV ' Destiny ').' Gad is *Fortune* and Meni *Destiny*. The name has been correlated with the Arabic *Maniyyat*, and with a supposed Babylonian god *Manu*. *Mānāh* in Hebrew means ' to number ' (cf AV ' unto that number '), and so ' to apportion.' See GAD. W. F. C.

MENNA.—An ancestor of Jesus (Lk 3[31]).

MENUCHAH, Jg 20[43] (AVm).—See NOHAH, **1.**

MENUHAH, Jg 20[43] (RVm).—See NOHAH, **1.**

MENUHOTH.—See MANAHATHITES.

MEONENIM.—See DIVINER'S OAK.

MEONOTHAI.—Son of Othniel, 1 Ch 4[13f].

MEPHAATH.—A city of Reuben, Jos 13[18]; assigned to the Levites, 21[37], 1 Ch 6[79]; a Moabite city in Jer 48[21]. In the 4th cent. A.D. it is said to have been the station of a Roman garrison. It is perhaps modern *Tell el-Jâwah*, near *Kh. Nefaʿa*, which preserves the ancient name.

MEPHIBOSHETH—1. A son of Jonathan (2 S 4[4]). The original form of the name, given in 1 Ch 8[34] 9[40], was **Merib-baal**, ' Baal defends (my) case '; Mephibosheth is an intentional corruption of this, with *bōsheth* ('shame') substituted for ' Baal.'

Mephibosheth was five years old when Saul fell on Mt. Gilboa, and in the flight of the royal household after the battle he was so seriously injured by a fall as to become lame in both feet (2 S 4[4]). When David succeeded to the throne, he inquired if any one was left of Saul's house, that he might show him kindness for the sake of Jonathan (2 S 9[1ff]). He was informed by **Ziba**, who had been Saul's steward, that Mephibosheth was in Lo-debar, E. of the Jordan. David then restored to Mephibosheth all the estates of Saul, Ziba became his steward, and Mephibosheth himself was maintained as a permanent guest at David's table (2 S 9[13]). Mephibosheth's lameness prevented him from becoming a real rival of David, which no doubt further inclined the latter to mercy. When David handed over Saul's surviving descendants to the Gibeonites for execution (2 S 21[7ff]), he spared Mephibosheth because of his oath to Jonathan.

When David fled from Jerusalem after Absalom's rebellion, Ziba met him on the Mount of Olives with provisions. He also stated that his master had remained in Jerusalem in hope of obtaining the kingdom of Saul. Apparently believing him, David said ' Behold, all that belonged to Mephibosheth is now yours ' (2 S 16[4]). On David's return Mephibosheth came out to meet him, and declared that Ziba had accused him falsely, taking advantage of his lameness. David seems to have doubted the truthfulness of Mephibosheth or did not wish to alienate Ziba, who had also been faithful, and divided the land of Saul between the two. Mephibosheth expressed his willingness that Ziba should have all, ' since my lord the king has come safely home ' (2 S 19[30]).

From 2 S 9^{12} we learn that Mephibosheth had a son, Mica, whose descendants are listed in 1 Ch 8^{35ff} 9^{41ff}.

2. One of the sons of Saul's concubine Rizpah, slain by the Gibeonites (2 S 21^{8}). W. F. B.—**J. Br.**

MERAB.—The elder daughter of Saul, promised to the slayer of Goliath (1 S 17^{25}), and then to David personally as a reward for prowess against the Philistines (1 S 18^{17}), but given as wife to Adriel the Meholathite. In 2 S 21^{8} her sons are said to have been given over to satisfy the Gibeonites (AV, RV here read ' Michal,' with Heb. ; RSV corrects to ' Merab,' with 2 Heb. MSS and LXX^{L}).

MERAIAH.—The head of a priestly house, Neh 12^{12}, where the name is probably a corruption of **Amariah** (so Syriac and LXX^{L}).

MERAIOTH.—**1.** Son of Ahitub and father of Zadok, 1 Ch 9^{11}, Neh 11^{11}. **2.** A Levite, 1 Ch 6^{6f}, Ezr 7^{3}, 2 Es 1^{2} (AV, RV **Marimoth**) ; called **Memeroth** in RV in 1 Es 8^{2} (AV **Meremoth** ; RSV omits with LXX^{B}). **3.** A priestly house in the days of Joiakim, Neh 12^{15} ; called **Meremoth** in v.^{3}.

MERAN, Bar 3^{23} (AV).—See MERRAN.

MERARI, MERARITES.—**1.** The third son of Levi, to whom a division of the Levites traced their descent (Gn 46^{11}, Ex 6^{16}, Nu 3^{17}, 1 Ch $6^{1, 16}$ 23^{6}). The title ' Merarites ' is found only in Nu 26^{57} ; elsewhere they are called ' sons of Merari ' (Ex 6^{19}, Nu 3^{20} $4^{29, 33, 42, 45}$ 7^{8} 10^{17}, Jos $21^{7, 34, 49}$, 1 Ch $6^{19, 29, 44, 63, 77}$ 9^{14} $15^{6, 17}$ 23^{21} 24^{27} 26^{19}, 2 Ch 29^{12}, Ezr 8^{19} [cf HANANIAH, **11**]). They were subdivided into two groups, the **Mahlites** and the **Mushites** (Nu 3^{33} 26^{58}), each being traced to a ' son ' of Merari (Ex 6^{19}, Nu 3^{20}, 1 Ch $6^{19, 29, 47}$ 23^{21}). From these families fragments of genealogies remain, some branches being traced through the daughters of Mahli (see 1 Ch 23^{22}).

Very little is related of the Merarites after the Exile. Certain Merarites are mentioned in 1 Ch $9^{14, 16-18}$ = Neh $11^{15, 17-19}$ as dwelling in Jerusalem immediately after the Return, and certain others as accompanying Ezra to the city (Ezr 8^{18f}). But Peter and the Chronicler introduce the family into the earlier history. (1) During the desert wanderings the Merarites were on the north side of the Tent (Nu 3^{35}) ; their duty was to carry the less sacred parts of it, the ' boards ' (or rather frames), pegs, cords, etc. (3^{36f} 4^{31f} 10^{17}), for which they were given four wagons and eight oxen (7^{8}) ; and they were superintended by Ithamar, the youngest son of Aaron (4^{33}). (2) After the settlement in Palestine, twelve cities were assigned to them (Jos $21^{7, 34-40}$ = 1 Ch $6^{63, 77-81}$). (3) In David's reign the Chronicler relates that the Temple music was superintended partly by Ethan, or Jeduthun, a Merarite, and his family (1 Ch 6^{44-47} 16^{41f} $25^{1, 3, 6, 9, 11, 15, 19, 21f}$; and see $15^{6, 17-19}$). David divided the Levites into courses ' according to the sons of Levi ' (23^{6} ; Merarites, vv.$^{21-23}$ 24^{26-30}), and particular offices of certain Merarites are detailed in $26^{10-13, 16-19}$. (4) They took part in the cleansing of the Temple under Hezekiah (2 Ch $29^{12, 14}$). Cf also KOHATH.

2. The father of Judith (Jth 8^{1} 16^{7}). A. H. McN.

MERATHAIM.—A symbolic name for Babylon, Jer 50^{21}. A play on words, meaning ' double rebellion,' with an allusion to Akkadian *marrâtim*, the region in S. Babylonia near the Persian Gulf.

MERCHANDISE, MERCHANT.—See MARKET, TRADE AND COMMERCE.

MERCHANTMAN.—This English word is now used only of a trading vessel. In AV it means ' merchant, tradesman ' : it occurs in Gn 37^{28} (so RV, RSV ' trader '), I K 10^{15} (RV ' chapman,' RSV ' trader '), Mt 13^{45} (RV ' man that is a merchant,' RSV ' merchant '). In each case the earliest editions of AV have two separate words.

MERCURY.—See HERMES.

MERCY, MERCIFUL.—Mercy (French *merci*) is traced, through ecclesiastical Latin, to *merces* (reward) ; it seems to have got its meaning from the exclamation of the alms-receiver, ' Merci ! ', *i.e.* ' Reward to you (in heaven) ! ' ' May God reward you ! '—the expression passing from the acknowledgment made to the bounty given, and then to the spirit prompting it. Thus **mercy** is by derivation allied to *merit*, *merchant*, *mercenary*, *amerce*.

1. In the OT, noun and adjective stood in AV for two different Hebrew roots, but in RSV they are used comparatively rarely for either. (1) The root *rāḥam* occurs as noun, adjective, or verb (' have mercy,' ' show mercy ') with the translation ' mercy ' over sixty times. The noun means primarily ' bowels ' (see Gn 43^{30}, 1 K 3^{26}), then ' compassion,' ' yearning.' In five cases the word ' pity ' is used, and in seventeen ' compassion.' In RSV rather less than half of all these remain as ' mercy,' and ' pity,' ' compassion ' are the regular renderings. This is as it should be, because the root is used mostly of God's compassion and pity for weak and suffering humanity. (2) *Ḥesedh* is a familiar word, and in AV it was rendered forty-three times by ' kindness ' (often on the part of men), and thirty times by ' loving-kindness ' (always of God, and mostly in Psalms), by ' mercy ' some 150 times, with other occasional renderings. RV generally substituted ' loving-kindness,' which was Miles Coverdale's word, but in RSV almost everywhere we find ' steadfast love ' (of God) and occasionally ' loyalty,' ' kindness ' (of men). The translation ' mercy ' is comparatively rare. This change is good, because the Hebrew *ḥesedh* has a basic meaning of ' strength ' and it comes to be used for the proper attitude which each party to a covenant should maintain towards the other. When it is used of God's attitude to the people of His covenant, the word means ' steadfast love.' G. A. Smith's rendering was ' leal-love.' This is because of God's determined and persistent love for a wayward people. In LXX the usual rendering is *eleos*, and in the Vulgate it is *misericordia*. This is the origin of the ' mercy,' ' kindness ' of AV, and the translation arose because in practice God had to exercise continual mercy and forgiveness towards this people Israel. The word *ḥesedh* is associated frequently with ' covenant,' but more often still with ' truth,' so that in AV we get the phrase ' mercy and truth.' It is better to render this ' steadfast love and reliability,' or ' troth and truth,' because both words are used to describe God's faithfulness and loyalty in the Covenant he has made with Israel. (3) A third root (*ḥānan*), the noun of which is translated ' grace ' (q.v.) and its adjective ' gracious ' appears in the verb sixteen times as ' be gracious ' or the like, and sixteen times as ' have ' or ' show mercy ' in AV (Dt 7^{2}, Ps 4^{1} etc.), thrice as ' pity.' This distribution is maintained in RSV. The main difference between this root and (2) is that this root is used of good favour where there is no covenant obligation, whereas *ḥesedh* becomes essentially a covenant-word, and is used in cases where there is a bond between the two parties. The LXX rendering of *ḥanan* is *charis*, which is the NT Greek word for ' grace.' But the NT ' grace ' is a combination of (2) and (3). It is the ' steadfast love ' of the covenant with the ' middle wall of partition ' broken down, so that God's saving love is available for all mankind, combined with the ' good favour ' which He persistently shows to all the undeserving. See GRACE.

2. Mercy in NT plays a subordinate part to that of love (q.v.). It represents a pair of Greek synonyms, both chiefly, but not exclusively, applied (in Scripture) to God. (*a*) *eleos*, used in LXX in its noun-form to represent the Hebrew *ḥesedh*, but the corresponding adjective and verb stand more often for (3) of the Hebrew roots indicated above, and less frequently for (1). Thus this word is retained in RSV in all quotations from OT (Mt 9^{13} etc.) where the Hebrew has *ḥesedh* and the RSV has changed in the OT to ' steadfast love.' Apart from such cases, the NT ' mercy ' does actually mean ' mercy, compassion, pity ' and the like. (*b*) *oiktirmos* is used in LXX chiefly to represent (1) and this usage is carried over into NT. In AV the regular renderings were ' mercy, compassion,' but in RSV some of these have been replaced by ' love.' G. G. F.—**N. H. S.**

MERCY SEAT.—See TABERNACLE, **7** (*b*).

MERED.—A Judahite, 1 Ch 4[17] (AV and RV, also v.[18]).

MEREMOTH.—**1.** The head of the 7th course of priests, Ezr 8[33], Neh 3[4, 21] 10[5], 1 Es 8[62] (AV, RV **Marmoth**). **2.** One of the sons of Bani who had married a foreign wife, Ezr 10[36]; called **Carabasion** in 1 Es 9[34]. **3.** A priestly house, Neh 12[3]; called **Meraioth** in v.[15]. **4.** 1 Es 8[2] (AV); see MERAIOTH, **1.**

MERES.—One of the seven princes and counsellors of Ahasuerus, Est 1[14].

MERIBAH.—See MASSAH AND MERIBAH.

MERIBAH-KADESH.—AV or AVm for **Meribath-kadesh** (q.v.).

MERIBAH OF KADESH.—RV for **Meribath-kadesh** (q.v.) in Dt 32[51].

MERIBATH-KADESH.—See MASSAH AND MERIBAH.

MERI(B)BAAL.—See MEPHIBOSHETH.

MERIBOTH-KADESH.—RV for **Meribath-kadesh** (q.v.) in Ezk 47[19].

MERODACH.—The name of the city-god of Babylon, worshipped, after the establishment of Babylon as capital of the Babylonian empire, as chief god of Babylonia. The Babylonian name was *Marduk*, older form *Maruduk*. He gradually absorbed the attributes of other gods once supreme through the influence of their city seats of worship, particularly Enlil the old Bēl, or lord supreme of Nippur. Hence he was in later times the **Bēl** of Babylonia. Merodach is a Hebraized form occurring only in Jer 50[2], but the Bēl of the Apocryphal Bēl and the Dragon and of Is 46[1] and Jer 51[4] is the same deity. Nebuchadrezzar was specially devoted to his worship, but the Assyrians reverenced him no less; and even Cyrus, on his conquest of Babylon, treated him with the deepest respect. The name occurs in many Babylonian proper names, and appears in the Bible in *Merodach-baladan* and *Evil-merodach*, and probably in *Mordecai*. C. H. W. J.

MERODACH-BALADAN.—A Babylonian usurper, mentioned in Is 39[1] and in 2 K 20[12] (AV and RV **Berodach-baladan,** following the mis-spelling of MT). In Assyrian the name is *Marduk-aplā-idin*, and means ' Marduk has given a son.' For his history see ASSYRIA AND BABYLONIA, II. 2 (*e*).

MEROM, THE WATERS OF.—The scene of Joshua's victory over the northern kings, after which he is said to have destroyed Hazor (Jos 11[5ff]). The Waters of Merom have generally been identified with Lake Huleh in the Upper Jordan Valley, and the proximity of Hazor might seem to corroborate this location. There is, however, a strong trend of modern opinion in favour of the village of *Meirûn* near *Ṣafed* in Upper Galilee. Here there is no considerable *tell*, though Late Bronze, Iron Age, Hellenistic, and Roman sherds attest a history which corresponds with that of Merom, which is mentioned for the first time in the conquest-lists of Thothmes III. (15th cent.). Y. Aharoni, in an archaeological survey of Galilee, has noticed the encroachment of settlement in the Iron Age from Lower Galilee on the more fertile plateau of Upper Galilee, which was more thickly populated in the Canaanite period. He regards the Battle of the Waters of Merom as the last effort of the king of Hazor and his allies from the Plain of Esdraelon and the Plain of Acco to resist Israelite penetration. The strategic situation of *Meirûn*, or the somewhat more northerly *Marûm er-Râs*, on the plateau at the head of the *Wâdī el-ʿAmûd*, which gives access to Upper Galilee from the Plain of Chinnereth, is a strong argument for this location of the Waters of Merom. W. E.—**J. Gr.**

MERONOTHITE.—A designation applied in the OT to two men: **1.** Jehdeiah, 1 Ch 27[30]. **2.** Jadon, Neh 3[7]. Meronoth was apparently close to Gibeon and Mizpah (cf Neh 3[7]), but it cannot be identified.

MEROZ.—A place which the angel of Yahweh bids men curse, together with its inhabitants, because they did not come to fight Yahweh's battle against Sisera. It is mentioned only in Jg 5[23], and probably owes its mention merely to the fact that it ' lay in the line of Sisera's flight ' (Moore).

MERRAN.—Bar 3[23] only (AV **Meran**). Probably *d* was misread *r* in the Semitic original, and the name = **Midian** (cf Gn 37[28], Hab 3[3, 7]).

MERUTH, 1 Es 5[24] (AV).—See AMARIAH, **7,** IMMER, **1.**

MESALOTH.—See ARBELA.

MESHA.—**1.** Son of Shaharaim, a Benjamite, 1 Ch 8[9]. **2.** Firstborn of Caleb (so AV, RV), 1 Ch 2[42] (RSV **Mareshah,** following Gr.). **3.** See next article.

MESHA.—Place name in Gn 10[30], marking one limit of the *habitat* of the sons of Joktan, brother of Peleg and son of Eber of the lineage of Shem. The other limit was **Sephar** (q.v.), the mountain of the E. In the present text the sons of Joktan include the peoples of Yemen. But there is reason to believe that the text has been expanded in 10[26–29] and that the Yahwistic source did not extend the Joktanids so far. In P Sheba is counted among the sons of Ham (10[7]) and that may have been J's view too. The analogous formulation in Gn 25[18] (J) ' from Havilah to Shur ' thinks of the remoter point before the nearer. Mesha is thus probably the farther limit of the sons of Joktan. Since the name can be vocalized **Massa** (q.v.), which is linked with Tema (q.v.) in Gn 25[14–15], it is quite possible that this was what the original writer intended. It would then lie in the *Jauf* area of N. Arabia. After the expansion of text this no longer fitted and brought about the different vocalization. E. G. K.

MESHA.—A king of Moab in the 9th cent. B.C. He was a tributary of Ahab of Israel, but rebelled at the death of the latter. Jehoram mobilized for war and Jehoshaphat of Judah joined in the campaign, as did the king of Edom. The prophet Elisha was with the Israelite army. The siege of Kir-hareseth (*el-Kerak*) could not be prosecuted to a successful conclusion (2 K 3). The whole situation gained new vividness through the accidental discovery on the surface of the ground at *Dhībân* (ruined site of Dibon) of a stela of King Mesha himself. It was found by a German missionary named Klein in 1868. Unhappily a rivalry ensued to get possession of the stone, and this led the Arabs to break it up and sell the pieces. A squeeze made before this happened has made possible the restoration of some of the lacunae, and the patched together monument is in the Louvre. Strange to say there was debate about whether the inscription was not a forgery. The stela was dedicated to the Moabite God Chemosh and was evidently raised up after Mesha had successfully maintained his independence. It records that Omri had subjected the Medeba territory. Ataroth, still farther S., had apparently been held by the Israelite tribe of Gad in the face of the rise of Moabite power under Mesha's father Chemosh-melech. That king had succeeded in pushing as far as Medeba. Mesha calls himself the Dibonite (cf how the Edomite king list mentions the places where the kings came from, Gn 36[31–39]). His stela was erected at a new high-place at the city he built—the otherwise unknown *Ḳrḥh*. The stone, therefore, must have later been brought to Dibon for reasons unknown. Israelite prisoners had to hew out the cisterns for the new town. Mesha carried on a war of extermination against some Israelite cities, such as Ataroth, Nebo and no doubt Jahaz, in the case of which this is not explicitly said. The text is translated in *ANET*, pp. 320 f. E. G. K.

MESHACH.—The name **Mishael,** by which one of Daniel's three companions, one of the children of Judah, was originally called, was changed by the prince of the eunuchs into *Meshach*, Dn 1[7] 2[49] 3[12ff]. Such changes of name were not uncommon; they marked the fact that a new state of life had now begun. The meaning of the name is quite uncertain.

MESHECH.—**1.** The name of a people of Asia Minor mentioned after **Tubal** as among the sons of Japheth, Gn 10[2], 1 Ch 1[5], These two peoples, possibly kindred, appear almost always in conjunction in OT; so even in Is 66[19], where read 'Meshech' instead of 'that draw the bow' (the word for 'bow' being a supplementary gloss). In Ps 120[5] Meshech and **Kedar** appear as types of barbarous and warlike people, just as Meshech and Tubal are represented in Ezk 32[26] 38[2] 39[1]. In the Assyrian annals the *Tabali* and *Mushki*, who are undoubtedly the same as Tubal and Meshech, are found again together (as fierce opponents of Assyria in the 12th cent. B.C.), the former lying to the NE. of Cilicia and the latter eastward between them and the Euphrates. The *Tibareni* and *Moschi* of the classical writers must stand for the same two peoples. Ezk 27[13] names them as trading in slaves and articles of bronze. **2.** In 1 Ch 1[17] 'Meshech' is written by mistake for '**Mash**' (cf Gn 10[23]).

MESHELEMIAH.—The eponym of a family of Korahite doorkeepers, 1 Ch 9[21] 26[1f. 9]; called **Shelemiah** in 26[14], **Shallum** in 9[17, 19, 31], and **Meshullam** in Neh 12[25].

MESHEZABEL.—**1.** One of those who helped to repair the wall, Neh 3[4]. **2.** One of those who sealed the covenant, Neh 10[21]. **3.** The father of Pethahiah, Neh 11[24].

MESHILLEMITH.—A priest, 1 Ch 9[12]; called **Meshillemoth** in Neh 11[13].

MESHILLEMOTH.—**1.** An Ephraimite, 2 Ch 28[12]. **2.** See MESHILLEMITH.

MESHOBAB.—A Simeonite, 1 Ch 4[34].

MESHULLAM.—**1. 2. 3.** Three Benjamites, 1 Ch 8[17] 9[7f]. **4.** A Gadite, 1 Ch 5[13]. **5.** The grandfather of Shaphan, 2 K 22[3]. **6.** The father of Hilkiah, 1 Ch 9[11], Neh 11[11]. **7.** Another priest of the same family, 1 Ch 9[12]. **8.** A Kohathite, 2 Ch 34[12]. **9.** A son of Zerubbabel, 1 Ch 3[19]. **10.** One of the 'chief men' whose services were enlisted by Ezra to procure Levites, Ezr 8[16], 1 Es 8[44] (AV **Mosollamon, RV Mosollamus**). **11.** A Levite who opposed Ezra's proceedings in connexion with the foreign marriages, Ezr 10[15], 1 Es 9[14] (AV **Mosollam**, RV **Mosollamus**). **12.** One of those who had married foreign wives, Ezr 10[29], 1 Es 9[30] (AV, RV **Olamus**). **13.** Son of Berechiah, one of those who helped to repair the walls of Jerusalem, Neh 3[4, 30]. His daughter was married to Tobiah, To 6[18]. **14.** Son of Besodeiah. He helped to repair the old gate, Neh 3[6]. **15.** One of the company that stood at Ezra's left hand during the reading of the Law, Neh 8[4]. **16. 17.** A priest and a chief of the people who sealed the covenant, Neh 10[7, 20]. **18.** One of the princes of Judah who marched in procession at the dedication of the walls of Jerusalem, Neh 12[33]. **19. 20. 21.** Two heads of priestly houses and a porter in the time of the high priest Joiakim, Neh 12[25], called **Meshelemiah** (q.v.) in 1 Ch 9[21] etc.

MESHULLEMETH.—Wife of king Manasseh and mother of Amon, 2 K 21[19].

MESOBAITE, 1 Ch 11[47] (AV).—See MEZOBAITE.

MESOPOTAMIA = Aram-naharaim (see ARAM).

MESS.—A mess is any dish of food *sent* to the table (Lat. *missum*, Old Fr. *mes*). The word occurs in AV and RV in Gn 43[34] (RSV 'portion'), 2 S 11[8] (RSV 'present'), Sir 30[18] (RSV 'offerings'), and RV introduces it at He 12[16] (AV 'morsel of meat,' RSV 'single meal').

MESSIAH.—**1. General.**—The word Messiah (sometimes Messias, following the Hellenized transcription) represents the Hebrew *māshîaḥ*, or *māshûaḥ* 'anointed,' from the verb *māshaḥ* 'anoint.' It is exactly rendered by the Greek *christos* 'anointed.'

The etymological background of the term is thus quite simple. Considerable terminological difficulties appear, however, when we try to relate ourselves to modern English usage of 'Messiah' and still more of the corresponding adjective 'Messianic.' In modern usage *futurity* or *expectation* is commonly taken to be essential to the meaning of 'Messiah' or 'Messianic.' Thus in the shorter *OED* the only definition given speaks of 'a promised deliverer of the Jewish nation, and hence Jesus of Nazareth as such deliverer.' Hence the word 'Messianic' is sometimes loosely extended to apply to any expectations of a golden age or realm of perfection lying in the future. In numerous books on the subject, when the question is raised 'What truly Messianic passages are there in the OT?', this is tacitly or explicitly taken to mean 'Which passages in the OT refer to a future and expected deliverer, or even to Jesus of Nazareth, or to an age of final plenty and welfare such as such a deliverer might be expected to initiate?'

This modern usage is, however, somewhat misleading. The concept of the *māshîaḥ* in Israel begins not with persons expected in the near or distant future but with persons now living. Saul was a *māshîaḥ* and was recognized by David as such. This article hopes to show how the expectation of the future *māshîaḥ* arose from the acknowledgement of the present *māshîaḥ*. But the conceptions of the first period, when the *māshîaḥ* is a person now living, are determinative and formative in a high degree for the later time. To define 'Messiah' as essentially futurist in sense is therefore to make a damaging split in what is one stream of thought. It means the peculiar assumption that Saul or David was called *māshîaḥ* but that they were not Messiahs or Messianic. The English versions of the Bible often rather obscure the linguistic facts here by using 'the anointed' where living persons are concerned. Justified as this may be in many ways, it is unfortunate in its disconnecting 'anointed' from 'Messiah,' when these are in fact the same word in Hebrew.

This is not to say that we can easily and conveniently reverse modern usage and say 'Messiah' or 'Messianic' without explanation every time the Hebrew says *māshîaḥ*. What is important is that an inadequate modern usage should not be allowed to impose a false delimitation or narrowing of the scope of the subject. The scope of the subject here will be taken as the whole range of meaning and association of Hebrew *māshîaḥ*, Greek *christos*. Where the terms 'Messiah' and 'Messianic' are used, an attempt will be made to make clear their meaning in the context concerned, if there is a danger of misunderstanding. For further discussion of this terminological question see Mowinckel, *He That Cometh*, ch. 1; Bentzen, *King and Messiah*, pp. 35–38 ('The King as the Present Messiah'); Anderson, in H. H. Rowley (ed.), *The O.T. and Modern Study*, p. 305. In general, the discussion about the sense of the terms has been so varied and so indecisive in recent years that it seems we cannot any longer take any sense for granted as axiomatic or as justified by tradition.

2. Oriental kingship.—We shall see that for the study of Israelite Messianism we must begin with the Israelite kingship. It is therefore convenient at this point to make a brief survey of kingship in the Ancient Near East. For this there is plentiful evidence from Egypt and Mesopotamia, while for Syria/Palestine the most important evidence is that now available from Ugarit. In addition it may be said that the whole field of kingship and its connexion with many aspects of religion has in recent years attracted much attention in anthropological study for many areas of the world (for a recent collection of essays over a wide range, see *La Regalità Sacra—The Sacral Kingship*, Leiden, 1959).

In general, we may say that the mythology embraces the world of the gods and the structure and needs of human society. The king is to some considerable extent the centre and pivot of human society, and is thus specially related to the world of the gods. He may have a superhuman descent or be born by a divine birth; or be adopted as son, the chosen or favourite of a god. Kingship as an institution is part of the divine order for the world, and may be traced back, as in the Sumerian King List, to the primeval times. On the other side the needs of society and their satisfaction are related by the gods to the king—order and justice, the defence of the oppressed; fertility and prosperity, victory in war and the establishment of peace. The king is thus a focus of the ordered and productive world in contrast to the chaos which constantly threatens it.

It is clear that all this is not mere theory, but embraces

and informs the actual processes of administration, justice, and warfare—what we would call political and economic matters. But on the other hand the mythology has its expression in ritual, for ritual is the re-enaction of the primal cosmic events in which the divinely-given order is established. Ritual involves such elements as the combat against hostile and chaotic powers, expiation of evil and dangerous elements, the promotion of fertility. The king as the focus of society's relation to the gods may have a priestly, dramatic, or representative part in such ritual. Recent study has had a special interest in the rituals of the New Year's Days in this connexion, because with the annual cycle of life in the great agricultural civilizations they seemed not unnaturally to have a specially important part in the ideas of re-establishment of the primal order and reintegration of society with the divine harmony. Within such types of thinking it is clear that salvation and well-being for a people would be closely related to their king; and this fact has led some scholars to suggest that the term 'Messianism' could be used without impropriety of this ideology or form of thought.

What has been said above is a considerable generalization, which seems broadly true for the mythological cultures of the Ancient Near East, but cannot be applied in an identical way in every situation. A notable contrast has been drawn in particular between Egypt and Mesopotamia. Although both are mythologically moulded cultures in which there is a certain similarity in the centrality of kingship, Egyptian thought differs from Mesopotamian in its underlying structure and not only in details within a common structure; and there are correspondingly great differences in the position of the king. It is in fact only by isolating certain features of kingship from the relevant culture as a whole that one can arrive at a common 'pattern' of kingship which can then be supposed to prevail in the same way in different cultural centres. In particular, certain important differences between Egypt and Mesopotamia have been abundantly demonstrated by recent study (see especially H. Frankfort, *Kingship and the Gods*). In Egypt the king was a god, the embodiment of Horus; he was, in fact, Horus. He is one with all gods. The mode of his union with deity includes both what we would call metaphysical and physical aspects. He is not only the symbol but the embodiment of the *ma'at* or divine right, justice, order, and harmony, by which the land, and indeed the world, is held in fruitfulness, peace, and life. Pharaoh was not a man at all, but totally belonged to the world of the gods. In Mesopotamia on the other hand the king was a man, but one greater than other men because he was the chosen of the gods, their favourite, one whom they had fashioned from the womb and upon whom they had laid the burden of government. Where the king is a 'son' of a god, this is meant in the sense mainly of choice, favouritism, adoption. Only at certain periods and in certain centres is the king's name preceded by the determinative indicating 'deity.' These cases are probably to be understood not as an innate divinity inhering in the king but rather as the occasional deification of him, *i.e.* the taking up of the human king into a closer association with the company of the gods—in Frankfort's opinion, mainly when a goddess chooses the king to be her bridegroom (*op. cit.* pp. 295–312). Although Mesopotamian government begins with the city-state, its theoretical scope becomes wider, and the kings call themselves kings of 'the land' or of 'the universe.' The institution of kingship on the other hand is traced back to the earliest times in the Sumerian King List, which begins 'when kingship was lowered from heaven.'

For Ugarit in northern Syria we also have good evidence of a kingship closely integrated with myth and religion. 'First and foremost in the society of ancient Canaan as exemplified at Ugarit stood the king in all the strength of his unique sacral status, the son of former rulers and the father of rulers to come, who was celebrated in the Ugaritic saga as suckled by the goddesses Atherat and Anat. . . . In the more primitive age to which the Krt and Aqht texts refer the king, realizing in his person the sacramental union of his people and their god, personally represented the people as their priest and mediated the divine revelation' (J. Gray, *The Legacy of Canaan*, 1957, p. 160). Essential to the kingly office is the administration of justice, in particular the vindication of the widow, the orphan, and the oppressed. But kingship does not maintain itself on the formal grounds of the institution; it requires the kingly power to be manifested in the splendour of the palace, the sexual vigour of the king, his begetting of sons to follow him and maintain his name.

This Ugaritic evidence is of special value to us for our purpose because of its nearness to Palestine. But it would be dangerous to assume that the situation of Late Bronze Ugarit was uniformly reproduced all over Syria/Palestine. Ugarit's position in the far north, near to Hurrian and other non-Semitic cultures, may have developed the older Semitic tribal inheritance in a special direction. It may, however, be taken as very probable that, although thought and practice were not uniform, a form of kingship closely integrated with myth and religion was widespread in the settled culture of Canaan during the first centuries of the Israelite settlement.

3. Israelite kingship.—(*a*) *The historical traditions.*—It was clearly realized in Israel that the monarchy, associated as it was with the will of God, did not go back into primeval times but had a historical origin of which a fairly good tradition was preserved; and that one of the most formative times in the Divine activity towards Israel, namely the story of the patriarchs, the Exodus, the giving of the Law, and the conquest of Palestine, had all been before the institution of kingship began, although it was well known to have existed among other peoples. Cf occasional remarks like Gn 36^{31}, Jg 21^{25}.

The story of the beginnings and the formative period of the kingdom is given in the books of Samuel. It has long been noticed that different estimates of the kingdom are represented in the different traditions brought together here. In some it is represented as a rejection of God by the people that they have demanded a king, so 1 S 8. But even in these passages God agrees to the demand which He has called a rejection of Himself, and the king is chosen and installed in a sacral act. In other passages the king is seen as foreknown and chosen by God. This aspect of the predestination of the kingship is hinted at frequently during the story of Samuel himself; *e.g.* the song of Hannah is related to the 'anointed one,' 1 S 2^{10}, and the future fall of the house of Eli is prophesied not because of its relevance to Samuel but because of the future priesthood of Zadok which shall be related to the anointed of the Lord, *i.e.* to David, 1 S 2^{35}. In their present composite form, which must have been attained while the Judaean kingdom was still in being, the story somewhat paradoxically combines the idea of a Divine purpose and foreordination with the element of human rebellion in the making of the kingdom.

The first kings, Saul and David, are initiated into kingship through anointing by a sacred official, and this remained the practice afterwards (Saul—1 S 10^{1}; David—1 S $16^{1,12-13}$; Solomon—1 K 1^{45}). The anointing may probably be taken as a ritual representation of life, health, and plenty as concentrated in the person anointed. It cannot be certainly said what place anointing had in Israelite religious practice before the first kings. We hear of the anointing of a *maṣṣēbhāh* or standing stone by Jacob, Gn 31^{13}, probably an application of oil, fat, or blood as forces of life to the deity. The numerous references in the Priestly documents of the Pentateuch to the anointing of priests may with some probability be taken as a practice later than and derived from the anointing of kings. It is likely, then, that the use of anointing as an installation was a Canaanite practice adopted by Israel, and its first mention is in Jotham's parable spoken at Shechem where a city-state kingship of the Canaanite type was established, Jg $9^{8,15}$.

At any rate, whatever other places anointing may have had, we can be certain that within the lifetime of the first king the title *m^eshîaḥ Yahweh* 'the anointed of Yahweh,' was amply recognized as a proper title for the king chosen and established by God (*e.g.* 1 S 16^{6-13} 24^{6} 26^{11}). Though the story represents Saul as having been rejected by Yahweh, nevertheless David cannot but continue to see him as the anointed one and therefore sacrosanct, in spite of his fierce enmity to David.

One cannot say that during Saul's time the status of the anointed one carried with it distinct lineaments of function, power, and authority. Saul was able to summon the men of Israel to arms in emergency, but it is not clear how far his activity in this went beyond the action of charismatic deliverers like Gideon. Pressure from the Philistines, the lack of a solid foundation for personal power, the inertia and unadaptability of older institutions, and Saul's own inner instability, contributed to prevent him from building a new and positive tradition round the status he held. How far Canaanite ideals of the kingly office were known to and adopted by Saul we can hardly tell from our evidence; but in general he seems to have adhered to the older Israelite traditions and not to have moved far towards assimilation with the Canaanites; cf, for example, 2 S 21^{2}.

With David, however, the kingly power assumes forms quite clearly distinct from those of the older deliverers. There is a personal royal domain of some extent and a professional army, small indeed but devoted to the king's interests; there is a kingly initiative in policy and planning; from the capture of Jerusalem onwards the royal city, the king's property, is the capital. There the palace is built, and the royal sanctuary becomes the centre of older Israelite traditions when the Ark is brought to rest there; there is also probably some assertion of continuity with older pre-Davidic Jerusalem tradition (Melchizedek) and of priest-kingship. And, perhaps most important of all, a dynastic principle is asserted; this was never established beyond doubt under Saul, who in some of his moments himself, as there is no reason to doubt, came to believe that David would succeed him (1 S 24^{20}), an expectation which his son Jonathan certainly held. What it means to be 'the anointed of Yahweh' is thus shown with much more positive content by David. Yet the very negativity of the picture of Saul which our sources give, rejected by Yahweh and rather a failure among men, makes all the more emphatic the fact that David still calls him 'the anointed of Yahweh.' The part of Saul cannot be neglected in any assessment of what is Messianic.

For in fact an important theme of the Books of Samuel in their present form, if not indeed their main theme, is the relation between Saul and David, not simply as historical persons, but as anointed ones; and between the house of Saul and the house of David, the two Messianic houses—using the word in the sense of the families chosen and marked out by the distinction of anointing given to their head and whose destinies are so different and yet so intimately interwoven. The dramatic tension of the story is worked out by the tracing of a number of subsidiary themes which run through the story. These can only be indicated in outline here. They include: the contrast of Saul's disobedience which brings disaster and David's sins which are turned to good; the attachment of Jonathan to David and David's promise to care for his descendants after his death, and the sequel; the marriages of David with daughters of Saul, which in the end never produce a child belonging to both families; the bitter and tragic strife and rebellion within David's family; the twin prophecies of Nathan, that there should always be a king of David's house, and that there should always be a sword against that house; and above all the question of guilt, with the strong sense that the Anointed should not avenge himself and bring guilt upon his house, but should allow Yahweh to take vengeance for him, and the repeated profit given to David by deeds of blood which are needed in his interest but which he cannot condone or accept as his guilt. And thus we have twin narratives of expiation in 2 S 21^{1-14} and 24^{1-25}, the first for the guilt of the house of Saul now laid to rest, and the second for a sin of David, with the place of expiation now established for the future.

It seems clear that this narrative, though much of it based on eye-witness experience, has its real interest in the characters as those to whom in that first and formative period the status of 'anointed of Yahweh' was given, along with their families. On the other hand we may expect that this story may have been fruitful in effects on later thought.

Although the term 'Messiah' has scarcely been used in this section, we must reiterate that 'Messiah' is merely a transliteration of the word we have translated as 'Anointed.' We are therefore justified in speaking of David and Saul as Messianic figures and their families as Messianic houses so long as we can understand the term 'Messianic' as equivalent to the *māshîaḥ* 'anointed' of the passages. The sense is not of future deliverers but of present chosen representatives of Yahweh. But a certain future element is now introduced in the story of David which is potentially important—the promise of the permanent future continuance of the Davidic house in the kingship before Yahweh (2 S 7). It is this element which more than any other gives an opening for the growth of Messianism in the future sense.

Meanwhile we may point to one or two famous passages which have traditionally been regarded as 'Messianic' in the sense of pointing towards the future deliverer or towards Jesus Christ, but which are better taken as related to David and his reign. The first is the famous 'Shiloh' prophecy in the blessing of Judah, Gn 49^{10}. Jacob sees the sceptre of primacy in the hands of Judah, to remain there until it is finally exercised by the prince to whom nations owe allegiance—'until he comes to whom it belongs' (so RSV), or perhaps 'until his ruler, *i.e.* Judah's ruler, comes' (Akk. *shelu* or *shilu*, 'ruler'). The second is the Balaam prophecy of the Star, Nu 24^{17}, which shall come from Jacob and overcome the people of Moab and Edom. It was, of course, David who first subjected these areas to Israelite domination. It is quite possible that both these passages are not purely *vaticinia ex eventu*, *i.e.* pseudo-prophecies produced in David's time to refer to events which have already come to pass, but are built on older pre-Davidic material which already asserted the excellence of Judah and the hope of victory over the surrounding nations. But it is clear that in their present form their fulfilment is supposed to lie in David; they are then Messianic in the sense of seeing Judah as the tribe from which the reigning Messianic house of David has come, and of seeing the nature of this Messianic calling fulfilled in domination over the surrounding nations. In later times, however, both passages are taken Messianically in the sense of prophesying the *future* deliverer, and this interpretation is confirmed from Qumrân.

(*b*) *The Psalms*.—In contrast with an earlier generation, which relegated many or most of the Psalms to a post-exilic or even a Maccabaean setting, most scholars now are prepared to assign a substantial proportion of them to the time of the monarchy. In this case the Psalter can be used with due care as evidence for the liturgical practice and the associated world of thought in the Solomonic Temple.

The Jerusalem Temple stood in the closest relation to the royal family. The city was royal property and the sanctuary was part of the palace complex. We hear of ritual actions on the part of the kings from time to time (David in 2 S 6^{16ff}; Solomon in 1 K 8); and there is no reason to doubt the statement of 2 S 8^{18} that 'David's sons were priests' although it is not clear how their priesthood is related to that of Zadok and Abiathar. It has indeed been suggested that the king played a major part in ritual, participating in coronation ceremonies and ritual combats. We cannot enter into this here, but may regard it as probable that the association of the king with the ritual was effective in fixing, stylizing and giving permanence to the forms of poetical expression. Some characteristic themes may now be mentioned:

(1) The victory of the king over his enemies and the submission to him of the kings of other nations (*e.g.* Ps 2, 110).

(2) The distress, affliction, and humiliation of the king, which nearly brings him into the realm of chaos and the underworld; and his vindication through his appeal to Yahweh (*e.g.* Ps 18, probably also Ps 22).

(3) The divine birth, choice, and installation of the king (Ps 2, 110).

(4) The maintenance of justice and the defence of the weak (*e.g.* Ps 72).

(5) The blessing of fertility and abundance given to the nation through the righteousness, strength, and life of the king (Ps 72).

(6) The continuance of the name, the strength and the dynasty of the king (*e.g.* Ps 72, 89, 132).

In these passages the term *māshîaḥ* ' the Anointed ' refers not to a future deliverer but to the reigning king (Ps 105^{15} is a rather exceptional extension of it figuratively to the patriarchs). For the people the anointed one is ' our shield ' (Ps 84^{9}); for God to look favourably on His anointed is to convey blessing and prosperity to the people.

We must also mention the Psalms of the kingship of Yahweh, which in many cases contain the formula ' Yahweh reigns ' or ' Yahweh has come to reign,' *e.g.* Ps 47, 93, 95, 96, 97, 98, 99. It is now widely held that these were used in a part of the autumn or New Year feast, in which the reigning king took some part to express the kingship of Yahweh. Whether this be so or not, we must notice a common theme of these Psalms—the thought of the creation of the world as an act of Yahweh's kingship, and along with that its defence against the forces of chaos which threaten it; and the suggestion of the coming or nearer approach of Yahweh with the dawning or beginning of a new era. This new era is not meant as a distant and future ' end of the world,' but is something immediately introduced and inaugurated in the celebration. It is not probable that the kingship of Yahweh is a contrast or opposition to the position of His anointed representative (in Ugarit also there is kingship among the gods, as there is among men); but certainly in the songs of the kingship of Yahweh the human king recedes from the centre of attention, whether because he is representing Yahweh's kingship or not. Nevertheless the themes of Yahweh's kingship may coincide with those associated with the earthly king, *e.g.* cf Ps 47 and Ps 2, Ps 98–99 and Ps 72.

In general then it would appear that the kingship as we know it in the Psalms is an institution central in the impartation of Yahweh's gifts and blessing to the people. Its centrality is something which can hardly be derived from the old pre-Conquest traditions of Israel, and must to some extent be attributed to Canaanite influence. But a good deal of transformation has also taken place; we may mention (1) reference to the historical realities of the Davidic house, its afflictions and its triumphs; (2) the influence of the older Israelite traditions; (3) in particular, the force exerted by the traditional Israelite conceptions of God and man, so that Yahweh is the only deity given positive recognition, the characteristic polytheistic patterns of mythology are weakened, and a limit is set to the mythological understanding of a person like the king. The divine birth and sonship of the king is probably not to be understood as a sharing in the Divine essence but as a belonging to the Divine work and purpose by predestination, election and adoption.

There are, then, a series of aspects and functions of the present reigning king which we may be justified in calling ' Messianic.' The ' Anointed ' or ' Messiah ' in the Psalms probably nowhere means a deliverer to come in the future. There are, however, a number of aspects which involve a future interest of some kind, namely (1) the promise of dynastic continuity, (2) the promise of victory over enemies and exaltation over all other kings, and (3) the initiation of a new time of right and prosperity, associated with the nearness and the kingship of Yahweh, which could be the starting point for an increasing futurist development.

4. Kingship and the classical prophets.—The Davidic settlement was not permanent, and after Solomon the northern kingdom not only broke away from the house of David but appears to have forsaken also the dynastic system; at any rate no dynasty succeeded in establishing itself for very long in fact. The tradition understands this whole matter theologically: Solomon followed other gods, and must lose most of his kingdom; only because of the promise to David is he left with Judah. But going farther back, we can see that the community between Israel and Judah, which David had to a fair extent himself achieved, had already been severely disturbed by events in David's reign provoked by the tragic strife in the royal family itself (2 S 19–20) and especially by David's own reliance (after the Absalom rebellion) on the loyalty of Judah to a Judaean king.

For the two centuries after Solomon we have little evidence to trace the conceptions held of the kingship of David's line; the great prophets of the 9th cent. worked mainly in the N. But it is clear that in part they are taking a stand on a revived old Israelite tradition and from it attacking the syncretistic religion and the more absolute claims of power of certain kings. In the 8th cent. the prophets are still more emphatic in their criticisms of contemporary life, more radical in the judgment and destruction they see as impending, more hostile to the security found in religious practices, in the supposed special place of the nation in the plans of God, and in the expected favourable aspect of the ' Day of Yahweh.'

The main interest in the Davidic kingship is found, however, in the Jerusalem prophet Isaiah, who had much to say about the related subjects of the Davidic line and the city of Jerusalem. His message is closely related to the political history of the time, with the renewed Assyrian pressure towards the W., and the planning of defensive alliances in Syria and Palestine.

Is 7 concerns an incident when the northern alliance tries to force Ahaz to join them, and failing that to replace him on the Judaean throne by a king of non-Davidic line. The use of the term ' house of David ' in vv.[2, 13] show that it is the king as representative of the anointed house, and not just in himself, who is being tested here. The prophet asks for trust in God. By the old dynastic promises the Davidic house is to be ' constant ' or ' established ' (2 S 7^{16} etc.); but this continuance is now to depend upon trust. Ahaz's refusal to ask a sign is probably taken as a refusal to trust in Divine action here. God will therefore give His own sign, the child Immanuel to be born. Although scholars are deeply divided over the interpretation of this, it seems to the writer reasonable to take the Immanuel as an ideal kingly child of the Davidic house, who will fulfil indeed what the actual Davidic line in its representative Ahaz is failing to do. He is thus a Messianic child, soon to be born, who will be what the true Anointed should be, the representative or embodiment of the presence of God with His people. For the name Immanuel, ' God with us,' we may compare the frequent thought of Yahweh's being ' with ' David, and the curds and honey may with some probability be taken as food of paradise (cf ch. 11). This interpretation is best supported by comparing the passage Mic 5^{2-4}, a passage which, in spite of the judgment of many older scholars, may very probably be taken as a genuine prophecy of Micah, and therefore close in time and situation to Isaiah. The Micah passage speaks of the birth of the true Davidic ruler whose origin lies in the primeval times. We have thus now come to the idea of a Messiah in the more usual sense, of a coming deliverer, although his coming may be expected soon, certainly in the Isaiah passage. But it is clear that this expectation of a coming Messiah is an extension into the future of the forms of thought surrounding the reigning Anointed.

Is 9^{1-7} is also in all probability genuinely Isaianic; it comes from the time when certain northern areas of

Israel (v.^{1}) were incorporated as provinces in the Assyrian Empire ; some of these were areas first brought under Israelite domination under David, and now that they are ' in darkness ' the prophet sees the Messianic child, the new David, born to establish right and prosperity. Is 11^{1-9} can less certainly, but still with considerable probability, be taken as the work of Isaiah. The coming king and judge of David's line will be richly endowed with the Spirit of Yahweh ; righteous judgment will be his function, as in the older kingly ideal ; but in this time there will be a state of innocence and peace as in the primeval paradise. That kingly rule had sometimes been associated with the paradise is seen from Ezk 28^{12-13}, and of course the element of the primeval man's rule over the other creatures is seen in Gn 1, cf Ps 8.

In Isaiah's work then we may see clearly the emergence of one who is of the Davidic house but is other than the reigning king, and who will represent far more fully the ideals of the kingly office.

A century later the next of the great prophets, Jeremiah, is also concerned with the standing and the destiny of the Davidic house. Jer 22^{1-8} reiterates the demand for obedience by the king to the norms of justice, and points out that if this obedience is given the Davidic dynasty is assured of continuance ; otherwise Yahweh is prepared to destroy it ; oracles about various kings follow ; Jehoiachin is rejected and exiled, and none of his offspring will succeed him on the Davidic throne. The next passage (23^{1-8}) speaks of how the evil shepherds will be punished and careful shepherds put in their place ; and in coming days God will raise up a ' righteous Branch ' as king ; the name ' Yahweh our righteousness ' (*Yahweh ṣidhḳēnû*) is a pun on and a contrast with the name of similar meaning of Zedekiah, the last of the Davidic line. The genuineness of this passage as a Jeremianic oracle has been much disputed, and it has been held to be dependent on Zec 3^{8} 6^{12} (*e.g.* Mowinckel, *He that Cometh*, pp. 19 f, 164, 456). In view of the interest of Jeremiah in the Davidic dynasty as expressed in ch. 22, however, it would seem reasonable to take 23^{1-8} as being in substance his thought, and to suppose that like Isaiah he looked for one who should be more truly a representative of anointed kingship then the present rulers were, and that the visible tottering of the dynasty in the early 6th cent. lent stimulus to this thought. Another form, perhaps rather later, of the same idea is Jer 33^{14-26}, probably spoken after 586 but not necessarily long after ; it includes the priestly family of the Levites with the royal house of the Davidides. Cf also 17^{19-27}, which envisages the continuance of the Davidic line on condition of obedience to the law of the Sabbath (this passage also is often taken as not Jeremiah's, wrongly in the writer's opinion). In general, Jeremiah contributed less of real originality to the understanding of the kingship and the development of the expectation of the coming true or ideal king than did Isaiah ; but his thought on the matter is sharpened by the impending disaster of the monarchy. The book of Jeremiah in its present form sees special significance in Jeremiah as the prophet who lived through and continued after the fall of Jerusalem, and this is one reason for the addition of historical material about this period (39–44) and about the later return to favour of Jehoiachin (52^{31-34}).

A not dissimilar position is occupied by the contemporary Ezekiel. In Ezk 21^{25-27} we have a prophecy of the dethronement and profanation of the king, probably Zedekiah ; there is to be a state of ruin (there are some obscurities here) until ' he comes whose right it is,' *i.e.* the rightful king to whom the royal emblems and dignity are to be restored. The wording here may perhaps be a hint at or an interpretation of the ' Shiloh ' passage of Gn 49^{10}. A number of modern scholars hold this passage to be part of the post-exilic supplementation of Ezekiel, but this seems improbable to the writer. The following passages belong either to the later period of Ezekiel when, after the fulfilment of the disaster which like Jeremiah he had expected and pronounced, his message turned to a new note of hope and restoration for his people or to a later supplementer of his work : 17^{22-24}, the tender sprig to be plucked from the cedar and planted on the heights of Israel ; 34^{23f}, where David, *i.e.* a true offspring of David's line, will be the one and faithful shepherd of Israel (cf the thought of Jer 23) ; 37^{22-28} looks forward to the reunion of Israel and Judah under ' my servant David.' In the programme of restoration and reform in Ezk 40–48, however, the central emphasis is on the priestly Temple service, and the ' prince ' is noticed mainly as responsible for the provision of the offerings, 45^{16-17} ; the holy city lies within his territory, 48^{21-22}.

Something of the aura which continued to attach to the kingship at and after its end, in spite of the criticisms of the later prophets, can be seen in the meditation on Zedekiah's fate, La 4^{20}—' The breath of our nostrils, the Lord's anointed, was taken in their pits, he of whom we said, " Under his shadow we shall live among the nations ".'

The later centuries of the kingdom also saw a rise in the importance of the priesthood, a tendency which is regarded by some scholars as a ' democratization ' of a function originally belonging to the kings, and in particular the great prominence of a ' chief ' or ' high ' priest. It is in post-exilic documents that we hear of this person also with the title ' anointed ' (*e.g.* Lv 4^{3}). By this time the high priest is deemed to be of the tribe of Levi and of Zadokite or Aaronic family. We have here the datum point from which is later developed the idea of the priestly, Levitical or Aaronic, Messiah.

It will be observed that the position of the king throughout this period cannot be simply characterized in the modern categories of ' religious ' and ' political.' He is not purely one or the other, nor can his functions be separated between the one and the other. Even as ' political ' ruler of Israel, his relation to other kings and to the rest of the world goes beyond ' practical ' and ' realistic ' policies. He is a man, the man whom Yahweh has chosen ; but in certain circles of tradition he may be traced back also to a Divine, a primeval or a superhuman origin.

5. The Exile and after.—The tendencies which we have traced in the greater prophets, and in particular the expectation of one who would fulfil the true calling and nature of the Davidic kingship more truly than the reigning king, was immensely strengthened and popularized by the end of the monarchy. The expected restoration of Israel included the restoration of the Davidic house and the rebuilding of the Temple ; and more widely, the vindication of Israel against the heathen nations, the establishment of peace, the renewal of fruitfulness, and the acknowledgement by the world of the dominion of Yahweh. ' Messiah ' in this case means clearly the expected Davidic ruler of the days of restoration ; the total expected restoration can be spoken of as the Messianic age.

Considerable variety of thought remains possible, however. In particular the unknown prophet of the exilic period whom we call Deutero-Isaiah, and the group of Servant Songs which are woven into his work, show original and unusual features. First we must mention the characterization of the Persian Cyrus as the anointed of Yahweh, Is 45^{1}, cf 44^{28} and 41^{25ff} 46^{11}. Along with this goes a noticeable absence of interest in the restoration of the Davidic house, although the return of Israel from exile and the rebuilding of the Temple are clearly spoken of. It would be perhaps reasonable to say that this prophet follows the line shown in Jeremiah of regarding the great heathen king rather than the Judaean monarch as the central active instrument of Yahweh ; Jeremiah called Nebuchadnezzar Yahweh's ' servant ' (Jer 27^{6}), Deutero-Isaiah goes on to call Cyrus ' anointed.' The function of Cyrus is the bringing of judgment on Babylon and the restitution of Jerusalem ; he does not himself understand or know the God of Israel (45^{4-5}) ; 45^{3} probably does not mean that the prophet expects Cyrus to become a worshipper of Yahweh in the fullest sense.

A more positive place in Deutero-Isaiah is taken by the 'servant,' both the general thought of Israel as the servant in the prophet's work and the more particular picture of the servant, seen at least sometimes as a single person, in the 'Servant Songs.' How far is the 'servant' of these passages to be understood as a Messianic figure? Some scholars recently have pointed to traits in the songs which are related to aspects of the royal theology, *e.g.* affliction and vindication, the maintenance of right, the representation of the people; and stylistically Deutero-Isaiah seems to have used to some extent the poetical forms of the royal cult. On the other hand it is clear that there are traits in the servant which point towards a prophetic rather than a kingly figure. It may be suggested that in Deutero-Isaiah there is a splitting apart of the royal theology; the task of armed vindication falls to Cyrus; but while there is no cultivation of the royal Davidic line as central to the future of Israel, the servant figure, itself composed from prophetic, patriarchal and kingly ideals, occupies the place of centrality which the Messianic house of David otherwise held and thus received a certain likeness of pattern to it. The servant figure therefore is not so much Messianic as something that takes the place of, and assumes some part of the forms of, the Messianic. Its reference seems to be past, in that some passages look back on a life of hardship and suffering, but also future in that a vindication from God is expected, and in that the form of the servant is expected to remain influential in the mission of Israel.

The thought of the Messianic line in a more traditional form, however, was given new life when Zerubbabel, a true descendant of the Davidic line, became for a short time prince of the revived Judaean community under Persian rule. With him was associated Joshua the high priest, and they are the two anointed ones (literally, 'sons of oil') of Zec 4^{14}. Zerubbabel's Messianic position as the son of David now actually reigning, and expected to introduce a new era of blessing, is expressed in Hag 2^{23}, Zec 3^{8-10} 4^{7} 6^{9-14}. This last passage has been taken by many scholars to have represented originally the coronation as Davidic king of Zerubbabel, by whose throne the priest (in fact Joshua) would stand; subsequently the name of Zerubbabel dropped out of the text. The peaceful concord between the two bearers of Messianic dignity, priest and prince, is emphasized. In fact the time of Zerubbabel was a very difficult one, and ushered in no age of perfection; its great achievement was the restoration of the Temple, but Zerubbabel himself had only a brief period of prominence, and then disappeared from history; perhaps he was considered dangerous by the Persian authorities, but he may have continued for some time in his modest position as governor, for he never had real independence. After him we know no more of members of the Davidic house upon whom similar hopes could be placed. With the departing of that modest but real reproduction of the Davidic pattern which Zerubbabel represented, the expectation of the coming Messiah revived and remained powerful; many of the later prophetic passages probably came from this period. In such as Zec 9^{9-10} the influence of the old kingship pattern is clear; the incident is pictured probably as a coronation procession.

Unlike the time of Zerubbabel, that of Ezra and Nehemiah is marked by a sober attention to law and organization and an absence of Messianic concentration; these men may have expected the future Messiah, but their main contribution to Judaism lay elsewhere. In any case, as later Judaism settled down in its concentration on the law, there occurred also an efflorescence of futurist and eschatological thought. From this period come prophecies like Malachi, the later parts of Zechariah, and certain late portions incorporated in the book of Isaiah. The interest in the future is not only in a restoration of the Davidic kingdom over Israel, but in the approach of Yahweh for judgment, victory over the final enemies of His people, the punishment of the wicked and the vindication of the righteous, and the healing and renewing of creation. In such eschatological passages the Messiah often does not appear, and often Yahweh is seen as carrying out His final purpose without any mediation. The Messiah is by no means essential to any expression of the future hope.

Finally this late prophecy turns into apocalyptic. This form of thought is more conscious of the larger sweep of history than the older prophecy, and commonly works with the periodization of history. Past time is interpreted as an episode awaiting the inauguration of the new; there is a strong sense that the new period is soon to begin, and a feeling of present crisis; a period of strong transitional woe and pain opens the way to the final age.

In apocalyptic, too, the future expectation can be developed with no mention of the Messiah. It is so for example in most of Daniel. The anointed ones of 9^{25-26} are probably (1) Zerubbabel or Joshua and (2) Onias the high priest—persons of the past when Daniel was written, although represented as future by the predictive form of writing. The eschatological kingdom of God is mentioned in 2^{44}, but no Messianic king. *Jubilees* has little to say of the Messiah, and the *Assumption of Moses* does not mention him.

The figure 'like a son of man' in Dn 7^{13} is probably not intended as the Messiah. Modern scholarship has frequently interpreted him as merely a figurative representation of Israel or the pious Israelites; it has also connected him with the idea of a Primordial Man, connected with paradise, glorious and wise, hidden in heaven but to be revealed at the end. The writer would prefer to understand him as an angelic figure, charged with the guardianship of God's kingdom (see J. Barr, 'Daniel,' *Peake Commentary*[2], ed. Black and Rowley). In any case the one like a son of man is a heavenly and eschatological figure, coming with clouds and heralding the last stage in the apocalyptic periodic scheme. 'Son of man' itself means 'a human being' (cf Ps 8^{4}), and it can be misleading to give it capitals and the definite article at this stage, since it is not really a title (the same applies in places to the usage of 'The Messiah'). It seems unlikely to the writer that a completely independent figure entitled 'the Son of Man' ever existed.

Until recently it has commonly been held that the next development was to be found in the 'Similitudes' of Enoch, to which the 'Elect One' (the common title for the Messiah in this work) is introduced as 'that Son of Man' in a passage closely following Daniel. The view that Enoch therefore developed the term 'Son of Man' much farther than Daniel, and in particular united it with the Messiah, in the 2nd cent. or so B.C., is now very doubtful, because no fragments from this section of Enoch have been found at Qumrân, though much has been found from outside the Similitudes. It seems likely, therefore, that this section of Enoch is post-Christian, and may represent syncretistic Judaistic Christianity. Certain other apocalyptic works in which the cosmic and heavenly dimension of eschatology was emphasized can also no longer be deemed pre-Christian, *e.g.* 2 Bar.

The literary type of 'Testaments of Patriarchs' was also known at Qumrân, but the developed *Testament of the Twelve Patriarchs* is probably a Christian writing which used such earlier testaments. *The Testament of the Twelve Patriarchs* is an important source for the picture of the double Messiahship of Davidic king and Aaronic/Levitical high priest together; we have already said something of the beginnings of this picture. In the present stage of study it is, however, difficult to use actual passages of the existing version of the Testaments as evidence for the pre-Christian period. But in view of the Qumrân evidence (see below) we may be fairly sure that an expectation of the two Messianic figures was current in the early circles to which the Testaments go back. We have seen that at least one of the 'anointed ones' of Dn 9 was a high priest, and *Jub* 31 promises princely dignity to both Levi and Judah, with the emphasis rather on Levi. It has been held that the importance of the Levitical Messiah arose from the power of the Hasmonaean house, who were themselves priests and not of Judahite stock. It now seems more probable that, though the Hasmonaean dynasty may have had some influence, the idea has its origin in older tradition, in the co-ordination of king and priest, and that the importance of priestly influence in this period, and of the centrality of the Temple for atonement and liturgy, was the main influence working for the prominence of Levi.

From Rabbinic sources in the 2nd cent. A.D. and after we hear of a distinction of two Messiahs, the Messiah of Joseph or Ephraim, and the Messiah of David or Judah; the former was to fight in the final conflict with God's enemies and perish. The origin of this distinction is imperfectly understood. The absence of all mention of it from Qumrân strengthens the common opinion that it did not arise until post-Christian times.

Scriptural interpretation was also at work interpreting of the Messiah many passages from the OT. Unfortunately, apart from the Qumrân texts, most of our sources are in the Christian era. The Targum interpreted Is 53 of the Messiah, but did not understand the Messiah to suffer as the Servant in the original did. By the 3rd cent. the reference to the Messiah of the 'one like a son of man' in Daniel could be taken for granted by the Rabbis. Messianic force was given to many other passages. The more conservative and modest picture of the Messiah is that in *Ps Sol.* 17–18, which very largely follows the type of Ps 2.

It seems probable that the idea of a Messiah making atonement by suffering was not common or normal in this period. It is true that the Messiah could be thought of as one who would die, but this is because he shares in the lot of mortal humanity. He might be thought to suffer in the sense of being involved in the great conflicts or woes of the last time. But this would not be thought of as principally vicarious in purpose or atoning in result, although any suffering might have a certain meritorious and beneficial effect. We have already seen how the Targum to Is 53 understands the Servant there as the Messiah but removes the idea of vicarious and atoning suffering. It sees the Messiah as interceding for the forgiveness of the people; he is, like the ancient king, their powerful representative before God; but his work is more the overcoming of enemies than the removal of sin.

We also hear of other persons than the Messiah who are connected with the coming of the last days. The return of Elijah is mentioned in Mal 4^{5}, though no Messiah is mentioned there. Taken along with the expectation of the Messiah, he becomes a forerunner; Moses sometimes has the same function. Dt 18^{15} leads either to the expectation of Moses or of some other prophet as forerunner. Indeed the Prophet may become the main figure of expectation. The Messiah also may assume some prophetic characteristics, such as discernment and wisdom, and ability to pronounce on legal and interpretative questions.

With the periodization of world history in apocalyptic, it was possible to calculate the time of the end, and many chronological schemes were directed towards this. But there was also the school of thought which held that this could not be known, and that the coming of the Messiah was dependent on various other circumstances, such as the obedience of Israel or the culmination of wickedness. In spite of the woes and conflicts which were to surround the coming of the Messiah, he would be a man among men, and his Messiahship might be hidden even as he lived on earth until the moment of its manifestation. We thus find around the turn of the era numerous pretenders to Messianic dignity, of whom the most notable was Simon bar Cochba, military leader of the Second Jewish Revolt. Much of this popular Messianism during the Roman period had a distinct revolutionary and nationalistic air; Josephus (*BJ* VI. v. 4 [312 f]) mentions Messianic excitement as a main cause of the drift to war in A.D. 66.

The Samaritans also had Messianic expectations of a kind (Jn 4^{25}). Later we hear of a figure called the Taheb, the human agent of God in ushering in the time of Divine favour. According to J. Bowman, however (*JJS* vi [1955], p. 72), the Samaritans never really developed the Messianic idea and often continued to think of God alone as active in the end.

6. The Messiah at Qumrân.—'And they (*i.e.* the men of the sect) shall be judged by the first statutes, by which the men of the community began to be disciplined, until there come a Prophet and the Messiahs of Aaron and Israel' (1*QS* ix. 10–11). This may be taken as the basic text for the Messianism of Qumrân. There remains a certain amount of doubt about its relation to statements in *CDC* and other Qumrân texts; and upon this depends the question whether there was a quite uniform doctrine of the Messiah(s) throughout the life of the sect. It is interesting that in an early copy of this same Rule the paragraph of which the above sentence is part does not occur (Milik, *Ten Years of Discovery*, p. 123).

The passage refers to two persons, the priestly and the royal (or lay) Messiahs, as well as their forerunner the prophet. It thus follows the old tradition which envisages the restoration jointly of king and priest. Another interpretation, that 'Aaron and Israel' are to be taken together, giving the sense that the Messianic figure(s) will arise from within the sect which calls itself 'Aaron and Israel,' now seems less likely, although it is quite possible on other grounds that the anointed ones were expected to appear from the community.

Along with this we should take a text (1*QSa*) which, after other regulations, gives the order for a session and feast 'when God begets the Messiah' (the word 'begets' has been emended to 'brings' by a number of scholars, but in the writer's opinion this change of text is very precarious). First 'the priest' enters and sits, the other priests ranging themselves before him; after this the Messiah of Israel takes his seat, and the chiefs of the clans before him. No one is to touch the food before the priest; he must bless it and touch it; only then shall the Messiah of Israel touch it; afterwards the others also bless it.

In our first passage 'Aaron' came before 'Israel,' and in this we find the precedence of the priest over the (royal or Davidic) Messiah. Does this mean an absolute superiority in rank of the priestly Messiah? This has frequently been affirmed, but seems doubtful to the writer. The order 'Aaron and Israel' is used simply because of the general precedence of priests over laity, and is used apart from the Messianic reference, *e.g.* *CDC* vi. 2. The precedence at the sacral feast emphasizes the essential place of the priest in giving the benediction and beginning the meal; it is the guarding of a priestly function, rather than an assertion of an absolute superiority. Further, there are a number of passages where 'the Messiah' in the singular is used and is understood of the lay or Davidic ruler (*e.g.* the passage about his begetting quoted above). In other words, the term in the singular, 'the anointed one,' was still taken to refer to the Davidic ruler as in the Jewish tradition generally; but used in the plural, or with the word 'priest' (as 'the anointed priest') it would include the coming high priest whose functions accompanied those of the ruler and took precedence of them in some ways. Further, it has been widely held, and perhaps prematurely, that all meals of the community were representations or anticipations of this Messianic feast. The idea of the great eschatological banquet was no doubt developed from passages in the prophets like Is 25^{6-8} 55^{1-5}.

The fragmentary series of Blessings (1*QSb*) is in four sections, covering the people, the chief or anointed priest (this unfortunately much damaged), the priests in general, and the 'prince of the congregation'; the relation of priest and prince is like that in Ezk 40–48, and for the arrangement cf that of Lv 4. The page of Testimonia from Cave 4 quotes from Dt 18 (the Prophet like Moses), from Nu 24 (the Star of Jacob and Sceptre of Israel), and from Dt 33 (Moses' blessing to Levi). These are taken as testimonies to the coming Prophet and either to the royal Messiah (the Star) and the priestly Messiah

(Levi) or to the priestly and royal Messiahs (Star and Sceptre respectively) and to the priesthood (Levi). The Star and Sceptre are interpreted separately in *CDC* vii. 18–20. We may notice in passing how Bar Cochba regarded himself as Messiah of Israel and associated with himself the priest Eleazar; in this case Bar Cochba seems to have held the primacy. Gn 49[10] was interpreted of the Davidic Messiah, and Is 10–11 probably of his victorious warfare against the enemies of God. The priestly and military leaders in the War scroll may with some probability be identified in the same way.

In general the distinction between the two Messianic figures may be seen mainly as a difference in function rather than an absolute difference of superiority and inferiority. The sect is itself strongly determined by priestly conceptions and by the superiority of priesthood to laity as a whole, and lays great emphasis on the work of the priests and the eschatological high priest. The work of the royal Messiah is primarily the overcoming of the enemies of God. It is an exaggeration born of modern concepts, however, to say that he is a purely worldly and political figure; as in the OT, the work of establishing the kingdom and defending it in righteousness is a sacral office.

In *CDC* a difficulty remains, in that the singular is used—'the Messiah of Aaron and Israel' (*CDC* xiv. 19, cf xix. 11, xx. 1). For a time it was thought that this singular was an error of mediaeval copyists but it has now been found on an early copy from Qumrân. On present knowledge this difference from other texts cannot yet be fully explained; it may go back to a uniting of the double Messianic concept by some sections of opinion in the community. In general, the relation of *CDC* to 1*QS* is still uncertain in many ways.

The Messianic expectation of Qumrân does not seem to be closely integrated with the cosmic eschatology of the end of the world, and in this respect is somewhat simple and conservative. While a new and final age is strongly expected, the relation of the Messiahs to its coming was mainly the re-establishment (and vindication in war) of a right religious constitution in obedience to the law as interpreted by the sect's teacher. Qumrân agrees with much of traditional Judaism in that the Messiahs, great as is their importance, are in some ways overshadowed by the Law and are hardly as central as seems natural to Christians with their conception of Messiahship formed from the NT. Thus the passages about the Messiahs in 1*QS* and *CDC* are often brought in incidentally, not in order to tell about the Messiahs but to indicate a time limit up to which certain statutory requirements are inescapable. Basically the Messiahs of Qumrân are the restored chief priest and king. Some passages (*e.g.* 4*Q* Florilegium) emphasize the exposition of the Law as the primary task of the one who appears along with the royal Messiah in the end.

Some further points remain to be mentioned. A passage in a thanksgiving hymn (1*QH* iii) mentions a birth in great travail; the child born of the woman is called 'wonderful counsellor' (from Is 9[6]); it is possible that this is the Messianic birth and that as in some other circles the humanity of the Messiah is combined with a highly-coloured and wondrous origin and birth (cf also the passage about the begetting of the Messiah in 1*QS*a). But it may be, and seems the opinion of a majority of scholars at present, that the passage has nothing to do with the Messiah. *CDC* xiv. 19, mentions the 'Messiah of Aaron and Israel' in the same line as a verb expressing 'making atonement for iniquity,' but the text is not yet certain. There are also places where 'anointed ones' is used of persons in the past, in fact of the prophets of classical Israel (*CDC* vi. 1; cf ii. 12). Similarly in the War Scroll xi. 7–8, we hear of 'thine anointed ones, seers of testimonies' by whom the ordering of God's battles has been made known. The usage here follows the style of Ps 105[15].

A more complicated problem is that of the relation of the two Messiahs to the Righteous Teacher or Teacher of Righteousness. The place of the Teacher is fixed in the beginning of the establishment of the sect by passages like *CDC* i. 11, xix. 34; the latter mentions his 'being gathered,' *i.e.* his death. As founder of the sect his position towards the Messiahs might be expressed as that of a forerunner; but he is probably different from the Prophet who is associated with the Messiahs, and is himself a priestly expositor rather than a prophet. On the basis of *CDC* vi. 10–11 it is possible but uncertain that the return of the same Righteous Teacher in the end time was expected. If he were to return, it might be taken that he would return as the priestly Messiah; but this seems to the writer unjustified on present knowledge.

The problem of suffering and its atoning value depends somewhat on the above question. We have good evidence of the suffering of the Teacher, his persecution by the Wicked Priest, the refusal of help to him by the House of Absalom, and, in the opinion of some scholars, of his martyr death. But unless we make the identification of Teacher and Messiah this does not mean Messianic suffering. And it seems doubtful whether a special connexion between suffering and atonement, or suffering and Messiahship, was made, beyond the commonly held beneficent and meritorious value of suffering. The priestly Messiah, as chief priest of the end time, would like existing priests naturally be in charge of rites of atonement, but this is rather different. The Hebrew term *kipper*, 'make conciliation, pardon,' is found used with God as subject in passages like *CDC* iii. 18, iv. 10, 1*QS* xi. 14, and with no relation either to Messianic persons or to suffering; rather it refers to the special Divine favour shown to the sect as those who repent and follow the law in truth. *CDC* xiv. 19 mentions the 'Messiah of Aaron and Israel' in the same line as the verbal phrase 'make atonement for iniquity' but since the text is much damaged it is not clear that the Messiah is the subject of the verb; elsewhere in *CDC* its subject is God.

7. The New Testament.—In the NT the Messianic theme becomes much more all-embracing, central and determinative than in the OT or other Jewish literature. The term *Christos* becomes a common title or indeed a proper name for Jesus of Nazareth in the post-resurrection church. That this Jesus who was crucified was indeed the Christ was the central article of the apostolic preaching. This interest was dominant or at least extremely important in the formation of the tradition which led to our written gospels. John (20[31]) explicitly states that his material has been presented with this intention, 'that you may believe that Jesus is the Christ.' It follows that there is an importance for the Messianism of the NT in many passages where the characteristic Messianic terms are not discussed or even mentioned. The comprehensiveness of Messianism in the NT thus means that we cannot hope to discuss the whole material here (rather see article JESUS CHRIST) but can only summarize the ways in which the lines already traced in the OT and Judaism are continued and adapted in the NT.

The term *Messias*, a Greek transliteration of the Hebrew/Aramaic term, occurs only in Jn 1[41] 4[25], and both times with the Greek translation *Christos*. *Christos* itself is of course extremely frequent, but it is far from evenly distributed, the Gospels and in particular the Synoptics using it much more sparingly than Paul.

The starting point of a study of the Messiah in the NT must be the very noticeable fact that in the Synoptic Gospels Jesus refrains almost entirely from using the term 'Messiah' directly and unambiguously of Himself. The characteristic term used by Jesus in speaking of Himself is 'Son of man.' He is recognized, however, as the Christ or Messiah by the exorcized demons (*e.g.* Lk 4[41], Mk 1[34] some MSS), although the phrase actually spoken by the demons is often another (*e.g.* 'Son of God,' Lk 4[41]; 'Holy One of God,' Mk 1[24] etc.). In such cases Jesus commands the demons to be silent and not make Him known. A turning point in the Gospels is reached when Jesus challenges the disciples to say who He is in their judgment, and Peter pronounces Him to be the

Christ (Mk 8$^{27-29}$ and ||s); here again Jesus commands that this knowledge should not be communicated. At the trial of Jesus one of the accusations affirmed to have been made was that He called Himself the Christ or King Messiah (Lk 23^{2}); this before Pilate. The Jewish authorities likewise demanded an affirmation whether He was the Christ (Mk 14^{61}, Mt 26^{63}, Lk 22^{67}). In Matthew and Luke the answer is oblique, but the definite affirmation 'I am' is given in Mark (most MSS); this may perhaps be deemed the most accurate historically, as best explaining what follows. In all three traditions a statement about the Son of Man follows. The passion story includes challenges to the crucified Jesus to prove Himself Christ, Mk 15^{32} and ||s etc.

This avoidance by Jesus of direct use of the term 'Messiah' of Himself (and it can hardly be doubted that the picture presented by the Gospels is accurate historically in this respect) has often been interpreted as a desire to avoid the worldly, political and nationalistic associations of the popular Jewish Messianic concept of the time. To the writer this seems to be only one rather minor aspect of the truth. The procedure of Jesus in the use of the Messianic title is part of the wider method of His self-communication to men; this is intended to elicit trust in Him by challenging men with the enigma of His person and deeds; only by trusting in Him do men know who He is. This approach is inconsistent with a mere and plain laying down of Messianic claims in straightforward assertion. There is much uncertainty about the sense of the 'Son of Man' in the speech of Jesus. It is not probable that this was a recognized Messianic term and therefore just a kind of alternative to 'the Messiah'; nor is it very likely that Jesus, turning away from the popular Messianic concept, replaced it with a 'Son of Man' or 'Heavenly Saviour' concept, for it is not clear that in the 1st cent. the term 'Son of Man' had a rich content of its own of this kind. Though the term has contact with OT usage, and especially with Daniel, in Jesus' speech it seems to be used primarily as a designation of Himself in His humanity, as He is, as the human being from whom the problems start out. The interpretation of 'Son of Man' as a collective figure, representing the holy community as a whole, has been popular in recent years and is based on the interpretation of Dn 7, but is in the writer's judgment a wrong interpretation of that passage and still less likely to be true for the NT.

The Messianic presentation of Jesus, then, takes place not in particular sayings affirming that He is the Christ but in the total series of the events of the gospel. The Gospel writers apply the title 'Christ' occasionally to Jesus as an accepted designation for Him, *e.g.* Mt 1$^{16-17}$ 11^{2}, Mk 1^{1}. Also the avoidance of the term 'Christ' in the speech of Jesus and with some implication of a reference to Himself is not absolute, *e.g.* Mt 23^{10}, Mk 9^{41}. The discussion of the meaning of the Davidic descent of the Christ (Mk 12$^{35-37}$ and ||s) is probably not, as some have held, a repudiation of the idea of the Davidic Messiah, but a question pointing to the enigma of Jesus and the possibility of His being Messiah. Numerous incidents in the stories are designed to point to the Messiahship of Jesus. Such, for example, is the entry to Jerusalem, with explicit reference to the Davidic kingdom by the crowds (Mk 11$^{1-11}$ and ||s); the fact that the crowds will later prove to have misunderstood Jesus' Messiahship does not affect the witness of this incident.

In this incident and many others special importance must be attached to the fulfilment of prophecy involved, *e.g.* Mt 21$^{4-5}$. Jesus is fulfilling Zechariah's vision of the restoration and coronation of the Davidic king. There is no reason to doubt that in this and some other cases the original connexion with OT prophecy is in the mind of Jesus, who saw His life patterned before Him in the figures of the OT, and reintegrated and actualized these figures in His action. This method of interpreting the OT descended from Him, however, to His disciples, and certain of the fulfilments of prophecy discerned in the events of His life are to be traced to certain schools within the early Church. The question how far the passages appealed to are really Messianic depends on the definition of this term. Some passages like Zec 9^{9} (quoted Mt 21$^{4-5}$) are Messianic in the sense of heralding the restoration of the Davidic anointed house, and predictive in the sense of seeing this as an event of the future. In other cases like Is 7^{14} (quoted Mt 1^{23}) the passage is again Messianic in the sense of being intrinsically and specially related to the fate of the Davidic house, but goes back to a time before a long eschatological perspective into the future was opened up; so roughly also the passages quoted at Mt 2^{6} 4^{15}. But sometimes even where the passage is Messianic in this sense the fulfilment lays emphasis on something that was quite secondary in the original, so Is 7^{14} and Mt 1^{23}. Other passages again, such as those from Ps 22 quoted in the passion story (Mk 15$^{24, 29, 34}$ etc.) have been held by some to be from royal lamentations in the first place, and in this limited sense connected with the Messianic office; but there was no predictive element in the original sense. Still other passages are not at all concerned with the Messianic-Davidic theme in the OT, but are related to other themes of the OT history, *e.g.* the Exodus in Mt 2^{15}. It is indeed characteristic of the NT that though Messianism is the centre of its scriptural interpretation the Messianic theme is integrated in new ways with other themes and patterns of the OT.

In John there are some differences, in that Jesus' recognition as Messiah by some of His disciples occurs at the beginning (1^{41}); in 4^{25} Jesus claims Messiahship in His words with the Samaritan woman, and cf 17^{3}. But the use of 'Son of Man' continues as in the Synoptics, and causes uncertainty (12$^{23, 34}$). The miraculous deeds of Jesus suggest His Messiahship, 4^{29} 7^{31}. But the fact that Jesus' origin is known is a difficulty, for the origin of the Christ would be mysterious, 7^{26f}. The failure of Jesus to make a direct affirmation of His Messiahship irritates the Jews, 10^{24}. Thus there is considerable agreement between John and the Synoptics about the way in which the Messiahship of Jesus was presented.

This presentation has its culmination in the passion and resurrection; though the Cross seemed to many to be inconsistent with Messiahship, the Gospels mean that it is the fullness of Messianic dignity. With the completion of the drama of this ministry, the peculiar presentation of Jesus by Himself comes to an end, and in particular the secrecy about the Messiahship. The term 'Christ' is regular and frequent in the Apostolic period, and 'Son of Man' is hardly used (only Ac 7^{56}). In the epistles and later works of the NT the term 'Christ' becomes very frequently attached to Jesus' name in 'Christ Jesus' or 'Jesus Christ.' This does not mean that the original Messianic sense was altered or lost (for the contrary view, see *Theological Word Book of the Bible*, ed. Richardson, s.v. Christ), but rather that the OT history of preparation could be assumed and compressed.

It is clear in the NT, whatever be the case at Qumrân, that there is only one Messiah, the Judaean/Davidic; though it may be that the relatedness of Mary to the Aaronic Elizabeth is taken to indicate the uniting of the Davidic and Aaronic lines. Among other passages which may be uniting the royal and priestly Messianic themes we may note the royal or holy priesthood of 1 P 2$^{5-10}$ and the interpretation of Jesus' death as a sacrifice as in Eph 5^{2}. But the most important of all is the letter to the Hebrews, which concerns itself especially with showing how Jesus the Judaean-Davidic Messiah is in fact the fulfilment of the priesthood and its service, and this by belonging to a greater priesthood than the Aaronic.

The NT also concentrates a much greater amount of significance in this one Messianic figure Jesus. The NT is not legalistic like Qumrân, and makes salvation depend exclusively on man's relation to the Christ in a way impossible at Qumrân. The direct interpretation of the Messianic task as the resumption of the religio-political rule of the Davidic house (still a possibility in the minds of the disciples as late as Ac 1^{6}) is avoided, and this makes His claims on another plane all the deeper and more comprehensive. Faith is essentially faith in the Christ and atonement is the work of the Christ. It has commonly been held that one of the main contributions of Jesus in this regard was to integrate with the concept of the Messiah that of the Suffering Servant from Deutero-Isaiah. The special importance of the Isaianic passages in the thought of Jesus and the NT has been questioned, however (cf Hooker, *Jesus and the Servant*, 1959). Whatever the truth about this may be, it seems clear that Jesus saw His suffering as part of His redemptive task (Mk 10^{45} etc.) and that when the suffering comes it appears to the onlookers to contradict the Messiahship but to the eye of faith paradoxically to fulfil it.

The Gospels agree with other historical sources in depicting the time of Jesus as one of vivid Messianic expectation, although as one would expect there is no complete uniformity in it. Along with the Messiah or before him there was expected Elijah the forerunner, and also 'the Prophet,' *i.e.* the prophet like Moses of Dt 18. In Jn 1^{20-23} John the Baptist says he is neither Christ nor Elijah nor Prophet; but by another tradition (Mt 11^{14}) he is Elijah in some sense. According to Mk 8^{27-29} and ||s the people say that Jesus is the Baptist, or Elijah, or one of the ancient prophets *redivivus*; Peter recognizes Him as the Christ. In Jn 7^{41} the crowd's opinion is divided between the Prophet and the Christ. In general it has been noticed how similar to the position of the Qumrân sect was the procedure of John as a radical teacher announcing the coming of the Messianic time and preparing for it a repentant people.

The provenance of the Christ was also much discussed. Could Messiahship be reconciled with Galilean origin (Jn 7^{41}), or with the fact that Jesus' origin (Jn 7^{27}) and even His family (Mk 6^{3}) were familiar? From whence was the Christ the son of David? Was not the Christ to remain for ever (Jn 12^{34}, a passage which if reliable must be set against the other tradition of the mortality of the Messiah)? Detailed stories of the birth of Jesus are given in Matthew and Luke, and strongly emphasize the fulfilment of the Israelite heritage in His coming. The idea of the marking out of time down to the coming of the Christ is worked out in the genealogy of Matthew (1^{17}). With the death and resurrection of Jesus the continuing triumphant life of the Christ becomes important.

So far we have mentioned only key passages in which for the most part the term 'Christ' is explicitly employed; but the number of incidents in which the Gospel writers would wish us to see some Messianic significance is much larger, and would include, for example, the Baptism of Jesus, the contest of Jesus with the Devil, some healing and other miracles, some aspects of His teaching (for example the presentation of the teaching as that of a new Moses), the Transfiguration (cf the appearance of Moses and Elijah there), and the Last Supper. Part of the genius of the Gospels is their richness in Messianic manifestation accompanied by the reserve of Jesus in making direct Messianic assertions. The question is often asked, how far was Jesus conscious of Messiahship? In view of what is now known of Messianic currents in His time, there is no reason to doubt that Jesus believed Himself to be the Christ whose coming was foreshadowed in the OT. But it should be emphasized that the NT documents are not interested in penetrating into the inner consciousness of Jesus and speak rather of what He said and did than of what He thought or felt.

For the significance of particular NT episodes see the relevant articles, *e.g.* BAPTISM, TRANSFIGURATION, etc.; and for the general questions of Christology, especially in the Epistles, see CHRISTOLOGY, JESUS CHRIST. J. Ba.

METE.—'To mete' is 'to measure,' and a 'mete-yard' (Lv 19^{35} AV and RV; RSV 'measures') is a merchant's measuring stick.

METERUS, 1 Es 5^{17} (AV).—See BAITERUS.

METHEG(H)-AMMAH.—A place mentioned in **2 S 8^{1}** (AV, RVm, RSV; RV 'the bridle of the mother city'). As a place name it is unknown. It has been thought that 'the bridle of the mother city' means the authority of the capital, *i.e.* the suzerainty exercized by the Philistines. In the parallel 2 Ch 18^{1} the text has 'Gath and her daughters' (reading *mtg* as *gt*), and it is probable that the text here is corrupt.

METHUSAEL, Gn 4^{18} (AV).—See METHUSHAEL.

METHUSELAH (? 'man of the dart' or 'man of Shelah').—A Sethite, the father of Lamech, Gn 5^{21ff}, 1 Ch 1^{3}, Lk 3^{37} (AV **Mathusala**); called **Methushael** (q.v.) in Gn 4^{18} (AV **Methusael**). He is said to have lived to the age of 969—a greater age than anyone else in the Bible.

METHUSHAEL ('man of El').—A Cainite, the father of Lamech, Gn 4^{18} (AV **Methusael**); called **Methuselah** (q.v.) in Gn 21^{5ff}.

MEUNIM.—One of the Nethinim (q.v.) whose descendants returned with Zerubbabel, Ezr 2^{50} (AV **Mehunim**), Neh 7^{52}. In 1 Es 5^{31} RSV has **Meunites** (AV **Meani**, RV **Maani**). See MAONITES and MINAEANS.

MEUNITES.—See MAANI and MAONITES.

MEUZAL, Ezk 27^{19} (AVm).—See UZAL.

ME-ZAHAB ('waters of gold').—Father of Matred and grandfather of Mehetabel the wife of Hadar (Hadad), one of the kings of Edom, Gn 36^{39}, 1 Ch 1^{50}. The name *Me-zahab* is much more like that of a place than of a person. Holzinger suggested that it is the same name as appears in a corrupted form in Dt 1^{1} as **Dizahab** (q.v.).

MEZOBAITE.—One of David's heroes is called 'Jaasiel the Mezobaite' (AV **Mesobaite**) in 1 Ch 11^{47}. The meaning is unknown, and the text is doubtful.

MIAMIN.—**1.** Ezr 10^{25} (AV); see MIJAMIN, **1.** **2.** Neh 12^{5} (AV); see MIJAMIN, **2.**

MIBHAR.—In 1 Ch 11^{38} one of David's heroes appears as 'Mibhar the son of Hagri.' The parallel passage 2 S 23^{36} reads 'of Zobah, Bani the Gadite,' which is probably the correct text.

MIBSAM.—**1.** A son of Ishmael, Gn 25^{13}, 1 Ch 1^{29}. **2.** A Simeonite, 1 Ch 4^{25}.

MIBZAR ('fortification').—A 'duke' of Edom, Gn 36^{42}, 1 Ch 1^{53}.

MICA.—**1.** Son of Merib-baal (Mephibosheth), 2 S 9^{12} (AV **Micha**); called **Micah** in 1 Ch 8^{34f} 9^{40f}. See MICAH, **3.** **2.** Son of Zichri, 1 Ch 9^{15} (AV **Micah**), Neh $11^{17, 22}$ (AV **Micha**); called **Micaiah** in Neh 12^{35}. **3.** One of those who sealed the covenant, Neh 10^{11} (AV **Micha**).

MICAH, MICAIAH ('Who is like Yahweh?').—This name, which occurs at least twelve times in the OT, and is a woman's name (the sole example, *Micaiah* in 2 Ch 13^{2}, is textually questionable; see MAACAH, **4**) as well as a man's, is spelt in different ways: the full form *Micayahu* is shortened to *Micajehu*, *Micaiah*, and *Micah*. *Mica* may be a variant spelling of *Micah* or an abbreviation of *Michael* ('Who is like God?'). The more important of those who bore this name are the following:

1. *Micah*, a dweller in the hill-country of Ephraim; he stole from his mother eleven hundred pieces of silver, which, however, he returned on hearing the curse which his mother pronounced against the thief. With part of the returned silver his mother causes an image to be made, which Micah sets up in his house; he then consecrates one of his sons a priest. But a Levite, named Jonathan, comes to the house of Micah while journeying; Micah induces him to be his priest instead of the son whom he had first consecrated. During this time the Danites send out five men to search for a suitable locality wherein to settle down; these five men come to the house of Micah, and while staying there they recognize the Levite. On their return they report that they have found a place for their tribe to dwell in. The whole 'family' of the Danites then set out, and come to take possession of the district they intend to make their home. On their coming into the neighbourhood of Micah's dwelling-place, the five men who had already been there come and persuade Micah's Levite to join them, and to bring with him Micah's ephod, teraphim, and graven image. Micah follows after them; but protests in vain, for he is warned that if he attempts to regain his priest and lost treasures by force he will lose his goods and his life; he therefore returns home without them (Jg 17, 18). This very interesting narrative has undoubtedly a basis in fact: it records—though later editors have somewhat altered its original form—how the sanctuary in Dan first came to be established (see especially Jg 18$^{29-31}$).

2. *Micaiah, the son of Imlah*; a prophet of Yahweh who is called by Ahab, at the request of Jehoshaphat, king of Judah, to prophesy concerning the result of a projected expedition against the Syrians. In reply to Ahab's inquiry Micaiah first prophesies smoothly; but Ahab bids him speak nothing but the truth; thereupon he foretells the disaster that is to befall the allied armies of Israel and Judah if they go up to Ramoth-gilead to battle. The parable which the prophet then utters is a terrible indictment against the 'lying prophets' of Israel; the blow which one of them thereupon gives him is answered by a further prophecy, this time directed against the false prophet who gave the blow. Micaiah is then commanded to be imprisoned until the king returns in peace; but undaunted, the prophet replies, 'If you return in peace, the Lord has not spoken by me.' The sequel showed Micaiah to have prophesied truly (1 K 22).

3. *Micah*, the son of Meribbaal (1 Ch 8^{34f} 9^{40f} [2 S 9^{12} **Mica**]). **4.** *Micaiah*, one of the teachers sent by Jehoshaphat to teach the commandments of Yahweh in the cities of Judah (2 Ch 17^{7}). **5.** *Micaiah*, the son of Gemariah, and a contemporary of Jeremiah, who heard Baruch reading out the prophecies of Jeremiah, and then spoke of them to the princes who were assembled in the scribe's chamber (Jer 36$^{9-13}$), perhaps identical with the *Micaiah* of 2 K 22^{12} and the *Micah* of 2 Ch 34^{20}. **6.** One of the priests who took part in the dedication of the wall (Neh 12^{41}). Other less important bearers of the name are mentioned in 1 Ch 5^{5} 9^{15} (AV; see MICA, **2**) 23^{20} (cf 24^{24f}); 2 Ch 13^{2} (see MAACAH, **4**), 12$^{35, 41}$ (**Micaiah**; see MICA, **2**), Jth 6^{15} (AV **Mica**). For the prophet Micah see the following article.

W. O. E. O.—**W. C. K.**

MICAH.—The Morashtite, one of the four prophets of the 8th cent. whose words are preserved for us in the Bible. The book which bears his name stands in EV (and the Hebrew Bible) sixth in order of the so-called Minor Prophets. In the LXX, however, it stands third, being preceded only by Hosea and Amos.

1. The Man and His Times.—Of Micah's life we know no concrete details whatever. His name, a shortened form of *Micayahu*, means 'who is like Yahweh?' He was probably a native of Moresheth-gath (cf 1^{14}), a village of SW. Judah located in the Shephelah near the edge of the Philistine plain. His prophecies indicate profound concern for the plight of the peasant landholders, of whose number he presumably was, and at the same time awareness of conditions in the capital city, Jerusalem, which we may presume he visited frequently. Much of his preaching, indeed, seems to have been done in Jerusalem, his words on occasion (cf 3^{12}, Jer 26^{18f}) reaching the ear of the king. According to the superscription of the book (1^{1}) Micah was active during the reigns of Jotham (742–735), Ahaz (735–715) and Hezekiah (715–687). Though some would restrict his activity entirely to Hezekiah's reign, this seems hardly correct, since certain passages (*e.g.* 1^{6ff}) are best understood as having been uttered at least before the fall of Samaria in 721. That he was still alive in Hezekiah's reign is, however, certain both from Jer 26^{18f} and because some of his words (1^{10ff}) appear to reflect the invasion of Sennacherib in 701, or that of Sargon in 711.

Micah's career thus fell in the generation after that of Amos and ran in good part parallel to that of his more famous contemporary, Isaiah. These prophets lived in a time which found their nation in a continuing emergency. The decades following the death of Jeroboam II. (746) and of Uzziah (742) saw the end of the period of prosperity which Amos addressed and the beginning of the westward expansion of Assyria under Tiglath-pileser III. (745–727). In 735–732, when attacked by Israel and Damascus for his refusal to join them in a defensive alliance against Assyria, Ahaz made himself a vassal of Tiglath-pileser and appealed for his aid (2 K 16$^{5-7}$); the latter responded by crippling and reducing Israel and destroying Damascus. A few years later, because of further rebellion, Samaria was taken (by Sargon II. in 721) and the N. state ended altogether. Judah, meanwhile, survived as a dependency of Assyria. As a vassal of the Assyrian king, Ahaz was forced to recognize his overlord's gods, and a place was made for their cults within the Temple itself (2 K 16$^{10-18}$). Since Ahaz likewise permitted all sorts of pagan practices, including human sacrifice, to flourish (2 K 16^{3f}), his reign was remembered as one of unexampled apostasy. This was accompanied, as both Isaiah and Micah let us see, by a social and moral decay for which, moreover, the official religion had no effective rebuke. Hezekiah, to be sure, reversed his father's policy and both attempted to regain his independence and to institute sweeping reforms. In this last the preaching of Micah (and of Isaiah) was influential. Hezekiah was, however, betrayed into relying on Egyptian help in his bid for independence, and this (in 701) brought the Assyrian army down on his country, with disastrous consequences. Though Judah survived, independence was not regained, while Hezekiah's reforms were cancelled by his son Manasseh. How long Micah's activity continued we do not know—possibly as late as 701.

2. The Book of Micah.—Reconstruction of Micah's message is complicated by the critical problems attaching to his book, which are of a magnitude far out of proportion to its size. The book falls into certain clearly marked divisions: chs. 1–3, which contain (except for 2^{12f}) exclusively prophecies of judgment on the national sin; chs. 4–5, which consist almost entirely of words of promise for the future; and chs. 6–7 which (except for 7$^{8-20}$, a poem of hopeful tone composed on a liturgical pattern) again contain words in which the note of judgment predominates. Though the first of these sections (except for a few verses such as 2^{12f}) is generally conceded to consist of genuine utterances of Micah, there is little agreement among scholars concerning the rest. While some allow almost none of chs. 4–7 to Micah, others, equally competent, would retain the greater part. There is, indeed, scarcely a passage in chs. 4–7 which is not questioned by some and defended by others.

The problem arises chiefly because of the apparent irreconcilability between Micah's message of uncompromising doom as we see it in chs. 1–3 (cf Jer 26^{18}) and passages which offer the nation hope for the future, as well as from the commonly held opinion that much of the material in chs. 4–5, 6–7 reflects later circumstances than those of the 8th cent. Like the other pre-exilic prophetic books, that of Micah came into being through a complex process of transmission and collection; it contains the remembered words of Micah as these were treasured, handed down and collected in circles sympathetic to the prophetic preaching. Since the compilation of the Book of the Twelve Prophets, of which Micah is a part, was not completed until the 4th cent. (or later), the possibility, indeed the likelihood, that it contains later material is to be reckoned with. Nevertheless, caution is indicated. While the book apparently contains exilic or post-exilic touches, it is unlikely that such large portions of it come from a late period as more extreme critics have supposed. Indeed, the bulk of the material of chs. 4–5, 6–7, though one certainly cannot prove that it comes from Micah himself, could be held to represent a type of prophetic preaching current in the late 8th cent.

In 4$^{1-5}$ we have a poem describing the future blessedness of Israel under Yahweh's rule which appears in somewhat shortened form in Is 2$^{2-4}$. Since the piece sits loosely in context in both books, it is difficult to say in which it is more original. The probability is that it was treasured by disciples of both prophets and so drawn into the books of both. But reasons adduced for assigning it to a post-exilic date are scarcely convincing, while its presence in the collections of two 8th cent. prophets might indicate that it represents future hopes current in prophetic circles at about that time. The same can be said of the famous oracle concerning the future Davidic king in 5^2ff, which is remarkably similar to certain oracles in Isaiah (9^2-7 11^1-9) the genuineness of which there is no adequate reason to question. Whether Micah's or not, it fits well in the theology of the 8th cent. Indeed, it is not excluded—and many so believe—that it comes from Micah himself. In 4^8ff there are, to be sure, exilic touches, as the mention of Babylon in v.^10 indicates. But if this one line be regarded as a gloss (which many scholars believe it to be) adjusting an earlier prophecy to a later situation, nothing in the passage forbids relating it to the 8th cent. In short, with the possible exception (and this not certain) of 3^12f 4^6f 5^7f, little in chs. 1–5 need be regarded as of exilic date.

As for chs. 6–7, with the possible exception of 7^8-20 (and this again contested by some), the same can be said. The material in 6^1–7^6 is certainly basically pre-exilic, and little objective reason exists for denying it to Micah himself. Some to be sure on the basis of the allusion to infant sacrifice in v.^7, place 6^1-8 in the reign of Manasseh. This would not, of course, even if correct, *a priori* deny it to Micah, who could still have been living at the time. But the suggestion is entirely unnecessary. Infant sacrifice was practised by certain of Israel's neighbours at all periods and, during Ahaz's reign, had been known in Judah. Moreover, though the passage implies knowledge of the custom, it certainly does not require that it was actually being practised in Judah at the time the oracle was uttered. Further discussion of critical issues is impossible here; the commentaries should be consulted for details. The safest conclusion would seem to be that the book of Micah consists basically of the words of Micah himself, plus expressions of the theology of those prophetic circles of his day which transmitted them, together with some (but not as many as frequently supposed) later glosses, expansions and additions.

3. The Message of Micah.—The message of Micah, like that of Isaiah, must be understood against the background of the socio-economic deterioration and the religious laxity which was encouraged by the policy of Ahaz, and which presumably continued until somewhat checked by the reforms of Hezekiah. While there is evidence that neither the infiltration of paganism nor social decay had gone as far as it had in the northern Israel addressed by Amos and Hosea, it is clear that similar tendencies were at work. The aristocracy of Jerusalem was taking advantage of the economic plight of the small landholders and were dispossessing them, often enough by dishonest means (2^1f, 9). The judges being unscrupulous and venal, the poor had no redress (3^1-4, 9f). Meanwhile the official cult, being supported by the state and in no position to criticize the nobles who guided the national policy, offered no effective rebuke but, by its stress upon cultic externals (cf Is 1^10-17), fostered the notion that Yahweh's demands could be met by ritual and sacrifice alone. Indeed, the clergy as Micah depicts them (3^5, 11) were corrupt, the priests being concerned chiefly for their livings, the prophets ready to trim their oracles to the size of the fee. It is clear that the nature of the Mosaic covenant with its stringent moral demands had been forgotten in Judah, as it had been in Israel. In fact, the official theology of the state cult which affirmed Yahweh's eternal choice of Zion and of the Davidic dynasty (*e.g.* Ps 89, 132, 2 S 7) stressed a notion of covenant in which Yahweh's promises to the nation were unconditional (cf 3^11); it may be supposed that this notion of covenant had largely overlaid the Mosaic covenant in the popular mind.

Micah felt it as his call (3^8) to attack these abuses as sins against the covenant God, and this he did fully in the tradition of Amos some decades earlier. It seemed to him (6^1-8) that Yahweh had entered His case against His people because they had forgotten His gracious acts towards them in the past and had imagined that the stipulations of covenant could be satisfied by heightened religious activity alone. Going beyond Isaiah, he rejected the confidence implicit in the official theology utterly and declared that Jerusalem would for its sins be ploughed like a field and the Temple left a ruin (3^12). Though he met opposition (2^6), his words reached Hezekiah's ear (Jer 26^18f) and helped to spur that king in his efforts at reform. That Micah had no hope for his nation (especially since Hezekiah heeded his words) is unlikely. The oracle in 5^2ff, at least, fits well in the context of 8th-cent. theology, and could well be his. If so, he (or those disciples who preserved his words), though affirming the Divine judgment on Jerusalem and its corrupt rulers and cult, held fast to the hope that God would rescue a remnant of His people (4^8ff) and bring out of Bethlehem an ideal scion of David's line under whom the age of promise would be ushered in.

J. Br.

MICAIAH.—See Micah, and Mica, 3.

MICE.—See Mouse, and Magic.

MICHA.—**1.** 2 S 9^12 (AV); see Mica, **1.** **2.** Neh 10^11 (AV); see Mica, **3.** **3.** Jth 6^15 (AV); see Micah, **6.** **4.** Neh 11^17, 22 (AV); see Mica, **2.**

MICHAEL ('Who is like God?').—**1.** Father of the Asherite spy, Nu 13^13. **2. 3.** Two Gadites, 1 Ch 5^13f. **4.** A Levite, ancestor of Asaph, 1 Ch 6^40. **5.** Name of a family in Issachar, 1 Ch 7^3 27^18. **6.** A Benjamite, 1 Ch 8^16. **7.** A Manassite chief who joined David at Ziklag, 1 Ch 12^20. **8.** A son of king Jehoshaphat, 2 Ch 21^2. **9.** The father of Zebadiah, Ezr 8^8 (cf 1 Es 8^34). **10.** The archangel. See next article.

MICHAEL ('the archangel').—Although reference to angels and their visitations is common in the OT, especially during transition periods (*e.g.* the period of the Judges and that of the Captivity are specially noticeable for angelic appearances), the name *Michael* is not found until the later period, when the angelic office was divided between functions, which were assigned to individual angels. In the Rabbinical traditions Michael figures considerably. He is connected with many incidents in the history of Moses, especially his burial (cf Dt 34^6), when he disputed with Satan, who claimed the body by reason of the murder of the Egyptian (Ex 2^12). In the OT he is alluded to several times in the book of Daniel (10^13, 21 12^1) as 'one of the chief princes,' 'the prince,' and 'the prince who has charge of your people,' and he is opposed to the prince-angels of Persia and of Greece. He is here regarded as the guardian of the Israelites in their opposition to polytheism and foreign innovations.

In the NT Michael is found fighting in heaven (Rev 12^7) against the dragon 'who is called the Devil and Satan,' and is typical of the warfare which is the special work of the Church on earth. In the passage in Jude (v.^9) a definite reference is made to the tradition already mentioned, 'When the archangel Michael, contending with the devil, disputed about the body of Moses, he did not presume to pronounce a reviling judgment upon him, but said "The Lord rebuke you"' (cf Zec 3^1 for a similar incident).

T. A. M.

MICHAIAH.—AV spelling of **Micaiah, 4, 5, 6.** Cf Maacah, **4.**

MICHAL ('Who is like El').—Younger daughter of Saul, offered to David, as a snare, on condition that he would slay one hundred Philistines. The popularity of David led Saul to seek his life. He had David's house surrounded, but Michal deceived the messengers, and contrived David's escape by the window (1 S 19^11-17). Saul then gave Michal to Paltiel. When Abner negotiated with David to deliver Israel to him, the king stipulated for Michal's return. This was accomplished, though the record does not make it clear whether directly from Ishbaal (Ishbosheth) at the instance of David, or through Abner (2 S 3^14f). Paltiel followed weeping, but was rudely dismissed by Abner. The closing scene between Michal and David is pathetic. David's dance before the

Ark was unseemly in the eyes of Michal, and she rebuked him. His answer was equally curt. The statement that Michal died childless may mean that she was divorced (2 S 6^{16f}). The estrangement was probably due to the numerous wives that now shared David's prosperity and Michal's authority. In 2 S 21^{8} ' Michal ' (so AV, RV, following Heb.) is an error for ' Merab ' (so RSV, with 2 Heb. MSS and LXX^{L}). See MERAB.

MICHEAS (2 Es 1^{39} AV) = the prophet Micah.

MICHMAS.—Ezr 2^{27}, Neh 7^{31}, 1 Es 5^{21} (AV, RV **Macalon**) = **Michmash** (q.v.).

MICHMASH.—A place (not enumerated as a town) in the territory of Benjamin, and in the mountains of Bethel, It comes into prominence in connexion with the daring raid of Jonathan and his armour-bearer on a garrison of the Philistines holding a position nearby (1 S 13, 14). It was one of the smaller places to which the returning exiles belonged, contributing only 122 men to the enumeration of Ezra (Ezr 2^{27}) and Nehemiah (Neh 7^{31}). Nehemiah further alludes to it as a border town of Benjamin (11^{31}). Indications of its position may be obtained from the Jonathan story and also from Isaiah's description of the Assyrian advance on Jerusalem (Is 10^{28}), which indicate its location at the modern village of *Mukhmâs* standing high above the E. bank of the *Wâdī Ṣuweinîṭ* at the head of the *Wâdī Qelt*, a wild stony region E. of the watershed of the hills of Palestine. It was occupied for a time by Jonathan the brother of Judas Maccabaeus to counteract the Seleucid garrison at Bethel (1 Mac 9^{73}). R. A. S. M.—**J. Gr.**

MICHMETHAH, Jos 16^{6} 17^{7} (AV).—See MICHMETHATH.

MICHMETHATH.—An Ephraimite town, on the boundary of Manasseh, Jos 16^{6} 17^{7} (AV **Michmethah**). It is possibly modern *Kh. Juleijil*, E. of *Nāblus*.

MICHRI.—Eponym of a Benjamite family, 1 Ch 9^{8}.

MICHTAM.—AV and RV form of **Miktam**; see PSALMS, **2.**

MIDDIN.—A town in the wilderness of Judah, Jos 15^{61}. It is perhaps modern *Kh. Abū Ṭabaq*.

MIDIAN, MIDIANITES.—A nomadic tribe or group of tribes, said by an early genealogy (Gn 25^{2}) to be descended from Abraham by Keturah, of which the Kenites were a part. They lived in ancient times in N. Arabia, E. of the Gulf of *'Aqaba*. Hab 3^{7} mentions them beside Cushan, Gn 25^{4} and Is 60^{6} beside Ephah. Ptolemy (*Geogr.* VI. 7) and Arabic geographers know of a place called ' Madian ' in NW. Arabia. First, they appear in the Bible as caravan leaders and traders, who sold Joseph into Egypt (Gn 37$^{28, 36}$). Later, Moses came in contact with them in the Sinai peninsula and married the daughter of a Midianite priest (Ex 2$^{15-21}$). After the Exodus this priest met the Israelites at the mountain of God and partook with their leaders in a sacrificial meal (Ex 18$^{1-12}$). Seeing Moses' predicament he counselled him to appoint judges (Ex 18$^{13-27}$). As Jethro, Moses' father-in-law, is also said to be a Kenite (Jg 1^{16}), probably the Kenites were a part of the Midianites. They were afterwards absorbed by the tribe of Judah (Jg 1^{16}, 1 S 15^{6}).

Some Midianites seem to have been located also in the territory of Moab, since Gn 36^{35} contains the information that a King of Edom smote Midianites in the field of Moab. These northern Midianites were also partly responsible for the apostasy of Israel at Baal-Peor (Nu 25$^{6, 15}$), and had hostile encounters with the invading Israelites (Nu 25$^{16-18}$ 31$^{1-12}$).

In the period of the Judges, the camel-riding Midianites invaded the territory of central Palestine in hordes, and were put to rout by Gideon and his three hundred men (Jg 6–8). Gideon so completely ruined the power of the Midianites that his victory was long remembered as ' the day of Midian ' (cf Is 9^{4} 10^{26}, Ps 83^{9}). From this blow the tribe never recovered, and disappears from history. G. A. B.—**S. H. Hn.**

MIDRASH.—See COMMENTARY.

MIDWIFE.—See MEDICINE.

MIGDAL-EDER.—See EDER, **1.**

MIGDAL-EL.—A town of Naphtali, between Yiron and Horem, Jos 19^{38}. The site is unknown.

MIGDAL-GAD.—A town in the lowland, in the territory of Judah, Jos 15^{37}. It is possibly modern *Kh. el-Mejdeleh*, SE. of *Tell ed-Duweir*.

MIGDOL (' tower,' a Semitic word borrowed by the Egyptians of the New Kingdom, and common as a word and in place-names).—**1.** A place on the border of Egypt near the spot where the Israelites crossed the Red Sea, Ex 14^{2}, Nu 33^{7}; probably a mere guardhouse on the road. **2.** A place mentioned in Ezk 29^{10} 30^{6} (AV, RV ' tower '). Here Migdol is in the NE. extremity of Egypt, as Syene is the S. It may be identical with *Magdolo* in a Roman itinerary, perhaps at the now deserted site of *Tell el-Ḥêr*, 12 miles S. of Pelusium. **3.** An Egyptian town mentioned with Tahpanhes and Memphis, Jer 44^{1} 46^{14}; probably the same as **2.** F. Ll. G.

MIGRON.—**1.** One of the places mentioned in Isaiah's description of the march of the Assyrians on Jerusalem, Is 10^{28}. It would appear to be N. of Michmash (q.v.) and of the *Wâdî eṣ-Ṣuweinîṭ*, which is the ' pass ' of Is 10^{29}. The name perhaps survives in *Makrûn*, a ruined site situated a mile or two NW. of Michmash. **2.** In 1 S 14^{2} Saul, whose army was encamped S. of the *Wâdī eṣ-Ṣuweinîṭ*, is said to have dwelt ' under the pomegranate tree which is at Migron.' This is probably *Tell Miryam*, SW. of Michmash. Some would identify **1.** with this site, and regard Is 10^{28} as not giving an orderly geographical route. But this does not seem likely.

MIJAMIN.—**1.** One of those who had married a foreign wife, Ezr 10^{25} (AV **Miamin**), 1 Es 9^{26} (AV, RV **Maelus**). **2.** Eponym of the 6th of the priestly courses, 1 Ch 24^{9}. This family returned with Zerubbabel, Neh 12^{5} (AV **Miamin**); it was represented at the sealing of the covenant, 10^{7}. The name appears as **Miniamin** in 12^{17}.

MIKLOTH.—**1.** A son of Jeiel, 1 Ch 8^{32} 9^{37f}. **2.** An officer of David, 1 Ch 27^{4} (AV, RV, RSVm; RSV omits).

MIKNEIAH.—A gate-keeper for the Ark, 1 Ch 15$^{18, 21}$.

MIKTAM.—See PSALMS, **2.**

MILALAI.—The eponym of a priestly family, Neh 12^{36}.

MILCAH.—**1.** Daughter of Haran and wife of Nahor, Gn 11^{29}. The names of her children are given in 22^{20ff}. Rebekah was her granddaughter, 24$^{15, 24, 47}$. **2.** Daughter of Zelophehad, Nu 26^{33} 27^{1} 36^{11}, Jos 17^{3}.

MILCOM.—The national deity of Ammon. Solomon established a sanctuary for him on the Mount of Olives, which seems to have continued till it was destroyed by Josiah (1 K 11$^{5, 33}$, 2 K 23^{13}). In 2 S 12^{30} (cf RVm), 1 Ch 20^{2} (cf RVm), Jer 49$^{1, 3}$ (RV), Zeph 1^{5} (RV; AV **Malcham**) **Malcam** (' their king ') is probably an incorrect vocalization of *Milcom* (so RSVm in 2 S 12^{30}, 1 Ch 20^{2}, RSV in Jer 49$^{1, 3}$, Zeph 1^{5}). The name is from the common Semitic root *malk*, *melekh* (' king ' or ' prince'), probably with an inflectional termination. The traditional identification of Milcom with **Molech** is based only upon 1 K 11^{7}, a verse which is probably corrupt. See MOLECH. W. M. N.

MILDEW (*yērāḳôn*), Dt 28^{22}, 1 K 8^{37}, 2 Ch 6^{28}, Am 4^{9}, Hag 2^{17}, is a disease of grain due to various fungi; it is produced by damp, and is in the above passages associated with *shiddāphôn*, ' **blasting** ' the opposite condition produced by excessive drought.

MILE.—See WEIGHTS AND MEASURES.

MILETUS.—The southernmost of the twelve colonies forming the Ionian confederacy of Asia Minor. It lay on the S. coast of the Latonian Gulf, which penetrated Caria S. of the peninsula of Mycale, and received the waters of the Maeander. See Map 16. The silt of this river filled up the gulf, and Miletus is now 5 miles from the sea, while the former island of Lade, which helped to make its harbour, is now a hill rising in the alluvial plain.

Two visits of St. Paul to Miletus are mentioned. The

first (Ac 20[15]) took place when he was returning to Jerusalem at the end of the Third Missionary Journey. He stayed long enough to send for the elders of Ephesus, and give them the farewell charge recorded in Ac 20. This probably needed two days. A second visit is mentioned in 2 Ti 4[20] ' Trophimus I left ill at Miletus.' This must have been between St. Paul's first and second imprisonment at Rome, *i.e.* if there were two imprisonments. In neither case are we told of any attempt to found a church at Miletus. Miletus was already unimportant by comparison with Ephesus, which now received the trade of the Maeander valley, and shared with Smyrna the trade that came along the great road through the centre of Asia Minor. Ephesus was recognized by the Romans as the southern capital of the province of Asia. Formerly Miletus had led Ionia. Its trade was mainly in wool, and it had founded numerous colonies on the Black Sea and Propontis (Sinope, Trapezus, Abydos, Cyzicus), besides Naucratis in Egypt. It had led the Ionian revolt, the fate of which was determined by the battle of Lade and the capture of Miletus, 494 B.C. It had defended itself on behalf of the Persian power against Alexander in 334 B.C. Its ruins are now called *Palatia*. They seem to include few Christian remains, but Miletus was a bishopric, and from the 5th cent. an archbishopric. A. E. H.—**F. C. G.**

MILK.—Milk was at all times an important article of diet among the Hebrews, and by ben Sira is rightly assigned a prominent place among the principal things necessary for man's life (Sir 39[26]). It was supplied by the ' herd ' and the ' flock,' the latter term including both sheep and goats (Dt 32[14], where render ' sour milk or curds (RSV) [*ḥem'āh*] of the herd, and milk [*ḥālābh*] of the flock '), probably also by the milch camels (Gn 32[15]). At the present day goats' milk is preferred to every other.

In Bible times, as now, milk slightly soured or fermented was a favourite beverage. The modern Bedouin prepares this sour milk, or *leben*, as it is called, by pouring the fresh milk into a skin (cf Jg 4[19] ' she opened a skin [AV and RV ' bottle '] of milk and gave him a drink '), to the sides of which clots of sour milk from a previous milking still adhere. The skin is shaken for a little, when the process of fermentation speedily commences, and the milk is served ' with that now gathered sourness which they think the more refreshing ' (Doughty, *Arabia Deserta*, i, 263). Such was the refreshment with which Jael supplied Sisera. ' He asked water, and she gave him milk ; she brought him curds (*ḥem'āh*) in a lordly bowl ' (Jg 5[25], where AV and RV have ' butter,' but one does not *drink* butter ; cf 4[19] cited above).

In several OT passages, however, this word, *ḥem'āh*, does evidently signify **butter**, as in Pr 30[33] ' the churning (literally as RSV and RVm ' pressing ') of milk bringeth forth butter.' So Ps 55[21] RV, ' his mouth was smooth as butter,' where ' sour milk ' is clearly out of place. The former passage suggests the procedure of the Arab housewife whom Doughty describes (*op. cit.* ii, 67) as ' rocking her blown-up milk-skin upon her knees till the butter came ; they find it in a clot at the mouth of the skin.' Butter cannot be kept sweet under the climatic conditions of Palestine, but must be boiled, producing the *samn* or clarified butter universally prized throughout the East.

Cheese is mentioned three times in our EV (1 S 17[18] 2 S 17[29], Job 10[10]) ; in each case the original has a different word. The clearest case is the last cited ; the text of 2 S 17[29], on the other hand, is admittedly in disorder, and we should perhaps read, by a slight change of consonants, ' dried **curds** ' ; these, when rubbed down and mixed with water, yield a refreshing drink much esteemed at the present day. From the Mishnah we learn that rennet and the acid juices of various trees and plants were used to curdle (Job 10[10]) milk. After being drained of the whey—' the water of milk '—the curds were salted, shaped into round discs, and dried in the sun. The Tyropoeon valley in Jerusalem received its name, ' the valley of the cheesemakers,' from the industry there carried on.

There has been a good deal of discussion as to the origin of the popular expression **' flowing with milk and honey,'** so frequently used in OT to describe Palestine as an ideal land abounding in the necessaries and delicacies of life. Many scholars have demurred to the traditional view that this is expressed by the words ' milk and honey,' on the principle of the part for the whole, and favour a more recondite origin in a forgotten Palestinian mythology. This explanation would bring the phrase in question into line with the equally familiar ' nectar and ambrosia ' of Greek mythology.

The thrice repeated command : ' You shall not boil a kid in its mother's milk ' (Ex 23[19] 34[26], Dt 14[21]) has been established as reflecting a ritual practice. It occurs as a positive command in the Râs Shamra tablets, and is prohibited in OT ' to avoid its heathen associations ' (J. W. Jack, *The Râs Shamra Tablets*, p. 32). A. R. S. K.—**B. J. R.**

MILL, MILLSTONE.—1. Three methods of preparing **flour** were in use in Palestine in Bible times, associated with the **mortar** and **pestle** (see MORTAR AND PESTLE), the **rubbing-stone,** and the quern or **handmill.** The most primitive apparatus was the rubbing-stone or corn-rubber, which consisted really of two stones. The one on which the corn was ground was a substantial slab, often 2½ feet long, and about a foot wide, slightly concave and curving upwards, like a saddle, at both ends (illustrated in Macalister, *Bible Sidelights*, etc., fig. 28). The other, the rubbing-stone proper, was a narrow stone from 12 to 18 inches long, pointed at both ends and also slightly curved, one side being plain and the other convex. In manipulating the rubber, the woman grasped it by both ends and ground the grains of wheat or barley with the convex side. Cf Macalister's description in *PEFSt*, 1903, p. 118, with Schumacher's photograph reproduced by Benzinger, *Heb. Arch.*[3] (1927) 63, and the Egyptian statuette in Erman's *Ancient Egypt*, 190. Vincent in his *Canaan d'après l'exploration récente* (405, fig. 282) shows a corn-rubber of flint from the palaeolithic age !

2. The more familiar apparatus for the same purpose was the handmill or quern. As in so many instances (see, *e.g.* LAMP), excavations have now enabled us to trace two distinct stages in the evolution of the Palestinian handmill. The Gezer specimens described in detail in *PEFSt*, 1903, 119, belong to the earlier type, which is distinguished from the later form by the absence of a handle for rotating the upper stone. The quern-stones ' are always small, rarely being as much as a foot across.' The lower stone, the ' nether millstone ' of Job 41[24], was always more massive than the ' upper millstone ' (Dt 24[6]), and was apparently fitted with ' a narrow spindle ' sunk into the stone. The upper stone was pierced right through, and by this hole the mill was fed. According to Macalister, ' the upper stone was grasped with both hands (the fingers clasping the edge, the thumbs being between the spindle and the stone), and worked through about one-third of a rotation, backward and forward.' For varieties of this type, see *PEFSt*, 1903, 119 f.

In the later and more effective type of handmill, which was that in use in NT times, the stones were larger, although the lower stone was still considerably wider than the upper (*Baba bathra*, ii. 1). As in the querns of the present day, the latter was fitted with a wooden handle (*yādh* in the Mishnah) in the shape of an upright peg inserted near the outer edge. The mill was fed, as before, through a funnel-shaped cavity pierced through the upper stone, which was rotated by the handle through a complete circle. Sometimes, as appears from Mt 24[41], two women worked the mill, seated opposite each other, and each turning the upper stone through half a revolution, as may still be seen in the East.

By the first century of our era a larger and different form of mill had been introduced, apparently, to judge by the names of the various parts in the Mishnah (see article 'Mill' in *EBi* iii, 3093), under Graeco-Roman influence. In the larger specimens of this type, the upper millstone, in the shape of two hollow cones, as described in detail, *loc. cit.*, was turned by an ass, and is the 'great millstone' of Mt 18[6] RV, RSV (literally as RVm 'a millstone turned by an ass').

3. The work of the mill belonged at all times to the special province of the women of the household (Mt 24[41]). In large establishments, it fell to the slaves, male (Jg 16[21]) and female (Ex 11[5]), particularly the latter, hence the figure for the slavery of captivity in Is 47[2].

The finer varieties of meal, the 'fine flour' of OT, were got by repeated grinding, or by sifting with sieves, or by a combination of both processes.

How indispensable the handmill was considered for the daily life of the family may be seen from the provision of the Deuteronomic legislation forbidding the creditor to take in pledge the household mill (so rightly RV and RSV), or even the upper millstone, 'for he taketh a man's life to pledge' (Dt 24[6]).

Since Professor Kennedy's article was written the number of actual millstones recovered from archaeological sites has increased, as have also details about their size and the way they functioned. But a comprehensive survey of them has still to be undertaken. A useful source of information is Dalman, *Arbeit und Sitte in Palästina*, i–vi. 5, 1928–1939.

A. R. S. K.—**B. J. R.**

MILLENNIUM.—A period of a thousand years, during which, according to Rev 20[2–7], Satan (the Dragon, the old serpent) is to be confined in the abyss, while the martyrs, having been raised from the dead, are to reign with Christ as priests and judges. The locale is apparently earth (20[3, 8f]), though this is disputed. The period begins with this first resurrection, and at its end, Satan, prior to his destruction, is to be released for a time to deceive the nations and war against the saints in the beloved city (20[9]).

This reference in Revelation is unique in the NT, but behind it evidently lie older hopes, *e.g.* Dn 7[9ff], Ezk 38 f, Apoc. Bar 73[3], 2 En 32 f, 4 Ezr 7[27ff]. Enoch speaks of a millennial 'sabbath of rest,' and it is possible to trace this conception in Persian sources. Zoroastrian parallels, however, are hardly relevant for understanding John's vision. His Christian martyrs are singled out for special distinction as the reward for fidelity and suffering (cf Rev 2[11, 26f] 3[21]), because the situation at the time made it imperative to show that martyrdom would not be in vain. The glorious status of 1[6] 5[10] is reaffirmed, and with it responsible functions in the Divine economy, but no details are worked out (cf 1 Co 6[2f] for the thought). The second coming of Satan is perhaps a counterpart to the parousia of Christ. Good powers, and evil, spring up like geysers, and complacency is dangerous; yet there will be an End when Death and the Devil are finally conquered. This corresponds to 1 Co 15[24–26], Col 1[13], though Paul nowhere makes explicit a connexion of Christ's rule with a millennium.

In the history of the Christian Church the doctrine of the Millennium has played a considerable rôle, but Chiliasm (q.v.) has been opposed by most of the great theologians. In modern times the pre-millenarians hold that all Christians will be raised, not only martyrs, when Christ returns before the millennium begins. Such an interpretation distorts the texts and is over-literal, for apocalyptic vision has its own peculiar ideas about Time. On the other hand, the symbolism of Revelation is sometimes dismissed too readily, and thus also its positive message (cf Mt 19[28], Lk 22[30] for Jesus' teaching about the thrones; note Mk 13[32]). The fundamental difficulty in erecting the pre-millennial view into a doctrine of essential Christianity is that it presupposes conditions and expectations, carried over from Judaism, which the course of history has shown to be most unlikely. Nevertheless, the idea that the created order will be ultimately perfected through the absolute triumph of our God and his Christ remains part and parcel of the genuine Christian Hope.

S. M.—**G. J.**

MILLET.—Mentioned only in Ezk 4[9] as an ingredient in bread. It is probably *Sorghum vulgare*. See Food, **2.**

MILLO.—Properly **Beth-millo** (Jg 9[6, 20]), a place in the Shechem area, the inhabitants of which were closely associated with those of Shechem in the coronation of Abimelech. It is commonly identified with the 'Tower of Shechem' (Jg 9[46ff]), and probably was the fortified acropolis in the upper city of Shechem (cf B. W. Anderson, *BA*, xx [1957], 15). Another possibility is that it was a military outpost some distance from the city proper (cf J. Simons, *The Geographical and Topographical Texts of the Old Testament* [1959], p. 143). It was destroyed by Abimelech *c* 1100 B.C. Joash was slain at a 'Beth-millo on the way that goes down to Silla' (2 K 12[20]). An identification with the Shechem Millo is unlikely; neither the identification nor the location of either place mentioned here has been determined. On the 'Millo' of 2 S 5[9], 1 K 11[27] etc. see Jerusalem, ii, **4.**

R. A. S. M.—**D. N. F.**

MINAEANS.—A S. Arabian people. It is doubtful whether they are mentioned in the OT. The Septuagint translators identified them with the **Meunites** mentioned in 1 Ch 4[41], 2 Ch 26[7] and also by correction of text 2 Ch 20[1]. Strabo lists the Minaeans as one of the four major peoples of Arabia in his day, and says the name of their capital was Karna (see Sheba). The Minaean inscriptions give it as *Qrnw*, generally vocalized as *Qarnāwu*. The ruined site has been known only as *Maʿîn* in more recent times. Halévy and Glaser collected numerous inscriptions there. It is in the area called the *Jauf*. For a long time scholars thought that the Minaean hegemony in Arabia antedated the Sabaean (see Sheba). But recent explorations and studies have disproved that. Palaeographic criteria, made available through the publication of actual photographs of Minaean inscriptions, play an important rôle. Three main groups of kings of the Minaeans are known. The first, beginning with Ilyafiʿ Yithiʿ reigned 400–200 B.C.; the second group held control over **Dedan** (q.v.) and ruled from 200–75 B.C.; the third seems to have been vassal of Qataban, and under it the Minaean kingdom ended, between 50 and 25 B.C. Other cities of the Minaeans were *Yathil*, *Nashk*, *Neshan*, *Harim* and *Kamna*. The Minaean chief gods were *ʿAthtar*, *Wadd*, *Nakrah*, and *Shams*. Minaean inscriptions from Dedan speak of the dedication to the god Wadd of persons designated as *lawi'u* and *lawi'atu*. A connexion with the name of the priestly tribe of Levi in Israel seems possible. Cultic terms similar to Hebrew ones also occur in these texts.

E. G. K.

MIND.—See Psychology.

MINIAMIN.—**1.** A Levite in the days of Hezekiah, 2 Ch 31[15]. **2.** Neh 12[17]; see Mijamin, **2.** **3.** A priest who took part in the ceremony of the dedication of the walls, Neh 12[41].

MINING AND METALS.—Though Palestine proper is deficient in mineral resources, yet these were present to some extent on its borders, and were not only abundantly found, but even largely developed, in other parts of the ancient East. The Scripture references to mining, accordingly, though not very numerous, are sufficiently definite. Such a passage as Dt 8[9] (cf 33[25]) holds good for the eastern side of the Jordan Valley and the Arabah where remains of extensive iron and copper mines have been found. The ore removed from these mines was processed at Solomon's great port on the Red Sea, Ezion-Geber. For a description of the mines and the vast refinery at Ezion-Geber, see Nelson Glueck's *The Other Side of the Jordan* (1940), chs iii and iv. The passage may also refer to the Lebanon district, or the region of Sinai, especially at Serābîṭ el-Khâdim where the Egyptians operated important turquoise mines. These were worked by Semitic slaves who left some of the earliest alphabetic inscriptions known (from the 15th cent. B.C., in a West-Semitic dialect akin to Hebrew). The classical description of the miner's life in Job 28 is evidently based on observation. It depicts the adventurous and toilsome character of the quest, the shafts sunk and the galleries tunnelled in the rock, the darkness, the waters that have to be drained away, the hidden treasures of precious stones and metals that reward the effort and the ingenuity of man.

The list of metals in Nu 31[22] includes all those that are mentioned in Scripture, viz. gold, silver, 'brass,' iron, tin, and lead. All these are again enumerated in Ezk 27[12f, 22] as articles of Tyrian commerce.

Brass.—This English word, as late as 1611, denoted **copper** or **bronze** (an alloy of copper and tin) rather than the modern brass (an alloy of copper and zinc). Hence, where 'brass' occurs in EV, copper or bronze is to be understood (see RVm on Gn 4[22], and article, BRASS).

Copper occurs once in AV (Ezr 8[27], RV 'bright brass,' RSV 'bright bronze'). But see on 'Brass' above and 'Steel' below.

Gold is a metal the use of which can be traced back to the earliest times of civilization. As a medium of currency it was reckoned by weight, in shekels and talents, coinage being unknown among the Jews before the Exile. While it figured in the history of Israel from the beginning (see the spoils of Egypt [Ex 12[35]], Midian [Nu 32[52], Jg 8[26]], and Jericho [Jos 7[21]]), it became specially plentiful in Palestine in the time of Solomon (1 K 10[14, 21]), the main sources of it being Ophir (1 K 9[28] 10[11]), Tarshish (1 K 10[22]), and Sheba (1 K 11[2], Ps 72[15]). Another gold-producing country was Havilah (Gn 2[11]). Of these localities Havilah and Sheba were Arabian. Ophir (q.v.) may have been the same, though its situation has also been sought in India and S. Africa. For **goldsmiths** see Neh 3[18, 21, 32], Is 40[19] 41[7] 46[6], also (RV, RSV) Jer 10[9, 14] 51[17]. The products of their art comprised beaten work (Ex 25[18] 37[17, 22], Nu 8[14] 37[7], 1 K 10[16f], 2 Ch 9[15f]), plating (Ex 25[11, 24] 26[29, 32] 30[3]), and wire or thread for embroidery (Ex 39[3]).

Iron appears to have come into use later than copper or bronze. Its ores are found in the Lebanon district, in the region of Sinai, and sparsely in Egypt. The most famous ancient seat of its manufacture was among the Chalybes in the Highlands of Assyria. Mining for the ore is mentioned in Job 28[2]; the 'iron furnace' in Dt 4[20], 1 K 8[51], Jer 11[4]; and the forge in Is 44[12]. In modern times iron is separated from its ores as cast iron, from which wrought iron and steel are subsequently prepared. But in ancient times the temperature necessary to melt iron was unavailable, and it must have been produced as wrought iron, which is still obtained by primitive smelting processes in various parts of the world. The uses of iron alluded to in Scripture are very varied, but call for no special comment. In Dt 3[11] and possibly in Am 1[3] 'iron' means black basalt.

Lead is mentioned in Jer 6[29], Ezk 22[18–22] in connexion with the smelting of silver (see 'Silver' below). Its weight is referred to in Ex 15[10]. The 'ephah' in Zec 5[7f] had a leaden covering. Rock-cut inscriptions were made more durable by having the chiselled letters filled up with lead (Job 19[24]).

Silver, like gold, was a very early medium of exchange (Gn 23[15f]). The Hebrew and Greek words for silver are often rendered 'money' in EV. There are frequent references in OT to the use of this metal for vessels and ornamental work. In NT there is special mention of the guild of **silversmiths** at Ephesus, and of the 'shrines' or models of the temple of Diana which were their most profitable article of trade (Ac 19[24]). Among the sources of the metal, Arabia (2 Ch 9[14]) and Tarshish (2 Ch 9[21], Jer 10[9], Ezk 27[12]) are named. The commonest ore of silver is argentiferous galena, which contains a large quantity of lead, and in which other metals may also be present. In the course of smelting the lead combines with the other impurities to form a heavy 'slag,' which separates by its weight from the molten silver, leaving the latter pure. This process is referred to, usually in a figurative moral sense, in Ps 66[10] (cf Is 48[10]), Pr 17[3] 25[4] 27[21], Zec 13[9], Mal 3[3], and especially in Jer 6[28–30] and Ezk 22[17–22]. In the last two passages lead is the most prominent impurity, the others being 'brass', iron, and tin. The mixture of these was the refuse or 'dross' of silver (see also Is 1[22, 25]).

Steel (2 S 22[35], Job 20[24], Ps 18[34], Jer 15[12]) is a mistaken translation in AV of the words elsewhere rendered 'brass.' RV has 'brass' in these passages, and RSV has 'bronze.' Only in Nah 2[3] is 'steel' a possibly correct rendering of *pᵉlādhôth*; but RSV renders 'flame.' Steel is a form of iron containing more carbon than wrought iron. It is capable not only of being welded but also cast, and tempered to various degrees of hardness and elasticity.

Tin derived its importance from its use as a constituent of bronze (an alloy of copper and tin). It is mentioned as an article of Tyrian commerce in Ezk 27[12], and as an impurity in silver in Ezk 22[18] (cf Is 1[25]; RVm, RSV '**alloy**'). Its earliest sources are uncertain, but it appears to have come to the East from the West. It is known that the Phoenicians obtained it from the Scilly Isles and Cornwall.

Flint is a form of silica, and occurs abundantly, in the form of nodules, in many of the limestone rocks of Palestine. It is exceedingly hard, and its property of sparking when struck on steel or on another flint provided a very ancient and common means of obtaining fire (2 Mac 10[3]). Flint has a sharp edge when broken or chipped, and was used for primitive weapons and instruments of many kinds—arrow-heads, knives, etc. For the latter see Ex 4[25] (RV, RSV), Jos 5[2f] (RV, RSV). In other Scripture references to flint its hardness is chiefly in view (Dt 32[13], Job 28[9] RV, Is 5[28] 50[7], Ezk 3[9]).

Marble is limestone (carbonate of lime), hard and close-grained enough to be polished. The purest forms are white, but many coloured varieties are highly valued. Marble was among the materials prepared by David for the Temple (1 Ch 29[2]). Josephus (*Ant.* VIII. iii. 2 [64]) says that Solomon's Temple was built of white stone from Lebanon, but the stones exposed in the Jews' Wailing Place appear to be from the neighbourhood of Jerusalem, probably from the quarries under Bezetha. Marble supplies a simile in Ca 5[15], and is mentioned among the merchandise of 'Babylon' in Rev 18[12].

J. Pk.—**D. N. F.**

MINISH.—The modern form is 'diminish.' 'Minish' occurs in AF and RV in Ex 5[19] (RSV 'lessen'), Ps 107[39] (RSV 'diminish'), and in RV in Is 19[6] (RSV 'diminish'; AV 'be emptied'), Hos 8[10] (RSV 'for a little while'; cf AV).

MINISTER.—The word 'minister' comes from the Latin *minister* = '**servant,**' and generally it may be said that wherever it is found in the Bible, whether in OT or in NT, its original meaning is its primary one, service being the idea it is specially meant to convey.

1. In OT it is used (corresponding to the same Hebrew word in each case) of Joshua as the personal attendant of Moses (Ex 24[13], Jos 1[1]), of the servants in the court of Solomon (1 K 10[5]), of angels and the elemental forces of nature as the messengers and agents of the Divine will (Ps 103[21] 104[4]; cf He 1[7, 14]), but, above all, of the priests and Levites as the servants of Yahweh in Tabernacle and Temple (Ex 28[35], 1 K 8[11], Ezr 8[17], and constantly). At first an Abraham as *paterfamilias* might sacrifice to God (Gn 12[7f]); later, holy men like Samuel were set apart (1 S 9[13]). Scholars are sharply divided on the prophets' relation to the cult, but kings certainly were sacral personages (2 S 1[14], 1 K 8[12ff], Zec 6[13]; cf He 7[1]), for they were God's servants and 'sons' (Ps 2[7] 89[20]). The secular uses show that the Hebrew word was not in itself a priestly term. Ministry was not necessarily a priestly thing, though priesthood was one form of ministry.

2. In NT several Greek words are translated 'minister,' three of which call for notice. (1) *Hypēretēs*, frequently for officer or guardsman (Mt 5[25], Jn 18[3] etc.), is found in Lk 1[2] 4[20], Ac 13[5] 26[16], 1 Co 4[1]. At Lk 4[20] RSV has properly substituted '**attendant**' for 'minister' to avoid misconception. The servant of the synagogue at Nazareth to whom Jesus handed the roll was the *ḥazzān*, a paid official, some of whose duties corresponded to those of an English verger or a Scots beadle. ' Minister ' is used by RSV only in Lk 1[2], and in the other cases it has ' to assist,' ' to serve,' and ' servants.' In Lk 1[2], Ac 26[16], and 1 Co 4[1] *hypēretēs* describes the minister of Christ or of the word in a sense that is hardly distinguishable from that of *diakonos* (see below).

(2) *Leitourgos*, and its cognates, refer in classical Greek to one who renders special services to the commonwealth, without any suggestion of a priestly ministry. But in the LXX they are regularly applied to the ministry of priests and Levites in the sanctuary. No NT writer, however, by his usage ever suggests the discharge of special priestly functions on the part of an official Christian ministry. Either the reference is to the old Jewish ritual (Lk 1[23], He 9[21] 10[11]), or the word is employed in a transformed sense (Ro 15[16], Ph 2[17]; cf Col 1[28], He 9[9f]) ; or, again, it is applied to a service of Christian charity (2 Co 9[12], with *diakonia* ; Ph 2[25, 30]) or of prayer (Ac 13[2f]) from which ideas of priestly ritual seem to be absent. At Ro 13[6] even political authorities are called ' ministers of God.'

(3) *Diakonos.*—It is significant that *diakonos* and *diakonia* are found instead of the *leitourgos* group when the ideas of minister and ministry are to be expressed. This corresponds with the fact that the priesthood of a selected class has been superseded by Christ's as High Priest (Hebrews, *passim* ; cf Col 1[22], Eph 5[27]) and by the universal priesthood of the Church, his Body (1 P 2[9]). It corresponds also with the fact that a ministry of lowly and devoted service (which *diakonia* particularly implies, Lk 17[7ff] ; cf ' slaves ' applied by St. Paul to himself and his colleagues, Ph 1[1] etc.) has replaced the old ministry of exclusive privilege and ritual performance. *Diakonia* is the distinctive Christian word for ' ministry,' and *diakonos* for ' minister ' (Ac 1[17, 25], Ro 12[7], Col 1[7], 1 Th 3[2]). These nouns and the related verb have a wide range of application in NT. The personal services rendered to Jesus by devout women (Lk 10[40], cf 8[3], Jn 12[2], Mt 27[55]), and to St. Paul by Timothy and others (Ac 19[22], Phn[13]) are described as forms of ministry. The true disciple of Jesus is his *diakonos* (Jn 12[26]), for Jesus is Master as well as Teacher (Jn 13[13] 15[15]). Nor will the minister of Christ fail to minister also to the brethren, since his gifts have been provided by the Spirit for the common good (1 Co 12[5, 7], 1 P 4[10]). The example of Jesus evoked obedience, inspiring His followers (Ro 15[8] ; cf Jn 13[15], Ph 2[7]), and our Lord explicitly presented Himself as the minister of His Father (Mk 10[45], Lk 22[27], ' I am among you as one who serves,' Jn 4[34]). Again, His disciples are related to Him as He is to the Father (Mt 10[40], Lk 10[16], Jn 13[20] 20[21] 21[15–17], 1 P 2[25]), and before them is set the glory and the greatness of service (Mk 9[35], ' If any man would be first, he must be last of all and servant of all '). The Body of Christ, however, had special organs of Ministry from the first, made possible by endowments of the Spirit (Ro 12[6–11], 1 Co 12[4–11, 28–30]), and all united in the bond of love (1 Co 12[31]–14[1], Col 3[14]). There were differences of function, indeed, and, above all, the distinction between those who were ministers of the word (apostles, prophets, and teachers, Ac 6[4], 1 Co 12[28], 2 Co 3[6], Eph 3[6f] 4[11]) and those whose contribution lay in gracious acts of benevolence or in administration (Ac 6[1ff] 9[36], Ro 12[8], 1 Co 12[9f, 28]). Whatever might be the ' varieties of service ' (and the variety is important), the word *diakonos* covered them all (1 Co 12[5]) because spiritual qualities outweighed formal status. At a later stage in Paul's lifetime the word *diakonos* is already appropriated to the **deacon** (q.v.) as distinguished from the presbyter-bishop (Ph 1[1] ; cf 1 Ti 3[1–13]). Eph 4[11] marks a trend toward regarding ministries as offices, perhaps. But even in the later NT period *diakonos* still continues to be used in its wider sense, for the Paulinist author of the Pastorals exhorts ' Timothy,' an apostolic delegate with diocesan authority, to be ' a good minister (*diakonos*) of Christ Jesus ' (1 Ti 4[6]).

J. C. L.—**G. J.**

MINISTRY.—The foregoing article has sufficiently dealt with the general idea of ministry, but more must be said about the official Christian ministry as it begins in the NT period.

1. Jesus called Twelve as colleagues, and they are described as ' apostles ' (Mk 3[14] 6[7, 30] and ||s, Jn 6[67] 20[21–23]). In Ac 1[26] Judas' place is filled by Matthias and to the teaching and fellowship of the Apostles the converts adhere (Ac 2[42]). The primary apostolic vocation is to preach the word (Ac 6[2]) but Philip, one of the Seven, is such a preacher (Ac 6[5] 8[5] 21[8]) ; so were Barnabas and Saul (Ac 9[15, 20, 29] 11[26] where their teaching should not be limited to doctrinal instruction). Hence we find others than the Twelve called ' apostles ' (Barnabas, Ac 14[14] ; James the Lord's brother, Gal 1[19] ; Andronicus and Junias, Ro 16[7]), though sometimes the term may be restricted, as in Ph 2[25] (Epaphroditus) and 2 Co 8[23]. There were also false apostles (2 Co 11[13] 12[11] ; cf Rev 2[2]). Technically, an *Apostle* is one of the Twelve companions of Jesus, reinstated by the Easter appearances (1 Co 15[5–7]) ; or one divinely commissioned through a similar vision (1 Co 15[7–9] 9[1]) ; and one whose calling is attested by spiritual gifts in his converts (1 Co 9[2], 2 Co 12[11]). Such status conferred authority (2 Co 13[10]) which Paul exercised to purify congregations, to extirpate heresy, and to maintain genuine Christian traditions (2 Th 2[15], 1 Th 4–5, Gal 1[6–9], 1 Co 5, 11[23] 15[3]). Later the Church was regarded as being grounded on the apostolic witness (Eph 2[20] 3[5], 2 Ti 3[10f], He 2[3], 2 P 1[12ff] 3[2], Jude [17], Rev 21[14]) and its scriptural canon enshrined their legacy (cf Lk 1[2], 2 P 3[15f]). Clearly very few could qualify as companions of Jesus, but there had to be many to whom might be granted, through the Spirit, authority like Paul's. This apostolic succession appears in the ' Timothy ' and ' Titus ' of the Pastorals and in local ministries. Charismatic gifts were much emphasized, and there were *prophets*, *teachers*, and (rarely) *evangelists*, whose work could not have been confined to one congregation (1 Co 12[28f], Eph 4[11] ; for prophets, see also Ac 11[27] 15[32] 21[10] ; for evangelists, Ac 21[8], 2 Ti 4[5] ; for teachers, Ac 13[1], 1 Ti 2[7], 2 Ti 1[11], Ja 3[1]). That the prophetic ministry in its various forms was a ministry rather of function than stated office may be shown by the fact that the same person might be at once apostle, prophet, and teacher (cf Ac 13[1] 14[14], 1 Co 14[18f], 1 Ti 2[7], 2 Ti 1[11]). Spiritual gifts, however, were not confined to those thus described : 1 Co 12 has both a local and a universal reference (cf Eph 4[12], ' to equip the saints for their ministerial work ').

2. Jerusalem had *elders* as well as Apostles, doubtless on the Synagogue model, and the pattern is repeated in the great Gentile Mission (Ac 11[30] 14[23] 20[17, 28]). James may have become president of the Christian elders, but note the distinction of Peter (Mt 16[18]). Pauline evidence corroborates Acts : see 1 Th 5[12], 1 Co 16[15f], Col 1[7] 4[12, 17], Phn [1f], Ph 1[1] (bishops and deacons) 2[25] 4[3]. ' *Elder* ' and ' *bishop* ' are synonyms (Ac 20[17, 28]). Thus, local churches were governed by a presbytery of bishops whose authority derived from the Spirit (Ro 12[6–8]) in conformity with apostolic tradition and to edify the faithful (1 Co 12[7], 2 Co 13[10]). Definite functions are stated only in Ac 20[28] (to be overseers and to feed the flock), with which compare the Qumrân overseers (*m[e]bhakkēr*, *pāḳîdh*, 1*QS* 6[12, 14, 20], *CD* 9[18] 13[7] 14[8]). Institutional and charismatic elements coexisted, but Paul demanded control of the latter by love (1 Co 14). The Seven (Ac 6) are variously regarded ; for Luke they may have been prototypes of the deacons, but they may have been simply *ad hoc* servants.

3. Presbyter-bishops continued for some time (1 P 5[1–5], Ja 5[14]). The beginnings of monepiscopacy may be seen in 2, 3 Jn and the Pastorals. Their duties remained to feed the flock and help the weak, to visit and pray for the sick, to rule and teach, to discipline heretics. Professionalism appears in 1 P 5[2] and possibly 1 Ti 5[17] (cf also Gal 6[6], 1 Co 9[3–7]). The *deacons* seem to have been assistants (1 Ti 3[8–13]), though we must wait until Justin Martyr for more precise details. Little is said about the liturgical duties of ministers (see Ac 10[48], 1 Co 1[17], 1 Ti 2[1f, 8] 4[5, 13] 5[22]). The *deaconess* (possibly Ro

16[1], but not 1 Ti 3[11]) is a vague figure, and the order of widows (1 Ti 5[9ff]) was probably not ministerial. Tension between the charismatic prophet and the local ministry is attested by the *Didache* (10[7] 13[3]), a source of very dubious value. NT makes no real break between clergy and laity. See, further, APOSTLE, BISHOP, DEACON, EVANGELIST, LAYING ON OF HANDS, PROPHET IN NT.

J. C. L.—**G. J.**

MINNI.—A people named in Jer 51[27] along with the Armenians ('Ararat') and Scythians ('Ashkenaz') as coming assailants of Babylon. They are the *Mannai* of the Assyrian inscriptions, who dwelt between the lakes Van and Urmia. J. F. McC.

MINNITH marks the direction in which Jephthah pursued the defeated Ammonites from Aroer, Jg 11[33], *i.e.* Aroer, **1** (q.v.). The site has not been recovered. That indicated in the *Onomasticon*, 4 miles from Heshbon on the way to Philadelphia, seems too far to the S. Minnith appears to have been famous for the high quality of its wheat, Ezk 27[17] (AV, RV; RSV emends the text and renders 'wheat, olives'); cf 2 Ch 27[5].

MINT (Gr. *hēdyosmon*, Mt 23[23], Lk 11[42]).—One of the trifles which were tithed; primarily, perhaps, peppermint (*Mentha piperita*), but including also allied plants, such as the horse mint (*M. sylvestris*), which grows wild all over Palestine. E. W. G. M.

MIPHKAD, GATE OF, Neh 3[31] (AV).—See MUSTER GATE.

MIRACLES.—A miracle is any event regarded as an act of God.

1. Translations.—The word miracle as it occurs in the English Bible represents a variety of terms in the original languages. The most common Hebrew words are *'ōth, mōphēth, pele'*, and *niphlā 'ôth*. Greek uses *sēmeion, teras, ergon, dynamis*. The Vulgate translates these words as *signum, ostentum, mirabilium, miraculum, portentum, virtus*, and *prodigium*. In its renderings of the different terms the AV makes frequent use of *sign* and *wonder*, as do most of the other English translations, but it has used *miracle* five times in the OT and thirty-two times in the NT, a total of thirty-seven times in the Bible. The ASV completely eliminated the word miracle from the OT, but used it eight times in the NT (Lk 23[8], Ac 4[16] 4[22] 8[13] 19[11], 1 Co 12[10] 12[28] and Gal 3[5]). The RSV reinstates *miracle* three times in the OT (Ex 4[21] 7[9], Ps 78[11]), but uses it only six times in the NT (Ac 8[13] 19[11], 1 Co 12[10] 12[28], Gal 3[5], He 2[4]), deleting it in Lk 23[8], Ac 4[16] and 4[22], but restoring it in He 2[4].

The five OT passages in which AV uses miracle are Ex 7[9], Nu 14[22], Dt 11[3] 29[3] and Jg 6[13]. The Hebrew words in these respective passages are *mōphēth, 'ōth, 'ōth, mōphēth*, and *niphlā'ôth*. ASV has translated these words as *wonder, sign, sign, wonder*, and *wondrous works*. RSV has *miracle, sign, sign, wonder*, and *wonderful deeds*, thus reinstating *miracle* in Ex 7[9]. But RSV has also introduced *miracle* in Ex 4[21] for *mōphēth*, which both AV and ASV give as *wonder*. The LXX translated it as *teras*, and the Vulgate as *ostentum*. In the five passages where AV uses *miracle* LXX has *sēmeion* or *teras* for Ex 7[9], and *sēmeion, sēmeion, teras*, and *thaumasion* for the others.

The Hebrew noun *pele'*, or the verb from which it is derived, occurs three times in Is 29[14], which AV translates, 'I will proceed to do a marvellous work among this people, even a marvellous work and a wonder.' The Vulgate says, 'Admirationem faciam populo huic miraculo grande et stupendo.' RSV renders it, 'I will again do marvellous things with this people, wonderful and marvellous.' In Ex 15[11] *pele'* is translated by LXX as *teras* and by Vulgate as *mirabilium*; by AV, ASV and RSV as *wonder*.

A wide vista of meaning for *niphlā'ôth* opens in Job 9[10], where it refers to all the wonderful phenomena of the natural world as acts of God. The LXX says here *mirabilia*; AV, *wonders*; ASV and RSV, *marvellous things*. In Ps 78[11], where it refers to wonders of the Exodus, RSV translates it *miracles*.

In twenty-three of the thirty-one times in the NT where AV uses *miracle* the Greek is *sēmeion*; in eight it is *dynamis*. ASV uses *miracle* for *sēmeion* three times in the NT; for *dynamis* five times. In the NT, RSV has consistently rendered *sēmeion* as *sign* and *dynamis* as *miracle*, with the exception of Ac 2[22], where it is *mighty work*.

None of the translations here considered has dealt adequately with *ergon* in such passages as Jn 5[20] 5[36] 6[28] 7[21]. Literally of course it means work. The Vulgate renders it as *opus*; AV, ASV, and RSV as *work*. But in 7[21] RSV translates it *deed*. The context makes it clear, however, that the work is a miracle.

Thus there is a tendency in recent English versions to avoid *miracle* and to differentiate the Hebrew and Greek words more frequently by resorting to *signs, wonders, wondrous works*, etc. But it is doubtful that this effort has been more successful than AV. For it is obvious that all of these terms as they occur in the Bible are intended to indicate Divine action. The words *sign, wonder*, and *wondrous work* have become so secularized in English that they no longer carry the full miraculous content of the originals. *Miracle*, on the other hand, denotes Divine activity with less ambiguity than any other word in English. With respect to miracles AV is superior to its successors.

2. Definition of Miracle.—The widely prevalent idea that a miracle is a historical event which violates the laws of nature is unsatisfactory in several respects. First, because many persons believe that nature itself is the work of God; and that it would be out of character for God to do exceptional things which violate the procedures which He ordinarily follows; for faith must hold a concept of God which is consistent with itself. Again, the view is superficial in assuming that there is an order of nature and that we know all of its laws, so that we can recognize a miracle when it occurs. Both this mechanistic view of nature and that extent of man's knowledge of it are unjustified at the present time.

The view that a miracle is an external sensible event inexplicable by laws known to us, but not a violation of laws of nature, while less objectionable, still leaves much to be desired. It is arbitrary in limiting miracles to external events, whereas faith is more concerned with the inner life than with external things. The view is unacceptable also in saying that a miracle is inexplicable by laws known to us. The fact is that we are learning new laws all the time. Therefore, as scientific research progresses faith might lose its support in miracles entirely.

Another view of miracle is that it is simply an expression of a law which is unknown to us, but which we might finally discover. This is a possibility, but the objection to this view, just as to that above, is that with the advance of science religion might be deprived of the miracles by which it lives. The view allows that all events of whatever kind might in time be restricted to a realm of nature which operates according to mechanistic laws. In such an order miracles could not exist, at any rate as they are popularly conceived.

St. Augustine (A.D. 354–430) was one of the first great Christian theologians to be concerned with the question of miracles. In his *City of God* he is sharply critical of the view expressed even in his time that nature is a closed mechanistic system. He points out numerous events which he thinks refute such a view. While some of the examples he cites would not be acceptable to us, his main point is still valid. For him the answer to the question of miracles is in God, who creates and controls the universe. Whatever happens is His will. This applies to miracles as well as to what are usually called natural phenomena. Since both types of events are expressions of the will of God, there can be no conflict between them. There is no problem of belief in miracle if you believe in God. All nature is therefore miraculous. In other words, everything in the universe is a miracle, although there are of course familiar and unfamiliar miracles.

The view of St. Thomas Aquinas (1225–1274) was that

MIRACLES

there is an order of nature, and that miracles are outside of that order, but that they are not in violation of it. He differs from Augustine by giving more place to the emerging scientific idea with its concept of a rigid natural order, and by restricting miracles to events which God causes to take place outside of the order of nature. His position continues to our time to be the most popular concept of nature and miracle in theological thought. The weakness of this view, however, is that it tends to exile God from the natural world and to deprive faith of its support in the wonders of nature.

René Descartes (1596–1650) stated the question of miracle with original insight when he said : *Tria mirabilia fecit Dominus* : *res ex nihilo, liberum arbitrium et hominem Deum.* ' The Lord has performed three miracles : the universe out of nothing, the free will, and the Incarnation.' The strength of Descartes' view is that it affirms those miracles which are the essence of Christian faith. Whether other miraculous events have occurred, or may occur, is thus not of primary concern. If historical research should indicate that some of the miracle stories are legends, that would also be no threat to faith. Descartes thus made a profound clarification of the concept of miracle.

Baruch Spinoza (1632–1677) also made an important contribution to religious thought, although he actually denied that miracles occur. Nature was for him a closed system. He thought of everything in terms of universal law, outside of which nothing could happen. Therefore no miracle could conceivably take place. Spinoza either reduced all miracles to legends, or to events which occurred according to natural law. But he was a truly religious man. He had a reverent view of the world of nature and was moved by the marvels which he saw there. His faith was not based on miraculous events outside the world of nature. This position is unacceptable to us insofar as it views nature as a closed system ; nevertheless modern theological thought is indebted to him. He made it possible for many persons who had lost their faith, which was based on what they had come to regard as legends, to recover their belief in God through contemplating the wonders of the universe itself.

David Hume (1711–1776), who is widely known for his scepticism, also actually gave assistance to theology, but in a negative way. He demonstrated that the person who attempts to follow reason alone as his guide will probably end up as a sceptic. While he doubted that miracles have ever occurred, his position tends to confirm the Biblical teaching that man walks by faith, not by sight.

3. Miracles and science.—All through the centuries, whenever miracle has created a problem for faith, it has been as a result of scientific and philosophical theories about the nature of the world. Science by its very nature assumes that the world with which it deals is orderly. It describes the cosmos in terms of universal laws and of interlocking causal chains which traverse it, so that everything that happens can be interpreted in terms of cause and effect. This view is inevitable. Otherwise, its experiments have no validity, and scientific knowledge is not real. While such a position is necessary for science, it obviously undermines the basis of moral character and religious faith. It denies morality by reducing personality to the influence of forces of heredity and environment over which man has no control. Man is therefore a product of universal determinism. He could not be other than what he is. Therefore he is not responsible for his actions. This view yields a materialism of which man is a part, and from which there is no escape.

We do not need to deny that there is order in the universe, and that there are mechanistic elements in nature with which science can deal. Heredity affects personality ; so does environment ; but to recognize a measure of determinism in the world is not to say that the universe as a whole is deterministic. Studies of science itself seem to refute the view that nature is a completely deterministic system controlled by inexorable laws.

A notable example of this has resulted from the discoveries of atomic physics. The ancient belief that the atom is an indivisible particle of solid matter has been abandoned in favour of an electronic concept. It is now conceived of as an elemental quantum of vibrant energy, which is composed of still smaller electric particles that constitute its nucleus. The movements of these particles in the nucleus of the atom conform to no observable pattern. Here we stand before what appears to be an example of discontinuity in nature. This discovery has led to a new concept of the order of the natural world. In atomic nuclei, which are the basis of all physical objects, only disorder is to be seen. So we have the paradox in the physical world of order emerging out of disorder. The order is of a statistical kind. It is an order of averages, and it is in fact only approximate.

Biology presents a similar picture. Views of evolution are based on the theory of mutation. A new form appears which is different from anything which has preceded it. It possesses a new character, and is able to become the first example of a new species because it has the ability to reproduce this unique character. Such a form is called a ' mutant.' While the biologist can recognize one when it appears, he cannot explain why it appears. All that he knows is that it has appeared. He can see no necessity in laws of heredity that requires its appearance. Discontinuity seems therefore to be basic also in living matter.

A third and more important example of discontinuity is mind itself. The unique thing that differentiates man from all other creatures is his intelligence. By means of mind, man is not only able to study the world about him, and to use it for his own purposes, but he can also observe himself. He is conscious of himself as a person, and can analyse himself. By means of the freedom which he thus possesses he is able to a considerable extent to transcend the limitations both of the world about him and of himself. It is also this freedom which enables him to choose between good and evil and thus become a moral person. So man possesses the freedom necessary to become a scientist, a philosopher, an artist, as well as to hold a faith.

If we define the natural world as the mechanistic area of the universe with which science is concerned, and in which its experimental procedures can operate, then those areas in which mechanism is transcended, where freedom prevails, should be regarded as supernatural. Thus in the atomic nucleus, in biological mutation, which is the mystery of life, and in the transcendent power of mind, which is able to recognize and contemplate these wonders and to worship the Power which they manifest, science itself draws back the curtain from the continuing miracles of our world. It appears that there is no segment of the universe, not even a small one, over which absolute mechanism ultimately holds dominion.

4. Biblical Miracles.—The miracles of the Bible fall naturally into different categories. (1) *The resurrection of Jesus.*—This is the supreme miracle for Christians because of its uniqueness. The evidence for it is recorded in the Gospels and the Acts of the Apostles, but the earliest record of it is the account by Paul in 1 Co 15^{4-8}, which was probably written about fifteen years earlier than Mark, the oldest Gospel. Here Paul affirms that his message to the Corinthians had stated that ' he [Christ] was buried, that he was raised on the third day according to the scriptures, and that he appeared to Cephas, then to the twelve. Then he appeared to more than five hundred brethren at one time, most of whom are still alive, though some have fallen asleep. Then he appeared to James, then to all the apostles. Last of all, as to one untimely born, he appeared also to me.' For Paul, resurrection is understood in a spiritual sense. There is no reference to an empty grave or a physical body. Paul goes on to make it clear in 15^{50} that, according to his view, ' flesh and blood cannot inherit the kingdom of God.' His testimony is based on the testimony of eyewitnesses who are still alive when he writes. He is overwhelmingly convinced that Christ arose from the tomb.

There can be no doubt that this faith was the foundation and inspiration of the Christian Church. It is clear, however, that some statements in the Gospels present the resurrection of Jesus as a physical event. It was also understood in this way in some of the later traditions, and this view has continued in many sections of the Church through the centuries.

(2) *The miracle of faith.*—This is the primordial miracle of the individual spiritual life. It is the foundation of Biblical religion. In Gal 3^{6} Paul traces it back to Abraham. The author of Hebrews in 11^{4} carries it all the way to Abel. Their insight is correct. All of the devout people of the Bible were familiar with this miracle. In the OT one finds it at its best in the Psalms, but there is abundant evidence of it elsewhere also. It has led both Jews and Christians to feel that they are children of God. In Gal 4^{5-6} and Ro 8^{15} Paul describes this experience as the spirit of adoption, which causes one to cry out, 'Abba! Father!' while Jn 3^{3-8} goes so far as to call it a new spiritual birth. This miracle of faith is the only miracle which a person knows at first hand. It makes it possible for him to believe in other miracles. It is the one irrefutable datum of religion. But it is not something which can be demonstrated by science or history; one can only bear testimony to it. Eph 2^{8} calls it a gift of God.

(3) *Miracles in nature.*—We have already seen how science opens up some of the wonders of nature which it is unable to penetrate. But is this not similar to the admiration and awe and the apprehension of God which the authors of the creation stories of Genesis felt as they looked out upon the physical world? Does it not remind us of the Biblical writers who saw the glory of God in the heavens, in fire, wind, rainfall, lilies of the field, and the conception and birth of children? Paul was so impressed that he felt that atheism has been without excuse ever since the world was created (Ro 1^{19-20}).

(4) *Miracles of history.*—It is assumed as a matter of course in the Bible that God is the sovereign of history. This view appears inescapable for mature monotheism. It is manifested first in the intense conviction of the Hebrews that God was in control of their destiny. They were convinced above all that it was God who delivered them from Egypt and led them into Canaan. But Amos affirmed (8^{7}) that God had also led the Philistines and Syrians in the same way; and all of his great successors saw the judgments of God in the rise and fall of all the nations. This is the inevitable view of history as it is seen with eyes of faith.

(5) *Miracles of healing.*—Both OT and NT record miraculous cures of disease. In the OT these cures are associated mainly with Elijah and Elisha; in the NT they are attributed often to Jesus, but also to a considerable extent to His disciples. Miraculous cures have continued to be reported in various sectors of Christianity down to our own time. Pagan religions also have reported divine healing. Among the Greeks and Romans the temples of Aesculapius specialized in curing disease. Records of such cures have been found in the ruins of temples at Epidaurus and Rome. It seems evident that faith in God is a therapy which sometimes can cure disease; also that Biblical people had no monopoly of it. This is an area in which one must be on guard against legends. We have no way of controlling either the diagnosis or the cures of the ancient ailments.

There seems no doubt that Jesus was successful in curing various types of disease. Some of the cases, such as the healing of leprosy, or of blindness from birth, and the raising of the dead, are beyond our understanding and power to confirm, but we should not deny that God has power to do these things. Exorcism of demons falls more nearly within our ability to understand. The vocabulary and practice of exorcism were probably only the ancient way of dealing with neuroses and psychoses. Mk 9^{14-29} shows epilepsy; Mk 1^{23-28} and Ac 16^{16-18} are probably the psychosis of hysteria; the demoniac in Mk 5^{1-20} and King Saul in 1 S 16^{14f} and 18^{10f} are examples of the manic-depressive psychosis (cf my *By the Finger of God,* New York: Macmillan, 1951). Other examples of demon possession in the Bible are not described fully enough to allow diagnosis. That Jesus and the disciples were able to relieve such cases is supported by the achievements of contemporary psychiatrists. There is no good reason to doubt the essential authenticity of records of this type.

(6) *Signs and Wonders.*—While these two topics are treated more fully elsewhere, they are mentioned here for completeness. They are the type of phenomena found in the various ancient religions, where they are usually called omens, portents, or prodigies. They may be movements of heavenly bodies, earthquakes, storms, eclipses, strange births, signs observed in sacrificial victims, etc. Such things had little place in the lives of the great prophets of the OT, and Jesus Himself refused to give a sign to validate His mission (Mk 8^{12}, Mt 4^{1-11}). But more popular traditions of the OT, such as those of the Exodus, and later elements in the Gospels and Acts, made a considerable use of phenomena of this type. We have no way of either proving or disproving that they occurred, but for that very reason they are an unsubstantial basis for faith.

(7) *Allegories.*—Biblical writers were gifted storytellers. The allegory was one of their specialities. The problem of miracle in some cases will be resolved when we recognize that the story was written as an allegory. The saga of Samson is a good example, which portrays with humour and pathos the struggle between Hebrews and Philistines. The story of Jonah, with its lesson about the universality of God, is another. This is the most likely approach also to the cycle of stories in Daniel; and some of the miracles of Jesus, especially in the Gospel of John, carry an allegorical meaning. The truth presented by an allegory does not depend for its validity on whether the story itself actually occurred.

5. Miracles as evidence.—This is the question of how faith comes; and in turn one must ask, What is the nature of faith? Is it the same as historical information, or scientific data, or the result of philosophical thought? The answer is No. It is more than any or all of these together. History, science, and philosophy are expressions of reason. The truth which they discover is an achievement of reason. Faith does not turn its back upon reason, but it goes beyond. It has more of the nature of intuition. Even the rational disciplines of history, science, and philosophy are based on postulates which are themselves not discovered by reason, but are the intuitions of faith. How faith is related to miracle stories in the Bible, it is difficult to say. But once faith is achieved, one is immediately able to understand many statements in the Bible about God's acts in nature, history, and human personality. Experiences of Biblical people have been a strong support to the faith of later generations. Faith has often been acquired by reading the Bible. But it is more often acquired from other persons, especially in the family, among friends, and in the Church. The birth of faith in the heart is a mystery which we do not understand.

There is probably no definition of miracle which will be entirely satisfactory. What one person sees as a miracle will be regarded by another as merely a natural event. The concept of miracle rests on the presupposition of God. Unless one believes in God he will see no miracle. Once he has achieved faith in God, however, the problem of miracle vanishes. As an intelligent person he will, of course, recognize that some miracle stories are legends, but of the possibility of miracle, of the existence, power, and activity of God in the world he will have no doubt. God was the presupposition of Biblical people, just as nature is the presupposition of secular thought in our time. In order to understand the experience of miracle we must first break the shackles which secular philosophy has bound upon us. It is necessary for us to rediscover that the natural world, history, and human personality were originally and still are God's creation; and that the wonders which we see in them all are His miracles. See SIGNS, WONDERS. S. V. McC.

MIRIAM.—**1.** The sister of Moses and Aaron, probably older than either. It was she who watched Moses in the ark of bulrushes, Ex 2^{4ff}. She is called 'the prophetess,' and led the women in the song of victory at the Red Sea, Ex 15^{20f}. In the course of the wilderness wanderings she combined with Aaron against Moses, and was punished by leprosy, which was healed in answer to the prayer of Moses, Nu 12^{1-15}. She died in Kadesh towards the end of the wilderness journey, Nu 20^{1}. Her story is referred to in Dt 24^{8-9} in connexion with the ceremonial law of leprosy, and in Mic 6^{4} she is spoken of along with Moses and Aaron as a leader of the people. The name Miriam is perhaps of Egyptian derivation (Gardiner suggests 'beloved of Amūn'); in Greek it became Mariam and Mariamme, whence Maria and Mary. **2.** A man (or woman) of the family of Caleb, 1 Ch 4^{17}.

MIRMA, 1 Ch 8^{10} (AV).—See MIRMAH.

MIRMAH.—Eponym of a Benjamite family, 1 Ch 8^{10} (AV **Mirma**).

MIRROR.—See GLASS.

MISAEL.—**1.** 1 Es 9^{44} (AV, RV); see MISHAEL, **2.** **2.** Ad. Dn 3^{66} (AV, RV); see MISHAEL, **3.**

MISGAB.—Mentioned in AV and RV along with Nebo and Kiriathaim in the oracle against Moab, Jer 48^{1}. Perhaps it is not intended as a proper name (RSV 'the fortress'; cf RVm). The same Hebrew term occurs in Is 25^{12}, where AV and RV render 'high fort' and RSV 'high fortifications.'

MISHAEL.—**1.** A Kohathite, Ex 6^{22}, Lv 10^{4}. **2.** One of Ezra's supporters, Neh 8^{4}, 1 Es 9^{44} (AV, RV **Misael**). **3.** See MESHACH.

MISHAL.—A town of Asher, Jos 19^{26} (AV **Misheal**); given to the Gershonite Levites, 21^{30} (in the parallel 1 Ch 6^{24} called **Mashal**). The site is unknown.

MISHAM.—Eponym of a Benjamite family, 1 Ch 8^{12}.

MISHEAL, Jos 19^{26} (AV).—See MISHAL.

MISHMA.—**1.** A son of Ishmael, Gn 25^{14}, 1 Ch 1^{30}. **2.** The eponym of a Simeonite family, 1 Ch 4^{25f}.

MISHMANNAH.—A Gadite chief, 1 Ch 12^{10}.

MISHNAH.—See TALMUD.

MISHRAITES.—A family of Kiriath-jearim, 1 Ch 2^{53}.

MISPAR.—One of the exiles who returned with Zerubbabel, Ezr 2^{2}, 1 Es 5^{8} (AV, RV **Aspharasus**); called **Mispereth** in Neh 7^{7}.

MISPERETH.—See MISPAR.

MISREPHOTH-MAIM.—From the waters of Merom the defeated Canaanites fled to Great Sidon, and unto Misrephoth-maim, Jos 11^{8}. It marks the S. boundary of the Sidonians, who had not been driven out by Joshua, 13^{6}. The ladder of Tyre formed a natural limit to the territory of the Sidonians. It is probably modern *Kh. el-Musheirefeh.*

MITE.—See MONEY, **7.**

MITHCAH, Nu 33^{28f} (AV).—See MITHKAH.

MITHKAH.—One of the stopping-places on the wanderings, Nu 33^{28f} (AV **Mithcah**). The site is unknown.

MITHNITE.—An else unknown gentilic applied to one of David's officer's in 1 Ch 11^{43}.

MITHRADATES, 1 Es $2^{11, 16}$ (RV).—See MITHREDATH, **1, 2.**

MITHREDATH ('a gift of Mithra').—**1.** The Persian treasurer, whom Cyrus commanded to deliver to Sheshbazzar the sacred vessels, Ezr 1^{8}; **Mithridates** in 1 Es 2^{11} (RV **Mithradates**). **2.** Apparently a Persian officer stationed in Samaria. Together with his colleagues he wrote to Artaxerxes I to hinder the re-building of the walls of Jerusalem, Ezr 4^{7}; **Mithridates** in 1 Es 2^{16} (RV **Mithradates**).

MITHRIDATES.—See MITHREDATH, **1, 2.**

MITRE.—With the exception of Zec 3^{5} (AV, RV; RVm, RSV '**turban**' for which see DRESS, **5** (*a*) where it represents the Hebrew *ṣānîph*, and Ezk 21^{26} (RV, AV '**diadem,** 'RSV 'turban'), on which see below, 'mitre' is used in AV and RV exclusively of the characteristic headdress of the Jewish high priest. It is always replaced by 'turban' in RSV. The mitre (Heb. *miṣnepheth*, from the same root as *ṣānîph*, signifying to 'wind round,') was an elaborate species of turban, composed of a long swathe of 'fine linen' (Ex 28^{39}) 16 cubits in length, according to the Talmud. Its precise form, however, is uncertain; the descriptions given by Josephus of the high-priestly mitre of his day, besides being obscure in themselves, agree neither with one another nor with the OT text.

On the common assumption that the Priests' Code originated in Babylonia, it is probable that the mitre was intended to have the conical form characteristic of the tiara of the Babylonian kings. For ornament it had a 'plate of gold' on which were engraved two Hebrew words signifying 'holy to the Lord,' Ex 28^{36}, Lv 8^{9} (cf Sir 45^{12}). The plate rested on the front of the mitre, and was kept in position by a blue-purple ribbon (Ex 28^{37} 39^{31}), which probably served as a fillet and was tied behind perhaps with the ends hanging down, as in the case of the jewelled diadem or fillet worn by the Assyrian kings. Hence the fillet could be described as 'the holy crown' (Lv 8^{9}), and by ben-Sira as 'a gold crown upon his turban' (AV, RV 'mitre'). The royal crown of Judah, according to Ezekiel (21^{26}), consisted of the same two parts. This passage is our warrant for saying that the headdress prescribed for the high priest in the Priests' Code, consisting of mitre and diadem, is intended to signify that the high priest shall unite in his person the highest office in both Church and State.

The headdress of the high priest is always distinguished from that of his subordinates, for which see BONNET. A. R. S. K.

MITYLENE was the chief town of Lesbos on its E. coast, subsequently giving its name to the whole island. It was one of the early Aeolian colonies, and one of the earliest homes of Greek lyric poetry—the birthplace of Sappho and Alcaeus. It attained great naval power, and founded colonies such as Sigeum and Assos. It took a prominent part in the Ionian revolt, but helped Xerxes against Greece. It joined the Athenian alliance, but revolted in 428 B.C. and was nearly annihilated. After opposing Rome in the Mithridatic War, it was made a free city. It has belonged to the Turks since A.D. 1462. Its mention in Ac 20^{14} is merely incidental; St. Paul's ship spent a night there. A. E. H.

MIXED MULTITUDE.—A description given (1) to certain persons who joined Israel in the Exodus from Egypt (Ex 12^{38}), and who fell a lusting at Kibroth-hattaavah (Nu 11^{4} AV, RV; RSV 'rabble'); (2) to those who were separated from the Israelites after the return from the captivity, Neh 13^{3} (AV, RV; RSV 'those of foreign descent').

In Ex 12^{38} those referred to are probably strangers of non-Israelite or half-Israelite origin. The Hebrew consonants (differently pointed) mean either 'mixed' or 'Arabian,' and some have suggested that we ought here to translate 'Arabians.' The same Hebrew word is translated in RV (cf AV) 'mingled people' in Jer 25^{20} (RSV 'foreign folk') 50^{37} (RSV 'foreign troops'), Ezk 30^{5} (RSV 'Arabia'), where it has been thought to refer to foreign mercenaries. In Ezk 30^{5} 'Arabians' gives a better meaning. The Hebrew word in Nu 11^{4} is a different one, and is probably a contemptuous term, signifying the mob, the rabble.

The context in Neh 13^{3} leaves no doubt as to the meaning. The reference is to the strangers with whom the Israelites had intermarried and the children of such alliances. W. F. B.

MIZAR.—Apparently the name of a hill in Ps 42^{6}. If so it must be a peak of the Hermons, otherwise unknown. Alternatively, it may be an appellative, 'the little.' Some read *har* (' O hill ') for *mēhar* (' from the hill ') and render ' O thou little hill,' *i.e.* Zion.

MIZMOR.—See PSALMS, **2.**

MIZPAH, MIZPEH.—These words (from *ṣāphāh*, to 'look out,' especially as a watchman) mean ' outlook point.' They are the names of several places and towns located both E. and W. of the Jordan River, all presumably situated on elevated spots, and all probably ancient sacred places. The sites of several are, however, uncertain. Both names are usually preceded by the Hebrew article; the Hebrew consonants are the same and the final vowel alone differs. RSV regularly transliterates the name as Mizpah except in four instances (Jos 11[8] 15[38] 18[26], 1 S 22[3]) where *Mizpeh* is used.

1. Mizpah in Gn 31[49], where Jacob and Laban made their covenant together, and where the name is explained by a popular etymology, from the words used by Laban in the so-called Mizpah benediction : ' The Lord *watch* between you and me, when we are absent one from the other ' (and interpose, it is implied, if either attempts to take advantage of the other). The name has not been preserved, and hence the site cannot be located with certainty. On the strength of v.[48] where the ' heap of witness ' called Galeed (q.v.) may be another designation of Mizpah, it has been argued that the latter did not designate a town but a memorial cairn or pillar. However, since Jacob's itinerary from Haran must have taken him through the territory later designated as Gilead, some scholars have proposed that this Mizpah must be identical with the **Ramath-mizpeh** of Gad (Jos 13[26]), and Mizpah of Gilead (Jg 10[17], 11[29]). A location at *Khirbet Jel'ad*, S. of the Jabbok River has been suggested (see L. H. Grollenberg, *Atlas of the Bible* [1957],p. 157).

2. The ' land of Mizpah,' at the foot of Hermon, in Jos 11[3], probably the same as ' the valley of Mizpeh ' in v.[8]. This ' Mizpah,' or ' Mizpeh,' has been identified with the Druse village of *Mutallah* (the ' climbed up to '), on a hill 200 feet high, at the S. end of the broad and fertile plain called the *Merj 'Ayūn* (the ' meadow of *'Ayūn*,' overlooking the basin of Lake Huleh, a little N. of *Abil*, and 8 miles WNW. of *Bāniyās* (Robinson iii, 372 f). This, however, is thought by some to be not far enough to the E. (notice ' under Hermon ' v.[3] and ' eastward ' v.[8]) ; and Buhl (*GAP*, 240) conjectured that it may have been the height on which are now the ruins of the Saracenic castle *Qal'at es-Subēbē*, 2 miles above *Bāniyās*, on the NE. In the former case the ' land ' of Moab would be the *Merj 'Ayūn* itself, between the rivers *Liṭânī* and *Ḥāṣbānī* ; in the latter, it would be the plain stretching down from *Bāniyās* towards Lake Huleh.

3. Mizpeh in Jos 15[38], in the Shephelah, or ' lowland ' of Judah, mentioned in the same group of cities as Lachish (q.v., now identified with *Tell ed-Duweir*, about 25 miles SW. of Jerusalem). According to Eusebius (*Onom.* 279), there was a Mizpeh in the district of Eleutheropolis (*Beit-Jibrîn*, 23 miles SW. of Jerusalem), on the N., and another on the road from Eleutheropolis to Jerusalem. The former of these descriptions would suit *Tell eṣ-Ṣāfiyeh*, on a hill of white chalk 7½ miles NNW. of Beit-Jibrîn, with a commanding view that recalls the early meaning of the name ' Mizpah.'

4. The Mizpah of Jg 10[17] 11[11, 34], Jephthah's home—apparently, to judge from the narrative, not very far from the Ammonite territory, and (11[33]) the Aroer in front of Rabbath-ammon (Jos 13[25], see RABBAH). The exact location is uncertain. Several scholars have proposed the *Jebel Osha'*, about 16 miles NW. of *'Ammân*, the highest point of the mountains (*c* 3600 ft.) S. of the Jabbok River, commanding a view of almost the whole Jordan Valley, as well as of much of the country opposite, on the W. of Jordan (Conder, *Heth and Moab*, 186f). If the ' Mizpeh of Gilead ' and ' Ramath-mizpeh ' (see above at **1**) are actually the same city, which was also the meeting place of Jacob and Laban, and the home of Jephthah, then *Khirbet Jal'ad*, as suggested above, may be the location. The Mizpah mentioned by Hosea (5[1]) is usually understood as referring to a city E. of the Jordan River ; the fact that he mentions it without identifying it more specifically may be an indication that there was only one Mizpah near the Jabbok River and that it was a city which, in Hosea's day, had reverted to paganism, although in earlier times it had sacred associations with the Hebrews.

5. Mizpeh of Moab (1 S 22[3]—' Mizpeh ' is perhaps also to be read in v.[5] for ' stronghold ' although a proper name here requires an unlikely emendation of the Hebrew and is not supported by the LXX), the residence of the king of Moab when David consigned his own parents to his care. It must have been situated on some elevated site in Moab, but its exact location is unknown.

6. The Mizpah, on the W. of Jordan, mentioned in Jg 20[1, 3] 21[1, 5, 8], 1 S 7[5ff] 10[7] as a meeting-place of Israelites on important occasions ; in 1 K 15[22] (2 Ch 16[6]) as fortified by Asa ; in 2 K 25[23, 25], Jer 40[6, 8], and several times besides in Jer 40, 41, as the residence of Gedaliah, the governor appointed by Nebuchadnezzar over Judah after the capture of Jerusalem in 586 B.C. ; and in Neh 3[7, 15, 19] which suggests that Mizpah served as a capital of a district in Judah after the Babylonian Exile. The same place appears to be intended by the ' Mizpah ' of 1 Mac 3[46] (AV **Maspha, RV Mizpeh** ; Gr. *Massēpha*, as often in LXX for ' Mizpah,' *e.g.* Jg 20[1, 3]), ' opposite Jerusalem,' and formerly a ' place of prayer ' (*i.e.* ' sanctuary ') for Israel ; here the faithful Israelites assembled after Antiochus Epiphanes had desecrated the Temple and stopped all worship in it. The allusions to Mizpah discussed thus far indicate that one city of this name is involved and that it must have been located N. of Jerusalem in the region of Gibeah and Gibeon which are often mentioned with it as if they were not far away.

This Mizpah was identified by Robinson (i, 460) with *Nebi Samwîl*, a hill 4½ miles NW. of Jerusalem, 2935 feet above the Mediterranean, and some 500 feet above the surrounding plain (notice ' gone *or* came up ' in Jg 20[3] 21[5, 8]), with a commanding view of the surrounding country (*ibid.* 457 f). Although other sites for Mizpah have been proposed, many scholars have followed Robinson in his identification. *Nebi Samwîl* is 3 miles WNW. of Gibeah (cf Jg 20[1, 3ff]), 2 miles S. of Gibeon (q.v., cf Neh 3[7]), and a little W. of the present road from Jerusalem to Ramallah. It is the actual point from which travellers ascending by the ancient route through the pass of Beth-horon caught their first glimpse of the interior of the hills of Palestine. ' It is a very fair and delicious place, and it is called Mount Joy, because it gives joy to pilgrims' hearts ; for from that place men first see Jerusalem ' (Maundeville, cited in *SP*, p. 214). Its present name, *Nebi Samwîl* (the ' Prophet Samuel '), is due to the Moslem tradition that it was Samuel's burial-place (cf 1 S 7[6, 16], where Mizpah is mentioned as one of Samuel's residences) ; and the mosque there—once a Crusaders' church—contains a cenotaph revered by the Moslems as his tomb.

Many scholars, however, locate Mizpah at *Tell en-Naṣbeh*, an important mound about 5 miles NE. of *Nebi Samwîl*. During four seasons of excavations at *Tell en-Naṣbeh*, between 1926 and 1935, conducted by W. F. Badé, evidence was uncovered which demonstrated that the site had been occupied during the periods when OT Mizpah was occupied. The results of the excavations have been published in 2 vols., C. C. McCown (with contributions by J. Muilenburg, J. C. Wampler, D. von Bothmer and M. Harrison), *Tell en-Nasbeh, I, Archaeological Results*, and J. C. Wampler, *Tell en-Nasbeh, II, The Pottery*, Berkeley, California and New Haven, Connecticut (1947). According to these reports, *Tell en-Naṣbeh* was not extensively occupied prior to the settlement of the Hebrews there shortly after 1200 B.C. No traces of a sanctuary have been found that can be dated to the period of Samuel, although it is not impossible that the hill was used as a temporary place of worship. The absence of evident Philistine occupation would be in accord with the Biblical record to the effect that the Israelites occupied Mizpah during the time of their wars with the Philistines. An impressive stone wall enclosing about 8 acres was found. Almost half a mile in length and more than 15 feet in thickness, this wall was buttressed with towers which added to its effectiveness as a city defence. There is some question as to the date of the city's defence, but there is a possibility that some of the building can be attributed to Asa (see above) who fortified Mizpah. *Tell en-Naṣbeh* continued to be occupied to the Maccabaean period although it apparently ceased to be an important city about 300 B.C. A seal of 'Jaazaniah, servant of the king,' is of considerable interest because of its possible naming of the officer associated with Gedaliah (2 K 25^{23}; Jer 40^{8}) who governed Mizpah and was slain there. For further discussion of the identification of Mizpah with *Tell en-Nasbeh*, see C. C. McCown, *op. cit.*, pp. 23–63. 'To put it briefly, there are no serious difficulties in applying all of the historically respectable biblical data (about Mizpah) to the site of Tell en-Nasbeh' (p. 58). Because no inscription was found naming the *tell* as Mizpah, any doubt that remains concerning this identification cannot be removed until excavations have been conducted at *Nebi Samwîl* and Ataroth-addar (q.v.) and other *tells* in this vicinity of *Tell en-Naṣbeh*. S. R. D.—**W. L. R.**

MIZRAIM.—The name of **Egypt** (q.v.), and especially of Lower Egypt. Mizraim (AV, RV; RSV **Egypt**) was son of Ham and father of Ludim, Anamim, Lehabim, Naphtuhim, Pathrusim (*i.e.* the inhabitants of Upper Egypt), Casluhim, and Caphtorim, Gn $10^{6, 13f}$. Cf also article, PATHROS.

MIZZAH.—A 'duke' of Edom, Gn $36^{13, 17}$, 1 Ch 1^{37}.

MNASON.—A Cypriot Christian, one of the early disciples, with whom Paul and his companions lodged (Ac 21^{16}), just conceivably in Jerusalem (so the Vulgate and Chrysostom), more likely on the way from Caesarea to Jerusalem. The text of the passage is muddled and the grammar difficult. The Western text, whether original or not, is probably a correct interpretation, making it explicit that the party halted at a village *en route*. The commoner route *via* Shechem-Neapolis was well over 100 miles. The coast road by way of Lydda and Diospolis is rather shorter but far longer than a single day's journey. Nothing further is known of Mnason. J. L.

MOAB, MOABITES.—Moab occupied the lofty tableland to the E. of the Dead Sea. It was bounded on the E. by the Arabian desert, on the S. by the river Zered (the northern boundary of Edom), on the W. by the Dead Sea and the Jordan Valley. Its N. boundary fluctuated at different periods between the Arnon and an indistinct line some distance N. of Heshbon. This tableland is elevated some 3000 feet above the level of the Mediterranean, and about 4300 feet above the Dead Sea. It is traversed by several valleys of which the middle one, the Arnon, frequently mentioned in the Bible, is the deepest. The northern portion of Moab consists of broad stretches of rolling country. Its reddish soil is fertile. In the southern portion more hills are found, and the deep wrinkles there interfere with agriculture. In the winter months the rainfall is adequate, and renders the country very desirable in comparison with the deserts on its border.

This area was originally occupied by a people known from the Bible as Rephaim, whom the Moabites are said to have called Emim (Dt 2^{10f}). Another name of a people preceding the Moabites is found in the Balaam oracles as 'sons of Sheth' who stand parallel to Moab (Nu 24^{17}). They occur in the Egyptian execration texts of the 19th cent. B.C. as *Šwt*(*w*), and in cuneiform records as *Sūtū* (Albright, *BASOR*, 83 [1941], 34; *JBL*, lxiii, [1944], 220). The narrative of Gn 19 tells the story of the origin of the Moabites from Lot and their relationship with the Ammonites. It also explains the name in popular etymology from *mē'ābhî*, 'from my father' (Gn 19^{37}), but its real meaning is disputed. That story, furthermore, shows that the Israelites recognized the Moabites as their kinsmen. That they really were such, their language, religion, and customs, so far as known to us, also testify.

Originally nomads, the Moabites became a settled people about 1300 B.C. At the time of the approach of the Hebrews to Palestine they were so strongly entrenched in their land that the invaders avoided all conflict with them (Dt 2^{9}, Jg 11^{15}, 2 Ch 20^{10}), although they conquered the land of king Sihon, who had subdued all of Moab N. of the Arnon (Nu 21^{21-31}, Dt 2^{24-35}). The Moabites viewed the coming of Israel with alarm, and desired to attack them, but did not dare (Nu 22–24, Dt 23^{4}, Jg 11^{25}). The Israelites secured at this time the territory N. of the Arnon; but the narratives differ as to whether its cities were all assigned to Reuben (so Jos 13^{15-21}), or whether some of the most southerly (Dibon, Ataroth, and Aroer) were assigned to Gad (Nu 32^{34ff}). The Gadites apparently obtained some of the southern cities, and the Reubenites some of the northern. Probably the conquest was not complete.

Early in the period of the Judges, the Moabites not only regained control of all this territory, but extended their power into western Palestine so as to oppress the Hebrews (Jg 3^{12-30}). This led to the assassination of Eglon, king of Moab, by Ehud. In course of time the Moabites absorbed the tribe of Reuben.

According to the Book of Ruth, friendly intercourse existed between Moab and Israel at some time during the period of the Judges. Saul fought with the Moabites (1 S 14^{47}), and they aided David against Saul towards the end of his reign (1 S 22^{3ff}). David subjugated Moab, and rendered the country tributary to Israel (2 S $8^{2, 12}$). This subjugation apparently continued during the reign of Solomon, who also took Moabitish women into his harem, and built a shrine for Chemosh, the god of Moab (1 K $11^{1, 7}$).

After the reign of Solomon, Moab apparently gained its independence. Our next information comes from the so-called '**Moabite Stone**,' an inscription of Mesha, king of Moab, found in 1868 at ancient Dibon, and now preserved in the Louvre. Mesha states that Omri, king of Israel, conquered Moab, and that it continued subject to Israel till the middle of the reign of his son. Then Chemosh enabled him (Mesha) to win victories over Israel and regain his country's independence. These affairs are described in detail. A narrative parallel only in parts is found in 2 K 3^{3ff}. Jehoram, Ahab's successor, undertook, with the aid of Jehoshaphat of Judah and the king of Edom, to reconquer Moab. The campaign almost succeeded. The country was overrun, the capital besieged and reduced to great extremity, when the king of Moab sacrificed to Chemosh his firstborn son on the city wall in sight of both armies (2 K 3^{27}). The courage which this aroused in the Moabites, and the superstitious dread which it excited in the besieging army apparently secured a victory for the former. It appears from 2 K 13^{20} that after this Moabites occasionally invaded Israel.

Amos (2^{1-3}) in the next century reproved Moab for barbarities to Edom. Tiglath-pileser III. of Assyria enumerates Salamanu, the king of Moab, among his tribute-payers (*ANET*, p. 282a). Sennacherib, about 700 B.C., received tribute from Kammusunadbi, king of Moab (*ANET*, p. 287b), and the country remained subject to Assyria during the following reigns of Esarhaddon and Ashurbanipal, who mention the Moabite kings Musuri (*ANET*, pp. 291a, 294a) and Kamashaltu (*ANET*, p. 298b) among their vassals.

Moabites aided Nebuchadnezzar against Jehoiakim at the end of the latter's reign (2 K 24^{2}). Is 15, 16, Zeph 2^{8-11}, Jer 48, and Ezk 25^{8ff} contain prophecies against Moab, but provide no historical information. Jer 48 indicates that a great calamity was impending over them. In Neh 4^{7} Arabians rather than Moabites are allies of the Ammonites (cf also 1 Mac 9^{32-42} and Jos. *Ant.* XIII. xiii. 5 [374], XIV. i. 4 [15]). We know that the Nabataeans were in possession of this country a little later, and it is probable that by the time of Nehemiah they had already brought the Moabite power to an end. Some infer from Jeremiah's prophecy that Moab rebelled against Nebuchadnezzar as Israel and Ammon did, and that he carried enough of them captive to weaken them and render them an easy prey to the Nabataeans. This is possibly true, but no more than an attractive hypothesis.

The language of the Moabites was, as the Moabite Stone shows, identical with that of Israel. That peculiar construction known as *waw consecutive* is found, outside of Biblical Hebrew, only in the Moabite Stone and in a few Phoenician inscriptions.

The religion of the Moabites was somewhat similar to that of early Israel. The references to Chemosh in Mesha's inscription parallel those to Yahweh in Israelitish writings of the same period. The name Ashtar-Chemosh indicates that the worship of the feminine divinity known to the Babylonians as Ishtar, and to the Phoenicians as Astart, was also mingled with the worship of Chemosh. Traces of the repellant nature of this worship appear in the OT (Nu 25^{5} 31^{16}, Jos 22^{7}, Ps 106^{28}). No great ethical prophets, such as elevated the religion of Israel, rescued the religion of Moab from the level of its barbaric origin.

G. A. B.—**S. H. Hn.**

MOADIAH.—See Maadiah.

MOCHMUR.—A wady apparently SE. of Dothan (Jth 7^{18}).

MODIN.—In the Talmud *Môdheʿîm.* A village in the Shephelah, never mentioned in the OT, but of great importance as the home of the Maccabees. Here Mattathias, by slaying a Seleucid official and a Jew who conformed to the paganizing commands of Antiochus, struck the first blow for Jewish religious freedom (1 Mac 2$^{1-28}$). He was buried at Modin (2^{70}), as were his sons Judas (9^{19}) and Jonathan (13^{25}). Simon here built an elaborate monument with seven pyramids, commemorative of his father, mother, and four brethren, with great pillars around, and bas-reliefs of military and naval triumphs. This splendid monument could be seen at sea. It stood for about 500 years, after which it seems to have disappeared; and with it was lost all recollection of the site of Modin. Guérin rightly identified it with *el-Midyeh*, near *Lidd*. There are numerous rock-tombs about, some of them traditionally known as *Qubūr el-Yehûd*, or 'the Jews' tombs,' but nothing remains of the Maccabaean mausoleum. Hatred of the Maccabees or of the Jews as such will have led to its obliteration.

R. A. S. M.—**E. G. K.**

MOETH.—See Noadiah.

MOLADAH.—A city reckoned to Judah in Jos 15^{26}, and to Simeon in Jos 19^{2}, 1 Ch 4^{28}; it was resettled after the exile, Neh 11^{26}. It is possibly modern *Tell el Milḥ*.

MOLE.—**1.** Hebrew *tinshemeth*, Lv 11^{30} (AV; RV, RSV **chameleon,** q.v.); to be distinguished from the bird *tinshemeth*, mentioned in Lv 11^{18}, Dt 14^{16} (see Owl, **5**). **2.** Hebrew *ḥᵃpharpārāh* (read *laḥᵃpharpārôth* for MT *laḥpōr-pērôth*), Is 2^{20}. The true insectivorous mole does not occur in Palestine, but the rodent *Spalax typhlus*, the mole rat, is very common. It lives entirely underground, has most rudimentary eyes, and makes very long burrows. It is gregarious, and large areas are sometimes covered thick with its hillocks. It is possible that the word (which is derived from a root meaning 'dig') may apply to rats, mice, jerboas, etc.

E. W. G. M.

MOLECH, MOLOCH.—A term associated with the practice of child sacrifice. The term occurs eight times in the OT (Lv 18^{21} 20$^{2-5}$, 1 K 11^{7}, 2 K 23^{10}, Is 30^{33}, Jer 32^{35}). The special centre of this practice was just outside Jerusalem, at a place in the Valley of Hinnom called the Topheth (q.v.). Molech worship was introduced, according to 1 K 11^{7}, by Solomon. This can hardly be correct, however; the text of 1 K 11^{7} should read *lᵉmilkōm*, 'to Milkom' (the god of the Ammonites; see v.^{5} and v.^{23}) rather than *lᵉmōlekh*.

The term Molech has long been explained as the title of a foreign god, applied also to Yahweh. It has been assumed that the original vocalization was *melekh*, 'king,' altered to Molech by the use of the vowels of the Hebrew word *bōsheth*, 'shame.' Judgments have differed as to the original homeland of this god; the Tyrian god Melkart has been proposed most frequently, since it is known that child sacrifices were common in the Phoenician homeland and in Carthage. Attention has also been called to the name of a city of the Benjamites of Mari, *Ilum-Muluk*. References to deities by the term *melekh* are common in the Semitic literature.

It is more probable, however, that Molech is a technical term for child sacrifice. In the majority of its occurrences the word, on this view, originally would have been vocalized *lᵉmōlekh*, 'for a Molech (child sacrifice),' rather than *lammōlekh*, 'to Molech' (the god Molech or Melek). A vivid picture of such a sacrifice is given by Isaiah (30^{33}) in his symbolic portrayal of Yahweh's preparations for the destruction of Assyria: 'For Topheth has long been prepared; yea, for a Molech (sacrifice) it is made ready, its pyre made deep and wide, with fire and wood in abundance; the breath of Yahweh, like a stream of brimstone, kindles it.'

The practice of child sacrifice was not unknown in early Israel (Gn 22$^{1-19}$, Ex 22$^{29\ (\text{Heb. } 28)}$, Jg 11$^{29-40}$). Archaeological discoveries of the skeletons of infants, often in earthen jars, are not to be taken as evidence for the wholesale offering of children to the gods of the Canaanites. Most of these are probably instances of the burial of infants. The mortality rate of children was very high in the ancient world. Nevertheless, in Canaan as in early Israel, children were occasionally offered to the deity. Ex 22$^{29\ (\text{Heb. } 28)}$ indicates clearly that the first-born son was considered to belong in a special sense to Yahweh. Some first-born sons were dedicated to the service of Yahweh, perhaps in fulfilment of this obligation (1 S 1$^{11,\ 27\text{f}}$). The common practice was, from early days, the substitution of an animal for the child. The sacrifice of the first-born was resorted to only in extreme circumstances, as the final effort of a family or community to secure the favour of the deity. Mesha, king of Moab, is reported to have offered his first-born as a burnt offering upon the wall (2 K 3^{27}), bringing 'great wrath upon Israel.' Prophetic protests against this practice are not numerous, probably because the practice itself only became widespread under Ahaz and Manasseh (see Mic 6^{7}, 2 K 16^{3} 21^{6}). The reform of Josiah, under the influence of the tradition of Deuteronomy, brought the practice to a decisive end (2 K 23^{10}). W. J. Ha.

MOLI, 1 Es 8^{47} (AV).—See Mahli.

MOLID.—The name of a Judahite family, 1 Ch 2^{29}.

MOLOCH.—See Molech.

MOLTEN SEA.—See Temple, **6** (*c*) **'Brazen Sea.'**

MOMDIS, 1 Es 9^{34} (AV, RV).—See Maadai.

MONEY.—**1.** *Antiquity of a metallic currency: weights and values.*—That the precious metals, gold and silver, and to a lesser extent copper, were the ordinary media of exchange in Palestine from a time long prior to the appearance there of the Hebrews, is amply attested by evidence from Egypt and Babylonia, and also from the soil of Palestine itself. The predominance of silver as the metal currency for everyday transactions among the Hebrews long before the introduction of coined money is perhaps further shown by the constant use of the word for 'silver' (*keseph*) in the sense of 'money,' as *e.g.* at Gn 42^{28} 'My money (*lit.* 'silver') has been put back; here it is in the mouth of my sack': and 1 K 21^{2} 'I will give you its value in money.'

Coined money begins in Palestine only in the Persian period. Mr. Raphael Loewe sees the earliest Biblical allusion to coined money in Hag 1^{6} (*PEQ*, 1955, pp. 141 ff). For most of the OT period therefore the understanding of money depends upon the recognition, which is not always possible, of the various systems of weights adopted for the weighing of the precious metals. Originally money must be weighed; cf 2 K 12$^{10\text{f}}$: 'And whenever they saw that there was much money in the chest, the king's secretary and the high priest came up and they counted and tied up in bags the money that was found in the house of the Lord. Then they would give the money that was weighed out into the hands of the workmen who had the oversight of the house of the Lord . . .' The introduction of coined money did not of course entirely supersede the counting of money by weight which is still in use in modern banks, but coins facilitated all day to day transactions. Before coins, money could be ' told ' or counted by being weighed. Hence the great emphasis on the just balance at Pr 16[11] : ' A just balance and scales are the Lord's ; all the weights in the bag are his work ' ; Pr 20[23] : ' Diverse weights are an abomination to the Lord, and false scales are not good ' ; cf Dt 25[13-15]. Scales were an essential in day to day transactions, as at Jer 39[9f] : ' And I bought the field at Anathoth from Hanamel my cousin, and weighed out the money to him, seventeen shekels of silver. I signed the deed, sealed it, got witnesses, and weighed the money on scales.'

All the weight-systems of W. Asia, and even of Europe, had their origin in Babylonia (for fuller details see WEIGHTS AND MEASURES). There, as required by the sexagesimal system of reckoning, the ancient unit of weight, the *manu* (Heb. *māneh* : in RSV **mina** as at Ezk 45[12], plural **minas** ; in AV, RV **pound,** except *maneh* at Ezk 45[12]) or **mina** was divided into sixty **shekels,** while sixty minas went to the higher denomination, the **talent.** A weight of stone (British Museum 91005) of one *mina* (*i.e.* sixty shekels) on which is ' an inscription stating that it is an exact copy of a weight made by Nebuchadnezzar II. (605–562) after the standard fixed by Shulgi (king of the Third Dynasty of Ur, about 2000 B.C.) ' is illustrated in Pritchard, *ANEP*, 118 : it weighs 978.3 grammes. Another weight, of bronze, with cuneiform inscription ' Palace of Shalmaneser (v.) king of Asshur, two-thirds mina of the king ' and Aramaic inscription ' Two-thirds [mina] of the land ' (British Museum 91230), described in Pritchard, *ib.* 119, weighs 665.795 grammes. Heavy and light Babylonian standards may be recognized. As the weight system spread westward with the march of Babylonian civilization and commerce, it came into conflict with the decimal system of calculation, and a compromise was effected, which resulted in the mina being reduced to fifty shekels, while the talent remained at sixty minas, although reduced in weight to three thousand shekels. That the Hebrew talent by which the precious metals were weighed contained three thousand, and not three thousand six hundred shekels may be seen by a simple calculation from Ex 38[25ff]. That the heavy Babylonian shekel of 16.329 grammes in theory remained in use among the Hebrews for the weighing of gold until NT times, we have the express testimony of Josephus *Ant.* XIV, vii. 1 (105), who equates the Hebrew *mina* with 21 Roman pounds giving a shekel of 16.37 grammes the exact weight of the heavy Babylonian shekel of the common or trade standard. Elsewhere (*Ant.* II. iii. 3 [33]), however, Josephus loosely equates the *mina* with the Hebrew shekel, and the value of his witness is accordingly uncertain.

For the weighing of silver, however, this shekel was discarded for practical reasons. Throughout the ancient E. the ratio of gold to silver was 13⅓ to 1, so that a shekel of gold could buy 13⅓ times the same weight of silver. In ordinary commerce, however, this ratio of exchange was extremely inconvenient. To obviate this inconvenience the weight of the shekel for weighing silver was altered so that a gold shekel might be exchanged for a whole number of silver shekels. This alteration was effected in two ways. On the one hand, along the Babylonian trade routes into Asia Minor the light Babylonian silver shekel of 8.16 grammes was raised to 10.88 grammes so that ten such silver shekels now represented a single gold shekel. On the other hand, the great commercial cities of Phoenicia introduced a silver shekel of 14.51 grammes, fifteen of which were equivalent to one heavy Babylonian shekel of 16.32 grammes. This 14.51 grammes silver shekel is accordingly known as the Phoenician standard. It was on this standard that the sacred dues of the Hebrews were calculated (below **3**). In Ex 30[13] and elsewhere this shekel is said to consist of 20 **gerahs** which the Greek translators identified with the small silver obol of Greek coinage, 20 of which yield a shekel of 14.51 grammes. Sixty **shekels** go to the **mina** (Ezk 45[12]), three thousand shekels to the **talent** (Ezk 38[25f]).

No self authenticating equivalents with modern money in purchasing power can be proposed. The reader can only meditate on Gn 23[15f] (a ' field ' bought for 400 silver shekels), Ex 21[22] (thirty silver shekels for damages by a goring ox), 1 K 10[29] (six hundred shekels of silver for a chariot, a hundred and fifty for a horse) etc.

It must be regarded as certain that other standards also were in use in Palestine for weighing the precious metals, in historic times (see WEIGHTS AND MEASURES).

2. *Money in the pre-exilic period.*—Throughout the whole of this period, as has already been emphasized, in every transaction involving the payment of considerable sums, the money was paid by weight. Accordingly when Abraham bought the field and cave of Machpelah he ' weighed out for Ephron the silver which he had named in the hearing of the Hittites, four hundred shekels of silver, according to the weights current among the merchants ' (so RSV justly renders Gn 23[16]). In view of what has been noted about the variety of standards in use in Palestine in early times, it would be unwise in the present state of knowledge to pronounce on the value of the price paid in this transaction. Similarly the price paid by David for the threshing-floor of Araunah (2 S 24[24]) is fifty shekels of silver. But by whose standard shekel? Tribute however paid by Hebrew kings in gold (*e.g.* 2 K 18[24]) will have been on an international standard common to Palestine and Assyria and represented very considerable sums. It is interesting to note that Solomon paid his large debts to Hiram of Tyre not in money but in territory (1 K 9[10-14]). A noteworthy feature also of the pre-exilic literature is the disappearance of the *mina* from calculations, sums being stated in terms of shekels and talents exclusively.

In this period the precious metals circulated in three forms. The shekel and its subdivisions (the half-shekel : Ex 38[26] ' a beka a head [that is, half a shekel, by the shekel of the sanctuary] ' ; note, **3** below, that an actual coin labelled **' beka '** is now known from the Persian period ; the quarter-shekel : 1 S 9[8] ' I have with me the fourth part of a shekel of silver ' ; and smaller multiples) had the form of ingots of metal, without any stamp or other mark, so far as our evidence goes, as a guarantee of their purity and weight. Larger values were made up in bars, such as Schliemann discovered at Troy and Macalister found in Gezer. The **bar** (literally ' tongue ' : AV, RV **wedge) of gold** which Achan appropriated from the loot of Jericho (Jos 7[21]) was probably such a thin bar of gold. Further Rebekah's nose-ring of half a shekel of gold and her bracelets of ten shekels (Gn 24[22]) represent a third form which the early period metal currency might assume. The bowls and other vessels of gold and silver so often mentioned in ancient tribute lists also probably represented definite weights and values.

The shekel was so exclusively the unit in all ordinary transactions that Hebrew writers frequently omit it from statements of price.

The discovery of Hebrew weights inscribed with the word **pim** has improved the possibilities of translating 1 S 13[21] where RSV should be followed (see PIM).

3. *Money in the Persian period : introduction of coins.*—In this period the money of the small Jewish community of *Yehud* was still, as before the Exile, mainly ingots and bars of the precious metals, without official mark of any kind. The addition of such a mark by the issuing authority serves as a public guarantee, still verifiable of course by the use of scales, of the purity of the metal and the weight of the ingot, and so transforms the ingot into a coin. Coined money, whether a Greek, or as Herodotus states (Herodotus i. 94 ; for the Greek ' competitors ' for this distinction see Pollux, *Onom.* ix. 83) a Lydian, invention has already a considerable history before the western expansion of Persian power brought the Biblical lands into momentously closer contact with more western communities. It is not probable that any coins reached Palestine, except perhaps as travellers' curiosities, before the Persian period. Under the Persians we see the beginnings of the transition from uncoined to coined currency which was only completed in the Biblical lands under the successors of Alexander. The two systems existed, during the centuries of transition, side by side. After the conquest of the Lydian King Croesus, the Persians appear to have continued to strike Lydian 'sigloi' in the early years of their rule. Later, certainly from the time of Darius I., they issued their own gold '*daric*' (average weight 8.354 grammes), and silver '*siglos*' or 'siklos' = 'shekel' (average weight 5.6 grammes). In the time of Darius I. twenty sigloi went to the daric on the old ratio of gold tc silver of 13.3 to 1. Later modifications in this ratio may be detected. The Persian darics and sigloi, for use principally in Persian Asia Minor rather than in the old Biblical lands, continued in series until the Persian power was broken by Alexander the Great (see G. F. Hill, *Catalogue of the Greek Coins of Arabia, Mesopotamia, and Persia, in the British Museum*, 1922, pp. cxx–cxl, and 148–175; and the very important study by Sydney P. Noe: *Two Hoards of Persian Sigloi*, American Numismatic Society, Numismatic Notes and Monographs, No. 136, 1956). In addition there were notable issues of coins by the satraps in Asia Minor, some for occasional causes, some, especially *e.g.* in Cilicia, in long series (see especially G. F. Hill, *Catalogue of the Greek Coins of Lycaonia, Isauria, and Cilicia in the British Museum*, 1900). The engravers of the dies for these satrapal coinages were Greek. The legends were in Greek, except in Cilicia where there are some bilingual legends, and some in Aramaic only, especially from the mint of Tarsus. Attention may be drawn to issues of silver coins (Hill, *Lycaonia*, etc., p. 170, No. 48) at Tarsus by the satrap Mazaeus, who lived to fight and later to serve Alexander, while he was satrap of 'Over-the-river' (the trans-Euphratesian satrapy in which lay the Jewish community of *Yehud*) and of Cilicia. The reverse legend reads, in Aramaic, 'Mazdai who is over "over the river" and Cilicia.' The title of the satrapy 'over-the-river' coincides, with one minor spelling variation, with the Biblical 'province Beyond the River' at Ezr 4[10] etc. (Ezr 4[10] is in Aramaic).

The Persians do not seem to have interrupted the older system of weight currency in Mesopotamia and Egypt by the introduction of coins. However, Greek money was flowing E. in large quantities, especially to Egypt where it was used to foster revolt. It is, *e.g.*, instructive to note that a deed of sale which dates itself 402 or 401 B.C. in Aramaic on an Elephantine papyrus quotes the price of a house as 'one karsh, three shekels' and adds the Greek equivalent 'and in the money of Yawan six staters, one shekel' (E. G. Kraeling, *The Brooklyn Museum Aramaic Papyri*, 1953, Papyrus 12). Athenian coin dies have been found in Egypt (J. H. Jongkees in *Numismatic Chronicle*, 1950, pp. 298–301) from which no doubt revolting Pharaohs struck pay for their mercenary soldiers. Some coins were even struck, no doubt for the same purpose, with Egyptian types and legends (in hieroglyphs), in the 4th cent. B.C. The discovery of a coin with a demotic inscription suggests an Egyptian coinage for Egyptians (G. K. Jenkins in *Numismatic Chronicle*, 1955, pp. 144 ff). But nearer home, in the modest district of *Yehud*, the Jews in the Persian period were within the circulation range of noteworthy series of silver coins issued from the Phoenician maritime cities (Aradus, Gebal, Sidon, Tyre) either by the satraps or sometimes, as it seems, by the local subject ruler. The issue of coins in the precious metals in antiquity may always be assumed to be an indication of privilege, even of autonomy, or of a claim to autonomy. What degree of privilege or autonomy these 'native' Phoenician silver issues indicates is not clear (for examples see G. F. Hill, *Catalogue of the Greek Coins of Phoenicia in the British Museum*, 1910, under the cities concerned). The types used on these coins testify to a lively and self-conscious Phoenician culture, and provide us with some of the few remarkable and attractive coin types of the ancient world of which the inspiration and workmanship is not Greek. Further S., there is a 'Philisto-Arabian' and 'an Egypto-Arabian' series of coins in silver awaiting elucidation. They are obviously much under the influence of far away Athens and perhaps their story belongs to that of persistent Athenian pressure to revolt against Persia. But it has become evident, since the first edition of this Dictionary was published, that some small silver coins were, at some time in the Persian period (or at latest during the transition to Ptolemaic rule), struck for the Jewish authorities in *Yehud*, either in the Holy Land itself, or elsewhere for the same authorities. This conclusion is irresistible from the four coins listed as 1a, 1, 2, and 3 in A. Reifenberg, *Ancient Jewish Coins*[2], 1947. Their legends are in Hebrew (1a) *beqaʿ* (one-half) Reifenberg dates in mid-5th cent.: (1) has '*Yehud*'; (2) has two legends of which one is '*Hezekiah*,' probably the name of a high priest (was he the high priest who knew Ptolemy I.?); (3) has again the name of the district '*Yehud*.' Another specimen (G. F. Hill, *Catalogue of the Greek Coins of Palestine in the British Museum*, 1914, p. 181, No. 29) of this last coin has been known for many years, and after long controversy it was generally agreed that the legend should be read as 'Yahu' and was in fact the name of the Hebrew God. The type which goes with the legend is of a bearded male deity, a solar Zeus. The question arose was there here an identification of the Hebrew God with Zeus, perhaps made by Jewish or non-Jewish syncretists, anticipating the position of the 'Hellenisers' in the time of Antiochus IV.? This is possible. The problem of the deity on the coin remains. But in spite of at least one eminent authority the older reading of the legend must be abandoned, and the reading 'Yehud' must be recognized as right. It may be added that there is nothing distinctively Jewish in any of the types shown on these coins. The types and weights have Athenian affinities. It is the legends which point to the Jews as the issuing authority wherever the coins may have been minted for them. In conjunction with other evidences scholars now rightly argue from these coins that the Persian authorities allowed the high priests considerable local autonomy from time to time. That is the direction in which the coins point. But there are problems about them (they do not necessarily all belong together) which will not be solved until more archaeological discoveries have shed light on that obscure period. Was there a time, however short, even then, when the Jew could pay his Temple tax in Jewish money? We do not know. The rabbinic tradition is that for payments 'according to the value of the shekel of the sanctuary' (cf Lv 27[25]: 'Every valuation shall be according to the shekel of the sanctuary . . .') Tyrian money should be used (Mishnah, *Bekhoroth*, viii. 7). If this ruling be valid as far back as the Persian period, the silver coins of Tyre (Hill, *Phoenicia*, pp. 227 ff) alluded to above are the numismatic representatives of 'the shekel of the sanctuary' in the Persian period. They were struck on a 'native' Phoenician standard giving a normal shekel of about 14.5 grammes. It is on this same standard that the Jewish skekels of the First Revolt (see below **5**) were struck. It is idle to speculate on equivalents in modern money in terms of purchasing power.

In several passages in Chronicles, Ezra, and Nehemiah, the RSV and RV have substituted '*darics*' for AV 'drams' (1 Ch 29[7], Ezr 2[69], Neh 7[70-72]). In the second and third of these passages the Hebrew form certainly suggests 'drams' or 'drachms,' but presumably Persian money is meant. Perhaps a weight system was in mind. The problem may be merely that the writers wrote in the Greek period. The 'forty shekels of silver' at Neh 5[15] may be either sigloi or Phoenician shekels.

4. *Money in the Greek period.*—The transition to coined money was completed in the Bible lands by

Alexander and his successors. Alexander himself issued coins in gold, silver, and 'brass.' An impressive survey of his coinage which seemed to be aimed at the introduction of 'a world currency' will be found in Charles Seltman, *Greek Coins*[2], 1955, pp. 203–217. His coins were struck, with Greek types and Greek legends, at many mints, among them, *e.g.* Tarsus of Cilicia, Myriandros, Aradus, Byblos (Gebal), Berytus, Ake (the Biblical *Acco* of Jg 1[31], later *Ptolemais*), Sidon, Alexandria (his new creation in Egypt), Damascus, and Babylon. The 'successors' continued according to this beginning, and (with the exceptions in small change noted below, **5**), from Alexander until the Hellenistic East was absorbed by Rome the Greek coinages of the Ptolemies in Egypt or of the Seleucid kings of Syria, or of the cities which achieved political independence in the decline of Seleucid power (notably Tyre), would be the coins of the Jews (To 5[14], 2 Mac 4[19] 12[43]) whether in Judaea or in dispersion in Egypt or Mesopotamia. When the Parthians absorbed Babylonia and incidentally the Jewish communities there they too issued coins of Greek type, according to the practice of their Seleucid predecessors. The Athenian standard of the Alexander coins was continued by the successors, but a slightly reduced Syrian and Phoenician standard later emerges, as perhaps a reversal to the preferences of an earlier period. A Jew who paid his half-shekel **Temple tax** in Tyrian money (cf above, **3**) could pay it with a **didrachm** (q.v.), or two could join, as Jesus and His disciple did at Mt 17[24-27], to pay one 'shekel.' The 'didrachm' is the regular Septuagint equivalent of the Biblical half-shekel of the tax. If two paid together they would use a silver 'stater' (or tetradrachm), (translated 'shekel' at Mt 17[27] in RSV). 'The didrachm' comes to mean in Jewish Greek the holy didrachm of the annual payment, as is evident from Mt 17[24] (RSV 'does not your teacher pay the *tax*': Greek '*t. didrachma*') and various passages in Philo who speaks of 'the holy didrachm.' From Alexander until the end of the 3rd cent. B.C.—when the Seleucids wrested the Phoenician cities and Palestine from the Ptolemies—Ptolemaic silver from the mint of Tyre was available. Thereafter Tyre continues as a Seleucid mint. From the time of its autonomy in 126–125 B.C. until at least A.D. 69 there was a continuation in the name of the city itself. It is presumably this autonomous Tyrian coinage that was acceptable for the Temple payment in the time of Christ. The 'stater' of Mt 17[24-27] is thus a Tyrian 'shekel' (for Tyrian 'shekels' see Hill, *Phoenicia*, pp. 233 ff, and for half-shekels' *ib.* pp. 250 ff). The types were: obverse, head of 'Herakles' or 'Baal' and reverse, Eagle on prow and the legend, 'of Tyre, the holy and inviolate,' was in Greek. (On the Alexander coinage see Seltman, *op cit.* and the works cited there, especially those of E. T. Newell; no copious and satisfactory account of the Ptolemaic coinage is available in English but the reader may commence the study from Seltman, *op. cit.* and two small works by E. T. Newell, namely *Royal Greek Portrait Coins*, 1937, and *Standard Ptolemaic Silver*, 1941. E. T. Newell has also written the standard works on the Seleucid coinage; see especially his *The Coinage of the Eastern Seleucid Mints*, 1938, and *The Coinage of the Western Selucid Mints*, 1941, which takes the subject down to Antiochus III., the Great, and occasionally beyond his reign. See also Newell's 'Seleucid Mint of Antioch' reprinted from *The American Journal of Numismatics*, li, 1918, which includes the coins of Antiochus IV. minted at Antioch, which are important for the study of the books of Maccabees.)

5. *The coinage of the Maccabaean rulers.*—According to 1 Mac 15[6] the Seleucid King Antiochus VII. (Sidetes) granted Simon 'the priest and ethnarch of the Jews' an important concession (which he subsequently rescinded, v.[27]): 'I permit you to mint your own coinage as money for your country . . .'—'The thorniest question of all Jewish numismatics' as it has been called, is the question whether, and if so to what extent Simon availed himself of this privilege while it lasted. A well-known series of silver shekels, half-shekels, and quarter-shekels, on the Phoenician standard, bearing dates from 'year 1' to 'year 5' has from time to time been attributed to Simon Maccabaeus. They show on the obverse and reverse respectively a cup or chalice, and 'a spike of a lily with three flowers.' The legends in old Hebrew letters on the shekels are: obverse: 'Shekel of Israel,' reverse: 'Jerusalem the holy' (see details and illustrations in Hill, *Palestine*, pp. 269ff and Plate xxx: or in Reifenberg, *op. cit.* pp. 57, 58 and Plate x). It was argued by A. R. S. Kennedy in the first edition of this Dictionary—and other well-known numismatists were already on his side of the question—that these coins belong not to Simon Maccabaeus but to the *First Revolt*. That conclusion, already then irresistible, has since been established by definitive new evidence from coin hoards. The reader should refer to the survey of the whole problem by the distinguished Hebrew numismatist, Leo Kadman, 'The Coins of the First Revolt' (the article is in English) in *Congrès International de Numismatique*, 1957, ii, pp. 239–248, which settles the matter decisively, with full evidence and references. The controversy is over. These silver coins belong to the first revolt. To the first revolt also belong some 'brass' coins hitherto associated with them.

With the mysterious exception therefore of the four 'Jewish' silver coins of the Persian period (see above, **3**), the first 'native' Jewish coins are the coins of the Maccabaean rulers. There are brass coins of various sizes, usually very small, of John Hyrcanus I. (135–104 B.C.), Judas Aristobulus (104–103 B.C.), Alexander Jannaeus (103–76 B.C.), Jonathan Hyrcanus II. (67 and 63–40 B.C.) and Antigonus Mattathias (40–37 B.C.). For these see Hill, *op. cit.* pp. 188 ff, or Reifenberg, *op. cit.* pp. 40 ff. There are no known silver coins of any of these rulers. In general it may be observed (1) that the characteristic types are, with one exception, not distinctively Jewish. They represent a continuation of Seleucid small change, and the only distinctively Jewish feature is that the representation of pagan deities or animals, alike repulsive to Judaism, is very naturally avoided. The exception, the one positively Jewish type, is a representation of the seven branched lampstand on coins of Antigonus Mattathias (Hill, *Palestine*, p. 219, No. 56: Reifenberg, p. 42, Nos. 23 and 24). (2) The legends are in Hebrew in the older writing, and in Greek. Some of the coins have only Hebrew legends, some only Greek, some are bilingual. (3) The legends provide valuable information about the titles adopted by these rulers. This information contains no surprises, except that it seems that it is from coins alone that we know that the Hebrew name of Antigonus II. whom the Parthians made King in Jerusalem in 40 B.C. was Mattahias. John Hyrcanus I.'s coins bear in Hebrew the legend '*John, the high-priest and the commonwealth of the Jews*' (the precise meaning of the word here translated *commonwealth* is uncertain). The title of *King* first appears on the coins of Alexander Jannaeus—'*Jonathan the King*'—who also first introduced a Greek, in addition to a Hebrew, legend.

6. *Money in Palestine under the Romans.*—From a numismatic point of view Judaea may be said to have formed part of the Roman dominions from 63 B.C. when Pompey entered Jerusalem. Besides the local coinages of the autonomous cities which were suffered to continue the Roman coinage became certainly 'legal tender' in Syria and Palestine. The silver **denarius** was almost equal in weight to the Syrian Attic drachm (the silver unit of Seleucid times) and henceforward the two coins were regarded as of equal value, and four *denarii* were regarded in ordinary business as the equivalent of a tetradrachm of Antioch.

The Roman answer to the Parthian action in making Antigonus Mattathias King in Jerusalem in 40 B.C. was to declare **Herod** King of the Jews. In 37 B.C., with the help of a Roman army under Sosius he entered Jerusalem his royal city. This king, Herod the Great (37–4 B.C.), continued the 'brass' coinage of the Maccabaean rulers with some new types (not distinctively Jewish, but avoiding, on the whole, positive affront to Jewish feelings except for some issues showing an eagle) and they are described in Hill, *Palestine*, pp. 220 ff, and Reifenberg, *op. cit.* pp. 42 ff. All the legends are in Greek. For larger coins the Roman gold and silver of the empire as a whole, and the silver from the Roman mint of Antioch (which was not plentiful), and above all the good silver of the still ' autonomous ' city of Tyre could be used in Palestine. After the death of Herod there are local ' brass ' coinages of his successors. After the new settlement of A.D. 6 the Roman procurators issued a local small ' brass ' coinage, with trifling variations, except for the brief reign of Agrippa I. (A.D. 37–44) continuously until the beginning of the First Revolt in A.D. 66. It may be said in general that the Procurators wisely avoided offending Jewish feelings in their choice of types, with the single exception of Pontius Pilate (A.D. 26–36) who placed a *simpulum* on some and a *lituus* on others of his Palestinian issues. It has been pointed out by Miss E. M. Smallwood (*Latomus*, xix, p. 328), and less soberly by other writers, that these symbols of pagan worship would probably give offence (for the coins of the Procurators see Hill, *Palestine*, pp. 248 ff, Reifenberg, *op. cit.* pp. 54 ff). Agrippa I. issued ' brass ' coins (Hill, *Palestine*, pp. 236 ff: Reifenberg, *op. cit.* pp. 46 ff) of which the Greek legends emphasize his loyalty to his imperial masters (he is ' philokaisar,' Caesar's friend; why he was also ' Great King ' has not been satisfactorily explained). The fact that some of his coins bear what can only be his own portrait (*e.g.* Reifenberg, *op. cit.* p. 46, No. 58) reminds us that his subjects included many non-Jews, and that there are other indications that this notable and engaging adventurer thought of himself as playing two parts, that of a King of the Jews in Jerusalem, and that of a Hellenistic god-king among his non-Jewish subjects (see M. P. Charlesworth, *Five Men*, 1936, pp. 23–35). The coin portraits would be consistent with this. Other members of this remarkable family showed portraits of themselves on their coins (A. Reifenberg, *Portrait Coins of the Herodian Kings*, 1935).

7. *The money of the NT.*—Here we may add a few notes on the various denominations mentioned in the NT. The currency was in three metals: ' Take no gold, nor silver, nor copper in your belts ' (Mt 10[9] RSV). Following this description we have (*a*) the Roman gold *aureus*, here referred to only indirectly, representing twenty-five denarii, and varying in weight in NT times from approximately 8.16 to 7.77 grammes. (*b*) The silver coin most frequently mentioned is the **denarius** (AV and RV **' penny,'** RV, more correctly, ' shilling,' RSV sometimes even better **' denarius '** and plural **' denarii '**). It was the day's wage of a Jewish labourer (Mt 20[2]). A typical denarius of our Lord's day, with which Roman dues were paid (22[19]), would have on its obverse the head of the reigning Emperor, Tiberius, and **' superscription '** or **' inscription '** (RSV) the following legend in Latin ' Tiberius Caesar, the son of the deified Augustus, (himself) Augustus ' and on the reverse Livia seated as *Pax* and in continuation of the Emperor's entitlements the legend in Latin ' High Priest,' and would be minted in far away Lugdunum in Gaul (see H. Mattingly, *Coins of the Roman Empire in the British Museum*, i, 1923, p. 125, No. 34, and *ib.* Plate 22, No. 22). (*c*) The silver **drachm** is named only at Lk 15[8] ' Or what woman, having ten silver coins, if she loses one coin ' (so RSV, adding the note ' The drachma, rendered here by *silver coin*, was about sixteen cents: AV, RV have **' pieces of silver '**). In ordinary usage (above **6**) it was the equivalent of the denarius. The 50,000 ' pieces of silver ' (literally **' silverlings '**) of Ac 19[19] were denarius-drachms. (*d*) The silver **didrachm** is mentioned only once, Mt 17[24] (AV ' tribute money,' RV and RSV ' the half-shekel '). This was a two-drachm piece on the Phoenician standard and minted at Tyre (above **3** and **4**). (*e*) The **shekel** (RSV), or ' piece of money,' in the original text **stater,** was a silver *tetradrachm* or four-drachm piece also of the mint of Tyre (and so acceptable for payment of Temple tax, above **3** and **4**). The ' thirty pieces of silver ' (Mt 26[15]) for which Judas betrayed his Lord were probably also Tyrian tetradrachms.

Passing to the copper coins of the Gospels, we find three denominations in the original, the *lepton*, the *kodrantes*, and the *assarion*. There are great difficulties in identifying these among the copper coins which have come down to us. (*f*) The *lepton*, the widow's **mite** of Mk 12[42] (RSV ' *two copper coins* ') and Lk 21[2], was the smallest coin in circulation and is to be looked for amongst the small ' brass ' of Pontius Pilate the procurator (above **6**). (*g*) The *kodrantes* (Latin, *quadrans*) was worth two *lepta* (Mk 12[42]) and was the ' *uttermost farthing* ' (or, in RSV, ' the last penny ') of Mt 5[26], was either the actual Roman *quadrans* or its equivalent among the local ' brass ' coins. (*h*) The *assarion* is the **farthing** (RSV *penny*) associated with the price of sparrows (Mt 10[29], Lk 12[6]) and was a small ' brass ' coin on the Greek system, probably the *dichalkus*, of which in ordinary business twenty-four went to the denarius-drachm. The relative value of the three coins may be expressed as $\frac{1}{16}$, $\frac{1}{8}$, and $\frac{1}{4}$ of a unit respectively.

There remain the two larger denominations, the talent and the ' pound ' or mina, neither of which was any longer, as in the earlier period, a specific weight of bullion, but a definite sum of money. (i) The *talent* now contained 6000 denarius-drachms, which made 240 aurei (Mt 18[24] to which RSV adds the note ' this talent was probably worth about a thousand dollars '). It is not always realized, perhaps, how vast was the difference in the amounts owing in this parable (18[23ff]). The one servant owed 100 denarii, the other 10,000 talents or sixty million denarii. The one debt, occupying little more space than 100 English sixpences, could be carried in the pocket; for the payment of the other, an army of nearly 8600 carriers, each with a sack 60 lb. in weight, would be required. If these were placed in single file, a yard apart, the train would be almost 5 miles in length. (*j*) The **mina** finally of another parable (Lk 19[13ff]) was the sixtieth part of a talent, or 100 denarius-drachms, and is translated in RSV and in AV and RV by **pound.**

In addition to the fundamental work of Hill, *Palestine*, and to Reifenberg's *Coins of the Jews*, to which reference has been made, for the later Jewish coins (which were confined to the two periods of revolt against Rome in A.D. 66–70 and 132–135, and included silver as well as brass) see, especially for discussion of the distinctively Jewish types adopted, Paul Romanoff, *Jewish Symbols on Ancient Jewish Coins*, 1944, and Erwin R. Goodenough, *Jewish Symbols in the Greco-Roman Period*, 1953, i, pp. 268–279. See also *The Dating and Meaning of Ancient Jewish Coins and Symbols*, Numismatic Studies and Researches, ii, 1958. A writer in the *Journal of Theological Studies*, 1952, pp. 172–198 (with six plates) has assembled illustrations of important coins with types and legends alluding to the Jews, struck by the Romans. For the coins struck at Jerusalem after Hadrian's new dispensation had turned it into a pagan city with the new name of Aelia Capitolina see Hill, *Palestine*, and Leo Kadman, *The Coins of Aelia capitolina*, 1956. A. R. S. K.—**H. St. J. H.**

MONEY-CHANGERS.—How indispensable were the services of the **' money-changers '** (Mt 21[12], Mk 11[15], Jn 2[14]) and **' bankers '** (Mt 25[27]) in the first century of our era in Palestine may be seen from the varied currencies of the period alluded to in the preceding article (**6, 7**). The Jewish money-changer, like his modern counterpart the *ṣarrāf* (see *PEFSt*, 1904, pp. 49 ff for a well known and graphic account of the complexity of exchange in modern times) changed the larger denominations into the smaller, giving denarii, for example, for tetradrachms, silver for gold, and so forth. An important department of his business was the exchange of foreign money and even money of the country on any non-Phoenician standard for shekels and half-shekels on this standard, the latter alone being acceptable in payment of the Temple dues (cf MONEY, **4, 6**). It was no doubt mainly for the benefit of the Jews of the Dispersion that the changers were allowed to set up their tables (in Greek they are 'table-men') in the outer court of the Temple (Mt 21[12ff]). Some members of the profession, the **bankers** of Mt 25[27] (cf Lk 19[23]) received money on deposit for purposes of investment, on which usury was paid (see USURY).

The money-changers had constantly to be on their guard against false money (to which there are many references in ancient literature, especially *e.g.* by Philo). This gives weight to the often quoted unwritten saying (*agraphon*) of our Lord to his disciples 'show yourselves expert money-changers'—be skilful in distinguishing true doctrine from false. A. R. S. K.—**H. St. J. H.**

MONTH.—See TIME.

MONUMENT.—In Is 65[4] AV, 'which remain among the graves and lodge in the monuments' (RV, RSV 'secret places'; literally 'in the guarded places') means 'among the tombs.' In the Rhemish Version 'monument' is the usual word for tomb or sepulchre, after Vulgate *monumentum*. The reference in Isaiah is to the custom of obtaining oracles by incubation, that is, spending the night in subterranean sacred places.

MOOLI, 1 Es 8[47] (RV).—See MAHLI.

MOON.—The moon is 'the lesser light to rule the night' of the cosmogony of Genesis (1[16]). Its importance was in part due to the recurrence of its phases, which formed a measure for time. Each **new moon**, as it appeared, marked the commencement of a new period, and so in Hebrew the word for 'moon' and 'month' is the same. Sun and moon occur side by side in passages of Scripture, and to the moon as well as to the sun is ascribed a fertilizing power over and above the gift of light which comes from them to the earth. Just as we have in Dt 33[14] 'the choicest fruits of the sun,' so we have there 'the rich yield of the moons' (RSV 'months'). As a consequence of this, the re-appearance of the new moon was eagerly looked for, and trumpets were blown and sacrifices offered on the day of the new moon. The coupling of the new moon with 'sabbath' in Is 1[13] *et al.* as the occasion for religious festivals makes it probable that the 'sabbath' in these passages was a moon-festival, and not the Jewish sabbath. In Ps 81[3] a 'full moon' festival is mentioned, but the word used is of uncertain derivation and only occurs elsewhere in Pr 7[20]. The Assyrian word *kusē'u*, 'head-dress,' or 'cap' is also used for 'full moon,' perhaps as tiara of the moon-god. The moon took its part with the sun in one of Joseph's dreams when it 'made obeisance' to him (Gn 37[9]); and it stood still, 'in the valley of Aijalon,' at the command of Joshua, at the battle of Gibeon (Jos 10[12f]; cf Hab 3[11]). Language which must have been derived from the appearances of the moon during **eclipses** is used by the prophets. The moon is to be darkened or turned into blood (Jl 2[10, 31]) before 'the day of the Lord'; and similar language is used by our Lord (*e.g.* Mk 13[24]). We are told of the redeemed Zion that the light of the moon is to be as the light of the sun (Is 30[26]), and that there is to be no need of the moon, because the glory of God is to be the light of His people (Is 60[19]; cf Rev 21[23]). Cautions against the worship of the moon, and punishment by death for the convicted worshippers, are to be found in Dt 4[19] 17[3]; whilst a superstitious salutation of the moon by kissing the hand, not quite unheard of even in our own day, is mentioned in Job 31[26f]. Moon-worship by the burning of incense was offered in Jerusalem, and put down by Josiah (2 K 23[5]).

In the OT we meet more than once with crescent-shaped ornaments (Jg 8[21], Is 3[18]); whether these are an indication of the worship of the moon is uncertain.

It has been always considered baneful in the bright clear atmosphere of the warmer regions of the earth to sleep exposed to the rays of the moon (Ps 121[6]). The influence of the earth's satellite has long been considered hurtful. Our word **'lunatic'** reproduces the idea of the Western world of our Lord's time, that lunacy was due to the influence of the moon: the Greek word used in Mt 4[24] 17[15] shows this. In the RV the word is translated 'epileptic.' There are many still to be found who believe that the violence and recurrence of epileptic fits vary with the phases of the moon.

H. A. R.—**S. H. He.**

MOOSIAS, 1 Es 9[31] (AV).—See MAASEIAH, **4.**

MOOSSIAS.—See MAASEIAH, **4.**

MOPH.—See MEMPHIS.

MORALITY.—See ETHICS.

MORASHTITE.—A gentilic used in RV to designate the prophet Micah, Mic 1[1], Jer 26[18] (AV **Morasthite**; RSV 'of Moresheth'); probably derived from Morsheth-gath (q.v.). Cf MICAH.

MORASTHITE, Mic 1[1], Jer 26[18] (AV).—See MORASHTITE.

MORDECAI.—1. A cousin (?) of queen Esther, who thwarted Haman's plot against the Jews, Est 2[5] etc. In Ad. Est 10[4] etc. he is called **Mardocheus** in AV and RV. **2.** One of those who returned with Zerubbabel, Ezr 2[2], Neh 7[7], 1 Es 5[8] (AV, RV **Mardocheus**).

MOREH, the Hiph'il participle from *yārāh*, means 'teacher' or 'one who gives direction' (2 K 17[28], Is 30[20] etc.), and so is applied to a prophet (Is 9[15]). Sitting in the shelter of a sacred tree, the priest or seer delivered his direction or 'oracles.' **1. The oak** (AV, wrongly, 'plain') **of Moreh** (Gn 12[6]) may have been so named from the theophany vouchsafed to Abraham there. The same spot may be indicated by the oak of Moreh in Dt 11[30], mentioned as indicating the position of Ebal and Gerizim. From their conjunction with Gilgal it has been suggested that the *gilgāl* ('stone circle') and the terebinths were parts of the same sanctuary. There may be a reference to this place in Gn 35[4], in Jos 24[26], possibly also in Jg 9[6]. Gilgal (Dt 11[30]) may be *Kh. Jiljûliyeh*, fully 1½ miles E. of Jacob's Well. But this would not fix with certainty the position of the sanctuary of the terebinth. **2. The hill of Moreh** (Jg 7[1]) seems to have lain to the N. of the position occupied by Gideon, in the direction of the camp of the Midianites. Taking the narrative as it stands, the Midianites 'encamped in the Valley of Jezreel' (6[33]), while Gideon held the lower spurs of Gilboa towards Jezreel. The 'spring of Harod' is with some probability identified with *'Ain Jālûd*. The conspicuous hill on the other side of the vale, *Jebel ed-Daḥī*, popularly now called Little Hermon, round the W. flanks of which, and northward in the plain, the Midianites would spread, may be almost certainly identified with the Hill of Moreh. The article with Moreh suggests the presence of a sanctuary on the hill. This may be represented by the modern shrine of *Nebī Daḥī*. Questions have been raised by the condition of the Hebrew text, but no more probable identification has been suggested. Cf MORIAH. W. E.

MORESHETH-GATH.—A place mentioned in Mic 1[4]. It was probably the birthplace of the prophet Micah, Mic 1[1], Jer 26[18]. The *Onomasticon* locates it E. of, and near to, Eleutheropolis. It is possibly modern *Tell el-Judeideh*.

MORIAH.—1. The name.—in Gn 22[2] Abraham was commanded to go 'to *the land of the Moriah*,' and to sacrifice Isaac upon 'one of the mountains' of which God would tell him. The derivation of the name is uncertain. The Peshitta (Syriac) reads 'the Amorites' in place of 'the Moriah.' This may be correct, although it does not help to locate definitely the region involved. It is probable that the Syriac and the Greek ('the high country') were deliberately indefinite because of uncertainty about the rival claims of the Samaritans and the Jews concerning the location of this sacred mountain. The narrator (E), in v.[14] engages in a play on words in which 'the Moriah' is derived from a verb. Which verb is involved is uncertain as indicated by the fact that it has been rendered variously as 'to provide' (cf RSV), 'to see' (with some of the early translators in their rendering of the name in v.[2]), and 'to fear' (with the

Targumists who emphasized the *worship* of Abraham at the spot).

2. The place.—The Chronicler (2 Ch 3[1]) leaves no doubt concerning the Jewish tradition that Mount Moriah was the Temple hill where Solomon built the house of the Lord in Jerusalem and the place of David's theophany. Efforts to identify the source of this tradition have been unsuccessful, although it persists among Jews, Christians, and Moslems, who now locate Mount Moriah at the Dome of the Rock where the Temple once stood. There is some similarity between the names of Moriah and 'Moreh,' the latter located near Shechem (Gn 12[6], Dt 11[30]) and Mount Gerizim. And it may have been owing to this that the Samaritans have claimed Gerizim as Abraham's mountain (cf Jn 4[20]). Gn 22[4] has been often cited to suggest that Gerizim, a mountain visible for some distance, must be the Moriah of Abraham because he 'lifted up his eyes and saw the place afar off.' However, on the strength of the reference in the same verse to Abraham's arrival at the place on the third day of his journey, presumably from Beer-sheba (21[33]), some scholars have proposed a location for Moriah on a mountain near Hebron. Because the place of origin of the journey is not stated in Genesis, it is best to conclude that evidence is not available for locating Moriah of Abraham's time and that by the time of the Chronicler (see CHRONICLES) tradition identified it with the Temple hill in Jerusalem. A. H. McN.—**W. L. R.**

MORNING.—See TIME.

MORROW AFTER THE SABBATH (Lv 23[11, 15]).—See PASSOVER.

MORTAR (AV 'morter').—See HOUSE, **1**, **4**, and cf BITUMEN.

MORTAR AND PESTLE.—The use, from the earliest times, of the mortar and pestle for crushing the grains of the cultivated cereals, for the preparation of spices, and probably, as at the present day, for pounding meal and vegetables (see commentaries on Pr 27[22]) is attested by the constant occurrence of these articles in the remains of places excavated in Palestine. The mortars found at Gezer, as elsewhere, 'are simply heavy stones, a foot or two across, in whose upper surface a hemispherical hollow is cut. The pestles are cylindrical, with convex bases, which not infrequently display marks of rough treatment' (*PEFSt*, 1903, 118).

The manna is expressly said to have been beaten in mortars as well as ground in mills (Nu 11[8]). Their use is implied for pounding certain spices (Ex 30[36]) and for the 'crushed new grain' for the meal-offering of the first-fruits (Lv 2[14] RSV). Copper mortars are also mentioned in later literature, and in Herod's Temple the incense was pounded in mortars of gold. From the Mishnah (*Baba bathra*, iv. 3) we learn that it was customary to have larger mortars fixed into the floor of the house.

In Babylon, when a house was built, the seller handed the pestle of the house-mortar to the purchaser, in token of the conveyance of the house to its new owner. Hence the frequent occurrence, in deeds of sale, of the words 'the pestle has been handed over.' Cf article SHOE.

A. R. S. K.

MORTAR, THE.—See MAKTESH.

MORTGAGE.—The word 'mortgage,' used of the pledging of real estate in return for a loan, is found only in Neh 5[3]. See DEBT.

MORTIFY.—'To mortify' is in AV metaphorically 'to put to death.' Early writers could use it literally also, as Erasmus, *Commune Crede*, 81, 'Christ was mortified and killed in dede, as touchynge to his fleshe: but was quickened in spirite.'

MOSAIC.—Hebrew *riṣpāh* is rendered 'mosaic pavement' by RSV in Est 1[6], since the context indicates a variety of stones used for it. There is no necessary idea of 'mosaic' in the word itself, and elsewhere it is rendered simply 'pavement' (2 Ch 7[3], Ezk 40[17f] 42[3]).

MOSERAH, MOSEROTH.—Moserah is named in Dt 10[6] as the place where Aaron died and was buried; Moseroth in Nu 33[30f] as a stopping-place on the route to Mount Horeb. Its location is quite uncertain.

MOSES.—1. Name.—The Hebrew narrator regards *Mōsheh* as a participle from the verb *māshāh*, 'to draw' (Ex 2[10]). Josephus and Philo derive it from the Coptic *mo* 'water,' and *ushe* 'saved'; this is implied in their spelling *Mousēs*, also found in LXX and NT. It is more plausible to connect the name with the Egyptian *mes*, *mesu*, 'son.' Perhaps it was originally coupled with the name of an Egyptian deity—cf *Ra-mesu*, *Thoth-mes*, and others—which was omitted under the influence of Israelite monotheism.

2. History.—(i) *The narrative of J.*—Moses killed an Egyptian, and rebuked one of two Israelites who were striving together, and then he fled to Midian. There he helped seven daughters of the priest of Midian to water their flocks, dwelt with him, married his daughter Zipporah, and had one son by her, named Gershom (Ex 2[11–22]). The king of Egypt died (2[23a]), and at Y″'s bidding Moses returned. On the way, Y″ smote him because he had not been circumcised before marriage; but Zipporah saved him by circumcising the child, and thus circumcising Moses by proxy (4[19, 24–26]; these verses must be put back to this point). Y″ appeared in the burning bush and spoke to Moses. Moses was to gather the elders, give them Y″'s message, and demand permission from Pharaoh to sacrifice in the wilderness. Moses was given two signs to persuade the Israelites, and yet a third if the two were insufficient (3[2–4a, 5, 7, 8a, 16–18] 4[1–9]). Y″ was angry at his continued diffidence. Moses spoke to the elders and they believed; and then they made their demand to Pharaoh, which led to his increased severity (4[10–12, 29–31] 5[3, 5, 23] 6[1]). Plagues were sent, the death of the fish in the river (7[14, 16, 17a, 18, 21a, 24f]), frogs (8[1–4, 8–15a]), flies ([20–32]), murrain (9[1–7]), hail ([13, 17f, 23b, 24b, 25b–34]), locusts (10[1a, 3–11, 13b, 14b, 15a, c, 16–19]). See PLAGUES OF EGYPT. Pharaoh bade Israel go with their families, but refused to allow them animals for sacrifice; so Moses announced the death of the firstborn (10[24–26, 28f] 11[4–8]). At a later time Israelite thought connected with the Exodus certain existing institutions. The ordinances relating to them were preserved by J, but their present position is due to redaction, and the result is a tangled combination in chs. 12, 13 of ordinance and narrative: the ritual of the Passover (12[21–23, 27b]), the death of the firstborn and the hurried flight of the Israelites (12[29–34, 37–39]), commands concerning the Feast of Unleavened Cakes (13[3a, 4, 6f, 10]), and the offering of firstlings (13[11–13]), Y″ went before the people in a pillar of cloud and fire (13[21f]), the water was crossed (14[5f, 7b, 10a, 11–14, 19b, 21b, 24, 25b, 27b, 28b, 30]), and Moses sang praise (15[1]). Moses made the water at Marah fresh (15[22–25a]), and thence they moved to Elim (v.[27]). Fragments of J's story of Massah are preserved (17[3, 2c, 7a, c]), and parts of the account of the visit of Moses' father-in-law, which it is difficult to separate from E (18[7–11]). The narratives attached to the delivery of the laws at Sinai are in an extraordinarily confused state, but with a few exceptions the parts which are due to J can be recognized with some confidence. The theophany occurred (19[18]), and Moses was bidden to ascend the mountain, where Y″ gave him directions respecting precautions to be taken (19[20–22, 24, 11b–13, 25]) [v.[23] is a redactional addition of a remarkable character; due to [11b–13] having been misplaced]. Moses stayed 40 days and nights on the mountain (34[28a]); Y″ descended, and Moses 'invoked the name of Y″' (v.[5]). The laws given to him are fragmentarily preserved (vv.[10–26]). Y″ commanded him to write them down (v.[27]), and he obeyed (v.[28b]).

The reason for the insertion of the laws so late in the book was that the compiler of JE, finding laws in both J and E, and noticing the strong similarity between them, considered the J laws to be the *renewal* of the covenant broken by the people's apostasy. Hence the editorial additions in 34^{1} (from ‘ like the first ’) and in v.^{4} (‘ like the first ’).

A solemn ceremony sealed the covenant (24$^{1f, 9-11}$). Something then occurred which roused the wrath of Y″ ; it is doubtful if the original narrative has been preserved ; but J has inserted a narrative which apparently explains the reason for the choice of Levites for Divine service (32$^{25-29}$). Moses interceded for the people (the verses to be read in the following order, 33$^{1-4a, 17, 12f, 18-23}$ 34$^{6-9}$ 33$^{14-16}$). Y″ having been propitiated, Israel left the mountain, and Moses asked Hobab to accompany them (Nu 10$^{29-36}$). Being weary of manna, they were given quails, which caused a plague (11$^{4-15, 18-24a, 31-35}$). Dathan and Abiram rebelled (ascribed by different commentators to J and to E, 16$^{1b, 2a, 12-15, 25f, 27b-32a, 33f}$). Fragments of the Meribah narrative at Kadesh appear to belong to J (20$^{3a, 5, 8b}$). Moses sent spies through the S. of Palestine as far as Hebron. Caleb alone encouraged the people, and he alone was allowed to enter Canaan (13$^{17b, 18b, 19, 22, 27a, 28, 30, 31}$ 14$^{1b, 8f, 11-24, 31}$). Moses promised that Hebron should be Caleb's possession (Jos 14$^{6-14}$). The Canaanites were defeated at Hormah (perhaps a later stratum of J, Nu 21$^{1-3}$). Israel marched by Edom to Moab, and conquered Heshbon and other cities (21$^{16-20, 24b, 25, 31f}$). The story of Balaam (parts of 22–24). Israel sinned with the Moabite women, and Moses hanged the chiefs (25$^{1f, 3b, 4}$). Moses viewed the land from the top of Pisgah, and was buried in Moab (parts of Dt 34$^{1-6}$).

(ii) *The narrative of E.*—The midwives rescued Israelite infants (Ex 1$^{15-20a, 21}$). Moses' birth ; his discovery and adoption by Pharaoh's daughter (2$^{1-10}$). Moses was feeding Jethro's sheep in Midian, when God called to him from a bush at Horeb, and told him to deliver Israel. He revealed His name ‘ Ehyeh,’ and promised that Israel should triumphantly leave Egypt (3$^{1, 4b, 6, 9-12, 13f, 21f}$). Moses returned to Egypt, meeting Aaron on the way ; they made their demand to Pharaoh, and were refused (4$^{17f, 20b, 27f}$ 5$^{1f, 4}$). Moses, by means of his Divinely given staff, brought plagues—the turning of the river to blood (7$^{15, 17b, 20b, 23}$), the hail (9$^{22, 23a, 24a, 25a, 35}$), the locusts (10$^{12, 13a, 14a, 15b, 20}$), the darkness ($^{21-23, 27}$). Moses was bidden to advise the Israelites to obtain gold, etc., from the Egyptians (11$^{1-3}$), which they did (12^{35f}). They departed, taking with them Joseph's mummy (13$^{17-19}$). They crossed the water (fragments are preserved from E's account, 13$^{7a, c, 10b, 15a, 16a, 19a, 25a}$), and Miriam sang praise (15$^{20, 21}$). On emerging into the desert, they were given manna ; it is possible that E originally connected this event with the name *massah*, ‘ proving ’ (15^{25b} 16$^{4, 15}$). Then follows E's Meribah narrative combined with J's Massah narrative (17$^{1b, 2a, 4-6, 7b}$). Israel fought with Amalek under Joshua's leadership, while Aaron and Hur held up Moses' hands with the sacred staff (17$^{8-16}$). Jethro visited the Israelites with Moses' wife and two sons ; he arranged sacrifices, and a sacrificial feast, in which the elders of Israel took part (18$^{1a, 5f, 12}$). Seeing Moses overburdened with the duty of giving decisions, he advised him to delegate smaller matters to inferior officers ; and Moses followed his advice. Jethro departed to his own home (18$^{12-27}$). Preparations were made for the theophany (19$^{2b, 3a, 9a, 10, 11a, 14f}$), which then took place ($^{16f, 19}$ 20$^{18-21}$). Laws preserved by E and later members of his school of thought are grouped together in chs. 20–23 (see Exodus, Law). In the narratives in which the laws are set, two strata, E and E^{2}, are perceptible, the latter supplying the narrative portions connected with the Ten Words of 20$^{1-17}$. E relates the ceremony which sealed the covenant (24$^{3-8}$) ; the usual practice of Moses with regard to the ‘ Tent of Tryst,’ where God used to meet with any one who wished to inquire of Him (33$^{7-11}$) ; and the people's act of repentance for some sin which E has not preserved (33^{6}). E^{2} relates as follows : Moses told the people the Ten Words, and they promised obedience (19^{7f} ; this must follow 20$^{1-17}$). Moses ascended the mountain to receive the written Words, leaving the people in the charge of Aaron and Hur (24^{13-15a} 31^{18b}). During his absence Aaron made the golden bull, and Moses, when he saw it, broke the tablets of stone and destroyed the image ; Aaron offered a feeble excuse, and Y″ smote the people (32$^{1-6, 15a, 16-24, 35}$). Moses' intercession has not been preserved in E, but it is supplied by a late hand in 32$^{30-34}$. We here resume the narrative of E. After the departure from Horeb a fire from Y″ punished the people for murmuring (Nu 11$^{1-3}$). At the ‘ Tent of Tryst ’ Y″ took of Moses' spirit and put it upon 70 elders who prophesied, including Eldad and Medad, who did not leave the camp ; Joshua objected to the two being thus favoured, but was rebuked by Moses (11$^{16f, 24-30}$). Miriam and Aaron spoke against Moses for having married a foreign woman and then for claiming to have received Divine revelations ; Miriam became leprous, but was healed at Moses' intercession (12). On Dathan and Abiram (16) see above, under J. Miriam died at Kadesh (20^{1}). Twelve spies were sent, who brought back a large cluster of grapes, but said that the natives were numerous and powerful (13$^{18a, c, 20, 23f, 26b, 27b, 29, 33}$). The people determined to return to Egypt under another captain (14$^{1b, 3f}$). [Here occurs a lacuna, which is partially supplied by Dt 1$^{19-46}$, probably based on E.] Against Moses' wish the people advanced towards Canaan, but were routed by the Amalekites and other natives (14$^{39-45}$). Edom refused passage through their territory (20$^{14-21}$). Aaron died at Moserah, and was succeeded by Eleazar (Dt 10^{6}). Serpents plagued the people for their murmuring, and Moses made the serpent of bronze (Nu 21^{4b-9}). Israel marched by Edom to Moab, and vanquished Sihon (21$^{11b-15, 21-24a, 27-30}$) ; the story of Balaam (part 22–24). Israel worshipped Baal-peor, and Moses bade the judges hang the offenders (25$^{1a, 3a, 5}$). Y″ warned Moses that he was about to die, and Moses appointed Joshua to succeed him (Dt 31$^{14f, 23}$). Moses died in Moab, and his tomb was unknown. He was the greatest prophet in Israel (Dt 34$^{5, 6b, 10}$).

(iii) *The narrative of D* is based upon the earlier sources, which it treats in a hortatory manner, dwelling upon the religious meaning of history, and its bearing upon life and morals, and Israel's attitude to God. There are a few additional details, such as are suitable to a retrospect (*e.g.* 1$^{6-8, 16f, 20f, 29-31}$ 32$^{1f, 23-28}$), and there are certain points on which the tradition differs more or less widely from those of JE. But D supplies nothing of importance to our knowledge of Moses' life and character.

(iv) *The narrative of P.*—Israel was made to serve the Egyptians ‘ with rigour ’ (Ex 1$^{7, 13, 14b}$). When the king died, Y″ heard their sighing, and remembered His covenant (2$^{23-25}$). He revealed to Moses His name Yahweh, and bade him tell the Israelites that they were to be delivered (6$^{2-9}$). Moses being diffident, Aaron his brother was given to be his ‘ prophet ’ (6$^{10-12}$ 7$^{1-7}$). [The genealogy of Moses and Aaron is given in a later stratum of P, 6$^{14-25}$.] Aaron turned his staff into a ‘ reptile ’ before Pharaoh (7$^{8-13}$). By Aaron's instrumentality with Moses plagues were sent—all the water in Egypt turned into blood (7$^{19, 20a, 21b, 22}$) ; frogs (8$^{5-7, 15b}$) ; gnats or mosquitoes (vv.$^{16-19}$) ; boils (9$^{8-12}$). [As in J, commands respecting religious institutions are inserted in connexion with the Exodus : Passover (12$^{1-13, 24, 28, 43-50}$). Unleavened cakes (vv.$^{14-20}$), Dedication of firstborn (13^{1f}).] The Israelites went to Etham (13^{20}) and thence to the Red Sea. The marvel of the crossing is heightened, the waters standing up in a double wall (14$^{1-4, 8f, 15b, 16b-18, 21a, c, 22f, 26, 27a, 28a}$). In the wilderness of Sin the people murmured, and manna was sent ; embedded in the narrative are fragments of P's story of the quails (16, except vv.$^{4, 15}$). They moved to Rephidim (17^{1a}), and thence to Sinai (19$^{1, 2a}$). After seven days Y″ called Moses into the cloud (24$^{15b-18a}$) and gave him instructions with regard to the Tabernacle and its worship (25–31^{17}), and also gave him the Tablets of the Testimony (31^{18a}). [Other laws ascribed to Divine communication with Moses are collected in Leviticus and parts of

Numbers.] When Moses descended, his face shone, so that he veiled it when he was not alone in Y″'s presence (34^{29-35}). A census was taken of the fighting men preparatory to the march, and the writer takes occasion to enlarge upon the organization of the priestly and Levitical families (Nu 1–4). The cloud which descended upon the Tabernacle was the signal for marching and camping (9^{15-23}), and the journey began (10^{11-28}). With the story of Dathan and Abiram (see above) there are entwined two versions of a priestly story of rebellion—(1) *Korah* and 250 princes, all of them laymen, spoke against Moses and Aaron for claiming, in their capacity of Levites, a sanctity superior to that of the rest of the congregation. (2) *Korah* and the princes were Levites, and they attacked Aaron for exalting priests above Levites (parts of 16). The former version has its sequel in 17; Moses and Aaron were vindicated by the budding of the staff for the tribe of Levi. In the wilderness of Zin Moses struck the rock, with an angry exclamation to the murmuring people, and water flowed; Moses and Aaron were rebuked for *lack of faith* [the fragments of the story do not make it clear wherein this consisted], and they were forbidden to enter Canaan (parts of $20^{1a, 2-13}$). Joshua, Caleb, and ten other spies were sent from the wilderness of Paran; the two former alone brought a good account of the land, and they alone were permitted to enter Canaan; the other ten died by a plague (parts of 13, 14; see above under J and E). Aaron died at Mount Hor (20^{22b-29}). Israel marched by Edom to Moab (20^{22} $21^{4a, 10, 11a}$). Phinehas was promised 'an everlasting priesthood' for his zeal in punishing an Israelite who had brought a Midianite woman into the camp (25^{6-15}). All the last generation having died except Joshua and Caleb, a second census was taken by Moses and Eleazar (26). Moses appointed Joshua to succeed him (27). The Midianites were defeated and Balaam was slain (31). Moses died on Mount Nebo, aged 120 (Dt $34^{1a, 7-9}$).

3. Historicity.—In the OT, there are presented to us the varying fortunes of a Semitic people who found their way into Palestine, and were strong enough to settle in the country in defiance of the native population. Although the invaders were greatly in the minority as regards numbers, they were knit together by an *esprit de corps* which made them formidable. And this was the outcome of a strong religious belief which was common to all the branches of the tribe—the belief that every member of the tribe was under the protection of the same God, Yahweh. And when it is asked from what source they gained this united belief, the analogy of other religions suggests that it probably resulted from the influence of some strong personality. *The existence and character of the Hebrew race require such a person as Moses to account for them.* But while the denial that Moses was a real person is scarcely within the bounds of sober criticism, it does not follow that all the *details* related of him are literally true to history. What S. R. Driver says of the patriarchs in Genesis is equally true of Moses in Exodus, Numbers: 'The basis of the narratives in Genesis is in fact *popular oral tradition*; and that being so, we may expect them to display the characteristics which popular oral tradition does in other cases. They may well include a substantial historical nucleus; but details may be due to the involuntary action of popular invention or imagination, operating during a long period of time; characteristic anecdotes, reflecting the feelings, and explaining the relations, of a later age may thus have become attached to the patriarchs; phraseology and expression will nearly always be ascribed rightly to the narrators who cast these traditions into their present literary shape' (article 'Jacob' in *DB* ii, 534^{b}).

Moses is portrayed under three chief aspects—as (i) a Leader, (ii) the Promoter of the religion of Y″, (iii) Lawgiver, and 'Prophet' or moral teacher.

(i) *Moses as Leader.*—Some writers think that there is evidence which shows that the Israelites, who went to Egypt at the time of the famine, did not comprise the whole nation. Whether this be so or not, however, there is no sufficient reason for doubting the Hebrew tradition of an emigration to Egypt. Again, if Israelites obtained permission—as foreign tribes are known to have done—to occupy pasture land within the Egyptian frontier, there could be nothing surprising if some of them were pressed into compulsory building labour; for it was a common practice to employ foreigners and prisoners in this manner. But in order to rouse them, and knit them together, and persuade them to escape, a leader was necessary. If, therefore, it is an historical fact that they were in Egypt, and partially enslaved, it is more likely than not that the account of their deliverance by Moses also has an historical basis. It is impossible, in a short article, to discuss the evidence in detail. It is in the last degree unsafe to dogmatize on the extent to which the narratives of Moses' life are historically accurate. In each particular the decision resolves itself into a balance of probabilities. But that Moses was not an individual, but stands for a tribe or group of tribes, and that the narratives which centre round him are entirely legendary, are to the present writer pure assumptions, unscientific and uncritical. The minuteness of personal details, the picturesqueness of the scenes described, the true touches of character, and the necessity of accounting for the emergence of Israel from a state of scattered nomads into that of an organized tribal community, are all on the side of those who maintain that *in its broad outlines* the account of Moses' leadership is based upon fact.

(ii) *Moses as the Promoter of the religion of Yahweh.*—Throughout the OT, with the exception of Ezk 40–48, the forms and ceremonies of Y″ worship observed in every age are attributed to the teaching of Moses. It is to be noticed that the earliest writer (J) uses the name 'Yahweh' from his very first sentence (Gn 2^{4b}) and onwards, and assumes that Y″ was known and worshipped by the ancestors of the race; and in Exodus he frequently employs the expression 'Y″ the God of the Hebrews' (3^{18} 5^{3} 7^{16} $9^{1, 13}$ 10^{3}). But, in agreement with E and P, he ascribes to Moses a new departure in Y″ worship inaugurated at Sinai. E and P relate that the Name was a new revelation to Moses when he was exiled in Midian, and that he taught it to the Israelites in Egypt. And yet in 3^{6} E represents Y″ as saying to Moses, 'I am the God of thy father' [the God of Abraham, the God of Isaac, and the God of Jacob (unless this clause is a later insertion, as in $^{15f, }4^{5}$)]. And in 6^{3} P states categorically that God appeared unto Abraham, Isaac, and Jacob, but He was not known to them by His name 'Yahweh.' All the sources, therefore, imply that Moses did not teach a totally new religion; but he put before the Israelites a new aspect of their religion; he defined more clearly the relation in which they were to stand to God: they were to think of Him in a peculiar sense as *their* God. When we go further and inquire whence Moses derived the name **'Yahweh,'** we are landed in the region of conjectures. Two points, however, are clear: (1) that the God whose name was 'Yahweh' had, before Moses' time, been conceived of as dwelling on the sacred mountain Horeb or Sinai ($3^{1-5, 12}$ 19^{4}); (2) that He was worshipped by a branch of the Midianites named Kenites (Jg 1^{16} 4^{11}), of whom Jethro was a priest (Ex 3^{1} 18^{1}). From these facts two conjectures have been made. Some have supposed that Moses learned the name 'Yahweh' from the Midianites; that He was therefore a foreign God as far as the Israelites were concerned; and that, after hearing His name for the first time from Moses in Egypt, they journeyed to the sacred mountain and were there admitted by Jethro into the Kenite worship by a sacrificial feast at which Jethro officiated. But it is hardly likely that the Israelites, enslaved in Egypt, could have been so rapidly roused and convinced by Moses' proclamation of an entirely new and foreign deity. The action taken by Jethro in organizing the sacrifice might easily arise from the fact that he was in his own territory, and naturally acted as host towards the strangers. The other conjecture, which can claim a certain plausibility, is that Y″ was a God recognized by Moses' own tribe of Levi. From Ex 4$^{24, 27}$ it is possible to suppose that Aaron was not in Egypt, but in the vicinity of Horeb, which he already knew as the 'mountain of God.' If Moses' family, or the tribe of Levi, and perhaps (as some conjecture) the Rachel tribes, together with the Midianite branch of Semites, were already worshippers of Y″, Moses' work would consist in proclaiming as the God of the whole body of Israelites Him whose help and guidance a small portion of them had already experienced. If either of these conjectures is valid, it only puts back a stage the question as to the ultimate origin of the name 'Yahweh.' But whatever the origin may have been, it is difficult to deny to Moses the glory of having united the whole body of Israelites in the single cult which excluded all other deities.

(iii) *Moses as Prophet and Lawgiver.*—If Moses taught the Israelites to worship Y″, it may safely be assumed that he laid down some rules as to the method and ritual of His worship. But there is abundant justification for the belief that he also gave them injunctions which were not merely ritual. It is quite arbitrary to assume that the prophets of the 8th cent. and onwards, who preached an ethical standard of religion, preached something entirely new, though it is probable enough that their own ethical feeling was purer and deeper than any to which the nation had hitherto attained. The prophets always held up a lofty ideal as something which the nation had *failed to reach*, and proclaimed that for this failure the sinful people were answerable to a holy God. And since human nature is alike in all ages, there must have been at least isolated individuals, more high-souled than the masses around them, who strove to live up to the light they possessed. And as the national history of Israel postulates a leader, and their religion postulates a great personality who drew them, as a body, into the acceptance of it, so the ethical morality which appears in the laws of Exodus, and in a deeper and intenser form in the prophets, postulates a teacher who instilled into the nucleus of the nation the germs of social justice, purity, and honour. Moses would have been below the standard of an ordinary sheikh if he had not given decisions on social matters, and Ex 18 pictures him as so doing, and 33$^{7-11}$ shows that it was usual for the people to go to him for oracular answers from God. It is in itself probable that the man who founded the nation and taught them their religion, would plant in them the seeds of social morality. But the question whether any of the codified laws, as we have them, were directly due to Moses is quite another matter. In the life of a nomad tribe the controlling factor is not a *corpus* of specific prescriptions, but the power of custom. An immoral act is condemned because 'it is not wont so to be done' (Gn 34^{7}, 2 S 13^{12}). The stereotyping of custom in written codes is the product of a comparatively late stage in national life. And a study of the history and development of the Hebrew laws leads unavoidably to the conclusion that while some few elements in them are very ancient, it is impossible to say of any particular detail that it is certainly derived from Moses himself; and it is further clear that many are certainly later than his time.

4. Moses in the NT.—(i) All Jews and Christians in Apostolic times (including our Lord Himself) held that Moses was the *author* of the Pentateuch. Besides such expressions as 'The law of Moses' (Lk 2^{22}), 'Moses enjoined' (Mt 8^{4}), 'Moses commanded' (Mt 19^{7}), 'Moses wrote' (Mk 12^{19}), 'Moses said' (Mk 7^{10}), and so on, his name could be used alone as synonymous with that which he wrote (Lk 16$^{20, 31}$ 24^{27}).

(ii) But because Moses was the representative of the Old Dispensation, Jesus and the NT writers thought of him as something more. He was a historical personage of such unique prominence in Israel's history, that his whole career appeared to them to afford parallels to spiritual factors in the New Covenant. The following form an interesting study, as illustrating points which cover a wide range of Christian truth: The 'glory' on Moses' face (2 Co 3$^{7-18}$), the brazen serpent (Jn 3^{14}), the Passover (Jn 19^{36}, He 11^{28}, 1 Co 5^{7f}), the covenant sacrifice at Horeb (Mt 26^{28}, Mk 14^{24}, Lk 22^{20}, 1 Co 11^{25}; see also He 9$^{18-20}$, 1 P 1^{2} with Hort's note), the terrors of the Sinai covenant (He 12$^{18-24}$), the crossing of the sea (1 Co 10^{2}), the manna (Jn 6$^{30-35, 41-58}$), the water from the rock (1 Co 10$^{3, 4}$), Moses as a prophet (Ac 3^{22} 7^{37}, Jn 1$^{21-23}$; and see Jn 6^{14} 7^{40} [Lk 7^{39}]), the magicians of Egypt (2 Ti 3^{8}), the plagues (Rev 8$^{5, 7, 8}$ 9$^{2-4}$ 15$^{6-8}$ 16$^{2-4, 10, 13, 18, 21}$), and 'the song of Moses the servant of God' (Rev 15^{3}). A. H. McN.

MOSOLLAM, 1 Es 9^{14} (AV).—See MESHULLAM, **11.**

MOSOLLAMON, 1 Es 8^{44} (AV).—See MESHULLAM, **10.**

MOSOLLAMUS.—1. 1 Es 8^{44} (RV); see MESHULLAM, **10. 2.** 1 Es 9^{14} (RV); see MESHULLAM, **11.**

MOST HIGH (*'Elyôn*) occurs as an epithet of *'El* 'God' (Gn 14$^{18-20, 22}$, Ps 78^{35}) or *Yahweh* (Ps 7^{17}); or it stands by itself as a title of God (Nu 24^{16}, Dt 32^{8}, Ps 21^{7}, etc.). We find it first in Gn 14, where **Melchizedek** is described as 'priest to the Most High God' (*'El 'Elyôn*), and since in later times the Salem where he lived was generally identified with Jerusalem, the double function of priest and king ascribed to him caused him to be regarded by the Jews as a type of the ideal king, and by the Christians as the type of Christ. Hence the name of the God whom he worshipped (*'El 'Elyôn*), which may possibly, in the first instance, have had reference merely to the lofty situation of Jerusalem, became in later generations a mysterious and exalted title of Yahweh. According to Philo of Byblos the Phoenicians worshipped a deity of this name (cf Eusebius, *Praep. Evang.* I. x. 14), and he is probably to be identified with the *Aleyin* of the Râs Shamra texts. The corresponding Greek word, *Hypsistos*, is frequent in inscriptions of the Graeco-Roman period, and was applied especially to Zeus. It is therefore clear that *'Elyôn* was originally a deity distinct from Yahweh (cf O. Eissfeldt, *JSS* i, 1956, 25 ff), whose title was transferred to Yahweh. Whatever the origin of the title *'Elyôn*, it never occurs in strictly prose passages of the OT, though we find it in the Songs of Balaam (Nu 24^{16}), Moses (Dt 32^{8}), and David (2 S 22^{14}). The Aramaic equivalents are fairly frequent in Daniel (3^{26} 4^{34}, etc.).

The uses of the Greek rendering in the NT are instructive. In the story of the Annunciation it is ordained that the child whom Mary is to bear shall be called Son of the Most High (Lk 1^{32}); and a little later on (v.^{76}) John the Baptist is spoken of as prophet of the Most High. The contrast is completed in the Epistle to the Hebrews, where Melchizedek is brought forward as priest of the Most High (cf 7^{1} with v.^{28}). It is worth noting, too, that the title is twice found in the mouth of demoniacs (Mk 5^{7}=Lk 8^{28}, Ac 16^{17}). The word, then, does not belong to the language of everyday life: it is reserved for poetry and elevated style, and it seems by its origin to have suggested something archaic and mysterious, whether it referred to the lofty dwelling-place or to the majestic nature and attributes of God.

H. C. O. L.—**H. H. R.**

MOTE.—The word chosen by Wycliffe and Tyndale, and accepted by subsequent versions as the translation of Gr. *karphos* in Mt 7^{3f}, Lk 6^{41f} (RSV '**speck**'). The root of *karphos* is *karphō* 'to dry up,' and it signifies a bit of dried stick, straw, or wool, such as, in the illustration, might be flying about and enter the eye. In its minuteness it is contrasted by our Lord with *dokos*, the **beam** that supports (*dechomai*) the roof of a building.

MOTH.—Hebrew *'āsh*, Job 4^{19} 13^{28}, Ps 39^{11}, Is 50^{9} 51^{8}, Hos 5^{12}; Greek *sēs*, Mt 6^{19f}, Lk 12^{33}, Ja 5^{2}. All these references are to the clothes-moth, which is ubiquitous and extremely plentiful in Palestine. It is almost impossible to guard against its destructiveness, except by constantly using clothes, shawls, carpets, etc. Such goods, when stored for long, are found to be reduced almost to powder on being removed (cf Job 4[19] etc.). In Job 27[18] AV and RV have ' moth,' but RSV emends to ' spider ' (cf RSVm). E. W. G. M.

MOTHER.—See FAMILY, **3.**

MOTHER-OF-PEARL.—See JEWELS AND PRECIOUS STONES, PEARL.

MOUNT.—An earthwork in connexion with siege-craft (Jer 6[6] AV, RV ; RSV ' siege mound ' ; so also elsewhere), also rendered **bank** (2 S 20[15] RV ; AV ' mount,' RSV ' mound '). In 1 Mac 12[36] RV has ' mound ' (AV ' mount ' ; RSV ' high barrier '). See, further, FORTIFICATION AND SIEGECRAFT.

MOUNT, MOUNTAIN.—Although on the whole a mountainous country, Palestine has few striking or commanding peaks to show ; consequently, though we find frequent mention of mountains in the Bible, there are comparatively few names of individual summits. ' Mountain,' as well as its cognate ' mount,' is used both of isolated elevations and of extensive districts of lofty ground—such as Sinai, Horeb, Carmel on the one hand, Mount Seir or the Mountain of Gilead on the other.

Mountains served various functions to the ancient inhabitants of the land. (1) They were *dwelling-places*, for which the numerous caves, natural and artificial, excavated in their soft limestone sides, well fitted them : thus Esau dwelt in Mount Seir (Gn 36[8]). (2) They served the purpose of *landmarks* : thus Mount Hor was indicated (Nu 34[7]) as a boundary of the Promised Land. (3) They were used as *platforms*, for addressing large crowds of people, as in the famous ceremony at Ebal and Gerizim (Jos 8[30ff]), in the address of Jotham to the Shechemites (Jg 9[7]), and that of Abijah to the Ephraimites (2 Ch 13[4]). (4) They were *burial-places* (' the tombs there on the mount,' 2 K 23[16]). (5) They served as *refuges* (Gn 14[10], Mt 24[16]) ; (6) as *military camps* (1 S 17[3]) ; (7) as *sources of stone, wood and plants* (2 Ch 2[18], Neh 8[15], Hag 1[8]) ; (8) as *watch-towers and look-out stations* (Ezk 40[2], Mt 4[8]) ; (9) as *pasturage* (Ps 50[10], Lk 8[32]) ; (10) as *fortresses* (Ps 125[2]). Their obvious fitness for typifying strength and endurance gives rise to metaphors and comparisons to be found in almost every book of both Testaments.

But it is in their aspect as *holy places* that mountains are of the deepest interest to the student of the Scriptures or of Palestine. In modern Palestine almost every hill a little loftier or more striking than its fellows is crowned by a domed shrine, *now* regarded as the tomb of a Moslem saint, but no doubt the representative of a sacred precinct that goes back to the earliest Semitic inhabitants of the land. Sinai, Horeb, Carmel occur to the memory at once as mountains consecrated by a theophany. The worship at **' high places '** was so deeply engrained in the Hebrews that no amount of legislation could eradicate it ; the severe discipline of the Exile was needed for its destruction. R. A. S. M.

MOUNT OF THE ASSEMBLY.—See CONGREGATION.

MOUNTAIN SHEEP.—See CHAMOIS.

MOURNING CUSTOMS.—The oriental expression of grief has a twofold relationship. Towards God it is marked by silent and reverent submission symbolized by placing the hand on the mouth. ' The Lord gave, and the Lord has taken away ' (Job 1[21]) ; ' I am dumb . . . for it is thou who hast done it ' (Ps 39[9]). But towards the relatives and neighbours the case is altogether different. It is now an event that has to be announced as quickly and publicly as possible, and a loss which love has to deplore with passionate abandonment and an accumulation of conventional ceremony. At the moment of death a loud shrill **wail** is raised by those present. Its meaning is understood only too well. As the piercing, tremulous shrieks are repeated, a few inquiries are made as to the locality and circumstances, and the rapidly increasing cry is accepted as an invitation and claim to proceed to the house of mourning. Immediately after death the body is washed and robed for the **burial,** which usually takes place within twenty-four hours. In addition to the successive outbursts of grief by members of the family, who have to be comforted and pleaded with and led away from the prostrate figure of the dead, the sustained ceremony of mourning is attended to by the neighbours. These, usually assisted by **hired mourners,** arrange themselves around the **bier,** or on opposite sides of the room, and keep up the lamentation without intermission. In this way they afford the preoccupation of a recognized routine, and give the relief of physical outlet to feelings that either are, or are considered to be, beyond control. At times one of the chief mourners leans over the body, wringing her hands or wiping away the fast falling tears, and asking why he has left them, and who will discharge the duties that belonged to him alone, pleading for love's sake to hear only once more the music of the voice now silent, or begging forgiveness on account of selfishness and imperfect service in the days that will never return. Meanwhile the band of mourners redouble their wailing, with beating of the breast and frantic clutching at their hair and clothes. As such paroxysms cannot last, the skilled mourners, usually women, endeavour to moderate and sustain the feeling of desolation by a plaintively descending chant. Among the singers there are usually one or two who are specially skilful in leading off with metrical phrases and rhymes of sympathetic appeal, which the others take up and repeat in concert. The invariable subject is the good qualities of the departed, and the extent of the loss which the family has been called upon to bear. In addition to the above allusions, new springs of tenderness are opened by referring to other members of the same family recently departed, and the loved one whose death they are lamenting is asked to bear messages of greeting to them. As the intimation of the bereavement reaches more distant parts of the town, or is carried to the neighbouring villages, companies of sympathizing friends come to show their regard for the dead. They announce their arrival by loud weeping and exclamations of grief; and as they enter the house the lamentation of the mourners in the room breaks out afresh. To the Western visitor unacquainted with the temperament and traditions of Oriental people, the whole scene is deeply distressing, and he has to check the feeling of repugnance by reminding himself that they would be equally shocked by the apparent callousness and ordered formality of our procedure on similar occasions. With cruel yet merciful swiftness the hour arrives for interment. The lamentation that was passionate before now becomes tumultuously defiant. Relatives lose all self-control, and, refusing to let the bearers discharge their sad office, have to be forcibly removed. The procession is then formed, and on the way to the cemetery is increased by those who join it to show their respect towards the family, and also to share the merit which the Lord attaches to service performed for those who can no longer reward it. Among the Jews, during the prescribed days of separation following upon a death in the family, the mourners are daily visited by the Rabbi, who reads the portions of Scripture and the prayers appointed by the synagogue. Over the door of the cemetery is inscribed in Hebrew ' The House of Eternity ' or ' The House of the Living.' The explanation given in regard to the latter term is either that the life beyond the grave is the real life, or, according to others, that the grave is the place of habitation to which all the living must come.

The references to mourning in the Bible show that the custom of to-day in Palestine is the same as in ancient times with regard to the house of mourning, although special features of liturgical form now belong to the Synagogue, the Church, and the Mosque. There is the same announcement by wailing (Mic 1[8], Mk 5[38]). Friends come to condole (Job 2[11-13]), and there is the same language of commendation and affectionate regret (2 S 1[17-27] 3[33, 34]). The exclamations of to-day were then used (1 K 13[30], Jer 22[18]). Hired mourners are alluded to (Jer 9[17, 18], Am 5[16]) ; and such manifestations as the **beating of the breast** (Is 32[12]), **tearing of the**

garments (2 S 3[31]), **fasting** (1 S 31[13], 2 S 3[35]), the putting of **ashes** on the head and the wearing of **sack-cloth** (Gn 37[34]). Remarkable indeed is the forbearance of David who discarded all signs of mourning after the death of his son (2 S 12[20]), out of quiet resignation to the irrevocable will of God. Ezekiel devoutly refrained from formal mouring after the death of his wife (Ezk 24[15-24]).

The form of lamentation for the individual is applied to afflicted Israel (Jer 9[1], La 1[16] 3[48f]), and to the historical extinction of Tyre (Ezk 27[28-36]). It was also applied to the supposed death of vegetation gods at the beginning of the dry season in the spring of the year: **Tammuz** (Ezk 8[14]), **Hadad-rimmon** (Zec 12[11]), **Baal** (Hos 7[14]). Resurrection of the god in the autumn brought the return of rain and of fresh vegetation. A long drought indicated the failure of the god to return from the netherworld (1 K 18[27]).

Dramatic display of sorrow carried with it the peril of insincerity and self-righteousness, hence Christ's note of warning (Mt 6[16-18]). The Apostle Paul commends as a Christian duty the showing of sympathy towards those in affliction (Ro 12[15]), but intimates that in Christ the familiar phrase of greeting to the afflicted, 'Hope is cut off!' has been made obsolete by the resurrection of the Lord Jesus (1 Th 4[13]). One of the features to which the New Jerusalem owes its title is the absence of mourning and tears (Rev 7[17]). G. M. M.—W. H. Br.

MOUSE.—Hebrew *'akhbār*. Probably a generic term including field-mice, hamsters, dormice, and even jerboas. The male of the last named is called *'akbâr* by the Arabs. All these small rodents are exceedingly plentiful in Palestine. The hamster (*Cricetus phoeus*) and the jerboa, of which three varieties have been found in the land, are eaten by the Arabs (cf Is 66[17]). Metal mice as amulets have been found in the Palestine plain (cf 1 S 6[4f]). The mouse was forbidden food to the Israelites (Lv 11[26]). E. W. G. M.

MOUTH.—Several Hebrew words are so translated. **1.** *gārôn* (literally 'throat'), Ps 149[6] (AV, RV; RSV 'throat'). **2.** *ḥēkh* (literally 'palate'), Job 12[11] (AV; RV, RSV 'palate'). **3.** *'adhî* (literally 'ornaments'), Ps 32[9] (AV; RV 'trappings,' cf RSV), Ps 103[5] (AV, RV; RSV emends to yield 'as long as you live'). **4.** *peh*, the most usual word for 'mouth,' meaning also 'edge,' *e.g.* of the sword (Ex 17[13] etc.), or 'border,' *e.g.* of a garment (Ps 133[2], AV, RV 'skirt'; RSV 'collar'). **5.** *pûm*, Aramaic=Hebrew *peh*, Dn 7[5] etc. **6.** *pānîm* (literally 'face'), Pr 15[14]. **7.** *t^era'*, Aramaic (literally 'door'), Dn 3[26] (RSV 'door'). **8.** Greek *stoma*, in NT. Frequently in Scripture 'mouth' is used figuratively for 'speech,' of which it is the organ. W. E.

MOZA.—**1.** Son of Caleb, 1 Ch 2[46]. **2.** A descendant of Saul, 1 S 8[36f] 9[42f].

MOZAH.—A town of Benjamin, Jos 18[26]; possibly modern *Kh. Beit Mizzeh*, close to *Qalôniyeh*, W. of Jerusalem.

MUFFLER, Is 3[19] (AV, RV).—See SCARF.

MULBERRY TREES.—**1.** 2 S 5[23f], 1 Ch 14[14f]; see BALSAM TREES. **2.** Ps 84[6] (AVm); see BACA, VALLEY OF.

MULE.—**1.** *peredh* (m) and *pirdāh* (f), in all passages except the following. **2.** *rekhesh*, Est 8[10, 14] (AV; RV 'swift steeds,' RSV 'swift horses'), 1 K 4[28] (AVm; AV 'dromedaries'; RV, RSV 'swift steeds'). In Mic 1[13] for the same word AV has 'swift beast,' RV 'swift steed' and RSV 'steeds.' There is no reason to think mules were intended. **3.** *yēmîm*, Gn 36[24] (AV; RV, RSV 'hot springs'). 'Mules' is certainly a wrong translation.

The breeding of mules was forbidden to the Israelites (Lv 19[19]), but from David's time (2 S 13[20] 18[9]) onwards (1 K 1[33] 10[25] 18[5]) they appear to have been increasingly used. The returning Israelites brought 245 mules with them (Ezr 2[66]). Mules are preferred in Palestine to-day as pack animals (cf 1 Ch 12[40], 2 K 5[17]); they are hardier, subsist on less food, and travel better on rough roads. A well-trained mule is a favourite riding animal with the highest officials in the land. E. W. G. M.

MUNITION occurs in a few passages of AV in the sense of a fortified place, *e.g.* Is 29[7], where RV and RSV have 'stronghold.' In Is 33[16] AV and RV have 'munitions,' but RSV 'fortresses.' Similarly in Nah 2[1] AV and RV have 'munition,' while ARV has 'fortress' and RSV has 'ramparts.' In 1 Mac 14[10] for AV and RV 'all manner of munitions,' RSV has 'the means of defence' (cf 10[11] AV and RSV 'fortifications,' RV 'defence,' for the same Greek word).

MUPPIM.—A son of Benjamin, Gn 46[21]; called **Shuppim** in 1 Ch 7[12, 15], and **Shephupham** in Nu 26[39] (AV **Shupham**), and **Shephuphan** in 1 Ch 8[5].

MURDER.—See CRIMES, **7**; REFUGE [CITIES OF].

MURRAIN.—See PLAGUES OF EGYPT.

MUSHI.—A son of Merari, Ex 6[19], Nu 3[30], 1 Ch 6[19, 47] 23[21, 23] 24[26, 30]. The patronymic **Mushites** occurs in Nu 3[33] 26[58]. See MERARI, **1.**

MUSIC AND MUSICAL INSTRUMENTS.—**1. Probable character of early Hebrew music.**—Since the Dispersion, the music of the Jews has always borne the impress of the peoples among whom they have settled. Synagogue ritual thus affords us no clue to the music of early times, and we must accordingly fall back on Scripture and tradition. From these we gather that Hebrew music was of a loud and piercing nature, far removed from the sweetness which modern taste demands. There is no real evidence that the players ever advanced beyond unison in their combinations of notes, apparently reproducing the air on successively rising or falling octaves of the scale. We may suppose, however, that they would hardly fail to discover that certain combinations were pleasing to the ear, and would thus learn to strike them either simultaneously or successively (*arpeggio*). How far, however, they grasped the nature of a chord or of harmony must remain obscure, in spite of the attempts to solve this question, some of them altogether baseless guesses. For example, even the Hebrew accents, though of comparatively late origin, and always confined in Jewish use to acting as guides in the proper recitation of the text, have been pressed into the service, as though employed for the purpose of a kind of 'figured bass,' and thus indicating an acquaintance with musical harmony. Unfortunately, even those who have maintained this theory differ considerably as to the details of its application.

2. Rendering of Hebrew music.—It seems clear at any rate that an antiphonal setting was in use for many of the Psalms (*e.g.* 13, 20, 38, 68, 89); but the chanting must not be taken as resembling what we now understand by that term. The account we have in 1 Ch 15[16ff] of the elaborate arrangements for conducting the musical services of the Temple, appears to indicate a somewhat complicated system, and to suggest that there entered a considerable element of flexibility into the composition. It is, for instance, quite possible that the long reciting note which with us may do duty on occasion for as many as twenty, thirty, or even more syllables, played no such monotonous part, but was broken up and varied to an extent suggested by the length of the verse as well as by the character of the sentiment to be conveyed.

3. Occasions on which music was used.—Hebrew religious melody had a popular origin, and was thus closely connected with the religious life of the nation. Apart from such references to song as those in Gn 31[27] and Job 21[12], we find in the headings of certain Psalms (*e.g.* 22, *'Ayyeleth hash-Shaḥar*, 'the hind of the morning') traces of what are in all probability in some, if not in all, cases secular songs. So *'Al Tashḥēth*, 'Destroy not,' prefixed to Pss 57, 58, 59, 75, may well be the first words of a vintage song (cf Is 65[8]). A parallel may be found in directions prefixed to Ibn Gabirol's hymns and those of other celebrated Jewish poets, when these compositions were adapted to music in the Spanish

(Sephardic) ritual (see D. J. Sola, *Ancient Melodies, etc.*, 1857, Pref. p. 13). Amos (6⁵) speaks of music performed at feasts, and in 1 S 18⁶ we read of its use in Saul's time in connexion with processions. As in this last case, so in general it may be supposed that music and dancing were closely connected and had a parallel development. David's careful elaboration of the Levitical music, vocal and instrumental, was employed, according to 2 Ch 5¹², with impressive effect at the dedication of Solomon's Temple. The reformations under both Hezekiah and Josiah included the restoring of the musical ritual belonging to David's time (2 Ch 29²⁵ᶠᶠ 35¹⁵). Later the descendants of Heman and other Levitical leaders of music were among the exiles of the Return from Babylon, and under them the services were reconstituted as of old (Neh 12²⁷, ⁴⁵ᶠᶠ).

4. Hebrew musical instruments.—Here our information is somewhat fuller, though involving a good deal of uncertainty in details. We may for clearness' sake divide under three heads, viz. stringed, wind, and percussion instruments.

(1) *Stringed instruments.*—Chief among these are the *kinnôr* and the *nēbhel*, **'lyre'** and **'harp'** (RV **'harp'** and **'psaltery'**), which were evidently favourites among the Jews. It is plain, in spite of doubts which have been expressed upon the point, that the two names were not used indifferently for the same instrument. The LXX in nearly all cases is careful to distinguish them (*kithara* or *kinyra*, and *psaltērion, nablē*, or *nabla* respectively). Both, however, were used in the main, and perhaps exclusively, to accompany songs, and those of a joyous nature. Both occur in the Dead Sea Hymn Scroll along with *ḥālîl* (see below) in this aspect. (They were unsuitable for times of mourning; see Ps 137², a passage which further shows that the instrument must have been, unlike a modern harp, easily portable). They were doubtless the chief, if not the sole, instruments employed in the Temple services. In Solomon's time they were made from almug (algum) trees, doubtfully identified with sandal wood. The strings, originally of twisted grass or fibres of plants, were afterwards formed of gut, and subsequently from silk or metal.

(*a*) The *kinnôr* (an onomatopoetic word, derived from the sound of the strings) is the only stringed instrument mentioned in the Hexateuch, where (Gn 4²¹) its invention is attributed to Jubal, son of Lamech. The *nēbhel* is first mentioned in 1 S 10⁵, as used by the prophets who went to meet Saul. The *kinnôr* (*kithara* or **lyre** [in 1 Mac 4⁵⁴ the AV renders **'cithern,'** RV and RSV **'harp'**]) consisted of a sound-box at the base, with wooden side-arms and a crossbar connected by the strings with the box below. The early and widespread use of this type of instrument in the Middle East is well attested from Assyrian reliefs, while the wooden harp, decorated with a copper cow's head, discovered at Ur testifies to the actual structure. Egyptian tombs also provide evidence, *e.g.* one shown on a tomb in Egypt, dating from about the 30th cent. B.C. (12th Dynasty). A tomb at Thebes in the same country (dating between the 12th and 18th Dynasties) exhibits a similar form, which was sometimes modified later in the direction of more artistic construction and sloping of the crossbar downwards, so as to vary the pitch of the strings. Jewish coins of Maccabaean date furnish us with a close resemblance to the Greek *kithara*. Josephus (*Ant.* VII. xii. 3 [306]) distinguishes the *kinnōr* as a ten-stringed instrument struck by a plectrum; the *nabla*, on the other hand, being, he says, played with the fingers. This need not necessarily conflict, as has been thought by some, with the statement (1 S 16²³) that David played the *kinnôr* 'with his hand'; and Josephus's evidence in such a matter should carry much weight.

(*b*) The *nēbhel.*—It has been sought to identify this with various instruments; among them, the **lute** (so RV in Is 5¹² [AV **viol**; RSV **'harp'**]; 'lute' is also RV and RSV translation of Greek *kinyra* in 1 Mac 4⁵⁴), guitar, and **dulcimer**. In support of the last it is urged that the Arabic name for that instrument, *sanṭîr*, is a corruption of the Greek *psaltērion*, by which, as has been said, the LXX sometimes render *nēbhel*. Having regard, however, to the testimony of Josephus (see above) that the *nēbhel* had twelve strings, and was played by the hand without a plectrum, we are safe in taking it to be a kind of **harp**, an instrument of larger size than the *kinnôr*, and used (Am 6⁵, Is 5¹² 14¹¹) at the feasts of the rich. The Dead Sea 'War' scroll mentions a *nēbhel* of ten(?) strings. So also Ps 33² 144⁹ (RV 'psaltery of ten strings'; RSV 'harp of ten strings' or 'ten-stringed harp'; AV adds 'and,' rendering 'psaltery and an instrument of ten strings'). We find, on the other hand, that it was not too large to be played by one who was walking (see 1 S 10⁵, 2 S 6⁵). The above argument from *sanṭîr* = *psaltērion* is weakened by the fact that the Greek word was used *generically* for stringed instruments played with one or both hands without a plectrum. We may note further that the *nabla* (see above for this as a LXX rendering of *nēbhel*), known to the Greeks as of Sidonian origin, was played according to Ovid (*Ars Amat.* iii. 327) with both hands.

Egyptian monuments show us portable harps, varying in form, bow-shaped, rectangular, or triangular, though all constructed on the same general principle, and having the sound-box above, not, as the *kinnôr*, below. Seven of these harps, of a triangular shape, and used by a Semitic people in Assyria, are to be seen on a bas-relief found at Kuyunjik. We may add that several early Church writers (Augustine on Ps 42; Jerome on Ps 149³; Isidore, *Etym.* iii. 22, 2) support the above identification of *nēbhel* with a harp.

(*c*) There is little that can be asserted with confidence as to the nature of other instruments of this class mentioned in the Bible. In Dn 3⁵ᶠᶠ, besides the *psantērîn* (Greek *psaltērion*) and *kitharis* (Greek *kithara*) with which we have already dealt, we have the *śabbᵉkhā* (AV, RV **sackbut**); RSV has **'trigon,'** 'a triangular instrument with four strings and bright tone' (*KB*). This is evidently the Greek *sambykē*, but the latter has been variously described as a large harp of many strings and rich tone, similar to the grand Egyptian harp, and as a very small one of high pitch. After all, both descriptions may be true, if referring to different periods of its existence.

Nᵉghînôth has sometimes been taken as the name of an instrument, but is much more probably a general term for stringed music. So in Ps 68²⁵ (Heb ²⁶), we have a contrast between the singers (*shārîm*) and the players on strings (*nōghᵉnîm*), which the Dead Sea Hymns scroll confirms.

Gittîth, the heading of Pss 8, 81, 84, has also, but somewhat doubtfully, been referred to instruments named after Gath: so the early Jewish paraphrase (Targum), 'the harp which David brought from Gath.'

(2) *Wind instruments.*—(*a*) The *ḥālîl*, 'flute' (AV, RV **pipe**; RSV 'pipe' or **'flute'**) seems to have been the instrument of this class in most common use. It was played in coming from and going to the high place (1 S 10⁵, 1 K 1⁴⁰ 'pipes'). It accompanied festal processions of pilgrims (Is 30²⁹). It was used in mourning (Jer 48³⁶, cf Mt 9²³), and in the ritual of twelve solemn annual occasions. According to Is 5¹², the feasts of the drunkards were enlivened by it. It may have been a simple **flute**, *i.e.* a mere tube with holes, played by blowing either into one end or into a hole in the side. It is possible, on the other hand, that it may have been a reed instrument, either, as the modern oboe, with a double and vibrating tongue, or, as the clarinet, with a single tongue. Neighbouring nations were, we know, familiar with **reed pipes**, as they also were with double flutes, which, for anything we know to the contrary, the *ḥālîl* may have been. On the other hand, the keyed flute is of decidedly later origin, and in the times with which we are dealing the fingers must have done all the work.

(*b*) The *'ûghābh*, 'pipe,' rendered uniformly in the AV as **'organ,'** an instrument which was not known even in rudimentary form in OT days, seems to have become an obsolete word even in LXX times, as shown by the variety of renderings which it has there received. The instrument known as 'Pan's pipes' (Gr. *syrinx*, Lat.

fistula) is perhaps the best conjecture that can be offered. RSV renders by ' pipe ' in Gn 4[21], Job 21[12] 30[31]. (*c*) The *mashrôḳîthā*, ' pipe ' (RSV ; AV and RV **flute**) may have been similar ; while (*d*) the *sumpōnyâ* (cf the Italian *zampugna* or *sampogna* for ' bagpipes ') may well have corresponded to the modern **bagpipes,** as developed from the double flute ; a good example of a double instrument is in a relief from Karatepe (Hittite), where also a ' bagpipe ' appears. (*e*) The *shōphār*, **' horn,'** ' trumpet ' is mentioned seventy-two times in the OT. It is not a musical instrument as such, but is used to give a loud sound (1 Ch 15[28], 2 Ch 15[14], Ps 98[6], Hos 5[8] ; AV and RV **cornet,** RSV ' horn '). It was a curved horn of a cow or ram, used mainly, and till later OT times exclusively, for secular purposes, such as to give signals in war (*e.g.* Jg 3[27] or to announce important events (*e.g.* 1 K 1[34, 39]). It is still employed by the Jews at solemn festivals. For 2 S 6[5], AV ' cornets,' see (3) (*c*) below.

The *ḥªṣōṣªrāh*, on the other hand—the one instrument of which we have an undoubtedly authentic representation, viz. on the Arch of Titus at Rome in front of the table of the showbread—was a long, straight, metal **trumpet,** used mainly for religious purposes, especially in later times (2 K 12[13], 1 Ch 13[8] ; LXX renders by *salpinx*, see BUGLE). *Ḥªṣōṣªrôth* are prominent in the Dead Sea ' War ' scroll.

(3) *Percussion instruments.*—(*a*) The *tōph*, **' tabret '** or **timbrel** (2 S 6[5], plural ' *tuppîm*,' **tambourines**), was a small hand-drum, represented on Egyptian and Assyrian monuments. In these instruments, unlike the modern drum, the parchment was probably rigidly fixed, and thus incapable of being tightened or loosened so as to regulate the pitch. In the ancient Sumerian ritual for the New Year festival a sacred bronze drum with drumsticks of hard wood was used and revered. (*b*) *mªṣiltaim* and *ṣelṣªlîm* were **cymbals.** Two shapes are found in Egypt and Assyria, the one consisting of two flat plates, played by being clashed together sideways, the other of two cones with handles at the peak, one cone being brought down on top of the other. (*c*) *mªna'an'îm*, **' castanets '** (so RV and RSV ; AV wrongly ' cornets ' ; RVm *sistra*, 2 S 6[5]) were formed of two thin metal plates with holes, through which were passed rods with loose metallic rings at their ends. (*d*) *shālishîm* in 1 S 18[6] ' instruments of music ' (RSVm ' triangles, or three-stringed instruments,' so also RVm) has been thought, from the apparent connexion of the word with the third Hebrew numeral, to be a triangle, but this is quite uncertain. It is more probable that it was a particular kind of *sistrum*. It may, however, be *groups of three* playing and singing as they dance, v.7.

A. W. S.—**R. A. B.**

MUSICIAN, THE CHIEF.—See PSALMS, **2.**

MUSTARD (Gr. *sinapi*).—The seed of this plant is used proverbially for anything exceedingly small. In this sense it occurs in the Gospels (Mt 17[20] etc.) and the Talmud. Jesus compares the Kingdom of heaven to the mustard seed (Mt 13[31] etc.), thus contrasting the tiny beginnings and the great result of the proclamation of the Gospel of the Kingdom. The plant intended is the *Sinapis nigra* (Arab. *khardal*), which grows wild in Palestine, and is a familiar sight on the shores of Gennesaret. It is also found under cultivation, and in the gardens it reaches a great size, being often from 10 to 12 feet in height. An annual, growing from seed, it is naturally compared with other garden herbs, which, although it springs from the smallest seed, it quite outgrows. It bears a profusion of minute seeds, of which the birds are very fond, sitting (' lodging ') on the branches as they eat. Although it is not properly ' a tree ' (Lk 13[19]), it quite accords with Oriental use to describe as such a great plant like this. And Plutarch even described a heather ' tree ' (*Isis and Osiris*, 357a).

E. W.—**F. C. G.**

MUSTER GATE.—A gate on the NE. side of Jerusalem, Neh 3[31] (AV **gate of Miphkad,** RV **gate of Hammiphkad**). Many attempts have been made to locate it, but as the course of this part of Nehemiah's wall has not been revealed by excavation, they are conjectural. Vincent believes it is the same as the **Gate of the Guard** (q.v.), Neh 12[39]

MUTH-LABBEN.—See PSALMS, **2.**

MUTILATION.—See CRIMES AND PUNISHMENTS, **9.**

MYNDOS (AV **Myndus**) was a city in Caria at the extremity of the peninsula on the S. side of which lay the city of Halicarnassus. It was strong enough to resist an assault of Alexander, but played no great part in history. It is mentioned separately in 1 Mac 15[23] as one of the places to which, in 139 B.C., the Romans sent messages on behalf of the Jews. Hence it is assumed that it was independent of the Carian confederacy ; and its native population seems to have descended from the race of the Leleges, and to have always maintained its independence against the Carians. A. E. H.

MYRA was a city of Lycia (q.v.) situated 2½ miles from the coast, but the same name is often applied to its harbour of Andriaca. In Greek times **Patara** (q.v.), 40 miles to the W., surpassed it, but in Roman times Myra became the chief seaport of Lycia, and was recognized by Theodosius as the capital. It grew especially through the Alexandrian grain-trade with Italy. The Alexandrian ships did not coast round the Levant, but took advantage of the steady west winds to cross direct between Lycia and Egypt. These winds made it easier for a ship sailing from Egypt to make for Myra, after which it could make its way across the Aegean, N. of Crete, and then the Ionian Sea, with the help of the N. wind, and up the W. coast of Italy with a westerly or southerly. A ship sailing to Egypt would be sailing more before the wind by taking a line from Patara. Doubtless this was the usual custom. In Ac 27[6] we read that the centurion in charge of St. Paul found at Myra ' a ship of Alexandria sailing for Italy ' ; whereas in Ac 21[1] Paul took ship direct from Patara to Tyre (though the Bezan text makes this ship touch at Myra). Myra retained its importance into the Middle Ages. Its bishop in the time of Constantine was St. Nicolas, and he became the patron saint of sailors in the E. Mediterranean, doubtless taking the place of a Lycian god to whom the sailors paid their vows on landing at Myra. There are splendid ruins on the site of Myra.

A. E. H.—F. C. G.

MYRRH.—**1.** *mōr* (Arab. *murr*), the dried gum of a species of balsam (*Balsamodendron myrrha*) growing in Arabia and India. It has a pleasant, though faint, smell, Ps 45[8], Est 2[12], Pr 7[17], Ca 1[13] 3[6]. It is used still in medicine (cf Mk 15[23]). It was used in embalming (Jn 19[39]), and was a valuable gift (Mt 2[11]). According to Schweinfurth, the myrrh of the OT was a liquid product of the *Balsamodendron opobalsamum*, known as balsam of Mecca. Ex 30[23] and Ca 5[5, 13], where the ' myrrh ' appears to have been liquid, support this view. See also OINTMENT.

2. *loṭ*, translated ' myrrh ' in Gn 37[25] 43[11], is a fragrant resin from the *Cistus* or ' rock rose,' a common Palestine shrub. In Arabic this is called *lâdan* (Lat. **ladanum**. so RVm). As a product of Palestine it was a likely substance to send to Egypt. E. W. G. M.

MYRTLE.—Hebrew *hªdhas*, Is 41[19] 55[13], Zec 1[8, 10f], Neh 8[15] ; also as a name *Hadassah* = Esther (Est 2[7]). *Myrtus communis* is an evergreen shrub much prized in Palestine. It grows wild in the mountains, especially on Carmel and in Gilead, but is also widely cultivated. It sometimes reaches a height of ten feet, but is usually much less. Its dark green leaves, pretty white flowers, and dark berries, which are eaten, are all much admired. It is still regularly used by the Jews in the Feast of Tabernacles (cf Neh 8[15]). E. W. G. M.

MYSIA was a district in the NW. of Asia Minor, S. of the Propontis and Hellespont. It derived its name from the Mysi, a Thracian tribe who probably entered Asia with the Phrygians. At no period were its boundaries strictly defined. It formed part of the dominions of the Persians and of Alexander. From 280 B.C. it was part of the kingdom of Pergamum, and therefore fell to the Romans in 133 B.C., becoming part of the province of Asia. The only mention of it in the Bible is Ac 16[7f], where St. Paul passed through it on his second missionary journey. A tradition assigned the evangelization of part of Mysia to a certain Onesiphorus, who was martyred at Parium when Adrian was proconsul of Asia, A.D. 109–114. See ASSOS, TROAS, ADRAMYTTIUM, all of which places were assigned to Mysia. A. E. H.

MYSTERY.—Several passages in the NT speak of (*e.g.*) 'the mystery of the gospel' (Eph 6[19]), and the question has been raised whether this use of the term 'mystery' is explicable from the Semitic background of the NT or if it reflects the influence of the Hellenistic mystery-religions. The mysteries are a group of ancient cults with a fairly wide following in the Hellenistic age. In the Greek world the mysteries of Demeter at Eleusis ranked as the oldest and most eminent, while in the second place stood the cult of the Cabiri of Samothrace, concerning which not much is known. Mystery-cults of non-Greek origin came in later: Mithras from Persia, Isis and Osiris from Egypt, Attis and Cybele from Phrygia, Adonis from Syria. The characteristic of all these cults was to regard their rites as a secret only revealed to initiates, who were forbidden to disclose the ceremonies and solemn formulas to the uninitiated. The ceremony of initiation was normally unrepeatable. Moral demands varied, but in some cases at least were fairly high (see Origen, *c. Celsum*, iii. 59). The initiate shared in the god's grief and joy, and was assured of immortality.

The mystery-religions present certain analogies, both in general and in particular, with the theology and practices of early Gentile Christianity. These analogies may have been overworked as an explanation of the latter, but they are not to be set aside as wholly irrelevant; they only need to be treated with restraint and caution. Paul's doctrine of the sacraments, for example, owes more to OT typology (cf 1 Co 10[1ff]) than to the mysteries, and there is a remarkable, probably conscious, avoidance of characteristic mystery-vocabulary in the NT. Nevertheless, there was probably some degree of influence, as is to be expected if the missionaries were using ideas and language intelligible to their audience. Heterodox forms of Christianity undoubtedly fell under the direct power of the mysteries; the language of Col 2[18] provides evidence for the heretics combated by Paul at Colossae. The second-century Ophites freely plagiarized the Mithraic routine for the soul's passwords, to be recited when ascending through the seven planetary spheres after death. The Naassenes manifest similar syncretistic phenomena. The Gnostic, for whom all was myth and symbol, for whom the particularity of the Word made flesh in time and space was incomprehensible, was more generous in his welcome to pagan myth and religion than the orthodox defender of an exclusive faith. Even so, Justin Martyr remains largely unembarrassed by the Mithraic use of bread and wine for a sacramental meal; and Clement of Alexandria delights to present Christianity as the supreme mystery-religion, God's esoteric secret that has at long last been revealed, Christ being the hierophant.

In the Septuagint the word 'mystery' is used in late writings (*e.g.* Wis 12[5] 14[15, 23]) in a manner that is broadly allusive to the pagan cults, but such passages are rare. In Dn 2[28f, 47], the word means a veiled hint of future events planned by God. It is understood that God reveals His hidden plans by His servants the prophets (cf Amos 3[7]), who possess insight into the counsels of the heavenly assembly (1 K 22[19ff]). This secret plan is unknown to false prophets (Jer 23[18, 21–22]). The apocalyptic writings naturally develop this notion, with their love of obscurity and claim to disclose the providential plan underlying terrible and meaningless events. The 'mystery' is the eschatological secret. This kind of language is reflected in the Qumrân *Manual of Discipline* (iii. 20–23, iv. 18), and in the book of *Hymns*, with special reference to the mystery of Divine providence in allowing evil. This background of apocalyptic usage is of pre-eminent importance for that of the NT, and is apparent, *e.g.* in 2 Th 2[7] 'the mystery of lawlessness,' and Rev 10[7]. In Mark 'the mystery of the kingdom of God' becomes a leading theme (cf Mk 4[11f]), being linked to the author's thesis of the messiahship of Jesus being a carefully guarded 'secret' and of the incarnation as a Divine incognito that can only be penetrated by those to whom it is granted so to do.

Similarly Paul can use the word 'mystery' of esoteric insight into the 'mystery of Christ,' only granted to the spiritual man, not to the psychic man or even to the cosmic powers which failed to comprehend the significance of the cross (1 Co 2[6–16]). In Col 1[25–27] and Eph 3[2f] it is explained that the 'mystery' of God, the secret at long last revealed through Paul as apostle of the Gentiles (cf Ro 16[25] which may be non-Pauline), is the extension of the gospel to the Gentile world. Paul also uses the word in referring to anything specially esoteric, like the resurrection of the saints (1 Co 15[51f]) or the symbolism of the marriage of Adam and Eve (Eph 5[32]). (The fact that the Latin *sacramentum* can mean either an esoteric symbol or a soldier's oath, and was used in the Vulgate to render *mystērion* in this last passage, among others, became important in post-Reformation debates about the sacramental status of marriage.) But in the NT esotericism is not cultivated for its own sake. In Christ God's secret stands revealed; the mystery of the gospel is that message which is now to be proclaimed. See ROME, **8.** H. C.

MYTH AND RITUAL.—The use of the expression 'Myth and Ritual' is intended to draw attention to one particular aspect of myth, namely, its relation to ritual and its function in ritual. The late Jane Harrison, in her studies in early Greek religion, especially in her book *Themis* (1912), was the first to bring into prominence the fact that the *mythos* (the spoken part), and the *drōmenon* (the done part), were the essential constituents of a valid ritual. At that time, however, little was known of the nature of early Semitic ritual, and she was not able to show that much of early Greek myth and ritual had its roots in a still earlier myth and ritual pattern discovered in Mesopotamia. The Scandinavian scholar S. Mowinckel, in his *Psalmenstudien* (especially ii: *Das Thronbesteigungsfest Jahwäs*, 1922), was the first to apply the knowledge of Babylonian rituals to Hebrew religion. In England, the publication of the symposium *Myth and Ritual* (1933) drew the attention of English OT scholars to this element in the religion of Israel. Since then this line of research has been most actively pursued by Scandinavian scholars. It has long been recognized that a relation of some kind existed between the origin stories in the first eleven chapters of Genesis and the Sumerian and Babylonian myths of Creation and the Flood. It is also admitted that various references in the OT to the victory of Yahweh over a dragon (Ps 74[13f], Is 51[9]) must be related to the Babylonian myth of the conquest of the chaos dragon Tiamat by the god Marduk. But since the latter myth formed an important part of the ritual of the New Year Festival in Babylon, the question arose whether a similar New Year Festival formed part of the pattern of the religion of Israel at any time during its history, and whether, if such a festival existed, it owed anything to the Babylonian festival. Into this controversy a fresh feature has entered, namely, the part played by the king in the Jerusalem cultus. Attention was first drawn to this aspect of the problem by an article contributed to the volume entitled *The Labyrinth* (1935) by Professor A. R. Johnson, and since followed up by him in his book *Sacral Kingship in Ancient Israel* (1955). In this book the view is advocated, based mainly on a detailed study of the royal and kingship psalms in the Hebrew Psalter, that, during the Davidic monarchy at Jerusalem there was a New Year Festival celebrated in the month Tishri, in which the king played an important part. The ritual consisted of a dramatic representation of the victory of Yahweh over hostile forces attacking Jerusalem. The 'myth,' or spoken part of this ritual was embodied in the kingship psalms which described the actions of the various participants in the ritual.

The question of the relation between myth and ritual has been extended to the field of NT studies. This aspect of the subject was first discussed by Professor E. O. James in his book *Christian Myth and Ritual* (1933), and has been followed up by other studies, such as Riesenfeld's *Jésus Transfiguré* (1947). Professor James suggests that the outlines of the myth and ritual pattern can be traced in the drama of redemption that is re-enacted annually at the Easter Festival and daily in the Liturgy at the Altar. S. H. He.

N

NAAM.—A Calebite family, 1 Ch 4^{15}.

NAAMAH.—**1.** Sister of Tubal-cain, Gn 4^{22}. **2.** Mother of Rehoboam, 1 K 14$^{21, 31}$, 2 Ch 12^{13}. **3.** A town of Judah in the lowland, Jos 15^{41}. There is no notice of it elsewhere. Zophar the **Naamathite**, Job 2^{11} etc.; there is nothing, however, to connect him with this town. It is possibly modern *Kh. Fered.*

NAAMAN (the word means 'pleasantness,' or, as an epithet, as is probable, of Adonis or Tammuz, 'darling'; cf the Adonis plantations referred to in Is 17^{10} [cf RVm]. The Arabs of the present day still call the red anemone, which blooms in the spring, at the time at which one of the Adonis festivals used to be held, the 'wounds of the darling, or Naaman'; the name of the flower probably comes from 'Naaman'; see W. R. Smith in the *English Historical Review*, April 1887). As a proper name, it is a good Syrian name, and is to be found in one of the Ugaritic genealogical tablets.—**1.** A name given to three different persons, who are described as the descendants of Benjamin; in Gn 46^{21} the name of one of the sons of Benjamin, in Nu 26^{40}, 1 Ch 8^{4} son of Bela, son of Benjamin, and in 1 Ch 8^{7} son of Ehud (or Abihud), grandson of Benjamin. It is difficult to assess the trustworthiness of these lists, but it may be assumed that it was a popular name among the Benjamites. Nu 26^{40} refers to the 'family of **Naamites** (*i.e.* Naamanites), and therefore they probably formed a clan belonging to the tribe of Benjamin.

2. A Syrian general who came to **Elisha** to be healed of leprosy. The story is told in 2 K 5, and belongs to the cycle of stories connected with Elisha. The incident must have taken place during a period of cessation of hostilities between Damascus and Israel, and has been described as 'brilliant in its representation of the international manners of the age.' Through an Israelite slave-girl Naaman hears of the man of God who works miracles, and in the hope of being cured, he is sent by the Syrian king to the king of Israel. When Elisha learns of the king's confusion, he requests that Naaman be sent to him, in order that he may learn that 'there is a prophet in Israel.' On his arrival Naaman receives a message to the effect that he is to wash in the river Jordan seven times; his objection that the prophet ought to work the miracle 'in the name of the Lord his God' seems very justifiable; upon the advice, however, of his servants he dips himself seven times in the Jordan, and is healed. His first words to the prophet, thereupon, are, 'Behold, I know that there is no God in all the earth, but in Israel.' On Elisha's refusing the gift offered to him, Naaman asks for two mules' burden of Israelitish soil upon which to worship the God of Israel; this is in entire accordance with the ideas of the time that a god of a country cannot be worshipped properly excepting upon his own soil (cf 1 S 26$^{19, 20}$). Quite natural, too, according to the beliefs of the time, is his wish to bow down in the house of Rimmon; for apart from the necessity of this on account of his attendance on the king, there is the fact that religious syncretism was considered not only permissible, but, under various circumstances, commendable. (For the unworthy conduct of the prophet's servant **Gehazi**, and the punishment inflicted on him see GEHAZI.) W. O. E. O.—**E. R. R.**

NAAMATHITE.—See NAAMAN, **1.**

NAAMITES.—See NAAMAN, **1.**

NAARAH ('girl').—**1.** One of the wives of Ashhur the 'father' of Tekoa, 1 Ch 4^{5f}. **2.** A town of Ephraim, Jos 16^{7} (AV **Naarath**); called **Naaran** in 1 Ch 7^{28}. It is possibly *Tell el-Jisr*, near *'Ain Dûq.*

NAARAI.—One of David's heroes, 1 Ch 11^{37}; called **Paarai** 'the Arbite' in 2 S 23^{35}.

NAARAN.—See NAARAH, **2.**

NAARATH, Jos 16^{7} (AV).—See NAARAH, **2.**

NAASHON, Ex 6^{23} (AV).—See NAHSHON.

NAASSON, Mt 1^{4}, Lk 3^{32} (AV).—See NAHSHON.

NAATHUS.—One who married a foreign wife, 1 Es 9^{31}; apparently corresponding to **Adna** in Ezr 10^{30}.

NABAL.—A wealthy but churlish sheep-owner 'in Maon, whose business was in Carmel,' 1 S 25^{2}. David, while living as an outlaw and freebooter, demanded at Nabal's sheep-shearing his reward for defending his flocks, 1 S 25^{5ff}. Nabal, inflamed with wine, returned an insolent answer, and David was prevented from wreaking terrible venegeance only by the timely arrival of Abigail, Nabal's wife, with large gifts and abundant flattery. The word *Nabal* means 'fool,' and Abigail, with wifely candour, says to David, 'Fool is his name and fool is he.' The next day Nabal was informed of all that had happened, and the shock of discovery brought on an apoplectic seizure, which caused his death. Abigail then became David's wife. W. F. B.

NABARIAH.—1 Es 9^{44} (AV, RV **Nabarias**) = **Hashbaddanah** (q.v.), Neh 8^{4}.

NABARIAS, 1 Es 9^{44} (AV, RV).—See NABARIAH.

NABATAEANS (1 Mac 5^{25} 9^{35}).—See ARABIA, ARETAS, EDOM, NEBAIOTH.

NABATHAEANS.—RV form of **Nabataeans** (q.v.).

NABATHITES.—AV form of **Nabataeans** (q.v.).

NABOTH.—A man of Jezreel, owner of a vineyard adjoining the palace of Ahab (1 K 21^{1}). The king, desiring to add the vineyard to his lands, offered to buy it or exchange it for another. Naboth, however, refused to give up 'the inheritance of his fathers.' Jezebel, Ahab's wife, by using the royal authority with the elders of the city, had Naboth accused of treason and blasphemy, and stoned to death. As Ahab went to take possession of the vineyard, he was met by Elijah, the prophet, who pronounced doom on him and his house. The murder of Naboth seems to have deeply impressed the popular mind, and the deaths of Joram and Jezebel near the spot were regarded as Divine retribution on the act, 2 K 9^{25f}. W. F. B.

NABUCHODONOSOR, the Greek form of the name Nebuchadnezzar (q.v.) retained in AV and RV in 1 Es 1^{40ff}, Ad. Est 11^{4}, Bar 1^{9ff} (RSV **Nebuchadnezzar**).

NACHON, 2 S 6^{6} (AV).—See NACON.

NACON.—The name of the threshing floor where Uzzah died, 2 S 6^{6} (AV **Nachon**); called **Chidon** in 1 Ch 13^{9}.

NADAB.—**1.** The eldest son of Aaron, Ex 6[23], Nu 3[2], 26[60], 1 Ch 6[3] 24[1]; he accompanied Moses to Sinai, Ex 24[1, 9f], and was admitted to the priestly office, Ex 28[1]; on the day of his consecration (cf Lev 10[12ff] with v.[9]) he and Abihu perished for offering 'unholy fire,' Lv 10[1f], Nu 3[4] 26[61], 1 Ch 24[2]. Wherein the transgression of Nadab and Abihu consisted is not clear. It is often suggested that 'unholy' fire means fire taken from a common source instead of from the altar (cf Lv 16[12], Nu 16[46]). **2.** A Jerahmeelite, 1 Ch 2[28, 30]. **3.** A Benjamite, 1 Ch 8[30] 9[36]. **4.** The ungrateful foster-son of Ahikar, To 14[10] (AV, RV **Aman**); in the Aramaic, Syriac, and Arabic forms of the **Ahikar** (q.v.) story, his name appears as **Nadan.** **5.** Apparently the nephew of Achiacharus (AV, RV; RSV **Ahikar**), who was the nephew of Tobit (To 11[18]; AV **Nasbas**). He came with Achiacharus to the wedding of Tobias. About his identity there is some little uncertainty. The Vulgate speaks of him as brother of Achiacharus, while others have regarded the two as identical. It has been suggested also that he is the same as Aman or Nadan, the ward of Achiacharus (To 14[19]), in which case the uncle adopted the nephew and brought him up as his son. **6.** Son and successor of Jeroboam I. as king of Israel, 1 K 14[20]; he reigned two years and was assassinated by Baasha, one of his generals, who became king, 1 K 15[25ff]. T. A. M.

NADABATH.—An unidentified town (?), east of the Jordan, in the neighbourhood of which a wedding party of the sons of Jambri was attacked, and many of them slain, by Jonathan and Simon, 1 Mac 9[37ff] (AV **Nadabatha**).

NADABATHA, 1 Mac 9[37] (AV).—See NADABATH.

NADAN.—See NADAB, **4.**

NAGGAI.—An ancestor of Jesus, Lk 3[25] (AV **Nagge**); cf the Hebrew name **Nogah.**

NAGGE, Lk 3[25] (AV).—See NAGGAI.

NAHALAL.—A town of Zebulun, Jos 19[15] (AV **Nahallal**); given to the Levites, 21[35]. Its inhabitants were not expelled by the Zebulunites, but were made tributary, Jg 1[30] (here called **Nahalol**). Alt has suggested the identification with *Tell en-Naḥl*; an alternative suggestion is with *Ma'lûl.*

NAHALIEL.—A stopping-place in the journey from the Arnon to Jericho, Nu 21[19]. The location is unknown.

NAHALLAL, Jos 19[15] (AV).—See NAHALAL.

NAHALOL.—See NAHALAL.

NAHAM.—The brother of Hodiah's wife, 1 Ch 4[19].

NAHAMANI.—One of the twelve heads of the Jewish community, Neh 7[7]; omitted in Ezr 2[2]. In 1 Es 5[8] **Eneneus** replaces him in RV (AV **Enenius**), for which RSV substitutes **Bigvai,** who stands further down in Neh 7[7].

NAHARAI.—The armourbearer of Joab, 2 S 23[37] (AV **Nahari**), 1 Ch 11[39]. In the latter he is called a Berothite (AV, RV), for which we should read Beerothite (RSV 'of Beeroth'), as in the former.

NAHARI, 2 S 23[37] (AV).—See NAHARAI.

NAHASH.—**1.** A king of Ammon, who demanded the surrender of the men of Jabesh-gilead, with the loss of the right eye of each, 1 S 11[1f]. So sure was he of their helplessness that he allowed them seven days' respite in which to appeal for help. Saul, newly designated as Israel's future king, was ploughing in the fields when the news was brought to him. He sacrificed the oxen, sent parts of the sacrifice to his fellow-countrymen with a command to muster, and promptly destroyed the Ammonites. Probably this is the Nahash who was kind to Saul's enemy David (2 S 10[2], 1 Ch 19[1f]), and whose son Shobi (2 S 17[27]) brought supplies to David at Mahanaim. **2.** The father of Abigail, and Zeruiah, if the text of 2 S 17[25] is correct, which is doubtful. According to Buchanan Gray, 'daughter of Nahash' may have crept into the text from 'son of Nahash' in v.[27]; cf 1 Ch 2[16]. J. H. St.

NAHATH.—**1.** A 'duke' of Edom, Gn 36[13, 17], **1** Ch 1[37]. **2.** A Kohathite Levite, 1 Ch 6[26]; perhaps called **Toah** in v.[34], and **Tohu** in 1 S 1[1]. **3.** A Levite in the time of Hezekiah, 2 Ch 31[13].

NAHBI.—The Naphtalite spy, Nu 13[14].

NAHOR.—**1.** Father of Terah and grandfather of Abraham Gn 11[22–25], 1 Ch 1[26], Lk 3[34]. **2.** Grandson of the preceding and brother of Abraham and Haran, Gn 11[26f]; cf Jos 24[2]. He is said to have married Milcah, daughter of Haran (Gn 11[29]), and twelve sons are enumerated, eight by Milcah and four by Reumah his concubine (Gn 22[20–24]). In Gn 24[10] we read of the 'city of Nahor,' *i.e.* Haran, where Rebekah was found. Laban, in making a covenant with Jacob, swears by the 'God of Abraham and the God of Nahor' (Gn 31[53]). The sons ascribed to Nahor (Buz, Uz, Aram, etc.) are for the most part names of tribes. It has been questioned if Nahor is a historical character at all. Some think we have, instead, the name of a lost tribe once resident in the neighbourhood of Haran, from which the Aramaean tribes were descended. While Abraham appears as the common ancestor of the Israelites and Edomites, Nahor is represented as the father of the Aramaeans. W. F. B.

NAHSHON.—Brother-in-law of Aaron, Ex 6[23] (AV **Naashon**); a descendant in the fifth generation from Judah, 1 Ch 2[10f], and prince of the tribe of Judah, Nu 1[7] 2[3] 7[12–17] 10[14]. He is mentioned as one of the ancestors of David, Ru 4[20], 1 Ch 2[10f]; and hence of Christ, Mt 1[4], Lk 3[32] (AV **Naasson**).

NAHUM.—I. THE MAN.—The word *Nahum* means 'full of comfort' and is probably a contraction of a longer Hebrew term meaning 'God (or Yahweh) is a comforter.' Of the man so named nothing is certainly known. He is called 'the **Elkoshite,**' but the exact meaning of the term cannot at present be determined. It is made in the Targum a kind of patronymic, recording the assumed descent of the prophet from an unknown ancestor *Koshi.* It is more likely to preserve the name of the prophet's birthplace or place of residence, of which the identification is still lacking. Three or four conjectures have been made.

(1) The prophet's tomb is shown at *Elkosh,* 24 miles to the N. of Nineveh; and accordingly he is said to have lived there, a descendant of a member of the ten tribes who was deported in 721 B.C. But the tradition that buries Nahum there is not met with before the 16th cent., and is sufficiently accounted for by the interest in Nineveh shown by the prophet.

(2) *Capernaum* is really a transliteration of Hebrew words which mean 'village of Nahum.' But a Galilaean origin for our prophet is unlikely (Jn 7[52]), and is not supported by any allusions in the prophecy.

(3) The same objection applies to Jerome's identification of *Elkosh* with a village *Elkozeh* in North Galilee, which on other grounds is precarious.

(4) The most probable tradition associates Nahum with *Elkosh* 'of the tribe of Simeon,' and locates the hamlet near *Beth-Gabre,* the modern *Beit-Jibrîn,* about half-way between Jerusalem and Gaza. The tradition occurs in a Syriac version of the biographies of the prophets, ascribed to Epiphanius, bishop of Salamis in Cyprus towards the close of the 4th cent., but probably of much later date.

II. THE BOOK.—**1. Analysis of contents.**—In the analysis of the book, a line of division can best be drawn at the close of 2[2]. The latter section is the actual prophecy or oracle. It is preceded by a psalm or proem of two parts, of which the one is general in its assertion of God's universal judgment, the other particular in its specific messages to Judah and to Assyria. Yahweh as the jealous Avenger is the opening theme. This fact holds good of His administration (1[3]); and as He passes on to the overthrow of the wicked, physical proofs of His power become evident everywhere (1[4–6]). Tenderness towards those who take refuge in Him, but an overwhelming flood upon His enemies (1[7–10]), are the two great characteristics of His rule. 'What do you plot against the Lord?' (1^{9}) is the point of passage to the section dealing with His particular acts, in which section either there are editorial additions, or the two messages, of deliverance to Judah ($1^{12f, 15}$ 2^{2}) and of vengeance upon some nation ($1^{11, 14}$ 2^{1}), were meant to be involved in repeated antitheses. Already the bearer of the good news is speeding over the hills (1^{15}; cf Is 52^{7}, Ro 10^{15}).

The oracle proper consists also of two sections, corresponding with the division into chapters. The second chapter is a swift and vivid description of the siege of Nineveh, its capture and sack, with the complete desolation that followed.

A second oracle is contained in the third chapter, of which the unity in theme and sequence of thought is conspicuous. The mention of the bloody city, full of lies and booty, is followed by one of the most vivid battle-pictures in Hebrew literature (3^{2f}). The cause of destruction is to be found in the diplomatic harlotry, whereby nations and races had been lured and sold; and so richly merited will be the woe, that none will be left or disposed to pity or bemoan Nineveh (3^{7}). The analogy of No-amon (Thebes) makes it certain that a similar fate is awaiting the Assyrian city (3^{8ff}). Her outposts and defences are already falling before the invader, just as the first-ripe figs fall at the mere shaking of a fig-tree; and her troops have become women (3^{12f}). The time to prepare for the siege is past, adds the prophet, with his sarcastic appeal, 'Tread the mortar, take hold of the brick mould!' The swarming merchants, the princes, and the scribes or marshals, are like locusts or grasshoppers, that camp in the hedges and walls, but vanish with the sunrise. Finally, the prophet addresses the king of Assyria himself, and on the eve of the destruction of the city proclaims her disappearance from history amidst the joy of all who had suffered under her tyranny: 'There is no assuaging your hurt . . . all who hear the news of you clap their hands over you.'

2. Authenticity of the first chapter.—Nahum's authorship of the two oracles is hardly open to question, but doubt has been thrown on the authenticity of the prologue, since Gunkel published an article on it in *ZAW*, 1893. The first ten verses of chapter 1 constitute an alphabetic acrostic poem (like La 1, 2, 3, 4, Pr 31^{10-31}, Ps 9–10, 25, 34 etc.) which is far more artificial and mechanical than the poetry of the second and third chapters; also, it is more abstract and theological in tone than the concrete and vivid descriptions of those chapters. The mention of Bashan, Carmel, and Lebanon in 1^{4} is not suitable to an ode on the downfall of Nineveh. This acrostic poem makes use of the first fifteen letters of the Hebrew alphabet, but they are not all in correct order: the N verse is in 2*b*; the beginning of 4*b* seems to be lost; and the L and M verses in 9 are transposed. According to the opinion of many critical scholars, this acrostic poem was found by an editor of the work of Nahum who prefixed it to the prophet's poetry. This editor did not know, or did not copy, the poem correctly or fully; or it has been imperfectly transmitted by copyists. While not the work of the prophet Nahum, its thought is not inconsistent with his. In chapter one, verses 11 and 14 may well be from the prophet; they are apparently addressed to the Assyrian king. $1^{12f, 15}$ and 2^{2} have as their common theme comfort and hope for Judah, which is promised that it will not have to suffer again at the hands of wicked Assyria. These are probably interpolations by an editor, possibly the one who prefixed the acrostic poem. 1^{15} seems to be dependent upon Is 40^{9} 52^{7}.

Thus, we may conclude that the work of Nahum the prophet is $1^{11, 14}$ $2^{1, 3-13}$ 3^{1-19}.

3. Date.—Nahum the prophet composed a prophecy which is exclusively concerned with the downfall of Nineveh. He must therefore have lived near the time of the fall of that city in 612 B.C. The Babylonian Chronicle records the capture of Nineveh in the late summer of that year under the combined attack of the Babylonians and Medes. They turned the city into ruins and heaps of debris and captured many prisoners, but the king of Assyria and his army escaped (see *ANET*, pp. 304 f).

Did Nahum prophesy before, during, or after the fall of Nineveh? Did he predict its fall, or only describe it after the event? Scholars are divided on the answers to these questions. Some of the verses use the Hebrew imperfect, and seem to point to the future, such as 2^{13} $3^{5-7, 11, 15}$. Other verses are so vivid and realistic in their description of the attack on the city and its downfall that they appear to have been written after Nineveh's capture, such as $2^{1, 3-10}$ $3^{1-4, 12f, 18f}$. Under the principles of Hebrew syntax, the imperfect verbs may be translated by the English present tense. It is to be considered as possible that Nahum began to write, or to proclaim his message orally, before or during the siege of Nineveh and completed it after the successful capture. The last two verses (which are considered secondary by some scholars) appear to look backward rather than forward.

According to A. Haldar, the book of Nahum originated in an association of cult prophets who employed ancient mythical and ritualistic themes for the purpose of propagandizing against Assyria and holding out hope of national restoration for Judah. The poems were composed shortly before 612 B.C.; though they made use of ritualistic themes, they were not intended for use in the Temple liturgy (Haldar, *Studies in the Book of Nahum*, 1947). According to P. Humbert, the book was a prophetic liturgy which was composed after the fall of Nineveh to be used at the Jewish New Year Festival in the autumn of 612 ('Le problème du livre de Nahoum,' *RHPR* xii, 1932, 1–15). P. Haupt even proposed the theory that the book is a liturgy composed for the celebration of Nicanor's Day in 161 B.C., incorporating two poems which had been written by an eyewitness of Nineveh's fall ('The Book of Nahum,' *JBL* xxvi, 1907, 1–53). This last theory is extreme and has no evidence to support it. Nahum could have been a Temple prophet; he was at any rate an ardent nationalist who did not criticize his fellow Hebrews and their institutions.

4. Literary character and religious value.—Picturesqueness and force have been described as the most prominent characteristics of Nahum's poetry. Compact thought, vivid description (2^{3-5} 3^{2f}), and effective imagery (2^{11f} 3^{17f}) separate him sufficiently from the prophets of the Chaldaean period, and give him a position not far behind that of Isaiah. His poetry is indeed among the best to be found in the OT.

If Nahum is not a religious teacher like Micah or Isaiah, he focuses upon the truth of God's moral government of the world, concentrating the light upon a single typical instance. Where he differs chiefly from the other prophets is in the complete outwardness of his gaze. He has no eye for the shortcoming or sin of Judah, and no revelation to make of the inner history or moral character of his own generation. In this respect he contrasts especially with his contemporary Zephaniah, who also looked for the collapse of the Assyrian kingdom, but saw clearly a similar fate about to overtake the sinners of Israel. For Nahum, Nineveh fills up the whole canvas. The prophecy is a stern song of war, a shout of triumph over the conquered and slain. It stands in contrast with the temper and spirit of the NT, in which no citation from the book occurs. The Assyrians were known in antiquity as one of the most cruel and ruthless of all nations. The prophecy of Nahum is a rebuke of militarism and illustrates the NT principle, 'They that take the sword shall perish with the sword' (Mt 26^{52}).

R. W. M.—**J. P. H.**

NAHUM.—An ancestor of Jesus, Lk 3^{25} (AV **Naum**).

NAIDUS.—One who married a foreign wife, 1 Es 9^{31}; possibly corresponding to **Benaiah** in Ezr 10^{30}.

NAIL.—1. Among the ancient Arabs it was the custom for a widow to allow her nails to grow during her term of mourning. To pare them was a formal indication that this period was at an end. From Dt 21^{12} and 2 S 19^{24} (LXX) it may be inferred that such was the custom among the Hebrews. The former passage, however, refers only to the case of a foreign captive whom a Hebrew might take to wife after a month's seclusion, during which the care of the person was neglected in token of mourning for the captive's condition. The latter passage in its Greek form (see *Cent. Bible*, *in loc.*) tells us that Mephibosheth showed his sympathy with David by, *inter alia*, omitting to trim his 'toe-nails and his finger-nails' during the latter's absence from Jerusalem.

2. The Hebrew word most frequently rendered 'nail' is properly a tent-peg, or, as in Jg 4^{21} RV **tent-pin** (AV 'nail'; RSV 'tent-peg'). This is also the better rendering in Zec 10^{4} (AV, RV 'nail'; RSV 'tent-peg'), where it is synonymous with 'corner-stone,' both terms signifying the princes or leading men of the State as its supports. The figure of Is $22^{23, 25}$, on the other hand, is derived from the custom of driving a nail (RSV 'peg') into the house-wall upon which to hang (v.^{24}) domestic utensils or the like. A. R. S. K.

NAIN.—From Hebrew *Na'îm*. The town where Jesus raised the widow's son to life (Lk 7^{11}). The name is found in the modern *Nēn*, a village six miles SE. of Nazareth on the N. slope of the so-called 'Little Hermon.' The summit of the hill is 1690 feet high, with a white-domed sanctuary, the tomb of the saint from whom the mountain takes its modern name, *Jebel ed-Dahi*. The village is 744 feet above the sea. Ruins stretch to the N., showing that the place was once of some importance; but they are comparatively modern. The rock-cut tombs to the E., however, bespeak a much higher antiquity. The small sanctuary, *Maqām Sīdna 'Isa*, 'Place of our Lord Jesus,' on the north, doubtless commemorates the visit of the Saviour. The spring lies on the W. side of the town. In this quarter sherds of both Israelite and Roman times are said to have been found. The site commands an interesting view. Across a narrow bay of Esdraelon rises Mount Tabor, over the eastern shoulder of which the white summit of Hermon is visible; while to the NW. and W. the eye ranges over the hills of Lower Galilee, and the rolling breadths of the great plain, to Mount Carmel by the sea. W. E.—**E. G. K.**

NAIOTH.—A place 'in Ramah,' where there was a 'company of the prophets.' Here David fled to Samuel after Saul had attacked him with a javelin; hither Saul pursued him, and was seized with an ecstatic fit of some kind, 1 S 19^{18-24}. Nothing is known of the situation of the place. It is not even absolutely certain that *Naioth* is a proper name; but opinions differ respecting its possible meaning. R. A. S. M.

NAME, NAMES.—**1. The names of God.**—See God.

2. Personal names.—From the earliest times the name given to a child was supposed to indicate some characteristic of the person; of the circumstances, trivial or momentous, connected with his or her birth; of the hopes, beliefs, or feelings of the parents. This is evident from the etymologies (Gn $21^{3, 6}$ 27^{36}, Ex 2^{10}, 1 S 4^{21} 25^{25} etc.), not always reliable, but testifying to the impression that name and facts should correspond. There are many indications of the persistence of this idea. For instance, there is the frequency of names denoting personal qualities, *Adin*, *Amasai*, *Jaddua*, *Korah*, *Solomon*, etc.; or pointing to occupations, *Asa Sophereth*, etc. Again, an Isaiah (7^{3} 8^{3}) or a Hosea ($2^{4, 6, 9}$) is quite ready to bestow symbolical names on his children; a Jeremiah (20^{3}) predicts the change from *Pashhur* to *Magor-missabib*, because the latter will more accurately correspond to the surroundings; and the same prophet sums up all his hopes for the future in the title which he bestows on the Messianic King and the holy city (23^{4} 33^{16}; cf Rev 19^{13}). The new name promised to the faithful (Rev 2^{17}) corresponds to the fresh glory bestowed on him, which differs in each recipient and is known only to himself (Rev 14^{1}).

Analogous convictions prevailed among other Eastern nations. *Nomen et omen* was an influential conception. When a man was wanted to milk a camel, Mohammed disqualified one applicant after another till a man came whose name meant 'Long Life'; if one of his converts was called 'Rough,' he called him 'Smooth'; he was even guided in his strategy by the names of the places *en route* (Margoliouth, *Mohammed*, pp. 61 f).

Generally the name was fixed immediately after birth, as it still is with the Arabs. The mother usually exercised this privilege (Gn 4^{25} 19^{37f} 29^{32ff} $30^{6ff, 18ff}$ 35^{18}, 1 S 1^{20} 4^{21}, Is 7^{14}), sometimes the father (Gn 4^{26} 16^{15} 17^{19} 21^{3}, Ex 2^{22}, 2 S 12^{24}, Hos 1^{4ff}), occasionally other interested persons (Ru 4^{17}, Lk 1^{57-63}). Some names were bestowed indifferently on men and women: *Abiah* (1 K 14^{31}, 1 Ch 2^{24}); *Abihail* (Nu 3^{25}, 1 Ch 2^{29}); *Zibiah* (2 K 12^{2}, 1 Ch 8^{9}).

Beginning at a fairly early date, there are a moderate number of names derived from the vegetable world: *Elah* ('terebinth'), *Zuph* ('sedge'), *Tamar* ('palm-tree'), etc. The majority, however, belong to more recent documents: *Asnah* ('bramble'), *Coz* ('thorn'), *Hadassah* ('myrtle'), *Susannah* ('lily'), *Shamir* ('thorn'), etc. Other natural objects are also drawn upon: *Geshem* ('rain'), *Barak* ('lightning'), etc.; curiously enough, *Jorah* ('autumn-rain,' Ezr 2^{18}) is identical with *Hariph* ('autumn,' Neh 7^{24}). A few, of peculiarly difficult interpretation, point to family relationships: *Ahab* = 'father's brother,' but the question is whether it signifies 'uncle' or whether it is an indication that the child closely resembles his father or is to be as a brother to him. *Ahban* = 'brother is son,' *Ahiam* = 'a maternal uncle,' belong to this class. But *Moses*, if, as is most probable, of Egyptian origin and signifying 'son,' is a shortened form of a theophorous name; cf Moses, *ad init.*

Names which have a religious import are more characteristic of the Semite races than of ours, and this is especially true of the Israelites all through their national life. A certain number of those found in the OT have heathen associations: *Anath* (transferred to a man from a well-known goddess worshipped in Syria, etc.), *Ahishahar* ('Shahar [*i.e.* 'Dawn'] is brother'), *Baal* (1 Ch 5^{5} 8^{30}), *Bildad* (Job 2^{11}), *Balaam*, *Obed-edom* ('servant of [the god] Edom'), *Reu* and *Reuel* (Gn 11^{18}, Ex 2^{18}). Among the earliest clan names are those of animals: *Rachel* ('ewe'), *Hamor* ('ass'), *Caleb* ('dog'), etc. This may well be a survival from a pre-historic age of totemism. In David's day we find individuals, possibly members of such clans, called *Eglah* ('calf'). *Laish* ('lion'), *Bichri* (from *becher*, 'a young camel'). And the curious recrudescence of words of this class in and about the reign of Josiah (*Huldah*, 'weasel,' *Shaphan*, 'rock-badger,' etc.), might be accounted for on the supposition that animal-worship had considerable vogue during that age of religious syncretism (cf Ezk 8^{10-12}). Names like *Hezir* ('swine'), *Achbor* ('mouse'), *Parosh* ('flea') favour this explanation. At the same time, it must be admitted that animal-names were in many instances bestowed as terms of endearment, or as expressions of a wish that the child might have swiftness, strength, gracefulness, or whatever might be the creature's peculiar quality.

There is an important class of compounds in which relationship—originally conceived as physical—with the god of the nation or clan is asserted: *Ammiel* ('kinsman is El'), *Abijah* ('father is Jah'), *Ahijah* ('brother is Jah'). These compounds ceased to be formed long before the Exile, owing, no doubt, to the sense that they infringed on the Divine dignity. Others now appear, containing an element which referred to the Divine sovereignty: *Adonijah* ('Jah is lord,' like the Phoen. *Adoneshmun*, 'Eshmun is lord'), *Malchiah* ('Jah is king'), *Baaliah* ('Jah is *baal*' [or 'lord']). Turning now to the two great groups in which *El* or *Yahweh* forms part of the name, it is to be noted that the former had the first run of popularity. From David until after the Exile, *Jah*, *Je*, or *Jeho* is more common. From the 7th cent. B.C. onwards *El* is seen to be recovering its ground. Altogether there are 135 names in *El*, and according to Gray (*HPN*, p. 163), 157 in one of the abbreviations of *Yahweh* [Jastrow (*ZAW* xvi, p. 2) has sought to reduce the latter number to about 80]. Abbreviations of both these classes are fairly common: *Abi*, for *Abijah*; *Palti*, for *Paltiel*; *Nathan*, for *Jonathan* or *Nathanael*, etc. The nations which were related to the Hebrews acknowledged or invoked their gods in the same fashion: Babylonian and Assyrian proper names containing the elements, *Bel*, *Ashur*, *Nebo*, *Merodach*, etc.; Phoenician having *Ashtoreth*, *Bel*, *Eshmun*, *Melech*, etc.; Aramaic, *Hadad*, *Rimmon*, etc.; Palmyrene Sabaean, and Nabataean exhibit the same features.

Special mention ought perhaps to be made of the curious words found in the Books of Chronicles. Ewald observes that they remind us of the nomenclature affected by the English Puritans of the 17th cent. They were meant to express the religious sentiments of the Chronicler and those like-minded. Thus we have *Jushab-hesed* ('kindness is required'). *Tob-adonijah* ('good is the Lord Yahweh'), *Elioenai* ('to Yahweh are mine eyes'), *Hazzelelponi* ('Give shade, Thou who turnest to me'; cf the Assyr. *Pān-Bēl-adagal* ['I look to Bel'] and *Pān-Aššūr-lāmur* ['I will look to Ashur']). But the climax is reached in 1 Ch 25^{4}, where, with very slight alteration, the list which begins with *Hananiah* reads, 'Be gracious unto me, Yahweh! Be gracious unto me! Thou art my God! Thou hast given great and exalted help to him who sat in hardship. Thou hast given judgments in multitudes and abundance.' These phenomena differ from the *Shear-jashub* and *Maher-shalal-hash-baz* of Isaiah, in that the latter were formed for the express purpose of symbolical prediction. We have, however, something resembling them in other late documents. P gives us *Bezalel* ('in the shadow of God'; cf Bab. *Ina-ṣilli-Bēl*, 'under the protection of Bel'), Ex 31^{2}, and *Lael* ('to God'; cf Bab. *Sha-Bēl-at-ta*, 'thou belongest to Bel'), Nu 3^{24}. And Neh 3^{6} has *Besodeiah* ('in the counsel of God').

From about the close of the 4th cent. B.C. it was a common practice to call children after their relatives (Lk 1^{59-61}). When we read such a list as this: *Hillel*, *Simon*, *Gamaliel*, *Simon*, *Gamaliel*, *Simon*, *Judah*, *Gamaliel*, *Judah*, we get the impression that the grandfather's name was more often adopted than the father's (cf To 1^{9}, Lk 1^{59}; Jos. *Ant.* XIV. i. 3 [10]). To the same period belong the Aramaic names *Martha*, *Tabitha*, *Meshezabel* (Bab. *Mushizib-ilu*), and those with the prefix *bar*, of which we have many examples in the NT. Foreign names abound in Josephus, the Apocrypha, and the NT. In some instances a person has two separate designations: *Alcimus*, *Jacimus*; *John*, *Gaddis*; *Diodotus*, *Tryphon*, etc. 'Saul, who is called Paul' (Ac 13^{9}), is a typical case. In some of the examples the reason for the second choice is obscure; in others there is an obvious similarity of sound or meaning. Double names were now frequent: *Judas Maccabaeus*, *Simon Zelotes*, etc. Non-Jewish names were substituted for Jewish: *Jason* for *Jesus*; *Simon* for *Simeon* (Deissmann, *Bible Studies*, p. 315, note).

After the birth of a son an Arab father will adopt an honorific name (*kunya*). If he had been called *Abdallah*, he is henceforth *Abu Omar*, or the like. There is no trace of this custom in Hebrew family life, but the idea of a distinguishing and honourable **surname** is not altogether wanting; see Is 44^{5} 45^{4}, Job 32^{21}, and some of the familiar double names. It is also possible that the Hebrew original of Sir 44^{23} signified 'I gave him the surname Birthright.' And the sense of Sir 47^{6} is 'They gave him the surname The Ten Thousand.'

3. Place Names.—The majority of these were no doubt fixed by the tribes whom the Hebrews dispossessed. From their great antiquity and the alterations to which they have been subjected, it is sometimes impossible to determine the meaning. Many places, however, got their designation from a salient natural feature, a well (*beer*), a fountain (*en*, in *En-gedi*), a meadow (*abel*), a vineyard (*karmel*), woods (*jearim*, in *Kirath-jearim*), a hill (*Gibeah*, *Gibeon*, *Ramah*), trees (*Bethphage*, *Beth-tappuah*, *Anab*, *Abel-hasshittim*, *Elah*, *Allon-bacuth*); from some circumstance belonging to the history or legends of the locality, an encampment (*Mahanaim*), a watch-tower (*Migdal*, *Megiddo*, *Mizpah*), a village (*Hazer*), a temporary abode of shepherds (*Succoth*), a place of refuge (*Adullam*), a vision (*Beer-lahai-roi*); from the clan which dwelt there (*Samaria*). Of the fifty-three names of animals in Gray's list (pp. 88–96), twenty-four are applied to towns or districts. On the totem-theory this would mean that the clan bestowed the name of its totem-animal on the place of its abode. Other names evidently imply the existence of local sanctuaries, some of which must have been pre-Israelite: *Beth-anath*, *Anathoth*, *Bethel*, *Gilgal*, *Kedesh-naphtali*, *Migdal-el*, *Migdal-gad*, *Neiel*, *Penuel*, *Beth-shemesh*. Almost all the compounds with *Baal* belong to this class: *Baal-beer*, *Bamoth-baal*, *B.-dagon*, *B.-hamon*, *B.-hazor*, *B.-meon*, *B.-perazim*, *B.-shalisha*, *B.-tamar*. One, *Baal-judah* (the correct reading of 2 S 6^{2}; cf 1 Ch 13^{6}), is clearly of Hebrew origin, *Baal* here being a name for Yahweh. Special interest attaches to the names of two clans in the S. and centre of Palestine, *Jacob-el* and *Joseph-el*, mentioned by Thothmes III. (*c* 1500 B.C.) in his inscription at Thebes. Corresponding with these forms are *Israel*, *Ishmael*, *Jezreel*, *Jabneel*, *Jiphtah-el*, *Jekabzeel*, *Joktheel*, in the OT. The *el* of the termination was the local deity, invoked (Gray, pp. 214 ff), or declared to have conferred some boon on his worshippers (Meyer, *ZAW*, 1886, p. 5).
J. T.

NANAEA (2 Mac $1^{13, 15}$; Gr. *Nanaia*).—The present consensus is that a remote divine ancestress of the Maccabaean Nanaea was the very ancient Sumerian goddess Nana, 'lady of the temple E-anna' and special protectress of the city of Uruk (Erech), who was recurrently invoked by name in Babylonian litanies. Records and remains of Nana-Nanaea cults have been recognized in Phoenicia, Syria, Mesopotamia, Iran, Bactria, Armenia, and in other parts of Asia Minor.

By the Greeks this goddess was identified sometimes with Artemis, sometimes with Aphrodite. She seems to have represented the productive powers of nature. In 2 Mac 1^{10-17} we have a legendary account of the death of Antiochus IV. Epiphanes, who is said to have attempted to plunder a temple of Nanaea in Persia, and to have been treacherously killed in the temple by the priests. According to 1 Mac 6^{1-4}, it was the wealthy Persian city of Elymais, its temple filled with treasure left there by Alexander the Great, which Antiochus attempted to plunder.
H. R. W.

NAOMI.—The wife of Elimelech the Ephrathite, of Beth-lehem-Judah, who was driven by famine into the land of Judah. After the death of her husband and her two sons, she returned, accompanied by Ruth, to her own land. Her return was a matter of surprise to the people of Bethlehem, and they said, 'Is this Naomi?' Her answer included a play of words on her own name, 'Call me not Naomi ('pleasant'), call me Mara ('bitter'): for the Almighty has dealt very bitterly with me' (Ru 1^{2ff}).

NAPHATH-DOR.—See DOR.

NAPHOTH-DOR.—See DOR.

NAPHISH.—A son of Ishmael, Gn 25^{15}, 1 Ch 1^{31}. In all probability it is his descendants who are mentioned in Ezr 2^{50} as 'the children of **Nephisim**' (RV and RSV) or **Nephusim** (AV and RVm). In the parallel passage (Neh 7^{52}) the reading is **Nephushesim** (RV and RSV) or **Nephishesim** (AV and RVm). In 1 Es 5^{31} RSV has **Nephisim** (AV and RV **Naphisi**).

NAPHISI, 1 Es 5^{31} (AV, RV).—See NEPHISIM.

NAPHTALI.—The second son of Bilhah, Rachel's handmaid, and the sixth son of Jacob (Gn 30^{7ff} J). The tradition connects the story in a vague way with the word 'twist, wrestle': *naphtûle 'elōhîm niphtaltî*—'With great wrestlings have I wrestled (and have prevailed),' Rachel exclaimed when Naphtali was born, 'and she called his name Naphtali.'

P ascribes to Naphtali four sons when Jacob and his family entered Egypt (Gn 46[24]), and these are said to have developed into families at the time of the Exodus, their number being given as 53,400 in the Sinai census (Nu 1[42]), and 45,000 in that in Moab (26[48]). None of these clan-names given here, except Guni, appears again outside of the genealogy repeated in 1 Ch 7[13]. In the march through the desert Naphtali is associated traditionally with Dan and Asher in 'the Camp of Dan' with a total of 157,000 men of war. Apart from Scriptural genealogies, the fact that Dan chose to migrate to the vicinity of Naphtali suggests a bond of kinship. Their descent from the concubine Bilhah indicates that they were tribes of minor significance in the national development.

Naphtali was the sixth to receive its lot (Jos 19[32-39]). Its territory is somewhat more precisely defined than the others, though few of the places can be certainly identified. Nineteen towns are mentioned in its territory, most of which are not found again in the OT, partly due to the fact that much of the highland of Naphtali was off the main thoroughfares of history and partly to the fact that the national history was enacted mainly in the regions further south. The district reached on the N. to the Anti-Lebanon and almost to the Lebanon. Southward it extended along the Jordan until it reached the confluence of the *Wâdī Bireh* and Jordan S. of the Sea of Galilee. The greater part lay NW. of the Sea of Galilee. The soil and climate of the district are both favourable, with abundant rainfall. Upland plains and pockets of earth, both in Upper and Lower Galilee yield corn, and the hillside vines, olives, and other fruits, while the lakeside, if somewhat enervating, is prolific in semi-tropical growth. The couplet on Naphtali in the 'Blessing of Jacob' (Gn 49[21]) seems to allude to this fertility (reading *'elāh shᵉlûḥāh*, 'a spreading oak,' after LXX, for *'ayyālāh shᵉlûḥāh*, EV 'a hind let loose,' and *nōthᵉnāh 'ᵃmīrê shāpher*, 'which puts forth beautiful branches,' for *hannōthēn 'imrê shāpher*, RV 'who gives goodly words'). Though much of Naphtali lay off the beaten track, trade-routes ran through the district from Bethshan northwards, from the E. end of the Plain of Jezreel northwards by *Tūrʿân* and *Lûbiyeh*, and from the W. through the Plain of the *Baṭṭûf* and so to the Plain of Chinnereth and northwards by Hazor and onwards to Damascus over Jordan or northwards to the *Biqāʿ* and so to *Ḥamā*.

Though the 'Blessing of Jacob' and the 'Blessing of Moses' (Dt 33[23]) note only the productivity of Naphtali, its heroism and warlike daring was sung in the Song of Deborah (Jg 5), and in the prose version recording the conflict against Sisera the leader Barak is derived from Kedesh-Naphtali. Hiram, the worker in metal, whom Solomon brought from Tyre to work on the Temple, was a man of Naphtali (1 K 7[14]; cf 2 Ch 2[14], which states that he was from Dan). Otherwise few names of prominence from Naphtali appear in connexion with the national life. After the rise of the kingdom of Damascus after the death of Solomon, Naphtali must have suffered much through her exposure in the far north, and the strength of her chief fortress, Hazor, bears witness to the strategic significance of this district. Under the Syrian king Benhadad especially, Naphtali seems to have suffered (1 K 15[20]). On the collapse of Damascus Naphtali bore the brunt of Assyrian assault and her strongholds were captured by Tiglath-pileser III. in 734 B.C., when there was wholesale depopulation (2 K 15[29]), the district being organized as an Assyrian province, called Megiddo after its administrative centre.
J. A. C.—**J. Gr.**

NAPHTHA.—See NEPHTHAR.

NAPHTUHIM.—Fourth son of Mizraim, Gn 10[13], 1 Ch 1[11]. It stands for the people of Lower Egypt (see *KB*). The name appears to be in Ashurbanipal's *Annals* in the form *Nathu*, probably in Lower Egypt.

NAPKIN (*soudarion*).—The cloth in which the unprofitable servant wrapped the money of his lord (Lk 19[20]); used to cover the face of the dead (Jn 20[7], but 11[44] 'a cloth'); carried, possibly as indicated by the name (Lat. *sudarium*), to wipe off perspiration (Ac 19[12]). The Arabic renders *mandîl*, which may be either 'towel,' 'napkin,' 'veil,' or 'head-band.' See also DRESS, **5** (*a*), **8**.
W. E.

NARCISSUS.—St. Paul, in Ro 16[11], salutes among others 'those in the Lord who belong to the family of Narcissus,' *i.e.* the Christian members of the slave household of Narcissus. The name is common among slaves and freedmen in the imperial age, but the expression seems to point to a well-known person, and if so the most probable identification is with a rich and powerful freedman named Narcissus in the service of the Emperor Claudius, referred to by several contemporary authors, who was put to death in the first year of Nero's reign, shortly before this Epistle was written. The normal custom would have been for his household to pass into the hands of the Emperor, retaining the name of the former owner. J. L.

NASBAS, To 11[18] (AV, RV).—See NADAB, **5.**

NASI, 1 Es 5[32] (RV).—See NEZIAH.

NASITH, 1 Es 5[32] (AV).—See NEZIAH.

NATHAN.—**1.** Third son of David by Bath-sheba (2 S 5[14], but note 2 S 12[24]). In Zec 12[12] the Nathan who is recognized as head of a house is probably David's son. In Lk 3[31] the genealogy of Jesus is traced through Nathan to David. **2.** The prophet, a confidential adviser of David. The king desired to build the Temple, and Nathan at first agreed, but later received a revelation forbidding the enterprise (2 S 7). The next appearance of Nathan is in connexion with the parable of the ewe lamb, by which David was self-convicted of his sin with Bath-sheba (2 S 12[1-15]). Later, in token that an atonement has been made, he adds to Solomon's name the significant title *Jedidiah* ('beloved of Jah').—The third service was rendered alike to David and to Solomon. Adonijah had planned a *coup* by which to grasp the sceptre, now falling from the hands of his aged father. It was Nathan's watchfulness that discovered the plot, and his ingenuity that saved the kingdom for Solomon (1 K 1). His service to Solomon was recognized by the king, who appointed his sons, Azariah and Zabud, to important offices (1 K 4[5]). **3.** Father of Igal, one of David's heroes (2 S 23[36]). The text of 1 Ch 11[38] reads, 'Joel brother of Nathan.' **4.** One of the chief men who returned with Ezra (Ezr 8[16], 1 Es 8[44]). **5.** One of the Bani family, who had taken strange wives (Ezr 10[39]); called in 1 Es 9[34] **Nethaniah** (AV, RV **Nathanias**). **6.** A Judahite (1 Ch 2[36]). J. H. St.

NATHANAEL.—**1.** A Greek form subsequently used in the Septuagint for the Hebrew name Nathanel. There it refers to a variety of minor figures (Nu 1[8] 2[5] 7[18, 23] 10[15], 1 Ch 2[14] 15[24] 24[6] 26[4], 2 Ch 17[7] 35[9], 1 Es 1[9] (AV, RV; RSV **Nethanel** [q.v.]) 9[22] (see NETHANEL, **8**), 2 Es 10[22] 22[21], Jth 8[1]). **2.** A disciple of Jesus mentioned only in the Gospel of John. There he appears twice, once in a dramatic account of his call to discipleship (Jn 1[45-49]) and again after the resurrection in a scene by the Sea of Tiberias (Jn 21[2]). In the latter passage he is said to be 'of Cana in Galilee.' Many fruitless attempts have been made to link him with one of the twelve disciples listed in the Synoptic Gospels (especially Bartholomew) and even with other personages. W. R. S.

NATHANIAS, 1 Es 9[34] (AV, RV).—See NATHAN, **5.**

NATHAN-MELECH.—An official in the reign of Josiah, whose name is used to designate one of the halls or chambers of the Temple, 2 K 23[11].

NATIONS.—In many places where in the AV we have '**Gentiles**' and '**heathen,**' RV and RSV have rightly substituted 'nations,' and might with advantage have carried out the change consistently.

The Hebrew (*gôy*) and Greek (*ethnos*) words denote invariably a nation or a people, never a person. Where in the AV (only NT) we find 'Gentile' in the singular (Ro 2[9f]) the RV, RSV have 'Greek,' following the original. In nearly every example the singular ' nation ' stands for ' Israel,' though we have a few exceptions, as in Ex 9^{24} (of Egypt), Pr 14^{34} (general), and Mt 21^{43}. It is often applied to Israel and Judah when there is an implication of disobedience to God, sinfulness, and the like: see Dt 32^{28}, Is 1^{4} etc. This shade of meaning became very common in the later writings of the OT. Quite early in Israelitish history the singular as a term for Israel was discarded for the word translated **' people '** (*'am*), so that *'am* (' people ') and *gôy* (' nation ') came to be almost antithetic terms=' Israelites ' and ' non-Israelites,' as in Rabbinical Hebrew. For the reason of the change in the use of *gôy* (' nation '), see below.

In the AV **' Gentiles '** often corresponds to ' Greeks ' in the original, as in Jn 7^{35}, Ro 3^{9} etc. In the RV, RSV the word ' Greeks ' is rightly substituted, though the sense is the same, for to the Jews of the time Greek culture and religion stood for the culture and religion of the non-Jewish world.

The two words (Hebrew and Greek) translated ' nation ' have their original and literal sense in many parts of the OT and NT, as in Gn 10$^{5, 20}$ etc., Is 2^{4} (=Mic 4^{2f}), Job 12^{23}, Ac 17^{26}, Gal 3^{14}. In other passages this general meaning is narrowed so as to embrace the descendants of Abraham, *e.g.* in Gn 12^{2} 18^{18} 17$^{4ff, 16}$. But it is the plural that occurs by far the most frequently, standing almost invariably for non-Israelitish nations, generally with the added notion of their being idolatrous and immoral: see, *e.g.* Ex 9^{24} 34^{10}, Lv 25^{44ff}, Nu 14^{15}, Dt 15^{6}, 1 K 4^{31}, Is 11$^{10, 12}$. These are contrasted with Israel ' the people of Yahweh ' in 2 S 7^{23}, 1 Ch 17^{21} etc.

This contrast between Israel (united or divided into the kingdoms of Israel and Judah) as Yahweh's people, and all the rest of the human race designated ' nations,' runs right through the OT. Such a conception could have arisen only after the Israelites had developed the consciousness of national unity and of being a special people under the covenant. At first, even among the Israelites, it seems that there was current the belief that other gods existed besides Yahweh and that each nation was justified in worshipping its own deity. Under the covenant, however, Israel was not permitted to worship any god but Yahweh (see Ex 20^{3}, Dt 32^{4} 10^{17}, 1 S 26^{19}, 1 K 8^{23}, Is 19^{1} etc.). As long as this idea prevailed there could be no necessary antagonism between Israelites and **foreign nations,** except that which was national, for the nation's god was identified with the national interests. But when the belief in Yahweh's absolute and exclusive claims possessed the mind of Israel, as it began to do in the time of the earliest literary prophets (see Am 9^{7}, Mic 7^{18}, Is 2$^{2-5}$), the nations came to be regarded as worshippers of idols (Lv 18^{21}), and in Ps 9$^{5, 15, 17}$ (cf Ezk 7^{21}) ' nations ' and ' wicked people ' are, as being identical, put in parallelism. It will be gathered from what has been said, that the hostile feelings with which Israelites regarded other peoples varied at different times. At all periods it would be modified by the laws of hospitality (see article STRANGER), by political alliances (cf Is 7^{1ff}, and 2 K 16^{5ff}, Ahaz and Assyria against Israel and Syria), and by the needs of commerce (see Ezk 27^{11} [Tyre], 1 K 9^{28} 10^{11}, 2 K 16$^{5-7}$).

The reforms instituted by king Josiah in the Southern Kingdom (2 K 22^{1ff}), based upon the Deuteronomic law newly found in the Temple, aimed at stamping out all syncretism in religion and establishing the pure religion of Yahweh. This reformation, as also the Rechabite movement (Jer 35), had a profound influence upon the thoughts and feelings of Israel, as the people of God, widening the gulf between them and **alien** nations. The teaching of the oldest prophets also had looked in the same direction (see Am 2^{11} 3^{15} 5$^{11, 25}$ 6^{8} 8^{5}, Hos 2^{19} 8^{14} 9^{10} 10^{13} 12^{7ff} 14^{4}, Is 2^{6} 10^{4} 17^{10}, Zeph 1$^{8, 11}$, Jer 35^{1ff} 37^{6f} etc.).

But the Deuteronomic law (the basis of Josiah's reform, 621 B.C.) made legally obligatory what earlier teachers had inculcated. Israelites were not to marry non-Israelites (Dt 7^{3}), or to have any except unavoidable dealings with them.

The feeling of national exclusiveness and antipathy was intensified by the captivity in Babylon, when the prophetic and priestly instructors of the exiled Jews taught them that their calamities came upon them on account of their disloyalty to Yahweh and the ordinances of His religion, and because they compromised with idolatrous practices and heathen nations. It was in Babylon that Ezekiel drew up the programme of worship and organization for the nation after the Return, laying stress on the doctrine that Israel was to be a holy people, separated from other nations (see Ezk 40–48). Some time after the Return, Ezra and Nehemiah had to contend with the laxity to which Jews who had remained in the homeland and others had yielded; but they were uncompromising, and won the battle for nationalism in religion, thereby protecting themselves against pagan influences.

Judaism was in even greater danger of being lost in the world-currents of speculation and religion soon after the time of Alexander the Great. Indeed, but for the brave Maccabaean rising in the earlier half of the 2nd cent. B.C., both the religion and the language of the Jew might, humanly speaking, have perished.

The Apocrypha speaks of the ' nations ' just as do the later writings of the OT. They are ' uncircumcised,' ' having sold themselves to do evil ' (1 Mac 1^{15}); they break the Sabbath, offer no sacrifice to Yahweh, eat unclean food and such as has been offered to idols (1 Mac 1^{43} 2$^{15f, 23, 44}$ 6^{21}, 2 Mac 5^{18} 15^{1f}).

The NT reveals the same attitude towards foreign nations on the part of the Jews (see Ac 10^{45} *et passim*). In Rabbinical writings Jewish exclusiveness manifested itself even more decisively (see *SB*, iv, 353–414). But, as in the OT a broader spirit shows itself constantly, culminating in the universalism of Christianity, so enlightened and broadminded Jews in all ages have deprecated the fanatical race-hatred which many of their compatriots have displayed. T. W. D.—H. S. G.

NATURAL.—The contrast between ' natural ' (Gr. *psychikos*; RSV ' physical ') and ' spiritual ' (*pneumatikos*) is drawn out by St. Paul in 1 Co 15$^{44-46}$. The natural body is derived from the first Adam, and is our body in so far as it is accommodated to, and limited by, the needs of the animal side of the human nature. In such a sense it is especially true that ' the unspiritual man does not receive the gifts of the Spirit of God ' (1 Co 2^{14}). Man derives his spiritual life from union with Christ (' the last Adam '), but his present body is not adapted to the needs of this spiritual existence; hence the distinction made by St. Paul between the natural body (called the ' body of death,' Ro 7^{24}) and the spiritual body of the resurrection. The transference from the one to the other begins in this life, and the two beings are identical in so far as continuity creates an identity, but otherwise, owing to the operation of the union with Christ, distinct.

For the non-theological use of ' natural ' see Ja 1^{23}. T. A. M.—F. C. G.

NATURE.—The term ' nature ' is not used in the OT, nor was the conception current in Hebrew thought, as God alone is seen in all, through all, and over all. The idea came with the word *physis* from Hellenism. Swine's flesh is commended for food as a gift of *nature* in 4 Mac 5^{7}. In the NT the term is used in various senses: (1) the forces, laws, and order of the world, including man (Ro 1^{26} 11$^{21, 24}$, Gal 4^{8}); (2) the inborn sense of propriety or morality (1 Co 11^{14}, Ro 2^{14}); (3) birth or physical origin (Gal 2^{15}, Ro 2^{27}); (4) the sum of characteristics of a species or person, human (Ja 3^{7}), or Divine (2 P 1^{4}); (5) a condition acquired or inherited (Eph 2^{3} ' by nature children of wrath '). What is contrary to nature is condemned. While the term is not found or the conception made explicit in the OT, Schultz (*OT Theol.* ii, 74) finds in the Law ' the general rule that nothing is to be permitted contrary to the delicate sense of the inviolable proprieties of nature,' and gives a number of instances (Ex 23^{19} 34^{26}, Lv 22^{28} 19^{19}, Dt 22$^{9-11}$, Lv 10^{9} 19^{28} 21^{5} 22^{24}, Dt 14^{1} 23^{2}). The beauty and the order of the world are recognized as evidence of Divine wisdom and power (Ps 8[1] 19[1] 33[6f] 90[2] 104, 136[6ff] 147, Pr 8[22-30], Job 38, 39)) ; but the sum of created things is not hypostatized and personified apart from God, as in much current modern thinking. God is Creator, Preserver, and Ruler. He makes all (Is 44[24], Am 4[13]), and is in all (Ps 139). His immanence is by His Spirit (Gn 1[2]). Jesus recognizes God's bounty and care in the flowers of the field and the birds of the air (Mt 6[26, 28]) ; He uses natural processes to illustrate spiritual, in salt (5[13]), seed and soil (13[3-9]), and leaven (13[33]). The growth of the seed is also used as an illustration by Paul (1 Co 15[37, 38]). There is in the Bible no interest in nature apart from God, and the problem of the relation of God to nature has not yet risen on the horizon of the thought of the writers. Nor is there anything like the ethical maxim of the Stoics, ' Follow Nature,' to be found in the NT. Instead, ' the creation was subjected to futility ' (Ro 8[20]), and the natural order is subject to the will of God only in a limited way : viz. it reflects the Divine power more clearly than it does the Divine purpose (Ro 1[20], 1 Co 15[20-28]). A. E. G.—**F. C. G.**

NAUGHT.—' Naught ' is ' nothing ' (from A.S. *na* ' not ' and *wiht* ' a whit *or* a thing '). Sometimes the spelling became ' nought ' (perhaps under the influence of ' ought '). In the earliest editions of AV there is no difference between ' naught ' and ' nought ' ; but in the edition of 1638 a difference was introduced, naught being used in 2 K 2[19], Pr 20[14] (so RSV), because there the meaning is ' bad ' ; ' nought ' everywhere else, but with the meaning ' worthlessness.' This distinction was preserved by Scrivener in his *Cambr. Par. Bible*, and is found in most modern English Bibles. RSV has the spelling ' naught ' at Ezk 12[22] and Hab 2[13], but elsewhere ' nought,' apparently without distinction (cf ' comes to naught,' Ezk 12[22], and ' comes to nought,' Ps 112[10], Pr 10[28] 11[7] ; and ' for naught,' Hab 2[13], and ' for nought,' Jer 51[55]).

' Naughty,' however, is simply ' worthless,' as Jer 24[2] ' very naughty figs ' (RV, RSV ' bad '). But **' naughtiness '** always means ' wickedness,' as Pr 11[6] ' transgressors shall be taken in their own naughtiness ' (RV ' mischief,' RSV ' lust '), and 1 S 17[28] ' the naughtiness of thine heart ' (so RV ; RSV ' evil ').

NAUM, Lk 3[25] (AV).—See NAHUM.

NAVE.—The form in which (possibly by a primitive error in transcription of the Greek) the Hebrew name **Nun** appears in AV of Sir 46[1].

NAVY.—See SHIPS AND BOATS.

NAZARENE, NAZORAEAN.—So Jesus is called in the Greek text (Mk 1[24] 10[47] 14[67] 16[6], Lk 4[34] 24[19]), for *Nazarēnos* is evidently intended to mean ' the one from Nazareth,' as *Magdalēnē* (Jn 20[18]) is ' the one from Magdala.' It is questionable, however, whether the form *Nazōraios* (used of Jesus in Mt 2[23] in connexion with the settlement of his parents at Nazareth, and in Mt 26[71], Lk 18[37], Jn 18[5, 7] 19[19], Ac 2[22] 3[6] 4[10] 6[14] 22[8] 26[9] and in the plural of Christians, Ac 24[5]) is a variant of *Nazarēnos*. Mt 2[23] vaguely alludes to prophecy ; the Evangelist may have in mind the passage about the ' branch ' (Is 11[1], Heb. *nēṣer*). However, this is merely a reflection on the name. The possibility that *Nazōraios* was a sectarian name (a formation like *Pharisaios*= Pharisee) cannot be discounted. In the translations ' Nazarene ' or ' of Nazareth ' is used. E. G. K.

NAZARETH.—The place from which Jesus came (Mk 1[9]), where He was reared (Lk 4[16]), where his parents lived (Lk 1[26] 2[4]) or settled (Mt 2[23]), and with which His name was associated (see NAZARENE). It is described as ' in Galilee ' (Mt 2[23]). The name-form is variously written in the Greek MSS : Nazerath, Nazaret, and Nazara also occurring. The correct form philologically must have been *Nāṣerāth*—a formation similar to that of Daberath (Jos 19[12]). The place is not mentioned in the OT or the Talmud or Josephus ; the oldest allusions to it are those in the Gospels. Its insignificance is reflected in Nathanael's remark (Jn 1[46]). The tenacious survival of the name in *en-Nāṣira* is noteworthy. That the Christians of Palestine should have lost sight of a town so prominently mentioned in the Gospels seems incredible, and so the tradition seeking it at *en-Nāṣira* is doubtless correct. The town seems to have been exclusively non-Christian until Constantine's time. Byzantine and Crusader structures here were later obliterated. The present Christian identification of holy places at Nazareth is mainly due to the Franciscan monks, who endured much persecution here at the hands of Islam. Christian interest has centred particularly on the Well of Mary as a point certain to have been frequented by Jesus' mother. However, it seems very probable that this spring was too remote from the ancient settlement, which probably lay farther south. The location of the synagogue in which Jesus preached (Lk 4[16]) invites interest owing to the local description attending His ejection from the city (v.[29]). However, it cannot be said that traditional identifications of the site of the synagogue or of the ' brow of the hill ' are satisfactory. The archaeology of Nazareth in the time of Christ awaits probing by the spade at various points where soundings are desirable and feasible. The place is so built up that this is difficult. It is now under Israeli control. Population : 20,000. E. G. K.

NAZARITE.—The AV form of Nazirite (q.v.).

NAZIRITE (AV **Nazarite**).—The primary meaning of the Hebrew verb *nāzar* is to separate. Hence the *nāzîr* is ' the separated,' ' consecrated,' ' devoted.' Joseph is ' the Nazirite,' *i.e.* the consecrated prince, among his brethren (Gn 49[26]) ; the nobles of Jerusalem bear the same title (La 4[7]) ; the untrimmed vine, whose branches recall the long hair of the Nazirite proper, is called ' thy Nazirite ' (Lv 25[5, 11]). But, above all, the name belongs to a class of persons devoted by a special vow to Yahweh (Am 2[11f], Jg 13[5, 7] 16[17], Nu 6, Sir 46[13], 1 Mac 3[49-53]). According to Jg 13 and Nu 6, the details of outward observance covered by the vow were : (1) abstinence from the fruit of the vine, (2) leaving the hair uncut, (3) avoidance of contact with the dead, and (4) of all unclean food.

Opinions differ as to whether the abstinence from wine or the untrimmed hair was the more important. Am 2[11f] mentions only the former. 1 S 1[11], on the other hand, refers only to the latter (the LXX ' and he shall drink no wine or strong drink ' being an interpolation). If we look outside the OT, we see that among the ancients generally the hair was regarded as so important an outcome of the physical life as to be a fit offering to the deity, and a means of initiating or restoring communion with Him. There is evidence for this from Syria, Arabia, Egypt, Greece, Rome, and, in recent times, even among the Maoris. This, then, seems to have been the original observance. If Am 2[11f] does not mention it, the reason is that the most attractive temptation was found in the wine. Jg 13[7] states that Samson's mother was bidden to abstain, but the same is not affirmed of Samson himself ; all the stress, in his case, is laid on the hair being untouched (Jg 16[17]). Nu 6[3f] puts the abstinence first, but even here the significance of the other point appears in the directions for the ceremonial shaving and oblation of the hair (Nu 6[18]). The vine stood for the culture and civilization of Canaan, and was specially associated with the worship of the nature-gods. Hence it was a point of honour with the zealots of Yahweh to turn away from it utterly. The luxury and immorality connected with a more advanced civilization threatened the simplicity of Israel's life and faith. Martial devotion coalesced with the ascetic spirit to produce such men as Jonadab, son of Rechab, who resembled the Nazirites very closely (2 K 10[15], Jer 35[6f]).

It may be remarked that the regulations concerning what von Rad has called ' the Holy War ' are closely related to the institution of the Naziriteship. Those who dedicated themselves to the Holy War allowed their hair to grow (Jg 5[2], where most authorities agree that the

Hebrew *pᵉrōaʿ pᵉrāʿôth* should be rendered 'for the loosing of locks,' *i.e.* allowing the hair to remain unshorn), and refrained from sexual intercourse (cf 1 S 21^{4f}) during the campaign.

The Nazirite vow was originally a life-long obligation. Young and enthusiastic men were moved by the Spirit of God to take it up, as others were inspired to be prophets, and it was an offence against Him to tempt them to break it (Am 2^{11f}). Women were divinely bidden to devote their promised offspring (Jg 13^7). Others prayed for children and promised that they should then be consecrated to this service (1 S 1^{11}; it is noteworthy that in the Hebrew and Syriac of Sir 46^{13}, Samuel is expressly called a Nazirite). In course of time, however, a great change came over the purpose and spirit of the institution. The vow was now taken to gain some personal end—protection on a journey, deliverance from sickness, etc. Women, too, became Nazirites. And the restrictions were only for a certain period. Nu 6 represents this stage, but the information which it gives needs supplementing. For instance, it fails to prescribe the manner in which the vow should be entered on. The Talmud asserts that this was done in private, and was binding if one simply said, 'Behold, I am a Nazirite,' or repeated after another, 'I also become one' (*Nazir*, i. 3, iii. 1, iv. 1). Nu 6 does not determine the length of these temporary vows. Here, again, a rule had to be made, and it was decided that the person himself might fix the period; otherwise, it should be thirty days (*Nazir*, i. 3, iii. 1; Jos *BJ* II. xv. 1 [313]). In case of accidental defilement, the Nazirite had to undergo seven days' purification, cut off his hair on the seventh day and have it buried (*Temurah*, vi. 4), on the eighth day bring two turtle-doves or two young pigeons, one for a sin-offering, one for a burnt-offering, as well as a lamb for a guilt-offering, and thus begin the course of his vow afresh (cf *Nazir*, iii. 6). At the expiration of the time he was brought to the door of the sanctuary, with a he-lamb for a burnt-offering, a ewe-lamb for a sin-offering, a ram for a peace-offering, ten unleavened cakes and ten unleavened wafers anointed with oil, a meat-offering, and a drink-offering. When the sacrifices had been offered his hair was shaved and he put it in the fire which was under the peace-offering, or under the cauldron in which the latter was boiled (*Nazir*, vi. 8). Then a wave-offering was made, consisting of the sodden shoulder of the ram, a cake, and a wafer. The fat was then salted and burned on the altar, and the breast and the foreleg were eaten by the priests, who also ate the waved cake and the boiled shoulder: the rest of the bread and meat belonged to the offerer (Maimonides, *Hilchoth, Maase ha-Corbanoth*, ix. 9–11). A free-will offering followed (Nu 6^{21}). In the second Temple there was a chamber in the SE. corner of the women's court, where the Nazirites boiled their peace-offerings, cut off their hair and cast it into the cauldron.

The following historical notices are of some interest: (1) 1 Mac 3^{49-53} enables us to realize the importance which came to be attached to the punctilious performance of every one of the ceremonies. Just before the battle of Emmaus, the Nazirites, being shut out of Jerusalem, could not offer the concluding sacrifices there. Evidently this was regarded as a serious public calamity. (2) The important tractate of the Talmud entitled *Berakhoth* tells a story of slightly later date than the above, which illustrates the ingenuity which the Rabbis displayed in finding reasons for releasing from their vows persons who had rashly undertaken them (vii. 2). (3) John the Baptist has been claimed as a Nazirite, but this is doubtful; we read nothing about his hair being untouched. (4) A custom grew up for wealthy people to provide the requisite sacrifices for their poorer brethren. Thus, when Agrippa came from Rome to Jerusalem to enter on his kingdom, 'he offered many sacrifices of thanksgiving; wherefore also he ordered that many of the Nazirites should have their heads shaven' (Jos. *Ant.* XIX. vi. 1 [294]). This throws light on Ac 21^{23-26}. (5) Eusebius (*HE* ii. 23) appears to represent James the Just as a lifelong Nazirite: 'He was holy from his mother's womb. Wine and strong drink he drank not, neither did he eat flesh. A razor passed not over his head.' But the further statement that he alone was permitted to enter the Holy of Holies is so improbable as to lessen our confidence in the narrator.

J. T.—**S. H. He.**

NEAH.—A place in Zebulun, Jos 19^{13}. It is possibly modern *Tell el-Wâwiyât*.

NEAPOLIS.—The harbour of Philippi, at which St. Paul landed (Ac 16^{11}) after sailing from Troas. It lay on the coast of Macedonia opposite Thasos, being situated on a promontory with a harbour on each side. It was about ten miles from Philippi. The Via Egnatia from Dyrrhachium, after passing through Thessalonica, Amphipolis, and Philippi, reached the coast again at Neapolis, and the regular course of travellers to Asia was not to continue farther by land, but to cross by ship to Troas. The modern name of Neapolis is *Kavalla*. A. E. H.

NEARIAH.—**1.** A descendant of David, 1 Ch 3^{22f}. **2.** A Simeonite, 1 Ch 4^{42}.

NEBAI.—One of those who sealed the covenant, Neh 10^{19} (RV **Nobai**). See NEBO, **3.**

NEBAIOTH.—An important tribe of North Arabians. In Gn 25^{13} (AV **Nebajoth**), 1 Ch 1^{29} Nebaioth is the eldest son of **Ishmael**; also the representative of the Ishmaelite tribes in Gn 28^9 36^3 (AV **Nebajoth**). The people of Nebaioth have an important place among the Arabian tribes subdued by Ashurbanipal of Assyria, named by him along with the people of **Kedar** (q.v.), just as in the genealogy of Genesis. It is about this date (650 B.C.) that they come into prominence among the competing tribes of the peninsula—a position which they retained for centuries. Their exact location cannot be definitely determined, but the inscriptions tell us that they were very remote from Assyria, and their place at the head of the tribes of Ishmael, as well as their affiliation with the **Edomites** (Gn 28 and 36) makes it probable that they were well known to the Hebrews. Hence they are to be sought for not far from the south-eastern borders of Palestine. The time when they flourished agrees with the fact that in the Bible they are mentioned only in the late Priestly Code and by the 'Third Isaiah' (Is 60^7). They are usually, but wrongly, identified with the **Nabataeans** (q.v.). J. F. McC.

NEBAJOTH, Gn 25^{13} 28^9 36^3 (AV).—See NEBAIOTH.

NEBALLAT.—A town inhabited by Benjamites, Neh 11^{34}; probably the modern *Beit Nebâlā*, 3½ miles NE. of Lydda.

NEBAT.—Father of Jeroboam I. (1 K 11^{26} and onwards). The constant designation of Jeroboam I. as 'ben-Nebat' is probably the usage of a writer later than Jeroboam ben-Joash. It is intended, doubtless, to distinguish the two kings.

NEBO (Assyr. *Nabū*, 'Announcer').—A Babylonian deity who presided over literature and science. The cuneiform system of writing was credited to his invention. He was the son and messenger of Bel-Marduk; whose will to mortals he interpreted. The planet Mercury was sacred to Nebo. The chief centre of his worship was the temple of E-zida in Borsippa, between which and the temple of Marduk in Babylon took place the great annual processions of which we find a reminiscence in Is 46^{1f}. The name Nebo appears as an element in many Babylonian names—Nebuchadrezzar, Nebuzaradan, Abed-nego (properly Abed-nebo), etc. W. M. N.

NEBO.—The name of a mountain in Moab, a Moabite town, and possibly a town in Judah. The etymology of the name is uncertain. According to one view, these places were named after the Babylonian deity Nebo (see preceding article), an indication of the influence of this Babylonian cult at a remote period both E. and W. of the Jordan. Other scholars, pointing out that there is no proof that the Hebrews and Moabites used the name of a foreign deity in this way (cf Nu 32^{38}), suggest that the name corresponds to the Arabic *naba'a*, denoting a high place or elevation. If the latter is correct, the Moabite town may have received its name from the mountain which had served in primitive times as a place of worship for various deities.

1. Mount Nebo is the traditional site of Moses' view of Canaan (Dt 34^{1f}) and of his death (Dt 32^{50}). It is described as being in the land of Moab, opposite Jericho, in the mountains of Abarim (Nu 33^{47}, Dt 32^{49}). Although the Hebrew of Dt 34^{1} is not clear, the phrase 'from the plains of Moab to Mount Nebo, to the top of Pisgah' may indicate that Nebo was the summit of Pisgah (q.v.), or another name for Pisgah (cf Dt 3^{27}). There can be no question that this description implies some point on the edge of the great plateau of Moab, which drops steeply some 4000 feet to the Jordan Valley or the Dead Sea. From several peaks in the region an admirable view can be had of ancient Gilead, the Jordan valley and the mountains of Canaan, but from none of them is there a view of the Mediterranean Sea, as Dt 34^{2} suggests was visible from Mount Nebo. If this verse is not interpreted literally, there appears to be good reason for identifying Mount Nebo with the peak now called *Jebel en-Nebā*, the Arab name of an elevation of about 2700 feet. This identification might be regarded as certain if we could feel sure that *Nebā* is really an ancient name, and not merely, as it may be, the name attached to the summit after tradition had claimed it as the Nebo of the Bible. *Nebā* lies about 12 miles almost due E. of the Jordan at the point where the river enters the Dead Sea, and is one of the summits that can be ascended from the steppes of Moab. Although it is not the highest peak in the region, it fits the geographical description of Mount Nebo in Dt 32^{49} 34^{1f} as well as any other. The presence of Iron Age sherds (*c* 1200 B.C.) on the slopes near *Nebā* is archaeological evidence of occupation during OT times (cf Nelson Glueck, *The Other Side of the Jordan* [1940], pp. 143–145). Surface exploration has added greatly to our knowledge of this Moabite region (cf *AASOR*, xv [1935], 109–111), but the exact burial place of Moses remains unknown. An early Christian tradition identified Mount Nebo with *Râs Siyâghah*, an elevation joined by a 'saddle' to the summit of *Nebā*. Extensive excavations were carried out on *Râs Siyâghah* from 1933 to 1937 by the Franciscans of Jerusalem (see S. Saller, *The Memorial of Moses on Mount Nebo*, Part I, The Text; Part II, The Plates [1941]). Several buildings, including the remains of Byzantine churches, were uncovered, indicating that Christian worship was conducted at the place from late Roman times to the early Arabic period. However, no remains from OT times were discovered that would identify *Siyâghah* with Mount Nebo. The most that can be claimed is that early Christian tradition attempted to preserve the memory of Moses at *Siyâghah* (cf *Quart. of the Dept. of Antiq. in Palestine*, vi [1938], 220 f), that Mount Nebo must have been in this region, *Jebel en-Nebā* being the most probable site.

2. The Moabite town called Nebo was located near or on Mount Nebo, and is listed among other Moabite towns where grazing of cattle was possible and in which the people of the tribes of Gad and Reuben hoped to settle (Nu 32$^{1-5}$). The Reubenites built (or rebuilt) the town of Nebo (Nu 32^{37f}); it was the scene of a Hebrew encampment (Nu 33^{47}), and later tradition associated it with the descendants of Reuben (1 Ch 5^{8}). According to the Moabite Stone (see Moab), Mesha king of Moab (*c* 850 B.C.) conquered the town: 'And Chemosh said to me, "Go, take Nebo from Israel!"' (l. 14), and following the attack, put to death all its inhabitants. Nebo is also mentioned among other Moabite towns in oracles against Moab (Is 15^{2}, Jer 48$^{1, 22}$). Uncertainty concerning the date and historical allusions of these oracles makes it impossible to determine whether Nebo was reconquered by the Hebrews or destroyed by other enemies of the Moabites such as the Babylonians. The site which best fits the description of the town is *Khirbet el-Mekhayyeṭ*. It is located less than two miles SE. of traditional Mount Nebo. The presence of the ruins of an ancient fortress and early Moabite sherds are evidence for its identification with the town of Nebo (see *AASOR*, xv [1935], 110–111).

3. The possible existence also of a town in Judah called Nebo depends on the interpretation of Ezra 2^{29} 10^{43} (cf 1 Es 9^{35}, Gr. **Nooma,** and so RV; AV **Ethma**), and Neh 7^{33}. In these passages which list the names and numbers of the Jews who returned to Judah following the Babylonian exile, the word Nebo could be the name of a person (see also Hebrew of Neh 10^{19} where **Nebai** [RV **Nobai**] is listed as a signatory to the covenant), the name of the Moabite town where the ancestors of the repatriated Jews had lived, or the name of a village in Judah. On the strength of the latter possibility and the similarity of the modern and ancient names, some scholars have located this Nebo at *Beit Nûbâ*, about 12 miles NW. of Jerusalem (cf L. H. Grollenberg, *Atlas of the Bible* [1957], p. 158). G. B. G.—**W. L. R.**

NEBUCHADNEZZAR.—See next article.

NEBUCHADREZZAR.—The *Nabū-kudur-uṣur* of the Babylonians, for which 'Nebuchad*n*ezzar' (the familiar form often retained in the pr sent work) is an error, was son and successor of Nabopolassar, founder of the Neo-Babylonian empire (604–561 B.C.). The fall of Nineveh gave Egypt a chance to reclaim Syria, and Pharaoh Neco made an attempt to regain it. Josiah fell in a vain effort to repel him (2 K 23^{29}), but Nebuchadrezzar defeated him at Carchemish (605 B.C.). He then recovered the whole of the West and seems to have been threatening Egypt when recalled to Babylon by news of his father's death. In 601 B.C. he led an unsuccessful expedition against Egypt. In a subsequent campaign in 597 B.C. he first captured Jerusalem (Dn 1^{1f}). We know little of his wars from his own inscriptions, which deal almost entirely with his buildings and pious acts at home. According to classical historians, he made Babylon one of the wonders of the world. He fortified it with a triple line of walls and a moat; he restored temples and cities throughout his kingdom. A fragment of his annals records that in his thirty-seventh year he fought against Amasis in Egypt (cf Jer 46$^{13-26}$, Ezk 29$^{2-20}$). For his relations with Judah. see Jehoiakim, Jehoiachin, Zedekiah, Gedaliah. He certainly was the greatest king of Babylon since Hammurabi. For his madness, see Medicine. C. H. W. J.—**C. J. M. W.**

NEBUSHASBAN, Jer 39^{13} (AV).—See Nebushazban.

NEBUSHAZBAN.—Rab-saris (q.v.) at the capture of Jerusalem, Jer 39^{13} (AV **Nebushasban**); Babylonian *Nabū-shezib-anni* means 'Nabu save me.' C. H. W. J.

NEBUZARADAN.—Captain of Nebuchadrezzar's bodyguard, 2 K 25$^{8-20}$, Jer 39^{9ff} 40^{10} 52^{30}: he was charged with the pacification of Judah after the fall of Jerusalem. Babylonian *Nabū-zēr-iddin* means 'Nabu has given seed.' C. H. W. J.

NECHO.—AV spelling of **Neco** (so RV, RSV) in 2 Ch 35$^{20, 22}$ 36^{4}, Jer 46^{2}.

NECHOH.—AV spelling of **Neco** (so RSV) in 2 K 23$^{29, 33ff}$.

NECK.—The most usual words are *'ōreph* and *ṣawwār* in Hebrew, and *trachēlos* in Greek. Chains upon the neck were a common ornament Pr 1^{9} etc., Ezk 16^{11}). To fall upon one another's neck has from old time been an affectionate form of greeting in the East (Gn 33^{4} etc.). The neck under yoke meant subjection and servitude (Dt 28^{48} etc.); breaking of the yoke meant deliverance (Gn 27^{40}, Jer 30^{8}). Stiff or hard of neck (Dt 31^{27} etc.) signified one difficult to guide, like a hard-necked bullock in the furrow. To put the foot upon the neck of a foe, meant his utter overthrow (Jos 10^{24} etc.). To put the neck to work (Neh 3^{5}) was a phrase equivalent to our own 'put a hand to.' W. E.

NECKLACE.—See Ornaments, **3.**

NECO.—The second king of the 26th Dynasty of Egypt, in modern works spelt *Necho* (but RSV uniformly Neco) after the Greek form of his name. He was the son of Psammetichus I. and reigned 609–594 B.C.

He tried to restore Egypt's empire in Asia and he continued his father's policy of supporting Assyria against the rising power of Babylon. The year after his accession he marched into Palestine to assist Ashur-uballiṭ, and not to attack him, as 2 K 23^{29} has been thought to imply. He defeated Josiah of Judah, who had allied himself with Babylon, at **Megiddo.** Josiah was killed in the battle and the people made Jehoahaz, his son, king in his stead. On his return from Megiddo, Neco deposed Jehoahaz and made his elder brother Eliakim king, changing Eliakim's name to Jehoiakim (2 K 23^{33f}). Heavy tribute was exacted from the new king at the expense of the people (2 K 23^{35}). Neco soon overran Syria and penetrated as far as the Euphrates. Nabopolassar, king of Babylon, sent his son Nebuchadrezzar against him and a severe defeat was inflicted on the Egyptian army at **Carchemish** in 605 B.C. (Jer 46^{2}). Neco lost all his gains in Asia. In 601 B.C. Nebuchadrezzar met Neco in another engagement in which there were heavy losses on both sides, but after which Nebuchadrezzar was forced to withdraw (see D. J. Wiseman, *Chronicles of Chaldaean Kings*, 1956).

T. W. T.

NECODAN, 1 Es 5^{37} (AV).—See NEKODA, **2.**

NECOH.—RV spelling of **Neco** (so RSV) in 2 K 23$^{29,\ 33ff}$.

NECROMANCY.—See MAGIC, DIVINATION AND SORCERY.

NECTAR.—In Ca 4^{11} RSV renders 'your lips distil nectar.' Elsewhere it renders Hebrew *nōpheth* by 'honey' (cf Pr 5^{3} 'the lips of a loose woman drip honey,' where the Hebrew is the same) or 'drippings from the honeycomb' (Pr 24^{13}).

NEDABIAH.—A descendant of David, 1 Ch 3^{18}.

NEEDLE'S EYE.—See CAMEL.

NEEDLEWORK.—See EMBROIDERY.

NEESING.—The verb 'to neese' (modern 'sneeze') occurs in the 1611 edition of AV at 2 K 4^{35}, 'the child neesed seven times.' But the 'neesing,' Job 41^{18} (AV, RV; RSV 'sneezings') of leviathan (the crocodile) means hard breathing, snorting, and does not come from the same A.S. verb as 'neese' meaning 'to sneeze.'

NEGEB, originally meaning 'the dry land,' is in most passages in the OT the name of a definite geographical area (Dt 1^{7} 34^{3}, Jos 10^{40} 12^{8} etc.); the word is, however, also used in the sense of **'South'** (Gn 13^{14}). The Negeb was often the scene of Abraham's wanderings (Gn 12^{9} 13$^{1,\ 3}$ 20^{1}); here Hagar was succoured by an angel (Gn 16$^{7,\ 14}$); Isaac (24^{62}) and Jacob (37^{1} 46^{5}) both dwelt there; through this district passed the spies (Nu 13$^{17,\ 22}$). In Nu 13^{29} the Negeb is described as belonging to the Amalekites. Later it was allotted to Simeon, and its cities are enumerated (Jos 19$^{1-9}$), some of which they shared with Judah (Jos 15$^{21-32}$). David was stationed by Achish at Ziklag just NW. of Beersheba on the borders of the Negeb (1 S 27^{6}). At this time the Negeb is described as of several parts, the Negeb of Judah, of the Jerahmeelites, and of the Kenites (1 S 27^{10}); while in 1 S 30^{14} we read of the Negeb of the Cherethites and of Caleb. Jeremiah prophesied trouble as coming on the cities of this region, but on return from captivity they too were to participate in the blessings (32^{44} 33^{13}).

The district in question was an ill-defined tract of country lying S. of Hebron, and extending some seventy miles to the *Tih* or desert. It was bounded on the E. by the Dead Sea and the Arabah, while W. it faded into the maritime plain. It was a pastoral region, wedged between the cultivated lands on the N. and the wilderness, and formed a most efficient barrier to the land of Israel on the S. Attacks of large armed forces could not come from this direction, but only by the Arabah from the SE. (*e.g.* Gn 14), via Gaza on the SW. or by the E. of the Jordan. The country consists of a series of mountainous ridges running in a general direction E. and W., with open wadis in which a certain amount of water collects even now. The OT, in the stories of Saul's and David's captures from the Amalekites (1 S 15^{9} 27^{9}), witnesses to a great wealth of cattle. Recent archaeological survey work by Glueck has, in fact, established that the region was much more settled in the 2nd millennium B.C. and in the Hebrew Monarchy than was previously thought, though it must be emphasized that settlement in the Israelite period was mainly confined to the lines of communication with the copper-mines of the Arabah and the open cultivable wadis extending about seventy miles S. of Beersheba. The area was settled in the early Christian period by the Nabataeans, and again in Byzantine times, when it was a frontier area, it reached its maximum development in antiquity. In this period several considerable towns flourished, such as Elusa (*Khalsa*), Mampsis (*Kurnub*), Eboda (*ʿAbda*), and Subaita (*Sbeiṭa*), where excavations have revealed the remains of three large churches and a monastery. There are many traces of channelling of hillsides and cisterns for collection and storage of water, damming of wadis and terracing of slopes against erosion of soil, while regular small piles of stones once served as vine-props. After the Arab invasion the region lost its significance as a frontier area and experienced a rapid decline. In the state of Israel, however, the chemical industry at the S. end of the Dead Sea, the strategic significance of Elath on the Gulf of ʿAqaba, water piped in for irrigation, and above all a greatly swollen population, are rapidly developing the the Negeb to capacity.

E. W. G. M.—**J. Gr.**

NEGINAH, NEGINOTH.—See PSALMS, **2.**

NEHELAM.—See NEHELAMITE.

NEHELAMITE.—An epithet applied to Shemaiah, a false prophet who opposed Jeremiah, Jer 29$^{24,\ 31f}$ (AV, RV). According to analogy the word should mean 'of **Nehelam**' (so RSV), but there is no place of that name mentioned in the Bible.

NEHEMIAH.—1. One of the twelve heads of the Jewish community, Ezr 2^{2}, Neh 7^{7}, 1 Es 5^{8} (AV, RV **Nehemias**). **2.** One of those who helped to repair the wall of Jerusalem, Neh 3^{16}. **3.** See the following article.

NEHEMIAH.—Son of Hacaliah and cupbearer to Artaxerxes. Our sole source of information regarding this great Jewish patriot is the book that bears his name. According to this, in the twentieth year of Artaxerxes (*i.e.* Artaxerxes I. Longimanus 465–424 B.C., q.v.), December 446 B.C., Nehemiah is at Susa, the chief city of Elam and the winter residence of the Persian court. In consequence of a report brought to him by his brother Hanani and certain men from Judah concerning the ignominious situation of the people in Jerusalem, the wall of the city broken down and its gates burned, Nehemiah, after prayer and fully conscious of Divine guidance in the matter, is able some months later (2^{1}, *i.e.* March-April 445) to obtain permission of the king to go to Judah, appointed as governor (*peḥāh*—though this is mentioned first in 5^{14}). A limited leave of absence is granted to him by the king, letters sent to the governors of the province 'Beyond the River' and to Asaph the keeper of the king's forest ordering the supply of timber for the Temple gates, for the city walls, and for a house for Nehemiah himself. He was also provided with an escort. On his arrival, he inspected the walls secretly by night, and then, revealing his intentions and the ways in which God had blessed his undertaking, he encouraged the people to build with him. By energetic measures and sharing of the work with the aid of men from surrounding villages, he completed the walls in fifty-two days. This was not achieved without opposition, from Sanballat and others (2^{10}), who accused Nehemiah of rebellious intentions, and subsequently attempted by various means to frustrate the enterprise (Neh 1–4, 6). He had also to deal with depression among the workers (4^{10ff}). The work was completed on the twenty-fifth day of the sixth month (6^{15}—presumably September-October, 445). The dedication of the walls is described in 12$^{27-43}$, and this was followed by certain reforms—reorganization of Temple stores, tithes, etc. and the making of provision for the Levites. As a result of a reading of the law (13^{1}) a separation was made from Israel of those of foreign descent.

This narrative is interrupted by various other sections. 1) Chapter 5 describes Nehemiah's measures to relieve economic distress. Many of the people were forced through poverty to mortgage their property and to sell their children as slaves. Nehemiah persuaded those who were lending money and grain to follow his example and charge no interest, and to restore land, money, and produce. It is also stated that Nehemiah himself, unlike former governors, not only took no allowances for himself and his associates, but in fact provided food daily for a large number of men out of his own resources. The date of this section can hardly be ascertained. (2) 7$^{1-4}$ contains provisions for guarding the city and may be linked with 11$^{1-2}$ where this matter is continued by showing how extra population was obtained for the sparsely inhabited city. (3) 7^{5-73a} contains a list also recorded in Ezr 2. (4) 7^{73b}–10 contains the narrative of Ezra's reading of the law and of the making of a new covenant. In this narrative Nehemiah is mentioned only in 8^{9} and 10^{1}, and the lack of real inter-relationship between the work of Nehemiah and Ezra—presented in the Biblical narrative as contemporaries—has led many scholars to believe that Ezra came later, either at the end of the reign of Artaxerxes I. or in the reign of Artaxerxes II. (see EZRA). At all events, the position of the reading of the law here can hardly be correct, since it allows a lapse of thirteen years between Ezra's coming to Jerusalem and his carrying out the main task for which, according to the narrative (Ezr 7^{25f}), he was sent.

The exact sequence of events is thus uncertain and similarly there is some difficulty concerning the chronology of the whole period of Nehemiah's first stay in Jerusalem. The only clues are provided by 5^{14} and 13^{6}; the former records twelve years as the period of Nehemiah's governorship, the latter, referring to certain events, states that Nehemiah was not present in Jerusalem at the time, and it thus appears that the 'on that day' of 12^{44} 13^{1} and the 'now before this' of 13^{4} provide no coherent chronological sequence. Nehemiah had apparently returned to Susa in the thirty-second year of Artaxerxes, *i.e.* 434 B.C. Some time later (13^{6b}), he obtained permission to return and found various abuses and internal disorders rampant in the community. Eliashib 'the priest' had provided Tobiah with quarters in one of the Temple-chambers (13^{4f}), the Levites had not received their dues, the Sabbath was openly desecrated in and around Jerusalem (13^{15f}). Various measures were adopted: Tobiah was turned out and the room he had occupied restored to its proper use. The tithes were reorganized and sabbath trading prevented. Moreover, the problem of foreign marriages (cf 13$^{1-3}$) was again acute, with children unable to speak 'the language of Judah.' By somewhat violent measures (13^{25}) Nehemiah exhorted the people to abandon the evil practice. One of the priestly family, who had married the daughter of Sanballat, was chased out, and the final statement is of the cleansing of the people, proper ordering of priests and Levites, and provision of the wood offering and first fruits (13^{30f}).

The Book of Nehemiah (see next article) is composite in character, and the narrative, as has been indicated, is in part fragmentary, its chronology uncertain. Some scholars have suggested that Nehemiah was active in the period of Artaxerxes II. Mnemon (404–358 B.C.), but the references in the Elephantine papyri to the sons of Sanballat in 407 B.C. indicate that he is likely to have been Nehemiah's opponent in the middle of the 5th cent. Josephus (*Ant.* XI. v. 6 [159]) places Nehemiah in the time of Xerxes.

The personality of Nehemiah, as revealed in his memoirs, is in many respects attractive. He appears as a gifted and accomplished man of action, well versed in the ways of the world, and well equipped to meet difficult situations. He is also deeply religious, as is to be seen in the prayer of ch. 1 and the measures adopted in chs. 12 and 13. The combination of strength, generosity, fervent patriotism and religious zeal contributed to form a personality of striking forcefulness. He rendered services of incalculable value to the cause of Judaism, and his work, together with that of Ezra, was one of the important factors in the preservation of the values of the ancient faith in the later Hellenistic period, when the temptation to religious compromise was particularly strong.

Like all great men, he has become the subject of legend. The recovery of the sacred fire from the altar, hidden during the captivity in Persia (*sic*), is attributed to him (2 Mac 1^{18ff}), and also that he 'founded a library and collected the books about the kings and prophets, and the writings of David, and letters of kings about votive offerings' (2 Mac 2^{13}). He is praised by ben Sira (Sir 49^{13}), who does not, however, mention Ezra; and by Josephus (*Ant.* XI. v. 8 [183]): 'He was a man of good and religious character, and very ambitious to make his own nation happy; and he hath left the walls of Jerusalem as an eternal monument of himself.'

G. H. B.—**P. R. A.**

NEHEMIAH, BOOK OF.—The two books, separated in our Bible and appearing as *Ezra* and *Nehemiah*, originally formed a single book (as appears from the Talmud, the LXX and from internal evidence), and constituted the last section of the work of the Chronicler. The book of Ezra in fact begins with words which overlap the ending of 2 Chronicles (2 Ch 36^{22f}=Ezr 1^{1-3a}). The whole work—1 and 2 Chronicles, Ezra, and Nehemiah—presents the history of the people from Adam to Nehemiah's second visit to Jerusalem. It is usual to refer to the author as the Chronicler, though the probability is that more than one hand may be discerned in the work. That part of this great work which now bears the title *Nehemiah* is so called because it deals largely with the career of the Jewish patriot whose name it carries, and embodies excerpts of considerable extent from his personal memoirs.

1. Extracts from the memoirs embodied in Nehemiah.—(*a*) 1^{1}–7^{4}(^{5}). At the outset we meet with a long section where the first person singular is used throughout. These chapters are authentic extracts from Nehemiah's personal memoirs (cf below on the nature of these). They are distinguished by individual characteristics which help us to form a distinct idea of his personality (see NEHEMIAH). From 5^{14} it is clear that the narrative cannot have been put into its present form until some years after the events recounted. Doubts have been raised as to the authenticity of 6^{15} (the walls finished in fifty-two days): Josephus (*Ant.* XI. v. 8 [179]) gives two years and four months, but it is probable that this rests upon an error in the Greek text he used. 6^{16} makes it plain that to Nehemiah and his contemporaries the speed of the building was a cause for wonder, and could only be ascribed to Divine assistance. 3$^{1-32}$, the list of builders, may well be an addition to the original narrative. 7^{5} now provides an introduction to a list which also appears in Ezr 2 (see below).

(*b*) 11$^{1-2}$ provides the continuation of 7$^{1-4}$ and indicates briefly the measures undertaken to increase the population of the city. It is followed by another list (11$^{3-36}$) which appears also in part in 1 Ch 9$^{3-17}$, probably not an original part of the memoirs, but possibly representing a contemporary record.

(*c*) 12$^{27-43}$. The account of the dedication of the walls continues the narrative in the first person singular (vv.$^{31, 38, 40}$) and should presumably be linked to 6^{15f}.

(*d*) 13$^{4-31}$. Another extract from the memoirs, giving details of a time some twelve or more years later than that referred to in the earlier extracts. It deals with Nehemiah's second visit.

2. Passages in Nehemiah not derived from the memoirs.—(*a*) 7^{6-73a}. This list of returned exiles appears also in Ezr 2 with slight differences. Opinion differs as to whether it is original to the one place or the other. 7^{5b} provides an easy link which makes it seem not impossible that it was placed here at an early stage, and subsequently included in Ezr 2 because its contents refer to the earlier period.

(*b*) 7[73b]–10[39]. This long section breaks the connexion between the main parts of the Nehemiah memoirs, and clearly belongs with Ezr 7–10. Since part of the Ezra material is in the first person singular (so Ezr 7[27]–9) and part in the third person singular (so Ezr 7[1-11] 10), there seems good reason to believe that the section in Nehemiah is also part of the same corpus. The prayer of 9[6-37] is ascribed to Ezra (so RSV, following LXX) and 9[38] 10[30-39] contains a covenant which appropriately concludes the reading and exegesis of the law. These last verses have sometimes been regarded as part of the Nehemiah memoirs, but there seems no entirely appropriate place for them in that narrative. Included in the section is a list (10[1-27]) of those adhering to the covenant.

(*c*) 11[3-36] and 12[1-26], two lists, of which the former (see above) may well be a record contemporary with Nehemiah, and the latter is a list of priests and Levites who returned with Zerubbabel. The priestly genealogy, however, is carried down to Jaddua in the reign of Darius the Persian (12[11, 22]), possibly Darius III. Codomannus (336–330 B.C.). According to Josephus (*Ant.* XI. viii. [304 ff]), Jaddua was a contemporary of Alexander the Great.

(*d*) 12[44]–13[3] contains firstly an account of various religious ordinances in the time of Nehemiah (and Zerubbabel 12[47]), and secondly an account of a reading from the law which resulted in the exclusion of foreigners. The chronology of these two sections, and their origin, are uncertain.

3. Historical value of the Book.—It is clear that the question of historicity can only be resolved after careful analysis of the material, and the recognition of its chronological problems. The separation of the Ezra material (for which see above and EZRA) and of certain other passages, leaves the Nehemiah memoirs as a document of primary importance. It is, however, necessary to recognize the kind of material this is. Mowinckel's view that the memoirs are a memorial, written to preserve the memory of a great man and to denounce the wickedness of his opponents, has much to commend it. Their style is reminiscent of ancient royal inscriptions, and the repeated prayers for remembrance (*e.g.* 5[19] 13[14, 22, 31]) emphasize the purpose of the work. Possibly it was designed to be placed in the sanctuary to keep before God the remembrance of this great national leader. Such a work might be produced by the hero himself or more probably by a scribe on his behalf. Though order and chronology are not always clear—in such a memorial the desire for emphasis may dictate the arrangement—yet the whole work sheds much light upon the period. The dating of Nehemiah in the reign of Artaxerxes I. may now be accepted as established (see previous article).

The literary problems are, however, difficult, and in many ways the most satisfactory suggestion appears to be that the Nehemiah material did not form an original part of the Chronicler's work. Later insertion would make the chronological confusion more intelligible, and unlike other parts of the work, the marks of the Chronicler's style are very little in evidence here. To some extent the traditions concerning Ezra and Nehemiah are parallel (cf the action in foreign marriages, and the later traditions concerning the OT scriptures, 2 Mac 2[13] and 2 Es 14). Such parallelism is not in itself surprising (cf Elijah and Elisha), and it may be that their actual work was somewhat less similar than it now appears.

G. H. B.—**P. R. A.**

NEHEMIAS.—**1.** 1 Es 5[8] (AV, RV); see NEHEMIAH, **1.** **2.** 1 Es 5[40] (AV, RV); see NEHEMIAH, **3.**

NEHILOTH.—See PSALMS, **2.**

NEHUM.—One of the twelve heads of the Jewish community, Neh 7[7]; perhaps a copyist's error for **Rehum** (see REHUM, **1**).

NEHUSHTA.—Wife of king Jehoiakim and mother of Jehoiachin, 2 K 24[8]. She was taken a prisoner to Babylon with her son in 597, 2 K 24[12].

NEHUSHTAN.—See SERPENT (BRAZEN).

NEIEL.—A town in Asher, Jos 19[27]; possibly modern *Kh. Ya'nîn.*

NEIGHBOUR.—In Hebrew there is a paucity of pronouns, and hence in a number of passages in the OT 'neighbour' is employed in a periphrasis for a reciprocal pronoun (Jer 22[8] 23[27] 31[34]). Elsewhere it stands for a fellow-Israelite (Ex 20[17], Lv 19[18]), though the command to love one's neighbour as oneself is extended to include the resident alien (Lv 19[33f]). In the NT this command is extended by Jesus in the Parable of the **Good Samaritan** (Lk 10[29-37]) to include Samaritans, who were regarded by Jews as outside the pale (Jn 4[9]). It is in this universalizing of the concept of 'neighbour' that Jesus brought a new meaning to the ancient command.

NEKODA.—**1.** Eponym of a family of Nethinim, Ezr 2[48], Neh 7[50], 1 Es 5[31] (AV, RV **Noeba**). **2.** Name of a family which returned from the Exile, but were unable to prove their Israelitish descent, Ezr 2[60], Neh 7[62], 1 Es 5[37] (AV **Necodan**, RV **Nekodan**).

NEKODAN, 1 Es 5[37] (RV).—See NEKODA, **2.**

NEMUEL.—**1.** A son of Simeon, Nu 26[12], 1 Ch 4[24]; called **Jemuel** in Gn 46[10], Ex 6[15]. The patronymic **Nemuelites** occurs in Nu 26[12]. **2.** A Reubenite, Nu 26[9].

NEPHEG.—**1.** Son of Izhar and brother of Korah, Ex 6[21]. **2.** One of David's sons, 2 S 5[15], 1 Ch 3[7] 14[6].

NEPHEW.—In AV 'nephew' means 'grandson.' It occurs in Jg 12[14], Job 18[19], Is 14[22], 1 Ti 5[4] (cf RV and RSV).

NEPHILIM.—A Hebrew word of uncertain etymology, retained by RV in the only two places where it occurs in OT (AV '**giants**'). In Gn 6[4] we read: 'The Nephilim were on the earth in those days, and also afterward, when the sons of God came in to the daughters of men, and they bore children to them. These were the mighty men that were of old, the men of renown.' The verse has the appearance of an explanatory gloss to the obscure mythological fragment which precedes, and is very difficult to understand. But we can hardly be wrong in supposing that it bears witness to a current belief (to which there are many heathen parallels) in a race of heroes or demigods, produced by the union of divine beings ('sons of God') with mortal women. The other notice is Nu 13[33], where the name is applied to men of gigantic stature seen by the spies among the natives of Canaan. That those giants were popularly identified with the demigods of Gn 6[4], there is no reason to doubt. See also article GIANT. J. S.

NEPHIS, 1 Es 5[21] (AV).—See MAGBISH.

NEPHISHESIM, Neh 7[52] (AV).—See NEPHISIM.

NEPHISIM.—A family of Nethinim (q.v.) who returned from exile, Ezr 2[50] (AV, RVm **Nephusim**), 1 Es 5[31] (AV, RV **Naphisi**); called **Nephushesim** in Neh 7[52] (AV, RVm **Nephishesim**).

NEPHTHAI.—See NEPHTHAR.

NEPHTHAR.—The name given by Nehemiah to a 'thick liquid' which was found in a dry pit after the return from Babylon (2 Mac 1[18-36]). The legend relates how certain priests, before the Captivity, took the sacred fire and hid it. On the Return, when a search was made, there was found in its place this highly inflammable substance, which seems not to have differed much from the naphtha (v.[36]) of commerce. Some of it was poured over the sacrifice, and was ignited by the great heat of the sun and burned with a bright flame. The name *nephthar* or **nephthai** (v.[36], RSV '**naphtha**') has not been satisfactorily explained, although it is said by the writer to mean 'purification.' T. A. M.—**F. C. G.**

NEPHTOAH.—A town on the boundary between Judah and Benjamin, Jos 15[9] 18[15]; generally identified with *'Ain Liftā.*

NEPHUSHESIM.—See NEPHISIM.

NEPHUSIM, Ezr 2[50] (AV).—See NEPHISIM.

NER.—The father of Abner, 1 S 14[50] 26[5, 14] etc.

NEREUS.—A Roman Christian, to whom, along with his sister, St. Paul sends greeting in Ro 16[15]. The expression 'and all the saints who are with them' seems to point to some community of Christians accustomed to meet together.

NERGAL.—The god of the city of Cuthah in Babylonia, hence worshipped by the captive Cuthaeans who were transplanted to Samaria by Sargon, 2 K 17[30]. In the Babylonian-Assyrian pantheon he was a god of war and pestilence, and of hunting, and the planet Mars was sacred to him. The name Nergal is probably of Sumerian origin, namely, *Ner-gal*=' great warrior.' W. M. N.

NERGAL-SHAREZER.—The Rab-mag (q.v.) who, with Nebuzaradan and Nebushazban, released Jeremiah from prison, Jer 39[3, 13]. Babylonian *Nĕrgal-shar-uṣur* means 'Nergal preserve the king.' It is tempting to think that he was the *Nĕrgal-shar-uṣur* who married a daughter of Nebuchadrezzar, and later came to the throne of Babylon, and is known from classical writers as Neriglissar (559–556 B.C.). C. H. W. J.

NERI.—An ancestor of Jesus (Lk 3[27]).

NERIAH.—The father of Baruch, Jer 32[12, 16] 36[4, 8] etc., Bar 1[1] (AV, RV **Nerias**).

NERIAS, Bar 1[1] (AV, RV).—See NERIAH.

NERO is not mentioned by name in the NT, but his connexion with St. Paul's trial (Ac 25–28, where 'Caesar' is Nero), the mention of his household (Ph 4[22]), and the general opinion that the 'number of the beast' (Rev 13[18]) is a cypher referring to him in some way, are sufficient reasons for including him here. Lucius Domitius Ahenobarbus was born on December 15, A.D. 37, son of Gnaeus Domitius Ahenobarbus (consul in A.D. 32, † A.D. 40) and Agrippina, daughter of Germanicus (nephew of the Emperor Tiberius), who married her uncle the Emperor Claudius in A.D. 48. On adoption by his stepfather in A.D. 50 he received new names, by one of which, Nero, he has since been known. His reign began on the murder of Claudius in A.D. 54, and during it he was officially known as Imperator Nero Claudius Caesar Augustus Germanicus. His death took place on June 9, A.D. 68.

Nero inherited evil qualities from his father and mother, which for the first five years of his rule were kept in check by his tutors, Burrus an experienced soldier, and the philosopher Seneca. When of age to throw off all restraints, he plunged into follies and excesses which suggest that madness had unhinged his mind. His defects, however, seem to have done little more than scandalize and amuse Rome; the prosperity of the provinces continued, thanks to the excellence of the bureaucratic machine. The constant problem of the eastern frontier demanded settlement in Nero's time, especially with reference to the strategic importance of Armenia, which the Romans could neither annex nor abandon to the Parthians. After ten years of fighting, mainly under the able general Cn.Domitius Corbulo, the Parthian Tiridates was recognized in Armenia as a Roman vassal. The long peace which followed is to the credit of Corbulo's generalship and Nero's diplomacy. The Roman hold on Britain, obtained by Claudius, was extended under Nero; the justly aroused rebellion of Boudicca (better known by the incorrect form Boadicea) was crushed by the governor Suetonius Paulinus (A.D. 60). The German and Danubian frontiers also received attention in Nero's time.

Nero was fond of the arts, especially music and poetry, but never attained more than a respectable standard in either. At Rome he exercised a wise care for the grain and water supplies. But on July 19, A.D. 64, a fire broke out and raged for nine days, leaving large parts of the city in ashes. On the evidence Nero must be acquitted of all connexion with the fire, which was due to chance. The populace, however, suspected the emperor, and were anxious to bring retribution on the originators of the fire. Nero selected the Christians as scapegoats, and he may have believed them guilty, as some were understood to have confessed. They were subjected to every variety of cruel death—not so much, says the historian Tacitus, on the original charge as for 'hatred of the human race," which probably means general disaffection to the imperial system and rejection of the state cults. This persecution was probably brief and local, but the precedent remained that determined profession of Christianity was punishable, the situation reflected for instance in 1 Peter.

A conspiracy against the emperor's life failed in A.D. 65; the effect on Nero's mind led to a reign of terror against the Roman aristocracy and its intellectual leaders. Misgovernment in Judaea led to the Jewish revolt in A.D. 66, the bloody suppression of which by Vespasian (q.v.) and Titus (q.v.) extinguished the Jewish commonwealth. In A.D. 68 the revolt of Vindex in Gaul was the prelude to Nero's overthrow and suicide; his life of ease and luxury had weakened a nature never inured to hardship. Not long after his death the rumour arose in the East, which had generally seen only his best side, that he had come to life, or had not really died, and would return. Several 'false Neros' arose to disturb the public peace. His eastern wars, and this *Nero redivivus* story, may provide some of the imagery of Revelation (cf Rev 13[12] 16[12]).

Tradition reports, probably correctly, that Peter and Paul suffered martyrdom at Rome under Nero (though probably not in the persecution of A.D. 64). Of the earlier trial of St. Paul we know nothing certain. His 'appeal to Caesar' was probably heard either before a committee of the emperor's privy council, or before his deputy, the prefect of the city. A. So.—**E. R. H.**

NEST (*ḳēn*).—Used literally of birds' nests (Dt 22[6] 32[11], Job 39[27], Ps 84[3] 104[17], Pr 27[8], Is 16[2]); metaphorically for a lofty fortress (Nu 24[21], Jer 49[16], Ob [4], Hab 2[9]); Job refers to his lost home as a nest (29[18]); in Gn 6[14] the '**rooms**' of the Ark are (see RVm) literally 'nests' (*ḳinnîm*). In Mt 8[20], Lk 9[58] our Lord contrasts His wandering, homeless life with that of the birds which have their 'nests' (*kataskēnōseis*, RVm 'lodging-places'). E. W. G. M.

NETAIM.—A place situated probably in the lowland of Judah, 1 Ch 4[23] (RV, RSV). The site is unknown. See GEDERAH.

NETHANEEL.—The AV spelling of Nethanel in all OT passages.

NETHANEL.—**1.** The leader of Issachar, Nu 1[8] 2[5] 7[18, 23] 10[15]. **2.** One of David's brothers, 1 Ch 2[14]. **3.** A priest in the time of David, 1 Ch 15[24]. **4.** A Levite, 1 Ch 24[6]. **5.** One of Obed-edom's sons, 1 Ch 26[4]. **6.** A 'prince' sent by Jehoshaphat to teach in the cities of Judah, 2 Ch 17[7]. **7.** A chief of the Levites under Josiah, 2 Ch 35[9], 1 Es 1[9] (AV, RV **Nathanael**). **8.** A priest who had married a foreign wife, Ezr 10[22]; called **Nathanael** in 1 Es 9[22]. **9.** A priest in the time of Joiakim, Neh 12[21]. **10.** A Levite musician, Neh 12[36].

NETHANIAH.—**1.** The father of Ishmael the murderer of Gedaliah, 2 K 25[23, 25], Jer 40[8, 14] etc. **2.** An Asaphite, 1 Ch 25[2, 12]. **3.** A Levite, 2 Ch 17[8]. **4.** The father of Jehudi, Jer 36[14]. **5.** One who had married a foreign wife, 1 Es 9[34] (AV, RV **Nathanias**); corresponding to **Nathan, 5,** in Ezr 10[39].

NETHINIM.—The word is a late form of a passive participle *neṯhûnîm*, and denotes 'men who are *given*.' In early days, when sacrifices were offered in the open air, there was little difficulty occasioned by the odour and dirt arising from the blood, fat, and ashes. But when they were offered within the walls of a temple, and offered with great frequency and with large numbers of victims, some very disagreeable drudgery was always necessary. The chopping of wood, lighting of fires, sharpening of knives, drawing of water, the cleansing not only of the altar and its surroundings and utensils, but of the whole of the Temple precincts, and the performance of many menial offices for the priests, required a large staff of servants. The analogy of other lands suggests that these offices would be performed by slaves, procured either by purchase or capture. The Greeks had *hierodouloi*, 'temple slaves,' and the Mohammedans at Mecca similarly. It is not known at what date the practice arose in Israel; but there seem to have been three stages in the history of Temple servants. (1) They were slaves in the strict sense; (2) they were admitted to Israelite privileges, being circumcised, and treated as free men holding an official position in the Church; (3) they rose in standing and prestige so as to become practically equivalent to the Levites.

1. The name *Nethinim* is not used before the Exile. Ezr 8^{20} speaks of the Nethinim as those 'whom David and the princes had *given* for the service of the Levites, which shows, at least, that common belief traced their origin back to David. A very similar class of persons, 'the children of **Solomon's servants,'** is mentioned in Ezr $2^{55,58}$ Neh $7^{57,60}$ 11^{3}; their descent was evidently traced to the non-Israelite slaves employed by Solomon in connexion with his buildings, some of whom must have laboured in the new royal sanctuary (cf 1 K 9^{19-21}). This employment of foreign slaves in the Temple continued till the beginning of the Exile (Ezk 44^{6f}).

2. A change in the status of these men was brought about by the Exile. When the people were far from their land, every one who had held any sort of position in the Temple must have gained a certain prestige. The former Temple-slaves seemed to have formed themselves into a guild. By the very fact of their exile, they were freed from their slavery to the Temple, and thus when they and their sons returned to Jerusalem, they returned as free men, who were recognized as part of the nation. As a guild, they acquired for themselves the title Nethinim, owing to their traditional origin. In Ezr $2^{43-58,70}$=Neh $7^{46-56,73}$ are given the names of the Nethinim who are reported to have returned with Zerubbabel; and they are mentioned together with priests, Levites, singers, and porters. Some of the names in the list are undoubtedly of foreign origin. Again, Ezra relates (8^{20}) that on his return, 220 Nethinim from Casiphia accompanied him. After a time we find them so completely established as a sacred official class that privileges are accorded to them. They shared with priests, Levites, singers, and porters, immunity from taxation (Ezr 7^{24}). They lived in a special quarter of the city, named Ophel, *i.e.* the southern and eastern slope of the Temple hill, or more particularly that part of it which reached to the **Water-gate** on the east and to the tower projecting from the royal palace (Neh 3^{26}). They were thus near the Temple, and Bishop Ryle (*Ezra*, etc., p. lviii) points out the appropriateness of assigning to 'drawers of water' the position by the Water-gate, which communicated with the Virgin's Spring. And v.^{31} mentions 'the house of the Nethinim,' which must have been an official building used by them during their periods of duty. They were under the command of two chiefs—of whom one, at least, was a member of their own body—Ziba and Gishpa (Neh 11^{21}); the former is the first in the list, in Ezr 2^{73}=Neh 7^{46}, and Gishpa may possibly be the same as Hasupha, the second name. Further, only a portion of them, like the priests, Levites, singers, and porters, dwelt in Jerusalem; the others 'dwelt in their cities' (Ezr 2^{70}=Neh 7^{73}, 1 Ch 9^{2}). And so far were they from being regarded as foreign slaves, that they joined, as full members of the community, in the oath that they would not (among other things) allow their sons and daughters to marry any but Israelites (Neh 10^{28-30}).

3. From this point the Nethinim gradually rose in official position, until they were indistinguishable from the Levites. In 1 Ch 23^{28} the Levites are spoken of in such a way as to suggest that the term included all Temple-servants. And conversely, since singers and doorkeepers (who are quite distinct from Levites in Ezra–Nehemiah) were explicitly reckoned by the Chronicler as Levites (1 Ch 15^{16} 26^{1-19}), it is probable that the same was the case with the Nethinim. Finally, in 1 Es 1^{3} the Levites, and in $8^{22,48}$ the Nethinim, are described by the same term, *hierodouloi*. A. H. McN.

NETOPHAH.—A town, the name of which first occurs in the list of the exiles who returned under Zerubbabel, Ezr 2^{22}, Neh 7^{26}, 1 Es 5^{18} (RV **Netophas**). It is possibly modern *Kh. Bedd Fālûḥ*, near *'Ain en-Nāṭûf*, which preserves the old name. The gentilic **Netophathite** occurs in 2 K 25^{23}, 1 Ch 9^{16}, Jer 40^{8}.

NETOPHAS, 1 Es 5^{18} (RV).—See NETOPHAH.

NETS were used in taking wild animals (see HUNTING), and birds (see SNARES); but their main use has always been in **fishing.** Fish were taken along the Mediterranean coast with 'line and hook' (Job 41^{1}, Is 19^{8}, Am 4^{2}), and the 'fish-spear' or 'harpoon' (Job 41^{7}). But sufficient quantities for commercial purposes could be obtained only by means of nets. (*a*) Heb. *mikhmār* (Is 51^{20}) and *makhmōr* (Ps 141^{10}) and the feminine forms *mikhmōreth* (Is 19^{8}) and *mikhmereth* (Hab 1^{15f}) is probably =Greek *sagēnē* (Mt 13^{47}), the Arabic *jarf*, **'drawnet.'** It is as much as 400 metres long, 20 feet deep, and of fine mesh, so that it sweeps everything before it. From the stern of a boat it is paid out in a great semicircle, the lower edge carried down by lead sinkers, the upper sustained by cork floats. It is then drawn ashore, with its contents, by ropes attached to the ends. Fishermen swim behind, diving to ease it over stones and other obstructions. This would account for Peter's being stripped (Jn 21^{7}). (*b*) Hebrew *ḥērem* (Ezk 26^{5}, Hab 1^{15} etc.), Greek *amphiblēstron* (Mt 4^{18}, Mk 1^{16} *v.l.*), the modern *shabakeh*, **'cast-net.'** It is circular, of close mesh, with a cord attached to the centre. The fisherman gathers it together, arranges it on his arm and shoulder, and moves or wades stealthily along the shore until he sees signs of fish within reach; then, with a skilful cast, the net flies out and drops full circle on the water; lead beads round the circumference carry it to the bottom, enclosing the fish, which are then secured at leisure. (*c*) A fishing-net which is used to-day consists of three nets strung on a single rope, the two outer being of wide, the inner of close, mesh. It is let down in fairly deep water, parallel with the shore. The fish pass through the outer net, pushing the inner before them through the wide meshes on the other side, thus being entangled. The net is pulled up and emptied into the boats. (*d*) Greek *diktyon* (Mt 4^{20} etc.) is a term used for nets in general. In the LXX *amphiblēstron* and *sagēnē* are used indiscriminately as translated alike of *ḥērem* and *mikhmār*, etc.

Fishing, which is being developed by the Israeli Government, is still an important industry on the Sea of Galilee, En Gev on the east shore of the lake being a noted centre. W. E.—**E. T. R.**

NETTLE.—1. Hebrew *ḥārûl*, Job 30^{7}, Pr 24^{31}, Zeph 2^{9}. Probably a generic name for thorn bushes growing in the wilderness, such as the *Zizyphus* and varieties of acacia. **2.** Hebrew *ḳimmôś*, Is 34^{13}, Hos 9^{6}, and *ḳimmᵉśônîm*, Pr 24^{31} (EV **thorns**). These words all refer probably to nettles, which are abundant in deserted places in Palestine. E. W. G. M.

NETWORK.—1. Hebrew *ma'ᵃśeh resheth* in Ex 27^{4} 38^{4} describes the bronze grating of the altar in the Tabernacle. **2.** Hebrew *śᵉbhākhāh* describes the ornamentation of parts of the pillars which Solomon set up in the Temple (1 K $7^{18,20,41f}$, Jer 52^{22f}). **3.** Hebrew *ḥôray* is rendered 'networks' in AV in Is 19^{9}. The root meaning of the word is 'to be white,' however, and RSV renders 'white cotton' (cf AVm 'white works,' RV 'white cloth'); LXX has *byssos*.

NEW BIRTH.—See REGENERATION.

NEW ENGLISH BIBLE.—See ENGLISH VERSIONS, **38.**

NEW GATE.—See JERUSALEM, GATES OF.

NEW MOON.—See FEASTS, **2,** and MOON.

NEW TESTAMENT.—See Bible, Canon of NT; Text of NT.

NEZIAH.—The name of a family of Nethinim, Ezr 2^{54}, Neh 7^{56}, 1 Es 5^{32} (AV **Nasith,** RV **Nasi**).

NEZIB.—A town in the lowland of Judah, Jos 15^{43}. It is probably modern *Kh. Beit Naṣîb.*

NIBHAZ.—An idol of the Avvites, 2 K 17^{31}. But the text is perhaps corrupt.

NIBSHAN.—A city in the desert of Judah, Jos 15^{62}. The site is unknown.

NICANOR.—**1.** Son of Patroclus, a Syrian general who was engaged in the Jewish wars (1 Mac 3^{38}). He was sent by Lysias in 166 B.C. against Judas Maccabaeus, but was defeated. Five years later he was sent on the same errand by Demetrius; this time he endeavoured to win by strategy what he had failed to gain by force. Again he was compelled to fight, and was twice defeated, once at Capharsalama (1 Mac 7^{26-32}), and again at Adasa, where he lost his life (vv.$^{39-50}$). The day of his death was ordained to be kept as a festival as '**Nicanor's Day.**' The account in 2 Mac (especially 14^{12-30}) differs in several details. **2.** One of the 'Seven' (Ac 6^{5}).
T. A. M.

NICODEMUS.—Nicodemus is mentioned only in the Gospel of John. There he appears as a Pharisee and a member of the Sanhedrin (Jn 3^{1} 7^{40}) and is addressed by Jesus as 'the teacher of Israel' (Jn 3^{10}). He was perhaps an old man (Jn 3^{4}) and evidently rich (Jn 19^{39}). He figures three times in the Gospel: once in a discussion with Jesus about baptism (Jn 3^{1-21}), a second time in a discussion with other Pharisees in which he attempts to soften their hostility towards Jesus (Jn 7^{45-52}), and finally in the burial scene after the crucifixion (Jn 19^{38-42}).

The name Nicodemus was frequently used by both Jews and Gentiles. The connexion which has sometimes been found between the Nicodemus of John and the Nicodemus of the Talmud is very tenuous.

The location of his place of origin, if Arimathea (Jn 19^{38}), is unknown. W. R. S.

NICOLAITANS.—See next article.

NICOLAS.—AV and RV for **Nicolaus** (q.v.).

NICOLAUS.—Among the 'Seven' (Ac 6^{1ff}) was 'a proselyte of Antioch,' Nicolaus; probably the other six were of Jewish birth. Nicolaus was circumcised; uncircumcised Gentiles first became members of a Christian community later on at Antioch. In Rev $2^{6, 15}$ the members of a sect seem to be called 'Nicolaitans.' Irenaeus and Hippolytus assert that Nicolas (or Nicolaus) had founded it. But that was only a guess. Possibly the sect claimed to have been founded by him. E. H.

NICOPOLIS, or the 'city of victory,' was founded by Augustus in 31 B.C., on the spot where he had had his camp before the battle of Actium. It was made a Roman colony, and was peopled by citizens drawn from various places in Acarnania and Aetolia.

In Tit 3^{12} St. Paul writes, 'Do your best to come to me at Nicopolis, for I have decided to spend the winter there.' It may be taken as certain that this means Nicopolis in Epirus, from which doubtless Paul hoped to begin the evangelization of that province. No other city of the name was in such a position, or so important as to claim six months of the Apostle's time.

The importance of Nicopolis depended partly on the 'Actian games,' partly on some commerce and fisheries. It was destroyed by the Goths, and, though restored by Justinian, it was supplanted in the Middle Ages by Prevesa, which grew up a little farther south. There are extensive ruins on its site. A. E. H.

NIGER.—The second name of **Symeon,** one of the prophets and teachers of the Church of Antioch (Ac 13^{1}). His name Symeon shows his Jewish origin, and Niger was probably the Gentile name which he assumed. Nothing further is known of him. M. St.

NIGHT.—See Time.

NIGHT HAG, Is 34^{14} (RSV).—See Owl and Lilith.

NIGHT HAWK.—Lv 11^{16}, Dt 14^{15} (EV); see Owl.

NIGHT MONSTER, Is 34^{14} (RV).—See Owl and Lilith.

NILE.—The Greek name of the river, of uncertain derivation. The Egyptian name was *Ḥapi*, later *i(t)rw-ʿꜣ* (Copt. *yero*), 'Great River,' but the Hebrew generally designates the Nile by the term *yᵉʾōr*, derived from the ordinary Egyptian word for 'river,' *i(t)rw* (Copt. *yoor*). The word *shîḥôr* (Is 23^{3}, Jer 2^{18}) is also employed, a derivative of Egyptian (*pꜣ*) *š-Ḥr*, 'the lake of Horus,' which designates an eastern arm of the Nile.

Rich in fish, it was the home of the crocodile and hippopotamus. It bore most of the internal traffic of Egypt; but it was pre-eminently the one source of water, and so of life and fertility, in a land which, without it, would have been desert. The White Nile sends down from the Central African lakes a steady stream, which is greatly increased in summer and autumn, when the half-dry beds of the *Baḥr el-Azraq* and the *ʿAtbarah* are filled by the torrential rains annually poured on the mountains of Abyssinia. The waters of these tributaries are charged with organic matter washed down by the floods, and this is spread over the fields of Egypt by the inundation.

The height of the Nile rise was measured and recorded by the Egyptians from the earliest times: on it depended almost wholly the harvest of the year, and a great excess might be as harmful as a deficiency. The rise begins about June 19, and after increasing slowly for a month the river gains rapidly until September; at the end of September it becomes stationary, but rises again, reaching its highest level about the middle of October. This annual inundation is referred to in Am 8^{8} 9^{5}. The crops were sown as the water retreated, and on the lower ground a second crop was obtained by artificial irrigation. Canals and embankments regulated the waters in ancient times. The water was raised for the irrigation of the fields by *shadūfs*, i.e. buckets hung from the end of dipping poles, and handscoops, and carried by small channels which could be opened or stopped with a little mud and cut herbage: by this means the flow was directed to particular fields or parts of fields as might be required. Water-wheels were probably introduced in Greek times.

The Nile had seven mouths, of which the western (the Canopic) and the eastern (the Pelusiac) were the most important. The former secured most of the traffic with Greece and the islands, the latter with the Phoenicians. The Pelusiac arm, on which Tahpanhes and Pi-beseth lay, would be best known to the inhabitants of Palestine. Now the ancient mouths are silted up: only a western (Rosetta branch) and a central one (Damietta branch) survive. The worship of the Nile-god must have been prominent in popular festivals, but has not left much monumental trace.

The Egyptians, knowing nothing of the sources of the Nile, regarded it as gushing out from two springs at the First Cataract, fed by the subterranean waters. They also thought of rain as the result of a Nile in heaven pouring its waters down upon earth. The 'seven lean years' in Gn 41 are paralleled by an Egyptian tradition from the Ptolemaic period of a much earlier seven years' famine under the 3rd Dynasty, and years of famine due to insufficient rise of the Nile are referred to in more than one hieroglyphic text. F. Ll. G.—**R. J. W.**

NIMRAH.—See Beth-nimrah.

NIMRIM, THE WATERS OF.—These are mentioned in Is 15^{6}, Jer 48^{34}, along with Zoar and Horonaim. They must therefore be sought in the S. of Moab. The *Onomasticon* places it ('Nemerim') to the N. of Zoar. It is probably modern *Wâdī Numeirah*, near the S. end of the Dead Sea.

NIMROD (Gn 10^{8-12}, 1 Ch 1^{10}, Mic 5^{6}).—A legendary personage, described in Gn 10^{8ff} as the first of the 'mighty men,' 'a mighty hunter before the Lord,' the ruler of four ancient Babylonian cities, and the founder of the Assyrian Empire. In the statement that he was begotten by Cush we have probably a reference to the *Kasshu* who conquered Babylonia about the 17th cent. B.C., and set up a dynasty that lasted about 600 years; the rise of Assyria dated from the decline of Babylonia under the later Kassite kings. The name Nimrod is almost certainly a corruption of Ninurta. Probably Tukulti-Ninurta I. (the Greek *Ninos*), king of Assyria, is meant. Much less likely is Nazimaruttash, king of Babylonia. The combination in Assyrian kings of warlike prowess with a passion for the chase is illustrated by the numerous war and hunting scenes sculptured on the monuments; and it may well be imagined that to the Hebrew mind Nimrod became an ideal personation of the proud monarchs who ruled the mighty empires on the Euphrates and the Tigris. J. S.—**C. J. M. W.**

NIMSHI.—Grandfather of king Jehu, 1 K 9^{16}, 2 K 9$^{2, 14, 20}$, 2 Ch 22^{7}.

NINEVEH (Assyr. *Ninâ, Ninûa*) is said in Gn 10^{11} to have been founded by Nimrod in Assyria. There was a village here in the 5th millennium B.C. At the close of the 3rd millennium kings of Ur dominated Urbilum (*i.e.* Arbela) and probably Nineveh. Nineveh was included in the dominions of Hammurabi, who restored the temple of Ishtar there. It was early an important city, and is frequently referred to in the royal inscriptions, but Sennacherib first raised it to the position of capital of Assyria. It lay on the E. of the Tigris, opposite the modern Mosul. Its chief remains are buried beneath the mounds of Kuyunjik and Nebī Yūnus, but the outline of the old walls can be traced. They enclosed some 1800 acres, with a circumference of about 8 miles. The mound of Kuyunjik is separated from the mound of Nebī Yūnus by the Khoser, and overlies the palaces of Sennacherib to the N., and Ashurbanipal to the S. The southern mound, Nebī Yūnus, covers palaces of Sennacherib and Esarhaddon. The Nineveh of Sennacherib's day lay largely outside this area, and included the *Rebit Ninûa*, or Rehoboth-ir, which extended as far as Khorsabad, where Sargon built a great city, Dur-Sharrukin. The traditions of its great size may be due to a reminiscence of this outer girdle of inhabited country. The fall of Nineveh (612 B.C.) is referred to by Nahum and Zephaniah (2$^{13-15}$). 2 K 19^{36} and Is 37^{37} know it as the city of Sennacherib. For Jonah's mission, see JONAH. Later, Tobit (1$^{10, 17}$ etc.) and Judith (1^{1}) refer to it, and the **Ninevites** are named in Mt 12^{41}, Lk 11$^{30, 32}$. C. H. W. J.—**T. F.**

NIPHIS, 1 Es 5^{21} (RV).—See MAGBISH.

NISAN.—See TIME.

NISROCH.—An Assyrian deity in whose temple Sennacherib was worshipping when assassinated, 2 K 19^{37}, Is 37^{38}. It is difficult to identify this god, and various suggestions have been made. Gesenius compared the name with the Arabic *nisr* ('eagle'), and conjectured that it referred to one of the eagle-headed divinities that appear in the bas-reliefs. Others have thought of Marduk, the god of Babylon, and Montgomery (see *ICC, ad loc.*) thinks this is the most probable. Against the objection that this is incongruous, since Sennacherib was the enemy of Babylon, Montgomery cites the Nabonidus inscription which says that the Assyrian king 'took the hand of Marduk, and brought him to Assyria,' and notes that Esarhaddon styles himself 'worshipper of Nabu and Marduk.' The most favoured identification is with Nusku, the god of light and fire, associated particularly with the moon god, and Sin, who was worshipped at Harran. Here the objection that Nusku did not occupy a sufficiently prominent place in the Assyrian pantheon is beside the point. Assyrian kings doubtless went to the temples of many gods, and the assassins would not be concerned with the importance of the deity in whose temple they carried out the murder.

NITRE, in its modern usage, denotes *saltpetre,* nitrate of potash, but the *nitron* or *nitrum* of the ancients was a different substance, *natron,* carbonate of soda. 'Nitre' occurs twice in AV. In Pr 25^{20} the effect of songs on a heavy heart is compared to the action of vinegar upon 'nitre' (AV, RV; RVm 'soda'; RSV 'a wound,' on the basis of Greek). Vinegar has no effect upon saltpetre, but with carbonate of soda it produces effervescence. In Jer 2^{22} 'nitre' (RV, RSV **lye**) is referred to as a cleansing agent. Here, again, natron rather than the modern nitre suits the connexion.

NO (Jer 46^{25}, Ezk 30$^{14-16}$).—The name of **Thebes** (Diospolis Magna), Egyptian *niw.t,* 'city,' *i.e.* the city *par excellence*; also **No-Amon** (Nah 3^{8}), 'the city of Amon.' Nahum seems to imagine Thebes as resembling the cities of the less remote Delta surrounded by canals, which were their chief protection. In reality it lay on both banks of the Nile, with desert bounding it on either side, and water probably played little part in its defence. Thebes was of no importance until the Middle Kingdom Dynasties 11–12), during which the royal families were much connected with it. It was the capital of the local 17th Dynasty, struggling against the Hyksos (q.v.) in the name of its god Amon. The great warriors of the succeeding 18th Dynasty enriched Thebes with the spoils of conquest, built temples there that surpassed all others in size and magnificence, and made it the greatest city of the Empire. Under the 19th and 20th Dynasties Amon was still the national god, and Thebes the capital of Egypt. Later, Memphis again took the first place, but Thebes was at least the religious centre of the widespread Amon worship, and the temples retained much of their wealth until the sack of the city by king Ashurbanipal (*c* 664 B.C.), referred to in Nah 3^{8}.

The temples of Thebes continued to be added to until insurrections under the Ptolemies led to its destruction and final abandonment as a city. In Jer 46^{25} (RSV) 'I am bringing punishment upon Amon of Thebes (No), and Pharaoh, and Egypt and her gods and her kings,' Amon is probably not taken as the representative god of Egypt, a position which he no longer held in the 6th cent. B.C.: the passage rather indicates the completeness of Egypt's fall by the punishment of the remote Thebes, which could not be accomplished till Lower Egypt was prostrate. The Theban Amon was often entitled 'Amon-Rē, king of the gods,' being identified with the sun-god Rē. His figure is that of a man, generally coloured green. The ram was his sacred animal. In Ethiopia he was adopted as the national god, and his worship was established in the Oases, especially in the Oasis of Amon (Siwa), where his oracle was visited by Alexander. See Sir A. H. Gardiner, *Ancient Egyptian Onomastica* (1947), ii. 24*–26*. F. Ll. G.—**R. J. W.**

NOADIAH.—1. A Levite in the time of Ezra, Ezr 8^{33}; called **Moeth** in 1 Es 8^{63}. **2.** A prophetess who opposed Nehemiah, Neh 6^{14}.

NOAH.—1. *Nōaḥ,* 'rest.' The name is explained in Gn 5^{29} by a play on *niḥam,* 'to comfort'; but perhaps the reading supported by the LXX should be adopted, 'This same shall *give us rest.*' In one tradition Noah is the hero of the Flood, and answers to **Ut-napishtim** in the Babylon legend. See DELUGE. Ut-napishtim was translated to immortality; and this is perhaps referred to in 6^{9b} (cf 5^{24} and see ENOCH). In another tradition he is the discoverer of the art of making wine (9$^{20-27}$). Elsewhere in the Bible, besides the references to the Flood, Noah is mentioned in 1 Ch 1^{4}, Ezk 14$^{14, 20}$, Lk 3^{36}. **2.** *Nō'āh* (Nu 26^{33} 27^{1} 36^{11}, Jos 17^{3}). One of the daughters of Zelophehad, of the tribe of Manasseh. They claimed their father's inheritance because he had died leaving no sons. It was given to them, on condition that they were not married into another tribe. A. H. McN.

NO-AMON.—See No.

NOB.—A place of this name is mentioned in three passages—1 S 21, 22, Neh 11^{33}, Is 10^{32} (text not quite certain). The context in the two latter passages points

.o a place near Jerusalem. In 1 Samuel, David passes Nob, which has become 'the city of priests' after the destruction of Shiloh, on his way from Saul (in Gibeah, q.v.) to Gath: this would suit a site near Jerusalem, though it does not demand such a position, unless, indeed, we infer (cf 1 S 20[6]) that David went to Nob with the intention of proceeding to Bethlehem (5 miles S. of Jerusalem). There is no strong reason against assuming that in all three passages the same place is referred to. In Neh 11[33] and Is 10[32] Nob is closely connected with Anathoth, 2½ miles N. of Jerusalem. Since in Is 10[32] Nob is the last point reached by the Assyrian army and the place from which it threatens Jerusalem, the site is best sought for on an eminence a little N. of the city, perhaps in particular (with S. R. Driver) on 'the Râs el-Meshārif, about 1½ miles SW. of Anathoth, the ridge from the brow of which the pilgrim along the north road still catches his first view of the holy city.' Specifically we may locate Nob at *Râs Umm eṭ-Ṭalaʿ*, on the E. slopes of Mount Scopus N. of the Mount of Olives (*Jebel eṭ-Ṭûr*). The name has not survived; and the identification suggested stands or falls with the correctness of the Hebrew text of Is 10[32].
G. B. G.—**D. N. F.**

NOBAH.—1. The clan name of the Israelites who conquered the city of Kenath (q.v.), Nu 32[42]. **2.** A place named with Jogbehah in the account of Gideon's pursuit of Zebah and Zalmunna, Jg 8[11]. It was near Jogbehah (q.v.), but its exact location is unknown.

NOBAI, Neh 10[19] (RV).—See Nebai, Nebo, **3.**

NOD.—According to Gn 4[16], the country in which Cain the fratricide took up his abode after his sentence of banishment. The place is unknown. It is probably connected in some way etymologically with the epithet *nādh* of v.[14] ('wanderer'). The addition 'eastward of Eden' is of little help for its location. J. F. McC.

NODAB.—The name of a tribe mentioned in 1 Ch 5[19], along with Naphish and Jetur, as among the foes encountered and subdued by the Reubenites. A comparison with the various readings of LXX shows that the vowels of the word are uncertain. An identification with the Nabataeans is excluded both on phonological grounds and by the fact that the latter, whose position was in any case too remote from Reuben, did not appear in history till long after the tribal period of the Hebrews had come to an end. The location of the tribe is unknown. J. F. McC.

NOE.—AV form of **Noah, 1** (q.v.) in Mt 24[37], Lk 3[36] 17[26f].

NOEBA, 1 Es 5[31] (AV, RV).—See Nekoda, **1.**

NOGAH.—One of David's sons, born at Jerusalem, 1 Ch 3[7] 14[6].

NOHAH.—1. A place mentioned in Jg 20[43] (AVm **Menuchah**, RVm **Menuhah**); possibly the same as **Manahath, 1** (q.v.), or possibly connected with **2. 2.** A Benjamite clan, 1 Ch 8[2].

NOISOME.—'Noisome' is literally 'annoy-some.' The adjective means 'offensive,' 'injurious' in AV and RV (Ps 91[3], Ezk 14[15, 21], Rev 16[2]); the word is now rather rarely used, but when it is used it means 'loathsome' rather than 'hurtful.' RSV substitutes 'deadly,' 'wild,' 'evil,' and 'foul' in the passages noted.

NON, 1 Ch 7[27] (AV) = **Nun** (q.v.).

NOOMA, 1 Es 9[35] (RV).—See Nebo, **3.**

NOPH.—See Memphis.

NOPHAH.—An unknown place mentioned in MT in Nu 21[30] (so AV, RV). The text is very uncertain, and for 'Nophah which' RSV has 'fire spread.'

NORTH COUNTRY, LAND OF THE NORTH.—A phrase of somewhat vague application, but denoting in a general fashion—**1.** The source or region from which dangerous foes were to come upon Palestine (so in Jer 6[22] 10[22], Zec 6[6, 8]). **2.** The regions to which the people of Israel or Judah had been exiled, and whence they were to be restored (so in Jer 3[18] 16[15] 23[8] 31[8], Zec 2[6]). **3.** Northern Syria (so Jer 46[10]). The last-named instance explains itself. The other applications of the term may be further illustrated by the usage of the word 'north' generally in OT. Here it is sufficient to recall the general fact that, while in the early history of Israel the land was invaded by many small peoples from the east and south, after the rise of the Assyrian and Chaldaean powers the attacks were made by larger armies which came in the course of their march down through Syria or the Mediterranean coast-land, the eastern desert route being impossible. Deportations of captives were naturally effected by the same routes, and by the same routes they would return. Thus, though Babylonia was in the same latitude as Palestine, it was included among the countries of the 'north.'
J. F. McC.

NORTHEASTER.—See Euraquilo.

NOSE, NOSTRILS.—Hebrew *'aph*, dual *'appayim*, is the usual word; *nᵉḥîrayim* dual, only in Job 41[20]; *naḥar* only in Job 39[20] AV (RV, RSV correctly 'snorting').—To have a flat (AV), or more probably slit (RV), nose (Lv 21[18]; the word 'nose' is not here expressed in the text, and RV renders 'a mutilated face'), disqualified a man for the making of offerings. The nose is the organ of the breath by which men live (Gn 2[7] etc.). The breath is easily stopped or expelled, hence the fact signifies the transiency of human life (Is 2[22]). Excited breathing, with distention of the nostrils when moved by indignation, led to the nose being used figuratively for anger (Gn 27[45], and very often). Ezk 8[17] refers to the custom of putting a twig to the nose, apparently in idolatrous worship, the significance of which is now obscure. For 'nose-ring,' see Ornaments, **2.** W. E.

NOUGHT.—See Naught: and notice, further, the phrase 'set at nought,' Ps 1[25] (AV, RV; RSV 'ignore'), Mk 9[12] (AV, RV; RSV 'treat with contempt'). 'To set' is 'to value' and 'nought' is 'nothing,' so the phrase means to reckon of no value.

NOVICE.—In 1 Ti 3[6] it is enjoined that the bishop must not be a 'recent convert' (AV 'novice'). The Greek word (*neophytos*, literally 'newly planted') was afterwards used in the technical sense of one who has not yet taken religious vows. Here it is general—one newly introduced into the Christian community.

NUMBER.—1. Notation.—The decimal scale of notation was used by the Israelites, Assyrians, Babylonians, Egyptians, Greeks, Romans, and, so far as we know, by the other nations mentioned in the Bible, *i.e.* they reckoned by units, tens, hundreds, etc.

2. Variety and range of numerical terminology.—The Hebrew language expressed the integers from one to any amount by words denoting units, tens, a hundred, two hundred, a thousand, two thousand, ten thousand, twenty thousand, and by combinations of these words. Thus the highest number expressed by a single word is twenty thousand, the word used meaning double ten thousand. The word 'millions' in AV of Gn 24[60] is a mistranslation; it should be 'ten thousands' as in RV and RSV. The number referred to in this verse, 'thousands of ten thousands,' for the descendants hoped for from Rebekah, and the number of the angels in Dn 7[10], a 'thousand thousands served him, and ten thousand times ten thousand stood before him' (cf Rev 5[11]), if taken literally, would be the largest numbers mentioned in the Bible, but they are merely rhetorical phrases for countless, indefinitely large numbers. In Rev 7[9] the redeemed are 'a great multitude which no man could number' (cf Gn 13[16])—the nearest approach which the Bible makes to the mathematical idea of infinity.

The largest literal number in the Bible is the number of Israelites fit for warlike service, ascertained by David's census as 1,100,000, in addition to the men of Judah 470,000 (1 Ch 21[5]). In 2 S 24[9], however, the numbers are 800,000 and 500,000 respectively. Close to this comes the army of Zerah (2 Ch 14[9]), 'a thousand thousand,' *i.e.* 1,000,000; and in 2 Ch 17[12ff], Jehoshaphat has an army in five divisions, of 300,000, 280,000, 200,000, 200,000, 180,000 respectively. The number of fighting men amongst the Israelites is given in Nu 2^{32} as 603,550; and later on in Nu 26^{51} as 601,730.

Hebrew also possessed a few special forms for the ordinals, first, second, etc., and to denote 'seven times,' etc.; in other cases, especially for the higher numbers, the cardinals are used. There are also a few words for fractions, 'a third,' 'a quarter.'

The Biblical Greek calls for no special comment; the writers had at their disposal the ordinary resources of Hellenistic Greek. We may, however, call attention to the disputed rendering in Mt 18^{22}, where RV and RSV have 'seventy times seven,' RVm 'seventy times and seven,' RSVm 'seventy-seven times.'

3. Symbols.—In the Hebrew text of the OT, and also for the most part in the Greek text of the NT, numbers are denoted by words. This method is also the only one used in the two ancient Hebrew inscriptions—the Moabite Stone (rather later than Ahab), and the Siloam inscription (usually ascribed to the time of Hezekiah). As the Assyrians, Egyptians, and Phoenicians used figures as well as words to denote numbers, it is possible that the Israelites also had arithmetical figures; but at present there is no positive evidence of such a usage. In the Elephantine papyri units are denoted by vertical strokes and tens by horizontal.

In later times the Jews used consonants as numerical signs; the units from one to nine were denoted by the first nine letters, the tens from ten to ninety by the next nine, and the hundreds from one hundred to four hundred by the remaining four letters. Other numbers were denoted by combinations of letters. A curious feature of this system is that the natural combination for 15, viz. *Yôdh*=10, *Hê*=5, was not used because '*Yodh, He*,' or *Yah* was a form of the sacred name *Yahweh*, which might not be pronounced; accordingly *Teth*=9 and *Waw*=6 were substituted. This system is still commonly used to number the chapters and verses in Hebrew Bibles. A similar system was also used by the Greeks, and is occasionally found in the NT; thus the Number of the Beast, 666, in Rev 13^{18}, is written by means of three letters.

4. Arithmetic.—There is no evidence of proficiency in arithmetic beyond the simplest operations, but we have examples of addition in connexion with the census in the wilderness, the numbers of the separate tribes being given first and then the total (Nu 1^{22ff} 26^{7ff}); subtraction is referred to in Lv 27^{18}; an instance of multiplication is Lv 25^{8}, $7 \times 7 = 49$; and Lv 25^{50} implies a kind of rule of three sum.

5. Round Numbers.—As in other languages, 'round numbers,' exact tens, hundreds, thousands, etc., must often have been used by the Israelites, on the understanding that they were only approximately accurate; and in the same way smaller numbers were sometimes used indefinitely for 'a few'; cf our 'half a dozen.' For instance, the exact ten thousands of Jehoshaphat's armies given above are doubtless round numbers. Again, in Lv 26^{8}, 'five of you shall chase a hundred,' merely means, 'a handful of you shall put to flight many times your own number.' This indefinite use of a small number is specially common where two consecutive units are given as alternatives, *e.g.* Is 17^{6}, 'two or three,' 'four or five.' A variety of this idiom is the use of two consecutive units to introduce emphatically the higher of the two; *e.g.* Pr 30^{21} 'Under three things the earth trembles; under four it cannot bear up'; then four things are enumerated. In addition to hundreds and thousands and ten thousands, the most common number used in this approximate way is 'forty': people constantly live or reign for 'forty years' or multiples of forty years. It is a matter of opinion how far the numerous 'sevens,' 'tens,' and 'twelves' were originally intended as exact numbers. Probably, however, in many cases what were originally round numbers were taken afterwards to be exact. For instance, David's reign is given as 40 years, 2 S 5^{4}; in the next verse this period is explained as made up of 7½ years at Hebron and 33 at Jerusalem—an explanation which implies that, apart from some odd months, the 40 years were the actual length of the reign. There are some indications, too, that the various 40's and 80's were added in with other numbers to obtain a continuous chronology. Again, in Nu 3^{39} the census gives 22,000 Levites, which one would naturally understand as a round number; but in vv.$^{43-51}$ it is taken as an exact number, inasmuch as it is ordained that because the 22,273 firstborn exceed the Levites by 273, redemption-money shall be paid for the surplus.

In view of the references to captains of thousands, hundreds, fifties, and tens in Dt 1^{15}, it has been suggested that these terms are sometimes not numerals, but names corresponding to our regiment, company, squad, etc., and denoting bodies of men whose numbers varied. '**Thousand**' especially has been held to be a term denoting 'tribe' or 'clan' (see Jg 6^{15} [cf RVm]; 1 S 10^{19}); so that 'a thousand' might contain comparatively few men. This view has been applied to make the census in the Book of Numbers more credible by reducing the total amounts; but it is clear that the narrative as it stands intends 'thousand' to be a numeral, and does not use the word for a 'clan.'

6. Accuracy of numbers.—Without attempting an exhaustive consideration of the accuracy of numbers as given by the original authors, we may point out that we should not expect a large measure of mathematical accuracy even in original numbers. Often as we have seen, they are apparently given as round numbers. However, in the case of large numbers they would seldom be ascertained by careful enumeration. The numbers of armies—especially hostile armies—of slain, and so forth, would usually be given on a rough estimate; and such estimates are seldom accurate, but for the most part exaggerated. Moreover, primitive historical criticism revelled in constructing hypothetical statistics on the slightest data, or, to put the matter less prosaically, the Oriental imagination loved to play with figures, the larger the better.

But apart from any question as to the accuracy of the original figures, the transmission of the text by repeated copying for hundreds of years introduces a large element of uncertainty. If we assume that numbers were denoted by figures in early times, figures are far more easily altered, omitted, or added than words; but, as we have seen, we have at present no strong ground for such an assumption. But even when words are used, the words denoting numbers in Hebrew are easily confused with each other, as in English. Just as 'eight' and 'eighty' differ only by a single letter; so in Hebrew, especially in the older style of writing, the addition of a single letter would make 'three' into 'thirty,' etc. And, again, in copying numerals the scribe is not kept right by the context as he is with other words. It was quite possible, too, for a scribe to have views of his own as to what was probable in the way of numbers, and to correct what he considered erroneous.

A comparison of the various manuscripts, versions, etc., in which our books have been preserved, shows that numbers are specially subject to alteration, and that in very many cases we are quite uncertain as to what numbers were given in the original text, notably where the numbers are large. Even where the number of a body of men, the length of a period, etc., are given twice over or oftener in different passages of the Bible itself, the numbers are often different; those in Chronicles, for instance, sometimes differ from those in Samuel and Kings, as in the case of David's census mentioned above. Then, as regards manuscripts, etc., we may take one or two striking instances. The chief authorities for the text of the Pentateuch are the Hebrew text in Jewish MSS, the Hebrew text in Samaritan MSS, and the Greek translation, the Septuagint. Now the numbers connected with the ages of the patriarchs are largely different in these three authorities; *e.g.* in the Jewish text Methuselah lives to the age of 969, and is the longest lived of the patriarchs; in the Samaritan he lives only to be 720, and is surpassed by many of the other patriarchs; and the interval from the Creation to the Flood is 2262 years in the Septuagint, 1656 in the Jewish text, 1307 in the Samaritan text. Again the number of persons on board the ship on which St. Paul was shipwrecked is given in some MSS as 276, and in others as 76 (Ac 27^{37}; cf RSV and RSVm); and similarly the number of the Beast is variously given as 666 and as 616 (Rev 13^{18}; cf RSV and RSVm).

The probability that many mistakes in numbers have been introduced into the Bible by copyists in the course of the transmission of the text has long been admitted. For instance, in the fifth edition of Horne's *Introduction to the Critical Study of Knowledge of the Holy Scriptures*, published in 1825, a thoroughly old-fashioned apologetic work, we are told that 'Chronological differences,' *i.e.* discrepancies, 'do undoubtedly exist in the Scriptures. . . . Differences in chronology do not imply that the sacred historians were mistaken, but they arise from the mistakes of transcribers or expositors'; and again, 'It is reasonable to make abatements, and not always to insist rigorously on precise numbers, in adjusting the accounts of scriptural chronology' (i, 550 f).

7. Favourite numbers and their symbolism.—Naturally the units, and after them some of the even tens, hundreds, and thousands, were most frequently in use, and came to have special associations and significance, and a fraction would in some measure share the importance of its corresponding unit, *e.g.* where 'four' occurred often we should also expect to meet with a 'fourth.'

One, suggesting the idea of uniqueness, self-sufficiency, and indivisibility, is specially emphasized in relation to the Divine Unity: 'Yahweh our God, Yahweh is one' (Dt 6^{4}); and similarly Eph 4^{5f} 'one Lord, one faith, one baptism, one God and Father'; and other like passages.

Two.—There were two great lights; men frequently had two wives (Lamech, Jacob, Elkanah); two sons (Abraham, Isaac, Joseph); two daughters (Lot, Laban, Saul). Or again, where a man had one wife, there was a natural couple; and so with animals; in one account of the Flood they go in 'two by two.' Two men often went together, *e.g.* Joshua's spies (Jos 2^{1}); and the Twelve and the Seventy went out by twos. The fact that men have two eyes, hands, etc., also gave a special currency to the number. Two objects or animals are often required for ritual purposes (*e.g.* Lv 14^{22}). There were two tables of stone. Similarly, a half would be a familiar fraction; it is most common in 'the half tribe of Manasseh.'

As sets of two were common in nature and in human society, so in a somewhat less degree were sets of three, and in a continuously lessening degree sets of four, five, etc. In each case we shall refer only to striking examples.

Three.—Three is common in periods; *e.g.* David is offered a choice between three days' pestilence, three months' defeat, and three years' famine (1 Ch 21^{12}; 2 S 24^{13} has seven years, cf RSVm); Christ is 'three days and three nights' in the tomb (Mt 12^{40}, cf Jn 2^{19}).

Deities often occur in groups of three, sometimes father, mother, and child: *e.g.* the Egyptian Osiris, Isis, and Horus. There are also the Babylonian triads, *e.g.* Bel, Anu, and Ea. Division into three is common; an attacking army is often divided into three parts, *e.g.* Gideon's (Jg 7^{16}; cf also Rev 8$^{10, 12}$).

Four.—The square, as the simplest plane figure, suggests four, and is a common shape for altars, rooms, etc.: hence four corners, pillars, the four winds, the four quarters of the earth, N., S., E., W. Irenaeus argues that there must be four canonical Gospels because there are four cherubim, four winds, and four quarters of the earth.

Five, *Ten*, and multiples obtain their currency through the habit of reckoning in tens, which again is probably derived from counting on the ten fingers. The fraction tenth is conspicuous as the tithe; and fifth and tenth parts of measures occur in the ritual.

Six, *Twelve*, and multiples are specially frequent in reference to time: 12 months, and its half, six months, 12 hours, sixth hour, etc., partly in connexion with the 12 signs of the Zodiac, and the approximate division of the solar year into 12 lunar months. It has been suggested that the number 12 for the tribes of Israel was fixed by the Zodiac; in the lists the number 12 is obtained only by omitting Levi or Dan, or by substituting Joseph for Ephraim and Manasseh. When the number 12 was established for the tribes, its currency and that of its multiples were thus further extended; *e.g.* the 12 Apostles, the 144,000 of the Apocalypse, etc.

Seven and multiples.—A specially sacred character is popularly ascribed to the number seven; and although the Bible does not expressly endorse this idea, yet it is supported by the frequent occurrence of the number in the ritual, the sacred seventh day, the Sabbath; the sacred seventh year, the Sabbatical year; the Jubilee year, the year following seven times seven years; the seven-branched candlestick; sevenfold sprinkling (Lv 4^{6} etc.); seven lambs offered (Nu 28^{11ff}); forgiveness till 70 times 7 (Mt 18^{22}); the seven churches of Asia; seven angels; seven stars, etc.; fourteen generations (Mt 1^{17}); 70 descendants of Jacob (Ex 1^{5}); 70 years captivity, etc. (Jer 25^{11}, Dn 9^{2}, Zec 7^{5}); 70 missioners (Lk 10^{1}). A similar use of 'seven' is found in the Egyptian, Assyrian, and Persian religions, and is often derived from astral worship of the seven heavenly bodies, the sun, moon, and the five planets known to the ancients. It is also connected with the seven-day week as roughly a quarter of the lunar month, seven being the nearest integer to the quarter of $29\frac{1}{2}$. The Pleiades also were thought of as seven (cf Am 5^{8}).

Eight.—There were eight persons in the ark; a boy was circumcised on the eighth day. Ezekiel's ritual has a certain predilection for the number eight.

Forty.—This number apparently owes its vogue to the view that 40 was the approximate or perhaps average length of a generation; at least this is a common view. It is a little difficult to reconcile with the well-known Oriental custom of early marriage. The number might perhaps be obtained by taking the average of the years of a man's age at which his children were born, though such an explanation does not appear very probable. Or the use of 40 for a generation might be a relic of the period when the youngest born succeeded to the family tent and *sacra*. At any rate 40 is well established as a moderate round number between 'a few' and 'a very great many.' Thus, in addition to the numerous reigns, oppressions, and deliverances of 40, 80 years etc., Isaac and Esau marry at the age of 40; there are 40 years of the wandering; Ezekiel's 40 years' captivity (29^{11}); 40 days was the period Moses spent in the Mount, Elijah and Christ fasted in the wilderness, etc.

A certain mystical value is attached to numbers in later Jewish and Christian philosophy and superstition, perhaps due partly to the ideas suggested by the relations of numbers to each other, and to the practical power of arithmetic; the symbols which aided men so effectually seemed to have some inherent force of their own. Or, again, if 'seven' is sacred, to pronounce a formula seven times must be more effective than to pronounce it six or eight times.

Great importance is attached to numbers in the mediaeval Jewish mystical system, the *Kabbala*. There are ten *s^{e}phîrôth* or primary emanations from God, one original *s^{e}phîrâh*, and three derivative triads; there are twelve channels of Divine grace; 613 commandments, etc.

8. Gematria, a Hebraized form of the Greek *geometria*, used to mean 'reckoning by numbers,' was a late development of which there are traces in the OT. It consisted in indicating a word by means of the number which would be obtained by adding together the numerical values of the consonants of the word. Thus in Gn 14^{14} Abraham has 318 'trained servants,' 318 is the sum of the consonants of the name of Abraham's steward Eliezer in its original Hebrew form. The number is apparently constructed from the name.

The Apocalyptic **number of the Beast** is often explained by Gematria, and 666 has been discovered to be the sum of the numerical values of the letters of some form or other of a large number of names written either in Hebrew, or Greek, or Latin. Thus the Beast has been identified with hundreds of persons, *e.g.* Mohammed, Luther, the Pope, Napoleon I., Napoleon III., etc., each of whom was specially obnoxious to the ingenious identifier. Probably by a little careful manipulation, any name in some form or other, in Hebrew, Greek, or Latin, could be made by *Gematria* to yield 666. The two favourite explanations are *Lateinos*=*Latinus* (the Roman Empire or Emperor), and *Nero Caesar.* The latter has the special advantage that it accounts not only for 666, but also for the variant reading 616 mentioned above; as *Neron Caesar* it gives 666, and as *Nero Caesar*, 616.

W. H. Be.

NUMBERS, BOOK OF.—The fourth book of the *Torah*, the first division of the Hebrew Canon. It continues the history of the Israelites from the stay at Sinai till the arrival at the plains of Moab. The name 'Numbers' is due to the repeated numberings in chs. 1, 3, 4, 26. The book is a conflation of two major documents. The older of these is the JE narrative of the journey from Sinai/Horeb to the E. of the Jordan, a continuation of the JE material in Exodus. The other is the post-exilic document known as the priestly code, consisting of laws from various sources fitted into a narrative framework, the continuation of Leviticus. The only deuteronomic material in the book is 21^{33-35} (=Dt 3^{1-3}). Although the narrative of the book begins at Sinai and ends in Moab, the period of the traditional forty years wandering in the desert (14^{33f}) is a blank, the events recorded occurring either in the second (1^1 10^{11}), or in the fortieth year (35^{38}) after the exodus. The book consists of three parts: 1^1–10^{10}, 10^{11}–21^9, 21^{10}–36^{13}.

A. **1^1–10^{10}**, from P. Ch. 1 records the first census. The reference to this by anticipation in Ex 36^{26} (cf Ex 30^{12}) suggests that it belongs to a stratum of the narrative framework of the post-exilic code older than the supplementary material standing in Ex 35–40 (see LEVITICUS). In the list of the tribes Gad comes third (v.^{24}), the position held by Levi in the tradition preserved in Gn 29^{31}–30^{24}. Levi however had long since ceased to be reckoned as one of the secular tribes when this list was drawn up (cf vv.^{47ff}). The choice of Gad to fill his place may be due to the influence of the tradition of the pre-monarchical twelve-tribe federation. The numbers given, 603,550 adult males in all (v.^{47}; cf Ex 12^{37}), are of course quite artificial; they represent the device used by the post-exilic writer to stress the historical importance of Israel. Vv.$^{47-54}$, explaining the exclusion of the Levites from the census, point ahead to chs. 3 f. Ch. 2 tells how the tribes were arranged in relation to the tent of meeting, both in camp and on the march. The arrangement is based upon the same principle as that in Ezk 48, and reflects the idealistic thinking of the Babylonian Jewish community for whom Israel was more of a theological than an historical entity. 3^{1-13} records the setting apart of the Levites as the servants of the priests, the sons of Aaron. This completely ignores the conception of Deuteronomy in which Levite and priest are synonymous terms, and the representation of Ezk 44 (cf also the comment on ch. 16 below) that the Levites had once been priests, but, with the exception of the family of Zadok, had been degraded to the rank of assistants to the priests because they had lapsed into idolatry. According to Nu 4 they never were priests, and their position as assistants was due not to their having been deposed from the higher office but to the fact that Yahweh had claimed them in lieu of the first-born of Israel which had been consecrated to him on the day he 'slew all the first-born in the land of Egypt' (vv.$^{11-13}$). Vv.$^{14-39}$ record the numbering of the Levites and the positions of the three families, Kohath, Gershom, and Merari, in the camp, to the west, south, and north of the Tabernacle, respectively, Moses, Aaron, and his sons being on the east. The designation of the sanctuary as the Tabernacle in vv.$^{7f, 23-26}$ etc., suggests that this section, unlike Lv 1 and 3 (see LEVITICUS) depends directly upon Ex 25–29, 35–40. Vv.$^{40-51}$ record that a census disclosed that the number of the firstborn males in Israel exceeded that of the Levites by 273, for each of whom a payment of five shekels was required as redemption money. It is impossible to say whether this reflects a claim made by the priesthood at some time subsequent to the composition of vv.$^{14-37}$, or whether it represents an attempt at a quasi-historical realism. Ch. 4 details the transport duties of the three Levitical families to be performed by those between the ages of thirty and fifty (vv.$^{3, 23, 30}$ etc.; contrast 8^{23-26} where the period of service is from twenty-five to fifty). Again, the numbers in chs. 3 f are quite artificial and would seem to be based on nothing more than the writer's imagination. 5^{1-4} commands the exclusion from the camp of three classes of unclean persons (cf Lv 14 f, Nu 19). Vv.$^{5-8}$, requiring restitution for wrong done to another and dealing with cases in which the injured party is dead, would seem to be derived from the same code as Lv 6^{1-9}, to which the summary regarding priestly dues (vv.^{9f}) also belongs. Vv.$^{11-31}$ describe the ordeal of jealousy—obviously an ancient practice—by which a woman suspected by her husband of adultery is compelled to prove her innocence or her guilt. Of importance for an analysis of the post-exilic code are the facts that in this chapter (*a*) the sanctuary is referred to only once and is called the Tabernacle (v.^{17}), not the tent of meeting, and (*b*) there is no mention of Aaron and his sons. In the law of the Nazirite (6^{1-21}), however, also ancient, the reference is to the tent of meeting (vv.$^{10, 13, 18}$; cf Lv 1^3), though here again there is no mention of Aaron. But the priest's formula of blessing (vv.$^{22-27}$) is connected with Aaron. This would seem to belong to the narrative framework; it may once have come before Lv 9^{22}. 7^{1-88}, describing the offerings, identical in each case, of the twelve tribal princes, is probably a supplement to this framework. V.^{89} implicitly refers back to Ex 25^{21f}; at the same time it disregards both the distinction in Ex 26^{33} between the holy place and the most holy and the implication of Lv 16 that the most holy was to be entered only by Aaron once a year, on the Day of Atonement—points of importance for the tracing of the development of the P tradition. 8^{1-4}, describing the lamp stand, appears to be a supplement to Lv 24^{1-4}. 8^{5-26}, telling of the purification of the Levites at the beginning of their ministry, scarcely presupposes, and so seems to be earlier than, the account of their numbering in 3^{14}–4^{49}; and vv.$^{16-19}$ repeat the substance of 3^{11-13}. 9^{1-14} records an apparent modification of passover customs in that it permits people who were precluded from keeping the feast on its appointed day because they were ritually unclean through contact with a dead body, or because they were absent from home, to keep it on the fourteenth day of the second month. 9^{15-23} is an anticipatory summary of the way in which the movements of the Israelites were determined by the cloud which hovered over the Tabernacle. It should be noted, however, that the section is not without a certain ambiguity: vv.^{18a} and ^{23} state that the people of Israel would set out and encamp 'at the command of the Lord.' Furthermore, if 10^{1-10}, commanding the making of two silver trumpets, had known anything of the cloud it would presumably have said that the signal to break camp would be sounded when the cloud moved; and vv.$^{11-28}$, recording the first movement of the camp, after mentioning the cloud states that 'they set out for the first time at the command of the Lord by Moses' (v.^{13}); finally there is no further reference to the cloud in the narrative following. It would thus appear that 9^{15-23} belongs to one of the latest strata of the book—an adaptation of an earlier command of which vv.^{18a} and ^{23} alone survive.

B. **10^{11}–21^9.** 10^{11-36} recounts the departure from Sinai; vv.$^{11-28, 34}$ are derived from the post-exilic

NUMBERS, BOOK OF

narrative from which the preceding material was taken; to this 11^{35} and 12^{16} also belong. $10^{29-33, 35f}$ come from the older (JE) tradition. Hobab's reply to Moses' request in 10^{31f} has been omitted, doubtless because of the representation of vv.$^{33, 35f}$, derived from another strand of the tradition, that the Ark miraculously guided the Israelites on their journey; it is probable, however, in view of Jg 1^{16}, that Hobab consented to accompany them. Chs. 11 and 12, recording incidents which occurred on the way from Sinai to Kadesh, are also from the older account of Israel's life in the desert. 11^{1-3} is an aetiological fragment accounting for the place-name, Taberah. 11^{4-34} is a fusion of four originally independent traditions: the provision of manna (vv.$^{7-9}$; cf Ex 16); the giving of the quails (vv.$^{4-6, 10-15, 18-23, 31f}$); Kibroth-hattaavah (vv.^{33f}); and the inspiration of the seventy elders (vv.$^{16f, 24-30}$). The first three of these are purely legendary; the fourth was to support the claim of the elders that they were the inheritors of the authority of Moses; it thus reflects a controversy in historical times between the elders and the priesthood. Ch. 12, stressing the unique position of Moses and telling of the rebellion of Aaron and Miriam against him, also appears to have a controversial background.

Chs. 13 f are a fusion of two accounts of Moses' sending out spies to find out conditions in Canaan, in preparation for an invasion of the land. The earlier account told only of the reconnaisance of the Negeb as far as Hebron; in the post-exilic narrative the whole country was covered. In both narratives the spies in their report stressed the strength of the Canaanites, with the result that the people, despite the insistence of Caleb and Joshua that they could conquer the land, refused to advance, and prepared to return to Egypt. Yahweh in anger condemned them to forty years' wandering, until all the then adults except Caleb and Joshua were dead. According to the earlier narrative (vv.$^{39-45}$) the people then regretted their folly and, ignoring Moses' protest against this fresh manifestation of disobedience, decided to move on the land at once, which they did, only to be defeated. This JE story, of which the post-exilic narrative is obviously a revision, itself represents an attempt to reconcile two independent traditions, one of which told of an entry into the land from the south, and the other of an entry from the east, across the Jordan. Both these traditions had an historical basis, but they preserved the memory of the movements of two different groups of tribes. To reconcile them the story was told that all the tribes on one occasion did attempt an invasion from the south, and when this was unsuccessful they moved round Edom to the east side of the Jordan, and entered the country in the vicinity of Jericho. One effect of this 'reconciliation' was the omission from the record of the actual entry from the south, which however is still reflected, though obscurely, in Jg 1^{1-20}.

15^{1-16}, derived from the post-exilic code, lays down the amount of flour, wine, and oil required with various animal sacrifices; it is a later and more carefully graduated system than that in Ezk $46^{5-7, 11, 14}$. 15^{17-21} commands that a cake made of the first meal from the newly harvested grain shall be offered to the Lord (cf Ex 34^{26a}, Lv 23^{14}). 15^{22-29} prescribes the offerings to be made for sins committed unwittingly; it is thus a parallel to Lv $4^{13-21, 27-31}$. It should be noted, however, that in Leviticus an unwitting sin on the part of the whole congregation requires a young bull for a sin-offering, and the tent of meeting is referred to; here a burnt offering of a young bull is required, together with a male goat for a sin-offering, and no mention is made of the tent of meeting. Vv.$^{22-26}$ would thus seem to be from another code than Lv 4^{13-21}. The compiler of the post-exilic code included both laws, reconciling them by implying that that in Numbers was to come into force after the settlement (Nu $15^{2, 17}$). The story of the man who was executed for breaking the sabbath (15^{32-36}) is similar in style to Lv $24^{10f, 23}$, and like the latter may have been part of the narrative framework. 15^{37-41} requires tassels to be worn on garments (cf Dt 22^{12}). The law refers explicity to (ritual) holiness (v.^{40}) and ends with the formula 'I am the Lord your God'; it may, accordingly, have been derived from the code upon which Lv 18–23, 25 depends. In view of the fact that in Deuteronomy the command follows upon the prohibition of the mingling of diverse kinds (Dt 22^{9-11}) this version of it may once have followed upon Lv 19^{19}; if so, it will have been torn from its context by the compiler of the post-exilic code and placed after the account of the sabbath-breaking incident (vv.$^{32-36}$). It is probable that in the post-exilic narrative the material in ch. 15 came before the account of the sending out of the spies (13^{1ff}), the present arrangement being due to the compiler of the book who favoured the order of events in JE where the spies story followed immediately upon those in chs. 11 and 12.

Ch. 16 is a fusion of two stories: the first, derived from the earlier history, that of a revolt of some Reubenites against the authority of Moses; it is likely that in its original context the incident was located in the territory of Reuben east of the Jordan and that the story reflects some political or religious tension between the Reubenites and the west Jordan tribes. The second story is from the narrative framework of the post-exilic code. In its primary form it told of a revolt of Korah and two hundred and fifty princes, representing all the secular tribes, against the special sanctity claimed for the Levites. Challenged by Moses, they offered incense at the entrance of the tent of meeting, and fire came forth from the Lord and consumed them. The next day the people assembled and charged Moses and Aaron with the death of the rebels. A plague broke out, which was checked by Aaron who put incense in his censer and made atonement, standing between the living and the dead. Into this story later passages have been interpolated ($16^{8-11, 16f}$) which represent Korah's company as Levites in revolt against the superior sanctity claimed for Aaron. This development of the story is further evidence that underlying the present narrative framework is an earlier schematization in which the Levites were still recognized as priests (cf Ezk 44). The sole priesthood of Aaron and his family is thus a secondary element in the post-exilic schematization. The same development appears in 17^{1-11}. Originally it was the rod of Levi that budded—to indicate the Divine choice of that tribe to be the ministers of the sanctuary; in its present form the tale authenticates the unique position of Aaron. Even in its primary form the tale appears to have been an addition to the main narrative of which 17^{12f} is obviously the conclusion. 18^{1-7} clarifies the relation of the Levites to the priests and belongs to the Aaron stratum of the framework. 18^{8-20} lists the dues to which Aaron was entitled, summarizing the provisions of Lv 2^{6f}, Dt 18^{4} and clarifying Ex 22^{29} 23^{19} 34^{26}. The statement that Aaron has no inheritance or portion in Israel (v.^{20}) is elsewhere made of Levi (v.^{24} Dt 10^{9} 12^{12} $14^{27, 29}$; cf Dt 18^{1}, Jos 13^{33}, Ezk 44^{28}), and this raises the question whether in its original context this list did not refer to the Levites. 18^{21-24} assigns the tithe to the Levites (cf Lv 27^{30}), who, in the supplementary vv.$^{25-32}$, are required to give a tithe of the tithe to the priests. Ch. 19 lays down the procedure to be followed in the purification of anyone who is unclean through contact with the dead. Although the references to Eleazar (vv.^{3f}) and to the Tabernacle (v.^{13}) indicate that the regulations in their present form belong to the latest stratum of the post-exilic material, they obviously reflect ancient practice, and the fact that they come here, at the end of the ritual laws, may suggest that they were taken over from another sanctuary than Jerusalem at a relatively late date.

20^{1} records the arrival of the Israelites at Kadesh 'in the first month.' The style indicates that it comes from the post-exilic framework. The year is not given, but from the fact that Aaron who was eighty-three at the time of the exodus (Ex 7^{7}) died on the first day of the fifth month at the age of one hundred and twenty-three (33^{39}), it must be the fortieth year after the exodus. It has been omitted here in the interest of the narrative in 20^{14}–21^{4}, which in its original context followed immediately upon ch. 14 (21$^{1-3}$ being a variant to 14$^{40-45}$). That is to say, whereas in the post-exilic framework the forty years had elapsed before the Israelites arrived at Kadesh, in the present narrative the traditional forty years in the wilderness are tacitly represented as having elapsed between 20^{13} and 20^{14}. 20$^{2-13}$, telling of water brought from the rock, is an adaptation of the story in Ex 17$^{1-7}$, used here to account for the fact that neither Moses nor Aaron reached the promised land. It is part of the post-exilic framework, the continuation of the Korah story in ch. 16. 20$^{14-21}$, describing the unsuccessful negotiations with the king of Edom for passage through his country, resume, as already noted, the older narrative broken off at 14^{45}. Vv.$^{22-29}$, recording Aaron's death on Mount Hor, are from the post-exilic framework; according to the older tradition, Aaron died at Moserah (Dt 10^{6}). 21$^{1-3}$ is another version of the tradition embodied in 14$^{40-45}$; in its original context it may have been followed by the account of the conquest of the Negeb underlying Jg 1$^{1-21}$ (see comment on chs. 13 f above). The story of the bronze serpent (21$^{4-9}$) may have been told to explain the existence of the bronze serpent in the Temple, later destroyed by Hezekiah (2 K 18^{4}).

C. **21^{10}–36^{13}.** 21^{10}–22^{1} records the progress of the people round Edom to the plains of Moab; it is a conflation of the itinerary of JE, part of which is preserved in Dt 10^{6f}, and that of the post-exilic framework, vv.$^{33-35}$ being an addition from Deuteronomy. 22^{2}–24^{25}, the story of Balaam, is from the older history, and is doubtless an adaptation and elaboration of legends current east of the Jordan about a local seer with whom certain Israelite tribes had on some occasion come into contact. In the post-exilic narrative he appears to have been associated with Midian (cf 25^{6ff} 31^{8}); hence the mention of 'the elders of Midian' in 22^{4,7}. 25$^{1-5}$, also from the older history, tells of the seduction of Israelites by Moabite women, leading to idolatry; it was probably followed by an account of a plague (cf vv.^{8f} 26^{1}), which has been displaced by the post-exilic material in 25$^{6-18}$, which tells how perpetual priesthood was promised to the family of Phinehas for his zeal in slaying an Israelite and the Midianite woman whom he had brought into the camp. This is a re-writing of the Peor story in 25$^{1-5}$. Its original continuation is now found in ch. 31, the account of the war with Midian, from which it is clear that in this tradition Balaam was represented not as the seer who had blessed Israel but as the evil instigator of the people's apostasy. In their original context the events recorded in 25$^{6-18}$ and ch. 31 must have been located in Midian, presumably in the course of the journey from Kadesh to the plains of Moab. The present arrangement of the material is due to the compiler of the book, who, to unify the two forms of the Balaam tradition, severed 25$^{6-18}$ from its continuation, making it an episode in the apostasy of Peor. He continued this with the events recorded in chs. 26–30, which the post-exilic narrative had represented as occurring in Moab, and then reverted to the conclusion of the Midian story in ch. 31. In 25$^{6-18}$ the promise to Phinehas tacitly ignores the fact that, being a descendant of Aaron, he was already a priest. It is not unlikely that we have here an echo of the fiction by which the family of Phinehas—apparently a Palestinian figure (cf Jos 24^{33})—came to be reckoned as descendants of Aaron; if so, the story throws further light upon the development of the post-exilic tradition.

Ch. 26 records the taking of a second census in which it was found that every man of those numbered at Sinai was now dead. The names of the various clans of the several tribes are given—possibly derived from an official record; and the total was 601,730 as against 603,550 in the earlier census (1^{46}); the Levites were 23,000 as against 22,273 (3^{43}). 27$^{1-11}$ records the circumstances under which it was decreed that the daughters of a man dying without a son should inherit his property. In 27$^{12-23}$ Moses is commanded to prepare for death by having Joshua commissioned as his successor by Eleazar the priest. 28$^{1-8}$ prescribes the offering of a lamb, with a cereal offering and a drink offering, every morning and evening; it repeats Ex 29$^{38-42}$. Vv.^{9f} prescribe an additional sacrifice of two lambs every sabbath, and vv.$^{11-15}$ the sacrifices for the beginning of each month. 28^{16}–29^{39} specifies the sacrifices for each of the appointed feasts; it is in the nature of a supplement to Lv 23$^{4-37}$. 30^{1f} affirms the binding character of a vow made by a man; vv.$^{3-16}$ lay down the conditions upon which a woman's vow is binding.

The basic material in ch. 31 was, as has been suggested above, originally the continuation of 25$^{6-18}$. In its present form the story provides a concrete instance of the application of the rules for the removal of uncleanness through contact with the dead (vv.$^{19-24}$) and for the distribution of the spoils of war (vv.$^{25-54}$). Ch. 32, derived from the earlier history, accounts for the fact that Reuben, Gad, and the half-tribe of Manasseh were settled east of the Jordan, and at the same time insists that the tribes are nevertheless true members of Israel. 33$^{1-49}$ recapitulates in the form of an itinerary the present narrative of Ex 12^{37}–Nu 22^{1}. 33^{50}–36^{13} contains instructions relative to the settlement in Canaan. The inhabitants are to be driven out and their cult objects destroyed (33$^{50-56}$). The land, the boundaries of which are delineated, is then to be divided among the several tribes by lot under the supervision of leaders named by Yahweh (ch. 34). It is then laid down that the Levites are to have their own cities, already referred to in Lv 25$^{32-34}$, forty-eight in number, together with the pasture lands surrounding them (35$^{1-8}$), a provision impossible to reconcile with the oft repeated statement that the Levites have no inheritance or portion in Israel (Dt 10^{9} etc.). Six of these cities will be cities of refuge, to which a man who kills another may flee to be safe from the avenger until it is determined whether or not the killing was intentional. If it was intentional, the avenger shall put the murderer to death; if it was not intentional, the slayer will be protected from him so long as he remains in the city of refuge. Only at the death of the reigning high priest may he return to his home (35$^{9-34}$). The earlier laws of asylum are given in Ex 21$^{12-14}$, Dt 19$^{1-13}$. Ch. 36 requires heiresses to marry within their own tribe so that land may not pass from one tribe to another; it is a supplement to 27$^{1-11}$.

The material derived from the older JE tradition is marked by its spontaneity and its portrayal of character. The personality of Moses is artlessly delineated: *e.g.* his humble piety (12^{3}), his trust in Yahweh (10$^{29-32}$), his faithfulness and intimacy with Him (12$^{6-8}$), his affection for his people (11$^{2,10-15}$ 21^{7}), his generosity (11$^{25-29}$ 12). And the character of the people is portrayed with equal vividness—their dislike of restraint, their selfish murmurings, their vehement repentance followed by wilful self-assertion. In these narratives there is, despite their legendary character, a strong sense of history. Events were under Divine control and so revealed the Divine purpose. But the control was exercised not arbitrarily and artificially from without the process but from within, through men inspired to see the meaning of events and to make adequate and selfless response thereto. The portrayal of character was thus not an incidental but a primary element in the work of those responsible for the ordering of the diverse traditions of which the narrative was composed. The post-exilic narrative is far more artificial and selfconscious. Though cast in the form of history, it is rather a distillation of what had been revealed and apprehended through events in the past. For these writers, Israel was less an historical than a theological concept, less a nation than a worshipping community. And their concern was with the cult, that it should remind the people constantly of the mystery of the Divine holiness and should be an adequate means of approach to God. Thus, in its origin this concern was not ecclesiasticism in the pejorative sense of the word. It was an expression of a necessary phase in the development of the idea of Israel. But if self-centred ecclesiasticism was to be avoided it was essential that those to whom it fell to administer the code should be as sensitive to changing conditions and changing needs as its compilers had been in their day. It was, in part, to meet such changing conditions that the code was ultimately conflated with the older tradition, to form the Pentateuch; and in the years that followed Jerusalem was the centre from which the light shone forth to lighten the Gentiles. Nevertheless, the NT provides abundant evidence that by the 1st cent. the vision had faded, to be recovered only when the universal approach to God was thrown open by one 'who has become a priest, not according to a legal requirement concerning bodily descent but by the power of an indestructible life' (He 7[16]). A. H. McN.—**C. A. Si.**

NUMENIUS.—One of an embassy sent (*c* 144 B.C.) by the Jews to Rome and Sparta (1 Mac 12[1-18]). He visited Rome on a similar errand a few years later (1 Mac 14[24] 15[15-24]).

NUN.—The father of Joshua, Ex 33[11], Nu 11[28], Jos 1[1] etc.

NUN.—Fourteenth letter of Hebrew alphabet, and so used to introduce the fourteenth part of Ps 119, every verse of which begins with this letter.

NURSE.—Healthy women among the Hebrews in ancient times were accustomed to suckle their own children, Gn 21[7]. As in Palestine to-day, the child was suckled for a long time, sometimes for as much as three years, 1 S 1[23f], 2 Mac 7[37]. Weaning was the occasion of a joyful feast, Gn 21[8], 1 S 1[24]. But the nurse was also found in olden times in Israel, and was often held in great affection and honour, Gn 24[59] 35[8], Ex 2[7], 2 K 11[2], Is 49[23], 1 Th 2[7]. The nurse, *mêneḳeth*, must be distinguished from the *'ōmeneth*, translated 'nurse' in Ru 4[16], 2 S 4[4], which means the attendant in charge of the child. W. E.

NUTS.—1. Hebrew *'ᵉghôz*, Ca 6[11]. This is without doubt the fruit of the walnut-tree (*Juglans regia*) called to-day in Arabic *jauz*. **2.** Hebrew *boṭnîm*, Gn 43[11]. This means **pistachio nuts** (so RVm, RSV), the fruit of *pistacia vera*, a tree widely cultivated in Palestine. The nuts, known in Arabic as *fistuq*, are very great favourites; they are eaten raw, and also made into various sweets and confectionery. E. W. G. M.

NYMPHA(S).—An influential Colossian Christian (Col 4[15]), whose house was used as a meeting-place for Christians. The question of the correct reading is a difficult one, and it is uncertain whether it should be Nymphas (so AV, RV) or **Nympha,** a man or a woman. Nothing further is known of the person named. RSV reads 'Nympha and the church in her house.'

O

OABDIUS, 1 Es 9[27] (RV).—See ABDI.

OAK.—1. Hebrew *'ēlāh*, Gn 35[4], Jg 6[11, 19], 2 S 18[9f, 14], 1 K 13[14], 1 Ch 10[12], Is 1[30], Ezk 6[13], Hos 4[13]; 'Valley of Elah' (RVm 'terebinth'), Is 6[13] (AV **teil tree**); Hebrew *'allāh*, a slight variant, Jos 24[26].

2. Hebrew *'ēlîm*, perhaps plural of *'ēlāh*, Is 1[29] (RVm 'terebinth') 57[5] (AV 'idols'; AVm, RV, RSV 'oaks') 61[3] (AV, RV 'trees'; RSV 'oaks'). These words, *'ēlāh*, *'allāh*, and *'ēlîm*, all apparently refer to the **terebinth** (q.v.).

3. *'allôn*, cannot be the same as *'ēlāh*, because it occurs with it in Is 6[13], Hos 4[13]; it is found also in Gn 35[8], Is 44[14], Am 2[9]. In Is 2[13], Ezk 27[6], Zec 11[2] the *'allônîm* ('oaks') of Bashan are mentioned. In Jos 19[33] (AV) *'allōn* is treated as a proper name.

4. *'ēlôn*, probably merely a variation of *'allōn*, is in Gn 12[6] 13[18] 14[13] 18[1], Dt 11[30], Jg 4[11] 9[6, 37], 1 S 10[3], translated 'plain' in AV, but 'oak' in RV and RSV, with RVm 'terebinth.' *'allôn* and *'ēlōn* apparently refer to the oak.

Oaks have always been relatively plentiful in Palestine. Even to-day, in spite of the most reckless destruction, groves of oaks survive on Carmel, Tabor, around Banias, and in ancient Bashan; while whole miles of country are covered with shrub-like oaks produced from the roots of trees destroyed every few years for fuel. Among the nine recognized varieties of oak in Syria, the evergreen *Quercus coccifera* or 'holm oak' is the finest—it is often 30 to 35 feet high. Its preservation is usually due to its being situated at some sacred *wely*. **'Abraham's oak'** at Hebron is of this kind. Other common oaks are the Valonia oak (*Q. Aegilops*), which has large acorns with prickly cups, much valued for dyeing; and the oriental gall oak (*Q. cerris*), a comparatively insignificant tree, especially noticeable for the variety of galls which grow on it. Both these latter are deciduous, the leaves falling from late autumn to early spring. Oak wood is used for tanning skin bottles and also as fuel, while the acorn cups of the Valonia oak and the galls of the various oak trees are both important articles of commerce in N. Syria. E. W. G. M.

OAR.—See SHIPS AND BOATS.

OATHS.—How the need of oaths must first have arisen can be seen in such a passage as Ex 22[10f]: 'If a man delivers to his neighbour an ass or an ox or a sheep or any beast to keep, and it dies or is hurt or is driven away, without anyone seeing it, an oath by the Lord shall be between them both to see whether he [the custodian] has not put his hand to his neighbour's property; and the owner shall accept the oath, and he [the custodian] shall not make restitution.' As there is no witness to substantiate the innocence or prove the guilt of the suspected person, God is called to witness.

An oath is really a conditional curse, which a man calls down upon himself from God, in case he should not speak the truth or keep a promise. The use of oaths was not restricted to judicial procedure, but was also connected with a variety of everyday matters. To swear by Yahweh was regarded as a sign of loyalty to Him (cf Dt 6[13], Is 48[1], Jer 12[16]).

There are two words in Hebrew for an oath: (1) *shᵉbhūʿāh*, which apparently comes from the same root as the word for 'seven' (*shebhaʿ*); the Hebrew verb meaning 'to swear' represents the same root, and may mean something like 'to do a thing seven times' or 'to come under the influence of seven things.' Seven was the most sacred number among the Hebrews (cf *shābhūaʿ*, 'week' of seven days), and among the Semites generally; likewise to a considerable extent among the Persians and Greeks. Among the Babylonians the seven planets each represented a god. Hence there is good reason for supposing a connexion between the sacred number and the oath. (2) *'ālāh*, which, strictly speaking, means a 'curse' and was a stronger form of oath. The combination of both words ('the oath of the curse') was used on especially solemn occasions, *e.g.* Nu 5[21] (cf Peter's denial by curse and oath, Mt 26[74]).

There were various forms used in taking an oath, *e.g.* 'God do so to me and more also if . . .' (1 K 2[23]); the punishment called down in case the oath is not observed is left indeterminate in this form. This is to be explained from the fact that there was a fear lest the mere mention of the curse should *ipso facto* bring it to pass—a remnant of animistic conceptions (*i.e.* there was the fear that a demon might think his services were required).

In later times, however, the nature of the curse is sometimes mentioned, *e.g.* 'The Lord make you like Zedekiah and Ahab, whom the king of Babylon roasted in the fire' (Jer 29^{22}; cf Is 65^{15}, Zec 8^{13}). Another form was: 'God is witness between you and me' (Gn 31^{50}), or, 'May the Lord be a true and faithful witness against us if . . .' (Jer 42^{5}). A more common form is: 'As the Lord lives' (Jg 8^{19}), sometimes varied by the addition of a reference to the person to whom the oath was made: 'As the Lord lives and as your soul lives' (1 S 20^{3}, cf 2 S 15^{21}). Still another form was: 'God . . . judge between us' (Gn 31^{53}). God Himself is conceived of as taking oaths: 'By myself I have sworn' (Gn 22^{16}).

The usual gesture in taking an oath was to raise the arm towards heaven (Dt 32^{40}, Dn 12^{7}), the motive being to point to the dwelling-place of God; to 'raise the hand' became a synonym for 'to swear' (Ex 6^{8}, Nu 14^{30}, not apparent in EV). Another gesture is referred to in Gn 24^{2} 47^{29}, *viz.*, putting the hand under the thigh; the organ of generation was regarded as peculiarly holy by the Hebrews.

With regard to the breaking of an oath, see Lv 6$^{1-7}$; and for the use of oaths in ratifying a covenant, see Gn 21$^{27-31}$ 26^{28} 31^{53}, Jos 9^{15}, 2 K 11^{4}.

W. O. E. O.—**W. F. S.**

OBADIAH ('servant of Y″').—A name of a type common among the Semitic peoples; it occurs frequently in the OT, for the most part as the name of persons of whom little or nothing is known. It has also been found on an ancient Hebrew seal. **1.** The author of the Vision of Obadiah: see following article. **2.** Ahab's steward, the protector of Yahweh's prophets against Jezebel, 1 K 18$^{3-16}$. This person lived in the 9th cent. B.C. **3.** A descendant of Saul, 1 Ch 8^{38}; he lived, to judge from his position in the genealogy, about 700 B.C. On the probable genuineness of the genealogy see G. B. Gray, *Studies in Hebrew Proper Names*, pp. 241 f. **4.** An Issacharite, 1 Ch 7^{3}. **5.** A descendant of David in the 5th cent. B.C., if the Hebrew text (1 Ch 3^{21}) correctly makes him a grandson of Zerubbabel, but in the 4th if the LXX is right and he belonged to the sixth generation after Zerubbabel. **6.** The head of a family who returned with Ezra, Ezr 8^{9}, 1 Es 8^{35} (AV, RV **Abadias**). **7.** A priestly contemporary of Nehemiah, Neh 10^{5}. **8.** A doorkeeper, Neh 12^{25}. **9, 10, 11, 12, 13.** Various persons in the genealogies or stories of the Chronicler, 1 Ch 9^{16} (called **Abda** in Neh 11^{17}) 12^{9} 27^{19}, 2 Ch 17^{7} 34^{12}. On the Chronicler's use of such names, see G. B. Gray, *op. cit.*, pp. 170–190. G. B. G.

OBADIAH.—This short prophetic book is fourth in the Book of the Twelve, or the Minor Prophets. Its position suggests that the editors of the prophetic books held it to be the work of a pre-exilic prophet. Since no clue as to identity or time of Obadiah was preserved in the superscription they may have been as much at a loss as we are. Since there is an affinity between Obadiah and a chapter of Jeremiah (Ob $^{1-4}$=Jer 49$^{14-16}$; Ob ^{5f}=Jer 49$^{9, 10a}$) they may have reasoned that Jeremiah was dependent on Obadiah. However, the material in Jer 49 is hardly authentic. Even so the pre-exilic origin of at least a part of Obadiah's prophecy has still found defenders in recent decades. Most scholars, however, favour post-exilic origin and doubt that the book is the work of one writer.

The work is composed of two sections. The concluding couplet of the first has been misplaced and put after the opening line of the second. The division thus is vv.$^{1-14, 15b}$ and $^{15a, 16-21}$. The first section is concerned with the fall of Edom and the question is whether it is genuinely predictive or mirrors the actual happening. In the former case the poem must have been written while the Jews were still mindful of the rôle played by the Edomites at the time of the fall of Judah in 586 B.C. (cf La 4^{21} etc.). In the latter case it could be considerably younger. According to Glueck's archaeological exploration of Edom that region was without sedentary occupation in the Persian period. The downfall of Edom was certainly complete by about 450 B.C. Malachi looks back on the event (1$^{2-5}$). Arab invasions seem to have brought it about. The second poem, vv.$^{15a, 16-21}$, is predictive of the Day of Yahweh that is to bring judgment on the nations, especially on Esau-Edom. The question here is whether vv.$^{19-21}$ are not a younger elaboration of the preceding ones. The fact that they are prose rather than poetry lends support to such a view. The region south of Judah is now 'Mount Esau,' not the old homeland NE. of the Gulf of ʿAqaba E. of *el-ʿArabah*. There is an interesting allusion to the Jewish dispersion in Sepharad, which according to the inscriptions is Sardis in Lydia, but perhaps here stands broadly for Asia Minor. This is clearly the group transplanted from Babylonia to Lydia and Phrygia by Antiochus III., *c* 205 B.C. (Jos. *Ant.* XII. iii. 4 [147]). Who the 'saviours' are that are to go up to Mount Zion remains obscure; the versions suggest the possibility of reading 'those who have been saved' instead of 'saviours.' The book of Obadiah is nationalistic prophecy and hence of very minor importance.

E. G. K.

OBAL.—Son of Joktan, Gn 10^{28}; called **Ebal** (q.v.) in 1 Ch 1^{22}.

OBDIA, 1 Es 5^{38} (AV, RV).—See HABAIAH.

OBED.—**1.** The son of Boaz and Ruth, the father of Jesse and grandfather of David (Ru 4^{17}), and an ancestor of our Lord (Mt 1^{5}, Lk 3^{32}). **2.** A descendant of Sheshan, 1 Ch 2^{37ff}. **3.** One of David's heroes, 1 Ch 11^{47}. **4.** A son of Shemaiah, 1 Ch 26^{7}. **5.** The father of Azariah, 2 Ch 23^{1}. **6.** One who returned with Ezra, 1 Es 8^{32} (AV, RV **Obeth**); called **Ebed** in Ezr 8^{6}.

OBED-EDOM.—**1.** A Philistine, a native of Gath, who lived in or near Jerusalem. In his house David deposited the Ark after the death of Uzzah, and here it remained three months, bringing a blessing by its presence, 2 S 6^{10f}, 1 Ch 13^{14}. **2.** The eponym of a family of doorkeepers and singers in the Temple, 1 Ch 15$^{18, 21, 24}$ 16$^{5, 38}$ 26$^{4, 8, 15}$. **3.** The son of Jeduthun and a doorkeeper in the Temple, 1 Ch 16^{38}. **4.** One who had charge of the vessels in the Temple in the days of Amaziah, 2 Ch 25^{24}.

OBEDIENCE.—Used in the EV to translate the Hebrew *shāmaʿ* meaning literally 'hear,' 'listen' (hence the title Shemaʿ for the Jewish confession of faith, Dt 6^{4}). For the Hebrew, to hear is to hearken, to be persuaded (hence the Greek term *peithomai* is used commonly to render the Hebrew 'hear' in the LXX and NT). The term is used of man's relationship to his fellows, children to parents (Dt 21^{18}, Eph 6^{1}), wives to husbands (1 P 3^{16}), slaves to masters (Eph 6^{5}), subjects to rulers (Gn 49^{10}, cf Ro 13), and in the NT Christians to their leaders (2 Th 3^{14}, Ph 2^{12} etc.). More often it refers to man's relationship to God (Dt 4^{30}, Jos 24^{24} etc.). Indeed the OT prophets encourage rebellion from a king who has himself disobeyed God (and see Ac 5^{29}). Obedience is superior to sacrifice (1 S 15^{22}). It is connected with the covenant (Ex 19^{5}, Dt 4^{30f}, Jer 11^{1ff}), and by obedience to God's accompanying commands the nation will prosper (Dt 11^{13}, 1 K 6^{12}, Is 1^{19} etc.). Yet the history of Israel is a persistent reiteration of disobedience and rebellion (*e.g.* Dt 8^{20}, Jer 7^{24}, Ac 7^{39}). With the perfect obedience of Jesus (Ro 5^{19}, Ph 2^{8}, He 5^{8}) the old pattern has been broken. Man through faith and love can now in Christ obey God and be saved (Jn 14^{15}, Ro 6^{17}, 1 Jn 5^{2}). Since Christ's obedience is primary, man's obedience takes the form of believing in His saving work; hence we have the expression, 'obedience to the faith' (Ro 1^{5} 16^{26}, Ac 6^{7}; cf He 11^{8}). Accordingly the NT, in contrast to the OT, stresses belief rather than obedience as such. C. C. Ro.

OBEISANCE.—A word derived from the French word for obedience, and used in the OT only as an occasional translation of the Hebrew *shāḥāh* 'bow down,' 'prostrate.' It is the gesture of homage or reverence before a king or superior ; the act of worship before a god. C. C. Ro.

OBELISK.—See Pillar, **2** (*c*).

OBETH, 1 Es 8^{32} (AV, RV).—See Ebed, **2.**

OBIL.—The overseer of David's camels, 1 Ch 27^{30}.

OBLATION.—See Sacrifice and Offering.

OBOTH.—A stopping-place on the wanderings, Nu 21^{10f} 33^{43f}. It is possibly modern *ʿAin el-Weiba*, S. of the Dead Sea.

OBSERVE.—Mk 6^{20} ' Herod feared John, knowing that he was a righteous and holy man, and kept him safe ' (AV ' observed him '). The meaning of the English word ' observed ' is ' reverenced.' Tyndale's translation is ' gave him reverence.' Cf Shakespeare's 2 *Henry IV.* iv. iv. 30, ' he is gracious, if he be observed.' But the more probable meaning of the Greek is ' protected him,' or, as RV and RSV, ' kept him safe.'

OCCUPY.—The ' occupier ' of Ezk 27^{27} (AV, RV ; RSV ' dealer ') is a ' trader,' and ' to occupy ' in Ezk 27^{9} (AV, RV ; RSV ' barter '), Lk 19^{13} (AV ; RV, RSV ' trade ') is ' to trade.' The original meaning of the English word is to be engaged in anything.

OCHIEL.—See Jeiel, **5.**

OCIDELUS, 1 Es 9^{22} (AV, RV).—See Gedaliah, **4.**

OCHRAN.—Father of Pagiel, Nu 1^{13} 2^{37} 7$^{72, 77}$ 10$_{9}$ (AV **Ocran**).

OCIDELUS, 1 Es 9^{22} (AV, RV).—See Jozabad, **6.**

OCINA.—Taking the towns mentioned in order as fearing the advance of Holofernes (Jth 2^{28}), Sidon and Tyre are well known. With some certainty Sur may be identified with *Umm el-ʿAmūd*, S. of *Iskanderūna*, which seems to have been formerly called *Turān*. The next step takes us naturally to Acre, in later times known as *Accon*, in which we may find an echo of the earlier Ocina. W. E.

OCRAN.—AV form of **Ochran** (q.v.).

ODED.—**1.** The father of the prophet Azariah, 2 Ch 15^{1}. In v.^{8} ' Oded ' of MT is a mistake, perhaps through the omission of ' Azariah the son of ' (cf RSV). **2.** A prophet who successfully protested against the proposal to enslave Judahites, 2 Ch 28^{9ff}.

ODOMERA.—A chief, slain by Jonathan (1 Mac 9^{66}).

OF.—As already noted, under By, the preposition ' of ' is generally used in AV for the agent, as Mt 2^{16} ' He was mocked of the wise men.' But there are other obsolete or archaic uses of ' of,' which should be carefully observed. Thus (1) it sometimes means *from* (the proper meaning of the A.S. ' of '), as Mk 11^{8} ' Others cut down branches of the trees,' Jn 15^{15} ' All things that I have heard of my Father,' Jn 16^{13} ' He shall not speak of himself ' ; (2) *concerning*, as Ac 5^{24} ' They doubted of them, whereunto this would grow,' Mt 18^{13} ' He rejoiceth more of that sheep than of the ninety and nine,' Jn 2^{17} ' The zeal of thine house ' ; (3) *with*, Ca 2^{5} ' I am sick of love.'

OFFENCE.—The Greek word *skandalon* properly means a ' trap.' The word is used in the Gospels (Mt 18^{7}, Lk 17^{1}) of offences (so AV ; RSV ' temptations to sin ') in the form of hindrances to the faith of believers, especially of Christ's little ones. The context makes it clear what kind of **stumbling-blocks** are referred to. In the corresponding passage in the Sermon on the Mount (Mt 5^{29f} ; cf Mk 9$^{45, 47}$) the right eye and right hand are given as instances of the kind of offences that may arise. The members here cited are not only in themselves good and serviceable, but necessary, though they are capable, in certain circumstances, of becoming the occasion of sin to us. In the same way the Christian may find pursuits and pleasures, which in themselves are innocent, bringing unexpected temptations and involving him in sin. The possible applications of this are numerous, whether the warning be referred to artistic gifts (the ' hand ' and ' eye '), or abuses of certain kinds of food and drink, or any other circumstances which may lead a man from the higher life or divert him from his aims. All these may be compared to the stumbling-blocks which cause a man to fall. Such things must be dispensed with, for the sake of entering the ' eternal life,' which is the Christian man's goal. The RSV uses ' offence ' only as a translation of Greek *skandalizō* in the sense ' take ' or ' give offence,' *e.g.* Mt 11^{6} 17^{27}. T. A. M.—**F. W. G.**

OFFERING.—See Sacrifice and Offering.

OFFICER.—By this somewhat indefinite expression are rendered some eight or ten different Hebrew and Greek words, several of which seem to have had an equally wide application. Of the Hebrew words the commonest is *shōṭēr*, from a root which in Assyrian means ' to write.' The *shōṭēr*, accordingly, was originally, it would seem, a subordinate official attached to the higher military, civil, and judicial officers of the State for secretarial purposes (see Driver's summary of their duties in his commentary [*ICC*], on Dt 1^{15}). In the narrative of the oppression of the Hebrews in Egypt, the ' officers ' are the Hebrew subordinates of the Egyptian taskmasters (see Ex 5^{14}) ; one of their duties, it may be assumed, was to keep account of the tale of bricks made by each of their compatriots.

In Gn 37^{36} and elsewhere ' officer ' is the translation of the usual word for **' eunuch '** (q.v.), but, as 39^{1} shows, the original (*sārîs*) must here signify, more generally, a court official. Still another word, rendered ' officer ' in 1 K 4$^{5, 7}$ etc., denotes the heads of the twelve administrative districts into which Solomon divided his kingdom.

In NT ' officer ' is, with one exception (Lk 12^{58}), the translation of a Greek word of equally wide application. In the account of our Lord's betrayal and capture the ' officers ' are members of the Temple police (Jn 7^{32} etc.), as also in the account of the imprisonment of Peter and John (Ac 5$^{22, 26}$; cf 4^{1}). The same word is elsewhere rendered ' minister,' either in the more general sense of ' attendant ' (so Ac 13^{5} RV), or in the special sense of the ' minister ' (RV and RSV ' attendant ') or officer of the Jewish synagogue (Lk 4^{20}), for whom see Synagogue. A. R. S. K.

OG.—The king of Bashan, who, with his children and people, was defeated and destroyed by the Israelites at Edrei, directly after the defeat of Sihon. His rule extended over sixty cities, of which the two chief were Ashtaroth and Edrei (Jos 12^{4}). The whole of his kingdom was assigned to the tribes of Reuben, Gad, and half-Manasseh (Dt 3$^{1-13}$, Nu 32^{33} ; see also Dt 1^{4} 4^{47} 31^{4}, Jos 2^{10} 9^{10} 13$^{12, 30}$). The conquest of this powerful giant king lingered long in the imagination of the Israelites as one of the chief exploits of the conquest (Ps 135^{11} 136^{20}). The impression of the gigantic stature of Og is corroborated by the writer of Dt 3^{11}, who speaks of the huge ' iron bedstead ' (or sarcophagus) belonging to him. According to the measurements there given, this sarcophagus was nine cubits long and four cubits broad. It is, however, impossible to estimate his stature from these dimensions, owing to the tendency to build tombs unnecessarily large in order to leave an impression of superhuman stature. The ' iron ' of which the sarcophagus was made, probably means black basalt. Many basaltic sarcophagi have been found on the east of the Jordan. T. A. M.

OHAD.—A son of Simeon, Gn 46^{10}, Ex 6^{15}.

OHEL.—A son of Zerubbabel, 1 Ch 3^{20} ; but the text is doubtful.

OHOLAH AND OHOLIBAH (AV **Aholah, Aholibah**). —Two sisters who were harlots (Ezk 23). The words appear to mean ' tent ' and ' tent in her,' the allusion being to the tents used for idolatrous purposes. The passage is figurative, the two harlots representing, the one Samaria and the other Jerusalem. Though both were wedded to Yahweh, they were seduced by the gallant officers of the East, Samaria being led astray by Assyria and Jerusalem by Babylon. The whole of the allegory is a continuation of ideas already expounded in chs. 16 and 20, and is intended as a rebuke against

Israel for her fondness for alliances with the great Oriental empires, which was the occasion of new forms and developments of idolatry. The main idea of the allegory seems to have been borrowed from Jer 3$^{6-13}$.

T. A. M.

OHOLIAB.—The chief assistant of Bezalel, Ex 31^{6} 35^{34} 36^{1f} 38^{23} (AV **Aholiab**).

OHOLIBAH.—See OHOLAH.

OHOLIBAMAH (AV **Aholibamah**).—**1.** One of Esau's wives, Gn 36$^{2, 5, 14, 18, 25}$. **2.** An Edomite 'duke,' Gn 36^{41}, 1 Ch 1^{52}.

OIL.—With one exception (Est 2^{12} 'oil of myrrh') all the Scripture references to oil are to **'olive oil,'** as it is expressly termed in Ex 27^{20} 30^{24} etc., according to the more correct rendering of RV and RSV. Considering how very numerous these references are—some two hundred in all—it is surprising that there should be so few that throw light on the methods adopted in the preparation of this indispensable product of the olive tree.

1. *Preparation of oil.*—By combining these meagre references with the fuller data of the Mishnah, as illustrated by the actual remains of oil-presses, either still above ground or recently recovered from the soil of Palestine, it is possible to follow with some minuteness the principal methods adopted. The **olives** were either shaken from the tree or beaten down by striking the branches with a light pole, as illustrated on Greek vases (illustrated in Vigouroux, *Dict. de la Bible*, article 'Huile'). The latter method supplies Isaiah with a pathetic figure of Israel (17^{6} RVm, RSV).

The finest quality of oil was got by selecting the best berries before they were fully ripe. These were pounded in a mortar, after which the pulp was poured into a basket of rushes or wickerwork. From this, as a strainer, the liquid was allowed to run off into a receiving vessel. After the oil had floated and been purified, it formed **'beaten oil,'** such as had to be provided for the lighting of the Tabernacle (1 K 5^{11} RSV; cf Ex 27^{20}, Lv 24^{2}).

In the preparation of the oil required for ordinary domestic use, however, the methods adopted closely resembled those for the making of **wine.** Indeed, it is evident that the same apparatus served for the making both of wine and of oil (see WINE for the names of the parts, and note the phrase, Jl 2^{24}, 'the vats shall overflow with wine and oil'). From evidence, literary and archaeological, it is clear that there were various kinds of oil-presses in use in different periods. A very common, if not quite the simplest, type consisted of a shallow trough hewn in the native rock, from which, as in the similar, if not identical, wine-press, a conducting channel carried the expressed liquid to a slightly lower trough or oil-vat. In early times it appears as if a preliminary pressing was made with the feet alone (Mic 6^{15}).

In the absence of a suitable rock-surface, as would naturally be the case within a city of any antiquity, a solid block of limestone—circular, four-sided, and eight-sided (Megiddo) are the shapes recovered by recent explorers—was hollowed to the depth of a few inches, a rim being left all round save at one corner. Such presses were found at Taanach (illustrated, Sellin, *Tell Ta'annek*, 61, reproduced in Benzinger's *Heb. Arch.*^{3} [1927] 148), and elsewhere. In these the olives were crushed by means of a large round stone. The liquid was either allowed to collect in a large cup-hollow in the surface of the trough, from which it was baled out by hand (*PEFSt*, 1903, p. 112), or it was run off into a vessel placed at the corner above mentioned (see Sellin's illustration, and *op cit.* 60 f, 93). At a later period, as we learn from the Mishnah, a stone in the shape of the modern millstone was used. Through the centre a pole was inserted, by which it was made to revolve on its narrow side round the circular trough—a method still in use in Syria (illustrated, Galling, *Biblisches Reallexikon* [1937] 402).

From the oil-mill, as this apparatus may be termed, the product of which naturally, after purification, produced the finer sort of oil, the pulp was transferred to the **oil-press** properly so called. Here it was placed in baskets piled one above the other. Pressure was then applied for the extraction of a second quality of oil, by means of a heavy wooden beam worked as a lever by ropes and heavy weights, or by a windlass. Details of the fittings of these 'press-houses,' as they are named in the Mishnah, and of another type of press formed of two upright monoliths with a third laid across, the whole resembling the Greek letter π, have been collected by the present writer in the article 'Oil' in *EBi* iii, 3467, and may now be controlled by the account of the elaborate underground 'press-house' described and illustrated by Bliss and Macalister in *Excavations in Palestine*, pp. 208 f and plate 92 (cf *ib.* 196 f and Index).

The expressed liquid, both from the oil-mill and from the oil-press, was collected either in a rock-cut vat or in separate jars. In these it was allowed to settle, when the oil rose to the top, leaving a bitter, watery liquid, the *amurca* of the Romans, and other refuse behind. Oil in this fresh state is distinguished in OT from the refined and purified product; the former is *yiṣhār*, so frequently named along with 'new wine' or must (*tîrôsh*, see WINE, **1**) and corn as one of the chief products of Canaan; the latter is always *shemen*, but the distinction is not observed in our versions. The fresh oil or *yiṣhār* was refined in the same manner as wine, by being poured from vessel to vessel, and was afterwards stored in jars and in skins. A smaller quantity for immediate use was kept in a small earthenware pot—the vial of 1 S 10^{1} and of 2 K 9$^{1, 3}$ RV (RSV 'flask'; AV 'box')—or in a horn (1 S 16$^{1, 13}$, 1 K 1^{39}).

2. *Uses of oil.*—Foremost among what may be called the secular uses of oil may be placed its daily employment as a **cosmetic,** already dealt with under ANOINTING (see also OINTMENT). This was the oil that made the face to shine (Ps 104^{15}). As in all Eastern lands, oil was largely used in the **preparation of food**; familiarity with this use of it is presupposed in the comparison of the taste of the strange manna to that of the familiar 'cakes baked with oil' (Nu 11^{8} RSV; see, further, MEALS, **1**, end). Oil was also indispensable for the **lighting** of the house after nightfall. In addition to the universal olive oil, the Mishnah (*Shabbath*, ii. 1 f.) names a variety of other oils then in use, among them oil of sesame, fish oil, castor oil, and naphtha. That used in the Temple (1 Ch 9^{29}) was no doubt of the finest quality, like the 'beaten oil' for the Tabernacle above described. The **medicinal** properties of oil were early recognized (Is 1^{6} RSV); the Good Samaritan mixed his with wine (Lk 10^{34}), producing an antiseptic mentioned also in post-Biblical Jewish writings.

Oil has a prominent place in the **ritual** of the Priests' Code, particularly in the preparation of the 'cereal offering' (Lv 2$^{1, 4}$ etc.). It also appears in connexion with the leprosy-offering (14^{10ff}) and in other connexions, but is absent from the sin-offering (5^{1ff}) and the jealousy-offering (Nu 5^{11ff}). For the special case of the 'sacred anointing oil' (Ex 30$^{23-25}$), see OINTMENT.

As might have been expected from the extensive cultivation of the olive by the Hebrews, oil not only formed an important article of inland **commerce,** but was exported in large quantities both to the West, by way of Tyre (Ezk 27^{17}), and to Egypt (Hos 12^{1}).

This abundance of oil furnished the Hebrew poets with a figure for material prosperity in general, as in Dt 33^{24} 'and let him dip his foot in oil.' From its being in daily use to anoint the heads of one's guests at a festive meal (Ps 23^{5} etc.), oil became by association a symbol of joy and gladness (Ps 45^{7}=He 1^{9}, Is 61^{3}).

A. R. S. K.—W. D. McH.

OIL TREE (*'ēṣ-shemen*, 1 K 6$^{23, 31-33}$ plural *'aṣê-shemen*), AV 'olive tree,' margin 'oily,' Hebrew 'trees of oil,' RSV 'olivewood'; Neh 8^{15} AV 'pine,' RSV 'wild olive'; Is 41^{19} AV and RV 'oil tree,' RVm 'oleaster,' RSV 'olive'). The precise nature of the 'tree of oil' is difficult to determine. Some kind of pine has been suggested (cf Neh 8^{15} AV), the resin of the tree being regarded as its oil or the heartwood being regarded as fat enough to entitle it to the name. The oleaster (*Eleagnus angustifolia*), a beautiful and common shrub, would suit, except that it is difficult to see how it could ever have furnished a block of wood sufficient for the two cherubim 'each ten cubits high' (1 K 6[23]). The Oxford *Hebrew and English Lexicon* has '*oil tree*, usually explained as wild olive, *oleaster*' (1032a). The name Oleaster was formerly used of the wild variety of *Olea europea*, with which has been identified the *agrielaios* ('wild olive' RSV) of Ro 11[17, 24]. That the 'oil tree' is the 'olive' is unlikely from Neh 8[15] where the olive tree is mentioned just before, but that it may be the 'wild olive' is not ruled out by the argument that the leaves of the cultivated and wild varieties are so alike that the one would hardly be specified after the mention of the other. E. W. G. M.—**W. D. McH.**

OINTMENT.—With two exceptions, 'ointment' in our EV is the rendering in OT, of the ordinary word for 'oil,' and in some passages the ointment may have consisted of oil only. In most of the references, however, **perfumed oil** is undoubtedly meant. The two are distinguished in Lk 7[46] 'You did not anoint my head with oil, but she has anointed my feet with ointment (*myron*).' The extensive use of *myron* in NT in the sense of 'ointment' shows that **myrrh** was then the favourite perfume. The dead body, as well as the living subject, was anointed with this ointment (Lk 23[56]). Another 'very costly' unguent is described as 'ointment of pure nard' (Mk 14[3], Jn 12[3] RSV; 'spikenard' RV); see SPIKENARD. These much-prized unguents were kept in pots of alabaster, as in Egypt, where they are said to retain their fragrance for 'several hundred years' (Wilkinson, *Anc. Egyp.* i, 426, with illustration).

In the Priests' Code there is repeated reference to a specially rich unguent, **'the holy anointing oil,'** the composition of which is minutely laid down in Ex 30[23-25]. The ingredients, in addition to a basis of olive oil, are rendered in RSV as 'liquid myrrh,' sweet cinnamon, sweet calamus, and cassia. The penalty for the unauthorized manufacture and sacrilegious use of this sacred chrism was excommunication.

A. R. S. K.—**W. D. McH.**

OLAMUS, 1 Es 9[30] (AV, RV).—See MESHULLAM, **12.**

OLD GATE.—See JERUSALEM, GATES OF.

OLD LATIN VERSION.—See TEXT (OT and NT).

OLD TESTAMENT.—See BIBLE, CANON OF OT, TEXT OF OT.

OLIVE (*zayith*, cf Arabic *zeit* 'oil,' and *zeitūn* 'olive tree').—This tree (*Olea europea*) is the first-named 'king of the trees' (Jg 9[8f]), and is, in Palestine at any rate, by far the most important. The scantily covered terraced hillsides, the long rainless summer of blazing sunshine, and the heavy night moisture of late summer afford climatic conditions which appear in a very special degree favourable to the olive. This has been so in all history; the children of Israel were to inherit 'oliveyards' which they planted not (Jos 24[13], Dt 6[11]), and the wide-spread remains of ruined terraces and olive-presses in every part of the land witness to the extent of olive culture that existed in the past. A large proportion of the fuel consumed to-day consists of the roots of ancient olive trees. The peculiar grey-green foliage with its silver sheen, and the wonderful twisted and often hollow trunks of the trees, are very characteristic of Palestine scenery. The OT writers admired the beauty of the olive (see Hos 14[6], Ps 52[8] 128[3], Jer 11[16]). The cultivation of the olive requires patience, and presupposes a certain degree of settlement and peace: perhaps for this reason it was the emblem of peace. Destruction of a harvest of cereals is a temporary loss, but when the vines and, still more, the olives are destroyed, the loss takes many years to make good (Rev 6[5f]).

The olive tree, grown from a slip taken from below the grafted branches of a selected fruitful olive, has to **be grafted** when three years old, but it does not bear fruit for some three or four years more, and not plentifully until it is about seventeen or eighteen years old; it may then, when well cared for, continue bearing for many years. The soil, however, must be carefully ploughed and manured every spring, and on the hill-sides the water of the early rains must be conducted to the very roots by carefully arranged channels. When after some years, the stem becomes too hollow from rotting of the wood, and the crop fails, it is sometimes cut sharp off at the root, and new shoots are allowed to spring up, which, after re-grafting, become a fruitful tree. Cf article GRAFTING.

The **wild olive** is a kind of reversion to the primitive plant—such as occurs also with the fig and the almond —and it takes place whenever the growth of the olive is neglected. Thus the little shoots which grow around the main trunk (perhaps the origin of Ps 128[3]) are of the wild variety, and also those growing from the self-sown drupe.

In most neglected olive groves numerous little bushes of the 'wild olive' may be seen, which, though very unlike the cultivated tree—having a shorter, smaller, and greener leaf and a stiffer, more prickly stem—are nevertheless derived from it. As a rule the wild olive is but a shrub, but it may grow into a tree and have small but useless 'berries.' Where groves of wild olives are found in Palestine, they are probably always the descendants of cultivated trees long ago destroyed.

The young wild olive trees, scattered over the mountains in Galilee, are gathered by the *fellahîn* and sold for olive plantations. Such plants are grafted three years after transplantation, and always in the late spring or early summer.

The **'olive berries'** (Ja 3[12] AV) ripen in the autumn, and are harvested in November or December. They are beaten from the trees with a long pole (Dt 24[20]), and collected in baskets. Olives are eaten pickled in brine, either when green and unripe or when soft and black. They are universally eaten by the *fellahîn* with bread—sometimes the oil is eaten instead, much as butter is used in our home lands. The oil is also used extensively for making soup, for frying meat, and for illumination. See OIL. E. W. G. M.—**W. D. McH.**

OLIVES, MOUNT OF.—The heights E. of Jerusalem, separated from the Temple mountain by the Kidron Valley. It is rarely mentioned in the OT. David crossed it when fleeing from Absalom (2 S 15[30]). Here branches were cut to make booths for the Feast of Tabernacles (Neh 8[15]). Ezekiel (11[23]) and Zechariah (14[4]) make it the scene of ideal theophanies: the literal interpretation of the latter prophecy has given rise to many curious and unprofitable speculations.

The chief interest of the mountain, however, is its connexion with the closing years of our Lord's life. Over this He rode on His triumphal entry to Jerusalem; and wept over the city as it came into view (Lk 19[41]); and during the days when He lodged in Bethany and visited Jerusalem He must necessarily have passed over it daily (Lk 21[37]). The fig-tree which He cursed (Mt 21[19]) was most probably on the mountain slopes; and here He is said to have delivered to His disciples the great eschatological discourse (Mk 13, Mt 24, 25). On the side of the mountain was Gethsemane (q.v.), where took place the first scene of the final tragedy.

The ridge, of which the mount is a part, is formed of hard cretaceous limestone, surmounted by softer deposits of the same material. It is divided, by gentle undulations and one comparatively deep cleft, into a series of summits. The name **Olivet** (Ac 1[12] [RSV], 2 S 15[30] [AV]) from Latin *Olivetum* 'olive grove,' probably applied only to the one opposite the Temple, still called *eṭ-Ṭūr* 'the mount,' by the Arabs.

Ecclesiastical tradition, as might be expected, has been busy with the whole ridge opposite the city. The places pointed out have by no means remained unaltered through the Christian centuries, as becomes evident from a study of the writings of the pilgrims. To-day are shown the tomb of the Virgin; the grotto of the Agony; the Garden of Gethsemane; the chapel of the Ascension

(a mosque, with a mark in the floor said to be the 'footprint of Christ'); the site of Christ's weeping over the city; the place where He taught the Lord's Prayer; the place where the Apostles' Creed was composed, etc. The Ascension chapel is on the site of the *Inbomon*, an unroofed octagonal structure built about A.D. 380 for celebration of the Ascension. Remains of the Basilica built by Constantine's mother have been found in the court of the Carmelite Convent; it marked the scene of Christ's eschatological discourse (Mk 13[3], Mt 24[3]).
R. A. S. M.—**E. G. K.**

OLIVET.—See preceding article.

OLYMPAS.—The name of a mid-first cent. Christian of Rome [or Ephesus] greeted by St. Paul in Ro 16[15]. This is all that is known about him. Originally his short name was an abbreviation from some longer compound name such as 'Olympiodorus'—to cite a very familiar Hellenistic example. H. R. W.

OLYMPIAN.—An epithet of Zeus derived from Mount Olympus in Thessaly, the legendary home of the Greek gods. Antiochus IV. Epiphanes caused the Temple at Jerusalem to be dedicated to Zeus Olympius in 168 B.C. (2 Mac 6[2]), and the setting up of his altar there was the 'abomination of desolation' (Dn 9[27] 11[31] 12[11]).

At this very time Antiochus was contributing lavishly to the restoration of the stupendous Olympieion in its vast precinct just north-east of the Acropolis in Athens. Eventually this gigantic temple of Zeus Olympius became one of the greatest and richest sanctuaries of Olympian religion in the Graeco-Roman world.
A. E. H.—**H. R. W.**

OLYMPIUS.—See OLYMPIAN.

OMAERUS, 1 Es 9[34] (AV).—See AMRAM, **2.**

OMAR (?'eloquent').—A grandson of Esau, Gn 36[11, 15], 1 Ch 1[36].

OMEGA.—See ALPHA AND OMEGA.

OMENS.—See MAGIC, DIVINATION AND SORCERY.

OMER.—See WEIGHTS AND MEASURES.

OMRI.—**1.** See following article. **2.** A descendant of Benjamin, 1 Ch 7[8]. **3.** A Judahite, 1 Ch 9[4]. **4.** A prince of Issachar, 1 Ch 27[18].

OMRI was one of the most important kings of Israel, and the founder of a dynasty. He was one of the generals of the army under Elah, son of Baasha. This king was assassinated by Zimri, another of the officers. Omri was at the siege of Gibbethon at the time, and his troops acclaimed him king instead of his rival. A civil war of some duration followed, in which (apparently after the death of Zimri) one Tibni took part, himself aspiring to the throne. Omri finally prevailed, and for a time occupied the old capital Tirzah (1 K 16[16ff]). But he had the intelligence to perceive the advantages of the central and commanding position of Samaria as a site for his capital, which he founded and raised to great political importance.

Omri's political measures included an alliance with the Phoenicians, in which he had the example of David and Solomon, though subsequent generations condemned him for it. The alliance was cemented by the marriage of Ahab and Jezebel, so important for the later history. Omri seems to have been an able soldier, and he subdued Moab to Israel. This is acknowledged by the Moabite king Mesha in his inscription on what is known as the Moabite Stone (see MOAB). The wars with Damascus were not so successful. The Assyrians first became acquainted with Israel in the time of Omri, and they called the country 'the house of Omri' even after the extinction of his dynasty. The length of this king's reign is given as twelve years, but his rule was more important than we should infer from the brief record we have of his achievements in the OT.
H. P. S.—**H. S. G.**

ON.—A Reubenite associated with Dathan and Abiram, Nu 16[1]. But the text is doubtful.

ON (Gn 41[45, 50] 46[20]).—The Egyptian city of **Heliopolis**, situated on the E. border of the Delta, 7 miles NE. of Cairo. The Hebrew name is an accurate reproduction of the Egyptian *iwnw* (Copt. *ōn*), but has been intentionally misvocalized as **Aven**, 'idolatry,' in Ezk 30[17]. In Jer 43[13] it is called **Beth-shemesh**, 'House of the Sun,' like its Greek name *Hēliopolis*, 'City of the Sun.' The reference in Is 19[18] to the 'city of destruction' (AV, RV) or 'city of the Sun' (RSV) may refer to Heliopolis (see IR-HA-HERES).

As the centre of the worship of the sun-god in Egypt, its temple was of the highest importance: it was favoured by the kings and served by the most learned priesthood in the land. Tradition makes Plato and other Greek philosophers study in Heliopolis; later, the foundation of the Alexandrian library, on the one hand, deprived Heliopolis of the glory of learning and, on the other, the old traditions of royal descent from the sun-god had little weight with the Ptolemies. Early in the Roman period Heliopolis is described by Strabo as almost deserted. Besides enclosure walls of crude brick and mounds of rubbish, the site of the temple is now marked by one conspicuous monument, an obelisk set up by Senwosret I. *c* 1950 B.C. See Sir A. H. Gardiner, *Ancient Egyptian Onomastica* (1947), ii, 144*–146*.
F. Ll. G.—**R. J. W.**

ONAM.—**1.** The eponym of a Horite clan, Gn 36[23], 1 Ch 1[40]. **2.** A son of Jerahmeel, 1 Ch 2[26, 28].

ONAN.—A son of Judah, Gn 38[4] 46[12], Nu 26[19], 1 Ch 2[3]. After the decease of his elder brother, Er, he was instructed by his father to contract a levirate marriage with Tamar. The device by which he evaded the object of this marriage 'was displeasing in the sight of the Lord, and he slew him,' Gn 38[8ff].

ONESIMUS.—The slave from Colossae who, having become associated with Paul during one of the latter's imprisonments, became a Christian under the Apostle's influence. We do not know how Onesimus happened to be with Paul. It is usually surmised that he was a runaway slave who either happened to meet Paul or sought him out for help. Paul sent him back to his owner with what we know as the Epistle to Philemon. In this letter Paul explains that Onesimus has become not only very dear to him but also very useful, and he virtually asks the owner of the slave to release him for Paul's service. Since the letter was preserved, it may be supposed that this request was granted. If so, it is not surprising that the Bishop of Ephesus, when Ignatius wrote his Epistle to the Ephesians a generation or so later, was named Onesimus and that there are grounds for identifying the two men. See PHILEMON, EPISTLE TO. J. K.

ONESIPHORUS.—The name of a Christian mentioned twice in Second Timothy (2 Ti 1[16–18] and 4[19]). From the first reference we learn that he showed special kindness to Paul during his imprisonment at Rome, when others, from whom he might have expected sympathy and help, held aloof from him; from the second we infer that he and his family lived at Ephesus. From the expression 'the household of Onesiphorus,' it has been inferred that Onesiphorus himself was dead, and this text has been urged in proof of the lawfulness of prayers for the dead. M. St.

ONIAS.—Four high priests bore this name. **Onias I.** was son of Jaddua and father of Simon the Just (Sir 50[1], where, however, the Hebrew reads *John* in place of *Onias*). In his time a letter was said to have come from the Spartan king Areus I. claiming kinship and suggesting alliance (1 Mac 12[7f] [RV, RSV **Arius**]; cf Jos. *Ant.* XII. iv. 10 [225]).—**Onias II.** was the son of Simon the Just. His reluctance to pay the tribute of twenty talents to Egypt would have led to great trouble if his shrewd and self-seeking nephew Joseph had not conciliated Ptolemy (*Ant.* XII. iv. 2 [160 ff]).—**Onias III.** was son of Simon II., and entered on his office about 198 B.C. According to 2 Mac 3[1]–4[38], he ruled the city well. A dispute arose between him and a man named Simon. The latter persuaded king Seleucus to send **Heliodorus** (4 Mac 4[1–14] substitutes **Apollonius**) to seize the Temple treasury. Heliodorus being supernaturally repulsed, Onias went to

Antioch to defend himself. He was deposed from his office. In 171 B.C. he was murdered (Dn 9[26]). The esteem in which his memory was held appears from 2 Mac 15[12-14].—His son **Onias IV.** fled to Egypt and was welcomed by Ptolemy Philometor, who gave him a disused temple in Leontopolis, which he rebuilt after the model of the one in Jerusalem, to serve as a centre of unity for the Hellenistic Jews (*Ant.* XIII. iii. 1, 3 [62 ff, 72 ff], *BJ* I. i. 1 [33], VII. x. 2 [421]). J. T.

ONIONS.—Hebrew *beṣālîm*, Nu 11[5]. The onion (*Allium cepa*, Arab. *baṣal*) is and always has been a prime favourite in Palestine and Egypt.

ONO.—A Benjamite city, 1 Ch 8[12]; named with Lod and Hadid (Ezr 2[33] etc.), to which his enemies invited Nehemiah to conference (Neh 6[2]). It was reoccupied after the Exile, Neh 7[37] 11[35], 1 Es 5[22] (AV, RV **Onus**). It is identified with *Kefr ʿAnā*, to the N. of Lydda.

ONUS, 1 Es 5[22] (AV, RV).—See ONO.

ONYCHA.—Hebrew *sheḥēleth*, Ex 30[34]. One of the ingredients of the sacred composition which gave a sweet smell when burned; mentioned also in Sir 24[15] (AV, RV **onyx**). Onycha was obtained from the claw-like (hence the name from Greek *onyx* ' nail ') operculum of some mollusc of the genus *strombus*. A similar product is still used in Upper Egypt for fumigations. E. W. G. M.

ONYX.—See JEWELS AND PRECIOUS STONES, ONYCHA.

OPHEL.—See JERUSALEM, I, 1.

OPHIR.—A region famed for its gold (Job 28[16]), which was brought to Solomon by his Red Sea navy (1 K 9[28]). Jehoshaphat made an abortive attempt to revive this trade (1 K 22[48]).

The location of Ophir is uncertain. It is located in Gn 10[29] between Sheba and Havilah, hence in South Arabia. The mention of apes and baboons (EV ' peacocks ') among Solomon's cargoes from Ophir, however, suggests remoter regions, which have been sought in Africa and India. Since such a trading voyage lasted three years (1 K 10[22]), it is suggested that Ophir must have been further away than South Arabia or Somaliland (Punt), which is known in Egyptian inscriptions as a source of gold. In favour of East Africa is the known Phoenician contact with the region between the Zambesi and the Limpopo. The Sanskrit origin of the word for apes, however, suggests contacts with India. In view of the Biblical tradition that Ophir was in Arabia (known to the Phoenicians as auriferous, Ezk 27[22]), it is safest to regard Ophir as in South Arabia, and as an important entrepot for merchandise from further East and also from East Africa. Doubtless the three-year duration of Solomon's trading ventures is to be explained by incidental coasting trade, and the fact that sailing, both from Ezion-geber to South Arabia and from more distant regions to South Arabia, was confined to a part of the year.

The LXX version of Ophir with an initial Σ has suggested *Sofala*, some 200 miles from the famous ruins of Zimbabwe in East Africa and *Supara* in Goa on the Malabar Coast. This probably reflects the sea-borne trade with India in Ptolemaic times. R. A. S. M.—**J. Gr.**

OPHNI.—A town of Benjamin, Jos 18[34]; possibly modern *Jifnā*.

OPHRAH.—**1.** A town in Benjamin, Jos 18[23]; it was near Michmash, and is only once elsewhere referred to, as an indication of the direction of a Philistine raid. 1 S 13[7]. Jerome states that it was 5 Roman miles E, from Bethel. It is perhaps modern *eṭ-Ṭaiyibeh*. **2.** Ophrah ' which belonged to Joash the Abiezrite '—*i.e.* to a member of a sept of the tribe of Manasseh (Jos 17[2]), was the native village of Gideon. It is not mentioned except in connexion with the history of him and of his son Abimelech (Jg 6–9). No satisfactory identification has been proposed. **3.** A name in the genealogy of the tribe of Judah, 1 Ch 4[14].

ORACLE.—See MAGIC, etc., TEMPLE.

ORAL TRADITION.—**1. Old Testament.** The phrase may have two references, (*a*) the Cabbala (Heb. *ḳabbālāh*, ' received '), originally the detailed application and elaboration of the written Torah (cf Neh 8[7f]) which also, it was claimed, went back to Moses, and which in effect attained a superior authority (cf Mt 15[1-6]). This Cabbala eventually crystallized into written form as Massorah and Talmud. (The name Cabbala also attaches to a mediaeval esoteric mystico-magical system of philosophy.) (*b*) More commonly the phrase refers to a theory of the mode of transmission of the words of Scripture from their first publication until finally written down in their definitive form.

No one would deny that some sections of the OT subsisted orally for at least a short period; but it has recently been maintained that ' the written OT is a creation of the post-exilic Jewish community; what existed before was certainly only in small part fixed in writing ' (H. S. Nyberg, *St. z. Hoseabuche*, 1935). This would fit in with the tradition that Ezra's amanuenses wrote out the whole OT at his dictation (2 Es 14[19-48]); but the more ' official ' view of Josephus (*c. Ap.* i. 7 [38-42]) and the Talmud (*Baba Bathra*, 14b–15a) does not describe him as custodian of an *oral* tradition, and Esdras attributes Ezra's knowledge to an *ad hoc* Divine revelation, not to a retentive memory. At the same time critical scholarship has until recently hardly given sufficient prominence to the probable rôle of oral transmission in Israel: a rôle illuminated by comparison with other ancient cultures (see Nyberg, *op. cit.*; H. Birkeland, *Z. hebr. Traditionswesen*, 1938; I. Engnell, *Gamla Testamentet. En traditionshistorisk inledning*, i, 1945; but also the more cautious attitude in S. Mowinckel, *Prophecy and Tradition*, 1946, and A. Bentzen, *Intro. to the OT*, i, 1948, pp. 102 ff. Strong counter-arguments are put forth in G. Widengren, *Literary and Psychological Aspects of the Hebrew Prophets*, 1948. E. Nielsen, *Oral Tradition*, 1954, accepts very largely Engnell's position).

There is as yet no generally agreed solution to the Oral *v.* Written Transmission controversy, but the following points must be given their due weight: (1) Comparative studies (Arabian, Celtic, Norse, Polynesian, etc.) show the amazing powers of memorization possessed by the professional memorizer (Arab. *qaṣṣ*, Irish *shanachie* and *fili*; there is no Hebrew term whose equation has yet been proved), whose repertoire might last for weeks or even months of oration. (2) Writing, like reading, was the province mainly of the specialist, who for obvious reasons was likely to be attached to the palace or the temple—no doubt like the official memorizer (might this have been the function of the Hebrew *mazkîr*?). (3) The OT as we have it is entirely a written work; literary criticism is therefore indispensable, though some features may be more easily explicable on the theory of a preceding oral transmission, than on principles of strictly literary criticism. (4) In the pre-exilic period it is not necessary that either form should have been exclusively used; oral transmission might easily have proved the more customary for one type of material, written transmission for another. Nielsen (*op. cit.*, p. 32) envisages the possibility of an alternation. (5) On the score of reliability there does not seem to be much to choose in the given circumstances between the two methods: each has its advantages and disadvantages.

There seem to be grounds for naming the 7th cent. as the period when the main emphasis shifted from oral to written literature; nevertheless, in a largely illiterate society, books are of limited use, and the nation as a whole must have depended on well stocked memories not only for entertainment, but for more serious guidance from the past. If, as might well be possible, the sack of Jerusalem in 586 B.C. destroyed many of the books represented in our OT, there were probably those who could reproduce verbatim from the storehouse of memory all that had been burnt. The question of the reliability of Scripture is not really affected one way or the other by this problem.

2. New Testament. Here there is comparatively a very limited field for oral tradition. Written transmission was by now the norm; 'Oral Literature' in the NT must be confined to possible catechetical instruction (partly of Judaic origin?) incorporated in the Epistles, to the sources of the Gospels and Acts, with perhaps some of the imagery of Revelation: apart from the last, therefore, the period covers scarcely more than a generation, which must also have been one of constant reiteration, thus avoiding the great foe of oral transmission, lack of an audience. [See further, V. Taylor, *The Formation of the Gospel Tradition*, 1933; E. B. Redlich, *Form Criticism*, 1939; P. Carrington, *The Primitive Christian Catechism*, 1940; E. G. Selwyn, *The First Epistle of Peter*[2], 1947.] See CRITICISM, **4.** D. R. Ap-T.

ORATOR.—The term (Gr. *rhētōr*, RSV 'spokesman') applied in Ac 24[1] to Tertullus, who was the advocate for the high priest and elders against St. Paul. Men of this class were to be found in most of the provincial towns of the Roman Empire, ready to plead or defend any cause, and generally possessed of a certain amount of glib eloquence, with a due admixture of flattery. M. St.

ORCHARD.—Hebrew *pardēs*, a Persian loan-word, Ec 2[5] (AV; RV, RSV 'park'), Ca 4[13] (AV, RV, RSV; RVm 'paradise'). The same word is found in Neh 2[8] (AV, RV, RSV 'forest'; RVm 'park'). See PARADISE.

ORDEAL.—See MAGIC, **B, 2** (*b*).

ORDER.—See PRIEST (in NT).

ORDINANCE.—See DECREE.

ORDINATION.—See LAYING ON OF HANDS.

OREB AND ZEEB.—Two princes of Midian in the invasion of Israel, mentioned in Jg 7[25] 8[3], Ps 83[11] (cf Is 10[26]). The meaning of the names is 'raven' and 'wolf.' Associated with the invasion put down by Gideon these two princes were killed by the men of Ephraim, who rose at Gideon's suggestion and intercepted the princes and their followers at the river Jordan. That their death, so briefly narrated in Judges, was accompanied by great slaughter may be inferred from the incidental references by the writers of Ps 83 and Is 10. Isaiah compares the destruction to that of the Egyptians in the Red Sea, while the Psalmist compares the flying Midianites to the whirling dust or chaff driven before the wind. The rock Oreb and the winepress Zeeb took their names from this incident. T. A. M.

OREN.—A son of Jerahmeel, 1 Ch 2[25].

ORGAN.—See MUSIC, etc. **4** (2) (*b*).

ORION.—See STARS.

ORNAMENTS.—**1.** The custom of wearing ornaments either as personal adornment or as amulets, or for both purposes combined, is almost coeval with the appearance of man himself. In historical times in Palestine, as elsewhere, these ornaments were chiefly of gold, silver, bronze, and paste, but the excavations have shown that in the neolithic age a favourite ornament was a string of sea-shells. The Hebrews, especially the Hebrew women, shared to the full the Oriental love of ornaments, which are denoted in OT by two comprehensive terms, *kᵉlî*, generally rendered 'jewels' (Gn 24[53], Ex 3[22] and often), and *'ᵃdhî*, rendered 'ornaments' (Ex 33[4, 6], Ezk 16[11] etc.). Lists of individual ornaments are found in such passages as Ex 35[22], Nu 31[50], Is 3[18ff], Ezk 16[11f], Jth 10[4], although the identification of each article is not always certain.

2. Ear-rings, always of gold or silver where the material is stated, are frequently named, from Gn 35[4] onwards. In this passage their character as amulets is clearly implied. Among the Hebrews ear-rings were apparently confined to women, and to children of both sexes (Ex 32[2]), for the '**rings**' of Job 42[11] RV and RSV are not necessarily ear-rings as AV. The only men expressly mentioned as wearing them are Midianites (Jg 8[24ff]). For illustrations of gold ear-rings found at Gezer see Macalister, *Bible Sidelights from Gezer*, Fig. 32, reproduced in Benzinger, *Heb. Arch.*[3] (1927) 91. The 'earrings' of Is 3[20] AV rightly appear in RV and RSV as '**amulets**' (see AMULET). The **pendants** of Jg 8[26] RV and RSV (AV '**collars**') and Is 3[19] RV and RSV (AV '**chains**'), to judge from the etymology of the original term, had the form of drops or beads, although it is unknown whether they were worn in the ears or as a necklace.

The custom still observed by the Beduin women of wearing a ring through the right nostril (Doughty, *Arab. Deserta*, i, 340; ii, 220, 297) was also in vogue among the Hebrew women. Such was the **nose-ring** presented to Rebekah, wrongly given in AV as an earring (Gn 24[22], note v.[47]), as also the '**nose jewels**' worn by the ladies of Jerusalem (Is 3[21]). Although Ezk 16[21], as correctly rendered by RV and RSV, cannot be cited in support of wearing ornaments on the forehead as AV suggests ('a jewel on thy forehead'), this practice is attested by the figure in Ex 13[16], Dt 6[8] 11[18], where the word rendered '**frontlets**' (between the eyes) really denotes a jewel or amulet (see Hastings' *DB* iii, 872, confirmed by Smend's reading of the Hebrew text of Sir 36[3]). For a real frontlet, see **6** below.

3. Several varieties of neck ornament occur, but here again the precise nature of each escapes us. The '**chains**' (RV) of Pr 1[9], Ca 4[9] are clearly **necklaces**; the same word is used of the chains hung as amulets about the necks of the Midianite camels (Jg 8[26]). The 'strings of jewels' of Ca 1[10] RV and RSV were probably a necklace of beads. A special form of necklace or breast ornament was composed of **crescents** of gold (Jg 8[26], Is 3[18], RV and RSV). Cf AMULET, and illustration in *PEFSt*, 1905, 314, Pl. IV. The wide-spread custom of wearing a gold chain of office on neck and breast is met with in Egypt (Gn 41[42]) and Babylon (Dn 5[7, 16, 29]).

4. Like other Eastern peoples, the Hebrews were fond of decking the arms and hands with ornaments. The term most frequently used for the **finger-ring** (*ṭabba'ath*) properly denotes a signet-ring, as in Gn 41[42] RV, RSV, Est 3[12], for which see SEAL. From the use of an engraved **cylinder** for this purpose was developed a form of ring found in the excavations, consisting of a small cylinder of stone or paste, or of more than one, fitted into a ring of silver or gold (see illustration in *PEFSt*, 1905, Pl. IV., and Benzinger, *op. cit.* 90, from Sellin's work cited in **6**). Ordinarily, however, *ṭabba'ath* denotes a plain finger-ring (Ex 35[22], Nu 31[50], Is 3[21], Lk 15[22]) such as those found at Taanach (**6**).

Of the various terms rendered **bracelet** in AV, the most common is *ṣāmîdh*; Rebekah's weighed 10 shekels, and was of gold (Gn 24[22, 30, 47]; cf Nu 31[50], Ezk 16[11] 23[42]). The bracelets of Is 3[19] seem to have been made of twisted strands of gold wire. The word 'bracelet' in 2 S 1[10] more probably denotes an **armlet** or arm-band, worn on the upper arm. It is rendered '**ankle-chains**' in Nu 31[50] RV, while a cognate word of the same meaning occurs in Is 3[20] (AV 'ornaments of the legs'), and in the emended text of 2 K 11[12], where the crown and the arm-band (EV '**testimony**') are named as insignia of royalty. Similarly, the bracelet worn 'upon the right arm' (Sir 21[21] EV) is an armlet, as is seen from the list of Judith's ornaments, who 'decked herself bravely' with her anklets (AV, RV 'chains'), 'and her bracelets, and her rings, and her ear-rings, and all her ornaments' (Jth 10[4]). The nature of the ornament given in AV as **tablets** and in RV and RSV as 'armlets' (Ex 35[22], Nu 31[50]), is quite uncertain. RV and RSV rightly find **anklets** in Is 3[18]; these the ladies of Jerusalem rattled as they walked (v.[16] *end*).

5. In a separate category may be placed such articles as, in addition to being ornamental, served some useful purpose in connexion with dress. Among these may be reckoned the gold **brooches** of Ex 35[22] RV and RSV (AV 'bracelets,' literally 'hooks'), and the '**buckle** of gold' of 1 Mac 10[89] etc. There seems to be no reference in OT to the ornamental pins in gold, silver, and bronze which are found in considerable numbers at Gezer and elsewhere. For illustrations of typical pins and brooches found at Gezer, see Macalister, *op. cit.* Fig. 34.

6. This article would be incomplete without a fuller reference to the countless specimens of ancient jewellery, recovered from the sands of Egypt and the soil of Palestine, which serve to illustrate the ornaments above mentioned. The jewellery of the early Egyptian goldsmiths (Ex 3[22]), as is well known, has never been surpassed in variety and delicacy of workmanship. The excavations at Gezer, Taanach, and Megiddo have revealed an unexpected wealth of gold and silver ornaments. One of the most remarkable of these finds is that described by its fortunate discoverer, Dr. Sellin, in his *Nachlese auf dem Tell Taʿannek*, 1906, 12 ff (cf *PEFSt*, 1905, 176). Beneath the debris of a Canaanite house were found the remains of a mother and her five children, and beside the former the following ornaments: a gold band for the forehead, 8 gold rings, of which 7 were simple bands of gold wire, while the eighth was of several strands of wire, 2 silver rings, 2 larger bronze rings, perhaps bracelets, 2 small cylinders of crystal, 5 pearls, a scarab of amethyst and another of crystal, and finally a silver fastener (all illustrated *op. cit.* Pl. IV. and Fig. 16).

The ornaments found in still greater variety in the mounds of Gezer are described and illustrated in the *PEFSt* from 1902 onwards. A special interest attaches to certain graves, probably of Philistine origin and of a date *c* 1000 B.C., in which a profusion of jewellery has been found similar in character and workmanship to the ornaments of the Mycenaean age found in Cyprus and Crete. For a description of the armlets, bracelets, anklets, rings, etc., found in these graves, see *PEFSt*, 1905, 318 ff and Pl. VI.; 1907, 199 ff and Pl. I., 240 ff.

A. R. S. K.

ORNAN.—See ARAUNAH.

ORPAH.—A Moabitess, sister of Ruth and daughter-in-law of Naomi. When the latter was returning to her own country, Orpah, following Naomi's advice, elected to go back to her own people and to her god (or gods), while her sister went with her mother-in-law, Ru 4[14].

ORPHAN.—The orphan is frequently linked with the widow in appeals to the charity of men (*e.g.* Dt 14[29], Is 9[17]), in demands for justice (Dt 24[17], Is 1[11]), or in denunciations of the oppression of those who took advantage of these defenceless persons (Is 10[2], Job 22[9] 24[3]). It is nowhere clear that the word means one who has lost both parents, and EV render 'fatherless' in most of its occurrences.

ORTHOSIA (1 Mac 15[37]).—Placed by the Peutinger Tables 12 Roman miles N. of Tripoli, and 30 S. of Antaradus. The name has not been recovered.

OSAIAS, 1 Es 8[48] (AV, RV).—See JESHAIAH, **5.**

OSEA, 2 Es 13[40] (AV, RV)=king **Hoshea** (q.v.).

OSEAS, 2 Es 1[39] (AV, RV)=**Hosea** (q.v.).

OSEE, Ro 9[25] (AV)=**Hosea** (q.v.).

OSNAPPAR (so RSV and RV Ezr 4[10], following some MSS; **Asnapper** of AV, or **Asenapper** represents a better transliteration). A distorted form of **Ashurbanipal** —possibly accidentally shortened—last great king of Assyria (669–*c* 632 B.C.), son of Esarhaddon, grandson of Sennacherib. A man of great ability and wide range of interests, claiming for himself ability to read Sumerian and Akkadian literature as well as being proficient in the handling of weapons and horses. He gathered a rich collection of Sumerian and Akkadian literature in his library at Nineveh, aiming at preserving this literature by having careful copies made. Their recovery in modern times has provided valuable material for study. His palace was also richly ornamented with reliefs. His choice as heir, rather than his elder brother Shamash-shum-ukin, is indicative of his greater energies and gifts. But his reign nevertheless marked a decline of Assyrian power. Egypt was lost by 656 B.C., and an attempt at reconquest failed. In 652 B.C. his brother Shamash-shum-ukin, ruler in Babylon, rebelled in alliance with Elamites and others; but Ashurbanipal was able to deal with the rebels piecemeal. Babylon fell in 648 B.C. after a two-year siege, and Elam was only conquered after a long struggle in 639 B.C., and it must have been after this event that Elamites from Susa, the capital, were deported to Samaria and its vicinity (Ezr 4[9f]). According to 2 Ch 33[11], Manasseh, king of Judah, was brought in fetters to Babylon, and this event, if historical, must presumably have fallen within the reign of Ashurbanipal. On this see MANASSEH. J. F. McC.—**P. R. A.**

OSPRAY (AV).—See OSPREY.

OSPREY (*ʿozniyyāh*, Lv 11[13], Dt 14[12]).—The Hebrew *ʿozniyyāh* is traditionally identified with the 'fish-eating eagle' (LXX, Vulgate), osprey or ossifrage (*pandion haliaetus*); but this does not suit its position in the list of unclean birds, and it is probably otherwise called (see OSSIFRAGE). If the name is derived *per metathesim* from the √ *ʿNZ* (hence Akk. *enzu*=Heb. *ʿēz*=Arab. *ʿanzu*, 'goat'), it may be the 'bearded vulture' (*gypaetus barbatus*), which has a goat-like beard. This etymology is quite uncertain (see OSSIFRAGE), and very possibly the 'short-toed eagle' (*circaetus gallicus*), which comes between vultures and hawks in size, is meant. This is far the commonest eagle in Palestine which it visits in the summer; it is a magnificent, large and heavy, bird which sits on a tree or rock all day watching (hence perhaps translated *ʿār*, 'watcher,' in the Targum) for lizards or serpents, which constitute its sole diet. Cf also GIER EAGLE. G. R. D.

OSSIFRAGE.—Lv 11[13] (AV, RSV), Dt 14[12] (AV; RSV 'vulture'). The Hebrew *peres*, 'smasher,' is probably not the 'gier-eagle' (RV, with LXX and Vulgate), but the 'bearded vulture' (*gypaetus barbatus*) or perhaps the black or 'Arrian's vulture.' Both the bearded vulture and the true ossifrage (of which 'ospray' or 'osprey' is a corruption) drop their victims repeatedly from a great height on to a rock or stone until their bones are thoroughly smashed when they extract the marrow, which they consume as well as the flesh.

G. R. D.

OSTRICH.—Three Hebrew words are commonly taken as designating the ostrich. The first is *bath yaʿanāh* (found in Lv 11[16], Dt 14[15], Job 30[29], Is 13[21] 34[13] 43[20], Jer 50[39], Mic 1[8]), which, however, is most probably an owl (AV; see OWL), not the ostrich (RV, RSV). The second is *yᵉʿēnîm*, which properly means 'greedy ones' (cf Syr. *yaʿîn*, 'greedy') and certainly connotes 'ostriches' (LXX, Symmachus, Vulgate), so called in consequence of their swallowing anything and everything whether edible or inedible (*e.g.* stones, nails, bullets), a habit engendered by their hard life in the sterile wilderness. They are mentioned *eo nomine* only once in the OT as a symbol of maternal cruelty (La 4[3]). The third is *rᵉnānim*, a name which means 'shouts of joy; rattlings' or the like (cf Heb *rānan*, 'shouted with joy,' and Arabic *ranna*, 'twanged; rattled') and seems to have been given to the ostrich (Vulgate; so RV, RSV; AV 'peacocks') either on the principle of *lucus a non lucendo* because of its hard and dreary desert life (like the Arab. *naʿâmatu*, 'delight; wilderness; ostrich') or as echoing the loud dolorous and stridulous cries which it emits at night. In the OT this word occurs only once, where it refers to the hen-ostrich, which is depicted as unable with her atrophied wings and deficient plumage to give proper care to her eggs and chicks and so brainless as to go careering across the wilderness like her mate when she ought to be caring for her brood (Job 39[13–18]). The myth of her lack of maternal instinct is based on a misunderstanding of the bird's habits. The ostrich is polygamous, and a group of three or four hens, jealously guarded by a cock, lay ten or twelve eggs each in a common nest, covering them carefully with sand; by day the sun's heat suffices as an incubator, and the birds leave them to go in search of food, but at night they take turns in keeping the eggs warm. A few scattered eggs are also laid round the nest,

whether by accident or design, and these are left to be used as food by the chicks when hatched. The neglect of these eggs and the abandonment of the nest by day, as well as the parents' habit of deserting the poults when closely pursued by an enemy (which is necessary for self-preservation in country where no cover is available), are between them responsible for the fiction that the ostrich is deficient in natural affection. The ostrich (*Struthio camelus*) still maintains a precarious existence in diminishing numbers in the Syrian wilderness. (In Job 39^{13b} AV ' ostrich ' is a mistranslation. See STORK.)
E. W. G. M.—**G. R. D.**

OTHNI.—A son of Shemaiah, 1 Ch 26^{7}.

OTHNIEL.—According to Jos 15^{17} and Jg 1^{13} the son of Kenaz, Caleb's younger brother. As a reward for taking Kiriath-sepher, he receives Achsah, the daughter of Caleb, for his wife. Othniel is the first mentioned among the ' Judges ' of Israel; Cushan-rishathaim (q.v.), king of Mesopotamia, had oppressed the Israelites for eight years when Yahweh ' raised up a deliverer ' in the person of Othniel, who fought against the oppressor and overcame him, thus bringing rest to the land. W. O. E. O.

OTHONIAH, 1 Es 9^{28}.—See MATTANIAH, **5.**

OTHONIAS, 1 Es 9^{28} (AV, RV).—See MATTANIAH, **5.**

OUCH.—The word ' ouch ' is used in AV and RV (Ex $28^{11, 13f}$ etc.) for the setting (so RSV) of a jewel, but it is also used in Old English for the jewel itself. See BREASTPIECE (of the High Priest).

OVEN.—See BREAD.

OWL.—Six Hebrew words are rendered ' owl ' in the English Bible: (1) *bath yaʿanāh* (AV; but **' ostrich '** (q.v.) in RV, RSV); (2) *yanshûph*, ' owl ' or ' great owl ' (AV and RV; but **' bittern '** in RVm in Is 34^{11}; RSV **' ibis '** in Lv 11^{17}): (3) *kôs*, ' owl ' or ' little owl '; (4) *ḳippōz*, ' great owl,' Is 34^{15} (AV; ' owl ' in RSV; but **' arrowsnake '** (q.v.) in RV); (5) *tinshemeth*, ' horned owl ' (RV; but **' swan '** in AV and **' water hen '** in RSV); (6) *lîlîth*, **' screech owl '** (AV; but **' night monster '** in RV and **' night hag '** in RSV). Owls are extremely common in Palestine, and the exact identification of several of those mentioned in the Bible must remain in doubt for lack of information; indeed, some of the words may be alternative or local names for the same bird. There appear in fact to be eight terms designating owls, arranged in descending order by their sizes, in the list of unclean birds (Lv 11^{13-19}, Dt 14^{11-20}), in which as *raptores* they are naturally included; for they consume the blood with the flesh of their victims. (i) The *bath yaʿanāh* ' daughter of the wilderness,' usually but wrongly translated **' ostrich '**; for this does not require water (Is 43^{20}; cf 34^{13}), does not haunt ruins (Is 13^{21}, Jer 50^{39}) and does not wail (Mic 1^{8}); such are habits of owls. This owl, the first and therefore the largest in the list, is probably the **' eagle-owl,'** a large owl numerous in Palestine in semi-desert districts covered with scrub and feeding on partridges, hares, and rodents; in Egypt it haunts precipitous cliffs and temples whether intact or ruined. (ii) The *taḥmās* (Lv 11^{16}, Dt 14^{15}; EV **' night hawk '**), whose name means ' robber ' (cf Aram. *ḥamas* ' robbed ') is translated ' owl ' by the earliest versions (LXX, Vulgate); it may be the ' short-eared owl,' a middling one which takes small rodents and birds alive, though rare (perhaps only a visitor in winter) in Palestine. (iii) The *shaḥaph* (Lv 11^{16}, Dt 14^{15}), wrongly translated **' sea gull '** (LXX, Vulgate; so RSV; AV **' cuckow,'** RV **' seamew '**), is likely from its position to be another owl, possibly the ' long-eared owl,' described as a very thin owl with a body very attenuated when at rest (cf Arab. *saḥufa* ' was thin, lean, emaciated '). (iv) The *kôs*, Lv 11^{17} (EV ' little owl '), Dt 14^{16} (AV, RV ' little owl,' RSV ' owl '), Ps 102^{6} (EV ' owl '), is by general consent an owl (LXX, Peshitta, Vulgate), being so called from its cry of ' chu-chu-chu '; its measurements and position in the list suggest the ' tawny owl ' (cf German *Kauz*, ' tawny owl '), which is seldom seen but whose unmistakeable hoot is often heard at night. The *kôs* is mentioned only once as an ' owl of desolate places ' (Ps 102^{6}); so the tawny owl haunts lonely woods and forests. (v) The *shālākh*, Lv 11^{17}, Dt 14^{17}, whose name comes from a root denoting plunging or the like (cf Arab. *salaka* ' went forward, entered '), has been taken for some plunging or diving bird (LXX, Vulgate), usually the **' cormorant '** (EV), which is impossible in view of its position amongst the owls; it is described as drawing up fish from the sea (Peshitta, Targum) and may therefore be the ' fisher owl,' although this bird is not common in Palestine. (vi) The *yanshûph*, or *yanshōph*, translated **' ibis '** in the earliest versions (LXX, Vulgate; so RSV in Lv 11^{17}, but ' great owl ' in Dt 14^{16}, and ' owl ' in Is 34^{11}), though not found in Palestine, is probably another owl (Peshitta, Targum; AV, RV ' great owl ' in Lv 11^{17}, Dt 14^{16}, and ' owl ' in Is 34^{11}); for its name means ' hisser ' (cf Heb. *nāshaph* ' blew, hissed '), which agrees with the owls' well-known habit of breathing heavily or panting. It may be the ' screech-owl,' a very nocturnal bird which though seldom seen by day is abundant in Palestine; it emits a long-drawn but not very loud hissing, puffing, or snoring, sound and a raucous shriek or snaps its bill and hisses; it breeds in hollow trees, buildings, and ruins, but always in darkness, and the young birds snore in the nest. (vii) The *tinshemeth* (Lv 11^{18}, Dt 14^{16}, AV **' swan,'** RV **' horned owl,'** RSV **' water hen '**), whose name similarly means ' panter ' (cf Heb. *nāsham* ' panted '), may perhaps be the ' little owl,' whose low wailing note is very often heard at sunset; it is the most widely distributed owl in Palestine, haunting thickets by the water-side and wells, tombs, and desolate mounds of ruined cities, whence it is called *'umm al-khirāb* ' the mother of ruins ' by the Arabs. (viii) The *ḳāʾāth* is almost certainly the **' scops-owl,'** though long wrongly taken to be the **' pelican '** (q.v.). The *lîlîth*, formerly translated ' screech-owl ' (AV) or ' night-monster ' (RV; RSV ' night hag '; cf Milton's ' night-hag ') is probably the **' night-jar '** or **' goat-sucker '**; for it is mentioned beside he-goats as a symbol of desolation (Is 34^{14}) and so seems in time to have come to be regarded as a demon haunting ruins. Several species of goat-sucker are found in the desolate parts of Egypt and the desert fringe of Palestine; the Egyptian goat-sucker (*caprimulgus aegyptius*) lives exclusively in desert sandy land, skulking in the day but coming out in search of food at twilight, and the Palestinian goat-sucker (*caprimulgus tamaricis*) frequents tamarisk-bushes and other desert shrubs in the most desolate regions at either end of the Dead Sea. The name may come from its nocturnal habits (cf Heb. *laylāh* ' night ') or from its weaving circular flight (cf Heb. *liwyāh* ' chaplet,' Arab. *lawā* ' twisted '; Eth. *lēlaya* ' twined oneself about ' and *lōlawa* ' flicked and twisted '). That it is named next to the goat in the prophet's description of the desolation of Edom is due to the legend that it sucks the milk of she-goats, although the story reported by both Aristotle and Aelian is quite untrue. G. R. D.

OX.—An ancestor of Judith (Jth 8^{1}).

OX, OXEN, HERD, CATTLE.—The essential difference between sheep and cattle-keeping in the Bible is seen in the way terms relating to the former distinguish clearly between male and female, young and old (see SHEEP), whereas the dozen or so words for cattle are, in general, almost interchangeable. They include *miḳneh*, which corresponds to our ' stock,' *beh ēmāh*, ' domestic animals '; *bāḳār*, ' oxen ' in general which may be subdivided to *'eleph* and *shôr*, the male working ox, *par*, ' the bull ' and *pārāh* ' cow,' and *ʿēghel*, ' heifer.' Oxen were used for sacrificial purposes, and their cultic significance may be seen also in the twelve brazen oxen beneath the Sea in Solomon's Temple (1 K $7^{25, 44}$). In everyday affairs they were the beasts of draught and burden, and consequently they were not allowed to roam about in search of pasture. They did the heavy work on the land. They ploughed in pairs, not, however, by decree, yoked to an ass though this is a common sight in Jordan to-day, and, apparently, always has been. In Israel, oxen are still occasionally to be seen ploughing, but normally they have been replaced by the tractor. They threshed the corn, unmuzzled, either by treading out the corn on the threshing-floor, or by dragging a threshing sledge. Apart from the Israeli stock, which compares favourably with that of any land, the Palestinian cattle are still very degenerate. They are rarely milked or slaughtered for meat. They are small, light brown in colour: they normally drop their calves in March–April, but breed at most only in two out of three years. Because of their traditional cultic use, bones of cattle have been recovered from ancient shrines everywhere, *e.g.* the Gezer excavations have produced them at all levels, and they all show the beasts to have been better nourished than they are to-day. B. J. R.

OX-GOAD.—See AGRICULTURE, **1.**

OZEM.—**1.** An elder brother of David, 1 Ch 2^{15}. **2.** A son of Jerahmeel, 1 Ch 2^{25}.

OZIAS.—**1.** 1 Es 8^{2} (RV); see UZZI, **1.** **2.** 2 Es 1^{2} (AV, RV); see UZZI, **6.** **3.** 1 Es 5^{31} (RV); see UZZA, **2.** **4.** Jth 6^{15} 7^{23} $8^{10, 25, 35}$ 10^{6} (AV, RV); see UZZIAH.

OZIEL.—An ancestor of Judith (Jth 8^{1}).

OZNI.—Eponym of a Gadite family, Nu 26^{16}; called **Ezbon** in Gn 46^{16}. The patronymic **Oznites** is found in Nu 26^{16}.

OZORA, 1 Es 9^{34} (AV).—See EZORA.

P

PAARAI.—See NAARAI.

PACE.—See WEIGHTS AND MEASURES.

PACHON (month).—See TIME.

PADDAN, PADDAN-ARAM (the former in Gn 48^{7} only).—The name used by P for the region (or part of it) designated by J **Aram-naharaim** (see ARAM): see Gn $28^{2, 5, 7}$ 31^{18} $35^{9, 26}$ 46^{15}. *Padanu* in Assyrian denotes a measure of land.

PADDLE occurs only in Dt 23^{13}, where it is used of a wooden tool for digging, a spade (RSV 'stick'). In earlier English a small spade used for cleaning the ploughshare was called 'a paddle' which explains the choice of this word in the Geneva Bible, whence it reached AV and RV.

PADON.—A family of Nethinim (q.v.) who returned with Zerubbabel, Ezr 2^{44}, Neh 7^{47}, 1 Es 5^{29} (AV, RV **Phaleas**).

PAGIEL.—Chief of the tribe of Asher, Nu 1^{13} 2^{27} $7^{72, 77}$ 10^{26}.

PAHATH-MOAB.—The name of a Jewish clan which consisted of two branches, Jeshua and Joab. Part of it returned with Zerubbabel, part with Ezra and part remained in Babylon, Ezr 2^{6} 8^{4}, Neh 7^{11}, 1 Es 5^{11} (AV, RV **Phaath Moab**) 8^{31} (RV **Phaath Moab**). The word has been read to mean 'governor of Moab,' and referred to a dominion once exercised over Moab. It is, however, more probable that we have a corrupted text.

PAI.—The capital city of Hadad (1 Ch) or Hadar (Gn), 1 Ch 1^{36}, Gn 36^{39} (in the latter called **Pau**). The site is unknown.

PAINFULNESS.—In Ps 73^{16} AV 'When I thought to know this, it was too painful (so RV; RSV 'a wearisome task') for me,' as well as in 2 Es 7^{12} AV (RV 'charged with great toils,' RV 'involved in great hardship') and 2 Mac 2^{26} AV (so RV; RSV 'toil' for 'painful labour'), 'painful' means 'laborious.' So in 2 Cor 11^{27} AV 'painfulness' (RV 'travail,' RSV 'hardship') means 'laboriousness.' Hooker says 'The search of knowledge is a thing painful, and the painfulness of knowledge is that which maketh the will so hardly inclinable thereto.'

PAINT.—In Jer 22^{14} occurs the only reference to house painting in the Bible. Here the colour vermilion was used. In Ezk 23^{14} the same colour is mentioned for portrayal of images of the Chaldaeans. See also ART. For **eye-paint** see EYE.

PALACE.—Primarily 'palace' denotes a large house (cf Jer 22^{14}), and especially a grouping of a number of rooms around a central courtyard. The distinction between a large house and a 'palace' (even now not easy to define) was only gradually made so that the ordinary OT term for 'palace' in its strict sense of 'royal residence' is 'the king's house' or simply 'his house' (1 K 7^{1} 9^{10}). This included not only the royal residence, but also the buildings required by court officials. The only royal residence of which we have any details in the Bible is Solomon's palace (1 K 7^{1-12}), which took thirteen years to build. The description is adapted to its literary setting and is therefore technically incomplete. This included 'the house of the forest of Lebanon,' a great hall 100 cubits long, 50 broad, 30 high, with four rows of pillars; a 'porch of pillars' 50 cubits by 30; the 'porch of the throne' for a court of justice; a dwelling-house for Solomon himself, and another for Pharaoh's daughter. Round about the whole was a great court of hewn stones and cedar beams. It somewhat overshadowed the house of Yahweh which adjoined it. Ezekiel (43^{8}) protested against this contiguity. There is now no trace of the houses built by David and Solomon.

Archaeologists have been able to investigate:

(a) Two large houses of the courtyard type in the ruins of Bethel and Bethshemesh. It is believed that these belong to the period of the Judges.

(b) The palace-fortress built by Saul in his home town of Gibeah. This was two storeys high, the family living on the second floor. It was built of roughly shaped stones. The corners of the surrounding wall were protected by towers. The whole area was at least 169 by 114 feet.

(c) The palaces of Samaria, and especially that of Omri and Ahab, which was part of a later, much larger complex of buildings. These conform, in general, to the oriental pattern familiar in the Assyrian royal palaces.

Belonging to the Persian period, there is the palace of *Tell ed-Duweir*; and to the Roman period, the palace of the Herods in Jerusalem.

In AV the word is sometimes used of the fortified part of the palace, or keep. See CITADEL. D. R. J.

PALAL.—The son of Uzai, Neh 3^{25}.

PALANQUIN.—This word is found only in RV and RSV in Ca 3^{9} (AV 'chariot'). It renders Hebrew *'appiryôn*, a word of non-Semitic derivation, whose origin is uncertain.

PALESTINA.—See next article, **1.**

PALESTINE.—**1. Situation and name.**—The land of Palestine is the territory which lies between the Mediterranean Sea and the Arabian Desert as E. and W. boundaries, and whose N. and S. boundaries are approximately at 31° and 33° 20′, N. Lat. respectively. These boundaries have not always been clearly fixed; but the convention is generally agreed upon that Palestine is separated from Egypt by the *Wâdī el-ʿArîsh* or 'River of Egypt,' and from Syria by the *Qasmîyeh* or Lîṭânî River, the classical

Leontes. Biblical writers fixed the limits of the territory by the towns Dan and Beersheba, which are constantly coupled when the author desires to express in a picturesque manner that a certain event affected the whole of the Israelite country (*e.g.* Jg 20[1]). The name 'Palestine' (AV in Jl 3[4]; in Ex 15[14], Is 14[29, 31] **Palestina**; RV, RSV **Philistia**), being derived from that of the *Philistines*, properly belongs only to the strip of coastland, S. of Carmel, which was the ancient territory of that people. There is no ancient geographical term covering the whole region now known as Palestine: the different provinces—Canaan, Judah, Israel, Moab, Edom, etc.—are enumerated separately when necessary. The extension of the word to include the entire Holy Land, both W. and E. of the Jordan, is subsequent to the introduction of Christianity.

2. Geology and geography.—The greater part of the country is of a chalky limestone formation, which overlies a layer of red sandstone that appears on the E. shore of the Dead Sea and elsewhere. Under the red sandstone are the archaean granitic rocks which form a large part of the Sinai Peninsula. Above the chalk is a layer of nummulitic limestone, which appears on some mountains. Volcanic rock, the result of ancient eruptions, appears in the Ḥaurân, Galilee (especially in the neighbourhood of *Ṣafed*), and elsewhere. For fuller information on the geology of the country, see article GEOLOGY. With respect to the surface, Palestine divides naturally into a series of narrow strips of country running from north to south, and differing materially from one another in character. (*a*) The first of these is the *Maritime Plain* running along the coast of the Mediterranean from the neighbourhood of Sidon and Tyre southward, and disappearing only at the promontory of Carmel. This plain widens southward from Carmel to a maximum breadth of about 20 miles, while to the N. of that promontory it develops into the great plain of Esdraelon, which intersects the mountain region and affords the most easy passage into the heart of the country. This plain is covered with a most fertile alluvial soil. (*b*) The second strip is the mountainous ridge of Judaea and Samaria, on the summit of which are Hebron, Jerusalem, and other important towns and villages; and which, with the single interruption of the plain of Esdraelon, runs continuously from the S. border of the country to join the system of the Lebanon. (*c*) The third strip is the deep depression known as the *Ghôr*, down which runs the Jordan with its lakes. (*d*) The fourth strip is the great plateau of Bashan, Moab, and Edom, with a lofty and precipitous face towards the W., and running eastward till it is lost in the desert.

3. Water supply, climate, natural products.—There is no conspicuous river in Palestine except the Jordan and its eastern tributaries, and these, being for the greater part of their course in a deep hollow, are of little or no service for irrigation. In consequence, Palestine is dependent as a whole for its water supply on springs, or on artificial means of storage of its winter rains. Countless examples of both exist, the former especially in Galilee, parts of which are abundantly fertile by nature, and would probably repay beyond all expectation a judicious expenditure of capital. The case of Judaea is a little different, for here there are extensive tracts which are nearly or quite waterless, and are more or less desert in consequence.

The climate of Palestine is, on the whole, that of the sub-tropical zone, though, owing to the extraordinary variation of altitudes, there is probably a greater range of average local temperature than in any other region of its size on the world's surface. On the one hand, the summits of Hermon and of certain peaks of the Lebanon are covered with snow for the greater part of the year; on the other hand, the tremendous depression, in the bottom of which lies the Dead Sea, is practically tropical, both in climate and in vegetation. The mean local temperature is said to range from about 62° F. in the upland district to almost 100° F. in the region of Jericho.

Rainfall is confined to the winter months of the year. Usually in the end of October or November the rainy season is ushered in with a heavy thunderstorm, which softens the hard-baked surface of the land. This part of the rainy season is the 'former rain' of the Bible (as in Jl 2[23]). Ploughing commences immediately after the rains have thus begun. The following months have heavy showers, alternating with days of beautiful sunshine, till March or April, when the 'latter rain' falls and gives the crops their final fertilization before the commencement of the dry season. During this part of the year, except by the rarest exception, no rain falls; its place is supplied by night dews, which in some years are extraordinarily heavy. Scantiness of the rainfall, however, is invariably succeeded by poverty or even destruction of the crops, and the rain is watched for as anxiously now as it was in the time of Ahab.

Soon after the cessation of the rains, the wild flowers, which in early spring decorate Palestine like a carpet, become rapidly burnt up, and the country assumes an appearance of barrenness that gives no true idea of its actual fertility. The dry summer is rendered further unpleasant by hot east winds, blowing from over the Arabian Desert, which have a depressing and enervating effect. The south wind is also dry, and the west wind damp (cf 1 K 18[45], Lk 12[54]). The north wind, which blows from over the Lebanon snows, is always cold, often piercingly so.

As already hinted, the *flora* displays an extraordinary range and richness, owing to the great varieties of the climate at different points. The plants of the south and of the Jordan Valley resemble those found in Abyssinia or in Nubia; those of the upper levels of Lebanon are of the kinds peculiar to snow-clad regions. Wheat, barley, millet, maize, peas, beans, lentils, olives, figs, mulberries, vines, and other fruit; cotton, nuts of various species; the ordinary vegetables, and some (such as *solanum* or 'egg-plant') that do not, as a rule, find their way to western markets; sesame and tobacco—which is grown in some districts—are the most characteristic crops produced by the country. The prickly pear and the orange, though of comparatively recent introduction, are now among its staple products. The *fauna* includes (among wild animals) the bat, hyaena, wolf, jackal, wild cat, ibex, gazelle, wild boar, hare, and other smaller animals. The bear, cheetah, lion, and hippopotamus are now extinct. Among wild birds, the eagle, vulture, and partridge are still found, and there is a great variety of smaller birds. Storks are seen in great numbers during the migration periods. Among the domestic animals, cows, sheep, and goats are herded, and the horse, donkey, mule, and camel are used as draught animals.

4. History, races, and antiquities.—Remains dating from the Palaeolithic period have been found fairly widely over Palestine, mainly in caves and shelters. In caves on the western slope of Mount Carmel have been found deposits which cover the greater part of the Middle and Upper Palaeolithic. The skeletal remains suggest that the inhabitants of Palestine were allied to Neanderthal man of Europe, and the connexions between Western Asia and Europe seem to have been fairly close. With the end of the Ice Age, and the accompanying pluvials of the Mediterranean, the connexions with Europe seem to have become less close, though there are broad similarities between the Palestinian and European Mesolithic.

Palestine is one of the few places in which a development can be traced from the hunting and food-gathering Mesolithic stage to the firmly settled Neolithic stage, with agricultural communities. This succession is seen at Jericho (q.v.). Side by side with the settled communities at Jericho and comparable sites which are to be presumed but are not yet known, other groups, using the same types of flint implements, still continued to live a simple life, largely based on hunting, in caves and in open sites. This stage covers the period from the eighth to the 6th millennium B.C.

In the 5th millennium groups allied to the village

communities which had been growing up in N. Syria, seem to have established themselves in Palestine. For this and most of the subsequent millennium, there is evidence of a number of village groups.

It was during the 3rd millennium that town life seems to have spread over Palestine. It is presaged by the entry into Palestine of a number of groups at the end of the 4th millennium, and the coalescing of these groups in the 3rd millennium produced the population which founded many of the towns known in the Biblical period. It is usually presumed that this population was Semitic, though there is little direct evidence to that effect. This is the period of the Old Empire of Egypt, and it is probable that some Egyptian control was exercised over at least the coastal towns.

This civilization of the Early Bronze Age was completely blotted out, probably *c* 2300 B.C. by an invasion of nomads, who occupied the whole land during the Intermediate Early—Middle Bronze period (sometimes called Middle Bronze I). The newcomers can be identified with great probability as the Amorites. In Jos 10[6], the Amorites are recorded as being in the hill country and the Canaanites on the coast and the plains. The Amorites are therefore probably pastoralists. Archaeological evidence shows them to have been loose federations of tribes, with no interest in town life.

About 1900 B.C., a fresh wave of immigrants brought a renewed civilization in the Middle Bronze Age. The links of the newcomers are with the Phoenicians of the Syrian coast, and they are probably to be identified with the Canaanites of the Biblical record. The civilization they established, based on numerous well-defended and closely built-up towns, lasted without a break until *c* 1200 B.C.

But though the basic culture remained the same, Palestine was affected by a number of political events. The sway of the Middle Empire of Egypt certainly extended to at least part of the country, and widespread finds of Egyptian scarabs and of furniture, alabaster, and other objects imitating Egyptian originals, show that Egyptian cultures had a considerable influence. About 1730 B.C. the Middle Empire of Egypt fell before the attacks or infiltration of the Hyksos. The Hyksos are probably best to be identified as warrior bands partly of Semitic origin and partly Ḫurrian. These bands must have passed through Palestine, and probably established a warrior aristocracy, of which evidence is found in the Ḫurrian names of rulers of towns in the 14th cent. Archaeological evidence is probably to be found in a new type of fortification, consisting of a great bank crowned by a wall. About 1580 B.C. the alien rulers were expelled from Egypt, and some towns were apparently destroyed when the Egyptians chased them back into Palestine.

The recoil of the Hyksos from Egypt may have introduced some new foreign elements into Palestine, and some of the destroyed towns, for instance Jericho and *Tell Beit Mirsim*, were not immediately reoccupied, but there was no major cultural break with the beginning of the Late Bronze Age. Egypt's suzerainty was probably only gradually re-established, and was not effective until the campaigns of Thothmes III. in the early 15th cent. During the next century, contacts with Egypt were close, and the stability introduced by the New Empire of Egypt stimulated trade in the Eastern Mediterranean, of which imports from Cyprus and the Aegean are evidence.

The weakening of Egyptian power under the heretic king Akhenaten early in the 14th cent. coincided with raids from the Ḫabiru which are the cause of appeals for help from rulers loyal to Egypt in the correspondence found at Tell el-Amarna. The philological identity of Hebrew with Ḫabiru is probable, but the relationship of the Biblical Hebrews to the Ḫabiru is not yet entirely clear. It is probable that some of the components of the later Israelite tribes were drawn from the groups which entered the country at this time. Archaeological evidence of the tribes that took part in the Exodus, and of the events of the conquest of the country as described in the Book of Joshua, is inconclusive. A destruction and subsequent abandonment of Jericho in the second half of the 14th cent., and a destruction of Hazor somewhat later, is probable. It is however clear that there was no major cultural break, though a deterioration in culture may reflect disturbed conditions. There was certainly no immediate conquest of the whole country under one leader, but more probably a gradual infiltration as suggested in Jg 1.

A major break is however suggested by archaeological evidence about 1200 B.C. One cause of this was the invasion and settlement of the Peoples of the Sea, groups probably derived from Anatolia and the Aegean, which established the Philistine towns on the coast, and cut off the interior from contacts with the Mediterranean. No Philistine town has been thoroughly excavated, but their characteristic pottery is found over the coastal plain and the Shephelah.

In the hill-country a general cultural amalgamation of the descendants of the Ḫabiru invaders and the indigenous Canaanites under the followers of Yahweh, with their tradition of the Exodus, was gradually taking place. By the end of the 11th cent., the Israelites were strong enough to defeat the Philistines, and the capture of Jerusalem, *c* 1000 B.C., at last enabled the north and the south to be united under David.

The history of the short-lived United Monarchy and of the subsequent kingdoms of Judah and Israel need not be traced in detail. Archaeological finds provide evidence of a simple way of life in most of the towns, and in the finds of fertility figurines and other heathen cult objects, shows that the fulminations of the prophets against the back-slidings of the people had ample justification. Of Jerusalem during the time it was capital of the United Monarchy and subsequently of Judah, there is little evidence. Excavations at Samaria and Megiddo, however, have given evidence of the grandiose lay-out of royal cities in the Northern Kingdom; in each case the whole summit of the hill was laid out as a royal quarter, and building styles and ivory carvings show the employment of Phoenician masons and craftsmen.

In 722–720 B.C., the Northern Kingdom fell before the attack of the Assyrians. Samaria and Tirzah (*Tell el-Fârʿah* near *Nâblus*) have provided evidence of the destruction of the towns, and the appearance of Assyrian types of pottery there and elsewhere is evidence of the introduction of foreign settlers. At Jerusalem the Assyrian threat, *c* 700 B.C., is reflected by the construction of the Siloam Tunnel by King Hezekiah, to bring the water of the Virgin's Fountain within the city wall. The Assyrian attack on Lachish (*Tell ed-Duweir*) is portrayed in reliefs in the palace of Sargon.

The Southern Kingdom however survived the Assyrian threat, and did not succumb till the attack of the Babylonians, successors of the Assyrians in the Mesopotamian empire, in 597 and 586 B.C. The Babylonian attacks are vividly illustrated in the destruction of Lachish, and the last hours of the town are described in the Lachish ostraca in language reminiscent of the Book of Jeremiah.

The Second Exile marks the effective end of the old Jewish culture. Only the poorest in the land were allowed to remain; and even after the return of the descendants of the captives carried off into Babylonia, permitted by Cyrus in 538 B.C., archaeological evidence suggests a poor and struggling existence. In the area of the Northern Kingdom, there was much racial admixture with the settlers planted by the Assyrians, and the resettled Jews in Jerusalem would not admit the northerners as pure Jews; from the northerners the modern sect of the Samaritans is descended. The rebuilding of Jerusalem and the Temple by the returned captives is recorded in the Books of Ezra and Nehemiah, but no archaeological evidence of this survives.

In 333 B.C. Syria fell to Alexander the Great after the battle of Issus. After his death followed a distracting and complicated period of conflict between his successors, which, so far as Palestine was concerned, had the effect of opening the country for the first time to the influence of Greek culture, art, and religion. From this time onward we find evidence of the foundations of such buildings as theatres, previously quite unknown and other novelties of western origin. Although many of the Jews adopted the Greek tongue, there was a staunch puritan party who rigidly set their faces against all such Gentile contaminations. In this they found themselves opposed to the Seleucid princes of Syria, among whom Antiochus Epiphanes especially set himself deliberately to destroy the religion of Judaism. This led to the great revolt headed by Mattathias the priest and his sons, which secured for the Jews a brief period of independence that lasted during the second half of the 2nd cent. B.C., under John Hyrcanus (grandson of Mattathias) and his successors. The kingdom was weakened by family disputes; in the end Rome stepped in, Pompey captured Jerusalem in 63 B.C., and henceforth Palestine lay under Roman suzerainty. Several important tombs near Jerusalem, and elsewhere, and a large number of remains of cities and fortresses, survive from the age of the family of Mattathias. The conquest of Joppa, under the auspices of Simon Maccabaeus, son of Mattathias (1 Mac 13^{11}), was the first capture of a seaport in South Palestine throughout the whole of Israelite history.

The Hasmonaean dynasty gave place to the Idumaean dynasty of the Herods in the middle of the 1st cent. B.C., Herod the Great becoming sole governor of Judaea (under Roman suzerainty) in 40 B.C. It was into this political situation that Christ was born in 4 B.C. Remains of the building activities of Herod are still to be seen in the sub-structures of the Temple, the Herodian towers of Jerusalem, and (possibly) a magnificent tomb near Jerusalem traditionally called the Tomb of Mariamme. Many public buildings were also constructed at Samaria, renamed Sebaste in honour of Augustus. Herod died shortly after Christ's birth, and his dominions were subdivided into tetrarchies, each under a separate ruler: but the native rulers rapidly declined in power, and the Roman governors as rapidly advanced. The Jews became more and more embittered against the Roman yoke, and at last a violent rebellion broke out, which was quelled by Titus in A.D. 70, when Jerusalem was destroyed and a large part of the Jews slain or dispersed. A remnant remained, which about sixty years later again essayed to revolt under their leader Bar Cochba: the suppression of this rebellion was the final deathblow to Jewish nationality. After the destruction of Jerusalem many settled in Tiberias, and formed the nucleus of the important Galilaean Rabbinic schools, remains of which are still to be seen in the shape of the synagogues of Galilee. These interesting buildings appear to date from the 2nd cent. A.D.

After the partition of the Roman Empire, Palestine formed part of the Empire of the East, and with it was Christianized. Many ancient settlements, with tombs and small churches—some of them with beautiful mosaic pavements—survive in various parts of the country: these are relics of the Byzantine Christians of the 5th and 6th cent. The native Christians of Syria, whose families were never absorbed into Islam, are their representatives. These, though Aramaean by race, now habitually speak Arabic, except in Maʿlūl and one or two other places in North Lebanon where a Syriac dialect survives.

This early Christianity received a severe blow in 611, when the country was ravaged by Chosroës II., king of Persia. Monastic settlements were plundered, their inmates massacred, and the country reduced to such a state of weakness that without much resistance it fell to Omar, the second Caliph of Islam. He became master of Syria and Palestine in the second quarter of the 7th cent. Palestine thus became a Moslem country and its population received the Arab element which is still dominant within it. It may be mentioned in passing that coins of Chosroës are occasionally found in Palestine; and that of the early Arab domination many noteworthy buildings survive, chief of which is the glorious dome that occupies the site of the Hebrew Temple at Jerusalem.

The Moslem rule was at first by no means tyrannical; but, as the spirit of intolerance developed, the Christian inhabitants were compelled to undergo many sufferings and indignities. This, and the desire to wrest the holy places of Christendom from the hands of the infidel, were the ostensible reasons for the invasions of the Crusaders, who established in Jerusalem a kingdom on a feudal basis that lasted throughout the 12th cent. An institution so exotic, supported by men morally and physically unfit for life in a sub-tropical climate, could not outlast the first enthusiasm which called it into being. Worn out by immorality, by leprosy and other diseases, and by mutual dissensions, the unworthy champions of the Cross disappeared before Saladin, leaving as their legacy to the country a score or so of place names; a quantity of worthless ecclesiastical traditions; a number of castles and churches, many of which have been converted into mosques. In 1516, Palestine was conquered by the Turks, and formed part of the Turkish provinces of Syria, until the Ottoman Empire disintegrated during the 1914–18 war. At the end of the war, Palestine was placed under the British Mandate by the League of Nations, with its eastern boundary formed by the river Jordan; east of the river the Emirate of Transjordan was established under the Emir Abdullah of the Hashemite house.

Some Jewish groups had continued to live in Palestine probably right through the Moslem domination, and in the later years of Turkish rule new settlers had entered the country. During the Mandate, as a result of the Balfour Declaration, new Jewish colonies were established, mainly in the coastal plain. The persecution of the Jews in Germany by the Nazis led to greatly increased immigration, and growing friction between Arabs and Jews started outbreaks of violence by the Arabs in 1936. During the European war, an uneasy truce existed, but at the end of the war illegal Jewish immigration led to a renewed outbreak of violence. Great Britain resigned the Mandate in 1948, and there was open warfare between the Jews and Arabs. When a truce was ultimately established in 1949, a purely artificial boundary was created running from ʿAqaba up the ʿArabah and part of the W. side of the Dead Sea, swinging between Beersheba and Hebron, with a re-entrant to touch the walls of the Old City of Jerusalem, then W. again to run along the western edge of the hill country, and E. once more a little S. of the Plain of Esdraelon to the Sea of Galilee. To the W. of this line was established the state of Israel. The enclave of the old Palestine to the E. of this line was incorporated with Transjordan, to form the Hashemite Kingdom of the Jordan. In Jordan, the greater part of the 800,000 Arab refugees from Israel are now housed in camps or new villages. R. A. S. M.—**K. M. K.**

PALLET.—Found only in RVm and RSV for AV and RV 'bed' in the stories of the paralytic in Mk 2 and of the cripple in Jn 5, and in Mk 6^{55}, Ac 5^{15}.

PALLU.—One of the sons of Reuben, Gn 46^{9} (AV **Phallu**), Ex 6^{14}, Nu $26^{5,8}$, 1 Ch 5^{3}. The patronymic **Palluites** occurs in Nu 26^{5}. We should probably read *Pallu* for **Peleth** in Nu 16^{1}.

PALM TREE (Heb. *tāmār*, Gr. *phoinix*).—The date palm (*phoenix dactylifera*) is identified in the Midrash *Bereshith Rabba* 15 as the 'tree of life' (Gn 2^{9}); the prophetess Deborah 'sat' under a noted palm tree (Jg 4^{5}); at the feast of Tabernacles *Lûlābhîm* made of palm, myrtle and willow branches were carried and waved (Lv 23^{40}, *Sukkah* iv, 5; cf 1 Mac 13^{51}, Jn 12^{13}, Rev. 7^{9}); it was a decorative and probably symbolic feature of sacred architecture (1 K 6^{29}, Ezk 40^{16} 41^{18})—a use also attested in Egypt and Mesopotamia (see *ANEP* Index s.v.) as well as on Jewish coins and synagogues (*e.g. Tell Ḥūm*=Capernaum). The palm was also a metaphor of stateliness (Ps 92^{12}, Ca 7^{7}), and a girl's name (2 S 13^{1}). These references indicate the important rôle of the date palm in the ancient as in the modern Near East.

Although not yet restored to its former abundance in Palestine itself—Jericho was known as the 'city of palms' (Dt 34[3], Josephus *BJ* IV. viii. 2–3 [451 ff])—the palm is still one of the most useful trees of Egypt, Mesopotamia and the desert oases (Ex 15[27], Nu 33[9]), its fruit being a staple diet and providing a substitute for sugar in the form of *dibs* or date honey, while its plaited leaves furnish mats and baskets, the bark is made into rope, and the kernels into fodder. Its cultivation goes back well into the third millennium, and there is a relief from *Tell Ḥalâf* (Gozan), which shows a man pollinating the female date-bearing flowers by hand to increase its prolificity.

E. W. G. M.—**D. R. Ap-T.**

PALMA CHRISTI.—See JONAH, 2.

PALMER-WORM.—Old English for 'caterpillar,' see LOCUST.

PALON.—See AHIJAH, 7, HELEZ, **1**, **2**, and PELONITE.

PALSY.—The modern form of this word is 'paralysis.' See MEDICINE.

PALTI.—**1.** The Benjamite spy, Nu 13[9]. **2.** The man to whom Michal, David's wife, was given by Saul, 1 S 25[44] (AV **Phalti**); called **Paltiel** in 2 S 3[15] (AV **Phaltiel**).

PALTIEL.—**1.** The prince of Issachar, Nu 34[26]. **2.** See PALTI, **2**.

PALTITE.—A native of **Beth-pelet** (q.v.). To this town belonged Helez, one of David's thirty heroes, 2 S 23[26]. In 1 Ch 11[27] he is called a **Pelonite.**

PAMPHYLIA.—The name of a district on the S. coast of Asia Minor, lying between Lycia and Cilicia. Strictly speaking, it consisted of a plain 80 miles long and (at its widest part) 20 miles broad, lying between Mt. Taurus and the sea. After A.D. 74 the name was applied to a Roman province which included the mountainous country to the N., more properly called Pisidia, but until that time it was used only in the narrower sense. The plain was shut in from all N. winds, but was well watered by springs from the Taurus ranges. Through lack of cultivation in modern times it has become very malarious, and in ancient times, though better cultivated, the district was never favourable to the development of a vigorous population. Moreover, it was very isolated except by sea, for the mountains to the N. had no good roads, and were infested by brigands. Even Alexander had to fight his way through them.

The name is probably derived from the *Pamphyli*, one of the three Dorian tribes, and it is likely that Dorian settlers entered Pamphylia at the time of the other Dorian migrations. But the Greek element never prevailed, and though Side and Aspendos were half-Greek cities in the 5th cent. B.C., the Greek that they spoke was very corrupt and was written in a corrupt alphabet. Side is said to have earned its prosperity as the market of Cilician pirates. The town of Attalia was founded in the 2nd century. But more important was the native town of **Perga**, situated inland and apparently having a port of its own on the river Cestrus at a distance of 5 miles. It was a religious centre, where a goddess 'Artemis of Perga' was worshipped, her rites corresponding to those associated with Artemis of the Ephesians, and being therefore more Asiatic than Greek. The ruins of the city date from the period of the Seleucid kings of Syria. Pamphylia was in turn subject to Persia, Macedonia, Syria, Pergamum, and Rome. Archaeological excavations are being conducted at Perga and Side by the Turks.

Paul and Barnabas on their first missionary journey crossed from Cyprus to Perga, but seem to have gone straight on to Antioch without preaching. It was at Perga that John Mark left them (Ac 13[13]). On the return journey, before taking ship at Attalia, they preached at Perga (Ac 14[25]), but by this time they had definitely determined to 'turn to the Gentiles' (cf 13[46]). Christianity was slow in taking root in Pamphylia, and this was probably due partly to the backwardness of the district. In Ac 2[10] Pamphylian Jews hear the Pentecostal 'speaking with tongues.' The presence of Jewish communities in Pamphylia is presupposed in 1 Mac 15[23] for *c* 137 B.C. A. E. H.—**E. G. K.**

PAN.—See HOUSE, **9**.

PANELLED, PANELLING.—See CEILED, CEILING.

PANNAG.—A word of doubtful genuineness occurring only in Ezk 27[17], in a list of articles which had a place in the commerce of Judah and Israel with Tyre. RV simply transliterates the word, and RVm observes 'perhaps a kind of confection.' AV had understood the word as a place name, 'wheat of Minnith and Pannag.' Three MSS have the reading 'paggag,' 'early figs' and RSV so renders.

PAPER.—See WRITING, **6**.

PAPER REEDS.—See MEADOW, REED.

PAPHOS was the name of two cities in the W. of Cyprus, Old Paphos about a mile from the sea, New Paphos (now Baffo) about seven miles NW. of this (Strabo, XIV. vi. 3). The Phoenician origin of the former need not be doubted; the latter was by tradition a Greek settlement, but in both the chief object of worship was the 'Paphian goddess,' undoubtedly of Syrian origin, and worshipped under the form of a conical stone, though identified by the Greeks with Aphrodite. Old Paphos was desolate in the time of Jerome. New Paphos was the centre of the Roman administration in Cyprus. It was here that St. Paul encountered the Roman proconsul Sergius Paulus in his first missionary journey—the first presentation of Christianity before Roman authorities (Ac 13[6–12]). A. E. H.

PAPYRI AND OSTRACA.—**1. Modern discoveries.**—Until almost the end of the 19th cent., the most important records of antiquity, apart from the authors, that had been preserved for literary reasons, were the inscriptions on stone and metal. Published in great collections, and utilized by scholars of all civilized countries, they have given new life to all branches of the study of antiquity, to history in the widest sense of the word, and in particular to the history of states, law, economics, language, and religion. The age of modern epigraphy has been extraordinarily productive of knowledge that never could have been discovered from the authors alone. And the end has not yet come. The researches and excavations of European and American archaeological institutes and of special archaeological expeditions in which the governments of almost all civilized countries and many wealthy individuals have taken part, bring to light innumerable inscribed stones every year. Then there are the engineering enterprises for opening up the countries of the Levant to traffic and commerce. In the construction of railways particularly, but also in other similar undertakings, a quantity of epigraphical material is discovered and made accessible to scholars.

These epigraphical records were reinforced in the last quarter of the 19th cent. by two quite new groups of records, both of which have ushered in a new epoch in the science of antiquity, viz. the *Papyri* and the *Ostraca*. Both have led to the development of entirely new branches of study. In comparison with the inscriptions they not only constitute an enormous quantitative increase of our materials, but also qualitatively they are of quite special importance: they allow us to see into the private life of the men of antiquity—their most private life, in fact—much deeper than we could ever have done by aid of the authors and the inscriptions.

Suppose for a moment that chance excavations in an absolutely dry mound of rubbish were to lead to the discovery of whole bundles of original private letters, contracts, wills, judicial reports, etc., relating to our own ancestors of the 10th cent. A.D.—what a wave of excitement would run through the whole of the learned world! How few are the documents that we do possess of the private life of those times! History preserves the old inscribed stones, the archives of kings, the chanceries of the great churches and municipalities, but suffers the written memorials of peasants, soldiers, women, artisans, to disappear after a few years without a trace. It was exactly the same in antiquity. The tradition that had come down to us was on the whole the tradition preserved in the history of what was great—the history of nations, potentates, the intellectual leaders in art, science, and religion; and that is true in great measure of the inscriptions, which for the most part owe their origin to princes, cities, and wealthy individuals.

Only those rare inscriptions that originated in the middle and lower classes of ancient society had to some extent counterbalanced the one-sidedness of the materials available as sources. The papyri and ostraca, however, have remedied the defect in a most unexpected manner. Rubbish mounds such as that which we just now assumed hypothetically to be discoverable in our own country, but which in reality, owing to the dampness of our climate, probably do not exist anywhere in the West, occur in large numbers in Egypt. In ancient times the dumping grounds for rubbish and refuse were on the outskirts of the cities, towns, and villages. Whole bundles of documents that were too old to be worth preserving were thrown on these rubbish heaps by the authorities, instead of being burned; and private persons did the same when they wished to get rid of written matter that had accumulated and was considered valueless. The centuries have covered these ancient rubbish-dumps with layers of dust and sand, and this covering has united with the great dryness of the climate to preserve most excellently the old sheets of papyrus and the inscribed fragments of pottery. Of course, these texts, when rediscovered in our own day, throw a flood of light upon the upper cultivated class, but for the most part they are documents of the middle and lower classes.

It had long been known that papyrus was in antiquity a very popular writing material. The pith of the papyrus plant, which thrives excellently in the damp levels of the Nile, was cut into strips, and from these strips, laid cross-wise, horizontally and vertically, upon each other, the sheets of papyrus were manufactured by pressing these strips together. Perishable as the material seems, it is in reality excellent. We possess Egyptian papyri of the time of king Assa (*c* 2600 B.C., according to Eduard Meyer's chronology); and most of the papyri now in our museums have lain more than 1500 years in the soil of Egypt.

The first discoverers of written papyri must have been Egyptian *fellahîn*, digging in the old rubbish mounds for good earth and treasure. In the year 1778 a European noticed a number of papyrus documents in the hands of some of these peasants; he bought one, and watched them burn some fifty others in order that they might enjoy the aromatic smoke. The one document came to Europe; it is the Charta Borgiana, the decipherment of which marks the first beginning of papyrology. Though a good number of papyri reached the European museums in the course of the 19th cent., only a few scholars took any trouble to cultivate papyrology further, until in 1877, a hundred years after the acquisition of the Charta Borgiana, many thousands of papyri came to light from the rubbish mounds near the 'City of Crocodiles' or 'City of the Arsenoites,' the old capital of the province of el-Fayyum in Middle Egypt.

This was the beginning of a new epoch that has led to a gigantic development of the science of papyri. The period of chance discoveries, the harvest of which used from merely financial considerations to be scattered hither and thither, has been succeeded by a period of systematic excavations carried out by highly trained specialists, who keep together the documents they discover and publish them in collected form. British scholars particularly have performed signal services by discovering and publishing papyri. Flinders Petrie obtained magnificent specimens from mummy-wrappings which had been made by sticking papyri together. Grenfell and Hunt carried out splendid excavations at Oxyrhynchus and other places, and published their treasures with a rapidity and accuracy that placed them in the front rank of editors, as the world of scholarship acknowledges. Besides these there are many other editors, and every year adds to the army of workers on the texts; philologists and historians, lawyers, and theologians, all have found and are finding abundant work. This science found a centre in the *Archiv für Papyrusforschung*, a journal published from 1900 to 1920.

2. Literary texts.—The papyri fall into two great classes according to the nature of their contents, viz. literary texts and non-literary texts.

Literary texts have come to light in large numbers, though generally only in fragments. They comprise not only very ancient MSS of well-known authors, but also a large number of lost authors; and lost writings by known authors have been partially recovered. These finds would suffice to show the extreme importance of the papyrus discoveries. And many scholars have considered these literary finds to be the most valuable.

But for scholarship as a whole the second group, the non-literary texts, is no doubt the more important. As regards their contents, they are as varied as life itself. Legal documents of the most various kinds, *e.g.* leases, accounts and receipts, contracts of marriage and divorce, wills, denunciations, notes of trials, and tax-papers, are there in innumerable examples; moreover, there are letters and notes, schoolboys' exercise-books, horoscopes, diaries, petitions, etc. Their value lies in the inimitable fidelity with which they reflect the actual life of ancient society, especially in its middle and lower strata.

The oldest papyri date from *c* 2600 B.C., and are among the most precious Egyptological records. To the 5th cent. B.C. belong the Aramaic papyri from Elephantine, published by Sayce and Cowley in 1906, by Sachau in 1911, and by Kraeling in 1953 (see ELEPHANTINE PAPYRI)—documents that have furnished astonishing information relative to the history of Judaism. In the 4th cent. B.C. the main stream, as it were, begins, consisting of Greek papyri, and extending from the time of the Ptolemies till the first centuries of the Arab occupation, *i.e.* over a period of more than 1000 years. Associated with them there are Latin, Coptic, Arabic, Hebrew, Persian, and other papyri—so that, taken all together, they confer an immense benefit, and at the same time impose an immense obligation, upon the science of antiquity.

What is the importance of the papyri to Biblical science? It is twofold. In the first place, they increase our stock of Biblical MSS in a most gratifying manner; and secondly, they place new sources at the disposal of the philological student of the Greek Bible.

Beginning then with Biblical MSS, and first of all MSS of the Hebrew Bible, we have in the Nash Papyrus a very ancient copy of the Ten Commandments. As regards the Greek OT, the first decades of exploration turned up numerous fragments (*e.g.* the Leipzig fragments of the Psalms, the Heidelberg fragments of the Minor Prophets), together with isolated remains of other translations. More recent discoveries include the Rylands Papyrus 458—fifteen verses of Deuteronomy 23–24 from the middle of the 2nd cent. B.C.; the Chester Beatty Papyri—parts of nine OT books of the 3rd to 4th cent. A.D.; the Berlin Genesis and the Freer Minor Prophets of the 3rd cent. A.D. There are also papyrus MSS among the Dead Sea Scrolls (q.v.).

For the NT, we now possess over 70 items from the middle of the 2nd cent. A.D. on. The earliest is a small fragment of the Gospel of John in the Rylands library, but much the most significant are the Beatty Papyrus of Paul (P^{46}), and the Bodmer Papyri: John (P^{66}), Luke and John (P^{75}), Jude and 1 and 2 Peter (P^{72}), an early Bohairic John and important patristic material. But besides these we have acquired quite new material, in particular the various remains of lost Gospels and two papyrus fragments and one vellum fragment with sayings of Jesus, some of which are not to be found in the NT. Of course, with such finds as these it is always a question how far they contain ancient and genuine material; and the opinions of specialists, *e.g.* with regard to these

PAPYRI AND OSTRACA

sayings of Jesus, are at variance. But in any case, even if, as is not at all likely, they should prove to be of quite secondary importance as regards the history of Jesus, they would be valuable documents in the history of Christianity.

Quite a number of the papyri throw fresh light on early Christianity as a whole. Fragments of the Fathers, Apocryphal and Gnostic writings—including the great collection of Coptic Gnostic MSS found at Nag Hammadi in 1947—liturgical texts, homiletic fragments, remains of early Christian poetry, have been recovered in large numbers, both in Greek and Coptic. But to these must be added the large number of non-literary documents, both Jewish and early Christian, which are to be reckoned among the oldest relics of our religion. From the time of the persecution of the Christians under the Emperor Decius, we possess, for example, scores of *libelli* issued to *libellatici*, *i.e.* official certificates by the authorities responsible for the pagan sacrifices, that the holder of the papyrus had performed the prescribed sacrifices. To the time of the Diocletian persecution belongs probably the letter of Psenosiris, a Christian presbyter in the Great Oasis, relating to a banished Christian woman named Politike. Then comes a long series of other early Christian original letters in Greek and Coptic, from the 3rd cent. until late in the Byzantine period. Centuries that had long been supposed to be knowable only from the folios of Fathers of the Church are made to live again by these original documents—documents of whose complete *naïveté* and singleness of purpose, there can be no doubt.

3. Non-literary texts.—The direct value of the papyri to Bible scholarship and ecclesiastical history is thus very considerable. Less obvious, however, but none the less great, is the indirect value of the papyri, and chiefly the non-literary documents of private life.

This value is discoverable in two directions. The papyri, as sources of popular, non-literary Late Greek, have placed the linguistic investigation of the Greek Bible on new foundations ; and, as autograph memorials of men of the ancient world from the age of the great religious revolution, they enable us better to understand these men—the public to whom the great world-mission of Primitive Christianity was addressed.

As regards the first, the philological value of the papyri, these new texts have caused more and more the rejection of the old prejudice that the Greek Bible (OT and NT) represents a linguistic entity clearly determinable by scholarship. On the contrary, the habit has arisen more and more of bringing ‘ Biblical ’ or ‘ New Testament ’ Greek into relation with popular Late Greek, and it has come to be realized that the Greek Bible is itself the grandest monument of the popular (*koinē*) language.

The clearest distinctive features of a living language fall within the province of phonology and accidence. And in the phonology and accidence we see most readily that the assumption of a ‘ Biblical ’ Greek, capable of being isolated from other Greek for purposes of study, was wrong. The hundreds of morphological details that strike the philologist accustomed only to classical Attic, when he begins to read the Greek Bible, are found also in the contemporary records of the ‘ profane ’ popular language, especially in the papyri and ostraca. The *Grammars of the NT*, by James Hope Moulton, Ludwig Radermacher, and Debrunner's revision of Blass have furnished an extremely copious collection of parallel phenomena. Helbing's *Grammar of the Greek Old Testament* (Septuagint) does the same. The Septuagint was produced in Egypt, and naturally employed the language of its surroundings ; the Egyptian papyri are therefore magnificent as parallel texts, especially as we possess a great abundance of texts from the Ptolemaic period, *i.e.* the time when the Septuagint itself originated. The correspondence between them goes so far that Mayser's *Grammar of the Greek Papyri of the Ptolemaic Period* might in many particulars be used as a Septuagint Grammar.

Questions of Biblical orthography, which seem unimportant to the layman, but cause much worry to an editor of the Biblical text, are of course illumined by the contemporary papyri. The matter is not unimportant to the scientific scholar, who must work with the fidelity of the wise steward.

In the same way problems of syntax and of style are considerably advanced by the papyri. It is possible, for example, to place the whole theory of the prepositions on a new basis. The use of the prepositions in Late Greek is very interesting. To mention but one small point, we are now able to make much more exact statements with regard to those prepositions in the NT which denote a vicarious relation (*e.g. hyper* and *peri*). The syntactical peculiarities of the NT, which used often to be traced back to Semitic influence, can also as a rule be paralleled from the papyri. The treatment of Semiticisms has been revolutionized. Formerly, when the NT used to be ‘ isolated ’ far too much, the question was generally answered in such a way that the influence of the so-called ‘ genius ’ of the Hebrew or Aramaic language, especially on the Primitive Christians, was greatly exaggerated. Linguistic phenomena that could not be found recorded in the ordinary Greek grammars were described summarily as Semiticisms. It was forgotten that the NT and the Septuagint are for the most part documents of the popular language, and that the popular language in Greek and in Semitic has much in common. For example, the so-called ‘ paratactic ’ style of St. John's Gospel and St. John's Epistles, which used generally to be pronounced strongly Semitic, is in fact simply popular style, and has its parallels in inscriptions and papyri which certainly are not under Semitic influence. The existence of Semiticisms in the Greek Bible is of course not denied by recent Biblical investigators—in the books translated from Semitic originals they are really numerous—but the number of Semiticisms has been considerably reduced, and in proportion as the Semitic character of the NT recedes, its popular character is made to advance. The emphasis upon the popular character of NT Greek was itself at first exaggerated. Then reaction produced a new recognition of Semitic influence, as in W. F. Howard's study ‘ Semitisms in the NT ’ in Part Two of J. H. Moulton's *Grammar*, and in Matthew Black's *An Aramaic Approach to the Gospels and Acts*. Again E. C. Colwell's *The Greek of the Fourth Gospel* checked extreme claims for translations of that Gospel from a Semitic original.

It is lexicography, perhaps, that derives most benefit from the new documents. Late Greek is rich in new words and new meanings of old words : the virgin soil of the life of the people is inexhaustible. Grammarians of a later age—the so-called Atticists—lured by Attic Greek of the classical period as by a phantom, fought against these new words and meanings, branded them as ‘ bad,’ and tried to root them out. A number of *littérateurs* suffered themselves to be bound by the rules of the Atticists, as if they had been living in the 5th cent. B.C. This unhistorical, pedantic, and dogmatic tendency left the men of the NT practically untouched. Men of the people themselves, they spoke as the people spoke, and in the Gospels, for example, they for the first time introduced the language of the people with vigour into literature. By reason of its popular character, the language of the first Apostles is pre-eminently a missionary language, and this language it was that really enabled Christianity to rise to a world-religion. All this is confirmed most amply by the new discoveries. Words that we used formerly to regard as specifically ‘ Biblical ’ or ‘ New Testament,’ we find now in the mouth of the people. Besides the papyri, the inscriptions also are rich sources. Illustrative quotations from the papyri are for us particularly lifelike, because we can generally date them even to the day. Turn over, for example, the pages of the second volume of *Oxyrhynchus Papyri* published by Grenfell and Hunt, and you find that the non-literary examples are almost exclusively documents of the 1st cent. A.D., *i.e.* the exact time in which the NT grew up. These and scores of other volumes of papyri and inscriptions have led to the remaking of the lexicons of the NT. J. H. Moulton and G. Milligan's *The Vocabulary of the Greek Testament* was the pioneer in this field in English, as Deissmann's publications were in German. Walter Bauer's *Wörterbuch zu den Schriften des Neuen Testaments und der übrigen urchristlichen Literatur* (4th ed., 1952) was the first lexicon to incorporate fully this new knowledge, and the work by W. F. Arndt and F. W. Gingrich, *A Greek English Lexicon* of the NT (1957), when added to R. W. Frank's translation of Blass-Debrunner, *A Greek Grammar* of the NT and other early Christian Literature (1961), at long last makes the lore from the non-literary sources available to those who do not know German.

Thus we see the justification of the statement that the new texts of popular Late Greek have placed the linguistic investigation of the Greek Bible on new foundations. In yet another direction they yield an important harvest to theology. The more we realize the missionary character of Primitive Christianity, and the more clearly we grasp the greatness of the Apostle Paul working among the proletariat of the great centres of the world's commerce—Ephesus, Corinth, etc.—the more we shall feel the necessity of studying the men to whom the gospel was preached, *i.e.* of obtaining, where possible, insight into their life, not only into their economic position and their family life, but into their very soul. As regards Egypt, we now possess wonderful documents among the papyri, especially in the numerous private letters, which were not intended for publicity but reflect quite naïvely the mood of the moment. As they have made clearer to us the nature of the non-literary letters of St. Paul—and this alone constitutes a large part of the value of the papyri to NT study—so they make live again for us the men of the middle and lower classes of the age of the Primitive Christian mission to the world, especially for him who has ears to hear the softer notes between the lines. But we may assume that the civilization of the Imperial age was tolerably uniform throughout the whole range of the Mediterranean lands and that if we know the Egyptians of the time of St. Paul, we are not far from knowing the Corinthians and the men of Asia Minor of the same period. And thus we possess in the papyri, as also in the inscriptions, excellent materials for the reconstruction of the historical background of Primitive Christianity.

4. Ostraca.—In conclusion, reference may be made once more to the fact that recently, in addition to the papyri, a great number of similar ancient texts, written on fragments of pottery, have been discovered in Egypt, *viz.* the *Ostraca.* As the potsherd cost nothing (anybody could fetch one from the nearest rubbish heap) it was the writing material of the poor man, and revenue officials were fond of using it in transactions with the poor. The ostraca, which are also numbered by thousands, are on the whole even more ' vulgar ' than the papyri, but for that very reason valuable to us in all respects already specified with regard to the papyri. The real founder of the study of ostraca on the great scale was Ulrich Wilcken, who collected, deciphered, and historically elucidated the Greek ostraca. Next to him W. E. Crum rendered similar services to the Coptic ostraca. To show that the ostraca, besides their indirect importance, have also a direct value for the history of Christianity, we may refer to the potsherds inscribed with texts from the Gospels, or the early Christian legal documents discovered at the town of Menas, but chiefly to the Coptic potsherds containing numerous Christian letters and illustrating particularly the inner history of Egyptian Christianity.

The whole study of papyri and ostraca is now mature, but the flood of publications continues, and secondary studies of great value are still to be expected. The layman also who loves his Bible may still expect much light from the wonderful texts from the period of the origin of the Septuagint and the NT, and there is no need to fear that the Light of the world (Jn 8^{12}) will pale before the new lights kindled for us by research. The more we set the NT in its own contemporary world, the more we shall realize, on the one hand, the contact between it and the world, and the more we shall feel, on the other hand, the contrast in which it stands with the world, and for the sake of which it went out to contend with and to conquer that world. A. D.—E. C. C.

PAPYRUS.—A plant which grew plentifully by the Nile. See RUSH. From it were made light boats (see REED, **5**) and also writing material (see WRITING, **6**). The name was also given to texts written on papyrus ; see PAPYRI AND OSTRACA.

PARABLE (IN OT).—The word is a translation of the Hebrew *māshāl* normally translated *parabolē* in LXX, but given a variety of translations in EV, *e.g.* parable, proverb, byword, allegory, taunt (song), and even (Nu 21^{27} RSV) **ballad.** The verbal form means ' to be like,' and this meaning is supported by cognate words in other Semitic languages. A verb with the same spelling means ' to rule ' (cf Gn 3^{16}) and this has suggested the original meaning as being ' an acted spell.' This is possible although few of the occurrences in the OT would naturally fit this derivation.

Since the verb means ' to be like ' and the noun is normally translated into Greek as ' *parabolē* ' (juxta-position, comparison), we may take this as a starting point. We may note that the translation ' *allēgoria* ' is never used, although RSV translates **allegory** at Ezk 17^{2} 20^{49} (21^{5}) 24^{3}. In many instances the sense of comparison is obvious, but it is comparison with a purpose, viz. to quicken the mind of the hearer so that he makes a true assessment of the situation, or his own actions. The prophet Ezekiel is seeking to awaken his people to the realities of the situation ; what has befallen them is not merely a political disaster but the work of their God. The result of this understanding would be penitence and the dawn of a new hope. Other parables in Ezekiel are those of the foundling girl (Ezk 16) and Oholah and Oholibah (Ezk 23). Parables (though not specifically described as such) occur in other parts of the OT ; cf 2 S 12^{1-6} the Ewe Lamb, 2 S 14^{5-11} the Reprieved Murderer, 2 K 14^{9} the Thistle and the Cedar, Is 5^{1-7} the Vineyard.

The parable is equated with the riddle in Ps $49^{4(5)}$ 78^{2}, and is not a mode of instruction appropriate to fools Pr $26^{7, 9}$. It requires mental alertness and stimulates to right judgment, cf Pr 1^{6}. This may indicate the significance of its use as a title for Proverbs (*mᵉshālîm*), much of whose contents is not ' proverbial ' in character, but short pithy sentences designed to quicken right understanding of the issues of life, cf Lk 4^{23}. Of a similar character are the passages 1 S 10^{12} $24^{13(14)}$, Ezk 12^{22} 18^{2f}, not all of which are proverbial in character but are intended to arouse insight. The use of the word in Dt 28^{37}, 1 K 9^{7}, Ps $44^{14(15)}$ $69^{11(12)}$, Ezk 14^{8}, is instructive. The fate of Israel, the people of God, at the hand of God is intended to move the Gentiles to reflect on their own state and to say ' If it was so with them, how shall it be with us ? ' The use of the word in taunt songs may well indicate that the utterance was accompanied by some mimetic actions, and the implied words would be, ' So shall it be with you ' (cf Is 14^{4}, Mic 2^{4}, Hab 2^{6}). There are many examples of acted parables in the OT, *e.g.* 1 K 11^{29ff}, Is 8^{1ff} 20^{2}, Jer 27^{2f} 32^{6ff} 28^{1ff}, Ezk 4^{1}–5^{4}. Whether the parable be spoken or acted, it is full of an energy of fulfilment ; it is intended to stimulate the mind of the hearer or observer to recognize that ' So it is ! ' or ' So shall it be ! ' and to lead to an acceptance of the Divine judgment. Only the insensitive would remain unaffected by the parable. Finally we may note that this mode of teaching continued in post-biblical Jewish teaching, and was brought to its finest expression in the teaching of Jesus. See also RIDDLE. A. S. H.

PARABLE (IN NT).—1. *Meaning and form.*—The English word, parable, is derived from the Greek, *parabolē,* which is the LXX translation of the Hebrew *māshāl* meaning comparison. In Hebrew usage the term was applicable to a wide variety of picturesque forms of expression including simile, proverb, metaphor, illustrative story, similitude, allegory, and riddle. By such means it was sought to illuminate unfamiliar ideas by reference to something analogous in the experience of those addressed. Disinclined as he was to discursive exposition, the Semite practised the art of persuasion by thus skilfully appealing to the imagination. All the forms of Hebrew parable except the riddle are found in the NT, chiefly in the Synoptic Gospels. In the Gospel of John and in the epistles of Paul, apart from simple metaphors, the parables which occur are in the form of *allegories* (*e.g.* Jn 10^{1-5}, the Shepherd and the Sheep; 15^{1-5}, the Vine and the Branches; Gal 3^{15-18}, the Promises to Abraham; 4^{21-31}, Abraham's Two Sons). In the allegory each item of the story has a hidden meaning, so that all have to be decoded. Without the key supplied either by the historical context (see below on Mk 12^{1-12}) or verbally, as in the above examples, the reader could not arrive at the meaning intended. The allegory is therefore an artificial method of instruction by contrast with the other forms of parable in which the meaning is apparent in the terms of the parable itself. It may well be that the Johannine and Pauline examples had an influence on the practice of the Church, which for centuries treated all the parables as allegories. In effect, this resulted in Jesus' parabolic teaching being transmuted into Christian theology. By exercising his ingenuity, the allegorizer completely ignored the obvious meaning of such a parable as the Good Samaritan and found support in it, instead, for his own theological position, as St. Augustine did.

It was not until Adolf Jülicher wrote his famous *Die Gleichnisreden Jesu* (1888-1899) that the fallacy of such a method of interpretation was generally accepted by scholarly opinion. Jülicher did not rule out all allegorical explanations but argued that they were legitimate only to a very limited extent, and that, where Mark and Matthew added allegorical explanations to certain parables of the kingdom, they were among the first to fall into this error. It is now recognized that, in addition to metaphors and short picturesque comparisons or similes, there are three kinds of parabolic utterance in the Synoptic Gospels, in none of which is the meaning recondite. These are the similitude, the parable proper, and the illustrative story. In the similitude the comparison is of a detailed kind, as in the Seed Growing of Itself (Mk 4^{26-29}); in the parable proper the point is to be found in the immediate context, as in the Importunate Householder (Lk 11^{5-10}); the illustrative story conveys its own meaning directly, the lesson being brought out in the story as a whole, as in the Good Samaritan (Lk 10^{29-37}).

2. *Problems of Interpretation.*—Awareness of the fallacy of allegorizing was an important advance, but many problems of interpretation still remained for the following reasons:

(1) There is a tendency, especially observable in Luke, to add to the parable in such a way as to shift the emphasis. The result is confusing, for the intention of the embellishment is plainly different from that of the parable itself. Two examples are the Lucan version of the New Cloth on the Old Garment (Lk 5^{36}) and the illustrative story of the Unjust Steward (Lk 16^{1-9}). In the former case the emphasis should be on the worsening of the rent in the garment, as in Mark's version. The meaning, derived from the context, is that any attempt to reconcile the new (Christian) order with the old (Judaism) is fruitless and only results in further evidence of the decay of the old order. In Luke this forthright denunciation is watered down to the statement that the new does not match the old and that the attempt to bring them together will result in the spoiling of the new—a thought which is not in the Marcan rendering at all. There is no parallel to the Unjust Steward, for comparison, but in v.[8] the thought appears to be that in a time of crisis the worldly man often exhibits more common sense than religious people (sons of light) are manifesting in the impending crisis of the kingdom of God. V.[9] must be regarded as a commentary involving a rather questionable diversion of thought.

(2) Another tendency, again appearing mostly in Luke, is the addition of sayings suggested by the parables but embodying other meanings. These confuse the reader, unless he is aware of this literary characteristic. Examples are the New Wine in the Old Wineskins (Lk 5^{37-39}) and the comments following the Unjust Steward (Lk 16^{10-13}). In the former case v.[39]. 'And no one, after drinking old wine, desires new; for he says: "The old is good,"' contradicts the point of the parable. If it is a genuine saying of Jesus its meaning is lost for lack of the proper context. Apparently Luke added it here because of the accidental similarity to the parable in the use of the figure of wine. The series of comments in the second example deal with the question of faithfulness in positions of trust, intended perhaps to counteract any false conclusions which might be drawn from the commendation of the rascal in the parable. These verses are derived from various sources (v.[13] is parallel to Mt 6^{24}), and have nothing to do with the parable to which they are appended.

(3) While the early Church cherished the teachings of Jesus which had been handed down, it shifted emphases to a degree, and here and there added Christian expositions to fit the later interests and conditions of the Church. Form Criticism has performed a valuable service in demonstrating the inevitability of adapting the primitive traditional teaching, almost from the first, to the pragmatic needs of the Christian community. There was no sense of disloyalty to Jesus' teaching in making such applications. The Church was confronted with the problems of missionary work, and sayings of Jesus were strained to give authority to what the leaders believed to be the course of action which accorded with His spirit. By the time the Gospels were written there was some dismay at the delay of the Parousia. Could Jesus' eschatological teaching, therefore, have been as simple as it had seemed? The problem of unworthy members in the Church loomed large. Could help be found in solving this problem in any of Jesus' parables of the kingdom? In short, the message which in the ministry of Jesus had been directed to individuals, whether opponents or friends, was now transferred to the community, confronted with the prosaic problems which always arise in the long pull of practical endeavour. The parables, which constituted so large a part of Jesus' teaching, did not escape such reconstruction.

Examples: (*a*) The interpretation of the parable of The Sower in Mk 4^{13-20} changes the point from the assurance of the triumph of God's rule to the different kinds of responses that were being made to the gospel. The parable was allegorized in order to yield that meaning. Such an exposition is recognizable as the product of the Church's early missionary endeavours. (*b*) The allegorical interpretation of The Parable of the Weeds in Mt 13^{36-43} is likewise an example of the application of a parable to the situation in the early Church. It alters the point from the certainty of the consummation, when all evil will be overthrown, to a warning addressed to all evil doers in view of the approaching end. (*c*) The parable of The Wicked Tenants in Mk 12^{1-12} probably owes its allegorical form to the same tendency, in this case the purpose being to castigate Israel for the killing of the Messiah. The growing animosity between the Church and Judaism supplies the clue to the allegory. It is difficult to recover the parable as spoken by Jesus. The kernel of it could be the persistent refusal of God's chosen people to heed His revelation in the past, down to Jesus' own time. In its present form it is quite certainly an elaboration of the original. (*d*) The parable of The Thief in the Night (Mt 24^{42ff} ∥ Lk 12^{39f}), which carries the point of the unexpectedness of the great crisis approaching, is altered into a parable of The Watchful Householder. The emphasis is shifted to what may have seemed the more important point brought out in

PARABLE (IN NT)

Matthew's introductory verse, 'Watch therefore, for you do not know on what day your Lord is coming.'

(4) There follows from the last point the problem of determining the actual life situations which prompted the telling of the various parables. More definitely than is apparent on the surface, the Jewish leaders are attacked for their lack of spiritual perception. However, all the known circumstances under which Jesus carried on His work must be taken into account in determining the context of any particular parable.

(5) The Secret of the Kingdom of God, Mk 4^{10ff} and parallels. This celebrated saying has caused great difficulty because it seems to mean that only the Twelve had true perception, and that the parables were uttered in order to mystify the public. This would lend support to the allegorical interpretation, which has been prevalent in the Church until recent times. With the modern awareness of the true significance of the parables, various attempts have been made to explain the passage along other lines. Wellhausen regarded it as a later insertion. Many have followed him in the belief that there were two factors at work in the Church giving rise to this inauthentic pronouncement: (*a*) The fact that the Jewish people as a whole had not accepted the Gospel; (*b*) The prevalence of the idea of mystery (translated 'secret' in RSV) in the gentile world so that it was natural to apply the term to the gospel. J. Jeremias renders vv. 11 f as follows; 'To you has God given the secret of the Kingdom of God; but to those who are without everything is obscure, in order that they (as it is written) may "see and yet not see, may hear and yet not understand, *unless* they turn and God will forgive them"' (*The Parables of Jesus*, p. 15). He concludes that the saying refers not to the parables specifically but to the teaching in general, which the great majority did not accept; and yet, if they repented, God would still mercifully forgive them. V. Taylor, in his commentary on Mark, believes that the passage is a modification of the original saying. He conjectures that Jesus was impressed by the similarity of his own experience to that of Isaiah and so made use of the prophet's ironic words. Like Jeremias, he holds that the word 'parables' should read, 'riddles' (*i.e.* obscure sayings), a possible translation; it therefore does not refer to the parables which Jesus spoke. However, he does not accept Jeremias' substitution of the word 'unless' for 'lest.' In conclusion, it must be stated that there is no unanimity of opinion in regard to this perplexing saying. It is agreed, however, that, whatever it means, the parables stand in their own inherent right as a means of clarifying the message of Jesus.

(6) The theme of the Kingdom of God, *passim*. What did it mean? Many of the parables are introduced with the words, 'The Kingdom of God is like . . .' Frequently these words are inept if taken literally. For example, in Mt 13^{45f} the kingdom is clearly not like the merchant, as stated, but is like the pearl. Account must be taken of the Semitic use of the dative so that the meaning would be, 'It is the case with the Kingdom as with . . .' The Kingdom being so central to Jesus' teaching, parabolic and otherwise, it is necessary to inquire what the conception meant to Jesus. (See KINGDOM OF GOD.) Here, for the explanation of the parables, it is necessary to note only a few important points. (*a*) The thought of the Kingdom was the focal point of Jesus' faith and teaching. (*b*) He divested it of all traces of Jewish national aspirations which were commonly an integral part of the idea. (*c*) He laid the stress on individual repentance as a necessity for belonging to the Kingdom; merit was not enough, for all fall short. (*d*) God is loving and merciful but also stern in His condemnation of unrepentant men. (*e*) Pride and avarice or over-concern with material possessions were especially singled out as obstacles to man's acceptance of his true position in the sight of God. (*f*) A note of urgency is prevalent in the record; at the least the premonitory signs of the Kingdom were present for those who had eyes to see; the power of Satan was already broken in heaven and was being destroyed on earth. (*g*) The Kingdom of God had brought Jesus with it; He had not come to establish the Kingdom, but to be its herald and, if need be, to die for its sake.

3. *The Message of the Parables*. In a thorough study of the parables, they must be considered one by one, taking into account the context and the possibility of accretions and changes. Here only a broad classification of the principal parables is made, with brief notations of the point of each, as a directive for such a study.

(1) Parables of assurance regarding the Kingdom. (*a*) The Sower, Mk 4^{3-8}: The certainty of the Kingdom's establishment in spite of some partial failures. (*b*) The Seed Growing Secretly, Mk 4^{26-29}: Man's part is to proclaim the message; God insures the outcome. (*c*) The Mustard Seed, Mk 4^{30f}: Small beginnings must not deceive one in regard to the final great consummation. (*d*) The Leaven, Mt 13^{33} || Lk 13^{20f}: Not a progressive advance, which is an Occidental idea, but the miraculous character of the results of so small a beginning. Perhaps also a hint of the hidden manner of God's operation.

(2) God in His relation to sinful men. (*a*) The Lost Sheep, Lk 15^{4-7} || Mt 18^{12-14}, and The Lost Coin, Lk 15^{8ff}. God is not only merciful toward the repentant sinner, as in rabbinic Judaism, but He actively seeks to win the sinner to Himself. The contrast is like that between transcendence and immanence in modern theistic beliefs. (*b*) The Prodigal Son, Lk 15^{11-32}. A contrast between the puritanical rectitude of the older son and the love of God which casts a mantle of charity over all defects of human character. (*c*) Labourers in the Vineyard, Mt 20^{1-6}. What God confers is not a reward for something earned but is given of His free grace to all who will accept it, regardless of the amount of service rendered Him.

(3) Forgiven men in their relation to God. (*a*) The Two Debtors, Lk 7^{41ff}. It is possible that the greater the sin, the more grateful the sinner will be when he experiences forgiveness. (*b*) The Unjust Judge, Lk 18^{1-8}, and The Friend at Midnight, Lk 11^{5-8}. To maintain a relationship to God through prayer, the individual must be earnest and persistent. It need scarcely be added that the end-result will be the elimination of petty ambitions and desires and the acceptance of God's will as in Jesus' prayer in Gethsemane. (*c*) The Pharisee and the Publican Lk 18^{9-14}. The first requisite in establishing a relationship with God is a recognition of one's unworthiness.

(4) The Challenge of the Kingdom. (*a*) The Hidden Treasure, Mt 13^{44}, and The Pearl, Mt 13^{45f}. This pair have the point that the Kingdom is of supreme worth and that every other concern is insignificant by comparison. The unexpected discovery in the first and the discovery after a long search in the latter are secondary differences between the parables. (*b*) The Faithful and Unfaithful Stewards, Lk 12^{42-46} || Mt 24^{45-51}; The Pounds and the Talents, Lk 19^{12-27} || Mt 25^{14-30}; The Doorkeeper, Mk 13^{33-37} || Lk 12^{35-38}. These parables denounce the religious leaders for their failure to fulfil the trust committed to them. Their seeking of selfish advantage, their inertia, their obtuseness in failing to recognize the coming of the Kingdom, are excoriated. (*c*) The Marriage Feast, Mt 22^{1-10} and The Great Supper, Lk 14^{16-24}. Undoubtedly the first readers of the Gospels would understand these similar parables as referring to the failure of the Jews to accept the gospel whereas the Gentiles had done so. As Jesus used the analogy, He would be thinking of the religious leaders in contrast to the simple people who paid heed to His teaching.

(5) Discipleship—the way of life in the kingdom. (*a*) On Defilement, Mk 7^{14f}. A categorical statement that what defiles a man is wrong moral and spiritual attitudes, not the failure to fulfill the outward requirements of religion. (*b*) The Mote and the Beam, Lk 6^{41f}. A charitable attitude toward others in view of our own weaknesses of character is inculcated. (*c*) The Tree and the Fruit, Lk 6^{43ff} || Mt 7^{16-20}. Good deeds are genuine only when the inner disposition is right, *i.e.* dedicated to God. (*d*) The Unmerciful Steward, Mt 18^{23ff}. God's forgiveness will produce a willingness to forgive; else we are

not really forgiven but condemned. (*e*) The Two Sons, Mt 21^{28-31}. The superficial confession by contrast with genuine conversion after initial refusal. (*f*) The Good Samaritan, Lk 10^{29-37}. Love knows no limitations of class or race ; it is boundless. (*g*) The Rich Fool, Lk 12^{16-21}, and Dives and Lazarus, Lk 16^{19-31}. The danger of being engrossed in material possessions. The former emphasizes their ephemeral character, the latter the result in the drying up of human sympathy. (*h*) The Difficulty of the Way, Lk 13^{24-30} ‖ Mt 7^{13f}. Great effort is required and many fail. W. S.

PARACLETE.—See ADVOCATE, PAUL, JOHN.

PARADISE.—A Persian word (*pairi-daēza*) for an enclosing wall, and then the space enclosed, a park, a garden, a pleasure ground (see ORCHARD). Used in later Jewish and Christian thought (*pardēs, paradeisos, paradisus*), it appears in religious language as God's garden, where man was placed at first by his Creator. Lost or hidden since the Fall, it will be regained at the end, whilst it may already mean, in the intermediate era, the abode of the blessed dead.

1. In the OT.—While the word *pardēs* occurs only three times in the Hebrew Bible (Ca 4^{12}, Ec 2^5, Neh 2^8) and then in the usual sense, with no reference to the *Garden of Eden*, it is unquestionable that Eden serves as the basis for the later conception. The transition from the usage of Genesis to one less literal is to be seen in Ezk 28^{13ff} and 31^{8ff}, which reflect the influence of Babylonian conceptions. These, undoubtedly, are also to be seen in the Genesis picture of Eden. The significance of Ezekiel's standpoint is that it shows the anticipation of eschatological and apocalyptic conceptions, both Jewish and Christian.

The shift from the secular to the religious sense appears more largely in the *Greek Bible* (LXX). *Paradeisos* is used there more than thirty times, especially in Genesis, where it means God's garden or Eden. The tendency to idealize grows in the apocryphal and pseudepigraphical writings (Sir 24^{25-30}, Ps. of Solom. 14^2).

2. In later Judaism.—In the apocalypses, there are elaborate descriptions (particularly 1 Enoch 23–28, Apoc. Bar 4, 2 Es 8^{52}, Test. Levi 18^{10f}) of Paradise as the opposite of *Gehenna*. (See P. Volz, *Eschatologie der jüdischen Gemeinde*, §49, 4.) In the Rabbinical conception of the universe, Paradise is the abode of the blessed dead. Here is the tree of life, and here also the righteous feast for ever. Gehenna and Paradise are, according to the rabbis, close together, being separated only by a handbreadth. This view, however, is difficult to harmonize with other conceptions, and an adjustment has been proposed by assuming the view of a twofold Paradise, one in Sheol and the other in Heaven. Such a view would harmonize with the conception that the righteous are to rise from the nether Paradise to the heavenly. But it looks hopeless to seek for much logic or harmony in the medley of rabbinic ideas and dreams. Although contrasting violently with the reserve and sobriety of Scripture, they have often crossed the Christian border.

3. In the NT.—The term *paradeisos* occurs only three times in the NT (Lk 23^{43}, 2 Co 12^4, Rev 2^7). The first instance is a word from the Cross, in Jesus' promise to the robber. Does it mean there the *lower* Paradise of Jewish conceptions, the Paradise of an 'intermediate state,' as some theologians have argued? Would it be identical with the 'Abraham's bosom' of Lk 16^{22f}, in a parable where Jesus obviously uses, in a symbolical and perhaps ironical way, the crude imagery of popular eschatology? Anyhow, the reference of Paul (2 Co 12^3) is undoubtedly to the *upper* Paradise—that is the third heaven. Here again, however, it is not safe to derive dogma from what may be a merely conventional expression, or a relic of archaic cosmology.

Paradise is often used in modern language, as the symbol less of a place than of a state and life of blessedness. H. Cl.

PARAH.—A city in Benjamin, Jos 18^{23}. It is now *Kh. el-Fârah*, near the head of the valley of Michmash.

PARALYSIS, PARALYTIC.—See MEDICINE.

PARAN.—A desert region settled by Ishmael (Gn 21^{21}) and traversed by Israel after the Exodus (Nu 10^{12} 12^{16} 13^{3-26}). It is associated with the '**wilderness of Zin,**' from which the spies went up to Palestine (Nu 13, 26), and in which Kadesh was located (Nu 20^1 27^{14}). Generally, the region of Paran apparently corresponds to the inland part of the North Sinai desert, of which Kadesh was the centre. The association of the mountain(s) of Paran with Seir in Dt 33^2 and with Teman in Hab 3^3 perhaps indicates specifically the E. edge of the plateau of *et-Tīh*, though Teman may mean the south generally. 1 K 11^{18} also indicates that Paran was contiguous with Edom and Midian. The district Paran, where David fled after the death of Samuel (1 S 25^1, where LXX reads *Maan* [Heb. *Maon*]), supports this location, though the action is located somewhat further north. Hence the particular location of 'Mount Paran' at *Jebel Maqrāh*, *c* 29 miles S. of *'Ain Qedeis*, has little to recommend it. El Paran, which Gn 14^6 visualizes on the southern limit of Mount Seir, has been identified by some with Elath, just N. of *'Aqaba*, but this depends on the LXX reading 'the terebinth (*'ēlôn*) of Paran.' The Hebrew El Paran indicates a sanctuary. J. Gr.

PARAPET.—See HOUSE, 5.

PARBAR.—In 2 Ch 26^{18} AV and RV treat this as a proper name, while RSV renders 'the parbar' with marginal note that its meaning is unknown. In a slightly different form, *parwārîm*, the same word is probably to be found in 2 K 23^{11} (AV '**suburbs**'; RV, RSV '**precincts**'). It is possible that the original text read *parwādhîm* (so 6 MSS), and *parbādh*, and that these are two forms of a word of Persian origin, meaning **forecourt.** H. H. R.

PARCHED CORN.—Hebrew *ḳālî*, Lv 23^{14}, Ru 2^{14}, 1 S 17^{17} 25^{18}, 2 S 17^{28}; *ḳālûy*, Jos 5^{11}; or more fully *'ābhîbh ḳālûy bā'ēsh*, Lv 2^{14}. This is often made on the harvest field by holding a bundle of ears in a blazing fire or by roasting them over a piece of metal. Cf FOOD, **2.**

PARCHED GRAIN.—See FOOD, **2,** PARCHED CORN.

PARCHMENT.—See PERGAMUM, WRITING.

PARDON.—See FORGIVENESS.

PARENTS.—See FAMILY.

PARK.—See ORCHARD.

PARLOUR.—See HOUSE, **5.**

PARMASHTA.—Seventh son of Haman, put to death by the Jews, Est 9^9.

PARMENAS.—One of the 'Seven' (Ac 6^5). Otherwise unknown.

PARNACH.—The father of Elizaphan, Nu 34^{25}.

PAROSH.—The name of a post-exilic family, Ezr 2^3, Neh 3^{25} 7^8 8^3 $10^{14, 25}$, 1 Es 5^9 (AV, RV **Phoros**) 8^{30} (AV **Pharez,** RV **Phoros**) 9^{26} (AV, RV **Phoros**).

PAROUSIA.—**1. Meaning of the term.**—The Greek word parousia is used in Christian teaching for Jesus Christ's **coming** or appearance at the end of the world, *i.e.* His return in glory and power. In the NT, as in general Greek usage, it means primarily 'presence' or 'arrival.' Paul uses the word in telling the Corinthians of his joy over the 'coming' of Stephanus (1 Co 16^{17}); and he voices the hope (Ph 1^{26}) to 'visit' the community in Philippi, following his release from prison (see also 2 Co 7^{6f} 10^{10}, Ph 2^{12}). Elsewhere in the NT the word bears the special meaning of Christ's 'coming' in the series of eschatological events. Thus it is always identified by the addition 'of the Son of Man' (Mt $24^{27, 37, 39}$) or 'of [our or the] Lord Jesus Christ' (1 Th 2^{19} 3^{13} 4^{15} 5^{23}, 2 Th $2^{1, 8}$, Ja 5^{7f}, 2 P 1^{16} 3^4) or simply 'of Christ' (1 Co 15^{23}). In the English translations the term is uniformly rendered by 'the coming.'

2. Eschatological connotations.—The content of the term *parousia* may readily be gathered from the passages just cited. In the synoptic apocalypse (Mk 13 and parallels), the Parousia of the Son of Man refers to the figure in Dan 7^{13} who ' comes ' on the clouds of heaven (Mk 13^{26}; see also 14^{62}). In 1 Th 4^{16} Paul speaks similarly of the ' descent ' of the Lord from heaven. According to 1 Th 3^{13} his ' revelation ' is accompanied by the appearance of the heavenly court (the angels). The ' sign ' of this event will be given by God Himself through a word of command and the sounding of the trumpet (1 Th 4^{16}, 1 Co 15^{52}). The date of this event is not given in the NT (cf Mk 13^{21}). Paul was convinced that it would take place during his lifetime (1 Th 4^{15}). This view was shared by most early Christians; in consequence the death of some of their number created a serious problem, which required an answer (1 Th 4$^{13-17}$). For the later writings of the NT (Luke-Acts and 2 Peter) the Parousia of Jesus has been postponed to the remote future, and Paul himself appears (in Ph 1^{23} and probably in 2 Co 5^{1ff}) to have given up the expectation of an immediate coming. The temptation to calculate ' the time of the end ' was generally resisted by the early church. The question of the exact day and hour was sharply cut short: ' As were the days of Noah, so will be the coming of the Son of Man '—Jesus' Parousia will be equally sudden and unexpected, for the whole world (Mt 24^{36f}, Mk 13^{32}). The same idea is found in the comparison of His coming with that of a thief in the night (1 Th 5^{2ff}, Mt 24^{43}). The point of these two comparisons is not exhausted in criticism of speculations and calculations of the date of the Last Day, such as were current in the neighbourhood of the early church, *viz.* in the apocalyptic type of Judaism, which began with the Book of Daniel (see also Lk 17^{20}). Their rich and positive significance, for the church itself, lay in the exhortation to be ready and watching for the Lord to appear (Mk 13^{33}). Every day must be lived as if it were the last!

3. Consequences.—The early church looked forward to the Parousia as the full and final realization of the hope of salvation. Hence it is no accident that 1 Co 15^{23} views the resurrection of Christians as accompanying the Parousia of Christ. His victory over Death, ' the last enemy ' (1 Co 15^{26}), which is now hidden and visible only to faith, will then be open and obvious to all the world. Paul testifies to the same belief in 1 Th 4$^{13-17}$, where he also speaks of the ' catching up ' of those still living ' to meet the Lord in the air '—*i.e.* the descending Christ. Clearly this states the goal toward which the primitive community faced: final reunion with the transfigured, glorified Christ. And it gives the meaning for personal salvation which was seen in the event (cf also 2 Th 2^{1}). When, on the other hand, 2 Th 2^{8f} speaks of the destruction of Satan by Christ, it is clear that the hope of the Parousia included the idea of the Judgment (see also Mt 25^{31ff}, Ro 2, 2 Co 5^{10}). This is vividly expressed in Mt 24^{40ff}, while in the Johannine admonition (1 Jn 2^{28}) it naturally remains more in the background: ' Abide in him [Christ], so that when he appears we may have confidence and not shrink from him in shame at his coming.' Closely connected with this is the frequent (*e.g.* 1 Th 3^{12}) reference to the Parousia in strong exhortations to Christian duty.

This is about the order in which the meaning of the Greek word *parousia* is unfolded in the NT. The primitive Christian hope of the coming End of the Age is most clearly attached to it, though not originally so connected. For this eschatological hope really had its roots in the OT and in contemporary Judaism, where the term *parousia* (with reference to the coming of God and—or—the revelation of the Messiah) is never used. Instead, the terminology is: ' the day of the Lord ' (1 Th 5^{2}), ' the day of Christ ' (Ph 1$^{6, 10}$ 2^{16}), ' that day ' (Mt 7^{22}). The Revelation of John pictures the approaching End without once using the term *parousia*; and it may be assumed that Jesus Himself never used it, though He referred to the future coming or appearance of ' the Son of Man ' (*e.g.* Mk 8^{38}). The passages referred to above (Mt 24$^{27, 37, 39}$ and parallels) can scarcely be attributed to Jesus, according to historical criticism. Since the development of Messianic expectation in the primitive community was independent of the use of the term *parousia*, the question of its origin therefore becomes inescapable.

4. Origin of the term.—For this we must turn to the world of Hellenistic culture. Here, in addition to the well-attested primary significance of the word, a special use had grown up which possessed a two-fold significance. (1) For Hellenism, *parousia* meant chiefly the epiphany of a god or goddess, either as a special miracle or in the setting of a cultic celebration—his or her glorious self-manifestation following a period of absence or invisibility. This use of the term is also found in the Jewish historian Josephus who describes the Divine manifestations of the OT with the word *parousia*. (2) The second important usage found in Hellenism belonged to the language of court etiquette or ceremonial. The official visit of an emperor or a king to a province was a *parousia*. It is hard to say which of these two meanings led the earliest Christians to apply the term to Christ's future ' coming,' especially since the sacral and the regal were not sharply distinguished. The example of Josephus shows how close at hand it lay for the earliest Christian community to use the term with reference to Christ's future ' appearing ' in power and glory. Clear also is the reason why at first the incarnation—or the appearance of Jesus in history—was not understood as a *parousia*: Jesus' power and glory were still hidden and their final disclosure before all the world was—according to early Christian belief—still to take place at the End of the Age. It was for this latter event that the technical Hellenistic term *parousia* seemed specially appropriate. In adopting this term, the primitive church declared its essentially eschatological outlook, its belief that the decisive event in the process of salvation, its final fulfilment, still lay in the future.

5. Later usage.—In the period following the NT, the meaning of *parousia* received a clear and characteristic revision. The hope that Christ would soon appear in power and glory had not been realized. This experience led to a new emphasis upon and interpretation of what had taken place already in the appearance of Jesus upon earth, His earthly life and ministry. As early as the Gospel of John, the life of Jesus is described as a revelation of His glory, as the epiphany of the Son of God (1^{14} cf 2^{11}). Hence it is not surprising that Ignatius of Antioch, who in other respects shares the point of view of the Fourth Evangelist, characterizes the Incarnation as the ' Parousia ' of Christ (*Philad.* 9^{2}). Clement of Alexandria (*c* 200 A.D.) uses the word in a similar way. Justin (*c* 150) combines the two lines of development, the eschatological and the historical, and distinguishes between the ' first ' and the ' second ' *parousia* of the Saviour (*Dial.* 14^{8} 40^{4} 118^{2}, *Apol.* 52^{3}). Irenaeus (*c* 180) also shares this view. But Justin also refers (*Dial.* 118^{2}) to the ' second ' *parousia* as the ' coming again.' This is the terminology which was destined to prevail in the end—a usage which must be clearly dissociated from that of the NT, with which it fails to correspond and for which the NT provides no basis. G. I.

PARSHANDATHA.—The eldest son of Haman, put to death by the Jews, Est 9^{7}.

PARSIN.—See MENE.

PARTHIANS.—The founders of a powerful dynasty in Persia which threw off the yoke of the Seleucids in 248 B.C. and maintained itself against all external powers till A.D. 226, defying even the Romans. At the beginning of the reign of Herod the Great (40 B.C.) the Parthians overran Syria and Asia Minor, including Palestine, spreading havoc and terror during their brief depredation. Originally the ' Parni,' nomads living N. of Hyrcania, to the E. of the Caspian Sea, and in Alexander's time found farther S., on the borders of the Salt Desert, they eventually spread out from the Euphrates to the Indus, thus occupying much of the eastern part of the Seleucid empire. Their religion was the current Iranian Mazdaism, but they were tolerant of other religions. They absorbed Greek culture readily, though their main interests were not intellectual or artistic; they formed a military aristocracy of land-owners, whose chief diversions were horsemanship and hunting. In battle their cavalry, both light and heavy, were irresistible. In A.D. 10 a new regime replaced the Arsacids, and the nation repudiated its former friendship with the West, re-emphasized the Mazdaean religion, and undertook to control to its own advantage the growing trade between Roman Syria and China. The Jews referred to in Ac 2⁹ presumably lived E. of the Euphrates.

J. F. McC.—**F. C. G.**

PARTIALITY.—See CRIMES, **5**, JUSTICE, **1** (*c*).

PARTRIDGE.—**1.** Only the Hebrew *ḳôrē'* is translated 'partridge' in the English Bible. This is the 'chukar' or 'rock-partridge' (*caccabis chukar*), whose call being given as 'girrah' or 'cok-cok-cokrr' explains its name, which has been assimilated to a well-known Semitic verb (Heb. *ḳāra'* 'called'). Its cry may be heard all over Palestine, and large coveys may be met in the autumn. This is the bird meant when the prophet describes it as gathering young which it has not brought forth (Jer 17¹¹); he alludes to a curious belief, which also the Arab writer al-Damîr mentions, that the hen visits a neighbour's nest and taking the eggs incubates them but that the chicks, so soon as they fly, return to their own mother. The story seems to have arisen from the fact that the chukar lays two clutches of eggs, one for herself and another for the cock. This bird is still used by Arabs, as by the ancient Hebrews, as a decoy-bird (Sir 11³⁰). The same Hebrew word is loosely used in comparison of Saul pursuing David to Engedi to hunting a partridge in the mountains (1 S 26²⁰); but the bird here meant is the **'sand-partridge'** or 'Hey's partridge' (*ammoperdix heyi*); for this, though not distinguished by a distinct name, is the only partridge found round the Dead Sea, where it is very numerous. **2.** The *ḳippōz*, whose name is derived from a verb meaning 'hopped, leapt' (Syr. *qᵉphaz*=Arab. *qafaza* 'leapt, sprang') cannot be the **'hedgehog'** or **'porcupine'** (LXX, Vulgate) which cannot leap, nor the **arrow-snake** which does not incubate although it frequents desert sites (Is 34¹⁵); it may therefore be a variety of the sand-partridge (*caccabis sinaica*), which lives in small parties in dry and unattractive places in the valley of the Jordan and round the Dead Sea, spending the day under the shadow of a boulder and, when disturbed, making away at great speed, hopping with great agility from rock to rock. **3.** The patriarch Jacob has an animal totem-name, as the Arabic *ya'qûbu* 'black partridge, francolin' shows; this, a bird widely spread in Palestine, is so called from the strong but blunt spurs on its heels (Heb. *'ēḳebh*= Aram. *'iqbâ*=Arab. *'aqibu* 'heel'). The meaning of the root has obviously inspired the stories woven round the name. **4.** Another word for the partridge is *ḥoghlāh* 'female partridge' as the Syriac *ḥaglâ*=Arabic *ḥajalu* 'partridge' from *ḥajala* 'hopped' shows; but the Hebrew word occurs only as the name of a woman and of a place on the borders of Benjamin and Judah (Jos 15⁶ 18¹⁹· ²¹). As only three species of partridge are found (nowadays, at any rate) in Palestine, the word may imply the settlement of a clan or tribe of Arab origin in southern Palestine, where other place-names (*e.g.* Eltekeh, Eltekon, Eshtaol, Eshtemoa) reflect Arabic-speaking settlements.

G. R. D.

PARUAH.—Father or clan of Jehoshaphat, Solomon's prefect in Issachar, 1 K 4¹⁷.

PARVAIM.—A region whence, according to 2 Ch 3⁶, the gold was obtained which was used for ornamenting the Temple of Solomon. It cannot be certainly identified. The name is most plausibly identified with *Farwa* in Yemen, or SW. Arabia. It was possibly from this place that the 'gold of Sheba' (Ps 72¹⁵; cf Is 60⁶) was in part derived.

PASACH.—An Asherite, 1 Ch 7³³.

PASCHAL LAMB.—See PASSOVER.

PAS-DAMMIM.—See EPHES-DAMMIM.

PASEAH.—**1.** A descendant of Judah, 1 Ch 4¹². **2.** The father of Joiada, Neh 3⁶. **3.** The eponym of a family of Nethinim (q.v.) who returned with Zerubbabel, Ezr 2⁴⁹ Neh 7⁵¹ (AV **Phaseah**), 1 Est 5³¹ (AV **Phinees**, RV **Phinoe**).

PASHHUR (AV **Pashur**).—**1.** A son of Malchiah, a prince of Judaea in the time of Jeremiah (Jer 38¹⁻¹³). He is probably identical with the Pashhur mentioned in 1 Ch 9¹², Neh 11¹² as the ancestor of Adaiah. **2.** The son of Immer, a Temple official and priest, who caused Jeremiah to be beaten and put in the stocks after he had predicted the fall of Jerusalem. The prophet told him his name was not Pashhur but **Magor-missabib** (q.v.), and added that he would die in Babylon, Jer 20¹⁻⁶. **3.** The father of Gedaliah mentioned in Jer 38¹. He may be either **1** or **2**, or neither. **4.** The head of a priestly family, 'the sons of Pashhur' mentioned in Ezr 2³⁸, Neh 7¹¹, Ezr 10²², 1 Es 5²⁵ (AV **Phassaron**, RV **Phassurus**), 9²² (AV, RV **Phaisur**). **5.** A priest who signed the covenant with Nehemiah, probably identical with **4**, or used of the clan as a whole (Neh 10³).

W. F. B.

PASHUR.—See PASHHUR.

PASSENGERS, Ezk 39¹¹ (AV).—See ABARIM.

PASSION.—In Ac 14¹⁵ 'We also are men, of like nature (AV 'passions') with you,' 'passion' means 'feeling *or* emotion.' But in Ac 1³ 'He presented himself alive after his passion,' the word means 'suffering,' as in Wycliffe's translation of He 2⁹ 'Ihesus for the passioun of deeth, crowned with glorie and honour.'

PASSOVER AND FEAST OF UNLEAVENED BREAD.—These two feasts were originally two separate ceremonies whose time of celebration came to coincide and they were welded, together with the ceremony of the waving of the barley sheaf, into a single composite festival.

1. OT references.—(1) *Law and Ezekiel.*—The first certain reference to the feast is in Ex 12²¹⁻²⁷ (J). These verses have become an integral part of the whole chapter, which may be regarded as the legend of the Passover festival. They are, however, probably the earliest part of the account and record two features: (*a*) a lamb is to be slain and its blood sprinkled on the lintel and door posts of the houses; (*b*) it is to celebrate the deliverance of the Israelites when the firstborn of the Egyptians were slain. There are two brief references in Ex 23¹⁸ and 34²⁵ which prohibit using leavened bread with the Passover, or leaving anything over till the morning. The festival takes place during the night.

In Dt 16¹⁻⁸ the Passover is directed to be observed in the month Abib (April), in commemoration of the Exodus from Egypt. The sacrifice is not to be offered in private dwellings, but 'in the place which Yahweh shall choose to place his name there.' With the Passover meal, and during seven days, no leavened bread was to be eaten. None of the flesh was to be left till morning. After the meal the worshippers were to go to their homes; the seventh day was to be a solemn assembly, and this period (v.⁹) was treated as opening the seven weeks' 'joy of harvest,' commencing from Abib, when the corn would be coming into ear. We may notice here: (*a*) the Passover is regarded as part of the Feast of Unleavened Bread (**Mazzoth**), the two being apparently blended into one; (*b*) the sacrifice, though composed of individual sacrifices, is to be offered only at the central sanctuary; (*c*) the offering may be taken from flock or herd.

In Ezk 45²¹⁻²⁴ the date is precisely assigned as 14th Abib. The feast lasts seven days, and unleavened bread only is to be eaten. The prince is to offer a bullock as a sin-offering for himself and the people, and a he-goat on each of the seven days, as well as seven bullocks and seven rams daily, with other offerings of meal and oil. All takes place at the central sanctuary; there is no mention of a lamb, and the Passover is part of the Unleavened Bread festival.

Lv 23⁵⁻¹⁴ ordains the Passover for the evening of

14th Abib. The Feast of Unleavened Bread is treated separately; it lasts seven days, a holy convocation is to be held on the first and seventh days; and 'on the morrow after the sabbath' a sheaf of new corn is to be waved before the Lord, a he-lamb is to be offered as a burnt-offering with other offerings; and till this is done, no bread or parched corn or green ears may be eaten. This is a harvest rite. It is not clear what is meant by the 'morrow after the sabbath'; later tradition associated it with the sabbath of Passover and Unleavened Bread.

According to Ex 12^{1-13}, the current month of the Exodus is to be regarded as the first month of the year. On the tenth day a lamb or a kid is to be taken for each family or combination of families, according to their size. It is to be slain at even on the fourteenth, and the door posts and lintel are to be stained with its blood. It is to be roasted intact, and eaten with unleavened bread and **bitter herbs.** Nothing of it is to remain till morning. It is to be eaten in haste, the partakers prepared as for a journey; it is a sign of the Lord's 'pass-over.' This account is clearly meant to draw out the commemorative element in the celebration and is probably to be ascribed to the priestly editing of the tradition.

Ex 12^{43-49} forbids any foreigner or hired servant or sojourner to eat the Passover unless he first submits to circumcision.

Nu 9^{1-14} records that some men were unable to keep the Passover on the first anniversary of the Exodus because of ritual uncleanness. Arising from this it was laid down that in such cases the men should keep the Passover on the fourteenth day of the next (the second) month.

In Nu 28^{16-25} the Passover is distinguished from the Feast of Unleavened Bread. The first and seventh days of the latter are to be days of holy convocation. On each of the seven days two bullocks, a ram, and seven lambs (with special offerings of meal and oil) are to be sacrificed, and a goat for a sin-offering.

(2) *Historical and Prophetical books.*—No certain reference is found previous to the date of the discovery of Deuteronomy. In the prophets there are a few references to festivals (Hos 2^{11} 9^{5} 12^{9}, Am 5^{21} 8^{10}) but nothing specific about Passover or Unleavened Bread. The observance in 2 K 23^{21-23} is stated to have conformed to the regulations of 'this book of the covenant' (doubtless Dt 16^{1-8} is meant) and to have been novel in character. 2 Ch 30 records a celebration in the reign of Hezekiah. It was a month late owing to ritual hindrances. 2 Ch 35^{1-19} records the celebration in Josiah's day. Both these accounts reflect usages of the Chronicler's own time. In Ezr 6^{19-22} the priests and Levites play the prominent part in the sacrifice, and the Feast of Unleavened Bread is distinguished from the Passover.

Many of the Passover rites are undoubtedly very ancient; but Deuteronomy tends to emphasize the historical connexion of the festival with the Exodus. The various regulations and allusions in the OT are not consistent with each other, and different ideas were probably associated with the feast at different periods of the national history. Thus Ezekiel lays most stress on its aim as a collective expiatory sacrifice. It is likely that the feast was observed during the Exile, and that its commemorative significance was then made more emphatic. This would explain the underlying conception of the account in the Priestly Code. But the Chronicler shows preference for the Deuteronomic version, perhaps owing to the growing centralization of worship at one sanctuary in his time.

2. Origin and primitive significance.—If we set aside the waving of the barley sheaf, which is mentioned in only one record in the OT (Lev 23^{10-12}), there are two basic rites in this combined festival. They represent two separate ceremonies, each with its distinctive purpose. The one is the sacrifice and eating of the lamb; an integral part of this is the smearing of the blood on the door posts and lintels. The other is the eating of unleavened bread for seven days. The first is a pastoral practice: it was timed to take place on the night of the full moon nearest to the spring equinox. In the original, and probably pre-Yahwistic, ceremony the lamb was sacrificed to ensure that the god of flocks (or of fertility in general) would receive his share and would be prevailed upon to guarantee the continued fertility of the flock. The lamb was eaten as an act of communion between the worshippers and their god. The smearing of the blood was an apotropaic act to protect the shepherds, their homes, and their flocks, from every kind of unseen evil.

The second is an agricultural practice: it reflects the belief that when the new crop began to be used there must be no risk of contamination from the old leaven, especially where it was the practice to mix a lump of old dough with each fresh mixture. To ensure this there was a complete break in the use of leaven for seven days. It so happened that the rites came to be observed at the same time of the year, and the Hebrews, with their genius for taking up the old in the service of Yahweh and weaving it into their worship of Him, combined the two rites into a single festival and transformed these ancient practices into solemn ceremonies commemorating Yahweh's sparing of the Israelites in Egypt when the Egyptian firstborn were killed and His rescuing them from bondage in Egypt at the Exodus.

The association of the festivals with the Exodus is seen to be very natural when we remember that the Israelites asked leave of Pharaoh to sacrifice to their God (Ex 3^{18} 7^{16}). This may well have been a request to celebrate the ancient festival which was subsequently reshaped into Passover. It is conceivable that at one time the slaughtered lamb was the first lamb of the season and if this were so it would be easy to think of it both as a thank-offering for the sparing of the Israelite firstborn and also as a substitutionary sacrifice for them. Unleavened bread was associated with the Exodus events through the story of the taking of unleavened bread by the people in their haste to leave Egypt (Ex $12^{34, 39}$).

3. Post-exilic observances.—The Samaritans continued to observe the detailed ordinances of Ex 12. But the Jews learned in time to disregard some of the details, as applicable only to the first or Egyptian Passover. Such details were the choice of the lamb on the tenth day, its slaughter at home, the sprinkling of the blood on the house-door, the admission of the unclean, the posture and attire of the partakers, etc. Various alterations and elaborations were introduced. The month Adar was devoted to a thorough purification of lands and houses, sepulchres being whitened, roads and bridges repaired. On the evening of 13th Abib all leaven was sought out. On the 14th the Passover was offered by indiscriminate companies of ten to twenty people. It was slain in relays at the Temple, and the blood thrown before the altar by the priests. The lambs were then dressed, and the fat offered, while the Levites chanted the Hallel (Pss 113–118). The lambs were taken home and roasted; each of the guests brought four **cups of red wine,** and the meal was eaten with **bitter herbs** and **unleavened cakes.** The posture at the meal was recumbent (as a token, according to the Pharisees, of the rest which God had given to His people). A blessing was said over the first cup (perhaps implied in Lk 22^{17ff}). Then followed the washing of hands and offering of prayer. At the second cup came the son's question as to the significance of the feast, and the father's explanation. This was succeeded by the singing of Pss 113 and 114. Grace was said over the third cup, and with the fourth came the singing of Pss 115–118. Large numbers assembled at Jerusalem for the feast, and such occasions were always carefully supervised by the Romans for fear of insurrection. Hence perhaps would come the custom of releasing a selected prisoner; but we have no hint of the origin of the custom.

A. W. F. B.—L. H. B.

PATARA.—A great seaport on the coast of Lycia, a few miles (60 stadia) SE. of the mouth of the Xanthus. The valley of this river is the best part of Lycia, and doubtless from early times Patara had a local trade, but its importance depended on its convenient position for the trade between the West and the Levant. The prevailing winds in this part of the Mediterranean are from the west (especially in the autumn), and ships sailing from the Aegean or from Italy to Phoenicia or Egypt would often risk the voyage straight across the sea from Patara. Thus we find St. Paul on his last journey to Jerusalem (Ac 21^{2}), after coasting in a slow vessel along the Aegean, taking a vessel that was sailing straight from Patara to Tyre. Cf MYRA.

Lycia was never definitely colonized by Greeks, and the Lycians spoke a non-Aryan language, which they abandoned for Greek in the 3rd cent. B.C. when they were ruled by the Ptolemies. Patara had an early culture—its coins date from 400 B.C.—and the chief Lycian god was identified with Apollo, whose celebrated oracle at Patara gave him the title Patareus (Hor. *Od.* III. iv. 64). A. E. H.—**F. C. G.**

PATHEUS, 1 Es 9^{23} (AV, RV).—See PETHAHIAH, **2.**

PATHROS (Is 11^{11}, Jer $44^{1, 15}$, Ezk 29^{14} 30^{14}).—The name of Upper Egypt, in Egyptian *p3-t3-rś*, 'the south-land,' comprising both the Thebaid and Middle Egypt from somewhat S. of Memphis to Syene at the First Cataract. '**Miṣraim**' was generally limited to Lower Egypt, *i.e.* the Delta and some distance up the valley to include the nome of Memphis. This division of Egypt was very ancient, corresponding, at least roughly, to the two kingdoms before Menes. While Lower Egypt was familiar to both Greeks and Hebrews, Upper Egypt was comparatively unknown, as witness Herodotus' woeful ignorance of Egypt above the Fayyum, and Nahum's description of No-Amon (see NO). Yet there is abundant evidence in the Aramaic papyri from Elephantine of an important settlement of Jews at the southernmost extremity at Syene before 525 B.C. (cf SYENE, ELEPHANTINE PAPYRI); and the passages in which Pathros is mentioned refer to Jews in the Upper Country more than half a century before that, after the destruction of Jerusalem. So also Greek and Phoenician mercenaries had reached Syene, and even *Abū Simbel*, far south in Nubia, in the 6th or 7th cent. B.C.: soldiers and traders of many nations must have passed frequently up and down the Nile in those days, yet without giving to their fellow-countrymen at home any clear idea of the Upper Country. In Gn 10^{14} the **Pathrusim** are the people of Pathros. They are represented as begotten of Egypt (*Miṣraim*). F. Ll. G.

PATHRUSIM.—See PATHROS.

PATIENCE.—See LONGSUFFERING.

PATMOS.—An island W. of Caria, now called *Patino*, with an area of 16 square miles and a population of about 4000. In the Middle Ages its palms gained for it the title of Palmosa, but it is no longer fertile. Its Cyclopean remains show that it was very early inhabited. It is the traditional place to which **St. John** (q.v.) was banished by Domitian, and in which he wrote the Apocalypse (Rev 1^{9}). The 'Cave of the Apocalypse' is still shown in which the Apostle is said to have seen the visions. The chief remaining interest of the island is the monastery of St. John, founded in the 11th cent. It once contained a valuable library, from which was purchased in 1814 the 9th cent. codex of Plato now in the Bodleian. It also contained a number of Biblical MSS. A. E. H.—**F. C. G.**

PATRIARCH.—This term is usually applied to (1) the antediluvian fathers of the human race; (2) the three great progenitors of Israel—Abraham, Isaac, Jacob (see separate articles); (3) in the NT it is extended to the sons of Jacob (Ac 7^{8f}), and to David (Ac 2^{29}).

PATRIMONY.—The meaning of the expression which stands in Dt 18^{8} is very uncertain (see S. R. Driver, *Deut.* [*ICC*], p. 218). All that can be said is that it denotes some private source of income.

PATROBAS.—The name of a member of the Roman Church greeted by St. Paul in Ro 16^{14}.

PATROCLUS.—The father of Nicanor (2 Mac 8^{9}).

PATTERN.—This word is used to render several Hebrew and Greek terms in OT and NT, some of which denote a *model*, as in Ex $25^{9, 40}$ of the building model of the Tabernacle shown to Moses on the mount (cf Nu 8^{4}—a different original—and ARTS AND CRAFTS, **3**), others a *copy* of the original model as He 8^{5} RV (AV, RSV 'pattern'). See, for a full examination of the different passages, Hastings' *DB*, *s.v.* A. R. S. K.

PAU.—See PAI.

PAUL THE APOSTLE.—1. The Authorities.—The primary source for a reconstruction of the life of Paul is the corpus of epistles bearing his name, nine of which (Romans, 1 and 2 Corinthians, Galatians, Philippians, Colossians, 1 and 2 Thessalonians, Philemon) are now almost universally recognized as genuine. The authenticity of Ephesians is still a matter of dispute, but this letter contains little historical information and few of its theological ideas are without parallel in the other nine. The Pastoral Epistles, written by a disciple of Paul, may incorporate genuine fragments of Pauline correspondence, but provide no clear indication of the period of the apostle's life to which these fragments belong. The valuable evidence of the epistles, however, yields by itself no connected narrative, and for this we have to rely on the secondary source, the Acts of the Apostles. The collation of evidence from these two sources produces a number of acute problems, to which there is at present no agreed solution, and leaves some considerable gaps which we have no means of filling. Where there is a conflict, the primary source is to be preferred; but these conflicts are neither so frequent nor so serious as to impugn the general veracity of Acts. It must be assumed, however, that the speeches in Acts are Thucydidean, *i.e.* that they are free compositions by the author, based perhaps on tradition or reminiscence, in which he puts into the mouths of others words which he himself considers suitable to the speaker and to the occasion.

2. Early Life and Training.—The placard which was nailed to the Cross, written in Hebrew and Greek and Latin, is a constant reminder of the three streams of history and culture at whose meeting-place Christianity had its origin; and of all the early Christians Paul most clearly belonged to each of the three streams.

He was a Jew. His parents, with the Jewish enthusiasm for genealogies, could trace their descent back to the tribe of Benjamin, and had named their son Saul after the most famous member of that tribe (Ph 3^{5}). Although they lived outside of Palestine they had adopted the voluntary but rigorous discipline of the Pharisees, and brought their son up to live by the same rule (Ph 3^{5}, Ac 23^{6} 26^{5}). So successful were they in imparting to him their own devotion to the Law, that he went to Jerusalem to study under Gamaliel, one of the greatest of the 1st-cent. Rabbis (Ac 22^{3}), and there he managed to outstrip his contemporaries in zeal for the traditions of the past (Gal 1^{14}). He had a fierce pride of race which in later life was to survive the repeated onslaughts of his Jewish adversaries (Ro 9^{1-5}, 2 Co 11^{22}, Ph 3^{5}). His native language was Greek and he habitually read the Scriptures in the LXX version but he could also speak fluent Aramaic (Ac 22^{2}). Throughout his epistles his Jewish antecedents make themselves apparent in his constant appeal to the OT, in his Rabbinic exegesis (*e.g.* Gal 4^{21-31}), in his use of midrashic legends (1 Co 10^{4}, Gal 4^{29}), in his apocalyptic expectations, and in the unquestioned assumptions of his theology.

He was a Greek. Tarsus in Cilicia, his native city (Ac 21^{39}), was a perfect example of the cosmopolitan Hellenism in which the classical culture of Greece had become blended with the unbridled vigour of the ancient Orient. It was a centre of commerce, situated on the great trade route which ran from the East through the Cilician Gates to the Aegean. It was a university city and the birthplace of some of the leading Stoic philosophers. Probably Paul never received a formal, Greek education—his upbringing was too strictly Jewish for that—but he certainly underwent the liberal education of life in a Greek city. As an Israelite he automatically divided mankind into Jews and Gentiles, but as a citizen of Tarsus he was equally accustomed to dividing them into Greeks and barbarians (Ro 1[14], Col 3[11]). Like Socrates, he belonged in the city and was a stranger to the countryside, so that most of his metaphors are drawn from city life—the stadium (1 Co 9[24], Ph 3[14]), the theatre (Ro 1[32], 1 Co 4[9]), the law-courts (Gal 4[1-2]), the processions (2 Co 2[14], Col 2[15]), the market (2 Co 1[22] 5[5]). Without betraying any profound influence of philosophy on his thinking, he nevertheless shows acquaintance with the terminology of Stoic popular teaching—' nature ' (Ro 1[26] 2[14, 27] 11[24], 1 Co 11[14], Gal 2[15] 4[8]), ' conscience ' (Ro 2[15] 9[1] 13[5], 1 Co 8[7, 10, 12] 10[25, 27ff], 2 Co 1[12] 4[2]), ' sufficiency ' (2 Co 9[8], Ph 4[11]). He had some superficial familiarity with the language of the mystery cults (Ph 4[12]). In Tarsus, too, he must first have become aware of the darker side of city life, the moral corruption which, when he met it elsewhere, seemed to him to be the working out of God's wrath against idolatrous religion (Ro 1[18-32]).

He was a Roman. He had inherited the coveted Roman citizenship from his father, who presumably had been awarded it for outstanding public service (Ac 16[37] 22[25, 28]). As a Roman he must have had the threefold Roman name. His *praenomen* and *nomen* are unknown to us, but his *cognomen* was Paulus, the name by which he is most commonly called. His Roman citizenship was one of his most prized possessions, and he seems to have found it easy to be on good terms with Roman officials. He understood what Rome was trying to do for the world in providing a world-wide commonwealth of law, order, and peace, and not only approved of it as a task ordained by God (Ro 13[1-7]), but found in it the model for the Divine commonwealth to which his own aspirations reached forward (Ph 3[20]). During his missionary work he concentrated on the great centres of Roman influence and was not content until he reached Rome itself (Ro 1[13] 15[22-29]). All this powerfully suggests that he worked with a missionary strategy which aimed at nothing less than the winning of the Roman world for Christ (' Their voice has gone out to all the earth, and their words to the ends of the world,' Ro 10[18]). The vision of a united Empire under the sole dominion of Caesar had conjured up in his mind the corresponding vision of a single empire of the spirit in which Christ should reign until all his enemies submitted to his authority (1 Co 15[25]).

It has sometimes been supposed that Paul had an unhappy adolescence. This supposition has its basis in Ro 7, interpreted as an autobiographical account of an actual event in Paul's childhood, when his first awareness of the Law's demands brought to a close the age of innocence and condemned him to a perpetual and fruitless struggle with an uneasy conscience. Elsewhere, however, Paul gives us the impression that his pre-Christian life had been entirely free from guilty qualms and inner tension : ' I advanced in Judaism beyond many of my own age among my people, so extremely zealous was I for the traditions of my fathers ' (Gal 1[14]) ; ' . . . as to righteousness under the law blameless ' (Ph 3[6]). It is likely, therefore, that Ro 7 represents not what Paul actually experienced in his youth but his pre-Christian life seen through Christian eyes, a Christian evaluation of the unregenerate life, described in terms reminiscent of the fall of Adam. In this case we have no reason to suppose that Paul the Jew had any other than the normal Jewish experience of rejoicing in the Law of the Lord and of self-congratulation at his place in the Divine favour (Ro 2[17-20]). It was not dissatisfaction with the Law that prepared the way for the experience of Christ ; rather, it was Christ who for the first time revealed to him the inadequacy of the Law.

3. Conversion.—Even as a Pharisee Paul must have had some acquaintance with the Christian church and its teaching. It is, indeed, unlikely that he ever saw Jesus during His earthly ministry—his remark about having known Christ after the flesh is correctly interpreted by the RSV to mean that his former estimate of Christ had been based on worldly standards (2 Co 5[16]). But he became a violent persecutor of the church, and no man persecutes anything unless he knows enough about it to fan the flames of his hatred (Gal 1[13], Ph 3[6] Ac 8[3]). He must have had opportunity to hear Christians on trial examined concerning the nature of their beliefs. Above all we know that he listened to Stephen and approved of his death. At this time his attitude to Christianity was plain and uncompromising. He believed that Jesus had been condemned—and justly—as a blasphemer and a breaker of the Law. Convinced of the reality of God's justice, he saw in the Cross the seal of Divine disapproval on an ungodly life, the proof of the curse of God which rests on the condemned criminal (Dt 21[23], Gal 3[13]). As long as the Jerusalem church was content to remain loyally within the framework of Judaism, observing the Law and attending Temple and synagogue, Paul could afford to acquiesce in Gamaliel's policy of leaving the new movement to the judgment of history (Ac 5[38-39]). But when Stephen began to develop those aspects of the teaching of Jesus which had earned him the enmity of the Pharisees, Paul determined that the Christian Way was a menace to all that he counted most dear.

No doubt Paul's conversion was prepared by his contact with Christians, by the logic of their Scriptural arguments, by the dynamic quality of their lives, by their confidence and fortitude under persecution. Luke clearly indicates his own opinion that the martyrdom of Stephen led straight to the conversion of Paul (Ac 8[1-3] 9[1-9] ; cf Bengel : ' Si Stephanus non orasset, Ecclesia Paulum non habuisset '). But according to Paul himself, as well as the three accounts in Acts (9[1-9] 22[3-16] 26[4-18]), the episode on the road to Damascus was a great act of God which by itself sufficiently explained the change it produced in his life. God the Creator who had said, ' Let there be light,' had performed a new act of creation (2 Co 4[6] 5[17]). He ' was pleased to reveal his Son in me ' (Gal 1[16]). Christ had arrested him and made him His own (Ph 3[12]). Christ had appeared to him, not in a vision which could be classed with Paul's later visions and ecstasies (2 Co 12[1-4], Ac 16[9]), but in an event which was comparable to the resurrection appearances to Peter, James, and the other apostles (1 Co 15[3-8]).

This event produced in Paul three convictions which were to dominate his thoughts and actions from that time forward. He was convinced that Christ was alive and that he must therefore revise his whole estimate of Christ's life and teaching and especially of his death : and out of this profound disturbance of his religious assumptions came his gospel of Christ crucified (Gal 1[11-12]). He was convinced that God had called him to be an apostle and throughout his life he constantly reiterated that his apostleship was neither of human origin nor received through human mediation (Gal 1[1], Ro 1[1, 5], 1 Co 1[1] 9[1] 15[10]). He was convinced that the purpose of his call was to bring in the Gentiles into the new people of God (Ro 11[13] 15[16], Gal 1[16] 2[7], Eph 3[8]). In the three accounts of Paul's conversion in Acts, three different versions of this commission are given : in Ac 9 the call to preach to the Gentiles is given through Ananias at Damascus ; in Ac 22 it comes in a subsequent vision in the Temple at Jerusalem ; in Ac 26 it is spoken by the Lord Himself as Paul lay by the roadside, blinded by the light from heaven. But these variations do not really conflict with Paul's settled habit of associating his call as apostle to the Gentiles with his conversion.

4. From Damascus to Antioch.—The immediate sequel to Paul's conversion involves one of the problems already mentioned. Paul tells us that the three years prior to his first Jerusalem visit were spent partly in Arabia (Nabataea ?) and partly in Damascus (Gal 1[17-18]). In Acts we are told that a prolonged stay in Damascus was brought to an end by a Jewish plot, from which Paul escaped by being lowered over the wall in a basket (9[23-25]). In another letter Paul mentions this incident without associating it with any definite period of his career, but seems to imply that it happened at a time when Damascus was under the rule of the Nabataean king Aretas (2 Co 11^{32}). Damascene coinage proves that in A.D. 33–34 the city was under the direct rule of Rome, and in view of Aretas' feud with Tiberius many scholars have felt it to be unlikely that it should have been transferred to him before the accession of Caligula in A.D. 37; but to place Paul's first visit to Jerusalem as late as this involves serious difficulties for the chronology of his subsequent career, and is unjustifiable on such problematic evidence.

After a brief visit to Jerusalem (Gal 1^{18-19}, Ac 9^{26-30}) he returned to his native province, and there for a time we lose sight of him. But in view of his forceful character, his apostolic commission, and his explicit statement in Gal 1^{21-23}, we can assume that these years were packed full of missionary activity in Syria and Cilicia. Almost certainly we must allocate to this period many of the hardships and trials enumerated in 2 Co 11^{23-27}, which must have occurred before the writing of the epistle in A.D. 56, but which cannot reasonably be fitted into the detailed account of the missionary journeys in Acts. The visionary experience of 2 Co 12^{1-4} also belongs to this period. These 'hidden years' came to an end when Barnabas arrived in Tarsus to invite Paul to return with him to Antioch to help lead the Gentile mission which had spontaneously opened up in that city (Ac 11^{25-26}).

5. The Second Visit to Jerusalem [A.D. 46?].—At this point we are confronted with the most puzzling of all Pauline conundrums, the question of his visits to Jerusalem. Acts recounts five visits in all (9^{26} 11^{30} 15^{2} 18^{22} 21^{15}), while Paul, writing to the Galatians an exhaustive list of his contacts with other apostles, mentions only two (Gal 1^{18} 2^{1}). In spite of minor differences we have already equated the first visit in Galatians with the first visit in Acts, but the second visit in Galatians has been variously identified with the second, third or fourth visit in Acts. On the whole it may be said that the equation of Gal 2^{1} with Ac 11^{30} is the simplest solution which leaves fewest loose ends and results in the most satisfactory and convincing reconstruction of events; and this is the solution here adopted.

According to this theory, then, the admission of Gentiles to full membership of the Christian fellowship at Antioch raised in the minds of some of their Jewish-Christian brethren a question about the conditions of church membership, a group of them holding the opinion that before a Gentile could become a Christian he must first become a Jew by the rite of circumcision. Paul and Barnabas, having been commissioned by the church in Antioch to carry a famine relief fund to Jerusalem (Ac 11^{30}), took the opportunity to hold a private conference with Peter, James and John, where Paul expounded his gospel of justification by faith in Christ crucified, which left no room for the Law as a way of salvation; and the Jerusalem apostles agreed that this was substantially the same gospel as their own and that Gentile converts should not be required to submit to the regulations of the Jewish Law (Gal 2^{1-10}).

This private agreement between the apostles did not, however, solve the problem of social contact between Jewish and Gentile Christians, since a Jew could not eat with a Gentile without incurring ceremonial defilement, unless the Gentile had himself avoided defilement by observing certain provisions of the Law. The church in Antioch solved the problem by ignoring it, and Jew and Gentile joined in the fellowship meals and communion services of the one church, a practice which had the support of Barnabas and Peter as well as Paul. But when news of this reached Jerusalem, it proved an embarrassment to the church there, which was desperately trying by meticulous observance of the Law to keep open the possibility of missionary work among the Jews. Some members of the Jerusalem church came to Antioch to suggest that the embarrassment could be avoided if Jewish and Gentile Christians would hold separate meals and separate celebrations of the Lord's Supper. Peter and Barnabas agreed, but Paul resisted the proposal on the ground that it was tantamount to forcing the Gentiles to accept Jewish practices, since even this would be preferable to a breach in the fellowship of the one body of Christ (Gal 2^{11-14}). This controversy necessitated a further conference to decide the terms on which Jewish and Gentile Christians could enter into table-fellowship without involving the Jewish Christians in a violation of their national tradition; and such a conference is described in Ac 15.

6. The First Missionary Journey, Ac 13–14 [A.D. 47–48].—In the meantime the church of Antioch, under prophetic guidance (Ac 13^{1-3}; cf 1 P 1^{12}, Eph 3^{5-6}), decided to embark on a new programme of missionary expansion throughout the Gentile world, and commissioned Paul and Barnabas as their first missionaries. Taking with them Barnabas's cousin, John Mark (Col 4^{10}), they set out for Barnabas's native Cyprus (Ac 4^{36}) and traversed it from Salamis to Paphos, where they had an interview with the governor, Sergius Paulus (Ac 13^{4-13}). Crossing to the mainland of Pamphylia, they landed at Perga. Here Mark left them to return home, perhaps because he had agreed to go only to Cyprus and had not bargained for any further extension of the tour; whatever his reasons may have been, Paul regarded his departure as a desertion (Ac 15^{38}).

We do not know what Paul's intentions were at this point, though in view of his subsequent career it is reasonable to suppose that he was heading for the cities of the Aegean seaboard. Assuming the S. Galatian theory to be sound, however, we can say that at Perga he suffered an illness which compelled him to change his plans and to go for the sake of his health into the highlands of Pisidia (Gal 4^{13}). This was probably a bout of a recurring illness which he refers to elsewhere as his 'thorn in the flesh' (2 Co 12^{7}). The once common suggestion that it was epilepsy has nothing to commend it; Ramsay's suggestion of malaria is much more plausible.

The revised plan brought the apostles first to the Roman colony of Antioch, where Paul formulated what was to be his regular missionary practice, preaching first in the synagogue, until this was made impossible by Jewish hostility, and then concentrating on a mission to the Gentiles (Ac 13^{46} 17^{2} 18^{6} 19^{8-10}, Ro 1^{16}). Persecution drove them on to Iconium, where they were able to preach for a long time before a threat of violence caused them to continue their journey. At Lystra they were first mistaken for local deities, but subsequently Paul was stoned and left for dead. Only at Derbe were they allowed to work unmolested. But the threats must have been short-lived, for they were able to return on their tracks and visit again all the churches they had founded, before returning to their base at Antioch.

This tour was followed by a third visit to Jerusalem for the Apostolic Council (Ac 15), which, unlike the private discussion described in Gal 2^{1-10}, was a public meeting of the whole Jerusalem church. According to Acts, this meeting began by opening again the debate about circumcision which the apostles had already settled among themselves, but ended with the issuing of a statement concerning the terms of table-fellowship between Jewish and Gentile Christians. The Gentiles were asked to meet their Jewish brethren halfway by observing certain of the Jewish rules of ceremonial purity.

7. The Second Missionary Journey, Ac 15^{36}–18^{22} [A.D. 49–52].—When a new missionary tour was projected, a sharp quarrel arose, because Barnabas wished to take Mark with them and Paul refused to do so on account of his earlier defection. Accordingly, Barnabas and Mark set out for Cyprus and Paul chose as his new companion Silas, a Jerusalem Christian who had had a share in drawing up the official statement of the Apostolic Council (Ac 15^{28}). Apart from his other accomplishments Silas had one very useful qualification that, like Paul himself, he was a Roman citizen (Ac 16^{37}). Paul was accustomed to refer to him by his Roman name Silvanus (1 Th 1^{1}, 2 Th 1^{1}).

The missionaries first visited the churches of Syria and

PAUL THE APOSTLE

Cilicia and then crossed the Taurus by the Cilician Gates to Derbe and Lystra, where they were joined by Timothy, a young Christian of mixed Jewish and Greek parentage. Paul now intended (for the second time?) to carry his missionary activity into the rich province of Asia, but was 'forbidden by the Holy Spirit' (Ac 16^{6}), speaking perhaps by the mouth of the prophetic Silas. They therefore turned N. through that part of the old kingdom of Phrygia which now belonged to the Roman province of Galatia, making for the large Roman cities on the Black Sea coast. (On the N. Galatian theory they made a lengthy detour through the territory which was ethnically Galatian, inhabited by tribes which had broken away from the main Celtic migration into Europe, and there founded the churches to which the Epistle to the Galatians was later written. This theory grew up in the early patristic period when the boundaries of the province of Galatia had been altered to exclude the southern territory in which Antioch, Iconium, Lystra and Derbe were situated, so that it did not occur to the fathers that the Epistle to the Galatians could have been written to the churches in these towns.) At the borders of Bithynia the Spirit again intervened to bar their further advance, and they turned westward to Troas, where Paul had his vision of a man of Macedonia asking him to come and help them. At this point the narrative of Acts changes from the third to the first person, which is usually taken to mean that the author here joined the party (16^{10}).

The Macedonian mission began at the Roman colony of Philippi, where a church was founded which of all Paul's churches was to give him most satisfaction and least anxiety. It was also the only church that attempted to share in his missionary work by making contributions to his travelling expenses (Ph 4^{15-16}). The work here, however, was interrupted by the cure of a clairvoyant slave-girl whose masters brought against Paul and Silas a charge of non-Roman activities, though the real reason for their enmity was financial. The missionaries made their escape by appealing to their Roman citizenship and moved on to Thessalonica. Here they were able to preach for three weeks in the synagogue before the Jews incited the city mob to an anti-Christian riot and lodged a charge of treason against Paul, Silas and their host, Jason. At Beroea there seemed to be a better chance of success (Luke rather naïvely remarks that there was a better class of Jews there), had not the Jews of Thessalonica pursued them there with accusations.

Paul now proceeded alone to Athens where he preached before the Council of the Areopagus and won a mere handful of converts, including one member of the Council. It has been thought that Paul's failure to found a church at Athens was due to an attempt on his part to resort to philosophic arguments to convince the educated Athenians, and that at Corinth he forswore this mistaken strategy and 'decided to know nothing among you except Jesus Christ and him crucified' (1 Co 2^{2}). But this theory depends on the very doubtful assumption that the speech assigned to him in Acts is an accurate report of what he said and not a free composition of the author, after the manner of the Greek historians. A much more likely explanation is that Paul was sick with anxiety about the church of Thessalonica which he had been forced to abandon to the threat of imminent persecution (cf his anxiety about the church of Corinth which prevented him from grasping an opportunity for effective work at Troas, 2 Co 2^{12-13}), and that he also had an attack of his recurrent illness. He tells us (1 Th 2^{18}) that at Athens he repeatedly formed the intention of returning to Thessalonica but was hindered by Satan (cf 2 Co 12^{7}, 'a thorn was given to me in the flesh, a messenger of Satan'). He had been joined at this time by Timothy, but so great was his distress of mind that he was 'willing to be left behind at Athens alone'—a small concession if he had been fit, but a very large one for a sick man—and sent Timothy back to Thessalonica to discover what the situation there actually was.

As soon as he was able Paul went on to Corinth 'in weakness and in much fear and trembling' (1 Co 2^{3}). Here he found lodgings with a Jewish couple, Aquila and Priscilla, who, like himself, were tent-makers, and who were to be among his most intimate friends. Under an edict of Claudius in A.D. 49 they had been compelled, along with other Jews, to leave Rome. Nothing is said about their being converted by Paul; on the contrary, when we next hear of them at Ephesus, they are already instructing Apollos in the Christian faith. We must assume, therefore, that they were Christians before they came to Corinth and that there was a church in Rome before A.D. 49.

Before long Silas and Timothy arrived in Corinth bringing a report from Thessalonica. In general the report was better than Paul had dared to expect, but there were one or two disquieting features about it. The Jews were now trying to undermine Paul's work by a campaign of systematic slander, insinuating that his preaching was based on hallucinations and moral corruption, that he was a charlatan, a smooth-tongued rascal whose motives were gain and self-assertion (1 Th 2^{3-6}). Within the church Paul's preaching about the return of Christ had caused some confusion and perplexity. On hearing this news Paul wrote his first letter to the Thessalonians, and some weeks later, when his messenger reported that the nervous anticipation of the Parousia had become more serious, he wrote a second letter in a sterner vein.

Altogether, Paul remained a little over eighteen months in Corinth. Towards the end of this period an event occurred which is of great importance for us, because it provides us with our only certain date in the life of Paul. When Gallio became proconsul of Achaea, the Jews laid before him an accusation against Paul. The Gallio inscription at Delphi provides enough data to show that Gallio must have entered on his year of office on July 1, A.D. 51. Paul, then, must have arrived in Corinth in the early months of A.D. 50. Shortly after the dismissal of his case he left the city to travel via Ephesus to Caesarea, to pay his fourth visit to Jerusalem, and to remain for a brief period at Antioch.

8. The Third Missionary Journey, Ac 18^{23}–21^{16} [A.D. 52–57].—After a prolonged tour through Galatia and Phrygia Paul came at last to Ephesus, which he made his headquarters for almost three years. The only incidents which Acts assigns to this period are daily lectures in the school of Tyrannus, the discomfiture of a Jewish exorcist and his seven sons, and a riot provoked by the guild of metalworkers because they found that Paul's preaching was adversely affecting their trade. We can, however, fill in a few more details from the epistles. At some time during these three years Paul was 'utterly, unbearably crushed,' whether by illness or persecution, so that he 'despaired of life itself' and felt that he 'had received the sentence of death' (2 Co 1^{8-10}). On this or some other occasion Aquila and Priscilla 'risked their necks for my life' (Ro 16^{3}). In 2 Co 11^{23} Paul refers to repeated imprisonments and elsewhere speaks of kinsmen who have shared a prison cell with him (Ro 16^{7}). One or more of these imprisonments must have occurred during his Ephesian mission.

During this same three-year period Paul had prolonged and complex dealings with the church in Corinth. First he wrote a letter to the church which has not survived (1 Co 5^{9}), unless a fragment of it is preserved in 2 Co 6^{14}–7^{1}. In reply he received a letter from the church (1 Co 7^{1}), asking for instruction on a number of difficult subjects—marriage and divorce, the eating of meat which had been sacrificed to a pagan god, the veiling of women, speaking with tongues, and the resurrection of the body. At about the same time he had some visitors from Corinth whom he calls 'Chloe's people' (1 Co 1^{11}), who reported the existence of serious disorders in the church—the division of the congregation into rival factions, tolerance of blatant immorality, litigation between church members in the public lawcourts, and unseemly conduct at the Lord's Supper. To deal with all this Paul wrote a second letter which we know as 1 Corinthians. Next, there arrived in Corinth with letters of recommendation from another church (perhaps Jerusalem) certain men whom Paul was to describe in the heat of argument as 'super-apostles' (2 Co 3[1] 11[5]). The result of their coming was the growth of opposition to Paul's authority and criticism of his doctrine, and the disturbance seems to have had its centre in one man (2 Co 2[5-11]). On hearing of this Paul changed his plans. He had intended to spend the following summer travelling through Macedonia to Corinth, there to make another prolonged stay. Now instead he paid a flying visit, presumably by sea. He calls it a 'painful visit' (2 Co 2[1] 13[1]), which suggests that it was not a success. His opponents taunted him with being humble when face to face and bold when away, and said, 'His letters are weighty and strong, but his bodily presence is weak, and his speech of no account' (2 Co 10[1, 10]). Having returned in chagrin to Ephesus, Paul wrote a third letter, a severe and bitter letter full of angry reproaches, sent it off by the hand of Titus, and immediately regretted that he had done so (2 Co 2[1-4] 7[8]). Some scholars think that 2 Co 10–13 is a part of this letter. Titus had been told to return by the overland route, and Paul was so anxious that he set out to meet him at Troas. Not finding him there, he pressed on to Macedonia, and there Titus met him with the news that the troubles in Corinth were now satisfactorily resolved. In a fervour of affection and gratitude Paul wrote his fourth letter, which is 2 Corinthians (with or without chs. 10–13).

Another activity to which Paul had devoted much thought and energy since his last visit to Palestine was the organizing of a collection for the relief of the penurious church of Jerusalem. Galatia, Asia, Macedonia, and Achaea were all included (1 Co 16[1-4], 2 Co 8–9, Ro 15[25-32]). Paul set great store by this collection as a symbol of church unity, believing that it would bring home to his converts their debt to the mother church and their responsibility towards her, and that it would prove to the sceptical Christians of Jerusalem the value of his Gentile mission.

Perhaps it was during his journey through Macedonia that Paul made the excursion into Illyricum to which he refers in Ro 15[19] (cf Tit 3[12]). Here we are in the realm of conjecture. But we know that he arrived in Corinth for his final visit early in A.D. 57 and during his three months' stay wrote the Epistle to the Romans. [See CHRONOLOGY OF THE NEW TESTAMENT.] This was the only letter he ever wrote to a church which neither he nor his associates had founded, and he had a special reason for writing it. He had long desired to visit Rome and now had hopes of realizing his desire. His immediate purpose was to travel to Jerusalem along with the representatives of the churches who were to carry the collection, but once this duty had been discharged he intended to go to Rome and hoped that the Roman Church would sponsor him on a new missionary venture in Spain (Ro 1[11-15] 15[23-24]). To this end he wrote, setting before the church a systematic exposition of the gospel which he preached.

After leaving Corinth, Paul celebrated the Passover at Philippi and completed the rest of his journey in haste, so as to be in Jerusalem by Pentecost (Ac 20[6, 16]). He was accompanied by the representatives of the churches, Sopater of Beroea, Aristarchus and Secundus of Thessalonica, Tychicus and Trophimus from Asia, Gaius of Derbe and Timothy of Lystra, together with Luke who perhaps was the representative of Philippi. They held a midnight Eucharist at Troas, at which a young man named Eutychus fell unharmed from an upstairs window; had a farewell meeting with the elders of Ephesus at Miletus, stayed for a week at Caesarea with Philip the evangelist; and so came to Jerusalem.

9. Arrest and Imprisonment, Ac 21[17]–28[31] [A.D. 57–62].—On the advice of James, Paul attempted to allay Jewish suspicions by undertaking a vow in company with four Jerusalem Christians and paying their Temple expenses. But the advice turned out badly, for some Jewish pilgrims from Asia found him in the Temple, having previously seen him in the city accompanied by Trophimus of Ephesus, whom they had recognized as a Gentile; and they accused him of violating the sanctity of the Temple by bringing Gentiles into it. A riot followed from which Paul was rescued by soldiers of the Roman cohort from the barracks nearby, who took him into protective custody. After two unsuccessful attempts to free himself from the charges laid against him, first before the mob, then before the Sanhedrin, Paul learnt through his nephew of a plot against his life. He informed the tribune, Claudius Lysias, who promptly sent him to Caesarea to the governor, Felix. Felix heard the case, but was unwilling either to commit an injustice by condemning Paul or to antagonize the Jews by acquitting him; he therefore left Paul in prison. His successor, Festus, reopened the case, and Paul, fearing that he was to be sent to Jerusalem to stand trial, exercised his rights as a citizen by appealing to Caesar. Festus had no option but to send him to Rome, but first held an examination, attended by Agrippa and Bernice, to try to find a reasonable way of presenting the case to the Emperor. See JUSTICE, 3, ROMAN PUBLIC LAW, 2.

The journey to Rome was begun in late autumn, interrupted by a shipwreck which delayed the party for three months on the island of Malta, and completed in the spring of the following year. At Rome Paul was allowed to live under guard in his own rented house for the two-year period prescribed by Roman law as the limit within which the prosecutors must come to Rome to present their case after an appeal to the Emperor. At this point the story of Acts comes to an end with the implication that the Jewish plaintiffs allowed the case to go by default. There is, however, no positive evidence that Paul was ever released from prison. As long as the Pastoral Epistles were believed to be Pauline the historical references they contain provided the basis for a theory that Paul was twice imprisoned in Rome and that between his two imprisonments he carried on missionary work in Greece, Macedonia, Epirus, Asia Minor, and Crete. But this interpretation of the evidence has had to be abandoned along with the Pauline authorship of the Epistles. All we can say is that Paul almost certainly died a martyr's death in Rome during the reign of Nero (Clem. 1 *Cor.* 5; Tert. *Scorp.* 15; Eus. *HE* iii. 1), and that 2 Ti 4[6-8] is probably a portion of his last letter.

From the genuine imprisonment epistles of Paul (Colossians, Philemon, Philippians, and ? Ephesians) we can fill in a few details of his sojourn in Rome. He had two contacts with the church of Colossae. The first was Onesimus, a slave who had run away from the household of Philemon, after helping himself to some of his master's property. He found his way to Rome, where he became a convert and a close friend of Paul. Not daring to take the risk of harbouring a runaway slave, Paul reluctantly sent him back to his master with the request that he receive him 'no longer as a slave but more than a slave, as a beloved brother' (Phm 16). The second visitor from Colossae was Epaphras, one of the leaders of the church, who came to consult Paul about an outbreak of heretical teaching. To deal with this heresy Paul wrote the Epistle to the Colossians and dispatched it and his letter to Philemon by the hand of Tychicus. At the same time he wrote a letter to Laodicea (Col 4[16]) and (if it is his work) the Epistle to the Ephesians.

From the church of Philippi came Epaphroditus with a gift of money to relieve the hardships of Paul's imprisonment. While he was in Rome he suffered a serious illness from which he nearly died. Epaphroditus had intended to stay with Paul, but Paul, hearing that his friends in Philippi were anxious about him, sent him home and wrote the Epistle to the Philippians to send with him.

10. Appearance and Character.—The historical romance called *The Acts of Paul and Thecla* (see *The Apocryphal NT*, translated by M. R. James, 1924, 273 ff) contains a description of Paul which may well go back to a genuine 1st-cent. tradition: 'a man little of stature, thin-haired upon the head, crooked in the legs, of good state of body, with eyebrows joining, and nose somewhat hooked, full of grace: for sometimes he appeared like a man, and sometimes he had the face of an angel.' His unprepossessing appearance is borne out by the contemptuous remarks of the opposition at Corinth (2 Co 10^{10} 11^{6}). His excellent physique could have been deduced from the story of his missionary journeys, which even as a physical achievement excites our admiration, especially when we remember that his health was under constant attack from his recurrent illness and from persecution, and that he could show on his body 'the marks of Jesus' (Gal 6^{17}). His grace is attested by his long lists of friends and by the willingness of many of them to risk their lives on his behalf (Ro 16^{3}, Ph 2^{30}, Gal 4^{15}).

He was a man of immense vitality and determination. At everything he must excel: as a Pharisee in zeal for the Law, as a Christian in zeal for his Lord, as a missionary in quest of new fields of endeavour, as a thinker in exploring the unsearchable riches of Christ (Gal 1^{14}, Ph 3^{8}, Ro 15^{20}, Ph 3^{12-14}). But what in the Pharisee had been an unlovely self-assertion became in the Christian a winsome whole-heartedness which others found infectious. The personal sections of his letters reveal a vast capacity for friendship, and not the least part of his secret was that he treated others as equals and expected from them something of the excellence he demanded from himself. He could also be a relentless opponent, and much of his teaching was hammered out in the heat of controversy. He had a keen, sensitive nature, and numbered among his spiritual endowments the gifts of tongues, vision, and prophecy (1 Co 14^{18}, 2 Co 12^{1-4}, Ac 13^{1}). But his most remarkable accomplishment was to combine enthusiasm with common sense, sanity with profundity. He was able to discuss practical problems in such a way as to elucidate the eternal principles that underlay them; he was able also on occasion to rise above argument and explanation to the region of poetry, content at the limits of human understanding to bow before the mysteries of God (Ro 11^{33-36}). G. B. C.

PAUL'S THEOLOGY.—The epistles of Paul are not systematic theology, nor can we assume that they contain the whole of his thinking on the themes of Christian faith and practice. They are genuine correspondence, written to deal with specific problems in particular churches. They presuppose the apostle's missionary preaching, but give no account of it except in sporadic references, as circumstances demanded (*e.g.* 1 Th 1^{9-10}, 1 Co 2^{2}). They allude in tantalizing fashion to other letters which have not survived (1 Co 5^{9}, 2 Co 7^{8}, Col 4^{16}) and to conversations which were never recorded (2 Th 2^{5}; cf 1 Co 4^{17}). If there had not been a singular lack of decorum in the worship of the Corinthian church, we might not have had a word from Paul about the meaning of the Lord's Supper (1 Co 11^{17-34}); and we cannot help asking whether there were other aspects of the life of the early church about which he was silent simply because they raised no problems. Besides omissions, there are contradictions; for Paul wrote often in the heat of controversy, always with the Semitic temperament which is at home in extremes and paradoxes, and never expecting that what he wrote would be subjected to the minute analysis of modern critical scholarship.

When all this has been said, however, the fact remains that the Paul who emerges so clearly from the pages of his writings was at all times a theologian. Everything he experienced, everything he taught, was measured against his fundamental belief in God. His own life, consciously or unconsciously, had been under the direction of God, who had set him apart before his birth (Gal 1^{15}), who had shone in his heart at his conversion (2 Co 4^{6}), who had made him by grace what he now was (1 Co 15^{10}). It was God who had called him to be an apostle (1 Co 1^{1}, Gal 1^{1}), who constantly directed his steps (Ro 1^{10}, 1 Th 3^{11}), who spoke to others through him (2 Co 5^{20}), who had even a hand in the humbling incapacity of his thorn in the flesh (2 Co 12^{7}). But what was true of Paul's individual life was true also of the life of mankind as a whole. Behind the whole of human history lay the hidden wisdom of God, the gracious mystery of the eternal purpose which had now been disclosed in Christ (1 Co 2^{7}, Ro 8^{29}, Col 1^{26-27}, Eph 3^{10}). For this disclosure God had prepared the way by promise (2 Co 1^{20}, Ro 1^{2}, Gal 3^{17-29}), discipline (Gal 3^{24}, 1 Co 10^{1-11}) and wrath (Ro 1^{18-32} 13^{4}, Col 3^{6}, 1 Th 2^{16}). In the fulness of time He had sent forth His Son (Gal 4^{4}), indeed He Himself had been in Christ working out man's redemption (2 Co 5^{19}, Col 2^{9}, Ro 8^{3}). It was God who had delivered Christ up to death for the sins of men (Ro 3^{25} 4^{25} 5^{8}) and had raised Him up to triumph and glory (Ro 6^{4}, 1 Co 15^{15}, 2 Co 4^{14}, Gal 1^{1}, Ph 2^{9}). It was God who had chosen and called men into the fellowship of His Son (1 Th 1^{4}), so that even the humble station of His people was the result of His choice (1 Co 1^{26-29}). It was God who shaped their lives to bring them into conformity with His purpose (Ro 8^{28}, 1 Co 3^{9} $12^{6, 28}$, Eph 2^{10}, Ph 2^{13}); and in the steadfastness of His mercy lay their sole confidence for the future (Ro 3^{4} $11^{1, 29}$). Paul's Christian experience began with the Christ who apprehended him (Ph 3^{12}), and there was a sense in which Christ remained the centre of his faith. But his thinking about his experience was theological: it began and ended with God. 'All this is from God, who through Christ reconciled us to himself' (2 Co 5^{18}).

1. Originality and Dependence.—Paul emphatically asserts that the gospel which he preached came to him, like his apostleship, from no human source and without the mediation of human teaching. It was a part of the revelation of Christ which he received at his conversion (Gal 1^{11-12}). This experience convinced him that Christ was alive, vindicated by God, and that His death must therefore be interpreted as an act of God's grace and a proof of God's love. It convinced him that he was accepted by God apart from any merit of his own and in spite of his hostility to Christ, so that the Law which had urged him to the pursuit of merit and had prompted him to persecute Christ through His disciples could no longer be regarded as the way of salvation. It convinced him that a salvation which depended not on man's will or effort but on God's mercy must be meant for all the world and that God had appointed him to carry it to the world. It convinced him that a world reconciled to God by God's own act of love was what the Creator had planned from the beginning.

His gospel was so thoroughly his own that he could refer to it as 'my gospel' (Ro 2^{16} 16^{25}). But he was well aware that his gospel was not radically different from that preached by the other apostles. Indeed, as there was but one Christ, so there could be but one gospel. Had it proved to be otherwise, he would have felt that he 'had run in vain' (Gal 2^{2}). He was glad, therefore, to be able to record that the other apostles had given full recognition both to his gospel and to his apostleship (Gal 2^{9}).

Paul's claim to originality, then, must not be pressed beyond its proper limits. It must be balanced by the clear evidence of his epistles that he owed much to those who were in Christ before him. He had at his disposal a collection, whether oral or written, of the sayings of Jesus (1 Co $7^{10, 25}$), and a detailed comparison of his epistles with the Synoptic Gospels shows that he used it to the full. He refers to kerygmatic traditions which he had received and handed on (1 Co 11^{23} 15^{3}; cf Ro 10^{8-9}). He mentions also a pattern of ethical teaching which he assumes to be the common possession of all churches, including the church of Rome which he has not yet visited (Ro 6^{17}); and it is a plausible conjecture that this pattern is the one which appears in his later letters (Col 3^{8ff}, Eph 4^{22ff}), with parallels in 1 Peter and James. His choice and interpretation of OT texts coincide at so many points with the general usage of the other NT writers that we may safely assume that he shared with them a common principle of scriptural exegesis. The two sacraments of baptism and the Lord's Supper were also part of his inheritance, and in the case of baptism he seems to have felt that not only the rite but the interpretation of it was shared by the whole church (Ro 6[3]).

2. The Divine Plan.—' I did not shrink from declaring to you the whole counsel of God ' (Ac 20[27]). The words are the words of Luke, but the thought is the thought of Paul. In a variety of terms Paul is constantly asserting that the ministry, death and resurrection of Jesus and the founding of the church are the revelation and realization of a secret and eternal, Divine purpose, that in Christ we have the clue to the whole intention of the Creator. We are told of ' the mystery which has been kept secret for long ages, but now is disclosed ' (Ro 16[25]; cf 1 Co 2[7-8], Col 1[26-27], Eph 1[9] 3[3f, 9f]), a mystery which involves the overthrow of all evil and divisive forces and the reconciliation of all men to God and to one another in a new fellowship of which Christ is the head. We hear of the ' gracious pleasure ' of God (Col 1[19], Gal 1[15], 1 Co 1[21], Ph 2[13], Eph 1[5, 9]), by which Paul means His free self-determination to act according to His essential character of love. We hear of His ' selective purpose ' (Ro 9[11]; cf 8[28], Eph 1[11] 3[11]), whereby, with sovereign freedom and without regard to man's deserts or capacities, He chooses one rather than another to be the agent of His will.

As a Jew Paul had believed that he already possessed ' the whole counsel of God,' revealed in the Torah, which had lain on the knees of God before the creation of the world (Ro 2[17-20]). The whole world had been called into existence for the sole purpose that out of the rest of mankind God might fashion for Himself a holy people, dedicated to the observance of all the rules and institutions of the Mosaic Law. Paul the Christian, who had come to realize that his zeal for the Law had blinded him to the presence of God in the person of Christ (2 Co 3[14] 4[4]), discovered even in the Scriptures something more ultimate than the Mosaic code—the promise of blessing given to Abraham and through him to mankind (Gal 3[14-18], Ro 4[13-21]). The promise represented God's real and permanent disposition towards men and was not annulled by the Law, which came after it and represented only God's reaction against sin. The Law, in fact, was only a temporary and provisional dispensation to keep sin within restraint until the promise should be fulfilled by the coming of Christ.

The heart of God's plan was that men should ' be conformed to the image of his Son, that he might be the first-born among many brethren ' (Ro 8[29]). Christ was the only Son of God, enjoying a unique relationship with the Father, but it was God's purpose to bring others into the same relationship, to teach them to regard Him as Father and to live as members of His family, at peace with Him and with one another. This new community was to have all the intimacy of the family circle but also the vast inclusiveness of a world-wide commonwealth (Ph 3[20], Ro 10[19]). Paul believed passionately in God's election of himself and his fellow-Christians to their place in this family and to citizenship in this commonwealth, because he was convinced that his conversion was all of God's doing and none of his own, and that the cause of it was therefore to be found entirely in the free choice and mercy of God. But at the same time he refused to set any limits to the Divine mercy. ' God has consigned all men to disobedience, that he may have mercy upon all ' (Ro 11[32]). Indeed, the soaring vision of the apostle could not rest even with the hope of mankind redeemed. The sub-human creation, too, must be liberated from the bondage of decay to share in the glorious liberty of the sons of God (Ro 8[21]), and the spiritual powers of evil in the heavenly sphere must be reconciled to God by the Cross (Col 1[16-20], Eph 3[10]), in order that the whole of creation might be summed up in Christ (Eph 1[10]).

3. The Human Need.—The one barrier to the fulfilment of this magnificent, universal plan was sin. Paul took a thoroughly realistic view of the moral depravity of the world he lived in, and recognized that, for all his claims to superiority, the Jew was not exempt from its taint (Ro 1[18]–2[4]). But he did not identify breaches of the moral law with sin. These were the symptoms of a disease, the consequences of a tyranny to which God had abandoned those who refused to acknowledge Him. The basic sin was to ' suppress the truth ' of God's claim on us and our dependence on Him, just as the basic virtue was faith, which means accepting God and allowing Him to shape our lives (Ro 14[23]: ' whatever does not proceed from faith is sin ').

The archetypal sin was the sin of Adam, who wanted to be equal with God (Ph 2[6]). Paul thought of Adam in three distinguishable but closely related ways. He was the first man, the progenitor of the human race. He was the typical man whose story was re-enacted in the life of Everyman—' as sin came into the world through one man and death through sin, and so death spread to all men because all men sinned . . .' (Ro 5[12]). He was the head of the corporate unit we call mankind, so that to be ' in Adam ' meant to share the common nature and therefore the common sinfulness of all mankind. Paul further indicates that there are two ways in which men are involved in the sin of Adam—imitation and implication (Ro 5[14]). Because to some extent every man is his own Adam, men commit sins which are ' like the transgression of Adam ' *i.e.* deliberate and witting breaches of a known commandment. But because sin, once it has been introduced into human life, exercises an influence far wider than the transgression of individual men and invades both their habitual character and the fabric of their social institutions, all men, even against their will, become implicated in the general sinfulness. Thus by imitation of Adam all men add to the total sin of mankind and increase its power to dominate their common life, and by implication they come under the tyranny of sin and therefore of death, which is the wages of sin (Ro 6[23]).

To describe human nature in its unredeemed state Paul frequently uses the word ' flesh.' In one sense ' the flesh ' means simply the natural, psycho-physical life of man, life in Adam; and, like Adam, it denotes the solidarity of mankind. But because in Adam all men sin, the flesh takes on a further, sinister significance. To set one's mind on the flesh or to live according to the flesh means to live only for worldly or selfish ends, to live under the control of sin. ' The works of the flesh are plain; immorality, impurity, licentiousness, idolatry, sorcery, enmity, strife, jealousy, anger, selfishness, dissension, party spirit, envy, drunkenness, carousing, and the like '(Gal 5[19-21]). In this condition all men are children of wrath (Eph 2[3]), for ' on account of these the wrath of God is coming upon the sons of disobedience, among whom you also once walked ' (Col 3[6-7]). This wrath represents the recoil of God's holiness from all that is incompatible with it, and it is manifested partly in the abandonment of men to the consequences of their disobedience (Ro 1[24, 26, 28]), partly in the visitation of temporal punishments (1 Th 2[16]) which may be imposed by the authority of the state (Ro 13[4]), and partly in the running up of a long reckoning against the day of judgment (Ro 2[5]).

The Jewish Law was powerless to release men from the domination of sin and the threat of Divine wrath, and nobody had a better right to testify to this fact than the Pharisee who had devoted all his zeal to the way of the Law. Just because he took it with the utmost seriousness, he saw that to those who broke it the Law offered only condemnation and a sentence of death (2 Co 3[7-11]). Paul discovered that a legal religion actually exacerbated man's condition in three ways. Since God asks that man should live in the childlike dependence of faith, and since the independence of pride is the root of all sin any system which bids man achieve his own salvation by obedience to a code will only inflame his pride. It substitutes self-righteousness for the righteousness which comes from God (Ro 10[2]). Again, it is possible to sin unwittingly; but those who live under a code of law sin against the light, so that the law actually turns sin into trespass (Ro 5[20] 7[13]). And finally, by the power of suggestion, the Law actually induces men to break its own commandments (Ro 7[7]). Paul describes this last process most forcefully in a passage in which he writes in the first person, as though it had been a part of his own spiritual biography, but identifying his own experience with that of Adam. Just as the serpent took God's commandment and turned it into a temptation which brought about Adam's fall from innocence into the dominion of sin and death, so in Paul's case sin took the commandment against covetousness and used it as a base of operations. Thus, without Christ, man lives under a triple tyranny in which sin, death and law all have their part. 'The sting of death is sin, and the power of sin is the law' (1 Co 15^{56}).

Elsewhere Paul speaks of the same tyranny as a reign of principalities and powers, elemental spirits of the universe, rulers of this age. These are angelic beings who have been given authority by God over various aspects of His creation, but who, because of the universally pervasive sin, exercise that authority in a distorted and despotic fashion. They include the angelic guardians of the pagan state and social order (1 Co 2$^{7-8}$ 6^{3} 11^{10}), the angelic guardians of the Jewish Law (Gal 3^{19} 4$^{3-4, 8-9, 21}$), and what we should call the powers of nature, including decay and death (Ro 8$^{38-39}$, 1 Co 15$^{24-26}$). These angelic beings shared in the paradox of the Law. For, like the Law, they had been created by God as the agents of His will and endowed by Him with a measure of His own authority; but men had exalted this partial and delegated authority into a position of supreme importance in their lives, and so had corrupted it and transformed it into a tyrannical power.

4. The Son of God.—God's remedy for universal sin was to send His Son. Paul believed in the full humanity of Christ, 'born of a woman' (Gal 4^{4}), 'descended from David according to the flesh' (Ro 1^{3}). He took 'the form of a slave, being born in the likeness of men' (Ph 2^{7}), *i.e.* in accepting the human form He accepted all its conditions, including the bondage to the angelic powers and involvement in the general sinfulness of men. Paul actually goes so far as to say that God sent 'his own Son in the likeness of sinful flesh and for sin' (Ro 8^{3}), and by this he means, not that there was anything incomplete or unreal about Christ's humanity, but that, without Himself actually committing sin, He shared the common nature that makes all men kin, and so was able, by His obedience to God, to break the tyranny of sin not only over His own life but over the lives of others as well.

In another sense it could be said that Christ was more fully human than any other man, even Adam. For Christ alone lived human life as God had meant it to be lived. God had made Adam in His own image and had intended him to be a constant reflexion of His own glory and the representative of His own authority over the whole creation (Gn 1$^{27-28}$, Ps 8$^{5-8}$). Adam and all others after him had 'sinned and fallen short of the glory of God' (Ro 3^{23}), and had also lost the divinely ordained dominion over creation and had fallen under the reign of tyrannical powers. But Paul had seen 'the glory of God in the face of Jesus Christ' (2 Co 4^{6}), and he believed that God had exalted Him to universal lordship (Ph 2$^{9-11}$) in a heavenly reign which would continue until all His enemies were put under His feet (1 Co 15^{25}). In this connexion he quotes from Ps 8 to show that Christ's lordship is nothing other than the fulfilment of God's destiny for man. Christ was thus 'the image of God' in a sense in which Adam never was (2 Co 4^{4}). 'The first man was from the earth, a man of dust; the second man is from heaven' (1 Co 15^{47}). He was the pattern of which Adam was only the copy, and in Him could be seen the purpose for which God made man in His own image. But because man was the centre and crown of God's whole purpose of creation, it followed that He who embodied the purpose of human life embodied also the purpose of all creation. 'He is the image of the invisible God, the first-born of all creation; for in him all things were created, in heaven and on earth, visible and invisible, whether thrones or dominions or principalities or authorities—all things were created through him and for him. He is before all things, and in him all things hold together' (Col 1$^{15-17}$).

Thus Paul arrived at a most elevated conception of Christ simply by taking seriously His true humanity, and for this reason he never had any problem over the relation of His two natures. God had created man for precisely that intimate communion with the Divine which was exemplified in Christ, so that Christ was more and not less truly human because 'in him dwells the whole fulness of deity bodily' (Col 2^{9}). This is not to deny the uniqueness of Christ, since it is only in union with Him that men can 'put on the new nature, which is being renewed in knowledge after the image of its creator' (Col 3^{10}). He is uniquely the Son of God, and other men become sons only by adoption (Gal 4$^{4-7}$, Ro 8$^{14-17}$). 'He was in the form of God . . . but emptied himself' (Ph 2$^{6-7}$); 'though he was rich, yet for your sake he became poor, so that by his poverty you might become rich' (2 Co 8^{9}). He was the Lord whom Paul served as a slave, to whom he prayed for help (2 Co 12^{8}; cf 1 Co 1^{2}, Ro 10^{13}), and on whom he bestowed every Divine honour except the name of God.

It is significant, however, that Paul never thinks of the pre-existent Christ or the incarnate Christ as an object of worship. This is a dignity to which He attains only by the resurrection (Ro 1^{4}, Ph 2$^{9-11}$). For in spite of His heavenly origin, Christ possesses no static divinity, but has a real and developing history. He is in the form of God; He assumes human form, not in any temporary or docetic sense, but permanently; and as man He passes through death and resurrection into new life. Then and only then does God bestow on Him the exalted title of Lord and make Him the recipient of all worship. Then and only then does He become 'a life-giving spirit' (1 Co 15^{45}), able to dwell in others as God has dwelt in Him (Ro 8$^{9-10}$, 2 Co 3^{17}). Nor is His history finished: for there remains the final crisis of His Parousia. See also CHRISTOLOGY, 3.

5. The Gospel of Salvation.—Paul nowhere gives us a systematic doctrine of the Atonement. Instead he uses a wide variety of metaphors, drawn from many fields of human activity—the lawcourt, the slave-market, the home, the Temple worship, the battlefield—to express the wealth of meaning and power which he found in the Cross of Christ. These terms have one thing in common, that they all have a threefold reference to the past, present, and future, so that it is difficult to select any words from Paul's own vocabulary to distinguish these three aspects of Christ's saving work.

The explanation of this is twofold. On the one hand, Paul, in common with the whole of the early church, believed that he was living in the very middle of the last act of God's drama of redemption. Upon them the ends of the ages had come (1 Co 10^{11}). God had promised to visit and redeem His people, and the day of salvation had arrived (2 Co 6^{2}). The resurrection and the gift of the Spirit both belonged, according to the OT prophets, to this dénouement of history, and both had begun to happen. For Paul regarded the Resurrection of Christ as inseparable from the general resurrection (1 Co 15$^{12-19}$). He was 'the first fruits of those who have fallen asleep,' and His followers were living in the period between the offering of the first sheaf and the ingathering of the whole harvest. The Spirit had been given them as a down-payment on the inheritance which would ultimately be theirs (2 Co 1^{22} 5^{5}; cf Ro 8^{23}). The whole period from the birth of Christ to the Parousia appeared to them to be a single great act of God, and because they stood in the midst of it, it was bound to present itself to them in a threefold guise. On the other hand, there was a sense in which God's act was already complete. For Christ was not merely the first of many brethren, but also their inclusive representative. As Messiah He had embodied in Himself the whole of Israel and in Him the nation had reached its appointed destiny. He was the last Adam in whom the whole of mankind had passed vicariously through death and resurrection. Paul even found it possible to say that in the Cross the whole creation had already been reconciled to God (Col 1[20]). All that followed would simply be the appropriation of that which had already been accomplished in Christ. Thus from one point of view it is correct to describe Paul's conception of the new age as 'inaugurated eschatology,' from another point of view as 'realized eschatology.'

Salvation, then, is past, present, and future. Christians have been saved once for all, as an accomplished fact (Ro 8[24] 10[10] 11[11], Eph 2[8]); but they are also being saved (1 Co 1[18] 15[2], 2 Co 2[15] 6[2], Ph 2[12]), and look forward to a salvation which is yet to come (Ro 13[11]). They have been justified (Ro 5[1]), but justification is also the state within which they live (Gal 2[21]), and the hope of their calling (Gal 5[5]). They have been emancipated (Ro 6[7] 8[2], Gal 4[4], Col 1[13]), but must stand fast in their new freedom (Gal 5[1]), acting as free agents (Phm [14]), and waiting also for their final liberation (Ro 8[23]). They have been glorified (Ro 8[30]), are being transformed into the likeness of Christ's glory (2 Co 3[18]), and live in hope of a glory to be revealed (1 Co 15[43], Ph 3[21], Col 3[4]). God has reconciled them to Himself (Ro 5[10], 2 Co 5[18], Eph 2[16], Col 1[22]), but they must continue to seek reconciliation with Him (2 Co 5[20]), and expect to participate in the fuller reconciliation that is to come (Ro 11[15]). Christ has won a decisive victory over the powers of evil (Col 2[15]), but the battle goes on (Ro 8[37], 1 Co 15[57], Eph 6[12]) until the ultimate triumph is achieved (1 Co 15[24-28], 2 Th 2[8]). Christians are God's building, God's workmanship, and He who has begun a good work in them 'will bring it to completion at the day of Jesus Christ' (1 Co 3[9], Eph 2[10], Ph 1[6] 2[13]; cf Ro 5[1-2] 6[22]).

6. The Fact of Salvation.—In the first place, then, Paul believed that man's salvation was a fact, already accomplished in the life, death, and Resurrection of Christ, and already appropriated once for all by the believer at his baptism.

Christ was the bringer of salvation because He had revealed the love of God and His merciful ways of dealing with men (Ro 5[8]). Hitherto men had been blinded to the truth of God, either by their own passions or by the mistaken notion that the Law enshrined the whole character of God (Ro 1[21], 2 Co 4[4]). They were 'ignorant of the righteousness that comes from God' (Ro 10[3]). But in the gospel 'the righteousness of God is revealed' (Ro 1[17]). 'Righteous' and 'justify' are metaphors drawn from the lawcourt, where it is the duty of the judge to justify one of the two litigants, *i.e.* to declare him to be in the right (righteous). What then must a man do to be righteous in the eyes of God, to be justified or acquitted by the Judge of all the earth? Judaism answered that he must obey the commandments of the Law, and Paul points out with the help of Scripture that by this standard no one is righteous (Ro 3[20]). The answer of Paul's gospel, which he found already foreshadowed in the story of Abraham, is that the one thing God requires in man is faith and that He justifies the man who has it. God's righteousness is thus not the stern justice with which He metes out to each according to his deserts, but rather His saving power whereby He rescues from the slavery of evil powers those who trust Him to do so; and goodness is not something achieved by human merit but a free gift bestowed eagerly by God on all who are ready to receive it.

In revealing this righteousness of God Christ also revealed the true nature of the powers by which men were enslaved. For God's purposes had been misunderstood and misrepresented by 'the rulers of this age' who 'crucified the Lord of glory' (1 Co 2[6-8]), *i.e.* by the angelic guardians of pagan state and Jewish religion, the spiritual representatives of the established order. In bringing about the crucifixion these rulers thought that they were protecting the existing order of things and their own divinely ordained authority in particular. They did not know that God had sent Christ to make common cause with sinful men, even to the point of dying the death of a criminal, so that the guilty might be redeemed by the vicarious suffering of the innocent. The Cross showed that they were only partial and imperfect representatives of God's will, doomed to be reduced to impotence once Christ had revealed the agelong secret of God's saving grace.

Christ was the bringer of salvation also because He was willing to identify Himself with men in their humiliation, in order that they might be identified with Him in His glory. We have already seen how complete Paul believed this identification to be. Christ accepted all the conditions of the life men live, including 'the likeness of sinful flesh,' the curse which the Law pronounces on the evildoer, and the death which is the wages of sin (Ro 8[3], Gal 3[13], Ro 6[23]), in order that thenceforward nothing in all creation should separate men from the love of God which found its perfect expression in Him (Ro 8[38-39]). Because He did not have the mind of the flesh, did not earn the curse of the Law by His own misdoings, did not submit to the dominion of sin and death, humanity in Him took a new beginning. The powers of evil did their best to subjugate Him and in the end killed Him, not realizing that death would carry Him for ever beyond their clutches and so put the seal on His victorious life. He died 'to the elemental spirits of the universe' (Col 2[20] RSV; a more literal translation would be 'out from under the elemental spirits'). His Cross was a victory, and since He lived and died as the representative of men, it was a victory which could be shared by all. 'We are convinced that one has died for all: therefore all have died' (2 Co 5[14]). The same solidarity of mankind which in Adam made possible the universal spread of sin and death enabled men to find in Christ the universal conquest of sin and death; with this difference that in Adam all men are one by nature and without option, but in Christ all are one by grace and by the voluntary response of faith. For faith means accepting what God has done in Christ, saying: 'Christ has identified himself with me; I accept that identification: I am a man in Christ.' The sign and seal of this acceptance is baptism, which shares in the once-for-all character of the Cross. 'Do you not know that all of us who have been baptized into Christ Jesus were baptized into his death? We were buried with him by baptism into death, so that as Christ was raised from the dead by the glory of the Father, we too might walk in newness of life' (Ro 6[3-4]; cf Col 2[12]).

Christ was the bringer of salvation because He dealt effectively with sin. Paul is aware that the doctrine of justification by faith is open to misconstruction and finds it necessary to assert vehemently that it does not mean the overlooking of sin, as if sin did not matter (Ro 6[1, 15]). There had indeed been times in the past when God had passed over sins with patient forbearance, but there was no passing over of sin in the Cross of Christ, 'whom God put forward as an expiation by his blood' (Ro 3[25]). An expiation is a means of removing the taint of sin so that it does not bar men from entry into the Divine presence, and Paul is here saying that the barrier has been decisively removed by the act of God Himself. Similarly, when the barrier is described as enmity, it is removed by God who 'was in Christ reconciling the world to himself' (2 Co 5[18]; cf Ro 5[10], Eph 2[16], Col 1[22]). Christ took upon Himself the consequences of sin and so drew its sting, exhausted the curse of the Law, drew off on to Himself men's enmity and neutralized it by forgiving love (2 Co 5[21], Gal 3[13], Ro 5[10]).

Finally, Christ was the bringer of salvation because He lived a life of complete obedience (Ro 5[19], Ph 2[8]); and on this point the other three points all depend. For whatever Paul might say about the Law as an inadequate way of salvation, he believed that there was such a thing as 'the just requirement of the law' (Ro 8[4]). 'Christ is the end of the law' as a way of salvation (Ro 10[4]), but upholds it and fulfils it as a statement of God's demands (Ro 3[31] 13[10]). Holiness is not a condition of man's acceptance by God, but it is God's design for man (1 Co 6[9] 7[19]). Christ could not have revealed God to man unless He Himself had been fully attuned to God's purpose. It would have availed nothing for Him to identify Himself with men, unless in Him men could find a new life, free from all the disabilities of the old life in Adam. His death was a victory only because sin had no dominion over Him. The Cross was an expiation and a reconciliation only because He had done nothing to deserve it.

7. The Experience of Salvation.—Man's salvation has been fully accomplished by the act of God in Christ, and into that salvation Christians have entered by the response of faith. They have been illuminated by the new revelation of God, acquitted before His judgment seat, emancipated from the tyranny of sin, admitted to a new life and fellowship, made partakers of the glory and victory of Christ. But the implications of all this have still to be worked out; and, as Paul is writing to Christians with a pastoral concern for their spiritual welfare, this is naturally the aspect of salvation which bulks largest in his letters. The Christian life must be a life of progress from religious infancy to maturity (1 Co 3^{1-3} 14^{20}). It must be a life consistent with the faith on which it rests (Col 2^{20} 3^{1}, Gal 5^{25}), and worthy of the God who is its source (1 Th 2^{12}, Ph 1^{27}).

Christians 'have obtained access to this grace in which we stand' (Ro 5^{2}; cf Eph 2^{8} 3^{12}). They may enter 'with unveiled face' into the presence of God (2 Co 3^{12-18}). And the God to whom they come is not the God of law but the God of love and mercy. Paul has much to say about the responsibility of the Christian for his own conduct under the new régime, so that it is well to establish clearly from the outset that he regards Christian progress as God's work, no less than conversion. 'Work out your own salvation with fear and trembling, for God is at work in you, both to will and to work for his good pleasure' (Ph 2^{12-13}, Ro 8^{28}). Grace is always freely given, never earned (Ro 11^{6}), and to come to God with any claim of merit or achievement is to fall away from grace (Gal 5^{4}; cf 1 Co 15^{1-2}).

By the grace of God Christians have been 'called into the fellowship of his Son' (1 Co 1^{9}). In their initial act of faith and in the symbolism of baptism they have accepted identification with Christ and union with Him in the new life which He represents. But this identification and union must be realized in experience: they must become in fact what they already are by faith. 'We know that our old self was crucified with him so that the sinful body might be destroyed, and we might no longer be enslaved to sin' (Ro 6^{6}; cf Gal 2^{20}, Col 2^{20} 3^{3}); but we must still put to death what is earthly in us, and reckon ourselves dead to sin and alive to God (Col 3^{5}, Ro 6^{11}). 'As many of you as were baptized into Christ have put on Christ' (Gal 3^{27}); 'you have put off the old nature with its practices, and have put on the new nature, which is being renewed in knowledge after the image of its creator. . . . Put on then . . . compassion, kindness, etc. . . .' (Col 3^{9-12}). Indicative and imperative go hand in hand. Paul speaks of his converts as 'children with whom I am again in travail until Christ be formed in you' (Gal 4^{19}). They are to be transformed by the renewing of their mind (Ro 12^{2}), to reflect the glory of Christ until stage by stage His image becomes permanently fixed upon their character (2 Co 3^{19}), to be fashioned anew by the hand of the Creator (2 Co 5^{17}, Gal 6^{15}), by whom they have been predestined to be conformed to the image of His Son (Ro 8^{30}). This process of transformation and renewal is a secret one and may be belied by outward appearances. Paul was aware that his own life appeared, to those of his critics who looked only to the things that are seen and temporal, to be burdened with an appalling load of affliction, but he was confident that to those who looked to the things that are unseen and eternal the burden would appear as an eternal weight of glory (2 Co 4^{7-18}). 'Your life is hid with Christ in God' (Col 3^{3}).

Life in Christ is also life in the Spirit, and Paul frequently declined to draw any distinction between the indwelling Christ and the indwelling Spirit (2 Co 3^{17}, Ro 8^{9-11}, 1 Co 15^{45}). As a sphere of life the Spirit is contrasted with the flesh, for the flesh is a source of weakness which lays men open to the attacks of sin, but the Spirit is the power of God which supplies the dynamic for the new life. The gifts and graces of the Christian life are produced as spontaneously by the Spirit as fruit grows on a tree (Gal 5^{22}). Some of these gifts are spectacular evidences of Divine power (1 Co 12^{8-10}), but the same power is active in a more permanently effective way in the development of Christian character, and above all in the gift of love (Ro 5^{5}, 1 Co 12^{31}). The Spirit is the fountain of all genuine conviction (1 Co 12^{3}), and in particular of the conviction that God is a Father who calls men to be His children and to live as members of His family (Gal 4^{6}, Ro 8^{14-17}). In this connexion Paul contrasts the Spirit of adoption with the spirit of slavery. Those who live under the Law are slaves, because the authority which governs their lives is the external authority of the written code which never succeeds in subduing the impulses of the flesh (2 Co 3^{6}, Ro 7^{22-23}). But those who live by the Spirit have their controlling authority within them, enabling them to act spontaneously in accordance with the will of God. It follows therefore that 'where the Spirit of the Lord is, there is freedom' (2 Co 3^{17}); for moral freedom consists in having one's ethical standards within oneself, and not dictated from without. Paul strenuously resisted any attempt to make the Mosaic code obligatory on Christians, because he saw that the ethics of law and the ethics of liberty are mutually incompatible. To live by rule is to silence the guiding voice of the inner Spirit. It is true that Paul recognized the validity of certain external guides to ethical decision: the words of the Lord (1 Co 7^{10}), the pattern of traditional teaching (Ro 6^{17}), the usage of the churches (1 Co 11^{16} 14^{33}); but none of these constituted a legal code or a substitute for the renewed mind. 'I give my opinion as one who by the Lord's mercy is trustworthy.' 'We have the mind of Christ' (1 Co 7^{25} 2^{16}).

The Christian life is, further, a life lived in the community of the church. God is the Father 'from whom every family in heaven and on earth is named' (Eph 3^{15}), and those who are led by the Spirit of God to call Him Abba must be members of the large family in which Christ is 'the first-born among many brethren' (Ro 8^{29}). Every fellow-Christian is therefore 'the brother for whom Christ died' (1 Co 8^{11}; cf Ro 14^{15}). Even when the Corinthians are behaving in a most unbrotherly manner Paul still addresses them as brethren (1 Co 1^{10}), and he appeals to Philemon to receive back the runaway Onesimus 'no longer as a slave but more than a slave, as a beloved brother' (Phn ^{16}).

The church was also the people of God, continuous with the old Israel, though transformed by Christ. The word *ecclesia* was a constant reminder of this continuity, for it had been used in the LXX to denote the congregation of Israel. To use this word was to claim that all the privileges and responsibilities of God's people have now devolved upon the church. The church is 'the Israel of God' (Gal 6^{16}), because Christ has fulfilled all the promises made to Abraham (Gal 3^{16}, 2 Co 1^{20}). Christians, therefore, whether they come of Jewish or of Gentile stock, are heirs of the promises made to Abraham, because they share the faith in God which had been counted to Abraham for righteousness (Gal 3^{29}, Ro 4^{16}). In Ro 9–11 Paul argues at some length to prove two points: that membership in the people of God has never been a matter of physical descent or historic transmission, but always of God's free and unconditioned calling, so that God is not being inconsistent when he excludes some Jews from the church and includes Gentiles instead; and that the Gentile Christians must nevertheless be aware that the people of God to which they now belong is rooted in Jewish history. They are wild olive branches, grafted on to the olive tree of Israel. 'So then you are no longer strangers and sojourners, but you are fellow citizens with the saints and members of the household of God' (Eph 2^{19}; cf 3^{6}, Ro 3^{29}, Gal $3^{9,28}$, Col 1^{27}, 3^{11}).

PAUL'S THEOLOGY

Paul frequently calls Christians saints, but he never uses the word in the singular; they are holy only insofar as they belong to God's holy people.

The church is the body of Christ. This metaphor is peculiarly Pauline and he uses it for a variety of purposes: to show how a multiplicity of functions can be combined within the one organic unity of the church (1 Co 12[12-27]), to draw attention to the mutual interdependence of Christians (Ro 12[4-5]), and to indicate their common dependence on Christ who is their head (Col 1[18], Eph 1[22]). It is not at all clear from what source Paul drew this picture of the church. It is unlikely that he was merely adapting a pagan fable. More probably it was the result of the fusion in his own mind of two ideas: that Christians are in Christ in the same way as all men are in Adam, and that Christ had called the eucharistic bread 'my body.' Both of these ideas are prominent in the earliest epistle in which Paul uses the metaphor of the body. There are two occasions when he uses the word Christ where we should have expected him to speak of the church. When he is commenting on the division of the Corinthian church into rival factions, he asks, 'Is Christ divided?' (1 Co 1[13]). The church is so completely identified with Christ that it can no more be divided than He can. Because there is one Christ there is one church, and to be a Christian is to belong to this one, indivisible fellowship. Later in his letter we read, 'Just as the body is one and has many members, and all the members of the body, though many, are one body, so it is with Christ' (1 Co 12[12]). The argument proceeds from the idea that Christ, like the human body, exemplifies multiplicity in unity to the idea that the church is the body of Christ. But Paul certainly had in mind also the parallel between the body of Christ which is the church and the body which is the eucharistic bread: 'because there is one loaf, we who are many are one body, for we all partake of the same loaf' (1 Co 10[17]). When he comes to write of the disorders at the Lord's Supper, he accuses the Corinthians of 'not discerning the body,' because, in disregarding the poorer members of the church they have failed to see in the sacramental loaf the symbol of their unity in Christ (1 Co 11[29]).

The church is the fellowship of the Holy Spirit (2 Co 13[14]). What Paul means by this phrase he explains fully in Ph 2[1-11]. It is the unity of mind and soul which the Spirit creates in those who take Jesus for their pattern. Paul hardly mentions the organization of the church (there is one reference in Ph 1[1] to bishops and deacons without any indication of their function). He does not prescribe a structure for the local church nor a fixed order for its worship: an organism does not require to be organized. To him the striking fact about the Christian community was the spontaneous emergence of a common life in people of multifarious backgrounds and interests, transcending differences of race, class and sex but allowing for divergence of capacity and function (Gal 3[28], 1 Co 12[4, 11]).

The marks of this common life are brotherly affection (Ro 12[10]), mutual strengthening and forbearance (Ro 1[11], Eph 4[2]), the bearing of one another's burdens (Gal 6[2]), the care of the strong for the weak, even at the sacrifice of individual freedom (Ro 15[1-2], 1 Co 8[9-13]; cf Ro 12[16]), and above all 'love which binds everything together in perfect harmony' (Col 3[14]). Jealousy and strife destroy the temple of God which is the church: love alone builds it up (1 Co 3[16-17], Eph 4[16]). Love is the one gift of the Spirit without which all other gifts are of no avail (1 Co 13[1-3]). This one gift comprehends in itself the whole experience of salvation. For faith finds its active expression in love (Gal 5[6]), through love men come to the knowledge of God (Col 2[2], Eph 3[17]), and the love of Christ becomes in them an inner constraint (2 Co 5[14]) which takes the place of the outward constraint of the Law and perfectly fulfils all the Law's requirements (Ro 13[8-10]). It is in fact the whole duty of man, and a possible duty because it is the gift and fruit of the Spirit (Ro 5[5], Gal 5[22]).

8. The Hope of Salvation.—Paul shared the commonly accepted belief of the apostolic age that the Parousia of Christ would occur within a generation. Some of his friends would die before that day, but he himself hoped to be among those who would live to see it (1 Th 4[17], 1 Co 15[51]). Even when his own personal survival was a matter of doubt, he still retained the same expectation (Ph 2[20-23] 3[21]), which was nourished, no doubt, by the regular celebrations of the Lord's Supper, when the church, with the prayer Maranatha, kept the memory of the Lord's death until He should come (1 Co 16[22] 11[26]). Yet, firmly as he held this notion of the imminence of the End, there is only one place in his letters where it has influenced his teaching. In his teaching on marriage Paul, as a Jew who had no sympathy with asceticism, started from the assumption that marriage is the natural and normal state for men and women (1 Co 9[5]) but his instructions on this subject were dictated by the belief that 'the appointed time has grown very short' and that 'the form of this world is passing away' (1 Co 7[29, 31]). During this final period worldly ties and troubles were likely to interfere with a man's loyalty, so that 'in view of the present distress it is well for a person to remain as he is' (1 Co 7[26]). Elsewhere Paul found it necessary to dissociate Christian ethics from the expectation of an imminent Parousia. Preaching at Thessalonica, he had urged his converts 'to serve a living and true God, and to wait for his Son from heaven' (1 Th 1[9f]), and they had taken this injunction so literally that many of them had ceased to do anything else. Paul had to write two letters to persuade them that Christian conduct is governed not by the future but by the past, by the fact that in Christ they have already become 'sons of light and sons of the day' (1 Th 5[5]). He never abandoned his belief in an imminent Parousia, but as his work developed it came to bulk less and less in his thoughts, and its place was taken by a new and broader vision of the missionary task of the church. From the first he had held that the coming of the End would be determined not by the mere passage of time but by the maturing of the purposes of God (2 Th 2[3-12]), and before long he came to realize that those purposes involved the bringing of all men within the scope of God's mercy (Ro 11[32]).

For the Christian the Parousia was chiefly associated with the resurrection of the body. Paul believed that Christ had died and risen as the inclusive representative of all men, so that men by faith might be united with Him here and hereafter in His death and resurrection (1 Th 5[10]). This union, however, had one qualification: resurrection had been for Christ both a spiritual and bodily triumph; for His followers resurrection as a spiritual experience came with baptism, but the resurrection of the body was still in the future. Chronic illness, the rigour of his travels and the harsh treatment he received at the hands of religious and civil authorities made Paul profoundly sensitive to bodily weakness, and although he turned this weakness to good account (2 Co 4[11] 11[30] 12[9]), his faith would not have been complete without the assurance that salvation would culminate in the redemption of the body (Ro 8[23]). He seems also to have had a thoroughly Greek horror of the decay to which the whole natural order was subject, and to have felt that, because Adam was 'from the earth, a man of dust,' man's physical body was one with the sub-human creation in its bondage to decay, so that man's redemption must carry with it the liberation of nature as a whole (Ro 8[21]). The resurrection of the body was for Paul no naïve or materialistic hope. He states quite clearly that 'flesh and blood cannot inherit the kingdom of God, nor does the perishable inherit the imperishable' (1 Co 15[50]). The physical body has to be transformed into a body of spirit or glory (1 Co 15[44], Ph 3[21]) to make it fit for the heavenly life to which it goes. But this physical transformation is only the climax of an inner change which has been going on secretly in the life of the Christian all along: 'your life is hid with Christ in God. When Christ who is our life appears, then you also will appear with him in glory' (Col 3[3-4]). In one passage Paul actually seems to suggest that each Christian has waiting for him in heaven a body which corresponds to the character which God has built up in him during his life of faith (2 Co 5^{1-11}).

For all men the Parousia means judgment. In the case of the Christian the verdict of this judgment is already known: 'there is therefore now no condemnation for those who are in Christ Jesus' (Ro 8^{1}). Whatever else the judgment may mean in terms of purgation and recompense, it does not affect the ultimate salvation of those who have believed in Christ (1 Co 3^{13-15} 5^{5}, 2 Co 5^{10}). With regard to the fate of others Paul's opinion changed during his ministry. At first he brought over into Christianity his Jewish particularism with only a slight modification. As a Jew he had believed that the judgment meant acquittal for the faithful Israelite and condemnation for all others, and in his early years as a Christian he simply substituted the word Christian for Israelite. The judgment would bring 'vengeance upon those who do not know God and upon those who do not obey the gospel of our Lord Jesus. They shall suffer the punishment of eternal destruction and exclusion from the presence of the Lord' (2 Th 1^{8-9}). His change of attitude was caused in part at least by his wrestling with the problem of unfaithful Israel (Ro 9–11). Israel had been God's chosen people upon whom He had lavished all the favours of the old covenant; and many of these, Paul's kinsmen by race, were among the unbelievers whom he had been ready to consign to perdition. But was this a fate for Israel with which God could rest content? Would God go back on His promises? 'For the gifts and call of God are irrevocable' (Ro 11^{29}). Moreover, God had saved Paul, the most intransigeant of all the enemies of the Cross of Christ, so that no limits could be set to the extent of His mercy. By such considerations as these Paul advanced to the mystery of universal salvation: 'A hardening has come upon part of Israel, until the full number of the Gentiles come in, and so all Israel will be saved. . . . For God has consigned all men to disobedience, that he may have mercy upon all' (Ro $11^{25f, 32}$).

Above all, the Parousia meant the final victory of Christ over His enemies, the principalities and authorities—those angelic beings who stood for worldly power, derived indeed from God but in revolt against Him. In this connexion also Paul's expectations were modified as he came to a larger conception of the scope of God's plan for salvation. In his earlier letters he was content that these powers should be defeated and destroyed. Writing in A.D. 50, only ten years after Caligula had given orders for his statue to be set up in the Temple at Jerusalem, he thought of Roman imperial authority as the embodiment of a mystery of lawlessness which would finally manifest itself in a man of lawlessness, whom Jesus would slay with the breath of His mouth and destroy by His appearing and His coming (2 Th 2^{3-12}). The rulers of this age who had been responsible for the crucifixion were being reduced to impotence and would in the end be destroyed, along with man's last enemy, death (1 Co 2^{6-8} 15^{24-26}). But with his growing experience of its administration in many parts of the world Paul came to have a deeper appreciation of the Roman Empire, so that when he wrote his letter to Rome he could speak of the Divine institution of its authority without any qualification (Ro 13^{1-7}). The Empire with its capital in Rome and its colonies and citizens dispersed throughout the provinces helped to evoke in his mind the picture of a Divine commonwealth with the Jerusalem above for its capital and with every church on earth a colony of heaven (Ph 3^{20}). Thus in his later letters when he had developed the cosmic implications of the Cross, and had come to see the salvation of man as the centre of a universal redemption, Paul was able to include even the heavenly powers within the redemptive purposes of God (Ph 2^{10}). In Christ was the source and purpose of their being, and therefore in Christ was the possibility of their restoration to the place which God had designed for them in His universal plan. 'In him all things were created, in heaven or on earth, visible and invisible, whether thrones or dominions or principalities or authorities—all things were created through him and for him . . . in him all the fulness of God was pleased to dwell, and through him to reconcile to himself all things, whether on earth or in heaven, making peace by the blood of his cross' (Col 1^{16-20}).

Paul's complete picture of the Parousia, then, is that with the appearing of Christ in glory the hidden life of Christians will be manifested in the glory of the resurrection body; the fulness of the Gentiles and all Israel will be brought by the inscrutable ways of God into the kingdom of His mercy; the physical creation will be liberated from the bondage of decay; the powers of heaven will be reconciled to their Creator; because God from the beginning has planned to sum up all things in Christ, things in heaven and things on earth (Eph 1^{10}). G. B. C.

PAULUS, SERGIUS.—Proconsul of Cyprus when Paul and Barnabas visited the island on the 'first missionary journey'; spoken of in Ac 13^{7} as 'a man of intelligence' (RSV). Cyprus, annexed to Rome in 58 B.C., was made an imperial province in 31 B.C. and a propraetor was appointed governor. In 22 B.C. because of more settled conditions it was transferred to the Senate and thereafter was administered by a proconsul (q.v.). This Sergius Paulus received his appointment in A.D. 46. The elder Pliny cites him twice as authority for matters concerning Cyprus. No coins have been discovered bearing his name, but it appears on an inscription. Of his alleged conversion (Ac 13^{12}) there is no supporting evidence. J. S. K.

PAVEMENT.—See GABBATHA, PEDIMENT.

PAVILION is formed (through Fr. *pavilion*) from Latin *papilio*, which meant a 'butterfly,' and also (from the resemblance to a butterfly's outspread wings) a 'tent.' 'Pavilion' is the translation in AV of *sōkh* in Ps 27^{5} (RSV 'shelter'), and of *sukkāh* in 2 S 22^{12} (RSV 'canopy'), 1 K $20^{12, 16}$ (RSV 'booths'), Ps 18^{11} (RSV 'canopy') 31^{20} (RSV 'shelter'), and to these RV adds Job 36^{29} and Is 4^{6} for AV 'tabernacle.' RSV has 'pavilion' in Job 36^{29} and Is 4^{6}, but nowhere else. *sukkāh* is of frequent occurrence, and is often rendered 'booth' or 'tabernacle,' once 'tent' (2 S 11^{11} AV). Besides these, *shaphrîr* is translated 'royal pavilion' (AV, RV; RVm 'glittering pavilion,' RSV 'royal canopy'). RV has also given 'pavilion' in Nu 25^{8}, with marginal **alcove** for AV 'tent' (RSV 'inner room'). It is possible that the Hebrew *ḳubbāh* in this passage is a mistake for *ḥuppāh*, 'nuptial tent.'

PE.—Seventeenth letter of Hebrew alphabet, and so used to introduce the seventeenth part of Ps 119, every verse of which begins with this letter.

PEACE.—1. The word 'peace,' as it is used in the OT, renders the Hebrew *shālôm* (Arab. *salām*), of which the fundamental sense is wholeness, health (*i.e.* hale-th), security (cf Gn 43^{27}, Ps 73^{3} etc.). The word has several uses: (1) it is the common formula of courteous well-wishing, employed both at meeting and at parting (cf Gn 43^{23}, 1 S 1^{17}, Ps 122^{7f}, Mt 10^{12f}); (2) it means 'peace' in the sense of freedom from war and conflict and the resultant social solidarity and political stability, all of which are secured in permanency only by the reconciliation of man with man and people with people; and (3) it can mean 'peace' in the religious sense of reconciliation of man with God and the experience of God's grace (cf Nu 6^{26}, Ps 29^{11} 85^{8ff} 122^{6}, Jer 16^{5} etc.). The peace of the Messianic Kingdom of God (q.v.) comprehends (2) and (3) by its expectation, on the one hand, that swords will be beaten into ploughshares and spears into pruning-hooks, and, on the other, that the old, harmonious order of nature will be restored and hostilities will have an end (cf Ps $72^{3, 7}$, Is 2^{4} 9^{5-7} 11^{6-9}, Hag 2^{9}, Zec 9^{10}). Sometimes its use in the OT approximates to its subjective NT signification, implying tranquillity of heart, as in Ps 4^{8} 119^{165}, Is $48^{18, 22}$.

2. It is said in the NT (Mt 10^{34}) that, owing to the challenge which the Gospel of Christ offered to orthodox and deeply-rooted ways of religious thought and practice,

His own conception of the immediate effect of His own work was that it would bring not peace, but a sword; but His purpose is to bring the abiding peace which comes only when every cause of strife and barrier of division is removed. The Greek *eirēnē* has much the same range of meaning as the Hebrew *shālôm*, being found in its broadest sense conspicuously in the (Hebraistic) Benedictions (cf Mk 5[34], Lk 7[50] 24[36], Jn 14[27], Ja 2[16] etc.) and in the epistolary Salutations. In the latter formulas, 'peace' comprehends the sum of blessing experienced, as 'grace' the sum of blessing bestowed, from God in Christ. The Messianic peace (**1** above) reappears in Lk 1[79] 2[14], Mt 10[34]; and the peace of harmony with God in Jn 16[33], Ac 10[36], Ro 8[6] 15[33], Ph 4[7] etc. These uses are gathered up into the specific NT doctrine of peace, of which Paul is the exponent and Ro 5[1] the classical text (cf v.[10] and 2 Co 5[18-21], Eph 2[13-18], Col 1[20]; and see the article on JUSTIFICATION): 'peace with God through our Lord Jesus Christ' is the state and the experience of those who have been 'reconciled' to the Father through the sacrifice offered by His Son in love, whose 'trespasses' are forgiven and in whose heart 'the spirit of adoption' dwells. Reconciled to God, we are enabled to accept in faith the vexatious experiences of life and the hostilities of the world; by His cross Christ 'has slain' at a blow 'the hostility' between God and man, and between race and race (Eph 2[16]). 'Peace on earth' is to flow from 'the peace of Christ' that 'rules in' Christian 'hearts' (Col 3[15]). G. G. F.—**J. Ma.**

PEACE-OFFERING.—See SACRIFICE AND OFFERING, **12**.

PEACOCKS.—1. Hebrew *tukkiyyîm*, 1 K 10[22], 2 Ch 9[21]. The word may be from the Tamil *tokei* meaning 'peacock' but from the fact that the LXX has in 1 K 10[22] 'carved stones' and that in 2 Ch 9[21] the word is omitted, the translation is doubtful. Alternatively, it has been thought that it comes from a word meaning *guinea-hen*, while Albright (*ARI*, 212) holds that it means 'ape' and has an Egyptian derivation. **2.** *rᵉnānîm* is translated 'peacock' in AV in Job 39[13] (RV, RSV **ostrich**, q.v.).

PEARL.—References in OT are uncertain. In Job 28[18] *gābhîsh* is translated 'pearls' in AV, but 'crystal' in RV and RSV, while *pᵉnînîm* in the same verse is translated 'rubies' in AV and RV, but 'pearls' in RVm and RSV. In Est 1[6] *dar* should be rendered 'pearl' or 'mother of pearl' (so RSV). In NT pearls (Gr. *margaritai*) are mentioned in Mt 7[6] 13[45f], 1 Ti 2[9], Rev 17[4] 18[12, 16] 21[21]. The last reference must be to mother-of-pearl. Pearls are a pathological production of the mollusc *Avicula margaritifera*. See also JEWELS AND PRECIOUS STONES. E. W. G. M.

PECULIAR PEOPLE.—This expression is found several times in AV to denote that Israel is the chosen people of God, 'peculiar' to Himself, *i.e.* belonging exclusively to Him. See ELECTION.

PEDAHEL.—The prince of Naphtali, Nu 34[28].

PEDAHZUR.—The father of the prince of the tribe of Manasseh, Nu 1[10] 2[20] 7[54, 59] 10[23].

PEDAIAH ('Y″ has redeemed').—**1.** Father of Joel, ruler of Manasseh, W. of the Jordan, in the time of David, 1 Ch 27[20]. **2.** 'Of Rumah,' father of Zebudah the mother of Jehoiakim, 2 K 23[36]. **3.** Son of Jeconiah, 1 Ch 3[18]; in 1 Ch 3[19] called the father of Zerubbabel who, however, is otherwise represented as the son of Pedaiah's brother Shealtiel. **4.** A man of the family of Parosh, who repaired the wall of Jerusalem, Neh 3[25]. **5.** One of those who stood by Ezra when he read the Law to the people, Neh 8[4], 1 Est 9[44] (AV **Phaldaius**, RV **Phaldeus**). He is perhaps the same as **4**. **6.** A Levite, Neh 13[13]. **7.** A Benjamite, Neh 11[7]. W. F. B.

PEDIAS, 1 Est 9[34] (RV).—see BEDEIAH.

PEDIMENT.—This word stands only in RSV in 2 K 16[17], where it renders Hebrew *marṣepheth* (AV, RV **pavement**). Here it is clearly the more appropriate translation. A kindred word, *riṣpāh*, is elsewhere rendered 'pavement' by RSV as well as the older versions (2 Ch 7[3], Ezk 40[17f]).

PEEP.—To 'peep' (Is 8[19] 10[14]) is to 'cheep' as nestlings do. RV and RSV mistakenly have 'chirp.'

PEKAH was one of the last kings of Israel. The country was unsettled, and there was great discontent on account of the heavy tribute paid to Assyria. Pekah made himself the organ of the dissatisfaction, and murdered his king **Pekahiah** (2 K 15[25]). He needed the help of only fifty soldiers or bravos to accomplish his purpose. Once on the throne he set on foot a movement against the Assyrians in which all the kingdoms of Syria were to unite. When the king of Judah held out against it, Pekah and Rezin invaded that country, as is set forth in the article AHAZ. The Assyrians were prompt in meeting the coalition, and the issue can hardly have been doubtful, except to those who were blinded by patriotism. The fall of Damascus was followed by the ravaging of the districts of Israel N. and E. of Samaria, and the transportation of their inhabitants to remote portions of the empire. The capital would no doubt have been besieged had not the party friendly to Assyria got the upper hand and removed Pekah by the usual method of assassination (v.[30]). The leader in this movement, **Hoshea** by name, had an understanding with the Assyrian king, and was perhaps from the first a creature of his. Abject submission on his part saved Samaria for the time being. The length of Pekah's reign is given as twenty years which is difficult to reconcile with other data at our command. The true period cannot have been more than five years. H. P. S.

PEKAHIAH, son of Menahem, was king of Israel for a short time in the troubled period which preceded the fall of Samaria. The record tells us nothing about him except that he displeased Yahweh by walking in the sins of Jeroboam I., and that he was assassinated by **Pekah**, one of his officers (2 K 15[23-26]). H. P. S.

PEKOD.—Mentioned in Ezk 23[23], Jer 50[21]. It probably represents the Babylonian *Pukūdu*, a people settled in Lower Babylonia, possibly of Aramaean race. Their seat was near the mouth of the Uknu River.

PELAIAH.—1. A son of Elioenai, 1 Ch 3[24]. **2.** A Levite who helped Ezra to expound the Law, Neh 8[7], 1 Est 9[48] (AV **Biatas**, RV **Phalias**): he was one who sealed the covenant, Neh 10[10].

PELALIAH.—A priest, Neh 11[12].

PELATIAH.—1. A 'prince of the people,' Ezk 11[1]; he died as the prophet delivered his message, v.[13]. It is difficult to decide whether Pelatiah's death is to be understood as actual or merely symbolical. **2.** A grandson of Zerubbabel, 1 Ch 3[21]. **3.** A Simeonite, 1 Ch 4[42]. **4.** A signatory to the covenant, Neh 10[22].

PELEG.—A descendant of Shem in the fourth generation, according to the table of peoples given in Gn 10[25], 1 Ch 1[19]. In Lk 3[35] he stands a generation further off through the interpolation of Cainan from the LXX. The etymology of the name is uncertain. Its reference may be geographical, or racial, or, as the word means ordinarily 'a water-course,' it may denote a land cut up by streams. W. F. C.

PELET.—1. A son of Jahdai, 1 Ch 2[47]. **2.** A Benjamite chief who joined David at Ziklag, 1 Ch 12[3].

PELETH.—1. See PALLU. **2.** A Jerahmeelite, 1 Ch 2[33].

PELETHITES.—See CHERETHITES AND PELETHITES.

PELIAS, 1 Est 9[34] (AV).—See BEDEIAH.

PELICAN.—The Hebrew *ḳā'āth* has generally been thought to be the pelican, being explained from *ḳî'* 'to vomit'; for the pelican was thought to throw up its food to feed its young. Although, however, two species of this bird, the white pelican (*pelicanus onocrotalus*) and the Dalmatian pelican (*pelicanus crispus*), occur in Palestine, neither can be meant; for these birds always live close to water and feed on fishes, whereas the *ḳā'āth* is expressly said to haunt ruins (Zeph 2[14], where the AV has '**cormorant**,' which is impossible for the same reason) and desert land (Ps 102[6]) and is regarded as a symbol of desolation (Is 34[11]); further, it is in no sense an unclean bird, as the *ḳā'āth* is said to be (Lv 11[18] Dt 14[17]). The name is best explained as an onomatopoeic attempt to represent the owl's hoot; for Symmachus' *nuktikorax* 'long-eared owl' suggests some such bird. It is perhaps rather the 'scops-owl,' which is very common about olive-groves and old ruins in Palestine. This bird's cry is given as 'kiu-kiu' monotonously repeated at regular intervals, and *ḳā'āth* may be easily taken as a participial formation from an otherwise unknown *ḳî'* 'to cry kiu-kiu.' Such a bird, being a *raptor*, will have been classified as unclean because of its habit of taking live prey; for eating the blood with the flesh was prohibited and what eats ritually unclean food may not itself be eaten for fear of conveying ceremonial contagion. See also VULTURE, 5. G. R. D.

PELONITE.—A designation applied to Helez, one of David's thirty heroes, 1 Ch 11[27], where it is probably a scribal error for **Paltite** (cf 2 S 23[26]); also of Helez, David's officer for the seventh month, 1 Ch 27[10], an Ephraimite. In the latter case it is possibly a gentilic from an unknown locality Palon. See HELEZ, 2. In 1 Ch 11[36] for 'Ahijah the Pelonite' we should probably read 'Eliam the Gilonite' (cf 2 S 23[34]).

PELUSIUM.—'The stronghold of Egypt,' Ezk 30[15f], must be Pelusium (so RSV; AV, RV **Sin**), the Egyptian name of which is not clearly known, or some fortress in its neighbourhood. In the list of governors appointed by Esarhaddon and Ashurbanipal, while native princes were retained elsewhere, Sin is the only city put in charge of an Assyrian; no doubt he was placed at Pelusium to keep the gate of Egypt open for the Assyrian king. F. Ll. G.

PEN.—**1.** Hebrew *ḥereṭ* in Is 8[1] (AV, RV) is a stylus for writing on a tablet. For 'with the pen of a man' RVm and RSV have 'in common characters,' but this is free interpretation. In Ex 32[4] the same word is rendered 'graving tool.' **2.** Hebrew *'ēṭ* Jer 8[8], Ps 45[1]) is probably a reed pen for writing on a scroll (cf Jer 36[2]). It also denotes an iron tool for use on stone (Job 19[24]), and sometimes it had a diamond point (Jer 17[1]). **3.** Hebrew *shēbheṭ* in Jg 5[14] (AV) is a rod or staff. Hence RV and RSV have 'marshal's staff' for 'pen of the writer.' It is more probable, however, that it denotes the symbol of office of the muster officer. **4.** Greek *kalamos* (3 Jn 13) is a reed pen. It is used in LXX to render **2** in Ps 45[1].

PENCIL.—See ARTS AND CRAFTS, **1**: LINE, **6**.

PENDANTS.—See AMULETS, ORNAMENTS, **2**.

PENIEL.—See PENUEL.

PENINNAH.—The second wife of Elkanah, 1 S 1[2, 4].

PENKNIFE.—Mentioned only in Jer 36[23]. Orientals use a reed pen in writing, and always carry a knife for the purpose of sharpening it.

PENNY.—See MONEY, **7**.

PENSION.—Only AV of 1 Es 4[56] (AVm 'portions of land,' RV 'lands'). This archaism is first found in the Geneva version, and is used in the original sense of 'payment' (Lat. *pensio*). RSV 'land and wages.'

PENTATEUCH.—The first five books in the OT, corresponding to 'The Law' (*tôrāh*), the first of the three divisions of the Hebrew Bible, commonly called by Jews 'the five-fifths of the Law.' Christian scholars as early as Tertullian and Origen adopted the name *Pentateuch* as a convenient title for these books. 'The Law' was regarded by the Jews as a unique and authoritative exposition of all individual and social morality; a wide gulf seemed to separate it from the book of Joshua, the first of the series of historical books known as 'The Former Prophets.' Such a division may be artificial and many scholars are of the opinion that the 'sources' apparent in the Pentateuch can be traced at least into Joshua. Hence the term *Hexateuch* for the books Genesis to Joshua, though the term is not in such common use as it was at the turn of the century. The Pentateuch contains not only 'The Law' proper but some account of the beginnings of the world and of civilization, and of the origins of Israel. But the giving of the Law at Sinai and its recapitulation (in Deuteronomy) by Moses, immediately prior to the entry into Canaan, were felt, with some justification, to be the climax of a long preparation of the chosen people.

I. THE PROBLEM OF AUTHORSHIP.—That Moses was the author of the Pentateuch was for long unquestioned. The basis of this belief was the Jewish tradition of its origin which the Church took over with the books themselves. Although it is nowhere said in the OT that Moses wrote *the whole of* the Pentateuch, there is little doubt that the words 'the book of the law of Moses' (Neh 8[1], and cf Chronicles, Ezra, Nehemiah, *passim*) were, by the beginning of the Christian era, understood to imply that he did. Similarly, the NT takes Moses' authorship for granted and it can hardly be denied that our Lord shared the common view.

When the first edition of this Dictionary was published, scholars trained in critical methods were well-nigh unanimous in denial of the Mosaic authorship, while the great majority of unacademic Christians still took the traditional view for granted. The situation to-day is somewhat different. Not all the learning is on one side. There are scholars who confidently affirm Mosaic authorship, notwithstanding that they have read all that is to be said to the contrary. For the 'fundamentalist'—to use the word without disparagement—the problem seems, in the last resort, to be largely one of conscience: to deny Mosaic authorship is to impugn the authority and plenary inspiration of Scripture, and even of our Lord himself. To this the 'critic,' in all good faith, replies that our Lord's 'knowledge' of questions of this kind was that of His contemporaries, and that the acceptance of such limitations was one condition of a true incarnation.

Such notes as 'At that time the Canaanites were in the land' (Gn 12[6]) and 'These are the kings who reigned in the land of Edom, before any king reigned over the Israelites' (Gn 36[31]), can hardly have been written by Moses. Nor is it probable that Moses wrote, 'Now the man Moses was very meek' (Nu 12[3]), and the account of his own death (Dt 34, especially vv.[10f]). But such occasional sentences or paragraphs are not proof that *the whole* Pentateuch is post-Mosaic. They could conceivably be later additions to a work which, *as a whole*, is by Moses. Indeed, this explanation of them is not uncommon among conservative scholars.

The Pentateuch nowhere claims to have been written by Moses, nor does it, on the whole, read as if it was. The bulk of Deuteronomy purports to be an address, or series of addresses, by Moses, and 31[9] says that 'Moses wrote this law.' But other references to Moses 'writing' certain sections (Ex 17[14] 24[4]) rather imply that he did not write the whole of the five books. The remainder of this article will attempt briefly to summarize: II. The Composition of the Pentateuch; III. The History of Criticism; IV. The Graf-Wellhausen Hypothesis; V. Characteristics of the Documents; VI. Recent Discussions.

II. COMPOSITION OF THE PENTATEUCH.—(*a*) There are in the Pentateuch—not including the Decalogue (Ex 20[1-17], Dt 5[1-21]), whose promulgation it is now very usual to assign to Moses—at least three collections of *laws*. They are (i) The Book of the Covenant (=C), Ex 21–23; (ii) 'The statutes and ordinances' of Dt 12–26 (=D); (iii) Laws relating to sacrifice, ritual 'cleanness' and 'uncleanness,' and the like, which occupy the bulk of Leviticus and large sections of Exodus and Numbers, and to which the name Priestly Code (=P) is often given.

(i) The laws of C are directed to the simple needs of an *agricultural* community. This is not in itself proof that they were not promulgated by Moses, since Moses is represented as giving to Israel laws which should be operative after the settlement in Canaan. In them three annual festivals are prescribed during which all male

Israelites must present themselves at a sanctuary. The preamble to the laws (Ex 20^{24f}) appears to say that a sanctuary, with an altar of earth or unhewn stones, might be built in any place where Yahweh had authentically revealed Himself.

(ii) Everything in D points to a more advanced civilization. There are seven festivals and their original agricultural character is subordinated to their religious significance. Many of the laws deal with the same matters as those of C and sometimes there is disagreement between them: *e.g.* in Ex 21$^{1-11}$ only male slaves are to be released after six years, but in Dt 15$^{12-18}$ female slaves are also to be manumitted. The most striking difference between C and D is that in the latter sacrifice may only be offered at one single sanctuary (Dt 12 *et passim*).

(iii) The laws in C and D deal largely with what we should call civil law; those in P are mainly concerned with matters ritual and ecclesiastical and do not, in general, conflict with C and D. Except in one important particular: in D all Levites are priests ('the Levitical priests,' Dt 18^{1} *et passim*); in P a clear distinction is made between the 'priests,' who must be descended from Aaron (Nu 3$^{1-4}$), and the Levites, who are descended from Levi (Nu 3$^{14-37}$) but not through the Aaronite branch of the tribe. The Levites are acolytes to the priests (Nu 3$^{5-10}$), a kind of third order in the descending scale High Priest, Priests, and Levites.

(*b*) Not only are there three collections of laws in the Pentateuch, there are three types of *narratives*. These correspond roughly, both in style and vocabulary, and in theological outlook and background, to the three corpora of laws. There is no mistaking this in Deuteronomy, which is throughout homogeneous in style, a style of which there are few or no traces elsewhere in the Pentateuch.

(i) This leaves us with Genesis, and the narrative portions of Exodus and Numbers. (The few narrative parts of Leviticus are in the same style as the laws.) In Genesis there are two distinct accounts of creation. In the first (1^{1}–2^{4a}) God is called *Elohim* (God) and the order of creation is vegetation, aquatic creatures and birds, mammals, and finally mankind (male and female together). In the second (2^{4b-24}) God is called *YHWH* (Yahweh) and the order is a man, vegetation, animals, and finally a woman. In the story of the Flood (6^{5}–9^{19}) some sections have Elohim, others Yahweh. In the Elohim sections Noah is told to take into the ark a single pair of each species of animals, 'clean' and 'not clean' alike (7$^{6-9}$); in the Yahweh sections (7$^{1-5}$) he is told to take seven pairs of 'clean' and one pair only of animals 'not clean.' The reason for this appears to be that the extra 'clean' animals would be required for the sacrifice to Yahweh (8^{20f}) after the Flood. It looks as if two narratives have been woven together instead of being put side by side as in Gn 1–2.

(ii) There are three stories of the 'sister-wife' (12$^{10-20}$, Yahweh; 20, Elohim; 26$^{6-11}$, no Divine name, and Isaac, not Abraham). In the story of Joseph as it now stands (Gn 37), Midianite traders take Joseph out of a pit and sell him to a caravan of Ishmaelites (v.^{28}). Yet the Midianites sell him to an Egyptian, Potiphar (v.^{36}). Notwithstanding, in 39^{1} Potiphar bought him from the Ishmaelites. The contradictions are resolved if one story told how, at the suggestion of Reuben, Joseph was cast into a pit from which he was stolen by the Midianites (37$^{22-24,\ 28a}$), while in the other (37$^{25-27,\ 28b}$) Judah persuaded his brothers to sell Joseph to the Ishmaelites. In v.^{28} the two narratives have crossed: originally the Midianites 'lifted' and Joseph's brothers 'sold' him. For the details of the passages mentioned above, and for examples of other dual narratives in Genesis, Exodus (*e.g.* the plagues), and Numbers (*e.g.* the spies, 13 f, and the rebellion of Korah, Dathan, and Abiram, 16 f), the reader is referred to the standard Introductions and Commentaries.

More often than not, the *Elohim* sections of Genesis agree in their catalogical style, in their fondness for dates and genealogies, and in their theological conceptions, with the 'P' laws: *e.g.* the absence of any sacrifice and, by implication, of 'spare' pairs of 'clean' animals, from the Elohim account of the Flood, agrees with the theological standpoint of P, according to which there was no animal sacrifice until God gave to Moses the rubrics of sacrifice (Lv 1). (The name Yahweh in Leviticus occasions no difficulty, since after Ex 6^{2} 'P' does not scruple to call God 'Yahweh.')

(iii) Almost invariably in Genesis any mention of a patriarch sacrificing is associated with *Yahweh*. But Gn 22$^{1-13}$ tells of a sacrifice, presumably to *Elohim* (though note *Yahweh* in vv.$^{14-18}$). The story of Abraham's offering of Isaac has more in common with the Yahweh (generally denoted by the symbol J = Yahwistic) stratum of the Pentateuch, than it has with the Elohim story of creation and genealogical paragraphs like those in Gn 5. There thus appear to be two *Elohim* strata in Genesis, one related to P and the other more akin to J. J and the non-P (= E) narratives are sometimes called 'JE,' and after Ex 3^{13f} it is often difficult to separate J from E. There is no decisive evidence of any relation between the JE stories and the C laws; but if the 'P' materials in Genesis should go with the P laws, and the narrative portions in Deuteronomy with the D laws, it is probable that the JE stories were current in the milieu of the C laws. There are many indications of this: *e.g.* the altars of Ex 20$^{24-26}$ were almost certainly to be found in places where the patriarchs were reputed to have sacrificed, such as Shechem (Gn 12^{7}), Bethel (Gn 12^{8} 28^{18} 35^{1}), and Beersheba (Gn 21^{33} 26$^{23-25}$).

III.—History of Criticism.—(*a*) The first writer to deal with the problem in a systematic way was Jean Astruc, physician to Louis xiv., who in 1753 published a short monograph of which the English title would be 'Conjectures on the memoirs which Moses appears to have used in composing the book of Genesis.' Astruc did not deny the Mosaic authorship. He noted the alternation of the Divine names Elohim and Yahweh, and conjectured that there were two main sources in Genesis. This became known as the **Documentary Hypothesis.** Next, Eichhorn observed that the variation of Divine names was regularly accompanied by characteristic differences of language and historical standpoint. Further investigation revealed the presence of two 'Elohim' sources [see II. (*b*) (iii) above].

(*b*) It was only a question of time before the methods of critical analysis should be applied to the other books of the Pentateuch (and Hexateuch). But the absence of the criterion of the two Divine names (after Ex 6^{2}) made progress difficult. Added difficulty was presented by the bewildering variety of laws and stories associated with the transactions at Mount Sinai. Vater (1802), a German, held that the frequent repetitions and varying phraseology could only be explained on the assumption that we are dealing with an agglomeration of unconnected fragments, subsequently collected and not inharmoniously patched together by an industrious student of Israel's early literature and antiquities. He supposed that Deuteronomy originated in the time of David and that it formed the kernel round which the rest of the Pentateuch was gradually added. This was known as the **Fragment Hypothesis.**

(*c*) The weakness of the Fragment Hypothesis was that it ignored the indications of a unifying principle and definite plan which are revealed by the Pentateuch as a whole. This was made abundantly clear by de Wette, who sought to supplement purely literary by historical criticism. Accordingly, he made a comparison between the Pentateuchal laws and the materials in the historical books. This convinced him (1805) that Deuteronomy presented a picture of Israelite life and worship unknown before Josiah's reformation. It was only a short step from this to the identification of D with the lawbook discovered in the Temple in the reign of Josiah and adopted by that king as the basis for his reforms. But again there was reaction, this time from exclusively historical and back to literary methods of

PENTATEUCH

investigation. This resulted in establishing the connexion between the first Elohist [=' P ' above, II. (*b*) (i)] of Genesis and the P legislation of Exodus, Leviticus, and Numbers. This corpus of materials was taken to be the *Grundschrift* or primary document, which was supposed to have been supplemented and revised by the Yahwist (J). This is known as the **Supplement Hypothesis.** The difficulty it had to encounter was that of placing the Yahwist in the category of a mere supplementer. The more his work is studied the more is he seen to have been a writer of outstanding originality and genius.

(*d*) This brings us back to some form of **Document Hypothesis.** The position as it stood about the middle of the 19th cent. may be summarized : (1) There are two 'Elohistic' sources in Genesis–Numbers, *viz.* P and E ; (2) P, with its detailed chronology and genealogies, is the framework into which the other materials have been fitted ; (3) The Yahwist, no less than P and E, must be regarded as an independent source ; (4) D is to be dated 7th cent. B.C. ; (5) It was assumed that P, which provided the framework and whose distinctive vocabulary and theological conceptions can be easily identified throughout Genesis to Numbers, is the earliest of the ' documents.' That would give a probable order in time of P, JE, D.

IV. THE GRAF-WELLHAUSEN HYPOTHESIS.—So far little had been done to inquire into the mutual relations of the documents. A provisional solution had been reached as to the extent of the several sources, but it had hardly occurred to anyone that P, JE, and D were the embodiments, so to speak, of historical processes through which Israel passed during a period of centuries. Graf (1866) made a comparison between the sources themselves, and, assuming the identity of D with Josiah's lawbook as a fixed point of departure, concluded that while D presupposes the laws in Ex 20–23 (C) and 34, the bulk of the P laws (and that would imply also the P *Grundschrift*) must have been unknown to D. Testing this result by the external evidence of books outside the Pentateuch, he concluded that P could not have been produced before the Exile, and that in all probability it was compiled by Ezra.

Graf's theory was adopted and worked out in detail by Wellhausen, whose *Prolegomena zur Geschichte Israels* (1883 ; English Translation, *History of Israel*, 1885) came to be widely regarded as a final solution of the problem. In Wellhausen's opinion a comparison of the laws with the evidence supplied by the prophetical and historical books shows that ' the three great strata of laws embodied in the so-called books of Moses are not all of one age, but correspond to three stages in the development of Israel's institutions.' He pointed out that there are no valid grounds for distinguishing between the legal and the historical sections : JE, which is mainly narrative, embodies the C legislation ; D gives a full historical presentation ; P supplies the framework of the whole. The chronological order of the documents is JE, D, P. Such was the regnant hypothesis when the first edition of this *Dictionary* was published. Full details of it may be found in S. R. Driver, *An Introduction to the Literature of the OT* (1891 ; 9th ed. 1913), which is still a standard work and easily accessible.

V. CHARACTERISTICS OF THE DOCUMENTS.—(*a*) **D.**—It is convenient to begin with Deuteronomy, since it is more self-contained than the other sources. It also exhibits, more immediately than they, evidence of independent thought and language, and its date, in the opinion of most scholars, can be determined with something approaching certainty.

From 2 K 22 f we learn that ' the book of the law ' discovered in the Temple created consternation, and provided the basis for the reformation undertaken by King Josiah in 621 B.C. The theory that this book was the Pentateuch, composed centuries before, long fallen into oblivion, accidentally rediscovered, and now adopted as the rule of national conduct, is quite unrealistic. It is incredible that the whole Pentateuch should have been lost and forgotten, and the reason why the book made so great an impression was that to everyone concerned it brought an entirely *new* message. Nor is it possible that ' all the words of the book ' could be read aloud in one day (23^{2}), if the book was the whole Pentateuch. And nothing in the story suggests that only selections from the book were read.

If negative evidence shows that the lawbook was only a part of the Pentateuch, positive reasons leave little room for doubt that it was some form of Deuteronomy, whether the whole book, or the central corpus of laws (12–26) plus, almost certainly, ch. 28, with its blessings and curses. Josiah's reformation followed the requirements of the lawbook. It consisted in an entire reform of Israelite religion, the abolition of local sanctuaries and the centralization of all sacrificial worship in the Jerusalem Temple. It closed with a celebration of the Passover, by the entire people (2 K 23^{21f}), in accordance with the ceremonies prescribed in the book (Dt 16).

The language and style of Deuteronomy are very marked. It contains comparatively few unusual words, but the repetitions of words, phrases, and even entire clauses, gives it a distinctive colouring, so that even the reader who knows no Hebrew can immediately recognize a passage of Deuteronomic authorship or written under Deuteronomic influence ; *e.g.* much in the books of Kings.

Theologically, the distinctive feature of D is the law of the one sanctuary, which is repeatedly enforced with solemn warnings. (That the law of the one sanctuary was unknown in Elijah's time is clear from 1 K 18^{30} 19^{10}.) But the modern reader is more likely to be struck by the emphasis on Yahweh's love for and ' choice ' of Israel, coupled with the demand for Israel's responsive love for Yahweh. With this there goes the frequent exhortation to humane treatment of the poor, of slaves, the widow and the orphan, and the ' sojourner.' This was a legacy from the teaching of the prophets. The influence of the prophets is also to be seen in the doctrine of moral retribution, so prominent in all the Deuteronomic writings.

(*b*) **P.**—If D is a prophetic reformulation of the laws of C, P shows how, in the period following the Exile, when theocracy was embodied in priestly ideals, the early history of Israel was once more reinterpreted. The law of the one sanctuary in D was a practical application of Isaiah's doctrine of the sanctity and inviolability of Zion ; P's distinction between priests and Levites is really the outcome of Ezekiel's solution (Ezk 44) of the difficulty which arose when the high places were suppressed, and the priests who had served them were deprived of livelihood. It was Ezekiel's plea that the Levites should forfeit full priestly status because of their participation in the idolatry which had characterized worship at the high places, and be degraded to the performance of the menial duties of the Jerusalem Temple. (Ezekiel would have confined the priesthood to the Zadokite branch of the Aaronites—cf 1 Ch 6^{8} ; P admitted all who claimed descent from Aaron.) A comparison of the theology and the historical situation presupposed by P shows that it originated later than Ezekiel : *e.g.* there is no mention anywhere in the historical books of the Day of Atonement (Lv 16), which in post-exilic times became the most important day in the calendar. This refers only to the literary formulation of P, not to all its contents, much of which (*e.g.* the ' Law of Holiness,' Lv 17–26, and the antique conception of quasi-physical ' holiness,' Lv 6^{27f}) is plainly derived from more ancient sources. But P is much more than rubrics dealing with ritual. It aims at giving, from the priestly standpoint, a systematic account of the ' origins,' both political and religious, of Israel. Accordingly, chronological lists, enumerations of names, and other statistics are a prominent feature of its narrative, and by these signs throughout the Pentateuch it is easy to distinguish it. As a rule, it is content to give a bare outline of the history, except where it is necessary to explain the origin of some ceremony or institution (*e.g.* Gn 17). In representing God's dealings with men, P shrinks from the forcible language of earlier writers. Anthropomorphisms are rare, angels and dreams are not mentioned. On the other hand, P nowhere deals with those deeper spiritual problems—the origin of evil, the purpose of election, the universal mission of Israel—which were sympathetically, if not systematically, treated in other sources of the Pentateuch.

The style of P is scarcely less distinctive than that of D. It is 'stereotyped, measured, and prosaic,' with frequent repetitions of stated formulas. There is little doubt that it is the literary and historical framework of Genesis–Numbers; but the first assumption that it was therefore the earliest document has not been borne out by later investigation. It is incredible that in the early days of the monarchy sacrifices were offered at one single sanctuary served by High Priest, priests, and Levites—such was the organization in post-exilic and down to NT times—and that *later* (so we should have to conclude from JE) the single sanctuary principle was abandoned to permit a multiplicity of altars served by nondescript orders of priests. In that case, how did the Aaronite priests and the Jerusalem Temple regain the control they undoubtedly exercised in post-exilic times? In other words, the history is intelligible if the order is JE–D–P, but unintelligible if the order is P–JE–D, or P–D–JE. At the same time, although P 'assumed finally the shape in which we have it in the age subsequent to Ezekiel, it rests ultimately upon an ancient traditional basis. . . . The laws of P, even when they included later elements, were still referred to Moses—no doubt because in its basis and origin Hebrew legislation was actually derived from him, and was only modified gradually' (Driver, *op. cit.*, 154).

(*c*) **JE.**—We now come to the non-P (=JE) sections of Genesis–Numbers, to which should be added the closing chapters (32–34) of Deuteronomy. Critical analysis of this material has already suggested that it is composite, embodying two distinct traditions, J and E [see *supra*, II. (*b*) (iii)]. Both strands cover much the same ground and were probably composed at about much the same time. The whole is characterized by a superficial homogeneity and by the same general religious beliefs and hopes. Yet the original independence of the two strands is so manifest that it has become a generally accepted conclusion of criticism. J and E are distinguishable in three ways: they often tell a different story, they employ different language, and convey a different message.

It is in the stories of the patriarchs that we first become aware of different accounts, neither of which can be assigned to P, of the same incidents. The use of 'Yahweh' by J, and 'Elohim' by E, provides a simple criterion, though this is not always available, especially after Ex 3^{13f}. Other differences, not sufficient in themselves to prove diversity of authorship, are yet sufficiently numerous to lend support to the two-sources hypothesis. These differences are not due merely to literary artifices. E's interest in the northern sanctuaries points to North Israelitish origin; for a similar reason J is almost certainly of Judahite provenance. Along with this, in J Judah, in E Reuben, is the leader among the sons of Jacob.

J is a patriot who takes a pride in Israel's early history. But he does more than tell a story, he presents what may, with some justification, be called a theology of history. He embodies in his narrative reflections on the origin of sin and on its dire consequences. He realizes that Yahweh's call to Abraham is according to purpose, a purpose that embraces mankind; that Israel has a mission *in*, if not yet *to*, mankind. He is a creative artist who gave permanent shape to an interpretation of history which was only elaborated in the framework of P. His style is flowing and picturesque. His psychological verisimilitude and insight are unsurpassed in the epic- and saga-literature of the world. When he speaks of Yahweh he is uninhibited by theological scruples, and uses anthropomorphic and even anthropopathic language without reserve.

E is more restrained, more didactic, and more theological. That he wrote after the beginnings of the prophetical movement is obvious: Abraham is called a prophet, Miriam a prophetess. Moses is a prophet in all but name; the seventy elders receive prophetic inspiration (Nu 11). The importance of high moral standards is emphasized. God reveals Himself in dreams and the forceful language of J is toned down to the demands and fears of a more timorous reverence. E ignores Israel's mission in the world, has little or no interest in other peoples, or in the universal significance of Israel's history. His work may be said to draw from the early history of Israel's ancestors a much needed lesson for the age in which he wrote, a lesson of the importance of ethical standards and of the reverence due to Elohim.

There is general agreement that both J and E, in their present written forms, date from after the establishment of the monarchy, say the 9th cent. B.C. E, which is the more ethically sophisticated, may be somewhat later than J. It has long been recognized that the stories they tell are not their own free invention and that centuries of oral tradition lie behind them. Indeed, archaeology has demonstrated that some of the details in the patriarchal stories accord with the cultural milieu of the 2nd millennium B.C., in which the patriarchs are represented as living, rather than with that of the 1st millennium in which the older critics supposed they were 'written.'

VI. Recent Discussions.—Since the publication of the First Edition of this *Dictionary* the sources hypothesis as outlined in the foregoing paragraphs has been vigorously challenged. In outlining the position as it stands to-day it seems best to take the sources in the order in which they have been characterized in V. above, and finally to review the problem as a whole.

(*a*) **D.**—Attempts have been made to date D considerably earlier than the 7th cent. B.C. (A. C. Welch), or after the exile (G. Hölscher, R. H. Kennett). Neither of these suggestions has met with any widespread approval.

Another suggestion is that D was not originally a component part of a 'Pentateuch' but the first of a series of writings—'The Deuteronomic History'—which included the historical books Joshua to Kings (M. Noth). This would leave us with a *Tetrateuch* rather than a Pentateuch. It has already been noted that D, although it obviously takes up and revises the C laws, has hardly any literary affinity—except in chs. 32–34, which may once have stood at the end of Numbers—with Genesis–Numbers. On the other hand, Deuteronomic influence on Joshua–Kings (especially Judges and Kings) is unmistakable. There is much to be said for Noth's thesis, which does not negate the conclusion that the chronological order of the laws is C, D, P.

(*b*) **P.**—The early critics had to base their conclusions almost entirely upon the internal evidence of the OT. This was because external evidence of the kind furnished by archaeology (excavations in Bible lands) was, to say the least, meagre. But they were always ready to admit that although P, as a written 'document,' was post-exilic, it nevertheless contains much that has its roots in conceptions which are much older; in other words that not everything in P is the *ad hoc* invention of its author(s). This has been abundantly confirmed by archaeology. P is the product of a kind of counter-reformation, in which a good deal of what D would have stigmatized as heathenish had, with the final triumph of Yahwism over the Baal-principle, been rendered innocuous and could therefore be given a place in the Temple ritual without inviting a relapse into heathenism. Much in P is in line with Ezekiel, for whom ritual 'cleanness' and moral holiness were indivisible. At the same time it is probable that P's conception of the 'atoning' efficacy of *all* sacrifice (cf Lv 1^4), and his emphasis on sin- and guilt-offerings, was new; pre-exilic sacrifice was eucharistic, not penitentiary, and the staple sacrifices were the peace-offering and the burnt-offering.

(*c*) **JE.**—There are some evidences that J, at least in

the primeval history (Gn 1–11), is not homogeneous. Some passages (Gn 4[16–24] 6[1–4] 11[1–9]) seem to know nothing of the Flood. Accordingly it has been common to distinguish two strands in it, J^1 and J^2. Otto Eissfeldt (1922) called the first of these L (=*Laienschrift* or 'Lay-document,' as being at the other extreme from the priestly source P) and he traced it throughout the Hexateuch. But the general tendency has been to reduce, rather than increase, the emphasis on 'documents.' Reference to any tabulation of the documents will show that E is more fragmentary than J. This may be either because the original E was briefer than J—there are no certain evidences of it in Gn 1–11—or because much of it was sacrificed when J and E were combined. However that may be, P. Volz and W. Rudolph (1933) proposed that 'E' is no more than so much supplement to J. Even if this were so, we should have to take account of the supplementary materials in writing a history of OT religion.

A more radical challenge to the documentary hypothesis has come from Scandinavia (J. Pedersen, 1931; Ivan Engnell 1945). According to Engnell it is in principle wrong to look for continuous parallel documents in the (for him) Tetrateuch. Such 'documents' never existed. Little of what we have, except legal sections like C, was deposited *in writing* until after the Exile. It received its present shape in *a traditionist circle* whose ideas were, by and large, those of the writer known to the critics as P. For the rest, the 'JE' of the critics must be taken as we have it, without attempting to separate it out into different strands. These non-P materials had long been current in oral tradition, and oral tradition can have all the fixity of written documents. Indeed, we can even speak of 'oral "literature."' No reliance, it is said, can be placed on the Divine names criterion, because 'the LXX shows inescapably that the variation in the divine names in the Hebrew text must be the result of a later process of unification; the variation is not original.' (Engnell, article 'Mosebӧckerna' in *Svenskt Bibliskt Uppslagsverk*, II, 1952, 329a.)

These contentions may be answered briefly: (1) Since, in its use of the Divine names, the Samaritan Pentateuch agrees with the Hebrew in over three hundred cases and differs from it in only eight or nine, the Hebrew text-tradition is obviously more reliable than the Greek; (2) If 'oral "literature"' can have all the fixity of 'written,' it is quite proper to apply source-critical methods to it. That means that we are more or less where we were.

To conclude, as matters now stand, there is less confidence than there was in assigning this or that word or half verse to Document X or Redactor Y. We are not to think of editors or redactors who sat at desks spread with manuscript documents, which they proceeded to dovetail together in the manner of Tatian composing his *Diatessaron.* Nevertheless, it would appear that the foundations of the sources-hypothesis were well and truly laid by Wellhausen and his predecessors. They may—inevitably in the circumstances, and working, as they did, with little help from archaeology—have been too much influenced by the then dominant theory of evolutionary progress; but the history of OT religion and institutions which they saw epitomized in the Pentateuch has a verisimilitude which is not to be easily gainsaid. It is often said that 'the Pentateuch is an epitome of the history of Israel's religion' (Peake's *Commentary on the Bible*, 1919, 130a). Christianity is committed to the faith that God has revealed Himself in history. Pentateuchal criticism is not an end in itself, or a pastime engaged in by scholars 'who like that sort of thing.' Its function is the ancillary but nevertheless important function of helping to clarify the history of the revelation which was mediated through history.

E. A. E.—**C. R. N.**

PENTECOST, FEAST OF.—1. The name for this feast in Israel was **the Feast of Weeks** (Ex 34[22], Dt 16[10]) or the **Feast of Harvest** (Ex 23[16]); it was also called the **Day of First-fruits** (Nu 28[26]). It marked the end of the barley harvest and the beginning of the wheat harvest, and was, almost certainly, a midsummer feast taken over by the Israelites from the ancient Canaanites. Otherwise little is known about it in the early days. It became one of the three pilgrimage feasts (Dt 16[16]), but, only once mentioned outside the Law (2 Ch 8[13]), it clearly played a much smaller and less important part than Passover or Tabernacles. It was calculated, according to Dt 16[9], seven weeks after the sickle had been put to the standing grain. In the priestly law, it was calculated seven weeks or fifty days after the Sabbath that followed Passover (Lv 23[15f]); it involved rest from work and was marked by the note of joy; it lasted one day (though the later Jews allowed two for it, because in the Dispersion, it was difficult to determine accurately the Palestinian month). Two leavened loaves of wheaten flour were waved before the Lord; two yearling lambs were also waved as a peace-offering; seven lambs, one bullock, and two rams were offered as a burnt-offering, and one kid of the goats as a sin-offering (Lv 23[17–21]). In Nu 28[27] the burnt-offerings are given as two bullocks, one ram, and seven lambs. These, perhaps, were supplementary to the offerings prescribed in Lv 23, where possibly only the sacrifices connected with the loaves are specified. Lv 23[22] also prescribes freewill offerings for the poor and the stranger, while Dt 16[10f] ordains a freewill offering for the sanctuary, and states that the festal joy is to be shared by all classes. Some scholars think that Dt 26[2–11] refers to this feast (though others find obstacles to the identification). If they are right, then Dt 26 provides a form of confession and thanksgiving that had been in use probably for centuries before the promulgation of the law of Deuteronomy in 621 B.C., and shows, particularly in the *credo* of vv.[5ff], how far the Canaanite agricultural feasts had been historicized at a very early date.

2. In later Judaism, the Pharisees and Sadducees disagreed over the interpretation of Lv 23[15], the Pharisees reckoning always fifty days after 16th Nisan. For both, the feast of Weeks came to be regarded as 'the concluding feast of Passover.' It partially retained the character of a harvest festival, as is shown by the fact that the book of Ruth was among the appointed lections, and the firstfruits of the priests were offered with a reading of Dt 26[3–10]. Yet the description 'concluding feast' and the Greek name 'Pentecost' (the fiftieth day) show that it largely lost its original meaning and importance. As a consequence of the destruction of the Jerusalem Temple in A.D. 70, this harvest festival was reinterpreted to commemorate the giving of the Law at Sinai. Passover and Tabernacles were already connected with the Exodus and Wilderness traditions respectively. The giving of the Law was thought, on the basis of Ex 19[1] to have taken place fifty days after the Exodus. The first reliable witness to this interpretation is *c* A.D. 150 (it is not found in Philo or Josephus); and the fact that the reading of the law in the sabbatical year took place at the Feast of Tabernacles and not at Pentecost, points to the late origin of the interpretation.

3. In the Christian Church Pentecost was the occasion on which the outpouring of the Holy Spirit occurred (the fiftieth day after the Resurrection, Ac 2[1]). The presence of multitudes at Jerusalem shows the generality of the observance which the Jews paid to this feast. It became one of the Church's great festivals, as the anniversary of the spiritual first-fruits procured through Jesus Christ's sacrifice. By the close of the 2nd cent. it was established as an occasion of Christian rejoicing. No fasting or kneeling in prayer was allowed during this feast, and it was especially a season for baptisms. It became known popularly as Whitsunday, and now ranks, after Easter, as the second of the festivals of the Christian Church.

A. W. F. B.—**D. R. J.**

PENUEL (once, Gn 32[30], **Peniel**).—A place E. of the Jordan at a ford of the Jabbok, at which Jacob wrestled

with the angel (Gn 32[24ff]), and said to be called Peniel (or Penuel), *i.e.* 'Face of God,' because Jacob said, 'I have seen God *face to face* . . .' (The mention of the 'face of God' in Gn 33[10] makes it possible that another explanation of the place-name is there alluded to.) If the name signifies 'Face of God' an analogy might be the headland known to Greek geographers as *Theou prosōpon* just S. of Tripoli in Phoenicia. It is probably mentioned in the list of the conquests of the Pharaoh Sheshonk, the contemporary of Jeroboam I., being there called Per-nu-al. Penuel is mentioned also in the history of Gideon, as a place with a strong tower, or fort, which Gideon destroyed (Jg 8[8f, 17]); it may be inferred from this passage that Penuel was a little E. of **Succoth** (q.v.) and on higher ground. Penuel was fortified by Jeroboam after the Disruption (1 K 12[25]), doubtless to secure Gilead, which, incidentally, had remained loyal to David in Absalom's revolt. Merrill, followed by Albright and Glueck, has identified Penuel with *Tulûl edh-Dhahab* ('the mounds of gold'), so called from the yellow metaliferous sandstone of which they are composed, two conical hills, about 250 feet high, round which the Jabbok forms a loop about 5 miles E. of the Jordan. Glueck has located Penuel particularly at the eastern mound, where he found Early Iron Age potsherds, and there is no good reason to doubt this location.
S. R. D.—**J. Gr.**

PEOPLE.—This is the translation used in AV for a large number of Hebrew and Greek terms. In some cases ambiguity occurs, as the plural **'peoples'** is not used in AV except in Rev 10[11] 17[15]. Thus 'people' is used sometimes of the people of Israel and often of heathen nations. RV and RSV use 'peoples' freely, and this makes the meaning much clearer in such passages as Ps 67[4], Is 55[4] 60[2] etc. (see NATIONS, also preface to RV).

A special phrase **'the people of the land'** occurs frequently in the OT, especially in Jeremiah, Ezekiel, 2 Kings, and 2 Chronicles. In most of these cases it means the general body of the people, the common people as opposed to the courtiers or the ruling class. In Gn 23[7, 12f], Nu 14[9] the term is applied to non-Israelites. In the books of Ezra and Nehemiah the 'people of the land' are the half-heathen, half-Jewish population with whom the less scrupulous Jews intermarried, but who were avoided by the stricter party represented by Ezra and Nehemiah (Ezr 10[2, 11], Neh 10[30f]; cf Ezr 9[1f], Neh 9[30]). The same phrase was used by the Rabbis to describe the common people who were lax in observing the Mosaic law (Jn 7[49]; RSV 'this crowd'). W. F. B.

PEOR.—**1.** A mountain E. of the Jordan to which Balak led Balaam, Nu 23[28]; its exact location is uncertain, but it was near Beth-peor (q.v.) in the neighbourhood of Mount Nebo. **2.** It stands for **Beth-peor** in Jos 22[17] (so RSV; AV, RV 'the iniquity of Peor,' see **3**). **3.** It stands for **Baal-peor** (q.v.) in Nu 25[18] 31[16] (also in Jos 22[17] in AV, RV). **4.** A place in Judah not far from Bethlehem, mentioned in LXX in Jos 15[59] (absent from Hebrew); modern *Khirbet Faghûr*.

PERAEA.—The region called by Josephus 'the Peraea' is referred to in the NT as 'beyond the Jordan' (Mt 19[1], Mk 3[8]) in obvious dependence on OT usage (Gn 50[10] etc.). When Josephus says that it stretches from Machaerus to Pella, and from Philadelphia ('Ammân) to the Jordan, he probably gives political boundaries, excluding Decapolis (*BJ* III. iii. 3 [46]). The name seems to have covered the ancient 'Land of Gilead,' what is now known as *Jebel 'Ajlūn*. But Josephus also uses it in a broader sense when he calls Gadara its capital (*BJ* IV. vii. 3, 6 [413, 439]).

Transjordan had become strongly Hellenistic under the Seleucids. Judas Maccabaeus found it necessary to remove the Jews from the northern areas (1 Mac 5[45]). Later the Jews sought to destroy the Hellenistic cities and make the area Jewish. Alexander Jannaeus held sway over most of Transjordan at the time of his death. But Pompey rehabilitated the Hellenistic cities. (See DECAPOLIS.) In 23 B.C. Augustus conferred Trachonitis, Batanaea and Auranitis on Herod, and several years later augmented this with the tetrarchy of Zenodorus, composed of Ulatha, Paneas, and the region adjacent to the Sea of Galilee. Herod was also permitted to name his brother Pheroras tetrarch of Peraea (*Ant.* XV. x. 3 [362] etc.). Later it came to Herod Antipas (XVII. viii. 1 [188]). From Peraea, Simon made his ill-starred raid upon Jericho (XVII. x. 6 [273ff]). It was part of the jurisdiction of Felix (*BJ* II. xii. 8 [247]). Manasseh was made governor after the disaster to Cestius (II. xx. 4 [566]). Placidus effected its final subjugation to the Romans (IV. vii. 3, 6 [413, 439]). It was attached by the Moslems to the province of Damascus. Subsequently it was under Kerak.

The Mishnah recognizes the land beyond the Jordan as a province of the land of Israel, ranking with Judaea and Galilee on the W. According to Mk 10[1] and Mt 19[1] (but not Luke) Jesus' final journey to Jerusalem was through Peraea, and according to Jn 10[40] he retired 'across the Jordan to the place where John at first baptized'—*i.e.* in Peraea. It was probably on the border of Peraea that Jesus was baptized. W. E.—**E. G. K.**

PERAZIM.—A mountain mentioned in Is 28[21]; see BAAL-PERAZIM.

PERDITION.—The word is used twice in the NT in the ordinary sense of 'destruction,' with special reference to the destruction of the soul (Rev 17[8, 11]). It is also found twice in the phrase **son of perdition**—a Hebrew expression denoting close connexion between product and producer (cf 'sons of thunder,' 'sons of light,' etc.). In Jn 17[12] the phrase is applied to Judas Iscariot, while in 2 Th 2[3] it is used of the 'man of sin,' or Antichrist. In the latter context a great deal of discussion has centred round the meaning of the reference (see article ANTICHRIST). It will suffice here to point out that the phrase in 2 Th 2[3], 'the son of perdition,' combined with certain passages in the Apocalypse (ch. 13), points to a constant tradition in the Christian Church of the Apostolic Age, which appears, from the passages alluded to, to have conceived not of a foreign potentate alien to the Church, but rather of a false Messiah who should be 'sent to them that are perishing' (namely, the Jews), and was expected to make his appearance at Jerusalem. The phrase 'son of perdition' suggests not so much the power of destruction exerted upon those coming under the sphere of the evil influence, as the effect of wickedness upon the soul of the individual to whom the phrase, in each case, is applied. T. A. M.—**F. W. G.**

PERES.—See MENE.

PERESH.—A 'son' of Machir, 1 Ch 7[16].

PEREZ ('breach').—Son of Judah and Tamar, and twin brother of Zerah, Gn 38[29] (AV **Pharez**), 1 Es 5[5] (**Phares**); patronymic **Perezites**, Nu 26[20] (AV **Pharzites**). His importance consists in his being the ancestor of David through Boaz and Ruth, Ru 4[18-22], and then of Jesus Christ, Mt 1[3] (AV **Phares**). His descendants were in all probability the most numerous among the families in Judah; hence the blessing of the elders on Boaz: 'May your house be like the house of Perez,' Ru 4[12]. According to Gn 46[12], Perez had two sons, Hezron and Hamul. From Hezron, according to 1 Ch 2, came Jerahmeel and Ram and Caleb, and through Ram was traced the line of the royal house of David, Ru 4[19].
W. F. C.—**H. H. R.**

PEREZ-UZZA.—1 Ch 13[11]; see PEREZ-UZZAH.

PEREZ-UZZAH ('breach of Uzzah').—Name given to the place where Uzzah (q.v.) died, when the Ark was being conveyed to Jerusalem, 2 S 6[8], 1 Ch 13[11] (**Perez-uzza**).

PERFECTION.—**1. The Unique Biblical Conception.**—The kind of perfection which chiefly concerns the Biblical writers is, in the broadest sense, moral—the perfection of human character. In order to understand their use of the term, one must first divest it of meanings imported from other kinds of perfection. One of its common, non-moral meanings, for example, is ' conformity to a prescribed pattern,' as when a dancer executes a ' perfect ' pirouette, or a student answers a question ' perfectly.' Some moralists have attempted to conceive human perfection in the same way. In their view, human beings qualify for virtue like animals in a livestock show. The champion is the one that most nearly approximates the ideal model. Candidates for this kind of perfection are obliged to eliminate every mark which might differentiate them. Any residual, private characteristic constitutes a blemish. As all converge toward perfection, they become progressively indistinguishable from one another, like coins struck from the same die. Following its logic to the bitter end, advocates of this view have condemned individuality itself as an obstacle to perfection.

For the Bible, on the contrary, differentiation is a positive good (*e.g.* 1 Co 12, Eph 4[7, 12-13]). The Biblical writers complain that, instead of fulfilling their true destinies as unique, unrepeatable personalities, men yearn for stereotypes with which to mask themselves, from the totem of primitive tribe to the blue print of academic moralist. The stereotype thus usurps the rôle which belongs to God alone; it provides the frame of reference for the individual's whole life. According to the psalmist, men become as impersonal as the false gods they worship (*e.g.* Ps 115[8] 135[18]), whether the cycles and rhythms of nature, symbolized by the cult of Baal; the sophisticated abstractions of philosophy; or the leviathans of scientific technology.

The Biblical God, however, is Himself a Personality. Indeed, as has often been remarked, His is the most vivid of all the graphic portraits in OT. Bearing a proper name (see NAME), the sign of uniqueness, He likewise addresses each man by name: Samuel (1 S 3[4-10]), Elijah (1 K 19[9]), Amos (Am 7[8]), Mary (Jn 20[16]), Saul (Ac 9[4]). To respond is to abandon the security of anonymity and venture, like Abraham, into unknown territory (Gn 12[1]). One is promised, in partnership with God, a personality in one's own right; not a copy, but a ' new creation ' (2 Co 5[17]).

2. Relation to Rules.—Perfection of a non-moral kind can generally be achieved by following certain rules. Many thinkers have plausibly concluded that moral problems may be approached in the same way. Benjamin Franklin, for example, tells in his *Autobiography* how he hoped to arrive at moral perfection by adding one virtue to another, until the list was complete. Such a conception appears somewhat stultifying in comparison with that of the Biblical writers, who correlate perfection with *life*, in the fullest sense (*e.g.* Dt 30[15], Mt 19[17]). Their answer to all such legalistic systems is: ' If a law had been given which could make alive, then righteousness would indeed be by the law ' (Gal 3[21]). Hence they carefully limit the rôle of moral laws as guides to perfection. Taken as ends in themselves, such rules are all lumped together as ' the letter that killeth ' (AV 2 Co 3[6]), and the actions issuing from them are branded ' dead works ' (He 6[1] 9[14]). Although NT is more emphatic on this point than OT, the difference between them is often exaggerated. The NT polemic against ' works of law ' (see LAW [NT]) is really against a contemporary Jewish legalism, which itself missed the spirit of OT. NT writers make their case by appealing to OT itself.

The Hebrew word *tôrāh*, generally translated ' law,' might better be rendered ' ways of the Lord ' (see WAY). When the psalmist sings, ' Teach me thy ways,' he is not asking for legislative enactments, but for acquaintance with his Maker. The ' morals ' of OT are really more like manners. They can be transposed into extended adverbial clauses with a two-fold function: first, to disclose what ' manner ' of Person God is; and second, to infer what ' manner ' of life is appropriate to a living relationship with such a God: ' What does the Lord require of you but to do justice, and to love kindness, and to walk humbly with your God? ' (Mic 6[8]). The ' good works ' which the Bible enjoins have the same purpose as all manners. Negatively, they protect society from carelessness and ill will. Positively, they can become sacramental: a joyful participation in the life of God Himself.

Where Franklin's view of moral perfection was quantitative, the Bible's is qualitative—a style of life, rather than a sum of all the virtues. The most conclusive illustration is the Incarnation, which implies that God could put aside His infinite power and knowledge without altering His personality, and therefore without diminishing His perfection. A quantitative view of perfection, such as is implied by the Greek word *teleiōtes*, connotes a static condition, a finished, completed state. The surest axiom of Greek thought declares perfection to be incompatible with change. Once the goal is reached, further progress is impossible. Any change would be a change for the worse. A person imbued with these Greek presuppositions easily misses the whole point of the Biblical concept of ' walking in the ways of the Lord.' He assumes that the only persons who ' walk ' are those who have not yet arrived. The need to walk is a sign of imperfection.

He might support his interpretation by citing St. Paul's statement: ' Not that I have already obtained this or am already perfect; but I press on . . . toward the goal ' (Ph 3[12, 14]). Granted the element of ' straining forward to what lies ahead ' (Ph 3[13]) in the life of Jew and Christian, the crucial issue concerns the nature of ' the goal ' itself. Is it a static, immutable state? The answer completely contradicts the Greek: God Himself is active. The words with which the Bible describes Him are nearly all verbs: create, love, promise, judge, redeem, forgive, speak. St. Paul's goal is to enter more fully into dynamic, living relationship with such a God. Indeed, as he explicitly says a few lines earlier, what impedes him is precisely the tendency to define perfection in quantitative terms. To attain the goal is to shed the last remnants of a static ' righteousness . . . based on law ' (Ph 3[9]).

3. Perfection attainable.—Some interpreters of Christianity have concluded that the Bible, in common with many pagan philosophies, regards perfection as unattainable on earth. The very conditions of finite existence—space, time, and matter—are impurities which adulterate even the highest human achievement. Just as the champion show dog always bears some telltale imperfection, so human beings are doomed for ever to strive, and for ever to fall short. Perfection, being an ' ideal,' repels the ' actual,' by its very definition.

Here again, the Bible differs. Perfection is not beyond man's reach, but is ' very near you, . . . so that you can do it ' (Dt 30[14]). St. Paul, often cited in support of the post-biblical notion of ' original sin,' quotes this passage with approval (Ro 10[6-8]). His purpose is to show that heaven and earth are not disjunctive, that perfection is compatible with finite existence. To be sure, no man is without sin (q.v.). But sin is far more serious when perfection is a live option. That it is a live option for St. Paul is clear from his injunction, ' Be imitators of God ' (Eph 5[1]), which simply paraphrases Jesus' own words, ' You therefore, must be perfect, as your heavenly Father is perfect ' (Mt 5[48]). Since perfection is qualitative, a way rather than a state, a man can be progressively transformed ' from glory unto glory ' (2 Co 3[18] AV). A foretaste of the resurrected life is possible here and now (*e.g.* Ro 8[23], 2 Co 1[22]).

4. Relation to Love.—If Biblical perfection has appeared to some as unattainable in this life, the explanation may lie in still another connotation imported from non-Biblical sources. Outside Biblical thought, it is nearly universally agreed that the highest perfection is completely sufficient unto itself. Since the Bible emphatically denies that a man can gain perfection by himself alone, it might seem to suggest an intrinsic weakness of human nature. The Bible's aim, however, is not to disparage human nature, but to redefine perfection. Biblical perfection is the opposite of self-sufficiency. It consists in a special kind of relationship between man and man, and between men and God, translated, for want of a better word, as ' love ' (q.v.).

Love satisfies all the foregoing requirements of Biblical perfection. It is not an archetypal pattern, but the avenue to fulfilled, individual personality; not a quantitative accumulation of virtues, but an orientation of the heart; not attained by following rules, but rather the maker and judge of all rules; not static, but an active, living relationship; not self-sufficient, but mutual. To speak of attaining this kind of perfection by oneself alone is a contradiction in terms. It takes two to love. In fact, according to the Bible, it takes three. For when love is abandoned to purely human resources, without constant nurture and renewal by God, it disintegrates. The Bible therefore prefers to speak of perfection as something which happens to men, at the Divine initiative, rather than as a purely human achievement: 'God's love has been poured into our hearts by the Holy Spirit which has been given to us' (Ro 5^{5}). The perfection of man, though it requires his voluntary co-operation, is also the crowning handiwork of God. E. L. C.

PERFUMER.—The Oriental liking for odoriferous substances has always rendered the function of the perfumer an important one. The materials used in Bible times were gums, resins, roots, barks, leaves; and these were variously combined according to the skill and fancy of the perfumer. In Neh 3^{8} we read of a guild of perfumers. In several passages we should read 'perfumer' for '**apothecary**' of AV and RV (see APOTHECARY) or for '**confectionary**' (see CONFECTION). Further references to perfumes are Is 3^{20} (AV 'tablets') ^{24} 57^{9}, Pr 7^{17} 27^{9}, Ca 3^{6}.

PERGA.—An inland city of Pamphylia, about 12 miles from Attalia on the coast, but possessing a river harbour of its own on the Cestrus 5 miles away. Its walls date from the 3rd cent. B.C. It was the chief native city of Pamphylia, and never seems to have come much under Greek influence, but it had a coinage of its own from the 2nd cent. B.C. to A.D. 276. 'Artemis of Perga' was the chief object of worship, and she resembled 'Artemis of the Ephesians' in her rites and images, being sometimes represented like the Greek Artemis as goddess of the chase, but more often by a pillar of stone, the top of which was rounded or roughly carved to represent a head. Her worship was more Asiatic than Greek. Her temple probably possessed the right of sanctuary. The 1955–1956 excavations revealed part of the central colonnaded street of the city and soundings were made in the near-by agora. North of the triumphal arch behind the city gate, statues to Divus Nerva and others were discovered.

St. Paul passed through Perga twice on his first missionary journey. See PAMPHYLIA. But Christianity did not take root there easily. Perga is not mentioned in early martyrologies. When the Empire became Christian, it was the seat of a metropolitan bishop, but after the blow suffered by the Byzantine Empire at the battle of Manzikert, A.D. 1071, Perga seems to have fallen into the hands of the Turks. In A.D. 1084 we find Attalia made a metropolitan bishopric. The modern name of the site of Perga is *Murtana*.

A. E. H.—**E. G. K.**

PERGAMOS, Rev 1^{11} 2^{12} (AV) = **Pergamum** (q.v.).

PERGAMUM, or **PERGAMUS** (Gr. *Pergamon*, or *Pergamos*), to-day *Bergama*, was an ancient city of Mysia, the seat of an independent kingdom from about 280 to 133 B.C., when the last of the Attalid rulers bequeathed it to Rome, and the capital of the Roman province of Asia from 133 B.C. until the 2nd cent. A.D. It lay in the Caicus valley about 15 miles from the sea, and its acropolis rose between two tributary streams 3 miles N. of the Caicus. As the capital of a kingdom, Pergamum had acquired a considerable importance. But it stood on no great trade route, and under the Romans it slowly lost all but the official pre-eminence in the province. Its kings had been champions of Greek civilization and arts, and it still remained a centre of conservative culture. But Ephesus was now the centre of trade, and it was at Ephesus that West and East met together, creating a medley of all philosophies and all religions. At Pergamum there were splendid temples of Zeus and Athene, where these gods were worshipped in the ordinary Greek way, but others also of Dionysus and Asklepios. Its library rivalled Alexandria's and was largely transferred to that city by the Romans (see ALEXANDRIA). **Parchment** made from sheepskin or goatskin gets its name from Pergamum, and was allegedly invented by King Eumenes, founder of the library.

The only allusion to Pergamum in the NT is in the Apocalypse, where (1^{11} 2^{12}) it is included among the seven churches of Asia. The message to it (2^{12-17}) speaks of Pergamum as the place 'where Satan's throne is.' While it is possible that this refers to it as the chief seat of heathen worship in general, it is more probable that it refers to the worship of Rome and Augustus, participation in which had become a test of loyalty, and therefore a frequent ground of Christian martyrdom. Christians would be brought to Pergamum for trial from any northern part of the province, and the mention of one martyr, **Antipas,** as having suffered there does not prove that he belonged to Pergamum. The Church at Pergamum is charged with having 'some there who hold the teaching of **Balaam,** who taught Balak to put a stumbling-block before the sons of Israel, that they might eat things sacrificed to idols and practice immorality'; and also 'some who hold the teaching of the Nicolaitans.' We must gather from this that a definite section of the church at Pergamum maintained that, inasmuch as heathen ceremonies meant nothing (cf 1 Co 8^{4} 10^{19}), they were at liberty to join in idolatrous feasts, and thus to maintain their social position and justify their loyalty in the sight of the law. Important excavations were conducted at Pergamum by a German expedition in 1879–1886 and again from 1901 on. The great acropolis with its temples and palaces was dug up. Marvellous works of art were recovered—notably a great altar with sculptures of the Gigantomachy. A. E. H.—**E. G. K.**

PERIDA.—A family of 'Solomon's servants,' Neh 7^{57}: called **Peruda** in Ezr 2^{55}, 1 Es 5^{33} (AV **Pharira,** RV **Pharida**).

PERIZZITES.—They occur in numerous lists as one of the (mostly six) pre-Israelitish nations of Palestine (Ex $3^{8,17}$ 23^{23} 33^{2} 34^{11}, Dt 20^{17}, Jos 3^{10} 24^{11} etc.). Sometimes the term 'Canaanites and Perizzites' (Gn 13^{7} 34^{30}, Jg 1^{4}) seems to be a standard expression to designate the whole population of early Canaan. The Perizzites, however, do not appear anywhere definitely in history. Because in Gn 15^{20} and Jos 17^{15} they are mentioned with the Rephaim, some have inferred that they were one of the pre-Semitic tribes of Palestine. On the other hand it has been suggested that they were Canaanite agriculturists, living in unwalled towns, and not a separate tribe, since the name 'Perizzite' (in AV and RV of 1 Es 8^{69}, 2 Es 1^{21}, and AV of Jth 5^{16} **Pherezite[s]**) is in Hebrew almost identical with a word meaning 'dweller in an unwalled village.' Others have pointed out that the name seems to be of Hurrian origin, since the name of a messenger of King Tushratta in an Amarna Letter was *Pirizzi*, hence the Perizzites may have constituted a Hurrian clan. G. A. B.—**S. H. Hn.**

PERJURY.—See CRIMES AND PUNISHMENTS, **5.**

PERSECUTION.—According to the Gospels Jesus frequently warned His disciples that persecution would be the lot of all who followed Him (Jn $15^{18,20}$). So far from being dismayed at this, it should be a cause of rejoicing (Mt 5^{11f}). The early Church had not long to wait for the experience. Stephen's martyrdom (Ac 7^{58}) was followed by the scattering of the Hellenists (Ac 8^{1}). Saul of Tarsus was the moving spirit in this matter, until, on his way to Damascus to proceed against the disciples there. 'Christ's foe became His soldier.' The conversion of Saul seems to have ended the persecution. The attempt of Caligula to set up his statue in the Temple at Jerusalem (*c* A.D. 40) also diverted the attention of the Jews from all else. Hence 'the churches had rest' (Ac 9^{31}).

Another persecution was begun by Herod Agrippa I., who put to death the Apostle St. James, and would have done the same to St. Peter had he not been delivered. Herod's motive was probably to gain a cheap popularity, but the persecution was ended by his own sudden and terrible death (Ac 12^20–23^). For the most part the earliest persecutions were acts of mob violence.

At first Christianity was tolerated by the Roman magistrates as a Jewish sect, and what persecution there was came largely from Jewish authorities and from anti-Semitic pagan mobs (as mainly in the case of St. Paul's afflictions). The decision of Ac 15 brought the church out in the open. The persecution of Nero resulted in the martyrdoms of St. Peter (Jn 21^{19}, 2 P 1^{14}) and St. Paul (2 Ti 4^{6} and see 3^{12} for prediction of general persecution). That of Domitian is probably reflected in Revelation ; the church had now come into conflict with the cultus of Rome and the emperor (see EMPEROR WORSHIP). The dates and circumstances of He 10^{32ff} and 1 P 2^{19ff} are not certain. C. C. Ro.

PERSEPOLIS.—The chief capital of the ancient kings of Persia, chosen as such by Darius Hystaspis (521–486 B.C.). Imposing ruins still mark its site about 30 miles NE. of Shiraz. It is named in 2 Mac 9^{2} in connexion with the unsuccessful attempt of Antiochus Epiphanes to plunder its temples and palaces.

PERSEUS.—'King of Kittim,' *i.e.* Macedonia (1 Mac 8^{5}). His kingdom was brought to an end with his defeat by the Romans at Pydna (168 B.C.).

PERSIA, PERSIANS.—The Persians were the southern branch of the Iranian invaders who moved westwards and occupied the areas to the N. and E. of Mesopotamia during the 2nd millennium B.C. They were closely connected with the **Medes** (q.v.) who became dominant to the north and who are referred to in the 9th cent. B.C. The Persians are themselves not mentioned before the time of Cyrus. In the early 7th cent., Achaemenes established himself NE. of Susa and his son Teispes took Anshan from the Elamites. Phraortes of Media subdued him, and although subsequently he was able to gain control of the area called Persis, the Persians again came under Median control in the reign of Cyaxares in the latter half of the same century. In the 6th cent., however, their prince **Cyrus II.** (the Great, 559–529 B.C.), king of Anshan, threw off the Median yoke and deposed his overlord Astyages in *c* 549 B.C. Nabonidus of Babylon at first welcomed the weakening of the Medes, but soon the reality of Cyrus' threat to him became clear and an alliance of Babylon, Lydia, Egypt, and the Spartans faced Cyrus. In 546 B.C. he defeated Croesus of Lydia, and the Greek cities of the coastline of Asia Minor soon fell under Persian control. In 539 B.C. Nabonidus was defeated and Babylon surrendered to Cyrus' general Gobyras without fighting. Babylon thenceforth became one of the Persian capitals and the Babylonian empire was added to the already extensive Medo-Persian. Military superiority and skilled generalship combined to give these successes, and they were followed in the next years by further extensions of territorial control—to Egypt under Cambyses, and into the Greek mainland in the reign of Xerxes, where, however, he met with major defeat.

The Persian rulers styled themselves 'king of kings' and 'king of the lands'—rulers of the whole civilized world. They viewed their task as one of governing and unifying, and to this end pursued a policy much more humane and tolerant than that of earlier empires. Subject peoples occupied a tolerably independent position. Unification of the empire proceeded by provincial organization under satraps and by colonization, and throughout the west the Aramaic language was generally used (cf Elephantine papyri and Persian coinage). Persian readiness to adopt foreign customs (cf Herodotus i. 135) may be seen in their taking over of the Median culture, and in Cyrus' ascription of his rise to power to Marduk of Babylon—and, in other propaganda, to the deities of other nations (cf Ezr 1^{2-4} 6^{3-5}, Is 41^{1ff}). Later Persian rulers may be seen taking a similar interest in the religious affairs of their peoples. So Darius I. encouraged the native religion of Egypt and an inscription from Asia Minor shows him ordering scrupulous observance of the privileges of a sanctuary of Apollo. The OT provides evidence of similar generosity towards the Jews (cf Ezr 6^{6-12} 7^{11ff}, Neh 2^{1-10}. Cf also the Elephantine papyri [q.v.]). Persian religion, though strongly influenced by the reforming zeal of Zoroaster, remained tolerant and accommodating, and the old Persian gods were readily assimilated to the deities of the older near eastern civilizations.

The Jews, whose rebuilding of the Temple at Jerusalem and whose re-establishment as a community in Judah as part of the satrapy 'Beyond the River,' are attributed to the benevolence of Persian rulers, came into contact with various of the kings. Apart from Cyrus, the OT mentions Darius I. Hystaspis (522–486 B.C.), his son Xerxes (486–465 B.C., the 'Ahasuerus' of Esther), and Artaxerxes (I. Longimanus, 465–424 B.C.—so Neh 2^{1}, and possibly II. Mnemon, 404–358 B.C.—cf Ezr 7^{1}). See these names in their alphabetic places. To these we may perhaps add Darius III. Codomannus (336–330 B.C., cf Neh 12^{22}), the last ruler of Persia, who was overthrown by Alexander the Great. With this, the Persian empire came to an end, and much of its area subsequently came under the control first of the Seleucids and then of the Parthians. Other references to Persia in the OT are comparatively few, but it may well be that some allusions to Elam (cf Is 21^{2} 22^{6}, Jer 25^{25} 49^{34-39}, Ezk 32^{24}) should be interpreted as referring to Persia, since Elam became a Persian province, its capital Susa being one of the Persian capitals. J. F. McC.—**P. R. A.**

PERSIS.—A Christian woman saluted in Ro 16^{12}.

PERSON OF CHRIST.—See CHRISTOLOGY.

PERUDA.—See PERIDA.

PESTILENCE.—See MEDICINE.

PESTLE.—See MORTAR.

PETER.—Simon, surnamed Peter, has been justly called the Prince of the Apostles. His father was named Jona or John (Mt 16^{17}, Jn 1^{42} 21^{15ff}). In the Fourth Gospel he is said to have come from Bethsaida (Jn 1^{44}), probably a village of fishermen on the northern shore of the Lake of Galilee E. of the Jordan (cf Mk 6^{45} 8^{22}). According to the Synoptic Gospels he lived in Capernaum with his wife (cf 1 Co 9^{5}), his mother-in-law, and his brother Andrew (Mk 1^{29-31}=Mt 8^{14f}=Lk 4^{38f}). He and Andrew were fishermen on the Lake of Galilee (Mk 1^{16}=Mt 4^{18}) in partnership with Zebedee and his sons (Lk $5^{7,10}$, Mt 4^{21}).

In the Johannine tradition Simon first met Jesus at Bethany beyond the Jordan (Jn 1^{28}), the scene of the Baptist's ministry (Jn 1^{35-42}). He had journeyed there with other Galileans to participate in the movement of religious reform then in progress. Jesus was there ; and Andrew, one of the Baptist's disciples, having been directed by his master to Jesus as the Messiah, told Simon of his discovery and brought him to Jesus. Jesus 'looked at him,' and he became a disciple from that moment. Jesus seemed to know at once both what Peter was then and what with God's help he could become, and He gave him a surname prophetic of the moral and spiritual strength he would eventually demonstrate. 'So you are Simon the son of John? You shall be called Cephas' (Jn 1^{42}). Cephas was the Aramaic equivalent of the Greek *petros* or *petra*, which means rock. It is thus given as a descriptive title and not as a proper name. He was not yet Peter but only Simon, impulsive and vacillating ; and Jesus bestowed upon him the new name before he had earned it so that it might be an incentive to him to realize what Jesus had expected. The designation of Simon as the rock is assumed in the Synoptic Gospels (Mk 3^{16}=Lk 6^{14}), and once there is a pointed reference to this play on words (Mt 16^{18}). In the Synoptic tradition, however, there is no agreement as to when Jesus gave this title to Simon.

Paul used the word Peter in only one passage (Gal 2^{7f}), preferring Cephas. In the Gospels we find Simon, Peter, or Simon Peter. On a number of occasions Jesus pointedly addressed him by the old name Simon, seemingly in order to prod him gently to greater endeavour (cf Mk 14^{37}, Lk 22^{31}, Jn 21^{15ff}).

In the Synoptic Gospels Peter with Andrew was the first disciple to be called by Jesus after the beginning of the Galilean ministry (Mk 1^{16ff} = Mt 4^{18ff}, Lk 5^{1-11}). James and John, also fishermen, were called soon thereafter; and the apostolic band was begun. When Jesus commissioned and sent out the Twelve to preach and heal, he arranged them in pairs and coupled Simon Peter and Andrew (Mk 6^{7}, Mt 10^{2}).

The distinction of Peter lies less in the qualities of his mind than in those of his heart. He was impulsive, and often he spoke inadvisedly so that he incurred rebuke. This, however, was only the weakness of his strength, and it was the concomitant of an enthusiastic and generous affection. Peter's spontaneous love for his Master appeared on several remarkable occasions. (1) According to John, following the feeding of the five thousand at Bethsaida, Jesus delivered (at Capernaum) His discourse on the Bread of Life, full of hard sayings designed to test the faith of His disciples by shattering their dream of a worldly Messiah (Jn 6^{22-65}). Many were offended and 'drew back and no longer went about with him.' Even the Twelve were doubtful. 'Will you also go away?' he asked; and it was Simon Peter who, speaking in the name of the Twelve, assured Jesus of their loyalty (Jn 6^{66-69}). (2) In the Synoptic Gospels we find that during His retirement at Caesarea Philippi in the last year of His ministry, Jesus, anxious to ascertain whether they had recognized in Him the long-expected Messiah, asked the Twelve: 'Who do you say that I am?' Again it was Peter who answered, in the more primitive form of confession: 'You are the Christ' (Mk 8^{29} = Mt 16^{16} = Lk 9^{20}). Jesus then told them of His approaching suffering, and once more it was Peter who expressed the feeling of the Twelve: 'God forbid, Lord! This shall never happen to you' (Mt 16^{22}). Even here it was love that spoke. (3) A week later Jesus went up a mountain with Peter, James and John, and was 'transfigured before them,' communing with Moses and Elijah, who 'appeared in glory' (Mk 9^{2-8} = Mt 17^{1-8} = Lk 9^{28-36}). Though confused and fearful, Peter cried out: 'Lord, it is well that we are here; if you wish, I will make three booths here, one for you and one for Moses and one for Elijah' (Mt 17^{4}). It was a foolish and unconsidered remark (Mk 9^{6} = Lk 9^{33}), but it breathed a spirit of tender affection. His idea was: 'Why return to the ungrateful multitude and the malignant rulers? Why go to Jerusalem and die? Stay here in this holy fellowship.' (4) When Jesus washed the disciples' feet in the Upper Room, it was Peter who protested (Jn 13^{6-9}). He could not allow his Lord to perform that menial office for him. (5) At the arrest in Gethsemane it was Peter who, seeing Jesus in the grasp of the soldiers, drew his sword and cut off the ear of Malchus (Jn 18^{10}).

Peter (always first), James, and John constituted the inner circle of Jesus' closest friends (Mk 5^{37} 9^{2} 14^{33}, cf Mk 13^{3}). The name of Peter appears first in all four of the NT lists of the Twelve (Mk 3^{16-19}, Mt 10^{2-4}, Lk 6^{14-16}, Ac 1^{13}). Throughout the Gospel narrative Peter stands in the foreground and consistently serves as spokesman for the band (cf Mk 10^{28} 11^{21}, Mt 15^{15} 18^{21}, Lk 8^{45} 12^{41}). Following Peter's confession at Caesarea Philippi, Jesus said: 'You are Peter, and on this rock I will build my church, and the powers of death shall not prevail against it' (Mt 16^{18f}). In this much debated passage, which is found in Matthew alone but which may well be a genuine utterance of Jesus, Peter is promised leadership in the early Church and is given the Power of the Keys (q.v.). Whether the rock is the faith of Peter which has seen Jesus as Messiah or the person of Peter, he did in fact emerge as the first leader of the Church. It is impossible to discover here any reference to successors of Peter.

The blot on Peter's life-story is his three-fold denial of Jesus in the courtyard of the high priest's palace (Mk 14^{66-72} = Mt 26^{69-75} = Lk 22^{56-62}, Jn $18^{15-18, 25-27}$). It was a terrible disloyalty, yet not without extenuations. (1) The situation was a trying one. It was dangerous just then to be associated with Jesus, and Peter's excitable and impetuous nature was prone to panic. (2) It was his devotion to Jesus that exposed him to the temptation. He was the only one who rallied from the dismay in Gethsemane (Mt 26^{56b}) and followed his Lord to the trial (Mk 14^{54} = Mt 26^{58} = Lk 22^{54}). According to the Fourth Gospel 'another disciple' (John?) also followed with Peter (Jn 18^{15}). (3) If he sinned greatly, he sincerely repented (Mk 14^{72} = Mt 26^{75} = Lk 22^{62}). He could never forget the look of his Master (Lk 22^{61}). (4) He was completely forgiven. According to 1 Co 15^{5}, Peter is the first one to whom the Lord appeared after His resurrection. In a subsequent appearance by the Lake of Galilee, Peter played a prominent part (Jn 21). On discovering that the stranger on the beach was Jesus, Peter, impatient to reach his Master, sprang overboard from the boat and swam ashore (cf his action in Mt 14^{28-31}). When the disciples were gathered together, Jesus gave Peter a three-fold commission to care for the Christian flock which stands in deliberate contrast to Peter's earlier triple denial. The episode points not to a rebuke of Peter but to Jesus' forgiveness and confidence in him.

Peter figured conspicuously in the history of the Apostolic Church. The Book of Acts makes it clear that Peter assumed a unique position in the primitive Jerusalem Church and was recognized as the leader. It was on his motion that Matthias (q.v.) was appointed as successor to Judas, between the Ascension and Pentecost (Ac 1^{15-26}), and it was he who acted as preacher on the day of Pentecost (2^{14-36}). He worked miracles in the name of Jesus (3^{1-10} 5^{15} 9^{32-42}). He fearlessly proclaimed the Lord to the Jewish leaders in Jerusalem (4^{1-13}). As head of the Church he administered discipline to wrongdoers (5^{1-11} 8^{14-24}), his authority extending even into Samaria. For his boldness in the face of opposition he suffered imprisonment and scourging (5^{17f} 12^{1-5}).

The persecution which followed the martyrdom of Stephen scattered the believers and inaugurated a fresh development of Christianity, involving a bitter controversy. Since the refugees preached wherever they went, the question arose, on what terms the Gentiles should be received into the Church. Must they first become Jews and observe the details of the Mosaic Law? Being appointed with John to examine into the matter, Peter approved Philip's work among the hated Samaritans, invoked the Holy Spirit upon his converts, and before returning to Jerusalem made a missionary tour among the villages of Samaria (Ac 8^{14-25}). He overcame his Jewish prejudice and took a position of first importance as a missionary to the Gentiles by his vision at Joppa and the subsequent conversion of Cornelius and his company at Caesarea; and when taken to task by the Judaistic party at Jerusalem for associating with uncircumcised Gentiles, he vindicated his action and gained the approval of the Church (10^{1}–11^{18}).

The controversy became acute when the Judaizers, becoming alarmed at the missionary activity of Paul and Barnabas, went to Antioch and insisted that the converts there be circumcised. The question was referred to a council of the Church at Jerusalem. Peter's plea for Christian liberty was heeded when, at the suggestion of James the Lord's brother, it was agreed that the work of Paul and Barnabas should be approved and that nothing should be required of the Gentiles beyond abstinence from things sacrificed to idols, blood, things strangled, and fornication (Ac 15^{1-29}; cf Gal 2^{1-10}). Later, Peter visited Antioch, and, though adhering to the decision at the outset, was intimidated by certain Judaizers. Together with Barnabas he separated himself from the Gentiles and would not eat with them, incurring an indignant and apparently effective rebuke from Paul (Gal 2^{11-14}).

After his imprisonment in Jerusalem by Herod

Agrippa I., Peter ' departed and went to another place ' (12[17]). The leadership of the Jerusalem Church apparently passed to James, the Lord's brother, and Peter is mentioned again in Acts only in connexion with the Jerusalem Conference. He may have become a missionary to the Jews of the Dispersion. The First Epistle of Peter (1[1]) may refer to his preaching activity in Asia Minor. He visited Antioch (Gal 2[11]) and may also have gone to Corinth (cf 1 Co 1[12] 3[22]).

There are copious traditions about Peter. It is highly improbable that he founded the Church at Rome, although it is most likely that he preached there (cf 1 P 5[13]). According to Papias of Hierapolis (*c* 130), as reported in Eusebius, our Second Gospel is based upon information derived by Mark from Peter's preaching, presumably in Rome. The First Epistle of Clement (*c* 96) provides indirect evidence of Peter's martyr death in Rome. Support for this tradition is also given by Gaius, a Roman presbyter (*c* 200) quoted in Eusebius, and by early Roman liturgical calendars which contain statements regarding the date and place of the martyrdom. According to Eusebius, Origen (*c* 225) wrote that Peter was at his own request nailed to a cross head downwards, since he deemed himself unworthy to be crucified in the same manner as his Lord.

Since 1938 systematic excavations have been carried on under St. Peter's Basilica in Rome, in an attempt to determine the site of Peter's martyrdom and burial. It now appears that some weighty consideration must have determined the precise location of Constantine's basilica on such a costly and troublesome building site in a pagan cemetery. Below the level of the Constantinian Church and directly under the present high altar have been found traces of a columnar monument (from *c* 150–170) which may have been erected to mark either the spot of Peter's martyrdom or his burial place. The finding of a large number of votive coins in the area suggests that it was from an early date an important object of pilgrimage. Present inconclusive archeological evidence tends to support the early tradition connecting Peter's death with the Vatican Hill. D. S.—**H. M. S.**

PETER, FIRST EPISTLE OF.—1 Peter attempts to make clear to a number of young congregations which have been oppressed by slander and persecution that precisely in such suffering lies ' the true grace of God.' A further concern of the letter is to show its readers what their duty in this situation is, namely, not to grow weary even in suffering, but to do good. For thus Christ also suffered and has thereby made available an imperishable hope.

1. Contents.—The epistle is addressed by Peter the apostle to the elect sojourners of Pontus, Galatia, Cappadocia, Asia, and Bithynia. (*a*) After this salutation the author offers up thanks and praise to God for his salvation (1[3-12]). He tells us that this salvation is (i) an imperishable inheritance through the Resurrection of Christ (vv.[3-5]) and (ii) the reason for joy even in suffering, for suffering purifies faith and directs it to its goal, the salvation of souls (vv.[6-9]); (iii) all this had only been dimly foreseen by prophets and angels while now it has been actually proclaimed to the readers (vv.[10-12]).

(*b*) This salvation contains within itself exhortations to the readers (1[13]–2[10]): (i) to separate themselves from the world as obedient children through holy living (vv.[13-16]); (ii) to walk in fear as those who have been redeemed through the precious blood of Christ (vv.[17-21]); (iii) to love each other as those who have been born again through God's Word (vv.[18-25]); (iv) to grow in faith by desiring like newborn children the pure milk of the word (2[1-3]); and (v) to build themselves up as a holy temple upon the living stone, Christ, who for unbelievers is a rock of offence, but who has called believers that He might possess them as His people (vv. [4-10]).

(*c*) Conduct within earthly institutions (2[11]–3[17]). The heading of this section is (i) an exhortation to the readers to keep themselves pure from fleshly lusts and to lead an exemplary life before the world (vv.[11-12]). Particular exhortations follow: (ii) free men, be subject to the government (vv.[13-17]); (ii) slaves, be obedient even to harsh masters, showing your possession of Divine grace and your discipleship to Jesus, being like Him whose unmerited death has brought us salvation (vv.[18-25]); (iii) women, exercise a quiet and gentle spirit like true mothers in Israel, submitting to your husbands in the hope that if they are heathen they may be won to the faith by your Christian way of life. Likewise, husbands, you must honour your wives, who equally with yourselves are heirs of life (3[1-7]); (iv) finally, you must all be at peace among yourselves, showing humility and love also to your enemies, as that brings with it the blessing of Ps 34[13-17] (vv.[8-12]).

(*d*) Conduct under oppression (3[13]–4[6]): (i) do not be afraid of suffering, be ready to defend yourselves with a good conscience (vv.[13-17]); (ii) you are like the small number saved with Noah when the whole world perished at the time of the Flood, but remember that Christ because of His suffering also preached to that godless generation (vv.[18-22]); (iii) prepare yourselves therefore for suffering which separates you from sin and this brings upon you the antagonism of your former friends (4[1-6]).

(*e*) Exhortations for the life of the congregation (4[7]–5[5]): (i) be sober, love one another, serve one another with the gifts that have been granted to each (vv.[8-11]). (ii) There follows a digression which again deals with oppression: be happy to share the suffering of Christ, do not suffer as evildoers. Your suffering is a sign of the coming judgment. Commend your souls to God by doing good (vv.[12-19]). (iii) Thereupon advice is given to the old and the young in the congregation (5[1-5]).

(*f*) Conclusion (5[6-14]): (i) Humble yourselves under God's hand, be sober, resist the devil. There follows a promise of blessing: God will strengthen you (vv.[6-11]). (ii) The epistle ends with a glance back over the letter and a greeting (vv.[12-14]).

2. Readers.—The epistle is directed to those who have only recently been converted (2[2, 10] 3[21] 4[2-4]). That they were formerly Gentiles may be deduced from 4[3] (idolatries) and 4[4], for ' to be surprised that you do not now join them in the same wild profligacy ' could only be said of Gentile converts; for Jews, as everyone then knew, held themselves scrupulously aloof from Gentiles. That the readers in 1[1] are addressed as the elect who are sojourners in the Dispersion does not prove that they are Jewish Christians. This form of address is simply intended to make clear to Gentile Christians that they became strangers in the world when they became Christians and that they dwell as a scattered people among the heathen. Similarly the phrase ' sojourners and pilgrims ' in 1 P 2[11] is used metaphorically.

The young congregations to which 1 Peter is directed live in the provinces of Pontus, Galatia, Cappadocia, Asia, and Bithynia (1[1]). As far as we know, Paul founded congregations only in Asia (*i.e.* the large province in the western part of Asia Minor) and Galatia. Concerning Pontus and Bithynia we learn from a letter of Pliny to the emperor Trajan, written in A.D. 111–112, that Christianity was so widely disseminated there by that time that the sale of animals for heathen sacrifices had appreciably fallen off. We are still a long way from this state of affairs at the time of 1 Peter. All that we learn from 1 Peter is that Christianity had a bad reputation. It is impossible to say whether this was already the case before these congregations arose or whether their renunciation of pagan ways was the cause. There is no agreement on the question, so important for the dating of the letter, as to whether proceedings had been initiated against the Christians by the state. The letter speaks at first only of slander (2[12] 3[16]), of reviling (3[16]), of ignorance (2[15]), of insults (4[4]), and reproach (4[14]). This does not suggest the interference of the state. Only 4[15f] is exceptional: ' to suffer as a murderer or thief ' presupposes state or municipal justice, and since ' to suffer as a Christian ' is contrasted with it, that suggests official jurisdiction also in the latter case. Nowhere, however, does it become clear that capital punishment has been inflicted, but 4^{19}, 'commit your souls in well-doing unto him, as unto a faithful Creator,' indicates that the possibility of such a verdict is reckoned with. One must assume then that the suffering of the Christian congregations in 1 Peter consists of ill-will, slander and annoyances in everyday life: in addition there is danger that accusations will be made before the authorities or that such accusations have already been made. The Roman government, however, does not yet seem to have taken a hand in the affair.

3. The literary character and the unity of the letter.—The unity of the letter has been questioned because of the passage beginning at 4^{12} (*a*) since at that point the problem of persecutions is again taken up after it has already been dealt with in 3^{13ff} and (*b*) because the first part of the letter speaks of persecutions only in a hypothetical manner (1^{6}: 'if need be'; 3^{14}: 'if ye should suffer'; 3^{17}: 'if it should be the will of God') while 4^{12ff} speaks of actual oppression (4^{13}), of sharing in the passion of Christ (4^{19}) and of present suffering. Many therefore (Perdelwitz, Jülicher, Beare) have seen in 1 Peter a reworking of two letters which stem either from situations distinctly separated from one another in time or from two closely related circumstances, perhaps even from the same author. To this question is related another as to whether we have in 1 Peter instead of a real letter an address which only later was issued in the form of a letter. This address is then regarded as a baptismal homily (Perdelwitz, Bornemann, Beare, Preisker, Cross). This thesis has been worked out in the greatest detail by Preisker who sees in 1 Peter an early Christian liturgy: the first part (1^{3}–4^{11}) contains a baptismal homily which begins with a prayer in psalm form (1^{3-12}) and an informative address (1^{13-21}). It is assumed that the rite of baptism takes place between 1^{21} and 1^{22}. There follows a baptismal vow (1^{22-25}), a hymn (2^{1-10}), an exhortation (2^{11}–3^{12}), a revelation (3^{13}–4^{7a}), and a closing prayer (4^{7b-11}). In this part of the service it is only natural that the persecution and suffering which baptism may occasion should be spoken of in hypothetical form. But 4^{12ff} is to be viewed as a short conclusion to the service in which the whole congregation participates and in which reference is made to the suffering which the congregation as a whole has already experienced. After an eschatological revelation (4^{12-19}), this part closes with an exhortation (5^{1-9}), a blessing (5^{10}), and a doxology. The whole liturgy to which the address and final greeting were added was then sent to the congregations of Asia Minor by the Roman congregation in which it took place. The assumption that the letter contains a baptismal homily makes it possible to account for the striking lack of an exhortation addressed to masters of slaves (an exhortation which is not lacking in any other 'table of duties' in the NT) by supposing that by chance no masters were present at this baptism.

Now it must be granted that the addressees are likened to newborn children (2^{2}), that the author speaks of their conversion as having taken place 'now' (2^{25}) and of their baptism as possessing saving effect 'now' (3^{21}), that reference is made to their pagan way of life as a condition not far removed in time (most clearly 4^{3f}, but see also $1^{14, 23}$ 2^{1} 4^{2}), and that baptism and the rebirth given with baptism are mentioned in various passages in the letter ($1^{3, 23}$ 3^{21}); yet that is not enough to give the letter or a part of it the character of a baptismal homily. In particular it is impossible to think that baptism took place between 1^{21} and 1^{22}; the active 'ye have purified your souls' (1^{22}) rules that out. In baptism one does not purify one's soul, rather the soul is purified. Every expression mentioned above is understandable if we keep in mind that the letter concerns itself with young congregations. For that reason it can speak of their conversion as having taken place 'now.'

The theory that the letter arose out of two originally separate parts certainly contains an element of truth in it. But that in itself does not make the theory acceptable. In substance, the part of the letter which begins at 4^{12} is closely related to the first part; 4^{13} is reminiscent of 1^{6-8} and the term 'well doing' (AV) or 'doing right' (RSV) in 4^{19} is a frequent catchword in the preceding sections ($2^{12, 14f, 20}$ $3^{6, 17}$). The main argument, however, against dividing 1 Peter is that the suffering mentioned in the first part is not spoken of in hypothetical terms because it has not yet come upon them, but because it has not affected all the congregations in the same way. That sufferings and persecutions have in many different ways also come upon those addressed in the first part of the letter is made clear by $2^{12, 19f}$ 3^{16} 4^{4}. Note that the 'if' of 3^{1} is not hypothetical in the sense that something is possible though as yet unrealized, but in the sense that something has happened, not everywhere, but here and there. In the same way the persecutions mentioned in the first part of the letter have already taken place in many of the congregations and have become realities.

It is correct, however, that 4^{12ff} is a striking passage in that the theme of suffering is again taken up and we hear of persecutions that have affected all the congregations. To be sure the word 'if' also appears here (4^{16}); but the following verse (4^{17}) goes on to explain why the congregations must *all* suffer. Yet it is not by chance that even those who wish to divide 1 Peter into two parts are unwilling to separate these parts too far from one another. But the complete unity of the letter must be maintained against all such views, for 4^{7-11} and 5^{1-5} belong together: they are both concerned with the congregation and its government. Since the writing of letters in the ancient world was a matter which consumed not only hours, but days, it is a fair assumption that the author interrupted himself at 4^{12} perhaps because he received new information or perhaps because he himself felt the need once more to go into the matter of suffering, and with greater emphasis.

4. The goal and thought of the letter.—Thus 1 Peter is a real letter, a circular letter addressed to a number of newly formed congregations in Asia Minor. The situation in which these various congregations find themselves is different. They experience different degrees of contempt, of hate, of slander, of daily persecution at the hands of Gentiles, but all feel oppressed and reckon with the possibility of interference from municipal authorities, behind which stands the threat of the Roman army. In this situation Peter directs the minds of his readers to the 'living hope through the resurrection of Jesus Christ from the dead' (1^{3}), to the imperishable inheritance (1^{4}), to the 'outcome of faith, the salvation of souls' (1^{9}), to the grace which the revelation of Jesus Christ brings (1^{13}). The exhortations of the apostle to these congregations point in two directions: in the first place he sets forth the basic demand that they be holy even as He who calls them is holy (1^{15}), remembering that they were redeemed through the precious blood of Christ (1^{18f}), and that as newborn men and women they are to build themselves up into a living temple (2^{5ff}) and soberly to withstand the assaults of the devil (5^{8f}).

In the second place Peter wishes to give them practical direction as to how they are to behave in the midst of persecution. In this connexion two catchwords constantly recur in the letter: be subject and do good. Both are closely related to one another, for to be subject is in reality an essential part of doing good; it entails the subjection of everyone to the government, the obedience of slaves even to arbitrary (2^{18}: froward, overbearing) masters, the submission of wives even when their husbands are still pagans, and the humility of all before one another; it involves not cursing enemies, but blessing them; it demands gentleness, fear and good conscience (3^{15f}). Such subordination joined with the doing of good may convince the heathen of your 'good behaviour in Christ' (3^{16})—though it will not necessarily do so. In this connexion reference is twice made to the example of Christ: 2^{21ff} in the exhortation to slaves and 3^{18-22} where it serves to underpin the sentence that it is better to suffer for doing right than for doing wrong. This difficult passage has the following sense : at the time of the Flood only eight persons including Noah were rescued. All others died in their disobedience. Yet even they obtained Christ's mercy since after His suffering (and precisely because of His suffering) He descended into Hades and preached to them. Thus Christians who like Noah and his family are a small band in the midst of many unbelievers ought not to give up hope for their adversaries but to persist in doing good to them following the example of Christ. This missionary hope does not however prevent Peter from seeing in persecution the power of Satan who would destroy these congregations and their members, or from seeing the end of all things as near at hand (4^{7}) when the great judgment on unbelievers will take place (4^{17f}).

5. Literary Relationships.—(*a*) OT. In its frequent quotations from and in its allusions to the OT this letter consistently uses the LXX and betrays no knowledge of the Hebrew text. The (partial) relationship with Paul when there is a departure from the LXX is striking (cf 1 P 2^{6-8} with Ro 9^{32f}). It is important to note that there are frequent echoes of Is 52–53 (cf 1^{18-19} $2^{22, 24f}$; for other references to the book of Isaiah cf 1 P 2^{6ff} with Is 28^{16} and Ps 118^{22}, 1 P 1^{24f} with Is 40^{6f}). In addition the book of Proverbs is frequently cited (cf 4^{8} with Pr 10^{12} ; 4^{18} with Pr 11^{31} ; 5^{5} with Pr 3^{34}). There are also frequent echoes of Ps 34 (cf v.^{9} with 1 P 2^{3} ; v.^{6} with 1 P 2^{4} ; vv.$^{13-17}$ with 1 P 3^{10-12}) though one is not to view the letter (with Bornemann) as a baptismal homily based on this psalm.

(*b*) Enoch. The book of Enoch often speaks of ' spirits in prison ' ($10^{4f, 12f}$ 64^{2}) though this does not mean that Peter necessarily knew the book. In fact he understands the expression differently.

(*c*) NT. 1 Peter has points of contact with many NT passages. (i) Direct citations from the Gospels are certainly lacking, and the conclusion based on 1 P 5^{1} (a witness of the sufferings of Christ) that the author was an *eye*witness of the suffering of Christ cannot be drawn with certainty. The expression may also signify that the author has borne witness to the suffering of Christ before these congregations and continues to do so. Yet 1P 2^{12} contains an echo of Mt 5^{16}, 1 P 3^{14} and 4^{14} an echo of Mt 5^{11f} and 1 P 3^{9} an echo of Mt 5^{44}. 1 P 2^{4-8} has a connexion with the parable of the evil tenants (Mk 12^{1-12}, especially v.^{10}). The use of Is 53 in 1 P 2^{22-25} is reminiscent of Mt 9^{36} 12^{18ff} and the speeches of Peter in the first part of Acts (God's servant : $3^{13, 26}$ $4^{27, 30}$). (ii) Some expressions are reminiscent of Romans : ' not to be conformed ' to the world (Ro 12^{2}, 1P 1^{14}), ' sincere ' in reference to love (Ro 12^{9}, 1 P 1^{22}), ' reasonable (spiritual) ' sacrifices or worship (Ro 12^{1}, 1 P 2^{5}) ; Ro 12^{3-13} has many echoes in 1 P 4^{8-11} ; Ro 12^{17a} reappears in 1 P 3^{9a} ; the passages concerning the government (Ro 13^{1ff}, 1 P 2^{13-17}) are close not only in the exhortation to be subject to the government, but also in the reason given for such subjection, viz. that the function of the state is to punish the wrongdoer and to approve of that which is good (Ro 13^{4}, 1 P 2^{14}) ; the departure from the LXX in Ro 9^{33} is reflected in 1 P 2^{6}. There is a close relationship between the ' table of duties ' in Colossians, Ephesians and 1 P 2^{18}–3^{8}. 1 P 1^{12} is especially reminiscent of Eph $3^{5, 10}$, 1 P 2^{4-6} is reminiscent of Eph 2^{20-22}, both letters begin with praise to God and both show a particularly close relationship in joining together the concept of Christ's ascension with that of the destruction of the demonic powers (1 P 3^{22}, Eph 1^{20f}). (iii) 1 Peter is related to Hebrews in its emphasis on the estrangement of Christians in the world (1 P 1^{1} 2^{11}, He 11 13^{12f}), through its use of cultic symbols (1 P 1^{2} : sprinkling of the blood of Jesus Christ, He 9^{14} 10^{22}) and by its pointing to the example of the passion of Christ (1 P 2^{21-23} 4^{1}, He 11^{26} 12^{1-3} 13^{13}). (iv) 1 P 1^{1} is reminiscent of Ja 1^{1} (dispersion), 1 P 1^{6f} of Ja 1^{2f} (joy in suffering, suffering as a trial of faith), 1 P 1^{23} of Ja 1^{18} (new birth through the word). The same quotation from Pr 3^{34} is found in both 1 P 5^{5} and Ja 4^{6}.

All these relationships between 1 Peter and other books of the NT do not, however, prove that Peter was acquainted with them. In recent decades it has become increasingly clear that the major elements of the tradition concerning matters of faith and life were common property in the primitive church (Carrington, Selwyn, Lohse, Nauck). For example, the primitive Church had to settle the question of its relationship to the government in order to dissociate itself from the Zealot movement ; but its solution of the problem also contained an evaluation of the Roman government which was distinguished from the view of the Pharisees who saw in the government only God's rod of affliction. The basic ideas which appear in Ro 13^{1ff} and 1 P 2^{12ff} therefore reach far back into the earliest Church. When the Law lost ground as an ethical norm, the question of the relationship to earthly institutions was immediately raised, and at least in the Gentile mission one may assume that a tradition arose as we find it preserved in the ' tables of duties ' ; yet this rejection of libertinism with its contempt for human institutions is to be traced back to the Palestinian scene (Mt 5^{17ff}) and may also lie behind the apostolic decree of Ac 15 (A. Schlatter). It is further true that since from its beginning the primitive Church had to reckon with opposition of all kinds, the evaluation of persecution and suffering as grounds for joy was common opinion among the early Christians (Ac 5^{41}). One must also reckon with a certain fund of OT passages which were understood in a peculiarly Christian manner, and so interpreted were common property in the primitive Church. And it is natural that the Greek-speaking part of the Church relied on the LXX in its use of the OT.

We cannot, therefore, conclude that Peter unquestionably knew other NT documents, since there are relationships between them and 1 Peter. We can only cautiously point out that we meet ideas and concepts in 1 Peter which we never or almost never find in Paul, but rather perhaps in the primitive Church : (i) ' soul ' used for the ' self ' (1 P $1^{9, 22}$ $2^{11, 25}$ 4^{19}, cf Mk 8^{35-37} ; in Paul only in 2 Co 12^{15}) ; (ii) cultic concepts used to elucidate the work of Christ (1 P 1^{2}, cf He 9^{14} ; the use of Is 53 also belongs in this category, especially the description of Christ as the lamb—this description appears only once in Paul, 1 Co 5^{7} ; in fact Is 53 plays a remarkably small rôle in Paul, but appears frequently in Matthew (see **5** (*c*)) ; (iii) the emphasis on Christians as aliens in the world (we already hear an echo of this in Stephen's speech in Ac 7 ; the theme is stressed in Hebrews, a document which used Palestinian tradition) ; (iv) the metaphor of ' girding up the loins ' is found in 1 P 1^{13} and Lk 12^{35} (in Eph 6^{14} the metaphor is used differently !) ; (v) the form of greeting (1 P 1^{2} : ' be multiplied ') is Semitic. On the other hand there is no question that many distinctive Pauline concepts are missing (dying and rising with Christ, Paul's whole doctrine of justification, the concept ' in Christ ' which is found only in 1 P 3^{16}) ; but there are also usages in 1 Peter which cannot be claimed without question as the teaching of the Palestinian Church : the pre-existence of Christ (1 P $1^{11, 20}$), the congregation as a spiritual house, a spiritual sacrifice (1 P 2^{5}, Ro 12^{1}, Eph 2^{21f}), the ' authorities and powers ' (1 P 3^{22}, cf Eph 1^{20f}).

If Jewish-Christian tradition is strong in Matthew, James, and Hebrews, then 1 Peter stands for the most part in the same context. That also becomes clear in his description of the ' constitution ' of the congregations addressed in his letter : 1 P 5^{1-5} distinguishes only ' elders ' and those who are ' younger.' When we are told that the ' elders ' are to exercise their office not by constraint but willingly, we may assume that they received their office not by being chosen for it, but because of their age ; when they are exhorted not to exercise their office ' for shameful gain ' (AV ' for filthy lucre '), that does not presuppose payment, but precisely the contrary, for all such ideas are thereby excluded. We have before us a clear and simple form of congregational life which can be understood on the basis of the Jewish evaluation of old age and which is also clearly coming into being in Ac $5^{6, 10}$ and in Ja 5^{14}.

Add to all this that the expectation of a speedy end to the world is still alive in 1 Peter ($4^{7, 17}$), and it becomes clear that the Epistle leads us back into the first generation of the Church and has strong connexions with the Palestinian tradition.

6. Author, place and time of writing.—1 Peter claims to have been written by the apostle Peter ' through Silvanus ' (5^{12}). If the letter is genuine, this can only mean that Silvanus was responsible for the wording of the letter; otherwise the addition ' a faithful brother as I regard him ' would be unintelligible. The first certain quotation of 1 Peter is found in the letter of Polycarp of Smyrna to the Philippians (*c* A.D. 117) and according to Eusebius Papias is also supposed to have used it. From the end of the 2nd cent. the Church fathers universally regard it as a recognized part of the canon; it is only in the Muratorian Canon that it is missing. Surprising as this omission is, no objection can be raised against the letter's authenticity on that ground.

But the majority reject Petrine authorship. The reasons are as follows: (i) the author's language is simple yet easy Greek, (ii) he uses only the LXX, (iii) the persecution mentioned in the letter presupposes a situation that could only have arisen after the death of the apostle, (iv) Peter could not have written to Gentile congregations located in the area of Paul's missionary activity, (v) personal recollections of the words and the life of Jesus could not be so completely lacking if the letter had been composed by Peter, (vi) the letter contains theological ideas which can only be understood as resulting from Paul's work, and such dependence of Peter on Paul is out of the question, (vii) the letter shows literary dependence on Paul's letters, particularly Romans and Ephesians, and this sets it in the subapostolic age.

Those who assume that the letter is not genuine have come to no agreement concerning the date of composition (A.D. 80–110) or the way in which it was written. In particular they have not succeeded in making intelligible the mention of Silvanus in 5^{12}. A second consideration which weighs against this theory is the marked restraint with which the claim to apostolic authority is made; a forger can hardly avoid falling into the temptation of making his forgery quite apparent, as 2 Peter shows. Moreover the reasons brought forward against the genuineness of the letter are not particularly convincing: (i) and (ii) can be easily explained by taking seriously Silvanus' share in the composition of the letter; as far as (iii) is concerned see **2** above; (v) fails to recognize that it was Good Friday, Easter and Pentecost which made Peter an apostle; (vi) and (vii) overlook the fact that 1 Peter has stronger connexions with the tradition of the primitive Church than with Paul (see **5**). Furthermore, one must also reckon with the fact that Silvanus played a rôle in the writing of the letter.

But the decisive question is whether a unified and understandable picture of 1 Peter results if we assume that it is genuine.

To answer this we must begin with (iv). Paul finished his work in Asia Minor in the middle of the fifties of the 1st cent., travelled to Jerusalem and was arrested. He remained in prison for a long time in Caesarea. Then he was taken to Rome under guard on a dangerous journey which lasted over six months. There he stayed for a year and a half under a sort of house arrest. Whether he then went to Spain (Ro $15^{24, 28}$) we do not know with certainty, but it is possible. If the Pastorals are genuine, we later find him once more in the Eastern provinces of the Roman empire. It is not only completely understandable, but also almost certainly the case that during this long period Christianity spread from western Asia Minor and Galatia to Pontus, Cappadocia and Bithynia, and also that new congregations arose in Asia and Galatia. We do not know where Paul's most intimate colleague, Timothy, was during these years. In any event one must conclude from 1 Peter (assuming that it is genuine) that Silvanus felt himself responsible for these new congregations. As a member of the primitive Church and as a colleague of Paul on his second missionary journey he played a rôle in the Gentile mission and was at the same time in touch with Peter. He therefore requested Peter to send an apostolic message to the new congregations. Our letter, 1 Peter, is this message and in its composition Silvanus probably played a part that went beyond the mere translating of Peter's Aramaic speech into Greek. This message has a double goal: to tell the congregations that oppression and persecution are ' the true grace of God ' and to exhort them to stand fast therein (5^{12}). On the other hand, however, the letter contains the exhortation to be subject and to do right. Thereby the danger was avoided which also arose in the Pauline congregations, namely, the danger of ' using your freedom as a pretext for evil ' (2^{16}). It is in this connexion that the ' table of duties ' plays its rôle. For it contains the first elements of instruction which for the most part were orally transmitted, but which appear in the letters directed to congregations not personally founded by Paul: Colossians and Ephesians and so also in 1 Peter. If Peter granted Silvanus' request to send such a message to the young Gentile congregations in central Asia Minor, that is no encroachment upon Paul's missionary territory when Paul (and perhaps Timothy as well) were not available.

Now it must be granted that this solution presupposes one thing that is almost universally rejected by scholars, namely, that the term ' Babylon ' in 5^{13} does not refer to Rome. It is certain that Babylon could be used at that time as a pseudonym for Rome and was so used (? Rev 17–20). But this does not make it necessary to assume that such was the case here. Whether one accepts the genuineness of the letter or not, there was nothing to compel the writer to avoid the mention of Rome. If, on the other hand, Peter was in Rome when he wrote 1 Peter, then it is difficult to imagine where Paul is supposed to have been, for Silvanus would surely have done better to turn to him. So then if Babylon = Rome, the letter can only with difficulty be regarded as genuine (for this would mean that Paul had died before Peter, a theory which one can hardly accept). But it is not only possible that Peter went from Palestine to Babylonia to fulfil his mission to the circumcised (Gal 2^{9}), it ought to be confidently maintained—though the contacts of Silvanus with Babylon are difficult to make out. He could hardly feel justified in neglecting the large number of Aramaic speaking Jews in Mesopotamia. That we have no mention of it is not surprising when the state of the tradition is taken into account. It is understandable then that Silvanus turned to Peter who was not too far away in Babylonia when he wanted to have an apostolic message for the young congregations. Whether by Babylon is meant the city or the country cannot finally be settled. 1 Peter was written therefore about the year A.D. 60. The situation presupposed in 1 Peter is fully conceivable, clear and understandable, if the letter is assumed to be genuine. W. F.

PETER, SECOND EPISTLE OF.—This Epistle cannot rank with 1 Peter as a Christian classic, but it nevertheless deserves our careful attention as a witness from about the turn of the 1st cent.

1. Contents.—**(a)** The greeting (1^{1f}). The apostle, who calls himself Symeon Peter in a formal Hebraizing manner, writes to those who ' have obtained a faith of equal standing with ours ' and expresses the wish that they may share richly in grace and peace through the knowledge of God and of Jesus Christ. (*b*) The apostle and his readers (1^{3-21}). In the ' us ' of verse three Peter includes himself along with the other apostles to whom everything has been given that leads to piety and spiritual life so that those to whom the letter is directed may share in the Divine nature while escaping the corruption that is in the world because of evil desires (vv.$^{3-4}$). Therefore the readers are counselled to let virtue, knowledge, self-control, steadfastness, godliness, brotherly affection and love flow from their faith (vv.$^{5-7}$). These things will prevent them from being unfruitful in the

PETER, SECOND EPISTLE OF

knowledge of faith (vv.[8-9]). Thus they are to confirm their calling that they may be provided with an entrance into the Kingdom of God (vv.[10-11]). Peter constantly reminds them of these things in view of his coming death so that even after he has departed they may recall what he has told them (vv.[12-15]). Peter claims that he proclaimed the power and the coming of Christ to the readers as an eye-witness of the transfiguration (vv.[16-18]). Thus the apostles have firm possession of the prophetic word. The readers are to pay attention to it and to realize above all that no prophecy of Scripture is a matter of one's own interpretation. For men of God spoke as they were moved by the Holy Spirit (vv.[19-21]). (*c*) Future heretics (2[1-12]). (i) Just as false prophets arose among the Jewish people, so will they also arise among the readers. They will cause destructive divisions and deceive many (vv.[1-3a]). (ii) The judgment upon them will not fail to take place just as the judgment upon the angels of Gn 6[1ff], upon the generation at the time of the Flood and upon Sodom and Gomorrah did not fail to take place (vv.[3b-6]). (iii) The example of Lot shows that God can preserve the righteous even when they live among sinners and at the same time can punish the sinners (vv.[7-9]). (iv) The heretics are described in 2[10-22]. (*aa*) They are immoral; they despise 'lordship' (RSV 'authority'); they blaspheme 'glories' (RSV 'the glorious ones')—a thing which mighty angels did not dare to do; they are like animals and will be destroyed (vv.[10-14]). (*bb*) They are like Balaam who loved unrighteous gain, but was rebuked by his ass; they are like waterless springs (vv.[15-17]). (*cc*) They deceive many with their empty words; they proclaim freedom and are themselves slaves to their passions (vv.[18-19]). (*dd*) When they learned of Christ, they left evil behind, but now they have gone back to their evil ways; it would have been better for them had they never known the way of righteousness (vv.[20-22]). (*d*) Doubt concerning the second coming of Christ (3[1-16]). (i) Peter points out that he is writing this letter to remind his readers of the words of the prophets and of the word of Christ given them through the apostles (vv.[1-2]). (ii) For mockers will come who will say, 'Since the death of our fathers everything has remained the same; the promised coming has not taken place' (vv.[3-4]). (iii) As the world perished at the time of the Flood through water, so also the present heaven and earth will perish through fire (vv.[5-7]). (iv) A thousand years are with God as a day; the day of the Lord will come as a thief in the night; but God is delaying it out of mercy (vv.[8-11]). (v) Thus the reader must await the Second Coming in holy living; then the heavens will perish and a new heaven and a new earth will appear where righteousness will dwell (vv.[12-13]). (vi) Therefore the readers must strive to be found guiltless and count God's patience as salvation. The writer adds that such things were also written to them by Paul. Nevertheless, since his letters like all other Scriptures are hard to understand, they have been twisted by many to their own destruction (vv.[14-16]). (e) The close of the letter is made up of an exhortation to the readers not to let themselves be deceived, but to grow in the grace and knowledge of Christ. There follows a doxology (vv.[17-18]).

2. Literary affinities.—(*a*) 1 Peter. The differences between first and second Peter are numerous and striking. Already the author's name is different: the Hebraizing form, Symeon Peter, is found elsewhere only in Ac 15[14] and (for other bearers of the name than Peter the apostle) in Lk 2[25, 34] 3[30], Ac 13[1], Rev 7[7]. 1 Peter is written in fluent Hellenistic Greek while the style of 2 Peter is almost pseudo-literary, and its words are often quite uncommon. 1 Peter quotes largely from the LXX, the use of which can hardly be detected in 2 Peter. The Divine names are different. Whereas in 1 P 3[19f] Christ is said to have preached to the generation that had died at the time of the Flood, in 2 P 2[5] these people are only mentioned as objects of God's judgment. Naturally the changed situation can explain many of the differences. Thus it is understandable that Is 53 and the example of Christ's suffering should play a large rôle in a letter to congregations which are oppressed, while they do not appear in a letter directed against libertines and those who deny the Second Coming. But it cannot be denied that in 2 Peter knowledge takes the place of hope and piety that of holiness. (*b*) The difference in the use of the OT is also significant: in 1 Peter there are many quotations; such quotations are missing in 2 Peter and in their place the author strings together references to OT narratives for the sake of illustration. That there are echoes of the OT also in many passages of 2 Peter (Ps 90[4] in 3[8] and Pr 26[11] in 2[22]) is no peculiarity of the letters of Peter. (*c*) A peculiarity of 2 Peter is the direct reference to the synoptic account of the transfiguration (1[16-18]). Echoes of OT passages and the eschatology of the Synoptics are found in 2 P 3[10-13]. But the extent of direct influence cannot be established. (*d*) It is remarkable that 2 Peter knows of a collection of Pauline letters (3[15f]). but only indistinct echoes of them can be heard (2 P 1[13] = 2 Co 5[1]: the body as a tabernacle). 2 Peter shows astonishingly little evidence of their influence. (*e*) Jude. All the more striking are the points of contact between 2 Peter and Jude. They are to be found especially in the second chapter. In the whole NT it is only 2 Peter and Jude which use the method of drawing up a list of OT stories and figures to characterize their opponents. Moreover the majority of OT examples are common to both letters and are used in the same order. The numerous other points of contact between the two letters are also found in the same order: denying the Lord (2[1] = Jude [4]; the term *despotēs*, *i.e.* Lord, which is rarely used of Jesus, is found in both passages in this sense)—the fall of the angels, the destruction of Sodom and Gomorrah (2[4-6] = Jude [6f])—defilement of the flesh, contempt of 'lordship,' blasphemy of the 'glories' (2[10] = Jude [8]; the same order in both cases!)—the opposite behaviour of the angels which is worthy of emulation (2[11] = Jude [9])—the comparison with the animals (2[12] = Jude [10])—carousing together (2[13] = Jude [12])—Balaam (2[15] = Jude [11])—the comparison with the waterless clouds or springs and the reservation of the nether gloom for the heretics (2[17] = Jude [12f]—) proud speech (2[18] = Jude [16]). At the same time it is only once that a whole sentence is word for word the same in each (2[17c] = Jude [13c]). On the whole the one is not a simple transcription of the other. Rather we find that one of the letters is a new edition or a complete reworking of the other. The echoes of 2 Peter in Jude go beyond the second chapter (1[12], 'though ye know' them = Jude [5], and Jude [17f] is very closely related to 2 P 3[2f]).

3. Authorship and date.—In view of the mutual relationship that exists between the two letters the question arises as to whether 2 Peter is an expanded revision of Jude or whether Jude is an abridged edition of 2 Peter. These are the only two possibilities. When the question is put in this way, there can be no doubt as to what the right answer is: there is no reason why a letter written by Peter should be reissued in a shortened form under the name of Jude whose authority was so much less significant than that of Peter. But it is immediately comprehensible that the letter of Jude should be expanded by entering in upon the question of the delay of the Second Coming and should be reissued under the name of Peter to assure it of greater influence. And it is also immediately clear that 2 Peter cannot stem from the apostle Peter. For he would not have been dependent on Jude in this way. This is irrefutably proven by 3[4] ('since the fathers fell asleep'). The 'fathers' are the first generation of Christians to which Peter belonged. Now Peter probably died in A.D. 64; in any event he did not, like John, outlive the first generation. Hence Peter was no longer alive when the letter was written. For 2 Peter was written at least after the year A.D. 70, a date which may be taken as representing roughly the time at which the first generation died out. The fact that 2 Peter already knows a collection of Pauline letters possessing almost canonical authority (3[16]) points to the same period of time after A.D. 70. Whether by the term 'other Scriptures' the author means the Synoptics and Acts for example and not only the OT cannot be decided with confidence. In any event, in 2 Peter we find ourselves in the subapostolic age, an age in which the canon was beginning to take shape.

That 2 Peter is secondary to Jude may also be gathered from certain other observations: (*a*) the examples in 2^{4-6}, unlike the examples in Jude, have been put in chronological order; (*b*) the quotation from Enoch and the reference to the Ascension of Moses (Jd ^{14f} and ^{9}) have been dropped; (*c*) the opponents in 2 Peter are more clearly described (they proclaim freedom, 2^{19}, and pose a grave danger for the congregations, $2^{2, 14, 18}$); (*d*) the judgment against them is sharper (2^{19-22}).

Some further observations show that 2 Peter is pseudonymous: (*a*) The future tense used in the description of the heretics in 2^{1ff} imperceptibly gives way to the present in v.^{10} and to the past in v.^{15}. This is an indication that the attempt of the author to speak from the point of view of Peter is only a fiction; (*b*) in 1^{15} the author himself says that the letter is intended for the time after his death; (*c*) 2 Peter consciously attempts to emphasize the assumed authorship of Peter (1^{13-19} 3^{15}). Borrowed authority must seek to give itself an air of genuineness. It is here (*d*) that the reference to 1 Peter in 3^{1f} also belongs. It does not really suit 1 Peter and the theory that the allusion is to a genuine letter of Peter which has not come down to us (Zahn) is simply a weak attempt to get around a difficulty. Rather the real author is here betraying himself. And nothing speaks for the idea that he was a disciple of Peter.

For the date of the letter we have no other clue than that it was written after Jude. Full-blown Gnostic systems cannot be recognized in it. One may date it roughly in the years A.D. 90–110.

4. Testimony of later Christian Literature.—Until the 3rd cent. the traces of 2 Peter are very few. Perhaps it was known to the author of the *Apocalypse of Peter* (*c* A.D. 150), but it is missing in the Muratorian Canon. The first certain quotation is found in Firmilian of Caesarea in Cappadocia (*c* 250); probably it was used by Clement of Alexandria; and Origen knew it, but doubted its genuineness. While Eusebius himself did not accept the Epistle, he placed it, in deference to general opinion, among the 'disputed' books. It is not referred to by the scholars of Antioch, nor is it in the Peshitta, the common version of the Syrian Church. The oldest Latin versions also seem not to have contained it; possibly it was absent from the original of Codex B, but it is found in the Egyptian versions. Jerome, and afterwards Erasmus and Calvin, harboured doubts about its genuineness.

5. Readers and purpose.—According to 1^{16} Peter (and his fellow apostles) are supposed to have gained for Christianity those to whom the letter is directed. But that belongs to the trappings of the letter and means nothing. The salutation mentions no definite congregation. Only from one passage does it appear probable that the readers are to be sought for among Gentile Christians (2^{20-22}: the opponents are said to have come from a heathen life of defilement and to have returned to it). Since in this passage it is a question of gross and notorious sins, one can hardly think that the readers of the letter had a Jewish past. Probably the fact that 2 Peter was addressed to Gentile Christians helps to explain the reason for the re-editing of Jude under the name of Peter, for while it is hardly likely that Jude had any particular authority among Gentile Christians, Peter doubtless had. Now since Jude was used by 2 Peter, it is to be expected that the readers of both letters did not live far apart, *i.e.* they are to be looked for in Syria or Asia Minor. The meagre witness to 2 Peter in the ancient Church speaks for a small circle of readers.

The first purpose of the author in reworking Jude was to put his readers on their guard against those who preached libertinism under the cloak of freedom. But to this was joined a new concern, namely, to oppose doubts about the Second Coming. Such doubts were probably brought forth by the same people who represented libertinism; we see also in 1 Co that doubt concerning the resurrection of Christ is joined with doubt concerning his return.

Jude exhorts his readers to fight for the faith handed on once and for all (v.^{3}). 2 Peter develops this theme in the first chapter. Everything that belongs to piety and spiritual life has been given to the apostles and they have handed it on. He points out in particular that the power and the coming of Christ are not 'cunningly devised fables,' but that the proclamation of these things rests upon the revelation of the glory of Christ in the transfiguration. Thus the apostles are those who have firm possession of the prophetic word to which the readers are to pay attention (1^{16-19}). But the author has a wider purpose than that of simply upholding religious authoritarianism. Behaviour marked by self-control and patience, and the knowledge of Christ and the Second Coming belong indissolubly together for him: behaviour is fruitful for knowledge, *i.e.* for faith (1^{8}); one's calling and election is confirmed by one's behaviour (1^{10}); the Second Coming which will bring a new heaven and a new earth in which righteousness will dwell is to spur one on to be found guiltless (3^{14}); the delay of the Second Coming is to be regarded as God's holy forbearance which increases fruitful conduct. By the example of Lot the author shows that God can preserve the righteous even in the midst of sinners (2^{7-9})—a situation in which the readers found themselves. Even though 2 Peter borders on a certain moralism and has brought in Greek ideas strange to the NT (1^{4} 'partakers of the divine nature'; $3^{7, 12}$ the cosmic 'conflagration'), such thoughts deserve to be given a hearing. W. F.

PETHAHIAH.—1. The head of the nineteenth priestly course, 1 Ch 24^{16}. **2.** A priest who had married a foreign wife, Ezr 10^{23}, 1 Es 9^{23} (AV, RV **Patheus**). **3.** A Levite, Neh 9^{5}. **4.** A Judahite officer, Neh 11^{24}.

PETHOR.—Mentioned in Nu 22^{5} and Dt 23^{4} as the home of Balaam, in N. Mesopotamia, when he was called by Balak to curse Israel. With this indication agrees the repeated statement by king Shalmaneser II. of Assyria regarding a certain city which he calls *Pitru*, that it lay on the river *Sāgūr* (modern *Sājûr*) near its junction with the Euphrates. Thus Pethor would seem to have lain a little S. of Carchemish, on the W. of the Euphrates. J. F. McC.

PETHUEL.—The father of the prophet Joel, Jl 1^{1}.

PETRA.—See SELA.

PEULLETHAI.—The eighth son of Obed-edom, 1 Ch 26^{5} (AV **Peulthai**).

PEULTHAI, 1 Ch 26^{5} (AV).—See PEULLETHAI.

PHAATH MOAB, 1 Es 5^{11} (AV, RV) 8^{31} (RV).—See PAHATH-MOAB.

PHACARETH, 1 Es 5^{34} (AV, RV).—See POCHERETH-HAZZEBAIM.

PHAISUR, 1 Es 9^{22} (AV, RV).—See PASHHUR, **4.**

PHALDAIUS, 1 Es 9^{44} (AV).—See PEDAIAH, **5.**

PHALDEUS, 1 Es 9^{44} (RV).—See PEDAIAH, **5.**

PHALEAS, 1 Es 5^{29} (AV, RV).—See PADON.

PHALEC, Lk 3^{35} (AV) = **Peleg** (q.v.).

PHALIAS, 1 Es 9^{48} (RV).—See PELAIAH, **2.**

PHALLU, Gn 46^{9} (AV).—See PALLU.

PHALTI, 1 S 25^{44} (AV).—See PALTI, **2.**

PHALTIEL.—1. 2 S 3^{15} (AV); see PALTI, **2. 2.** The 'chief of the people,' 2 Es 5^{16} (AV **Salathiel**).

PHANUEL.—The mother of Anna (Lk 2^{36}).

PHARACIM, 1 Es 5^{31} (AV).—See PHARAKIM.

PHARAKIM.—A family of Nethinim, 1 Es 5^{31} (AV **Pharacim**).

PHARAOH.—The later Egyptian royal title, *pr-'3*. 'Great House,' adopted into Hebrew. Originally designating the royal establishment in Egypt, it gradually became the appellative title of the king (like the Ottoman Turkish *Sublime Porte*), and from the 22nd Dynasty (*c* 940–730 B.C.) onwards was regularly attached to the king's name in popular speech. The Hebrew Pharaoh Neco (2 K 23^{29}, Jer 46^{2}) and Pharaoh Hophra (Jer 44^{30}) are thus precise renderings of Egyptian. Shishak also was so entitled in Egyptian, but apparently Hebrew had not yet adopted the novel fashion, and so gave his name without Pharaoh (1 K 11^{40} 14^{25}). Tirhakah is not entitled Pharaoh as in Egyptian documents, but is more accurately described as king of Cush (2 K 19^{9}).

The following Pharaohs are referred to without their names being specified: **1.** Pharaoh of Abram (Gn 12^{10-20}), impossible to identify. The title Pharaoh and the mention of camels appear to be anachronisms in the story. **2.** Pharaoh of Joseph (Gn 39 etc.). The proper names in the story, viz. Potiphar, Potiphera, Asenath, Zaphenath-paneah are at once recognizable (when the vocalization is discounted) as typical names (Petepre, Esneit, Zepnetefonkh) of the late period beginning with the 22nd Dynasty (*c* 940 B.C.), and ending in the reign of Darius I. (*c* 500 B.C.). It has been conjectured that the Pharaoh of Joseph was one of the Hyksos kings, but it is not advisable to press for historical identifications in this beautiful legend. **3.** and **4.** The Pharaohs of the Oppression and the Exodus. The name of **Raamses** (q.v.), given to a store-city built by the Hebrews (Ex 1^{11}), points to one of the kings named Ramesses in the 19th–20th Dynasties as the pharaoh of the Oppression. The chief of these was Ramesses II. (*c* 1290–1223 B.C.), after whom several towns were named. He was perhaps the greatest builder in Egyptian history. His son Merenptah might be the Pharaoh of the Exodus: but from the fifth year of Merenptah there is an Egyptian record of the destruction of 'Israel,' who, it would seem, were already in Palestine. At present it is impossible to ascertain the proportion of historical truth contained in the traditions of the Exodus. **5.** 1 Ch 4^{17}, 'Bithiah, daughter of Pharaoh': no clue to identity. Bithiah is Hebrew, and not like an Egyptian name. **6.** 1 K 3^{1} $9^{16, 24}$ 11^{1}, Pharaoh, the father-in-law of Solomon, was possibly Sheshonk I. (see SHISHAK; *c* 940–919 B.C.) of the 22nd Dynasty, but more probably one of the feeble kings of the end of the 21st Dynasty, such as Siamun (*c* 990–974 B.C.) or his successor Psusennes II. (*c* 974–940 B.C.). **7.** 1 K 11^{18-22}, the Pharaoh who befriended Hadad the Edomite in the last days of Solomon, and gave him the sister of his queen Tahpenes. Though not identified, he was probably Siamun. (At this point in the narrative Shishak comes in: he is never called Pharaoh; see above.) **8.** Pharaoh, king of Egypt in 2 K 18^{21}, Is 36^{6} etc., perhaps as a general term for the Egyptian king, not pointing to any individual. In the time of Sennacherib and Hezekiah, Tirhakah or some earlier king of the Ethiopian Dynasty would be on the throne. **9.** For Jer 37, Ezk 29, see HOPHRA. F. Ll. G.—**R. J. W.**

PHARATHON.—Named, with Timnath and Tephon, high walls and gates and bars,' 1 Mac 9^{50} (AV **Pharathoni**). Some authorities read with LXX 'Timnath-pharathon,' as indicating one place. Conder suggested *Fer'ōn*, about 15 miles W. of Nāblus. This seems to be too far to the north, as the towns mentioned are all 'in Judaea.' It may possibly be *Far'ata*, 6 miles SW. of Nāblus, although the same difficulty exists in a modified degree. Cf PIRATHON. W. E.

PHARATHONI, 1 Mac 9^{50} (AV).—See PHARATHON.

PHARES.—AV form of the name **Perez** (q.v.) in Mt 1^{3}, Lk 3^{33}, where RV, RSV have **Perez.** In 1 Es 5^{5} AV, RV, RSV all have Phares.

PHAREZ.—**1.** AV form of the name **Perez** (q.v.) in Gn 38^{29} 46^{12}, Nu 26^{20f}, Ru $4^{12, 18}$, 1 Ch 2^{4} 4^{1} 9^{4}; in 1 Ch 27^{3}, Neh $11^{4, 6}$ AV has Perez, as RV and RSV in all cases. **2.** 1 Es 8^{30} (AV); see PAROSH.

PHARIDA, 1 Es 5^{33} (RV).—See PERIDA.

PHARIRA, 1 Es 5^{33} (AV).—See PERIDA.

PHARMACIST.—Sir 38^{8} (RSV); see APOTHECARY.

PHARISEES.—Hebrew *Pᵉrûshîm*, 'separatists.' From the Aramaic emphatic *Pᵉrûshāyâ* came the Greek *Pharisaioi*. A religious society, chiefly of laymen, frequently mentioned in the NT. The movement derived from the tendency toward religious puritanism, marked in the Priestly and Holiness codes and stimulated by the reformation of Ezra and Nehemiah. (Cf Sifra to Lv 19^{2}; Mekilta to Ex 19^{6}.) *Pārûsh* is equivalent to *Nibhdāl* in Ezr 6^{21} and Neh 10^{29}, where it characterizes one 'who separated himself from the ritual uncleanness of the gentiles of the land' and from the Jewish 'people of the land' (*'ammê hā-'āreṣ*) to follow the law of God.

Closely related to the Hasidim, the Pharisees branched out as a separate body after it became evident that mingling with the heathen and the secular trends of the Maccabaean state and of the priestly aristocracy, the **Sadducees** (q.v.), endangered the distinctive character of the Jewish people. Including **Scribes** (q.v.) in their ranks, they made the study of the Law and the scrupulous regard for its requirements the chief goal of their piety. Accordingly, they figure in Rabbinic literature as *Ḥakhmê Yiśrā'ēl*. In the account of their break with John Hyrcanus, Josephus names them Pharisees, while the Talmudic parallel of this incident, linked with Alexander Jannaeus, designates them *Ḥakhmê Yiśrā'ēl* (*Kidd.* 66a; Jos. *Ant.* XIII. x. 5–6 [288 ff]). Early Rabbinic literature knows them also as *Ḥᵃbhērîm*. The word *ḥābhēr*, originally a common expression for companion or associate, through its connexion with the Pharisaic associations for worship, for religious meals and for study of Torah, acquired the special meaning of Pharisee. Kohut traces this usage to Ps 119^{63} (see *Aruch Completum, Ḥābhēr*). In the Mishnah *hābhēr* is used to distinguish a person from *'am hā'āreṣ* and is synonymous with *pārûsh* and *talmîdh ḥākhām*. It reflects the Pharisaic method of extending their teaching and practice. 'Form groups and engage in the study of Torah, for the Torah may not be acquired save through association' (*Ber.* 63b). 'Provide theyself with a teacher and acquire a companion (*ḥābhēr*)' (*Aboth* 1^{6}).

The Pharisees drew their following from all sections of the people irrespective of economic, social, and hereditary distinctions. They included priests and even members of the high priestly families. Their influence radiated not from the market place, but from the synagogue as the centre of the threefold activity of study, worship, and works of charity.

Their chief distinction derived from their attitude toward the Law. As the word of God, the Torah, they believed, must be adequate for all times and circumstances. Accordingly, they devoted themselves to the interpretation of the scriptural text in such a way as to find with it light for all conditions of changing times. 'Turn it and turn it again, for everything is within it' (*Aboth* 5^{22}). They linked useful popular customs and ancient traditions with the text of the Law, and by a subtle exegesis (often eisegesis), they were able to find within it grounds for needed institutions and reforms in Jewish life (*Ant.* XIII. x. 5 [288 ff]). They thus developed the doctrine of the dual character of the Torah, one Written and the other Oral, and maintained that the written Law must be understood in the light of the Oral tradition (*Aboth* 1^{1}). The Sadducees, on the other hand, rejected the doctrine of the Oral Law as well as the obligatory character of the observances which were not expressly included in the written word. (Cf Dt 13^{1}.) While the exegesis of the Pharisees appears artificial, it served the purpose of keeping the spirit of the Law as a living force and made for progress in Judaism.

As the party of the people, the Pharisees did not set themselves against the priests, but rather insisted on paying the priests the tithes and offerings due to them in accordance with the Law. At the same time they insisted that the priests act as the servants of God and as ministers of the people rather than as their masters (*Yoma* 1^{5}). They sought to democratize Judaism by raising the people to the level of the priests in accordance with the Divine command: 'And ye shall be to me a kingdom of priests and a holy nation' (Ex 19^{6}). Thus they applied the laws of priestly purity to the people as a whole. They extended the requirements of priestly ablutions to all the people (Ex 30^{17-21}). The holiness of the Temple they would carry into the home of the Jew, turn his table into an altar, and render him an officiating priest in the domestic sanctuary. Thus they took over the mode of slaughtering of sacrificial animals at the Temple for private use, and adapted the washing of hands and grace at priestly meals to their own meals.

The Pharisees, continuing Ezra's reformation, evolved the rules of conduct that translated the general requirements of the Law into a specific way of life (Halakhah). As the interpreters and guardians of the Law, they set up 'hedges' for its preservation, and defined the minutiae of its application to everyday conduct. This tendency brought them into conflict with the those groups that refused to submit to their rigorous standards, such as strictness in tithing, ritual purity, Sabbath observance, etc. These are classed in rabbinic literature as *'ammê hā'āreṣ* (see above), a term covering various classes and stations. Among their chief opponents, as we noted, were the Sadducees, who rejected their claims of the democracy of all Jews and their doctrine of the Oral Law, maintaining that only the observances prescribed in the Law were binding upon people but not those which the Pharisees 'derived from the tradition of the forefathers' (*Ant.* XIII. x. 6 [293 ff]). The Pharisees also drew the antagonism of Jesus and His disciples and particularly of Paul whose messianic claims and antinomist teachings they rejected. In consequence they were branded as bigoted formalists, hair-splitting legalists, and crafty hypocrites, devoid of charity and spirituality (Mk 7^{1-23}, Mt 23, Lk 11^{38-54} etc.). This view still colours many treatments of the Pharisees, but it is being corrected by scientific research, both Christian and Jewish. While unenviable characters were doubtless found in their ranks as among all bodies of men, they cannot be identified with these 'virtuosi of religion.'

The Pharisees are seen at their best when contrasted with the party of **Zealots** (q.v.) on the one side and the **Herodians** (q.v.) on the other. Unlike the latter, they were deeply in earnest with their ancestral religion. Again and again at critical times they showed the vigour and temper of fearless Puritanism. Unlike the former, they held back from the appeal to force, believing that the God of the nation was in control of history, that in His own good time He would grant the nation its desire; that, meanwhile, the duty of a true Israelite was wholehearted devotion to the Torah, joined to patient waiting on the Divine will. This nobler side of Pharisaism could find itself in Ps 119. The Pharisees were in a sense Churchmen rather than statesmen. And they emphasized spiritual methods. Their interests lay in the synagogue, in the schooling of children, in missionary extension amongst the heathen. Hence we are not surprised when we learn that, after the conflicts with Rome (A.D. 66–135), Pharisaism became practically synonymous with Judaism. One great war (the Maccabaean) had defined Pharisaism. Another war, even more terrible, gave it the final victory. The two wars together created the Judaism known to Europeans and Americans. And this, allowing for the inevitable changes which a long and varied experience bring to pass in the most tenacious race, is in substance the Pharisaism of the 2nd cent.

A wide historical study discovers moral dignity and greatness in Pharisaism. The Pharisees, as contrasted with the **Sadducees** (q.v.), represented the democratic tendency. As contrasted with the priesthood, they stood both for the democratic and for the spiritualizing tendency. The priesthood was a close corporation. No man who was unable to trace his descent from a priestly family could exercise any function in the Temple. But the Pharisees and the Scribes opened a great career to all the talents. Furthermore, the priesthood exhausted itself in the ritual of the Temple. But the Pharisees found their main function in teaching and preaching. So Pharisaism cleared the ground for Christianity. And when the reader goes through his NT with this point in mind, and when he notes the striking freedom of the NT from ritualistic and sacerdotal ideas, he should give credit to Pharisaism as one of the historical forces which made these supreme qualities possible.

We have not yet exhausted the claims of the Pharisees on our interest and gratitude. It was they who, for the most part, prepared the ground for Christianity by taking the Messianic idea and working it into the very texture of common consciousness. Pharisaism was inseparable from the popularization of monotheism, and the universal acceptance by the nation of its Divine election and calling. The Pharisees made idealized nationalism, based upon the monotheism of the prophets, the pith and marrow of Judaism. It was they who wrote the great Apocalypses (Daniel and Enoch). It was they who made the belief in immortality and resurrection part of the common consciousness. H. S. N.—**S. S. C.**

PHARPAR.—A river of Damascus mentioned with the **Abana** (2 K 5^{12}) by Naaman as contrasting favourably with the Jordan. Its identification is by no means so certain as that of Abana with the *Baradā*. The most probable is that suggested by Thomson, namely, the *Nahr el-A'waj*, a river rising E. of Hermon. A wady near, but not tributary to, one of its sources is called the *Wâdī Barbar*, which may possibly be a reminiscence of the ancient name. The principal obstacle to this identification is the distance of the river from the city; but Naaman was perhaps thinking as much of the fertile plain of Damascus as of the river itself. R. A. S. M.

PHARZITE.—See PEREZ.

PHASEAH, Neh 7^{51} (AV).—See PASEAH, 3.

PHASELIS is mentioned 1 Mac 15^{23} as a city to which the Romans in 139 B.C. sent letters on behalf of the Jews. It was at the E. extremity of the coast of Lycia, a Rhodian colony founded early in the 7th cent., which apparently endeavoured to maintain its independence of the rest of Lycia, though not immune to larger political changes. It was taken by Alexander the Great and ruled by the Ptolemies from 309 to 197 B.C., when it was captured by Antiochus III. Its early importance was due to its position in the trade between the Aegean and the Levant. Its alliance with Cilician pirates caused it to be captured by Servilius Isauricus in 78 B.C., and it seems never to have recovered its former importance. Under the Roman empire it was a member of the Lycian League. It was a bishopric in the Byzantine period. There was also a city named Phaselis in Palestine. It was built by Herod the Great in honour of his brother Phasael, and lay in the Jordan valley N. of Jericho.

A. E. H.—**F. C. G.**

PHASIRON.—A Nabataean tribe (1 Mac 9^{66}); unknown.

PHASSARON, I Es 5^{25} (AV).—See PASHHUR, **4.**

PHASSURUS, 1 Es 5^{25} (RV).—See PASHHUR, **4.**

PHEBE, Ro 16^{1} (AV).—See PHOEBE.

PHENICE.—**1.** Ac 27^{12} (AV) = **Phoenix** (q.v.). **2.** Ac 11^{19} 15^{3} (AV) = **Phoenicia** (q.v.).

PHENICIA, Ac 21^{2} (AV) = **Phoenicia** (q.v.).

PHEREZITE.—See PERIZZITES.

PHICHOL.—AV form of **Phicol** (q.v.).

PHICOL.—Abimelech's captain, Gn $21^{22, 32}$ 26^{26} (AV **Phichol**).

PHILADELPHIA was a city in Lydia, *c* 30 miles from Sardis (q.v.), in the valley of the Cogamus, a tributary of the Hermus, and conveniently located for handling the trade between the great central plateau of Asia Minor and Smyrna (q.v.). The district known as *Katakekaumenē* (Burnt Region), because of its volcanic character, rises immediately to the NE. of the city; this was a great vine-growing district.

Philadelphia was founded and named by Attalus II.

Philadelphus of Pergamum (159–138 B.C.). It was liable to severe earthquakes (for some time after A.D. 17 it lay in ruins), but nevertheless remained an important centre of the Roman province of Asia, receiving the name of Neo-Caesarea from Tiberius, and later on, the honour of the Neocorate (*i.e.* the wardenship of the temple for emperor worship). There is no record of the beginning of the church at Philadelphia, but in the Apocalypse it is one of the seven churches to which, as heads of districts, special messages were sent. In its message (Rev 3^{8-13}) it is said to have ' but little power ' (which perhaps refers to its recent origin), and to have before it ' an open door ' (which seems to refer to the opportunity to spread the gospel in the centre of Asia Minor. In 3^{9} ' the synagogue of Satan who say they are Jews and are not ' may perhaps mean that the Jews of Philadelphia had been lax, and had conceded too much to Gentile ways ; on the other hand, as in 2^{9} (Smyrna) they were persecutors of the Christians, and their non-Judaism was perhaps not so much laxity as affiliation with the persecuting authorities (see W. Bousset, commentary). The passage contains no reproach against the Christians, though they are bidden to hold fast what they have, and the promise to him who conquers is that ' I will make him a pillar in the temple of my God [not the heathen imperial shrine] . . . and I will write on him the name of the city of my God, the new Jerusalem . . . and my own new name.' Perhaps there is a reference here, as in the message to Pergamum, to the new name taken at baptism and apparently sometimes kept secret.

A marble stele from the 1st cent. B.C. sets forth the rules of a private mystery cult (Dittenberger, *Syllbge* 985 ; translation in F. C. Grant, *Hellenistic Religions*, pp. 28 ff). It is one of the most impressive examples of real piety and of ethical idealism from the ancient pagan world.

Philadelphia was the seat of a bishop but was not a metropolis until about A.D. 1300 when the importance of Sardis had declined. In the 14th cent., when the Greek empire retained nothing on the mainland of Asia except a strip of territory opposite Constantinople, Philadelphia still continued to resist the Ottoman army, though far from the sea and almost forgotten by the emperors. The date of its final capture is uncertain—probably A.D. 1391. Its modern name is *Alashehir*, and a considerable portion of the population is Christian.

There was also a city named Philadelphia in Palestine, a member of the Decapolis (q.v.). A. E. H.—**F. C. G.**

PHILARCHES, 2 Mac 8^{32} (AV).—See PHYLARCH.

PHILEMON.—Known only as the person first addressed in the Epistle to Philemon (q.v.). This epistle of Paul's is concerned with the treatment to be accorded a returning Colossian slave, Onesimus, who has become a Christian under the Apostle's influence. It has usually been supposed that Philemon was the owner of the slave. That individual, however, may well have been Archippus, also addressed in the letter, in which case it would be most plausible to see in Philemon, whom Paul calls his ' fellow-worker,' one of the Apostle's coadjutors in the Laodicea-Colossae-Hierapolis area. But see PHILEMON, EPISTLE TO. J. K.

PHILEMON, EPISTLE TO.—A brief, skilfully written, warmly personal, and unquestionably authentic letter of Paul, now found as the final epistle in the Pauline corpus in our canon. It is addressed : ' To Philemon . . . , Apphia . . . , Archippus . . . and the church [that meets] in your house.' After the salutation to all of these, Paul speaks to one person only in the rest of the letter except for the final benediction, where the second personal pronoun again occurs in the plural. The letter, then, is concerned to convey a message to one person, but in the hearing, so to speak, of two others and even of the church to which presumably all three individuals belonged and which met in the house of the one principally involved.

1. Purpose.—The occasion of the letter is the return of a slave to his master. The slave, whose name is Onesimus, has in some way fallen in with Paul during one of the latter's imprisonments. Perhaps the meeting was accidental ; perhaps Onesimus sought the Apostle out for help ; perhaps (although this is less likely) he came on some errand from his master. It has usually been said that he was a runaway ; but the letter gives no real support to such a view, unless a hint that the slave has not been very useful to his master (despite his name, which means ' useful ' or ' profitable '), and may even have done his master some wrong, is taken to require such an inference. However this may be, it is clear that Onesimus has become a Christian under Paul's influence, has proved himself to be very ' useful ' to the Apostle, and has also won a very warm place in his affections. Paul says that sending Onesimus back is like sending his very heart. It is obvious that he wants to keep him and that he had thought of doing so without more ado. Actually, however, he has decided not to keep him without the owner's full consent. He therefore sends him to his master (also a Christian) with this letter. We could not know from this letter (from which all of this story has been derived) where Onesimus and his master lived, but the Epistle to the Colossians, written at the same time, refers to Onesimus as ' one of yourselves.' The letter then was sent to Colossae. Where Paul himself was at the time we can only guess. We know only that he was in prison. Most scholars favour Rome, others Caesarea, and others still Ephesus. The time of writing is equally, and correspondingly, uncertain.

2. Philemon or Archippus ?—It is to be assumed that the owner of the slave and of the house in which the church met was one of the three individuals named in the salutation of the letter. But it is not equally clear which of the three he was. The traditional view, obviously based on the order of the names, is that Philemon was this person. But this is not necessarily true, and a strong case can be made for the hypothesis that the owner was Archippus, who is mentioned in closest connexion with the church. If Archippus was the owner of both house and slave, and Paul's request was addressed to him, we have a clue to understanding Col 4^{17} : ' Say to Archippus, " See that you fulfill the ministry which you have received in the Lord ".' The term here for ' ministry ' is the same Greek term used in the Epistle to Philemon when Paul speaks of wanting to have Onesimus with him that ' he might serve me in your place.' The letter referred to in Col 4^{16} as ' from Laodicea ' would, in that event, be our Philemon. Perhaps Philemon himself, to whom the letter would first come, belonged in that city.

3. Later History.—On the basis of the ordinary view that Onesimus was simply a returning runaway slave and that the letter to Philemon was primarily an appeal for clemency, it is hard to understand its preservation, its incorporation among the collected letters of Paul and its eventual canonization. But if the letter marks the moment when a very useful man became permanently associated with Paul's work, quite a different prospect appears. Onesimus may well have become an important figure among the Pauline churches in the generation after the Apostle's death. In Ignatius' letter to the Ephesians (*c* 110) some allusions to Onesimus, Bishop of Ephesus, and some reminiscences of the language of the Epistle to Philemon give good ground for the identification of Onesimus the one-time slave with Onesimus the later bishop. Since the letters of Paul were almost certainly first gathered together and published in Ephesus in this same period, the preservation of the Epistle to Philemon and its place in the corpus of the Pauline writings is fully explained. J. K.

PHILETUS.—Mentioned in Second Timothy (2 Ti 2^{17}) as one of those who were doing harm by their false teaching on the subject of the resurrection of the body. For them the resurrection was past. *I.e.* their view may have been that the resurrection was spiritual, from sin to holiness and hence there was no future resurrection of the body, no life to come. Cf HYMENAEUS.

PHILIP (Apocr.).—**1.** Father of Alexander the Great

(1 Mac 1[1] 6[2]). **2.** A friend or courtier (2 Mac 9[29]) of Antiochus Epiphanes, who received the charge (previously given to Lysias) of bringing up the young Antiochus Eupator (1 Mac 6[14–17]). On the death of Antiochus Epiphanes, Lysias took upon himself to proclaim young Eupator king (164 B.C.). The jealousy over this matter led to open hostilities between Lysias and Philip. Philip was overcome by Lysias at Antioch and put to death. He is by many regarded as identical with—**3.** A Phrygian who (in 168 B.C.), when left in charge of Jerusalem by Antiochus Epiphanes, was remarkable for the cruelty of his government (2 Mac 5[22] 6[11]). Little more is known of him unless the details of his life be filled up by assuming his identity with the former Philip. **4.** A king of Macedonia (220–179 B.C.) overthrown by the Romans (1 Mac 8[5]). T. A. M.

PHILIP (NT).—**1. The Apostle.**—The Synoptic Gospels and Acts have handed down only Philip's name in the lists of the twelve apostles (Mk 3[18], Mt 10[3], Lk 6[14], Ac 1[13]). John tells us 1[43ff] that Philip was called by Jesus after Andrew and Peter, that he, like them, was of Bethsaida, and that he found Nathanael. Philip is mentioned in 6[5, 7], then in 12[21] and 14[8f]. John does not sketch Philip's personal character; he is, rather, a representative well meaning but not yet illuminated disciple. Later legend related that he had laboured in Asia Minor and was buried at Hierapolis.

2. The Evangelist.—This Philip was one of the 'Seven' (Ac 6[5] 21[8]), the leaders of the Hellenistic, Greek-speaking group in the early Christian community at Jerusalem. He seems to have been an effective missionary in Samaria (Ac 8[5ff]) and on the Palestinian coast from Ashdod to Caesarea (Ac 8[40]). There he resided at last. When St. Paul visited Caesarea on his last journey to Jerusalem, he stayed with him. By converting the chamberlain of Candace, the queen of Ethiopia, Philip was the first to cross the frontiers of Jewish Christianity (Ac 8[26ff]). His four unmarried daughters 'prophesied' (21[9])—later on there were no prophetesses in the Christian Church.

3. Herod Philip.—See HEROD. D. S.—E. H.

PHILIPPI was a city situated E. of Mt. Pangaeus, on the E. border of Macedonia, about 10 miles from the coast. It was originally (under the name of Crenides) a settlement of Thasians, who mined the gold of Mt. Pangaeus; but one of the early acts of King Philip II. of Macedon was to assure himself of revenue by seizing these mines and strongly fortifying the city, to which he gave his own name (358 B.C.). The mines are said to have yielded him 1000 talents a year. Philippi passed with the rest of Macedonia to the Romans in 168 B.C. Until 146 B.C. Macedonia was divided into four regions (see TETRARCH), with separate governments, and so divided that a member of one could not marry or hold property in another. But in 146 it received the more regular organization of a province. In 42 B.C. Philippi was the scene of the great battle in which Antony defeated M. Brutus and Cassius. The great Eastern road of the Roman Empire, the Via Egnatia, after crossing the Strymon at Amphipolis, kept N. of Mt. Pangaeus to Philippi and then turned SE. to Neapolis, which was the port of Philippi. Philippi stood on the steep side of a hill, and immediately S. of it lay a large marshy lake.

The Church at Philippi was founded by St. Paul on his second missionary journey, the first Christian community in Europe, as far as our records show. With Silas, Timothy, and Luke he landed at Neapolis, and proceeded to Philippi, which the book of Acts describes as 'the leading city of the district of Macedonia, and a Roman colony.' Philippi was not the capital city of either of the regions into which Macedonia had been divided in 168 B.C., but the most natural explanation of the phrase 'first of the district' (if the text is correct; see Haenchen in the Meyer commentary) is that the province had at this time a division for official purposes of which we do not know. Other explanations are that it means 'the first city we arrived at' (which the Greek could scarcely mean), or that Philippi claimed a pre-eminence in much the same way that Pergamum, Smyrna, Ephesus all claimed to be the 'first city' of Asia. It had become a Roman colony after the battle of Philippi, 42 B.C., when Octavian and Antony, having vanquished Brutus and Cassius, settled a number of their veterans there. Another body of veterans was settled there after Actium, 31 B.C., when Octavian made it a colony (Ac 16[12]) for partisans of Antony evicted from Italy. As a colony its constitution was modelled on the ancient one of Rome, and its two chief magistrates had not only lictors (AV, RV **serjeants**, q.v.; RSV 'the police'), but also a jurisdiction independent of that of the governor of the province. It was the first essentially Roman town in which St. Paul preached. There was no synagogue, but on the Sabbath, says Ac 16[13], 'we went outside the gate to the riverside where we supposed there was a place of prayer.' At this place, therefore, St. Paul found a number of women assembled, Jewesses or proselytes, one of whom named **Lydia** (q.v.), a dealer in purple goods from Thyatira, was immediately converted and baptized. For the subsequent incidents see PAUL, PYTHON, MAGISTRATE, etc.

Some scholars believe that the Church at Philippi was left in charge of St. Luke, for at this point in the narrative of the Acts the first person is dropped until St. Paul passes through Macedonia on his return from the third missionary journey (*i.e.* between 16[17] and 20[5]). The Church flourished, and always remained on terms of peculiar affection with St. Paul, being allowed to minister to his needs more than once. See article PHILIPPIANS [EPISTLE TO], which was probably written during his imprisonment at Rome. From 1 Ti 1[3] it has been inferred that Paul paid a later visit to Philippi.

Before A.D. 117 Ignatius passed through Philippi on his journey from Antioch to his martyrdom in Rome. He was welcomed by the Church, and they wrote a letter of consolation to the Church of Antioch and another to Polycarp of Smyrna, asking for copies of any letters that Ignatius had written in Asia. Polycarp wrote his Epistle to the Philippians in answer. In the 4th and 5th cents. the bishop of Philippi was present at Councils, but apart from this the Church passes out of history.

A. E. H.—F. C. G.

PHILIPPIANS, EPISTLE TO.—1. The Church of Philippi.—St. Paul visited Philippi (q.v.) on his second missionary journey, and founded there his first Church in Europe. The names in Ph 4[2f], probably those of early converts, lead us to infer that the Gentile element continued strong from the days when the Church began in the households of Lydia and the jailor (Ac 16[12–40]). It is only by the exercise of much imagination that the character of the city—a Roman colony enjoying the *jus Italicum*, and therefore with a sense of its own importance—can be discerned in the letter, though probably the fact that St. Paul was a Roman citizen, and the virtual apology with which he was sent away by the praetors, may have had some effect on the subsequent treatment of the Christians. As one of the Churches of Macedonia referred to in 2 Co 8[2ff], it was doubtless in deep poverty, but is held forth along with them as a model of liberality. St. Paul seems to have treated the Philippians in an exceptional way, by accepting from them support which he ordinarily refused (2 Co 11[7ff], Ph 4[15]). He must have visited Philippi at least three times (Ac 16[12], 2 Co 2[13], Ac 20[6]), and he always found his own love reciprocated by the Church, and experienced a unique joy in their fellowship with him for the furtherance of the gospel (Ph 1[3–8]). The Apostle's ascendancy in the Church was never questioned, as in Corinth. There were, it is true, rivalries in the congregation, especially, it would seem, among some of the active women of the Church, and St. Paul does not hesitate to use the most powerful of Christian motives to give force and direction to the shaft that he aims at discord (2[1–11]). But, unlike the Churches of Galatia, Philippi had not been disturbed by a severe attack from the Judaizers, though the Apostle sees threatening indications of their approach (3[2, 18f]). The Church was organized with bishops (q.v.) and deacons (q.v.), from whom St. Paul seems to have received the people's gift (1[1]), which they sent by Epaphroditus, probably with a letter. In no part of his missionary field, so far as we know, did he find such a pure Christian life. They were 'lights in the world' (2[15f]), and the Apostle's 'joy and crown' (4[1]).

2. Situation of St. Paul.—The Apostle is a prisoner (1[7, 13f, 17]). It appears that his imprisonment had become more rigorous since the Philippians received their first word concerning him; and it must have been of some duration, because there had been several communications between them (2[25–30] 4[10]). They are distressed by the fear that the gospel will suffer through his strict confinement and possible martyrdom. But this imprisonment, instead of hindering the gospel, has really led to a much more zealous preaching of Christ by the Christians of the city. The motive of this increased activity was sometimes an unworthy emulation of the Apostle, and there must have been those in the Church who refused to acknowledge his leadership, being aroused by the success with which 'his bonds became manifest throughout all the Praetorium and to all the rest' (1[12–18]). He has come to be recognized as no mere disturber of the peace (Ac 24[5] 25[8]), but as a preacher of a religion different from that of the Jews, and one which had already reached Caesar's household (Ph 4[22]). His defence has been partly made, and he is full of hope of a speedy acquittal (1[25ff]), though the possibility of martyrdom hangs like a cloud in his sky, bright to his own view, but casting a shadow upon his readers' joy (1[19–30]).

It has usually been assumed that Philippians, together with the other so-called 'Imprisonment Letters,' was written during the apostle's imprisonment at Rome that is described in Ac 28[16, 20, 30], and that it is to be grouped with the 'later letters' of St. Paul. The greetings in 4[23] from 'those of Caesar's household' and the reference in 1[13] to 'the whole praetorian guard' were believed to identify Rome, beyond any reasonable doubt, as the letter's place of writing. But it is now known that 'Praetorium' in the days of the Roman Empire could designate the residence of any provincial governor and that 'Caesar's household' could refer to the royal entourage at any provincial capital as well as at Rome.

According to the Book of the Acts, Paul was imprisoned for two years at Caesarea, and it is possible to argue that it was from this Palestinian city that Paul wrote the letter. However, the apostle's references in 1[15–26] and 2[20–24] to serious rifts in the church, to the disloyalty even of intimate friends, and to the danger of imminent death that beset him have no reflection in the narrative in Acts of his Caesarean imprisonment. Furthermore, Paul's hopes of shortly revisiting his congregation at Philippi would be difficult to understand in light of his belief while at Corinth that his work in Macedonia and in Achaia was finished and his plans at that time to go on to Spain by way of Rome (Ro 15[23–29]).

In recent times the possibility has been raised that Paul had suffered an imprisonment at Ephesus of which there is no indication in Acts. 2 Co 1[8–10], written shortly after the apostle's departure from the capital of the Province of Asia, implies that he had undergone some nerve-racking experience late in his stay at Ephesus that seemed at one time to threaten his very life and from which he believed himself to have been delivered only by the direct intervention of God. Paul's remark in 1 Co 15[32] that he had 'fought with beasts at Ephesus' can be interpreted as an oblique reference to an actual ordeal as a prisoner. On the hypothesis that Ro 16 was originally a letter addressed to the church at Ephesus, it can be argued that the Apostle's references to Prisca and Aquila in vv.[3–4] as having 'risked their necks' for his life and in v.[7] to Andronicus and Junias as his 'fellow prisoners' lend further support to the hypothesis of an Ephesian imprisonment. An early 'Marcionite' prologue to Colossians attests that the belief was current in the church, perhaps as early as the 2nd cent., that Paul had been imprisoned at Ephesus and that Colossians (and therefore in all probability also Philippians) had been written from that city.

If an Ephesian imprisonment be assumed, the suggestion that Philippians was written at Ephesus certainly lies close at hand and is attractive. If the letter is to be dated before the second visit to Philippi about which we are told in the Book of the Acts, Paul had not yet concluded that his work in Macedonia and Achaia was finished and had not yet decided to turn westward to Italy and Spain, as was the case when he wrote the Epistle to the Romans (15[23–29]), and the expression of his hope of revisiting his Philippian converts (Ph 1[23–27] 2[24]) raises no problems for the critical reader. If Paul was imprisoned at Ephesus when Epaphroditus visited him as an emissary of the Philippian church (2[25–30] 4[18]), we do not have to think of the long and difficult journey by land and sea from Philippi to Rome (almost 800 miles), but of the relatively short and easy one from Philippi to Ephesus.

Nevertheless, it must be kept in mind that the hypothesis of an Ephesian imprisonment remains a hypothesis, and to support it by arguments based on another, that of the Ephesian origin of the 'Imprisonment Letters,' is questionable critical procedure. Since the objections to Rome as the place in which Philippians was written are not insuperable, it appears to this writer that the older hypothesis of Roman origin is preferable to the other possibilities that have been raised.

If Philippians was written from Ephesus it would be earlier than 2 Corinthians and Romans, possibly earlier also than Galatians, and would have to be dated sometime before A.D. 54. If it is a letter from Rome it must be dated sometime after A.D. 57 and may possibly be the latest of the letters of Paul that has been preserved by the church. (For dates based on a different relative chronology, see article CHRONOLOGY OF THE NT.)

3. Contents of the Epistle.—

(i) *Greeting*, 1[1f]. Paul and Timothy salute the saints of Philippi, together with their bishops and deacons.

(ii) *Introduction*, vv.[3–11]. St. Paul is constantly moved to thanksgiving for their generous fellowship with him in the furtherance of the gospel from the beginning, and they are all ever on his heart where Christ dwells. His prayer for them is that their love may abound in knowledge and insight as to what befits the Christian life, that so they may live sincere and blameless lives until Christ comes.

(iii) *The present condition of St. Paul*, vv.[12–26]. His imprisonment has, contrary to expectation, led to the spread of the gospel, partly by his being chained to the Praetorian guards, partly through a new courage among his friends and partly through envious rivalry. He, however, rejoices because he is assured that in answer to their prayers the Spirit of Christ will enable him to glorify his Lord whatever be the issue of his imprisonment; he does not know what to desire, though he believes that he will be acquitted and will work for their Christian welfare.

(iv) *Exhortations to the Philippians to walk worthily of the gospel*, 1[27]–2[18]. No hostility must deter them from maintaining the gospel in a spirit of unity, for ability to suffer for Christ is a sign of Divine grace to them and of ruin to their enemies. An appeal is also made to them, by all that they have experienced of Christian love, to complete his joy by living in fellowship, and to exhibit that unselfish mind which prompted Christ to come to earth and die for them. Wherefore He is now exalted to be worshipped by every creature. By reverent obedience let them work with God and effect His will of good towards them, so that at the last day the Apostle and his beloved Philippians may rejoice in what the gospel has done for them.

(v) *The promise to send Timothy, and the commendation of Epaphroditus to the Philippians* (2[19–30]).

(vi) *Christian progress through the knowledge of Jesus Christ*, 3[1]–4[1]. To sum up his letter, the Apostle would say, 'Rejoice in the Lord.' But, as though suddenly reminded of a danger, he returns, even at the risk of wearying them, to a warning against the Judaizers—dogs, evil workers, mutilators of the flesh. He who believes in Christ alone as a sufficient Saviour is the true Israelite. St. Paul, who had enjoyed every Jewish privilege, knows of how small value they were for attaining true righteousness, and now he boasts only in Christ. For personal knowledge of Him he will gladly lose all else, in order that he may get the righteousness which is from God by faith, and in close union with Him may realize the meaning of His sufferings, death, and resurrection. Christian perfection is still in the distance, but all who have been laid hold of by Christ must respond by striving eagerly for perfect fellowship with Him. The mature Christian must keep on in the path of progress, and not be misled by teaching which will end in an earthly goal and the rejection of the cross. St. Paul and his followers are to be their example, for their Commonwealth and its ideals are above, whence Christ will soon come to transfigure them into His likeness. Wherefore let this Church, which will be his crown at that day, stand fast in the Lord.

(vii) *Conclusion*, 4^{2-19}. (*a*) Exhortations to individuals to unity (vv.^{2f}). Possibly 'yoke-fellow' (v.^{3}) refers to Epaphroditus; possibly it should be translated 'Synzygus' (q.v.), a proper name. (*b*) St. Paul their example for Christian joy and conduct (vv.$^{4-9}$). (*c*) Thanks for their gifts and for their many past favours. Contented as he is with whatever God sends, he might have done without them, but they will add interest to the account of the Philippians, and he gives them a receipt in full which God will acknowledge (vv.$^{10-19}$).

(viii) *Doxology and final greetings* (vv.$^{20-23}$).

4. Purpose and Characteristics.—Epaphroditus had fallen sick at Rome before his work of love for St. Paul was done, and the news, having reached Philippi, cast the Church into anxiety; Epaphroditus in his turn having heard of their alarm has grown home-sick. St. Paul uses the occasion of his return to set their mind at rest about his own imprisonment for the gospel, and to deal with some affairs about which they had informed him. The letter is so thoroughly personal that it has no plan or any single aim. He thanks the Philippians for their gift, crowning many acts of generosity towards him, and yet, lest they should feel that he was too dependent upon them, he reminds them that it is their spirit that he values most. Again he warns them against a Judaistic gospel, and is urgent in seeking to compose personal jealousies of two of the women workers. His gospel is the only one, and it is the gospel of love. His union with Christ fills him with love and contentment, and thrills the lonely prisoner with *joy*, which may be called the note of the Epistle, and he hopes by this letter to impart some of this spirit to the Philippians also. Should the view that St. Paul was not acquitted be correct, this letter might be called 'his last testament to his beloved Church'; but there is good reason to believe that his hope of release was fulfilled.

Philippians is an excellent example of the Pauline method of sustaining Christian life by doctrinal truth which is the outcome of personal experience. Human thought has made few nobler flights into the mystery of redemption than Ph 2^{5-11}, but it is used to exalt the homely duty of sacrifice in the ministry of fellowship. Like 2 Co 8^{9}, the dynamic of the truth lies not in an intellectual interpretation of the mystery of Christ's personality, for little is told further than that He was in His nature essentially Divine, and enjoyed the prerogatives of Divinity; but it lies in the fact that St. Paul had learned from his own intercourse with the risen Christ His extraordinary power and grace as the eternal, Divine Son of God. Everything earthly becomes worthless in comparison with the excellency of the knowledge of Jesus Christ, his Lord. The contrast between His earthly life of suffering and death and the eternal, glorious existence involved in the vision of the risen Lord, has become the religious motive of supreme efficacy. Similarly in $3^{8-11, 20f}$ the doctrine is deduced from experience, and is to be wrought into character. The emphasis on the practice of virtue, especially in 4^{8-12}, is said to reflect the finest contemporary teaching of the pagan world, but the form is pervaded with the purest Christian spirit.

5. Authenticity and Integrity.—Objections once urged against the authenticity of this Epistle are not seriously regarded to-day, and have been abandoned by all but a few extremists. The recurrence of the motives, ideas, and language of the great Pauline Epistles, and the external evidence of its use from the early sub-Apostolic age, make it unnecessary to consider them in detail. More plausibility attaches to the theory that the Epistle, as we now have it, consists of two letters, which are joined at 3^{2}, the last two chapters being probably earlier and addressed to different readers. Much has been made of what are described as 'abrupt breaks' after 3^{1} 3^{16} 4^{3} and 4^{9}, and it is argued that 3^{1} originally marked the end of a letter and ought to be translated: 'Now, my brothers, goodbye, and the Lord be with you' (Goodspeed). In support of this hypothesis, appeal is made to Polycarp's letter to the Philippians (iii. 2), where the words 'who also wrote you letters' are held to prove that they had not then been united. But Polycarp, who knew apparently only our letter, may either have heard of others which St. Paul wrote to the Philippians or have employed the term loosely; or perhaps he was referring to a collection of St. Paul's Epistles used widely for edification by all the Churches. The abruptness noted above may be explained by the fact that St. Paul is expressing himself freely in an intimate letter to his friends, and perhaps it was partly due to something in their letter to him which he suddenly remembered. R. A. F.—**S. M. G.**

PHILISTIA.—See PHILISTINES and PALESTINE.

PHILISTIM, Gn 10^{14} (AV) = **Philistines** (q.v.).

PHILISTINES.—The inhabitants of the Maritime Plain of Palestine (cf article PALESTINE, **1**) from the period of the Judges onward to the 6th cent. or later. They are said to have come from Caphtor (Am 9^{7}, Jer 47^{4}, Dt 2^{23}), which is with much probability identified with Crete. At all events they came from over the sea.

Rameses III. of the 20th Egyptian dynasty encountered a piratical sea-faring people on the borders of Syria, whom he called *Purusati* (=*Pulista* or 'Philistines'). They afterwards made incursions on the northern coast of Egypt as well as on the coast of Palestine. In the latter country they gained a permanent foothold, owing to its disorganized condition. When Wenamon made his expedition to Lebanon for a king of the 21st Dynasty (*c* 1100), a Philistine kingdom existed at Dor. (For these facts cf Breasted, *Ancient Records*, iv. 274 ff, and *History of Egypt*, p. 513.)

The Philistines first make their appearance in Biblical history late in the period of the Judges, when Samson, of the tribe of Dan, is said to have waged his curious single-handed combats with them (Jg 13–16). These conflicts were the natural result of the impact of the Philistines upon Israel's western border. The reference to the Philistines in Jg 3^{31} is a later insertion (cf ISRAEL, I, **11**). During the time of Eli these invaders were trying to make their way into the central ridge of Palestine, and in one of the battles captured the Ark of Yahweh, which a pestilence (probably bubonic plague) induced them to return (1 S 4–6).

When Saul became king the Philistines tried to break his power, but were defeated through the bravery of Jonathan (1 S 13 f). Saul did not permanently check their progress, however, as by the end of his reign the whole of the rich plain of Jezreel was in their possession, including the city of Bethshean at its eastern end (1 S 31^{10}). David early in his reign inflicted upon them a severe defeat (2 S 5^{22ff}), afterwards reducing them to vassalage (2 S 8^{1}). Down to this time Philistine power was concentrated in the hands of the rulers of the five cities of Gaza, Ashkelon, Ashdod, Ekron, and Gath. The rulers of these cities are called by a peculiar title, which is translated 'lords of the Philistines' (q.v.).

After the reign of David, probably at the division

of the kingdom, the Philistines regained their independence, for we find the kings of Israel in the 9th cent. trying to wrest from them Gibbethon, a town on the border of the Maritime Plain (1 K 15[27] 16[15]). Late in the same century the Assyrian king Adad-nirari III. took tribute of Philistine kings (*KIB* i. 190), and began the long series of Assyrian interferences in Philistine affairs. Amos (1[6-8]) denounces Philistine monarchies as among the independent kingdoms of his time.

The position of the Philistines exposed them to every approach of the Assyrians and Egyptians, and during the last third of the 8th cent. and the whole of the 7th their history is a series of conquests, conspiracies, and rebellions. It is possible to follow these with much fulness in the Assyrian inscriptions, but full details cannot be given here. Tiglath-pileser III. received tribute from Philistines (*KIB* ii. 20). They became Sargon's vassals the year that Samaria fell, 722 B.C. (*KIB* ii. 54), but ten years later a rebellion was led by Ashdod (Is 20[1]; *KIB* ii. 64 ff). At the beginning of the reign of Sennacherib another effort was made to shake off the Assyrian yoke. In this Hezekiah of Judah took part by imprisoning Padi, the Philistine king of Ekron, who remained faithful to Sennacherib. The allies thus brought together were defeated at Eltekeh (*KIB* ii. 92 ff), and the siege of Jerusalem by Sennacherib was the result (2 K 18 f). Esarhaddon (*KIB* ii. 148), and Ashurbanipal (*KIB* ii. 240) marched across the Philistine territory and held it in subjection. With the decline of Assyria the Philistines began to suffer from the rise of Egypt under the 26th Dynasty. Psammetichus I. took Ashdod after a siege of 29 years (Herod. ii. 157). Neco II., a contemporary of Josiah of Judah, captured Gaza (Herod. ii. 159). It is probable that the Philistines suffered at the hands of Nebuchadnezzar, but no record of his doings among them has been preserved. The Assyrians call the Philistine rulers 'kings.' The older title, 'lords of the Philistines,' has disappeared.

When Cambyses made his expedition into Egypt (525 B.C.), Gaza opposed him (Polyb. xvi. 40). The Sidonian king Eshmunazar claims that Dor and Joppa were added to the dominions of Sidon. Gaza in 332 held out against Alexander the Great, and his siege of it is famous (Diod. Sic. XVII. xlviii. 7). The Ptolemies and Seleucids often fought over Philistine territory. It finally passed under Roman rule, and its cities had then an important history.

The Philistines cease to be mentioned by this name after the time of the Assyrians. Some infer from the fact that Herodotus (iii. 5) speaks of the Arabians as being in possession of the coast in the time of Cambyses, that the Philistines had even then been supplanted. It is probable that in the ebb and flow of the nations over this land they were gradually absorbed and lost their identity.

Probably the Philistines adopted in the main the religion and civilization of the Canaanites. Their chief god, Dagon (1 S 5[2ff]), was a Semitic deity. He appears in the el-Amarna letters and also in Babylonia (cf Barton, *Semit. Or.*, 229 ff). There was also at Ashkelon a temple of Astarte (Herod. i. 105). If their religion was Semitic, so also were probably the other features of their civilization. If they brought other customs from beyond the sea, they are not described in our scanty records.

G. A. B.

PHILO OF ALEXANDRIA, often called Philo Judaeus to distinguish him from Philo of Larissa († 79 B.C.) who became the teacher of Cicero. He was born *c* 20 B.C. and died sometime after A.D. 40. His voluminous works, chiefly the allegorical or philosophical exegesis of the OT, are incomplete, as large sections have perished; those which remain were preserved by Christians, not Jews. Yet he is the first philosopher after Aristotle to be represented by a large quantity of writings. The chief questions relating to his place in history are these: (*a*) How representative was he of contemporary Judaism, especially of Hellenistic Judaism? (*b*) What was his influence upon Christianity and how early did it begin? His influence—or that of his 'school'—upon the Epistle to Hebrews is unquestionable; but upon Paul and John it is less certain. His influence upon the Alexandrian church fathers, especially Clement and Origen, was enormous, and through them upon early Christian theology.

1. Life.—Almost the only surviving data for the life of Philo are to be found in his two works, *Against Flaccus* and the *Embassy to Gaius*. These relate to the anti-Jewish outbreak in A.D. 38, when the Prefect of Egypt, A. Avillius Flaccus, had attempted to set up cult images of the mad emperor Gaius in the Jewish synagogues. (A similar attempt was made to set up a colossal statue of him in the Temple at Jerusalem in A.D. 40.) When the Jews resisted, Flaccus ordered troops to search Jewish homes and synagogues for arms, with the result that both homes and synagogues were sacked and rifled and all who resisted were cut down. Philo was sent to Rome as head of a delegation of protest. Though nothing came of the protest, the problem was solved within a few months by the death of Gaius.

Philo's prominence in the Jewish community is evident from this important commission. His brother Alexander was 'alabarch' or 'ethnarch' of the Jews in Alexandria, and he was said to be one of the richest men in the world. Philo had a thorough Greek education and wrote Greek fluently and effectively. He was familiar with Greek philosophy, and was especially influenced by Plato, Aristotle, and the Stoics. Modern historians of Greek philosophy (*e.g.* Zeller, Wolfson) have accorded him a prominent place in the record, not only as the transmitter of Platonic-Stoic doctrines (*e.g.* of the *Logos*) but as an independent thinker whose contributions influenced later generations all the way to mediaeval scholasticism and even beyond. But Philo was not primarily a philosopher; he was an exegete, and aimed to bring out the secret inner meaning of the Jewish Law (*Torah*=teaching) by showing its compatibility with Greek philosophy: if truth is one, and both are true, they must agree. He would not admit any disagreement between the external requirements of the Law and its inner meaning (contrast Paul's interpretation). Theosophical speculation about the Law's inner meaning was no excuse for lax observance of the religious rules, and both eclectics and dilettantists were discouraged from attendance upon his lectures. Many of his interpretations were in close agreement with the exegesis, *i.e.* the *halakhah*, of the Palestinian rabbis and their successors; but there also were wide divergences, which show that Philo (like Paul) was not a thorough and consistent disciple of the Tannaim. It has even been questioned whether, or to what extent, Philo was familiar with Hebrew. Like Paul, once more, he read the Jewish Scriptures in the LXX translation, not in Hebrew—though obviously, like any Diaspora Jew, then or now, he was familiar with certain technical words or 'tags.' Like Paul, moreover, and like many others since, Philo viewed the LXX as inspired, equally with the Hebrew original. The question of accuracy in text or translation seems never to have arisen for either interpreter.

2. Writings.—Philo's surviving works include apologetic as well as exegetical and philosophical writings. (*a*) The *Flaccus* and *Embassy to Gaius* were clearly meant for general reading, as was also his *Apology for the Jews*, fragments of which are preserved in Eusebius, *Praep. Evang.* viii. 11. His famous work *On the Contemplative Life* may belong to this treatise; it is especially important for its description of the 'Therapeutae,' an Egyptian Jewish group similar to the Essenes in Palestine (see DEAD SEA SCROLLS and ESSENES). Another apologetic work was his *Life of Moses*, which describes the lawgiver in terms designed to appeal to Gentiles, especially those who accepted the Stoic ideal of kingship.

(*b*) His works of exegesis include the *Exposition of the Law*, a series of studies *On the Creation of the World*, *On Abraham* [*On Isaac* and *On Jacob* are now lost], *On Joseph*, *On the Decalogue*, *On Special Laws*, *On Virtues*, and *On Rewards and Punishments*. This series is also, apparently, addressed to Gentiles, and attempts to correlate the OT conceptions of religion with those of Greek philosophy, especially those of Plato. However, Philo goes far beyond Plato in his description of the **Logos** as the agent or power of God in creation and also as the underlying synthetic force of law and order in nature—a conception close to that of the early Stoics, *e.g.* Cleanthes (see his famous *Hymn to Zeus*), and also to the NT idea of Christ (Col 1[17]). The conception of law set forth in these writings is also akin to the Greek (Platonic-Stoic), not as an agreed convention in human society, designed to do away with barbarism, or as the expressed will of the more powerful, or as the 'customs of the ancestors' (the Roman *mos maiorum*), but as the eternal harmony embedded in the very nature of the universe, prior to all codes and conventions. It is the inspired source of heroic virtue as seen in the lives of the noblest men, who have lived by conscience rather than mere precept or command. Obviously Philo (like Paul) was striving for a more satisfactory conception of law as based upon an inner principle or obligation and not mere external commandment. Philo viewed the Ten Commandments as the central and basic expression of this eternal and unchanging system of law.

(*c*) A third group of writings is the series since called the *Allegories of the Sacred Laws*. Of these works only eighteen survive. The views set forth in the earlier *Exposition* are here assumed, but the analysis of the text (chiefly of Genesis) is definitely addressed to more advanced (Jewish or Gentile) students. Like the writings of Aristotle these treatises may represent Philo's lectures to his school, who are addressed as 'initiates.' In content, however, the series is more a collection of meditations on the great themes which Philo found allegorically set forth in the narratives of the patriarchs.

(*d*) Another and similar series is the *Questions and Answers in Genesis and Exodus*, now extant in fragments, chiefly in the Armenian version (translated by Ralph Marcus in the Loeb Classical Library edition of Philo). Its form is a verse by verse midrashic commentary, giving both the literal and the allegorical (or 'spiritual') interpretation.

(*e*) Various philosophical writings survive, chiefly of the then popular essay type, including one *On the Indestructibility of the World* (an introduction to a much longer treatise); there are also essays entitled *That Every Virtuous Man is Free, On Providence*, and *Alexander*, or *On the Question Whether Dumb Animals Possess the Power of Reason.* The titles remind us of those of the 2nd-cent. eclectics, Plutarch, Dion of Prusa, Maximus of Tyre.

3. Teaching.—Philo may be studied either as a philosopher or an exegete, as a systematic metaphysical thinker or a religious teacher and homilist. Among modern expositors Wolfson takes the former view, Goodenough the latter. Philo's philosophy is really eclectic, based on Plato, Aristotle, and the Stoics—all as understood and interpreted in the 1st cent. He evidently made no attempt (at least in his surviving works) to set forth a system of philosophy. His interests were predominantly religious, not philosophical, and apologetic or expository rather than systematic. Moreover, his mystical type of thought enabled him to embrace views which, at least in origin, carried with them diverse and incompatible connotations.

The background of Philo's thought was the widespread Hellenistic tendency (or effort) to reinterpret and re-evaluate ancient myth, legend, and belief, in the direction of a more 'spiritual' understanding of religion, and especially of a recognition of the superior reality of the immaterial world (the world of pure thought) to the physical cosmos which is its copy (cf 2 Co 4[18]). This tendency formed the background of several movements of religious thought in later Hellenism and under the early empire: Euhemerism, Stoic allegorization of the classical myths, Neo-Pythagoreanism, Gnosticism, Neo-platonism, and the 'Christian Platonism' of the Alexandrian church fathers, especially Clement and Origen. The source of all being is God, who creates the world by fiat (as in Gn 1), *i.e.* through His 'word.' But this 'word,' his *logos*, is more than a mere utterance (as in Ps 33[6]); it is almost a part of His own being: so Goodenough, who uses the word 'Stream' for this divine effulgence. The language of He 1[1-4] is close to Philo's thought, though the word Logos is not used. The Platonic source of this whole conception is obvious, especially in Plato's *Timaeus*; but Plato never adopted the view that the Ideas were independent forces or hypostases, or even 'thoughts in the mind of God'—though this step was taken by later Platonism, especially perhaps after Posidonius and the Middle Platonists. The divine effulgence was not only the source of creation and revelation, but also of divine grace, resulting in human reflection of the divine attributes. The noblest concepts of virtue include not only the four virtues of traditional classical ethics but also the Biblical values of purity, mercy, and compassion. As Hellenistic philosophers allegorized the pagan myths and idealized the heroes (*e.g.* Heracles) and gods (*e.g.* Mithras), so Philo allegorized the OT myths and legends, and idealized the characters of the patriarchs, describing both them and their wives as paragons of wisdom and virtue: pure reason or intelligence was attributed to the men—since *logos* is masculine—and wisdom to their wives, since *sophia* is feminine. Whether or not Philo viewed Judaism as 'a mystery cult,' it is clear that he (like Paul) used language derived from the mysteries, and that he found in his ancestral faith values equal to and indeed far superior to those discovered by many of his pagan contemporaries in the ancient cults. He could even describe one of the psalmists as an initiate of Moses (*thiasōtēs, De Plant.* 39=ch. 9, cf *De Cherub.*, 48 f=ch. 14, and Paul's phrase, 'baptized into Moses,' 1 Co 10[2]).

Philo described the **Logos** as the mediator between God and the world, between God and mankind, and between God and Israel. His classic statement is in *Who is the Heir of Divine Things*, 206=ch. 42: 'I [the Logos] stand between the Lord and you [as Moses stood, Dt 5[5]], I who am neither uncreated like God nor created like you, but midway between the two extremes, a hostage to both sides.' Whether Philo thought of the Logos as *personal*, or only as an aspect of the divine nature—the 'manward aspect of God'—and whether or not he viewed the Logos as a supernatural being, a divine *hypostasis*, is uncertain. Obviously Philo was so understood and interpreted by those Christian theologians who made use of his teaching. But his language was cautious, and he was a Jew as well as a philosopher, deeply concerned for monotheism and not required to explain and account for a second divine existence, being, or person. The point of view and angle of approach in early Christian theology is entirely different from that of Philo, whose real problem was the rational, philosophical, and religious interpretation of the OT, not to explain the Incarnation.

Whether or not Philo influenced the NT is another unanswered question. The contacts between Philo and Paul are clear, but their respective dates seem to rule out a direct influence; at most, both drank from a common spring of philosophical Diaspora Judaism, the 'school' presupposed by Philo and Alexandrian Judaism (see Zeller's *Philosophie der Griechen*, v, 242 ff, or *Grundriss*=*Outline*, § 77). But where is the evidence for Paul's dependence upon this 'school'? His exegesis of the story of man's creation (in Gn 1–2) is very different from that of Philo, who could not have maintained that 'the second man [rather than the first] is from heaven' (1 Co 15[45-49]). Contacts with the Epistle to Hebrews are clearer and far more numerous: scores of words, phrases, turns of thought in Hebrew are like those in Philo (see Moffatt's commentary in *ICC*). Contacts with John and 1 John have been often pointed out; but the contrasts are even clearer. Though the Logos, according to Philo, was often manifested in human character and virtuous deeds, it was quite impossible, indeed inconceivable, that the Logos should ever have become ' flesh ' (Jn 1[14]). F. C. G.

PHILOLOGUS.—A Christian greeted in Ro 16[15].

PHILOSOPHY.—This word occurs in EV only in Col 2[8], where it refers to an unsound and pernicious form of teaching. The history of ancient philosophy falls outside the scope of the present work. Some points of contact between it and the Bible will be found in such articles as GNOSTICISM, LOGOS, ECCLESIASTES, WISDOM; cf also PHILO, PLATO, PLATONISM, EPICUREANS, STOICS.

PHINEAS.—1 Es 8[2, 29] (RSV) = **Phinehas, 1** (q.v.).

PHINEES.—**1.** 1 Es 5[5] 8[2, 29], 2 Es 1[2a] (AV, RV); see PHINEHAS, **1.** **2.** 2 Es 1[2b] (AV, RV); see PHINEHAS, **2.** **3.** 1 Es 8[63] (AV, RV); see PHINEHAS, **3.** **4.** 1 Es 5[31] (AV); see PASEAH, **3.**

PHINEHAS.—**1.** The son of Eleazar, who was the third son of Aaron. Both his name and that of his mother Putiel are perhaps of Egyptian origin. The only certain occurrence of the name in a pre-exilic writing is in Jos 24[33]; a hill in Ephraim was named after him, where his father and (LXX) he himself were buried. In P and the Chronicler he rises into great prominence. He succeeded Eleazar as chief priest (Ex 6[25], 1 Ch 6[4, 50], Ezr 7[5], 1 Es 8[2], 2 Es 1[2]), and was the superintendent of the Korahite Levites (1 Ch 9[20]). The succession of the priesthood in his line was assured to him when he showed his zeal at Shittim in Moab, when Israel ' joined themselves unto Baal-peor.' An Israelite brought into the camp a woman from the Midianites who had beguiled the people into foreign worship. Phinehas slew the man and the woman (Nu 25). This is referred to in Ps 106[30f], Sir 45[23-25], 1 Mac 2[26, 54]. As priest he accompanied the expedition to punish the Midianites (Nu 10[8f]). He was the spokesman of the western tribes concerning the altar which the eastern tribes had erected (Jos 22[13, 30-32]. See ED). The war between Benjamin and the other tribes occurred in his high priesthood (Jg 20[28]). After the Exile a clan of priests, ' the sons of Phinehas,' claimed descent from him (Ezr 8[2], 1 Es 5[5] 8[2, 29], 2 Es 1[2a] [AV. RV **Phinees**]). **2.** The younger son of Eli (1 S 1[3], 2 Es 1[2b] [AV, RV **Phinees**]). See HOPHNI AND PHINEHAS. **3.** The father of a priest named Eleazar (Ezr 8[33], 1 Es 8[63] [AV, RV **Phinees**]). **4.** The last High Priest of Jerusalem before the destruction of the city in A.D. 70 was Phineas ben Samuel, Jos. *BJ* IV. iii. 8 (155). **5.** The last Treasurer of the Temple, who at the fall of Jerusalem handed over some of the Temple treasures to the Romans, Jos. *BJ* VI. viii. 3 (390 f).

A. H. McN.—**A. S. H.**

PHINOE, 1 Es 5[31] (RV).—See PASEAH, **3.**

PHLEGON.—The name of a Christian greeted by St. Paul in Ro 16[14].

PHOEBE.—The bearer, apparently of the Epistle to the Romans, Ro 16[1] (AV **Phebe**). She was ' deaconess ' of the church at Cenchreae. See DEACONESS.

PHOENICIA, PHOENICIANS.—Greek designations for the country and the people on the coast of Syria. The term Phoenicia is sometimes used very broadly by the geographers, but generally the area W. of the Lebanon and of Galilee is meant. The name *Phoinikes* is to be explained from Greek *phoin* (os) plus the suffix *-ik*, used in ethnic names. As the word means ' dark red,' ' purple,' it described the Phoenicians as the ' purple-men ' or vendors of the fine cloth dyed in this colour, made from the glands of the *murex* shell-fish of the Syrian Coast. The Phoenicians themselves seem to have called their region ' Canaan.' That name, which appears in the OT as a term for western Palestine, is found in the *Tell el-Amarna* letters as *Kinakhni* (with variants of spelling). Some scholars hold that the name obtained the *-ni* under Hurrian influence, and that the main element means ' purple,' in which sense *kinakhu* appears in the cuneiform texts from Nuzi. If that were true the name would, indeed, have applied to Phoenicia at first, and been secondarily extended inland, just as ' Palestine ' was a millennium later. In the Amarna letters *Kinakhni* already has a broad use, including Palestine.

Phoenicia was a particularly desirable object for a great civilized country like Egypt to control, since the lumber of the Lebanon was a much desired product and could be transported by water. The city we hear of most is **Gebal** (q.v.) which the Greeks later called Byblos. Thither journeyed the Egyptian ambassador Wen Amon *c* 1100 B.C., at a time when Egyptian prestige was low. Gebal was still important in the days of King Ahiram, whose sarcophagus and inscription, dating from about the time of Solomon, were found by French excavators in 1923 at *Jebeil.*

The Phoenicians, having only a narrow hinterland were forced out on the sea by population pressure and commercial opportunity. They were able to step into the vacuum created by the downfall of Cretan sea-power about the middle of the 2nd millennium B.C. In the OT ' Sidonians ' sometimes appears as name for the Phoenicians or at least for a portion of them that included Tyre (cf 1 K 16[31], Is 23[2, 4, 12]). Similarly in the Homeric poems, where Tyre is never mentioned, Sidonians is the name for Phoenicians, and their skill in producing finely decorated metal ware is especially noted. This terminology evidently reflects a period of Sidon's leadership either prior to Hiram of Tyre or at a later juncture. Both Homeric and Biblical criticism have to be heeded here. In Graeco-Roman times people of Sidon claimed for their city the original leadership in Phoenicia, and even the founding of Tyre. The truth of such claims cannot be taken for granted. Essentially Phoenician history becomes the history of **Tyre** (q.v.) and of **Sidon** (q.v.), which managed to have periods of hegemony when Tyre was in the dust.

The Phoenicians carried out a remarkable activity in colonizing places throughout the Mediterranean. Their ' Tarshish ships ' sailed as far as Spain (see TARSHISH). Phoenician inscriptions have been found in many places, including the Nora stone of the 9th cent. from Sardinia and several inscriptions from Cyprus, one of equal age. Their most important and lasting colony was Carthage; the inscriptions from there are commonly called ' Punic.' A living descendant of the Phoenician language is Maltese, for Malta was colonized by them. The Phoenician control of the seas was, however, imperilled by the rise of Greek sea-power. The Phoenicians must have welcomed Persian backing, and indeed made possible Persia's attempt to subdue Greece. Their turning against Persia under Artaxerxes III. Ochus in 351 B.C. was premature, as Tyre's adherence to Persia at Alexander's coming in 331 B.C. was catastrophic.

The search for metal for the use of their metal-workers was a factor in Phoenician exploration and colonization. The word Tarshish means ' smelter.' Spain was especially rich in metals (see Strabo iii. 2, 8). The joint venture of Phoenicians and Hebrews in Red Sea commerce (1 K 9[26f]) involved among other things the quest of gold. It seems probable that Phoenician mariners got as far W. as the coasts of England in order to obtain tin. Pharaoh Neco employed Phoenicians to circumnavigate Africa (Herod. iv. 42). Strabo affirms that they had always been superior to all other peoples in seamanship (xvi. 2, 23).

The Greeks, probably in the 10th cent. B.C., received their alphabet from the Phoenicians (Herod. v. 58), but this author's words leave room for positing an earlier script. Cretan Linear B, deciphered by Ventris, has proved this an actuality. The Râs Shamra texts have shown that there was a cuneiform alphabet, written on clay tablets, in use at Ugarit in the 15th cent. But the alphabet of the Sinaitic inscriptions of which specimens have also been found in Palestinian excavations, was the predecessor of the Canaanitic alphabet, of which the Phoenician is an example. That the Sinaitic was developed from the hieroglyphs of Egypt seems certain. The Phoenicians wrote the alphabet more gracefully than did the Hebrews. Some very fine Phoenician inscriptions are extant, notably from Byblos and Sidon (cf Pritchard, *ANET*, p. 502). At Byblos early Phoenician ' Pseudo-hieroglyphic' inscriptions of *c* 1800 B.C. were also found by Dunand in 1929, which Dhorme has attempted to decipher.

Among the fine products of Phoenicia which were in great demand in the world were the carved ivories, used for inlay purposes on furniture. Remarkable specimens of this have been found in Spain, Palestine (Megiddo and Samaria) and Mesopotamia (notably at Calah, modern *Nimrûd*). Of Phoenician metal work the finest specimens were found at Râs Shamra (q.v.), hence from a time antedating the classic Phoenician period. Phoenician glass ware was also famed in antiquity.

The Phoenicians were engulfed in the Hellenistic civilization after Alexander's conquest, and continued to thrive, especially after Rome took over the E. in 63 B.C. Philo of Byblos, a writer of about A.D. 100, undertook to relate Phoenician history to the Greeks, based for the older period on a writer called Sanchuniathon (whose existence some have doubted). The quotations preserved by Eusebius and Porphyry have been much discussed, but only become clear as texts like those from Râs Shamra lend aid, for Greek transcriptions of Semitic words are often difficult to analyse, especially when corrupted by copyists.

Phoenician religion was no uniform thing, but rather represents the diverse cults of the Phoenician cities. Underlying, of course, was a common Canaanite religious heritage. A triad of gods, father, spouse and son or daughter, seems to have been favoured in most cities. At early Ugarit the god El, the goddess Ashirat, and the virgin Anat were prominent. But there were further deities in considerable number. At Byblos the chief deities were the Baʿalat Gebal, or 'lady of Gebal,' El and Adonis, the latter the youthful god, whose dying and rising was the object of celebration; we can see from Egyptian inscriptions that El was once more important at Byblos than his spouse. Sidon had Astarte, Baal and Eshmun for its gods; the last named was a youthful figure and originally a god of healing. At Tyre the god Melkarth ('king of the city'), whom the Greeks identified with Heracles, was the 'Baal of Tyre,' but at the same time a dying and rising god, with Astarte for consort. The importation of this Tyrian Baal into Israel by Jezebel led to fanatical opposition by the Hebrew element in the country, but of course pleased the old Canaanite element, which formed a substantial part of the population of the chief Israelite cities (cf Jg 1^{27-33}). The religion of the Carthaginians was basically that of the Phoenicians, and the sources for the former shed light on the general picture. The invasion of basically Phoenician heathenism into Judah is vividly reflected in the references to the offerings of Molech (2 K 23^{10}, Jer 32^{35}), whether that word be taken as a title of god or understood as 'sacrificial vow' in the light of Punic inscriptions (so Eissfeldt). The great popularity of Heracles in the Greek world in those times might suggest that his counter-part the god Melkarth of Tyre is meant. Phoenician and Punic personal names give many indications of the religious ideas of the people. The sacrificial cult of Israel and of the Phoenicians has much terminology in common. A Phoenician deity that was readily equated with Israel's God on the one hand and Zeus Olympios on the other hand was *Baal-shāmēm*, 'lord of the heavens,' *i.e.* god of the sky (but not sun-god). Antiochus IV. Epiphanes introduced his worship in Jerusalem (Dn 9^{27} 12^{11}, but with 'Baal' corrupted or veiled by editors). E. G. K.

PHOENIX was a good harbour on the S. coast of Crete. It has been identified almost certainly with *Loutro*, which is said to be the only harbour W. of Fair Havens where a ship of such size as that by which St. Paul travelled (it was a cargo ship, but had crew and passengers on board numbering altogether 276—though B and Sah. read 76) could find shelter. Strabo (x. iv. 3) speaks of Phoenix as being on an isthmus (*i.e.* a narrow part of the island), and apparently as being in the territory of Lappa, which was not far from Loutro. Other authorities speak of it as if it were near Aradena, which is only a mile from Loutro. The identification would therefore be certain but for Luke's description of the harbour of Phoenix as looking 'towards the SW. and the NW.' (Ac 27^{12} RSV: 'NE. and SE.'; margin, 'SW. and NW.'), whereas the harbour of Loutro looks towards the East. Hence some identify Phoenix with a small harbour, Phineka, a little farther W., but we have no evidence that it could accommodate so large a ship. It is perhaps more probable that Luke makes a mistake in his description of a harbour which was never reached. The RV understands the Greek to mean 'in the direction in which the SW. and NW. winds blow,' and therefore translates 'looking NE. and SE.' This may have been a sailor's way of expressing it, but we have no authority for it. See Map 16. A. E. H.—**F. C. G.**

PHOROS, 1 Es 5^{9} (AV, RV) 8^{30} (RV) 9^{26} (AV, RV).—See PAROSH.

PHRURAI.—See PHURIM.

PHRYGIA.—The Phrygians were a European race who seem to have had their first home in Thrace, and to have crossed into Asia Minor, *c* 1100 B.C., through the same southward movement of tribes that had brought the Hellenes into Greece. In Asia Minor they occupied at one time the greater part of the country W. of the Halys, probably absorbing an earlier race from whom they may have learned the worship of Cybele. We must regard Homer's Trojans as part of the Phrygian race, and the Trojan War may have been a contest between them and Greek settlers from Thessaly (*Iliad* iii. 184–189). In more historical times the name Phrygia applies to an inland region varying in extent at different times, but bounded at its widest by the Sangarius on the N., the Halys on the E., the Taurus range on the S. It thus covered the W. part of the great plateau of Asia Minor and the upper valleys of the rivers Maeander and Hermus. It was a region fruitful in oil and wine, exporting also wool, gold, marble, and salt.

When the Romans inherited the kingdom of Pergamum (q.v.) in 133 B.C., a part of Phrygia was included in the province of Asia, but the southern portion towards Pamphylia was not included. This portion was in the hands of the dependent king of Galatia when Augustus constituted Galatia a province in 25 B.C., and was therefore included in the new province which extended from Lycia on the SW. almost to the mouth of the Halys on the NE. Hence this portion of Phrygia, with its cities of Antioch and Iconium, came to be known as Phrygia Galatica.

This country was included by St. Paul in the work of his first missionary journey (Ac 13^{14}–14^{24}). From Perga he and Barnabas made their way N. along the difficult mountain road to Antioch, here called 'Pisidian Antioch' (see PISIDIA). On his second missionary journey Paul (now accompanied by Silas) began with the churches of Cilicia and then passed through Derbe and Lystra, where he took Timothy into his company. The narrative then proceeds (Ac 16^{6}): 'And they went through the region of Phrygia and Galatia [Gr. 'the Phrygian and Galatian region'], having been forbidden [AV 'and were forbidden'] by the Holy Spirit to speak the word in Asia [=the province of Asia]. And when they had come opposite Mysia they attempted to go into Bithynia, but the Spirit of Jesus did not allow them; so, passing by Mysia, they went down to Troas.' The natural interpretation of this is that from Lystra they traversed *Phrygia Galatica*, from Antioch took the road leading N. to Dorylaeum, where they would be near Bithynia, and from there were directed W. to Troas. Attempts have been made, however, to find here an evangelization of Galatia proper with its towns of Pessinus and Ancyra. But against this we must set (1) the form of the Greek phrase 'the Phrygian and Galatian region'; (2) the strange silence of St. Luke about a work that must have taken a considerable time; (3) the geographical consideration that the travellers could not have crossed the desert of the Axylon straight from S. to N. and must in any case have used the road to

Dorylaeum. See, further articles GALATIA and GALATIANS [EPISTLE TO] for this and the further question whether the Epistle to the Galatians can have been written to the churches of Phrygia Galatica. If it was, we have an interesting glimpse of how in the churches first founded by St. Paul his authority was very soon (perhaps A.D. 50) assailed by Judaizers, who disputed his Apostolic credentials and declared his doctrine to be an imperfect form of Christianity, neglecting its Jewish basis and the necessity of full observance of the sacred Law.

The third missionary journey likewise began with 'the region of Galatia and Phrygia' (Ac 18^{23}), or 'the Galatian region and Phrygia.' Here the reference is probably to the same churches, but the order of words is doubtless meant to include the churches of Lycaonia first—these were in the province of Galatia, but were not in Phrygia. The order is in any case strongly against the inclusion of Galatia proper. The journey was continued 'through the upper country to Ephesus' (19^{1}), *i.e.* along the direct route which passed through the higher country from Metropolis to Ephesus, instead of the high road which followed the valley of the Lycus. See PAUL. A. E. H.—**F. C. G.**

PHURAH, Jg 7^{10f} (AV).—See PURAH.

PHURIM.—In Ad. Est 11^{1} (AV) the Book of Esther is called 'the epistle of Phurim' (*i.e.* 'Purim' [q.v.]). RV has **Phrurai**. RSV, Ad. Est, *ad fin.*, 'Letter of Purim.'

PHUT, Gn 10^{6}, Ezk 27^{10} (AV) = **Put** (q.v.).

PHUVAH, Gn 46^{13} (AV).—See PUAH, 2.

PHYGELLUS, 2 Ti 1^{15} (AV) = **Phygelus** (q.v.).

PHYGELUS.—Mentioned in company with Hermogenes in 2 Ti 1^{15}, as those in Asia who, among others, had turned away from the Apostle. See HERMOGENES.

PHYLACTERIES, FRONTLETS.—1. Among the charges brought against the Pharisees we read: 'They do all their deeds to be seen by men; for they make their phylacteries broad and their fringes long' (Mt 23^{5}). The word 'phylactery' (Gr. *phylactērion*) literally signifies a 'safe-guard,' as protecting the wearer against the attacks of harmful spirits and other malign influences such as the evil eye—in other words, an amulet.

2. This identification has been rejected by a small number of scholars, on two grounds. First, too little is known of tephillin in the days of Jesus to permit a firm identification, and what we do know suggests that 'broadening the phylacteries' is a senseless phrase. There is little about the tephillin to justify describing them as amulets. Secondly, the intention in Matthew is obviously a slur, and therefore hardly consistent with the expected attitude towards a revered custom. Accordingly, Goodspeed (*Problems of NT Translation*, pp. 35–36) translates: 'They wear wide Scripture Texts as charms.'

Though the identification is unlikely, the word 'phylacteries' has come into such frequent use for 'tephillin' that the latter merit description. Modern Jewish usage agrees in all essential points with allusions in the Mishnah. Then, as now, they consisted of two small square cases or capsules of leather, 'two finger-breadths' according to the Talmud, say 1½ inch, in the side, one of which was worn on the forehead, the other on the left upper arm. The leather had to be prepared from the skin of a ritually 'clean' animal, and was coloured a deep black.

The case for the forehead, which was termed the 'head-tephillah,' was distinguished from the 'arm-' or 'hand-tephillah' by its being shaped so as to give four small but distinct compartments, while its fellow consisted of a single compartment. In each of the four compartments of the former was placed a narrow strip of parchment, also from the skin of a 'clean' animal, having carefully written on it one of the Pentateuch passages, which were regarded as the Scripture warrant for the institution of the phylacteries (see **4**). These were Ex 13^{1-10} 13^{11-16}, Dt 6^{4-9} 11^{13-21}. The companion capsule, on the other hand, contained the same four passages written on a single strip of parchment. Each case was then closed by folding back the lower half of the square of stout leather from which it projected, space being left at the fold for the passing of a long strap, blackened on the upper side, by which each phylactery was kept in position when properly 'laid.' The strap of the head-phylactery was tied behind the head into a knot having the shape of the Hebrew letter *dāleth*. On the two sides of the capsule were impressed the letter *shin*, on one side with the usual three prongs, on the other with four prongs. The corresponding loop of the phylactery for the arm was supposed to form the letter *yōdh*, the three letters together giving the sacred name *Shaddai*, 'Almighty.'

3. From the Mishnah we learn further that women, slaves, and minors were exempted from the obligation of wearing, or in technical phrase 'laying,' the tephillin, a duty still incumbent on all male Israelites, from the age of thirteen years and a day, during the recital of morning prayer, on all days save Sabbaths and festivals. These, being themselves 'signs,' rendered the tephillin unnecessary for this purpose (Ex 13^{9}; cf **4** below.)

In putting on the tephillah, that of the hand is 'laid' first, to the accompaniment of a prescribed prayer, and must lie on the inner side of the left arm, which must be bare, a little above the elbow, so that the case with the Scripture passages may rest upon the heart (Dt 11^{18}). The strap is then drawn tight and wound round the arm and the middle finger of the left hand a prescribed number of times. (For details see Hastings' *DB* iii. 870.) The head tephillah is next laid, its position being the middle of the forehead, 'between the eyes' (Ex 13^{9} etc., see **4**), with the knot above described at the back of the head, and the two ends of the strap brought forward to hang down over the breast in front. The phylacteries are taken off in the reverse order. When not in use, they are kept in a bag, which is often made of superior material richly ornamental (see illustration in *Jewish Encyc.*, *s.v.* 'Phylacteries').

4. The Scripture warrant for this institution of Judaism is found in the four passages, Ex $13^{9, 16}$, Dt 6^{8} 11^{18}. Of these Dt 6^{3} may be quoted as the most explicit: 'And thou shalt bind them'—*i.e.* 'these words which I command thee this day,' v.^{6}—'for a *sign* upon thine hand, and they shall be for *frontlets* between thine eyes.' These words and their parallels in the other passages, it is maintained by Jewish and some Christian scholars, are intended by their authors to be taken literally.

Others have, however, concluded that the intent of Scripture was only figurative. If the literal interpretation is followed, we should have to recognize another of the numerous instances in the Hebrew legislation, in which a deeply rooted and ineradicable practice of heathen origin and superstitious associations was adopted and given a religious signification, precisely as was done with the kindred sign of the tassels on the corners of the mantle (see FRINGES, end).

5. The date at which this literal interpretation was first adopted and the wearing of the phylacteries introduced cannot be determined with certainty. The fact that the institution is unknown to the Samaritans shows that it must have arisen after the date of the Samaritan schism. A passage in Ecclesiasticus seems to imply that the figurative interpretation still held the field. On the other hand, the writer of the famous *Letter of Aristeas* (scarcely later than 90 B.C.) distinctly mentions (§ 159) the binding of 'the sign upon the hand' (see Thackeray's translation in *JQR* xv, 368 f). We may, therefore, with some confidence regard the broad use of tephillin as already established in the second pre-Christian century.

In the earlier Middle Ages there was no complete uniformity among Jews on the wearing of tephillin. Some influential Jewish exegetes maintained that the cardinal passages in the Pentateuch were to be taken figuratively. In the later Middle Ages uniformity increased. In more modern times, the practice of 'laying the tephillin,' became standard and is now universally approved by Orthodox Jews, and practised by the Orthodox faithful. Reform Judaism has largely abandoned the custom.

A. R. S. K.—S. S.

PHYLARCH (2 Mac 8^{32}).—A military title for either a cavalry officer or a commander of auxiliary troops. In AV taken as a proper name, Philarches.

PHYSICIAN.—See MEDICINE.

PI-BESETH.—Egyptian city mentioned in Ezk 30^{17}, known to the Greeks by the name Bubastis, one of the greatest cities in Lower Egypt. The name means 'House of Bast,' and the city was especially the residence of the 22nd Dynasty, which was founded by Shishak. The goddess Bast (or Bastet) was usually figured with a lion's head, but she was of a mild character, and her sacred animal in late times was the cat. The ruins of the city are now called *Tell Basṭah*, lying near Zagazig, in the E. of the Delta. The temple described by Herodotus was excavated by Naville, yielding monuments of every period from the 4th Dynasty to the 30th. F. Ll. G.

PICK.—See HARROW.

PIECE.—*Piece* is used in AV for (1) a measure equal to a firkin (1 Es 8^{20} 'an hundred pieces of wine'; RV 'firkins'; RSV 'baths'); (2) an instrument of war (1Mac 6^{51} 'pieces to cast darts' [so RV]; RSV 'machines to shoot arrows').

PIETY.—See HOLINESS, PERFECTION, SANCTIFICATION.

PIGEON.—See DOVE.

PI-HAHIROTH.—Mentioned in connexion with the camping of the Israelites, Ex 14^{2,9}, Nu 33^{7}. It was 'between Migdol and the sea, in front of Baal-zephon' (Ex 14^{2}). This definition does not enable us to fix its site, for these other places are themselves unknown. In Nu 33^{8} the name is simply **Hahiroth** (so RV and RSV, following MT: AV Pi-hahiroh).

PILATE.—Pontius Pilatus, a Roman of no known family, succeeded Valerius Gratus as procurator of Judaea in A.D. 26. He possibly owed his appointment to Sejanus, and his administration, as described from the Jewish standpoint, shows either that he shared the anti-Jewish feelings of Sejanus or that he failed to understand the temper of the people with whom he had to deal. His first offence was, in contrast with his predecessors, in not allowing the soldiers to remove the images from their standards on entering Jerusalem. These images were worshipped by the soldiers, and were therefore symbols of idolatry. A deputation of Jews waited on Pilate for five days, and refused to desist though threatened with instant death. He was compelled to give way, but subsequently put up on the walls of Herod's palace (which was now the procurator's residence when in Jerusalem) certain golden shields bearing the name of the Emperor (Philo, *Legatio ad Gaium*, 38); this was taken to be an attempt to introduce the Caesar-worship already flourishing elsewhere in the Empire. Only an order from Tiberius, after a Jewish delegation had presented its appeal to him, compelled Pilate to yield a second time. He gave still further offence by a more justifiable action. The need of water in the city was much felt at the time of festivals, and Pilate proceeded to construct a new aqueduct at the expense of the Temple treasure. The Sanhedrin might have ordered such a work, but as Pilate's act it caused a riot which was not quelled without bloodshed. To these incidents we must add the massacre of some Galilaeans at the very altar of sacrifice, referred to in Lk 13^{1}, but not otherwise explained. The end of Pilate's rule was brought about by a disturbance in Samaria. Tradition said that the vessels of the Tabernacle had been buried on Mount Gerizim, and a band of armed men escorted thither an impostor who promised to reveal them. Pilate sent troops to the spot, who, after a massacre, dispersed the multitude. Complaint was made to Vitellius, the *legatus* of Syria, who seems at this time to have had authority over the governor of Judaea. Pilate was ordered to justify himself at Rome (A.D. 36), but before he arrived there Tiberius had died (March, A.D. 37), and he was not re-appointed (Jos. *Ant.* XVIII. iii. 1–iv. 2 [55–89]). Eusebius states that he committed suicide. The 'Acts of Pilate' and his letters to the Emperor are late forgeries. Their main interest lies in the fact that they usually represent an attempt to exonerate Pilate and even to Christianize him, thus incriminating the Jews still further.

Pilate would therefore be to us only one of a series of unsuccessful procurators, but for the fact that his years of office covered the period of Jesus' ministry. From the Passion Narratives in the Gospels we learn more of him than from any other source.

Except at the times of the great feasts the governors usually stayed at Caesarea; but Pilate was probably present with reinforcements to repress any disorder during the Passover, and had his headquarters in the fortress known as the Castle of Antonia, which adjoined the Temple on the N. side. The **praetorium** (q.v.) formed part of this fortress, and on this occasion, while the prisoner was led inside, the accusers remained below the steps which led into the hall, lest they should be rendered unclean for the feast by entering a building defiled by leaven (Jn 18^{28}). Pilate examined Jesus inside the hall, and came outside each time he wished to speak to the accusers. Jesus had been brought to him to be condemned to death, this penalty being out of the power of the Sanhedrin; and at first—according to John—they expected Pilate to pass sentence on their simple statement that he was 'an evildoer' (Jn 18$^{28-32}$). Pilate was too Roman for this—penalties in their power they might inflict, but if he was to add his authority he required a reason. Therefore (the charge of blasphemy, Mk 14^{64}, is not mentioned) they accused Jesus of 'forbidding tribute' and calling himself 'Christ, a king' (Lk 23^{2}). Pilate returned inside, and by questions assured himself that the prisoner claimed only what he would have called a 'philosophical kingship'—an idea familiar to him, if only from the Stoics. Hardly believing that truth was attainable (as he showed by the scornful answer, 'What is truth?'), he was yet prepared, like many Romans of his day, to patronize one who thought he had attained to it (Jn 18$^{33-38}$). From this time onwards (as the situation is reflected in the Gospels, if one may attempt to harmonize them) we must regard the trial as a series of attempts on Pilate's part to release Jesus without too great offence to the Jews. (1) Hearing that He came from Galilee—according to Luke—he sends Him to **Herod Antipas**, who was at Jerusalem for the feast. If Herod had claimed jurisdiction over the prisoner he might have released Him, but he had no more power to condemn a man to death in Jerusalem than the Jews had. The courtesy reconciled Herod and Pilate, their former enmity being due to the fact that Herod sent private reports to Rome and was regarded as the Emperor's spy. But when Herod failed to get either reply or miracle from Jesus, he sent Him back to Pilate (Lk 23$^{6-12}$). (2) It was a custom (whether Jewish or Roman in origin) to release a prisoner in honour of the Passover. (We have no further imformation about this custom, beyond what is contained in the Gospels.) Pilate proposed to release Jesus, but, persuaded by the priests, the multitude clamoured for Barabbas (Mt 27$^{15-21}$, Mk 15$^{6-11}$, Lk 23$^{13-19}$, Jn 18^{39f}). (3) After solemnly washing his hands, as if absolving himself of responsibility for condemning an innocent man (according to Mt 27^{24f}), Pilate hoped to satisfy the rancour of the accusers by scourging the prisoner. 'I will chastise him and release him' (Lk 23^{16,22}). But when Jesus came forth from the scourging, the Jews for the first time brought forward the cry that He 'made himself the Son of God' (Jn 19^{7}). To such as Pilate, Greek mythology would make it not incredible that 'the son of a god' should be on earth, and in the decadence of their own religion the Romans were lending a ready ear to the religions of the East. Moreover, according to Matthew, Pilate's superstitious fear had already been aroused by the report of his wife's dream (Mt 27^{19}). Again, therefore, he questioned Jesus. But at length the priests prevailed with the cry, 'If you release this man, you are not Caesar's friend' (Jn 19^{12}). The threat that the province would accuse him at Rome for treason overcame Pilate's scruples. An accusation for 'treason' might mean death, under Tiberius. Pilate gave way, caused his throne or tribunal to be brought on to the tessellated space in front of the praetorium (called 'Gabbatha' in Aramaic), and there pronounced final judgment. But in the taunting words, 'Here is your king!' and 'Shall I crucify your king?' as well as in the inscription on the cross, which he refused to alter in spite of protest, he again showed his contempt for his Jewish subjects, to whose clamours he had been forced to yield (Jn 19$^{17-22}$). In this powerfully dramatic account in the Fourth Gospel, one may note the tragic irony of Pilate's words and deeds. Like Caiaphas, the priestly head of the Jewish nation (cf Jn 11$^{49-53}$ 18$^{14, 28}$) he, Rome's highest representative, bears his unconscious witness to the Christ, the Saviour, the Man, the King. And so, in spite of a rough sense of justice tempering his arbitrary exercise of authority, and with angry reluctance and disdain, the procurator finally yields to the pressure of the Jerusalem hierarchy and consents to the carrying out of their plot.

In this unjust complaisance we have an illustration of one danger in the strict supervision which Augustus and Tiberius maintained over provincial government. In the main it was a great benefit, but it enabled the provincials to intimidate a weak governor. The weak points in Pilate's character stand out strongly. He seems to have been a sceptic in principle, but not free from superstition, in this resembling perhaps most of the upper class among the Romans in his day. He had probably not taken the trouble to understand the fierce passions of the people whom he was sent to govern, and when worsted by them in early encounters, the scorn which Romans felt for Jews became in him something like hatred, and a strong desire to be avenged on their leaders at all costs save one, namely, disgrace at Rome. For above everything else he seems to have considered his own personal position and career.

But it is very unlikely that Tiberius, who was jealous for good provincial government, would have allowed Pilate to remain procurator for ten years if his administration had been as bad as our knowledge of him based on the Passion Narratives would imply. It is easy to underestimate the difficulties of his post. The province of Judaea included not only Judaea proper, but Samaria and Idumaea; and in addition to its normal population there was at the time of great feasts, particularly the Passover, an influx of Jews from other provinces, which made the temporary population of Jerusalem (according to Jos. *War* vi. IX. 3 [423–425]) approximated 2,700,000. And this population was animated, as no other people was, by a religious fervour capable of passing on occasion into political excesses difficult to cope with, since in the eyes of a large minority submission to foreign rule was religious apostasy. But the province ranked only as a 'minor Imperial province'; its governor was a procurator, not a *legatus* or *praefectus*, and to control the difficult elements in the population he had only 3000 troops, quartered usually at Caesarea, besides small detachments used to garrison Jerusalem and Sebaste (see Schurer, *GJV*^{4}, i. 461). The governor usually went up to Jerusalem for the Passover time, but he must have felt that in face of a sudden national movement he would be powerless; and it is no small testimony to Roman skill in administration that for sixty years the series of procurators in Judaea managed to postpone more serious conflicts. The fault would seem to rest with the central authority, which did not realize that in administering the small province of Judaea it had to deal not with the province alone, but with all the millions of Jews scattered throughout the Empire, profoundly earnest in religious convictions, regarding Judaea as the holy centre of all they held dearest, and maintaining direct communication with the Sanhedrin, to which the Romans themselves had allowed a certain authority over all Jews throughout the Empire. Hence, mistaking the nature of the task, they sent as procurators second-rate men, who were often (like Pilate) nominees of Imperial favourites, and who were probably looking forward to their promotion from the moment that they landed in Caesarea. Had Judaea been definitely attached to the province of Syria, it would at any rate have been governed by men with a wider outlook. A. E. H.—**H. Cl.**

PILDASH.—One of the sons of Nahor, Gn 22^{22}.

PILEHA, Neh 10^{24} (AV).—See PILHA.

PILHA.—A signatory to the covenant, Neh 10^{24} (AV **Pileha**).

PILL.—In Gn 30^{37f} 'to pill' means 'to peel' (so RV, RSV), *i.e.* to remove the bark.

PILLAR.—**1.** The term 'pillar' in OT is usually the translation of two distinct Hebrew terms, *'ammûdh* and *maṣṣēbhāh*. The former denotes in most cases—for a conspicuous exception see JACHIN AND BOAZ—a pillar or column supporting the roof or top part of a building (Jg 16^{25f}, 1 K 7^{2f}), also the pillars from which the hangings of the Tabernacles were suspended (Ex 26^{32} and often). In this sense is probably to be understood the column of smoke (Jg 20^{40}), and the **'pillar of cloud'** and the **'pillar of fire'** of the Exodus and the Wanderings (Ex 13^{21} etc.). For the figurative use, which prevails in NT (Gal 2^{9}, 1 Ti 3^{15}, Rev 3^{12} 10^{1}), cf Job 9^{6} 26^{11}—passages which reflect an antique cosmogony in which the pillars of earth and heaven were actual supports.

2. The term *maṣṣēbhāh* is much more difficult. It is derived from a Semitic root *nṣb*, 'to stand.' The word thus refers to something 'set up' on end, in particular an upright stone, whether it be a megalithic monument such as the stones known to archaeologists as *menhirs*, or to a less imposing funerary stele.

(*a*) Some pillars were erected to mark a grave. The word *maṣṣēbhāh* is regularly used in Phoenician inscriptions to designate tomb-pillars. Jacob erected such a pillar over the grave of Rachel (Gn 35^{20}). Such a pillar was probably intended as a memorial to 'keep one's name alive,' as was the case of Absalom (2 S 18^{18}).

(*b*) Other pillars were erected to commemorate some important event. Jacob set up a stone as a 'pillar' to commemorate his pact of friendship with the Aramaeans at Galeed in Transjordan (Gn 31$^{43-54}$). Such commemorative stones are also mentioned in connexion with the establishment of the Shechem covenant (Jos 24^{27}), the 'stones for a memorial' of the crossing of the Jordan at Gilgal (Jos 4^{7}), as well as the 'stone of help' (Ebenezer) set up by Samuel (1 S 7^{12}), though in none of these cases is the actual word 'pillar' used.

(*c*) The most common use of the term is for the cultic pillar. When Jacob fled from the wrath of his brother Esau he slept one night at a holy place where God appeared to him in a dream (Gn 28^{16ff}). Since this was a numinous place Jacob took the stone which had been his pillow, set it up as a 'pillar,' **anointed** it with oil, and called it a Bethel, 'house of God' (cf also Gn 31^{13}). Apparently a 'pillar' was a monument of God's presence.

Actually this may well be the dominant significance of all such cultic pillars. Of interest is a passage describing Jacob's safe return to Palestine when he paid the vow made on the occasion of the Bethel theophany (Gn 35^{14}). It is expressly called 'the place where he (God) had spoken with him.' Jacob there 'poured out a drink offering on it, and poured oil on it.' It has now become a place of theophany and thus a legitimate place for sacrifice. See HIGH PLACE.

Such pillars were often built in proximity to an altar (Ex 24^{4}; cf Hos 10^{1f}). The worship of Baal involved 'pillars of Baal' (2 K 3^{2} 10^{26}), and the Israelites were commanded to tear down the altars and pillars of the indigenous peoples of Canaan (Ex 23^{24} 34^{13} and throughout the Deuteronomic legislation). Because of their Canaanite cultic connotations such pillars were condemned for the Israelites by the Deuteronomic Code (*e.g.* Dt 16^{22}) as well as by the Deuteronomic historians

(1 K 14[23], 2 K 17[10] 18[4] 23[14]). AV commonly renders by the misleading term 'image,' for which RV and RSV have substituted 'pillar,' with RVm **'obelisk'** (cf Ex 23[24] 34[13], Dt 7[5] 16[22] etc.). In Ezk 26[11] AV renders by 'garrison' (q.v.).

In the early days of Palestinian archaeology, archaeologists confidently identified every large upended stone as such a pillar. For example, the so-called high place at Gezer contains ten large pillars varying from five and a half to ten and a half feet in height. These pillars were enthusiastically called *maṣṣēbhōth*. Comparison with such sites as the Dagon temple at Ugarit and the 'stele field' of Ashur has now resulted in the identification of this 'high place' as a mortuary shrine founded in the Early Bronze period (cf W. F. Albright, *The Arch. of Palestine*, 104; A. G. Barrois, *Man. d'Arch. Biblique* ii, 358 ff). In fact, many such stone pillars found in Israelite sites which were once identified as *maṣṣēbhôth* are now known to have been ordinary features of Iron Age house construction.

Actual *maṣṣēbhôth* have been found at Beth-shean, Megiddo, and especially at Byblos where about twenty columns or obelisks of unequal height were found. The earliest datable 'pillar' found thus far is at Mari (from the Old Akkadian period; *c* 2300 B.C.).

One can only guess at the purpose served by such 'pillars.' Apparently libations were offered on them and they were commonly associated with altars. In the patriarchal tales a 'pillar' might mark a place of theophany, but this can hardly have been its sole meaning in view of the Byblos pillars. They were condemned as marks of pagan worship throughout the Hebrew law codes since they were associated in people's minds with Canaanite worship. They are not, however, evil in themselves, since a 'pillar to Yahweh' is to be erected in Egypt as a sign of God's good presence in the day of Egypt's predicted confusion (Is 19[19]).

A. R. S. K.—**J. W. W.**

PILLAR, OAK OF THE.—In Jg 9[6] we read that the men of Shechem made Abimelech king 'by the oak (RV, RSV; AV 'plain') of the pillar.' The correct translation is undoubtedly 'the terebinth of the pillar' (so RVm), the meaning being the sanctuary of Shechem. The 'pillar' refers to the sacred stone, originally a fetish, which was often found in holy places along with the sacred tree (see preceding article).

PILLAR, PLAIN OF THE, Jg 9[6] (AV).—See PILLAR, OAK OF THE.

PILLOW.—The 'pillow' of Mk 4[38] (AV) is the **cushion** (so RV, RSV) used by rowers. See also BOLSTER and HOUSE, **8.**

PILOT.—**1.** Hebrew *ḥōbhēl*, in Ezk 27[8, 27ff], is the man who pulls the rope (*ḥebhel*). It denotes some category of sailor, but the rendering 'pilot' is doubtful. In Jn 1[6] *rabh ḥōbhēl* is rendered 'captain' (AV and RV 'shipmaster'). **2.** Greek *euthynōn*, in Ja 3[4] (RSV; AV 'governor,' RV 'steersman'), means 'the one who guides straight.'

PILTAI.—A priestly house, Neh 12[17].

PIM.—This word, occurring in 1 S 13[21], is now definitely known from inscriptions on weights from Palestinian excavations to be a term of standard weight, probably two-thirds of a shekel. The ancient Sumerian weight *šanabu*, amounting to two-thirds of a shekel, was apparently adopted in the Semitic North of Mesopotamia and was known also at Râs Shamra as *šinipu*. The knowledge that the weight was *two* third-units caused the misapprehension that the *šin* element was the Semitic root meaning 'two,' hence the dual form *payim* was assumed and came into common use, appearing unvocalized on the weights as *pym*. Long after the original significance of the word had been forgotten the Massoretes vocalized it as *pîm*. J. Gr.

PIN.—**1.** The 'pins' used in the Tabernacle (AV and RV in Ex 27[19] 35[18] 38[10, 31, 40], Nu 3[37] 4[32]) were wooden 'pegs' (so RSV), and similarly the 'pin' of Ezk 15[3] (AV, RV; RSV 'peg'). **2.** The 'pin' of Jg 16[13f] (here in RSV also) is the stick used for beating up the woof in the loom. **3.** 'Crisping pins,' Is 3[22] (AV); see BAG.

PINE TREE.—**1.** *ʿēṣ-shemen*, Neh 8[15] (AV; RV, RSV 'wild olive'); see OIL TREE. **2.** *tidhhār*, Is 41[19] 60[13] (AV, RV; RSV 'plane'); see PLANE TREE. **3.** *teʾashshûr*, Is 41[19] 60[13] (RSV; AV, RV 'box'), Ezk 27[6] (RSV; AV 'Ashurites'; RV 'boxwood'); see BOX TREE. **4.** *berôth*, Ca 1[17] (RSV; AV, RV 'fir'); probably the Aramaic form of *berôsh*; see CYPRESS, **1.**

PINNACLE.—This word has been adopted by our EV from the Vulgate of Mt 4[5] (*pinnaculum*) to indicate the spot within the Temple enclosure from which the devil tempted our Lord to cast Himself down. The precise nature and location of '*the* pinnacle of the temple' (Mt. *l.c.*, Lk 4[9] [both RV, RSV]), however, are nowhere indicated. The context and the use of the word usually employed for the whole complex of buildings as opposed to that which denotes the Temple proper (see plan in article TEMPLE, **12**) rather favour the view that the 'pinnacle' is to be sought in the neighbourhood of the SE. corner, where the royal 'porch' met that of Solomon. Here, as Josephus informs us—and the excavations corroborate his testimony—a spectator looking down into the valley of the Kidron 'would turn giddy, while his sight could not reach down to such an abyss' (*Ant.* xv. xi. 5 [412]). Many authorities, on the contrary, favour some part of the roof of the Temple building itself. A. R. S. K.

PINON.—An Edomite 'duke,' Gn 36[41], 1 Ch 1[52]. The place **Punon** (q.v.) may bear the same name.

PIPE.—See MUSIC, etc., **4** (2) (*a*).

PIRAM.—The king of Jarmuth, defeated by Joshua at Beth-horon and afterwards put to death, Jos 10[3ff].

PIRATHON.—An Ephraimite city, and the home of Abdon, one of the judges, Jg 12[13, 15]; also of Benaiah, one of David's heroes, 2 S 23[30], 1 Ch 11[31] 27[14]. The gentilic **Pirathonite** occurs in Jg 12[13, 15]. In NT times it was called **Pharathon** (q.v.); it is possibly modern *Farʿata*, about 6 miles SW. of *Nāblus*.

PISGAH.—A mountain in the region of Moab, with a commanding view over both the desert (Nu 21[30]) and W. Palestine. Hither the Israelites journeyed from Bamoth and there took place the extraordinary episode of Balaam who on top of Pisgah built seven altars, Nu 23[14]. Its principal distinction, however, is its being the scene of Moses' vision of the Promised Land (Dt 3[27] 34[1]) and of his death. It lay within the territory of Reuben, Jos 13[20] (AV **Ashdoth-pisgah**; RV, RSV 'slopes of Pisgah'; cf Dt 3[17] 4[49], Jos 12[3]). It is probably modern *Râs es-Siâghah*.

An alternative name for Pisgah is **Nebo** (q.v.) referred to in Dt 32[49] as the scene of the death of Moses. The latter name is preserved by *Jebel Nebā*, a range whose summit reaches a height of 2643 ft. and commands a view of a large part of W. Palestine. It is 5 miles SW. of Heshbon, and runs westward from the Moabite plateau. R. A. S. M.

PISHON.—See EDEN (GARDEN OF).

PISIDIA.—The name applied to a district about 120 miles long and 50 miles broad, immediately N. of the plains of Pamphylia. It is entirely occupied by the numerous ranges into which the Taurus here breaks, with the deep intersecting valleys. The name was not applied to a definite political division, and nothing is known of the race inhabiting Pisidia. Until the time of Augustus they were wild mountaineers and brigands. Augustus began their reduction about 25 B.C. by establishing a chain of Roman posts which included on the N. side Antioch and Lystra, reconstituted as colonies. The name 'Pisidian Antioch' (Ac 13[14] RSV, Antioch of Pisidia) would seem to record this fact, since Antioch (q.v.) was never included in Pisidia. The civilizing of the district seems to have been completed by about A.D. 74. Until then it was dealt with as part of the province of Galatia, but at that date Vespasian attached a considerable portion of it to Pamphylia, in which province no great military force was maintained. During the 2nd cent. numerous small cities grew up and prospered.

Paul and Barnabas traversed the district twice in the first missionary journey (Ac 13^{13} 14^{24}). It was probably still a dangerous locality, and it is plausibly conjectured that St. Paul refers to it when he speaks of 'dangers from robbers' (2 Co 11^{26}). The route which they followed is uncertain, but the most likely theory is that of Prof. Ramsay (see *Church in the Roman Empire*, ch. ii. 2), that they went through Adada, the ruins of which bear the name Kara Bavlo (*i.e.* Paulo). The dedication of the church to St. Paul may have been due to some surviving tradition of his passing by that way, but we are not informed that he preached at all in Pisidia. There is no evidence that Christianity made any progress in Pisidia before the time of Constantine. From the time of Diocletian we find the name Pisidia applied differently, namely, to a Roman province including Phrygia Galatica, Lycaonia, and the part of Phrygia round Apamea. See PAUL. A. E. H.—**F. C. G.**

PISON.—AV form of **Pishon** (q.v.).

PISPA.—An Asherite, 1 Ch 7^{38} (AV, RV **Pispah**).

PISPAH, 1 Ch 7^{38} (AV, RV).—See PISPA.

PISTACHIO NUTS.—See NUTS.

PIT.—Of the dozen Hebrew words, besides two Greek words in NT, rendered 'pit' in EV, the following are the most important.

1. The term *bōr* is responsible for nearly half of all OT occurrences. It is the usual word for the cistern with which almost every house in the towns was supplied (see CISTERN). Disused cisterns in town and country are the 'pits' mentioned in Gn 37^{20ff} (that into which Joseph was cast [cf PRISON]), 1 S 13^{6} (RSV, RVm 'cisterns') etc. In some passages, indeed, the context shows that 'cistern' not 'pit' is the proper rendering, as in Lv 11^{36}, Ex 21^{33f} with reference to an uncovered and unprotected 'cistern' (so RSV), cf Lk 14^{5} (RSV, RV 'well' for AV 'pit'). The systematic exploration of Palestine has brought to light many series of underground caves which were used at various periods as catacombs (cf Ezk 32^{23}) and dwelling-places (cf 1 S 13^{6}); hence by a natural figure, 'pit' became a synonym of **Sheol**, the underworld (Is 14^{15}, Ps 28^{1}, Pr 1^{12}, etc.; cf Rev 9^{1ff} and SHEOL).

2. A second word rendered 'pit' (*shaḥath*) seems to have denoted originally a pit in which, after concealing the mouth by a covering of twigs and earth, hunters trapped their game (Ezk 19$^{4, 8}$). Like the preceding, it is frequently used in a figurative sense of the underworld; so five times in Job 33 (AV four times).

3. A hunter's pit, denoted by *paḥath*, also supplied the figure of Is 24^{17f} and its parallels Jer 48^{43f} and La 3^{47} RV—note the association with 'snare.' Such a pit served as a place of concealment (2 S 17^{9}) and of burial (18^{17}).

4. In Mk 12^{1} RSV, RV rightly recognize 'a pit for the winepress,' where the reference is to what the Mishnah calls 'a cement-vat,' *i.e.* a pit dug in the soil for a winevat (cf Mt 25^{13}, where the same expression 'digged,' RSV 'dug,' is used), as contrasted with the usual rock-hewn vats (see WINE AND STRONG DRINK, **2**).

A. R. S. K.—**D. R. Ap-T.**

PITCH.—See BITUMEN.

PITCHER.—The earthenware jar (cf La 4^{2} AV and RV 'earthen pitchers') in which in all ages the women and maidens of Palestine have drawn and carried the water from the village well (Gn 21^{14ff}). In wealthy households this task was performed by a slave or other menial (Mk 14^{13}, Lk 22^{10}). RSV replaces 'pitcher' by 'pot' or 'jar' everywhere save in Ec 12^{6}, but introduces 'pitcher' in Jer 25^{5} for AV 'pot' and RSV 'bowl.'

PITHOM.—One of the two 'store-cities' said to have been built for the Pharaoh of the oppression by the Hebrews (Ex 1^{11}). The name occurs in the Papyrus Anastasi VI. in the reign of Seti II. (*c* 1205 B.C.). The site has been identified by Gardiner with *Tell er-Reṭâbeh*. A town called Pithom (Pi-Tum, *i.e.* 'the house of the god Tum'), existed in Ramesside times in the *Wâdī Ṭûmilât*, a district which corresponds to the Biblical description of the land of Goshen. Naville's identification of Pithom with *Tell el-Maskhûṭeh* is no longer accepted. S. H. He.

PITHON.—A grandson of Merib-baal, 1 Ch 8^{35} 9^{41}.

PITY.—This word is entirely synonymous with **compassion** both in OT and NT, except, perhaps, in 1 P 3^{8}, where 'sympathetic' would better express the meaning of the original word (see RVm and RSV). Pity was regarded by OT writers as holding an essential place in the relations of God and His people (see Ps 78^{38} 86^{15} 103^{13} 111^{4} 112^{4} 145^{8}, Is 63^{9}; cf Ja 5^{11}). One of the ways in which this Divine feeling became active on their behalf reveals an incipient belief in the dealings of Yahweh with nations other than Israel; for He is often represented as infusing compassion for His chosen into the hearts of their enemies (cf 1 K 8^{50}, 2 Ch 30^{9}, Ps 106^{46}, Ezr 9^{9}, Neh 1^{11}, Jer 42^{12}). An objective manifestation of the feeling of pity in the heart of God was recognized in the preservation of His people from destruction (La 3^{22f}), and in the numerous instances which were regarded as the interventions of mercy on their behalf (cf Ex 15^{13}, Nu 14^{19}, Dt 13^{17} 30^{3}, 2 K 13^{23}, 2 Ch 36^{15}). The direct result of this belief was that Israelites were expected to display a similar disposition towards their brethren (cf Mic 6^{8}, Is 1^{17}, Jer 21^{12}, Pr 19^{17}). They were not required, however, to look beyond the limits of their own race (Dt 7^{16}, Zec 7^{9}) except in the case of individual aliens who might at any time be living within their borders (see Ex 22^{21} 23^{9}, Dt 10^{18f} etc.).

In the parable of the Unmerciful Servant, Jesus inculcates the exercise of pity in men's dealings with each other, and teaches the sacredness of its character by emphasizing its identity with God's compassion for sinners (Mt 18^{33}; cf Lk 6^{36}, Mt 5^{7} 9^{13}). The teaching of Jesus, moreover, broadened its conception in the human mind by insisting that henceforth it could never be confined to the members of the Jewish nation (cf the parable of the Good Samaritan, Lk 10$^{25-37}$). At the same time His own attitude to the thronging multitudes surrounding Him was characterized by profound pity for their weaknesses (Mt 15^{22}=Mk 8^{2}; cf Mt 9^{36} 14^{14}). Under His guidance, too, Divine pity for the world was perceived to spring from that Eternal Love which resulted in the Incarnation (Jn 3^{16}). Side by side with this development, and in exact correspondence with it, Jesus evolves out of human pity for frailty the more fundamental, because it is the more living, quality of love, which He insists will be active even in the face of enmity (Mt 5^{43f}, Lk 6^{27ff}). J. R. W.

PLACE OF TOLL.—See TAX OFFICE.

PLAGUE.—See MEDICINE.

PLAGUES OF EGYPT.—There are not many references in the Bible to the plagues outside the Book of Exodus. They are epitomized in Ps 78$^{44-51}$ and 105$^{28-36}$. In Ro 9$^{14-24}$ God's treatment of Pharaoh is dwelt upon, to show His absolute right to do what He will with the creatures of His own handiwork. In Rev 8, 9, 16 much of the imagery in the visions of the trumpets and the bowls is based upon the plagues—hail and fire (8^{7} 16^{17f}), water becoming blood, and the death of the creatures that were in it (8^{8f} 16^{3f}), darkness (8^{12} 16^{10}), locusts (9$^{1-11}$), boils (16^{2}), frogs (16^{13}).

The narratives of the plagues demand study from three points of view: (1) their literary history; (2) the relation of the several plagues to natural phenomena; (3) their religious significance.

1. The sources.—For a full discussion of the theories of documentary analysis reference must be made to commentaries. It is probable that the original account of JE contained *eight* and not ten plagues. The third and fourth are insect pests, the former *kinnîm, kinnām, i.e.* **gnats** or **mosquitoes** (P), the latter *'ārōbh, i.e.* **swarms of flies** (J). These may with some probability be considered duplicates. Similarly the fifth and sixth, **plague** (J) and **boils** (P).

2. Relation to natural phenomena.—The hostility which used to exist between religion and natural science is rapidly passing away, as it is becoming more clearly recognized that science is concerned solely with the observation of physical sequences, while religion embraces science as the greater includes the less. Nothing can lie outside the activity of a God who is both a transcendent Person and an immanent sustaining Power in the universe. Therefore to point out a connexion between some of the ' miracles ' of Scripture and ' natural phenomena ' does not eliminate from them the Divine element; it rather transfigures an unreasoning ' faith in the impossible ' into a faith which recognizes the ' finger of God ' in everything. Thus the following discussion of the plagues may claim to be entirely constructive; it seeks to destroy nothing, but aims at showing it to be probable that the providence of God worked in Egypt by means of a series of natural phenomena, upon which the religious instinct of the Hebrew writers unerringly seized as signs of God's favour to their forefathers, and of punishment to their oppressors. This religious conviction led in process of time to accretions and amplifications; as the stories were handed down, they acquired more and more of what is popularly called the miraculous.

1st Plague.—This consisted in the smiting of the river which was turned to blood, and the consequent death of the fish, causing the necessity of obtaining water by digging in the neighbourhood of the river. Two suggestions have been made as to the natural phenomena which might give rise to the story. When the Nile rises in June, its waters become discoloured from fragments of vegetable matter, which gradually turn to a dull red colour as the river rises to its height in August. This is confirmed by many travellers, who also speak of offensive odours emitted at the later stage. Others refer the reddening of the water to enormous quantities of minute organisms. The ease with which the belief could arise that the water was turned to blood is illustrated in 2 K 3[23]. In P's final amplification, every drop of water in Egypt was turned to blood (7[19]).

2nd Plague.—From whatever cause the river became fetid, a mass of organic matter and of animal life would be collected. These conditions would be suitable to the rapid multiplication of **frogs.** Plagues of frogs were not unknown in ancient times; and Haggard tells of a plague in the upper Nile valley in modern times (*Under Crescent and Star*, p. 279). Frogs are most plentiful in Egypt in September.

3rd and 4th Plagues.—The mass of dead frogs collected in heaps (8[14]) would lead to the breeding of innumerable insects. In J, Yahweh Himself sends **' swarms of flies '**; in P, through the stretching out of Aaron's staff (as elsewhere in P), ' all the dust of Egypt became **gnats'** (AV, RV **' lice '**). The ' gnats ' cannot have been, according to any natural sequence, distinct from the ' swarms '; P particularizes the general statement of J. Stinging gnats of various kinds are common in Egypt about October. The insects come to maturity after the waters of the Nile inundation have receded, and the pools in which the larvae have lived have dried up. Note that in Ps 105[31] the ' swarm ' and the ' gnats ' are coupled in one sentence; Ps 78[45] omits the ' gnats ' altogether.

5th and 6th Plagues.—The decomposing bodies of the frogs would produce pestilential effects, and bacteriological research shows that some insects are a serious factor in the spread of disease. Thus the **plague** (AV, RV **' murrain '**) (J) is amply accounted for. In the preceding narrative J relates that Goshen enjoyed complete immunity from the insects. It is not impossible that the direction of the wind or other natural causes, under God's guidance, prevented them from reaching the Israelite territory. If the insects, which spread disease, did not enter Goshen, the statement that the plague did not touch the cattle of the Israelites is also explained. P, on the other hand, departs from natural causes. Moses and Aaron flung soot into the air, which became **boils** on man and beast. Cattle plagues, causing enormous mortality, are reported in Egypt. One such in A.D. 1842 killed 40,000 oxen.

7th Plague.—Thus far the series of plagues have followed one another in a natural sequence. At this point a new series begins with a destructive thunderstorm, accompanied by **hail.** Such storms are rare in Egypt, but are not without example. Those which have been reported in modern times have occurred about January; and that is the point of time defined in 9[31f], ' the barley was in the ear, and the flax was in bud, but the wheat and the spelt . . . were late in coming up.' Thus the cattle plague had lasted about two months and a half (November to the middle of January) when the storm came; and the first five plagues (reckoning 3, 4 and 5, 6 as duplicates) occupied a period of about five months.

8th Plague.—The atmospheric conditions which resulted in the storm also led to other plagues. A strong east wind (the sirocco) brought a dense mass of **locusts.** The lightness and fragility of the locusts rendered them helpless before a wind (cf Ps 109[23b]), so when the wind shifted to the west, they were completely swept away to the ' Sea of Reeds '; cf Jl 2[20].

9th Plague.—The **darkness** may have been a further consequence of the west wind. Dr. A. Macalister (article, ' Plagues of Egypt ' in Hastings' *DB* iii) writes: ' The condition of darkness referred to is strikingly like that brought about by the severer form of the electrical wind *Khamsin.* This is a S. or SW. wind that is so named because it is liable to blow during the twenty-five days before and the twenty-five days after the vernal equinox (*Khamsin* = 50). It is often not so much a storm or violent wind as an oppressive hot blast charged with so much sand and fine dust that the air is darkened. It causes a blackness equal to the worst of London fogs, while the air is so hot and full of dust that respiration is impeded. . . . Denon says that it sometimes travels as a narrow stream, so that one part of the land is light while the rest is dark.' He adds, that three days is not an uncommon duration for the *Khamsîn.*

10th Plague.—Malignant epidemics have at all times been the scourge of Bible lands; and it is worthy of note that many authorities state that pestilence is often worst at the time of the *Khamsîn* wind. In the Hebrew narratives, however, all thought of a ' natural ' occurrence has passed away. Only the **firstborn** are smitten, as a just retribution for Pharaoh's attempt to destroy the firstborn of the Israelites.

3. Religious value.—This is manifold. Considered from the point of view of natural phenomena, the narratives teach the all-important truth that God's providential care of men is not confined to ' miracles ' in the commonly accepted sense of the term, else were God's providential actions unknown to-day. The lifting of Moses' staff to bring the plagues, and his successive entreaties for their removal, teach that prayer is not out of place or unavailing in cases where natural laws can be co-ordinated and guided by God to bring about the wished-for result. From whatever point of view the plagues are regarded, the same great facts shine through the narratives—that Yahweh is supreme in power over the world which He made; that He has an absolute right, if He so wills, to punish Pharaoh in order to show forth in him His power; that He does so, however, only because Pharaoh is impenitent, and consequently ' made for destruction,' for Yahweh is a God who hates sin; that if a man hardens his heart, the result will be as inevitable as results in the natural world—so inevitable that it may truly be said that Yahweh hardens his heart; that the sin of Pharaoh, and so of any other man, may entail sufferings upon many innocent men and animals; and finally, that Yahweh is mindful of his own, and delivers them from the ' deadly pestilence,' ' the pestilence that stalks in darkness,' and ' the destruction that wastes at noonday,'

so that 'no scourge can come near their tent' (Ps 91).
A. H. McN.—**R. J. W.**

PLAIN.—This word is to be found in the Bible as a rendering of seven different terms, six Hebrew and one Greek; it is found more frequently in AV than in RSV.

(1) *biḳ'āh*, being from a verb meaning 'to split or cleave,' is commonly rendered as **'valley.'** But it often designates a broad, open valley between hill ranges, so that in RSV the translation is 'plain' in Gn 11², Neh 6², Is 40⁴, Ezk 3²²ᶠ 8⁴, Dn 9¹; and in the margin of Ezk 37¹ᶠ. In Ps 26¹² 'level ground' is found. The word was used of certain notable localities, such as the plain of Megiddo (2 Ch 35²², Zec 12¹¹); but in Jos 11¹⁷ and 12⁷ the pass between Lebanon and Hermon is named the valley of Lebanon.

(2) *mîshôr* means an area with a flat, even surface, without indicating whether it is fertile or desert. It is variously translated: 'plain' in 1 K 20²³, ²⁵, Zec 4⁷; 'a level path' in Ps 27¹¹ 143¹⁰, and 'level' in Ps 26¹², Is 40⁴. But in such passages as Dt 3¹⁰ 4⁴³, Jos 13⁹ 20⁸ 'table-land' is used and the reference is to the plateau E. of the Jordan between the Arnon and Heshbon.

(3) *'ᵃrābhāh* designates an arid area, a desert or steppe. The rendering 'plain' or 'plains' is given in Nu 22¹, Jos 4¹³ 5¹⁰, Zec 14¹⁰ etc., particularly as designating specific localities such as the plains of Jericho or of Moab; at other times the translation is 'desert' (*e.g.* Is 33⁹ 35¹, ⁶, Jer 17⁶, Job 24⁵), or 'wilderness' (*e.g.* Jer 50¹²), or 'steppe' (*e.g.* Job 39⁶). But often the word is used as a proper noun to indicate the area W. of the lower Jordan and the Dead Sea, or, with wider reference, the whole Jordan valley, or the whole depression from the Jordan valley in the N. to the Gulf of 'Aqaba; in all such cases RSV uses the term Arabah.

(4) *kikkār*, 'a round,' should fundamentally signify an area around a specified centre. In Neh 3²² and 12²⁸ it does mean the district around Jerusalem, and in the latter case RSV gives the rendering **'circuit.'** It is thus a word which characterizes, not the surface of the locality to which it is applied, but its shape. Most often it is used of the plain around the lower reaches of the Jordan and around the city of Jericho, but it is translated in this connexion by 'valley' (*e.g.* Gn 13¹⁰, ¹² 19¹⁷, ²⁵, ²⁸ᶠ, Dt 34³) or 'plain' (*e.g.* 2 S 18²³, 1 K 7⁴⁶, Neh 3²²). In Gn 13¹⁰ RVm has 'circle.'

(5) *shᵉphēlāh* is the name applied to the low foothills on the W. of the Judaean hill country, flanking the coastal plain, although Jos 11² implies that it could be applied to the lowland near the coast N. of Carmel. The translation 'plain' is not given in RSV, the usual terms in use being **'lowland'** (*e.g.* Dt 1⁷, Jos 9¹, Zec 7⁷) or the transliterated form 'Shephelah' (*e.g.* Jer 17²⁶ 32⁴⁴ 33¹³, 2 Ch 26¹⁰).

(6) *'ēmeḳ* (literally 'a deep place') is the word used in Jos 17¹⁶, Jg 6³³, Hos 1⁵ of the valley of Jezreel; but 1 K 20²⁸, when compared with 20²³, ³⁵, shows that it had sometimes almost the value 'plain.' In Jg 1¹⁹, ³⁴ the translation 'plain' is actually given.

(7) The only place where the word 'plain' is used in the NT is Lk 6¹⁷ (AV) in the account of one of our Lord's discourses, which the account in Matthew (5¹) says was delivered on a mountain; but for the term 'plain' RSV uses 'level place.' J. Ma.

PLAIN, CITIES OF THE.—These were five in number, namely, Sodom, Gomorrah, Admah, Zeboiim, and Bela (or Zoar), situated in the plain ('circle') of Jordan. Their inhabitants being guilty of great wickedness, the first four of the above-named five were overthrown by fire. Lot, the nephew of Abraham, who had made his home in Sodom, was warned by the Lord to withdraw from the city before it was destroyed; and he accordingly escaped to Zoar, which, at his entreaty, was spared the fate of its neighbours (Gn 18, 19).

The situation of the five cities has been variously placed at the N. and the S. end of the Dead Sea. The Biblical statements seem generally to favour the former site, which is supported by the facts: (1) that the circle of the Jordan, which is also called the circle of the valley of Jericho (Dt 34³) is appropriate only to the broad basin of the Jordan, near its mouth; (2) that it was visible from near Bethel (Gn 13³⁻¹⁰); (3) that the cities were N. of Hazazon-tamar (usually identified with En-gedi), since this place was passed by Amraphel when he marched from Kadesh against the king of Sodom and his allies (Gn 14⁷ᶠ). For the most recent statement of the case for the northern location, see J. Simons, *The Geographical and Topographical Texts of the Old Testament* (1959), pp. 222–229. On the other hand, (1) it is implied in Ezk 16⁴⁶ that **Sodom** was on the right (*i.e.* south) of Jerusalem, whereas if it were at the N. end of the Dead Sea it would be almost due E.; (2) **Zoar,** which must have been near the other cities (Gn 19²⁰), is placed by Josephus in Arabia (*BJ* IV. viii. 4 [482]), and by Eusebius at the opposite end of the Dead Sea to Jericho; (3) the same *Sodom* is generally identified with *Jebel Usdûm*, a cliff of rock-salt near the SW. corner of the Dead Sea; (4) Hazazon-tamur may be, not En-gedi, but the Tamar of Ezk 47¹⁹, which has been identified with a locality 20 miles WSW. of the lake, and therefore on the road between Kadesh and Sodom if the latter were at its S. end. In addition, W. F. Albright has adduced impressive evidence in support of the southern hypothesis, on the basis of archaeological surveys in the area S. of the Dead Sea. He located the cities under water at the southern tip of the Dead Sea. Early occupation of sites in this area has been confirmed by exploration, while the thorough-going depopulation of the region early in the 2nd millennium suggests a date for the catastrophe described in Gn 18–19 (cf Albright, *The Archaeology of Palestine and the Bible*³, 1935, ch. iii. 2; for a detailed presentation of the southern hypothesis, see J. P. Harland, *BA* v [1942], 17–32).

The nature of the catastrophe which destroyed the cities can only be conjectured. Harland plausibly suggests that a great earthquake, accompanied by an electrical storm, may have overthrown the cities, and at the same time ignited a terrible conflagration, which was partly fuelled by seepages of bitumen (cf *BA* vi [1943], 41–54). G. W. W.—**D. N. F.**

PLAISTER, PLASTER.—**1.** See ARTS AND CRAFTS, 4; HOUSE, 4. **2.** The 'plaister' (Is 38²¹ AV, RV) which Isaiah prescribed for Hezekiah's boil was a fig-poultice, according to the text of 2 K 20⁷, but the parallel passage above cited reads literally 'let them take a cake of figs and apply it to the boil' (so RSV).

PLANE.—Carpenter's tool, Is 44¹³ only; see ARTS AND CRAFTS, 1.

PLANE TREE.—**1.** *'armôn*, Gn 30³⁷, Ezk 31⁸ (RV, RSV; AV 'chesnut tree'). There is no doubt that RV and RSV are correct. The chestnut tree is only an exotic in Palestine, but the plane (Arab. *dilb*) is one of the finest trees of the land. It attains great development; a wonderful specimen, which has a small room or shop within its hollow trunk, is to be seen in one of the streets of Damascus. The plane (*Planus orientalis*) peels its outer layers of bark annually, leaving a white streaky surface. It flourishes specially by watercourses (Sir 24¹⁴). **2.** *tidhhār*, Is 41¹⁹ (RVm, RSV; AV, RV 'pine') 60¹³ (RSV; AV, RV 'pine'). This is an unidentified species of tree. From similarity to the Syriac *daddār* ('elm'), it has been supposed to be the **elm,** but this is improbable, and it is more likely that it was some kind of **pine.** Alternatively the **ash** has been proposed. E. W. G. M.

PLANETS, 2 K 23⁵ (AV).—See STARS.

PLASTER.—See HOUSE, 4.

PLAT, 2 K 9²⁶ (AV, RV).—Obsolete for 'plot of ground' (so RSV).

PLATO, PLATONISM.—Although the philosophy of Plato, unlike Stoicism and Epicureanism, is not mentioned in the Bible, its influence upon the background of religious thought is clear from the Book of Wisdom, from Paul, the Epistle to Hebrews, and the Gospel of John. Plato (427–347 B.C.) was a disciple of Socrates (469–399 B.C.), whose martyr death led to his veneration by all later schools of philosophy. From Socrates' teaching, Plato learned his method of dialectic, the questioning of common assumptions ; from his character he gained the conviction of the indispensable primacy of ethical goodness in all the relations of life : there is no higher value than goodness or virtue, which must be pursued at whatever cost. Thus ' the good ' is independent of all other considerations, political, economic, or even religious. In his earliest writings, the so-called Socratic Dialogues, Plato carried somewhat further the thought of his master, though presumably intending only to portray accurately what Socrates thought and said. But in his later writings he developed an independent set of convictions, though not a systematic philosophy. His greatest influence upon later religious thought was in his fundamental contrast between (*a*) the external world of passing sensation with its unreliable flux of ' opinion ' based thereon and (*b*) the inner world of unchanging reason and harmony, the realm of the eternal ' ideas ' of goodness, truth, and beauty (cf 2 Co 4^{18}). The soul, he held, is immortal by nature, and therefore pre-existent (see PRE-EXISTENCE OF SOULS) ; the universe itself is eternal, without beginning or end, an outward and visible manifestation of divine harmony, if not of deity (cf Ro 1^{20}).

The tendency of Plato's thought as a whole was deeply religious. His influence upon later generations was not limited to the succession of teachers in the Academy, which he founded at Athens, but spread widely among kindred minds throughout the world. Many of the later Stoics were influenced by his teaching, as were Posidonius and the Eclectics, the Neopythagoreans, Philo Judaeus, and finally the Neoplatonists. A subterranean stream of modified Platonism nourished the soil of Hellenism for several centuries and was an important factor in the ' preparation for the gospel.' (See LOGOS, PHILO, HEBREWS, JOHN [THEOLOGY OF], PAUL [THEOLOGY OF].) Plato's influence upon early Christian theology, both in the East (especially Alexandria, *e.g.* Clement and Origen) and the West (*e.g.* Augustine), attests its reality and power during the preceding period, despite the lack of adequate literary evidence. He was ' the prophetic thinker, who pointed upward toward the supersensible world of the mind, the eternal home of the soul ' (Eduard Zeller, *Grundriss der Gesch. der griech. Philosophie*, § 41). F. C. G.

PLATTER.—RSV has replaced ' platter ' of AV and RV by ' plate ' in Mt 23^{25f}, and by ' dish ' in Lk 11^{39}, but in Mt 14$^{8, 11}$, Mk 6$^{25, 28}$ it has replaced the obsolete ' charger ' of AV and RV by ' platter.'

PLAY.—See GAMES, MUSIC.

PLEAD.—In AV ' plead ' always means to ' argue for or against a cause ' as in a court of justice, never to ' pray ' or ' beseech.' The substantive ' pleading ' is used in the same sense in Job 13^{6} ' Hearken to the pleadings of my lips.' In RSV ' plead ' has the meaning ' beseech ' in Jer 15^{11} ; cf ' pleading ' in Jer 3^{21}.

PLEASANT PLANTS.—See ADONIS.

PLEDGE.—The taking of a pledge for the repayment of a loan was sanctioned by the Law, but a humanitarian provision was introduced to the effect that, when this pledge consisted of the large square outer garment or cloak called *śimlāh*, it must be returned before nightfall, since this garment often formed the only covering of the poor at night (Ex 22^{26f}, Dt 24^{12f} ; cf Am 2^{8}, Job 22^{6} 24^{9}, Ezk 18$^{7, 12, 16}$ 33^{15}). It was forbidden also to take the mill or the upper millstone as a pledge (Dt 24^{6}). In Is 36^{8} the reference is to a pledge to be forfeited if a wager is lost (cf RVm, RSV ' make a wager with '). In 1 S 17^{18} ' take their pledge ' probably means ' bring back a token of their welfare ' (cf RSV).

PLEIADES.—See STARS.

PLEROMA.—The transliteration of a Greek word which is generally rendered ' fulness ' in the NT. *Plērōma* is derived from the verb *plēroun*, which means either (*a*) ' to fill ' or (*b*) ' to fill up,' hence ' to fulfil.' The corresponding meanings of the noun are (*a*) ' fulness,' (*b*) ' fulfilment.'

1. Pleroma = ' that which fills ' (corresponding to the verb *plēroun* = fill, *e.g.* Ro 15^{13}, Ac 13^{52}). It is used in this sense in 1 Co 10^{26} (= Ps 23^{1} LXX) ' The earth is the Lord's, and every thing in it ' ; Mk 6^{43}, ' twelve baskets full of broken pieces ' (cf Mt 14^{20}) ; Mk 8^{20}. Perhaps this is also the meaning of Eph 1^{23}, where it is said of the Church, ' which is his (sc. Christ's) body, the fulness of him who fills all in all.' According to this interpretation the relation between Christ and the Church is considered as reciprocal : as the Church, the pleroma of Christ, builds up His body, so the Church in turn is built up by Him who fills all in all. In this case the verb is middle and is used to indicate that Christ will do this for Himself (but see below **2**).

2. Pleroma = ' that which is filled,' ' fulness.' In this sense Ro 15^{29} : ' And I know that when I come to you I shall come in the fulness of the blessing of Christ.' Also Jn 1^{16} : ' And from His fulness have we all received, grace upon grace ' ; cf v.^{14} where the incarnate Word is depicted as ' full of grace and truth.'

In the religious philosophy of the Hellenistic age many formations from the stem *pler-* (' fill ') are used in a context of cosmological and theological speculation to characterize the plenitude of the world or the sphere of the divinity. Pleroma here often means the totality of reality rather than numerical completeness. This is the case, *e.g.*, in Philo of Alexandria, in the *Odes of Solomon*, in the Hermetic writings and the Neoplatonists. In Gnostic literature the term (in absolute usage) means the sphere of the Aeons, the upper pneumatic world to which the Gnostic is substantially related and into which he hopes to ascend after his death. Thus the concept pleroma changed from a merely formal conception of fulness to a material conception of divine essence.

Some passages in the NT show this modified usage. This applies perhaps to Jn 1^{16} (see above), but especially to some passages of Colossians and Ephesians. In Col 1^{19} pleroma is used absolutely : ' in him (sc. Christ) all the fulness was pleased to dwell.' The RSV adds ' (fulness) of God,' as in Col 2^{9} we find : ' For in him dwells the fulness of deity bodily.' These statements are probably intended as a contradiction to gnostic speculations. We meet the same meaning of pleroma in Eph 3^{19} : ' that you may be filled with all the fulness of God.' Perhaps in Eph 1^{23} pleroma must also be understood in this sense (see above **1**). For Eph 4^{13} see below **4**.

The sense ' fulness ' may also be applied to time (corresponding to the use of the verb ' fill ' in the passive voice, *e.g.* Mk 1^{15}, Lk 21^{24}, Jn 7^{8}). This is the case in Gal 4^{4} : ' but when the time has fully come,' literally translated in AV : ' but when the fulness of the time was come.' Also Eph 1^{10}, where the purpose of God is described ' as a plan for the fulness of time ' (literally ' of the times '). These expressions are not simply chronological statements, but they refer to the source of time as determined by God.

3. Pleroma = ' that which fills up,' *i.e.* that which makes complete (corresponding to the use of the verb ' fill,' *e.g.* Mt 23^{32}, Rev 6^{11}). Is this sense Mk 2^{21} where pleroma means ' patch ' : ' the patch tears away from it ' (sc. the garment) ; cf Mt 9^{16}.

4. Pleroma = ' the completed whole,' ' totality.' It seems that this is the sense in Ro 11^{25} : ' A hardening has come upon part of Israel, until the full number of the Gentiles come in.' The sense in Ro 11^{12} cannot be explained with certainty ; perhaps it is the same as 11^{25} : ' If their (sc. Israel's) failure means riches for the Gentiles, how much will their full inclusion (literally ' their fulness ') mean.' Some interpreters think that pleroma here means ' fulfilment ' (sc. of the Law ; see below **5**), because ' pleroma ' contrasts with ' *hēttēma* ' which may mean ' failure ' (RSV) or ' diminishing ' (AV). Doubtful is also the interpretation of Eph 4^{13} : ' until we attain . . .

to the measure of the stature of the fulness of Christ.' It seems that this phrase is intended to explain the preceding figure of speech: 'to a perfect man' (thus correctly in AV, while RSV says: 'to mature manhood'). In the given context (cf especially v.15) it would seem preferable to interpret according to AV: The perfect man is Christ in all His fulness; into Him the Christians shall grow up so that his body, *i.e.* the Church, shall be built (cf v.12).

5. Pleroma = 'fulfilling' (corresponding to the use of the verb 'fill' *e.g.* Ro 8⁴, 13⁸, Gal 5¹⁴). In this sense Ro 13¹⁰: 'Love is the fulfilling of the Law.' It is possible to understand Ro 11¹² in this sense; see above **4.**

R. B.

PLOUGH.—See Agriculture, 1.

PLUMBLINE. PLUMMET.—The latter is a diminutive of 'plumb,' from Latin *plumbum*, 'lead,' and denotes the combined cord and weight, by suspending which against a wall it can be seen whether or not the latter is perpendicular. On the strength of Zec 4¹⁰ (literally 'the stone, the tin,' not 'lead'; cf AVm), it has been inferred that the Hebrew masons used a plumb-bob of lead, but the text of this passage is undoubtedly corrupt. The Hebrew plummet (2 K 21¹², Is 28¹⁷) more probably consisted of a stone (Is 34¹¹ AV; RV, RSV 'plummet') suspended by a cord, the 'plumbline' of Am 7⁷ᶠ. Cf Arts and Crafts, 3.

A. R. S. K.

POCHERETH-HAZZEBAIM.—Among the 'children of Solomon's servants' who returned with Zerubbabel, Ezr 2⁵⁷, Neh 7⁵⁹ (AV '**Pochereth of Zebaim**'), 1 Es 5³⁴ (AV 'the sons of Phacereth, the sons of Sabi'; RV 'the sons of Phacereth, the sons of Sabie').

POCHERETH OF ZEBAIM, Ezr 2⁵⁷, Neh 7⁵⁹ (AV).—See Pochereth-Hazzebaim.

PODS (*keratia*, Lk 15¹⁶) are almost certainly the pods of the **carob** tree (*Ceratonia siliqua*), commonly called the **locust** tree. This common Palestine tree is distinguished by its beautiful dark glossy foliage. The long pods, which ripen from May to August according to the altitude, are even to-day used as food by the poor; a confection is made from them. But they are used chiefly for cattle. The name 'St. John's bread' is given to these pods, from a tradition that these and not locusts, composed the food of St. John the Baptist but see Food, **8.**

E. W. G. M.

POETRY.—1. The Nature of Poetry.—Poetry is the work of imagination, feeling, and reflection. As the Greek word *poiētēs* suggests, the poet is the maker: he employs his inventive and creative powers to order words in varied forms and patterns, to associate sounds in such a way as to produce a desired effect, and to stimulate the mind to range and explore beyond the barriers of literal fact. The origins of poetry lie deeply embedded in the elemental rhythms of life which find their expression in such activities as marching, singing, playing of musical instruments, and dancing. Perhaps at a very early period singing was antiphonal, the response of person to person, of words to words (Ex 15²⁰⁻²¹, 1 S 18⁶⁻⁷, Is 6³); there is much to suggest that some of the psalms were so rendered.

2. Poetry in the Bible.—The presence of poetry in the Bible has long been recognized. In an early and beautifully written fragment of Dt 32 among the Dead Sea Scrolls each stichos or colon appears on a separate line. Philo of Alexandria (*de vita Mosis*, i. 5 = 23) and Josephus (*Ant.* ii. xvi. 4 [346]; iv. viii. 44 [303]; vii. xii. 3 [305 f]) comment on the metrical forms of Biblical poetry, and their views are perpetuated for the most part among the Fathers. Origen, in a scholion on Ps 118¹ (LXX), writes of the two stichoi in a metrical unit and of the measurement of meter by the number of accented syllables (G. B. Gray, *The Forms of Hebrew Poetry*, p. 12), while Eusebius, in the *Praeparatio evangelica* (xi. v. 5) follows in the main the views of Josephus. Jerome, too, turns to the subject on several occasions, especially in his *Prologue to Job*. Among the great medieval rabbis, Ḳimḥi and Ibn Ezra stand out as the most independent and discriminating interpreters of Hebrew metrical form. But it was not until 1753, when Bishop Richard Lowth published his epoch-making word *de sacra poesi Hebraeorum praelectionis academicae*, that the true character of Hebrew poetry was correctly grasped, and this work was followed in 1778 by a more detailed and discriminating treatment of the subject in his translation and notes on *Isaiah*. With the exception of Ḳimḥi and Ibn Ezra, all previous work lay too much under the domination of Greek critical norms and models, with the result that the form and structure of Hebrew poetry was greatly obscured.

While a substantial and impressive literature on the nature of Hebrew poetry has arisen since the time of Lowth, the greatest advance has come from the recovery of the literatures of the ancient Near East. It is now clear that behind our earliest Hebrew compositions there lay a long and established literary tradition among the peoples of Egypt, Mesopotamia, and Canaan in which we recognize the same literary phenomena as we encounter in the poetry of the OT. That Canaanite literary practice exercised a profound influence upon ancient Israel cannot be doubted. The Ugaritic inscriptions (see Râs Shamra) often display the same syntactical phenomena, lexical usage, and literary structure. The rhetorical features are much the same, the formal patterns show similar affinities, and the basic modes of composition and construction are identical. The Ugaritic poems reveal the same rich and varied metrical structures as Hebrew poetry, and their epic style conforms to that of many Hebrew compositions.

Despite the strong feeling for cadence and rhythm among the King James translators, especially in the Psalter and Job, the presence of poetry is unrecognized in the printed text. In the RSV more than 35 per cent. of the literature is given in its proper poetic guise, and there are not a few other passages which should probably be printed as poetry, notably Jotham's fable (Jg 9⁸⁻¹⁵), Malachi, and more of Ezekiel. The issue here is not merely theoretical. The poetic form makes it possible for us to gain a deeper appreciation of the aesthetic qualities of Hebrew literary compositions, but more than that it often provides us with an indispensable instrument for the proper interpretation of the text. Failure to recognize the formal patterns of Hebrew poetry has often been responsible for fanciful and mistaken exegesis. Poetry must be interpreted as poetry.

3. The poetry of the OT.—Many poetic pieces lie scattered throughout the Pentateuch and historical books. These were doubtless transmitted from generation to generation in oral tradition by the professional singers (*mōshᵉlîm*, Nu 21²⁷), and were later reduced to writing in such collections as the *Book of Jashar* (Jos 8¹², 2 S 1¹⁸) and the *Book of the Wars of Yahweh* (Nu 21¹⁴). Among the Cain traditions appears the Song of Lamech (Gn 4²³⁻²⁴), breathing the nomad's unbridled passion for revenge. Like so many other early poems its rhythm and parallelism are flawless, and the assonance is accentuated by the rhyme of its pronominal suffixes. From this early time come also curses and blessings, both from the primordial period (*e.g.* Gn 9²⁵⁻²⁷) and from the time of the patriarchs (Gn 12¹⁻³ 27²⁷ᵇ⁻²⁹ 27³⁹⁻⁴⁰). The crossing of the Sea of Reeds was celebrated in the triumphant Song of Miriam (Moses?) in Ex 15²¹, which may be the *incipit* of the extensive version given in vv.¹ᵇ⁻¹⁸. The Song of the Well (Nu 21¹⁷⁻¹⁸), the taunt against Heshbon (Nu 21²⁷⁻³⁰), and the marching song along the boundaries of Moab (Nu 21¹⁴⁻¹⁵), as well as the cultic Ark songs (Nu 10³⁵⁻³⁶), are ascribed to the wilderness period. From the age of the Conquest comes the superb Song of Deborah (Jg 5), unrivalled in poetic feeling, rhetorical power, and literary craftsmanship in the poetry of early Israel. From about the same time we have Jotham's fable, a literary type paralleled only once elsewhere in the OT, but common among the Sumerians and other ancient Near Eastern peoples. Here, too, we have the raucous riddles of Samson (Jg

POETRY

14[4, 18] 15[16]). The period of the United Monarchy produced an extensive literature, as rich and powerful as it is diverse. Among its supreme poetic monuments, David's Lament over Saul and Jonathan (2 S 1[19–27]) holds a secure place. To this time belong also the Blessing of Jacob (Gn 49), the oracles of Balaam (Nu 23–24), and possibly the Blessing of Moses (Dt 33), and Ps 18 (=2 S 22). The power that popular poetry could exert in Israel is illustrated by the little couplet sung about Saul and David (1 S 18[7] 21[11 (Heb 12)] 29[5]).

The prophetic books of the OT are largely poetic. They contain a great variety of literary types and forms as well as great diversity in literary style. Here the well-known dictum of Buffon applies: *le style est l'homme même*, for the prophets reflect their own background, temper, and experience. Of the three so-called books of poetry, *Psalms*, *Proverbs*, and *Job*, the first is a product of the devotional and cultic life of ancient Israel, spanning many centuries, and containing precipitates from a wide diversity of cultic situations; the second belonging to the Wisdom literature has striking affinities with the sapiential literatures of other peoples, especially the Egyptian *Proverbs of Amenemope*; the third, an elaborate poetic dialogue, towers high among the great literary achievements of the Near East, and in certain sections, as in the Divine discourse from the whirlwind (chs. 38–41), rises to the height of sublimity.

4. The poetry of the Apocrypha and Pseudepigrapha.—*Ecclesiasticus* or *Ben Sirach*, belongs to the Wisdom literature; here proverbs and wise sayings are often expanded into miniature 'essays,' full of keen observation, shrewd insight, and fervent piety. The *Wisdom of Solomon* is of quite a different strain, reflecting the influence of Greek philosophy, especially Stoicism. The historical book of *I Maccabees* includes within it several laments (2[8–12] 3[45]) and eulogies (3[3–9] 14[6–15]). The didactic romance of *Tobit* concludes with a prayer of adoration (13[1–18]) and that of *Judith* with a hymn of thanksgiving (16[2–17]). In the pseudepigraphical literature, the narrative of *Jubilees* is broken here and there by poetical sections (*e.g.* 12[3–5, 18–20] 20[6–10] 22[11–23]), most of it belonging to the literature of *blessing*; similarly the *Testaments of the Twelve Patriarchs* (Test. of Simeon 2[1–4], Levi 4[1–6], Joseph 1[2]–2[7]), where the poetic portions usually appear at the beginning of the patriarch's instructions. The *Apocalypse of Enoch* contains large sections of poetry, as in the opening and closing chapters, much of the Parables (chs. 36–71), and the miscellaneous materials of 92[1]–100[9]. *Fourth Ezra* and the *Syriac Apocalypse of Baruch* also have substantial poetic material, some of it of a very high order. The *Psalms of Solomon* are poetic throughout. In this connexion mention may be made of the collection of psalms of thanksgiving, the *Hodayoth*, among the Dead Sea Scrolls, and the longer prayer at the close of the *Manual of Discipline*. Much of this poetry is very moving, though taken as a whole it does not rise to the level of the canonical psalms.

5. The poetry of the New Testament.—In striking contrast with the OT, there is relatively little poetry in the NT, and often where we do meet it the influence of the OT is apparent, as in the infancy hymns (Lk 1[47–55, 68–79] 2[14, 29–32, 34b–35]) and in the exultant heavenly adorations of the Apocalypse (Rev 5[9f] 7[15–17] 15[3b–4] 19[1b–3, 5b, 6b–8]) as well as in its great laments (18[2b–3, 4b–8, 21b–24]). In the Gospels especially we encounter many brief poetic effusions, and they reveal the same formal characteristics as the OT compositions. Synonymous parallelism is illustrated in Mt 7[6] 10[41], Lk 12[48], Jn 6[35,] 13[16] antithetic in Mk 2[27] 8[35], Mt 7[17] 10[39] 15[11], Jn 3[6, 18]; stair-like or ascending in the manner of the Psalms of Ascent (Pss 120–135) in Mk 9[37] (cf Mt 10[40] 18[5], Lk 9[48] 10[16], Jn 13[20]). The Prologue to John's Gospel is a notable example of this style (1[1–18] with possible excision of prose elements). The tricola constructions are of special interest; as in the OT the third line constitutes the impressive climax (Mt 7[7–8], Lk 11[9–10], Mk 2[27–28], Mt 6[24], Lk 16[13], Jn 3[18] 4[22] 6[32–33]). Examples of rhythm are also evident as in the Lord's Prayer (Mt 6[9–13]); the admonitions of Lk 6[27–29] and vv.[36–38]. Blessings, too, are present in remarkably sententious form (Mt 5[3–11]; cf Lk 6[20–22]) as are also prophetic invectives (Mt 23[29–33], Lk 6[24–26]) and threats (Mt 23[34–36]). In certain sections of the Pauline letters the language rises to a great elevation approximating poetry as in 1 Co 13.

6. The characteristic features of Hebrew poetry.—How, then, shall we define the characteristic features of Hebrew poetry? It is to be observed, first of all, that the language was peculiarly suited as a vehicle for poetic utterance. Abstractions are relatively rare; the ancient Hebrew thinks and speaks concretely. Words appeal to the senses and evoke images. Nouns and verbs predominate, pronouns are generally attached to the verb and the pronominal modifiers to the noun, adjectives are used sparingly, the conjunction 'and' is used with great frequency where we should employ subordinate connectives. Sentences are short. The speech is concentrated, reduced it would seem to its minimal essentials. Modern translations often employ more than twice the number of words to render the Hebrew original. The verb plays a central rôle. Nouns are usually derived from the verbs. 'They are as it were living beings, extracted and moulded, while their radical source itself was in a state of living energy' (J. G. Herder, *The Spirit of Hebrew Poetry*, p. 29). The most characteristic features of Biblical poetry are action, imagery, passion, music, rhythm, simplicity, vigour, concreteness.

a. Parallelism. The basic element of Hebrew poetry is the line or colon. It has no independent status however; it exists only *in relation*, most frequently to a second line but sometimes also to a third. The bicola is then the characteristic unit of Hebrew poetic speech. The essential words of one line are parallel with the essential words of the other, words parallel words in at least three ways: (1) *Synonymous parallelism.* The second line restates the first, not merely by repetition, however, as in many of the Near Eastern liturgies, but by enriching, deepening, and even transforming it with new words, by adding fresh nuances, and by giving it a symmetry and balance, as in

O Lord, who shall sojourn in thy tent?
Who shall dwell on thy holy hill?—(Ps 15[1])

or

The heavens are telling the glory of God;
and the firmament proclaims his handiwork.
—(Ps 19[1])

(2) *Antithetic parallelism.* The second line is contrasted with the first, as frequently in the Book of Proverbs:

A son who gathers in summer is prudent,
but a son who sleeps in harvest brings shame.
—(Pr 10[5])

(3) *Climactic parallelism.* The lines are related to each other in an ascending climax, normally of three members. This form is familiar in the Ugaritic texts, and is illustrated in the OT by Ps 92[9 (Heb 10)]:

For lo, thine enemies, O Lord,
for lo, thine enemies shall perish;
all evil-doers shall be scattered.

Akin to climactic parallelism is the so-called *stair-like* construction of the Psalms of Ascent (120–135).

Parallelism assumes many forms and modes, many of them complicated. Some scholars speak of complementary parallelism, but it is best to confine this form to comparisons, such as

As a hart longs
for flowing streams,
So longs my soul
for thee, O God.—(Ps 42[1])

b. Meter. A second formal feature of Hebrew poetry is meter. But unlike Western poetry generally the accent is determined not by the measured succession of syllables, but by meaning. Therefore such terms as iambic, anapaestic, *etc.* are to be avoided. The number of unstressed syllables is irrelevant ; it is only the stress of the thought that is important. Parallelism and meter are closely associated ; the number of stressed syllables in one colon is related to the number in its parallel. The bicola is the true unit. Usually the cola are of equal length, *i.e.* they have the same number of stressed syllables. The meter can then be expressed as follows : 2′ 2′ or 3′ 3′ or upon occasions 4′ 4′. The first is to be found in many poems, as in the Song of Miriam (Ex 15[21]) :

Sing to Yahweh
for he has triumphed mightily ;
the horse and his rider,
he has hurled into the sea.

This meter is present in many Canaanite poems. The 3′ 3′ meter also appears frequently :

The glory of Lebanon shall be given to it,
the majesty of Carmel and Sharon.—(Is 35[2])

Often, however, the bicola are unequal in length, most frequently in the so-called ' lamentation ' or *ḳînāh* meter, which is illustrated by much of *Lamentations*, Is 53[1-9], and many of the poems of the Psalter :

God looks down from heaven
upon the sons of men
to see if there are any who are wise,
who seek after God.—(Ps 53[2])

The metrical scheme is frequently very irregular, however, and different meters are employed in the same poem ; indeed this variety prevents the poem from becoming monotonous.

c. Strophic structure. The poem is normally divided into strophes or stanzas. They may be of equal length, but more often they are not. In the acrostic poems such as Pss 9–10, 25, 34, 119, and La 1–4, the divisions are plainly marked by the Hebrew letters with which the lines open. Where refrains are present the division is also clear (Is 9[8]–10[4] and 5[24-25], Pss 99, 107). At other times the division can be detected by the climactic lines, or by the change of person, or by striking words such as *behold, therefore, and now*, or by the presence of key words in the opening or closing lines. Often the poems are composed of two strophes (Ps 1), more frequently of three (Pss 2, 46, Is 42[5-17]) ; sometimes of five (Is 52[13]–53[12]), or even seven (Ps 107), or nine (Jer 3[1]–4[4] with deletion of prose additions ; 4[3-4] is the coda).

d. Literary genres or types. The recognition of literary forms in the OT is due primarily to the pioneering work of Hermann Gunkel. Before a poem can be understood, it is necessary to determine its genre. Unfortunately our nomenclature for the various types is still unsatisfactory, and the Hebrews, while employing a number of such terms, like *song, oracle, parable, proverb, lamentation,* and *prayer*, were imprecise in their designations. Among the numerous literary types the following may be mentioned : *blessings* (Gn 22[16-18] 27[27a-29] 49, Dt 33), *taunt songs* (Nu 21[27-30], Is 47) ; *love songs* (Ca 1[7-8, 9-17] 2[8ff]) ; *laments* (2 S 1[19-27], Am 5[2], Jer 9[17ff] (Heb 16ff), Ezk 19[2-14], Is 53[1-9]) ; *hymns* (Pss 19, 23, 103, 136, 146–150) ; *royal hymns* (Pss 2, 20, 21, 45, 72, 110) ; *pilgrim songs* (Pss 84, 122) ; *thanksgivings* (Pss 18, 30, 41, 118) ; *invectives* and *threats* (Am 1[3]–2[16], Is 5[8-23], Hab 2[9-20]). As in the case of parallelism, meter and strophic structure, the forms are often fluid and tend to coalesce. Many types have their own peculiar terminology, especially in their openings, words such as *blessed* (*bārûkh*), *cursed* (*'ārûr*), *woe* (*hôy*), *therefore* (*lākhēn*), *how* (*'ēkhāh*), *praise* (*hôdhû*), ' I will sing ' (*'āshîr*).

e. Style. We have called attention to the major features of Hebrew literary style : simplicity, vigour, passion, rhythm, concreteness, variety and versatility of composition. The ancient Hebrew was sensitive to sound ; he was fond of euphony and disliked cacophony. His choice of words was often determined by their assonance. The confessional lament of Is 53[1-9] is a superb example of the literary effects of constantly recurring words and sounds. Repetition, too, was a major feature of Hebrew poetic rhetoric, as almost any poem in the OT will show. But the most significant feature of Hebraic poetic style is imagery. Such books as Isaiah, Jeremiah, Hosea, Psalms, and Job are alive with vivid images and figures. They are drawn from a wide variety of sources : light and darkness, thunder, rain, cloud, snow, mountains, sea, fire, death, sowing, harvest, the life of the shepherd, ploughman, and vintner, the heavenly bodies, etc. Similes, metaphors, personifications, apostrophes, parables, allegories, and many other figures abound throughout the poetic portions of the OT. The poet's descriptive powers can at times attain the highest levels of literary power, as in Job's incomparable lines on the ostrich (39[13-18]), the horse (39[19-25]), the hawk (39[26-30]) and above all of Leviathan (ch. 41), or Jeremiah's lament about death coming through the windows (9[21]). Indeed, the Hebrew poet observed everything about him with all his senses attent, and then gave expression to his religious faith by laying hold on all the imaginative resources granted him in his created universe. J. Mu.

POLE (SACRED).—See ASHERAH, 3.

POLICE.—RSV translation in Ac 16[35, 38] (AV, RV '**serjeants**') of Greek *rhabdouchoi* (=' rod-bearers '), which represents the Latin *lictores* (RVm **lictors**), officials whose duty it was to attend the Roman magistrates, to execute their orders, and especially to administer the punishments of scourging or beheading. For this purpose they carried, as their mark of office, the *fasces*, a bundle of rods with an axe inserted. Cf PHILIPPI.

Temple police, under the charge of a captain (Ac 4[1] 5[24, 26] ; cf Jos. *Ant.* xx. vi. 2 [131] ; *BJ* VI. v. 3 [294]), were responsible for the maintenance of order in the Temple. They had to see that no one entered the part of the Temple to which he or she was not entitled to go and to close the gates at night. They consisted of priests and Levites, and the captain, himself a priest, ranked as second in dignity to the High Priest. Cf *SB* ii, 628 ff.

POLL.—' By the poll ' (Nu 3[47] AV and RV ; omitted in RSV as superfluous) is ' by the head.' Cf Shakespeare, *Hamlet*, IV. v. 196, ' All flaxen was his poll.' The idea in the Hebrew word is ' roundness,' and so to ' poll ' the head is to give it the appearance of roundness by cutting off the hair. Cf More, *Utopia*, Arber's edition, p. 49, ' Their heads be not polled or shauen, but rounded a lytle about the eares.'

POLLUX.—See DIOSCURI.

POLYGAMY.—See FAMILY, MARRIAGE.

POMEGRANATE.—Hebrew *rimmôn* (Arab. *rummân*) tree and fruit, Ex 28[33f] 39[24ff], Nu 13[23] 20[5], Dt 8[8], 1 S 14[2], 1 K 7[18, 20, 42], 2 K 25[17], 2 Ch 3[16] 4[13], Ca 4[3, 13] 6[7, 11] 7[12] 8[2], Jer 52[22f], Jl 1[12], Hag 2[19]. The pomegranate (*Punica granatum*) is one of the familiar fruit trees of the OT ; it is usually a shrub, but may attain the height of a tree (1 S 14[2]) ; it was much admired for its beauty (Ca 4[3] 6[11]), and its flower was copied in ornamentation (Ex 28[33], 1 K 7[18]). Its dark green leaves and brilliant scarlet blossom make it a peculiarly attractive object, especially when growing in orchards (Ca 4[13]), mixed with trees of other shades of green ; its buds develop with the tender grapes (Ca 7[12]), and the round, reddish fruit, with its brilliant, crimson, juicy seeds, ripens at the time of the vintage. The fruit is a favourite food, and the bark a valued astringent medicine. E. W. G. M.

POMMEL.—See BOWL.

POND.—See POOL.

PONTUS.—In the earliest times of which we have any knowledge, this name, meaning ' sea ' in Greek and Latin, was used by Greeks to indicate vaguely country bordering on or near the Black Sea. From its importance for the grain supply of Greece, the Black Sea and the land around it came to be known as ' the sea ' *par excellence*. As time went on the term gradually became confined to the country to the *south* of the Black Sea.

It was not till about 302 B.C. that a kingdom was formed here. In that year consequent upon the troubles due to the early death of Alexander the Great, Mithridates II. was able to carve out for himself a kingdom beyond the river Halys in NE. Asia Minor, and about 281 B.C. he assumed the title of king. We cannot define the exact extent of the territory ruled by him and his descendants, but it is certain that it included part of the country previously called Cappadocia, some of the mountain tribes near the Black Sea coasts, and part of Paphlagonia; and also certain that its extent varied from time to time. Acting with Nicomedes of Bithynia he succeeded in settling down the Galatians (who were Gauls, *i.e.* Celts) in Phrygia. The Mithridatic dynasty lasted till 63 B.C., when Mithridates VI., 'the Great,' died, defeated by Pompey. In the preceding year the kingdom ceased to exist, and part of it was incorporated in the Roman Empire under the name Pontus, and this district henceforth constituted one-half of the combined province Bithynia-Pontus, which was put under one governor. The remaining portions of the old kingdom were distributed in other ways. The civil wars helped Pharnaces, a son of the last Mithridates, to acquire the whole of his father's kingdom, but his brief reign ended in his defeat by Julius Caesar (47 B.C.). The narrowed kingdom of Pontus was reconstituted by Mark Antony in 39 B.C., and given in 36 B.C. to Polemon, who founded a dynasty, which ruled over this kingdom till A.D. 63. The daughter of this Polemon, Queen Tryphaena, is mentioned in the apocryphal book, *The Acts of Paul and Thecla*, as having been present at a great imperial festival at Pisidian Antioch in the reign of the Emperor Claudius, whose blood-relation she was. This statement is no doubt founded on fact. These *Acts* relate that she protected the Christian maiden Thecla, and was converted, through her instrumentality, to Christianity. As tradition connects Bartholomew also with the Polemonian dynasty, it is probable that there were some Christians among them. In A.D. 63 the kingdom of Pontus had been brought to a sufficiently high pitch of civilization to be admitted into the Roman Empire; the western part was made a region of the province Galatia, and the eastern was added to Cappadocia. The dispossessed Polemon was given a Cilician kingdom, and it was as king of part of Cilicia that he (later than A.D. 63) married Berenice (q.v.).

In the 1st cent. A.D., therefore, the name Pontus had various significations, and a strict nomenclature was available for their distinction. The province was Pontus, Polemon's kingdom was Pontus Polemoniacus (incorporated into the province of Galatia A.D. 63), the part of Mithridates' old kingdom incorporated in the province Galatia (3–2 B.C.) was Pontus Galaticus, and the regions that lay E. of Pontus Polemoniacus, between the Black Sea and Armenia, were known as Pontus Cappadocicus. From about A.D. 78 to 106 Pontus Galaticus and Pontus Polemoniacus were included in the combined provinces Galatia and Cappadocia, and after A.D. 106 they constituted permanent parts of the province Cappadocia. In 1 P 1^1 Pontus means clearly the Roman province. There is little doubt that the adjective *Pontikos*, applied to **Aquila** in Ac 18^2, means that, though a Jew, he was a native of the Roman province, and it is interesting in connexion with this to mention that an inscription has been found which refers to one Aquila at Sinope, one of the principal cities of the Roman province of Pontus. The only remaining NT reference to Pontus (Ac 2^9) cannot be so easily explained. It must be left uncertain whether the name Pontus there is used strictly of the province, or more loosely of the kingdom, or of the kingdom and the province together.

Christianity was not brought to Pontus by St. Paul, if we can trust the silence of Acts, and it is best to do so. From 1 Peter it is clear that by the date of the Epistle there were Christians in that country, and these converts from paganism to Christianity probably came there from the Asian coasts or from Rome. There is a well-known and valuable testimony to the prevalence of Christianity in the province, belonging to the period A.D. 111–113. At that time the younger Pliny was governor of the province Bithynia-Pontus, and addressed inquiries to the Emperor Trajan on the manner in which Christians ought to be treated by the administration. He reports that many men and women of all ages and of every rank in town and country were Christians, and that some had abandoned the faith twenty or twenty-five years before (see Pliny, *Epp.* x. 96 f). After Pliny's time Pontus continued to be a stronghold of Christianity. From here came the famous **Marcion** (born about 120 at Sinope), and of this province **Aquila**, a translator of the OT into Greek, was a native. A. So.—**F. C. G.**

POOL, POND.—Hebrew *'ᵃgham*, a collection of standing water, is distinguished from *miḳweh*, a place into which water flows, or is led (Ex 7^{19}). The former may denote the water left in the hollows when the inundation of the Nile subsides, and the latter, reservoirs (cf Gn 1^{10}, Lv 11^{36}). AV translates *'ᵃgham* 'pond' in Ex 7^{19} 8^5; RV and RSV uniformly 'pool' (Is 14^{23} etc.), except Jer 51^{32} (AV and RV 'reeds,' RSV 'bulwarks; cf RVm). *bᵉrēkhāh* (2 S 2^{13} 4^{12} etc.) is = Arabic *birkeh*, an artificial pond or tank. It is applied to great reservoirs constructed to furnish water for cities, or for irrigation, like that at Gibeon, 2 S 2^{13}), those at Hebron (2 S 4^{12}), and at Jerusalem (2 K 18^{17}), etc.; and also to large basins, such as lend freshness to the courts of the houses in Damascus. The usual LXX equivalent is *kolumbēthra*, the word used in NT for the pools of Bethesda and Siloam (Jn 5^2 9^7). In Is 19^{10} read with RSV 'all who work for hire will be grieved' (cf RV). See also HESHBON. W. E.

POOR.—See POVERTY.

POPLAR.—Hebrew *libhneh* (from a root meaning 'white'), Gn 30^{37} (RVm 'storax'), Hos 4^{13}. In Hos 14^5 RSV conjecturally reads *libhneh* for MT *lᵉbhānôn*, 'Lebanon' (so AV, RV). The Hebrew is very similar to Arabic *lubna* meaning 'storax,' which is the LXX translation in Gn 30^{37}; on the other hand, in Hos 4^{13} the LXX has *leukē* ('white'), *i.e.* the 'poplar.' The poplar may easily have furnished Jacob with white rods. There are two kinds of poplar in Syria, *Populus alba* and *P. euphratica*; they both flourish round Damascus, where their trunks are much used in making supports for the mud roofs. E. W. G. M.

PORATHA.—Fourth son of Haman, put to death by the Jews, Est 9^8.

PORCH.—This word is a doublet of 'portico' (from Lat. *porticus*), both originally denoting a covered entrance to a building. When the front of this entrance is supported on pillars, the porch becomes a portico. *Porticus*, like the Greek *stoa*, was extended to signify a roofed colonnade running round a public building such as a temple, or enclosing an open space, like the cloisters of a mediaeval monastery. The most famous of these 'porches'—a sense in which the word is now obsolete—were the 'painted porch'—the Porch *par excellence*—at Athens, and Solomon's porch at Jerusalem (see below).

In the OT a porch is named chiefly in connexion with the Temple (see below), or with the **palace** (q.v.) of Solomon. The pillars of the temple of Dagon at Gaza which Samson pulled down, or rather slid from their stone bases, were probably two of those supporting the portico, as ingeniously explained by Macalister, *Bible Sidelights*, etc., ch. 7 (see HOUSE, **5**). The word rendered 'porch' in AV and RV in Jg 3^{23} (RSV 'vestibule') is of quite uncertain meaning and even of doubtful authenticity.

In the NT, in connexion with the trial of Jesus, mention is made in Mk 14^{68} of a 'porch' or, as RVm, 'forecourt' (RSV 'gateway'), as distinguished from the 'court' (v.^{66} RV; RSV 'courtyard') of the high priest's palace, for which Mt 26^{71} (EV 'porch') has a word elsewhere rendered 'gate.' In both cases the covered gateway leading from the street to the court is probably meant.

Solomon's porch (Jn 10^{23}, Ac 3^{11} 5^{12}; RSV 'portico') was a covered colonnade or cloister running along the east side of the Temple enclosure (for details see *Exp T*, November 1908, p. 68). A similar colonnade enclosed the pool of Bethesda (Jn 5^{2}). A. R. S. K.

PORCUPINE.—Mentioned in Is 14^{23} (RV) 34^{11} (RV, RSV), Zeph 2^{14} (RV); AV has 'bittern' in all cases, RSV 'hedgehog' in Is 14^{23}, Zeph 2^{14}. See also BITTERN, JACKAL.

PORPHYRY.—Found only in AVm, RVm, RSV in Est 1^{6}, where AV and RV have 'red marble.' It renders Hebrew *bahaṭ*, the meaning of which is not certainly known. See JEWELS AND PRECIOUS STONES.

PORPOISE.—In RVm **porpoise skins** are mentioned in Ex 25^{5} 26^{14} etc., as used for the covering of the Tabernacle (AV 'badgers' skins,' RV 'sealskins,' RSV '**goatskins**'), and in Ezk 16^{10} as used for making sandals (AV 'badgers' skin,' RV 'sealskin,' RSV '**leather**'). The Hebrew *tāḥāsh* may be connected etymologically with Arabic *tukhas*, 'dolphin' or 'porpoise,' but porpoise-skin is an improbable material for this use. Goatskin is a more likely material for the covering of the Tabernacle, and for this Delitzsch found an Assyrian etymology. But perhaps the word simply means 'leather,' as Egyptian *ṯḥś*.

PORT.—The port of Neh 2^{13} AV is a 'gate' (so RV, RSV), the same Hebrew word being translated 'gate' in the same verse. Cf Pr.-Bk. version of Ps 9^{14} 'Within the ports of the daughter of Sion.'

PORTER in AV and RV has always the sense of 'doorkeeper' (see HOUSE, **6**) or 'gatekeeper' (see FORTIFICATION AND SIEGECRAFT, under **gates**), and RSV always substitutes one or other of these words. In Jn 10^{3} the porter is the man left in charge of a sheepfold by the shepherd or shepherds whose sheep are there housed for the night. In private houses the doorkeeper might be a woman (2 S 4^{6} as restored from LXX, Ac 12^{13}). In OT, however, porters are most frequently named in the Books of Chronicles, Ezra, and Nehemiah in connexion with the Temple (1 Ch 9^{17f} onwards), where they had charge of the various gates (see TEMPLE, **6**, PRIESTS AND LEVITES, **2** (*c*)). The same word is rendered **doorkeepers** in AV 1 Ch 15^{22f}, and in several other places in RV (15^{18}, etc.). It is to be regretted that this term was not substituted throughout (RSV has 'gatekeepers' in these cases). In Ps 84^{10}, where AV, RV and RSV have 'doorkeepers,' the original is different, and should probably be rendered: 'I had rather be (standing or lying) at the threshold in the house of my God.' A. R. S. K.

POSIDONIUS.—An envoy sent by Nicanor to Judas (2 Mac 14^{19}).

POSSESSION.—1. Meaning of the term.—The central idea in the word is the coercive seizing of the spirit of a man by another spirit, viewed as superhuman, with the result that the man's will is no longer free but is controlled, often against his wish, by this indwelling person or power. In Scripture the idea is associated with both phases of moral character; and a man may be possessed by Christ or the Holy Spirit, or by *a* or *the* devil. Later usage has confined the word mainly, though not exclusively, to possession by an evil spirit. Of the better possession there are several kinds of instances in both Testaments. It is sometimes represented, according to the more material psychology of early times, as the seizure of a man by an external power, though the internal occupation is implied, and the control is none the less complete (1 S 10^{10}, Is 61^{1}; cf the frequent 'the hand of the Lord was upon' him, 1 K 18^{46}: so of an evil spirit, 1 S 18^{10}). The inspiration of the prophets is in some places described as effected by a supernatural agency occupying the seat of personality within the prophet, and controlling or moving him (Lk 1^{70}, 1 P 1^{11}, 2 P 1^{21}, 2 Es 14^{22}). In personal religion not only is the transference of authority within to the indwelling Christ spoken of (Jn 17^{23}, Gal 2^{20}), but the Holy Spirit also may seize and possess a man (Ac 2^{4}, Lk 1^{15}, Ro 8^{9}, Eph 5^{18}), and should rule in him (Eph 4^{30}). But this involves a welcome and glad submission to the sway of a spirit within, though personal wishes may be thwarted or crossed (Ac 16^{7}). Demoniacal possession, on the other hand, is characterized by the reluctance of the sufferer, who is often conscious of the hateful tyranny under which he is held and against which his will rebels in vain.

2. Features of demoniacal possession. — In such possession two features may generally be traced. It is allied with and yet distinct from physical disease, and there is almost always something abnormal with respect to the physical development or defect of the sufferer. It is given as the explanation in cases of dumbness (Mt 9^{32}, Lk 11^{14}), of deafness and dumbness (Mk 9^{25}), of dumbness and blindness (Mt 12^{22}), of curvature of the spine (Lk 13^{11}), and of epilepsy (Mk 1^{26}). Elsewhere such complaints are referred to as merely disease, and no suggestion is made that they were caused or complicated by the action of an evil spirit (Mt 15^{30}, Mk 7^{32}, Lk 18^{35}). Sometimes possession and disease are even distinguished by different enumeration (Mt 10^{8}, Mk 1^{32}, Lk 6^{17f} 7^{21} 13^{32}); and once at least epileptics (or lunatics) and palsied occupy a different category from demoniacs (Mt 4^{24}). The right conclusion seems to be that the same disease was in some cases ascribed to ordinary causes and in others to possession, the distinguishing feature being possibly intractability due to the violence or permanence of the symptoms. Evidence that the disorder was at the same time of a psychical or nervous character is plentiful. According to Arab belief, something abnormal in the appearance, such as a strange look in the eyes or an unusual catching in the throat, was an invariable symptom, and both are indications of nervous excitement or alarm. The will was paralysed (Mk 9^{18}), and the sufferer was under the influence of illusions (Jn 7^{20}). He identified himself with the demons, and was averse to deliverance (Mk 1^{24} 5^{7}). In such cases Jesus does not follow His usual course of exciting faith before He heals, but acts as though the sufferer were not in a fit state to believe or to trust, and must be dealt with forcibly first of all. Some confident and majestic word is spoken, of which the authority is immediately recognized; and only then, when the proper balance of the mind has been restored, is an attempt made to communicate religious blessing.

3. Our Lord's belief.—Two opinions have been held as to whether Jesus shared the views popular in His day, which views had been growing more common for two or three centuries as a result of the general 'demonizing' of religion in the Eastern Mediterranean world. That He did so is attested on almost every page of the Synoptic Gospels; but in the Fourth Gospel there is no mention of either demons or belief in them—save for the arch-demon and evil spirit Satan. Paul, although he represents Christ's death and resurrection as a victory over the evil powers, does not suggest that Jesus practised exorcism. (*a*) One view holds that our Lord merely accommodated Himself to the views common in Galilee in His day: but this seems to make unreal and untrue his strong pronouncements upon the fall of Satan, the casting out of demons by the Spirit of God, and the serious challenge He set before men to resist the power of the evil one (Lk 9^{49f} 10$^{17-20}$ 11$^{14-26}$). (*b*) The other view holds that in this respect He shared completely the outlook of His own time and place. Even the Pharisees were credited with practising exorcism (Mt 10^{8} 12^{27f}, Lk 11^{19f})—the popular modern idea that Jewish exorcism was a later development is untrue, as the oldest rabbinic sources make clear. The religion of the Incarnation certainly assumes the reality of Jesus' human nature, and His share in the mind of His times. Moreover, the phenomena described as demonic possession represent a widespread ancient popular diagnosis, which was all but universal at one time, and survived for many centuries, in fact down to the rise of modern scientific medicine and psychology. Homer held that a wasting sickness was caused by a demon, and the Greek dramatists generally attributed madness and religious frenzy to demonic (or divine) possession. The Egyptians located a demon in each of the thirty-six members of the body; their presence was the cause of disease, which was healed by their expulsion. Seven evil spirits are grouped in Babylonian mythology (cf Mt 12^{45}, Mk 16^{9}, Lk 8^{2} 11^{26}), and these with their subordinate genii kept men in continual fear and were thought to be able to occupy the body and produce any kind of disease (see also *Testaments of the XII Patriarchs*, Reuben 2–3). In almost every civilization, ancient as those of the E. or rude as those of central Africa, a similar conception has prevailed; and this points toward a certain rudimentary truth about which even the most advanced modern researches have not yet reached an agreement. The exploration of man's inner world is still far from ended. Even to-day there are mental and physical states which can hardly be better described (not diagnosed) than as apparent possession by an evil spirit or spirits. By the same token, in areas where demonic possession is a common belief, the phenomena are likely to be more commonly found; the power of mass suggestion must be taken into account, especially in regions and at times of unusual tension, terror, oppression or persecution, or among peoples commonly given to superstition, or persons suffering from spiritual torpor and ennui. See also article, DEMONS AND DEMONOLOGY; SATAN, **4**. R. W. M.—F. C. G.

POST.—Used in AV and RV for 'a bearer of despatches,' 'a runner,' in 2 Ch $30^{6, 10}$, Est $3^{13, 15}$ $8^{10, 14}$, Job 9^{25}, Jer 51^{31}; RSV has 'courier' save in Job 9^{25} and Jer 51^{31}, where it has 'runner.' The 'runners' were chosen from the king's bodyguard, and were noted for their swiftness, whence Job's simile in 9^{25}.

POST, DOORPOST.—See HOUSE, **6**.

POT.—See HOUSE, **9**.

POTIPHAR.—A high Egyptian official in the story of Joseph (Gn 37^{36} 39^{1}). The more correct form of the name is probably **Potiphera** (Joseph's father-in-law, Gn $41^{45, 50}$ 46^{20}) which means 'He whom Re' has given.' The name has not been found in Egyptian documents, but many names occur which are formed in a similar way, *e.g.* Pa-di-Amun 'He whom Amun has given.' They are first encountered in the 21st Dynasty and are very common in the 22nd Dynasty. The other two Egyptian names in the Joseph story, Asenath and Zaphenath-paneah, likewise belong to the later periods, and all three are specially frequent in the 22nd Dynasty (950–730 B.C.), *i.e.* about the time of the composition of the J and E documents and centuries after the events of the Joseph narrative could have taken place. Potiphar was entitled 'captain of the guard' and 'officer' of Pharoah, the office which he held under him has not been precisely identified. Joseph was sold to Potiphar, whose wife attempted to seduce him: she accused him falsely and he was cast into prison. A story with a similar motif, known as the 'Tale of the Two Brothers' was current in Egypt in later times and has often been compared with the story of Joseph and Potiphar's wife.

T. W. T.

POTIPHERA.—The father of Joseph's wife **Asenath** (q.v.) and priest of On, *i.e.* probably high priest of Re', the Sun-god, Gn $41^{40, 45}$ 46^{20}. He would thus be the head of the most learned sacerdotal college in the country, and of high rank. The consonants in the Hebrew are an almost exact transcript of the Egyptian *Petepré'*, 'Given by Re',' a late name found from the 22nd Dynasty onwards; only the letter *w* (represented by English *o*) is puzzling. F. Ll. G.

POTIPHERAH.—AV form of **Potiphera** (q.v.).

POTSHERD.—See POTTERY.

POTSHERD GATE.—The name of a gate in Jerusalem leading to the Valley of Hinnom, Jer 19^{2} (RV 'the gate **Harsith**,' RVm 'the gate of potsherds,' *i.e.* where they were thrown out. AV deriving the word from *ḥeres* 'sun,' has 'the east gate'; AVm 'the sun gate').

POTTAGE.—See FOOD, **3**.

POTTER, POTTERY.—The potter is mentioned frequently in Scripture. He is the 'former' or 'fashioner' (*yōṣēr*), cf Is 29^{16} 41^{25}, Jer $28^{2-4, 6}$, La 4^{2}, 1 Ch 4^{29}). The term thus arose when hand-moulding was still customary, and covered not only the making of pots but also the related activity of making clay figurines. Hence the deity is imagined as 'forming' man out of 'dust from the ground' (Gn 2^{7}, mention of clay, *ḥōmer*, *ṭīṭ*, *ḥeres*, being avoided because of the desired link with man's final returning to dust, Gn 3^{19}). In Zec 11^{13}, however, the potter is not meant, though it was so understood in Mt 27^{7}, but rather the smelter of metal. The occupation of the potter required skill and we hear of families or groups residing in several Judaean villages, who carried on this craft in the royal service (1 Ch 4^{23}).

The technique of pottery making was at first that of moulding over a form, or building up with coils of **clay** in a gradual process, leaving each coil time to harden. American Indians never got beyond this level. The discovery of the potter's **wheel** (Jer 18^{3}) greatly improved the product. Here a ball of clay is placed at the centre of the wheel, which is swiftly turned by the potter or a helper, and acts upon the clay. Models and portrayals of the potter at work at the wheel have been found in Egyptian tombs. Baking in a kiln followed the fashioning. The chief methods used for decorating pottery were the slip, burnishing, and painting; glazing was never achieved by Canaanites or Israelites. The slip is simply putting a veneer of finer grade clay over the visible part of the object made of coarse clay; this made possible the attainment of a different colour as well. The 'wash' is the veneer put on after the object has been baked and is the cheapest process. Burnishing is effected by pressure of a tool against the vessel, as it is turned on the wheel, for the purpose of sealing the pores; it does not remove substance as does the polishing of pottery. Painting of pottery was done before baking, and required considerable skill to prevent blotting.

Earthenware vessels were easily broken, and so the pieces or **potsherds** (Jer 18^{1} 19^{1f}; **sherds** for short), are found in great numbers in the ancient moulds of cities of the Near East. Little attention was paid to them until Sir Flinders Petrie in his 1890 excavations at *Tell el-Ḥesī*, a 'mound of many cities' (as his successor in the excavations there called it), recognized that each period had its distinct pottery. With the help of datable objects known from Egypt he was able to set up a rough pottery chronology. But it was not until after the First World War that this great archaeological key to the history of the occupation of ancient ruin mounds was properly exploited. The excavations carried on 1926–32 by Albright at *Tell Beit Mirsim*, a site occupied from late 3rd millennium to the Exile, first set up an accurate and elaborate chronology for Palestinian pottery. Numerous other Palestinian excavations have since then greatly enriched the picture, especially for the periods antedating this city. The excavations in other Near Eastern lands naturally created the question of the extent of territory over which certain styles of pottery ranged at the same periods. With this and all other matters of craft, art, and architecture, archaeology has become so intricate a study that it has emancipated itself from the control of theologian and philologist and become an independent speciality.

Pottery making, as revealed by the excavations, goes back to Chalcolithic times and earlier. In the Early Bronze Age (Period I) there was a different pottery style prevalent in northern Palestine (both E. and W.) from that in southern. The band-slip ware with criss-cross patterns prevailed in the north; the painted pottery (red and brown colours being used) with parallel or wavy lines in the south. About the time of the 1st Egyptian Dynasty Palestine was in the Period II of Early Bronze. At this time we find hardware, covered with burnished red slip, prevailing. The designs sometimes are quite intricate. Early Bronze III is synchronous with Egypt's 3rd-5th Dynasties. This is the time of the red and black burnished *Khirbet Kerak* ware, ornamented with geometrical designs and spirals, sometimes ribbed and fluted. Toward the end of Early Bronze the 'envelope ledge-handle' provides a characteristic criterion. Middle Bronze I begins *c* 2000 B.C. At this period there prevailed the calciform pottery, which seems to have spread to Palestine from Syria. It gets its name from the chalice-type of vase. In Middle Bronze II red or cream slip was used and burnished to give a metallic lustre to pottery; shapes were very graceful and finely curved. The *Tell el-Yehûdîyeh* pear-shaped jug, burnished black and with geometric designs, has long been recognized as a characteristic product of the Hyksos Age. In the Late Bronze Age a great deal of **Mycenaean ware** was imported (*c* 1400–1250 B.C.). Cypriote ware with a base-ring and usually black, brown, or dark grey also occurs. Typical Philistine pottery dates from 1150–1000 B.C. It consists notably of **bowls** with two handles, buff in colour with a creamy grey wash. In the Iron Age I the large storage jar with a collared rim, which yielded to a different rim *c* 1000 B.C., is the characteristic ware. Pottery, with wheel-burnished red slip over light buff clay, such as was found at Samaria, dates from Iron II. In Iron III Greek influence becomes apparent, and Ionian and Attic black-figured pottery appears on the scene. In the 5th cent. Ionian black-figured ware yielded to Attic red-figured ware.

It is worthy of note that **jar handles** of the Persian period have been found in Judah that were stamped with a word and a circle (indicating royal Persian property). The word is most often *Yhd* (Judaea), sometimes *Jerusalem*. Uncertain is the meaning of *mṣh*, with a line under the second letter; some hold it to stand for *Mizpah*. Of great interest is the pottery of the Maccabaean and Roman periods found at the *Qumrân* settlement, notably the jars with covers in which the scrolls of Cave 1 were stored (cf Jer 32[14]); the larger ones are 28⅓ inches high and have a maximum diameter of about 10 inches. The smaller type has small looped handles. E. G. K.

POTTER'S FIELD.—See AKELDAMA.

POUND.—See MONEY, 7; WEIGHTS AND MEASURES, III.

POVERTY.—1. In the OT.—The character and degree of the poverty prevalent in a community varies with its social development. Poverty is more acutely felt, and its extremes are more marked, where city-life and commerce have grown up than where the conditions of life are purely nomadic or agricultural.

The *causes of poverty* referred to in the OT (apart from those due to individual folly) are especially (*a*) bad seasons, involving failure of crops, loss of cattle, etc. (cf 2 K 8[1–7], Neh 5[3]); (*b*) raids and invasions; (*c*) land-grabbing (cf Is 5[8]); (*d*) over-taxation and forced labour (cf Jer 22[13f]); (*e*) extortionate usury, the opportunity for which was provided by the necessity for meeting high taxation, and the losses arising from bad harvests (cf Neh 5[1–6]).

Amongst nomads, only the simplest forms of personal property existed; all else, particularly the cattle, belonged to the clan. Within the clan, the sense of kinship was powerful; all shared the same food, wore the same kind of clothes, and lived in tents. In the earlier period of Israel's history, when the tribal system flourished, there was, accordingly, little distinction between rich and poor. But as a settled society developed, this distinction became more pronounced. Nathan's parable (2 S 12[1–6]) implies that in the time of David, there were rich men capable of oppressing the poor, though there was little permanent poverty. Matters were maintained in a state of equilibrium so long as the land system, under which all free Israelite families possessed a patrimony (cf Naboth and his vineyard) remained in working order. In the earlier legislation of JE (cf especially the Ten Commandments, Ex 20[1–17], and the 'Book of the Covenant,' Ex 20[23]–23[33]), the few references that do occur (*e.g.* Ex 22[25] 23[6]) do not suggest that poverty was very widespread or acutely felt. Neither riches nor poverty are a problem in the older literature of Israel. During the period of the later monarchy, however, commerce, city-life and luxury grew apace, and the greed and heartless oppression of the rich, the corruption and perversion of justice which this state of things brought in its train, were constantly denounced, especially by the great prophets of the 8th cent. (cf, *e.g.* Is 1[23], Am 4[1] 6[1ff], Mic 2[1ff]).

The Deuteronomic legislation (7th cent.) bears eloquent testimony to the prevalence of poverty under the later monarchy (cf Dt 10[17–19] 14[28–29] 15, 23[19–20] 24[10–21] 26[12–15]), and in one famous sentence predicts its permanence ('the poor shall never cease out of the land,' 15[11]; cf Mk 14[7]).

The classes of poor more particularly mentioned are widows, orphans, and the sojourners, or resident strangers, who possessed no landed rights (*gērîm*). The Levites also are specially referred to in Deuteronomy as an impoverished class (cf 12[12–19] 18)—a result of the centralization of worship in the one sanctuary at Jerusalem. All classes of the poor are the objects of special solicitude and consideration in the Mosaic legislation, particularly in the Priestly Code (cf, *e.g.* Lv 5[7, 11] 19[9–15] etc.).

For a long time after the Exile and the Return the Palestinian community remained in a state of miserable poverty. It was a purely agricultural society, and suffered much from contracted boundaries and agricultural depression. The 'day of small things' spoken of by the prophet Zechariah (4[10]) was prolonged. A terrible picture of devastation (produced by a locust plague) is given by the prophet Joel (ch. 1), and matters were aggravated during the last years of Persian rule (down to 332), and by the conflict between the Seleucids and Ptolemies for the possession of Palestine, which raged for considerably more than a century (312–198). During the earlier part of the post-exilic period, the wealthy Jewish families for the most part remained behind in Babylon. In the later period, after the conquests of Alexander the Great (from 322), prosperous communities of Jews grew up in such centres as Antioch and Alexandria (the Greek 'Dispersion'). Slowly the Palestinian community grew in importance; for a time under the Maccabees there was a politically independent Jewish state. A certain amount of material prosperity ensued. Jerusalem, as being a centre of pilgrimage, received large revenues from the Jewish pilgrims who thronged to it: a Temple-tax swelled the revenues of the priesthood. The aristocratic priestly families were very wealthy. But the bulk of the priesthood still remained comparatively poor. The Jewish community of Palestine was still mainly agricultural, but more prosperous under settled government (the Herods and the Romans); while Galilee became a hive of industry, and sustained a large industrial population (an artisan class).

In dealing with poverty, the Jewish legislation displays a very humane spirit. Usury is forbidden: the poor are to have the produce of the land in Sabbatical years: and in Deuteronomy tithes are allotted to be given them (14[28], etc.); they are to have the right to **glean** (24[15, 21]), and in the Priestly Code there is the unrealized ideal of the Jubilee Year (Lv 25; cf Dt 15[12–15]). All these provisions were supplemented by **almsgiving**, which in later Judaism became one of the most important parts of religious duty. See ALMS, ALMSGIVING.

On the whole Israelite thinkers attach no intrinsic value to the economic state of poverty, though riches and injustice are often closely linked. As riches were a blessing, poverty was an evil (Pr 10[15] 31[7]); and it was therefore a problem of faith when poverty overtook the righteous. In later Judaism it is understood that both the rich and poor are tested, the rich as to whether they will open their hands to the poor, the poor as to whether they will accept their sufferings without murmuring.

The parallel terms *'ānî* and *'ānāw* (poor, humble), in the Psalms, are typical descriptions of the man who suffers from some form of social oppression, and who displays a proper humility before God in the time of his need. These psalms, no doubt composed specially for the use of such people at the sanctuary, are the best indication of the religious understanding of poverty in the OT.

The voluntary and deliberate acceptance of poverty, practicable only in celibate, community life, was a characteristic of the Qumrân community. The (probably) earlier Damascus Covenanters made no such renunciation of property or marriage. But at Qumrân, according to the *Manual of Discipline*, those who 'dedicated themselves' brought all their property into 'the community of God,' in order that it might be regulated 'according to his righteous counsel' (vi. 20). The novice continued technically to own his property for the period of his novitiate, but in the second year renounced it. Josephus gives similar information about the Essenes (whom many scholars associate with the Qumrân sect).

2. In the NT.—In the NT period, conditions were not essentially altered. The exactions of tax-collectors seem to have been acutely felt (notice especially the collocation 'publicans and sinners'), but **almsgiving** (q.v.) was strongly inculcated as a religious duty, the early Christians following in this respect the example set by the synagogue (cf Ro 12^{13}); Jesus Himself reinforced the Jewish insistence on almsgiving (Lk 12^{33}), which presupposes private property. He nowhere taught the absolute renunciation of property, but frequently stressed the importance of indifference to possessions. The term 'poor' is found prominently in His teaching with the religious connotation characteristic of the Psalms. 'Blessed are you poor' (Lk 6^{20}) is correctly paraphrased in Mt 5^{3} as 'poor in spirit.' The experiment by which the Jerusalem Church pooled and shared its wealth (Ac 2^{44} 4$^{34-37}$) has little to do with 'communism.' It was rather an economic expression of the fellowship of the early believers who expected Christ's Second Coming at any moment. Some scholars have thought that the experiment involved a realizing of capital which was economically disastrous, and caused the impoverished church to be dependent on St. Paul's 'collections' for 'the poor saints at Jerusalem' (Ro 15^{26}, Gal 2^{10}). The early generations of Christians were drawn mostly from the poorer classes (slaves or freedmen), but the immediate disciples of our Lord belonged rather to what we should call the lower middle class—sturdy Galilaean fishermen, owning their boats, or tax-collectors. St. Paul said to the Corinthians: 'Not many of you were powerful, not many were of noble birth' (1 Co 1^{26}); on the other hand, it is plain from Acts that some Christians were well-to-do. Jesus Himself claimed to have nowhere to lay His head and seems to have been dependent on hospitality. St. Paul recognized that His whole life was, in a profounder sense, a voluntary acceptance of poverty for the enrichment of mankind (2 Co 8^{9}). See also WEALTH. G. H. B.—**D. R. J.**

POWER.—In general the word (Gr. *dynamis*) means ability for doing something, and includes the idea of adequate strength, might, skill, resources, energy, and efficiency, either material, mental, or spiritual, to effect intended results. Strictly speaking, there is no real power or authority in the universe, but that which is ultimately of God (Ps 62^{11}, Jn 19^{11}, Ro 13^{1}). But this Almighty One has originated innumerable subordinate powers, and some of these are possessed of ability to perform acts contrary to the will and commandments of the Creator. And so we may speak of the power of God, or of man, or of angel, or of demon, or of powers inherent in things inanimate. Inasmuch as in the highest and absolute sense 'power belongeth unto God,' it is fitting to ascribe unto Him such doxologies as appear in 1 Ch 29^{11}, Mt 6^{13}. In Mt 26^{64} the word 'power' is employed for God Himself, and it is accordingly very natural that it should be often used to denote the various forms of God's activity, especially in His works of creation and redemption. Christ is thus the power of God both in His Person and in His gospel of salvation (1 Co 1$^{18, 24}$, Ro 1^{16}). The power of the Holy Spirit is also another mode of the Divine activity. By similar usage Simon the sorcerer was called 'that power of God which is called Great' (Ac 8^{10}), *i.e.* a supposed incarnation of the power of God. The plural **powers** is used in a variety of meanings. (1) In Mt 7^{22}, Lk 10^{13}, Ac 2^{22} 8^{13} (here 'miracles' RSV), 'powers,' or 'mighty works,' along with 'signs and wonders,' are to be understood as miracles, and were concrete manifestations of supernatural power. (2) 'The powers of the heavens' (Mt 24^{29}, Mk 13^{25}) are understood by some as the forces inherent in the sun, moon, stars, and other phenomena of the heavens, by virtue of which they 'rule over the day and over the night' (Gn 1^{18}); by others these heavenly powers are understood to be the starry hosts themselves conceived as the armies of the heavens, or the astral beings which control them. (3) Both good and evil angels are designated by the terms '**principalities and powers**' in such passages as Eph 1^{21} 3^{10} 6^{12}, Col 1^{16} 2$^{10, 15}$, 1 P 3^{22}. The context of each passage must show whether the reference is to angels or demons. In Eph 2^{2} Satan is called '**the prince of the power of the air,**' and these powers are further defined in 6^{12} as 'world-rulers of this darkness, the spiritual hosts of wickedness in the heavenly places.' These are thought of as so many ranks of evil spirits who are ever at war with God's hosts, and seek to usurp the heavenly regions. (4) In Ro 13^{1} civil magistrates are called 'the higher powers' ('governing authorities' RSV) because of their superior rank, authority, and influence as officers ordained of God for the administration of justice among men (cf Lk 12^{11}, Tit 3^{1}). (5) 'The powers of the age to come' (He 6^{5}) are best understood of all supernatural gifts and spiritual forces which belong to the age or dispensation of the New Covenant, of which Jesus is the Mediator (cf He 9^{15}). The supernatural forces of the Age to Come, now conceived as near at hand, are already being manifested in the present age, which is approaching its end. They doubtless include the 'greater works' (Jn 14^{12}) which Jesus assured His disciples they should do after His going to the Father and sending them the Spirit of truth. See AUTHORITY, KINGDOM OF GOD.

M. S. T.—**F. W. G.**

POWER OF THE KEYS.—See KEYS [POWER OF THE] and PETER.

PRAETOR.—See MAGISTRATE, PROVINCE.

PRAETORIAN GUARD.—See next article and GUARD.

PRAETORIUM (Gr. *praitōrion*) occurs only once in AV (Mk 15^{16}). Elsewhere it is represented by 'common hall' (Mt 27^{27}, RV '**palace**'), 'judgment hall' (Jn 18$^{28, 33}$ 19^{9}, Ac 23^{35}; RV in all '**palace**') and 'palace' (Ph 1^{13}, RV '**praetorian guard**'). But RSV consistently reads 'praetorium' (Mk 15^{16}, Mt 27^{27}, Jn 18$^{28, 33}$ 19^{9}, Ac 23^{35}, Ph 1^{13}—praetorium or praetorian guard). The word at first denoted the officers' headquarters in a Roman camp, a space within which stood the general's tent, the camp altar, the *augurale*, and the *tribunal*; then it came to mean the military council meeting there. Thus the term praetorium has two aspects, a local and a military one. The meaning of the word depends on which aspect is emphasized. It may mean the praetorian cohorts or their barracks (Suet. *Tib.* 36, *Nero*, 9; Tac. *Hist.* ii. 11). There is, however, no example for these military meanings in Koine Greek, where the local aspect is stressed. Praetorium usually signifies the residence of the 'praetor' or of another provincial governor (Mt 27^{27}=Mk 15^{16}, Jn 18$^{28, 33}$ 19^{9}) as the centre of his political and judicial authority (Ac 23^{35}). It can also refer to the official residence of provincial officials or to the villas of high officials in Italy, especially the Emperor's residence outside Rome. In the Gospels *praetorium* perhaps (but see PILATE) stands for the palace of Herod the Great, occupied by Pontius Pilate—a splendid building, probably in the western part of the city. Ph 1^{13} probably refers to the praetorium as the judicial court where Paul gives witness 'that his imprisonment is for Christ'; but a reference to the barracks of the praetorians, the Imperial bodyguard, is not impossible. Originally the *Cohors Praetoria* was a company attached to the commander-in-chief in the field. Augustus retained the name, but raised the number to ten cohorts of 1000 each, quartering only three cohorts in the city at a time. Tiberius brought them all to Rome, and placed them in a fortified camp, at the northern extremity of the Viminal. Under Vitellius their number was raised to 16,000. W. E.—**J. C. B.**

PRAISE is the recognition and acknowledgment of merit. Two parties are involved: the one possessing at least supposed merit, the other being a person who acknowledges the merit.

Men may praise men. Forms of praise may be used without genuine feelings of praise, and extravagent praise may be rendered intentionally, because of the advantage that will be gained thereby. This is downright hypocrisy, and the whole burden of the moral teaching of the Bible, and especially of Christ, is against hypocrisy. Again, the estimate of values may be so completely false that praise may be felt and expressed genuinely in cases where it is undeserved. And Jesus' whole influence is directed towards the proper appreciation of values so that only the good shall appear to us good.

In its common Biblical use, however, *praise has God for its object.* This restriction does not involve an essential difference either in the praise or in the sense of moral values. The difference lies rather in the greater praiseworthiness of God. Praise of God is of course called forth only as He reveals Himself to men, only as men recognize His activity and His power in the event or condition which appears to them adequate to call out praise. Men praise God in proportion as they are religious, and so have conscious relations with God. The praise-worthiness of a god is involved in the very definition of a god. If men postulate a god at all, it is as a being worthy to be praised. Every thought and act by which men come into relation with God is a thought and an act of praise. Petition is justifiable only if behind it is the belief that God is worthy of such approach. If the act is confession of sin, the same is true, for confession is not made to a being who does not hold a place of honour and praise. If some active service is rendered to God, this subjugation of ourselves to Him can be explained only by the conviction that God is in every way entitled to service.

Moreover, as in the case of praise of men, there is a very clear distinction to be drawn between genuine and hypocritical ascription of praise to God. The temptation to the latter is extreme, because of the immense gain presumably to be secured by praise; but the hypocrisy and the sin of it are equally great. Indeed, the seriousness of the offence is evident when one reflects that he who praises God knows full well the praiseworthiness of God, so that if he praises while the genuine feeling is lacking and the sincere act of praise is unperformed, only moral perversity can account for the hypocrisy.

In order to genuineness, praise must be *spontaneous.* It may be commanded by another human being, and the praise commanded may be rendered, but the real impelling cause is the recognized merit of God. God may demand praise from His creature in commands transmitted to them through prophets and Apostles, but if man praises Him from the heart, it is because of the imperative inseparable from the very being and nature of God.

We are prepared, then, to find that in the Bible praise to God is *universal* on the part of all who acknowledge Him. It is the very atmosphere of both dispensations. It is futile to attempt to collate the passages that involve it, for its expression is not measured by special terms or confined to special occasions. The author of Gn 1, like every reader of the chapter, finds the work of creation an occasion for praising God. The chapter is a call to praise, though the word be not mentioned. We have but to turn to the Psalms (*e.g.* Ps 104) to find formal expression of the praise that the world inspires.

The legal requirements of the Law likewise depend for their authority with men upon the recognition of the merit of the Law-giver. 'Ye shall be holy, for I Yahweh your God am holy,' has no force except for him who acknowledges holiness in God who commands; and obedience is the creature's tribute of praise to the holy God.

The whole history of Israel, as Israel's historians picture it, has in it the constant element of praise to Israel's God: we turn to the Psalms (*e.g.* Ps 102) or to other songs (*e.g.* Ex 15), and find the praise of the heart rising to formal expression.

In the NT, praise of Christ and of God in Christ is the universal note. It is the song of those who are healed of their sicknesses, or forgiven their sins; of Apostles who meditate on the gospel message and salvation through Christ; of those who rehearse the glories of the New Jerusalem as seen in apocalyptic vision.

We are also prepared by this universality to find that praise cannot form a topic for independent treatment. There is no technical terminology to be examined in the hope that the etymology of the terms used will throw light upon the subject, for in this case etymologies may lead us away from the current meaning of the common words employed. The history of praise in the OT and the NT is the history of worship, Temple, synagogue, sacrifice, festivals. The literature of praise is the literature of religion, whether as the product of national consciousness or of personal religious experience.

It will suffice to mention one or two points of interest which the student may well bear in mind as he studies the Bible and consults the articles on related subjects.

The Hebrew word oftenest used for praise is *hillēl*, perhaps an onomatopoetic Semitic root meaning 'cry aloud.' An interesting feature is the use of the imperative in ascriptions of praise. Taken literally, these imperatives are commands to praise; but they are to be taken as real ascriptions of praise, with the added thought that praise from one person suggests praise from all. Cf the doxology 'Praise God from whom all blessings flow,' which consists solely of four imperative sentences.

The imperative of the Hebrew verb, followed by the Divine name, gives us **Hallelujah**, *i.e.* 'Praise ye Jah.' The word is used at the beginning and end of Psalms, apparently with liturgical value. Cf also the Hallel Psalms (113–118, 136). The noun from the same root appears as the title of Ps 145. See HALLEL.

The form which praise took as an element of worship in Israel varied with the general character of worship. It was called forth by the acts of Yahweh upon which the Israelites were especially wont to dwell in different periods. For personal and family favours they praised Him in early times with forms of their own choosing. When the national consciousness was aroused, they praised Him for His leading of the nation, in forms suitable to this service. As worship came more and more to conform to that elaborated for, and practised in, the royal sanctuary—the Temple at Jerusalem—the forms of praise could not fail to share the elaboration and to become gradually more uniform. To what extent these modifications took place is to be studied in the history of OT religion.

Praise was certainly a part of the varied service rendered by the Levites in the Temple ritual of later Judaism, and an examination of that ritual will show how far praise was given over to them, and how much was retained by the congregation. The Psalms are certainly adapted to antiphonal rendering. Did the people respond to the priests, or were there two choirs? [This word occurs in EV only in RVm of Neh 12^{8}, where RSV has 'songs of thanksgiving.'] The element of praise in the synagogue worship is an interesting and disputed question. Cf also ADORATION, HYMN.

O. H. G.

PRAYER.—Prayer in the Bible commonly means communion with God, and that implies the belief that God is a person who seeks such approach from man and has ordained it as the way by which man comes to know Him, and to know himself as a creature made by

Him and endowed with spiritual capacities. But prayer can be made by a man before he is aware of the possibility of such communion, or even has thought of the possibility of it. His prayer may be a cry of distress such as 'Oh, my God,' a cry, and nothing but a cry. Or it may be an outcry for help when 'human helpers fail and comfort flees' (*e.g.* Ps 130^{1}).

If there are tokens that such prayer is answered, the man who makes it comes to believe in it and practise it. If he believes that he gets no answer, he may conclude there is no God and that such prayer is a wishful act that can bring no help for a man's need. But man cannot easily rest in unbelief. The rhythm of nature, for example, upon which his livelihood depends, appears to him to be ruled by a god or God, and he makes prayer or an offering that the beneficent rhythm of nature may continue unbroken. Even if he speaks no word, but simply makes his offering on an altar, such as an offering of the first fruits of his fields or of his flocks and herds, that is an acted prayer which expresses the petition of the worshipper who offers it.

It is said that the prayer of a wicked man is an abomination to the Lord (Pr 15^{29} 28^{9}), but that is not wholly true. When a wicked man offers a prayer formally or hypocritically, like those who, for a pretence, make long prayers (Mt 23^{14}, Mk 12^{40}), it is true. But in the case of one like the publican who cried, 'God be merciful to me, a sinner' (Lk 17^{13}), it is not true. The cry, 'O God, if there be a God, hear my cry' may arise out of unbelief and unhoping hope; but it may be a heart-cry from a wicked man who has found life empty, and may be the first step in his return to God and to repentance. But thereafter prayer to God arises from knowledge of God on the one hand and of human need on the other, and it may express itself in many forms.

1. Terminology.—(*a*) In the OT the most usual word (*t^{e}phillāh*) and the related verb are possibly derived from a root meaning 'to cut,' which would have reference to a cultic act going back to the days when devotees cut their flesh in ecstatic frenzy (cf 1 K 18^{28}). It has been conjectured by some that the Jewish *t^{e}phillîn* (phylacteries) originated as substitutes for such marks of laceration, but *t^{e}phillāh* may mean merely intervention. In the NT it is the classical Greek word (*proseuchomai*) which is commonly used. Unlike most OT words, this is used for prayer to God only. The simple form of the verb (*euchomai*) means by itself little more than 'wish' (*e.g.* Ro 9^{3}), and needs supplementing to mean pray (*e.g.* 2 Co 13^{7}). The corresponding noun (*euchē*) usually means 'vow' (*e.g.* Ac 18^{18}), but 'prayer' in Ja 5^{15}.

(*b*) Several words are used which mean 'to call.' 'To call on the Name' is to call upon God, to worship Him (*e.g.* Gn 4^{26}). Others mean to call for the redress of wrongs (*e.g.* Jg 3^{9}), or for help in trouble (*e.g.* Ps 72^{12}). Another means to utter a ringing cry of joy or of sorrow (*e.g.* Ps 17^{1}). In the NT 'to call on the Name' is to invoke God in prayer (*e.g.* Ac 9^{14}).

(*c*) It is natural in this connexion to find words which mean to 'seek' (*e.g.* Am 5^{4}; a different verb is used in Hos 5^{15} 'to seek God's face'), 'ask' (*e.g.* Ps 105^{40}), although some of these verbs (for instance 'seek' as in Am 5^{4}) are not used exclusively of seeking God.

In the NT the verbs meaning 'to seek' and 'to ask' may be used of requests or inquiries made to man (*e.g.* Ac 8^{34}), and do not of themselves connote worship. One word denotes the request of the *will* (*e.g.* Mt 6^{8}); another the request that arises out of the awareness of a *need* (*e.g.* Ac 8^{22}); another denotes the *form* of the request (*e.g.* Jn 17^{9}; cf RVm).

(*d*) Some verbs are notably anthropomorphic in meaning, *e.g.* 'to encounter' or 'fall upon' in order to supplicate or intercede (*e.g.* Jer 7^{16}); 'to make the face of God soft or pleasant,' *i.e.* 'to smooth His face,' to appease Him or gain His favour (*e.g.* Ex 32^{11}), or to seek God's favour (*e.g.* Dt 3^{23}, 1 K 8$^{33, 47}$, Ps 30^{9} 142^{2}, etc.).

(*e*) Other verbs have reference to the suppliant's state of mind: prayer is an 'outpouring of the soul' (*e.g.* Ps 62^{8}) or a 'meditation' (*e.g.* Job 15^{4} RVm); or 'complaint' (*e.g.* Ps 142^{2}); or the original connotation may be physical, 'to bow down,' 'to bow to the ground,' 'to whisper' (Ezr 6^{10}, cf Eph 3^{14}, Is 26^{16} RVm).

It should be noted that symbolic action was often used as an act of prayer, or as a reinforcement of a said prayer. Water was poured upon an altar as an acted or representative prayer for rain. The first fruits of the field or the flock were offered as a prayer for the full increase of the fields or of the flocks. When Moses held his arms outstretched above him while the Israelites battled with Amalekites, it was at once a prayer for their victory and a posture that represented the communication of his great spirit to his people.

2. Place, time and circumstance.—(*a*) Place.—There were from early times in Israel's history certain sanctuaries which stood out prominently, and which must have been frequented by worshippers, *e.g.* Shiloh, where the Ark rested (1 S 1^{9f}), Mizpah (1 S 7^{5}, 1 Mac 3^{46}), Gibeon (1 K 3^{4ff}). At these sanctuaries the annual festivals were celebrated (cf Ex 23$^{14-17}$, etc.), and the great acts of communal worship took place. These festivals were related to the agricultural seasons, and at them the people made the prescribed offerings and the priest or king, representing the people, fulfilled the traditional ritual that the bounty of nature might be continued. But at a later period the festivals became associated with decisive periods or events in Israel's history, and so became commemorative of them. After the fall of the northern kingdom in 721 B.C. and, more especially, after the reformation of Josiah in 621 (cf 2 K 22–23), the Jerusalem sanctuary came to be a place of supreme importance in the religious life of the people. Thereafter the Temple was the place 'where' (Is 37^{14ff} 56^{7}) or (for the Jews of the diaspora) 'toward which' prayer was offered (1 K 8^{29f}, etc., Ps 28^{2}, Dn 6^{10}, 1 Es 4^{58}). The destruction of the Temple in 586 B.C. and the diaspora of the Jews in Babylon and Egypt caused the development of the synagogue as a place of prayer and instruction in the Law. Where there was no synagogue, a spot outside the town was chosen, near some stream, for hand-washing before prayer (Ac 16$^{13, 16}$). In the NT we find Apostles going to the Temple (Ac 3^{1}); and St. Paul attended the synagogue on his mission journeys (Ac 17^{1f}). Distinctively Christian worship was held in ordinary buildings (Ac 1^{13f} 4^{23f} 12^{12}, Col 4^{15})—a practice made natural by Jewish arrangements for private prayer (Dn 6^{10}, Jth 8^{5} 10^{2}, Mt 6^{6}, Ac 10$^{9, 30}$) or for Passover celebration (Mt 26^{18}).

(*b*) Time.—The occasions of the great festivals have already been mentioned. Private prayer at a sanctuary or in a home could be made at any time in the choice of the worshipper, but it became a custom to pray thrice daily, *i.e.* at the 3rd, 6th and 9th hours (cf Dn 6^{10}, Ac 3^{1} 10$^{9, 30}$; cf 2^{15}). For instances of grace before meat cf 1 S 9^{13}, Mt 15^{36}, Ac 27^{35}, and the Paschal meal.

(*c*) Circumstance.—(i) *Attitude*: standing (*e.g.* Gn 18^{22}, 1 S 1^{26}, Neh 9^{5}, Mk 11^{25}, Lk 18$^{11, 13}$ [the usual Jewish mode, not followed by the early Christian Church save on Sundays and the days between Easter and Whitsun]); kneeling (Ps 95^{6}, Is 45^{23}, 1 K 8^{54}, Ezr 9^{5}, Dn 6^{10}, Lk 22^{41}, Ac 7^{60} 9^{40} 20^{36} 21^{5}, Eph 3^{14}); prostrate, face to the ground (Ex 34^{8}, Neh 8^{6}, 1 Es 8^{91}, Jth 9^{1}, 2 Mac 13^{12}, Mt 26^{39}); face between knees (1 K 18^{42}); sitting (? 2 S 7^{18}); hands uplifted (Ps 28^{2} 63^{4} 134^{2}, La 2^{19} 3^{41}, 2 Mac 3^{20}, 1 Ti 2^{8}); or extended [symbol of entreaty to God or reception by God?] (Ex 9^{29}, 1 K 8^{22}, Is 1^{15}, Ezr 9^{5}, Ps 77^{2}).

(ii) *Forms of Prayer*: Set forms of prayer are mentioned (Dt 21^{7f} 26$^{5-15}$) and, of course, there is the Lord's Prayer in the NT (Mt 6$^{9-13}$, Lk 11$^{2-4}$); there is allusion to John the Baptist's instructions to his disciples on prayer (Lk 11^{1}) which is given as the reason why Christ's disciples likewise asked for instruction; there is reference to Christ's repeated prayer (Mt 26^{44}); and such words as 'ask and ye shall receive, seek and ye shall find, knock and it shall be opened unto you' (Lk 11^{9}) emphasize the need for persistent prayer. But there is a condemnation of vain repetitions (cf Mt 6^{7}, Sir 7^{14}).

3. Prayer in the OT.—(*a*) There are many references

to the prayers of ordinary people, but they are incidental references, and little information is given about the nature of such prayers. But there are many passages in the OT which describe leaders of the community at prayer. In these the belief is often exemplified that the prayer of a righteous man is energized with his own spiritual power and therefore may avail for others; and inasmuch as the righteous man knows God and is known of God, his prayer comes before Him with acceptance. Abraham pleads for the cities of the plain, that the righteous in them might not be destroyed with the wicked (Gn 18[23ff]). Moses, at the burning bush, when engaged in an act of worship at an ancient sanctuary received his Divine command to be the leader and deliverer of his enslaved people in Egypt (Ex 3), and thereafter he is represented in the Pentateuchal narrative in communion with God (Ex 4, 5[22] 6[1, 10, 12, 28–30], Dt 3[23–26]), making appeal to God in crises (Ex 5[22], Nu 11[11]), and interceding time after time for his people in their need or in their rebelliousness (*e.g.* Ex 8[12, 30] 32[11, 13, 32], Nu 14[13–19]; cf Jer 15[1]), and in the prophetic blessing (Dt 33[6–11]). Joshua prays after the defeat at Ai (Jos 7[7–9]) and in battle (10[14]); there is reference to Gideon's colloquy with God (Jg 6[11–24]); and there are references in the Book of Judges to the Israelites' frequent cry for help (Jg 3[9, 15] 6[6], etc.).

Samuel, like Moses, was a leader and prophet to his people, and time after time interceded on their behalf (1 S 7[5, 8f] 8[6, 10, 21] 12[23] 15[11]).

(*b*) David (leaving out the evidence from the Book of Psalms) makes prayer for guidance (1 S 23[2, 4] 30[8]), of confession (2 S 24[17]) of adoration (2 S 7[18–29]), although probably his most memorable prayer is that which he offers after the death of Bathsheba's child, which he interprets as an act of punishment inflicted on him because of the circumstances of his marriage with Bathsheba, a prayer which ends with the words 'I shall go to him but he shall not return to me' (2 S 12[23]).

Solomon's great prayer for wisdom is recorded (1 K 3[5ff]) and his intercession at the dedication of the Temple (1 K 8[22–53], 2 Ch 6[12–42]).

(*c*) In the period of the divided kingdom, the prophets come into prominence as men of prayer. There is the record of Elijah's great intercessory act on Mount Carmel (1 K 18[36f]), and, subsequently, of his communion with God on Mount Horeb (19[9–11]); so also Elisha (2 K 4[33] 6[17]). Intercession in attitude, action, and word characterizes the canonical prophets. The reason lay in the prophet's Divine call, his vision of the Divine. will, and his proclamation of the Divine message, so that he was not only a prophet for God to the people, but an intercessor before God on behalf of the people. Hence a prophet can intercede to avert national disaster (*e.g.* Am 7[2f, 5f], Is 63[9–17], and vividly, Jer 14, 15, in which there is persistent intercession by the prophet despite Divine discouragement). But such intercession for the people is shown particularly in the Book of Jeremiah in those passages which are commonly called the confessions of that prophet. And it is in the Book of Jeremiah that the prophet is bidden not to make intercession for his people because they are now wicked beyond salvation (Jer 7[16] 11[14] 14[11]), and in the same book there occur the words 'If Moses and Samuel stood before me as intercessors, my mind could not be towards this people' (15[1]).

(*d*) During the Exile prayer had a large place among the Jews owing to the cessation of sacrificial worship and the recognition that the judgment of God foretold by the prophets had come upon them. Consequently confession and a humble sense of dependence are prominent. The following passages are of particular importance in this respect: Is 63[7] 64[12], Ezr 9[5–15], Neh 1[4–11] 9[5–38], Dn 9[4–19]. In the post-exilic period, especially with the development of the worship of the synagogue, prayer comes to have a very much greater place, and in the restored Temple the sin offering, which is an acted prayer, comes to great prominence; and morning and evening prayers are a regular practice in the Temple.

(*e*) The Book of Psalms might be properly called also the Book of Prayers (five only are so described specifically in title: 17, 86, 90, 102, 142, but cf 72[20], Hab 3[1]). Throughout the Psalms, prayer—whether of the Psalmist as an individual or as representing the people—is specially an outpouring of the varied experiences, needs, desires, and aspirations of the human heart, and the Psalms often exhibit quite sudden transitions of thought and alterations of mood (*e.g.* 6[7–10] 42, 69[20, 27, 30] 77[9–11] 109[23–30]). The blessing sought is sometimes material or external, like deliverance from trouble or punishment; but often there is some spiritual aim, Ps 51 being an outstanding example, and Ps 119 being notable for repeated requests for inward enlightenment and quickening. The suitability of many of the Psalms as vehicles of prayer is indicated by the use of them made in the Christian Church to-day. In estimating Psalms which express vindictive and imprecatory sentiments, we should note that they express abhorrence of evil, and are not the utterance of private malice. But even if that interpretation could not be given in some instances of this element in the Psalms, it could be regarded as an illustration of human desire breaking into the act of prayer and throwing into sharp relief the gospel temper and teaching.

(*f*) In the Book of Job, Job himself often appears expostulating with God, and crying out for an opportunity to plead his cause and state his case before God; and his spiritual conflict culminates in the colloquy between God and Job, after which Job expresses his reverent submission of faith (42[1–6]). And when thereafter the others are told to prepare a sacrifice that God's anger against them may be turned away, 'My servant Job will pray for you; for him I will accept' (42[8]).

(*g*) The examples so far quoted of intercession describe intercessory prayer, but there are passages in the OT which speak of an intercessor, or interposer, who is willing to pay the price of the reconciliation to God of those for whom he prays, to bear the penalty and, by his own suffering—by his own death, if need be—to bring forgiveness and peace to others, removing their guilt and bearing their punishment. In some passages it is said that no ransom at all is possible (*e.g.* Ps 49[7f]); and in the Book of Ezekiel it is said repeatedly that 'though these three men, Noah, Daniel, and Job, were in the land, they should deliver only their own soul by their righteousness, they could not save the land' (Ezk 14[14, 16, 18, 20]). But Dt 1[37] leaves it to be inferred that Moses, by his exclusion from the promised land, interposed for his people and bore the penalty of their disobedience (Ex 32[32], Dt 3[36] 4[31ff]); and in Ezk 22[30] (cf 13[5]) 'And I sought for a man among them, that should make up the hedge, and stand in the gap before me for the land, that I should not destroy it; but I found none,' *i.e.* none was found to interpose, to be a saviour, who, by his righteousness could turn away the punishment, or by his labour and self-sacrifice could bear the burden and pay the price (cf Is 59[16]).

(*h*) The greatest intercessor of the OT is, of course, the Suffering Servant, as described in Is 53. Moses and David, for instance, aware of their own sin, offered to bear the penalty due to their people. The Servant was without sin, and gave Himself willingly that his sacrifice might avail for others. He suffers for the community, and the community suffers in him.

4. Prayer in the Apocrypha.—The Apocryphal books—of fiction, fable, history, and apocalyptic and sapiental writings—are of unequal value, but contain many examples of prayers. Various kinds are represented, sometimes even an unworthy kind such as prayer for utterly selfish or evil ends (Jth 9, 11[17f] 13[4f]); prayers in time of national peril (1 Mac 3[46–53] 4[10, 24, 30–33, 40, 55] 7[36–38, 41, 42], 2 Mac 1[24–29] 10[16, 25, 38] 13[10–12, 14] etc.); confession (cf 2 Es 3[4–36] and Bar 1[15]–3[8]); and supplication (cf Jth 4[9–15]); and thanksgiving (cf 1 Es 4[58–60], To 8[15–17] 11[14–17] 13). In Bar 1[11] there is a notable example of prayer on behalf of heathen rulers. 2 Mac 12[44f] speaks of the efficacy of the prayers of the living on behalf of the dead, a practice not mentioned in the canonical Scriptures; and 15[12-14] speaks of the prayer of the dead on behalf of the living. Particular note should be taken of the Apocryphal book entitled 'The Prayer of Manasseh,' which expresses deep and genuine religious feeling, and is arranged in fine liturgical form. In the Book of Sirach also, prayer reaches notable heights of devotion; true prayer is heard of God (35[13-17]); prayer is made in time of sickness (38[9, 14]); for deliverance from sin (23[1-5]). For prayer and alms, see 7[10]; for prayer and revenge, 28[1-4]; for national prayer against a foe, 36[1-17]; for thanksgiving, 50[21-24]; and for the closing prayer of the book, 51[1-12].

Reference has sometimes been made to two passages in 4 Maccabees which speak of the work of an intercessor: (*a*) The passage in 6[28f]: 'Be merciful to Thy people, accepting our punishment on their behalf. Make my blood a purification for them, and take my life as a substitute for their life.' These are the words of a Maccabaean martyr as he delivered himself to the fire for the sake of the Law. (*b*) 17[21f] speaks thus of the blood of the Jewish martyrs: 'They have become, as it were, a substitute for the sin of the nation, and through the blood of these pious ones and their propitiatory death, divine providence preserved Israel, which formerly had been evenly entreated.'

5. Prayer in the NT.—I. EXAMPLE AND TEACHING OF JESUS CHRIST.—Of the Synoptics, Luke is especially instructive as to prayer (cf Acts also), and the special character of the Fourth Gospel should be kept in mind. For the LORD'S PRAYER, see separate article.

(i) CHRIST'S EXAMPLE.—Christ lived His life in communion with God, so that the attitude of prayer was for Him a permanent attitude. His meat was to do the will of Him who sent Him. Reference is made on several occasions to His departure into a desert place for refreshing and solace of spirit (cf Mt 14[13], Mk 6[32], Lk 4[42]). But there is mention especially of His prayers at great junctures in His life and ministry: baptism (Lk 3[21]), the call of His disciples (Lk 6[12f]), on the occasion of many of His miracles (Lk 9[16]; cf Jn 6[23], Mk 7[34] 9[29], Jn 9[30-33] 11[41f]), transfiguration (Lk 9[29]), and especially Gethsemane (Lk 22[39-46]), crucifixion (Mt 27[46], Lk 23[46]); in Jn 17 there is the great prayer for unity; Lk 22[32] records His prayer for Peter, and 23[34] for the soldiers; for His intercession in glory, see below II (i).

(ii) CHRIST'S TEACHING.—The range of prayer is chiefly for spiritual blessing (cf Lord's Prayer and especially Mt 6[33]), but not exclusively so ('daily bread' in Lord's Prayer and Mt 24[20]). The conditions and requisites of prayer are numerous: (*a*) *Earnestness* (Lk 11[5-13]); and His attitude to the Syro-phoenician seems to teach urgency of petition (Mk 7[27]). (*b*) *Humility* (Lk 18[9-14]); the juxtaposition with the preceding parable is suggestive. (*c*) *A forgiving spirit*, as in Sirach (see above **4**). (*d*) *Privacy*: it is recommended that prayer should not be made in a public place lest the element of ostentation enter in, but in a private room (cf Christ's own example of solitary prayer; Lk 6[12]). (*e*) *Without vain repetition*; see above **2** (*c*) (ii), where the references show that the repetition discouraged is that of mere mechanical prayer or of pretence (Mk 12[40]). (*f*) *With faith*; Mk 11[23] contains such hyperbole as would appeal to an eastern mind and would enforce the value of prayer; while the seeming paradox of v.[24] must be taken along with this and understood in the light of Christ's general teaching. The need of faith is further illustrated by Christ's attitude to those seeking aid (*e.g.* Mt 8[13] 9[28], Mk 5[36] 9[23], Lk 8[48]). (*g*) *Agreement*. Where two or three are gathered together for prayer, there is awareness of human community, and selfish prayer does not easily enter in (Mt 18[19f]). (*h*) *In His Name* (Jn 14[13] 15[16] 16[23f, 26]). This phrase, which is characteristic of the Fourth Gospel, implies that men should ask in prayer only those things which they can ask in the spirit of Jesus Christ.

II. CUSTOMS AND IDEAS IN APOSTOLIC TIMES.—Evidence is given by Acts (where the prominence given to prayer is natural if Luke wrote it, see above I), and by the Epistles, whose writers had inherited the best traditions of Jewish piety and had assimilated their Master's teaching (even if they did not always grasp all of it fully) and had followed His example. A glimpse of availing prayer may be afforded by such passages as Ac 3[16] 4[31] 9[40] 10[4] 12[5, 12] 16[25] 28[8]. One or two detailed points have already been considered, but it may be well now to collect, from Acts to the Book of the Revelation, some passages showing the practice and teaching as to prayer in the Apostolic Church.

(i) Prayer is found in connexion with: (1) *Laying on of hands*: (*a*) in healing (Ac 28[8]; cf 9[17] (see below (3)); (*b*) after baptism (Ac 8[14-17]; cf 19[6]); (*c*) on appointment to office (Ac 6[6] 13[3]), with which also prayerful lot-casting is associated (Ac 1[24, 26]; cf Pr 16[33]). (2) *Public worship* (1 Ti 2): (*a*) prayer and gift of tongues (1 Co 14[14f], where it is suggested that the head as well as the heart is concerned with prayer); (*b*) prayers for the community in the Apostolic Church (1 Ti 2[1f]; cf **4**). (3) *Sickness* (Ja 5[13-16], where notice conjunction of prayer and outward means [for unction cf Mk 6[13]] with confession; physical and spiritual healing are associated, and both with prayer; see above, **4**).

(ii) (1) A distinctive idea in NT prayer is *the work of the Holy Spirit*. He aids us in prayer (Ro 8[14-16], Eph 6[18], Jude [20]); and when words fail us and we cannot pray for ourselves, He intercedes for us with groanings that cannot be uttered (Ro 8[26]). Christ also, who, in His own life and death has interposed for us, intercedes on our behalf (Ro 8[34], He 7[25]; cf presentation of prayer to God in Rev 5[8] 8[4]). By Christ we enjoy free access to God (Gal 4[4-7], Eph 2[18] 3[12], He 4[15f] 10[19-22]; see above, **5** I (ii) (*h*); prayer is offered to Christ direct (Ac 7[59f] 9[14] (?), 1 Co 1[2] (?). (2) *Prayer needs faith* (Ja 1[6-8], 1 Ti 2[8] RVm, He 10[22]), must have right aims (Ja 4[3]), and be backed by conduct (1 Jn 3[22]). Such prayer succeeds (Ja 5[16-18], 1 Jn 3[22] 5[14f]). Prayer for temporal gifts is not very conspicuous in NT, but see Ro 1[10], 2 Co 12[8], Ph 4[6]. (3) *Exhortations to prayer* (Ro 12[12], Col 4[2], 1 Th 5[16], 1 P 4[7], Jude [20]). (4) *Reminiscences of OT* occur in prayer as colloquy (Ac 9[13-16] 22[17-21]; cf **3**), as struggle (Ro 15[30], Col 2[1] 4[12]; cf Gn 32[24]), as cry for vengeance (Rev 6[9f]; cf 1 Ti 2[8]). (5) *Intercession*, which in OT is specially characteristic of the prophetic office, is here a general duty, and is very prominent: Apostles for converts (Ro 10[1] 15[5], 2 Co 13[7], Eph 1[16] 3[14], Ph 1[4, 9], Col 1[9] 2[1], 1 Th 1[2] 2 Th 1[11], Phn [4], 3 Jn [2]); converts for Apostles (Ac 12[5], Ro 15[30], 2 Co 1[11] 9[14], Col 4[3], 2 Th 3[1], Phn [22]); for one another (Ja 5[16], 1 Jn 5[16] [within limit]). (6) *Thanksgiving* abounds (Ro 1[8], 1 Co 1[4], 2 Co 2[14] 8[16], Ph 1[3], Col 1[3], 1 Th 1[2] 2[13], 2 Th 1[3] 2[13], 1 Ti 1[12], 2 Ti 1[3]). (7) Note also the *salutation and blessing* at the beginning and close of Epistles. The NT closes with a threefold prayer for Christ's coming (Rev 22 [17, 20]).

H. F. B. C.—**J. Ma.**

PRAYER OF MANASSEH.—See APOCRYPHA, **13**.

PREACHING.—1. In Judaism.—In the OT the verb 'preach' occurs merely as an occasional variant to the more common 'prophesy,' and consequently does not designate a distinct activity. Preaching as a regular part of the service of public worship was a comparatively late development. Its real beginning can be traced back to the custom attributed to Ezra of reading a part of the 'Law' or 'Torah' at the Sabbath-day assemblages of the people, and on other holy days. On these occasions the lesson from the Law was read in the original Hebrew, and explained in the form of a paraphrase in the Aramaic vernacular by a *m^e^thûrg^e^mān* (dragoman) or interpreter. Such translations were called Targums. It was from this practice that preaching in the synagogue developed.

The title 'preacher' (*darshān*) occurs from the 1st cent. B.C. on. He was supposed to prepare his sermon (*d^e^rāshāh*) carefully in advance, and present it in an appealing way. He usually reproduced the Scripture lesson or parts of it, interspersing exhortations, warnings and comfort, as suggested by the text. The gist of such a sermon preached by Rabbi Eleazar ben Azarja around A.D. 100 was as follows: ' From all your sins you shall be clean before the Lord ' (on the Day of Atonement, Lev 16^{30}). What has taken place between you and God is forgiven (by God) to you (on the Day of Atonement); but what has taken place between you and your neighbour is forgiven to you only when you have reconciled yourself with your neighbour (*Siphra Lev.* 16^{30}; 324a). Philo reports concerning the synagogue service: ' The people sit decorously, keeping silence and listening with the utmost attention out of a thirst for refreshing discourse, while one of the best qualified stands up and instructs them in what is best and most conducive to welfare, things by which their whole life may be made better ' (*de spec. Legg.* ii. 62). An indication of special skill was the ability to construct a chain of abstrusely related scriptural texts.

2. In the NT.—Thus by NT times preaching had become an integral part of the ordinary synagogue service (Ac 15^{21}), and provided the occasion for much of the preaching of Jesus and Paul. The practice of opening the exposition of the Torah with an appropriate passage from the prophets had led to the introduction of a second lesson, taken from the prophets, prior to the sermon. It is this second reading which is given by Jesus according to Lk 4^{16ff}, where, as in Ac 13^{14ff}, the sermon comes immediately ' after the reading of the law and the prophets.' However, the synagogue sermon is not constitutive of the NT concept of ' preaching.' Rather Jesus is often spoken of as ' teaching ' in the synagogue, and Paul as ' arguing ' there, while their ' preaching ' frequently takes place outside the context of the synagogue service, as at the seaside or in the marketplace. Nor can the worship service discussed in 1 Co 14 be derived from the synagogue, but rather has its nearest analogies in the practices of certain Hellenistic cults.

The NT term for ' preaching ' is *kērygma.* It referred originally to the proclaiming done by a herald or announcer, and to the content of his message. The latter meaning is rare in the NT (1 Co 1^{21}), and consequently *kērygma* did not become a technical term as did ' gospel.' Only in modern theology has it come to be so used. Hence the nature of the NT ' kerygma ' cannot be derived from the term, but only from an analysis of preaching in the primitive church.

Jesus preached the imminence of the eschatological Kingdom of God (Mt 4^{17}), calling upon His hearers to repent of their way of life built upon the ' present evil aeon,' and offering them a life to be lived out of the reality of the future Kingdom. This preaching was itself the last and decisive sign of the Kingdom's imminent coming (Lk 11^{29-32}). Hence one's response to Jesus' preaching determined one's ultimate destiny (Mk 8^{38}). Thus Jesus' preaching is prominent among the actions comprising His eschatological rôle (Mt 11^{4-6}), and to this extent implies a Christology. This implied Christology became still more evident when His death completed the radical break with the power of evil which he preached, and when on Easter the reality of the life of transcendence which He offered was revealed to His disciples in His own person. Thus the one who had originally been the preacher of an eschatological message became Himself the content of the Christian sermon, without any basic disjunction in underlying meaning. Herein resides the validity of the primitive church's procedure of interpreting Jesus' sayings in terms of their Easter faith, and even of placing their kerygma on His lips.

3. The early church.—The gist of the preaching in the primitive church can be detected in various ways: The material in the Synoptic Gospels reflects the setting in the life of the church in which it was transmitted, and this setting of the oral tradition may often have been the sermon. Luke made use of various early fragments of tradition in composing his sermons in Acts, so that fragments of primitive preaching may have been preserved in Ac $2^{22-24, 32-36}$ $3^{13-15, 19-21}$ 4^{10} 5^{30-32} 10^{36-43} (13^{23-33}). Paul quotes early hymns (Ph 2^{6-11}; cf also Col 1^{15-20}), confessions (1 Co 12^{3}, Ro 10^{9}), credal formulae (Ro 1^{3f}, 1 Co 8^{6}), and other traditions, both explicitly (1 Co 11^{23ff} 15^{3ff}) and tacitly (Ro 3^{24f} 4^{24f} 8^{32ff}). Such material can be identified and disengaged from the Pauline text by establishing its non-Pauline nature and its stylized liturgical form. In content though not in form this material doubtless reflects the evangelistic preaching of the primitive church. The content of Paul's own preaching may be inferred from specific allusions on his part, such as Gal 3^{1}, 1 Co 1^{23} 2^{2}, 2 Co 5^{11-21}, 1 Th 1^{9f}. His homiletical style may be inferred from his letters, which in various respects recall the informal give-and-take of the ' diatribes ' delivered by the wandering Cynic and Stoic street preachers.

4. The sermons in Acts.—The relative stability of the primitive Christian message centering in Jesus' death and resurrection, His humiliation and exaltation, His suffering and glory, provides considerable justification for the modern custom of speaking of *the* kerygma. Yet it would probably be historically inaccurate to extend this insight into the hypothesis of a universally accepted outline of the primitive Christian sermon dating from the very beginning. Such a fixed outline only becomes visible toward the end of the 1st cent., in the sermons Luke composed to illuminate the narrative of Acts. For, in spite of occasional omissions, repetitions, and transpositions, the pattern used for the first sermon is followed fairly consistently throughout:

(*a*) Address to the audience appropriate to the situation: Ac 2^{14b} 3^{12b} 4^{8b} 13^{16b} 14^{15a} 17^{22b}; it is sometimes repeated: 2^{22a} 3^{17} $13^{26a, 38a}$.

(*b*) A call upon them to hearken, sometimes expressed only indirectly: Ac 2^{14c} 4^{10a} (10^{36a}) 13^{16b} (14^{15c} 17^{23c}); it is sometimes repeated: 2^{22a} 13^{38a}.

(*c*) A misunderstanding on the part of the audience: Ac 2^{15} 3^{12c} 4^{9} (5^{29} $10^{25f, 34b-35}$) 14^{15a} $17^{22b-23ab}$.

(*d*) Scriptural quotation: Ac 2^{16-21} 3^{13a} 5^{30b} $10^{38a, 39b}$ (13^{17-25}) 14^{15d} 17^{24a}.

(*e*) Christological kerygma: Ac 2^{22b-24} 3^{13b-15} 4^{10b} 5^{30-31a} 10^{37-42} 13^{27-31}; it is sometimes repeated: 2^{32f} $3^{19b-21a}$. It has its centre in the theme: you crucified Jesus ($2^{23, 36}$ $3^{13, 15}$ 4^{10} 5^{30} 10^{39}), but God raised Him from the dead ($2^{24, 32}$ 3^{15} 4^{10} 5^{30} 10^{40}).

(*f*) Proof text: Ac 2^{25-31} 3^{18} 4^{11} 10^{43a} 13^{32-37} (17^{28}); it is sometimes repeated: 2^{34f} 3^{21b-24}.

(*g*) Apostolic witness to the resurrection: Ac 2^{32} 3^{15} 5^{32} $10^{(39a), 41}$ $13^{31, (32)}$ (14^{15c} 17^{23c}).

(*h*) Solution of the misunderstanding: Ac $2^{33b, 36}$ 3^{16} 4^{10c} 14^{15b} 17^{29}.

(*i*) Call for repentance and proclamation of salvation: Ac 2^{38} 3^{19a} 4^{12} 5^{31b} 10^{43b}.

(*j*) Specific application to the audience: Ac 2^{39} 3^{25f} ($10^{36, 44}$) $13^{26b, 40f}$ 17^{30f}.

In the sermons in Acts one can detect older traditions, especially the christological statements and the use of the proof texts. Yet the sermons do not seem to depend upon a specific preacher or occasion. For the preacher's individuality is in terms of Luke's understanding, as is most apparent in the one case where Luke's presentation can be compared with the preacher's own presentation: Paul. In Ac 13^{31f} ' Paul ' presents Luke's view of the apostolic office, which excludes Paul (cf 1 Co 9^{2}); in 13^{38f} Luke succeeds only in presenting a garbled version of Pauline theology, while the sermon on the Areopagus (17^{22ff}) is simply Luke's theology. Hence it is Luke who has given each sermon its distinctiveness, in terms of the rôle it plays in his narrative. This is most apparent in the programmatic sermons at the founding of the church (2^{14ff}), the admission of the first Gentiles (10^{34ff}), the opening of the Pauline mission (13^{16ff}), and the encounter with Greek culture (17^{22ff}). Consequently the major divergences between the sermons derive not from the preachers, but rather from the way the audience is envisaged. Luke seems to think that the Jerusalemites are consistently involved in misunderstanding and the need for repentance, while both traits disappear in sermons to ‘ God-fearers ’ (10^{2} $13^{16, 26f}$). To audiences which are purely pagan one preaches the doctrine of God (14^{16f} 17^{24-27}) rather than the christological kerygma, which is either omitted or relegated to the position of an appendix (17^{31}).

5. Ethical exhortation.—The evangelistic preaching of the primitive church was of course supplemented with catechetical instruction at baptism, and continuing ethical exhortation in the life of the church. The nature of this exhortation can be deduced from the ethical sections of the NT epistles, especially where they incorporate traditional patterns current in the life of the church : lists of virtues and vices (Gal 5^{19-23}, Col $3^{5-8, 12}$ etc.), and tables of household regulations (Col 3^{18}–4^{1}, 1 P 2^{13}–3^{7}, Tit 2), taken over from the Hellenistic world ; the Ten Commandments, and the description of the ‘ two ways ’ (*Barnabas* 18–20, *Didache* 1–6), taken over from Judaism ; and collections of Jesus' teaching (the Sermon on the Mount). This material tended to become ‘ kerygmatized ’ : Jesus' teachings were readdressed to the present situation by the heavenly Lord (1 Th 4^{15}, 1 Co 7^{10}, Ac 20^{35}, and the Gospels) ; household relationships were ‘ in the Lord,’ *e.g.* the conduct of the slave was that of the Suffering Servant (1 P 2^{21-25}) ; the contrast between one's way of life then and now corresponded to the shift in aeons proclaimed by the kerygma (Gal 4^{4}, Tit 3^{3-7}, Ro 6^{17f}, 1 Co 6^{9-11}). Actually the survival of kerygmatic fragments in the NT is largely due to their incorporation in ethical exhortation.

Primitive Christian preaching made considerable use of the Jewish and Hellenistic thought forms of the day, just as preaching to-day makes use of modern patterns of thought. Hence if modern preaching is to convey to the world of to-day the message of primitive Christian preaching, it must do so by means of a translation of thought forms as well as of words. This process of translation is currently designated ‘ demythologizing,’ since it often consists in stating in modern terms a theological meaning which was originally stated in terms dependent upon a mythological world view.

J. M. R.

PRECINCTS.—See Parbar.

PRECIOUS STONES.—See Jewels and Precious Stones.

PREDESTINATION.—The English word ‘ predestinate ’ in the AV is, in the few cases in which it occurs (Ro $8^{29, 30}$, Eph $1^{5, 12}$), exchanged in the RV for ‘ **foreordain,**’ a return to the usage of the older Versions (cf RSV). The Greek word (*proorizō*) conveys the simple idea of defining or determining beforehand (thus, in addition to above, in Ac 4^{28}, 1 Co 2^{7}). The change in rendering brings the word into closer relation with a number of others expressing the same, or related, meanings, as ‘ foreknow ’ (in pregnant sense, Ac 2^{23}, Ro 8^{29} 11^{2}, 1 P $1^{2, 20}$), ‘ determine ’ (Ac 17^{26}), ‘ appoint ’ (1 P 2^{8}), ‘ purpose ’ (Eph 1^{9}), in the case of believers, ‘ choose ’ or ‘ elect ’ (Eph 1^{4} etc.). In the OT the idea is expressed by the various words denoting to *purpose*, *determine*, *choose* (*e.g.* Is 14^{24-27} 46^{10f}), with the abundance of phrases extolling the sovereignty and immutability of God's counsel in all the spheres of His operation (see below ; so in NT). The best clue to the Scripture conception will be found in tracing it as it appears in these different spheres of the Divine action.

1. In its most general aspect, **foreordination** is coextensive with the sphere of God's universal providence, is, in fact, only another name for the eternal plan, design, purpose, counsel of God, which executes itself in providence. The **election** (q.v.) of believers, to which ‘ predestination ’ is sometimes narrowed, is but a specific case of the ‘ purpose ’ of Him ‘ who accomplishes *all things* according to the counsel of his will ’ (Eph 1^{11}). It is in this wider regard, accordingly, that foreordination must be studied first. It cannot be reasonably doubted that all Scripture—OT and NT—represents God as exercising in and over the world a providence that is absolutely universal. Nothing, great or small—operations of nature or actions of men—is left outside its scope. This does not happen blindly, but in accordance with a plan or purpose, equally all-embracing, which has existed from eternity. As Plato says in his *Parmenides* that nothing, not even the meanest object, is unpenetrated by the idea, so even the minutest details, and seemingly most casual happenings, of life (the numbering of hairs, the fall of a sparrow, Mt 10^{29f}) are included in the Divine providence. Free agency is not annulled ; on the contrary, human freedom and responsibility are everywhere insisted on. But even free volitions, otherwise mere possibilities, are taken up in their place into this plan of God, and are made subservient to the accomplishment of His purposes. The Bible does not trouble itself with solving difficulties as to the relation of the Divine purpose to **human freedom,** but, in accordance with its fundamental doctrine of God as the free personal Creator of the world and absolutely sovereign Ruler in the realms both of matter and of mind, working through all causes, and directing everything to the wisest and holiest ends, it unhesitatingly sees His ‘ hand ’ and His ‘ counsel ’ in whatever is permitted to happen, good or bad (Ac 2^{23}). It need not be said that there is nothing arbitrary or unjust in this ‘ counsel ’ of God ; it can be conceived of only as the eternal expression of His wisdom, righteousness, and love.

Texts are almost superfluous in the case of a doctrine pervading the whole of Scripture—history, prophecy, psalm, epistle—but an instance or two may be given. The history is a continual demonstration of a Divine teleology (*e.g.* Gn 45^{8} 50^{20}). God's counsel stands, and cannot be defeated (Ps 33^{1} 46^{10f}) ; all that God wills He does (Ps 115^{3} 135^{6}, Dn 4^{35}) ; it is because God purposed it, that it comes to pass (Is $14^{24, 27}$ 37^{26}) ; God is the disposer of all events (2 S 17^{11f}, Job 1^{21}, Pr 16^{33}) ; man may devise his way, but it is the Lord who directs his steps (16^{9}) ; even the hearts of men are under His control (21^{1}) ; God sends to man good and evil alike (Am 3^{6}, Is 45^{7}). It has already been pointed out that the same doctrine is implied in the NT (*e.g.* Ac 4^{28} 15^{18} 28 [story of Paul's shipwreck], Eph 1^{11}, Rev 4^{11} etc.).

2. A universal, all-pervading purpose of God in creation, providence, and human life, is thus everywhere assumed. The end of God's **purpose,** as regards humanity, may be thought of as the establishing of a moral and spiritual kingdom, or Kingdom of God, in which God's will should be done on earth, as it is done in heaven (cf Mt 6^{10}). But this end, now that sin has entered, can be attained only through a *redemption.* The centre of God's purpose in our world, therefore—that which gives its meaning and direction to the whole Biblical history, and constitutes almost its sole concern—is the fact of redemption through Jesus Christ, and the salvation of men by Him. To this everything preceding—the call of Abraham, the Covenant with Israel, the discipline and growing revelation of Law and Prophets—leads up (on predestination here, cf Gn 18^{18f}, Lv $20^{24, 26}$, Is $43^{1, 7}$ etc.) ; with this begins (or, more strictly, continues) the ingathering of a people to God from all nations and races of mankind, who in their completeness, constitute the true Church of God, redeemed from among men (Eph 5^{25-27}, 1 P 2^{9f}, Rev 1^{5f} 14^{1-5} etc.). The peculiar interest of the doctrine of foreordination, accordingly, in the NT, concentrates itself in the calling and salvation of those described as the ‘ chosen ’ or ‘ elect ’ of God to this great destiny (Eph 1^{4} etc.). The doctrine of foreordination (predestination) here coalesces practically with that of election (q.v.). Yet certain distinctions arise from a difference in the point of view from which the subject is contemplated.

Election, in the NT, as seen in the article referred to, relates to the eternal choice of the individual to salvation. As little as any other fact or event in life is the salvation of the believer regarded as lying outside the purpose or pre-determination of God ; rather, an eternal thought of love on God's part is seen coming to light in the saved one being brought into the Kingdom (2 Th 2[13, 15]). There is the yet deeper reason for seeing in the believer's calling and salvation the manifestation of a Divine purpose, that, as lost in sin, he is totally incapable of effecting this saving change in himself. He owes his renewal, his quickening from spiritual death, to the gratuitous mercy of God (Eph 2[1-8]; see REGENERATION). Every soul born into the Kingdom is conscious in its deepest moments that it is only of God's grace it is there, and is ready to ascribe the whole glory of its salvation to God (Rev 7[10]), and to trace back that salvation to its fountainhead in the everlasting counsel of God. Thus regarded, 'election' and 'foreordination' to salvation seem to have much the same meaning. Yet in usage a certain distinction is made. It may perhaps be stated thus, that 'election' denotes the Divine choice simply, while 'foreordain' has generally (in sense of 'predestine') a reference to the end which the foreordination has in view. Thus in Eph 1[4f] 'Even as he chose us in him before the foundation of the world . . . having destined us in love to be his sons' (where 'destined,' as Meyer rightly says, is not to be taken as prior to, but as coincident in point of time with, 'he chose'); and in v.[11] 'destined and appointed to live for the praise of his glory' (v.[12]). In Ro 8[29], again, where 'foreknew'—which seems to take the place of 'chose' (it can hardly be foreknowledge of the faith which is the result of the later 'calling')—comes before 'predestined' the latter has the end defined: 'to be conformed to the image of his Son.' Those 'foreknown' are afterwards described as God's 'elect' (v.[33]). This striking passage further shows how, in foreordaining the end, God likewise foreordains all the steps that lead to it ('foreknew'—'predestined'—'called'—'justified'—'glorified').

3. Predestination is always a mystery. This is because it is an act of God, and if there were no mystery about God's action, there would be nothing to adore. But it is not all mystery; much has been unveiled in Christ, through whom we know that God's purpose is 'to unite all things in him, things in heaven and things on earth' (Eph 1[9f]). Yet though the end is clear, we cannot discern all the workings of God on the way. Because we are creatures in time and He is eternal, and because our justice is at best ineffective and imperfect while His is effective and perfect, we cannot without blasphemous presumption pretend to know who are predestined to glory and who not. But what we already know of the forgiving love of God in Christ assures us that the end will not deny the central act of mercy and redemption, any more than it will deny the judgment of it. Somehow in the end justice and love, mercy and judgment will be seen to have been brought together.

The language of predestination is essentially religious; it is also temporal. When the Christian yields to Christ he does a voluntary act. But he knows, or comes to know, that such voluntary action is fundamentally an act of God in him. But we cannot relate God's action with metaphysical accuracy by using temporal prefixes. To say that God *pre*-destined us to salvation is an accurate enough transcript of a religious experience that we do not save ourselves, and that somehow God works before we act. But the words are not an accurate transcript of the temporal relationship of God's act and our own, because we are in time while God transcends it. It is always wrong therefore to erect hard metaphysical doctrines on the believer's religious language. If we do, blemishes are unavoidable: for we must say either that God will save all and so make nonsense of our conceptions of justice, or that some will be damned and God's universal purpose thus frustrated. Against this it must be said that what we know of God's purpose and love in Christ sufficiently assures us that at the end we shall find both mercy and justice perfectly fulfilled and satisfied.

Some difficulties can be cleared away by observing, *e.g.*, that in Ro 9–11 Paul is dealing with God's election of men in history, and not with their eternal salvation. In history it appears arbitary that God should choose Jacob rather than Esau until we know that such arbitary choices appear reasonable in the light of the final inclusion of all men in both condemnation and mercy: 'God has consigned all men to disobedience, that he may have mercy upon all' (Ro 11[32]). If Calvin, and even more his disciples, had grasped this distinction between the intra-historical and the extra-historical election of God, we might have achieved long since a doctrine of predestination in which, with a due sense of mystery, the mercy and judgment of God were seen as equal partners in His love at the end. J. O.—**J. Mar.**

PRE-EXISTENCE OF SOULS.—The idea is common in many religions, especially Indian (but not in Buddhism or Islam), and in the Greek tradition it is prominent in Pythagoreanism and Platonism. In Biblical documents it appears only in the Hellenized Wisdom of Solomon (8[19-20]). The fact that it did not otherwise find its way into canonical books does not mean that it was unknown in Judaism, as is evident from Philo, from Josephus' account of the Essenes, and from allusions in Talmud and Midrash. In the NT the notion is presupposed in the question of Jn 9[1] whether the man was born blind because of his sin, Jesus' reply to which takes the form of a critique of the question. The doctrine was maintained by Gnostics such as Basilides with a special interest in theodicy, and by Origen who, however, denied the idea often associated with pre-existence, namely transmigration of souls. It is this Platonic association of the two related ideas which no doubt explains much of the resistance of Christian orthodoxy to the doctrine of pre-existence, apart from the negligible support given in Scripture, and the difficulty of reconciling it with the doctrines of Divine creation and bodily resurrection. H. C.

PREFECT.—Found only in RSV in Dn 2[48] 3[2f, 27] 6[7] where it renders Aramaic *s^e^ghan*. AV has 'governors,' while RV has the same except in 6[7], where it has 'deputies.' See PROCURATOR, PROVINCE, ROMAN PUBLIC LAW.

PREPARATION (Gr. *paraskeuē*).—A term applied by the Jews to the day preceding the Sabbath, or any of the sacred festivals, especially the Passover (cf Mt 27[62] ||, Jn 19[14, 31, 42]).

PRESBYTER (Gr. *presbyteros*, 'elder').—The word occurs as a RV marginal alternative for **'elders'** in Ac 20[17]; the Greek *presbyteros*, which is of frequent occurrence, being otherwise invariably rendered 'elder.' For treatment of the subject of the presbyter, see BISHOP and also next article.

PRESBYTERY (Gr. *presbyterion*).—In AV of NT the word occurs only in 1 Ti 4[14], where it denotes the body of *Christian* presbyters or elders (possibly those belonging to the church at Lystra; cf Ac 16[1-4]) who laid their hands upon Timothy before he set out on his labours as St. Paul's missionary companion. In the Greek text, however, the word *presbyterion* is found in two other passages, viz. Lk 22[66] (AV 'elders,' RV 'assembly of the elders') and Ac 22[5] (AV and RV 'estate of the elders,' RSV 'council of elders'), as an expression for the body of *Jewish* elders who with the 'chief priests' and the scribes composed the Sanhedrin. This twofold use of the word (like the corresponding twofold use of 'elder' q.v.) affords a strong confirmation of the view, which is otherwise most probable, that the presbytery of the Christian Church finds its roots in the eldership of the Jewish *ecclesia*.

The presbytery was at first a purely local body (cf the *Letters* of Ignatius, *passim*), which may have included those persons whose functions are also described as 'overseers,' 'guardians,' or 'bishops' (Ac 20[28]). But early in the post-Apostolic age the bishop was clearly distinguished from the presbyters in office. (Cf 1 Ti 5[17], 'Let the elders who rule well be considered worthy of double honour, especially those who labor in preaching and teaching'). The bishop as we meet him in the *Letters* of Ignatius (*e.g.* Eph 4) is a congregational bishop, the president of a body of congregational presbyters. See BISHOP.

What was involved in the **laying on of the hands of the presbytery** in the case of Timothy it is impossible to say with certainty. Probably it was an act corresponding to ordination to office (see LAYING ON OF HANDS), St. Paul himself being associated with the presbytery in the action (cf 2 Ti 1^{6}). On the other hand, it may have been no more than a commendation of Timothy to the grace of God for strength and guidance in his new work as a missionary, analogous thus to the action of the prophets and teachers of Antioch in the case of Barnabas and Saul (Ac 13^{1-3}). The laying on of St. Paul's hands (2 Ti 1^{6}) may really have been a separate incident, comparable again to the laying on of the hands of Ananias on himself (Ac 9^{17})—not an official act but a gracious benediction (cf Lindsay, *Church and Ministry*, p. 143n.). St. Paul without doubt received a consecrating grace from the hands both of Ananias and of those prophets and teachers of the Church at Antioch, but he claimed to be an Apostle 'not from men, nor through man, but through Jesus Christ and God the Father, who raised him from the dead' (Gal 1^{1}). J. C. L.—M. H. S.

PRESENCE OF GOD.—See SHEKINAH.

PRESENCE-BREAD.—See SHOWBREAD.

PRESIDENTS.—Aramaic *sārᵉkhîn*, in Dn 6^{2ff}, denotes officials of the Persian empire. It is probable that it is a loan-word from Persian.

PRESS, PRESSFAT.—The former occurs in AV for the usual **winepress** in Pr 3^{10} (RV 'fats,' RSV 'vats'), Is 16^{10} (where alone it is retained in RV, RSV), and Jl 3^{13} (RV, RSV 'winepress'). 'Pressfat' is found only in Hag 2^{16} AV (RV 'winefat,' RSV 'winevat'). For the ancient winepresses, see WINE AND STRONG DRINK, **2.** A. R. S. K.

PREVENT.—To 'prevent' in the English of AV is to 'be before,' 'anticipate,' 'forestall,' as Ps 119^{147} 'I prevented (so RV; RSV 'rise before') the dawning of the morning.' Sometimes it is to forestall for one's good, as Ps 59^{10} 'The God of my mercy shall prevent me' (so RV; ASV, RSV 'My God . . . will meet me'); and sometimes for one's hurt, as Ps 18^{5} 'The snares of death prevented me' (RV 'came upon me,' RSV 'confronted me'), but the modern idea of merely 'hindering' never occurs in AV.

PRICK.—**1.** Hebrew *śēkh*, Nu 33^{55}, means a 'thorn.' **2.** Ac 26^{14} (AV; RV, RSV 'goad'); see AGRICULTURE, **1.**

PRIDE.—As humility (q.v.) is commended in the Bible, pride is condemned (Jer 13^{15}). The wicked are frequently denounced for their self-confident pride (Ps 10^{2ff} 73^{6}, Job 35^{12}), and humiliation is promised them (Pr 11^{2} 16^{18}, Is $2^{11,17}$ 14^{11}, Ob ^{4}) or recorded as experienced by them (2 Ch 26^{16} 32^{25}, Dn 4^{30ff}). In the NT the Pharisees are condemned for their pride and ostentation (Mt 6^{5} 23^{5}, Lk 18^{9ff}), and all social pride is castigated by Christ (Mt 23^{6f}, Lk 14^{7ff}), who rebukes His disciples for place seeking and makes service the criterion of honour (Mk 10^{35-45}). So, too, Paul rebukes the Corinthians for spiritual pride (1 Co 4^{6ff}).

There is, nevertheless, a commendable pride, but it is in God (Ps 34^{2}, Jer 9^{23f}) or in the gospel (Ro 1^{16}), or in the privilege of serving God (Ro 15^{17}, 2 Co 11^{10ff}).

PRIDE OF JORDAN.—See JORDAN, **5.**

PRIESTS AND LEVITES.—Every ancient society has produced a class of persons whose task is to guard the sanctuary and preserve the sacred traditions, thereby constituting the most conservative and stabilizing element in the community. Such was the priesthood in Israel, averse to change, yet itself developing in the course of its history, and capable of longer survival than either kingship or prophecy.

Little is known of the priesthood in Palestine before the Settlement. The existence of sanctuaries in the time of the patriarchs implies priests, though, with the exception of the enigmatic figure of Melchizedek in Jebusite Salem (Gn 14), they receive no mention in the OT. The Krt and Aqht texts from Râs Shamra, reveal that in Canaan the priesthood was bound up with kingship, and the king performed priestly functions. The administrative texts show that, in the 2nd millennium, there had grown up, in connexion with the sanctuaries in Ugarit, hereditary guilds of priests (*khnm*—cf Heb. *kōhᵃnîm*) and sacred persons (*qdšm*) in a hierarchy comparable in principle with that of later Israel.

1. The Levitical Priesthood.—The origins of Israel's priesthood are obscure, and involved in the uncertainties of the early history of the tribe of Levi.

(*a*) Probably the earliest evidence of the tribe is the so-called Blessing of Jacob in Gn 49^{5-7}, where there is no allusion to priestly functions. Levi is regarded on the same level as vanished Simeon, and its scattered life a punishment for violence against the Canaanites. On the basis of the discovery of Minaean inscriptions, in which the term *l(a)w(i)* seems to indicate a cultic official, some scholars have disregarded the evidence of Gn 49, and concluded that Levites were priests from the first. But if this is so, Gn 49 becomes unintelligible, and no one has yet offered an adequate explanation how such a tradition could have arisen about a group *ex hypothesi* priestly. Levi must therefore be regarded as originally a secular tribe. Whatever may have been the reason for Levi's loss of tribal territory, the OT tradition suggests that its possession of the priestly office was ultimately due to a specially strong zeal for Yahweh worship.

(*b*) There follows a period of wandering, in the period of the Judges, corresponding perhaps to the more general change from nomadism to a sedentary way of life. The transition period is illustrated by the story of Micah's Levite in Jg 17–18. The point of the story is to account for the origin of the sanctuary of Dan. It shows that, at this time, the head of a household might offer sacrifices. There is, on the other hand, a preference for a young man, so that Micah installed one of his sons as priest of his shrine. But when a Levite can be obtained, there is special blessing. 'Now I know that the Lord will prosper me, because I have a Levite as priest.' Micah's Levite had previously been a sojourner (*gēr*) in Bethlehem. Thus a homeless Levite became a private priest when required. Later the Danites took him to their new territory, and he founded a new line of priests at the northern sanctuary of Dan. No doubt this represents at least one way in which Levite communities arose in tribes and families.

(*c*) In the same period, which sees the growth and organization of the Israelite confederation of Twelve Tribes, the Levites seem to have become key figures in the practice of war. The guardianship of the Ark was assigned to them, and they would accompany it into battle. Examples of their exhortations to Israelite forces preparing for battle, are probably preserved in the Book of Deuteronomy, and it is highly likely that Levitical circles were responsible for the transmission of much of the older amphictyonic material contained in that book. It is clear that, at a very early date, the Levites developed that care for sacred learning which has been one of the distinguishing marks of priesthood in all ages.

It may well be that the **Levitical cities** of Nu 35^{1-8}, usually interpreted as a late unhistorical institution, belong originally to this period, when the Levites were scattered about the land, often in need, and not necessarily attached to recognized sanctuaries. But precisely how this provision was made, it is impossible to deduce from the late account, which may owe its present form to arrangements of the period of the Second Temple.

(*d*) The so-called Blessing of Moses (Dt 33^{8-11}) describes the character and rôle of the tribe of Levi probably in the period of the early monarchy. Levi is now a priestly group, chiefly noted for the possession of the sacred oracle Urim and Thummim, and charged with responsibility for teaching the law. The offering of sacrifice is mentioned last, and is a consequence of

Levi's primary concern with the law. Clearly, the principal function of the Levites was the giving of oracular direction, and this was done in these two ways. The sacred lot required a question to be posed in a form demanding a simple negative or affirmative answer. The law (*tôrāh*) implied a legal code, comprehending both civil and religious law and custom. The priestly office was understood to be a *teaching* office (cf Mic 3^{9-12}, Hos 4^{1-4}, Zeph 3^{4}, Jer 18^{18}, Ezk 22^{26}, Hag 2^{10ff}), and the priest as much a medium of revelation as the prophet. He differed from the prophet mainly in the *way* he he secured oracular direction. When the sacrificial function had become predominant, still the priest was expected to be an assiduous teacher, as is shown in Mal 2^{7}

The lips of a priest should guard knowledge
And men should seek instruction from his mouth,
For he is the messenger of the Lord of hosts.

The Chronicler (2 Ch 15^{3}) regarded a teaching priest and the knowledge of the law as indispensable if Israel was to know 'the true God.'

The story of the infant Samuel shows how a man might become a priest. The technical expression for ordination was 'to fill the hand,' and is either a term meaning simply 'to appoint,' like the parallel Assyrian expression which was no longer understood in its literal sense; or else it alludes to the portions assigned to the priests for their maintenance. A priest might be called 'father' (Jg 17^{10} 18^{19}), was marked outwardly by wearing the **linen ephod** (1 S 2^{18}, etc.), and usually lived, like Eli and Samuel, at the sanctuary. It is noteworthy that Samuel was not a Levite, and Levitical monopoly was only gradually achieved. The ancient stories about the priestly progenitors and families suggest that the growth of the priesthood was attended by deep jealousies and rivalries.

2. The Zadokite Priesthood.—The inception of the Davidic monarchy was momentous for the development of Israel's priesthood. This was inevitable, by reason of the close connexion between priesthood and kingship everywhere in the ancient, near-eastern world. Royal temples and the royal cult meant that priests were, in some sense, the king's assistants.

(*a*) Two leading priests appear in the time of David. Abiathar apparently belonged to the already existing, privileged priesthood of the Israelites (1 K 2^{27}). Zadok, on the other hand, the newcomer who continued in the possession of the Jerusalem priesthood after the expulsion of Abiathar by Solomon, seems to have boasted no such pedigree. Indeed, the balance of probability is that Zadok was the pre-Davidic priest of the ancient Jebusite shrine in Jerusalem. Some scholars have supposed that he was priest-king, and that David, after the capture of Jerusalem, took over the kingship with its attendant cultus, leaving to Zadok something of his priestly status. But how this could have happened defies the imagination. Neither David nor a defeated king would behave in this way. It is better to suppose that Zadok was priest of the 'Most High,' 'of the order of Melchizedek' (cf Ps 110^{4}, which is probably a royal acknowledgment of Zadok's status), and that he was willing to assist David in adapting the ritual and mythology to Israel's purposes. The resultant royal cult is reflected in certain psalms, which may be conveniently studied in this connexion in A. R. Johnson's *Sacral Kingship in Ancient Israel.* At first, Abiathar and Zadok were joint custodians of the Ark. After David's death, Zadok won sole possession, and the prophecy of 'the faithful priest,' who 'shall go in and out before my anointed for ever' (1 S 2^{35}) was understood to refer to him and his line. This new priesthood was bound to become the more important. Later the house of Zadok was understood to be a family within the house of Levi, and the genealogies adapted accordingly. A connexion was thus created between the priesthood of Jerusalem and the earlier Israelite priesthood.

There thus emerged in the time of David a royal establishment of king and priest, which took its place alongside the Levitical priesthood, and was destined to increase in power and influence. In the beginning it owed its prestige to the king who retained a priestly character (2 S 6^{17f}, 1 K $8^{5, 62ff}$, 2 K 16^{12f}), even as the importance of the priests in the royal temples of the north was also dependent upon their connexion with the king. Yet, although the disaster of 586 B.C. was interpreted as a spurning of 'king and priest' (La 2^{6}), the priesthood steadily gained in independent power and authority, so that, unlike the monarchy, it was strong enough to survive the Exile.

It was the head of the Jerusalem priesthood who, before the Exile, might be described as 'chief priest' or 'high priest' or simply 'the priest.' Although his authority does not seem to have extended beyond the sphere of the Jerusalem Temple, he is plainly the precursor of the '**high priest**' of the post-exilic theocracy.

(*b*) Towards the close of the monarchical period the inevitable tension between the Jerusalem priesthood and the Levitical priesthood generally, seems to have been resolved temporarily by the ascendancy of the Levites. Thus, although the historical difference between the Jerusalem priesthood and the country Levites is perhaps reflected in the use of the term 'Levite(s)' alone of the latter (rather than 'the priests the Levites') in the Book of Deuteronomy, yet in 10^{8} (cf 21^{5} 33^{8-10}) it is the tribe of Levi as a whole who are specifically designated as bearers of the highest sacerdotal dignity. 'The Lord set apart the tribe of Levi to carry the ark of the Covenant of the Lord, to stand before the Lord to minister to him and to bless in his name, to this day.' That is to say, while the older strata in the book of Deuteronomy betray the historical division between the Jerusalem priesthood and the country Levites, undoubtedly the work as it stands in its final form, intends to teach that all Levites are priests in the fullest sense. On the other hand Josiah's reform had the undesigned effect of hardening the division. The 'priests of the high places' in Samaria were slaughtered (2 K 23^{20}) and the priests of the cities of Judah did not come up to the altar of the Lord at Jerusalem, thus frustrating the unifying provision of Dt 18^{6-8}. It is plain that Deuteronomy attempted to limit the exclusiveness of the Jerusalem priests and failed.

The prophets, by their comments on the priesthood, direct and indirect, give a picture of overwhelming influence and vested interest at this time. Theoretically the priests were to be without inheritance in the land (Dt 18^{1ff}), although personal ownership was not excluded (18^{8}, cf Abiathar, 1 K 2^{26}, Jer 32^{16ff}). And that there were rich and poor among the priests is shown by the fact that they were among the usurers in the time of Nehemiah (5^{12}). But in fact great numbers of them were unpropertied and reckoned among the *gērîm* (Dt 18^{6}). They were dependent upon the dues and offerings of the people. To them belonged, for example, the shoulder, cheek and maw of all offerings in cattle and sheep (18^{3}), together with the first-fruits of corn, must, oil, and sheepwool (18^{4}). Under them in the Temple were attendants or slaves who might be foreigners (cf Jos 9^{23}).

(*c*) Ezekiel, in his blue-print for the post-exilic theocracy (chs. 40–48), wished to strengthen the division between the Zadokite priests and the Levites, which growing Levitical power had tended to obliterate. He stipulated that none but the Levitical priests, the sons of Zadok (44^{15f} 43^{19}) should perform the priestly office in the Temple, on the ground that the Zadokites had kept the service of Yahweh pure when the Levites were guilty of apostasy. The latter were to take the place of foreigners (now to be banished from the Temple), to perform the menial tasks of the Temple, such as keeping the gates, slaughtering the victims, and cooking the sacrifices for the people. This represents the aggravation of an ancient division. The Levites had always enjoyed full priestly dignity and prerogatives outside Jerusalem. Now their former sanctuaries were denied to them and they were to be permitted no corresponding status in Jerusalem. Moreover, their inferior status was now written into a dogma. Henceforth, even if the limits were to be differently prescribed in P, there were to be exclusive grades within the priesthood. A strict hierarchy had come into being.

The disappearance of the king was of critical importance. The high priest had not yet succeeded to the priestly functions of the monarchy. But tradition required that the king should have place in the cultus. Ezekiel therefore speaks of a 'prince' (*nāśî'*) who is to stand in the inner gate and prostrate himself while the offerings are made by the priests. The priestly privilege is now inalienable, and the royal person merely has the right to be present.

(*d*) The achievement of the Jerusalem priesthood is often underestimated. After the fall of Samaria, it is probable that many of the traditions of the north came into their hands. Ultimately the whole Pentateuch and the historical narratives were preserved and taught by them. Ezra is described as a Zadokite (7^{1}), and if the law brought to Jerusalem by him and promulgated (Neh 8) may be identified with the legal part of the Priestly Code, we have a clue to the unremitting activity of these priests in Exile.

3. The Aaronite Priesthood.—The return from Exile affected the priesthood, as it affected every Israelite institution. At first there remained a hope of re-establishing the pre-exilic situation. The prophets Haggai and Zechariah thought of Zerubbabel and Joshua as succeeding to the royal and priestly prerogatives, although in fact Zerubbabel seems to have occupied a place more like Ezekiel's 'prince.' They are the two 'sons of oil' of Zec 4^{14}. In the reconstructed text of Zec 6^{9-14} they sit on thrones together, and there is 'peaceful understanding between them both.' History did not confirm this dream, and the present text of Zec 6 reflects the disappearance of the royal figure, and the inheriting by the high priest of all the priestly functions of the king. A succession of foreign regents made it impossible to allow the *de facto* ruler of the country to occupy the traditional position of the king in the Temple. Nehemiah thought it improper to enter the sanctuary (6^{11}).

Despite struggles for power, reflected in the priestly genealogies and legends (*e.g.* the story of Korah in Nu 16 etc.), the distinction between priests and Levites was made absolute, though not in the way that Ezekiel expected. The hardly won equilibrium is reflected in the Priestly Writing of the Pentateuch, which presents the highly organized, hierarchical system of the Second Temple, in terms of a comprehensive theory of its origin.

(*a*) The Jerusalem priesthood became exclusively Aaronic. That is, other families were co-ordinated with the Zadokites, although the main body of Levites remained subordinate. The new emphasis on Aaronic lineage was inevitable both theoretically and practically, and far-reaching in its implications. *Theoretically*, it meant that the priesthood could be regarded as Mosaic. It was Moses who installed Aaron and his sons (Ex 28^{41} 29^{44} $40^{12\text{ff}}$), Eleazar and Ithamar who perpetuated the family. It was Moses who ordained their vestments, functions, and rules in detail. This does not rule out the possibility that Aaron was, by long tradition, an early Israelite progenitor of priests, and there are a few signs that he may have belonged to Ephraim. The figure of Aaron also provided the type of the **high priest**, second only to Moses. *Practically*, it meant an adjustment to the contemporary situation. The theory fitted the facts. It is not improbable that when the Zadokite priesthood of Jerusalem had been exiled, the priests of Bethel took advantage of this situation to entrench themselves in Jerusalem. Bethel escaped the disaster of 586 B.C. It has been suggested with great plausibility that these priests traced their descent to Aaron, who was, in the tradition, responsible for making the golden calf, and thereby connected with the worship of Bethel and Dan. The Aaronites must have come into favour after 586 B.C., and it is probable that the underlying text of Zec 7^{1-3} $8^{18\text{f}}$ reflects this change. At the rebuilding of the Temple, men *sent to Bethel* to inquire whether the fast commemorating its destruction should be discontinued. Plainly the priesthood of Aaron had prestige. When the Zadokites returned to Jerusalem, all they could do was to secure a place alongside the entrenched Aaronites. The glorification of Aaron was tolerable because the theoretical advantages were protected by the criticism of the northern cultus implied in the story of the golden calf. This explains the careful preservation of so injurious a story about so important a figure. Aaron was received, but on stringent terms.

Now finally the priests became cultic specialists, whose primary task was the carrying out of sacrificial duties. Their teaching office, never wholly forgotten, was taken over more and more by the Scribes. It was the function of the Aaronite priests to perform the exclusively priestly tasks, as, for example, the sprinkling of blood in the sanctuary (Lv $1^{5,11,15}$), and to pronounce the priestly blessing (Nu $6^{22\text{f}}$). They were installed in office by a solemn rite of consecration. Anointing came to be restricted to the consecration of the high priest, a sign of high priestly succession (Ex 29^{7}). They were to be free from all bodily defects, and in a state of perfect ritual purity. Neh 12^{1-7} mentions twenty-two '**courses**' of priests for the time of Zerubbabel and Joshua. 1 Ch 24 has twenty-four divisions. The *War of the Sons of Light with the Sons of Darkness* has twenty-six divisions. The difference between the two latter is probably due to a difference in the calendar. The intention is the same, viz. that a priest would serve twice a year in the Temple for a period of one week. For the rest of the year he might live where he pleased. Supremely the priests existed to make atonement for sin, and, in the service of the cult, to maintain communion between the holy God and His people.

(*b*) Aaron at once became the type of the high priest, who was the characteristic expression of the power and significance of the priesthood in the post-exilic period. He was a phenomenon of Judaism. It was the **high priest** 'who secures through the cultus the strength for the people which it had previously been the duty of the king to create' (Pedersen). He had special vestments and exclusive duties. He alone was entitled to carry Urim and Thummim. He alone entered the Holy of Holies on the Day of Atonement, and made atonement for his own guilt, that of his house and of the people. His role of mediator was symbolized by the names of the children of Israel, which he bore upon his breastplate (Ex 28^{29}). As 'the priest who is greater than his brethren,' he was subject to stricter laws of purity. Later history shows that the narrower Zadokite family succeeded in claiming the high priesthood to itself. The Hebrew of Sir $51^{12\text{c}(9)}$ may reflect this *c* 200 B.C. The disturbances which preceded the Maccabaean Revolt broke this hold, and the Hasmonaean kings arrogated the high priesthood to themselves. If the Sadducees of NT times are Zadokites, it seems that the traditional Jerusalem priesthood regained control until they disappeared with the priesthood for ever in A.D. 70.

(*c*) The non-Aaronite Levites were now servants of the priests, on the theory that they had been given (*nᵉthûnîm*) to Aaron and his sons. They were divided into the three families of Gershon, Kohath, and Merari. That the **Kohathites** had charge of carrying the Tabernacle and its vessels when on the march (Nu $4^{5\text{ff}}$) probably means that they were entrusted with the honourable task of fetching and carrying in the sanctuary. When Levites are described as 'guardians' of the dwelling-place of Yahweh (Nu $3^{28,32}$ 31^{30-47}), this is probably the application of ancient terminology to door-keeping. We are not told plainly what the Levites have to do *when* the permanent sanctuary is set up. But it seems clear that their function was intermediate between the congregation and the priests. They were exempt from military service, installed by a solemn rite of laying on of hands (Nu $8^{5\text{ff}}$), and eligible for office, presumably at different times, from their thirtieth, twenty-fifth, and twentieth year (Nu 4^{3} 8^{24}, 1 Ch $23^{3,24,27}$) to their fiftieth year. They, like the priests, were supported by the carefully graded dues of the people.

The Chronicler emphasized the importance of **Singers** and **Doorkeepers** among the Levites. The three families of singers, Heman, Asaph, and Ethan (Jeduthun) were distributed among the Levite families Gershon, Kohath, and Merari (1 Ch $6^{18\text{ff}}$). Among them were the last remnants of the cultic prophets. From the period of the early monarchy, prophets had been closely associated with the priests at the sanctuaries, with similar functions. Both were experts in giving oracular direction; they differed in their *method* of seeking it. The greater mass of prophets, consistently denounced by the great canonical prophets for prophesying peace when there was no peace, had fatally lost prestige, when Jerusalem fell and the exile followed. The people were disillusioned. But the priesthood suffered no such embarrassment. All the conditions of the post-exilic period favoured their rise to complete power. It is probable that the remaining cultic prophets were absorbed into the minor orders of the priesthood, and are at any rate in part, to be identified with the personnel of the Temple choirs. And if in the time of Jeremiah, prophets and priests seem to share an equal dignity under the superintendent priest in the Temple (Jer 29^{24-28}), in the time of the Chronicler (*c* 300 B.C.) the prophet has become completely subordinate to the priest. On the other hand these guilds of singers will not be underestimated when it is realized that in these circles the psalms were preserved, collected, arranged and compiled, used in the Temple worship, and perhaps a few of them, composed. Some of the more menial work of the Levites was, by the time of the Chronicler, devolved upon a group known as **Nethinim** (q.v.). These are always distinguished from the Levites and are said, in a note of the Chronicler's, to have been given by David to the Levites, just as in P the Levites are said to have been given (*nᵉthûnîm*) to the priests (Ezr $2^{43\text{ff}}$ 8^{20}).

4. The Priesthood in the Intertestamental Period.—Within the last two centuries B.C., the power of the priests diminished, as the leadership of the people passed into the hands of the Scribes and Pharisees, now the effective teachers of the people. As late as *c* 200 B.C. it was natural for Ben Sira to glorify Aaron as the founder of the priestly line ($45^{6\text{ff}}$), and to sing a panegyric on Simon II., the son of Onias 'the great priest' who died in 195 B.C. This family, down to the murdered Onias III., was Zadokite. The passing of the reality of power from the priests is connected with the events that follow. The hellenizing designs of the Antiochene kings found a response in a succession of scheming claimants to the high priesthood, and finally in 152 B.C. Jonathan, the Hasmonaean king, assumed the high priesthood for himself and his successors.

Here the *Damascus Document* and the sectarian texts found at Qumrân are likely to throw new light on this part of the history of the Jewish priesthood. Where reconstruction must be tentative, and confidence is premature, it is possible only to suggest an interpretation which commands substantial agreement. Both the *Damascus Document* and the *Manual of Discipline* exhibit a strong Zadokite stamp. referring repeatedly to 'the sons of Zadok, the priests, the keepers of the Covenant,' and it is highly probable that the Teacher of Righteousness belonged to this family. It may be claimed that the following account does justice to a maximum amount of the evidence. The community which produced this literature first came into existence as a result of the menace of Hellenism and the resultant threat to the Jewish faith and institutions between 200 and 170 B.C., and the Teacher of Righteousness came into prominence probably at the time of the revolt against Antiochus Epiphanes. All the literature suggests that this was mainly a group of priests, loyal to the house of Zadok, organized to preserve their sacred traditions and privileges, distinguished from the Hasidaeans precisely by their Zadokite loyalty and character. The *War of the Sons of Light with the Sons of Darkness* suggests that they began by supporting the Maccabees. But they finally severed all connexion with them when, in 152 B.C., Jonathan seized the high priesthood. It was this event which transformed the community into a dissident sect. The Teacher of Righteousness with his followers went into exile, and later settled in Damascus, in the conviction that they were the 'community of the New Covenant in the land of Damascus.' To those years of exile belong some of the *Hymns*, the *Damascus Document*, and perhaps the *Habakkuk Commentary*. When the Hasmonaean dynasty came to an end, and they returned to Jerusalem, they found that the possessors of real influence were the lay Pharisees, while the Jerusalem priests were those priests who had been prepared to compromise, and for some reason not altogether clear, were now known as Sadducees. Their own future lay primarily at Qumrân where they established their centre. The Sadducees successfully retained control of the Jerusalem priesthood, together with the outward but unsubstantial trappings of power. See also DEAD SEA SCROLLS.

5. The Theological Contribution of the Priests.—(*a*) In the post-exilic period, the priesthood was responsible for a profound change of emphasis in the religion of Israel, with a corresponding change in the function of the priest himself. Judaism has been defined as 'a state constituted by the close alliance of race and religion, of civil and religious legislation under the same law, by the exercise of single authority in the hands of the high priest' (Lagrange). What the priests did was to mould the institutions and traditions of Israel into an impressive whole, designed for the maintenance of holiness in the community. This was understood to be given and directed by God, in every part, through his servant Moses (P), and again through David (the Chronicler), and therefore binding every detail upon every faithful Israelite. The principle of legitimacy was fundamental. Schism was abhorrent. Hence the Samaritans, who built their temple on Gerizim probably towards the end of the 4th cent., were regarded as outside the covenant community, and their priesthood illegitimate. Fundamental to the thought of the priests was the conception of sin everywhere implicit in the law and the cult, and the atonement which was dependent upon the hierarchy and its service. Ancient conceptions of holiness and sin, and the sacrificial ritual appropriate to them (ultimately Canaanite and indeed common to the near-east), were adjusted to more characteristically Israelite (Mosaic) principles of the moral law and of the character of the Living God, without a satisfactory unity ever being achieved. Nevertheless, the priests made sure that holiness and sin would be taken seriously. They understood that atonement must always be costly. They penetrated in the heart of their ritual to the mystery of vicarious sacrifice. Thus they understood man's need and the *principles* of the Divine method of meeting it, providing the terms, thought-forms and images with which to describe the more excellent way of the NT.

(*b*) The mediatorial rôle of the priest was also a principle of permanent importance, applied already within the OT to the place of Israel as a whole in the purpose of God. As a priest is to Israel, released from ordinary toil to concentrate on priestly ministry, so shall Israel be to the nations, which shall release her from manual toil for her ministry to the whole world (Is $56^{6\text{f}}$, cf Ex 19^{6}, 1 P 2^{4}).

(*c*) The high priest especially was regarded as a mediator and intercessor on behalf of the people. And just as the expectation of a perfect kingly rule was projected into the future in the form of a messianic hope, so later Judaism became familiar with the figure of a priestly advocate, who performed the high priestly function of intercession and mediation in heaven (*e.g.* Michael, Enoch, Elijah, Metatron). Whereas it might be expected that the demise of the monarchy and the dominant position of the high priest might influence the form of the messianic hope, in fact there was persistent resistance to the confusion of the royal and sacerdotal rôles. As it has been said, 'Judaism almost consistently refuses to portray a priest-messiah.' Test. Levi 18 is the main exception, and even this is not free of difficulties, since it may have come down to us in a Christian form, which understands both the priest of Levi and the king of Judah to be realized in the single figure of Jesus. Elsewhere and far more frequent in the Testaments is the double picture of an eschatological high priest from Levi and a Messiah from Judah, and the eschatological high priest takes precedence (Test. Jud. $21^{2, 4}$). It is undoubtedly this circle of ideas which provided the key-conception of the heavenly intercession of Jesus for the author of the Epistle to the Hebrews.

The Zadokites of Damascus abandoned the idea of a Messiah of Judah altogether. They speak of a Messiah 'from Aaron and Israel,' a phrase which sums up their own identity as the true Israel, mainly but not exclusively composed of priests. Messiah would be a priest of their own number. D. R. J.

PRIESTS (in NT).—'Priest' (Gr. *hiereus*) is employed in the NT to denote anyone whose office it is to minister in sacred rites, including sacrifice. **1.** It is used of a *Gentile* priesthood in Ac 14^{13} ('the priest of Zeus'), and also in Hebrews, in a transferred sense, as applied to the 'order of Melchizedek' ($5^{6, 10}$ 6^{20} 7^{1ff}), for Melchizedek, it is evident, was not merely a pre-Aaronic but a Gentile priest.

2. It is constantly employed to denote the members of the *Jewish* priesthood in their various ranks and functions. The ordinary officiating priests of the Temple come before us discharging the same offices of which we read in the OT. They burn incense (Lk $1^{5, 8}$), present the sacrificial offerings (Mt 12^{5}, cf Nu 28^{9f}), effect the ceremonial cleansing of the leper (Mt 8^{4}=Mk 1^{44}=Lk 5^{14}, cf 17^{14}). As in the OT, the priests are still the teachers of religion, though in the NT period this function has been largely taken over by the scribes (q.v.). The high priest (*archiereus*) appears as president of the Sanhedrin (Mt 26^{57} ||, Ac 5^{27} 7^{1} 23^{2} etc.) and as entering every year on the Day of Atonement into the Holy Place (the Holy of Holies; see TEMPLE) with his offering of blood (He 9^{25}). Most frequently of all the word occurs in the plural form 'chief priests' (*archiereis*), an expression that probably designates a high-priestly party consisting of the high priest proper, the ex-high priests, and the members of those privileged families from which the high priests were drawn (see *e.g.* Mk 15^{1}).

3. In the Epistle to the Hebrews *Christ* is described as both priest and high priest, but the fact that **Melchizedek** (q.v.), the chosen type of His eternal priesthood, is also described by the same two terms (cf 5^{6} with v.^{10}, 6^{20} with 7^{1}) shows that no distinction in principle is to be thought of, and that Christ is called a high priest simply to bring out the dignity of His priesthood—he is superior to angels, to Moses, and to Aaron. This conception of Christ as a priest is clearly stated in no other book of the NT, though suggestions of it appear elsewhere. In Hebrews it is the regulating idea in the contrast that the author works out with such elaboration between the Old and the New Covenants. He thinks of a mediating priest as essential to a religion, and his purpose is to show the immense superiority in this respect of the new religion over the old. He finds certain points of contact between the priesthood of **Aaron** and that of Christ. This, indeed, was essential to his whole conception of the Law as having a shadow of the good things to come (10^{1}), and of the priests who offer gifts according to the Law as serving 'a copy and shadow of the heavenly sanctuary' (8^{5}). Christ, *e.g.*, was Divinely called and commissioned, even as Aaron was (5^{4f}). He too was taken from among men, was tempted like His fellows, learned obedience through suffering, and so was qualified by His own human sympathies to be the High Priest of the human race (4^{15ff} 5^{1ff}). But it is pre-eminently by way of antithesis and not of likeness that the Aaronic priesthood is used to illustrate the priesthood of Christ. The priests of the Jewish faith were sinful men (5^{3}), while Jesus was absolutely sinless (4^{15}). They were mortal creatures, 'many in number, because they were prevented by death from continuing in office' (7^{23}), while Jesus 'holds his priesthood permanently, because he continues for ever' (v.^{24}). The sacrifices of the Jewish Law were imperfect (10^{1ff}); but Christ 'by a single offering . . . has perfected for all time those who are sanctified' (10^{14}). The sanctuary of the old religion was a worldly structure (9^{1}), and so liable to destruction or decay; but Christ enters 'into heaven itself, now to appear before the face of God for us' (9^{24}).

And this contrast between the priesthood of Aaron and the priesthood of Christ is brought to a head when Jesus is declared to be a priest—not after the order of Aaron at all, but after the order of Melchizedek (7^{11ff}). **'Order,'** it must be kept in mind, does not here refer to ministry, but to the person of the high priest—a fact which, when clearly perceived, saves us from much confusion in the interpretation of this Epistle. The distinctive *order* of Christ's priesthood is found in His own nature, above all in the fact that He is 'a priest for ever.' Christ as high priest is conceived as performing the same kind of priestly function as was discharged by the high priests of the house of Aaron, *i.e.* mediation, intercession, cleansing, the removal of sin and guilt—in brief, a ministry of atonement and reconciliation with God; but both His nature and the quality of His Person are quite different, and this completely alters the character of His acts, raising them from the realm of copies and shadows to that of absolute reality and eternal validity.

It is a mistake, therefore, to distinguish between an Aaronic priesthood exercised by Christ on earth and an eternal Melchizedekian priesthood exercised by Him in heaven; it is equally a mistake to attempt to confine His priestly ministry to a work of mediation and intercession that begins only after His exaltation. No doubt it is true that His priestly work is not consummated until He enters God's presence in the heavenly places, but all that the writer has previously set forth about His priesthood must be borne in mind. It was by His life on earth, by the obedience He learned and the human sympathy He gained, that Christ was qualified to be the high priest of men. Moreover, every high priest 'is appointed to offer gifts and sacrifices; hence it is necessary for this priest also to have something to offer' (8^{3}); this 'something' was Himself, yielded up on earth in a life of perfect obedience (5^{8f}) and an atoning death of spotless self-sacrifice ($9^{11-15, 28}$). It was with this priestly offering of His life and death, and in virtue of it, that Jesus entered into the presence of God (9^{24}) as the 'mediator of a new covenant' (v.^{15}) and the ever-living intercessor (7^{25}), and so secured for us our access with boldness to the throne of grace (4^{16} 10^{19-22}).

4. According to Hebrews, Revelation and 1 Peter, *the Church* is a priestly institution, and Christians are themselves priests. The OT idea that Israel was 'a kingdom of priests and a holy nation' (Ex 19^{6}) is transferred in precise terms to God's people under the New Dispensation. They are 'a royal priesthood' (1 P 2^{9}); Christ has made them to be 'a kingdom, priests to his God and Father' (Rev 1^{6} 5^{10}). Again, they are referred to by these same two writers as 'a holy priesthood' (1 P 2^{5}), 'priests of God and of Christ' (Rev 20^{6}). And though the author of Hebrews does not so describe them in set language, it follows from his way of speaking that he regards all Christ's people as priests. When he says in the passage last cited (10^{19-22}) that they have boldness to enter into the sanctuary by a new and living way through the curtain, it seems evident that he is thinking of those who draw near to God, by the blood of Jesus and in fulness of faith, as a company of worshipping priests; for under the old dispensation, which serves him at so many points as a type of the new, it was priests alone who could pass through the curtain into the Holy Place. It is the same idea, probably, that meets us in St. Paul when he speaks of our 'access' (Ro 5^{2}), our 'access in one Spirit to the Father' (Eph 2^{18}), our 'access in confidence through our faith' in Christ (3^{12}). And it is nothing more than a carrying out of this same conception that all believers belong to a holy priesthood, when the author of 1 Peter writes of the 'spiritual sacrifices' which they are called to offer up (1 P 2[5]); and Paul bids his readers to present their bodies a living sacrifice (Ro 12[1]); and the author of Hebrews bids his hearers offer to God the sacrifice of praise (13[15]), or declares that God is well pleased with such sacrifices as kindly deeds and gifts of Christian liberality (v.[16]); and the seer of the Apocalypse speaks of the prayers of all the saints as rising up like incense from the golden altar before the throne (Rev 8[3]).

5. It is a noteworthy fact that the NT never describes *the Christian ministry* as a priesthood, or the individual minister as a priest; there is no trace in the NT of the later idea that in the Lord's Supper a sacrifice of propitiation is offered to God, much less that this sacrifice is presented through the mediation of an official priesthood. The two terms 'presbyter' (*presbyteros*) and 'priest' (*hiereus*), which came in time to be identified, were at first kept absolutely distinct. Thus, as far as the NT is concerned, it is only in an etymological sense that it can be said that 'New presbyter is old priest writ large.' J. C. L.—**F. C. G.**

PRINCE.—This is the translation of a considerable number of Hebrew, Aramaic and Greek words, expressing different shades of meaning, *e.g.* 'chieftain,' 'ruler,' 'king,' 'governor,' 'noble,' 'deputy.' The rendering of these as 'prince' is to be found more frequently in AV than in RV and RSV. The main terms are: **1.** *śar* (cf Akk. *šarru*=king, in plural=viceroys). It is used for foreigners, *e.g.* representatives of a king (Gn 12[15], of Pharaoh), chieftains (Nu 22[8], of Moab), as leaders (1 K 20[14], RSV 'district governors'), and also of the chief butler and baker (Gn 40[2]), the keeper of the prison (Gn 39[23]), taskmasters (Ex 1[11]), chief eunuch (Dn 1[7]). With reference to Israelites, it is used of notables and chiefs (*e.g.* 2 S 3[38]), of officials of a town (Jg 8[6], of Succoth, RSV 'officials'). Later it is used of angelic beings (Dn 10[13, 20f] of the guardian angels of the nations; 12[1], of Michael). The feminine form *śārāh* is used of the wives of Solomon (1 K 11[3]), of Jerusalem 'princess among the cities' (La 1[1]), and is translated 'ladies' in Jg 5[29], Est 1[18] (in the latter RV has 'princesses'), and 'queens' in Is 49[23].

2. *naśî'*, 'one lifted up,' perhaps originally of tribal representatives (*e.g.* Gn 17[20] 25[16] and frequently in Numbers). It is applied to Abraham (Gn 23[6]), Shechem (34[2]), Sheshbazzar (Ezr 1[8]), and in Ezekiel to the rulers of Judah and other nations, and to the future head of the ideal state (34[24] of David, and cf 45, 46, 48). RSV sometimes uses 'leader'; AV, RV 'ruler.'

3. *nāghîdh*, 'one who is high, conspicuous,' is used frequently of a divinely appointed leader of Israel, *e.g.* David (1 S 9[16]), Jeroboam I. (1 K 14[7]). It is also used of the ruler of Tyre (Ezk 28[2]), the 'crown prince' (2 Ch 11[22]), the high priest (Dn 9[25]), the palace governor (2 Ch 28[7]), the keeper of the treasury (1 Ch 26[24]), the chief officer of the Temple (1 Ch 9[11], 2 Ch 31[13]). AV sometimes 'captain' or 'ruler,' once 'noble.'

4. *nādhîbh*=willing, hence 'a noble,' often used in the plural (*e.g.* 1 S 2[8], Ps 47[9] 107[40], etc.), and sometimes translated 'nobles.'

5. Other less frequent terms are *nāsîkh* 'anointed' or 'installed' (AV wrongly in Dn 11[8] for 'molten images'); *rāzôn* (Pr 14[28], cf the proper name Rezon, 1 K 11[23]) and the plural form *rōzᵉnîm* (from 'be weighty'); *rabh* meaning 'chief,' as in 'chief officers' (Jer 39[13]), and in titles *Rabshakeh, Rabsaris, Rabmag*; *rabhrᵉbhān* 'lords' (Dn 5[2f]); *shālîsh*, either Hittite *šalliš*=great, or 'third man in chariot,' often=adjutant (2 K 9[25]); *ḳāṣîn*, (cf Cadi), 'judge' or 'leader' (Jephthah); *sᵉghānîm*, of Assyrian or Babylonian officials, and of the heads of the Jewish community (Ezr 9[2], Neh 2[16]); *partᵉmîm* (Persian *fratama*), 'nobility.'

In Dn 3[2f, 27] 6[2, 4, 7] *'aḥashdarpᵉnayyā'* (Persian *kshathrapān*)=satraps (so RSV, RV; AV 'princes'); Ps 68[31] *ḥashmannîm*=bronze (so RSV; AV, RV 'princes'); Job 12[19] *kōhēn*=priest (so RSV, RV; AV 'prince').

The NT terms are **1.** *archēgos*, applied to Christ, Ac 3[15] (RSV 'author'), 5[31] (RSV 'Leader'), He 2[10] 12[2] (RSV 'pioneer'). **2.** *archōn*, used of Beelzebub (Mt 9[34] 12[24], Mk 3[22]), the princes of the Gentiles (Mt 20[25]; RV, RSV 'rulers'), the princes of this world (1 Co 2[6, 8]; RV, RSV 'rulers'), the prince of the power of the air (Eph 2[2]), and of Christ, prince of the kings of the earth (Rev 1[5]; RV, RSV 'ruler'). **3.** *hēgemōn*, used of Bethlehem (Mt 2[6]; AV, RV 'princes,' RSV 'ruler,' cf Mic 5[2] 'clans'; AV, RV 'thousands').

W. F. B.—**P. R. A.**

PRINCIPALITY.—This word is found in OT once only, in AV of Jer 13[18], where this meaning is improbable. AVm and RV have 'headtires' and RSV revocalizes the Hebrew and renders 'from your heads.' In NT 'principalities' is used in AV in Tit 3[1] of human authorities (RV and RSV 'rulers') and in AV, RV, and RSV in Ro 8[38], Eph 3[10] 6[12], Col 1[16] 2[15] of supramundane powers. The former use is found in AV in 2 Mac 4[27] (RV and RSV 'office') 5[7] (RV 'office,' RSV 'control of the government') and the latter also in AV in Eph 1[21] (RV and RSV 'rule') and in AV and RV in Col 2[10] (RSV 'rule'). In Jd [6] AVm and RV have 'principality' where AV has 'first estate' and RSV 'position,' in an allusion to the myth of the fallen angels.

PRISCA, PRISCILLA.—See Aquila and Priscilla.

PRISON.—Imprisonment, in the modern sense of strict confinement under guard, had no recognized place as a punishment for criminals under the older Hebrew legislation (see Crimes and Punishments, **9**). The first mention of such, with apparently legal sanction, is in the post-exilic passage Ezr 7[26]. A prison, however, figures at an early period in the story of Joseph's fortunes in Egypt, and is denoted by an obscure expression, found only in this connexion, which means 'the Round House' (Gn 39[20, 23] 40[3, 5]). Some take the expression to signify a round tower used as a prison, others consider it 'the Hebraized form of an Egyptian word,' but it may be from the Akkadian '*sa'ru*' (ring). Joseph had already found that a disused cistern was a convenient place of detention (Gn 37[24]; see Pit). The same word (*bôr*) is found in Ex 12[29] and Jer 37[16] in the expression rendered 'dungeon' and 'dungeon cells' respectively; also alone in 38[6] where it is rendered 'cistern' (RV 'dungeon'), Zec 9[11] 'pit.'

The story of Jeremiah introduces us to a variety of other places of detention, four being named in 37[15–16], all of which imply rigorous imprisonment. The first used denotes literally 'house of fetters' and is rendered as a verb in RSV 'imprisoned,' whereas AV, RV render 'in prison'; cf also Jg 16[21, 25], where Samson is bound with 'bronze fetters.' The second word is literally 'house of restraint' rendered 'prison,' as also in vv.[4, 18] 52[31]. The third is literally 'house of the pit,' or 'cistern' and is rendered 'dungeon,' qualifying the fourth word rendered 'cells' (AV 'cabins') probably 'vaulted room' (so *KB*). Some textual students treat the first and the fourth as glosses.

Jeremiah had already had an experience of an irksome form of detention, when placed in the stocks (20[2]; cf Ac 16[24]), an instrument which, as the etymology shows, compelled the prisoner to sit in a crooked posture. 2 Ch 16[10] 'in the stocks, in prison' is literally 'a house of the stocks' (so RVm; AV 'prison house'), while Jer 29[26] associates with the stocks (so RSV and RV for AV 'prison') an obscure instrument of punishment, variously rendered 'shackles' (RV), 'pillory' (*Oxf. Heb. Lex.*), 'collar' (RSV), and 'iron-collar, pillory' (*KB*).

In NT times Jewish prisons doubtless followed the Greek and Roman models. The prison into which John the Baptist was thrown (Mt 14[3, 10]) is said by Josephus to have been in the castle of Machaerus. The prison in which Peter and John were put by the Jewish authorities (Ac 4[3] 'in custody'; RV 'in ward'; AV 'in hold') was doubtless the same as the 'common prison' of 5[18] (AV, RSV; RV 'the public ward'). St. Paul's experience of prisons was even more extensive than Jeremiah's (2 Co 6[5]), varying from the mild form of restraint implied in Ac 28[30], at Rome, to the severity of 'the inner prison' at Philippi (16[24]), and the final horrors of the Mamertine dungeon.

For the *crux interpretum*, 1 P 3[19], see DESCENT INTO HADES. A. R. S. K.—**R. A. B.**

PRISON GATE, Neh 12[39] (AV).—See GUARD, GATE OF THE.

PRIZE.—See GAMES.

PROCHORUS.—One of the 'Seven' appointed by the Apostles (Ac 6[5]). Nothing more is known of him.

PROCONSUL.—The governor of a senatorial *province* (q.v.); the title usually means 'ex-consul.' It was originally two words—*pro consule*, meaning a magistrate with the insignia and powers of a consul. When the kingship was abolished in Rome it gave place to a rule of two men, not called by the now detested name, but named *praetores* ('generals') or *consules* ('colleagues'). As the Roman territory increased, men of praetorian or consular rank were required to govern the **provinces** (q.v.). During the Empire all governors of senatorial provinces were called proconsuls, whether they were ex-consuls and governed important provinces like Asia and Africa, or merely ex-praetors, like Gallio (Ac 18[12] AV **deputy**), who governed a less important province, Achaia. Except for the important provinces of Africa and Asia, it was only a title of courtesy.

A. So.—**J. S. K.**

PROCURATOR.—Meaning originally a steward of private property, a procurator had become the man to whom the Emperor assigned some special task. The task could vary from administering an important province to collecting a single tax. Whether the responsibility was great or small, he served as the personal representative of his master. And because procuring, whether of taxes or other property, was the chief function of this class of imperial servants, they were chosen from the *equites*, the knighthood of Rome, who in the early days of the Empire still retained a monopoly of skill as bankers and entrepreneurs. Until the days of Claudius (A.D. 41–54), when freedmen began to replace knights as functionaries, this class formed the mainstay of the principate.

Extreme differences of calibre were found among the procurators. Notably the governor of Egypt had to be a man of rich experience and sensitive to the diversified folkways of the people whom he governed. Egypt was the only imperial province administered by a procurator. Choice of an equestrian rather than a member of the senatorial class, as for all the other provinces, was due to exploitation of Egypt as the ruler's private estate much as in the days of the pharaohs and Ptolemies. Because of the importance of his office, the procurator commissioned to Egypt bore the distinctive title 'prefect.'

Ability to handle money was often the sole requirement of a procurator. Thus if he were assigned to collecting the tribute in an imperial province such as Syria he would not even need experience as a military commander; such a man could always ask help from the governor. With the title of *legatus*, 'legate,' the governor of such a province was of senatorial rank and had a strong force of legionaries under his command (see PROVINCE). But there were situations in which the procurator himself might be in command of an army contingent—if not of legionaries, at least of auxiliaries. That would likely be the case when the governor was a native whose loyalty could not be wholly trusted.

This was precisely the situation in Palestine during the period before the debacle of A.D. 70, except during intervals and in areas where Herodian princes performed the duties both of governor and procurator. Despite the tense situation, the Emperor's agents were often men with little sympathy for Jewish customs. Their choice and tenure seems to have been largely determined by the hope of curbing the rapacity for which their equestrian class was notorious. Of procurators mentioned in the NT, Pontius Pilate showed his contempt for Jewish custom by bringing the imperial standards with their images of Caesar into the Holy City and by minting coins with offensive symbols. Moreover, as a creature of Sejanus, commander of the praetorian guard and traitor to the Emperor, the matter of rapacity does not seem to have entered into his appointment. This factor should be considered in assessing the likelihood that Joseph of Arimathaea paid him a substantial bribe to obtain illegal custody of the body of Jesus. Felix and Festus, who figure in the narrative of the Apostle Paul, are among the officials cited by Josephus as responsible for stirring the Jews to revolt.

The misleading title 'governor' is given these procurators by the NT writers. It occurs also in Josephus and in the Hebrew of the Mishnah. The term is correct after A.D. 70 when procurators did indeed have these enlarged powers; thus its use in these writings is a hint as to the date when they were compiled. But during the earlier period the actual governor was not the procurator but the high priest. The relation between the two was much like that formerly in India between British 'resident' and maharajah. The high priest outranked the procurator even when, as with Caiaphas and his two predecessors, he himself was an appointee of the procurator. When in Rome the procurator remained a mere knight, but the high priest received the courtesy honours of a Roman senator. Therein the status of Judaea was comparable to that of other Roman provinces.

The procurator of Judaea had in addition to his duties as chief tax collector the curbing of sedition, for which he was given the *jus gladii*, 'power of the sword.' To make this power effective he was given command of one or more cohorts of auxiliaries. The high priest was in no way thereby deprived of his former rights to execute those who offended against Jewish law. Indeed the appointment of procurators carried with it an enlargement of the powers of the high priest. What is meant by bestowing *jus gladii* on the procurator is that transference of the governorship of the province from Herodian princes to the Jewish high priest did not include also the task of repressing sedition that they had possessed. Thus the handing over of Jesus to the procurator for execution signified that his offence was not covered by Jewish religious law but concerned imperial security. See ROMAN PUBLIC LAW. J. S. K.

PROFANE.—'To profane' is 'to make ceremonially unclean,' 'to make unholy.' And so a 'profane person' (He 12[16]) is an 'ungodly person,' a person of common, coarse life, not merely of speech. RSV "irreligious.'

PROGNOSTICATOR.—See MAGIC, DIVINATION AND SORCERY, and STARS.

PROMISE.—1. Despite the lack in Biblical Hebrew of a word specifically denoting 'promise,' the idea is strongly present in the OT with its reiterated emphasis upon Yahweh's devotion (*ḥesedh*) and faithfulness (*'ᵉmûnāh*) and upon the fulfilling of the covenant (*bᵉrîth*) obligations. The verbs 'to say' (*'āmar*) and 'to speak' (*dibber*) together with their nouns 'speech' (*'ōmer*) and 'word' (*dābhār*) were in themselves sufficient to convey the force, in such theocentric and ethically focussed literature, of a solemn promise, cf 2 S 7[28], '. . . thou art God, and thy words are true, and thou hast promised (literally 'spoken') this good thing.' Of special significance in this connexion is the use of the verbs 'to keep' (*shāmar*) and 'to do' (*'āśāh*), cf Dt 23[23], 'You shall be careful to perform (literally 'you shall keep and do') . . . what you have promised (literally 'spoken') with your mouth.' The adequacy of what is thus solemnly uttered is further supported in Mt 5[37] (cf Ja 5[12] and T. W. Manson, *The Sayings of Jesus*, 1949, 159), and is noteworthy in view of the tendency in Hellenism and Rabbinic Judaism to use a stronger form of expression, cf the employment of ‘ to trust ’ (*bāṭaḥ*) in the sense of ‘ to promise,’ which also has been taken over into modern Hebrew.

2. Whilst instances thus occur of man’s promises to man (*e.g.* Neh 5^{12f}, Est 4^{7}) and of man’s promises to God (*e.g.* Dt 23^{23} and cf Dt 26^{17f}, where the assurance is reciprocal), of paramount interest are God’s promises to man. These are especially to be noted in the instances of the words spoken respectively to Abraham, to Israel, and to David. In the case of Abraham the Divine promise has a threefold reference—to a numberless posterity, to the gift of Canaan as the ‘ promised land ’ and to the blessing of his descendants (Gn $12^{2f,\,7}$ 13^{14-17} 15^{18} 17^{4-8} 22^{17f}, cf its reiteration to Isaac and Jacob in Gn 26^{3-5} and 28^{13-15}). Under the terms of the Sinaitic covenant with the tribal brotherhood of Israel at the mountain of God (Sinai according to J and P ; Horeb according to E and D) Yahweh promises that they shall be his ‘ own possession ’ if they will obey His voice and keep His covenant (Ex 19^{5}). To this Old Covenant also the prophets refer (*e.g.* Jer 7^{23}, Ezk 16^{8} Am 3^{1f}), and Yahweh’s faithfulness to His promise is frequently affirmed (*e.g.* Dt 4^{31}, cf Ex 34^{6}) as well as His power to fulfil His promises (*e.g.* Ps 93^{5}, where for ‘ testimonies ’ or ‘ promises ’ RSV renders ‘ decrees ’). The promise to David relates to an ‘ *everlasting* covenant ’ with Yahweh, whereby His throne was to be established for ever, a promise eventually to be fulfilled in the coming of the true Messiah of the House of David, His descendant and ideal successor, cf *e.g.* 2 S $7^{12,\,16}$ 23^{5}, Ps $89^{3f,\,19-29}$ 132^{11} and note the important discussion of these and related passages in A. R. Johnson, *Sacral Kingship in Ancient Israel*, 1955, 14–27, 58 (where ‘ testimonies ’ (*‘ēdhôth*) is shown to be synonymous with ‘ promises ’), 97 f, 118 f. Elsewhere in the OT the promises to Abraham and to David are echoed and occasionally connected (*e.g.* Jer 23^{5f}, Ezk 37^{24-2}). The Prophetic writings are of their very nature shot through with the promises of God, and two others of them which call for mention here concern the New Covenant (Jer 31^{31-34}) and the pouring out of God’s spirit on all flesh (Jl 2^{28-32}).

3. The principal term in the NT for ‘ promise ’ (verb *epangellesthai*—there used only in the middle voice, noun *epangelia*) in classical Greek means ‘ announce,’ often in the sense of giving prior notice of intention, which in the setting of public life may have reference, *e.g.* to the proclamation of authority, to the threat of legal proceedings, or to the promise by a magistrate on taking office of a distribution of food. Almost invariably it there appears to have been limited to human declarations, whereas, apart from a few instances (*e.g.* Mk 14^{11}, 2 P 2^{19}), in NT usage it has to do with the assurances of God, an emphasis which may well have come about through the kind of phraseology current amongst the rabbis in their discussions concerning the Divine promises. cf G. Dalman, *The Words of Jesus*, translated by D. M. Kay, 1909, 103.

4. The OT promises outlined above, and thus far not realized (*e.g.* He 11^{13}, cf 1 P 1^{10ff}), are in the NT regarded as being fulfilled in Jesus Christ (2 Co 1^{20}, cf Ro 15^{8}), an emphasis which informs the primitive preaching (*i.e.* the *kērygma*, cf C. H. Dodd, *The Apostolic Preaching and Its Developments*,[2] 1944, 7–35), being indeed central in NT apologetic (*e.g.* Ac 2^{39} 13^{32f}, Ro 1^{1f}). A distinctive note of the First Gospel is that Jesus is the Messiah of prophecy, the events in the life of Christ being regarded as having taken place ‘ to fulfil what the Lord had spoken by the prophet ’ (Mt 1^{22} 2^{15}, cf $2^{17,\,23}$ 8^{17} 12^{17} etc.). Of special importance here is the promise made to David (Ac 2^{30}, cf Ps 132^{11}), Peter arguing on the basis of Ps 16^{10} that David ‘ foresaw and spoke of the resurrection of the Christ ’ (Ac 2^{31}), and Paul declaring that of David’s ‘ posterity God has brought to Israel a Saviour, Jesus, as he promised ’ (Ac 13^{23}, cf Ro 1^{3}). Earlier in his speech at Pentecost (Ac 2^{16-21}) Peter accounts for what has just taken place as the fulfilment of Jl 2^{28-32}, and in conclusion of his speech makes it clear that ‘ this gift of the Holy Spirit ’ is the ‘ promise ’ (cf Eph 1^{13}, ‘ the promised Holy Spirit ’) made available for such as repent and are baptized in the name of Jesus Christ (Ac 2^{38f}). The promise made to Abraham occupies a prominent place in Paul’s consideration of faith. Abraham was ‘ fully convinced that God was able to do what he had promised ’ (Ro 4^{21}), in the matter both of a multitudinous posterity (Ro 4^{17f}) and of the gift of Canaan (Ro 4^{13}, where ‘ the world ’ in current Rabbinic thought was but an extension of ‘ the promised land ’), and ‘ his faith was “ reckoned to him as righteousness ” ’—so ‘ It will be reckoned to us who believe in him that raised from the dead Jesus our Lord ’ (Ro 4^{22ff}). Likewise regarding the third constituent of this promise (Gal 3^{8}), the condition for receiving the blessing of Abraham is faith (Gal 3^{9}), a blessing which is extended in Christ Jesus to the Gentiles and equated as it were with ‘ the promise of the Spirit ’ (Gal 3^{14}), the argument being clinched in Gal 3^{29}. In He 8^{8-12} the author quotes *in extenso* Jer 31^{31-34} as the ‘ better promises ’ on which is enacted the better covenant which Christ mediates (He 8^{6}), surpassing the promises underlying the Old Covenant of Sinai, cf He $8^{7,\,13}$. Special attention also is in this epistle given to the promise as having an eschatological reference under the aspects of entering God’s rest (He 4^{1-11}, arguing from Ps 95^{7-11}), of the heavenly city (He 11^{8-10}, on the basis of Gn 12^{1-8}), and of the ‘ kingdom that cannot be shaken ’ (He 12^{26ff}, citing Hag 2^{6}). Eschatological expectation similarly underlies the ‘ precious and very great promises ’ of 2 P 1^{4}, relating to ‘ new heavens and a new earth in which righteousness dwells ’ (2 P 3^{13}, cf Is 65^{17} 66^{22}).

E. T. R.

PROPHECY, PROPHETS.—The more scholars learn about OT prophecy—and their knowledge has grown immensely during the last fifty years—the more they feel its unique power. Psychology, anthropology, sociology, archaeology, the history of religions, and other relevant disciplines have helped us to understand various aspects of prophecy, but they have not solved the riddle of prophecy itself. The theologian who knows how to use the resources of history and linguistics is still the best interpreter of prophecy. Our aim here is to summarize what is known about (1) the history of OT prophecy, (2) the prophet as a religious functionary (3) prophetic inspiration, (4) the distinctive beliefs and attitudes expressed in the prophetical literature, and (5) the transition from OT prophecy to NT prophecy.

1. History.—The four books of ‘ canonical ’ prophecy —Isaiah, Jeremiah, Ezekiel, and the Minor Prophets —are a definitive collection recognized as Scripture early in the 2nd cent. B.C. and not subject to structural alteration after that time. Presumably the terminal editing was accomplished about 200 B.C. The material appears to have been produced between the 8th and the 3rd cents. B.C. Thus, on the one hand, G. E. Wright’s confident assertion that the Latter Prophets ‘ were completed in their present form at least by the fourth century B.C.’ cannot command unqualified assent, and, on the other hand, extensive insertions in the 2nd cent. or later are precluded.

The finest declarations of the OT prophets belong, on the whole, to the earlier half of the five-century period we have indicated, and in the latter half apocalyptic, a derivative form of prophecy, comes increasingly to the fore. Both individually and collectively the canonical prophets were creative in the highest degree, and much that they taught has lasting value and admits of universal application ; yet they are not, save in the broadest way, comparable with modern thinkers, critics, and reformers. They did not invent prophecy, nor did prophecy cease with them. Hence its history consists of three parts : (1) the pre-canonical, (2) the canonical, and (3) the post-canonical.

(1) What we are told about **pre-canonical prophecy** is rarely history in the strict sense. In the historical books the prophet is doubtless often a stock figure who speaks at the narrator’s bidding and in the narrator’s words. We need not question the historicity of the more sharply

defined pre-canonical prophets, such as Samuel, Nathan, Elijah, and Micaiah, but the complete authenticity of the utterances ascribed to them is not assured. Despite these difficulties, it is evident that prophecy is an ancient institution in Israel. Amos' words (2^{11-12}) imply that there were legitimate prophets before him; and, in fact, something like a continuous line may have extended as far back as to Moses (Dt 34^{10}), though scarcely still farther to Abraham (Gn 20^7). Probably the Israelites, like the peoples around them, made no absolute distinction between the prophet on the one hand and the priest, the diviner, the poet, and the charismatic political leader on the other. Such prophets as Miriam, Aaron, Deborah, Samuel, Nathan, Elijah, and Elisha illustrate the combination of several gifts or functions in one person. The cultic connexions of prophecy have been emphasized in many modern studies and the division of primitive Semitic prophets into two classes, the interpreters of signs and the ecstatics, has met with some favour. It has been suggested that the more obviously ecstatic practices were learned from the Canaanites. Exercises of this type are particularly conspicuous in the Samuel-Saul complex of traditions, and there may be some significance in the simultaneous appearance of prophetic communities known as **'sons of the prophets,'** for a more suitable means of promoting ecstatic prophecy cannot readily be imagined. Pre-canonical group prophecy is one of the enigmas of the OT. If it preserved Yahwistic traditions and effected a synthesis of ecstatic and non-ecstatic prophecy, it was also in a position to foster an infatuated nationalism and to sponsor a perilous syncretism. In the absence of positive information one suspects that it had a multiple influence, with both good and bad results.

(2) The exact number of prophets represented in the **canonical** collection cannot be determined. Most of the books contain considerable material of unknown authorship, but this supplementary matter is now handled less cavalierly than was formerly the custom. Whereas it was once thought that the application of critical axioms could separate the genuine nucleus from the accretions that had obscured it, less confidence is felt to-day in a documentary criticism based on Western presuppositions. Form criticism and traditio-historical method have established new objectives for research in the prophetical writings; the compilation of the books is viewed more as an organic process than as a series of accidents; and the present interest in theology has helped to stop undue fragmentation. The OT cares more about content than about authorship, and we are slowly learning to follow its lead. Even when the author of a prophecy can be named with almost complete certainty, we know relatively little about him.

Malachi sounds like a fictitious name formed by the simple capitalization of *mal'ākhî* 'my messenger' in Mal 3^1. The book itself may be assigned to the first half of the 5th cent. There was a prophet Jonah in the days of Jeroboam II. (?782/81–753 B.C.), but he did not write the Book of Jonah, which is a late polemical tract (4th cent.), aimed at the rigidities of prophecy in its decadence. Save for these, the names attached to the prophetical books presumably represent historical persons, each of whom is likely to have had some part in the production of the book with which he is credited. Amos, a Judaean, prophesied in the Kingdom of Israel, and for all we know, elsewhere as well, close to the middle of the 8th cent. At the same time or shortly thereafter Hosea's voice was heard. Isaiah's career covers roughly the latter half of the 8th cent., and the most suitable setting for Micah's prophecies is the crisis of 701 B.C. The dangers and calamities of 627–586 B.C. bred a diversity of prophets: Zephaniah, Nahum, and Habakkuk, all of whom prophesied before the close of the 7th cent.; Jeremiah, whose work spans the whole unsettled era; and Ezekiel, who, according to the dates given in his book, was active from 593–571 B.C. Cyrus' conquest of Babylon in 539 B.C. is the key to the dating of the Second Isaiah's oracles, which survive in Is 40–55. Haggai's prophecies were uttered in 520 B.C. and Zechariah's (Zec 1–8) in 520–518 B.C. About 400 B.C. will serve as an approximate date for the Third Isaiah (Is 56–66). Obadiah's book was written in the 5th cent., Joel's in the 4th, and Zechariah 9–14 in the 3rd. Insofar as the prophets and their annotators have supplied the material with dates, the information given appears to be substantially correct. Where definite chronological intelligence is lacking, only an inferential date is possible, and therefore further debate may be expected.

The difference between canonical prophecy and 'false' prophecy cannot be defined with precision. The notion of **'false' prophets** originates in the conflict between 'true' prophets and their opponents. The record was written by the 'true' prophets and their sympathizers. Are the 'false' prophets misrepresented? Judged by the disasters they assisted in precipitating, they deserved all that the canonical prophets said of them. They had, nevertheless, their own kind of sincerity and their own way of being loyal to the covenant. They simply mistook the clamour of their own desires for the promptings of the Divine Spirit. Jeremiah and Ezekiel acutely brought to light the nature and source of the self-deception that characterized false prophecy. The evil may have been aggravated by reckless reliance on drugs, strong drink, and auto-suggestion for the simulation of ecstasy. In any event, the externals of behaviour were not decisive. It was the prophet's dedication that counted, and when we try to measure it, the OT rules of thumb (Dt 13^{1-5} 18^{21-22}) are of limited assistance.

(3) In 1 Maccabees (4^{46} 9^{27} 14^{41}) prophecy is dormant, if not extinct. This was perhaps the general belief regarding it in the 2nd cent. Eventually the true date of its supposed termination was forgotten. Josephus (*Against Apion*, I. 7 [40, 41]) recognizes no prophets, and indeed no Scripture, after Artaxerxes I. (464–424 B.C.). Subsequent opinion is vague, but at least some authorities (*Baba Bathra* 12ab) conclude the prophetic age with the destruction of the First Temple (586 B.C.). The effect of these artificial views was that **prophecy no longer appeared under its own name.** He who would formerly have assumed the character of a prophet was now an apocalyptist, a psalmist, or a sage. To be sure, we read of an occasional prophet (Josephus, *The Jewish War*, II. xiii. 5 [261–263], VI. v. 2 [285–288]), but such figures were never taken seriously by the nation as a whole. The Book of Daniel, written some decades after the adoption of the prophetical canon, illustrates the real interests of those who still practised some semblance of prophecy. Eschatology had become their main concern. Preoccupation with its intricacies had a regrettable influence on the study of prophecy. For example, the interpretation given the canonical prophets in the Dead Sea commentaries is dictated by the convictions and expectations of a sect, to the total disregard of what the oracles might have meant when they were delivered. Nevertheless, even eschatological interpreters are prophets in a manner of speaking. Thus, attenuated rather than extinguished, OT prophecy closed its career.

2. The prophet as a religious functionary.—The priest is inescapably attached to the cult, apart from which, no matter what the origin or theory of his office, he cannot act as a priest. In contrast, despite the resourceful arguments of many very competent writers in the present century, the prophet's dependence on the cult is still somewhat less than self-evident. If the respective vocations and interests of priests and prophets are no longer represented as totally incompatible, scholarship should be grateful for the more correct view that now prevails, but OT theologians cannot be altogether comfortable when some of their colleagues seem bent on assimilating prophecy completely to priesthood or, if they do not go quite so far, converting prophecy into an almost purely cultic activity.

There are, admittedly, many passages that appear to indicate a more than casual relation between prophets and the cult. Indeed, the information we have is so copious and so various that it rules out at the start a radical simplification of the question. Reserving the pentateuchal references to prophecy for later consideration, we shall limit ourselves here to the post-Mosaic history. Joshua, as the successor of Moses, has direct communication with Y″. The absence of prophets from the traditions about Joshua is not difficult to explain, for he exercises the essential faculties of prophecy and is in fact what we have learned to call a ‘ sacral king.’ The word ‘ prophet ’ as applied to Deborah (Jg 4[4]) and the anonymous prophet of Jg 6[8] is more an adjective than a noun and in any case indicates no link with the cult. The record is remarkably silent regarding prophecy in the age of settlement and consolidation. At the end of this time, however, the volume of data abruptly increases.

The traditions assembled in 1 Samuel present a composite portrait of Samuel, some features of which seem at first sight more historical than others. Efforts to separate the historical from the legendary and tendentious have had little success, in the absence of really reliable criteria. The narrative as a whole is credible, consistent, and intelligible if we regard it as a reflection of the period in which Samuel led the nation. It is not impossible that he actually was everything from an obscure village seer to an omnicompetent ‘ sacral king.’ At any rate, much of the OT vocabulary of prophecy is applied to him: various traditions describe him as a ‘ man of God ’ (1 S 9[6]), an apprentice priest who experiences an audition (1 S 3), a *rō'ēh* ‘ seer ’ (1 S 9[11]), an intercessor (1 S 7[8] 12[19–25]), and finally a *nābhî'* ‘ prophet ’ (1 S 3[20]) familiar with groups of ecstatic prophets (1 S 10[5]) and on one occasion conducting or supervising a session of ‘ prophesying ’ (1 S 19[20]). This diversity suggests that in Samuel's time two kinds of prophecy were coalescing. On the one hand, there was traditional Hebrew prophecy, divisible into (*a*) cult-bound and cult-controlled divination, for example inquiry by means of the ‘ ephod ’ (1 S 23[9–12]), and (*b*) ‘ psychic ’ forms of prophecy—second sight, nocturnal visions and auditions, and the like—which could be, and probably often were, practised independently of the cult. On the other hand, the impact of a more manifestly ecstatic prophecy, foreign to the old Yahwism, was being felt; and while this variety of prophecy may long have had an assured place in the Canaanite cults, its association with the Yahwistic cult was new, incomplete, and tentative. The conflict between the old prophecy and the new was to continue until the end of the monarchy. Thus the editorial observation in 1 S 9[9], notwithstanding the sceptical view that some scholars take of it, may accurately represent the truth. It is true, as the note states, that in popular usage the term ‘ prophet ’ eventually supplanted the term ‘ seer,’ but we must add that the meaning of ‘ prophet ’ was altered in the process.

With the introduction of the monarchy the structure of the state assumes a more recognizable form, in which a place should have been assigned to the prophets if they were cultic functionaries. Prophets are absent from the lists of the court officials of David (2 S 8[15–18] 20[23–26]) and Solomon (1 K 4[2–19]); priests, on the contrary, are included. The frequent Deuteronomistic phrase ‘ the priests and the prophets ’ (2 K 23[2], Jer 26[7f, 11, 16] 29[1]), so far from proving that the position of the prophets was comparable throughout with that of the priests, could with equal justice be held to demonstrate the opposite. ‘ Prophets ’ and ‘ priests ’ balance each other in Hebrew verse or are coupled for rhetorical purposes (Is 28[7], Jer 4[9] 5[31] 6[13] 23[11], Hos 4[4–5], Mic 3[11], La 4[13]), but this means no more than that the two groups belong to the same society. The prophets constituted a class or order in the commonwealth without, for that reason, possessing a more cultic character than the people, the princes, the elders, or the wise men (Is 3[2], Jer 18[18] 26[12] 29[1]). The use of the Temple for prophecy is well attested. There the least sacerdotal of the prophets could count on an atmosphere and an audience, and that is doubtless, in the main, why the Temple—or some local sanctuary—is so often the scene of prophecy. So far as we can determine, the prophets did not normally live in the Temple or any other sanctuary: if ‘ the sons of Hanan the son of Igdaliah, the man of God ’—apparently a prophetic group—had a chamber in the Temple (Jer 35[4]), so had Tobiah the Ammonite (Neh 13[4–9]), and both cases were exceptional. If our sources are trustworthy, the prophets who frequented the holy places were, at least in certain instances, under the supervision of the priests (Jer 20[1–6] 29[24–28], Am 7[10–17]), who manifest a professional hostility to them. To be sure, a priest or a member of a priestly family could also be a prophet, witness Jeremiah, Ezekiel, and probably Zechariah. After the Exile canonical prophecy is much more friendly towards the cult than before. For all that, the existence of a stylized cultic prophecy (reflected, it is alleged, in some of the Psalms) and the eventual absorption of prophecy into the Temple music are to be viewed as interesting matters of speculation rather than certainties of science. In short, if prophecy has a cultic setting much of the time, there are also occasions on which the cultic background cannot be discerned (2 S 12[1–15], 1 K 21[17–29] 22[5–28], 2 K 22[14–20]), and therefore while, for quite patent reasons, prophecy utilizes cultic facilities, it remains an essentially autonomous force, never wholly explicable in cultic terms.

Coming as it does from different periods and sources, the evidence scattered through the Pentateuch is of varied character. In the complex figure of Balaam (Nu 22–24) several prophetic techniques are combined, the most fundamental and original of which is perhaps the art of the poet and the orator, the masters of cursing and blessing. Possibly Miriam was a prophetess (Ex 15[20]) primarily in the sense that she possessed the power to curse Israel's enemies. However, it is much more likely that the details of such narratives do not rest wholly on a factual acquaintance with the methods of early prophecy, but conform in part to later patterns. The most interesting example of the blend of old and new is, of course, Moses. It is quite credible that the historical Moses had all the recognized charismata, including that of prophecy. At all events, a wide range of powers is attributed to him. Moses' peculiar intimacy with God is emphasized even in one of the most primitive pentateuchal traditions (Ex 33[7–11]); hence there may be some historical basis for the claims made in Ex 7[1–2], Nu 12[6–8], Dt 34[10], as well as in a fourth passage, Nu 11[24–30], which differs from the others in being deeply coloured by a late conception of the manner in which prophets were inspired. Private divination and like practices are vehemently condemned (Ex 22[18], Lv 19[26, 31] 20[6, 27], Dt 18[10–14]) in the pentateuchal codes, which significantly ignore prophecy proper save in Dt 13[1–5] 18[15–22]. If prophecy was mainly a cultic affair, one is at a loss to find a reason for this curious silence, which contrasts strikingly with the numerous instructions given to the priests.

Semantic analysis affords a second approach to prophecy. The basic word for ‘ prophet ’ in the OT as a whole is *nābhî'*, and its normal Greek equivalent is *prophētēs*, which means essentially ‘ one who tells forth, announces, proclaims.’ *Nābhî'* has precisely this sense in Ex 7[1], where Aaron's task is to utter the words that Moses has given him. Here the term is purely functional and implies neither the existence nor the non-existence of special endowments in Aaron. It is not improbable that this is the oldest sense of the word, which accordingly is best viewed as an active (‘ crier,’ ‘ announcer,’ ‘ messenger ’), not a passive (‘ a person who is called,’ ‘ recipient of a vocation ’), noun derived from the Akkadian *nabū*, ‘ call.’ From the noun a Hebrew verb has arisen. Two stems of the verb occur, the niph'al and the hithpa'el, and it is impossible to detect any radical difference of meaning between them. Each of these stems has the double sense of ‘ to act like a prophet ’ and ‘ to act as a prophet.’ One can act like a prophet by exhibiting or simulating the curious behaviour that is regarded as evidence of the possession of the Spirit. This aspect of prophecy is, however, not always prominent, and the verb can mean merely ‘ to do the work of a prophet,' 'to prophesy.' The nipḥ'al is transitive in Jer 14^{14} and other passages in the same book, the hithpa'el in Jer 14^{14} and 1 K 22$^{8, 18}$.

While there is really no synonym for 'prophet,' parallel terms have a limited currency. Examined singly they give us little insight into prophecy, but in the aggregate they prove to be surprisingly instructive. For example, Elijah is directed to anoint his successor Elisha (1 K 19^{16}), and a later prophet commends himself to his audience on the ground that Yahweh has anointed him for the work he is doing (Is 61^{1}). For this reason or in consequence of some specific call or commission, the prophet is the deity's confidential 'servant' (1 K 14^{18} 15^{29}, 2 K 9^{36} 10^{10} 14^{25}, Is 20^{3} 42^{1} 49$^{3, 5f}$ 52^{13} 53^{11}), and in the plural the title repeatedly designates the prophets as a class (2 K 9^{7} 17$^{13, 23}$ 21^{10} 24^{2}, Jer 7^{25} 25^{4} 26^{5} 29^{19} 35^{15} 44^{4}, Ezk 38^{17}, Am 3^{7}, Zec 1^{6}, Ezr 9^{11}, Dn 9$^{6, 10}$). The word 'messenger' (2 Ch 36^{15f} Hag 1^{13}) characterizes the prophet a little more sharply. In Jer 23$^{18-22}$ it is asserted, if only indirectly, that the true prophets have access to Yahweh's presence and hear His decisions; they are the first to learn of His secret intentions (Am 3^{7}). They have even more exalted status in terrestrial courts, where as mentors and critics of the king and his subordinates they are at times among the most powerful of public figures. Seeing what is hidden from other men, they can be called 'seers' (*ḥôzîm, rô'îm*) as well as 'prophets' (Is 29^{10} 30^{10}), and occasionally a prophet of considerable eminence is styled 'the Seer' (2 S 24^{11}, 2 Ch 16$^{7, 10}$ 19^{2}). The phrase 'man of God' is commonly applied to prophets: Samuel (1 S 9^{10}), Shemaiah (1 K 12^{22}), Elijah (1 K 17, 2 K 1), Elisha (2 K 4, 5, 6, 7, 8, 13), and unnamed prophets. The sense 'prophet' probably still clings to this expression when it is used of an angel (Jg 13$^{6, 8}$), Hanan (Jer 35^{4}), Moses (1 Ch 23^{14}, 2 Ch 30^{16}, Ezr 3^{2}, Ps 90^{1}), and David (2 Ch 8^{14}, Neh 12$^{24, 36}$). 'Man of (? the) Spirit' is employed as a parallel to 'prophet' in Hos 9^{7}.

One way of getting help in a crisis was to approach or summon a prophet and address a question to him (Jer 38^{14}) or inquire of him (1 K 22^{7}). The folk-prophets may normally have prophesied in response to a particular inquiry. We have no means of ascertaining what proportion of canonical prophecy originated in this manner. In any case, for the canonical prophets and their aggressive predecessors the delivery of 'words,' 'burdens,' and 'oracles' was rather a response to God than a reply to His people, and therefore, more often than not, the prophet takes the initiative and transmits the message, regardless of the mood of the recipients (Ezk 2$^{5, 7}$ 3^{11}).

Another form of aid rendered by the prophets in time of difficulty was their expert **intercession**. The prophet's familiarity with God and His concerns gave him a special competence in the delicate business of restoring Israel's 'rightness' (*ṣᵉdhākāh, ṣedhek*), which could be impaired by disloyalty on the part of the people. The procedure of the law courts furnished a model for prophetic mediation, which was directed towards the vindication of the just party by his own demonstration of his 'justness' and not by the mere verdict of a judge acting as an administrator of objective law. Yahweh is, to be sure, the ultimate judge in all tribunals, but He may also be the plaintiff, the injured party, whose interests the prophet, as judge, is bound to protect. In accordance with this conception of justice, the prophet, while still in some fashion the judge who brings the litigants together, is free either to double as the voice of the prosecution and state Yahweh's case (*rîbh*) against His people (Hos 4$^{1-6}$ Mic 6$^{1-5}$, Is 5$^{1-4}$) or to take the part of the defendant in an effort to obtain for him the clemency that will remit or mitigate the penalty (Gn 18$^{22-33}$ 20$^{7, 17}$, Ex 32$^{11-14, 31-34}$, Dt 9$^{25-29}$, 1 S 12$^{19-25}$, Jer 7^{16} 11^{14} 14$^{11-12}$). Many immaterial variations of the prophet's rôle are possible; for example, in Hab 1$^{2-4, 12-13}$ 2$^{1-4}$ he pleads for the deliverance of the righteous from the injustice they suffer at the hands of the ungodly, in Jl 2$^{12-17}$ he urges the people to contrition, and in Hos 11$^{8-9}$ he is the spokesman of Yahweh's compassion. So strong was the belief in the efficacy of the prophets' intercession that reliance on the advocacy of the prophets Moses and Samuel (Jer 15^{1}) and the quasi-prophetic mediators Noah, Daniel, and Job (Ezk 14^{14}) could go too far. If at times people leaned too heavily on the prophets, the excess was understandable. Save perhaps for the king, nobody in the community was comparable with the prophet. It meant a great deal that he knew, or could find out by some means or other, what was going to happen; but his service was not complete when he had done a thing that, after all, the least remarkable diviner or necromancer was credited with the power to do: besides being a man whose vision triumphed over the restrictions of time and space, he was capable of interpreting the future that God had shown him and so guiding the people back to 'the ancient paths, where the good way is' (Jer 6^{16}) and can always be found by penitents who seek it resolutely. He was the custodian of the national conscience and the guardian of those virtues by which the covenant was maintained.

One cannot help perceiving the intimate tie that exists between the office of prophet and the office of king. They may at one time have been identical, that is to say they may have originated, as separate offices, in a division of functions formerly combined in the same person, the charismatic head of the community, whatever the name by which he was known. The king's sacerdotal functions, delegated to full-time priests for the ordinary operation of the cult, were exercised by the king himself in extra-ordinary circumstances (2 S 6$^{12-15}$, 1 K 8). By an analogous differentiation, the actual practice of prophecy may have fallen increasingly into the hands of qualified functionaries until the bond between king and prophet became purely vestigial. Hence Saul's association with the prophets (1 S 10$^{11-12}$ 19^{24}) and David's prophetic endowments (2 S 23$^{1-2}$) are conceivably relics of an earlier time, when prophecy was concentrated in the king's person. If the king was in theory the chief of prophets as well as the chief of priests, we need no longer be puzzled by the royal habit of overruling and disregarding the prophets. Notwithstanding the hypothetical character of these observations, they are in general agreement with views that are held widely to-day, and there are at least some grounds for postulating the emergence of prophecy from a primitive organic totality that embraced kingship, priesthood, and prophecy.

In a survey of the entire range of prophetical functions, with their ideological concomitants, a touch of the Hebrews' unaffected realism is helpful. The prophet was a person who possessed certain powers and skills that enabled him to serve as an intermediary between God and the people. No ancient society could have done without him. Some of the OT prophet's traits, habits, and methods were common to prophets, diviners, soothsayers, and magicians the world over. His gifts were an accepted reality, and his fellow Israelites found them useful, dangerous, or merely distasteful, according to the requirements and interests of the moment. At its ordinary level, prophecy was a distinct, but not tightly organized, profession, into which men were drawn, as they were into other occupations, by aptitude, association, opportunity, and training. It had points of contact with, if not a recognized position in, the national cult, and it is extremely unlikely, despite the relative silence and obscurity of the OT on this point, that prophecy lacked forms of initiation, admission, and consecration. The prophetical art was a combination of technique and inspiration, either of which might eclipse the other in a given prophet. Yet technique was never wholly uninspired, and inspiration of a sort could be induced by means of technical devices. Thus, the importance attached to a personal vocation cannot easily be estimated. The most eminent of the canonical prophets appear to have been called to the prophetic life as individuals, but a specific vocation may not have been

PROPHECY, PROPHETS

considered indispensable. In any event a man proved that he was a prophet by doing what was expected of a prophet, and if he played the part convincingly, he was probably not often asked how he had come to assume it. The prophet, in brief, was an acknowledged organ of society, and prophecy was an established institution. The traditional conception of prophecy both aided and hindered the canonical prophets.

3. Prophetic inspiration.—Prophetic inspiration received a certain amount of critical attention while the OT was still being written. Almost from the very start, the representatives of the movement that has given us the prophetical books of the OT were challenged by practitioners of a different sort of prophecy. The former found theological and ethical reasons for condemning the latter: intemperance (Is 28[7]), venality (Mic 3[5, 11]), irresponsibility (Zeph 3[4]), untruthfulness (Jer 5[31]), and plagiarism (Jer 23[30]) are among the offences of which the unfaithful prophets are said to be guilty; and on the theological side it will suffice to mention the severe denunciations attributed to Jeremiah and Ezekiel, according to which the prophets in question are devoid of authority (Jer 5[13] 23[21] 27[15]) and, so far from being Yahweh's accredited agents, have been misguided by Him (Ezk 14[9], cf Jer 23[15]). There is also a psychological verdict: false prophecy is self-deception, and the word that is passed off as Yahweh's is really the product of the prophet's own psyche (Jer 14[14] 23[26, 31], Ezk 13[2f, 17]). In its own way, the OT has anticipated the main drifts of subsequent discussion, which has pursued either the inspired word or the inspired person, but rarely both. Patristic, mediaeval, and reformation writers were content to trace the design implicit in the prophetic word. Criticism, textual, literary, and historical, and psychology, experimental and analytical, have taught us the importance of the minds and personalities that operate in prophecy. We have much to gain from a synthesis of the two ways of thinking about prophetic inspiration.

On prophetic premisses, **inspiration** presupposes an inspirer. A simple and immovable certitude with regard to the covenant underlies all the utterances of prophecy. They came from Y″, and the mark of their authenticity was their agreement with the faith long since defined by what God had done to and for the nation. The originality of the most gifted and devoted prophets, and of the 'true' prophets generally, consists in the conclusions they drew from axioms that neither they nor their hearers questioned. The covenant, with its boundless implications for the dedicated and obedient, was not the only criterion by which inspiration could be tested. The prophetic mind was capable of unsparing self-criticism and exercised a vigilant censorship over the ideas and impulses that came to it. It is to a prophet's credit that he is cautious and hesitant in his response to Yahweh's approach (Ex 3[11] 4[1, 10, 13], 1 S 3[2-9]) and shrinks from his vocation (Is 6[5], Jer 1[6, 17]). Jeremiah denies himself the gratification of an immediate retort to Hananiah and does not reply until Yahweh has unmistakably spoken (Jer 28[11-12]). Here we have an arresting contrast between the 'false' prophet's precipitate opportunism and the 'true' prophet's patient submission to the discipline Yahweh imposes on those whom He inspires. A second proof of inspiration was therefore to be found in the prophet's sincerity, his self-denying identification of himself, on the one hand, with Yahweh and, on the other, with the people; his personal suffering and the violence done to his private inclinations were a guarantee against the aberrations of desire and pride. With the corroboration he received from the covenant and from his own commitment, the prophet had all the confirmation his oracles required. The only language that will adequately convey what has happened to the prophet is the language he habitually employs: 'thus saith Yahweh,' 'Yahweh made it known to me' (Jer 11[18]), 'the word of Yahweh came to me' (Jer 1[4], Ezk 3[16], Zec 4[8]), 'Yahweh said to me' (Hos 3[1]), 'Yahweh spoke thus with me' (Is 8[11]), 'I saw Yahweh' (Am 9[1]), 'Yahweh showed me' (Am 7[1, 4, 7] 8[1], Zec 3[1]), 'Yahweh took me' (Am 7[15]), 'the Spirit entered into me' (Ezk 2[2]), 'lifted me up' (Ezk 3[12]), 'fell upon me' (Ezk 11[5]). In speaking of his inspiration he may trace it to the Word or to the Spirit; but these are not necessarily antithetical terms, whatever the preference of the prophet or the period. How intricate the problem of prophetic inspiration is on its purely historical side anyone can discover by turning to Mic 3[5-8], where the prophet lumps together prophet, seer, and diviner in a comprehensive denunciation and then describes himself as 'filled with strength (? that is), the Spirit of Yahweh, and judgment, and power, to tell Jacob his transgression and Israel his sin.' Whether or not the words meaning 'that is *or* with the Spirit of Yahweh' are original, Micah has his own equations, his own locutions, and his own antipathies. It would be rash to generalize concerning any term from the use that is made of it in this passage. In Mic 3[5] probably three voices are represented: Yahweh speaks to the prophet, the prophet speaks for Yahweh, and the editor speaks for the prophet. To indicate, here and in scores of other places, the limits and degrees of inspiration is a task of surpassing delicacy, and we have no mind to attempt it. It seems sufficient to say that the prophetical books, like the OT generally, spring from a prophetic community, in which men who are widely separated by history may yet do a common work.

The entire psyche apprehends the word, which is spoken of as seen (Am 1[1], Is 2[1], Jer 38[21], Hab 1[1]), felt (Jer 20[9]), and even tasted (Jer 1[9] 15[16], Ezk 3[1-3]). So far as the subject matter is an index to the appositeness of technical terms, the word *ḥāzôn* 'vision' could often be exchanged, without perceptible loss, for a word having primary reference to the sense of hearing (Is 1[1], Jer 23[16], Hos 12[10], Ob 1[1], Hab 2[2f]). *Rā'āh* 'see' tolerates as its object 'what [Yahweh] will speak' (Hab 2[1]). The niceties of sense are not important to the prophet, who is indifferent to Yahweh's mode of approach and welcomes the 'word,' the 'vision,' or any other communication as a rational imperative.

The **psychological study of prophecy** might teach us something about the human aspect of inspiration were it not for the severe handicaps under which all such effort labours. The prophets are too remote from us to be studied with modern devices. The qualified psychologist normally has no training in the Biblical disciplines. Thus far we have had nothing but fragmentary suggestions that for the most part leave prophetic inspiration where they found it and make us feel that the enigmas of the prophet's inner life still await clarification: Allwohn's psychoanalytical explanation of Hosea in terms of repressed sexuality, displacement, ecstatic identification with Yahweh, and, in the end, sublimation; Broome's verdict that Ezekiel, 'a true psychotic (unrecognized in his day and looked upon as an ecstatic) capable of great religious insight,' was afflicted with 'paranoid schizophrenia'; Jung's characterization of the prophets as intuitive introverts; Hölscher's Wundtian treatment of prophetic phenomena; Povah's discoveries in the depth psychology of the prophets; and odd bits of scholarship in which it is argued that the prophets were psychotics, geniuses, mystics, poets, or something else.

A candid inquirer cannot dismiss cavalierly the possibility that some of the prophets—indeed perhaps all of them—had psychic gifts. The question arises very forcibly with respect to Samuel (1 S 9[20]), Jeremiah (Jer 28[16-17]), and Ezekiel (Ezk 11[13]), and they are only three of the many who are reported to have exercised what the relatively new science of parapsychology calls the 'psi capacities.' Regrettably, the usefulness of parapsychology in the exploration of the prophetic psyche is not as yet very evident. The fulfilment of the parapsychologist's most enthusiastic dreams of scientific achievement would simply open the vast question of the relation between the prophet's extrasensory knowledge and other factors in the complex phenomenon of prophecy. Prediction is not the whole of prophecy, and although the prophets may have been favoured with a natural aptitude for penetrating the future, they do not stand or fall by this alone, nor do they permit us to doubt that the future they see is the moral consequence of a present and a past that have been put to unworthy uses. The OT forecasts could be proved inferior, as regards accuracy, to modern prognostications made under parapsychological observation, and the prophets would still be the prophets. Prophecy offers an interpretation, not a photograph, of things to come.

It can easily be shown that the prophets do not exhibit psychotic symptoms. The psychopath is a person who has repudiated the world that the rest of us recognize and has devised a way of living and thinking in defiance of facts. So far from being indifferent to what is happening about them, the prophets respond promptly and appropriately to changes in their surroundings. They deal with life on the widest scale and yet are never betrayed by the immensity of their commissions into regarding themselves as the centre of all things. Their personalities do not deteriorate, their utterances do not become fantastic, and their reactions to adversity are balanced and constructive. Genuine disorders of the mind—schizophrenia, paranoia, involutional melancholia, and manic-depressive insanity—simply do not appear in any convincing fashion. Ezekiel, the prophet who comes closest to being demonstrably a psychotic, is vindicated by the conventions of prophecy, which are not violated in his wildest flights. The prophet's fellow-Israelites expected him to be queer, unpredictable, and histrionic, and there were times when, in order to teach his lesson, he had to meet this expectation in a very extravagant manner. Unlike the psychotic, he always knew how far he was permitted to go and where dramatics ended and madness began. In the context of their faith, their vocation, and their culture, the prophets were as normal as a man can be without ceasing to be creative, and this may be taken to mean that if they were measured by our standards of psychic health, which are of debatable relevance here, substantially the same judgment would follow.

Two terms now current among psychologists are possibly of considerable relevance: *autism* (in the good sense) and *eidetic imagery*. The former enables us to visualize the prophet as a man who is preoccupied, at a certain time, with certain specific interests, and, much like a modern scientific or artistic observer, but with different presuppositions, is apt to find a pertinent communication in any object or incident, that is, to see what he is looking for in what comes his way. Sometimes the prophet will experience, at the slightest sensory stimulus or even without an external stimulus, a vision of some duration and intensity, and we can say that one of the reasons why this has happened to him is that he needed it, wanted it, and expected it. To make such a statement is not to preclude inspiration, but merely to indicate what we should probably observe in an inspired prophet if we knew him well enough and had been with him long enough. A closely related phenomenon has been discovered in the eidetic images that some people have the ability to produce. These images are, save for the use they make of sensory memories, independent of the senses. A prophet who had a talent for eidetic imagery could construct a vision that for him would be as lifelike as an actual spectacle and would therefore be as truly seen. The two phenomena here discussed go far to explain a third phenomenon, **ecstasy**.

Enthusiastic prophecy, in the literal sense of the adjective, has already come to our notice. In extreme instances, it appears to be a profound psychophysical disturbance, in which the prophet's volition is completely suspended and he becomes the helpless organ of the deity that has taken hold of him. Ordinarily this is what we mean by 'ecstasy.' The scholars who maintain that it is indigenous to Syria and Asia Minor are probably right in their interpretation of the scanty evidence we possess, much of which (*e.g.* the contributions of Justin, Celsus, Lucian, and Apuleius) is from the first few centuries of the Christian Era and therefore can serve only indirectly to fix the locality in which ecstasy was an original part of religious practice. A little information can be garnered from more ancient sources, but for the most part we must rely on our sense of what is primary and what is secondary in OT religion. Wen-amon, writing in the 11th cent. B.C., relates that while he was at Byblos a member of the king's entourage—apparently not a professional prophet—remained a whole night (?) under the influence of the god and delivered a message that opened the way to the completion of Wen-amon's business. The hieroglyphic determinative employed in the text represents a man in an attitude that an ecstatic prophet might well assume. The Mari specimens of prophetic utterance may belong to the same species of prophecy. *Maḫḫu* priests, who seem to have been ecstatics of a sort, are mentioned in Akkadian documents; of the content and style of their oracles we are totally ignorant. The Ugaritic literature contains no undisputed evidence of prophecy. The OT is far more informative than any of the extrabiblical sources. When Ahab's prophets (1 K 22$^{5-28}$), approximately 400 in number, are set side by side with the 450 prophets of Baal (1 K 18$^{17-40}$), it requires no great acumen to perceive that both bands are ecstatic. These, of course, are not the only passages in which the ecstatic state can plainly be discerned. The Hebrews can scarcely have been acquainted with it before their migration to Canaan, where they adopted it, to a considerable extent, out of deference to Canaanite culture. This, at any rate, is a tenable opinion as to the genesis and growth of ecstatic prophecy. In the absence of a better hypothesis, we shall have to be content with it.

The earliest examples of ecstatic prophecy among the Israelites long antedate the first of the canonical prophets; hence, insofar as ecstasy became normal in Hebrew prophecy, its assimilation was completed by the time canonical prophecy arose. There were doubtless many folk-prophets who regarded it as indispensable and carefully cultivated it. So close an attachment to it is not the rule with the canonical prophets. Their stand, if they had one, must be inferred partly from their oracles, partly from their beliefs regarding their respective vocations, and partly from their controversies with the folk-prophets. Some oracles reflect violent emotion (Is 21$^{1-10}$, Jer 4$^{19-29}$) or frenetic activity (Ezk 21$^{14-22}$); they compel us to grant that canonical prophecy may occasionally be ecstatic prophecy. At the same time, no canonical prophet adduces his ecstasies as such in confirmation of his claim to be accepted for what he believes himself to be, nor does he taunt his adversaries with their possession or lack of any psychic gift, but only with its misuse. The truth is that modern scholarly interest in ecstasy would have been puzzling to any prophet, true or false.

If we are to retain the word at all, the utmost semantic latitude is desirable. Achelis' comprehensive definition of ecstasy as 'the peculiar intensification of our psychic powers above the normal level' accommodates all the forms that occur in normative OT prophecy. The most characteristic form in canonical prophecy is a devout preoccupation with the affairs of the covenant, a concentration of the prophet's psychic forces that gives him a rare receptivity and unifies his scattered and conflicting human capacities. Ecstasy is any psychophysical condition that is compatible with inspiration. The two terms must not be used loosely to mean the same thing. Ecstasy is something man feels. Inspiration is something God does.

4. The distinctive beliefs and attitudes expressed in the prophetical literature.—All prophetic teaching is occasional or existential teaching. It is given under the stimulus of a situation and is meant primarily to show how the corporate righteousness is to be maintained in face of the unfamiliar difficulties of the situation. Hence the total teaching of the prophets does not appear in any single place, and prophetic doctrine is never presented as a carefully articulated whole.

There is only one God in prophecy. The Second

Isaiah's vigorous assertions of Yahweh's uniqueness make it plain that this prophet was a monotheist of the most uncompromising sort. The monotheistic language interpolated in the writings of the pre-exilic prophets may have been influenced by his lively satire. His predecessors were perhaps not his equals as theologians, but their rejection of other gods was as vehement as his. The man-made character of the idols is emphasized in Am 5[26], Hos 8[5] 13[2] 14[3], Is 2[8, 20] 31[7], Hab 2[18–19], Jer 1[16] 16[19–20], and in these and like passages we are told again and again that the idols are things of wood and stone or gold and silver ; the prayers offered to them are futile ; they have no life ; they are worthless ; they are helpless ; and they can neither supply man's common needs nor succour him in distress. The only conclusion we can draw from the evidence before us is that the prophets, despising idols as impotent and allowing the divinities they represented no existence save insofar as a name was thought to give a semblance of reality, utterly repudiated the common ancient belief in a multiplicity of gods. The prophets concede nothing to idols (Is 41[24, 29]) : they exhaust the resources of the Hebrew tongue in support of their conviction that all gods but Yahweh are false, illusory, and altogether less real than the vain devotion of their worshippers.

God is depicted—necessarily and therefore without apology and without explanation—as a Person whose behaviour is broadly similar to man's. This does not mean that He is merely a magnified human being. Quite as little does it mean that man is an incomplete god. There is a generic difference between God and man, and we are confronted with a forcible statement of it in Is 31[3] :

> The Egyptians are men, and not God ;
> And their horses are flesh, and not spirit.

The Divine spirit withers defenceless flesh as a hot wind withers grass (Is 40[7]). It is precisely this spirit that is absent from the idols (Jer 10[14], Hab 2[19]). Man is not master of his own affairs, but must appeal to God to rectify his blunders (Jer 10[23–24]). God is familiar with the operations of man's mind and conscience, as man is not (Jer 17[9–10]). His thoughts and ways are higher than mortal thoughts and ways (Is 55[8–9]). His presence embraces the most distant parts of the universe (Jer 23[23–24]). Like the Hound of Heaven He pursues man to the bounds of the created world (Am 9[2–4]). Rare are the gifts of the Prince of Tyre, but he is still ' a man and no god ' (Ezk 28[2, 9]).

The presupposition underlying all the rich diversity of prophetic speaking and writing is that Yahweh, the only God, possesses unique power, goodness, and devotion. The prophets cast no light on the origin or signification of His personal name. Its linguistic history did not interest them. Far more were they concerned with the God who had long ago revealed Himself under this name, and the individuality of the name blocked any tendency they may have had to convert Him into a Prime Mover or an impersonal cosmic Law. They had, in fact, no such inclination. Nowhere do they resolve Him into an abstraction. The Second Isaiah's sublime poems are perhaps the best example of the essential concreteness of prophetic thought. No matter how deep his awareness of what we should call God's transcendence, God remains for him the paramount Person (Is 40[21–23]). Antinomies were reconciled by a stubborn insistence on God's wholeness.

Yahweh has demonstrated His power by making the world, and He continues to demonstrate it by governing the world. The prophetic teaching with regard to creation will occupy us presently. What must now be stressed is the complete absence of recognized limits, physical or moral, to God's power as the prophets know it (Is 40[12–17]). Nations are judged, but it is God who judges them, and He Himself is never measured by any standard. He can do anything, He may do anything, and He has the right to do anything. The problems arising out of the Divine omnipotence, unpredictability, and unanswerability go for the most part unnoticed in the prophetical literature. At times a modern conscience is gravely disquieted by the apparently unreflecting and unblushing vigour of the language the prophets employ when they want unresponsive Israel to understand that God can be terrifying in His fury and irresistible in the defence and vindication of His honour, majesty, and glory. The prophets acknowledge Yahweh as the wielder of supreme and universal power. They do not question the ethics of His self-glorification. He is free to choose His own means of making the nations realize that He is Yahweh (Ezk *passim*). The Assyrian, the rod of Yahweh's anger, will suffer punishment in his turn (Is 10[5–19]). Babylon is utilized for a certain end and then cast aside. God is accountable to nobody but Himself for conduct that in a human being would be called ruthless ; but God is God, and the prophets see no reason why He should not exercise the prerogatives of the universal King (Is 6[5] 33[22] 43[15] 44[6], Zeph 3[15], Jer 10[10], Ob [21], Mal 1[14], Zec 14[9, 16f]). They are not very fond of the title *King*, perhaps because they were too familiar with kings and had often been disappointed in them ; yet there was no better way to designate Yahweh if one wanted to emphasize His sovereign authority. When sheer power was the primary consideration, the prophets found a vehicle for their meaning in the image of the potter and the clay. The clay does not talk back to the potter ; it owes everything to him and may not presume to question his creative will (Is 29[16] 45[9–13], Jer 18[6]). The language of Jer 27[5] may not be Jeremiah's, but the idea belongs to him and to the prophets in general : ' *I* have made the earth—more particularly, the men and the beasts that are on the face of the earth—by My great strength and by My outstretched arm, and I will give it to whom I see fit.'

It is no denial of this absolute power, nor even a qualification of it, to testify that goodness always accompanies it. Here again God and man are far apart :

> Man is bowed down, and men are brought low,
> And the eyes of the haughty are humbled.
> But Yahweh of hosts is exalted in justice,
> And the holy God shows Himself holy in holiness.
> —(Is 5[15–16])

There can be only one reason for God's unfailing goodness : '. . . let him who glories glory in this, that he understands and knows Me, that I, Yahweh, practise devotion, justice, and righteousness in the earth ; for in these things I delight, says Yahweh ' (Jer 9[24]).

As Yahweh's righteousness, in a manner of speaking, softens His power, so His devotion softens His righteousness. He is not strictly, unbendingly just with His people. This is not a weakness, but rather a loyalty that looks in vain for a comparable steadfastness on the part of Israel. The reason for Israel's election lies concealed in the inscrutability of a God who does not have to justify Himself in the eyes of humanity. There may have been in Israel some recollection of covenants offered to other nations and rejected by them. Amos (9[7]) may have something of the sort in mind when he holds all the nations of his narrow world to one basic law of justice (1[3]–2[16]). Yet even Amos knows, so far as we can see, of no enduring historical covenant save the one linked with the exodus from Egypt (2[9–10]). Election is, in any case, the distinguishing mark of Israel, and the prophets perpetually exhort God's people to be worthy of God's favours. God's anger springs from frustrated love, a love that can be likened to a father's attachment to his son (Hos 11[1], Jer 31[20] ; Yahweh's love is like a mother's [Is 49[15]]) or a husband's to his wife (Hos 1–4, Ezk 16[23]). It is ' an everlasting love ' (Jer 31[3]) that can never be wholly extinguished (Hos 11[8–9]), even when Israel wantonly forgets it and exploits it. The prophets, in their frank anthropomorphism, do not shrink from portraying God as an almost doting Lover who, in the very act of enumerating His kindnesses and Israel's offences, pleads for the gratitude and the fidelity that are His due. If the tie is

PROPHECY, PROPHETS

weakened or dissolved, it is not God who is at fault (Mic 6[3]). There is an organic relation between the Divine love and the Divine power. Only a God who can do as He wills can will to love in this fashion (Hos 11[9]). At the moment we need not inquire into the ultimate implications of Yahweh's love for creation as a whole. The special position of Israel is candidly accepted by the prophets for what it is. What is it but the least explicable of mysteries, a gift bestowed with unbelievable generosity on a people who must forever be reminded that they have never deserved it?

A brief way of putting what we have said in the last few paragraphs is to confess that Yahweh is 'the Living God.' He has imparted, and is continually imparting, His life to all things :

. . . the spirit takes its departure from Me,
And I am the Maker of the breath each creature breathes.
—(Is 57[16])

Rarely and then only in passages that may be secondary (Hos 1[10], Is 37[4, 17], Jer 10[10] 23[36]), do the prophets characterize Him as 'the Living God,' but, whether or not they used the phrase, they were enthusiastic exponents of the idea. They have a mature doctrine of creation in which Yahweh as the Giver of life is central and exclusive. The Second Isaiah, with his technical term for 'create' (*bārā'*) and his repeated claim for Yahweh's recognition as the sole creator, is introducing no novelties. Centuries before, if not at the very beginning, Israel had learned to worship Yahweh as Creator. Many indeed had confused Him with the forces of nature. Among the capital achievements of the prophets was their correction of this pantheistic tendency. They declared that Yahweh was not merely the producer and dispenser of nourishment for living things : He was also a God of justice and devotion. Life was not simply survival. For human beings it was participation in the ethical (Am 5[14]), affective, and purposive aspects of creation (Is 40[28–31]). Yahweh had made the world primarily to be the seat of human life and culture (Is 45[18–19]) and the scene of guided events. The Canaanites, and innumerable Israelites with them, imagined that the created world was a gigantic womb made fruitful by the recurrent, unvarying exertions of the gods, unless the gods by some accident were negligent. According to the prophets it was the sphere of Divine action directed towards an end that man could understand (Is 40[27–28]) and obediently seek. Life in its fulness, therefore, is lost by alienation from the unique absolute Possessor of life (Jer 2[13]), and there is but one way to renew it : seek Him and live (Am 5[4]). Estrangement from God, even though it may not issue immediately in physical death, is an aimlessness that is worse than death. Creation has a goal, and the proper rôle of man is to contribute to the attainment of the goal. God is the author of the evil as well as the good of creation (Is 45[7]). How evil can exist without malice on the part of the Creator the prophets are at no pains to inform us. Their realism is satisfied to deal with the world as it is and to derive all things from God. Things happen as they do because God causes them to happen that way. If we look closely enough, we can see what He is about. We can discern Him behind everything. The prophets must have realized that God sometimes acts indirectly. It remains true that they habitually skipped the multitude of intermediate causes and traced each new impulse in creation to Yahweh.

In a universe completely subject to Yahweh man cannot occupy an independent position. The prophets have no distinctive creation myth, notwithstanding the glimpses of such myths we get in Ezekiel (28[12–15]) and the Second Isaiah (Is 45[12, 18] 48[13] 51[3, 9, 13, 16]). The traditional anthropology is part of the prophetic heritage. The origin of sin is a speculative problem about which the prophets show no curiosity. Ignoring it, they concentrate on man's corruptibility in small things and large. Again and again, on the petty scale and on the grand scale, man is exposed as a creature gifted with a fatal ability to foul the world that God has given him. His boundless perversity supplies the prophets with inexhaustible material for their denunciations. It is a theme from which man's actual conduct and condition never allow them to turn. Isaiah handles it with brilliant eloquence. Among the prophets he has no peer in the art of contrast, as anyone can discover by reading his skilful description of degenerate Jerusalem (1[21–23]) and his punning Song of the Vineyard (5[1–7]). The latter rises to a superb climax, the force and compactness of which are merely suggested by this feeble rendering :

And he expected honesty, but behold homicide
And righteousness, but behold wretchedness.
—(Is 5[7])

Isaiah's authorship of Is 2[22] is debatable :

Have done with man,
In whose nose is breath,
For what does he amount to?

He may have used this extreme language in a moment of bitterness, but despair of man is not really characteristic of the prophets. Any such abandonment of man would have been a betrayal of the God who had sent them, not only to rebuke the sinner, but also to recall him to a forgotten allegiance. God desired the repentance of the offenders, not their death (Ezk 18[32]). He would not relinquish the ideal for the sake of which He had created them. No matter what they were actually, they were always potentially what He had at the beginning designed them to be. He would betroth them to Himself in righteousness, justice, devotion, mercy, and faithfulness (Hos 2[19–20]). They might eventually comprehend that He cared more for them than for anything they possessed (Hos 6[6]). Man as such is neither perfect nor perfectible. Man as the servant and son of God has incalculable possibilities. The prophets are not pessimistic about him.

Surely these considerations have some bearing on the mystery of **election**, and here we can go completely astray if we are not extremely wary. The canonical prophets were not shallow nationalists to whom the service of the national deity was a crass matter of *quid pro quo*. We are unjust to them if we make no distinction between prophetic Yahwism ana popular Yahwism, but we do them a greater injustice when we confuse them with the internationalists and humanitarians of our own day and underrate their loyalty to nation, land, state, and cult. All four were organs of the covenant. Israel rightly cherished them as assurances that Yahweh was implementing election and giving it concrete effect. Yahweh's preference for Israel is taken for granted by all the prophets, even by Amos (3[2]), who in this question as in most others seems, of all the prophets, the least prone to sentiment. It was not for them to determine whether or not Yahweh had chosen Israel. The service they could and did render was to confront Israel with the inexhaustible commitment to which the nation was obligated by Yahweh's choice. Israel was not a party to a contract ; the covenant was a personal relation between Yahweh and Israel, due allowance being made for the disparity of their respective positions, Yahweh the master and Israel the servant. The covenant was unilateral in the sense that it originated with Yahweh and was subject to His will. Yahweh had forged the bond, was free to break it, and in Hos 1[6] seemed to declare it broken, whether or not He regarded the breach as permanent. Howbeit, Hosea himself tells us that Yahweh is reluctant to take this extreme step, which, as human language had to put it, would cause Him pain (11[8–9]). Did the prophets then resign themselves to the dissolution of the covenant as a practical possibility? If an unqualified reply is demanded, it must assume a negative form. If we have to choose between complete, unmitigated doom and an overthrow that still did not preclude renewal and restoration, we must grant that the latter was the expectation of the prophets from Amos to Jeremiah. They might be

PROPHECY, PROPHETS

prepared to abandon the bulk of the nation as irrevocably lost, but they could not surrender the hope that some small part of Israel would survive the worst disaster. Only the Israel that had, by misuse, forfeited the security of the covenant and therefore did not really belong to Yahweh would perish. This could not happen to the whole of Israel, and no prophet envisaged the possibility, save that a few may have done so in an occasional moment of unrelieved dejection. Likewise, the land, though polluted by Israel's infidelities, was Yahweh's inheritance (Jer 2^{7} 3^{2}), and to be removed from it was a bitter punishment (Am 7$^{10-17}$, Jer 22$^{10, 28}$); the state, with Yahweh's anointed at its head, offended the prophets only when it failed in its appointed duties; and the cardinal objection to the cult was not that it was superfluous, but that it substituted the forms of devotion for devotion itself (Am 2$^{7-8}$ 4$^{4-5}$ 5$^{21-27}$, Is 1$^{10-17}$ 58, 66^{3}, Jer 6^{20} 7). What the prophets believed is at least partially to be seen in their influence on the devout of later generations. Post-exilic Israel, revering the prophets as they had never been revered when they were alive, nevertheless restored nation, land, state, and cult in the fullest practicable measure. Thus, for historical as well as for psychological reasons, it is very unlikely that the prophets contemplated the irremediable extinction of these things.

What Yahweh proposes to do with a co-operative Israel in relation to all mankind does not come to the surface in a prophet of the type of Amos. The future is too obscure and present problems are too pressing. The first task of prophecy is to break the people's faith in the ritual stereotype of destiny (conquest, prosperity, and honour under Yahweh) and to declare that the nation fulfils its destiny by being faithful to the character Yahweh has impressed upon Israel alone. Its place in the world is its supreme destiny, to which all programmes and missions are secondary and on which the issue of the nation's life depends. Amos takes Yahweh's world-wide dominion out of the realm of ceremonial illusion—at best a dignified, socialized kind of magic—and sets it firmly on a groundwork of ethical fact (5$^{18-20}$). The universalism of the prophets expresses itself here generously and there narrowly, its emphasis determined by the man and the moment. Not all can climb to the sublimities of the Second Isaiah, nor do all sink to the fury of Nahum, which is only a step from the coarsest passion for revenge. Beneath the variety of individual attitudes, the prophets' confidence in Israel's unique historical office abides unshaken. To them more than to its other teachers the nation owes its tough, enduring sense of destiny.

The destiny of the individual is not a fundamental theme of prophecy. Threats and promises affecting individuals are invariably confined to this world (Am 7$^{11, 17}$, Is 7$^{3-17}$ 22$^{15-25}$, Jer 20$^{3-6}$ 21^{7} 22$^{10-12, 24-27, 30}$ 28^{16} 29$^{21, 32}$ 35$^{18-19}$ 39$^{16-18}$). The one hint of a resurrection appears in the Isaiah Apocalypse (Is 26^{19}) and scarcely belongs to prophecy in the proper sense. Whatever beatitude the individual is to enjoy is awarded to him through, and because of, his participation in the destiny of his people. The faithful proselyte will have a happy life in the beloved community, but the best that the prophets can offer him thereafter is 'an everlasting name' (Is 56^{5}). What happens to the individual after death is beyond the horizon of the prophets. This apparent omission was in reality the providential postponement of a question that might have been mishandled if it had arisen prematurely. Only after Jeremiah and Ezekiel had diligently explored the individual conscience was it safe to consider the matter of man's deliverance from death. It could then be examined on solidly ethical premisses.

The prophets are beyond compare in their grasp of human motivation. They transferred sin from its traditional place in nature and events to its real seat, which is man's conscience. They investigated the heart and found the malice that is the essence of all sin. No longer could sin be dismissed as the result of mischance and error. They coined a multitude of terms for it and in each name they gave it exhibited some facet of man's blameworthy misuse of a precious personal relation. Sin is rebellion (Am 1$^{3, 6, 9, 11, 13}$ 2$^{1, 4, 6}$, Is 1^{2}, Ezk 2$^{3, 5, 6, 7}$ 3$^{9, 26, 27}$ 12$^{2, 3, 9}$ 17^{12} 24^{3} 44^{6}), obstinacy (Jer 3^{22}), wilfulness (Hos 8^{4}), arrogance (Is 9^{9}), pride (Is 5^{24}), self-reliance (Am 6^{13}, Is 5^{21}). It is desertion (Jer 2^{17}), deviation (Hos 7^{13}), forgetfulness (Jer 18^{15}), stupidity (Jer 4^{22}), and indifference (Is 5^{20}). It is infidelity (Hos 4^{1}), adultery (Hos 1^{2} 2^{2}), and a breach of confidence (Hos 5^{7}). It is anything that impairs righteousness, the visible assurance of Israel's stability and acceptability. Before the days of the prophets, *righteousness* meant, at bottom, correctness or normality. It was the state of the man or nation that was 'all right,' but not necessarily all right because completely good. Goodness was included without any objective analysis of its motivation and basic direction. It was still conceived of in part as an external thing, compatible with self-interest. When the prophets had finished with sin, the primitive, naïve idea that man was only vaguely responsible for it had been demolished forever. Righteousness could not be righteousness unless it proceeded from a whole and submissive heart. These concepts must be learned and made operative before religion can become a field in which the individual freely commits himself to the pursuit of transcendent ends.

The range of sin is broad, and so is the range of punishment. Here again the prophets inherit a concept and transform it. They do not work out a nicely adjusted scale of penalties. If there is collective sin, there is also collective punishment, from which the righteous are not necessarily exempt (Ezk 21^{3}). Ultimately, of course, the relation between sin and punishment is clarified with a wonderfully delicate logic (Jer 31$^{29-30}$, Ezk 3$^{16-21}$ 14$^{12-20}$ 18). Prophecy can then make two affirmations that are more true when they are combined than when each stands alone: 'The person who sins shall die' (Ezk 18^{4}) and 'The righteous shall live by his faithfulness' (Hab 2^{4}).

Prophecy would have stultified itself if it had not been from the start a summons to repentance. The prophets continually exhort the people to 'return' (Hos 7^{10} 14$^{1, 2}$, Is 9^{13} 10^{21} 31^{6}, Zec 1^{3}) to God. Amos' recollection of calamities that have failed to convert the people does not wholly discourage him (4$^{6-12}$): he can still extend the invitation 'Seek me and live' (5^{4}). Appropriate comparisons underline the renewing effect of repentance. There are no more powerful recommendations of repentance than Isaiah's 'Wash yourselves; make yourselves clean' (1^{16}) and Jeremiah's 'Circumcise yourselves to the Lord, remove the foreskin of your hearts' (4^{4}).

Forgiveness is not granted grudgingly. It is liberally offered and earnestly pressed upon the iniquitous nation. 'I will speak compassionately' (Hos 2^{14}) to Israel, says Yahweh, who has no 'pleasure in the death of the wicked' (Ezk 18^{23}). He welcomes contrition (Is 57^{15}) and brings punishment to an end when it has done its work (Is 40^{2}). The prophets speak of repentance in different accents, but none of them would have denied that the 'wicked man' who 'turns away from all his sins' (Ezk 18^{21}) receives forgiveness.

Punishment and forgiveness, which can and do take place in the world as it is, are assimilated in the long run to judgment, redemption, and recreation, which appertain rather to the world as it will be. Judgment exhibits a curious duality, with Yahweh sometimes in the character of judge (Is 2^{4} 3$^{13-15}$ 33^{22} 51^{5}, Jer 11^{20}, Ezk 11$^{10-11}$ 34^{20} 35^{11}, Jl 3^{12}) and at other times in the rôle of litigant (Hos 2^{2} 4^{1}, Is 5^{3}, Mic 6$^{1-5}$). Redemption is Yahweh's complete repossession of a nation alienated from Him by its own failure. He has never surrendered it; hence redemption is not His success in a contest with some rival power. Redemption belongs to the same circle of ideas as righteousness, salvation, and sanctification. They are all aspects of a reconstituted nation in a re-energized universe. The new heavens and the new earth are not radically different from the old. The hope that is typical of prophecy in the period of its greatest courage and originality is centred in the present world, which Yahweh's touch can convert into a habitation of peace and holiness. The old universe need not be discarded for a fresh one. God will not suddenly return to a creation that He has long since abandoned to evil forces. He has never left that creation and has conceded nothing to those evil forces.

In one sense it would be correct to say that prophecy has no **eschatology** at all ; in another, that it has two eschatologies. The pre-exilic prophets, surfeited as they are with the excesses of a degenerate cult, have little liking for the eschatological features of the ' ritual pattern.' Beyond the catastrophes they foretell they can merely see a nebulous remnant (Am 3^{12} 4^{11} $5^{3, 14-15}$, Is 7^{3}, Zeph $2^{7, 9}$ 3^{13}, Zec $8^{6, 11, 12}$) surviving to play an as yet undetermined part in some sort of reconstruction. This eschatology, if it deserves the name, could doubtless from time to time develop considerable enthusiasm for a concrete cause, such as national unity or the Davidic monarchy, but we shall never be certain that it did in fact lend its voice to the projected revival of Israel's shattered institutions, which for the moment must have seemed discredited and incapable of being salvaged. Subsequently other prophets, less daring than their forebears, sponsored the re-establishment of the cult and reintroduced into eschatology the remains of the ancient cultic mythology, and these fragments were the primary material of apocalyptic. Prophetic eschatology was first demythologized and then remythologized, neither process terminating in thorough alteration. Both trends were phenomena of the sort nobody is disposed to push to a rigid conclusion. See also MESSIAH.

The universal and the particular in prophecy are inseparable. Neither is intelligible by itself. We cannot distil any colourless eternal verities from the utterances of prophecy. It has nothing to say to a merely curious humanity. Its particularities must be accepted, and when they are, it is discovered that they are susceptible of infinite enlargement. The reason for this is that prophetic truth, in all possible extensions and applications, radiates from the central reality of a Living God. We know about God more than the prophets knew, but we should know nothing at all if we had not first learned what they had to teach us. They are the masters who initiated us into the mysteries of life under God, and we have progressed by remembering their instruction and following the direction they indicated.

5. The transition from OT prophecy to NT prophecy.— In the NT and in the oldest patristic literature there are three varieties of prophecy : glossolalia, charismatic prophecy, and the prophetic interpretation of the Scriptures. We shall confine ourselves here to an evaluation of Justin Martyr's claim that the Christians have taken over the Jewish ' gifts of prophecy ' (*Dialogue with Trypho*, 82). We are all prepared to grant that this is true theologically. What we have to determine is how true it is historically.

Glossolalia, ' speaking with tongues,' which is either spontaneous or of pagan origin, presents itself to St. Paul as a new phenomenon, and his attitude towards it shows that he has not referred it to any OT prototype. In his masterly discussion of glossolalia and prophecy (1 Co 13–14) he frankly attaches greater value to the latter than to the former, but he appears to have no scriptural reason for his opinion. In the only place where he cites Scripture (1 Co 14^{21-25}), he handles it very freely, and his argument is obscure. Nothing clearly identifiable with glossolalia occurs in the OT. The sounds to which Isaiah refers in his warning against ' the mediums and the wizards who chirp and mutter ' (8^{19}) may have been glossolalic, but it is equally possible that they were only artistic preliminaries to intelligible utterance. The entire question would, of course, be much less baffling if we had a few authentic specimens of primitive Christian glossolalia. See TONGUES, SPEAKING WITH.

So far as we can judge, the charismatic prophecy practised among Christians bore little resemblance to the best of canonical prophecy. The former was normally concerned with prediction (Ac 11^{27-28} 21^{10-11}), though many of the ' revelations ' must have been similar to the ' guidance ' of the First Century Christian Fellowship (Ac 13^{1-2}, 1 Ti 1^{18} 4^{14}, cf St. Ignatius, *To the Philadelphians* 7). The Judaism in which Christianity arose had long since forgotten the true nature of OT prophecy. The existence of a prophetical canon implied that prophecy had run its course. In theory all Jews looked for Elijah (Mal 4^{5}) and ' that prophet ' (Dt 18^{15}) ; nevertheless ' until a faithful prophet should arise ' meant ' forever ' (1 Mac 14^{41}). John Hyrcanus, uniting in his person the king, the priest, and the prophet (Josephus, *The Jewish War* I. ii. 8 [68], Test. Levi 8^{15}), was in no sense the successor of Isaiah or Jeremiah. The interests of apocalyptic, for all its cosmic sweep, are narrower and more intense than those of OT prophecy, which, moreover, is subjected to a diversity of treatment in the numerous Jewish schools and parties of the time. In this by no means simple situation Christianity could, and did, borrow whatever suited its purpose. Its prophets were probably not governed by any discerning admiration for the OT prophets. They were obliged to recognize, when they considered the matter, that the Spirit now inspiring them had formerly inspired the prophets of Israel, but there was no deliberate, formal imitation of OT prophecy.

Prophecy lingered on in its interpreters, and when they claimed a peculiar gift of interpretation they came close to declaring that they themselves were prophets. T. H. Gaster holds that this was the case with the Qumrânites (see DEAD SEA SCROLLS), whose succession of authoritative interpreters (Gaster prefers ' right-teacher ' to ' Teacher of Righteousness ') quite possibly begins soon after the concluding redaction of the Latter Prophets and their canonization. About the same time a teacher whose devotion to the Law has none of the Qumrânite sectarianism associates himself in some degree with the prophets when he writes, ' Yet will I pour forth doctrine as prophecy ' (Sir 24^{33}). For the NT treatment of OT prophecy precedents of a sort were not lacking, and in tracing the prophetic testimony that pointed to Christ inspired writers who believed that Christianity had inherited the promises of prophecy were doing what Jewish exegetes, each in accordance with his leanings, had done before them.

Bibliography.—O. Eissfeldt, ' The Prophetic Literature ' (*The Old Testament and Modern Study*, ed. H. H. Rowley [Oxford, 1951], pp. 115–161) ; A. Guillaume, *Prophecy and Divination among the Hebrews and other Semites* (London, 1938) ; A. Haldar, *Associations of Cult Prophets among the Ancient Semites* (Uppsala, 1945) ; J. Hessen, *Platonismus und Prophetismus*, 2nd edition (Munich, 1955) ; G. Hölscher, *Die Profeten* (Leipzig, 1914) ; A. R. Johnson, *The Cultic Prophet in Ancient Israel*² (Cardiff, 1962) ; W. C. Klein, *The Psychological Pattern of Old Testament Prophecy* (Evanston, 1956) ; H. H. Rowley, ' The Nature of Prophecy in the Light of Recent Study ' (*The Servant of the Lord* [London, 1952], pp. 89–128) ; E. Troeltsch, ' Glaube und Ethos der hebräischen Propheten ' (*Gesammelte Schriften* [Tübingen, 1925], IV, pp. 34–65). W. C. K.

PROPHET (in NT).—Among Jewish teachers in NT times it was commonly believed that prophecy had come to an end, though apocalyptic writers continued to prophesy, using pseudonyms taken from the OT. At Qumrân, *e.g.*, the coming of a prophet like Moses was expected on the basis of Dt $18^{15, 18}$. In the NT this prediction is found fulfilled in Jesus (Ac 7^{37}, probably Jn 6^{14} ; Ac 3^{21-24} is different). The coming of Jesus is attested by Zechariah, a priest who prophesies (Lk $1^{5, 67ff}$), by the prophetically inspired Simeon (2^{25ff}), by the prophetess Anna (2^{36}), and by John the Baptist, generally regarded as a prophet (Mk 11^{32}=Mt 21^{26}=Lk 20^{6}, Mt 14^{5}), though Jesus calls him ' more than a prophet ' (Mt 11^{9}=Lk 7^{26}). If Jesus referred to Himself as a prophet, He did so only rarely (Mk 6^{4} = Mt 13^{57} = Lk 4^{24}, Lk 13^{33}), though there is an obvious continuity between His gospel and that of the major OT prophets, in form as well as in content. He was regarded as a prophet by the people (Mk 6^{15}, Lk 7^{16}; cf Mk 8^{28}). It is in Luke-Acts that the prophetic ministry of Jesus and of the Church is most strongly emphasized, and in Ac 2^{16ff} the prediction of prophecy as a gift to all (Jl 2^{28f}) is depicted as fulfilled at Pentecost in Christians' ability to speak ' in other tongues,' by some regarded as speaking in foreign dialects (Ac 2^{5ff}), by others as talking incoherently (2^{13-15}). Apparently prophecy took two forms, one incoherent and ecstatic, the other coherent and rational. In Acts we seem to encounter only the coherent prophets (Agabus in 11^{28} 21^{10}; others at Antioch, 13^{1ff}; Judas and Silas, 15^{32}; the daughters of Philip, 21^{9}; note that Paul too can prophesy, 20^{29f} 27^{22ff}), though an absolute distinction cannot be drawn. Different problems engaged Paul's attention in regard to prophets. Writing to the Thessalonians (1 Th 5^{19ff}) he tells them not to quench the Spirit or despise prophesying but to test everything. Writing to the Corinthians (1 Co 12, 14), on the other hand, he has to insist on the diversities of Spirit-given functions (12^{10}) and on the subordination of prophets to apostles (12^{28ff}). He also draws a distinction between prophecy, which is rational and builds up the community, and ecstatic speech, which is addressed only to God (14^{2f}). Ideally, all are to prophesy ($14^{24, 39}$), but actually it is more likely that there will be two or three prophets in the Church; their spirits are to be subject to themselves (14^{32}) and prophetesses are not to speak (14^{34}; a self-styled prophetess is mentioned in Rev 2^{20}). Paul does not deny the significance of prophets; in 1 Corinthians as in Ephesians (2^{20} 3^{5} 4^{11}) they rank second only to apostles. But their utterances need to be tested (1 Th 5^{21}, 1 Co 14^{29}; cf 1 Jn 4^{1}; false prophets in Mt 7^{15} $24^{11, 24}$), in spite of the *Didache's* command not to test them (11^{7}). The *Didache*, probably written well before the end of the 1st cent., reflects Jewish-Christian enthusiasm for prophecy; the prophets of the community are its high priests (13^{3}). Somewhat later, the problem presented by false prophets is clearly stated in the *Shepherd* of Hermas (*Mand.* 11), also Jewish-Christian. Although prophecy was revived later in the 2nd cent., in Gnosticism and Montanism, in the Church as a whole the function of the prophet was assumed by the bishop (Ignatius of Antioch spoke ' with God's voice ' and said what the Spirit told him, *Philad.* 7^{1}), partly by the martyr. The dangers presented by tendencies toward heresy and schism resulted in a certain ' institutionalizing ' of the work of the prophet. R. M. G.

PROPHETESS.—1. The courtesy title of a prophet's wife, Is 8^{2}. **2.** The OT title of women in whom the promise was fulfilled: ' your daughters shall prophesy ' (Jl 2^{28}). ' The term is of course not to be misunderstood, as if it referred merely to predictions relating to the future; the reference is in general to inspired instruction in moral and religious truth ' (Driver, *Camb. Bible, in loc.*). The title is given to Miriam (Ex 15^{20}), Deborah (Jg 4^{4}), Huldah (2 K 22^{14}, 2 Ch 34^{22}), and Noadiah (Neh 6^{14}). **3.** The NT gift of prophecy was bestowed on women (Ac 21^{9}, 1 Co 11^{5}). Anna (Lk 2^{36}) is the only ' prophetess ' mentioned by name, except Jezebel (Rev 2^{20}), who was probably not the wife of the angel of the church (RVm), but a temptress of the Christians at Thyatira to whom was given the name of Israel's wicked queen. J. G. T.

PROPITIATION.—In English usage the difference between propitiation and expiation is as follows: one propitiates or appeases an angry or offended person, god or man, but one expiates sin or guilt. The difference is then in the directing of the verbal action towards a person or an offence.

Certain Greek words were translated as ' propitiation ' by AV in a few places, *e.g.* Ro 3^{25}, 1 Jn 2^{2} 4^{10}. Since the direction of the action in these cases seems to be toward sins rather than toward God, the RSV has translated ' expiation,' and the passages are so treated here (see EXPIATION). There remain, however, for our consideration some passages where the fact of propitiation seems to appear although the word itself is not used.

Propitiation of one man by another appears clearly in Gn 32^{20}, where Jacob plans to placate his offended brother with a gift (literally, ' I will wipe his face,' using the verb *kippēr*, commonly = ' expiate '). The same verb appears in Pr 16^{14}, where the deadliness of a king's anger is noticed, and ' a wise man will appease it.'

The passages where an appeasement of God is intended are mostly concerned with the smelling of sacrifice by God. So 1 S 26^{19}, ' If it is the Lord who has incited you against me, let him accept an offering ' (literally, smell a gift). The impression given is not that a sin is thought of, to be expiated, but that the incitement is the act of a God irritated without evident reason. This case is a rather isolated one, and the smelling of sacrifice appears much more frequently in the phrase *rēaḥ nîḥōaḥ*, in the sense ' smell of appeasement ' or ' soothing smell ' (RSV ' pleasing odour '), frequent in the priestly sacrificial codes.

In view of the frequent appearance of this formula, almost by routine, in sacrificial laws, it is remarkable that precisely in the codes for those sacrifices which concern especially the expiation of sin, the so-called sin and guilt offerings, the formula occurs only once (Lv 4^{31}), and it is reasonable to suppose its occurrence there to be accidental or at any rate secondary. The frequent cases of the formula in sacrifices other than the expiatory makes it likely that, although the origin may probably lie in the appeasement of an angry, offended, or arbitrary deity, its present sense in the codes as they are is the pleasure of God in being worshipped rightly. It was thus understood by the LXX (' a smell of pleasant odour '), and so RSV. It occurs in narrative in Gn 8^{21}, where the sense is not the appeasement of the Divine anger by the sacrifice (for the Flood has already abated), but the Divine pleasure at the resumption of right worship.

It seems, then, that the technical sacrificial terminology refers rather to expiation of sin than to propitiation of an angry God. But in a number of cases it is also clear that the anger of God falls on Israel when the sin is not expiated, so that expiation has a certain apotropaic aspect; it alone turns away the anger of God (Nu 16^{41-50} 25^{6-13}). In a number of stories it is therefore difficult to carry out the clear distinction of expiation and propitiation, *e.g.* the related stories of 2 S 21^{1-14} 24^{1-25}.

We conclude that the propitiation or appeasement of an angry or fickle deity appears at an early stage in Israelite religion, but that in the developed sacrificial terminology expiation is more important; but that even expiation can be understood as necessary for turning away the anger of God. For the question how far this fits into the general Biblical understanding of atonement, see ATONEMENT. J. Ba.

PROSELYTE.—1. The character and the history of the proselyte.—The character and the history of the proselyte are somewhat obscured by the fact that the name ' proselyte ' occurs only in the NT, and there in the final meaning of a convert to Judaism, as if he were a product of NT times alone. But the same Greek word that stands for ' proselyte ' in the NT is very largely used in the LXX, where EV has ' stranger.' Even the Hebrews themselves are described by the LXX as ' proselytes ' in Egypt (Ex 22^{21} 23^{9}, Lv 19^{34}, Dt 10^{19}). The ' stranger ' of the OT becomes the ' proselyte ' of the NT. For the history that lies behind the use of the word, see STRANGER. By the 4th cent. B.C. the ' stranger ' had become a member of the Jewish community—a proselyte in the technical sense.

Other expressions are used in the NT to indicate a more or less close sympathy with Jewish religious thought and life without implying absolute identity with and inclusion in Judaism. These are ' fearers of God ' (*phoboumenoi ton Theon*, Ac $10^{2, 22}$ $13^{16, 26}$ etc.) and 'worshippers of God' (*sebomenoi ton Theon*, Ac 16[14] 17[4, 17] etc.). They had been drawn from heathenism by the higher ideals and purer life of Judaism. Dissatisfied with the traditional religious beliefs of paganism, they had found in Judaism an intellectual home and a religious power which they had sought in vain elsewhere. But a study of Ac 10, 11, especially 11[3], shows that these were not proselytes; they refused to take the final step that would have carried them into Judaism—*viz.* circumcision (see A. Harnack, *Expansion of Christianity*, i, p. 11). They lived on the fringe of Judaism and were, it seems (Lk 7[5], Ac 10[2]), often generous benefactors to the cause that had lifted them nearer to God and truth.

The view that the 'proselytes of the gate' were half-Jews, and formed a group neither pagan nor Jewish, is completely mistaken. One was either a Jew or he was not.

2. Proselytizing activity of the Jews.—Up to the time of the Exile and for some time after, the attitude of the Hebrews towards 'strangers' was passive: they did not invite their presence in their community, and did not encourage them to be sharers of their beliefs and practices. But by the 3rd cent. B.C. a change of outlook and national purpose had taken place, which had converted them into active propagandists. There appear to have been three reasons for this change. (1) The Hebrews were no longer concentrated in one narrow land where a homogeneous life was followed, but were now scattered over all parts of the civilized world, and found themselves in contact with peoples who were religiously far inferior to themselves, and who excited both their disdain and their pity. (2) Many of those in the Gentile world who were dissatisfied with the intellectual results and the religious conditions of their time saw in Judaism, as lived and taught before their eyes, something finer and nobler than they had found elsewhere; and they were drawn to its practical teaching and life without committing themselves to the rites and practices that offended their sense of fitness and even of decency. (3) The Hebrews themselves seem to have responded to their opportunity with a quickened enthusiasm for humanity and a higher ideal of their national existence, in the providence of God, among the nations of the earth. It does not appear that the Hebrews have ever been so powerfully moved towards the peoples lying in darkness as in this time subsequent to the Exile. They were convinced of the claim of God to the homage of men everywhere, the universalism of their revelation of truth and duty, and their own calling to bring the world to God. The needs of the world moved them powerfully, and the thoughts that found expression in such passages as Ps 33[8] ('Let all the earth fear the Lord, let all the inhabitants of the world stand in awe of him'), 36[7-9] 64[10] 65[8] etc. filled them with a burning zeal to make the world their offering to God. Perhaps we may not be wholly wrong in regarding the Septuagint as a product of, as it certainly was an aid to, this missionary effort.

This spiritual enthusiasm for God's honour and man's salvation continued till about the time of the Maccabees, when as a consequence of pagan persecution the tenderer springs of missionary zeal were dried up, and the sword became the instrument of national idealism, and whole cities and tribes were given the option of circumcision or exile, if not slaughter (1 Mac 2[46] 13[48] 14[14, 36]; Jos. *Ant.* XIII. ix. 1 [254 ff], xi. 3 [318], xv. 4 [395–97]). Of course, this was a means not available outside their hereditary home. This zealous propaganda, attested by Jesus (Mt 23[15]) went on till the 1st cent. of our era, when the unrest of the Palestinian Jews with the Roman occupation culminated in insurrection. In their conflict with Rome their numbers were greatly reduced by slaughter, and their power of religious expansion was checked by the decree of Hadrian, modified later by Antoninus in forbidding circumcision. By this time, however, Judaism had won a large following in every town of size and importance (cf Ac 2[9-11], Jos. *BJ* VII. iii. 3 [43 ff], *c. Apion.* ii. 11, 40 [125 ff, 287 ff]; Seneca, *ap.* August. *de Civitate Dei* vi. 11; cf 'victi victoribus leges dederunt'; Schürer, *HJP* II. ii. 304 ff). But now bloodshed and persecution produced the twofold result of closing and steeling the heart of Judaism to the outside world, so that proselytes were no longer sought by the Jews, and the tenets and the practices of Judaism became crystallized and less amenable to Hellenistic influences, and so less fitted to win Gentile converts.

3. Admission of the Proselyte.—The ritual conditions imposed on the proselyte on entering Judaism were three: (1) circumcision, (2) cleansing or baptism, (3) sacrifice. Baptism took place after the healing of the wound caused by circumcision. The requirement of cleansing or baptism lay in the very nature of Judaism: the heathen was unclean, through his lifelong contact with idolatry, and had to be cleansed by washing in water before admission into Judaism. Sacrifice was both an expression of thanksgiving and the convert's own participation in Jewish worship. With the fall of the Temple, sacrifice lapsed, though at first the proselyte was required to lay aside enough to pay for the sacrifice, should the Temple again be restored; but even this demand was in course of time allowed to lapse, as the prospect of restoration faded. These three conditions seem to have been of early origin, though we may not have specific reference to them till the 2nd cent. A.D. By his initiation the proselyte became a full member of the Jewish community (except for some few rights), and was bound to keep the whole Mosaic Law.

Among individual Jewish teachers there was for a time a difference of opinion as to the necessity of circumcision and baptism, but all early usage seems to confirm their actual observance. It is true that Izates, king of Adiabene, for a time refrained from circumcision under the guidance of his first Jewish teacher, Ananias; but this counsel had been given not because it was at the time deemed unnecessary for a proselyte to be circumcised, but because circumcision might alienate the sympathies of his people from Izates and endanger his throne. And Ananias wisely laid greater stress upon the moral than upon the ritual side of conversion. (Jos. *Ant.* xx. ii. [17 ff].) The 'God-fearers' were allowed to continue for some time in that state; but according to the rabbis they had to make a final decision for or against admission to Judaism by the end of twelve months. A 'lapsed' God-fearer was viewed as a pagan. It does not appear that conversion enhanced the popular reputation of the proselytes; for although they could not but gain esteem by their higher moral life, they seemed to many to display a type of daily life lacking in domestic reverence and in civic and national patriotism (Tac. *Hist.* v. 5, 8; Juv. xiv. 103–4).

4. Place of the proselyte in the growth of the Christian Church.—Proselytes upon embracing Judaism seem also to have accepted the attitude of the Jews generally towards Christianity. Most of them opposed it. If the experience of Justin is an indication of the general attitude of the proselytes to the Church, they must have deemed it a duty to their adopted faith to manifest a violence of speech and an aggressiveness of action unsurpassed by the Jews themselves; for he says, 'The proselytes not only do not believe, but twofold more than yourselves blaspheme [Christ's] name, and wish to torture and put to death us who believe in Him' (*Dial.* 122, 2). The idea, popular a generation ago, *viz.* that Christianity spread widely and rapidly throughout the Roman world chiefly because multitudes of proselytes and God-fearers swept into it, is not borne out by the facts. As Justin said, a century later, reviewing the whole story of the relations of Jews and Christians, the great majority of converts to Christianity were Gentiles (*First Apology*, 53, 5). At most, the God-fearers had responded in some degree to the moral and religious teaching of the synagogue, and had thus become acquainted with the Hebrew Scriptures in the Greek translation.

The proselytes must always have formed a small minority of those among the Gentiles who had lent an ear to Jewish teaching. There were many who were attracted to the synagogue by the inspiration of its worship and the purity of its teaching, but who could not meet the requirements for admission, especially circumcision, which to anyone reared in the world of Graeco-Roman culture meant a mutilation of the human body—like the barbarities practised in the jungle. Among these the gospel had a different reception; it was rapidly accepted and eagerly followed. They found in it all that drew them to the synagogue, and more. With historical Judaism they had little to do, and loyalty and nationality did not appeal to them as motives to maintain it against Christianity. It is easy to understand how quickly the gospel would be adopted by these adherents of Judaism. Every synagogue would thus become the seed-plot of a Christian church. And so it was specially to these that St. Paul addressed himself on his missionary journeys, and from them he formed the beginnings of many of his churches (Ac $13^{16, 43}$ 16^{14f}). One can easily understand with what feelings of combined jealousy and resentment the Jews would see these worshippers detached from the synagogue and formed into a church (Ac 18^{12-17}). But Judaism had nothing to offer the Gentile that was not now provided by the Christian Church. In consequence the Jews, especially after the terrible Second Revolt, under Hadrian (A.D. 132–135), restricted their vision to their own people and abandoned their interest in the conversion of the rest of the world. J. Gi.—**W. C. v. U.**

PROSTITUTION.—See Crimes and Punishments, 3.

PROVENDER.—1. Hebrew *mispô*, Gn $24^{25, 32}$ 42^{27} 43^{24}, Jg 19^{19}, a general name for cattle food. **2.** *blîl*. Job 6^5 (EV **fodder**); *b*ᵉ*lîl ḥāmîṣ*, Is 30^{24}, 'salted (RVm, RSV; AV 'clean,' AVm, RV 'savoury') provender,' *i.e.* fodder mixed with salt or aromatic herbs. The ordinary food of cattle in Palestine—besides pasturage—is *tibn* (broken straw), *kursenneh* (the vetch, *Vicia ervilia*), bran (for fattening especially), and sometimes hay made from the flowering herbs of spring.

E. W. G. M.

PROVERB.—1. Meaning.—In the Bible there is no essential difference between the proverb and the **parable** (q.v.). The Hebrew *māshāl* and the Greek *parabolē*, meaning 'resemblance,' were applied indiscriminately to both. The value arising from this likeness was twofold. In the first place, as the moral truth seemed to emerge from the observed habits of animals, objects in nature, familiar utensils, or occurrences in daily life, such juxtaposition gave to the ethical precept or fact of conduct the surprise and challenge of a discovery. Thus the whole influence of example and environment is compressed into the proverb, 'Like mother, like daughter' (Ezk 16^{44}). The surprise was intensified when the parable product contradicted ordinary experience, as in the statement, 'One sows and another reaps' (Jn 4^{37}). Definite labour deserves a definite reward, yet the unexpected happens, and, while man proposes, there remains an area in which God disposes. Out of such corroboration grew the second value of the proverb, namely, authority. The truth became a rule entitled to general acceptance. The proverb usually has the advantage of putting the concrete for the abstract. Among the modern inhabitants of Palestine, when a letter of recommendation is asked, it is customary to quote the proverb, 'You cannot clap with one hand.' Of a dull workman without interest or resource in his work it is said, 'He is like a sieve, he can do only one thing.'

2. Literary form.—(1) Next to the fact of resemblance was the essential currency to the unpremeditated exclamation, 'Is Saul also among the prophets?' (1 S 10^{11f}). When the proverb consisted of two parts, rhetorical emphasis was secured either by repeating the same thought in different words (Pr 3^{17}) or by the introduction of contrasting particulars (3^{33}). (2) *Rhythmic measure* was also studied, and there was often an untranslatable felicity of balance and repeated sound. The final mark of literary publicity was conferred by a rhetorical touch of picturesque hyperbole, as in the reference to a camel passing through the eye of a needle (Mt 19^{24}). (3) The fact that a wise saying was meant for the wise encouraged the use of *elliptical form*. This carried the complimentary suggestion that the hearer was able to understand a reference that was confessedly obscure. On this account proverbs were called 'the words of the wise' (Pr 22^{17}). Hence the note of surprise and unexpectedness in Christ's words, when He said that the mysteries of the Kingdom had been hidden from the wise and understanding and revealed unto babes (Mt 11^{25}, Lk 10^{21}). (4) The *obscurity* referred to was sometimes made the leading feature and motive of the proverb, and it was then called an 'enigma' or '**dark saying**' (Ps 49^4, Pr 1^6 30^{15-31}). Its solution then became a challenge to the ingenuity of the interpreter. Both the prophets and Christ Himself were charged with speaking in this problematical manner (Ezk 20^{49}, Jn 16^{29}). **Riddles** (q.v.) were introduced at festive gatherings as contributing an element of competitive acuteness and facetious exhilaration. Instances resembling Pr 30^{15-31} are common among the modern Arabs and Jews in Syria, as when it is said: 'There are three chief voices in the world, that of running water, of the Torah, and of money.' An enigma for the study of books is: 'Black seeds on white ground, and he who eats of the fruit becomes wise.'

3. Subject-matter.—This is summarized in Pr 1^{1-6}. The reference is generally to types of character, the emotions and the desires of the heart, and the joys and sorrows, the losses and gains, the duties and the relationships of human life. Amid these the proverb casts a searching light upon different classes of men, and points out the path of wisdom. Hence the name 'words of truth' (Pr 22^{21}).

4. Authority.—Proverbial literature is more highly esteemed in the East than in the West. While the popularity of proverbs is partly due to literary charm and intellectual force, and the distinction conferred by the power of quoting and understanding them, the principal cause of their acceptance lies in their harmony with Oriental life. The proverb is patriarchal government in the region of ethics. It is an order from the governing class that admits of no discussion. The proverb is not the pleading of the lawyer in favour of a certain view and claim, but the decision of a judge who has heard both sides and adjudicates on behalf of general citizenship. Such authority is at its maximum when it not only is generally current but has been handed down from previous generations. It is then 'a parable of the ancients' (1 S 24^{13}). The quotation of an appropriate proverb in a controversy always carries weight, unless the opponent can quote another in support of his claims. Thus, to the careless and inattentive man in business who says 'Prosperity is from God,' it may be retorted 'He that seeketh findeth.' Beneath some commendable social qualities belonging to this attitude there is a mental passivity that seeks to attain to results without the trouble of personal inquiry, and prefers the benefits conferred by truth to any sacrifice or service that might be rendered to it. G. M. M.

PROVERBS, BOOK OF.—The title of the book which stands second in the 'Writings' is *Mish*ᵉ*lê Sh*ᵉ*lōmôh ben-Dāwîdh melekh Yiśrā'ēl*. It is the most characteristic example of the Wisdom Literature in the OT. The word *Māshāl* rendered here by proverb has a somewhat extended meaning. It is applied to the oracles of Balaam (Nu 24^{15}) and is rendered by the RSV as 'discourse,' while in Is 14^4 it refers to the taunt-song against the king of Babylon and is rendered by RSV as 'taunt.' It is also used of parables and allegories and of the short, pungent, pithy saying (see Proverb). Accordingly the contents of this book are as varied as the meaning of the title-word *Mish*ᵉ*lê* (Gr. *paroimia*, Lat. *Proverbia*). The book is ascribed to Solomon in accordance with the Hebrew custom which derived all Law from Moses, all sacred songs from David, and all Wisdom from Israel's wisest king. But that the book consists of separate collections from different authors and various periods is clearly indicated by the fact that several different authors and sources are mentioned throughout the book (24[23] 30[1] 31[1]).

1. We may adopt the division of the book made by the headings in the Hebrew text as follows:

I. 1[1]–9[18]. The Proverbs of Solomon, son of David, king of Israel.
II. 10[1]–22[16], The Proverbs of Solomon.
III. 22[17]–24[22], The Words of the Wise.
IV. 24[23–34], These also are the Sayings of the Wise.
V. 25[1]–29[27], These also are proverbs of Solomon which the men of Hezekiah king of Judah copied.
VI. 30[1–33], The Words of Agur.
VII. 31[1–9], The Words of king Lemuel.
VIII. 31[10–31], Praise of the Virtuous Woman.

Section I. is probably the latest part of the book and may not be dated before the 4th cent. B.C. The first six verses seem to be an introduction to the whole book: the material here consists mainly of short essays interspersed with an occasional briefer wisdom saying. In 8[1ff] occurs the remarkable personalisation of Wisdom which may be one of the main sources of the Johannine thought of the Word made flesh. Section II. is the oldest part of the book and here may be found much pre-literary material. Here are 375 single proverbs, generally discrete and separate, but frequently connected by a common viewpoint or formal likeness (10[2f, 4f, 6f] 16[10–15] 11[9–12], where four verses begin with the letter 'B'). These proverbs are concerned mainly with the efforts of the sages to increase the number of the wise and reduce the number of the fools of whom there seems to have been quite an overplus. Some Aramaisms occur in this section (14[34] 17[10] 18[24] 19[20] etc.) and though the section contains ancient material the collection may not be dated before the Exile. The third section may be subdivided into 22[17]–23[14] and 23[15]–24[22]. The former of these sections is clearly connected with *the Wisdom of Amenemope*, the text of which dates from about the 8th cent. B.C. The 'excellent things' of Pr 22[20] (AV) is properly rendered in RSV by 'thirty sayings.' The writer has treated his source somewhat independently, but about one third of this material is taken directly from the Egyptian source. 23[13f] is from Ahikar. The date of this collection is not earlier than 700 B.C. and may be considerably later. Section IV. consists of five brief sayings warning against partiality and laziness: Oesterley holds it to be closely connected with III. but the section gives no hint as to date. The fifth collection is assigned to the period of Hezekiah and, while later than section II., it seems to be from the pre-exilic period. It contains 139 verses of which 128 are single verse sayings. The sixth section is attributed to the unknown Agur: it contains some thoughts that are reminiscent of the book of Job (Job 40[5] 42[6]). Some editors allow no more than vv.[1–6] to Agur and judge the remainder to be added. Section VII. belongs to another Massaite, Lemuel, and contains salutary sayings regarding wine and women. To this is appended (31[10–31]) an acrostic poem in praise of the virtuous woman. These last four sections occupy a different position in the LXX and this would indicate that they were added at a period subsequent to the completion of the book. The date of the compilation must be later than the date of its latest main source, and in Proverbs the latest section is the first. Thus we have here a post-exilic work but a work which includes authentic ancient material.

The Wise Men do not claim revealed wisdom. They are the Hebrew Humanists. They stand on the *terra firma* of everyday life and seek to articulate the lofty prophetic ideals in the common workaday life of men. They count nothing human alien to their interest and sympathy: the whole world is their parish. The book of Proverbs may be regarded as a Manual of Conduct or, as Bruch called it, 'an anthology of gnomes.'

J. Pn.

PROVIDENCE.—The word is not found in the OT. In the NT it is used only once; in the introduction of his address to Felix, the orator Tertullus says: '. . . by your *Provision* (AV and RV 'providence') . . . reforms are introduced on behalf of this nation . . .' (Ac 24[2]). Here providence (or provision) simply means foresight, as in 2 Mac 4[6], 'the King's providence' (RV; RSV 'attention').

The first appearance of the word 'providence' (Gr. *pronoia*) in Jewish literature is in Wis 14[3], where God is represented as making for a ship 'a way even in the sea'; the author, borrowing the expression from the Stoic philosophers, says: 'Your providence, Father, pilots it' (Goodspeed). In another passage, recognizing the sterner aspect of the truth to which the OT also bears witness, he contrasts the destinies of the Hebrews and Egyptians and describes the latter, when they were 'prisoners of darkness,' as 'exiled from the eternal providence' (17[2]).

Although the OT does not contain the word 'providence,' the idea of God's guidance of His people runs like a thread in each type of Biblical literature. Legal materials and the traditions of the conquest of Palestine reflect the constant impression that through social experience God's guidance of the Hebrews is made known. Narrators picture the gradual accomplishment of His purpose concerning the chosen people and the world at large (Gn 50[20], Ex 8[22], Dt 32[8ff]; cf Ps 74[12ff]); poets delight to extol Him whose 'compassion is over all that he has made' (Ps 145[9]; cf 29[3ff] 104 136); prophets point to the proofs of God's guidance in the past in order that the people may gain wisdom for the present and courage for the future (Dt 32[7ff], Hag 2[9], Is 51[2], Mal 4[4ff]). Job, sometimes called the 'book of providence,' offers several solutions for the problems of God's dealings with men and emphasizes the necessity of unyielding faith in His guidance.

Belief in Providence presupposes the conviction that God speaks and moves through history and nature. The ancient problems which perplexed Greek philosophers and Hebrew sages still challenge the modern mind to reconcile its trust in Divine providence with the reign of law in the universe and with the existence of pain and evil. The Gospels picture Jesus as teaching that the laws of nature are the established methods of His heavenly Father's working and that they fulfil as well as reveal His will (Mt 6[25ff] 10[29ff], Jn 5[17]). Christian belief in providence suggests trust in God who clearly revealed His will in Jesus Christ in order that men should know that history and nature serve moral and spiritual ends in this life and that God's eternal purposes extend beyond it (Ro 8[28], 2 Co 4[11ff], 1 P 1[6ff]).

J. G. T.—H. H. H.

PROVINCE.—The Persian Empire included the '127 provinces from India to Ethiopia' (Ad. Est 13[1]), or, better, the twenty satrapies, each of which was governed by a satrap under the Great King. This principle of political organization was inherited by the Romans. In Latin, the word *provincia*, of unknown derivation, originally meant simply 'a sphere of (magisterial) duty,' and was applied, for example, to the duty of the *praetor urbanus*, who was never permitted to leave Rome. With the extension of the Roman Empire, and the consequently much increased number of spheres of duty outside Rome and Italy, the word came gradually to have a territorial application also. It is in this derived sense that the word is taken here. It was part of the Roman policy throughout to be in no unnecessary hurry to acquire territory and the responsibility connected with it, and it was not till the year 227 B.C.—hundreds of years after the foundation of the Roman State—that the first province was taken over. In that year Sardinia and Corsica became one province, Western Sicily another, and each, after the details of government had been settled by special commissioners, was put under an additional **praetor** elected for the purpose. Behind this step, as behind the annexation of most

Roman provinces, there lay long years of warfare. Province after province was annexed, until in the time of Christ the Romans were in possession of the whole of Europe (except the British Isles, Norway, Sweden, Denmark, most of Germany, and Russia), all Asia Minor, Syria, Egypt, and the north-west of Africa. Most of this vast territory had been acquired during the Republic, but certain portions had not been annexed till the time of the first Emperor, Augustus. During the Republic the governors of these provinces were appointed by the Roman senate from among their own number, generally after a period of service as praetor or consul, as the case might be. They were unpaid, and had heavy expenses to bear. Few resisted the temptation to recoup themselves at the expense of the long-suffering provincials, and the vast sums required by an extortionate governor in his one year's governorship may be estimated from the fact that Cicero, a just and honest man, acquired £18,000 during his tenure of the province Cilicia. The trial of Verres, the infamous governor of Sicily, and Cicero's orations against him, illustrate one of the worst examples of tyranny, embezzlement, and plunder by governors during the later years of the Republic. Under the Empire conditions considerably improved, though Tiberius found it necessary to order at least one official to return to his province and live among those he had robbed; another was told to 'shear my sheep, not flay them.'

During the Empire the provinces were treated according to a notable settlement made between the Senate and the Emperor Augustus on January 1, 27 B.C. On that date it was arranged that those provinces which were peaceful and did not require the presence of an army should be under the control of the senate, who would appoint their governors; while the disturbed provinces that did require the presence of an army were to be under the Emperor himself, who was generalissimo of all the forces of the State. At the same time the Emperor retained financial interests even in senatorial provinces. The following thus became senatorial (or public) provinces: Asia (*i.e.* roughly the western third of Asia Minor), Africa (*i.e.* practically Tunis), Gallia Narbonensis, Hispania Baetica, Achaia, Cyprus, Creta et Cyrenaica, Macedonia, Sicilia, Bithynia, Illyricum, Sardinia et Corsica. The first two were senatorial provinces of the first rank, and were governed each by an ex-consul with the title of proconsul, and three *legati* under him. The others were senatorial provinces of the second rank, and were governed each by an ex-praetor, also with the title **proconsul**. All the rest of the Roman world outside Italy, namely, three-fourths of the whole, was made up of imperial provinces, including the following: Egypt (where the Emperors, as successors of the Ptolemies, ruled as kings), Judaea, Syria-Cilicia-Phoenicia, Galatia (established 25 B.C.), Thracia, Pamphylia (established 25 B.C.), Galliae tres (Aquitania, Lugudunensis, Belgica), Britannia (established A.D. 43). Every new province naturally came under the Emperor's authority. He governed his more important provinces (*e.g.* Syria, Galatia) through a *legatus pro praetore* in each—a man of consular or praetorian rank, who was paid a fixed salary in and after the time of Tiberius—and his less important provinces through a **procurator** (*e.g.* Judaea) or *praefectus* (*e.g.* Egypt). The period of senatorial governorships was one year, that of imperial indefinite. Each province was governed according to a definite statute, which determined the administrative procedure and defined the privileges of individual cities in it. The inhabitants were disarmed and taxed. Judaea became a province in A.D. 6, when procurators were appointed to rule it. The Roman soldiers in Palestine, under the procurators, were auxiliary troops, *i.e.* native, though non-Jewish, recruited from the neighbouring peoples who were enemies of the Jews. This no doubt goes far to explain the constant friction and finally the unbearable burden of Roman occupation of the country, which led to the two revolts of A.D. 66 and 132. But speaking of the Roman imperial administration in general, the oppressive and unjust rule of the Republic was exchanged for a much better during the Empire; and the provinces, at least during the first three centuries of our era, were prosperous and contented.

Accordingly, in NT times there were two kinds of provinces, senatorial and imperial. Senatorial provinces in the East were Asia (comprising the western third of Asia Minor), Bithynia, Cyprus, and Crete-Cyrene. Imperial provinces in the East consisted of Egypt, Syria, Judaea, Galatia, and Moesia (into which were now merged Achaea and Macedonia). The distinction rested on the gesture made by Octavian in 27 B.C. whereby he restored the authority of the Senate except in areas which because of unsettled conditions or exposed frontiers required large bodies of soldiers. But the gesture was illusory. In addition to the three-fourths of the Roman world outside of Italy that he retained under his immediate control, within the senatorial provinces the Emperor controlled tax collection, employed armies as they were needed, and issued advice that had the force of law—as in the famous Cyrene inscriptions (7-4 B.C.).

Governors of senatorial provinces were chosen by lot and served for a single year with the title of *proconsul*. They were indeed ex-consuls in the important provinces of Asia and Africa; elsewhere, being only ex-praetors, they were 'proconsul' only by courtesy. Imperial provinces were administered by the Emperor's personal representatives: a *legatus* of senatorial rank for important areas such as Syria and Galatia; elsewhere by a *procurator* (q.v.) of equestrian rank.

Within the province, authority rested primarily in the *polis*, the traditional city organization of the Hellenistic world. To each city was given the maximum of autonomy compatible with Roman rule. Tribal centres and assimilated temple states were transformed into *poleis*, and new cities were founded in rural areas. Thus fragmented provinces were powerless for joint political action. What semblance of unity they achieved was in relation to the person of the Emperor. Each province had its assembly of notables (*synedrion*) and at its head a provincial high priest. The supreme responsibility of this body was to promote loyalty. As symbol of that loyalty it offered sacrifices—in Jerusalem *for* and elsewhere *to*—Rome and Augustus. Through this body the Emperor communicated his wishes to the aristocracy of each province, and from it received regular reports concerning internal affairs and the conduct of his agents. See ROMAN PUBLIC LAW, and Map 16. A. So.—**J. S. K.**

PROVOKE.—'To provoke' is now 'to try to call forth evil passions,' but in AV it is used in the sense of inciting to any action, good or evil, as 2 Co 9[2] 'Your zeal hath provoked very many'; RV and RSV 'your zeal has stirred up most of them.' 'Provocation,' however, always occurs in a bad sense. It is used in AV in Ps 95[8] (RV, RSV 'Meribah'), He 3[15] (so RV; RSV 'rebellion') of the conduct of the children of Israel towards God in the wilderness.

PSALMS.—1. Title and place in Canon.—The Book of Psalms is a collection of sacred poems, in large part liturgical in character and intended to be sung. The book belongs to the *Kethubim* or 'Writings,' *i.e.* the third and last group of the Jewish Scriptures. The order of the Writings was much less fixed than the order of the Law and the Prophets, the other two groups of Scriptures; but the Psalms in all cases come near the beginning of this group, and in the modern Hebrew printed Bibles, which follow the great majority of German MSS, they stand first. In placing the Psalms, together with the rest of the Writings, before the ('Latter') Prophets, the EV have followed the Greek version; but in the internal arrangement of the writings the English and Greek versions differ from one another.

The title of this collection of poems is derived from the Greek version, in which the book is entitled in some MSS *Psalmoi*, in others *Psaltērion* (in NT 'Psalms,' and 'Book of Psalms,' Lk 20[42] 24[44], Ac 1[20]). *Psalmos* in classical Greek signified the twanging of strings, and especially the musical sound produced by plucking the strings of a stringed instrument; as used here it means poems sung to the music of (stringed) instruments. The Greek word thus corresponds closely to the Hebrew *mizmōr*, of which it is the translation in the titles of individual Psalms (*e.g.* 3^1). The Hebrew title for the whole book is 'Praises,' which refers to the subject-matter of the poems rather than their musical character, although not all of them consist of praise.

The Psalter contains, according to the division of the Hebrew text followed by EV, 150 poems; the Greek version contains 151, but the last of these is described as 'outside the number.' This number does not exactly correspond with the number of different poems. On the one hand, there are one or two clear cases of a single Psalm having been wrongly divided into two; thus Psalms 9 and 10 are shown by the continuance of the acrostic scheme through the latter Psalm (cf ACROSTIC) to have once formed, as they still do in the Greek version, a single poem. So Pss 42, 43 are shown by the recurrence of the same refrain ($42^{5, 11}$ 43^5) to be one poem. But the Greek version is scarcely true to the original in making two distinct Psalms out of each of the Psalms numbered 116 and 147 respectively in the Hebrew text and EV. Probably in a larger number of cases, owing to an opposite fortune, two poems originally distinct have been joined together under a single number. A clear instance of this kind is Ps 108, which consists of two Psalms or fragments of Psalms (viz. 57^{7-11} 60^{5-12}). Among the more generally suspected instances of the same kind are Pss 19 (=vv.$^{1-6}$+$^{7-14}$) 24 (=vv.$^{1-6}$+$^{7-10}$) 27 (=vv.$^{1-6}$+$^{7-14}$) and 36 (=$^{1-4}$+$^{5-12}$); but caution is necessary here, for changes in metre and thought may be due to the liturgical setting of the Psalm (see below).

The Psalter does not contain quite the whole of what survives of Hebrew literature of this type. A few psalms not included in the Psalter are found in other books: see, *e.g.* Ex 15^{1-18}, 1 S 2^{1-10}, Is 12, 38^{10-20}, Hab 3. And we have other smaller collections in the 'Psalms of Solomon' written about 63 B.C. and the more or less contemporary hymns of the Dead Sea Scrolls. These, with such NT psalms as Lk $1^{46-55, 68-79}$, are important as showing that the period of psalm composition extended to the beginning of the Christian era.

2. Origin and history.—(1) *Reception into the Canon.*—The history of the Psalms and the Psalter is obscure; and many conclusions with regard to it rest, and for lack of other independent evidence must rest, on previous conclusions as to the origin and literary history of other Hebrew and Jewish literature. Conclusive external evidence for the existence of the Psalter *in its present extent* does not carry us very far back beyond the close of the Jewish Canon (see CANON OF OT); but the mode of allusion to the Psalms in the NT renders it very unlikely that the book was still open to additions in the 1st cent. A.D.; and the fact that none of the 'Psalms of Solomon' (see **1**, end) gained admission, and that this collection by its title perhaps presupposes the canonical 'Psalms of David,' renders it probable that the Psalter was complete, and not open to further additions, some time before 63 B.C. Other evidence (cf Hastings' *DB* iv, 147), such as that derived from the substantial agreement of the Greek version with the Hebrew text, does not carry the proof for the existence of the Psalter in its present extent much further. The net result is that, if not impossible, it is unsafe, to place the completion of the Psalter much below 100 B.C.

(2) *Previous history.*—Behind that date lies a long history; for the Psalter represents the conclusion of a complex literary growth or development. We may note, first, two things that prove this general fact, that the Psalter is neither a simple edition of the poems of a single man or a single age, nor the first collection of its kind. (1) At the close of Ps 72 stand the words: 'The prayers of David, the son of Jesse, are ended.' This is intelligible if the remark once closed an independent collection, and was taken over with the collection by the compiler of a larger work. But apart from some such hypothesis as this it is not intelligible; for the remark is not true of the Psalter as we have it; the prayers of David are not ended, other Psalms actually entitled 'prayers' and described as 'of David' are Pss 86 and 142; and several subsequent Psalms assigned to David are, without being so entitled, actually prayers. (2) The same Psalm is repeated in different parts of the Psalter with slight textual or editorial variations: thus Ps 14 = Ps 53; 40^{13-17}=70; 108=57^{7-11}+60^{5-12}. The Psalter, then, was composed by drawing on, and in some cases incorporating, earlier collections of Psalms.

Our next questions are: How many collections earlier than the Psalter can be traced? How far can the methods of the editor who drew on or combined these earlier collections be discerned? The first clue to the first question may be found in the titles referring to persons and their distribution; the more significant features of this distribution may be shown thus—

1. Pss 1, 2 are without title.
2. Pss 3–41 are all entitled 'of David,' except Ps 10, which is a continuation of Ps 9 (see above), and Ps 33.
3. Pss 42–49 are all entitled 'of the sons of Korah,' except Ps 43, which is a continuation of Ps 42 (see above).
4. Ps 50 is entitled 'of Asaph.'
5. Pss 51–72 are all entitled 'of David,' except Pss 66, 67, 71, 72.
6. Pss 73–83 are all entitled 'of Asaph.'
7. Of Pss 84–89, four (Pss 84, 85, 87, 88) are entitled 'of the sons of Korah,' one (Ps 86) 'of David,' and one (Ps 89) 'of Ethan.'
8. Pss 120–134 are all entitled (according to RSV), 'A Song of Ascents.'

The remaining forty-six Psalms (90–119, 135–150) are either without title, or the titles are not the same in any considerable number of consecutive Psalms (but note 108–110 and 138–145 entitled 'of David').

Now, if it stood by itself, the statement at the close of Ps 72 could be explained by a single process—the incorporation of a previous collection consisting of Pss 1–72 by an editor who added these to Pss 73–150 derived from other sources. But within Pss 1–72 we have two occurrences of the same Psalm (Ps 14=Ps 53), which in itself indicates that in Pss 1–72 at least two hymn-books are combined. Again, Ps 53 differs from Ps 14 by the entire absence from it of the name 'Yahweh' and the use in four places of the name 'God,' where Ps 14 uses 'Yahweh' (EV 'the LORD'). So also in Ps 70=Ps 40^{13-17} 'Yahweh' is twice retained, but twice, if not thrice, it is replaced by 'God.' But the editorial activity thus implied proves on examination to have affected the entire group of Pss 42–83; for the difference in the use of the names 'Yahweh' and 'God' between Pss 1–41, and Pss 42–83 is remarkable: in Pss 1–41 'Yahweh' occurs 272 times, 'God' (absolutely) 15 times; in Pss 42–83 'Yahweh' 43 times, but 'God' 200 times (see Driver, *LOT*^{9}, 371). Now this Elohistic Psalter, as Pss 42–83 are termed on account of the marked preference which is shown in them for the term *Elohim*='God,' is one of the earlier collections embodied in our Psalter; but it is itself in turn derived from different sources; for it includes the group of David's Psalms which closes with the statement that the prayers of David are ended—a statement which, though not true of the whole Psalter, is true of this earlier Psalter, for between Pss 73–83 no prayer of David occurs. It also includes Psalms 'of the sons of Korah' and 'of Asaph.' Very possibly this Elohistic Psalter has not reached us in its original condition; for (1) the untitled Psalms may have been subsequently inserted; and (2) the Psalms entitled 'of Asaph' may have once stood all together: at present Ps 50 stands isolated from the rest (Pss 73–83).

In addition to the occurrences of Psalms in two recensions and the occurrence of similar titles or groups, another feature points to earlier independent books of Psalms: this is the occurrence of a doxology or suitable concluding formula at certain points in the Psalter, viz. 41^{13} at the end of the first group of Psalms entitled 'of David'; 72^{18f} immediately before the statement that the prayers of David are ended; and 89[52]. See also 106[48] and 150, which last Psalm in its entirety may be taken as an enlarged doxology at the close of the completed Psalter. The doxologies at the end of Pss 41 and 72 occur at points which we have already found reason for regarding as the close of collections; that at 89[52], however, occurs not at the close of the Elohistic Psalms, but six Psalms later. Now five of these six Psalms are drawn from the same sources as supplied the Elohistic editor, viz. from the 'prayers of David' (Ps 86) and the book 'of the sons of Korah.' In Pss 42–89 we not improbably have the original Elohistic Psalter (Pss 42–83), enlarged by the addition of an appendix (Pss 84–89), in which the name 'Yahweh' was left unchanged, and consequently the form 'Elohim' ceases to predominate.

From the evidence thus far considered or suggested (it cannot here be given in greater detail), we may infer some such stages as these in the history of the Psalms before the completion of the Psalter:—

1. Compilation of a book entitled 'of David' and including Pss 3–41 (except the untitled Ps 33).
2. Compilation of a second hymn-book entitled 'of David' (Pss 51–72, with exceptions).
3. Compilation of a book entitled 'of Asaph' (Asaph being the name of a guild of singers, Ezr 2[41]).
4. Compilation of a book entitled 'of the sons of Korah' (also probably a guild of singers; cf 2 Ch 20[19]).
5. Compilation of 'the Elohistic Psalter' out of Psalms derived from 2, 3, 4, by an editor who generally substituted 'Elohim' ('God') for 'Yahweh' (EV 'the LORD').
6. Enlargement of 5 by the addition of Pss 84–89.
7. Compilation of a book with some such title as 'Songs of the Ascents.'

Can we detect the existence of other earlier Psalters? So far we have taken account mainly of titles of one type only and of titles which occur in groups. C. A. Briggs (*ICC*, 1906–7) carried the argument from titles to the existence of collections of Psalms further. He inferred that there was a collection of **Miktams** (a Heb. term of uncertain meaning), whence Pss 16, 56–60, and Is 38[9-20] were drawn; a collection of **Maskils** (another Heb. term of uncertain meaning), whence Pss 32, 42–45, 52–55, 74, 78, 88, 89, 142 were derived; another collection of Psalms proper, of poems set to music, whence the fifty-seven Psalms described in the titles as **Mizmor** (EV 'psalm') were derived: and yet another collection which bore the name of the musical director or choir master (AV, RV **'the chief musician'**; RSV **'the choirmaster'**), whence the fifty-five Psalms so entitled were derived. If this be the case, then the composite titles enable us to see that many Psalms stood successively in two or three collections before they obtained their place in the completed Psalter; *e.g.* Ps 19—entitled 'of (or belonging to) the chief musician, a Psalm, of (or belonging to) David'—had previously been included in three distinct collections; and so also Ps 44—entitled 'of the chief musician, of the sons of Korah, Maskil.' Perhaps the strongest case for these further collections is that of the chief musician's Psalter; in any case, the English reader must be warned that the preposition prefixed to 'the chief musician' is the same as that prefixed to 'David' or 'Asaph' or 'the sons of Korah,' though in the first case RV renders 'for' (RSV 'to') and in the latter cases 'of' (RSV *id.*). Consequently, since in many cases it is impossible, owing to intervening words (*e.g.* in Pss 12, 45), to interpret such a combination as 'of the chief musician, of David,' 'of the chief musician, of the sons of Korah' of *joint* authorship, we must see in them either conflicting ascriptions of authorship placed side by side, or, far more probably, as just suggested, the titles of collections of Psalms or hymn-books to which they had previously belonged. It is then highly probable that in the first instance such titles as **'of David,' 'of Asaph,' 'of the sons of Korah,'** were neither intended nor understood to name the *author* of the Psalm in question. But if this was so, we can also see that before the final stage in the growth of the Psalter they were misunderstood; for the title 'of David' clearly implied authorship to the author(s) of the longer titles in Pss 7 and 18: it is scarcely less clear that the title implied authorship to the authors of other titles that suggest an historical setting (see, *e.g.* Pss 3, 57).

Titles of the Psalms.—Inasmuch as the terms occurring in the titles to the Psalms are not explained elsewhere in this Dictionary, it will be convenient to give here brief notes on those which have not already been discussed. It may be said in general that great obscurity enshrouds the subject, and that, in spite of the many ingenious speculations to which the terms in question have given rise, it is hazardous to base, on any particular theories of interpretation, far-reaching conclusions. With few exceptions the titles of the latter part of the Psalter (Pss 90–150) are free from these terms.

Apparently we have in the titles not only notes indicating the source whence the Psalm was derived (see above), but also in some cases notes defining the character of the Psalm (see below 12 and 13 and [?] 19), or some circumstances of its use. Thus Ps 92 was to be used on the Sabbath, Ps 30 at the Feast of the Dedication (1 Mac 4[56], Jn 10[22]), celebrated from the time of the Maccabees onward; and Ps 100 on the occasion of offering thank-offering; so also 'to bring to remembrance' (AV, RV) in Pss 38 and 70 may rather mean 'at the time of making the offering called *'azkārāh* (RV 'memorial,' *e.g.* Nu 5[26]) as RSV 'for the memorial offering'; see also 5 (below). This type of note is more frequent in the LXX, which assigns Ps 24 for the use of the first day of the week, Ps 48 for the second, Ps 94 for the third, Ps 93 for the day before the Sabbath. Other titles, it is supposed, name, by the opening words of songs sung to it or otherwise, the tune to which the Psalm was to be sung (on *'Ayyeleth hash-shaḥar*, *'Al-tashḥēth*, *Yônath-ēlem-reḥōḳîm*, *Shōshannîm*; see below), or the instruments which were to accompany the singing of the Psalm (? *Neḥîlôth*, *Neghînôth*).

For ease of reference we give these and other relevant terms of a like kind in alphabetic order.

1. **'Ayyeleth hash-shaḥar** (Ps 22) is a transliteration of Hebrew words which mean 'the hind of the dawn' (cf RSV; AV **Aijeleth Shahar,** RV **Aijeleth hash-Shahar**); the Hebrew consonants might equally well mean 'the help of the dawn.' These words are preceded by the Hebrew preposition *'al*, which, among many others, has the meaning 'in accordance with,' and here and in other similar titles not improbably means 'set to' (RV). The whole note, then, may mean that the Psalm was to be sung to the tune to which the song beginning 'the hind (or 'the help') of the dawn' had been accustomed to be sung. With this title cf below 3, 7, 9, 10, 14, 20 (not all equally probable instances).

2. **Alamoth** (Heb. *'alāmôth*) (Ps 46). This term and **Sheminith** (Heb. *Shemînîth*) (Pss 6, 12) must be treated together. They are preceded by the same preposition *'al* discussed under 1, and accordingly RV renders 'set to the Sheminith,' etc. But it is hardly likely in view of 1 Ch 15[19-21], that these terms are names of tunes, though they obviously have some reference to the music. The usual meaning of *shemînîth* in Hebrew is 'eighth,' of *'alāmôth* 'young women'; so that the titles run 'upon' or 'according to' or 'set to the eighth' or 'the maidens.' 'The maidens,' it is conjectured, means 'the voices of maidens,' and that, it is further conjectured, stands for 'the falsetto voice of males'; so that the whole phrase 'set to the maidens' would mean 'to be sung with soprano voices,' Thence, it is inferred, 'set to the eighth' means 'sung with the bass voice.' All this, though it has found considerable acceptance and has sometimes been stated with little or no qualification, possesses no more than the value of an unverified and perhaps unverifiable guess.

3. **Al-tashheth** (Heb. *'al-tashḥēth*) (Pss 57, 58, 59, 75 RV; AV **Al-taschith**). The words mean 'destroy not' (cf RSV), and may be the beginning of a vintage song cited in Is 65[8] 'Destroy it not, for a blessing is in it.' Then the note presumably directs that the

Psalms shall be sung to the tune of this song (cf 1). But the omission of the preposition *'al* used in similar cases is suspicious.

4. **The Chief Musician** (or Choirmaster). See preceding page.

5. **' Ascents '** (RV, RSV ; **' degrees '** AV), **a song of** (Pss 120–134). The Hebrew may also be the plural of a compound expression, and mean ' Songs of Ascent.' In the latter case the title of the whole collection has been prefixed to each Psalm (see above). ' Songs of Ascent ' *might* mean ' Songs of the Ascent ' (cf Ezr 7⁹) from Babylon, but more probably ' Songs of the Ascent ' to Jerusalem on the occasion of the great yearly festivals. On the supposition that the meaning is ' A song of Ascents ' (plural), the phrase has been explained with reference to the 15 ' ascents ' or ' steps ' (such is the meaning of the Hebrew word in Ex 20^{26}, 1 K 10^{19f}), that led from the Women's Court to that of the men in the Temple area ; it has been inferred that one of each of these 15 Psalms was sung on each of the 15 steps. (Cf the Mishnah tractate *Middoth*, ii. 5.)

6. **Dedication of the House** (or Temple) (Ps 30). See above and DEDICATION [FEAST OF THE].

7. **Gittith** (Pss 8, 81, 84). The word is the feminine of the adjective derived from *Gath*. In the three titles it is preceded by the preposition *'al* (see under 1, and the phrase has been supposed to mean that the Psalm was to be sung to the accompaniment of the Gittite instrument (cf 15 and ? 16), whatever that may have been, or to the Gittite tune (cf 1). If the word was originally pronounced ' Gittôth ' (plural of *gath*, ' a wine-press '), the note may direct that the Psalms were to be sung to some vintage melody (cf 3).

8. **Higgaion** (Heb. *Higgāyôn*).—The word thus transliterated in 9^{16} (EV) is *translated* in 92^{3} ' a solemn sound ' (AV, RV), ' melody ' (RSV), and in 19^{14} ' meditation ' (EV). In 9^{16} it seems to be a musical note.

9. **Jeduthun** (Heb. *Yᵉdhûthûn*).—On the analogy of ' of David,' etc. (see above), the title in Ps 39 should run ' of Jeduthun.' In Pss 62, 77 the preposition prefixed to the term is *'al* (cf 1), and by analogy Jeduthun might be the name of a tune or an instrument. But this is very uncertain ; see JEDUTHUN.

10. **Jonath-elem-rehokim** (Heb. *yônath 'ēlem rᵉḥōḳīm*) (Ps 56 RV ; AV **Jonath-elem-rechokim**). The Hebrew consonants are most naturally translated ' the dove of the distant terebinths ' (cf RSV) ; less probably, but as the tradition embodied in the vocalized Hebrew text suggests, ' the dove of the silence of them that are distant.' The note is to be explained as 1.

11. **Mahalath** (Heb. *maḥᵃlath*) (Ps 53), **Mahalath Leannoth** (Heb. *maḥᵃlath lᵉ'annôth*) (Ps 88). The words are very ambiguous and obscure, but the fact that in both Psalms the preposition *'al* precedes, relates these notes to the group which of 1 is typical.

12. **Maskil** (Pss 32, 42–45, 52–55, 74, 78, 88, 89, 142). The term is usually thought to describe the character of the Psalm, for etymologically it may be held to denote a carefully composed, didactic or meditative poem ; but its precise meaning remains uncertain.

13. **Miktam** (Pss 16, 56–60, also perhaps in the original text of Is 38^{9}) is a term like the last, but of still more uncertain meaning. S. Mowinckel (*Psalmenstudien IV* [1923], 4 f, *Offersang og Sangoffer* [1951], 492 f) suggests on etymological grounds that it may indicate a Psalm composed with an expiatory purpose. The Rabbinical interpretation—a *golden* (*poem*)—is quite unconvincing.

14. **Muth-labben** (Ps 9). The Hebrew consonants may mean ' Death whitens ' or ' Death of a son,' and this may have been the commencement of a song which gave a name to a tune ; cf 1. But it is not unreasonable to suspect the text, as many have done.

15. **Neginoth** (Heb. *nᵉghînôth*) (AV in Pss 4, 6, 54, 55, 67, 76) and **Neginah** (Heb. *nᵉghînāh*) (Ps 61). The words thus, in excess of caution, transliterated by AV are correctly *translated* by RV, RSV ' stringed instruments ' (RV singular in Ps 61), and so even by AV in Hab 3^{19}.

16. **Nehiloth** (Heb. *Nᵉḥîlôth*) (Ps 5, AV, RV), often supposed to mean ' wind instruments,' *e.g.* ' flutes ' (RSV) (cf 15). But this is quite doubtful. Uncertain, too, is the view that the word indicates a tune ; the preposition (*'el*) that precedes is not the same as that which generally introduces what appear to be names of tunes elsewhere (cf 1) ; but cf 20.

17. **Selah.** See SELAH.

18. **Sheminith.** See 2.

19. **Shiggaion** (Heb. *Shiggāyôn*) (Ps 7). The plural of this word occurs in Hab 3^{1}, **Shigionoth** (Heb. *Shigyōnôth*). The root from which the word is derived means ' to go astray ' or ' to reel ' (as *e.g.* from drunkenness). Hence, since Ewald, many have conjectured that *Shiggaion* means a ' wild, passionate song, with rapid changes of rhythm ' (*BDB*) ; but better, perhaps, a wildly emotional ' lament ' or ' dirge ' (cf *KB*).

20. **Shoshannim** (Pss 45, 69), **Shushan Eduth** (Heb. *Shûshan-'ēdhûth*) (Ps 60), and **Shoshannim Eduth** (Heb. *Shôshannîm 'ēdhûth*) (Ps 80) appear to be different ways of citing the same song to the tune of which these Psalms were to be sung. The preposition used before these words is *'al* (cf 1), except in Ps 30, where it is *'el*, which in some cases is used interchangeably with *'al*. It is curious that Psalms so different as 45 and 69 should be set to the same tune. It has been thought that Ps 80 cites the first two words of the poem, ' (Like) lilies (or rather anemones) is the Testimony (or Law) ' ; Pss 45, 69 the first word only, while Ps 60 was variant, ' (Like) a lily ' (singular for plural), etc.. but this is by no means certain.

Is it possible to determine the dates at which any of these collections of Psalms were made? Obviously they are earlier than the completion of the Psalter, *i.e.* than about 100 B.C. (see above) ; obviously also the *collections* were later than the *latest* Psalm which they originally contained. One or more Psalms in all the collections show more or less generally admitted signs of being post-exilic. The various collections therefore which we have in the Psalter were compiled between the 6th and the 2nd cent. B.C. ; and this, apart from the dates of individual Psalms, is significant for the part which continued to be played by the Psalms in the religious life of the post-exilic community.

3. Character of the contents.—This is not to say that all the Psalms in the foregoing collections were themselves a product of the post-exilic age. Indeed a more sympathetic understanding of the forms of worship in ancient Israel and a growing recognition that the canonical prophets need to be studied against a background of worship which can be reconstructed, in part at least, from the Psalter are amongst the most important developments in recent study of the OT. The credit for this must go, in the first place, to Hermann Gunkel, who at the turn of the century began to stress the importance of studying the Psalms according to (*a*) their literary types or ' classes ' (*Gattungen*), and (*b*) the particular ' situation in life ' (*Sitz im Leben*) which had brought each Psalm into being. At the same time he rightly insisted upon the importance of doing so in the light of the similar material from the religious literature of early Egypt and Mesopotamia ; and to this we must now add the mythological texts from Râs Shamra (Ugarit). (See especially *Die Psalmen* [1926] and, with the co-operation of J. Begrich, *Einleitung in die Psalmen* [1933] ; also, for the Ugaritic material, J. H. Patton, *Canaanite Parallels in the Book of Psalms* [1944].) Gunkel admitted that, for the most part, the different types of Psalm had their origin in cultic circles ; but he maintained that most of the Psalms themselves, although showing the influence of the corresponding cultic types, were composed independently of such an association and, as such, were more spiritual in character. It is to the credit of Sigmund Mowinckel, who widened the field of comparative study so as to include the religious rites of the so-called ' primitive ' peoples of our own day, that it is now increasingly recognized that the majority of the Psalms were designed from the first for use in worship and, in some respects, worship of no mean spiritual order, and that their authors are to be sought, for the most part, among the Temple personnel, specifically the cultic prophets and their associates in the so-called musical guilds (such as that of Asaph: cf **2** (2), *ad init.*), which figure so prominently in the post-exilic records, *e.g.* 1 Ch 25[1ff]. (See, *e.g. Psalmenstudien I-VI* (1921–24), *Offersang og sangoffer* (1951).)

A few of the Psalms, of course, defy any such classification, unless one is prepared to admit a very broad definition for the different types; but the following groups may easily be distinguished.

A. *Hymns*, some of a processional character, which in many cases extol Yahweh for the assurance of His power and majesty in the realm of nature and, above all, the tokens of His providential care for Israel in the great events of the nation's history. *E.g.* 24, 29, 46–48, 68, 76, 78, 81, 82, 84, 87, 93, 95–100, 103–106, 113–115, 145–150. Of these, Pss 93 and 95–99, which celebrate in a very special way the universal Kingship of Yahweh, must be singled out as indicative of the changing climate of opinion concerning the history of Israel's faith and worship. Under Mowinckel's influence more and more students of the OT are refusing to see in these Psalms evidence of dependence upon Is 40–55; instead, stress is laid on the greater degree of probability attaching to the view that these and other, seemingly related, Psalms have as their original 'setting in life' the celebration of Yahweh's Kingship at the autumnal festival of the Jerusalem Temple in the pre-exilic period, and that the Psalms in question have themselves had a marked effect upon the message of this prophet.

B. *Communal Laments*, which were composed under the constraint of some calamity, *e.g.* famine or war, which threatened the well-being of society as a whole. *E.g.* 44, 74, 79, 80.

C. *Communal Songs of Thanksgiving*, which express the gratitude of the worshippers for some mark of the Divine favour such as a successful harvest or victory in battle. *E.g.* 67, 124.

D. *Individual Laments*, which reveal the worshipper as suffering from sickness or other ills and, in some cases, subject to slander, false accusation or, indeed, active persecution. *E.g.* 3, 5–7, 13, 17, 22, 25, 26, 28, 31, 35, 38, 39, 42 and 43, 51, 54–57, 59, 61, 63, 64, 69–71, 86, 88, 102, 109, 120, 130, 140–143. Occasionally these Psalms are marked by a sudden change of tone which indicates the worshipper's assurance of answered prayer, and it has been suggested that this corresponds to some element in the ritual, for example a prophetic oracle or sign, which would be indicative of Yahweh's favourable response. *E.g.* 6, 22, 28, 31, 51, 55, 57, 63, 69, 71. The recognition of this type of Psalm, like that of the next group, is indicative of the strong reaction which has set in against the theory that the 'I' who speaks in so many of the Psalms is not an individual in the strict sense of the term but a personification of the community (cf Pss 124, 129).

E. *Individual Songs of Thanksgiving*, which correspond in principle to the second part of those Individual Laments which end with an assurance of answered prayer. *E.g.* 18, 30, 32, 34, 41, 66, 92, 116, 118, 138 (cf Is 38[10-20], Jon 2[2-9]). In some cases from each of these two groups it is clear that the words of thanksgiving are linked with an act of sacrifice which marks the fulfilment of a vow. *E.g.* 22, 54, 56, 66, 116 (cf Jon 2[2-9]). In others, however, no such reference occurs; and indeed in more than one case the normal ritual of sacrifice is evidently regarded with some misgiving, although it is equally clear that the worshipper is offering thanks in public and thus bearing due witness within a cultic setting to Yahweh's power and willingness to save those who call upon Him (see below, **6** (5)).

While it is of value to distinguish Psalms of the foregoing types, it is possible and indeed helpful to use different criteria for distinguishing other types which may cut across this classification and, indeed, may do so in the case of one another. The most important of these are:

F. *Royal Psalms, i.e.*, obviously pre-exilic Hymns, Laments or Songs of Thanksgiving, which find their focus in the person of a king either as the leader of his people and, therefore, with special responsibility towards Yahweh or in a more individual capacity as one who is about to enjoy marriage or is obviously subject to ordinary human ills. *E.g.* 2, 18, 20, 21, 28, 45, 61, 72, 101, 110, 118, 132, 145 (see below, **4**, **6** (3)). In fact it is conceivable that far more of the Psalms in the two immediately preceding groups should also be classified in this way; but one cannot be certain of this.

G. *Oracular Psalms, i.e.* compositions which wholly or in part communicate to the congregation or to an individual worshipper, especially the king, what is Yahweh's will and pleasure in a given connexion. *E.g.* 2, 12, 50, 60, 75, 81, 82, 85, 91, 95, 110 (cf 121).

H. *Wisdom Psalms, i.e.* reflective or didactic poems which may be of a simple, proverbial kind or may represent the more personal struggle of one who is haunted by life's cruelty, suffering and injustice. *E.g.* 1, 37, 49, 73, 112, 127, 128, 133. The possible connexion between the Psalms of this class and those of a more obviously cultic type (*e.g.* 78) remains to be determined in the light of our increasing knowledge of the comparatively early appearance of Wisdom literature in the ancient Near East and the relationship which evidently existed between scribal school and temple.

4. Dates of individual Psalms.—This is a difficult question which allows scope for considerable divergence of opinion; and the only comparatively straightforward arguments in favour of (*a*) a pre-exilic, and (*b*) an exilic or post-exilic date are (*a*) the obvious existence of royal Psalms which cannot satisfactorily be explained in terms of the post-exilic period, *e.g.* a foreign monarch or one of the Hasmonaean rulers, and (*b*) allusions to the Exile or the desolation of Zion. It is now generally conceded that clear examples of (*a*) are those which celebrate the founding of the Davidic dynasty and its royal sanctuary on Mount Zion (132), a king's enthronement (2, 101, 110) or some similar anniversary (21, 72), a royal wedding (45), a king's departure on a military campaign (20) and his victorious return (18). In the case of (*b*) an obvious example is Ps 137, and other likely examples are Pss 102 and 147. On the other hand Ps 50, for instance, serves to show that apparently an earlier Psalm could be adapted to an exilic or post-exilic situation by the incorporation or addition of new lines. Moreover, special caution is required on the part of the English reader, for it is now quite clear that the expression which is traditionally rendered by some such words as 'turn (*or* restore) the captivity' really means 'restore the fortunes (*or* well-being),' and thus, while not inapplicable to the conditions of the Exile, is not in itself sufficient evidence for an exilic or post-exilic date. Compare, *e.g.* AV and RV with RSV in the case of Pss 85 and 126; and, for the significance of the above expression, see Job 42[10]. For the rest, grave doubts attach to arguments for an exilic or post-exilic date which are based upon (i) literary style and language; (ii) imagined allusions to social and political conditions, such as the frequent division of the Jews into religious parties, with the use of terms like 'the poor,' 'the pious' (*ḥᵃsîdhîm*) as party names; and (iii) supposed dependence upon exilic and post-exilic writings (cf **3** A, above).

If, as the previous remarks should have suggested, it is in many cases only possible to determine whether a Psalm is pre-exilic or post-exilic on evidence which is, at best, somewhat widely applicable, it should be clear that the attempt to fix the authorship or dates of Psalms very precisely must generally prove fruitless. Are there *any* that can be referred, even with great probability, to a particular occasion as that of their origin, or to a particular writer? The mere fact that a Psalm may appear to be suitable to a particular occasion, as, *e.g.* Ps 46 to the deliverance from Sennacherib in 701, does not necessarily prove that it even refers to it, still less that it was written at the time; the question arises, is the occasion in question the *only* one to which the terms of the Psalm are applicable, or are those terms sufficiently specific to render it improbable that the Psalm might have fitted other occasions unknown to us, or but partially known? Thus Pss 44, 74, 79 presuppose conditions which resemble what is known of the period of the Maccabaean revolt (cf 1 Maccabees) more closely than what is known of any other period, and on that ground they were once commonly assigned to the Maccabaean period : the question is, are the descriptions so specific that they might not also correspond to the conditions of, say, the Persian period, the Babylonian period, or even the Assyrian period (to which other scholars have referred one or another of these Psalms), if we were equally well informed with regard to these? The position is further aggravated by the possibility that in some cases, *e.g.* Pss 18, 46, 48, 89 and 118, the absence of any specific historical allusions may be due to the Psalm's having its original setting in a form of ritual drama, and that we should think in terms of what Mowinckel would describe as cultic reality rather than simple historicity.

5. The question of Davidic Psalms.—On the whole the question of authorship retains an interest only with reference to David. The theory that David was the author of Psalms can be traced back as far as the time (not to be dated precisely, but centuries at least after David's time) when the historical notes were added in certain Psalms to the title 'of David' (see above). Whether it goes back further to the time of the origin of the collection entitled 'of David' is less clear, for it is by no means certain that the similar title 'of the chief musician (*or* choirmaster)' referred to authorship (see above); and, indeed, as we shall see, the same is true of the expression 'of David.' Still, we may consider the argument which, based on the assumption that 'of David' implies authorship, is to the effect that, if so many Psalms (as seventy-three in the Hebrew text, more in the Greek text, and all in later Jewish tradition) were attributed to David, some must actually be his, though many so entitled are demonstrably and admittedly not. In a word, where there is much smoke, there must have been some fire. The argument at best does not seem to justify more than a strong probability that David wrote psalms; and possibly the fact that David was a famous poet, even though all his poems more nearly resembled 2 S 1^{19-27} than the Psalms, coupled with his fame as a zealous worshipper of Yahweh, may be the extent of the historical fact underlying the late traditions. But even granted that the evidence were strong enough to justify the statement that some Psalms of David are preserved in the Psalter, the most important problem still remains to be solved, viz. which Psalms in particular are David's? No doubt there are some Psalms which in whole or in part may not be incompatible with what we know of David's life, but the allusions are too general to enable us to deny that they are equally applicable to many other lives. In fact it will be found on examination that the positive reasons assigned for regarding any particular Psalm as David's are inconclusive; they often amount to nothing more than an argument that there is nothing in such and such Psalms which *forbids* us to ascribe them to David, the simplest and, perhaps, most obvious example being Ps 23.

Moreover it must be borne in mind that, while it remains uncertain that the name 'David' is derived from a god 'Dod,' it was almost certainly the regnal name assumed by Elhanan (cf A. M. Honeyman, *JBL*, lxvii (1948), 23 f), and, as such, it was to prove of developing significance in its application to the founder of the Davidic dynasty; for in Israelite thinking the house of David would be as much 'David' as, say, the nation 'Israel' was the continuing embodiment of the patriarch whose name it bore. This being the case, it may well be that the expression 'of David' sometimes had the meaning 'Davidic' in the sense that the Psalms in question were in general use in connexion with the royal ritual and mythology of Solomon's Temple, for this was undeniably a royal sanctuary intimately associated with the Davidic dynasty. The likelihood of this is reinforced by the fact that in the mythological texts of the 14th cent. B.C. from Râs Shamra (Ugarit) the heading 'of Baal,' for example, is used to indicate that the tablet in question belongs to the cycle of texts which have the adventures of Baal as their leading motif.

6. Religious value and influence of the Psalter.—Probably no book of the OT has exercised a more profound and extensive influence over succeeding ages than the Psalms. Among the Jews, indeed, the Law has received a more persistent and greater attention; but the place of the Psalms in the history of the Christian Church and in Christian experience is typified by the frequency with which they are quoted in the NT. To trace this influence or to illustrate it as R. E. Prothero did so excellently in *The Psalms in Human Life* (1904), falls outside the scope of this article. All that can be attempted, and even that but very inadequately, is to indicate some of the leading ideas, some of the striking religious qualities of the Psalms. And in doing this it is necessary to emphasize clearly the fact that such ideas and qualities are by no means common to all the 150 or more poems which were written by an indefinite number of writers, and were gathered together in our Psalter. What alone is aimed at here is to draw attention to some of the qualities that are at least frequently present, and some of the ideas which frequently or strikingly appear—to the ideas and qualities which have in large measure been the cause of the great and persistent influence which the Psalms have exercised.

(1) We turn first to the Psalmists' *belief in God*: and here it must suffice to draw attention to two features —the breadth of the conception, and the intensity of the consciousness, of God. The early belief of Israel that other gods besides Yahweh existed has left vivid traces in the Psalter (*e.g.* 29, 82, 89, 97), and there can be no reasonable doubt that originally, so far as some of the Psalms are concerned, this reflects the standpoint of the pre-exilic period. Even so it is equally clear from these Psalms that Yahweh was regarded as the supreme God, in fact the Divine King, to whom all other gods were subservient. As such He was not only the Creator and Sustainer of man's habitable world but the Lord of History. In short, the recognition of His control in the realm of nature could not be divorced from that of His interest in the realm of man's behaviour. Indeed, as King of the gods, Yahweh's authority was such that the gods themselves were ultimately answerable to Him for their failure to establish justice upon earth (82); for the standpoint is obviously that of Dt 32^{8f} (LXX), which tells us that the gods of the nations were granted jurisdiction over their particular territories by Yahweh Himself, who, in virtue of His supremacy, was able not only to do this but to adopt the Hebrews as His own chosen people (see below (2)). In Israel the monotheistic idea sprang, not from an abstraction of what was common to many gods previously or still worshipped, but from the expansion of the thought of the same one God whom alone Israel had previously worshipped. While Israel believed the gods of the other nations to be real beings set over against Yahweh, it was natural for them to feel a peculiarly close relation to Yahweh, to look upon Him as their possession just as they felt themselves to belong closely to Him; the belief in other gods perished, the sense of Yahweh as a close and intimate Personality survived; and not a little of the enduring power of the Psalms is due to the vivid apprehension of God that resulted. Yahweh was the 'Living God' as opposed to the comparative nonentities worshipped by other peoples (cf 42, 84: and see A. R. Johnson, *The Vitality of the Individual in the Thought of Ancient Israel* (1949), 88–107); and an important factor in this development was, no doubt, the contrast which was drawn from the first between the imageless worship of Yahweh and the image worship which was characteristic of other nations. (Cf H. H. Rowley, *The Faith of Israel* [1956], 76 ff.)

(2) This thought of the peculiarly intimate relationship

which existed between Yahweh and Israel finds familiar expression in terms of *the covenant at Sinai-Horeb*; but it must be emphasized that the way in which this idea dominates the Psalter as something vital to the well-being of the nation—king and commoner alike—can only be appreciated in full by the Hebraist, who is made aware of its presence in language which goes far beyond the comparatively rare use of the simple Hebrew term which is commonly rendered as 'covenant.' (Cf N. H. Snaith, *The Distinctive Ideas of the Old Testament* [1944], 94 ff). Time and again, by the use of certain Psalms in the regular worship of the festivals or, it may be, in some form of service designed to secure Divine aid in meeting the more serious challenges of life, the worshipper is reminded or, as sometimes happens, seeks to remind Yahweh of the momentous occasion at Sinai-Horeb, when God and people entered into a mutual pledge of loyalty to one another and to the common good. Lessons may be drawn for all and sundry from the chequered history of the intervening years with their eloquent testimony to that which happens to a faithful or an apostate people (*e.g.* 77, 78, 81, 95, 105, 106, 136); or the individual, faced with his own more personal problems, may plead with Yahweh for the help which he is led to expect as a member of this covenant people whose ties are so close with Him who is not merely the God of Israel but the 'Living God' with supreme power over all the issues of life and death (*e.g.* 6, 13, 16, 25, 26, 30–32; and so on).

(3) This brings us to another feature of the Psalms which has contributed to the influence exercised by them —the hope that is in them, *their Messianic outlook*. While it may be true that the original sense of many passages has been obscured by specific applications to the life of Christ, applications which in some instances have been built on a very questionable Hebrew text or an illegitimate translation, closer examination of the so-called Royal Psalms has brought into proper perspective, not only the lofty ideal which was associated with the Davidic dynasty at its best, but also the fact that this ideal had its roots in a covenant between Yahweh as the national God and David as the founder of the dynasty, and that this covenant was to be the means of realizing the ideal already enshrined in the covenant which had been mediated through Moses at Sinai-Horeb (89, 132; cf 2 S 23^{1-7}). In short, there is reason to believe that some of these Royal Psalms, like those which celebrate the Kingship of Yahweh (see above, **3** A), look forward to a future when this ideal of righteousness will be realized not only within the boundaries of Israel but also amongst the other peoples of the earth; and this will be brought about by a scion of the House of David who, as the true Messiah in virtue of his proven loyalty to the Davidic covenant and *ipso facto* to the purpose of the covenant at Sinai-Horeb, will enable Israel to fulfil its mission to the world. (Cf A. R. Johnson, *Sacral Kingship in Ancient Israel* (1955).) Even so it remains true that Israel occupies a central position, and Zion is to become for the whole world what it comes to be for Israel—the centre of religion, the place where Yahweh will be worshipped. No Psalmist has attained to the standpoint of our Lord's teaching in Jn 4^{21ff}.

(4) From the thought of the Psalmists about God and their hope in Him, we may turn to their thought of men, which is for the most part primarily of Israel, and in particular to their *sense of sin*. Judged by their attitude towards sin, the Psalms fall into two great groups: the extreme representatives of each group are very different in thought, tone, and temper; the less extreme (and they are in the majority) approximate more or less closely to one another. In the one group the writers claim for themselves, and, so far as they identify themselves with Israel, for their nation, that they are righteous, and in consequence have a claim on God's righteousness to deliver them from their present afflictions (so *e.g.* Pss 7, 17, 26, 28, 44, 86). In the other group, confession is made of great iniquity; the appeal for help, if made, can be made to God's compassion and willingness to forgive (see Pss 25, 32, 40, 51, etc.). The view taken of sin in both groups of Psalms is best appreciated by noticing how, with all their differences, they are yet related. Some sense of sin is perhaps never altogether absent from the Psalms that lay claim to righteousness, and a strong sense of relative righteousness generally accompanies the most fervent confession of sin. Even in such Psalms as the 32nd and the 51st, where the difference is most clearly felt between God's standard and man's performance, the sense is also present of a sharp difference between those who, in spite of sin, yet pursue after righteousness, and those who constitute the class of 'the wicked' or 'the transgressors.' This attitude towards sin might doubtless without much difficulty become that of the Pharisee in the parable; but it is also closely akin to the highest Christian consciousness, in which the shadow of sin shows darkest in the light of the righteousness and love of God as revealed in Christ, and which leads the truest followers of Christ, with all honesty, to account themselves the chief of sinners. And it is because the 'penitential' Psalms are confessions, not so much of grosser sins open to the rebuke of man, but of the subtler sins which are committed in the sight of and against God only, of the sins which stand in the way of the nation called of God fulfilling its missionary destiny, that these Psalms have played so conspicuous a part in forming the habit and moulding the form of the confession of the Christian man and the Christian Church.

(5) Allied to this is the more spiritual attitude to *sacrifice* which is discernible in the Psalter. It comes to the fore in one of the most spectacular of the Oracular Psalms (50), where emphasis is laid upon the fact that, if sacrifice is to be acceptable to Yahweh, it must be a genuine expression of gratitude on the part of those who are in covenant with Him. If figures even more prominently, however, in the Individual Laments and Songs of Thanksgiving with their stress on the need to bear witness in public to Yahweh's willingness and power to help those who put their trust in Him. Several of these Psalms make it clear that the offering of sacrifice was a recognized means of thanksgiving for answer to prayer (*e.g.* 22, 54, 56, 66, 116); but in other Psalms from these groups the thought of ordinary animal sacrifice as a suitable mode of expressing such thanks to Yahweh is definitely rejected; in fact, man's proper sacrifice is that of 'a broken spirit' or 'a broken and a contrite heart' (51; cf 69). Thus the Psalter offers evidence to show that something like a purist movement appears to have arisen within the cultus itself, and, while it lies outside the scope of this article to discuss the degree to which one or another of the canonical prophets may have contributed to this movement, it is clear that there is here a line of thought which is akin to that of Jeremiah's vision of a new covenant which would be written upon the heart (Jer 31^{31ff}); so that, here again, we see something of that long spiritual travail which ultimately gave birth to the new Israel of the Christian Church. G. B. G.—**A. R. J.**

PSALMS OF SOLOMON.—See PSEUDEPIGRAPHA, 3.

PSALTERY.—See MUSIC, etc., **4**.

PSEUDEPIGRAPHA.—The word *pseudepigrapha* means 'false or spurious writings,' especially those which purport to be written by Biblical characters or in Biblical times. In accordance with conventional usage of the word, the present article will deal with certain pseudepigraphic works of Jewish or Jewish-Christian origin, dating from the centuries just before and just after the beginning of the Christian era. Besides those mentioned here, scores of other pseudepigrapha are known to have been circulated among various early Jewish and Christian sects.

One of the literary forms which is characteristic of the pseudepigrapha is the *apocalypse* (a work which purports to reveal what is hidden). Its ultimate origins have been disputed by scholars, but among the Hebrews its forerunner was the description of the **Day of Yahweh**. On that day, the prophets taught, Yahweh was to punish the enemies of Israel and to establish His people as a world power. In the course of time this conception was supplemented by the further expectation of a judgment for Jews as well as for heathen (Am 2^{6-8} 3^{9-15} 5^{10-13}, Zec 1^{2-18} 2^{4-15}, Jl 2^{18-28}, Ezk 30^{2f}). The first approach to the apocalyptic method is probably to be seen in Zec 9–14. It was in the same period that the tendencies towards the aesthetic conceptions which had been inherited from the Babylonian exile were beginning to be realized under the influence of Hellenistic culture. Because of their religion, literature was the only form of aesthetic expression (except music) which was open to the art impulses of the Jews. In the apocalypse we thus can see a union of the symbolism and myths of Babylonia with the religious faith of the Jews, under the influence of Hellenistic culture. By its very origin it was the literary means of setting forth by the use of symbols the certainty of Divine judgment and the equal certainty of Divine deliverance. The symbols are usually animals of various sorts, and frequently involve composite creatures whose various parts represented certain qualities of the animals from which they were derived.

Apocalyptic is akin to prophecy. Its purpose was fundamentally to encourage faith in Yahweh on the part of those who were in distress, by 'revealing' the future. Between genuine prophetism and apocalyptic there existed, however, certain differences not always easy to formulate, but appreciable to students of the two types of religious instruction. (*a*) The prophet, taking a stand in the present, so interprets current history as to disclose Divine forces at work therein, and the inevitable outcome of a certain course of conduct. The writers of the apocalypse, however, seem to have had little spiritual insight into the providential ordering of existing conditions, and could see only present misery and miraculous deliverance. (*b*) Assuming the name of some worthy long since dead, the apocalyptist re-wrote the past in terms of prophecy in the name of some hero or seer of Hebrew history. On the strength of the fulfilment of this alleged prophecy, he forecast, though in very general terms, the future. (*c*) Prophecy made use of symbol in literature as a means of enforcing or making intelligible its Divinely inspired message. The apocalyptists employed allegorically an elaborate machinery of symbol, chief among which were sheep, bulls, birds, as well as mythological beings like Beliar and the Antichrist.

The parent of apocalyptic is the book of Daniel, which, by the almost unanimous consensus of scholars, appeared in the Maccabaean period (see DANIEL [BOOK OF]). From the time of this book until the end of the 1st cent. A.D., and indeed even later, we find a continuous stream of apocalypses, each marked by a characteristic combination of pessimism as to the present and hope as to the future yet to be miraculously established. These works are the output of one phase of Pharisaism, which, while elevating both Torah and the Oral Law, was not content with bald legalism, but dared trust in the realization of its religious hopes. The authors of the various works are utterly unknown. In this, as in other respects, the apocalypses constitute a unique national literature.

1. The Enoch Literature.—The Enoch literature has reached us in three forms: (*a*) The Book of Enoch (sometimes called Ethiopic Enoch or 1 Enoch); (*b*) The Slavonic Book of the Secrets of Enoch; and (*c*) Third Enoch. The three works indicate the widespread tendency to utilize the story of the patriarch in apocalyptic discourse.

(*a*) *The Book of Enoch* is a collection of apocalypses and other material written during the last two centuries before Christ. It was written in Hebrew or Aramaic, and then translated into Greek, and from that into Ethiopic and Latin. As it now exists, the collection is a survival of a widespread Enoch literature, and its constituent sections have been to a considerable extent edited by both Jews and Christians. Critics, while varying as to details, are fairly well agreed as to the main component sources, each probably representing a different author or school.

(i) The original ground-work of the present book is to be found in chs. 1–36 and 72–104, in the midst of which are, however, numerous interpolations (see iv below). These chapters were probably written before 100 B.C. Chs. 1–36 deal chiefly with the portrayal of the punishment to be awarded the enemies of the Jews and sinners generally on the Day of Judgment. The eschatology of these chapters is somewhat sensuous as regards both the resurrection and rewards and punishments. In them we have probably the oldest piece of Jewish literature touching the general resurrection of Israel and representing Gehenna as a place of final punishment (see GEHENNA).

The dream visions (chs. 83–90) were probably written in the time of Judas Maccabaeus or John Hyrcanus. By the use of symbolic animals—sheep, rams, wild beasts—Hebrew history is traced to the days of the Hasmonaean revolt. The years of misery are represented by a flock under seventy shepherds, who, in the new age about to dawn, are to be cast with the evil men and angels into an abyss of fire. The Messiah is then to appear, although His function is not definitely described. In ch. 91 the future is somewhat more transcendentally described.

In the later chapters of this oldest section the new eschatology is more apparent. In them are to be found representations of the sleep of the righteous, the resurrection of the spirit of the Messiah, though human, as God's Son (105^{2}), the Day of Judgment, and the punishment of the wicked in hell.

(ii) Whether or not the second group of chapters (37–71), or the *Similitudes*, is post- or pre-Christian has been thoroughly discussed. The general consensus of scholars is that the *Similitudes* were probably written sometime before the reign of Herod. The most remarkable characteristic of these *Similitudes* is the use of the term 'Son of Man' for the Messiah. But it is not possible to see in the use of this term any reference to the historical Jesus. More likely it marks a stage in the development of the term from the general symbolic usage of Dn 7^{13} to the strictly Messianic content of the NT. In the *Similitudes* we find described the judgment of all men, both alive and dead, as well as of angels. Yet the future is still to some extent sensuous, although transcendental influences are very evident in the section. The Messiah pre-exists and is more than a man. The share which he has in the reorganization of the world is more prominent than in the older sections.

(iii) Interspersed throughout the book are sections which Charles calls 'the book of celestial physics.' These sections are one of the curiosities of scientific literature, and may be taken as a fair representative of the astronomical and meteorological beliefs of the Palestinian Jews about the time of Christ.

(iv) Interpolations from the so-called *Book of Noah*, which are very largely the work of the last part of the pre-Christian era, although it is not possible to state accurately the date of their composition.

The importance of Enoch is great for the understanding of the eschatology of the NT and the methods of apocalyptic.

Except for occasional references in the Church Fathers to the existence of a book of Enoch, full knowledge of the work was first brought to Europe in 1773 when James Bruce, the great Abyssinian traveller, returned to Britain with an Ethiopic Manuscript of 1 Enoch. Portions of the text have been preserved also in a Latin manuscript. At Qumrân by the Dead Sea eight manuscripts of part of 1 Enoch in Aramaic have come to light.

(*b*) The (Slavonic) *Secrets of Enoch*, which presupposes the existence of 1 Enoch, first came to the attention of Western scholars in the late 19th cent. Originally written in Greek, which is no longer extant, the work is preserved in two Slavonic recensions of unequal length. The longer text is the product of the fantasy of Slavonic redactors of the 15th and 16th cent. The shorter text appears to be an epitome of the original and may have been made in the 10th cent. When the original Greek work was composed has been vigorously debated by scholars, who have argued for dates as widely separated as the 1st and the 7th Christian centuries. The author gives a detailed account (chs. xxv–xxx) of the six days of Creation. As the world was made in six days, so its history is to be accomplished in six thousand years (cf Ps 90[4]). At the close of the six thousand years, the new day, or Sabbath of the thousand years, is to begin. The *Secrets of Enoch* is a highly developed picture of the coming age and of the structure of the heaven, which, it holds, is seven-fold. Here, too, are the Judgment, though of individuals rather than of nations, the two aeons, the complete renovation or destruction of the earth. There is no mention of a resurrection, and the righteous are upon death to go immediately to Paradise.

(*c*) *Third Enoch*, a heterogeneous work extant in several Hebrew manuscripts, was first edited in its entirety in 1928. Its contents represent a direct continuation in development from the earlier Enochic literature, with influences on the one hand from Gnosticism and on the other from Rabbinic traditions developed during the Tannaitic period. To a central core of the book there were added at later times various sections akin to the mysticism which is also reflected in the Cabbala. The author describes many angels and their activities. He also supplies an account of the divine Chariot (cf Ezk 1[14]) and the destinies of Metatron, *i.e.* the Divine servant who in I Enoch is identified with the Elect One and the Son of Man.

2. The Book of Jubilees is a Haggadist commentary on Genesis, and was probably written in the Maccabaean period. At Qumrân by the Dead Sea five manuscripts of Jubilees were discovered preserving parts of chs. i–ii, xxi–xxiii, xxv, xxxii–xl, written in a good style of Hebrew. From these it can now be shown that the Latin and Ethiopic versions faithfully translate the original.

In this writing angelology and demonology are well developed. While there is no mention of the Messiah, the members of the Messianic age are to live a thousand years, and are to be free from the influence or control of Satan. The book contains no doctrine of the resurrection ; but spirits are immortal. While there is punishment of the wicked, and particularly of evil spirits and the enemies of Israel, the Judgment is not thoroughly correlated with a general eschatological scheme. The chief object of the book is to incite the Jews to a greater devotion to the Law, and the book is legalistic—rather than idealistic.

The ' new age ' was to be inaugurated by wide-spread study of the Law, to which the Jews would be forced by terrible suffering. Certain passages would seem to imply a resurrection of the dead and a renewing of all creation along with the endless punishment of the wicked.

3. The Psalms of Solomon—a group of noble songs, written by a Pharisee (or Pharisees) probably between 70 and 40 B.C., the dates being fixed by reference to the Roman conquest of Jerusalem and the death of Pompey (Ps-Sol ii. 30, 31). The collection is primarily a justification of the downfall of the Maccabaean house because of its sins. Its author (or authors) was opposed to monarchy as such, and looked forward to the time when the Messiah would really be king of Judaea. The picture of this king as set forth in Pss 17–18 is one of the noblest in Jewish literature. He is to be neither sufferer nor teacher, pre-existent nor miraculously born. He is not to be a priest, or warrior. He is to be sinless, strong through the Holy Spirit, gaining his wisdom from God, conquering the entire heathen world without war, ' by the word of his mouth,' and to establish the capital of the world at Jerusalem. All the members of the new kingdom, which, like the Messiah, is miraculous, are to be ' sons of God.'

4. The Assumption of Moses was probably written in the opening years of the 1st cent. A.D., and narrates in terms of prophecy the history of the world from the time of Moses until the time of its composition, ending in an eschatological picture of the future. As it now stands, the writing is hardly more than a fragment of a much larger work, and it exists only in an old Latin translation. The most striking characteristic is the importance given to Satan as the opponent of God, as well as the rather elaborate portrayal of the end of the age it narrates. The Judgment is to be extended to the Gentiles, but no Messiah is mentioned, the Messianic kingdom rather than He being central. Further, the writer, evidently in fear of revolutionary tendencies among his people, says distinctly that God alone is to be judge of the Gentiles.

5. The Testaments of the Twelve Patriarchs is a composite work purporting to preserve the last words of the twelve sons of Jacob. Because of the presence of many passages that are obviously Christian in outlook, the book in its present form seems to date from the 1st or 2nd cent. of our era. Much of the material, however, reflects Jewish traditions of a pre-Christian period. Several Aramaic fragments of the Testament of Levi were discovered in the Cairo Genizah and at Qumrân. In literary character the Testaments resemble homilies illustrated with much legendary material, including descriptions of demons and Beliar their leader. The new age is not distinctly described but apparently involves only earthly relationships. God's judgment on wicked men and demons is, however, elaborately pictured, sometimes in terms hard to reconcile with the less transcendental accounts of the blessings assured to the Jewish nation. Each of the patriarchs is represented as dealing with that particular virtue or vice with which the Biblical account associates him, and also as foretelling appropriate blessings or curses. The work is preserved in Greek and Armenian translations.

6. The Ascension of Isaiah is a composite book which circulated largely among the Christian heretics of the 3rd cent. At its basis lies a group of legends of uncertain origin, dealing with the Antichrist and Beliar. These in turn are identified with the expectation that Nero would return after death. The book, therefore, in its present shape is probably of Christian origin, and is not older than the 2nd cent., or possibly the latter part of the 1st. The Isaiah literature, however, was common in the 1st cent., and the book is a valuable monument of the eschatological tendencies and beliefs of at least certain groups of the early Christians. Particularly important is it as throwing light upon the development of the Antichrist doctrines. It exists to-day in four recensions—Greek, Ethiopic, Latin, and Slavonic.

7. The Apocalypse of Ezra (Second Esdras, chs. 3–14 ; see APOCRYPHA, THE, **2**), written about the time of the destruction of Jerusalem. It is the most complete expression of Pharisaic pessimism. Written in the midst of national misery, it is not able to see any relief except in the creation of a new world. The age was coming to an end, and the new age which was to belong to Israel would presently come. The judgment of Israel's enemies was presently to be established, but not until the number of the righteous was complete. The book is no doubt closely related to the *Apocalypse of Baruch*, and both apparently reproduce the same originally Jewish material. It has been considerably affected by Christian hopes. Both for this reason and because of its emphasis on generic human misery and sin, with the consequent need of something more than a merely national deliverance, it gives a prominent position to the Messiah, who is represented as dying. As Second Esdras the book has become part of the Apocrypha of the OT, and has had considerable influence in the formation of Christian eschatology. In vii. 30–98 is an elaborate account of the general Resurrection, Judgment, and the condition of souls after death ; and it is this material quite as much as the Messianic prediction of chs. xii–xiv that make it of particular interest to the student. It is possessed, however, of no complete unity in point of view, and passes repeatedly from the national to the ethical (individual) need and deliverance. The separation of these two views is, however, more than a critical matter. As in Mk 13, the two illustrate each other.

8. The Apocalypse of Baruch is a composite work which embodies in itself a ground-work which is distinctly Jewish, and certain sections of which were probably written before the destruction of Jerusalem. Criticism, however, has not arrived at any complete consensus of opinion as regards its composition, but there can be little doubt that it represents the same apocalyptic tendencies and much of the material which are to be seen in 2 Es. Just what the relations are between the two writings, however, has not yet been clearly shown. The probability is that the Apocalypse of Baruch, as it now stands, was written in the second half of the 1st cent. A.D. and has come under the influence of Christianity (see especially chs. xlix–li). Like 2 Esdras, it is marked by a despair of the existing age, and looks forward to a transcendental reign of the Messiah, in which the Jews are to be supremely fortunate. It exists to-day in Greek and Syriac versions, with a strong probability that both are derived from original Hebrew writing. This apocalypse, both from its probable origin and general characteristic, is of particular value as a document for understanding the NT literature. In both the Apocalypse of Baruch and 2 Esdras we have the most systematized eschatological picture that has come down to us from Judaism of the early Christian centuries.

9. The Sibylline Oracles are the most important illustration of the extra-Palestinian-Hellenistic apocalyptic hope. As the work now exists, it is a collection of various writings dealing with the historical and future conditions of the Jewish people. The most important apocalyptic section is in Book iii. 97–828, written in Maccabaean times. In it the punishment of the enemies of the Jews is elaborately foretold, as are also the future and the Messianic Judgment. This third book was probably edited in the middle of the 2nd cent. by a Christian. In general, however, this Sibylline literature, although of great extent, gives us no such distinct pictures of the future as those found in the Ezra-Baruch apocalypses.

10. Third Maccabees is a religious novel written in Greek by an Alexandrian Jew sometime between 100 B.C. and A.D. 100. Its title is misleading, for the book has nothing to do with the Maccabees. The subject matter deals with the triumph of the Jews over their enemies through Divine intervention during the reign of Ptolemy Philopator (222–204 B.C.). The book contains incredible yarns characterized by grotesquely fabulous details, and the style of the author is rhetorical and bombastic. It is included in most manuscripts of the Septuagint, including the two uncials A and V.

11. Fourth Maccabees is a composition resembling an extended sermon on the theme of the supremacy of pious reason over the passions. This Stoic doctrine is reinforced by recounting with exaggerated and gruesome details the horrible persecutions experienced by the Maccabean martyrs (2 Mac 6^{18}–7^{42}). The author was probably an Alexandrian Jew who lived sometime shortly before or shortly after the beginning of the Christian era. As regards literary style and rhetorical power, the work is superior to 2 Maccabees, on which it depends. The personal earnestness and zeal of the writer are obvious at every point. He is an ardent and orthodox Jew who is thoroughly acquainted with the Hebrew Scriptures. Under the influence of Is 53, the author teaches that in their death the martyrs ‘ became as it were a ransom for our nation's sin ’ (xvii. 21 f). In xviii. 6 ff we have very interesting glimpses of Jewish family life of the writer's own day.

12. The Lives of the Prophets is a collection of extra-biblical traditions concerning the history, activities, manner of death, and place of burial of these famous men. Probably written in Hebrew sometime during the first Christian century, the work has been preserved in five Greek recensions, as well as in Syriac, Latin, and Ethiopic versions. The list, which varies in the several sources, includes the biographies of the four major and the twelve minor prophets, followed by those of Nathan, Ahijah, Joed, Azariah, Zechariah the son of Jehoiada, Elijah, and Elisha. Except for the briefest allusions, no attempt is made to repeat what is recorded in the canonical Scriptures. The amount of new material varies from two or three sentences in some cases to more than two or three pages. Some of the legendary details include the following. Jonah was a son of the widow of Zarephath (1 K 17^{8-24}). Ezekiel was killed in Babylonia by one of the Jewish exiles, ‘ for they had opposed him all the days of his life.’ Daniel interceded for Nebuchadnezzar, who had been changed into an animal having the fore parts of a bull and the hind parts of a lion. When Elisha was born at Gilgal, a seat of idol worship, ‘ the golden calf bellowed so loudly that the shrill sound was heard at Jerusalem.’ Isaiah met his death by being sawn in two (see He 11^{37}). Among Christian additions is the prophecy of Jeremiah to the Egyptian priests that ‘ their idols would be shaken and their gods made with hands would all collapse, when a virgin bearing a child of divine appearance [Jesus] should arrive in Egypt.’

13. The Testament of Solomon is a Christianized reworking of a kernel of Jewish legends pertaining to Solomon's super-human powers in curing diseases and exorcizing demons which plagued his favourite workman during the building of the Temple. The book contains a great amount of magical, astrological, and demonological matter drawn from a wide variety of sources—pagan, Jewish, and Christian. It is extant to-day in several recensions, the oldest of which may date from about the fourth Christian century, and the latest of which betrays late Mediaeval additions.

S. M.—B. M. M.

PSYCHOLOGY.—The Bible does not contain a science of psychology in the modern sense ; but it abounds in examples of shrewd psychological insight, and there is a definite and consistent view of man's nature from the religious standpoint. This being recognized, the old dispute, whether it teaches the bipartite or the tripartite nature of man, loses its meaning, for the distinction of **soul** and **spirit** is not a division of man into soul and spirit along with his body or **flesh**, but a difference of point of view—the one emphasizing man's individual existence, the other his dependence on God. The account in Gn 2^7 makes this clear. The breath or spirit of God breathed into the dust of the ground makes the living soul. The living soul ceases when ‘ the dust returns to the earth as it was, and the spirit returns to God who gave it ’ (Ec 12^7). The soul is not, as in Greek philosophy, a separate substance which takes up its abode in the body at birth, and is released from its bondage at death, but is matter animated by God's breath. Hence no pre-existence of the soul is taught (except in Wis 8^{19f}), nor is the future life conceived as that of a disembodied soul. Man is the unity of spirit and matter ; hence the hope of immortality involves the belief in the resurrection of the body, even though in St. Paul's statement of the belief the body raised is described as *spiritual* (1 Co 15^{44}). The OT has not, in fact, a term for the body as a whole ; the matter to which the spirit gives life is often referred to as ‘ flesh.’ This term may be used for a man as *finite earthly creature* in contrast with God and His Spirit. Man is ‘ flesh,’ or ‘ soul,’ or ‘ spirit,’ according to the aspect of his personality it is desired to emphasize. The varied senses in which these terms are used are discussed in the separate articles upon them ; here only their relation to one another is dealt with. These are the three principal psychological terms ; but there are a few others which claim mention.

Heart is used for the inner life, the principles, motives, purposes (Gn 6^5, Ps 51^{10}, Ezk 36^{26}, Mt 15^{19}, 2 Co 3^3), without precise distinction of the intellectual, emotional, or volitional functions ; but it can never, as the preceding terms, be used for the whole man. Nevertheless, according to the vivid Hebrew notion of such things, any organ may become, for the moment, the seat, instrument or symbol of man's energy or personality, whether the underlying idea be called 'diffusion of consciousness' (Robinson) or synecdoche (Johnson). St. Paul, influenced probably by Greek philosophy, uses *nous* for **mind** as man's intellectual activity (Ro 7^{23-25}), and even contrasts it with the ecstatic state (1 Co 14^{14f}), and adopts other terms used in the Greek schools. Another Greek term, *syneidēsis*, rendered '**conscience**,' is used in the NT consistently for what Kant called the practical reason, man's moral consciousness (Ac 23^{1} 24^{16}, Ro 2^{15} 9^{1} 13^{5}, 1 Co $8^{7,10,12}$ $10^{25,27ff}$, 2 Co 1^{12} 4^{2}, 1 Ti $1^{5,19}$ 3^{9} 4^{2}, 2 Ti 1^{3}, Tit 1^{15}, He $9^{9,14}$ 10^{22} 13^{18}, 1 P 2^{19} $3^{16,21}$), and is an instance of the influence of the Stoic ethics on 'the moral vocabulary of the civilized world at the time of the Christian era.' This distinction of the intellectual and the moral functions of personality anticipates some types of modern psychological thinking, and other parallels to scientific psychology could easily be found; but the NT really knows nothing of these subtleties. Its psychology is principally of OT origin, and what is not Hebrew is derived from the popular thought and speech of the Greek world.

A. E. G.—**W. C. K.**

PTOLEMAIS (Ac 21^{7}).—The same as **Acco** (Jg 1^{31}), now the port *'Akkā*, called in the West, since Crusading times, *Acre* or *St. Jean d'Acre*. The city of early times lay at *Tell el-Fukhkhâr*, E. of the present port; sherds of 2200–900 B.C. are found there. Acco received the name Ptolemais some time in the 3rd cent. B.C., probably in honour of Ptolemy II., but although this name was in common use for many centuries, it reverted to its Semitic name after the decline of Greek influence. Although so very casually mentioned in OT and NT, this place has had as varied and tragic a history as almost any spot in Palestine. On a coast peculiarly unfriendly to the mariner, the Bay of *'Akkā* is one of the few spots where nature has lent its encouragement to the building of a harbour; its importance in history has always been as the port of Galilee and Damascus, of the Hauran and Gilead, while in the days of Western domination the Roman Ptolemais and the Crusading St. Jean d'Acre served as the landing-place of governors, of armies, and of pilgrims. So strong a fortress, guarding so fertile a plain, and a port on the highroad to such rich lands to north, east, and south, could never have been overlooked by hostile armies, and so we find the Egyptian Thothmes III., Seti I., and Rameses II., the Assyrian Sennacherib, Esarhaddon, and Ashurbanipal, and several of the Ptolemies engaged in its conquest or defence. It is much in evidence in the history of the Maccabees—a queen Cleopatra of Egypt holds it for a time, and here some decades later Herod the Great entertains Caesar. During the Jewish revolt it is an important base for the Romans, and both Vespasian and Titus visit it. In later times, such warriors as Baldwin I. and Guy de Lusignan, Richard Coeur de Lion and Saladin, Napoleon I. and Ibrahim Pasha are associated with its history.

In the OT Acco is mentioned only as one of the cities of Asher (Jg 1^{31}), while in Ac 21^{7} Ptolemais occurs as the port where St. Paul landed, 'greeted the brethren and stayed with them for one day,' on his way to the new and powerful rival port, Caesarea which a few decades previously had sprung up to the south.

The modern *'Akkā* (16,000 inhabitants) is a city, much reduced from its former days of greatness, situated on a rocky promontory of land at the N. extremity of the bay to which it gives its name. The sea lies on the W. and S. and somewhat to the E. The ancient harbour lay on the S., and was protected by a mole running E. from the S. extremity, and one running S. from the SE. corner of the city. Ships of moderate dimensions can approach near the city, and the water is fairly deep. The walls, partially Crusading work, which still surround the city, are in the ruined state to which they were reduced in 1840 by the bombardment by the English fleet under Sir Sidney Smith. Extending from Carmel in the S. to the 'Ladder of Tyre' in the N., and eastward to the foothills of Galilee, is the great and well-watered 'Plain of Acre,' a region which, though sandy and sterile close to the sea, is of rich fertility elsewhere and is dotted with ancient tells. The two main streams of this plain are the *Nahr Na'mān* (R. Belus), just S. of 'Akkā, and the Kishon near Carmel.

Under modern conditions, *Ḥaifā*, with its better anchorage for modern steamships, and its railway to Damascus, has usurped the place of *'Akkā*.

E. W. G. M.—**E. G. K.**

PTOLEMY V. (Epiphanes).—'Ptolemy' was the dynastic name of the Macedonian kings who ruled over Egypt 305–31 B.C.; during the whole of this period Egypt was an independent country; it was not until the great victory of Augustus at Actium (31 B.C.) that Egypt again lost her independence and became a province, this time under Roman rule. Ptolemy V. reigned 205–182 B.C. He married Cleopatra, the daughter of Antiochus III. the Great; this matrimonial alliance between the Ptolemies and the Seleucids is alluded to in Dn 2^{43}. During his reign Palestine and Coele-Syria were lost to Egypt, and were incorporated into the kingdom of Syria under Antiochus III.; this is probably what is alluded to in Dn 11^{12-16}; see Jos. *Ant.* XII. iii. 3 [131].

W. O. E. O.

PTOLEMY VI. (VII.) (Philometor).—Son of the foregoing, who reigned 182–146 B.C.; in 170 the kingdom was divided between him and his brother Ptolemy VII. (Physcon); peace was made between them by the Romans and they continued as joint kings. In the year 170, while Ptolemy VI. was still sole king, he attempted to reconquer the Syrian provinces which had been lost during his father's reign; the attempt was, however, abortive, and he was defeated by Antiochus IV. It was only through the intervention of the Romans that Antiochus was prevented from following up this victory by further conquests. References to Philometor are to be found in 1 Mac 1^{18} 10^{51ff} 11^{1-18} 15^{16-24}, Dn 11^{25-30}; and see Jos. *Ant.* XIII. iv. 5–9 [103 ff].

W. O. E .O.

PUA, Nu 26^{23} (AV).—See PUAH, **2.**

PUAH.—1. One of the Hebrew midwives, Ex 1^{15}. **2.** Father of Tola, Jg 10^{1}. In 1 Ch 7^{1} he is Tola's brother. He is called **Puvah** in Gn 46^{13} (AV **Phuvah**), Nu 26^{23} (AV **Pua**). The gentilic **Punites** occurs in Nu 26^{23}.

PUBLICAN.—This term is a transliteration of a Latin word (used in the Vulgate) which meant a member of one of the great Roman financial companies, which farmed the **taxes** of the provinces of the Roman Empire. Under the Republic, the Roman State relieved itself of the trouble and expense of collecting the taxes of the provinces by putting up the taxes of each in a lump to auction. The auctioneer was the *censor*, and the buyer was one of the above companies, composed mainly of members of the equestrian order, who made the best they could out of the bargain. The abuses to which this system gave rise were terrible, especially as the governors could sometimes be bribed to wink at extortion; and in one particular year the provincials of Asia had to pay the taxes three times over. These companies required officials of their own to do the business of collection. The publicans of the Gospels appear to have been agents of the Imperial procurator of Judaea, with similar duties. Under the Empire, the system of tax-farming by *publicani* was abolished and the Emperor had a procurator (q.v.) in each province whose business it was to supervise the collection of revenue. They were also employed in collecting the customs dues on exports. Some Jews found it profitable to serve the Roman State in this way, and became objects of detestation to such of their fellow-countrymen as showed an impotent hatred of the Roman supremacy. The Gospels show clearly that they were coupled habitually with 'sinners,' a word of the deepest contempt. A. So.—**J. C. B.**

PUBLIUS (Gr. *Poplios*).—The 'chief man' of Malta, whose father was cured by St. Paul of fever and dysentery by laying on of hands (Ac 28^{7f}). The title *Prōtos* ('first man') at Malta is attested by inscriptions; it occurs also at Pisidian Antioch (Ac 13^{50}, cf 25^{2}). A. J. M.

PUDENS.—Mentioned in 2 Timothy as sending greetings from Rome to Timothy (2 Ti 4^{21}; 'Pudens and Linus and Claudia'). For the suggested relationship of these persons and identification of the first and of the last, see CLAUDIA. Pudens is a common Roman name. A. J. M.

PUHITES, 1 Ch 2^{53} (AV).—See PUTHITES.

PUL.—**1.** See TIGLATH-PILESER. **2.** In Is 66^{19} **Pul** (so AV and RV following MT) is probably a slip for **Put** (q.v.); so RSV.

PULSE.—Hebrew *zērô'îm*, Dn 1^{12}; *zēr'ônîm*, v.^{16}. AV and RV render 'pulse' (RVm 'herbs') and RSV 'vegetables.' The food may have been garden produce. The English word 'pulse' belongs to leguminous grains specially, but it is doubtful whether the meaning of the Hebrew can be so restricted. In 2 S 17^{28} RV 'pulse' is supplied after 'parched,' but 'corn' (AV) or 'grain' (RSV) is better. See also FOOD, **3.** E. W. G. M.

PUNISHMENTS.—See CRIMES AND PUNISHMENTS, **8–11**, REWARD.

PUNITES.—See PUAH, **2.**

PUNON.—A stopping-place on the wanderings, Nu 33^{42f}; it is modern *Kh. Feinân*. See also PINON.

PUR.—See PURIM.

PURAH.—Gideon's servant or armour-bearer, Jg 7^{10f} (AV **Phurah**).

PURGE.—To 'purge' in AV is simply to 'cleanse *or* purify,' as Ps 51^{7} 'Purge (so also RV, RSV) me with hyssop and I shall be clean'; Mk 7^{19} 'purging all meats,' *i.e.* making all food ceremonially clean (cf RV, RSV).

PURIFICATION.—See CLEAN AND UNCLEAN.

PURIM.—**1. In the OT.**—On the 14th and 15th of the month Adar (March) fell the celebration of the Feast of *Purim* or Lots. This commemorated the deliverance of the Jews from Haman, who in 473 B.C. had plotted their extermination throughout the Persian empire (Est 3^{7} 9^{15-32}). In 2 Mac 15^{36} it is called **'Mordecai's day.'** The observance of this festival was probably not at first universal, but Josephus mentions the annual festival after telling the story of Esther (*Ant.* XI. vi. 13 [295]). At first no special religious services were enjoined to mark it, nor was there any prohibition of labour. It was a time of feasting and joy, of the giving of presents and alms. In later times it was celebrated by a synagogue meeting on the evening of the 13th and the morning of the 14th, when the Book of Esther was read through, special prayers and thanks were offered, and the congregation recited curses on Haman and blessings on Esther and Mordecai. The rest of the feast was given up to good cheer and boisterous enjoyment of an almost Bacchanalian character. In 1 Mac 7^{49} and 2 Mac 15^{36}, as also in Josephus, the 13th of Adar is recorded as a feast-day in commemoration of the defeat of the Syrian general Nicanor in 161 B.C. But later ages observed it as the Fast of Esther (cf Est 9^{31} 4^{3}), the celebration taking place on the 11th, if the 13th happened to be a Sabbath.

The origin of the Purim feast is a matter of dispute. It is difficult to identify any known Persian word with **pur** (Est 3^{7} 9^{26}), which gave the festival its name; it may be a word of Akkadian origin. Various theories have been put forward, of which the most noteworthy are: (*a*) that which derives it from a Persian spring festival; (*b*) that which regards it as a transformation of an old Zoroastrian festival of the dead; (*c*) that which traces its origin to a Babylonian New Year's festival.

2. In the NT.—Some have supposed that the nameless feast mentioned in Jn 5^{1} was Purim. But this is not convincing, for (*a*) Purim was never one of the great national solemnities which called for attendance at Jerusalem: it was observed locally and not only at the capital; (*b*) Christ would naturally go up for the Passover in the next month. And it is more probable that the Passover is the feast here intended. A. W. F. B.—L. H. B.

PURITY.—In Israelite thinking, and especially in priestly thinking, persons and things can be arranged as holy or common, pure (clean) or unclean. Things common can be clean or unclean, but nothing unclean can be holy or can approach the holy. Impurity is conveyed like a contagion (and is indeed more contagious than holiness, Hag 2^{11ff}) and especially comes from contact with the mysterious sources of life and death—*e.g.* childbirth (Lv 12), sexual and other discharges from the body (Lv 15), dead bodies (Nu 19); also certain animals (Lv 11). After contraction of impurity a period of waiting is normal, and often sacrifices and other rituals of purification are required (*e.g.* Lv 12, cf Jesus' parents in Lk 2^{22ff}). Purity is specially important for ritual and sacral occasions, and impure persons are excluded from such; warfare was a sacral occasion in early times (cf 1 S 21^{4-5} for early times) and Dt 23^{9ff} has laws for the purity of the war-camp. For priests as holy persons constantly in touch with the holy it was specially important to observe rigorous rules of purity (Lv 21^{1}–22^{16} etc.). Washing was one of the main elements in maintaining purity, and the washing of priests for Temple service, and their donning of new clothes, is prescribed.

In late Judaism we find the Pharisees observing strict purity among lay people, and their ablutions are frequently mentioned in the NT. The interest in purity was also very great in the Qumrân community. Discussion of purity of foods and purification by water is carried on in the *Zadokite Documents*, and the community is spoken of as 'camps' in the fashion of Dt 23. In the *Manual of Discipline* we hear of purification by water frequently; in v. 13 'he shall not enter the water to touch the purity of the holy men'; in vi. 16–7 'he shall not touch the purity of the masters (or, of the many) until he has been examined.' It has quite often been held that this 'purity' is a sacred meal, though this is perhaps being too precise; but various degrees of purity are involved, and are especially important in matters of food.

In the Gospels we find Jesus criticising the Pharisaic interest in purity as external, hypocritical, and based on human tradition rather than Divine law (*e.g.* Mk 7^{1-23}). With the beginning of Gentile entry into the Church, the problem of purity created difficulties at first (Ac 10, Gal 2^{12}), but only minimal demands were made by the council of Ac 15. The tradition of purity and purification from defilement continued in the Church, however, but is used with a deepened ethical meaning, of an inward cleansing. It applies to the sacrificial purification of Temple and people by Christ, and to baptism, which sprinkles the heart from an evil conscience and washes the body in pure water (He 10^{19-22}, 1 P 3^{21}, etc.). We also have renewed images of the Church as a royal priesthood (1 P 2^{9}) and as a pure virgin, cleansed by water and word. With this goes purity of heart in the individual Christian, 1 Ti 1^{5}, etc. J. Ba.

PURPLE.—See COLOURS, **5.**

PURSE.—See BAG.

PURSLAIN.—See PURSLANE.

PURSLANE.—RSV in Job 6^{6} renders '(is there any taste in) the slime of purslane' (cf RVm 'in the juice of purslain'), where AV and RV have 'in the white of an egg.' The meaning of the Hebrew word is uncertain, and while many scholars take the view of RSV, E. Dhorme (Comm. on Job, *ad loc.*) thinks AV and RV more appropriate.

PUT, PHUT.—A people counted amongst the sons of Ham (Gn 10^{6}, 1 Ch 1^{8}), and frequently mentioned in the prophets as an ally of Egypt (Jer 46^{9}, Ezk 27^{10} 30^{5} 38^{5}, Nah 3^{9}). It has been suggested that it represents: (1) the people of Punt (rather *Pwēnet* in Egyptian), *i.e.* the African coast of the Red Sea with Somaliland, etc.; warriors may perhaps have been obtained thence for Egypt; or (2) Libya, whose people were called in Coptic *Phaiat* (certainly not to be identified with Put): Put is rendered by 'Libyans' in the LXX version of Jer 46[9], Ezk 27[10] 30[5] 38[5]; however, the Libyans are mentioned along with Put in Nah 3[9]; or (3) the bow-bearing allies called in Egyptian *pdtyw* (from which Put cannot be derived); or (4) the Carians or other pre-Hellenic peoples of Asia Minor or the Aegean islands, since Put is generally associated with Lud = Lydians (in Nah 3[9] Lubim). F. Ll. G.—**R. J. W.**

PUTEOLI (modern *Pozzuoli*).—In ancient times an important harbour and emporium, especially for Eastern trade, on the W. coast of Italy near Naples. It was founded by Greeks at a very early period. Such cities were specially sought by Jews and other foreigners, and Christians would early be living there, as St. Paul and his party found them on reaching this port at the end of their voyage from the East (Ac 28[13]). A. So.

PUTHITES.—A family of Kiriath-jearim, 1 Ch 2[53] (AV **Puhites**).

PUTIEL.—A father-in-law of Eleazar, Ex 6[25].

PUVAH.—See PUAH, **2**.

PYGARG.—The Hebrew *dîshôn* is an otherwise unknown word which appears as the name of a clean animal listed amongst the deer (Dt 14[5]); it is variously translated *pygargos* (LXX) or *pygargus* (Vulgate), 'wild goat' (unknown Greek translator), 'aurochs' (Targum), and '**ibex**' (Saʿadya; so RSV). It is perhaps the 'pygarg' (AV, RV), *i.e.* 'white-rumped' or 'white-tailed **antelope**' (*antilope addax*, Tristram), which has long backwards twisting horns (hence called *strepsiceros* by Pliny) and a white tail; it is well-known to the Arabs and approaches the E. and S. frontiers of Palestine. The 'bubale' (*antilope bubalis*, Tristram) or 'wild cow' of the Arabs, which resembles the South African *hartebeest*, is perhaps included under the same name; it roams the Arabian wilderness, certainly has been seen till the last century on the E. borders of Gilead and Moab and has been reported drinking at the head-waters of the streams flowing into the Dead Sea. Whether the Akkadian *didānu, ditānu* 'bison' (?) is the same word is doubtful. G. R. D.

PYRE.—This word is found only in RSV in Is 30[33], where it renders Hebrew *m*ᵉ*dhûrāh*, which means 'a pile of wood.' In Ezk 24[9] RSV renders the same word by 'pile.'

PYRRHUS.—A man of Beroea, father of Sopater, according to the best text (Ac 20[4] RSV). For the unusual insertion of the patronymic, see article SOPATER. A. J. M.

PYTHON.—In Ac 16[16] we read of a young girl at Philippi who had 'a spirit, a Python' (this is the reading of all the best MSS); RSV, 'a spirit of divination.' Pytho was a district close to Delphi; and Python was the serpent at that place slain by Apollo (Strabo ix. 3–12), who therefore was called 'the Pythian.' Hence the priestess at Delphi was called 'the Pythia.' This seems to be the connexion of the name with divination. Plutarch says (*de def. Orac.* ix. 414 E) that ventriloquists in his day (2nd cent. A.D.) were called 'Pythons.' Their powers were considered to be due to spiritual influence, and to include prediction. The girl at Philippi, then, was probably a ventriloquist, who brought her masters gain by soothsaying. She proclaimed aloud for many days that Paul and his companions were slaves of the Most High God; and the Apostle at last drove out the spirit 'in the name of Jesus Christ.' Her masters thereupon, having lost their source of profit, denounced Paul and Silas to the magistrates. See the article in Bauer's *Lexicon*, and Haenchen, *ad loc.* A. J. M.—**F. C. G.**

Q

QERÊ or **KERÊ.**—See TEXT OF OT, **5**.

QESITA.—Given in RSVm in Gn 33[19], Jos 24[32] as the Hebrew word rendered '**piece of money**'; in RSVm in Job 42[11] spelt **Kesitah**, and so in RVm in all three passages. No clue has yet been found to the weight, and therefore the value, of the *kesitah*; but that it was an ingot of precious metal of a recognized value is more probable than the tradition represented by several ancient versions, which render it by '**lamb**' (so AVm at Gn 33[19], Jos 24[32].)

QUAIL.—The Hebrew *ś*ᵉ*lāw*, which is composed of a sibilant *ś* followed by a liquid *l* and a weak letter, is the 'quail' (*coturnix communis*), which is said to emit a 'very liquid' sound. This bird migrates annually in vast numbers from SE. Europe by way of Sinai to the N. African coastal countries and back again. In the course of their migration the quails reach the wilderness of Sinai, carried with the wind, flying very low and indeed often just skimming the surface of the ground (never towering like the sand-grouse, with which the *ś*ᵉ*lāw* has sometimes been wrongly identified) and so exhausted that they can be taken by hand in any number (Nu 11[31-32], where the relevant words must be translated 'they fluttered over the camp . . . all round the camp and about two cubits above the ground'). The birds were brought to the Israelite camp in spring, during their migration northwards, *i.e.* back to Europe, when they followed the coast of the Red Sea until they reached its bifurcation by the Sinaitic peninsula; then, helped by a favouring wind, they crossed the water at its narrowest part, resting near the shore before continuing their journey (Ex 16[13], Ps 105[40]). Thus what was a miracle to the Israelites was in fact exactly in harmony with the quail's migratory habits. The flesh is fatty and considered a delicacy (unlike that of the sand-grouse, which is dry), though apt to disagree if taken in excess, especially if inefficiently preserved. E. W. G. M.—**G. R. D.**

QUARREL.—The original meaning of this English word (from Lat. *querela*) is a 'complaint.' This is its meaning in Col 3[13] AV 'if any man have a quarrel (RV, RSV 'complaint') against any.' Then it came to mean any cause of complaint, or any case that had to be stated or defended, as Mk 6[19] 'Herodias had a quarrel (RSV 'grudge') against him'; so Lv 26[25] (RSV 'vengeance'), 2 K 5[7] (RSV 'quarrel').

QUARRY.—In the story of the slaughter of Eglon by Ehud (Jg 3) we are told (v.[19]) in AV and RV that Ehud turned back from the 'quarries that were by Gilgal,' while after the assassination he 'escaped while they tarried, and passed beyond the quarries' (v.[26]). An alternative translation 'graven images' is given in AVm and RVm, while other versions, *e.g.* LXX and Vulgate, read 'idols.' The Hebrew word *p*ᵉ*silîm* is applied to images of gods in wood, stone or metal (Dt 7[5, 25] 12[3], Is 21[9] 30[22], 2 Ch 34[4]). Moore suggests the translation 'sculptured stones (probably rude images).' RSV renders by 'sculptured stones.' Probably they were the stones set up by Joshua to commemorate the crossing of the Jordan (Jos 4).

'Quarry' occurs also in RV and RSV of 1 K 6[7]. The stones used for the Temple building are said to have been prepared 'at the quarry.' AV reads 'before it was brought thither,' RVm 'when it was brought away.' The translation 'quarry' is probably correct. RSV has 'quarry' in Is 51[1] for AV and RV 'hole of the pit,' and uses the verb 'quarry' in 2 Ch 2[2, 18], Ec 10[9].

QUART.—This measure figures only in RSV in Rev 6[6] (AV, RV 'a measure') for Greek *choinix*, which renders Hebrew *bath* in Ezk 45[10f]. See WEIGHTS AND MEASURES.

QUARTUS.—Mentioned as joining in St. Paul's greeting to the Church of Rome (Ro 16[23]).

QUARTERMASTER.—A word found only in RVm and RSV in Jer 51[59] (RV 'chief chamberlain'). The Hebrew is *śar m^enûḥāh*, which means 'prince of rest' or 'of resting place. In 1 Ch 22[11] *'îsh m^enûḥāh* is rendered 'man of peace,' and AV renders 'a quiet prince' in Jer 51[59].

QUATERNION.—A guard of four soldiers (Ac 12[4]), one for each quarter (or 'watch') of the night. RSV 'squad.'

QUEEN.—The functions of a queen reigning in her own right would be identical with those of a **king** (q.v.). The queen as the wife of a monarch in Israel held a position of comparatively little importance, whereas that of a dowager queen ('queen-mother') commanded great influence (cf the cases of Bathsheba, Jezebel, Athaliah).

QUEEN OF HEAVEN (Heb. *m^elekheth hash-shāmayim*).—An object of worship to the people of Jerusalem (Jer 7[16-20]) and the Jewish exiles in Egypt (44[15-30]). The Massoretes evidently took the first word as *m^ele'kheth* ('work,' 'creation')—supposing that the silent 'aleph (') had been omitted—and considered the expression a synonym for 'Host of Heaven' (*ṣ^ebhā' hash-shāmayim*, Jer 8[2] 19[13], Zeph 1[5], Dt 4[19] 17[3], etc.). The correct reading is almost certainly *malkath* ('queen') and is to be understood as referring to the worship of the mother goddess. In Assyrian inscriptions Ishtar is called *Bēlit Shamē* ('lady of heaven') and *Sharrat Shamē* ('queen of heaven'). In Ugaritic texts the mother goddess is referred to as *rbt aṯrt ym* ('Lady Asherat of the Sea'). The worship of the mother goddess had particular appeal to the women, who had little place in the official worship of Israel. In Jer 44[19] we learn that the cakes made for the queen of heaven were fashioned in her likeness, perhaps in the form of a woman like the clay figurines of earlier times, perhaps in the form of a star (Venus). The worship of the queen of heaven was probably a borrowing from the Assyrians during the reign of Manasseh. Stamped out in connexion with Josiah's reform (2 K 23), it appears to have returned to prominence after his death. The worshippers of the queen of heaven persist in their practice, against the warnings of Jeremiah, because they believe that the fall of Jerusalem has come about as a result of their having ceased to honour the mother goddess (Jer 44[15-19]). In the Jewish-Aramaean community at Elephantine in Upper Egypt, the goddess *Anat-bethel*, also called *Anat-Yaho*, appears as the consort of Yaho (=Yahweh) and is perhaps to be identified with the Queen of Heaven.
W. M. N.—**W. J. Ha.**

QUICK, QUICKEN.—In AV 'quick' frequently means 'living,' and 'quicken' means 'bring to life.' The phrase 'the quick and the dead' occurs in Ac 10[42] 2 Ti 4[1], 1 P 4[5].

QUICKSANDS.—See SYRTIS.

QUIRINIUS (AV **Cyrenius**).—In Lk 2[1-3] we are first met by a grammatical difficulty. V.[2] may be translated either: 'this was the first enrolment that took place (and it took place) while Quirinius was governing Syria' (so RSV); or: 'this was the first of two (or more) enrolments that took place while Quirinius was governing Syria.' The first statement is probably true, but it may be that the second is what the author meant, because it is certain that a **census** took place during the governorship of Syria by Quirinius (A.D. 6–9), when Judaea was incorporated in the province Syria (Jos. *War*, II. viii. 1 [117]; VII. viii. 1 [253]). This latter census was a basis of taxation, and was made according to the Roman method: it thus aroused the rebellion of Judas (Ac 5[37]). The fact that enrolments took place every fourteen years in Egypt has been absolutely proved by the discovery of numerous papyri there, containing returns made by householders to the government. One of the dates thus recovered is A.D. 20. There is also evidence in the ancient historians of enrolments held in certain other provinces. The truth of Luke's statement in 2[2] need not therefore be doubted. The real difficulty lies in the statement that Quirinius was governing Syria at the time the first census of all was made. It is quite certain that he could not have been governing Syria, in the strict sense of the term governing, both at the time of the birth of Christ and in A.D. 6–9. This is contrary to all ancient procedure, and the rules as to such appointments were rigid. Further, we have ancient authority that the governor of Syria from 9–7 B.C. was Sentius Saturninus, and from 6–4 B.C. was Quinctilius Varus. After 4 B.C. we know nothing till the succession of P. Sulpicius Quirinius in A.D. 6, but it is possible that an inscribed stone may yet turn up to enable us to fill the gap. Yet an inscription exists, which all authorities agree refers to P. Sulpicius Quirinius, stating that he governed Syria twice. Theodor Mommsen considered that the most probable period for his earlier governorship was 3–1 B.C., but admitted serious doubts. Sir Wm. Ramsay discussed the whole problem afresh, following out the clues offered by the ancient historians, and adopted as most probable the conclusion that Quirinius was given command of the foreign relations of Syria during the critical period of the war with the Cilician hill tribe the Homonadenses. Roman history provides analogies for such a dual control of a province at a time of crisis. The date at which this position would have been held by Quirinius was about 6 B.C. The Greek word used (*hēgemoneuontos*) is a general term applied to the Emperor, a proconsul, a procurator, etc., and is quite consistent with this view. The mention of Quirinius by Luke is merely intended to give a date. The enrolment itself, as it took place in Herod's kingdom, would be superintended by him at the orders of Augustus, who had suzerainty over the kingdom of Herod, which constituted part of the *Imperium Romanum* in the full sense of the term. The census, however, was not carried out by the Roman method, but by tribes, a method less alien to Jewish feeling than the Roman method by households. Cf also LUKE-ACTS, **9**, and CHRONOLOGY OF THE NT. A. So.—**J. C. B.**

QUIT.—The adjective 'quit' (from Lat. *quietus*) means 'free from obligation,' as Ex 21[19] 'Then shall he that smote him be quit.' The verb 'to quit' (from Lat. *quietare*) is used in AV reflexively—quit oneself, *i.e.* discharge one's obligations, as 1 Co 16[13] 'Quit you like men.' RSV, 'be courageous.'

QUIVER.—See ARMOUR, **1** (*d*).

QUMRAN.—See DEAD SEA SCROLLS.

QUOTATIONS (IN NT).—The NT contains quotations from at least five sources: (1) the OT; (2) non-canonical Jewish writings; (3) non-Jewish sources; (4) letters to which a writer is replying; (5) earlier Christian documents or traditions. Those in class 1, far outnumbering the sum of all the others, are the main concern of this article; see below. The single explicit reference under class 2 is Jd [14] to 1 Enoch 1[9]; otherwise there are some twenty-five more or less probable allusions (see Ryle, article 'Apocrypha' in Smith's *DB*[2]; Woods, article 'Quotations' in Hastings' *DB*; index of Charles' *Apocrypha and Pseudepigrapha*). In the absence of any OT source for Mt 5[43b] some propose an influence (perhaps indirect) from the Dead Sea 'Manual of Discipline' i. 4, 10. Only three definite quotations from pagan literature (class 3) are known: Ac 17[28], 1 Co 15[33], Tit 1[12] (see Nestle's margin *in locc.*). Hellenistic models, but not specific sources, probably lie behind Luke's two prologues, Paul's frequent diatribe-style (cf Bultmann:

QUOTATIONS (IN NT)

Der Stil der paulinischen Predigt und die stoisch-kynische Diatribe), the vice and virtue catalogues in the epistles (cf Dibelius' commentaries in Lietzmann's *Handbuch*) and the household codes in Colossians, Ephesians, and the pastorals (cf Weidinger, *Die Haustafeln*). As to class 4, 1 Corinthians contains quotations from the lost letter of the Corinthians to Paul; 6^{12} and 8^{1} are the most likely. 2 Co $10^{1f, 10}$ probably contain (ironical) quotations. Matthew and Luke, separately or together, 'quote' (class 5) almost all of Mark; Ephesians seems to quote much of Colossians, as 2 Peter does Jude. Hymnic inlays are alleged or more or less convincingly demonstrated to lie behind 1 Co 13 (Paul quoting himself from a more formal context?), Ph 2, Col 1, Eph 5^{14} 1 Ti 3^{16}, 1 P 3, while the portions of the heavenly liturgy in Revelation are probably adaptations of earthly (Christian) liturgies. At least twice (1 Co 11^{23} 15^{3}) Paul quotes formed tradition; the Gospels and Acts directly or indirectly do so constantly.

The NT writers bear eloquent witness to the fundamental importance of the OT by the frequency and the way in which they quote it. Swete counted a hundred and sixty passages, with or without formulas of quotation, as directly quoted from the OT. Westcott and Hort reckoned the total number of quotations and allusions to the OT at 1279. Nestle, with some subtractions and additions to their list, exhibits about the same number by his bold-face type. The great majority of these are derived directly from the LXX even in the frequent cases where some liberty is taken in the quoting. Among NT books Hebrews shows the strongest LXX influence and Matthew the least. According to Westcott (Com. p. 479), fifteen quotations in Hebrews agree with both LXX and MT, eight with LXX against MT, three with neither, and three are free renderings. Westcott recognized that 'the writer . . . nowhere shows any immediate knowledge of the Hebrew text.' Matthew at the other extreme certainly shows other knowledge of the OT text than is supplied by the LXX. Not that its author neglects the LXX! Where Mark or Q underlies Matthew, he usually leaves the embedded OT quotations (about fifty-seven in number) in their predominantly LXX-form. Indeed, he alters eighteen of these into even closer conformity with LXX. (The reverse tendency, though less prominent, also occurs [six times]: Mt 4^{6} 10^{35} 15^{4} 21^{13} $22^{32, 37}$; Mark has in these cases altered away from LXX but not uniformly toward the Heb.) Even of the quotations peculiar to Matthew (numbering about forty-three), eleven agree word for word with some LXX MSS cited by Swete. The remaining thirty-two quotations differ from all known Greek versions, nearly always in the direction of closer conformity to MT. The 'author' used either both the LXX and the MT directly or the LXX and a lost Greek translation closer to the MT than the LXX. It is possible that the 'author' was not an individual but a Christian rabbinic school operating with the MT. The quotations in John and Paul are derived in the main from LXX and show surprisingly little clear acquaintance with the MT. (On the singular fact that LXX quotations show a special similarity to the type of LXX text found in Codex A, see Swete, *Introduction to OT in Greek*, p. 395.) Revelation shows constant literary influence from the OT but contains no explicit or argumentative quotation from it.

As to the nature and extent of the influence exerted by the OT in passages which may be called quotations in the broad sense indicated above, there are several distinguishable classes, though it is sometimes difficult to draw the line sharply. We may recognize: (1) *Argumentative quotations*. The OT passage is quoted, with recognition of its source, and with intention to employ the fact or teaching or prophecy for an argumentative purpose. Passages so quoted may be: (*a*) historical statements which are supposed to contain in themselves an enunciation of a principle or precept, or to involve a prediction, or to tend to prove a general rule of some kind: cf Mk 2^{25f}, Mt 2^{18}, Jn 19^{24}, Mt 15^{7-9}, He 7^{1-10}; (*b*) predictions; cf *e.g.* Ac 2^{17ff}; (*c*) imperative precepts, quoted to enforce a teaching; Mk 12^{29ff}, 1 Co 9^{9}; or (*d*) affirmations interpreted as involving a general principle of Divine action or a general characteristic of human nature; Mk 12^{26}, Mt 9^{13}, Lk 4^{11}, Ac 7^{48f}, Ro $3^{4, 10-13}$, Ja 1^{10f}, 1 P 1^{24f}. (2) *Quotations made the basis of comment*. In this case the language of the OT is not cited as supporting the statement of the speaker or writer, but is itself made the basis of exposition or comment, sometimes with disapproval of its teaching or of the teaching commonly based on it; Mt $5^{21, 27, 31}$ etc., Ro 4^{9f}, Ac 8^{32}. (3) *Quotations of comparison or of transferred application*. The OT language is employed, with recognition of it as coming from the OT and with the intention of connecting the OT event or teaching with the NT matter, but for purposes of comparison rather than argument. The language itself may refer directly and solely to the OT event, being introduced for the sake of comparing with this event some NT fact (simile); or the OT language may be applied directly to a NT fact, yet so as to imply comparison or likeness of the two events (metaphor); Mt 12^{40f}, Lk 11^{29f}, Ac 28^{26f}, Mt 21^{42f}, 1 Co 10^{7f}. Closely allied to these, yet perhaps properly belonging to the class of argumentative quotations, are cases of quotation accompanied by allegorical interpretation: cf *e.g.* Gal 4^{21-31}. (4) *Literary influence*. In the cases which fall under this head the language is employed because of its familiarity and its applicability to the matter in hand, but without intention of affirming any other connexion than this between the OT thought and the NT fact or teaching. The writer may be conscious of this influence of the OT language or not, and the interpreter often cannot determine with certainty which is the case; Mt 5^{5} 10^{35}, Gal 6^{16}, Eph 1^{20}, Rev 5^{1} 7^{1} 9^{14} 14^{8} 21^{11}.

As to their method of interpretation and their attitude toward the OT, there is wide difference among the speakers and writers in the NT. Within the Synoptic Gospels there is a distinct difference, which must rest upon reliable tradition, between the method of OT interpretation which they almost uniformly ascribe to Jesus and the method which they themselves employ. Jesus is represented as quoting the OT almost exclusively for its ethical and religious teaching (exceptions: Mk 12^{35-37} ||, Mt 12^{40} ||), rather than for any predictive element in it, and interprets what he quotes with insight and sobriety. The author of Matthew, however, quotes the OT mainly for specific predictions which he (or the tradition behind him) conceives it to contain, and allows his interpretation to be controlled by the proposition which he wishes to sustain rather than by the actual sense of the original—much as in the *pesher*-comments of the Habakkuk Commentary among the Dead Sea Scrolls. The one quotation not within the words of Jesus but common to all three Synoptics has the same general character (Mk 1^{3} ||). In general the other writers of the NT stand in this respect somewhere between these two methods, showing less sobriety and discernment toward the OT than the Synoptics ascribe to Jesus, yet often showing more than Matthew commonly does.

E. de W. B.—**K. G.**

R

RAAMA.—See Raamah.

RAAMAH.—Son of Cush and father of Sheba and Dedan, Gn 10[7]; called **Raama** in 1 Ch 1[9] (AV **Raamah**). In Ezk 27[22] Raamah is associated with Sheba as trading with Tyre. The locality of this Arabian tribe is not yet ascertained. Opinion is divided between the *Regma* of Ptolemy, on the W. of the Persian Gulf, and the *Rammanitae* of Strabo in S. Arabia, NW. of Ḥadramaut (see Hazarmaveth) and E. of the ancient Sheba. The latter is the more probable identification. J. F. McC.

RAAMIAH.—One of the twelve chiefs who returned with Zerubbabel, Neh 7[7]; called **Reelaiah** in Ezr 2[2], and **Resaiah** in 1 Es 5[8] (AV **Reesaias, RV Resaias**).

RAAMSES, RAMESES.—One of the store-cities built by the Israelites in Egypt, and the starting-point of the Exodus (Ex 1[11] 12[37], Nu 33[3, 5]). The site is not quite certain, but it was probably the city called in Egyptian, *Pi-Raʿmesse*, 'House of Ramesses,' the Delta capital of Ramesses II. and his successors. In Gn 47[11] Joseph, by Pharaoh's command, gives to Jacob's family 'a possession in the land of Egypt, in the best of the land, in the land of Rameses.' It thus lay in the Land of Goshen (q.v.), and is probably to be identified either with *Qanṭir*, or more probably Tanis. See Sir A. H. Gardiner, *Ancient Egyptian Onomastica* (1947), II. 171*–175*, 278*–279*. F. Ll. G.—**R. J. W.**

RABBAH.—The capital city of the Ammonites (q.v.), and the name of a town in Judah.

1. The name is derived from the Semitic word meaning 'great.' In Hebrew it appears as 'Rabbah' (Jos 13[25]) but more frequently as 'Rabbah (AV, **Rabbath,** Dt 3[11], Ezk 21[20]) of the Ammonites' (2 S 16[26], Jer 49[2] etc.), *i.e.* the chief city or capital of the Ammonites. Rabbah was situated on the upper sources of the River Jabbok on the site of the modern *ʿAmmân*, a name which preserves the ancient name of the country of Ammon. The city was located about 25 miles E. of the River Jordan and on the main caravan route which extended from Damascus to Medeba, Dibon, Kir and other cities to the S. The Ammonite city was situated on the hill-top to the N. of the river now called *Wâdī ʿAmmân*. From its position it commanded a wide view in all directions, but especially extensive to the NW. Rabbah is mentioned in Dt 3[11] as the place where Og's 'bedstead' might still be seen. This is thought by some to be a reference to a large dolmen still visible not far from *ʿAmmân*. In Jos 13[25] Rabbah is mentioned in defining the boundaries of the tribe of Gad. The chief event connected with Rabbah which the OT relates is its siege by Joab, in connexion with which Uriah the Hittite, by the express direction of King David, lost his life (see 2 S 11[1] 12[26, 27, 29], 1 Ch 20[1]). The city was at this time confined apparently to the hill mentioned above; since the sides of the hill are precipitous, the task of capturing it was difficult, and the siege was stubborn and prolonged. These conditions gave Joab his opportunity to carry out David's perfidious order (2 S 11[14ff]).

From 2 S 12[26–29] it appears that the city consisted of two parts, one of which was called the 'royal city' (v.[26]) or the 'city of waters' (v.[27]). This Joab captured, after which David came and captured Rabbah itself. What relation this 'royal city' bore to Rabbah proper, it is difficult now to conjecture. On the supposition that the Hebrew of vv.[26–27] is in error and that Joab captured only one district of the city which was 'the city of waters,' it has been proposed that David's general, like Antiochus III., and Herod in later centuries, captured the covered passage by which the people went to a cistern for water, or the fort which defended it, and so compelled a surrender to David. A large cistern was discovered by Conder (see *Survey of Eastern Palestine*, pp. 34 ff). Then David's accomplishment was that of conquering the citadel or 'royal city.' It is equally possible that the Hebrew of vv.[26–27] is correct and that Joab captured two districts, one of which was the 'royal city' or the citadel, and the other the 'city of waters,' *i.e.* the region adjacent to the river, leaving the slopes of the hills and the rest of the valley to be captured by David. The conquest of the upper and lower sections of a city recalls Abimelech's victory at Shechem (Jg 9[45, 49]), although in this case it was the Tower or citadel which was the last to be taken, a situation which can be explained by a difference in terrain at Shechem and Rabbah.

The Israelites did not occupy Rabbah, but left it in the possession of the Ammonite king, who became David's vassal. When David later fled to Mahanaim, E. of the Jordan, because of Absalom's rebellion, the Ammonite king was residing in Rabbah (2 S 17[27]).

Later the Ammonites regained full possession of their city, and in the time of Amos (*c* 750 B.C.), judgment was pronounced upon the city because of the transgressions of the Ammonites (Am 1[13–14]). Although the dates of the prophecies of Jeremiah and Ezekiel against the Ammonites and Rabbah are uncertain, it has been proposed that they refer to Nebuchadnezzar's punishment of the city for a rebellion by the Ammonites. Whether or not this monarch besieged and captured Rabbah we do not know, but it is possible; only cities situated like Tyre, which was partly surrounded by water, could withstand the might of that monarch.

For a time the city (one of the Decapolis group) bore the name *Philadelphia*, given to it by Ptolemy Philadelphus 285–247 B.C.), but finally it received its modern name, *ʿAmmân*. The Greek name is still preserved in the name of the modern Hotel Philadelphia located in the city near the impressive remains of a Roman theatre. Although no large-scale excavations have been conducted in the city, many tombs and the remains of numerous buildings have been uncovered in the course of the erection of many modern buildings. These ruins, some of which were uncovered during the construction of the modern Museum on the Citadel, opened in 1951, are evidence of occupation since early OT times. After existing for centuries as a small caravan town, *ʿAmmân*, following World War I, became the capital of Transjordan. At the partition of Palestine in 1948, the city became the capital of the Hashemite Kingdom of the Jordan which included territory W. of the Jordan River. From this region came an increased population, and new financial resources which resulted in the rapid transformation of *ʿAmmân* into a thriving metropolis joined by paved highways and an airline with the other cities of the Near East. The *Haj* railway, completed from Damascus as far as Maʿân in the direction of Mecca, passes near ʿAmmân, which has a station on the line.

2. Rabbah, a city in Judah, named in Jos 15[60] with Kiriath-jearim (q.v.), was apparently in the same region near Jerusalem, and important enough to have dependent villages. It has been suggested that the city corresponds to the Rabbah of Egyptian historical texts and the Rubutu of the Tell el-Amarna tablets; the exact location is unknown. G. A. B.—**W. L. R.**

RABBATH.—See Rabbah.

RABBI.—The transliteration of a Hebrew word meaning 'my master.' This term of respectful address with which the learned were greeted came to be used as a title, the pronominal suffix 'I' losing its significance. As a title it was not known before the 1st cent. (A.D.), and was first applied as a token of ordination to the disciples of Hillel and Shammai, attesting their fitness to participate in the Sanhedrin, which had come under Pharisaic control (thus eliminating the *'Ammê Hā-'āreṣ*). The rabbi held no office in the synagogue and received neither stipend nor perquisite. His presence was required in the local courts and especially in the Sanhedrin as an expert in the law. In the conduct of the synagogue he enjoyed no special prerogatives beyond those accruing to him by virtue of his knowledge and character.

The head of the Sanhedrin or *Nasi*, 'Prince,' was distinguished by the title *Rabban* (an Aramaic form of *Rab* with suffix in the first person plural), corresponding to *Patriarch*. Gamaliel the Elder was the first bearer of this title. Judah Hanasi was called simply *Rabbi* and *Rabbenu*, 'our master.' The term was applied affectionately to Moses ('Mosheh Rabbenu,' in *Sifre Dt* 305; cf Assumption of Moses).

The Gospels use the term as an honorary designation of Jesus. He is so addressed by His disciples (Mt $26^{25, 49}$; Mk $9^{5, 25}$ 11^{21} 14^{45}, Jn $1^{38, 49}$ 4^{31} 9^{2} 11^{8}) and by others (Jn 3^{2} 6^{25}). **Rabboni** in Jn 20^{16} and Mk 10^{51} is a Palestinian Aramaic form of the word. Jn 3^{26} applies the title also to John the Baptist. Mt 23^{8-10} limits the use of the title to Jesus, as the 'one teacher,' but his disciples were 'not to be called rabbi.' Inasmuch as the title did not exist in the time of Jesus, its use in the Gospels may be anachronistic (so H. Graetz, *Geschichte*, IV, 431), and probably represents a later addition to the evangelic tradition. S. S. C.

RABBITH.—A town of Issachar, Jos 19^{20}; perhaps we should read **Daberath** (q.v.).

RABBONI.—See RABBI.

RAB-MAG.—The title of Nergal-sharezer (q.v.), a Babylonian official present at the taking of Jerusalem, Jer $39^{3, 13}$. For various conjectures as to the origin of the title, see Hastings' *DB*, *s.v.* The view that it means 'chief magus' is unlikely, and it is more probable that it was a military official title. It occurs in an Aramaic-Greek bilingual text as the equivalent of *stratēgos*, 'general.'

RAB-SARIS.—**1.** The title of an Assyrian official who was sent by Sennacherib to Hezekiah to demand the surrender of Jerusalem, 2 K 18^{17}. **2.** The title borne by two Babylonian officials, one of whom is recorded to have been present at the capture of Jerusalem by Nebuchadnezzar, while the other is mentioned among the officials who ordered the release of Jeremiah after the capture of the city, Jer $39^{3, 13}$. *Rab-sārîs* is the transcription, both in Hebrew and Aramaic, of the Assyrian and Babylonian title *rabû* (or *rubû*)-*sha-rēshu*, borne by a high court-official, who may perhaps have been the 'chief eunuch,' though this office cannot be determined with absolute certainty. L. W. K.

RAB-SHAKEH.—The title of an Assyrian officer, who with the **Tartan** (q.v.) and the **Rab-saris** (q.v.) was sent by Sennacherib to Hezekiah to demand the surrender of Jerusalem, 2 K 18 f, Is 36 f. The word is the Hebrew transcription of the Assyrian *rab-shaḳû*—a title borne by a military officer of high rank, subordinate to the Tartan. L. W. K.

RACA, which occurs only in Mt 5^{22} (AV, RV), is a word of uncertain origin and meaning. The MSS vary in spelling between *racha* and *raka*. Should the former be the correct form, the word would seem to occur in a Zenon papyrus from Egypt dated 257 B.C. where it is used in much the same sense as in the Gospel. Thus both *racha*, a shortened form of *rachistēs* 'empty braggart,' and the following *mōre* 'thou fool,' would be Greek words used colloquially as abusive epithets. If, however, *raka* is the correct form, it is most simply explained as a Galilean Aramaic word cognate with the Jewish *rēqā* used as a term of contempt for empty-headed, frivolous people of uncertain morals. In this case the following *mōre* would probably be another local Aramaic word of abuse. In either case it is apparent that both words meant something much worse that our 'empty-headed braggart' and 'fool' suggest. Thus Jesus is saying that those who use to their brothers such foul words of abuse are in danger not only of punishment by the authorities in this world, but of more serious punishment in the world to come. Chrysostom, Augustine, and Jerome all had information that *Raca* was a word of abuse in the colloquial Levantine speech, though by their times it may, as in Edessene Syriac, have come into the language from the NT. A. J.

RACAL in 1 S 30^{29} (AV **Rachal**) is probably a mistake for 'Carmel' (**1**).

RACE.—See GAMES.

RACES.—In Gn 10 we have a list of the names of mankind known to the writer, divided into the descendants of the three sons of Noah. Complex, and in some cases still unresolved, problems arise in classifying the races mentioned in the Bible, and while race and language do not necessarily belong together, we are often mainly guided by language in our classification. The following classification shows the groupings of the main races of the Bible:

I. ARYANS.—**1. Greeks. 2. Javan** (Ionian Greeks). **3. Hittites. 4. Philistines. 5. Persians. 6. Medes** (Madai). **7. Parthians. 8. Romans.**

II. HAMITES.—**1. Egyptians. 2. Cushites** (Nubians, Ethiopians). **3. Libyans** (Put).

III. SEMITES.—A. **North Semites:** (*a*) *Eastern Branch*—**1. Babylonians. 2. Assyrians. 3. Amorites.** (*b*) *Western branch.*—**1. Ugaritians. 2. Phoenicians. 3. Israelites. 4. Ammonites. 5. Moabites. 6. Edomites. 7. Jebusites. 8. Aramaeans.** B. **South Semites:** (*a*) *Northern branch.*—**1. Amalekites. 2. Ishmaelites. 3. Midianites.** (*b*) *Southern branch.*—**Sabaeans** (Sheba).

IV. RACES WHICH DO NOT FIT INTO THESE GROUPS.—**1. Cimmerians** (Gomer). **2. Elamites. 3. Hurrians** (Horites). G. A. B.—H. H. R.

RACHAL, 1 S 20^{39} (AV).—See RACAL.

RACHEL.—Gn $29^{6, 10}$ *et al.* The younger daughter of Laban, and Jacob's second wife, mother of Joseph and Benjamin. She died on the way back from Paddan-aram at Ephrath and was buried there. Her grave is mentioned as a landmark in 1 S 10^{2}. There are two divergent traditions in the OT with regard to the site of the grave. (*a*) According to Gn 35^{16}, 1 S 10^{2}, and Jer 31^{15}, Ephrath lay on the N. border of Benjamin, about 10 miles N. of Jerusalem. (*b*) According to later Christian tradition, resting on the gloss in Gn 35^{19}, it was a mile N. of Bethlehem. The gloss rests on a confusion between Ephrath, and the clan-name Ephratah, which is always connected with Bethlehem. The former is undoubtedly the true site. The name in Hebrew means 'ewe,' and like the name Caleb ('dog'), has been used to support the now rejected view that totemism formed an element in the early religion of the Hebrews. The early history of the Rachel tribes is obscure. The group was probably first known as 'the house of Joseph,' then, in the process of settlement, Ephraim, Manasseh (Machir), and Benjamin, filled the gap in central Palestine left by the dispersal and disappearance of Reuben, Simeon, and Levi; then, with the rise to power of Judah, Benjamin was absorbed into Judah, and Ephraim confronted Judah as a successful rival for the hegemony of Palestine. See also RAMAH, **3.**
S. H. He.

RADDAI.—The fifth son of Jesse, 1 Ch 2^{14}.

RAFTS.—See SHIPS AND BOATS.

RAGAE.—See RAGES.

RAGAU.—**1.** Jth $1^{5, 15}$ (AV, RV); see RAGES. **2.** Lk 3^{35} (AV); see REU.

RAGES.—*Ragā* in the Old Persian inscriptions. The modern *Rei*, 6 miles SE. of Teheran, one of the seats of the ancient Iranian civilization, but now a mass of fallen walls and stupendous ruins covered with mounds of *débris.* Its position near the Caspian Gates gave it great strategic importance. It was the capital of Media before Ecbatana, and has the distinction of having been the home of the mother of Zoroaster. Alexander visited it in his pursuit of Darius III. Seleucus I. rebuilt it and called it Europos. It is mentioned in the Apocrypha. In Tobit (1[14] 4[1, 20] 5[5] 6[12] 9[2]) it was visited by the angel Raphael, and there he recovered for Tobias the deposit of silver which his father had placed there. In Judith (1[5, 15]) it is said that in **Ragae** (AV, RV **Ragau**)—evidently the same place—Nebuchadnezzar slew in battle 'Arphaxad' prince of the Medes. In To 6[9] read *Ecbatana* for *Rages* (so RSV). The Parthians called it Arsacia and made it the residence of their kings in the spring. Under the Sassanians it was the seat of a Christian bishop. It was destroyed by an earthquake in A.D. 863, but again played a rôle in the 15th century.

J. F. McC.—**E. G. K.**

RAGUEL.—1. See Reuel, **2. 2.** The father of Sarah, the wife of Tobias (To 3[7, 17f] 14[12]).

RAHAB.—1. The story of this woman, called a harlot, of Jericho is given in Jos 2. The two spies sent out by Joshua to view the land of Canaan come first to the house of Rahab, in Jericho. The king hears of it, and bids Rahab bring them forth; but she asserts that they have left her house, and that she does not know where they have gone; she had, however, previously hidden them among stalks of flax upon the roof. After their pursuers have left, Rahab comes to them, professes her belief in Yahweh, and adjures them to spare her and her kinsfolk when the attack on Jericho is made; this they promise shall be done; and after arranging that a scarlet thread is to be hung from her window, in order to denote which house is to be spared when the sack of the city took place, the two spies escape from her house by a rope. The promise is duly kept, and Joshua spares her when the city is burned (6[22-25]). The whole story has a clear aetiological atmosphere. In Mt 1[5] Rahab is mentioned in the genealogy of our Lord.

2. The term Rahab (Heb. *Rahabh*, to be distinguished from Rahab considered above, which is *Rāḥābh* in Heb.) is used for a mythological monster, the **Dragon**, and applied also to Egypt. In most passages where the term Rahab occurs, there is an allusion to the myth of Creation, the battle with the Dragon of Chaos, Leviathan, or Rahab. In the Biblical literature, this myth has been transferred to Yahweh, and the purpose is to affirm that the God who has performed such a wonder will strengthen and help His people in their distress, cf Ps 74[12-14] 87[4] 89[10], Job 9[13] 26[12]. The myth was also historicized and used metaphorically to describe Yahweh's great victories in history, especially over Pharaoh's army at the time of the Exodus. Hence the term Rahab is applied to Egypt; cf Is 30[7] 51[9]. Then it was developed in an eschatological way to describe God's victories over his enemies in the great Day to come, cf Is 27[1], and in the NT, Rev 21[1].

W. O. E. O.—**E. R. R.**

RAHAM.—A descendant of Caleb, 1 Ch 2[44].

RAHEL, Jer 31[15] (AV) = **Rachel** (q.v.).

RAIMENT.—See Dress.

RAIN.—The Palestine year is divided into two parts—the rainy and the dry. Of these the dry summer is the more regular, and lasts from May 15 to September 15. At either end is a six-week transitional period, marked by the *sirocco*, and possibly a light shower. A heavy storm of rain during October, which would permit early planting, or in early April, when it helps to swell the grain, is particularly valuable. Hence the importance in the Bible of the **former** and **latter rains** (Dt 11[14], Jer 5[24], Hos 6[3], Jl 2[23]). The true rainy season usually lasts from early November to the end of March, and in a very good year rain falls regularly about once a week. In other years it is more intermittent, and may be interrupted for as long as a month or more. If this happens when the grain is still young the result may be disastrous. Equally bad is a late start to the season, which in Jerusalem may be delayed until Christmas, and E. of the Jordan until mid-January. The first rainfall, upon which the beginning of ploughing is absolutely dependent, is often in the form of thunderstorms and sometimes very limited in area. One village may have rain, and another, 5 miles away, have none (Am 4[7-8]).

Rainfall decreases from north to south, and also from west to east, that is with increasing distance from the sea, though this may be modified by the presence of higher land. The lee slopes of hills are usually in a marked rain-shadow. This is very clearly seen in the Rift Valley (Tiberias 16 inches, Beisan 12, Jericho 4, Dead Sea 2). The rainfall of the Coast Plain and the Western Plateau does not differ greatly in amount (Haifa and Jerusalem both have 24 inches), but that of the Coast Plain is usually less variable, and the rainy season starts earlier. On the Eastern Plateau the season usually starts late, though the plateau edge may have surprisingly heavy rain (*Es-Salṭ* 31 inches), but this dies away rapidly to the east (*'Ammân* 13 inches, and *Zerqā*, 10 miles away, only 5 inches). The total rainfall in most parts of Palestine is very variable from year to year, and unfortunately this is especially true of the marginal areas between the Desert and the Sown. A. D. B.

RAINBOW.—This word never occurs in OT; even where it is obviously implied (Gn 9[13f, 16], Ezk 1[28]), EV translate Hebrew *ḳesheth* literally with **'bow'** (cf LXX *toxon*). In NT it renders *iris* (Rev 4[3] 10[1]). The latter passages clearly presuppose the former, combining the rainbow as a symbol of (divine) glory and splendour (Ezk 1[28], cf Sir 43[11] 50[7]) with its use as a symbol of merciful forbearance (Gn 9[13ff]), a promise of the old dispensation now realized and assured in the new, in Christ and His gospel. There is no trace here of the personified *Iris*, messenger of the gods in Greek mythology.

In the sequel (Gn 9[8-17]) to the story of the universal flood the bow of Yahweh is set in the clouds as a proof to the people and a reminder to Yahweh that no deluge shall again destroy the earth. The writer seems to have used an ancient nature myth which explained the rainbow as God hanging up his 'rain-bow,' and made it a token of the Noachic covenant, as was circumcision of the Abrahamic (Gn 17[10]). No parallel to this symbolic interpretation of the rainbow has yet been discovered in ancient Near Eastern literature, but the bow is of course a common weapon of the warrior gods (*e.g.* Marduk, in the Bab. Creation Epic IV. 35); and in the Ugaritic literature the breaking of Aqhat's bow seems to be followed by a drought (*Aqhat* I. i. 1 ff). Ps 7[12f] 21[12] mention Yahweh's war bow; Ps 77[18], Hab 3[9, 11], Zec 9[14] show that his arrows were the lightning; Job 38[25f], Ps 135[7] attribute rain to the effect of lightning ('puncturing' the rain-clouds). These passages together may help to elucidate both the point of the rainbow as a 'sign' in Gn 9, and the 9th cent. picture of an Assyrian god (Ashur?) drawing a bow at heavy rainclouds (see *ANEP*, fig. 536). The Noachic covenant, with the rainbow as the sign of God's magnanimity towards mankind as a whole, seems to be overshadowed in Biblical theology by the Abrahamic covenant with the Hebrew race, and the Mosaic one with the Twelve Tribes; but in popular religion it may have played a larger rôle owing to the phenomenological character of its sign, which has assured the rainbow of attention in the mythologies of most races (see *e.g.* J. Skinner, *Genesis* [I.C.C.], p. 173).

C. W. E.—**D. R. Ap-T.**

RAISINS.—Hebrew *ṣimmûḳîm* (from root meaning 'to dry up'), 1 S 25[18] 30[12], 2 S 16[1], 1 Ch 12[40]; Hebrew *'ashîshāh*, 2 S 6[19], 1 Ch 16[3], Ca 2[5], Is 16[7], Hos 3[1] (RV and RSV; AV **'flagon'** [q.v.] in all cases, save Is 16[7], where it has 'foundations'); Hebrew *'anābhîm yebhēshîm*, Nu 6[3], literally 'dried grapes' (so EV). Raisins are now, as of old, prepared in great quantities in the Holy Land; the bunches are dipped in a strong solution of potash before being dried. *Es-Salṭ*, across the Jordan, has long been famous for its stoneless raisins. E. W. G. M.

RAKEM.—See Rekem, 3.

RAKKATH.—A 'fortified city' of Naphtali, Jos 19^{35}; possibly modern, *Tell Eqlāṭîyeh.*

RAKKON.—A town of Dan, Jos 19^{46}; possibly modern, *Tell er-Reqqeit.*

RAM.—**1.** An ancestor of David, Ru 4^{19}, 1 Ch 2^{9f}, and so of Jesus, Mt 1^{3f} (RV, RSV; AV **Aram**); in Lk 3^{33} he is called **Arni** (RV, RSV; AV **Aram**). In 1 Ch 2^{9} he is called the *brother* of Jerahmeel, but in vv.$^{25, 27}$ his *son.* **2.** The family to which Elihu belonged, Job 32^{2}. Some have thought *Ram* is a contraction of **Aram.**

RAM.—See Sheep, and (for battering-ram) Fortification and Siegecraft.

RAMAH.—The name of several places in Palestine, so called from their 'loftiness,' that being the radical meaning of the word. These are as follows:

1. A city of Naphtali (Jos 19^{36}) not otherwise known, perhaps *er-Râmeh,* Acco and Damascus, WSW. of *Ṣafed.* **2.** A city of Asher (Jos 19^{29}) not elsewhere mentioned, and identified not improbably with *er-Râmiah,* near Tyre. **3.** A city of Benjamin (Jos 18^{25}) between which and Bethel was the palm of Deborah (Jg 4^{5}); one of the alternatives which the Levite of Bethlehem had to choose for a lodging on his fatal journey (Jg 19^{13}); yielded with Geba 621 men to the post-exilic census of Ezra (Ezr 2^{26}, 1 Es 5^{20} [AV **Cirama,** RV **Kirama**]); re-settled by Benjamites (Neh 11^{33}). Its place is indicated between Geba and Gibeah in Isaiah's picture of the Assyrian advance (10^{29}). A tradition placed here the site of **Rachel's tomb**; this explains the allusions in 1 S 10^{2}, Jer 31^{15} (quoted in Mt 2^{18}). Here Jeremiah was loosed from his chains (40^{1}). The name, and not improbably the site, of this place is preserved by a little village on a hillside N. of Jerusalem known as *er-Râm,* which answers the geographical requirements of these incidents. Near it are some remarkable ancient monuments, known locally as 'The Graves of the Children of Israel,' which possibly are the 'tomb of Rachel' of the ancient tradition. This town was probably the home of Shimei, the **Ramathite,** David's vine-dresser (1 Ch 27^{27}). **4.** A place in the district called **Ramathaim-zophim** (1 S 1^{1}), a (corrupt) name probably='the two heights of the Zuphites.' The latter ethnic can hardly be dissociated from the name of the great high place of **Mizpah** (*Nebi Samwîl*). Its chief distinction is its connexion with Samuel. It was in 'the hill country of Ephraim,' but might have been over the S. border of the tribe. Here Elkanah lived, and here was the headquarters of Samuel throughout his life (1 S 1^{19} 2^{11} 7^{17} 8^{4} 15^{34} 16^{13} $19^{18, 23}$ 20^{1} 25^{1} 28^{3}). This is probably the Ramah fortified by Baasha against the Judahite kingdom (1 K 15^{17}, 2 Ch 16^{1}), rather than the Benjamite Ramah: the latter being actually within Judahite territory would not have been accessible to him. This Ramah appears also in 1 Mac 11^{34} as **Ramathaim.** It is perhaps modern, *Rentis.* **5.** By the name *Ramah* allusion is made to **Ramoth-gilead** (q.v.) in 2 K 8^{29} and the parallel passage 2 Ch 22^{6}. **6. Ramath-lehi,** the scene of Samson's victory over the Philistines with the jawbone (Jg 15^{17}) is unknown. See Lehi. Ramath here is probably a common noun, and we ought to render it 'the height of Lehi.' **7. Ramath-mizpeh** (Jos 13^{26}). See Mizpah, **1, 4. 8. Ramah** (AV **Ramath**) **of the Negeb** (AV, RV **of the South**), Jos 19^{8}. A town in the tribe of Judah, given to Simeon, to which David sent the spoil of Ziklag, 1 S 30^{27} (**Ramoth**). It is quite unknown. R. A. S. M.

RAMAH OF THE NEGEB.—See Ramah, **8.**

RAMAH OF THE SOUTH, Jos 19^{8} (RV).—See Ramah, **8.**

RAMATH OF THE SOUTH, Jos 19^{8} (AV).—See Ramah, **8.**

RAMATHAIM, RAMATHAIM-ZOPHIM.—See Ramah, **4.**

RAMATHITE.—See Ramah, **3.**

RAMATH-LEHI.—See Ramah, **6.**

RAMATH-MIZPEH.—See Mizpah, **4.**

RAMESES.—See Raamses.

RAMIAH.—One of the sons of Parosh who had married a foreign wife, Ezr 10^{25}, 1 Es 9^{26} (AV, RV **Hiermas**).

RAMOTH.—**1.** A Gershonite Levitical city in Issachar, 1 Ch 6^{73}, apparently=**Remeth** of Jos 19^{21} and **Jarmuth** of Jos 21^{29} (see Jarmuth, **2**). **2.** For **Ramoth of the Negeb,** 1 S 30^{27}, see Ramah, **8. 3.** For **Ramoth in Gilead,** Dt 4^{43} etc., see Ramoth-Gilead. **4.** Ezr 10^{29} (AV); see Jeremoth, **8.**

RAMOTH-GILEAD, or **'Ramoth in Gilead,'** was the centre of one of Solomon's administrative districts which extended N. of the Yarmuk (1 K 4^{13}), and was one of the cities of refuge (Dt 4^{43}, Jos 20^{8}) assigned to the Merarite Levites of Gad (Jos 21^{38}, 1 Ch 6^{80}). It was a key fortress in the wars between Israel and Aram, and Ahab was killed there (1 K 22^{3-24}, 2 Ch 18). There Jehu was anointed (2 K 8^{28} 9^{1-14}, 2 Ch 22^{5}). The *Onomasticon* sites it near the Jabbok 15 miles W. of Philadelphia (*'Ammân*), visualizing either *Es-Salṭ* or *Khirbet Jil'ād.* The narrative of the Aramaean wars, however, and the fiscal list of Solomon indicate a site further N. The dominating site of *Ḥuṣn 'Ajlûn* is suggested by Albright and Dalman, and the period of occupation of this site as ascertained by Glueck certainly indicates the feasibility of this suggestion. An alternative suggestion is *Er-Remtheh* (Aramatha of Jos. *Ant.* viii. xv. 3 [398]; ix. vi. 1 [105]), but the open situation of this place hardly suggests the obviously commanding situation of Ramoth-Gilead in the wars between Israel and Aram.

R. A. S. M.—**J. Gr.**

RAMOTH OF THE SOUTH, 1 S 30^{27} (RV).—See Ramah, **8.**

RAMOTH, SOUTH, 1 S 30^{27} (AV).—See Ramah, **8.**

RAMPART.—See Bulwark, Citadel.

RANGES in AV of 2 K $11^{8, 15}$, 2 Ch 23^{14}='ranks' (RV, RSV).

RANSOM.—See Redeemer, Redemption.

RAPE.—See Crimes and Punishments, 3.

RAPHA.—**1.** A Benjamite, 1 Ch 8^{2}. **2.** 1 Ch 8^{37} (AV); see Rephaiah, **4.**

RAPHAEL ('God has healed').—Does not appear in the Bible except for Tobit in the Apocrypha. (In 1 Ch 26^{7} EV have the form Rephael as a personal name.) He is a prominent figure in Enoch as well as in the post-biblical literature. In To 3^{17} he is sent to *heal* Tobit, by restoring his sight; to give Sarah, daughter of his kinsman Raguel, to his son Tobias for wife; and to prevent the demon Asmodaeus from adding him to the seven husbands he has already killed. In 5^{4ff} he appears as 'brother **Azarias**' to accompany Tobias on his journey to Media. Tobit despatches them with the parting 'May [God's] angel go with you' (v.^{16}, cf v.^{21}), and they start with their dog (a favourite subject with the great painters). In 6^{3ff} he directs Tobias to take the heart, liver, and gall of a fish, manages the marriage, binds the demon, fetches money from Rages, and heals Tobit. 12^{12-20} gives his description of himself, a passage which probably became the groundwork of later speculations. (1) He is one of the seven 'angels of the presence' (Lk 1^{19}, Rev 8^{2} [1^{4}?], 1 Enoch 90). So in Enoch 20^{3} he is one of the 'watchers,' the 'angel of the spirits of men.' The conception is usually traced to Persian influence; cf the seven 'princes of light' of Zoroastrianism. (2) He is an intermediary, bringing the memorial of prayers before God (Rev 8^{3}). The doctrine of the Divine aloofness made it hard to conceive that man could have direct access to the ear of God, any more than a subject could enter into the presence of an Oriental monarch, or that He could interfere directly in the petty affairs of men. See Angels. (3) He is also a guardian angel, being present at Tobit's good deeds, and the companion of Tobias. The long-maintained disguise is a unique feature; the 'eating and drinking' is explained as an illusion (12^{19}). (4) He is true to his name, 'the healer'; cf 1 Enoch 10^{7}, where he is ordered to bind Azazel (so 54), and *heal* the earth which the angels have defiled; and 40[5], where he is 'set over the diseases and wounds of the children of men.' (5) In 1 Enoch 22 he is a guide in Sheol; in 32, in Paradise.

C. W. E.—**C. C. Ro.**

RAPHAH.—See REPHAIAH, **4**, REPHAIM.

RAPHAIM.—An ancestor of Judith (Jth 8[1]).

RAPHON.—A city of Bashan (1 Mac 5[37]), the *Raphana* of Pliny (*HN*, v. 16); possibly *er-Râfeh*, 33 miles E. of the Lake of Galilee.

RAPHU.—The father of the Benjamite spy, Nu 13[9].

RAS SHAMRA TABLETS.—The excavation of *Râs Shamra*, ancient Ugarit, which was occupied from the Neolithic Age (before *c* 3500 B.C.) to the end of the Bronze Age (*c* 1200 B.C.), certainly inaugurated a new epoch in OT research. This nexus of trade routes near the North Syrian coast about 12 miles N. of *Latakia* abounded in texts in several scripts, including Egyptian hieroglyphic inscriptions, business documents and political and legal texts in Akkadian syllabic cuneiform, alphabetic texts in the language of the non-Semitic Hurrians (possibly Biblical Horites) of the Anatolian foothills, Sumerian-Akkadian and Sumerian-Akkadian-Hurrian vocabularies, and texts in the linear Cypriot script, and also Hittite elements even in Semitic texts. More directly relevant to the OT are a large number of official documents from the palace archives and myths and sagas in alphabetic cuneiform from the Late Bronze Age stratum (*c* 1400 B.C.) of the library of the temple of Baal. The former are vital for the study of Canaanite society and institutions; the latter, of epic style and often of epic proportions, comprise a substantial torso of the literature of Canaan on the eve of the Hebrew settlement.

The administrative and legal documents indicate that the subjects were listed for military service or for provision of arms, and that taxes were levied in silver, produce, or labour, recalling Solomon's levies in Israel (1 K 5[13ff] 9[15ff] 11[25]). A fact that further suggests Solomon's administration (1 K 4[7-19]) is that, though there are traces of a social order based on families, the population was organized by districts, guilds, and classes, the chief class being the *mariannu*, known already from contemporary Egyptian records as equestrian feudatories, who specialized in chariot warfare. The conception of a professional military class owing their status and property solely to the king was adopted by Israel in the early monarchy (1 S 14[52] 18[13] 22[7]).

The themes of the myths are:

1. Baal's triumph over Chaos.
2. Baal's struggle with Death.
3. The Birth of Dawn and Evening (star).
4. The Marriage of Nikal (moon-goddess).

Three fragmentary texts describe how Order in Nature is menaced by the insolence of 'Prince Sea, yea Judge River,' against whom the 'divine assembly' is apparently impotent. Baal, however, undertakes to engage the unruly waters, and eventually prevails, and so gains 'his eternal kingship.' This is obviously the local variant of the myth of the conflict of Cosmos and Chaos, best known in the Babylonian New Year myth *enuma elish*, the leading motifs of which it exhibits. The theme and the imagery recur in the OT in passages in the Prophets relating to God's kingship and judgment, and in the 'Enthronement' Psalms, notably Ps 93. In the Râs Shamra texts, however, there is no extension, as in the OT, of the Reign of God into the field of history or the moral order. The various indications of the association of such passages in the OT with the autumnal new year suggest a similar association of the Canaanite myth, though of this there is no conclusive proof.

The rest of the Baal-mythology reflects the tension between fertility and sterility in the Canaanite peasant's year. The chief themes are the death of **Baal**, the vengeance of his sister **Anath,** his resurrection, the building of his 'house,' his final victory over death. Baal here is the vegetation-god, the local variation of Mesopotamian Tammuz, Egyptian Osiris, and the Greek Dionysus, and there are certain features in the myth which suggests its relation to seasonal rituals. Anath's mourning for the dead Baal suggests the weeping for Tammuz by the women of Jerusalem, presumably in the sixth month (Ezk 8[14]); her vengeance on Death, cutting him with a sickle, winnowing him, parching him with fire, grinding him, etc., obviously suggests the Hebrew rite of the first sheaf (Lv 2[14]); the building of the 'house' of Baal in the season of heavy rains suggests an analogy with the dedication of Solomon's Temple in the seventh month, *Ethanim*, the 'Regular Rains' (1 K 8[2]). This was also the season of the Feast of Tabernacles, and the 'house' of Baal may well be the prototype of the booths, or bivouacs, which the Hebrews seem to have taken over from the Canaanites. Though we do not doubt that these myths were related to rites of imitative magic, which they were designed to make doubly effective, they have undergone a long process of elaboration and have an intrinsic literary value.

The sagas or legends concern two ancient kings **Keret** and **Dan'el,** and they also have a direct bearing on OT study. Both kings are without prospect of heir, and both probably, and certainly Dan'el, go into ritual incubation (cf Solomon at Gibeon, 1 K 3[5]), and in dreams receive assurance of issue. In the case of Dan'el the son is described with relation to his social and religious duties—an invaluable passage for the study of Canaanite society—and Keret is given instructions and assurance in his task of finding a new wife—again an important text for sociological study. The Keret text continues in mutilated form, describing domestic history. The text, on three tablets, is but the torso of a much fuller text, and its undoubted value is to be realized by detailed study. The Dan'el text suffered also, but the story is much more intelligible. Dan'el's son **Aqhat** receives a bow from the divine craftsman, which, intended for gods, not men, incites the desire of the goddess Anath, who uses her allurements to procure it. Aqhat repulses her with scorn, and is in consequence struck down. Blood violently shed and uncovered by the earth occasions sterility (cf Gn 4[11-12], Nu 35[33]), so, to maintain congruity with this disaster, Dan'el puts a ban upon the winter and later summer rain-clouds, the summer dew, and the subterranean water (cf David's curse on the mountains of Gilboa, 2 S 1[21]). We note the close association of the primitive king with the fertility of nature, of which we find indications also in the Keret text. Dan'el then performs rites designed to transmit fertility through the season of drought and dearth to a new phase of fertility, when he anticipates his son Aqhat performing the rite of the ingathering, an instance of dramatic irony. Subsequently Dan'el learns that the slain man is his own son. He recovers his remains, and mourns and buries him. The coincidence of Aqhat's death with harvest is noteworthy, and it is suggested that in Aqhat we have the personification of the genius of the corn, which was symbolically killed to make the new crop available for public use; cf the death and dismemberment of Death in the Baal-myth. Thus the Dan'el text, in spite of its human protagonists, was probably a composite work, where an originally historical theme had already passed into a myth, incorporating a variety of seasonal themes.

The study of these texts in detail in the original reveals many more points of contact with the OT, the language of which they largely employ. Their value for the study of the OT is manifold. They document very fully the Canaanite fertility-cult, by which the Hebrews were influenced and against the grosser aspects of which their leaders reacted. The legends directly document the institution of kingship. These texts and the many anthropomorphisms in the myths give insight into social practices and values in the Canaanite environment of Israel, and the administrative and legal texts from the palace give a clue to the structure of society. The language and imagery of the texts enhances the appreciation of many nuances in the OT, notably in Prophets, Psalms, and the Book of Job, and indicates the extent to which the Hebrews knew and used the mythology of Canaan. The Râs Shamra texts are of great value for textual criticism of the OT. Many a word in the OT, suspect and rejected as a *hapax legomenon*, has been found in several contexts in the Râs Shamra texts, the rather rigid parallelism fixing the meaning of the word beyond all doubt, so that the Massoretic Text is often supported. The Canaanite prototype of certain passages in the OT, however, occasionally suggests emendation. Such cases are notably fewer than those where the standard Hebrew text is corroborated. J. Gr.

RASSES, Jth 2^{23} (AV, RV).—See RASSIS.

RASSIS.—A people subdued by Holofernes, Jth 2^{23} (AV, RV **Rasses**).

RATHUMUS, 1 Es 2^{16} (AV, RV).—See REHUM, **2.**

RAVEN.—The Hebrew *'ôrēbh* and the Greek *korax* seem to be names based on the cry of the bird which they represent, *i.e.* the 'cruck-cruck' or 'pruck-pruck' or 'whurk-whurk' attributed to the raven. The *'ôrēbh* designates *omne corvinum genus* (Jerome) including crow, raven, and rook. It is black (Ca 5^{11}) and haunts ravines (1 K $17^{4,6}$), and it or its young plucks out the eyes of its victim (Pr 30^{17}), a habit to which Aristophanes (*Birds* 582, *Acharnians* 92) refers. Both crow and raven are black, both commonly build their nests on rocks or cliffs overhanging wadis, both attack and kill sickly beasts as large as lambs, while the Mediterranean hooded crow begins the destruction of its victim by picking out eyes and tongue while it is still alive. Both feed on carrion and refuse, which explains why they are counted unclean (Lv 11^{15}, Dt 14^{14}). The raven also haunts the wilderness (Is 34^{11}), and its habit of storing food in hiding places for future consumption perhaps lies behind the story of those that fed Elijah by the brook Cherith (1 K 17^{4-6}). Why the raven, as also the dove, is connected with the Flood is not clear; but that 'it went to and fro until the waters were dried up from the earth' (Gn 8^{7}) may be based on some recollection of scavenger birds searching for carrion left by the receding waters of a flood. In Job 38^{41} (where the young ravens are said to croak for lack of food), Ps 147^{9}, Lk 12^{24} God is said to feed the raven. G. R. D.

RAVEN, RAVIN.—The verb 'to raven,' *i.e.* prey upon, and the substantive 'raven' or 'ravin,' *i.e.* prey, both occur in AV. We find also the adjective 'ravening' (Ps 22^{13}, Mt 7^{15}) as well as the form 'ravenous' (Is 35^{9} 46^{11}, Ezk 39^{4}). 'Ravening' is used as a substantive in Lk 11^{39}, 'Your inward part is full of ravening and wickedness' (RV 'extortion'). RSV retains 'ravening' in Ps 22^{13} and introduces it at Jer 2^{30} (AV, RV 'destroying'), but has 'ravenous' in Mt 7^{15}.

RAZIS.—The hero of a narrative in 2 Mac 14^{37-46}.

RAZOR.—A razor for removing the hair (q.v.) of the head or beard is referred to in Nu 6^{5} 8^{7}, Jg 13^{5} 16^{17}, 1 S 1^{11}, Is 7^{20}, Ezk 5^{1}, especially in connexion with the Nazirite (q.v.). In Ps 52^{2} it is used as a simile for the tongue.

REAIA, 1 Ch 5^{5} (AV).—See REAIAH, **2.**

REAIAH.—**1.** A Calebite family, 1 Ch 4^{2}; called **Haroeh** (q.v.) in 2^{52}. **2.** A Reubenite family, 1 Ch 5^{5} (AV **Reaia**). **3.** A Nethinim family name, Ezr 2^{47}, Neh 7^{50}, 1 Es 5^{31} (AV **Airus,** RV **Jairus**).

REAPING.—See AGRICULTURE, 3.

REBA.—One of the five kinglets of Midian slain by Moses, Nu 31^{8}, Jos 13^{21}.

REBECCA.—Form of the name Rebekah (q.v.), found in Ro 9^{10}.

REBEKAH.—The wife of Isaac (Gn 24), daughter of Bethuel the son of Nahor (Gn 24^{15}), Abraham's brother. There is a divergence in the sources about the original home of Rebekah. According to the Yahwist's narrative in Gn 24, Eliezer, Abraham's steward, whom he sends to find a wife for Isaac, finds Rebekah and her family living in Haran, in Aram-naharaim (*i.e.* Mesopotamia); but in Gn 29^{1} Jacob finds Laban and Rebekah's father Bethuel living in 'the land of the children of the east.' Now, in OT usage, this expression always denotes the inhabitants of the NW. part of the Arabian desert, and in the genealogical list in Gn 22^{20-24} the names of Nahor's children are place-names or tribal names belonging either to the Syro-Arabian desert, or to the settled regions in North Syria. Hence, behind the beautiful story of the finding of Rebekah, and the story of Jacob's adventures in his search for a wife, there lies the historical fact that an important part of what was to become the people of Israel consisted of Aramaean stock which had originally lived both in NW. Mesopotamia and in North Syria.

The only feature of the Isaac saga which concerns Rebekah is the account of how Isaac went down to Gerar and Rebekah was taken into Abimelech's house, which is clearly a duplicate version of the story of Abraham in Gerar and Sarah's being taken by Abimelech (Gn 20^{1-18}). The rest of the Rebekah story forms part of the Jacob-Esau cycle of sagas. She plays a part in two of the episodes in this cycle. Before the birth of Esau and Jacob she goes to 'enquire' (*bḳsh*) of Yahweh, which, under the conditions of that time, means that she sought an oracular response from the Canaanite shrine at Hebron. She receives a poetic oracle which reflects the traditional enmity between Edom and Israel, and the fact that Edom (Esau) was a nation before the birth of national consciousness in Israel (cf Gn 36^{31}). In the other episode Rebekah secures the fulfilment of the oracle by a stratagem, making Jacob impersonate Esau and so deceiving Isaac into giving Jacob the blessing of the firstborn. No account is given of Rebekah's death, but in Gn 49^{31} Jacob tells Joseph that Isaac and Rebekah were buried in the cave of Machpelah. S. H. He.

RECAH.—An unknown place name, 1 Ch 4^{12} (AV **Rechah**).

RECEIPT OF CUSTOM.—See TAX OFFICE.

RECHAB, RECHABITES.—**1. Jehonadab,** the son of Rechab, appears in 2 K 10^{15-28} as a fervent supporter of Jehu's attack on the house of Ahab and his endeavour to root out the idolatrous worship which that dynasty had allowed. That his influence was a matter of some importance is clear from the prominent place which the new ruler gave him (2 K $10^{16,23}$). The principles which actuated him are to be gathered from Jer 35, according to which Jehonadab's descendants refused to drink wine because he had told them to abstain from it, build no houses, sow no seed, plant no vineyard, but live in tents all their lives. He evidently held that civilization and settled life inevitably led to apostasy from Yahweh, the ancestral Deity of his tribe. And the peril was a very real one because of the inveterate popular belief that the local *baals* were the dispensers of all blessings pertaining to field and vineyard (Hos $2^{5,10-12}$). Hence it seemed to more than one of the prophets that the early, simple period of the nation's life, before it became immersed in the Canaanite civilization, was preferable to all later developments. Again, the self-restraint of the Rechabites reminds us of the Nazirite vow (see NAZIRITE). But the latter did not include so many taboos. It permitted the cultivation of land and the building of houses. It was also not binding on an entire clan. A genuine tradition is probably embodied in the Chronicler's statement (1 Ch 2^{55}) that the clan of the Rechabites was connected with the **Kenites.** Subsequently to Jeremiah we do not find more than two Biblical allusions to the Rechabites, and one of these is doubtful. Neh 3^{14} reports that Malchijah, the son of Rechab, the ruler of part of Beth-haccherem, assisted in refortifying Jerusalem. But if he was a Rechabite by descent, he must have abandoned the principles of the clan. The men whom Jeremiah approached were but temporary sojourners, driven into the city through dread of the invader. This Malchijah was doubly a townsman, living in a country town and interested in the metropolis.

The title of Ps 71 in the LXX is : 'Belonging to David. Of the sons of Jehonadab and of the earliest captives,' as though the exiles and the Rechabites agreed in appropriating this poem of sorrow and hope. Finally, it may be noted that later Rabbis found the fulfilment of Jer 35[19] in those marriages of Rechabite maidens into priestly families from which later priests sprang. Hegesippus relates that one of the Rechabite priests interceded in vain for the life of James the Just (Eusebius, *HE* ii. 23).

2. Rechab and his brother Baanah, two guerilla captains, treacherously murdered Ishbosheth, their king, and met with the due reward of their deed at David's hands (2 S 4). J. T.—**T. J. M.**

RECHAH, 1 Ch 4[12] (AV).—See Recah.

RECOMPENSE.—See Reward.

RECONCILIATION.—The word 'reconciliation,' with its cognates, is a Pauline one, and is not found in the NT outside St. Paul. The chief passages in which it and related terms are employed are Ro 5[10, 11] (RV), 2 Co 5[18–20], Eph 2[16], Col 1[20–21]. In He 2[17], where the AV has 'to make reconciliation for the sins of the people,' the RSV reads, more correctly, 'to make expiation.' OT usage, where the word occasionally translated 'reconcile' (Lv 6[30] etc.) is again more correctly rendered in RSV 'make atonement,' throws little light on the NT term. The *effect* of expiation is to remove the variance between God and man, and so bring about 'reconciliation.' The means by which this result is accomplished in the NT is the reconciling death of Christ (Col 1[20–22]). On the special questions involved, see Atonement, Expiation, and Redemption.

Perhaps better than any other, this term brings out in vivid form St. Paul's conception of the gospel. As proclaimed to men, the gospel is a message of 'reconciliation' (2 Co 5[18–20]). It is a misunderstanding of the Apostle's meaning in such passages to suppose that the need of reconciliation is on man's side only, and not also on God's. Man, indeed, does need to be reconciled to God, from whom he is naturally alienated in his mind in evil works (Col 1[21]). 'The mind of the flesh is enmity against God' (Ro 8[7]), and this enmity of the carnal heart needs to be overcome. On this side, the 'ministry of reconciliation' is a beseeching of men to be reconciled to God (2 Co 5[20]). But the very ground on which this appeal is based is that 'God was in Christ reconciling the world to himself, not counting their trespasses against them' (v.[19]). It is an essential part of the Apostle's teaching that sinners are the objects of a Divine judicial wrath (Ro 1[18]). They lie under a condemnation that needs to be removed (3[19ff]). They are described as 'enemies' in two passages (5[10] 11[28]) where the word is plainly to be taken in the passive sense of *objects* of wrath (cf, in Ro 11[28], the contrast with 'beloved'). It is this barrier to God's reconciliation with men that, in the Apostle's doctrine, Christ removes by his expiatory death (Ro 3[25], Col 1[20]). The ground on which men are called to be reconciled to God is : 'Him who knew no sin he made to be sin on our behalf ; that we might become the righteousness of God in him' (2 Co 5[21] RV). Believers 'receive' a reconciliation already made (Ro 5[11] RSV). The gospel reconciliation, in other words, has a twofold aspect—a Godward and a manward ; and peace is made by the removal of the variance on both sides. See articles above referred to. J. O.—**A. R.**

RECORDER.—See Asaph, **1**, and King, **2** (7).

RED.—See Colours, **3**.

RED HEIFER.—The ashes of a 'red heifer'—more correctly a red *cow*—added to 'running water,' formed the most powerful means known to the Hebrews of removing the defilement produced by contact with a dead body. The method of preparing the ashes and the regulations for the application of the 'water of impurity' (see below) are the subject of a special section of the Priests' Code (Nu 19). It will be advisable to summarize the contents of the chapter, in the first place, and thereafter to inquire into the significance of the rite in the light of recent anthropological research.

1. The chapter above cited consists of two parts ; the first part, vv.[1–13], gives instructions for the preparation of the ashes, and (vv.[11–13]) for the removal by their means of the defilement contracted by actual contact with the dead body. The second part, vv.[14–22], is an expansion of vv.[12f], extending the application of 'the water of impurity' to uncleanness arising from a variety of sources connected with death.

The animal whose ashes acquired this special virtue had to be of the female sex, of a red, or rather reddish-brown, colour, physically without blemish, and one that had never borne the yoke. The duty of superintending the burning, which took place 'without the camp,' was entrusted to a deputy of the high priest. The actual burning, however, was carried through by a lay assistant, which fact, taken along with the detail (v.[5]) that every particle of the animal, *including the blood*, was burned, shows that we have not to do here with a ritual sacrifice, as might be inferred from the EV of v.[9]. The word there rendered 'sin-offering' properly denotes in this connexion (cf 8[7]) 'a purification for sin' (*Oxf. Heb. Lex.* 310[a] ; cf Sacrifice, **14**). The priest's share in the ceremony was confined to the sprinkling of some of the blood 'toward the front of the tent of meeting' (v.[4] RV and RSV), in token of the dedication of the animal to Y″, and to the casting into the burning mass of a piece of cedar wood and a bunch of hyssop bound with a piece of scarlet cloth (such, at least, is the regulation of the Mishnah treatise dealing with this subject).

A third person—the priest and his assistant having themselves become 'unclean' through contact with these sacred things (see below)—now gathered the ashes and laid them up 'without the camp in a clean place,' to be used as occasion required. The special name given to the mixture of 'running water' (v.[17], literally 'living water,' *i.e.* water from a spring, not a cistern) and the ashes is properly 'water of impurity' v.[9, 13, 20f]—so RVm ; ASV and RSV 'water for impurity' ; AV and RV **water of separation**), *i.e.* water for the removal of impurity or uncleanness. This powerful cathartic was applied to the person or thing to be cleansed, either by being thrown over them (see Gray, *Com.* on v.[13]), or by being sprinkled with a sprinkler of hyssop (v.[18]). This was done on the third and seventh days, after which the defiled person washed his person and garments, and was then restored to the privileges of the cult and the community. The only other reference to 'the water of impurity' is in the late passage, Nu 31[23].

2. The clue to the significance of the rite above described is found in the primitive conception of uncleanness, as this has been disclosed by modern anthropological research (see Clean and Unclean). In all primitive societies a dead body in particular is regarded as not only unclean in itself, but as capable of infecting with uncleanness all who come in contact with it or are even in proximity to it. The Semites shared these ideas with primitive communities in every part of the world. Hence, although the literary formulation of the rite of the Red Heifer in Nu 19 may be late, the ideas and practices thereof are certainly older than the Hebrews themselves.

While the central idea of the rite—the efficacy of **ashes** as a cathartic, due probably to their connexion with fire (cf Nu 31[23], and Farnell, *The Evolution of Religion*, 101 n.)—has its parallels elsewhere, the original significance of several of the details is still very obscure. This applies, for example, to the red colour of the cow, and to the addition to her ashes of the 'cedar wood and hyssop and scarlet' (for various suggestions see, in addition to Gray, *op. cit.*, Hastings' *DB* iv, 208 ff ; Bewer in *JBL* xxiv (1905) 42 ff, who suggests that the cow may have been originally a sacrifice to the dead).

The value of the chapter for the student of Hebrew ritual lies in the illustration it affords of the primitive conceptions of uncleanness, especially of the uncleanness of the dead, and of the 'contagiousness of holiness,' the nature of which has been so clearly expounded by Robertson Smith (see *RS*2 446 ff 'Holiness, Uncleanness, and Taboo'). The ashes of the red heifer and the water of impurity here appear, in virtue of their intense 'holiness,' as 'a conducting vehicle of a dangerous spiritual electricity' (Farnell, *op. cit.* 95), and have the same power as the dead body of rendering unclean all who come in contact with them (see vv.[7ff, 21f] and CLEAN AND UNCLEAN).

There are no inventions in ritual, it has been said, only survivals, and in the rite under review we have one of the most interesting of these survivals. The remarks made in a previous article (ATONEMENT [DAY OF]) are equally applicable to the present case. As reinterpreted by the compilers of the Priests' Code, the rite conveys, in striking symbolism, the eternal truth that purity and holiness are the essential characteristics of the people of God. A. R. S. K.

RED SEA.—The body of water, over 1200 miles in length, which divides Africa from Arabia, and whose two northern projections or arms, the Gulf of Suez and the Gulf of ʿAqaba, embrace the Sinai Peninsula. Its width varies from about 250 miles in the S. half to 130 miles at the N. where it divides. The mean depth of the Red Sea is about 1600 feet, varying from the shallow depth of the Gulf of Suez to a maximum of 7200 feet in the main basin. This is formed structurally by a system of rift valleys, the best known of which represents the Gulf of ʿAqaba in the great depression extending from the Lebanon mountains, through the Jordan Valley, the Dead Sea, the Wâdī ʿArabah, and into Africa.

The origin of the Hebrew name, *Yam Sûph*, 'sea of reeds' (Ex 10[19] 15[4] etc.) which is usually rendered in English as 'Red Sea' is uncertain. Some scholars have thought that *Yam Sûph* was originally a designation of the region of lakes where reeds thrive at the N. of the Gulf of Suez, through which the Hebrews passed in their flight from Egypt (*see* Wright and Filson, *The Westminister Historical Atlas to the Bible* [1956] pp. 38 f). On this supposition, the designation later came to be applied to the present Gulf of ʿAqaba (Nu 21[4]), and possibly also to the entire body of water now known as the Red Sea, stretching from the *Râs Muḥammad* southward to the straits, and perhaps even to the Persian Gulf (Ex 23[31]). *Yam Sûph* was translated into Greek by *erythra thalassa*, literally Red Sea (LXX, Ex 15[4, 22]; Herodotus, Josephus, He 11[29]; Lat. *Rubrum*). No satisfactory explanation of the term 'red' (*erythra*) has been found. Two proposals have been made: (1) the name came from the red or copper-skinned people such as the Edomites and others who lived near the Red Sea; (2) it was descriptive of the reddish colour of the corals and weathered limestone along its shores and may have suggested to early voyagers the name Red Sea.

The Gulf of Suez, or some part or ancient projection of it at the N. figures in the accounts of the Exodus which refer to *Yam Sûph*. It was formerly thought that the Gulf extended further N. in Moses' time, but with the discovery of an Egyptian settlement on the shore of the Sinai Peninsula near *Abū Zeneimeh*, and the excavation of Ezion-geber (q.v.), modern *Tell el-Kheleifeh*, near modern ʿAqaba, near the shore of the Gulf of ʿAqaba, it became certain that the water level has not receded appreciably in the last 3000 years. However, since the construction of the Suez Canal, one lake in the region has disappeared, and it is possible that the *Yam Sûph* crossed by the Israelites was a lake near the present Lake Menzaleh. In such a case, the 'exodus' would not involve the present Red Sea except as the stations on the early part of the journey to Mount Sinai may have been located near its shore (see EXODUS, SINAI).

The Gulf of ʿAqaba, about 100 miles in length and about 15 miles in width, must have been known to the Hebrews both before and after the conquest of Canaan. According to Nu 33[35-36], Dt 2[8] the Hebrews under the leadership of Moses encamped at Ezion-geber which, with Elath, was located near the northern shore of the Gulf of ʿAqaba. The former has been excavated by the American Schools of Oriental Research (see Nelson Glueck, *The Other Side of the Jordan* [1940], pp. 89–113) and proved to be not only an important seaport, but also a thriving copper-smelting centre in the time of Solomon. The latter operated a fleet of ships at Ezion-geber (1 K 9[26]) with the help of Phoenician seamen, and it is thought that his navy may have made it possible for him to carry on commercial relations with India. Jehoshaphat attempted to revive this use of the Red Sea, but the ships were wrecked at Ezion-geber (1 K 22[48]), doubtless by the periodic violent winds which blow down the Arabah from the N. creating insufferable sand-storms in the vicinity of the ancient Hebrew seaport.

Later references to the Red Sea, without designating any specific region of it, make mention of it in connexion with a denunciation of Edom (Jer 49[21], literally 'Reed Sea'), and in recalling the marvellous deliverance at the time of the Exodus (Neh 9[9], Ps 106[7, 9, 22] 136[13, 15], Ac 7[36], He 11[29]). H. L. W.—**W. L. R.**

REDEEMER, REDEMPTION.—'Redemption' means deliverance, properly by payment of a *price* or *ransom*. In the OT, besides the passages in the Law where it is used in the strict sense, it is often used of deliverance simply, either of Israel or of the individual. Occasionally it is stated or implied to be deliverance from *sins* (Ps 130[8], Is 44[22]; but it may be deliverance from the consequences of sins that is meant); elsewhere it is from physical calamity, including captivity, sickness, and death. The typical OT redemption was the exodus from Egypt, when the Lord redeemed Israel 'to be his people' (1 Ch 17[21]). The fact of redemption is stressed, rather than the price. Deutero-Isaiah, proclaiming a similar deliverance from Babylon, states (Is 45[13]) that Cyrus will receive no recompense; elsewhere (43[3-4]) he states that other nations are given in exchange.

Two words, with their derivatives, are used in the OT to express the idea. The one, *gāʿal* (from which *gōʿēl*, 'redeemer'), is used technically of redemption of an inheritance, of tithes, and of brethren from slavery; in a wider sense it is a favourite term in the later Psalms and Deutero-Isaiah. The other, *pādhāh*, is used technically of redeeming the first-born of men or beasts by sacrifice, or of compounding for certain offences by a payment in money; in the more general sense it is frequent in Deuteronomy and the earlier Psalms. The *gōʿēl* is the kinsman who has the right to redeem; the term is used also for the 'avenger' of blood (Nu 35[12], etc.); elsewhere (Job 19[25], Ps 19[14], etc. and especially Deutero-Isaiah) it denotes Yahweh as the vindicator, deliverer, and avenger of His people (cf Is 41[14] 43[14]). The LXX properly renders these verbs by *lutroomai* (from *lutron*, 'ransom'), but sometimes is content to use general words meaning 'deliver,' without any hint of ransom or payment; the most common of these is *ruomai* ('rescue') used *e.g.* for 'the Redeemer' (*gōʿēl*) in Deutero-Isaiah.

Two further points must be noticed before the NT teaching can be fully understood. First, Judaism in the time of Christ had a strong hope of God's intervention to deliver His people not only from Gentile oppressors, but from Satan's bondage; this hope was general among the Jews, and is characteristic of apocalyptic (see PSEUDEPIGRAPHA). Neither the Jews nor Jesus' disciples made a clear distinction between the political and the religious aspects of the Messianic hope, and this uncertainty is reflected in the use of the word 'redemption.' (Cf Lk 1[68-75] and also 24[21], read in the light of Ac 1[6]). Secondly, slavery was widespread in the ancient world, and the longing for freedom familiar. The word for 'ransom' (*lutron*, usually in the plural) was used in this connexion, particularly in the so-called 'sacral manumission,' whereby it was arranged that the slave should be purchased by some temple, regarded as the property of the god, and thus set free from human owners. St. Paul's word for 'redemption' (*apolutrōsis*) is used in an inscription at Cos to denote such a manumission.

Christ plainly teaches that by His work the power of Satan was broken, and the day of release was dawning (cf Lk 4[18] 10[18] 11[17-20] 13[16]). His salvation is no longer political, but wholly religious. He connects it with His coming and person and in certain well-known passages with His death (Jn 3[14-16] 6[51-56], Mt 26[26-28] ||, etc.); in one of these (Mt 20[28] || Mk 10[45]) He states that He came 'to give his life as a ransom (*lutron*) for many.' These words seem to echo Is 53[11-12], and the word 'many' denotes the whole body of those who benefit by His work; it should not be pressed either to give, or to exclude, the meaning 'all' (in 1 Ti 2[6] the phrase is echoed in the words 'as a ransom, *antilutron*, for all').

In the apostolic teaching, besides the derivatives of *lutron*, *agorazō* ('buy,' 'purchase') is used, and these words are commonly rendered 'redeem,' 'redemption,' in the EV. But to be understood they must be seen in the light of what has been said above about God's deliverance and the prevalence of bondage and must be set alongside other words that render the general ideas of God's deliverance (*e.g.* 'deliver,' 'set free,' 'loose,' 'escape') and God's 'purchase' of His people.

1. The NT writers constantly stress the bondage from which deliverance is needed, and the release now made possible. Through Christ deliverance is given 'from the present evil age' (Gal 1[4]), 'from the dominion of darkness' (Col 1[13]), from the hopeless impotence and slavery to the passions which was men's lot under the law (Ro 7[6] 8[2], Gal 4[5]), and from the bondage to the devil which results from the fear of death (He 2[14-15]). Ultimately death itself will be destroyed (1 Co 15[26]), and the created world set free from its bondage to decay (Ro 8[23]).

The Hellenistic world saw the material as inherently evil, and looked for deliverance from the finite. The NT, while agreeing that decay and transitoriness are a consequence and sign of evil and at times all but reflecting the Hellenistic outlook (*e.g.* 2 P 1[4] 2[20]), nevertheless sees *sin*, not finitude, as the ultimate evil. The word 'redemption' is explicitly connected with the forgiveness of past sins (Col 1[14] Eph 1[7], He 9[15]; cf also Ro 3[21-26]) and the break with the old sinful life and all iniquity (1 P 1[18], Tit 2[14]). Sometimes the reference is to the redemption already achieved through Christ's completed work (Ro 3[24], Col 1[14], Eph 1[7]), sometimes to the deliverance still to come when death is finally conquered (Ro 8[23], Eph 4[30]). Deliverance from God's 'wrath' or final judgment is certainly part of the NT teaching (Ro 5[9], 1 Th 1[10]), but it would be hazardous to claim it as the key to the concept of redemption, since it is never explicitly connected with that word. (In Gal 3[13], which comes closest, redemption is from the curse of the Law.)

2. Parallel to the idea of deliverance *from* sin, etc., is the positive assurance that God has purchased or acquired a people *for* Himself. Echoes of the OT are clear and important (1 P 2[9-10]). Here too the 'redemption' language is used alongside other words. Christ has 'ransomed men *for God*' (Rev 5[9] 14[3f]). St. Paul twice reminds the Corinthians that they were 'bought with a price' (1 Co 6[20] 7[23]), and his point, reminiscent of some of the pagan manumission inscriptions, is that they now belong to the Lord, not to men, nor yet to themselves. (Cf also 2 P 2[1].)

3. Deliverance or redemption is through Christ and His death; and in a few passages the death is stated (1 P 1[18]) or implied (1 Co 6[20] 7[23], 1 Ti 2[6]) to be the ransom-price. This glances back to Christ's own saying that He came 'to give his life as a ransom for many.' But although the NT brings out the many aspects of man's bondage, it does not explain *how* Christ's death is a ransom. Attempts to explain it by postulating that some price was due either to the devil or to the demands of God's justice go beyond the explicit words of the NT, and it seems preferable not to press the analogy of ransom to the point of asking *to whom* the money is paid. Better insight into the efficacy of Christ's death is achieved by turning to other lines of explanation, especially the language of sacrifice (q.v.); the language of ransom and sacrifice are linked in the OT Law (Ex 13[13], etc.), in Christ's saying (Mk 10[45] || Mt 26[28]), and in the NT generally (Ro 3[24-25], 1 P 1[18], Rev 5[9]). Some expositors have linked the price language with the law-court language (condemn, justify), and have held that by dying Christ endured men's *punishment*. But the NT never says exactly this, although it is clearly held that Christ stepped between men and the *consequences* (which for them would be punishment) of their sins (Gal 3[13]). The NT teaching is the product of the OT and Jewish preparation, of Christ's own words and work, and of the apostles' experience. Other religions have contributed something to the expression, but little to the substance. Some have claimed the NT doctrine of a redeemer to be indebted to a postulated pre-Christian Gnosticism; but its character and even its existence remain speculative.

4. A fuller picture of the *positive* blessings implied in redemption may be found in other words, such as 'eternal life,' 'sonship,' 'fellowship,' 'joy,' 'peace,' etc. (q.v.).

G. M. S.

REED.—1. *ḳāneh*, translated 'reed,' 1 K 14[15], 2 K 18[21], Is 36[6] 42[3]; 'stalk,' Gn 41[5, 22]; 'sweet cane' (RVm '*calamus*'), Is 43[24], Jer 6[20]; 'calamus,' Ca 4[14], Ezk 27[19]; 'reeds,' Ps 68[30] (so RV, but AV 'spearmen'); also metaphorically used as 'socket' of the arm, Job 31[22] (probably bone of the upper arm); 'scales' (the arm of 'a balance' AV, RV), Is 46[6]; and 'shaft' of a candlestick, Ex 25[31], and 'branches,' Ex 25[32]. The *ḳāneh* is probably the familiar *qasāb* (*Arundo donax*), which flourishes on the banks of all the streams and lakes of the Jordan Valley. Miles of it are to be seen at the *'Ain Feshkhā* oasis on the Dead Sea shore, and at the Huleh marshes. It is a lofty reed, often 20 feet high, brilliantly green in the late summer, when all around is dry and bare; but dead-looking, from a distance, in the spring, when it stands in full flower and the lofty stems are crowned by beautiful silken pannicles. In the district mentioned the reeds are cleared from time to time by fire, that the young and tender shoots may grow up to afford fodder for cattle. The covert of the reeds is often the only possible shade (Job 40[21]). The bruised reed, Is 42[3], which, though standing, a touch will cause to fall and lie bedraggled on the ground, is a familiar sight (2 K 18[21], Is 36[6], Ezk 29[6-7]). A reed forms a most convenient **measuring-rod**, being straight and light (Ezk 40[3, 5], Rev 11[1] etc.). In certain passages where *kāneh* is translated **'calamus,'** or **'sweet cane,'** some imported aromatic cane or bark is meant. For the use of reeds as pens, see PEN, 4, WRITING, 6.

2. *'ārôth*, Is 19[7] translated 'bare places' (AV **'paper reeds,'** RV 'meadows'). See MEADOW.

3. *'agammîm*, literally 'pools' (see POOL), is in Jer 51[32] translated 'bulwarks' (AV, RV 'reeds'). For bulrushes see RUSH.

4. *'āḥū*, Gn 41[2, 18] 'reed grass'; Job 8[11] 'reeds'; Hos 13[15] 'the reed plant' (emendation of Heb. 'among brethren,' so AV, RV). See MEADOW.

5. *'ēbheh*, Job 9[26] 'reed' (boat). The reference is to light skiffs of papyrus. E. W. G. M.—**R. A. B.**

REELAIAH.—See RAAMIAH.

REELIAH, 1 Es 5[8] (AV **Reelius**, RV **Reelias**), corresponds in position to **Bigvai** in Ezr 2[2], Neh 7[7]; the form of the name may be due to a duplication of **Reelaiah** in the same verse of Ezra.

REELIAS, 1 Es 5[8] (RV).—See REELIAH.

REELIUS, 1 Es 5[8] (AV).—See REELIAH.

REESAIAS, 1 Es 5[8] (AV).—See RAAMIAH.

REFINER, REFINING.—The ancient Egyptians purified gold by putting it into earthen crucibles with lead, salt, a little tin, and barley bran, sealing the crucibles with clay, and then exposing them to the heat of a furnace for five days and nights. Refining silver by cupellation is a very old process. The silver mixed with lead is put into a crucible made of bone earth, and placed in a reverberatory furnace. As the oxide of lead forms, it is blown off by bellows, and towards the end of the process the thin covering of oxide becomes iridescent and soon disappears, and the pure bright surface of the silver flashes out. This process of refining silver is referred to in Jer 6[29]. The reference in Mal 3[2f] is to the purifying influence of affliction on the people of God ; their sinful impurities gradually disappear, and at last the Divine image is reflected from the soul, as the face of the refiner from the surface of the purified silver.

REFUGE, CITIES OF.—1. Origin of the right of asylum.—The story of Cain and Abel illustrates the fact that the man who shed blood committed an offence against God (cf Gn 4[10]). That was because of the ancient idea that the life was in the blood and God is the giver of the mysterious life-force. Having no city of refuge to which he could resort, Cain saw that his fate was inescapable. Therefore, the man who had shed blood, whether the deed had been done accidentally or intentionally, was under penalty ; he had done a wrong that could be atoned for only by blood ; he had done violence to the community of blood that existed between a god and his people. On the other hand, the god chose certain places where he manifested himself and there it was customary for his people to meet and worship him. Within the precincts claimed by his presence all life was sacred, and so it came about that even a **murderer,** if he escaped to such a sacred place, could be safe from those to whom he had forfeited his life and remained safe so long as he remained there. The murderer thus escaped the penalty of his crime, but in the process he became socially ineffective and separated from his tribe or people ; if ever he left the asylum he had found, he was at the mercy of the **avenger of blood,** so that by this practice both the tribe or people and the offender himself were punished. This primitive usage still prevails in certain communities, but, while it guards against the possibility of savage, reckless revenge on the part of the offended community, it enables a murderer to escape the full penalty of his offence.

2. Development of asylum in OT.—According to the OT, asylum could be found only by the man who had shed blood unintentionally, the man into whose hand 'God let the victim fall' (Ex 21[13]). A man who wilfully attacked another and treacherously stained his hands with blood, could not find refuge at God's altar ; he could be taken from it to his death (Ex 21[14]) or he could be put to death at the altar, as happened to Joab (1 K 2[30f, 34]). The community, as a whole or through accredited representatives, came between the fugitive and the avenger of blood, and decided whether he should be handed over to death. In other words, what we would term a proper administration of justice came into being and every case was duly heard and tried. It is possible to trace three stages of development of this right of asylum in the OT.

(1) In the first stage any **altar** or **sanctuary** could provide a place of refuge and give protection to the man who had unintentionally taken the life of another ; but he had to justify his claim to protection by showing to the authorities of the sanctuary, or to the leaders of the community which the sanctuary served, that his deed had been unintentional. If he succeeded in doing that, he was allowed to remain within the sacred precincts. Thus he could not return home and, presumably, had to earn his living where he was, in a condition of virtual confinement. Whether his family could join him in his place of asylum and whether there were circumstances or conditions in which he could regain freedom of movement, cannot be answered. This stage of development is represented in the OT in Ex 21[13f], 1 K 1[50] 2[28, 34]. The story of Joab shows that he was aware that he could be put to death even at the altar (1 K 2[30]), and it is not likely that this could be done only in virtue of the king's authority.

(2) When the local altars outside Jerusalem were suppressed in terms of Josiah's reformation in 621 B.C., the question of asylum for the **manslayer** had to be urgently considered. Dt 19[1-9] states that three cities were to be set apart for the purpose on the west side of the Jordan, and, if the people prospered and their territory was expanded, three more cities were to be set apart. These cities were conveniently situated, so that each served a district ; Dt 19[3] seems to imply that the roads to them were kept in good condition to facilitate escape to them. The fugitive had still to justify his claim to protection by establishing before the elders of the city his plea that he had not wilfully taken life. Any one who failed to sustain such a plea was handed over to the elders of his own city. The fact that they in turn surrendered him to the avenger of blood for the execution of the sentence of death shows that this concession at least continued to be made to primitive practice ; but the administration of justice was in the hands of properly constituted and recognized authorities (Dt 19[12f]).

(3) The passages which may be presumed to give evidence concerning post-exilic usage are Nu 35[9-25] and Jos 20[1-9]. The six cities of asylum remained in use and the judicial procedure continued to follow the same pattern as formerly, except that the congregation, presumably the Jerusalem community, had the responsibility of determining the innocence or guilt of the fugitive ; this may have become possible owing to the contraction of the territory occupied by the Jews at this time. It is interesting that Nu 35[16-21] sets forth, for the guidance of the congregation, circumstantial evidence which may be taken as establishing murderous intent ; and Jos 20[4] states that the fugitive has to establish his claim for asylum at the gate before the elders to qualify for permission to enter the city ; this may have been a provisional inquiry before the official trial of the case at Jerusalem. One important development is to be noted : the man who had been granted asylum had not to spend all his days in confinement within the area of asylum, but was free to return home upon the death of the high priest of the time (Nu 35[25, 28], Jos 20[6]). The high priest in the post-exilic period was the only constituted authority that Jewish law could recognize.

3. Number of the cities of refuge.—The relevant evidence is contained in Nu 35[11, 13-15], Dt 4[41-43] 19[7-10], Jos 20[2, 7f]. Dt 4[41-43] states that the first to be established were three on the E. side of Jordan ; Dt 19[2, 7] speaks of three in Palestine, W. of Jordan, with v.[9] allowing for the later addition of three more cities. Does that mean that a total of nine was at least contemplated (so G. Ernest Wright, *Interpreter's Bible*, ii, 452) or are we to assume that there has arisen a certain confusion in the evidence as it is now extant, and that the full number was six? The latter is generally accepted. The common view is that these cities came into use for the purposes of asylum in the time of king Josiah and that in his days, with Judah but of small extent, the three on the W. side of the Jordan sufficed ; but when in post-exilic times the Jews covered a wider area, there naturally arose the need for more cities and that was the occasion for the coming into use of the full number of six cities stated in Nu 35 and Jos 20. According to this interpretation additions made to the text in Dt 4[41-43] and 19[8] suggest that the six had been envisaged from the beginning. These six were Kedesh, Shechem, and Hebron W. of the Jordan, places which were known to have possessed ancient sanctuaries from early times, and Golan, Ramoth, and Bezer E. of it.

This interpretation is not without difficulty, apart from possible textual confusion, for at least two reasons : Ex 21[12-14], part of the ancient Book of the Covenant, speaks of the intention to establish places of asylum for the manslayer, so that their use may have gone back to much earlier times than those of Josiah, although they may have had little prominence so long as the provincial sanctuaries remained available ; W. F. Albright puts their institution in the time of David or Solomon (*ARI*, p. 121). And, secondly, it is not easy to maintain that the Jewish territorial expansion in post-exilic times was such as to warrant the provision of three additional cities of refuge, especially in the area E. of the Jordan. It seems more probable that these cities of refuge were designated at an early period of Israel's history in order to control the practice of unrestrained blood revenge and that they came prominently into use in the conditions which obtained subsequent to the reformation of Josiah. J. Gi.—**J. Ma.**

REFUSE.—The verb ' to refuse ' has lost much of its vigour. In AV it often means ' to reject.' Thus Ps 118^{22} ' The stone which the builders refused ' (RV, RSV ' rejected '). Cf Tyndale's translation of Mt 24^{40} ' Then two shalbe in the feldes, the one shalbe receaved, and the other shalbe refused.'

REGEM.—The eponym of a Calebite family, 1 Ch 2^{47}.

REGEM-MELECH.—One of the deputation sent to the prophet Zechariah, Zec 7^{2}.

REGENERATION.—In the language of theology ' regeneration ' denotes that decisive spiritual change, effected by God's Holy Spirit, in which a man, naturally estranged from God and ruled by evil powers, is renewed in character, becomes the subject of holy affections and desires, and enters upon a life of progressive sanctification, the issue of which is complete likeness to Christ. The actual term, however, to which this word corresponds (Gr. *palingenesia*), occurs only twice in the NT (Mt 19^{28}, Tit 3^{5}). In the former instance it is translated ' the new world ' in RSV, because it concerns, not the renewal of the individual, but the eschatological restoration of all things to their original perfection at the Parousia (cf Ac 3^{21}, 2 P 3^{13} ; see RESTORATION). In the other passage (Tit 3^{5}), the expression ' the washing of regeneration ' connects ' renewal in the Holy Spirit ' with the action of baptism, which is its outward sign and seal (see below). The doctrine, nevertheless, is a thoroughly Scriptural one and the change in question is expressed by a great variety of terms and phrases : ' born,' ' born anew,' ' new creation,' ' renewed,' ' quickened,' etc., to which attention is directed below. The basic need of regeneration is recognized in the OT as well as in the NT (*e.g.* Ps 51^{10f}, though of course the prophets speak more frequently of national or eschatological renewal rather than of individual (*e.g.* Is 65$^{17-25}$ 66^{22}, Jer 31^{31ff} 32$^{38-40}$, Ezk 36$^{25-28}$, Hos 6$^{1-3}$, etc.).

The classical passage on the *need* of regeneration is Jn 3$^{3-7}$. Men born of the flesh do not have by nature the life of the Spirit (v.^{6}). Hence the declarations : ' Unless one is born anew (*or* from above), he cannot see the kingdom of God ' ; ' Unless one is born of water and the Spirit, he cannot enter the kingdom of God . . . Do not marvel that I said to you, you must be born anew ' (vv. $^{3, 5, 7}$). The miracle is wrought by the Spirit of God, whose action is sovereign (v.^{8}). Many do marvel, like Nicodemus, at the strangeness and universality of this demand of Christ ; yet the strangeness will disappear, and the need of a supernatural agent to effect the change will be felt, if due consideration is given (1) to the vastness of the change, and (2) to the actual condition of our human nature in which the change is to be made.

(1) It is sufficient, to show the vastness of this change, to reflect that here, and elsewhere, regeneration—which, after all, is only the Latin for ' being born again '—means nothing less than a revolution of such a kind as results in bringing the whole man round from his ordinary worldly way of thinking, feeling, and willing, into harmony with God's mind and will ; truly being brought round to God's point of view, so that now he sees things as God sees them, feels about things as God would have him feel, judges matters as God judges them, loves what God loves, hates what God hates, sets God's purposes before him as his own. Who can doubt, if this is the nature of the change, that it does not lie in man's own powers to produce it ; that it can be effected only through a higher power entering his being and working the change?

(2) The need of a supernatural agency in the change is further evident from the condition of the human nature in which the change is wrought. The testimony of Scripture is uniform that man has turned aside from God (Ps 14$^{1-3}$, Ro 3^{9ff}), and that his nature has undergone a terrible depravation (Gn 6^{5} 8^{21}, Ps 51^{5}, Is 1$^{2-4}$, Ro 7^{14ff}, Eph 2$^{1-3}$ 4^{17f} etc.) ; that the bent of the will is away from God (Ro 8^{7f}) ; that the love of God has been replaced by love of the world and the self-seeking principles connected therewith (1 Jn 2$^{15-16}$, cf Jn 5$^{42, 44}$) ; that the better nature is in bondage to a law of sin which works lawlessness in thought, feeling and desire (Ro 7^{22f}, 1 Jn 3^{4}). Is it not obvious, leaving out of account altogether the darker forms in which evil manifests itself, that this is a condition of the soul which only a Divine power can rectify?

Nothing, therefore, is more plainly taught in Scripture than that this spiritual change, which we call regeneration, is one which nothing short of Divine power can effect. It is spoken of as being born of God (Jn 1^{12f} 3^{5}, 1 Jn 3^{9} etc.) ; as a new creation (2 Co 5^{21}) ; as a being raised from the dead (Eph 2^{5f}). It is likened to the miraculous work of God in raising Christ from the dead (Eph 1$^{19, 22}$, 2$^{1, 6}$). It is a complete transfiguration or renewal of the inner man (Ro 12^{2}, Eph 4^{23}, Col 3^{10}, Tit 3^{5}, 1 P 1^{22f}). It is the counterpart or anticipation within the individual of the cosmic restoration or renewal of all things, which shall take place at the End ; and it is the result of the pouring out of the Holy Spirit in the latter days (Joel 2^{28f} etc.) which has now taken place (Ac 2^{16f}). Though it is visible only to faith, it is the earnest of the great change that will transform us from glory to glory in the likeness of Christ at his Parousia (2 Co 3^{18}). Thus, regeneration, whether we consider it from the cosmic or from the individual aspect, is an eschatological event, not a natural evolutionary development within the historical order ; it happens to us now, because the Last Things are already here, made present in us even now by the operation of the outpoured Spirit. Though regeneration is not a natural work, it is nevertheless not a *magical* work ; it is not effected *ipso facto* by the recitation of formulas and the performance of ceremonies. Despite this unquestionable truth, regeneration in the NT is closely connected with *baptism* (*e.g.* Ro 6^{4}, 1 Co 6^{11}, Col 2^{11f}, Tit 3^{5}, 1 P 3^{21}). What indeed is being ' born of water and the Spirit ' (Jn 3^{5}) except a characteristically Johannine allusion to Christian baptism and an implicit assertion of its necessity? The receiving of the Spirit, which is the regenerating power of God within us, was from apostolic times connected with the baptismal action (Ac 2^{38} 19$^{2-6}$, etc.) ; and it is probably more correct to say that baptism, the ' seal ' of the Spirit (see BAPTISM, 3), was the efficacious sign of regeneration, than to say that it is only a symbol of it. At the same time one should hesitate to say that baptism is the absolutely necessary precondition of regeneration (see, *e.g.* Ac 10$^{44-48}$) ; what can be said without risk of contradiction is that baptism in NT times was the *normal* means of entry into the sphere of regeneration, the Church, the eschatological community of the new creation in Christ.

The instrument by which, according to the NT, the work of regeneration is begun in us is the *word*, which is ' quickened ' or brought to life in our hearts by the life-giving Spirit. The preaching of the word, that is, the declaration of God's saving action in Christ on behalf of each one of us, is made to bear fruit within us by the inner witness of God's Holy Spirit ; the work of conversion, leading to regeneration, is always a Divine work, even though human sowers of the word have been co-workers with God in his quest for man's salvation (1 Co 3^{6f}). This is part at least of what is meant when it is said that regeneration is effected not magically but by rational means, for words are functions of rational beings ; although it must not be implied that infants, or others whom rational address cannot touch, are beyond the outreach of God's grace. What is affirmed is, as regards whose who have come to years of discretion, that God's normal dealing with them is through the word. The OT equally with the NT extols the saving, converting, quickening, cleansing, sanctifying power of the word of God (*e.g.* Pss 19^{7ff} 119). Jesus declares the word to be the seed of the Kingdom of God (Lk 8^{11}). He prays,

'Sanctify them in the truth ; thy word is truth' (Jn 17^{17}). Conversion, regeneration, sanctification, are connected with the word (Ac 11^{19-21}, Eph 1^{13}, Col 1^{5}, 1 Th 2^{13}, 2 Th 2^{13}, Ja 1^{18}, etc.). In this connexion 1 P 1^{23-25} is particularly relevant: 'You have been born anew . . . through the living and abiding word of God . . . That word is the good news which was preached to you.'

If this, then, is the nature of regeneration, there is a definite process which is experienced by those who undergo it. The Spirit of God doubtless has innumerable ways of dealing with men's souls ; still, if we look closely, it will be found that there are certain elements which *do* in some degree enter into all experience of regeneration, and furnish to this extent a test of the reality of the change. There is first, of necessity, the awakening of the self out of its customary spiritual torpor—out of that deep insensibility to spiritual things in which ordinarily the natural man is held (Eph 1^{18} 5^{14}, cf Ro 14^{11f}). Especially there comes into view here the peculiar awakening of the soul through the conscience, which takes the form of what is called *conviction of sin* towards God (Lk 5^{8}, Jn 16^{8f}). Probably no one can undergo regeneration without in some degree being brought inwardly to the realization of his sinful condition before God and to the sincere confession of it (Ps 51^{4}). The law of God has its place in producing this conviction of sin, but law alone will not produce genuine contrition. (See REPENTANCE.) For this there is needed the exhibition of mercy. Hence the next stage in this spiritual process is that described as *enlightenment*—growing enlightenment in the knowledge of Christ. This also, like the preceding stages, is a Divine work (Jn 16^{13-15}, 2 Co 4^{4}). Even with this, however, the work of regeneration is not complete. The will of God for man's salvation has not only to be understood ; it has also to be obeyed. There is the *will* to be laid hold of—the centre and citadel of our being. So the work of the Holy Spirit is directed, finally, to the renewing of the will. To this end the Spirit works first of all by *persuasion*, for He does nothing by violence or coercion. Everything that God does is accomplished in accordance with the nature He has given us ; but God most graciously, most lovingly, brings His persuasions to bear upon our wills, and by the power of appropriate motives draws us to the acceptance of Christ (Jn 6^{44}). With this there goes, in the next place, what may be called the *enabling* of the will—the imparting to it of the power to lay hold on Christ with full and firm faith (Eph 4^{16}). Last of all, this work of regeneration is completed when the self is brought to the point of absolute *surrender* to Christ—when, drawn and persuaded, and at length enabled by the Spirit, it yields itself up entirely to Christ as Saviour, and lays hold on Christ for a complete salvation. There is now union with Christ by faith and by baptism into his Body, and, with that, entrance into the life of the new-created people of God as a new-born child of God. 'If any one is in Christ, he is a new creation ; the old has passed away, behold, the new has come' (2 Co 5^{17}). J. O.—**A. R.**

REGISTER (*i.e.* genealogical record).—See GENEALOGY, **2.**

REHABIAH.—A Levitical family, 1 Ch 23^{17} 24^{21} 26^{25}.

REHOB.—1. A town or district at the northern end of the valley of the Jordan, marking the limit of the journey of the spies, Nu 13^{21}. It is named also in 2 S 10^{8} where it must be the same as **Beth-rehob** of v.^{6}. It is therefore probably to be identified with Beth-rehob, near Laish, Jg 18^{28}. Its site is unknown. **2. 3.** Two Asherite towns, Jos $19^{28, 30}$. One of these was a Levitical city, Jos 21^{31}. 1 Ch 6^{75}. The latter is perhaps to be located at *Tell el-Gharbī* or *Tell Berweh*. **4.** The father of Hadadezer, 2 S $8^{3, 12}$. **5.** A signatory to the covenant, Neh 10^{11}.

REHOBOAM, son of Solomon, is said to have reigned seventeen years. The statement that his mother was Naamah, the Ammonitess (1 K 14^{21}) has nothing improbable about it. The LXX (1 [3] K 12^{24a}) calls her a daughter of Hanun, the son of Nahash, the Ammonite king. In the history of Rehoboam the chief point is his indiscreet treatment of the tribes at his accession—treatment which resulted in the revolt of the best part of the nation and the establishment of a rival kingdom in the North (1 K 12). The coherence of the tribes was evidently imperfect under Solomon. Ephraim, which had always been conscious of its own strength, was not minded to recognize the young king without some concessions on his part. Shechem, a traditional place of meeting, was the town chosen by 'all Israel' for the formal recognition of Rehoboam as Solomon's successor. Here the hereditary chiefs demanded that he should lighten the yoke. In this they had reference particularly to the forced labour exacted by Solomon. Rehoboam's arrogant answer is well known, and as a result the kingdom was split.

It was natural that an effort should be made to reduce the rebel tribes to subjection. But Rehoboam seems not to have had either adequate resources or military capacity. The brief notice that there was war between Rehoboam and Jeroboam continually is all that we are told. Besides this, the Biblical author describes the religious condition of the people in this reign in dark colours. A disastrous event in the history of the time was the invasion of the country by Shishak (Sheshenk, Sheshonk), the first pharaoh of the 22nd Dynasty of Egypt. This monarch claims to have reduced the whole country to subjection, probably reviving ancient claims to suzerainty. The editor of our Books of Kings is chiefly concerned at the Egyptian's plundering the Temple (1 K 14^{26}), while the Chronicler (2 Ch 12) makes an edifying story out of the incident. H. P. S.—**H. S. G.**

REHOBOTH.—1. A well dug by the servants of Isaac and finally conceded to him, after two others, dug also by them had become a subject of quarrel with Abimelech, king of Gerar, Gn 26^{22}. It is possibly modern *Ruḥeibeh*, about 20 miles S. of Beersheba. **2.** An Edomite king is called Shaul 'of Rehoboth by the River' Gn 36^{37}, 1 Ch 1^{48}. 'The River,' which usually stands for the Euphrates (so RSV here) is more probably here the 'River of Egypt' (see EGYPT [RIVER OF]), as an Edomite site is indicated. Its location is unknown. J. F. McC.—**H. H. R.**

REHOBOTH-IR ('broad places of the city').—One of the four cities of Assyria built by Nimrod, Gn 10^{11} (AV 'the city Rehoboth'). It immediately follows Nineveh, and might mean a suburb of that city, originally separate from it, but later annexed and containing some of its most spacious streets or market-places. It is unidentified.

REHUM.—1. One of the twelve heads of the Jewish community, Ezr 2^{2}, 1 Es 5^{8} (AV, RV **Roimus**) ; in Neh 7^{7} called **Nehum,** perhaps by a copyist's error. **2.** The 'commander' (AV, RV 'chancellor') in the time of Artaxerxes, Ezr $4^{8f, 17, 23}$, 1 Es $2^{16, 25}$ (AV, RV **Rathumus**). See BELTETHMUS. **3.** A Levite who helped to repair the wall, Neh 3^{17}. **4.** One of those who sealed the covenant, Neh 10^{25} (Heb. 26). **5.** The eponym of a priestly family, Neh 12^{3}, where it is perhaps a miswriting of **Harim** (q.v.).

REI ('Y" is a friend').—This name is given to one of the supporters of Solomon at the time of Adonijah's attempt to secure the throne, 1 K 1^{8}. He is mentioned along with Shimei, and was probably an officer in the royal guard. These troops seem to have had an enormous influence in determining the succession to the throne. The reading, however, is not above suspicion, and Josephus (*Ant.* VII. xiv. 4 [346]) reads 'Shimei, the friend of David,' and thus gets rid of Rei as a personal name (so, differently, Lucian). W. F. B.

REINS.—See KIDNEYS.

REKEM.—1. One of the five kinglets of Midian slain by Moses, Nu 31^{8}, Jos 13^{21}. **2.** A Calebite family, 1 Ch 2^{43}. **3.** A clan of Machir, 1 Ch 7^{16} (EV **Rakem,** but this is simply the pausal form of the Hebrew name). **4.** An unidentified city of Benjamin, Jos 18^{27}.

RELIGION.—The word ‘ religion,’ wherever it occurs in AV, signifies not the inner spirit of the religious life, but its outward expression. It is thus used of one form of religion as distinguished from another ; as in 2 Mac 14[38], where the same word is translated in the middle of the verse ‘ Judaism,’ and in the end of it ‘ the religion of the Jews ’ (RSV has simply ‘ Judaism ’). It is also used by St. James (1[26f]) to contrast religious acts with ritual forms.

REMALIAH.—The father of Pekah, 2 K 15[25ff] 16[1, 5], 2 Ch 28[6], Is 7[1ff] 8[6].

REMEMBRANCE.—Sons were regarded as of great importance in Israel to keep alive the memory of a man's name, and hatred of enemies might be expressed in the desire that their name should be blotted out and forgotten (Ex 17[14], Dt 25[19], Ps 109[13]). In the absence of sons a man might erect a pillar to preserve his name (2 S 18[18]). Great events might be kept in remembrance by the erection of a cairn (Gn 31[46f]) or stone (Gn 35[14], 1 S 7[12]), or of an altar (Jos 22[10]).

Remembrance is not always preserved by visible things or persons. The righteous are to be remembered for honour (Pr 10[7]), just as the anointing of Jesus was to be (Mt 26[13]). The names of those who feared the Lord are said to be recorded in a book of remembrance (Mal 3[16]), but this, like the book of life (Rev 3[5] 20[12, 15] 21[27]), is not thought of as on earth.

Remembrance of the mighty works of God is an abiding duty (Dt 5[15] 8[2] 16[3], Ps 105[5]), not merely as a private memory, but as something to be expressed in religious rites (Dt 26[1ff], Lv 2[2, 9]). Such remembrance is a summons to renewed loyalty and obedience, just as the remembrance of the Sabbath (Ex 20[8]), of God's commandments (Nu 15[39f], Ps 103[18]), or of the law of Moses (Mal 4[4]), is a call to observe them. Similarly in the NT Christians are exhorted to remember the words of Jesus (Ac 20[35]), or the resurrection (2 Ti 2[8]), not merely as an exercise in memory, but for response to their meaning. The reconciling ministry of Christ is to be remembered (Eph 2[12ff]), that the heart may be stirred to gratitude and devotion. The death of Jesus is remembered in the Eucharist (1 Co 11[23f]), in order that its power might be renewed in the heart of the believer. The poor are to be remembered (Gal 2[10]), that their need might be met. In all these cases, therefore, remembrance has a practical purpose.

Frequently God's remembrance is spoken of in the Bible. In mercy He remembered Rachel (Gn 30[22]) and Hannah (1 S 1[19]). Jeremiah cries to be remembered and helped (Jer 15[15]), and so also Israel (La 3[19]). God is ever mindful of His Covenant and faithful to His promise (Gn 9[15f], Ex 2[24], Lv 26[42], Ps 105[8] 106[45]). He remembers His love for Israel (Ps 98[3] ; cf 25[6]), or His promise (Ps 105[42]). He is besought to remember David (2 Ch 6[42]), those who bring offerings (Ps 20[3]), those who intercede (Jer 18[20]), and His remembrance is always thought of in terms of grace and help. In sadness He remembers the devotion of Israel in her youth (Jer 2[2]), when she has wantonly turned from Him. He remembers sin to visit it upon the sinner (Ho 7[2], Jer 14[10]). Sometimes the psalmists cry to Him not to remember their sins (Ps 25[7]) or those of their fathers (Ps 79[8]), though man should ever remember his own sin (Ps 51[3]) that he may be stirred to penitence. Jeremiah looked forward to the New Covenant, when the sins of the past would be remembered no more (Jer 31[34]) in the loyalty of the present.

H. H. R.

REMETH.—See Ramoth, 1.

REMMON, Jos 19[7] (AV).—See Rimmon, 3.

REMMON-METHOAR, Jos 19[13] (AV).—See Rimmon, 4.

REMNANT.—This thought is found throughout Scripture and the Remnant is always presented as a token of the Divine mercy. The idea undergoes development in the prophetic writings and it gives rise to a definite coherent doctrine, closely allied with the doctrine of Election (q.v.). ‘ It is the bridge binding the threat of punishment to the hope of restoration ’ (De Vaux, *RB* xlii, 538). It is a direct derivative from Israel's thought of God who is righteous altogether and whose mercy endureth for ever. ‘ The gifts and call of God are irrevocable ’ (Ro 11[29]). The doctrine reconciles the righteousness of God with His faithfulness and truth.

The terms used to express the idea are *sh'r* and its derivatives (220 times in OT), *plṭ* (escape away) and its derivatives (80 times in OT) and *śrd* (panic flight) and its derivatives (29 times in OT). *Ythr* with its derivatives appear 103 times but is slightly less fitted to express the idea. These terms are frequently combined or used in parallelism to give the thought of an ‘ escaped remnant ’ while in Jer 44[14] a threefold combination heightens the effect. In the majority of instances these terms have their natural meaning of something left over or surviving from a scattering or general destruction (E. W. Heaton, *JThSt*, 1952, 27–39). But it may not be denied that there remain many instances where a special meaning is attached to the term and it refers to a group—not necessarily righteous (Am 3[12])—spared by the mercy of God. Through this group the privileges and promises of the Election are conveyed to later generations. Israel had failed in its response to Election and God reacts in righteousness against this failure. But the redemptive purpose of God will not be finally thwarted. Through a remnant of His own choosing the inheritance will be preserved. This thought of God's selective action may be seen in the case of Noah (Gn 7[1f]), the sons of Isaac (Gn 27[1]), Joseph in Egypt (Gn 45[7]), the remnant of 7000 in Elijah's time (1 K 19[18]). The idea and the terms used were commonly known and understood by all. ‘ The remnant of Joseph ’ (Am 5[15]) or ‘ Shear-jashub ’ (Is 7[3]) were intelligible to the hearers and needed no explanation. The idea may have been embedded in the cult (Mowinckel) and the ‘ Day of the Lord ’ may have signified Israel's V-day when all her foes would be overthrown and Israel left as a remnant. But to the prophets ‘ the Day of the Lord ’ signified judgment day, the day when the God of all good order would hold assize and sift His people (Am 9[9]) and only a remnant would survive (Am 3[12]). There is threat here : ‘ only a remnant ’ (Is 6[13] 10[22] 17[5f]), and there is promise : ‘ a remnant shall survive ’ (Ob [17], Mic 4[6f] 7[18]). In the divine Epiphany judgment and mercy are joined and mercy finally triumphs over judgment.

The development of this idea is due mainly to Isaiah. Despite textual difficulties the thought is seen in Is 6[13] and it is further developed in 7[3f] where the remnant is seen to be a faithful remnant (cf Am 5[15], Is 8[16] 10[20–22], Zeph 2[3], 1 K 19[18]). As set apart for God it is a ‘ holy remnant ’ (Is 4[3] 6[13] 62[12]). The idea of ‘ Israel after the Spirit ’ begins to appear and through this remnant God's purpose will be achieved (Is 4[3] 27[5] 37[31], Mic 5[5–7 (Heb. 6–8)], Ezk 36[22–25]). The formation of Isaiah's group of disciples (8[16]) is the foundation stone of the Church (W. R. Smith, *Prophets of Israel*, p. 275). In Jeremiah the emphasis may seem to be on total destruction (5[1f] 6[27–30] 4[23–25]), but Jer 31[31f] 23[3f], showed that he shared this hope.

As to the *locus* of the Remnant the earlier prophets centre on Jerusalem (Is 17[5f] 37[31f]). To Jeremiah and Ezekiel the hope of Israel lay with the Exiles (Jer 24, Ezk 5[1f] 22[30]), and while they viewed the remnant there, not yet clean and unsullied but requiring purgation and sanctification, as the nucleus of the new Israel, both prophets looked for a return to Zion (Jer 29[10f], Ezk 11[13f]). The remnant is not the débris of the inglorious and unfaithful past but the germ of a new and glorious Israel (Ezk 37[12]). To the post-exilic prophets the Remnant is the community of Ezra and the New Covenant and the Messianic age is about to dawn (Ezr 9[8, 13–15]).

New Testament.—Whether Jesus thought of the Church as the Remnant may be open to question ; it may be that in the selection of the twelve disciples He signifies His intention of creating a new People of God (cf Is 8[16]).

In the thought of Paul the Church fulfils the function of the faithful Remnant and he contrasts 'Israel after the flesh' with the 'Israel of God' which is the Church (Ro 9^{27}, Gal 6^{16}) and his interpretation follows the doctrine of OT. In Ja 1^{1} the scattered Christian Church is identified with the true Israel, while in 1 P 2^{9} the Church is called 'God's own people.' In He 8$^{8-12}$ the Church is identified with the people of the New Covenant (Jer 31^{31f}) and in Eph 2$^{4-10}$ it is regarded as Ezekiel's new and true Israel risen from the dead. In Ro 3^{24} it represents the 'ransomed' of Deutero-Isaiah while in 1 Co 1^{2f} it appears as Daniel's 'people of the saints of the Most High' (Dn 7^{27}). All this is not mere rhetoric but the purposed interpretation of prophetic doctrine.
J. Pn.

REMPHAN.—See Rephan.

REPENTANCE.—Two words are used commonly in the OT for repent, *nāḥam,* literally 'pant' or 'groan,' and *shûbh,* 'turn, return' (in particular, to God). The NT equivalents are *metanoia,* 'change of mind,' and *epistrephein,* 'turn.' The OT usage is often morally neutral, meaning a change of purpose or attitude. In this sense it can be used of God (Gn 6^{6}, Ex 32^{14}, etc.) although a number of passages deny 'repentance' to Him (Nu 23^{19}, 1 S 15^{29} but cf v.^{35}, Ezk 24^{14}). The prophets command the people to repent and turn from evil, with the implication that man can do this of himself (Is 1^{16f} 55^{6}, Jer 3^{12}, Ezk 18^{30}, Hos 6^{1}, Jl 2^{12}, Am 5^{4}). In the later literature it is God Himself, however, who must create the new heart (Ps 51^{10}, Ezk 36^{25}; but cf 18^{31}) and initiate the whole process of man's repentance.

We find this same contrast in the NT. Both John the Baptist and Jesus begin their ministry with the call to repent (Mt 3^{2} 4^{17} etc.). This is also the apostolic message (Ac 2^{38} 3^{19} 17^{30}). Yet repentance is regarded as the gift of God rather than the act of man (Ac 5^{31} 11^{18}, Ro 2^{4}, 2 Ti 2^{25}). The solution is to be found in the work of Christ who came to call sinners (Mk 2^{17}, Lk 4^{18} and see the parables in Lk 15). Repentance is to be preached in His name (Lk 24^{47}, 2 Ti 1^{9ff}). Hence repentance goes hand in hand with faith (Mk 1^{15}, Ac 20^{21}, He 6^{1}). It is the product of godly sorrow (2 Co 7^{10} where St. Paul contrasts a worldly sorrow that produces death; cf Mt 27^{3ff}) and leads to forgiveness of sins (Mk 1^{14}, Ac 2^{38} 3^{19} etc.). It brings forth worthy fruits (Mt 3^{8} ‖ Lk 3^{8}, Ac 26^{20}). Yet Christian repentance is more than grief for the past and resolution for the future. It involves a change of the whole person. It is creative, a positive, affirmative act rather than a mere negative turning away from sin. Accordingly St. Paul thinks in terms of death and resurrection with Christ into the new life of the Spirit (Ro 6^{2}, Col 2^{12}), and the Johannine literature completely replaces the terminology of repentance with that of the new birth (Jn 3^{3}). C. C. Ro.

REPHAEL.—A family of gatekeepers, 1 Ch 26^{7}.

REPHAH.—An Ephraimite family, 1 Ch 7^{25}.

REPHAIAH.—**1.** A Judahite, 1 Ch 3^{21}. **2.** A Simeonite chief, 1 Ch 4^{42}. **3.** A descendant of Issachar, 1 Ch 7^{2}. **4.** A descendant of Saul, 1 Ch 9^{43}; called **Raphah** in 8^{37} (AV **Rapha**). **5.** One of those who helped to repair the wall, Neh 3^{9}.

REPHAIM.—A name given in several Biblical passages to some pre-Israelitish people. In Gn 14^{5} they are said to have dwelt in Ashteroth-karnaim. Gn 15^{20} classes them with Hittites and Perizzites (similarly Jos 17^{15}). Dt 2^{11,20} calls certain peoples 'Rephaim' whom the Moabites and Ammonites called respectively '**Emim**' and '**Zamzummin.**' Dt 3^{11} says that Og, king of Bashan, alone remained of the Rephaim (so also Jos 12^{4} 13^{12}), while Dt 3^{13} says that Argob was a land of Rephaim. A valley near Jerusalem was also called the '**Vale of Rephaim**' (see 2 S 5^{18,22} 23^{13}, 1 Ch 11^{15} 14^{9}, Is 17^{5}). Because Dt 2^{11} counts them with the **Anakim,** who were giants, and 2 S 21$^{16-22}$ says that the sons of a certain **Raphah** (AV, RV 'giant'; RSV 'giants') were giants, it has been supposed by some that *Rephaim* means 'giants,' and was given to a race as their name by their neighbours because of their stature. Cf Giant.

The word *r^{e}phā'îm* in the OT and in Phoenician inscriptions means also 'shades' in the insubstantial Semitic afterlife. At least it used to describe the dead, as in Ps 88^{10}. Schwally is probably right, therefore (*Leben nach dem Tode*, 64 ff and *ZAW*, xviii, 127 ff), in holding that the word means 'shades,' and that it was applied by the Israelites to people who were dead and gone, and of whom they knew little.

In the Râs Shamra texts the Rephaim almost certainly denote a high-caste guild associated with fertility-ritual, which was anciently a royal office, two ancient kings, Dan'el and Keret, having apparently this significance.

The connexion between the dead and fertility is not unfamiliar in antiquity, *e.g.* Osiris, with whom the dead Pharaohs were identified, was also the giver of fertility; cf the connexion between the chthonic cult and fertility at Eleusis. In Hebrew tradition, however, it is the chthonic aspect of the Rephaim which has survived, though for the Hebrews these have become a departed race. There are two cases in administrative texts from Râs Shamra where the root appears as apparently a gentilic, but in the longer texts above mentioned, they are not a race, but a guild. G. A. B.—**J. Gr.**

REPHAN (AV **Remphan**).—A word which replaces **Chiun** of the Hebrew text of Am 5^{26}, both in the LXX and in the quotation in Ac 7^{43}. The generally accepted explanation of this word is that *Rephan* (the preferable form) is a corruption and transliteration of *Kaiwan* (q.v.) —*r* having somehow mistakenly replaced *k*, and *w* (the Heb. *waw* or *vav*) having been transliterated *ph* (the Gr. *phi*). W. M. N.

REPHIDIM.—A stage in the Wanderings, between the wilderness of Sin and the wilderness of Sinai (Ex 17^{1,8} 19^{2}; cf Nu 33^{14f}). Here water was miraculously supplied, and Israel fought with Amalek. The site has not been identified. Those who accept the traditional Sinai generally place Elim in *Wâdī Gharandel*, and Rephidim in *Wâdī Feirān*, about four miles N. of Mount Serbal. Scholars who place Sinai E. of the Gulf of 'Aqaba look for Rephidim in that area, while those who identify Horeb with one of the mountains near Kadesh-barnea find Rephidim in one of the oases in that district. See for a discussion of the various locations Kraeling, *Bible Atlas*, pp. 107–113. W. E.—**S. H. Hn.**

REPROBATE.—The Hebrew word so rendered in Jer 6^{30} (AV; RSV 'refuse') has its meaning explained by the context. 'Refuse silver they are called, for the Lord has rejected them.' Like metal proved to be worthless by the refiner's fire (v.^{29}), they are thrown away (cf Is 1^{22}). In the NT, in accordance with the meaning of the Greek word (*adokimos*), 'reprobate' is used of that which cannot abide the proof, which, on being tested, is found to be worthless, bad, counterfeit, and is therefore rejected. 'A reprobate (RSV 'base') mind' in Ro 1^{28} (with tacit reference to the previous clause, 'they did not see fit to acknowledge God') is, as the context shows, a mind depraved and perverted by vile passions. To such a mind God abandoned those who wilfully exchanged His truth for a lie (v.^{25}). In 1 Co 9^{27}, St. Paul declares that he 'pommels' and 'subdues' his body lest, having preached to others, he himself should be rejected ('disqualified' RSV). The figure is that of an athlete who, through remissness in training fails in the race or fight (for the opposite figure, cf 2 Ti 2^{15}). In 2 Co 13$^{5-7}$ the word occurs three times, in each case as opposed to genuine, true ('failing to meet the test' RSV). Christ is in them, except they be reprobates, *i.e.* false to their profession, hence rejected by God. Let them 'examine' themselves by this test (v.^{5}). St. Paul trusts that they will find out that he has not failed in it; let them think of him what they will, if only they themselves do what is right (v.^{7}). 'Reprobate' here is contrasted with what is 'approved,' 'honourable'; it is identified with 'doing evil.' In 2 Ti 3^{8}, certain are described as 'corrupted in mind, reprobate concerning the faith '(' rejected as regards the faith' RSV 1946 ; ' men of corrupt mind and counterfeit faith', RSV 1955), where both moral corruption and false speculation as the result of this corruption seem intended. They fail, brought to the rest of ' sound ' or ' healthful ' doctrine (1^{13f} 4^{3}). Similarly Tit 1^{16} speaks of those who, denying God by their works, are ' unto every good work reprobate ' (' unfit for any good deed,' RSV). Their hypocrisy is brought home to them by their wicked lives. ' Professing that they know God,' they are proved by their works to be counterfeits, impostors. The word occurs, finally, in He 6^{8}, where those whom it is impossible ' to renew again to repentance ' are compared to ground which, receiving the rain oft upon it, and being tilled, brings forth only thorns and thistles, and is ' rejected ' (' worthless ' RSV). From all this we may conclude that ' reprobate,' generally denotes a moral state so bad that recovery from it is no longer possible ; there remains only judgment (cf He 6^{8}). It is only to be added that the term has no relation in Scripture to an eternal decree of reprobation ; at least, to none which has not respect to a thoroughly bad and irrecoverable condition of its objects. ' Reprobate ' is not used in the NT of the RSV ; in the OT, only Ps 15^{4}. Cf Predestination. J. O.—**F. W. G.**

RESAIAH.—See Raamiah.

RESAIAS, 1 Es 5^{8} (RV).—See Raamiah.

RESEN.—The last of the four cities built by Asshur, or, according to the RV, by Nimrod, and described as lying between Nineveh and Calah (*i.e. Quyunjiq* and *Nimrûd*), on the E. bank of the Tigris, Gn 10^{12}. Its site is unknown. That the words ' that is the great city ' should refer to Resen alone seems unlikely—more probably Nineveh, Rehoboth-ir and Calah are included, the two latter forming, with Resen, suburbs of the first.

RESH.—Twentieth letter of Hebrew alphabet, and so used to introduce the twentieth part of Ps 119, every verse of which begins with this letter.

RESHEPH.—An Ephraimite family, 1 Ch 7^{25}.

REST.—The conception of rest as a gift of God runs through the Bible, the underlying idea being not idleness, but the freedom from anxiety which is the condition of effective work. It is promised to Israel in Canaan (Ex 33^{14}, Dt 3^{20}), and Zion is the resting-place of Y″ (Ps $132^{8, 14}$) ; the Temple is built by ' a man of rest ' (1 Ch 22^{9} AV and RV [RSV ' a man of peace '] ; a contrast is implied with the desert wanderings in Nu 10^{33-36}). At the same time no earthly temple can be the real resting-place of Y″ (Is 66^{1}, Ac 7^{49}). The rest of the Sabbath and the Sabbatical year are connected with the rest of God after creation (Gn 2^{2}, Ex 20^{11}, Lv 25^{4} ; see Sabbath). The individual desires rest, as did the nation (Ps 55^{6}) ; it is not to be found in ignoble ease (Gn 49^{15} Issachar), but in the ways of God (Ps 37^{7}, Jer 6^{16}) ; it is the gift of Christ (Mt 11^{28}). Sinners fail to find it (Is 28^{12} 57^{20}), as Israel failed (Ps 95^{11}). He 4 develops the meaning of this failure, and points to the ' sabbath rest ' still to come. This heavenly rest includes not only freedom from labour, as in OT (Job $3^{13, 17}$ [in Ps 16^{9}, see RV]), but also the opportunity of continued work (Rev 14^{13}). C. W. E.

RESTITUTION.—See Crimes and Punishments, **8.**

RESTORATION.—Although the term *apokatastasis* connotes the eschatological idea of a final restoration of all things to their primal perfection (Gn 1^{31}), the real starting point for the NT conception of restoration is the realization of *newness in Christ* : we walk in newness of life (Ro 6^{4}), we serve in the new life of the Spirit (Ro 7^{6}). Christ has become the ' new man ' in us (Ro 5^{12-21}) to transform us into a new creation (Eph 2^{15}) which begins here (2 Co 5^{17}) and will end in the *eschaton*. There will be a new heaven and a new earth (Rev 21^{6}, 2 P 3^{13}, Ro 8^{18-25}), a new Jerusalem (Rev 21^{2} 3^{12}), a new song (Rev 5^{9} 14^{3}), a new name (Rev 2^{17} 3^{12}). This new aeon, already begun with Christ, will come to fulfilment with the eschatological meal (Mk 14^{25}), when God will ' make everything new ' (Rev 21^{5}), after the final separation of good and evil (Mt 13^{40} 25^{32}), when heaven and earth will have passed away (Mk 13^{31}, Rev 21^{1}). Jesus did not expect the *parousia*, the coming of the Lord (Mt $24^{3, 27}$) to take place during His lifetime ; but it began with His resurrection and will be fulfilled in His second coming (2 Th 2^{19}), when each in his order will receive a new life (1 Co 15^{23}). Ac 3^{21} uses the term *apokatastasis*, which is used elsewhere in ancient literature in various connexions, *e.g.* for the return of the stars to their original constellations after their great cycles. Here it refers to the establishing of ' all things that God spoke by the mouth of his holy prophets ' (RSV) ; the text can also be translated, ' until the times of the establishing [or re-establishing] of all things, of which [times] God spoke . . .' God has promised from of old that He will re-establish the cosmos both physically and spiritually in its pristine state, when ' he saw everything that he had made, and behold, it was very good.' But this does not represent a universalist doctrine of the final salvation of all, whether good or evil, sinner or faithful. The very definite Pauline stress on the total aspect of salvation in Christ (Ro 5^{18} 11^{32}, 1 Co 15^{22}, Col 1^{20}) must be understood in terms of the kerygmatic preaching of the apostle, as spoken by a *homo sub gratia* proclaiming salvation to Corinth and Rome, and not as an expression of a theological speculation—like that of Origen, *e.g.*, though Origen was more careful in stating this conception than is generally realized. Paul's outlook is bright : the salvation to come will include nature (Ro 8^{21}) as well as men ; but the NT still keeps men under the tension of a final judgment in which the sheep will be separated from the goats (Mt 25^{31-45}). S. L.

RESURRECTION.—1. In the OT.—On the doctrine of the resurrection the NT presents a striking development as compared with the OT. Clear and explicit references to the resurrection are rare in the OT ; the NT gives the resurrection a central place. We have here a particularly impressive example of the way God gradually led His people to grasp certain important truths.

Two ancient alternatives to a real doctrine of resurrection receive no support in the OT. Its writers are not content with the cyclical pattern of an annual resurrection, or the seasonal rising of a vegetation god from the dead. This is in part the significance of the bitter, continual prophetic attack on Baal worship. This type of worship was linked with nature. It was a fertility cult, practised to ensure fertility in crops, in flocks and herds, and even in human family life. Annual observance was inherent in such a cult. Wherever vegetation and fertility were linked with a god or goddess, the idea of the dying and rising of the god easily entered the picture. This entire pattern, prevalent throughout the Near East, was denounced by the prophets and finally rejected by Israel. The faith in resurrection did not arise by simple application of a resurrection pattern derived from annual fertility and renewal rites.

The other possible alternative to a true resurrection faith was the idea of the immortality of the soul. On this view, the body is at best a transient unworthy instrument of the pure and eternal soul. Death sets the soul free to enjoy without hindrance its true life. This road to blessedness seems not to have confronted Israel at an early date, and with rare exceptions it was rejected as soon as it was faced. What prevented such an idea from taking root in Israel was the firm faith, which reached far back into the early history of that people, that their God, the Giver of life, was the Creator and so the Lord of the whole earth. He had made the world, and saw that ' it was very good ' (Gn 1^{31}). The body of man therefore was not a negligible or an evil part of his life ; it was an integral part of the man ; man was a living body. Israel could accept no conception of future blessedness which ignored the material world and rejected the goodness of God's work as Creator.

The usual early OT view did not teach the complete extinction of the person at physical death. It thought rather that after death came a shadowy and unsatisfying existence in Sheol, where king and subject, rich and poor, might still be aware of their former class distinctions but none had a really happy or complete life. This idea reflected the importance attached to the body in the life of man; without the body life could not be normal, full, or satisfying. From that state there is no return; 'he who goes down to Sheol does not come up' (Job 7⁹). In this prevailing early view there was no real tie with God; 'in death there is no remembrance of thee; in Sheol who can give thee praise?' (Ps 6⁵). 'For Sheol cannot thank thee, death cannot praise thee; those who go down into the pit cannot hope for thy faithfulness' (Is 38[18]).

Yet two ideas already led Israel to the verge of the idea that God could bring His people back even from Sheol. One was the grateful testimony of those who in sickness or danger had come dangerously near to death; they had gone to the very gates of Sheol, but had been saved and brought back by God; 'my life draws near to Sheol' but 'thou dost not give me up to Sheol' (Ps 88[3] 16[10]). The other ray of hope is the conviction that even in Sheol God is not absent; 'If I make my bed in Sheol, thou art there!' (Ps 139[8]). The presence and so the power of God are there; perhaps, then, the dead are not beyond the reach of His saving work.

It is not possible to trace clearly the factors that led Israel to affirm faith in resurrection. Figurative statements, such as those which speak of God's miraculous snatching of individual people from death, may have had their influence. It may have been felt that God is not helpless before Sheol; He can save not only from the very gateway of Sheol but from the actual domain of the dead. Figurative expressions which described the bringing back of Israel from the death of captivity may have had their influence (cf Ezk 37). Increased interest in God's dealings with individuals may have led men to ask whether God's goodness could maintain the life of His loyal saints beyond death. Sheol was just what the wicked deserved (Ps 49[14]), but could not God give His faithful people a better lot? And God's own rôle was restudied. Since the lot which the good and the wicked receive in this life is often not in accord with what they deserve, men might feel the need of a future situation in which God's justice finds full expression, and so might be led to think that there must be a resurrection.

The OT passages which express clear faith in a resurrection are amazingly few. The taking up of Enoch and Elijah to fellowship with God (Gn 5[24], 2 K 2[11]) does not express it, but these stories could stimulate men to think that God's people will have a permanent privileged position in living touch with Him. The raising of a child by Elijah and by Elisha (1 K 17[17-23], 2 K 4[32-36]) created an atmosphere congenial to the idea of a permanent resurrection of the body. Is 53[10-12] is not clear; some, who interpret the Servant to be an individual, find here a hint that he will have some form of satisfying life after death. Job 14[14f] raises the question, but is rather despairing; Job 19[25-27] is an obscure text whose original wording is difficult to determine, but it is more hopeful. The two most explicit passages are (1) Is 26[19], where Israel is promised a resurrection which seems not expected for their oppressors (v.[14]); and (2) Dn 12[2], where no universal resurrection is expected, but the loyal righteous who have suffered from the oppressor (11[32ff]) and the apostate Jews who have collaborated with him will rise to receive their respective rewards, 'everlasting life' and 'shame and everlasting contempt.' Thus there is in the OT no clear statement that all men will rise in a general resurrection. But the basis is provided for such a more developed view.

2. In the Apocrypha.—In the period between the writing of the Book of Daniel (fourth decade of the 2nd cent. B.C.) and the ministry of Jesus, a development of thought occurred, but it was not uniform or shared by all Jews. This may be seen first in the Apocrypha and other Jewish writings of the period, and then in the position taken on this subject by the Jewish sects.

Three chief positions are represented in the Apocrypha. (1) The composite work Ecclesiasticus reflects for the most part the lack of any expectation that there will be a resurrection or even a rich future existence. 'A son of man is not immortal' (according to the probable text of 17[30]), but it can be said that a man's 'name will live for ever' (37[26]). It is not certain what 46[12] and 49[10] mean; the former verse may mean that a man receives new life in his sons; in any event, Ecclesiasticus as a whole has no expectation of a resurrection, and if these passages express such an expectation, they differ from 17[30] and from the general tenor of the book. (2) The Wisdom of Solomon, in 2[23] and 3[1ff], expresses a clear expectation of a future life, but probably in the form of immortality apart from the body, in a manner akin to Greek thought. (3) 2 Maccabees repeatedly expresses confident faith in the bodily resurrection of those who suffer under the oppressor of God's people (7[9] 12[43-45] 14[46]).

3. In other late Jewish writings.—It is difficult to state what the Book of Enoch teaches; it is a composite work, its present form is late, and it may contain Christian interpolations or Christian passages. In an early portion, 22[9-13], there are divisions in Sheol between the righteous and the wicked, and some of the wicked will not rise. In the later Similitudes (chs. 37–71), there appears to be a clear expectation of a general resurrection (51[1]). In 90[33] 91[10] the resurrection of the righteous is expected; 103[4] raises a question whether this means a bodily resurrection or only a revival of the surviving spirit of the righteous dead. This question is not clearly answered in the Psalms of Solomon; 3[16] says that 'they that fear the Lord shall rise to life eternal,' and this sounds like definite resurrection teaching, but the exact nature of the resurrection state is not indicated.

Both the Apocalypse of Baruch and IV Ezra are decades later than the time of Jesus. They express a clear expectation of bodily resurrection. In *Apoc. Bar.* 30[2] only the rising of the righteous is mentioned, but it is clear from 50[2-4] and 51[1-6] that all will be raised just as they were before death, and the wicked will then be given a worse form of existence and the righteous a more glorious form. A new idea appears when the reign of the Messiah for 400 years (?; the text varies as to the number) is followed by his death and by a general resurrection (2 Es 7[28-30]). This thought of an intermediate kingdom or period appears in the Book of Revelation, ch. 20.

The Jewish sects of the time of Jesus—if we accept the report of Josephus (*BJ* II. viii. 2–14 [119–166]; *Ant.* XVIII. i. 3–5 [12–22])—reflect the same three positions which we found in the Apocrypha. (1) The Sadducees denied the resurrection (Ac 23[8]) and tried to trap Jesus into conceding their contention (Mk 12[18-27] and parallels). Josephus declares that they held the soul to die with the body. (2) The Pharisees expected a resurrection (cf Ac 23[6-8]) and so on grounds of principle could not deny the possibility of Jesus' resurrection. Josephus says they expected the resurrection only of the righteous. (3) The Essenes, according to Josephus, believed in the immortality of the soul. However, Hippolytus (*Refutatio*, IX. 27) says they believed in the resurrection; if he is right, they agreed essentially on this matter with the Pharisees. The Dead Sea Scrolls of the Qumrân sect do not settle this question; they clearly expect a final judgment and a blessed life for the righteous, but it is not clear whether they imply a resurrection of the body or simply the immortality of the soul. The careful burial of the dead by this sect may imply that a resurrection was expected. If so, this is significant, for the Qumrân sect was an Essene type of religious fellowship.

4. The Teaching of Jesus.—(*a*) *The Synoptic Gospels.*—Since Jesus taught by act as well as by word, it is noteworthy that He is said to have restored to life certain individuals who had just died (Mk 5[35-43], Mt 9[23-26], Lk 7[11-17] 8[49-56]), and that He instructed His disciples to raise the dead (Mt 10[8]). This means restoration to life in the present conditions of physical existence; it does not describe a resurrection that gives man a form of life fit for the eternal Kingdom of God. But it does show that Divine saving power can reach even into the realm of the dead.

Jesus almost never refers to the resurrection of all men; Mt 25^{31-46}, however, clearly describes a general resurrection. Jesus usually emphasizes God's gift of life and blessedness to His faithful people at the resurrection; attention centres on the 'resurrection of the just,' in which the 'sons of God' or 'sons of the resurrection' enter into eternal and full fellowship with God (Lk 14^{14} 20^{36}). The one detailed discussion of the resurrection is in Mk 12^{18-27}, Mt 22^{23-33}, Lk 20^{27-40}. Here Jesus explicitly opposes the Sadducees' denial of resurrection; He argues that the Scripture, *i.e.* the OT, teaches that there will be a resurrection, and He asserts that the power of God is adequate to effect this. He argues from Ex 3^{6}; God spoke to Moses of Abraham, Isaac, and Jacob as in living relation to him, though they had died long before the time of Moses. This does not in itself establish the certainty of resurrection. It affirms that the patriarchs, though they have experienced physical death, still live and are in living fellowship with God; Jesus apparently infers that at the last day the Divine power on which this survival and continued privilege rests will raise the patriarchs and give them eternal blessedness.

That He expected an actual resurrection becomes clearer from His predictions of His own resurrection. This thrice repeated prediction (Mk 8^{31} ‖ Mt 16^{21} ‖ Lk 9^{22}; Mk 9^{31} ‖ Mt 17^{23}; Mk 10^{34} ‖ Mt 20^{19} ‖ Lk 18^{33}) is often described as a prediction of His passion, but these predictions end (Lk 9^{44} does not) with the explicit though brief promise of the resurrection. The mention of 'after three days' or 'on the third day' shows that more is meant than the soul's survival of death; the phrase implies a definite act of resurrection, giving a new form and power of life. The gathering of the elect 'from the four winds' seems to anticipate that they will first be raised in the places where they had lived and died (cf Mk 13^{27} ‖ Mt 24^{31}). That the form of the resurrection life will be fully personal appears in the expectation that God's people will share fellowship with one another and with God, and will enjoy the Messianic banquet (Mt 8^{11}, Lk 13^{29}), which was a traditional Jewish picture of final privilege and blessing.

(*b*) *The Fourth Gospel*.—The Gospel of John rarely speaks about the resurrection of the wicked, but 5^{29} shows that it was expected. As in the Synoptic Gospels, attention centres almost entirely on the resurrection of believers to a privileged life with God and Christ. Jesus as the Son of God is the active agent in raising the dead ($5^{25, 28f}$ $6^{39f, 44, 54}$); He is 'the resurrection and the life' (11^{25}), which means not only that 'in him was life' (1^{4}) but also that He gives life now (3^{36}) and through the resurrection of the dead at the last day. The climactic miracle and sign of the Fourth Gospel, the raising of Lazarus from the dead (ch. 11), is an acted parable of this resurrection power which the Father has given to Jesus to exercise during His ministry and at the final day. This Gospel emphasizes strongly the present gift of life to all who believe, but it does not discard the common early Christian theme of the gift of true, perfect, and endless life by the resurrection at the end of history.

5. The Resurrection of Jesus.—The NT teaching concerning the resurrection centres in the key event of the entire NT history, the resurrection of Jesus Himself. For every NT preacher and writer resurrection is not merely an inherited doctrine, an intellectual inference, or a wistful hope; it is an assured fact, placed beyond doubt by the resurrection of Jesus Christ from the dead by the power of God. Both the OT message and the teaching and cross of Jesus are understood in the light of this central act of God. The present life of the believer and the future work of God are likewise understood in the light of the solid fact that Christ is risen and is the living Lord of His Church.

This confident affirmation of the resurrection of Jesus was a key item in the original apostolic message. The disciples rallied after the crucifixion because they became convinced that God had raised Jesus from the dead. The rise, growth, and courage of the Church finds its one adequate explanation in the fact of the resurrection. It thus is no surprise that the apostolic preaching centred in this fact. The apostle chosen to succeed Judas was to 'become with us a witness to his resurrection' (Ac 1^{22}). The key affirmation of the Pentecost message was: 'This Jesus God raised up, and of that we all are witnesses' (Ac 2^{32}). This preaching aroused the opposition of the priestly leaders of the Jews, and motivated the persecution of the apostles (Ac 3^{26} 4^{2}). The Apostolic Church was not built upon Jesus as a prophet or martyr; from the beginning the Church was the Church of the risen Christ, the living Lord of His followers and the destined Lord of all.

When therefore the Gospels tell that Jesus rose from the dead they share the common theme of all NT preachers and writers. Paul illustrates this fact; in 1 Co 15^{4-8} he tells of the appearances of the risen Christ, and he indicates that except for his own encounter with the risen Christ these appearances were basic Christian tradition delivered to him within a very few years after the event.

The Gospels raise questions by their narratives. (1) Where did the risen Christ first appear to His disciples? In Galilee (Matthew, Mark by implication) or in Jerusalem (Luke, Jn 20)? Appearances no doubt occurred in both places, but it may be that the Eleven first saw the risen Christ in Galilee and then returned to Jerusalem. (2) In what form did the risen Christ appear to the disciples? In the same physical body He had during His earthly ministry or in a transformed body? The somewhat baffling details of the resurrection narratives suggest a real identity of person with a decisive transformation of mode of existence. (3) Is the finding of the empty tomb part of the original resurrection story? All four Gospels tell of finding the tomb empty; the phrase 'after three days' or 'on the third day' clearly describe an event which left the tomb empty; the Jews never produced the dead body of Jesus because they could not do so; the tomb was empty. God's resurrection act had transformed the body of Jesus. This is what the Gospels mean; it is what Paul teaches in 1 Co 15; it is implied throughout the NT (*e.g.* 1 P 1^{21}), where the resurrection of Jesus is followed by an exalted state of glory.

The NT never presents the resurrection of Jesus as merely the subjective recovery of faith and courage by the disciples, or as merely the survival of death by Jesus, so that His soul proved immortal while His dead body was discarded. The resurrection meant first of all the bringing back of Jesus to renewed and higher life, in a form continuous with but no longer identical with His earthly physical life. He came back to personal contact and relationships with His closest followers. Yet it was not mere restoration to former relations; the disciples in every case sensed an exaltation, a higher form of life, and their meetings with the risen Christ were limited in number and in duration. The new status of Christ transcended the physical and spatial limitations of His earthly ministry. After the resurrection He possessed the same body or form of personal presence and activity that He will have for all time to come.

6. The Resurrection of Mankind.—The expectation of a general resurrection was not new in first-century Judaism; probably by that time most Jews held such a view. But the Apostolic Church held the expectation in a special form, and could not be frightened or shamed by either Sadducean opposition (Ac 4^{2}) or Hellenistic scepticism (Ac 17^{32} 25^{19} $26^{8, 23f}$). The risen Christ is to be the 'judge of the living and the dead' (Ac 10^{42}, 2 Co 5^{10}). This involves the resurrection of all the dead in order that they may be judged. The focus of attention in the NT is on the resurrection of believers in Christ, but some passages specifically refer to the resurrection of both wicked and righteous or by mention of a general judgment make it clear that a general resurrection is expected (Mt 8^{11f} 25^{31-46}, Jn 5^{28f}, Ac 10^{42} 24^{15}, Ro 2^{6-10}, Rev 20^{11-15}).

But on the whole the resurrection of the wicked receives scant attention in the NT and little light is thrown on how they are to be raised. Emphasis rests rather on the promise—a certainty in the light of the resurrection of Christ—that faithful believers will be raised. The close link between Christ and His followers will not be broken by death ; it will hold fast and lead to their resurrection (Ro 6^{5}, 1 Co 15^{22}, 1 Th 4^{14-18}).

This hope of resurrection at the last day was never abandoned ; it was a constant and integral part of the Christian hope. The assertion that ' the resurrection is past already ' (2 Ti 2^{18}) was roundly condemned as an attack on an essential Christian conviction. Nevertheless, for Christians the resurrection doctrine no longer had a purely future reference. For one thing, Christ had been raised and was the living Lord of the Church ; He was henceforth ' the first fruits of those who have fallen asleep ' (1 Co 15^{20}) ; the new age had begun to dawn. Now, through faith, those who believed in Him knew the transforming Divine power which effected a changed life. This ' newness of life ' was a present fact ; Christians were already ' raised with Christ ' (Ro $6^{4,11}$, Co 3^{1}). It is not clear how widely the present Christian life was definitely described as a risen life, but the sense of thrilling newness, the awareness of the Spirit's inspiring and transforming presence, and the references to rebirth (Jn 3^{3-6}, Ti 3^{5}, Ja 1^{18}, 1 P 1^{3}) show that the Church knew the power of the new age to be already active in a preliminary way. The eschatological sequence pictured by the Apostolic Church was not limited to purely future events ; it began in the work and resurrection of Christ, continued in the lives of loyal believers, and would reach dramatic and full expression at the last day, when the resurrection, judgment, and final establishment of the eternal Kingdom would mark the completion of the purpose of God.

There are rare suggestions that the resurrection of mankind will be realized in two stages, with the righteous dead rising first and the wicked later. Some have seen this pattern in 1 Co 15^{23f} ; on this view ' the end ' in v.^{24} is the time for the resurrection of the wicked. Rev 20^{4-6} is sometimes interpreted along this line, but while it speaks of two resurrections, the first does not include all the righteous, but only the martyrs for Christ ; they will be raised and given a special privilege of unhindered fellowship with Christ before the final defeat of Satan and the resurrection of the rest of mankind. Some of those raised in the second resurrection will be saved, but since they were not martyrs they will not be included in the first resurrection. As a general rule, however, the NT makes no such distinction ; it almost always speaks simply of the resurrection, with no indication that it will occur in two stages.

The form of life after the final resurrection is discussed in detail only in 1 Co 15. Paul's views in this chapter probably represent the usual Christian view of the Apostolic Age. In response to those at Corinth who, probably in the interest of a doctrine of the immortality of the soul, disowned the common Christian idea of the resurrection of the body, Paul insisted that just as Christ had really been raised and given a spiritual body, so His followers would be raised and given a new and perfect form of existence. There would be a real continuity with the former physical body, yet ' flesh and blood cannot inherit the kingdom of God ' (v.^{50}), and so the new body will be a spiritual body, fit for the perfect life of the eternal Kingdom. He thus asserts continuity of personal life, perfect form of existence in the future life, free fellowship with God and Christ (as 1 Th 4^{17} says, ' we shall always be with the Lord ') and with other redeemed people. This social fellowship is probably part of the meaning of the table fellowship expected (Mt 8^{11}) ; this figurative language need not imply a literal physical body and physical eating in the final Kingdom. As in 1 Co 15, so also in Ph 3^{21} Paul expects Christ to ' change our lowly body to be like his glorious body.' No doubt some believers thought of the resurrection in literally physical terms, but the common conviction that the body of Jesus had been transformed and made glorious would imply what Paul specifically asserts, that the Christians also are to be given a higher form of existence, a new body, a perfect instrument of full spiritual life and fellowship.

For the resurrection of Jesus see further JESUS CHRIST **17**. F. V. F.

REU.—Son of Peleg, Gn 11^{18-21}, 1 Ch 1^{25}, Lk 3^{35} (AV **Ragau**).

REUBEN.—The eldest son of Jacob, by his wife Leah (Gn 29^{32} JE, or L). The etymology of the name is obscure. From the forms of the name in Josephus and the Peshitta it has been inferred that the original form of the name was Rubil or Rubel. This might be either an animal name, from the Arabic word for a lion, or a theophorous name compounded with Baal. The Hebrew derivation is an artificial one, intended to connect the name with the circumstances of Reuben's birth.

The incidents recorded in Genesis of Reuben's personal history are (*a*) he finds mandrakes in the field (Gn 30^{14}) ; this provides the occasion for a barter transaction between Leah and Rachel, and an explanation for the name of Issachar ; (*b*) he lay with Jacob's concubine, Bilhah (Gn 35^{22}), an incident which is said to have brought upon him his father's curse (Gn 49^{4}) ; (*c*) he intervenes to prevent Joseph's brethren from killing him (Gn 37^{21}). How far these episodes are to be taken as evidence for the existence of Reuben as an historical character is open to question. The second episode is made the explanation for the chequered history of the tribe of Reuben, and it is with the history of Reuben as a tribe that most of the remaining references to Reuben are concerned.

The first point to be noted is the grouping of the tribes in the various tribal lists (Gn 49, Nu 26, Nu 1). In each of these lists the same group of six tribes comes first, headed by Reuben, Simeon, and Levi. Of these three, Reuben is said to have suffered a diminution of population ; Simeon disappears as a tribe, and is apparently absorbed by Judah ; while Levi also disappears as a territorial tribe, and becomes the priestly tribe. The second point is that in the narratives of the settlement of the tribes, Reuben, Gad, and the half-tribe of Manasseh (Machir), are associated as a group located on the E side of the Jordan (Nu 32, Jos 13^{15-31}). Thirdly, the Song of Deborah (Jg 5^{15-16}) seems to picture Reuben as settled in pasture-land in Canaan W. of the Jordan ; and a tradition in Jos 15^{6} 18^{17} mentions a place called ' the stone of Bohan, the son of Reuben,' situated to the S. of Jericho. Noth suggests (*History of Israel*, p. 64) that as Hebrew *bōhen* means ' thumb,' the name of the place was originally ' thumbstone,' and that Bohan was later taken to be a personal name and connected with a tradition that Reubenites had lived in the district. Lastly, the Reubenite family of Carmi (1 Ch 5^{3}) is assigned in Jos 7^{1} to the tribe of Judah, from which it may be inferred that the Reubenites who lived in the neighbourhood of Judah were ultimately absorbed into the tribe of Judah. From these various elements of tribal tradition it may be inferred that in the earliest stages of settlement Reuben, Simeon, and Levi occupied some part of the central territory W. of the Jordan, and had then, for reasons which are not clear, dispersed, migrated, and made room for the Ephraim tribes which occupied that district later. Reuben probably never had any definite tribal boundaries W. of the Jordan, and when the scattered elements of the tribe migrated to the E. of the Jordan, they shared the territory already occupied by Gad (Gilead).

There is much to recommend Noth's theory that the six tribes previously referred to had, in the early period of settlement, constituted a tribal society or league with its religious centre at Shechem. (For the arguments in support of this theory cf Noth. *History of Israel*, pp.

86–89). A tradition is preserved in 1 Ch $5^{10, 18-22}$ that in the time of Saul the Reubenites made war on the Hagrites (q.v.), *i.e.* the Ishmaelites, and occupied their territory until the captivity, by which is meant the invasion of Tiglath-pileser III. in 734 B.C. when most of the northern tribes were carried away to Assyria. Whether Reuben had maintained its separate identity as a tribe to so late a date is open to doubt. S. H. He.

REUEL.—**1.** A son of Esau, Gn $36^{4, 10, 13, 17}$, 1 Ch $1^{35, 37}$. **2.** The father-in-law of Moses, Ex 2^{18}, Nu 10^{29} (AV in the latter **Raguel**). See HOBAB and JETHRO. **3.** Nu 2^{14} (AV, RV); see DEUEL. **4.** A Benjamite, 1 Ch 9^{8}.

REUMAH.—The concub ıe of Nahor, Gn 22^{24}.

REVELATION.—**1. Modern use of the word.**—A common modern usage has been to speak of 'revelation and reason' as the two possible forms of access to the knowledge of God. For Biblical study this contrast has a double disadvantage; firstly that this contrast and the definition of its terms are not drawn from Biblical thought, and secondly that it implicitly lumps together all human knowledge of God apart from direct Divine action as 'reason' and all human knowledge which depends upon such action as 'revelation.' Twentieth-century theology in fact makes much less use of this contrast. In many circles, however, it continues to speak of revelation as a comprehensive term for all forms of Divine self-communication. Almost any kind of Divine action or utterance is thus treated as 'revelation.' The use of the word in the Bible is, however, considerably less comprehensive and more particular, and the use of the word as a blanket term may only obscure the sense of particular occurrences.

2. Method of this article.—We shall proceed here therefore strictly from the Biblical usage of words meaning 'reveal,' and shall not discuss such traditional problems as 'revelation and reason,' 'general revelation,' or 'revelation in nature' except in so far as they are forced on us by the Biblical statements. For the other method, readers are referred to the articles 'Revelation' in Richardson, *Theological Word Book of the Bible*, and Allmen, *Vocabulary of the Bible*. A strict investigation of the word 'reveal' may help us to judge whether the above problems are, in the light of Biblical thinking, correctly and appropriately posed. We shall not accept as material any terms for Divine communication in general, such as 'to speak' or 'to make known.'

3. Biblical words for revealing.—The English word is derived from a Latin word meaning to unveil or uncover, and this sense adequately represents the Greek *apokalyptō*, the noun from which is *apokalypsis*, apocalypse. Similar to this Greek word is the Hebrew root *gālāh* to uncover, of which it is the usual translation in the Septuagint; the related compound *anakalyptō* also represents *gālāh* quite frequently.

Of other terms that which may be most closely associated with our subject is the group 'manifest' (Gr. *phaneros*), 'to make manifest' (*phaneroun*) etc. Members of this group do a few times represent Hebrew *gālāh* 'uncover' in the LXX, so that the possibility has to be considered that in the NT 'reveal' and 'manifest' may occasionally be roughly synonymous. An examination of the passages, however, suggests that they are not usually interchangeable without shift of sense or reference. Occurrences of 'manifest' will not therefore be normally adduced here.

4. Common uses in the OT.—A basic and frequent use of 'uncover' in the OT is with reference to the human body. Ruth 'uncovers the place of the feet' to lie down near Boaz (Ru 3^{4}). The uncovering of the body is often strongly associated with shame and impropriety; so Is 47^{2f}, part of the humiliation of Babylon. In particular, some of the law codes describe incest or intercourse with a menstruous woman as 'uncovering of nakedness' and peculiarly abominable. This lies in a tradition of custom where propriety demands that certain things should not be uncovered, a tradition also expressed in the story of paradise where after man's disobedience he felt shame for his nakedness and God mercifully gave him a covering.

The word can also be used for a document which is left open and not sealed.

We also find the usage of 'to uncover the ear,' hence to disclose—my father, says Jonathan, does nothing great or small without uncovering my ear, 1 S 20^{2}. This leads on to—

5. Usage in the prophets.—The prophets are granted special sensitivity in vision and audition. So Samuel's ear is uncovered, 1 S 9^{15}, and Nathan's, or David's through Nathan, 2 S 7^{27}. He whose ear is uncovered by God receives a message from God. Similarly, the eyes are uncovered in the case of Balaam, so that he sees a vision of God (Nu $24^{4, 16}$). These ways of speaking are not, however, common in the classical prophets.

More important and characteristic for the classical prophets is Amos's affirmation (3^{7}): 'Surely the Lord God does nothing without revealing his secret to his servants the prophets.' 'Secret' is rather too precise here; it means the private discussion in which God's mind has been made up, on the basis of which He will act. What God uncovers to the prophet is His decision and purpose; hence the validity and the urgency of the prophetic message. The wisdom literature warns against the gossip who discloses private discussion (Pr 20^{19} etc.); but God discloses His private counsel to His servants. Amos is probably using a rather original metaphor here, for 'revealing' did not become a technical term among the prophets for the source of their message, and it appears elsewhere among the prophets only of Samuel (1 S $3^{7, 21}$) and Isaiah (22^{14}) apart from the uncovering of eye or ear already mentioned. The prophet, speaking of the source of his message, usually says not 'God revealed,' but 'I saw' and 'I heard.'

6. God and His revealing.—The assertion that God reveals Himself is infrequent, and of the many Divine appearances in the Pentateuch it is used only once, Gn 35^{7}; also in the Samuel and Isaiah traditions, 1 S 3^{21}, Is 22^{14}. These are, however, sufficient to indicate that God is covered or hidden from normal human access, but hardly to show how far this hiddenness is complete or absolute. The revealing is at the will of God and is not conditioned by human effort.

Some important cases also occur where it is the glory (Is 40^{5}) or the deliverance or vindication (Is 56^{1}, Ps 98^{2}) of God which is to be revealed. The important thing in these is that the revealing is in the future or is the impending or immediately past appearance of something new, such as the judgment of the world in righteousness. A purpose or status which has not been hitherto clear or properly recognized is now to be made evident.

We also find a significant usage in which it is sin or evil that is uncovered or revealed, Ezk 21^{24}, Hos 7^{1}, Is 26^{21}. One may conceal or ignore evildoing, but in the time of God's visitation it becomes evident. The sky reveals the iniquity of the wicked man, Job 20^{27}; secret evil passions will be exposed, Pr 26^{26}, Sir 1^{30}. The prophets should have uncovered the sin of Jerusalem, but failed to do so, La 2^{14}.

Rather exceptional is Jer 11^{20} 20^{12}, where Jeremiah expects God's vengeance on his enemies, 'for to thee have I revealed my case' (RSV 'committed my cause'). Here man uncovers or discloses to God.

God's power may be seen when he uncovers elements of the world which are inaccessible to men, Job 12^{22}, Ps 18^{15}.

It is commonly suggested that God revealed Himself in His 'mighty acts' in the history of Israel, and especially in the Exodus complex; but curiously not a single certain case exists of a use of the word 'reveal' for the events of the Exodus and Mount Sinai. 1 S 2^{27} refers not to the Exodus story but to a particular revelation to the ancestors of the house of Eli. To say that these mighty acts are the centre of revelation in the OT would seem therefore incongruous with actual usage. Dt 29^{29} would seem to mean that the sphere of human obedience is the world open and accessible to man, unlike the hidden world which is reserved to God (cf 30^{11-14}).

7. Apocalyptic literature.—' To reveal mysteries ' is a frequent phrase in Dn 2, and the theme of the chapter is that ' there is a God in heaven who reveals secrets.' The depth of the mystery is apparent because the king cannot tell the dream which is to be interpreted ; but also because the content of the secret, once known, is the scheme of the sequence of the earthly kingdoms which in due time are succeeded by the kingdom of God. The contribution of this class of literature is to heighten the sense of deep mystery which has to be broken through, and on the other hand to discern a movement through a number of historical epochs to a culmination ' in the latter days.' The treatment in Daniel is in some ways related to the Israelite Wisdom conception ; yet it is made clear that Daniel's success is not the result of his own wisdom, 2^{30}. Similarly, in a writing of similar date, God reveals His secrets not to the lofty but to the meek, Sir 3^{19}.

The Book of Enoch uses the phrase ' reveal secrets ' more liberally than Daniel, and in other connexions. There are cosmological secrets of the skies, secrets of invention which the evil angels revealed to men, the name of the Son of Man which is to be revealed. Enoch's commission is to reveal the hidden things for a future generation. But the content of the secrets is less connected with a historical movement than in Daniel, and the atmosphere is more otherworldly and fantastic.

8. General NT usage.—The simple sense ' to uncover ' of a body or the like is not found, and usage is therefore more specialized in a theological direction. Some cases with a fairly general sense ' disclose ' appear, as Mt 10^{26}, ' Nothing is covered that will not be revealed,' cf Lk 12^{2}, both apparently in warnings against the insincerity of enemies and so in the OT tradition of Pr 26^{26} and the like. Mk 4^{22} gives a different setting and slant to the saying, using ' manifest ' rather than ' reveal.' In Lk 2^{34-35} the coming of Jesus will create unrest in Israel and uncover the secret thoughts of many, again a development of the OT tradition, and for the sense cf He 4^{12-13}. Lk 2^{32}, ' a light for revelation to the Gentiles ' may rather be a linking of Is 42^{6} and 49^{6} and mean ' a light for the bringing forth of the nations to the light.'

9. The Father revealed.—The phrases ' God reveals himself ' and ' the revelation of God,' remarkably enough, do not occur, and the passage which comes nearest thereto is Mt 11^{25-27}, Lk 10^{21-22}, where ' no one knows the Father except the Son and any one to whom the Son chooses to reveal him.' Father and Son are known only to each other, but the Son may reveal the Father to whom He wishes. Nothing is said of revealing the Son ; nor do we hear that the Son is the revelation of the Father. The central point is the reciprocity of Father and Son, and within this theme the unique place of the Son, to whom ' all things have been delivered,' as having sovereign authority to reveal the Father. Two verses earlier we hear of the Father hiding ' these things ' from the wise and revealing them to babes. ' These things ' may perhaps be the Divine counsel as in Am 3^{7}, announced by John the Baptist or the seventy disciples, and disclosed to the simple as Sir 3^{19}.

It is appropriate to take along with this Mt 16^{17}, where the content of the revealing is the recognition of Jesus as the Christ. The source of this disclosure is not within humanity but is ' My Father who is in heaven.' That Jesus is the Christ is not evident and unmistakable, especially when He does not declare Himself as such, and is a secret which must be broken through. This only the Father grants. Mt 11^{27} and 16^{17} might reasonably be taken together as complementary. The Son alone reveals the Father. The Father does not reveal the Son, He discloses who Jesus is. The examples here cannot be generalized as cases of ' divine revelation,' since they are significant only within the schema of Father and Son in which they are given.

10. Future revelation.—A much more frequent usage in the NT is to indicate something that is hidden for the present time but will be uncovered in the end-time. In that time the Son of Man will be revealed, Lk 17^{30} (cf ' the coming of the Son of Man,' Mt 24^{37}). The Day of Judgment itself is to be revealed, 1 Co 3^{13} (probable meaning). We speak of ' the revelation of Jesus Christ ' precisely because He is the one whom we now do not see but love and trust, 1 P 1^{7-8}, so 1^{13}. This way of speaking is frequent in 1 Peter, where we have also ' a salvation ready to be revealed in the last time ' (1^{5}).

This usage is found notably in connexion with the revealing of ' glory.' We now share in the sufferings of Christ, but later will share in His glory which is to be revealed, 1 P 4^{13} 5^{1}. Paul also knows of this future glory ; its revelation is ' the revealing of the sons of God ' in their glory, Ro 8^{17-21}. Cf the thought in Col 3^{3-4}, where the term ' manifest ' or ' appear ' is used.

Future revelation is not only of Christ and the glory of His followers, however, but also of the ultimate expression of evil, the ' man of lawlessness ' of 2 Th $2^{3, 6, 8}$. Evil is now at work, but is at least to some extent veiled in secrecy ; but its true nature must be disclosed in order that it may be destroyed. Cf the uncovering of sin by the Divine visitation in the prophets, and the eliciting of the enemies of Israel to their destruction, Ezk 38–39.

11. Mystery and Spirit.—The term ' mystery ' in the sense of a secret Divine purpose embracing the ages and culminating in the establishment of the Divine kingdom is inherited in the NT from Apocalyptic. This mystery was not known to other generations as ' it has now been revealed to his holy apostles and prophets by the Spirit ' (Eph 3^{5}) ; its content here in particular is the place of the Gentiles in the Divine purpose, in 1 Co 2^{6-10} it is the hidden meaning of the death of Christ. The precise reference in Ro 16^{25} is not easy to fix, but probably is the respective places of Jew and Gentile as in Eph 3^{5}. The sense of the word ' mystery ' in the NT seems to go beyond this, but this seems to cover those cases where the word is used with ' reveal ' or ' revelation.' The verb ' make to know ' is more frequent.

The place of the Divine Spirit in uncovering mysteries is also found in Daniel ($4^{8f, 18}$ $5^{11, 14}$). The place of the Spirit in these NT passages just discussed may be understood from the general work of the Spirit as giving a foretaste of future realities still inaccessible to ordinary contact. The full meaning of the Divine plans becomes evident only at the end, but the Spirit reveals or discloses them even now to chosen people.

12. Direct revelation.—What has just been said leads us on to notice how often ' revelation ' in the NT refers to a particular reception by a person at a particular time. When the church assembles, each has a hymn, a lesson, or a revelation (1 Co 14^{26}) ; when one is speaking, revelation may come to another who is sitting (14^{30}). This is a direct personal revelation as it is understood to come to prophets, as it came also to the OT prophets (1 P 1^{12}) ; the book of Revelation is intended as an example of this, and is so entitled (Rev 1^{1}). Such direct revelations are frequently mentioned by Paul. One of them may well coincide with his conversion experience, the ' revelation of Jesus Christ ' (Gal $1^{12, 16}$) ; another seems to be special guidance (Gal 2^{2}). The revealing of the mystery of Gentile participation in the plan of God is also of this kind (Eph 3^{3}) ; other revelations are of the heavenly world (2 Co $12^{1, 7}$). The strong presence of, or possession by, the Spirit is characteristic of this type of revelation (Rev 1^{1}) and they come among the ' spiritual gifts ' of 1 Co 12–14.

13. Righteousness and wrath.—Ro 1^{17-18} speak of the righteousness of God being revealed in the gospel, and go on to say that the wrath of God is revealed from heaven against the ungodliness of man. The first phrase is close to Ps 98^{2} (see above), and the sense in general that the righteousness of God is not something naturally self-evident, and Paul's unashamed attachment to the gospel is because in it this righteousness is disclosed. The revealing of wrath lies somewhat in the

REVELATION, BOOK OF

prophetic tradition of the uncovering of evil at the approach of God, but goes farther in that it suggests not that the evil was hidden but that the Divine reaction of anger was hidden.

14. General and Conclusion.—It can scarcely be doubted that 'reveal' is a very important word of Biblical vocabulary. It is not, however, extremely frequent, and its distribution is uneven (*e.g.* no cases in Mark except in the Freer MS ending, and none in the Johannine literature). And as soon as we go beyond the general sense 'uncover,' which seems to be common to all occurrences, it is doubtful whether we can identify any 'Biblical concept of revelation' with which all cases would fit. In particular, it is doubtful whether the common theological use of 'revelation' for the Divine self-communication is appropriate in the light of the Biblical usage. In usage, 'reveal' has certain quite definite and particular connexions in which it appears, and these are an important part, but not the whole, of the Divine communication with man.

Whether traditional problems such as 'revelation and reason,' 'general revelation' or 'revelation in nature' are to be posed depends therefore on whether we wish our language to be conformed to Biblical usage or not. If we do so wish, we have no reason to suppose that anything like 'reason' or 'nature' was ever thought of in connexion with, or as a contrast to, revelation; and as for 'general revelation,' all the Biblical evidence is for revelation as special and particular, with its own content of communication in each situation. The now common theological use of 'revelation' for divine self-communication in general needs to be criticized wherever it has grown too far away from the Biblical usage. See also INSPIRE, INSPIRATION. J. Ba.

REVELATION, BOOK OF.—This is the only apocalypse in the NT. Like other apocalypses Revelation shows dependence on various other religious writings, borrowing 245 times from the OT, 9 times from the NT, and suggesting inferences in many places from the Apocrypha and the Pseudepigrapha. It is mostly in prose; only 37 of its total 394 verses are in poetry ($4^{8, 11}$ 5^{9f} 7^{15-17} 11^{17f} 13^{10} 15^{3f} 16^{5-7} $18^{2-8, 10, 14, 16, 19-20, 21-24}$ $19^{1-5, 6-8}$). Its language is shrouded with mystery, its ideas are clothed in imagery, symbolism, myth, and numerology. The number 'seven' is used 54 times as applied to such objects as the churches, seals, heads, trumpets, angels, bowls, and plagues. Multiples of 12 and 1000 are used: the names of the faithful are 144,000; the crown has 12 stars; there are 12 gates around the New Jerusalem; the city is 12,000 stadia in length, breadth, and height. The Roman emperor cult is symbolized as a beast with 10 horns and 7 heads; the number of the beast is 666; the time of terrible persecution is to be 42 months, 3½ years, 'time, times, and half a time.' The word 'apocalypse' means 'revelation' or 'uncovering.' Hence as the student interprets the truths hidden amid the mysterious figures the purpose of Revelation is unfolded.

1. Outline of the Book.—With the author's artistic use of the numbers 'seven' and 'ten' the book fits naturally into seven acts and ten scenes, exclusive of the Prologue and the Epilogue:

Prologue 1^{1-8}

Act I First Vision, 1^{9}–3^{22}. *The Son of God in the Earthly Church*
- Scene 1, Setting for John's Initial Vision (1^{9-20})
- Scene 2, Letters to the Seven Churches (2, 3)

Act II Second Vision, 4^{1}–8^{1}. *God's Plan for History*
- Scene 3, John's Vision of the Court of Heaven (4^{1}–5^{14})
- Scene 4, Opening of the Seven Seals (6^{1-17}) [The first parenthesis, Vision of the Redeemed (7^{1-17}); Silence in Heaven (8^{1})]

Act III Third Vision, 8^{2}–11^{19}. *The Church Faces Trouble*
- Scene 5, Blowing of the Seven Trumpets (8^{7}–9^{21}) [The second parenthesis, Vision of the Book (10^{1-11}); Prophecy Regarding Israel's Repentance (11^{1-13}); Voices Speak from Heaven (11^{14-19})]

Act IV Fourth Vision, 12^{1}–14^{20}. *The Battle Won by the Righteous in Heaven is Transferred to Earth*
- Scene 6, The Third Parenthesis: The Oracles about the Last Judgment (12^{1}–14^{20})

Act V Fifth Vision, 15^{1}–16^{21}. *God's Wrath Visits the World*
- Scene 7, Pouring of the Seven Bowls: The Last Plagues (15^{1}–16^{21})

Act VI Sixth Vision, 17^{1}–20^{10}. *Judgment Visits 'Babylon'*
- Scene 8, Vision of the Fall of the Great Harlot (17^{1}–18^{24})
- Scene 9, Vision of the Return of the Victorious Christ (19^{1}–20^{10})

Act VII Seventh Vision, 20^{11}–22^{5}. *God's Purpose is Consummated in the 'New Jerusalem'*
- Scene 10, Vision of the New Jerusalem (20^{11}–22^{5})

Epilogue 22^{6-21}

2. Canonicity.—R. B. Y. Scott views Revelation as written in Hebrew and translated into Greek. C. C. Torrey believes it was written in Aramaic and translated into Greek. Most present-day scholars assume that Revelation was originally composed in Greek, agreeing with Dionysius of Alexandria that the Greek in Revelation is unusual, with no parallel in the NT.

The Revelation was not universally accepted by the early Church as canonical. There is no evidence of its existence worthy of consideration in the writings of the Apostolic Fathers, although it is just possible that Papias may have known of it. By the middle of the 2nd cent., however, Revelation is well known, and is declared by Justin to be by the Apostle John (*Dial.* lxxxi. 15). It is also used, among others, by Melito, Tertullian, Clement of Alexandria, and Origen, and attributed to the Apostle John by the first-named as well as by Irenaeus. The fact that it appears in the Canon of the Muratorian Fragment is evidence that by the middle of the 2nd cent. it was accepted in the West. After its defence by Hippolytus its position was never seriously questioned except in the East. Jerome is, in fact, the only Western theologian of importance who doubts it, and he puts it among those books which are 'under discussion,' neither canonical nor apocryphal.

In the East, as might be expected, it was rejected by Marcion, and, because of disbelief in its Apostolic authorship, by Dionysius of Alexandria (middle of the 3rd cent.). Palestinian and Syrian authors (*e.g.* Cyril of Jerusalem) generally rejected it, in large measure because of the struggle with the Montanists, by whom Revelation was used as a basis of doctrine. It does not appear in the lists of the Synod of Laodicea, the *Apostolic Constitutions*, Gregory of Nazianzus, Chrysostom, the *Chronography* of Nicephorus, the 'List of the Sixty Books,' or in the Peshitta version of the NT. It was included by the Gelasian Decree at the end of the 5th cent. as canonical, and was finally recognized by the Eastern Church. Yet as late as 692 a Synod could publish two decrees, the one including the Apocalypse in the Canon, the other excluding it. It was not held in high repute by the Reformers Carlstadt, Luther, Zwingli, all of whom doubted its apostolicity. Luther placed Revelation along with Jude, James, and Hebrews in an Appendix.

3. Integrity.—In our earliest NT manuscripts the entire Book of Revelation is found in Codex Sinaiticus and Codex Alexandrinus. Codex Ephraemi has the following lacunae: 3^{19}–5^{14} 7^{14-17} 10^{10}–11^{3} 16^{13}–18^{2} 19^{5}–22^{21}. Several views, however, have been suggested regarding the composition of the book.

(1) One view is that the work, while essentially a literary unit, is *a Christian redaction of a Jewish writing.* This view would attribute to the Christian redactor the first three chapters and important sections like 5^{9-14}

7^{9-17} 13^{11ff} 22^{6-21}, in addition to separate verses like 12^{11} $14^{1,5}$ $12^{13,15}$ 16^{15} 17^{14} $19^{9,10,13b}$ 20^{4-6} 21^{5b-8}. The difficulties with this position are not only those which must be urged against any view that overlooks the evidences of the composite authorship of the work, but also the impossibility of showing that ch. 11 is Jewish in character.

(2) *Theories of composite origin.*—These are of various forms—(*a*) The theory according to which an original work has been interpolated with apocalyptic material of various dates ($7^{1-8,9-17}$ 11^{1-13} $12^{1-11,12-17}$ 13^{17}) and subjected to several revisions. (*b*) The view that Revelation is a Christian book in which Jewish apocalypses have been framed. (*c*) The theory according to which Revelation is composed of three sources, each of which has subdivisions, all worked together by a Christian redactor. (*d*) Notwithstanding the difficulty in determining the sources, critics are fairly well agreed that, as the book now stands, it has a unity which, though not inconsistent with the use of older material by its author, is none the less easily recognized. Some of this older material, it is now held, undoubtedly represents the general stream of apocalyptic that took its rise in Babylonian mythology. The structural unity of the book appears in the repetition of sevenfold groups of episodes, as well as in a general grammatical and linguistic similarity. In achieving this remarkable result, the redactor so combined, recast, and supplemented his material as to give the book an essentially Christian rather than Jewish character.

(3) While Revelation borrows from the OT, the book as a whole in its literary development seems to have unity. The consistency of the texts found in codices Sinaiticus, Ephraemi, and Alexandrinus points to the fact that interpolations or deletions from the original text were slight and negligible.

4. Date.—Various dates have been assumed for the writing of Revelation: (1) in the latter part of Nero's reign (A.D. 54–68); (2) during the days immediately preceding the fall of Jerusalem in A.D. 70; (3) during the reign of Vespasian (A.D. 69–79), after the fall of Jerusalem; (4) in the latter part of Domitian's reign (A.D. 81–96), about A.D. 95. Irenaeus, Clement of Alexandria, and Pliny support the date A.D. 95. The myth of Nero's suicide and resuscitation and the expectation of his return with his soldiers from Parthia also fit smoothly into the latter part of Domitian's reign.

5. Authorship.—Dionysius of Alexandria said that John Mark was possibly the author. Eusebius described him as John the Elder. Irenaeus designated John the disciple of the Lord as its author. Justin Martyr viewed the work as written by John the Apostle. While we are not certain as to which John wrote the book, we note certain characteristics about him: (1) he was possibly a Jew well versed in the Scriptures; (2) he had perhaps learned Greek rather late in life, as is evidenced by his often awkward Greek style; (3) he was a church leader, well known to the seven churches of the Province of Asia; (4) he was a deeply religious man, with great faith in the ultimate victory of the Christian religion over the demonic forces of the world; (5) he was not an eyewitness of Jesus, for he never refers to personal reminiscences of Jesus' life, and never indicates himself as an apostle or disciple; he refers to himself as a servant (1^{1}) and a brother (1^{9}); (6) he was a literary genius, his skilled artistry giving us one of the most important and beautiful of the apocalypses.

6. Interpretation.—Revelation was written from Patmos, a small, rocky, sparsely populated island in the Aegean Sea, fifteen miles SW. of Ephesus; today it is known as Patino. It was originally addressed to the seven churches of Asia, to encourage them to be faithful during the impending persecution under Domitian and thus prepare themselves for the great reversal on the Day of Judgment and for citizenship in the New Jerusalem. But it has been interpreted in a variety of ways: (1) Some view it as a book to be ignored, with no value or significance for a scientific age. (2) Others hold to the *futurist* interpretation, believing that it accurately foretells what will happen in the last days of history before the end of the world. (3) The *preterist* interpretation sees many of its predictions already fulfilled in the fall of Jerusalem in A.D. 70 and the downfall of the Roman Empire in 476. (4) The *continuous-historical* view, for which Revelation depicts important historical events in the time of various Popes, Martin Luther, Napoleon, Kaiser Wilhelm, Mussolini, Hitler and others. However, since the Church has already passed through these events, this interpretation is not highly esteemed today by many people. (5) The *timeless-symbolic* interpretation, which holds that the author had no specific historical situation in mind, but sets forth a philosophy of history wherein Christian forces are continuously meeting and conquering the demonic forces of evil. Its symbols describe this everpresent conflict. (6) The *demythologizing* approach sees the religious ideas in Revelation clothed in myth—such as the Roman emperor cult, symbolized as a beast with ten horns and seven heads. We must now 'demythologize' the book and try to find the underlying truths which lie beneath the mythological symbols. (7) Incorporating much of the demythologizing interpretation of Revelation is the *religious-historical* method. It asks the reader first to study Revelation in the light of events in Domitian's time, when the return of Nero was expected, and to learn what the book had to say as an encouragement to the faithful Christians of that time. Then the reader must come back to the present day, and partly by demythologizing the symbols of the book and partly by unravelling its initial religious truths, ask what religious teaching it contains for the contemporary world. As the reader discovers the message which encouraged Christians to be faithful to God and Christ, when the forces of evil tried to dominate the world, its present religious value becomes clear. It assures us that God, through the fidelity of Christians, will overcome the demonic forces in the world, and that God will reward His martyrs and faithful followers at the end of this age with citizenship in the New Jerusalem.

The first beast with ten horns and seven heads (13^{1-10}) symbolizes the ten Roman emperors from Tiberius (A.D. 14–37) to Domitian (A.D. 81–96); the second beast (13^{11-17}) symbolizes the priesthood of the Roman emperor cult who, with the aid of Roman soldiers, are forcing the Christians to worship the emperor as a deity. The 'number of the beast,' 666 (13^{18}), probably refers to Nero, who was rumoured to have been revived after his suicide in A.D. 68, hurried to Parthia, and from there with ten Parthian satraps was expected soon to return to the Roman Empire—though later it was thought he would be released from Sheol where he was imprisoned until the final battle at Armageddon against Christ and His faithful followers. The *Nero redivivus* myth—'the beast that you saw was, and is not, and is to ascend from the bottomless pit and go to perdition' (17^{8})—fits best into the period of Domitian's reign. It was amid the threatening circumstances of Domitian's time that the Book of Revelation encouraged its readers to be faithful to God and to Christ, rather than yield to pressure and worship Domitian as 'Lord and God.' Such a book, through the long centuries and still today, has continued to encourage faith and loyalty despite the demonic forces which have repeatedly threatened to dominate the world.

S. M.—T. S. K.

REVENGE.—See Avenger of Blood, Kin (Next of).

REVERENCE.—See Fear.

REVISED STANDARD VERSION.—See English Versions, **37**.

REVISED VERSION.—See English Versions, **35**.

REVIVE.—In 1 K 17^{22}, 2 K 13^{21}, Neh 4^{2}, Ro 14^{9} (RV, RSV 'live again'), 'to revive' is literally 'to come to life again,' as in Shakespeare, 1 *Henry VI*, I. i. 18—'Henry is dead, and never shall revive.' We thus see the force of Ro 7^{9}, 'When the commandment came, sin revived, and I died.'

REWARD.—In the Bible God is conceived of as inflexibly just, and so as punishing the evil and rewarding the good (Is 62^{11}, Pr 1^{31} 24^{12}, Ob ^{15}, Mt 16^{27}, Eph 6^{8}, 2 Ti 4^{14}, He 2^{2f} ; cf Rev 18^{6}). He punishes the sin of Adam and Eve (Gn 3$^{16-19}$), of the generation of Noah (Gn 6$^{5-7}$), of the people of Sodom (Gn 18^{20f}), of those who violate His Covenant (Ezk 17^{19}), of Israel (2 K 17^{23} and often), and of foreign nations (Am 1^{3}–2^{3}, Is 10^{12}). His **punishment** is conceived for the nation in terms of defeat at the hands of enemies or of natural disasters (Dt 28$^{15-68}$), or for the individual in terms of death (Ezk 18^{4}, Ro 6^{23}) or misfortune (2 Ch 26^{20}, Jer 11^{11} 28^{16}). Nevertheless, God's justice is often tempered with mercy, and while He never exceeds desert in punishment, He may spare the sinner all he deserves (Ps 103^{10}). To those who keep His Covenant He gives reward (Ps 19^{11}, Am 5^{4}), usually conceived in the OT in terms of material blessing (Dt 28$^{1-14}$). In Dn 7 those who suffer through their loyalty to Him are promised the reward of authority and power (cf Mt 19^{28}, 2 Ti 2^{12}). There are, however, passages in the OT which penetrate to a deeper understanding. In Ps 73 the psalmist envies the prosperity of the wicked, and then comforts himself with the thought that their prosperity is fleeting, but finally realizes that since he has God he has the true reward which he would not change for their prosperity. Similarly Job ceases to cry out against God when he finds in his very suffering an experience of God that surpasses all he had known before as sight surpasses hearsay (Job 42^{5f} ; cf 2 Co 12^{9}). In the NT the reward is commonly looked for in the future (Mt 25$^{34-40}$, Lk 14^{14}, 2 Ti 4^{8}, Rev 7$^{14-17}$), where it is conceived in terms of bliss in the presence and service of God rather than in self-indulgence and sensuous enjoyment. The punishment of the evil is to be evil, and the reward of the holy is to be holy (Rev 22^{11}).

H. H. R.

REZEPH.—A city mentioned in the message of the Rabshakeh of Sennacherib to Hezekiah, 2 K 19^{12}, Is 37^{12}. It is the *Raṣappa* or *Raṣapi* of the Assyrian inscriptions, the modern *Ruṣâfeh*, between Palmyra and the Euphrates. This district belonged for several centuries to the Assyrians, and many of the tablets show it to have been an important trade-centre. Between 839 and 737 B.C. the prefects who had authority in the place were, to all appearance, Assyrians, only one, of unknown but apparently late date, having a name which may be West Semitic, namely Abda', possibly a form of Abda or Obadiah.

T. G. P.

REZIA, 1 Ch 7^{39} (AV).—See RIZIA.

REZIN.—From the ancient versions and the cuneiform inscriptions it is clear that the form should be *Razon* or *Razin*.

1. The last king of Damascus. Towards the close of the 8th cent. B.C. Damascus and Israel were under the suzerainty of Assyria. Tiglath-pileser III. enumerates the articles paid him in tribute by *Raṣunnu* of Damascus and Menahem of Israel (738 B.C.). **Pekah**, one of Menahem's successors, joined Rezin in the attempt to throw off the yoke. Failing to secure the co-operation of Ahaz, they turned their arms against Judah (734 B.C.). (2 K 16^{6} mentions, among the incidents of the campaign, that ' Rezin, the King of Aram, recovered Elath for Aram, and drove the men of Judah from Elath.' This statement originated in a scribal error, the *r* of *Aram* having been substituted for the *d* of *Edom*, with which it is almost identical, and Rezin's name having been added later [cf 2 Ch 28^{17}]. RSV corrects the error and renders ' the King of Edom recovered Elath for Edom '). The two allies besieged Jerusalem, greatly to the alarm of the populace, and Isaiah strove in vain to allay the terror (Is 7–9). Ahaz implored aid from Tiglath-pileser, to whom he became tributary (2 K 16^{8}). On the approach of the Assyrians, Pekah was murdered by his own subjects. Damascus sustained a siege of more than a year's duration, but was eventually taken (732 B.C.) ; Rezin was slain (2 K 16^{9}), and his kingdom became subject to Assyria (cf *ANET*, p. 283).

It is not known who **' the son of Tabeel '** (Is 7^{6}) was. Winckler proposed to identify him with Rezin (*Alttest. Untersuchungen*, pp. 74 f), but this is most improbable. Tabeel seems rather to be a place name (cf Albright, *BASOR* 140, December 1955, pp. 34 f). The ' son of Tabeel ' would then be a Tabeelite whom the confederates purposed to seat on the throne of Judah.

2. The ' sons of Rezin ' are mentioned as a family of Nethinim (q.v.) in Ezr 2^{48}, Neh 7^{50}, 1 Es 5^{31} (AV, RV **Daisan**—another confusion of *r* and *d*). They may have been of foreign descent.

J. T.—H. H. R.

REZON.—According to 1 K 11$^{23-25}$, Rezon, son of Eliada, was one of the military officers of that Hadadezer, king of the little realm of Zobah (cuneiform, *Subiti*), S. of Damascus and not far from the Sea of Tiberias, whom David overthrew, 2 S 8^{2ff}. For some unknown reason he deserted Hadadezer, gathered a band of freebooters, seized Damascus, and founded there the dynasty which created the most powerful of the Syrian kingdoms. He was a thorn in Solomon's side, and his successors were bitter adversaries of Israel. The text seems to be in some disorder. The LXX omits vv.$^{23-25a}$ and for v.^{25b} reads ' This is the evil which Hadad did ; and he abhorred Israel, and reigned over Edom,' and this is probably correct. The story appears, with some variations, in the LXX after v.^{14a}, where it is quite out of place. There is no reason to doubt that it is ancient and authentic. The suggestion that Rezon should be identified with **Hezion** (q.v.) of 1 K 15^{18} is accepted by many.

J. T.—H. H. R.

RHEGIUM (now *Reggio*) was an old Greek colony near the SW. extremity of Italy, and close to the point from which there is the shortest passage to Sicily. Messana (modern Messina) on the opposite side is but six miles distant from Rhegium. The whirlpool of Charybdis and the rock of Scylla are in this neighbourhood, and were a terror to the ancient navigators with their small vessels. Rhegium was in consequence a harbour of importance, where favourable winds were awaited. The situation of the city exposed it to changes of government. In the 3rd cent. B.C. Rome entered into a special treaty with it. Soon after 90 B.C. it acquired municipal status. In NT times the population was mixed Graeco-Latin. Greek was spoken here throughout imperial times. St. Paul's ship waited here one day for a favourable S. wind to take her to Puteoli. Ac 28^{13} describes how the ship had to tack (' make a circuit ') to get from Syracuse to Rhegium, owing to the changing winds.

A. So.—F. C. G.

RHEIMS VERSION.—See ENGLISH VERSIONS, **29.**

RHESA.—A son of Zerubbabel (Lk 3^{27}).

RHODA.—The name of the maid-servant in the house of Mary, John Mark's mother, when St. Peter came there on his release from prison by the angel (Ac 12^{13}).

A. J. M.

RHODES was one of the most important and successful cities in ancient Greece, at the NE. corner of the island of the same name, which is 43 miles long and 20 miles wide at its widest. In 408 B.C., during the war with Athens, it became the federal capital of the island by the union of three Dorian city-states, Ialysus, Lindus, and Camirus. The situation was admirable, and the people were able to take advantage of it and to build up a splendid position in the world of commerce. It reached the summit of its prosperity in the 2nd cent. B.C., after the settlement with Rome in 189 made it mistress of great part of Caria and Lycia. Its fleet was one of the most famous in the ancient world, and its maritime law had wide influence. Rome's trade interests were seriously threatened by this powerful rival, and in 166 B.C. Rome declared the Carian and Lycian cities independent, and made Delos a free port. Its conspicuous loyalty to Rome during the first Mithridatic War was rewarded by the recovery of part of its former Carian possessions. It took the side of Caesar in the civil war, although most of the East supported Pompey, and suffered successive misfortunes, which reduced it to a common provincial town, though it remained a free city in Paul's time, and retained its fine harbours, walls, streets, and stores. Paul touched here on his way from Troas to Caesarea (Ac 21^{1}), as it was a regular port of call on that route. Rhodes is mentioned in 1 Mac 15^{23} as one of the free States to which the Romans sent letters in favour of the Jews. Ezk 27^{15}, according to the LXX, reads 'sons of the Rhodians': this is probably correct (so RSV; AV, RV **Dedan**); cf Gn 10^{4} (LXX) and 1 Ch 1^{7} (LXX) where the Hebrew is Dodanim and Rodanim. The famous *Colossus* was a statue of the sun-god at the harbour entrance, 150 feet high. It stood only from 280 to 224 B.C. The Temple Chronicle of Lindus is important for the history of Hellenistic religion.

A. So.—**F. C. G.**

RHODOCUS.—A Jewish traitor (2 Mac 13^{21}).

RIBAI.—The father of Ittai or Ithai, 2 S 23^{29}, 1 Ch 11^{31}.

RIBBAND.—Found only in AV in Nu 15^{38} in the expression 'ribband (RV, RSV 'cord') of blue.' In the same expression it is rendered 'lace' in Ex $28^{28,\,37}$ $39^{21,\,31}$ in AV, RV and RSV.

RIBLAH.—**1.** An important town (modern *Ribleh*) and military station on the eastern bank of the Orontes, 50 miles S. of Hamath. It is mentioned in the Bible only in the literature of the Chaldaean period, and was apparently the headquarters of Nebuchadrezzar the Great for his South-Syrian and Palestinian dominions. From this position the Phoenician cities of the coast were within easy command, as also were Coele-Syria and the kingdom of Damascus, along with the land-routes leading farther S. Here judgment was pronounced upon Zedekiah and his officers (2 K $25^{6,\,20f}$, Jer 39^{5f} 52^{9ff}).

The statement of 2 K 23^{33}, that Pharaoh Neco put Jehoahaz in bonds at Riblah in the land of Hamath, is to be corrected by the parallel passage 2 Ch 36^{2}, where the transaction is said to have taken place in Jerusalem itself. The true reading is, 'and Pharaoh Neco removed him from reigning in Jerusalem' (cf also the LXX). It was the later action of Nebuchadrezzar with regard to Zedekiah, above referred to, that suggested the change in the text. The phrase 'in the land of Hamath' (2 K 25^{21}) is to be compared with the 'nineteen districts of Hamath' enumerated in the Annals of Tiglath-pileser III.

Riblah should be read for **Diblah** (RV, AV Diblath) in Ezk 6^{14} (so RSV). See **2.**

2. Riblah (with the article) is, if the reading is correct, mentioned as one of the eastern boundary marks of Israel in Nu 34^{11}. The place intended was not far NE. of the Sea of Galilee, but the exact site is unknown.

It was, of course, not the Riblah on the Orontes. It is remarkable, however, that this Riblah is mentioned in connexion with the 'approach to Hamath' (v.^{8}), which, as Winckler has shown, was on the SW. of Mount Hermon, and the centre of the kingdom of Hamath of the time of David. Cf Ezk 6^{14} as above corrected.

J. F. McC.—**J. Gr.**

RICHES.—See WEALTH.

RIDDLE.—The Hebrew *ḥîdhāh* means a perplexing or obscure observation, and it includes what we mean by 'riddle.' It is rendered 'riddle' in AV only in Jg 14^{12ff}, Ezk 17^{2}. Elsewhere it is rendered '**dark saying**' (Ps 49^{4} 78^{2}, Pr 1^{6}), 'dark speech' (Nu 12^{8}), 'dark sentence' (Dn 8^{23}), or 'hard question' (1 K 10^{1}, 2 Ch 9^{1}). RV agrees in all cases, but has 'riddle' in margin in Pr 1^{6}. RSV has 'dark saying' in Ps 78^{2}, 'dark speech' in Nu 12^{8}, and 'hard question' in 1 K 10^{1}, 2 Ch 9^{1}, but 'riddle' in all the other passages. In Hab 2^{6}, for *m^{e}lîṣāh ḥîdhôth* AV and RV have 'taunting proverb' (with RVm 'taunting riddle'), and RSV 'scoffing derision.' The word is commonly rendered in LXX *ainigma.* This word is found in Wis 8^{8} (AV 'dark sentences,' RV 'dark sayings,' RSV 'riddles'), Sir 39^{3} (AV 'dark [parables],' RV 'dark sayings [of parables],' RSV 'obscurities [of parables]') 47^{15} (AV and RV 'dark [parables],' RVm '[parables of] riddles,' RSV '[parables and] riddles'). In NT *ainigma* is used once, in 1 Co 13^{12} (AV and RV 'darkly,' AVm and RVm 'in a riddle,' RSV 'dimly'). See also PARABLE (IN OT).

RIE (the AV spelling of '**rye**') occurs twice (Ex 9^{32}, Is 28^{25}) in AV as rendering of *kussemeth,* which in Ezk 4^{9} is rendered 'fitches.' In all three passages RV and RSV have '**spelt.**' Whatever *kussemeth* was, it was neither true rye, which is a cereal unknown in Palestine, nor spelt. See FITCHES.

RIGHTEOUSNESS.—I. IN OT.—'Righteousness,' 'righteous' (except in a few passages) stand in EV for some offshoot of the Semitic root *ṣdḳ* which, in Arabic, originally appears to have meant either 'straightness' (Nöldeke, Delitzsch) or 'hardness' (Skinner). The former is probably the sounder. The Hebrew words are the adjective *ṣaddîḳ,* and the nouns *ṣedheḳ* and *ṣ^{e}dhāḳāh* (indistinguishable in meaning) and the verbal forms *ṣādhaḳ, hiṣdîḳ,* etc. This group of words is represented in EV in about 400 passages by 'righteousness,' 'righteous' and the like: in the remainder, about one-fifth of the whole, by 'just,' 'justice,' 'right,' 'salvation.' RSV has made more use of such a rendering as 'innocent,' particularly in forensic contexts.

The material can conveniently be arranged under two heads: (1) 'righteousness' in common speech; (2) 'righteousness' in religious terminology. It has been held that the development of the idea of righteousness in OT moves in the opposite direction to that traversed by the idea of holiness, *i.e.* from man to God rather than from the Divine to the human, and there is some truth in this.

1. 'Righteousness' in common speech.—(*a*) It is perhaps safest to begin with the forensic or juristic application. The plaintiff or defendant in a legal case who was in the right was 'righteous' (RSV 'innocent,' Dt 25^{1}, Is 5^{23}), and his claim resting on his good behaviour was 'righteousness' (1 Kg 8^{32}). A judge who decided in favour of such a person gave 'righteous judgment,' literally 'judgment of righteousness' (Dt 16^{18}), judged 'righteously' (Dt 1^{16}). The Messianic King was to be the ideal judge, and this meant he would be 'swift to do righteousness' (Is 16^{5}) and 'with righteousness he shall judge the poor' (11^{4}), and 'righteousness shall be the girdle of his waist' (v.^{5}). A court of justice was, in theory, 'the place of righteousness' (Ec 1^{16}). The purified Jerusalem would be 'a city of righteousness' (Is 1^{26}). On the other hand, corrupt judges 'cast down righteousness to the earth' (Am 5^{7}), and 'deprive the innocent of his right' (Is 5^{23}: RV 'take away the righteousness of the righteous from him'). (*b*) From the forensic use is readily developed the general meaning 'what is right,' 'what ought to be,' though some scholars reverse this order and think that the idea of 'rightness' comes first. Indeed, it is probably better to take the earlier idea to be 'in the right,' 'conforming to the norm,' 'conforming to the standard.' Balances, weights, and measures which came up to the required standard were 'just balances,' etc., literally 'balances of righteousness' (Lv 19^{36}), whilst their converse were 'wicked scales' and 'deceitful weights' (Mic 6^{11}) or 'false balances' (Am 8^{5}). (*c*) Righteous speech also, *i.e.* truthful speech, came under the category of 'righteousness.' 'Righteous lips,' literally 'lips of righteousness,' 'are the delight of a king' (Pr 16^{13}).

2. Righteousness in religious terminology.—(*a*) For the ancient Hebrew, 'righteousness' was especially *correspondence with the Divine will.* This is why it is better to think of the original idea as 'in the right,' 'conforming to the norm,' especially when we remember that the thought of God was perhaps never wholly absent from the mind of the Hebrew when he used the word. Note, for this conception of righteousness, Ezk 18^{5-9}, where doing 'what is lawful and right (*ṣ^{e}dhāḳāh*)' is illustrated by a number of concrete examples followed up by the general statement, 'walks in my statutes, and is careful to observe my ordinances —he is righteous.' The Book of Ezekiel has many references to righteousness thus understood. (*b*) As the Divine will was revealed in the Law, 'righteousness' was thought of as *obedience to its rules* (Dt 6^{25}). Restoration of a pledge at sun-down was 'righteousness'

(Dt 24^{13}). The avenging deed of Phinehas was ‘reckoned to him as righteousness’ (Ps 106^{31}). And so ‘the Lord is righteous, he loves righteous deeds’ (Ps 11^{7}: literally ‘righteousness’). (*c*) In most of the passages quoted, and in many places in Ezekiel, Job, Proverbs, and Ecclesiastes, the righteousness of the individual is referred to; but in others Israel (Ps 14^{5} 97^{11} 118^{20} etc., Is 41$^{8-11}$ and other parts of Deutero-Isaiah, Hab 1^{13} etc.), or a portion of Israel (Is 51$^{1, 7}$ etc.) is represented as ‘righteous.’ (*d*) Since righteousness is conformity to the Divine will, and since Israel was often unrighteous, the righteousness of God would then be revealed only in judgment (Is 1^{37} 5^{16} 10^{32}), and in nationalistic contexts it was revealed in judgment on their heathen oppressors (Ps 40^{9f} 98^{2} etc.). (*e*) On the other hand, beginning with Amos, a fundamental element in the ethical teaching of the prophets is a special consideration for the poor and the unprivileged. This is because if righteousness and justice are to be established there must be most said in cases where they do not exist. God’s righteousness is therefore particularly concerned with the poor and those who have no helper. Thus *ṣᵉdhāḳāh* tends to pass over from being a barely ethical word into the vocabulary of salvation. *Ṣᵉdhāḳāh* stands primarily for the establishment of God’s will on earth. It becomes a wider term than justice. God has a particular regard for the helpless. Thus, already in OT, there is ‘a righteousness which is better than that of the scribes’ (Dalman). In the Targums and the Talmud, the Hebrew *ṣᵉdhāḳāh* and the corresponding Aramaic *ṣidhḳāh* most frequently mean ‘almsgiving’ and ‘benevolence,’ so that in modern Hebrew a benevolent deed is a *ṣᵉdhāḳāh*. This development of *ṣᵉdhāḳāh* to suggest mercy, benevolence, leads to the fact that in a number of passages, especially in Is 40–66, ‘righteousness’ is practically synonymous with ‘salvation’ (Is 45^{8} 46^{13} 51^{5f} 58^{8} 59^{9} 61^{11} 62^{1}; many passages in Psalms [22^{32} 24^{5} etc.], Mal 4^{2} [Heb 3^{20}]). In addition we have such a passage as Ex 9^{27}, where Pharaoh says, ‘The Lord is in the right (*ṣaddiḳ*),’ meaning ‘victorious’; this passage, combined with the idea of ‘salvation,’ gives the translation ‘whom victory (*ṣedheḳ*) meets at every step’ (Is 41^{2}). For more on this subject cf Justification.

II. In NT.—The Greek equivalents of *ṣaddiḳ*, *ṣedheḳ*, etc., are *dikaios* (81 times), ‘righteous,’ ‘just’; *dikaiōs* (5), ‘justly,’ ‘righteously’; *dikaiosynē* (92), ‘righteousness’; *dikaioō* (39), ‘justify’; *dikaiōma* (10), etc.

In the teaching of Jesus (Mt 5$^{6, 10, 20}$ 6$^{1, 33}$ 21^{32}, Jn 16$^{8, 10}$), and in NT generally, ‘righteousness’ means, as in OT, conformity to the Divine will, but with the thought greatly deepened and widened. In Mt 6^{1} the Textus Receptus has *eleēmosynē* (pity, almsgiving, charity), and the alternative reading is *dikaiosynē* (‘righteousness,’ RSV ‘piety’), a plain case of the benevolent meaning of the Hebrew *ṣᵉdhāḳāh*. For a fuller treatment, cf Justification, since the Greek words are usually translated ‘justification,’ ‘justify.’

W. T. S.—N. H. S.

RIMMON (god).—‘The Thunderer,’ cf Akkadian *ramânu*, ‘to roar.’ The deity whom Naaman the Syrian and the King of Damascus worshipped in his temple, probably at Damascus (2 K 5^{18}). The god was known to the Assyrians as *Ramanu*, a title of **Hadad** (q.v.), the god of storm, rain, and thunder, called in Syria Baʿal, *i.e.* ‘the lord.’ The identity of Rimmon with Hadad and his significance in the religion of the Aramaeans of Damascus is confirmed by the fact that Hadad occurs as an element in the theophoric name Benhadad, borne by several kings of Aram, and Tabrimmon, the father of Benhadad, the contemporary of Asa of Judah (1 K 15^{18}). (On the particular features of this god and his cult in Palestine as Hadadrimmon, see Hadad.)

J. Gr.

RIMMON.—**1.** A Beerothite, 2 S 4$^{2, 5, 9}$. **2.** The rock whither the remnants of the Benjamites fled, Jg 20$^{45, 47}$ 21^{13}. It has been identified with a lofty rock or conical chalky hill, visible in all directions, on the summit of which stands the village of *Rammûn* about 3 miles E. of Bethel. **3.** A city in the south of Judah, towards the border of Edom, Jos 15^{32}; in 19^{7} (AV **Remmon**; RSV **En-rimmon**), 1 Ch 4^{32} counted to Simeon. In all these three passages Rimmon is preceded by ‘Ain,’ which should probably be combined with it to yield **En-rimmon** (q.v.). In Zec 14^{10} Rimmon is named as lying S. of Jerusalem. **4.** A city of Zebulun, Jos 19^{13} (AV **Remmon-methoar**); called **Dimnah** (probably a copyist’s error for *Rimmonah*) in Jos 21^{35}, and **Rimmono** in 1 Ch 6^{77} (AV **Rimmon**); modern *Rummâneh*.

RIMMONO.—See Rimmon, **4.**

RIMMON-PAREZ, Nu 33^{19f} (AV).—See Rimmon-Perez.

RIMMON-PEREZ.—A stopping-place on the wanderings, Nu 33^{19f} (AV **Rimmon-parez**). It is possibly modern *Naqb el-Biyâr*, W. of *ʿAqaba*.

RING.—See Ornaments, **2**, **4**. In Ca 5^{14} for AV and RV ‘ring’ we should read ‘**cylinder,**’ with RVm. The comparison is either with the fingers of the hand, or with the arm, as RSV ‘His arms are rounded gold.’

RINGSTRAKED.—See Colours, **6**.

RINNAH.—A Judahite, 1 Ch 4^{20}.

RIPHATH.—One of the sons of Gomer, Gn 10^{3}; called **Diphath** in 1 Ch 1^{6} (RV, RSV; AV **Riphath**).

RISSAH.—A stopping-place on the wanderings, Nu 33^{21f}. It is possibly modern, *Kuntilet el-Jerâfi*.

RITHMAH.—A stopping-place on the wanderings, Nu 33^{18f}. The site is unknown.

RIVER.—For the meaning and use of *ʾāphîḳ*, *yᵉʾōr*, and *naḥal*, sometimes rendered ‘river,’ see Brook. *Yûbhal* (Jer 17^{8}), *ʾûbhal* (Dn 8$^{2f, 6}$), are from the root *yābhal*, ‘to flow.’ *Pelegh*, ‘division,’ signifies an artificial water-channel, used for irrigation (Ps 1^{3} etc.). It is used poetically of the stream bringing the rain from the great storehouse on high (Ps 65^{9}). *Tᵉʿālāh* (Ezk 31^{4}) is properly a ‘channel’ or ‘conduit’ (so 2 K 18^{17} 20^{20}, Is 7^{3} 36^{2}, also Job 38^{25} RV). The usual word for river in OT is *nāhār* (Job 40^{23}, Ps 46^{4} etc.). It is often used of rivers that are named: *e.g.* the rivers of Eden (Gn 2^{10} etc.), the Euphrates (Gn 15^{18} etc.), the rivers of Damascus (2 K 5^{12}). The Euphrates is called ‘**the river**’ (RSV ‘the Euphrates,’ Gn 31^{21} etc.), and ‘**the great river**’ (Gn 15^{18}, Dt 1^{7}), a title given also to the Tigris (Dn 10^{4}). *Aram-naharaim* (Ps 60 [title], also Heb. Gn 24^{10}, Dt 23^{4}), ‘Aram of the two rivers,’ is Mesopotamia. The word appears to have been used like the Arabian *nahr*, only of perennial streams. It is applied, indeed, to the Chebar (Ezk 1^{1}) and the Ahava (Ezr 8^{21}), while in Ps 137^{1}, Nah 2^{6}, Ex 7^{19} 8^{5}, canals seem to be intended. The NT word is *potamos* (Mk 1^{5} etc.).

In the figurative language of Scripture the rising of a river in flood signifies the furious advance of invading armies (Jer 46^{7f} 47^{2}, Is 8^{7}). The trials of affliction are like the passage of dangerous fords (Is 43^{2}). The river is significant of abundance (Job 29^{6} etc.), and of the favour of God (Ps 46^{4}). To the obedient, peace is exhaustless as a river (Is 48^{18}; cf 30^{28}). Prevailing righteousness becomes resistless as an overflowing stream (Am 5^{24}). And in several at least semi-eschatological passages the ideal Jerusalem is pictured as the source of a life-giving river, or rivers, which will flow down to fertilize barren places (Ps 46^{4}, Is 33^{21}, Ezk 47^{1}, Jl 3^{18}, Zec 14^{8}, Rev 22^{1}).

Palestine is not rich in rivers in our sense of the term. The Jordan is perhaps the only stream to which we should apply the name. Apart from the larger streams, the *wādy* of the mountain is sometimes the *nahr* of the plain before it reaches the sea, if in the lower reaches it is perennial. The location and modern names of the 17 or so main ‘rivers’ may be found on any good physical map of Palestine.

The rivers may be crossed today, as in ancient times, by **fords**. When the rivers are in flood, tragedies at the fords are not infrequent. Possibly this gave rise to the old belief in an antagonistic river-deity, which seems to lie behind the story of Jacob's wrestling-match at Penuel (Gn 32^{22ff}). The rivers that open into the Mediterranean have their main fords at the mouth. The sand washed up by the waves forms a broad bank, over which the water of the stream spreads, making a wide shallow.

W. E.—**D. R. Ap.-T.**

RIVER OF EGYPT.—See EGYPT (RIVER OF).

RIZIA.—An Asherite, 1 Ch 7^{39} (AV **Rezia**).

RIZPAH.—Daughter of Aiah, concubine of Saul, seized by the ambitious Abner after he had placed Ishbosheth (Ishbaal) on the throne. When accused by the king, Abner, who was the real ruler of Israel, promptly proffered the Northern Kingdom to David, 2 S 3^7. A three years' famine was divined to be due to the displeasure of Yahweh at the slaughter of the Gibeonites by Saul. When David inquired what expiation he should make, the Gibeonites refused money compensation, but demanded descendants of Saul to expose before Yahweh. The king gave them two of Rizpah's, and three of Michal's (RSV Merab's) sons, who were slain and exposed on Mount Gibeah, 2 S 21^{1-14}. Rizpah spread sackcloth on the rock—a sign that the land repented—and watched the dead till the anger of Yahweh relented, and the rain came. Her vigil ended, she was at liberty to perform the rite of burial.

J. H. St.

ROADS AND TRAVEL.—In RSV 'road' is frequently the rendering of Hebrew *derekh*, for which AV and RV normally have 'way.' 'Highway' renders Hebrew *m^esillāh*, which means a raised road or embankment (from *sālal*='cast up'). For the chief trade routes through Palestine, see TRADE AND COMMERCE, **7.** '**Byways**' in Jg 5^6 should rather be 'roundabout ways.' In Jer 18^{15} '**bypaths**' (RV, RSV) are opposed to the old tracks.

ROBBERS OF CHURCHES.—See CHURCHES [ROBBERS OF].

ROBE.—See DRESS.

ROBOAM, Mt 1^7 (AV) = **Rehoboam** (q.v.).

ROCK represents various Hebrew words, which, generally speaking, have the same ideas as the English—strength, security, height, etc. (cf Stanley, *SP*, Appendix). The rocks named in OT are Oreb (Jg 7^{25}, Is 10^{26}), Etam (Jg 15^8), Rimmon (20^{45} 21^{13}), the crags Bozez and Seneh (1 S 14^4), Sela-hammahlekoth (23^{28} AV, RV; RSV 'Rock of Escape'). In 2 K 14^7, Is 16^1 42^{11} 'the Rock' (RV and RSV '**Sela**') is a proper name, Sela or Petra, the rock-city *par excellence*; in Jg 1^{36} (RVm and RSV 'Sela') the identification is doubtful. Rocks were the haunt of the eagle (Job 39^{28}), of the wild goat (v.^{1}), or the coney (Pr 30^{26}); cf Ps 104^{18}. Pr 30^{19} refers to the mysterious gliding of the serpent over a rock; Am 6^{12}, to the proverbial impossibility of horses running over crags. Dt 32^{13} emphasizes the fact that in Palestine even the rocks are the home of bees (cf Ps 81^{16}, Is 7^{19}), and the rocky soil produces olives (Job 29^6). Besides this natural marvel, we have the miracles of Ex 17^6, Nu 20^8 etc. In 1 Co 10^4 St. Paul follows a wide-spread Jewish *haggādhāh*, which can be traced to the 1st cent. A.D., according to which the rock (perhaps originally *the well*) followed Israel; when the Tabernacle was pitched, the water gushed out afresh, the princes singing the song of Nu 21^{17}. The epithet 'spiritual' does not deny the literal reality of that to which it refers; the manna was literal to St. Paul, and the water and rock must have been so too. He sees in the literal fact a foreshadowing of the Christian sacraments. Further, he identifies the rock with Christ, implying His pre-existence and care for His people; cf Philo's identification of it with the Wisdom and Word of God.

Rocks, particularly the soft sandstone of Edom, were primitive dwelling-places (Job 24^8 30^6), and were used for sepulchres (Is 22^{16}, Mk 15^{46}). Job 19^{24} refers to the permanence of the rock inscription; 28^9 (a somewhat unusual word, 'flinty rock' RV and RSV) to mining. In Jg 6^{20} 13^{19} the rock is a natural monolithic altar; in 6^{26} translate 'strong-hold' with RV and RSV. Rocks as dangers to ships are mentioned in Ac 27^{29}, and metaphorically in Jude ^{12} RV (but RVm and Bigg retain 'spots' of AV [cf RSV 'blemishes'], which has the support of the parallel 2 P 2^{13}). The barrenness and desolation of a rock is the point of Ezk $26^{4, 14}$, with a pun on *Tyre* (=rock); cf the unfruitful 'rock' (Lk 8^6), or 'rocky ground' (Mt 13^5 RSV; cf RV) of the parable of the Sower; *i.e.* rock with a thin layer of earth. The rock meets us continually as a place of refuge, literal or metaphorical (Nu 24^{21}, 1 S 13^6, Is 2^{19}, Jer 48^{28} 49^{16}, Ob ^{3}); cf 'feet on rock' (Ps 27^5 40^2); in Is 32^2 it is a shade from the heat. And so it is a frequent *title for God*, as the unvarying strength and support of His people (Dt 32^{4ff} [6 times], Ps 18^2 etc., Is 17^{10} 30^{29}, Hab 1^{12}). It is often represented by 'God,' and vague terms ('help,' etc.) in the ancient versions, as well as AV and Prayer Book (*e.g.* Ps 95^1). A sufficient explanation of the use is found in the natural scenery of Palestine. It is doubtful how far 'Rock' (*Ṣûr*) was a definite name for God. It has been found in compounds in S. Arabian inscriptions, and occurs in the proper names of Nu $1^{5f, 10}$ 3^{35}. 'Great Rock' is a common title of Ashur and Bel in Assyria. In Dt 32^{31}, Is 31^9 the title is given to heathen gods, but in the latter passage the word *Ṣela*, is used. And the fact that this word is freely employed in this connexion side by side with *ṣûr* rather contradicts the supposition that the latter was technically a proper name. Convulsions of nature and the power of God are connected with breaking the rock (1 K 19^{11}, Job 14^{18}, Jer 23^{29} Nah 1^6, Mt 27^{51}), and in Jer 5^3 it is a symbol of obstinacy. In Mt 7^{24} it represents the sure foundation; cf Mt 16^{18} and POWER OF THE KEYS. The name 'Peter' is a translation of the Aramaic **Cephas**, the Hebrew form of which is used Jer 4^{29}, Job 30^6 (see PETER). For the 'rock of offence *or* stumbling,' see Is 8^{14} 28^{16}, Ro 9^{33}, 1 P 2^6. Precipitation from a rock was a form of execution (2 Ch 25^{12}; cf Lk 4^{29}).

C. W. E.

ROCK BADGER.—See BADGER.

ROCK OF ESCAPE.—A rock or cliff in the wilderness of Maon, to which Saul returned from pursuing after David, 1 S 23^{28} (AV, RV **Sela-hammahlekoth**). It is possibly modern *Wâdī el-Malâqi*.

ROD.—The rods, sticks, staves, and clubs carried or otherwise used by the Hebrews were probably as varied in size and shape as those in use among the inhabitants of Palestine at the present day, of which a minute description, with illustrations, is given by Baldensperger in *PEFSt*, 1905, 35 ff. No hard-and-fast distinction can be made out between the *maṭṭeh*, the *shēbheṭ*, and the *makḳēl*—all three rendered in EV by 'rod' or 'staff.' The context must generally decide which of the two is the better rendering. For example, the twigs which Jacob peeled in the device recorded in Gn 30^{37ff} are true rods; but in 32^{10} the same word (*makḳēl*) is properly rendered '**staff.**' On the other hand, Moses' 'rod' (so EV) is rather his shepherd's 'staff' (Ex 4^2 etc.).

For the rod as an instrument of punishment, *shēbheṭ* is more frequently employed than *maṭṭeh*, as in Pr 10^{13} 13^{24} 26^3, although both are not seldom employed in parallel lines (Is 10^{24} 30^{31f} etc.). The former also denotes the shepherd's **club** (q.v.; described and figured in Hastings' *DB*, iv, 291^a, *PEFSt*, 1905, 36), as in Ps 23^4, Lv 27^{32} (AV, RV 'rod,' RSV 'staff') etc. See also SCEPTRE.

A. R. S. K.

RODANIM.—See DODANIM.

ROE, ROEBUCK.—**1.** *ṣ^ebhî* and *ṣ^ebhiyyāh*; see GAZELLE. **2.** *ya'^alāh*, Pr 5^{19} (RV, RSV **doe**); see 'Wild Goat' under GOAT. **3.** *'ōpher*, Ca 4^5 7^3 (AV 'young roe'; RV, RSV '**fawn**'). **4.** *yaḥmûr* (literally 'red'), Dt 14^5, 1 K 4^{23} (AV '**fallow deer**'; RV, RSV 'roebuck'). The true fallow-deer is the *'ayyāl* or hart; see HART. In the LXX *yaḥmûr* is translated *boubalos*, the bubale; but it is much more probable that it is the roebuck (*Cervus capreolus*), still called the *yaḥmûr* by some Arabs. It is a gazelle-like animal with three-branched upright horns.

E. W. G. M.

ROGELIM.—The native place of Barzillai the Gileadite, 2 S 17[27] 19[31]; possibly modern *Bersîniyâ*.

ROHGAH.—An Asherite, 1 Ch 7[34].

ROIMUS, 1 Es 5[8] (AV, RV).—See REHUM, **1.**

ROLL.—See WRITING, **6.**

ROMAMTI-EZER.—A son of Heman, 1 Ch 25[4, 31].

ROMAN PUBLIC LAW.—1. Jurisdiction.—The juridical capacity of the governors of Judaea differed in no known respect from that of governors of other provinces under the control of the emperor. The equestrian *procuratores* and *praefecti* of the smaller provinces such as Judaea, Thrace, and Noricum, were given powers equivalent to those held by the senators who as legates of Caesar technically held *imperium pro praetore.* (Cf Tacitus, *Ann.* xii. 60. Jos. *BJ* II. viii. 1 [117]). This gave its holder unrestricted powers of judgment in cases of civil law and of punishment for all criminal offences committed by persons of ordinary provincial status (*peregrini*). Nominally the governors held the same powers over Roman citizens in their provinces unless these exercised their right of appeal to the emperor (see below). Only the governor himself could exercise the supreme criminal jurisdiction, which unlike the civil could not be delegated to assistants. Governors gave jurisdiction either at their capital or on an annual tour of assize centres.

Minor criminal offences, which involved fines and beatings rather than such sentences as expulsion, exile, hard labour, or death, were handled not by imperial judges but by municipal courts in which the magistrates were the annually elected civic authorities (see below). These were expected to refer cases beyond their competence to the governor for trial.

The jurisdiction of the governors in the 1st cent. A.D. was remarkably unfettered either by statute laws or by rules of procedure. They might, but were not bound to, follow the definitions and penalties provided by the Roman system, or *ordo* of *leges publicae*, for the major criminal and political offences such as murder, forgery, treason, and public violence. These laws operated in Italy, and formed the *ordo iudiciorum publicorum.* Many forms of crime were outside their scope, since they were largely concerned with the offences of officials. The governor's jurisdiction was mostly '*extra ordinem*' or outside the schedule. He was left generally free to make his own definitions of crimes and penalties. Hence there were remarkable differences even in the later empire between the criminal codes of different provinces. The only check on freedom of jurisdiction lay in the consideration that excessive cruelty in the use of *imperium* might lay the governor open to complaints by the provincials to the emperor or Senate and to a prosecution under the Roman extortion law when his office had expired.

Governors were expected but not compelled to follow a customary procedure inherited from the Republican period. Initiation of charges and conduct of prosecutions were left to independent prosecutors, who might be either private persons or municipal representatives, but who were in no sense officials of the Roman government. Parties might speak for themselves or be represented by advocates. The governor sat as judge, but was expected to take the advice of a *consilium* or committee, which he selected from among his personal friends and assistants, or notable personalities of the province. This was not a jury, and he was not bound to follow its advice, but commonly he gave sentence in accordance with its opinion: '*e consilii sententia*.'

The prosecution of Roman citizens took the same form as the above with two exceptions. First, the accused, by exercising his right of appeal to the emperor (see below) could avoid provincial jurisdiction in serious charges altogether. Second, in certain provinces, which contained large numbers of Roman citizens, the Italian system of independent jury courts (*quaestiones*) was introduced for crimes covered by the *ordo*. This system did not last long in the provinces, and is clearly documented only in Cyrenaica. But on its disappearance the governors seem to have been left with the power of sentencing Roman citizens for crimes within the *ordo*, without appeal.

Such was the normal method when charges were brought to the notice of the governors by third parties. In times of riot and crisis governors and their assistants freely exercised repressive police powers of arrest and chastisement (*coercitio*) under the general authority of their *imperium*. But the tendency was only to punish summarily the man caught in the very act of crime, or accused of a minor offence. The account of the various arrests and trials of St. Paul in the *Acts* and of Christ in the *Gospels* can be explained simply according to this system. Earlier discussions have been apt not to recognize the informality of Roman procedure, and hence to create unreal difficulties and to pose unreal questions about the details of the jurisdiction of the procurators.

In the various trials of Christ and Paul either private individuals or members of the Sanhedrin acting as private prosecutors try to persuade the procurators to construe something that was an offence under Jewish law as a capital crime under his own jurisdiction (*cognitio*). The details are clearest in the accusation before Gallio, proconsul of Achaea (Ac 18[12-16]). He refused jurisdiction in terms that underlined the freedom of his tribunal: 'I do not wish to take cognisance of such matters.' So too the town clerk of Ephesus insists accurately: 'If Demetrius and his fellow craftsmen have any complaint against him, there are assizes and proconsuls. Let them plead against each other' (Ac 19[38]). The long story of the prosecution of Paul before Felix and Festus is clear in its main features. Sundry Jews were trying to involve Paul in a charge based on the contravention of Jewish custom before the tribunal of the procurator, who correctly declared: 'I will hear your case when the accusers also are present' (Ac 23[35]; cf 22[1, 30] 23[29-30] 25[9]). So too Festus later (Ac 25[16]): 'It is not the custom of the Romans to condemn a man before the accused has faced his accusers and has had opportunity to defend the charge.' But the story is confused in two sections. In the opening phase the activities of the tribune Lysias have been misunderstood. He arrested Paul in the course of an open riot under the impression that Paul was the troublemaker. Hence the prisoner was chained and scourged before questioning (Ac 21[33] 22[24]). Lysias so far was exercising *coercitio* as the subordinate officer of the procurator. Even so he was not prepared to punish the man without further investigation. The revelation of the Roman status of Paul at this moment changed the mode but not the substance of the procedure. The following scene before the Sanhedrin was not a trial, as has sometimes been supposed, but an attempt to establish the charges by gentler means, as the letter of Lysias to Felix makes clear (Ac 22[30] 23[10] 24[26-30]). The second confusion arises when the Jews, after Festus succeeded Felix as procurator, tried to have the case heard not at Caesarea but at Jerusalem (Ac 24[1-11]). Strictly, this is represented as a trial 'before,' *i.e.* 'by,' the procurator, though in an atmosphere unfavourable to Paul. But the author also implies that such a trial would amount to the mere ratification by Festus of the sentence of the Sanhedrin, as in the trial of Christ. Nothing in Roman law prevented Festus from using the Sanhedrin as his *consilium* if he so wished, provided that the actual accusers were kept distinct.

Paul was asked if he would accept this proposal. The question was political rather than legal. A Roman citizen had no right to determine the form of his trial except by the exercise of his right of appeal. Paul objected: 'I stand at the tribunal of Caesar where I ought to be judged' (Ac 25[10]). This meant only that he was prepared to accept the independent judgment of the procurator as the officer—but not strictly the delegate—of Caesar. The words were immediately followed by Paul's formal 'appeal to Caesar,' by which he altogether avoided the risk of a virtual trial by the Sanhedrin. See also JUSTICE, 3.

Apart from these two obscurities the Acts give the normal procedure of the Roman criminal jurisdiction *extra ordinem*. The narrative continually mentions or implies in a non-technical manner the presence of accusers, charges, advocates, speeches in defence, and even the *consilium* of the procurator. The account of the trial of Christ before Pilate in the Gospels is much less precise. In Mt 27$^{11-15}$ and Mk 15$^{1-6}$ the charges are not mentioned, though they may be inferred from Pilate's references to Christ as a king. Pilate hears the accusers and invites Christ to reply. His silence, from the Roman aspect, left Pilate no option but to condemn him: 'Do you answer nothing? Why, what charges they make against you' (Mk 15^{4}). In Lk 23$^{1-16}$ political charges are formulated—'stirring up the people,' 'forbidding the payment of tribute to Caesar,' 'calling himself a king'—which Pilate rejects as baseless. In these three accounts the real basis of the condemnation is left obscure. Only John (18^{31} 19^{6}) suggests directly that Pilate confirmed the sentence given by the Sanhedrin on religious grounds. There is nothing in the four accounts that contradicts ordinary Roman provincial usage: it was a long established custom to allow the subject peoples to 'use their own laws' when possible.

2. Provocatio.—The 'appeal to Caesar' of the Roman citizen in the Empire derived from the *provocatio ad populum* guaranteed by the protective powers of the Tribunes of the Plebs, which existed throughout the Republican period. In the late Republic the citizen in Italy was protected from arbitrary beating or execution at the hands of a Roman official, and could only be sentenced to such punishment by regular jury courts established by *leges publicae*. By the time of Augustus a *lex Iulia de vi publica* had guaranteed to the Roman citizen in the provinces the privileges which he enjoyed in Italy under the laws of *provocatio*. The emperor, whose powers included an extensive form of the tribunician authority (*tribunicia potestas*), took the place of the college of tribunes and of the jury courts as the effective organ of appeal. So much may be inferred from the legal text, *Sententiae Pauli*, v. 26, 1, where the original wording of the *lex* is given in part: 'Whoever kills, orders to be killed, tortures, beats, sentences, or bids to be set in bonds a Roman citizen who exercises his right of appeal, as formerly to the People, so now to the emperor, etc.' The author of Acts is aware that it was dangerous for a governor to bind or beat a Roman citizen in any circumstances, though twice he speaks loosely as if it was lawful to beat after condemnation in a court (Ac 22^{29} 16$^{37-39}$ 22^{25}).

It is possible that the right of appeal only operated outside the sphere of crimes regulated by *leges publicae* (see above), and that governors in the Empire were empowered to execute Romans condemned for crimes within the *ordo*, either at their own tribunal or at the provincial jury courts (see above). Several examples are known of such sentences (cf Pliny, *Epp*. II. xi. 8; x. lviii. 3; Suetonius, *Galba*, ix. 1). Appeals to the emperor would then have been operative only for charges *extra ordinem*, such as those made against Paul. Hence the Jews attempted to show that Paul was also guilty of recognized crimes such as treason and sedition; the author of Acts might be right in implying that a Roman could be punished in such cases after due condemnation. In a later age governors tended automatically to send Roman citizens direct to Rome for trial, without waiting for their formal appeal (cf Pliny, *Epp*. x. xcvi. 4). The *lex Iulia* quoted above confirms Acts in the suggestion that the procurator could try and sentence Roman citizens if they did not exercise their right of appeal (Ac 27^{32}). The words of Festus should not be pressed technically against this: 'Since he has appealed to Caesar I have *determined* to send him (*sc*. to Rome)' (Ac 25^{25}). The trial could not be continued after the appeal because the *lex Iulia* did not allow any form of sentence, even to a non-capital form of punishment such as expulsion from the province, after appeal had been made. Festus consulted his advisers at this juncture because he was not familiar with the procedure (Ac 25^{12}, see below). No known rules controlled the moment at which appeal might be made.

The dispatch of prisoners in chains and under guard to Rome for trial is well documented, both for Romans and for provincial subjects (cf Josephus, *Vita*, 76 [424]; *BJ* I. xxix. 3 [577]; II. xiii. 2 [253]; Pliny, *Epp*. x. lvii. 2; S. Riccobono, *Fontes Iuris Romani Antejustiniani*, I., No. 68, 2, lines 45–50). The Prefects of the Praetorian Guard were normally in charge of such prisoners; the 'prefect of the camp' mentioned in Ac 28^{16} should be one of them. The trial might not come before the emperor himself. Later emperors commonly nominated a senior senator, or an official such as the City Prefect or the Praetorian Prefect, to hear such cases in their stead (cf Pliny, *Epp*. VII. vi. 8–11).

That Paul remained 'two whole years' without trial (Ac 28^{30}) may well be due (as is suggested in Foakes-Jackson and Lake, *Commentary*, cited below) to the failure of their accusers to appear. It is possible that he was then discharged. But the suggestion that there was a legal rule at this time allowing discharge automatically in such cases after two years is not probable. The intention of enactments of this period about absent prosecutors was to compel the absentees to complete their actions, under severe penalties—not to let the accused escape trial (cf Riccobono, *F.I.R.A.*, I., No. 44, col. ii. Generally, Marcian, *Digest*, 48, 16, 1, 7–14, on the *Senatus Consultum Turpilianum*). The edict quoted in support of this theory belongs to a much later age (*F.I.R.A.*, I., No. 91). The *lex Iulia* quoted above allowed the withdrawal of a charge only on special grounds (*Dig*. 48, 2, 3, 4).

3. Local Administration.—Control of local affairs in Roman provinces was vested in municipal authorities who enjoyed a large measure of independence. There were magistrates elected annually by assemblies of local citizens, and town councils composed either of aldermen holding office for life, as most commonly, or of persons elected annually. These authorities governed the territory surrounding and belonging to their communes with little interference from the Roman governors, except in matters affecting the upper criminal and civil jurisdiction, imperial taxation, and public disorders (cf Ac 19^{40}). The forms of government in the eastern provinces were commonly Greek, derived from the Hellenistic civilization, but pre-Greek native institutions survived in many areas, particularly in village administration, and notably in Judaea, which was an area of mingling cultures. It was Roman policy to encourage the spread of Greek forms of city government in the East, and the family of Herod supported this policy in their principalities. Caesarea, Samaria, Tiberias, and the cities of the Decapolis, were notable centres of Hellenistic influence. Acts rightly depicts Paul on his travels as much more frequently in conflict with civic authorities than with Roman governors, as at Pisidian Antioch, Iconium, Thessalonica, and Ephesus (Ac 13^{50} 14^{5} 16$^{19-23}$ 17$^{6-10}$ 19$^{29-40}$). Special privileges were enjoyed by a few cities in the East which received settlements of Roman veteran legionaries in the time of Caesar and Augustus (*coloniae civium Romanorum*). Hence the designation of Philippi in Macedonia as 'First city and colony' (Ac 16^{12}). Corinth and Pisidian Antioch were also colonies, but are not so noted in Acts (18$^{1-17}$ 13^{14}). The Roman element, which provided the governing class of such cities, was apt to be submerged by a large population of Greeks, who formed the mass of the inhabitants. Except in frontier provinces the governors seldom had effective forces for police duties. Hence the civic authorities were responsible for the ordinary maintenance of public order, and had powers of arrest and minor punishment, but serious charges, even at Roman colonies, were reserved for the tribunal of the governors (Ac 16$^{19-23, 35}$ 17^{9} 18$^{12-15}$ 19$^{38-39}$). No municipal magistrate in the Roman empire could sentence a man to death, except in a small number of cities known as 'free states' (*civitates liberae*) and 'states free by treaty' (*civitates foederatae*). Even these could not sentence Roman citizens, and appeals from their courts came to be allowed in other cases also to the governors and to the emperor. Among cities visited by Peter and Paul in Acts, Syrian Antioch, Thessalonica, and Athens were thus 'free.' So too were Tarsus itself, and probably Tyre and Sidon (Ac 12[20]).

But local government in Palestine and southern Syria differed from most of the empire. Greek city-government existed in many coastal cities, in the Decapolis, and in the new foundations of Herod at Tiberias and Samaria. But the rest of the kingdom of Herod had a centralized Hellenistic bureaucracy similar to that of Ptolemaic and Roman Egypt. Numerous 'toparchies,' or districts of villages, were administered by *strategi*. Each village had its clerk appointed by the king. This system survived in the tetrarchies and even under the Roman procurators. But before the rise of Herod the Romans had also divided the old Jewish kingdom into five large districts, including Galilee, Judaea proper, and the region of Samaria. These were set under the government of a Council or *Synhedrion* of gentry. Traces of this system survived the Herodian period, notably in the function of the Sanhedrin at Jerusalem. This acted or tried to act as the local authority for Jewish affairs in Jerusalem and throughout Judaea. The curious dispatch of Saul to deal with Jews at Damascus, an independent city over which the Sanhedrin had no power, suggests a claim to authority throughout the Diaspora. The procurators treated the Sanhedrin as the effective town council of Jerusalem, but because of the city's turbulence exercised closer control over its affairs than was normal in other provinces. Its control over public order was limited largely to the Temple precinct by the presence of a permanent Roman garrison under a military resident (Ac 5[17-18, 40] 21[31-32]). The Sanhedrin acted as a supreme court in matters of Jewish religious and civil law. But even its religious authority was hampered by the insistence of the Romans on keeping custody of the sacred vestments of the High Priest, which through a historical accident had fallen into their hands as part of the royal establishment when the kingdom became a province. Though this control was suspended from time to time, the claim was maintained *de iure* as a useful form of political pressure (Jos. *Ant*. xv. xi. 4 [398]; xviii. iv. 3 [91]; xx. i. 2 [12]). In lacking the power of capital punishment the Sanhedrin was in the same condition as most local authorities throughout the empire. Such incidents as the stoning of Stephen and the attempt to kill Paul at Jerusalem were violations of the Roman order, like the stoning at Lystra (Ac 7[57-60] 14[19] 21[30-31]). The special power of executing persons who violated the Temple sanctuary was a deliberate exception for particular reasons (Jos. *BJ* vi. ii. 4 [126]; OGIS 598).

In initiating prosecutions and complaints in the interest of the province, the Sanhedrin acts like other provincial councils of the Empire. These, composed of annually elected representatives of the provincial communes, acted as intermediaries between the province and the Roman authorities, though otherwise their functions were very different, since they had no responsibility for municipal administration, and were closely associated with the politico-religious cult of the emperor. of which their presidents were high priests. But in Roman eyes the two institutions were analogous. The Asiarchs who made trouble for Paul at Ephesus were either deputies or ex-presidents of the council of the Asian province (Ac 19[31]).

4. Procurator and province.—The procurators of Judaea were not men experienced in provincial government. For most of them it was their first post in the administrative service following tenure of a military command at the intermediate level, as military tribune of a legion and prefect of a regiment of the auxiliary army (see below). Their training was limited to military administration and courts martial. Hence they depended greatly on the advice of their cabinet or *consilium* (see above) (cf Ac 25[12, 23]). Hence too the tendency frequent in Judaea to leave difficult matters to Rome or to the legate of Syria, or to take the advice of local dynasts (Ac 25[25-27], Lk 23[6-12]; cf Jos. *Ant*. xviii. iv. 2–3 [88–95]; 8, 2 [261 ff]; *BJ* ii. xii. 6 [241–244]). The title, before Claudius, was probably *praefectus*, not *procurator*.

The procurator of Judaea had four or five regiments of infantry and at least one of cavalry at his disposal. This was an extremely large force by Roman standards for police duties within a province that had no problems of frontier defence. The men were not Roman legionaries but local provincial levies. The imperial army consisted in roughly equal proportions of (*a*) legions of infantry—divisions composed of Roman citizens recruited in Italy or the provinces with a paper strength of about 5550 men—and (*b*) auxiliary troops—regiments of infantry (*cohortes*) and of cavalry (*alae*)—levied mostly from the native, and often the most barbarous, inhabitants of the provinces. The cohorts had a nominal strength of either 500 or 1000 men, and the cavalry of 1000 troopers. Their commanders were entitled *praefectus* or (for the cohorts at double-strength) *tribunus*. In and after the period of Acts these officers were, like the procurators, drawn from the Roman 'equestrian' or upper and middle class. They were commonly commissioned in their thirties and might hail either from Italy or from citizen families in the provinces (see below). Sometimes they were promoted from the centurionate of the legions. The company officers of the auxiliary regiments were centurions commanding a unit of about 90 infantrymen, or *decuriones* commanding a squadron of cavalry. These officers do not correspond, as is commonly believed, to the non-commissioned officers of modern army system. Socially they belonged to the class that filled the town councils of the municipalities. They were often promoted from within the auxiliary units, though some were transferred from the legionary army. By this system men might rise socially from the proletarian to the middle class of Roman and provincial society. Auxiliary centurions were not always Roman citizens (unless they were ex-legionaries), but like the rankers of the auxiliary army they received the Roman citizenship after twenty-five years' service.

The units in Judaea were mostly recruited locally from the population of Samaria and Caesarea, according to Josephus (*BJ* ii. xiii. 7 [268]; *Ant*. xix. ix. 1 [357]; xx. viii. 7 [176]). But the *cohors secunda Italica civium Romanorum*, which is probably the unit meant in Ac 10[1], belonged to a special group of units originally raised in Italy from freed slaves; for this unit see the inscription in Dessau, *Inscriptiones Latinae Selectae* 9168. The *cohors Augusta* of Ac 27[2] is less certainly identifiable among several units so named.

It was held even by Mommsen that procuratorial Judaea was not a *provincia populi Romani* before the Jewish rebellion of A.D. 66–70, and that the procurator was simply a substitute for the expropriated king, managing the kingdom in the interests of the Emperor. The point is of little practical importance, but it can hardly be maintained. Judaea in every respect resembles other kingdoms, such as Thrace, Mauretania, and Cappadocia, which were turned into provinces of the Roman empire in the time of Tiberius and Claudius, and governed by equestrian *praefecti* and *procuratores* when the former ruling house failed to produce satisfactory heirs. The reason for the use of equestrian instead of senatorial men as governors lies in the internal politics of Rome, and not in the status of the regions concerned. The introduction of Roman forms of taxation, with the attendant census, of Roman jurisdiction, and permanent military occupation, is decisive. Such kingdoms had been part of the Roman empire before they became territorial provinces; they had been at the absolute disposition of the Romans, who rearranged the principalities as they saw fit at the death or even during the lifetime of the rulers.

The procurator administered Judaea with full power akin to that of the proconsuls and *legati propraetore* of the greater provinces. But his authority (*potestas*) was subordinate to that of the *legati* of Syria, who exercised a general supervision over Judaean affairs. Both before and after the creation of the province the legates of Syria frequently intervened at times of crisis and insurrection in Judaea. This was probably enjoined in their general instructions (*mandata*) from the emperor; they had similar authority in the affairs of Cappadocia and Armenia. When unusual complaints were made against the procurator Pilate and, later, Cumanus, a special commission was given to the legate of Syria to investigate the matter and to send the offending procurators back to Rome (Jos. *Ant.* XVIII. iv. 2 [89]; XX. vi. 2 [132]; *BJ* II. xii. 6–8 [244–249]; Tacitus, *Ann.* XII. liv). But in ordinary administration the procurator was independent of the legate. He was not the deputy but the representative of the emperor, holding a power absolute in itself. Strictly the appeal of Paul from the jurisdiction of Festus to that of Caesar was not from a lower to a higher but to a different tribunal. Once sentence had been given by a provincial governor it could not normally be reversed by another court.

5. Taxation.—The procurator was responsible for supervision of the collection of the imperial taxes. The principal tax was the land tax, *tributum soli*, a percentage tax on real estate. There was also a poll tax (*tributum capitis*) and there were indirect taxes of which the customs dues, or *portorium*, was the chief. Land values were assessed by the Roman census, first made in Judaea at the establishment of the province in A.D. 6. All inhabitants were required to register their real property, if any, their persons and those of their families, in accordance with a set formula. The provincial census was usually repeated at long intervals, but nothing is known of a second census between A.D. 6 and 66. The work was organized on a municipal basis, and supervised by military officers under the authority of an imperial legate, much as described in Lk 2¹⁻³ (there, however, there is a notorious difficulty about the date, which seems to have been displaced by obscurities in the chronology of the life of Christ, since Josephus dates the census under Quirinius in A.D. 6, *Ant.* XVII. xiii. 5 [355]; XVIII. i. 1 [1]). Taxes were collected by the use of tax farmers or *publicani* who probably managed the taxes of subdivisions of the province, either municipal territories or toparchies. The cities also collected local taxes for their own purpose, such as customs and sales taxes. Hence 'publicans' mentioned in the NT may be collecting either Roman or local taxes. After the Jewish revolt the emperor Vespasian confiscated the levy which Jews throughout the Diaspora paid to the Temple at Jerusalem, and treated it as an additional poll-tax on all persons of Jewish faith.

The main items of the provincial budget were the cost of armed forces and the salary and establishment of the governor. His staff were drawn from the personnel of his army. Within the client kingdoms, large and small, these expenses fell upon the local rulers, who were not required to make any direct contribution to the Roman treasury (Jos. *Ant.* XVII. xi. 4 [317–20]; XIX. viii. 2 [343–52]). But their armed forces were placed at the disposal of the legate of Syria or the procurator of Judaea in time of need.

Considerable tracts of land in the provinces were owned by the emperors. These were administered as private estates by agents of equestrian class who also bore the title of procurator, but in public law they formed part of the province in which they lay. Such was the former small principality of Jamnia from the time of Tiberius onwards. Their rents formed part of the private revenues of the emperors.

6. Roman citizenship.—All free-born inhabitants of Italy (except resident aliens) and of official Roman colonial settlements overseas were Roman citizens. In the early empire the Roman citizenship was also given to numerous native communities in the western provinces, and to individuals who either as common soldiers from the working classes or as leading men in municipalities had served Rome well. In the eastern provinces citizenship was given only to individuals and in the latter manner. Such grants were authorized by the emperor in edicts published at Rome. To secure citizenship a recommendation from an official or notable Roman was necessary, which might be secured by merit, personal influence, or bribery (as in Ac 22²⁸). Such grants were relatively common in the Greek-speaking provinces. Service in the auxiliary army (see above) opened the privilege to members of the urban and rural proletariat. Paul's family at Tarsus seems to have belonged to the commercial class of the city and might have secured the citizenship for political or economic services. Citizenship descended to all a man's children born of a legal wife who was also a Roman citizen. Births of Romans were legally registered, and certificates of birth existed, by which a man might prove his claim. New citizens were often furnished with a copy of the edict which made them citizens. False claims were liable to the death penalty. The legally freed slaves of Roman citizens also became Roman citizens, but their rights were restricted to those of private life.

The advantages of citizenship to a provincial were social and legal rather than political. The Roman citizens were the upper crust of provincial society. They enjoyed special advantages in criminal jurisdiction (see above), and in civil law their property could not be disposed arbitrarily by governors but was treated according to the rules of Roman jurisprudence. Citizenship was the key to lucrative professions. Common service in the army was a well paid employment for the toiling peasantry, and the wealthy few could enter the service of the Roman state, as military tribunes and prefects, and even rise to the governorship of provinces. Three of the twelve procurators of Judaea, including Antonius Felix, were Roman citizens who originated in the eastern provinces. The son of such a procurator might hope to enter the Roman Senate and reach the highest rank of the Roman administration. Thus Gallio, the proconsul of Achaia, originated from an 'equestrian' family in Spain.

7. Religious duties of Roman citizens.—Nominally Roman citizens were required to maintain the cults of the gods upon whose favour the safety of the state depended. They were not allowed to worship foreign deities unless their cult had been officially sanctioned by a decree of the Senate or later the emperor. This principle was only enforced when such worship was associated with immoral behaviour (*flagitia, scelera*) or led to civil disturbances. In the early empire the cults and followers of Isis, Magianism, and Judaism were occasionally expelled from Italy and Druidism was suppressed in Gaul on such grounds. Otherwise Romans were free to follow private religions, and in the provinces the official religions of local communities were protected. Judaism not only in Judaea but throughout the Diaspora was protected by a series of decrees which dispensed the Jews from certain obligations ordinarily required of provincial subjects but incompatible with Judaism. Hence even devout Jews like Paul found no difficulty in holding the Roman citizenship. The cults and ceremonies of the Roman gods were entirely in the hands of official priesthoods and magistracies, both national and municipal. No active co-operation was required of the private citizen. So too the new political cult of the emperor, often combined with that of *Roma* as a deity, which in various forms was encouraged throughout the provinces as a bond of loyalty, was not obligatory on private individuals. The apostles had no difficulty in bidding the faithful to 'honour the king.'

In Judaea the Roman governors took great pains to avoid thrusting the polytheistic ceremonies and symbols of the Roman state upon the notice of the Jews. The only violation of this policy was the unfortunate insistence of the third emperor, Gaius Caesar (Caligula), that his statue should be set in the Temple at Jerusalem, in conformity with the usual practice of the non-Jewish provincial communities.

The magistrates of the Roman colony of Philippi fairly represented the theory and practice of Rome in Ac 16$^{20-21}$: ' These men who are Jews *disturb our city* and introduce customs which it is not lawful for us as Roman citizens to take up.' Throughout Acts the Christian preachers have trouble with Roman authorities only in so far as they are thought to cause civil disturbances. The Romans, regarding them as Jews, were indifferent to their religious activity.

Apart from specific decrees about particular cults on special occasions, there were no legal enactments controlling the religious activities of Roman citizens or provincial subjects ; there was no need for them. In the post-Apostolic generation, when the distinction between Jews and Christians became apparent (particularly through the claim of Jewish Christians to exemption from the new poll-tax), Christians came to be sporadically prosecuted, as earlier sects had been, for the immoral activities (infanticide, incest) supposed to be associated with their cult—*flagitia cohaerentia nomini Christianorum.* This is first clearly documented in the letter of the Younger Pliny to the emperor Trajan about the Christians of Pontus written about A.D. 110-112 (Pliny, *Epp.* x. xcvi f). Such prosecutions were sanctioned by no general enactment, but depended upon the loosely defined power of provincial governors to punish malefactors, in the system of jurisdiction *extra ordinem* (see above), for any behaviour deemed criminal by the governor. The notion that the Christians were opposed to the Roman government developed only when it was found that Christians like Jews (from whom it was never required) objected to making sacrifices to the images of the emperors. But not till the end of the 2nd cent., in the writing of Tertullian, does this appear as the main charge against the Christians.

8. Right of Assembly.—In republican Rome it was illegal to hold any public meeting except under the presidency of an official of the State. In the empire there was similar objection to the holding of private assemblies ; hence the agitators at Ephesus tried to transform their demonstration into a meeting of the civic assembly, to the dismay of the city magistrates (Ac 19$^{31-32, 40}$). This general principle appears mainly in rules controlling the formation of societies and groups —*collegia, sodalitates*—which might tend to become subversive political organizations. Some types of these, particularly those concerned with certain crafts, or those attracting men of substance, required authorization by Senate or emperor. But from the time of Claudius or Nero onwards, small associations of working men, usually connected with religious cults—*collegia tenuiorum religionis causa*—were dispensed from such necessity. In Roman eyes the early ' churches ' were hardly distinguishable from such groups. Hence the Christians had no legal difficulty in holding their meetings for the agapê, preaching, and eucharist. Besides, it is improbable that the legislation controlling clubs was applied extensively in the eastern provinces before the end of the 2nd cent. A.D. In practice its serious enforcement was beyond the scope of the governors' administrative machinery in most provinces, though the civic authorities might succeed in detecting major violations.

A. N. S.-W.

ROMANS, LETTER TO THE.—1. Occasion, purpose, and character.—From beginning to end, Paul's letter to the Romans is permeated with the pastoral concern of a missionary ' to all the nations ' (1$^{5-6}$ 15$^{14-16}$). In it every man stands before God as a sinner with nothing to plead but guilty. But the judge, by sheer grace, through the death and resurrection of His Son Jesus Christ, leads him to repentance, reckons his faith as righteousness, forgives him, and changes his status from criminal in court to son and heir in his eternal kingdom of righteousness and peace and joy in the Holy Spirit. ' Justification by faith ' is the Latin for this saving activity of God. Paul's Greek is *dikaiosynē tou Theou,* ' the righteousness of God,' which means that God vindicates His righteousness by loving sinners and putting them into right relationship with Himself on the basis of faith in Christ. This creative act of forgiveness sets men free from their slavery to the flesh, which rebels and defeats even their best efforts to make themselves acceptable to God by credit for obedience to His law. But God's grace-gift of life in Christ brooks no licence to keep on sinning, as if being right with God through faith were separable from doing right. Those who accept it die in baptism with Christ, who died to sin : transformed and led by the Spirit of God, they must present themselves as a living sacrifice in spiritual service in this present world, looking to the perfect righteousness which will be theirs when God sets His whole creation free from its bondage to decay. This is the gospel which Paul preaches in his letter to the Christians in Rome.

The occasion can be inferred from the letter itself in the light of Luke's narrative in Acts. Paul had long wanted to visit Rome, but his work in Asia, Macedonia, and Greece prevented. At last he was ready to turn west to Spain. But first he must go to Jerusalem with delegates from the churches in Macedonia and Achaia to make sure that the fund they had raised for the poor would be delivered and accepted in a spirit that would break down the separation between Jew and Gentile and foster unity between the Jewish Christians and their Gentile brethren. Since he was risking death at the hands of unbelievers in Judaea, his plans might once again be thwarted ; and so, as he set out for Jerusalem, he wrote, telling the Romans of his intention to visit them on his way to Spain, to be refreshed by their company and then to be sped on his way by them (1$^{8-15}$ 15$^{14-32}$). The steadfastness of his fellow believers was part of his very life (1 Th 3^{8}), and the faith of the Christians in the capital was being proclaimed throughout all the Roman world. He needed strength from them and they from him, so that he and they might be mutually encouraged, each by the other's faith. His plea for their prayers and support was written sometime during his three months in Greece following the riot of the silversmiths which had ended his work in Ephesus (Ac 19^{21} 20^{3}). The year is not certain ; Corinth in the spring of A.D. 55 comes closest to satisfying the chronological data, but it may have been A.D. 56 or 57. (See CHRONOLOGY OF NT and PAUL.)

Paul's boldness in addressing a church which others had founded grew out of his debt to preach to all men and to bring Jewish and Gentile believers into one body in Christ (1$^{1-17}$ 12$^{3-8}$). He needed the influence of the Roman church on all the other churches he was labouring to knit together by his visits and his letters. But his Jewish opponents might prejudice the Roman Christians by impugning the truth of his interpretation of the gospel and misrepresenting his motives for preaching it. His extension of God's kingdom to all men on equal terms of faith apart from works of law seemed to degrade God's chosen people, who regarded themselves as ' sons of light,' to the level of the Gentile ' sons of darkness,' who were usurping the throne of David (2$^{25-29}$ 3$^{27-31}$). He was doing this at the very time when thousands of these sons of light, goaded to apocalyptic fury by their worsening situation under the Roman procurators, were planning the Messianic war which would set their feet upon heaps of the slain and make their oppressors lick the dust of their feet (1 *QM* xii. 10–15). The rejection of Christ by the majority of the Jewish nation was cited against Paul's gospel, and Jewish Christians were under patriotic pressure to regard Jesus not as the Saviour who had died to reconcile all men to God (5$^{6-11}$), but as a national Messiah who was going to subjugate or destroy all but the remnant whom God had predestinated for life in the Age to Come. The temper of the times can be judged from what happened to Paul when he arrived in Jerusalem (Ac 21$^{27-36}$). The strategic position of the Roman Christians in this struggle for the integrity, freedom, and universality of the Christian gospel explains why Paul made this exception to his rule not to build on another man's foundation (15^{14-21}).

Romans is therefore not to be interpreted as a general treatise on systematic theology abstracted from the historical process through which it originated. Paul was addressing the members of a particular church under stress of a specific situation in which he and they and his world mission were involved at the moment of writing. As an apostle to all the nations, he aimed to free the Christian gospel from the double constriction of legalism and Jewish nationalism without cutting it loose from God's special revelation to Israel and turning it into a cult of antinomians who would not make responsible use of their freedom by living according to the indwelling Spirit of God (8^{12-14}). Every Christian whose conduct fell below the righteousness set by the Law could be used by Paul's Jewish opponents to discredit his faith that good works are not the condition but the result of God's grace. They too recognized their dependence on God's mercy and power, but their remedy for the weakness of the flesh which had defeated Paul was not to despair of law observance as God's acceptable way of salvation but to ask His help to obey it more strictly (*e.g.* 1 *QS* i. 1–15; xi. 7–10; 1 *QH* ix. 2—xi. 27). The function of law in Christianity thus became a question of sharp debate. Some, fearing God's wrath, continued to observe certain food taboos and holy days to which they had been accustomed, and became self-righteous in judging others, who had abandoned them; while the latter, considering themselves strong in faith, regarded their critics as weak. Not all these 'weak' Christians were Jews: some were Gentiles from cults in which salvation depended upon the observance of law; and the 'strong' likewise came from both groups. The Gentiles, who constituted the majority of the Roman church, had to be warned against unbrotherly treatment of the Jews (11^{17-24}). Before they could set a valid example to all the other churches, they must learn to live in harmony (15^{5-6}). Roman governmental restrictions on private religious associations made it hard enough without these 'disputes over opinions' (14^{1}) to give these Christians, who met in isolated groups in the homes of their respective members, the sense of belonging to a church which embraced them all. Pleading for conduct befitting their new status as sons and heirs of God, Paul bids them welcome each other as Christ has welcomed them (15^{7}). He bases his appeal on his theology, but he treats only those subjects which are required by his theme in relation to his purpose in writing this letter.

In stating his theme, Paul interprets Hab 2^{4} to prove that 'The righteous shall live by faith' (1^{17} RV; RSVm). 'By faith' is not only reliance on the grace of God for life in the age to come but also a way of living in this present world. Habakkuk's faith was inseparable from his faithfulness in doing God's will, and the Greek *pistis* which translates his Hebrew word for it includes both faith and faithfulness. Ro $8^{12-14, 28-29}$, 1 Co 13^{2}, Gal 5^{16-25}, and many other passages show that Paul's repudiation of salvation by merit does not allow Christians to divorce the faith which trusts God for His grace from the faithfulness which bears the fruit of His Spirit. But when the RSV changes the translation to 'He who through faith is righteous shall live,' it obscures this inseparability of faith from faithfulness and blunts the ethical edge of Paul's insistence that the faith which accepts God's grace-gift of life is faith energized by the Spirit for creative living (Gal 5^{6}). The argument for the change is that Paul's purpose in adapting Hab 2^{4} was to persuade his readers to stop seeking life by claiming their own righteousness instead of trusting 'the righteousness of God' to accept sinners for the sake of Christ. This is true, and it is also true that, by reason of his own previous experience, Paul must have had the opposition between these two ways of salvation in mind when he wrote Ro 1^{17}. But the order of the words in his Greek sentence favours 'The righteous shall live by faith.' A reader of Ro 1^{1-17}, who was familiar with Habakkuk in the Septuagint, but who had never heard of Paul and his gospel before, could not have read all this argument for the RSV into Paul's quotation from Hab 2^{4} until he came back to it after going on to the end of the letter.

2. Argument and content..—The content of Romans was not the flash of the moment of writing, but had been taking shape in Paul's personal living and public debate for many years. Therefore what he is writing in one part of his letter cannot be separated from what he has written, or is going to write, in another part. Sometimes he will start to answer an objection only to break off and leave it suspended for fuller treatment later; examples are 3^{1-4}, which is continued in chs. 9–11 and 3^{5-8}, which is developed in chs. 6 and 8 and 12^{1}–15^{13}. The extreme difficulty of maintaining the priority of Israel as God's chosen people while insisting that every man's salvation is based on grace and that grace is for all leads his argument into some broken sentences which have affected the transmission of the text and have helped to produce important differences of theological interpretation. In this letter Paul's preaching passes into dialogue in the manner of the Stoics, and there are Hellenistic as well as Semitic ideas and forms of expression, together with liturgical elements which indicate that what he is writing has long been a matter of private prayer and public worship. Although clarity requires us to divide Romans into sections with appropriate headings, one must be careful not to cut the thread of the theme which runs through it from beginning to end. Justice to Paul also requires the analysis to make clear that his faith includes not only entrustment of himself solely to God's grace but also faithfulness in living the new life in Christ by the power of the Spirit. His argument proceeds through four stages:

(1) Man's sin and God's righteousness (chs. 1–4).
(2) The new life in Christ: its basis and its character (chs. 5–8),
(3) God's lifegiving purpose for *all* men, Gentiles as well as Jews (chs. 9–11), and
(4) Living in accord with Christ in this present age (chs. 12–15^{13}).

(1) Introducing himself as an apostle called to preach Christ among all the nations, Paul thanks God for the faith of the Christians in Rome and tells why he is eager to visit them (1^{1-15}). Stating his theme (1^{16-17}), he proceeds to show that *all* men are sinners. The Gentiles do not have righteousness to set themselves right with God, and their lack is their own fault. God has shown them all that can be known about Himself; but, instead of worshipping Him as their Creator, they made images of His creatures. Therefore God gave them up to their lusts, so that they not only do all manner of wickedness but approve others who do the same, even though they know they deserve death (1^{18-32}). Presuming on God's kindness and forbearance, which are meant to lead them to repentance, they store up wrath for the day of judgment, when God will render impartially to every man according to His works (2^{1-11}).

Turning to the Jews, Paul reminds them that they too lack righteousness to make them acceptable to God. Since it is not hearers but doers of the law who are righteous before God, the Jew who sins will be judged by the law he has, while the Gentiles, who do not have this law, will be judged according to their own conscience for having done or not done by nature what the law requires (2^{12-16}). The Jews, who are sure that they are the light of the world, are causing God's name to be blasphemed among the Gentiles by breaking his law. Consequently their circumcision becomes of no value, and the Gentiles, who are not circumcised but who keep the precepts of the law, will condemn the Jews who break it. Real circumcision is spiritual, and not literal (2^{25-29}).

Then what advantage has the Jew, and why not do evil in order to magnify God's glory by giving occasion for His grace to abound in coping with it? These objections come from patriotic Jews who charge Paul with fostering sin and regard his gospel as an affront to their nationalism. Paul repudiates the charge as slander and says those who make it will get what they deserve. He agrees that the Jews have the advantage of being the recipients of God's Torah. But then, reading this revelation as God's preannouncement of the gospel of Christ, he quotes from it (*a*) to show that the faithlessness of some of God's people cannot nullify the faithfulness of God ; (*b*) to vindicate God's justice in punishing those who thus presume on His grace ; (*c*) to clinch the charge that *all* men are slaves of sin ; and (*d*) to prove that no man will be justified by works of the law (3[1–20]). On the contrary, this same revelation bears witness to God's universal salvation, open without distinction to all who believe. Since all men have sinned, God accepts them by His grace through faith in Christ Jesus, whom He has offered as an expiation, and who frees them from slavery to sin. In this way, without compromising His own righteousness, God acquits sinners and passes over the sins of the people who lived before Christ (3[21–26]). And since this God is *one* and not many gods, He will accept both the Jews and the Gentiles on the same basis of faith. All human boasting is excluded, and Paul's gospel, to which the law points, does not overthrow but fulfills the law (3[27–31]).

But Paul's opponents, quoting Gn 15[6], claim that Abraham had been obeying God all his life previous to his circumcision, and that his act of believing God's promise to make him and his descendants heirs of the world was one of the meritorious deeds that were reckoned to him *as* but not *instead* of the righteousness necessary to make him acceptable to God. Paul replies that Abraham's circumcision was simply a sign and seal of the righteousness which he had by faith while he was still uncircumcised ; otherwise God would not have been exercising grace but paying wages. God's purpose in making His promise depend on faith apart from works of law is in order that the uncircumcised who share the faith of Abraham may enjoy the blessedness of the man to whom the Lord will not reckon his sin (Ps 32[1–2]), and may grow strong in Abraham's invincible faith in the God who gives life to the dead and calls into existence the things that do not exist (4[1–25]).

(2) Having shown that all men are guilty and justified only by faith in Jesus Christ, Paul is ready to describe the new life in Christ (chs. 5–8). This is a life of peace with God based on His reconciling love through His Son, who died for us while we were yet sinners ; of faith that trusts God and gratefully accepts His gift of acquittal and access to Himself ; of reliable hope produced by character which develops through joyful endurance of suffering ; of God's love poured into our hearts through His Holy Spirit ; of victory over the sin of Adam, which brought condemnation and caused death to reign over all men because all men sinned. Contrasted with life under the law, which could only increase man's trespass, life in Christ is one of abounding grace reigning through righteousness to eternal life (5[1–21]).

In answer to those who charge him with saying, 'Let us do evil that good may come,' Paul explains that, since Christians are united in baptism with Christ in a death like His, which was death to sin, and since they expect to be united with Him in a resurrection like His, they must consider themselves dead to sin and alive to God. Free from sin, whose wages is death, they are now slaves of God, whose free gift is eternal life (6[1–23]). Under grace they can yield themselves to righteousness for sanctification, because they are as free from the old written code, which can only arouse rebellion and sinful passions, as a woman whose husband has died is free to marry another (7[1–6]).

Speaking now in the first person singular, Paul describes his own and everyman's enslavement to sin, which keeps man from becoming righteous in God's sight. The law itself is holy and just and good, but because of the weakness of man's flesh it cannot give life. When the law said, 'You shall not covet,' Paul rebelled, and sin, which had lain dormant within him, sprang up and took him prisoner, forcing him to do the evil he abhorred and thwarting his best efforts to do the good he approved (7[7–25]). But God set him free from this law of sin and death to live according to the Spirit, whose mind is life and peace, and who frees men from fear and bears witness with their spirits that they are children and heirs of God (8[1–17]). The struggle to put to death the deeds of the body that are dictated by the sin that dwells in it, and to become what children of God ought to be, continues ; but it is no longer hopeless. Nor are the sufferings of this present time worth comparing with the glory that will result when God's whole creation, now groaning for release from bondage to decay, obtains the glorious liberty of the children of God (8[18–25]). Meanwhile, the indwelling Spirit of God bears the burden with us, intercedes for us, teaches us how to pray ; and God is working all things for good with those who love Him, whom He has called and predestined to be conformed to the image of His Son. Since God is for us, nothing in all the universe, past, present, or future, will be able to separate us from His love in Christ Jesus (8[26–39]).

(3) But in view of God's lifegiving purpose for all men, what of the future of God's covenant people? In chs. 9–11, Paul explains Israel's rejection of Jesus as the working of God's sovereign power to harden Pharaoh, to choose Isaac and not Ishmael, and to say, 'Jacob I loved, but Esau I hated.' In reply to the objection that God is unjust in punishing those whom He has chosen to harden, he says that the pot is not in position to talk back to the Potter, and that Israel's stumbling was also their own fault (9[1–33]). But Paul's own abiding love for his stumbling kinsmen leads him to seek a better answer. He recognizes their zeal for God but calls it unenlightened, because they do not see that righteousness based on faith does not depend on human striving to bring it down from heaven or up from the abyss, but is in the heart of everyone who calls upon Jesus and confesses that He is Lord. But since believing requires hearing and hearing requires preaching, Christ must be preached to all the nations if all men are to be saved. God's purpose in hardening all but a remnant of Israel is not to destroy them but to make their opposition His means of thrusting His preachers into all the world. When the rejecters see the blessings Christ is bestowing on all the other nations, they will be moved to jealousy and accept Him (10[1–21]). Therefore Paul magnifies his ministry to the Gentiles, who are being grafted as wild olive branches into God's tree. But Gentile Christians must not deride the Jewish branches that have been cut off because of their unbelief ; for unless they continue in God's kindness, they too will experience God's severity. He has consigned all men to disobedience in order that He may have mercy upon all : He can graft the broken branches in again, and in the end all Israel will be saved (11[1–32]). Recognizing that God's ways are inscrutable, Paul turns this insoluble mystery of Divine predestination and human responsibility into a doxology (11[33–36]).

(4) Having described the nature and future of this new life in Christ, Paul appeals to his brethren in Rome to live it, beginning now in this present world (12[1]–15[13]). Presenting themselves as a living sacrifice transformed by the renewing of their minds, they will discern and do the good and acceptable and perfect things that constitute the will of God. They will be zealous, joyful, hopeful, patient and prayerful, generous and hospitable, each thinking soberly of himself and exercising his spiritual gift for the harmonious functioning of the community. They must aim at peace with all men, feeding their enemies and overcoming evil with good (12[1–21]). They will obey the governing authorities and owe no one anything except to fulfil the whole law by loving one another as themselves. Since God's new age is at hand, they must cast off the works of darkness and clothe themselves with the character of Christ (13[1–14]). Christians are free with respect to holy days and food taboos, but since the

kingdom of God is not eating and drinking but righteousness and peace and joy in the Holy Spirit, and since Christ did not please Himself but fulfilled the Scriptures by enduring the reproaches of men, the strong ought to bear with the weak, each pleasing his neighbour for his good. They will live in such harmony that all, both Jews and Gentiles, may with one voice glorify God; and Paul prays that the God of hope may fill them with all joy and peace in believing (14^{1}–15^{13}). The remainder of ch. 15 explains why Paul is writing.

3. Chapter 16 and the original form of Romans.—Ch. 16 consists of a letter commending Phoebe, a deaconess from Cenchreae; greetings from Paul and his fellow workers to members of the church to which Phoebe is taking the letter; a warning against teachers who flatter, deceive and create dissension; and a doxology 'to the only wise God,' who is now disclosing His long-hidden mystery to all nations. Textual variations, however, raise the question whether this chapter belongs to Romans. In most manuscripts the words 'The grace of the Lord Jesus Christ be with you all. Amen' occur twice, once as 16^{20b} and again as 16^{24}; but some omit them at 16^{20} and others at 16^{23}, while a few have them after 16^{27}. The doxology in vv.$^{25-27}$ also shifts its position. Sometimes it stands at the end of ch. 14 and sometimes it follows $16^{23(24)}$, while a few manuscripts give it at both places. But the 3rd cent. papyrus codex P^{46} puts it at the end of ch. 15, then continues with 16^{1-23}. Manuscript G (9th cent.), which lacks the address *en Rōmē* in $1^{7,15}$, does not have the doxology at all but leaves a space which would be large enough for it after 14^{23}. These textual variations indicate that there were two forms of Romans, one consisting of chs. 1–14, the other of chs. 1–16. Tradition attributes the short form to Marcion but cannot explain why he made the cut at 15^{1} rather than at 15^{14}; and the same difficulty faces the hypothesis that chs. 15 and 16 were omitted because they were not of general interest when the letter began to circulate elsewhere than in Rome. The shifting position of the words of grace and the doxology does not disprove the genuineness of ch. 15, but the case for ch. 16 is complicated with historical questions which illustrate the effect of the circulation and use of Paul's letters upon their text.

The principal points urged against the genuineness of ch. 16 are (*a*) the residence in Rome of so many of Paul's friends, particularly Prisca and Aquila, whom he had left in Ephesus only a few months before (Ac 20^{1}); (*b*) the designation of Epaenetus as the first convert in Asia, which would be more natural for Ephesus than for Rome; (*c*) the harsh warning in vv.$^{17-20}$, for which the reader of chs. 1–15 is unprepared, but which would be in keeping with the situation in Ephesus described in Ac 20^{28-30}; and (*d*) the difference in language and ideas between vv.$^{25-27}$ and the doxologies in the undisputed letters of Paul. But the attempt to solve these difficulties by supposing that this chapter was a separate letter, or fragment of a letter, addressed to the church in Ephesus does not explain satisfactorily how so short a letter consisting mainly of personal greetings came to be added to *Romans*; and the view that Ro 1–15 was written as a theological circular of which Phoebe was taking a copy to Ephesus is only conjecture. Another hypothesis, which holds that ch. 16 was written and added in Paul's name in order to claim his authority for the Roman church against such heretics as Marcion, raises difficulties at least as formidable as the textual and historical problems it is designed to solve. But since the view that Paul wrote this chapter as the conclusion of his letter to the Romans also leaves some questions without satisfying answers, any deductions from it that go beyond what can be inferred from chs. 1–15 must be regarded as uncertain and tentative. For this reason no reference has been made to ch. 16 in the account of the occasion, purpose and character of Romans in section one; if accepted, this chapter will supplement, but if rejected it will not invalidate what is there said concerning the historical context of Paul's purpose. One would expect him to appeal for co-operation to every person then living in Rome with whom he had worked elsewhere, and his missionary planning may even have had something to do with their going there. In view of the mobility of the peoples of the Roman world, the residence of so many of his friends in its capital is not fatal to the hypothesis that vv.$^{1-23}$ of this chapter belong to his letter to that city. Afterthoughts and sudden changes in tone as in vv.$^{17-20}$ are not unusual in Paul's letters; but vv.$^{25-27}$, which, in the form of a doxology, also serve as a summary description of the theme and content of the letter, may be later than Paul.

The fact that Romans stands first in the canonical order of Paul's correspondence measures its pre-eminence in capacity to function throughout the centuries in the shaping of Christian life and theology. Although written to a particular church in a specific situation in the middle of the first Christian century, its recognition of the futility of man's efforts to conquer the evil drive within himself and to reconcile his alienation from God by observance of God's law, its acceptance and sole reliance on God's way of effecting this reconciliation by His grace through faith in Christ, and its resulting incentive to live the new life in Christ make it both relevant and of ultimate concern to every man in every age. Permeated throughout by Paul's trinity of faith, hope, and love, its gospel abides forever, making those who accept it 'more than conquerors' in the midst of ceaseless change (8^{37-39}). R. T. S.

ROME.—1. The City.—The beginnings of Rome are shrouded in obscurity. The city was situated on the left bank of the Tiber, about 18 miles from its mouth. Though it is known as the city of the seven hills, the original Rome was built on one hill only, the Palatine; but the neighbouring hills were successively included, and about the middle of the 6th cent. B.C., according to tradition, a wall was built to enclose the enlarged city. The whole circuit of this wall was about 5 miles, and it was pierced by nineteen gates. Within the walls was a large area of vacant spaces, which were gradually built on later, and at the beginning of the Empire (roughly middle of 1st cent. B.C.) not only was the city congested with buildings, but large areas without the wall were also covered with houses. The Roman Forum, an open space measuring over 300 feet in length, and about 150 feet in breadth, was the centre of political, legal, and commercial life. At one end was the *rostra* or platform, from which speeches were delivered to the public; at the other end were shops. It was flanked by the senate-house and law-courts. On the top of the Capitoline Hill was the *Capitolium*, or great temple dedicated to Jupiter, Juno, and Minerva, and on the Palatine Hill the principal residence of the Emperor, and the Temple of Apollo, containing the public libraries, Greek and Latin. In the Imperial period four additional *fora* were built, devoted entirely to legal, literary, and religious purposes—the *Forum Iulium* begun by Julius Caesar, the *Forum Augustum* built by Augustus, the *Forum Transitorium* completed by Nerva, and the *Forum Traiani* built by Trajan—the most splendid work of Imperial times. Near the Viminal Gate in the E. lay the camp of the Praetorian guard (since Tiberius), to which Paul must have been conducted. On the 'Vatican Mount' W. of the Tiber lay the *Circus of Gaius and Nero*, where Peter may have been martyred. Various estimates of the population of Rome in the 1st cent. have been given: 2,000,000 seems not unlikely. All nationalities in the Empire were represented—among them many Jews, who were expelled by Claudius in A.D. 50, but returned at his death four years later. Slaves constituted a great part of the population.

2. Early history.—The Romans began as one of the members of the Latin league, of which, having become presidents, they eventually became masters. After conquering Latium they were inevitably brought into conflict with the other races of Italy, over most of which they were sovereign by about the middle of the 3rd cent. B.C.

The Roman State was at first ruled by kings, but these gave place to two rulers, known later as *consuls.* Their powers were gradually circumscribed by the transfer of some of their duties to other magistrates. The period of steady accession of territory was coincident with a bitter struggle between the patrician and the plebeian classes, both of which comprised free citizens. The contest between the orders lasted for about two centuries, and at the end of that period all the offices of State were open equally to both. This was not, however, the establishment of a real democracy, but the beginning of a struggle between the governing class and the mass of the people, which eventually brought the Republic to an end. The civil wars, which during the last century of its existence had almost destroyed it, had shown clearly that peace could be reached only under the rule of one man.

3. Expansion of territory.—The rise of Rome to almost universal power represents a remarkable history of diplomatic and military triumphs. After lower Italy had been subjugated (by 266 B.C.) Rome faced the power of Carthage, which held Sicily. The latter was swiftly taken in the First Punic War (264–241 B.C.) and in 238 B.C. Sardinia and Corsica were also seized. In the second Punic War (218–201 B.C.) Hannibal from his base in Spain crossed the Pyrenees and the Alps and invaded Italy. He was eventually defeated at Zama in Africa (202 B.C.). In 201 B.C. Carthage had to cede Spain to Rome and hand over its navy. The Romans now turned their attention toward the East. At Cynoscephalae they defeated Philip V. of Macedon, who had supported Carthage. The effort of the Seleucid king, Antiochus III., to establish himself in control of the straits leading to the sea of Marmora led to a clash with Rome that ended with his defeat at Magnesia in 190 B.C. and involved the loss of all Seleucid possessions W. of the Taurus. In the second Macedonian war king Perseus was defeated at Pydna in 168 B.C. and the country annexed. Greece now was also subjugated and Corinth brutally destroyed (146 B.C.). In the third Punic War (149–146 B.C.) Carthage was destroyed by Scipio Africanus. In 133 B.C. Attalus of Pergamum bequeathed his realm to Rome. The attempt of Mithridates of Pontus, from 95 B.C. on, to expand the influence of his realm into western Asia Minor and Greece led to Sulla's victories in Greece and to a temporary peace in 85 B.C. After Sulla's death in 78 B.C. Pompey, as leader of the Senatorial party, came to the fore. He was given extraordinary powers to put down the piracy rampant on the Asia Minor coast, and then became commander in the East, where he concluded the third war with Mithridates of Pontus in 64 B.C. and gave the *coup de grâce* to the Seleucid realm. He created Bithynia and Pontus as a province, and also Syria as another province. It was at this time (64 B.C.) that he took a hand in the affairs of Judaea.

4. Dictatorship and Empire.—The two-consul system which Sulla had replaced with dictatorship was restored under Pompey and Crassus in 70 B.C. But Pompey became sole consul in 52 B.C. Meanwhile Caesar had become a great factor through the successes he had won in his campaigns. In 49 B.C. came his break with the Senate and the beginning of a civil war. His victory over Pompey at Pharsalus in 48 B.C. and his success in the Egyptian War in 48–47 B.C. led to his being made dictator for ten years in 46 B.C. and for life in 44 B.C. His assassination robbed him of the fruits of his great achievements. Mark Antony sought to succeed to his rôle, but Caesar's adopted son Octavian, with Senatorial aid, forced the creation of a triumvirate. Antony took command in the East, and Octavian, who soon ousted the triumvir Lepidus, had control in the West. In the battle of Actium (31 B.C.) Octavian won the supremacy. He was given the title of Augustus and in addition bore the family name of Caesar. He ruled as autocrat under constitutional forms: the appearance of a republic was retained, but the reality was gone, and the appearance itself gradually disappeared also. The *Imperium Romanum* now had at its head an *Imperator* (whence our words Empire and Emperor).

5. The Provinces.—For the city of Rome the Empire was a time of luxury and idleness, but the provinces entered upon an era of progressive prosperity. The Emperor was responsible for the government of all provinces where an army was necessary (for instance, Syria), and governed these by paid deputies of his own. The older and more settled provinces were governed by officials appointed by the Senate, but the Emperor had his financial interests attended to by procurators of his own even in these. Under the Empire the provinces were much more protected against the rapacity and cruelty of governors than in Republican times. The Emperors themselves stood for just as well as efficient administration, and most of them gave a noble example by strenuous devotion to administrative business.

The resident Romans in any of the forty-two provinces consisted of (1) the officials connected with the Government, who were generally changed annually; (2) members of the great financial companies and lesser business men, whose interests kept them there; (3) citizens of *coloniae* (or military settlements), which were really parts of Rome itself set down in the provinces; (4) soldiers of the garrison and their officers; (5) distinguished natives of the province, who, for services rendered to the Roman State, were individually granted citizenship. Such must have been one of the ancestors of St. Paul. The honour was not conferred on all free male inhabitants of the Empire till A.D. 212, and in NT times those who possessed it constituted the aristocracy of the communities in which they lived.

6. The Jews and Rome.—Under the Maccabaean rulers the Jews had become virtually independent of the moribund Seleucid realm. In their rise the diplomacy of the Romans, who aided and abetted all enemies of the Seleucids, may have played a rôle. In 1 Mac 8 is vividly reflected the impression made on the Jews by Rome. Whether there was any historical basis for the alleged treaty with the Romans at the time of Judas Maccabaeus or not, the sending of an embassy to Rome to seek their support is plausible enough. A renewal of the treaty is claimed for the time of Jonathan (1 Mac 12$^{1-4}$) and again of Simon (1 Mac 14^{24} 15$^{15-24}$). Hyrcanus (134–104 B.C.), too, had Roman support (*Ant.* XII,. ix. 2 [259 ff]; XIV. x. 22 [190 ff]). The quarrel between the sons of Alexander Jannaeus (103–76 B.C.) was judged by Pompey in 63 B.C., and as Aristobulus acted suspiciously Pompey seized Jerusalem and terminated the kingship of the Hasmonaean house. During Caesar's campaign in Egypt (48–47 B.C.) Antipater, an Idumaean, and his son Herod (q.v.) succeeded in gaining the favour of Caesar and were given control of the Jewish kingdom. The favour of Antony and subsequently of Augustus led to the kingship of Herod (37–4 B.C.) over all Palestine and adjacent northern districts. In his testament, Herod divided his realm. The division was approved by Augustus, but Archelaus, who had the most important share, was soon deposed (A.D. 6) and Judaea put under imperial government. The procurator resided at Caesarea. One of the incumbents of the office was Pontius Pilate (q.v.).

Under Caligula (A.D. 37–41), Herod Agrippa was made king, and for a few years (A.D. 41–44) the situation existing in the days of Herod the Great was virtually restored. At Agrippa's death, however, Rome again took over direct control of Judaea. Rising Jewish terrorism led to open rebellion in A.D. 66, and this to the campaign of Vespasian and Titus which resulted in the devastation of Palestine and the destruction of Jerusalem in A.D. 70. The arch of Titus in Rome is a surviving monument of this event, as are the *Judaea capta* coins. A tax, the so-called *Fiscus Judaicus*, was imposed on all Jews of the realm in place of their old Temple-tax. Under Domitian (A.D. 81–96) strict measures against the Jews continued. Under Nerva (A.D. 96–98) things were less strict; there was even a coin bearing an inscription that accusations based on the annual Jewish tax were now set aside (*Fisci Judaici calumnia sublata*).

Under Trajan (A.D. 98–117), however, it became apparent that the Jews were a menace to the Empire. In his effort to subdue the Parthians the Jews of Mesopotamia offered strong resistance, and Jewish revolts broke out in Egypt, Cyrene, and Cyprus. It required the sending of strong military forces to master the situation. Lucius Quietus carried on a war of destruction against the Jews of the Euphrates-Tigris lands and Martius Turbo in Egypt and Cyrene. In Cyprus the Jews were exterminated and their kin forbidden the island. The synagogue of Alexandria, famed for its beauty, was destroyed. Quietus was about to proceed against the Jews in Palestine, where they had again become numerous, when Trajan died and Hadrian (A.D. 117–138) succeeded him. The new ruler was inclined to moderation, and held friendly talks with the Jewish Patriarch, Joshua. After the latter's death, Akiba, a proponent of active rebellion, came to the fore, and leagued himself with the political leader and insurrectionist Barcochba (*c* 132 ; his real name and title, preserved in a papyrus from Wâdī Murabbaʿât near the Dead Sea, were ' Simeon ben Kosebah, Prince of Israel '). Even the Samaritans and pagan mercenaries participated on the side of the Jews in this fantastic venture. The Roman commander Tineius Rufus was unable to control the situation. Hadrian recalled one of his best generals, Julius Severus, from Britain, and sent him to Palestine with the necessary troops. The country was subjected, the final tragedy taking place at Beth-ter (*Bittir*) S. of Jerusalem. Tineius Rufus was again put in charge of the region, and no Jew was allowed to set foot in *Aelia Capitolina*, the newly founded city on the site of Jerusalem. A temple of Aphrodite was built on the site of Golgotha, a temple of Jupiter on the site of the Jewish Temple in Jerusalem and also one in place of the Samaritan temple on Mount Gerizim. With the accession of Antoninus Pius, A.D. 138, Roman policy became more tolerant. While Aelia was still closed to them many Jews returned to the land of their fathers and devoted themselves to peaceful pursuits. Circumcision, which had been forbidden, was again allowed.

7. The Christians and Rome.—Christians were at first considered a Jewish sect by the Romans. But when the Jews disowned them this posed a difficult situation. Anti-Christian actions by the Roman authorities arose chiefly out of the refusal of Christians to worship the deified past emperors and the state gods. Nero's persecution was local and represented a whim rather than a policy. Domitian was the first emperor to claim divinity for himself. A persecution in his time in the province of Asia is reflected in the Revelation of St. John. Under Trajan occurred the martyrdom of Symeon of Jerusalem and Ignatius of Antioch, as well as the persecution in Bithynia under Pliny the Younger (see his *Epistles*, x. 96–97). Hadrian in an order issued to the governor of Asia discouraged active attempts to bring Christians to trial. Antoninus Pius (A.D. 138–161) discouraged anti-Christian tumults, but various martyrdoms occurred in his time, notably that of the aged Polycarp of Smyrna (A.D. 156). Marcus Aurelius (A.D. 161–180) renewed the law against superstitious cults, thus causing a state of danger for Christians. In his time Justin was martyred at Rome (A.D. 165), and there were martyrs in Asia Minor and in Gaul. Under Commodus (A.D. 180–192) there were scattered persecutions in N. Africa, Asia Minor, and Rome. The period from Decius (A.D. 249–251) on was one of planned persecution. That ruler, as well as Valerian (A.D. 253–260) and Diocletian (A.D. 284–305), vainly sought to destroy Christianity. The victory of Constantine over the usurper Maxentius in A.D. 312 paved the way for the edict of Milan (A.D. 313), in which Christianity was recognized as a legitimate religion (*religio licita*). The sons of Constantine abandoned the tolerant attitude and proceeded to persecute heathenism. After a heathen revival under Julian the Apostate (A.D. 361–363), Theodosius the Great and Gratianus from A.D. 381 on engaged in the destruction of heathenism and in the creation of a state-church.

8. The Religion of Rome.—The old Roman religion was one of fear and awe in the presence of mysterious divine powers, coupled with methodical efforts to placate them. Even before Rome's founding Jupiter (' heaven-father ') was worshipped in that vicinity and he remained the highest god to the end. His temple on the Capitol was the religious centre of both the Republic and the Empire. He was storm-god and guardian of law and order. Other gods were Mars, god of war ; Saturn who guarded the crops and Ceres who nurtured them, along with Faunus, patron of the herds. Vesta, goddess of the hearth and Janus, god of the door, were worshipped in every home, but also cultivated by the State. The temple of Vesta had its six vestal Virgins, whose task it was to keep the sacred flame burning. The Romans had a tendency to develop specialized gods as patrons of all manner of activities. Those of the household were included in the general name Penates (*penus*, ' store-room '). Certain concepts were even deified *e.g. pietas*, ' reverence for one's parents.' Considerable change was wrought in Roman religion by the wars with Hannibal and the fierce Gauls. They struck fear into people's hearts and a desire to appease the anger of the gods. Much new Greek and eastern lore was introduced through the attention given the Sibylline books. The Sibyls were the oracle-priestesses of the Apollo-cult in S. Italian cities. The books of the Sibyl of Cumae were even brought to the Capitol and their advice was seriously consulted. This could even lead to the introduction of new cults, as when the goddess Cybele, the *magna mater*, was imported from Pergamum in 204 B.C. With the rise of the Empire and of emperors a cult of emperor-worship (q.v.) arose. It served to make the provincials conscious of their dependence and of the blessings they enjoyed through the protection of Rome. In the cult of Mithras, which came to Rome in the time of Trajan and flourished under Commodus (A.D. 180–192) and after, Christianity faced a formidable rival. Other Hellenistic mystery cults also had their devotees, with the result that the picture of Roman religion under the Empire is one of great diversity.

See articles on the Emperors : AUGUSTUS, TIBERIUS, etc. ; PROVINCE, PROCURATOR, ROMAN PUBLIC LAW.

A. So.—**E. G. K.**

ROOF.—See HOUSE, **5.**

ROOM.—See HOUSE, **2.** For the ' upper room,' see *ib.* **5**, and for the now obsolete use of ' room ' in the sense of place at table, as 'the chief room ' (Lk 14^{7}) the ' highest room ' (v.^{8}—RV in both cases ' chief seat ' ; RSV ' place of honour '), or ' the uppermost room ' (Mt 23^{6}, Mk 12^{39}, RV ' chief place ' ; RSV ' place of honour '), see MEALS, **6.** A. R. S. K.

ROPE.—See CORD.

ROSE.—Hebrew *ḥᵃbaṣṣeleth*, Ca 2^{1} **(rose of Sharon)**, Is 35^{1} (AV, RV ; RSV **crocus**). All authorities are agreed that the translation ' rose ' is incorrect. The *ḥᵃbaṣṣeleth* appears to have been a bulbed flower. The RVm suggests ' autumn crocus ' (*colchicum autumnale*) ; on the other hand, many good authorities suggest the much more striking and sweeter-scented plant—the narcissus, which is a great favourite to-day in Palestine. Two species are known—*N. Tazetta* and *N. serotinus*. In Wis 2^{8}, Sir 24^{14} 39^{13} 50^{8} we have mention of *rhodon* (Gr.). Whether this is, as Tristram maintains, the Rhododendron or the true rose is uncertain ; both occur in parts of Palestine. E. W. G. M.

ROSH.—**1.** A descendant of Benjamin, Gn 46^{21} (but the text is doubtful). **2.** In Ezk 38^{2f} 39^{1} the word *Rosh* is thought by many interpreters to refer to a people (so RV), otherwise unknown, but coupled with *Meshech* and *Tubal* (q.v.). It is possible, however, that the word meaning ' head ' is used as a preposition ' over,' so that the phase here applied to Gog (q.v.) simply means, ' prince over Meshech and Tubal (cf AV and RSV ' chief prince of '). J. F. McC.

RUBY.—See JEWELS AND PRECIOUS STONES.

RUDDER.—See SHIPS AND BOATS, **2** (2).

RUE (Lk 11[42]).—The rue of Palestine is *Ruta chalepensis*, a variety of the officinal plant, which is cultivated as a medicine.

RUFUS.—**1.** The brother of Alexander and son of Simon of Cyrene (Mk 15[21] only). **2.** A Christian at Rome greeted by St. Paul (Ro 16[13]) as 'eminent in the Lord,' together with 'his mother and mine.' It has been conjectured that these two are the same person, that Simon's widow (?) had emigrated to Rome with her two sons, where they became people of eminence in the Church, and that this is the reason why the brothers are mentioned by St. Mark, who probably wrote in Rome.

RUG.—Found in Jg 4[18] (AVm, RV, RSV; AV 'mantle'). The meaning is uncertain.

RUHAMAH.—The second child (a daughter) of Gomer, Hosea's wife, was called **Lo-ruhamah,** 'unpitied,' Hos 1[6, 8] (RSV 'not pitied'). The name was given symbolically to indicate that God had ceased to pity Israel, and given her over to calamity. The return of God's mercy is indicated in Hos 2[1] 'Say ye unto your brethren, *Ammi* (RSV 'My people,' in opposition to **Lo-ammi,** 'not my people'); and to your sisters, *Ruhamah* (RSV 'She has obtained pity'). A similar play on the word is found in Hos 2[23] 'I will *have mercy on* her that had not obtained mercy (*lô-rūhāmāh*).'
W. F. B.

RULE.—See Arts and Crafts, **1.**

RULER OF THE FEAST.—See Governor, Meals, **6.**

RULER OF THE SYNAGOGUE.—See Synagogue, **5.**

RULERS OF THE CITY.—EV translation in Ac 17[6, 8] of the Greek *politarchai*, which was the special local title of the magistrates or city councillors of Thessalonica. They were five or six in number. RSV 'city authorities.'

RUMAH.—The home of Pedaiah, the maternal grandfather of Jehoiakim, 2 K 23[36]. Josephus (*Ant.* x. v. 2 [83]) reads *Abouma*, no doubt a scribal error for *Arouma*, which may be the **Arumah** of Jg 9[41] near Shechem. There was another Rumah in Galilee (Jos. *BJ* iii. vii. 21 [233]), perhaps the modern *Kh. er-Rûmeh* near Nazareth; and Pedaiah may have been a Galilean.
W. F. B.

RUNNEL.—This word is used only in RSV in Gn 30[38, 41] for watering troughs (AV, RV 'gutter'). In Ex 2[16] the same word is rendered 'trough' in AV, RV and RSV.

RUNNERS.—See Footman, Guard, and Post.

RUSH, RUSHES.—**1.** Hebrew *gōme'*, Ex 2[3] (EV **bulrushes**; RVm 'papyrus'), Job 8[11] (AV, RV 'rush'; RVm, RSV 'papyrus'), Is 8[2] (AV 'bulrushes'; RV, RSV 'papyrus'); 35[7] (EV 'rushes'). This was probably the once famous plant the papyrus (*Cyperus papyrus*, Arab. *babîr*), which now flourishes in the Huleh swamps. The bulrush (*Scirpus maritimus*) and other species may have been included in the Hebrew name *gōme'*. **2.** Hebrew *'agmôn*, Job 41[2] (AV 'hook'; RV, RSV 'rope'; RVm 'a rope of rushes') 41[20] (AV 'caldron'; RV, RSV '[burning] rushes'), Is 9[14] 19[15] (both AV, RV 'rush'; RSV 'reed') 58[5] (AV 'bulrush'; RV, RSV 'rush'). There are some twenty kinds of rushes in Palestine, but it is impossible to fit the references to any one kind and, indeed, some kind of reed (q.v.) is quite as probable, especially in Is 58[5].
E. W. G. M.

RUTH.—A woman of Moab, who, like her mother-in-law Naomi, and her sister-in-law Orpah, was left a widow. On Naomi's desiring to return to her own people in Bethlehem-Judah—which she had left with her husband owing to a famine—Ruth refused to leave her, and the two returned to Bethlehem. Here she became the wife of **Boaz,** and bore him Obed, who became the father of Jesse; she therefore figures in the genealogy of Christ (Mt 1[5]). See, further, the next article.
W. O. E. O.

RUTH (Book of).—**1. Contents.**—The book is a short story, told in a very charming manner; indeed it is often cited as a perfect example of its literary *genre*. It tells how Naomi, a Judaean, after the death in Moab of her husband and two sons, started to return to Bethlehem, leaving her Moabite daughters-in-law. Orpah returned to her family, but Ruth loyally remained with Naomi. Subsequently Ruth was married to a kinsman, Boaz, and bore a son, who was the grandfather of David. Naomi, Ruth, and Boaz are all represented as wholly admirable characters, and there is no villain in the narrative.

Though a charming story, this book presents many difficulties in interpretation. Why was it written? Many interpreters say it was composed as a protest against the narrow nationalism which prevailed in the time of Ezra and Nehemiah, or at some other time. Was it written to plead for a wider interpretation of levirate marriage than was customary? Was it intended to present the story of a beautiful friendship between a mother-in-law and her daughter-in-law? Some scholars believe it was written only to entertain, and with no other motive. Some think it developed from an ancient fertility myth of Bethlehem. Rabbinic Judaism saw in Ruth the example of a perfect proselyte. It is not probable that the story was told only to entertain; any adequate view of its purpose must take into consideration the fact that Ruth, the central character, is a Moabitess by birth, but is represented as being completely loyal to her mother-in-law and her adopted nation, and as an ancestress of the great king David.

Much interest has been aroused by the legal customs reflected in the book, especially in 4[1-12]. These do not correspond precisely to the known customs of any period of Hebrew history. The legal transaction of ch. 4 seems to combine features both of levirate marriage (Dt 25[5-6]) and of redemption of property (Lv 25). The curious custom of drawing off the sandal (4[8]) may represent a token payment for the rights of the nearest of kin.

2. Date.—The language of the book and other considerations point to the post-exilic period as the time of composition of the book in its present form. It may draw upon a very ancient tale, which was used by the author for his own purpose. In the Hebrew canon Ruth is one of the Hagiographa, or Writings. More precise dating depends upon the view one takes of the purpose of the story and of the legal customs involved in it. A date between 450 and 250 B.C. is probably correct.
J. P. H.

RYE.—See Rie.

S

SABACHTHANI.—See Eloi, Eloi, etc.

SABAEANS.—See Sheba.

SABAN, 1 Es 8[63] (AV).—See Binnui, **2.**

SABANNEUS, 1 Es 9[33] (RV).—See Zabad, **6.**

SABANNUS, 1 Es 8[63] (RV).—See Binnui, **2.**

SABAOTH.—See Lord of Hosts.

SABAT, 1 Es 5[34] (A.V.).—See Shaphat, **6.**

SABATEAS, 1 Es 9[48] (AV).—See Shabbethai.

SABATEUS, 1 Es 9[48] (RV).—See Shabbethai.

SABATHUS, 1 Es 9[28] (RV).—See Zabad, **5.**

SABATUS, 1 Es 9^{28} (AV).—See ZABAD, **5.**

SABBAIAS.—One who married a foreign wife, 1 Es 9^{32} (AV, RV **Sabbeus**); perhaps the same as **Shemaiah, 18.**

SABBATEUS, 1 Es 9^{14} (RV).—See SHABBETHAI.

SABBATH.—1. Origin of the Sabbath.—The name 'Sabbath' (Heb. *shabbāth*, from a verb *shābhath*, meaning 'to desist') might be applied to any sacred season as a time of cessation from labour, and is so used of the Day of Atonement, which was observed annually on the tenth day of the seventh month (Lv 16^{31} 23^{32}). But in usage it is almost confined to the day of rest which closed each week of seven days, the cycle running continuously through the calendar without regard to the month or the year. The origin of this institution and its early history among the Israelites are involved in much obscurity. That it has affinities with certain Babylonian observances is obvious; but the differences are very marked, and a direct dependence of the one on the other is difficult to understand. It is known that in two months (possibly in all) the 7th, 14th, 21st, and 28th days (those in which the moon enters a new phase), and also the 19th (the 7×7th $=$ 49th from the beginning of the previous month), were regarded in Babylonia as days of ill omen, on which certain actions had to be avoided by important personages (king, priest, physician). The name *shapattu* has also been found in the inscriptions, where it is explained as *ūm nuḥ libbi* 'day of the appeasement of the heart' (of the deity)—in the first instance, therefore, a day of prayer or atonement. But that the five days of ill omen mentioned above were called *shapattu* has not been proved, and is indeed, rendered improbable by the more recent discovery that *shapattu* was a name for the day of the full moon (the 15th of the month). When we turn to the early references to the Sabbath in the OT, we find a state of things which seems at first sight to present a parallel to the Babylonian usage. It is a singular fact that except in the expansions of the Fourth Commandment in Ex 20^{9-11} and Dt 5^{13-15} (which are evidently no part of the original Decalogue), there is nothing in the pre-exilic literature which explicitly indicates that the word 'Sabbath' denoted a weekly day of rest. In the kernel of the Decalogue (Ex 20^{8}, Dt 5^{12}), the observance of the Sabbath is enjoined; but neither the manner of its observance nor the period of its recurrence is prescribed. Where, on the other hand, the weekly rest is inculcated (Ex 23^{12} 34^{21}), the name 'Sabbath' does not occur. In the prophetic and historical books 'Sabbath' and 'new moon' are associated in such a way as to suggest that both were lunar festivals (Am 8^{5}, Ho 2^{11}, Is 1^{13}, 2 K 4^{23}); and the attempt has been made to trace the transition from the Babylonian institution to the Hebrew Sabbath by the hypothesis that originally the Sabbath in Israel was the feast of the full moon, just as in Babylonia. This theory, however, is little but an ingenious paradox. It is arbitrary to deny the antiquity of Ex 23^{12} or 34^{21}; and if the word 'Sabbath' is not found in these passages, yet the related verb *shābhath* is used in both, as is rarely the case except in connexion with the Sabbath. Moreover, the way in which the Sabbath is isolated from all other sacred seasons (Decalogue, 2 K 11^{5ff}, 16^{18}) goes far to show that even in the pre-exilic period it was a festival *sui generis*, and had already acquired something of the prominence which belonged to it in later times. It is not too much to say that the Israelite origins of the institution are to be traced to Moses himself (Ex 20^{8} 23^{12} 31^{15} 34^{21}) and that the later prophetic interpretations of its true significance have their source in the Mosaic traditions. The most reasonable conclusion is that the weekly Sabbath is everywhere presupposed in the OT, and that, if it be connected historically with Babylonian institutions, the development lies behind the range of Israelite tradition, and in all probability was a feature of Canaanitish civilization when the Hebrews settled in the country. It must be remembered, however, that the hypothesis of a Babylonian origin does not exhaust the possibilities of the case. It has often been asserted that a regularly recurring day of rest is neither necessary nor possible for pastoral nomads, but it must be pointed out that the Israelites were semi-sedentary and it is quite conceivable that some form of Sabbath observance depending on the phases of the moon, was practised by the Hebrews in the desert, and that the transformation of this primitive lunar festival into the Sabbath as we find it in the OT was due to the suppression of its superstitious associations under the influence of the national religion of Israel.

2. Religious significance of the Sabbath.—The distinctive characteristics of the Hebrew Sabbath were mainly these two: it was, first, a day sacred to Yahweh, and second, a day of rest. In the earlier period cessation from labour may have been merely a consequence of the festal character of the day; although the reinforcement of the ceremonial sanction by humanitarian motives in the legislation (Ex 23^{12}, Dt 5^{14}) shows that already the religious mind of the nation had grasped the final justification of the Sabbath as an institution made for man, and not one for which man was made. This conception of the Sabbath underwent a radical modification in the age of the Exile. It is hardly accurate to say that the change was entirely due to the fact that the Sabbath was one of the few religious ordinances by which the Israelite in a foreign land could mark his separation from heathenism. The idea of the Sabbath as a covenant between Yahweh and Israel, which is elaborated in Ezekiel and the code called the Law of Holiness, is foreshadowed in Dt 5^{15}; and even the more imposing conception of it as a memorial of the Creation finds expression in Ex 20^{11}, which is quite possibly of older date than the Priestly account of Creation in Gn 1. The truth is that in this, as in many other cases, the real turning-point was not the deportation of the people but the suppression of the popular ritual by Josiah's reformation. None the less it is important to observe that, for whatever reason, a profound transformation of the character of the Sabbath emerges in writings of the Exilic and post-exilic period. The obligation of rest, from being a necessary concomitant of acts of worship, or a means to a higher end, becomes an end in itself, a form of self-denial, pleasing to the Deity as an act of implicit obedience to His positive command. The whole of the subsequent legislation proceeds from this point of view. In Ezekiel and the Law of Holiness the Sabbath (as has just been observed) is conceived as an arbitrary sign of the covenant between Yahweh and Israel, and of the individual's fidelity to that covenant. The Priestly Code not only exalts the Sabbath by making it the impressive climax of its account of the creation of the universe and by basing its sanction on the example of the Creator (Gn 2^{2-4}, Ex 31^{17}), but seeks to enforce its observance by the imposition of the death penalty (Ex 31^{14}, Nu 15^{32-36}), and sets the example of guarding its sanctity by prohibitive regulations (Ex 35^{3}). The memoirs of Nehemiah reveal at once the importance attached to the Sabbath as a mark of the distinction between the faithful Jews and their heathen neighbours (10^{31} 13^{15}), and the stern determination which was necessary to compel obedience (13^{17ff}). In post-exilic prophecies there are several allusions to Sabbath observance as a supreme religious duty, and a condition of the fulfilment of the Messianic expectations (Jer 17^{19ff}, Is 56^{2ff} 58^{13f} 66^{23}). At the commencement of the Maccabaean revolt, regard for the Sabbath was so ingrained in the mind of the people that strict Jews allowed themselves to be slaughtered by their enemies rather than use arms for their own defence (1 Mac 2^{31ff}); though after one incident of this kind the maxim laid down that defensive operations in war were legitimate on the Sabbath (v.^{41}).

3. Sabbath in the NT.—The Gospels show that by the time of Christ the casuistry of the scribes had hedged round the Sabbath with many of those petty and vexatious rules which are preserved in the Rabbinical literature. The scribal interpretation of the Sabbath law was one of the subjects of controversy between Jesus and the Pharisees (see Mt $12^{1ff, 10f}$, Lk 13^{14ff} 14^{1ff}, Jn 5^{5ff} 7^{23} 9^{14ff} etc.). As regards our Lord's own attitude it is enough to say that it combined reverence for the ordinance, in so far as it served religious ends (Lk 4^16 etc.), with a resolute vindication of the principle that 'the Sabbath was made for man and not man for the Sabbath' (Mk 2^27). Similarly, in the Pauline Epistles the Sabbath is relegated, either inferentially (Ro 14^5f, Gal 4^9ff) or expressly (Col 2^16f), to the category of things morally indifferent, with regard to which each man must follow the dictates of his conscience. It is significant also that the decree of the Council of Jerusalem does not impose the observance of the Sabbath on the Gentile Churches (Ac 15^29). On the later Christian observance of the first day of the week, and its assimilation to the Jewish Sabbath, see LORD'S DAY. J. S.—**J. Mu.**

SABBATH DAY'S JOURNEY.—See WEIGHTS AND MEASURES, 1.

SABBATHEUS, 1 Es 9^14 (AV).—See SHABBETHAI.

SABBATICAL YEAR (including **year of Jubilee**).—**1. OT references.**—In a consideration of the regulations connected with the Sabbatical and Jubilee years, it is of the greatest importance to keep distinct the various stages of the Jewish legislation on the subject. The various ordinances differ greatly in character and detail; and in order to comprehend the diversity it is necessary to assume as granted the main conclusions of OT criticism, and to admit at any rate that a separation in time and difference in spirit characterize the several parts of the 'Mosaic Law.'

Exodus. In 23^10f an entire cessation of all fieldwork is ordered to take place in every seventh year. This is said to be dictated by a regard for the poor and the beasts of the field. In effect the gift of one year's produce to the poor is prescribed, that the landless may enjoy a share in the produce of the soil. In 21^2-6 it is laid down that a Hebrew slave can be kept in bondage only for six years. After this period he was automatically emancipated, though his wife and children must remain in servitude, if he had married after his term of service began. But provision was made for cases where a slave might desire to remain in this condition. A public ceremony took place which signified his acceptance of the position in perpetuity. Nothing is here said which leads us to suppose that there was one simultaneous period of emancipation all over the country, and no reference is made to redemption of land or remission of debts.

Deuteronomy. In 15^1-3 the seventh year is assigned as the period at which all the liabilities of a Jew were suspended (or possibly, as Josephus supposes, entirely cancelled); this provision was to be of universal operation. 15^12-18 repeats the ordinances of Ex 21 with regard to the emancipation of slaves; here again no simultaneity of redemption can be inferred. 31^10-13 prescribes that the Law is to be read every seventh year (the 'year of release') at the Feast of Tabernacles (cf Neh 8^13-18). Nothing is said in Deuteronomy about a possible redemption of land.

Leviticus. In 25^1-55 provision is made for a seventh-year fallow; but there is no mention of the poor. The reason assigned is that the land, being Yahweh's land, must keep Sabbath, *i.e.* the Sabbath principle is extended to cover nature as well as man. We also find here the jubilee ordinances. After forty-nine years had elapsed, every fiftieth year was to be inaugurated as a jubilee by the blowing of the trumpet (Heb. *yōbhēl,* hence the name jubilee) on the Day of Atonement. All slaves were to be emancipated (this may be a modified substitute for the earlier provisions with regard to emancipation after seven years); no mention is made of the possibility of perpetual slavery, but it is ordained that the Hebrew slave of a foreigner may be redeemed by a relative, all Jews being essentially Yahweh's servants. The land was to be fallow. Providential aid was promised to ensure sufficient food while crops could not be gathered when the land lay fallow (presumably both for the jubilee year, vv.^11f, and for the seventh year, vv.^20-22). Here also we find elaborate directions for the redemption of land in the jubilee year. They may be thus summarized: (1) No landed property may be sold, but only the value of the series of crops up to the next jubilee, and the price must be calculated by the distance from that period. (2) A kinsman may redeem land thus mortgaged, or (the meaning may possibly be) exercise a right of pre-emption upon it. (3) The mortgager may redeem at the selling price, less the yearly proportion for the time elapsed since the sale. (4) House property in walled towns (not in villages) may be sold outright, and is redeemable only during one year. Such property was presumably regarded as human and artificial, whilst all land was essentially the property of Yahweh. (5) The Levitical possessions were redeemable at any time, and did not come under the jubilee provisions. (6) Nothing is said in Leviticus as to the remission of debts, but there is a general prohibition of usury. (7) In Lv 27^16-25 a field devoted to Yahweh must be valued by the priest with reference to the number of crops before the next jubilee and might be redeemed at this price with the addition of one-fifth. If not redeemed by the jubilee it became sacred property; no redemption of it was thereafter possible.

2. Purposes of the Sabbatical rules.—The purposes underlying the ordinances above catalogued may be classified under four heads; but it is practically impossible to assign any certain priority of time to any one of the classes. (*a*) *The periodical fallow.* This is a very common provision in agriculture, and the seven years' period is still observed in Syria. Since the fallow year was not at first everywhere simultaneous, the earlier historical books are silent about it; and indeed it cannot have been generally observed. The seventy years' captivity and desolation of the land was regarded as making up for the unobserved Sabbaths of the land (2 Ch 36^21, cf Lv 26^34, 43). The reference in Neh 10^31 may be to the periodical fallow or to the remission of debts. But 1 Mac 6^49, 53 shows that the fallow year was observed later. (*b*) *The emancipation of slaves* (cf Jer 34^8f). Such a provision must have been very difficult to enforce, and we find no other possible reference to it. (*c*) *The remission or suspension of debts.* The only reference is the dubious one in Neh 10^31. (*d*) *The redemption of real property.* The kind of tenure here implied is not uncommonly found in other countries, and Jer 32^6ff, Ru 4, Ezk 7^13 show that something akin to it did exist in Palestine (cf also Ezk 46^17). But that it was in no sense universal may be inferred from Isaiah's and Micah's denunciations of land-grabbing; on the other hand, 1 K 21^3f furnishes an instance of the inalienability of land.

In general we have no sign that the sabbatical and jubilee provisions were ever strictly observed in Biblical times. Their principles of rest and redemption, though never practised as a piece of social politics, were preached as ideals, and may have had some effect in discouraging slave-owning, land-grabbing, and usury, and in encouraging a more merciful view of the relations between Jew and Jew. Thus Is 61^1-3 is steeped in the jubilee phraseology, and Christ adopted this passage to explain His own mission (Lk 4^18ff). A. W. F. B.—**L. H. B.**

SABBEUS, 1 Es 9^32 (AV, RV).—See SABBAIAS.

SABI.—**1.** 1 Es 5^28 (RV); see SHOBAI. **2.** 1 Es 5^34 (AV; 1611 ed. **Sabie**); see POCHERETH-HAZZEBAIM.

SABIAS, 1 Es 1^9 (AV).—See HASHABIAH, 6.

SABIE, 1 Es 5^34 (RV).—See POCHERETH-HAZZEBAIM.

SABTA, SABTAH.—In the genealogical list of Gn 10^7 (**Sabtah**) and 1 Ch 1^9 (**Sabta**) a son of Cush, named between Havilah and other Arabian districts. It was probably a region on or near the east coast of Arabia, but in spite of several conjectures it has not been identified with any historical tribe or country. The relationship with Cush is to be accounted for on the ground that the Cushites were held to have extended across the Red Sea from Nubia north-eastward over the great peninsula.
J. F. McC.

SABTECA.—The youngest son of Cush according to Gn 10^{7}, 1 Ch 1^{9} (AV **Sabtecha**). The only identification at all plausible has been made with *Samydake* on the E. side of the Persian Gulf. But this is improbable, since that region did not come within the Cushite domain, as judged by the names of the other sons of Cush. Possibly *Sabteca* is a mis-writing for **Sabtah** (q.v.). J. F. McC.

SABTECHA, Gn 10^{7}, 1 Ch 1^{9} (AV).—See SABTECA.

SACAR.—1. 1 Ch 11^{35} (AV, RV) ; see SACHER. **2.** A family of gatekeepers, 1 Ch 26^{4}.

SACHER.—The father of Ahiam, 1 Ch 11^{35} (AV, RV **Sacar**).

SACHIA.—A Benjamite, 1 Ch 8^{10} (AV, RV **Shachia**).

SACKBUT.—See MUSIC, etc., **4** (*c*).

SACKCLOTH.—The sackcloth of OT was a coarse dark cloth woven on the loom from the hair of goats and camels. In the OT it has the following uses: (*a*) a sack for grain (Gn 42^{25}, Lv 11^{32}) ; (*b*) a garment worn in mourning, or spread out to lie upon (2 S 21^{10}, 1 K 21^{27}). It may also have been a waist-cloth, if the frequently occurring expression ' to gird sackcloth upon the loins ' is to be understood in that sense. But it need not imply more than that the garment of sackcloth was to be fastened about the waist (2 S 3^{31} *et al.*). The wearing of sackcloth is associated with rending of the clothes and putting ashes upon the head, as signs of grief and penitence. These customs have been interpreted by anthropologists as remains of rites practised by primitive peoples caused by fear of the dead, with the intention of disguising themselves from recognition by the spirits of the dead. In Jon 3^{8} the Ninevites are said to have put sackcloth upon their animals, where the sackcloth can hardly be understood as a waistcloth. It is even said to have been put upon the altar (Jth 4^{11}), where it can still less be a waist-cloth. See MOURNING CUSTOMS. S. H. He.

SACRAMENTS.—1. The term.—Although applied by common consent to certain institutions of the NT, the word ' sacrament ' (Lat. *sacramentum*) is not a Scriptural one. In classical Latin *sacramentum* (from *sacrare*, ' to consecrate ') is used especially in two senses: (*a*) passively, as a legal term, to denote a sum of money deposited by the parties to a suit, which was forfeited by the loser and appropriated to sacred uses ; (*b*) actively, as a military term, to denote the oath taken by newly enlisted soldiers. When it came to be applied to Christian uses, the word retained the suggestions of both of these earlier employments. A sacrament was something set apart for sacred purposes ; it was also, in certain cases, of the nature of a vow of self-consecration, resembling the oath of the Roman soldier (cf Tertullian : ' We were called to the warfare of the living God in our very response to the sacramental words,' *ad Mart.* iii.). But the application and history of the word in the Christian Church were determined chiefly by the fact that in the Old Latin and Vulgate it was repeatedly employed (*mysterium*, however, being employed more frequently) to render the Greek *mystērion*, ' a mystery.' Thus Vulgate translated St. Paul's ' This mystery is great ' (Eph 5^{32}) by ' Sacramentum hoc magnum est '—a rendering that had not a little to do with the subsequent erection of marriage into a sacrament. See also RSV, ' This is a great mystery.' This identification of the idea of a sacrament with that of a mystery was carried still further by Tertullian (see article MYSTERY). Tertullian (end of 2nd cent. and beginning of 3rd) is the first writer to apply the name ' sacrament ' to Baptism, the Eucharist, and other rites of the Christian Church.

When Pliny (*c* A.D. 112), in his account of the worship of the Christians of Bithynia, describes them at their morning meetings as ' binding themselves by a *sacramentum* to commit no kind of crime ' (*Epp.* x. xcvi), it has been suggested by some that he was using the word in the Christian sense, and was referring either to the baptismal vow or to participation in the Eucharist. The probability is that Pliny intended it in the old Roman sense of an oath or solemn obligation.

2. Nature and number.—(1) Though used especially of Baptism and the Eucharist, the application of the term by Christian writers was at first exceedingly loose, for it was taken to describe not only all kinds of religious ceremonies, but even facts and doctrines of the Christian faith. The prevailing notion is illustrated by Augustine's remark that ' signs pertaining to things Divine are called sacraments,' and by his well-known definition of a sacrament as ' the visible form of an invisible grace.' It is otherwise illustrated by the fact that Hugo of St. Victor (12th cent.) enumerates about thirty sacraments that had been recognized in the Church. The Council of Trent defined the nature of a sacrament more closely, by laying it down that not all signs of sacred things have sacramental value, and that visible forms are sacraments only when they *represent* an invisible grace and become its channels. It further delimited the sacramental area by re-enacting in its seventh session (1547) a decision of the Council of Florence (1439) in which effect was for the first time authoritatively given to the suggestion of Peter Lombard (12th cent.) and other Schoolmen that the number of the sacraments should be fixed at seven, namely, Baptism, Confirmation, the Eucharist, Penance, Extreme Unction, Orders, and Matrimony—a suggestion that was evidently influenced by the belief that seven was a sacred number.

(2) In the Reformed Churches criticism of this scheme was based on the fact that the number 7 is arbitrary. While, therefore, the Reformers retained the term ' sacrament,' for ' an outward and visible sign of an inward and spiritual grace given unto us,' they found the distinguishing mark of a sacrament in the fact of its being instituted by Christ Himself and enjoined by Him upon His followers. **Baptism** and the **Lord's Supper** are the only two rites for which they could make this claim. The uniqueness that belongs to these as resting upon Christ's personal appointment and being bound up with His own words (Mt 28^{19}, Mk 16$^{[16]}$; Mt 26$^{26-29}$||, 1 Co 11$^{23-25}$) justified them in separating these two from all other rites and ceremonies. A justification of this segregation of Baptism and the Lord's Supper from all other rites, and their association together under a common name, is furnished in the NT by Ac 2^{41f} and 1 Co 10$^{1-4}$. A further justification may perhaps be found in the fact that St. Paul traces an analogy between Circumcision and the Passover—the two most distinctive rites of the Old Covenant—on the one hand, and Baptism (Col 2^{11}) and the Lord's Supper (cf 1 Co 5^{7} with 11^{26}) respectively, on the other.

See BAPTISM, CONFIRMATION, EUCHARIST, LAYING ON OF HANDS, LORD'S SUPPER. J. C. L.—**M. H. S.**

SACRIFICE AND OFFERING.—1. TERMINOLOGY OF SACRIFICE.—(*a*) *General.* Since every sacrifice was an offering, but not all offerings were sacrifices, this preliminary study of the usage of these two important terms may start from the more comprehensive ' offering.' It is true that in the majority of the occurrences of ' offering ' it is simply a synonym of ' sacrifice.' This is the case more particularly in the extensive nomenclature of the various sacrifices, *e.g.* ' burnt offering ' (which also appears in AV as ' burnt sacrifice ') or ' cereal offering.' Names of this type would be more correctly joined by a hyphen as in American RV : ' burnt-offering,' etc ; for as will presently appear (**2**), the compound expression in such cases represents but a single word in the original, which is the technical term for the particular sacrifice.

In the remaining occurrences, however, ' offering,' or its synonym ' oblation,' is used in a more extended application to denote a gift offered to God, as opposed to a secular gift, in the form of a present, bribe, or the like, to a fellow-creature. Such ' holy gifts ' (Ex 28^{38}) or offerings may be divided into three classes, namely, (1) altar-offerings, comprising all such offerings as were brought into contact with the altar (cf Mt 23^{19}), mostly for the purpose of being consumed thereon ;

(2) the stated sacred dues, such as tithes, first-fruits, etc.; and (3) special votive offerings, *e.g.* those specified in Nu 7. In this comprehensive sense of the term, 'offering' or—as almost uniformly in RV—'oblation,' corresponds to the Hebrew *ḳorbān*, a word peculiar to Ezekiel and the priestly legislation. It is the **Corban** of Mk 7[11], 'that is given to God' (AV literally, 'a gift'), and means 'something brought near,' *i.e.* to the altar, or at least presented at the sanctuary, in other words, a present to God. The term, as has been said, appears late in the history of OT sacrifice (Ezk 20[28] 40[43] and the various strata of P *passim*), the nearest corresponding term in the older literature being *minḥāh*, for which see **2.**

The classification of OT offerings above suggested serves, further, to bring into relief the relation of 'sacrifice' to 'offering.' The former may be defined as *an offering which is consumed, in whole or in part, upon the altar*, or, more briefly, as an altar-offering. It is in this more restricted sense of altar-offering that 'sacrifice' and 'offering' are employed synonymously in our English nomenclature of sacrifice.

'Sacrifice' is the common translation for Hebrew *zebhaḥ*, which is the characteristic designation of an **animal** offering. Literally it means 'slaughter'; the verb is originally to slaughter generally, then specially to immolate the sacrificial victim, to sacrifice. Hence comes also the word for **'altar,'** *mizbēaḥ*, literally the place of slaughter (for sacrifice). In a number of passages this word is coupled with *minḥāh*, which in the early literature could mean any offering to God but later was specialized to mean the non-animal offerings of cereal, oil, etc. In late occurrences of the phrase 'sacrifice and offering' we then have animal and cereal types taken together; such will certainly be the sense in Dn 9[27]. In some other passages it is doubtful if we can give the second noun the later precise meaning, and the phrase may be taken as meaning altar-offerings in all their various forms; so Ps 40[6], 1 S 3[14], Is 19[21] (in this last RSV certainly mistranslates with 'burnt offering').

2. TERMINOLOGY OF SACRIFICE.—(*b*) *Special.* To the foregoing study of the more general terms may now be added a brief review of the more specific renderings of the names of the principal altar-offerings, reserving for later sections the examination of their characteristic features. Following the order of the manual of sacrifice, Lv 1–5, we have (1) the **burnt offering**—AV uses also 'burnt sacrifice'—Hebrew *'ōlāh*, literally 'that which goes up' (on the altar). A derivation meaning 'that which is cooked' has also been suggested. The name is supposed to point to the feature by which the *'ōlāh* was distinguished from all other sacrifices, viz., the burning of the whole victim as a holocaust upon the altar. This characteristic is more explicitly brought out by the rare designation (2) *kālîl*, the **'whole burnt offering'** of Dt 33[10] and Ps 51[19].

(3) **Cereal offering** (AV 'meat offering,' RV 'meal offering') translates *minḥāh* in its normal sense in the Levitical code. The word could in earlier times be used of any gift or present, *e.g.* that of Jacob to Esau (Gn 32[13]) or that which a king would expect to receive from his subjects (1 S 10[27]). When used of a gift to Yahweh it could include both animal and cereal offerings, as in the case of Cain and Abel (Gn 4[3ff]). When it was specialized to the sense of 'cereal offering,' its place as a general term for sacred gifts was taken by *ḳorbān*. With the cereal offering may be taken (4) the **drink offering** or **libation** (Gn 35[14], Nu 15[1–10] etc.).

(5) **Peace offering** is at best only a token translation for the term *shelem*, nearly always in the plural *shᵉlāmîm*. In the Levitical system the distinguishing feature of this sacrifice is the eating of the main part of the animal by the offerer and his family or friends after the choice portions have gone to the altar and the priests. The name of the sacrifice may be connected with *shālôm* 'peace,' to reflect the harmonious relations of worshipper and worshipped expressed in the sacrifice. Even in this case the reader should not interpret the name 'peace offering' as an offering to make peace, a kind of propitiation, as sometimes in colloquial English, which is certainly not the meaning. It is perhaps better to take the word in the sense 'completeness' (a general meaning of the root, and one which could well fit this particular use). When several types of animal sacrifice follow in series, the 'peace offerings' come at the end, and the sense 'final offering' has in fact been suggested. We may note that two of the three sub-divisions of this sacrifice in the Levitical code suggest the completion of something, a blessed event or a vow. These three are: (6) the *tôdhāh*, or **thank offering** (RSV usually 'thanksgiving'), Lv 7[13], Jer 17[26], Ps 107[22]; (7) the **votive offering** (AV, RV 'vow'), clearly a sacrifice vowed and performed when the time or occasion is fulfilled, and (8) the **freewill offering**, offered from no other special motive than the desire to offer at this time. These two types appear together in Lv 7[16], Nu 15[3].

The probable meaning of the difficult terms rendered (9) **sin offering**, and (10) **guilt offering** (AV **trespass offering**) will be more profitably discussed when the precise nature and object of these offerings are under consideration (**14** f). All the various offerings (1) to (10) are explicitly or implicitly included in a favourite term of the Priestly legislation namely (11) *'ishsheh*, **fire offering**, RSV 'offering by fire.' The fire offering is also mentioned in Dt 18[1] and 1 S 2[28] (a Deuteronomic passage).

Two other significant terms may be taken together, namely, the **heave offering** and the **wave offering.** The former is the rendering, in this connexion, of (12) *tᵉrûmāh*, which would apparently signify not something 'heaved up' (so Ex 29[27]), but rather 'what is *lifted off* a larger mass, or separated from it for sacred purposes.' The Hebrew word is used in a variety of applications—gifts of agricultural produce, of the spoils of war, etc., and in these cases is rendered 'offering' or 'oblation' (see Driver, *DB* iii. 588, and *Com. on Deut.* 142, who considers 'that "contribution" is perhaps the English word which . . . best suggests the ideas expressed by the Hebrew *tᵉrûmāh*'). In connexion with sacrifice, however, it denotes certain portions 'taken or lifted off' from the rest and assigned to the priests as their due, in particular the 'heave thigh' (Lv 7[34] RV), or 'the thigh of the heave offering' (Ex 29[27f]). 'Heave offering' accordingly in the sacrificial terminology is the equivalent of 'priest's portion' (cf Lv 6[17], where, however, a different word is used). RSV translates this term variously as 'priests' portion' (*e.g.* Ex 29[27–28]) or 'that is offered' (*e.g.* Lv 7[34] 10[14]) or 'an offering' (Lv 7[32], and often in non-sacrificial contexts).

(13) With the *tᵉrûmāh* is closely associated the *tᵉnûphāh* or **wave offering.** The Hebrew word denotes a movement to and fro, swinging, 'waving,' the priest lifting his share of the victim and moving it to and fro in the direction of the altar, thus symbolizing the presentation of the part of Yahweh, and Yahweh's return of it to the priest. It is applied specially to the breast of the sacrificial victim, hence termed 'the breast of the wave offering' (Ex 29[26f]), or more tersely 'the breast that is waved' (Lv 7[34] 10[14f]). Further, like *tᵉrûmāh*, *tᵉnûphāh* is also used in the more general sense of 'offering' (Ex 35[22]; cf Nu 8[11, 13] of the Levites, where the change from 'offering' (AV) to 'wave offering' (RV, RSV) is not an improvement).

(14) **Memorial portion,** or memorial, is the translation usual for *'azkārāh*, which is the handful of the cereal offering burned by the priest on the altar (Lv 2[2, 9] etc.), and also the incense accompanying the bread of the presence (24[7]). The meaning may originally have been 'the odorous part'; but it was later interpreted from the root *zākhar* 'remember' in the sense 'memorial.'

3. SACRIFICE AND OFFERING IN THE PRE-EXILIC PERIOD.—The history of OT sacrifice, like the history of the religion of Israel of which it is a characteristic expression, falls into two main divisions, the first embracing the period from Moses to the end of the monarchy (586 B.C.), the second the period from the Babylonian exile to the destruction of the Temple in A.D. 70. For the latter period we have the advantage of the more or less systematic presentation of the subject in the various strata of the complex legislation of P (especially Lv 1–7); for the former we must have recourse to the numerous references to sacrifice in the non-Priestly sources of the Pentateuch, in the early narratives of the historical books, and in the writings of the pre-exilic prophets.

It should not, however, be supposed that the Levitical system of sacrifice is something wholly new, appearing for the first time after the Exile. When we bear in mind the common conservatism of practice in such matters as sacrifice, it is likely that the Levitical system has a long development behind it, and that many aspects of it were already in operation some centuries before our literary evidence first appears. For example, the element of expiation is much less clearly marked in pre-exilic texts than in Ezekiel and Leviticus; yet it is by no means convincing to attribute this to a growth in the sense of sin as a result of the Exile. In fact the sense of a need for expiation is in some ways a primitive one, and there are many aspects of the expiatory ceremonies of the Levitical system which look very ancient and are most unlikely to have been the invention of the priests returned from exile. It will be convenient, however, to speak first of the material from pre-exilic texts and secondly to deal with the post-exilic system, although we leave it open that some elements of the latter may have been already working in the earlier period.

The sacrificial worship of the earlier differs from that of the later period mainly in the greater freedom regarding the occasion and in particular the place of sacrifice. As for the place of sacrifice, first of all, every village appears to have had its sanctuary or 'high place' with its altar and other appurtenances of the cult. Not that sacrifice could be offered at any spot the worshipper might choose; it must be one hallowed by the tradition of a theophany: 'in every place where I record my name I will come unto thee and I will bless thee' (Ex 20^{24} RV). With the abolition of the local sanctuaries by Josiah in 622–621 B.C., the Temple at Jerusalem became, and henceforth remained, the only legitimate place of sacrifice, as required by the legislation of Deuteronomy (12^{2ff}).

The **occasions of sacrifice** were manifold, and in the days of the local sanctuaries, which practically means the whole of the period under consideration, these occasions were naturally taken advantage of to an extent impossible when sacrifice was confined to the Temple of Jerusalem. Only a few of such occasions, whether stated or special, can be noted here. Of the regular or stated occasions may be named the daily sacrifices of the Temple—a burnt offering in the morning followed by a cereal offering in the afternoon (2 K 16^{15}, cf 1 K $18^{29, 36}$, which, however, may refer to one or more of the large sanctuaries of the Northern Kingdom, *e.g.* Bethel or Samaria), the 'yearly sacrifice' of the various clans (1 S 20^{6}), those at the recurring festivals, such as the new moon and the three agricultural feasts (Ex 23^{14ff} 34^{22ff}), at which the oldest legislation laid down that 'none shall appear before me empty' (23^{15} 34^{20}), that is, without an offering in token of gratitude and homage. Still more numerous were the special occasions of sacrifice—the installation of a king (1 S 11^{15}), the arrival of an honoured guest, family events such as the weaning of a child, a circumcision, a marriage, the dedication of a house (Dt 20^{5}): no compact or agreement was completed until sealed by a sacrifice (Gn 31^{54} etc.); at the opening of a campaign the warriors were 'consecrated' by a sacrifice (1 S 13^{9ff}, Is 13^{3}). One of the most fruitful occasions of sacrifice was undoubtedly the discharging of a vow, of which those of Jacob (Gn 28^{20-22}), Jephthah (see **5**), Hannah (1 S 1^{11}), and Absalom (2 S 15^{7}) may be cited as typical specimens, just as in Syria to-day, among *fellahin* and *bedouin* alike, similar vows are made to the *welys* of the local shrines by or on behalf of sick persons, childless women, or to avert or remove plague or other threatened calamity.

4. THE VARIETIES AND MATERIAL OF SACRIFICE IN THIS PERIOD.—Three varieties of sacrifice are met with in the older Hebrew literature, viz. the **burnt offering,** the **'peace' offering,** and the **'cereal offering.'** The two former, appearing sometimes as 'burnt offerings and sacrifices' (Ex 18^{12}, Jer 7^{22} etc.), sometimes as 'burnt offerings and peace offerings' (Ex 24^{5}, 1 S 13^{9} etc.), exhaust the category of animal sacrifices, the special 'sin' and 'guilt' offerings being first definitely named by Ezekiel (see **13–15**). The typical animal offering in the pre-exilic period is that now termed 'sacrifice' (*zebhaḥ*) simply, now 'peace offering' (Am 5^{22}) to differentiate it more clearly from the burnt offering, now still more explicitly 'sacrifice of peace offerings.' Almost all the special offerings and most of the stated ones were of this type. Its distinguishing feature was **the sacrificial meal,** which followed the sacrifice proper. After the blood had been returned to the Giver of life (we have no details as to the manipulation of the blood in the earliest period, but see 1 S 14^{32-34}), and the fat burned upon the altar (1 S 2^{15}; cf Is 1^{11}), the flesh of the victim was eaten at the sanctuary by the sacrificer and his family (1 S 1^{3-7}) or, in the case of a communal sacrifice, by the representatives of the community (9^{22-25}). The last passage shows that a special 'guest-chamber' was provided at the 'high place' for this purpose.

It is this kind of sacrifice, more than any other, that is susceptible of interpretation primarily as a form of communion with God, the interpretation championed especially by Robertson Smith. The worshippers were the 'guests' (Zeph 1^{7}) of God at His sanctuary, and as such secure of His favour. It is probably, however, too crude and one-sided an interpretation to say that the worshippers were sharing a common meal with the deity. The characteristic Deuteronomic phrase is 'ye shall eat (and drink) before the Lord your God' (Dt 12^{7}; not 'eat with him') and 'ye shall rejoice before the Lord your God' (the note of joyousness emphasized in Deuteronomy and noticeable in the early sources frequently). It is rather more probable that the common eating of the group is the increase and sustenance of their strength and welfare as a group, family or cultic or both, by partaking in the presence of God ('before him') of a victim sanctified to Him, whose life force has been set free, sanctified by application of the blood to the altar, and released for the benefit of the worshippers.

Much less frequent in the older documents is the mention of the **burnt offering,** more precisely the 'whole' offering (see above, **2**). The fact that the whole was consumed upon the altar enhanced its value as a 'holy gift,' and accordingly we find it offered when the occasion was one of special solemnity (Gn 8^{20}, 1 K 3^{4} etc.), or was otherwise extraordinary, as *e.g.* 1 S 6^{14}. In most cases the burnt offering appears in conjunction with the ordinary 'sacrifice' above described (Ex 18^{12}, 1 S 6^{15}, 2 S 6^{17}, 2 K $16^{13, 15}$; cf Is 1^{11}, Jer 7^{22} 17^{26}).

Apart from the special offering of the **first-fruits,** the cereal offering is rarely mentioned as an independent offering in this period, but is frequently named along with the two more important offerings discussed above, as Jg 13^{23}, Am 5^{22}, Jer 14^{12} (with the burnt offering), 1 S 2^{29} 3^{14}, Is 19^{21} and often. 'When the Hebrew ate flesh, he ate bread with it and drank wine, and when he offered flesh on the table of his God, it was natural that he should add to it the same concomitants that were necessary to make up a comfortable and generous meal' (*RS*², 222). The various forms which the meal offering might assume are attested for a later period by Lv 2, for which see **11.** One form occurring there is undoubtedly ancient, viz. parched ears of corn (2^{14}; cf FOOD, **2**).

Another very ancient form of offering, although not an altar-offering in the strict sense (yet strangely reckoned among the fire offerings, Lv 24^{9}), is that named 'the **bread of the Presence'** (AV, RV 'shewbread'). It is clear that this is connected with the old idea of a meal for the deity, but equally clear that this cannot explain the custom in its present form. The bread was in fact eaten normally by the priests (or others who are properly sanctified in earlier times, 1 S 21[4-6]) and only a small portion was offered to God (Lv 24[5-9]). The idea is rather the exposure of the bread in the presence of God than His partaking of it. The mention of 'its flagons and bowls with which to pour libations' (Ex 25[29]) shows that, as for an ordinary meal, the holy bread was accompanied by a provision of wine, in other words by a libation. This species of offering occurs as an independent offering only in Gn 35[14]. The skins of wine mentioned in 1 S 1[24] 10[3] doubtless served in part for a drink or 'wine offering' (Hos 9[4]), in part, like the accompanying flour and loaves, for the sacrificial meal. More explicit reference to the wine of the drink offering as an accompaniment of animal sacrifice is found in Dt 32[38] (cf the early reference, Jg 9[13], to wine 'which cheereth God'). For the ritual of the later drink offering, see **11**. It is significant of the predominant part played by the drink offering in early Babylonian ritual, that the word for libation (*niqu*) has there become the usual term for sacrifice.

A brief reference must suffice for **oil** in early ritual (Gn 28[18], Jg 9[9], Mic 6[7]—for the later ritual, see **11**). A **water** offering appears only in the isolated cases 1 S 7[6], 2 S 23[16], but emerges as an interesting survival in the rites of the Feast of Tabernacles (q.v.). **Honey**, although offered among the **first-fruits** (2 Ch 31[5]), was excluded, along with milk, from the altar (Lv 2[11]), on the ground that both were liable to fermentation (see also Leaven).

5. Material and ritual of sacrifice in this period.—From the details just given it is evident that 'among the Hebrew offerings drawn from the vegetable kingdom, meal, wine, and oil take the chief place, and these were also the chief vegetable constituents of man's daily food' (*RS*[2], 219). The same remark holds good of the animal sacrifices, which were drawn chiefly from 'the herd,' *i.e.* neat cattle, and from the 'flock,' *i.e.* sheep and goats. Excluded from the altar, on the other hand, were not only all unclean animals, but also game and fish, which, not being reared by man, were probably regarded as God's special property, and therefore inadmissible as a present from man. This idea that only what was a man's 'very own' constituted an appropriate sacrifice is reflected in David's words to Araunah, 2 S 24[24] (offerings 'which cost me nothing'). Males of the various species—a heifer is mentioned in connexion with ordinary sacrifice only 1 S 16[2] (Gn 15[9], Dt 21[3ff], 1 S 6[14] do not belong to this category).—and of these, yearlings, as in the later legislation, were doubtless the commonest victims, although we read of 'a bullock of three years old' (1 S 1[24], following reading of LXX and Qumrân; 'seven years' is mentioned in Jg 6[25], and seems to be the true reading, though the text of the other words may be confused).

The complicated question of **human sacrifice** cannot be fully discussed here. 2 K 3[27] reports a human sacrifice by the Moabite king, a burnt offering of his son with propitiatory and apotropaic intent. 1 K 16[34] is probably a foundation sacrifice. The existence of these types is supported for Canaanite culture by archaeological evidence. The chief appearance of human sacrifice in Israel is, however, the 'passing through the fire' of children in the non-Yahwistic Moloch-worship, so powerful in the later kingdom. The case of Jephthah's daughter in Jg 11 is certainly a human sacrifice and made to Yahweh, but is hardly to be interpreted as a normal case even in the early times from which it comes. The understanding of the human first-born as one whose life was forfeit and must therefore be returned to God by killing was at a very early date in Israel superseded or alleviated by the practice of substitution or redemption (Ex 34[20]), and the story of Isaac's imminent sacrifice by his father (Gn 22[1-14]) is a narrative related to this substitutionary practice. Though the practice of human sacrifice was probably well known from experience of what other peoples did, and may well have satisfied certain traditional instincts which found fulfilment in the Moloch worship of the late kingdom, there is no evidence that it was a normal or regular part of Yahwism in the historical period. Indeed the tradition suggests the opposite, that the Yahwistic law put the life and blood of man on a different level from the life and blood of beasts from an early date.

As regards the ritual of sacrifice in this period, we have little information, 1 S 2[13-16] being the only passage that touches definitely on this subject. This much is certain, that much greater latitude prevailed while the local sanctuaries existed than was afterwards the case; and also, that the priest played a much less conspicuous part in the rite than he does in the developed system of the priestly laws. The chief function of the priest in the earliest times was to give 'direction' (*tôrāh*) by means of the oracle, and to decide in matters pertaining to the sphere of 'clean and unclean.' The layman—as father of the family or head of the clan, still more the anointed king—offered his sacrifice without the intervention of the priest. The latter, however, as the custodian of the sanctuary, was entitled to his due (see 1 S 2[13-16], Dt 18[3]). At the more frequented sanctuaries—Jerusalem, Bethel, Beersheba, etc.—a more or less elaborate ritual was gradually evolved, for which the priest, as its depositary, became indispensable.

But even from the first the deity had to be approached with due precaution. The worshippers 'sanctified' themselves (1 S 16[5]), by washing (Ex 19[10]) or changing their garments (Gn 35[2]); for only those who were ceremonially 'clean' could approach the altar of Yahweh. The sacrificer then entered the high place and immolated the sacrificial victim, originally, it would appear, upon the altar itself (Gn 22[9], 1 S 14[33f]), so that the blood ran over it; later, near to the altar, care being taken that the blood was caught and poured out at its base. The victim was next cut up and the fat of the viscera removed. In the case of an ordinary sacrifice (*zebhaḥ*), to judge from 1 S 2[16], the flesh was boiled for the sacrificial meal, and not until the latter was ready was the fat, Yahweh's special portion, burned upon the altar. By this simultaneous consumption of the sacrifice the table-fellowship of Yahweh and His guests was more strikingly realized, the latter 'eating and drinking before the Lord' as the 'sweet smoke' (*ḳᵉṭōreth*) ascended from the altar, an 'odour of soothing (EV 'sweet savour') unto the Lord.'

While the normal attitude of the worshippers on such occasions was one of rejoicing, as became those who, by thus renewing their covenant relation to Yahweh in the way appointed, felt themselves secure of His favour and protection, a more serious note, implying a sense of alienation and the need of propitiation, is not infrequently found even in pre-exilic sacrifice, as will appear in a later section (**13**).

6. The developed sacrificial system of the post-exilic period—its general features.—The first fact of importance for the new situation is the concentration of sacrificial worship at Jerusalem. Hitherto any slaughter of a domestic animal for the entertainment of a guest or to celebrate an event was a form of sacrifice. Henceforth this is no longer so, and Dt 12[15-16] permits slaughter of animals for eating 'within your gates,' *i.e.* without the journey to the one place of sacrifice at Jerusalem, on the one condition that the blood be not eaten.

The transference of all worship to Jerusalem made it possible for a more uniform sacrificial procedure to develop and become normative. Though we have little definite evidence, it is probable that considerable divergences in procedure and terminology existed in different parts of the country. The cultus now assumes a much more official character, and the Levitical sacrificial codes are not so much an innovation planned and later put into effect as a hardening into system of long-established procedures. With the one sanctuary also the sacrifices are an affair for the whole national community, and the initiative of tribe and family recedes somewhat, although even in the fully developed system regularity by no means ousts the opportunity for the worshipper voluntarily to bring his offering.

We also have a greatly increased emphasis on the **priesthood** as the ministers of sacrifice. In Ezekiel only the sons of Zadok can serve the altar; in P only the sons of Aaron—the Levites are their assistants but cannot perform the one peculiarly priestly task, the bringing of the sacrifices to the altar and the manipulation of the blood. In the priestly conception of holiness special and inviolable holiness belongs to the sanctuary, and within that to the ministry, and within it to the priesthood and the altar which they served; still more to the most holy place, entered by the high priest once a year only. The sacrificial service is part of the sustenance of the holiness of the sanctuary, and must be properly continued at all times. Beyond immolating the victims, the laity are no longer competent to perform the sacrificial rites, although the participation of the laity remains by his laying on of hands on the victim.

Priestly thinking was characterized by its clear, regular and systematic care for the proper categories, and it is to this interest in clarity, developed probably in centuries of the giving of priestly instruction or *tôrāh*, that we owe the systematic presentation of the Levitical laws. It is notable on the other hand how reserved these codes are in any statement of the value or effectiveness of the sacrificial ceremonies.

The relative importance of the two older animal sacrifices, the *'ōlāh* and the *zebhaḥ*, is now reversed. The typical sacrifice is no longer the latter with its accompanying meal, but the 'continual burnt offering,' an act of worship performed every morning and evening (Nu 28^{1-8}) in the Temple in the name of the community. Also characteristic of the late sources is the special treatment given to the expiatory sacrifices, the sin and guilt offerings. The new importance of these is commonly ascribed to the humiliating and disillusioning effect of the Exile and the deepened sense of sin. It is perhaps more probable that the expiatory interest and the special rituals of these sacrifices were ancient, but that they are not brought into prominence until the Levitical codes give precision to their terminology and status. The lack of specific mention in early sources is probably because these sacrifices more than any other were the special concern of the priests and of the inner holiness of the sanctuary.

7. THE FIVE KINDS OF ALTAR-OFFERINGS IN P.—The numerous altar-offerings mentioned in the various strata of the Priestly legislation are divided by Josephus into two classes: (i) those offered 'for private persons,' and (ii) those offered 'for the people in general'—a classification corresponding to the Roman *sacra privata* and *sacra publica* (*Ant.* III. ix. 1 [224]). The public sacrifices were either stated or occasional, the former and more important group comprising the daily burnt offering (see **10**) and the additional sacrifices at the stated festivals—Sabbath, New Moon, New Year, the three great feasts, and the Day of Atonement.

Since it is impossible within present limits to attempt to enumerate, much less to discuss, the multifarious varieties and occasions of public and private sacrifices, it will be more convenient to follow, as before, the order of the five distinct kinds as given in the systematic manual, Lv 1–7. These are (1) the burnt offering, (2) the cereal offering, (3) the peace offering, and the two expiatory sacrifices, viz. (4) the sin offering, and (5) the guilt (AV 'trespass') offering. Arranged according to the material of the offering, these fell into two groups represented by the terms 'sacrifice' and 'offering' (cf **1**); in other words, into animal and vegetable or cereal offerings (including the drink offering). The four animal or bloody offerings may be classified according to the destination of the flesh of the victim, thus (cf below)—

(i) The flesh entirely consumed upon the altar—the burnt or whole offering.

(ii) The flesh not consumed upon the altar—the peace offerings and the two propitiatory offerings.

The second group may again be subdivided thus—

(*a*) The flesh, apart from the priest's dues, assigned to the offerer for a sacrificial meal—the peace offering.

(*b*) The flesh assigned to the priests to be eaten within the sanctuary—the guilt offerings and the less important of the sin offerings.

(*c*) The flesh burned without the sanctuary—the more important sin offerings.

8. THE MATERIAL OF SACRIFICE IN P.—'*Holy*' *and* '*most holy*.'—The material of all these remains the same as in the pre-exilic period (**5**), with the addition of pigeons and turtle-doves to meet the needs of the poor, but the victim for each special kind of sacrifice, and its qualifications, are now definitely prescribed. As regards neat and small cattle, the victims must be males for the most part, entire and without blemish (see Lv 22 for list of imperfections—an exception, however, was made for the freewill offering, v.^{23}). For the peace offering both sexes were equally admissible (3^{1}), and a female victim is specially prescribed for the less important sin offerings ($4^{28, 32}$). The animals were eligible for sacrifice from the eighth day onwards (22^{27}), but the typical sacrifice was the yearling. For the material of the cereal offering see below.

Here may be noted an interesting contrast between such offerings as were regarded as merely 'holy' and those reckoned 'most holy.' The limits of the former category are somewhat vague, but it certainly included firstlings and **first-fruits,** the tithe and the portions of the peace offerings falling to the priests, whereas the show-bread (Lv 24^{9}), the sacred incense (Ex 30^{36}), the meal offering (Lv 2^{3}), and the sin and guilt offerings ($6^{25, 29}$ $7^{1, 6}$) are all classed as 'most holy.' One practical effect of the distinction was that the 'most holy things' could be eaten only by the priests, and by them only within the Temple precincts ($6^{16, 26}$, Nu 18^{10}; cf Ezk 42^{13} 46^{20}). As charged with a special potency of holiness, which was highly contagious, the 'most holy things'—there were many other entries in the category, such as the altar and the high priest's dress—rendered all who came in contact with them 'holy,' (Lv $6^{18, 27}$). The 'holy things,' on the other hand, might be eaten by the priests and their households, if ceremonially clean, in any 'clean place,' *i.e.* practically in Jerusalem (10^{14} $22^{3, 10-16}$, Nu 18^{11ff}).

9. THE RITUAL OF POST-EXILIC SACRIFICE.—This is now, like all else, a matter of careful regulation. The ritual, as a whole, doubtless continued and developed that of the pre-exilic Temple, where the **priest** had long taken the place of the lay offerer in the most significant parts of the rite. After the offerer had duly 'sanctified' himself as explained in **5**, and had his sacrifice examined and passed by the Temple officials, the procedure comprised the following 'actions':—

(1) The formal presentation of the victim to the priest officiating at the altar.

(2) The *s^{e}mîkhāh* or laying on of hands; the offerer leaned his right hand—both hands were used by the high priest on the scapegoat on the Day of Atonement, Lv 16^{21}—upon the head of the victim. The meaning of this is characteristically not stated, but it may most probably be interpreted as an act of identification accepted or sought.

(3) The immolation of the victim, on the north side of the altar (Lv 1^{11} 6^{25}), by severing the arteries of the neck. In private sacrifices this was always done by the person presenting them.

(4) The manipulation of the blood by the priest. This, the central action of the whole rite, varied considerably for the different sacrifices. After being caught by the priest in a large basin, the blood was in most cases tossed against the sides of the altar. In sin offerings the blood was also 'sprinkled' (a different word) before (on the Day of Atonement, within) the veil of the most holy place, and blood was applied to the horns of the altar. Generally it may be said that the more pronounced the expiatory character of the sacrifice, the nearer the blood was brought to the presence of the deity (see **14**), the climax being reached in the blood-rite of the Day of Atonement (16^{14}, see ATONEMENT [DAY OF]).

(5) The skinning and dismemberment of the animal,

SACRIFICE AND OFFERING

including the removal of the internal fat, as specified 3^{3f} and 4^{8f}. The hide fell to the officiating priest, except in the case of the sin offering, when it was burned with the flesh (Ex 29^{14}).

(6) The arrangement of all the pieces upon the altar in the case of the burnt offering, of the specified portions of ' the inwards ' in the case of the others ; and finally—

(7) The burning—literally the turning into ' sweet smoke '—of these upon the altar of burnt offering, the fire on which was kept continually burning (Lv 6^{13}).

Of these various elements of the ritual, those requiring contact with the altar as a ' most holy thing,' viz. (4), (6), and (7), represent the priest's, the rest the layman's, share in the rite of sacrifice. In Ezekiel's plans the slaying of the victim was to be done by those Levites who were not of the Zadokite house and had gone far from Yahweh (Ezk 44^{11}).

10. The burnt offering (Lv 1^{1-17} 6^{8-13}, Ex 29^{15-18}).—The first place in the manual of sacrifice, Lv 1–7, is occupied by the sacrifice which alone was entirely consumed upon the altar, a feature which constituted it the typical honorific sacrifice, the fullest expression of homage to Yahweh on the part alike of the community and of the individual. The victim from the flock and the herd was always a male—young bull, ram, or he-goat. The turtle-dove and the young pigeon of the poor had their special ritual (1^{14-17}). The most important of the stated sacrifices in the period under review was the **' continual burnt offering '** (Ex 29^{38-42}, Nu 28^{3-8}), so called because it was presented every morning and evening along with a cereal oblation by the particular ' course ' of priests on duty in the Temple. The victim was a yearling lamb, which was offered on behalf of the whole community of Israel throughout the world. An interesting survival of the primitive anthropomorphic conception of sacrifice, as affording a complete meal to the deity, is seen in the provision that every burnt offering (as also every peace offering) must be accompanied by both a meal offering and a drink offering (see **11**).

11. The cereal offering (Lv 2 6^{14-23}, Nu 15^{1-16} etc.).—As pointed out in an early section, the term *minḥāh*, which originally was applicable both to an animal and to a cereal offering, is in the later legislation limited to the latter species. As such it appears in a large variety of forms, and may be either an independent offering, as contemplated in Lv 2, or, as in most cases, an accompaniment of the burnt and peace offerings (Nu 15^{1-16}). One of the oldest form of the *minḥāh* was, undoubtedly, the ' cereal offering of **first-fruits**,' as described Lv 2^{14-16} ; another antique form survived in the unique offering of barley meal in the **offering of jealousy** (Nu 5^{15}). As an ordinary altar-offering the *minḥāh* consisted of ' fine flour,' and was presented either cooked or uncooked, as prescribed in detail in Lv 2^{1-7}. The flour was placed in a vessel and mixed with oil, the equivalent of our butter in culinary matters, and salted, an indispensable accompaniment of this type of offering (2^{13}). The dough was then covered with incense, when it was ready for presentation at the altar. The priest took off all the incense, then removed a handful of the dough, and proceeded to burn the latter with the incense on the altar ; this was the *'azkārāh* or memorial portion (**2**). The remainder fell to the priests and was eaten by them as a ' thing most holy.' The cereal offerings of the priests themselves, on the other hand, were wholly burned (Lv 6^{23}).

In Nu 15^{1-16} and elsewhere, minute instructions are given as to the precise amounts of fine flour, oil and wine, which should accompany the burnt and peace offerings (cf Ezk 46^{5-14} and the tabular comparison of the quantities in the two passages in Gray, ' Numbers ' [*ICC*], 170). These were regulated by the importance of the animal sacrificed, the **libation** of wine (Hos 9^4), for example, being uniformly $\frac{1}{2}$ hin for a bullock, $\frac{1}{3}$ hin for a ram, and $\frac{1}{4}$ hin for a lamb—the hin may be taken approximately as 12 pints.

No instructions have been preserved as to how the wine was to be offered, but from later evidence it appears that, like the blood, it was ' poured out at the foot of the altar ' (Sir 50^{15} ; cf Jos. *Ant.* III. ix. 4 [234]). For the importance of incense in the later ritual, see INCENSE.

12. The **peace offering** (Lv 3^{1-16} $7^{11-21, 28-34}$ 17^{1-9} 22^{21-33} etc.).—Its distinguishing feature continued to be the sacrificial meal which followed. For the three subdivisions of this offering, the thank offering, the votive offering, and the freewill offering, see above under **2.** The freewill offering admits of certain imperfections in the victim (Lv 22^{23}), probably because it alone depends purely on the worshipper's initiative and not on a previous sacred sanction like a vow or a Divine intervention such as would motivate a thank offering. As a fourth variety may be reckoned the priests' **installation** or consecration offering of a ram (Ex 29^{19-26}).

The *modus operandi* was essentially the same as for the burnt offering—female victims, however, being admitted equally with males. Special instructions are given as to the removal of the fat adhering to the inwards, along with the appendage of the liver (held by G. F. Moore to be the caudate lobe) and the two kidneys. The parts falling to the priests, the breast and the right hind leg—these varied at different times, cf Dt 18^3 with Ex 29^{26}, Lv 7^{31f}—were symbolically presented to and returned by Yahweh, by being ' waved ' towards the altar (see **2** for this ceremony, and for the expressions ' heave offering ' and ' wave offering '). The fat was then salted and burned, while the remainder of the flesh furnished the characteristic meal. Both sexes, if ceremonially clean, might partake of this meal, but only on the day of the sacrifice or the day following (Lv 7^{16-18} 19^{5-8}). The flesh of the special thanksgiving offering (*tôdhāh*), however, had to be eaten on the day it was offered (7^{15} 22^{29f}).

13. THE SPECIAL EXPIATORY SACRIFICES.—The **sin offering** and the **guilt offering**.—Although we have no very early texts mentioning these offerings by name, it has already been suggested that they, and the expiatory interest which they serve, have probably a long history before their precise formulation in the Levitical codes, and that the common theory of their origin in the dark days of the dying monarchy or during the exile is not a probable one. Some more precise arguments may now be given :

Firstly, it is in any case admitted that concepts of expiation or propitiation are associated with sacrifice in early times and during the kingdom (*e.g.* 1 S 3^{14} 26^{19}, 2 S 24^{25}, Mic 6^{6-7} ; see the articles EXPIATION and PROPITIATION). The removal of sin is, without doubt, one of the principal motives for sacrifice in Semitic culture, and was well established in Mesopotamia long before our period. Certainly the early Israelite sources quoted above do not name any special kind of sacrifices for the expiatory purpose, but we do not have a precise vocabulary for Israelite sacrifice before Ezekiel, and special expiatory techniques may well be concealed by familiar words.

Secondly, there is certain internal evidence in the OT for the antiquity of the expiatory offerings. We may first mention 2 K 12^{16}, which mentions certain moneys which were not brought into the Temple but went direct to the priests. This was the money of *'āshām* and of *ḥaṭṭā'ôth*, the terms used for the guilt and sin offerings. This does not mean money deposited to buy sacrificial victims. But in spite of the powerful arguments of G. B. Gray (*Sacrifice in the Old Testament*, pp. 61 f) and others, it seems most likely that the passage intends not merely monetary payments of restitution totally unconnected with sacrifices, but such payments made to the priests in connexion with special rituals of expiation (we do not go so far as to argue that the rituals must have been identical with those of Leviticus), and most probably payments to the priests for their service, just as in Punic sacrificial tariffs payments to the priests are appointed (though in that case for all types of sacrifice). That the money in this case went to the priests is naturally to be connected with the fact that in Leviticus it is the expiatory offerings in which the main share goes to the priests.

The date of the events of 2 K 12 is about 814 B.C. To this we may add that Ezekiel, usually taken to be the first literary source for our terms as technical words for offerings, shows no sign of speaking of innovations or unfamiliar entities (Ezk 40^{39} etc.). Further, we have already pointed out that certain aspects of these rituals bear every mark of high antiquity, *e.g.* the goat 'for Azazel' on the day of Atonement, and one has to bear in mind the considerable conservatism common in sacrificial matters.

Thirdly, some interesting evidence exists in the Punic sacrificial tariffs of Carthage and Marseilles (see especially R. Dussaud, *Les origines cananéennes du sacrifice israélite*, 2nd edition, 1941). In these three types of animal sacrifice are treated, and while for one kind nothing goes to the priest but the money payment which applies in all cases, for another they receive certain parts of the animal while the remainder goes to the offerer, and in the third nothing is recorded as going to the offerer but a stated weight of flesh goes to the priest. In none of these does the name of the Israelite expiatory offerings appear, and while some of the names of sacrifices are related to Israelite names, they do not appear to mean the same thing or apply to the same procedures. But it does appear that three modes of disposal of sacrificial flesh exist here, as in the Levitical system, and one of them is that special mode in which the main part of the flesh goes to the priests. If there is something in common between the Levitical code and the Punic tariffs, it can only be by connexion through a common and remote ancestry. Ugaritic literature does not seem to have yielded much definite evidence (see J. Gray, *The Legacy of Canaan*, pp. 143–7).

From the point of view of ritual, the chief points of difference between the sin offering and the guilt offering are these: (1) In the guilt offering the manipulation of the blood agrees with that prescribed for the older sacrifices; in the sin offering, on the other hand, the blood ritual is more complicated and varies in intensity according to the theocratic and social position of the offerer. This feature alone is sufficient to distinguish the sin offering as *par excellence* the sacrifice of expiation and atonement. (2) For the guilt offering the victim is uniformly a ram ('the ram of atonement,' Nu 5^{8}); for the sin offering the victim varies according to the same principle as the blood ritual: the higher the position of the offerer in the theocratic community the more valuable the victim. On the other hand, both agree as compared with the other sacrifices: (1) in the disposal of the flesh of the sacrifice in so far as it was neither entirely burned on the altar as in the whole offering, nor assigned to the offerer for a sacred meal as in the peace offering, but was otherwise disposed of (see below); and (2) in the absence of the cereal and wine offerings which were the regular accompaniments of the other animal sacrifices.

14. The sin offering (Lv 4^{1}–5^{13} 6^{24-30}, Ex 29^{11-14}, Nu 15^{22-29} etc.).—Leaving aside the question of the relation of these sections to each other as to origin and date—all-important as this is for the evolution of the sin offering—we find from a comparison of Lv 4, 5^{7-13}, the most systematic as it is probably the latest exposition of the subject, with other sections of the code where this special sacrifice is required, that the latter was the prescribed medium of expiation for two main classes of offences. These are (1) sins committed in ignorance or by inadvertence ($4^{2, 13, 22}$, Nu 15^{24-29}) as opposed to sins committed 'with an high hand' (v.^{30} RV), *i.e.* in conscious and wilful defiance of the Divine law, for which no sacrifice could atone; (2) cases of defilement or uncleanness, contracted in various ways and having no connexion with 'sin' in the modern sense of a breach of the moral law, such as the defilement of childbirth and of leprosy, the uncleanness of the altar and the like.

At this point it will repay us to examine the origin of the term *ḥaṭṭā'th*, omitted from **2**, as likely to afford a clue to the true significance of the sacrifice. Derived from the verb signifying 'to sin' in the sense of 'to miss (the mark or the way),' *ḥaṭṭā'th* denotes sin, then a sacrifice for sin. It may be questioned, however, whether this transference of meaning was as direct as is usually implied. The intensive stems of the root-verb are repeatedly used in the 'privative' sense best expressed by 'to unsin' (German, *entsündigen*) by some rite of purification, as Lv 8^{15} Ezk 43^{20-23}, of 'unsinning,' *i.e.* purifying or purging the altar; Nu 19^{19}, of 'unsinning' a person defiled by contact with a corpse; 8^{21} 'the Levites unsinned themselves (RV purified themselves from sin) and washed their clothes,' where the 'sin' of RV refers only to ceremonial uncleanness. From this use of the verb, *ḥaṭṭā'th* itself acquired the secondary sense of 'purification,' *e.g.* Nu 8^{7} (AV rightly 'water of purifying'—RV 'expiation') and 19^{9-17}, where the red heifer and her ashes are described as a *ḥaṭṭā'th*, that is, as the means of removing the uncleanness caused by the dead. It follows from the above that 'purification offering' better expresses to the modern mind the purposes of the *ḥaṭṭā'th* than does 'sin offering,' with its misleading association.

On the other hand we see that the distinction between moral and ritual offences is one foreign to priestly thinking. Even what is committed 'in error' is not mere accident, but may be the infatuation or blindness of one possessed, for the same word is used for the infatuation of the lover, the uncontrolled words and deeds of the drunkard, or Saul's fanatical pursuit of David. God's holiness is not in fact ethical perfection, but includes His awesomeness as the mysterious source of life and the one to whom life returns; and many of the 'ritual offences' are points of human life which approach too closely to the mystery of life and death which belongs to God alone. Holiness requires obedience of heart and observation of the due limits which God has set for men, and which must be observed throughout His sacral community. This shows why there is a gradation in the rituals of the sin offering for different persons; the closer the person to God as the centre of holiness, the more dangerous and comprehensive the contagion of his offence, and the more deeply the inviolable holiness of God is threatened.

Returning to Lv 4^{1}–5^{13}, we find that, apart from the gradation of the prescribed victims already referred to, the distinguishing feature in the ritual of the sin offering is the more intense application of the blood. In this respect two grades of sin offering are distinguished, a higher and a lower. In the higher grade, which comprises the offering of the high priest and that of the 'whole congregation,' the blood is carried by the officiating priest into the Holy Place of the Tent of Meeting—in practice the Temple. There some of it is sprinkled with the finger seven times before the veil, and some applied to the horns of the altar of incense, while the rest is poured out at the base of the altar of burnt offering. The victim in both cases is a young bull, the flesh of which is so sacrosanct that it has to be burned without the camp.

In the lower grade, part of the blood was smeared upon the horns of the altar of burnt offering, while the rest was poured out, as before, at its base. It is interesting to note, as bearing on the evolution of the ritual, that in a presumably older stratum of P (Ex 29^{11-14}), the blood ritual, even for the high priest's offering, does not exceed that of the lower grade of Lv 4. The flesh of the latter, which was also 'most holy,' was eaten by the priests within the sanctuary (6^{24-30}). To meet the requirements of the poor man, provision was made for the admission of 'two turtle-doves or two young pigeons,' and in cases of extreme poverty of 'the tenth part of and ephah of fine flour' (about 7 pints), offered without oil and without incense (5^{11-13}).

15. The guilt offering (AV trespass offering; Lv 5^{14}–6^{7} 7^{1-7}, Nu 5^{5-8}).—This offering, the *'āshām*, is prescribed in the Levitical system for cases involving restitution, *e.g.* when a man finds something lost and keeps it, refuses to return a deposit, or swears falsely in property questions (Lv 6^{1-6}). In these cases restitution is made (with an addition of one-fifth as compensation), and the restitution is accompanied by the guilt offering to Yahweh. We note also from a much earlier time the guilt offering of the Philistines when they make restitution of the Ark to Israel, in this case a gift of restitution rather than a sacrifice (1 S 6^{1-9}). Even in the priestly legislation we find *'āshām* being used (Nu 5^{8}) for the 'restitution for wrong,' *i.e.* the property wrongly possessed and now to be restored, which in the case where the rightful owner is no longer accessible goes 'to Yahweh,' *i.e.* to the priest. Another connexion with property restitution appears in that a valuation of the sacrificial victim by the priest is normal for most cases of the guilt offering (Lv 5^{18} 6^{6}).

The occasion of the sacrifice may then reasonably be held to be restoration or reintegration to normality after an offence. In this case the offences are mostly what we would call moral offences, but the distinguishing of the moral nature of the offence is no more the point here than in the sin offering. The interpretation of the sacrifice as one of reintegration fits with such passages as Ezr 10^{19} (for priests after putting away foreign wives), Nu 6^{12} (for the Nazirite as he resumes his period of consecration after its interruption by contact with the dead), Lv 14 (restoration of the leper). In Lv 19^{20-22} the offering is explicitly connected with cleansing or forgiveness of 'the sin which he has committed' (intercourse with a slave woman betrothed to a man; in this case the guilt offering probably applies since it is regarded as a property matter, but the man is punished first of all by flogging, since this is the probable meaning in Lv 19^{20} rather than 'an inquiry shall be held' as RSV puts it; cf Mishnah *Ker.* ii 4). The phrase declaring forgiveness is recurrent in Lv 4–5. In Lv 5^{17-19} the guilt offering is related like the sin offering to sins of which the person does not know. Provision is made for a public confession in some cases, Nu 5^{7}. Normally the victim is a ram, and the ritual is like that of the ordinary sacrifices, but the flesh is eaten, like that of the lower grade of sin offerings, only by the priests 'in a holy place.' In the case of the restoration of the leper, however, a 'male lamb' is specified, and a special blood ritual is carried out.

It should be mentioned at this point also that in one quite isolated but very important passage, the Servant Song of Is 53 (v.^{10}), the Servant's life or person is mentioned as being made a 'guilt offering' (most translations 'an offering for sin' presumably understanding that the reference to sacrificial ceremonies is quite vague and general), cf the references to 'sin-bearing' in vv.$^{11-12}$. It is difficult to know how far the precise characteristics of the Levitical guilt offering are understood to apply in Is 53.

For the expiatory offerings in general, see EXPIATION.

16. Combinations of sacrifices.—On solemn occasions we may have a combination of various categories of sacrifice, and then the order is normally (1) the expiatory offerings (2) the burnt offerings (3) the peace offerings. This full sequence appears in Lv 9. In many places we have only the elements (2) and (3), while in mainly expiatory rituals the peace offerings are often not mentioned, so that the elements are (1) and (2), *e.g.* the cleansing of the leper in Lv 14 or the Day of Atonement, Lv 16. The Day of Atonement is built up from sin-offerings, followed by the scapegoat release, followed by burnt offerings. Where the full series appears it is reasonable to see a thought of expiation as the first need on approaching Yahweh, followed by the burnt offerings as the culmination of worship to Him, followed by the peace offerings as the sharing of the community by its partaking in the sacrificial meal. A cereal offering accompanied the burnt and peace offerings, but not the expiatory type. For the occasions of various types of sacrifice, see ATONEMENT [DAY OF], NAZIRITE, TITHE, VOW, etc.

It should further be remembered that while this article has confined itself for the most part to sacrifice understood as what is brought to the altar and offered there, it is difficult or impossible to make an absolute distinction between such sacrifices and certain other rituals. The killing of the passover, for example, is not treated here, because it required neither priest nor altar, but it was a *zebhaḥ* or animal killing like the altar sacrifices, and one can hardly say the translations are wrong in rendering this as 'sacrifice of the passover' (Ex 12^{27}). Similarly Ex 13^{15} uses the verb 'sacrifice' for the killing of the first-born. On the other hand, the sacrificial system shares many conceptions and procedures with other offerings which were not in any part consumed on the altar, but were only presented at the altar or in the Temple premises. See therefore PASSOVER, FIRST-BORN FIRST-FRUITS, TITHE, etc.

17. THE SIGNIFICANCE OF SACRIFICE IN THE OT.—The question may first of all be asked, how far the sacrificial system of the OT is the peculiar property of Israel, and how far it is shared with the religion of sister Semitic peoples. A comparison in detail cannot be entered upon here, and in any case no such fullness of data is available for Israel's neighbours as we have in the OT, although much material is known for Mesopotamia. The Punic (Carthaginian) tariffs have been mentioned, but offer only a small fraction in quantity of the OT's sacrificial codes. It may be said in general that Israelite sacrifice had large elements in common with widespread Semitic practice, and it is not probable that any large proportion of its procedures are specifically Yahwistic innovations. Sacrifice was, of course, common property of most or all ancient religions, and though the OT represents its sacrificial practice as being commanded to Moses and Aaron by God, it also knows in certain of its traditions of sacrifice offered to God by the earliest men (Gn 4^{3}) and by Noah, the father of all existing men and not of Israel only (Gn 8^{20}). Nevertheless Israelite sacrificial procedure, however much of it was inherited, came to be integrated in the national consciousness, and we can see how well it fits into other expressions of religious life. In certain cases special connexions can be seen; *e.g.* the avoidance of milk and honey in altar offerings is probably to be understood in their liability to fermentation like leaven—though honey is included in offerings of first-fruits, Lv 2^{11-12}.

It has already been noted that the Levitical sacrificial codes are very reserved towards any statement of the theory or theology behind sacrifice, and confine themselves to a large extent to formal statements of procedure. Even where they use terms which might help us to understand their theory of the effect of sacrifice, such as 'a pleasing odour,' 'it shall be accepted for him,' 'to make expiation,' these terms are not themselves explained further. In some cases the formulae themselves may well be traditional and may no longer be understood in the sense suggested by their etymology. Important as must be the study of the origins of sacrifice, we must remember that these lie far in the prehistory of Israel, and the meaning of a custom for Israel may be quite a different one from the intention which gave rise to it.

The formal expression of the laws should not lead us to assume that Israel held a mechanical view of the efficacy of sacrifice. Sacrificial thinking should not be classified under 'magic,' nor did the Hebrews have the clear hard understanding of 'cause and effect' by which one would interpret the sacrifice as a cause which once set in motion could not fail to effect the good will of God. Terms like 'validity,' 'efficacy' and '*ex opere operato*' are inappropriate to OT thinking. Even those abuses in sacrificial worship which the prophets criticized were not so much 'mechanical' as syncretistic, un-Yahwistic, and separated from the ethical traditions of the covenant. Now that the Psalter is being dated in many parts much earlier than scholars were formerly willing to do, it becomes possible to use sections of it with care as being the sung liturgy which was used in the Temple and accompanied the sacrificial service. In certain Psalms we find the reception of sacrifice a matter of prayer (*e.g.* Ps 20^{3}); the need of inward worship is emphasized (4^{5}), and it is proclaimed that sacrifice is not something needed by God (Ps 40 and 50). Passages like these should probably not be ascribed to an anti-cultic reform atmosphere which wishes to replace the sacrifices by a spiritual worship, but rather may be taken as a complement to the sacrificial worship. Similarly in

Ps 51^{15-17} inward cleanliness is demanded by God, and sacrifices are not a substitute for it; the paradox of the ending of this Psalm should not be too easily evaded by regarding the last two verses as a secondary addition. The Psalter with its emphasis on God's mercy, love, freedom and judgment is a balance to the more formal sacrificial laws.

One interpretation of sacrifice which is almost certainly archaic for developed Israelite thought is that which speaks of it as the 'food' of God (Lv 3^{11} 21^{6}, Ezk 44^{7}). See also above, on the bread of the Presence. That God eats the flesh of animals is denied and mocked by Ps 50^{12-13}. It is probable that with the thought of God as the one God and universal creator the idea of His needing nourishment dies away. But its effect remains not only in the phrase 'food of God' but in the use for sacrificial material of the normal foods. On the other hand it is relevant that food is the source of strength, and is itself composed of animal and vegetable life; and in accordance with the common Hebrew conception of holiness and increase by deprivation, it may have been felt that the taking of so much strength in the form of food from the community and its devotion to the centre of life and holiness is a building up of increased life and welfare. Such a construction would fit well the continual offering which was made twice daily in the later ritual. In this sense it is possible to give more real content to the sacrificial use of the word 'food.'

The 'communion theory' of sacrifice has already been mentioned, and was supported especially by Robertson Smith (see **4** above). He saw in it the main force of sacrificial religion. It was, however, in his exposition (*The Religion of the Semites*) linked with the institution of totemism among the Semites; the absence of evidence for the latter has greatly weakened his case. His case applied best to the peace offerings and could not explain the burnt offering well. It has already been suggested above that the peace offering or communion type may be best understood as the increase and sustenance by the worshippers of their welfare as a group, by partaking in the presence of God (not partaking 'with him,' still less 'of him,' but 'before him') of a victim sanctified to Him, of which the blood and fat have been applied to the altar.

It has equally been maintained that the basis of sacrifice is to be found in the conception of a gift given to God; though even G. B. Gray, the most scholarly supporter of the gift theory for the OT (in his *Sacrifice in the Old Testament*), readily admitted that it did not explain *all* sacrifice, and in particular of course not the peace offering, where the worshippers ate the main part of the victim. The strength of this explanation is in certain terms, such as *minḥāh*, which may be used of any present from man to man as well as being a principal sacrificial term, and also that it brings the sacrificial worship of the altar into line with certain other rituals which are not related to the altar and are undoubtedly to be understood as gifts. Its weakness as an overall theory is perhaps that it does not explain enough; for even where much, or most, sacrifice is a gift, it is not therefore immediately clear why the gift is given. The proper extension of the gift theory may be partly in what was said above about the 'food of God,' partly in conceptions of propitiation and expiation, and perhaps most generally in the conception that God wills to be worshipped with the returning to Him of life and strength.

The reader of the NT will often have the impression that the main purpose of the OT sacrifices was expiatory, and some interpretations of sacrifice have in fact so concentrated on the expiatory function as to obscure the existence of sacrifices such as the peace offering or the cereal offering which cannot easily be thus explained. The group of sacrifices which may be specially called expiatory have already been discussed, and for the more general concept of expiation see EXPIATION, PROPITIATION, ATONEMENT. It should, however, be mentioned here that the Hebrew phrase *kipper* 'make expiation' is applied in the sacrificial codes not only to the expiatory sacrifices proper but to certain others: in particular to burnt offerings (Lv 1^{4}), and to any sacrificial blood (Lv 17^{11}).

It is in fact probable that the purpose or intention of Israelite sacrifice was complex, and that no one motivation can be built into a theory which will explain the most part of it. Central to all animal sacrifices is the application of the blood to the altar or the presence of Yahweh, which may be understood as returning of life to God for the increase of the living force of the community which has the sanctuary as its centre, and also as expiatory of offences by the life which is in the blood. Where part of the sacrifice remains to be consumed by worshipper or priest, the application of the blood or the burning of the other parts constitutes a sanctifying of the portion to be consumed, its introduction within the sphere of deep holiness related to the altar. The leaning of the hand on the victim seems to mean an identification in which the worshipper enters into the act of sacrifice, for increase of his life and strength and for expiation of his sin.

A sacrifice like the peace offering stresses more the increase of life and prosperity for the group; the expiatory type is concentrated on the removal of sin. All sacrifice is worship in the sense of the proper action of man before God; sacrifice can indeed be a form of prayer or supplication. God is pleased to be properly worshipped (this is the probable meaning ascribed in historical times to the phrase 'for a pleasing odour,' see PROPITIATION). Where there is sin unexpiated, God's anger will speedily visit people and land; in such a case the expiation is a turning away of anger and catastrophe. In later Judaism, with the concentration of piety on the obedience of the Law, the motives for sacrifice were rather simplified, for the final reason for sacrificing was simply enough that God had commanded Moses that sacrifice should be made in such and such a way.

A. R. S. K.—**J. Ba.**

SACRILEGE.—In Ro 2^{22} AV and RVm have 'commit sacrilege' where RV and RSV have 'rob temples.' On the other hand, RSV has 'sacrilegious' in Ac 19^{37} where AV and RV have 'robbers of churches (or temples).' In 1 Mac 1^{54}, Mt 24^{15}, Mk 13^{14} RSV has 'desolating sacrilege' for AV and RV 'abomination of desolation.'

SADAMIAS, 2 Es 1^{1} (AV).—See SHALLUM, **6.**

SADAS, 1 Es 5^{13} (AV).—See AZGAD.

SADDEUS, 1 Es 8^{45} (AV).—See IDDO, **1.**

SADDUC, 1 Es 8^{2} (AV).—See ZADOK, **8.**

SADDUCEES.—Probably the name 'Sadducee' is derived from the name Zadok, a notable priest in the time of David and Solomon (2 S 8^{17} 15^{24}, 1 K 1^{34}). His descendants long played the leading part among the priests, so that Ezekiel regarded them as the only legitimate priests (Ezk 40^{46} 43^{19} 44^{15} 48^{11}). The name indicates the fact that is most decisive for the right understanding of the Sadducees. About the year 200 B.C., when party lines were beginning to be drawn, the name was chosen to point out the party of the priests. That is not saying that no priest could be a Pharisee or a Scribe. Neither is it saying that all the priests were Sadducees. In the time of Jesus many of the poor priests were Pharisees. But the higher priestly families and the priests as a body were Sadducees. With them were joined the majority of the aristocratic lay families of Judaea and Jerusalem. This fact gives us the key to their career. It is wrapped up in the history of the high priesthood. For two centuries after the Exile the high priesthood earned the right to the leadership of the Jewish nation. But in Jesus' time its leadership lay far back in the past. Its moral greatness had been undermined on two sides. On one side it had lost touch with what was deepest in the being of the Jews. For the most part this was due to its aristocratic bias. The Levitical priesthood was a close corporation. No man not born a priest could become a priest. More and more, as the interests of the nation widened and deepened, the high priesthood failed to keep pace. Its alliance with the aristocratic families made things worse.

The high priesthood and the people drifted apart. No great institution can do that and remain great.

From another side also—the political—the high priesthood was undermined. Owing to the mixture of Church and State the high priests were necessarily in politics all the time. Consequently the historical process, which ended by incorporating Palestine in the Roman Empire, drained away from the high priesthood much of the moral responsibility involved in the handling of large affairs. So, undermined on two sides, the high priesthood lost the right to lead. And the party which grew up about it—the Sadducees—became the party of those who cared more for their own well-being and for the maintenance of things as they were than for the Kingdom of God.

When we turn to the tenets of the Sadducees, it is still the contrast with the *Pharisees* that puts them in an intelligible light. Pharisaism, with all its faults, was the heart and soul of the nation, the steward of its treasures, the Holy Scriptures, the trustee of its vitalizing hope. The Sadducees stood for the tenaciously conservative tendencies in the nation. They lay under the curse which rests upon all aristocracies, the inability to realize that the best things must grow. In contrast to the Pharisees they had clung to the letter of the Law, refusing to modify it in any form. Thus they insisted on applying the *lex talionis* literally. In cases that were not clearly covered by Pentateuchal law, the Sadducees, when in power, enacted new laws of their own. As the latter accumulated, they tended to push the old Law into the background. Further, the draconic character of their laws outraged the people. According to *Megillath Ta 'anith* iv, the day upon which the Sadducean code was abrogated was observed as a holiday by the people. They denied the Pharisaic doctrine of the resurrection of the body (Mk 12^{18}, Mt 22^{23}, Lk 20^{27}, Ac 23^{8}). The NT is a better guide in this field than Josephus, who affirms (*BJ*, II. viii. 14 [165], *Ant.* XVIII. i. 4 [16]) that they denied the immortality of the soul. Josephus overstated things in his desire to make the Jewish parties look like the philosophical schools of Greece. The Sadducees did not deny the immortality of the soul. But they lingered in the past, the period when the belief in immortality was vague, shadowy, and had not yet become a working motive for goodness. They did not accept the developed faith in immortality which was part and parcel of the Pharisaic teaching regarding the Kingdom of God. And this meant that their nation had outgrown them. The Sadducees also denied the Pharisaic doctrine regarding angels and ministering spirits (Ac 23^{8}). Thereby they maintained a certain sobriety. They even emancipated themselves from a considerable amount of superstition bound up with Pharisaism. But they paid for it by a wholly disproportionate sacrifice of vital piety.

From this sketch we can see why Jesus had almost no dealings with the Sadducees during His ministry. His interests were with the common people. This brought Him into continual conflict with the Pharisees. It was not until His popularity seemed to threaten the peace of Jerusalem that the high priest, with the Sadducees at his back, was moved to decisive action. We can also see why the Apostolic Church, in her first years, had most to fear from the Sadducees (Ac 4 and 5).

As the party of the priestly aristocracy bound up with the Temple and the sacrificial cult, the Sadducees sustained a death blow by the tragic events of the year A.D. 70. Only remnants lingered on and finally merged with the Karaitic movement in the 8th cent. H. S. N.—**S. S. C.**

SADDUK, 1 Es 8^{2} (RV).—See ZADOK, **6.**

ṢADHE.—See TZADE.

SADOC.—**1.** 2 Es 1^{1} (AV, RV); see ZADOK, **6.** **2.** Mt 1^{14} (AV, RV); see ZADOK, **7.**

SAFFRON.—Hebrew *karkōm*, Ca 4^{14}. This is identical with the Arabic *kurkum* or *zaʿfarân* (whence is derived the English 'saffron'), the name of a variety of crocus (*Crocus saticus*), of which the yellow styles and stigmas are used for dyeing and for flavouring food. A similar dye, also called saffron, is more commonly derived from the florets of the *Carthamus tinctorius* (*Compositae*) cultivated everywhere in Palestine for this purpose.

E. W. G. M.

SAHIDIC VERSION.—See GREEK VERSIONS OF OT, **11**, and TEXT OF NT, **27.**

SAILS.—See SHIPS AND BOATS.

SAINTS.—See HOLINESS, II, and SANCTIFICATION.

SAKKUTH.—A word which is found in parallelism with Kaiwan in Am 5^{26}. The AV and RV forms are 'Siccuth' and 'Chiun,' as in the Massoretic Text, due to the Massoretic combination of the consonants with the vowels of *shiḳḳūs* ('abomination'). Sakkut is another name for the Assyrian god Ninurta, god of the planet Saturn; thus Sakkuth and Kaiwan are synonymous. See STARS. W. M. N.—**C. J. M. W.**

SALA.—**1.** Lk 3^{22}; see SALMON, **1.** **2.** Lk 3^{35} (AV); see SHELAH, **2.**

SALAH, Gn 10^{24} 11$^{13-15}$ (AV).—See SHELAH, **2.**

SALAMIEL.—An ancestor of Judith, Jth 8^{1} (AV **Samael**).

SALAMIS, in Cyprus, which must not be confused with the scene of the great battle between Xerxes and the Greeks in 480 B.C., was the first place visited by Paul and Barnabas on the first missionary journey (Ac 13^{5}). It is already mentioned in 7th-cent. Assyrian inscriptions. A whole line of its kings is known. It attained great power under Evagoras (410–373 B.C.). It was besieged by the Persians (381 B.C.). The royal house ended in 310 B.C. In Roman times it remained a flourishing commercial city, and the eastern half of the island was governed from there. There were very many Jews in Cyprus. Christianity was early preached there (Ac 11^{19f}), and among early converts were Mnason (Ac 21^{16}) and Barnabas (Ac 4^{36}). Under Trajan (A.D. 116–117) the Jews made an uprising and destroyed the city. They were annihilated, and Jews were henceforth not allowed on the island. A. So.—**E. G. K.**

SALASADAI, Jth 8^{1} (AV).—See SARASADAI.

SALATHIEL.—**1.** 1 Es 5$^{5, 48, 56}$ 6^{2} (AV, RV) and Mt 1^{12}, Lk 3^{37} (AV); see SHEALTIEL, **1.** **2.** 2 Es 3^{1} (AV, RV); see SHEALTIEL, **2.** **3.** 2 Es 3^{15} (AV); see PHALTIEL, **2.**

SALCAH, Jos 12^{5} 13^{11}, 1 Ch 5^{11} (AV).—See SALECAH.

SALCHAH, Dt 3^{10} (AV).—See SALECAH.

SALECAH.—The most easterly of the towns claimed by Israel; it was assigned to Gad and is always described as being on the eastern frontier of Bashan, Dt 3^{10} (AV **Salchah**), Jos 12^{5} 13^{11}, 1 Ch 5^{11} (AV **Salcah**). It is better indicated less theoretically as being in the extreme SE. of the Ḥauran. On account of its commanding position it has always been of strategic importance; but it was probably never permanently occupied by any of the Israelitish people. It was a Nabataean and Roman stronghold, and a station on the great trade and military road from Gadara and Edrei eastward through the desert to the Persian Gulf. It is now inhabited by Druses, and bears the name *Salkhad*.

SALEM.—1 Es 8^{1} (RV); see SHALLUM, **6.**

SALEM.—The name of the city where the mysterious **Melchizedek** (q.v.) was king and priest (Gn 14^{18}; cf He 7^{1f}). Modern scholarship has inclined toward the view that Salem is **Jerusalem** (q.v.). This identification appears to be supported by references to the city as *Urusalim* in the Tell el-Amarna tablets of the patriarchal period, and as *Ur-sa-li-im-mu* in Assyrian records from the time of Hezekiah. Josephus clearly makes this identification, stating that 'they afterwards called Salem *Jerusalem*' (*Ant.* I. x. 2 [180]). An important confirmation of this view appears in one of the Dead Sea Scrolls which was first called the Lamech Scroll, later the Genesis Apocryphon, col. XXII. lines 13–14, where it is reported that Abram 'came to Salem, that is Jerusalem. And Abram camped in the Valley of Shaveh, that is the King's Dale, the plain of Beth-karma (*bkʿth byth krm*').' The meaning of the last phrase, which does not occur in the Genesis account, is uncertain, but in the light of the geographical information preceding, and references to Beth-kerem in the Mishnah (*Midd.* iii. 4, *Nidd.* ii. 7) and in Jer 6[1] to Beth-haccherem (*byth hkrm*, 'house of the vineyard'), it must have been located in the vicinity of Jerusalem.

The likelihood that Melchizedek came from Jerusalem is supported by the statement that his meeting place with Abraham and the king of Sodom was 'at the Valley of Shaveh (that is, the King's Valley),' Gn 14[17]. This valley directly E. of Jerusalem is referred to in connexion with Absalom (2 S 18[18]), and Jehoshaphat Jl 3[2, 12]). Also, Jerusalem is alluded to in Ps 76[2] where the name *Salem* is used. Although neither name appears in Ps 110, the references to Zion (v.[2]) and Melchizedek (v.[4]) suggest the traditional association of the latter with Jerusalem. The Samaritans did not accept this identification but claimed that Salem or Salim of the Abraham story was located near Shechem. The LXX reads *Salem* for *Shiloh* (q.v.) in Jer 41[5], although most translators consider this an erroneous reading. Since the name was from a common Hebrew root, it came to be applied to other places. The early Christians knew of a Salem S. of Beth-shean. The valley of Salem is mentioned in Jth 4[4] and has been understood to be in the Jordan Valley, but this is uncertain. However, the two OT references to Salem (Gn 14[18], Ps 76[2]) support the view that Salem was another name for Jerusalem.

R. A. S. M.—**W. L. R.**

SALEMAS, 2 Es 1[1] (RV).—See SHALLUM, **6.**

SALIM, near to which was **Aenon** (Jn 3[23]), lay on the W. of Jordan (cf 1[28] 3[26] 10[40]). Aenon is placed by the *Onomasticon* eight Roman miles S. of Scythopolis (*Beisān*), 'near to Salim and Jordan.' This points to the neighbourhood of the ruin *Umm el-ʿAmdân*, with Tell er-Ridhghah on the N., where the tomb of Sheikh Selim probably preserves the ancient name. *Aenon*, 'place of springs,' we may find in the seven copious fountains near by. In the 1st cent. the district belonged probably to Scythopolis, not to Samaria. The difficulties of other suggested identifications can be got over by doing violence to the text or to the sense. W. E.

SALIMOTH, 1 Es 8[36] (RV).—See SHELOMITH, **5.**

SALLAI.—**1.** A Benjamite, Neh 11[8]. **2.** A priestly family, Neh 12[20]; called **Sallu** in v.[7].

SALLU.—**1.** A Benjamite family, 1 Ch 9[7], Neh 11[7]. **2.** See SALLAI, **2.**

SALLUMUS, 1 Es 9[25] (AV,RV); See SHALLUM, **11.**

SALMA.—**1.** One of the sons of Caleb the son of Hur and 'father' or founder of Bethlehem, 1 Ch 2[51, 54]. **2.** See SALMON, **1.**

SALMAI, Neh 7[48] (RV).—See SHALMAI.

SALMANASAR, 2 Es 13[40] (AV, RV) = **Shalmaneser** (q.v.).

SALMON.—**1.** The father of Boaz, Ru 4[20f]; in the direct line of the ancestry of our Lord, Mt 1[4f], Lk 3[32] (in the last **Sala** in RSV); called **Salma** in 1 Ch 2[11]. **2.** Ps 68[14] (AV); see ZALMON, **1.**

SALMONE.—A promontory at the NE. end of Crete, now *Cape Sidero*. St. Paul's ship, after reaching Cnidus with difficulty, was met by a powerful NW. wind, which forced the captain to alter the course. Off Salmone (Ac 27[7]) he decided to work his way westward under the lee of Crete. A. So.

SALOAS, 1 Es 9[22] (RV).—See ELASAH, **2.**

SALOM.—**1.** Bar 1[7] (AV, RV); see SHALLUM, **6. 2.** 1 Mac 2[26] (AV); see SALU.

SALOME.—**1.** The daughter (unnamed in NT) of Herodias who according to Mk 6[17-29], Mt 14[3-11] danced before Herod Antipas and received as a reward the head of John the Baptist. **2.** One of the women who were present at the crucifixion (Mk 15[40]) and who afterwards visited the sepulchre (16[1]). Mt 27[56], compared with Mk 15[40], shows that Matthew identified Salome with 'the wife of Zebedee' whom he had mentioned in 20[20]. W. F. B.—**E. H.**

SALT.—Salt is rightly included by Ben-Sira among the things 'basic to all the needs of man's life' (Sir 39[26] RSV). The Hebrews of the Southern Kingdom, at least, had access to inexhaustible stores of salt, both in the waters of the Dead Sea ('the Salt Sea,' Dt 3[17] and elsewhere), whence it could easily be obtained by evaporation, and in the deposits of *Jebel Usdum* (Arabic for Mount of Sodom) at its south-western extremity. References to 'salt pits' are found in Zeph 2[9], 1 Mac 11[35]. One hundred pounds of water from the Dead Sea are said to yield 24½ lb. of salt, compared with 6 lb. obtained from the same quantity of water from the Atlantic Ocean.

In addition to its daily use as a condiment in the preparation of food (cf Job 6[6]), and its important place in the sacrificial ritual, salt was employed by the Hebrews in an even greater variety of ways than it is among ourselves. Newborn infants, for example, were rubbed with salt (Ezk 16[4])—a practice in which a religious, rather than a hygienic, motive may be detected. A grain of salt placed in the hollow of a decayed tooth was considered a treatment for toothache (Mishnah, *Shabbath*, vi. 5). In other tractates of the Mishnah we find frequent references to the use of salt for preserving fish, for pickling olives, vegetables, etc. The salting of meat for preservation is referred to in the 'Letter of Jeremiah' (Bar 6[28]). The modern Jewish custom of laying meat in salt for the purpose of more thoroughly draining it of the blood was doubtless observed in Bible times. In Palestine, under the Seleucids, salt formed a government monopoly (1 Mac 10[29] 11[35]), as it did in Egypt under the Ptolemies.

As regards the presence of salt in the ritual of sacrifice, the words of Mk 9[49] AV, 'every sacrifice shall be salted with salt,' although omitted by RV and RSV following the best authorities, are nevertheless true to fact. The legislation of the Priests' Code, at least, expressly ordains: 'with all your offerings you shall offer salt' (Lv 2[13]). This passage specifies that the cereal offerings ('meal offerings' in RV; 'meat offerings' incorrectly in AV) as well as the more important animal sacrifices had to be salted (cf Ezk 43[24]). A special 'salt chamber' is mentioned among the rooms adjoining the Priests' Court in the description of Herod's Temple given in the Mishnah (*Middoth*, v. 3). The sacred incense also had to be 'seasoned with salt' (Ex 30[35] RV and RSV); likewise the showbread ('bread of the Presence' in RSV), according to the Greek text of Lv 24[7]. Probably the idea behind all this was that since salt was an indispensable accompaniment of man's food, it could not be absent from the 'bread (or food) of God,' as the sacrifices are termed in Lv 21[6, 8, 17, 22].

In the developed priestly legislation, however, there can be little doubt that the presence of salt had a symbolic significance. From its use as a preservative, reflected in our Lord's figure, 'You are the salt of the earth' (Mt 5[13]), and as an antidote to decay, it is natural that salt should become a symbol of permanence, and even of life as opposed to decay and death. From this symbolical standpoint we probably reach the true explanation of the striking expression 'a covenant of salt' (Nu 18[19], 2 Ch 13[5]), which denotes a covenant that is inviolable and valid in perpetuity. Therefore the presence of salt with every sacrifice may have come to symbolize the irrevocable character of Yahweh's covenant with Israel (see commentaries on Nu 18[19]; cf Ezr 4[14]).

In marked contrast to the employment of salt as a symbol of life, stands its parallel occurrence as a symbol of barrenness, desolation, or death (Dt 29[23] and elsewhere). This is partly due to the fact that land saturated with salt, such as that around the Dead Sea, is barren like a desert (cf Jer 17[6]). By this aspect of the symbolism of salt it has been usual to explain the treatment meted out by Abimelech to the city of Shechem, Jg 9[45]: 'He razed the city and *sowed it with salt*.' It is possible,

however, in harmony with the fundamental conception of the ban (see BAN) to regard the strewing of a city with salt as symbolizing its complete dedication to a deity.
A. R. S. K.—**W. F. S.**

SALT, CITY OF.—A city of Judah, Jos 15^{62}. It may be inferred to have been somewhere near the Dead Sea on the W. side, but the location is unknown.

SALT SEA.—See DEAD SEA.

SALT, VALLEY OF.—The scene of memorable victories of David over the Edomites, 2 S 8^{13}, 1 Ch 18^{12}, Ps 60 Heading; at a later period Amaziah here defeated the same enemies, 2 K 14^{7}, 2 Ch 25^{11}. It is probably modern *Wâdī el-Milḥ*, which still bears the same name.

SALTWORT, Job 30^{4} (RV).—See MALLOWS.

SALU.—The father of Zimri, Nu 25^{14}, 1 Mac 2^{26} (AV **Salom**).

SALUM.—**1.** 1 Es 8^{1} (AV); see SHALLUM, **6. 2.** 1 Es 5^{28} (AV, RV); see SHALLUM, **8.**

SALUTATION (or **greeting**) is a serious matter in the East; some knowledge of immemorial practice is necessay in dealing with Orientals. The subject salutes his king by prostration; the humble his superior by touching the ground with his hand, and then his lips and brow. The young salutes the aged, the rider the footman, etc. In crowded streets only men of age, rank, and dignity need be saluted (Mt 23^{7} etc.). Common forms of salutation are, 'Peace be upon you'; response, 'And upon you': 'May your day be happy'; response, 'May your day be happy and blessed': and, in the highway, 'Blessed be he that cometh' (Jg 18^{15}, Mt 10^{12}, Lk 24^{36} [AV, RV, RSVm]. Ps 118^{26}, Mt 21^{9} etc.). Salutations are frequently prolonged, and repeated inquiries after health and welfare extremely tedious (2 K 4^{29}, Lk 10^{4}). See also GESTURES, KISS. W. E.

SALVATION, SAVIOUR.—'Salvation' is the generic term employed in Scripture to express the idea of any gracious deliverance of God, but specially of the spiritual redemption from sin and its consequences predicted by the OT prophets, and realized in the mission and work of the Saviour Jesus Christ.

1. In the OT.—The root meaning of the principal OT words for 'save,' 'salvation,' 'saviour' is, *to be broad, spacious*; salvation is enlargement. As illustrations of this OT meaning of salvation may be taken the words of Moses at the Red Sea, 'Stand firm, and see the salvation of the LORD' (Ex 14^{13})—'He has become my salvation' (15^{2}); or the avowal of the psalmist, 'This poor man cried, and the LORD heard him, and saved him out of all his troubles' (Ps 34^{6}). Y″ is said to have given 'saviours' to Israel in the time of the Judges (Neh 9^{27}). Victory in battle is 'salvation' (Ex 14^{14}, 1 S 14^{45}, Ps 20 etc.). Salvation, or deliverance, of this kind is sometimes national, but sometimes also individual (cf of David, 2 S 22, Ps 18). Such external deliverances, however, it is to be observed, are never divorced from spiritual conditions. It is the righteous or penitent alone who are entitled to look to God for His saving help; no others can claim Him as the rock of their salvation (Ps 18^{1-3}, cf 4^{1}). When, therefore, the people had turned their backs on Y″, and abandoned themselves to wickedness, salvation could come only through a change of heart, through repentance. The chief need was to be saved from the sin itself. In the prophets, accordingly, the perspective somewhat changes. External blessings, deliverance from enemies, return from exile, are still hoped for, but the main stress is laid on a changed heart, forgiveness, restoration to God's favour, righteousness. In the pictures of the Messianic age it is these things that come to be dwelt on (cf Jer 31^{31-34}, Ezk 36^{26-28}, Hos 14 etc.). As the idea of salvation becomes more spiritual, it likewise becomes more universal; the Gentiles are to share its blessings (Is 45^{23f} 49^{8-12} 60^{1-12}).

The teaching of the prophets bore fruit in the age preceding the advent of Jesus in deepening ideas of the future life, of resurrection and a future perfected state, of the connexion of prosperity with righteousness—though mostly in the sense of outward legal obedience the very error against which the prophets declaimed—and in more concrete representations of the Messiah. But there never failed a godly kernel, who cherished more spiritual hopes, and waited in patience and prayer for 'the consolation of Israel' (Lk 2^{25}).

2. In the NT.—In the NT the word 'salvation' (*sōtēria*, from *sōtēr*, 'saviour') is sometimes applied to temporal benefits, like healings (*e.g.* Mt 9^{22} 'your faith has made you well,' literally 'saved you'), but most generally it is employed as a comprehensive term for the spiritual and eternal blessings brought to men by the appearance and redeeming work of Jesus Christ. The name *Jesus* was given Him because 'it is he that shall save his people from their sins' (Mt 1^{21} RV); He is distinctively the 'Saviour' (Lk 2^{11}); His work on earth was 'to seek and to save the lost' (Lk 19^{10}); His death and resurrection were a means to salvation (Ro 5^{9f}); He is exalted 'as Leader and Saviour' to give repentance and forgiveness of sins (Ac 5^{31}); 'and there is salvation in no one else' (4^{12}). In Apostolic usage, therefore, salvation is the all-embracing name for the blessings brought by the gospel (cf 'the gospel of your salvation,' Eph 1^{13}; 'the message of this salvation,' Ac 13^{26}; 'a repentance that leads to salvation,' 2 Co 7^{10} etc.). To expound fully the contents of this term, accordingly, would be to expound the contents of the gospel. Enough here to say that it includes deliverance from all sin's evils, and the bestowal of all spiritual blessings in Christ (Eph 1^{3}). It begins on earth in forgiveness, renewal, the bestowal of the Holy Spirit, enlightenment, guidance, strengthening, comfort; and is perfected in the blessedness and glory, in which body and soul share, of the life everlasting. The fact never to be forgotten about it is, that it has been obtained at the infinite cost of the redeeming death of God's own Son (cf Rev 5^{8}). For further elucidations, see ATONEMENT MEDIATOR, REDEMPTION. J. O.—**N. H. S.**

SAMAEL, Jth 8^{1} (AV).—See SALAMIEL.

SAMAIAS.—1. 1 Es 1^{9} (AV, RV); see SHEMAIAH, **14. 2.** 1 Es 8^{39} (AV, RV); see SHEMAIAH, **16. 3.** 1 Es 8^{44} (RV); see SHEMAIAH, **15. 4.** To 5^{13} (AV); see SHEMAIAH, **28.**

SAMARIA.—A city built on a hill purchased by Omri, king of Israel, from a certain **Shemer,** and by him made the capital of the Israelite kingdom (1 K 16^{24}). We gather from 1 K 20^{34} that Ben-hadad I., king of Syria, successfully attacked it soon afterwards, and had compelled Omri to grant him favourable trade facilities. Ahab here built a Baal temple (1 K 16^{32}) and a palace of ivory (22^{39}). Ben-hadad II. here besieged Ahab, but unsuccessfully, and was obliged to reverse the terms his father had exacted from Omri. Jehoram attempted a feeble and half-hearted reform, destroying Ahab's Baal-pillar, though retaining the calf-worship (2 K 3^{2}) and the *'ᵃshērāh* (13^{6}). The city was again besieged in his time by Ben-hadad II. (2 K 6, 7). After this event the history of Samaria is bound up with the troublesome internal affairs of the Northern Kingdom, and we need not follow it closely till we reach 724 B.C., when Shalmaneser IV. besieged Samaria in punishment for king Hoshea's disaffection. It fell three years later; and Sargon, who had meanwhile succeeded Shalmaneser on the Assyrian throne, deported its inhabitants, substituting a number of people drawn from other places (2 K 17). In 331 B.C. it was besieged and conquered by Alexander, and in 120 B.C. by John Hyrcanus. Herod carried out important building works here large portions of which still remain. He changed the name to *Sebastē* in honour of Augustus. Philip preached here (Ac 8^{5}). The city, however, gradually decayed, fading before the growing importance of Neapolis (Shechem). The Crusaders established a bishopric here.

Extensive remains of ancient Samaria still exist at the mound known as *Sebasṭîyeh* (Sebaste), a short distance from *Nâblus*. It is one of the largest and most important mounds in ancient Palestine. Excavations under the auspices of Harvard University were carried out 1908–1910, and there were joint expeditions 1931–1933 and 1935. Amongst the discoveries were the palace of Ahab or Jeroboam II., a number of ostraca, and many ivories. See J. W. Crowfoot, *et al., Samaria-Sebaste*, 3 vols.

R. A. S. M.—**J. Bo.**

SAMARITAN, GOOD.—See NEIGHBOUR.

SAMARITANS.—Religio-ethnic Hebrew sect whose laity claim descent from the Joseph tribes, but their priesthood from Phinehas. The OT reference (2 K 17^{29}) to Samaritans over-emphasizes non-Hebraic racial admixture and reflects the later enmity between Jew and Samaritan. This enmity was a continuation of the pre-720 B.C. Ephraim versus Judah strife. After 586 B.C. the north had the advantage this time over Judah and made the returning exiles aware of this. In the 5th cent. Sanballat the Horonite (Aaronide ?; in Samaritan sources Sanballat is regarded as Levitical) was the native ruler of Palestine under the Persians; at first Samaritan obstructionism was political, after Ezra's purging of the priesthood it was also religious. The Jews only in the time of John Hyrcanus (the end of the 2nd cent. B.C.), with his destruction of the Samaritan Temple on Gerizim, were able to retaliate, but the Samaritans (who maintained their national entity until the time of Justinian, A.D. 527) never recognized Jerusalem and Mount Zion as the chosen place for God's sanctuary; in their eyes the chosen place was Mount Gerizim, which had been an Israelite Holy place before Jerusalem. The question is not when the Samaritan Temple was first built on Gerizim, but when it was first regarded as their only sanctuary; this was probably after Ezra's rebuff.

The Holy Book of the Samaritans is the Torah, the perfect recension of which they hold they and not the Jews have; their one prophet is Moses. Their religion and life is still under the control of their priests, very much as in post-exilic Judaism prior to the emergence of the Pharisaic rabbis. Since the Samaritan priesthood is Zadokite it is not surprising that resemblances can be found between some Samaritan practices and those of Sadducees and Dead Sea Sectaries. There are no heathen beliefs or practices in Samaritanism. The Jewish attitude to the Samaritans is reflected in the various attitudes of the Gospels. Matthew is hostile, Mark ignores them, Luke, while fair, is distant. John is more conciliatory. The Talmud's attitude varies with the individual opinion cited, yet the only heresies were belief in Mount Gerizim and alleged denial of the resurrection of the dead (cf Tractate *Kuthim*). At least for the first millennium of our era, Samaritans were divided into two groups the Sabbuai and the Dositheans. The former were conservative and orthodox, the latter influenced by Gnosticism.

There is a large Samaritan literature in Hebrew, Aramaic, and Arabic, the bulk of which still awaits investigation and is important for the study of the text of the Bible and the Targum. Their liturgical, exegetical, midrashic, and halakhic works are important for the study of Sectarian Judaism.

The Samaritan Diaspora once widespread is now represented by seventy Samaritans at Holon in Israel, the rest of the sect live at *Nâblus*, successor to the ancient Shechem.

J. Bo.

SAMATUS, 1 Es 9^{34} (AV, RV).—See SHALLUM, **12,** and SHEMAIAH, **29.**

SAMECH.—Fifteenth letter of Hebrew alphabet, and so used to introduce the fifteenth part of Ps 119, every verse of which begins with this letter.

SAMEIUS, 1 Es 9^{21} (AV).—See SHEMAIAH, **17.**

SAMELLIUS, 1 Es $2^{16f, 25, 30}$ (RV).—See SHIMSHAI.

SAMEUS, 1 Es 9^{21} (RV).—See SHEMAIAH, **17.**

SAMGAR-NEBO.—One of the Babylonian princes who, at the taking of Jerusalem by Nebuchadnezzar, in the eleventh year of Zedekiah, came and sat in the middle gate, Jer 39^3. There has been much discussion concerning this name, due to the varying forms of the Greek version. The most probable explanation is that of Schrader, namely, *Shumgir-Nabû*, a name meaning 'Be gracious, O Nebo.' As, however, *Rab-saris* and *Rab-mag* are titles. the question arises whether *Samgar-nebo* may not be one also. If so, it may be a corruption of *sangu Nebo*, 'the priest of Nebo'—an office possibly held by **Nergal-sharezer,** who, if identical with king Neriglissar, was closely connected with E-zida, the temple of Nebo at Borsippa. His daughter married a priest of E-zida in the first year of his reign. Other textual reconstructions have been attempted, resting on the comparison of the text here with v.[13], but no satisfactory solution has been reached.

T. G. P.

SAMI, 1 Es 5^{28} (AV).—See SHOBAI.

SAMIS, 1 Es 9^{34} (AV).—See SHIMEI, **11.**

SAMLAH.—An Edomite king, Gn 36^{36f}, 1 Ch 1^{47f}.

SAMMUS, 1 Es 9^{43} (AV, RV).—See SHEMA, **3.**

SAMOS was an important island in the Aegean Sea off the coast of Ionia. It was a centre of luxury, art, and science. In 84 B.C. it was united to the province of Asia, and in 17 B.C. was made a free state by Augustus. This it was when St. Paul touched here (Ac 20^{15}) on his way home from his third journey. There were many Jewish residents on the island, and it was one of the places addressed by the Romans in favour of the Jews (1 Mac 15^{23}).

A. So.

SAMOTHRACE.—An island S. of Thrace and NW. of Troas, from which place St. Paul had a straight run to it (Ac 16^{11}). It was a regular stop for vessels sailing between Syria and the Hellespont (see *Ant.* XVI. ii. 2 [23]). The town of the same name was on the N. side of the island. Herod gave the people of Samos generous presents (Jos. *BJ* I. xxi. 11 [425]). The island is mountainous and has a summit nearly a mile above the sea level. Samothrace played little part in Greek history, but was famous as the seat of the mysterious cult of the divinities known as Cabiri (see Herod. ii. 51).

A. So.—**E. G. K.**

SAMPSACES, 1 Mac 15^{23} (AVm, RVm) = **Sampsames** (q.v.).

SAMPSAMES.—One of the places to which the Romans wrote in favour of the Jews (1 Mac 15^{23}); often identified with *Samsun*, which however was called Amisus then, a seaport town on the Black Sea. AVm and RVm with Vulgate, have **Lampsacus.**

SAMSON.—The form of the name in EV is from LXX and Vulgate; Hebrew *Shimshôn* suggests a derivation from *shemesh*, 'sun,' and the meaning 'sun-man.' His birthplace, Zorah, was close to Beth-shemesh, 'house of the Sun.' The account of Samson occurs in Jg 13–16 and he is alluded to in He 11^{32}.

1. The story of Samson need not be recapitulated; but it falls into two well-defined parts: Jg 13^{1-24}, The Birth of Samson; Jg 13^{25}–16^{31}, The Exploits of Samson. The birth is supernaturally foretold to a hitherto childless couple; the scene is the Danite territory before the enforced migration of that tribe northward. He is to be a Nazirite, *i.e.* a dedicated man in the nomadic tradition, from birth. The religious motif of the story is similar to that of Jg 6^{11-24}. The exploits are of a different character, and show the marks of stories long preserved in the oral traditions of the district. They are practically devoid of religious interests, though they reflect a belief in God who works for His people even through the waywardness of men. It seems reasonable to suppose that these popular stories were gathered together by the author of Jg 13^{2-24} and that the whole cycle was given literary form in the Deuteronomic circle, when the opening and closing comments were added (Jg 13^1 16^{31b}). If the stories existed in oral form, this may well account for the formal inconsistencies and additions.

It is evident that 'his father and mother' have been added at $14^{5, 6b, 10a}$. The original story would have told of Samson's request to his parents for a marriage of the normal kind, but with a Philistine woman. This was refused, and Samson arranged a marriage of the ṣadiḳa type (cf Marriage), in which the bride remains as a member of her own clan as do the children of the marriage. Hence the friends of the bridegroom, 14[11], are Philistines and not Danites. The ' linen garments ' (14[12]) are pieces of fine linen (Pr 31[24], Is 3[23]) and the ' festal garments ' are gala dress suitable for the occasion (cf 2 K 5[5, 22f]). For ' before the sun went down ' we should read ' before he entered the bridal chamber ' (14[18]). In 16[13f] the words '. . . and make it tight with the pin, then I shall become weak, and be like any other man. So while he slept, Delilah took the seven locks of his head and wove them into the web ' have been restored to the text from LXX. Delilah wove Samson's hair into the cloth that was being woven on the loom ; but when Samson was aroused, he pulled up the whole loom as it was thus fastened to his hair. When he was finally captured and made to grind at the mill in the prison, it was the ultimate dishonour that the strong man of the Hebrews should be condemned to a woman's work. Dagon (v.[23] ; cf 1 S 5) was a Semitic corn deity.

2. Origin and nature of the story.—It may be hazardous to assign the narrative to the J source in the Pentateuch, and perhaps misleading to think of it as a ' document ' before its incorporation into the complex of the book of Judges. It would appear that we have here a series of popular stories about a local hero, Samson, preserved in the district of Mahaneh-dan. It is possible that we have preserved a selection from a much wider series of stories. As we have it, the narrative falls into three clearly defined sections : (*a*) the birth narrative, ch. 13, the most distinctively ' religious ' section, which may well have been associated with a local sanctuary ; (*b*) a series of exploits, chs. 14 and 15, in which the ' religious ' motif is least apparent ; and (*c*) the account of Samson's downfall and humiliation, through which the defeat of Israel's enemies is brought about in the very house of their god. In this last section we may feel that the religious interest, though never obtrusive, is most profound. It is said that he began ' to deliver Israel from the hand of the Philistines ' (13[5]), and that he ' judged Israel twenty years ' (15[20] 16[31]). There is, however, no suggestion in the stories that he was recognized as the leader of his people, and he was certainly not so acknowledged by the men of Judah (15[10-13]). His actions are prompted by selfish interests and private revenge ; the events are of local significance. Parallels can be found in many parts of the world, particularly among peoples who have known oppression and foreign domination. It is therefore impossible to assert or to deny, on the basis of evidence, the factual historicity of the events associated with Samson. Yet the obvious antiquity of the stories is evidence for an attitude of mind among the Israelites which was to come to clearer expression under Saul, and to victory under David. The name Samson has suggested that the stories associated with the hero have their origin in a solar myth, but attempts to identify certain elements in the story with known sun-myths are hardly convincing. His long hair (rays of the sun), the burning of the crops, the name of his paramour Delilah (worshipper or devotee, *sc.* of Ashtart), and certain similarities between the Samson and Gilgamesh stories have been cited in support of this suggestion. But these features, with a great deal that has no possible solar connexion, are integral to the story and they serve no mythic function. It is possible that vague memories of the Gilgamesh myth have coloured the incidents, but there is no suggestion that Samson is ' two-thirds god and one third man ' ; he has no traffic with the deities and there is nothing to correspond to Enkidu. Similarly, the association of the jaw-bone incident with Ramath-lehi (the height of Lehi) would naturally suggest the throwing away of the jaw-bone (*lᵉḥî*), while En-hakkore (Partridge-spring) would call to mind the occasion when Samson called (*ḳārā'*) on the Lord. In other words, these place names have conditioned the form of the stories, but have not created them. In fact the stories are told with artless simplicity and rustic humour and reflect the historical situation and local customs. Parallels with the Hercules cycle have been noted, but they are not close enough to suggest identity of origin. It is a fact of experience that great heroes have killed wild beasts, suffered thirst, and sometimes been unwise in their choice of a mate. The incidents in the Samson story find their natural explanation as belonging to a historical situation as preserved in local tradition.

3. Historical value.—From this point of view the great importance of the stories lies in their portrayal of the political and social conditions of the time. The southern part of Canaan is completely under Philistine control ; what is described is not a condition of war but of domination against which the inhabitants of the districts bordering on the Maritime Plain have no thought of rebelling (15[10f]). Samson himself leads no political revolt ; his actions are the result of private quarrels. There is no suggestion of Philistine objection to intermarriage ; although it is offensive to Israelite tradition. There appears to have been no restriction of movement imposed by the Philistines on the inhabitants of the district. The Philistines have successfully established control and the process of assimilation has begun. It is to be noted that the Philistines have adopted a Semitic corn deity. We gain from the story a clear picture of early *marriage* customs, accompanied by lavish feasting lasting for a week and gifts of clothing. The riddle is of greater significance than it would be among us. It is a test, not of mental agility, but of wit and ability to find the answer which could only be known to the questioner. The solution, however dubiously obtained, brought ' honour ' to the answerers.

4. Religious significance.—This can be recognized at two levels ; first that which is inherent in the stories themselves, and second, that which arises from the use made of these stories by the deuteronomic editor. The religious emphasis on the birth of Samson is evident. The birth is a miracle, not in the modern sense of something abnormal, but in the Biblical sense of an event in which Divine activity is apparent. He is to be a Nazirite from the time of his conception : the rules for a Nazirite in Nu 6 agree with what we find in Jg 13—clear evidence of the high antiquity of some of the material found in the Priestly Code. The consecration of the hair, regarded as a seat of life, was particularly associated with war regarded as a religious activity (Dt 32[42], Ps 68[21]). The prohibition against fermented drink is a negative side of the same consecration, since the mysterious phenomenon of fermentation was regarded as evidence (to the man of the desert tradition) of the activity of an alien deity. This applies also to ' unclean ' food. The exceptional thing about Samson was that he should be a life-long Nazirite. Samson's strength was particularly associated with his hair : but at times he was seized with a demonic frenzy, when the Divine energy ' struck ' him (13[25]) or ' came powerfully upon him ' (14[6, 19] 15[14]). The sequel to Ch 13 can only be regarded as a degradation of a life specially equipped for a high purpose. But this association may well indicate the high art as well as the profound religious insight of the deuteronomist. For the writing of this whole story in its present form could only have taken place after the reform of King Josiah, and perhaps during the Exile period. Its parallel to the life of Israel then becomes obvious. Yet, in spite of Israel's waywardness, the Divine purpose will be accomplished, even in Israel's humiliation and death. Samson was, even in his ignorance, an exponent of Israel's deepest faith. It may be that this is intended in the reference to him in He 11[32].

C. W. E.—**A. S. H.**

SAMUEL.—The figure of Samuel is similar to that of Moses in that no single one of the sacral institutions of Israel, *e.g.* the offices of prophet, seer, judge, or sacrificial intercessor, can be used to characterize his position. Both men combine the traits of several of these offices in the tradition we have of them. This makes it hard to determine their precise historical position. In the case of Samuel it is possible to see that different sections of the tradition have seen him in a different way, or attached to his name different examples of sacred life and action. These different traditions can probably not be separated by pure literary criticism which would seek to identify various 'documents' or 'sources'; rather we may discern the special interest of various parts of the narrative, as cherished in various centres and circles of tradition.

1 S 1–3 is probably from the tradition of Shiloh and tells how Samuel's birth was an answer to prayer and a reversal by God of human weakness (the theme of the song of Hannah, 1 S 2[1–10]); and how the child was dedicated to God and became the established mouthpiece of the Divine word at Shiloh, at a time when the priesthood of the house of Eli is falling into decadence and destruction. Samuel is here seen as a prophet, a prophet established at the sanctuary, receiving and transmitting oracles of the future will of Yahweh. It has long been noticed that the etymologizing interpretation of the name of the child (1 S 1[20, 27–28]) as 'lent, asked' (Heb. *Shā'ûl*) fits not the name of Samuel but the first king Saul. But if so only the particular theme of the naming has been transferred from Saul to Samuel, probably because of the interest in the Divine calling and sending of Samuel; it is not credible that the whole of 1 S 1–3 originally belonged to Saul.

1 S 7[3–14] displays Samuel rather as a war-leader or deliverer on the pattern of earlier 'judges' like Gideon. The tradition here has come from Mizpah and is interested in the stone Ebenezer where the Philistines were said to have been defeated. The story of the victory is a rather flat and featureless one, and the most interesting thing is Samuel's act of intercession by sacrifice. In later times the few references to Samuel outside the books that bear his name remember him as a great intercessor like Moses (Jer 15[1], Ps 99[6]).

The following passage (7[15]–8[3]) sees Samuel as a judge in the proper sense, a guardian and interpreter of the sacred law, who went round the great sanctuaries of Israel. His sons, appointed as colleagues and successors, lead by their corrupt ways to a demand for monarchical government.

The place of Samuel in the traditions of the origin of the kingdom is a complicated one. In chs. 8 and 12, Samuel makes more or less the standard Deuteronomic criticisms of the kingdom, with Solomon's rule as the standard bad example; even here, though it is held that Israel has done wrong to ask for a king, it is admitted that God has appointed them a king. Chs. 9–10 represent Samuel as a seer, who can be asked for guidance in a case of lost asses, who is given Divine guidance for the choosing out of the man to be king, who can tell what Saul will meet on his way as he departs. From certain unevennesses in the narrative it seems likely that traditions of different localities have been fused together. We see the emphasis on Samuel as director in sacrificial worship (9[13] 10[8]) and we have mention of bands of ecstatic prophets, among whom Samuel appears as a leader at Ramah in 1 S 19[18–24]. 1 S 10[17–27], on the other hand, shows Samuel convoking an assembly of all Israel and installing Saul as king on the basis of the sacred lot; this is again the Mizpah tradition, and at the sanctuary there Samuel deposits the 'book' of the rights and duties of the kingship. 11[14] probably speaks not of 'renewing' but of 'inaugurating' the kingdom in the original sense, and is the tradition of the rise of Saul to kingship after his successful Ammonite campaign, and its sanctification by Samuel at Gilgal—perhaps the most historically probable of these traditions. In its present place it is no doubt intended as a renewal of the kingship.

Two incidents at Gilgal, 13[8–15] and 15[10–31], indicate hard opposition between Samuel and Saul. The first is connected with war against the Philistines (and is rather an interruption to the story of the war), and Samuel is represented as claiming exclusive rights, or priority of rights, in the offering of sacrifice. The second concerns the non-execution of the ritual destruction of the booty in the Amalekite war. In the first case Samuel pronounces the non-continuance of the kingdom of Saul rather than his rejection; in the latter the opposition is sharper and goes on to rejection. Both passages show that Saul's motives were either reasonable or religious or both. 1 S 15[22–23] contains a passage about the value of sacrifice which suggests the prophecy of the 7th cent. rather than Samuel's time. The stories show how the older premonarchic sacral leadership, represented by Samuel, was able to resist the freedom for innovation by the first king and to interpret his innovations as disobedience to Yahweh. The story indicates also that Samuel was not lacking in personal sympathy for Saul (15[35] 16[1]).

1 S 16[1–13] tells how Samuel chose David on God's behalf out of the family of Jesse, and anointed him as king. The story again shows Samuel's special place in sacrificing. Other stories of the rise of David are independent of Samuel. We find David during his flight from Saul taking refuge with Samuel at Ramah, 1 S 19[18]. But from this time Samuel has no central place in the tradition. His death is mentioned in 25[1], and 28 is devoted to the story of how his ghost is called up by Saul; the ghost repeats the accusation of disobedience in the case of Amalek, and prophesies the defeat by the Philistines in which Saul perished.

The different traditions about Samuel have been fairly carefully put together and in spite of occasional unevennesses may be read as one story. Samuel is in this context seen as destined to be the last of the 'judges' and the human mediator to Israel of the origin of the kingship and its messianic line, along with the dark and mysterious choice and rejection of the first king and the ambiguity of the Divine judgment of the kingdom.

We have no exact data for the chronology of the life of Samuel or for his age at his death; but his life certainly lay within the approximate limits 1070–1000 B.C. If we can take as historical the accounts of his activity as a 'judge,' and there is no reason to doubt them, his work as a guardian of the sacred law in a number of centres must have done much to consolidate the unity of Israel, to provide a certain minimal administration of the ancient law, and to keep alive the knowledge of the God of Israel upon whose action the law, the covenants and the traditions depended.

Samuel was of Ephraimite family, and it is only the later genealogical interest which tries to make him a Levite, in conformity with the later rules of priesthood (1 Ch 6[28]). J. Ba.

SAMUEL, BOOKS OF.—1. Title.—The two Books of Samuel are really parts of what was originally one book. This is shown not only by the fact that the narrative of Book I. is continued without the slightest interruption in Book II., and that the style, tone, point of view, and purpose are the same throughout, but also by their appearance as one book bearing the simple title 'Samuel' in the oldest known Hebrew MSS. The division of the Hebrew text into two books was first made in print by Daniel Bomberg in his Hebrew Bible (2nd edition, 1517). In doing so he was in part following the text of the Septuagint and the Vulgate, in which the Books of Samuel and Kings are described as the First, Second, Third, and Fourth Books of Kingdoms (LXX), or Kings (Vulgate). The title 'Samuel,' less accurately descriptive of the contents than that of 'Kingdoms' or 'Kings,' owes its origin to the prominent place held by Samuel in 1 S 1–16. A late Jewish interpretation regarded it as declaring Samuel's authorship of the narrative; but this is impossible, in view of the fact that the history extends through the reign of David, long after the death of Samuel (1 S 25[1]).

2. Contents.—The period covered by the Books of Samuel extends from the birth of Samuel to the close of David's reign, *i.e.* approximately from 1070 B.C. to 961 B.C. The narrative can conveniently be divided into seven sections which are roughly marked off by content and by the history of the tradition they contain. These are (largely following Hertzberg, *Die Samuelisbücher*, *ATD*, 1956): 1. The childhood of Samuel and his relation to the Eli priesthood at Shiloh (1 S 1–3); 2. The

Ark and its wanderings (1 S 4¹–7²), with which 2 S 6 is closely connected; 3. The story of Samuel, the beginnings of the kingdom, and the conflict of Saul with Samuel (1 S 7–15); 4. The story of Saul and David, from the anointing of David down to the defeat and death of Saul by the Philistines (1 S 16–2 S 1); 5. David as king, first in Hebron over Judah and then in Jerusalem over all Israel; his establishment of Jerusalem as capital, the question of a house there for Yahweh, the promise to the Davidic dynasty, and his imperial conquests (2 S 2–8); 6. The 'Succession Story' of David, in which the central interest and architectonic theme is the question who should follow David as king (2 S 9–20); 1 K 1–2 belong originally to this narrative, and relate how Solomon was established on the throne after David. The division after 2 S 20 is, however, an old one, and the editors of the Book of Kings have taken the extreme old age of David (1 K 1¹) as their starting point; 7. A series of appendices (2 S 21–24). These are six in number, and appear to have been placed inside one another in such a way that the first and sixth, the second and fifth, and the third and fourth should be taken together. Thus we have three pairs: (1) Two stories of divinely-sent catastrophe and its ending by apotropaic ceremonies, 2 S 21¹⁻¹⁴ and 24. (2) Stories of heroic deeds against giant enemies, and lists of heroes, 21¹⁵⁻²² and 23⁸⁻³⁹. (3) Two poems, a 'song of David' (identical with Ps 18 except for small details) and the 'last words of David,' 2 S 22 and 23¹⁻⁷ respectively.

3. Text and Versions.—It has long been recognized by many scholars that Samuel is a book where the LXX presents at many points a better text than the traditional Hebrew text. The RSV indicates in its margin numerous cases where it has followed the Greek reading where it affords better sense than the Massoretic; the reader may compare 1 S 1²⁴⁻²⁵ 9²⁵ 14⁴¹ in the RSV text with the translation of the Hebrew text in the AV or the RSV margin. The value of the LXX in Samuel has now been substantially reinforced by the texts discovered at Qumrân which in some cases give a Hebrew text superior either to the Greek or to the Massoretic. An impression for a passage of some length may be got from Allegro, *The Dead Sea Scrolls*, pp. 57–65, and cf Cross, *The Ancient Library of Qumrân*, pp. 133–145. This does not mean that the Massoretic text is always 'wrong' when it disagrees with LXX or Qumrân. Decisions about the best reading, *i.e.* the one nearest to the original writing of the passage, have to be made on their own merits for each passage. The value of the new evidence is that it sets us free from limitation to a very narrow line of witness such as the Massoretic text affords.

The other versions of the book, Latin, Syriac and so on, also present differences from the MT, but these are less striking than those of the LXX. For those passages of Samuel which are repeated in Chronicles it is now possible to take into consideration also the value of the Chronicles text. Cross (*op. cit.*, p. 141) points out that a Qumrân text of Samuel contains a phrase which appears in the MT of Chronicles (1 Ch 21¹⁶, 'standing between earth and heaven, and his sword drawn in his hand'). The evaluation of evidence of this kind must in many cases await more complete publication of the texts discovered.

4. Sources and Date.—It is probable that the Books of Samuel are not a single composition made at one time, but have drawn at various stages from different circles and settings of tradition. The evidence for this is to be found not so much in the existence of inconsistencies and doublets, although these occur (*e.g.* the two accounts of David's introduction to Saul in 1 S 16¹⁷ᶠᶠ and 17⁵⁵ᶠᶠ, or the inconsistency of 1 S 7¹³⁻¹⁴ with 1 S 13). The evidence lies rather in the differing 'interest' in which the various blocks of tradition handle the material. Something of this should be evident from our summary of contents, where we note that 1 S 4–6 is interested in the Ark, while for the long composition 2 S 9–20 the interest is the problem of succession to David. See also SAMUEL.

It is, however, improbable that sources can be separated by purely literary-critical methods. That is to say, this book cannot be satisfactorily explained as the product of two or more parallel sources in written form put together more or less mechanically by an editor. The attempt made by many earlier scholars to trace the Pentateuchal documentary sources J and E through Samuel must be regarded as a complete failure, and few scholars would try such a method to-day.

In a number of cases we can discern the setting of the tradition quite easily. This is so especially when an important sanctuary is involved in the story, and it is extremely likely that the story relates the event as it was remembered at that place. So the first group of traditions about Samuel (1 S 1–3) is centred at Shiloh and concerns the fate of its priesthood; it was almost certainly cherished by later priestly circles after the fall of Shiloh. The story of how the kingdom began was related at Mizpah, and we have that form of the story in 1 S 10¹⁷⁻²⁷; the Gilgal form appears in 11¹²⁻¹⁵. We have already mentioned the Ark's own tradition, and this would be cultivated at Jerusalem after the Ark came there (2 S 6). Other aspects of the tradition would form part of the cult story of the Jerusalem holy place, *e.g.* David's plan to build a temple there, and the story of the purchase of the threshing floor as a sanctuary (2 S 24). Some passages came from official records (such as the lists of officials) and some would be handed down in official or military groups (heroic deeds of David's men).

But for the story of Saul and David we can safely say that most was handed down by simple reminiscence by eye-witnesses of the events. In these cases the stories reached their present form when they were still quite fresh from the historical actuality. David in particular was a great centre of popular interest and veneration, and from an early stage in his conflict with Saul he had with him his band of men who shared his present experiences and learned of his earlier ones. These men later came to official position in Jerusalem, the royal city. For most of the David story, then, we may be fairly sure of eye-witness material reaching its present form while David was still alive or in the reign of his successor Solomon. The long Succession Story of 2 S 9–20 may confidently be taken to have been composed by a contemporary; we can only guess who he may have been.

In the stories of Samuel there is a bigger gap probably between the original event and the present form of its narration, and the tradition was handed down longer in a plastic form. Alive as it must have been in David and Solomon's time, it may not have been till the 9th cent. that the different traditions had grown together, and certain aspects in their handling would suggest that the incipient Deuteronomic school had had some effect on them (*e.g.* Samuel's speech in 1 S 12); this would suggest they were still fluid in the 8th cent., and the same applies to the similarities to the prophets in passages like 1 S 15²²⁻²³.

In any case it is not likely that the books of Samuel were subjected to a heavy editorial revision in late times, nor were its early stories fitted within a chronological or other framework, as happened in both Judges and Kings to some extent. For the most part the old stories were left to tell their own tale.

On the other hand, the interest of those who retold and remoulded the stories was in some ways orientated in a new way, towards the origin of the kingdom as the messianic house. Within their general outlook some of the inconsistencies of the present narrative would not be inconsistencies so much as proper expressions of different aspects in a reality itself ambiguous and mysterious. Such a case is the estimate of the value of the monarchy. It is true that different traditions have been more or less willing to welcome it or to criticise it. But the circles of the late tradition were willing to include both, and they did not try to suppress one of them. And the opposition between the sources should not be exaggerated, for even those which regard the call for a king as rejection of God do not dispute that God did in fact give a king in answer to this call. Nor does any source which criticises the kingdom suggest that all would have gone well if no demand for a king had arisen; and though Samuel is seen in 1 S 7 as one who could deliver from the Philistine menace, 8^{1-3} go on to tell how Samuel's form of rule could not lead on to satisfactory government, for his own sons were corrupt.

In general, then, we may regard it as probable that much of the material of these books had reached substantially its present form by about 940–930 B.C., and the remainder gradually fell into shape between that time and perhaps 700 B.C. Of really late material there is very little sign.

5. Historical and religious value.—As historical sources those sections of the Books of Samuel which rest very nearly on contemporary or eye-witness accounts must be estimated highly, and a passage like the Succession Story is as good a historical source as we find anywhere in the OT. Even contemporary accounts are, however, not without their own special interest and viewpoint. The Succession Story is not an attempt to write a history of David's reign, but a study of the vicissitudes of the succession. Even where this is accurate there will be many things left out or unsaid because they are not part of the interest of the narrative. An appreciation of the literary interest of documents like the Succession Story is therefore necessary before a judgment can be made how far they are adequate as historical sources.

Where accounts are more remote from contemporary experience, as in parts of the Samuel story appreciation is more difficult. It is not easy from the varied traditions of the origin of the kingdom to state what the historical circumstances in fact were. It is rather arbitrary to accept one account as the earliest and brush the others aside completely. In fact all or nearly all of the narratives are not simply historical information but theologically interested history, and have to be interpreted first to see what is their religious and theological interest (which has preserved, selected, and moulded the stories); only after that can an assessment of historical accuracy be begun. On the other hand even stories of predominantly theological character have embedded in them all sorts of accurate remembrance of old customs and events. In this it is a great help that the books of Samuel were not subjected to an extensive editing in late times, so that many primitive customs and events remain unchanged.

The same applies to these books as a source for the history of religion in this period. Editors have not been at work excising the references to early practices which were later abnormal or unorthodox, and very many of the religious practices mentioned may be taken accurately as having existed in the time of Saul or David. As examples we may give: the sacrificial practice at Shiloh (1 S 2^{12-17}); the sacrificial intercession of Samuel (7^{8-11}); the use of the term 'seer' (9^{9}); the kind of activity one would expect from a band of prophets (10^{5-6} 19^{18-24}); the general shape of the image or *teraphim* (19^{11-17}); the use of the ephod in divination (23^{9-13}). We cannot, however, take absolutely everything contained in these books as certainly expressing the religion of the period, *e.g.* Samuel's words in 1 S 15^{22-23} are not likely to be the atmosphere of the 11th cent. B.C.

In any case we should remember that the books are not intended as a survey of religion as it was in that time. Their own religious interest is not that of producing a history of religion. The interest ultimately is in the history of Israel as a history governed and guided by God, and more particularly in the series of events by which God initiated or permitted the rise of the monarchy and the way in which that institution became the possession of the house of David, the messianic house, to whom was recorded the promise that a son of its family would never be lacking, to sit on the throne of his father David.

J. M. P. S.—**J. Ba.**

SANAAS, 1 Es 5^{23} (RV).—See SENAAH.

SANABASSAR, 1 Es 2^{12} (AV, RV).=**Shesh-bazzar** (q.v.).

SANABASSARUS, 1 Es $6^{18, 20}$ (AV, RV)=**Shesh-bazzar** (q.v.).

SANASIB, 1 Es 5^{24} (AV, RV).—See ANASIB.

SANBALLAT (Ass. *Sin-uballiṭ*, 'Sin gives life').—The most inveterate of Nehemiah's opponents, Neh $2^{10, 19}$ 4^{1ff} 6^{1ff} 13^{28}. He is called a Horonite, which probably means a native of Beth-horon. From the Elephantine Papyri we know that he was Governor of Samaria in 407 B.C., when he seems to have been an old man, since affairs were apparently left in the hands of his sons. The fact that these sons bore names compounded with Yahweh, Delaiah, and Shelemiah, suggests that he was a worshipper of Yahweh, and this is borne out by the fact that his daughter married the son of the Jerusalem High Priest, Neh 13^{25}. When Nehemiah came to Jerusalem to repair the walls, Sanballat, with his allies **Tobiah** (q.v.) and **Geshem** (q.v.) met him with derision; and after the work was well under way he stirred up the garrison of Samaria and planned an attack against the builders. This was prevented by the watchfulness of Nehemiah and the workmen. Several devices aimed against the life of Nehemiah were also thwarted by the sagacity of the latter. On Nehemiah's second visit he banished Sanballat's son-in-law from Jerusalem, Neh 13^{28}. It is sometimes supposed that the Samaritan schism dates from this time; but see H. H. Rowley, *BJRL*, xxxviii, 166 ff. J. F. McC.—**H. H. R.**

SANCTIFICATION, SANCTIFY.—'Sanctify' (Latin, from the Vulgate)=the native English 'hallow' (*i.e. make, count, keep holy*), the latter word being in use somewhat the loftier. AV uses 'hallow' thirty-five times in OT and twice in NT (Mt 6^{9} ‖ Lk 11^{2}), 'sanctify' one hundred and ten times in OT and twenty-six times in NT—for identical Hebrew and Greek terms. For the same Hebrew and Greek terms, in the same passages, RSV uses 'hallow' twelve times, 'sanctify' fifty-five times, 'consecrate' fifty-six times, 'dedicate' ten times, and verbal phrases containing 'holy' or 'holiness' thirty-one times. For the meaning of the root word 'holy,' see article HOLINESS. The noun 'sanctification' —denoting first the *act* or *process* of making holy (hallowing), then the resultant *state* (hallowedness)—appears only in NT. RSV retains it in 1 Co 1^{30}, 1 Th 4^{3}, 2 Th 2^{13}. For the same Greek noun, AV uses 'holiness' in Ro $6^{19, 22}$, 1 Th 4^{7}, 1 Ti 2^{15}, He 12^{14}; RSV retains 'holiness' except in Romans, where it uses 'sanctification,' and it changes to 'holiness' in 1 Th 4^{4}. In all these passages the *state* rather than the process is implied. In 1 P 1^{2}, however, 'sanctification' stands for the act or process, and RSV uses verbs rather than nouns: 'chosen and destined by God the Father and sanctified by the Spirit for obedience to Jesus Christ and for sprinkling with his blood.'

1. In the Israelite as in other ancient religions, that is 'holy' which is set apart for Divine use, so that the 'sanctified' is the opposite of the 'common,' secular, profane. Is 65^{2-7} 66^{17} illustrate the application of this term in heathenism. With this broad signification it is applicable to whatever is devoted to the public service of the Lord: to persons—priests, Nazirites, etc.; to sacrifices; to vessels, garments, buildings, days (especially the Sabbath). In Jl 3^{9}, Jer 6^{4} (see RVm) even 'war' is 'sanctified'; in Is 13^{3} the warriors are 'my sanctified ones' (RV 'consecrated ones'); in Nu 21^{14} we hear of 'The Book of the Wars of the Lord.' The numerous Levitical and other kindred uses of the verb bear this formal sense. But as 'holy' came to designate the specific character of the Lord—'the Holy One of Israel' (see Isaiah *passim*)—in distinction from heathen gods, 'sanctify' acquired a corresponding ethical connotation; holiness came to imply a *character* (actual or ideal) in the holy people, accordant with its status. For Israel, being the Lord's servant, is 'brought near' to Him (Ex 19^{4-6}, Dt 4^{7}, Jer 2^{2}, Ps 65^{4} 73^{27f} 148^{14}; contrast Ex 19^{12-24}, Jer 2^{13}, Hos 9^{1} etc.), and such proximity necessitates congeniality—that congruity of nature whereof circumcision and the ceremonial cleansings were

SANCTIFICATION, SANCTIFY

symbolical (Ps 15, 24^{3-6}; cf Is $1^{4,16f}$ 3^{8} 6^{3-8}, Jer 4^{1-4}, Hab 1^{12f}, Ezk 36^{16-28}, Ps 51 etc.). The refrain 'I am the Lord' resounds through the Law of Holiness in Lv 17–26; this code blends the ritual and the moral in the holiness it demands from Israel, which is the corollary of the Lord's own holiness. Such is the OT doctrine of sanctification. The prophets, it is said, taught an ethical monotheism—which is to say, in effect, they *ethicized holiness*. The sanctification binding Israel to the Lord was, in a sense, reciprocal: 'You shall not profane my holy name (cf Ex 20^{7}, Lv 19^{22} 22^{2}, Am 2^{7}, Mal 1^{11f}), but I will be hallowed among the people of Israel; I am the Lord who sanctify you' (Lv 22^{32}); to sanctify the Lord or his 'name' is to recognize and act towards Him as holy, to 'make him holy' in one's thoughts and attitude (Is 8^{13}). This expression is characteristic of Isaiah (5^{16} 29^{23}) and Ezekiel (20^{41} $28^{22,25}$ 36^{23} $38^{16,23}$ 39^{27}), who regard the Lord as 'sanctified' when His awe-awakening judgments bring men to acknowledge His Deity and character. The Lord is said to sanctify Himself or His 'great name' when He vindicates His holiness and makes Himself known in the sight of many nations for what in truth He is. RSV expresses the Divine initiative more clearly in these texts; where AV has 'be sanctified' RSV has 'shows himself holy' (Is 5^{16}), 'manifest my holiness' (Ezk 20^{41} $28^{22,25}$), 'vindicate my holiness' (Ezk 36^{23} 38^{16} 39^{27}).

2. In the NT we must distinguish the usage of our Lord, of the author of the Letter to the Hebrews, and of the Apostle Paul.

(1) Adopting the language of Lv 22^{32} and of the prophets, Jesus bids the disciples pray, 'Our Father . . . *hallowed* be thy name . . . on earth' (Mt 6^{9f} ‖ Lk 11^{2}). To bring about this 'hallowing' is the very work of Jesus, who for this end 'makes known' the Father's 'name' (Jn $1^{14,18}$ 14^{7-9} $17^{6,25f}$, Mt 11^{27}; cf Jn 17^{3}, 2 Co 4^{6}, also Jer 9^{23f} 31^{34}). In (*a*) Jn 10^{36} and (*b*) 17^{17-19} our Lord makes Himself the object of the verb—in the second instance the subject also. (*a*) The Father 'consecrated' Him for His world-mission (a pre-incarnate destination; see 1^{18}, 1 Jn $4^{9,14}$; cf Jer 1^{5}); (*b*) at the Last Supper the Son endorses that consecration in view of its dread issue, and proposes to share it with His disciples, as He dedicates Himself to the sacrifice of the cross. Thus in the Person of Jesus Christ sanctification assumes a new and very definite character; as *Christian* holiness, general consecration to the service of God becomes a specific consecration to the mission of redemption.

(2) The Letter to the Hebrews builds upon the OT conception of holiness. Its doctrine of sanctification is found in 2^{11} 9^{11-13} $10^{10-14,19-22}$ 12^{14} 13^{11-12}. Being 'the pioneer of their salvation' and 'high priest' of mankind, it is the office of Jesus to 'sanctify' His brethren, *i.e.* to consecrate them to God's service, for which as sinners they have been disabled (5^{1} 10^{22}). This He effects God-ward by making expiation for their sins (2^{17}), and man-ward by cleansing their conscience with the virtue of His blood—by removing the sense of personal guilt before God—even as the animal sacrifices 'sanctified' the Israelites 'for the purification of the flesh,' and made their ritual worship possible (9^{11-14}). The chasm which sin has opened between man and God was bridged by the mediation of Jesus Christ; no longer is he kept aloof from the Divine presence, but is bidden to 'draw near with confidence to the throne of grace' (4^{16} 10^{19-22}). 'Once for all' this access has been secured, this qualification bestowed on 'the people' whom Jesus sanctified 'through his own blood' (9^{26} 13^{12}): 'we have been sanctified' according to 'the will of God,' which Jesus embraced and whose demands He met on our behalf with perfect loyalty, in 'the offering of his body' (10^{5-10}). By that one offering 'he has perfected for all time those who are sanctified'—He has assured, for all who will accept it, till the world's end, a full qualification for fellowship with God (10^{14}). Hebrews supplies the link between the 'I consecrate myself' of Jesus and 'that they also may be consecrated in truth' (Jn 17^{19}). With the writer of Hebrews 'purify' and 'sanctify' define, on the negative and positive sides, all that St. Paul means by 'justification' and 'sanctification'; only, the second term is here made more prominent and wider in meaning than with the Apostle. St. Paul sees the sinner confronted by the Law of God, guilty and impotent; his fellow-teacher sees him standing outside the Temple of God, defiled and banned. Sanctification means, for the former, engagement to God's service (Ro 6^{12-22}); for the latter, empowerment for God's worship. That this grace imports, however, in Hebrews more than a status once conferred, is evident from 12^{14}; it is a state to be increasingly realized, an ideal to be pursued to the end.

(3) St. Paul addresses his readers constantly as 'saints' (see article, HOLINESS): once as 'sanctified in Christ Jesus' (1 Co 1^{2})—a phrase synonymous with 'called saints,' *i.e.* made holy by God's call which they obeyed, when He summoned them into His Kingdom (1 Co $1^{9,26-30}$, 1 Th 1^{4} 2^{12}). The former expression points to the completed act of God by which they have become His saints (1 Co 6^{11}, Ac 20^{32} 26^{18}). That sanctity, with St. Paul, is a term of relationship, not primarily of character, is evident from 1 Co 7^{14}, where the unbelieving husband or wife is said to be 'consecrated' through the Christian wedded partner, so that their offspring are 'holy': the person of the unbeliever, under the marriage-bond, is holy in the believer's eyes, as indeed every possession and instrument of life must be (see 1 Ti 4^{3-5}). In the case of the believer himself, who 'in Christ Jesus' is brought into immediate personal contact with God (Col 3^{3}), destination and use imply moral condition—the vessels of the Lord must be clean and 'ready for any good work' (2 Ti 2^{19-22}; cf **1** above, touching the OT Law of Holiness); so that, while 'sanctity' does not denote character, it normally connotes this; all virtue comes under the category of what 'is fitting among saints' or 'is fitting in the Lord' (Eph 5^{3}, Col 3^{12-18} etc.). Accordingly, in 1 Th 4^{3-8} 'sanctification' and 'holiness' are opposed specifically to 'lust' or 'uncleanness.'

Sanctification completes justification (q.v.); together, these constitute the present work of salvation, the re-instatement of the sinful man before his Maker, his instatement into the Christian standing and condition (see 1 Co 6^{11}, and the connexion between chs. 5 and 6 of Romans). In principle the former depends on the latter, in experience they are concomitant (Ro $6^{6f,22}$). They are alike acts of God, dealing with men in His grace through Christ (Ro $8^{30,33}$, I Th 5^{23f}, Jn 17^{17}; cf Lv 22^{32f}). The language of 2 Co 1^{21f}, while referring formally to baptism, substantially describes sanctification, since God consecrates the believer for His use and marks him in baptism with His 'seal.'

As the writer of Hebrews shows in his own way—see (2) above—Christ is the mediator of sanctification no less than of justification. He 'bought' men with the 'price' of His blood—the body along with the inner self—so that we are no longer our own and may not live for ourselves, but are, from the hour we know this, men living for God in Christ Jesus; and Christ 'presents' His redeemed to God as 'holy' and makes them God's 'own possession' destined 'to the praise of His glory' (1 Co 6^{19f}, Ro 6^{11-14} 12^{1}, Col 1^{22}, Eph 1^{14}, 1 P 2^{9}, Rev 1^{6} etc.). Once, in relation to the Church His bride, Christ is Himself called the sanctifier (Eph 5^{26}; cf He 13^{12}). Being our Head and Representative before God, dedicating all His own (Jn 17^{10}) to the Father in the offering of Calvary, Jesus virtually accomplished the sanctification of His people, with their justification, once for all (1 Co 1^{30}): Paul's saying, 'I have been crucified with Christ' (Gal 2^{20} 6^{14}), implies that he has been, by anticipation, included in the perfect sacrifice; he thus unfolds the implicit doctrine of Jn $17^{9f,17-19}$ (see (1) above; cf He 10^{14}).

Collectively, believers were sanctified in the self-devotion of their redeeming Lord; individually, they are sanctified when they accept the Redeemer's sacrifice and personally endorse His action. From the latter point of view, sanctification is the man's own deed ; he presents himself to God as ' brought from death to life ' (Ro 6[13, 18]) ; but the sinner is never, as in OT phrase, said to ' sanctify himself.' The Holy Spirit is, with much emphasis, identified with the work of sanctification ; Christian believers are ' sanctified in the Holy Spirit ' (Ro 15[16], 1 Co 6[11] ; also 1 Th 4[7f], Eph 4[30] ; cf 1 P 1[2] etc.). To receive the gift of the Spirit and to be sanctified are the same thing ; when God takes possession of the believer, his ' body ' becomes a ' temple of the Holy Spirit ' (1 Co 6[19])—then he is a holy man ; and to possess the Spirit is, in effect, to have Christ dwelling in the heart (Eph 3[16–19]). This twofold identity (' sanctified '=' in the Spirit '=' united to the Lord ') holds alike of the Church and of the individual Christian (1 Co 3[16f] 6[17], Eph 2[21f] ; cf 1 P 2[9]). Faith conditions this experience (Ac 26[18], Eph 1[13f]). Like the author of Hebrews, Paul recognizes a progressive holiness based upon the fundamental sanctification of the believer, the former being the growing and finally complete realization of the latter. Holiness is the starting-point, perfect holiness the goal of the Christian course—the progress ' is a growth *in* holiness rather than *to* holiness ' (Bartlet). Hence in Ro 6[19–22] the aim of one's service to God and righteousness is found in ' sanctification ' ; and in 1 Th 5[23f] the Apostle prays that God will sanctify his readers wholly, who are still lacking in many respects (3[10]), so that their ' spirit, soul, and body may be kept sound and blameless at the coming of our Lord Jesus ' (3[13]). This prayer touches the ideal life in Christ ; but it is an ideal to the present Christian state, and is not to be relegated to the visionary or the celestial : ' He who calls you is faithful, and he will do it ' (1 Th 5[24]).

St. John does not employ in his Letters either ' sanctify ' or ' sanctification,' but their whole substance is there. 1 Jn 1[3, 6f] 2[1f] recall the teaching of Hebrews in speaking of ' the expiation ' made by our ' Advocate,' whose ' blood cleanses us from all sin ' and thus brings the sinner into ' fellowship with the Father.' Paul's doctrine of holiness is resumed in such passages as 3[23f] 4[13f] 5[3f, 20], setting forth union with Christ through the indwelling Spirit as the spring of a new, eternal life for the man, in the strength of which God's commandments are kept in love, sin and fear are cast out, and the world is overcome.

G. G. F.—L. A. W.

SANCTUARY.—See HIGH PLACE ; TABERNACLE, 7 (*b*) ; TEMPLE.

SAND.—Minute particles of silex, mica, felspar, etc., easily rolled before the wind ; hence, probably, its Hebrew name *ḥôl*. It lies in great stretches along the Palestinian and Egyptian sea-board—an apt symbol of the incalculably vast or numerous (Gn 22[17] 41[49], Jer 33[22] etc.). For ' sand,' in Job 29[18], some would read, with RVm, ' phoenix.' This goes back to the Talmud (*Sanhedrin*, 108b), but no evidence that *ḥôl* had this meaning is known, and no derivation can be provided. However compact and firm, sand at once becomes soft at the touch of water (Mt 7[26f] etc.).

SAND FLIES.—See LICE.

SAND LIZARD.—See LIZARD.

SANDAL.—See DRESS, **6.**

SANHEDRIN.—The Greek word *synedrion* (EV council) was so familiar to the Jews that they adopted it in the form ' Sanhedrin,' which occurs very frequently in the Talmud where it is the title and subject of a tractate. Accurate information about the Sanhedrin, its history, its composition, and its authority is elusive. Statements about it in the Mishnah and in the NT need careful weighing, for they are both internally inconsistent and also mutually contradictory. The material in the Mishnah may well reflect a later age which attributed its own procedures to the earlier Sanhedrin of which it had only hazy recollections.

1. According to Rabbinic tradition the Sanhedrin was created by Moses in obedience to Divine command (cf Nu 11[16]), and existed, and exercised judicial functions, throughout the whole period of Biblical history right up to Talmudic times. However, this cannot have been the case. King Jehoshaphat is mentioned as having instituted the supreme court at Jerusalem (2 Ch 19[8]). This court cannot have been identical with the Sanhedrin of later times, for the latter had governing powers as well as judicial functions, while the former was a court of justice and nothing else. It is possible that the **' elders '** (q.v.) mentioned in the Book of Ezra (5[5, 9] 6[7, 14] 10[8]) and ' rulers ' in the Book of Nehemiah (2[16] 4[8 (14), 13 (19)] 5[7] 7[5]) constituted a body which to some extent corresponded to the Sanhedrin properly so called. The Sanhedrin is often referred to as a *Gerousia* (*i.e.* an aristocratic, as distinct from a democratic, body), and as such it is not mentioned before the time of Antiochus the Great (223–187 B.C.) ; it is reasonably certain that, in its more developed form at all events, it did not exist before the Greek period. The Sanhedrin is referred to under the name *Gerousia* (EV **senate**) in 2 Mac 1[10] 4[44], Jth 4[8] 11[14] 15[8] and elsewhere in the Apocrypha, in Ac 5[21], and frequently in Josephus, *e.g. Ant.* IV. viii. 14 [218].

The Sanhedrin was conceived of mainly as a court of **justice**, and it is in this sense that it is usually referred to in the NT (see, *e.g.* Mt 5[22] 26[59], Mk 15[1], Lk 22[66], Jn 11[47], Ac 4[15] 5[21] 6[12] 22[30] etc.). Sometimes in the NT the terms *Presbytērion* and *Gerousia* are used in reference to the Sanhedrin (Ac 5[21] 22[5]). A member of this court was called a *bouleutēs* (' councillor '). Joseph of Arimathaea was one (Mk 15[43], Lk 23[50]). The Sanhedrin disappeared after the destruction of Jerusalem (A.D. 70), and was replaced by the Beth Din, the court of law.

2. Regarding the composition of the Sanhedrin, the hereditary high priest stood at the head of it, and in its fundamental character it formed a sacerdotal aristocracy, and represented the nobility, *i.e.* predominantly the Sadducaean interest ; but under Herod, who favoured the Pharisaic party in his desire to restrict the power and influence of the old nobility, the Sadducaean element in the Sanhedrin became less prominent, while that of the Pharisees increased. During the Roman period the Sanhedrin contained representatives of two opposed parties, the priestly nobility with its Sadducaean sympathies, and the learned Pharisees. According to the Mishnah, the Sanhedrin consisted of seventy-one members (*Sanhed.* i. 6) ; when a vacancy occurred the members co-opted some one ' from the congregation ' to fill the place (*Sanhed.* iv. 4), and he was admitted by the ceremony of the laying on of hands. The reliability of the Mishnah at this point is often challenged.

3. The extent of the Sanhedrin's jurisdiction varied at different times in its history. In a certain sense it exercised civil jurisdiction over all Jewish communities, wherever they existed, but the extent to which Jewish communities outside of Judaea were willing to submit to such orders depended entirely on how far they were favourably disposed towards the central authority ; it was only within the limits of Judaea proper that real authority could be exercised by the Sanhedrin (Ac 9[2] 22[5] and 26[12] attribute to the Sanhedrin the power to extradite Jewish Christians from Damascus ; the historical reliability of the right, and of the passages in Acts, has been questioned). It was the supreme native court, as contrasted with the foreign authority of Rome ; to it belonged all such judicial matters as the local provincial courts were incompetent to deal with, or as the Roman procurator did not attend to himself. Above all, it was the final court of appeal for questions connected with the Mosaic Law ; its decision having once been given, the judges of the lower courts were, on pain of death, bound to acquiesce in it.

The NT offers some questionable though interesting examples. Jesus appeared before it on a charge of blasphemy (Mt 26[57], Jn 19[7]), Peter and John were accused before it of being false prophets and deceivers of the people (Ac 4[5ff]), Stephen was condemned by it because of blasphemy (Ac 7[57f]), and Paul was charged with transgression of the Mosaic Law (Ac 22[30]). It had independent authority and right to arrest people by its own officers (Mt 26[47], Mk 14[43], Ac 4[3] 5[17f]) ; it had also the power of finally disposing, on its own authority, of such cases as did not involve sentence of death (Ac 4[5-23] 5[21-40]). It was only in cases when the sentence of death was pronounced that the latter had to be ratified by the Roman authorities (Jn 18[31]); the case of the stoning of Stephen must be regarded as an instance of mob-justice.

While the Sanhedrin could not hold a court of supreme jurisdiction in the absence, or, at all events, without the consent, of the Roman procurator, it enjoyed, nevertheless, wide powers within the sphere of its extensive jurisdiction. Recent interpreters have sought to harmonize the conflicting data in NT and Rabbinic literature by various devices, principally by assuming that there were two Sanhedrins, one political-civil (which would accord with NT data), the other religious (which would accord with Talmudic data). Such harmonizations are ingenious but not persuasive.

4. The Sanhedrin, according to Rabbinic sources, met in the Temple, in what was called the *Lishkath-hag-Gāzîth* (the 'Hall of hewn-stones') as a general rule, though an exception is recorded in Mt 26[57ff], Mk 14[53ff]. The members sat in a semicircle in order to be able to see each other; in front stood clerks of the court, and behind these, three rows of disciples of the 'learned men.' The prisoner had always to be dressed in mourning. When anyone had spoken once in favour of the accused, he could not afterwards speak against him. In case of acquittal the decision might be announced the same day, but a sentence of condemnation was always pronounced on the following, or later; in the former a simple majority sufficed, in the latter a majority of two-thirds was required. W. O. E. O.—**S. S.**

SANSANNAH.—A town of Judah in the Negeb, Jos 15[31]; modern *Kh. esh-Shamsâniyât*.

SAPH.—One of four Philistine champions slain by David's heroes, 2 S 21[18]; called **Sippai** in 1 Ch 20[4].

SAPHAT.—**1.** 1 Es 5[9] (AV, RV); see SHEPHATIAH, **2.** **2.** 1 Es 5[34] (RV); see SHAPHAT, **6.**

SAPHATIAS, 1 Es 8[34] (AV, RV).—See SHEPHATIAH, **2.**

SAPHETH, 1 Es 5[33] (AV).—See SHEPHATIAH, **3.**

SAPHIR, Mic 1[11] (AV).—See SHAPHIR.

SAPHUTHI, 1 Es 5[33] (RV).—See SHEPHATIAH, **3.**

SAPPHIRA.—See ANANIAS, **1.**

SAPPHIRE.—See JEWELS AND PRECIOUS STONES.

SARA, He 11[11], 1 P 3[6] (AV) = **Sarah** (q.v.).

SARABIAS, 1 Es 9[48] (AV, RV).—See SHEREBIAH.

SARAH.—**1.** The wife of Abraham. In Gn 11[29] she is called Sarai, and in Gn 17[15], in connexion with the promise of the birth of Isaac, Y" is said to have changed her name to Sarah. There is no philological significance in the change, Sarai being an archaic form of the feminine Sarah, meaning 'princess.' Her parentage is not given in Gn 11[29], but in the E narrative of Abraham's sojourn in Gerar (Gn 20[1-18]), Abraham is said to have told Abimelech, the king of Gerar, that Sarah was his half-sister. According to the J genealogy in Gn 11[29], Abraham's brother Haran's daughter Milcah married Nahor, the other brother of Abraham. Apparently among the Terahites marriage between near relations was the rule (cf Gn 20[12] 24[3ff] 29[10]). It is noteworthy that in the Terahite genealogy the two female names Sarah (princess) and Milcah ('queen') correspond to two deities in the pantheon of Harran; Sarratu being the title of the moon-goddess, the consort of Sin, and Malkatu a title of Ishtar, who was also worshipped there. Those passages in the Abraham sagas which give definite statements about the ages of Abraham and Sarah are usually assigned to P, and they raise some difficulty by contrast with other elements in the sagas, such as the description of Sarah's great beauty at the age of sixty-five (Gn 12[14]). However, the Yahwist's purpose in using the saga material before him was to present a picture of Abraham as the typical man of faith; hence he uses the tradition of the birth of Isaac when both Abraham and Sarah were past the natural age of expectation as the supreme example of the Divine response to faith. According to the P narrative in Gn 23, Sarah died in Hebron at the age of 127, and was buried by Abraham in the cave of Machpelah which he bought from the Hittites for that purpose. In He 11[11] Sarah is also included among the examples of faith, although in Gn 18[13-14] she is rebuked by Yahweh for her incredulity with regard to his promise of a son. In the NT she is mentioned in Ro 4[19] 9[9], He 11[11], 1 P 3[6], Gal 4[21]-5[1].

2. Sarah, daughter of Raguel and wife of Tobias (To 3[7, 17] and elsewhere).

3. Nu 26[46] (AV); see SERAH. G. R. B.—**S. H. He.**

SARAI.—See SARAH, **1.**

SARAIAS, 1 Es 5[5] (AV, RV), 8[1] (AV), 2 Es 1[1] (AV, RV).—See SERAIAH, **2.**

SARAMEL, 1 Mac 14[28] (AV).—See ASARAMEL.

SARAPH.—A descendant of Shelah, 1 Ch 4[22].

SARASADAI.—An ancestor of Judith, Jth 8[1] (AV **Salasadai**).

SARCHEDONUS, To 1[21f] (AV, RV) = **Esarhaddon** (q.v.).

SARDEUS, 1 Es 9[28] (AV).—See AZIZA.

SARDINE STONE.—Found in AV in Rev 4[3], where RV has '**sardius**' and RSV '**carnelian.**' See JEWELS AND PRECIOUS STONES.

SARDIS was the capital of the ancient kingdom of Lydia on the western coast of Asia Minor, and in the 6th cent. B.C. one of the most powerful cities of the world. It stood on one of the alluvial hills between Mount Tmolus and the sea, about 1500 feet above and S. of the great plain of the river Hermus, and was inaccessible except by a neck of land on the S. The situation was ideal for an early fortified capital of a kingdom. As time advanced, extension was necessary, and a lower city was built on the W. and N. sides of the original city, near the little river Pactolus, and probably also on the E. side. The older city now acted as acropolis, or citadel, for the latter. This rich Oriental city, whose wealth depended on well-cultivated land and incessant commerce, was for centuries to the Greek the type of an Oriental despotism, under which all must sooner or later bend. Its absorption was not without its effects on the conquerors, and Sardis became the home of a newer Hellenism, different from the old.

Croesus was king of Lydia in the second half of the 6th cent. B.C., and planned a campaign against Cyrus, the Persian king. He proceeded with the greatest caution, and crossed the river Halys. There he was completely defeated. He returned to prepare a second army, but Cyrus pursued him in haste, and besieged him in Sardis before he could get it ready. The citadel was captured by means of a climber who worked his way up by an oblique crevice in the perpendicular rock. The city was similarly captured by Antiochus the Great from Achaeus late in the 3rd cent. B.C. The patron deity of the city was Cybele, but she was conceived as possessing different attributes from those usually associated with the name. A special characteristic was the power of restoring life to the dead. Sardis is mentioned in Ob 20 as Sepharad (Assyrian *Saparda*). The late passage presupposes the Jewish dispersion in Asia Minor. Jews of Sardis are referred to in *Ant.* XIV. x. 24 [259 ff]. The city suffered greatly from an earthquake in A.D. 17, and received a large donation as well as a remission of five years' taxation from the Emperor Tiberius. The greatness of the city under the Roman empire was due entirely to its past reputation. The acropolis ceased to be inhabited, being no longer necessary for purposes of defence. Its use was revived in the earlier Turkish days, but for long there has been no settlement at Sardis. Its place is taken by Salikli, above 5 miles to the E.

The letter addressed by the writer of the Apocalypse to Sardis (Rev 3[1-6]) shows that the church at that place was practically dead. Most of the Christians had fallen back to the pagan level of life. The few noble ones shall have their names enrolled in the list of citizens of heaven. But Christianity survived at Sardis. It was the capital of the province of Lydia, instituted about A.D. 295. The bishop of Sardis was metropolitan of Lydia, and sixth in order of precedence of all the bishops subject to the patriarch of Constantinople. Important excavations have been conducted at the site of Sardis.

A. So.—E. G. K.

SARDITES, Nu 26[26] (AV).—See SERED.

SARDIUS.—See JEWELS AND PRECIOUS STONES.

SARDONYX.—See JEWELS AND PRECIOUS STONES.

SAREA.—One of Ezra's swift scribes (2 Es 14[24]).

SAREPTA.—See ZAREPHATH.

SARGON (Assyr. *Šarru-kēn(u)*, 'the king is legitimate'). Although mentioned in the Bible only in Is 20[1], this king of Assyria (722–705 B.C.) is now well known from Assyrian inscriptions and letters. At the death of Shalmaneser v., he seized the throne with the support of the disaffected priesthood of the cities Ashur and Harran and took the name of the famous Sargon who had ruled the empire of Akkad almost two thousand years earlier. Shortly after usurping the throne, he reaped the harvest of Shalmaneser's three-year siege of Samaria by taking as booty 27,290 prisoners and re-populated the city with peoples from other countries. In 720 B.C. Sargon captured Qarqar and Hamath in Syria, which had revolted, and put down a rebellion on the part of Hanno of Gaza, who had been aided by the Egyptians. Carchemish, a strategic commercial centre, which with the aid of King Midas of Phrygia had plotted a revolt, was captured in 717 B.C. (cf Is 10[9]). In his eleventh year, 711 B.C., Sargon abolished the rule of Azuri, king of Ashdod, who had refused to send tribute, and placed his pro-Assyrian brother Ahimiti on the throne. When the people of Ashdod revolted and made a Greek their king, Sargon secured by extradition the custody of the rebel Greek ruler who had fled to Ethiopia. After conquests in Syria, Palestine and Armenia, Sargon set out to extend his empire to the E. and S. in his twelfth year (710 B.C.). He entered Babylon as a liberator and a restorer of religious freedom. Mardukapaliddin (Biblical Merodach-baladan), a Chaldaean who had been the master of the S., was defeated and his town Bit-Iakin taken. Sargon proclaimed himself as the governor of Babylon. During his reign Sargon extended the borders of Assyria from the Caucasus to Egypt and from Elam to Cyprus—the largest area of Assyrian domination until his time. Toward the end of his reign he constructed a magnificent palace and temple complex at Dûr-Sharrukîn (Sargonsburg), the modern Khorsabad, to the NE. of Mosul. The remains of this capital city, excavated by the French a century ago, are the principal sources for our knowledge of this important king. He was killed in battle during an expedition to the region of western Iran and was succeeded by his son Sennacherib. J. B. P.

SARID.—A border town of Zebulun, Jos 19[10, 12]. Probably *Sarid* is a copyist's error *Sadud* (so Gr. MSS and Pesh.); modern *Tell Shadûd*, to the N. of the plain of Esdraelon.

SAROTHIE.—A family of 'Solomon's servants' (1 Es 5[34]).

SARSECHIM.—A Babylonian official, Jer 39[3]; but the versions—*Nabousachar*, *Nabousarach*, *Sarsacheim*—suggest that the text was early corrupt. There is no known Babylonian name which exactly corresponds to any of these variants, and it is impossible to identify the person intended. The word is absent from v.[13] and some have attempted to reconstruct the text to bring the two verses into closer accord. C. H. W. J.

SARUCH, Lk 3[35] (AV).—See SERUG.

SASH.—This occurs in RV and RSV in Is 3[20] (AV 'headband' q.v.). In Jer 2[32] the same Hebrew word is rendered 'attire,' where it refers to the girdle of a bride (cf Is 49[18], where the cognate verb is used).

SATAN.—1. In the OT.—The term *Satan* is Hebrew and means 'adversary.' In the earlier usage of the language it is employed in the general sense of 'adversary,' personal or national: (cf *e.g.* Nu 22[22], 2 S 19[22], 1 K 5[4] 11[25] etc.). In such passages no trace of a distinct being designated 'Satan' is to be seen. Such a being meets us for the first time in the OT in the prologue (chs. 1 and 2) of the Book of Job, in the person of one of 'the sons of God' who bears the title of 'the Satan.' Here Satan appears as a member of the celestial council of angelic beings who have access to the presence of God. His special function is to watch over human affairs and beings with the object of searching out men's sins and accusing them in the celestial court. He is thus invested with a certain malevolent and malignant character; but it is to be observed that he has no power to act without the Divine permission being first obtained, and cannot, therefore, be regarded as the embodiment of the power that opposes the Deity. In Zec 3[2] essentially the same view of 'the Satan' is presented. But in 1 Ch 21[1] ('And Satan stood up against Israel, and incited David to number Israel') the personality of this being is more distinct: he appears now as 'Satan' (a proper name without the article), the tempter who is able to provoke David to number Israel. This is the Chronicler's (4th or 3rd cent. B.C.) reading of the incident which in the earlier narrative (2 S 24[1]) is ascribed to the direct action of God Himself. Here (in Chronicles) the work of Satan is apparently conceived of as more or less independent of, and opposed to, the Divine action.

2. In the extra-canonical literature of the OT.—In the later (apocryphal) literature of pre-Christian Judaism the dualistic tendency becomes more pronounced—a tendency powerfully affected by Persian influence, it would seem, which is also apparent in the development of an elaborate Jewish angelology and demonology. This is most clearly visible in the *apocalyptic literature.* In the oldest part of the Book of Enoch (chs. 1–36), dating, perhaps, from about 180 B.C., the origin of the demons is traced to the fall of the angelic watchers, the 'sons of God' who corrupted themselves with the 'daughters of men' (Gn 6[1f]). It was from the offspring of these sinful unions—the 'giants' or *nephilim*—that the demons were sprung. Of these demons the **Asmodaeus** of the Book of Tobit (3[8, 17]) seems to have been regarded as the king (Bab. Talmud, *Pes.* 110*a*). The name *Asmodaeus* (or in Heb. *Ashmedai*) has plausibly been connected with the ancient Persian *Aeshma daeva*, *i.e.* 'the covetous or lustful demon'; in its Hebrew form it suggests the meaning 'destroyer' or 'bringer of destruction,' and this demon may be intended by 'the destroyer' of Wisdom 18[25] and by the **Apollyon** (='Destroyer') of Rev 9[11]. In the latest part of the Book of Enoch, however, the so-called 'Similitudes' (chs. 37–71), which perhaps dates from about 64 B.C., 'the fallen watchers' (and their descendants) are carefully distinguished from the Satans, who apparently belong to 'a counter kingdom of evil' which existed before the fall of the watchers recorded in Gn 6[1], the latter, in consequence of their fall, becoming subject to the former. Apparently these 'Satans' are ruled by a single chief, who is styled 'Satan' in one passage (Enoch 54[6]). 'Their functions were threefold: they tempted to evil (69[4, 6]); they accused the dwellers upon earth (40[7]); they punished the condemned. In this last character they are technically called "angels of punishment" (53[3] 56[1] 62[11] 63[1])' (R. H. Charles).

In the Book of Wisdom (2[24]: 'by the envy of the devil death entered into the world') we already meet with the identification of the **Serpent** of Gn 3 with Satan, which afterwards became a fixed element in belief, and an allusion to the same idea may be detected in the Psalms of Solomon 4[11], where the prosperous wicked man is said to be 'like a serpent, to pervert wisdom, speaking with the words of transgressors.' The same identification also meets us in the Book of the Secrets of

Enoch (? 1st cent. A.D.), where, moreover, satanology shows a rich development (the pride, revolt, and fall of Satan are dwelt upon). Cf FALL.

The secondary Jewish (Rabbinical) literature which is connected with the text of the OT (especially the Targums and the Midrashim) naturally reflects beliefs that were current at a later time. But they are obviously connected closely with those that have already been mentioned. The Serpent of Gn 3 becomes 'the old serpent' who seduced Adam and Eve. The chief of the Satans is Sammael, who is often referred to as 'the angel of death'; and in the Secrets of Enoch he is prince of the demons and a magician. It is interesting to note that in the later Midrash one of the works of Messiah ben-Joseph is the slaying of Sammael, who is 'the Satan, the prime mover of all evil.' In the earlier literature his great opponent is the archangel Michael. The Rabbinic doctrine of the 'evil impulse' (*yēṣer raʿ*), which works within man like a leaven (*Berak.* 17*a*), looks like a theological refinement, which has sometimes been combined with the popular view of Satan (Satan works his evil purpose by the instrumentality of the 'evil impulse').

3. In the NT.—In the NT, Satan and his kingdom are frequently referred to. Sometimes the Hebrew name 'Satan' is used (*e.g.* Mk 3^{26} 4^{15} etc.), sometimes its Greek equivalent (*diabolos*: cf our word 'diabolical'), which is translated 'devil,' and which means 'accuser' or 'calumniator.' In Mt 12$^{26, 27}$ (cf 10^{25}) Satan is apparently identified with **Beelzebul** (q.v.) (or Beelzebub), and is occasionally designated 'the evil one' (Mt 13$^{19, 38}$ etc.; so, perhaps, also in the Lord's Prayer: 'deliver us from *the evil one*').

The demonology that confronts us in the NT has striking points of contact with that which is developed in the Enochic literature. The main features of the latter, in fact, reappear. The 'angels that did not keep their own position' (Jd ^{6}, 2 P 2^{4}) are the angelic watchers whose fall through lust is described in Enoch 6–16. Their punishment is to be kept imprisoned in perpetual darkness. In Enoch the demons, who are represented as the evil spirits which went forth from the souls of the giant offspring of the fallen watchers, exercise an evil activity, working moral ruin on the earth till the final judgment. In exactly the same way the demons are described in the NT as disembodied spirits (Mt 12$^{43-45}$, Lk 11$^{24-26}$). The time of their punishment is to be the final judgment (cf Mt 8^{29}: 'Have you come here to torment us *before the time*?'). They belong to and are subject to Satan. As in the Book of Enoch, Satan is represented in the NT as the ruler of a counter-kingdom of evil (cf Mt 12^{26}, Lk 11^{18} 'if Satan casts out Satan, how then will his kingdom stand?'); he led astray angels (Rev 12^{4}) and men (2 Co 11^{3}); his functions are to tempt (Mt 4$^{1-12}$, Lk 22^{31}), to accuse (Rev 12^{10}), and to punish (1 Co 5^{5}: impenitent sinners delivered over to Satan for destruction of the flesh). It should be added that in the Fourth Gospel and Johannine Epistles the lesser demonic agencies disappear. Opposition is concentrated in the persons of Christ and the devil. The latter is the ruler of this world (Jn 16^{11}), and enslaves men to himself through sin. The Son of God is manifested for the express purpose of destroying the devil's works (1 Jn 3^{8}).

Both in St. Paul (cf Ro 16^{20}, 2 Co 11^{2f}) and in the Apocalypse Satan is identified with the **Serpent** of Gn 3. It is also noteworthy that St. Paul shared the contemporary belief that angelic beings inhabited the higher (heavenly) regions, and that Satan also with his retinue dwelt not beneath the earth, but in the lower atmospheric region; cf Eph 2^{2}, where 'the prince of the power of the air' = Satan (cf also Eph 6^{12} and Lk 10^{18} 'I saw Satan fallen as lightning *from heaven*'). For Satan's rôle in the Apocalypse see ESCHATOLOGY. See also DEMONS AND DEMONOLOGY.

4. The attitude of our Lord towards the Satan-belief.—Our Lord, as is clearly apparent in the Synoptic tradition, recognized the existence and power of a kingdom of evil, with organized demonic agencies under the control of a supreme personality, Satan or Beelzebul. These demonic agencies are the source of every variety of physical and moral evil. One principal function of the Messiah is to destroy the works of Satan, and his subordinates (Mk 1$^{24, 34}$ 3$^{11f, 15}$ etc.). Maladies traced to demonic possession play a large part in the Synoptic narratives (see EXORCISM, POSSESSION especially **3**). In the expulsion of demons by Himself and His disciples, Jesus sees the overthrow of Satan's power (Lk 10^{18} 11^{20}). The evil effected by Satanic agency is intellectual and moral as well as physical (Mk 4^{15}, Mt 13$^{19, 39}$; cf 2 Co 4^{4}). That our Lord accepted the reality of such personal agencies of evil cannot seriously be questioned; nor is it necessary to endeavour to explain this fact away. The problem is to some extent a psychological one. Under certain conditions and in certain localities the sense of the presence and potency of evil personalities has been painfully and oppressively felt by more than one modern European, who was not prone to superstition. It is also literally true that the light of the gospel and the power of Christ operate still in such cases to 'destroy the works of darkness' and expel the demons.

G. H. B.—**J. Macq.**

SATCHEL.—See BAG.

SATHRABUZANES (1 Es 6$^{3, 7, 27}$ 7^{1}) = **Shethar-bozenai**, Ezr 5$^{3, 6}$ 6$^{6, 13}$.

SATRAPS.—RV and RSV translation of *'ᵃḥashdar-pᵉnîm* (and its Aram. form), Ezr 8^{36}, Est 3^{12} 8^{9} 9^{3} (AV **lieutenants**), Dn 3$^{2f, 27}$ 6^{1ff} (AV **princes**). The term stands for the Persian *khshatrapân* (= 'protector of the realm'). The satrap was the governor of a whole province, and he held the position of a vassal king. His power, however, was checked by the presence of a royal scribe, whose duty it was to report to the 'great king' on the administration of the province.

SATYR.—The Hebrew word *'sāʿîr*, means primarily 'he-goat,' but the plural, *sᵉʿîrîm*, is translated 'satyrs' in Lv 17^{7}, 2 Ch 11^{15} (AV 'devils,' RV 'he-goats'), Is 13^{21} 34^{14} (RVm 'he-goats'). Possibly too in 2 K 23^{8} *shᵉʿārîm* ('gates') should be *śᵉʿîrîm*, and translated 'satyrs.' In these passages some 'hairy' demon is to be inferred, to whom 'sacrifices' were made (Lv 17^{7}), 'high places' erected (2 K 23^{8}), and 'priests' set apart (2 Ch 11^{15}). The association of these creatures with the mythological **Lilith** (q.v.) in Is 34^{14} is specially noticeable.

E. W. G. M.

SAUL.—**1.** First king of Israel who reigned at Gibeah in Benjamin. Historically dependable information about his reign and achievements is meagre. The digest of information given in 1 S 14$^{47-52}$ suggests that lost sources reported a great deal more about him, and that achievements of David were wrongly ascribed to him in some quarters. A new order began with him. He was essentially king of a small territory whose leadership was acknowledged by the Hebrews of other tribes or territories both W. and E. of the Jordan. However, it does not seem that he had the capacity to organize a kingdom and bring the various tribes or districts under firm control. Theirs was only a loose allegiance for the duration of a crisis. Nor can we say how far his power extended in any direction, except perhaps the S.

Main interest of the surviving narratives about Saul centres on his attainment of the kingship. Stories of conflicting viewpoint contained in two or three narrative strands as in the Hexateuch, have been combined by a compiler, and the first task is to disengage them. According to 1 S 8 the popular desire for a king was regarded as apostasy. Samuel accedes to it, however, and convokes the people at Mizpah, where a king is chosen by lot (10$^{17-27}$). In 1 S 9^{1}–10^{16} a much-pleased Samuel discovers the right man for the kingship and anoints him secretly. Saul, imagined as a youth from Gibeah, returns home and says nothing about this. On the way, however, he experiences happenings that Samuel had predicted and which therefore confirm his belief in his own election. It seems probable that the event which led Saul to reveal himself as leader and king has been omitted by the source or by the compiler, for Chapter 11 gives a third explanation of how Saul became king. Here the Philistine crisis is forgotten and there is no thought of Samuel except in the probably interpolated v.[14]. The plea for deliverance by Jabesh comes to Saul at Gibeah. He goes to the rescue and defeats the Ammonites. He thereupon is made king at Gilgal. While the deliverance of Jabesh is certainly historical, the account can scarcely be reliable in connecting it with the rise of Saul. A mobilization and foreign war in the midst of the Philistine occupation is too improbable. Since 1 S 13–14[46] assumes that Saul already is king and has an adult son Jonathan, whose act at Gibeah (slaying of the Philistine prefect?) touches off the events leading to the liberation from Philistine oppression, it is apparent that no dependable account of Saul's rise exists. That he attained power by his own efforts is the view of the author of 1 S 14[47].

The story of the war of liberation of 1 S 13–14 into which the compiler has introduced the Gilgal excursion (especially 13[7b–15a]), is very much interested in Jonathan, and in the pursuit episodes already makes Saul a rather sinister figure. The initial events centering about Geba (not Gibeah !) and Michmash show good local knowledge.

That Saul not only ousted the Philistines from Benjamin and probably also from the Ephraimite and Manassite regions and held them off at the Danite-Judaean border to the W. is the presupposition of such a narrative as that of David and Goliath (1 S 17) and other David stories. Valuable information about his subjection of the Amalekites, implying his control of Judah, is offered by 1 S 15, a narrative that in other respects is governed by the theocratic ideal and tells of the break between Samuel and Saul (a theme already occupying the material in 1 S 13[7b–15a]).

That Saul maintained a small mercenary force is stated in 1 S 14[52]. A Judaean from Bethlehem, David, gained his favour and Saul gave him one of his daughters to wife. But Saul was soon consumed by jealousy and sought David's life. Saved by the loyal friendship of Jonathan David fled and became an outlaw, whom Saul vainly pursued. Saul, however, is only a secondary figure in this group of narratives, the hero of which is David. That Saul became mentally disturbed, as they imply, cannot be doubted. The fearful vengeance he took on the priests of Nob for aiding David (1 S 20–21) shows up his ferocity. In the David-Saul stories Saul is the Lord's Anointed for David, and hence untouchable. This presupposes a different view of how Saul assumed office from that of the narratives discussed above presented.

Perhaps we come closest to historical realities in the final narrative about Saul, 1 S 28 and 31. It assumes that Saul had control of the Manassite area, though the status of the great old Canaanite cities is not clarified. The Philistines invade the Esdraelon plain, while Saul is encamped on the slopes of Mount Gilboa. His nocturnal journey to the witch of Endor ; the battle in the forest ; his death by suicide ; the hanging of his and his sons' bodies on the walls of Beth-shean ; the rescue of these bodies by the men of Jabesh, are plausibly and impressively told. The elegy ascribed to David (2 S 1[19–27]) suggests that Saul's reign brought great economic prosperity (v.[24]). It is thus incredible that his reign should have lasted only two years, as the very uncertain text of 1 S 13[1] states. Years later the bodies of Saul and Jonathan were transferred to Zela in Benjamin (2 S 21[13]). That evidently was the real home of Saul, before he established himself at Gibeah. The excavations at the latter place have shown that Saul built himself a palace there. **2.** Gn 36[37f] (AV) ; see SHAUL, **1.** **3.** Saul of Tarsus ; see PAUL. E. G. K.

SAVIAS.—A descendant of Aaron, 1 Es 8[2] (AV, RV) ; omitted from RSV with LXX[B], and not in the parallel passage in Ezr 7[4].

SAVIOUR.—See SALVATION.

SAVOUR.—The word ' savour ' is used in AV and RV literally for *taste*, as in Mt 5[13] ' If the salt have lost his savour ' (RSV ' taste '), and for *smell*, as 2 Es 2[12] ' an ointment of sweet savour ' (RSV ' fragrant perfume '). It is also used figuratively in the sense of *reputation*, Ex 5[21] ' Ye have made our savour to be abhorred (RSV ' us offensive ') in the eyes of Pharaoh ' (literally ' our smell to stink ' as AVm). The verb ' to savour ' is either ' to taste *or* smell of,' as in Preface to AV ' to savour more of curiosity than of wisdom ' ; or ' to seek out *or* to search by tasting or smelling,' used figuratively in Mk 8[33] AV ' Thou savourest not the things that be (RV ' thou mindest not the things,' RSV ' you are not on the side ') of God.

SAW.—See ARTS AND CRAFTS, **1.**

SCAB.—See MEDICINE.

SCALES.—See BALANCE.

SCALING LADDER.—See FORTIFICATION AND SIEGECRAFT.

SCALL.—See MEDICINE.

SCAPEGOAT.—See AZAZEL, ATONEMENT [DAY OF].

SCARF.—The word as rendered occurs only in Is 3[19] (AV, RV ' muffler '), as an article of female attire. The cognate verb, in the sense of ' veiled,' is applied in the Mishnah (*Shabbath*, vi. 6) to Jewesses from Arabia. A close veil of some sort, therefore, is evidently intended by Isaiah.

SCARLET.—See COLOURS, **4.**

SCEPTRE, as translation of *shēbeṭ*, may stand either for a short ornamental sceptre such as appears in some representations of the Assyrian king, or for a long staff reaching to the ground, which characterizes some portrayals of the Persian monarchs. The long sceptre is simply an ornamented **staff,** the short one is a development of the **club** or *mace*. On Gn 49[10] see LAWGIVER and SHILOH. On the difficulty of approaching the presence of the Persian kings referred to in Est 4[11], cf also Herodotus, iii. 118, 140.

SCEVA.—In antiquity the Jews had the reputation of being the best exorcists. At Ephesus where Paul worked ' special powers ' (Ac 19[11ff]), seven sons of a Jewish ' chief priest ' Sceva tried to exorcise a demoniac saying : ' We adjure you by Jesus whom Paul preaches.' But the evil spirit answered : ' Jesus I know, and Paul I know ; but who are you ? ' And he attacked and wounded them and threw them all out of the house.

There are two difficulties in this story. The minor one is linguistic. The Greek text seems to say : ' He threw them out, " both of them " (*amphoterous*).' But this word could, in colloquial Greek, mean ' all,' for small numbers. The major difficulty is to get the gist of the story. This narrative tells us that Jesus with his supernatural power is unique, and that the best of non-Christian exorcists—the sons of the Jewish high priest, who had learned from him the secret name of God and were therefore able to do the most powerful miracles—could not equal, let alone rival, Him.

Professor Ramsay thinks that the whole passage is unworthy of Luke (*St. Paul the Traveller*, pp. 272 f). But it is unsafe to judge first-century thought by that of our own day. The Apostolic age firmly believed in possession by evil spirits ; and there is really nothing in this chapter unlike what we read elsewhere in NT. A. J. M.—E. H.

SCHISM.—See HERESY.

SCHOOL, SCHOOLMASTER.—' School ' occurs in AV only in Ac 19[9] for the lecture-room (RSV ' hall ') of an Ephesian rhetorican (cf EDUCATION) ; ' schoolmaster ' only in AV in Gal 3[24f] for which RV has **' tutor '** and RSV ' custodian.' The original is *paidagōgos*, literally ' child-conductor,' ' pedagogue '—an old and trusty slave, who accompanied the Greek child to and from school and ' was bound never to lose sight of him, to carry his lyre and tablets, and to keep him out of mischief ' (Gardner and Jevons, *Manual of Gr. Antiq.* 303). He had nothing to do with the *teaching*, as is suggested by both earlier English renderings. The same word is rendered ‘instructors’ in 1 Co 4^{15} AV (RV, as before, ‘tutors’; RSV ‘guides’). In AV the latter word is found only in Gal 4^{2} as the translation of an entirely different word, correctly rendered ‘guardians’ by RV, RSV. For the duties of guardians in Greek law see *op. cit.* 552 f.

A. R. S. K.—F. C. G.

SCHOOLS.—See Education.

SCIENCE.—The word ‘science’ occurs in AV only twice, Dn 1^{4} (so RV; RSV ‘learning’), 1 Ti 6^{20} (RV, RSV ‘knowledge’); in both places it simply means ‘knowledge’; as in Barlowe's *Dialoge*, p. 109, ‘There is no truthe, no mercye, nor scyence of god in the yerth.’

SCIMITAR.—See Fauchion and Armour, Arms, **3.**’

SCORPION.—Hebrew *‘aḳrābh*, Dt 8^{15}, Ezr 2^{6}; Greek *skorpios*, Lk 10^{19} 11^{12}, Rev $9^{3, 5, 10}$. The scorpion belongs to the *Arachnidae* or spider family. It occurs plentifully in Palestine, ten species being known; it is nocturnal in its habits, and kills small insects, spiders, etc., for food, by means of the poisonous sting at the end of its tail. The effect of the poison on human beings is severe pain, and sometimes collapse and even death, the latter in young children only. The ‘scorpions’ 1 K $12^{11, 14}$, 2 Ch $10^{11, 14}$ are clearly used only figuratively. It is possible, but hardly likely (see Hastings' *DCG*, article ‘Scorpion’), that the language of our Lord in Lk 11^{12} is suggested by the egg-like form of the ‘scorpion’ when at rest. More probably He has in mind some such form of proverb as was current among the Greeks: ‘Instead of a perch, a scorpion.’ E. W. G. M.

SCOURGING.—See Crimes and Punishments, **9,** and Crucifixion, **4.**

SCREECH OWL, Is 34^{14} (AV).—See Owl and Lilith.

SCREEN.—See Hanging, Hangings.

SCRIBE.—See King, **2** (7), Writing, **5.**

SCRIBES.—The scribes were the *sōphᵉrîm*, *i.e.* writers, copyists, ‘bookmen,’ and consequently the interpreters of the sacred writings of the OT, as their professional occupation gave them unusual familiarity with these books. In Greek, *grammateus* usually meant secretary or recorder, though ‘scribe’ covered both its basic meaning and its acquired significance in the 1st cent. Among the forerunners of the scribes were also to be reckoned the ‘wise’ teachers of Israel who produced and handed on a body of oral teaching and eventually created the Jewish Wisdom Literature (see Wisdom). Sir 38–39 contains a classic description of the ideal scribe who is both student and teacher of ‘the Law of the Most High.’ (See G. F. Moore, *Judaism*, Int., ch. 3) The successors of the scribes, in turn, were the rabbis (q.v.) in the period following the two wars with Rome, when the Jewish schools were reorganised and the Oral Tradition was cultivated, transmitted, and eventually written down in Mishnah and Talmud.

After the Exile, the scribe tended to take the place of the priest as teacher of the Law (see Neh 8^{9} ‘Ezra the priest the scribe’). In the Gospels the scribes are sometimes referred to as ‘lawyers’ (*e.g.* Lk 10^{25}), *i.e.* experts in the sacred Mosaic Law which was in theory the sole legislation, civil and religious, governing the Jewish people. They were usually associated with the Pharisees (*e.g.* Mt 12^{38} Mk 7^{5} Lk 6^{7}); in Mk 2^{16} we read of ‘the scribes of the Pharisees,’ which must mean scribes who belonged to the Pharisaic party (not the Pharisees' secretaries!). This connexion was most natural, for the Pharisees (q.v.), who originated among the Pious (*Ḥᵃsîdhîm*) in Maccabaean days, were a lay society devoted to the fullest possible observance of the Law as expounded by the scribal experts. In turn many of the scribes became members of the Sanhedrin, the highest legal and administrative body in the Jewish theocratic state. Among them were Gamaliel in Ac 5, Nicodemus in Jn 3 and 7. They sat ‘on Moses' seat’ (Mt 23^{2}) as official interpreters of the Law. The later rabbis also administered the Law, especially after the destruction of Jerusalem. They thus had the power of ‘binding and loosing,’ *i.e.* of issuing authoritative judgments or decisions upon the legality or illegality of actions.

Among them were many noble characters, like Hillel and Shammai, early in the 1st cent., and Gamaliel (Ac 22^{3}) who spoke for fairplay and against persecution ($5^{34\text{ff}}$). Their services, both educational and judicial, were rendered freely and without compensation. Unless he possessed independent means the scribe had to earn a livelihood in other ways and then teach as an avocation. It has been suggested that the rule grew out of the danger of bribery, cited in Ex 23^{8}, Dt 16^{19} where ‘judges’ were ordered not to accept fees or gifts. Presumably there must have been exceptions. Yet the ideal was ennobling (cf the rule for Christian evangelists, Mt 10^{8b-9}), and it must have inspired devotion to their calling. At the same time, as with all professional clergy, their position encouraged a certain amount of pride and vanity. They stood on their prerogatives as ‘Teachers’ and they loved the title ‘Rabbi’ (‘Master’)—see Mt 23^{5-7}; the title was forbidden the Christian scribes or teachers (23^{8-10}).

It is true that criticism of the scribes (and Pharisees) may be found in their own literature, which is profoundly human. They criticized one another freely. But the invective set forth in Mt 23, in seven formal strophes which read like a quasi-poetical tirade of the kind to be found elsewhere in Oriental polemics, may reflect the crisis in feeling which arose between Christians and Jews toward the end of the 1st cent. It was the time when the Christians were excommunicated from the synagogue and when the malediction against the apostates (*mînîm*) was inserted in the *Shemoneh Esreh*. Other sections in the Gospels, even in Matthew, take a far friendlier view of the scribes, their teaching and practice (*e.g.* Mk 12^{34}). Moreover, the methods of interpreting Scripture (q.v.) in the Jewish schools and among the Christians were entirely different, and led to inevitable conflict, the scribes (now rabbis) upholding their traditional views, interpretations, and methods, and sharply repudiating the methods and conclusions of the Christians.

It was inevitable that a religion based upon a sacred Law should require legal interpreters and casuists. It was also inevitable that the evangelical, prophetic, eschatological movement of early Christianity should collide squarely with the traditional legalism associated with scribal teaching and practice. The same tension has characterized the Christian church almost from the beginning. The opposing poles are legalism (or nomism) and anarchy (total absence of law and administration, following the free guidance of ‘the Spirit’ in all things). But the most wholesome religious life and thought appear to flourish at some distance from both extremes. And it is quite unfair to label other Christians or members of other religions with polemical titles which, doubtless true of individuals here and there, certainly in ancient times, scarcely fit whole groups or even religious bodies and justify their condemnation or exclusion from fellowship. From a strictly historical point of view, the wholesale condemnation of the scribes which we find in some Christian books is far too harsh, too sweeping, and too one-sided. F. C. G.

SCRIP.—See Bag.

SCRIPTURE.—**1.** The word ‘Scripture’ (Lat. *scriptura*, ‘a writing,’ ‘something written’) is used for the Bible as a whole, more often in the plural form ‘Scriptures,’ and also more properly for a passage of the Bible. It appears as translation of the Greek *graphē*, which is used in the singular for a portion of the OT (*e.g.* Mk 12^{10}), and also for the whole OT (Gal 3^{22}), and more frequently in the plural (*hai graphai*). The specific idea of Scripture contains an element of sanctity and authority. Thus it becomes usual to refer to Holy Scripture, or the Holy Scriptures (*en graphais hagiais*, Ro 1^{2}). See also Bible.

2. This specific conception of Scripture as distinguished from ordinary writing is due to the reception of it as a record of the word of God, and is therefore associated with inspiration (q.v.). The earliest reference to any such record is in the narrative of the finding of the Book of the Law by Hilkiah the scribe in the time of Josiah (2 K 22^{8ff}). Since this book is now known to have been Deuteronomy or part of it, we must reckon that this was the first book treated as Scripture. Still greater sanctity was given to the enlarged and more developed Law in the time of Ezra, and from that time the whole Pentateuch, regarded as the Law given by God to Moses, is treated as especially sacred and authoritative. The special function of the scribes in guarding and teaching the Law rested on this Scriptural character attached to it, and in turn rendered it the more venerable as Scripture. Later the reception of the *Hagiographa* and *the Prophets* into the Canon (q.v.) led to those collections being regarded also as Scripture, though never with quite the authority attached to the Law.

The Rabbis cherished great veneration for Scripture, and ascribed to it a mechanical inspiration which extended to every word and letter. Philo (q.v.) also accepted plenary inspiration, finding his freedom from the bondage of the letter in allegorical interpretations.

Unlike the Palestinian Rabbis, in this respect followed by most of the NT writers, who quote the various OT authors by name, Philo quotes Scripture as the immediate word of God, and in so doing is followed by the author of Hebrews. Thus, while St. Mark says, ' as it is written in Isaiah the prophet ' (Mk 1^2), and St. Paul, ' David says ' (Ro 11^9), in Hebrews we read, ' He (*i.e.* God) says ' (He 1^7), ' the Holy Spirit says ' (3^7), or, more indefinitely, ' it is said ' (3^{15}), which is quite in the manner of Philo. Still, the technical expression ' It is written ' (*gegraptai*) is very common, both in the Gospels and in St. Paul's Epistles. As a Greek perfect, it has the peculiar force of a present state resulting from a past action. Thus it always conveys the thought that Scripture, although it was written long ago, does not belong to the past, but is in existence to-day, and its inherent present authority is thus emphasized as that of a law now in force. The impersonal character of the passive verb also adds dignity to the citation thus introduced, as something weighty on its own account.

3. No NT writings during the Apostolic age are treated as Scripture—a title, with its associated authority, always reserved by the Apostles for the OT. There is an apparent exception in 2 P $3^{15, 16}$, where the Epistles of ' our beloved brother Paul ' are associated with ' the other scriptures ' ; but this is a strong argument in favour of assigning 2 Peter to a late period in the 2nd cent. Apart from this, we first meet with the technical phrase ' it is written ' attached to a NT passage in Barn. iv. 4 ; but here it is a Gospel citation of a saying of Christ : ' As it is written, Many are called but few chosen.' Thus the authority of Christ's words leads to the record of them being cited as Scripture. In Polycarp (*Phil.* xii. 1) we have the title ' Scripture ' applied to the source of a NT quotation, but only in the Latin translation (*his scripturis*). In 2 Clem. ii. 4 a saying of Christ is cited as Scripture. But, apart from these rare instances, no writer previous to the second half of the 2nd cent. appeals to the NT as technically Scripture. Clement of Rome, Barnabas (with the one exception referred to), Hermas, and even Justin Martyr use the title for the OT only. Theophilus of Antioch (*c* 180) cites passages from St. Paul as ' the Divine word ' (*ad Autol.* iii. 14). Irenaeus (185), on the other hand, constantly treats NT passages as the word of God and authoritative Scripture. For an explanation of this remarkable development, see CANON OF NT.

W. F. A.—**F. C. G.**

SCROLL.—See WRITING.

SCROLLS, DEAD SEA.—See DEAD SEA SCROLLS.

SCULPTURE.—See ART.

SCURVY.—See MEDICINE.

SCYTHIANS.—A wandering race of the Indo-European stock who lived between the Danube and the Don, and spread over the territory between the Caucasus and the Caspian. They were a cruel and savage people, of huge build. The Athenians employed them as police. In Col 3^{11} they are mentioned as a degree worse than barbarians. The latter word simply connoted those who spoke neither Greek nor Latin. A. So.

SCYTHOPOLIS.—See BETH-SHEAN.

SEA in Scripture generally means the Mediterranean, variously called ' the Sea ' (Nu 33^8, Ezk 26^{17f} etc.), ' the **Great Sea** ' (Nu 34^6, Ezk 47^{10} etc.), ' the **sea of the Philistines** ' (Ex 23^{31}), and ' the **western sea** ' (Jl 2^{20}, Zec 14^8). The Dead Sea is known as ' the **Salt Sea** ' (Gn 14^3, Nu 34^{12} etc.), ' the **eastern sea** ' (Jl 2^{20}, Zec 14^8), or ' the **Sea of the Arabah** ' (2 K 14^{25} etc.). Names for the Sea of Galilee are ' the **Sea of Chinnereth** ' (Nu 34^{11}, Jos 13^{27} etc.), ' the **Lake of Gennesaret** ' (Lk 5^1), and ' the **Sea of Tiberias** ' (Jn 6^1 21^1). ' The Sea of Reeds ' (Ex 10^{19}, Nu 14^{25} etc.) is rendered by ' **Red Sea** ' (so LXX), although it more properly refers to the marshes in the vicinity of Lake Timsāḥ.

The term ' sea ' is also used for large rivers, specifically the Euphrates (Is 21^1, Jer 51^{36}) and the Nile (Is 18^2, Na 3^8). Since the Mediterranean forms the W. boundary of Palestine, ' sea ' is a common expression for ' West ' (Gn 12^8 etc.).

The influence of the Babylonian and Canaanite (Ugaritic) myths of the conflict of the gods with the primeval sea may be traced in certain Scripture representations of the sea (Job 7^{12}, Ps 74^{13f} etc. See article ' Cosmogony ' in Hastings' *DB*). *Tᵉhôm* (RSV ' deep ') of Gn 1^2 etc., is related etymologically to Babylonian *Ti'āmat*. By the dismemberment of this monster the ordered world is produced (Gn 1^6).

The turbulent and dangerous character of the sea is often referred to in Scripture (Ps 46^2 89^9, Is 17^{12}, Jer 49^{23} etc.). From the sea came up the monsters of Daniel's vision (7^{2ff}) ; so also in the Apocalypse (13^1). If in the literature of the Hebrews there is manifest a certain horror of, and shrinking from, the sea, which seem strange to a sea-faring people, we must remember that, as a nation, Israel never knew the sea ; nor need we wonder if, viewed from their mountain heights, stretching vast and mysterious into the far horizons, it seemed to them the very home of storms and vague terrors. So when the Jewish seer depicts the future home of the blessed there is ' no more sea ' (Rev 21^1). Cf DUALISM, **1**, RAHAB, **2**.

The word ' sea ' was further employed to describe a huge bronze basin in the court of the Solomonic Temple (1 K 7^{23-26}) designed to contain water for the use of the priests. See C. C. Wylie, *Bib. Arch.* xii (1949), 86–90.

W. E.—**R. J. W.**

SEA (BRAZEN).—See TEMPLE, **6** (*c*).

SEA OF GALILEE.—See GALILEE (SEA OF).

SEA GULL, Lv 11^{16}, Dt 14^{15} (RSV).—See OWL.

SEA OF GLASS.—One of the features of the heavenly scene described in Rev 4^6 15^2. By its side stood those who had been victorious in the struggle with the beast, singing to the glory of God. Its location was apparently before the throne of God. The symbolism here intended is difficult to make out. The probability is, however, that there is no distinct symbolism whatever, but that the reference is rather to the brilliancy of the waters as one element in the supremely beautiful land of heaven. Some scholars have supposed the author's imagination thus recorded the view of the surrounding sea at Patmos (Rev 1^9). But he was an exile, and 21^1 *ad fin.* surely reflects his feeling more accurately. S. M.—**F. C. G.**

SEAH.—See WEIGHTS AND MEASURES, **2**.

SEAL, SIGNET.—Sealing was done primarily to authenticate documents or to provide objects with a label. For the former purpose a seal must be different from every other. Where the seal was first developed is not clear. It appears on the scene very early in the Near East, and is made of semi-precious stone such as agate, steatite, chalcedony. The cylinder seal, of which upwards of 10,000 have been preserved, consists of a stone cylinder perforated in its whole length and usually engraved with a pictorial scene on its surface. When gods or men are portrayed the style of dress gives ready indication of the period. In Babylonia and Elam this type of seal remained in constant use through millennia. This was because it was well adapted to the sealing of clay tablets; the witnesses to a business deal or a legal matter could take the seal which they wore on a string around the neck (Herod. i. 195) and unroll it on the tablet or its 'envelope' or casing. The stamp form of seal is characteristic of Hittite tablets from Asia Minor and Syria.

When papyrus or leather was used as writing material, as was the case in Israel, a seal could only be employed in connexion with a string around the rolled and folded document and a lump of clay covering the knot. A small seal of scaraboid and sometimes of conical shape thus arose about the 9th cent. in Palestine and Syria. On these there were engraved the owner's name (and station, if any) and occasionally an emblem of a figure, whether divine, human, mythical or animal. Particularly famous is the seal (found 1904 at Megiddo) '(Belonging) to Shema', the servant of Jeroboam' (II), with its life-like engraving of a roaring lion. The owner was thus an official of some sort. The seal (from *Tell en-Naṣbeh*) inscribed to 'Jaazaniah, servant of the king' has the figure of a fighting cock under the inscription. The owner may be the individual mentioned in 2 K 25[3]; the date is *c* 600 B.C. Pictureless, but with a dividing double line between two lines of inscription, is the seal of 'Eliakim, servant of Yaukin' (*i.e.* King Jehoiachin) found at *Tell Beit Mirsim*. From Lachish comes a seal of *c* 600 B.C. belonging 'To Gedaliah who is over the house'—thus confirming the title borne by some OT personages such as Shebna (Is 22[15]). A seal-impression from Beth-zur gives the name of a Judaean prince: 'Gealyahu son of the king.' Six seals bearing the names of women are extant. In all about 150 seals of this general type are known, dating from *c* 800–500 B.C. From the Persian period on the seals are generally without Hebrew inscriptions, and Greek influence on their design becomes important.

The seal engraver used a tool with diamond point (Jer 17[1]). His patience, skill, and industry aroused admiration (Sir 38[27]). The Hebrew seal was either pierced and hung on a string or set in the bezel of a ring. It was worn around the neck (Gn 38[18]), or on the arm (Ca 8[6]), or on the right hand (Jer 22[24]). It was used to seal documents (Jer 32[10, 14], Is 8[16] 29[11]) and letters (1 K 21[8]), and even for special purposes such as Dn 6[7], Mt 27[66]. Numerous papyri from Egypt, with strings and seals still intact, illustrate how sealing must have been done in biblical times. A document sealed with seven seals (Rev 5[1f]) is, however, a product of fancy.

E. G. K.

SEALSKIN.—See PORPOISE.

SEAMEW, Lv 11[16], Dt 14[15] (RV).—See OWL.

SEA-MONSTER.—See DRAGON, LEVIATHAN, RAHAB, SEA.

SEBA.—The eldest son of Cush in Gn 10[7], 1 Ch 1[9], named along with **Sheba** in Ps 72[10], and with Egypt and Cush in Is 43[3] 45[14] (the gentilic **Sabaeans** in the latter). In Is 45[14] its people are referred to as of high stature. A comparison with Is 18[2] points to a supposed connexion with the tall Cushites or Nubians, though there is no evidence which directly associates either the people or the country with Nubia proper, in the region of the Nile. More specific seem to be the references by Strabo and Ptolemy to a seaport *Saba* and *Sabat*, near the modern Massowa on the west of the Red Sea. This location, nearly opposite the ancient Sheba, gives some colour to the hypothesis that *Seba* is an African differentiation of **Sheba** (q.v.), the latter being naturally the parent community.

J. F. McC.

SEBAM.—A place in the east-Jordan territory of Reuben, Nu 32[3] (AV **Shebam**); elsewhere the name appears in the feminine form **Sibmah**, Nu 32[38] (AV **Shibmah**), Jos 13[19], Is 16[8f], Jer 48[32]. The 'vine of Sibmah' is mentioned by Isaiah and Jeremiah as one of the possessions of Moab on which destruction was to fall. The location is uncertain.

SEBAT, Zec 1[7] (AV) = **Shebat** (q.v.).

SECACAH.—A Judahite town in the wilderness, Jos 15[61]. It is possibly modern *Kh. Samroh*.

SECHENIAS.—1. 1 Es 8[29] (AV, RV); see SHECANIAH, **3. 2.** 1 Es 8[32] (AV, RV); see SHECANIAH, **5.**

SECHU, 1 S 19[22] (AV).—See SECU.

SECOND COMING.—See PAROUSIA.

SECOND DEATH.—In Rev 2[11] 20[6, 14] 21[8] reference is made to the 'second death,' from which the righteous shall be preserved, but which shall overtake the wicked.

SECOND QUARTER.—See COLLEGE.

SECOND SABBATH AFTER THE FIRST.—This expression is found in AV in Lk 6[1], but the word *deuteroprōtos* is found nowhere else and is of doubtful meaning. Many MSS omit the word, and so RV and RSV ('on a sabbath').

SECRET.—See MYSTERY.

SECT.—See HERESY.

SECU.—A place-name which appears only in the late narrative of 1 S 19[22] (AV **Sechu**) in connexion with Ramah, Samuel's home, and especially with the 'great well.' Its site is unknown. Some Greek and Old Latin texts read 'the well of the threshing-floor which is on the bare height,' and it is possible that it is not a place-name.

SECUNDUS.—A man of Thessalonica who accompanied St. Paul on his journey to Jerusalem (Ac 20[4]), perhaps as a delegate to carry alms from the church in his city. The verse is somewhat obscure, but the meaning probably is that Aristarchus and Secundus and those mentioned afterwards went directly from Troas to Corinth and waited there for the Apostle, who came with Sopater by way of Macedonia. See SOPATER.

A. J. M.—F. C. G.

SECURE.—To be secure, in the language of AV, does not mean to be free from danger; it means not to anticipate danger. Thus, Jg 8[11] 'Gideon smote the host, for the host was secure.' The verb 'to secure' occurs in Mt 28[14] 'And if this come to the governor's ears, we will persuade him, and secure you,' where the Greek means literally *make you free from care*, *i.e.* make it all right for you, or 'keep you out of trouble' (RSV).

SEDECIAS.—1. Bar 1[1] (AV); see ZEDEKIAH, **5. 2.** Bar 1[8] (AV) = **Zedekiah, 6** (q.v.).

SEDEKIAS.—1. Bar 1[1] (RV); see ZEDEKIAH, **5. 2.** 1 Es 1[46], Bar 1[8] (RV) = **Zedekiah, 6** (q.v.).

SEDGE.—See WEED.

SEDUCTION.—See CRIMES AND PUNISHMENTS, **3.**

SEED, SEEDTIME.—As an essential part of agricultural routine, sowing the seed looms large in the Bible, and has its natural place in the proverbs of both Testaments, as, to choose at random, Dt 11[10], Job 4[8] 31[8], Ps 126[5], Pr 11[18] 22[8], Ec 11[4, 6], Hos 8[7], 2 Co 9[6], Gal 6[7], and many of the proverbs have become part of our common heritage.

There were three main times of sowing main crops, corresponding to the rainy seasons. The first was in October, before the early rains; the second, and most important, during the heavy rains of November, preferably, according to Hesiod, before the setting of the Pleiades in the middle of the month (cf Pr 20[4], which has an exact parallel in modern Arabic). In the third season, as we are reminded in Ja 5[7], the farmer does not ignore the latter rains of January–February, but not only are cereals sown then where the crop has failed, but also, as will be noted, there were a number of minor crops which were kept for this season. During February 1958, it was pathetic to see Jordan peasants ploughing in the sparse growth of the main sowing because the latter rains had failed. Ploughing for the late sowing was always deeper than for other crops.

The main cereals, sown early, were barley and wheat, but there was also extensive sowing of leguminous crops—beans (*pôl*), fitches (Talmud *karshīnāh*), lentils (*ʿadhāshāh*), flax (*pesheth*). Late crops include millet (*dôḥan*), sesame (introduced from Egypt into Palestine in Ptolemaic times), and *kussemeth* (translated 'spelt' in Ex 9[32], Is 28[25], Ezk 4[9]; indigenous to Egypt, but possibly 'bearded wheat' which still grows wild in Palestine).

Seed, *Zeraʿ*, is also the word used for *semen virile*, hence, 'offspring,' and in this sense it was commonly used metaphorically and even typologically, especially in the NT. B. J. R.

SEER.—See Israel, II, 3 (8), Prophecy, 2.

SEETHE.—This verb, which means to *boil*, occurs occasionally in AV and RV, especially in the command (Ex 23[19] etc.), 'Thou shalt not seethe (RSV 'boil') a kid in his mother's milk.' The past tense was **sod**, Gn 25[29], 'Jacob sod (RSV 'was boiling') pottage'; and the past participle, **sodden**, as La 4[10] 'The hands of the pitiful women have sodden (RSV 'boiled') their own children.' RSV retains 'seethe' only in Ezk 24[5].

SEGUB.—**1.** The youngest son of Hiel who re-built Jericho, 1 K 16[34]. He died, or less probably was sacrificed by his father, when the gates were set up. See House. **2.** Son of Hezron, 1 Ch 2[21f].

SEIR ('hairy' or 'goat').—**1.** Eponym of a Horite clan, Gn 36[20f], 1 Ch 1[38]. **2.** The name of a mountainous district E. of the Arabah, peopled by the Edomites, Gn 36[8f], Dt 2[5], Jos 24[4]. **3.** Seir is also used for the district S. of the Dead Sea (cf Dt 1[44]), and is practically synonymous with Edom (cf Gn 32[3]). The district was formerly occupied by Horites (Gn 14[6]), who were later incorporated into Edom (cf **1** above). **4.** A mountain mentioned in Jos 15[10] among the points defining the boundaries of Judah; possibly modern, *Sārîs* preserves the name.

SEIRAH.—The place to which Ehud escaped after killing Eglon, king of Moab, Jg 3[26] (AV **Seirath**); the location is unknown.

SEIRATH, Jg 3[26] (AV).—See Seirah.

SELA means 'rock,' 'crag,' or 'cliff,' and as a common noun is of frequent occurrence in Hebrew. In a few passages (Jg 1[36], 2 K 14[7] (AV **Selah**), Is 16[1], and, according to some, Is 42[11]), the word appears to be a proper name, though it is generally used with the definite article. In Jg 1[36] a site in the Arabah S. of the Dead Sea is required by the context, which would also satisfy the requirements of 2 K 14[7] and Is 16[1]. But it is not improbable that more than one place was so designated, and indeed Glueck attests one such place *Es-Selaʿ*, with traces of Iron Age occupation on a rocky site N. of Petra. Generally, however, as probably in 2 K 14[7] and Is 16[1], Sela signifies the capital of Edom, named by Amaziah after its capture Joktheel (2 K 14[7], 2 Ch 25[12]), which the *Onomasticon* identifies with the celebrated **Petra** ('Rock'), about 50 miles SSE. of the Dead Sea in an impressive sandstone canyon of the *Wâdī Mûsā* entered by the long, narrow *sîq* between cliffs towering 500 ft. high. The Early Iron, or Edomite, settlement has been located specifically by the work of Horsfield and Head at *Umm el-Bayāra*, an impressive height of *c* 3500 ft. comparatively isolated. The monuments of the more extensive site of Petra are great ornamental and smaller tombs, mortuary chapels, at least one temple, and two theatres, cut out of the grained sandstone rock, and the two 'high places,' or open-air sanctuaries on mountain-tops. The last date back probably to Edomite times, but the other monuments are of the Nabataeans, a virile mercantile people from N. Arabia, who occupied Edom in the 5th cent. B.C. Petra was the capital of this mercantile kingdom, one of whose rulers was Aretas IV. (9 B.C.–A.D. 40), the father-in-law and later enemy of Herod Antipas and the ruler of Damascus at the time of St. Paul's escape. Petra under the Nabataeans defied the Seleucids and Romans until A.D. 106, when it was taken by Trajan and incorporated in Provincia Arabia. It continued to be a populous caravan city, but declined with the rise of Palmyra in the 3rd cent. A.D. Most of its monuments show Hellenistic as well as Nabataean features, and are in consequence hard to date accurately. G. B. G.—**J. Gr.**

SELAH, 2 K 14[7] (AV).—See Sela.

SELAH.—A Hebrew liturgical-musical term of uncertain meaning. It occurs (*a*) in the OT, (*b*) in the Psalms of Solomon, and (*c*) in the Jewish (Synagogue) Liturgy.

In the OT the term occurs 74 times altogether in the Hebrew text, viz. 71 times in the Psalter, and 3 in the Prayer of Habakkuk (Hab 3). In the Greek translation of the OT (the LXX) the Greek equivalent (*diapsalma*) does not always appear in the same places as in the Hebrew text; the number of occurrences is also rather larger in the LXX. Possibly in some cases 'Selah' has fallen out of the Massoretic text accidentally. In the *Psalms of Solomon* 'Selah' occurs twice (17[31] and 18[10]), and in the oldest parts of the Jewish Liturgy (apart from the canonical Psalms, which are incorporated in it) 5 times (3 in the 'Eighteen Blessings' and 2 in the morning Benedictions preceding the *Shemaʿ*).

Various explanations have been proposed as to the etymology and meaning of the term. Perhaps the least improbable of these is that which regards it as a liturgical direction intended to indicate the place for *lifting up* the voices in a doxology at the close of a section; such a doxology might have been sung at the end of a psalm or section of a psalm which liturgically was separated from the following (cf the use of the 'Gloria' at the end of Psalms or [in the case of the 119th] at the end of sections of the Psalm in Christian worship). Or it may have been a direction to the orchestra—'Lift up! loud!'—to strike in with loud music (after the soft accompaniment to the singers' voices) during a pause in the singing. Other theories, such as that it represents a Hebrew transliteration of a Greek word (*e.g. psalle*) or an acrostic of three words directing a change of voices or *da capo*, have little probability. The meaning of the LXX rendering (*diapsalma*) is as uncertain as that of the Hebrew word itself. G. H. B.—**J. Mu.**

SELA-HAMMAHLEKOTH, 1 S 23[28] (AV, RV).—See Rock of Escape.

SELED.—A Jerahmeelite, 1 Ch 2[20].

SELEMIA.—One of Ezra's swift scribes (2 Es 14[24]).

SELEMIAS, 1 Es 9[34] (AV, RV).—See Shelemiah, **2.**

SELEUCIA.—Commonly called Seleucia Pieria (after the mountain on its N. side) to distinguish it from other cities of the same name. It was on the coast of Syria, above the mouth of the Orontes River. It was founded by Seleucus I. as his capital, but, lacking control of the sea, he subsequently shifted his government to a new place farther up the river (Antioch). But he was buried at Seleucia. Seleucia was a great fortress. In the second Syrian war Ptolemy Euergetes established himself here (1 Mac 11[8]) and it remained in Egyptian hands for 27 years. Antiochus III. the Great retook it in 219 B.C. Ptolemy VI. again seized it when he sided with Demetrius against Alexander Balas. It formed a league with Antioch, Apamea, and Laodicea. When Tryphon occupied Antioch, Seleucia was the seat of Demetrius II. From here Antiochus VII. Sidetes reconquered the realm. Faithful to Antiochus VIII. Grypus, it was given its freedom. It locked out Alexander Zabinas (123–122 B.C.) and it alone resisted the Parthian Tigranes (83–69 B.C.). Pompey awarded it liberty. Its greatness and importance for trade increased in imperial times. Important remains exist, and some work has been carried on there by the Princeton University Antioch Expedition. E. G. K.

SELEUCUS.—**1. Seleucus I.** (*Nicator*), originally a cavalry officer of Alexander the Great, became satrap of Babylon on the death of the king. After some vicissitudes his position there was securely established in 312 B.C., from which date the Seleucid era was reckoned (1 Mac 1[16]). The battle of Ipsus, 301 B.C., made him master of Syria and great part of the E. He founded Antioch (q.v.) and its fortified port Seleucia (1 Mac 11[8]), and is said by Josephus (*Ant.* XII. iii. 1 [119]) to have conferred on the Jews the privileges of citizenship. He is the 'one of his [*i.e.* the king of Egypt's] princes' (Dn 11[5]). He died 280 B.C.—**2. Seleucus II.** (*Callinicus*, 246–226 B.C.), son of Antiochus *Soter*, is entitled the 'king of the north' in the passage (Dn 11[7-9]) which alludes to the utter discomfiture of the Syrian king and the capture of Seleucia.—**3. Seleucus III.** (*Ceraunus*, 226–223 B.C.), 'one of his (Seleucus II.'s) sons' (Dn 11[10]), was murdered during a campaign in Asia Minor: the struggle with Egypt was continued by his brother Antiochus (Dn 11[10-16]).—**4. Seleucus IV.** (*Philopator*; but Jos., *Ant.* XII. iv. 10 [223], calls him *Soter*), son of Antiochus *The Great*, reigned 187–176 B.C. He it was who despatched Heliodorus to plunder the Temple (2 Mac 3[1-40], cf Dn 11[20]).—**5. Seleucus V.** (125–124 B.C.) and **VI.** (95–93 B.C.) are not of importance to the Biblical student. The four first-named belong to the 'ten horns' of Dn 7[24]. J. T.

SELF-CONTROL.—See TEMPERANCE.

SELF-SURRENDER.—Jesus told His disciples that they must deny themselves (Mk 8[34]) if they were to follow Him; and, as this verse and Jesus' own example alike show, there is no limit to what may be required in this surrender of oneself; it may mean death. But whatever it means in any given case, the practice of self-surrender or self-denial is never an end in itself; it is a presentation of oneself to God so that one may be used for His purposes. This presentation of oneself is described in the OT in language drawn from the servant's attendance on his lord (*e.g.* Job 1[6], Dn 7[10, 13], Zec 6[5]); and as the OT worshipper, when he presented himself before Yahweh at His shrine or Temple, had to be pure and to present an unblemished offering, so St. Paul exhorts his readers to present *themselves* as pure offerings to God (Ro 12[1]; cf 6[12-19]). With the Christian, as with His Lord, the offering called for is nothing less than himself. But this is only possible for men because Christ makes it so; hence it is He who is described as presenting the Colossians 'blameless and irreproachable' before God (Col 1[22]) and as presenting the Church in splendour before Himself (Eph 5[27]). To surrender ourselves to God, which is life in its true sense (cf He 12[9]), we must surrender ourselves first to Christ, by dying with Him that we may live with Him (Ro 6[1ff]); by being born again (Jn 3[3, 5]) into the Kingdom of the Son who has completely surrendered Himself to the Father (He 10[9], Jn 4[34] etc.). So St. Paul can sum up the origin and the consequences of self-surrender to God in the words: 'I have been crucified with Christ; it is no longer I who live, but Christ who lives in me' (Gal 2[20]). R. S. B.

SEM, Lk 3[36] (AV) = **Shem** (q.v.).

SEMACHIAH.—A Korahite family of gatekeepers, 1 Ch 26[7]. Perhaps the same name should be substituted for **Ismachiah** in 2 Ch 31[13].

SEMEI.—**1.** 1 Es 9[33] (AV, RV); see SHIMEI, **11. 2.** Ad. Est 11[2] (AV); see SHIMEI, **12. 3.** Lk 3[26] (AV); see SEMEIN.

SEMEIAS, Ad. Es 11[2] (RV).—See SHIMEI, **12.**

SEMEIN.—The father of Mattathias, Lk 3[26] (AV **Semei**).

SEMEIS, 1 Es 9[23] (RV).—See SHIMEI, **11.**

SEMELLIUS, 1 Es 2[16] (AV).—See SHIMSHAI.

SEMIS, 1 Es 9[23] (AV).—See SHIMEI, **11.**

SENAAH.—The children of Senaah, or more correctly **Hassenaah** (q.v.), were a clan or family who, according to Ezr 2[35], Neh 7[38], 1 Es 5[23] (AV **Annaas, RV Sanaas**), were among the exiles of the first Restoration under Zerubbabel, and had a share in rebuilding the walls, Neh 3[3]. They are elsewhere unknown, unless they should be classified with **Hassenuah** (q.v.), a clan of Benjamin, 1 Ch 9[7], Neh 11[9]. The latter would then be the correct reading. Other conjectures are less probable. J. F. McC.

SENATE is the translation of Greek *gerousia* in Ac 5[21], where 'all the senate of Israel' is intended to explain the preceding **'council'** (*synedrion*). See SANHEDRIN. It is the Jewish 'senate' that is meant likewise in 2 Mac 1[10] 4[44]. The Roman senate is alluded to in 1 Mac 8[17ff].

SENEH.—A rocky crag on one side of the Michmash gorge, opposite Bozez, 1 S 14[4].

SENIR.—The name of **Hermon** among the Amorites, according to Dt 3[9], but in Ca 4[8] and 1 Ch 5[23] distinguished from Hermon. It was famous for its large fir trees, Ezk 27[5]. The Amorite name was, naturally enough, the one in vogue among the Babylonians and Assyrians. In Deuteronomy it appears, like Hermon and Sirion, to designate the whole of Anti-Lebanon. When taken more strictly it stood, we may assume, for the northern portion. The Arab geographers gave the name to that part of the range lying between *Ba'albek* and *Ḥomṣ*. J. F. McC.

SENNACHERIB (Ass. *Sīn-aḫê-erība, i.e.* 'Sin has replaced the brothers'), son of Sargon, became king of Assyria on the 12th of Ab, 705 B.C. He first made Ashur his capital and later in 701 B.C. raised Nineveh to the position of capital city; at the latter site have been found Sennacherib's most famous monuments. In 703 B.C. he was faced with trouble in Babylon. Merodach-baladan had regained the throne from which he had been removed a few years before by Sargon. In a decisive victory Sennacherib subdued the Babylonian insurrection and placed Bêl-ibni of royal seed upon the throne as a vassal king. After wars against the Kassites and Yasubigallai, E. of the Tigris, Sennacherib turned his attention to rebellions in Syria and Palestine. Luli, king of Sidon, fled overseas; Ethba'al was placed as king over the Phoenician cities, which submitted to the Assyrian king. Kings to the south hastened to send gifts of tribute; among them were the kings of Ashdod, Beth-Ammon, Moab, and Edom. Sennacherib moved southward, where he captured Ashkelon and the surrounding cities. He set up a former pro-Assyrian king and imposed tribute. At Eltekeh he met and defeated the Egyptian and Ethiopian armies which had been summoned by the revolutionists at Ekron, who had thrown their former king Padi into fetters and given him over to Hezekiah, king of Judah, After capturing Eltekeh, Timnah, and Ekron, Sennacherib brought back Padi from Jerusalem and restored him to his throne. He next captured forty-six of the strong cities of Hezekiah and carried away 200,150 prisoners. Siege was laid to Jerusalem and Hezekiah himself was shut up 'like a bird in a cage.' Sennacherib records in his royal inscription tribute from Hezekiah amounting to 30 talents of gold and 800 talents of silver, as well as other precious materials. According to 2 K 18[14ff]. Hezekiah paid Sennacherib 300 talents of silver and 30 talents of gold while he was in Lachish. Lachish fell to Sennacherib; his artists later decorated the royal palace in Nineveh with pictures of the storming of the city and of the king sitting on his throne as 'passed in review the booty of Lachish.' The Assyrian Tartan (commander-in-chief), Rabsaris, and Rabshakeh went to Hezekiah in Jerusalem to demand surrender of the city (2 K 18[17ff]) but Hezekiah refused. A second embassy (2 K 19[9ff]) from Sennacherib likewise failed. According to 2 K 19[35-36] the siege of Jerusalem was lifted by the miraculous death of 185,000 Assyrians; from the Assyrian account it is clear that Jerusalem was not captured. There is some reason to think that certain Biblical narratives in 2 Kings (and their duplicates in Is 36–37) may refer to another campaign of Sennacherib towards the end of his reign. In 700 B.C. he marched again to Babylon, captured Bêl-ibni and pursued his old enemy Merodach-baladan, who had fled by ship to Elam. Sennacherib placed his own son Ashurnadin-shumu on the Babylonian throne. In 694 B.C., with a fleet constructed by Phoenician shipbuilders, Sennacherib again invaded the south to attack the Babylonians and the Elamites. After indecisive battles in the south, Babylon was finally taken in 689 B.C. and wiped out. The remaining eight years of his reign were relatively quiet, to judge from the scant records we have. In 681 B.C. Sennacherib was murdered by two of his sons (2 K 19[37]), who escaped, and Esarhaddon, another son, reigned in his stead. J. B. P.

SENUAH, Neh 11[9] (AV).—See HASSENUAH.

SEORIM.—The name of the fourth priestly course, 1 Ch 24[8].

SEPARATE PLACE.—A space at the end of Ezekiel's Temple, Ezk 41[12ff] 42[1, 10, 13] (AV, RV; RSV 'temple yard').

SEPARATION, WATER OF.—See RED HEIFER.

SEPHAR.—Mentioned as a boundary of the descendants of Joktan in Gn 10[30]. The site is unknown.

SEPHARAD.—A country in which was a community of exiles from Judah in the days of the prophet Obadiah, Ob [20]. Targum and Peshitta render 'Spain,' and Vulgate 'Bosphorus.' It is probable that it was a district of Asia Minor, possibly Sardis.

SEPHARVAIM.—A city mentioned in 2 K 18[34] 19[13], Is 36[19] 37[13] among those captured by the Assyrians, all apparently in Syria; also in 2 K 17[24, 31] as the name of a place whose inhabitants were deported to Samaria. Its location is unknown. It is possibly to be identified with **Sibraim** (q.v.).

SEPTUAGINT.—See GREEK VERSIONS OF OT, **1.**

SEPULCHRE.—See TOMB.

SERAH.—A daughter of Asher, Gn 46[17], Nu 26[46] (AV **Sarah**), 1 Ch 7[30].

SERAIAH.—**1.** 2 S 8[17]; see SHAVSHA. **2.** High priest in the reign of Zedekiah, who was put to death, with other distinguished captives, by order of Nebuchadrezzar at Riblah, 2 K 25[18, 21], Jer 52[24, 27]. He is mentioned in the list of high priests, 1 Ch 6[14]. Ezra claimed descent from him, Ezr 7[1], 1 Es 8[1] (AV **Saraias**, RV **Azaraias**), 2 Es 1[1] (AV, RV **Saraias**). He is also named in 1 Es 5[5] (AV, RV **Saraias**). **3.** One of the 'captains of the forces' who joined Gedaliah at Mizpah, 2 K 25[23], Jer 40[8]. **4.** Second son of Kenaz, father of Joab, and brother of Othniel, 1 Ch 4[13f]. **5.** A Simeonite, 1 Ch 4[35]. **6.** One of the twelve leaders who returned to Jerusalem, Ezr 2[2], 1 Es 5[8] (AV **Zacharias**, RV **Zaraias**); called **Azariah** in Neh 7[7]; he sealed the covenant, Neh 10[2] 12[1], and is perhaps the same as the head of the priestly house named in Neh 12[12]. **7.** The grandson of Meshullam, Neh 11[11]; called **Azariah** in 1 Ch 9[11]. **8.** One of those sent to apprehend Jeremiah, Jer 36[26]. **9.** Son of Neriah, Jer 51[59ff]. He held the office of quartermaster.

SERAPHIM.—The seraphim are mentioned in only one passage in Scripture (Is 6[2ff]). In Isaiah's inaugural vision these constitute the celestial adorants who sing the Trisagion in antiphonal chorus. They are described as having six wings, one pair for veiling their eyes, another for covering their body (euphemistically called 'feet'), and one, for flying. These creatures had human hands and voices (vv.[6f]), but whether they had human bodies is not known. Their function was Yahweh's service, both in adoration and protecting Him from the approach of the profane and unholy. Though not mentioned as such in NT the four living creatures of Rev 4[8] are an obvious reflection of this passage and of Ezk 10.

Later Jewish tradition suggests that the Seraphim were serpentine (1 En 20[7] 61[10] etc.). This accords with the use of the singular *sārāph* (Nu 21[8], Dt 8[15], Is 14[29] 30[6]) for **fiery serpent**, also found in the plural (and thus identical with our word) at Nu 21[6]. The word is derived from a root meaning 'to burn.' An interesting relief on stone from Tell Halaf (Oppenheim, Plate 32A) shows a goddess with six wings holding a serpent in each hand. Whether this has anything to do with the Hebrew seraphim is, of course, undemonstrable.

J. A. K.—**J. W. W.**

SERAR, 1 Es 5[32] (RV).—See SISERA, **2.**

SERED.—A son of Zebulun, Gn 46[14], Nu 26[26]; the gentilic **Seredites** occurs in Nu 26[26] (AV **Sardites**).

SERGIUS PAULUS.—See PAULUS (SERGIUS).

SERJEANTS.—See POLICE.

SERMON ON THE MOUNT.—The first of the five major discourses in Matthew (5–7), paralleled by a briefer discourse in Luke (6[20–49]) which was delivered on the 'plain' or 'level place.' Because of its location, Luke's sermon is sometimes described as 'the ordination sermon to the Twelve'; but its contents, like those of Matthew, are general in application; Matthew's sermon is delivered to the disciples, but the crowd is also present. Like Matthew's other discourses, the material in chs. 5–7 has been collected and arranged by the author in order to set forth Jesus' teaching on one leading subject; here it is the 'new righteousness' or practice of religion (6[1]) which must not fall short but even exceed the religious practice of the Pharisees (5[20]). In view of the parallel in Luke, it is probable that such a collection of Jesus' sayings (though briefer) on discipleship, love of enemies, the criteria of true devotion, and the distinction between 'hearing' and 'doing' the word, was to be found in their common non-Marcan source (Q). Most of the material found in Mt 5–7 but not in Lk 6[20–49] is to be found elsewhere in Luke; *i.e.* it also belongs to this early gospel source, or to similar sources (*e.g.* 'M').

1. Structure.—Both 'sermons' begin with the Beatitudes (q.v.), 9 in Mt, 3 in Lk, where they are matched by the three 'Woes' setting forth the contraries. The new piety, which is required of Jesus' true followers or disciples, is 'perfectionist' and absolute in its demands. 'The poor' must be 'poor in spirit,' according to Matthew, not only in earthly possessions, as in Luke; *i.e.* they must be poor in their own self-esteem, helpless and dependent upon God rather than upon themselves; the 'meek' (or gentle) will inherit 'the land' (from Ps 37[11] LXX, possibly a later addition to the original series of Beatitudes); the 'mourners' will be comforted in the Age to Come, and the 'hungry' will be filled with good things (cf Lk 1[53])—here again Matthew adds an explanatory phrase, '(hunger) for righteousness,' in order to make sure the religious reference. Luke's bare 'you that hunger now,' which was perhaps the original form of the saying in Q, could easily be understood in a social revolutionary sense. The merciful, the pure in heart, the peacemakers, the persecuted (these verses are not in Luke) are those who supremely exhibit the devout character required by God: this was the teaching of Judaism (see especially the Psalms) as well as of Jesus and the earliest Christians. The appended Beatitude in Mt 5[11f] sums up and applies the teaching of the whole series to the early Christian situation. As C. F. Burney demonstrated, the Aramaic original underlying the Matthaean Beatitudes was probably metrical, and the explanatory glosses in vv.[3] and [6] overload the lines. It is also probable that the arrangement and form were meant for easy memorization, and may go back to Jesus Himself. Their outlook, not only in Luke but also in Matthew, is eschatological. 'Blessed' means more than 'happy' here and now (as in classical macarisms), *e.g.* as possessing true peace of mind; it is a felicitation pronounced upon—almost an apostrophe (Hail!) addressed to—those who are to be the inheritors of the Kingdom of Heaven.

2. Purpose.—The Beatitudes supply the clue to the purpose of the Sermon, which is to expound the meaning of the New Piety, that of Jesus' disciples, in contrast with the Old, that of the scribal teachers of the Law and their Pharisaic followers and supporters. The Sermon was therefore designed for reading and study, perhaps for memorization, like most of Jesus' teaching in Matthew, and certainly for practice in the Christian church of Matthew's time. The true disciples of Jesus are truly pleasing to God; they are 'the salt of the earth,' 'the light of the world,' 'a city built on a hill'; their only purpose in life is to serve God humbly and proclaim and exemplify the gospel (5[13–16]). Such 'righteousness' is not only superior to the ordinary, but far excels it, and in fact carries out to its full realization the basic teaching of both the Law and the prophets (5^{17-20}); here Matthew specifically aligns Jesus' teaching with the traditional religion of his people (cf 23^{2f}). Anti-Pharisaism must not be allowed to go the length of irreligion, or anti-nomism to become antinomianism. Following this statement of the underlying principle of Jesus' interpretation of the Law (see other examples: *e.g.* Mk 7^{9-13} 10^{2-12} where He preserves the fundamental teaching but rejects the traditional interpretation), the Sermon proceeds to examine the teaching of the Law at six points: murder, adultery, divorce, oaths, revenge, and the treatment of enemies (5^{21-48}), concluding with the summary requirement, which is also 'perfectionist,' 'You therefore must be perfect, as your heavenly Father is perfect.' The Sermon then turns to the customary Pharisaic practice of religion, with three examples, the 'pious deeds' of almsgiving, prayer, and fasting, and warns against ostentation in their performance (6^{1-18}); here the model prayer of Jesus (see LORD'S PRAYER) is included in vv.$^{9-13}$. Following this formal examination of the traditional norms of piety, the Sermon continues with various sayings of Jesus on laying up treasure (6^{19ff}) and the importance of singleness of purpose (the parable of the eye, and the saying on serving one master, ^{22ff}). Then follow a series of warnings against anxiety, which destroys faith in God ($^{25-34}$), and against censoriousness (7^{1-5}) which invites a judgment upon oneself; the sayings on assurance in prayer ($^{7-11}$), the narrow gate (^{13f}, which may belong with the sayings on loyalty and sincerity, above); the warning against false (Christian) prophets without ($^{15-20}$) and self-deception within ($^{21-23}$). The Sermon concludes with the great parable of the Two House Builders who built, one upon sand, the other upon rock ($^{24-27}$), a sublime climax to a sermon on the practice of religion which stressed repeatedly the actual doing as opposed to the mere casual hearing of the words of the true Teacher.

Into this sequence of thought have been inserted two verses which are difficult to explain, and by some are thought to be derived from Matthew's 'M' material: 7^6, the warning against desecrating sacred things, which may refer to the teaching of the gospel, with its transcendent requirements, to those who will only reject and ridicule it or revile the teacher; and 7^{12}, the Golden Rule, which was already known in Judaism and is sound enough as far as it goes but seems out of place where it stands in Matthew. It may belong after 7^{1-5}, having been separated from that pericope by the insertion of $^{6-11}$.

3. Sources.—The basis of the Sermon was the combination of Q and M material, following the pattern just described. Into this combination Matthew inserted some material from Mark. The central section of Q was on discipleship, that of M was on the new interpretation of the Law. It is characteristic of Matthew that he often introduced sayings in groups of three, adducing two further sayings in support or elucidation of the one which provided the topic of the pericope. The background of the Sermon is the religious tradition of the Palestinian or Syrian church toward the end of the 1st cent., totally uninfluenced by 'Paulinism' with its repudiation of the Jewish Law. For Matthew, the Law was more binding than ever, now that its fundamental principles had been revealed by Jesus, the 'Second Moses.' His view resembles that of Philo (q.v.), for whom the Law is the expression of the eternal moral order which undergirds the universe.

4. Interpretation.—Although the Sermon on the Mount (in Matthew) has often been viewed as a brief, summary statement of the whole gospel of Jesus, this would not have been the view of Matthew, who supplies four or five other discourses setting forth other aspects of the Lord's teaching: the Mission of the Disciples (9^{35}–10^{42}), the Hidden Teaching of the Parables (13^{1-52}), Church Administration (17^{24}–18^{35}), the Discourse against the Scribes and Pharisees (23^{1-39}) followed by the Discourse on the Parousia (24^1–25^{46}). See MATTHEW, GOSPEL OF. Understood as Matthew doubtless meant it to be understood, *i.e.* as Jesus' programmatic discourse on the New Piety *versus* the Old, the Sermon yields rich insights, both into Jesus' teaching as a whole and into the religious life, beliefs, and even worship of the early Palestinian or Syrian Christians. Hence the modern interpretations of the Sermon must be appraised from the vantage point of critical scholarship. The Sermon is scarcely 'Christ's legislation' (Sir John Seeley, *Ecce Homo*, 1865; cf Thomas Aquinas's phrase, the *nova lex*), nor his programme for social betterment or the achievement of an ideal society (so the Ritschlians, more or less, and the 'social gospel' school earlier in this century), nor pure religious ethics (so Bishop Charles Gore, *The Sermon on the Mount*, 1900, who reduced Jesus' 'heroic' ethics to 'a safe life is better than a complete one'). Martin Dibelius (*The Sermon on the Mount*, 1940) and others influenced by modern continental theology have viewed it as setting forth 'the pure will of God,' regardless of whether or not it could be put in practice: if not, the result would be to force men in penitence to acknowledge their sinfulness and helplessness and to fling themselves down before God, crying for mercy and grace; but of this 'mirror of perfection' purpose the Sermon itself contains no suggestion. Hans Windisch (*Der Sinn der Bergpredigt*, 1929, 2nd edition 1937, English translation, 1951) compared the ancient Jewish religious ethics, with their similar strain of perfectionism (see the Testaments of the XII Patriarchs, the ethical sections in 1 and 2 Enoch, Pirke Aboth, etc.); evidently Jesus assumed that His disciples would put His teaching in practice. Apart from that assumption the Sermon (both in its Lucan and Matthaean form) would have been meaningless.

F. C. G.

SERON.—A Syrian commander defeated by Judas Maccabaeus at Beth-horon (1 Mac $3^{13, 23f}$).

SERPENT.—**1.** *nāḥāsh*, generic name (cf Arab. *ḥanash*), Gn $3^{1, 3}$ etc., the most commonly used word, occurs frequently.

2. *'eph'eh* (root 'to groan, hiss,' cf Arab. *af'a*) is applied to the viper (Job 20^{16}, Is 30^6 59^5).

3. *'akhshûb*, parallel to *nāḥāsh* in Ps 140^3. This word is a *hapax legomenon* in the OT, and is probably a textual error for *'akkābhîsh*, 'spider.'

4. *pethen*, translated 'asp,' Dt 32^{33}, Job 20^{14}, Is 11^8; translated 'adder' in Ps 58^4, where it is referred to as the favourite of the snake-charmer.

5. *shᵉphîphôn*, Gn 49^{17} 'viper' (RSV; AV, RV 'adder,' AVm 'arrowsnake,' RVm 'horned snake'); cf Arabic *shiffûn*, 'the one who looks askance,' though the Hebrew word is possibly cognate with the Arabic *siff*, 'speckled serpent.'

6. *ṣepha'*, Is 14^{29}, perhaps an onomatopoeic word meaning 'hisser.'

7. *ṣiph'ônî*, Pr 23^{32} 'adder'; so RSV in Is 11^8 59^5, Jer 8^{17} (AV 'cockatrice,' RV 'basilisk').

8. *ḳippôz*, Is 34^{15} 'owl' (RSV; AV 'great owl,' RV 'arrowsnake'). This is probably cognate with Arabic *qiffaza*, 'the arrowsnake,' from the verb *gafaza*, 'to leap,' *i.e.* out of a tree upon its victim. See OWL.

9. *sārāph*, Is 14^{29} 30^6, 'fiery serpent,' coupled with *nāḥāsh* in Nu 21^6, Dt 8^{15}.

10. *zōḥᵃlê 'āphār*, Dt 32^{24}; *zōḥᵃlê 'ereṣ*, Mic 7^{17}, creatures that glide on the dust or the earth, so probably serpents, cf the Stone of Zoheleth (1 K 1^9), where *zōḥeleth* means 'serpent' if the adjacent well of En-rogel is the 'Dragon's Well' of Neh 2^{13}. Cf WORM, **5.**

11. *tannîn*, translated 'serpent,' Ex $7^{9f, 12}$ (RVm 'any large reptile'), Ps 91^{13} (AV and RV 'dragon'); cf Neh 2^{13}, where RSV has 'jackal' (AV, RV 'dragon'). See DRAGON.

12. (Greek) *echidna*—any poisonous serpent (Mt 3^7 12^{34} 23^{33}, Lk 3^7, Ac 28^3).

Serpents are very common in Palestine and the wilderness to the south, over thirty species being known. Though the great majority are really harmless, all are dreaded by the natives, and several kinds are most deadly, fatal snake-bites being by no means uncommon.

The Egyptian cobra (*naja ḥaji*) is found, but fortunately is not common. It is the favourite with snake-charmers, and is very probably the *pethen* (*v. supra*, **4**). It was held in much veneration by the ancient Egyptians, and a little bronze serpent found in Macalister's excavations at Gezer was of this form, and was probably an object of worship in pre-Israelite Palestine. Another very dangerous snake is the horned sand-snake (*Cerastes hasselquistii*), supposed to be the 'asp' of Cleopatra. It lies in ambush (Gn 49^{17}) in depressions of the road and bites the passers-by. It is called by the Arabs *shiffûn* (*v. supra*, **5**). Other poisonous Palestinian snakes belonging, like the last mentioned, to the viper family are *Vipera euphratica*, *V. ammodytes*, *Daboia xanthina*—a large nocturnal species—and the small *echis arenicola* which haunts the sandy deserts. These vipers are all included under the Hebrew *'ephʿeh* (*v. supra*, **2**). The viper of Ac 28^{3} was probably the *Vipera aspis*, which is common on most of the larger Mediterranean islands, though extinct in Malta. The expression 'fiery serpent' probably refers to the burning sensation produced by the bite; in Ps 140^{3} their poison is supposed to reside in their tongues (but cf *supra*, **3**).

Some of the references to serpents do not apparently refer to any natural object. Apart from the 'cockatrice' and 'basilisk' of the English versions—the former a monster with the head and body of a cock and the tail of a serpent ending in a sting, and the latter properly the golden serpent on the royal headdress of Egypt—which almost certainly refer to local serpents in the original Hebrew, there are references to mythological monsters. The reference in Am 9^{3} to the serpent (*nāḥāsh*) at the bottom of the sea probably refers to the Canaanite myth of the conflict of Cosmos (Baal) and Chaos, represented by various sea-monsters including *tnn* and *ltn*, Hebrew Leviathan (see DRAGON and LEVIATHAN), a local variant of the Babylonian myth of the conflict of Marduk and Tiamat.

The serpent is found in association with the mother-goddess *Asherat* in pendant reliefs at Râs Shamra and on clay-moulded incense-altars of the pre-Israelite period at Bethshan. This association may have suggested the rôle which the serpent plays in the Fall in Gn 3 (see FALL and SATAN). E. W. G. M.—**J. Gr.**

SERPENT, BRAZEN.—Nu 21$^{4-9}$ relates that Moses was commanded by God to make a bronze serpent and to set it on a pole in view of the people, in order that those who had been bitten by the fiery serpents (*i.e.* serpents whose bite caused a burning inflammation) might look upon it and be healed. Among many ancient peoples the serpent was regarded as sacred. The belief in its healing power was widespread (cf especially the serpent of the Greek god of healing, Asklepios). Serpent figures have been found in Palestine in such circumstances as to indicate that they represented the *vis genetrix* in a context of fertility cults. The serpent symbol, **Nehushtan,** in Jerusalem (2 K 18^{4}), which was destroyed by Hezekiah, may have been a pre-Davidic symbol which was taken over by the Israelites when they captured the city, or it may have been a well-known symbol in Palestine which they adopted for use in Yahweh worship. In either case the point of the story in Nu 21$^{4-9}$ was probably to show that healing comes from God and not from any magical properties inherent in the symbol. Jn 3^{14} says that, as the Israelites in the wilderness looked to the bronze serpent on the pole for healing, so men must look in faith upon Christ upon the cross (cf Sir 16$^{5-7}$).

J. T.—**J. Ma.**

SERUG.—Son of Reu, Gn 11$^{20-23}$, 1 Ch 1^{26}, Lk 3^{35} (AV **Saruch**).

SERVANT.—See next article and SLAVE.

SERVANT OF THE LORD.—In this phrase, as is usual in EV of the OT, 'LORD' is substituted for 'Yahweh,' the proper name of the God of Israel, which stands in the Hebrew text.

1. Originally the term 'Servant' (Heb. *ʿebhedh*) was simply correlative to such words as 'lord,' 'master,' which the Hebrews, like other Semites, applied to their God. In the first instance 'the servant of Yahweh' meant one who acknowledged, *i.e.* worshipped, Yahweh as his God. It could stand in antithesis to a phrase in which the name of another god takes the place of Yahweh. Thus, in 2 K 10^{23} a distinction is made between 'the servants (*ʿabhᵉdhê*) of Yahweh' and 'the worshippers (*ʿôbhᵉdhê*) of Baal.' But there is little doubt that the original expression was 'the servants (*ʿabhᵉdhê*) of Baal'; so some MSS and LXX. The Massoretes made a conventional distinction between 'servants' of Yahweh and 'worshippers' of Baal, on the principle that only Yahweh could have 'servants.' Originally, of course, 'servant' and 'worshipper' in such expressions meant much the same.

2. Any Israelite might be called a servant of Yahweh and this is reflected in the name Obadiah, originally (as in LXX) Abdiyah. (There are no fewer than thirteen Obadiahs in the OT.) Similar names are found outside Israel, *e.g.* Ebed-melech = 'servant of (the god) Melek' (Jer 38^{7}), and Abd-Melkart, Abd-Eshmun, Abd-Manat, typical Phoenician and Nabataean names, servants of Melkart, Eshmun, and Manat respectively.

3. Much as modern terms like 'Christian' or 'believer' may differ greatly in the fulness of their meaning, so 'the servant of Yahweh' might imply a higher degree, or more special form, of service than is necessarily implied in the proper name Obadiah, or in the distinction between 'servants of Yahweh' and 'servants of Baal.' Such fuller significance is apparent when prophets (Am 3^{7}, 2 K 9^{7}, Jer 7^{25} and often) or priests and Levites (Ps 134^{1}) are called 'the servants of Yahweh'; so also when particular individuals are so described. Among individuals called 'the servant of Yahweh' (or 'my servant' when Yahweh Himself speaks) are Abraham (Gn 26^{24}), Moses (Ex 14^{31} and nearly forty times), Joshua (Jos 24^{29}), Caleb (Nu 14^{24}), Job (1^{8}), David (2 S 3^{18} and about thirty times), Hezekiah (2 Ch 32^{16}), and Zerubbabel (Hag 2^{23} and Zec 3^{8} 6^{12}, where 'the Branch,' a messianic title, refers to Zerubbabel).

4. In Is 40–55 there are passages in which the nation Israel is called 'my/his (*i.e.* Yahweh's) servant.' They are 41^{8f} 44$^{1f, 21}$ 45^{4} 48^{20}. Israel is also, in all probability, 'my servant' in 42^{19} 43^{10}. This calling of Israel 'my servant' is unusual and deserves more attention than it has generally received. It appears that Deutero-Isaiah was the first, as he is also almost the last, to equate 'the servant of Yahweh' with Israel. Of the two passages outside Is 40–55 which identify the servant with Israel, Ps 136^{22} is late, and Jer 30^{10} (not in LXX) = 46^{27f} cannot with any confidence be assigned to Jeremiah. (In Ezk 28^{25} 37^{25} 'my servant Jacob' is the patriarch of the past, not the nation of the present.) How Deutero-Isaiah came to equate the servant with Israel can only be decided from the contexts in which the equation occurs. In them the leading motif is that Yahweh 'chose' Israel. This brings the concept into close relation with the doctrine of the Divine 'election' of Israel, so prominent in Deuteronomy. The reason for the Divine choice is probably that Jacob-Israel is 'the offspring of Abraham, my friend' (41^{8}, cf 51^{2}).

5. Although the particular character of 'the servant of Yahweh' in which Israel is personified is almost confined to Deutero-Isaiah, similar personifications are common enough in OT, and are sometimes so remote from our habits of thought and expression that EV have sacrificed the figure for the sake of intelligibility, as, *e.g.* in Jos 9^{7}, which is literally 'And the man of Israel said to the Hivite, "Perhaps thou art dwelling in my midst; how then can I make a covenant with thee?"' Other examples of what has come to be called 'corporate personality' are Hos 11^{1}, 'When Israel was a child, I loved him, and out of Egypt I called my son,' and Ps 129^{1ff} 'Sorely have they afflicted me (Israel) from my youth, yet they have not prevailed against me. The ploughers ploughed upon my back; they made long their furrows' (cf Is 50^{6}).

6. Within Is 40–55 there are four passages, generally

called ‘The Servant Songs,’ which describe a servant of Yahweh, his call and mission, sufferings, death and resurrection, in much fuller detail than do the texts enumerated in **4** above. They are 42$^{1-4\,(9)}$ 49$^{1-6\,(13)}$ 50$^{4-9\,(11)}$ 52^{13}–53^{12}. (The figures in brackets indicate the outside limits of the ‘Songs’; the majority of scholars limit them to the unbracketed figures.) In them the Servant is anonymous, except that in 49^{3} he is called Israel. Until the end of the 18th cent. the almost unanimous Christian view was that these ‘Suffering Servant’ passages were predictions of the sufferings, death, and resurrection of Christ. Jewish scholars meantime held that the Servant was the Jewish people, as elsewhere in Is 40–55. Since the end of the 18th cent., when the view gained currency that Is 40–55 was the work of ‘Deutero-Isaiah,’ an anonymous prophet who lived during the Babylonian exile, many Christian scholars have maintained that the Servant everywhere in Deutero-Isaiah is Israel.

7. It is only since the end of the 19th cent. that the designation ‘The Servant Songs’ has been current. Their authorship has been much discussed, some maintaining that they are, others that they are not, from Deutero-Isaiah. Those who think they are not, generally date them about a century later than he. To judge from their style and vocabulary, the argument that they are *not* from Deutero-Isaiah is difficult to sustain, certainly as regards the first three, while the fourth is more like the work of Deutero-Isaiah than it is to the work of any other OT writer. On the whole, the view that Is 40–55, including the Songs, is substantially a unity, has steadily gained ground. At the same time, the differences between the Israel of the Songs—if the Servant in them is Israel—and the Israel of the rest of the prophecy is marked. Put summarily, outside the Songs Israel has suffered, deservedly, for his own sins; the Servant of the Songs suffers, undeservedly, for the sins of others. His is a character nobler than that of any individual figure in the OT, let alone of Israel.

8. It is therefore not surprising that many Christian scholars have abandoned the view that the Servant of the Songs is Israel. The many theories of who the Servant was, or whom the author took as his ‘model,’ may be briefly summarized. (*a*) Some who maintain a collective interpretation go so far as to admit that the Servant is not the deaf and blind (42^{19}) Israel of the Exile, but a pious ‘kernel’ of the nation, who constituted a kind of ‘ideal’ as distinct from the actual Israel. The most attractive form of this view is that based on the concept of corporate personality (see **5** above). In ancient Israel, as in the ancient world generally, it is said, thought could pass quickly from community to individual and back again, so that ‘Israel’ (49^{3}) could be said to have a mission to ‘Israel’ (49^{5f}). (*b*) Among historical individuals who have been suggested as models for the Servant are Isaiah, Hezekiah, Uzziah, Jeremiah, Zerubbabel, Jehoiachin, Moses, and even Cyrus. Variants of the theory are (i) that the Servant was an anonymous contemporary of Deutero-Isaiah, or an otherwise unknown teacher who lived about a century later than he; (ii) that he was Deutero-Isaiah himself. This view presupposes either that the prophet wrote about his own death, or that the last Song was written by one of his disciples. None of these historical individual theories has any strong following. (*c*) It has been suggested that the Servant is the future Messiah depicted in the category of the pre-exilic Davidic kings, who, it is conjectured, annually ‘suffered’ certain ‘penances’ in the New Year Festival ritual. This is sometimes coupled with the view that the king embodied in his person some of the functions of the dying and rising nature god Tammuz (see Tammuz), and is generally supported with reference to the words ‘He shot up like a young plant’ (Is 53^{2}). But precisely similar language is used of Achilles by his mother, the sea-nymph Thetis (*Iliad*. xviii, line 437), and Achilles cannot have had any association with Tammuz. The complexity of the problem and the difficulties encountered in sustaining any one theory to the exclusion of others, has resulted in attempts to combine two or even more views in synthesis, as that the Servant is at once collective and individual, or historical and ideal.

9. To suppose that the prophet intended *in the Songs* to describe more than one figure—as that the Servant is at once Israel, *and* the Messiah, *and* himself—can only result in confusion, though it may well be that the Servant is a composite figure in the sense that more than one individual, say Moses and Jeremiah, or type, say king and prophet, has contributed to the (ideal) portrait. That Deutero-Isaiah thought of Israel as the Servant of Yahweh is undisputed (see **4** above); but he may well have envisaged another Servant in the Songs, without laying himself open to the charge of muddled thinking. There is insufficient textual evidence to delete ‘Israel’ in 49^{3}, yet since this ‘Israel’ is distinguished from Israel (vv.^{5f}), he cannot be Israel *simpliciter*. And notwithstanding corporate personality, the Servant in 52^{13}–53^{12} leaves the almost overwhelming impression that an individual is in mind. The most likely solution of a very difficult problem is that the prophet started with the equation the Servant = Israel, and came at last to see that the perfect Servant of God is such an one as no nation, not even Israel, can ever be, one who by the sufferings, culminating in death, which are the inevitable lot of the perfect Servant of God in ‘this naughtie world,’ would reconcile both Israel and the world to God. In this sense the Servant of 52^{13}–53^{12} and the related passages foreshadows the sufferings, death, and resurrection of Christ, as tradition has affirmed, and as Christ Himself appears to have divined. And no matter what view any individual Christian scholar may hold about who the original Servant was, his last word on the subject is almost invariably that the only person in history who has ever completely embodied in Himself the person and mission of the Servant, is Jesus Christ. This is always said in all good faith, not as a concession to traditional orthodoxy or to conventional piety.

G. B. G.—C. **R. N.**

SESIS, 1 Es 9^{34} (AV, RV).—See Shashai.

SESTHEL.—See Bezalel, **2.**

SET.—‘Set at’ is *valued at*, as 2 K 12^{4} AV, ‘The money that every man is set (RV ‘rated,’ RSV ‘assessed’) at.’ ‘Set at nought’ means *treat with contempt*, as Lk 23^{11} AV and RV, ‘Herod, with his men of war, set him at nought’ (RSV ‘treated him with contempt’). ‘Set by’ is to *value, esteem*, as in 1 S 18^{30}. ‘His name was much set by’ (RSV ‘was highly esteemed’). ‘Set to’ means to *affix*, as in Jn 3^{33} AV, ‘He that hath received his testimony hath set to his seal (RV, RSV ‘sets his seal to this’) that God is true.’

SETH.—The third son of Adam, Gn 4^{25f} 5^{3ff}, 1 Ch 1^{1} (AV **Sheth**), Lk 3^{38}. In the first of these passages J assigns a characteristic etymology for the name, Eve being made to say, ‘God hath set (*shāth*) for me another seed instead of Abel,’ for which reason she called him *Shēth* (*i.e.* ‘setting’ or ‘slip’). In Sir 49^{16} Seth is coupled with Shem as ‘honoured among men.’

SETHUR.—The Asherite spy, Nu 13^{13}.

SETTLE.—Found in AV and RV in Ezk 43$^{14,\,17,\,20}$ 45^{19} (RVm, RSV ‘ledge’) as translation of *ʿazārāh*, which is used of the two ledges between the base and the hearth of the altar.

SEVEN.—See Number, **7.**

SEVENEH.—See Syene.

SEVENTY.—See Number, **7.**

SHAALABBIN.—See next article.

SHAALBIM (‘place of foxes’).—A town mentioned with Mount Heres and Aijalon as being occupied by the Amorites (Jg 1^{35}). It was, with Makaz and Beth-shemesh, in the district of one of Solomon's commissariat officers (1 K 4^{9}); and if it be the same place as **Shaalabbin,** it is mentioned with Aijalon and Beth-shemesh in Jos 19^{42}. It is probably identical with **Shaalbon,** the home of one of David's heroes who is called ‘the **Shaalbonite**’

(2 S 23^{32}, 1 Ch 11^{33}). It may perhaps be identified with *Selbît*, about 8 miles N. of Beth-shemesh.

SHAALBON, SHAALBONITE.—See SHAALBIM.

SHAALIM, LAND OF.—A district in the hill country of Ephraim, 1 S 9^{4} (AV **Shalim**).

SHAAPH.—**1.** The son of Jahdai, 1 Ch 2^{47}. **2.** A son of Caleb by his concubine Maacah, 1 Ch 2^{49}.

SHAARAIM (' two gates ').—**1.** A town of Judah, in the Shephelah, mentioned in Jos 15^{36} (AV **Sharaim**); mentioned in connexion with the pursuit of the Philistines after the death of Goliath, 1 S 17^{52}. The site is unknown. **2.** A town of Simeon, 1 Ch 4^{31}; called **Sharuhen** in Jos 19^{6}; and **Shilhim** in Jos 15^{32}. It is probably modern *Tell el-Fâr'ah*, S. of Gaza.

SHAASHGAZ.—A chamberlain of Ahasuerus, Est 2^{14}.

SHABBETHAI.—A Levite who opposed Ezra in the matter of the foreign marriages, Ezr 10^{15}, 1 Es 9^{14} (AV **Sabbatheus**, RV **Sabbateus**); cf Neh 8^{7} 11^{16}, 1 Es 9^{48} (AV **Sabateas**, RV **Sabateus**).

SHACHIA, 1 Ch 8^{10} (AV, RV).—See SACHIA.

SHADDAI.—See GOD, **4** (d).

SHADRACH.—The name given to **Hananiah**, Dn 1^{7}.

SHAFTS.—See ARMOUR, ARMS, **1** (*d*).

SHAGE, 1 Ch 11^{34} (AV).—See SHAGEE.

SHAGEE.—A Hararite (q.v.) mentioned in 1 Ch 11^{34} (AV **Shage**). See SHAMMAH, **3.**

SHAHARAIM.—A Benjamite, 1 Ch 8^{8}.

SHAHAZIMAH, Jos 19^{22} (AV).—See SHAHAZUMAH.

SHAHAZUMAH.—A town allotted to Issachar, Jos 19^{22} (AV **Shahazimah**). Its location is unknown.

SHALEM.—In Gn 33^{18} AV we read ' Jacob (on his return from Haran) came to Shalem a city of Shechem ' (RV ' in peace to the city of Shechem '; RSV ' safely to the city of Shechem '; similarly Luther in his German translation). The word *shālēm* means ' peace,' and the preposition *b* ' in ' may have fallen out owing to the final letter of Jacob. Otherwise we must suppose Shalem to be a small town (in the neighbourhood of Shechem), which has been identified with a village called *Salim.*
W. F. B.

SHALIM, 1 S 9^{4} (AV).—See SHAALIM, LAND OF.

SHALISHA.—A region through which Saul travelled with his servant in search of the lost asses, 1 S 9^{4} (RV **Shalishah**). The route as given probably describes a circuitous journey, to the NW., the E., and finally S. through Benjamin. This would place the ' land of **Baal-shalishah** ' (q.v.) somewhere on the hills W. of Shiloh. **Baal-shalishah** (2 K 4^{42}) was doubtless a place in the same district.

SHALISHAH, 1 S 9^{4} (RV).—See SHALISHA.

SHALLECHETH.—See JERUSALEM, GATES OF.

SHALLUM, an inhabitant of Jabesh, was nominally king of Israel for one month in the period of anarchy which preceded the extinction of the nation. As he assassinated his predecessor, Zechariah, so in turn he was ' removed ' by his successor **Menahem** (2 K 15^{10ff}).
H. P. S.

SHALLUM.—**1.** See preceding article. **2.** See JEROAHAZ, **2. 3.** The husband (or son, LXX in 2 Kings) of Huldah, 2 K 22^{14}, 2 Ch 34^{22}. **4.** A Judahite, 1 Ch 2^{40f}. **5.** A descendant of Simeon, 1 Ch 4^{25}. **6.** A high priest, 1 Ch 6^{12f}, Ezr 7^{2}, 1 Es 8^{1} (AV **Salum**, RV **Salem**), 2 Es 1^{1} (AV **Sadamias**, RV **Salemas**, Bar 1^{7} (AV, RV **Salom**). **7.** A son of Naphtali, 1 Ch 7^{13}; called **Shillem** in Gn 46^{24}, Nu 26^{49}; gentilic **Shillemites** in Nu 26^{49}. **8.** The eponym of a family of gatekeepers, 1 Ch 9^{17}, Ezr 2^{42}, Neh 7^{45}, 1 Es 5^{28} (AV, RV **Salum**); perhaps the same as **Meshullam** in Neh 12^{55}. **9.** A Korahite gatekeeper, 1 Ch 9$^{17, 19, 31}$; called **Meshelemiah** in 26$^{1f, 9}$ and **Shelemiah** in 26^{14}. It is not at all unlikely that this name should be identified with the preceding. **10.** Father of Jehizkiah, and Ephraimite chief, 2 Ch 28^{12}. **11.** One of the porters who had married a foreign wife, Ezr 10^{24}, 1 Es 9^{25} (AV, RV **Sallumus**). **12.** One of the sons of Bani who had committed the same offence, Ezr 10^{42}; perhaps the same as **Shemaiah** in 1 Es 9^{34} (AV, RV **Samatus**). **13.** The son of Hallohesh, Neh 3^{12}. **14.** The uncle of Jeremiah, Jer 32^{7}. **15.** Father of Maaseiah, Jer 35^{4}. **16.** The son of Col-hozeh, Neh 3^{15} (AV, RV **Shallun**).

SHALLUN, Neh 3^{15} (AV, RV).—See SHALLUM, **16.**

SHALMAI.—A family of Nethinim (q.v.), Neh 7^{48} (RV **Salmai**); called **Shamlai** in Ezr 2^{46} (AV **Shalmai**), 1 Es 5^{30} (AV, RV **Subai**).

SHALMAN.—This name occurs only in the clause ' as Shalman spoiled **Beth-arbel** (q.v.) in the day of battle,' Hos 10^{14}. *Shalman* may be a contraction for *Shalmaneser*, but it is impossible to say which, if any, of the four kings of Assyria bearing that name suits the connexion. It has been suggested that the Moabite king Salmanu (mentioned in Tiglath-pileser's triumphal inscription, II Rawl. 67, line 60) may be the person referred to by the prophet. The Vulgate version seems to think of the slaughter of Zalmunna by Gideon (Jg 8). Some scholars read *Shallum* for *Shalman* (cf 2 K 15$^{10, 15}$). W. F. B.

SHALMANESER (Assyr. *Šulmān-ašarēd, i.e.* ' Shulman is First '), son of Tiglath-pileser III., king of Assyria (727–722 B.C.), known now as Shalmaneser V. He also ruled Babylon, where he was known as Ululai. When Hoshea, king of Israel, with the king of Egypt conspired against Assyria and refused tribute (2 K 17$^{3-4}$), Shalmaneser marched to Palestine and brought Hoshea into subjection. He began the siege of Samaria, which later fell to Sargon II. On the occasion of a revolution instigated by the priests of Ashur and Harran, Shalmaneser was murdered and the throne was seized by the usurper Sargon II.
J. B. P.

SHAMA.—One of David's heroes, 1 Ch 11^{44}.

SHAMBLES.—See ARTS AND CRAFTS, **7**, FOOD, **11**, MARKET.

SHAME.—**1.** In the first Biblical reference to this emotion (Gn 2^{25}; cf 3^{7}) ' shame ' appears as the ' correlative of sin and guilt '; it is, within a man's own inner experience, ' the overpowering feeling that inward harmony and satisfaction with oneself are disturbed ' (Delitzsch, *Com., in loco*); and it means disgrace in the social sense of the loss of the esteem of one's fellow men, and in the religious sense of the loss of the favour and fellowship of God. From the OT point of view the crowning shame is idolatry : ' They say to a tree, you are my father ' (Jer 2^{26}; cf Is 42^{17} 44^{11}). The all-inclusive promise to those who trust in God is ' none that wait upon thee shall be ashamed ' (Ps 25^{3} RV; cf 119$^{6, 80}$, Is 45^{16f} 54^{4f}, Jer 17^{13}, Jl 2^{26f}, Ro 5^{5} 9^{33} 10^{11}). The absence of shame is always regarded as an aggravation of sinful conduct : Job (19^{3}) reproaches his friends because they are ' not ashamed ' of dealing hardly with him; the climax of Jeremiah's complaint (6^{15}) against those who had ' committed abomination ' is that ' they were not at all ashamed, neither could they blush ' (cf 8^{12}, Zeph 3$^{5, 11}$). The culmination of shamelessness is seen in those ' who glory in their shame ' (Ph 3^{19}); but in this passage, as elsewhere (Is 50^{6}; cf Pr 10^{5} 25^{8}), ' shame ' is, by a natural transference of ideas, applied not to the inward feeling, but to its outward cause. The degradation of those ' whose god is their belly ' is seen in their boasting of conduct which ought to have made them ashamed of their perversion of gospel liberty into sinful licence. The return of shame is a sign of repentance : ' then you will remember your ways and be ashamed ' (Ezk 16^{61}; cf Ezr 9^{6}).

2. The consciousness of shame varies with the conventional standards adopted in any society. In the sense of violation of propriety St. Paul applies the word to men who wear their hair long and to women who wear it short (1 Co 11$^{6, 14}$; cf 6^{5} 14^{35}). Poverty (Pr 13^{18}), leprosy (Nu 12^{14}), widowhood (Is 54^{4}) are viewed as involving ' shame ' when these conditions are regarded as tokens of the loss of God's blessing or as penalties for sin. St. Paul describes God's ideal ' workman ' as one ' who has no need to be ashamed ' (2 Ti 2^{15}).

3. In the NT *sin* is pre-eminently the shameful thing (Ro 6^{21}, Ph 3^{19}, Eph 5^{12}, Jd ^{13}, 1 Jn 2^{28} ; cf 3^{5}). But the distinguishing characteristic of the early Christian use of the word is occasioned by the fact that Jesus Christ releases men from the guilt and bondage of sin by ' becoming sin ' for men (2 Co 5^{21}) ; he ' endured the cross, despising the shame ' (He 12^{2}). When St. Paul says ' I am not ashamed of the gospel ' (Ro 1^{16}), he means that the ' offence ' of the Cross has become the ground of his glorying (Gal 6^{14}, 1 Co 1^{31}, 2 Co 10^{17} 12^{9f}). ' To suffer as a Christian ' and ' not (to) be ashamed ' is to ' glorify God ' (1 P 4^{16} ; cf 2 Ti $1^{8f, 12, 16}$). The Son of Man, in the day of judgment, will be ashamed of all who are now ashamed of Him and of His words (Mk 8^{38}, Lk 9^{26}) ; but St. John's assurance is that those who abide in Christ ' may have boldness and not be ashamed before him at his coming ' (1 Jn 2^{28}). Of them who desire a heavenly country ' God is not ashamed . . . to be called their God ' ; for the city He has prepared, they are being prepared by the sanctifying grace of Him ' who is not ashamed to call them brethren ' (He 11^{16} 2^{11}).

J. G. T.—**J. Ma.**

SHAMED, 1 Ch 8^{12} (AV).—See SHEMER, **3.**

SHAMER.—1. 1 Ch 6^{46} (AV).—See SHEMER, **2. 2.** 1 Ch 7^{34} (AV) ; see SHEMER, **3.**

SHAMGAR smote 600 Philistines with an ox-goad, Jg 3^{31}. There is no mention of his judging Israel, or of the duration of his influence. The exploit belongs to the latest redaction of the book ; 4^{1} continues the story of 3^{30}. Nothing is known of any Philistine dominion at so early a period, and in some Greek MSS the verse follows 16^{31}. His exploit resembles that of Shammah in 2 S 23^{11} (cf 21^{15-22}), and may have been attached to him as an expansion of the reference in the song of Deborah, Jg 5^{6}, There, however, he appears to be a foreign oppressor. and the connexion of the two passages is obscure, the song having to do with Caananite oppression in the N. The name is foreign, Hittite or Assyrian. He is ' the son of **Anath.**' *Anati* occurs in the Tell el-Amarna tablets, and *Anatu* is an Assyrian goddess. From the Râs Shamra texts we have now a considerable knowledge of her place in Caananite mythology. Her name appears in the place-names Beth-anath, Beth-anoth, and Anathoth (q.v.).

C. W. E.—**H. H. R.**

SHAMHUTH.—One of David's officers, 1 Ch 27^{8} ; called **Shammah** in 2 S 23^{25}. See SHAMMAH, **4.**

SHAMIR.—1. A Kohathite, 1 Ch 24^{24}. **2.** A town in the hill-country of Judah, Jos 15^{48}. It is perhaps *Kh. el-Bîreh*, near *Kh. Sumara*, which preserves the ancient name. **3.** The home and burial-place of Tola, Jg 10^{1f}. It was possibly later the site of Samaria.

SHAMLAI.—See SHALMAI.

SHAMMA.—An Asherite, 1 Ch 7^{37}.

SHAMMAH.—1. Son of Reuel, son of Esau, a tribal chief, Gn 36^{13}, 1 Ch 1^{37}. **2.** Third son of Jesse, present when Samuel sought a successor to Saul, 1 S 16^{9} ; with Saul on the battlefield when David visited the camp, 17^{13} ; called **Shimeah,** father of Jonadab, in 2 S 13^{3}, **Shimea** in 1 Ch 2^{13} (AV **Shimma**), and **Shimei,** father of Jonathan who slew the giant, in 2 S 21^{21}. In 1 Ch 20^{7} Jonathan is called son of Shimea. **3.** Son of Agee, a Hararite (q.v.), one of the three mighty men of David, 2 S 23^{11}. Alone he held the field against the Philistines. The parallel passage, 1 Ch 11^{12f}, attributes the feat to Eleazar. In 1 Ch 11^{34} ' son of **Shagee** ' should probably read ' son of **Shammah** ' (cf 2 S 23^{32f}, where the right reading appears to be ' Jonathan the son of Shammah '). In 2 S 23^{11} Lucian reads ' Ela ' for ' Agee,' and if this is right, perhaps **Shimei** the son of Ela (1 K 4^{18}) is the same as Shammah. **4.** A Harodite (q.v.), one of David's heroes, 2 S 23^{25} ; called **Shammoth** in 1 Ch 11^{27} and **Shamhuth** in 1 Ch 27^{8}. He is probably the same as **3.**

J. H. St.

SHAMMAI.—1. A Jerahmeelite, 1 Ch $2^{28, 32}$. **2.** The ' son ' of Rekem and ' father ' of Maon, 1 Ch 2^{44f}. **3.** A Judahite, 1 Ch 4^{17}.

SHAMMOTH.—One of David's heroes, 1 Ch 11^{27} ; called **Shammah** in 2 S 23^{25}. See SHAMMAH, **4.**

SHAMMUA.—1. The Reubenite spy, Nu 13^{4}. **2.** One of David's sons, 2 S 5^{14} (AV **Shammuah**), 1 Ch 14^{4} ; called **Shimea** in 1 Ch 3^{5}. **3.** A Levite, Neh 11^{17} ; called **Shemaiah** in 1 Ch 9^{16}. **4.** The head of a priestly family, Neh 12^{18}.

SHAMMUAH, 2 S 5^{14} (AV).—See SHAMMUA, **2.**

SHAMSHERAI.—A Benjamite, 1 Ch 8^{26}.

SHAPHAM.—A Gadite, 1 Ch 5^{12}.

SHAPHAN (' rock-badger ').—**1.** The secretary of Josiah in 621 B.C., who laid before the king the law-book discovered by Hilkiah (q.v.) in the Temple, 2 K 22^{3ff}, 2 Ch 34^{8ff}. Shaphan appears to have been the chief lay-leader in the execution of Josiah's reforms. His family for two following generations played a worthy part as servants of Yahweh, and friends of the prophet Jeremiah ; the Ahikam of 2 K 22^{12-14}, 2 Ch 34^{20-22} and Jer 26^{24}, the Gemariah of Jer $36^{12, 25}$, and Elasah of Jer 29^{3}, were Shaphan's sons ; the Micaiah of Jer 36^{11f}, and Gedaliah (q.v.), whom the Chaldaeans made governor of Judaea after the Captivity of 586 B.C., his grandsons. **2.** The ' Jaazaniah, son of Shaphan,' denounced in Ezk 8^{11} as ringleader in idolatry, was possibly, but not certainly, a son of the same Shaphan.

G. G. F.

SHAPHAT.—1. The Simeonite spy, Nu 13^{5}. **2.** The father of Elisha, 1 K $19^{16, 19}$, 2 K 3^{11} 6^{31}. **3.** A name in the royal genealogy of Judah, 1 Ch 3^{22}. **4.** A Gadite, 1 Ch 5^{12}. **5.** One of David's herdsmen, 1 Ch 27^{29}. **6.** A family which returned with Zerubbabel, 1 Es 5^{34} (AV **Sabat,** RV **Saphat**) ; omitted in the parallel list in Ezra and Nehemiah.

SHAPHER, Nu 33^{23f} (AV).—See SHEPHER.

SHAPHIR.—A city, probably on the Philistine plain, Mic 1^{11} (AV **Saphir**). It is probably modern *Kh. el-Kôm*, W. of Hebron.

SHARAI.—One of those who had married a foreign wife, Ezr 10^{40} ; omitted in the parallel list in 1 Es 9^{34}.

SHARAIM, Jos 15^{36} (AV).—See SHAARAIM.

SHARAR.—A Hararite (q.v.) mentioned in 2 S 23^{33} ; called **Sacher** (q.v.) in 1 Ch 11^{35}.

SHAREZER corresponds to Assyrian *Šar-uṣur*, which as a personal name is incomplete. **1.** In 2 K 19^{37} = Is 37^{38} Sharezer is a son of Sennacherib, who with **Adrammelech** (q.v.) murdered his father. The Assyrian records speak of only one son as the murderer of Sennacherib and do not name him. **2.** Sharezer appears in Zec 7^{2} (AV **Sherezer**), but there is a possibility that the full name here is Bethel-Sharezer, as in certain Non-Babylonian documents.

J. B. P.

SHARON.—1. *hash-shārôn*, literally ' the plain,' 1 Ch 27^{29}, Ca 2^{1}, Is 33^{9} 35^{2} 65^{10} ; Greek *ho Sarōn*, whence AV **Saron,** Ac 9^{35}. This is the great Maritime Plain extending from Jaffa, or a little S. of it, to Mount Carmel in the N. Though called a plain, it is of an undulating character, and was in parts, particularly towards the N., a forest of oaks (Is 35^{2}). Although but poorly cultivated, it has a great depth of rich soil and is capable of much development ; it yields annually a magnificent crop of beautiful wild flowers. It has always been a pasturage of flocks (1 Ch 27^{29}, Is 65^{10}). Around Ramleh and Ludd are forests of olives, and the orange gardens of Jaffa are too well known to need more than a passing reference ; wherever the hand of man has been diligent, there the soil has bounteously responded. Over a great part of the plain, especially near the sea, water may be tapped at no great depth. Its rivers are the marshy *Nahr ez-Zerqā* or Crocodile River, just below Carmel, *Nahr el-Mefjir*, *Nahr Iskanderûneh*, and *Nahr el-ʿAujā*, the last mentioned close to Jaffa. The chief town of Sharon was in ancient days Dor (Jos 11^{2}

12^{23}, 1 K 4^{11}), in NT times Caesarea, and in later Crusading times (1218–1291) the fortified port of Athlīt. In Jos 12^{18} **Lasharon** is mentioned as one of the royal cities of Canaan; as ' the king of ' is omitted in the original, the passage may read ' king of Aphek in the Sharon.' For ' rose of Sharon ' see Rose.

2. A second Sharon (*Saronas*) is mentioned by Eusebius and Jerome as between Mount Tabor and Tiberias, and this is to-day represented by the village of *Sārôna* in the *Arḍ el-Ḥamma* NE. of Tabor. This may be the place mentioned in Jos 12^{18} (see above).

3. The suburbs (RSV ' pasture lands ') of Sharon (1 Ch 5^{16}) are mentioned as among the possessions of Gad along with Gilead and Bashan. E. W. G. M.

SHARUHEN.—See Shaaraim, **2.**

SHASHAI.—One of the sons of Bani who had married a foreign wife, Ezr 10^{40}, 1 Es 9^{34} (AV, RV **Sesis**).

SHASHAK.—A Benjamite family, 1 Ch $8^{14,\,25}$.

SHAUL.—**1.** A king of Edom, Gn 36^{37f} (AV **Saul**), 1 Ch 1^{48f}. **2.** A son of Simeon, Gn 46^{10}, Ex 6^{15}, Nu 26^{13}, 1 Ch 4^{24}. The clan of which he is the eponym was of mixed Israelite and Canaanite descent, hence Shaul is called in Gn 46^{10} and Ex 6^{15} ' the son of the Canaanitess.' In Nu 26^{12} the patronymic **Shaulites** occurs. **3.** An ancestor of Samuel, 1 Ch 6^{24}; called **Joel** in v.^{36}.

SHAVEH, VALLEY OF.—A broad valley (*'ēmek*), known also as **the king's valley** (Gn 14^{17}), which was near Salem. Here Absalom set up a pillar or monument, 2 S 18^{18}. Shaveh was possibly the broad open head of the valley of Hinnom which, lower down, contracts to a ravine.

SHAVEH-KIRIATHAIM (' the plain of Kiriathaim ').—The place where the Emim were smitten by the allied kings from the E. Gn 14^{5} (AV **Shaveh-Kirjathaim**). It probably derived its name from **Kiriathaim, 1.**

SHAVSHA occurs in the list of David's officers in 1 Ch 18^{16} as secretary, an office made necessary by the growth of the court and relations with other states. His name, and the fact of his father's not being mentioned, make it probable that he was a foreigner chosen to deal with foreign correspondence. His name was evidently unfamiliar; in the list of 2 S 20^{25} it appears as **Sheva**; in that of 8^{15-18} (otherwise identical with Chronicles) **Seraiah** has been substituted; LXX varies greatly in all passages. It is generally held that *Shavsha* is correct. Apparently in Solomon's time he was succeeded by his sons (1 K 4^{3} **Shisha** being probably only another variation of the name). It has been suggested that the name is the equivalent of *Shamsha*, the Sun-god. C. W. E.

SHAWL.—See Wimple.

SHEAL.—One of those who had married a foreign wife, Ezr 10^{29}, 1 Es 9^{30} (AV **Jasael, RV Jasaelus**).

SHEALTIEL.—**1.** The father of Zerubbabel, Ezr 3^{28} 5^{2}, Neh 12^{1}, Hag 1^{1-12} etc., 1 Es $5^{5,\,48}$ etc. (AV, RV **Salathiel**), Mt 1^{12}, Lk 3^{37} (AV **Salathiel**). According to 1 Ch 3^{17}, Shealtiel was the eldest son of king Jeconiah. In v.^{19} the MT makes **Pedaiah** (a brother of Shealtiel) the father of Zerubbabel. **2.** Another name for Ezra, 2 Es 3^{1} (AV, RV **Salathiel**).

SHEARIAH.—A descendant of Saul, 1 Ch 8^{38} 9^{44}.

SHEARING-HOUSE, THE.—See Beth-Eked.

SHEAR-JASHUB (' a remnant shall return ').—A symbolical name given to a son of Isaiah to signify the return of the remnant to God after the punishment at the hands of the Assyrians, Is 7^{3}; cf 8^{18} 10^{20f} and 7^{14} 8^{1-4}.

SHEATH.—See Armour, Arms, **1** (*c*).

SHEBA.—Spelt differently from the geographical name. **1.** A rebel against David's return to power (2 S 20^{1ff}). Exponent of N. Israelite secession. His revolt was nipped by speedy action led by Joab and Abishai. He took refuge in Abel-beth-maacah (q.v.). The inhabitants escaped punishment by throwing his head over the wall. **2.** A Gadite (1 Ch 5^{13}). **3.** A supposed place in Jos 19^{2}, but an error for Shema (15^{26}). See Shema, **4.** J. T.—E. G. K.

SHEBA.—The ancient name for what is now the heart of Saudi-Arabia. (Not to be confused with **Seba** q.v.) According to the ancients four peoples inhabited S. Arabia: the **Minaeans** (q.v.), the **Sabaeans**, with capital at Mariaba (*Marib* near *Ṣan'ā*) the **Qatabanians** with capital Tamna, and the **Chathramothites** (Heb. Hazarmaveth, q.v.), or people of *Ḥadramaut*, with capital Shabata (see Strabo, xvi. iv. 2). The Sabaeans or people of Sheba were the most important of these in Strabo's time. They controlled the S. Arabian trade in frankincense, myrrh, cinnamon and other much desired articles, and being protected by remoteness and intervening deserts from rapacious powers, waxed rich thereby.

In OT Sheba is considered a descendant of Shem in younger materials of Yahwistic stratum (Gn 10^{28}) but of Ham in P (Gn 10^{7}; cf 1 Ch 1^{9}). They are considered sons of Keturah in Gn 25^{3}. The visit of the Queen of Sheba (see next article) to Solomon has glamourized the country's name. Aside from this the allusions to Sheba are all relatively late. Import of frankincense and cinnamon for the Jerusalem cult is mentioned by Jeremiah (6^{20}). The Sabaeans traded with Tyre, bringing spices, precious stones and gold (Ezk 27^{22}). Sheba is mentioned as a remote point in Ezk 38^{13}. Along with the Nabataeans they carried raids into Syria until the Roman conquest of the latter region (Strabo, xvi. iv. 21), an item illustrating Job 1^{15}. Their caravan trade is mentioned in Job 6^{19}; their slave-trade in Jl 4^{8}. They are among the Arabian peoples that will bring gold and frankincense to Jerusalem in the Messianic times (Is 60^{6}), and their kings will be tribute-bearers (Ps 72^{10}).

The Assyrian inscriptions provide what is probably the oldest testimony to Sheba's existence. Tiglath-pileser iii. (745–727 b.c.) records receiving tribute from It'amara king of the land of the Sabaeans. Sargon (721–705 b.c.) lists a king of that name as tributary. Under Sennacherib (704–681 b.c.) a *Karibīlu* of Sheba sent his present when the foundation of a *Bīt-akītu* was laid at Asshur.

Since the great expedition of Carsten Niebuhr (1761–1764) brought basic information about Arabia to Europe a number of explorers sought to penetrate into Yemen. The hostility and fanaticism of the people made this difficult. There are innumerable inscriptions there, written in characters resembling the Ethiopic (which was derived from the S. Arabian script), and some of these were copied or squeezes made of them. Great numbers of texts were obtained by Halévy (1869) and above all by Eduard Glaser (1882 f); many of the latter's are still unpublished. More recently the explorations of the *American Foundation for the Study of Man* under Wendell Phillips succeeded in doing some excavating at Marib in 1952, but the undertaking had to be abandoned very suddenly.

Yemen is superior to the rest of Arabia in climate and soil. The central district is a highland region with mountains attaining a height of some 8000 ft. above sea level. The air is comparatively cool. Ṣan'ā is on the southernmost of three great plateaux and Marib lies NE. of it between the rich valleys of the W. and Ḥadramaut. Particularly striking at Marib are the remains of a great dam, which burst about a.d. 450. Glaser published important inscriptions referring to the event. Photos of the remains of the dam were published by Ahmed Fakhri in his *An Archaeological Journey to Yemen* (pt. 3, 1951).

It has recently been recognized that the Sabaean kingdom antedates that of the Minaeans (contrary to the beliefs of Glaser and Hommel). There are three palaeographically distinct groups of inscriptions of the **Mukarribs** or priest-kings of the Sabaeans, all of which antedate 450 b.c. One may tentatively date the third group from 525–450 b.c., the second group with at least ten *mukarribs* from 675–525 b.c.; the first group in very archaic characters, with at least 5 *mukarribs* represented, from *c* 800 b.c. to 675 b.c. A radio-carbon date of charcoal, from a beam found in excavations at *Ḥajar bin-Ḥumeid* in the Western Aden Protectorate, helps to put a monogram on a storage jar in the script of the first group before 700 B.C.

It seems probable that the last king of the first group, *Karib'il Watar son of Dhimri'lay*, is the *Karibīlu* who sent presents to Sennacherib, because he built a *kutallum*, which is presumably a loan-word from Assyrian *bit kutalli*, 'arsenal.' Evidently the Sabaean king was impressed by the one that Sennacherib built. The It'amara of Sargon is probably his predecessor, as yet unrepresented by any inscription.

Most of the inscriptions of the *Mukarribs* are from *Ṣirwaḥ*. This seems to have been their residence. However, a new period of Sabaean history began about 525 B.C., contemporaneously with the rise of the Achaemenid empire. Marib now became the capital of the *kings* of Sheba (the *mukarrib* title is no longer used). In the Ptolemaic period sea-traffic between Egypt and India was opened up, and thereby the Sabaean position in the world of trade was damaged. The power over Sheba passed into the hands of the Himyarites, a tribe in the SW. corner of Arabia. The new rulers call themselves 'kings of Sheba and of Raidan' (the latter being their original centre). At this time, *c* 115 B.C., the kingdom of Qataban seems to have ceased. Some 26 Himyarite rulers are known from inscriptions, and the period lasted till about A.D. 300. In the year 26 B.C. a Roman expedition under Aelius Gallus was sent to subject the Sabaeans. He was a friend of the geographer Strabo, who reports in detail on the disastrous expedition (XVI. iv). Around this time, however, the Abyssinians—originally S. Arabians who had emigrated to Africa—established a foothold in S. Arabia, and soon came to have increased power. They seized control about A.D. 300, inaugurating a new period of Sabaean history. The rulers call themselves 'kings of Sheba and of Raidan, of Ḥadramaut and of Yemen.' After the destruction of Jerusalem by Titus in A.D. 70 great numbers of Jews came to S. Arabia. They made common cause with the Himyarites and ousted the Abyssinian rulers. A new Jewish-Sabaean kingdom was established, whose outstanding ruler was Dhu Nuwas. But the Christian Abyssinians of Africa, desiring to get control of the wealth of Sheba and enjoying the aid and support of the Eastern Roman empire, overthrew Dhu Nuwas in A.D. 525. The pagan elements in the country called in the Persians, who overthrew the Christian Dynasty in A.D. 575 and installed a Persian governor in Yemen. Half a century later Islam triumphed completely in Arabia and therewith Sabaean history ended.

The S. Arabian religion is of considerable interest to the student of the OT. The chief gods of Sheba were *Athtar* (male), *Haubas*, *Almakūhu* and *Shams* (female). The religion gives particular importance to the moon—Haubas being the Sabaean appellative for the deity as 'the drier' or regulator of the tides. In Ḥadramaut he is called *Sin*, as in Babylonia. The Minaeans call him *Wadd* 'friend,' the Qatabanians *'Amm* 'paternal uncle.' Very often he is *Ilu* 'the god,' and in personal names like *Ili-kariba* 'my god has blessed,' *Ili-rapa'a* 'my god has healed' the moon-god is meant. *'Ammi-yadi'a* 'my uncle knows,' *Abi-amara* 'my father has commanded,' *Sumuhu-kariba* 'his name has blessed,' provide further examples of appellatives for the moon-god. The last instance reminds of the use of Hebrew *shēm* 'name' as substitute for mention of Yahweh (cf Lv 24^{11-16}) or of the more frequent hypostasized use. The kinship of S. Arabian nomenclature with that of the Amorite First Dynasty of Babylon (cf *Sumu-abum*, *Ammi-ṣaduga*, etc.), as well as with Hebrew names, is noteworthy. Numerous cultic terms of the Hebrew have equivalents in the Sabaean inscriptions.

E. G. K.

SHEBA, QUEEN OF.—A visit of a Queen of Sheba to Solomon is narrated in 1 K 10^{1-13}. The narrative was no doubt drawn from the source mentioned in 1 K 11^{41}. Its popular nature is indicated by the fact that the name of the queen is forgotten and by the idea that she made her journey to ask questions of Wisdom of that wisest of potentates. A historical account would have mentioned her name and the more practical economic or political concerns that govern such visits of royalty. The inscriptions from **Sheba** (q.v.) have not as yet furnished any information going back to the 10th cent. B.C. Early Sabaean history shows the region under the rule of men bearing the title *mukarribs* or priest-kings. Future discoveries may of course vindicate the existence of an earlier stage of history in which queens reigned. Meanwhile, however, one may well ask whether the name Sheba was not used anachronistically here in an extended sense warranted in the story-teller's time, when Sheba's control extended far northward and included the areas in N. Arabia where queens are actually found ruling in the second half of the 8th cent. B.C., and so may already have reigned there in the 10th cent. We hear of *Samsî*, queen of Aribi, of *Zabibî* and of *Ya-ti-'i-e* in the days of Tiglath-pileser, Sargon and Sennacherib. A N. Arabian queen would have had good reason to negotiate with a ruler by-passing the trade-routes with ships sailing from Ezion-geber (1 K 9^{26}). The Koran (Sura 27^{22-45}) gives a variant of the Biblical story, but provides a name for the queen of Sheba, *Bilqis*, and mentions the Sabaean capital Marib. In his *Lives of the Prophets* Tha'labi gives a further development of the legend. The Abyssinian *Kebra Nagast* seeks to justify the right of a new dynasty that began A.D. 1270 with the claim that it was descended from Menelik, son of Solomon by the queen of Sheba, who is given the name Makeda. The 'fact' was allegedly communicated to the council of Nicaea by the Patriarch Demetrius of Constantinople. E. G. K.

SHEBAH, Gn 26^{33} (AV).—See SHIBAH.

SHEBAM, Nu 32^{3} (AV).—See SEBAM.

SHEBANIAH.—1. A Levitical family, Neh 9^{4f} 10^{10}. **2.** A priest or Levite who sealed the covenant, 10^{4} 12^{14}; see SHECANIAH, end. **3.** Another Levite who sealed the covenant, 10^{12}. **4.** A priest, 1 Ch 15^{24}.

SHEBARIM.—A place mentioned (Jos 7^{5}) in the description of the pursuit of the Israelites by the men of Ai. Its location is unknown.

SHEBAT.—See TIME.

SHEBER.—A son of Caleb, 1 Ch 2^{48}.

SHEBNA (in 2 K $18^{18, 26}$ **Shebnah**: short form of **Shebaniah**; meaning uncertain, possibly connected with 'protection').—An official of Hezekiah, described as the steward, 'Over the house' (cf 1 K 4^{6}), the subject of a denunciation by Isaiah (Is 22^{15-25}). In 2 K $18^{18, 26, 37}$ 19^{2} = Is $36^{3, 11, 22}$ 37^{2} he appears as 'scribe' or 'secretary' whereas **Eliakim** (q.v.) is described as 'Over the house.' This may indicate the degradation of Shebna (Is 22^{19f}) and his replacement by Eliakim. P. R. A.

SHEBNAH.—See SHEBNA.

SHEBUEL.—1. A son of Gershom, 1 Ch 23^{16} 26^{24}; called **Shubael**, which is probably the original form of the name, in 1 Ch 24^{20}. **2.** A son of Heman, 1 Ch 25^{4}; called **Shubael** in v.^{20}.

SHECANIAH (Yahweh has taken up his abode).—**1.** Chief of the tenth course of priests (1 Ch 24^{11}). **2.** A priest in the time of Hezekiah (2 Ch 31^{15}). **3.** A descendant of Zerubbabel (1 Ch 3^{21f}; cf Ezr 8^{3}, 1 Es 8^{29} [AV, RV **Sechenias**]), father of Shemaiah, a builder of the walls with Nehemiah (Neh 3^{29}). **4.** The father-in-law of Tobiah the Ammonite (Neh 6^{18}). **5.** An exile returning with Ezra (Ezr 8^{5}, Es 8^{32} [AV, RV **Sechenias**]). **6.** A contemporary of Ezra, Ezr 10^{2}, 1 Es 8^{92} (AV, RV **Jechonias**). Also a priest of the time of Zerubbabel (Neh 12^{3}), but some manuscripts have **Shebaniah** (cf Neh 10^{4} 12^{14} and also 9^{4f} $10^{11, 13}$). The AV form in all OT passages is **Shechaniah**. P. R. A.

SHECHANIAH.—1. 1 Ch 3^{21f}, Ezr 8^{3} (AV); see SHECANIAH, **3. 2.** Ezr 8^{5} (AV); see SHECANIAH, **5. 3.** Ezr 10^{2} (AV); see SHECANIAH, **6. 4.** Neh 3^{29} (AV);

see SHECANIAH, **3.** **5.** Neh 6^{18} (AV) ; see SHECANIAH, **4.** **6.** Neh 12^{3} (AV) ; see SHECANIAH, end.

SHECHEM.—1. The 'son' of Hamor (q.v.), Gn 33^{19} 34$^{2, 4}$. **2.** A Manassite clan, the **Shechemites,** Nu 26^{31} ; cf Jos 17^{2}, 1 Ch 7^{19}. **3.** See next article.

SHECHEM.—An important town of Israelite and pre-Israelite days at the E. end of the pass between Mount Ebal and Mount Gerizim, placed as the neck between the shoulders (cf *shᵉkhem*, 'shoulder'), it was specifically associated with Jacob (Gn 33^{18}), whose well (Jn 4^{12}) is still shown. It was the scene of the violent reprisals of the tribes Simeon and Levi before the former migrated to the S. and the latter lost political status in Israel (Gn 34). This phase of the Hebrew settlement may correspond to the activities of the *Ḥabiru* which the Amarna Tablets note in the district of Shechem. A further association with the Hebrew patriarchs is the burial of Joseph in the vicinity (Jos 24^{32}), this tradition being commemorated by the Moslem shrine to 'the Prophet Yussuf' by *Tell el-Balâṭah*, the ruins of Shechem. The name ('Mound of the Oak') may perpetuate the tradition of the sacred tree under which Jacob buried his teraphim, or household images (Gn 35^{4}). Shechem, with its temple of Baal Berith, 'Lord of the Covenant' (Jg 9^{4}), and as the scene of Joshua's covenant with Israel (Jos 24), and with its status as a Levitical city of refuge (Jos 20^{7}), played an important part in Israelite religion. It is plausibly argued by M. Noth that it was the scene of the regular periodic recitation of the law in solemn assembly and of a renewal of God's covenant with Israel, which is the source of the narrative in Jos 24. No doubt Shechem played a much more prominent rôle in Israel than is immediately apparent, this having been obscured first by the concentration of the cult in Jerusalem under David and Solomon, second because of the predominance of Judahite tradition in the OT, and lastly because of the enmity of orthodox Judaism to the Samaritan sect. Noth's thesis is supported by the fact that on the death of Solomon Rehoboam met all Israel at Shechem, when the disruption of the kingdom was effected (1 K 12^{1}). Shechem was also the first capital of N. Israel after the Disruption (1 K 12^{25}). Even after the Hebrew occupation Shechem continued to be a stronghold of Canaanite influence and was the scene of the abortive attempt at kingship by Abimelech the son of Gideon by a local Canaanite woman (Jg 9).

Excavations at *Tell el-Balâṭah,* begun before the First World War, and continued at intervals since, have been again resumed under G. E. Wright, who has found traces of settlement from before *c* 3000 until the 2nd cent. B.C. There was a definite recession in the life of the city from about the 9th cent. to the 4th cent., no doubt because of the shifting of the capital to Tirzah in the vicinity of Shechem and then to Samaria, but Jeremiah (41^{5}) indicates that after 586 B.C. there was still an orthodox Israelite community at Shechem. It is significant that there was apparently no destruction of Shechem corresponding to the destruction of Hazor, *Tell Beit Mirsim, Tell ed-Duweir* (Lachish), and Bethel about the beginning of the Iron Age, a fact which indicates that Israelite elements had effected a symbiosis with the local Canaanites before the final phase of the Israelite occupation, as the Jacob tradition in Genesis suggests. In the Christian era occupation shifted slightly westward, especially with the foundation of *Flavia Neapolis* after A.D. 70, the name of which survives in *Nâblus*, a vigorous centre of political and religious life in Jordan. Here there is a small native Christian community and a few hundred survivors of the Samaritan sect with a modest new synagogue on the slopes of Mount Gerizim, on the summit of which they still hold their annual Passover, with slaughter of lambs, which has fallen into desuetude in orthodox Judaism. J. Gr.

SHEDEUR.—A Reubenite, father of Elizur, Nu 1^{5} 2^{10} 7$^{30, 35}$ 10^{18}.

SHEEP.—The generic term for 'flocks,' *sôn* in Hebrew, *probaton* in Greek, includes both sheep and goats (q.v.), and the word for a single sheep, as for a single goat, in Hebrew is *śeh*. But we have, for sheep, at least five Hebrew words and three Greek, which indicate different ages and sexes—ram, ewe, lamb, young suckling lamb, yearling for sacrifice.

The usual Palestinian sheep is the fat-tailed *ovis laticaudata*, a rather small animal but sturdy, with wavy fleece, a high, curved nose and broad, flopping ears. Its main feature is the tail, and though Herodotus' remark that the tail extends to three cubits or more is overdone, the rumps hanging in the butchers' stalls in Jordanian Jerusalem to-day weigh up to 8 or 10 lbs. That, of course, is the explanation for the broad tail—it is a mass of fat which spreads over the whole rump and down to the caudal extremity and then turns back on it like an appendix. This is the *'alyāh*, which is designated (cf Ex 29^{22}, Lv 3^{9} 7^{3} 8^{25} 9^{19} ; and probably 1 S 9^{24}) as the choice bit for sacrifice to the deity or hospitality for the guest. The rest of the carcase looks very meagre.

The shepherd was ever a heroic figure, and, though a nomad, he was cultured and very well versed in country lore. He was responsible for finding pasturage, and wandered, with his family, over the barren country-side of Palestine—sometimes for many miles. He lived in a tent made of sheets woven from goat-hair. Gn 31^{39f} gives a picture of the hazards of shepherding, and other passages (*e.g.* Job 1^{16}), and the frequent mention of marauding bands and wild beasts fill out the picture. The shepherd's rod and staff were for defence as well as for counting the sheep when they were folded, and the sling, too, was expertly used. The ability to throw a well-aimed stone was useful to head off a straying sheep, but on one occasion in 1947 a boy missed his aim, and the stone fell into a cave and resulted in the discovery of the Dead Sea Scrolls ! E. W. G. M.—**B. J. R.**

SHEEP GATE.—See JERUSALEM, GATES OF.

SHEEPCOTE.—Found in AV and RV in 2 S 7^{8}, 1 Ch 17^{7} (RSV 'pasture') and in 1 S 24^{3} (RSV 'sheepfold').

SHEERAH.—A daughter of Ephraim, 1 Ch 7^{24} (AV **Sherah**). She built the two Beth-horons and **Uzzen-sheerah** (q.v.).

SHEET.—See DRESS, **4** (*d*).

SHEHARIAH.—A Benjamite, 1 Ch 8^{26}.

SHEKEL.—See MONEY, WEIGHTS AND MEASURES, III.

SHEKINAH (from Heb. *shākhan* 'to dwell' meaning 'dwelling' [abstract] or 'that which dwells').—The word is not found in OT, but occurs often in other Jewish literature, always of God. The OT, particularly in certain of its writings, uses 'anthropomorphisms' freely, *e.g.* it speaks of God dwelling in a place or being seen. Later thought objected to this, as materializing the Divine nature ; hence in the Targums (Aram. paraphrases of the OT used, though not in their present form, by the 1st cent. A.D.) various devices were adopted to prevent popular misunderstandings. Paraphrases were used for the Divine name, 'the Word' (mêmrā'), 'Spirit,' or 'Wisdom' being substituted. One of the most important of these was 'the Shekinah.' 'God dwells' usually became 'the Shekinah rests' ; 'the Temple of God' became 'the house of S.' (note the Tabernacle was the *mishkān*, from the same root). Gn 28^{16} becomes 'the glory of the S. of Y″ is in this place' ; Is 6^{5} 'my eyes have seen the glory of the S. of the King of the world.' God's hiding His face is the removal of the S. Now the presence of God (especially in P and related writings) was often manifested by a fiery appearance, or a light in a cloud. It was so in nature (Ps 18^{11f}), on Sinai (Ex 24^{16}), in the wilderness and in the Tabernacle (16^{7} 29^{43} 40^{34}, Nu 14^{10}), in the Temple (1 K 8^{11}) ; cf Ezk 1^{28} etc. This glory was not God, but an effluence from Him, or from His Shekinah. For the S. was not 'the glory,' as is usually imagined, but the source and centre of it. It is a stage nearer to God Himself and, though often used in connexion with the physical manifestation, represents an invisible and universal presence. *E.g.* it is the source

of inspiration. Eli failed to recognize Hannah's condition because it had left him. It was present where three were gathered to administer justice. According to some it was inseparable from Israel, still hovering over the W. wall of the Temple. But it was commonly taught that it had always been absent from the second Temple, as had been 'the glory' (but cf Ezk 11^{23} 43^{2}); or again, that on the successive sins of Adam and his descendants it had been withdrawn from earth to the first heaven, and finally to the seventh. The conception, in fact, varied. It was disputed whether it was an entity distinct from God, or only the essence of God as manifested. Though at first regarded as impersonal and passive, as distinct from the Memra, the agent of creation, in the Talmud it becomes active and takes the place of the latter. The tendency to personification is significant. Insisting one-sidedly on the transcendence or aloofness of God, the Jew had to bring Him to earth again by such mediatorial agencies, which were semi-personal and Divine, but not God, and by the development of an elaborate angelology. In the NT the word '**glory**' seems often to refer to the Shekinah (cf Eth. Enoch 'Lord of glory' and 'the Great Glory,' as titles of God). Ro 9^{4} speaks of 'the glory' as a Jewish privilege; He 9^{5} of 'the cherubim of glory.' It was believed that the Shekinah would return with the Messiah; 'the glory of the Lord and the cloud will appear' (2 Mac 2^{8}). (*a*) It is connected with Christ (Lk 2^{9}, Mt 17^{5}; cf 2 P 1^{17} RVm and RSV, where the Shekinah is personified). In 1 P 4^{14} 'the spirit of glory' rests upon Christ, as upon the Tabernacle; in He 1^{3} He is 'the effulgence (RV; AV 'express image') of the glory' (RSV 'He reflects the glory'); in Ja 2^{1} He is apparently called 'the Shekinah.' Of special significance is Jn 1^{14}, which combines the expressions 'glory' and 'tabernacle' (Gr. *skēnoun*, probably intentionally chosen to represent 'Shekinah,' as in Rev 21^{3}). It connects the personal presence of God in Christ with the earlier presence in the Tabernacle; what was formerly symbol is now manifest 'in flesh.' The vagueness of the Jewish conception gives place to the definite presence of the personal Christ. Cf with Mt 18^{20} and 1 Co 11^{11}, sayings such as 'when two sit together and are occupied with the words of the Law, the Shekinah is with them,' or 'the man is not without the woman, nor the woman without the man, nor both of them without the Shekinah.' (*b*) It is connected with the Christian. The first of the six things lost by Adam was 'the glory,' *i.e.* the reflection upon him of the Divine glory, or perfection. Of this we fall short (Ro 3^{23}), but it is in process of being recovered by the Christian (5^{2} 8$^{18, 30}$, 2 Co 3^{18} 4^{6}; cf 2 Es 7^{97f}).
C. W. E.

SHELAH.—1. The youngest son of Judah by Shua, Gn 38$^{5, 11, 14, 26}$ 46^{12}, Nu 26^{20}, 1 Ch 2^{3} 4^{21}. The gentilic **Shelanites** occurs in Nu 26^{20}. Perhaps 'the Shelanite' should be read also for 'the **Shilonite**' in Neh 11^{5}, 1 Ch 9^{5}. **2.** The son of Arpachshad, Gn 10^{24} 11$^{13-15}$ (AV **Salah**), 1 Ch 1$^{18, 24}$, Lk 3^{35} (AV **Sala**). **3.** Neh 3^{15}; see SILOAM.

SHELEMIAH.—1. 2. Two of the sons of Bani, who married a 'strange' wife, Ezr 10$^{39, 41}$, 1 Es 9^{34} (AV, RV **Selemias**). **3.** Father of Hananiah, Neh 3^{30}. **4.** A priest, Neh 13^{13}. **5.** The father of Jehucal or Jucal, Jer 37^{3} 38^{1}. **6.** The father of Irijah, Jer 37^{13}. **7.** 1 Ch 26^{14}. See MESHELEMIAH. **8.** Ancestor of Jehudi, Jer 36^{14}. **9.** Son of Abdeel, Jer 36^{26}.

SHELEPH.—A son of Joktan, and therefore a tribe in Southern Arabia, Gn 10^{26}, 1 Ch 1^{20}. It has not been identified.

SHELESH.—An Asherite, 1 Ch 7^{35}.

SHELOMI.—Father of an Asherite prince, Nu 34^{27}.

SHELOMITH.—1. The mother of the man who was stoned to death for having blasphemed 'the Name,' Lv 24^{11}. **2.** Daughter of Zerubbabel, 1 Ch 3^{19}. **3.** One of the sons of Izhar, 1 Ch 23^{18}; called **Shelomoth** in 24^{22}. **4.** A son of Rehoboam, 2 Ch 11^{20}. **5.** A family which returned with Ezra, Ezr 8^{10}, 1 Es 8^{36} (AV **Assalimoth**, RV **Salimoth**). **6.** 1 Ch 26$^{25f, 28}$ (AV); see SHELOMOTH, **2. 7.** 1 Ch 23^{9} (AV); see SHELOMOTH, **3.**

SHELOMOTH.—1. See SHELOMITH, **3. 2.** A descendant of Moses, 1 Ch 26$^{25f, 28}$ (AV **Shelomith**). **3.** A Gershonite, 1 Ch 23^{9} (AV **Shelomith**).

SHELUMIEL.—Prince of the tribe of Simeon, Nu 1^{4} 2^{12} 7$^{36, 41}$ 10^{19}. See also SHEMUEL.

SHEM.—One of the three sons of Noah (Gn 5^{32}). The meaning of the word in Hebrew is 'name'; it also has the secondary meaning 'renown,' (cf Gn 6^{4}, *b^{e}nê shēm*, 'men of renown'). In the J genealogy of Shem he is the ancestor of Eber the eponymous ancestor of the Hebrews, and ultimately the ancestor of Abraham. For the Yahwist the line of Divine purpose descends through Seth, Shem, and Eber to Abraham. According to the P genealogy the 'sons' of Shem are Elam, Asshur, Arpachshad, Lud, and Aram, representing an ancient Hebrew tradition of the territorial distribution of peoples to the NE. of Palestine. Of these only two Asshur and Aram, are Semitic-speaking peoples, and Arpachshad and Lud cannot be identified with certainty. The designation Semite is derived from the name Shem.
S. H. He.

SHEMA' (Heb.—*Hear*).—The watchword of Jewish monotheism derived from the opening word of Dt 6^{4}, 'Hear, O Israel: The Lord our God, the Lord is one.' It consists of three sections: Dt 6$^{4-9}$ 11$^{13-21}$, Nu 15$^{37-41}$. Together with the Decalogue, it served as the core of Jewish worship at the Temple in pre-Christian times (Mishnah, *Tamid*, v. 1; cf W. F. Albright, 'The Nash Papyrus,' *JBL*, 1937, pp. 145–176), and was carried by itself into the reconstructed morning and evening liturgy of the Synagogue for public and private use (Mishnah *Berakoth*, i. 1–2). Affirming the unity of God, it has served as the Jewish confession of faith (cf Mk 12^{29f}) in the face of polytheism and Persian dualism against which Is 45^{7} protested. Its recitation morning and evening may have been stimulated by the Persian practice to hail the sun at its rising and setting (*Sacred Books of the East, Avesta*, II. p. 351; *Pahlavi Texts*, I. 156 ff). The benedictions, preceding and following its recitation, praised God as Creator, as giver of the Law and as redeemer. See SYNAGOGUE, **2** (*b*). S. S. C.

SHEMA.—1. A Reubenite, 1 Ch 5^{8}. See SHIMEI, **5. 2.** One of those who put to flight the inhabitants of Gath, 1 Ch 8^{13}; called **Shimei** (see SHIMEI, **14**) in v.^{21}. **3.** One of those who stood at Ezra's right hand, at the reading of the Law, Neh 8^{4}, 1 Es 9^{43} (AV, RV **Sammus**). **4.** A town of Judah, situated in the Negeb, Jos 15^{26}; called **Sheba** (see SHEBA, **4**) in 19^{2}. The site is unknown. It is probably this Shema that appears in 1 Ch 2^{43} as a 'son' of Hebron.

SHEMAAH.—A Benjamite, 1 Ch 12^{3}.

SHEMAIAH ('Y″ has heard').—**1.** The prophet who with Ahijah encouraged the revolution of the ten tribes from Jeroboam. In MT he appears after the revolution has begun (1 K 12$^{22-24}$, 2 Ch 11$^{2-4}$). In the second LXX account, however, he appears at the beginning, at the assembly in Shechem (1 K 12^{24o}). He is mentioned further in 2 Ch 12$^{5-8}$, and his history in 12^{15}. **2.** Son of Shecaniah, descendant of Zerubbabel, 1 Ch 3^{22}. **3.** Son of Shecaniah, 'keeper of the East Gate,' and assistant to Nehemiah in repairing the wall, Neh 3^{29}. **4.** A Simeonite, 1 Ch 4^{37}; perhaps **Shimei** of vv.^{26f}. **5.** A Reubenite, 1 Ch 5^{4}. **6.** A Merarite Levite dwelling in Jerusalem, 1 Ch 9^{14}, Neh 11^{15}. **7.** A Levite of the family of Jeduthun, 1 Ch 9^{16}; called **Shammua** (see SHAMMUA, **3**) in Neh 11^{17}. **8.** Head of the Levitical Kohathite clan of Elizaphan in the time of David, 1 Ch 15$^{8, 11}$. **9.** The scribe who registered the names of the priestly courses in the time of David, son of Nethanel, 1 Ch 24^{6}. **10.** A Korahite Levite, oldest son of Obed-edom, 1 Ch 26$^{4, 6f}$. **11.** A Levite, teacher of the Law in Judah under Jehoshaphat, 2 Ch 17^{8}. **12.** A Levite of the family of Jeduthun, engaged in purifying the Temple under Hezekiah, 2 Ch 29^{14}. **13.** A Levite 'over the freewill offerings of God,' 2 Ch 31^{15}. **14.** A chief of the Levites, 2 Ch 35^{9}, 1 Es 1^{9} (AV, RV **Samaias**). **15.** A chief man under Ezra, Ezr 8^{16}, 1 Es 8^{44} (AV **Mamaias**, RV **Samaias**). **16.** One of the family of Adonikam, Ezr 8^{13}, 1 Es 8^{39} (AV, RV **Samaias**). **17.** A priest of the family of Harim who married a foreign wife, Ezr 10^{21}, 1 Es 9^{21} (AV **Sameius**, RV **Sameus**). **18.** A layman of the family of Harim who did the same, Ezr 10^{31}; perhaps the same as **Sabbaias** in 1 Es 9^{32} (AV, RV **Sabbeus**). **19.** A prophet, son of Delaiah, hired by Sanballat and Tobiah to terrify Nehemiah, Neh 6^{10-14}. **20.** A priest who sealed the covenant, Neh 10^{8} $12^{6,18}$. **21.** A man present at the dedication of the wall, Neh 12^{34}. **22.** A priest, descendant of Asaph, Neh 12^{35}. **23.** A singer who took part in the dedication of the wall, Neh 12^{36}. **24.** Another, or perhaps the same, Neh 12^{42}. **25.** Father of Uriah the prophet, Jer 26^{20}. **26.** A prophet, called 'the Nehelamite' (q.v.), carried into captivity at Babylon with Jehoiachin, actively engaged in opposing Jeremiah, Jer 29^{24-32}. Jeremiah predicted the complete cutting off of his family. **27.** Father of Delaiah, who was a prince in the reign of Zedekiah, Jer 36^{12}. **28.** 'The great,' kinsman of Tobias, To 5^{13} (AV **Samaias**). **29.** One who had married a foreign wife, 1 Es 9^{34} (AV, RV **Samatus**); perhaps the same as SHALLUM, **12.** In several cases two of these may be the same individual. The identification has the most probability in reference to **2** and **3**, **8** and **9**, and **12** and **13**. G. R. B.

SHEMARIAH.—**1.** A Benjamite who joined David at Ziklag, 1 Ch 12^{5}. **2.** A son of Rehoboam, 2 Ch 11^{19}. **3. 4.** Two men who had married foreign wives, Ezr $10^{32,41}$.

SHEMEBER.—King of Zeboiim, Gn 14^{2}.

SHEMED.—See SHEMER, **4.**

SHEMER.—**1.** The owner of the hill purchased by Omri, 1 K 16^{24}. **2.** A Merarite, 1 Ch 6^{46} (AV **Shamer**). **3.** An Asherite, 1 Ch 7^{34} (AV **Shamer**); called **Shomer** in v.^{32}. **4.** A Benjamite, 1 Ch 8^{12} (AV **Shamed**; RV, RSV **Shemed**). The Hebrew MSS show here some confusion between *r* and *d* as the final letter of the name, though the majority have *r*. The ancient versions favour *d*.

SHEMIDA.—A 'son' of Gilead, according to Nu 26^{32}; called a 'son' of Manasseh in Jos 17^{2}; his descendants are enumerated in 1 Ch 7^{19} (AV **Shemidah**). The gentilic name **Shemidaites** occurs in Nu 26^{32}.

SHEMIDAH, 1 Ch 7^{19} (AV).—See SHEMIDA.

SHEMINITH.—See PSALMS, **2.**

SHEMIRAMOTH.—A Levitical family, 1 Ch $15^{18,20}$ 16^{5}, 2 Ch 17^{8}.

SHEMONEH ESREH.—See APOSTASY, SYNAGOGUE, **2.**

SHEMUEL.—**1.** The Simeonite appointed to assist in the dividing of the land, Nu 34^{20}. It is not improbable that the MT should be corrected to **Shelumiel** (q.v.). **2.** Grandson of Issachar, 1 Ch 7^{2}. **3.** 1 Ch 6^{33} (AV); see SAMUEL (so RV, RSV; cf 1 S 1^{1} 8^{2}).

SHEN ('the tooth' or 'crag').—Named in AV, RV in 1 S 7^{12} with Mizpah; but RSV amends the text to read **Jeshanah** (q.v.).

SHENAZ(Z)AR.—See SHESHBAZZAR.

SHEOL.—In OT the abode of the dead, the equivalent of the classical **Hades.** The derivation of the word is uncertain. AV translates it as 'grave,' **'hell,'** or occasionally 'pit'; RSV consistently reads 'Sheol' (in NT 'Hades').

Though the ancient Israelites had no doctrine of a future life, they did not think of death as extinction. Like the Semites generally, they believed that the dead passed into Sheol, where they continued to pursue a conscious, but pale and inactive existence. Sheol was thought of as in the underworld (Nu 16^{30ff}, Am 9^{2}), sometimes as if it were a huge grave where worms destroy the body (Is 14^{4ff}; cf v.^{11}). All men without distinction go there (Job 3^{11ff}). One's loved ones do not return from there, but there one must eventually join them (2 S 12^{23}). Hebrews looked upon Sheol with horror as a place without hope or communion with God (Ps 6^{5} 88^{4f}, Is 38^{18}). Though popular belief held that the dead could be brought back through necromancy (1 S 28), Israel's normative faith censured such practices (Dt 18^{9ff}, Is 8^{19}).

But inequality in this life made the lack of a doctrine of future awards a theological problem with which men increasingly wrestled. There were those who were confident that Yahweh rules also in Sheol and would vindicate them even there (Ps 139^{8} 49^{14f} 73^{23f}, Job 19^{25ff}). In a few late passages (Is 26^{19}, Dn 12^{2}) we see the beginnings of the notion of liberation from Sheol through resurrection, in the latter a selective resurrection both of righteous and wicked to bliss and to shame respectively. Belief in resurrection established itself among the Jews, although even in NT times the Sadducees rejected it. In late literature there is considerable speculation about Sheol: *e.g.* in 1 En 22^{1-14}, where Sheol is divided into compartments—for the righteous, for sinners who have gone unpunished on earth, and for sinners who have suffered somewhat. But Judaism had no consistent doctrine on the subject.

In NT the whole concept is transfigured in the light of the resurrection of Christ. His body did not see corruption in Hades (Ac 2^{31}); He has 'the keys of Death and Hades' (Rev 1^{18}). Yet the notion of Sheol as the abode of the dead pending the judgment continued. Dives suffers torment in Hades (Lk 16^{23}) while Lazarus rests in Abraham's bosom (NT, however, usually expresses punishment by **Gehenna**). Christ preached 'to the spirits in prison,' *i.e.* in Sheol (1 P 3^{19}). And in the end Death and Hades will yield their dead to the last judgment and themselves be destroyed (Rev 20^{13f}). J. Br.

SHEPHAM.—A place on the eastern boundary of the Promised Land, Nu 34^{10f}. The site has not been identified. Perhaps Zabdi, the **Shiphmite** (1 Ch 27^{27}) was a native of Shepham.

SHEPHATHIAH, 1 Ch 9^{8} (AV).—See SHEPHATIAH, **5.**

SHEPHATIAH ('Y" has judged').—**1.** One of David's sons, 2 S 3^{4}, 1 Ch 3^{3}. **2.** A family which returned with Zerubbabel, Ezr 2^{4}, Neh 7^{9}, 1 Es 5^{9} (AV, RV **Saphat**); also with Ezra, Ezr 8^{8}, 1 Es 8^{34} (AV, RV **Saphatias**). **3.** A family of the 'sons of Solomon's servants,' Ezr 2^{57}, Neh 7^{59}, 1 Es 5^{33} (AV, **Sapheth**, RV **Saphuthi**). **4.** A Judahite family, Neh 11^{4}. **5.** A Benjamite family, 1 Ch 9^{8} (AV **Shephathiah**). Either this or the preceding should perhaps be identified with **2** above. **6.** A contemporary of Jeremiah, Jer 38^{1}. **7.** A Benjamite warrior who joined David at Ziklag, 1 Ch 12^{5}. **8.** A Simeonite prince, 1 Ch 27^{16}. **9.** A son of Jehoshaphat, 2 Ch 21^{2}.

SHEPHELAH.—See PLAIN (5).

SHEPHER.—A stopping-place on the wanderings, Nu 33^{23f} (AV **Shapher**). It is possibly modern *Jebel 'Arâyif en-Nâqah*, S. of Kadesh.

SHEPHERD.—See SHEEP.

SHEPHI (1 Ch 1^{40}) or **SHEPHO** (Gn 36^{23}).—A Horite chief.

SHEPHUPHAM.—See MUPPIM. The gentilic **Shuphamites** is found in Nu 26^{39}.

SHEPHUPHAN.—See MUPPIM.

SHERAH, 1 Ch 7^{24} (AV).—See SHEERAH.

SHEREBIAH.—One of the Levites who joined Ezra (Ezr $8^{18,24}$, Neh 8^{7} 9^{4} $10^{12\ (\text{Heb. } 13)}$ $12^{8,24}$, 1 Es 8^{47} (AV **Asebebia**, RV **Asebebias**) ^{54} (AV **Esebrias**, RV **Eserebias**) 9^{48} (AV, RV **Sarabias**). See MAHLI.

SHERESH.—A Manassite clan, 1 Ch 7^{16}.

SHEREZER, Zec 7^{2} (AV).—See SHAREZER, **2.**

SHERIFF.—In Dn 3^{2f} 'sheriffs' is the AV and RV translation of Aramaic *tiphtāyē* (RSV 'magistrate').

SHESHACH.—A cryptic name of Babel found in the received text of Jer 25^{26} 51^{41} (AV, RV, RSVm; RSV substitutes 'Babylon'). It is formed by the method called Atbash, that is a substitution of *taw* for *aleph*, *shin* for *beth*, and so on. The word is, however, no part of the original text of Jeremiah, being a conceit of later editors. In both passages it is lacking in LXX. Cf LEB-KAMAI. J. F. McC.

SHESHAI.—A clan resident in Hebron, driven thence by Caleb, Nu 13[22], Jos 15[14], Jg 1[10].

SHESHAN.—A Jerahmeelite, 1 Ch 2[31, 34f].

SHESHBAZZAR.—This name is of Babylonian origin, most probably corresponding to Šin-ab-uṣur 'May Sin (moon-god) protect the father.' The name appears in various forms in LXX, and on the basis of some of these an alternative explanation connects it with the sun-god Šamaš, *i.e.* Šamaš-apla-uṣur. Sheshbazzar is described as 'the prince of Judah' and is said to have received from Cyrus' treasurer the sacred Temple vessels and to have taken them to Jerusalem (Ezr 1[8, 11] = 1 Es 2[12, 15]). These statements are repeated in Ezr 5[14] in the letter sent to Darius enquiring into the authority for rebuilding the Temple. Here Sheshbazzar is said to have been made governor (*peḥāh*) by Cyrus. He is also said to have laid the foundation of the Temple (Ezr 5[16]; cf 1 Es 6[18, 20]). The Persian title 'Tirshatha' ('Governor') in Ezr 2[63], Neh 7[65, 70] may refer to Sheshbazzar.

Since Ezr 3[8] describes Zerubbabel as laying the foundation of the Temple, Sheshbazzar and **Zerubbabel** have been identified by some scholars. The same person might bear two names (cf 2 K 23[34] 24[17], Dn 1[7]). But a comparison of Ezr 3[8] and 5[16], together with consideration of the intervening material, does not suggest that the two men are one and the same. In Ezr 4[4f, 24]—though there is clearly some confusion in the passage—it appears that such work as was begun by Sheshbazzar was then interrupted. The work began again in the time of Darius I. (cf Haggai) and Zerubbabel was then the governor. Either Sheshbazzar was responsible at the earlier period, under Cyrus, and Zerubbabel at the later—in which case Ezr 3[8] is merely a duplicate of 5[2]—or Zerubbabel was the actual builder at both periods and the work is attributed to Sheshbazzar in 5[16] because he was the governor. The latter would not be unnatural in an official report, though what the letter to Darius purports to record is the words of the Jewish leaders of whom Zerubbabel was presumably one; but it is strange that no reference is made to his own part in the earlier work. It is very probable that the Chronicler has confused the traditions concerning the two periods. The identifying of the two as different names of the same person is also improbable. In Dn 1[7] one name is Hebrew, and the other foreign, *i.e.* Daniel and Belteshazzar, whereas both Zerubbabel and Sheshbazzar are Babylonian names. The double naming of kings (as in 2 K 23, 24) may indicate the use of throne-names in Israel.

Sheshbazzar is likely to have been a Jew bearing a Babylonian name. He may be identical with **Shenazzar** of 1 Ch 3[18] (AV **Shenazar**), a son of Jehoiachin and uncle of Zerubbabel; and this would justify the title of 'a prince of Judah' given to him in Ezr 1[8]. The appointment of two men of the family of David as governors is exceedingly probable, but the family relationship again makes most probable the suggestion that Sheshbazzar belongs to the period of Cyrus and Zerubbabel to that of Darius I. W. F. B.—**P. R. A.**

SHETH.—'The sons of Sheth' are mentioned only in Nu 24[17] (AV, RVm, RSV), but RV translates the name 'sons of tumult.' A proper name is more in place as a parallel to Moab, but scarcely one so little known as Sheth. Albright identifies with the *Šwtw* of the Egyptian execration texts (*BASOR* 83, 1941, 34). For Sheth, 1 Ch 1[1] (AV), see SETH.

SHETHAR.—One of the seven princes who had the right of access to the royal presence Est 1[14].

SHETHAR-BOZENAI.—One of those who corresponded with Darius about the re-building of the Temple, Ezr 5[3, 6] 6[6, 13]; called **Sathrabuzanes** in 1 Es 6[3, 7, 27] 7[1].

SHETHAR-BOZNAI.—AV form of **Shethar-bozenai** (q.v.).

SHEVA.—**1.** A son of Caleb, 1 Ch 2[49]. **2.** See SHAVSHA.

SHEWBREAD.—See SHOWBREAD.

SHIBAH.—A name given to a well dug by Isaac, Gn 26[33] (AV **Shebah**); it gave its name to the town **Beersheba** (q.v.). The word means, according to the writer, 'an oath'; and *Beersheba* is 'the well of the oath,' so named from the swearing of the oath of friendship between Isaac and Abimelech, Gn 26[31]. In Gn 21[22–31] we have another account, according to which the well was dug by Abraham and received its name from the oath between Abraham and Abimelech. There is also a play on the word *shᵉbhûʿāh*, 'oath' and *shebhaʿ*, 'seven,' as a sacrifice of seven lambs was offered. Perhaps the name, however, was already in existence before Abraham's time, and the writer simply gives a more or less plausible explanation of the derivation. W. F. B.

SHIBBOLETH.—**1.** 'Ear of corn,' **2.** 'stream.' The only important occurrence of the word is in Jg 12[1–6] where, regardless of its meaning and on account of its initial sibilant alone, it serves as a test-word to distinguish between fugitive Ephraimites and Jephthah's revengeful Gileadites at the Jordan crossing. Commentators have mainly supposed that the dialectical differentiation was that the W.-Jordanian Ephraimites said, 'Sibboleth,' for 'Shibboleth'; but E. A. Speiser (*BASOR* 85 [1942]) has shown grounds for attributing the 'abnormality,' in fact, to the E.-Jordanian Gileadites, who pronounced the word in a 'non-Israelite' way, with an initial '*th*.' In either case the result was the same: exposure and execution of the heteroglot Ephraimites—though hardly 42,000 as the story now relates.
W. O. E. O—**D. R. Ap-T.**

SHIBMAH, Nu 32[38] (AV).—See SEBAM.

SHICRON, Jos 15[11] (AV).—See SHIKKERON.

SHIELD.—See ARMOUR, ARMS, **2** (*a*).

SHIGGAION.—See PSALMS.

SHIGIONOTH.—See PSALMS, **2.**

SHIHON, Jos 19[19] (AV).—See SHION.

SHIHOR in Is 23[3] (AV **Sihor**), Jer 2[18] (AV **Sihor**, RSV 'the Nile') seems to mean Egypt (?), the Nile (?), or the waters of Egypt; in Jos 13[3] (AV **Sihor**), 1 Ch 13[5], it is the SW. frontier of Canaan. If the name is Hebrew it may mean 'the Black,' in allusion to the dark waters or even to the black alluvial land itself: the Egyptian name of Egypt is *Kemi*, meaning 'black.' But, as Brugsch pointed out, *Shi-Ḥōr* is the Egyptian name of a stream or canal, possibly the Pelusiac branch of the Nile, on or near the eastern border of Egypt (see SHUR). The black alluvium might well be counted as the boundary of Canaan; but elsewhere the boundary is 'the Brook' (or 'River') of Egypt, *i.e.* the *Wâdī el-ʿArîsh.*

SHIHOR-LIBNATH.—One of the boundaries of Asher, Jos 19[26]. It stands apparently for a river, most probably the *Nahr ez-Zerqā*, the Crocodile River.

SHIKKERON.—A place on the northern boundary of Judah, Jos 15[11] (AV **Shicron**). The site is unknown.

SHILHI.—Father of Asa's wife, 1 K 22[42], 2 Ch 20[31].

SHILHIM.—A town of Judah, Jos 15[32]: probably the same as the Simeonite **Shaaraim** (q.v.).

SHILLEM, SHILLEMITES.—See SHALLUM, **7.**

SHILOAH.—See SILOAM.

SHILOH.—**1.** Here the Israelites are said to have assembled at the completion of the conquest, and erected the Tent of Meeting; portions were assigned to the still landless tribes, and cities to the Levites (Jos 18[1] etc. 21[1] etc.). At Shiloh the congregation deliberated regarding the altar built by the men of the eastern tribes in the Jordan valley (22[12f]). During the period of the Judges it was the central sanctuary (Jg 18[31]), the scene of great religious festivals and pilgrimages (21[19], 1 S 1[3]). On one of these occasions the Benjamites captured as wives the girls who danced among the vineyards (21[18f]). Here the youth of Samuel was spent, and from this narrative it appears that the 'tent' had given place to a permanent structure, a 'temple' (*hēkhāl*), under the care of the high priest Eli and his family. The loss of the Ark and the disaster to his sons proved fatal to Eli (1 S 4^{12f}), and Shiloh apparently ceased to rank as a sanctuary, being possibly destroyed by the Philistines (Jer 7$^{12, 14}$ 26$^{6, 9}$; cf Ps 78^{60}). At any rate Eli's descendants are afterwards found at Nob (1 S 14^{3} 22^{11}). The prophet Ahijah was a native, or possibly a member of a prophetic guild, of Shiloh (1 K 11^{29} 14$^{2, 4}$).

The original name, as shown by the gentilic **Shilonite**, was *Shîlōn*; cf modern *Seilûn*, a ruined site on a hill E. of the road from Jerusalem to Shechem, about 9 miles N. of Bethel and 3 miles E. of *Khan el-Lubbân* (Lebonah, Jg 21^{19}). Excavations by Kjaer and Schmidt demonstrated occupation in the first phase of the Iron Age (*c* 1200–1000), with destruction in the same period, possibly that to which Jeremiah alludes. No trace of the sanctuary was certainly identified, but a Byzantine church, the remains of which were discovered, presumably occupied the reputed site of the Israelite temple.

2. The real meaning of the clause translated in AV ' until Shiloh come ' (Gn 49^{10}) is disputed. The Targums (Onkelos, Jerusalem, and pseudo-Jonathan) all interpret this of the Messiah, but no ancient version does so. Three possible readings are given in RVm. (1) ' Till he come to Shiloh '; grammatically correct, and supported by many scholars, being taken to refer to Judah's laying down the leadership which he had presumably exercised, when, the conquest finished, Israel assembled at Shiloh. Apart from other objections, however, *shēbeṭ*, ' sceptre,' seems to denote more than a tribal supremacy, and it is not certain that Judah possessed even that pre-eminence. (2) ' Until that which is his (*shellô*) shall come '; so LXX ' till the things reserved for him come.' (3) ' Until he shall come whose it is ' (Peshitta, Targums as above; cf RSV). Another possibility which is admitted by Jerusalem Targum I. is that *shîlōh* means ' his progeny ' (cf Late Heb. *shilyāh*, ' afterbirth.' The most satisfactory solution seems to be that the word *shîlōh* is a lost Hebrew cognate of the Akkadian *šilu*, ' ruler.' The verse obviously reflects the ascendancy of the House of David, but finds an eschatological Messianic interpretation only later in the Targums.

Shilonite = ' belonging to Shiloh ' is used of—**1.** Ahijah (1 K 11^{29} etc.). **2.** A family dwelling at Jerusalem (1 Ch 9^{5}), though here the true reading may be **' Shelanite '** (cf Nu 26^{20}). See SHELAH, 1. W. E.—**J. Gr.**

SHILONITE.—1. See SHILOH, **2.** **2.** See SHELAH, **1.**

SHILSHAH.—An Asherite, 1 Ch 7^{37}.

SHIMEA.—1. 1 Ch 3^{5}; see SHAMMUA, **2.** **2.** A Merarite, 1 Ch 6^{30}. **3.** A Gershonite, 1 Ch 6^{39}. **4.** 1 Ch 2^{13}; see SHAMMAH, **2.**

SHIMEAH.—1. A Benjamite who dwelt in Jerusalem, 1 Ch 8^{32}; called **Shimeam** in 9^{38}. **2.** See SHAMMAH, **2.**

SHIMEAM.—See SHIMEAH, **1.**

SHIMEATH.—A name given to the father or mother of one of the murderers of Joash, 2 K 12^{21}, 2 Ch 24^{26}. The murderer himself is called **Zabad** in 2 Chronicles, and **Jozacar** in 2 Kings. Probably for *Zabad* in 2 Chronicles we should read *Jehozabad*, and doubtless *Jozacar* and *Jehozabad* are identical (the letters are easily confused in Heb.), and by scribal repetition (dittography) we have two really identical names of the murderers, with the varying names for the parent, *Shimeath*, **Shimrith** and **Shomer**. The descriptions ' Ammonitess ' and ' Moabitess ' in 2 Chronicles are certainly later embellishments of the story, and Shimeath was probably the father of the one murderer, Jehozabad, and an Israelite. The **Shimeathites** were a family or division of the tribe of Caleb, 1 Ch 2^{55}. W. F. B.

SHIMEI, SHIMEITES.—Shimei was a popular name among the Hebrews, being especially common in Levitical circles. Of most of the persons bearing it, absolutely nothing except the name is known. **1.** The personage of this designation, of whom the historian has given us some details, is a Benjamite of the clan of Saul. On account of his tribal and family connexions, it is quite natural for him to be David's bitter enemy. As the latter is fleeing before Absalom, Shimei meets him and heaps curses and insults on the fugitive monarch. David's triumphant return, however, brings him in abject penitence to the feet of his sovereign, who pardons him (2 S 16^{5ff} 19^{17ff}). Nevertheless, David in his dying charge is represented as enjoining Solomon to ' bring his hoar head to Sheol with blood.' After this Shimei is not permitted to go beyond the walls of Jerusalem on pain of death; but presuming three years later to go to Gath in quest of fugitive slaves, he is executed by Benaiah at the command of the king (1 K 2$^{8ff, 36ff}$). **2.** In the court intrigues connected with the royal succession, a courtier, Shimei (cf article REI) by name espoused the cause of Solomon (1 K 1^{8}). The official at the head of one of the prefectures which were erected by this monarch, is probably identical with him (1 K 4^{18}). **3.** A master of the vineyards under David (1 Ch 27^{27}). **4.** A prince of the Judaean royal house, a brother of Zerubbabel (1 Ch 3^{19}). **5.** The name occurs in the tribal genealogies of both Simeon and Reuben (1 Ch 4^{26f} 5^{4} [in v.^{8} **Shema**]). See SHEMAIAH, **4.** **6.** The grandson of Levi (Ex 6^{17} [AV **Shimi**], Nu 3$^{18, 21}$, 1 Ch 6^{17} 23$^{7, 9}$). **7.** A son of Merari (1 Ch 6^{29}). **8.** In the genealogy of Asaph (1 Ch 6^{42}). **9.** The tenth course of Levitical singers who were appointed by David (1 Ch 25^{17}). **10.** A Levite who took part in the cleansing of the Temple under Hezekiah, probably identical with one mentioned later as having charge of the tithes and oblations (2 Ch 29^{14} 31^{12f}). **11.** In post-exilic times the name appears among those who had married foreign wives (Ezr 10^{23}, 1 Es 9^{23} [AV **Semis, RV Semeis**], Ezr 10^{33}, 1 Es 9^{33} [AV, RV **Semei**], Ezr 10^{38}, 1 Es 9^{34} [AV **Samis**, RV **Someis**]). The individuals referred to in Ezr 10^{33} and ^{38} belong to the laity. In Zec 12^{13} the family of the **Shimeites** are mentioned as participants in the mourning for national guilt; they appear in this connexion as representatives of the Levites. **12.** The name occurs in the genealogy of Mordecai (Est 2^{5}, Ad. Est 11^{2} [AV **Semei**, RV **Semeias**]). **13.** Shammah, the brother of David, appears as **Shimei** in 2 S 21^{21}. **14.** 1 Ch 8^{21} (AV **Shimhi**) = **Shema** of v.^{13}. J. A. K.

SHIMEON.—One of the sons of Harim who had married a foreign wife, Ezr 10^{31}; called **Simon Chosamaeus** in 1 Es 9^{32}.

SHIMHI, 1 Ch 8^{21} (AV).—See SHIMEI, **14.**

SHIMI, Ex 6^{17} (AV).—See SHIMEI, **6.**

SHIMMA, 1 Ch 2^{13} (AV).—See SHAMMAH, **1.**

SHIMON.—A Judahite family, 1 Ch 4^{20}.

SHIMRATH.—A Benjamite, 1 Ch 8^{21}.

SHIMRI.—1. A Simeonite, 1 Ch 4^{37}. **2.** The father of one of David's heroes, 1 Ch 11^{45}. **3.** A family of gatekeepers, 1 Ch 26^{10} (AV **Simri**). **4.** A Levite, 2 Ch 29^{13}.

SHIMRITH.—See SHIMEATH.

SHIMROM, 1 Ch 7^{1} (AV).—See SHIMRON.

SHIMRON.—1. The fourth son of Issachar, Gn 46^{13}, Nu 26^{24}, 1 Ch 7^{1} (AV **Shimrom**). The gentilic **Shimronites** occurs in Nu 26^{24}. **2.** One of the towns whose kings Jabin called to his assistance, Jos 11^{1}; it was afterwards allotted to the tribe of Zebulun, Jos 19^{5}. It is perhaps modern *Kh. Semûniyeh*, W. of Nazareth.

SHIMRON-MERON.—A Canaanite town W. of Jordan, whose king was among those whom Joshua smote, Jos 12^{20}. Comparing its position in the list with that of **Shimron** (q.v.) in the list given in Jos 11^{1}, we may infer that the two places are identical. The LXX here separates the two parts of this name, and reads as two names.

SHIMSHAI.—The scribe or secretary of Rehum, Ezr 4$^{8f, 17, 23}$, 1 Es 2^{16} (AV **Semellius**, RV **Samellius**).

SHIN and SIN.—Twenty-first letter of Hebrew alphabet, and so used to introduce the twenty-first part of Ps 119, every verse of which begins with this letter.

SHINAB.—The king of Admah, Gn 14^{2}.

SHINAR.—The term employed in the OT for the greater part, if not the whole, of **Babylonia**, Gn 10^{10} 11^{2}

14[1, 9], Is 11[11], Dn 1[2], Zec 5[11] (also Jos 7[21] RV and RSV; AV 'Babylonish'). It has been suggested that it is the equivalent of the Sumerian *Shingi-Uri*='Sumer and Accad,' but the attempt to equate the name with Sumer has been generally abandoned. Some have thought of Accadian *Shankhar*, which represents a country other than Babylonia. Egyptian texts mention the same country by the name *Sngr*. There is evidence to connect this with modern *Jebel Singhar*, W. of Mosul (cf de Vaux, *RB* lv, 332 f). Whatever the origin of the name the use in the Bible as the equivalent of Babylonia is not in doubt.

SHINAR, MANTLE FROM (*'addereth Shinʿār*).—A garment stolen by Achan, Jos 7[21] (AV 'Babylonish garment'; RV 'Babylonish mantle'); probably a cloak of embroidered stuff. Babylonia was famous in classical times for costly garments, and the sculptures exhibit the most elaborately embroidered dresses. The Babylonian inscriptions enumerate a great variety of such garments, worked in many colours. C. W. H. J.

SHION.—A town of Issachar, Jos 19[19] (AV **Shihon**); possibly modern *ʿAiyûn esh-Shaʿîn*, about 3 miles E. of Nazareth.

SHIPHI.—A Simeonite prince, 1 Ch 4[37].

SHIPHMITE.—See SHEPHAM.

SHIPHRAH.—One of the two Hebrew midwives, Ex 1[15].

SHIPHTAN.—An Ephraimite prince, Nu 34[24].

SHIPS AND BOATS.—1. In OT and Apocrypha.—(1) *Among the Israelites.*—In spite of the long line of coast by which Palestine is bordered, the Israelites were an agricultural rather than a maritime people. In fact a large part of the coast was occupied by the Phoenicians in the N. and the Philistines in the S. It seems that in the earliest times the people as a whole were ignorant of navigation. Exceptions more or less to the rule in relatively ancient times were the tribes of Asher on the N., and Dan, before its emigration, on the S.

'And Dan, why did he abide with the ships?
Asher sat still at the coast of the sea,
settling down by his landings' (Jg 5[17]).

It is very doubtful whether **boats** were originally used, even by the Phoenicians and the Philistines, except for fishing, and perhaps for purely local traffic and communication. Sidon, the earliest Phoenician settlement, was, like its synonym Beth-saida, derived from a root meaning to catch prey, and was doubtless first noted as a fishing town. Again, the name of Dagon, the chief god of the Philistines, is derived from the word *dāgh*, meaning a fish.

At a somewhat later period we find Zebulun described as a '**haven for ships**' (Gn 49[13]), and later still, probably after the division of the kingdom, Issachar is mentioned with Zebulun as deriving wealth from naval commerce (Dt 33[19]).

In any case, it is not till the time of Solomon that we hear definitely of any important development of commercial enterprise. Under the direction, and with the co-operation, of the Phoenicians, cedar and cypress timbers from Lebanon were cut and floated down the rivers to the coast and formed into rafts, which carried the sawn stones to Joppa. Here they were broken up, and both were conveyed to Jerusalem for the building of the Temple 1 K 5[9] [AV 'float'], 2 Ch 2[16] [AV 'flote,' RV 'float']). Solomon had also a **navy** of ships navigated by Phoenician sailors. They were stationed at **Ezion-geber**, at the head of the Gulf of ʿAqaba, and traded in gold and precious stones (1 K 9[26-28]) with Ophir, which may have been in the S. or E. of Arabia or on the African coast of Punt, in the general region of Somaliland. While the 'ivory and apes and peacocks (or rather, baboons)' of 1 K 10[22] may have been imported from India, they could just as well have had their origin in Africa. In addition to this, there was a regular trade maintained with Egypt, whence Solomon imported chariots and horses (10[28, 29]).

The conflict between the Northern and Southern Kingdoms after Solomon's death put a stop to the commercial activities of the Israelites, and there does not appear to have been any attempt to revive them till the time of Jehoshaphat, whose fleet of ships made for trading for gold to Ophir was wrecked at Ezion-geber. An offer of Ahaziah to join in a renewal of the enterprise was afterwards rejected (1 K 22[48f]). The mention in Is 2[16] of 'ships of Tarshish' among the objects against which Y″'s judgment would be directed, makes it likely that there was again a revival of naval commerce in the prosperous reigns of Jotham and Uzziah. Finally, in the time of the Maccabees we read that Simon, the brother of Judas, made **Joppa** a seaport (1 Mac 14[5]). It was probably at this period that the Jews first began to have experience of **ships of war** (1 Mac 1[17] 15[3]; cf Dn 11[30]), though they must have been in use at a much earlier period. There are figures of such ships, with sharp beaks for ramming, in A. H. Layard's *History of Nineveh*, and Sennacherib in his expedition against Merodach-baladan had ships manned by Tyrians. In Is 33[21] the allusion is certainly to hostile ships, but the reference may be to ships of transport, rather than warships. In any case the distinction between a merchantman and a warship in early times was obviously not so definite as it afterwards became.

(2) *Among neighbouring nations.*—As early as 3000 B.C. men had learned to navigate the Nile, and great ships for this purpose were built in the 1st and 2nd Dynasties. In the 3rd Dynasty (2600–2550 B.C.) Snefru sent to Phoenicia 40 ships, which returned with cedars from Lebanon. In the 5th Dynasty Sahure built the first navy in the history of the world. Hatshepsut (1504–1482 B.C.) had a large fleet, which carried on an extensive trade with Punt by way of the Nile and the Red Sea. Ramses III. (1198–1167 B.C.) tells of a sacred barge at Thebes, which was 224 ft. long and built of enormous timbers of cedars of Lebanon. Also on the Euphrates there was navigation as early as 3000 B.C., and voyages were made from the upper Euphrates to Babylon. Unlike the Israelites, the Phoenicians were the great navigators of the ancient world. Their country was particularly favourable for such a development. Dwelling on a narrow piece of sea-board, unsuited for agriculture (they imported corn from Palestine, 1 K 5[11], Ac 12[20]), they had behind them the Lebanon range, famed for its great cedars, and a coast with good natural harbours. By the time of Solomon they would seem already to have had an extensive trade. The phrase '**ships of Tarshish,**' which probably meant originally ships accustomed to trade with Tartessus in Spain, had come to be used in a secondary sense, like our 'East-Indiaman,' of large vessels suited for such a trade. It is believed that by this time they had penetrated as far as Cornwall, and had even found their way to the Canaries. The rise of Phoenicia as an independent marine power may be dated in the 12th cent. B.C. The numerous colonies of the Phoenicians were the result of their commercial enterprises by sea; their earliest settlement in N. Africa was Utica (1100 B.C.), and Carthage was founded *c* 822 B.C. The form of their ships was, it would appear, a gradual development from the hollowed trunk of a tree to the vessel of three banks of oars, known among the Greeks as a trireme (see Hastings' *DB*, article, 'Ships'). With the Assyrians navigation seems to have been confined to the Tigris and Euphrates, where small timber boats, supported by inflated skins, and coracles of plaited willow, were largely in use (see *EBi*, article, 'Ships'). On the other hand, the Babylonians extended their voyages to the Persian Gulf, and even engaged in commerce with India since the 7th cent. B.C. The Egyptians used '**vessels of papyrus**' for the navigation of the Nile (Is 18[2]; cf Job 9[26]), but it is not quite certain whether they were boats constructed out of papyrus, or rafts composed of bundles of these reeds bound together. We learn from Egyptian monuments that they had also ships of considerable size. We have very little to guide us in determining the form or size of ships during these early periods, but it is probable that

while at first they appear to have varied greatly, they gradually approximated to the type of vessel used in the Levant in NT times. It is not possible to say at what time **sails** were first introduced. We find them, or more correctly the sail, in the one great sail mentioned in Ezk 27[7] in addition to the oars. In Is 33[23] the sail only is mentioned. In v.[21] the **'galley with oars'** is mentioned distinctively, and in contrast to the **'stately ship,'** which probably means the larger vessel provided with a sail.

(3) *In literature.*—That the Israelites, though generally speaking unused to navigation, had some acquaintance with and took an interest in shipping, is clear from the constant reference to ships in their literature. Is 33[23], in which Israel is compared to a disabled vessel, has been already alluded to. Ezekiel's famous comparison of Tyre to a ship in 27[4–11] gives a fair general idea of the different parts of a ship of that period, though some of them—the deck-planks of ivory, the sail of fine bordered linen, the awnings of blue and purple—are evidently idealized. The graphic picture in Ps 107[23–28] of the terrors experienced by those 'who went down to the sea in ships' was almost certainly written by one who had experienced a storm at sea. In Ps 104[26] the ships are, as much as leviathan, the natural denizens of the deep. Of special beauty is the simile of the ship that passes over the waves and leaves no pathway of its keel behind (Wis 5[10]), to express the transitoriness of human life and human hope. The danger of ship-faring is pointed out in Wis 14[5]. That people should commit their lives to a small piece of wood would be absurd but for Divine Providence.

2. In the NT.—We are concerned chiefly with our Lord's Galilaean ministry and St. Paul's voyages. (1) *On the Sea of Galilee.*—The Galilaean **boats** were used primarily for fishing, and also for communication between the villages on the Lake, and probably for local trade. At least four of our Lord's disciples were fishermen, and were called while engaged in their work. He frequently crossed the Lake with His disciples, and sometimes preached from a boat to the people on the shore (Lk 5[3], Mk 4[1]). Among the most picturesque incidents of His life as recorded in the Gospels are the miracle of stilling the tempest and the miraculous draughts of fishes. The boats were small enough to be in danger of sinking from a very large catch of fish, and yet large enough to contain our Lord and at least the majority of His twelve disciples, and to weather the storms which are still frequent on the Lake. It appears from the frequent use of the definite article, 'the boat,' that one particular boat, probably St. Peter's, was usually employed.

(2) *In the Levant.*—Ships played an important part in St. Paul's missionary journeys. It was frequently necessary for him to cross the Aegean, and sometimes to make longer voyages to and from Syria. That he was frequently exposed to great danger we learn not only from the detailed account of his shipwreck in Ac 27, but from an express statement in 2 Co 11[25], in which, writing *before this event*, he says 'Three times I have been shipwrecked; a night and a day I have been adrift at sea,' which certainly seems to mean that he drifted for this space of time upon the spar or some part of a wrecked ship. But our interest is centred chiefly in the account of his voyage from Caesarea to Puteoli in Ac 27, 28. From this we learn that the larger vessels were of a considerable size, that of the shipwreck containing, according to what is probably the correct text, 276 persons (27[37]; according to B about 76). It was impelled only by **sail**, the only **oars** mentioned being the paddles used as **rudders**, which were braced up, probably in order to allow the ship to be more easily **anchored** at the stern (vv.[29, 40]). This, a custom not infrequently resorted to when some special purpose was served by it, was to enable them to thrust the vessel into a favourable place on shore without the necessity of turning her round. In addition to the **mainsail**, the vessel had a **foresail** (*artemōn*), which was used for the same purpose, as more easily adapted for altering the ship's course (v.[40]). The vessel had one small **boat**, which was usually towed behind, but was taken up for greater security during the storm (v.[16]). Another remarkable practice is that described in v.[17] as 'using helps, under-girding the ship.' These **helps** or 'under girders' were chains passed under and across the ship, and tightened to prevent the boards from springing. It was a common practice of ancient times, and is not unknown even in modern navigation. **Soundings** were taken to test the near approach to land, much as they would be at the present day. Though ships had to depend mainly on one great square sail, by bracing this they were enabled to sail within seven points of the wind. In this case, allowing another six points for leeway, the vessel under a north-easter (*Euraquilo*, v.[14]) made way from Cauda to Malta, a direction considerably N. of W. As, however, the vessel could not safely carry the mainsail, or even the yard-arm, these were first lowered on deck, and then the vessel must have been heaved to and been carried along and steadied by a small storm-sail of some kind. Had she drifted before the wind she would inevitably have been driven on to the Syrtis, the very thing they wished to avoid (v.[17]). This has been shown very clearly by James Smith in his classical work, *The Voyage and Shipwreck of St. Paul*, ch. iii. The same writer draws attention to the thoroughly nautical character of St. Luke's language, and the evidence of its accuracy by a comparison with what is known of ancient naval practice; and, what is perhaps even more striking, the evidence of skilful navigation to which the narrative points. He justly observes that the chief reason why sailing in the winter was dangerous (27[9] 28[11]) was not so much the storms, as the constant obscuring of the heavens, by which, before the discovery of the compass, mariners had chiefly to direct their course.

The fact that two of the ships in which St. Paul sailed were ships of Alexandria engaged in the wheat trade with Italy (27[6, 38] 28[11, 13]; Puteoli was the great emporium of wheat), is especially interesting, as we happen to know more about them than any other ancient class of ship. In the time of Commodus a series of coins with figures of Alexandrian corn-ships was struck to commemorate an exceptional importation of wheat from Alexandria at a time of scarcity. One of these ships, moreover, was driven into the Piraeus by stress of weather. Lucian lays the scene of one of his dialogues (*The Ship* or *Wishes*) on board of her. From the coins and the dialogue together we get a very good idea of the ships of that time (2nd cent. A.D.) and their navigation. Lucian's ship was 180 ft. by 45 ft., with a calculated tonnage of about 1200. It is not surprising, then, that the *Castor and Pollux* was large enough to contain, in addition to her cargo and crew, the 276 persons of the shipwrecked vessel (Ac 28[11]). Josephus was wrecked in a ship containing 600. The ships had one huge square sail attached to an upright **mast** about the centre of the vessel, with a very long yard-arm. There was also a second small mast, set diagonally near the bow, and looking not unlike a modern bowsprit, which carried the foresail. On the principal mast there was also sometimes a small triangular topsail. Both ends of the vessel curved upwards and were pointed horizontally, and terminated, the former especially, in some sort of decoration, very frequently a swan. The two **rudder paddles**, the universal method of steering till about the 12th cent., were usually in the larger vessels passed through port-holes, which could also serve as hawser holes when the vessel was **anchored** by the stern. For pictures of ancient ships, see F. Vigouroux, *Dict. de la Bible*, iv, 1494–1515 and *ANEP*.

(3) *In literature.*—In the books of the NT, shipping provided the writers with some striking similes. In referring to the Christian hope (He 6[19]), the writer says: 'We have this as a sure and steadfast anchor of the soul, a hope that enters into the inner shrine behind the curtain.' Again, St. James compares the tongue, in the control which its constraint exercises on the character, to the very small **rudders** by which ships, though they be so great, are turned about (3[4]). F. H. W.—H. S. G.

SHISHA.—See SHAVSHA.

SHISHAK.—Egyptian, *Sheshonq I*, founder of the 22nd Dynasty (*c* 940–919 B.C.). He may have been the unnamed Pharaoh who became the father-in-law of Solomon (1 K 3^{1} $9^{16, 24}$ 11^{1}). Jeroboam fled to him (1 K 11^{40}), and he plundered Jerusalem in the fifth year of Rehoboam (1 K 14^{25}, 2 Ch 12^{2}). A list of 156 towns of Syria-Palestine was carved by Shishak on the S. wall of the temple of Karnak. Although Shishak claims to have captured these towns, it may be that they merely paid tribute. F. Ll. G.—**R. J. W.**

SHITRAI.—A Sharonite who was over king David's herds that fed in Sharon, 1 Ch 27^{29}.

SHITTAH TREE.—Hebrew *shiṭṭāh*, rendered 'shittah tree' in AV in Is 41^{19} (RV, RSV **acacia tree**); *ʿaṣê shiṭṭîm*, rendered 'shittim wood' in AV in Ex $25^{5, 10, 13}$ etc. (RV, RSV 'acacia wood'). The name *shiṭṭāh* was originally *shinṭāh*, and is equivalent to Arabic *sanṭ*, which is the *Acacia nilotica*; but the word no doubt included other desert acacias. The *seyâl* of the Arabs, which includes the gum-arabic tree (*A. seyal*), and *A. tortilis* would both furnish suitable wood. Both these trees are plentiful around the Dead Sea, particularly at *ʿAin Jidi* (En-gedi). E. W. G. M.

SHITTIM.—**1.** The last encampment of the Israelites on their journey from Egypt to Canaan (in Nu 33^{49} called 'Abel-shittim [the meadow of acacias] in the plains of Moab'), possibly identical with modern *Tell Kefrein*, *c* 14 miles E. of Jericho. Here the Israelites 'began to play the harlot' with the women of Moab and to worship the Baal of Peor (Nu 25^{1ff}); from here Joshua sent his two spies to reconnoitre Jericho (Jos 2^{1}) and later set out with the Israelites to cross the Jordan (Jos 3^{1}). Josephus identifies it with 'the city Abila, . . . a place full of palm-trees' (*Ant.* IV. viii. 2 [176]), which he locates about 7 miles E. of the Jordan (*ib.* V. i. 1 [4]). In Mic 6^{5}, 'remember . . . what happened from Shittim to Gilgal, that you may know the saving acts of Yahweh' (cf RSV), should be understood as a reference to the events that attended Israel's entry into Canaan, from their last encampment before crossing Jordan to their first encampment after crossing (cf Jos 4^{19ff}).

2. The 'valley of Shittim' (Jl 3^{18}), which is to be watered by the stream flowing from the Temple in Jerusalem (cf Ezk 47^{1ff}, Zec 14^{8}), is probably the Kidron Valley (modern *Wâdī en-Nâr*), which runs from the SE. of Jerusalem to the Dead Sea; others identify it with the Valley of Elah (modern *Wâdī es-Sanṭ*), which runs from Bethlehem towards Ashdod, but this is less likely. G. A. B.—**F. F. B.**

SHIZA.—Father of a Reubenite chief, 1 Ch 11^{42}.

SHOA.—A race named in Ezk 23^{23} along with Babylonians, Chaldaeans, Pekod, Koa and Assyrians. They are the *Sutū* of Accadian texts. These were nomads, frequently named in the same company by Assyrian and Babylonian writers, and among other seats inhabited the E. of the Tigris.

SHOBAB.—**1.** One of David's sons 2 S 5^{14}, 1 Ch 3^{5} 14^{4}. **2.** A Calebite, 1 Ch 2^{18}.

SHOBACH.—The captain of the host of Hadarezer, the Aramaean king of **Zobah** (q.v.), who commanded the forces of that king when he aided the Ammonites in their war with king David. David defeated him, and Shobach lost his life, 2 S 10^{16-18}. In 1 Ch 19^{16} the name is spelled **Shophach**. Perhaps because so little was known of Shobach, he played an important part in the later imaginative tradition. The Mishnah (*Sotah*, viii. 1) makes him a giant of the Ammonites equal to Goliath, while the Samaritan Chronicle tells a long tale concerning him (chs. 26–38), making him the son of Haman, a king of Persia whom Joshua had killed, and who stirred up a great coalition to avenge the death of his father. All authentic information concerning Shobach is contained in 2 S 10^{16-18}, which 1 Ch 19^{16} repeats. G. A. B.

SHOBAI.—A family of porters, Ezr 2^{42}, Neh 7^{45}, 1 Es 5^{28} (AV **Sami**, RV **Sabi**).

SHOBAL.—**1.** A 'son' of Seir the Horite, and one of the 'dukes' of the Horites, Gn $36^{20, 23, 29}$, 1 Ch $1^{38, 40}$. **2.** A Calebite family in the tribe of Judah; he is called a son of Caleb and father of Kiriath-jearim in 1 Ch 2^{50}, and a son of Judah in 4^{1f}. The name may be connected with **1.**

SHOBEK.—A signatory to the covenant, Neh 10^{24}.

SHOBI.—A son of **Nahash**, the king of Ammon, who, with Machir of Lo-debar, showed kindness to David when he fled to Mahanaim at the time of Absalom's rebellion, 2 S 17^{27}. He was perhaps the brother of Hanun, the son who succeeded Nahash, 1 Ch 19^{1f}.

SHOCHO, 2 Ch 28^{18} (AV).—See Soco, **1.**

SHOCHOH, 1 S 17^{1} (AV).—See Soco, **1.**

SHOCK, STACK.—'Shock' is used in AV in Jg 15^{5} and Job 5^{26}, and 'stack' in Ex 22^{6}. In all three cases RV has 'shock,' while RSV has 'stacked grain' in Ex 22^{26} and 'shock' in the others. The Hebrews did not set up their sheaves in shocks (*Scoticé* 'stooks'), but piled them in **heaps** for conveyance to the threshing-floor (AGRICULTURE, **3**). A. R. S. K.

SHOCO, 2 Ch 11^{7} (AV).—See Soco, **1.**

SHOE.—See DRESS, **6.** The shoes were removed before entering a temple, or other sacred precinct, in order to save the latter from defilement. Hence the priests performed their duties barefoot. The shoe played a part, further, in certain symbolical actions in Hebrew law. One who renounced the duty of levirate marriage (see MARRIAGE, **4**) had his shoe publicly pulled off by the widow, who also spat in his face, Dt 25^{9}. In Ru 4^{7f} Ruth was not present when the next of kin renounced her, and he drew off his own shoe. This may have been a later modification of the custom, or, more probably, was due to the more distant relationship of the kinsman, and the consequent lessening of the degree of reproach resting on him. This passage further implies that it was customary for the vendor to draw off his shoe and hand it to the buyer on completing a transaction. A similar custom is widely known. (In early Babylonian deeds of sale concerning house property we find the pestle [of the mortar] was so transferred.)

In the expression 'upon Edom I cast my shoe' (Ps 60^{8} 108^{9}) it is possible that there is an extension of this shoe symbolism, the taking possession of the property being symbolized by throwing a shoe upon it. Some prefer the sense of RVm 'unto Edom,' and see here a reference to Edom's servitude, it being the part of the slave to carry his master's shoes. A. R. S. K.—**H. H. R.**

SHOHAM.—A Merarite, 1 Ch 24^{27}.

SHOMER.—**1.** 1 Ch 7^{32}; see SHEMER, **3.** **2.** 2 K 12^{21}; see SHIMEATH.

SHOPHACH.—See SHOBACH.

SHOPHAN, Nu 32^{35} (AV).—See ATROTH-SHOPHAN.

SHOSHANNIM, SHOSHANNIM-EDUTH.—See PSALMS.

SHOVEL.—**1.** Ex 27^{3} 38^{3}, Nu 4^{14}, 1 K $7^{40, 45}$, 2 K 25^{14}, 2 Ch $4^{11, 16}$, Jer 52^{18}, of a utensil for removing the ashes from the altar. **2.** Is 30^{24}, for the broad, shallow, winnowing shovel with which corn after threshing was thrown up against the wind to clear it of the chaff.

SHOWBREAD (**Shewbread** (AV and RV), also rendered as **Bread of the Presence** (RSV) and **Presence-Bread** (RVm Ex 25^{30} 35^{13})).—There are various terms used in the Bible to describe this bread which was placed before God in the shrine. The expression 'bread of the presence' appropriately renders the Hebrew, literally 'bread of (the) face' (so in Ex 25^{30} 35^{13} 39^{36}, 1 S 21^{6}, 1 K 7^{48} || 2 Ch 4^{19}). In Nu 4^{7} the phrase is 'continual bread.' Corresponding to this, 2 Ch 2^{4} has 'ordering of continuity,' 'continual offering of the showbread' (RSV), 'continual shewbread' (RV). The technical expression 'ordering,' 'row,' 'setting in order' appears also in 1 Ch 9^{32} 23^{29}, Neh 10^{33}, all referring to the 'bread of the ordering'; 2 Ch 13^{11} reverses the words and has 'the ordering of (the) bread.' A different word for 'order' is used in Ex 40^{23}. In 1 S 21^4 'holy bread' is used.

The NT has two phrases, both rendered as 'bread of the Presence' (RSV), 'shewbread' (AV and RV). In He 9^2 RVm indicates the literal meaning as 'the setting forth of the loaves.' Mk 2^{26} and its parallels Mt 12^4, Lk 6^4 have the words in the reverse order: 'the loaves of the setting forth.' These two phrases correspond exactly to the usage of the Chronicler, and are found in LXX, which uses also a more literal rendering of the phrase 'bread of the face' (cf Vulgate, *panis facierum*, *panis propositionis*). The term 'showbread' (shewbread) is due apparently to Tyndale, and is found as early as 1526, though he also uses other terms, *e.g.* 'the halowed loves.'

Various OT passages give further information about this bread. In 1 S 21^{1-6} we are told of David's flight from Saul and his requesting bread from Ahimelech at the sanctuary at Nob. The bread is described as 'holy,' contrasted with common bread, and the priest was evidently concerned to know that those who were to eat it would be in a fit state. The bread is further described as that which is 'removed from before Yahweh so that hot bread is placed there on the day it is taken away.'

The two points here—the holiness of the bread and its periodic renewal—find further elaboration, and information is also given about the table upon which it is placed. Lv 24^{5-9} describes its preparation. Twelve loaves are to be made, each containing one fifth of an ephah (q.v.) of fine flour. The loaves are placed upon the table in two rows, six in each row, and pure frankincense upon each row. The frankincense was to be offered by fire and the bread to be set in order on the sabbath. The loaves then removed were to be eaten by the priests within the holy place, because this bread is 'most holy.' This latter provision is indicated also in Mk 2^{26} and parallels.

The table upon which the bread was to be placed is described in connexion with the Tabernacle (Ex 25^{23-30}; cf TABERNACLE). In 1 K 7^{48} a golden table (2 Ch 4^{19} has the plural 'tables' but no mention of gold) is included among the Temple furniture. This is sometimes identified—though hardly rightly—with the 'altar of cedar' (1 K 6^{20}; cf TEMPLE). Such an identification appears to be made in Ezk 41^{22}. The existence of the table in the second Temple is indicated by 1 Mac 1^{22}. The practice was restored by Judas Maccabaeus (1 Mac 4^{49-51}) and such a table is portrayed on Titus' triumphal arch after the destruction of A.D. 70 (cf also Jos. *BJ* VII. v. 5 [148]). Further information is provided by later writers, *e.g.* Josephus, who says that the incense was in golden platters (or cups, *Ant.* III. vi. 6 [143]) and burnt at the end of the week (*Ant.* III. x. 7 [255 f]). Rabbinic information may be found in *JE*, xi, 312 f and *SB*, iii, 719 ff. The Letter of Aristeas (51 ff) gives an elaborate description of the table.

Parallels to such an offering of loaves have been found among the Babylonians, who laid cakes of sweet (unleavened) bread before various deities, in twelves or multiples of twelve (cf Zimmern, *KAT*^{3} 600). In the Apocrypha, Bel and the Dragon (v.^{11}) provides indirect evidence of a similar kind, though here with a ridiculing of the crude notion that the deity himself fed upon the bread. We may also compare the cakes offered to the Queen of Heaven (Jer 7^{18} 44^{19}), and in the Râs Shamra texts there are references to deities eating bread, possibly set out for them by the worshipper (cf *SS*, i. 6). Comparison has also been made with the Roman custom of *lectisternia*, banquets for certain gods, a celebration of Greek origin. The number twelve may well have had astral significance originally.

In the OT, the original intention of providing food for the deity, or of sharing a meal with Him, may well still be detected (see SACRIFICE AND OFFERING). But the stress is now laid upon the covenant, the number twelve being associated with the twelve tribes, so that the offering is a 'pledge of the covenant between the twelve tribes and Yahweh' (de Vaux, *Ancient Israel*, 1961, p. 422; cf Lv 24^8). There may also be an allusion to the months of the year, and so perhaps to the dedication of the blessings of food to God who is the giver of them.

P. R. A.

SHRINE.—See ARTEMIS.

SHROUD.—This word is used in AV and RV in Ezr 31^3 in the general sense of 'shelter,' 'covering' (RSV 'forest shade' for 'shadowing shroud'), as in Milton's *Comus*, 147—'Run to your shrouds, within these brakes and trees.'

SHUA.—**1.** The father of Judah's Canaanite wife, Gn $38^{2,12}$ (AV **Shuah**); called **Bath-shua** in 1 Ch 2^3 (AV 'the daughter of Shua'). **2.** A daughter of Heber, 1 Ch 7^{32}.

SHUAH.—**1.** A son of Abraham and Keturah, Gn 25^2, 1 Ch 1^{32}. The tribe represented by this name may perhaps be the *Suchu* of the cuneiform *Shuḫu* on the right bank of the Euphrates. Bildad the Shuhite (Job 2^{11} 8^1 18^1 25^1 42^9) is probably intended to be thought of as belonging to this tribe. **2.** Gn $38^{2,12}$ (AV); see SHUA, **1.** **3.** 1 Ch 4^{11} (AV); see SHUHAH.

SHUAL ('jackal').—An Asherite, 1 Ch 7^{36}.

SHUAL, LAND OF.—A region referred to in 1 S 13^{17} as the destination of one of the three bands of Philistine raiders. The close connexion of Ophrah with the district named indicates that this was one of its towns. Its exact site is unknown.

SHUBAEL.—See SHEBUEL.

SHUHAH.—A brother of Chelub, 1 Ch 4^{11} (AV **Shuah**).

SHUHAM.—A son of Dan, Nu 26^{42}; called **Hushim** in Gn 46^{23}. The gentilic **Shuhamites** is found in Nu 26^{42f}.

SHUHITE.—See SHUAH.

SHULAMITE, Ca 6^{13} (AV) = **Shulammite** (q.v.).

SHULAMMITE.—See SHUNEM, SONG OF SONGS.

SHUMATHITES.—A family of Kiriath-jearim, 1 Ch 2^{53}.

SHUNAMMITE.—See next article.

SHUNEM.—A border town of Issachar (Jos 19^{18}) and the camping ground of the Philistines opposite Gilboa before Saul's last battle (1 S 28^4). It was identified already in the *Onamasticon* as *Suleim*, a site 5 miles S. of Tabor. The modern town of *Sôlam* or *Sûlam* lies on the W. slope of *Jebel Daḥī*. That the Shunem which was the scene of Elisha's miracle (2 K 4^{8ff}) is probably not the same site is suggested by the story itself which indicates that it lay on the way from Samaria to Carmel near which it must have been (v.^{25}).

The term **Shunammite** is applied to (1) the mother of the lad raised by Elisha (2 K 4^{12}) and (2) Abishag (1 K 1^3). Possibly the term is the original of the Shulammite of Ca 6^{13} (cf Shunem, Solam). This identification has given rise to theories that Abishag was the prototype of the Shulammite. On the other hand, the term may simply be the etymological counterpart to Solomon. It would thus have nothing to do with Shunem at all.

C. W. E.—**J. W. W.**

SHUNI.—A son of Gad, Gn 46^{16}, Nu 26^{15}; the gentilic **Shunites** occurs in Nu 26^{15}.

SHUPHAM, Nu 26^{39} (AV).—See MUPPIM.

SHUPHAMITES.—See SHEPHUPHAM.

SHUPPIM.—**1.** See MUPPIM. **2.** A door keeper, 1 Ch 26^{16}.

SHUR ('wall').—A place or district on the NE. border of Egypt, Gn 16^7 20^1 25^{18}, Ex 15^{22}, 1 S 15^7 27^8. It probably refers to the border of Egypt in the isthmus of Suez, held by a line of forts, and perhaps especially to the 'wall of *Thāru*' (Egyp. *th* corresponds to *sh* in Heb.), at *Tell Abū Seifeh*, near *Qanṭarah*.

SHUSHAN.—See SUSA.

SHUSHANCHITES.—The gentilic from **Shushan** (see SUSA), found in RV of Ezr 4^9, where RSV has 'men of Susa.' They are here included among the colonists settled by **Osnappar** (q.v.) in Samaria.

SHUSHAN-EDUTH.—See PSALMS, **2.**

SHUTHALHITES, Nu 26[35] (AV).—See SHUTHELAH, **1.**

SHUTHELAH.—**1.** One of the three clans of the tribe of Ephraim, Nu 26[35f], 1 Ch 7[20]. The gentilic **Shuthelahites** occurs in Nu 26[35] (AV **Shuthalhites**). **2.** A son of Zabad, and descendant of Ephraim, 1 Ch 7[21].

SHUTTLE.—Only Job 7[6], where it is doubtful whether the reference is to the shuttle-rod of the loom, or to the loom itself. The Hebrew word has the latter meaning in its only other occurrence, Jg 16[14]. See SPINNING AND WEAVING, **4** (*b*).

SIA.—A family of Nethinim (q.v.) who returned with Zerubbabel, Neh 7[47]; called **Siaha** in Ezr 2[44], 1 Es 5[29] (AV **Sud**, RV **Sua**).

SIAHA.—See SIA.

SIBBECAI.—The name of one of David's thirty heroes, 2 S 21[18] (AV **Sibbechai**), 1 Ch 11[29] 20[4] (AV **Sibbechai**) 27[11]; called **Mebunnai** in 2 S 23[27].

SIBBECHAI, 2 S 21[18], 1 Ch 20[4] (AV).—See SIBBECAI.

SIBBOLETH.—See SHIBBOLETH.

SIBMAH.—See SEBAM.

SIBRAIM.—A place on the ideal northern boundary of the Holy Land, Ezk 47[16]. Its location is unknown, but it would appear to be in the neighbourhood of Hamath.

SICCUTH, Am 5[26] (RV).—See SAKKUTH. For 'Sakkuth your King,' AV has 'the tabernacle of your Moloch'; cf Ac 7[43] 'the tent of Moloch' (RSV).

SICHEM, Gn 12[6] (AV)=**Shechem** (q.v.).

SICK, SICKNESS.—See MEDICINE.

SICKLE.—Hebrew *ḥermēsh*, Dt 16[9] 23[26]; *maggāl*, Jer 50[16], Jl 3[13]; Greek *drepanon*, Mk 4[29], Rev 14[14ff]; in 1 S 30[20] RSV restores *ḥermēsh* with LXX (AV, RV 'mattock'). The Hebrew sickles or reaping hooks were successively of flint, bronze (rarely found), and iron, and set in handles of bone or wood. In Palestine the flint sickle goes back to the later Stone age (see illustrations from Gaza in Galling, *BRL*, p. 475). Similar flint sickles, with bone hafts, have been found in Egypt. The ancient sickles were of two kinds, according as the cutting edge was plain or toothed; the modern Palestinian reaping-hook is of the latter kind and somewhat elaborately curved. In Jer 50[16] the reaper is described as 'one who handles the sickle' (AVm **scythe,** which is also wrongly given as an alternative in AVm of Is 2[4], Mic 4[3] for 'pruning hooks'). In Jl 3[13] we should read with RVm 'put ye in the sickle, for the *vintage* is ripe,' the context, the LXX rendering, and the same figure in Rev 14[19f] all show that the reference is to the smaller but similarly shaped **grape-knife,** expressly named *maggāl* in the Mishnah, with which the grape-gatherer cut off the bunches of ripe grapes. A. R. S. K.—**H. H. R.**

SICYON.—This was one of the numerous places written to by the Romans on behalf of the Jews in 139 B.C. (1 Mac 15[23]). It was situated on the Gulf of Corinth, about 18 miles W. of Corinth and was an important stopping place for vessels; it was held to be an 8 days' sail from here to Brundisium. It was distinguished in plastic art, and was in early times very important and wealthy, but sank to insignificance early in the Christian era. Some excavations have been carried on here.

A. So.—**E. G. K.**

SIDEBOARD.—See CUPBOARD.

SIDDIM.—The 'Valley of Siddim' (derived by some from Hittite *siyantas*, 'salt') is mentioned only in Gn 14, where it is the scene of the defeat of the kings of Sodom, Gomorrah and the other cities of the Jordan pentapolis by Chedorlaomer and his allies. It is identified with the 'Salt Sea' (v.[3]) and described as being 'full of bitumen (AV, RV 'slime') pits' (v.[10]). Most probably it was a well-watered and fertile region, S. of El-Lisân, which is now covered by the southward extension of the Dead Sea. Its submergence beneath the sea may have been due to a faulting of the rock formation, induced by earthquake action. The Dead Sea, especially in its southern part, still yields masses of bitumen, and it was its bituminous products that procured for it from the Greeks the name *Asphaltitis*. See J. P. Harland, 'Sodom and Gomorrah,' *BA*, v (1942), 17 ff, vi (1943), 41 ff.

G. W. W.—**F. F. B.**

SIDE, a Greek colony, was situated on the coast of Pamphylia, on a low promontory about 10 miles E. of the river Eurymedon. It had two harbours and was well fortified. The remains are extensive and interesting (*Eski Adalia*). It was one of the cities addressed on behalf of the Jews by the Romans in 139 B.C. (1 Mac 15[23]).

A. So.

SIDON.—About midway between *Beirût* and Tyre, on the edge of a fertile strip of plain stretching from the mountain to the shore, a small rocky promontory juts into the sea. Here stood the ancient city of Sidon. The site was chosen doubtless because of the excellent harbour formed by a series of small islets, a short distance from the shore, which protected shipping lying by the city. In old times the islets were joined together by artificial embankments. This harbour lay to the N.; on the S. was a second one, larger but less secure, known as the Egyptian harbour. Sidonians is sometimes used for Phoenicians in the OT (Gn 10[15], Jg 10[12] etc.) as regularly in Homer. Sometimes Sidon is called 'Great Sidon' (Jos 11[8] etc.). The Sidonians excelled in artistic metal work (cf Homer, *Il*, xxiii. 743–748) and in the products of the loom, the value of which was enhanced by the famous dye, used first by the Sidonians, but known to the later world as 'Tyrian purple.' The planting of colonies was a natural, and almost necessary, outcome of her commercial enterprise. Aradus (Strabo, XVI. ii. 13) and Carthage (Appian, *de Rebus Punicis*, 1, etc.) are said to have been founded by her, and she seems to claim on a coin to be the mother-city of Melita or Malta, as well as of Citium and Berytus. King Zimrida of Sidon appears in the Amarna tablets as rebel against Egyptian rule. Sidonian ascendancy succeeded the decline of the Egyptian power after Rameses II. How long it lasted we do not know. The Asherites, who had not dispossessed the Sidonians (Jg 1[31]), allegedly suffered oppression at their hands (10[12]). By the time of Solomon, however, **Tyre** had assumed the hegemony (Jos. *Ant.* VIII. v. 3 [141 ff], *c. Apion*, i. 18 [116 ff]). But Assyrian power was now expanding and Tiglath-pileser I. *c* 1100 B.C. had already assumed the heritage of the Hittites by coming to Arvad. In 877 B.C. Sidon, with other Phoenician cities, submitted to Ashur-naṣir-pal and 'sent him presents.' Sidon suffered under Shalmaneser III., Tiglath-pileser III., Shalmaneser V., and finally was subdued by Sennacherib who made Tubaal, a creature of his own, king. A revolt under Tubaal's successor led to the utter destruction of the city in 678 B.C. by Esarhaddon, who built a new city called by his own name. The attempt to gain Judah for the league against the growing power of Babylon brought an embassy to Jerusalem, in which the king of Sidon was represented (Jer 27[3]). A revolt joined in by Judah, was stamped out by Nebuchadrezzar in 597 B.C. Sidon's swift submission was due to devastating pestilence (Ezk 28[21ff]). The long resistance of Tyre led to her destruction and humiliation (Ezk 26[8ff]), Sidon once more assuming the leadership.

In the beginning of the Persian period the Phoenician cities enjoyed practical autonomy, and a time of great material prosperity. A friendly arrangement with Cambyses perpetuated this state of things, and in the Greek wars most valuable assistance was given by the Phoenicians to the Persians. The revolt of the Phoenicians, headed by Sidon, about 351 B.C., was remorselessly crushed by Artaxerxes Ochus. Sidon was betrayed into his hands by the despairing king, Tennes. The inhabitants burned the city, more than 40,000 perishing in the flames. Perhaps at this time Sidonians were settled at Shechem, where Alexander encountered a population claiming that name (Jos. *Ant.* XI. viii. 6 [344]). But the city rose again from its ashes, and regained something of its former prosperity. The son of Tennes became king and retained the sceptre till the advent of Alexander.

While Phoenicia then lost her predominance in the trade of the Mediterranean, Sidon retained considerable importance as the possessor of an excellent harbour, and as a seat of Phoenician industry. Lying in the territory often in dispute between Syria and Egypt, in the following centuries Sidon several times changed hands. Under the Romans she enjoyed the privileges of a free city. Sidon figures in the Gospel narratives (Mt 11[21f] 15[21], Mk 3[8] etc.). Jesus may have passed through territory belonging to the city (Mk 7[31]). It appears in Ac 12[20], and was touched at by St. Paul in his voyage to Rome (Ac 27[3]). It later became the seat of a bishop. Sidon suffered heavily during the Crusades. Under the Druse prince, Fakhreddin (1595–1634), its prosperity revived; but, in order to prevent the approach of the Turkish fleet, he caused the entrance to the harbour to be filled up, thus making it comparatively useless. The present walls of the city were built by Mohammed ʿAli of Egypt (1832–1840). The fortress, *Kal ʿat el-Baḥr*, 'Castle of the Sea,' dating from the 13th cent., stands on the largest of the islands, which is joined to the mainland by a bridge of 9 arches. The present population is about 11,000. The chief occupations are fishing, and the cultivation of the gardens and orange groves for which modern Sidon is famous. While the oldest existing building dates from the Middle Ages, there are many remains of great antiquity, traces of walls, hewn stones, pillars, coins, and the reservoirs cut out of the rock. The most important discoveries so far have been (1855) the sarcophagus of king Eshmunazar (early in the 4th cent. B.C.), with the well-known inscription, now in Paris; and (1887) the tomb containing 17 Phoenician and Greek sarcophagi, highly ornamented; among them that of Tabnit, father of Eshmunazar, and the so-called Alexander Sarcophagus—probably that of Abdalonimus, whom Alexander restored to the throne of his fathers. W. E.—**E. G. K.**

SIEGE.—See Fortification and Siegecraft.

SIEVE.—See Agriculture, **3**.

SIGN (Heb. *'ôth*; Gr. *sēmeion*).—The word occurs some 90 times in the OT and 74 in NT; also frequent in Hellenistic writers and with similar meanings.

1. A mark of identification: sun, moon and stars for signs of day, night and seasons (Gn 1[14]); military standards (Nu 2[2]); manger and swaddling clothes (Lk 2[12]); Paul's penmanship (2 Th 3[17]); Judas' kiss (Mt 26[48]).

2. Memorials: stones from the Jordan (Jos 4[6]); metal of censers (Nu 16[38]); Aaron's rod (Nu 17[10]); myrtle tree (Is 55[13]); passover (Ex 13[9]); pillar (Is 19[20]).

3. Pledge of a covenant: rainbow (Gn 9[12-17]); circumcision (Gn 17[11]); Sabbath (Ex 31[13-17], Ezk 20[12]).

4. Prophetic symbols: Isaiah and his children (Is 8[18] 20[3]); diorama of siege of Jerusalem (Ezk 4[3]).

5. Signs and wonders: a standard idiom often used of omens and portents associated with the Exodus (Ex 7[3] etc.), birth, life, death (Mt 27[45-54]), and resurrection of Jesus, preaching of the apostles (Ac 2[43]) and end of world (Mt 24[1-31]). Josephus (*War* VI. v. 3 [288–309]) lists portents which accompanied the fall of Jerusalem in A.D. 70.

6. Signs and wonders were also attributed to false prophets (Ex 7[11-12], Dt 13[2-3]), false Christs (Mk 13[22]), and Satan (2 Th 2[9]).

7. According to the earliest sources, Jesus Himself refused to give a sign to validate His ministry (Mk 8[12], Mt 4[1-11]), but later traditions (Mt 16[4] 12[40], Jn 20[30-31] etc.) ascribe many signs to Him. It may be, however, that John means that the signs he records are allegories, written to replace parables such as are found in the other Gospels. The attitude of Jesus indicates that although He healed many persons of their diseases, He did this out of compassion, not as signs; and that He did not consider such things as a necessary basis of faith.

Cf also Miracles, and Wonders. S. V. McC.

SIGNET.—See Seal.

SIHON.—A king of the Amorites at the time of the conquest of Canaan. His dominion lay beyond the Jordan, between Jabbok on the N. and Arnon on the S., extending eastward to the desert, Jg 11[22]. He refused to allow Israel to pass through his land, and was defeated at Jahaz, Nu 21[21-24], Dt 2[26-36], Jg 11[19-22]. **Heshbon,** his capital, was taken; and his land, along with that of Og, king of Bashan, became the possession of Reuben, Gad, and the half tribe of Manasseh. Frequent reference is made to his defeat, Nu 32[33], Dt 1[4], Jos 2[10], 1 K 4[9], Neh 9[22], Ps 135[11] 136[19] etc. In Jer 48[45] Sihon stands for Heshbon, the city of Sihon (RSV 'the house of Sihon' for AV and RV 'the midst of Sihon'). W. F. B.

SIHOR, Jos 13[3], Is 23[3], Jer 2[18] (AV).—See Shihor.

SILAS (Acts) and **SILVANUS** (Epistles).—Silas is the Greek form of the Aramaic name *shᵉ'îlâ* (='asked for'); Silvanus is a Latin name very similar in sound. The Jews liked to have Greek or Latin names of similar sound in addition to their Hebrew or Aramaic names. Silas, according to Ac 15[22] a Christian prophet at Jerusalem, was sent as a delegate to the community of Antioch; later on he accompanied St. Paul on the Second Journey (Ac 15[40]–18[50]). Then he disappears from the Pauline history in Acts.

In 1 Thessalonians, written during the Second Journey, Silvanus is named as sender besides Paul (and Timothy): 1[1]. St. Paul reminds the Corinthians of Silvanus's former preaching (2 Co 1[19]). In 1 P 5[12] Silvanus is represented as accompanying St. Peter. The words 'By Silvanus . . . I have written' have been interpreted in various ways: Peter has dictated the letter, or he has indicated only the main lines. But because the letter is probably postapostolic, this tradition concerning Silvanus remains uncertain. E. H.

SILK.—See Dress, **1**.

SILLA.—The servants of king Joash smote him 'in the house of Millo [read rather 'at Beth-Millo'] *on the way* that goes down to Silla,' 2 K 12[20]. What Silla may have been there is nothing to show. The LXX reads *Gaala* or *Gaallad.* R. A. S. M.

SILOAH, Neh 3[15] (AV).—See Siloam.

SILOAM.—The name survives in *Silwân*, the village on the steep E. slopes of the Kidron Valley stretching from opposite 'the Virgin's Fountain' (Gihon) to near *Bir Ayyûb* (En-rogel). The whole of the N. part of the village has been built upon in ancient times, and the whole area is riddled with cave-dwellings, cisterns, rock-cut steps and tombs, among which one, the defaced inscription of which intimates that it was that of a royal chamberlain and his slave-wife, may be that of the official Shebna, whose presumption in having such a tomb prepared for himself Isaiah (22[15ff]) stigmatizes. It may be considered as certain that in NT times there was a considerable village here. The 'tower' which fell (Lk 13[4]) may have been a building similar to many today built on the edge of the precipitous rocks above the Kidron. The source of the famous 'Pool of Siloam' is the above-mentioned 'Virgin's Fountain,' known to local Moslems as *ʿAin ed-Daraj* ('the Spring of the Stairway') see Gihon. In 1867 Warren discovered a vertical shaft on the E. slope of the Ophel Hill leading down to a tunnel which connected with the spring in the Kidron Valley, thus making water accessible from the shelter of the city wall. This work and other tunnels at Megiddo, Gezer, and Gibeon no doubt reflect the insecurity in Palestine on the eve of the Iron Age *c* 1200. A later development is a channel which follows the contour on the E. slope of Ophel, sometimes under the rock, but more often open, until it debouches into an open pool, the city cesspool in Turkish times, but now dry, called *Birket el-Ḥamrā*, in the depression between the Ophel and the W. hill of Jerusalem. This work, rather for irrigation than drinking, was practicable only in the security of Solomon's reign. This, rather than the Pool of Siloam, may be 'the canalized water' (EV 'waters of **Shiloah**') of Is 8[6], *Birket el-Ḥamrā*, insofar as it actually adjoined the city wall, being the 'Pool of Shiloah' (AV **Siloah**; RV, RSV **Shelah**) of Neh 3[15], and 'the King's Pool' of Neh 2[14].

The water supply under this arrangement being vulnerable, Hezekiah 'stopped the upper water-course of Gihon and brought it straight down to the west side of the city of David' (2 Ch 32^{30}; cf 32^{4}, 2 K 20^{20}), this being the famous **Siloam tunnel**. This runs in an extraordinary serpentine course for 1700 ft., debouching in the Tyropoeon Valley under the name of *'Ain Silwân* ('the Spring of Siloam') to feed *Birket Silwân*, the Pool of Siloam. Close to the lower opening of the tunnel was found in 1880 a Hebrew inscription giving an account of the completion of the work, but not naming its author, who was nevertheless probably Hezekiah.

The original Pool of Siloam, of which the present *birkeh* occupies but a part, was excavated by Bliss, and proved to have been a rock-cut reservoir 71 ft. N. to S. by 75 ft. E. to W. A covered arcade, 12 ft. wide had been built, probably about NT times, round the four sides of the pool, and a division ran across the centre to separate the sexes when bathing. Such was probably the condition of the pool at the events described in Jn 9^{7}. The water of *'Ain Silwân*, like that of its source (Gihon), is naturally brackish and impregnated with sewage; it runs intermittently, a feature which may be indicated in the name of its source, Gihon ('Gusher').

E. W. G. M.—**J. Gr.**

SILVANUS.—See SILAS.

SILVER.—See MINING AND METALS.

SILVERLING.—Only in Is 7^{23} AV and RV, where the original reads 'a thousand of silver,' the denomination to be supplied being 'shekels' (so RSV).

SIMALCUE, 1 Mac 11^{39} (AV).—See IMALKUE.

SIMEON (Lk 3^{30}, Ac 13^{1} 15^{14}; RV, RSV Symeon). —**1.** The second son of Jacob and Leah and the eponymous ancestor of one of the tribes of Israel. According to Gn 29^{33} he was named *Shim'ōn* by his mother because Yahweh 'has heard (*shāma'*) that I am hated'—an allusion to the fact that Rachel was Jacob's favourite wife. This association of the name with Leah's unhappiness is obviously legendary, though the derivation of it from *shāma'* will be correct if, as has been suggested by some scholars, it is an abbreviation of Ishmael (*Yishma'ēl*). Others have thought that it is connected with the Arabic *sim'*, the hybrid offspring of the hyena and the female wolf, which appears as a tribal name among the bedouin.

The fact that Simeon and Levi are specifically designated as 'Dinah's brothers' in Gn 34^{25}, and again in 49^{5} are referred to as brothers, points to a particularly close association of the two tribes and suggests that their eponyms may have been regarded as brothers and sons of Leah before the growth and articulation of the tribal traditions placed them among the sons of Jacob. If so, then it may be assumed that Simeon had its own history before it entered the federation of southern clans which ultimately coalesced to form the tribe of Judah. The fact that its eponym was included among the sons of Jacob indicates that it was at one time a more important group than the Kenites, the Jerahmeelites, the Othnielites and the Calibbites, whose eponyms never attained this status.

There is a reminiscence of some episode in its history in the story of the seduction of Dinah in Gn 34. In its present context the story locates the event in Shechem, but nowhere else in the OT is there any suggestion that the Simeonites ever reached as far N. as this; furthermore there are indications in the tale itself that in the earlier of the two narratives of which it was composed the scene was in the S. (*e.g.* the LXX reading of 'Horite' for 'Hivite' in v.^{2}; cf Gn 36^{20} where the Horites are implicitly located in Edom). According to the oracle in Gn 49$^{5-7}$ the tribes of Simeon and Levi were shattered as the result of some act of wanton violence. The terms in which this is described may suggest fratricidal warfare; they scarcely warrant the assumption that it was the treachery with which they are charged in Gn 34^{25f}, though this may well be appealed to as another instance of the ruthlessness and irresponsibility which brought about their destruction. By the time the oracle in Gn 49 took form—not later than the 9th cent. and probably considerably earlier—Simeon had already lost its tribal identity. But in the early tradition of the conquest preserved in Jg 1 it still appears as a separate entity though, significantly, in close association with Judah; and Jg 1^{17} would seem to imply that it was settled in the region of Zephath-Hormah, not far from Arad (cf Nu 21$^{1-3}$), some 17 miles S. of Hebron. In Jos 15^{30}, however, Hormah is mentioned as a city of Judah, and most of the cities assigned to Simeon in Jos 19$^{1-9}$ reappear elsewhere as cities of Judah (cf Jos 15$^{26-32, 42}$, 1 K 19^{3}, Neh 11$^{26-29}$, 1 S 27^{6} 30^{30}). The inference to be drawn is that following the disaster alluded to in Gn 49$^{5-7}$ the survivors of Simeon were absorbed into Judah; and the fact that Simeon does not appear among the southern clans mentioned in 1 S 27^{10} 30^{29f} suggests that the survivors were so few and so scattered that they could not maintain themselves even as a political sub-division of Judah.

Nevertheless, the memory of the tribe was kept alive in the national tradition. Simeon is named in the Joseph story (Gn 42^{24}) as the hostage detained in Egypt to ensure the brothers' return with Benjamin. He is not mentioned in the blessing of Moses (Dt 33) but the tribe is included in the census lists in Numbers (1^{22f} 26$^{12-14}$). A note in 1 Ch 4^{39ff}, appended to the genealogical register of Simeon, says that some 500 men of the tribe, being expelled from Gedor (LXX Gerar) in the time of Hezekiah, migrated to Mount Seir and there seized the land of the Amalekites. If this is based upon an authentic tradition it indicates, somewhat surprisingly in view of the silence elsewhere, that Simeon was still an entity of sorts in the 7th cent.

It has been thought by some scholars that Simeon appears in the inscriptions of Esar-haddon as the name of a district in the vicinity of Apku which they identify with Aphekah, near Hebron (Jos 15^{53}). But the reading Simeon is precarious; Samaria may be intended; and there is an Aphek in Asher mentioned in Jos 19^{30}, possibly identical with that in Jos 12^{18} and another in Jos 13^{4} on the border of the territory of Sidon.

2. The great-grandfather of Judas Maccabaeus (1 Mac 2^{1}). **3.** The righteous and devout man who took the infant Jesus in his arms and blessed Him when He was presented in the Temple (Lk 2^{25ff}). **4.** A descendant of David (Lk 3^{30}) mentioned in the Lucan genealogy of Jesus. **5.** A leader of the church at Antioch (Ac 13^{1}). **6.** The apostle Peter (Ac 15^{14}). J. A. C.—**C. A. Si.**

SIMON (a Greek form of *Simeon*).—**1.** Simon Chosamaeus, who was found to have a 'strange' wife (1 Es 9^{32} ∥ Ezr 10^{31} **Shimeon**). **2.** The subject of the encomium in Sir 50^{1ff}, the high priest, son of Onias—probably Simon II. (*grandson* of Onias I.) early in the 2nd cent. B.C. **3.** The Maccabaean high priest and ethnarch, son of Mattathias, slain by his son-in-law Ptolemy, 135 B.C. (1 Mac 16^{16}; see MACCABEES, **4**). **4.** A Benjamite, guardian of the Temple in the time of Onias III., who suggested to Apollonius, the governor, to plunder it (2 Mac 3^{4}). **5.** See PETER. **6.** See SIMON MAGUS. **7.** Simon the Cananaean, one of the Twelve (Mt 10^{4}, Mk 3^{18}). The surname is an Aramaic equivalent of 'Zealot' (Lk 6^{15}, Ac 1^{13}). **8.** See BRETHREN OF THE LORD. **9.** Simon the Leper, our Lord's host at Bethany (Mt 26^{6}, Mk 14^{3}; cf Jn 12^{2}), possibly husband or father of Martha, doubtless cured of his leprosy at some time before the anointing by Mary (cf MARY, **2**). **10.** The Pharisee who was our Lord's host when the penitent woman anointed Him (Lk 7^{40}). The contradictions between these two stories are so great that it is difficult to suppose that they relate the same event in different versions. Two such incidents may well have happened, and one may have suggested the other (cf MARY, **2**). **11.** Father, or brother, of Judas Iscariot, himself surnamed Iscariot (Jn 6^{71} 13^{26} 'Judas of Simon Iscariot,' 13^{2} 'Judas Iscariot son of Simon'). **12.** The Cyrenian who bore our Lord's cross (Mt 27^{32}, Mk 15^{21}, Lk 23^{26}); see ALEXANDER and RUFUS. The followers of Basilides in the 2nd cent.

said that Simon was crucified instead of Jesus. **13.** The tanner, Peter's host at Joppa (Ac 9^{43}). A. J. M.

SIMON MAGUS.—In the NT the Samaritan magician Simon appears only once (Ac 8$^{9-24}$). He is converted to Christianity largely because of the miracles performed by the evangelist Philip (q.v.), though he does not receive the Holy Spirit, given by the imposition of the apostles' hands. He offers money to Peter and John, but Peter condemns him and urges him to repent; Simon then asks Peter to pray for him. Luke apparently knows more about Simon than this story, for he says Simon called himself 'someone great' and the Samaritans acclaimed him with the words 'The man is that power of God which is called Great.' Evidently the Samaritans regard Simon as an angelic messenger or, less probably, as the Samaritan *Ta'eb* or Messiah; in the year A.D. 36 there was a Samaritan prophet who told the people he could recover the lost sacred vessels buried by Moses on Mount Gerizim (Jos. *Ant.* XVIII. iv. 1 [85–87]).

In later times there was a gnostic sect of Simonians which flourished in Samaria but also had representatives in Rome; this is attested by Justin and Irenaeus, who say that Simon claimed to be the supreme deity from whom emanated a 'first thought' through whom the universe was made; this 'thought' had fallen and was imprisoned in a succession of female bodies; Simon himself finally descended in order to save her. Irenaeus tells us that he regarded himself as Father, Son, and Holy Spirit. It is by no means clear that this Simonian doctrine actually goes back even to the end of the 1st cent., and many aspects of Simonian thought seem to be based on NT writings.

A different account, found in the Ebionite pseudo-Clementine literature traces Simon's spiritual descent back to a certain Dositheus (Dosthai), whose doctrines, as described by late sources, were very close to those of the Essenes as revealed by the Dead Sea Scrolls. According to the Pseudo-Clementines, both Simon and Dositheus were disciples of John the Baptist; after John's death Dositheus was head of the sect, but soon came to recognize that Simon was 'the standing one.' This account may be more reliable than that of the church fathers, with which it can hardly be reconciled.

Perhaps we can differentiate two stages in Simonian doctrine, the earlier reflected in the Pseudo-Clementines, the latter found in church writers. The account in Acts might then represent an intermediate stage, described from a hostile point of view. R. M. G.

SIMPLICITY.—In the OT 'simple' is almost always the translation of a word (*p^{e}thî*) which appears mainly in Proverbs, and can be used in a good or a bad sense. The simple are represented as on a level with the young (Pr 1^{4}) and the foolish (1$^{22, 32}$), the opposite of the 'prudent,' those who 'believe everything' and therefore 'acquire folly' (14$^{15, 18}$). On the other hand, Yahweh guards them (Ps 116^{6}) and His testimony makes them wise (Ps 19^{7}). In 2 S 15^{11} 'simplicity' means 'integrity' (*tōm*). In the Testaments of the Twelve Patriarchs (Issachar) the man of straightforward simplicity is vividly eulogized. In the NT 'simple' and 'simplicity' denote the same singleness of character (Gr. *haplotēs*) described in the Testament of Issachar, the attitude of 'sincere devotion' (as RSV translates the word in 2 Co 11^{3}) to Christ. The 'sound eye' of Mt 6^{22} (Gr. *haplous*) is a Semitic way of describing this type of character. Similarly, Jesus' disciples are told to be 'wise as serpents and innocent as doves' (Mt 10^{16}, cf Ro 16^{19}). Because the 'simple' man (in this good sense) is generous without ulterior motives the term 'simplicity' comes to mean 'generosity' (Ro 12^{8}, 2 Co 8^{2} 9$^{11, 13}$, Ja 1^{5}; cf Pr 11^{25} LXX). 'Singleness of heart' is another Semitic expression referring to purity in self-surrender (q.v.) to God (Eph 6^{5}, Col 3^{22}). R. S. B.

SIMRI, 1 Ch 26^{10} (AV).—See SHIMRI, 3.

SIN, Ezk 30^{15f} (AV, RV).—See PELUSIUM.

SIN.—The earliest OT writers (J tradition) no sooner mention man than they find themselves faced with the problem of sin. It arose out of disobedience (Gn 3^{11}) and it grew into falsehood, selfishness and defiance (Gn 4^{9}). From the second chapter of the Bible to the last chapter we read of man's persistent sin, of God's varied methods of dealing with it, and of the rewards and penalties of sin. The Bible is essentially realistic, but never more so than in dealing with this problem. Others may 'call evil good and good evil' (Is 5^{20}), but not the Bible writers. They condemn sin, they call sinners to repentance, they earnestly seek for a cure that no mortal man can provide, till finally God Himself in Christ provides the cure for 'every one who believes in' Christ.

I. THE OLD TESTAMENT.—**1. The early narratives.**—In the story of the Fall, not only does the writer (J) attribute sin to a positive act of conscious disobedience to God, but he regards it as an entity standing over against 'good' (2^{17}). In the same writer's narrative of the murder of Abel, sin is represented as the *rōbhēṣ*, the door-demon who lurks outside in the dark to catch the unwary (4^{7}). These stories are the beginning of the history of a long process of deterioration which culminated at the Flood. From individual acts of wrong-doing we are brought face to face with the condition, 'every imagination of the thoughts of his heart was only evil continually' (6^{5}). The growth and arrogance of sin in the human race became so pronounced and universal that God is said to have rejected man completely, and in His wrath to have destroyed His creation, which was infected by man's corruption. He is 'grieved to his heart' and sorry that he ever 'made man on the earth' (6^{6}). The same writer, in giving the current explanation for the diversity of human language, notes another racial rebellion against God, which was punished by the overthrow of Babel (11$^{1-9}$).

A change in the Divine method of dealing with sinful man is now noticeable. The writers lead gradually up to this, beginning with Noah, whose righteousness (7^{1}) stands in solitary contrast to the universal decadence. The elective principle enters into the relationship of God and man. A covenant is established by which this relationship is defined, and in consequence human consciousness of sin is gradually deepened. It is not always the patriarchs who lead the way. In individual cases outside the covenant we see, indeed, evidences of a higher standard of moral obligation (Gn 12^{18f} 20^{9f}). At the same time, the history of Esau furnishes us with proof that already glimmerings of a more profound ethical basis upon which to build human character than that recognized elsewhere, had begun to intrude themselves. If in the case of Abraham 'faith was reckoned as righteousness' (Ro 4^{9}), and belief in the fidelity of God's promises in the face of the most untoward conditions, constituted the foundation-stone of the patriarch's noble character, so in Esau's case it was the lack of this belief, with the consequent inability to appreciate the dignity to which he was born, that lay at the root of his great and pathetic failure. The secret of Joseph's power to resist temptation lay, not merely in his natural inability to be guilty of a breach of trust towards his master, but still more in his intense realization that to yield would be 'a great wickedness and sin against God' (Gn 39^{9}). Thus, while it is true to say that the dominating conception of sin in the OT is that it is the great disturbing element in the personal relations of God and man, it seems to have been realized very early that the chief scope for its exercise lay in the domain of human intercourse. The force of Abimelech's complaint against Abraham lay in the fact that the former was guiltless of wronging the latter, whereas he was in serious danger of sinning against God in consequence of the patriarch's duplicity.

2. The Sinaitic Law.—The next great critical point in the evolution of human consciousness of sin is reached in the promulgation of the Law from Sinai. Here the determinative process of Divine election is seen in its widest and most elaborate working. The central purpose of the Law may be considered as of a twofold character. Not only are the restrictions tabulated in order for the erection of barriers against the commission of sin ('God has come to prove you, and that the fear of him may be before your eyes, that you may not sin,' Ex 20[20]), but positive enactments regulating the personal communion of God and Israel provide frequently recurring opportunities of loving and joyful service (Ex 23[14ff]). The law of restitution, as given in Ex 21–22, may be regarded as harsh in some of its enactments, but it may be easily conceived as an immense stride forward on the road to 'the royal law . . . You shall love your neighbour as yourself' (Ja 2[8]). It cannot be said that restitution and mutual service are left out of sight in those chapters of Exodus which are universally recognized as containing the oldest part of the Mosaic Code. Although anthropopathic conceptions of God abound and are to be seen, for instance, in the idea of His jealousy being roused by idolatrous practices (Ex 20[5]), yet the promises are made to Israel that, in return for services to Y″, He will save His people in the face of their enemies (Ex 23[25ff]).

3. Deuteronomy and the Historical Books.—In the Deuteronomic summary of the Law, whatever be the date at which it was edited, a loftier ground of obedience is attained. Love of God and of their fellow-men is more explicitly dwelt on as the motive power of human life (Dt 6[5] 10[12] etc.), and the heart is again and again referred to as the seat of that love, both passively and actively (11[18] 6[6] 10[16]). The basis upon which it is rested is the fact of God's persistent love for them and their fathers evidenced in many vicissitudes and in spite of persistent waywardness and stubbornness to hinder its activity (4[37] 7[7f] 10[15]). Though there are numerous echoes of the older conception that the keeping of God's commandments is one side of a bargain which conditions men's happiness and prosperity (4[24, 40] 6[15]), yet we observe a lofty range of thought bringing in its train truer ideas of sin and guilt. The sternness of God is insisted on, but as having for its objective the ultimate good of His people (10[13] 6[24]). It is a necessary phase of His love, compelling them to recognize that sin against God is destructive of the sinner. The ultimate aim of the Deuteronomist is the leading of men to hate sin as God hates it, and to love mercy and righteousness as and because God loves them (cf Dt 10[18f], Lv 19[33f]), by establishing the closest relationship and communion between Him and His people (cf Dt 14[1f] 7[6] 26[18f] 27[9] 28[9] etc.).

One sin is specially insisted on by the Deuteronomist, namely, the sin of idolatry. We know in these days that Israel had no genius for religion except in continually turning aside to worship the gods of Canaan. The tablets found from 1927 onwards at Râs Shamra (Ugarit) have given us a picture of Canaanite religion, the kind of religious ideas and cults with which the Hebrews came into contact when they entered Canaan. It is against Canaanite cults such as this that the Deuteronomists are fighting, as indeed we realize most clearly when we read a statement such as that in Jer 44[17], that for generations the Queen of Heaven had been worshipped. In Deuteronomy and the historical books the national disasters which recur so frequently are always atrributed to this sin of idolatry, *i.e.* worshipping the gods of Canaan, while the return of the people under the guidance of a great representative hero or later under the government of a good king, is marked by the blessings of peace and prosperity. In the story of the Northern Kingdom the constant refrain meets us in each succeeding reign: 'He clung to the sin of Jeroboam the son of Nebat which he made Israel to sin' (2 K 3[2] 10[29] 13[2] etc.). During the vigorous and successful reign of Ahab and Jezebel, the seeds of national decay were sown, and the historian does not neglect to point out the source to which the later mournful decline may be traced (1 K 16[31]). The great rebellion against the Davidic dynasty which occurred at the death of Solomon is attributed to the stated declension of Solomon in his old age from the pure Y″ worship so zealously and consistently advocated by his father David. We are not, however, altogether limited to what is here inferentially taught as to national sin, with its consequent national punishment. Side by side with the introduction of foreign religious ideas, vices peculiar to Oriental despotism invaded the royal court and the nation of Israel. David himself is represented as guilty of a sin which marred his character as an individual, and the census (2 S 24) was regarded as a breach of that trust held by him as God's vicegerent on earth. Both these cases are of interest in the light they throw on the doctrine of sin and its consequences. In the case of Bathsheba, which was a purely personal transgression, the prophet Nathan comes not only as the bearer of a message of Divine pardon to the repentant sinner, but also as the stern judge pronouncing sentence of severe and protracted punishment. The death of the newly born child and the subsequent distractions arising out of the affair of Absalom are looked on as expressions of God's wrath and of retributive justice (see 2 S 12[10–18]). Whatever the contemporary reasons for regarding the taking of the census as sinful, and even the reckless Joab considered it an act of wanton folly, we find the same features of repentance and forgiveness, and the same inclusion of others in the suffering consequent on its commission. The prophet Gad comes to the king as the revealer of God's wrath and the messenger of God's pardon (2 S 24[1–25]). Into this narrative, however, another element is introduced, telling of the difficulty which was felt, or perhaps not yet felt, as to the origin of sin. God is said by the early historian of David's reign to have been the instigator of the king's act, because His anger 'was kindled against Israel' (2 S 24[1]). It is difficult to avoid the conclusion that at one stage of Hebrew thought God was looked on as, in some respects at least, the author of evil (cf Ex 4[21] 7[3] 14[8], Jg 9[23], 1 S 16[14] 18[10] 19[9]). Nor ought we to be surprised at this, for this problem is one which was sure to present itself very early to the minds of thoughtful men; while the numerous instances where the commission of a sin seemed to have been made subservient by God to the exhibiting of His power and love afforded presumptive **prima facie** evidence that He Himself willed the act as the minister of His glory (see the history of Joseph with the writer's comments thereon, Gn 45[5] 50[20], Ps 105[17]; cf Job 1[6–12] 2[1–7], Hos 2). It is interesting to note the advance made in speculative thought with regard to this still unsolved, and perhaps insoluble problem, between the time of the above-mentioned historian and that of the later Chronicler (1 Ch 21[1]). Here the name of Satan or 'Adversary' is boldly inserted as the author of the sin, a fact which reminds us of the categorical denial of the Son of Sirach, 'He hath not commanded any man to be ungodly; and he hath not given any man licence to sin' (15[20]). That the origin of sin continued to be debated and speculated upon down to a very late period is evidenced by the vehement warning of St. James against imputing to God the temptation to evil (Ja 1[13]), and by the counter assertion that God is the author of nothing but good (v.[17]).

4. The Prophets.—By far the most important stage in the history of the OT doctrine of sin is that which is marked by the teaching of the prophets. The four practically contemporary prophets of the 8th cent. are Amos, Hosea, Isaiah, and Micah. The first named reveals a growing outlook on the world at large, and a recognition of the prevalence and power of sin in other nations than Israel. Damascus, Philistia, Tyre, Edom, Ammon, and Moab, as well as Judah and Israel, all come under the displeasure of the prophet Amos. Each had been guilty of cruelty and wrong against the people of Y″. The characteristic faults of these heathen peoples—lust and tyranny of the strong over the weak—had invaded Israel too. The love of money, with its attendant evils of injustice and robbery of the poor by the wealthy, is inveighed against by both Amos and Hosea as deserving of the wrath of God (cf Hos 12[7f], Am 4[1] 8[4ff]). This degeneracy of the people of the Northern Kingdom during the reign of Jeroboam II. was as much in evidence in the ranks of the prophets and priests as among the other ruling classes, and to it, as the cause, is assigned the downfall which so speedily followed (Am 3[11] 6[1–7] 2[7] 9[1ff], Hos 4[9] 9[7f] 5[1], Mic 3[5, 11] etc.). Both Isaiah and Micah mourn over the same moral declension (Is 5[8] 1[16f], Mic 2[2] etc.), and it may be said that it is owing to the preaching of these four prophets that the centre of gravity, as it were, of sin is changed, and the principles of universal justice and love, as the fundamental attributes of Y″'s character and rule, are established. It was the prophetic function to deepen the consciousness of sin by revealing a God of moral righteousness to a people whose peculiar relationship to Y″ involved both immense privileges and grave responsibilities (Am 3^{2}, Hos 3^{5ff}, Mic 3^{1ff} etc.). Terrible, however, as were the denunciations, and emphatic as were the declarations of the prophets against the vices of greed, oppression and lust, they were no less clear in their call to repentance, and in promises of restoration and pardon (Is 1^{18f}, Mic 7^{18}, Hos 6^{1}, ? Am 9^{11f}). The later story of Jonah of Gath-hepher is the revelation of a growing feeling that the righteous dominion of Y″ was not, in the exercise of its moral influence, confined exclusively to Israel. The consciousness of sin and the power of repentance have now their place in the lives of nations outside the Abrahamic covenant.

Hitherto the prophetic teaching was largely confined to national sin and national repentance. It is not till the days of Jeremiah that the importance, in this respect, of the individual begins to manifest itself. The lament of Jeremiah, it is true, frequently expresses itself in terms of national infidelity (Jer 2^{5-37} 8^{7} 35^{14-17} 31^{28} 32^{32ff} etc.). At the same time an element of individualistic thought enters largely into his teaching (cf 17^{10} 32^{19}). On its darker side he notes how universally present sin is seen to be: he says ' from the least to the greatest,' or again, ' from prophet to priest ' all are infected (8^{10}, cf v.^{6}). It is impossible to find a man either just or truth-loving (5^{1}); and the explanation is not far to seek for sin is a disease which affects the individual heart, and therefore poisons the whole life of each man (cf 13^{7} 5^{23} 7^{24} etc.). The nature of the disease he characterizes as desperate is in the awful deceit which supervenes (17^{9}). A hopeless pessimism seems at times to have pervaded the prophet's teaching, and such of the people as were aroused by his appeals were smitten by a blank despair (10^{23} 2^{25} 18^{12} 13^{23} etc). As the prophet grows older, however, and gains a wider knowledge from his own bitter experiences, he discovers a way of escape from the overpowering influence of sin. As the heart is the seat of evil, it is found that the creative act of God can provide a remedy (31^{33} 32^{39} 24^{7}). A new heart straight from the hand of God, beating with new and holy impulses, is the sure, as it is the only, hope for men (32^{40}). Every individual, from the least to the greatest, in whom the Divine activity has been at work shall have the felicity of hearing the blessed sentence, ' I will forgive their iniquity, and I will remember their sin no more ' (31^{34}).

Following up and developing this tendency, Ezekiel is express in his declaration of the moral independence of each man. Repudiating, as Jeremiah did, the doctrine that the sin and guilt of the fathers are imputed to the children, he elaborates clearly and emphatically the truth, which seems to us axiomatic, that the father as an individual is independent of the son, with the terrible but inevitable corollary, ' the individual who sins, shall die ' (Ezk $18^{4,20}$; cf vv.$^{10-20}$). The profound truth which lies at the basis of the ancient belief in the close interaction of individual and racial guilt is, of course, valid for all time, and has been sanctified by the historical fact of the Incarnation. The life, work and death of Christ have their value in the re-establishment of this truth, and in the re-creation, as it were, of the concurrent truth of the solidarity of the whole human race (cf the expression ' we are all become like one who is unclean,' Is 64^{6}).

5. Psalms.—We turn now to the Psalms, and there find, as might be expected, the deepest consciousness of personal guilt on the part of the sinner. Of course, it is to be remembered that the Jewish Psalter is the product of different epochs in the national history, ranging probably from the time of David and the heyday of prophetic religion to the age immediately succeeding the Captivity, if not much later. It may be said, indeed, that this volume of sacred poetry constitutes a kind of antiphonal response to the preaching of the Prophets. Not only so, but there is a considerable consensus of opinion in modern times that here we have also the apparatus of a living cultus. Thus, from both points of view, the Psalter has its roots and was imbedded in the religious life of the people. Confession of and repentance for sin, both personal and national, constitute the prominent feature of the authors' attitude. A deep love for God breathes through the poems, and a profound hope that at some future date Israel may be restored once more to the favour of Y″.

The climax of confession, repentance and restoration of the sinner is to be seen in Ps 51. Early editors of the Psalter who sought wherever possible to find an occasion for the psalm in the life of David, associated this psalm with David's sin with Bathsheba and his subsequent repentance. The first two verses of the psalm are instructive in ideas of sin, not only for the Psalter, but for the whole of the OT. Here there are three words used for ' sin ': transgressions, iniquity, sin. The first is the Hebrew *pesha'*, which strictly means ' rebellion.' Sin is rebellion against God, and this is the characteristic idea of the prophets also. This means that sin is not the transgression of a code of morals so much as a personal rebellion against God. This conception of sin is important, and is one of the important contributions which prophet and psalmist make to true religion. The second word is *'āwōn*, which describes sin as a deliberate turning aside out of the way. Here is no mistake, nothing accidental, no weakness of humankind, but a deliberate choice. The third word is *ḥaṭṭâth*, which describes sin as missing the mark, missing one's way, the action of a man who goes astray, not wilfully, but because of the weakness of humankind. The first and the second types of sin are regarded as the most serious, cf Job 34^{37}, ' For he adds rebellion to his sin.' In this psalm also we get the conviction that all sin is against God (v.^{4}), and that sin is so imbedded in human nature that the psalmist says he was born like that. He knows that the only way of getting rid of sin is that God shall cleanse him through and through. God must create in him a clean heart and give him a new and right spirit. This repentance and consequent cleansing is to issue in joyful song and witness to God's saving grace and the psalmist is to offer to God what God most desires ' a broken and a contrite heart ' (v.^{16}). Throughout the Psalter we get this deep understanding of the serious nature of sin, and the growing conviction that God, and God alone, can cleanse and release him from this incubus which weighs him down to death and dominates him from the cradle to the grave. It is doubtless because in these matters the Psalter reflects the inner struggles of every man that it has maintained its unique place in the devotions of the Church through the ages.

6. The Priestly Code.—Here we have an elaborate and intricate system of legal and ceremonial obligations, all associated with the ritual of the second Temple. This code, found in Exodus, Leviticus, Numbers, does not deal with deliberate sin, ' with a high hand ' (Nu 15^{30}). For such sin, the Priestly Code has no remedy except that ' that person shall be cut off from among his people ' (Nu 15^{30}). The laws deal with unwitting sin, where a man commits a fault in ritual affairs or touches what is unclean. This includes accidental defilement due to circumstances over which a man has no control. The Priestly Code has taken over those taboos which are associated with primitive religion, ideas concerning the sacredness of blood and fat, taboos concerning certain animals, birds and insects, and taboos concerning all types of uncleanness. The good element in this was the attempt to include all the details of everyday life within the sphere of God's direct concern. The bad element was in the tendency for these things to be taken to comprise the whole of religion. For all offences mentioned an offering was due, either a sin-offering or a guilt-offering. First, cases where a sin-offering is due: they are mostly accidental and unconscious. The Hebrew word is *bishᵉghāghāh* (by error, inadvertence). A man does accidentally what is prohibited. The whole congregation errs and is not aware of it. When the ' sin ' is known, then a sin-offering is due. Or again (Lv 5) a man is silent when he is put on oath as a witness ; a man touches something unwittingly that is unclean of man or beast ; a man makes a rash oath and does not realize it till it is pointed out to him—all these are faults for which a sin-offering is required when the fault is made known to the person concerned. But a man who unwittingly makes a mistake over a holy-gift, that is a gift which becomes the perquisite of the priest, must offer a guilt-offering. This is a case where damage has been done, or a right infringed and the damage can be assessed. This case is extended in Lv 5^{17-19} to the man who does not know whether he has committed a fault or not, but wishes to offer a guilt-offering in case he has overstepped the mark. This was called the *'āshām tālûy* (' suspended guilt-offering '), and in the last days of the Temple men of the most scrupulous conscience used to bring such an offering daily, just in case by any possible chance, in spite of all earnest precautions, they had transgressed any rule in any detail, cf Job 1^5. The nearest approach to deliberate sin and conscious sin which we find in the Priestly Code is in Lv 6^{1-7}. This passage is concerned with such offences as dealing falsely with a neighbour in the matter of a deposit, a pledge or robbery, and of stealing by finding. The general opinion is that these are sins which would not have been known except for the offender's own confession. This was the interpretation of Rabbi Akiba in the 2nd cent. A.D., on the ground that lending or borrowing is done in the presence of a third person, but not depositing a pledge, and Rashi definitely says it is a matter that arises on the confession of the guilty party. The full use of the *'āshām tālûy* whilst the Temple was still standing makes this explanation likely, since in that case everything depended upon the confession of the person involved. This extension into the realm of deliberate fraud is probably an extension of the idea of not knowing. Other sin-offerings in the Priestly Code are concerned with cleansing from ceremonial uncleanness, either because of the impurity of any flow of blood or discharge from the genital organs, male or female, or in all skin diseases which are listed in Lv 3 under the head of ' leprosy.' They also include uncleanness from touching the dead, an unclean animal, etc.

In a general way all the sacrifices of the Priestly Code are ' to make atonement ' (Lv 1^4) for the worshipper, but the sin- and guilt-offerings are for ritual and inadvertent offences, whilst the general statement is that the Code can do nothing for deliberate and presumptuous sin.

7. Job, Proverbs, Ecclesiastes.—The confidence thus expressed is all the more remarkable because of the general belief in the universality of sin and of its effects (cf Ps 14^{2f} 51^5), a belief which was shared by the authors of the Book of Job (14^4 15^{14ff} 4^{17}), Proverbs (20^9), and Ecclesiastes (7^{20}, cf 1 K 8^{46}). In the Proverbs we have what might be described as an attempt to place the moral life on an intellectual basis. The antithesis of wisdom and folly is that which marks the life of the righteous man and the sinner. Ethical maxims, the compiled results of human experience, follow each other in quick succession, but the book is devoid of the bright, warm hopefulness so characteristic of the Psalms. The sinner is left to his fate, and the wise man is he who, ordering his own life aright, leaves the fool to pursue his folly and deserve his fate.

The author of the Book of Job sets himself to solve the problem of the connexion between sin and human suffering, and though he fails, as he was bound to fail, to clear up the difficulty, he makes it evident that the one cannot always be measured in terms of the other. The conviction of his own innocence—Job's most treasured personal possession—upholds his belief against the prevalent conception that sin is *always* punished here and now, and that righteousness is *always* rewarded in like manner. The end of this dramatic treatise, however, emphasizes the popular creed, though the experience of Job must have shaken its universal validity. The conception of sin is, of course, entirely ethical, but is very wide in its scope. In defending himself against the thinly veiled accusations of his friends, Job reveals his ideas of the range and depth of the ravages of sin in human life and conduct, and gives evidence of remarkable spiritual penetration (*e.g.* ch. 31, see R. A. Watson's commentary on this book in *The Expositor's Bible*). Mention may, perhaps, be usefully made here of Elihu's contribution to the discussion, in which he intervenes by a lengthened argument to prove that suffering may be looked on not merely as *punishment* for sin, but also as a means of *discipline*, and as designed by God as a *warning* against sin (cf chs. 33 ff).

J. R. W.—N. H. S.

II. Apocryphal Books.—**Sirach** and **Wisdom of Solomon.**—The intellectualism which is characteristic of Proverbs and Ecclesiastes finds a prominent place in Sirach and the Wisdom of Solomon. There are here two sharply defined classes of men (' in pairs, one the opposite of the other,' Sir 33^{15}), a dualistic conception which permeates all creation (cf 42^{24}). The sinner is to be dealt with unmercifully (' Give to the godly man, but do not help the sinner,' 12^4), for no good can come from him who refuses instruction. It is possible, however, for the sinner to return to the Lord and forsake his sins (17^{25f}). The only way in which righteousness may be pursued is by the cultivation of wisdom and instruction, and by paying heed to the experiences of daily life (34^9 39^{1-8} 14^{20ff}). Let reason be the guide of human action and all will be well (37^{16} ; cf 32^{19}). It is possible for the educated man to acquire such a command over his inclinations that he is able of himself to make the great choice between life and death (15^{17}), but for the fool there is little hope (15^7). Looking back on the centuries of human history, the writer discovers that sin has brought in its train all the great physical calamities which mark its progress (39^{28ff}). The relation is, however, external, and is a mark of Divine vengeance and wrath against sinners (cf 40^{9f}). There is no trace of the profound conception of spiritual sympathy between the different orders of creation, characteristic of the teaching of St. Paul (cf Ro 8^{19-22}).

The author of the Book of Wisdom displays the same fundamental thought that wisdom and sin are totally incompatible (Wis 1^{4f}). Ignorance and folly are identified with sin (2^{21f} 4^{15} 5^4 etc.), and not merely the causes of sin. The only way to attain to righteousness is by the careful, unremitting discipline of the reason (' Great are thy judgments and hard to describe ; therefore uninstructed souls have gone astray,' 17^1 ; cf 2^1 6^{15f}). Running like a thread of gold through the whole book, however, is the conception of the immortality of righteousness and of those who cultivate widsom (1^{15} 2^{23} 3^4 6^{18f} $8^{13, 17}$ etc.). In the beautiful personification of Wisdom (6^{12}–8^{21}) we find the writer not only speaking of the Spirit of God as being its Author and Diffuser, but practically identifying them with each other (cf 9^{17} 12^1 ; cf 2 Es 14^{22}). The universality of sin does not figure largely in his teaching, but, with regard to its effects on those under its thrall, he is no optimist. Of such he could believe ' that their origin was evil and their wickedness inborn, and that their way of thinking would never change '(12^{10}). Such is the penalty of ignorance. ' All men who were ignorant of God were foolish by nature ; and they were unable from the good things that are seen to know him who exists, nor did they recognize the craftsman while paying heed to his works ' (13^1). The author appears to suggest that some were born to be righteous and some to sin, the power of moral choice being really confined to the former (cf 8^{19ff} 7^{16f}).

III. The New Testament.—**1. Synoptists.**—The practical outcome of the teaching of the OT is seen in the fact that the first of the Synoptists continually emphasizes that the mission of Jesus was to forgive sin. The account of the angelic communication to Joseph (Mt 1^{21}) is significant, ' You shall call his name Jesus, for he will save his people from their sins.' This is the feature of Jesus' work upon which the apostles laid particular stress, in their earliest as in their latest teaching. The preparatory work of the Baptist aroused in the breasts of the multitudes who thronged to hear him an active consciousness of sin, together with the necessity for repentance and the possibility of consequent forgiveness (Mk 1^{4}). The preaching of John, however, lacked the new power that the life and work of Jesus brought, giving men the gift of repentance (Ac 5^{31}; cf 11^{18}), and enabling them to turn from their wickedness (Ac 3^{26}). It is significant that the recorded teaching of Jesus reveals little direct and abstract instruction regarding sin. At the same time, we must not forget the scathing denunciation hurled by Him at the legalistic conceptions of sin found among the scribes of His time (Mt 23^{1-28}, Mk 7^{9ff}), or the positive, authoritative declarations by which He drew from the ancient laws of Sinai the essential ethical ideas therein enshrined (Mt 5^{21-48}, where the teaching is not so much an extension of the area of sin as a plumbing of its depths). For Him 'the law and the prophets' had an abiding significance (Mt 5^{17-20}, 7^{12}), but their interpretation and application were inadequate. Outward and physical behaviour was, for Jesus, a poor index of the sin against which the Law was meant to be a deterrent and the preaching of the prophets was a persistent and solemn protest (cf Lk 11^{38-44}). Sin, whether inward or outward in appearance, is lodged in the deepest part of man's being. It destroys upward growth by poisoning the life at its roots, and here the language of Jesus assumes its most formidable prophetic severity. There are certain classes of sins, however, against which He uttered His most solemn warnings. Their common characteristic is that of wilful and deliberate rejection of truth and goodness. Remarkable amongst these is 'blasphemy against the Spirit' (Mt 12^{31f}; cf Mk 3^{29}, Lk 12^{10}), which St. Mark designates 'an eternal sin.' Taking into consideration the circumstances in which the words were spoken, it is clear that Jesus was pointing to a condition when man loses the ability to retrace his steps, when, because he has rejected the Spirit and described Jesus' exorcisms as due to collusion with 'Beelzebul,' he has put himself into a position where he is cut off from the one power that might move him to repent and thus turn back for forgiveness. The sin of unreality, which could so easily be a stage toward this graver sin, was one to which the Pharisees were specially addicted, and to it, therefore, He drew their attention constantly (Mt 23^{5-7}, Mk 12^{38f}, Lk 11^{43} 20^{45f}; cf Mt 6^{1-16} 5^{20}).

Every sin is bound to exercise influence, not only on the life and character of those immediately guilty, but also on a circle outside. There is, however, a species having for its special object the dragging down of those who would otherwise be innocent. The terms of the emphatic warning against leading others astray, either by positive interference or by the force of example (cf Mk 9^{42}, Mt 18^{6}, Lk 17^{2}), remind us of the sad presage by which Jesus foreshadowed the traitor's end (Mt 26^{24}). The word used to denote this sin is also employed in speaking of sin in its relation to the guilty individual. The fact that Jesus deals with both aspects at the same time shows how strongly He felt the impossibility of any sin remaining, in its working, a purely personal offence. There is always here in activity a force which may be described as centrifugal, inevitably bringing harm to those within the circle of its movement (cf Ro 14^{7f}). Nor did Jesus hold Himself to be free from this danger of contamination ('You are a hindrance to me,' Mt 16^{23}), while He points to the ideal Kingdom of the Son of Man where nothing causing men to stumble shall be allowed a place (Mt 13^{41}). It is interesting to remember here that St. Paul uses the same word to express the result of the preaching of 'Christ crucified' to the Jews (1 Co 1^{23}; cf Gal 5^{11}, Ro 9^{32f}, 1 P 2^{8}). This was, indeed, a contingency foreseen by Jesus Himself, as will be seen in His answer to the messengers of the imprisoned Baptist (Mt 11^{6}). Doubtless these words were intended to convey a gentle warning to the prisoner against permitting the untoward circumstances of his life to overcome his once firm faith in the Messiahship of One whom he had publicly proclaimed as 'the Lamb of God' (Jn 1^{29}). A direct reference to an OT example of this sin occurs in Rev 2^{14}, where the conduct of Balaam is held up to reprobation.

In the parable of the Pharisee and the Publican, Jesus taught the necessity for the realization of personal guilt on the part of the sinner in order to obtain forgiveness and justification in the sight of God (Lk 18^{13}). In the same way, it was the lack of this sense by the Pharisees, so far as they were themselves personally concerned, that constituted the great obstacle to their conversion (Jn 9^{41}).

A prominent feature of Jesus' teaching has to do not so much with active, deliberate sins as with what may be termed 'sins of omission.' It seems as if He wished to inculcate, by repeated emphasis, the truth that the best way to combat temptation with success is to be active in the pursuit of good. The spiritual side of this doctrine He enshrined in the form of a parable, in which He pointed out the danger to the soul arising from neglect to invoke the active agency of the Holy Spirit, even though the 'unclean spirit' had been exorcized and banished 'out of the man' (see Mt 12^{43-45} ‖ Lk 11^{24-26}). In the discourse descriptive of the General Judgment, Jesus marks the crucial test by which men shall be tried: 'As you did it not to one of the least of these, you did it not to me' (Mt 25^{45}). The same thought is conveyed frequently in parabolic form, as for example in the parables of the Ten Virgins (Mt 25^{1-13}), the Talents (25^{14-30}) in which is emphasized the profound lesson, 'from him who has not, even what he has will be taken away' (cf Mt 13^{12}), Dives and Lazarus (Lk 16^{19-31}); while much of the teaching in the Sermon on the Mount is based on the same principle (cf Mt 5^{38-44}).

2. St. Paul.—The presentation of the gospel message to the world outside the Jewish nation led St. Paul to review in detail the origin, cause, scope, and result of sin. Starting from his own individual experience, which was that of a sinner profoundly conscious of his position (cf 1 Co 15^{9} 9^{27}, Ro 7^{18ff}, 1 Ti 1^{15}), and conscious also of the remedy inherent in Christ's gospel (2 Co 12^{9}), he insists on the universality and power of sin, in order to establish the co-ordinate universality and power of 'the righteousness of God through faith in Jesus Christ' (Ro 3^{21f}; cf the expression 'where sin increased, grace abounded all the more,' 5^{20}). The central feature of St. Paul's teaching is the activity of God's grace in forgiving, restoring, and justifying the sinner; and for the purpose of establishing the reasonableness and the necessity (cf 1 Co 9^{16}) of bringing the gospel before the world, it was needful first to establish the guilt of all for whom it was intended, and to create, so to speak, in men a consciousness of moral failure and helplessness. This he does in the opening chapters of his Epistle to the Romans. Here, although he deals separately with Jews and Gentiles, he maintains the proposition that all alike are sinners (Ro 5^{12}; cf Eph 2^{3}). It is true that the Jew was the recipient of the Law; and as such he occupied the position of the moral teacher of mankind. But instead of proving the means whereby a true 'knowledge of sin' (Ro 3^{20}; cf 5^{13}) is gained, it became, through abuse, a hindrance rather than a help to his spiritual advancement (see 2^{17ff}). And just as the Jews stultified the Divinely given Law, by the exaltation of its merely transitory elements at the expense of its essential moral ideals, so the Gentiles defied 'the law written in their hearts, testified to by their conscience' (Ro 2^{15}).

This reduction of all mankind to the same level in the sight of God is further incidentally pressed by the establishment of a definite relationship between the sin of Adam and racial guilt ($5^{12, 18}$). What precisely were St. Paul's opinions as to this connexion it is impossible to discover. It is doubtful whether, in face of the intensely practical work in which he was engaged, he stopped to work out the problem of **'original sin.'** It is enough for him that 'sin came into the world through one man' and that 'by one man's disobedience many were made sinners' (see Sanday-Headlam, *Romans* in *ICC*, pp. 136 ff).

Different interpretations have been given to the words translated 'because all men sinned' (5^{12}). Some have tried to affirm that St. Paul is here asserting the freedom of the will, and is stating the plain proposition that all men have sinned as a matter of fact, and of their own choice. This, however, breaks up the parallelism with Christ and is, indeed, a notion foreign to Paul's thought as a whole. Others have seen in these words an explicit statement that the whole race was involved generically in Adam's sin. It is more constructive, however, to seek a synthesis of these two ideas. (See Nygren, *Romans ad loc.*) As a result of Adam's transgression sin obtained an entrance and a sphere of action in the world, and not only so, but a predisposition to sin was inherited, giving it its present power over the human will. At the same time, the simple statement 'all sinned,' explaining as it does the universality of death, includes the element of choice and freedom. Even those whose consciousness of sin was weakened, if not obliterated, by the absence of positive or objective law, were subjected to death. Paul assumes that physical death is the result of sin and that, therefore, because death is universal, sin is universal (cf 1 Co 15^{22}). Then, passing from physical death to that of which it is but a type, spiritual or moral death, he shows the awful depth to which sin has sent its roots in man's nature (Ro 6^{21ff}; cf v.^{8ff} 2^{7ff}).

Mention has been made above of the power of choice, where sin is concerned, inherent in human personality. Into the very seat of this power, however, sin has made an entrance, and has found a powerful ally in 'the flesh' (7^{18}). The will to resist is there, but its activity is paralized. Though St. Paul makes 'the flesh' or 'the members' of the body the seat of sin, he is far from teaching that human nature is essentially evil. The flesh may be crucified with its 'passions and desires' (Gal 5^{24}; cf 1 Co 9^{27}, Ro 6^{19}), and the bodily members instead of yielding a foothold to impurity may be given up to righteousness with sanctification as the end (cf E. D. Burton, *Spirit, Soul and Flesh*, also article, 'Flesh' in Hastings' *DCG*). An important feature of St. Paul's doctrine of sin consists in his exposition of the function of law in revealing and arousing the consciousness of sin. The expression 'the mind that is set on the flesh' (Ro 8^{7}) emerges in this connexion, and the impossibility of its 'submitting to God's law' is insisted on. 'Apart from the law sin lies dead,' but, once the law came, sin sprang into life, its presence and power were revealed (cf 1 Co 15^{56}), and by it man was confronted with his own moral weakness.

In spite of his belief in the all-pervading character and strength of sin, St. Paul's gospel is the reverse of a gospel of despair. If, on the one hand, there is a death which connotes moral corruption and slavery to sin, on the other hand there is a *death unto sin* which is not only a realization of, but a participation in, the death of Christ. The fact of his employing the same word and idea in senses so completely contrasted lends force and finality to his teaching on the remedial and restorative effects of Christ's work (cf Ro 6^{2-14}, Eph 2^{1-10}). Paul often uses the figure of crucifixion. The believer in Christ has crucified his 'old self' (Ro 6^{6}), 'the flesh with its passions and desires' (Gal 5^{24}; cf 2^{20}). This is the end of the redemptive work of Christ. The experience of St. Paul forbade him to believe that the state of being 'dead to sin' is fully realized here and now. His continuous references to the Christian life as one of warfare, in which it behoves the follower of Christ to be armed with weapons offensive and defensive, shows that his conception of the struggle against sin is that of an unceasing age-long conflict, issuing in victory for the individual, as for the race, only when the Kingdom of Christ is established in a peace that is everlasting (Eph 6^{1-17}, 1 Ti 1^{18} etc.).

3. St. John.—(*a*) In order to understand St. John's presentation of Jesus' teaching on sin, it will be useful to see his own individual doctrine as given in his *Epistles*. Here it is stressed that Christ's mission was to take away sins (1 Jn 3^{8}; cf Jn 1^{29} 16^{11}), and 'abiding in him' is regarded as the guarantee of safety against sin (1 Jn 3^{6}; cf Jn 15^{4ff}) as it also affords power to live the active, fruitful life of righteousness. Further, there is a law which expresses the Divine ideal for man, and whoever violates it, by wilfully putting himself in opposition to this law, is guilty of sin, for 'sin is lawlessness' (3^{4}). Another aspect of this law has to do with the mutual relationship of Christians who should be bound together by a love which is the reflection of the eternal love of God for men (1 Jn 4^{7-21}). If the law of love is neglected or broken, even in the matter of intercessory prayer for brethren who have sinned, wrongdoing is present, and 'all wrongdoing is sin' (5^{13-17}). From this we see how intensely real was St. John's belief in the presence and power of sin amongst men. Indeed, one of the tests by which a man's sincerity may be discovered is his power of realizing this fact. He, moreover, gives as his reason for writing this Epistle, 'that you may not sin' (2^{1}). The need of 'an advocate' who is also 'the expiation for our sins' is insisted on as being the special creation of Christ in Christian consciousness (1 Jn 2^{1f}; cf Jn 14^{16}). All this brings into clearer relief and greater prominence his doctrine of the sinlessness of the professing follower of Jesus Christ. The Christian as such 'cannot sin because he is born of God' (1 Jn 3^{9}; cf 5^{18}, 3 Jn^{11}), and, on the other hand, 'he that commits sin is of the devil' (1 Jn 3^{8}). The Christian abides in Christ (cf Jn 15^{4ff}), and because he does so he does not sin (3^{6}), whereas the committal of sin is the sure guarantee that he has neither seen nor known Him. The secret of his safety lies in the promise of Jesus that He 'keeps' (cf Jn 17^{12}) His own so that 'the evil one does not touch him' (1 Jn 5^{18}). The paradox in which St. John thus clothes his doctrine of sin reveals his profound conception of its character. Any sinful act by the Christian interrupts, and mars so far, his fellowship with God. If, however, the act be not the outcome of the man's habit or character, he cannot be said to do 'sin' in the sense of realizing sin in its completeness. The fruit of Divine fellowship is developed in the Christian's inner or central life from which sin is banished; and this reminds us somewhat of St. Paul's view of the crucifixion of the flesh with its 'passions and desires.'

A peculiar reference is made by St. John to 'sin which is mortal.' It is not any specific act or acts that he so characterizes. The saying must rather refer to sinful deeds of a character which wholly separates from Christ, and thus tends to death. In so far as it springs from a heart which wilfully and with contumely rejects Christ, it may be identified with the sin against the Holy Ghost (cf Mk 3^{29}, Mt 12^{31f}, Lk 12^{10}). The writer's refusal to insist on intercessory prayer for one thus guilty calls to mind the warnings in the Epistle to the Hebrews against the sin of apostasy or wilful sin after the reception of 'the knowledge of the truth' (cf He 6^{4-6} 10^{26}). It is probable that St. John has in his mind a class of sins which combines within itself the characteristics of both those mentioned (see article, 'Sin' in Hastings' *DB*, iv, p. 535^{b}). One feature of 1 John connects this Epistle very closely with the Fourth Gospel, revealing itself in those passages which identify sin with falsehood, and righteousness with truth. It seems as if the writer traced all sin back to the spirit which leads men to deny 'that Jesus is the Christ' (1 Jn 2^{22} 4^{3}). On the other hand, the acceptance of this belief carries with it the assurance of God's abiding presence, wherein is the sure guarantee of the realization of His purpose in us—'that we might live through him' (1 Jn 4^{9}; cf 4^{2} 5^{1}).

(*b*) *Fourth Gospel*.—It is this last aspect of sin that is the dominant note of the teaching of St. John's Gospel. Indeed, this writing may be said to be a record of the sad rejection foreshadowed in the general terms, 'He came to his own home, and his own people received him not' (1^{11}). This was more particularly true of the Jews of Jerusalem and Judaea, where the story of Jesus' ministry as told in this Gospel is for the most part laid. It is thus significant that in His last great discourse with His disciples, occurring as it did in Jerusalem, the centre of the activity hostile to His claims, Jesus lays special stress on the sin of unbelief in Him (' He will convince the world of sin . . . because they do not believe in me' Jn 16^{8f}). The revelation of the Divine life, with its manifold evidences of love and mercy in and by Jesus, took away whatever excuse men might have in the presence of God's judgment. The real reason for the rejection of Jesus by the Jews lay in their hatred of ' the Father' (Jn 15^{24}; cf v.[22]). Indeed, it is this very revelation designed by God as the eternal remedy against sin (Jn 1^{29}), which in its process and achievement affords further possibilities to sin and its consequences (Jn 9^{41}; cf Lk 12^{47f}).

Nor must we omit to note that in this Gospel sin is regarded as a species of slavery. The reference to this aspect occurs but once (Jn 8^{34}), but that it occupied an important place in early Christian teaching is evident from the incidental notices found scattered throughout the NT (cf Ro 6^{16-20}, Tit 3^{3}, 2 P 2^{19} etc.).

The popular belief in the connexion between sin and physical suffering is noticed also in the Fourth Gospel, where Jesus is represented as denying its universal applicability (Jn 9^{3}). At the same time He recognized that in certain cases the belief was justified (Jn 5^{14}). It was, perhaps, His profound knowledge of a similar but a deeper relationship than this—the relationship of sin to the whole life—that gave to the words and actions of Jesus that exquisite tenderness in His treatment of individual sinners so noticeable in this Gospel (cf Jn $8^{11, 15}$); a tenderness which he would fain impart to His followers in their dealings with fellow-sinners (cf Jn 7^{24}, Mt 7^{1ff}).

We are thus enabled to see that the view of sin held and taught by Jesus is profounder and graver than any as yet existing, for it is an offence against One who is at the same time a righteous and loving Father and a just and holy God (Mt 5^{48}, Lk 15^{18}, Jn 3^{16ff} etc.). The life of Christ is the object lesson which Christians are invited to imitate in their daily relationships and life (Mt 11^{29}, Jn 13^{15}, 1 Jn 2^{6}, Ph 2^{5}, 1 P 2^{21} etc.), and St. John has pointed out to us, as the words of Jesus Himself, the standard to which His followers are asked to aspire when He challenged His enemies to convict Him of sin (Jn 8^{46}).

4. St. James.—The author of this circular letter views sin in its practical bearings on the daily life of men. Nevertheless, his conception of its character and results is as far-reaching as we have seen it to be in both the Pauline and the Johannine teaching. Its origin he traces to the surrender of the individual's will to ' desire' (Ja 1^{14f}). Desire is not of itself evil, but it becomes sin as soon as a man who knows the higher law of duty yields to the lower attraction. ' When indulged desire bears its natural fruit, first sin, then, ultimately, death' (J. H. Ropes, *The Epistle of St. James* in *ICC*, p. 157). The writer combats the idea that God is the author of evil by insisting on the fact that each man may make a good or a bad use of temptation. As a morally free agent he stands or falls, and the result of this freedom may be the promised ' crown of life' (1^{12}) or hopeless ' death' (1^{15}). We are here reminded of the ' sin which is mortal' (1 Jn 5^{16}) referred to already, for sin, when it has become complete, fully developed, fixed and determined, inevitably brings forth death, its baneful fruit. This Epistle betrays its Jewish origin in the attitude of the writer to the Law; for him the result of the Christian revelation has been the transmuting of the Mosaic Law into ' the perfect law, the law of liberty' (1^{25}; cf 2^{12}), ' the royal law' (2^{8}). It may be said that he sometimes merely echoes the well-known opinion of the Rabbis about transgressing the minutest commandment of the Law. At the same time it must be admitted that his conception of sin, even when it finds expression in the seemingly trivial case of ' partiality' (2^{9}), is founded on a true spiritual view of the relation of man to God. The law of love is the essential guiding principle of all Christian life, and where this law is transgressed in the social relations of that life, the expression in our Epistle ' you commit sin' (literally ' you work sin,' 2^{9}) is not too strong or emphatic.

A further point in connexion with St. James' teaching occupies the closing passages of his Epistle. In this, as in the whole of his writing, he deals with it from the point of view of the daily life. In his exhortation to mutual confession of sins and intercessory prayer for forgiveness he is incidentally dwelling on the truth that all real Christian life is conditioned by its adherence, both in word and in deed, to the principle of love (cf 2^{15f}). The same may be said of his advice with regard to the corporate prayer of the Church, on behalf of one who is physically sick (5^{14f}). It is probable that our author held the common Jewish belief that sin and disease were connected as cause and effect, and his conviction that ' the prayer of faith' reaches out in its power to the whole man, extending even to the forgiveness of his sins by God, is based on his belief in the solidarity of human life as well as of the law to which it owes its allegiance. As in the case of the member of the community whose bodily and spiritual needs are ministered to by the active intervention of the Church, so he urges each individual member to prayer on behalf of his erring brother. The twofold blessing promised to this act of brotherly love may well be taken as an expression of his conviction that the individual lives of the members of the Christian community are knit so closely together that no single act of sin can be committed without so far bringing death within range of all, and that no act of love can be exercised without so far bringing mercy and forgiveness to all, and thus ' covering a multitude of sins' (cf 1 P 4^{8}).

5. Hebrews.—It cannot be said that there is any special doctrine of sin in this Epistle. Its readers were well acquainted with OT conceptions and teaching, and the writer deals mainly with the superiority of the New Covenant over the Old in supplying means whereby there shall be no longer ' any consciousness of sin' (He 10^{2}; cf Westcott, *The Epistle to the Hebrews*, Additional Note on 9^{9}). The central feature of this writing is the stress laid on the discovery by Christianity of ' the new and living way' (10^{20}) by which we have direct access to God. It is by the removal of guilt in the forgiveness of sins by the sacrifice of Jesus that this way is opened ' once for all' (10^{10}; cf v.[18] 9^{12} etc.). Special emphasis is therefore laid on the failure of the Mosaic institutions to ' take away sins' (10^{11}; cf 9^{9}), and on the awful character of the danger of harbouring ' an evil, unbelieving heart' (3^{12}).

The temptation to which the ' Hebrews' were exposed was that, under stress of persecution, they would reject the final revelation of God in Christ, or revert, under the influence of the Hellenistic Judaizers, to the somewhat eclectic faith of the latter. This wilful sin the writer characterizes as crucifying the Son of God afresh (6^{6}) and as treading Him under foot (cf 10^{29}). In warning them against the dangers to which they would be exposed during the time of suffering and trial now imminent, he points out to them that these trials may become in their own hands the means of their spiritual advancement. Instead of being the sole outcome of sin, suffering is often the chastisement of a loving Father ' that we may share his holiness' (12^{10}). The great Example, whose solution of an age-long problem we are asked to study, was Jesus, ' who for the joy that was set before him endured the cross, despising the shame' (12^{2}) and who though ' in every respect . . . tempted as we are, yet without sinning' (4^{15}), was nevertheless made ' perfect through suffering' (2^{10}).

See also articles, Atonement, Expiation, Forgiveness, Guilt, Propitiation, Redemption, etc.

J. R. W.—**W. D. S.**

SIN, WILDERNESS OF (name probably derived

from the moon-god Sin).—A region on the route of the Hebrews from Egypt to Mount Sinai. It is probably to be identified with modern *Debbet er-Ramleh*, and is not to be confused with the Wilderness of **Zin** (q.v.).

SINA, Ac 7[30, 38] (AV) = **Sinai** (q.v.).

SINAI.—The name of a mountain which, according to Hebrew tradition, was the scene of the theophany of Y″ and the giving of the Law. The connexion of the name with the Moon-god Sin is very doubtful, and Meyer's suggestion that there may be a connexion between the name Sinai and the unusual Hebrew word for the burning bush, *seneh*, is worth noting. The location of the Sinai of Hebrew tradition is very uncertain for several reasons. In the first place, the Christian tradition placing the site of Sinai in the SW. of the Sinai peninsula is late. Early in the 4th cent. A.D. it was identified with *Jeb. Serbāl*, and from the 6th cent. with *Jeb. Mûsa*. Secondly, the fact that Hebrew sources use two names for the sacred mountain, Sinai and **Horeb**, is more than a literary peculiarity. Behind the literary difference lie the traditions of the various tribes which passed through the wilderness experiences. As Professor Rowley has said, ' We have to distinguish between the history behind the tradition and the tradition as it is modified by combination with the traditions of the various tribes.' Thirdly, the weight of early Hebrew tradition connects the original home of Y″ with Mount Seir and Edom (cf Jg 5[4], Dt 33[2], Hab 3[3]) ; moreover the early episodes of the wilderness sojourn are placed at or near Kadesh, and that place is not in the SW. of the Sinai peninsula. Fourthly, in spite of efforts to disprove it, the phenomena connected with the theophany at Sinai-Horeb are clearly volcanic, and geological evidence has shown that there are no signs of volcanic activity in the SW. corner of the peninsula, but there is abundant evidence of such activity in the region to the S. of Edom. Hence, although *Jeb. Mûsa* may have been a sacred mountain and a place of pilgrimage long before the Christian era, the weight of probability is against it as the site of the theophany of Y″ and the giving of the Law.

For the allegorical use of ' Sinai ' in Gal 4[25] see article, HAGAR. S. H. He.

SINAI (Peninsula).—The triangular tongue of land intercepted between the limestone plateau of the *Tih* desert in the N., and the Gulfs of Suez and *'Aqaba*, at the head of the Red Sea, on the SW. and SE. It is a rugged and waste region, little watered, and full of wild and impressive mountain scenery. Except at some places on the coast, such as Tor, there is but little of a settled population.

This region was always, and still is, under Egyptian influence, if not actually in Egyptian territory. From a very early period it was visited by emissaries from Egyptian kings in search of turquoise, which is yielded by the mines of the *Wâdī Maghârah*. There sculptured steles were left, and scenes engraved in the rock, from the time of Semerkhet of the 1st Dynasty, and Sneferu of the 3rd—dated by Professor Petrie in the 5th and 6th millennia B.C. These sculptures remained almost intact till recent years ; till a party of English speculators, who came to attempt to re-work the old mines, wantonly destroyed many of them (see Petrie, *Researches in Sinai*, p. 46). What these vandals left was cut from the rock and removed for safety, under Professor Petrie's direction, to the Cairo Museum. A remarkable temple, dedicated to Hathor, but adapted, it would appear, rather to Semitic forms of worship, exists at *Serâbiṭ el-Khadim*, not far from these mines. It was probably erected partly for the benefit of the parties who visited the mines from time to time.

Geologically, Sinai is composed of rocks of the oldest (Archaean) period. These rocks are granite of a red and grey colour, and gneiss, with schists of various kinds —hornblende, talcose, and chloritic—overlying them. Many later, but still ancient, dykes of diorite, basalt, etc., penetrate these primeval rocks. Vegetation is practically confined to the valleys, especially in the neighbourhood of water-springs. R. A. S. M.

SINCERE.—The English word ' sincere,' as it occurs in 1 P 2[2] ' the sincere milk of the word,' is used in its old sense of ' unmixed,' ' pure ' (RV ' without guile '). RSV reads ' pure.'

SINEW.—In Gn 32[32] there is preserved the traditional origin of a special food-taboo (cf FOOD, **10**), the result of which was that the Hebrews abstained from eating the sciatic muscle (AV ' the sinew which shrank ' ; RV and RSV ' the sinew of the hip ') of animals otherwise clean. The prohibition is not mentioned in any of the legislative codes of the Pentateuch. A. R. S. K.

SINGERS.—See PRIESTS AND LEVITES, **3** (*c*).

SINIM.—The ' land of Sinim ' (Is 49[12] AV and RV) must, from the context, have been in the extreme S. or E. of the known world. In the S. Sin (*Pelusium*, Ezk 30[15f]) and Syene (Ezk 29[10] 30[6]) have been suggested, and RSV reads the latter. This is favoured by discoveries of papyri (cf SYENE). The LXX favours the view that a country in the E. was intended, and some modern commentators have identified Sinim with China, the land of the Sinae, but this is generally abandoned to-day.

SINITES.—A Canaanite people, Gn 10[17], 1 Ch 1[15]. Their identification is quite uncertain.

SIN-OFFERING.—See SACRIFICE AND OFFERING, **13.**

SION.—**1.** A name of **Hermon**, Dt 4[48] (AV, RV, following Heb.). It is doubtless a textual error for **Sirion** (q.v.) ; so RSV. **2.** See ZION.

SIPHMOTH.—One of the places to which a portion of the spoil of the Amalekites was sent after David's return to Ziklag, 1 S 30[28]. The site is unknown.

SIPPAI.—See SAPH.

SIRACH.—See APOCRYPHA, **7.**

SIRAH, THE WELL OF.—The place at which Joab's messengers overtook Abner, 2 S 3[26]. It lay on the road from Hebron to Jerusalem, and is now probably *'Ain Sâreh*, near Hebron.

SIRION.—The name said to be given by the Sidonians to Mount Hermon, Dt 3[9] ; also 4[48] in RSV (AV, RV **Sion,** q.v.). Like **Senir,** it may originally have been the designation of a particular part of the mountain. Cf SION, **1.**

SISAMAI, 1 Ch 2[40] (AV).—See SISMAI.

SISERA.—**1.** In Jg 4[2ff] Sisera is represented as captain of the host of **Jabin,** a Canaanite king ; his army is overcome by the Israelites under Barak. In his flight after the battle, Sisera, overcome by fatigue, seeks refuge in the tent of **Jael,** who treacherously kills him while asleep. In an earlier account of the same episode (the Song of Deborah, Jg 5) Sisera appears as an independent ruler, and Jabin is not even mentioned ; the two accounts differ in a number of subsidiary details, but in two salient points they agree, namely, as to the defeat of Sisera and as to the manner of his death. It is clear that in Jg 4 two traditions have been conflated ; the story of Jabin's defeat apparently has been drawn from the record of Joshua's conquest of Hazor (Jos 11[1-15] ; cf Jg 4[2]). In order to harmonize them Sisera has been made Jabin's captain (see BARAK, DEBORAH, etc.). **2.** A family of Nethinim (Ezr 2[53], Neh 7[55], 1 Es 5[32] AV **Aserer,** RV **Serar**). W. O. E. O.—**D. N. F.**

SISINNES.—The governor of Coele-Syria and Phoenicia under Darius (1 Es 6[3, 7, 27] 7[1]). In Ezr 5[3] etc., he is called **Tattenai** (q.v.).

SISMAI.—A Jerahmeelite, 1 Ch 2[40] (AV **Sisamai**).

SISTRUM.—See MUSIC, **4** (3) (*c*).

SITH.—' Sith,' *i.e.* ' since,' occurs in Ezk 35[6] AV and RV (RSV ' because ').

SITHRI.—A grandson of Kohath, Ex 6[22] (AV **Zithri**).

SITNAH (' strife ').—The name given to a well dug by the herdmen of Isaac in the region of Gerar, Gn 26[21]. The site is uncertain.

SIVAN.—See TIME.

SKIFF.—Found only in RSV in Job 9[26] 'skiffs of reed' (AV, RV 'swift ships'). See REED, **5.**

SKIRT.—See DRESS, **4** (*b*).

SKULL, PLACE OF A.—See GOLGOTHA.

SLANDER, TALEBEARING.—Both noun and verb 'slander' are used of malicious gossip of varying degrees of heinousness. The references are all to the slandering of persons, except Nu 14[36] AV 'a slander upon (RV, RSV 'evil report against') the land.' The expression 'going about with slanders' (Jer 6[8]; cf 9[4], Lv 19[16]) is in the original identical with 'going about as a talebearer' (Pr 11[13] 20[19] [here RSV 'gossiping']; cf Ezk 22[9]). The element of falsehood in the gossip is seen in 2 S 19[27], where 'slandered' is synonymous with 'falsely accused.' 'Of no sin and wickedness are there so many complaints in OT as of slander and false accusation—whereof the Psalms are witness' (Cornill, *Jeremia*, 89). See, further, CRIMES AND PUNISHMENTS, **5.** A. R. S. K.

SLAVE, SLAVERY.—The Hebrew *'ebhedh*, usually translated **'servant,'** has a variety of meanings, between which it is not always easy to distinguish. *E.g.* in 2 S 9[2] 'servant'=retainer, in v.[10b]=bondman, in v.[11]=a polite expression of self-depreciation (cf 2 K 4[1] and 1 K 9[22]). In a discussion of Hebrew slavery only those passages will be dealt with in which the word probably has the sense of **bondage.**

1. *Legally the slave was a chattel.* In the earliest code (Book of the Covenant [=BC]) he is called his master's money (Ex 21[21]). In the Decalogue he is grouped with the cattle (Ex 20[17]), and so regularly in the patriarchal narratives (Gn 12[16] etc.). Even those laws which sought to protect the slave witness to his degraded position. In the BC the master is not punished for inflicting even a fatal flogging upon his slave, unless death follows immediately. If the slave lingers a day or two before dying, the master is given the benefit of the doubt as to the cause of his death, and the loss of the slave is regarded as a sufficient punishment (Ex 21[21]). The *jus talionis* was not applicable to the slave as it was to the freeman (cf 21[26ff] with [22ff]); and it is the master of the slave, not the slave himself, who is recompensed if the slave is gored by an ox (Ex 21[32]). In these last two instances BC follows the Code of Hammurabi [=CH] (196–199, 252).

In *practice* the slave as a chattel was often subject to ill usage. He was flogged (Ex 21[20], Pr 29[19]), and at times heartlessly deserted (1 S 30[11ff]). Though the master is here an Amorite, the cases of runaway slaves in Israel bear testimony to their sufferings even at the hands of their fellow-countrymen; cf the experiences of the churl Nabal (1 S 25[10]), of the passionate Shimei (1 K 2[39]), and of Sarah (Gn 16[6]); the implications as to the frequency of such cases in the law of Dt 23[15ff] and in later times (Sir 33[24–31]). The position of the **maid-servant** was in general the same as that of the man-servant. In the BC it is assumed that the maid-servant is at the same time a concubine (Ex 21[7ff]; cf Hagar, Zilpah, and Bilhah in the patriarchal narratives). Even in P the idea of the slave-girl as property is still retained (Lv 19[20]). Here the punishment for the violation of a slave-girl was almost certainly a fine to be paid to the master, if we may judge from the analogous law in Ex 22[16]=Dt 22[38]; *i.e.* it is an indemnity for injury to property. In practice the maid-servant, though the concubine of the master, is often the special property of the mistress (Gn 16[6a, 9] 25[12] 30[3]), at times having been given to her at marriage (Gn 24[59] 29[24, 29]). She is subject to field labour (Ru 2[8ff]) and to the lowest menial labour (1 S 25[41], figurative, but reflecting actual conditions).

Slaves were *recruited* (1) principally from war, at least in earliest times. Captives or subject populations were often employed not only as personal attendants, but also as public slaves at the Temple (Jos 9[23, 27] [21 a gloss], Neh 7[57–60], and see NETHINIM) or on public works in the *corvée* (Jos 16[10], Jg 1[28ff], I K 9[20–22]=2 Ch 8[7–9]), while captive women were especially sought as concubines or wives (Dt 21[10–14]). (2) From the slave-trade, of which the Israelites undoubtedly availed themselves (cf the implications in Gn 37[28] 17[12], Lv 25[44]). This trade was mainly in the hands of the Phoenicians and Edomites (Am 1[6, 9], Ezk 27[13], Jl 3[6]). (3) From native Israelites who had become enslaved as a punishment for theft (Ex 22[1–4]), whether for other crimes also is not stated; Josephus (*Ant.* XVI. i. 1 [3]) knows of no other. (4) From native Israelites who, through poverty and debt, had been forced to sell themselves (Ex 21[2], Am 2[6] 8[6], Dt 15[12], Lv 25[39], Pr 11[29] [?] 22[7] [?]) or their children (Ex 21[7], 2 K 4[1], Neh 5[5, 8], Is 50[1], Job 24[9]) into servitude. (5) Possibly from the exposure of infants and the kidnapping of minor children, as in Mesopotamia. The latter is rather clearly implied by Ex 21[16], Dt 24[7]; that the exposure of infants was sometimes practised is suggested by Ezk 16[5].

Whether the creditor had the right to force the debtor into slavery against his will is not clear. Ex 21[2] and 2 K 4[1] (cf Mt 18[25]) rather favour this view. The reflexive verb in Lv 25[39a] and in Dt 15[12], where the same verbal form should probably be again translated by the reflexive, not by the passive as in RV, favours voluntary servitude. But probably the later codes are modifications of the earlier practice. Neh 5[5] is ambiguous.

As to the *number* of slaves we have no adequate data. Gn 14[14] refers to retainers rather than slaves. The numbers in 1 K 5[13, 15] must include native Israelites subject to *corvée*; it may not refer to state slaves at all, as 1 K 9[21] does. The prosperous retainer of Saul has 20 servants (2 S 9[10]). The proportion of slaves to freemen in Neh 7[66ff] is 1 to 6.

The *price* of slaves naturally varied, but BC (Ex 21[32]) fixes the average rate at 30 shekels, which apparently was maintained at later times (cf 2 Mac 8[11]; *Ant.* XII. ii. 3 [25]; Mt 26[15]). In CH the average price is 20 shekels (116, 214, 252).

It seems probable that the number of slaves in Israel was never high, certainly not as high as in Greece and Rome. In the economy of Palestine it was probably at most times cheaper to hire day labour than to buy and support slaves, except in domestic service. State slaves could be used in very large operations requiring much unskilled labour, such as Solomon's mining and building operations. In the time of Hammurabi in Babylonia, it is estimated that the price of a slave, 20 shekels, was equivalent to three or four years' wages of hired labour (I. Mendelsohn, *Slavery in the Ancient Near East*, p. 118). In Palestine the situation was probably even less favourable for slave-holding (but cf Dt 15[18]). In the ancient Near East in general the basis of the economy was not slavery, but the free tenant and share-cropper in agriculture, and the free artisan and day labourer in industry (*ibid*, pp. 121 f). In Israel, most of the privately owned slaves were probably in domestic service; at certain times state slaves were used on large public works (in addition to the *corvée*), and temple slaves performed menial duties in the temples.

2. But while the slave was a chattel, nevertheless certain *religious and civil rights and privileges* were accorded him. *In law* the slave was regarded as an integral part of the master's household (Ex 20[17]), and, as such, an adherent of the family cult (cf the instructive early narratives in Gn 24 and 16). Accordingly the BC (Ex 23[12]) and the Decalogue (Ex 20[10]) guarantee to him the Sabbath rest. Deuteronomy allows him a share in the religious feasts (12[12, 18] 16[11, 14]), the humanitarian viewpoint being chiefly emphasized. In P the more primitive idea of the slave as a member of the family, conceived as a religious unit, is still retained and utilized in the interest of religious exclusiveness. Thus, while the *gēr* (sojourner) cannot partake of the Passover unless circumcised, the slave must be circumcised and so is entitled to partake (Ex 12[44]; cf the narrative Gn 17[12ff]). Again, while the *gēr* in a priest's family, or even the daughter of a priest who has married into a non-priestly family, may not eat of the holy things, the priest's slave is allowed to do so (Lv 22[10ff]).

As to civil rights : In the BC, murder of the slave as well as of the freeman is punishable with death (Ex 21[12] = Lv 24[17] ; the law is inclusive). If death results from flogging, the master is also punished, conjecturally by a fine (Ex 21[20ff]). If the slave is seriously maimed by his master, he is given his freedom (Ex 21[26ff]). At this point the BC contrasts very favourably with the CH. The latter does not attempt to protect the slave's person from the master, but only provides for an indemnity to the master if the slave is injured by another (199, 213, 214). While a man could be sold into slavery for debt (see above), **man-stealing** is prohibited on pain of death (Ex 21[16] = Dt 24[7]). Deuteronomy interprets the Exodus law correctly as a prohibition against stealing a fellow-countryman. Deuteronomy also forbids returning a slave who has escaped from a foreign master (Dt 23[15ff]). If the slave in this case were a non-Israelite (which, however, is not certain), the law would be a remarkable example of the humane tendencies in Deuteronomy and would again contrast favourably with CH, which prescribes severe penalties for harbouring fugitive slaves (16, 19). The humane law for the protection of captive wives (Dt 21[10-14]) is also noticeable.

But *practice* often went far beyond law in mitigating the severity of servitude. Indeed, slavery in the ancient East generally was a comparatively easy lot. The slave is grouped with wife and child as part of the master's household (Ex 20[17]). Children are property and can be sold as well as slaves (Ex 21[7] ; cf 22[16] = Dt 22[28] where the daughter is regarded as the father's property). Children are flogged as well as slaves (Pr 13[24]). Wives were originally bought from the parents, and wives and concubines are often almost indistinguishable. Hence the lot of the slave was probably not much harder than that of wife or child (cf Gal 4[1]), and the law implies the possibility of a genuine affection existing between master and man (Ex 21[5] = Dt 15[16]). Accordingly we find many illustrations of the **man-servant** rising to a position of importance. He may be entrusted with the most delicate responsibilities (Gn 24), may be the heir of his master (Gn 15[1-4]), is often on intimate terms with and advises the master (Jg 19[3ff], 1 S 9[5ff]), the custom of having body-servants (Heb. *na'ar*, Nu 22[22], 1 K 18[43], 2 K 4[12], Neh 4[22] etc.) favouring such intimacies, and he may even marry his master's daughter (1 Ch 2[34ff] ; cf similar cases in CH 175 ff). Especially servants of important men enjoy a reflected dignity (1 S 9[22], 2 K 8[4]). The rise of servants into positions of prominence was so frequent as to be the subject of proverb-making (Pr 14[35] 17[2] 19[10] 30[22a]).

Whether a servant could own property while remaining a servant is not clear. The passages adduced in favour of it (1 S 9[8] [a gratuity], 2 S 9[2ff] 16[1ff] [Ziba is a retainer], Lv 25[49b] [not a real servant]) are not pertinent. Dt 15[13] makes against it, but not necessarily, and the fact that in Arabia and Babylonia (CH 176) the slave could own property awakens a presumption in favour of the same custom in Israel.

Under a good house-wife the **maid-servant** would be well taken care of (Pr 31[15]). At times she also seems to be the heir of her mistress (Pr 30[23b] [?]). The son of the slave-concubine might inherit the property and the father's blessing (Gn 16[1ff] 21[13] 49[1ff]), but this depended on the father's will (Gn 25[6]), as in Babylonia (CH 170 ff). The effect of occupying such positions of trust was often bad. Proverbs fears it (19[10] 30[21-23]), and such passages as 2 K 5[20ff], Neh 5[15], Gn 16[4] justify the fear. Servants also tended to become agents of their master's sins (1 S 2[13-15], 2 S 13[17]).

3. Thus far no *distinction between native and foreign slaves* has been observed either in law or in practice, except possibly by implication at Ex 21[16] = Dt 24[7], and Dt 23[15ff]. The view that the protective laws in Ex 21[20ff, 26ff, 32] apply only to the native slave is without exegetical justification, and Gn 17[12], Ex 12[44], Gn 15[2] [if the text can be trusted] 39[1ff] [probably equally applicable to conditions in Israel], 1 Ch 2[34ff] and Gn 16[1ff] show that the foreign man- or maid-servant may enjoy all the advantages of the native Israelite.

The distinction drawn between the subject Canaanites and the Israelites at 1 K 9[20ff] = 2 Ch 8[7ff] is clearly incorrect (cf 1 K 5[13]) and belongs to a later development in the ideas of slavery (see below). The distinction drawn in P between the ' home-born ' slave and the one ' purchased with money ' (Gn 14[14] 17[12] etc.) does not refer to the two classes of foreign and native slaves.

In apparently but one particular, though this is of vital importance, the native slave is legally better off than the foreign-born, namely, in the right to *release*. Already in CH (117) provision was made for the release, after three years, of a wife or children who had been sold for debt. In the BC (Ex 21[1-6]) this idea was associated with the Sabbath idea, and a release was prescribed after 6 years of servitude, but the law was extended to cover every Israelite man-servant. Yet in the specifications of the law (vv.[3, 4]) the rights of the master still noticeably precede the rights of the husband and father. Provision is also made for the slave to remain in servitude if he prefers to do so. In this case the servant is to be brought to the door of the master's house, not of the sanctuary (the rite would then lose its significance), and have his ear pierced with an awl (a wide-spread symbol of servitude in the East), when he would become a slave for life.

The phrase **' unto God '** (v.[6a]) can scarcely refer in this connexion to the local sanctuary, as has usually been held. It signifies the adoption of the slave into the family as a religious unit, and probably referred originally to the household gods (or ancestors ?).

In the case of the **maid-servant** (Ex 21[7-11]) no release was permitted under ordinary circumstances (v.[7]), for it is assumed that the slave-girl is at the same time a concubine, and hence release would be against the best interests both of herself and of the home. Yet she is not left without protection. Her master has no right to sell her to a family or clan not her own (' foreign people,' v.[8b], probably has this restricted significance, sale of an Israelite to a non-Israelite being out of the question), but must allow her to be redeemed, presumably by one of her own family. Failing this, he may give her to his son, in which case she is to be treated as a daughter (v.[9]). If neither of these methods is adopted, a third way is provided. He may take another (concubine or wife), but must then retain the first, provide for her maintenance and respect her marital rights (v.[10]). If the master refuses to adopt any one of these three methods (' these three,' v.[11], refers to the three methods in vv.[8-10], not to the three provisions in v.[10]), then, and then only, the maid-servant has a right to release.

The Deuteronomic re-formulation of the Law of Release (Dt 15[12-18]) is noteworthy. (1) Release is extended to the maid-servant. Consequently the specifications in Ex 21[3, 4, 7-11] are allowed to lapse, and in the awl-rite only the possibility of the slave continuing in servitude through love of his master is considered. This change is due to the increasing respect for the marriage relation. The slave-husband's rights over the wife are now superior to the master's rights, and it is apparently no longer assumed that the maid-servant as such is the concubine of her master. Where concubinage does not exist, the maid-servant can be released without prejudice to the marital relation. (2) In Deuteronomy the awl-rite is clearly only a domestic rite. This confirms the interpretation of the rite given above. The Deuteronomist, who localizes all religious observances at the central sanctuary, consequently drops the ' unto God ' of Ex 21[6a]. (3) The characteristic humanitarian exhortation (vv.[13, 14]) is added, and the reasonableness of the law defended (vv.[15, 18]).

Jer 34[8-17] describes an abortive attempt to observe the law in its Deuteronomic formulation. The law had evidently not been observed in spite of its reasonableness, and was subsequently again allowed to become a dead letter.

A third version of the Law of Release is found at Lv 25[39-55]. Three cases are considered: (1) That of the Israelite who has sold himself, because of poverty, to his fellow-countryman (vv.[39-43]). Such an one is not to be regarded as a real slave but as a hireling, and is to be released in the year of Jubilee. (2) Actual slaves are to be obtained only from non-Israelite peoples (cf 1 K 9[20]). For them there is no release (vv.[44-46]). (3) If an Israelite sells himself to a *gēr*, he may be redeemed at any time by his next of kin or by himself (power to acquire property assumed), but in any case he must be freed at the year of Jubilee (vv.[47-54]). The redemption-price is proportioned to the number of years he had yet to serve from the time of his redemption to the Jubilee year, in other words, to the pay he would receive as an hireling during that period. Thus the possibility of an Israelite becoming an actual slave is again obliterated. The differences between this law and the earlier legislation are marked. (*a*) It formulates the growing protest against the idea that an Israelite could be a slave (cf Neh 5[5, 8]). (*b*) Through the institution of the Jubilee year it provides that even the *quasi*-servitude which is admitted should not be for life, and consequently it ignores the awl-rite.

A difficulty emerges at this point. The Levitical law, which postpones release till the 50th year, seems to work a greater hardship at times than the earlier laws, which prescribe release in the 7th year. Here three things are to be remembered: (*a*) the earlier law had probably become a dead letter long before the present law was formulated (cf Jer 34, above); (*b*) the Jubilee law is the result of a theological theory (cf vv.[23, 42, 55]), and never belonged to the sphere of practical legislation; (*c*) as such it is to be construed, not in antithesis to the 7th year of the earlier laws, but to the life-long period of servitude often actually experienced. It will not lengthen the time until the year of release, but will theoretically abolish all lifelong servitude. This theoretical point of view so predominates that the prolongation of the time of servitude, if the law had ever become actually operative, is left out of account. The fact that the Israelite in servitude to another Israelite is really worse off than an Israelite attached to a *gēr*, who could be redeemed at any time, also shows that we are not dealing with practical legislation.

4. In these three laws of release we have three clearly marked stages in the recognition of the slave's personality. The BC provides for the release of the Israelite man-servant. Deuteronomy, with its humanitarian tendencies, extends this privilege to the maid-servant. Leviticus, on the basis of its theological conceptions, denies that any Israelite can be an actual slave. But all these laws remain within nationalistic limitations. *One step more must be taken.* The rights of the slave as a man, and not simply as a fellow-countryman, must be recognized. The growing individualism which accompanied the development of the doctrine of monotheism prepared the way for this final step, which was taken by Job in the noble passage 31[13-15]. In the same spirit Joel universalizes the primitive conception of the necessary attachment of the slave to the family cult, and makes him share equally with all flesh in the baptism of the Spirit of God (2[29]).

Note.—The relationship of servant to master is a favourite figure in the OT for the relationship of man to God (especially in the Psalms). The nation, Israel, is also often thought of as the servant of Yahweh (cf Is 41[8ff])—a thought which finds its most profound expression in Is 42[1-4] 49[1-6] 50[4-10] 52[13]–53[12]. Cf article, Servant of the Lord.

5. In the NT it is only the attitude of Jesus and St. Paul towards slavery that demands attention. Jesus was not a political agitator, or even a social reformer. In nothing is this fact more strikingly illustrated than in His allusions to slavery. He refers to it only for purposes of illustration (*e.g.* Mk 12[2, 4], Mt 24[45], Jn 8[35] etc.). He never criticises it, even when it violates, as He must have realized, His own principles of love and brotherhood (Mt 18[25], Lk 17[7ff]; contrast the figurative picture in Lk 12[37]). But, as Christianity reached into the world and developed into a social force, it became increasingly necessary to consider what its attitude towards slavery should be, especially as many slaves became Christians (in Ro 16[10f], 1 Co 1[11], Ph 4[22] ' those of Caesar's household ' may include slaves). In this connexion St. Paul enunciates just one great principle—in Christ all the distinctions of this world disappear; the religion of Jesus knows neither bond nor free (1 Co 12[13], Gal 3[28], Col 3[11]). But he did not use this principle to overthrow the institution of slavery. On the contrary, at 1 Co 7[21-23] he counsels one who has been called (into the Christian life) while a slave not to mourn his lot. He even advises him, if the opportunity to become free is offered, to remain in servitude (v.[21], but the interpretation is doubtful), the near approach of the Parousia (v.[29]) apparently throwing these external conditions of life into a perspective of insignificance for St. Paul. The Apostle does not seek ' to make free men out of slaves, but good slaves out of bad slaves ' (Eph 6[5-9], Col 3[22]–4[1]; cf 1 P 2[18]). In these passages the corresponding duties of **master** to man are also insisted upon, as there is no respect of persons with Christ. It is significant that in the later Pastoral Epistles (1 Ti 6[1ff], Tit 2[9-11]) the exhortations to the masters are omitted. It would seem as if some slaves had taken advantage of the Christian principle of brotherhood to become insubordinate. In Philemon we have the classical illustration of St. Paul's attitude towards slavery exemplified in a concrete case. Here again he does not ask Philemon to free Onesimus; and it is clear from 1 Ti 6[1ff] and the subsequent history of the Church that Christians in good standing owned slaves. But in Phn[16] the slave is transfigured into a brother in Christ. For further discussion of this point see Philemon.

Though the Church recognized slavery, it is a remarkable fact that in the epitaphs of the catacombs the deceased is never spoken of as having been a (human master's) slave, though often described as a slave of God. In death, at least, the Christian ideal was fully realized. The slave becomes with the master only the slave of God. Contrast the gloomy equality in Job 3[19].

K. F.—**J. P. H.**

SLEDGE, THRESHING.—Found only in RSV for AV and RV ' threshing instrument '; see Agriculture, **3.**

SLEEVES.—See Dress, **2** (*d*).

SLEIGHT.—The word translated ' sleight ' in Eph 4[14], ' by the sleight of men,' means literally *dice-playing*. Tyndale uses ' wylynes,' which is more intelligible now than ' sleight.' RSV reads ' cunning.'

SLIME.—See Bitumen, Siddim [Vale of].

SLING.—See Armour, Arms, **1** (*e*).

SLOTHFULNESS.—See Work.

SLUICE.—Found only in Is 19[10] AV (cf RVm), where RV and RSV have ' (who work for) hire.' AV here follows Targum and Vulgate and Jewish commentators; LXX and Peshitta render by ' strong drink,' which represents a different vocalization of the Hebrew.

SMELTING.—See Mining and Metals.

SMITH.—See Arts and Crafts, **2.**

SMYRNA (also and more strictly *Zmyrna*) was founded as a colony from Greece before 1000 B.C., but the early foundation, which had been Aeolian, was captured by its southern neighbours the Ionian Greeks and made an Ionian colony. This second foundation became a powerful State, possessing territory far to the E., and as late as the 7th cent. B.C. fought as a member of the Ionian Confederacy against the great Lydian power (see Sardis). It gradually gave way, however, and was captured and destroyed in 627 B.C. by Alyattes, king of Lydia. It now ceased to be a Greek city, and it was not till the 3rd cent. B.C. that it became so again. There was a State called Smyrna between 600 and 290 B.C., but it was mainly a loose congeries of villages scattered about the plain and the surrounding hills, and not in the Greek sense a *polis* (city-State). Alexander the Great intended to re-found the city, but did not carry out his plan. It was left for his successors, Lysimachus and Antigonus, who accomplished it in 290 B.C. The old city had been on a steep high hill on the N. side of the extreme eastern recess of the gulf; the new was planted on the SE. shore of the gulf, about 2 miles away. The object of the change was to obtain a good harbour and a suitable starting-point for the land trade-route to the E. There were in reality two ports—a small inner one with a narrow entrance, and a mooring ground; the former has gradually filled up through neglect. Its maritime connexion brought it into contact with the Romans, who made an alliance with Smyrna against the Seleucid power. In 195 B.C. Smyrna built a temple to Rome, and ever afterwards remained faithful to that State, through good fortune and bad. Rome showed a thorough appreciation of this friendship and loyalty, and in A.D. 26 this city was preferred before all others in Asia as the seat of the new temple to be dedicated by the confederacy of that province to Tiberius.

The city was of remarkable beauty. Its claim to be the chief city of Asia was contested by Ephesus and Pergamum, but in beauty it was easily first. In addition to its picturesque situation it was commended by its handsome and excellently paved streets, which were fringed by the groves in the suburbs. The city was well walled, and in the *pagos* above possessed an ideal acropolis, which, with its splendid buildings in orderly arrangement, was known as the crown or garland of Smyrna. The protecting divinity of the city was a local variety of Cybele, known as the Sipylene Mother, and the towers and battlements of her head-dress bore an obvious resemblance to the appearance of the city. (The Greeks identified her with Nemesis, who here only in the Greek world was worshipped, and not as one but as a pair of goddesses.) There was one street known as the Street of Gold. It went from W. to E., curving round the sloping hill, and had a temple on a hill at each end. For its length and fine buildings it was compared to a necklace of jewels round the neck of a statue. The life of the city was and is much benefited in the hottest period of the day by a west wind which blows on it with great regularity, dying down at sunset. This was counterbalanced by a disadvantage, the difficulty of draining the lowest parts of the city, a difficulty accentuated by this very wind. Smyrna was a centre of learning, especially in science and medicine, and boasted that it was the birthplace of Homer, who had been born and brought up beside the river Meles. This stream is identified by local patriotism with the Caravan Bridge River, which flows northwards till it comes below the *pagos*, then flows round its eastern base and enters the sea to the NE. of it. But this is a mistaken view. The Meles is undoubtedly to be identified with the stream coming from the Baths of Artemis and called Chalkabounar, as it alone satisfies the minute description of the Smyrnaean orator Aristides (2nd cent. A.D.) and other ancient writers. It rises in the very suburbs of the city, and is fed by a large number of springs, which rise close to one another. Its course is circle-shaped at first, and afterwards it flows gently to the sea like a canal. Its temperature is equable all the year round, and it never either overflows or dries up. The city has suffered from frequent earthquakes (for instance, in A.D. 178), but has always risen superior to its misfortunes. It did not become a Turkish city till Tamerlane captured it in A.D. 1402. It has always been an important place ecclesiastically.

The **letter to the Church at Smyrna** (Rev 2^{8-11}) is the most favourable of all. The writer puts its members on a higher plane than any of the others. They have endured persecution and poverty, but they are rich in real wealth. They are the victims of calumny, but are not to be afraid. Some are even to be sent to prison as a prelude to execution, and to endure suffering for a time. If they are faithful unto death, they will receive the crown of eternal life. The church was dead and yet lived, like the city in former days. The Jews in Smyrna had been specially hostile to the Christians, and had informed against them before the Roman officials. Most of them were probably citizens of Smyrna, and had become merged in the general population, since the Romans ceased to recognize the Jews as a nation after A.D. 70. The hatred of the Jews there can perhaps be explained by the supposition that many of the Christians were converted Jews. Similarly they helped in the martyrdom of Polycarp (A.D. 155). In *c* A.D. 112 Ignatius of Antioch, on his way to martyrdom at Rome, visited the church in Smyrna and later, from Troas, sent them a letter, which survives. The city and its Christians have survived all attacks. A. So.—**F. C. G.**

SNAIL.—1. *ḥōmeṭ*, Lv 11^{30} (AV; RV, RSV 'sand lizard'); see LIZARD. **2.** *shabbᵉlûl*, Ps 58^{8} 'like the snail which dissolves into slime.' But G. R. Driver has shown that the word means 'a miscarriage,' before the foetus is old enough for its sex to be known (*JThS* xxxiv, 41 f); cf 'an untimely birth' in the parallel line.

SNARES.—A cord with running noose (*môḳēsh*, Am 3^{5} etc.; cf *yāḳôsh* 'one who lays snares,' **'fowler,'** Hos 9^{8}) was used to catch ground game and birds. The fowler also used a **net** (*resheth*, Pr 1^{17}, Hos 5^{1} etc.), under which he tempted birds by means of food, and then, concealed near by, pulled it down upon them. The *paḥ* (Ps 124^{7}, Pr 7^{23}, Ec 9^{12} etc.) probably corresponded to the Arabic *fakhkh*, a trap made of bone and gut, with tongue and jaws on the principle of the common rat-trap. It is light, and the bird caught by the foot easily springs up with it from the ground in its vain efforts to escape. Of this Amos gives a vivid picture (3^{5}). In later times the fowler used decoys to lure birds into his cage (Sir 11^{30}). Both *môḳēsh* and *paḥ* are several times rendered in EV by **gin.** The NT *pagis* (Ro 11^{9} etc.), and *brochos* (1 Co 7^{35}; but cf RSV), may mean 'snare,' 'net,' or 'trap'; whatever seizes one unawares. W. E.

SNOW.—Every winter snow falls occasionally in the mountainous districts of Palestine, but seldom lies for more than a few hours—at most for a day or two. For the greater part of the year, however, snow, glistening on the shoulders of Great Hermon, is easily seen from most of the higher hills in the country. It is frequently used as a symbol of whiteness and purity (Ex 4^{6}, Ps 51^{7}, Is 1^{18}, Mt 28^{3} etc.). It stands for the cold against which the good housewife provides (Pr 31^{21}). From Mount Hermon snow has been carried since olden times to great distances, to refresh the thirsty in the burning heat of summer (Pr 26^{1}). Water *mithl eth-thilj* ('like the snow') for coolness, is the modern Arab's ideal drink. W. E.

SNUFFERS, SNUFF DISHES.—The former of these are the 'tongs' of Ex 37^{23} (RV; AV, RSV 'snuffers'), the latter the vessels in which the burnt portions of the wicks were deposited (RSV 'trays'; AV, RV 'snuff-dishes'). See FIREPAN and TABERNACLE, **6** (*b*).

SO.—The 'king of Egypt' with whom Hoshea corresponded (2 K 17^{4}) shortly before he openly revolted against Assyria in 725 B.C. So, written *Sw'* in the Hebrew text, is almost certainly to be identified with the Sib'u of the Annals of Sargon and with the Sib'e of Sargon's 'Display Inscription.' The name should therefore probably be vocalized Siw'e. In the Display Inscription Sargon says: 'Hanuno, king of Gaza, and Sib'e, the commander-in-chief of Egypt, advanced to Rapihu to make a direct attack and to battle with me. I defeated them. Sib'e fled . . . I received tribute from Pir'u of Muṣuru. . . .' If 'Pir'u of Muṣuru' is 'Pharoah of Egypt,' as seems most probable, though this identification has been disputed by some scholars, then So would appear to have been not the 'king of Egypt,' but a general under him. At the time of the battle of Raphia, where Sib'e was defeated, Piankhi, the founder of the Ethiopian (25th) Dynasty, was ruler of Egypt and Nubia, but the 'Pir'u of Muṣuru' of the Assyrian inscriptions is probably Bocchoris, one of the vassal princes whom he allowed to reign in Lower Egypt. Some scholars have identified So = Sib'e with Shabaka, who succeeded Piankhi and reigned 716–701 B.C. In favour of this view it can be said that Shabaka, as crown prince, might well have been a commander of the Egyptian army and that the termination -ka, the main philological objection to the equation of the two names, is found with other royal names of the period. The identification is, however, very uncertain and few modern scholars accept it. T. W. T.

SOAP (*bōrîth*) occurs in EV (AV **'sope'**) only in Jer 2^{22} (washing of the person) and Mal 3^{2} (operations of the fuller). Properly *bōrîth* denotes simply 'that which cleanses.' The cognate word *bōr* is commonly rendered 'cleanness,' but in Job 9^{30}, Is 1^{25} RVm and RSV have **'lye.'** Soap in the modern sense of the word was unknown in OT times, and we do not know what precisely is referred to by *bōrîth*. As in Jer 2^{22} *nether* (AV 'nitre' q.v. ; RV, RSV 'lye'), a mineral alkali, is set in antithesis to *bōrîth*, it is supposed that the latter was some kind of vegetable alkali which, mixed with oil, would serve the purposes of soap. This may be confirmed by the fact that in Jer 2^{22} and Mal 3^{2} LXX renders *bōrîth* by *poia* = 'grass.' J. C. L.

SOBRIETY.—See Temperance, **1.**

SOCHO, 1 Ch 4^{18} (AV).—See Soco, **4.**

SOCHOH, 1 K 4^{10} (AV).—See Soco, **3.**

SOCKETS.—See Tabernacle, **4** (*a*).

SOCO.—1. A fortified town in the lowland of Judah, mentioned with Adullam and Azekah in Jos 15^{35} ; the Philistines gathered here (1 S 17^{1}), and later raided here (2 Ch 28^{18}) ; it was fortified by Rehoboam, 2 Ch 11^{7} ; probably modern *Khirbet ʿAbbâd.* The **Sucathites** (1 Ch 2^{55} [AV **Sucathites**]) are perhaps inhabitants of Soco. **2.** A city of Judah in the hill country, mentioned with Jattir and Debir in Jos 15^{48} ; modern *Khirbet esh-Shuweikeh,* SSW. of Hebron, a Byzantine site known to Eusebius and Jerome, the earlier site being indicated by Iron Age potsherds at *Khirbet ʿAbbâd* (see **1**, above), on a spur a little further W. **3.** A city in Solomon's 3rd district, mentioned in 1 K 4^{10} ; modern *Tell er-Râs,* WNW. of Samaria. **4.** In 1 Ch 4^{18} Heber is said to be the father of Soco, where one of these towns may be meant. In the earlier editions of RSV (as in RV) the name was given as Soco in 1 Ch 4^{18}, 2 Ch 11^{7} 28^{18}, and Socoh elsewhere, but in later editions it is Soco in all places ; AV employs the spellings Shocho, Shochoh, Shoco, Socho, Sochoh, Shocoh (q.v.). E. W. G. M.—**J. Gr.**

SOCOH, Jos $15^{35, 48}$ (AV).—See Soco, **1, 2.** This spelling is also found in some passages in RV and in early editions of RSV. See Soco (end).

SOD, SODDEN.—See Seethe.

SODERING.—AV form of 'soldering' in Is 41^{7}.

SODI.—The father of the Zebulunite spy, Nu 13^{10}.

SODOM.—See Dead Sea, Plain [Cities of the].

SODOM, SEA OF, 2 Es 5^{7} = the **Dead Sea** (q.v.).

SODOM, VINE OF.—See Vine.

SODOMA, Ro 9^{29} (AV) = **Sodom** (q.v.).

SODOMITISH SEA, 2 Es 5^{7} (AV, RV) = **Dead Sea** (q.v.)

SODOMY.—See Crimes and Punishments, **3,** and Homosexuality.

SOJOURNER.—See Stranger.

SOLDERING.—Found only in Is 41^{7} for the joining up of the metal plates covering an idol.

SOLDIER.—See Army, Legion, War.

SOLEMN, SOLEMNITY.—The adjective 'solemn' frequently occurs in EV, always with *assembly* or *meeting* or some such word, and always in its early sense of 'regular' or 'public.' Thus **'**a solemn feast**'** means simply 'a stated feast'; there is no corresponding word in the Hebrew. In the same way 'solemnity' means 'public occasion.' How much this word, as used in EV, differs from its modern meaning, may be seen from Shakespeare, *Midsummer Night's Dream,* v. i. 376 :

> 'A fortnight hold we this solemnity,
> In nightly revels and new jollity.'

SOLEMN ASSEMBLY.—See Congregation.

SOLOMON.—1. Sources.—1 K 1–11 (cf 11^{41}), with parallels in 2 Ch 1–9 (add references in closing chs. of 1 Ch). In Chronicles the character of Solomon, as of the period as a whole, is idealized ; *e.g.* nothing is said of the intrigues attending his accession, his foreign marriages and idolatry, or his final troubles, even with Jeroboam. Details are added or altered in accordance with post-exilic priestly conceptions (5^{12f} 7^{6} 8^{11-15}) ; 1^{3} (cf 1 K 3^{4}) makes the sacrifice at Gibeon more orthodox ; the dream becomes a theophany ; in $7^{1, 3}$ fire comes down from heaven. In 9^{29} reference is made to authorities, possibly sections of 1 Kings ; there is no evidence that the Chronicler was able to go behind 1, 2 Kings for his materials. The books of OT and Apocrypha ascribed to Solomon are of value only as giving later conceptions of his career. Josephus (*Ant.* viii. i.–viii.) cannot be relied on where he differs from OT ; the same holds good of the fragments quoted by Eusebius and Clemens Alexandrinus. Later legends, Jewish and Mohammedan, are interesting, but historically valueless ; the fact that they have in no way influenced the OT narrative is an evidence of its general reliability ; only two dreams and no marvels are recorded of Solomon. Archaeological research and discovery in recent years has greatly increased our knowledge of his reign.

2. Chronology.—His reign is to be dated *c* 969–922 B.C. (*BASOR* 100, 16–23) and the reign of Shishak may be set *c* 940–920 B.C. while the reign of Hiram of Tyre should be placed *c* 969–936 B.C. The origin and interpretation of the 480 years in 1 K 6^{1} are very doubtful. The 'little child' (*naʿar ḳāṭôn*) of 3^{7} (cf Jer 1^{6}) does not imply the tradition that Solomon was only 12 years old at his accession ; more probably he was near 20 years of age. The 40 years of his reign, as of David's, would seem to represent a generation.

3. Early years.—Solomon was the son of David and Bathsheba (2 S 12^{24f}), presumably their eldest surviving child ; his position in the lists of 5^{14}, 1 Ch 3^{5} 14^{4} is strange, perhaps due to emphasis. The name means 'peaceful' (Heb. *Shelōmōh* ; cf *Irenaeus, Friedrich*), indicating the longing of the old king (1 Ch 22^{9}) ; cf *Absalom* ('father is peace'). The name given him by Nathan (2 S 12^{25}), **Jedidiah** ('beloved of Y″,' the same root as *David*), is not again referred to, perhaps as being too sacred. It was the pledge of his father's restoration to Divine favour. We have no account of his training. 'The Lord loved him' (2 S 12^{24}) implies great gifts ; and v.^{25} and 1 K 1 suggest the influence of Nathan. His mother evidently had a strong hold over him (1 K 1 2).

4. Accession.—The appointment of a successor in Eastern monarchies depended on the king's choice, which in Israel needed to be ratified by the people (1 K 12) ; where polygamy prevails, primogeniture cannot be assumed. 1^{13} implies a previous promise to Bathsheba, perhaps a 'court secret'; the public proclamation of 1 Ch 22^{2-19}, if at all historical, must be misplaced. Adonijah, 'a very goodly man' (1 K 1^{6}), relying on the favour of the people (2^{15}) [it is doubtful whether he was the eldest surviving son], made a bid for the throne, imitating the method of Absalom and taking advantage of David's senility. He was easily foiled by the prompt action of Nathan and Bathsheba ; Solomon himself was evidently young, though soon able to assert himself. The careful and impressive ritual of the coronation was calculated to leave no doubt in the people's mind as to who was the rightful heir. The young king learned quickly to distinguish between his friends and enemies, as well as to rely on the loyalty of the Cherethites, his father's foreign bodyguard. The sparing of Adonijah (1 K 1^{53}) suggests that he was not a very formidable competitor ; his plot was evidently badly planned. His request to Bathsheba (2^{13}) may have been part of a renewed attempt on the kingdom (as *heir* he claims his father's wives), or may have been due to real affection. At any rate the king's suspicion or jealousy was aroused, and his rival was removed; Canticles suggests that Solomon himself was believed to have been the lover of Abishag. The deposition of Abiathar, and the execution of Joab and Shimei, were natural consequences; and in the case of the two last, Solomon was only following the advice of his father ($2^{5,8}$). He thus early emphasized his power to act, and as a result 'his kingdom was established greatly' at a cheap cost. We shall hardly criticise the removal of dangerous rivals when we remember the fate which he himself would have met if Adonijah had succeeded (1^{21}), and the incidents common at the beginning of a new reign (2 K 11^1; cf Pr 25^5).

5. Policy.—The times were singularly favourable to Solomon at the time of his accession to the throne. The government of Egypt was in the hands of the last weak rulers of the Tanite Dynasty and they were incapable of any large enterprises. Assyria under Tiglath-pileser II. (966–935 B.C.) could stage no major effort and Sidon, with its capital at Tyre, was too heavily engaged in large commercial enterprises to give heed to Palestinian politics. The Aramaeans had been conquered by David and no signs of their resurgence appeared. It was an era of peace favourable to the policy of Solomon whose main aim was to surround his kingdom with all the outward signs of a great power. With this view he gathered to himself a very large harem, though the figures given may appear somewhat exaggerated (1 K 11^3, Ca 6^8). The buildings which he erected were something new in the way of luxury and extravagance: they included a Temple that rivalled in splendour the richest shrines of Phoenicia and Egypt. No serious military operations found place in his reign but Solomon set himself in a position of strength by establishing a powerful standing army, and particularly a chariot force which his father had steadfastly refused to employ. The figures given as to the size of this force vary but it seems probable that he had 1400 chariots, 4000 stalls for chariot horses, and some 12,000 horses. This seems a large and expensive establishment but it does not seem improbable: at the battle of Qarqar about a 100 years later Ahab's chariotry force almost equalled that of Hadadezer of Damascus. The earlier custom of hamstringing horses was abandoned by the Hebrews and archaeology has revealed that certain cities were chariot cities where the corps had headquarters. Such cities seem to have been Megiddo, Taanach, Gezer, Hazor: these are attested by archaeology and doubtless there were others. At Megiddo the excavators have uncovered stalls for 450 horses with space for about 150 chariots. As to how this corps was raised we learn from 1 K 10^{28}: this is quite unclear in the AV but the obscurity is cleared up in RSV. We translate with Albright (*ARI*, p. 135): 'And Solomon's horses were exported from Cilicia: the merchants of the king procured them from Cilicia at the current price; and a chariot was exported from Egypt at the rate of 600 shekels of silver and a horse from Cilicia at the rate of 150: and thus (at this rate) they delivered them by their agency to all the kings of the Hittites and the kings of Aram.' Solomon also developed a strong system of fortifications and fortified such towns as were of strategic or commercial importance—Hazor and Megiddo on the Egypt-Damascus road, Beth-horon and Gezer (probably also Baalath) guarding the approaches to Jerusalem, and Tamar, in Judah, protecting the road leading to the Dead Sea. In Jerusalem he built the Millo, a block of fortifications intended to 'close up the breach of the city of David' (1 K 11^{29}), that is, to fill in the ravine which formerly divided Zion hill from the site of the new royal palaces and the Temple. In addition to these measures Solomon strengthened himself by foreign alliances. Early in his reign he married the daughter of the Pharaoh and received Gezer as her marriage portion (1 K 3^1). He also entered into alliance with Hiram of Tyre and this opened up large opportunities for commercial expansion. Solomon became a great trader and the sources tell us of commercial dealings with Phoenicia, Egypt, S. Arabia, and adjacent regions, and with the more remote regions of Hittite N. Syria and Cilicia (see above). In this period the commercial expansion of Phoenicia had developed to a high degree and trading posts were established as far W. as Sardinia and Cyprus. We cannot say whether Phoenicia had expanded as far as Spain but it is not improbable. Archaeological discoveries have revealed that the term *Tarshish* was applied in the following century to *Nora* in southern Sardinia, and, as Albright has shown, the term *Tarshish* seems to have the general significance of 'refinery' (*ARI*, p. 136). The researches of Nelson Glueck (*The Other Side of Jordan*; also *BASOR* 90, 13 f) have shown how, with Phoenician co-operation, Solomon exploited the copper mines in the Ghôr and established great refineries at Ezion-geber (*Tell el-Kheleifeh*). Here the copper ore was smelted—probably by slave-gangs—to yield metal for his great building projects and for purposes of trade. Ezion-geber was formed into a great maritime trading centre from which ships sailed to SW. Arabia and probably the African coast to return with 'gold, silver, ivory, apes and monkeys,' (1 K 10^{22}). This maritime trade may well have cut into the overland caravan trade within Arabia, and it may well be that the visit of the Queen of Sheba was prompted not only by religious interest but by real economic concern. No permanent success attended these maritime ventures and we are later informed that Jehoshaphat failed to keep the enterprise in being (1 K 22^{48}). The Jews did not take naturally to the sea and such enterprises remained with the Phoenicians.

6. Internal condition of the kingdom.—Solomon sought to centralize authority in the crown by weakening tribal ties and increasing his control of the hierarchy. For purposes of administration the tribal divisions were replaced by 12 prefectures cutting across tribal boundaries (1 K $4^{2\text{f}}$). Under both David and Solomon there was a fundamental conflict between the tribal separatism of early Israel and the centralizing tendencies of the crown. The prefectures were in charge of prefects whose sole loyalty was to the crown and their royal patron. Two of them are reported to have been married to daughters of Solomon (1 K $4^{11,15}$): the system was a close corporation and bureaucracy. It has been thought that Judah was exempted from this system but 1 K $4^{19\text{f}}$ seems to deny any such preferential treatment. It was the duty of those prefects to care for the provisioning of the royal household, each being responsible for one month. That this was no light burden is clear from 1 K 4^{22} (Heb $5^{2\text{f}}$) where we learn that each district had to supply annually 5000 bushels of flour, 10,000 bushels of meal, 900 oxen, 3000 sheep. For districts of less than 100,000 population this must have been a crushing burden. The Samaritan Ostraca, found in the palace of Jeroboam II. at Samaria, give evidence of the system of taxation: many traces of 10-gallon jars have been found bearing the inscription 'for the king'—somewhat like O.H.M.S. These were evidently used in paying taxes in kind, mainly wine and oil. Archaeology has disclosed the fact that certain cities were 'store cities' (Lachish, Beth-shemesh, etc.). 'The king's mowings' (Am 7^1) would seem to imply a royal claim on the first cut grass for the army horses. The kind of impact made on the people may be gauged from the words describing the monarchy and its heavy exactions in 1 S 8^{11-17}. These words were written after sad experience of the institution. Nothing could be more grievous to the sons of the desert than to be pressed into a system of forced labour (*mas*, the same word as is used of Israel's hard labour in Egypt). There was conscription for the army and there was conscription for labour. Thirty thousand males were pressed into labour gangs and these were taken one month in every three to hew lumber in Lebanon. That is equal to 4 per cent. of the population: in Britain it would mean 2,000,000 people working four months each year on government building projects. In addition women were conscripted for palace service; such a system must have involved serious dislocation of life's normal activities. Had Jeremiah lived in the days of Solomon he might well have excoriated him as he did Jehoiakim (Jer 22[18]). To Solomon we owe the building of the Temple, but this did not at that time become the only legitimate centre of worship in Israel. As the royal chapel it assumed a high place in the religious life of the people. In its building we can discern the influx of Canaanite culture and alien religious ideas. It does not really set forth an example of authentic Israelite worship. There is little wonder that when the city fell in 586 B.C. Jeremiah did not feel an irreparable blow had been struck at religion: the prophet did not believe it was essential for the survival of the Hebrew faith.

7. His wisdom was the special gift of God (3[5]). His 'judgment' (v.[16ff]) is the typical instance. It presumably took place early in his reign (cf the contemptuous laughter of the people in Jos. *Ant.* VIII. ii. 2 [32]), and simply shows a shrewd knowledge of human nature; many parallels are quoted. It proves his fitness for judicial functions, and 4[29–34] gives the general idea of his attainments. He was regarded as the father of Jewish proverbial (or gnomic) wisdom; 'wisdom books' existed in Egypt long before, but it seems impossible to distinguish in our present 'Proverbs' (*c* 250 B.C.) what elements may be due to him. Sirach and Wisdom have no title to his name. 1 K 4[29, 33] suggest general and poetical culture, parables drawn from nature, rather than the beginnings of science. Ps 72 may possibly belong to his age, but not Ps 127 or Canticles. Later tradition added much; the solving of 'riddles' held a large place in the wisdom of the East and we hear of the 'hard questions' of the queen of Sheba (10[1]), and of a contest between Solomon and Hiram (Jos. *Ant.* VIII. v. 3 [143]). Josephus also speaks of his power over demons; Rabbinical legend of his control over beasts and birds, of his 'magic carpet,' and knowledge of the Divine name. Examples of the legendary material are accessible in Farrar's *Solomon*.

8. Character.—Solomon evidently began his reign with high ideals, of which his dream (3[5]) was a natural expression. His sacrifice at Gibeon (v.[4]) gives another aspect; his religion was associated with external display. So the magnificence of the Temple, the pageantry and holocausts of its dedication (8), certainly ministered to his own glory, no less than to God's. His prayer, however, if it be in any sense authentic, is full of true piety, and he seems to have had a real delight in religious observances (9[25]). His fall is connected with his polygamy and foreign wives (11, cf Neh 13[26]). He not only allowed them their own worship, a necessary concession, but shared in it; the memory of his 'high places,' within sight of his own Temple, was preserved in the name 'Mount of Offence.' This idolatry was, in fact, the natural syncretism resulting from his habitual foreign intercourse. Self-indulgence and the pride of wealth evidently played their part in his deterioration. Of his actual end nothing is known; he was an 'old man' (1 K 11[4]) at sixty years, but Jeroboam's flight suggests that he could still make his authority felt. Ecclesiastes gives a good impression of the 'moral' of his life; but whether he actually repented and was 'saved' was warmly debated by the Fathers. Dt 17[16f] criticises his Egyptian alliance and harem. his love of horses and of wealth, and Sir 47[12–21] is a fair summary of the career of one whose 'heart was not perfect with the Lord his God, as was the heart of David his father' (1 K 11[4]). His wisdom could not teach him self-control, and the only legacy of a violated home-life was a son 'ample in foolishness and lacking in understanding.' C. W. E.—**J. Pn.**

SOLOMON, PSALMS OF.—See PSEUDEPIGRAPHA, 3.

SOLOMON'S PORCH or PORTICO.—See PORCH, TEMPLE.

SOLOMON'S SERVANTS.—See NETHINIM.

SOMEIS, 1 Es 9[34] (RV).—See SHIMEI, **11.**

SOMETIME, SOMETIMES.—There is no difference in the use of these two forms in AV, and except in Sir 37[14] ('For a man's mind is sometime wont to tell him,' etc.), where the meaning is 'occasionally,' as now, both forms are used in the sense of 'once upon a time.'

SON.—See CHILD, FAMILY.

SON OF GOD, SON OF MAN.—See CHRISTOLOGY.

SONG OF SONGS (or **CANTICLES**).—**1. Place in the Canon.**—The Song of Songs is one of the *Kᵉthûbhîm*, *Hagiographa*, or Writings, the third of the three classes into which the Jewish Canon was divided. Printed copies of the Hebrew OT follow the arrangement of the German and French MSS in placing it at the head of the five *Mᵉghillôth* or Rolls—the short books which are read at the great annual feasts of Passover, Pentecost, the 9th of Ab, Feast of Booths, and Purim. Probably it owes its position to the fact that the Passover is the earliest festival of the year. But there is reason for believing that a more ancient order survives in the LXX, where it stands by the side of Proverbs and Ecclesiastes, the two other works to which Solomon's name was attached.

Grave doubts were long entertained by the Rabbis respecting the canonicity of **Canticles** (a common name of the book, from Vulgate *Canticum Canticorum*), the school of Shammai opposing it, while the more liberal school of Hillel favoured its inclusion in the Canon.

The Synod of Jamnia (A.D. 90–100), after some discussion, decided in favour of its reception, and Rabbi Akiba (A.D. 135) lent to this conclusion the weight of his great influence: 'All the Hagiographa are holy, but the Song of Songs is the most holy, and the whole world is not of such importance as the day on which it was given.' The opening words of the Targum are equally strong: 'Songs and praises which Solomon the prophet, the king of Israel, spoke by the Holy Spirit before Yahweh, the Lord of the whole world. Ten songs were sung in that day, but this song was more to be praised than they all.' The Midrash asserts that 'Canticles is the most excellent of songs, dedicated to Him who one day will cause the Holy Spirit to rest on us; it is that song in which God praises us and we Him.'

2. Interpretation.—(*a*) The earliest type of interpretation was the *allegorical*. This type of exegesis undoubtedly explains its eventual inclusion in the Canon. According to its earliest form, the book is understood as symbolizing the relations of Yahweh (the bridegroom) and Israel (the bride) from the Exodus to Messianic times. In its Christian version the bridegroom and the bride became Christ and the Church (or the individual believer). The Jewish form persisted throughout the mediaeval period (Rashi, Saadia b. Joseph and Ibn Ezra), but eventually it became unpopular among Jewish scholars. To-day it is almost limited to orthodox circles.

Among Christians various forms of symbolism have been seen in the book. Origen, Jerome, Augustine, and others felt the book to refer to the love relation between Christ and the Church, an interpretation which still exists in certain Christian circles. Others such as Gregory of Nyssa and Bernard of Clairvaux felt that it referred to the relations of Christ and the individual believer. Some Roman Catholic writers interpreted the book as dealing with the incarnation, the Virgin Mary being the bride. Luther saw in the bride the state, with the songs being Solomon's thanksgivings for the blessings bestowed on his kingdom. Mystics have naturally found in the book reference to the mystical union. Still others see in the book reference to Wisdom (cf Pr 8 and 9). On the whole, most modern scholars do not follow an allegorical interpretation.

(*b*) *Dramatic.*—Origen already felt that on the surface the Song was a nuptial poem honouring Solomon's marriage to Pharaoh's daughter, though the real meaning was to be found in allegory. The dialogue nature of the Song was also indicated in early Greek MSS (Cod. Sinaiticus and Alexandrinus, with marginal notes indicating change of speakers) and Vulgate MSS (cf the rubrics prefixed to various verses in Cod. Amiatinus: 'Voice of the Church,' 'Voice of Christ,' 'Voice of Mary Magdalene to the Church'). It was, however, not until modern times that a dramatic interpretation was fully worked out. The two main characters are Solomon and the Shulammite. Various attempts at dividing the book into acts were made, but it is difficult to promote any dramatic development with only two characters. Within the poem there is no movement towards a climax. Matters are as far advanced at 1^4 and 2^4 as at 8^5.

Somewhat more popular has been the three character dramatic interpretation (Solomon, the Shulammite, and the shepherd). The Shulammite and the shepherd are lovers, but Solomon has abducted the Shulammite for his harem, and tries to win her love. She resists her royal suitor, remaining true to her rustic lover. It is not fully clear why such an ancient version of the eternal triangle which places the great Solomon in a very bad light should have been incorporated into the canon. Furthermore, if this book were written as drama the speakers would certainly have been noted (as in the case of Job).

(*c*) *Wedding Cycle*.—On the basis of Wetzstein's *Die syrische Dreschtafel*, many felt the book to be composed of a number of originally detached pieces which were eventually brought together. Wetzstein noted, while living in Syria, that the peasant bridegroom and bride are entitled king and queen for the first week of married life ; they are attended by a vizier, have their throne on the threshing-floor, and receive the homage of the whole countryside. Songs and dances are executed by the 'friends of the bridegroom,' the bystanders, and the newly married pair. Some of these songs, especially those which enumerate the charms of the bride, are of exactly the same character as certain sections of Canticles, and 7^{1ff} corresponds precisely with the *waṣf* (' description ') which the bride sings as she goes through the sword-dance on her wedding night. These facts have induced a large number of expositors to believe that Canticles is a collection of love-songs, composed expressly for, or at any rate suitable for use at, marriage festivals. Budde in particular held to this view and presented it with such persuasion that it dominated the scholarly world for many years. Unfortunately, no Judaean counterpart to such *waṣfs* has ever been found, nor are the Syrian customs really parallel to Canticles. The bride is never called ' queen ' : the motifs of sword-dance and threshing floor are absent ; nor is it reasonable to assume that such secular ditties would have been attributed (wrongly to be sure) to Solomon.

(*d*) *Secular love songs*.—Many believe Canticles to be a group of (possibly unrelated) secular love songs. This was already held by Theodore of Mopsuestia (A.D. 360–429). Due to von Herder's able defence of this interpretation it is widely followed to-day. Its ablest modern defence is that of Gordis who divides the book into twenty-eight poems, ranging in origin from the 10th to the 5th cents. Chief objections to this approach which have been raised are the reference to Solomon, the presence of the daughters of Jerusalem, the forwardness of the bride in pressing her love for the shepherd, and its inclusion in the Canon.

(*e*) *Liturgical*.—According to this theory, Canticles is an anthology of liturgies which in their original form were part of the ancient Hebrew New Year festivals in which the change of seasons, particularly that of springtime, was celebrated in dramatic form as the marriage of the Sun God with the Mother Goddess. These liturgies are then survivals of one of the forms of the ancient fertility cult as it was practised in Palestine. According to T. J. Meek, ablest and most vigorous exponent of this theory, there are numerous traces of such liturgical usage : the prominent rôle of the ' daughters of Jerusalem,' the separation of the lover and the beloved, the unnamed speakers, the rôle of the king (playing the part of the Sun God ?), the repetitious nature of the speeches, its adjurations by animals known to be sacred to the fertility cult, certain cultic terms, and the use of the term ' Beloved' (the name of a fertility god). It must be admitted that a cultic background to Canticles best explains its continued usage by the Jews in connexion with Passover as well as its inclusion in the Canon. Meek also appeals to its elusive geographical background with its greater prominence to places in the north than in the south, but it is not clear why this fact should support any particular theory. Chief objections to this theory deal mainly with its speculative character and the slightness of any particular points cited in its favour. It should be added, however, that its proponents do maintain that these folk liturgies have been reworked to such an extent that in their present form they practically amount to secular love songs. But it is argued that only some original religious usage could have brought about acceptance of the work as canonical on the one hand, and the dominance of the allegorical interpretation on the other.

3. Its style.—The Hebrew of this book is unique in its consistent use of the short 1st singular pronoun as well as of the relative particle *she* (except for 1^1, on which cf below). Its vocabulary is unusual, full of *hapax legomena* and difficult words which defy certain translation. Phonologically the Hebrew is dialectally different from the Jerusalem dialect which dominates the OT. Syntactically it also presents a number of peculiar features such as the preponderance of the masculine, even where the feminine might be expected, the use of the pronoun with the finite verb, as well as other features, all of which have led scholars to feel that the basic substratum of the language of Canticles is the Northern dialect. Further support for this might be found in the allusions to Tirzah, Lebanon, Hermon, and Gilead.

4. Authorship and date.—According to a Southern (Jerusalem ?) editor the book was attributed to Solomon (1^1). That the attribution is historically false is soon apparent. He is himself a character in the work. Its setting is mainly Northern with a later Judaean reworking of the poems to make them more suitable to a Southern context. On the other hand, the attribution was probably made because Solomon is mentioned (1^5 $3^{7, 9, 11}$ 8^{11f}), and because of his reputed wisdom, writing of Wisdom Literature, and his harem. Whether Canticles be simply love poetry or cultic in origin, it is probably folk song in character, and nothing can be said further concerning authorship.

The book in its present form contains evidence of late (3rd cent. ?) rewriting. To be noted are the use of a Persian word *pardēs* in 4^{13} and *'appiryōn*, a Greek word, in 3^9. There are also a number of Aramaic spellings of words which suggests a late textual form. The original form of the poems was, however, much earlier. A number of place-names are mentioned which imply early authorship. Tirzah as Northern capital (6^4) implies a pre-Omrid (early 9th cent.) composition. Heshbon (7^4) and Gilead (4^1 6^5) were lost to Israel during the 8th cent. J. T.—**J. W. W.**

SONG OF THE THREE YOUNG MEN.—See Apocrypha, **10.**

SONS OF GOD.—See Children of God.

SONS OF THE PROPHETS.—See Prophecy.

SOOTHSAYER.—See Magic, Divination, and Sorcery.

SOP.—See Meals, **5.**

SOPATER, SOSIPATER.—These are two forms of the same name ; Luke, as usual, adopts the more colloquial. **1.** In Ac 20^4 we read that Sopater of Beroea, the son of Pyrrhus, accompanied Paul on his journey towards Jerusalem as far as Asia (if these last words are part of the true text), *i.e.* Troas [see Secundus]. The mention of the father's name, unusual in NT, is thought by Blass to denote that Sopater was of noble birth. **2.** Sosipater (RSV), a ' kinsman,' *i.e.* fellow-countryman [see Jason], of Paul, who sends greetings in Ro 16^{21}. It seems unlikely, but not impossible, that these two men are the same. A. J. M.—**F. C. G.**

SOPE.—See Soap.

SOPHERETH.—A family of Nethinim, Neh 7^{57} : also Ezr 2^{55} (AV ; RV, RSV **Hassophereth,** q.v.).

SOPHONIAS, 2 Es 1[40] (AV, RV) = **Zephaniah** the prophet (q.v.).

SORCERY.—See Magic, Divination, and Sorcery.

SOREG.—See Temple, **11** (*b*).

SOREK, VALLEY OF (perhaps = 'valley of the *śōrēḳ* vine' [cf Vine]).—The valley or Wady in which Delilah lived, Jg 16[4]. Eusebius and Jerome connect the valley with *Capharsorec*, a village to the N. of Eleutheropolis and near Saraa, that is Zorah, the home of Samson's father. Capharsorec is now *Kh. Surîk*, to the N. of *Wâdī eṣ-Ṣurâr*, which is identified with 'the valley of Sorek,' and not far from *Ṣarʿah*. See also Zorah.

SORREL.—See Colours, **3.**

SOSIPATER.—See Sopater.

SOSTHENES.—**1.** Ruler of the synagogue at Corinth, whom 'they all' laid hold on and beat when Gallio dismissed the case against Paul (Ac 18[17]). He probably succeeded Crispus as ruler when the latter became a Christian (v.[8]), and the hostility of the rabble to the Jews showed itself when they were worsted in the courts. **2.** The 'brother' associated with Paul in addressing the Corinthians (1 Co 1[1]), and therefore probably a native of Corinth who had special relations with the Church there. If both references are to the same man, he must have been converted after the Gallio incident. A. J. M.

SOSTRATUS.—The governor of the citadel at Jerusalem under Antiochus Epiphanes (2 Mac 4[27 (28), 29]).

SOTAI.—A family of 'Solomon's servants,' Ezr 2[55], Neh 7[57]; omitted in the parallel 1 Es 5[33].

SOUL.—The Biblical concept of soul appears in the Hebrew *nephesh*, which in various contexts may be rendered 'soul,' 'life,' or 'self.' It can be usefully compared with *bāśār*, 'flesh.' The soul is not an entity with a separate nature from the flesh and possessing or capable of a life of its own. Rather it is the life animating the flesh. The soul of the flesh can thus be identified with the blood (Lv 17[14]). Soul and flesh therefore do not go different ways, but the flesh (or a part like the eye or the hand) expresses outwardly the life or soul. When the soul thirsts for God, the flesh faints for him (Ps 63[1]). Soul is thus the living being. 'Flesh' can be lifeless, but *nephesh* in its normal usage is alive. Adam was made of the dust, but when God gave him breath he *became* (not obtained) a living *nephesh*. Man does not 'have' a soul, he is a soul. So are the beasts, for they too are 'living *nephesh*' (Gn 1[24]). Notice that in such cases the singular is usual, not the plural. Sometimes the word means what we would express by 'persons.' 'All the soul of those who came forth from Jacob's loins were seventy souls,' *i.e.* seventy persons (Ex 1[5], literally); in English we also talk sometimes of the number of 'souls' on board a ship or the like. 'Spirit' differs from soul in that it is commonly understood to belong to God; it is the breath of God by which human life is made possible, informed and guided. But it becomes possible for a man to speak of 'my spirit' also, and the lines between the anthropological concepts are not clearly drawn at every point.

In the NT the term *psychē* 'soul, life' follows many of the usages of the OT, though it is perhaps somewhat more individualized as the centre of the vital choices and decisions by which destinies are determined. Men can kill the body but not the *psychē*, Mt 10[28]; this is hardly a statement of the natural immortality of the disembodied soul, but means rather that the life of the self is a matter between man and God or man and devil. Nothing is more precious to man than his *psychē*, Mk 8[35-37]; it is beyond price, yet by seeking to guard it you can lose it, and by losing it you can save it. The contrast here is not between body and soul but between self or life and the world and possessions. The *psychē* is soul as centre of emotion and decision, *e.g.* Mt 26[38], Jn 12[27]; it can even be addressed and congratulated on its possessions, Lk 12[19]. The salvation of the faithful can often be called 'salvation of the soul' (1 P 1[9], He 10[39]), and the faithful have a will to serve 'from the soul' (Eph 6[6], RSV 'from the heart') and care for the soul of one another (3 Jn [2]). It should be remembered, however, that these are complementary, and not opposed, to statements about the body of Christ, the redemption of the body, and the body of the resurrection. J. Ba.

SOULS, PRE-EXISTENCE OF.—See Pre-existence of Souls.

SOUTH.—See Negeb.

SOWER, SOWING.—See Agriculture, **1**, Seed.

SPAIN.—The country to which the name Spain or Hispania was given by the Romans, but which Greek writers called Iberia (country of the River Ebro); Paul shows Roman influence in using the Roman name of the region. The name Hispania really originated in the city of Hispalis (Seville). From that territory it was extended to cover the whole country now known as Spain. In the earliest times of which we have any knowledge it was inhabited, at least in part, by a race supposed to be a mixture of the aboriginal Iberian population with immigrant Celts. In 236 B.C., Hamilcar, father of the great Hannibal, invaded the country from Carthage, and after nine years of conquest was succeeded by his son-in-law Hasdrubal, who in turn was succeeded by Hannibal, under whom about 219 B.C. the conquest of the country was practically completed. Hannibal used it as his base in the Second Punic War against Rome. The Romans first invaded Spain in 218 B.C., and after various successes and reverses constituted two provinces there in 197 B.C., known for centuries afterwards as *Hispania Citerior* (Tarraconensis) and *Hispania Ulterior* (Baetica), separated from one another by the Ebro. The mountainous districts in the NW. were not actually subdued till the time of the Emperor Augustus (20 B.C.). The country was valued for its agricultural products as well as its precious metals. Much of Rome's power and wealth came from the control of this rich land. Vast numbers of enslaved Greeks had been sent to Spain, and it must have been they who attracted Paul to the area, for his mission was to Greeks. In Rome he only proposed to stay for a brief visit with Greek-speaking Christians (Ro 15[24, 29]) while en route to Spain. It is not known whether he carried out his plan. Spain claims more honoured names in Roman literature than any other country in the 1st cent. A.D., having been the birthplace of the two Senecas, Columella, Mela, Lucan, Martial, and Quintilian. A. So.—**E. G. K.**

SPAN.—See Weights and Measures.

SPARROW (*ṣippôr*, Ps 84[3] 102[7]). The Hebrew word is probably equivalent of Arabic *ʿaṣfûr*, and includes any 'twittering' birds; generally translated 'bird' or 'fowl.' See Bird. In the NT references (Mt 10[29], Lk 12[6f]) *strouthion* evidently refers to the sparrow, which to-day is sold for food as cheaply as in NT times. E. W. G. M.

SPARROW-HAWK.—See Hawk.

SPARTA, SPARTANS.—See Lacedaemonians.

SPEAKING, EVIL.—See Evil Speaking.

SPEAR.—See Armour, Arms, **1.**

SPEARMEN.—The rendering of AV in Ps 68[30] 'the company of spearmen' is quite indefensible, and we should certainly render the 'beasts that dwell among the reeds' with RSV (cf RV). In Ac 23[23] the word rendered 'spearmen' in AV, RV, and RSV is *dexiolaboi* (Codex A has *dexioboloi*), which is of uncertain meaning. It may possibly denote a bowman or slinger. Cf Arndt and Gingrich, *Lexicon*, s.v.

SPECK.—See Mote.

SPECKLED BIRD.—Jer 12[9] (only). If the MT of this passage is correct, the translation can hardly be other than 'Is my heritage to me (*i.e.* to my sorrow) like a speckled bird of prey? Are the birds of prey against her round about?' (RSV; cf RV). The people of Israel is compared to a bird of *prey*, just as, on account of its hostility to Yahweh, it is compared in v.[8] to a lion. But, as a speckled bird attracts the hostile attention of other birds, Israel becomes a prey to the heathen. The rendering proposed by some, 'mine heritage is unto me **the ravenous hyena**,' rests on an emended text.

SPELT.—See FITCHES, RIE.

SPICE, SPICES.—1. *bāśām*, Ca 5[1], RVm **'balsam'**; *bōśem* [once, Ex 30[23], *beśem*], plural *beśāmîm*. In Ex 30[23] is a list of various aromatic substances included under the name *beśāmîm*. These were stored in the Temple (1 Ch 9[29]), and in Hezekiah's treasure-house (2 K 20[13]); they were used for anointing the dead (2 Ch 16[14]), and also as perfumes for the living (Ca 4[10] etc.). **2.** *sammîm*, Ex 30[34] 'sweet spices'; and, along with 'incense,' Ex 30[7] 40[27], Lv 4[7], Nu 4[16] etc. (RSV 'fragrant incense'; for RV 'incense of sweet spices'). In the first passage the 'sweet spices' are enumerated as stacte, onycha, and galbanum (qq.v.) in RV (RSV 'liquid myrrh,' 'sweet smelling cinnamon,' and 'aromatic cane'). **3.** *nekhō'th*, Gn 37[25] 'spicery' (RVm 'gum tragacanth *or* storax'; RSV 'gum'), 43[11] (RV 'spicery'; RSV 'gum'). The gum **tragacanth** is the product of the *Astragalus gummifer*, of which several species are known in Syria. The **storax** (*Styrax officinalis*), a shrub with beautiful white flowers, also affords an aromatic gum valued by the ancients. Whether *nekhō'th* corresponded definitely to one of these, or was a generic term for 'perfumes,' is an open question. **4. 5.** Greek *arōmata* (Mk 16[1], EV 'spices') and *amōmon* (Rev 18[13], RVm **'amomum'**; RV and RSV 'spice'; AV omits) are probably both generic. E. G. W. M.

SPIDER.—1. *śemāmith*, Pr 30[28] AV (RV, RSV **lizard**). See LIZARD. **2.** *'akkābhîsh*, Job 8[14], Is 59[5]. Both references are to the frailness of the spider's web.

SPIKENARD (*nērd*, Ca 1[12] 4[13f]; also Gr. *nardos pistikē*, Mk 14[3], Jn 12[3]; RSV 'pure nard').—The fragrant oil of an Indian plant, *Nardostachys jatamansi*, which grows with a 'spike.' The Arabic name *sunbul hindi*, Indian spike, preserves the same idea. The perfume when pure was very valuable (Jn 12[3]).

About the meaning of the Greek epithet *pistikē* there has been much speculation. See note in RVm at Mk 14[3] ('liquid nard') and cf article, 'Spikenard' in Hastings' *DCG*. E. W. G. M.—**F. C. G.**

SPINDLE.—See SPINNING AND WEAVING, 3.

SPINNING AND WEAVING.—1. *The raw material.*—In all periods of Hebrew history the chief textile materials were **wool** and **flax**, and to a less extent **goats' hair**. As for the last named, St. Paul's native province was famed for its goats' hair (*cilicium*) woven into coarse cloth used for tent furnishing such as curtains, rugs, as well as cloaks. Ac 18[3] suggests that the Apostle practised this trade in Corinth, being 'chargeable to no man' (2 Co 11[9], AV). The RSV punctuation of this verse (a comma in place of the colon of AV and RV), rather suggests that his needs were met by the friends of Macedonia. The Greek word '*skēnopoioi*' of Ac 18[3] is correctly '*tentmakers*' etymologically, but most modern scholars consider that its meaning at this time was '*leather-worker*' (see *e.g.* E. Haenchen, *Die Apostelgeschichte* [1956], 476, in Meyer's Krit. exeg. K.u.d. NT). Eleven curtains of goats' hair made a 'tent over the tabernacle' (Ex 26[7]). The preparations of the various materials for the loom differed according to the nature of each. Wool before being spun, was thoroughly scoured and carded, by means of the bow-string, the age-long method of E. and W. until the introduction of modern methods. In the case of flax, the stalks were rippled and exposed to the sun till thoroughly dry, frequently on the roofs of the houses (Jos 2[6]); thereafter by repeated processes of steeping, drying and beating, the fibres were ready for the 'heckling' or combing. Representations of these processes are preserved in the tombs of Egypt.

Is 19[5-10] shows how the failure of the Nile waters can cause distress in the flax industry on its banks affecting the women combers and the men weavers of cotton, the other great cloth industry of Egypt. The translation of v.[9], however, is difficult, and the weavers may refer to those who work the finest *white* linen rather than white cotton. In Palestine itself, flax appears to have been an important crop near Gezer. The agricultural calendar found there in 1908 speaks of the 'month of pulling flax' (so J. Mauchline in *Documents from O.T. Times*, ed. D. Winton Thomas [1958], p. 121).

2. *Spinning.*—The spinning was done, as all the world over, by means of the **distaff** and **spindle**, and was pre-eminently women's work (Ex 35[25f], 2 K 23[7], Pr 31[19]). Both men and women, on the other hand, plied the loom. The distaff probably consisted, as elsewhere, of a piece of cane slit at the top to hold the wool. The spindle was generally a round shank of wood (sometimes stone, bronze or ivory), 9–12 inches in length, furnished with a hook at the top for catching the wool or flax, and having its lower end inserted into a circular or spherical whorl of clay, stone or other heavy material to steady the rotary motion of the spindle. Many forms of spindles and whorls have been excavated (see R. J. Forbes, *Studies on Ancient Archaeology*, iv [1956], pp. 152 ff for description and illustration). Sometimes a piece of broken pottery served as a whorl (*PEFSt* 1902, 338). Distaff and spindle are named together in Pr 31[19] (AV reverses the renderings). In 2 S 3[29] 'who holds a spindle' (literally 'one taking hold by the spindle') expresses the wish that Joab's descendants may be womanish and effeminate. The AV rendering 'one that leaneth on a staff' suggests a cripple in this context.

3. *The three variations of loom.*—**'Loom,'** which does not occur in AV, is found in RSV twice, viz., Jg 16[14] (see below **4** (*c*)), and Is 38[12] (so also RV) but RVm is 'thrum,' which rather describes the threads of the warp remaining on the loom when the web has been cut (see below **5**). Three varieties of loom were in use around the Mediterranean in ancient times—the horizontal loom and two varieties of the upright loom, distinguished by the Romans as the *tela pendula* and the *tela jugalis*.

(*a*) The horizontal loom is at least as old as the twelfth Egyptian Dynasty, and probably goes back to pre-historic times. A pottery dish found in a woman's tomb at Badari depicts a ground-loom with warp stretched between two beams with four pegs at the corners (Brunton and Caton Thompson, *The Badarian Civilisation*, plate 28). This type of horizontal ground-loom fits the Samson-Delilah incident (see below **4** (*c*)). It is still, with modifications, the loom in use in parts of the Arab world, India and farther E.

(*b*) The oldest variety of the upright loom is that familiar to classical students from the well-known representation on a Greek vase, of Penelope's loom. It consisted of two uprights joined at the top by a cross-beam, from which, or from a second beam below, depended the threads of the warp. These were kept taut by having small stone weights attached to their lower ends, hence the name *tela pendula*. In view of the numerous 'weavers' weights' unearthed at various places in the present century (Megiddo, Jericho, Gezer, Lachish, and elsewhere) it is clear that this form of the upright loom was used in Palestine from the earliest age.

(*c*) The second and later variety of the upright loom had for its distinguishing features a second cross-beam at the foot of the uprights, which served as a **yarn-beam** or as a cloth-beam capable of revolving; a web of much greater length could be woven than if the latter were confined to the height of the loom. The loom in ordinary use in NT times was of this type, as is evident from many passages in the Mishnah.

4. *OT references to the processes of weaving.*—In its simplest form the art of weaving consists in interlacing a series of parallel threads, called the **warp**, with another series called the **weft** or **woof** or filling, in such a way that each thread of the weft passes alternately over and under each thread of the warp. In the beginnings of the art this interlacing was laboriously done by the fingers of the spinner as in plaiting of which weaving is only a more complicated variety. The first process is to stretch the threads of the warp (Lv 13[48ff]) evenly between the upper and lower beams of the loom. Behind the Hebrew *shāthōthēhā* of Is 19[10], rendered in RSV 'those who are the pillars of the land,' may be the word *sh'thî*, 'warp,' which would give an emended translation 'those who lay the warp'; elsewhere this process is used in a metaphorical sense, as Job 10[11] 'knit me together' (so also RV, but AV 'fenced,' AVm 'hedged'), Ps 139[13] RSV and RVm, and the difficult passage Is 30[1] 'and who make a league,' which is also one of the three readings of RVm. But the first of the RVm is best, 'weave a web,' or, better still, 'warp a warp.' an apposite figure for commencing a new 'web' of political intrigue (cf the similar metaphor 59[6]). The Hebrew law forbade the use of wool and linen, the one as warp, the other as woof or filling, in the same web (Dt 22[11]).

In the process of uniting warp and woof there are 'the three primary movements,' as they are called, to be considered. These are (1) shedding, *i.e.* dividing the warp into two sets of odd and even threads for the passage of the weft; (2) passing the weft through the 'shed' by means of a rod or a shuttle; and (3) beating up the weft to form with the warp a web of uniform consistency. These three processes, so far as applicable to the Egyptian and Hebrew looms, are described in detail in Kennedy's article 'Weaving' in *EBi* iv, 5282–87 (with illustrations). Certain OT references require special mention.

(*a*) The formation of the shed was effected by at least two leash-rods or shafts, the Roman *liciatoria*, suspended from the upper cross-beam (see illustration Wilkinson, *Anc. Egyp.* ii, 171) or otherwise, connected by loops or leashes with each of the odd and even warp-threads respectively. The two sets of threads were alternately brought forward (or raised in the horizontal loom) by pulling the leash rods, thus forming a shed for the passage of the shuttle-rod carrying the weft. With a heavy warp, the rods must have been of considerable thickness—a stout branch of a tree serves as a leash-rod, for example, in a modern Anatolian loom figured in Smith's *Dict. of Gr. and Rom. Ant.*[3] ii, 179. Accordingly when the shaft of Goliath's spear is compared to a weaver's *mānôr* (1 S 17[7], 2 S 21[19], 1 Ch 20[5]; cf 11[23]), it is not to either of the 'beams' of the loom but to a 'weaver's shaft' or leash-rod that the comparison applies. The original term above given, it may be added, is from the same root as *nîr*, one of the Mishnah terms for the leash-rod (cf Jerome's true rendering, *quasi liciatorium texentium*).

(*b*) The weft or **woof** (Lv 13[48ff]) was passed through the shed by means of a staff or rod on which the **yarn** was wound. Homer, however, was already familiar with a shuttle-rod at one end of which was a revolving spool from which the weft-thread unrolled itself in its passage. A needle-shuttle with point at one end and hole at the other is among the finds at Ghassûl to be dated about 3rd millennium B.C. (Mallon, Koeppel, and Neuville, *Teleilât Ghassûl* [1934]). It is uncertain whether Job 7[6], the only EV occurrence of **shuttle,** refers to a shuttle-rod, or to the loom as a whole.

(*c*) The weft was beat up at each passage of the shuttle-rod by a thin lathe or pin, or batten, or, as later, by a special comb.

In Egypt, however, under the Middle Empire, it would appear that the more efficient 'reed,' still used in modern weaving, had already been invented for this purpose (Garstang, *Burial Customs of Anc. Egyp.* [1907], 133 ff with illustration); the two reeds there figured are 27 and 29 inches in length, showing approximately the width of the web. The Bedouin women of Moab still weave their curtains in strips about 5 yards long and from 16 to 20 inches wide, according to Jaussen (*Coutumes des Arabes*, etc. [1908], 74).

The Hebrews in early times used a 'pin' simply to beat up the weft. In the Samson-Delilah story, Jg 16[13–14], the completeness of the weaving of Samson's locks into the warp of the web already begun on the loom is shown by the phrase 'and she made them tight with the pin' (v.[14] RV 'she fastened it with the pin'; literally 'and she beat it with the pin'). Thus the slack of the hair in the weft was beaten in, so that it was one with the web. This sense is brought out by the RSV restoring to the text at the end of v.[13] and at the beginning of v.[14] sentences based on the Greek text here. The words lacking in the RV and AV are 'and make it tight with the pin, then I shall become weak, and be like any other man. So while he slept, Delilah took the seven locks of his head and wove them into the web.' For Delilah, seated on the ground beside her *horizontal* loom with Samson's head upon her knees (cf v.[19]), it was an easy matter to use his flowing locks as weft and to weave them into the warp of her loom. When she gave the alarm-call, Samson raising his head sharply to get up, wrenched the loom from the peg which fastened it to the ground. The RV and AV of v.[14b] seems to have in mind the same 'pin' as in v.[14a], assumed to be fastening the web 'to the wall' (so Greek text, *eis ton toichon*, [14a], and *ek tou toichou*, [14b]). The rendering '*beam*,' properly '*loom*' (as already noted) may indicate the warp-beam.

With Penelope's type of loom, the web could be woven only from the top downwards. This was also the Jewish custom in NT times with the other form of upright loom. Our Lord's tunic, it will be remembered, 'was without seam, woven from top to bottom' (Jn 19[23]; AV, RV 'from the top throughout'). For the weaving of such **seamless robes,** which were in vogue in Egypt under the later dynasties at least, it was necessary to mount a double warp and to weave each face of the warp with a continuous weft (see *EBi* iv, 5289).

5. When the web was finished, the weaver cut it off 'from the loom' (Is 38[12]) by severing the ends of the warp threads, and rolled it up. These two processes are the source of the figures for premature death in the passage cited (see also **3**). The 'unshrunk' cloth of Mt 9[16], Mk 2[21] (AV 'new,' RV 'undressed'), was not fulled, that is, cloth fresh from the loom. The milling or fulling was the work of the fuller (ARTS AND CRAFTS, **6**).

6. *Special kinds of fabrics.*—By appropriate arrangements of the warp, woof, and leash-rods, striped, checked, and other varieties of cloth were produced. The cloth intended by the '**chequer work**' of Ex 28[4] is quite uncertain. The Revisers probably mean by the phrase a species of check, produced by alternating different coloured bands in the warp, or in the woof, or in both. The examination of the linen textiles used for wrapping and packing of the now famous '*Dead Sea Scrolls*' shows something of this special type of weaving (see Crowfoot, *Linen Textiles from the Cave of Ain Feshkha*, *PEQ*, 1951, 5 ff and illustrations). Ex 26[1–6] describes the fine quality expected in the Tabernacle curtains, including '*cherubim skilfully worked*,' v.[1] (RV 'work of the cunning workman'); whether this refers to embroidery or **tapestry** work is uncertain. For Pr 7[16] 31[22], the RSV prefers '*coverings*' to the AV and RV 'tapestry.' The use of colours is evident in both places 'coloured spreads of Egyptian linen,' Pr 7[16], and 'fine linen and purple,' Pr 31[22].

A weft of gold thread was employed for the high priest's robes (Ex 28[5f] 39[2ff]; cf Jth 10[21], 2 Mac 5[2] 'cloth of gold,' 2 Mac 5[2] RV 'robes inwrought with gold'). Herod Agrippa's 'royal robes' (Ac 12[21]) are said by Josephus to have been woven throughout of silver thread.

In OT times the finer textile fabrics were imported from Babylonia, 'Shinar' (Jos 7[21]), Phoenicia (Ezk 27[16f]), Egypt, and in NT times even from India for the high priest's dress (Mishnah, *Yoma*, iii. 7). In the days of the Chronicler the weavers formed a trade guild (1 Ch 4[21]), and so continued in later times. As a class they were held in disrepute by the mass of the people, so much so that the Talmud declares weaving to be 'the lowest of crafts,' an opinion also held, it seems, in ancient Egypt.

A. R. S. K.—**R. A. B.**

SPIRIT.—See HOLY SPIRIT.

SPIRITS IN PRISON.—See DESCENT INTO HADES.

SPIRITS, UNCLEAN.—See DEMONS.

SPIRITUAL GIFTS.—**1. The term.**—A special Greek word, *charismata*, is used in NT for spiritual gifts. It usually stands alone, but in Ro 1[11] it is coupled with the adjective *pneumatikon* (' spiritual '). It means concrete, dynamic manifestations of the grace (*charis*) of God in the life of the Christian and is almost a technical term, though in Ro 6[23], 2 Co 1[11] it is used generally of the free gift of God. The principal passages which deal with spiritual gifts are Ro 12[6ff], 1 Co 12, 13, 14, Eph 4[7ff], 1 P 4[10]. The gifts may be divided into the following categories: (*a*) the power of speech and understanding: *i.e.* speaking with tongues (see TONGUES, GIFT OF), and their interpretation, prophecy, the receiving of revelations and the discerning of spirits, exhortation, teaching, utterances of wisdom and knowledge; (*b*) the power of healing and working miracles (by faith), where we may instance exorcism ([Mk] 16[17], Ac 16[18] 19[12]), and the punishment of offenders (Ac 5[1-11] 13[9], 1 Co 4[21] 5[5]); (*c*) the powers of administration and help in the life of the congregation: *i.e.* to be an official (*e.g.* an apostle) in the church, or to render services, such as almsgiving and hospitality; (*d*) the power of continence and self-surrender (1 Co 7[7] 13[3]). A list of the fruits of the Spirit, as shown in the Christian life, is given in Gal 5[22-23], but it differs somewhat, in its ethical setting, from the specific *charismata*.

2. Their nature.—Endowment with the power of the Divine Spirit is characteristic of the religious heroes and prophets of the OT, such as Gideon (Jg 6[34] 11[29]), Saul (1 S 10[6, 9ff]), Ezekiel (Ezk 2[2]). The Messianic age was conceived of as being distinguished above all by the outpouring of the Spirit, resulting in prophecy, miracles, and a marked intensification of life (Is 61[1ff], Jl 2[28f]; cf Lk 4[18f], Ac 2[17]).

In an analogous way the ministry of Jesus is described, in the Gospels, as a continuous manifestation of an inherent spiritual power, which revealed itself in the authority of His words and deeds (*e.g.* Mk 1[22, 27] 6[2]). The mission of the Twelve in Galilee also implies an endowment of the disciples with special gifts of an authoritative and miraculous character (*e.g.* Mt 10). According to Ac 2 the Spirit's coming, after the resurrection of Christ, is conceived as that of God's breath taking violent action as in OT days, inaugurating the new order and age of the Church. Paul speaks of the dynamic activity of the Spirit in his own apostolic ministry as well as in the life of the local churches, and He 2[4] mentions miraculous gifts as a recognized characteristic of the first age of Christianity. In this period the first-fruits of the new life could be actually experienced, with all their encouragement and power, even by the humblest Christian.

The different gifts acted as a proof of the presence and the creative activity of the Spirit within the Church, enabling each member to perform some special service for the community. Some of the gifts appeared to be plainly supernatural; others seemed to be natural powers raised to a new and supernatural efficacy. As Rudolf Otto held (*Reich Gottes und Menschensohn*, 1934, p. 292), these *charismata* are not to be considered as magic forces, such as a wonder-worker in the Hellenistic world would have boasted; they consist rather in a mysterious intensification of talents and faculties already possessed by their bearers, a phenomenon which has its analogies in general psychology.

The Corinthian congregation, which according to 1 Corinthians was specially rich in spiritual gifts, made a wrong use of them. Failing to recognize the unity of the Church and the place of mutual service, and at the same time believing that the full freedom of the age to come had already been realized, the more highly gifted made their gifts an occasion of pride, as marks of superior sanctity. Others, on the contrary, felt themselves forgotten, and yielded to jealousy or despair. Thus rivalry led to disorder.

3. Hence the tone of **Paul's teaching as to their use.** (*a*) He insists on their *regulation*. The gifts may be intermittent or dynamic; none the less their use must be orderly (1 Co 14[40]); ecstasy is no excuse for loss of self-control (v.[32]). Each Christian must recognize the limitations of his powers and not attempt to transcend them (Ro 12[6]). Love is the norm by which the gifts are to be judged; without love, which is the mark of eternal life, they are useless (1 Co 13).

There arises the question of the relation of the *charismata* to the ministry. Some have maintained that there was originally no fixed ministry, but only unorganized *charismata*; others again have tried to assign a definite office to most of the *charismata*. The truer view would seem to be that the *charismata* and the official ministry existed side by side, but were by no means identical. All Christians were supposed to have their share in the gifts of the Spirit, though there were special endowments which would be looked for in the case of officers of the Church. Thus Paul characterizes himself as an apostle in Ro 15[18ff], 2 Co 12[12]. In 1 Ti 4[14], 2 Ti 1[6] a *charisma* is connected with ' the laying on of hands.'

(*b*) *The purpose of the gifts is the edification and the service of the whole body.* Chrysostom, in his homily on 1 Co 12, calls attention to the change of word in vv.[4f]. The ' gifts ' are also ' ministrations ' (*diakoniai*), *i.e.* opportunities of service; hence the greater the gift the greater the responsibility, and the harder the work to be done. And so Paul passes on to the doctrine of the one body, served in different ways by all its members. Similarly in Eph 4[11] the possessors of the endowments are themselves gifts ' given ' to the Church. The same truth is emphasized in Ro 12, 1 Co 14, 1 P 4, in fact in every place where the *charismata* are mentioned at any length; Paul's own object is always to ' impart ' to others (Ro 1[11], 1 Co 14[19]; cf Jn 7[38]). (See the modern commentaries on 1 Co 12–14.)

(*c*) *Relative importance of the gifts.*—The more startling gifts are consistently treated as subordinate to gifts of character and edification. The former, indeed, are not decisive as to their origin; they are not peculiar to Christianity, and may be the accompaniment of evil and falsehood (Mt 7[22] 24[24], 2 Th 2[9], 1 Co 12[3], Rev 13[13f]). Indeed, in an age when ecstasy was a common feature of different religions, and the pagan *mantis* or frenzied prophet was a familiar phenomenon, it was impossible to ascribe all ' powers ' or all ' inspiration ' to the Holy Spirit. The test is on the one side doctrinal (1 Co 12[2f], 1 Jn 4[1-3]); on the other it is the moral life (Mt 7[15ff], Ro 8[9], 1 Co 13) and the practical tendency to edification (1 Co 14). The ' discerning of spirits ' is itself an important gift (1 Co 12[10], 1 Th 5[21], 1 Jn 4[1]). It is, indeed, remarkable how steadily the NT concentrates attention on the inner gifts of character, which the popular mind would ignore; and if it does not disparage, it certainly does not exaggerate, those which at first sight seemed to give more direct evidence of the presence of the Spirit. As a fact of history these tended to degenerate and finally to disappear. Justin and Irenaeus mention them, and they played a large part in the Gnostic and Montanist movements; but after the 2nd cent. they practically died out as normal endowments of the believer, to be revived only sporadically in times of religious excitement. C. W. E.—**H. R.**

SPITTING.—See GESTURES.

SPONGE (Gr. *spongos*, Mt 27[48], Mk 15[36], Jn 19[29], used in the Crucifixion scene).—Sponges have been used from early times, and are common along the Syrian coasts of the Mediterranean.

SPOONS, Ex 25[29] (AV, RV).—RSV has ' dishes.' See TABERNACLE, **6** (*a*).

SPRINGS.—See FOUNTAIN, ISRAEL, II. **1** (6).

SPY.—See WAR, **3.**

SQUAD.—Found only in RSV in Ac 12[4] for AV and RV **' quaternion '** (q.v.).

SQUARE.—See CITY.

STACHYS.—A Christian greeted by Paul in Ro 16[9].

STACK.—See SHOCK.

STACTE.—Hebrew *nāṭāph*, Ex 30[34]; cf Sir 24[15] (RV, RSV; AV ' sweet storax '). The Hebrew word means literally 'drops.' It denotes some fragrant gum collected in drops, either *storax* or, more probably, myrrh.

STADIA.—See WEIGHTS AND MEASURES.

STAFF.—See CLUB, ROD, SCEPTRE.

STAIR.—See HOUSE, **5.**

STALL.—See MANGER.

STALLION.—Found only in RSV in Jer 5^{8} (rendering *sûs*, 'horse') 8^{16} 47^{3} 50^{11} (rendering *'abbîr*, 'mighty one'; rendered 'steeds' in RSV in Jg 5^{22}).

STANDARD.—See BANNER.

STAR OF THE MAGI.—The Gospel according to St. Matthew, after a brief reference to the birth and naming of Jesus, goes on to describe the visit of 'wise men' from the east who come to Jerusalem to worship Him that is born king of the Jews (Mt 2^{1ff}). The Magi (q.v.) explain their arrival on the ground that they have seen His star 'in the east,' or rather, 'at its arising.' It may not seem obvious why the appearance of a star should lead them to conclude that a Jewish ruler had been born, but the explanation is no doubt to be found in Nu 24^{17}, 'A star shall come forth out of Jacob, and a sceptre shall rise out of Israel.' Taken in its context Balaam's prophecy anticipates a military leader who will 'smite through the corners (or temples) of Moab,' but it may have been taken as promising some heavenly manifestation of a more literal kind, thus linking a celestial phenomenon with the birth of the Messiah. Matthew's story may also have been influenced, as was later Christian tradition, by Is 60^{3}, 'Nations shall come to your light, and kings to the brightness of your rising'; but the Gospel does not say that the wise men were kings.

Matthew does not imply that the star led the Magi from the east to Jerusalem, but only that they understood its appearance as a sign that a king had been born in Judaea; but in the continuation of the story the star reappears to lead them to the house in Bethlehem where the young child was. Thus the star is no longer a portent, but a guide, without which the wise men would have been unable to find the child and present their gifts. So it is essential to Matthew's theme that the sages of the Gentiles worshipped Him whom the rulers of His own people rejected and sought to kill.

Speculations as to the nature of the star are unprofitable, for no natural phenomenon could have behaved as did the star of Bethlehem. Matthew's narrative of the birth of Jesus must be taken as a whole and compared with that of Luke from which it differs in many particulars. Matthew evidently regards Bethlehem as the home of Joseph and Mary, who only settle at Nazareth after the death of Herod the Great (Mt 2^{23}). Luke, on the other hand, brings Joseph and Mary to Bethlehem for a short time only in connexion with the census, and after the birth of Jesus they return to their own city, Nazareth (Lk 2^{39}). Luke knows nothing of the Magi and their star, or of the massacre of the children, or of the flight into Egypt, and he leaves no room for these things in his narrative. Nor does Matthew leave room for the Presentation in the Temple. It is clear that various stories about the birth of Jesus were current in the 1st cent., of which Matthew adopts one cycle and Luke another. Both narratives are beautiful, display the simple devotion of early days, and have inspired Christian art throughout the ages; but they cannot be reconciled, and only in the broadest outline do they provide material for an objective history of the birth of Christ. P. G.-S.

STAR-GOD.—Am 5^{26} (RSV); see KAIWAN.

STARS.—The stars (Bab.-Ass. *kabkabu, kakkabu* = Syr. *kaukbhâ* = Heb. *kôkhābh* from a reduplicated root *kbb* 'to flicker'; cognate Bab.-Ass. *kabābu* 'to burn') were created by God (Am 5^{8}, Ps 8^{3} 136^{9}, Job 9^{7}) to give light (Gn 1^{16}, Jer 31^{35}, Sir 43^{9}), being bright (Dn 12^{2}) but differing in magnitude (1 Co 15^{41}) and numberless (Gn 15^{5}, and *passim*), high above earth (Is 14^{13}, Ob ^{4}) and loftier than man (Job 22^{12}) but lower than wisdom (Wis 7^{29}). God gave them their 'paths' according to fixed laws (Jer 31^{35}), keeping them in subjection to Himself (Job 9^{7}, Is 45^{12}, Ps 147^{4}, Bar 3^{34} 6^{60}), and called them by their names (Is 40^{26}); and they ever praise Him (Dn 3^{63}).

Occasionally reference is made to particular numbers of stars, *e.g.* to seven or twelve stars (Re 1^{16} 12^{1}), where the figures perhaps belong to the conventions of apocalyptic usage. Elsewhere, they may have special application: the 'eleven stars' which do obeisance to Joseph in his dream reflect not the eleven (twelve) Zodiacal constellations but the number of his brethren (Gn 37^{9}; cf 35^{23-27}), as 'the seven stars' correspond to the number of the seven churches (Rev 1^{20}), whereas the 'seven stars' of Amos are the *Pleiades*, for which it is an old English name (Am 5^{8} AV; see below). In poetry hyperbolical expressions are used of the stars: as at creation 'the morning stars sang together' (Job 38^{7}), so at the battle in Taanach by the waters of Megiddo 'the stars in their courses fought against Sisera' (Jg 5^{20}), where the implication is not perhaps that they were the host of Yahweh or the cause of the rainstorms that flooded the Kishon but that Israel's victory was not won by their own unaided efforts (Moore).

The appearance of an unusually bright star or comet (Heb. *shēbheṭ*, 'club' and 'comet' as shaped like a club; cf Arab *sabiṭa* 'was long, flowing,' of hair) was thought to portend the coming of some great personage: so Balaam prophesied that 'a star shall proceed out of Jacob, a comet arise from Israel' (Nu 24^{17}). This prophecy was afterwards applied to the Epiphany (Mt 2^{2}). In the Gospel 'the day of the Lord' will be heralded by 'signs in the sun and in the moon and in the stars' (Lk 21^{25}); and in apocalyptic literature 'they that turn many to righteousness shall shine as the stars for ever and ever' (Dn 12^{3}). Simon the high-priest is compared to 'the day-star in the midst of a cloud' (Sir 50^{6}; *astēr eōthinos*) and Jesus describes Himself as 'the bright, the earliest star' (Rev 22^{16}; *astēr orthinos*); and metaphorically the Christian is bidden to pay heed to the Gospel 'as unto a light that shineth in a dark place until the day dawn and the morning star arise in your hearts' (2 P 1^{19}, *phōsphoros*). Here these celestial bodies may be distinguished: the third is *Lucifer*, the morning and evening star (commonly the planet *Venus* but occasionally also other planets); the second is perhaps a star rising heliacally *i.e.* shortly before dawn; the third may be one which rises earlier but is noticeable for remaining visible while the sun comes up and perhaps also afterwards and which may sometimes be identical with the morning star. The distinction between the last two stars, however, is by no means certain, and what the 'early star' (Rev 2^{28}, *astēr prōinos*) is and how it differs from them is equally obscure; indeed, all three expressions may be synonyms. Contrariwise, the darkening of the stars was regarded as a presage of distress or disaster (Am 8^{9}, Job 2^{10}, and often elsewhere). Allusions also occur to 'wandering stars, for whom the blackness has been reserved for ever' (Jd ^{13}), *i.e.* shooting stars which come out of darkness and go back into it and can be seen on almost any night in Palestine and the neighbouring countries (cf Mt 24^{29}, Mk 13^{25}).

Isaiah, describing the downfall of the king of Babylon, says 'how are you fallen from heaven, O Day Star, son of Dawn' (Is 14^{12}), where the 'shining one' (Heb. *hêlēl*, here translated 'day-star'; RV, RSV) is usually supposed to be *Lucifer* (LXX, Vulgate and thence AV) or *Venus* as the morning star, in view of its brilliance when it is apparent and its total disappearance at times, while alternatively an allusion has been seen to the overpowering of the temporary brilliance of the morning star by the rays of the sun. No reason, however, for connecting this, though the brightest, planet with the Babylonian king is suggested, its daily disappearance is nowhere regarded as symbolic and is not likely to have become a symbol of total ruin since it regularly reappears next day, and the Assyrian *muštêlil* 'shining,' which is cited as an epithet of the same planet and so as evidence for the identification, is a *vox nihili* based on a misreading of a cuneiform tablet. That the new moon (Arab. *hilâlu* 'shining one' = 'new moon') or the waning crescent moon as seen at dawn is meant (Winckler) is equally improbable, as the moon is not commonly connected with royalty. What is meant is perhaps rather *Jupiter*, the largest but not the brightest planet which ancient astrologers connected with royalty and whose principal Babylonian name was *Marduk*, which it shared with the chief god of Babylon. Although, too, *Venus* is most commonly *lucifer*, *Mercury* and *Jupiter*, *Mars* and *Saturn*, can each (though rarely) be so. Further, *Venus* is probably the 'queen of heaven' (Jer 7[18] 44[17, 19, 25]), being described in Sumerian texts as 'queen of heaven and earth' and as 'bearded' (*i.e.* emitting rays); and while *Venus* can never be more than 47° away from the sun as seen from the earth, *i.e.* is never more than just over half-way from horizon to zenith, in the night-sky, *Jupiter* can appear at any angular distance from the sun and so be high in the night-sky; thus *Jupiter* rather than *Venus* fits the description of a star falling from a height to utter ruin. Lastly, *Jupiter* for about two months in every year is too near the sun to be visible and can also not be seen in the night-sky. Such periods of invisibility were regarded as especially dangerous for the Babylonian king; so, for example, an omen says 'when the *iku*-star (*Jupiter*) is present all day but at night-fall (?) enters the world below and is invisible all night, the king will die' (Virolleaud, *Astrologie Chaldéenne*, *Ishtar*, xxviii. 8). Possibly then Isaiah was using *Jupiter*'s descent into the world below and consequent invisibility as a symbol of the downfall of the king of Babylon and his disappearance from earth.

Individual stars are mentioned or named in various passages of the OT. In it God is pictured as sitting 'at the height of heaven,' *i.e.* the zenith, and contemplating 'the chief of the stars, high as they are' (Job 22[12]); this is most probably the pole-star (Budde), which lies at the centre of rotation and was *β Ursae Minoris* or 'Kochab' between 1500 B.C. and A.D. 300; but *Gemini* (*Castor* and *Pollux*), which were at their highest point *c* 700 B.C. (Kugler), and *Aires*, the first of the Zodiacal constellations and therefore described as *caput . . . ante omnia princeps* (Manilius, *Astronomicon*, ii. 456; cf i. 263), have also been suggested. The zenith is perhaps mentioned also in a corrupt passage which may mean 'the sun forgot to turn in his course and the moon stood still at her zenith' (Hab 3[10b, 11a]). The stars, as the work of God's hands, mark the changes of day and night, summer and winter. They rise about sunset to indicate the onset of night (Neh 4[21]), and the appearance of the day-star announces the dawn (2 P 1[19]). God is further described as 'he who has made the *Pleiades* and *Orion*, who turns darkness into morning and darkens day into night . . . who makes *Taurus* (Heb. *shôr* for MT's *shōdh* 'sudden destruction') rise after *Capella* (Heb. *'ēz* for MT's *'az* 'strong') and *Taurus* (*do.*) to set hard on the rising of *Vindemiatrix* (Heb. *m^{e}bhaṣṣēr* for MT's *mibhṣār* 'fortress'), as the text has been cleverly corrected and interpreted (Am 5[8–9]; Hoffmann); accordingly it means that God has made the alternations not only of day and night but also of summer and winter (for *Taurus* rises soon after *Capella* in May–June and sets soon after the rising of *Vindemiatrix*, namely ε *Virginis*, in October–November). Again, it is He who has made *Aldebaran* (commonly mistranslated *Arcturus* or the 'Bear'), *Orion* and the *Pleiades* (Job 9[9] 38[31–32]). Their names are easily explained. The Hebrew *'ayish*, *'āsh* is identical with the Syrian *'yûthâ*, namely, *Aldebaran* (Schiaparelli), which the cognate Arabic *ġaithu* 'rain, clouds' connects with the rainy season, and 'his sons' (AV; cf RSV) or 'his train' (RV) are the *Hyades*, the *nimbosa Hyas* (Claudian, *Carmina* xvi. 497–8) or rainy constellation (cf Gr. *hūein* 'to rain'), of which *Aldebaran* is the brightest member. The Hebrew *k^{e}sîl* 'stout, sturdy' denotes *Orion*, the magical hunter of gigantic strength and beauty, whom Aramaeans and Syrians as well as Arabs called the 'Giant' and whose 'strength' is often mentioned by the Greek poets from Homer onwards; the constellation consists of seven stars in the form of a colossal man with a narrow waist indicated by the three stars forming his 'belt' (Heb. *môshekheth* for MT *môsh^{e}khôth* = Arab. *masakatu* 'bracelet, anklet; fetter'). The Hebrew *kîmāh* 'cluster' (cf Assyr. *kīmtu* 'family,' Arab. *kûmu* 'herd' and *kûmatu* 'heap') is the *Pleiadum parvo glomeramine sidus* (Manilius *Astronomicon*, iv. 520) and the *thurayyâ* 'multitude' (namely the *Pleiades*) of the Arabs; the absurdly translated 'sweet influences' (Job 38[31] AV) of the *Pleiades* is a misrendering of a word which means 'cluster' (RV; Heb. *ma'^{a}dheneth* for MT *ma'^{a}dhannôth* = Ugar. *'dn* 'host' and Arab. *'adânatu* 'company, party of men,' from the same root as also the M.-Heb. *ma'^{a}dhān* 'bundle'), the *chorus Pleiadum* of the Latin poets. These three constellations, *Orion* with the *Pleiades* and *Hyades*, are mentioned together as in classical literature (Homer, *Iliad*, xviii. 486; Hesiod, *Works and Days*, 615); and so God asks Job whether he can bind, *i.e.* check the unleashing of, the rains when the *Pleiades* usher in the spring or 'unloose' *Orion*'s belt, *i.e.* release him from heralding the onset of winter, or whether he can 'guide,' *i.e.* control, the activity of *Aldebaran* and the *Hyades*, the seven stars whose rising simultaneously with the sun was held to portend wet weather.

God also asks Job 'canst thou bring forth *Mazzaroth* in their season?' (Job 38[32] RV, RSV); what the Hebrew *mazzārôth* means is disputed, but it is perhaps best taken as standing for *ma'^{a}zārôth* (cf *makkōleth* = *ma'^{a}khōleth* 'food-stuff, fuel') and so denoting 'girdling stars,' *i.e.* the Zodiacal circle, when the point of God's question is to imply that only He and no man can make the stars to rise and give their light in this great circle of constellations. Another term is 'the chambers of the south (*ḥadh^{e}rê têmān*),' which the Greek translator known as 'the Hebrew' explains as 'the encirclers (cf Wis 13[2]) of the south (*ḥôdhrê têmān*).' Babylonian astronomers divided the Zodiacal circle into six solar and six lunar 'houses,' *i.e.* groups of stars or constellations, which will correspond to the Hebrew 'chambers'; and these 'chambers of the south' will be the belt of stars or constellations lying roughly parallel to and to the S. of, *i.e.* below, the ecliptic (Zodiac), namely the Babylonian 'way of Ea' or *circulus austrinus* as classical writers (Eudoxus, Aratus, Hyginus, Martianus Capella) call it. Both Babylonian and classical lists vary: the former contain 12–15 stars amongst which 6 are commonly named (*Orion*, *Piscis*, *Austrinus*, *Aquarius*, *Ara*, *Centaurus*, *Canis Major*; if rightly identified); the latter contains 11–16 stars, of which 9 are constant (*Orion*, *Argo*, *Cetus*, *Eridanus*, *Piscis Austrinus*, *Hydrus*, *Ara*, *Centaurus*, *Procyon*).

Further, when Elihu says 'out of the chamber (*ḥedher*) comes the storm, and cold out of the north' (Job 37[9]; cf RV), he is referring to definite stars or constellations, not merely to the points of the compass. The former is not the same as 'the chambers of the south' (RV; cf Job 9[9]), but the principal constellation in that circle of stars, that which because of its circular configuration is called *alqubbatu* 'the tent' or 'vaulted chamber' by the Arabs (for the Heb. *ḥedher* is the same word as the Arab. *ḥidru* 'tent') and the Southern Cross (*Corona australis*) by western astronomers. When Job was written, though not now, this was visible on the extreme southern horizon of Palestine. The 'storm' coming from that direction is the sirocco. The latter name as it stands means 'scatterers' (cf RSV) and can hardly be explained; but if it be read *mizrayim* (so Schiaparelli), it can be translated as 'the two winnowing fans,' namely *Ursa Major* (which the Chinese call the Ladle) and *Ursa Minor* (which the Vulgate's *arcturus*, if taken with Grotius as an error for *arctus*, will support); the Greater Bear was much nearer the Pole in Job's time than now, the Phoenicians used the Lesser Bear to find the north, and the cold came to Palestine from that direction (Sir 43[20]).

God further asks Job whether he can bid dawn appear 'that it might take hold of the ends of the earth and the

Wicked be shaken out of it, when it is changed as clay under the seal and stands forth as a garment and their light is withholden from the Wicked and the High Arm is broken?' (Job 38[12–15]). Here 'the Wicked' are Orion's dogs, *i.e.* the Dog-stars (*Canis Major* and *Canis Minor*), of which one (*Sirius*, namely *α Canis Majoris*) was called the 'evil sign' (Homer, *Iliad* xxii. 29–30) because its rising in the torrid heat of late summer (July 13–August 10) was associated with sickness and plague and which was formerly thought to be nearest to earth because of its brilliance; and this suggestion is strengthened by a curious point in the Hebrew text which seems to suggest as an alternative reading 'hairy ones' (Heb. *śᵉʿîrîm* for *rᵉshāʿîm*), which will be the Dog-stars (cf Arab. *shiʿrā*=*canis major* and *alshiʿrâni*=*Sirius* and *Procyon*). Then the 'High Arm' will be what is sometimes called the 'Navigator's Line,' namely *Sirius—Procyon—Gemini* (*Castor* and *Pollux*), patrons of sea-farers (cf Ac 28[11]), which are extended like a bent 'arm' (Heb. *zᵉrôaʿ*; cf Arab. *dhirâʿu* 'arm'=*Gemini* when extended and *Canis Minor* when contracted) across the sky from the horizon to the zenith (*Sirius* the shoulder, *Procyon* the elbow, *Gemini* the fingers) and which from their brilliance are a principal aid to navigation. Accordingly, the picture is that of the sun as it rises extinguishing the light of the stars one by one and picking out the hills and valleys as its rays reach them, like the pattern on a seal or the folds of a dress (G. R. Driver in *JThS* N.S. iv, 208–212, vii 1–11).

The worship of the stars, commonly grouped together as the 'host of heaven,' is often mentioned (*e.g.* Jer 7[18] 19[13] 44[17], Ac 7[43]) and condemned (2 K 17[16], Jer 44[19, 25]), and those who practised it are threatened with death in the Law (Dt 4[19] 17[2–5]). Nonetheless, Manasseh introduced it (2 K 21[5]) but Josiah 'put down the idolatrous priests . . . and them that burned incense unto Baal, to the sun and to the moon and to the planets and to all the host of heaven' (2 K 23[5]; see Host of Heaven). The Hebrew *mazzālôth* in this passage has often been taken for the Zodiacal signs (LXX, Vulgate; cf Aram. *mazzālâ* 'Zodiacal constellation'), but these are not likely to have been objects of worship; the term is therefore preferably translated 'planets' (cf Aram. *mazzālāthâ*= Syr. *mauzalāthâ* 'planets'). The 'queen of heaven,' who was worshipped in Jerusalem immediately before the Captivity (Jer 7[18]) and to the neglect of whose worship the captives ascribed their disasters (Jer 44[19, 25]) was the Babylonian goddess Ishtar who, from early times, bore as one of her titles the Sumerian NIN-DAR-AN.NA 'bright mistress of heaven,' *i.e.* the Phoenician and Hebrew 'Ashtoreth'=Greek *Astartē* and Latin *Venus* (Gössmann, *Planetarium Babylonicum*, 120–122). A reference to the worship of the stars has also been found in 'ye have borne Siccuth (RSV 'Sakkuth') your king and Chiun (RSV 'Kaiwan') your images, the star of your god, which ye made to yourselves' (Am 5[26], RV), by reading 'Siccuth' as **sakkūth* and equating it with the Sumerian=SAG.KUD=Babylonian *Ninurta* god of war, and by reading 'Chiun' as **kaiwān*, which may then be taken as the Babylonian *Kaimānu* (cf Syr. *kewān*= Arab. *kaiwânu*) 'Saturn' (cf Ac 7[43], which is not necessarily decisive); but, although these two names occur together in a Babylonian incantation (Reiner, *Šurpu* ii. 180), they are not entirely in place here and are not supported by the earliest versions, which may accordingly be followed in reading 'but you shall now take up the shrine (Heb. *sukkath* for the MT *sikkūth*) of your idol-king and the pedestal(s) of your images, the star-gods which you have made for yourselves' to carry them into exile. Whether or how far the ancient Hebrews regarded the 'host of heaven' (which denotes also various heavenly beings) as the visible counterpart or image of the army of the angels (cf Is 24[21]) is disputed.

The OT also occasionally speaks of astrologers, called 'dividers of the heavens' (*i.e.* those who divide them into sections by constellations in order to 'contemplate' the movements of the heavenly bodies), the 'star-gazers' and the 'monthly prognosticators' (Is 47[13]), who professed a knowledge of future events based on a heavenly lore of which the prophet speaks with contempt, knowing them well from the experience of the Exile. They are the same as the 'Chaldaeans' and perhaps as the 'sooth-sayers' or rather 'determiners of fate' [not as the 'astrologers' (AV) or 'enchanters' (RV, RSV), who were rather 'exorcists' at the Persian court in Babylon] (Dn 5[7]); the term translated 'determiners of fate' may mean the same class of persons as the above-mentioned 'dividers of the heavens' (Gesenius), while 'Chaldaeans' is a general term for members of the Babylonian learned and priestly class who made astronomy or astrology one of their principal studies (S. R. Driver, *Daniel*, 12–16).

G. R. D., with help from L. C.

STATE OF THE DEAD.—See Death, Eschatology, Paradise, Sheol.

STATER.—See Money, **7.**

STATUTE.—See Decree.

STEALING.—See Crimes, **6, 'Theft.'**

STEEL.—See Mining and Metals.

STEERSMAN.—See Pilot.

STEPHANAS.—A Corinthian, apparently of some importance, whose household were baptized by Paul personally (1 Co 1[16]), and are called 'the first-fruits (='first converts' RSV) of Achaia' (16[15]). Stephanas himself had joined the Apostle at Ephesus when he wrote, and was of great assistance to him there.

A. J. M.

STEPHEN.—The story of Stephen, told in Ac 6 and 7, narrates the election of Stephen and six other men for superintending the distribution of alms. But Stephen is shown to be a miracle worker and a debater. His success resulted in a trial before the Sanhedrin. False witnesses accused him of blasphemy and of speaking against the Temple and the Law. In his long speech Stephen gave a survey of the history of Israel. He described Moses as the type of Christ and stated that the Temple had been built contrary to the will of God (7[48ff]). He accused the Jews of having persecuted the prophets, as they now had killed Jesus, and not keeping the Law themselves. His vision of the exalted Lord and his announcing of it exasperated the Jews. They cast him out of the city and stoned him. Thus Stephen became the first Christian martyr. His death led to a persecution of the whole community. Some of the dispersed disciples founded the Gentile Christian community of Antioch. In connexion with this persecution Saul of Tarsus was converted (9[1ff]).

This picture has been corrected by modern critics at two points: 1. It was not the whole community which suffered persecution, but only the Hellenistic group about Stephen. 2. Stephen himself was lynched by a fanatical mob; the trial before the Sanhedrin is merely a device of the writer of Acts which enables him to insert the long speech in ch. 7.

E. H.

STEWARD.—This term is found seven times in the OT. In Gn 43[16, 19] 44[1, 4] Joseph's steward is literally 'he who was over his house.' In 1 Ch 27[31] 28[1] 'stewards' is the translation of Hebrew *śārîm* ('overseers' would be a good rendering). Another word, *sōkhēn*, used in Is 22[15], receives clarification in vv.[21ff]. *Melṣar* found in Dn 1[11, 16] might well be translated 'guardian.'

The NT terms are (1) *epitropos*, 'steward' in Mt 20[8], Lk 8[3]; also translated 'guardians' in Gal 4[2]; (2) *architriklinos* in Jn 2[8f (twice)], which is quite possibly 'toastmaster,' 'master of the feast'; and (3) *oikonomos*, the usual term, 'one who manages a household.' This is used both literally and metaphorically; literally in Lk 12[42] 16[1, 3, 8], and metaphorically in 1 Co 4[1f], Tit 1[7], and 1 P 4[10]. The cognate noun, *oikonomia*, 'stewardship,' is used similarly; the verb, *oikonomein*, has a literal meaning in Lk 16[2].

W. F. B.—**J. H. Sc.**

STOCKS.—See Crimes, **9**; Prison.

STOICKS.—AV spelling of **Stoics** (q.v.).

STOICS.—When St. Paul met representatives of the Stoic philosophy at Athens (Ac 17^{18}), that school had been in existence for about three and a half centuries. The name came from the *Stoa* or Porch (Stoa Poikilē) in Athens where Zeno (*c* 340–265 B.C.), the founder of the school, had taught his followers. The system was partly religious in outlook from the start. One of its finest religious expressions was the *Hymn to Zeus* written by Cleanthes, Zeno's successor. It is preserved in Stobaeus, *Eclogae*, I. i. 12 (see H. von Arnim, *Stoicorum Veterum Fragmenta*, i, 537). According to Cleanthes, God 'knows to make the crooked straight, prune all excess, give order to the orderless,' and bring good out of evil. Another great Stoic teacher was Posidonius of Apamea (135–51 B.C.), who exercised a strong influence on the Middle Stoa, especially its theology. His was the most universal mind of his age; he was not an Eclectic, but combined a consistent system of Monism with deep religious feeling. He was interested in the occult, like many other philosophers of the Hellenistic age, and he defined philosophy as the knowledge of things divine and human and their causes. He believed that a universal 'sympathy' explains nature as a whole and its diverse phenomena—*e.g.* the tides, which follow the moon; and he thereby opened the way to belief in astrology and divination, even among the educated. He looked upon the sun as the source of 'vital energy,' which floods and energizes the universe. Even souls are derived from the sun and fill the region below the moon. God is thus a fiery breath. Both sleep (dreams) and ecstasy lead to intuition, and religion arose from the contemplation of the heavens by early men, who lived more closely in communion with the gods than their descendants have done. Such a writing as the pseudo-Aristotelian essay, *On the Cosmos* (1st cent. B.C.), is filled with Posidonius's teaching, and is a good example of the popular type of Stoicism which belongs to the background of the NT and is taken for granted in Ac 17.

The early Stoic teaching was organized under three headings, Logic (including epistemology, logic, and rhetoric), Physics (including ontology, physics, and theology), and Ethics. The leading Stoic maxim was, 'Live in harmony' (so Zeno), to which Chrysippus added, 'with nature.' Both in the physical universe and in man, nature is to be interpreted by its highest manifestation, Reason, which appears in the world as the all-pervading ethereal essence or spirit, forming and animating the whole; in man it appears as the soul. Hence virtue is based on knowledge (as Socrates had held); and hence only the Wise Man can be really virtuous. The World-Soul, Reason, or Spirit of the universe is God, for the Stoic teachers (*e.g.* Cleanthes). According to Ac 17^{28}, Paul quoted the words of a Stoic writer: 'We are indeed his offspring' (or, 'belong to his race'; cf Aratus, *Phaenomena*, 5). But the quotation, though apt, represents a parallel in language rather than in ideas: the theology of the Stoics was pure pantheism. The Stoic god had no independent or personal existence—at least as conceived by the majority of teachers.

The supremacy of reason in man was pushed to such an extreme that virtuous conduct demanded the entire suppression of man's emotional nature. This rigorous moral standard became, for practical reasons, considerably modified, as by Seneca and Epictetus; but Stoic morality was always marked by rigidity and coldness.

The great quality of Stoicism, which set it apart from Epicureanism (q.v.), and brought it into line with Christianity, was its *moral earnestness*. In his famous dissertation on 'St. Paul and Seneca' (published in his *Commentary on Philippians*, 1868), Bishop J. B. Lightfoot wrote: 'Stoicism was the only philosophy which could even pretend to rival Christianity in the earlier ages of the Church.' Following the decline of the Academic philosophy into scepticism and the endless 'suspense of judgment' (see Cicero's *Academics* and *On the Nature of the Gods*), Stoicism remained the noblest school of thought with which the majority of men were acquainted; as such it was brought into contact with St. Paul by the author of Acts. Elsewhere he shows little knowledge of the system; see A. Bonhöffer, *Epiktet und das NT* (1911), pp. 98–180. The real influence of Stoicism upon Christian thought came later than the NT.

W. M. McD.—**F. C. G.**

STOMACH.—This English word occurs in 2 Mac 7^{21} AV with the meaning of 'courage,' 'Stirring up her womanish thoughts with a manly stomach.'

STOMACHER.—The English word 'stomacher' was applied to that part of a woman's dress which covered the breast and the pit of the stomach. It was usually much ornamented, and was looked upon as an evidence of wealth. The word occurs in AV and RV in Is 3^{24} as translation of Hebrew *pᵉthîghîl* (RSV 'rich robe'). Its meaning is very uncertain.

STONE.—I. In OT.—1. Several different words are rendered 'stone,' but the one of by far the most frequent occurrence is *'ebhen*, which has the same wide range of application as its English equivalent. Palestine is a stony country, and the uses to which stone was put were numerous and varied. In its natural state a stone served for a pillow (Gn 28^{18}) or a seat (Ex 17^{12}), for covering the mouth of a well (Gn 29^{2ff}) or closing the entrance to a cave (Jos 10^{18}). The stone rolled on to the opening of Christ's grave, Mt 27^{60}, was probably not in its natural state, and in a number of archaeological sites in Palestine traces can still be seen of the tracks along which the stones were rolled, and, indeed, of the way in which they were levered into place. Out of it, again, might be constructed a vessel (Ex 7^{19}; cf Jn 2^{6}), a mill (Dt 24^{6}). Above all, stone was employed in architecture. Houses (Lv 14^{42} etc.), walls (Neh 4^{3}, Hab 2^{11}), towers (by implication in Gn 11^{3}), and especially the Temple (1 K 5^{17f} etc.), are referred to as built of stone. We read of foundation-stones (1 K 5^{17}), of a corner-stone (Ps 118^{22}), of a head-stone or finial (Zec 4^{7}); and in 2 K 16^{17} mention is made of a pavement of stone. Masonry was a regular trade (2 S 5^{11} etc.), and stone-hewing is frequently referred to (2 K 12^{12} etc.). Belonging to the aesthetic and luxurious side of life are precious stones and the arts of cutting and graving and setting them (Ex 28$^{9, 11}$ 31^{5} etc.); see, further, JEWELS AND PRECIOUS STONES. The profusion of stones made it natural to use them as missiles. Stone-throwing might be a mark of hatred and contempt (2 S 16$^{6, 13}$), or the expedient of murderous intentions against which provision had to be made in legislation (Ex 21^{18}, Nu 35^{17}). In war, stones were regular weapons of offence. Usually they were hurled with slings (1 S 17^{49}, 1 Ch 12^{2}), but, later, great stones were discharged by means of 'engines' (2 Ch 26^{15}, 1 Mac 6^{51}). **Stoning to death** was a natural and convenient method of execution. At first an expression of popular fury (Jos 7^{25}), it was afterwards regulated by law as an appointed means of capital punishment (Dt 17$^{5-7}$; cf Ac 7^{58f}). See, further, CRIMES AND PUNISHMENTS, **10.** The use of stones as memorials was common. Sometimes a single large stone, at other times a heap of stones, was raised (Gn 31^{45f}, Jos 8^{29} 24^{26}). Akin to this was their employment to mark a boundary (Jos 15^{6} etc.). Stones would be the ordinary landmarks between the fields of one person and another, the removal of which was strictly forbidden (Dt 19^{14} etc.). In religious worship stones were employed in the forms of the pillar (Gn 28$^{18, 22}$ 31^{45} 35^{14}) and the altar. The latter was at first a single great stone (1 S 6^{14f}), but afterwards was built of several stones, which must be unhewn (Ex 20^{25}, Dt 27^{5f}). See, further, PILLAR AND ALTAR. The use of stone for literary purposes (cf the Moabite Stone) is illustrated by the tables of stone on which the Decalogue was written (Ex 24^{12} etc.) and the inscribed stones of the altar on Mount Ebal (Dt 27^{2ff}, Jos 8^{30ff}).

2. Stones in Lv 21^{2}, Dt 23^{1} (AV, RV), Lv 22^{24} (RV) = testicles (so RSV).

II. In NT.—Here *lithos* is the ordinary word, and is found in most of the connexions already referred to. Noteworthy is the fact that Jesus, after quoting Ps 118^{22}, took the rejected and exalted stone as a symbol of Himself (Mt 21^{42ff}, Lk 20^{17f}). St. Peter adopts the symbol in his address to the Sanhedrin (Ac 4^{11}), and enlarges it, with further reference to Is 8^{14} 28^{16}, in his figure of the 'living stone,' which is at once the foundation of God's spiritual house and a stone of stumbling to the disobedient (1 P 2^{4-8}). The 'stone' (*petros*) of Jn 1^{42} (AV), should be 'rock' (as RSV) or Peter (RV); 'Stony' (*petrōdēs*) in Mt 13^{5}, Mk $4^{5, 16}$ (AV) should be 'rocky' (RSV). The 'white stone' of Rev 2^{17} represents *psēphos* 'a pebble,' and the reference, which has been variously interpreted, is best explained with Charles as 'an amulet engraved with . . . a name' (*Revelation*, ad loc.) a relic of the mystery cults which became transformed into a Christian symbol. J. C. L.—**B. J. R.**

STONE-SQUARERS.—Found only in 1 K 5^{18} [Heb. 32] AV; RV has **Gebalites** (RSV 'men of Gebal') as Jos 13^{5}, *i.e.* men of the Phoenician city of Gebal, or Byblos, mentioned in Ezk 27^{9}, where the elders and wise men of Gebal are referred to as caulkers of ships. It has been suggested that the gentilic had become an appellative in the sense of stonecutter (as Canaanite came to mean 'trader'), which is the meaning of AV. Others would emend the text (but cf Montgomery-Gehman, *ICC*, p. 140). A. R. S. K.

STONES, PRECIOUS.—See Jewels and Precious Stones.

STOOL.—'In older English (including AV) "stool" was used freely for any kind of seat' (*DB* iv, 621); similarly the Hebrew *kissē'* includes both chairs and stools, see House, **8.** In the difficult passage Ex 1^{16} the word rendered 'stools' (AV) in the sense of birth-stools (RV, RSV), *sella parturientis*, must be pointed to read 'stones' (*'abhnayim* for *'obhnayim*, both dual number), the reference being to the two stones or bricks on which a woman sat during her accouchement. This widely spread custom has been conclusively shown to have existed in ancient Egypt by Spiegelberg (*Aegypt. Randglossen*, 19–25), from the realistic representation preserved in an early hieroglyphic sign for birth confirmed by literary references. A. R. S. K.

STORAX.—See Poplar, Spice, Stacte.

STORK (*ḥ^asîdhāh*).—The Hebrew *ḥ^asîdhāh* is variously translated in the ancient versions, but the most likely renderings are 'heron' (Gr. versions and Vulgate often) and/or 'stork' (Peshitta in some places). The name means 'kindly,' and the stork has been called *ciconia pietaticultrix* (Petronius) for its parental affection; but the heron is equally assiduous in caring for its young. Therefore both birds, since they belong to the same order, may be denoted by the Hebrew word. Both the 'white stork' (*ciconia alba*) and the 'black stork' (*ciconia nigra*) as well as the 'common heron' (*ardea cinerea*) are well known in Palestine. The white stork nests both on houses and on trees, the black stork and the heron on trees, so that the reference to this habit (Ps 104^{17}) does not indicate which is meant. The common **heron** may be meant in some places, but the intended bird must be the white stork in two, namely when the expanse of its wings is in question (Zec 5^{9}), since it is far the largest and most conspicuous of these birds, and when its migratory habit is mentioned (Jer 8^{7}), since it is one of the very few birds which migrate in daylight, so that this habit must have been well known. The stork feeds on locusts and reptiles and is therefore highly valued, while the heron takes fish and reptiles and also frogs and water-rats; being predators, therefore, they are classed amongst unclean birds (Lv 11^{19}, Dt 14^{18}). The supposed reference to the *ḥ^asîdhāh* in connexion with the ostrich (Job 39^{13}) is certainly due to textual corruption, and 'are pinion and plumage lacking (*ḥās^erāh*)?' must be read (Hoffmann). G. R. D.

STORM.—See Galilee (Sea of), **3**; Whirlwind.

STORY (EV for 'storey').—See House, **5.**

STRAIT.—This English word is used in AV in the literal sense of 'narrow,' and in the figurative sense of 'strict' (of which it is simply another form). Once the verb 'strait' occurs, Sus ^{22} 'I am straitened on every side.'

STRAKES.—AV and RV in Gn 30^{37} where RSV has 'streaks,' and in Lv 14^{37} where RSV has 'spots.' In the former case the word comes from a root meaning 'to peel,' and in the latter from a root meaning 'to be hollow.'

STRANGE FIRE (AV RV).—RSV 'unholy fire'; see Nadab.

STRANGER.—This seems, on the whole, the most suitable English word by which to render the Hebrew *zār*, which is a participle denoting primarily one who turns aside, one who goes out of the way, *i.e.* for the purpose of visiting or dwelling in another country. It has frequently the meaning **foreigner,** in contrast to 'Israelite,' especially with the added notion of hostility (cf 'estranged'), and in antithesis to 'Israel' (*e.g.* Hos 7^{9} 8^{7}, Is 1^{7}, Ezk 7^{21} 11^{9}, Jl 3^{17}, Ob ^{11}, Ps 54^{3} etc.). In P the word takes on a technical meaning found nowhere outside the Hexateuch, and exclusively post-exilic. It means 'layman' (which might with advantage be substituted for EV 'stranger'), as opposed to a Levite (see Nu 1^{51} 18^{7}; RSV 'anyone else'), or to a priest proper, or Aaronite (see Ex 29^{33} 30^{33}, Nu $3^{10, 38}$ 18^{2}, Lv $22^{10, 12f}$ (H)).

The 'strange woman' of Pr 2^{16} etc. has the same technical sense as 'foreign woman' with which it stands in parallelism, viz. *harlot* (RSV 'loose woman').

Sojourner (sometimes the translation of *tōshābh*, 'settler [see below]) is frequently substituted by RV, RSV for the AV 'stranger,' as translation of *gēr*. The *gēr* was originally a man who transferred himself from one tribe or people to another, seeking, and usually obtaining, some of the rights of natives. A whole clan or tribe might be *gērîm* in Israel, as *e.g.* the Gibeonites (Jos 9), the Beerothites (2 S 4^{2}). The Israelites are themselves often spoken of as 'sojourners' in the land of Egypt (see Gn 15^{13}, Ex 22^{21} 23^{9}, Lv 19^{24} (H), Dt 10^{19} 23^{7} etc.). In the oldest Israelite code (the Book of the Covenant, Ex 21^{1} to 23^{13}), the *gēr* is protected against injustice and violence (21^{20} 23^{9}). The D code (*c* 620 B.C.) goes much further, for, besides making more explicit and urgent the duty of defending, helping, and even loving the 'sojourner' (Dt 10^{18} 14^{29} $24^{14, 19}$), and also securing to him his rights (24^{17} 27^{1-9}), the *gēr* was to be allowed to participate in the three great annual feasts (Dt 16^{11ff}; cf 5^{14} and Ex 23^{12}). He is not, however, compelled, though allowed, to follow his protector's religion (Dt 14^{29}, 1 K 11^{7}). That he occupies a status inferior to that of the born Israelite is indicated by the fact that he is classed with the widow and orphan as needing special consideration (10^{18} 14^{29} $29^{14, 19}$), and that the right of intermarrying is denied him (7^{1ff} 23^{4}). When, however, we come to P and to other parts of the OT which belong to the same stage of history and religion, we find the 'sojourner' almost on an equal footing with the native Israelite—he is fast becoming, and is almost become, the **proselyte** of NT and Rabbinical times. His position has now religious rather than political significance. He is expected to keep the Sabbath and to observe the Day of Atonement, as well as the three great feasts (Lv 16^{29}). He is to eat unleavened bread during Passover week (Ex 12^{19}; Passover and the Feast of Unleavened Bread are now blended), and, if circumcised (not otherwise), to keep the full Passover itself. But the *gēr* is not even yet the full equal of the Israelite, for he is not compelled to be circumcised, and no one can belong to the congregation who has not submitted to that rite (Ex 12^{47ff}, Nu 9^{14}); he has not yet received the right of intermarriage (Gn 34^{14}), and is prohibited from keeping Jewish slaves (Lv 25^{47ff}).

The closing of the ranks of Judaism, helped by the Samaritan schism, and consummated by the Maccabaean wars, led to the complete absorption of the 'sojourner.' The word *prosēlytos* (representing the Heb. *gēr*), common in classical Greek for one who has come to a place

(Lat. *advena*), acquired in Hellenistic Greek the meaning which meets us often in the NT (Mt 23[15], Ac 2[6] etc.) See PROSELYTE.

The indiscriminate use of 'stranger' with the meaning of 'sojourner,' and of '*alien*' and 'foreigner' is very confusing. 'Foreigner' is the proper rendering of Hebrew *nokhrî*. The Hebrew *tôshābh* (literally 'dweller') is a post-exilic substitute for *gēr* ('sojourner') in the original non-religious sense of the latter. For the sake of distinction it might be uniformly rendered 'settler' (EV 'sojourner,' 'stranger,' 'foreigner,' RSV 'sojourner,' 'stranger'). See, for the relations of Israel to foreigners proper, NATIONS. T. W. D.—**W. J. Ha.**

STRANGLING.—This is suggested as a mode of death, Job 7[15]. The cognate verb describes the manner of Ahithophel's self-inflicted death (2 S 17[23], EV 'hanged himself'; cf Mt 27[5] of Judas). The idea conveyed is death by suffocation, not necessarily produced by suspension. Elsewhere, where hanging is mentioned in EV as a mode of punishment, some form of impalement is intended (see CRIMES AND PUNISHMENTS, **10**). In the Mishnah strangling figures as one of the four kinds of death penalties inflicted by the court. The others are stoning, burning, and beheading (*Sanh.* vii. 1, 3, xi. i.).

In the pastoral letter sent down by the Council of Jerusalem to the early converts from heathenism, these are instructed to abstain *inter alia* 'from blood and from things strangled' (Ac 15[29], cf v.[20] 21[25]). Both belong to the category of Jewish food taboo (FOOD, **10**). The former refers to the prohibition against eating meat which had not been thoroughly drained of the blood, the second to the similar taboo affecting the flesh of animals not slaughtered according to the very minute Rabbinical rules then in force. Thus in the Talmudic treatise *Chullin*, specially devoted to this subject, it is laid down (i. 2) that 'any one may slaughter . . . with any instrument except a harvest-sickle, a saw, etc., because these strangle,' in other words, they do not make the clean incision required for proper slaughter. 'What is strangled' (Ac 15[20] RSV) or strangled meat is thus seen to be a current technical term of the Jewish *shᵉḥîṭāh* or ritual of slaughter. In modern phrase the Gentile converts were to eat only *kōsher* meat.

A. R. S. K.—**S. S. C.**

STRAW, STUBBLE.—In Hebrew the former is *tebhen*, the latter *ḳash*, and to Western ideas the one is as much 'straw' as the other. The distinction between the two is as follows: *tebhen*, the modern Arabic *tibn*, is the mixture of chopped straw and chaff, produced by the action of the threshing-drag and winnowed out by the fan (AGRICULTURE, **3**), as distinguished from the grains of wheat (so Jer 23[28] where 'straw' RSV, and 'chaff' AV are both inadequate). It is mentioned as the food of horses, asses, and camels. In reaping, as is still the custom, the stalks were cut knee-high or over; the length of stalk left standing is *ḳash*. Accordingly, when the Hebrews in Egypt 'gathered stubble for straw' (Ex 5[12]), what they did was to pull up the stalks of wheat left standing in the fields and cut them up into short pieces suitable for brick-making, instead of being allowed to procure the *tibn* ready to their hand from the local threshing-floors. Since the corn-stalks were usually burned as manure, 'stubble' is frequently found in metaphors suggested by this practice (Is 5[24] 47[14] etc.). In other passages containing reference explicit or implied to 'driven stubble' (41[2]), the smaller fragments of chopped straw which the wind blew away with the chaff from the threshing-floor may be intended.

A. R. S. K.

STREET.—The streets of ancient cities were very narrow (cf Jos. *Ant.* xx. v. 3 [111]) and followed no definite plan. In ancient times, as in modern, a feature of an eastern city was the collection of merchants or craftsmen dealing in the same commodities in the same streets or quarters. See ARTS AND CRAFTS, **10.**

STRENGTH OF ISRAEL.—The AV and RV translation of the Divine title *nēṣaḥ Yiśrā'ēl* in 1 S 15[29]. Probably a more accurate rendering would be 'Glory of Israel' (so RVm, RSV).

STRIPES.—See CRIMES, etc., **9**, **'Beating.'**

STRONG DRINK.—See WINE AND STRONG DRINK.

STRONGHOLD.—See CITADEL.

STUBBLE.—See STRAW.

STUD.—This word is found in RV and RSV only in Est 8[10], where it renders a word of uncertain meaning, perhaps = 'bred in the royal stud.' *KB* suggests that it means 'swift-running mares.' AV has 'young dromedaries.'

STUFF.—In Lk 17[31] and elsewhere in AV 'stuff' means 'furniture' or 'goods'; cf Udall's translation of Erasmus' *Paraphrase*, i. 7, 'All that ever they had about them of stuffe or furniture.'

STUMBLING-BLOCK.—The OT word, *mikhshôl*, 'that which causes one to trip' or 'stumble,' is used in the literal sense in Lv 19[14], elsewhere figuratively. It is used of Yahweh in Is 8[14] without the causative idea, viz., 'stumbling.' Of the two NT words, the commoner, *skandalon*, has an earlier form which means the movable stick in a trap, on which bait is placed. In the NT it has the connotation of 'pitfall,' 'trap,' but always in a figurative sense, meaning (1) enticement to sin, as in Mt 18[7], where it is so translated, or (2) that which causes offence, as in 1 Co 1[23]. Another word, *proskomma*, is usually the equivalent of *skandalon*; in Ro 9[32f], 1 P 2[8] it means simply the act of 'stumbling.' J. H. Sc.

SUA, 1 Es 5[29] (RV).—See SIA.

SUAH.—An Asherite, 1 Ch 7[34].

SUBA, 1 Es 5[34] (AV).—See SUBAS.

SUBAI, 1 Es 5[30] (AV, RV).—See SHALMAI.

SUBAS.—A family of 'Solomon's servants,' 1 Es 5[34] (AV **Suba**).

SUBURB.—This word is used in AV in two quite distinct senses. (1) In 2 K 23[11] a certain chamber, really within the Temple precincts, is said to have been 'in the suburbs' (Heb. *parwār*, RV and RSV 'precincts'). Practically the same original is retained as a proper name, **Parbar**, in 1 Ch 26[18] (RVm 'the Precinct'), where the reference is probably to the same spot as in the former passage. Modern scholars find in this mysterious *parbār* or *parwār* a designation of the western colonnade (or part thereof) of the Temple (see PARBAR).

(2) In all other instances 'suburbs' (so AV, RV) occurs only in connexion with the so-called Levitical cities, as the rendering—derived from the Vulgate *suburbana* (fields, etc. close to a city)—of a Hebrew word meaning 'pasture lands' (so RSV). Each of the 48 cities, according to Nu 35[2ff], is to be provided with a square tract of land measuring 2000 cubits—roughly 1000 yards—each way, which is to serve the Levites as a common pasture ground 'for their cattle and for their livestock and for all their beasts' (v.[3]; cf the lists in Jos 21[2-42], 1 Ch 6[55-81]).

A. R. S. K.

SUCATHITES.—See SOCO, **1.**

SUCCOTH.—**1.** A town of Gad (Jos 13[27]) in the Jordan Valley near the Jabbok by Zarethan (1 K 7[4-6]), commanding the ford of *ed-Dâmiyeh* (Jg 8[4-5]), said to have been so called by Jacob, who built 'booths' (*sukkôth*) there for his cattle on his journey from Penuel to Shalem in the district of Shechem (Gn 33[17]). *Tell el-Akhṣāṣ* ('Mound of Bivouacs'), 1½ miles N. of the *Zerqā* (Jabbok) and 7 miles NE. of *ed-Dâmiyeh* would suit the Biblical data, but, in view of the significance of Succoth, a better location is 1 mile further S. at *Deir 'Allah*, a considerable site with abundant Iron Age deposits. This may be an Arabic corruption of *Tar'ālāh*, where the Talmud locates Succoth.

2. The first station of the Israelites in the Exodus (Ex 12[37] (J) 13[20] (P) Nu 33[5f] (P)). There is probably a double tradition in the matter of the route of the Exodus, namely that of J, which supports a northern route by way of the Serbonian Bog (*Sabkhāt el-Bardawîl*), and that of E, followed by P, which depicts an Exodus

through the *Wâdī Ṭumilāt* and southwards by the Bitter Lakes. In the latter region Succoth has been credibly identified with *Tell el-Mashkûṭeh* in the old Egyptian district of *Ṭeku* towards the E. end of the *Wâdī Ṭumilāt*.
S. R. D.—**J. Gr.**

SUCCOTH-BENOTH.—A deity whose image was made and set up in Samaria by the colonists from Babylon, 2 K 17[30]. 'Benoth' (LXX *Banith*) suggests 'banitu' as it appears in the name *Ṣarpanîtu*—in the inscriptions *Ṣar-banitu*—the wife of Marduk, patron god of Babylon. It has further been suggested that *suk* is for *ṣar*, and that the name is a corruption of *Ṣarpanîtu*.

SUCHATHITES, 1 Ch 2[55] (AV).—See Soco, **1.**

SUD, 1 Es 5[29] (AV).—See Sia.

SUDIAS.—A Levite, 1 Es 5[26]; see Joda, **1.**

SUFFER.—In AV and RV, in addition to its usual meaning, 'suffer' is used in the sense of 'permit,' as in 'Suffer the little children . . . to come to me' (Mt 19[14], Mk 10[14], Lk 18[16]). RSV has 'let' in all these cases, and completely eliminates the obsolete use.

SUKKIIM.—The name of a tribe led by Shishak against Judaea, 2 Ch 12[3] (AV **Sukkiims**). They are unidentified.

SULPHUR.—Found only in RSV in Rev 9[17f], where AV and RV have 'brimstone' (q.v.). In v.[17] the Greek once has *theiōdēs*, found only here in NT, and once *theion*, which stands in v.[18]. The latter word is rendered 'brimstone' in RSV in Lk 17[29], Rev 14[10] 19[20] 20[10] 21[8].

SUMER, SUMERIANS.—Excavation of some sites in Lower Mesopotamia has revealed prehistoric levels of culture. The earliest material remains were found at Obeid immediately above virgin soil. The next in age, and immediately above the Obeid type, were found at Uruk (Erech). There is great difference between the material remains found in the earliest Obeid-Uruk levels and those which follow, *i.e.* Uruk IV and III. It is agreed that the latter, which have yielded the first *cylinder* seals and the first inscribed tablets, are remains of Sumerian culture. Opinion differs on the question whether the former also are Sumerian. and therefore on the question whether the Sumerians were the first settlers in Lower Mesopotamia. Their original home is uncertain. The Caucasus region, India and Iran have been suggested. Archaeological remains found principally at Ur, Uruk, Kish, Eridu and Lagash establish that from *c* 3000 B.C. they created in Lower Mesopotamia the earliest civilization known to us in the Ancient Near East. Anthropological data are not sufficient to determine their race, nor can their language be placed within any known family.

The cities of Sumer known to us lay in the alluvial plain between the site of modern Baghdad in the N. and the marshland barrier in the S. Tradition, preserved in later King lists, assigns kings to some of these cities before the Flood. Written and non-written remains limit the Sumerian timetable to the 3rd millennium B.C. From the period *c* 2600 B.C. to the end of the 3rd millennium B.C. comes most of the published evidence of the political, religious, social and economic life of the Sumerians. They lived under kinglets, with titles *ensi* or *lugal*, until the coming of the Semitic Akkadians who *c* 2400 B.C. established hegemony over Sumer. The Akkadian king Sargon I. carried war into Elam and Syria. After the Akkadians came the Guti, barbarians from the Zagros district, with disaster especially for the northern land of Akkad. The Sumerian culture and language survived this long interlude of almost 300 years. From Lagash, under Gudea, and from Ur of the 3rd Dynasty of Ur at the close of the 3rd millennium, come some of the best extant examples of Sumerian craftsmanship. Under the five kings of that Dynasty, Sumer, now unified politically under Ur, had more than 100 years of prosperity. The proportion of persons in office bearing Semitic names is considerable, and non-Sumerian deities appear in the pantheon. But the religious pattern of former days is unchanged. There was one king over many cities, years were everywhere dated by the same formula of event, but the god of the capital, Nanna, the moon god, reigned only in the capital, and it was the god of Nippur, Enlil, who 'called' kings to office. Polytheism was the mark of Sumerian religion, and death the limit of human horizons. The earth was the local lord's and the fulness thereof. Man's function was to serve the gods by supplying foods and abodes. The temple, *i.e.* the deity, had the monopoly of all wealth. Next to him, the royal family. Land was not sold but given as maintenance to officials and worked by organized labour, free and slave. A simple but effective system of book-keeping, recorded all income and expenditure. Records were inspected and stored. Merchants traded on behalf of the temple, and from Ur of the 3rd Dynasty, local metal work was transported abroad, and local products have been found in India and in Syria.

From Sumer, the script. cuneiform, was carried far beyond its borders. Originally pictographic, it came to denote mere syllabic sounds with no reference to the original picture. There is reason to believe that it was originally written from right to left, but, apart from a few words, the order of the signs is from left to right in the text. The same sign may have two or more phonetic values, and different signs may have the same phonetic value. More than 500 signs were in use in the late Sumerian age, to the majority of which exact phonetic values can be assigned, though the Semitic equivalents are sometimes unknown or doubtful. The language which the signs convey belongs to the type known as agglutinative, to which Hungarian, Turkish, and Finnish belong. Itself not Semitic, its vocabulary is known through later bilingual, *i.e.* Sumerian and Akkadian, word lists, and through Akkàdian texts which translate from the Sumerian which accompanies them. The verbal system, in respect of prefixes, infixes and postfixes provides the main area of debate amongst scholars. The literature comprises historical, legal, economic, religious texts written during the Sumerian age. The language survived through temple schools long after it ceased to be a spoken language, and was studied as late as the 3rd cent. B.C.
T. F.

SUN.—The first mention of the sun in the Bible is in Gn 1[16], as 'the greater light to rule the day.' It was looked upon as the greatest and most important of the heavenly bodies, and motion was attributed to it, as is still done in ordinary parlance. We read of the going down of the sun, and of its rising; of the increasing force of its heat as the day went on (Ex 16[21]), of its influence in the production of the crops of the ground ('the choicest fruits of the sun,' Dt 33[14]). The sun 'rises in his might' (Jg 5[31]). The situation of a place is spoken of as 'toward the sunrise,' *i.e.* to the east (*e.g.* Nu 34[15]). Things that were notorious and done openly were said to be 'before *or* in the sight of the sun.' But while the sun is strong, the power of God is greater still. This is expressed in Job's assertion (9[7]) that God 'commands the sun and it does not rise.' The power of the sun affects the complexion ('I go about blackened, but not by the sun,' Job 30[28]; cf Ca 1[6]), and even causes death. A case of death by **sunstroke** occurs in 2 K 4[18f], and this power is alluded to in Ps 121[6] 'The sun shall not smite you by day.' The light of the sun is cheering: 'it is pleasant for the eyes to behold the sun' (Ec 11[7]). Contrivances for measuring the length of the day by the shadow cast by the sun were invented: we have some kind of **dial,** of which steps formed a part, indicated in 2 K 20[9, 11], Is 38[8]. Though there is no actual mention of an **eclipse** in the Bible, part of the language used in describing the terrors of the day of the Lord both in OT and NT is derived from such an event: 'the sun shall be turned to darkness' (Jl 2[31]), 'the sun became black as sackcloth' (Rev 6[12]). On the other hand, the brilliance and glory of the future life is portrayed by comparison with the sun. 'Then the righteous will shine like the sun' (Mt 13[43]); 'The light of the sun will be sevenfold' (Is 30[26]); and even the sun will not be required, for, as in Ps 84[11] 'the Lord God is a sun,' so in Rev 21[23] (cf 22[5]) 'the city has no need of the sun . . . for the glory of God is its light.' The wonders of the day of Joshua's victory over the Amorites, when at his command the sun and moon are said to have stood still (Jos 10[12-14]), were long remembered by the Israelites (Hab 3[11], Sir 46[4]).

The power and influence of the sun over the natural world would soon lead to its being personified and worshipped, inasmuch as what was done upon earth was done 'under the sun.' In one of Joseph's dreams there is a personification of the sun (Gn 37[9]). In the Book of Deuteronomy (4[19]) there is a caution against **sun-worship,** and the punishment of death by stoning is assigned to the convicted worshipper of the sun (17[3]), whilst in Job (31[26]) there is an allusion to a superstitious salutation of the sun by the kissing of the hand. Sun-pillars, or obelisks used in the worship of the sun, are mentioned frequently in the OT, *e.g.* Ex 23[24] (RVm), Lv 26[30], 2 Ch 14[3], Is 17[8], Ezk 6[4] (RV; but cf RSV); and in Phoenicia, a solar Baal, Baal-Hammon, was worshipped. Sun-worship itself was, in the later days of the kingdom of Judah at any rate, one of the permitted forms of worship in Jerusalem. Sun-images are mentioned in 2 Chronicles (14[5] RV; RSV 'incense altars') as existing in all the cities of Judah as early as the reign of Asa. In Josiah's reformation those who burnt incense to the sun were put down (2 K 23[5]), while the chariots of the sun were burned with fire (after being hewn down according to 2 Ch 34[4, 7]), and 'the horses that the kings of Judah had given to the sun' were taken away (2 K 23[11]). There was a great chariot of the sun at Sippar in Babylonia. We gather from Ezk 8[16] that this sun-worship actually took place in the inner court at the door of the Temple, between the porch and the altar; the worshippers turned their backs upon the Temple itself, and worshipped the sun toward the east. Certain places where this worship appears to have been most popular took the name **Beth-shemesh** (q.v.), 'house of the sun,' from the fact.

We must not forget, in conclusion, that, in one Messianic passage (Mal 4[2]), the coming deliverer is spoken of as 'the sun of righteousness.' H. A. R.

SUN IMAGES.—See PILLAR.

SUNDAY.—See LORD'S DAY.

SUNSTROKE.—See SUN, MEDICINE.

SUPERSCRIPTION.—See TITLE, and MONEY, 7.

SUPH.—This occurs as a place-name in Dt 1[1] (AV 'the Red Sea,' elsewhere *yam sûph*; it is therefore assumed in AV that *yam* had fallen out). LXX and Vulgate understood as AV, which may be right. Otherwise Suph is unknown.

SUPHAH.—An unknown locality E. of Jordan, Nu 21[14] (AV 'the Red Sea').

SUPPER.—See MEALS; for Last Supper see EUCHARIST.

SUR.—**1.** An unidentified gate in Jerusalem, 2 K 11[6]. **2.** A town on the seacoast of Palestine, Jth 2[28]. Its site is unknown, unless it is a duplicate of Tyre.

SURNAME.—See NAME, 2.

SUSA.—For many centuries the capital of Elam, and afterwards one of the three capitals of the Persian empire. It is mentioned in Neh 1[1], Dn 8[2], Est 1[2] etc., where AV and RV have **Shushan.** In Ad. Est 11[3] AV, RV and RSV have 'Susa.' It is modern **Shush,** in SW. Persia.

SUSANCHITES.—AV form of **Shushanchites** (q.v.).

SUSANNA.—See APOCRYPHA, 5.

SUSI.—A Manassite, Nu 13[12 (Heb. 11)].

SWALLOW.—**1.** Hebrew *d*e*rôr*, Ps 84[3], Pr 26[2]. The allusion to the nesting of this bird in the sanctuary and its swift (unalighting) flight fits the swallow. **2.** Hebrew *'āghûr*, Is 38[14], Jer 8[7] (AV; RV, RSV **crane**); see CRANE. **3.** Hebrew *sûs, sîs*, Is 38[14], Jer 8[7] (RV, RSV; AV **crane**). Some species of swallow or swift, of which ten species are common in the Holy Land, is here indicated. See CRANE.

SWAN, Lv 11[18], Dt 14[16] (AV).—See OWL.

SWEARING.—See OATHS.

SWEET CANE.—See REED.

SWINE (*ḥ*a*zîr*).—Domesticated swine were probably kept in the East in the earliest historic times, when they appear to have been regarded as sacred. In a cave associated with the earliest place of sacrifice at ancient Gezer, in use certainly before 2000 B.C., large quantities of pigs' bones were found. It was the sacrosanct character of swine that lay at the root of the prohibition in Lv 11[7] and Dt 14[8]; and the eating of swine's flesh and offering of swine's blood (Is 65[4] 66[3, 17]) are clearly regarded as a sign of lapse into paganism. The heathen frequently tried to compel the Jews to eat swine's flesh (*e.g.* 2 Mac 6[18] 7[1]) and thus renounce their religion. The contempt felt for swine is shown by the proverbs quoted in Pr 11[22], Mt 7[6], and 2 P 2[22]. In the Talmudic writings the pig appears as the emblem of uncleanness, and those who keep swine are regarded with aversion. The same ideas colour the parable of the Prodigal Son (Lk 15[15]), where he is depicted as reaching the lowest depth of infamy in being sent to feed swine, and actually being reduced to covet their food; and also the narrative of the demoniacs, where the Gentile inhabitants of Gerasa lose their great herd of swine (Mt 8[30], Mk 5[13], Lk 8[32]).

In modern Palestine very much the same feeling survives. *Khanzîr* 'pig' is a common but very opprobrious appellation. Swine's flesh is loathed by Jews and Moslems; the latter, who otherwise eat the same food as Christians, are always very suspicious that any unknown food may be contaminated with it.

E. W. G. M.

SWORD.—See ARMOUR, ARMS, **1** (*c*).

SYCAMINE (Lk 17[6]).—*Sykaminos* is, strictly speaking, the black mulberry (*Morus nigra*, the *tût shâmi* of the Syrians), and it is probably this tree that is referred to in Lk 17[6] and in 1 Mac 6[34]. But *sykaminos* is also used in LXX in many passages as the equivalent of the *shiḳmîm* or **sycamore** (q.v.). E. W. G. M.

SYCAMORE (RV 'sycomore').—Hebrew *shiḳmîm*, 1 K 10[27], 1 Ch 27[28], 2 Ch 1[15] 9[27], Is 9[10], Am 7[14]; *shiḳmôth*, Ps 78[47]; Greek *sykomorea*, Lk 19[4]. This is the sycomore fig (*Ficus sycamorus*), a tree often 50 feet high, with an enormous trunk. It bears poor figs (Am 7[14]), but furnishes good timber. It is not to-day 'in abundance' as of old (1 K 10[27]), but considerable numbers flourish still in the plain around Jaffa. This tree must not be confused with the 'sycamore' (*Acer pseudo-platanus*) of our home lands, which is a species of maple. See also SYCAMINE. E. W. G. M.

SYCHAR.—'A city of Samaria,' near the parcel of ground that Jacob gave his son Joseph (Jn 4[5]). Jerome in *Onomast.* distinguishes Sychar from **Shechem,** but in *Ep. Paul.* and in *Quaest. Gen.* he identifies them, saying that the form *Sychar* is due to scribal error. The Old Syriac also reads *Shechem.* In A.D. 333 the *Itinerary of Jerusalem* places a *Sechar* one mile E. of Nāblus. Some authorities have suggested identification of Sychar with *'Askar*, a village on the skirt of Ebal, about 2 miles E. of Nāblus. An objection to this is the presence there of a copious spring, more than sufficient to supply the village; while from Jn 4[15] we learn that the woman of Sychar was accustomed to go to Jacob's Well for water. Ancient Shechem, we now know, lay at *Tell Balâṭah*, which bears evidence of occupation from the period of the Hebrew monarchy to Roman times. **Jacob's Well,** according to unanimous and unbroken tradition, lies about half a mile to the E. of *Tell Balâṭah*, on the S. edge of the plain, at the foot of Gerizim. It was formerly of great depth (Jn 4[11]). The sacred associations of the Well, and the 'lightness' of the water, compared with the hardness of that from the spring, would form attractions in early as in modern times. It seems certain that the story-teller meant Shechem. W. E.—**E. G. K.**

SYCHEM, Ac 7^{16} (AV) = **Shechem** (q.v.).

SYCOMORE.—See SYCAMORE.

SYELUS, 1 Es 1^{8} (AV).—See JEHIEL, **6.**

SYENE.—This is the Greek form of the name Seveneh. Egyptian *Sewen* 'mart,' to-day still Assuan (*Aswān*), a town on the E. bank of the Nile, below the first cataract). Behind it are the quarries from which the stone used in so much Egyptian sculpture was obtained. In the river opposite it lay the island the Greeks called *Elephantine* (translation of Egyptian *'Iēbew* 'Elephant place,' *Yeb* in the Aramaic texts). On the W. shore of the Nile there are ancient tombs of princes of the 6th Dynasty period (*c* 2350–2190 B.C.). Situated on the border of Nubia Seveneh had a considerable commercial and military importance. For the OT 'from Migdol to Syene' (Ezk 29^{10} 30^{6} according to LXX, RV, RSV; AV 'from the tower of Syene') indicates the northern and southern limits of Egypt. Reference to the 'Syenians' is also made in Is 49^{12}; here the 'land of Sinim' is to be read 'land of the *Swnyym*' according to Dead Sea Isaiah Scroll. In Persian times there was a foreign, Aramaic-speaking military colony at Elephantine and Syene. Among them were many Jews, who had a temple of Yahweh. The **Elephantine Papyri** (q.v.) give a vivid picture of their life. The Jewish temple antedated Cambyses (525 B.C.) and so the Jews must have been settled there earlier in the 6th cent. Temple and Jewish colony must have ended about 399 B.C.. with the accession of Nepherites I. E. G. K.

SYMBOL.—The prevalence of figurative language in the Bible is due partly to the antiquity and Oriental origin of the book and to the fact that its subject, religion, deals with the most difficult problems of life and the deepest emotions of the soul. The English word 'type,' as the equivalent of 'symbol' or 'emblem,' is sometimes confusing, as it has been used both for the fulfilment of the prototype and as that which points forward to the antitype. Like the proverb and parable the symbol, implies a connexion between two things of which one is concrete and physical, the other abstract and referring to intellectual, moral, and spiritual matters. The former, of course, is the symbol.

1. Symbols of similarity.—Here the connecting principle is one of recognized likeness between the material object and its counterpart. Thus 'a watered garden' is made the emblem of a satisfied soul (Jer 31^{12}). The similarity is that of supplied wants. In the same way the white garments of the priests and of the redeemed were emblematic of holiness (Ex 39^{27-29}, Rev 19^{8}). Marriage, as an Oriental relationship of purchased possession, was an emblem of Palestine in covenant with God, and of the Church as the bride of Christ. Thus also the Christian life was a race (He 12^{1}) and a warfare (Eph 6^{11-17}). An element of similarity entered into the dream-visions recorded in the Bible and into the symbolism of prophetic warnings (Is 5^{1-7}, Jer 13^{1-12}, Ezk 37^{1-11}). In the Epistles we meet with a rich variety of emblems created by the desire to interpret the Person and mission of Christ, and the relationship of the Christian believer to Him. The writers, being of Jewish origin and addressing communities which usually contained a number of Jewish Christians, naturally turned to the biographies, national history, and sacred institutions of the OT. Whatever was drawn from such a source would not only be familiar, but would seem to be part of an organic whole, and to possess a value of Divine preparation. Examples of these are the Second Adam, the Firstborn, the Chief Shepherd, the Chief Corner-stone. The journey to Canaan supplied Passover, manna, rock, redemption, better country, rest. From the Tabernacle and Temple were taken high priest, altar, sacrifice, veil, peace-offering, lamb, atonement.

2. Symbols of representative selection or Synecdoche.—The symbol is in this case the agent or implement, or some conspicuous accompaniment selected from a group of concrete particulars, so that the part represents the whole. Thus the insignia of office and authority are crown, sword, sceptre, seal, coin, robe, rod, staff. Various actions and relationships are symbolically indicated, such as the giving of the hand (compact), foot on the neck (conquest), bored ear (perpetual servitude), washing of the hands (innocence), bared or outstretched arm (energy), gnashing of teeth (disappointment and remorse), shaking the head (contempt and disapproval), averted face (angry repudiation), bread (hospitality), cross (suffering of Christ, and suffering for Him).

3. Memorial and mystical symbols.—These might belong to either of the above forms or be artificially selected, but the purpose was not so much to instruct and emphasize as to recall and perpetuate circumstances and feelings, or to suggest a meaning that must remain concealed. Such were the rainbow at the Flood, the stone Ebenezer, the symbolical names often given to children, as *Moses, Ichabod*, and the names in Jacob's family, the Urim and Thummim, the white stone, and the number of the beast, etc. Of this class were the sculptured emblems of the early Christians in the catacombs of Rome, such as the palm, dove, anchor, ship, fish, Alpha and Omega. Water, bread and wine, as the material elements in Baptism and the Lord's Supper, are the symbols of those Sacraments. The name 'symbol' is applied to the selection of generally accepted truths forming the Christian creed, or canon of belief. Certain characters in the Bible, such as Jonah, Mary Magdalene, Herod, Judas, have come to be identified with special types of character and conduct, and are said to be symbolical of those classes.

4. Dangers of symbolism.—(1) The act of transmitting spiritual and eternal truth through material and perishable media always involves *limitation and loss.* (2) The injudicious carrying out of symbolism into inferences not originally intended, leads into the opposite error of *irrelevant addition.* (3) The *scrupulous avoidance of symbolism* may itself become a symbol. (4) The external form which illuminates, emphasizes, and recalls is no guarantee of *inward reality.* The ceremony of purification is not purity, as the prophets so forcefully declared. Sheep's clothing may not be a robe of innocence, or rent garments indicate distress of soul. The cry 'Lord, Lord!' is not always raised by true discipleship. Hence Christ's message to the Samaritan woman concerning true worship, and His frequent protests against the ceremonial insincerities of the Pharisees. The condemnation of image-worship turned upon the total inadequacy of symbol to represent God. It might indicate man's thought of God, but it left untouched the constituent element of true religion, God's thought of man. 'Eyes have they, but they see not.'

G. M. M.

SYMEON (cf SIMEON, *ad init.*).—**1.** An ancestor of Jesus (Lk 3^{30}). **2.** A prophet and teacher at Antioch (Ac 13^{1}). **3.** Ac 15^{14} = Simon Peter (see PETER).

SYMMACHUS' VERSION.—See GREEK VERSIONS OF OT, **18.**

SYNAGOGUE.—**1. Meaning and History.**—Like its original *synagōgē* (literally a gathering, assembly—for its use in LXX see CONGREGATION), 'synagogue' is used in both rabbinic literature and NT in a double signification: (1) in the sense of a community organized for religious purposes, as Ac 6^{9} 9^{2} (cf Rev 2^{9} 3^{9}; *Aboth* 4^{11}, *Yoma* 7^{1}); and (2) to denote the building in which the community met for worship (Mt 4^{23} etc.; *Meg.* 3^{1}). Its Hebrew equivalent is *k^eneseth*, and in the latter sense, also *bêth k^eneseth* ('house of assembly'). As a place of worship, the synagogue is named *bêth t^ephillāh* (adopted from Is 56^{7}), *proseuchē* (Ac 16^{13}, 'place of prayer' RSV). In rabbinical literature *bêth hammidhrāsh*, 'house of study' is used (*Ber.* 4^{2}, *Demai* 7^{5}; cf Sir 51^{23}).

The origin of the synagogue as a characteristic institution of Judaism is hidden in obscurity. Most probably it took its rise in the conditions that followed the dispersal of the Jewish people after the destruction of the first Temple in 586 B.C. Hitherto worship had practically meant sacrifice, but sacrifice was impossible outside the Temple (cf Dt 12) and particularly in foreign lands (cf Hos 3^4 9^{3f}). There was still left, however, the living word of the prophet. From olden times it was customary to visit the man of God on Sabbaths and new moons and in times of stress for intercession and for counsel (2 K 4^{23}). Such visits to the priest-prophet Ezekiel by the elders of the captivity in Babylonia came to play a special rôle (Ezk 8^1 20^{1-3}). Some of his reflexions on the ways of God with His people were delivered at such gatherings. To similar gatherings in Palestine and in other lands the prophets addressed themselves (*e.g.* Zec 6–8, Is 58, Lv 26, Dt 28, etc.).

In Egypt, at Elephantine (before 526 B.C. and continuing till its destruction in 407 B.C.), a temple with sacrificial worship was maintained. During Maccabaean times, a rival sanctuary to that of Jerusalem was set up by Onias IV., in 160 B.C. These temples were in defiance of the Deuteronomic law which forbids sacrificial worship outside of Jerusalem. No question of legitimacy arose in connexion with the gathering places for instruction in the word of God and for prayer, which acquired the Greek name *synagogue*.

Archaeological discoveries have brought to light a record of the foundation of a synagogue at Alexandria in 308 B.C. and numerous inscriptions of the same sort from the following century (N. Bentwich, *Hellenism*, pp. 31 f). In every Jewish settlement of the expanding diaspora synagogues sprang up as rallying points of the Jewish people. In Palestine itself, due to the quickening of spiritual life in consequence of the reformation of Ezra–Nehemiah, religious assemblies outside of the rebuilt Temple increased. Psalm 74^8 suggests that religious meeting places had assumed a fixed character in pre-Maccabaean or probably in the Greek or even in the late Persian period. Around Christian times they were found in all cities and towns. A synagogue existed within the precincts of the Temple itself (*Tamid* v. 1 ; *Yoma* vii. 1).

2. Function of the Synagogue.—The three Hebrew names of the synagogue express the threefold function which it served in Jewish life.

(*a*) As a ' house of assembly,' it served as a meeting place for communal and philanthropic purposes. Thus it unified the Jews of each community and linked them with those of other communities in the diaspora and in Palestine. While all synagogues of Jewry were united by their common purpose, each synagogue enjoyed fairly complete autonomy. During Temple times, the synagogue functioned in an auxiliary capacity. After the fall of the Temple, it emerged as the sole agency for the preservation of Judaism.

(*b*) It is as a ' house of prayer ' that the synagogue ultimately replaced the Temple. Rabbinic tradition refers the beginnings of synagogue worship to the ' Men of the Great Synagogue ' (*Ber.* 33a). The reference to this unknown body (see below) points to the religious leadership during the Persian period, when Judaism came into contact with the Parsi religion, and when it acquired certain new elements (*e.g.* eschatology, angelology, etc.). Among them we note the recitation of prayers at sunrise. The Talmud reports that ' the pious (*ḥ^asîdhîm*) used to complete reciting the *Shema*ʿ at sunrise ' (Jer. *Ber.* ii. 1 ; Bab. *Ber.* 9b). That it was recited also in the evening is suggested by Is 45^7 and Ps 72^5. The usage may have been prompted by the Parsi practice of hailing the sun at its rising and setting, thus acknowledging Ahuramazda as creator (*Sacred Books of the East*, Pahlavi Texts, I. 156 ff ; K. Kohler, *Origins of the Synagogue and the Church*, 1929, ch. XII). The recitation of the Shemaʿ and the benediction *Yōṣēr* (' creator,' in the morning and a similar benediction in the evening, based on Is 45^7) aimed to emphasize the unity of God and to overcome the dualism suggested by the phenomena of light and darkness.

Among the followers of Ezra who carried forward the spirit of his reformation were the *scribes*. Drawn from both priestly and lay ranks, the scribes distinguished themselves not merely as scholars but also as men of devotion (Sir 39^{1-6}). Ben Sira exemplifies this type, combining mastery of sacred lore and tradition with worldly wisdom and proficiency in prayer. His influence on synagogue worship is marked.

The *ḥ^asîdhîm* were men of prayer par excellence. While they came to the fore as a militantly religious body at the outbreak of the Maccabaean revolt, their existence goes back to earlier times. Their spirit is reflected in numerous Psalms (*e.g.* 30, 50, 73, 149, etc.). Daniel typifies these saintly men, whose piety expressed itself in zeal for the Law and in the practice of thrice daily prayer (Dn 6^{11}). The Mishnah reports that they used to spend an hour in preparation for worship, and would not be interrupted in their devotions even if greeted by a king or if a snake coiled itself at their heels (*Ber.* v. 1). They were valued as leaders of worship, especially in times of distress and on fast days (*Taʿanith* ii. 2, iii. 8).

Synagogue Worship.—Two stages may be noted in the development of synagogue worship. During Temple times it supplemented the sacrificial ritual. 1 Ch 23^{30} refers to the prayer services of the Levites, morning and evening (cf Ps $55^{18\ (17)}$ $92^{3\ (2)}$). As part of the democratization of the Temple service itself, the daily burnt offerings were supplied at the expense of the entire people and not of any private person or high priest. The ordinance (Nu 28^2) was understood by the Pharisees to require the presence of all the people at these sacrifices. As this was impossible, it was instituted that the country be divided into twenty-four sections, corresponding to the number of the priestly and Levitical divisions (1 Ch 23^{6-24} 24^{4-18} 25^{31}), and that a committee of each section (*maʿ^amādh*) should go up to Jerusalem to stand, by the rotating course (cf Lk 1^8) of priests for one week in each half year, as representatives of all Israel during the sacrificial offerings. In turn, their brethren at home assembled in the synagogues of their respective towns and read verses from the first chapter of Genesis pertaining to the day of the week, and prayed for the various needs of the people (*Taʿanith* iv. 2 f, *Megillath Taʿanith* i).

An outline of the morning liturgy at the synagogue of the Temple is reported in *Tamid* v. 1, vii. 2. Following the preparations for the morning burnt offering, the priests would repair to the Chamber of Hewn Stones, which served as the Temple synagogue, for prayer. The liturgy began with a call to worship, modelled after the call of the Levites in the assembly of Ezra-Nehemiah (Neh 9^5). Then followed the recitation of the Decalogue, the three sections of the *Shema*ʿ (Dt 6^{4-9} 11^{13-21}, Nu 15^{37-41} ; cf Nash Papyrus), and three benedictions ; an affirmation of the faith, a petition for the acceptance of the worship, and a prayer for peace. After the prostrations, the high priest and his associates took their stations at the steps of the porch and pronounced the Aaronic benediction (Nu 6^{24-27}), without a pause as a unit. Outside the Temple, in the synagogues, it was pronounced as three blessings. In the Temple the Tetragrammaton (YHWH) was pronounced, but in the synagogues the substitute Adonai (Lord) was spoken. At the end of the offering, the Levites sang the Psalm of the day. (For a list, see end of Mishnah *Tamid*.)

With the destruction of the Temple, the worship at the synagogue entered at the second phase of its development. Whatever could be salvaged from the Temple ritual was carried into the synagogue. Worship now came to mean not sacrificial ritual but prayer, recited three times daily, corresponding to the times of the offerings at the Temple : *shaḥ^arîth* (morning), *minḥāh* (' meal offering ' corresponding to sacrifice at dusk), and *maʿ^arîbh* (' evening,' which had no exact equivalent in the Temple ritual, but was artificially connected with the time of burning the remnants of the sacrificial animals at the altar fire) ; cf Ps 55^{17}. An additional service of prayer (*mûsāph*) was provided for the festival days when additional sacrifices were offered at the Temple (Nu 28–29). On the Day of Atonement a fifth service was added to correspond to the closing of the gates (*n^eʿîlāh*).

Around the end of the 1st cent., Rabban Gamaliel II., as head of the reconstituted Sanhedrin at Jamnia, authorized a certain Simeon of Phecola to arrange a liturgy of prayer to replace the defunct sacrificial service. From the first stage of synagogue worship, the Shema' and its benedictions were carried into the new liturgy. The addition consisted of the *Eighteen Benedictions* (Shemoneh Esreh). Simeon did not create them anew, but only arranged the existing traditions of prayer and established their sequence. These short paragraphs go back to the Prophets, Psalms, Sirach, etc. Their number is said to correspond to the eighteen times that the name of God appears in Ps 29, and, according to another view in the Shema'. They were also linked with the prayer of Hannah in 1 S 2^{1-10} (cf Lk 1^{46-55}). The first three praise God as the possessor of heaven and earth, whose might sustains the living and revives the dead, and who is holy and awe-inspiring, beside whom there is no other God. The second section consists of twelve (subsequently expanded to thirteen) petitions, six personal and six national. The personal pray for understanding, repentance, forgiveness, redemption, healing and blessing the year with plenty. The national petitions ask for the ingathering of the dispersed, restoration of the theocracy, punishment of the apostates and destruction of the dominion of arrogance, the well-being of the righteous and the proselytes, the rebuilding of Jerusalem and the advent of the Davidic Messiah. The intermediary group ends with a petition for the acceptance of these prayers. For those who were prevented from reciting the Eighteen Benedictions, the intermediary group was subsequently contracted into one short prayer. The three closing benedictions ask for Divine favour, express thanks for God's goodness, and pray for peace. The whole is introduced with Ps 51^{15}. On the Sabbath and festivals the intermediary group is replaced with a benediction for the day, thus reducing the eighteen to seven. Within the framework of these benedictions room was left for variations of expression, but in course of time they became fixed. Nonetheless, different versions of the Eighteen Benedictions have come down from Palestine, Babylonia, Yemen and elsewhere. (See G. Dalman, *Die Worte Jesu*, i, 1898, pp. 299–304; L. Finkelstein, 'Development of the Amida,' *JQR*, xvi, 1925, pp. 130–170; A. Marmorstein, 'The Oldest Form of the Eighteen Benedictions,' *JQR*, xxxiv, 1943, pp. 137–159). Recited standing, the Eighteen Benedictions are known also as the *Amidah*. Such importance was attached to this composition that it is referred to as *T^ephillāh* (prayer) par excellence.

(*c*) As a 'house of study' the synagogue served as the fountain-spring of religious knowledge. While children were taught in special schools (*bêth sēpher* and *bêth 'ûlpānâ*), the synagogue represented the popular home of adult instruction in Torah. Instruction, as we noted, formed the original object of synagogue assemblies. The procedure at the great assembly of Ezra-Nehemiah set the pattern of these meetings: 'and they read from the book, from the law of God, clearly [or with interpretation], and they gave the sense, so that the people understood the reading' (Neh 8^{8}). Philo describes the 'prayer houses' in the cities as places of instruction in morality, piety and holiness (*Vita Mos.* ii. 168). The congregation listened in rapt attention to the teaching put forth by 'one most experienced' (*De Sept.* ii. 282 = *Spec. Leg.* ii. 62; see *Yalkut Shimeoni, Vayyākhel*). Josephus refers this phase of synagogue to Moses himself (*c. Ap.* ii. 17 [173 ff]). Similarly James declared, 'For from early generations Moses has had in every city those who preach him, for he is read every Sabbath in the synagogue' (Ac 15^{21}).

3. Scripture Reading.—Synagogue worship included a lesson from the Law. The five books were divided into 154 (or more) Sabbath pericopes or sections, so that the whole Pentateuch was read through in three years (or $3\frac{1}{2}$ years, half of a Sabbatic period). In Babylonia an annual cycle of Torah reading was adopted, a custom which spread to all parts of the Diaspora. The custom of calling up seven readers in succession—a priest, a Levite, and five others—may be as old as the 1st cent. After the Law came, at the Sabbath morning service only, a lesson from the Prophets, read by one person and left to his choice. It was the *haphtarah*, as the prophetic lesson was termed, that Jesus read in the synagogue of Nazareth (Lk 4^{16-20}). In course of time the haphtarahs were fixed. 'The Hagiographa, except Esther, were not at this period read at divine service. Even the Psalms had no place in the usual service' (Dalman).

In order that the common people might follow the lessons with intelligence, these were translated into Aramaic, the vernacular of Palestine, by an interpreter (*m^ethûrg^emān*—our 'dragoman' is from the same root). The unique position of the Law in the estimation of the time is shown by the fact that the Pentateuch lessons had to be translated a verse at a time, while the Prophets might be rendered three verses at a time. Reader and interpreter stood while at the reading desk.

At this point in the service, on the principal occasions of worship, a sermon was introduced. The preacher sat while giving his exposition (Lk 4^{20}), which is often described in NT as 'teaching' (Mt 4^{23}, Mk 1^{21} 6^{2} etc.). In the synagogue there was full 'liberty of prophesying.' Any member of the community was free to exercise his gift. When a likely stranger was present, he was invited by the ruler of the synagogue to address the congregation (Ac 13^{15}). The service was closed by a priest pronouncing *the priestly benediction* (Nu 6^{24-26}); if no priest was present, it is said that a layman gave the blessing in the form of a prayer.

On some occasions, at least, it was usual to ask the alms of the congregation (Mt 6^{2}) on behalf of the poor. The full service, as sketched above, was confined to the principal service of the week, which was held on the forenoon of the Sabbath. At the other services, such as those held daily in the larger towns, where ten 'men of leisure' were available to form the minimum legal congregation, and at the Monday and Thursday services, some of these items were omitted.

4. The synagogue building and its furniture.—Remains, more or less extensive, of Jewish synagogues still survive from the second and third, more doubtfully from the first, centuries of our era, chiefly in Galilee. (See F. L. Sukenik, *Ancient Synagogues in Palestine and Greece*, Schweich Lectures, London, 1934; H. G. May, 'Synagogues in Palestine,' *Biblical Archaeologist* vii, 1944, pp. 1–20; C. H. Kraeling, 'The Earliest Synagogue Architecture,' *Bulletin of the American Schools of Oriental Research*, 59, 1934, pp. 18–20). In plan and details of ornamentation these Galilaean synagogues display a general similarity. The buildings are rectangular in shape, and divided into three or five aisles by two or three rows of pillars. The entrance is almost always in the south front, and often consists of a large main, and two smaller side, entrances. The most elaborate was the synagogue of Capernaum, where, as elsewhere, traces were found of galleries running round three sides of the centre aisle. These were probably assigned to the women (for a similar arrangement in Herod's Temple, see TEMPLE, **11** (*b*)), although the question of the separation of the sexes in NT times is one on which the best authorities disagree.

As regards the furniture of the synagogue, the most important item was the chest or cupboard (*tēbhāh*, the 'ark'), in which the sacred rolls of the Law and the Prophets were kept. The synagogues of NT times were also doubtless provided with a raised platform (*bîmāh*), on which stood the reading-desk from which the Scriptures were read. The larger portion of the area was occupied by benches for the congregation, the worshippers facing southwards, in Galilee at least, towards the holy city. A few special seats in front of the *bîmāh*, and facing the congregation, were occupied by the heads of the community. These are the 'chief seats in the synagogues' coveted by the Pharisees (Mt 23^{6}). In front of the 'ark' a lamp burned day and night. [The excavations in Palestine and neighbouring lands have yielded evidence of a lost pictorial art of the ancient synagogue. The most notable group of

Biblical frescoes was unearthed at Dura-Europos, built in A.D. 244. See C. H. Kraeling, *The Synagogue*, 1956.]

5. The officials of the Synagogue.—The general management of the synagogue of a Jewish town, where it served also as a court of justice and—at least in the smaller towns and villages—as a school, was in the hands of the elders of the community. It had no special priest or '**minister,**' as will appear presently. The leader of the service (*Shᵉlîaḥ ṣibbûr*, 'representative of the congregation') held no official position. He was selected because of his religious character and familiarity with the ritual. A religious quorum consisted of ten males (*Meg.* 4[3]; cf Ru 4[2]; see PHARISEES). It was usual, however, to appoint an official called '**the ruler of the synagogue**' (Lk 8[41] etc.) to whom the authorities of the community committed the care of the building as well as the more important duty of seeing that everything connected with the public services was done 'decently and in order.' Hence the indignation of the ruler of Lk 13[14] at the supposed breach of the decorum of worship related in the preceding verses (vv.[10-13]). It lay with the ruler also to select the readers for the day, and to determine the order in which they were to be called up to the reading-desk. Occasionally, it would seem, a synagogue might have two or more rulers, as at Pisidian Antioch (Ac 13[15]).

The only other permanent official was the *ḥazzān* or *shammāsh*, 'the **attendant**' of Lk 4[20] RV and RSV (AV 'minister' in the same, but now obsolete, sense; cf Ac 13[5]). The duties of the synagogue 'officer' were somewhat varied. He was responsible for the cleaning and lighting of the building; and during service it was his special duty to convey the sacred rolls from the ark to the readers at the desk, and to restore them when the reading was over, as recorded in Lk 4[17, 20]. To him fell also the duty of scourging criminals condemned by the court (Mt 10[17] 23[34] etc.), but not, as is usually represented, the teaching of the school children (see EDUCATION, also art. 'Education' in *DB* i. 650a).

6. The influence of the Synagogue.—This article would be incomplete without a reference, however brief, to the influence of the synagogue and its worship not only upon the Jews themselves, but upon the world of heathenism. As to the latter, the synagogue played a conspicuous part in the *praeparatio evangelica*. From the outworn creeds of paganism many earnest souls turned to the synagogue and its teaching for the satisfaction of their highest needs. The synagogue of 'the Dispersion' (Jn 7[35], Ja 1[1], 1 P 1[1], all RSV) became in consequence the seed-plots of Christianity, as every student of the Book of Acts is aware.

The work which the synagogue did for Judaism itself is best seen in the ease with which the violent breach with the past, involved in the destruction of the Temple in A.D. 70 and the cessation of the sacrificial worship, was healed. The highest religious life of Judaism had already transferred its channels from the grosser and more material forms of the Temple to the spiritual worship of the synagogue.

Nor must a reference be wanting to the fact that the synagogue, and not the Temple, supplied the mould and model for the worship of the Christian Church.

7. The Great Synagogue.—In late Jewish tradition Ezra is alleged to have been the founder and first president of a college of learned scribes, which is supposed to have existed in Jerusalem until the early part of the Greek period (*c* 300 B.C.). To 'the men of the Great Synagogue,' or rather 'of the Great Assembly,' were ascribed the composition of some of the later OT books, the close of the Canon, and a general care for the development of religion under the Law. Recent writers, however, have in the main accepted the results of Kuenen's careful investigation in his *Gesammelte Abhandlungen* (German translation, 125–160), and now regard the Great Synagogue as unhistorical, the tradition of its existence having arisen from a distorted view of the nature and purpose of the great popular assembly of which we read in Neh 8–10. A. R. S. K.—**S. S. C.**

SYNOPTICS, SYNOPTISTS.—See GOSPELS, 3.

SYNTYCHE.—A Christian, perhaps a deaconess, at Philippi (Ph 4[2]); see EUODIA. A. J. M.

SYNZYGUS (literally 'yoke-fellow').—This is taken by some as a proper name in Ph 4[3] ('Synzygus truly so called'), but it is nowhere else found as such (see RSV 'true yokefellow'). It is more probably a way of describing the leader of the church at Philippi. Lightfoot (*Com., in loc.*) suggests Epaphroditus; Ramsay (*St. Paul*, p. 358), Luke; others, Barnabas or Silas or Timothy. An old tradition of the 2nd cent. (Lightfoot, *ib.*) makes the '**yoke-fellow**' to be the Apostle's wife—a most unlikely guess; Renan supposed that Lydia is meant, and that she had become his wife—an equally improbable conjecture. See 1 Co 7[8].

A. J. M.—**F. C. G.**

SYRACUSE, on the E. coast of Sicily, was the principal city in the island. It was originally a Greek colony of ancient date, which was powerful enough to defeat the famous Athenian Sicilian expedition (415–412 B.C.). Its kings were often men of distinction, even in literature, of which they were noted patrons. The city had a varied career, being sometimes a kingdom, sometimes a democracy. In 241 B.C. the Romans took the western half of Sicily from the Carthaginians, but remained in alliance with the kings of Syracuse. The last king of Syracuse intrigued with the Carthaginians; the city was besieged and captured by Marcellus in 212, and the whole island was henceforth under a praetor, who had two quaestors, one residing at Lilybaeum in the W., the other at Syracuse. The city continued prosperous till about the end of the 2nd cent. B.C. After that date it declined in importance, though it remained the capital of the eastern half of the island. In NT times a large number of the inhabitants were Roman citizens.

St. Paul's ship lay at anchor in the harbour for three days, when he was on his way from Malta to Rome (Ac 28[12]). He did not preach there. Christian memorials at Syracuse are not specially early. A. So.

SYRIA, SYRIANS.—See ARAM, ARAMAEANS.

SYRIA-MAACAH, 1 Ch 19[6] (AV).—See MAACAH.

SYRIAC VERSIONS.—See TEXT (OT, **15** (6), and NT, **11** ff), and GREEK VERSIONS OF OT, **11** (*c*).

SYROPHOENICIAN.—This is the designation of a 'Greek' (or Gentile) woman whose demoniac daughter Jesus healed when near Tyre (Mk 7[26]). She was undoubtedly Greek-speaking, but was descended from the old Phoenicians of Syria (|| Mt 15[22] has 'Canaanite'), or lived in that part of the new Roman province of Syria which had once been known as Phoenicia.

A. J. M.—**F. C. G.**

SYRTIS (Ac 27[17]).—The Syrtes, Major and Minor, are situated on the N. coast of Africa, in the wide bay between the headlands of Tunis and Barca. They consist of sandbanks occupying the shores of the Gulf of Sidra on the coast of Tripoli, and that of Gabes on the coast of Tunis or Carthage. They have been considered a source of danger to mariners from very early times, not only from the shifting of the sands themselves, but owing to the cross currents of the adjoining waters.

T

TAANACH (Jos 12[21], 1 K 4[12], 1 Ch 7[29]).—One of the royal Canaanite cities, mentioned in OT always along with **Megiddo.** Though in the territory of Issachar, it belonged to Manasseh; the native Canaanites were, however, not driven out (Jos 17[11–13], Jg 1[27]). It was allotted to the Kohathite Levites (Jos 21[25] [AV **Tanach**]). It was one of the four fortress cities on the 'border of Manasseh' (1 Ch 7[29]). The fight of Deborah and Barak with the Canaanites is described (Jg 5[19]) as 'at Taanach by the waters of Megiddo.' The 'waters of Megiddo' are to be identified with the 'torrent Kishon' which flows down the *Wâdī el-Lejjûn,* just S. of *Tell el-Mutesellim* (Megiddo), about 4 miles NW. of *Tell Ta'annak* (the modern name of Taanach). It is not clear why Taanach and the waters of Megiddo are linked in the poem, but it has been suggested that at the time of the Song of Deborah, Megiddo was in ruins, and that Taanach was therefore the nearest large city (implying a date around 1100 B.C. for the battle and the poem; cf Albright, *BASOR*, No. 62 [1936], 26–31). The tell was excavated by Professor Sellin of Vienna. Many remains of Canaanite and Israelite civilization were found, and also a considerable number of clay tablets with cuneiform inscriptions similar to those discovered at Tell el-Amarna in Egypt. See Sellin in *Mem. Vienna Acad.*, l (1904), lii (1905). E. W. G. M.—**D. N. F.**

TAANATH-SHILOH.—A town on the NE. boundary of Ephraim, Jos 16[6]. It is probably modern *Kh. Ta'nah el-Fôqā*, about 7 miles ESE. of *Nâblus.*

TABAOTH, 1 Es 5[29] (AV, RV).—See TABBAOTH.

TABBAOTH.—A family of Nethinim (q.v.) who returned with Zerubbabel, Ezr 2[43], Neh 7[46], 1 Es 5[29] (AV, RV **Tabaoth**).

TABBATH.—A place mentioned in Jg 7[22]; possibly modern *Râs Abū Ṭābât.*

TABEAL, Is 7[6] (AV).—See TABEEL, **1.**

TABEEL.—1. The father of the rival to Ahaz put forward by Rezin (q.v.) and Pekah, Is 7[6] (AV **Tabeal**). **2.** A Persian official, Ezr 4[7], 1 Es 2[16] (AV, RV **Tabellius**).

TABELLIUS, 1 Es 2[16] (AV, RV).—See TABEEL, **2.**

TABER.—Only in Nah 2[7] AV and RV 'her handmaids mourn as with the voice of doves, tabering upon (ARV, RSV 'beating') their breasts.' Beating the breast was a familiar Oriental custom in mourning (cf Is 32[12]). The Hebrew word here used means literally 'drumming' (cf Ps 68[25], translated 'playing,' its only other occurrence). The English word 'taber' means a small drum, usually accompanying a pipe, both instruments being played by the same performer. Other forms are 'tabor,' 'tabour,' and 'tambour'; and diminutive forms are **'tabret'** and **'tambourine.'**

TABERAH.—An unidentified stopping-place in the wilderness, Nu 11[3], Dt 9[22].

TABERNACLE.—1. The word is used in EV to translate three etymologically unconnected Hebrew terms: (*a*) *sukkāh* (and cognates) = 'booth,' as in Feast of Tabernacles (see next article), usually rendered **'Booths'** in RVm and RSV (except 2 Ch 8[13]); (*b*) *'ōhel* = 'tent' (so RV, RSV), especially in the phrase **'tent of meeting'**; (*c*) *mishkān* = 'dwelling place,' or 'habitation,' the place where Yahweh comes to dwell. It is with the last of these that this article deals. The rendering of the word by the Greek *skēnē* is appropriate by reason of its meaning and sound. This is less true of the Latin *tabernaculum,* anglicé 'tabernacle.' But since the Hebrew is in the main a highly technical cultic term, the English 'tabernacle,' which apart from its Biblical usage has no other content of meaning, may rightly be retained. The meaning of the Hebrew term, 'place of dwelling,' will determine its significance. It will be seen that, while there is a continuity of thought between the Tent (where first in the desert and later during the period of the monarchy Yahweh came to meet His people) and the Tabernacle, the latter is the term especially associated with the Jerusalem tradition. In P it virtually replaces the Tent. Thus it prepares the way for the later Jewish concept of **Shekinah** and the NT *skēnoun* (Jn 1[14]). In Ex 25 ff it is described as an elaborate portable sanctuary prepared according to Divine instructions as the place of worship for Israel, to be in the midst of the camp during the wilderness wanderings. This, however, is confined to the P tradition of the Pentateuch, characteristic of the exiled priests and their descendants, and is to be carefully distinguished from the simpler structure, the Tent, characteristic of the E tradition. The relation between these two sanctuaries will be considered in **9.**

2. The section of P devoted to the details of the fabric and furniture of the Tabernacle, and to the arrangements for its transport from station to station in the wilderness, fall into two groups, viz. (*a*) Ex 25–27, 30, 31, which are couched in the form of instructions from Y″ to Moses as to the erection of the Tabernacle and the making of its furniture according to the 'pattern' or model shown to the latter on the holy mount (25[9, 40]); (*b*) Ex 35–40, which tell *inter alia* of the carrying out of these instructions. Some additional details, particularly as to the arrangements on the march, are given in Nu 3[25ff] 4[4ff] and 7[1ff].

In these and other OT passages the wilderness sanctuary is denoted by at least a dozen different designations (see the list in Hastings' *DB* iv, 655). The most frequently employed is that also borne, as we have seen, by the sacred tent of E, **'the tent of meeting'** (so RV and RSV throughout). That this is the more correct rendering of the original *'ōhel mō'ēdh,* as compared with AV's **'tabernacle of the congregation,'** is now universally acknowledged. The sense in which the Priestly writers, at least, understood the second term is evident from such passages as Ex 25[22], where, with reference to the mercy-seat (see **7** (*b*)), Y″ is represented as saying: 'there I will *meet with you* and . . . will speak with you' (cf Nu 7[89]). This, however, does not exclude a possible early connexion of the name with that of the Babylonian 'mount of meeting' (Is 14[13], RSV 'assembly,' AV and RV 'congregation'), the *mō'ēdh* or assembly of the gods.

3. In order to do justice to the Priestly writers in their attempts to give literary shape to their ideas of Divine worship, it must be remembered that they were following in the footsteps of Ezekiel (chs. 40–48), whose conception of a sanctuary is that of a dwelling-place of the Deity (see Ezk 37[27]). Now the attribute of Israel's God, which for these theologians of the Exile overshadowed all others, was His ineffable and almost unapproachable holiness, and the problem for Ezekiel and his priestly successors was how man in his creaturely weakness and sinfulness could with safety approach a perfectly holy God. The solution is found in the restored Temple in the one case (Ezk 40 ff), and in the Tabernacle in the other, together with the elaborate sacrificial and propitiatory system of which each is the centre. In the Tabernacle, in particular, we have an ideal of a Divine sanctuary, every detail of which is intended to symbolize the unity, majesty, and above all the holiness of Y″, and to provide an earthly habitation in which a holy God may again dwell in the midst of a holy people. 'Let them make me a sanctuary, *that I may dwell in their midst*' (Ex 25^{8}).

4. Taking this general idea of the Tabernacle with us, and leaving a fuller discussion of its religious significance and symbolism to a later section (**8**), let us proceed to study the arrangement and component parts of P's ideal sanctuary. Since the tents of the Hebrew tribes, those of the priests and Levites, and the three divisions of the sanctuary—court, holy place, and the holy of holies—represent ascending degrees of holiness in the scheme of the Priestly writer, the appropriate order of study will be from without inwards, from the perimeter of the sanctuary to its centre.

(*a*) We begin, therefore, with 'the **court of the tabernacle**' (Ex 27^{9}). This is described as a rectangular enclosure in the centre of the camp, measuring 100 cubits from east to west and half that amount from south to north. If the shorter cubit of, say, 18 inches (for convenience of reckoning) be taken as the unit of measurement, this represents an area of approximately 50 yards by 25, a ratio of 2 : 1. The entrance, which is on the eastern side, is closed by a **screen** (27^{16} RV and RSV) of embroidered work in colours. The rest of the area is screened off by plain white **curtains** (EV **'hangings'**) of 'fine twined linen' 5 cubits in height, suspended, like the screen, at equal intervals of 5 cubits from **pillars** standing in sockets (AV, RV) or **bases** (RSV) of bronze. Since the perimeter of the court measured 300 cubits, 60 pillars in all were required for the curtains and the screen, and are reckoned in the text in groups of tens and twenties, 20 for each long side, and 10 for each short side. The pillars are evidently intended to be kept upright by means of **cords** or stays fastened to **pins** or pegs of bronze stuck in the ground.

(*b*) In the centre of the court is placed the **altar of burnt-offering** (27$^{1-8}$), called also **'the brazen altar'** and **'the altar'** *par excellence*. When one considers the purpose it was intended to serve, one is surprised to find this altar of burnt-offering consisting of a hollow chest of acacia wood (so RV and RSV throughout, for AV 'shittim')—the only wood employed in the construction of the Tabernacle—5 cubits in length and breadth, and 3 in height, overlaid with what must, for reason of transport, have been a comparatively thin sheathing of bronze. From the four corners spring the four **horns of the altar,** 'of one piece' with it, while half-way up the side there was fitted a projecting **ledge,** from which depended a network or **grating** (AV **'grate'**) of bronze (27^{4} 38^{4} RV and RSV). The meshes of the latter must have been sufficiently wide to permit of the sacrificial blood being dashed against the sides and base of the altar (cf the sketch in Hastings' *DB* iv, 658). Like most of the other articles of the Tabernacle furniture, the altar was provided with rings and poles for convenience of transport.

(*c*) In proximity to the altar must be placed the bronze **laver** (30$^{17-21}$), containing water for the ablutions of the priests. According to 38^{8}, it was made from the 'mirrors of the ministering women who ministered at the door of the tent of meeting'—a curious anachronism.

5. (*a*) It has already been emphasized that the dominant conception of the Tabernacle in these chapters is that of a portable sanctuary, which is to serve as the earthly dwelling-place of the heavenly King. In harmony therewith we find *the essential part of the fabric of the Tabernacle, to which every other structural detail is subsidiary*, described at the outset by the characteristic designation **'dwelling.'** 'You shall make the dwelling (EV tabernacle) with ten curtains' (26^{1}). It is a fundamental mistake to regard the wooden part of the Tabernacle as of the essence of the structure, and to begin the study of the whole therefrom, as is still being done.

The ten **curtains** of the dwelling (*mishkān*), each 28 cubits by 4, are to be of the finest linen, adorned with inwoven tapestry figures of cherubim in violet, purple, and scarlet (see Colours), 'skilfully worked' (26^{1ff} RSV). They are to be sewed together to form two sets of five, which again are to be 'coupled together' by means of **clasps** (RV and RSV; AV **'taches'**) and **loops,** so as to form one large surface 40 (10 × 4) cubits by 28 (7 × 4), 'for the dwelling shall be one' (26^{6}). Together the curtains are designed to form the earthly, and, with the aid of the attendant cherubim, to symbolize the heavenly, dwelling-place of the God of Israel.

(*b*) The next section of the Divine directions (26$^{7-14}$) provides for the thorough protection of these delicate artistic curtains by means of three separate coverings. The first consists of eleven curtains of goats' hair 'for a **tent** over the dwelling,' and therefore of somewhat larger dimensions than the curtains of the latter, namely 30 cubits by 4, covering, when joined together, a surface of 44 cubits by 30. The two remaining coverings are to be made respectively of rams' skins and goatskins (RSV; RV 'sealskins'; Hebrew *taḥash*) dyed red (v.^{14}).

(*c*) At this point one would have expected to hear of the provision of a number of poles and stays by means of which the dwelling might be pitched like an ordinary tent. But the author of Ex 26$^{1-14}$ does not apply the term 'tent' to the curtains of the dwelling, but, as we have seen, to those of the goats' hair covering, and instead of poles and stays we find a different and altogether unexpected arrangement in vv.$^{15-30}$. Unfortunately the crucial passage, vv.$^{15-17}$, contains several obscure technical terms, with regard to which the true exegetical tradition has probably been lost. The explanation usually given, which finds in the word rendered 'boards' huge wooden beams of impossible dimensions, has been shown in a former study to be exegetically and intrinsically inadmissible; see article 'Tabernacle' in Hastings' *DB* iv, pp. 563^{b} ff. To **7** (*b*) of that article, with which Haupt's note on 1 K 7^{28} in *SBOT* should be compared, the student is referred for the grounds on which the following translation of the leading passage is based. 'And thou shalt make the frames for the dwelling of acacia wood, two uprights (EV 'tenons') for each frame joined together by cross rails.' The result is, briefly, the substitution of 48 light **open frames** (see diagrams, *op. cit.*), each 10 cubits in height by 1½ in width, for the traditional wooden beams of these dimensions, each, according to the usual theory, 1 cubit thick, equivalent to a weight of from 15 to 20 hundredweights!

The open frames—after being overlaid with gold according to our present but scarcely original text (v.^{29})—are to be 'reared up,' side by side, along the south, west, and north sides of a rectangular enclosure measuring 30 cubits by 10 (3 : 1), the east side or front being left open. Twenty frames go to form each long side of the enclosure (1½ × 20 = 30 cubits); the western end requires only six frames (1½ × 6 = 9 cubits); the remaining cubit of the total width is made up by the thickness of the frames and bars of the two long sides. The two remaining frames are placed at the two western corners, where, so far as can be gathered from the obscure text of v.^{24}, the framework is doubled for greater security. The lower ends of the two uprights of each frame are inserted into solid silver **bases,** which thus form a continuous foundation and give steadiness to the structure. This end is further attained by an arrangement of **bars** which together form three parallel sets running along all three sides, binding the whole framework together and giving it the necessary rigidity.

Over this rigid framework, and across the intervening space, are laid the tapestry curtains to form the **dwelling,** the symbolic figures of the cherubim now fully displayed on the sides as well as on the roof. Above these come the first of the protective coverings above described, the goats' hair curtains of the **'tent,'** as distinguished from the 'dwelling.' In virtue of their greater size, they overlap the curtains of the latter, their breadth of 30 cubits exactly sufficing for the height and width of the dwelling (10 + 10 + 10 cubits). As they thus reached to the base of the two long sides of the Tabernacle, they were probably fastened by pegs to the ground. At the eastern end the outermost curtain was probably folded in two so as to hang down for the space of two cubits over the entrance (26^{9}). In what manner the two remaining coverings are to be laid is not specified.

This solution of the difficulties connected with the construction of the Tabernacle, first offered in *DB* iv, has been generally adopted; cf A. H. McNeile (WC), W. H. Bennett (CentB), and more recently F. M. Cross (*BA* x [1947], 46–68).

(*d*) The fabric of the Tabernacle, as described up to this point in Ex 26^{1-30}, has been found to consist of three parts, carefully distinguished from each other. These are (1) the artistic linen curtains of the **dwelling,** the really essential part; (2) their supporting **framework,** the two together enclosing, except at the still open eastern front, a space 30 cubits long and 10 cubits wide from curtain to curtain, and 10 cubits in height; and (3) the protecting **tent** (so called) of goats' hair, with the two subsidiary coverings.

The next step is to provide for the division of the dwelling into two parts, in the proportion of 2 to 1, by means of a beautiful portière, termed the **veil** (vv.^{31ff}), of the same material and artistic workmanship as the curtains of the dwelling. The veil is to be suspended from four gilded pillars, 20 cubits from the entrance and 10 from the western end of the structure. The larger of the two divisions of the dwelling is named the **holy place,** the smaller the **holy of holies,** or most holy place. From the measurements given above, it will be seen that the most holy place—the true presence-chamber of the Most High, to which the holy place forms the ante-chamber—has the form of a perfect cube, 10 cubits (about 15 feet) in length, breadth, and height, enclosed on all four sides and on the roof by the curtains and their cherubim.

(*e*) No provision has yet been made for closing the entrance to the Tabernacle. This is now done (v.^{36f}) by means of a hanging, embroidered in colours—a less artistic fabric than the 'skilfully worked' tapestry—measuring 10 cubits by 10, and suspended from five pillars with bases of bronze. Its special designation, 'a **screen** for the door of the Tent' (v.^{36} RV and RSV), its inferior workmanship, and its bronze bases, all show that strangely enough it is not to be reckoned as a part of the dwelling, of which the woven fabric is tapestry, and the only metals silver and gold.

6. Coming now to the furniture of the dwelling, and proceeding as before from without inwards, we find the holy place provided with three articles of furniture: (*a*) the table of showbread, or, more precisely, presence-bread (25^{23-30} 37^{10-16}); (*b*) the so-called golden candlestick, in reality a seven-branched lampstand (25^{31-40} 37^{17-24}); (*c*) the altar of incense (30^{1-7} 37^{25-28}). Many of the details of the construction and ornamentation of these are obscure, and reference is here made, once for all, to the fuller discussion of these difficulties in the article already cited (*DB* iv, 662 ff).

(*a*) The **table of showbread,** or presence-table (Nu 4^{7}), is a low table or wooden stand overlaid with pure gold, 1½ cubits in height. Its top measures 2 cubits by 1. The legs are connected by a narrow binding-rail, one hand-breadth wide, the 'frame' of Ex 25^{25}, to which are attached four golden rings to receive the staves by which the table is to be carried on the march. For the service of the table are provided the 'plates and dishes for incense, the flagons, and the bowls with which to pour libations' (25^{29}), all of pure gold. Of these the golden '**plates**' (AV, RV '**dishes**') are the salvers on which the loaves of the presence-bread (see SHOWBREAD) were displayed; the '**dishes**' (AV, RV '**spoons**') are rather cups for frankincense (Lv 24^{7}); the 'flagons' (AV 'covers') are larger, and the 'bowls' the smaller, vessels for the wine connected with this part of the ritual.

(*b*) The **golden candlestick** or lampstand is to be constructed of 'beaten work' (*repoussé*) of pure gold. Three pairs of arms branched off at different heights from the central shaft, and curved outwards and upwards until their extremities were on a level with the top of the shaft, the whole providing stands for seven golden lamps. Shaft and arms were alike adorned with ornamentation suggested by the flower of the almond tree (cf diagram in *DB* iv, 663). The golden lampstand stood on the south side of the holy place, facing the table of showbread on the north side. The '**tongs**' of 25^{38} (RV) are really '**snuffers**' (so RSV; cf AV 37^{23}) for dressing the wicks of the lamps, the burnt portions being placed in the '**snuff dishes.**' Both sets of articles were of gold.

(*c*) The passage containing the directions for the **altar of incense** (Ex 30^{1-7}) forms part of a section (chs. 30, 31) which, there is reason to believe, is a later addition to the original contents of the Priests' Code. The altar is described as square in section, one cubit each way, and two cubits in height, with projecting horns. Like the rest of the furniture it was made of acacia wood overlaid with gold, with the usual provision of rings and staves. Its place is in front of the veil separating the holy from the most holy place. Incense of sweet spices is to be offered upon it night and morning (30^{7ff}).

7. In the most holy place are placed two distinct yet connected sacred objects, the Ark and the propitiatory or mercy-seat (25^{10-22} 37^{1-9}). (*a*) P's characteristic name for the former is the '**ark of the testimony.**' The latter term is a synonym in P for the Decalogue (25^{16}), which was written on 'the tables of testimony' (31^{18}), deposited, according to an early tradition, within the Ark. The Ark itself occasionally receives the simple title of 'the testimony,' whence the Tabernacle as sheltering the Ark is named in P both 'the dwelling (EV 'tabernacle') of the testimony' (Ex 38^{21} etc.) and 'the tent of the testimony' (Nu 9^{15} etc.). The Ark of the Priests' Code is an oblong chest of acacia wood, 2½ cubits in length and 1½ in breadth and height ($5\times3\times3$ half-cubits), overlaid within and without with pure gold. The sides are decorated with an obscure form of ornamentation, the 'moulding' (AV, RV 'crown') of Ex 25^{11} (so probably; cf RVm 'rim *or* moulding'). At the four corners (v.^{12} AV; RV and RSV, less accurately, 'feet') the usual rings were attached to receive the bearing-poles. The precise point of attachment is uncertain, whether at the ends of the two long sides or of the two short sides. Since it would be more seemly that the throne of Y″, presently to be described, should face in the direction of the march, it is more probable that the poles were meant to pass through rings attached to the short sides, but whether these were to be attached at the lowest point of the sides, or higher up, cannot be determined. That the Decalogue or 'testimony' was to find a place in the Ark (25^{16}) has already been stated.

(*b*) Distinct from the Ark, but resting upon and of the same superficial dimensions as its top, viz. 2½ by 1½ cubits, we find a slab of solid gold to which is given the name *kappōreth*. The best English rendering is the **propitiatory** (vv.^{17ff}), of which the current **mercy-seat,** adopted by Tyndale from Luther's rendering, is a not inappropriate paraphrase. From opposite ends of the propitiatory, and 'of one piece' with it (v.^{19} RV and RSV), rose a pair of **cherubim** figures of beaten work of pure gold. The faces of the cherubim were bent downwards in the direction of the propitiatory, while the wings with which each was furnished met overhead, so as to cover the propitiatory (vv.$^{18-20}$).

We have now penetrated to the innermost shrine of the priestly **sanctuary.** Its very position is significant. The surrounding court is made up of two squares, 50 cubits each way, placed side by side (see above). The eastern square, with its central altar, is the worshippers' place of meeting. The entrance to the Tabernacle proper lies along the edge of the western square, the exact centre of which is occupied by the most holy place. In the centre of the latter, again, at the point of intersection of the diagonals of the square, we may be sure, is the place intended for the Ark and the propitiatory. Here in the very centre of the camp is the earthly throne of Y″. Here, 'from above the propitiatory, from between the cherubim,' the most holy of all earth's holy places, will God henceforth meet and commune with His servant, Moses (25^{22}). But with Moses only; for even the **high priest** is permitted to enter the most holy place but once a year, on the great Day of Atonement, when he comes to sprinkle the blood of the national sin-offering 'with his finger on the front of the mercy-seat' (Lv 16^{14}). The ordinary priests came only into the holy place, the lay worshipper only into 'the court of the dwelling.' In the course of the foregoing exposition, it will have been seen how these ascending degrees of sanctity are reflected in the materials employed in the construction of the court, holy place, most holy place, and propitiatory respectively. It is not without significance that the last named is the only article of solid gold in the whole sanctuary.

8. These observations lead naturally to a brief exposition of the religious symbolism which so evidently pervades every part of the wilderness sanctuary. Its position in the centre of the camp of the Hebrew tribes has already been more than once referred to. By this the Priestly writer would emphasize the central place which the rightly ordered worship of Israel's covenant God must occupy in the theocratic community of the future.

The most assured fruit of the discipline of the Babylonian Exile was the final triumph of monotheism. This triumph we find reflected in the presuppositions of the Priests' Code. One God, one sanctuary, is the idea implicit throughout. But not only is there no God but Yahweh; Yahweh, Israel's God, 'is one' (Dt 6^{4} RVm), and because He is one, His earthly 'dwelling' must be one (Ex 26^{6}; cf **5** (*a*)). The Tabernacle thus symbolizes both the oneness and the unity of Y″.

Nor is the perpetual striving after proportion and symmetry which characterizes all the measurements of the Tabernacle and its furniture without a deeper significance. By this means the author undoubtedly seeks to symbolize the perfection and harmony of the Divine character. Thus, to take but a single illustration, the perfect cube of the most holy place, of which 'the length and breadth and height,' like those of the New Jerusalem of the Apocalypse (21^{16}), 'are equal,' is clearly intended to symbolize the perfection of the Divine character, the harmony and equipoise of the Divine attributes.

Above all, however, the Tabernacle in its relation to the camp embodies and symbolizes the almost unapproachable holiness of God. This fundamental conception has been repeatedly emphasized in the foregoing sections, and need be re-stated in this connexion only for the sake of completeness. The symbolism of the Tabernacle is a subject in which pious imaginations in the past have run riot, but with regard to which one must endeavour to be faithful to the ideas in the mind of the Priestly author. The threefold division of the sanctuary, for example, into court, holy place, and holy of holies, may have originally symbolized the earth, heaven, and the heaven of heavens, but for the author of Ex 25 ff it was an essential part of the Temple tradition (cf TEMPLE, **7**). In this case, therefore, the division should rather be taken, as in **7** above, as a reflection of the three grades of the theocratic community, people, priests, and high priest.

9. We must return, in conclusion, to the question mooted in **2** as to the relation of the gorgeous sanctuary above described to the simple **'tent of meeting'** of the older Pentateuch sources. In other words, is P's Tabernacle historical? In the first place, there is no reason to question, but on the contrary every reason to accept, the data of the Elohistic source (E) regarding the Mosaic 'tent of meeting.' This earlier 'tabernacle' is first met with in Ex 33$^{7-11}$: 'Now Moses used to take the tent and to pitch it (the tenses are frequentative) outside the camp, far off from the camp . . . and everyone who sought the LORD would go out to the tent of meeting which was outside the camp.' To it, we are further informed, Moses was wont to retire to commune with Y″, who descended in the pillar of the cloud to talk with Moses at the door of the tent 'as a man speaks to his friend' (see also the references in Nu 11$^{16-30}$ 12^{1ff} 14^{10}).

It is not possible to reconcile the picture of this simple tent, 'far off from the camp,' with Joshua as its single non-Levitical attendant (33^{11}), with that of the Tabernacle of the Priests' Code, situated in the centre of the camp, with its attendant army of priests and Levites. Moreover, neither tent nor Tabernacle is rightly intelligible except as the resting-place of the Ark, the symbol of Y″'s presence with His people. Now, the oldest of our extant historical sources have much to tell us of the fortunes of the Ark from the time that it formed the glory of the Temple at Shiloh until it entered its final resting-place in that of Solomon (see ARK). But nowhere is there the slightest reference to anything in the least resembling the Tabernacle of **4–8**. It is only in the Books of Chronicles, in certain of the Psalms, and in passages of the pre-exilic writings which have passed through the hands of late post-exilic editors that such references are found. An illuminating example occurs in 2 Ch 1^{3f}, compared with 1 K 3^{2ff}.

The description of the Tabernacle in Ex 25 ff presents obvious difficulties, *e.g.* the brazen altar (**4** (*b*)), the great mass of silver and gold and the high degree of artistic skill hardly to be expected from recently liberated slaves. Neither does the worship associated with it appear to be appropriate to conditions in the desert, or to be discernible during the early period of Israel's history. The Tabernacle here described belongs to the Priestly stratum in the Pentateuch and can hardly have received its present form until the Persian period. It would appear that the elaboration of the picture arose among the exiled priests. Yet though it is an elaboration, it is not an invention or an innovation. It is evident from Ps 74^{7}, which describes conditions existing soon after 586 B.C., that a tabernacle was part of the pre-exilic Temple. Other Psalms point to the same conclusion, *e.g.* Ps 46$^{4 (\text{Heb. } 5)}$ 78^{60} 132^{5,7} etc. A tabernacle appears to be associated with the time of David (2 S 7^{6}). Here it is referred to together with a tent, and it seems hardly likely that two such dwellings for the same God were part of the same religious tradition (the recognition of this seems to have been responsible for RSV: 'a tent for my dwelling'—which is not a natural rendering of the Hebrew). Now the term *mishkān* appears, with *'ōhel*, in the Ugaritic texts as dwellings for the gods (Aqhat II. v. 31 f; Keret III. iii. 19). So too does the word *ḳeresh*, 'frame supports' (**5** (*c*)) (Baal I. i. 4; II. iv. 24; III. i. 7). In the Pentateuch this is a word peculiar to P (elsewhere only Ezk 27^{6}, apparently of some structure on the deck of a ship). This suggests the possibility that the Tabernacle belonged to the pre-Israelite Jerusalem sanctuary and that it was associated by David—as were other features of the ancient Jerusalem cultus—with the desert tradition, and in particular with the Tent. The Tabernacle appears to be peculiar to the Jerusalem tradition as reflected in the Psalter, Ezekiel, and P. It replaces the Tent in the ultimate form of that tradition, P, where what is described is an elaborated form of an earlier tabernacle, destroyed by the Babylonians. Every detail serves to glorify Him who is holy, unapproachable, yet dwelling in the midst (Ex 25^{8}). This may be more of a portrait of the shrine in the Temple-to-be than a reproduction between this portrait and the pre-exilic shrine, and, beyond that, the portable shrine of the Mosaic period. This is suggested by the conjoining of Tent and Tabernacle in Ex 26. Just as there is a living continuity of the post-exilic age and the people of God in the desert, so, and most importantly, there is a living continuity in worship. The externals may be modified to meet the conditions of changed circumstances; the confidence that the Lord their God dwelt with them remained. As if to express this, the cognate verb *shākhan*='dwell,' is used in the P tradition exclusively of God's coming to dwell in the midst of His people. A. R. S. K.—**A. S. H.**

TABERNACLES, FEAST OF.—1. OT references.—In pre-exilic times there was an autumnal feast, at the end of the Hebrew year, called the **Feast of Ingathering.** It was observed for seven days and it began on the night of the September full-moon (the Harvest Moon), Ex 23^{16} 34^{22}. In post-exilic times this feast became broken up owing to the change of calendar. Part of the feast, the strictly new-year element, gravitated to the 1st of the seventh month (Tishri); part to the 10th of Tishri and became the Day of Atonement, whilst the rest kept to the night of the Harvest Full-Moon and became the *Feast of Tabernacles*.

In Dt 16^{13-15} its name is given as the Feast of Tabernacles or **Booths**, probably referring to the use of booths of intertwined branches used in the vineyards during the vintage. It still is to last seven days; it is to be observed, not at every local shrine as in the earlier days, but at the Central Sanctuary, and it is to be an occasion of rejoicing. The association of penitence with the End of the Year Feast has gravitated to the ten days of Penitence, culminating in the Day of Atonement. In the 'year of release' (the sabbatical year), the Law is to be publicly read (Dt 31^{10-13}). The dedication of Solomon's Temple took place at the autumnal feast; in the account given in 1 K 8^{66} the seven-day rule of Deuteronomic and earlier times is observed; but the parallel narrative of 2 Ch 7^{8-10} reflects later custom and assumes that the eight-day rule of Leviticus was followed.

In Lv 23^{34ff} and Nu 29^{12-39} we find elaborate ordinances. The feast begins on 15th Tishri (September–October) and lasts for eight days, the first and the last being days of 'holy convocation,' presumably meaning that all are specially enjoined to be there. The people are to live in booths. A very large number of offerings is ordained; on each of the first seven days two rams and fourteen lambs, and a goat as a sin-offering; and successively on these days a diminishing number of bullocks, thirteen on the first day, twelve on the second, and so on till the seventh, when seven were to be offered. On the eighth day the special offerings were one bull, one ram, seven lambs, and a goat as a sin-offering. The feast is mentioned in Ezr 3^{4}, but nothing is said of the method of observance. The celebration in Neh 8^{16} follows the eight-day rule of Leviticus, with the eighth day as a 'closing-assembly,' and it is expressly stated that such had not been the case since Joshua's days.

2. Character of the Feast.—It was the Jewish harvest-home, both in the pre-exilic and the post-exilic periods. All the year's produce of every kind had been gathered in, and now last of all there came the vintage. Like the other feasts, it commemorated an event in the rescue from Egypt and the wanderings through the desert, that great saga of Israelite history. It was an occasion for great joy and was the most important of all the festivals, until perhaps in the last days of the second Temple, when Passover as the festival of the coming of Messiah took on increased importance. In Zec 14^{16} the future sign of Judah's triumph over all the world is that all nations shall come up yearly to keep this festival.

There has been a great deal of discussion on the observance of and the meaning of this Feast, particularly as it was observed in pre-exilic times. Many scholars maintain that there were elaborate ceremonies on the analogy of the Babylonian new-year feasts or of Canaanite annual festivals. The case for a close parallel between the pre-exilic Feast of Ingathering and the Babylonian Festival is to be found in *Myth and Ritual* (ed. S. H. Hooke), pp. 1–146. The general pattern involved a dramatic representation of the death and resurrection of the god, a recitation of the myth of Creation, a ritual combat in which the god overcomes his enemies, a sacred marriage and a triumphal procession. To what extent these and other details were observed in Old Israel is a matter of dispute, but scholars generally are agreed that some such annual festival of the utmost importance for the life and well-being of king and community was regularly observed through the time of the Kingdoms. Mowinckel maintained that such psalms as 93, 95–99, 47 were the apparatus of a living cult, and since his *Psalmenstudien* II (1921), many other psalms and passages from both the Law and the Prophets have been connected with this Feast.

3. Later customs.—We have many details of customs observed in the last days of the Temple. How many of these go back to very ancient times, it is impossible to say. There were daily processions round the altar and a sevenfold repetition on the 7th day; the singing of special psalms, a procession on each of the first 7 days to Siloam to fetch the water for the drink-offering, the illumination of the Court of the Women by the lighting of giant candelabra, and all-night dancing in the court whilst spectators looked on from galleries above.

A. W. F. B.—N. H. S.

TABITHA.—See DORCAS.

TABLE.—See HOUSE, **8**; MEALS, **3, 4.** For 'Table of Showbread' see SHOWBREAD, TABERNACLE, **6** (*a*); TEMPLE, **5, 9, 12.**

TABLE, TABLET.—**1.** Writing tablet is indicated by the Hebrew *lûaḥ*, which is also applied to *wooden* boards or planks (Ex 27^{8} 38^{7} in the altar of the Tabernacle, Ezk 27^{5} in a ship, Ca 8^{9} in a door) and to *metal* plates (in the bases of the lavers in Solomon's Temple, 1 K 7^{36}). It is, however, most frequently applied to tables of *stone* on which the Decalogue was engraved (Ex 24^{12} 31^{18} etc.). It is used of a tablet on which a prophecy may be written (Is 30^{8}, Hab 2^{2}), and in Pr 3^{3} 7^{3} and Jer 17^{1} figuratively of the 'tables of the heart.' In all these passages, when used of stone, both AV and RV translate 'table' except in Is 30^{8} where RV has 'tablet.' *lûaḥ* generally appears in LXX and NT as *plax* (2 Co 3^{3}, He 9^{4}). The 'writing table' (RV 'tablet') of Lk 1^{63} was probably of wax.

2. Some article of feminine adornment is indicated by Hebrew *kûmāz*, AV 'tablets' RV, RSV 'armlets' RVm 'necklaces' and 'beads' respectively at Ex 35^{22}, Nu 31^{50}.

3. The AV 'tablets' in Is 3^{20} is in RV, RSV 'perfume boxes,' literally houses 'of the *nephesh*.' Two alternatives may be suggested: (i) If *nephesh* here means 'throat,' the phrase may mean (gold or silver) collars; (ii) it may refer to a box into which the lover has breathed and so his 'soul' is kept by his beloved.

4. The 'tablet' (*gillāyôn*) in Is 8^{1} signifies a polished surface. The same word appears in Is 3^{23}, AV 'glasses,' RV 'hand-mirrors,' RSV 'garments of gauze.'

W. F. B.—A. S. H.

TABLELAND.—In a number of passages RSV has 'tableland' for AV and RV 'plain' (Dt 3^{10} 4^{43}, Jos $13^{9, 16f, 21}$ 20^{8}, Jer 48^{21}). Elsewhere it retains 'plain' (1 K $20^{23, 25}$, 2 Ch 26^{10}, Jer 21^{13} 48^{8}).

TABLETS.—See PERFUMER.

TABOR.—**1.** A town in the tribe of Zebulun, given to Levites descended from Merari, 1 Ch 6^{77}. It is perhaps modern *Kh. Dabûrah*, near Mount Tabor. **2.** A place near Ophrah, Jg 8^{18}. **3.** The Oak (AV 'plain') of Tabor was on the road from Ramah S. to Gibeah, 1 S 10^{3}. **4.** See next article.

TABOR (MOUNT).—A mountain in the NE. corner of the plain of Esdraelon, some 7 miles E. of Nazareth. Though only 1843 feet high, Tabor is, from its isolation and remarkable rounded shape, a most prominent object from great distances around; hence, though of much less size than the great mountain mass of Hermon (9232 feet high and 25 miles long), it was associated with it in popular thought (Ps 89^{12}). In Jer 46^{18} Nebuchadrezzar towers above men 'like Tabor among the mountains, and like Carmel by the sea.' Its Arabic name to-day is *Jebel eṭ-Ṭôr*, 'the mountain of the mount.' From its summit a magnificent outlook is obtained, especially to the W., over the plain of Esdraelon to the mountains of Samaria and Carmel.

It was on the common frontier of Zebulun and Issachar (Jos $19^{12, 22}$); it was an early sanctuary (Hos 5^{1}), being probably the mountain where peoples are convoked and right sacrifices offered in Dt 33^{19}. Here Barak mustered his forces before giving battle to Sisera (Jg $4^{6, 12, 14}$); here, too, in Gideon's day there was a clash between Midianites and Israelites (Jg 8^{18}). In later history Tabor figures mainly as a stronghold. In 218 B.C. Antiochus III. captured the city of Atabyrion on Tabor and fortified it. It was in Jewish hands from *c* 105 B.C. to the end of the Hasmonaean regime. Here in 53 B.C. Gabinius defeated the insurgent Alexander, son of Aristobulus II. In A.D. 66 Josephus fortified the hill against Vespasian, but it surrendered after the defeat of the Jewish troops by Placidus. During the Crusades it was for long in the hands of the Christians, but it fell to the Muslims after the battle of Hattin (1187), and was fortified in 1212 by Saladin's successor—a step which led to the abortive Fifth Crusade. At Mount Tabor Napoleon defeated a Turkish army in 1799.

The tradition that Tabor was the mountain of the **Transfiguration** has little evidence in its favour, although it is quite early. Its earliest form is that found in the 2nd-cent. 'Gospel according to the Hebrews,' where Jesus says : 'Even now my mother the Holy Spirit took me by one of my hairs and carried me up to the great mountain Tabor'—but this may be in origin an embellished variant of one of the Temptation incidents. Tabor was probably an inhabited spot at the time of Christ, while the requirements of the Biblical narrative of the Transfiguration (Mk 8^{27} 9^{2-10} and parallels) are met rather by a site near Caesarea Philippi, such as an isolated spur of Hermon.

Mount Tabor to-day is a well-wooded spot, groves of oaks and terebinths not only covering the hillsides but extending also over a considerable area of hill and valley to the N. ; game abounds in the coverts. On the summit the Greek Church has a monastery and the Franciscans have the Basilica of the Transfiguration, with a hospice attached. The Franciscans in particular have carried out extensive excavations ; the foundations of a great wall of circumvallation have been traced, many ancient tombs have been cleared, and the remains of several churches of the 4th and 12th cent. have been unearthed.

E. W. G. M.—**F. F. B.**

TABRET (see TABER) is the AV translation of *tōph* in Gn 31^{27}, 1 S 10^5 18^6, Is 5^{12} 24^8 30^{32}, Jer 31^4, Ezk 28^{13}. The same Hebrew word is translated **'timbrel'** in Ex 15^{20}, Jg 11^{34}, 2 S 6^5, 1 Ch 13^8, Job 21^{12}, Ps 81^2 149^3 150^4. RV substitutes 'timbrel' in 1 S 10^5 18^6, and RSV has 'tambourine' in Gn 31^{27}, 1 S 10^5, 2 S 6^5, 1 Ch 13^8, Job 21^{12}, but otherwise uses 'timbrel' (save Ezk 28^{13} where it has no reference to a musical instrument). It might have been well to drop both 'timbrel' and 'tabret,' neither of which conveys any clear sense to a modern ear, and adopt some such rendering as 'tambourine' or 'hand-drum.' The AV rendering of Job 17^6 'aforetime I was as a tabret,' has arisen from a confusion of *tōpheth* 'spitting' with *tōph* 'tambourine.' The words mean 'I am become one to be spit on in the face' (RV 'an open abhorring'; RSV 'a byword').

TABRIMMON.—The father of Benhadad, 1 K 15^{18}.

TACHES.—An old word of French origin used by AV to render the Hebrew *ḳᵉrāsîm*, which occurs only in P's description of the Tabernacle (Ex $26^{6, 11, 33}$ 35^{11} etc.). The Greek rendering denotes the rings set in eyelets at the edge of a sail for the ropes to pass through. The Hebrew word evidently signifies some form of **hook** or **clasp** (so RV, RSV) like the Roman *fibula*.

TACHMONITE.—See TAHCHEMONITE.

TACKLE in Is 33^{23} (AV, RV 'tacklings') simply means a ship's ropes ; in Ac 27^{19} (AV, RV 'tackling') it is used more generally of the whole gearing (RVm 'furniture').

TADMOR.—City on the route from Damascus to the Euphrates, which route, however, was little used until Roman times, when Tadmor became a very great place and was called **Palmyra**. But the older name survives in present *Tudmur*. The corruption of the name *Tadmyra > Palmyra is difficult to explain. The ruins of old Tadmor must have been wiped out when the metropolis of the caravan trade arose in this desert oasis, which is watered by a brook of clear but sulphurous water. The Assyrian inscriptions have shown that Tadmor existed already in the time of Tiglath-pileser I. (1100 B.C.), who mentions *Tadmar* of the land of *Amurrū* (the name for the western regions). It is quite probable that some Apocryphon, like the one on Genesis found among the Dead Sea Scrolls in Qumrân Cave 1, attributed to Solomon the rule over Tadmor, as 2 Ch 8^{3-4} does over Hamath and Zobah. It was not just a mistake if 2 Ch 8^4 says that Solomon built 'Tadmor in the desert,' but an attempt to get into the sacred text an important fact affirmed by outside tradition. The obscure **Tamar** in the (Judaean) desert mentioned in the corresponding passage of 1 K 9^{18}, was the place originally meant by the Chronicler, but excellently served the reviser's purpose, as it was so easily changed into Tadmor. In his time Palmyra had begun to be of some consequence, and it was worth knowing that Solomon had held it. Jewish travellers now often took that road in going to Babylonia.

The first mention of Palmyra by a classical writer is by Appian (*Bell. Civ.* v. 9), who tells how the wealth of this caravan city excited the cupidity of Mark Antony (41 B.C.). In the Age of Augustus a temple of *Belos* (or *Beelsamen* in Greek transliterations) was built there, as an examination of the ruins has shown. Trajan wrought destruction here, but Hadrian rebuilt the city, calling it Adrianopolis. It became a Roman colony under Septimius Severus (A.D. 193–211), or Caracalla (A.D. 211–217), and since that time fell heir to the importance previously held by Petra. Under the rule of Odenathus and his successor, Queen Zenobia, Palmyra became an important power, even conquering Egypt. Zenobia was defeated by Aurelian near Antioch and Emesa (Hamath) and captured (A.D. 272). Under Diocletian (A.D. 284–305) a portion of the city was turned into a camp for the army. In the 4th–5th cents. there were desolate areas in it in which Christians could erect Basilicas. Construction of a city wall under Justinian (A.D. 527–565) did considerable damage to important buildings and changed the plan of the city. The decline of Palmyra was primarily due to Diocletian's policy of making Mesopotamia (with Edessa, Amida, and Nisibis) the focal point for relations with the East. There are numerous Palmyrene inscriptions, written in a western Aramaic dialect, and many of them with accompanying Greek version. Of particular interest is the Tariff inscription of A.D. 173. (See Cooke, *A Text Book of North-Semitic Inscriptions* [1903], 313 f.) The inscriptions are also important for our knowledge of late phases of Semitic religion.

(For an interesting account of Palmyra see M. Rostovtzeff, *Caravan Cities*, 1932.) E. G. K.

TAHAN.—**1.** An Ephraimite clan, Nu 26^{35} ; the gentilic **Tahanites** occurs in Nu 26^{35}. **2.** A descendant of Ephraim in the fourth or fifth generation, 1 Ch 7^{25}.

TAHAPANES, Jer 2^{16} (AV).—See TAHPANHES.

TAHASH.—A son of Nahor, Gn 22^{24} (AV (**Thahash**).

TAHATH.—**1.** A Kohathite Levite, 1 Ch $6^{24, 37}$. **2. 3.** Two (unless the name has been accidentally repeated) Ephraimite families, 1 Ch 7^{20}. **4.** An unidentified stopping-place in the wilderness, Nu 33^{26f}.

TAHCHEMONITE (AV **Tachmonite**).—See HACHMONI.

TAHPANHES.—An Egyptian city mentioned in Jer 2^{16} (AV **Tahapanes**) 43^{7ff} 44^1 46^{14}, Ezk 30^{18} (**Tehaphnehes**), Jth 1^9 (AV **Taphnes**), the same as the Greek Daphnae, usually and most probably identified with the modern *Tell Defneh*, which lies on the Pelusiac branch of the Nile. The name means 'The Fortress of Penaḥse (*i.e.* the Negro).' Penaḥse was probably a powerful Theban general who lived in the 11th cent. B.C. and suppressed a rebellion in the north. Several cities were named after him, so effectively did he do his work. According to Herodotus, Daphnae was the frontier fortress of Egypt on the Asiatic side and was garrisoned by Greeks. *Tell Defneh* was excavated by Petrie at the end of the last century. In its ruins was found an abundance of Greek pottery, iron armour, and arrow-heads of bronze and iron, while numerous small weights bore testimony to the trade that passed through it. The garrison was kept up by the Persians in the 5th cent., and the town existed to a much later period.

F. Ll. G.—T. W. T.

TAHPENES.—The name of Pharaoh's wife, whose sister was given to Hadad the Edomite, 1 K 11[19f]. It has the appearance of an Egyptian name, and has been explained by Albright as for **T.-ḥu.t-p* (or *pr*)-*nsw* = ' she whom the king (or palace) protects ' (*BASOR* 140, p. 32). The name of her son **Genubath** is not Egyptian. The Pharaoh should be of the weak 21st Dynasty.

TAHREA.—A grandson of Mephibosheth, 1 Ch 9[41]; called **Tarea** (perhaps by a scribal error) in 8[35].

TAHTIM HODSHI, THE LAND OF.—A place E. of Jordan, which Joab and his officers visited when making the census for David, 2 S 24[6] (AV, RV). It is mentioned between Gilead and Dan-jaan. The MT, however, is certainly corrupt. In all probability we should read *ha-Ḥittîm Ḳādēshāh* = ' to the land of *the Hittites towards Kadesh* ; cf RSV ' to Kadesh in the land of the Hittites,' *i.e.* to Kadesh on the Orontes.

TALE.—' Tale ' in AV generally means ' number *or* sum,' as in Ex 5[18] ' Yet shall ye deliver the tale of bricks ' (so RV ; RSV ' the same number '). And the verb ' to tell ' sometimes means ' to number,' as Gn 15[5], AV and RV ' Tell (RSV ' number ') the stars if thou be able to number them.'

TALEBEARING.—See SLANDER.

TALENT.—See MONEY, WEIGHTS AND MEASURES.

TALITHA CUMI.—The command addressed by our Lord to the daughter of Jairus (Mk 5[41]), and interpreted by the Evangelist ' Little girl, I say to you, arise.' The relating of the actual (Aramaic) words used by Jesus is characteristic of St. Mark's graphic narrative (cf 7[11, 34] 14[36] 15[34]), and may have been embedded in the tradition he used.

TALMAI.—**1.** A clan resident in Hebron at the time of the Hebrew conquest and driven thence by Caleb, Nu 13[22], Jos 15[14], Jg 1[10]. **2.** Son of Ammihur, king of Geshur, and a contemporary of David, to whom he gave his daughter Maacah in marriage, 2 S 3[3] 13[37], 1 Ch 3[2].

TALMON.—The name of a family of Temple gatekeepers, 1 Ch 9[17], Ezr 2[42], Neh 7[45] 11[19] 12[25], 1 Es 5[28] (RV **Tolman**). See TELEM.

TALMUD (' learning ').—The principal literary production of post-Biblical Judaism. The collection is divided into two parts : the **Mishnah** (' second law '), corresponding chronologically to the NT and the Apostolic Fathers of the Christians ; and the **Gemara** (' completion '), corresponding in time to the ante-Nicene, Nicene, and post-Nicene Fathers. There are two Talmuds, the Jerusalem or Palestinian, and the Babylonian, the names being derived from the two centres of redaction (eastern and western), just as Christian patristic literature may be divided into Greek Fathers and Latin Fathers.

1. Origin and character of the Mishnah.—Jewish tradition draws a distinction between the ' Oral Law,' which was handed down for centuries by word of mouth, and the ' Written Law,' *i.e.* the Pentateuch or Five Books of Moses. Both, according to Rabbinical teaching, originated with Moses. It was an article of faith that in the Pentateuch there was no precept or regulation of which God had not given to Moses all explanations necessary for their application, together with the order to transmit them by word of mouth. This, of course, was only a tradition giving proper authority to the Oral Law. Actually the Oral Law, though containing elements of great antiquity—*e.g.* details of folklore—probably dates from the time when the Written Law was first read and expounded to the people (Neh 8[1-9]).

This oral expounding inevitably led to differing explanations. Hence in later times it was necessary to reduce to writing the explanations considered authoritative and correct. This process began in the time of Hillel and Shammai (end of 1st cent. B.C.) and came to be called *mishnah* (' repetition ' or ' second law '). Frequently, each teacher would compile his own Mishnah, as was done by Rabbi Aqiba, Rabbi Meir, and others (1st cent. A.D.). There were even rules without apparent Scriptural authority. The confusion created by this state of affairs necessitated some authoritative action, which was taken by Rabbi Judah ha-Nasi, when he understook his great redaction of the Mishnah. Judah was born about A.D. 135 and died about A.D. 220 ; his title, *ha-Nasi*, means literally ' the Prince,' but was used at that time to denote the Patriarch or presiding officer of the leading Rabbinical school (then in Galilee, the centre of Jewish life). This was an influential position, and Judah graced it so well that he was sometimes referred to as ' Judah the Holy ' ; usually, he is called in the literature simply ' Rabbi,' without further qualification, a unique distinction indeed.

Judah's work of redaction was complete by about A.D. 200. Owing to the skill and authority of his work, the Mishnah of Judah the Patriarch soon superseded all other collections, and became the only one used in the schools. The object that Judah had had in view, namely, of restoring uniform teaching, was thus achieved. The Mishnah as we now have it is not, however, quite as he first produced it. There were some further changes by his pupils during his lifetime, with his acquiescence ; there is also a reference to his death, mention of his sons, and a few references to teachers living shortly after his time. Moreover, in about thirty instances, his own teachings are referred to as those of ' Rabbi,' and the unsolved question arises as to whether he would have referred to himself in this way. Nevertheless, what we have is essentially his. It is written in Hebrew of a kind somewhat different from that of the OT, and is essentially the same in the two Talmuds, whereas the Gemara of both Talmuds is basically Aramaic in language, but otherwise very different as between the Babylonian and Palestinian versions.

The Mishnah is divided into six *Sedarim* (Hebrew for ' Orders,' often called ' Sections ' in English). Each *Seder* or Section contains a number of ' treatises ' or ' tractates ' ; each tractate is divided into chapters, and these again into paragraphs. In all there are sixty-three tractates, and it is to these, not to the Sections, that references are made, including the chapter and paragraph, in the fashion of a Bible reference, thus : *Nedarim* or *Ned.* (' Vows ') iii. 5. The names of the six Sections, which to some extent indicate their contents, are : (1) *Zeraim* (' Seeds '), containing eleven tractates, treating mostly of agricultural tithes and offerings ; (2) *Moed* (' Festival '), twelve tractates, having to do with the Sabbath, Passover, and the like ; (3) *Nashim* (' Women '), seven tractates, special regulations relating to women, marriage, divorce, etc. ; (4) *Nezikin* (' Damages '), ten tractates, on civil and criminal law ; (5) *Kodashim* (' Holy things '), eleven tractates, mostly on animal sacrifices ; (6) *Tohoroth* (' Ritually clean things '), twelve tractates, treating all phases of ritual impurity, how to avoid it and overcome it.

The accessibility of the Mishnah to readers of English has been enormously increased since the publication in 1933 of Herbert Danby's masterly translation, with introduction, notes, and appendices, all in one convenient volume. This work has been a boon especially to Christian students of the Bible who wish to inform themselves of what the Jewish teachers of the Mishnah (the so-called **Tannaim**) were saying during the first two Christian centuries. Also now available is *Mishnayoth*, an edition by Philip Blackman in seven volumes (1951–1956), with the Hebrew text, introductions, translation notes, appendices, etc. Available in German is the very competent edition entitled *Die Mischna*, by G. Beer, O. Holtzmann, and others (begun in 1912, now nearing completion), with text, translation, and detailed discussions.

Two of the better known or more discussed tractates (at least among Christians) are *Aboth* (' Fathers ') and

Middoth ('Measurements'). *Aboth*, also called *Pirke Aboth* ('Chapters of the Fathers') and Sayings of the Fathers, is a collection of moral maxims and sayings in praise of the law attributed to some sixty teachers living between 300 B.C. and A.D. 200. Because of the fine ethical content, this tractate is much admired by both Jews and Christians, and has several times been published separately. *Middoth* is a detailed description of the Temple, based to some extent on recollections of Herod's sanctuary destroyed in A.D. 70 (see TEMPLE) but also in part presenting an idealized picture of what a future Temple should be like. These tractates, however, are not of the usual kind. In general, the material of the Mishnah is strictly **Halakhah** ('usage'), *i.e.* details of Rabbinic law, mostly, but not necessarily, based on Scripture. In contrast to Halakhah is **Haggadah** or **Aggâdah** ('narrative'), exposition or interpretation of Scripture that aims at edification and includes a wide range of non-legal matter. There is little of this in the Mishnah except in *Aboth*.

Alongside the Mishnah, is a parallel collection, arranged in the same manner, known as the **Tosephta** ('addition' or 'supplement'). Some say it was intended as a supplement to the Mishnah, others that it contains material excluded from the Mishnah and therefore is a sort of apocryphal Mishnah. It presupposes the Mishnah, treats its material more freely, and contains more Haggadic elements. No English translation of the whole is available. An important edition of the text has been published by M. S. Zuckermandel.

Material of Mishnaic type and date is also found scattered through the two Gemaras in small fragments. Each instance of such material is called a **Baraitha** ('outside Mishnah'). These Baraithas are in Hebrew, while their surrounding context is Aramaic. They are also introduced by certain formulas, such as 'Our Rabbis have taught,' 'There is a tradition,' or 'Rabbi So-and-so taught.' Like the Tosephta, the Baraithas may be considered 'apocryphal' in relation to the Mishnah. Thus the Tosephta is essentially a collection of Baraithas.

2. The two Talmuds.—The Mishnah forms the basis of the Talmud; the **Gemara** is an expansion, by means of comment and explanation, of the Mishnah; thus the Talmud contains the Mishnah, with a great deal more additional matter. The Talmud is practically a mere amplification of the Mishnah by comments and supplementation; even those portions of the Mishnah which have no Gemara are regarded as component parts of the Talmud.

The two Talmuds, the **Palestinian** and the **Babylonian**, are known in Hebrew as *Yerushalmi* ('Jerusalemite,' though it was not written in Jerusalem, the Jews having been expelled from there in A.D. 70) and *Babli* ('Babylonian'). The material which went to make up *Yerushalmi* was prepared in the academies, the centres of Jewish learning in Palestine, chief among which was Tiberias. It was from here that Rabbi Yohanan issued *Yerushalmi* in its earliest form, during the middle of the 3rd cent. A.D. The first editor, or at all events the first compiler, of *Babli* was Rabbi Ashi (died about A.D. 430), who presided over the academy of Sura. Both these Talmuds were constantly being added to; *Yerushalmi* was not finally closed until the end of the 4th cent., *Babli* not until the beginning of the 6th. The teachers of the Gemaras, both Palestinian and Babylonian, are called **Amoraim** ('speakers,' 'interpreters') in contrast to the **Tannaim** ('repeaters,' 'teachers') of the Mishnah. By the time of the completion of the Talmuds, the centre of Jewish life had moved from Palestine to Babylonia (under the rule of the Sassanid Persians). Neither Talmud is complete, in the sense of containing an exposition of every tractate of the Mishnah; but *Babli* is much more voluminous, being about three times the size of *Yerushalmi*. The latter has always occupied a position of subordinate importance, while *Babli* may be said to have absorbed the thought and learning of all the Jewish teachers of the Talmudic age, and hence is sometimes called simply 'The Talmud.' On the other hand, *Yerushalmi* has certain values of its own, such as the early date of some of its material, its simplicity, and especially its rich store of Haggadah. In the Babylonian schools intellectual acumen reigned supreme; there was but little room for the play of the emotions or for the development of poetic imagination; these were rather the property of Palestinian soil. But the Haggadah, whether in *Yerushalmi* or *Babli*, occupies in reality a subordinate place, for in its origin, as we have seen, the Talmud was a commentary on the Mishnah, which was a collection of Halakhah; and although the Haggadic portions are of much greater human interest, it is the Halakhic portions that form the bulk of the Talmud, and that constitute its importance as the fountainhead of Jewish belief and theology.

In order to give some idea of Talmudic method, an abbreviated example may be cited. In the beginning of the Mishnah occurs this paragraph: 'During what time in the evening may the *Shema'* be recited? From the time when the priests go in (to the Temple) to eat their heave-offering until the first watch of the night, according to R. Eliezer. But the Sages say, until midnight. Rabban Gamaliel says, until the coming of the dawn.' This is the text upon which *Yerushalmi* then comments in three sections. The first section contains the following: a citation from a Baraitha with two sayings of R. Jose to elucidate it; remarks on the position of one who is in doubt whether he has read the *Shema'*; another passage from a Baraitha, designating the appearance of the stars as an indication of the time in question; further explanations and passages on the appearance of the stars as bearing on the ritual; other Rabbinical sayings; a Baraitha on the division between day and night, and other passages bearing on the same subject; discussion of other Baraithas, and further quotations from important Rabbis; a sentence of Tannaitic origin in no way related to the preceding matters, namely, 'One who prays standing must hold his feet straight,' and the controversy on this subject between Rabbis Levi and Simon, the one adding, 'like the angels,' the other, 'like the priests'; comments on the two comparisons; further discussion concerning the beginning of the day; Haggadic statements concerning the dawn; a conversation between two Rabbis; cosmological comments; dimensions of the firmament, and more Haggadic comments; a discussion on the night watches; Haggadic material concerning David and his harp. Then comes the second section, thus: a Rabbinical quotation; a Baraitha on the reading of the *Shema'* in the synagogue; other Rabbinical and Haggadic matter; further Haggadic sayings. Lastly, the third section gives R. Gamaliel's view compared with that of another Rabbi, together with a question that remains unanswered.

As with the Mishnah, the accessibility of the Babylonian Talmud to readers of English has been greatly eased by a new translation, the so-called Soncino Talmud, entitled *The Babylonian Talmud Translated into English*, edited by I. Epstein, in thirty-five volumes (1935–1952). This magnificent work also contains notes, introductions, glossaries, and other kinds of helpful material. There is a good German translation of *Babli* by L. Goldschmidt. The Palestinian Talmud is not as a whole available in English; there is a useful French edition by Moise Schwab, *Le Talmud de Jérusalem*, in twelve volumes (1932–1933).

Another category of Rabbinical literature that should be mentioned in this connexion is the **Midrash** (plural Midrashim). A Midrash is a sort of commentary on a book of the Bible, based directly on the Biblical text taken verse by verse. This literary form is vast, having flourished all the way from the 2nd to the 10th cent. A.D. The earliest, or Tannaitic, Midrashim are *Mekhilta*, on the legal part of Exodus (English translation by Lauterbach); *Siphra*, on Leviticus; *Siphre*, on most of Numbers and the whole of Deuteronomy (partial English translation by Levertoff). The most extensive and important collection of later Midrashim is that called the *Midrash Rabbah*, or Great Midrash, based on the Pentateuch and a few other OT books. There is an epochal translation of this, the Soncino Midrash, or *Midrash Rabbah Translated into English*, edited by H. Freedman and M. Simon, in ten volumes (1939). The earliest Midrashim are more Halakhic, the later mostly Haggadic.

Another important type of Rabbinic literature has a special article in this dictionary; see TARGUMS.

3. The authority of the Talmud in Judaism.—The Oral Law, which with its comments and explanations is what constitutes the Talmud, is regarded as of equal authority with the Written Law. Hence the Talmud is considered, at least by orthodox Jews, as the highest authority on all matters of faith. It is true that in the Talmud itself the letter of Scripture is always clearly differentiated from the rest; but, in the first place, the comments and explanations declare what Scripture means, and without this official explanation the Scriptural passage would lose much of its practical value for the Jew; and, in the second place, it is firmly believed that the oral laws preserved in the Talmud were also delivered to Moses on Mount Sinai. It is, therefore, hardly an exaggeration to say that the Talmud is of equal authority with Scripture in orthodox Judaism.

4. The Talmud and Christianity.—Much that is written in the Talmud was originally spoken by men who were contemporaries of Christ and the early Christians, as was pointed out at the beginning of this article. It is, moreover, well known that a conflict was waged in the infant Church regarding the question of the admission of Gentiles, the result of which was an irreconcilable breach between Jew and Gentile, and an ever-increasing antagonism between Judaism and Christianity. There is, therefore, a likelihood that references to Christ and Christianity could be found in the Talmud. In recent times a number of friendly and objective scholars on both the Christian and Jewish sides have studied this question in considerable detail. The great translations mentioned above have helped immensely in mutual understanding. Jewish scholars have studied the NT and related literature, and Christian scholars have made an approach to the immense difficulties of Talmudic and Rabbinic lore. The present conclusions seem to be that there are indeed a few genuine references to Jesus in early Rabbinic literature, though they are usually veiled and sometimes unfriendly, as might be expected; and that the much-discussed term *Minim* (' heretics ') in the Talmud does sometimes refer to the early Christians, but at other times to Jewish Gnostics or other Jewish heretics. There is no space here to discuss this important matter in detail; it must suffice to mention a few works available in English as indicators of what is being done and as guides to further study: R. T. Herford, *Christianity in Talmud and Midrash* (1903), and several later works on related subjects; J. Klausner, *Jesus of Nazareth* (1925); *idem, From Jesus to Paul* (1943); M. Goldstein, *Jesus in the Jewish Tradition* (1950), accurate, objective, and with an excellent, up-to-date bibliography. The most fruitful result of such study has not been the discovery by Christians of a few isolated references to Jesus and Christianity in the Talmuds or other Rabbinic literature, but the opening up of the Jewish background of Christianity to show the many features possessed in common by the two religions, as well as the differences. Outstanding in this respect is G. F. Moore, *Judaism in the First Centuries of the Christian Era* (3 vols., 1927–1930). Also useful in this connexion is J. Klausner, *The Messianic Idea in Israel* (1955). Unfortunately, H. L. Strack and P. Billerbeck, *Kommentar zum Neuen Testament* (4 vols., 1922–1928), the classic application of this method to NT exegesis, is not available in English. The best available introductory works are: W. O. E. Oesterley and G. H. Box, *A Short Survey of the Literature of Rabbinical and Mediaeval Judaism* (1920); M. Mielziner, *Introduction to the Talmud* (1925); H. L. Strack, *Introduction to the Talmud and Midrash* (1931). W. O. E. O.—**W. F. S.**

TALSAS, 1 Es 9^{22} (AV).—See ELASAH, 1.

TAMAH, Neh 7^{55} (AV).—See TEMAH.

TAMAR.—1. A Canaanite woman, married to Er and then to his brother Onan (see MARRIAGE, **4**). Tamar became by her father-in-law himself the mother of twin sons, Perez and Zerah, Gn 38^{6ff}, Ru 4^{12}, 1 Ch 2^{4}, Mt 1^{3} (AV **Thamar**). **2.** The beautiful sister of Absalom, who was violated and brutally insulted by her half-brother, Amnon, 2 S 13^{1ff}. **3.** A daughter of Absalom, 2 S 14^{27}. Cf MAACAH, **4. 4.** See next article.

TAMAR.—1. A city in the S. of Judah, mentioned as one of the cities rebuilt by Solomon, 1 K 9^{18} (AV **Tadmor,** which follows *Ḳᵉrê* and the Versions, is manifestly wrong; see TADMOR). It is probably to be identified with **Hazazon-tamar** (q.v.). **2.** The SE. boundary mark of the restored Kingdom of Israel in Ezk 47^{19} 48^{28}; perhaps the same as **1**.

TAMARISK.—Hebrew *'ēshel*, Gn 21^{33} (AV **grove,** AVm ' tree ') 1 S 22^{6} (AV ' tree,' AVm ' grove ') 31^{13} (AV ' tree '). There are some eight species of tamarisks in Palestine; they are most common in the Maritime Plain and the Jordan Valley. Though mostly but shrubs, some species attain to the size of large trees. They are characterized by their brittle feathery branches and minute scale-like leaves. RVm gives ' tamarisk ' for AV and RV **' heath '** in Jer 17^{6}, where a species of juniper is meant (RSV ' shrub '). E. W. G. M.

TAMBOURINE.—See TABRET.

TAMMUZ (Ezk 8^{14}) was a Babylonian god whose cult is one of the oldest in the world and still survives in Kurdistan. It spread rapidly in Palestine after *c* 700 B.C. The name is Sumerian, **Du-mu-zi** (' faithful son '). He was the youthful lover of Ishtar and was the vegetation god who died at the time of greatest heat, and returned the following spring. Ishtar descended into the Underworld to bring him back to life. His departure was celebrated by dirges, many of which survive. His ' weeping ' took place on the second of the month Tammuz (June–July). He was identified with the Phoenician Adon (Greek *Adonis*), and with the Egyptian Osiris. Cf Gn 35^{8}, Zec 12^{11}. N. H. S.

TANACH, Jos 21^{25} (AV).—See TAANACH.

TANHUMETH.—The father of Seraiah, one of the Hebrew captains who joined Gedaliah at Mizpah, 2 K 25^{23}, Jer 40^{8}.

TANIS (Jth 1^{10}) = **Zoan** (q.v.).

TANNER.—See ARTS AND CRAFTS, **5**.

TAPESTRY.—See SPINNING AND WEAVING, **6**.

TAPHATH.—Daughter of Solomon and wife of Ben-abinadab, 1 K 4^{11}.

TAPHNES, Jth 1^{9} (AV).—See TAHPANHES.

TAPHON, 1 Mac 9^{50} (AV).—See TEPHON.

TAPPUAH (' apple ').—**1.** A ' son ' of Hebron, 1 Ch 2^{43}. Probably the name is that of a town in the lowland, Jos 15^{34}. There was a **Beth-tappuah** (q.v.) in the hill country. Tappuah is possibly modern *Beit Nettîf*. **2.** A place on the boundary between Ephraim and Manasseh, Jos 16^{8} 17^{8} (cf **En-tappuah**, 17^{7}). It is probably modern *Sheikh Abū Zarad*. In 2 K 15^{16} Tappuah (so RSV, following Lucian's recension of the LXX, instead of AV, RV **Tiphsah**) is said to have been sacked by Menahem. **3.** One of the towns W. of Jordan whose kings Joshua smote, Jos 12^{17}. It was perhaps the same place as **2** above; but this is by no means certain. See also TIPHSAH and TEPHON.

TARAH, Nu 33^{27f} (AV).—See TERAH, **2**.

TARALAH.—An unknown town of Benjamin, Jos 18^{27}.

TAREA.—See TAHREA.

TARES (Gr. *zizania*, Arab. *zuwān*) are certain kinds of darnel growing plentifully in cornfields. The bearded darnel (*Lolium temulentum*) most resembles wheat. The seeds, though often poisonous to human beings on account of parasitic growths in them, are sold as chicken's food. When harvest approaches and the tares can be distinguished, they are carefully weeded out by hand by women and children (cf Mt 13[24–30]). RSV uses ' weeds.' E. W. G. M.

TARGET.—See ARMOUR, ARMS, **2.**

TARGUMS.—Originally the word *targum* meant ' translation ' in reference to any language; but it acquired a restricted meaning, and came to be used only of translation from Hebrew into Aramaic. As early as the time of Ezra we find the verb used in reference to a document written in Aramaic (Ezr 4[7]), though in this passage the addition ' in Aramaic ' is made, showing that the restricted meaning had not yet come into vogue. As early as the time of the Second Temple the language of the Holy Scriptures, Hebrew, was not understood by the bulk of the Jewish people, for it had been supplanted by Aramaic. When, therefore, the Scriptures were read in synagogues, it became necessary to translate them, in order that they might be understood by the congregation. The official translator who performed this duty was called the *methurgeman* or *targeman*, which is equivalent to the modern *dragoman* (' interpreter '). The way in which it was done was as follows:—In the case of the Pentateuch (the ' Law ') a verse was read in Hebrew, and then translated into Aramaic, and so on to the end of the appointed portion; but in the case of the prophetical writings three verses were read and then translated. Whether this sytem was the custom originally may be doubted; it was probably done in a less formal way at first. By degrees the translation became stereotyped, and was ultimately reduced to writing; and thus the Targums, the Aramaic translations of the Hebrew Bible, came into existence. The various Targums which are still extant will be enumerated below. While the texts of the official Targums may not have been fixed until the 5th cent. A.D., they were preceded by earlier written versions. There is a reference in the Talmud to a Targum of Job which Rabbi Gamaliel (*c* A.D. 50) ordered to be built into the wall of the Temple; the work must be earlier than this and probably there is a reference to it in the LXX at Job 42[17]. There is old pre-Christian material in the Jerusalem Targum, and this is now extant in a separate form in the manuscripts published by Paul Kahle in *Masoreten des Westens*, ii, pp. 1–65. Thus, although the evidence does not allow a definite date to be attached to the beginnings of written Targums, it is clear that the process of committing the translation to writing began very early. There are Targums to all the books of the Bible, with the exception of Daniel, Ezra, and Nehemiah; as these are to a large extent written in Aramaic, one can understand why Targums to these books should be wanting. Most of the Targums are mainly paraphrases; the only one which is in the form of a translation in the modern sense of the word is the Targum of Onkelos to the Pentateuch; this is, on the whole, a fairly literal translation. Isolated passages in the Bible which are written in Aramaic, as in Genesis and Jeremiah, are also called Targums. The following is a list of the Targums:

1. Targum of Onkelos to the Pentateuch, called also *Targum Babli*, i.e. the Babylonian Targum.
2. Old Palestinian Targum to the Pentateuch.
3. Jerusalem Targum to the Pentateuch.
4. Targum of Jonathan to the prophetical books (these include what we call the historical books).
5. Jerusalem Targum to the prophetical books.
6. Targum to the Psalms.
7. Targum to Job.
8. Targum to Proverbs.

9–13. Targums to the Five *Megilloth* (' Rolls '), namely: Song of Songs, Ruth, Lamentations, Ecclesiastes, Esther.

14. Targum to Chronicles.

For printed editions of these and references to literature, see Aage Bentzen, *Introduction to the Old Testament*, vol. I., pp. 68–72; B. J. Roberts, *The Old Testament Text and Versions*, pp. 307 ff. A. Sperber has recently published an edition of the Targum of Onkelos with superlinear vocalization, based on the BM manuscript Or. 2363 (Leiden, 1959), and an edition of the Targum of Jonathan on the Former Prophets, based on the BM manuscript Or. 2210, as the first parts of *The Bible in Aramaic*.

The *Targum of Onkelos* is the official, revised, Aramaic version of the Pentateuch, probably Palestinian in origin but in its present form a product of the 5th cent. Babylonian Jews, hence the title *Targum Babli*. It is for the most part a literal translation, only here and there assuming the form of a paraphrase. The Hebrew text behind it is very close to the MT. The name of this Targum owes its origin to a passage in the Babylonian Talmud (*Megillah*, 3*a*), in which it is said: ' The Targum to the Pentateuch was composed by the proselyte Onkelos at the dictation of Rabbi Eliezer and Rabbi Joshua '; and in the Jerusalem Talmud (*Megillah*, 71*c*) it is said: ' Aquila the proselyte translated the Pentateuch in the presence of Rabbi Eliezer and Rabbi Joshua.' That Aquila is the same as Onkelos can scarcely admit of doubt, but that this Aquila is to be identified with the Aquila who in the 1st cent. A.D. produced a literal Greek translation of the OT is not proved; and, though in the tractate *Abodah zarah*, 11*a*, we are told that this Onkelos was the pupil of Rabbi Gamaliel the Elder, who lived in the second half of the 1st cent. A.D., there is a strong probability that the names Onkelos and Aquila are but conventional labels; cf the names Jonathan and Theodotion. It is characteristic of the Targum of Onkelos that, unlike the other Targums, the Midrashic element is greatly subordinated to simple translation; when it does appear it is mainly in poetic passages, though not exclusively (cf Gn 49, Nu 24, Dt 32[33], which are prophetic in character). Though it has been said that ' the idea apparently was that greater licence was permitted in dealing with passages of this kind than with those in which the legal element predominated,' a more likely explanation is that this material represents an earlier stage in the history of this Targum, before the version was revised to bring it into closer conformity with the Hebrew. As with the Targums generally, so with that of Onkelos, there is a marked tendency to avoid anthropomorphisms and expressions which might appear derogatory to the dignity of God; this may be seen, for example, in Gn 11[4], where the words ' The Lord came down,' which seemed anthropomorphic, are rendered in this Targum, ' the Lord revealed Himself.' Then again, the transcendent character of the Almighty is emphasized by substituting for the Divine Person intermediate agencies like the *Memra*, or ' Word ' of God, the *Shekinah*, or ' Glory ' of God, to which a more or less distinct personality is imputed; in this way it was sought to avoid ascribing to God Himself actions or words which were deemed unfitting to the inexpressible majesty and transcendence of the Almighty. A good example of this, and one which will also illustrate the general character of this Targum, is the following; it is the rendering of Gn 3[8ff]; ' And they heard the voice of the Word (*Memra*) of the Lord God walking in the garden in the evening of the day; and Adam and his wife hid themselves from before the Lord God among the trees of the garden. And the Lord God called to Adam and said: " Where art thou? " And he said: " The voice of Thy *Word* (*Memra*) I heard in the garden, and I was afraid, because I was naked, and I would hide." '

The *Old Palestinian Targum*, which preceded the official Targum of Onkelos, exists in fragments of several MSS which came from the Geniza or lumber-room of the synagogue of Old Cairo and which were published by Kahle in *Mas. d. Westens* ii. This Targum is less literal than the official Targum and contains much more explanatory matter. Its text is related to the text of the Syriac Peshitta version, and its language is the current Aramaic of the people of Palestine, whereas by the time the Targum of Onkelos was finalised Aramaic was no longer current speech in Palestine and so an artificial literary form, the creation of the Babylonian Rabbis, was used. An interesting illustration of the difference between the interpretation of this pre-standard Targum and that later adopted officially may be perceived by comparing the RSV text at Ex 22[5f], which agrees with the official view, with that given in Smith-Goodspeed, *The Bible, an American Translation*, which here follows the interpretation of the Old Palestinian Targum.

Under the heading *Jerusalem Targum* come two forms of this Targum: one complete, the other in fragments. The latter, called also the *Fragment Targum*, exists also in two forms. The fragments have been gathered from a variety of sources, from MSS and from quotations in the writings of ancient authors. A copy of a Targum on the Pentateuch dating from the 15th cent. has been discovered in the Vatican Library (Neofiti 1), and it is claimed that this is a complete copy of the Fragment Targum (cf Díez-Macho, *Sefarad* xvii (1957), 117–121). Akin to these in language and outlook is the third Jerusalem Targum, sometimes erroneously called the 'Targum of Jonathan ben Uzziel on the Pentateuch.' But though this Jonathan was believed to be the author of the Targum to the Prophets which bears his name (see below), there was not the slightest ground for ascribing to him the authorship of this Targum to the Pentateuch. The mistake arose because this Targum was referred to as 'Targum J,' and the 'J,' which stood for 'Jerushalmi,' was in the 14th cent. wrongly taken to refer to Jonathan ben Uzziel. So tenaciously has the wrong name clung to this Targum, that a kind of compromise is made as to its title, and it is often known as the 'Targum of pseudo-Jonathan.' This Targum is like that of Onkelos in its avoidance of anthropomorphisms and in its desire not to bring God into too close contact with man; for example, in Ex 34[5] the words: 'And the Lord descended in a cloud, and stood with him there, and proclaimed the name of the Lord' are rendered by the Targum as: 'The Lord revealed Himself in the clouds of the glory of His Shekinah,' thus avoiding what in the original text appeared to detract from the dignity of the Almighty. This kind of thing occurs with great frequency, and it is both interesting and important, as showing the evolution of the idea of God among the Jews. But in other respects this Targum differs from that of Onkelos, especially in its being far less a translation than a free paraphrase. Mohammed's wife and daughter are mentioned in the Targum of pseudo-Jonathan, and, if the names are not a later insertion, this would date the Targum as not earlier than the 7th cent. A.D. But this applies only to its final form, and it is generally agreed that in the Jerusalem Targum 'there are elements of translation and Halakhah which go back to an early period' (B. J. Roberts, *op. cit.* p. 204).

As the Targum of Onkelos was the official version of the Pentateuch, so the *Targum of Jonathan to the Prophets* was also an official recension. It owes its name to an ancient tradition, according to which Jonathan ben Uzziel composed it 'from the mouths of Haggai, Zechariah, and Malachi' (*Megillah*, 3*a*); this is merely a figurative way of saying that the traditional interpretation, as supposed to have been handed down by these prophets, was embodied in written form by Jonathan. It is said of him that when he occupied himself with the study of the Law, every bird that happened to fly over his head got burned, the reason being that so many angels had gathered around him to hear the words of the Law from his mouth (*Sukkah*, 28*a*). Jonathan was a pupil of Hillel and therefore lived during the middle and end of the 1st cent. A.D. (*Baba bathra*, 134*a*). But the date of the Targum cannot be deduced from this, for Jonathan is the Hebrew form of Theodotion, the name of the author of a Greek version of the OT, and the Hebrew name may have been attached to the Targum under the influence of the name of the Greek author, and only later was the name Jonathan connected with Hillel's pupil. In language, origin, and history the Targum of Jonathan resembles that of Onkelos, which indeed is often quoted verbatim. While the official editing of the Targum must be placed in Babylonia not earlier than the 5th cent. A.D., it must contain older Palestinian material. An interesting example of the Targum's treatment of the Biblical text is afforded by Is 53, where 'it is curious to note that the passages which refer to the humiliation of the Servant are interpreted of the people of Israel, while those which speak of the glory of the Servant are referred to the Messiah' (Oesterley and Box, *The Religion and Worship of the Synagogue*, p. 49). Professor Pinhas Churgin explains the fact that the 'man of sorrows' appears in terms of pride and exaltation and the defeat of the enemies of Israel by supposing that the translation was made at the time of bar Cochba (*c* A.D. 135) and reflects the contemporary political situation.

The *Jerusalem Targum to the prophetical books* is extant only in fragmentary form, notably as glosses in the Karlsruhe *Codex Reuchlinianus* (A.D. 1105), edited in 1872 by P. de Lagarde. These resemble the Jerusalem Targum to the Pentateuch and may have a similar history and represent the pre-official translation.

The Targums to the Writings are of various types. The Targum to the Psalms is sometimes literal, sometimes paraphrastic, which may point to different origins; and there are also signs in it of editorial activity, for example, in the conflate reading at Ps 97[11]. The fact that Mt 27[46] quotes from the Aramaic form of Ps 22 is relevant to the discussion of the age of the Targum. Very similar in character is the Targum to Job, while that to Proverbs is based not on the Hebrew but the Peshitta. The Targums to the Megilloth are Midrashes of different dates; on Esther there are three, one more literal and the others elaborate paraphrases, that called *Targum Sheni* being very popular. Finally, the Targum to Chronicles is usually fairly literal but it contains also Haggadic passages, which suggests a varied origin. There is no official revision of the Targums to the Writings.

The Targums are important not only for the study of Jewish theology and the history of Jewish exegesis but also for the proper understanding of the NT writings.

W. O. E. O.—W. D. McH.

TARPELITES.—One of the peoples settled in the cities of Samaria, Ezr 4[9] (RSV 'the officials'). As a gentilic it is unknown.

TARSHISH.—1. See following article. **2.** A Benjamite family, 1 Ch 7[10] (AV **Tharshish**). **3.** One of the seven princes who had the right of access to the royal presence, Est 1[14]. **4.** The name of a precious stone, Ex 28[20] 39[13], Ezr 1[16] 10[9] 28[13], Ca 5[14], Dn 10[6]. See Jewels and Precious Stones.

TARSHISH.—1. A place far from Palestine (Jon 1[3] 4[2]), probably in the extreme W. of the Mediterranean. If Sheba and Dedan stand for the commerce of the East, Tarshish may stand for that of the West (Ezk 38[13]). It is mentioned in Jer 10[9] as the source of silver and, in Ezk 27[12], also of iron, tin, and lead. This indicates Spain and even the regions beyond the Straits. The Greeks were in touch with Tartessus in the 7th and 6th cents. B.C. (Herod. i. 163; iv. 152). The *Onomasticon* refers to *Tharseis hē Baitikē*, which points to the region of the Guadalquivir, anciently the *Baetis*. The name *Tarseion* occurs in a commercial treaty (Polyb. iii. 24) referring to a city of the Carthaginians in Spain.

The form of the word suggests a verbal noun derived from the root *ršš*. This is found in Akkadian in connexion with bright metals and mining products, so that Tarshish may have originally been a common noun, perhaps signifying 'metal refinery.' We may further note that one of the copper-smelting sites explored by Glueck in the Arabah is called *Mrashshash*. In any case it is significant that Tarshish and ships of Tarshish are generally mentioned in connexion with metal.

'Ships of Tarshish' did not necessarily belong to, or trade with, Tarshish, but signified large ocean-going ships voyaging primarily to the mines and refineries of the far West (Is 2[16] 23[1], Ezk 27[25], Ps 48[7]), but also as in the case of Solomon's navy (1 K 10[22]; cf 1 K 22[48]), sailing S. and E. *from* the copper refineries of Ezion-geber. W. E.—**J. Gr.**

TARSUS, the capital of the Roman province of Cilicia (Ac 22[3]) in the SE. of Asia Minor, and the birth-place of Paul, is a place about which much more might be known than is known if only the ancient city could be excavated in the way that Pompeii, Olympia, Pergamum, and other cities have been excavated. Tarsus, as a city whose institutions combined Oriental and Western characteristics, was signally fitted to be the birthplace and training ground of him who was to make known to the Gentile world the ripest development of Hebrew religion.

Tarsus (modern *Tersous*) is situated in the plain of Cilicia, about 70 to 80 feet above sea-level, and about 10 miles from the S. coast. The level plain stretches to the north of it for about 2 miles, and then begins to rise gradually till it merges in the lofty Taurus range, about 30 miles N. The climate of the low-lying city must always have been oppressive and unfavourable to energetic action, but the undulating country to the N. was utilized to counteract its effects. About 9 to 12 miles N. of the city proper there was a second Tarsus, within the territory of the main Tarsus, in theory a summer residence merely, but in reality a fortified town of importance, permanently inhabited. It was to periodical residence in this second city among the hills that the population owed their vigour. In Roman times the combined cities of Tarsus contained a large population.

The history of the Maritime Plain of Cilicia was determined by the mutual rivalries of the three cities, Mallus on the Pyramus, Adana on the Sarus, and Tarsus on the Cydnus. The plain is mainly a deposit of the second of those rivers, and contains about 800 square miles of arable land, with a strip of useless land along the coast varying from 2 to 3 miles in breadth. The site of Mallus has been rediscovered at *Kara-Tash*, S. of Adana. The other two cities retain their names and some of their importance to the present day. In ancient times Mallus was a serious rival of Tarsus, and was at first the great harbour and the principal Greek colony in Cilicia. The struggle for superiority lasted till after the time of Christ, but the supremacy was eventually resigned to Tarsus. The river Cydnus flowed through the middle of the city. This river, of which the inhabitants were very proud, was liable to rise very considerably when there had been heavy rains in the mountains, but inundation in the city was in the best period very carefully guarded against. Between A.D. 527 and 563 a new channel was cut to relieve the principal bed, which had for some time previously been insufficiently dredged, and it is in this new channel that the Cydnus now flows, the original channel having become completely choked. About 5 or 6 miles below the modern town the Cydnus flowed into a lake ; this lake was the ancient harbour of Tarsus, where were the docks and arsenal. At the harbour town, which was called Aulai, all the larger ships discharged, and in ancient times buildings were continuous between the north of this lake and the city of Tarsus. Much engineering skill must have been employed in ancient times to make a harbour out of what had been a lagoon, and to improve the channel of the river. This city lies on the road to one of the greatest passes of ancient times, the 'Cilician Gates.' Cilicia is divided from Cappadocia and Lycaonia by the Taurus range of mountains, which is pierced from NW. to SE. by a glen along which flows the Tchakut Su. This glen offers a natural road for much of its course, but there are serious difficulties to overcome in its southern part. A waggon road runs over the hills there, and a level path has been cut out of the solid rock on the western bank of the stream, perhaps already by the Hittite kings.

Shalmaneser III., king of Assyria, captured Tarsus about the middle of the 9th cent. B.C. as did Sennacherib. 696 B.C. Neriglissar campaigned in Ḫume (E. Cilicia) in 556 B.C. Afterwards kings ruled over Cilicia, with the Persian kings as overlords. In 401 B.C. there was still a king with the name or title Syennesis, but not in 334 B.C., when Alexander the Great entered the country. It then was governed by the Satrap Arsames. During the 4th cent. Tarsus was subject to the Greek kings of Syria of the Seleucid dynasty. It continued during the 3rd cent. in abject submission to them. The peace of 189 B.C. changed the position of Cilicia. Previous to that date it had been in the middle of the Seleucid territory. Now it became a frontier country. About 175–164 B.C. Tarsus was reorganized by Antiochus IV. Epiphanes as an autonomous city under the name Antioch-on-the-Cydnus (cf 2 Mac 4[30f, 36]). It is extremely probable that the exact date of this refoundation was 171–170 B.C. ; the new name lasted only a few years. Not only Tarsus, but a number of other Cilician cities also were reorganized at this time, but Tarsus received the most honourable treatment.

The population of this reconstituted Tarsus in addition to what remained of the earlier population, consisted of Dorian Greeks from Argos. That the Greek element in the population was mainly Dorian is proved by the fact that the chief magistrates bore the Dorian title *damiourgos*. A mythology was invented to prove that this Dorian element was much earlier. It is likely that a large body of Jews also was added to the population by Antiochus. These would be incorporated in a new tribe by themselves, to enable them to practise their own religion unhindered. St. Paul, and probably the 'kinsmen' of Ro 16[7, 11, 21], were citizens of Tarsus enrolled in the Jewish tribe. As the Seleucid empire decayed, the Greek element in Tarsus became weaker, and the Asiatic spirit revived. About 83 B.C. its influence swept over Cilicia with the armies of Tigranes, king of Armenia, under whose power Tarsus fell. For about twenty years it continued under Oriental domination, till the reorganization of the East by Pompey the Great in 65–64 B.C. The Roman province Cilicia had been instituted about 104 or 102 B.C., but Tarsus was not then included in it. It was established mainly to control piracy in the Levant, and included the S. and E. of Asia Minor, but was not sharply defined in extent. In 25 B.C. the province GALATIA (q.v.) was established by Augustus, and Cilicia in the narrow sense became a mere adjunct of Syria. Tarsus was the capital even of the large province Cilicia, and remained that of the smaller under the Empire, which brought many blessings to the provinces and their cities. Experience of the barbarian Tigranes caused a revulsion in favour of Hellenism, and the Tarsians were enthusiastic for the Empire, which carried on the work of Hellenism. Cassius forced them, in 43 B.C., to take his and Brutus' side against Octavian and Antony, but they returned to their former loyalty on the earliest opportunity. Tarsus was made a free city (that is, it was governed by its own laws) by Antony, who met Cleopatra here. This privilege was confirmed by Octavian in or after 31 B.C. It is likely that Pompey, Julius Caesar, Antony, and Augustus all conferred Roman citizenship on some Tarsians, and these would take new names from their benefactors : Gnaeus Pompeius from Pompey, Gaius Iulius from Julius Caesar or Augustus, Marcus Antonius from Antony. The Roman administration probably trusted more to the Jewish than to the Greek element. The latter was capricious, and was restrained by the Stoic Athenodorus, a Tarsian, who had the influence of Augustus behind him. The Oriental element seems to have thus become more assertive, and about A.D. 100 it was predominant. This Athenodorus lived from about 74 B.C. till A.D. 7. He was a Stoic philosopher, distinguished for his lectures and writings. He gained a great and noble influence over Augustus, who was his pupil, and he remained in Rome from 45 B.C. till 15 B.C. as his adviser ; in the latter year he retired to Tarsus. There he attempted by persuasion to reform local politics ; but being unsuccessful, he used the authority granted him by Augustus, and banished the more corrupt of the politicians. A property qualification was now required for possession of the citizenship. (Among these citizens the Roman citizens formed an aristocracy.) Athenodorus was succeeded by Nestor, an Academic philosopher (still living A.D. 19). These men had influence also in the university, which was more closely connected with the city than in modern times. A new lecturer had to be recognized by some competent body. There was a great enthusiasm in Tarsus and neighbourhood for learning and philosophy, and in this respect the city was unequalled in Greece. It was here that Paul learned sympathy with athletics, and tolerance for the good elements in pagan religion. The principal deity of Tarsus was Sandon (*Ba'al Tarz*), who was identified with Heracles. A. So.—**E. G. K.**

TARTAK.—An idol introduced by the Avvites into Samaria when Sargon of Assyria transported them thither, 2 K 17[31]. This deity is mentioned along with another called **Nibhaz,** and, according to the Babylonian Talmud, was worshipped in the form of an ass. In Assyro-Babylonian mythology no such deity is at present provable; moreover, the geographical position of the Avvites is uncertain, and their city may have been in one of the western States of Asia. A connexion with *Atargates* has been suggested. LXX[A] replaces *Tartak* by *Naibas*, but this may be merely a corruption of *Nibhaz*. T. G. P.

TARTAN.—The title borne by two Assyrian officers, one of whom was sent by Sargon to Ashdod (Is 20[1]), while the other, with the **Rab-saris** and the **Rab-shakeh,** was sent by Sennacherib to demand from Hezekiah the surrender of Jerusalem (2 K 18[17]). The word is a transcription in Hebrew of the Assyrian *tartânû* or *tardinnu*, the second in command of the army. L. W. K.

TARTARUS.—See GEHENNA.

TASSEL.—See FRINGES.

TATNAI, Ezr 5[3, 6] 6[6, 13] (AV).—See TATTENAI.

TATTENAI.—The name of the governor of Coele-Syria and Phoenicia under Darius Hystaspis, Ezr 5[3, 6] 6[6, 13] (AV **Tatnai**). He is called **Sisinnes** in 1 Es 6[3, 7, 27] 7[1]; this is simply a reproduction in Greek of a Persian name *Thithinaia* (original *Thathanaia*?), with aspirated *t*.

TATTOO.—Found only in RSV in Lv 19[28], where AV and RV have ' print.' The Hebrew word is found only here in OT.

TAU or **TAW.**—Twenty-second letter of Hebrew alphabet, and so used to introduce the twenty-second part of Ps 119, every verse of which begins with this letter.

TAVERNER'S BIBLE.—See ENGLISH VERSIONS, **21.**

TAVERNS, THREE (Lat. *Tres Tabernae*).—A name of uncertain origin, which might be translated ' three shops ' or ' three huts.' It was a station on the Appian Road (built 321 B.C.) which went from Rome to the S. along the W. coast. This was the principal road for all travellers to or from the S. and E., except those who embarked at Ostia at the mouth of the Tiber. The village was about 33 Roman miles from Rome, and to this point many Christians walked, or drove, to meet Paul on his arrival in Italy from the E. (Ac 28[15]). A. So.

TAW.—See TAU.

TAX COLLECTOR.—See PUBLICAN.

TAX OFFICE.—See CUSTOM(S). AV has ' receipt of custom,' and RV ' place of toll.'

TAXES, TAXING.—See KING, **2** (5), PUBLICAN, TRIBUTE, QUIRINIUS.

TEACHER, TEACHING.—See EDUCATION.

TEBAH.—A ' son ' of Nahor, Gn 22[24]; probably a tribal name. See TIBHATH.

TEBALIAH.—A Merarite gatekeeper, 1 Ch 26[11].

TEBETH.—See TIME.

TEHAPHNEHES (Ezk 30[18]).—See TAHPANHES.

TEHINNAH.—The father of Ir-nahash, 1 Ch 4[12].

TEIL TREE.—In Is 6[13] AV has this mistranslation for **terebinth** (q.v.), as in RV, RSV. See also OAK.

TEKEL.—See MENE MENE TEKEL AND PARSIN.

TEKOA (**Tekoah** in AV in 2 S 14[2, 49] and in RV in 1 Mac 9[33]; **Thecoe** in AV in 1 Mac 9[33]).—A fortress city on the edge of the wilderness to which it gave its name, 2 Ch 20[20]. From here came the ' wise woman ' sent by Joab to plead for Absalom, 2 S 14[2, 4, 9]. Rehoboam fortified it, 2 Ch 11[6]; and apparently it continued to be a fortress, Jer 6[1]. Amos was among the shepherds of Tekoa, Am 1[1]. Tekoa is mentioned also in LXX in Jos 15[59], and in the genealogies in 1 Ch 4[5–8]. The site is now *Kh. Teqû'*, an extended but shapeless mass of ruins crowning the summit of a hill (2790 feet above sea level), 5 miles S. of Bethlehem. It is on the extreme edge of the cultivated lands. Bethlehem, the Mount of Olives, and *Nebi Samwil* (Mizpah) are all visible from it. A. R. S. K.

TEKOAH.—See TEKOA.

TEL-ABIB (? ' hill of corn ').—A place on the Chebar, Ezk 3[15]. The site is unknown.

TELAH.—An Ephraimite, 1 Ch 7[25].

TELAIM (' the lambs ').—The place at which Saul concentrated his forces, and numbered his fighting men before his campaign against the Amalekites, 1 S 15[4]. The LXX reads *Gilgal* for Telaim, and Josephus (*Ant.* VI. vii. 2 [134]) also makes Gilgal the place of assembly. A more suitable locality for the place of assembly would, however, be in the Negeb, or South; and here lay **Telem** (q.v.), with which Telaim is probably identical.

TELASSAR (' Ashur's hill or mound ').—This city is mentioned with Gozan, Haran, and Rezeph and is spoken of as a place inhabited by ' the people (AV and RV ' children ') of Eden ' (2 K 19[12] [AV **Thelasar**], Is 37[12]). Assyrian inscriptions mention two places so called, one being *Til-Ashuri*, mentioned by Tiglath-pileser III., which had a renowned temple dedicated to Marduk and is stated to have been a Babylonian foundation. The other written *Til-Aššur*, is referred to by Esarhaddon as having been conquered by him (the people of Mihrānu, he says, called it *Pitānu*). It was inhabited by the people of Barnaki—a name which Delitzsch points out as similar to the Parnach of Nu 34[25]. This *Til-Aššur* is supposed to have lain near the land of Mitanni (Upper Mesopotamia), which would find support if *Mihrānu* be connected with the Mehri mentioned by Tukulti-Ninurta I. T. G. P.—**C. J. M. W.**

TELEM.—**1.** A gatekeeper who had married a foreign wife, Ezr 10[24], 1 Es 9[25] (AV, RV **Tolbanes**); perhaps the same as **Talmon** (q.v.). **2.** A town in Judah, Jos 15[24]; possibly the same as **Telaim** (q.v.). The exact site is unknown.

TEL-HARESHA, Neh 7[61] (AV).—See TEL-HARSHA.

TEL-HARSA, Ezr 2[59] (AV).—See TEL-HARSHA.

TEL-HARSHA.—A Babylonian town of unknown site, Ezr 2[59] (AV **Tel-harsa**), Neh 7[61] (AV **Tel-haresha**), 1 Es 5[36] (AV, RV **Thelersas**).

TELL.—See TALE.

TELL EL-AMARNA.—The modern name of Akhetaten, the city built by Akhenaten (*c* 1366–1350 B.C.) as the centre of his religious reform; on the E. bank of the Nile, about 190 miles S. of Cairo. The city lies in a great bay in the desert, 8 miles long, 3 miles wide, and is built around three roads parallel with the river. The principal units are: the South City, houses of nobles and a manufacturing quarter; Central City with the main temple, official and private palace, Foreign Office in which the Amarna Letters were found, and administrative offices; North Suburb, partly a merchants' quarter, partly a slum; the North City containing the palace to which Nefertiti was banished, offices, and a customs house. A mile to the E. of the main city was a small workers' village, and in the cliffs the tombs of the nobles. Included in the city was a large area on the W. bank that provided food for the inhabitants. Abandoned by Tutankhamun three or four years after the death of Akhenaten, all official buildings were destroyed by Haremhab and Ramesses II. and the site was never again inhabited. See AKHENATEN. H. W. F.

TEL-MELAH (' hill of salt ').—A Babylonian town of unknown site, Ezr 2^{59}, Neh 7^{61}, 1 Es 5^{36} (AV, RV **Thermeleth**).

TEMA.—A son of Ishmael, Gn 25^{15}, 1 Ch 1^{30}. The country and people meant are still represented by the same name—the modern Teimā, a large oasis about 200 miles SE. of the head of the Gulf of 'Aqaba, and the same distances due N. of Medina in W. Arabia. It was an important community in ancient times, mentioned in Assyrian annals of the 8th cent. B.C., and later inhabited in part by Aramaeans, who have left inscriptions. It was noted for its caravan traffic (Job 6^{19}, Is 21^{14}), as might be expected from its position on the great trade routes. In Jer 25^{23} it is mentioned with ' all who cut the corners of their hair.' J. F. McC.

TEMAH.—A family of Nethinim (q.v.) mentioned in Ezr 2^{53} (AV **Thamah**), Neh 7^{55} (AV **Tamah**), 1 Es 5^{32} **(AV Thomoi, RV Thomei).**

TEMAN.—A tribe (and district) of Edom, whose importance is indicated by its eponym being the eldest son of the eldest son (Eliphaz) of Esau (Gn $36^{11, 15}$, 1 Ch 1^{36}; cf Gn 36^{42}, 1 Ch 1^{53}) and by its being taken along with Bozrah (q.v.) to represent the whole land of Edom (Am 1^{12}; cf Ob ^{9}). Ezk 25^{13} implies that Edom stretches from Teman to Dedan, from which we infer that the former lay in the NE. of the territory claimed by Edom, that is, to the SE. of Moab. Its inhabitants were renowned for wisdom (Jer 49^{7}), and the chief of Job's counsellors was Eliphaz ' the **Temanite** ' (Job 2^{11}). J. F. McC.

TEMENI.—The ' son ' of Ashhur, 1 Ch 4^{6}.

TEMPERANCE.—**1.** In the RV ' temperance ' is the translation of the Greek word *enkrateia*, the root-meaning of which is ' power over oneself,' ' self-mastery.' It is a comprehensive virtue, and on this account **' self-control,'** the translation of RVm, RSV, is to be preferred (Ac 24^{25}, Gal 5^{23}, 2 P 1^{6}). The corresponding adjective is found only in Tit 1^{8}, and the verb only in 1 Co 7^{9} 9^{25}. The negative form of the adjective is translated ' without self-control ' (2 Ti 3^{3}), and of the noun ' excess ' (Mt 23^{25}), and ' incontinency ' (1 Co 7^{5}). The RV translates another Greek word (*nēphalios*) ' temperate ' in 1 Ti $3^{2, 11}$, Tit 2^{2}; its root-meaning points to the avoidance of intemperance in the form of drunkenness, but in actual usage it condemns all forms of self-indulgence. This extension of its significance must be remembered in expounding the passages in which the corresponding verb is found, for the RV (and RSV except 2 Ti 4^{5}) always translates it (*nēphein*) ' to be **sober** ' (1 Th $5^{6, 8}$, 2 Ti 4^{5}, 1 P 1^{13} 4^{7} 5^{8}).

2. From the philosophical point of view, ' self-control ' is mastery over the passions; it is the virtue which holds the appetites in check; the rational will has power to regulate conduct without being unduly swayed by sensuous appetites. From the NT point of view the grace of ' self-control ' is the result of the Holy Spirit's indwelling; it is the Spirit-controlled personality alone that is ' strengthened with power ' (Eph 3^{16}; cf 5^{18}) to control rebellious desires and to resist the allurements of tempting pleasures.

3. The NT passages in which reference is made to this virtue form an instructive study. To Felix, with an adulteress by his side, Paul discoursed on ' self-control,' directing his stern condemnation against the vice of unchastity (cf 1 Co $7^{5, 9}$). But to every form of ' excess ' (Mt 23^{25}) it is directly opposed. In 1 Ti 3^{3} ' not given over to wine ' (*paroinos*, RSV ' drunkard ') balances ' temperate ' (v.^{2}, cf v.^{8}), and from this chapter it is plain that the Apostle regards violent quarrelling (v.^{3}), false and reckless speech (v.^{8}), self-conceit (v.^{6}), greed of filthy lucre (v.^{8}), as well as fondness for much wine (v.^{8}), as manifold forms of intemperance by whose means men ' fall into reproach and the snare of the devil ' (v.^{7}).

4. ' Self-control,' in its widest sense, as including mastery over all tempers, appetites, and passions, has a prominent place in two NT lists of the Christian graces. In 2 P 1^{6}, faith is regarded as the germ of every virtue; it lays hold of the ' divine power ' which makes possible the life of godliness (v.^{3}). The evolution of faith in ' manliness, knowledge, self-control ' is the reward of its ' diligent ' culture (v.^{8}). This ' self-control,' as Principal Iverach says, ' grows out of knowledge, it is using Christian knowledge for the guidance of life ' (*The Other Side of Greatness*, p. 110). In Gal 5^{23}, ' self-control ' closes the list of the graces which are all ' the fruit of the Spirit,' just as ' drunkenness and revellings ' close the list of ' the works of the flesh ' (v.^{21}). The flesh and the Spirit—these, indeed, are ' contrary the one to the other ' (v.^{17}). The flesh triumphs when the Spirit is quenched; but the Spirit's victory is gained, not by suppressing, but by controlling, the flesh. Those who are ' led by the Spirit ' (v.^{18}), who ' live by the Spirit ' and ' by the Spirit also walk ' (v.^{25}) attain, in its perfection, the grace of complete ' self-control.'
J. G. T.—**J. Ba.**

TEMPEST.—See GALILEE [SEA OF], **3**; WHIRLWIND.

TEMPLE.—**1.** The first Temple mentioned in connexion with the worship of Y″ is that of Shiloh (1 S 1), ' where the ark of God was ' (3^{3}) in the period of the Judges, under the guardianship of Eli and his sons. It was evidently destroyed by the Philistines after their decisive victory which resulted in the capture of the Ark, as recorded in 4^{10ff}; for the descendants of Eli are found, a generation afterwards, acting as priests of a temple at **Nob** (21^{1ff} 22^{9ff}). With the capture of Jerusalem by David, and the transference thither of the Ark, a new political and religious centre was provided for the tribes of Israel.

2. SOLOMON'S TEMPLE.—*The site.*—The successive Temples of Solomon, Zerubbabel, and Herod were buildings of moderate dimensions, and were built, by every token, on one and the same site. Now, there is only one place in Jerusalem where this site is to be looked for, namely, on that part of the eastern hill which is now occupied by the large platform, extending to some 35 acres, known as the *Ḥaram esh-sharîf* or ' Noble Sanctuary ' (see JERUSALEM, and below, **11**). There has, however, been considerable difference of opinion in the past as to the precise spot within the Ḥaram area on which the ' holy house ' itself was reared. Thus a few British writers, among whom Fergusson, the distinguished architect, and W. Robertson Smith, in his article ' Temple ' in the *EBrit*^{9}, are the most influential, have maintained that the Temple and its courts occupied an area about 600 feet square in the SW. portion of the Ḥaram. But the great majority of scholars, both in Britain and abroad, are agreed in placing the Temple in close connexion with the sacred rock (*eṣ-Ṣakhra*) which is now enclosed in the mosque named after it ' the Dome of the Rock,' also, less appropriately, ' the Mosque of Omar.'

The remarkable persistence of sacred sites in the East, is a phenomenon familiar to all students of religion, and there can be little doubt that the Chronicler is right in identifying the site of ' the altar of burnt offering for Israel ' (1 Ch 22^{1}) with the spot ' by the threshing-floor of Ornan (in 2 S 24^{16} Araunah) the Jebusite,' where the angel of the plague stayed his hand, and on which David by Divine command erected his altar of commemoration (see further, **6** (*b*)). This being so, the location of the Temple *immediately to the west of the rock* follows as a matter of course. The only possible alternative is to regard the rock as marking the site, not of the altar of burnt-offering, but of ' the holy of holies ' of the successive Temples—a view beset with insuperable difficulties.

3. *The Temple building—Its arrangement and dimensions.*—The Temple and its furniture are described in 1 K 6^{1-38} 7^{13-51}—two passages which are, unfortunately, among the most difficult in the OT. This is partly by reason of the perplexing technical terms employed, but mostly because of the unsatisfactory nature of the received text. This latter difficulty seems to be due to the fact that the details of Solomon's Temple have been ' corrected ' by a scribe who knew the Second Temple and believed that the Second Temple was a replica of the First.

The most recent account of the Temple is A. Parrot, *The Temple of Jerusalem* (1957). Earlier books are G. A. Smith, *Jerusalem* (1908), vol. ii. (with plans), which deals fully with all the Temples, F. J. Hollis, *The Archaeology of Herod's Temple* (1934), Fathers Vincent and Abel, *Jerusalem II* (1926). Apart from the standard commentaries, the most useful of which for the textual difficulties is Burney's *Notes on the Hebrew Text of the Books of Kings* (1903), there are many articles, the chief of which are Vincent's articles in *RB*, 1907 and 1954, and G. E. Wright's articles in *BA*, 1941 and 1955.

The Temple proper was an oblong building, 60 cubits in length by 20 in breadth (1 K 6[2]), with a porch in front, facing eastwards, of the same width as the main building and 10 cubits in depth. These, however, are inside measurements, as is evident from vv.[20, 24, 27]. The corresponding outside measurements depend, of course, upon the thickness of the walls, which is nowhere stated. But inasmuch as Ezekiel, the Temple of whose vision is presumably, in part at least, a replica of that of Solomon, gives 6 cubits as the thickness of its walls (Ezk 41[5]), except the walls of the porch, which were 5 cubits thick (40[48]), those of the first Temple are usually assumed to have been of the same dimensions. Less they could scarcely have been, if, as will presently appear, rebatements of three cubits in all have to be allowed in the lower half, since a thickness of 3 cubits in the upper half seems necessary, in view of the thrust of a heavy roof of 20 cubits' span.

The interior was divided into two chambers by a transverse partition, implied in 6[31], but disregarded in the inside measurements given in v.[2]. The anterior chamber, called 'the **house**' and the *hêkhāl* (Temple), measured 40 cubits by 20. It has been equated by the editor with the **holy place** of the Second Temple. It was twice as large as the inner chamber, the *d^ebhîr* (EV 'oracle'), which was only 20 cubits by 20, and was identified by the editor with the **most holy place** (literally 'holy of holies'). The latter in fact formed a perfect cube, since its height was also 20 cubits, as compared with that of 'the holy place,' which was 30 cubits (6[2]). Assuming that this was also the height of the porch, the whole building, we may conjecture, was covered by a flat roof of uniform height throughout, leaving an empty space 10 cubits in height over the inner chamber.

On all sides, except the front which was occupied by the porch, the Temple proper was surrounded by a lateral building of three storeys, the whole 15 cubits high (so the emended text of v.[11]), each storey containing a number of small chambers for storage purposes. The beams forming the floors and ceilings of these **side chambers** were not let into the Temple wall, but were supported by making three successive rebatements of a cubit each in the wall (v.[6]). The chambers accordingly increased a cubit in width in each storey, from 5 in the lowermost storey to 6 and 7 in those above. The entrace to the side chambers was on the S. side of the building. The nature and position of the **windows** which were made 'for the house' are alike uncertain. Openings fitted with lattice work are probably intended (v.[4]). Their position was most likely in the side walls above the roof of the lateral building.

The question of the area covered by the complete building now described has usually been answered hitherto by a reference to Ezekiel's Temple, which was exactly 100 cubits by 50. But a careful comparison of the measurements of the two Temples makes it extremely probable that the numbers just given are due to Ezekiel's fondness for operating with 50 and its multiples. It is therefore most probable that the prophet has not only increased the depth of the porch from 10 to 12 cubits (Ezk 40[49] LXX), but has likewise added to the thickness of the walls of the side-chambers and of the interior partition wall. For if the former are taken as 3 cubits in thickness, as compared with Ezekiel's 5, *i.e.* of the same dimensions as the upper half of the Temple walls, and the partition as 1 cubit thick in place of 2 (Ezk 41[3]), we find the area of the whole building to be 96 cubits by 48, the same relative proportion (2 : 1), it will be noted, as is found in Ezekiel. Similarly, the outside width of the *naos* or sanctuary proper (32 cubits) stood to the total width as 2 : 3.

In the existing uncertainty as to the length of the cubit employed by Solomon's architects, it is impossible to translate these dimensions into feet and inches with mathematical exactness. If the long cubit of about 20½ inches employed by Ezekiel (see Ezk 40[5] and cf 2 Ch 3[3]) is preferred, the total area covered will be 164 by 82 feet, while the dimensions of 'the holy place' will be approximately 70 by 35 by 50 feet in height, and those of 'the most holy place' 35 by 35 by 35 feet. A serious objection to this adoption of the longer cubit, which was not foreseen when the article 'Weights and Measures' in Hastings' *DB* iv (see pp. 907 f) was written is presented by the detailed measurements of the interior of Herod's Temple in Josephus and the Mishnah (see below, **12**). These are numerically the same as those of the first Temple. but the cubit employed in the 1st cent. was the short cubit of 17.6 inches, and this has been shown by an inductive study of the Herodian masonry (*ExpT* xx. [1909], p. 24 ff). Now, it is certain that the *actual dimensions of Herod's Temple were not less than those of Solomon's*, as they would be if the cubits were in the ration of 6 to 7. It is more than probable, therefore, that the dimensions above given should be reduced by one-sixth—the Chronicler notwithstanding; in other words, 140 by 70 feet will be the approximate area of the building, 60 by 30 feet, and 30 by 30 feet—that of the 'holy' and 'most holy place' respectively.

4. *The interior of the Temple.*—The entrance to the Temple was through the open porch or vestibule on the eastern front. 'For the entering of the temple' was provided a large folding-door of cypress wood (6[34]), each leaf divided vertically into two leaves, one of which folded back upon the other. According to v.[35] in its present form, the leaves were ornamented with carved figures of cherubim, palms, and flowers, all overlaid with gold (but see below). The stone floor was covered with planks of cypress wood. That the latter should have been plated with gold (v.[30]) is scarcely credible. The walls of both chambers were lined with boards (literally 'ribs') of cedar wood, 'from the floor of the house to the rafters of the ceiling' (so read v.[15]). There is no mention in this verse, it will be noted, of any ornamentation of the cedar panels, which is first found in vv.[18] and [29]; but the former verse is absent from LXX, and vv.[28-30] are recognized by all as a later addition. The ceilings, as we should expect, were formed of beams of cedar (v.[9, 15]). Over all was probably laid an outer covering of marble slabs.

The inner chamber of the Temple (the oracle) was separated from the house, as has already been shown, by a partition wall, presumably of stone, which we have assumed above to have been a cubit in thickness. In it was set a door of olive wood, described obscurely in v.[31], which seems to say that its shape was not rectangular like the entrance door (see the Commentary on vv.[31, 33]), but pentagonal; in other words, the lintel of the door, instead of being a single cross-beam, consisted of two beams meeting at an angle. In the centre of the chamber, facing the entrance (2 Ch 3[13]), stood two **cherubim** figures of olive wood, each 10 cubits high, with outstretched wings. The latter measured 10 cubits from tip to tip, so that the two sets of wings reached from the north to the south wall of 'the most holy place' (1 K 6[23-28]). It is entirely in accordance with ancient practice that these symbolic figures should be overlaid with gold (v.[28]).

But with regard to the excessive introduction of gold plating by the received text throughout, including even the Temple floor, as we have seen, there is much to be said in favour of the view, first advanced by Stade, that it is due to a desire on the part of later scribes to enhance the magnificence of the first Temple. In the original text the gold plating was perhaps confined to the cherubim, as has just been suggested, or to these and the doors, which appear to have had a gold sheathing in the time of Hezekiah (2 K 18^{16}).

5. *The furniture of the Temple.*—If 1 K 7^{48-51} is set aside as a later addition (see the Commentary), the only article of Temple furniture is the **altar of cedar** introduced in the composite text of vv.$^{20-22}$. As there are good grounds for believing that a special altar of incense was first introduced into the second Temple (see **9**), the former is now identified by most writers with the **table of showbread** (see SHOWBREAD ; and TABERNACLE, **6** (*a*)). Its position is evidently intended to be in the outer chamber in front of the entrance to the inner shrine. The same position ' before the **oracle** ' (*d^ebhîr* 7^{49}) is assigned to the ten ' candlesticks,' properly **lampstands** (TABERNACLE, **6** (*b*)), five probably being meant to stand on either side of the entrance. Although, from the date of the passage cited, we may hesitate to ascribe these to Solomon, they doubtless at a later time formed a conspicuous part of the Temple furniture (cf Jer 52^{19}).

On the completion of the Temple, the sacred memorial of earlier days, the already venerable **Ark** of Y″ was brought from the tent in which David had housed it and placed within ' the oracle,' where it stood overshadowed by the wings of the cherubim (1 K 8^{5ff}). Another sacred object of like antiquity, the **brazen serpent** (see SERPENT [BRAZEN]), found a place somewhere within the Temple.

6. *The court of the Temple and its furniture.*—(*a*) *The court and gates.*—The Temple of Solomon formed part of a large complex of buildings, comprising an arsenal, a judgment-hall, the palace with its harem, and finally the royal chapel, the whole surrounded by ' the great court ' of 1 K $7^{9,12}$. Within this enclosure, at its upper or northern end, was ' the inner court ' of 6^{36} 7^{12} within

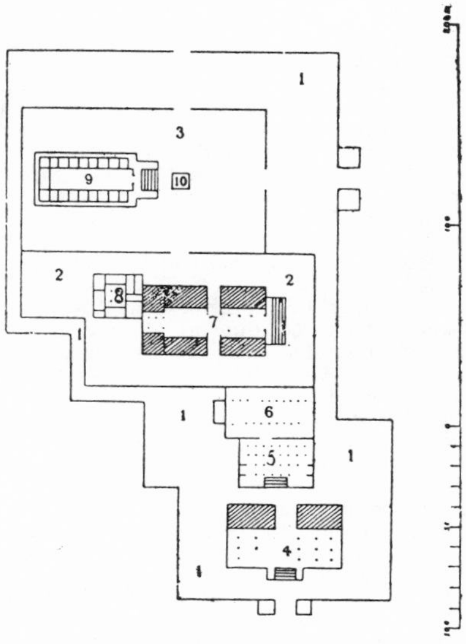

PLAN OF ROYAL BUILDINGS
(after Stade and Benzinger).

1. The great court. 2. The ' other ' or middle court. 3. The inner (or Temple) court. 4. House of Lebanon. 5. Porch of pillars. 6. Throne porch. 7. Royal palace. 8. Harem. 9. Temple. 10. Altar.

which, again, stood the Temple (8^{64}). It is of importance to note that this single **court of the Temple** was open to the laity as well as to the priests (8^{62}), as is specially evident from Jer 35^{1ff} 36^{10} etc.

Several **gates** of this court are mentioned by later writers, but their precise position is uncertain. The main entrance was doubtless in the east wall, and may be indicated by ' the king's entry without ' of 2 K 16^{18}, and ' the king's gate eastward ' of 1 Ch 9^{18}. The ' gate of the guard ' (2 K 11^{19}), on the other hand, may be looked for in the south wall separating the Temple court from ' the other court ' (1 K 7^{8}) in which the royal palace was situated (cf Ezk 43^{7f}). There were also one or more gates on the north side (Ezk 8^{3} 9^{2}, Jer 20^{2} **' gate of Benjamin,'** etc.). Cf JERUSALEM, GATES OF.

(*b*) *The altar of burnt-offering.*—It is surprising that no reference is made in the early narrative of 1 K 7 to the making of so indispensable a part of the apparatus of the cult. In the opinion of most critics, this omission is due to the excision from the original narrative of the relative section by a much later editor, who assumed that the brazen altar of the Tabernacle accompanied the Ark to the new sanctuary (but see Burney, *Notes on Heb. Text*, etc., 102 f). The Chronicler, whether informed by *his* text of 1 Kings or otherwise, tells us that Solomon's **altar of burnt-offering** (1 K 9^{25}) was of brass (cf the ' brazen altar,' 8^{64}), 20 cubits in length and breadth and 10 in height (2 Ch 4^{1}). Its position was on the site of the earlier altar of David (2 Ch 3^{1}), which, it may be asserted with confidence, stood somewhere on the sacred rock still to be seen within the Mosque of Omar (see **2** above). The precise position which the altars of the first and second Temples occupied on the surface of the rock, which measures at least some 50 by 40 feet, must remain a matter of conjecture. Herod's altar was large enough almost to cover the rock (**11** (*c*)). This question has been made the subject of an elaborate investigation by Kittel in his *Studien zur heb. Archäologie* (1908, 1–85). Solomon's altar was superseded in the reign of Ahaz by a larger altar of more artistic construction, which this sovereign caused to be made after the model of one seen by him at Damascus (2 K 16^{10-16}).

(*c*) *The brazen sea.*—In the court, to the south of the line between the altar and the Temple (1 K 7^{39}), stood one of the most striking of the creations of Solomon's Phoenician artist, Huram-abi of Tyre. This was **the brazen sea** (7^{23-26}, 2 Ch 4^{2-5}), a large circular basin or tank of bronze, 10 cubits ' from brim to brim ' and 5 in depth, with the enormous capacity of 2000 baths, or more than 16,000 gallons. Even should this prove an exaggerated estimate, the basin must have bulged very considerably in the middle, and the medial diameter must have been at least twice that of the mouth. The brim curved outwards like the calyx of a flower, and underneath it the body of the ' sea ' was decorated with two rows of gourd-shaped ornaments. The basin rested on the backs of twelve bronze oxen, which in groups of three, faced the four cardinal points. Notwithstanding 2 Ch 4^{6}, written centuries after it had disappeared (Jer $52^{17,20}$), recent writers are inclined to give the brazen sea a purely symbolical signification. But whether it is to be interpreted as a symbol of the primeval abyss (Gn 1^{2}) and of Y″'s power as Creator, or in the terms of the Babylonian mythology as symbolizing the upper or heavenly sea, bounded by the zodiac with its twelve signs (the 12 oxen), or otherwise, must be left to the future to decide (cf G. A. Smith, *Jerusalem*, ii, 65 f).

(*d*) *The brazen lavers.*—A similar symbolical significance is probably to be assigned to the ten **lavers** of bronze (1 K 7^{27-39}). These were smaller editions of the brazen sea, being only 4 cubits in diameter, holding only 40 baths (about 325 galls.), and resting on wheeled carriers, or **bases.** The peculiarly difficult description of the latter has been the subject of special study by Stade (*ZAW*, 1901, 145 ff, with which cf Haupt's *SBOT*), and more recently by Kittel (*op. cit.* 189–242). It must suffice here to say that each carrier was 4 cubits in length and breadth and 3 cubits in height. The sides were open frames composed of uprights of bronze joined together by transverse bars or rails of the same material, the whole richly ornamented with palm trees, lions, oxen, and cherubim in relief. Underneath were four wheels of bronze, 1½ cubits in diameter, while on the top of each stand was fitted a ring or cylinder on which the laver directly rested.

(*e*) *The pillars Jachin and Boaz.*—Nowhere is the symbolical element in these creations of Huram-abi's art more apparent than in the twin pillars with the mysterious names *Jachin* and *Boaz*, which were set up on either side of the entrance to the Temple porch. They have been discussed in the article Jachin and Boaz (where **'chapiter'** is explained) (see also Kittel's article 'Temple' in *PRE*³, xix [1907], 493 f).

7. *General idea and plan of Solomon's Temple.*—The building of the Temple occupied seven years and six months (1 K 6³⁷ᶠ). After standing for three centuries and a half it was burned to the ground by the soldiers of Nebuchadnezzar in 587–586 B.C., having first been stripped of everything of value that could be carried away. Before passing to a study of its successor, it may be well to note more precisely the purpose for which it was erected, and the general idea underlying its plan. As expressly implied by the term 'the house' (*bayith*) applied to it by the early historian, the Temple was intended to be, before all else, the dwelling-place of Israel's God, especially as represented by the Ark of Y″ (see, for this, 2 S 7²· ⁵ᶠᶠ). At the same time it was also the royal chapel, and adjoined the palace of Solomon, precisely as 'the king's chapel' at Bethel was part of the residence of the kings of Israel (Am 7¹³). There is no reason for supposing that Solomon had the least intention of supplanting the older sanctuaries of the land—a result first achieved by the reformation of Josiah (2 K 23).

As regards the plan of the new sanctuary as a whole, with its threefold division of court, holy place, and holy of holies (to adopt, as before, the later terminology), its origin is to be sought in the ideas of temple architecture then current not only in Phoenicia, the home of Solomon's architects and craftsmen, but throughout Western Asia. Syria, as we now know, was influenced in matters of religious art not only by Babylonia and Egypt, but also by the so-called Mycenaean civilization of the Eastern Mediterranean basin. The walled court, the porch, fore-room, and innermost *cella* are all characteristic features of early Syrian temple architecture. Whether or not there lies behind these the embodiment of ideas from the still older Babylonian cosmology, by which the threefold division of the sanctuary reflects the threefold division of the heavenly universe (so Benzinger, *Heb. Arch.*³, 328 f, following Winckler and A. Jeremias), must be left an open question. In certain details of the furniture, such as the wheeled carriers of the lavers and their ornamentation, may also be traced the influence of the early art of Crete and Cyprus through the Phoenicians as intermediaries.

8. The Temple of Ezekiel's vision (Ezk 40–43).—Although the Temple of Ezekiel remained a dream, a word may be said in passing regarding one of its most characteristic features, on account of its influence on the plan of the actual Temples of the future. This is the emphasis laid throughout on *the sacrosanct character of the sanctuary*—a reflection of the deepening of the conception of the Divine holiness which marked the period of the Exile. The whole sacred area covered by the Temple and its courts is to be protected from contact with secular buildings. One far-reaching result of this rigid separation of sacred and secular is the introduction of a second Temple court, to which the priests alone, strictly speaking, are entitled to access (Ezk 40²⁸ᶠᶠ). For the details of Ezekiel's sketch, with its passion for symmetry and number, see the Commentary and Witton Davies' article 'Temple' in Hastings' *DB* iv, 704 ff.

9. The Temple of Zerubbabel.—The second Temple, as it is frequently named, was built, at the instigation of the prophets Haggai and Zechariah, under the leadership of Zerubbabel. According to the explicit testimony of a contemporary (Hag 2¹⁸), the foundation was laid in the second year of Darius Hystaspis (520 B.C.)—a date now generally preferred to that of the much later author of Ezr 3⁸ᶠᶠ. The building was finished and the Temple dedicated in 516 B.C. We have unfortunately no description of the plan and arrangements of the latter, and are dependent for information regarding it mainly on scattered references in the later canonical and extra-canonical books. It may be assumed, however, that the **altar of burnt-offering,** previously restored by the exiles on their return (Ezr 3³), occupied the former site, now consecrated by centuries of worship, and that the ground-plan of the Temple followed as nearly as possible that of its predecessor (cf G. A. Smith, *op. cit.* ii, ch. xii).

As regards the furnishing of Zerubbabel's Temple, we have not only several notices from the period when it was still standing, but evidence from the better known Temple of Herod, in which the sacred furniture remained as before. Now, however scantily the former may have been furnished at the first, we should expect that after the introduction of the Priests' Code under Ezra, the prescriptions therein contained for the furniture of the Tabernacle would be carried out to the letter. And this is indeed to a large extent what we find. Thus only one **golden lampstand** illuminated 'the holy place' (1 Mac 1²¹) instead of ten in the former Temple. The **table of showbread** succeeded 'the altar of cedar' of 1 K 6²⁰ (for which see **5** above). The golden **altar of incense,** which belongs to a later stratum of P (Tabernacle, **6** (*c*), was most probably introduced at a somewhat late date, since pseudo-Hecataeus in the 3rd cent. B.C., quoted by Josephus (*c. Apion.* i. 22 [198 f]), knows only of 'an altar and a candlestick both of gold, and in weight two talents'—the former presumably the altar or table of showbread. There is no reason, however, to question the presence of the incense altar by the 2nd cent., as attested by 1 Mac 1²¹ᶠᶠ (cf 4⁴⁹), according to which Antiochus Epiphanes robbed the Temple of 'the golden altar and the candlestick of light . . . and the table of showbread,' where the first of these must be identified with the altar in question (see, against the scepticism of Wellhausen and others, the evidence collected by Schürer, *GJV*⁴ ii [1907], 342 f [=³ 285 f]).

In one point of cardinal importance the glory of the second house was less than that of the first. No attempt was made to construct another **Ark**; 'the most holy place' was empty. A splendid curtain or **veil** replaced the partition wall between the two divisions of the sanctuary, and is mentioned among the spoils carried off by Antiochus (1 Mac 1²²). In another way the second Temple was distinguished from the first; it had two courts in place of one, an inner and an outer (4³⁸· ⁴⁹ 9⁵⁴), as demanded by Ezekiel. This prophet's further demand, that the laity should be entirely excluded from the inner court, was not carried out, as is evident from the experience of Alexander Jannaeus. Having given offence to the people while officiating at the altar on the occasion of the Feast of Tabernacles, he was pelted with the citrons which they carried. Alexander in consequence had the altar and Temple railed off to keep the worshippers henceforth at a more respectful distance (Jos. *Ant.* xiii. xiii. 5 [372 ff]).

The altar was no longer of brass but of unhewn stone (1 Mac 4⁴⁷), as required by Ex 20²⁵, and attested by the earlier writer above cited (*ap.* Jos. *c. Apion., l.c.*), who further assigns to it the same dimensions as the Chronicler gives to the brazen altar of Solomon (**5** (*b*)). In 168 B.C., Antiochus iv., as already stated, spoiled and desecrated the Temple, and by a crowning act of sacrilege set up a small altar to Zeus Olympius on the altar of burnt-offering. Three years later, Judas the Maccabee, after recapturing Jerusalem, made new sacred furniture—altar of incense, table of showbread, the seven-branched candlestick, and other 'new holy vessels.' The stones of the polluted altar were removed and others substituted, and the Temple dedicated anew (1 Mac 4⁴¹ᶠᶠ). With minor alterations and additions, chiefly in the direction of making the Temple hill stronger against attack, the Temple remained as the Maccabees left it until replaced by the more ambitious edifice of Herod.

10. If only for the sake of completeness, a brief reference must be made at this point to *two other* *temples* for the worship of Y″ erected by Jewish settlers in Egypt during the period covered by the previous section. The earlier of these came to light through the discovery of certain Aramaic papyri on the island of **Elephantine** (q.v.). These describe this temple of Yāhū (Yahweh), which existed at Elephantine before Cambyses invaded Egypt in 525 B.C., and had been destroyed at the instigation of Egyptian priests in 411 B.C. It was probably rebuilt soon after 408 B.C. The story of the other, erected at **Leontopolis** in the Delta by Onias, son of the Jewish high priest of the same name, in the reign of Antiochus IV., has been told by Josephus, who describes it as a replica 'but smaller and poorer,' of the Temple of Zerubbabel (*BJ* VII. x. 2 ff [420 ff], *Ant.* XIII. iii. 1 ff [62 ff]). This description has recently been confirmed by the excavation of the site, the modern Tell el-Yehūdîyeh, by Flinders Petrie (Petrie and Duncan, *Hyksos and Israelite Cities*, 1906, 1927, with plans and models, plates xxiii.–xxv.); not the least interesting feature of this temple *in partibus infidelium* is the fact that it seems to have been built according to the measurements of the Tabernacle. This is altogether more probable than the view expressed by Petrie, that Onias copied the dimensions of the Temple of Jerusalem (*op. cit.* 24).

11. THE TEMPLE OF HEROD.—It was in the eighteenth year of his reign that Herod obtained the permission of his suspicious subjects to rebuild the Temple of Zerubbabel. The Temple proper was rebuilt by a thousand specially trained priests within the space of eighteen months; the rest of the buildings took years to finish, indeed the last touches were given only six or seven years before the final catastrophe in A.D. 70, when the whole was destroyed by the soldiers of Titus. For a fuller study of several of the points discussed in this section, see the articles on 'Some Problems of Herod's Temple' in *ExpT* xx (1908–09), 24 ff, 66 ff, 181 ff, 270 ff.

(*a*) *The outer court, its size, cloisters, and gates.*—It is advisable in this case to reverse the order of study adopted for the first Temple, and to proceed from the courts to the Temple proper. In this way we start from the existing remains of Herod's enterprise, for all are agreed that the Ḥaram area (see above, **2**) and its retaining walls are *in the main* the work of Herod, who doubled the area of Zerubbabel's courts by means of enormous substructures (Jos. *BJ* I. xxi. 1 [401 f]). There are good grounds, however, for believing that, as left by Herod, the platform stopped at a point a little beyond the **Golden Gate** in the eastern wall, its northern boundary probably running in proximity to the north wall of the present inner platform of the Haram. (The latter has been considerably extended in this direction since Herod's day, and is indicated by double dotted lines on the accompanying plan). This gives an area of approximately 26 acres compared with the 35 acres, or thereby, of the present Ḥaram. The measurements were, in round numbers, 390 yards from N. to S. by 330 yards from E. to W. on the north, and 310 yards E. to W. on the south. If the figures just given represent, with approximate accuracy, the extended area enclosed by Herod, the outer court, called in the Mishnah 'the mountain of the house,' and by later writers **'the court of the Gentiles,'** will have appeared to the eye as almost a square, as it is stated to be, although with divergent measurements, by our two chief authorities, the Mishnah treatise *Middoth* (literally 'measurements') and Josephus (*BJ* V. v., *Ant.* XV. xi. and elsewhere).

The climax of Herod's architectural triumphs was reached in the magnificent colonnades which surrounded the four sides of this court. The colonnade along the south wall, in particular, known as **'the Royal Porch'** (or portico, *stoa*), was exceeding magnificent' (1 Ch 22[5]). It consisted of four rows of monolithic marble columns of the Corinthian order, forming three aisles; the two side aisles were 30 feet in breadth and 50 feet in height, while the central aisle was half as broad again as the other two and twice as high (Jos. *Ant.* XV. xi. 5 [401 ff], but see *ExpT*, *l.c.*). The ceilings of the roofs were adorned with sculptured panels of cedar wood. On the other three sides of the court the colonnades had only two aisles, that along the east wall bearing the name of **Solomon's Porch** (Jn 10[23], Ac 3[11] 5[12]), probably from a tradition that it occupied the site of one built by that monarch.

The main approaches to the court were naturally on the west and south. The principal entrance from the west was by the **gate of Kiponos** (*Midd.* i. 3), the approach to which was by a bridge over the Tyropoeon, now represented by Wilson's arch. On the south were the two gates represented by the present 'double' and 'triple' gates, and named the **Huldah** (or 'mole') gates, because the visitor passed into the court by sloping tunnels beneath the royal porch. These ramps opened upon the Court of the Gentiles about 100 feet from the south wall (see plan and, for details, *ExpT*, *l.c.*).

(*b*) *The inner courts and their gates.*—The great court was open to Jew and Gentile alike, and, as we learn from the Gospels, was the centre of a busy life, and of transactions little in accord with its sacred purpose. The **sanctuary** in the strict sense began when one reached the series of walls, buildings, and courts which rose on successive terraces in the northern half of the great enclosure. Its limits were marked out by a low balustrade, the *sōrēgh*, which ran round the whole, and was provided at intervals with notices warning all Gentiles against entering the sacred enclosure on pain of death (cf Paul's experience, Ac 21[26ff]). From the *sōrēgh*, flights of steps at different points led up to a narrow terrace, termed the *ḥēl* (XYZ in plan), 10 cubits wide, beyond which rose a lofty retaining wall enclosing the whole sanctuary, to which Jews alone had access.

The great wall by which the sanctuary was converted into a fortress, was pierced by nine gateways—H 1–9 on the plan—over which were built massive two-storeyed gate-houses 'like towers' (Jos. *BJ* V. v. 3 [203]), four in the N., four in the S., and one in the E. wall. The most splendid of all the gates was the last mentioned, the eastern gate, which was the principal entrance to the Temple. From the fact that it was composed entirely of Corinthian brass, and had been the gift of a certain Nicanor of Alexandria, it was known as 'the **Corinthian gate**' (Jos.), and 'the **gate of Nicanor**' (Mish.). There is little doubt that it is also 'the **Beautiful Gate** of the temple' (Ac 3[2, 10]), as shown by Schürer in his exhaustive study (*ZNW*, 1906, 51–58). The other eight gates were 'covered over with gold and silver, as were the jambs and lintels' (Jos. *BJ* V. v. 3 [201]), at the expense of Alexander, the Jewish alabarch of Alexandria (*c* A.D. 20–40). All the gates were 20 cubits high by 10 wide, according to the Mishnah (Josephus says 30 by 15).

Entering by the 'Beautiful Gate,' H 5, one found oneself in the colonnaded **court of the women**—so called because accessible to women as well as men. This was the regular place of assembly for public worship (cf Lk 1[10]). The women were accommodated in a gallery which ran round the court (*Midd.* ii. 5), probably above the colonnades as suggested in the plan. Along by the pillars of the colonnades were placed thirteen trumpet-shaped boxes to receive the offerings and dues of the faithful. These boxes are **'the treasury'** into which the widow's mites were cast (Mk 12[42]).

The west side of this court was bounded by a wall, which divided the sanctuary into two parts, an eastern and a western. As the level of the latter was considerably higher than that of the eastern court, a magnificent semicircular flight of fifteen steps led up from the one to the other. At the top of the steps was an enormous gateway, 50 cubits by 40, allowing the worshippers an uninterrupted view of the altar and the Temple. The leaves of its gate were even more richly plated with silver and gold by Alexander than the others, and hence many have identified this gate with 'the gate that was called Beautiful' (but see Schürer, *loc. cit.* and *ExpT.* xx [1908–09]).

(*c*) *The court of the priests and the great altar.*—There is some uncertainty as to the arrangements of the western court, which we have now reached, owing to the divergent data of our two authorities, Josephus and the Mishnah. The simplest solution is perhaps to regard the whole western court as in one sense **the court of the priests,** 'the court' *par excellence* of the Mishnah (*Midd.* v. 1, etc.). Alexander Jannaeus, we learned (**9**), railed off the Temple and altar, and restricted the male Israelites to the outer edge of the then inner court. This arrangement was retained when the courts were laid out anew by Herod. In *Middoth* ii. 6 a narrow strip by the entrance—only 11 cubits in width, but extending the whole breadth of the court from N. to S.—is named the **court of Israel.** Josephus, however, is probably right in representing the latter as running round three sides of the western court (as on plan BBB). Its small size was a reminder that the laity—apart from those actually taking part in the sacrifices, who had, of course, to be allowed even within the still more sacred precincts of the priests' court—were admitted on sufferance to the western court; the eastern court, or court of the women, was, as has been indicated, the proper place of worship for the laity. Along the north and south walls of the enclosure were built chambers for various purposes connected with the Temple ritual (*Midd.* v. 3, 4), chambers and gatehouses being connected by an ornamental colonnade. Those whose location can be determined with some degree of certainty are entered on the plan and named in the key thereto.

The inner court is represented in the Mishnah as a rectangle, 187 cubits by 135, the outer or women's court as an exact square, 135 cubits by 135 (and so on most plans, *e.g. DB* iv, 713). But the rock levels of the Ḥaram, the oblique line of the east side of the platform—due probably to the lie of the rock required for the foundation of the massive east wall—and the repeated appearance of 11 and its multiples (note that $187 = 11 \times 17$) in the details of the totals in *Middoth* v. 1, all combine to justify a suspicion as to the accuracy of the figures. On the accompanying plan the whole inner court, B and C, is entered as 170 cubits long from E. to W., and 160 broad. The outer court, A, has a free space between the colonnades of 135 by an average of about 110. The total dimensions of the sanctuary, including the surrounding buildings and the terrace (*ḥēl*) are as follows: (1) length from W. to E. across the rock, 315 cubits or 462 feet; (2) width from N. to S. 250 cubits or 367 feet. The data on which these measurements are based will be found in the essays in the *Exp. Times*, already frequently referred to.

In the latest, and in some respects the best, plan of Herod's Temple by Waterhouse in Sanday's *Sacred Sites of the Gospels*, the data of the Mishnah are set aside, and a large 'court of men of Israel' is inserted in the western court *in addition to* those above described. Against this view it may be urged, (1) that it requires its author to remove the eastern court, which was an essential part of the sanctuary, from a place on the present inner platform of the Ḥaram; (2) the consequence of this is to narrow unduly the space between the Beautiful Gate and Solomon's Porch. If there is one statement of the Mishnah that is worthy of credit, it is that 'the largest free space was on the south, the second largest on the east, the third on the north, and the smallest on the west' (*Midd.* ii. 1). But, as the plan referred to shows, this is not the case if the court of the women is removed so far to the east by the insertion of a large 'court of Israel.' The plan is also open to criticism on other grounds (cf G. A. Smith, *op. cit.* ii, 508 ff).

The **altar of burnt-offering,** D, was, like that restored by Judas the Maccabee, of unhewn stone, and measured at the base 32 cubits by 32 (47 feet square, thus covering almost the whole of the sacred rock, see **6** (*b*)), decreasing by three stages till the altar-hearth was only 24 cubits square. The priests went up by an inclined approach on the south side in accordance with Ex 20[26]. To the north of the altar was the place where the sacrificial victims were slaughtered and prepared for the altar. It was provided with rings, pillars, hooks, and tables. A **laver,** O, for the priests' ablutions stood to the west of the approach to the altar.

12. *The Temple building.*—A few yards beyond the great altar rose the Temple itself, a glittering mass of white marble and gold. Twelve steps, corresponding to the height (12 half-cubits) of the massive and probably gold-covered stereobate on which the building stood, led up to the porch.

The porch was probably 96 cubits in height and of the same breadth at the base. The Mishnah gives its height, including the 6 cubits of the podium or stereobate, as 100 cubits. The real depth was doubtless, as in Solomon's Temple (**3**), 10 cubits in the centre, but now increased to 20 cubits at the wings (so Josephus). As the plan shows, the porch outflanked the main body of the Temple, which was 60—the Mishnah has 70—cubits in breadth, by 18 cubits at either wing. These dimensions show that Herod's porch resembled the pylons of an Egyptian temple. It probably tapered towards the top, and was surmounted by an Egyptian cornice with the familiar cavetto moulding (cf sketch below). The entrance to the porch measured 40 cubits by 20 (*Middoth*, iii. 7), corresponding to the dimensions of 'the holy place.' There was no door.

The **'great door of the house'** (20 cubits by 10) was 'all over covered with gold,' in front of which hung a richly embroidered Babylonian veil, while above the lintel was figured a huge golden vine (Jos. *Ant.* xv. xi. 3 [395], *BJ* v. v. 4 [210]). The interior area of Herod's Temple was, for obvious reasons, the same as that of its predecessors. A hall, 61 cubits long by 20 wide, was divided between the **holy place** (40 by 20, but with the height increased to 40 cubits [*Middoth*, iv. 6]) and the **most holy place** (20 by 20 by 20 high). The extra cubit was occupied by a double curtain embroidered in colours, which screened off 'the holy of holies' (cf *Midd.* iv. 7 with *Yoma*, v. 2). This is the **veil of the Temple** referred to in Mt 27[51] and ‖ (cf He 6[19] etc.).

As in Solomon's Temple, three storeys of side-chambers, probably 30 cubits in height, ran round three sides of the main building. But by the provision of a passage-way giving access to the different storeys, and making a third outside wall necessary, the surface covered by the whole was now 96 cubits in length by 60 in breadth, not reckoning the two wings of the porch. Over the whole length of the two holy places a second storey was raised, entirely, as it seems, for architectural effect.

The total height of the *naos* is uncertain. The entries by which the Mishnah makes up a total of 100 cubits are not such as inspire confidence; the laws of architectural proportion suggest that the 100, although also given by Josephus, should be reduced to 60 cubits or 88 feet, equal to the breadth of the *naos* and lateral chambers. On the plan the lowest side chambers are intended to be 5 cubits wide and their wall 3 (both as in **3**), the passage-way 3, and the outside wall 3, giving a total width of $14+6+20+6+14=60$ cubits (Jos. v. v. 4 [207 ff]; cf *DB* iv, 715 for the corresponding figures of *Midd.* iv. 7). The result of taking the principles of proportion between the various parts as the decisive factor when Josephus and the Mishnah are at variance, is exhibited in the diagram on p. 968, which combines sections through the porch and the holy place.

The furniture of 'the holy place' remained as in former days. Before the veil stood the altar of incense; against the south wall the seven-branched **golden lampstand,** and opposite to it the **table of showbread** (Jos. *BJ* v. v. 5 [216 f]). A special interest attaches to the two latter from the fact, known to every one, that they were among the Temple spoils carried to Rome by Titus to adorn his triumph, and are still to be seen among the sculptures of the Arch of Titus.

'The most holy place' was empty as before (Jos. *ib.*), save for a stone on which the high priest, who alone had access to this innermost shrine, deposited the censer of incense on the Day of Atonement (*Yōmā*, v. 2).

All in all, Herod's Temple was well worthy of a place

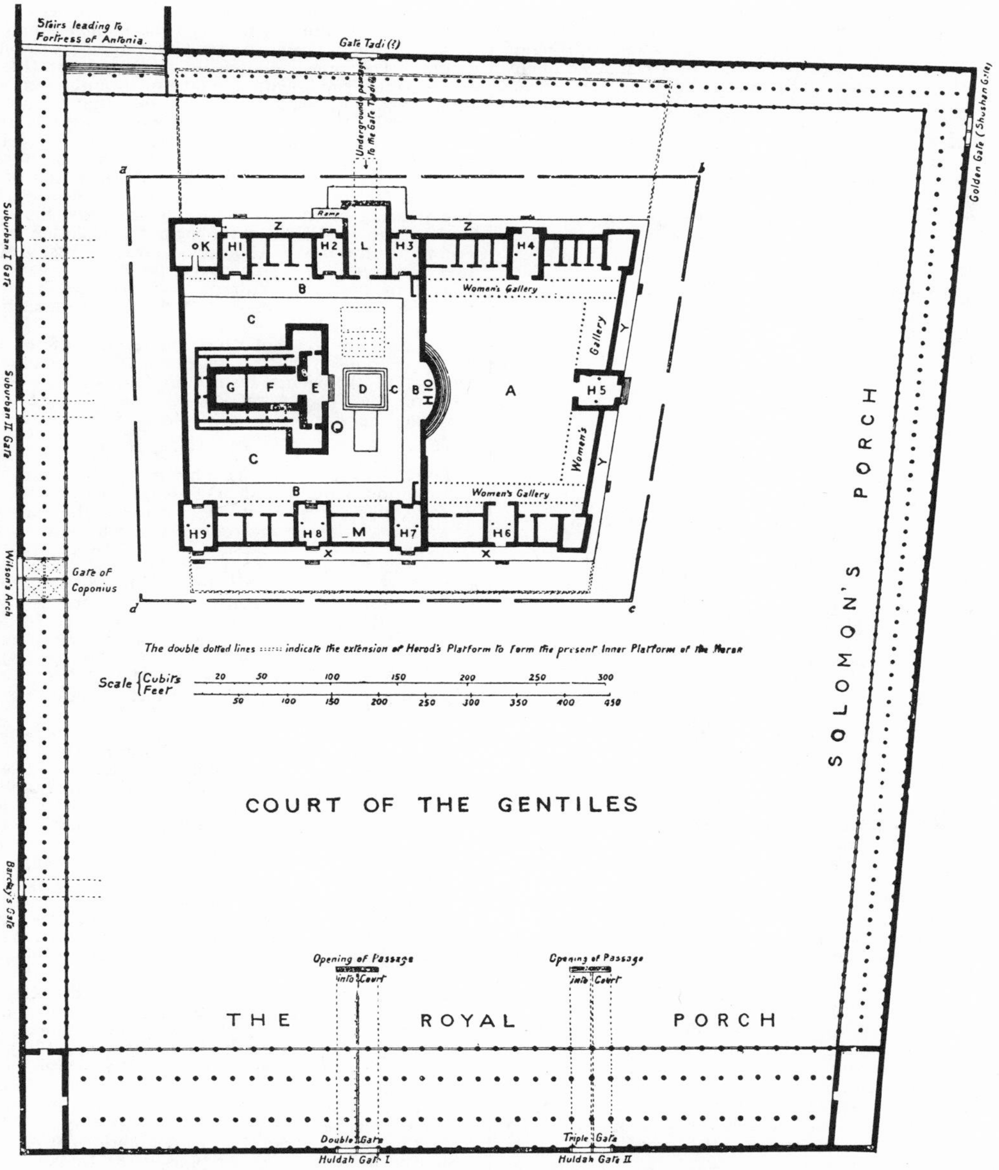

KEY TO PLAN OF HEROD'S TEMPLE AND COURTS

a b c d, the surrounding balustrade (*sōrēgh*). **X Y Z,** the terrace (*ḥēl*).

A, Court of the Women. **B B B,** Court of Israel. **C C C,** Court of the Priests.

D, altar of burnt-offering. **E F G,** porch, holy place, and holy of holies. **O,** the laver.

H, 1–9, Gates of the Sanctuary (*Middoth*, i. 4, 5), viz.: 1, gate of the House Moked; 2, Corban gate; 3, gate Nitsus; 5, the gate of Nicanor, or the Beautiful Gate; 7, the water gate; 8, gate of the firstborn; 9, the fuel gate; 10, the 'upper gate,' wrongly called the gate of Nicanor.

K, the guardhouse Moked (=hearth). **L,** the 'northern edifice that was between the two gates' (see *BJ* VI. ii. 7 [150]). Here, it is suggested, the sacrificial victims were examined by the priests, having been brought in either by the underground passage shown on the plan, or by the ramp also shown. The upper storey may have contained the important 'chamber of the councillors' (*parhedrin*) (*Yoma*, i. 1).

M, the chamber Gazith, in which the priests on duty assembled for prayer (*Tamid*, iv. end). There are not sufficient data for fixing the location of the other chambers mentioned in the Mishnah. Their distribution on the plan is purely conjectural.

among the architectural wonders of the world. One has but to think of the extraordinary height and strength of the outer retaining walls, parts of which still claim our admiration, and of the wealth of art and ornament lavished upon the porticoes and buildings. The artistic effect was further heightened by the succession of marble-paved terraces and courts, rising each above and within the other, from the outer court to the Temple floor. For once we may entirely credit the Jewish historian when he tells us that from a distance the whole resembled a snow-covered mountain, and that the light reflected from the gilded porch dazzled the spectator like ' the sun's own rays ' (Jos. *BJ* v. v. 6 [222]).

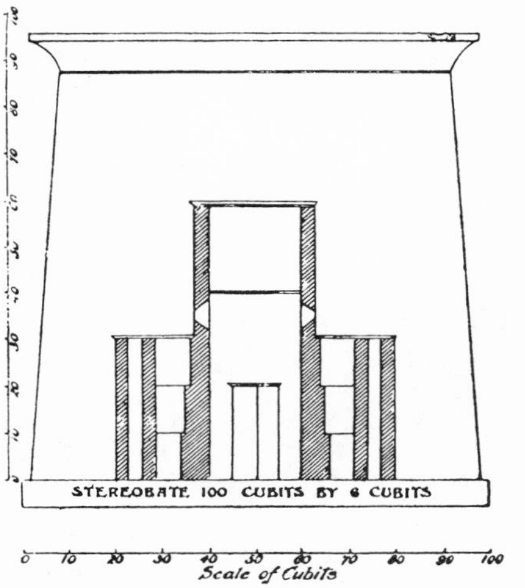

DIAGRAMMATIC SECTION OF TEMPLE AND PORCH

13. *The daily Temple service in NT times.*—This article may fitly close with a brief account of the principal act of Jewish **worship** in the days of our Lord, which centred round the daily or ' continual ' (Heb. *tamîdh*, Ex 29^{42}) burnt-offering, presented every morning and every evening or rather mid-afternoon,, throughout the year, in the name, and on behalf, of the whole community of Israel (see Ex 29^{38-42}, Nu 28^{3-8}). A detailed account of this service, evidently based on reliable tradition, is given in the Mishnah treatise *Tamid* (cf also the full exposition given by Schürer, *GJV*³ ii, 288–299 = ⁴345–357 [*HJP* II. i, 273–299]).

The detachment of priests on duty in the rotation of their ' courses ' (Lk 1^{8}) slept in the ' house Moked ' (**K** on plan). About cock-crow the priests who wished to be drawn for the morning service bathed and robed, and thereafter repaired to the chamber Gazith (**M**) in order to determine by lot those of their number who should ' officiate.' By the first lot a priest was selected to remove the ashes from the altar of burnt-offering, and prepare the wood, etc., for the morning sacrifice. This done, ' the presiding official said to them, Come and draw (to decide) (1) who shall slay, (2) who shall toss (the blood against the altar), (3) who shall remove the ashes from the incense altar, (4) who shall clean the lampstand, (5)–(10) who shall carry the parts of the victim to the foot of the altar [six parts are specified], (11) who shall prepare the (meal-offering) of fine flour, (12) the baked offering (of the high priest), and (13) the wine of the drink-offering ' (Mishnah, *Tamid*, iii. 1).

At the hour of dawn the preparations here set forth were begun, and the Temple gates thrown open. After the victim, a yearling lamb, had been slain, the incense altar prepared and the lamps trimmed, the officiating priests assembled in the chamber Gazith for a short religious service, after which there commenced the solemn acts of worship in which the *tāmîdh* culminated —the offering of incense and the burning of the sacrificial victim. The priest, chosen as before by lot (Lk 1^{9}), entered the Temple with a censer of incense, and, while the smoke was ascending from the altar within the Holy Place, the worshippers without prostrated themselves in adoration and silent prayer. After the priestly benediction had been pronounced from the steps of the porch (*Tamid*, vii. 2), the several parts of the sacrifice were thrown upon the altar and consumed. The pouring of the drink-offering was now the signal for the choir of Levites to begin the chanting of the Psalm for the day. At intervals two priests blew on silver trumpets, at whose sound the people again prostrated themselves. With the close of the Psalm the public service was at an end, and the private sacrifices were then offered.

The order of the mid-afternoon service differed from the above only in that the incense was offered after the burning of the victim instead of before. The lamps, also, on the ' golden candlestick,' were lighted at the ' evening ' service. **A. R. S. K.—N. H. S.**

TEMPLE SERVANTS.—See NETHINIM.

TEMPTATION.—1. The English words ' tempt ' and ' temptation ' are, in the OT—with the exception of Mal 3^{15}, where a synonym *bāḥan* is used—the translation of various forms of the root *nissāh*, which is properly rendered ' prove ' or ' test.' In Gn 22^{1} RV translates ' God did prove Abraham ' (RSV ' God tested Abraham '). RV (but not RSV) retains ' temptation ' for (*a*) God's testing of Pharaoh's character and disposition (Dt 4^{34}, RVm ' trials ' or ' evidences ' ; cf 7^{19} 29^{3}) ; (*b*) Israel's distrustful putting of God Himself to the proof (Dt 6^{16} ; cf Ex $17^{2, 7}$, Nu 14^{22}, Ps $78^{18, 41, 56}$). In Ps 95^{8} RV and RSV rightly keep ' Massah ' as a proper noun, the reference being to the historic murmuring at Rephidim (Ex 17^{1ff} ; cf Dt 33^{8}, Ps 81^{7}).

Driver (*ICC*, on Dt 6^{16}) points out that *nissāh* is a neutral word, and means to *test* or *prove* a person, to see *whether* he will act in a particular way (Ex 16^{4}, Jg 2^{22} 3^{4}), or *whether* the character he bears is well established (1 K 10^{1}). God thus *proves* a person, or *puts* him *to the test*, to see if his fidelity or affection is sincere (Gn 22^{1}, Ex 20^{20}, Dt 8^{2} 13^{3} ; cf Ps 26^{2}) ; and men *test*, or *prove* the Lord when they act as if doubting whether His promise be true, or whether He is faithful to His revealed character (Ex $17^{2, 7}$, Nu 14^{22}, Ps 106^{14} ; cf Is 7^{12}).' There appears to be a special meaning of ' testing ' in Ex 20^{20}, Dt 7^{19} 8^{2-16} 29^{3}, where the mighty works and theophanies of the Exodus story are to test the character of Israel.

2. In the intertestamental literature God's testing of Abraham (Gn 22^{1-19}) becomes a favourite theme and receives a special development, in that an evil angel tempts Abraham (*Apocalypse of Abraham* 12^{1ff}), and the angel Mastema suggests to God that Abraham (like Job) should be put to the test (*Jub.* 17–19). Isaiah is tempted at the time of his martyrdom to deny God and to obey the devil instead (*Martyrdom of Isa.* 5^{4ff}). Rabbinic tradition knows of ten temptations of Abraham (*Aboth* v. 4 ; cf the ten temptations of Joseph in *Test. Joseph* 2^{7}). In Ben-Sira, temptations are a part of God's testing of anyone who prepares to serve the Lord (Sir 2^{1-5}), but God will give help and rescue man from temptation (33^{1}). The idea is not unknown in pagan literature ; Seneca, *de Providentia*, iv. 12, says that God tests noble spirits with severity.

3. The Greek word *peirasmos* is the usual LXX rendering of *massāh*. This and its cognates *peirazō*, *peiraomai*, etc., are also ' neutral ' words. In pre-Christian Greek they cover the range ' attempt,' ' try,' ' make trial of,' ' put to the test,' ' tempt,' and ' seek to seduce.' In the NT the verb often retains the wider meaning of ' try,' ' test ' (*e.g.* Mk 10^{2}, Jn 6^{6}, Ac 16^{7}), but also frequently refers to enticement into sin (Mt 4^{1}, 1 Co 7^{5}, Ja 1^{13} etc. ; cf ' the tempter,' Mt 4^{3}, 1 Th 3^{5}).

In the RV it is almost always translated 'temptation,' with the occasional marginal alternative 'trial' (Ja 1[2], 1 P 1[6]); the exceptions are Ac 20[19], Rev 3[10], where 'trial' is found in the text. RSV substitutes 'try' or 'make trial of' ('trial') for 'tempt' ('temptation') wherever enticement to what is wrong is not evidently spoken of; but 'temptation' is retained in Mt 6[13] ‖ Lk 11[4], where the range of the petition cannot be thus limited; cf Ja 1[2].

4. In NT eschatology there is a persistent idea that the woes of the last days are a final trial of the faithful (Mk 13[11-22], Rev 3[10]), and A. Schweitzer believes that this was a feature of Jesus' own teaching; it is, however, for the most part an idea of the early Christian community. But the idea is also present, as in Ben-Sira, that God will rescue the faithful out of their trial (2 P 2[9]). The phrase in the Lord's Prayer 'lead us not into temptation' (Mt 6[13] ‖ Lk 11[4]) has been much debated, and the difficulty may be partly ascribed to the narrowing of the significance of the English word since 1611, so that it now most often has the sense of *provoking* or *enticing* a person so that he may act in a particular way. Perhaps the original meaning is 'preserve us from being put to the test.' At the same time, the Gethsemane saying (Mk 14[38]) seems to say that the disciples must watch and pray lest they enter into 'temptation.' The Epistle of James, however, argues (1[13f]) that God cannot be tempted to do evil and will not tempt anyone; temptation is due to one's own evil desires. Here the author may have in mind the Lord's Prayer with its difficult clause. Certainly it would seem unlikely that the prayer contemplates a situation in which the faithful are miraculously exempted from the normal trials and perplexities of the moral life. Although it is not said in so many words, the prayer may be for strength to overcome temptation. Paul teaches that God will not let the believer be tempted beyond his strength but with every temptation will provide a way to endure it (1 Co 10[13]). The Epistle to the Hebrews points to the temptation of Christ as a sign that the one who has thus been tempted is able to help others (2[18]). As in contemporary Judaism, the NT frequently ascribes to Satan rather than God the origin of temptation (1 Co 7[5], Rev 2[10]). The temptations of Christ include the temptation to put God to the test (Mt 4[5-7], Lk 4[9-12]); this is a familiar theme in the intertestamental literature and in Ac 5[9], 1 Co 10[9], He 3[9]. The stories of our Lord's temptations symbolize spiritual dangers which He faced at other points in His ministry. They have analogies in Jewish apocalyptic literature and in other religions, especially the temptations of the Buddha and Zoroaster. See Jesus Christ, 8. S. E. J.

TEN.—See Number, 7.

TEN COMMANDMENTS.—1. The traditional history of the Decalogue.—The 'ten words' were, according to Ex 20, proclaimed vocally by God on Mount Sinai, and written by Him on two stones, and given to Moses (Ex 24[12] 31[18] 32[15f]; cf Dt 5[22] 9[10f]). When these were broken by Moses on his descent from the mount (Ex 32[19], Dt 9[17]), he was commanded to prepare two fresh stones like the first, on which God re-wrote the 'ten words' (Ex 34[4, 28], Dt 10[2, 4]). This is clearly the meaning of Exodus as the text now stands. But many critics think that v.[28b] originally referred not to the 'ten words' of Ex 20, but to the laws of 34[11-26], and that these laws were J's version of the Decalogue. It must suffice to say here that if, as on the whole seems likely, v.[28b] refers to our Decalogue, we must distinguish the command to write the covenant laws in v.[27], and the words 'he wrote' in v.[28b], in which case the subject of the latter will be God, as required by 34[1]. The two stones were immediately placed in the Ark, which had been prepared by Moses specially for that purpose (Dt 10[1-5] [probably based on JE]). There they were believed to have permanently remained (1 K 8[9], Dt 10[5]) until the Ark was, according to Rabbinical tradition, hidden by Jeremiah, when Jerusalem was finally taken by Nebuchadrezzar.

2. The Documentary History of the Decalogue.—The Decalogue of Ex 20 can be compared with two different sets of commandments, (*a*) that of the above-mentioned J collection in Ex 34[14-28] and (*b*) that of Dt 5[6-21]. (*a*) Historically the comparison with the J *corpus* is the more important. It is difficult to establish the exact number of laws in it, or indeed to extract them from their accretions, but the following list may be suggested:

(i) You shall worship no other god (v.[14]).
(ii) You shall make for yourself no molten gods (v.[17]).
(iii) The feast of unleavened bread you shall keep (v.[18]).
(iv) All that opens the womb is mine (v.[19]).
(v) None shall appear before me empty (v.[20]).
(vi) Six days you shall work, but on the seventh day you shall rest (v.[21]).
(vii) You shall observe the feast of weeks, . . . and the feast of ingathering at the year's end (v.[22]).
(viii) Three times in the year shall all your males appear before the Lord (v.[23]).
(ix) You shall not offer the blood of my sacrifice with leaven (v.[25]).
(x) The sacrifice of the feast of the Passover shall not be left until the morning (v.[25]).
(xi) The first of the firstfruits of your ground you shall bring to the house of the Lord (v.[26]).
(xii) You shall not boil a kid in its mother's milk (v.[26]).

Marks of affinity with the Decalogue are obvious—no other gods, no idols, Sabbath observance; but the differences are equally obvious, and explain why the one version is called the Ritual and the other the Ethical Code. The primitive nature of the Ritual code over against the Ethical is also obvious. Ex 34, too, lacks the prestige of Ex 20, placed as the latter is, at the head of an identifiable collection, the Book of the Covenant and the Code of Deuteronomy.

(*b*) A comparison of the Decalogue in Ex 20 with that of Dt 5 renders it probable that both are later recensions of a much shorter original. The phrases peculiar to Dt 5 are in most cases obviously characteristic of D, and must be regarded as later expansions. Such are 'as the Lord your God commanded you' in the 4th and 5th 'word,' and 'that it may go well with you' in the 5th. In the last commandment the first two clauses are transposed, and a more appropriate word ('desire') is used for coveting a neighbour's house. Here evidently we have a later correction. Curiously enough Ex 20, while thus generally more primitive than Deuteronomy, shows signs of an even later recension. The reason for keeping the Sabbath, God's rest after creation, is clearly based on Gn 2[1-3], which belongs to the post-exilic Priestly Code (P). The question is further complicated by the fact that several phrases in what is common to Ex 20 and Deuteronomy are of a distinctly Deuteronomic character, as 'who is within your gates' in the Fourth Commandment, 'that your days may be prolonged' 'in the land which the Lord your God gives you' in the 5th. We see, then, that the Decalogue of Exodus is in all probability the result of a double revision (a Deuteronomic and a Priestly) of a much more simple original. It has been suggested that originally all the commandments consisted of a single clause, and that the name 'word' could be more naturally applied to such. In favour of this view, beyond what has been already said, it is argued that this short form would be more suitable for inscription on stone.

3. How were the 'ten words' divided?—The question turns on the beginning and the end of the Decalogue. Are what we know as the First and Second, and again what we know as the Tenth, one or two commandments? The arrangement which treats the First and Second as one, and the Tenth as two, is that of the Massoretic Hebrew text both in Exodus and Deuteronomy, and was that of the whole Western Church from the time of St. Augustine to the Reformation, and is still that of the Roman and Lutheran Churches. Moreover, it may seem to have some support from the Deuteronomic version of the Tenth Commandment. Our present arrangement, however, is that of the early Jewish and early Christian Churches, and seems on the whole more probable in itself. A wife, being regarded as a chattel, would naturally come under the general prohibition against coveting a neighbour's goods. If, as already suggested, the original form of the commandment was a single clause, it would have run, 'You shall not covet your neighbour's house.'

4. The contents of each table.—If, as suggested, the original commandments were single clauses, it is most natural to suppose that they were evenly divided between the two tables—five in each. This view is adopted without hesitation by Philo, and it is not contradicted by our Lord's division of the Law into the love of God and the love of one's neighbour. It would be difficult to class parents in the category of neighbour, whereas the reverence due to them was by the ancients regarded as a specially sacred obligation, and was included, by both Greeks and Romans at any rate, under the notion of piety.

5. Order of the Decalogue.—The Hebrew texts of Ex 20 and Dt 5 agree in the order—murder, adultery, theft—as the subjects of the 6th, 7th, and 8th Commandments. The LXX (best MSS) in Exodus have the order—adultery, theft, murder; in Deuteronomy—adultery, murder, theft. This last is borne out by Lk 18^{20}, Ro 13^{9}, and by the Nash Papyrus and Philo, and may possibly have been original.

6. Mosaic origin of the Decalogue.—The question has recently been thoroughly examined by H. H. Rowley ('Moses and the Decalogue,' *Bull. of the John Rylands Library*, 1951–52, pp. 81–118), and he concludes for the highly probable authenticity of Mosaic authorship of the Ethical Decalogue over against the Ritual *corpus*. The latter approximates to the pre-Mosaic form, but there are elements in the Ethical code which are more suitably attributed to Moses himself. The prohibition of images of Yahweh is consistent with the complete absence of proof that true Yahwism, which is demonstrably pre-Mosaic, had ever permitted an idol, and the once popular idea that the Ark of the covenant originally contained an image has no actual foundation. Weekly Sabbath observance, whatever it may have implied, goes consistently back to the very earliest form of the Decalogue, and a pre-Mosaic background is not unreasonable despite the nomadic life of the people. All this is common to both codes. The Ritual code is traced to the Kenite Yahweh worshipping groups with which Judah was associated. On the other hand, the Ethical Decalogue, in its simplest and most direct form, most probably belongs to the tribes which Moses himself led from Egypt to Sinai. 'The change from the primitive Decalogue to the Ethical Decalogue is most naturally to be associated with some great prophetic personality, and Moses would supply the personality, and the circumstances of the time the occasion, better than any other individual or time of which we have knowledge' (*op. cit.*, p. 100). This is a drastic and over-simplified statement of Rowley's survey, and although it is admittedly hypothetical it is unlikely that the conclusion will be denied unless some actual evidence to the contrary, such as the archaeological discovery of a post-settlement image of Yahweh among the orthodox Yahweh worshippers, is discovered to contradict it.

On the Decalogue in the NT see LAW (IN NT).

F. H. W.—**B. J. R.**

TEN-STRINGED HARP (or 'harp of ten strings,' or 'psaltery of ten strings').—See MUSIC, **4** (1) (*b*).

TENONS.—See TABERNACLE, **5** (*c*).

TENT.—Apart from the traditions of the patriarchs as 'quiet' men, 'dwelling in tents' (Gn 25^{27} RVm, RSV), the settled Hebrews preserved a reminder of their nomad ancestry in such phrases as 'going to one's tent' for 'to go home' (Jg 19^{9} RV, RSV, cf RVm), and in the recurring call, 'to your tents (*i.e.* to your homes), O Israel' (1 K 12^{16} etc.), as well as in a number of more figurative expressions, *e.g.* Job 8^{22}, Ps 132^{3}, Pr 14^{11}, Is 16^{5}, La 2^{4}. For an interesting case of adherence to the 'nomadic ideal' on religious grounds, cf Jer 35^{7ff} and see RECHABITES.

The Hebrew tent, even in later days, cannot have differed much from the simple Bedouin tent of to-day, made by sewing together strips of the native goats' hair cloth (cf Ca 1^{5} 'I am very dark . . . like the tents of Kedar'). These 'curtains' (Jer 4^{20}, Ex 26^{2} and often) are held up by poles, generally nine in number, arranged in three rows of three, and 6–7 feet high, which are kept in position by ropes—the **'cords'** of EV and the **'tent-cord'** of Job 4^{21} RV, RSV—attached to 'stakes' or **'tent-pins'** driven into the ground by a mallet (Jg 4^{21}). The larger the tent, the longer the cords and the stronger the stakes, according to the figure, Is 54^{2}. The tent, then as now, was probably divided into two parts by hanging a curtain from the three middle poles along the length of the tent—the front division open and free to all, the back closed and reserved for the women and the privacy of domestic life (Jg 15^{1}, Ca 3^{4}; cf Gn 18^{9f}). Adjoining such tents were tents for the cattle, cf 2 Ch 14^{14}, literally 'cattle-tents', and K. Galling, *Biblisches Reallexikon*, 1937, s.v. ZELT.

In time of war we read both of **booths** (2 S 11^{11}, so RV, RSV rightly for AV 'tents') and of tents (2 K 7^{7}, Jer 37^{10}). The Assyrian sculptures represent the soldiers' tents as conical in shape, supported by a central pole with two arms. On the famous bronze sheathing of the palace gates at Balâwât, representing every detail of the conduct of war, the royal **pavilion** (1 K 20$^{12, 16}$, RSV 'booths') is frequently represented. It was rectangular in shape, with ornamental wooden pillars with floral capitals at the four corners. The walls were probably of linen, and the roof evidently of tapestry or other rich material edged with tassels (see the plates in Billerbeck's *Die Palasttore Salmanassars* II., 1908).

In early times a special tent was pitched for a newly wedded pair (Ps 19^{5}, Jl 2^{16}; cf 2 S 16^{22}), as is still the custom among the Arabs. The **canopy** under which Jewish couples are married at the present day still retains the name, as it is a survival of the ancient *ḥuppāh* or bridal tent.

Priscilla and Aquila, as well as the Apostle Paul, were **tentmakers** (Ac 18^{2f}). See SPINNING AND WEAVING, **1**, **4** (*c*).

A. R. S. K.—**E. T. R.**

TENT OF MEETING.—See TABERNACLE, **1.**

TENT OF THE TESTIMONY.—See TABERNACLE, **7.**

TENTH.—See TITHES.

TEPHON.—One of the towns in Judaea fortified by Bacchides, 1 Mac 9^{50} (AV **Taphon**). Tephon was probably an old **Tappuah**; but whether it was Tappuah **1** or **2**, or Beth-tappuah, is uncertain.

TERAH.—The father of Abraham, Nahor, and Haran, Gn 11$^{24-32}$, 1 Ch 1^{26}, Lk 3^{34} (AV **Thara**). Along with his three sons he is said to have migrated from Ur of the Chaldees to Haran, where he died. In Jos 24^{2} it is said that he 'served other gods'—a statement which gave rise to some fanciful Jewish Haggadoth about Terah as a *maker* of idols. **2.** A stopping-place of the Israelites, Nu 33^{27f} (AV **Tarah**). Its location is unknown.

TERAPHIM.—See IMAGES, **2**; ISRAEL, II, **3** (7).

TEREBINTH.—The terebinth or **turpentine** tree (Sir 24^{16} AV) (*Pistacia terebinthus*, the *butm* of the Arabs) is one of the most imposing trees in Palestine. In almost every locality where it is allowed to attain its full growth—30 to 40 feet high—it is associated with a person or tomb (teacher's t. Gn 12^{6}, Dt 11^{30}, diviner's t. Jg 9^{37}, and as a burial place 1 Ch 10^{12}). Dwarfed trees occur everywhere among the oak brushwood. The tree has pinnate, lancet-shaped leaves, and small reddish clusters like immature grape clusters; it is also often covered with curious red galls—like pieces of coral. The dark overhanging foliage affords a grateful shade in summer, but in autumn the leaves change colour and fall off. It is this deciduousness (cf Is 1^{30}) which enables a distinction to be made between very similar Hebrew words, *'ēlāh* and *'ēlōn*, ' terebinth ' and *'allōn*, ' oak ' (see Oak). The distinction is clear in Is 6^{13} and Hos 4^{13}. The abundant branching and foliage of the terebinth is mentioned in the story of Absalom (2 S 18^{9}). The word does not occur at all in AV, and only three times in RV and RSV—in Is 6^{13} for AV's **' teil** tree,' in Hos 4^{13} for **' elm '** and in Sir 24^{16} for ' turpentine tree.' RV margin, and less often RSV margin, have terebinth as an alternative to oak in a few places. Tradition may also have lent confusion: the oak of weeping Gn 35^{8}, the palm tree of Deborah, Jg 4^{5}, and the terebinth of Tabor (? Deborah), 1 S 10^{3}, may all refer to the same tree. E. W. G. M.—**L. H. B.**

TERESH.—A chamberlain of Ahasuerus, Est 2^{21} 6^{2}; called in Ad. Est 12^{1} **Tharra.**

TERTIUS.—St. Paul's amanuensis who wrote Romans and added a personal salutation (16^{22}). It was the Apostle's custom to employ a scribe (no doubt dictating shorthand notes, a common practice), but to add a short autograph himself. The autographs probably are: Ro 16$^{25-27}$, 1 Co 16$^{21-24}$ (expressly), 2 Co 13^{13f} (or ^{11ff}) Gal 6$^{11-18}$ (expressly), Eph 6^{23f}, Ph 4$^{21-23}$, Col 4^{18} (expressly), 1 Th 5$^{25-28}$, 2 Th 3^{17f} (expressly). In the Pastoral Epistles and Philemon, which are personal letters, the presence of autograph passages is more uncertain. A. J. M.

TERTULLUS.—This name (a diminutive of *Tertius*) is that of the advocate hired by the Jews to speak for them against Paul before Felix (Ac 24^{1}). From his name we should judge him to be a Roman; probably he was not a Jew. It has been conjectured (Dean Milman) that his speech is a translation from the Latin, though Greek was allowed in the law courts. It is a gross piece of flattery, for the Jews were in constant opposition to Felix. It accuses Paul of stirring up disturbances, of being the ringleader of an unlawful sect, and of profaning the Temple (cf the reply in 25^{8}). A. J. M.

TESTAMENT.—The word is not found in the OT. In the NT, it occurs thirteen times in the text of the AV and only twice in the text of the RV and the ARV (He 9^{16f}). It never occurs in the text of the RSV. It is always used to translate the Greek word *diathēkē*, elsewhere rendered **' covenant '** (q.v.), in the AV, RV, and ARV. In the RSV, however in Gal 3^{15} and He 9^{16f}, *diathēkē* is rendered **' will '** with ' covenant ' in the margin. In He 9$^{15-20}$, *diathēkē* is always translated ' testament ' in the AV. In the same passage, it is translated ' covenant ' three times and ' testament ' two times in the RV and the ARV, and ' covenant ' three times and ' will ' two times in the RSV. An indication of the difficulty involved in its interpretation is given in a marginal note on all five occurences of *diathēkē* in He 9$^{15-20}$ in the RV and the ARV: 'The Greek word here used signifies both *covenant* and *testament*.' In the RSV, however, this note occurs only on the second occurrence of *diathēkē* in He 9^{15} and on its occurrences in He 9^{16f}.

In classical Greek, *diathēkē* means ' a testamentary disposition,' and *synthēkē* ' a covenant ' or ' a compact.' The latter word connotes an agreement between two persons regarded as being on an equal footing (*syn-*); hence it is unsuitable as a designation of God's covenants with men. Moulton and Milligan (*The Vocabulary of the Greek New Testament*, p. 148) pointed out that *diathēkē* ' is properly *dispositio*, an ' arrangement ' made by one party with plenary power, which the other party may accept or reject, but cannot alter (see Aristophanes, *Birds*, 439). A will is simply the most conspicuous example of such an instrument, which ultimately monopolized the word just because it suited its differentia so completely.' The LXX translators, because this monopoly was not yet established, were free to translate the Hebrew word for ' covenant ' (*b^{e}rîth*) by *diathēkē* which, in its primary sense (*dispositio*), was exactly the needed word.

By the time the NT documents were written, *diathēkē* had come to mean, in common usage, ' will ' or ' testament.' The NT writers, however, because of their knowledge of the LXX, also knew *diathēkē* in its primary sense (*dispositio*) and usually so used it. These two meanings of *diathēkē* made possible a meaningful play on words in Greek which is absolutely impossible in English. Both Paul and the author of the Epistle to the Hebrews took advantage of this fact in Gal 3^{15} and He 9^{16f}. In these verses, *diathēkē* is best translated by ' testament ' or ' will ' if these words are understood to signify ' last will and testament.' All other occurrences of *diathēkē* in the NT are best translated by ' covenant ' if it is understood to signify ' an " arrangement " made by one party with plenary power which the other party may accept or reject, but cannot alter.'

In the NT, *testamentum* is the uniform Latin translation of *diathēkē*. Usually, therefore, it means ' covenant.' This use of the Latin word is the explanation of the fact that, as early as the 2nd cent. of our era, the books of the Old and New Covenants were spoken of as the Old and New Testaments. J. G. T.—**M. M. P.**

TESTIMONY.—See Ark, **1**; Tabernacle, **7** (*a*); Witness; and, for 2 K 11^{12}, Ornaments, **4.**

TESTIMONY BOOKS.—Cyprian (A.D. 200–258) prepared a collection of Biblical proof-texts arranged under subjects and published it in Latin in three books as ' Testimonies ' or ' Ad Quirinum.' A similar collection in Greek has been attributed to Gregory of Nyssa. There are some later collections, particularly one by Bar Salibi (6th cent. A.D.) which survives in Syriac. These compilations are not original; the writers were obviously dependent on earlier works of a similar nature such as Tertullian's ' Adversus Judaeos,' Irenaeus' ' Against Heresies,' and Justin's ' First Apology ' and ' Dialogue with Trypho.' J. Rendel Harris (assisted by G. Vacher Burch) in ' Testimonies ' (Vol. I, 1916; Vol. II, 1920) attempted to prove that all these books were ultimately derived from a Testimony Book (or Books) which was just such a collection of OT prophecies arranged according to subject matter with brief notes of their sources. This was used to prove to the Jews that Jesus was indeed the Messiah. Harris thought that this was the ' Logia ' which Papias says Matthew prepared, and that Papias' own lost five books of ' Oracles of the Lord ' were a commentary on it. His method of proof was to collate and compare the use of OT quotations in the NT and the relevant patristic works with special attention to Justin, Irenaeus, and Cyprian. He thought that common argument, common order, community of error and similarity of text where there were divergencies from the LXX and the MT would prove his case. The evidences of the use of Testimony Books that he found in the NT were (1) wrong ascriptions, such as a text from Malachi being ascribed to Isaiah in Mk 1^{2}; (2) recurrent quotations, such as the passages about the Stone in Mk 12^{10} and parallels, Ac 4^{11}, 1 P 2^{7} *et al*; (3) chains of citation such as Ro 3$^{10-18}$ (previously investigated by E. Hatch); (4) editorial prefaces and comments, so common in Matthew; (5) peculiar texts such as Mt 15^{8f} quoting LXX of Is 29^{13} with variations; (6) anti-Jewish controversial matter, such as Ps 110^{1} quoted in Mk 12^{36} and parallels (cf Ac 2$^{34-35}$, He 1^{13}). The case for Testimony Books found some support from F. C. Burkitt, and more recently it has been restated by B. P. W. Stather Hunt and accepted by Archbishop P. Carrington; but it has been criticised by C. H. Dodd and K. Stendahl. Stather Hunt emphasizes the facts of the conflict of the early Church with Judaism, the Church's appeal to the OT, the motive behind the Gospels of relating the facts about Jesus to the Messianic prophecies, and that few people could afford a complete OT or even complete books of the OT; so that even before the rise of Christianity such selections, probably with a Messianic emphasis, must have been made. Confirmation of this theory has been found at Qumrân where a Messianic florilegium was discovered (published in 1955). The arguments, however, fall short of proving the existence of Testimony Books as written documents.

Dodd and other scholars have urged, first, that such an important work would surely have survived and have been included in the Canon, and second, that the quotation of OT passages in the NT is not necessarily accounted for by the postulate of Testimony Books. The composition of such books was the result, not the presupposition, of the work of early Christian Biblical scholars, and the wide use of NT quotations from the OT in the Fathers is indicative of the influence of the NT itself rather than of common use of a Testimony Book lying behind both the NT and the Fathers. Stendahl's careful investigation of different types of OT quotations in Matthew proves that Matthew's OT quotations come from both the LXX and the MT as well as other possible texts. Any peculiarities or community of error can be explained by the theory of oral tradition. The theory of Testimony Books, therefore, is one possible explanation of certain common features of the use of the OT in the NT and in the Fathers, but the case remains unproven, at least until further light can be shed on the subject by the progress of textual, source and form criticism. F. B.

TESTAMENTS OF TWELVE PATRIARCHS.—See PSEUDEPIGRAPHA, **5**.

TESTICLES.—See STONES, I. **2**.

TETA, 1 Es 5[28] (AV).—See HATITA.

TETH.—Ninth letter of Hebrew alphabet, and so used to introduce the ninth part of Ps 119, every verse of which begins with this letter.

TETRARCH.—Originally (in Macedonia) ' ruler of a fourth part,' the title was apt as applied to Herod Antipas, administrator of Galilee and Peraea (Mt 14[1], Lk 3[1, 19] 9[7], Ac 13[1]), and to his brother Herod Philip who administered Ituraea and Trachonitis (Lk 3[1]) because together they had inherited one half of the territory ruled by their father, Herod the Great (Jos. *Ant.* XVII. xi. 4 [317]). When applied to Lysanius of Abilene in Lk 3[1], it may be understood less literally as ' ruler of a district.' J. S. K.

TETRATEUCH.—See PENTATEUCH, VI (*a*).

TETTER.—See MEDICINE.

TEXT AND VERSIONS OF OT.—**1.** *Text of OT.*—In Hebrew the OT consists of three parts : the Pentateuch, the Prophets, and the Writings (or Hagiographa), which by the Jews are reckoned as twenty-four books. In the English Bible, which has a different order and method of counting, the same books form a total of thirty-nine. The OT was originally written in Hebrew except Gn 31[47] two words ; Jer 10[11] ; Ezr 4[8]–6[18]. 7[12–26] ; Dn 2[4b]–7[28], which are in Aramaic.

The Hebrew alphabet used by the OT writers consisted of twenty-two consonants : it contained no vowels, in this respect resembling the Phoenician, Moabite, Arabic and Syriac alphabets. The old Semitic alphabet was used in Phoenicia as far back as *c* 1500 B.C. The books of the OT were originally written in the older script, but in course of time the MSS were transliterated into the square characters now used in printed Hebrew Bibles. Our knowledge of the pronunciation of Hebrew words, as far as the vowels are concerned, depends on three main sources : (1) Jewish tradition, which is embodied in vowel signs written under, over, or in the consonants of the ancient text ; (2) the Greek versions, which transliterate a large number of Hebrew words, especially, but by no means only, the proper names ; (3) the Assyrian texts : these, being written in a language which expressed in writing vowel sounds as well as consonantal, give us the vowels of such Hebrew names as they cite.

Though in the Hebrew MSS of the Bible, which are of the mediaeval period, the consonants of the original text are accompanied by the vowels which express the traditional pronunciation, it is known that the written vowels formed no part of the original text ; they had to be supplied by the reader.

2. *Date of the addition of vowels of the OT text.*—The date at which the vowels were attached to the consonants of the Hebrew text can be determined only within broad limits. Neither the Talmud (*c* A.D. 500) nor Jerome (A.D. 420) knows anything about the written vocalization. C. D. Ginsburg says that the introduction of the graphic signs took place *c* A.D. 650–680 and that the work of the Massoretes was complete about A.D. 700. It must have been before the 10th cent., for the fully-developed system is employed in the earliest Hebrew Biblical MSS of Massoretic tradition, which date from the beginning of the 10th cent. (or, according to some, from the 9th cent.).

The received text of the Hebrew OT is called the Massoretic Text (MT), because in its present form it rests upon the **Massorah** (Hebrew *massōreth*, ' tradition '), which has been transmitted by Jewish scholars known as the Massoretes. Of special importance here is the insertion of vowel points to indicate the pronunciation. The determinative work was done in the first Christian millennium in two regions : (1) the East or Babylonia ; (2) the West or Palestine, whose chief centre was Tiberias, where the Ben Asher family for five or six generations (middle of the 8th cent. to the middle of the 10th) was eminent. Originally both the Babylonian and the Palestinian method of writing vowels was supralinear, but finally there was developed at Tiberias a more precise system of writing vowels and accents, which is still used in our printed Hebrew Bibles. In the first half of the 10th cent. Ben Naphtali was a rival of Ben Asher, but eventually the text of Ben Asher became the standard one.

3. *Earlier attempts to represent vowel sounds.*—Long before the invention of vowel points certain consonants had been used, though neither systematically nor consistently, to indicate the vowel sounds : thus *h* was used to indicate *a*, and sometimes *e* ; *w* to indicate *o* or *u*, *y* to indicate *i*. This practice in some measure goes back to the times, and doubtless also to the actual usage, of some of the writers of the OT ; but in many cases these consonants used to indicate vowels were added by scribes or editors. This we learn from the fact that passages which happen to occur twice in the OT differ in the extent to which, and the particular instances in which, these letters are employed. Ps 18 occurs not only in the Psalter, but also in 2 S 22 ; the Psalm expresses these consonants used vocalically where 2 Samuel does not ; *e.g.* 2 Samuel writes *'ppny* (v.[5]) and *ḳdmny* (v.[6]), where the Psalm writes *'ppwny* and *ḳdmwny*. In some cases Rabbinic discussions prove that words now written with these vowel letters were once without them ; so, *e.g.* it appears from a discussion attributed to two Rabbis of the 2nd cent. A.D. that in Is 51[4] the word *l'wmy* (' my nation ') was at that time written without the *w*, thus *l'my*. The importance of this fact for the textual criticism will appear later.

4. *Character of evidence for the text of OT.*—The text of the OT has been transmitted to us through circumstances singularly different from those which mark the transmission of the NT text. In this connexion we may confine our attention to the nature of the evidence for the text of the OT furnished by (1) Hebrew MSS, (2) ancient versions.

5. It has often been stated that one well-established result of the examination of Hebrew MSS is that all exisiting MSS are derived from a single edition prepared by Jewish scholars in accordance with a textual tradition which goes back substantially to the 2nd cent. A.D. In view of the number of variant readings in Hebrew MSS and the discovery of the Dead Sea Scrolls this view needs modification. Many MSS, however, have similar peculiarities, such as the occurrence at certain places of letters smaller or larger than the normal, of dots over certain letters, or broken or inverted letters. For example, the *h* in the word *bhbr'm* (Gn 2[4]) is written small in many Hebrew MSS ; it was doubtless written originally so by accident or owing to pressure of room ; but under the influence of a school of Jewish scholars, of whom R. Aqiba in the 2nd cent. B.C. was a leading spirit, all such minutiae of the Scripture came to acquire

TEXT AND VERSIONS OF OT

a mystic significance. Thus the word just cited really means 'when they were created,' but the small *h* was taken to mean that the words were to be translated 'in the letter *h* he (*i.e.* God) created them' (the heavens and the earth), and this in turn led to much curious speculation. As another illustration of this method of interpretation, which was so important in securing from the 1st or 2nd cents. A.D. onwards a remarkably accurate transmission of the text, the case of the word *wyyṣr* in Gn 2⁷ may be cited. The word means 'And he formed'; an alternative orthography for the word is *wyṣr* (with one *y*). Why, it was asked, was it here written with two *y*'s? Because, it was answered, God created man with two *yṣr*'s (*i.e.* two natures), the good nature and the bad. In order to secure the perpetuation of the text exactly as it existed, a mass of elaborate rules and calculations was gradually established; for example, the number of occurrences of cases of peculiar orthography were duly recorded on the margins of MSS of Scripture. The scribes or Sopherim counted all the letters in the OT. In every book they knew the middle letter, the middle word, and the middle verse. With such meticulous information was avoided the possibility of adding or removing words or verses. This textual tradition, known as the **Massorah,** also includes a certain number of variant readings; in this case the one reading (**Kᵉthîbh** 'written') stands in the text, but provided with vowels that do not belong to the consonants in the text, but to the consonants of the alternative reading (**Ḳᵉrê,** 'read,' 'to be read') given in the margin. These two words are Aramaic passive participles. In the Ginsburg text a word having a **Kᵉthîbh** and a **Ḳᵉrê** is left unvocalized in the text, while in a footnote two spellings are given with appropriate vocalization. *E.g.* in Job 9³⁰ the word *bmw*, which means 'with,' should, if vocalized, have the vowel *o* over *w*; but in the Hebrew text the vowel actually supplied to the word is *e* under *m*, which is the vowel that really belongs to the **Ḳᵉrê,** which has the letters *bmy* ('in, with the water of'). The value of the Massorah in perpetuating a form of the Hebrew text for many centuries has doubtless been great; but it has also long served to obscure the fact that the text which it has perpetuated with such slight variation was already removed by many centuries from the original text.

But in spite of the Massorah, certain minute variations have crept into the Hebrew MSS and even into the consonantal text. It must not be supposed, however, that all pre-Massoretic readings have been lost. A study of the variants collated by Kennicott (1776–80) and de Rossi (1784–88) shows that a large number of pre-Massoretic readings have been preserved in Hebrew MSS, and in numerous cases these variants find support in the Old Greek or LXX and the Origenian and Lucianic recensions; cf J. W. Wevers, 'Hebrew Variants in . . . Kings,' *ZAW* lxi (1945–48), 43–76. In the meanwhile, our knowledge of the proto-Massoretic text has been extended through the discovery of the Dead Sea Scrolls.

6. *The earliest MSS.*—(1) *The Dead Sea Scrolls.*—The discovery of the Dead Sea Scrolls (1947–55) has furnished material that carries Hebrew examples of the proto-Massoretic text back to the 2nd cent. B.C. and even earlier. Of prime importance in this connexion is the Isaiah MS (1 Q Isaᵃ), which probably is to be dated in the 2nd cent. B.C. It contains the entire book, and it may be noted that it has thirteen variants which have been accepted by the RSV and cited in the footnotes as from 'One ancient Ms.' In this connexion cf M. Burrows, *The Dead Sea Scrolls*, pp. 305 ff. It has a number of agreements with the LXX as well as various careless mistakes. In spite of all its variants, however, it tends to confirm MT. By using *w* and *y* to indicate vowels it has a rather full vocalization.

Another scroll of Isaiah, incomplete, is known as 1 Q Isaᵇ.

The Habakkuk Commentary (1 Qp Hab) on chs. 1–2 is a work which was probably composed in the 1st cent. B.C.

Among these scrolls are numerous fragments of Biblical MSS, which are of great value in tracing the textual history of the OT. The documents found so far represent copies from the 3rd cent. B.C. into the 2nd cent. A.D. Of Samuel, 4 Q Samᵃ is hardly later than 200 B.C., and 4 Q Samᵇ is probably from the end of the 3rd cent. B.C. The importance of the Samuel fragments is that they represent a text closely related to the LXX. The portions of Daniel are written in a script of the late 2nd cent. B.C., and accordingly this MS is no more than half a century younger than the autograph of the book. It is furthermore important to have fragments of the books of the Pentateuch as well as of the Major and Minor Prophets; at any rate, in the latter instance, such evidence rules out speculation about very late additions to prophetical works. All the canonical books of the Hebrew OT are represented in the Dead Sea fragments with the exception of the Book of Esther.

(2) *The Genizah Fragments.*—It is estimated that a total of 200,000 fragments of MSS was recovered from the Genizah in Cairo, many of which are Biblical. It was here that about two-thirds of the Hebrew text of the Book of Ecclesiasticus was found, which previously had been known only in Greek. The earliest of the Biblical fragments probably belong to the 5th cent. A.D.

(3) *The Nash Papyrus.*—Thanks to a discovery in 1902 we have this fragment, which apparently is not later than the 2nd cent. A.D.; Dr. W. F. Albright, however, has dated it in the Maccabaean period. It contains in Hebrew the Ten Commandments, in a text based on Exodus and Deuteronomy, and Dt 6⁴ᶠ. The order of commandments six and seven is reversed, and the Shemaʿ is introduced by a sentence lacking in MT, but present in the LXX. This papyrus was edited by S. A. Cook in *PSBA* (January 1903).

(4) There are a number of MSS which represent the tradition of the Ben Asher family; the oldest of these are:

(*a*) *British Museum, Oriental* 4445, of Pentateuch. The consonantal text was written probably A.D. 820–850, and the marginal notes cite Ben Asher as the authority.

(*b*) *Cairensis*, which contains the Former and the Latter Prophets, has a colophon, in which it is stated that it was copied by Moses Ben Asher in A.D. 895. It is now in the possession of the Karaite community in Cairo.

(*c*) *The Aleppo MS* of the first half of the 10th cent. It was copied by a scribe in the time of Aaron Ben Asher (A.D. 900–940), who supplied the punctuation and the Massorah. It was in the possession of the Jewish community in Aleppo, who would not permit it to be photographed for use in the preparation of the *Biblia Hebraica*, 3rd edition. It suffered damage in the destruction of the Old Synagogue at Aleppo, and to-day it contains only 294 folios of the presumable original number of 380. It is now being used at the Hebrew University of Jerusalem in the preparation of a new edition of the OT.

(*d*) *Leningradensis*. This MS of the entire OT was copied from the Aleppo MS in A.D. 1008, and accordingly it represents the Ben Asher tradition. It is kept in Leningrad, and it furnished the text for the *Biblia Hebraica*, 3rd edition.

(*e*) *The Petersburg MS of the Major and Minor Prophets*, at Leningrad, was copied in A.D. 916. It represents the text tradition of the West, but the eastern method of writing the punctuation is employed.

(5) The tradition of Ben Naphtali. *The Erfurt MSS*, E^1 (14th cent.), E^2 (13th cent.), E^3 (before A.D. 1000). The punctuation and the text in places follows the Ben Naphtali tradition, while in others there is only the influence of that text.

The Massoretic MSS in addition to having the vowels and accents written, also represent the sectional divisions of the text. In this connexion should be considered the open section (*pᵉthûḥāh*) and the closed (*sᵉthûmāh*), which signify a change of thought; of these the latter denotes a slighter transition than the former. In the Hebrew

TEXT AND VERSIONS OF OT

MSS these sections are indicated by a system of leaving vacant spaces in the text, but in some of the printed editions פ is placed in the text to show where the open section starts, while ס signifies the beginning of a closed one. *E.g.* in Gn 1 an open section begins at the end of v.[5]; likewise at the end of vv.[8, 13, 19, 23, 31]. Many MSS have a closed section in Gn 4[8]. This gap, however, is filled in the LXX and the Samaritan Hebrew with the sentence: 'Let us go out to the field.' In the editions by Ginsburg all these sections are represented by vacant spaces as in the MSS. There are also indicated in the margin of printed Hebrew Bibles the pericopes: the triennial (*s'dhārîm*) and the annual (*pārāshîyôth*). Frequently the pericopes coincide with an open or closed section. The verses are ancient divisions, which the Massoretes carefully marked. The chapters, however, are of Christian and not of Jewish origin. This system of enumeration was first applied to the Vulgate in the 13th cent., probably by Stephen Langton, Archbishop of Canterbury, and later was introduced into the Hebrew Bible for facility of reference.

7. *Critical editions of the Massoretic text.*—S. Baer and Franz Delitzsch published in separate parts the individual books except Exodus–Deuteronomy (Leipzig, 1869–95); the text was based on MSS and Massoretic sources. The received text of our standard editions of the Hebrew OT has been substantially that of Jacob ben Chayim in the Second Rabbinic Bible, Venice, 1524–25. C. D. Ginsburg edited two editions, the first of which was published in two volumes (London, 1894); the second in four volumes (British and Foreign Bible Society, 1926) has copious textual notes in Hebrew. He followed the text of Jacob ben Chayim as did R. Kittel in *Biblia Hebraica,* 1st edition, 1905; 2nd, 1912. The *Biblia Hebraica,* 3rd edition (1937), edited by P. Kahle, A. Alt, and O. Eissfeldt, represents the Leningrad MS; for the first time since the Reformation a MS is made the basis of an edition and Jacob ben Chayim is left aside. Mention may also be made of the *OT in Hebrew,* corrected according to the Massorah of Ben Asher, edited by M. D. Cassuto, 1953, and of the Hebrew Bible edited by N. H. Snaith, published by the British and Foreign Bible Society, 1958.

8. *The Samaritan Pentateuch.*—Before passing from the evidence of Hebrew MSS we have to note that for the Pentateuch we have a Hebrew text representing an entirely different recension. This is the **Samaritan Pentateuch.** The Samaritan Pentateuch is a form of the Hebrew text which has been perpetuated by the Samaritans. It is written in the Samaritan character, which far more closely resembles the ancient Hebrew characters than the square Hebrew letters in which the Massoretic MSS are written. There are no known MSS of the Samaritan Pentateuch older than the 10th cent. The MS at Nâblus purports to have been copied in the thirteenth year after the Conquest, but this date is not accepted by scholars. There is one in the John Rylands Library at Manchester, which is dated A.D. 1211–12. What is probably the oldest is in codex form and is kept at the University of Cambridge. It contains a note saying that it was sold A.D. 1149–50, and accordingly it may have been copied some centuries earlier. The value of the recension lies in the fact that it has descended since the 4th cent. B.C. in a different circle, and under different circumstances, from those which have influenced the Massoretic MSS. Though in some respects, as for example through expansion by insertion of matter from parallel passages, the Samaritan is more remote than the Jewish from the original text, it has also preserved better readings, often in agreement with the LXX. An instance is Gn 4[8]; here in the ordinary Hebrew MSS some words spoken by Cain have certainly dropped out; the Samaritan text and the LXX have the additional words 'Let us go into the field'; this is adopted by RSV: 'Let us go out to the field.'

9. *The Samaritan Targum.*—No thoroughly critical edition of the Samaritan Pentateuch at present exists. The material for establishing a critical text consists of the several MSS and also of the Samaritan Targum—a translation of the Samaritan recension into an Aramaic dialect.

10. *Versions: Earliest MSS.*—We come now to the second main branch of evidence for the text of the OT. The evidence of versions is of exceptional importance in the case of the OT. In the first place, the actual MSS of the versions are much older than the earliest Massoretic Hebrew MSS; in this respect, however, the Dead Sea Scrolls have made a great contribution to our knowledge of the Hebrew text. Not counting the papyri, there are Greek MSS of the OT of the 4th cent. A.D. and there is a Syriac MS of the greater part of the Pentateuch of the date A.D. 464. But secondly, and of even greater importance, the versions, and especially the LXX, represent different lines of tradition; in so far as the original text of the LXX itself can be established, it is a witness to the state of the text some two to four centuries before the date at which the stereotyping of the Hebrew text by the Massoretes took place.

The versions of the OT are either primary, *i.e.* made direct from the Hebrew text, or secondary, *i.e.* made from a version. Secondary versions are of immediate importance in establishing the true text of the primary version from which they are made; and only indirectly witness to the Hebrew text. Among them the Old Latin version is of exceptional importance in determining the text of the LXX. On this and other versions of the LXX, see GREEK VERSIONS OF OT, **11.**

11. *Brief account of the Primary Versions.*—The Primary versions of the OT, arranged in (approximately) chronological order, are as follows:—

(1) The earliest **Greek Version,** commonly known as the **Septuagint.** The earliest part of this version, namely, the translation of the Pentateuch, goes back to the 3rd cent. B.C. The remaining parts of the OT were translated at different later periods; but the version was probably, in the main at least, complete before the end of the 2nd cent. B.C. See GREEK VERSIONS OF OT.

(2) The **Targums.** These Aramaic versions may be considered next, inasmuch as they rest on a tradition earlier than the date of the versions yet to be mentioned; it is probable, however, that no Targum was actually committed to writing till some centuries later, after the later Greek versions, perhaps, too, after the Syriac version, had been made.

The Targums are in large part very free, and even diffuse, paraphrases rather than translations of the Hebrew text. They owe their origin to the custom of explaining the Hebrew passages of Scripture read in the synagogues in the language spoken by the people, which was Aramaic (cf Neh 8[8]). The earliest (as is most generally believed) and least paraphrastic of these versions is the **Targum of Onkelos** on the Pentateuch from Babylonia; it does not appear to have been committed to writing before the 5th cent. A.D., and is first mentioned by name by Saadia Gaon in the 9th cent. Far more paraphrastic is the Targum of the Pentateuch known as the **Targum of Pseudo-Jonathan,** or the **Jerusalem Targum.** Fragments of yet a third Targum of the Pentateuch survive, and are known as the **2nd Jerusalem Targum.** Quite distinct from these is the **Samaritan Targum,** which is a translation of the Samaritan recension of the Hebrew text (see **9**). The chief Targum of the Prophets is that known as the **Targum of Jonathan ben Uzziel**: it is also from Babylonia and was put into final form in the 5th cent. A.D. There are also fragments of an old Palestinian Targum preserved in seven MSS of the 7th–9th cents. recovered from the Cairo Genizah. A lost Targum of Job has been recovered (1956) in one of the Dead Sea caves. Targums of the Hagiographa (with the exception of Ezra, Nehemiah, and Daniel) exist, and there are two of the Book of Esther. Cf TARGUMS.

The text of the Targums will be found in Walton's (and other) polyglots, with a Latin translation. Onkelos has been separately edited by Berliner (1884–86), and the Prophets and Hagiographa by Lagarde (1872). A.

Sperber, *The Bible in Aramaic* (1959) contains: 1. The Pentateuch according to the Targum of Onkelos; 2. The Former Prophets according to the Targum of Jonathan. See, further, Hastings' *DB*, article 'Targum.' There is an English translation of the Targums of the Pentateuch by Etheridge (two vols., London, 1862–65).

(3), (4), and (5) The **Greek Versions** (which have survived in fragments only) of Aquila, Theodotion, and Symmachus, all of the 2nd cent. A.D. See GREEK VERSIONS OF OT, **15–18.**

(6) The **Syriac Version,** commonly called the Peshitta. The date at which this version was made is unknown; the Pentateuch may be as early as the 1st cent., while the rest of the books may be of the 2nd and perhaps some of the 3rd. The earliest extant MS of part of this version is, as stated above, of the year A.D. 464; and the quotations of Aphraates (4th cent. A.D.) from all parts of the OT agree with Peshitta. The character of the version varies in different books, being literal in the Pentateuch and Job, paraphrastic for example in Chronicles and Ruth. The text in the main agrees closely with the Massoretic Hebrew text, though in parts (*e.g.* in Genesis, Isaiah, the Minor Prophets, and Psalms) it has been influenced by the LXX.

(7) The **Vulgate.**—The **Old Latin Version** was a translation of the LXX. To Christian scholars acquainted with Hebrew the wide differences between the LXX and versions derived from it and the Hebrew text then current became obvious. As it seemed suitable to Origen to correct the current LXX text so that it should agree more closely with the Hebrew, so at the close of the 4th cent. Jerome, after first revising the Old Latin, making alterations only when the sense absolutely demanded it, prepared an entirely fresh translation direct from the Hebrew text. The Vulgate is derived from this direct translation of Jerome's from the Hebrew in the case of all the canonical books of the OT except the Psalms; the Psalms appear commonly in editions of the Vulgate in the form of the so-called Gallican Psalter; this was a second version of the Old Latin, in which, however, after the manner of Origen's Hexaplaric text, the translation was brought nearer to the current Hebrew text by including matter contained in the later Greek versions but absent from the LXX, and obelizing matter in the LXX which was absent from the later versions. Jerome's Latin version of the Psalms, made direct from the Hebrew, was edited by Lagarde (*Psalterium juxta Hebraeos Hieronymi*, 1874); the edition edited by J. M. Harden appeared in 1922. An elaborate edition of *Psalterium S. Hieronymi de Hebraica Ueritate interpretatum* has been published in *Biblia Polyglotta Matritensia*, 1960. On the extent to which editions of the Vulgate differ from Jerome's translation, see VULGATE. In some cases additional matter (*e.g.* 1 S 14[41], on which passage see **20**) has been incorporated from the Old Latin.

The effect of the substitution of Jerome's version from the Hebrew text for the Old Latin version of the LXX was to give the Church a Bible which was more elegant and intelligible and in much closer agreement with the Hebrew text current in the 4th cent. A.D.

12. *Two groups of versions. Pre-eminence of the Septuagint.*—Judged from the standpoint of their importance for recovering the original text of the OT, and for the kind of service which they render to OT textual criticism, the primary versions fall into two groups: (1) the LXX, (2) the rest. The LXX differs, and often differs widely, from the Massoretic text; the remaining versions closely agree with it; the LXX dates from before the Christian era and, what is more significant, from before the rise of the Massoretic schools; the remaining versions date from after the Christian era, and, with the *possible* exception of the Syriac, from after the close of the 1st cent. A.D. The agreement of these versions made direct from the Hebrew text at various dates subsequent to 100 B.C. confirms the conclusion that since that date the Hebrew text has suffered relatively little in course of transmission.

A fuller discussion of the versions of the OT other than the LXX would carry us into *minutiae* of the subject which do not belong to a brief sketch such as the present. On the other hand, the LXX claims further attention even here.

13. *The early history of the Hebrew text.*—The history of the Hebrew text since the 2nd cent. A.D. is uneventful; it is a history of careful transmission which has preserved the text from any serious deterioration since that date. But the fortunes of the text before that date had been more varied and far less happy. They cannot be followed completely, nor always with certainty. But the main fact is abundantly clear, that between the ages of their several authors and the 2nd cent. A.D. the Hebrew Scriptures had suffered corruption, and not infrequently very serious corruption. Nor is this surprising when it is remembered that the text in that period consisted of consonants only, that in the course of it the character of the writing was changed from the Old Hebrew to the square character still in use (the difference between the two being much greater than that between old black letter type and the Roman type now commonly used), that in the earlier part of the period copies of the books cannot have been numerous, and that in times of persecution copies were hunted for and destroyed (1 Mac 1[56f]). We are here concerned, of course, merely with such changes as crept into the text accidentally, or such minor changes as the introduction of the expressed for the implicit subject, which belong to the province of textual criticism. The larger changes, due to the editing and redacting or union of material belong to the province of higher criticism, though in the case of the OT it is particularly true that at times the line between the two is not sharply defined. Our chief clues to the earlier history of the Hebrew text, and to the solution of the problems connected with it, will be found in a comparison of MT and the Hebrew of the Dead Sea Scrolls with the Septuagint version, and in certain features of the Hebrew text itself.

14. *The Hebrew Text between c* 250 B.C. and *c* A.D. 100. *The LXX and the Massoretic Text.*—The materials for forming a judgment on the general character of the changes undergone during this period by the Hebrew text, and for the existence of early variant readings in particular passages, are to be drawn mainly from a comparison of the LXX with the various Hebrew texts extant. A much smaller amount of material is to be derived from the quotations in the NT and other early Jewish works, such as the *Book of Jubilees*, written, according to R. H. Charles, at the close of the 2nd cent. B.C.; but so far as it goes this material bears witness of the same general character as that of the LXX.

15. A current solution of the main problem here raised depends on three things: (1) the establishment of the original text of the LXX; (2) the detection of the Hebrew text which lay before the translators; and (3) in cases where the Hebrew text there recorded differs from the present Hebrew text, the determination of the original or older Hebrew reading. A complete solution of the problems will never be reached, for it will be no more possible to establish beyond dispute the original text of the LXX; the detection of the underlying Hebrew text must inevitably often remain doubtful; and when variants are established, there will be in many cases room for difference of opinion as to their relative value. But though no complete solution is to be hoped for, a far greater approximation to such a solution than has yet been reached is possible. A good beginning (though no more) towards the recovery of the original text of the LXX has been made (see GREEK VERSIONS OF OT, **13**), but of really systematic work on the recovery of the underlying Hebrew text there has been far too little. What commonly happens is that in particular passages where the *sense* of the LXX and of the Hebrew text differs, the Greek is retranslated without exhaustive reference to the methods of the translators, and retranslation thus obtained is cited as the variant. In many cases the true variant even thus has undoubtedly been obtained, but in many others a closer and more

TEXT AND VERSIONS OF OT

systematic investigation of the methods and idiosyncrasies of the translators has shown or will show that, through misinterpretation, the support of the LXX has been cited for variants which there is no reason for believing ever had any existence. See GREEK VERSIONS OF OT, **14.**

16. *Distinction between real and apparent variants.*—A difference in *sense* between the Greek version and the Hebrew text as subsequently interpreted by no means necessarily points to a variation in the Hebrew text that underlay the version.

For example, parts of the three Hebrew verbs *šbh* (*to lead captive*), and *yšb* (*to dwell*) and of *šwb* (*to return*) are indistinguishable in the Hebrew consonantal text; the letters *wyšb* may have among others the following meanings, *and he dwelt, and he returned, and he brought back, and he took captive.*

The substitution of one of these meanings for the other occasionally reduces the Greek version to nonsense; inconvenient as this must have been for those who used that version, or versions, like the Old Latin, made from it, it presents no difficulty to those who are attempting to recover the Hebrew original of the Greek version. It may sound paradoxical, yet it is to a large extent true, that for textual criticism the LXX is most useful when it makes least sense; for when a passage makes no sense in the Greek, but can be explained as a translation from the Hebrew, we have the best of reasons for believing that we have before us the original text of the Greek, and through it can recover a Hebrew text of early date. Copyists and translators do not *deliberately* turn sense into nonsense, and sense does not frequently, through mere accidents of transmission, become the particular form of nonsense that can be accounted for by a misunderstanding of a Hebrew original.

As a further illustration we may refer to the Greek translation of the letters *by*; these very commonly occur with the meaning *in me*, but they also represent a particle of entreaty *Oh!* or *I pray!* this particle occurs but rarely, about a dozen times altogether, and its existence was unknown to some of the Greek translators. In the Pentateuch and Joshua it is correctly rendered; but elsewhere it is rendered 'in me' with ridiculous results, as the English reader will see if he substitutes these words for 'Oh' in Jg 6^{13}, 1 S 1^{26}. But again, there is no difficulty in seeing beneath the nonsense of the Greek the true sense and the actual reading of the Hebrew. The ignorance of the translators is as useful to the textual critic as their knowledge.

17. *Euphemistic translations.*—But there are many variations in sense which point to no real textual variants, though both Hebrew and Greek in themselves yield a good sense.

The last clause of the 19th Psalm in the AV, 'O Lord, my strength and my redeemer,' reads admirably; but though the translators give us no clue to the fact, it is *not* a rendering of the Hebrew, it is a translation of the LXX. The Hebrew reads, 'My rock and my redeemer' (so RV, RSV). In this case the LXX rendering is due not to ignorance, but to religious scruple; their rendering is a euphemism. So in Gn 5^{24} the Greek version substitutes 'Enoch was well-pleasing to God' (hence He 11^{5}) for the anthropomorphic 'walked with God' of the Hebrew text; in these cases, if we had not also the Hebrew text we could not discover the original from the LXX with certainty, or, perhaps, even be sure that the translators were influenced by a theological approach. Cf GREEK VERSIONS OF OT, **14.**

18. *Relative values of Greek version and Hebrew text.*—These illustrations may suffice to show both that much care is required in using the LXX for the recovery of the Hebrew underlying it, and also that it is wide of the mark to depreciate the textual value of the version by emphasizing the ignorance of the translators. Before either the fullest or the securest use of the version can be made, an immense amount of work remains to be done; but the importance of doing this work is clear, for even the most cautious deductions have already proved that there are differences underlying the LXX and the present Hebrew text, and that in some instances the LXX text is superior. The relative values differ in the case of different books; and to avoid misunderstanding it should be added that in no case would a simple translation of the LXX bring us as near to the sense of the original document as a translation into English from the Hebrew text; nor would it be possible, unless the Hebrew text had survived, to detect by means of the LXX the correct text and the sense of the original. Perhaps the most important general point to remember is that neither the one nor the other would be nearly as valuable by itself as it is when used in combination with the other.

19. *Examples of important readings preserved by the Greek Version only.*—We may now pass to some illustrations of important variations in which the LXX has clearly preserved an earlier text than the Hebrew. These are much less numerous in the Pentateuch than elsewhere; probably the Law, as the most important Scripture, received at an early period something approaching that great care in transmission which was later extended to the entire OT. It is the more remarkable, therefore, that in one section of the Pentateuch (Ex 35–39) we find striking differences in the arrangement of sections in the Hebrew and Greek texts. Other instances of different arrangement or of marked differences in the extent of the material occur in the Books of Job and Jeremiah (see, further, Swete, *Introd. to the OT in Greek*, 231 ff).

20. In some cases matter subsequently lost (through *homoioteleuton* or otherwise), and now absent from the Hebrew text, survives in the Greek.

A striking illustration of this occurs in 1 S 14^{41}. The Hebrew text underlying the Greek version reads, 'Saul said unto Yahweh, the God of Israel [wherefore hast thou not answered thy servant to-day? If this iniquity be in me, or in Jonathan my son, O God of Israel, give Urim, but if this iniquity be in thy servant Israel], give Thummim.' The words in square brackets are absent from the Hebrew text, but certainly belonged to the original, and the origin of the error is clear: the scribe's eye accidently passed by parablepsis from the first occurrence of 'Israel' to the third, and the intervening words were lost. With the loss of these the sense of the last two words 'give Thummim' became obscure, and the punctuators, followed by RV, gave them an indefensible interpretation. In this case RSV emends the text in agreement with the LXX.

21. In other cases the Greek version is nearer to the original by its relative brevity; the additional matter now present in the Hebrew text was subsequently interpolated.

As an instance of this we may cite 1 K 6^{20f}, which RV, following the Hebrew text, renders, 'And he covered the altar [with cedar. So Solomon overlaid the house within with pure gold: and he drew chains of gold across] before the oracle; and he overlaid it with gold.' The bracketed words are absent from the Greek; it is probable that of these words 'with cedar' stood in the original text, but that the rest were absent. The Greek text has also for the first four words above (before the bracket) what appears to be the superior reading: 'And he made an altar.'

22. At times, when either the sense or the text of both the Hebrew and the Greek seems to be remote from the original it is possible. from a comparison between the two, to recover the original.

An interesting example of this is furnished by Is 37^{27f} =2 K 19^{26f}. RV, following the Hebrew text, renders, 'They were as the grass of the field . . . and as corn (Isaiah, 'a field of corn') blasted *before it be grown up.* But I know *thy sitting down* and thy going out and thy coming in.' RSV follows the same interpretation. The Hebrew text of the underlined words is *lpny ḳmh wšbtk*; the Hebrew equivalent of 'I know' stands much lower in the sentence, and though it may with difficulty be taken as in the RV, more naturally demands a different object. A reading of the Greek *Quinta* preserved only in a

TEXT AND VERSIONS OF OT

marginal note in the Syro-Hexaplar closes v.[26] with the phrase ' before thy rising up ' ; this presupposes Hebrew *lpny ḳmk wšbtk*, which differs from the present Hebrew text by one letter only. The first word, if vocalized as in the Hebrew text and by the Greek translators *liphnê*, means *before*, but if vocalized *lᵉphānay* it means *before me*. Adopting the latter vocalization, we recover (at least so far as the three words are concerned) the original sense, ' They were as grass of the field . . . and as corn that is blasted. Before me is thine uprising and thy down sitting (cf Ps 139[2]) and thy going out and thy coming in I know.' So great is the difference in sense that the corruption of a single letter may make in a text which contained only consonants, and no marks of punctuation whatever. What appears to have been the true reading of the Hebrew in this case was pointed out by J. Wellhausen, *Composition des Hex. u. d. hist.Bücher d.ATs.*[3], p. 282, n.l.

23. *The Hebrew text before the date of the Greek version.*—If the Hebrew text suffered to a very considerable extent in the ways just illustrated, during the three or four centuries that intervened between the time when the LXX version was made and the time when the Hebrew text was stereotyped and the later Greek versions were made, by nothing short of a miracle could the text have been preserved free from errors of transmission during the centuries that separate the original autographs from the date of the Greek version. This intervening period differs, of course, widely in length ; between the age of Isaiah and the Greek translation of the Book of Isaiah lay some six centuries ; between the age of Deborah (Jg 5) and the translation of Judges perhaps 900 years ; between the age of David (2 S 1[19ff]) and the translation of Samuel 800 years. On the other hand, between the final *compilation* of the Pentateuch and the LXX not more than two centuries elapsed, while in the case of the Book of Daniel the time was less than a half a century.

24. *Means of detecting early corruption of Hebrew text.*—Though the general fact that the present Hebrew text contains corruptions that date from these earlier centuries cannot reasonably be questioned, the detection of the actual cases of early corruption is necessarily difficult, and only within limits is it possible. We are obviously far worse situated in attempting to determine corruptions of this date than corruptions of later date ; the LXX often indicates the presence of the later corruptions, but we have no external clue to the earlier corruptions. We have to rely entirely on indications in the Hebrew text itself. One of these indications will of course be the occurrence of nonsense, for the original autographs were intended to convey an intelligible meaning. Another indication will be the occurrence of bad grammar—unless in the case of a particular writer there is reason for supposing that he was not master of the language which he wrote. An interesting illustration of the way in which the latter indication may serve is furnished by some of the references to the Ark.

The Ark is called in Hebrew *h'rn, the ark*, where the first letter is the Hebrew article ; or *'rn bryt YHWH, the ark of the covenant of the Lord* ; where a word in Hebrew is defined by a following genitive it cannot be preceded by the article, so in this second phrase we have *'rn*, not *h'rn*. Now, in certain passages (*e.g.* Jos 3[17]), our present Hebrew text has the grammatically impossible combination *h'rn bryt YHWH* ; some corruption then is present here ; and it is probable that the original text had only *h'rn, the ark*, and that the following words are due to the intrusion into the text of an annotator's explanation.

25. *Negative and positive judgments* : *the justification of conjectural emendation and its limitations.*—The ultimate task of textual criticism is to recover as far as possible the actual words of the original ; an intermediate task of the textual criticism of the OT is to establish all the real variants of the Hebrew text underlying the Greek version, and in each case to determine the relative value of the variants. In this way the text which was the common source of the Greek translators and that of the Jewish scholars of the 2nd cent. A.D. is as far as possible recovered. So far negative and positive judgments must necessarily accompany one another ; we say, Here the Hebrew text is right, and the Greek text wrong, or *vice versa*. But when we have recovered that common source of the Hebrew and Greek texts, it is wise to distinguish sharply between negative and positive critical judgments. The general fact that there are early errors in the Hebrew text must, as we have seen, be admitted ; and, further, no sound criticism of the Hebrew text can proceed far without being compelled to say, This or that is corrupt, even though the Greek version agrees with the Hebrew text or cannot be shown to have differed from it. In some cases where this negative judgment can be passed with confidence, it may be possible with scarcely less confidence to pass to the positive statement. These words are a corruption of these other words ; that is to say, the text in such cases can be restored *by conjecture* ; but in many cases where the first judgment—These words are not the original text—must be passed, the second judgment ought only to take the form—It is possible that such and such words or something like them were in the original text. In brief, we can more often detect early corruption than restore the text which has been corrupted. The reason should be obvious. We may assume that the scribes and Massoretes knew their Hebrew quite well, and emendation or conjectures should be adopted only as a last resort. Before considering any emendation MT should be carefully compared with the LXX and the other ancient versions. Nonsense (to take the extreme case) must be due to corruption, but the sense which it has obscured may altogether elude us, or, at best, we may be able to discern the general sense without determining the actual words.

There can be no question that it is nonsense to say, as the Hebrew text does, that Saul, who was anointed king to meet a national emergency, was a year old when he began to reign (1 S 13[1]) ; but it is impossible to say whether the original text attributed to him twenty, thirty, forty, or any other particular number of years. Nonsense is unfortunately more serious in the original language than in a version ; we may pass from nonsense in the LXX to the actual original consonants of the Hebrew text, which merely require when thus recovered to be correctly interpreted ; but if the Hebrew letters themselves yield nonsense, we are reduced to guessing, and frequently with little hope of guessing right.

26. The preceding paragraphs should have suggested the justification for occasional conjectural emendation in the textual criticism of the OT, and at the same time they should have indicated its limitations. As against a conjectural emendation, it is in no way to the point to urge that the Hebrew text and all the versions are against it ; for the agreement of the Hebrew text and the versions merely establishes the text as it was current about, let us say, 300 B.C.–A.D. 100. The principle of conjecture is justified by the centuries of transmission that the Hebrew text had passed through before that date. It may be worth while to notice also the degree of truth and the measure of misunderstanding involved in another common objection to conjectural emendations. Tacitly or openly it takes this form : Critics offer different emendations of the same passage ; not all of these can be right ; therefore the Hebrew text is not to be questioned. The real conclusion is rather this, The fact that *several* scholars have questioned the text renders the presence of corruption probable, that they differ in their emendations shows that the restoration of the original text is uncertain. The idiosyncrasy of a single scholar may lead him to emend the text unnecessarily ; the larger the number who feel compelled to pronounce it unsound, the greater the probability that it is unsound, however difficult or uncertain it may be to pass beyond the negative judgment to positive reconstruction of the text.

27. *Evidence of parallel texts within the OT.*—We have

TEXT AND VERSIONS OF OT

now to consider in what ways beyond those indicated in **24** the Hebrew text, taken by itself, gives indication of the presence of corruptions, or, on the other hand, of having been accurately preserved, and how it is to be used in order to approximate most closely to the original text, and through it to the original intention of the authors of the several books.

Of most importance, so far as it is available, is the evidence of double texts within the OT. There are certain passages that occur twice over in the OT: *e.g.* Ps 18 is found also in 2 S 22; Ps 14 recurs as Ps 53; 2 K 18^{13}–20^{19} is (for the most part) repeated in Is 36–39; 2 K 24^{18}–25^{21} and 25^{27-30} in Jer 52, and large parts of Samuel and Kings are incorporated in Chronicles. The variations between these parallel texts are of two kinds: some are due to the editor who incorporates in his own the matter common to his work and the earlier work from which he derives it; for example, in drawing on the Books of Samuel and Kings, the Chronicler often abbreviates, expands, or modifies the passages he borrows, with a view to adapting them to his special purpose; or, again, the editor who included the 14th Psalm in the collection in which Ps 53 stands, substituted 'God' for 'Yahweh' (PSALMS **2** (2)). With these changes, which it is the province of higher criticism to consider and explain, we are not here concerned. But the second type of variations is due to accidents of transmission, and not infrequently what is evidently the earlier reading is preserved in the later work; 'and the explanation is very simple: the earlier books were more read and copied: and the more a book is used the worse is its text' (Benzinger). In certain cases there is room for doubt as to the type to which particular variations belong, so, for example, in several variations as between 2 K 18–20 and Is 36–39.

28. *Evidence of mutilated literary forms.*—(1) *Acrostics.*—Thus the comparison of parallel texts furnishes one line of evidence of the way in which the Hebrew text had suffered in transmission before the date of the Greek version. Another proof may be found in the mutilated form in which certain fixed literary forms survive in the present Hebrew text. Most conclusive is the case of the acrostic poems (see ACROSTIC). At times two considerations converge to prove a particular passage corrupt. For example, the early part of Nah 1 consists of a mutilated acrostic: in the middle of v.4 a word beginning with *d* should occur; instead the word *'mll* beginning with ' is found: but this word *'mll* occurs again at the end of the verse. It is probable that *'mll* in the first has been accidentally substituted for a parallel word which began with *d.*

29. (2) *Rhythm and strophe.*—It is possible that further study of the laws of Hebrew rhythm or metre may give us a valuable instrument for the detection of corruption; much has already been attempted in this way, and in some cases already with results of considerable probability. Similarly, in some cases the strophic division of poems admits of conclusions that are again, if not certain, yet probable. Thus in Is 9^8–10^4 and 5^{26-29} we have a poem in five strophes marked off from one another by a refrain; for a discussion of this problem see the commentaries.

30. *Limited extent of corruption of text of OT.*—The considerations adduced in the two preceding paragraphs have a double edge. They show, it is true, that the Hebrew text has in places suffered considerably; but they also indicate certain limits within which corruption has taken place, or, to state it otherwise, the degree of integrity which the transmitted text has preserved. If in the ways just indicated we can detect the loss or intrusion of lines or words, or the substitution of one word for another, we can elsewhere claim a strong presumption in favour of a poem having preserved its original length and structure. For example, the majority of the acrostics have come down to us with little or no mutilation that affects their length or the recurrence at the right place of the acrostic letters. Similarly the very possibility of determining rhythm must rest on a considerable amount of the text having reached us free from far-reaching corruption. A further consideration of a different kind may be found in the fact that a large number of proper names (which are peculiarly exposed to transmissional corruption) as handed down in the Hebrew text have been paralleled in ancient material brought to light by modern discovery. In many cases it is beyond question that names have suffered in the course of transmission; but the correct transmission of rare, and in some cases strange, names is significant.

31. *Secondary nature of vowel letters: bearing on textual criticism.*—So long as we deal with parallel texts, we are not brought face to face with the question of how to deal with a Hebrew text resting on a single authority. Yet the great bulk of the OT is of this class. How, then, is it to be dealt with, especially when there is no control over it to be obtained from fixed literary forms? The first duty of sound criticism is to disregard, or at least to suspect, all vowel letters (see **3**). We cannot, indeed, assert positively that the original writers made no use of these letters, for we find them employed in certain cases in early inscriptions (Moabite stone, Siloam inscription); but in view of the evidence of the parallel texts of the Hebrew Bible of Isaiah (1 Q Isa[a]) for example, of the LXX, and of Rabbinic references, it is certain that in a large number of cases these vowel letters have been added in the course of transmission. The consequence is that we cannot claim any particular vowel letter for the original author; he may have used it, he may not; particularly in the case of earlier writers, the latter alternative is as a rule the more probable. In other important respects the form of the present Hebrew consonantal text differs from what there is reason to believe was its earlier form.

32. *Similarity of certain letters a source of confusion.*—We have seen above (**13**) that the alphabet in which existing Hebrew MSS are written differs widely from that in use at the time when the OT was written; the letter *yôdh*, proverbially the smallest (Mt 5^{18}) in the alphabet in use since the Christian era, was one of the larger letters of the earlier script. It is necessary in doubtful passages to picture the text as written in this earlier script, and to consider the probability of a text differing from the received text merely by letters closely resembling one another in this earlier script.

Thus the letters *d* and *r* are similar in most Semitic alphabets, in some they are indistinguishable; for example, in the Assuan papyri, documents from Egypt of the 5th cent. B.C. (see ELEPHANTINE PAPYRI), *d* and *r* cannot be clearly distinguished, and it was at first disputed whether a particular word which occurs several times is *dgl* or *rgl.* It becomes important, therefore, in dealing with the Hebrew text of the OT to consider the variants which arise by substituting D's for R's. The Hebrew words for Aram and Edom are *'rm* and *'dm* respectively; the context alone is really the only safe clue to the original reading in any particular passage, and the mere fact that the present Hebrew text reads the one or the other is relatively unimportant; thus, for example, the MT is obviously wrong in 2 S 8^{13}, and probably in 2 Ch 20^2 (in these cases RSV reads 'Edomites' and 'Edom'); cf Gn 10^4 Dodanim, where 1 Ch 1^7 has Rodanim; Is 15^9 where 1 Q Isa[a] has Dibon (accepted by RSV) for MT Dimon.

33. *Division of text into words secondary.*—Finally, it must be remembered that there is good reason for believing that the division of the consonants of one word from those of another had not been a constant feature of the text. Consequently we cannot safely assume that the present division always corresponds to that of the original writers.

34. *The starting-point of criticism in attempting to detect the earliest errors in the text.*—From all this it follows that sound criticism requires us to start from this position: the original writers wrote in a different script from the present, used no vowel signs, no marks of punctuation, and even vowel letters but sparingly; either they themselves or copyists wrote the text continuously without dividing one word from another, or at least without systematically marking the divisions. Consequently the canon that the history of the text justifies is that that division of consonants and that punctuation of clauses and sentences must in all cases be adopted which, everything considered, yields the most suitable sense; the Massoretic tradition, however, should always receive prime consideration. Emendations without justification in the LXX and other ancient versions should be adopted only when MT does not make sense or when its reading does violence to the context. And yet there are cases where the Hebrew text gives a division of consonants or clauses which are not the original, but have arisen from accident or particular theories of exegesis. Further, where no division of the existing consonants yields any sense, or but an improbable sense, it must be considered whether the substitution of similar consonants will. Whether the text thus obtained has very much probability of being the original will depend on many considerations.

35. *Illustrations of such errors.*—We shall conclude with some illustrations of the variations in text or sense that arise when the foregoing considerations are allowed due weight. It is not to be understood that in all cases the variations from the traditional interpretation (1–3) or text (4) are certainly the true interpretation or text, but they all may at least be seriously considered.

(1) In some cases simply a fresh punctuation of the sentences without any alteration of the consonants whatever gives an important variation in sense. A good instance is Is 1^{12-14}; even in the present text the denunciation of ritual worship is severe; probably it was once more severe. Thus, without any change in the text, we could render—

'When ye come to see my face,
Who hath required this at your hand?
No more shall ye trample my courts.
The bringing of oblations is a vain thing;
Incense is an abomination to me;
New moon and sabbath, the calling of assembly, I cannot away with.
Iniquity and the solemn meeting, your new moons and your appointed feasts my soul hateth.'

For *'wn, iniquity*, the Greek version has *ṣwm, fast(s)*. We probably have in the history of this passage a series of attempts to soften down the severity and absoluteness of the prophetic denunciation of the externalities of religion.

(2) In the Hebrew Bible the word for man, *'yš*, is distinguished from the word for *fire*, *'š*, by the insertion of the vowel letter *y*; but in the Moabite stone, the Siloam inscription (written in Jerusalem in the age, as is commonly supposed, of Isaiah), and in Phoenician inscriptions, it is regularly written without the *y*, and is thus indistinguishable from the word for 'fire.' Where either of these words occurs, therefore, we must decide by the context only which was intended. In Is 9^{19} did Isaiah mean, 'and the people are as the food (=fuel) of fire,' or 'as the food of man'? By the change of a single letter, *t* to *y*, in the word rendered 'food,' we obtain for the whole phrase 'like those that devour men,' *i.e.* like cannibals—a reading suggested by Duhm, and, in the parallelism at least, worthy of consideration; the LXX, however, does not favour the emendation. A clear instance of confusion of the two words *'yš* and *'š* is Ezk 8^2: for 'fire' RSV reads with LXX 'a man.'

(3) Mutilation of the sense of the original is sometimes occasioned by incorrect division of words in the present Hebrew text. For examples where RSV took this into account, see Gn 49^{20}, Ps 25^{17}, Hos 6^5, Jer 23^{33}. In Ps 73^4 a division of *l^{e}mōthām* into *lāmô tām* gives a reading better than the present text: (RSV) 'For they have no pangs; their bodies are sound and sleek.' Another variant of some importance appears when we divide the words in Is 8^8 differently (viz. *'rṣ k 'mnw 'l* instead of *'rṣk 'mnw 'l*). With this reading the verse closes not with a proper name in the vocative, but with a statement, as in LXX—'The outstretching of his wings shall fill the breadth of the land, for God is with us' (cf v.^{10}). In this connexion, however, it should be noted that the Massoretes may have intentionally given two readings in adjacent verses either to show two possible interpretations or to preserve two alternative traditions.

(4) Parallelism or the context often gives great probability to conjectural readings that differ from the Hebrew text by a letter or two, even though the change is not (clearly) supported by the Greek version. For example, in Dt 33^2 the word *mrbbt* may be an error for *mmrbt* (*m* having accidentally been written once instead of twice, and *b* twice instead of once); then the line would read 'from Meribath-kadesh,' which is a good parallel to 'Paran'; cf Meribath-kadesh (32^{51}).

36. *Alternative Readings.*—In spite of what is supposed to be a standard Hebrew text, the variations in the Dead Sea Scrolls, Kennicott, and de Rossi testify to the existence of alternative readings, which find support in the LXX and later Greek recensions. In this class should be noted the *K^{e}thîbh* and *Ḳ^{e}rê*, which in many cases make equally good sense. In this connexion should also be considered the *s^{e}bhîrîn* (conjectures), which have been preserved by the Massoretes. This, however, does not exhaust the alternative readings. Some of these may be discerned in MT itself, even though no annotations or outward indications are employed. Frequently the Massoretes combined two readings in one verse; *e.g.* Jer 31^{15}, where MT has *bānêhā* and *'ēnennū*. This use of the singular and plural in the same verse shows that there existed two readings for this verse: one where both words were singular, and another where both were plural. By making a conflation neither reading was lost. Synonyms may have been used and interchanged in adjacent verses. In Ezk 27^7 MT has *šēš* (LXX *byssos*) while, 27^{16} has *būṣ*. The error in LXX *tharseis* shows that there was a reading *šēš* in the Hebrew instead of *būṣ*; cf *The J. H. Scheide Bib. Papyri—Ezekiel*, edited by A. C. Johnson, H. S. Gehman, and E. H. Kase, Princeton, 1938, pp. 98–101.

A comparison of the LXX with MT proves that the Hebrew original of the Greek was closer to MT than the notes of many commentators would imply. A study of the variants and alternative readings in the Hebrew leads to the conclusion that for the most part MT represents a good and reliable tradition. With all the evidence available in MT, Hebrew MSS, and the ancient versions we may conclude that we know as much about the text of the OT as we do of that of Shakespeare. For alternative readings, cf O. H. Boström, *Alternative Readings in . . . Samuel*, Rock Island, 1918; J. W. Wevers, *op. cit.*; J. A. Armstrong, *A Study of Alternative Readings . . . Isaiah*, Princeton University dissertation, 1958.

Any study of the subject of this article naturally involves a knowledge of Hebrew. The best edition of the Hebrew Bible is the *Biblia Hebraica*, 3rd ed., and next in order is the text of Ginsburg. In addition to the articles in the larger dictionaries the following may be consulted: A. Bentzen, *Intro. to the OT* (1948); F. Buhl, *Canon and Text of the OT* (1892); M. Burrows, *The Dead Sea Scrolls* (1955) and *More Light on the Dead Sea Scrolls* (1958); F. M. Cross, *The Ancient Library of Qumran and Modern Biblical Studies* (1958); S. R. Driver, *Notes on the Hebrew Text of the Books of Samuel* 2nd ed. (1913), Introduction; C. D. Ginsburg, *Introduction to the Massoretico-critical Edition of the Hebrew Bible* (1897); R. Gordis, *The Biblical Text in the Making: a Study of the Kethib-Qere* (1937); P. E. Kahle, *The Cairo Geniza*, Schweich lectures of 1941 (1947); F. G. Kenyon, *Our Bible and the Ancient MSS.* Revised by A. W. Adams, with introduction by G. R. Driver; R. H. Pfeiffer, *Intro. to the OT* (1941); E. Würthwein, *The Text of the OT*, translated by P. R. Ackroyd (1957).

G. B. G.—H. S. G.

TEXT OF THE NEW TESTAMENT.—1. The text of the NT as read in ordinary copies of the Greek Testament, and as translated in the AV of 1611, is substantially identical with that printed by Stephanus (Robert Estienne) in 1550, and by the Elzevirs in their popular edition of 1624. To this text the Elzevirs in their next edition (1633) applied the phrase 'Textum ergo habes nunc ab omnibus receptum'; and by the name of *Textus Receptus* (TR) or Received Text, it has since been generally known. The edition of Stephanus was based upon the two earliest printed texts of the NT, that of Erasmus (published in 1516), and that of the Complutensian Polyglot (printed in 1514, but not published until 1522); and he also made use of 15 MSS, mostly at Paris. Two of these (Codd. D and L, see below, **7**) were of early date, but not much use was made of them; the others were minuscules (see **5**) of relatively late date. The principal editor of the Complutensian Polyglot, Lopez de Stunica, used MSS borrowed from the Vatican; they have not been identified, but appear to have been late, and ordinary in character. Erasmus, working to a publisher's order, with the object of anticipating the Complutensian, depended uncritically upon a single 12th cent. MS for the Gospels, upon one of the 13th or 14th for the Epistles, and upon one of the 12th for the Apocalypse, mutilated at the end. (Erasmus made good the lacuna by translating from the Latin Vulgate into Greek!) All of these were at Basle, and were merely those which chanced to be accessible.

The TR is consequently derived from (at most) some 20 to 25 MSS, dating from the last few centuries before the invention of printing, and not selected on any estimate of merit, but merely as being ready to the editor's hands. They may be taken as fairly representative of the great mass of Greek Testament MSS of the late Middle Ages, but no more. At present we have over 70 papyri, over 230 uncial MSS and nearly 2500 minuscules and about 1700 lectionaries. The oldest of these is a papyrus fragment of Jn 18, dated within the first half of the 2nd cent. The great Chester Beatty papyri of the Gospels and Acts and of Paul belong to the 3rd cent. and the oldest uncial codices to the following century. The history of **Textual Criticism** during the past three centuries has been the history of the accumulation of all this material (and of the further masses of evidence provided by ancient translations and patristic citations), and of its application to the discovery of the true text of the NT; and it is not surprising that such huge accessions of evidence, going back in age a thousand years or more behind the date of Erasmus' principal witnesses, should have necessitated a considerable number of alterations in the details of the TR. The plan of the present article is, first to set forth a summary of the materials now available, and then to indicate the drift of criticism with regard to the results obtained from them.

2. The materials available for ascertaining the true text of the NT, as of other works of ancient literature, fall into three classes: (1) Manuscripts, or copies of the NT in the original Greek; (2) Versions, or ancient translations of it into other languages, which were themselves, of course, originally derived from very early Greek MSS, now for the most part lost; (3) Quotations in ancient writers, which show what readings these writers found in the copies accessible to them. Of these three classes it will be necessary to treat separately, in the first instance, and afterwards to combine, the results of their testimony. It need not be stressed that the available material is only a tiny fraction of what existed once or that much of the material, especially the later material, though catalogued, has not been examined or collated fully.

3. Manuscripts.—It is practically certain that **papyrus** was used for the originals of the NT books, papyrus being in universal use for literary purposes in the Graeco-Roman world. Mark may have been written on a papyrus codex (*i.e.* in book form) but other NT books were written probably on papyrus rolls separately, and would at first circulate separately; and so long as papyrus continued to be used, it was impossible to include more than a single Gospel or a group of short Epistles in one volume. Consequently there could be no collected 'New Testament' at this early stage, and no question (so far as the conditions of literary transmission were concerned) of fixing a Canon of books to be included in such a collection. Papyrus is a material (made from the pith of the stem of the Egyptian water-plant of that name) which becomes brittle with age, and quite unable to resist damp; consequently papyrus MSS have almost wholly perished—from friction and use if they remained above ground, from moisture if they were buried beneath it. With a few exceptions buried papyri have survived only in Middle and Upper Egypt, where the soil is extraordinarily dry. Literary works and business documents have been dug up of late years in Egypt in very large numbers, ranging from about 500 B.C. to A.D. 700, so that the styles of writing in use at the time when the NT books were written are well known to us; but Christianity and its literature are not likely to have penetrated much beyond Lower Egypt in the first two centuries of their existence, and consequently it is perfectly natural that no MSS of the NT older than A.D. 140 are now extant. The 2nd-cent. papyrus codex fragment (P^{52}) of Jn 18^{31-34} and ^{37f} has been mentioned. Other NT papyri range from the 3rd cent. to the 7th. Of the 3rd-cent. papyri the most important are P^5, containing fragments of John; P^{20}, fragments of James; P^{37}, verses of Matthew; P^{45-47}, the Chester Beatty papyri, large parts of the Gospels and Acts, of Paul and of Revelation; P^{48}, fragments of Acts; P^{49}, verses of Ephesians; P^{53}, fragments of Matthew and Acts, and P^{64} (which Mr. C. H. Roberts places late in the 2nd cent.), fragments of Matthew. The recently discovered P^{66} (Bodmer) papyrus of John is also of the greatest importance. Its date is *c* A.D. 200.

4. Persecution ceased in the 4th cent. and official copies of Christian books were no more surrendered to pagans. The acceptance of Christianity by the Roman Empire gave a great impulse to the circulation of the Scriptures; and simultaneously papyrus began to be superseded by **vellum** as the predominant literary material. Papyrus continued to be used in Egypt until the 8th cent. for Greek documents, and, to a lesser and decreasing extent, for Greek literature, and for Coptic writings to a still later date; but the best copies of books were henceforth written upon vellum. Vellum had two great advantages over a papyrus roll: it was much more durable and those who used it followed the custom, made popular by Christians rather than pagans, of folding their material into book-form or codex so that it was possible to include a much greater quantity of matter in a single MS, to which also reference could be made more easily. Hence from the 4th cent. it became possible to have complete copies of the NT, or even of the whole Bible; and it is to the 4th cent. that the earliest extant Biblical MSS of any substantial size belong, apart from the Chester Beatty papyri.

5. Vellum MSS are divided into two classes, according to the style of their writing. From the 4th cent. to the 10th they are written in **uncials**, *i.e.* in capital letters, of relatively large size (so-called, probably, because they took up originally one twelfth of a line, not because they were one inch high), each being formed separately. In the first half of the 9th cent. a new style of writing was introduced, by the adaptation to literary purposes of the ordinary running hand of the day; this, consisting as it did of smaller characters, is called **minuscule**, and since these smaller letters could be easily linked together into a running hand, it is also commonly called **cursive**. In the 9th cent. the uncial and minuscule styles are found co-existing, the former perhaps still predominating; in the 10th the minuscules have decidedly triumphed, and the uncial style dies out. Minuscules continue in use, with progressive modifications of form (*e.g.* an increasing use of contractions is made), until the supersession of MSS by print in the 15th cent.; at first always upon vellum, but from the 13th cent. onwards sometimes upon paper. **Paper**, an early discovery in China, found its way into the West eventually through the Arabs, who used it from the 8th cent. onwards.

6. Uncial MSS being, as a class, considerably older than the minuscules, it is natural to expect that the purest and least corrupted texts will be found among them ; though it is always necessary to reckon with the possibility that a minuscule MS may be a direct and faithful representative (*e.g.* 1739) of a MS very much older than itself.

In an *apparatus criticus* of the NT some of the 230 uncial MSS are indicated, always by capital letters, first of the Latin, then of the Greek alphabet and one MS by the first letter of the Hebrew. Many uncial fragments are indicated by numerals preceded by O. Further, since comparatively few MSS contain the whole of the NT, it is found convenient to divide the material under four headings : (1) Gospels, (2) Acts and Catholic Epistles, (3) Pauline Epistles, (4) Apocalypse ; and each group has its own numeration of MSS. The uncial MSS which contain all of these groups, *e.g.* A and C, retain these designations in each group ; but when a MS does not contain them all, its letter is given to another MS in those groups which it does not contain ; *e.g.* D, Codex Bezae, for the Gospels and Acts is different from D, Codex Claromontanus, for Paul. The attempt made by von Soden to adopt a new and ' simpler ' system has not been successful ; Gregory, von Dobschütz, and Eltester have developed the old system started by Wettstein in 1751–1752.

7. A selection of the most important *uncial* MSS will now be briefly described, so as to indicate their importance in the textual criticism of the NT :

B. *Codex Vaticanus*, No. 1209 in the Vatican Library at Rome, where it has been since about 1481. One of our oldest and best MSS, its evidence was largely responsible for the changes of text embodied in the RV. It is written in a small, neat uncial, probably of the 4th cent., with three columns to the page. It originally contained the whole Bible (except the Books of Maccabees), possibly with additional books, as ℵ and A had, but it has lost everything from He 9^{14} to the end of the NT, including the Pastoral Epistles (but not the Catholic Epistles, which follow the Acts and hence have escaped) and Apocalypse.

ℵ. *Codex Sinaiticus* sometimes cited as ' S,' originally a complete codex of the Greek Bible. Forty-three leaves of the OT were discovered by Tischendorf in the monastery of St. Catherine at Sinai in 1844, and acquired by him for the University Library at Leipzig ; while the remainder (156 leaves of the OT, and the entire NT, with the Epistle of Barnabas and part of the ' Shepherd ' of Hermas, on 148 leaves) were found by him in the same place in 1859. It was given by the monks of Sinai to the Czar in 1862 and was bought for £100,000 for the British Museum from the Soviet Union in 1933. The Bible text is written with four columns to the page (the narrow columns being a survival from the papyrus period) ; and palaeographers are now generally agreed in referring the MS to the 4th cent., and it is ranked in importance close to B. Tischendorf attributed the original text of the MS to four scribes, one of whom he believed on rather dubious grounds to have been also the scribe of B ; and the corrections to six different hands, of whom the most important are $ℵ^{a}$ (about contemporary with the original scribe, and $ℵ^{ca}$ and $ℵ^{cb}$ (of the 7th cent.). The corrections of $ℵ^{ca}$ were derived (according to a note affixed to the Book of Esther) from a MS corrected by the martyr Pamphilus, the disciple of Origen and founder of the library at Caesarea. It has been held that ℵ itself was written at Caesarea, but this cannot be regarded as certain. Textually it belongs rather to the Alexandrian family ; see below **40 ff.**

Θ. *The Koridethi Codex* of the Gospels was discovered in 1906 by Bartholomée at Koridethi in Western Caucasia. The scribe, who seems to have known little Greek, lived approximately in the 8th cent. but worked on a text akin to that found in minuscules grouped as fam.[1] and fam.[13] especially for the text of Mark. It is usually classified as ' Caesarean ' ; see below.

W. *The Washington codex*, 4th or 5th cent., of the Gospels written in the Western order, Matthew, John, Luke, Mark. The text is almost protean, but the section, Mk 1^{1}–5^{30} gives valuable support to the Old Latin version. At Mk 16^{14f} it contains an apocryphal insertion hitherto known only from Jerome's *Adv. Pelag.* ii. 15, which quotes part of it.

A. *Codex Alexandrinus*, gives an ' Alexandrian text ' for Paul but not the Gospels, which are Byzantine. It was probably written at Alexandria in the 5th cent., and is now in the British Museum. From an uncertain, but early, date it belonged to the Patriarchs of Alexandria ; it was brought thence by Cyril Lucar in 1621, when he became Patriarch of Constantinople, and was presented by him to Charles I. in 1627, and so passed, with the rest of the Royal Library, to the British Museum in 1757. It contains the whole Greek Bible, with the exception of forty lost leaves (containing Mt 1^{1}–25^{6}, Jn 6^{50}–8^{52}, 2 Co 4^{13}–12^{6} ; it also contained originally the two Epistles of Clement and the Psalms of Solomon, but the Psalms and the conclusion of the Second Epistle have disappeared, together with one leaf from the First Epistle. The text of the NT is written by three scribes, with two columns to the page ; there are many corrections by the original scribes and an almost contemporary reviser (A^{a}).

D. *Codex Bezae*, in the University Library at Cambridge, to which it was presented in 1581 by Theodore Beza, who obtained it in 1562 from the monastery of St. Irenaeus at Lyons. It contains the Gospels and Acts, in Greek and Latin, the former occupying the left-hand pages and the latter the right. It is mutilated, Ac 29^{22}–end being lost, together with all, except a few words of the Catholic Epistles, which followed. It is generally assigned to 5th or early 6th cent. Its place of origin has been variously supposed to be southern France, southern or western Italy, Sardinia, or Egypt ; but the evidence is not decisive in favour of any one of these. Its text is very remarkable, containing a large number of omissions (especially in the Gospels) and a large number of additions (especially in Acts) as compared with the TR. In some places the Latin seems to have been accommodated to the Greek, in others the Greek to the Latin. There is affinity also with some Syriac readings and it has even been suggested that its Greek side is a retranslation from an Aramaic Targumizing version of the original Greek text. Its type of text is usually classed with those of the chief representatives of the Old Latin and Old Syriac versions.

D_2. *Codex Claromontanus*, in the Bibliothèque Nationale at Paris, written probably in the 6th cent., contains the Pauline Epistles in Greek and Latin, the latter being practically independent of the Greek. Preceding the Epistle to the Hebrews is a list of the books of the NT, with the number of *stichoi* (or normal lines of sixteen syllables each) in each of them, which must be descended from an early archetype, since it places the books in an unusual order and includes in the list several uncanonical books (cf descriptions of ℵ and A) ; the order is Matthew, John, Mark, Luke, Romans, 1 and 2 Corinthians, Galatians, Ephesians, 1 and 2 Timothy, Titus, Colossians, Philemon, 1 and 2 Peter, James, 1, 2, and 3 John, Jude, Barnabas, Apocalypse, Acts, Hermas, Acts of Paul, Apocalypse of Peter (Thessalonians, Hebrews, and Philemon being omitted). The MS was in the monastery of Clermont, whence it was acquired by Beza, who was also the owner of D. It may possibly have been written in Italy. Other Graeco-Latin MSS of the Pauline Epistles are E_3 F_2 G_3, which all go back to the same archtype as D_2.

E_2. *Codex Laudianus*, in the Bodleian Library at Oxford, contains Acts in Greek and Latin, the latter holding the place of precedence on the left. Probably of the 7th cent., it was in Sardinia at an early date, and may have been written there ; thence it came to England (probably with Theodore of Tarsus in A.D. 669) and was used by Bede. The Greek text is somewhat akin to that of **D** ; the Latin has been accommodated to the Greek, and is of little independent value. It is the

TEXT OF THE NEW TESTAMENT

earliest MS extant that contains Ac 8^{37}, though the verse was in existence in the time of Irenaeus (late 2nd cent.).

H_3. *Codex Coislinianus* 202, of the 6th cent., consists of forty-one leaves of Paul's Epistles, eight of which are in the original home on Mount Athos, twenty-two in Paris, three each in Moscow, Leningrad, and Kiev, and two at Turin. The MS represents the text of the Pauline Epistles as edited by Euthalius in the 4th cent.

L. *Codex Regius*, of the 8th cent., in the Bibliothèque Nationale in Paris, contains the Gospels. It is remarkable as containing both the shorter conclusion of Mark (see RSVm) as well as the usual longer one, 16^{9-20}, a note before each saying that it is found in some copies. Its readings often agree with those of **B** against TR.

N. *Codex Petropolitanus*, contains the Gospels, written in large silver letters on purple vellum, in the 6th cent. One hundred and eighty-two out of two hundred and twenty-eight leaves (the latter being slightly less than half of the original text) are in Leningrad. It is textually akin to **Σ** which was copied from the same original and not far distant from two other purple MSS **O** and **Φ**, all these MSS giving support to the 'Caesarean' clan, where their witness is not Byzantine.

Σ. *Codex Rossanensis*, at Rossano in Calabria, 6th cent. Contains Matthew and Mark, written in silver letters on purple vellum, with illustrations. See above on **N**.

O. *Codex Sinopensis*, in the Bibliothèque Nationale at Paris. 6th cent.; 43 leaves mainly of Mt 13–24, written in letters of gold on purple vellum with 5 illustrations like those of **Σ**.

Φ. *Codex Beratinus*, at Berat in Albania, 6th cent., contains Matthew and Mark in silver letters on purple vellum; is is textually akin to **N** and **Σ**, but not so closely related to them as they are to one another.

C. *Codex Ephraemi*, a 5th cent. palimpsest (in the Bibliothèque Nationale in Paris), *i.e.* a manuscript of which the original writing has been partially washed or scraped off the vellum in order to use it again to receive other writing. In this case the original writing was the text of the Greek Bible in one broad column to the page; and this was sacrificed in the 12th cent. in order to inscribe on the same vellum some treatises by St. Ephraem of Syria. Only 64 leaves of the OT now survive, and 145 of the NT (out of 238); and often it is impossible to decipher the original writing.

Δ. *Codex Sangallensis*, of about the 9th cent., at St. Gall, a Graeco-Latin text of the Gospels, the text of Mark being apparently unrevised and of the Alexandrian type; the Latin side, unfortunately, has been assimilated to the Vulgate.

Λ. *Tischendorfianus III*, in the Bodleian Library at Oxford, of the 9th cent., contains Luke and John. Matthew and Mark, written in minuscules, are in Leningrad. This MS is chiefly notable for a subscription stating that its text was derived 'from the ancient copies at Jerusalem.' Similar subscriptions are found in a group of 12 minuscule MSS.

T. A number of fragments from Egypt, mostly bilingual, in Greek and Coptic (Sahidic). The most important, T or T^a in the library of the Propaganda at Rome, consists of 17 leaves from Luke and John, of the 5th cent., with an Alexandrian text. $\mathbf{T^1}$ (otherwise **099**) has the double ending in Mark.

Ξ. *Codex Zacynthius*, a fragmentary palimpsest of Luke, in London, was written in the 8th cent. It alone has the same section divisions as **B** and where the text has not been assimilated to the Byzantine textual type, it is Alexandrian.

Ψ. *Codex Laurensis*, at Mount Athos, written in the 8th or 9th cent., contains Mk 9–end, Luke, John, Acts and Paul. Like **L** it has the double ending of Mark. For the rest of Mark it has been less assimilated to the Byzantine form of text than elsewhere and is Alexandrian.

046. *Codex Vaticanus 2066* at Rome, written in the 8th cent., contains the Apocalypse and textually stands at the head of some 40 minuscules, which diverge from both the textual type behind the uncial MSS and that of Byzantine MSS. This MS is sometimes quoted misleadingly as $\mathbf{B_2}$.

K. *Codex Cyprius*, in the Bibliothèque Nationale in Paris, written in the 9th cent., contains the four Gospels in a Byzantine text.

$\mathbf{P^5}$. (P. Ox. 208 and 1781), a 3rd cent. codex, perhaps a lectionary originally, containing fragments of John. It has many omissions; it agrees with **B** and **ℵ** against **D** and goes closely with **ℵ** (*e.g.* Jn 1^{34}) except in parts of Jn 16.

$\mathbf{P^{20}}$. (P. Ox. 1171), a late 3rd cent. codex, containing fragments of Ja 2–3, supporting the text of **B**, **ℵ** and **C**.

$\mathbf{P^{37}}$. A late 3rd cent. codex, containing fragments of Mt 26. The text supports that of **Θ**, **ℵ** and **B** in that descending order, rather than that of **D**.

$\mathbf{P^{45}}$. Chester Beatty Papyrus, a 3rd cent. codex of the Gospels and Acts (ed. by Sir F. G. Kenyon, 1933) contains large fragments of those books with hundreds of readings of the utmost importance textually. The text of the Gospels seems to be 'Caesarean,' oscillating between a **B**-type and a **D**-type but the text of Acts (*i.e.* of fragments of 4–17) supports the **B**, **ℵ** and **A** text on the whole.

$\mathbf{P^{46}}$. Chester Beatty Papyrus, a late 3rd cent. codex, containing large fragments of Pauline Epistles in the following order, which is unusual! Romans, Hebrews, 1 and 2 Corinthians, Ephesians, Galatians, Philippians, Colossians, 1 and 2 Thessalonians. There is no certain evidence that the Pastorals were included.

$\mathbf{P^{47}}$. Chester Beatty Papyrus, a late 3rd cent. codex, contains fragments of Rev 9–17.

$\mathbf{P^{48}}$. P. Soc. Ital. 1165, a 3rd cent. codex with a Western text of fragments of Acts.

$\mathbf{P^{49}}$. Yale P. 415, a 3rd cent. codex, having fragments of Eph 4–5, of an Alexandrian type textually.

$\mathbf{P^{52}}$. P. Rylands Gr. 457, fragment of a codex written in the first half of the 2nd cent., with portions of Jn 18 in an Alexandrian text.

$\mathbf{P^{53}}$. A 3rd cent. Michigan codex, with fragments of Mt 26 and Ac 9–10^{1} in an indeterminate type of text.

$\mathbf{P^{64}}$. At Magdalen College, Oxford, a codex written *c* A.D. 200 with fragments of Mt 26.

$\mathbf{P^{66}}$. The Bodmer papyrus codex containing about two-thirds of Jn 1^{1}–14^{26}, written *c* A.D. 200 with a text standing in the middle of the Alexandrian family. (Cf K. Aland, *TLZ*, lxxxii, 1957, 161–184 and *ZNW*, 1957, 157; A. J. F. Klijn, *New Testament Studies*, iii, 1937, 327–334, and F. Lasserre, *Revue de Théologie et de Philosophie*, 1957, 44–57. For Jn 14–21 cf Victor Martin, *Papyrus Bodmer II, Supplement*, 1958.)

$\mathbf{P^{67}}$. At Barcelona, 3rd cent. fragments of Mt 3 and 5, akin to **ℵ**.

$\mathbf{P^{72}}$. Papyrus Bodmer VII–VIII contain Jude and 1 and 2 P, published by M. Testuz, 1959.

8. Passing to the *minuscules*, we find the number of witnesses overwhelming, though they are but a small part in comparison with the MSS that have been lost. There are more than 2500 such MSS, most of them containing only the text of the Gospels many of these being in a fragmentary state. It is, of course, impossible to give any individual account of so great a mass of MSS, many of which have never been fully examined though more and more are being collated by the joint efforts of British and American scholars. It is true, however, that the minuscule MSS contain much the same type of text as that underlying the TR. The fact that over 90 per cent. of these MSS contain substantially the late Byzantine or ecclesiastical text may be taken as universally admitted, whatever may be the inferences drawn from it. The most noteworthy MSS are those which depart from this normal standard and ally themselves with some of the early Uncials. If a Byzantine reading is supported by an early papyrus, it is shown not to be the product of late scribal conflation or error unless it is coincidental.

For instance, in the Gospels 33 is akin to the text found in **B ℵ**. Ferrar noted the family group named after him or named Family[13] to which 13, 60, 124, 346, 348, 543,

TEXT OF THE NEW TESTAMENT

13, 788, 826, 828 and others belong; Lake noted Family[1] headed by 1, 118, 131, 209; Gregory separated Family[1424], Colwell, Family[2327], and K. W. Clark, Family[2412]. Other such families remain, no doubt, to be discovered and to be connected with particular localities, as the Ferrar group is with Calabria. Families[1] and [13] both seem to witness to the early form of the Caesarean text written probably in Egypt, apart, of course, from harmonization with the Byzantine text. (The numeration of these MSS is that of Gregory, adopted by Eltester and Aland, despite von Soden's alternative system.)

For the Pauline Epistles 33 and 1739 lend valuable support to the Alexandrian text and for the Catholic Epistles the following do the same, 6, 33, 81, 104 and 326; the last four of these, with 1175, support the same text of Acts.

In Apocalypse, where uncials are scarce and minuscules consequently more important, the following give a valuable non-Alexandrian text 2329, 2351, 69, 141; 598, 2302; 1, 2186, 181; 1732; 104.

9. One other class of MSS remains to be mentioned, namely the *Service-Books* or *Lectionaries*, in which the Gospels, Acts and Epistles were divided into portions to be read on each day throughout the ecclesiastical year. These books fall into two classes, according as they contain the lessons from the Gospels (*Evangelia* or *Evangeliaria*) or from the Acts and Epistles (*Praxapostoli*). There are over 1200 of the former and 300 of the latter. Over 100 of these are uncials, but with hardly an exception they are of relatively late date, unless some early papyrus fragments are from an Evangelia rather than from Tetraevangelia. Where it occurs, the uncial style is preserved because liturgical documents tend to be conservative, but the MSS are of comparatively late date, usually 9th cent. or later. Thanks chiefly to American scholars such as E. C. Colwell and D. W. Riddle, these MSS are beginning to be studied. It is hoped that light will be thrown on the history of the Byzantine or ecclesiastical text at least, if not on the older local and divergent textual types.

The standard lists of NT MSS are those of C. R. Gregory, *Prolegomena* to Tischendorf's *NT Graece*, ed. 8, 1864, reproduced in German, with additions, in his *Textkritik des NT*, 1900; of E. von Dobschütz, *ZNW* xxiii, 1924, 248–264; xxv, 1926, 299–306; xxvii, 1928, 216–222; and xxxii, 1933, 185–206; and of K. Aland, *ZNW* xlv, 1954, 179–217, and xlviii, 1957, 145–191.

10. The Versions.—The second class of authorities, as indicated in **2**, is that of the versions, or translations of the NT into languages other than Greek. It is only the earlier versions that can be of service in recovering the original text of the NT; modern translations are of importance for the history of the Bible in the countries to which they belong, but contribute nothing to textual criticism. The early versions may be divided into Eastern (Syriac, Coptic, Armenian, Arabic, Ethiopic, etc.) and Western (Latin and Gothic), but the distinction is of little importance. Age is a more important factor than locality, and the two oldest, and on the whole, most important (though not necessarily the most trustworthy) are the Old Latin and Old Syriac versions, which, moreover, are in many respects akin to one another. Next in importance are the Coptic versions and the Latin Vulgate; and the Armenian and later Syriac versions are also of considerable value. It will be convenient to describe the several versions under their respective countries in the first instance, and to defer the discussion of their characters and affinities until the tale of our authorities is complete.

A. Syriac Versions.—

11. *The Diatessaron.*—The question has been much debated whether the harmony of the four gospels made by Tatian, the Diatessaron, was older than the Syriac version of the separate gospels; in all probability it was, and it influenced them. Tatian, an Assyrian Christian and a disciple of Justin Martyr, compiled (probably about A.D. 170) his harmony either in Syriac or in Greek; the discovery in 1933 of a tiny fragment of the Greek Diatessaron at Dura Europos, written before A.D. 256, does not clinch the argument that Greek was the original language. Tatian's activity was mainly in the East; the Diatessaron circulated most extensively in Syria, where it was almost the sole form of the Gospels in use until the 5th cent.; and a commentary on it was written by the Syrian Father Ephraem. These facts suggest a Syriac origin. However, the Greek name for the Diatessaron and the variant in Mk 9[15] *proschairontes* for *prostrechontes*, unless it was a Tatianic variant with widespread influence, and the Dura fragment, point to a Greek original. It is also increasingly recognized that Latin and other harmonies found in the West depend on an early Latin recension of the Diatessaron, which was more probably a rendering from the Greek than the original of it. Tatian is likely to have used a form of the Greek text as his base, which was current in Rome (*c* A.D. 170), altering it occasionally to suit his own views. Until 1880 the Diatessaron existed only in name, and the very fact that it was a compilation from our four canonical Gospels was a matter of controversy. In that year, however, E. Abbott called attention to the fact that in 1876 G. Moesinger had published a Latin translation of an Armenian treatise which had been printed in 1836 and which was, in fact, St. Ephraem's Commentary on the *Diatessaron.* Subsequently two copies of an Arabic version were discovered and from these the text was published by Ciasca in 1888; since then, the Beyrouth fragments have come to light and a further MS was published by Marmadji in 1935, and an 18th and a 19th cent. codex have appeared, both based on older copies. These texts point to two forms of the Arabic text, which itself was altered, unfortunately, to make it agree with the Peshitta or Syriac Vulgate text (see below). A 16th cent. Persian MS based on a 13th-cent. copy was published by Messina in 1951; it is derived from a Syriac text and preserves many Tatianic readings but not Tatian's order of the sections of his harmony. Some of the Syriac Fathers, *e.g.* Aphraates, witness to Tatian's text, as does Ephraem's commentary, extant only in Armenian (see Leloir's edition).

On the Western side, Codex *Fuldensis* prepared by order of Bishop Victor of Capua (*c* A.D. 545) is a harmony based on Tatian's but made to conform first to an Old Latin, then to the later Latin Vulgate text. The 14th-cent. Liège MS, in Dutch, was published in the middle of the last century; other Dutch versions were collected and published by Plooij and others in 1929–1938. These all point back to one or more Latin harmonies of a Tatianic character, which had been subjected comparatively little to the influence of the Latin Vulgate. Also based on a Latin Diatessaron is the Italian evidence, which appears in Venetian and Tuscan form in MSS of the 13–14th cents. Traces of Tatian's influence have also been found in German, French, and English works; for an English one, see M. Goates' edition of the *Pepysian Gospel Harmony*, 1922.

The material for the reconstruction of the Diatessaron is now so extensive that only a team of scholars is capable of following up the work of Baumstark on this enterprise. It is tragic that the early MSS of the Diatessaron were destroyed. Bp. Theodoret of Cyrrhus in the 5th cent. could boast that he collected and destroyed two hundred copies, replacing them with the four separate Gospels.

Some slight traces of an ancient Syriac text of Acts and Paul exist in the *Liber Graduum* (edited by Kmosko, 1926) as well as in Aphraat's *Demonstrations* and in an Armenian translation of Ephraem's commentaries; whether Tatian was the author of this text is in doubt.

12. *The Old Syriac Version* (OS).—The evidence for the character, and even the existence, of the Old Syriac version is of comparatively recent discovery. Before 1842 the earliest extant Syriac version was the Peshitta (see below), to which, however, a much higher antiquity was assigned than is now admitted. In that year, however, W. Cureton discovered, among the MSS brought to the British Museum from the convent of S. Maria Deipara

TEXT OF THE NEW TESTAMENT

in the Nitrian desert in Egypt, an imperfect Gospel text very different from the Peshitta. This (which was not finally published by Cureton until 1858) was known for fifty years as the Curetonian Syriac, and the relative age of it and the Peshitta was a matter of controversy among scholars. In 1892 Mrs. A. S. Lewis and Mrs. Margaret Gibson from Cambridge discovered in the monastery of St. Catherine at Sinai a palimpsest MS, which was subsequently recognized from their photographs as containing a text closely akin to the Curetonian. Comparison of the two showed that they represented different recensions of the same version, the Lewis or Sinaitic MS (Syr.-Sin.) containing the earlier form of it. Neither is complete, though Bensly, Burkitt, J. R. Harris, and Hjelt added to the knowledge of it, Hjelt visiting Sinai in 1911 to check disputed readings and publishing his results in 1930. The Curetonian (Syr. Cur.) contains nothing of Mark except 16^{17-20}, just sufficient to show that the last twelve verses were present in this form of the version, though they are absent from Syr.-Sin.; of John it has only about five chapters, and there are large gaps in Matthew and Luke. Syr.-Sin. contains a large part of all four Gospels, but none is intact. Both MSS are assigned to the 5th cent., Syr.-Sin. probably being the earlier; but the version which they represent dates back probably to the 3rd cent., perhaps even to A.D. 200, as Burkitt maintained, ascribing it to Bishop Palut. It had widespread influence (denied by Burkitt) even after Bishop Rabbula's time at Edessa. The OS text, which tends to be short, has often an affinity with 'Western' MSS. Streeter took it to witness to a text-type of Antioch rather than to class it with the 'Western'; the scribes of the latter may have been Jewish Christians with a knowledge of Syriac.

13. *The Peshitta.*—Previous to the discovery of Syr.-Cur., the Peshitta was believed to be the oldest Syriac version and was sometimes regarded as the queen of all the versions, a title that has been given more justifiably to the Armenian. Its date was supposed to be referable to the 2nd cent. Even when the superior claims of the OS version came to be generally admitted, the Peshitta was assigned to the 4th cent. at latest, on the ground that traces of it were supposed to be found in the Biblical quotations of St. Ephraem, who died in A.D. 378. Since, however, it was shown (by Burkitt, *S. Ephraem's Quotations from the Gospels*, 1901) that the treatises in which the use of the Peshitta is observable are not the genuine work of Ephraem, this evidence falls to the ground, and there is nothing now to prove the existence of the Peshitta before the 5th cent. Vööbus has found traces of this version as early as A.D. 411 and he would not credit Rabbula of Edessa with its creation, as Burkitt and many others following him did. It was probably the gradual growth of a school rather than the work of one man. (But see M. Black on Vööbus' view, *The Bulletin of the John Rylands' Library*, xxxiii, 1951, 203 ff.) It did not completely supersede its predecessors, as is often alleged, but it appears in both branches of the Syrian Church (Nestorian and Monophysite) whose quarrel dates back to A.D. 431. The name Peshitta means 'the simple,' perhaps to distinguish it from the *Evangelion-da-Mehalletê*, 'the Gospel of the mixed' or the Diatessaron, and from the *Evangelion-da-Mepharreshê* or 'Gospel of the Separated,' *i.e.* four-fold Gospel. MSS of the Peshitta go back to the century of its origin, the 5th, unless its growth started in the 4th. There are over 180 Gospel MSS in this version, and over 150 of Catholic Epistles and Paul. One Gospel MS can be dated A.D. 463–464 and the British Museum possesses another (of Matthew and Mark) of the same century. The Apocalypse, with the four minor Catholic Epistles, was not included in the Syriac canon. The later MSS reproduce the earlier very faithfully, so that the modern edition by the British and Foreign Bible Society (1905–1920), based on the researches of Gwilliam and Gwynn, does not differ substantially from the first (A. Widmanstadt, 1555). Ropes maintains that for Acts the Peshitta preserves some early Western readings embedded in a text akin to that of our early Uncial MSS (*Beginnings of Christianity*, iii, pp. cxlix, 291 ff).

14. *The Philoxenian Syriac.*—Unlike the Latin Vulgate, the Peshitta was not entirely unchallenged in its supremacy. In A.D. 508 Philoxenus, Jacobite Bishop of Mabug in eastern Syria, caused a new translation of the NT to be made by one Polycarp; but of this nothing has come down to us except the four minor Catholic Epistles (which were incorporated into the Peshitta to fill the gap caused by their original omission there) and a single MS of the Apocrypha (at Trinity College, Dublin, published by Gwynn in 1897). The style of Philoxenus was free and idiomatic, and the Greek text on which it was based was that of the majority of the late MSS.

15. *The Harklean Syriac.*—On one view, a complete revision of Philoxenus was made in A.D. 616 by Thomas of Harkel, who converted its idiomatic freedom into extreme literalness, and added various readings in critical notes, which show an acquaintance with a Greek MS or MSS of Western character for Acts at least, second in importance only to that of Codex Bezae itself. About thirty-five MSS of Harkel are known, dating from the 7th and 8th cents. onwards. The Apocalypse, which is now incorporated with the Peshitta, is probably derived from this version. On the other, less likely, view, Thomas did no more than add marginal notes from a few Greek MSS to the version of Philoxenus.

16. *The Palestinian Syriac.*—Yet another Syriac version exists, but in a different version from those hitherto described; for, whereas they all belong to E. Syria, with its centre at Edessa, this is in the Western Aramaic characteristic of Palestine and its neighbourhood. For some decades now no new discoveries have been made of MSS in this version, apart from two fragments published by H. Duensing (*ZNW*, xxxvii, 1938, 42–46). The extant MSS, few in number, are mainly lectionaries. F. C. Burkitt argued that it owed its origin as a version to the efforts of Justinian and Heraclius to abolish Judaism in Palestine in the 6th cent., and that it came again into prominence in the 11th cent.

It has also been suggested that this version was preserved by the Melkites or Royalists after Chalcedon or even that this version rests on the primitive oral tradition of Palestinian Christianity which was not reduced to writing until the 5th cent. The three principal MSS of the version are dated in 1030, 1104, and 1118.

On the Syriac versions see especially articles by Woods and Gwilliam in *Studia Biblica*, vols. i. and iii.; A. S. Lewis, *The Four Gospels translated from the Sinaitic Palimpsest*, 1894; Gwynn, *Apocalypse of St. John in a Syriac Version*, 1897; F. C. Burkitt, *Evangelion da Mepharreshê*, 1904; B. M. Metzger, *The Evidence of the Versions for the Text of the NT*, in M. M. Parvis and A. Wikgren's *New Testament MS Studies*, 1950; A. Vööbus, *Neue Materialen zur Geschichte der Vetus Syra in den Evangelienhandschriften*, 1953, and his *Early Versions of the NT, MS Studies*, 1954, 67–131.

17. *The Armenian Version.*—The first state to accept Christianity as its official religion, Armenia, received the Gospel in Greek form from the West and in Syriac from the South; according to Lazar of Pharpi the written Armenian Gospels were derived from the Greek; according to Koriun and Moses of Chorene, from the Syriac. The latter tradition is probably correct, the earliest translation into Armenian having been undertaken by Sahak and Mesrop *c* A.D. 400 from a Syriac text. There is still doubt whether this was the Diatessaron or an OS text. Hints of this Arm[1] text, as it has been called, can be gleaned from the writings of some of the Armenian Fathers, such as Agathangelus, Koriun, Eznik, Pseudo-Gregory, and John Mandakuni (S. Lyonnet, *Biblica et Orientalia*, xiii, 1950). After A.D. 431, this version seems to have been revised with the help of Greek MSS received from Constantinople, perhaps akin to **B** and **ℵ**, and perhaps also of Greek MSS showing, for the Gospels at least, a Caesarean tendency. The

TEXT OF THE NEW TESTAMENT

printed text of Zohrab rests on this Arm[2] version. The earliest extant MSS usually omit the last twelve verses of Mark; but one, which has them, has a marginal rubric assigning them to the 'Elder Ariston' (Aristion?), the presbyter known to us by a mention in Papias; this rubric may be due, however, to the guess of a 10th-cent. scribe of this MS, E. 229, derived from the Armenian version of Eusebius, *HE* iii. 39 (4).

On the Armenian version see F. C. Conybeare, article in Hastings' *DB*; J. Armitage Robinson, *Euthaliana*, 1895; F. Macler, *Le texte arménien de l'évangile d' après Matthieu et Marc*, 1919; A. Merk, *Biblica*, vii, 1926, 40–70; E. C. Colwell, *Journal of Religion*, xvii, 1937, 48–61; S. Lyonnet, *Les origines de la version arménienne et le Diatessaron*, 1950, and L. Leloir, *S. Ephrem, Commentaire de l'évangile concordant, version arm.*, 1953 (*C.S.C.O.* 137).

B. Latin Versions.—

18. *The Old Latin Version* (OL).—As Christianity spread westwards, inevitably it came into contact with the Latin-speaking population of the Roman Empire; and a translation of the NT into Latin might naturally be looked for at an early date. Indeed, since the gospel was preached in Rome by St. Paul himself, it might seem reasonable to suppose that Latin versions of the Christian literature would have been required almost as soon as it came into being. Colour might be lent to this view by the theory that 'the magic square,' ROTAS-OPERA-TENET-AREPO-SATOR (which seems to point to 'Pater noster' with A and O written in the form of a cross), found at Pompeii implies that there were Latin-speaking Christians there before A.D. 79. Similarly, several scholars, working independently on the Diatessaron in its Western forms, have been led to postulate a primitive Latin Diatessaron, which may underlie even the OL text. At the same time, one cannot overlook the bilingual character of the Roman Empire, even in Italy. The educated classes spoke and wrote Greek freely; the uneducated classes were largely recruited from the East, and spoke Greek more naturally than Latin. The evidence of the predominantly Greek character of the primitive Roman Church is clear. St. Paul wrote to it in Greek. The names of those whom he salutes are mainly Greek (but was Ro 16 addressed originally to Ephesus?). All the early literature of the Church in Rome was Greek. It is no more than a tempting hypothesis that the Latinisms in the Pastoral letters and the absence of most of the Pauline particles from them point to an original Latin form of these letters. So far as we know, the Church in Gaul used Greek too: the report on the martyrdoms at Vienne and Lyons, which the Christians of that province sent to their brethren in other countries, was written in Greek. Irenaeus (*c* A.D. 135–202), the most famous representative of the Gallican Church in the 2nd cent., came from Asia Minor, and wrote his works in Greek; all the traditions of Gallia Narbonensis were Greek, not Latin. The first theologian to write at Rome in Latin was the 3rd cent. Novatian.

19. There was one large and important province in which Greek had no place, and where Latin was alike the literary and the spoken language. This was Africa, where the Mediterranean coast, and especially the district which is now Tunis, was inhabited by a large Latin-speaking population. When Christianity was first introduced into the province is uncertain; but in the 2nd cent. it was strong and flourishing there. The twelve Christians of Scillium, in pro-consular Numidia, were asked before their martyrdom what they had in their chest; they replied, 'the books and letters of Paul, a righteous man.' ('The books' included, doubtless, the Gospels, if not the prophets as well.) Tertullian (*c* A.D. 150–220) defended the faith hotly. Two lines of argument combine to show that the earliest Latin version of the NT known to us had its home in Africa. The first mention of the existence of a Latin version occurs in Tertullian; and that type of text which, of all those represented by our extant OL MSS, appears on internal grounds to be the earliest, is identical with the Biblical quotations in the writings of Tertullian's junior contemporary and compatriot, Cyprian (*c* A.D. 200–258). Whether the version was actually made in Africa cannot be determined with certainty. It is true that its Latinity agrees with that of certain African writers of the 2nd and 3rd cents. (Apuleius, Arnobius, Lactantius, besides Tertullian and Cyprian); but it so happens that there is very little non-African Latin of that period in existence for comparison with it. The kinship which the OL has with the Syriac has caused Antioch to be suggested (by Sanday) as the original home of the version, that being a metropolis where Syrian and Latin elements met, and whence versions of the Scriptures in either tongue might radiate from a common centre. But the strong general resemblance between the two versions may be due to ex-Jewish converts with a knowledge of Semitic languages and perhaps of Syriac MSS especially, which they may have taken far from Syria itself. There is also a considerable amount of divergence between the two versions in details, so that one cannot be dogmatic. That the original home of the OL was, after all, Rome is the recent plea both of G. Bardy and of C. Mohrmann; Bardy thinks that Latin versions of 1 *Clement*, the *Shepherd of Hermas*, and the *Didache* were soon made at Rome from the Greek and Miss Mohrmann points to the use of Latinisms in the *Shepherd*, *e.g.* 'statio.'

20. The extant MSS of the OL are mainly fragments; for after the supersession of this version by the Vulgate its MSS naturally fell into neglect, and survived only fortuitously. The number of them is a little over 40, and they are habitually indicated by the small letters of the Latin alphabet. The following are the most important:

a. Codex Vercellensis, at Vercelli, containing the Gospels (in the usual Latin order, Matthew, John, Luke, Mark), somewhat mutilated, assigned to the 4th cent.

b. Codex Veronensis, at Verona, containing the Gospels on purple vellum; 5th cent.

c. Colbertinus, at Paris, of the 12th cent., contains the whole NT, chiefly in a Vulgate text; but Mark and Luke mainly and in part Matthew and John (especially Jn 1–6) have escaped harmonization with the Vulgate.

d. The Latin text of *Codex Bezae* in the Gospels and Acts, and of *Codex Claromontanus* in the Pauline Epistles.

e. Codex Palatinus, at Vienna, considerably mutilated; 5th cent. One leaf is at Dublin. It contains the Gospels in silver letters on purple vellum. In the Acts, *e* is the Latin text of *Codex Laudianus*; in Paul, that of *Codex Sangermanensis*.

f. Codex Brixianus, at Brescia, of the Gospels, in silver on purple vellum; 6th cent.

ff[2]. *Codex Corbeiensis II*, at Paris, containing the Gospels, but imperfect, of the 5th or 6th cent.

g. Codex Gigas, at Stockholm; a complete Bible of the 13th cent., with Acts and Apocalypse in an OL text. Written in Bohemia, it is a remarkable example of a late survival of OL.

h. Palimpsestus Floriacensis, at Paris; palimpsest fragments, formerly at Fleury, of Acts, Catholic Epistles, Apocalypse, in an African text; see A. C. Clark's edition of Acts.

i. Codex Vindobonensis, at Vienna, with fragments of Luke and Mark in silver on purple vellum; of the 6th cent.

k. Codex Bobiensis, at Turin; contains Mk 8–16 (ending at 16[8]), Mt 1–15; 4th or 5th cent. Contains the OL in an early form with slight traces of the apocryphal Gospel of Peter; see A. Bakker's collation.

m. The *Speculum* of Pseudo-Augustine, which contains copious quotations from the NT. It is probably of Spanish origin, and should be reckoned with the Fathers rather than with the MSS.

q. Codex Monacensis, at Munich, containing the Gospels; 6th or 7th cent.

The remaining MSS are, for the most part, only small fragments, of a few leaves each. The Apocalypse is also found, almost complete, in the commentary of Primasius, written in Africa in the 6th cent.

21. With these MSS must be reckoned the *quotations of the early Latin Fathers*, notably Tertullian (who, however, appears often to have made his own translations, and is also too inexact to be of much service in this respect), Novatian, Cyprian, Hilary, Lucifer of Cagliari, Ambrose, Jerome, Augustine, Tyconius, Priscillian and (as just noted) Primasius. It is usual to classify all these authorities (MSS and Fathers) under three heads of (1) African, (2) European, (3) Italian and to assume that the African type of text is the earliest; it is certainly very rough in style and vocabulary. In both these respects the European is so far modified as to be supposed by some scholars to be the result of fresh translations. The 'Italian' is taken to be a revision of the European but its very existence is in doubt, the words of Augustine (*De Doctrina Christiana*, II, xv [22]; *PL* xxxiv, col. 46) having been challenged, 'In ipsis autem interpretationibus Itala ceteris praeferatur; nam est verborum tenacior cum perspicuitate sententiae.' Burkitt thought that by 'Itala' Augustine referred to the Vulgate; others have emended Augustine's 'Itala' to read 'illa' or 'Aquila.'

The problem of grouping the OL MSS is complicated by the fact that no two MSS represent quite the same type of text. All (except perhaps *k*) have undergone modification in some respect, either by the corrections introduced by scribes in early times, or by contamination with the Vulgate. Cyprian and *k*, so far as they go, represent the African text of the Gospels in what appears to be a fairly pure form; *e* and *m* come next to them; *h* is a good African authority in Acts and Apocalypse, and Priscillian, Tyconius and Primasius in the Epistles and Apocalypse. The leading representatives of the European family are *a* and *b* for the Gospels, with the Latin version of Irenaeus; in Acts, *d*, *g* and Lucifer; in the Pauline Epistles, the Latin texts of *Codex Claromontanus* (D), *Sangermanensis* (E), *Augiensis* (F), and *Boernerianus* (G); and *g* for the Apocalypse. For the 'Italian' group *f* is said to be the most pronounced and it has been taken by Wordsworth and White as the best representative of the OL text which Jerome had before him when he undertook his revision of the Latin NT. (Souter argued, however, that at least for Luke, Jerome used a text like *a*.) Next to *f* in this category *q* is placed—but this category should be subsumed perhaps beneath 'European.' The Latin texts in the bilingual MSS have to be used with caution, as they show signs of assimilation to the Greek. The remaining MSS are either too fragmentary to be of much service, or too mixed in their text to be classified definitely with any family.

In general character, as already indicated, the OL version (especially in its earliest form) belongs to the same class of authorities as the Old Syriac and Codex Bezae, the class, namely, which is distinguished by rather striking divergences from both the TR and the text represented by **B** and **ℵ**. The character and claims of this type of text will be considered later; here it will be sufficient to point out the high antiquity which can be established for it through the OL (and still more through the consensus, so far as it exists, between OL and OS), and the great amount of divergence which exists between the several MSS which contain it. It is not possible even approximately to reconstruct the original OL text; it is even a matter of dispute whether it had one original or more. What is certain is that it underwent constant revision and alteration, and that the few and fragmentary MSS which have come down to us, and of which no two agree even approximately with one another, do but reflect a state of textual confusion which was rampant in the Latin Bibles of the 4th cent.

22. *The Vulgate*.—This state of confusion is described in emphatic terms by the great Latin Fathers of the 4th cent., Jerome (*c* A.D. 345–420) and Augustine (A.D. 354–430) and it was to the former that the task fell of attempting to reduce the chaos to order. The credit of inspiring the work which was to become the Bible of the West for a thousand years is due to Pope Damasus (pope, A.D. 366–384). At his request, Jerome, the leading Biblical scholar of the day, who had devoted many years to the study of the Scriptures in the East in their original tongues, being a *vir trilinguis*, undertook, as he says in his preface to the NT, to 'make a new work out of an old one' by revising the existing Latin texts with reference to the original languages. He began with the Gospels, about the year A.D. 382; and at first his revision was on conservative lines. Where the existing text fairly represented the sense of the original, he let it stand, without enforcing complete accuracy; only where errors affected the sense did he feel bound to make alterations. The Greek MSS which he employed have been disputed; Wordsworth and White believed them to be akin to **B**, **ℵ** and **L**, von Soden to his reconstructed **I—H—K** text, and F. C. Burkitt to **B** and **A**, the latter being a late ecclesiastical text for the Gospels. The Gospels were revised by A.D. 383. Doubt has been cast on Jerome's authorship of the Epistles. De Bruyne suggested that the 'Vulgate text' of the Pauline Epistles was actually that of Pelagius, though the latter's text may have been assimilated to that of the Vulgate; Diehl suggested that it went back to Novatian's text. The Vulgate text of Acts has been shown by J. H. Ropes to approximate to that of A and OL MSS, and that of the Apocalypse by H. J. Vogels to the text of **ℵ**. Vogels thinks that the OL text(s) on which Jerome also based his work for the Gospels approximated to *b-c-ff-i-q*. At about the same time Jerome was beginning his work on the OT by a revision of the Psalter; but for the history of this, see TEXT OF THE OT, **11** (7), and VULGATE.

23. The later history of the Vulgate, as Jerome's version eventually came to be called, is the subject of a separate article. Here it is only necessary to mention that the received text of it, which is found in all ordinary Latin Bibles, is that which was officially sanctioned by Pope Clement VIII. in 1592, and that the critical edition of the NT has been produced by Bishop J. Wordsworth and Dean H. J. White, Dr. C. Jenkins, Dr. H. F. D. Sparks and Mr. A. W. Adams. In 1908 Pope Pius X. ordered the Benedictines to prepare a new edition, which in over 50 years has not progressed beyond part of the OT.

The principal MSS of the Vulgate include:

Σ. *Codex Sangallensis 1395*, of the 6th cent. Nearly half the text of the Gospels is extant on leaves used for bindings. According to C. H. Turner it is the oldest MS of the Vulgate.

A. *Codex Amiatinus*, at Florence, contains the whole Bible. It was written in the N. of England, at Wearmouth or Jarrow, by order of Ceolfrid, abbot of these monasteries, early in the 8th cent., and was taken by him in A.D. 716 as a present to Pope Gregory. Ceolfrid died on the way, but his companions completed the gift, and the MS has since remained in Italy; for some time it was at Monte Amiata, whence its name. Its text was probably derived from one or more MSS brought to England from Italy; it is regarded as among the best extant MSS of the Vulgate. Twelve leaves of a closely cognate MS are in England, one in the British Museum, eleven in private possession.

C. *Codex Cavensis*, at La Cava, near Naples; 9th cent. Contains the whole Bible, written in Spain in a Visigothic hand; it is reckoned among the best of the Spanish family of Vulgate MSS.

D. *Codex Dublinensis*, or *Book of Armagh*, at Dublin; 8th or 9th cent. Contains the NT in an Irish hand.

Δ. *Codex Dunelmensis*, in Durham Cathedral Library; 7th or 8th cent. Contains the Gospels, with a text akin to that of A.

F. *Codex Fuldensis*, at Fulda in Germany; between A.D. 541 and 546. Written by order of Bishop Victor of Capua. Contains the whole NT, the Gospels being arranged in the same manner as Tatian's Diatessaron, on the basis of a copy of a Latin version of that work accidentally found by Bishop Victor; unfortunately the actual text is harmonized with that of the Vulgate.

G. *Codex Sangermanensis*, at Paris; 8th or 9th cent.;

contains the whole NT, Matthew in an OL text. Its text of Acts is most valuable as a Vulgate text.

H. *Codex Hubertianus*, and Θ, *Codex Theodulfianus*, contain the edition of the Vulgate produced by Bishop Theodulf of Orleans, for which see VULGATE.

K. *Codex Karolinus*, and V, *Codex Vallicellianus*, of the 9th cent., represent the edition of Alcuin. (See *ib.*)

L. *Codex Lichfeldensis*, or *Gospels of St. Chad*, at Lichfield, 7th or 8th cent. Contains Matthew, Mark, and Lk 1¹–3⁹.

O. *Codex Oxoniensis*, in the Bodleian Library; 7th cent. Akin to X it contains the Gospels in a text affected by Irish influences.

Q. *Codex Kenanensis*, the *Book of Kells*, at Trinity College, Dublin; 8th cent. Contains the Gospels, lavishly decorated in the Celtic style. Its text, naturally, is of the Irish type.

S. *Codex Stonyhurstensis*, at Stonyhurst College; 7th cent. Contains John alone, in a text akin to that of A and Y. Formerly at Durham and probably written in that neighbourhood, it is connected with St. Cuthbert.

V. See K above.

X. *Codex Corporis Christi Cantabrigiensis*, at Cambridge; 7th cent.; contains the Gospels in a text akin to O. Both MSS at one time belonged to St. Augustine's, Canterbury.

Y. *Codex Lindisfarnensis*, in the British Museum; contains the Gospels; written at the end of the 7th cent., in honour of St. Cuthbert († A.D. 687), with beautiful Anglo-Celtic ornamentation. Some liturgical directions inserted in it show that it was copied from a MS written in Naples, no doubt one brought to England by Hadrian, abbot of a monastery near Naples, who came to England with Archbishop Theodore in A.D. 669. It is closely akin in text to A.

Z. *Codex Harleianus*, in the British Museum; 6th or 7th cent. An excellent copy of the Gospels with a text different from A's. Wordsworth and White relied on A, C, F, Θ, K, T, V in Acts, to which may be added:—

G. *Codex Sangermanensis*, at Paris; 9th cent. Contains the whole Bible, but is particularly good in Acts, so that Wordsworth and White state that their text agrees with it oftener than with any other MS.

O. *Codex Oxoniensis* or the *Selden Acts*, in the Bodleian Library; 8th cent. The text is of the Irish type.

24. The MSS may be grouped as follows:—

For the Gospels; A, S, Y, Δ (Northumbria); also F; Z, Σ (Italy); O and X (mixed Italian and Irish); D, L, Q (Ireland); C, T (Spain); K, V (Alcuin's edition); and Θ, H (correctors) (Theodulf's edition).

For Acts, the most valuable are G and O (Selden), C, A, F and D.

For Paul's Epistles, A, F, D, H; C; Θ, K, V.

For the Catholic Epistles and Apocalypse, A, F, D, V.

Since Jerome's revision was based on OL MSS as well as on Greek Uncials, some of which may have been ancient, his NT at least is of composite character. The historical importance of the Vulgate is dealt with in a separate article.

For the OL version see H. A. A. Kennedy in Hastings' *DB*; F. C. Burkitt, *The Old Latin and the Itala*, 1896; the prefaces by Wordsworth, Sanday, and White to their editions of *Old Latin Biblical Texts*; A. Jülicher, *Itala, das Neue Testament in altlateinischer Überlieferung nach den Handschriften*, 1938–1954 (Matthew, Mark, Luke); H. J. Vogels, *Evangelium Colbertinum*, 1953; M. J. Lagrange, *Critique textuelle, ii, La critique rationelle*, 240–281; B. M. Metzger, in Parvis and Wikgren's *New Testament MS Studies* 1950, 51–55; and A. Vööbus, *Early Versions of the NT*, 1954, 33 ff. On the Vulgate, see Westcott's article in Smith's *DB*, White's chapter in Scrivener's *Introduction*, 4th edition (which deals with both versions); the prefaces to Wordsworth and White's edition of the Vulgate 1899–1954; Lagrange, *op. cit.*, 281–312 and Vööbus, *op. cit.*, 53 ff.

C. COPTIC VERSIONS.—

25. Coptic is the literary form of the vernacular language of Egypt, the descendant of the ancient tongue which we know first in its hieroglyphic form, and later in its demotic, but differing from them in adopting the Greek alphabet, with the addition of certain letters to represent sounds not employed in Greek. Coptic is the outcome of the Greek settlement in Egypt, which took place under the empire of the Ptolemies and continued under that of Rome; and along with the Greek characters the native tongue adopted also a considerable number of Greek words. It is uncertain when this form of writing came into being. It appears in a primitive form in a certain pagan horoscope now in the British Museum, the date of which is probably A.D. 95; and it is reasonable to suppose that it became established as a literary medium in the course of the 2nd cent. It is quite possible that its growth was promoted by the need for it in making the Gospel known to native converts. Christianity was probably introduced into Alexandria or even into other parts of Egypt before the end of the 1st cent., to judge from the date of Greek papyri with a bearing on John. It would have come in the first instance to the Jews of Alexandria and to the Greek-speaking population generally. Even when it penetrated farther, and addressed the native population in its own tongue, its message is likely at first to have been oral, and the earliest Coptic versions of the NT may well have been merely oral paraphrases, such as were the earliest Anglo-Saxon versions. What is, no doubt, the first mention of Coptic Scriptures occurs in the Life of St. Anthony, who is said to have heard the Gospel (Mt 19²¹) read in church as a youth *c* A.D. 270; and since he was not acquainted with Greek, this must have been a Coptic version, whether oral or written. Early in the 4th cent. the monks of the order established by Pachomius were required by their rule to study the Scriptures. Also between *c* A.D. 300–320 the British Museum papyrus Or. 7594 was written, containing, oddly, a text of Deuteronomy, Jonah, and Acts. Towards the end of the 3rd cent., therefore, at the latest, and possibly by the end of the 2nd (as Hyvernat, Horner, and Thompson maintain), a Coptic translation of the NT (except the Apocalypse) was in circulation. The Coptic versions unquestionably have some very early characteristics, not due entirely to their peasant vocabulary.

26. The Egyptian language was not uniform throughout the country, but possessed various local dialects. Two of these are well marked, and possess a respectable quantity of literature, almost wholly theological. These are the Bohairic, or dialect of Lower (northern) Egypt, and the Sahidic, or dialect of Upper (southern) Egypt. Between the two lie several dialects collectively known as Middle Egyptian, viz. Fayumic, Memphitic, Achmimic, and sub-Achmimic.

27. *The Sahidic Version* (Sah., formerly called Thebaic).—At one time it was held that the Bohairic version (Boh.) was the first in point of age, since it was the version of Lower Egypt, which would have been the first to receive Christianity; but Coptic scholars are agreed that the order of precedence must be inverted. Lower Egypt was very largely Greek speaking, and the language in which the Septuagint was familiar would have been sufficient for a considerable time. In Upper Egypt, though there were considerable Greek communities there also, and in the principal towns Greek must have been generally understood, the population as a whole must have been more Egyptian, and an Egyptian version of the NT would have been required there sooner than in the neighbourhood of Alexandria. The characteristics of the Sahidic version also suit this hypothesis of an earlier date. It is rougher and less literary in style than the Bohairic, and its text is of an early date, akin in some details, though not as a whole, to the OL and the OS; in the OT its text is in some books pre-Origenian. Enough fragments of different dates exist for G. Horner to publish *The Coptic Version of the New Testament in the Southern Dialect* (1911–1924, with a valuable critical apparatus), making a mosaic, as it were, of the remains.

Since 1910 scholars have had access also to MS Morgan 569, a tetraevangelium of the 8th or 9th cent., published by Hyvernat; since 1924 to *The Gospel of St. John according to the earliest Coptic MS*, containing Jn 2^{12}–20^{20}, of the 4th–5th cent., in a Sahidic-Achmimic dialect, published by Sir Herbert Thompson. On the whole Cop.^{sa}, as it is often termed, agrees with B or with D, more often with the former than the latter, and seldom with the latter's peculiar additions (*e.g.* in Acts) or omissions.

28. *The Bohairic Version.*—This, which became ultimately the Bible of the Coptic Church, is better known than Sah., and is preserved in a considerable number of MSS. The date of its origin has been much debated. In favour of an early date is the fact that the Apocalypse was apparently not originally contained in it; this book seems to have been generally accepted after the end of the 3rd cent., but was regarded with some doubt before. A fragment of a 4th (or possibly 5th) cent. MS of Ph 3^{19}–4^{9} in sub-Bohairic, to which P. E. Kahle (jun.) drew attention, and the presence of Bohairic variants in the sub-Sahidic John mentioned above point to the probability that the Bohairic version was in existence during the 4th cent. If the date of the schoolboy's exercise in copying Ro $1^{1-8, 13-15}$ in Bohairic could also be confirmed as of the 4th cent., as Husselmann maintained, the probability would become certainty; but other scholars date the exercise as much as two centuries later. There seems no ground for accepting now Guidi's late date, in the 8th cent., nor on the other hand for asserting with W. H. Worrell that Boh. is older than Sah.

The Bohairic version follows the Greek very closely, being closer to Greek MSS such as L or other secondary Alexandrian Uncials than Sah., and comparatively uncontaminated by Western MSS (known to exist from an early date in Egypt). Divergent readings of the type represented by OL and OS, which are found not infrequently in Sah., are almost absent from Boh. An early Boh. MS of the Gospels is the Curzon Catena (an intermixture of text and commentary) in the Parham Library, which is dated A.D. 889; one of the oldest and best continuous MSS of the Gospels is Huntington MS 17, in the Bodleian, dated 1174. Many others are late and some have Arabic versions in the margin. G. Horner's edition of fragments of Boh. (1898–1905) needs to be supplemented by reference to more recent researches mentioned in W. Kammerer's *A Coptic Bibliography* (1950), especially those by J. H. Ropes, W. H. P. Hatch, P. L. Hedley and H. C. Hoskier.

29. *The Middle Egyptian Versions.*—Of these the Achmimic has left most traces, including fragments of three chapters of John, James and of Jude on one MS, and fragments of Ja 5^{17-20} on another; also a codex of Lk 12–18 of the 4tn or 5th cent. exists in fragments and an early 4th cent. fragment of Mt 11^{25ff}. The 'spread' of these fragments suggests that most of our NT existed once in Achmimic; but the date of the version, presumably before the end of the 4th cent.. is uncertain. This version may be an entirely different translation from the Sah. rather than an early form of it. Still less can be said about the Fayumic version. Fragments exist of 2 Thessalonians and of 1 Peter in it.

30. Other versions exist—Georgian, Ethiopic, Arabic, Persian, Sogdian, Nubian, Gothic and Old Slavic—but one cannot dwell at length on these; see B. M. Metzger (*op. cit.*) and A. Vööbus (*op. cit.*). Some of them throw welcome light on texts and versions already discussed, *e.g.* the Georgian seems often to depend on the Old Armenian and to witness to a 'Caesarean' streak in the Gospels; and the Gothic version, the work of Bishop Ulfilas, reflects an early form of the ecclesiastical or Byzantine text. The versions that are of first-rate importance are those that have been described above—the Syriac, Latin, and Coptic versions. Of these the Old Latin and Old Syriac take the first place, both on account of their age, and because they are the chief extant representatives of a very early and important type of text, as will be seen below. Next in textual importance are Sah. and Boh., which give us the evidence of Egypt, the country which has played, perhaps, the largest part in the history of the Greek Bible. Then follow the Latin Vulgate and the Syriac Peshitta, each just too late and too composite in character to be of first-rate importance as evidence of the primitive Greek text, but each the authorized Bible of a great Church. Finally, evidence of some value is to be obtained from the later Syriac and the Armenian versions.

For the Versions in general, see A. Vööbus, *Early Versions of the New Testament, Manuscript Studies*, 1954; cf B. M. Metzger, *New Testament Studies*, ii, 1956, 1–16.

For the Coptic version, see A. Vaschalde, *Le Muséon*, xlvi, 1933, 299 ff and W. Kammerer, *A Coptic Bibliography*, 1950; G. Horner, *The Coptic Version of the NT in the Northern Dialect*, 1898–1905; *idem*, *The Coptic Version of the New Testament in the Southern Dialect*, 1911–1924; H. Hyvernat, *A Check List of the Coptic MSS in the Pierpont Morgan Library*, N.Y., 1919; P. E. Kahle (jun.), *Le Muséon*, lxiii, 1950, 147 ff; J. H. Ropes and W. H. P. Hatch, *HTR*, xxi, 1928, 69 ff; Sir H. Thompson, *op. cit.* and *The Coptic Version of the Acts and the Pauline Epistles in the Sahidic Dialect*, 1932 and H. C. Hoskier's articles in the *Bulletin of the John Rylands Library*, vii and viii.

For the Georgian Version, see R. P. Blake, *Patrologia Orientalis*, xx, 1928, Mark; *ib.* xxiv, 1933, Matthew; *ib.* R. P. Blake and M. Brière, xxvi, 1950, John; *ib.* xxvii, 1955, M. Brière, Luke; R. P. Blake and S. Der Nersessian, *The Gospels of Bert' ay*, *Byzantion*, xvi, 1943–1944, 226 ff; V. Beneševič, *Quattuor Evangeliorum Versio Georgica Vetus*, i, 1909 (Matthew), ii, 1911 (Mark); J. Molitor, *Das Adysh-Tetraevangelium*, *Oriens Christianus*, xli, 1957, 1 ff; F. C. Conybeare, *The Georgian Version of the NT*, *ZNW* xi, 1910, 232–249; *ib.* (Acts) xii, 1911, 131–140; P. M. Tarchnišvili, *Geschichte der kirchlichen Georgischen Literatur*, *Studi e Testi*, clxxxv, 1955, 313 ff.

For the Ethiopic, see F. da Bassano, *NT aethiopice*, 1934, based on that of T. P. Platt and F. Prätorius, 1899; J. A. Montgomery, *HTR* xxvii, 1934, 169 ff (Acts); cf A. Vööbus, *Early Versions of the NT*, 1954, 243 ff.

For the Arabic, see I. Guidi, *Le traduzioni degli Evangelii in arabo e in etiopico*, Atti della R. Accademia dei Lincei, 1888, iv, i^{a}, 5–37; G. Graf, *Geschichte der christlichen arabischen Literatur*, i, 1944, *Studi e Testi*, 118, 138–185; R. H. Kilgour, 'Arabic Versions of the Bible,' *The Moslem World*, vi, 1916, 383–386; A. Ciasca, *Tatiani Evangeliorum Harmoniae Arabice*, 1888; J. H. Hill, *The Earliest Life of Christ*, 1894; A. S. Marmadji, *Diatessaron de Tatien*, 1935; A. F. L. Beeston, *The Arabic Version of Tatian's Diatessaron*, *The Journal of the Royal Asiatic Society*, 1939, 608 ff; Vööbus, *op. cit.*, 274 ff.

For the Persian, see B. Walton, *Biblia Sacra Polyglotta*, iv, 1657; B. M. Metzger, 'Tatian's Diatessaron and the Persian Gospel Harmony,' *JBL* lxix, 1950, 26 ff; G. Messina, *Diatessaron Persiano*, *Biblica et Orientalia*, xiv, 1951; W. J. Fischel, *The Bible in Persian Translation*, *HTR* xlv, 1952, 3 ff.

For the Sogdian, Nubian and Old Slavic, see B. M. Metzger, in Parvis and Wikgren's *NT MS Studies*, 1950, 49–51, 63–66; G. Bonifante and B. M. Metzger, *JBL* lxxiii, 1954, 217 ff.

For the Gothic, see G. W. S. Friedrichsen, *The Gothic Version of the Gospels*, 1926 and *The Gothic Version of the Epistles*, 1939; A. Wilmart, *RB* xxxvi, 1927, 46–61; F. Kauffmann, *Theologische Literaturzeitung*, 1927, 370 ff; Lagrange, *op. cit.*, 325 ff; W. Streitberg, *Die gothische Bibel*, 1950; Vööbus, *op. cit.*, 299 ff.

31. Patristic Quotations.—The third class of evidence available for textual purposes is that which is derived from the quotations from the NT in the writings of the early Fathers. If we can be sure that a writer is quoting from a MS lying before him, then his quotation gives us the reading of a MS which in many cases must have been earlier than any which we now possess. Sometimes we can be fairly sure of this, as when the quotation occurs in a continuous commentary on a single book; or when the writer expressly emphasizes a certain reading as against other variants; or when he quotes the same passage several times in the same way. In other cases it is impossible to be certain that he is not quoting from memory; and this makes quotations from the Synoptic Gospels especially fallacious, since it is so easy to confuse the wordings of the different Evangelists. There is always the danger also that a copyist may have assimilated the wording of a quotation to the form with which he was himself familiar. Consequently evidence of this class, though highly valuable when its surroundings guarantee it from suspicion, has to be handled with great caution. In one respect Patristic quotations have a special value, because they can be both dated and placed. The dates of the earliest MSS and versions are uncertain, within half a century or more, while the date of any given Patristic work can generally be fixed within a few years. The advantage of being assignable to a certain country is one which Patristic quotations share with versions, but it is of great importance in fixing the origin and range of certain types of text. In both respects it will be found that the evidence of the Fathers is of great value in elucidating the textual history of the NT. It is impossible to treat the subject at length here, but the names and dates of some of the most important fathers may be mentioned, and subsequent sections will show what sort of part they play in the operations of textual criticism.

32. The earliest Patristic writings, such as the Epistles of Clement, Barnabas, Ignatius, and Polycarp, and the 'Shepherd' of Hermas contain very few quotations from the NT, and those few are inexact (see *NT in Apost. Fathers* [Oxf. Soc. of Hist. Theol.]). In the third quarter of the 2nd cent. we have the writings of Justin Martyr and Tatian, and we know something of the Gospel text used by the heretic Marcion. From about A.D. 180 onwards the evidence becomes much fuller. Irenaeus (whose principal work was written between A.D. 181 and 189) worked mainly at Lyons, though his home was in Asia Minor. Western texts are also represented by Tertullian (*c* A.D. 150–220), Cyprian (*c* A.D. 200–258), and Hippolytus (flourished *c* A.D. 220); the two former being African writers, and the last named of Rome. In Egypt there are the two very important theologians, Clement of Alexandria (*c* A.D. 160–220) and Origen (A.D. 185–253), and the two scholars who succeeded to the latter's literary inheritance, and founded the library of Caesarea largely upon the basis of his works, Pamphilus († A.D. 309) and Eusebius (*c* A.D. 270–340). In Syria the most notable names are those of Aphraates (flourished *c* A.D. 340) and especially Ephraem († A.D. 378); in Asia Minor, Gregory Thaumaturgus († A.D. 265), Basil of Caesarea (A.D. 329–379), Gregory of Nyssa (flor. *c* A.D. 370), and Gregory of Nazianzus († A.D. 389); in Palestine, Cyril of Jerusalem (bishop, A.D. 351–386), and especially Chrysostom (A.D. 347–407). Returning to the West, the important writers, from a textual point of view as well as from others, are Hilary of Poitiers (bishop, A.D. 354–368), Lucifer of Cagliari († A.D. 371), Ambrose of Milan (bishop, A.D. 374–397), Tyconius (an African writer of the end of the 4th cent.), Priscillian (a Spaniard, † A.D. 385); and, finally, the two great Fathers of the Western Church, Jerome (*c* A.D. 345–420) and Augustine (A.D. 354–430). Later than the first quarter of the 5th cent. it is not necessary to go; for the settlement of the great issues in the textual history of the NT had taken place before this date.

A list of ecclesiastical writers and their principal works is given by Gregory (*Prolegomena* and *Textkritik*). An index of Patristic quotation was compiled by Dean Burgon and is now in the British Museum. Critical texts of the Latin and Greek Fathers have been and are being issued under the direction of the Vienna and Berlin Academies respectively. For the value of Patristic citations, cf K. Lake, *The Text of the NT*[6], 1953, 49 ff, and R. P. Casey in Parvis and Wikgren's *New Testament Manuscript Studies*, 1950, 69 ff; cf A. H. McNeile, *Introduction to the New Testament*, 1953, 413–415.

33. Such are the materials—MSS, Versions, Patristic Quotations—with which the textual critic has to deal; but it is only within the last century that his resources have become so extensive. Two centuries of diligent work were spent in the collection of the evidence of Greek MSS; the most important of all, the Codex Vaticanus (B), has become fully known only within the last ninety years and the next most important Alexandrian Uncial (א) was discovered only in 1859 and published in 1862. The Washington or Freer MS (W) was not acquired till 1906; the Koridethi MS (Θ) was not found and published till 1913, and the vast majority of paypri have not been known till the last thirty years. Of the two most important versions, the Old Syriac was wholly unknown before 1848, and quite inadequately known until 1894; while the Old Latin, though known and studied in the 18th cent. (when Sabatier published his *Bibliorum sacrorum Latinae versiones antiquae*, Rheims, 1743), cannot be said to have been rightly understood and classified before the publications of several scholars who are still living. For many of the Fathers, we still are without editions which can be trusted with regard to their Scripture quotations. The textual criticism of the NT, as now understood, is consequently a science of comparatively modern growth. As was shown above (**1**), the earliest editions of the Greek NT were in no sense critical texts. It is true that MSS were collated for them, but only such MSS as chanced to be easily at the disposal of the editor. No search was made for specially good or old MSS, and (except for a very slight use of Cod. Bezae by Stephanus) the TR was made and established before any of the great uncial MSS had been examined. This is the more remarkable because B was used as the main basis of the text which became the standard text of the Septuagint, that, namely, which was printed at Rome in 1587; but it chanced that no Roman edition of the NT was issued, and consequently the great Vatican MS was little known and less used until the 19th cent. was far advanced.

34. As stated in **1**, the TR of the NT took final shape in the editions of Stephanus in 1550 and the Elzevirs in 1624. It was not until after the latter date that the scientific collation of evidence began. The Codex Alexandrinus (A) was brought to England in 1627, and a collation of it (with D D_2, and several minuscules) first appeared in the great Polyglot Bible edited by **Brian Walton** in 1657. Walton's Polyglot (modelled, so far as its plan and scope were concerned, on the Antwerp Polyglot of 1571–1572, and the Paris Polyglot of 1630–1633, but greatly superior to both in its textual material) may be said to be the fountainhead of the textual criticism of the NT. It was followed during the next century and a half by a series of editions in which, while no attempt was made to modify the actual text, an increasing number of MSS was laid under contribution to supply materials for the *apparatus criticus*. The first of these was that of Dean Fell in 1675; the greatest was that of **John Mill** in 1707, which was remarkable not only for the number of Greek MSS quoted in it, but for its use of the versions, its collection (for the first time) of Patristic quotations, and its valuable *prolegomena*. In the 18th cent. Bentley (whose first appearance in the field of Biblical criticism was stimulated by Mill's great work) made large collections for a new edition, but was unable to make use of them. **J. J. Wetstein,** a Swiss assistant of Bentley, produced in 1751–1752 an edition in which our present notation of the MSS was first introduced; and the list was considerably extended by C. F. Matthaei (1782–1788), F. K. Alter (1786–1787), A. Birch (1788–1801), and, finally, J. M. A. Scholz (1830–1836), with whom the first stage of NT textual criticism may be said to have come to a close.

35. During this first, and most necessary, stage of the collection of evidence, which extends from 1657 to 1830, little was done in the way of classifying the materials thus obtained, or laying down the principles upon which

TEXT OF THE NEW TESTAMENT

they should be employed and interpreted. There are, however, some notable exceptions. Mill, in his *Prolegomena*, discussed the true reading of many passages. **J. A. Bengel,** in 1734, divided the MSS and versions into two families, which he called African and Asiatic, and asserted the superiority of the former, consisting of the few most ancient witnesses, over the latter, which included the great mass of later authorities. In this we find the germ of the principle of the classification of authorities, which is now the guiding principle of textual criticism, whether Biblical or classical. It was opposed by Wetstein, who anticipated the advocacy of the TR in our own time by Dean Burgon and others, maintaining that all the most ancient MSS had been contaminated from the Latin, and that only the later authorities were worthy of attention. J. S. Semler (1767) developed Bengel's theory, making a triple classification of authorities, as Alexandrian, Eastern (*i.e.* Antiochian and Constantinopolitan), and Western ; and this was elaborated by his pupil J. J. Griesbach (1774–1775), who adopted the same classification, but carried much further the assignment of the then extant MSS and versions to their several classes. Both in his classification and in his estimate of the characteristics of the various families Griesbach went far to anticipate the theory of Westcott and Hort, which is the foundation of contemporary criticism.

36. None of the scholars hitherto named, however, put his principles to the test by producing a reformed Greek text of the NT. This step, which marked the opening of a new era in textual criticism, was taken in 1831 by **K. Lachmann,** a distinguished classical scholar, who, like Bentley before him, but with greater success, resolved to apply to the text of the NT the principles which were admitted as sound in the case of the Greek and Latin classics. This method consisted of selecting some of the oldest authorities (MSS, Versions, and Fathers), and forming his text solely from them, while ignoring the great mass of later witnesses. In putting faith mainly in the most ancient witnesses, in spite of their numerical inferiority, Lachmann only did what every editor of a classical text would do ; but he departed from sound principle, first, by absolutely ignoring all evidence outside his selected group ; and, secondly, by adopting in all cases the reading given by the majority of his selected authorities, without regard to the internal probabilities of the various readings, or applying any of the tests which textual science provides for discriminating between alternatives the external evidence for which is approximately equal. Moreover, the knowledge of the earlier authorities at Lachmann's disposal was by no means so complete as that which we have at the present day. For these reasons Lachmann's text could not long hold its ground precisely as it stood ; nevertheless it did very great service in breaking the monopoly of the TR, and in preparing the way for further progress.

37. The next stage in this progress is marked by the names of Constantine Tischendorf and S. P. Tregelles. As the discoverer of the Codex Sinaiticus, **Tischendorf** achieved the most sensational success in textual history ; but he also did admirable service by his collation of almost all the uncial MSS of any importance (except that he was allowed only very limited access to B), and his collection of evidence in his successive editions of the NT (culminating in the 8th, published in 1869–1872) remains the fullest *apparatus criticus* to the present day. His own printed text of the NT fluctuated considerably from one edition to another, and his judgment between various readings was hardly equal to his industry in collecting them ; still, in the main he followed the best authorities, and his edition remains one of the principal examples of a text constructed on critical lines. The *prolegomena* to his 8th edition was compiled after his death by Dr. C. R. Gregory, and is a perfect storehouse of bibliographical information ; in its latest form (published as an independent work, in German, under the title of *Textkritik des neuen Testaments,* Leipzig, 1900) it is the standard book of reference on the subject.

38. Tischendorf's industry as a collator was rivalled by that of his English contemporary, **Tregelles,** who collated all the extant uncial MSS and some of the chief minuscules, so that his results serve to check and test those of Tischendorf. In his text (published in 1857–1872) he confined himself almost wholly to the uncials, with the versions and Fathers, completely ignoring the TR. In fact, he followed very much the same principles as Tischendorf, and his edition is serviceable chiefly as a means of testing Tischendorf's judgment, and of showing how far two scholars, working independently on the same evidence, arrive at the same results. Unfortunately his text of the Gospels was published before the discovery of ℵ, and his knowledge of B was even less than that of Tischendorf.

39. The evidence accumulated by Lachmann, Tischendorf, and Tregelles, aided by the public interest excited by such discoveries as those of the Codex Sinaiticus and the Curetonian Syriac, produced a general sense of dissatisfaction with the TR, and in England led to an increasing desire for a revision of the AV in the light of modern knowledge, culminating in 1870 in the appointment of the Committees which produced the RV (for which see article ENGLISH VERSIONS, **35–36**). Meanwhile two English scholars were at work on the text of the NT, whose results were destined not only to affect very greatly the revision of the English Bible, but also to lay the foundation of all the textual work of the succeeding generation, and whose influence remains paramount to this day. These were **B. F. Westcott** (afterwards Bishop of Durham) and **F. J. A. Hort.** Their joint work began as far back as 1853, when they were colleagues at Cambridge ; and it bore fruit in 1881, when their text of the NT appeared on May 12 (five days before the publication of the RV of the NT), and the *Introduction*, embodying the principles upon which their text was based, in the following September. This volume (written by Hort, but representing the views of both scholars) is the textbook of modern textual criticism as applied to the Greek Bible.

40. The principles of WH are an extension of those of Semler and Griesbach, as described above (**35**), and rest upon a classification of our authorities into families, and a discrimination between the merits of these families. It is in the Gospels and Acts that the textual phenomena are most plainly marked, and it is to them that the characteristics to be described apply most fully ; but they are likewise true, in a lesser degree, of the other books of the NT. If the *apparatus criticus* of the Gospels be studied, it will be found that certain MSS and versions tend to agree with one another, and to form groups distinguishable from other groups. Four such groups are in fact distinguished by WH, as follows ; the reasons for the names assigned to them will appear shortly. (α) The *Syrian* family, often headed in the Gospels by the manuscripts A and C, but more fully and characteristically represented by the later uncials, such as E, F, K, M, S, etc., and by the great mass of the minuscules, by the Peshitta version, and by most of the Fathers from Chrysostom downwards ; from this family, in its fully developed form, is descended the TR. (β) The *Neutral* family, of which the main representative is B, often supported by ℵ, by L, R, T, Z, by the minuscule Evan. 33, and some other minuscules in a lesser degree, by Boh. and sometimes Sah. and frequently by the quotations of Origen ; in Acts, Ephesians, and Apocalypse, A and C generally join this group. (γ) The *Alexandrian* family, a sort of sub-species of β, not continuously found in any one MS, but represented by the readings of some MSS of the β group when they differ among themselves, and especially when they differ from B ; L, T, and A, C, when they are not Syrian, may be taken as the leading members of the family. (δ) The *Western* family, headed by D among the uncials (with E_2 in Acts and D_2 in Paul) and Evan. 473 among a small group of minuscules, but most authentically represented by the Old Latin and Old

TEXT OF THE NEW TESTAMENT

Syriac versions, and especially by *k* and Syr.-Sin.; it also largely colours Sah., and is found in almost all the early Fathers, notably Justin, Irenaeus, Cyprian, and Clement.

41. These being the main divisions which are found to exist among our authorities, the next step is to discriminate between them, so as to determine which is the most generally trustworthy. Here it is (in addition to the greater minuteness of the examination and analysis of the individual authorities) that the original and epoch-making character of the work of WH is most conspicuous. The first proposition—and one which strikes at the root of the claims of the TR—is this, that *no specifically 'Syrian' reading occurs in the NT quotations of any Father before Chrysostom.* In other words, wherever the Syrian family marks itself off from the others by a reading of its own, that reading cannot be shown to have been in existence before the latter part of the 4th cent. The importance of this proposition is obvious, and it is note-worthy, as showing the value of Patristic evidence, that the proof of it rests wholly on the quotations found in the Fathers. The inevitable conclusion is that the Syrian text is a secondary text, formed (according to WH in Syria, and especially in Antioch) in the course of the 4th cent. This secondary character is also established by an examination of representative Syrian readings (for these, see especially J. O. F. Murray's article 'Textual Criticism of the NT' in Hastings' *DB*, Ext. Vol.). As compared with the rival readings of other groups, they show the ordinary signs of editorial revision, such as the modification of harsh or strange phrases, assimilation of one version of an incident with another, greater literary smoothness, and the like. A special proof of secondariness is found in what WH call *conflate* readings, when one group of authorities has one reading and another has a second, and the Syrian text combines the two. The shortest and simplest example is Lk 24[53], where ℵ, B, C, L, Boh. read *eulogountes ton theon*, D, OL, and Augustine *ainountes ton theon*, while A and the general mass of late uncials and minuscules have *ainountes kai eulogountes ton theon.* For other examples of this type see Hort's *Introduction*, and Murray, *loc. cit.*). The conclusion, therefore, is that the witnesses belonging to the Syrian family, although they predominate enormously in numbers, possess little intrinsic weight when opposed to witnesses of the other groups.

42. As between the remaining groups the discrimination is not so easy, and must be made by other methods. The Patristic evidence can show us that the Western text (originally so named because the principal representatives of it were the OL version, the Latin Fathers, and the bilingual MSS) was spread over all the principal provinces to which Christianity penetrated—Syria, Egypt, Rome, Gaul, Africa—and that it goes back as far as we have any evidence, namely to the middle of the 2nd cent. On the other hand, it points to Egypt as the special stronghold of the Neutral text, and the sole home of the Alexandrian. All, however, are of such antiquity that the preference can be given to none on this ground alone. It is necessary, therefore, to look at the internal character of the several texts. Of the Western text WH say (*Introd.* § 170): 'Any prepossessions in its favour that might be created by its imposing early ascendancy are for the most part soon dissipated by continuous study of its internal character.' The chief characteristics with which they charge it are a love of paraphrase; a tendency to interpolate words, sentences, and even paragraphs; free changes or insertions of conjunctions, pronouns, and prepositional phrases; and generally an extreme licence in handling the original text. Alexandrian readings, on the other hand, consist mainly of slight linguistic changes, made in the interest of literary style; they are thus comparatively unimportant, and give rise to little controversy. Over against these various divergences stands the text which WH call Neutral, because it shows few or none of the signs of aberration which characterize the other groups. This text is found predominantly in B, the character of which is so superior that its evidence always deserves the most careful consideration, even when it stands alone.

43. Such is, in briefest summary, the theory with regard to the textual history of the NT propounded by WH. On its first promulgation it was bitterly assailed by the advocates of the TR; but against these its triumph, in the opinion of nearly all students of the subject, has been decisive. More recently the tendency has been to depreciate the pre-eminence of the β or Neutral Text, as being merely the local text of Egypt, and to exalt the δ or Western family, on the ground of its wide and early diffusion and the apparently primitive character of some of its special readings. A further topic of criticism has been the terminology of WH. The term 'Syrian' has been condemned as liable to be confused with 'Syriac'; 'Western' as wholly misleading, since that type of text was widely prevalent in the East also, and probably took its rise thence; 'Neutral' as begging the question of the superior character of the family so described. These criticisms may be briefly dismissed; there is good foundation for them, but they are matters of form rather than of substance. 'Byzantine' might be substituted for 'Syrian' with advantage, and the Egyptian status of the 'Neutral' text might be admitted without abandoning its claims to superiority; but no good substitute for 'Western' has yet been proposed. In some ways it would be better to abandon epithets altogether, and to call the several families by the names of the α-text, the β-text, the γ-text, and the δ-text, as indicated in **40**; or the nomenclature of WH may be retained, but regarded simply as so many labels, devoid of any significant connotation.

44. It is more important to say something with regard to the comparative claims of the β and α texts in the first instance, and the β and δ texts subsequently. With regard to the former controversy, which raged with great warmth after the publication of the RV of the NT, the advocates of the α or Syrian or TR (chief among whom were Dean Burgon, his disciple and literary heir the Rev. E. Miller, and the Rev. G. H. Gwilliam, the editor of the Peshitta) rest their case mainly on the numerical preponderance of the manuscripts of this type, which they take as indicating the choice, deliberate or instinctive, of the early Church, and as implying the sanction and authority of Divine Providence. But to argue thus is to maintain that the textual history of the Bible is fundamentally different from that of all other books of ancient literature, and that the reasoning faculties given to us by God, which are generally recognized as guiding us to the truth with regard to the textual history of classical literature, are not to be employed with regard to the textual history of the NT. There is nothing strange or abnormal in the rejection of a relatively large number of late authorities in favour of a relatively small number of ancient authorities; on the contrary, it is a phenomenon common to nearly all works of ancient literature that have come down to us, the sole difference being that the NT manuscripts, early and late, are far more numerous than those of any classical work, so that the ordinary phenomena are exhibited on a much larger scale. If once it be admitted that the ordinary principles of literary criticism are to be applied to the NT, then the rejection of the TR in favour of one of the earlier families follows as a matter of necessity. It may be added that the course of discovery since the publication of WH's theory has furnished the best possible test of such a theory, that of wholly new and unforseen witnesses, and that it has received therefrom much confirmation and no refutation. The discovery of the Sinatic Syriac, the fuller scrutiny of the versions, the testing of the Patristic quotations (*e.g.* in the case of Ephraem Syrus, who was formerly supposed to have used the Peshitta), the papyrus and vellum fragments from Egypt and Sinai, the examination of more of the minuscule MSS, all these have brought additional support to readings of the β, γ, and δ families, for which the evidence previously available was sometimes very scanty, while they have done nothing to carry back the date of the distinctively Syrian readings beyond the period assigned to them by WH, namely, the age of Chrysostom.

45. One point remains to be dealt with in this connexion, namely, the question of the origin of this 'Syrian' or 'Byzantine' text, which thus dominated the NT tradition for considerably over a thousand years. The view of WH is that it was due to deliberate editorial revision, operating probably in two stages, the first revision taking place early in the 4th cent., the second at some time after the middle of that century. Against this hypothesis it has been objected that, if such revisions took place, we should have expected to find some record of them in early Christian literature. We know the names of several editors of the Greek OT during this very century (see GREEK VERSIONS OF OT); is it likely that two revisions of the NT could have been executed and yet have left no trace in history? It has been urged that there is no record of how another great textual change was carried out, namely, the substitution in the Greek OT of Theodotion's version of Daniel for that of the LXX; and it is no doubt true that where the whole available literature likely to deal with such a subject is so scanty, the argument from silence is very precarious. Still it must be allowed to carry some weight, and not a few critics would substitute for Hort's double revision a process of gradual change spread over a considerable period. Such a gradual change would be due to a general consensus of opinion as to the right way to deal with divergent texts, namely, to combine them when possible, and otherwise to soften down harshnesses, to harmonize contradictions, and to give greater smoothness to the literary style. In favour of this hypothesis it may be noted that the MSS themselves show signs of a gradual and progressive development of the *α* text. The earliest MSS which (in the Gospels) can be classed with this family, A and C, exhibit its characteristics sporadically, not continuously, and not infrequently side with MSS of the *β* and δ families against readings found in the overwhelming mass of later witnesses. The 6th-cent. MSS, N, *Σ*, *Φ*, show the *α* text in a somewhat more advanced stage; but it is not until we reach the later uncials, such as E, F, K, M, S, *Π*, that we find it fully developed in the form which we know as the TR. But whether we adopt the hypothesis of a definite revision or that of a gradual process of change in order to account for the existence of the *α* text, the *fact* of the existence of such a text remains, and its character as a secondary text of relatively late origin must be taken to be one of the established results of criticism.

46. The ordinary English student of the Bible is able readily to appreciate the points at issue in the controversy between the *α* and *β* texts, because they are substantially represented to him by the differences (so far as they are differences in text, and not merely in rendering) between the AV and the RV; for though the RV does not go the whole way with the 'Neutral' text, nevertheless its textual departures from the AV are in that direction, and give an adequate general idea of its character. In dealing with the δ text, however, there is no such ready means of realizing its character, since it is not embodied in any English version, or even in any edition of the Greek text. (A partial exception is furnished by Blass' texts of Matthew, Luke, and Acts, and A. C. Clark's and J. H. Ropes's editions of Acts.) Its features must be gathered by an inspection of the *apparatus criticus* of such works as the 'Variorum' edition of the English Bible, or the Oxford edition (with Sanday's appendixes) of the Greek. Even here it is not all plain sailing, since no one MS gives a full and consistent representation of the δ text, and the authorities which are predominantly of this character not infrequently disagree with regard to particular readings. Generally it may be said that the Old Syriac (especially Syr.-Sin.) and Old Latin (especially *k*, *e*, and Cyprian) represent the oldest form of the δ text, while Codex Bezae (D), its chief champion among Greek MSS, has it in a more advanced (and more extravagant) form.

From these some idea of its divergences from the *α* and *β* texts may be gathered (though it must be remembered that sometimes *α* and δ are found in agreement against *β*, owing to the eclectic compilers of *α* having adopted a δ reading from the alternatives presented to them; and sometimes, on the other hand *β* and δ concur in the preservation of some early reading which has been dropped or altered in *α*). Thus OL and OS (with ℵ, B) omit 'firstborn' in Mt 1^{25}, and the words 'bless them that curse you, do good to them that hate you' and 'despitefully use you' in Mt 5^{44}, while D in both cases has the omitted words; Syr.-Cur. has the doxology to the Lord's Prayer, while D and most OL MSS omit it; OS omits Mt 16^{2f} and 17^{21} (with ℵ, B), while OL and D retain both; in Mt 18^{11}, D, OL, and Syr.-Cur. agree with the *α* group in retaining the verse, while Syr.-Sin. sides with the *β* group in omitting it; after Mt 20^{28} a long additional passage (akin to Lk 14^{8-11}) is inserted in D, *Φ*, OL, and Syr.-Cur. (Syr.-Sin. is defective). Mk 16^{9-20} is omitted by *k* and Syr.-Sin., inserted by D, Syr.-Cur., and most MSS of the OL. At Lk 6^{5} D inserts the incident of the man working on the Sabbath day, but OS is defective here, and OL has no trace of it; in Lk 9^{55} the TR is derived from the δ text (D, OL, Syr.-Cur.), but Syr.-Sin. agrees with the *β* group in omitting the words 'and said, Ye know not what spirit ye are of,' etc.; D and some OL MSS omit Lk 22^{20}, while other OL MSS and OS transpose vv.^{17f} to this place; Syr.-Sin. omits Lk 22^{43f}, but D, OL, and Syr.-Cur. retain them; in Lk 23^{48} some words are added to the end by OS and g^{1}; in Lk $24^{6,12,36}$, where D and OL have remarkable omissions (which WH are inclined to accept, even against the testimony of B), both MSS of OS contain the omitted passages; but they concur with D and OL in omitting 24^{40}. These examples serve to show both the character of the δ text and the way in which its authorities are divided among themselves—a point of considerable importance; while in Acts the divergences of the δ text (here mainly represented by D and OL, the OS not being extant) are even greater, so much so as to have given rise to the hypothesis that it represents a different edition of the book, due to the author himself. (For a fuller list of notable δ-readings, both in the Gospels and Acts, see Kenyon, *Handbook*, pp. 76, 131–134, 293–299.) The vagaries of individual members of the δ group are occasionally still more striking than those which have been quoted; as when two OL MSS (*a* and g^{1}) insert in Mt 1^{15} the legend (apparently from the Ebionite Gospel) of the great light which flashed from Jordan at the baptism of Jesus, or when D, *c*, and Sah. state (at Lk 23^{53}) that the stone at the mouth of the sepulchre was 'such as scarce twenty men could roll.' In addition to these substantial additions to or alterations of the text, the verbal divergences are very numerous, proving that an excessive licence was taken by scribes or editors in dealing with the Gospel text.

47. Until quite recently, the special variants of the δ text were almost universally regarded as aberrations, which no one would think of accepting as readings of the original text. It is true that WH were disposed to believe that the passages omitted by the 'Western' authorities in the later chapters of Luke are no authentic part of the Evangelist's original work, but are additions made at a very early date; but this is the only case in which they accepted testimony of this class as superior to that of B and its allies, and few other scholars would at that time have gone even so far as they did. For some time after the promulgation of WH's theory, the conflict raged over the comparative merits of the *α* and *β* types of text; and it was only as the superiority of the latter was more and more established that scholars began to investigate more fully the characteristics and claims of the remaining family (ignoring *γ*, as merely a sub-species of *β*), for which a very high antiquity could be demonstrated. The claims of the δ text

TEXT OF THE NEW TESTAMENT

received a considerable stimulus from the publication of more of the OL MSS (especially *k*), and above all from the discovery of Syr.-Sin., which is perhaps the most important single member of the group. Further attention was attracted to it by Blass's attempt to show that the δ text in Luke and that in Acts represent different editions of those books, issued by Luke himself at different dates, though few now hold Blass's theory. In F. C. Burkitt's day, and due to his influence, not a few scholars were inclined to attach considerable weight to the evidence of this family, and to hold that the *β* text, no less than the *α*, is due to editorial revision, and that the original form of the NT text is to be looked for in the OL and OS to a much greater extent than was previously supposed possible.

48. The main argument in favour of the δ text is its great age and wide circulation, as demonstrated by the Patristic evidence of the 2nd and 3rd cents. It has to be borne in mind, however, that purity of text is due not so much to great age as to care in transmission, and that where such care has been wanting, corruption is both rapid and far-reaching. The papyrus MSS of the Greek classics, written in the first two centuries of the Christian era, which have recently come to light in large numbers, are almost always less accurate than the vellum MS of the 10th and 11th cents.; the reason no doubt being that the papyri are generally cheap copies, circulating among private individuals in the upper provinces of Egypt, while the vellum MSS represent the tradition of the great libraries, in which transcripts would be made more accurately and revised more carefully. So with regard to the early Christian literature: we can well imagine that during the century and a half following the composition of the books, when Christianity was an unauthorized religion, liable to persecution and the destruction of its books, and when Christians themselves looked for a speedy Second Coming of the Lord, there would be little care and little opportunity for the precise collation of manuscripts, and a great possibility of verbal and even material variation in transcription. It is quite intelligible, therefore, that through the greater part of the Christian world inaccurate copies would circulate, and that the more careful preservation of the true text would run in a comparatively narrow channel. And if there was one part of the world in which such care might more than elsewhere be expected it was Egypt, and especially Alexandria, the home of Greek textual criticism, and the home also of the Greek version of the OT. Hence, if the internal evidence points to the *β* text as the most accurate and authentic in character, the inference to be drawn therefrom is not materially shaken when we find signs that its birthplace was in Egypt, and that its early circulation was in that country, while texts of various shades of the δ type were prevalent elsewhere. That such was the character of the *β* text was the deliberate opinion of WH, who were perfectly aware of the early and wide attestation of the δ text; and their conclusion is supported by the quite independent investigations of B. Weiss, whose elaborate study (on very different lines) of the texts of the principal uncials led him to the conclusion that, whereas all the rest show marked indications of editorial revision in varying degrees, the text of B, though by no means free from scribal blunders, has the strongest signs of authenticity and originality. It is also to be remembered that it is impossible to form a coherent text of the δ type. The witnesses differ so much among themselves that it is easier to find a majority of them against any reading of that type than in favour of it. This appears even in Blass's attempt to form a δ text of Luke and Acts, and in the other books the task is still more hopeless. Readings of the δ type, in short, have much more the character of results of a common tendency, working more or less independently in different places under similar circumstances, than of the descendants from a common original.

49. Since Westcott and Hort, scholars have grouped minuscules together and related them, if possible, to Uncials; they have investigated the text of the versions and of some of the Fathers; and they have concentrated on splitting up the δ text, recognizing that the term 'Western' is a misnomer.

In *The Four Gospels*, 1924, B. H. Streeter advanced a theory of local texts of Alexandria, Antioch, Caesarea, Italy and Gaul, and Carthage for the Gospels. The primary authority of Alexandria was B; the secondary authorities ℵ, L, Sah., Boh.; and the Patristic, Origen, A.D. 230, and Cyril of Alexandria, A.D. 430. The primary authority of Antioch was Syr.-Sin., the secondary, Syr.-Cur. The primary authority of Caesarea was *Θ*; the secondary, fam.[1], fam.[13], 28, 565, 700 and W (for Mk 1[1]–5[30]); and the Patristic, Origen, A.D. 240, after his removal from Alexandria to Caesarea in A.D. 231, and Eusebius, A.D. 325. The primary authority for Italy and Gaul was D; the secondary, *b* and *a*; the Patristic, Tatian, A.D. 170, and Irenaeus, A.D. 185. The primary authority for Carthage was *k* for Mark and Matthew; the secondary, W for Mk 5[31]–end and *e*; and the Patristic, Cyprian, A.D. 250. For the Caesarean family, Sreeter was able to use the work of Ferrar, J. R. Harris, and K. Lake on the minuscules. Since 1924, P[45] has been discovered and should be added to the primary authority of Caesarea for the Gospels, not Acts, where it agrees with the Alexandrian family.

In 1935 T. Ayuso published his findings on the 'Caesarean' text (*Biblica*, xvi, 369 ff), splitting this family into a pre-Caesarean, which had its home in a remote part of Egypt, represented by P[45], W, fam.[1], fam.[13], and a Caesarean proper, represented by *Θ*, 565, 700, supported by Origen, Eusebius, Syr.-Sin., and the Old Armenian and Old Georgian; for in 1928, K. Lake, R. P. Blake and S. New had shown that Origen used a Caesarean text in Alexandria, then an Alexandrian text in Caesarea, and then a Caesarean text there. In 1935 also M.-J. Lagrange summed up many years' research (published in the *Revue Biblique*) in his *Introduction à l'étude du Nouveau Testament, Deuxième Partie: Critique textuelle, ii, La Critique rationelle*, 2nd ed. In this indispensable work, he made much the same grouping of the evidence for the Gospels as Streeter had done and proceeded with the evidence for the rest of the NT on the same lines, pointing out the lack of evidence for a 'Caesarean' family outside the Gospels. In 1951, W. H. P. Hatch produced his valuable *Minuscule Manuscripts of the New Testament*, in which he made the following grouping (p. 60)—(1) *Western*: D, W[Mk.] and the Pauline D, F, G; OL; Latin Vulgate in part; OS; Harklean margin; Irenaeus, Tertullian and Cyprian; (2) *Old Egyptian*: P[45] (Luke, John), P[46], P[37], P[38]; W (Mark in part and John); fam.[1], fam.[13], 28; Sah. in part; Harklean margin in part; Clement of Alexandria; (3) *Alexandrian*: (*a*) Proto-Alexandrian, P[45] (Acts), B, ℵ; (*b*) Later Alexandrian, C, L, T[a] (Luke, John), W (Luke, John), X, Z (Matthew), *Δ* (Mark), *Ξ* (Luke), *Ψ* (Mark, Acts, Epistles), A (Acts, Epistles), H (Paul), 33; Sah., in part; Boh. in part; Origen partly and Cyril Alex.; (4) *Caesarean*: P[45] (Mark), *Θ*, W (Mark), N, O, *Σ*, *Φ*, 565, 700; OS, Syr.-Pal. (?), Old Armenian, Old Georgian; Origen in part; (5) *Byzantine*: A (Gospels) and E, F, G, H for Epistles; S, U (mostly), W (Matthew, Luke), Y, *Ψ* (Luke, John); most minuscule MSS; Peshitta, Harklean text; Chrysostom.

In view of the trend of recent research towards grouping the evidence, it is difficult to accept P. L. Hedley's verdict, (*Church Quarterly Review*, cxviii, 1934, 222) 'All forms of text, with the possible exception of that known to us from [OS], are represented among our Egyptian authorities; and except in the case of [the Byzantine text], it is improbable that one occurred much before another.' Admittedly, the 'Western' text was found in Egypt at an early date, during the 2nd cent., and onwards, and some kind of compromise between it and a more Alexandrian form of text may well have led to the pre-Caesarean text there which spread later in Caesarea and later still through Origen to Cappadocia, Armenia, and Georgia.

The origin of the 'Western' text itself is unknown but it is tempting to connect it with a recognition of certain NT books as canonical during the 2nd cent., perhaps at Antioch. If a popular recension of such books was made between *c* A.D. 125–150, this would account for a hard core of such Western variants, some of which preserve the authentic text of the archetype lost in other streams of tradition, *e.g.* the Alexandrian. To this 'hard core,' found *e.g.* in the Western text of Acts, other 'Western' readings were added later. The origin of the Alexandrian family is also unknown but it seems to have been due to a slight revision of some good MSS preserved at Alexandria, where the textual standards of pagan scribes were of the highest order. An editor of the NT, though he would do well to trust the β family generally, is bound also to consider readings of the δ type on their merits; and that especially when support is found for them from more than one branch of the family. The Latin and Syriac clans or families often differ; but when they agree, the reading which they support may well go back to a very early date, unless the variant can be traced to Tatian. The Codex Bezae, the principal Greek member of the δ family, represents its characteristics in a somewhat extreme form, and readings supported by it alone must be regarded with much suspicion; but in combination with OL and OS, especially where Tatianic influence is not suspected, it becomes an important witness.

50. The great hopes placed in von Soden's work on the text were not realized when *Die Schriften des Neuen Testaments* appeared in 1902–1913. Not only were his new *sigla* for the MSS unpalatable but he also put too closely together the readings of D with *Θ*, and despite the enormous mass of material that he collected, his work has constantly to be checked (cf H. C. Hoskier, *JTS*, xv, 1914, 307 ff, and A. Souter, *Expositor*, x, 1915, 429–444). The history and bibliography of textual criticism are well set out in Scrivener's *Plain Introduction to the Criticism of the NT* (4th ed., 1894); and C. R. Gregory's *Textkritik des Neuen Testaments* (I, 1900; II, 1902; III, 1908). Shorter summaries of the historical matter, with fuller discussions of the textual problem as it stands since Westcott and Hort, will be found in Sir F. G. Kenyon's *Handbook to the Textual Criticism of the NT*, 2nd ed., 1926, his *Recent Developments in the Textual Criticism of the Greek Bible*, 1933, his *The Text of the Greek Bible*, 1937, and A. W. Adams' revised edition of his *Our Bible and the Ancient MSS*, 1958; cf K. Lake, *The Text of the NT*, 6th ed., revised by S. New, 1953; M.-J. Lagrange, *Critique textuelle*, ii, *La critique rationelle*, 1935; A. H. McNeile, *Introduction to the New Testament*, 2nd ed., 1953, 373–453; A. Souter, *The Text and Canon of the NT*, 2nd ed., 1954. See also A. F. J. Klijn, *A Survey of the Researches into the Western Text of the Gospels and Acts*, 1949, and B. M. Metzger, *Annotated Bibliography of the Textual Criticism of the NT*, 1914–1939, in *Studies and Documents*, xiv, 1955. Also of great value is B. Kraft, *Die Zeichen für die wichtigeren Handschriften des griechischen NT*, 1955. Hort's *Introduction* (forming vol. ii. of *The NT in the Original Greek* by B. F. Westcott and F. J. A. Hort, 1881, is the standard work for a statement of the principles of textual criticism, and for its exposition of the epoch-making theory of the two scholars.

The fullest *apparatus criticus* at present available is that in Tischendorf's *NT Graece*, 1869–72, supplemented by the *apparatus* in Horner's editions of the Coptic version. S. C. E. Legg's edition of Mark, 1935, is more accurate than his edition of Matthew, 1940, and his enterprise is being carried on along different lines by a group of British and American scholars. A. Souter, *Novum Testamentum Graece*, 2nd ed., 1947, and that of E. Nestle (and K. Aland), 22nd ed., 1956, or that of A. Merk, 2nd ed., 1935, or that of J. M. Bover, 1943, or the Greek NT published by the British and Foreign Bible Society, 2nd ed., 1958, would provide a student with a concise but good *apparatus criticus*.

E. G. K.—**C. S. C. W.**

THADDAEUS.—The lists of the 'Twelve' differ slightly: Thaddaeus (Mk 3[18], Mt 10[3]) is replaced by **Judas** the (son) of James in Lk 6[15], Ac 1[13]. Emanuel Hirsch (*Frühgesch d.. Ev.*, i, 21 f) gives the following explanation: The group of the Twelve was formed first by the paschal appearance of the Lord (1 Co 15[5]). When one tried to date this group back into the lifetime of Jesus, Judas the traitor was thought to have been a member of it. Hence one of the original Twelve had to be left out: either Judas' namesake Judas the son of James was omitted (Mk 3, Mt 10) or another one, namely Thaddaeus, of whom only his name was known.

The Codex Bezae (D) and a few other MSS have replaced Thaddaeus by **Lebbaeus**—perhaps one of the writers of this codex found in this name the 'Levi' of Mk 2[14]. Because the gospel had narrated his vocation, he had to be included among the Twelve. This Levi is called 'the (son) of Alphaeus' (q.v.) in Mk 2[14]. D has replaced these words by 'James the (son) of Alphaeus' here and in the parallel Lk 5[27]. St. Luke himself has left out the addition 'the (son) of Alphaeus' in 5[27] in order to avoid confusion with 'James the (son) of Alphaeus.' E. H.

THAMAH, Ezr 2[53] (AV).—See TEMAH.

THAHASH, Gn 22[24] (AV).—See TAHASH.

THAMAR, Mt 1[3] (AV).—See TAMAR, **1.**

THAMNATHA, 1 Mac 9[50] (AV).—See TIMNATH-SERAH.

THANK-OFFERING.—See SACRIFICE, **2, 12.**

THARA, Lk 3[34] (AV).—See TERAH, **1.**

THARRA.—See TERESH.

THARSHISH, 1 Ch 7[10] (AV).—See TARSHISH, **2.**

THASSI.—The surname of Simon the Maccabee (1 Mac 2[3]). The meaning of the word is quite uncertain. As likely an interpretation as any is 'the zealous.'

THEATRE.—The name is Greek (literally 'a place for viewing' [a spectacle]), and the thing appears to be of Greek origin also. From the cities of Greece proper, theatres spread all over the Greek and Roman world. The auditorium consisted regularly of a semicircular cavity cut on the side of a hill, much broader at the upper end than the lower. The seats were placed concentrically, being commonly carved out of the rock. The part level with the ground, the orchestra, was occupied by the chorus. The stage and scene were on the diameter, and were of artificial construction, being very often like the front of a temple. The theatres were used for public meetings, as being generally the largest buildings in the cities (Ac 19[29, 31]; cf also EPHESUS).

In Palestine as elsewhere drama held an important place in the cultural life of Hellenistic communities, a fact attested by impressive ruins. Of theatres built by Herod the Great, traces have been discovered of what appears to have been the one at Caesarea. But not even the site is known of the one at Jerusalem, so shocking to devout Jews. Along with a great amphitheatre it appears to have served especially the quadrennial Jerusalem Olympics, to which athletes, musicians, and other contestants thronged 'out of every nation' (Jos. *Ant.* xv. viii. 1 [267 ff]). A. So.—**J. S. K.**

THEBAIC VERSION.—See TEXT OF NT, **27.**

THEBES.—See No.

THEBEZ.—A fortified city in the reduction of which Abimelech met his death, Jg 9[50], 2 S 11[21]. It is described by Eusebius and Jerome as 13 miles from Neapolis, on the road to Scythopolis. This is almost certainly the present *Ṭûbâṣ*, a prosperous village in a fruitful open valley, 10 miles NE. of *Nâblus*, on the ancient highroad to *Beisân*. E. W. G. M.

THECOE, 1 Mac 9[33] (AV).—See TEKOA.

THEFT.—See CRIMES AND PUNISHMENTS, **6.**

THELASAR, 2 K 19[12] (AV).—See TELASSAR.

THELERSAS, 1 Es 5[36] (AV, RV).—See TEL-HARSHA.

THEOCANUS, 1 Es 9[14] (AV).—See TIKVAH, **2.**

THEODOTION.—See GREEK VERSIONS OF OT, **16.**

THEODOTUS.—1. One of the messengers sent by Nicanor to Judas Maccabaeus (2 Mac 14[19]). **2.** The author of a plot to assassinate king Ptolemy Philopator, which was frustrated by Dositheus (3 Mac 1[2]).

THEOPHILUS (literally 'beloved of God').—The person to whom St. Luke's two works are addressed (Lk 1[3], Ac 1[1]). That Theophilus stands for a real person and is not a general name for the Christian reader is made probable by the title 'most excellent,' which, when strictly used, implies equestrian rank (Ramsay, *St. Paul*, p. 388). It is used also of Felix (Ac 23[26] 24[2]) and of Festus (26[25]). Further, the name is common among Jews and Gentiles from the 3rd cent. B.C. But some take the title as a mere complimentary address, and therefore as telling us nothing of Theophilus himself. If it is used strictly, we may agree with Ramsay that Theophilus was a Roman official, and the favourable attitude of St. Luke to the institutions of the Empire is in keeping with this idea. So also is the whole purpose of Luke-Acts as an apologia for Christianity, addressed to educated Romans, possibly even to magistrates before whom Christians were being haled. A. J. M.—F. C. G.

THERAS (1 Es 8[41]) = **Ahava** (q.v.), Ezr 8[21, 31].

THERMELETH, 1 Es 5[36] (AV, RV).—See TEL-MELAH.

THESSALONIANS, FIRST EPISTLE TO THE.— 1. Occasion and Date.—According to the narrative of Ac 17[1ff], Paul, in the course of his second missionary journey, went from Philippi to Thessalonica, and reasoned there in the synagogue for three Sabbaths, with the result that 'some of them were persuaded, and consorted with Paul and Silas; and of the devout Greeks a great multitude, and of the chief women not a few' (v.[4]). There follows the account of a tumult of the Jews, and of an accusation against Jason, St. Paul's host, who is bound over to keep the peace. St. Paul is sent away by the brethren to Beroea, and thence again to Athens, leaving Silas and Timothy in Beroea. From Athens he sent for them, and waited for some time hoping they would join him there (17[15f]), but apparently he had reached Corinth before they arrived (18[5]). 1 Thessalonians confirms, on the whole, this general picture. Paul is presumably in Corinth, and Silas and Timothy are with him (1[1]). One would gather, however, that Timothy, who has just arrived (3[6]), has come, not from Beroea, but from Thessalonica, whither Paul had dispatched him from Athens under the pressure of the apostle's intense concern for his Thessalonian converts, whom he could not re-visit personally, for 'Satan hindered us' (1 Th 3[1f] 2[17f]). The discrepancy is probably due to a misunderstanding on the part of the author of Acts; but it is also possible that Silas and Timothy had rejoined Paul in Athens and that Paul had then sent Timothy back to Thessalonica.

At yet another point the Acts account is subject to question. The impression is conveyed by Acts that St. Paul's expulsion from Thessalonica followed immediately upon a three week's ministry in the synagogue, but there are indications in the Epistle of a longer stay (*e.g.* 2[7-12]). To these indications may be added the following considerations: (1) While in Thessalonica St. Paul received gifts more than once from his converts at Philippi (Ph 4[16]); and (2) the synagogue ministry does not account for his astonishing success among the Gentiles (Ac 17[4], 1 Th 1[9]). Some have held that the Acts narrative is to be interpreted as implying a brief and almost fruitless appeal to the Jews, followed by a longer and more successful ministry to the Gentile population (cf Ac 13[44-46]). It may be added that at Ac 17[4] there is considerable 'Western' authority for inserting 'and of' before 'Greeks,' thus giving *three* classes of converts besides the women—Jews, devout persons (*i.e.* proselytes), and Greeks (*i.e.* heathen). See also Ramsay, who constructs an 'eclectic' text (*St. Paul the Traveller*, pp. 226, note, 235, note 2).

The *occasion* of the letter, then, was the return of Timothy from his mission: its *date* falls within the eighteen months' period of Paul's sojourn in Corinth—as late as possible, to allow time for the history of the Church as sketched in the Epistle, and yet early enough to leave room for the circumstances of 2 Thessalonians, which is probably later than 1 Thessalonians but falls also in this period. The usual schemes of Pauline chronology assign for the departure from Corinth the spring of some year between A.D. 50 and 54; according to these schemes, perhaps A.D. 52 is the most probable date for 1 Thessalonians. With the possible exception of Galatians (which, if addressed to the churches of South Galatia, *may* have been written earlier), it is the earliest of extant Pauline writings.

2. Contents.—The Epistle does not lend itself to formal analysis. The least doctrinal and most personal of all St. Paul's letters to the churches, it is prompted largely by affectionate gratitude for the 'faith and love' of his recent converts, and for their 'good remembrance' of himself.

The tidings brought by Timothy that they 'stand fast' (3[5-8]) leads the Apostle to begin with an outburst of thankful memories of his mission. This 'thanksgiving,' interrupted by references to his intense longing to see his Thessalonian friends and to the visit and return of Timothy, forms the first and main section of the Epistle (chs. 1–3), the final words gathering up all its desires into a prayer (3[11-13]). Very simple yet profound expression is given to the Christian faith and hope (1[9f]); Jewish hostility is referred to (2[14-16]), but there is no controversial insistence on an anti-Judaic Christianity—a confirmation of early date. In ch. 4 there is warning against the besetting impurity of the Gentile world (4[1-8]), and against a fanatical detachment from the ordinary duties and responsibilities of life (vv.[9-12]). This is followed by a comforting assurance, rendered necessary by the belief in the speedy 'coming of the Lord' which St. Paul shared with his converts (v.[15]), that those of the brethren who have already died will have part in that event equally with those who are yet alive (vv.[13-18]). This theme is carried on to a warning to be watchful against the sudden coming of 'the day of the Lord,' as beseems 'sons of light and sons of the day' (5[1-11]). A general admonition to the Church to respect its leaders and to cultivate peace (vv.[12f]) leads out into a beautiful series of short exhortations, like a 'string of glittering diamonds' (vv.[14-22]), prayer and salutation (vv.[23-26]), the injunction that the letter be read to all the brethren (v.[27]), and the final benediction (v.[28]).

3. Authenticity.—(1) *External testimony.*—Echoes of 1 Thessalonians have been traced in Barnabas, Ignatius, Polycarp, the Didache—none of them, however, certain. It is contained in the Syriac and Old Latin Versions; it belonged to the Marcionite canon, and is named in the Muratorian Fragment. The earliest quotation is in Irenaeus, who attributes the Epistle to St. Paul, and specifies it as the 'First' to the Thessalonians: it is quoted by Clement of Alexandria, and frequently by Tertullian. If regard be had to the personal and non-theological character of the letter, this testimony is ample.

(2) *Internal evidence.*—The simplicity of the letter, the prevalence of the personal note over the doctrinal, its accord with the history in Acts (apart from the slight discrepancies already noted, which a pseudepigraph might have been expected to avoid), and the agreement with Philippians and 2 Corinthians in the writer's attitude of affectionate confidence towards these Macedonian Christians, all make strongly for genuineness, and the Epistle is, in fact, generally accepted by critics of all schools.

The assertion of an un-Pauline doctrinal standpoint (by Baur) takes for the standard of comparison the later Epistles—Galatians, Corinthians, and Romans—and ignores the gradual shaping of Pauline Christianity under stress of problems and controversies as yet hardly in sight. The Jewish opposition is not to St. Paul's distinctive teaching, but to his whole mission (2[14-16]): the declaration that because of persistent rejection of

 THESSALONIANS, SECOND EPISTLE TO

Christ 'God's wrath has come upon them at last' (2^{16}) does not need to imply that Jerusalem is already destroyed (A.D. 70). The rapid progress of the Church at Thessalonica reflects the first enthusiasm of the new faith, and such primitive organization as it exhibits (5^{12}) is consistent with other indications of how the primitive Pauline churches were organized.

There is really no reason to doubt that the Epistle gives a genuine and invaluable self-revelation of St. Paul the *man*. All the great Christian truths appear—the divinity of Christ, His death for men, and resurrection, the Christian's union with Him, the gift of the Holy Spirit—but less as doctrines than as vital elements of personal religion, the moving forces of St. Paul's own life and ministry. S. W. G.—**J. K.**

THESSALONIANS, SECOND EPISTLE TO THE.—1. Occasion and date.—Scattered indications fix the letter (if genuine) as written from Corinth, not long after the First Epistle, although some scholars have defended the priority of 2 Thessalonians (see, *e.g.* T. W. Manson in *BJRL*, xxxv, March 1953, pp. 428 ff). Timothy and Silas (Silvanus) are still with the Apostle (1^{1}, cf 1 Th 1^{1}), whereas in Acts there is no further mention of Silas after St. Paul left Corinth. The former letter seems to be referred to (2^{15}), and the allusions to St. Paul's ministry in Thessalonica suggest that this was almost as recent as when 1 Thessalonians was written. Very possibly 3^{2} is to be explained by the opposition encountered at Corinth, recorded in Ac 18. The reasons for a second letter are hardly evident in any considerable difference of subject-matter; they appear to consist in tidings which had reached St. Paul as to (1) some misunderstanding of his teaching about the Parousia (2^{1-3}); (2) increase of persecution (1^{4-10}); (3) disorderly conduct on the part of some members of the Church (3^{11}); (4) possible letters forged in the Apostle's name (2^{2} 3^{17}).

2. Contents.—Salutation (1^{1f}); thanksgiving (with prayer) for the Church's growth in faith and love in the midst of affliction patiently endured, with assurance of God's vengeance upon their persecutors (vv.$^{3-12}$); warning that the day of the Lord is not yet, but must be heralded by certain signs (2^{1-12}); renewed thanksgiving, exhortation, and prayer (vv.$^{13-17}$). St. Paul asks for his readers' prayers (3^{1f}), expresses his confidence in them (vv.$^{6-15}$); and between repeated benedictions authenticates the letter by his signature (vv.$^{16-18}$).

3. Authenticity.—(1) *External testimony.*—The evidence already cited for 1 Thessalonians applies also to 2 Thessalonians; the second letter is as well attested as the first.

(2) *Internal evidence.*—Circumstances have already been assigned to the letter, in themselves consistent and not improbable. To these may be added the close resemblance to 1 Thessalonians in subject-matter and phrasing, so obvious that it need not here be detailed. A *literary* dependence of 2 Thessalonians on 1 Thessalonians is practically certain, for the interval necessary to justify a second letter at all forbids the supposition of unconscious repetition. If 2 Thessalonians is by St. Paul, he must have re-read his former letter before writing this and the question naturally arises whether it is likely that he would so reproduce himself. Hence the resemblance to 1 Thessalonians is made an argument against the Pauline authorship of 2 Thessalonians. Moreover, along with the resemblance are found other features which are regarded as un-Pauline and post-Pauline, with the result that the Second Epistle is widely rejected by those who admit the first. The ground of this rejection must be briefly examined.

(*a*) *Style.*—It is freely admitted that this argument is hazardous and indecisive: those who rely upon it would not perhaps quarrel with Jowett's dictum that 'objections of this kind are, for the most part, matters of taste or feeling, about which it is useless to dispute.' The argument must also reckon with the fact that the close resemblance of this Epistle to 1 Thessalonians means the presence in it of some features of Pauline style and vocabulary, while what is exceptional may be due to the new subject-matter. Still, it may be argued that some of the passages which are most closely parallel to 1 Thessalonians show a loss of ease and simplicity which suggest that they have been worked over by another hand. One cannot but note a difference, hard to account for if the same writer is saying the same thing after so short an interval; nor is the change such as marks advance towards the style of St. Paul's later letters.

(*b*) *Subject-matter* (apart from 2^{1-12}).—As compared with 1 Thessalonians, very little appears in 2 Thessalonians that is new or convincingly Pauline: something, too, of the warmth and glow of personal feeling has gone. The severity of tone in 1^{6-9} cannot perhaps be objected to, in view of 1 Th 2^{15f}, while 3^{6-15} is sufficiently accounted for by an aggravation of the offence already rebuked (1 Th 4^{11} 5^{14}). The reference to an 'epistle as from us' (2^{2}) suggests an earlier correspondence of St. Paul with his churches, of which we have no knowledge, frequent enough to have already given rise to fraudulent imitation. This is not impossible, though the precaution of a certifying signature (3^{17}) may seem, perhaps, a little inadequate.

(*c*) *The passage* 2^{1-12}.—The objection that this contradicts the eschatology of 1 Th 5^{2f} cannot be sustained. The earlier passage speaks of a coming of 'the day of the Lord,' sudden and unexpected; if Paul believed that this had been misinterpreted to mean that the 'day' had already arrived (2 Th 2^{1-2}), with the result that the ordinary duties of life were being neglected, he might well, without inconsistency, remind the Thessalonians that he had warned them of certain signs which must precede the 'day' itself (2^{3-5}).

A more serious doubt is raised by the apocalyptic character of the passage, unique in Paul, and held to show both dependence on later writings and allusion to post-Pauline history. So far, however, as the thought is exceptional, the section may fairly be regarded as a pendant to the equally exceptional section 1 Th 4^{15-17}, and as more likely to be original than to have been attributed to Paul by a later imitator. The question rather is whether it can be accounted for by *contemporary* ideas, or betrays the facts and conceptions of a later time. The general thought is that the coming of Christ is to be heralded by an outburst of iniquity, described as the 'apostasy' ('falling away,' 2^{3}), either headed by or personified as 'the man of sin' (RVm 'the man of lawlessness'; RSV reverses text and margin), 'the son of perdition,' 'the lawless one' (vv.$^{3,\,8}$) whose character and coming are more fully described in vv.$^{4,\,9-12}$. Already 'the mystery of lawlessness' is at work (v.^{7}), but the crisis is delayed, as the Thessalonians know, by 'what is restraining' (v.^{6}), 'he who now restrains' (v.^{7}). In due season this restraint will be removed, that the lawless one may be revealed, to be slain by the Lord Jesus (vv.$^{6-8}$).

Now, of the elements of this conception, that of an 'apostasy' is not un-Pauline: it appears 2 Co 11^{13-15}, Ro 16^{17-20} (as well as Ac 20^{29-30}, and throughout the Pastoral Epp.), and is attributed to false teachers. The same idea occurs in Mt $24^{5,\,11f,\,24}$ ||, 2 Peter and Jude, 1 Jn $2^{18,\,22}$ 4^{3}, 2 Jn ^{7}. This wide prevalence of the thought in the NT writings, and the constant prediction of 'many' false teachers, false prophets, false Christs, antichrists (1 Jn 2^{18}), may suggest as regards our passage (1) that it draws upon a common stock of eschatological ideas; (2) that 'the man of sin' is not necessarily a person but a type (cf 1 Jn 2^{18}, '*many* antichrists,' but v.^{22} and elsewhere '*the* antichrist'), symbolizing tendencies and movements, and therefore only at grave hazard to be identified with any definite historical personage. Hence the appeal to the legend of 'Nero redivivus' (Tac. *Hist.* ii. 8), with its implication of A.D. 68–70 as the earliest possible date for 2 Thessalonians, is quite without warrant.

It is true that our passage has close affinities with Revelation (especially 13^{11-18} 19^{20f} 20^{10}), but this does not necessarily mean dependence. For Ezk 38 f, Dn 7–9

11 f, and later extra-canonical Jewish apocalyptic literature present, under varied historic colouring, the same conception of a final rally of the powers of evil before the last days, and of the triumph of Messiah over 'antichrist.' In *Test. XII Patr.*, this 'anti-christ' is 'Belial' or 'Beliar' (cf 2 Co 6[15]), in Revelation 'the beast' (symbol of the Roman Empire rather than exclusively of Nero), and it is not necessary to regard 'the man of sin' and equivalent expressions as more personal than these. What is really peculiar to 2 Thessalonians is the assertion of a *restraining power*, holding in check the mystery of lawlessness already *at work*. Can this be explained as historical colour given by St. Paul to current apocalyptic tradition under the circumstances of A.D. 53 or thereabouts?

One answer has been that the Apostle to the Gentiles had lately experienced the determined enmity of the Jews to his whole Christian mission, at Thessalonica, Beroea, and Corinth. Though the Parousia is not yet (2 Th 2[2]), St. Paul expects it within his own lifetime (1 Th 4[17]). The traditional 'antichrist' is therefore already to be looked for (2 Th 2[7]) and might well be discovered in Jewish hatred, bent on the very destruction of Christianity (1 Th 2[15f]), fortified by its secure hold of the national sanctuary (2 Th 2[4]), and held in restraint only by the forces of order seated on the Roman power, or, possibly, in the better elements of Judaism itself (2[6f]). Other explanations of the 'restraining' power have been offered—as, *e.g.* the view that the antichrist is being held back till the gospel can be preached to the Gentiles. However interpreted, the passage would be a development on apocalyptic lines of the outburst of 1[7-10], and no necessity would remain for the suggestion, quite unsupported by evidence, that 2[1-12] is either an interpolation or a genuine Pauline fragment worked up into a spurious Epistle.

So far, then, as doubts concerning 2 Thessalonians are reduced to argument, they can hardly prevail against the tradition of Pauline authorship. Whether misgivings as to style can be relieved by the suggestion that Timothy or Silas wrote in the Apostle's name is doubtful; certainly the repeated 'we' cannot be held to point to such co-operation (cf 1 Th 2[17]–3[1]). The trend of modern critical opinion is perhaps indicated in Jülicher's judgment, that the difficulties 'can after all be most easily solved' under the view that the Epistle was written by St. Paul. S. W. G.—**J. K.**

THESSALONICA (now *Thessalonikē*).—An important city of the Roman province Macedonia, situated on the Via Egnatia, the overland route from Italy to the East, and at the NE. corner of the Thermaic Gulf. Its buildings rose above one another in tiers on the slopes of the hills. The situation is in every respect admirable, and must have been occupied early. This city was founded about 315 B.C., and named after a stepsister of Alexander the Great. Its greatness under Macedonian rule was even extended under Roman rule. It became the capital of the Roman province Macedonia, constituted 146 B.C. It was made a 'free city' in 42 B.C. (Ac 17[5] knows this fact), and was ruled by its own magistrates under the rather rare title 'politarchs,' who were five or six in number. There were many Jews here, as the possession of a synagogue shows (Ac 17[1]), and a number of proselytes (Ac 17[4]). The enemies of St. Paul raised a cry of treason, and a serious riot resulted. Some of Paul's friends had to give security that this would not be repeated. This forced Paul to leave the city. Members of the church here were Jason, Gaius, Secundus, Aristarchus. See THESSALONIANS. A. So.

THEUDAS.—St. Luke makes Gamaliel mention Theudas as the leader of an unsuccessful rebellion of 400 men (Ac 5[36]). Josephus (*Ant.* xx. v. 1 [97 f]) speaks of a Theudas who gave himself out for a prophet. Theudas was decapitated and his followers killed or taken prisoners by a squadron of the procurator Fadus (A.D. 46–48), *i.e.* at least ten years later than the supposed speech of Gamaliel. In Acts Gamaliel goes on to say: 'After him Judas the Galilean arose in the days of the census'—*i.e.* forty years before Fadus (Jos. *Ant.* XVIII. i. 1, 6 [4–10, 23–25]; xx. v. 2 [102]; *BJ* II. viii. 1 [118], xvii. 8 [433]; VII. viii. 1 [253]) and thirty years before the supposed speech of Gamaliel. Apparently there is some chronological confusion in Gamaliel's speech, which various modern conjectures still leave unsolved. E. H.

THIGH (Heb. *yarēkh*, Gr. *mēros*).—The hollow of Jacob's thigh was strained as he wrestled at Peniel (Gn 32[25]), and to this is attributed the Jewish custom (enjoined in the Mishnah) of not eating 'the sinew of the hip' (v.[32]). See SINEW. On the thigh the sword was girded (Ex 32[27], Ps 45[3], Ca 3[8]); Ehud's on the *right* thigh because he was left-handed (Jg 3[16, 21]). Under the jealousy ordeal the woman's thigh falls away if she has been guilty of adultery (Nu 5[21ff]). To smite 'hip and thigh' (literally 'leg upon thigh') is a phrase denoting utter discomfiture accompanied by great slaughter (Jg 15[8]). Its origin is unknown, and its meaning much disputed. In Jer 31[19] and Ezk 21[12] smiting upon one's thigh is a gesture of sorrow or terror. In the Hebrew (cf AVm) of Gn 46[26], Ex 1[5], Jg 8[30] a man's children are described as coming out of his thigh. This explains the oath taken by placing the hand under the thigh (Gn 24[2, 9] 47[29]), a special sacredness being ascribed to the organs of generation. In NT 'thigh' occurs only in Rev 19[16], where perhaps the meaning is that the name was written on that part of the garment which covered the thigh. J. C. L.

THIMNATHAH, Jos 19[43] (AV).—See TIMNAH, **2.**

THISBE.—The place from which Tobit was carried away captive by the Assyrians (To 1[2]). Its position is described as being on the right hand (S.) of Kedesh-naphtali in Galilee above Asher. No trace of the site has yet been found. Some commentators maintain that Thisbe was the home of Elijah 'the Tishbite,' but this is very doubtful.

THISTLES.—See THORNS.

THOCANUS, 1 Es 9[14] (RV).—See TIKVAH, **2.**

THOMAS.—One of the twelve apostles. The Synoptic Gospels mention only his name in listing the apostles (Mt 10[3], Mk 3[18], Lk 6[15]; cf Acts 1[18]). But in the Gospel of John he plays an important rôle, particularly in connexion with the resurrection appearances of Christ (Jn 11[16] 14[5] 20[24-29] 21[4]). Probably as a result of this the importance of Thomas continued to grow in the apocryphal literature of the early Church. According to Eusebius he evangelized Parthia, while according to Jerome he went to Persia. Others ascribe to him the founding of Christianity in India.

The name Thomas appears to be related to an Aramaic word meaning 'twin.' The Greek name **Didymus** used of him by John (11[16] 20[24] 21[2]) also means 'twin,' and is meant to serve as a translation. But as far as we know the Aramaic word was never used simply as a surname and Thomas is itself a good Greek name. Apparently Aramaic speaking people used the Greek name and arbitrarily attached to it the Aramaic meaning which naturally suggested itself. The name gave rise to much speculation in the early Church as to the identification of Thomas and his twin. W. R. S.

THOMEI, 1 Es 5[32] (RV).—See TEMAH.

THOMOI, 1 Es 5[32] (AV).—See TEMAH.

THONG.—See LATCHET, DRESS, **6.**

THORNS, THISTLES, ETC.—So many words are used in the Hebrew for thorny plant, and they are so variously translated, that it will be convenient to consider them all in one group. In the great majority of cases it is impossible to identify the special species referred to.

1. *'āṭādh*, Jg 9[14f] AV, RSV **'bramble,'** AVm 'thistle,' RVm 'thorn,' Ps 58[9] AV, RV, RSV 'thorns.' In Gn 50[10f], Atad occurs as a proper name. The *'āṭādh* is probably the buckthorn (*Rhamnus palestina*) or *Lycium europaeum*, a lowly bush.

2. *barḳānîm* (Jg 8[7, 16] **'briers'**), some kind of thorn.

Arabic *berqān* is the *Centaurea scoparia*, a thorny-headed composite common in Palestine.

3. *dardar* (Gn 3[18], Hos 10[8]), some thistly or thorny plant. In modern Arabic *shauket el-dardar* is applied to the star thistles or knapweeds of which *Centaurea calcitrapa* and *Centaurea verutum* are common Palestine forms.

4. *ḥēdheḳ* (Pr 15[19] ' thorn,' Mic 7[4] **' brier '**; cf Arabic *ḥadaqa* ' to enclose '), some prickly plant used as a hedge (Pr 15[19]).

5. *ḥôaḥ* (RSV 2 K 14[9], 2 Ch 25[18], Is 34[13] ' thistle '; Ca 2[2] ' bramble '; 2 Ch 33[11], Job 41[2] ' hook '; Job 31[40], Hos 9[6] ' thorn '; 1 S 13[6] ' holes '), some shrub, species unknown, with very strong spines.

6. *m^e^śūkhāh*, a thorn hedge (Mic 7[4]).

7. *naʿaṣûṣ* (Is 7[19] ' thornbushes,' 55[13] ' thorn '), from Aramaic *n^e^ʿaṣ* ' to prick,' a general term for a thorn.

8. *sîrîm* (Ec 7[6], Is 34[13], Hos 2[6], Nah 1[10] ' thorn '). The reference to the ' crackling of thorns ' suggests the thorny burnet (*Poterium spinosum*), which is burned all over Palestine in lime-kilns. *sîrôth*, Am 4[2], means ' hooks.'

9. *sillôn* (Ezk 28[24] **' brier '**); *sallônîm* (Ezk 2[6] ' thorns ').

10. *sārābhîm* (Ezk 2[6] **' briers,'** literally ' rebels,' as in margin, but text doubtful); Sir 41[2] suggests ' obstinate.'

11. *sirpadh* (Is 55[13] **' brier,'** literally the ' burner,' hence perhaps ' nettle ').

12. *ṣinnîm* (Job 5[5], Pr 22[5] ' thorns '); *ṣ^e^nînîm* (Nu 33[55], Jos 23[13] ' thorns ').

13. *ḳôṣ* (Gn 3[18], Ex 22[6], Jg 8[7, 16] etc.), the commonest and most general word for ' thorns.'

14. *ḳimmôś* (Pr 24[31] ' thorns '), elsewhere (Is 34[13], Hos 9[6]) ' nettles.' See NETTLE.

15. *śikkîm* (Nu 33[55] ' pricks '), cf Arabic *shauk* ' thorn ' Akkadian *šakāku*, ' be pointed.'

16. *shayith*, only in Isaiah (5[6] 7[23f] 9[17] 10[17] 27[4]), always with *shāmîr* (**' brier '**), and translated ' thorns.'

17. *shāmîr*, in Isaiah (see above) always translated **' brier '**; cf Arabic *samur* ' a thorny tree.'

18. *rhamnos* (Gr.), Ep. Jer [71] (AV and RV ' thorn '; RSV ' thorn bush ').

19. *skolops* (Gr.), 2 Co 12[7] ' thorn ' (RVm ' stake '). See MEDICINE, **3**; PAUL, **7**.

20. *akanthai* (Gr.) = Hebrew *ḳôṣ*, Mt 7[16] 13[7, 22] 27[29] etc. ' thorns.'

21. *tribolos* (Gr.), Mt 7[16], He 6[8] ' thistle ' (AV ' briars ' in the latter).

The variety of words used to describe these prickly plants is not surprising, when it is remembered that such plants are ubiquitous throughout Palestine, and for many months of the year are almost the only living uncultivated vegetation. They form the common food of goats and camels; they are burned (Ec 7[6]), specially the thorny burnet (Arab. *billān*), in ovens and lime-kilns, large areas of land being diligently cleared every autumn for this purpose. Gigantic thistles, sometimes as high as a horse's head, cover whole acres of fallow land and have to be cleared by fire before ploughing can begin. ' Thorns ' of various kinds, *e.g.* brambles, oleasters, etc., are commonly used as hedges; and tangled masses of dead thorny branches from the *Zizyphus* and similar trees are used, particularly in the Jordan Valley, as defences round fields, flocks, or tents (Pr 15[11], Mic 7[4] etc.).

E. W. G. M.—**A. S. H.**

THOUGHT.—In I S 9[5], in Mt 6[25] (as well as in the following vv.[27, 28, 31, 34]), in 10[19], in Mk 13[11], and in Lk 12[11, 22, 25, 26] the English word ' thought ' is used in AV in the old sense of ' grief *or* anxiety.' Thus Mk 13[11] ' Take no thought beforehand ' does not mean *do not think or plan*, but ' do not be anxious beforehand ' (RSV).

THOUSAND.—See ARMY, **2**, NUMBER, **5**.

THRACE.—The name Thrace—it was not till A.D. 46 the name of a Roman province—was applied to all the country lying between the rivers Strymon and Danube. After the death of Lysimachus (281 B.C.—see THYATIRA), with whom the prospect of civilization for the country died, it continued barbarous, and was famous only for its severe climate and its soldiers. Of the latter there was a plentiful supply, and as soldiers of fortune they were to be found in the armies of the richer States. They were chiefly cavalry and light-armed infantry. (The name ' Thracian ' was hence applied to gladiators armed in a particular way). Kings who employed them in war frequently settled them in colonies after peace was declared. A Thracian horseman is mentioned in 2 Mac 12[35] (about 163 B.C.) as saving Gorgias, the governor of Idumaea under Antiochus Epiphanes, from capture.

A. So.

THRASAEUS (2 Mac 3[5] RV; AV **Thraseas**).—The father of Apollonius; but read with RSV ' Apollonius of Tarsus.'

THRASEAS, 2 Mac 3[5] (AV).—See THRASAEUS.

THREE.—See NUMBER, **7**.

THREE TAVERNS.—See TAVERNS, THREE.

THREE YOUNG MEN (AV, RV **CHILDREN**), **SONG OF.**—See APOCRYPHA, **10**.

THRESHING, THRESHING FLOOR.—See AGRICULTURE, **3**.

THRESHOLD.—See HOUSE, **6**.

THRONE.—The OT translation of Hebrew *kissē'* or *kissēh*. It is used of any seat of honour: *e.g.* of the high priest (1 S 1[9] 4[13, 18]), of a judge (Ps 94[20]; cf AV, RV), of a military officer (Jer 1[15]); but most frequently of a king (*e.g.* Pharaoh Ex 11[5], David and Solomon 1 K 2[12] etc.), and thus of God Himself (Ps 9[7] 11[4] 45[6], Is 6[1]). For a description of Solomon's throne see 1 K 10[18–20], 2 Ch 9[17–19]. Frequently ' throne ' is used metaphorically for *dignity*, *royal honour*, and *power*. Thus ' the throne of David ' often stands for the royal honour of David's house (2 S 7[16]). So God's ' throne ' is His sovereign power (cf Ps 45[6] 93[2]).

The NT term *thronos* [once (Ac 12[21]) *bēma*, ' judgment-seat,' is translated ' throne '] is similarly used. It is applied in Rev 20[4] to the thrones of the assessors of the heavenly judge (cf Mt 19[28] || Lk 22[30]); but is most frequently used of the throne of God or Christ (Mt 5[34] || 19[28] ||, Lk 1[32], Ac 2[30] 7[49], He 1[8] 4[16] 8[1] 12[2], Rev 1[4] 3[21] etc.). For ' thrones ' as a rank of angels, see DOMINION, and cf POWER.

W. F. B.

THROUGHLY.—This is the older spelling of ' thoroughly.' In modern editions of AV we find both forms used, ' thoroughly ' in Ex 21[19], 2 K 11[18], and ' throughly ' elsewhere; but in the original edition of 1611 the spelling is ' throughly ' everywhere. There was no distinction in earlier English between ' through ' and ' thorough,' ' throughly ' and ' thoroughly.' In the first edition of AV Ex 14[16] reads ' the children of Israel shall goe on dry ground thorow the mids of the Sea.'

THRUM.—See SPINNING AND WEAVING, **3**.

THUMB.—The thumb is associated with the great toe, and occurs in two different connexions. **1.** We are told that Adonibezek's thumbs and great toes were cut off (Jg 1[6]), and that he himself had practised this mutilation on seventy kings (v.[7]). The object seems to have been to render the vanquished monarchs unfit for war and thus for reigning in a warlike age. **2.** In the *ritual* of the consecration of Aaron, and his sons (Ex 29[20], Lv 8[23f]) blood was sprinkled on ' the tip of the right ear, upon the thumb of the right hand and the great toe of the right foot.' The cleansed leper was similarly sprinkled with blood and oil (Lv 14[14, 17, 25, 28]). The action seems to have symbolized the consecration (or purification) of the whole man, the *extremities* only being touched, just as only the horns of the altar were sprinkled with the blood.

W. F. B.

THUMMIM.—See URIM AND THUMMIM.

THUNDER.—Thunder occurs in Palestine only during the rainy season, particularly at the beginning and the end. In the eastern plateau region thunderstorms are often spectacular, but they may occur anywhere in the country, and are usually accompanied by magnificent cloud effects and torrential rain. In the early period God was believed to come from Edom in a thunderstorm to help His people, and the idea continues as a literary device in later writing (Jg 5^{4-5}, Hab 3^{3-15}). According to poetic and popular ideas, thunder was the *voice of God* (Ps 104^{7}, Job 37^{4} etc.), which a soul gifted with insight might understand and interpret (Jn 12^{28f}; cf Mk 1^{11}, Mt 3^{17} etc.). It is the expression of His resistless power (1 S 2^{10}, Ps 18^{13} etc.), and of His inexorable vengeance (Is 30^{30} etc.). Thunder plays a part in afflicting the Egyptians (Ex 9^{23ff}), at the delivery of the Law (19^{16} 20^{18}), and in discomfiting the Philistines (Is 7^{10}). It is not guided by caprice, but by the will of God (Job 28^{26} 38^{25}). It appears largely in the more terrible imagery of the Apocalypse. For 'Sons of Thunder,' see BOANERGES. W. E.—**A. D. B.**

THYATIRA.—There is a long valley extending northward and southward and connecting the valleys of the Hermus and Caicus. Down this valley a stream flows southwards, and on the left bank of this stream was Thyatira. An important road also ran along this valley, the direct route between Constantinople and Smyrna, and the railway takes this route now. Thyatira was also in the 1st cent. A.D. a station on the Imperial Post Road (overland route) from Brundisium and Dyrrhachium by Thessalonica, Neapolis (for Philippi), Troas, Pergamum, Philadelphia . . . to Tarsus, Syrian Antioch, Caesarea in Palestine, and Alexandria. In its connexion with **Pergamum** this road had always a great importance. Thyatira was built (in the middle of the valley, with a slight rising ground for an acropolis) by Seleucus, the founder of the Seleucid dynasty, whose vast kingdom extended from W. Asia Minor to the Himalayas. The city was garrisoned by Seleucus I. after the battle of Korupedion (281 B.C.). It had no strong location and hence was never a fortress, but only a military post. It held watch against Lysimachus, whose kingdom bordered that of Seleucus on the N. and W., and the colonists were Macedonian soldiers. In 282 B.C., Philetaerus revolted from Lysimachus and founded the kingdom of Pergamum. After the death of Lysimachus, Thyatira was a useful garrison to hold the road, in the interests first of the Seleucids and afterwards of the Pergamenians. The latter were safe from the former if they were in possession of Thyatira. The relation between Pergamum and Thyatira was thus of the closest.

The character of the city's religion is illustrated by the hero Tyrimnos, who is figured on its coins. He is on horseback and has a battle-axe on his shoulder. This hero is closely related to the protecting god of the city, whose temple stood in front of it (cf the temple in Ac 13^{14}). He was considered the divine ancestor of the city and its leading families, and was identified with the sun-god. He also had the title Pythian Apollo, thus illustrating the strange mixture of Anatolian and Greek ideas and names which is so common a feature in the ancient religions of Asia Minor. In conformity with this, he was represented as wearing a cloak fastened by a brooch, carrying a battle-axe, and with a laurel branch in his right hand, symbolizing his purifying power. The city had Pythian games on the model of those in Greece proper, and in the 3rd cent. A.D. the Emperor Elagabalus was associated with the god in the worship connected with them, showing the closer relation which had been effected between the popular and the Imperial religion. It is probable that Seleucus I. had settled Jews in Thyatira, as he certainly did in some of the cities in Asia. Lydia of Thyatira (Ac 16^{14}) had come within the circle of the synagogue, possibly in her native place.

Little is known of the history of the city. The name indicates that it was old Lydian in origin. Seleucid control ended in 190 B.C. It was Pergamene until 133 B.C. The pretender Aristonicus occupied it 133–132 B.C. Thereafter it was in the Roman province of Asia. It must have suffered severely and repeatedly during the fighting between Arabs and Christians, and Turks and Christians, in the Middle Ages. Its situation demands that it be captured and refortified by every ruling power. In Roman times it had been a great trading city, dating its greatest period of prosperity from about the time when the Seven Letters were written. There is evidence of more trade-guilds there than in any other Asian city: wool-workers, linen-workers, makers of outer garments, dyers, leather-workers, tanners, bronze-smiths, etc. **Lydia** probably belonged to one of those guilds. The purple in which Lydia dealt must have been a product of the region of Thyatira, and the well-known Turkey-red must therefore be meant. It is obtained from madder-root, which grows abundantly in that region. The name 'purple' had a much wider meaning among the ancients than among us. The bronze work of Thyatira was also remarkably fine (cf Rev 2^{18}). The ancient city lies buried under a modern town (*Akhissar*).

The **letter addressed to the Church at Thyatira** (Rev 2^{18-29}) is the most obscure of all the seven, as we know so little of local conditions at which it hints. The principles which their prophetess represented were regarded by the author as subversive of true Christianity (see NICOLAITANS). A. So.—**E. G. K.**

THYINE WOOD (Rev 18^{12} AV and RV; AVm 'sweet'; RSV 'scented') is the *citrus* wood of the Romans, used for the manufacture of costly furniture. The tree, *Thuia articulata*, in appearance like a cypress, about 25-feet high, was the source of this wood.

TIBERIAS.—A town built by Herod (A.D. 16–22) on the western shore of the Sea of Galilee (called the 'Sea of Tiberias' in Jn 6^{1} 21^{1}, and in modern Arabic), and named in honour of the Roman Emperor Tiberius. Allegedly it was erected over the site of an ancient graveyard (Jos. *Ant.* XVIII. ii. 3 [38]). This made it an unclean place to the Jews, and Herod was obliged to use force in order to obtain settlers. It was designed entirely on Greek models, and the fact that it was in spirit and civilization entirely foreign is perhaps the reason why it is hardly alluded to in the Gospels—the sole reference being Jn 6^{23}. There is no evidence that it was ever visited by Jesus. The city surrendered to Vespasian and by him was restored to Agrippa. After the fall of Jerusalem many of the Jews took up their abode in Tiberias, and by a strange reversal of fate this unclean city became a most important centre of Rabbinic learning. Here, late in the 2nd cent., lived Judah the Prince (*Nasî*) or the Holy, editor of Mishnah. Here the 'Jerusalem (*i.e.* Palestinian) Talmud' was compiled. Here the Massoretic vocalization of the Hebrew Scriptures was developed. In the neighbourhood are the tombs of Akiba and of Maimonides. Hadrian built himself a temple here, which is probably portrayed on coins of Tiberias of A.D. 119–120.

Constantine built a church and established a bishopric at Tiberias, but Christianity never flourished there. The Arabs seized it in A.D. 637; the Crusaders lost it to Saladin in 1187. The city was almost destroyed by a great earthquake in 1837. The principal objects of interest are the ruins of a large castle (possibly Herodian), a very ancient synagogue, and—half an hour's journey to the S.—the hot springs of *Emmaus* (the Hammath of Jos 19^{35}, not to be confused with Hamath-Gader, mentioned by Josephus and Pliny, at the railroad crossing over the Yarmuk river). Tiberias has a population of about 16,000.

For the **'Sea of Tiberias,'** see GALILEE [SEA OF].
R. A. S. M.—**E. G. K.**

TIBERIUS, whose designation as Emperor was Tiberius Caesar Augustus, was the son of Tiberius Claudius Nero (a Roman noble) and Livia whose second husband was the Emperor Augustus. He was born 42 B.C. and died A.D. 37. Augustus, as he grew old, appointed in succession four of his relatives as co-regents, or marked them out as his intended successors. It was clear that he did not desire the succession of his stepson Tiberius, who was reserved, morose, and unlovable. The successive deaths of his nominees compelled him to fall back upon Tiberius, who in A.D. 13 was made co-emperor. A year later he succeeded to the purple. The 'fifteenth year' in Lk 3^{1} may be counted from the first of these dates, but more probably from the second, thus meaning A.D. 28–29. Tiberius was an able general and a competent Emperor, but the unhappy experiences of his early life made him suspicious and timorous, and he put many of his rivals or supposed rivals to death. In his later years he was much under the influence of a villainous schemer Sejanus. He spent these years in retirement at Capri. A. So—**E. R. H.**

TIBHATH.—A city of Hadarezer, king of Zobah, 1 Ch 18[8]. The parallel 2 S 8[8] has **Betah,** but the original reading was perhaps **Tebah,** as in Peshitta (cf Gn 22[24], where this occurs as a tribal name). The site is unknown.

TIBNI.—A rival who disputed the throne with Omri for four years, 1 K 16[15, 21].

TIDAL.—The fourth of the four kings who carried out an invasion of Canaan in the time of Abraham (Gn 14[1]). He is called 'king of Goiim,' and the word 'goiim' in Hebrew means the heathen nations, or Gentiles. It is difficult to understand why this king should be called 'king of the nations,' unless it is an honorific title, like 'king of the four quarters,' assumed by Assyrian kings. Tidal has been identified with some probability as Tudhaliash I., the first of a line of kings who ruled the Old Hittite Empire. He may be dated *c* 1700–1650 B.C. S. H. He.

TIGLATH-PILESER (in 1 Ch 5[6, 26] and 2 Ch 28[20] corrupted to the form **Tilgath-pilneser**).—This Assyrian ruler, the *Tukulti-apil-ēsharra* of the monuments, was the third of the name. He began to reign about 745 B.C. (13th of Iyyar), and is supposed to have been a usurper. In the Babylonian chronological list he is called *Pulu*, the **Pul** of 2 K 15[19], and the *Poros* of the Canon of Ptolemy. His reign was a very active and important one. Five months after his accession he marched into Babylonia to overthrow the power of the Aramaean tribes. In 744 B.C. he went to Namri to punish the tribes who harassed the Assyrian border. In 743 B.C. he defeated the forces of Sarduris II. of Urarṭu at Arpad. Among those who gave tribute on this occasion were Rezin of Damascus, Hiram of Tyre, and Pisiris of Carchemish. Arpad, however, revolted again, and was for three years the objective of Tiglath-pileser's expeditions (742–740 B.C.). In 739 B.C. he went north to Ulluba, and the presence of his armies there enabled him, in 738 B.C., to make head against Syrian and Phoenician resistance. On this occasion he subjected Kullani, supposed to be the Calno of Is 10[9]. Rost suggests that Azriau or Izriau (Azariah) of Judah played some part in this expedition, and among those who gave tribute was Menahem of Samaria (2 K 15[19]). In 737 B.C. his objective was the Medes, in many of whose cities he set up bas-reliefs with the royal image. After this (736 B.C.) his forces were again engaged in hilly Nairi, and reached the mountain of Nal. This led the way to the conquest of Urarṭu in 735 B.C. In 734 B.C. the Assyrian army invaded Pilishtai (Philistia)—according to Rost, the Mediterranean coast-land S. of Joppa. Gaza was captured, and Hanun, the king, having fled, Tiglath-pileser mounted the throne and set up his image in the palace there. In 733 B.C. came the turn of Damascus and also of Israel, the immediate cause being affairs in Judah. Azariah had died, and after the short reign of his son Jotham, Jehoahaz or Ahaz came to the throne. Taking advantage of the change, Pekah of Israel made an alliance with Rezin of Damascus to attack Judah, and captured Elath (2 K 16[5ff]). Feeling that Judah would be compelled to submit to the allied powers in the end, Ahaz turned to Assyria, sending the best of his own treasures and those of the Temple at Jerusalem to make a worthy present to the Assyrian king (2 K 16[8]), who therefore came to his aid. Pekah and Rezin withdrew their forces from Judah, but, instead of uniting against the common foe, awaited the Assyrian king's attack each in his own territory. Marching by the coast-route, Tiglath-pileser assured himself of the submission of his vassals in N. Phoenica, and attacked N. Israel, capturing Ijon, Abel-beth-maacah, Janoah, Kedesh, Hazor, Gilead, Galilee, and all the land of Naphtali (2 K 15[29]). These names are not preserved in the annals, though 'the broad (land of) . . . -li' may be, as Hommel suggests, the last named. Pekah saved his land from further harm by paying tribute, but things went harder with Rezin, his ally, who shut himself up in Damascus. The siege which followed ended, in 732 B.C., in the capture of the city; 591 towns, including Hadara, Rezin's own city, were razed to the ground. An attack upon Samsi, queen of the Arabians, followed, the result being that a number of tribes—Sabaeans, Mas'aeans, etc.—hastened to propitiate the Assyrian king with gifts. Idi-bi'il, a N. Arabian prince, was made governor on the Muṣrian border. Meanwhile, a number of Israelitish nobles, with Hoshea as leader, revolted, and Pekah fled, but seems to have been murdered. Hoshea thereupon mounted the throne, and bought the recognition of the Assyrian king, who had continued to ravage Syria. Mitinti of Ashkelon, seeing the fate of Rezin of Damascus, seems to have gone mad. He was succeeded by his son Rūkipti, who tried to atone for his father's disaffection by sending tribute and gifts. Metenna of Tyre likewise became tributary. After the fall of the capital, Damascus became an Assyrian province. According to 2 K 16[9], the people were taken captive to Kir, and Rezin was slain. It was in Damascus that Ahaz made homage to the conqueror, and seeing there an altar which took his fancy, had one made like it. Tiglath-pileser, confident, seemingly, of his hold upon Palestine, did not again invade the country. Its States remained for many years more or less tributary to Assyria, according as that power seemed strong or weak. In 731 B.C. Tiglath-pileser was attracted by events in Babylonia. Ukīn-zēr, a Chaldaean prince, having seized the Babylonian throne, the Assyrian king besieged him in his capital Sapia, which he captured in 729 B.C., taking Ukīn-zēr prisoner. In 728 B.C. Tiglath-pileser became king of Babylon, but beyond 'grasping the hand of Bel' (Marduk) as its ruler, took part in no further important event. He probably died when making an expedition against a city whose name is lost; and Shalmaneser V. mounted the throne (25th of Tebeth, 727 B.C.). When at home, Tiglath-pileser resided in Nineveh or in Calah, where he restored the central palace, decorating it with bas-reliefs and the annals of his reign. This building was partly destroyed by Esarhaddon. T. G. P.—**T. F.**

TIGRIS.—Only in Gn 2[14] (RVm, ASV), Dn 10[4] (RVm, ASV, RSV), where both AV and RV have **Hiddekel** (q.v.), and in all EV in To 6[1], Jth 1[6], Sir 24[25]. The Tigris rises a little S. of Lake Gōljik and flows S. to Diarbekr. After passing Diarbekr it receives the eastern Tigris (which rises in the Niphates mountains) at Osman Kieui. Then it flows through narrow gorges into the plateau of Mesopotamia, where it receives from the east the Greater and Lesser Zab, the Adhem or Radanu, and the Diyaleh or Tornadotus. On the E. bank, opposite Mosul, was Nineveh and a little N. of the junction of the Tigris and Greater Zab, Kalah, and on the W. bank, N. of the Lesser Zab, was Assur (now Kalah Sherghat), the primitive capital of Assyria. The Tigris is about 1150 miles in length, and rises rapidly in March and April owing to the melting of the snows, falling again after the middle of May. Cf also EDEN [GARDEN OF].

TIKVAH.—**1.** The father-in-law of Huldah, 2 K 22[14]; called **Tokhath** in 2 Ch 34[22] (AV **Tikvath**). **2.** The father of Jahzeiah, Ezr 10[15], 1 Es 9[14] (AV **Theocanus,** RV **Thocanus**).

TIKVATH, 2 Ch 34[22] (AV).—See TIKVAH, **1.**

TILE, TILING.—The former occurs in AV and RV in Ezk 4[1] for 'brick'—the usual rendering of the original (so RSV here). For the plan of a city drawn on 'bricks' or 'tablets' of soft clay, which were afterwards baked hard, see Pritchard, *ANEP*, No. 260. **'Tiling'** is found only in Lk 5[19] AV, for which RV and RSV have 'through the tiles.' St. Luke seems here to have adapted the narrative of Mark (for which see HOUSE, **5**) to the style of roof covered with tiles, with which his Western readers were more familiar; or 'through the tiles' is here simply synonymous with 'through the roof' (cf our expression 'on the tiles'). A. R. S. K.

TILGATH-PILNESER.—See Tiglath-pileser.

TILON.—A son of Shimon, 1 Ch 4[20].

TIMAEUS.—The father of Bartimaeus (Mk 10[46]).

TIMBREL.—See Tabret, and Music, etc., **4** (3) (*a*).

TIME.—In EV 'time' serves as the translation, or as one element in the translation, of a number of different Hebrew and Greek words and expressions, the precise meaning of which in each instance depends on the context. Thus, duration of 'time' is referred to in such passages as Dn 11[24] ('. . . but only for a *time*'—Heb. *ʿēth*) or Ac 18[23] ('After spending some *time* there . . .'—Gr. *chronos*): or the reference may be to a particular moment of 'time' (*e.g.* Gn 21[22] 'At that *time* . . .'—Heb. *ʿēth*, Mt 2[7] '. . . what *time* the star appeared'—Gr. *chronos*), to a particular 'time' of day (*e.g.* Ex 9[18] 'to-morrow about this *time* . . .'—Heb. *ʿēth*), or of year (*e.g.* Mt 13[30] 'at harvest *time* . . .'—Gr. *kairos*): there are set 'times' for feasts (*e.g.* Dt 31[10] 'at the *set time* . . . at the feast of booths . . .'—Heb. *mōʿēdh*) and a 'time'-limit may be appointed for the fulfilment of a mission (*e.g.* Neh 2[6] 'So it pleased the king to send me, and I set him a *time*'—Heb. *zᵉman*): there is past 'time' (*e.g.* Is 9[1] 'In the former *time* . . .'—Heb. *ʿēth*) and future 'time' (*e.g.* Jos 22[24] '*in time to come* . . .'—Heb. *māḥār*): there is also eschatological 'time' (*e.g.* 1 P 1[5] '. . . in the last *time*'—Gr. *kairos*, 1 P 1[20] '. . . at the end of the *times*'—Gr. *chronos*); and in this eschatological connexion '*the* time' may be used absolutely as almost coterminous with 'the Day' (*e.g.* Mk 1[15] 'The *time* is fulfilled . . .', Rev 1[3] '. . . the *time* is near'—Gr. *kairos* in both cases). It should also be noted that in a few passages in Dan (4[16, 23, 25, 32] 7[25]) and in Revelation (12[14]—obviously dependent on Dn 7[25]) 'time' stands for 'year.'

Of 'Time' in our modern sense, as opposed to 'Eternity,' the Bible has little, if any, conception. For the Biblical writers 'time' was a continuum with several various natural divisions.

The most obvious of these natural divisions was that between **day and night**, brought about by the regular rising and setting of the sun (cf *e.g.* Gn 1[14–16], Jos 10[13]). As 'times of day' are mentioned **morning** (*e.g.* Ps 5[3], Mt 21[18]) and **evening** (*e.g.* Nu 9[3], Ac 4[3]), **dawn** (*e.g.* 1 S 9[26], Lk 24[1]) and **twilight** (*e.g.* Pr 7[9]—not in NT), and **noon** (*e.g.* Am 8[9], Ac 22[6]) and **midnight** (*e.g.* Ru 3[8], Lk 11[5]). To call midnight a 'time of day' reveals immediately the ambiguity in the use of the word 'day' both in the Bible and in current usage: in one sense 'day' includes 'night,' in the other it is contrasted with 'night' (the ambiguity may be conveniently illustrated by the verse 'God called the light Day, and the darkness he called Night. And there was evening and there was morning, one day'—Gn 1[5]). Among the Sumerians and Babylonians the day in the former sense ran from sunset to sunset, and there is reason to think that the OT day in this wider sense also began at sunset—at least in the pre-exilic period (cf *e.g.* Gn 1[5], Lv 23[32], Dt 16[4]). In the more narrow sense the Babylonians further divided, not only the day, but also the night, into twelve **hours** each: in the OT there is no mention of hours, though this does not necessarily mean that they were not known and used (the rendering of the Aram. *shāʿāh* as 'hour' by AV and RV in Dn 3, 4 and 5 is inexact and has been rightly abandoned by RSV). In the NT, apart from such general phrases as 'in that hour' (meaning 'at that time' or 'at the same time'—*e.g.* Mt 10[19]), there are a number of more specific references to hours—thus, there are said to be 'twelve hours in the day' (Jn 11[9]), the Crucifixion took place at 'the third hour' (Mk 15[25]), and the uproar at Ephesus went on 'for about two hours' (Ac 19[34]): there is also a reference at Ac 23[23] to 'the third hour of the night.' In both OT and NT we read also of **watches** as subdivisions of the night: in the OT there are three (as in Babylonia), the first (La 2[19]), the 'middle' (Jg 7[19]), and 'the morning watch' (Ex 14[24], 1 S 11[11]): in the NT, Matthew (14[25]) and Mark (6[48] 13[35]) plainly adopt the Roman system of four watches, while Lk 12[38] ('If he comes in the second watch, or in the third, and find them so') is reconcilable with either a three-fold or four-fold system.

Just as the regular rising and setting of the sun was responsible for the division between day and night, so the regular waxing and waning of the moon was responsible for the division into **months.** Of the two Hebrew words for 'month,' one (*yeraḥ*) is consonantally identical with the word for 'moon' (*yārēaḥ*), while the root meaning of the other (*ḥōdhesh*) is 'newness.' The new moon, accordingly, marked the beginning of the month, and its appearance was celebrated by a 'new-moon' feast: these feasts were observed both in pre-exilic (*e.g.* 1 S 20[5], Is 1[14]) and post-exilic (*e.g.* Nu 10[10], Ps 81[2]) times: they are mentioned also by St. Paul (Col 2[16]). When the Hebrews first settled in Palestine they adopted the local Canaanite names for the months, but only four of these names have survived in the OT. It may also have been the practice in the early period to designate the month by number (*e.g.* 1 K 8[2] 'in the month Ethanim, which is the seventh month,' or 1 K 12[32] 'And Jeroboam appointed a feast on the fifteenth day of the eighth month'—though to what extent such passages may be relied upon as preserving a genuine pre-exilic tradition is uncertain). In the exilic and post-exilic periods, however, designation by number became extremely common (*e.g.* Gn 7[11], 1 Ch 12[15], Ezk 24[1], Hag 1[1]), and the original Canaanite names were displaced by the Babylonian, which have retained their place in the Jewish calendar to the present day. A complete list of these Hebrew month-names (with details of their attestation in the OT) is as follows:

1. Canaanite name **Abib** (Ex 13[4] 23[15] 34[18], Dt 16[1]); Babylonian name **Nisan** (Neh 2[1], Est 3[7], 1 Es 5[6]). About the same time of year as our April; the month in which the Passover was celebrated.
2. Can. name **Ziv** (1 K 6[1, 37]); Bab. **Iyyar** (not in OT).
3. No Can. name has survived in OT; Bab. **Sivan** (Est 8[3]).
4. No Can. name; Bab. **Tammuz** (not in OT).
5. No Can. name; Bab. **Ab** (not in OT).
6. No Can. name; Bab. **Elul** (Neh 6[15], 1 Mac 14[27]).
7. Can. name **Ethanim** (1 K 8[2]); Bab. **Tishri** (not in OT).
8. Can. name **Bul** (1 K 6[38]); Bab. **Marchesvan** (not in OT).
9. No Can. name; Bab. **Chislev** (Neh 1[1], Zec 7[1], 1 Mac 1[54] 4[52, 59], 2 Mac 1[9, 18] 10[5]).
10. No Can. name; Bab. **Tebeth** (Est 2[16]).
11. No Can. name; Bab. **Shebat** (Zec 1[7], 1 Mac 16[14]).
12. No Can. name; Bab. **Adar** (Ezr 6[15], Est 3[7, 13] 8[12] 9[1] etc., 1 Mac 7[43, 49], 2 Mac 15[36]).

At 2 Mac 11[30] **Xanthicus**, the name for the first month in the Macedonian calendar, occurs; at 2 Mac 11[21] **Dioscorinthius** may represent a corruption of another Macedonian month-name; and at 3 Mac 6[38] two Egyptian months, **Pachon** (the ninth month) and **Epiphi** (the eleventh month), appear, the former being omitted in some texts. The NT provides no evidence of either the numbering or the naming of months.

The idea of the **week** seems to have arisen as a subdivision of the month. From the frequent occurrence of the tenth day of the month in the dating of events (*e.g.* Ex 12[3], Jos 4[19], 2 K 25[1]) it has been suggested that the month was at one time subdivided into three periods of ten days each. Whether this be so or no, subdivision into four periods of seven days each was undoubtedly more normal; and this is borne out by the fact that the ordinary Hebrew word for week (*shābhūaʿ*) means 'heptad' (cf Gn 29[27f], Lv 12[5], Dt 16[9f]). The classic OT statement of this seven-day week is to be found in Gn 1, where God works for six days and rests on the seventh. Here the practice of numbering the days of the week is followed, and this practice is attested elsewhere (*e.g.* Ex 12[15] 16[5, 22]) ; but the seventh day is more usually called the 'sabbath' (*e.g.* Ex 16[25f] 20[8, 11]). 'Sabbaths' were certainly observed as days of cessation from work in pre-exilic times (cf *e.g.* 2 K 4[23], Am 8[5], Is 1[13]—where in each case the 'sabbath' is mentioned immediately after the 'new moon'—and especially Ex 20[8-11] 34[21], and Dt 5[12-15]). In the post-exilic literature the Hebrew *shabbāth* is used to denote, not only the 'sabbath' proper (*i.e.* the seventh day), but also, occasionally, the 'week' (Lv 23[15] 25[8] ; cf Nu 28[10] and Is 66[23]). This latter usage became established in Aramaic, where *shabbethâ* regularly means 'week' as well as 'sabbath' ; and it is further reflected in Greek in the NT where *mia* [*prōtē*] *sabbatōn* [*-tou*] (Mt 28[1], Mk 16[2, 9], Lk 24[1], Jn 20[1, 19], Ac 20[7], 1 Co 16[2]) is rendered 'the first day of the week.' This 'first day' was known also to Christians as 'the Lord's day' (Rev 1[10]), and observed as a memorial of the Resurrection. Of other days of the week in the NT we hear only of the sabbath (*e.g.* Mk 1[21], Ac 13[14]) and of 'the day of Preparation, that is, the day before the sabbath' (Mk 15[42] ; cf Mt 27[62], Lk 23[54], Jn 19[31, 42]).

The root meaning of the Hebrew word for **year** (*shānāh*) is 'change,' and this suggests a concept based on observation of the alternation of the seasons and the agricultural operations associated with them (cf Gn 8[12]). Before the Exile, the year ran from harvest to harvest (Ex 23[16] 34[22]), and 'times of year' were indicated by reference either to the season (2 S 11[1], 1 K 20[22, 26]) or to the month (*e.g.* Ex 23[15], 1 K 8[2]), though what was the relation between the year and the months at this period is obscure. During the Exile, however, the influence of the Babylonian calendar made itself felt ; not only, as has been seen already, were the original Canaanite names for the months displaced by the Babylonian, but the months themselves now definitely became twelfths of the year (with an extra thirteenth month intercalated every two or three years, in order to make up the difference between the lunar and the solar year) : furthermore, the beginning of the year was transferred from the autumn to the spring—thus, the spring month, Abib, originally the seventh month, became Nisan, the first (Ex 12[2], Est 3[7]). Yet the Babylonian calendar did not win a complete victory. To-day the Jews distinguish between the 'ecclesiastical year' beginning with Nisan in the spring, and the 'civil year' beginning with Tishri in the autumn—a distinction which is at least as old as Josephus (*Ant.* I. iii. 3 [81]) : the origin of the 'civil year' may accordingly be explained as a survival of pre-exilic custom, and a stage in its development traced in the regulations for the observance of 'the first day of the seventh month' in the post-exilic Pentateuchal legislation (Lv 23[23-25], Nu 29[1-6]).

Duration (or lapse) of time, if specific, is expressed in the Bible by numbers attached to one of the natural divisions just discussed (*e.g.* 1 S 13[8], Rev 13[5]). Fixed points are similarly indicated, though of necessity in relation to other fixed points previously determined (*e.g.* Gn 7[11], Mk 9[2]) : in the case of 'dates,' the other fixed points are normally either well-known events (*e.g.* Am 1[1], Is 20[1]) or the year of a king's accession (*e.g.* 2 K 18[9], Lk 3[1]). Of instruments to measure time we hear of only one—'the dial of Ahaz' (2 K 20[8-11], Is 38[7f] [AV **sun-dial**]) : since it was called after Ahaz some twenty or more years after his death, the probability is that it was an innovation on his part, no doubt a foreign importation, and perhaps contemporaneous with the altar that he caused to be set up in the Temple as a replica of the altar that had caught his fancy in Damascus on his visit there to do homage to Tiglath-Pileser (2 K 16[10-16]).

H. F. D. S.

TIMNA.—1. A concubine of Eliphaz, son of Esau, Gn 36[12]. **2.** A woman of the Esau clan of Horites, Gn 36[22], 1 Ch 1[39]. **3.** A 'duke' of Edom, Gn 36[40], 1 Ch [51] (AV **Timnah**). **4.** A grandson of Esau, 1 Ch 1[36].

TIMNAH.—1. A town in the hill country of Judah SE. of Hebron, Jos 15[57]. It is possible that this was the Timnah visited by Judah at the time of sheepshearing, Gn 38[12ff] (AV **Timnath**). It is possibly modern *Kh. Tibneh*, W. of Bethlehem. **2.** A place on the N. frontier of the tribe of Judah between Beth-shemesh and Ekron, Jos 15[10]. At one time it was counted in the territory of Dan, Jos 19[43] (AV **Thimnathah**) ; at another it was in Philistine possession, Jg 14[1, 2, 5] (AV **Timnath**). Here Samson celebrated his marriage. His father-in-law is called the **Timnite**, Jg 15[6]. The town was held by the Hebrews in the reign of Uzziah, but was lost to the Philistines by Ahaz, 2 Ch 28[18]. It is now *Kh. Tibneh*, 2 miles SW. of Beth-shemesh. **3.** Gn 36[40], 1 Ch 1[51] (AV) ; see Timna, 3.

TIMNATH.—1. Gn 38[12ff] (AV) ; see Timnah, **1. 2.** Jg 14[1, 2, 5] (AV) ; see Timnah, **2. 3.** 1 Mac 9[50] ; see Timnath-Serah.

TIMNATH-HERES.—See Timnath-Serah.

TIMNATH-SERAH.—A city assigned to Joshua as an inheritance and burying-place, Jg 19[50] 24[30] ; called **Timnath-Heres** in Jg 2[9] and **Timnath** (q.v.) in 1 Mac 9[50] (AV **Thamnatha**). In the latter it is reckoned to Judaea, but in Jg 2[9] it is said to be in Mount Ephraim on the N. side of the hill Gaash. The *Onomasticon* identifies it with *Tibneh*, where there are remains of an important place, with a spring and ancient tombs, on the Roman road from Caesarea to Jerusalem, about 14 miles NE. of Lydda. The tombs are on the S. of the road. One, distinguished by size and workmanship, may be that pointed out as Joshua's in the time of Eusebius and Jerome. The Samaritans place the burial of Joshua at *Kefr Ḥâris*, a village some 10 miles S. of *Nâblus*, with two sanctuaries to the E., one of which, *Nebī Kifl* ('the prophet of the portion *or* lot'), may be associated with Joshua. In this case, only the second element in the name has survived. *Heres*, it will be observed, simply reverses the order of the letters in *Serah*. W. E.

TIMON.—One of 'the Seven' (Ac 6[5]).

TIMOTHEUS.—1. The AV form of Timothy, **1** (q.v.) everywhere in NT except 2 Co 1[1], 1 Ti 1[2], 2 Ti 1[2], Phn [1], He 13[23]. **2.** The AV and RV form of Timothy, **2** (q.v.).

TIMOTHY.—1. A native of Lystra, chosen while still a young man as companion and assistant to Paul, on the occasion of the Apostle's second visit to that city. He was the child of a mixed marriage, his father (probably dead at the time of his selection by Paul) being a Greek or Gentile and his mother a Jewess (Ac 16[1]). It is said that in his childhood he received training in the Jewish Scriptures from his mother *Eunice* and his grandmother *Lois* (2 Ti 1[5] 3[15]), although this statement is not probable on historical grounds—as B. S. Easton has shown. Probably he was converted during Paul's first sojourn at Lystra, for on the Apostle's second visit he was already 'a disciple' of some standing, 'well spoken of by the brethren' (Ac 16[1-2]). Indeed, Paul seems to claim him as a *personal* convert in 1 Co 4[17], describing him as his 'beloved and faithful child in the Lord.'

The selection of Timothy was due not only to the wish of Paul (Ac 16[3]), but also to the action of the Church at Lystra. In his case, as in the case of Paul and Barnabas (Ac 13[2]), the local prophets 'led the way' (1 Ti 1[18] RVm) to him ; the Pastoral Epistles contain two references which have been interpreted as describing his ordination. Paul caused him to be circumcised (Ac 16[3]), judging that, as his mother was a Jewess, his not having received the rite would prove an obstacle to his ministry among Jews, and, further, that from his semi-Jewish parentage, he did not come within the scope of the Church's decree which released Gentiles from circumcision.

Timothy at once accompanied Paul through Asia to Troas, and thence into Macedonia. He was left behind at Beroea when the Apostle moved on to Athens, but was summoned to rejoin him (Ac 17[14-15]). He was then sent back to Macedonia to strengthen the church at Thessalonica, and to bring news of its state to Paul. He rejoined the Apostle in Corinth and cheered him by a favourable report (1 Th 3^{1-8}, Ac 18^{5}). While in Corinth, Paul wrote his Epistles to the Thessalonians, and included Timothy in the greetings (1 Th 1^{1}, 2 Th 1^{1}). He is next mentioned at Ephesus with Paul, and thence is sent with Erastus to Macedonia in advance of the Apostle (Ac 19^{22}). Shortly after Timothy's departure, Paul dispatched by direct sea route his First Epistle to the Corinthians. In this he mentions that Timothy (travelling *via* Macedonia) would shortly reach them (1 Co 4^{17}); he asks a kindly welcome for him, and adds that he wishes him to return with 'the brethren' (*i.e.* probably the bearers of the Epistle) to Ephesus (1 Co 16^{8} and ^{10f}). Timothy may not have reached Corinth on this occasion, being detained in Macedonia; alternatively his visit may have been unsuccessful. The absence in 2 Corinthians of any mention of his being there would support either supposition. In any case he is found with Paul again when 2 Corinthians was written from Macedonia (2 Co 1^{1}). When Paul returned to Corinth Timothy was with him, for his name occurs among the greetings in the Epistle to the Romans which was written there (Ro 16^{21}). Those scholars who believe that the final chapter of Romans was a separate Epistle originally addressed to Ephesus might wish to assign this text to a different place and date. Timothy is again mentioned as being with Paul at Troas on the Apostle's journey to Jerusalem (Ac 20^{4-5}); this is the last reference to him in Acts.

In those Pauline writings which are sometimes called the Epistles of the Captivity, Timothy is named as a companion of the Apostle in his imprisonment (Col 1^{1}, Phn 1, Ph 1^{1}), and Paul considered sending him on a mission to Philippi (Ph 2^{19}). In the Pastoral Epistles it is indicated that Paul left Timothy as his delegate in Ephesus, giving him full instructions as to his rule of the Church during Paul's absence (1 Ti 1^{3} 3^{14-15}). In the other letter which bears his name, he is summoned to the Apostle's side, presumably in his final imprisonment at Rome. It is not possible to place any reliance upon these statements, for much that is said of Timothy in the Pastoral Epistles seems completely inconsistent with what is known of him from other sources, and the best explanation of these documents would appear to be that the name of one of Paul's subordinates has been chosen to represent the new leaders who were emerging in the third generation of the Church, and who stood in need of advice. Thus there is no certain knowledge of Timothy's life in the NT after the time covered by the Epistle to the Philippians. While there is a mention of his having recently been released in He 13^{23}, this says nothing of the place or circumstances of his imprisonment, and in fact tells no more than that he continued to be a faithful Christian or 'brother.'

2. A leader of the Ammonites who was defeated in many battles by Judas Maccabaeus, 1 Mac 5^{6ff} ^{34ff}, 2 Mac 8^{30} 9^{3} 10^{24-37} (AV and RV **Timotheus**).

C. T. P. G.—**J. H. W. R.**

TIMOTHY, EPISTLES TO.—These Epistles, together with that to Titus, form a special group to which Paul Anton gave the name 'Pastoral' in 1726. They are united by common objects and a common literary style. Each of them claims, in its opening words, to have St. Paul for its author, and this claim the Church has accepted throughout the greater part of its history. In recent decades, however, increasing numbers of Biblical scholars have been led to the conviction that these writings cannot be fitted into any period of the Apostle's life, and that they probably belong to the early 2nd cent. It is still debated whether 2 Timothy and Titus may contain genuine fragments of Pauline letters, but if this is so the verses in question have had little influence upon the purpose or teaching of the Epistles.

1. The *situation* presupposed in 1 and 2 Timothy is as follows. Paul, having to go into Macedonia, left Timothy in charge of the Church at Ephesus (1 Ti 1^{3}), and wrote telling him how to act during the prolonged absence of his chief (1 Ti 3^{14-15}). From other allusions in the Epistles it appears that the journey took Paul to Troas (2 Ti 4^{13}), Corinth and Miletus (2 Ti 4^{20}), and Crete (Tit 1^{5}), and that he proposed wintering in Nicopolis (Ti 3^{12}).

It is impossible to fit these visits into the period covered by Acts, and during Paul's two-year stay in Ephesus (Ac 19^{22}) it was Timothy and not the Apostle who went to Macedonia. Moreover, two years does not allow sufficient time for such journeys as these Epistles describe. Any such activity on the part of Paul would have to be referred to a period after release from the imprisonment in Rome with which Acts closes. For such a release there is no definite evidence, and the strongest argument in favour of it seems to be a hope expressed by the Apostle in Ph 2^{24}. Moreover, if he did regain his freedom, no doubt, as stated in the Muratorian Fragment, he fulfilled his wish of visiting Spain (Ro $15^{24,\,28}$), and the statement of Clement of Rome that he 'reached the bounds of the West' would imply work in the same area. In any period of liberty that Paul may have enjoyed after A.D. 61, there would not have been the opportunity for extensive work both in the western and eastern portions of the Mediterranean world. Accordingly, it seems certain that the names and places mentioned in the Pastoral Epistles all form part of a literary scheme devised to support the teaching of the author.

2. The *external evidence* in favour of Pauline authorship is strong, and includes Irenaeus, Clement, and Tertullian. Polycarp also quotes from 1 Ti $6^{7,\,10}$. On the other hand, the Michigan Beatty Codex of Paul apparently did not contain the Pastorals, for although it is defective its length is known, and these thirteen chapters could have been included only if the handwriting were incredibly compressed. Furthermore, the Muratorian Fragment places these after all the other Epistles, as if they were an addition. The full incorporation of the Pastorals among the other Pauline letters, so that they precede Philemon instead of following it, belongs to the 3rd cent. (see B. S. Easton, *The Pastoral Epistles*, pp. 31–32).

3. Discussion concerning the nature of the *heresies* attacked in these Epistles is affected by one's judgment about their authorship. Those who think of them as produced by Paul himself regard the false teaching as essentially Jewish in origin, citing such phrases as 'the circumcision party' (Tit 1^{10}), 'Jewish myths' (Tit 1^{14}), and 'quarrels over the law' (Tit 3^{9}), or the reference to those who desire to be 'teachers of the law' (1 Ti 1^{7}). On this theory the 'endless genealogies' of 1 Ti 1^{4} (cf Tit 3^{9}) would have to do with the legendary history of the Jewish patriarchs. Yet it is clear that the errors described find expression in an asceticism which condemns marriage absolutely, and prohibits the use of certain foods such as meat and wine (1 Ti $4^{1-4,\,8}$ 5^{23}). Such rejection of the world can be related more readily to Gnostic belief in the essential evil of matter than to anything which may be found in conventional Judaism, and the 'genealogies' can easily be explained as the long lists of emanations and aeons which were prominent in Gnostic cosmologies. In 2 Ti 2^{18} one heresy is distinctly named, the belief that the resurrection was already past; this opinion may have been the same as that which Paul condemned in 1 Co 15^{12} as a denial that there could be any material resurrection, but this view of an incorporeal immortality was Gentile and not Jewish. Within Paul's lifetime it is not likely that the Gnostic type of heresy would have made such progress in the Church, but early in the 2nd cent. there is incontrovertible evidence that such teaching had become common.

4. While these Epistles employ the common theological terms of the Pauline writings, the words are used with different emphasis. Thus *faith* describes the objective belief which the individual holds rather than the personal trust and affection which unites the soul to Christ. Similarly *righteousness* denotes a virtue to be reached by personal struggle instead of a relationship to God. While it must be admitted that *faith* occasionally bears an objective sense in Paul's writings (Gal 1^{23} and probably 1 Co 2^{5}), and that *righteousness* is sometimes spoken of as a virtue to be acquired (2 Co 9[10], Ro 8[10]), this is far less significant than the fact that the full Pauline use of *faith* as the justifying principle is conspicuously absent from the Pastorals, and that in 1 Ti 1[14] faith along with love is a *result* of justification instead of being its antecedent (Easton, *op. cit.* 203–204). Another distinguishing feature of these writings is the approach to a formulated creed seen in frequent quotations such as the five *sure sayings*, or the hymn of 1 Ti 3[16]. These facts are indications of a Church with a history behind it, of Christians of the third generation rather than the first.

5. In the Pastorals *Church Organization* is seen as a major interest. The picture presented is that of the Apostle or the author holding supreme control (1 Ti 1[20] 2[1, 8]), while 'Timothy' and 'Titus' serve as his delegates. This reflects the statements that the disciples whose names are used here did serve temporarily as representatives of Paul (1 Co 4[17], 2 Co 8[16–18], Ph 2[19]). Here the recipients of the letters appear to hold permanent commissions, and to be given the final word concerning the qualifications necessary in those appointed to the offices of bishop (or elder) and deacon. The bishop and elder are spoken of in similar terms (Tit 1[5–7]), except for the fact that bishop is always referred to in the singular and elders regularly in the plural (see M. Dibelius, *Pastoralbriefe*, 46 f). The distinction between the two offices (if any) is clearly not that drawn in the Ignatian Epistles between the monarchical bishop and the elders; at most the bishop is a permanent president of the body of elders. Thus one must suppose either that the Pastorals were written some time before A.D. 115, or in an area other than Asia Minor, and the latter alternative is the more probable. It may be argued strongly that they were written from Rome and addressed to smaller churches located in Italy.

Instructions are also given regarding 'women' in 1 Ti 3[11], and 'widows' in 1 Ti 5[3–16]. The former are mentioned in the midst of regulations regarding deacons, and scholars are divided as to whether these are deaconesses or the wives of deacons; in view of the fact that the duties later performed by deaconesses are assigned to the widows of 1 Ti 5[9–13], while the qualifications of the women in the earlier chapter are such as one might expect in 'well-managed households,' it seems likely that the AV translators were right in saying 'wives.' In Greek, as in many other languages, the same word does duty for both *wife* and *woman*. The social customs of the 1st and 2nd cents. made it desirable for the Church to appoint women to perform for women the functions that deacons discharged for men, and 1 Ti indicates that these were entrusted to the older widows. The care of indigent widows (1 Ti 5[3–8, 16]) engaged the Church from the first.

The absence of all instructions regarding *prophets* is in notable contrast to the *Didache*, which probably comes from the same period, and to the discussion concerning them in 1 Co 14[29–33]. It indicates a growing stress upon the regular functions of the ministry as contrasted with the extraordinary ones. The recipients of these directions regarding Church order and government are clearly subordinate to the writer of the Epistles. Their position may be compared to that of the *Chorepiscopi* of the 3rd to the 12th cents., men in full charge of particular congregations but under the authority of Church leaders of higher rank (see article 'Chorepiscopus,' *Oxford Dict. of the Chr. Ch.*, p. 273).

6. The literary style of St. Paul has had a marked influence upon these Epistles, but the differences are not less striking than the resemblances, and the result is what might be expected in a conscious imitation. Some 36 per cent. of the words of the Pastorals are not found in any other work ascribed to Paul. While expressions technically known as *hapax legomena* range in frequency from 3·3 per page in 2 Thessalonians to 6·2 per page in Philippians, in the three Pastorals the range is from 12·8 to 16·1. For comparison, in the plays of Shakespeare the variation is from 3·4 to 10·4. Words not shared with other NT writers appear in the Pastorals at the rate of 11·0 to 13·0 to the page, in the other letters from 3·6 to 6·8. On the other hand, the accepted Pauline writings share with the later Christian Apologists from 4·2 to 6·2 words per page, while in the Pastorals these figures are from 13·3 to 16·5. A comprehensive treatment of the stylistic issues can be found in P. N. Harrison, *The Problem of the Pastoral Epistles*, pp. 18–86, but these extracts from his argument should suffice to show that the works in question can scarcely be accounted genuine compositions of the Apostle.

Thus the judgment of most modern scholars is that the Pastoral Epistles are not the work of Paul, but of an admirer who wrote within the first decade of the 2nd cent. The probable sequence of the letters was 2 Timothy, Titus, 1 Timothy, and Easton treats them in that order in his commentary. The Pauline terms and references are literary rather than historical. Yet the works are not to be regarded as forgeries. Their first readers undoubtedly were aware of the true author's identity, and recognized that he was bringing the message of his hero up to date. In the ancient world, convention ascribed any vital teaching to the person who had been its original inspiration. Paul's work had inspired the Pastorals, and so they bear his name. The efforts of later Christians to fit them into the Apostle's own life have been the cause of misunderstanding of their message, and of confusion about the life of Paul himself.

J. H. W. R.

TIN.—See MINING AND METALS.

TIPHSAH ('crossing').—**1.** A place named as the NE. limit of the dominions of Solomon, 1 K 4[24]. It is the classical *Thapsacus*, the chief crossing-place on the middle Euphrates for caravans and armies, after the decline of Carchemish in the Persian period. It lay in the eastward bend of the river where it leaves its southerly course. It is the modern *Dibseh*. **2.** In 2 K 15[16] Tiphsah (AV, RV) should be corrected to **Tappuah** (q.v.) with RSV, following Lucian's recension of the LXX.

J. F. McC.—**H. H. R.**

TIRAS.—A son of Japheth, Gn 10[2], 1 Ch 1[5]. Ancient writers identified him with the ancestor of the Thracians, but this is generally abandoned. Others have thought of the *Turusha*, a piratical people who invaded Syria and Egypt in the 13th cent. B.C. The name has also been connected with *Tarsus* and even *Tarshish* (q.v.). Yet another view is that he was the progenitor of the people later known as the Etruscans.

TIRATHITES.—A family of scribes, 1 Ch 2[55].

TIRE.—See HEADTIRE and DRESS, **5.**

TIRHAKAH.—King of Cush (2 K 19[9], Is 37[9]) who, according to the Biblical narrative, marched out from Egypt against Sennacherib when the latter laid siege to Jerusalem in 701 B.C. The Egyptian and Assyrian armies did not come into contact, as Sennacherib was suddenly obliged to abandon his plans for the capture of Jerusalem. Herodotus preserves a version of the same event. Recently discovered Egyptian evidence shows that Tirhakah was only a boy of eight when this campaign took place and he could therefore hardly have been in command of an Egyptian army at that time. Possibly the author of the Book of Kings has telescoped two campaigns, one in 701 B.C. and the other in the period 689–686 B.C., and it was during the latter that Tirhakah led his army into Palestine. Tirhakah was the third king of the Ethiopian (25th) Dynasty and he reigned over Egypt and Nubia from 690–664 B.C. His whole reign was spent in plotting against the Assyrians and in conflict with them. When he succeeded Shabataka to the throne he moved his capital to the Delta in order to be nearer the Assyrian vassals in Tyre and Sidon and to foment revolt amongst them. Esarhaddon resolved to put an end to these intrigues and invaded Egypt in 671 B.C. He captured the Delta and the city of Memphis, and Tirhakah was forced to flee to Thebes. No sooner had Esarhaddon left Egypt than Tirhakah began to plot with the Egyptian governors appointed by the Assyrians, and he regained control over Egypt. His success was brief. After three years Ashurbanipal sent an expedition to Egypt and Tirhakah fled to Thebes a second time. He died two years later and was succeeded by his nephew Tanutamon. T. W. T.

TIRHANAH.—A son of Caleb, 1 Ch 2[48].

TIRIA.—A son of Jehallelel, 1 Ch 4[16].

TIRSHATHA.—A Persian word, corresponding in use to the Assyrian title *peḥāh* = '**governor.**' It is found in AV and RV in Ezr 2[63], Neh 7[65, 70] 8[9] 10[1], but RSV translates by 'governor' in all cases. In the first three of these passages it is used of Zerubbabel, and in the last two of Nehemiah. See also Attharates, Attharias.

TIRZAH.—**1.** One of the thirty-one cities captured by Joshua, according to Hebrew tradition (Jos 12[24]). It was the seat of Jeroboam I. after Shechem (1 K 14[17]) and his successors down to Omri (1 K 15[21] 16[6, 8, 15, 17, 23]). The doubtful reference in Ca 6[4] compares the Shulammite to Tirzah in beauty. Long disputed, the site seems now settled beyond doubt at *Tell el-Fâr'ah*, a well-watered and strategically significant site *c* 6 miles NE. of *Nâblus* and Shechem, commanding communications from Shechem to Bethshan and the Jordan Valley. The recent excavations of the Dominican fathers De Vaux and Stève have established occupation since the Chalcolithic Age, before *c* 3000 B.C., to the end of the Israelite kingdom. The burnt level which terminates the first stratum of Iron Age occupation may indicate the civil disorders before Omri came to power (1 K 16[18]). The reduction of the place from an important fortress to virtually an open town just at the time that Samaria was built strongly confirms the view that *Tell el-Fâr'ah* was the site of the old capital Tirzah. **2.** One of the five daughters of Zelophehad (Nu 26[33] 27[1] 36[11], Jos 17[3]). H. L. W.—**J. Gr.**

TISHBE.—In 1 K 17[1] Elijah is said to be of 'the inhabitants of Gilead' (AV; cf RV). Here RSV follows LXX in reading 'from **Tishbe**' (this involves no change of the Hebrew consonants), and this is certainly correct. Elijah is repeatedly designated the **Tishbite,** 1 K 17[1] 21[17, 25] etc. Tishbe is probably modern *Kh. Lisdib.*

TISHBITE.—See Tishbe.

TISHRI (month).—See Time.

TITANS.—In Hellenic mythology and literature Titans and Giants were primitive, pre-Olympian figures, defeated and disciplined only with the utmost difficulty by the Olympian gods of classical Greece. These two groups of monstrous deviates, though quite distinct in origin, became more and more associated and confused in Greek mythology and literary tradition.

In the LXX version of Samuel, the 'Vale of Rephaim' (2 S 5[18, 22]) is called the 'Vale of the Titans.' Here the word is used in the sense of 'giants,' for the same version of Chronicles translates this name in 1 Ch 11[15] 14[9] 'Vale of the Giants.' Thus in interpreting early Hebrew thought for Greek readers, the old shadowy Rephaim (q.v.) were identified with Titans and Giants.

Similarly in the song of victory in Jth 16[7] we read:

'For their mighty one did not fall by the hands of the young men,
nor did the sons of the Titans smite him,
nor did tall giants set upon him;
but Judith the daughter of Merari undid him.'

Here Greek mythology has been absorbed by Jewish.
G. A. B.—**H. R. W.**

TITHES.—There is no law of tithes (so-called) in the E or J documents though according to both northern (Gn 28[22]) and southern tradition (Gn 14[20]) Israel's patriarchs paid tithes. The custom thus seems to be very ancient. The laws in P (Nu 18[21–32], with corresponding practice in Neh 10[37f] and Lv 27[30f]) differ fundamentally from the laws in D (Dt 14[22–29]). A full discussion of these differences and apparently incompatible practices will be found in Pedersen, *Israel* I–II, 308 f and G. A. Smith, *Deuteronomy* (Cambridge Bible), pp. 196–197.

The institution of offering tithes of the fruits of the field and of the flocks is one which dates back to a period anterior to Israelite history. A tenth of the flocks, fruits, and possessions of all kinds, as well as of the spoils of war, was given to their gods by many peoples, not only of Semitic but also of Indo-Germanic race.

In the OT two ideas lie at the root of the custom: the more ancient—apart from its position in the Bible—is that which regards the offering of a tenth to the Deity as His due owing to His being the supreme owner of the land and its produce (Lv 27[30–33]). The underlying thought here is that of propitiation, the idea being that, if the supreme owner does not receive his due, his blessing will fail in the coming year. The other idea, obviously the later, is that of thankfulness for the blessings received (Gn 28[20–22]). The tithes were given in thanks for all the gifts received.

Among the Israelites this ancient custom was taken advantage of by the Levitical priests, who, as those employed in the sanctuary, claimed for themselves, on behalf of God, a tithe of all. It assumed the nature of a direct levy or tax. According to Nu 18[21–24] the Levites were to receive this in lieu of the inheritance of land which fell to all the other tribes, but they received the tithe on behalf of Yahweh: 'For the tithe of the people of Israel which they present as an offering to the Lord I have given to the Levites for an inheritance' (v.[24]). The 'heaving' or presenting of an offering *towards* the altar was the substitute for the actual consuming of it *upon* the altar. Although tithes were, of course, intended to be offered once a year (Dt 14[22]), it would appear from Am 4[4]—the words are ironical—that in their excess of 'religiosity' many worshippers brought them more frequently (the Hebrew is rather ambiguous). Though, generally speaking, tithes were offered only to the Deity yet it is clear that they might be given to, or levied by, a king (cf Gn 14[20], 1 S 8[17], He 7[2, 4]). W. O. E. O.—**J. Pn.**

TITIUS JUSTUS.—See Justus.

TITLE.—A *titulus* (Jn 19[19f]) might be inscribed on any material to designate the nature of an article, as when attached to a votive offering, a bottle of wine, or the neck of a slave who was placed on sale. Affixed to the top of the *arbor infelix*, it proclaimed the crime for which the suspended victim had been crucified. That inscribed 'King of the Jews,' which according to Mk 15[26] (here called '**superscription**' in AV and RV; RSV '**inscription**') epitomized the charge on which Jesus was put to death, is amplified by the other Evangelists; according to Jn 19[20] 'it was written in Hebrew [presumably Aramaic is intended], in Latin, and in Greek.' It signified that Jesus was leader of a movement that aimed at national independence, and was probably meant to be a warning to other revolutionists. J. S. K.

TITTLE.—See Jot.

TITUS.—Titus Flavius Sabinus Vespasianus, son of Vespasian (q.v.), later emperor, succeeded his father in command of the Roman forces in Judaea in A.D. 69, and in the following year captured Jerusalem and ordered the destruction of the Temple, the treasures of which are represented on the triumphal Arch of Titus at Rome. His brief reign, however, A.D. 79–81, left a memory of gentleness and goodness, perhaps in contrast with his father and his brother Domitian (q.v.). E. R. H.

TITUS.—A convert from heathenism (Gal 2[3]), said to have been won by St. Paul himself (Tit 1[4]). He is not directly mentioned in *Acts*, and all that is certainly known of him comes from the Epistles to Galatians and 2 Corinthians. The references in the Pastorals are dubious, for most scholars agree that they come from a later hand than Paul. Neither his age nor his place of birth is told us. We first hear of him when he accompanies St. Paul on his journey from Antioch to Jerusalem—a journey undertaken in connexion with the question of the circumcision of *Gentile* Christians (Gal 2[1]). He is thus included in the 'others' mentioned in Ac 15[2]. The Judaistic party within the Church wished to have Titus circumcised (Gal 2[3]); but the Apostle and those representing Gentile Christianity strenuously resisted (v.[5]), and one gathers that the decision of the Church was in their favour

(Ac 15^{28f}). The case of Titus thus seems to have been the *test case* in this controversy. From this time we may suppose that Titus continued with St. Paul as one of his missionary companions and assistants, but we have no other distinct reference to him until we turn to the Apostle's Corinthian letters. In 2 Corinthians Titus is mentioned nine times, and it appears that he visited Corinth as the Apostle's delegate—probably three times. On the first occasion, which was a year before the writing of 2 Co $8^{6, 10}$, he came with an unnamed brother (12^{18}), and on his arrival set on foot the necessary organization to secure the local contributions towards the collection for the poor Christians of Judaea, which the Apostle had inaugurated (1 Co 16^{1-2}). After his departure from Corinth serious trouble vexed the Church there, and he was sent a second time to reduce matters to order. Probably on this occasion he was the bearer of the letter referred to in 2 Co 2^{3ff} 7^{8ff}. St. Paul anxiously awaited at Troas the return of Titus (2 Co 2^{12}); but the journey took longer than was expected; and so the Apostle moved on into Macedonia, with a view to meeting him the sooner on his way. Here Titus ultimately reached him, and bringing good news from Corinth refreshed his spirit (v.^{14}). Titus was then despatched a *third* time to Corinth, bearing the letter in which St. Paul expressed his thankfulness for the solution of the difficulties in that Church (2 Co 1–9; cf 8^{16-24}). He was charged to complete 'the collection'—the organization of which he had begun the year before (8^{10}).

After these events we do not hear of Titus again, excepting in the Pastoral Epistle which bears his name. From this it has been argued that he accompanied the Apostle, after his release from Roman imprisonment, on a visit to Crete, and that he was left there by him 'to amend what was defective' and to 'appoint elders in every town' (Tit 1^5). There is, however, no satisfactory evidence that St. Paul obtained this release, or that he was ever able to undertake any work later than that mentioned in Acts. Indeed, since P. N. Harrison's study, *The Problem of the Pastoral Epistles* (1921), an increasing number of scholars have come to the conviction that the three Pastoral Epistles are pseudonymous, and that the names of Titus and Timothy have been chosen from among the associates of St. Paul to represent the leaders of Christian congregations at the beginning of the 2nd cent. The advice given in the Epistle to Titus is to maintain sound doctrine (2^1), to avoid unprofitable discussions (3^9 AV), and duly to assert authority (2^{15}). In what may well be a fragment from a personal letter of the Apostle addressed to Titus at Corinth, there is a statement that Paul intends to send Artemas or Tychicus to him, and bids him, when this occurs, to join him in Nicopolis, where he hopes to winter (3^{12}). If this verse is from a genuine Pauline communication, it should probably be dated in the course of the controversy in Corinth; but it may be no more than literary colouring. In 2 Ti 4^{10} there is a further reference to Titus as being with the Apostle in his final imprisonment, although temporarily absent in Dalmatia.

Titus and Timothy share the honour of being the most trusted and efficient helpers of St. Paul, and the fact that the former was chosen to deal with so sharp a crisis as presented itself at Corinth shows that prudence, tact, and firmness marked his Christian character.

C. T. P. G.—**J. H. W. R.**

TITUS, EPISTLE TO.—The Epistle claims Paul as its author (1^1), and is said to be addressed to Titus while the latter was acting as his delegate in Crete (1^5). As far as our records tell us, St. Paul never made a missionary visit to the island. While he had touched there on his way from Caesarea to Rome (Ac 27^{7-8}), on that journey he was a prisoner and probably would not have been allowed to leave his ship; certainly he would have no opportunity for effective evangelization. There might have been time for such a visit during the Apostle's stay at Corinth (Ac 18^{11}) or at Ephesus (Ac 19^{10}), but we have no proof that he made such a journey. Thus Crete may be described as a stage setting for the teaching which this author is concerned to present. The literary style of the Epistle marks it as belonging to the same group as 1 and 2 Timothy, and as being a revision of Paul's teaching for the early 2nd cent. (see TIMOTHY, EPISTLES TO).

The group of Churches to which the Epistle is addressed was evidently deficient in its organization, although a mission area of some years' standing. We read of several cities having congregations in need of supervision (1^5), and of elders to be chosen from among those who were fathers of 'believing' (*i.e.* Christian) families (1^6). The heresies dealt with are those that are *in opposition* to true doctrine, rather than such as might occur in a newly-founded Church through ignorance of it.

The general character of the Cretans was not high. Ancient writers describe their avarice, ferocity, fraud, and mendacity, and the Epistle itself quotes (1^{12}) Epimenides, one of their own poets, as saying, 'Cretans are always liars, evil beasts, lazy gluttons.' Such faults, however, were not confined to Cretans, and Christianity must always contend with them. Thus the author of this Epistle lays his chief emphasis upon the importance of personal holiness, and insists that right belief must issue in a useful, fruitful life (1^{15-16} 3^{14}). The chief opponents mentioned are unruly men, vain talkers, and deceivers who led men astray for base gain (1^{10-11}), men who professed that they knew God but denied Him by their deeds (1^{16}), and men who were 'factious' (RSV 3^{10}). The advice to avoid 'controversies, genealogies, dissensions' probably indicates some form of Gnosticism as the error to be opposed. The additional term contained in 3^9, 'quarrels over the law,' has led many interpreters to regard the opposition as Jewish, but the phrase may be no more than the author's effort to relate his own problems to those encountered by Paul (see Easton, *The Pastoral Epistles*, pp. 87 ff, 104). These false teachings resemble closely those of 1 Timothy, despite the Jewish origin ascribed to them here.

The ecclesiastical organization referred to is rudimentary. Elders (1^5) are to be appointed, as Paul had been accustomed to provide such officers for the churches which he founded (Ac 14^{23}). From Tit 1^7 it appears that there is no real distinction between elder and bishop. In this Epistle such appointments seem to be left entirely in the hands of the Christian leader who is represented by the name of 'Titus,' but some consultation with the congregations over whom the elders were to be appointed is implied in the charge (1^6) to select only those who are not liable to have any accusation brought against them (see Lock, *The Pastoral Epistles*). Further, the bishop or elder is spoken of as 'God's steward' (1^7), so that the authority committed to him was ultimately derived from God and not from man. No mention is made in this Epistle of deacons, deaconesses, or widows, a fact which shows less developed organization than in 1 Timothy.

While the letter claims to be written by St. Paul, the genuineness of that ascription is open to the same objections as in the case of 1 and 2 Timothy. For a discussion of the questions involved in this connexion, see TIMOTHY, EPISTLES TO. The conclusion of the Epistle (3^{12-15}), however, may well be a fragment from a personal note brought from the Apostle himself by Zenas or Apollos to Titus when the latter was in charge at Corinth. In that situation the verses would have been most appropriate. At a later date they could serve to crown another author's work with an authentic Pauline conclusion (P. N. Harrison, *The Problem of the Pastoral Epistles*, 115–118). C. T. P. G.—**J. H. W. R.**

TITUS JUSTUS.—See JUSTUS.

TITUS MANIUS.—See MANIUS.

TIZITE.—A designation, whose origin is unknown, applied to Joha, one of David's heroes, 1 Ch 11^{45}.

TOAH.—See NAHATH.

TOB.—One of the small Aramaean principalities founded to the S. of Mount Hermon and Damascus in the 12th century B.C., the others being Hamath, Zobah, Beth-rehob, and Maacah or Geshur. It was in Tob that Jephthah lived as an outlaw, Jg 11[3, 5]. Tob joined the rest of the Aramaeans, except those of Hamath (2 S 8[9f]), in helping the Ammonites in their war against king David, 2 S 10[6ff] (AV **Ish-tob**). Tob is perhaps to be identified with modern *eṭ-Ṭaiyibeh*, between Bozrah (see Bozrah, 3) and Edrei. It is mentioned in 1 Mac 5[13] (AV **Tobie**, RV **Tubias**), and probably its inhabitants are meant by the **Toubiani** of 2 Mac 12[17] (AV, RV **Tubieni**). J. F. McC.—**H. H. R.**

TOB-ADONIJAH.—One of the Levites sent by Jehoshaphat to teach in the cities of Judah, 2 Ch 17[8].

TOBIAH.—**1.** A family which returned from exile, but could not trace their genealogy, Ezr 2[60], Neh 7[62], 1 Es 5[37] (AV, RV **Ban**). **2.** The Ammonite who, in conjunction with Sanballat and others, persistently opposed the work of Nehemiah, Neh 2[10, 19] 4[3, 7] 6[17] 13[4, 8] etc.

TOBIAS.—**1.** The son of Tobit, To 1[9] and often. **2.** The father of Hyrcanus, 2 Mac 3[11].

TOBIE, 1 Mac 5[13] (AV).—See Tob.

TOBIEL.—The father of Tobit, To 1[1].

TOBIJAH.—**1.** One of the Levites sent by Jehoshaphat to teach in the cities of Judah, 2 Ch 17[8]. **2.** One of a deputation that came from Babylon to Jerusalem with contributions of gold and silver, Zec 6[10, 14].

TOBIT, BOOK OF.—See Apocrypha, **3**.

TOCHEN.—An unidentified town of Simeon, 1 Ch 4[32].

TOGARMAH.—The third son of Gomer, his brothers being Ashkenaz and Riphath, Gn 10[3], 1 Ch 1[6]. In Ezk 27[14] 38[6] mention is made of **Beth-togarmah** (q.v.), which traded for the wares of Tyre with horses and mules. Togarmah is identified with Accadian *Tilgarimmu*, Hittite *Tegarama*, and it lay between Samosata and Melitene.

TOHU.—See Nahath.

TOI.—See Tou.

TOKHATH.—See Tikvah, **1**.

TOLA.—The first of the five minor Judges, Jg 10[1f]. In Gn 46[13], Nu 26[23], 1 Ch 7[1] he appears as the son of Issachar; Tola was apparently the name of the leading clan of the tribe. It means 'a worm' (Ex 16[20]), from which came a crimson dye (Is 1[18]). His home and burial place was Shamir (q.v.).

TOLAD.—A Simeonite town, 1 Ch 4[29]; called **Eltolad** in Jos 19[4].

TOLBANES, 1 Es 9[25] (AV, RV).—See Telem, **1**.

TOLL.—See Tribute.

TOLMAN, 1 Es 5[28] (RV).—See Talmon.

TOMB, GRAVE, SEPULCHRE.—The disposal of the dead among the Israelites was always by **burial**. While spices were sometimes sprinkled among the grave-clothes, there was no religious motive for the embalming of the dead as in Egypt. **1.** The common grave must have been the usual opening in the ground with protective stones laid on the surface; or one prepared slab of stone either quite flat, or with the ridge of a sarcophagus lid, might be used. To judge by the custom of to-day, the grave would often be cut partly or altogether in rock, not because that was preferred, but because the village elders usually marked off for the cemetery a section of ground that was too rocky for purposes of cultivation. **2.** Tombs of a more important kind were made by excavating in the face of a rock to form a chamber about 8 or 9 feet on each side. At the opposite end and on the two sides were three narrow recesses, Hebrew *kôkhîm*, 6 or 7 feet long and about 2 feet wide, cut into the rock at right angles to each wall. Into one of these the dead body was inserted with the feet towards the entrance, which was then covered with a slab sealed around the edges with plaster. **3.** During the two centuries of Greek influence before the Christian era, a somewhat larger form of tomb came into use. The common chamber had on each of its three sides two, and occasionally three, shallow arched recesses, and in each recess a sarcophagus was laid along the line of the wall. The tradition preserved in Jn 20[12] appears to picture a tomb of this character. The tomb discovered N. of the wall of Jerusalem, 'the Garden Tomb,' is of this type. It can be seen to-day in something like its original setting. The opening to the central chamber was guarded by a large and heavy disc of rock which could roll along a groove slightly depressed at the centre, in front of the tomb entrance. Both the primitive Israelite sepulchre and its Greek successor might be of a compound form, having a passage leading from one chamber to another, each with its *kôkhîm* or *loculi*. The most extensive example of such tombs is found in the catacombs of Rome.

The Cult of the Dead, centring around burial rites and the libations and sacrifices at the tomb, was prominent in pre-Biblical Canaan and continued through Biblical times (Jer 16[5–8]) despite attempts to discourage the practices (Lv 19[28] 21[1–5, 10–11]). The pillar or *maṣṣēbhāh*, erected to a departed leader (Gn 35[20]), or even by a living person to assure his remembrance (2 S 18[18]), was supposed to contain the power or *mana* of the departed. There were probably shrines at the tombs of the judges and kings of Israel as there are to-day at the tombs of the Muslim *welis* in Palestine. The tombs of the martyrs came to be venerated in the early Christian Church and later the relics of the departed saint were deposited in the church dedicated to him (or her). This gave rise to the continuing practice of naming a Christian church for a saint. G. M. M.—**S. T.**

TONGS.—See Arts and Crafts, **2**; Tabernacle, **6** (*b*).

TONGUES, CONFUSION OF.—The belief that the world, after the Flood, was re-populated by the progeny of a single family, speaking one language, is reconciled in the Bible with the existing diversity of tongues by a story which relates how the descendants of Noah, in the course of their wanderings, settled in the plain of Shinar, or Babylonia, and there built of brick a city, and a **tower** high enough to reach heaven, as a monument to preserve their fame, and as a centre of social cohesion and union. But the Lord discerned their ambitious purposes, and, after consulting with the Divine beings who constituted His council and court (cf Gn 1[26] 3[22]), frustrated their design by confounding their speech, so that concerted action was no longer possible for them. In consequence, the name of the city was called **Babel** (see below), and its builders were compelled to disperse over the face of the earth (Gn 11[1–9]).

The story belongs to a class of narratives (of which there are several in the Bible) intended to explain the origin of various institutions, or usages, the existence of which excited the curiosity of a primitive race. Among these was the prevalence in the world of different languages, which contributed so greatly to produce between the various peoples, who were thus unintelligible to one another, feelings of mutual suspicion and fear (cf Dt 28[49], Is 28[11] 33[19], Jer 5[15]). The particular explanation furnished was doubtless suggested partly by the name of the city of *Babel*, or Babylon (which, though really meaning 'gate of God,' was by a popular etymology connected with the Hebrew word *bālal*, 'to confuse'), and partly by the presence, at or near Babylon, of the ruins of some great tower, which looked as though it had originally been designed as a means to scale heaven. Two such towers, or *ziqqurats*, were the temple of Merodach (or Marduk) in Babylon (supposed to be beneath the mound of *Babil*), and the temple of Nebo in Borsippa (the ruins of which form the mound of *Birs Nimrûd*); and knowledge of one or other of these may have helped to shape the narrative. The character of the narrative makes it impossible to consider it as real history: it bears on its surface manifest evidence that it is a creation of fancy. The question whether the various languages of mankind have really been derived from one common tongue cannot be separated from the question (into which it is unnecessary to enter here) whether the various *races* of men have sprung from a single stock, *i.e.* 'whether man appeared originally on the globe at one centre or at many centres.' It may be said, however, that philological research has proved that the numerous existing languages are members of a comparatively small number of *families of speech* (such as the Indo-European, the Semitic, etc.); but that between these families of speech, there is so great a difference of structure, that their descent from one original tongue seems highly improbable. At the same time, all languages must have arisen from certain faculties and instincts common to human nature; and the presence, in languages belonging to distinct families, of onomatopoetic, or imitative, words serves to illustrate the essential similarity of human tendencies in the sphere of speech all the world over. G. W. W.

TONGUES, GIFT OF.—1. A phenomenon (*glossolalia*, 'speaking with tongues') that sometimes accompanied the outpouring of the Holy Spirit in the NT. (See SPIRITUAL GIFTS.) Possession of the gift enabled the believer to give voice to ecstatic utterances in moments of high religious excitement. The two primary passages, Ac 2 and 1 Co 12–14, differ in one important respect. In Acts, the speech is in a foreign tongue and is understood by hearers from the appropriate country. In 1 Corinthians it is unintelligible. This difficulty is not insoluble and the passages represent not two distinct phenomena, but one.

Acts 2^{1-13}.—After being filled with the Holy Spirit at Pentecost, the disciples 'began to speak in other tongues, as the Spirit gave them utterance.' The news spread quickly and a crowd was soon outside the house. Jerusalem, at the time, was full of Jews and proselytes who had come from abroad for the feast. Some were bewildered, 'because each one heard them speaking in his own language,' telling 'the mighty works of God.' Others were not impressed. Peter then seized the opportunity to preach to the crowd.

1 *Co* 12–14.—Among the gifts of the Spirit known to the Corinthians (12^{8-10}), the gift of tongues seems to have been sought after most eagerly. Possessors of the gift would arise during worship and pour out a flood of excited but unintelligible speech. It was thought that they had been caught up into heaven by the Spirit to converse in the special tongues angels use (13^{1}. Each order of angels had its peculiar tongue. See *Testament of Job*, ch. xlvii). When the ferment was over, someone with the kindred gift of interpretation ($12^{10, 30}$ 14^{28}) explained the message, if he could.

Paul's advice is shrewd and practical. He claims the gift himself (14^{18}) and agrees that it should be sought with other spiritual gifts ($14^{5, 39}$), but he discourages it because speech in a tongue, though it is addressed to God (14^{2}), is unintelligible to speaker and hearers, and is unedifying to the Church (14^{4}). The 'outsider' does not even know whether to say 'Amen' (14^{16}). The gift is thus inferior to prophecy ($14^{1, 4}$). It is mentioned last in 12^{8-10} and 12^{28}. The danger is obvious. 'Tongues' were an ostentatious gift, giving unlimited opportunity for self-display (14^{4}) and the Corinthians, coming from various pagan traditions in which religious ecstasy was common, were peculiarly open to temptation. There was competition to possess the gift and rivalry in giving vent to it. The effect on fellowship and worship was ruinous. Paul insists that the unnoticed gift is often the most worthy (12^{22-25}), and he restores a sense of proportion with the 'hymn of love' in ch. 13. In ch. 14 he gives rules to keep the 'tongues' within bounds. No one should put this gift first ($14^{1-4, 19}$). Prophecy is to be preferred because it is self-explanatory (14^{24f}). In each service, not more than two or three should speak in a 'tongue.' They should do so in turn and with a pause for interpretation ($14^{13, 27f}$). (One can imagine the pandemonium if two or three spoke at once.) Tongues may be a sign for unbelievers (14^{22}), but the wild scenes at Corinth would excite ridicule, not faith (14^{23}). The first consideration must always be the edification of the Church (14^{12}).

2. Other references.—Other passages have little to add. A promise is made to the disciples that they would speak 'in new tongues' in Mk 16^{17}, but this passage is part of the later appendix to St. Mark. Cornelius and his friends spoke with tongues at their baptism (Ac 10^{46f} 11^{15}) and Peter regarded this as a repetition of the apostles' experience at Pentecost. There is a reference to 'tongues' at Ephesus (Ac 19^{6}) and there may be allusions in Ac 8^{17}, Ro $8^{15, 26}$, Gal 4^{6}, and 1 Th 5^{19}. Irenaeus († 202) and Tertullian refer to the gift but Chrysostom (A.D. 347–407) believed that, in his day, the practice had ceased.

3. Later evidence.—'Tongues' have occurred sporadically throughout the history of the Church, especially at times of crisis. In 1685, Louis XIV. began a persecution of French Protestants, some of the worst excesses taking place among the peasants of the Çévennes. Cruelty inspired retaliation, and soon there was widespread insurrection, waged and put down with equal severity. During twenty years of danger and suffering, many devout Huguenots, including women and children, had ecstasies in which they swooned, struggled, groaned and, most interesting, spoke also in pure French, free from their normal dialect. Early in the 19th cent. there were similar happenings in a church in London under the preaching of Edward Irving. Irving's great eloquence in setting forth his belief in the imminent return of Our Lord undoubtedly stimulated those in his congregation who spoke with 'tongues.' Their utterances were short, unintelligible, and usually followed by prophecy. Irving died in 1834, but some of his congregation formed a new Christian community, in which speaking with tongues was practised regularly. Crude and corrupt forms of the gift can still be found among certain minor Protestant sects.

4. Meaning of the gift.—Relying chiefly on Ac 2, most of the Fathers understand 'tongues' as a miraculous endowment to facilitate preaching. Sts. Cyril and Gregory of Nazianzus regarded it as the fulfilment of a prophecy in Ps 19^{3}. Others (Gregory of Nyssa, Chrysostom, Augustine) found in Pentecost the NT counterpart to and correction of the disaster of Babel, a view that is still maintained. Some commentators, ancient and modern, have suggested that whatever speech was used at Pentecost, the listeners *heard* in their own dialects. This explanation is far-fetched and unnecessary.

Most of the difficulties arise from the assumption that Ac 2 is normative and the Corinthian phenomenon a deviation. All other examples, however, including those in the NT, imply unintelligible speech. There is, therefore, a *prima facie* case for regarding the Corinthian type as normative and the account in Acts as misleading. This is a more satisfactory hypothesis.

Paul's description of *glossolalia* concurs with a type of religious ecstasy familiar to psychologists. It is well known that extreme excitement tends to inhibit the higher faculties and stimulate the lower ones. Vocal expression is an early development of the human mind, and the reasoning process a late one. Consequently men talk more and think less when they are excited. Similarly a series of meaningless sounds is an earlier development than intelligible conversation. A state of great animation may, therefore, subjugate thought and logical expression altogether and provoke meaningless, animal chatter, normally held in check. Foreign tongues will be used only if they are already hidden in the memory. Excitement may quicken recollection, which probably explains the 'tongues' of the Camisards, who knew the French of the Huguenot Bible. This type of ecstasy requires certain conditions. The first is extreme excitement, due to fear, expectation of the end, or the atmosphere of a revival service. The second is a not too high average mentality, for the disciplined mind is not easily inhibited. Though Edward Irving coveted the gift himself, it was denied him and given to uneducated members of his congregation. The third is some initial prompting. After the first occurrence, the sense of expectancy will promote further manifestations. Fourthly, a group of kindred spirits is necessary, some of whom, at least, are amenable to this kind of stimulus. The condition is highly contagious. It nearly always occurs in public. *Glossolalia* at Corinth is thus reasonably explained as a state of religious ecstasy in which the believer lost self-control and spoke incoherently at the prompting of subconscious impulses.

What relevance has this to Ac 2? First it must be noted that the list of nationalities is misleading. Sixteen names are mentioned but two languages, Greek and Aramaic, would be sufficient. The majority would speak Greek. Various dialects would be no barrier to understanding odd phrases. Secondly, there is no suggestion that more than odd phrases were uttered in 'tongues.' V.[13] is the end of a section. The comments of v.[7f] do not refer to the sermon that begins in v.[14]. The sermon itself makes no claim that the previous utterances were intelligible. Indeed, the fact that the sermon was necessary argues that the 'tongues' had done little more than excite curiosity. Thirdly, ordinary preaching in a foreign tongue would have evoked a different response. Even those present were not sure what was happening. Some were impressed, but others said, 'They are filled with new wine.' Fourthly, the gift of speech in a strange tongue, if such it was, has never been given a second time. Later manifestations of 'tongues' have all followed the Corinthian pattern. It seems reasonable then to suppose that Ac 2 describes a dramatic instance of *glossolalia* on the Corinthian pattern. The gift of the Holy Spirit induced emotional exaltation as well as devotional ardour. The apostles—one does not know how many, but it may have been more than twelve (2[1])—in rapt sincerity and faith spoke in 'tongues.' Probably their ejaculations included Greek words. The hearers were amazed and some, catching their spirit and recognizing the tones and perhaps the words of adoration, grasped that the burden of their speech was 'the mighty works of God.' Luke's account is, therefore, but a slight exaggeration. What was in fact a 'normal' example of *glossolalia* was, due to the accident of foreigners being present, misconstrued as a peculiar gift of speech in a foreign tongue.

5. Value of the gift.—Without detracting from the vivid experiences of apostolic times, it remains true that the religious application of subliminal phenomena is fraught with danger. Artificially stimulated utterances are not to be compared with the experience of Pentecost. 'For a modern man to indulge in this form of expression means that he must put himself in a state where the controlling apparatus of his mind is not functioning, and where the primitive reactions, which usually sleep in the unconscious, find their way to the surface and represent the individual' (G. B. Cutten). For this reason, and because of the danger of ostentation and self-display, the gift has never been cultivated in the larger Christian communions. It has little to offer either to worship or preaching. Paul's judgment has proved sound. 'Nevertheless, in church I would rather speak five words with my mind, in order to instruct others, than ten thousand words in a tongue!' (1 Co 14[19]). W. D. S.

TONSURE.—In Lv 21[5] RSV renders 'They shall not make tonsures upon their heads,' where AV and RV have the literal rendering 'baldness.' The reference is probably to the practice prohibited in Lv 19[27], *i.e.* the cutting off of the hair from the temples. Herodotus (*Hist.* iii. 8) says that Arab tribes cut the hair away from the temples as a religious rite.

TOOLS.—See Arts and Crafts.

TOPARCHY.—A compound word from Greek *topos* (place) and *archē* (rule), found only in 1 Mac 11[28] (cf 1 Mac 10[30, 38] 11[34] RSV 'districts') among the sacred books, but very many times in the papyri of Egypt (with reference to that country). It means a very small administrative division of territory. Three toparchies were detached from Samaria and added to Judaea in Maccabaean times. A. So.

TOPAZ.—See Jewels and Precious Stones.

TOPHEL.—A place mentioned only in Dt 1[1]. It is usually identified with *eṭ-Ṭafîleh*, SE. of the Dead Sea.

TOPHET, Jer 7[31f] 19[6, 11ff] (AV)=**Topheth** (q.v.).

TOPHETH.—A term of uncertain etymology, designating some locality in one of the valleys near Jerusalem, very possibly in the **Valley of Hinnom** (2 K 23[10]), or near the point of juncture of the three valleys of Jerusalem. It was there that the Jews under Ahaz and Manasseh performed the rites of human sacrifice (Jer 7[31–32]), offering children to Baal, Molech, and other heathen gods. It was defiled by Josiah as a part of his religious reformation, and so came to be an abominable place where the refuse was destroyed, and thus a synonym of **Gehenna** (q.v.). S. M.

TORAH.—See Law (in OT), **2**, **3**.

TORCH.—See Lamps, **1**; Lantern.

TORMAH.—In the margin of Jg 9[31] Tormah is given as an alternative rendering of the Hebrew word rendered 'craftily' in RV and 'privily' in AV. It is probable that the word is a corruption of **Arumah** (v.[41]), and RSV so renders.

TORTOISE.—Hebrew *ṣābh*, Lv 11[29] (AV; RV, RSV 'great lizard.') Several kinds of land and water tortoises are common in the Holy Land, but here the reference is probably to some kind of lizard. See Lizard.

TOU.—King of Hamath on the Orontes, who sent an embassy to congratulate David on his defeat of Hadadezer, 1 Ch 18[9f]. In the parallel passage (2 S 8[9f]) the name appears as **Toi** (so Heb., AV, RV; RSV **Tou**, with LXX[B]).

TOUBIANI.—See Tob.

TOW.—**1.** Hebrew *neʿōreth*, Jg 16[9], Is 1[31]. In the former passage its weakness as soon as it is touched by fire is indicated, and in the latter its ready consumption by fire. **2.** Hebrew *pishtāh* is rendered by 'tow' in AV in Is 43[17] (RV '**flax**'; RVm, RSV '**wick**'), but in Is 42[3] by 'flax' (so RV; RVm, RSV 'wick'). In Ex 9[31] the same word is used for growing flax. See Flax.

TOWER.—See Citadel. For 'Tower of Babel' see Tongues [Confusion of].

TOWN.—See City, Village.

TOWN CLERK.—In Graeco-Asiatic cities under the Roman Empire the *grammateus* (translated 'town clerk') was responsible for the form of decrees presented to the popular assembly. They were first approved by the senate and then sent to the assembly, which formally passed them. At Ephesus (Ac 19[35]) the clerk feared that he would have to account to the Roman governor for the irregularly constituted assembly. A. So.

TRACHONITIS.—Mentioned in Lk 3[1] as the name of the tetrarchy of Philip. It is to be identified with the lava region SE. of Damascus, known to the Greeks as *Trachon*, and to modern Arabs as the *Lejā*. An inscription discovered by Burckhardt in 1810 at Mismiyeh dispels all doubt as to the identity of this region with Trachon. It has ever been regarded as a refuge from invaders. Josephus frequently speaks of the inhabitants of these parts as predatory (*Ant.* xvi. ix. 1 [271 ff]). Augustus gave it to Herod in 23 B.C., along with Batanaea and Auranitis. To Herod the region owed a great deal (*Ant.* xvi. ix. 1 [271 ff]). In 4 B.C. it became the possession of his son Philip, whose rule is described as just and gentle (*Ib.* xviii. iv. 6 [106 f]). Trajan in A.D. 106 transformed Trachonitis into a new province, which he called 'Arabia,' making Bostra (=*Bozra*) its capital.
G. L. R.—**E. G. K.**

TRADE AND COMMERCE.—The participation of Palestine in the international trade of the Near East is attested by indirect, as well as by direct, evidence. The diffusion of oriental arts and techniques, and the existence of arms, jewels and painted pottery in, for example, both the tells of the Negeb and stratum II of Râs Shamra, show that as early as the 2nd millennium, there was considerable unification of artistic and industrial techniques. This means that there was commensurate commercial activity, and Palestine, situated between Asia Minor, NW. Mesopotamia and Egypt, could not remain outside the main currents. The Israelites seem to have become merchants only relatively late, and commercial dealings were for a long time in the hands of foreigners. Thus 'Canaanite' came to be synonymous with 'trader.' There is little *direct* evidence of any serious commerce with other peoples before 1050 B.C.; only the occasional Philistine or Syrian vase appears. Later, imports from Phoenicia and Cyprus become more common. The development of commercial relationships seems to have been due primarily to royal initiative, especially to Solomon, who was able both to encourage trade on a large scale and to levy contributions on the traffic of the surrounding nations. Solomon's meeting with the queen of Sheba was, no doubt, what would now be described as 'trade talks.' In the period of the divided kingdoms, trade was carried on within the limits of the local agricultural market. Ahab exercised an exceptional measure of control over the Syrian hinterland (1 K 20[34]). The 8th cent. was a period of economic expansion in N. and S. But independent international trade is a phenomenon of the Exile. In post-exilic Palestine, commerce was generally in the hands of foreigners—Phoenicians, Arabs or Idumaeans. In the early Christian era, the caravans were monopolized by Palmyrenes and Nabataeans. But the Jews of the Diaspora, forced to abandon their traditional, agricultural mode of life, turned more and more to independent commercial activity.

1. The **products of Canaan** were, in the main, agricultural, horticultural and pastoral, and some of these could be exported, Natural wealth consisted in grain, wine and olive oil (Dt 7[13], Neh 5[11]). Oil was sent to Egypt (Hos 12[1]) and Phoenicia (Ezk 27[17]); wine to Phoenicia (2 Ch 2[10]), as well as wheat, barley, oak timber (Ezk 27[6]) from Bashan, honey (or *dibs*) and balsam (Ezk 27[17]), and an unknown substance called *pannag*. Oil and cereals were among the deliveries to Hiram (1 K 5[11]). Other possible objects for exportation were sand for glass manufacture, bitumen, the purple-fish, wool and leather; and certain fruits and spices (Gn 43[11]).

2. Of national **industries** we hear little in the OT, but this little is now brilliantly illuminated by archaeology. In Saul's days, according to 1 S 13[19], there were no Israelite smiths—a fact there explained as due to the tyrannical precautions of the Philistines; but perhaps we should infer that the Israelites had as yet learned no crafts. Even in Solomon's time, when great progress had been made in other directions, artificers had to be imported for the building of the royal edifices. The place of industry had to be supplied by raiding, and Saul himself is praised for having stripped the finery of his enemies' women to put it on his own (2 S 1[24]). The heroic David fights with rustic weapons and without armour. The possibility of the peaceful progress which is the preliminary condition of trade would seem to have been provided by the first two kings.

Solomon can now be seen to have exploited this legacy to the full. He must be reckoned as a considerable exporter of copper in the ancient world. His port, Ezion-geber (1 K 9[26]) has been discovered to be the centre of a flourishing copper industry. Here is the largest smelting refinery yet found in the Near East. Nearby were the ships to convey the products to wherever they could be sold. Remains of copper furnaces, of the period of the Judges, have also been found at Beth-shemesh, Tell Qasîle and Tell Jemmeh. These, together with the discovery of smaller iron-smelting installations S. of Gaza, illustrate the otherwise puzzling description of the Holy Land as 'a land whose stones are iron and out of whose hills thou mayest dig brass' (Dt 8[9]).

The whole city of Debir seems to have been devoted to the weaving and dyeing industry, and contained up to thirty dye plants. There must have been a loom in nearly every home. There are not a few references to potteries, and there is evidence that Israel was capable of first-class craftsmanship, particularly after the 10th cent. It has been rightly said that 'the old view that the Israelite had no artistic skill must certainly be revised in the field of ceramics.' So far archaeologists have found no Astarte plaques or figurines in any early Israelite levels in central Palestine. This contrasts so strikingly with their frequent appearance in corresponding levels from the 9th cent. onwards, that it is necessary to find the explanation in the anti-idol character of Yahwism.

The housewife of Pr 31 not only makes her own clothes, but sells some to the 'Canaanite' or pedlar. In 1 Ch 4[21] there is mention of a Jewish family that owned a byssus-factory.

3. We have unfortunately no account of **the financial system** which must have been introduced with the foundation of the kingdom, though the prophecy of Samuel (1 S 8[11-17]) suggests that the king claimed a tithe of all produce, but in theory had a right to both the persons and possessions of his subjects. Before the end of David's reign we hear of permanent officials appointed by the king; and the need for steady sources of revenue, whence the stipends of such officials could be supplied, is sufficient to cause the erection of an elaborate financial system, with surveys and assessments, tax-gatherers and clerks. The 'numbering of the people,' which lived on in popular tradition as an iniquity earning condign punishment, doubtless belonged to the beginnings of orderly government. For Solomon's time we have something like the fragment of a budget (1 K 10[14f]), according to which it would appear that the king had three sources of revenue—one not further specified, but probably a land-tax; another, tribute from subject states, governed by satraps; and a third connected with commerce, and probably equivalent to excise and customs. The text implies that these various forms of revenue were paid in gold, which was then stored by the king in the form of shields and vessels. The figure 666 talents of gold is probably an exaggeration but v.[15a] is the earliest record we have of the taxation of international merchandise. Some potsherds discovered at Samaria prove to be 'administrative dockets recording shipments of wine and oil to Samaria from the towns and districts of western Manasseh, and in a way yet to be clarified, illustrate royal fiscal organization.'

The **gold** must all have been imported, as there are no mines in Palestine; and indeed we are told that it came, with other produce as well as silver, from the mysterious Ophir and Tarshish; and that the enterprise was a joint venture of Solomon and the king of Tyre, the latter probably supplying the vessels, the former the produce which was exchanged for these goods, unless indeed the gold was procured by raiding. If it was obtained in exchange for commodities, we must suppose either that the latter were identical with those of which we afterwards read in Ezekiel, or that the commodities to be exchanged were all supplied by the Phoenicians, the service by which the Israelites earned their share being that of giving the former access to the harbour of Ezion-geber. In favour of the latter supposition, it has been pointed out that the commodities known to have been exported from Palestine at one time or another were ill-suited for conveyance on lengthy voyages, and unlikely to be required in the countries where the gold was procured. There is in the OT no allusion to the practice of coining metal, and where sums of money are mentioned they are given in **silver**; the effect, however, of the quantities of gold brought into Palestine in Solomon's time was not, according to the historian, to appreciate silver, as might have been expected, but to depreciate it, and render it unfashionable. Yet the notice of prices in the time of Solomon (1 K 10[29]) suggests that silver was by no means valueless, whatever weight we assign to the shekel of the time. While it is clear that all silver in use must have come in by importation, the notices in the OT of transactions in which it would probably be employed are too scanty to permit of even a guess as to the amount in use; and though it is likely that (as in Eastern countries to this day) foreign coins were largely in circulation, there is little authority for this supposition.

4. If little is known of Israelite exports, many objects are mentioned in the OT which were certainly **imported** from foreign countries. These were largely objects of luxury, especially in the way of clothes or stuffs; the material called *'ēṭûn* (Pr 7[16], RSV 'linen') was imported from Egypt; the ivory to which reference is frequently made during the period of the kingdom (of which so much has been found in Samaria from Ahab's ivory house, 1 K 22[39]), from Ethiopia through Arabia or Egypt; spices and perfumed oils and incense from S. Arabia; gems from one or other of these countries. Cosmetic bowls, used to prepare colours for the face, have been found in considerable numbers in Israelite towns; they are of close-grained limestone and thought to have been imported from Syria. Iron was, before 1200, B.C. a monopoly of the Hittites of Asia Minor. The Philistines first used it in Palestine in the 12th and 11th cents. Only gradually did the Israelites break the Philistine monopoly (1 S 13[19-22]). The first iron implement which can be dated is a ploughpoint from Saul's fortress at Gibeah *c* 1010. It is improbable that enough iron was mined in Palestine itself, and ore had to be imported. Pottery came from the Aegean and Greece. The Palmyrenes brought silk in the Roman period, but by then the variety of imports must have been large. For later (Talmudic) times a list of 118 articles has been drawn up which came from foreign countries into the Palestinian market; this list contains many foods and food-stuffs, materials for wearing apparel and domestic utensils. We should rather gather that in pre-exilic times, food was not ordinarily imported, except in times of famine. Imports of raw materials must have been considerable as soon as the people began to settle in towns. Among the more important imports in Biblical times were horses. The notice of 1 K 10[26], that Solomon had '1400 chariots and 12,000 horsemen, whom he stationed in the chariot cities,' has been marvellously illustrated by the discovery of Solomon's stables at Megiddo (provision for 450 horses), and sheds of similar type at Taanach, Eglon, and perhaps Gezer. 1 K 10[28f] says that these horses were exported from Egypt and Cilicia (land of fine horses and horse-breeding), and that Solomon acted as a middleman, reselling the horses to the Aramaean kings to the north.

Of the **slave-trade** there are very few notices in the OT, and it may be that the reduction of the aboriginal population by the Israelites to serfs, and the almost continuous warfare leading to the constant capture of prisoners, rendered the importation of slaves ordinarily unnecessary. According to Joel (3[4-7]), the Phoenicians acted as dealers, purchasing prisoners of war (in this case Jews), and exporting them to foreign countries. The same may have been the fate of those persons who, for non-payment of debt, were assigned to their creditors (2 K 4[1]). Encampments in and around Ezion-geber are thought to be the location of Solomon's slaves. They were probably prisoners of war, taken in Solomon's successful wars. Solomon could hardly have carried out his enormous building projects without such slave-labour.

5. Persons engaged in commerce.—The words used in the OT for merchants are such as signify primarily 'traveller' (1 K 10[15], RSV 'traders,' 'merchants,' 'traffic'), and convey the idea of going around or to and fro. The use of the word 'Canaanite' for pedlar has been noticed. References to shop-keeping are rare before the exile. In the large cities we may suppose that men of the same trade would establish themselves in the same street. Thus in Jer 37[21] we are informed that the prophet was given daily 'a loaf of bread out of the bakers' street.' In Nehemiah's time different classes of dealers had their locations in Jerusalem—goldsmiths and grocers (3[32]), fishmongers (13[16]); but most articles of general consumption seem to have been brought in day by day by foreigners and others (13[20]), and sold in the streets. The distinction between wholesale and retail dealers perhaps first occurs in the Apocrypha (Sir 26[29] 37[11]). It is worth observing that in the prophetic denunciations of luxury we miss allusions to the shops or stores in which such objects might be supposed to be offered for sale (Is 3[18-24]). Moreover, the verse of Ezekiel (7[12]) 'let not the buyer rejoice nor the seller mourn' suggests that the latter operation was not ordinarily thought of as it is in communities a large portion of which lives by trade, but rather as a humiliation required at times by stern necessity; and there are few allusions to trade in the codes embodied in the Pentateuch, though such are not absolutely wanting. Perhaps, then, we are justified in concluding that the practice of trade was in pre-exilic times largely in the hands of itinerant foreigners; and it is only in NT times that merchandise is regarded as an occupation as normal as agriculture (Mt 22[5]). To the cumbrous process of bargaining there is an allusion in Pr 20[14].

Allusions to the **corn-trade** are rather more common than to any other business, and to certain iniquities connected with it—probably, in the main, forms of the practice by which corn was withdrawn from the market in the hope of selling it at famine prices: this at least seems to be the reference in Pr 11[26]. In Am 8[4-8] the reference is more distinct, and implies both the offence mentioned above and the use of deceitful measures, a wrong also condemned by Micah in a similar context (6[10]). The interpretation of these passages must remain obscure until more light is thrown on land-tenure in Israel, and the process by which the king's share in the produce was collected.

The **foreign commerce** conducted in king Solomon's time is represented in his biography as a venture of his own, whence the goods brought home were his own possessions; and the same holds good of commerce in the time of Jehoshaphat (1 K 22[48f]). There is no evidence that Israelitish commerce was conducted on any other principle before the Exile, after which isolated individuals doubtless endeavoured to earn their livelihood by trade ventures. The foreign commerce of which we occasionally hear in the OT was also conducted by communities (*e.g.* Gn 37[25, 28]), to be compared with the tribes whom we find at the commencement of Islam engaged in joint enterprises of a similar kind. In 1 K 20[34] there appears to be a reference to a practice by which sovereigns obtained the right to the possession of bazaars in each other's capitals—the nearest approach to a commercial treaty that we find in this literature. But at such times as the condition of the Israelitish cities allowed of the purchase of luxuries—*i.e.* after successful campaigns or long spells of peace, permitting of accumulations of produce—it is probable that the arrival and residence of foreign merchants were facilitated by the practice of 'protection,' a citizen rendering himself responsible for the foreign visitors, and making their interests his own—doubtless in most cases for a consideration. The spirit of the Mosaic legislation (like that of Plato's and Aristotle's theories) is against such intermixing with foreigners; and except for forces such as only powerful chieftains could collect, journeys whether on sea or land were dangerous. Of an expedient for commerce like the Arabian months of sacred truce the OT contains no hint.

6. The chief passage in the OT dealing with commerce is **Ezekiel's prophecy against Tyre** (ch. 27). Many commentators think that an editor, wishing to illustrate the glory of Tyre, has introduced into Ezekiel's poem, a prose passage (vv.[9b-25a]), which is more likely to have described originally the commercial relations of Egypt than those of Tyre. But however that may be, the passage remains an invaluable and unique record of Mediterranean commerce in the 6th cent. B.C. In a prophecy of the Book of Isaiah (ch. 23), Tyre is described as the great mart of the time, serving, it would seem, as the chief exchange and centre of distribution for goods of all kinds. Ezk 26[2] is sometimes interpreted as implying that Jerusalem was a competitor with Tyre for the trade of the world, but perhaps it means only that the taking of any great city led to the Tyrian merchants obtaining the spoil at low prices.

7. Trade-routes.—Palestine has no internal waterways,

and goods had to be brought to it either by sea or across desert. Caravans from Cappadocia, Asia Minor, the Caucasus, and the Caspian all came south to join the classic route of the patriarchs from the east, through Aleppo, Hamath, and Damascus. At Kadesh the route divided, the one going west to Byblos, Tyre, and Acco on the coast, passing inland through the plain of Esdraelon, and then through the depression of Samaria and Judaea to Gaza and the south. Another route at Kadesh connected with Palmyra; a third went due south to Damascus, whence it divided again, connecting both with Bethshean and the coast road, and with Rabbath Ammon and Petra which, in the Christian era, became the Nabataean capital and centre of the caravan trade. When Jerusalem became the capital of the country, goods were brought thither probably by the same routes as were in use until the construction of the railways. The unnamed place in 1 K 5[9], used as a port of Jerusalem in the time of Solomon, is in 2 Ch 2[16] identified with Joppa, probably by a good tradition. Elath (Ezion-geber) served as the port of Jerusalem on the NE. arm of the Red Sea, and after Solomon's time, was repeatedly taken out of the possession of the Jewish kings, and recaptured (2 K 14[22]). But the Hebrews do not seem to have understood or to have liked the sea. From the 2nd millennium, the ports were mainly in the hands of the Phoenicians. Indeed the Hebrews did not exercise effective control over the coast until Hellenistic times. Jaffa was occupied only under Simon (1 Mac 14[5]), the Hellenized cities of the coast only under Alexander Jannaeus (Jos. *Ant.* XIII. xv. 4 [395]). In the Tosefta, the coast was still not part of the 'clean' territory of the Holy Land.

Josephus (*Ant.* VIII. vii. 4 [187]) asserts that Solomon had the roads leading to Jerusalem paved with black stone, but his authority for this statement is unknown. On the whole, before the Romans, roads were simply the tracks made by constant use. The Romans revolutionized the whole system not only by building roads, but also by setting up mile-stones and by establishing military controls. It is possible that the familiar passage Is 40[3f] alludes to the process of road-making by mounding and excavating. On the other hand the word *m^esillāh* ('embanked road'), does not necessarily imply road-making, for the road from Bethel to Shechem, thus described in Jg 21[19], was simply part of the configuration of the natural ridge.

8. Transport.—Before the 11th cent. donkeys and mules were the main means of transport, and the movement of traders was restricted accordingly. The domestication of the camel in the 11th cent. was something of a revolution which for the first time enabled the nomad to cover great distances swiftly. It was the coming of these 'ships of the desert' that opened up the traffic in incense from S. Arabia along the 'incense road,' and brought S. Arabia into the Mediterranean world. The first appearance of camels in Palestine seems to have been when a Midianite invasion was repulsed by Gideon (Jg 6[5]). They are mentioned in connexion with goods brought from Arabia (1 K 10[2], Is 60[6] etc.), and even with such as were carried in Syria and Palestine (2 K 8[9], 1 Ch 12[40]). **Caravans** are mentioned in Jg 5[6], Job 6[18], Is 21[13]. Asses and mules remained the main means of day to day transport. Horses provided another means of swift travel, though their use was limited. Horse-breeding had been learned by the Hittites from the Kikkuli of the land of the Mitanni. They had used them mainly with light chariots of war, and probably this was their main use in Israel. It is probable that the ancients did not know the art of harnessing horses effectively, though Dussaud thinks the Assyrians had some form of breast-strap in the 8th cent. When wagons were used to carry commodities to market, they were drawn by yoked oxen.

9. Commercial instruments.—The money-lender appears at the very commencement of the history of the Israelitish kingdom, where we are told that David's followers were to some extent insolvent debtors; and the Jewish law allowed the taking of pledges, but not (it would seem) the taking of interest, except from foreigners. The result of similar legislation in Moslem countries is to make the rate of interest enormously high, and in Palestine it may have had the same effect. Deeds of loan appear not to be mentioned in the OT, though there is frequent reference to the danger of giving security. To the institution of banking there is a familiar reference in the NT (Mt 25[27]); the persons there referred to—like the bankers of modern times—undertook the charge of deposits for the use of which they paid some interest; the money-changers (Mt 21[12] etc.) were, as now, in a smaller way of business. Those who hoarded money more often put it 'under the stone' (Sir 29[10]) than entrusted it to bankers; and this is still probably the favourite practice all over the nearer East. Another common practice was to deposit money with trustworthy persons, to which there is a reference in Tobit (4[20] etc.). In most ancient cities the temples served as places of security, where treasure could be stored, and this is likely to have been the case in Israelite cities also. See, further, USURY.

10. Development of the Israelites into a commercial people.—The prophets appear to have expected that the exiles would carry on in their new home the same agricultural pursuits as had occupied them in Palestine (Jer 29[5]); and it would appear that until the taking of Jerusalem by Titus, and perhaps even later, agriculture remained the normal occupation of the Israelites. It was in exile, where many Jews were compelled to give up their traditional skills, that we find a number of them becoming independent traders and bankers. The first evidence of this is in the 5th cent. The Elephantine Papyri show that Jews in Egypt were active in trade and banking, and in the same period the firm of Murashu Sons at Nippur dealt with people bearing Jewish names. After the conquest of Alexander, *ghettos* began to be formed in the great Hellenistic cities, and the Roman conquests soon led to colonies of Jews settling yet farther west. D. S. M.—**D. R. J.**

TRADES.—See ARTS AND CRAFTS.

TRADITION.—See LAW (IN NT), **1.**

TRADITION, ORAL.—See ORAL TRADITION.

TRAGACANTH, Gn 43[11] (RVm).—See SPICE, SPICES.

TRAJAN.—Marcus Ulpius Traianus, adopted by the childless Emperor Nerva, succeeded him as emperor A.D. 98–117—second of the 'good emperors' who ruled the Roman world conscientiously from Nerva to Marcus Aurelius, A.D. 96–180. A distinguished soldier, Trajan was the last emperor to embark on considerable plans of expansion (probably unwisely), conquering territory N. of the Danube (Dacia, modern Transylvania) and E. of the Euphrates (Armenia and Mesopotamia, mostly abandoned at once by his successor, Hadrian). Preparations for the eastern campaign may account for the watch on possible subversive activities reflected in the correspondence of Pliny the Younger, governor of Bithynia in A.D. 111–112, including his report on trials of Christians and Trajan's reply approving their punishment when formally charged (*Epistles* x. 96–97). To the same period belong martyrdoms in the eastern provinces, such as those of Simeon, bishop of Jerusalem, and Ignatius of Antioch, made famous by the letters, important for church history and theology, written on his way to death at Rome. E. R. H.

TRANCE.—A condition in which the mental powers are partly or wholly unresponsive to external impressions while dominated by subjective excitement, or left free to contemplate mysteries incapable of apprehension by the usual rational processes. The word occurs in AV in the OT in Nu 24[4, 16] (but cf RV, RSV), and in all EV in the NT in Ac 10[10] 11[5] 22[17]. See, further, DREAMS, VISION. H. L. W.

TRANSFIGURATION.—The Transfiguration is a mysterious occurrence in the life of our Lord which conveyed to the three apostles who witnessed it the true authority of Him who six days before ('about eight days,' Lk 9[28]) had made the first announcement of His coming Passion. Silence regarding it is enjoined by Jesus, and practised by the disciples until the Resurrection, with which it is closely connected in significance. Indeed, many scholars have seen in the episode a pre-dated Resurrection appearance, associated as it is particularly with Peter. The event is referred to by Jesus Himself as a vision (*horama*, Mt 17[9]). It is vouched for by the three Synoptists (Mk 9[2-13], Mt 17[1-13], Lk 9[28-36]). Elsewhere in the NT it is referred to only in 2 P 1[16-18], whose author significantly sees in it a pledge of the Parousia. H. Riesenfeld (*Jésus Transfiguré*, 1947) persuasively connected the representation and many of its details with the Messianic enthronement of Jesus, and found a setting for this in the ideology and symbolism of the Feast of Tabernacles (note the three tabernacles, the six-day period after the Day of Atonement, the Messianic designation, etc.). The mountain in question is probably to be identified with Hermon.

Associated with Jesus are Moses and Elijah, who according to Lk 9[31] spoke of His coming *exodus*. These figures could well suggest not only Christ's imminent exaltation to heaven but also His fulfilment of the Law and the prophets. The cloud is associated with the Divine theophany (cf Ex 24 for this and other details), and the transfigured lineaments and apparel of Jesus with the body of light which the Rabbis and the early believers assigned to the Messiah and indeed to the saints in the New Age. The Divine voice in distinction from that at the Baptism concludes its witness to Christ as 'my beloved Son' with the admonition, 'Listen to him.' The great lesson for the disciples was that the dreadful shame of His cross was really glory, and that all suffering is ultimately radiant with heavenly beauty, being perfected in Him.

Mark, followed by the other Synoptists, offers us in this narrative a symbolic portrayal of the true nature and final victory of Christ as a kind of window in the story of the way to the Cross. Resting as it well may upon some momentary experience by the disciples of the transcendent majesty of the Nazarene, the recollection comes to us bodied forth in such visionary detail as quickened faith and insight would draw upon from the eschatological poetry of Israel. R. H. S.—**A. N. W.**

TRANSGRESSION.—See SIN.

TRAP.—See SNARE.

TRAVAIL.—The French *travail*, meaning 'labour *or* trouble,' was taken into English without alteration of meaning or spelling. This spelling is found in AV, and it is still sometimes used, especially for the labour of child-birth, and in RSV it is confined to this use, save in Is 53[11]. Thus in Nu 20[14] RSV has 'adversity' for AV and RV 'travail,' in Ec 4[4] 'toil' for AV 'travail' (RV 'labour'). In Ec 2[26] 'work' for AV and RV 'travail,' and in 1 Th 2[9] 'toil' for AV and RV 'travail.'

TRAVELLERS, Ezk 39[11] (RSV).—See ABARIM.

TRAYS.—See SNUFFERS.

TREASURE, TREASURY, TREASURER.—1. In OT 'treasure' and 'treasury' stand for various Hebrew terms, but both words usually render *'ôṣār*. This shows that 'treasure' and 'treasury' are not carefully distinguished in EV, or else that *'ôṣār* itself may stand for either. As a matter of fact the truth lies with both alternatives. Strictly, a treasure is a store of wealth, while a treasury is a storehouse, a place where treasure is kept. Sometimes, however, 'treasure' occurs in AV where 'treasury' is meant as Job 38[22] 'Hast thou entered into the treasures (RV 'treasuries'; RSV 'storehouses') of the snow?'; and, on the other hand, 'treasury' is sometimes found where 'treasure' would be the more correct rendering, as Jos 6[19, 24] and RV and RSV of Ezr 2[69]. The indeterminateness of *'ôṣār* is shown by its constant employment for 'treasure' and 'treasury' alike. The 'treasure (RV and RSV 'store') cities' of Ex 1[11] (cf 1 K 9[19], 2 Ch 8[4]) are cities in which provisions were stored up (cf Gn 41[48, 56]).

2. In NT we find a like ambiguousness in the use of 'treasure,' and also of the Greek *thēsauros* for which it stands. The treasures of the Magi (Mt 2[11]) and the treasure in heaven (Mt 19[21]) refer to precious stores; but it is out of his *treasury* rather than his *treasure* that the good man brings forth good things (Mt 12[35]), and the householder things new and old (13[52]). In Ac 8[27] 'treasure' renders *gaza*, a word of Persian origin. In Mt 27[6] 'treasury' represents *korbanas* (the depository of the 'corban' [q.v.]), the sacred treasury into which the chief priests would not put Judas's 30 pieces of silver. For the treasury of the Temple (*gazophylakion*) into which Jewish worshippers cast their offerings (Mk 12[41, 43], Lk 21[1]) see TEMPLE **11** (*b*). When Jesus is said to have spoken 'in the treasury' (Jn 8[20]), the meaning probably is that He was teaching in the colonnade of the Temple where stood the treasure-boxes into which the offerings were cast.

Treasurer occurs in OT in Neh 13[13], Ezr 1[8] 7[21], Is 22[15] (RSV 'steward'), Dn 3[2f], representing a different term in each writer. The word is found in NT only in RV and RSV of Ro 16[23] as substitute for AV 'chamberlain' (Gr. *oikonomos*), but the Ethiopian eunuch is said to have had charge of all the treasure of queen Candace. J. C. L.

TREE.—'Tree' is used as a name for the Cross in Ac 5[30] 10[39] 13[29], 1 P 2[24]; cf Gal 3[13]. For sacred trees see HIGH PLACE, **1**, ISRAEL, II, **1**. (6); and for the various trees of the Bible, see under their respective names.

TREE OF KNOWLEDGE.—In the story of Paradise in Gn 2 it is stated that Yahweh Elohim caused to grow out of the ground in the garden which He had planted in Eden, 'every tree that is pleasant to the sight and good for food, the tree of life also in the midst of the Garden, and the tree of the knowledge of good and evil' (Gn 2[9]). The story goes on to relate that, while it was permissible to eat of all the other trees in the garden, Adam was forbidden to eat of the tree of the knowledge of good and evil under pain of death. In ch. 3 Eve tells the serpent that it is the tree in the midst of the garden which is the forbidden tree. An explanation of the ambiguities in the story has been sought in the theory of two recensions which have been woven together by the editor of the J-E narrative; it was suggested by Budde, on the ground of grammatical anomalies in 2[9], that in the original form of the story there was only one tree, namely, the tree of the knowledge of good and evil. It is clear, however, that for the Yahwist there were two trees, and that the tree of life possessed different properties from those of the tree of knowledge (see TREE OF LIFE). In the mythology of the ancient Near East there are numerous examples of sacred trees guarded by dragons or serpents, and the cult of oracle-giving trees was wide-spread, and is found in Canaan, *e.g.* the terebinth of Moreh (Gn 12[6]). The main problem is the nature of the knowledge acquired by eating of the tree. The serpent tells Eve that they will become gods, knowing good and evil; and Yahweh is represented as saying (3[22]), 'Behold, the man has become like one of us, knowing good and evil.' In the Babylonian myth of Adapa, and similar myths, eating of the food of the gods conferred immortality, not knowledge; but in Babylonian magical texts the knowledge possessed by the god Ea and imparted by him to the priests was magical knowledge, the knowledge of spells and incantations which gave power over evil spirits. This was undoubtedly the kind of knowledge originally envisaged in the story. But to the Yahwist, who had transformed the ancient stories into symbols of the relation between God and man, the forbidden knowledge was of those 'secret things' which belonged only to Yahweh (Dt 29[29]). S. H. He.

TREE OF LIFE.—In the story of the garden of Eden in Gn 2 it is related that Yahweh Elohim planted two special trees among the other trees of the garden; one of these was the tree of life in the midst of the garden, and the other was the tree of the knowledge of good and evil, whose position in the garden is not stated (see TREE OF KNOWLEDGE). According to the form of the story as we have it, Adam was only forbidden to eat of the tree of knowledge, and no mention is made of the tree of life; hence it might be inferred that Adam and Eve were free to eat of that tree. But, in the description of the temptation of Eve by the serpent, Eve says that it is the tree in the midst of the garden of which they have been forbidden to eat. Hence it is possible to infer that for the Yahwist the tree of life was identical with the tree of knowledge; but against this is the statement at the end of the story which represents Yahweh as saying that since Adam has acquired the knowledge which makes him 'as one of us,' that is, by eating of the tree of knowledge of good and evil, he must be prevented from acquiring immortality by eating of the tree of life. In the Sumerian and Babylonian myths which underlie the Hebrew story, it is always immortality that man is represented as seeking, and which he is prevented by the jealousy of the gods from attaining. In the Gilgamesh Epic it is the secret of how to acquire immortality that the hero goes in search of in vain. It is generally agreed that the Yahwist has used two different versions of the myth, and to this is due the confusion between the two trees. But there is no confusion in the Yahwist's mind. From whatever source he has derived it, the inspired writer has used the ancient material to give in symbols the picture of God's design for man, to be His representative as head of His creation, in happy dependence upon the source of his life; drawing from the same source in the ancient myths which reflect so clearly man's ruined state, his despair and misery, the author has depicted in symbols the cause of that ruin, in 'man's first disobedience, and the fruit of that forbidden tree.' But, still in symbols, he has let in the light of hope, and God's purpose of redemption. So it is fitting that in Rev 2^7 the way to the tree of life is opened, and the victor is promised the reward of being permitted to eat of the tree of life, 'which is in the midst of the Paradise of God'; and in the final vision the seer sees the tree of life in the centre of the heavenly city by the banks of the river of the water of life (Rev 22^{1-2}). S. H. He.

TRESPASS-OFFERING.—See SACRIFICE, **15.**

TRIAL.—See TEMPTATION.

TRIBES OF ISRAEL.—The Israelite confederacy (nowadays often termed amphictyony) of tribes came to be regarded, ideally, as numbering twelve and as being descended from twelve sons of Jacob (1 K 18^{31}). In Gn 29^{31}–30^{24} and 35^{18} the following relationship of Jacob's sons is given:

Sons of Leah: Reuben, Simeon, Levi, Judah.
Sons of Bilhah (Rachel's maid): Dan, Naphtali.
Sons of Zilpah (Leah's maid): Gad, Asher.
Sons of Leah (additional): Issachar and Zebulun.
Sons of Rachel: Joseph and Benjamin.

Several facts emerge which must be considered in any reconstruction of the history of the tribes. (i) All the sons except Benjamin were born in Mesopotamia, which probably implies that these tribes were in existence before the occupation of Canaan and migrated from Mesopotamia. (ii) That Benjamin was said to have been born in Canaan separates that tribe at once from the rest and may mean that the tribe was only constituted after the occupation. (iii) The order of birth, and the distinction between the Leah and Rachel tribes on the one hand and between the Leah-Rachel tribes and the 'handmaid' tribes on the other, may betoken a difference of standing and priority within the confederacy. (iv) If the Joseph tribe be regarded as in effect two tribes, Ephraim and Manasseh, as it so regularly is, then the number would be thirteen, unless, or until, Levi is omitted from the reckoning because of its priestly status.

The several tribal lists bring further problems to be unravelled by the historian. (1) The Song of Deborah, Jg 5, enumerates ten tribes, separating Ephraim and Machir (Manasseh) as two tribes and making no mention of Judah, Simeon and Levi. Why these three are omitted is not known for certain. It is thought that Judah, although being placed by the birth stories among Leah's first group of children, was a late-comer in joining the tribes of Israel, indeed it may have been as late as David's time, when he became king in Hebron, that this happened. Simeon and Levi may have been regarded as outcasts, following upon the incident narrated in Gn 34 (cf Gn 49^7).

The position in the birth stories may suggest that Judah had had a long history before its incorporation in the confederacy. Its association with Hebron is explicit in Jg 1^{10} and implicit in Jg 1^{20} through Caleb which was an associate tribe within Judah.

(2) The Blessing of Jacob, Gn 49, lists twelve tribes, does not separate Joseph into two (22–28), deprives Reuben, the firstborn, of his pre-eminence, ascribes authority to Judah and links Simeon and Levi together in disgrace. (3) The Blessing of Moses, Dt 33, omits Simeon but retains the number twelve by separating Joseph into Ephraim and Manasseh (Ephraim being reckoned as the more important with tens of thousands over against Manasseh's thousands), recognizes the insignificance of Reuben, acknowledges the priesthood of Levi and prays for the reunion of Judah with the other tribes (indicating a date of composition after Jeroboam's rebellion). (4) Finally, there are two census lists, Nu 1^{20-43} and 26^{5-50}. Both lists agree in having twelve tribes, in omitting Levi and in listing Ephraim and Manasseh separately (in that order in Nu 1 and with Manasseh first in Nu 26). Levi is counted separately as a sacred priestly tribe. It is clear that tradition varied about the priority of Ephraim; there seems to have been an early ascendancy of Ephraim (Jg 8^1 12^1, reflected in Jacob's blessing of them Gn 48^{14}) and a later ascendancy of Manasseh, the firstborn.

Twelve was apparently a conventional number for tribal grouping as may be seen in the groups of Ishmael, Gn 25^{13-16}, Edom, Gn 36^{10-14}, and the Horites, Gn 36^{20-26}. There were, however, six sons of Leah who may have formed a half-size group. The Joseph and Judah tribes may also have been small groupings of tribes. It should be remembered that twelve was the ideal number and that probably at no time in history did the historical situation correspond with the ideal. It is clear that in Deborah's time the number was ten (which would be as suitable a number for a group as twelve would be). The tribes of Israel formed an ever changing group, subject to increase or loss as occasion dictated. Sometimes fusion took place, as with Judah and Caleb, or absorption, as with Judah and Simeon, and sometimes tribes would divide as did Joseph into Ephraim and Manasseh. Loss of tribes might come about by absorption (Simeon), or gradual lessening of strength and final disappearance as with Reuben, or complete change of status, as possibly with Levi from a secular to a priestly tribe. Opinion is divided about the original status of Levi.

The 'system' of Israelite tribes may well have been formed for the first time under the leadership of Moses, but it is not at all certain that the scheme of family relationships, tracing all the tribes to a common ancestor, was formulated at that time. The change of name from Jacob to Israel cannot be dated; it may have been a secondary process reflecting the consciousness of a reconstitution of the associated tribes, or it may have been the result of the fusion of two groups, one honouring the name Jacob as the eponymous ancestor and carrying a wealth of tradition about him, and the other, ultimately the more powerful, honouring the name Israel but carrying little or no tradition. L. H. B.

TRIBUTE, TOLL, TAXING.—**1. In OT** the subject is obscure. The Hebrew word *mas*, rendered in AV as 'tribute,' properly denotes a body of forced labourers (2 S 20^{24}, 1 K 9^{21} etc.), and then later 'forced service' (RSV 'forced labour' or 'forced levy')—the feudal *corvée*. Solomon had a regular system of levying provisions for the maintenance of the royal establishment (1 K 4[7-19]), and labourers for the execution of his vast building schemes (5[13ff] 9[15]), and also exacted toll from the caravans of merchants that passed through his kingdom (10[15]). After the fall of the Jewish State, tribute (Heb. *'ōnesh*—indemnity, fine) was imposed on the land by its foreign masters (2 K 23[33]). In Ezr 4[13] (cf v.[20] 7[24]) we read of 'tribute, custom, or toll,' but have no information as to the precise meanings of the terms and the distinctions between them. Cf TRADE AND COMMERCE, **3.**

2. In NT 'tribute' represents three Greek words. (1) *phoros* is properly a land tax; (2) *kēnsos* (originally a property register), a capitation or poll tax. Both were direct Imperial taxes payable by the Jews as Roman subjects; the former in kind, the latter in Roman money. In NT, however, the distinction is not carefully observed (cf Mt 22[17], Lk 20[22]). The RSV similarly tends to equate *phoros* and *kēnsos* by using 'tribute' and 'taxes' alternatively for both words. For the 'money for the tax' (AV 'tribute money') of Mt 22[19] see MONEY, **7** (*b*). (3) *didrachmon* (Mt 17[24], AV 'tribute money,' RSV 'the **half-shekel** tax') was the sum paid by every male Israelite to meet the cost of the daily services in the Temple. See MONEY, **7** (*d*). Toll (*telos*, RSV 'toll' [Mt 17[25]] and 'revenue' [Ro 13[7]]; AV 'custom,' *telōnion*, RSV 'tax-office,' AV 'receipt of custom'; RV 'place of toll') must be carefully distinguished from tribute (cf Mt 17[25], Ro 13[7]). It was not a direct tax like (1) and (2), but an impost on the value of exported goods. For details see CUSTOM(S), PUBLICAN. **Taxing** (*apographē*, RSV 'enrollment' [Lk 2[2]] and **'census'** [Ac 5[37], RV 'enrolment']) denotes a registration with a view to taxation for Imperial purposes. See QUIRINIUS. J. C. L.—**A. G. McL.**

TRIGON.—See MUSIC, **4** (1) (*c*).

TRINITY, THE.—The Christian doctrine of God (q.v.) as existing in three Persons and one Substance is not demonstrable by logic or by scriptural proofs, but is (like certain scientific and mathematical principles) a necessary hypothesis, above reason but not contrary to it. The term *Trias* was first used by Theophilus of Antioch (*c* A.D. 180), and although not found in Scripture was thereafter used as a brief designation for the doctrine which had been made necessary by the data of Scripture.

The chief trinitarian text in the NT (going beyond such suggestive summary formulae as 2 Co 13[14]) is the baptismal formula in Mt 28[19]: 'Go therefore and make disciples of all nations, baptizing them in the name of the Father and of the Son and of the Holy Spirit, teaching them to observe all that I have commanded you.' This late post-resurrection saying, not found in any other Gospel or anywhere else in the NT, has been viewed by some scholars as an interpolation into Matthew. It has also been pointed out that the idea of 'making disciples' is continued in 'teaching them,' so that the intervening reference to baptism with its trinitarian formula was perhaps a later insertion into the saying. Finally, Eusebius's form of the text ('in my name' rather than in the name of the Trinity) has had certain advocates. But the passage can readily be understood (like the rest of the Gospel of Matthew) from the Christian Jewish point of view. It sums up the experience of Christian Jews: their inherited conception of God as 'Father,' their new faith in Christ as the 'Son' (or 'Son of Man'), and their experience of the Spirit which has been given as the earnest and guarantee of the coming New Age. The formula is probably, therefore, not an addition to the text of Matthew. Nevertheless, though an integral part of the original text of Matthew, this does not guarantee its source in the historical teaching of Jesus. It is doubtless better to view the formula as derived from early Christian, perhaps Syrian or Palestinian, baptismal usage (cf *Didache* 7[1-4]), and as a brief summary of the Church's teaching about God, Christ, and the Spirit: God, who is the Father; Christ, who is the Son; the Spirit, who is holy, and one with the Father and the Son.

The stage of Christian teaching reflected in the letters of Paul assumes the subordination of the Son (1 Co 8[6] 11[3]), not only before the Incarnation (Ph 2[5-11]) but also at the Consummation and for ever after (1 Co 15[24-28]). Paul never thought out in detail the relations between the Son and the Father. The same is true of the author of John and the Johannine epistles, though the unity of the Father and the Son is repeatedly stressed (*e.g.* Jn 10[30]). In the Epistle to Hebrews the Son is pre-existent (1[1-4]), but no effort is made to work out a theological statement of the eternal relations within the Godhead. It may be said, very briefly, that the Christology of the NT (see CHRISTOLOGY) is neither 'binitarian,' as has been claimed, nor 'adoptianist.' These 2nd-cent. views were stages in the development which led eventually to the final formulation of the doctrine of the Trinity. The point of view of the NT as a whole is practical rather than speculative, and its formulae have to do with the daily teaching and practice of the Church—the instruction of converts, their baptism and pastoral supervision, the interpretation of the OT, weekly or daily worship, personal religion and the life of Christian piety, prayer, and fasting, the extension of the gospel to all mankind, and the constant expectation of fuller revelation at the Last Day and in the Age to Come. Its language reflects various aspects of Divine revelation and redemption, and also the on-going Christian experience which led eventually to the fullest possible expression of their implications, in creeds, liturgy, homilies and hymns, and in Christian preaching and interpretation of sacred Scripture. F. C. G.

TRIPOLIS.—An important town in northern Phoenicia, where Demetrius Soter landed when he made his successful attack against Antiochus v. (2 Mac 14[1]). It was formed by colonies from three cities—Tyre, Sidon, and Arvad—hence the name. The modern *Ṭarâbulus* is two miles inland, its fort occupying the site of the ancient city on the coast.
J. F. McC.—**E. G. K.**

TROAS.—A city of Mysia on the NW. coast of Asia Minor. It was in the Roman province Asia. It was founded by Antigonus, and re-founded in 300 B.C. by Lysimachus, who named it Alexandria Troas. For a time, under the Seleucid kings of Syria, it gained its freedom, and began to mint its own coins (examples exist from 164 to 65 B.C.). Its freedom continued under Pergamene and afterwards, from 133 B.C., under Roman rule. Augustus made it a Roman colony, and it became one of the greatest cities of NW. Asia. The Roman preference was partly explained by their belief in the early connexion between Troy and their own capital. This place was a regular port of call on coasting voyages between Macedonia and Asia. St. Paul, with Silas and Timothy, approached Troas from the Asian-Bithynian frontier near Dorylaeum or Cotiaeum (Ac 16[6-8]). He did not preach in Mysia on the first visit, though the Western text at Ac 16[6] makes him do so. On his third journey Paul stopped at Troas after leaving Ephesus, as may be seen from 2 Co 2[12], and on the return journey left the ship at Troas to go on foot to Assos (Ac 20[5, 13]).
A. So.—**E. G. K.**

TROGYLLIUM.—According to the AV (Ac 20[15]), which here follows the Western text, St. Paul's ship, after touching at Samos, and before putting in at Miletus, 'tarried at Trogyllium.' This statement is no part of the NT text as now commonly read, but it is not impossible, and perhaps embodies a real tradition. Trogyllium is a promontory which projects from the mainland and overlaps the eastern extremity of Samos, so as to form a strait less than a mile wide. There is an anchorage near, still called 'St. Paul's Port.' A. So.

TROPHIMUS.—A Gentile Christian, a native of Ephesus (Ac 21[29]), who, with Tychicus, also of the province Asia (20[4]), and others, accompanied St. Paul to Jerusalem. The Jews, seeing Trophimus with the

Apostle in the city, hastily concluded that St. Paul had brought him into the inner court of the Temple, separated from the outer 'Court of the Gentiles' by a barrier on which were inscriptions in Greek and Latin forbidding any non-Jew to enter on pain of death. This occasioned the riot which led to St. Paul's arrest. Some years later Trophimus was left at Miletus sick (2 Ti 4^{20}).
A. J. M.

TROW.—'To trow' was originally 'to trust,' with which it is connected in origin; but it came to mean no more than 'think *or* suppose.' This is the meaning in Lk 17^{9}, its only occurence in AV. The sentence is probably a gloss; RV and RSV omit.

TRUMPET.—See MUSIC, **4** (2) (*e*).

TRUMPETS, FEAST OF.—The first day of Tishri (October), the seventh month of the sacred year, was signallized by a 'memorial proclaimed with blast of trumpets' (Lv 23^{24}), to call both God and the people to remembrance of their reciprocal positions. It was a day of holy convocation, on which no servile work might be done. The trumpets blown were probably of a different kind from those used at the ordinary new-moon festivals. At the Feast of Trumpets special offerings (cf Lv 23^{24f}, Nu 29^{1-6}) were made: a burnt-offering of a bullock, a ram, and seven lambs, and a sin-offering of a kid of the goats; these in addition to the ordinary daily and monthly offerings. This was one of the lunar festivals of the Jewish calendar, and was the most important of the new-moon celebrations.
A. W. F. B.

TRUST.—See FAITH.

TRUTH.—In OT (*'ᵉmeth, 'ᵉmûnāh*).—*Firmness* or *stability* is the fundamental idea of the root, and to this radical thought most of the uses of the Hebrew nouns may be traced. Often they signify truth in the common meaning of the word, the correspondence, viz., between speech and fact (Dt 13^{14}, Pr 12^{17}). At first the standards of veracity were low (Gn 12^{11ff} 20^{2ff} 26^{7ff} 27^{18ff} etc.); but truthfulness in witness-bearing is a commandment of the Decalogue (Ex 20^{16}), and from the prophetic age onwards falsehood of every kind is recognized as a grave sin (Hos 4^{2}, Ps 59^{12}, Pr 12^{22}). See, further, LIE. Sometimes 'truth' denotes justice as administered by a ruler or a judge (Ex 18^{21}, Pr 20^{28}), and, in particular, by the Messianic King (Ps 45^{4}, Is 42^{3}). Frequently it denotes faithfulness, especially the faithfulness of a man to God (2 K 20^{3}) and of God to men (Gn 32^{10}). When God is described as a 'God of truth,' His faithfulness to His promises may be especially in view (Ps 31^{5}). But not far away is the sense of 'living reality' in distinction from the 'lying vanities' in which those trust to whom Yahweh is unknown (v.^{6}; cf Dt 32^{4}). In some later canonical writings there appears a use of 'truth' or 'the truth' as equivalent to Divine revelation (Dn 8^{12} 9^{13}), or as a synonym for the 'wisdom' in which the true philosophy of life consists (Pr 23^{23}). In the Apocryphal books this use becomes frequent (1 Es 4^{33ff}, Wis 3^{9}, Sir 4^{28} etc.).
J. C. L.

TRUTH.—In NT (*alētheia*).—The Greek word (which is employed in LXX to render both *'ᵉmeth* and *'ᵉmûnāh*) has the fundamental meaning of *reality*, as opposed to mere appearance or false pretence. From this the sense of veracity comes quite naturally; and veracity finds a high place among the NT virtues. The OT law forbade the bearing of false witness against one's neighbour; the law of Christ enjoins truth-speaking in all social intercourse (Eph 4^{25}), and further demands that this truth-speaking shall be animated by love (v.^{15}; cf v.^{25} 'for we are members one of another').

Special attention must be paid to some distinctive employments of the word. (*a*) In the Pauline writings there is a constant use of 'the truth' to describe God's will as revealed—primarily to the reason and conscience of the natural man (Ro $1^{18, 25}$), but especially in the gospel of Jesus Christ (2 Co 4^{2}, Gal 5^{7} etc.). 'The truth' thus becomes synonymous with 'the gospel' (Eph 1^{13}; cf Gal $2^{5, 14}$ etc., where 'the truth of the gospel' evidently means the truth declared in the gospel). In the Pastoral Epistles the gospel as 'the truth' or 'the word of truth' appears to be passing into the sense of a settled body of Christian doctrine (1 Ti 3^{15}, 2 Ti 2^{15} etc.). It is to be noted that, though the above usages are most characteristic of the Pauline cycle of writings, they are occasionally to be found elsewhere, *e.g.* He 10^{26}, Ja 1^{18}, 1 P 1^{22}, 2 P 1^{12}.

(*b*) In the Johannine books (with the exception of Revelation) *alētheia* is a leading and significant term in a sense that is quite distinctive (cf 'light' and 'life'). To Pilate's question, 'What is truth?' (Jn 18^{38}), Jesus gave no answer. But He had just declared that He came into the world to bear witness to the truth (v.^{37}), and the Fourth Gospel might be described as an elaborate exposition of the nature of the truth as revealed by Jesus, and of the way in which He revealed it. In John 'the truth' stands for the absolute Divine reality as distinguished from all existence that is false or merely seeming (cf 8^{40ff}, where Jesus contrasts His Father, from whom He had heard the truth, with 'your father the devil,' who 'has nothing to do with the truth, because there is no truth in him'). Jesus came from the bosom of the Father (Jn 1^{18}), and truth came by Him (v.^{17}) because as the Word of God He was full of it (v.^{14}). The truth is incarnated and personalized in Jesus, and so He is Himself the Truth (14^{6}). The truth which resides in His own Person He imparts to His disciples (8^{31f}); and on His departure He bestows the Spirit of truth to abide with them and be in them for ever (14^{17}). Hence the truth is in the Christian as the very groundwork and essence of his spiritual being (1 Jn 1^{8} 2^{4}, 2 Jn 1^{2}). It is there both as a moral and as an intellectual quality —standing midway, as it were, between 'life' and 'light,' two other ruling Johannine ideas with which it is closely associated. Primarily it is a moral power. It makes Christ's disciples free (Jn 8^{32})—free *i.e.*, as the context shows, from the bondage of sin (vv.^{33ff}). It has a sanctifying force (Jn 17^{17-19}); it ensures the keeping of the commandments (1 Jn 2^{4}) and the life of Christian love (3^{13f}). And, while subjectively it is a moral influence, objectively it is a moral vocation—something not only to be known (Jn 8^{32}) and believed (vv.^{45f}), but requiring to be done (Jn 3^{21}, 1 Jn 1^{6}). From this moral quality of the truth, however, there springs a power of spiritual illumination. The truth that is life passes into the truth that is light (Jn 3^{21}). Every one who is of the truth hears Christ's voice (18^{37}); if any man's will is to do His will, he shall know of the doctrine (7^{17}); the Spirit of truth, when He comes, will guide the disciples into all the truth (16^{13}).
J. C. L.—**W. D. S.**

TRYPHAENA.—Greeted along with **Tryphosa** by St. Paul in Ro 16^{12}, and described by him as workers in the Lord. They were probably sisters or near relations, 'for it was usual to designate members of the same family by derivatives of the same root' (Lightfoot). The common root makes their names signify 'delicate,' 'luxurious'— meaning which contrasts with their active Christian toil. Inscriptions in a cemetery used chiefly for the Emperor's servants contain both names; if we identify them with these, then they would be among 'the saints of Caesar's household' (Ph 4^{22}).

A Tryphaena plays a prominent part in the apocryphal *Acts of Paul and Thecla*.
C. T. P. G.

TRYPHO(N).—An officer of Alexander Balas, who, after the death of the latter, took advantage of the unpopularity of **Demetrius** (q.v.) to put forward Antiochus, the son of Balas, as a claimant to the throne (1 Mac 11^{39}). His real aim, however, was to gain the crown for himself, and this he accomplished after he had murdered in succession Jonathan the Maccabee (12^{39-50}) and Antiochus (13^{31f}). His rapacity led Simon to appeal to Demetrius (13^{34}). The latter was organizing an expedition against Trypho when he was himself made prisoner by Arsaces (14^{1-3}). In the end, Antiochus Sidetes, the brother of Demetrius, attacked Trypho, besieged him in Dor and pursued him when he escaped thence to Orthosia ($15^{10-14, 37-39}$). Trypho was finally shut up in Apamea, where he committed suicide (Strabo, xiv. v. 2; Jos. *Ant.* xiii. vii. 2 [224]; Appian, *Syr.* 68).

TRYPHOSA.—See Tryphaena.

TUBAL.—A country and people in Asia Minor mentioned only in association with **Meshech** (q.v.).

TUBAL-CAIN.—In Gn 4^{22} 'the forger of all instruments of bronze and iron,' *i.e.* the founder of the guild or profession of metal-workers. The name seems to be made up of *Tubal* (or the Tibareni, noted for production of bronze articles (Ezk 27^{13}) and *Cain* ('smith'), as the ancestor of the Kenites or 'Smiths.'

TUBIAS, 1 Mac 5^{13} (RV).—See Tob.

TUBIENI, 2 Mac 12^{17} (AV, RV).—See Tob.

TUMOUR.—See Medicine.

TUNIC.—See Dress, **2** (*d*).

TURBAN.—See Dress, **5**; Bonnet, Headtire, Mitre.

TURPENTINE TREE.—In Sir 24^{16} AV has this for **terebinth** (q.v.), as in RV, RSV.

TURTLE DOVE.—See Dove.

TUSK.—Ezk 27^{15} RSV, for AV and RV 'horn (of ivory).'

TUTOR.—See School.

TWELVE.—See Number, **7.**

TWIN BROTHERS.—See Dioscuri.

TWO.—See Number, **7.**

TYCHICUS.—A native of the province of Asia, like Trophimus, and a companion of St. Paul on the final journey to Jerusalem (Ac 20^{4}). He is named as the bearer of both Ephesians and Colossians (Eph 6^{21f}, Col 4^{7f}). According to the Pastoral Epistles, either he or Artemas was to have been sent to Crete, apparently to take Titus' place (Tit 3^{12}); but he was sent to Ephesus, probably instead of to Crete (2 Ti 4^{12}).

A. J. M.—**J. K.**

TYNDALE'S VERSION.—See English Versions, **12** ff.

TYRANNUS.—'The hall of Tyrannus' (Ac 19^{9}) was a lecture room, rented by St. Paul for his preaching at Ephesus. We do not know if Tyrannus was the former or actual owner of the building or if he was a lecturer himself or if the school only bore his name. Codex Bezae (D) and a few other MSS add the words 'from the fifth to the tenth hour,' *i.e.* from 11 a.m. to 4 p.m. This was the time of the mid-day meal and of the rest taken during the worst heat of the day. 'At 1 p.m. there were probably more people sound asleep than at 1 a.m.' (*BC* iv, p. 239). The glossator may have supposed that the rent for these hours was cheapest. E. H.

TYRE.—City of the Phoenicians (q.v.) situated on the Syrian coast, originally on a rocky island (hence its name *Ṣōr* 'rock,' which has survived to this day as *Ṣûr*). It lay some 22 miles S. of **Sidon** (q.v.) and 35 miles N. of the Carmel headland. It was no doubt settled very anciently. Herodotus (*c* 450 B.C.) was told it was built 2300 years ago (ii. 44). It is mentioned in an Egyptian Papyrus of the time of Rameses ii. (1301–1234 B.C.) as a city to which water has to be brought in ships and which is richer in fish than in sand. We hear of it first in the *Tell el-Amarna* letters of the time of Akhenaten (1377–1358 B.C.). Its king Abimilki, a loyal henchman of Pharaoh, complains that the king of Sidon had seized *Ushu*, the mainland suburb (later called *Palai-Tyros*, 'old Tyre,' by the Greeks). Tyre must soon have forsaken its loyalty to Egypt, for Seti i. (1317–1301 B.C.) subsequently subdued it. Under Rameses iii. (1197–1165 B.C.) it was again lost.

An early predominance of Sidon over Tyre must be assumed. However, the leadership of Tyre became definitely established about the same time as that of Jerusalem over the Hebrews. In the absence of inscriptions we are heavily dependent for the history of Tyre on the OT, the Assyrian inscriptions, and materials preserved by Josephus from Menander of Ephesus, a writer who apparently drew on official Tyrian records (Jos. *c. Apion*, i. 18 and 21 [116, 155]; *Ant.* viii. v. 3 [144]; ix. xiv. 2 [283]). Basic for the chronology is the statement that from Hiram i. to the founding of Carthage in the seventh year of king Pygmalion 155 years and 8 months had elapsed. As the founding of Carthage took place in 814 B.C., Hiram i. is to be dated 969–936 B.C., according to the king list of Menander. The date is of great importance for Hebrew chronology, as Hiram is the contemporary of David and Solomon. It is clear that Tyrians needed good relations with the Hebrews to gain strength against Sidon, and that Israel needed Tyrian neutrality in its warring with Philistines and Aramaeans. It is very doubtful whether the border of Israel ever extended to Palai-Tyros, as 2 S 24^{7} seems to imply (the reference to Tyre in Jos 19^{29} is probably a later addition). If the Hebrews managed to get a foothold in Phoenician territory they evidently found it expedient not to press it. Hiram, indeed, got the territory of Cabul from Solomon (1 K 9^{10f}), thus safeguarding or regaining the plain of Acre, and it may well be that the Hebrews soon lost the Mount Carmel region, which they seem to have had in their hands for a while, as the territory of Asher reached the sea S. of Dor (Jos 19^{26}). Hiram's power is shown by the fact that he is credited with having founded *Qart-ḥadast* 'New City,' predecessor of Kition, on Cyprus. He greatly enlarged the island area of Tyre by means of engineering operations, and built new temples for the chief god of the city, *Melqarth* ('king of the city') and *'Ashtart*, and set up a golden stela in the temple of *Baal-shāmēm* 'the lord of the heavens,' *i.e.* of the firmament. That he supplied the Hebrew king with the technical assistance necessary for building and equipping palaces and Temple and sold him the required lumber from the Lebanon Mountains is vividly reported in 1 Kings.

Under the divided monarchy we find Israel's king Ahab with a Tyrian princess for his queen—Jezebel, daughter of Ethbaal (887–856 B.C. according to Menander's figures). A regular covenant existed between Israel and Tyre, which the latter violated by delivering up a whole people to Edom (Am 1^{9}, but read *Aram* for Edom), *i.e.* deporting an entire Hebrew community. Already in the 9th cent. the Assyrian inscriptions begin to shed light on events. In 876 B.C. Ashurnaṣirpal received Tyre's tribute. Shalmaneser iii. likewise collected tribute in 842 B.C. and portrayed the scene on the gates of *Balawāt*, and Adadnirari iii. (809–782 B.C.) reports the same thing. Menander gives valuable information about King Elulaeus (725–690 B.C.). He again subjected Kition (which as we know from Assyrian inscriptions had been occupied by Sargon), but when Sennacherib (whose name has been corrupted to **Selampsas** in the Josephus text) came to Phoenicia the cities of Sidon, Acco, Ushu, and others deserted the Tyrian overlord. Tyre was vainly besieged for five years. Sennacherib mentions Elulaeus as *Luli* and misleadingly calls him king of Sidon. He says nothing about Tyre at all (to cover up his failure there) but reports that a whole series of cities rebelled against Tyre and submitted to him. Luli fled to Cyprus where he died. The Assyrian thus confirms Menander's report, and we see that Tyre was, indeed, holding sway over Sidon and the cities southward to Acre in this period. But Sennacherib now handed over the power to Sidon.

Tyre was, however, soon to come to the fore again after the fall of Sidon in 678 B.C. The Tyrian king conspired with the Egyptian Tirhakah, and the city underwent a five year siege by Esarhaddon. In 668 B.C. it submitted to Ashurbanipal. Tyre was involved with Pharaoh Hophra and Judah in resistance to Nebuchadrezzar in 586 B.C. and was besieged for thirteen years—a siege that ended in 572 B.C. with the surrender of its king Ithoba'al iii., who was carried off to Babylon. Subsequently we hear of Tyre being ruled by 'judges.' Descendants of the exiled king of Tyre were, however, allowed to reign again by Nabonidus.

The events of Nebuchadrezzar's time are most vividly reflected in Ezk 26–28[19] 29[17–21]. The description of the Ship Tyre unrolls a remarkable picture of Tyrian wealth and far flung connexions, but it is noteworthy that the Hebrew author's horizon is limited to the Near East; he has no clear idea of the vast Tyrian colonization (see PHOENICIA).

The rising power of the Greeks spelt the end of many of the Tyrian colonies. In Carthage (*Qart-ḥadast*), however, Tyre had a daughter city that still was to play a great rôle and that preserved ties with its parent.

In the Persian era the Tyrians naturally became very valuable to the Achaemenid rulers. They assisted Cambyses in his invasion of Egypt. Later we find them aiding the Persians in the wars with Greece. That brought new prosperity and concessions to Tyre and Sidon. The Phoenicians pushed their influence far southward in the Palestinian coastal plain. We hear of Tyrian fish merchants at the gates of Jerusalem (Neh 13[16]). But after the peace of Antalcidas in 387 B.C. the Tyrians (and Sidonians) went over to the side of Persia's enemies. Artaxerxes III. Ochus destroyed Sidon *c* 350 B.C. (cf Is 23[1f], Ezk 28[20f]), whereupon Tyre surrendered. It is uncertain whether the threat against Tyre and Sidon and the districts of Philistia in Jl 4[4–8] is from this period or a later one; it reveals Phoenician traffic in Hebrew slaves, and Jewish hopes of selling Phoenicians as slaves to the Sabaeans.

In 332 B.C. Alexander the Great appeared before Tyre, which refused to admit him. A great siege followed, to which according to some scholars Zec 9[3f] refers. The city was reduced by means of assault from land and sea. Land assault was made possible by the construction of a mole leading out to the island. Originally 200 feet wide the mole has now become an isthmus half a mile wide through sanding up. But Tyre's destruction and the slaughter or enslavement of its population was not the end. It was resettled soon and again became a great city. Strabo speaks of its many storeyed houses, higher than those in Rome, and of its two harbours—the southern, Egyptian one then being open and the northern one a closed harbour. We learn in an inscription of an era of Tyre that began 274–273 B.C. It became Seleucid possession in 198 B.C., but gained autonomy in 126 B.C. This was confirmed by Pompey in 65 B.C. Tyrian territory in the time of Christ extended to Kedesh in Galilee; hence Jesus did not have to go very far toward the city of Tyre to be in its sphere (Mk 3[8] 7[24–31], Lk 10[13]). Tyre (and Sidon) suffered from the anger of Herod Agrippa I. and sent an ambassador to pacify him (Ac 12[20]). There was a Christian church at Tyre, which Paul visited (Ac 21[3f]). Its Jewish or proselyte origin seems likely as there had been Jews there for centuries (see Ps 87[4]).

In subsequent centuries when heathenism was persecuted, a Christian Church was built on the site of the old temple of the god Melqarth. Origen died at Tyre in A.D. 254. Jerome (4th cent.) speaks of it as 'the most noble and beautiful city of Phoenicia.' It fell a prey to the Islamic conquest in A.D. 638, but was taken by the Crusaders in A.D. 1124. It produced a crusader-historian, William of Tyre. In A.D. 1291 the Crusaders gave up Tyre, where the evidences of their fortifications and other structures are still to be seen. These later buildings make excavation of Phoenician Tyre virtually impossible. Exploratory soundings carried on by Renan in 1860 and more recently by Lasseur (1921) have not produced any finds antedating 600 B.C. Poidebard's explorations rediscovered the mole of the Egyptian harbour in 1934, thus confirming Arrian's report that it was a closed one in Alexander's time. By Strabo's time it had evidently sanded up and so one must imagine the beach scene of Ac 21[5] as taking place on the one formed by Alexander's mole. E. G. K.

TYRUS.—Form of the name **Tyre** (q.v.) often found in AV.

TZADE or **ṢADHE.**—Eighteenth letter of Hebrew alphabet, and so used to introduce the eighteenth part of Ps 119, every verse of which begins with this letter.

U

UCAL.—See ITHIEL, **2.**

UEL.—One of the sons of Bani who had married a foreign wife, Ezr 10[34]; called **Joel** in 1 Es 9[34] (AV, RV **Juel**).

UGARIT.—See RAS SHAMRA.

UKNAZ.—In 1 Ch 4[15] AVm gives 'Uknaz' instead of 'even Kenaz' (AV) or 'and Kenaz' (RV). In all probability something has dropped out of the text, which had originally read 'the sons of Elah: . . . and Kenaz.' This is favoured by the plural 'sons.' RSV reads simply 'Kenaz.'

ULAI.—A large river of Elam, emptying into the Persian Gulf. According to Dn 8[2, 16] and the Assyrian inscriptions, it flowed past the city of Shushan (Susa). It is modern *Kārûn* which, however, does not now flow close to the site of Susa, but to the E. of it. Cf also HYDASPES.

ULAM.—**1.** A Manassite family, 1 Ch 7[16f]. **2.** A Benjamite family, specially noted as archers, 1 Ch 8[39f]; cf also 2 Ch 14[8].

ULCER.—Found in RSV in Dt 28[27] for AV and RV 'emerods,' RVm 'tumour' or 'plague boils.' The Hebrew has the word translated 'tumour' in 1 S 5[6]. See MEDICINE.

ULLA.—An Asherite family, 1 Ch 7[39].

UMMAH.—An Asherite city, Jos 19[30]; we should probably read with some Greek MSS **Acco.** See PTOLEMAIS.

UMPIRE.—See DAYSMAN.

UNCHASTITY.—See MARRIAGE, **7, 8.**

UNCLE.—Hebrew *dôdh* is frequently translated 'uncle' in EV (*e.g.* Lv 10[4] 25[49], 1 S 10[14ff], Est 2[7]), and occasionally more specifically as 'father's brother' (Nu 36[10]; also 2 K 24[17] AV and RV). Sometimes it may perhaps be used more widely of a 'kinsman' (so RVm and RSV in Am 6[10]; AV, RV 'uncle'). In Ca 1[13] and often it is used of the Shulammite's 'beloved.'

UNCLEAN, UNCLEANLINESS.—See CLEAN AND UNCLEAN.

UNCLEAN SPIRITS.—See DEMONS, POSSESSION.

UNCTION.—The same Greek word as that translated 'anointing' in 1 Jn 2[27] is in 2[20] rendered 'unction' (RV and RSV 'anointing'). It is used there metaphorically of the effect of the presence of the Holy Spirit upon the believer.

UNDERGIRDING.—See HELPS; SHIPS, **2** (2).

UNDERSETTER.—Only in 1 K 7[30, 34] (AV, RV), in the difficult description of Solomon's lavers (cf TEMPLE, **6** (*d*)). In older English it meant 'support' (so RSV); the Hebrew word is literally 'shoulders,' and denotes something of the nature of a strut or brace.

UNDERTAKE.—In AV of Is 38[14] 'undertake' has the meaning 'be surety for' (so R4; cf RSV).

UNICORN.—Hebrew *reʾēm*, Nu 23[22], Dt 33[17], Ps 22[21] etc.; *rêm*, Job 39[9f]; RV and RSV **wild ox** in all passages. This animal is undoubtedly the *rīmu* of the Assyrians, often figured on their sculptures. A fine bas-relief of this animal was uncovered by the excavations of Nineveh. It is probably identical with the aurochs or *Bos primigenius*, the *urus* of Julius Caesar. It was of great size and strength (Nu 23^{22} 24^{8}, Ps 22^{21}), very wild and ferocious (Job 39$^{9-12}$), and especially dangerous when hunted, because of its powerful double horns (Ps 92^{10}, Dt 33^{17}). In connexion with Is 34^{7} it is interesting to note the inscription of Shalmaneser II., who says 'His land I trod down like a *rîmu*.' The Arabic *ri'm*, the graceful *Antilope leucoryx* of Arabia is a very different animal.

E. W. G. M.

UNKNOWN GOD.—St. Paul walking along the streets of Athens, saw an altar bearing the dedication, 'To an unknown god' (Ac 17^{23}). He used this as the text of his sermon before the Areopagus. Ancient writers refer to the existence of such dedications (Pausanias, I. i. 4; V. xiv. 8, and see the illustration in Deissmann's *Paul*), although an exact parallel to this inscription in the singular is not known. To Paul, however, the point of the inscription lay in its singular usage, for it pointed to the One God of the OT whom he proclaimed.

A. So.—**J. C. B.**

UNLEAVENED BREAD.—See BREAD, LEAVEN, PASSOVER.

UNNI.—1. A Levitical family, 1 Ch 15$^{18, 20}$. **2.** See UNNO.

UNNO.—A family of Levites that returned with Zerubbabel, Neh 12^{9} (so RV, RSV with *Kᵉthîbh*; AV **Unni** with *Ḳᵉrê*).

UNTOWARD.—'Untoward' is 'not toward,' *i.e.* not well disposed. It occurs in AV in Ac 2^{40} 'this untoward generation' (RV, RSV 'crooked'). Cf 'untoward to all good . . . forward to evil'—*Judgement of the Synode at Dort*, p. 32. The substitute 'untowardness' occurs in the AV heading of Is 28, Hos 6. The word is still occasionally used, but in the more modern sense of 'unfortunate'—as an 'untoward accident.'

UNWRITTEN SAYINGS.—See AGRAPHA.

UPHARSIN.—See MENE MENE TEKEL AND PARSIN.

UPHAZ.—A supposed country or region mentioned in Jer 10^{9}, Dn 10^{5}, as a source of gold. Probably the word is miswritten for **Ophir** (q.v.).

UPPER GATE.—An unidentified gate of the Temple built by Jotham, 2 K 15^{35} (AV 'higher gate'), 2 Ch 27^{3} (AV 'high gate'). It is possibly the same as the 'upper Benjamin gate' of Jer 20^{2} (AV 'high gate of Benjamin').

UPPER ROOM.—See HOUSE.

UR.—Father of one of David's heroes, 1 Ch 11^{35}.

UR OF THE CHALDEES, whence Abraham set out upon his journey to Canaan (Gn 11$^{28-31}$ 15^{7}, Neh 9^{7}), is usually identified with the well-known city of *Uri* in southern Babylonia, the site of which is marked by the mounds of Muqayyar. Literary and non-literary remains on the site testify to high civilization and international trade. Excavation has shown that the city was in existence early in the 3rd millennium B.C., and became the seat of kings of three Dynasties, under whom arts and crafts attained a very high standard. The chief gods were the moon-god Nanna, *i.e.* Sin, and his consort Nin-gal. Samsu-iluna, son of Hammurabi, razed the walls and burnt the city which had rebelled against the rule of Babylon. Five hundred years later, Kurigalzu, a Kassite ruler, rebuilt local shrines. The last royal builder was Cyrus, king of Anshan and conqueror of Babylon. The latest tablets found *in situ* are of the 5th cent. B.C.

L. W. K.—**T. F.**

URBANE, Ro 16^{9} (AV).—See URBANUS.

URBANUS.—A Christian greeted by St. Paul in Ro 16^{9} (AV **Urbane**). The name is found several times in inscriptions, including some referring to members of the Imperial household at Rome.

J. L.

URI.—1. The father of Bezalel, Ex 31^{2} 35^{30} 38^{22}, 1 Ch 2^{20}, 2 Ch 1^{5}. **2.** Father of Geber, 1 K 4^{19}. **3.** A porter, Ezr 10^{24}.

URIAH.—1. One of David's 30 heroes, the husband of Bathsheba. He was a Hittite but, as the name indicates, doubtless a worshipper of Yahweh, 2 S 11, 12$^{9f, 15}$, 1 K 15^{5}, Mt 1^{6} (AV here **Urias**). After David's ineffectual attempt to use him for a shield for his own sin, he was killed in battle in accordance with the instructions of David to Joab. **2.** High priest in the reign of Ahaz; called 'a reliable witness' in Is 8^{2}, but subservient to the innovations of Ahaz in 2 K 16$^{10-16}$ (here called **Urijah**). The omission of the name in 1 Ch 6$^{4-15}$ may be due to textual corruption, since it appears in Jos. *Ant.* x. viii. 6 [153], which is based on Chronicles. **3.** A prophet, son of Shemaiah of Kiriath-jearim. His denunciations of Jerusalem and Judah in the style of Jeremiah aroused the wrath of king Jehoiakim. Uriah fled to Egypt, was seized and slain by order of Jehoiakim, and was buried in the common graveyard, Jer 26$^{20-23}$ (AV **Urijah**). **4.** A priest, the son of Hakkoz, Neh 3$^{4, 21}$ (AV **Urijah**). He was the father (or ancestor) of Meremoth, an eminent priest, Ezr 8^{33}, 1 Es 8^{62} (AV **Iri**, RV **Urias**). **5.** A man who stood on the right hand of Ezra when he read the Law, Neh 8^{4} (AV **Urijah**), 1 Es 9^{43} (AV, RV **Urias**).

URIAS.—1. Mt 1^{6} (AV); see URIAH, **1. 2.** 1 Es 8^{62} (RV); see URIAH, **4. 3.** 1 Es 9^{43} (AV, RV); see URIAH, **5.**

URIEL ('El is my light').—**1.** A Kohathite, 1 Ch 6^{24} 15$^{5, 11}$. **2.** Father of one of Rehoboam's wives, 2 Ch 13^{2}. **3.** The angel mentioned in 2 Es 4^{1} 5^{20ff} 10^{28} as coming to Salathiel (=Ezra) and rebuking his questioning of God's way by propounding various unanswerable questions. In 1 En 9^{1}, under the form Urjan, Uriel is the fourth of the four archangels, although 40^{9} and ch. 71 have Phanuel. It is possible that the **Jeremiel** of 2 Es 4^{36} is also to be equated with Uriel. In 1 En 19^{1} 20^{2} Uriel is one of the holy watchers; because of his connexion with fire, he is 'the angel over the world and Tartarus.' In the latter capacity he explains to Enoch the fate of the fallen stars and angels, 1 En 21, and the accursed, ch. 27 (and see *Sib. Orac.* ii. 228). A more auspicious function is to explain the names and movements of the stars, 33^{1f}, and the luminaries, ch. 72 ff. In later literature Uriel is the angel who helps to bury Adam and Abel in Paradise, and wrestles with Jacob.

C. C. Ro.

URIJAH.—1. See URIAH, **2. 2.** Jer 26$^{20-23}$ (AV); see URIAH, **3. 3.** Neh 3$^{4, 21}$ (AV); see URIAH, **4. 4.** Neh 8^{4} (AV); see URIAH, **5.**

URIM AND THUMMIM.—These denote the two essential parts of the sacred oracle by which in early times, the Hebrews sought to ascertain the will of God. The RVm (Ex 28^{30}) renders 'the Lights and the Perfections' thus reflecting the view of the late Jewish scholars to whom we owe the present vocalization of the OT text. In this instance the LXX renders by *tēn dēlōsin kai tēn alētheian*, but the Versions offer little help. The LXX varies in its rendering for Urim translating it by *dēlōsis* (manifestation), *dēloi* (*sc. lithoi*) (clear stones), *phōtizō* (to illumine or give light) (Ezr-Neh). Aquila, Symmachus and Theodotion render variously by *phōtismos, didachē*. Thummim in the LXX appears as *alētheia, hosiotēs, teleia*, while Symmachus and Theodotion give *teleiotētes*. OL and Jerome translate Urim by *doctrina, demonstratio, ostensio, doctus*, and for Thummim they give variously, *veritas, perfectio, sanctitas, perfectus, eruditus*. The oldest references to the sacred lot suggest that the words express two sharply contrasted ideas. Hence if Thummim denotes innocence Urim should signify guilt, and this term might well seem to be connected with *'ārar* (to curse). Winckler and his followers, however, start from 'light' as the meaning of Urim and interpret Thummim as 'darkness' (the completion of the sun's course). 'Urim and Thummim are life and death, yes and no, light and darkness' (Jeremias, *Das AT im Lichte des alt. Orients*, p. 450, Benzinger, *Heb. Arch.*^{3}, pp. 344 f). Muss-Arnolt (*JE* XII, 384–386) would associate Urim with the Assyrian *u'uru* (pi'el infinitive of *a'aru*) meaning 'to send forth' (an edict) from which root we have the forms *urtu* and *ertu*=a divine decision. Thummim he would derive from the Assyrian *tamu* (pi'el form *tummu*) with the noun form *tamatu*=an oracle. The two terms might thus constitute a hendiadys, as Engnell suggests (*SBU*, ii, col. 1517). This suggestion might find some support in the LXX renderings of *dēlōsis* and *alētheia* or *didachē* (Aquila, Symmachus, Theodotion) and the Latin variants *doctrina, demonstratio, ostensio* (OL and Jerome).

However obscure the meaning of the terms may be it seems clear that here we are dealing with something that was taken over from the pre-Mosaic period. Lindblom would associate it with the Kenites (*Israels Religion i G.T. tid*, p. 61) while Eichrodt holds it to have originated with the priests of Kadesh, and to have been a survival which disappeared after the institution of the monarchy (*Theology of OT*, 1961, 113 ff). According to Rabbinical tradition Urim and Thummim belong to the five things that disappeared at the time of the Exile (*Sotah* 48b, *Yoma* 21b, Jer. Talm., *Kidd.* 65b). Later references (Sir 23[3] 45[10], Josephus, *Ant.* III. viii. 9 [215 f], and Talmud, *Berak.* 17a) prove that no real or reliable tradition survived on the subject. References in Neh 7[65] Ezr 2[63] and 1 Es 5[40] show that Urim and Thummim were not in use in the post-exilic period. The occurrence of 'Ortom' in the Dead Sea Scrolls (1 QH iv. 6, 23 ; xviii. 29) is simply 'a play on the Biblical Urim and Thummim' (Gaster) and 'has nothing to do with the Urim and Thummim' (Nötscher, *Zur theol. Terminologie der Qumrân-texte*, 93).

The most instructive, as it is historically the oldest, passage dealing with Urim and Thummim is 1 S 14[41f]: the text is that of the LXX (confirmed by the Dead Sea Scrolls) and given by the RSV. 'Therefore, Saul said, O Lord God of Israel, why hast thou not answered thy servant this day? If this guilt is in me or in Jonathan my son, O Lord God of Israel, give Urim : but if this guilt is in thy people Israel give Thummim. And Jonathan and Saul were taken, but the people escaped.' A comparison of this passage with several others in the narratives of Samuel, *e.g.* 1 S 23[3f] 30[7f], 2 S 2[1], where mention is made of 'enquiring of the Lord' the following facts emerge : (1) The Urim and Thummim were two lots closely connected, in some fashion no longer intelligible to us, with the equally mysterious ephod (see EPHOD). (2) As there were only two lots only one question at a time might be put and the question was answered affirmatively or negatively according to the fashion in which 'the lot came out.' (3) To simplify matters in a complicated case, as in 1 S 14[41], it was necessary to decide beforehand the significance to be attached to the two lots. The Mishnah informs us in addition that 'they were not inquired of for a common person but only for a king, for the court, or for one of whom the congregation had need' (*Yoma* vii. 5).

As to the material, shape, etc., of the two lots and the method of manipulation we are left to conjecture. Oesterley and Robinson suggest that they were probably 'flat stones, white on one side, black on the other. If both fell white side upwards the answer was in the affirmative, if black side upwards then negative. If they differed no reply was vouchsafed to the question' (*Heb. Rel.*[2], p. 166 ; cf 1 S 28[6]). It has been suggested with less probability (Kautzsch *PRE*[3] xx, 328–336) that they were arrows and were used as in Babylonian rituals of divination (Ezk 21[21]). Were they contained within the hollow ephod-image which was provided with a narrow aperture so that it was possible to shake the image and yet neither lot 'come out'? To 'come out' or 'fall' seems here to be used in a technical sense (cf Jos 16[1] 19[1]). The early narratives show that the operation of the sacred lot was a special prerogative of the priests, as is expressly stated in Dt 33[8] (RSV) where the Urim and Thummim are assigned to the priestly tribe of Levi ; this is confirmed in Ezr 2[63]=Neh 7[65].

In the P document the Urim and Thummim are introduced in Ex 28[30], Lv 8[8], Nu 27[21] without any clue as to their nature beyond the inference as to their small size ; this inference may be drawn from the fact that they were to be inserted in the high priest's 'breastpiece of judgment.' But this seems merely to be an attempt on the part of P to divest these old-world mysteries of their association with ideas of divination now outgrown and forbidden by the Law. In placing them within 'the breastpiece of judgment' it is not impossible that the later writer was influenced by the analogy of the Babylonian tablets of destiny worn by Marduk on his breast. The analogy, as Muss-Arnolt points out, is close but not complete. No reference to Urim and Thummim is found in the Râs Shamra (q.v.) tablets but Virolleaud has suggested that the ephod was used in that ritual (*Syria*, 1934, pp. 318 f). This interpretation, however, is open to question and G. R. Driver renders the term, which occurs in B*I i. 5, by the general term 'robe' (*Canaanite Myths and Legends*, p. 103). A. R. S. K.—**J. Pn.**

USURY, INTEREST, INCREASE.—At the date of our AV 'usury' had not acquired its modern connotation of exorbitant interest ; hence it should be replaced in OT by 'interest,' as in RSV, and as the English Revisers have done in NT. The OT law-codes forbid the taking of interest on loans by one Hebrew from another, see Ex 22[25] (Book of the Covenant), Dt 23[19f], Lv 25[35-38] (Law of Holiness). Of the two terms constantly associated and in EV rendered 'usury' (*neshekh*) and 'increase' (*tarbîth*), the former, to judge from Lv 25[37], denotes interest on loans of money, the latter interest on other advances, such as food stuffs, seed-corn, and the like, which was paid in kind. In Dt 23[20] *neshekh* is applied to both kinds of loan. For the distinction in, *e.g.*, the laws of Eshnunna (*c* 2000 B.C.), see *ANET*, p. 162, §§ 20, 21 ; and in NT times, see Mishnah, *Baba Metzia* v. 1.

To appreciate the motives of the Hebrew legislators, it must be remembered that, until a late period in their history, the Hebrews were almost entirely devoted to agricultural and pastoral pursuits. The loans here contemplated are therefore not advances required for trading capital, but for the relief of a poor 'brother' temporarily in distress, who would otherwise be compelled to sell himself as a slave (Lv 25[47ff]). We have to do with an act of charity, not with a commercial transaction. In similar circumstances loans without interest were made from the Babylonian temple funds and by private individuals, as is still done by the Arabs (Doughty, *Arabia Deserta*, i, 318).

In NT times conditions had greatly changed, and capital was required for many trading concerns. Our Lord twice refers, in parables, to the investment of money with 'the bankers,' so as to yield a proper 'interest' (Mt 25[27], Lk 19[23], both RSV). The rate of interest in Israel is unknown ; in the ancient world generally it was very high. In Babylon a loan system was fully developed before 1700 B.C. : where the loan was of grain or provisions, it was one third ; where of money, it was one fifth. This is confirmed by fragments of the Code of Hammurabi (*ANET*, pp. 168–170, especially §§ 88 ff). See also some examples of the law in operation *ANET*, p. 217 C(3), p. 218 D(2), p. 221 I(3). In the Nuzi documents, interest is as high as a half of the capital.

The papyri from Elephantine in Egypt show members of the Jewish colony there already engaged in the characteristically Jewish business of money-lending (*c* 430 B.C.). Tablets of the business house of Murashu Sons at Nippur (455–403 B.C.) show that Jews did business with this firm, but it is not certain, as some think, that Murashu and his sons were themselves Jewish bankers (see *Documents from OT Times*, ed. D. Winton Thomas, pp. 95 f). For the question of guarantees and surety on loans, see DEBT and TRADE AND COMMERCE, **9.** A. R. S. K.—**D. R. J.**

UTA (1 Es 5[30] AV, RV).—See UTHAI, **3.**

UTENSILS.—See HOUSE, **9.**

UTHAI.—**1.** A family of Judah after the Captivity, 1 Ch 9[4]. **2.** One of the sons of Bigvai, Ezr 8[14], 1 Es 8[40]

(AV, RV **Uthi**). **3.** One whose sons returned under Zerubbabel, 1 Es 5[30] (AV, RV **Uta**). Ezra and Nehemiah omit.

UTHI, 1 Es 8[40] (AV, RV).—See UTHAI, **2.**

UZ.—1. A son of Aram, grandson of Shem (Gn 10[23] and 1 Ch 1[17] [in emended text]). **2.** A son of Nahor Gn 22[21], AV **Huz**), whose descendants are placed in Aram-naharaim (Gn 24[10]). **3.** One of the Horites in the land of Edom (Gn 36[28] [v.[21] and v.[30]], 1 Ch 1[42]). **4.** A region which is called the dwelling-place of the daughter of Edom (La 4[21]). **5.** A district containing a number of kings, situated between Philistia and Egypt, or, with a different pointing of the consonants of one word, between Philistia and the country of the Bedouin (Jer 25[20]: the name is not in LXX). **6. Job's** country (Job 1[1]). As the first three are probably tribal designations, all may be regarded as geographical terms. It is not certain that they all refer to the same region. Nos. **1** and **2** seem to point to Mesopotamia. Nos. **3** and **4**, and perhaps **5**, indicate Edom or its neighbourhood. The locality of No. **6** is obscure. Ancient tradition is threefold. In LXX of Job 42[19], Uz is affirmed, on the authority of ' the Syriac book,' to lie on the borders of Idumaea and Arabia. In v.[23] it is located on the borders of the Euphrates. Josephus (*Ant.* I. vi. 4 [145]) associates the *Uz* of No. **1** with Damascus and Trachonitis. The evidence of the Book of Job itself about its hero's home seems to favour the neighbourhood of Edom or N. Arabia. *Teman* (2[11]) was an Edomite district containing the city of Bozrah (Am 1[12]), and *Eliphaz* was an Edomite name (Gn 36[4]). The *Sabaeans* (Job 1[15] 6[19]) were a S. Arabian people who had settlements in the north. *Tema* (6[19]) lay in N. Arabia about 250 miles SE. of Edom. The description of Job, however, as one of ' the children of the East ' (1[3]) is most naturally understood to refer to the E. of Palestine. The cuneiform inscriptions have a name *Uzzai*, which has been identified with *Uz*, but the identification is extremely uncertain.

Modern tradition, which can be traced back to early Christian times, locates Job in the Ḥauran, where the German explorer J. G. Wetzstein found a monastery of Job, a tomb and fountain and stone of Job, and small round stones called ' worms of Job.' Another German explorer, Glaser, finds *Uz* in W. Arabia, at a considerable distance to the NW. of Medina. Decision at present is unattainable, both on the general question of the signification of *Uz* in OT and on the special question of its meaning in the Book of Job. All that can be said is that the name points to the E. and SE. of Palestine, and that the Book of Job appears to represent its hero as living in the neighbourhood of the Arabian or Syro-Arabian desert. W. T. S.

UZAI.—Father of Palal, Neh 3[25].

UZAL.—1. Gn 10[27], 1 Ch 1[21]. One of the sons of Joktan. The two sons of Eber, Peleg and Joktan, represent the two main divisions of the Semitic-speaking peoples, viz. the Aramaeans and the Arabs. The sons of Joktan are thirteen in the MT, but twelve in the LXX, which is probably the original number, intended to correspond with the twelve tribes of Israel. **2.** Ezk 27[19], where, instead of ' Vedan and Javan traded with yarn,' we should read, ' and wine from Uzal ' (RSV). Here Uzal is one of the places with which Tyre traded. It has been identified with *Ṣanʿā*, the capital of Yemen. ' Bright ' or ' wrought ' iron is mentioned as one of the exports of Uzal, and *Ṣanʿā* is still noted for its steel. It should, however, be noted that in Ashurbanipal's account of his expedition against the Nabataeans three places are mentioned together, Hurarina, Yarki, and Azalla, whose names bear a remarkable resemblance to Hadoram, Jerah, and Uzal. If Azallu is the same as Uzal, the latter would not lie as far S. as Yemen, but might be in the neighbourhood of Medina. S. H. He.

UZZA.—1. A Benjamite family, 1 Ch 8[7]. **2.** A family of Temple servants, Ezr 2[49], Neh 7[51], 1 Es 5[31] (AV **Azia,** RV **Ozias**). **3.** 1 Ch 13[7, 9ff]; see UZZAH. **4.** A ' garden of Uzza ' was attached to the palace of Manasseh, and in it Manasseh was buried, 2 K 21[18, 26].

UZZAH.—The driver of the cart on which the Ark was removed from Kiriath-jearim, 2 S 6[3, 6ff]; he is called **Uzza** in 1 Ch 13[7, 9ff]. His sudden death led to the temporary abandonment of David's project of transferring the Ark to Jerusalem, and the place of Uzzah's death was called **Perez-uzzah.** In the popular mind Uzzah's death was attributed to Y"'s anger at his presumption in handling the sacred emblem.

UZZEN-SHEERAH.—A place mentioned only in 1 Ch 7[24] (AV **Uzzen-sherah**); possibly modern *Beit Sîrā*, W. of Beth-horon.

UZZEN-SHERAH, 1 Ch 7[24] (AV).—See UZZEN-SHEERAH.

UZZI.—1. A descendant of Aaron, 1 Ch 6[5f, 51], Ezr 7[4], 1 Es 8[2] (AV **Ezias,** RV **Ozias**). In 1 Es 8[2] AV and RV add ' the son of Meremoth, the son of Zaraias, the son of Sarias,' which RSV, following LXX[B] omits (see RVm). **2.** A family of Issachar, 1 Ch 7[2f]. **3.** A Benjamite family, 1 Ch 7[7] 9[8]. **4.** A Levite overseer, Neh 11[22]. **5.** A priestly family, Neh 12[19, 42]. **6.** Father of Arna and an ancestor of Ezra, 2 Es 1[2] (AV, RV **Ozias**).

UZZIA.—One of David's heroes, 1 Ch 11[44].

UZZIAH.—1. A king of Judah. See next article. **2.** A Kohathite Levite, 1 Ch 6[24]; called **Azariah** in v.[36]. **3.** The father of an officer of David, 1 Ch 27[25]. **4.** A priest who had married a foreign wife, Ezr 10[21]; in 1 Es 9[21] he is called **Azariah** (AV, RV **Azarias**). **5.** A Judahite, Neh 11[4]. **6.** The son of Micah, Jth 6[15] 7[23] 8[10, 28, 35] 10[6] (AV, RV **Ozias**).

UZZIAH, also called **AZARIAH,** was king of Judah *c* 783–742 B.C., succeeding his father Amaziah as a lad of sixteen. Rather strangely the Book of Kings has little to say about him (2 K 15[1-7]), but his reign is quite fully treated in 2 Ch 26[1-23], and the account there can be taken as historical in the main, as verified by archaeology. In his reign Judah reached the height of its power and prosperity. He reorganized the army, and is credited with the introduction of the siege engine into Judah. The walls of Jerusalem were rebuilt and provided with towers. He conquered the northern and eastern part of the Philistine plain, thus gaining control over the important caravan routes there. He rebuilt Elath at the head of the Gulf of ʿAqaba and campaigned in Arabia to give him control of the land and sea routes to and from Arabia and the East. The revival in commerce that resulted helps to explain the prosperity of his reign, which was also furthered by his great interest in agriculture and the raising of live stock. He constructed cisterns throughout the country to collect the winter rains for irrigating the soil. Watch-towers were also built to give protection to the population on the land, for he was a patron of agriculture and a lover of the soil (2 Ch 26[10]). Politically Tiglath-pileser III. of Assyria regarded him as the head of the anti-Assyrian faction in the west. In any case, when Syria and Israel were in a more or less continuous state of internecine warfare, Judah was stable and prosperous, and was a leader in the west. It used to be thought, and still is by some, that the Azariah of Judah mentioned by Tiglath-pileser in one of his inscriptions refers to a prince in Northern Syria, but it is most unlikely that there would be an Azariah of Judah in the north and another at the same time in southern Palestine. Toward the end of his life, *c* 750 B.C., Azariah was stricken with leprosy, and his son Jotham became regent, but Azariah remained the power behind the throne until his death *c* 742 B.C. T. J. M.

UZZIEL (' El is my strength ').—**1.** A son of Kohath, Ex 6[18, 22], Lv 10[4], Nu 3[19, 30], 1 Ch 6[2, 18] 15[10] 23[12, 20] 24[24]; the gentilic **Uzzielites** occurs in Nu 3[27], 1 Ch 26[23]. **2.** A Simeonite, 1 Ch 4[42]. **3.** Founder of a Benjamite family, 1 Ch 7[7]. **4.** A musician of the sons of Heman, 1 Ch 25[4]; called **Azarel** in v.[18]. **5.** A Levite, of the sons of Jeduthun, 2 Ch 29[14]. **6.** A goldsmith who aided in repairing the walls, Neh 3[8].

V

VAGABOND.—In AV in Gn 4^{12} 'a fugitive and a vagabond shalt thou be,' *i.e.* a wanderer (so RV, RSV). So in Ps 109^{10} AV and RV 'Let his children be continually vagabonds' (RSV 'wander about'). Similarly in Ac 19^{13} AV 'certain of the vagabond Jews' (RV 'strolling,' RSV 'itinerant'). In all these places the word is used in its older and literal meaning (from Lat. *vagari*, to wander). RSV has 'vagabond' only in Pr 6^{11} 'poverty will come upon you like a vagabond' (AV 'as one that travelleth,' RV 'as a robber,' RVm 'rover').

VAHEB, Nu 21^{14} (RV).—See WAHEB.

VAIL, VEIL.—In AV this word is spelled 'vail' and 'veil'; in RV and RSV uniformly 'veil' (q.v.).

VAIZATHA.—Tenth son of Haman, put to death by the Jews, Est 9^{9} (AV **Vajezatha**).

VAJEZATHA, Est 9^{9} (AV).—See VAIZATHA.

VALE, VALLEY.—'Vale' is found in AV as the translation of two Hebrew words *'ēmeḳ* and *sh^{e}phēlāh*; 'valley' represents five Hebrew words, *biḳ'āh, gay', naḥal, 'ēmeḳ, sh^{e}phēlāh* and the Greek *phara[n]gx*. For *sh^{e}phēlāh* (a low-lying tract of ground) and *biḳ'āh* (a broad plain) see article PLAIN, and for *naḥal* (wady) see BROOK.

1. The word *gay'* (AV and RV always 'valley') refers to a narrow gorge, a *glen* or *ravine*. A considerable number of such are named in the OT, *e.g.* the valley of Hinnom, beside Jerusalem; of Iphtah-el, between Zebulun and Asher; of Zeboim, SE. of Gibeah; of Salt, etc., while several other valleys are mentioned without a special name being attached to them.

The reference in Ps 23^{4} to the 'valley of the shadow of death' may be simply figurative of a place of peril and loneliness, or, as Gunkel holds, the place through which the ancient Hebrew supposed the soul had to pass on the way to the underworld.

In the Apocrypha, 'valley' is the translation of *phara[n]gx* and *aulōn*, the former appearing in the NT (Lk 3^{5}).

2. The word *'ēmeḳ* (generally translated 'valley' but 'vale' in AV of Gn $14^{3, 8, 10}$ 37^{14} and also in RV of Gn 14^{17}, Jos 8^{13} 15^{8} 18^{16}, 1 S $17^{2, 19}$ 21^{9}; in RSV only of the Vale of Succoth, Ps 60^{6} 108^{7}) means literally *depression*, and is 'a highlander's word for a valley as he looks *down* into it, and is applied to wide avenues running up into a mountainous country like the Vale of Elah, the Vale of Hebron, and the Vale of Aijalon' (*HGHL* 384). Thus the *'ēmeḳ* is broader than a *gay'* and not so broad or extensive as a *biḳ'āh* (plain). A considerable number of vales are mentioned in the OT, *e.g.* of Siddim, of Shaveh, of Hebron, of Achor, of Aijalon, etc.

Other vales are mentioned without special names being attached to them. The fertility of the vale (1 S 6^{13}, Is 17^{5}) and its suitability for cavalry operations (*e.g.* Jos 17^{16}, Jg $1^{19, 34}$ etc.) are frequently referred to.

W. F. B.

VALLEY GATE.—See JERUSALEM, GATES OF.

VAMPIRE, Pr 30^{15} (RVm).—See LEECH.

VANIAH.—One of the sons of Bani, who had married a foreign wife, Ezr 10^{36}, 1 Es 9^{34} (AV, RV **Anos**).

VANITY.—The root-idea of the word is 'emptiness.' Skeat suggests that the Latin *vanus* (perhaps for *vac-nus*) is allied to *vacuus* 'empty.' In English literature 'vanity' signifies (1) emptiness, (2) falsity, (3) vainglory. The modern tendency is to confine its use to the last meaning. But 'vanity' in the sense of 'empty conceit' is not found in the English Bible.

1. In the OT.—(1) 'Vanity' is most frequently the translation of *hebhel*, 'breath' or 'vapour.' The RV rightly gives the literal rendering in Is 57^{13}: 'a breath (AV 'vanity') shall carry them all away' (cf RSV). The word naturally became an image of what is unsubstantial and transitory; In Ps 144^{4} man is said to be 'like a breath' (RVm, RSV), because 'his days are like a passing shadow.' In Ecclesiastes 'vanity' often occurs; it connotes what is fleeting, unsatisfying and profitless. 'Vanity of vanities' (1^{2} 12^{8}) is the superlative expression of the idea of the futility of life. Jeremiah regards idols as 'vanity' because they are 'a work of delusion' (10^{15}), 'lies and things wherein there is no profit' (16^{19}). (2) Another Hebrew word (*'āwen*) whose root-meaning is 'breath' or 'nothingness,' is twice rendered 'vanity' in the RV and is applied to idols (Is 41^{29} [RSV 'delusion'], Zec 10^{2} [RSV 'nonsense']). But *'āwen* generally describes moral evil as what is naughty and worthless; the RV therefore substitutes 'iniquity' for 'vanity' in Job 15^{35} [RSV 'evil'], Ps 10^{7} [so RSV]; cf Is 58^{9}. (3) More frequently, however, 'vanity' is the translation of *shaw'*, which also signifies 'what is naught.' In the OT it is used to set forth vanity as that which is hollow, unreal, and false. In Ps 41^{6} RVm 'he speaketh falsehood' is preferable; but the AV 'he speaketh vanity' [RSV 'utters empty words'] exemplifies the close connexion between vain or empty words and lies (cf Ps 12^{2} 144^{8}, Job 35^{13}, Pr 30^{8}, Ezk 13^{8} 22^{28}). (4) 'Vanity' occurs twice as the rendering of *rîḳ* 'emptiness,' and refers to what is destined to end in failure (Ps 4^{2} [RSV 'vain words'], Hab 2^{13} [RSV 'naught']). (5) In the RV it is used for *tōhū* 'waste,' but the marginal alternative in all passages but one (Is 59^{4}) is 'confusion' (Is 40^{17} [RSV 'nothing'], ^{23} [RSV 'emptiness'] 44^{9} [RSV 'nothing']).

2. In the NT.—'Vain' is the rendering of (*a*) *kenos* 'empty,' (*b*) *mataios* 'worthless.' When the former word is used, stress is laid on the absence of good, especially in essential qualities. The true thought is suggested by the RVm 'void' in 1 Co $15^{10, 14, 58}$. A partial exception is Ja 2^{20}—a rare example of the absolute use of the word [RSV 'foolish fellow']. The 'vain man' is not only 'one in whom the higher wisdom has found no entrance,' but he is also 'one who is puffed up with a vain conceit of his own spiritual insight' (Trench, *NT Synonyms*, p. 181). Even here the primary negative force of the word is clearly discernible; the man's conceit is 'vain,' that is to say, his conception of himself is devoid of real content. He is a 'man who cannot be depended on, whose deeds do not correspond to his words' (Mayor, *Com. in loc.*). *Kenos* is the word rendered 'vain' in the NT, except in the passages cited in the next paragraph.

When 'vain' is the translation of *mataios*, as in EV in Ja 1^{26} and AV and RV [RSV 'futile'] in 1 Co 3^{20} 15^{17}, Tit 3^{9}, 1 P 1^{18} (cf the adverb Mt 15^{9}, Mk 7^{7}), more than negative blame is implied. 'By giving prominence to objectlessness it denotes what is positively to be rejected, *bad*. . . . In Biblical Greek the word is, in the strongest sense, the expression of perfect repudiation' (Cremer, *Bib.-Theol. Lexicon of NT Greek*, pp. 418, 781). In 1 Co 15^{14} the reference (*kenos*) is to 'a hollow witness, a hollow belief,' to a gospel which is 'evacuated of all reality,' and to a faith which has 'no genuine content.' But in v.^{17} the reference (*mataios*) is to a faith which is 'frustrate' or 'void of result,' because it does not save from sin (cf Findlay, *EGT*, *in loc.*).

'Vanity' occurs only three times in the NT (Ro 8^{20}, Eph 4^{17} [both 'futility' in RSV], 2 P 2^{18} [RSV 'folly']); it is always the translation of *mataiotēs*, which is not a classical word, but is often found in the LXX, especially as the rendering of *hebhel* 'breath' (see above). When St. Paul describes the creation as 'subject to vanity' (Ro 8[20]), he has in mind the marring of its perfection and the frustration of its Creator's purpose by sin; nevertheless, the groanings of creation are, to his ear, the utterance of its hope of redemption. When he says that 'the Gentiles walk in the vanity of their mind' (Eph 4[17]), he is dwelling on the futility of their intellectual and moral gropings, which is the result of their walking in darkness (v.[18]). In 2 P 2[18] the intimate connexion between unreality and boastfulness in speech is well brought out in the graphic phrase, 'great swelling words of vanity.' How pitiful the contrast between the high-sounding talk of the false teachers who were themselves 'bond-servants of corruption,' and yet had the effrontery to 'promise liberty' to those whom in reality they were bringing into bondage (v.[19]). J. G. T.

VASHNI.—Samuel's firstborn son according to AV in 1 Ch 6[28] (following MT); RV and RSV follow the Syriac and one form of Greek and read 'and the second' for Vashni, and then supply **Joel** for the firstborn (cf 1 S 8[2]).

VASHTI.—The queen whom Ahasuerus repudiated, Est 1[9, 11] etc. See ESTHER, BOOK OF.

VAT.—See WINE, 2.

VAU or **WAW.**—Sixth letter of Hebrew alphabet, and so used to introduce the sixth part of Ps 119, every verse of which begins with this letter.

VEDAN.—In RV the name of a country or city that traded with Tyre, Ezk 27[19]. AV has 'Dan also.' The passage is certainly corrupt, and both names should probably go out. See UZAL.

VEGETABLES.—See FOOD, **1, 11.**

VEIL.—See DRESS, **5** (*b*), KERCHIEFS, TABERNACLE, **5** (*d*), and TEMPLE, **9, 12.**

VENISON.—See FOOD, **5.**

VERMILION.—See COLOURS, **4.**

VERSIONS.—See ENGLISH VERSIONS, GREEK VERSIONS OF OT, TEXT OF NT, TEXT AND VERSIONS OF OT, VULGATE, etc.

VESPASIAN.—Titus Flavius Vespasianus, appointed in A.D. 67 to command the Roman forces in the Jewish War, was the candidate of the eastern armies in the period of civil war that followed the death of Nero. He was proclaimed emperor at Alexandria on July 1, A.D. 69, his supporters were victorious by the end of the year, and he ruled with austere justice till his death in A.D. 79. Though personally unassuming, he was, as divine ruler, credited with two miraculous healings at Alexandria in A.D. 70; the pro-Roman Jewish historian Josephus claimed that his reign fulfilled the messianic prophecies. On his deathbed he is said to have murmured 'I think I am becoming a god' (*puto me deus fio*), in jesting reference to the deification which would follow. E. R. H.

VESSELS.—See HOUSE, **9**; MEALS, **5.** For the 'instruments' or 'vessels' (AV) of the tabernacle, RV has 'furniture' or 'instruments,' according to the context, and RSV uses such words as 'furniture,' 'instruments,' 'furnishings,' or 'accessories' (cf, *e.g.* Nu 1[50] with 3[36]). For the Temple cf 1 Ch 9[29] in AV, RV, and RSV. In Gn 43[11] 'vessels' (AV, RV) is equivalent to 'saddlebags' (RSV 'bags'). In 1 Th 4[4] for 'vessel' (AV, RV), RSV has 'wife,' for which some would understand rather 'body.'

VESTIBULE.—RSV substitutes 'vestibule' for AV and RV '**porch**' (q.v.) in all its OT occurrences.

VESTRY occurs only in 1 K 10[22] (AV and RV) 'him that was over the vestry,' where RSV has 'wardrobe'; cf 22[14].

VESTURE.—In AV this word occurs as the rendering both of words denoting dress or raiment generally, as Gn 41[42] (so RV; RSV 'garments'), Ps 22[18] 102[26] (so RV; RSV 'raiment'), and of special words for the plaid-like upper garment of antiquity, as Dt 22[12] (so RV; RSV 'cloak'; see FRINGES), Rev 19[13, 16] (RV 'garment,' RSV 'robe'), for which see DRESS, **4** (*a*). A. R. S. K.

VIAL occurs in OT in 1 S 10[1] (AV, RV, RSV) and 2 K 9[1f] (RV; AV 'box,' RSV 'flask'), for an oil-flask. In NT, RV and RSV have substituted 'bowl' for 'vial' throughout (Rev 5[8] 15[7] 16[1ff]). The *phialē* was a flat vessel, resembling a saucer, specially used for pouring libations of wine upon the altar of a deity.

VILLAGE.—For the OT villages and their relation to the 'mother' city, see CITY. In all periods of Hebrew history the cultivators of the soil lived for greater security in villages, the cultivated and pasture land of which was held in common. Solitary homesteads were unknown. The NT writers and Josephus also distinguish between a city (*polis*) and a village (*kōmē*), the distinction being primarily a difference not of size but of status. Thus in Mk 1[38] the word rendered '**towns**' is literally 'village-cities' (others render 'market-towns'), *i.e.* places which are cities as regards population but not as regards constitutional status. When Josephus tells us that 'the very least of' the villages of Galilee 'contained above 15,000 inhabitants' (*BJ* III. iii. 2 [43]), he is, *more suo*, drawing a very long bow indeed! A. R. S. K.

VINE, VINEYARD.—The usual Hebrew word for 'vine' is *gephen*, used of the grape-vine everywhere except in 2 K 4[39], where *gephen śādeh* (literary 'field vine') refers to a wild-gourd vine. Another word, *sōrēq* (Is 5[2], Jer 2[21]), or *sōrēqāh* (Gn 49[11]), refers to superior vines with purple grapes.

The vine (*Vitis vinifera*) is supposed to be a native of the shores of the Caspian, but has been cultivated in Palestine from the earliest times, as is witnessed by the extensive remains of ancient vineyards. The climate is peculiarly suited to the grape, which reaches perfection during the prolonged sunshine and the dewy nights of late summer. Vines specially flourish on the hillsides unsuited for cereals (Jer 31[5], Am 9[13]). In modern Jordan viticulture is practised almost solely by monks in Christian monasteries, for the Moslems are, by religion, teetotal. Israel, however, has in recent years forged ahead as a wine-producing, even wine-exporting country. The mountain-sides of Israel are newly terraced, intensively cultivated, and experiments with vines and wine-making are being vigorously carried out by Agricultural Institutes. Here, as in many other ways, the state of Israel is changing the countryside, and not always in accord with OT customs. As in the case of the olive, the culture of the vine needs a peaceful, settled population, as the plants require several years' care before bearing fruit (Zeph 1[13]), and constant attention if they are to maintain their excellence; hence to sit under one's 'own vine and fig tree' was a favourite image of peace (1 K 4[25], Mic 4[4], Zec 3[10]). In some districts to-day vines are trained over a trellis at the front door, making a cool summer resort. The Israelites found Palestine ready planted with vineyards (Dt 6[11], Jos 24[13], Neh 9[25]). The steps taken in making a vineyard are described in detail in Is 5[1-7]. The land must be fenced (cf Ps 80[9]), the stones gathered out, the choicest possible plants obtained. A **winepress** was cut in the rock, and a **watch tower** (Is 5[2], Mt 21[33]) was built to guard against intruders. These last included foxes (or jackals) (Ca 2[15]) and boars (Ps 80[13]). In such a tower the owner's family will probably pass all the grape season; during the vintage a large proportion of the people are to be found living in the vineyards. Every spring the soil between the vines must be dug or ploughed up and the plants pruned (Lv 25[3f], Is 5[6]); neglect of this leads to rapid deterioration of the grapes; only the slothful man could permit his vineyard to be overgrown with 'thorns and nettles' and 'the stone wall thereof to be broken down' Pr 24[30f]). The clusters of **grapes** are often enormous (cf Nu 13[23]). When the vintage is over and the leaves turn sere and yellow, the vineyards have a very desolate look (Is 34[4]). The failure of the **vintage** was looked upon as one of God's terrible punishments (Ps 78^{47}, Jer 8^{13}, Hab 3^{17}), and a successful and prolonged vintage as a sign of blessing (Lv 26^{5}). Of the vast quantities of grapes produced in ancient times a large proportion was, without doubt, converted into *dibs* (Arabic) or **grape honey** (cf Heb. *dᵉbhash* = ' honey '), a form of thick, intensely sweet grape juice, which is still made in considerable quantity in Syria, but which must have been much more important in the days when cane sugar was unknown. Many references to ' honey ' probably refer to this product rather than to that of the bee.

Israel is compared to a vine in Ezk 15, 17, Is 5, and Ps 80. The vine-leaf was a favourite design on Jewish coins. The numerous references to the vine in the NT (*e.g.* Mt 20^{1ff} $21^{28, 33ff}$, Jn 15) point to the continued importance of viticulture in those days.

Vine of Sodom (Dt 32^{32}).—If the reference is to any particular plant—which is very doubtful—the most probable is the colocynth (*Citrullus colocynthis*); see Gourd. The apple-sized fruit of the curious *'osher* (*Calotropis procera*) has been suggested; but though this answers well to the description by Josephus (*BJ* iv. viii. 4 [484]) of the ' fruits of Sodom ' which vanish into ashes, so substantial a tree, with its cork-like bark and large glossy leaves, could in no sense be called a vine.

E. W. G. M.—**B. J. R.**

VINEGAR.—The light wine of Bible times, in consequence of the primitive methods of manufacture then in vogue (for which see Wine and Strong Drink), turned sour much more rapidly than modern wines. In this condition it was termed *ḥōmeṣ* (literally ' sour [stuff] '), and was used, mixed with water, as a drink by the peasants (Ru 2^{14} AV and RV; RSV ' wine '). The Nazirite's vow of abstinence included also ' vinegar of wine ' and ' vinegar of strong drink,' *i.e.* of all intoxicating liquor other than grape-wine (Nu 6^{3} AV, RV and RSV). The Jewish *ḥōmeṣ* corresponded to the Roman *posca*, the favourite drink of the soldiers, which those charged with our Lord's crucifixion offered Him on the cross—EV ' vinegar ' (Jn 12^{29f}, but not Mt 27^{34}; see RV and RSV). A. R. S. K.

VIOL.—See Music, etc., **4** (1) (*b*).

VIOLET.—See Colours, **5.**

VIPER.—See Serpent.

VIRGIN, an unmarried girl, is in Hebrew *bᵉthûlāh* (fifty times). EV usually translate ' virgin,' sometimes ' maid ' or ' maiden.' In Jl 1^{8} the word is used of a young widow. The importance of virginity in a bride was stressed (Dt 22^{13f}; cf Gn 24^{16}) and in Dt 22^{25-29} there are laws for the protection of virgins. The word is used of countries, sometimes with the addition of ' daughter,' *e.g.* Israel (Am 5^{2}, Jer 18^{13}), Zion (2 K 19^{21}, La 2^{13}), Babylon (Is 47^{1}), Egypt (Jer 46^{11}). A less frequent word is *'almāh* (only Gn 24^{43}, Ex 2^{8}, Ps 68^{25}, Pr 30^{19}, Ca 1^{3}, 6^{8}, Is 7^{14}). AV renders ' virgin(s) ' in Genesis, Canticles, and Isaiah; RV in Canticles and Isaiah (RVm ' maidens '), but RSV only in Is 7^{14} (RSVm; text ' young woman '). Rebekah (Gn $24^{16, 43}$) is called both *bᵉthûlāh* and *'almāh*, but it does not appear that *'almāh* always implied virginity. The root meaning is probably ' to be (sexually) mature,' hence ' a girl of marriageable age,' and in one Aramaic dialect the word is used of prostitutes. LXX has *parthenos* (' virgin ') in Is 7^{14}, but later translations substituted *neanis* (' young woman '). For further discussion see Immanuel. The NT use of *parthenos* (RSV ' maiden(s) ' in Mt 25^{1-11}) is straightforward, except that in Rev 14^{4} it is used of men, probably implying chastity (RSV), not celibacy; cf 2 Co 11^{2}. Ac 21^{9} may be the scriptural basis of the later ' order ' of virgins. For **Virgin birth**, see Mary, **4**, Immanuel, **5**, Jesus Christ, **5** (3). C. W. E.—**C. R. N.**

VIRTUE.—In Mk 5^{30}, Lk 6^{19} 8^{46} (AV) the word ' virtue ' is used with the antiquated meaning of ' power,' or ' powerful influence ' (Gr. *dynamis*). RV and RSV read ' power.'

VISION.—1. In OT.—The usual Hebrew terms are *ḥāzôn* and *mar'eh*, but the verb *ḥāzāh*, from which the former comes, frequently has as its object *word* (Is 2^{1}, Am 1^{1}, Mic 1^{1}) or *oracle* (Is 13^{1}, Hab 1^{1}), suggesting that it had something of the double sense of the English *observe*. Through the vision the prophet felt himself admitted to the secrets of God (Am 3^{7}) or transported to the very council of God (Jer $23^{18, 22}$). It is often difficult to tell whether the vision came through an objective or a purely subjective experience, though in either case it involved Divine activity on the spirit of the seer (cf Is 6^{1ff} and Jer 1^{11ff}, Am 7^{7ff} 8^{1ff}). Frequently the vision is associated with the **dream** (q.v.), but it is always the medium of a Divine communication (cf Nu 12^{6}). Where vision and dream are mentioned together, the dream is rather the *form* and the vision the *substance* of the communication (cf Dn 1^{17} 2^{28} 4^{5}, Jl 2^{28}, 2 Mac 15^{11ff}). In the darkness, when the eye is closed (cf Nu 24^{3} RV; RSV ' opened ') and the natural faculties are suspended by sleep, God speaks to men (cf ' visions of the night,' Dn 2^{19}, Job 4^{13}, Gn 46^{2}). Prayer and fasting were believed to quicken spiritual discernment (Dn 10^{2-9}; cf Ac 10^{9-11}).

The content of the visions of the pre-exilic prophets was always some relevant message of religious and ethical import to contemporary society, reinforcing the constraint which the prophet felt to declare God's word to his fellows. In the book of Daniel the vision is a literary device to disclose in cryptic symbolism future events, or events that were hypothetically future to the persons to whom they were ascribed.

2. In NT.—The usual Greek terms are *optasia* and *horama*; in the book of Revelation *horasis*. Here the vision is always the medium of a revelation to the seer, rather than of a message for men given to him by its means. Paul receives visions in the night (Ac 16^{9} 18^{9}), while Stephen has one by day (Ac 7^{55}). Peter's vision is said to have come to him ' in a trance ' (Gr. ' in ecstasy,' Ac 10^{10} 11^{5}; cf Gn 15^{12} LXX), and Paul has a similar experience (Ac 22^{17}). Paul was apparently subject to visions (2 Co $12^{1, 7}$), and relates an ecstatic experience whose content could not be divulged (2 Co 12^{2ff}). His experience on the road to Damascus (Ac 9^{3ff} 22^{6ff} 26^{12ff}) had for him an objective character (Gal 1^{11ff}, 1 Co 9^{1} 15^{8}), though it was essentially subjective since it was not shared by those who were with him. Visions are recorded in Lk 1, 2, and the term is once applied to the Transfiguration (Mt 17^{9}). In the book of Revelation, as also in 2 Esdras, the vision becomes the literary medium of the disclosure of future events through cryptic symbolism as in Daniel. See also Trance. S. W. G.—**H. H. R.**

VOPHSI —The father of the Naphtalite spy, Nu 13^{14}.

VOWS.—As among most of the peoples of the ancient world, the making of vows was of frequent occurrence among the Israelites. The underlying idea in making a vow was to propitiate the Deity; this was done either by promising to do something for Him, or to please Him by the exercise of self-denial. Vows were made from a variety of motives: Jacob vows a vow according to which he will please Yahweh by becoming His worshipper, on condition that Yahweh will keep him safe during his journey and give him food and raiment (Gn 28^{20-22}). Jephthah vows to offer to Yahweh the first person he sees coming out of his house on his return from battle, provided he is victorious (Jg 11^{30f}). Hannah vows that if Yahweh gives her a son, she will dedicate him to the service of God (1 S 1^{11}). These cases are typical: in each something is promised to God, on condition that God will do something for him who makes the vow. But there was another class of vows which were of a more disinterested character, such as the vow of the Rechabites (q.v.) to abstain from wine. The most striking case here is the **Nazirite** vow, according to which a man undertook to lead a strenuously austere life, which was supposed to approximate to the simple life of the patriarchs; that was done out of protest against the current mode of life, which had been largely adopted from the Canaanites; indeed, the Nazarite vow implied, and was intended to be, a life of greater loyalty to Yahweh (see NAZIRITE).

There are two words in Hebrew for a vow—though they do not necessarily correspond to the two ideas just mentioned: *nedher*, which is a vow whereby a man dedicates something, even himself, to God; *'issar*, a vow by which a man binds himself to abstain from enjoyment, or to exercise self-denial, in honour of Yahweh.

Vows were clearly of very common occurrence in Israel; indeed it would almost seem as though at one time it was deemed generally incumbent on men to make vows; this would, at all events, explain the words in Dt 23[22], 'But if you refrain from vowing, it shall be no sin in thee.' A vow having once been made had to be kept at all costs (Dt 23[21, 23], Nu 30[2], Jg 11[35]); though, as regards women, they might be absolved by father or husband, under certain conditions, from fulfilling a vow (Nu 30[1-8]). Persons vowed to God might be redeemed (Lv 27[2ff]), as could unclean beasts (27[11ff]) or houses and fields (27[14ff]); but clean beasts could not be redeemed (27[9f]). From the expression used in connexion with the making of a vow, 'to bind the soul' (Nu 30[2]), it would seem that the idea was that if the vow was broken the life was forfeited to the Deity to whom the vow had been made; the warning, therefore, of Pr 20[25], Ec 5[4f], was needed.

In making a vow in which something was promised to Yahweh, only such things could be promised as were truly the property of him who vowed; for this reason a man might not promise a firstling or the like, as that was already the property of Yahweh (cf Lv 27[26-29]).

In later times the spirit in which vows were observed appears to have degenerated; Malachi speaks sternly of those who make a vow, and in fulfilling it sacrifice unto the Lord 'a blemished thing' (1[14]). Another, and still worse, misuse of vows meets us in the Gospels: the spurious piety of some men induced them to vow gifts to the use of the sanctuary, but they neglected, in consequence, the most obvious duties of natural affection; when a man uttered the word '**Corban**' in reference to any possession of his, it meant that it was dedicated to God. Money that should have gone to the support of aged parents was pronounced to be 'Corban,' the son felt himself relieved of all further responsibility regarding his parents, and took honour to himself for having piously dedicated his substance to God (see Mt 15[5], Mk 7[6ff]).

In NT we read that Paul made a vow to abstain from cutting his hair (cf Samson's dedication to be a Nazirite, Jg 13[5, 7]) for a period (Ac 18[18]; cf 21[23f]).

A special collective vow of destruction of enemy persons and property was sometimes made in war (see BAN). W. O. E. O.—**H. H. R.**

VULGATE.—1. The position of the Latin Vulgate, as a version of the original texts of the Bible, has been dealt with in the two articles on the Text of the OT and the NT. But its interest and importance do not end there. Just as the LXX, apart from its importance as evidence for the text of the OT, has a history as an integral part of the Bible of the Eastern Church, so also does the Vulgate deserve consideration as the Bible of the Church in the West. Although the English Bible, to which we have been accustomed for more than 300 years, is in the main a translation from the original Hebrew and Greek, it must be remembered that for the first thousand years of the English Church the Bible of this country, whether in Latin or in English, was the Vulgate. In Germany the conditions were much the same, with the difference that Luther's Bible was still more indebted to the Vulgate than was our AV; while in France, Italy, and Spain the supremacy of the Vulgate lasts to this day. In considering, therefore, the history of the Vulgate, we are considering the history of the Scriptures in the form in which they have been mainly known in Western Europe.

2. The textual articles above-mentioned have shown that, when **Jerome's** Biblical labours were at an end, about A.D. 404, the Latin Bible as left by him was a very complex structure, the parts of which differed very considerably in their relations to the original Greek and Hebrew texts. The Canonical Books of the OT, except the Psalms, were Jerome's fresh translation from the Massoretic Hebrew. The Psalms were extant in three forms—(*a*) the *Roman*, Jerome's slightly revised edition of the OL, which still held its own in a few churches; (*b*) the *Gallican*, his more fully revised version from the Hexaplar text of the LXX; and (*c*) the *Hebrew*, his new translation of the Massoretic text; of these it was the second, not the third, that was taken into general use. Of the deutero-canonical books, or Apocrypha, Judith and Tobit, with the additions to Daniel, were in Jerome's very hasty version; the remainder, which he had refused to touch (as not recognized by the Massoretic canon), continued to circulate in the OL. The Gospels were Jerome's somewhat conservative revision of the OL; the rest of the NT was a much more superficial revision of the same. The Latin Bible, therefore, which we know as the Vulgate was not wholly Jerome's work, still less did it represent his full and final views on the textual criticism of the Bible; and, naturally, it did not for a long time acquire the name of 'Vulgate.' The 'vulgata editio,' of which Jerome himself speaks, is primarily the Greek LXX, and secondarily the OL as a translation of it. It is not until the 13th cent. that the epithet is found applied to Jerome's version by Roger Bacon (who, however, also uses it of the LXX); and it was canonized, so to speak, by its use in the decree of the Council of Trent, which speaks of it as 'haec ipsa vetus et vulgata editio.' By that time, however, it differed in many points of detail from the text which Jerome left behind him; and it is of the history of Jerome's version during this period of some twelve hundred years that it is proposed to speak in the present article.

3. Jerome's correspondence and the prefaces attached by him to the several books of his translation (notably those prefixed to the Pentateuch, Joshua, Ezra and Nehemiah, Job, Isaiah, and the Gospels) sufficiently show the reception given to his work by his contemporaries. He complains constantly and bitterly of the virulence of his critics, who charge him with deliberate perversions of Scripture, and refuse to make themselves acquainted with the conditions of his task. Especially was this the case with the OT. In the NT Jerome had restrained his correcting pen, and made alterations only when the sense required it ['Ita calamo temperavimus ut his tantum quae sensum videbantur mutare correctis, reliqua manere pateremur ut fuerant' (*Praef. ad Damasum*)]; and though even these were sufficient to cause discontent among many readers, the openings given to adverse criticism were relatively insignificant. But in the case of the OT the basis of the OL rendering to which people were accustomed was the LXX, the differences of which from the Massoretic Hebrew are often very wide. When, therefore, readers found whole passages omitted or transposed, and the meanings of very many sentences altered beyond all recognition, they believed that violence was being done to the sacred text; nor were they prepared to admit as axiomatic the superiority of the Hebrew text to the Greek, the OT of the Jews to the OT of the Christians. Even Augustine, who recommended and used Jerome's revision of the Gospels, questioned the expediency of the far-reaching changes made in the OT.

4. Nor was Jerome's translation assisted by authority to oust its predecessor. Never until 1546 was it officially adopted by the Roman Church to the exclusion of all rivals. It is true that the revision of the Gospels was undertaken at the instance of Pope Damasus, and was published under the sanction of his name; and the Gallican version of the Psalms was quickly and generally adopted. But the new translation of the OT from the Hebrew had no such shadow of official authority. It was an independent venture of Jerome's, encouraged by his personal friends (among whom were some bishops), and deriving weight from his reputation as a scholar and from the success of his previous work, but in no sense officially commissioned or officially adopted. It was thrown on the world to win its way by its own merits, with the strong weight of popular prejudice against it, and dependent for its success on the admission of its fundamental critical assumption of the superiority of the Massoretic Hebrew to the LXX. It is not to be wondered at if its progress in general favour was slow, and if its text was greatly modified before it reached the stage of universal acceptance.

5. The extant evidence (consisting of occasional statements by ecclesiastical writers, and their ascertainable practice in Biblical quotations) is not sufficient to enable us to trace in detail the acceptance of Jerome's version in the various Latin-speaking countries. Gaul, as it was the first country to adopt his second Psalter, was also the first to accept the Vulgate as a whole, and in the 5th cent. the use of it appears to have been general there; but Gaul, it must be remembered, from the point of view of Christian literature, was at this time confined mainly to the provinces of the extreme south. Isidore of Seville, however, testifies to the general use of the Vulgate by all churches, as being alike more faithful and more lucid than its predecessors. In the 6th cent. it is probable that its use was general among scholars. Victor of Capua, about A.D. 541, finding a Latin version of the Diatessaron according to the OL text, and being desirous of making it generally known, had it transcribed, with the substitution of the Vulgate for the OL. Gregory the Great († A.D. 604) used the Vulgate as the basis of his commentary on Job, but speaks of both versions as existing and recognized by the Church ('Novam translationem dissero, sed, ut comprobationis causa exigit, nunc novam nunc veterem per testimonia assumo; ut, quia sedes Apostolica utraque utitur, mei quoque labor studii ex utraque fulciatur'). On the other hand, Primasius is evidence of the continued use of the OL in Africa and a considerable number of the extant fragments of OL MSS are of the 6th cent. or later date (see TEXT OF NT, **20**). In general it is probable that the old version was retained by the common people, and by such of the clergy as took little interest in questions of textual scholarship, long after it had been abandoned by scholars. In any case, it is certain that the Vulgate was never officially adopted in early times by the Roman Church, but made its way gradually by its own merits. The continuance of the OL in secluded districts is illustrated by the fact that Codex Colbertinus (*c* of the Gospels) was written as late as the 12th cent. in Languedoc, and Codex Gigas (*g* of the Acts) in the 13th cent. in Bohemia.

6. Although this method of official non-interference was probably necessary, in view of the fact that Jerome's version of the OT was a private venture, and one which provoked much hostile criticism, and although in the end the new translation gained the credit of a complete victory on its merits as the superior version for general use, nevertheless the price of these advantages was heavy. If the Vulgate had enjoyed from the first the protection of an official sanction, which Sixtus and Clement ultimately gave to the printed text, it would have come down to us in a much purer form than is actually the case. Under the actual conditions, it was peculiarly exposed to corruption, both by the ordinary mistakes of scribes and by contamination with the familiar OL. In some cases whole books or chapters in a Vulgate MS contain an OL text; for some reason which is quite obscure, Matthew especially tended to remain in the earlier form. Thus Codices g^1, *h*, r^2 all have Matthew in OL, and the remaining Gospels in Vulgate. Codex Gigas is OL in Acts and Apocalypse, Vulgate in the rest of the Bible. Codex *p* of the Acts is OL in Ac 1^1–13^6 28^{16-30}, while the rest of the book is Vulgate. Codices ff^1 and g^2 of the Gospels have texts in which OL and Vulgate are mixed in various proportions. Even where OL elements do not enter to a sufficient extent to be noteworthy, MSS of the Vulgate tend to differ very considerably. In the absence of any central authority to exercise control, scribes treated the text with freedom or with carelessness, and different types of text grew up in the different countries of Western Europe. It is with these different national texts that the history of the Vulgate in the Middle Ages is principally concerned.

7. During the 5th and 6th cents., when Jerome's version was winning its way outwards from the centre of the Latin-speaking Church, the conditions over a large part of Western Europe were ill fitted for its reception. Gaul in the 5th cent., was fully occupied with the effort first to oppose and then to assimilate the heathen Frankish invaders; and even in the 6th cent. it was a scene of almost perpetual war and internal struggles. Germany was almost wholly pagan. Britain was in the throes of the English conquest, and the ancient British Church was submerged, except in Wales and Ireland. Outside Italy, only Visigothic Spain (Arian, but still Christian, until about A.D. 596) and Celtic Ireland were freely open at first to the access of the Scriptures; and in these two countries (cut off, as they subsequently were, from central Christendom by the Moorish invasion of Spain and the English conquest of Britain) the two principal types of text came into being, which, in various combinations with purer texts from Italy, are found in the different MSS which have come down to the present day. From the Visigothic kingdom the Spanish influences made their way northward into the heart of France. Irish missionaries carried the Bible first into southern Scotland, then into Northumbria, then into northern France and up the Rhine into Germany, penetrating even into Switzerland and Italy, and leaving traces of their handiwork in MSS produced in all these countries. Meanwhile Rome was a constant centre of attraction and influence; and to and from Italy there was an unceasing stream of travellers, and not least between Italy and distant Britain. These historical facts find their illustration in the Vulgate MSS still extant, which can be connected with the various churches.

8. In the 6th and 7th cents. the primacy of missionary zeal and Christian enterprise rested with the Irish Church; but in the latter part of the 7th and the first half of the 8th cents. the Church of Northumbria sprang into prominence, and added to the gifts which it had received from Iona a spirit of Christian scholarship which gave it for a time the first place in Christendom in this respect. In the production of this scholarship the arrival of Theodore of Tarsus as archbishop of Canterbury in A.D. 669 happily co-operated, if it was not a chief stimulus; for Theodore and his companions brought with them from Italy copies of the Latin Bible in a purer text than Ireland had been able to provide. There is clear evidence to show that the celebrated Lindisfarne Gospels (Y in Wordsworth's numeration) was copied from one of these MSS, and the same was probably the case with another Northern copy of the Gospels now in the British Museum (Royal 1 B vii.). The great Codex Amiatinus (A) itself, the best single MS of the Latin Bible in existence, was written in Northumbria before A.D. 716, and must have been copied from MSS brought from Italy either by Theodore or by Ceolfrid of Jarrow, by whose order it was made. Other MSS (notably Δ and S), written in the north, are closely akin to these, and must be derived from the same source; and this whole group of MSS furnishes the best text of the Vulgate now available. The centres of English scholarship, to which this pre-eminence in Biblical study was due, were the twin monasteries of Wearmouth and Jarrow, of which the most famous members were Ceolfrid and Bede; but their influence spread widely over Northumbria, and was renowned in the more distant parts of England and western Europe.

9. To this renown it was due that, when a king at last arose in France with a desire to improve the religious education of his country, he turned to Northumbria for the necessary assistance to carry out the reform. The king was Charlemagne, and the scholar whom he invited to help him was **Alcuin** of York; and the record of their joint achievement constitutes the next chapter in the history of the Vulgate. Alcuin came to France in A.D. 781, and was made master of the schools attached to Charlemagne's court at Aix-la-Chapelle (Aachen). He was subsequently made titular abbot of Tours, and in A.D. 796 he obtained leave to retire to that monastery, where he spent the nine remaining years of his life († A.D. 805) in establishing the school of calligraphy for which Tours was long famous. His work in connexion with the Latin Bible falls into two stages. To the earlier part of his life at Aix belongs, in all probability, the beginning of a series of magnificent copies of the Gospels, of which several have survived to the present day. Certainly, they date from about this period, and have their home in the country of the Rhine and the Moselle. They are obviously modelled on the Anglo-Celtic MSS, of which the Lindisfarne Gospels is the most eminent example. Prefixed to each Gospel is a portrait of the Evangelist (in the Byzantine style), a full page of elaborate decoration, and another containing the first words of the Gospel in highly ornamental illumination. The English MSS excel their French successors in elaboration and skill of workmanship; but the French books have an added gorgeousness from the lavish use of gold, the whole of the text being written in gold letters, sometimes upon purple vellum. Hence the whole series of these books (the production of which continued through the greater part of the 9th cent.) is often described as the 'Golden Gospels.'

10. The importance of the 'Golden Gospels' group of MSS is artistic rather than textual, and although their dependence upon Anglo-Celtic models is obvious, their connexion with Alcuin personally is only hypothetical. It is otherwise in both respects with another great group of MSS, which are directly due to the commission given by Charlemagne to Alcuin to reform the current text of the Vulgate. About the end of A.D. 796, Alcuin established the school of Tours, and sent to York for MSS to enable him to carry out his work. On Christmas Day of A.D. 801 he presented to the king a complete Bible, carefully revised. Several descendants of this Bible are still in existence, and enable us to judge of Alcuin's work. They differ from the 'Golden Gospels' in being complete Bibles, and in being written in the beautiful small minuscule which at this time, under Charlemagne's influence, superseded the tortured and unsightly script of the Merovingian and Lombardic traditions, and of which Tours was one of the principal homes. The MS which appears most accurately to represent the edition of Alcuin at the present day is the Codex Vallicellianus at Rome (Wordsworth's V); with this Wordsworth and White associate the 'Caroline Bible' (Add. MS 10546 [Wordsworth's K] in the British Museum), and there are some eight or ten other MSS (written mostly at Tours), besides several others containing the Gospels only, which in varying degrees belong to the same group. In text, these MSS naturally show a great affinity to the Northumbrian MSS headed by the Codex Amiatinus, and there is no question that Alcuin introduced into France a far purer text of the Vulgate than any which it had hitherto possessed.

11. Alcuin's attempt, however, was not the only one made in France at this period to reform the current Bible text. Another edition was almost simultaneously produced in western France by **Theodulf,** bishop of Orleans and abbot of Fleury (*c* A.D. 795–821); but its character was very different from that of Alcuin. Theodulf was a Visigoth, probably from Septimania, the large district of southern France which then formed part of the Visigothic kingdom of Spain; and it was to Spain that he looked for materials for his revision of the Latin Bible. The MS which represents his edition most fully (Paris, *Bibl. Nat.* 9380) has a text closely connected with the Spanish type of which the Codices Cavensis and Toletanus are the most prominent examples, except in the Gospels, which are akin rather to the Irish type; and a contemporary hand has added a number of variants, which are often Alcuinian in character. With this MS may be associated a volume at Puy, and Add. MS 24124 in the British Museum, which are closely akin to the Paris MS, but follow sometimes its first and sometimes its second reading; the latter (especially in its corrections) has been used by Wordsworth and White along with the Paris MS to represent the Theodulfian edition. All are written in an extremely minute Caroline minuscule.

12. In spite, however, of the labour spent upon these attempts to improve the current text of the Vulgate, the forces of deterioration were more powerful than those of renovation. Theodulf's edition, which was a private venture, without the advantages of Imperial patronage, had no wide sphere of influence, and left no permanent mark on the text of the Vulgate. Alcuin's had, no doubt, much greater authority and effect; yet its influence was only transient, and even at Tours itself the MSS produced within the next two generations show a progressive departure from his standard. On the other hand, the study of the Scriptures was now definitely implanted on the Continent, and the number of copies of them produced in France and Germany shows a great increase. During the 9th cent. splendid copies of the 'Golden Gospels' continued to be produced in the valley of the Rhine, and Alcuinian texts at Tours; while a new centre of Scripture study and reproduction came into existence in Switzerland, at the famous abbey of **St. Gall.** The library and scriptorium of this monastery (many of the inmates of which were English or Irish monks) first became notable under abbot Gozbert (A.D. 816–836), and perhaps reached the height of their importance under abbot Hartmut (A.D. 872–883). Many copies of the Bible were written there, and the influence of St. Gall permeated a large portion of central Europe. Here, too, was produced by Walafridus Strabo, dean of St. Gall before A.D. 842, the original form of the *Glossa Ordinaria*, the standard commentary on the Bible in the Middle Ages.

13. After Alcuin and Theodulf no important effort was made to recover the original text of the Vulgate, though some attempt in this direction was made by Lanfranc, of which no traces seem to survive; but the history of its diffusion can to some extent be followed by the help of the extant MSS, which now begin to increase greatly in number. The tradition of the 'Golden Gospels' was carried into Germany, where copies of the Gospels were produced on a smaller scale, with less ornamentation, and in a rather heavy Caroline minuscule, which clearly derive their origin from this source. In France itself, too, the later representatives of this school are inferior in size and execution to their predecessors. Spain and Ireland had by this time ceased to be of primary importance in the circulation of Bible texts. In England a new departure was made, on a higher scale of artistic merit, in the fine Gospels and Service-Books produced at Winchester between about A.D. 960 and 1060, the chief characteristics of which are broad bands of gold forming a framework with interlaced foliage. These details, however, relate more to the history of art than to that of the Bible, and with regard to the spread of the knowledge of the Scriptures there is nothing of importance to note in the 10th and 11th cents. beyond the increase of monasteries in all the countries of western Europe, in the *scriptoria* of which the multiplication of copies proceeded apace.

14. In the 12th cent. the most noteworthy phenomenon, both in England and on the Continent, is the popularity of annotated copies of the various books of the Bible. The ordinary arrangement is for the Bible text to occupy a single narrow column down the centre of the page, while on either side of it is the commentary; but where the commentary is scanty, the Biblical column expands to fill the space, and *vice versa.* The main staple of the commentary is normally the *Glossa Ordinaria*; but this, being itself a compilation of extracts from pre-existing commentaries (Jerome, Augustine, Isidore, Bede, etc.), lent itself readily to expansion or contraction, so that different MSS differ not inconsiderably in their contents. The various books of the Bible generally form separate MSS, or small groups of them are combined. Simultaneously with these, some very large Bibles were produced, handsomely decorated with illuminated initials. Of these the best examples come from England or northern France. These are of the nature of *éditions de luxe*, while the copies with commentaries testify to the extent to which the Bible was at this time studied, at any rate in the larger monasteries; and the catalogues of monastic libraries which still exist confirm this impression by showing what a large number of such annotated MSS were preserved in them, no doubt for the study of the monks.

15. A further step in advance was taken in the 13th cent., which is to be attributed apparently to the influence of the **University of Paris,** then at the height of its renown and the intellectual centre of Europe. The present chapter division of the Bible text is said to have been first made by Stephen Langton (archbishop of Canterbury, 1207–1228), while a doctor at Paris; and the 13th cent. (probably under the influence of St. Louis) witnessed a remarkable output of Vulgate MSS of the complete Bible. Hitherto complete Bibles had almost always been very large volumes, suitable only for liturgical use; but by the adoption of very thin vellum and very small writing it was now found possible to compress the whole Bible into volumes of quite moderate size, comparable with the ordinary printed Bibles of to-day. For example, one such volume, containing the whole Bible with ample margins, measures $5\frac{1}{2}\times3\frac{1}{2}\times1\frac{3}{4}$ inches, and consists of 471 leaves. From the appearance of these Bibles (hundreds of which are still extant) it is evident that they were intended for private use, and they testify to a remarkable growth in the personal study of the Scriptures. The texts of these MSS seem to embody the results of a revision at the hands of the Paris doctors. *Correctoria*, or collections of improved readings, were issued at Paris about 1230, and at other places during this century, the best being the 'Correctorium Vaticanum,' so called from a MS in the Vatican Library. This revision, however, was superficial rather than scientific, and is of importance in the history of the Vulgate mainly because it established the normal text which was current at the time of the invention of printing. These small Bibles were produced almost as plentifully in England as in France, and in an identical style, which continued well into the 14th cent.

16. After the Parisian revision of the 13th cent. no important modification of the text or status of the Latin Bible took place until **the invention of printing** two centuries later. The first book to be printed in Europe was the Latin Bible, published in 1456 by Gutenberg and Fust (now popularly known as the Mazarin Bible, from the circumstance that the first copy of it to attract notice in modern times was that in the library of Cardinal Mazarin). In type this Bible resembles the contemporary large German Bible MSS; in text it is the ordinary Vulgate of the 15th cent. During the next century Bibles poured from the press, but with little or no attempt at revision of the text. Some MSS were consulted in the preparation of the Complutensian Polyglot; but the only editions before the middle of the 16th cent. which deserve the name of critical are those of Stephanus in 1540 and Hentenius in 1547, which laid the foundations of the modern printed Vulgate. It is, however, to the action of the **Council of Trent** that the genesis of an authorized text is ultimately due. Soon after its meeting, in 1546, a decree was passed declaring that the 'vetus et vulgata editio' of the Scriptures was to be accepted as authentic, and that it should be printed in the most accurate form possible. It was forty years, however, before this decree bore fruit. **Sixtus V.**, in his short pontificate of five years (1585–90), not only caused the production of an edition of the Greek OT (1587), but in 1590 issued a Latin Bible which he declared was to be accepted as the authentic edition demanded by the Council of Trent. This edition was the work of a board of revisers appointed for the purpose, but Sixtus himself examined their results before they were published, and introduced a large number of alterations (rarely for the better) on his own authority. The Sixtine edition, however, had hardly been issued when it was recalled in 1592 by **Clement VIII.**, at the instance, it is believed, of the Jesuits, with whom Sixtus had quarrelled; and in the same year a new edition was issued under the authority of Clement, with a preface by the famous Jesuit Bellarmine, in which (to avoid the appearance of a conflict between Popes) the suppression of the Sixtine edition is falsely stated to be due to the abundance in it of printers' errors, and to have been contemplated by Sixtus himself. The Clementine revisers in many instances restored the readings of Sixtus' board, which Sixtus himself had altered; and the general result of their labours was to produce a text resembling that of Hentenius, while the Sixtine edition was nearer to that of Stephanus. The bull in which the Clementine edition was promulgated forbade any future alteration of the text and any printing of various readings in the margin, and thereby stereotyped the official text of the Vulgate from that day until this.

17. Clement's bull practically closed the textual criticism of the Vulgate in the Roman Church, though Vallarsi was able to print a new text in his edition of the works of St. Jerome in 1734, and Vercellone published a collection of various readings in 1860–1864. The course of criticism outside the Roman communion can be briefly sketched. Bentley, with the help of his assistants, made large collections for an edition of the Vulgate, but was unable to carry through his task. Lachmann, in the second edition of his Greek NT (1842–1850), added a text of the Vulgate, based on a collation of the Codex Amiatinus and a few other selected MSS. Corssen in 1885 printed a revised text of Galatians as a sample of a new NT, but carried his enterprise no further. The Oxford edition of Wordsworth and White (1889–1954) gives a revised text of the Vulgate NT with a full critical apparatus and introductions; and the very handy *Editio Minor* (1911) reprints the text with a much abbreviated apparatus. In 1907 Pope Pius x. entrusted the Benedictine order with the revision of the whole Bible: Genesis was published in 1926 and the latest part to appear is the eleventh (containing Proverbs, Ecclesiastes, and the Song of Songs), published in 1957. Like Wordsworth and White's larger Oxford edition, the Roman edition offers, not only a revised text, but also a full critical apparatus. F. G. K.—**H. F. D. S.**

VULTURE.—1. *dā'āh*, Lv 11^{14} (AV; RV and RSV 'kite'); *dayyāh*, Dt 14^{13} (AV; RV 'kite,' RSV 'buzzard'), Is 34^{15} (AV; RV and RSV 'kite'). See Kite. **2.** *'ayyāh*, Job 28^{7} (AV; RV and RSV 'falcon'). In Lv 11^{14} the same word is rendered by 'kite' in AV, 'falcon' in RV and RSV, while in Dt 14^{13} it is rendered by 'kite' in AV and RSV, and by 'falcon' in RV. See Kite. **3.** *peres*, Dt 14^{12} RSV; AV 'ossifrage,' RV 'gier eagle.' In Lv 11^{13} AV and RSV have 'ossifrage,' RV 'gier eagle.' See Gier Eagle. **4.** *rāḥām* (*rāḥāmāh*), Lv 11^{18} RV and RSV; AV 'gier eagle.' In Dt 14^{17} RV has 'vulture,' RSV 'carrion vulture,' and AV 'gier eagle.' See Gier Eagle. **5.** *ḳā'āth*, Zeph 2^{14} (RSV; AV 'cormorant,' RV 'pelican'), Ps 102^{6} (RSV; AV and RV 'pelican'). In Is 34^{11} RSV has 'hawk,' AV 'cormorant,' and RV 'pelican'; in Lv 11^{18}, Dt 14^{17} AV, RV and RSV all have 'pelican.' See Pelican. **6.** Greek *aetos* in RVm in Mt 24^{28}, Lk 17^{37}. See Eagle.

W

WAFER.—See Bread, end.

WAGES.—Under the conditions of life in Palestine in OT times, work on the land, at all times the chief occupation, was done for the most part by the peasant and his family, assisted, in the case of the well-to-do, by a few slaves. The ' hired servants ' do not seem to have been numerous, and were sometimes aliens. We have no information about the wages of such field-labourers, as compared with the detailed information about different classes of ' hirelings ' in, for example, ancient Mesopotamia and Asia Minor. (See Johns, *Bab. and Assyr. Laws*, ch. xxv, Driver and Miles, *The Assyrian Laws*, pp. 271 ff, E. Neufeld, *The Hittite Laws*, pp. 157, 178.) Dt 15^{18} seems to say that a hireling cost the farmer twice as much as a slave, and since the latter received only his keep and a few clothes, it follows that the former will have earned the equivalent thereof, over and above, in wages. The first definite engagement—disregarding the special case of Jacob and Laban—with stipulated wages, is that of the Levite whom Micah hired as his domestic chaplain for 10 shekels a year, with ' a suit of apparel ' and his ' victuals ' (Jg 17^{10}). The next instance is Tobit's engagement of the angel Raphael as his son's travelling companion for a drachma (worth $\frac{1}{4}$ shekel) a day and all found (To 5^{14}). The story may be taken to reflect social conditions before and after 200 B.C. Dt 24$^{14-15}$ (cf Lv 19^{13}) is designed to protect the ' hired servant ' against the unscrupulous employer who is careless in the payment of wages, which, at least in cases of poverty, are to be paid daily.

In the parable of the Labourers in the Vineyard, the labourers are thus paid immediately after the day's work and each man receives a *denarius*. The denarius may be taken as the usual day's wage for a labourer in NT times. It was a silver coin rather more than $\frac{2}{3}$ the weight of a shilling, roughly equivalent to the drachma. The pay of a Roman legionary was $\frac{5}{8}$ denarius per day. A papyrus of A.D. 66 reveals that an apprentice weaver in Oxyrhynchus received five drachmae for food per month and, at the end of the year, twelve drachmae for clothes. The NT period is overshadowed by the evil of unemployment, particularly after the completion of Herod's Temple, when special public works were undertaken to absorb 18,000 unemployed (Jos. *Ant*. xx. ix. 7 [214]). Something like trade unions were not unknown. Thus in ancient times the whole city of Debir was given over to the weaving industry, presumably because craftsmen and merchants in ancient Palestine were organized in guilds. In a much later time, the Talmud, *Bab. B.* 9, permits tradesmen to combine to work on one or two days only in the week, in order to give sufficient employment to each workman. Details of the conditions of hire and the mutual obligations of master and servant are to be found in the Mishnah (*Baba Metzia* vi and vii).

Throughout the Bible there is an implicit assumption that wages are a proper reward for work done. Jesus gave direct instructions that His disciples, engaged on a mission, were to accept hospitality on the principle that ' the workman deserves his wages ' (Lk 10^{7}). St. Paul accepted this as authoritative direction for the practice of the early Church (1 Co 9^{14}; cf 1 Ti 5^{18}), and taught that Christian apostles had a right to material reward in return for spiritual ministrations (1 Co 9^{11}). This was contrary to the Jewish requirement that a rabbi should practise a trade. Paul and Barnabas in fact worked for their living (Paul having learned the craft of a tent-maker), and some at Corinth objected to the self-imposed freedom which the Apostle exercised in declining the support of the Corinthian church. There appear to have been special reasons why he needed to demonstrate his disinterestedness, and he declined money from any church except the Philippian (4^{15}). He makes it clear that he was waiving a right.

The same word (*misthos*) is used for both wages and reward in both LXX and NT, and, in line with the deuteronomic principle of retribution, becomes the expression both of a blessed reward in heaven (Mt 5^{17} 10^{41f}) and of retribution in the coming judgment. But while Jesus used the conception of wages, he radically transformed it. Wages or reward in the kingdom are, like the wages of the labourers in the vineyard, *not* according to strict justice or human reckoning, but according to Divine grace. The very point of the parable is that the freedom of grace cuts across the operation of the strict principle of retribution. So also St. Paul understood that, while the law of sin and death works ruthlessly and strictly (' the wages, *opsōnion*, of sin is death '), this is the very antithesis of the free grace of Christ (Ro 6^{23}; cf 4^{4}). Thus the idea of wages is used to demonstrate as much the difference as the similarity in the dispensing of rewards in the kingdom of God. The operation of a human right and an inflexible law is set in opposition to the freedom of the Divine sovereignty and love. A. R. S. K.—**D. R. J.**

WAGON.—See Cart, Agriculture, **3.**

WAHEB.—An unknown locality in Amorite territory, Nu 21^{14} (RSV; AVm, RV **Vaheb**); AV renders ' Waheb in Suphah ' by ' What he did in the Red Sea.' See also Dizahab.

WAILING.—See Mourning Customs.

WAIN, THRESHING.—Found only in Job 41^{30} RV, where AV has ' sharp pointed things ' and RSV ' threshing sledge.' See Agriculture, **3.**

WALL, BROAD.—See Jerusalem, Gates of.

WALLET.—See Bag.

WALLS.—In Palestine the principal cities were protected by surrounding walls, sometimes of great size. That of Gezer, for instance, was fourteen feet thick. These walls were built of stones set in mud, or else of brick. The walls of houses were generally ill-built structures of the same materials. The choice of material varied with the locality: Eglon (*Tell el-Ḥesī*), for example, was almost entirely a brick town; in Gezer brick is the exception. See also City, Fortification, House, **4.** For the walls of Jerusalem, which may be taken as typical of a city wall, see Jerusalem.

R. A. S. M.

WALLS, GATE BETWEEN THE TWO.—See Jerusalem, Gates of.

WANTONNESS.—See Lasciviousness.

WAR.—Many Biblical passages (especially in Deuteronomy) are dominated by the idea of the **Holy War**; and the religious character of ancient Israelite warfare is also otherwise clear. Israel's wars were ' the wars of the Lord ' (Nu 21^{14}); the Lord of Hosts was ' the God of the armies of Israel ' (1 S 17^{45} RV, RSV), and to Him belonged of right the population of a conquered city (see Ban)—an idea which explains the ruthless demand for complete destruction of the Canaanites and the other peoples in Palestine before the Conquest (see *e.g.* Dt 20^{16f}, and cf Nu 21^{1ff}, Jg 1^{17}, Dt 2^{34f}, Jos 6 f, 8$^{2, 26f}$). In describing warfare use is made of language familiar from the cult (see *e.g.* Nu 32^{20ff}, Jos 3^{5}); during the campaign the warriors adhered to certain rules of abstinence (cf *e.g.* Jg 20^{26}, 1 S 7^{6} 14^{24} 21^{5}, 2 S 11^{11}); Yahweh's presence was secured by the Ark accompanying the army in the field (2 S 11^{11}; cf 1 S 4^{3ff}). The soldiers were God's 'consecrated ones' (Is 13^{3} RV, RSV), and to open a campaign is in the Hebrew phrase 'to consecrate war' (Jl 3^{9}, Jer 6^{4}, in both of which passages RV and RSV translate by 'prepare'). The religious character of warfare is also evident in the way in which it was usual to 'enquire of the Lord' by means of the sacred lot (Jg 1^{1}, 1 S 23^{2} etc.) or by the mouth of a prophet (1 K 22^{5ff}), *e.g.* in order to ascertain the propitious moment for the start. The practice of anointing or oiling the shield, which is mentioned in Is 21^{5} (cf 2 S 1^{21}) may have a purely practical origin in the wish to make hostile weapons glance off more readily.

2. In the days before the monarchy the wars of the Hebrews were local and battles were fought by the individual tribes. Rarely, as in the case of the campaign against Sisera (Jg 4), was it necessary to summon a larger army from several tribes. From the days of Saul and David, with their long struggle against the Philistines (who were in military respect a highly organized people with superior weapons of iron), war became the affair of the whole nation, leading to the establishment of a **standing army** (cf already 1 S 13^{2} 14^{52}; see ARMY). David had a personal bodyguard (2 S 8^{18}), apart from the regular army (2 S 10^{10}), and archers appear to be in the infantry from about this time. In the reign of Solomon we hear of a complete reorganization of the kingdom (1 K 4^{7}), no doubt with a view, among other things, to the conscription of troops, and cavalry and chariots were introduced.

3. Early spring, after the winter rains had ceased, was 'the time when kings go out to battle' (2 S 11^{1}). The war-horn (EV 'trumpet'), sounded from village to village on the hilltops, was in all periods the call to arms (Jg 6^{34}, 1 S 13^{3}, 2 S 20^{1}). How far the exemptions from military service specified in Dt 20^{5-8} were in force under the kings is unknown; the first express attestation is 1 Mac 3^{56}. The **tactics** of the Hebrew generals were as simple as their strategy. As the army advanced scouts or **spies** were sent out to ascertain the enemy's position and strength (Jos 2^{1}, Jg 1^{24}, 1 S 26^{4}; cf Gideon's exploit, Jg 7^{10ff}). Usually the opposing forces would draw up in a line facing each other. At a given signal each side raised its **battle-cry** (Jg 7^{21}, Am 1^{14}, Jer 4^{19} [EV, in the last-mentioned passage, translate by 'the alarm of war']) as it rushed to the fray. It was a common practice for a general to divide his forces into three divisions (Jg 7^{16}, 1 S 11^{11}, 2 S 18^{2}, 1 Mac 5^{33}). A favourite piece of tactics was to pretend flight, and by leaving a body of men in **ambush**, to fall upon the unwary pursuers in front and rear (Jos 8^{15}, Jg 20^{32}). As examples of more elaborate tactics may be cited Joab's handling of his troops before Rabbath-ammon (2 S 10^{9-11}), and Benhadad's massing of his chariots at the battle of Ramoth-gilead (1 K 22^{31}). The recall was sounded on the war-horn (2 S 2^{28} 18^{16} 20^{22}). The tender mercies of the victors in those days were cruel, although the treatment which the Hebrews meted out to their enemies was, with few exceptions (*e.g.* 2 K 15^{16}), not to be compared to what Benzinger only too aptly describes as 'the Assyrian devilries.' (It should be noted here that 2 S 12^{31} should probably be translated as in RSV, and not as in RV.) The captives were sometimes sold as slaves. A heavy war indemnity or a yearly tribute might be imposed on the conquered people (2 K 3^{4}). The **booty** fell to the victorious soldiery, the leaders receiving a special share (Jg 8^{24ff}, 1 S 30^{26ff}). The men 'that tarried by the stuff,' *i.e.* those who were left behind as a camp-guard, shared equally with their comrades 'who went down to battle' (1 S 30^{24}), a law first introduced by David, but afterwards characteristically assigned to Moses (Nu 31^{27}). The returning warriors were welcomed home by the women with dance and song (Ex 15^{20f}, Jg 11^{34}, 1 S 18^{6f}). As long as the campaign lasted the general and his men would live in tents and booths (cf 2 S 11^{11}, 1 K $20^{12, 16}$), but we know very little of their military **camps**. The obscure term rendered by RV 'place of the wagons,' and by RSV 'encampment' (1 S 17^{20} $26^{5, 7}$) is derived from a root which justifies us in supposing that the Hebrew camps were round rather than square. Of the twenty Assyrian camps represented on the bronze plates of the gates of Balawât, four are circular, fourteen almost square, and two have their long sides straight and short sides curved outwards. Two gates are represented at opposite ends, between which a broad road divides the camp into two almost equal parts (see Billerbeck and Delitzsch, *Die Palasttore Salmanassars*, ii, p. 104). As regards the **commissariat**, the soldiers might receive provisions from friends, cf 2 S 17^{27ff}, or they might live on the booty; the arrangement by which 'ten men out of every hundred' were told 'to bring provisions for the people' (Jg 20^{10}) probably reflects a later development. The night was divided into three watches (Jg 7^{19}, 1 S 11^{11}).

A. R. S. K.—**P. W.-M.**

WARDROBE.—See VESTRY.

WARS OF THE LORD, BOOK OF THE.—A work quoted in Nu 21^{14f} to settle a point with regard to the boundary of Moab and Ammon. The quotations in vv.$^{17f, 27-30}$ are probably from the same original. This is the only mention of the book in the OT. It is not likely that the work is identical with the **Book of Jashar** (q.v.). It probably consisted of a collection of songs celebrating the victories of Israel. The song in Ex 15^{1-19} describing the Lord as 'a man of war' has been thought to be derived from it; also the poem in Jg 5. The date of the book is unknown. If it included Nu 21^{27-30} (cf Jer 48^{45f}), and if that poem refers to the wars of Omri, as some have thought, the collection will not have been completed before the 9th cent. Nu 21^{27-30} may, however, come from the heroic age as Jg 5 does and possibly Ex $15^{1-16, 18}$ (v.^{17} seems to presuppose the existence of the Temple); in this case the collection may have been made much earlier. W. F. B.—**C. A. Si.**

WASHBASIN.—Only Ps 60^{8} 108^{9}, as a figure of contempt. The pot (*sîr*) was also used for boiling (see HOUSE, **9**).

WASHPOT.—See WASHBASIN.

WATCH.—See TIME.

WATCHMAN.—A person who patrolled the streets in the night (Ca 3^{3} 5^{7}; cf Ps 127^{1}) or who was posted on watch duty on the walls of a city (2 S 18^{24}, 2 K 9^{17ff}, Is 62^{6}) or on watchtowers (2 Ch 20^{24}, Hab 2^{1}) or hilltops (Jer 31^{6}).

WATCH TOWER.—See VINE.

WATER.—The scarcity of water in the East lends it a special value. Its presence in some form is essential to life. The fruitfulness of the land depends on the quantity available for watering. The Jordan, with its great springs, is too low for the irrigation of anything but the valley. There are many fountains in Palestine, but most fail in summer. The average annual rainfall approaches 30 inches. But this is confined to the months from April to October; and the water would rush down the slopes to the sea, were it not caught and stored for future use. The limestone formation, with its many caves, made easy the construction of cisterns and reservoirs to collect the rain water: thence supplies were drawn as required during the dry months. Wherever water is found, there is greenery and beauty all through the year. In the Maritime Plain plentiful supplies of water are found on digging (Gn 26^{15ff}). To fill up the wells would make the district uninhabitable. From Egypt to Palestine the Egyptians had a series of wells to ensure the success of their military campaigns, and invading armies were at times reduced to sore straits by the stopping of wells (2 K $3^{19, 25}$), or diversion and concealment of a stream from a fountain (2 Ch 32^{3f}).

The earliest use of water was doubtless to allay the thirst of man and beast. Refusal of drink to a thirsty man would be universally condemned (Gn 24^{17f}, Jn 4^{7}). It is held a meritorious act to set a vessel of water by the wayside for the refreshment of the wayfarer, but already in Biblical times water was sold in the streets (cf Is 55^{1}), and for flocks water must often be purchased (Nu 20^{17ff}, Dt 2^{28}). Use and wont established certain regulations for the watering of animals, infringement of which frequently caused strife (Gn 29^{2ff}, Ex 2^{16ff}; cf Gn 26^{20} etc.). The art of irrigation (q.v.) was employed in ancient days (Ps 1^{3} 65^{10}, Ezk 17^{7} etc.), and reached its fullest development in the Roman period. To this time also belong many ruins of massive aqueducts, leading water to the cities from distant sources.

Cisterns and springs are not common property. Every considerable house has a **cistern** for rain water from roof and adjoining areas. Importance is attached to plunging in the buckets by which the water is drawn up, this preventing stagnation. The springs, and cisterns made in the open country, are the property of the local family or tribe (cf Gn 21^{25f} 26^{15ff}), from whom water, if required in any quantity, must be bought. The mouth of the well is usually covered with a great stone. Drawing water for domestic purposes is the work of women Gn 24^{11}, 1 S 9^{11}, Jn 4^{7}). In crossing the desert water is carried in skins (Gn 21^{14}).

In the various rites of purification water naturally plays an important part, see Ex $30^{18, 21}$ $40^{7, 30ff}$, Lev 11^{32} 14^{8f} 15^{5} etc. A special rite of drawing and pouring out water is mentioned in 1 S 7^{6}; a similar rite is alluded to in Is 12^{3}. According to later Jewish sources water from Siloam was poured out in the Temple at the Sukkoth festival—no doubt a very ancient rite. Water is furnished to wash the feet and hands of a guest (Lk 7^{44}). To pour water on the hands is the office of a servant (2 K 3^{11}).

According to Gn 1 the primeval, chaotic waters were divided (and thus brought under control) by the creation of the firmament, and the fear of water is reflected in many Scripture passages (*e.g.* Is 8^{7} 28^{17}, Jer 47^{2}, Ps 18^{16} 32^{6} 69^{2} 88^{17}.

The living, *i.e.* flowing, water of the **spring** is greatly preferred to the 'dead' water of the cistern, and it stands frequently for the vitalizing influences of God's grace (Jer 2^{13}, Jn 4^{10} etc.). Water is, in fact, alluded to in many Biblical passages in a metaphorical and figurative way, see *e.g.* (apart from some of the passages already mentioned) 2 S 5^{20} 14^{14}, Is $32^{2, 20}$ 58^{11}, Jer 17^{13} 31^{9}, Hos 5^{10} 10^{7}, Ps 23^{2} 36^{9} 46^{4} 58^{7} 63^{1} 66^{12} 79^{3}, Job 11^{16} 14^{11} 15^{16} 22^{11} 27^{20}, Pr 5^{15} 9^{17} 18^{4} 20^{5} 25^{25}. As for the abundance of water in the Messianic Age, see Is 30^{25} 35^{6f} 41^{18} 49^{10}, Jer 31^{9}, Ezk 47, Zech 14^{8}. See also City; Jerusalem, I. **2**, **4**. For 'water-gate' see Jerusalem, Gates of. W. E.—**P. W.-M.**

WATER HEN, Lv 11^{18}, Dt 14^{16} (RSV).—See Owl.

WATER OF BITTERNESS.—See Jealousy.

WATER OF SEPARATION.—See Red Heifer.

WATERPOTS.—See House, **9.**

WATERSPOUTS.—Only Ps 42^{7} AV and RV, 'Deep calleth unto deep at the noise of thy waterspouts' (RVm, RSV 'cataracts'). The reference is probably to the numerous noisy waterfalls in a stream swollen by the melting of the snow.

WAVE-BREAST, WAVE-OFFERING.—See Sacrifice, **2** (13), **12.**

WAW.—See Vau.

WAX.—See Education; Writing, **8.**

WAY.—1. OT usage.—(*a*) Of a road or journey (1 S 6^{9}, 2 K 3^{8}, Jer 2^{17}). (*b*) Figuratively, of a course of conduct or character (Job 17^{9} 22^{15}), either in a good sense as approved by God (Dt 31^{29}, Ps 50^{23}, Is 30^{21}), or in a bad sense of man's own choosing (Ps 139^{24}, Is 65^{2}, Jer 18^{11}). (*c*) Of the way of the Lord (AV), His creative power (Job 26^{14}), His moral rule and commandments (Job 21^{14}, Ps 18^{30}, Pr 8^{32}).

2. NT usage.—(*a*) In the literal sense (Mt 2^{12}, Lk 17^{11}, Ac 25^{3}). (*b*) Figuratively, as in OT of human conduct, or God's purpose for man (Mt 21^{32}, Ja 5^{20}). But the gospel greatly enriched the ethical and religious import of the word. Though Jesus was addressed as one who taught 'the way of God in truth' (Mt 22^{16}), He Himself claimed to show the way to the Father because He is 'the Way, the Truth, and the Life' (Jn 14^{4ff}). By Him 'the two worlds were united' (Westcott). This is equivalent to the Apostolic doctrine that Christ is the Gospel (Mk 1^{1}, Ro 15^{19}). In He 9^{8} 10^{20} there is the similar thought that Jesus by His life, death, and exaltation has opened a way whereby men may enter into the holy presence of God, and enables them also to walk therein. In Acts 'the Way' is used with the distinctive meaning of the Christian faith and manner of life, which is the only 'way' that leads to salvation (9^{2} $19^{9, 23}$ 24^{22}). This is the 'way of the Lord' so often referred to in the OT, of which Jesus became the final and perfect revealer. The development of the conception may be traced in Ac 16^{17} 18^{25f}. In Hellenistic and ancient Jewish literature the term was used of moral behaviour, a 'way of life': see Prodicus's Choice of Heracles (in Xenophon, *Memorabilia,* II. i. 21–34) and the Two Ways in the *Didache*, ch. 1 ff. R. A. F.—**F. W. G.**

WAYMARK.—In Jer 31^{21} 'virgin Israel' is called on to set up waymarks and make guideposts to mark the way for the returning exiles. The Hebrew word translated 'waymark' apparently means a small stone pillar, similar to our milestones, with an indication of routes and distances.

WEALTH.—1. Palestine is described in Dt 8^{7-9} as rich not only in cereal but also in mineral wealth. Recent excavations have shown that this is not a poetic description but simple truth. (See Trade and Commerce.) It is also frequently spoken of as 'flowing with milk and honey' (Ex 3^{8} etc.)—products which were in ancient times considered the marks of fertile lands. The wealth of Israel increased as the country developed; and under the monarchy it reached its height. The increased prosperity did not, however, lead to increased righteousness. If in the times of Isaiah the land was 'full of silver and gold,' it was also 'full of idols' (Is 2^{7f}): the ruling classes oppressed the poor (5^{8}, Mic 2^{2}), drunkenness (Is 5^{11}, Mic 2^{11}) and audacity of sin (Is 5^{18}) were rampant. The national poverty that followed upon the Exile had been removed before the birth of our Lord, as exemplified by the magnificent buildings of Herod. Throughout the OT and NT many instances of wealthy individuals occur: *e.g.* Abram (Gn 13^{2}), Nabal (1 S 25^{2}), Barzillai (2 S 19^{32}), Zacchaeus (Lk 19^{2}), Joseph of Arimathaea (Mt 27^{57}).

2. In the OT the possession of wealth is generally regarded as evidence of God's blessing and so of righteousness (Ps 1^{3f} etc.). In early Israel, blessing consisted primarily in the power of fertility, fertility in the family, the field, and the herd (cf Abraham, Gn 24^{35}), and this posed no urgent problem for faith. By the 9th cent., but more clearly in the 8th cent., the existence of wealth in the hands of unscrupulous rich men created a *social* problem which evoked prophetic denunciation. Accordingly rich men are again and again bad men (Am 2^{6f}, Is 1^{23} 31^{4f}, Pss 37, 49, 73). It became a *problem of faith* demanding theodicy in Jer 12, but especially in the Wisdom literature. Proverbs and Ecclesiasticus maintain the strict connexion between righteousness and blessing. Ecclesiastes is haunted by the vanity of riches in the perspective of life and death. The profoundest discussions (Ps 73, Job) lead to a humble and total trust in the Living God, despite the manifest disconnexion between wealth and righteousness. In the Book of Wisdom, the ungodly rich will be discomfited when they behold the immortality of the righteous (cf especially 5^{1-8}, 'What good has our boasted wealth brought us?'). In the NT full belief in a future life and the expectation of the imminent return of the Lord take the acid out of the problem. Nevertheless some connexion between righteousness and well-being is reaffirmed (1 Ti 4^{8}, cf Mt 6^{33}, Mk 10^{30}), while the necessity of complete detachment from wealth is repeatedly enforced.

3. *Our Lord's position regarding wealth* must be deduced from His practice and teaching. As regards His *practice*, it is clear that, until He commenced His ministry, He obtained His livelihood by labour, toiling as a carpenter in Nazareth (Mk 6^{3}). During His ministry, He and the Twelve formed a family with a common purse. This store, composed, no doubt, of the personal property of those of their number who originally had wealth, was replenished by gifts of attached disciples (Lk 8^{2f}). From it necessary food was purchased and the poor were relieved (Jn 4^{8} 13^{29}). Christ and His Apostles as a band, therefore, owned private property. When our Lord dispatched the Twelve on a special tour for preaching and healing, and when He sent the Seventy on a similar errand, He commanded them to take with them neither money nor food (Mt 10^{10}, Lk 10^{4}); but these were special instructions on special occasions, and doubtless on their return to Him the former system of a common purse was reverted to (cf Lk 22^{36}).

As regards Christ's *teaching*, it is important to balance those sayings which appear to be hostile to any possession of wealth, with those which point in the other direction. On the one hand, we find Him bidding a rich young man sell his all and give to the poor (Mk 10^{21}), and then telling His disciples that it is easier for a camel to go through a needle's eye than for a rich man to enter the Kingdom of God. He pictures a possessor of increasing wealth hearing God say, 'Fool! This night your soul is required of you' (Lk 12^{20}); He follows beyond the grave the histories of a rich man and a beggar, placing the rich man in a 'place of torment' and the poor man in Abraham's bosom (Lk 16^{19f}). But there is the other side; for we find that He sympathized deeply with those enduring poverty, assuring them of their Father's care (Mt 6^{32}), preaching especially to them the gospel (Mt 11^{5}), and pronouncing upon them in their sorrows a special benediction (Lk 6^{20}). He showed that He desired that all should have a sufficiency, by bidding all, rich and poor alike, pray for 'daily bread.' If He taught that riches were indeed an obstacle to entrance into the Kingdom of God, He also taught that it was the 'few' (whether rich or poor) that succeeded in entering it (Mt 7^{14}). If He told one young man to sell all that he had, clearly He did not intend this counsel to be applicable to all, for He assured of 'salvation' Zacchaeus, who gave but the half of his goods to the poor (Lk 19^{8f}). If the builder of larger barns is termed a 'fool,' his folly is shown not to have been mere acquisition of wealth, but that acquisition apart from riches 'toward God' (Lk 12^{21}); and if Dives is in Hades, it is evident that he is not there merely because of his riches, for Lazarus lies in the bosom of Abraham, the typical rich Jew. Further, in the parables of the Pounds and Talents (Lk 19^{12}, Mt 25^{14}) He teaches, under the symbolism of money, that men are not owners but stewards of all they possess; while in the parable of the Unjust Steward He points out one of the *true* uses of wealth—namely, to relieve the poor, and so to insure a welcome from them when the eternal tabernacles are entered (Lk 16^{9}).

From the foregoing we may conclude that, while our Lord realized that poverty brought sorrow, He also realized that wealth contained an intense peril to spiritual life. He came to raise the world from the material to the spiritual; and wealth, as the very token of the material and temporal, was blinding men to the spiritual and eternal. He therefore urged those to whom it was a special hindrance, to resign it altogether; and charged *all* to regard it as something for the use of which they would be held accountable.

4. In the Apostolic Church, in its earliest days, we find her members having 'all things common,' and the richer selling their possessions to supply the wants of their poorer brethren (Ac 2^{44f} 4^{34-37}). But this active enthusiasm does not necessarily show that the Church thought the personal possession of wealth, in itself, unlawful or undesirable; for the case of Ananias clearly indicates that the right to the possession of private property was not questioned (Ac 5^{4}). Later in the history of the Church we find St. James inveighing against the proud and heartless rich (Ja 2^{1-8} 5^{1-5}), and St. Paul warning men of the spiritual dangers incident to the procuring or possessing of wealth (1 Ti $6^{9f, 17-19}$; cf Rev 3^{17}). C. T. P. G.—**D. R. J.**

WEAPONS.—See Armour, Arms.

WEASEL.—Hebrew *ḥōledh*, Lv 11^{29}, an unclean animal. Since the Hebrew root *ḥāladh* means to 'dig,' and the Arabic *khuld* is the 'mole-rat,' it is practically certain that this latter is the correct translation of *ḥōledh*.

WEAVING.—See Spinning and Weaving.

WEDDING.—See Marriage.

WEDGE (of gold).—Jos $7^{21, 24}$ (AV, RV; RSV 'bar'). See Money.

WEEDS.—**1.** Hebrew *sûph*, Jn 2^{5}, referring to seaweeds (cf the designation *yam sûph* 'sea of weeds,' applied to the Red Sea [q.v.]). **2.** Greek *chortos*, Sir 40^{16} (RV 'sedge,' RSV 'reeds'), used in the same indefinite sense as English 'weeds.'

WEEK.—See Time.

WEEKS, FEAST OF.—See Pentecost.

WEEPING.—See Mourning Customs.

WEIGHTS AND MEASURES.—There never was, in Palestine, a system of weights and measures comparable with that of the great Mesopotamian empires from the 3rd millennium. Some systematization seems to have been attempted under the monarchy; and indeed, several systems seem to have been adopted at different times. The peasants who used stones and odd scraps of iron for weights were satisfied with approximate standards. Such weights as have been discovered provide no absolute measurements, and show how easy it must have been to 'make the ephah small, and the shekel great' (Am 8^{5}). Micah denounced the man with 'wicked scales and a bag of deceitful weights' (6^{11}), and in Proverbs, 'a false balance' and 'diverse weights' are contrasted with 'a just weight' (11^{1}; cf 20^{23}). Such weights as have been found (29 inscribed weights altogether) show that weights probably varied according to the region or to the goods sold (*e.g.* wool), or sometimes to both. The variation which is most plainly disclosed in the value of weights is probably true of other measures also. Measures of length, for example, were no doubt based on a more primitive and unscientific system than that of Egypt or Babylon.

I. Measures of Length.

The Hebrew unit was a cubit ($\frac{1}{6}$ of a reed, Ezk 40^{5}), containing 2 spans or 6 palms or 24 finger's breadths. The early system did not recognize the foot or the fathom. Measurements were taken both by the 6-cubit rod or reed and the line or 'fillet' (Ezk 40^{3}, Jer 31^{39} 52^{21}, 1 K 7^{15}).

The ancient Hebrew literary authorities for the early Hebrew cubit are as follows. The 'cubit of a man' (Dt 3^{11}) was the unit by which the 'bedstead' of Og, king of Bashan, was measured (cf Rev 21^{17}). This implies that at the time to which the passage belongs (apparently not long before the time of Ezekiel) the Hebrews were familiar with more than one cubit, of which that in question was the ordinary working cubit. Solomon's Temple was laid out on the basis of a cubit 'after the first (or ancient) measure' (2 Ch 3^{3}). Now Ezekiel (40^{5} 43^{13}) prophesies the building of a Temple on a unit which he describes as a cubit and a hand's breadth, *i.e.* $\frac{7}{6}$ of the ordinary cubit. As in his vision he is practically reproducing Solomon's Temple, we may infer that Solomon's cubit, *i.e.* the ancient cubit, was also $\frac{7}{6}$ of the ordinary cubit of Ezekiel's time. We thus have an ordinary cubit of 6, and what we may call (by analogy with the Egyptian system) the **royal cubit** of 7 hand's breadths. For this double system is curiously parallel to the Egyptian, in which there was a common cubit of 0·450 metres or 17·72 inches, which was $\frac{6}{7}$ of the royal cubit of 0·525 metres or 20·67 inches (these data are derived from actual measuring rods). A similar distinction between a common and a

WEIGHTS AND MEASURES

royal norm existed in the Babylonian weight-system. Its object there was probably to give the government an advantage in the case of taxation; probably also in the case of measures of length the excess of the royal over the common measure had a similar object.

We have at present no means of ascertaining the exact dimensions of the Hebrew ordinary and royal cubits. The balance of evidence is certainly in favour of a fairly close approximation to the Egyptian system. The estimates vary from 16 to 25·2 inches. They are based on: (1) *the Siloam inscription*, which says: 'The waters flowed from the outlet to the Pool 1200 cubits,' or, according to another reading, '1000 cubits.' The length of the canal is estimated at 537·6 metres, which yields a cubit of 0·525 to 0·527 metres (20·67 to 20·75 inches) or 0·538 metres (21·18 inches) according to the reading adopted. Further uncertainty is occasioned by the possibility of the number 1200 or 1000 being only a round number. The evidence of the Siloam inscription is thus of a most unsatisfactory kind. (2) *The measurements of tombs*. Some of these appear to be constructed on the basis of the Egyptian cubit; others seem to yield cubits of 0·575 metres (about 22·6 inches) or 0·641 metres (about 25·2 inches). The last two cubits seem to be improbable. The measurements of another tomb (known as the Tomb of Joshua) seem to confirm the deduction of the cubit of about 0·525 metres. (3) *The measurement of grains of barley*. This has been objected to for more than one reason. But the Rabbinical tradition allowed 144 barley-corns of medium size, laid side by side, to the cubit; and it is remarkable that a careful test made on these lines resulted in a cubit of 17·77 inches (0·451 metres), which is the Egyptian common cubit. (4) *Josephus*, when using the Jewish measures of capacity, etc., which differ from the Greek or Roman, is usually careful to give an equation explaining the measures to his Greek or Roman readers, while in the case of the cubit he does not do so, but seems to regard the Hebrew and the Roman-Attic as practically the same. The Roman-Attic cubit (1½ feet) is fixed at 0·444 metres or 17·57 inches, so that we have here a close approximation to the Egyptian common cubit. Probably in Josephus' time the Hebrew common cubit was, as ascertained by the methods mentioned above, 0·450 metres; and the difference between this and the Attic-Roman was regarded by him as negligible for ordinary purposes. (5) *The Mishnah*. No data of any value for the exact determination of the cubit are to be obtained from this source. Four cubits is given as the length of a *loculus* in a rock-cut tomb; it has been pointed out that, allowing some 2 inches for the bier, and taking 5 feet 6 inches to 5 feet 8 inches as the average height of the Jewish body, this gives 4 cubits = 5 feet 10 inches, or 17½ inches to the cubit.

The general inference from the above five sources of information is that the Jews had two cubits, a shorter and a longer, corresponding closely to the Egyptian common and royal cubit. The equivalents are expressed in the following table:—

	Royal System.		Common System.	
	Metres.	Inches.	Metres.	Inches.
Finger's breadth	0·022	0·86	0·019	0·74
Palm = 4 fingers	0·088	3·44	0·075	2·95
Span = 3 palms	0·262	10·33	0·225	8·86
Cubit = 2 spans	0·525	20·67	0·450	17·72
Reed = 6 cubits	3·150	124·02	2·700	106·32

Parts and multiples of the unit.—The ordinary parts of the cubit have already been mentioned. They occur as follows: the **finger's breadth** or digit (Jer 52[21], the *daktyl* of Josephus); the palm or **hand's breadth** (1 K 7[26] Ezk 40[5, 43] 43[13] etc.); the **span** (Ex 28[16] 39[9] etc.). A special measure is the *gōmedh*, which was the length of the sword of Ehud (Jg 3[16]), and is not mentioned elsewhere. It was explained by the commentators as a short cubit (hence EV 'cubit'), and it has been suggested that it was the cubit of 5 palms, which is mentioned by Rabbi Judah. The Greeks also had a short cubit, known as the *pygōn*, of 5 palms, the distance from the elbow to the first joint of the fingers. The **reed** (=6 cubits) is the only definite OT multiple of the cubit (Ezk 40[5]). This is the *akaina* of the Greek writers. The **pace** of 2 S 6[13] is probably not meant to be a definite measure. A 'little way' (Gn 35[16] 48[7], 2 K 5[19]) is also indefinite. Syrian and Arabic translators compared it with the parasang, but it cannot merely for that reason be regarded as fixed. A **day's journey** (Nu 11[31], 1 K 19[4], Jon 3[4], Lk 2[44]) and its multiples (Gn 30[36], Nu 10[33]) are of course also variable.

The **Sabbath day's journey** (Ac 1[12]) was usually computed at 2000 cubits. This was the distance by which the Ark preceded the host of the Israelites, and it was consequently presumed that this distance might be covered on the Sabbath, since the host must be allowed to attend worship at the Ark. The distance was doubled by a legal fiction: on the eve of the Sabbath, food was placed at a spot 2000 cubits on, and this new place thus became the traveller's place within the meaning of the prescription of Ex 16[29]; there were also other means of increasing the distance. The Mount of Olives was distant a Sabbath day's journey from Jerusalem, and the same distance is given by Josephus as 5 *stadia*, thus confirming the 2000 cubits computation. But in the Talmud the Sabbath day's journey is equated to the *mil* of 3000 cubits or 7½ furlongs; and the measure 'threescore furlongs' of Lk 24[13], being an exact multiple of this distance, seems to indicate that this may have been one form (the earlier?) of the Sabbath day's journey. In the Zadokite Document the Sabbath day's journey is limited to 1000 cubits (*CDC* x. 20).

In later times, a Byzantine writer of uncertain date, Julian of Ascalon, furnishes information as to the measures in use in Palestine ('Provincial measures, derived from the work of the architect Julian of Ascalon, from the laws or customs prevailing in Palestine,' is the title of the table). From this we obtain (omitting doubtful points) the following table:—

1. The finger's breadth.
2. The palm = 4 finger's breadths.
3. The cubit = 1½ feet = 6 palms.
4. The pace = 2 cubits = 3 feet = 12 palms.
5. the **fathom** = 2 paces = 4 cubits = 6 feet.
6. The reed = 1½ fathoms = 6 cubits = 9 feet = 36 palms.
7. The *plethron* = 10 reeds = 15 fathoms = 30 paces = 60 cubits = 90 feet.
8. The *stadium* or **furlong** = 6 *plethra* = 60 reeds = 100 fathoms = 200 paces = 400 cubits = 600 feet.
9. (*a*) The *milion* or **mile**, 'according to Eratosthenes and Strabo' = 8⅓ stadia = 833⅓ fathoms.
   (*b*) The *milion* 'according to the present use' = 7½ stadia = 750 fathoms = 1500 paces = 3000 cubits.
10. The present *milion* of 7½ stadia = 750 'geometric' fathoms = 833⅓ 'simple' fathoms; for 9 geometric fathoms = 10 simple fathoms.

We may justifiably assume that the 3000 cubits of 9 (*b*) are the royal cubits of 0·525 metres. The geometric and simple measures according to Julian thus work out as follows:—

	Geometric.		Simple.	
	Metres.	Inches.	Metres.	Inches.
Finger's breadth	0·022	0·86	0·020	0·79
Palm . . .	0·088	3·44	0·080	3·11
Cubit . . .	0·525	20·67	0·473	18·62
Fathom . .	2·100	82·68	1·890	74·49

Measures of area.—For smaller measures of area there seem to have been no special names, the dimensions of the sides of a square being usually stated. For land measures, two methods of computation were in use. (1) The first, as in most countries, was to state area in terms of *the amount that a yoke of oxen could plough in a day* (cf the Latin *jugerum*). Thus in Is 5[10] (possibly also in the corrupt 1 S 14[14]) we have '10 yoke' (*ṣemedh*) of vineyard. Although definite authority is lacking, we may perhaps equate the Hebrew **yoke** of land to the Egyptian unit of land measure, which was 100 royal cubits square (0·2756 hectares or 0·6810 acre). The Greeks called this measure the *aroura.* (2) The second measure was *the amount of seed required to sow an area.* Thus 'the sowing of a homer of barley' was computed at the price of 50 shekels of silver (Lv 27[16]). The dimensions of the trench which Elijah dug about his altar (1 K 18[32]) have also been explained on the same principle; the trench (*i.e.* the area enclosed by it) is described as being 'like a house of two seahs of seed' (EV wrongly 'as great as would contain two measures of seed'). This measure '**house of two seahs**' is the standard of measurement in the Mishnah, and is defined as the area of the court of the Tabernacle, or 100×50 cubits (*c* 1648 square yards or 0.1379 hectares). Other measures of capacity were used in the same way, and the system was Babylonian in origin; there are also traces of the same system in the West under the Roman Empire.

II. Measures of Capacity.

The terms '**handful**' (Lv 2[2]) and the like do not represent any part of a system of measures in Hebrew, any more than in English. The Hebrew 'measure' *par excellence* was the **seah**, Greek *saton.* From the Greek version of Is 5[10] and other sources we know that the ephah contained 3 such measures. Epiphanius describes the seah or Hebrew *modius* as a modius of extra size, and as equal to 1¼ Roman modius=20 sextarii. Josephus, however, equates it with 1½ Roman modius =24 sextarii. An anonymous Greek fragment agrees with this, and so also does Jerome in his commentary on Mt 13[33]. Epiphanius elsewhere, and other writers, equate it with 22 sextarii (the Babylonian ephah is computed at 66 sextarii). The seah was used for both liquid and dry measure.

The **ephah** (the word is suspected of Egyptian origin) of 3 seahs was used for dry measure only; the equivalent liquid measure was the **bath** (Gr. *bados, batos, keramion, choinix*). They are equated in Ezk 45[11], each containing $\frac{1}{10}$ of a homer. The ephah corresponds to the Greek *artabē* (although in Is 5[10] six artabai go to a homer) or *metrētēs.* Josephus equates it to 72 sextarii. The bath was divided into tenths (Ezk 45[14]), the name of which is unknown; the ephah likewise into tenths, which were called *ʿōmer* or *ʿiśśārôn* (distinguish from *homer*=10 ephahs). Again the ephah and bath were both divided into sixths (Ezk 45[13]); the $\frac{1}{6}$ bath was the *hin,* but the name of the $\frac{1}{6}$ ephah is unknown.

The **homer** (Ezk 45[11], Hos 3[2]) or **cor** (Ezk 45[14], Lk 16[7]; Gr. *koros*) contained 10 ephahs or baths, or 30 seahs (The term 'cor' is used more especially for liquids). It corresponded to 10 Attic *metrētai* (so Jos. *Ant.* xv. ix. 2 [314], though he says *medimni* by a slip). The word *cor* may be connected with the Babylonian *gur* or *gurru.*

The **lethech** (Ugaritic *lth̲*) occurs in Hos 3[2], and by Vulgate and EV is rendered by 'half a homer.' Epiphanius says the lethech is a large *ʿōmer* (*gomor*) of 15 *modii.*

The **hin** (Gr. *hein*) was a liquid measure=½ seah. In Lv 19[36] the LXX renders it *chous.* But Josephus and Jerome and the Talmud equate it to 2 Attic *choes*= 12 sextarii. The hin was divided into halves, thirds (=cab), quarters, sixths, and twelfths (=log). In later times there were a 'sacred hin'=¾ of the ordinary hin, and a large hin=2 sacred hins=$\frac{3}{2}$ ordinary hin. The Egyptian *hen,* of much smaller capacity (0·455 litres) is to be distinguished.

The **ʿomer** (Gr. *gomor*) is confined to dry measure. It is $\frac{1}{10}$ ephah and is therefore called *assaron* or *ʿiśśārôn* (AV '**tenth deal**'). Epiphanius equates it accordingly to 7$\frac{1}{5}$ sextarii, Eusebius less accurately to 7 sextarii. Eusebius also calls it the 'little gomor'; but there was another 'little gomor' of 12 modii, so called in distinction from the 'large gomor' of 15 modii (the lethech of Epiphanius). Josephus wrongly equates the *gomor* to 7 Attic *kotylai.*

The **cab** (2 K 6[25], Gr. *kabos*) was both a liquid and a dry measure. From Josephus and the Talmud it appears that it was equal to 4 sextarii, or ⅓ hin. In other places it is equated to 6 sextarii, 5 sextarii ('great cab' =1¼ cab), and ¼ modius (Epiphanius, who, according to the meaning he attaches to *modius* here, may mean 4, 5, 5½, or 6 sextarii!).

The **log** (Lv 14[10, 12]) is a measure of oil; the Talmud equates it to $\frac{1}{12}$ hin or $\frac{1}{24}$ seah, *i.e.* ¼ cab. Josephus renders the ¼ cab of 2 K 6[25] by the Greek *xestēs* or Roman *sextarius,* and there is other evidence to the same effect.

A measure of doubtful capacity is the *nēbhel* of wine (Gr. version of Hos 3[2], instead of **lethech** of barley). It was 150 sextarii, by which may be meant ordinary sextarii or the larger Syrian sextarii which would make it=3 baths. The word means 'wine-skin.'

We thus obtain the table on p. 1035 (showing a mixed decimal and sexagesimal system) of dry and liquid measures. Where the name of the liquid differs from that of the dry measure, the former is added in italics. Where there is no corresponding liquid measure, the dry measure is asterisked.

The older portion of this system seems to have been the sexagesimal, the *ʿōmer* and $\frac{1}{10}$ *bath* and the *lethech* being intrusions.

When we come to investigate the actual contents of the various measures, we are, in the first instance, thrown back on the (apparently only approximate) equations with the Roman *sextarius* (Gr. *xestēs*) and its multiples already mentioned. The *log* would then be the equivalent of the *sextarius,* the *bath* of the *metrētēs,* the *cab* (of 6 logs) of the Ptolemaic *chous.* If log and sextarius were exact equivalents, the ephah of 72 logs would=39·39 litres,=nearly 8⅔ gallons. This is on the usual assumption that the sextarius was 0·545 litres or 0·96 imperial pints. But the exact capacity of the sextarius is disputed, and a capacity as high as 0·562 litres or 0·99 imperial pint is given for the sextarius by an actually extant measure. This would give as the capacity of the ephah-bath 40·46 litres or 71·28 pints. But it is highly improbable that the equation of log to sextarius was more than approximate. It is more easy to confound closely resembling measures of capacity than of length, area, or weight.

Other methods of ascertaining the capacity of the ephah are the following. We may assume that it was the same as the Babylonian unit of 0·505 litres (0·89 pint). This would give an ephah of 36·37 litres, or nearly 8 gallons or 66·5 sextarii of the usually assumed weight, and more or less squares with Epiphanius' equation of the seah or ⅓ ephah with 22 sextarii. Or we may connect it with the Egyptian system, thus: both the ephah-bath and the Egyptian-Ptolemaic *artabē* are equated to the Attic *metrētēs* of 72 sextarii. Now, in the case of the *artabē* this is only an approximation, for it is known from native Egyptian sources (which give the capacity in terms of a volume of water of a certain weight) that the *artabē* was about 36·45 litres, or a little more than 64 pints. Other calculations, as from a passage of Josephus, where the cor is equated to 41 Attic (Graeco-Roman) modii (*i.e.* 656 sextarii), give the same result. In this passage *modii* is an almost certain emendation of *medimni,* the confusion between the two being natural in a Greek MS. There are plenty of other vague approximations, ranging from 60 to 72 sextarii. Though the passage of Josephus is not quite certain in its text, we may accept it as having the appearance of precise determination, especially since it gives a result not materially differing from other sources of information.

Homer or cor. . .	1											
* Lethech . . .	2	1										
Ephah, *bath* . . .	10	5	1									
Seah	30	15	3	1								
⅙ ephah, *hin* . . .	60	30	6	2	1							
'Omer or 'issaron, $\frac{1}{10}$ *bath*	100	50	10	3⅓	1⅔	1						
½ *hin*	120	60	12	4	2	1⅕	1					
Cab	180	90	18	6	3	1⅘	1½	1				
¼ *hin*	240	120	24	8	4	2⅖	2	1⅓	1			
½ cab, ⅙ *hin* . . .	360	180	36	12	6	3⅗	3	2	1½	1		
¼ cab, *log* . . .	720	360	72	24	12	7⅕	6	4	3	2	1	
* ⅛ cab	1440	720	144	48	24	14⅖	12	8	6	4	2	1

Name of Measure.	(1) Log=0·505 litre.		(2) Ephah=65 Pints.		(3) Log=0·99 Pint.		Rough Approximation on Basis of (3).
	Litres.	Gallons.	Litres.	Gallons.	Litres.	Gallons.	
Homer (cor) . .	363·7	80·053	369·2	81·25	405	89·28	11 bushels
Lethech . . .	181·85	40·026	184·6	40·62	202	44·64	5½ ,,
Ephah-bath . .	36·37	8·005	36·92	8·125	40·5	8·928	9 gallons
Seah	12·120	2·668	12·3	2·708	13·5	2·976	1½ pecks
Great hin . . .	9·090	2·001	9·18	2·234	10·08	2·232	2¼ gallons
Hin	6·060	1·334	6·12	1·356	6·72	1·488	1½ ,,
Sacred hin . . .	4·545	1·000	4·59	1·117	5·04	1·116	9 pints
'Omer . . .	3·637	0·800	3·67	0·813	4·05	0·893	7⅕ ,,
½ hin	3·030	0·667	3·06	0·678	3·36	0·744	6 ,,
Cab	2·020	0·445	2·05	0·451	2·25	0·496	4 ,,
¼ hin	1·515	0·333	1·53	0·339	1·68	0·372	3 ,,
½ cab	1·010	0·222	1·02	0·226	1·12	0·248	2 ,,
Log	0·505	0·111	0·51	0·113	0·56	0·124	1 pint
⅛ cab	0·252	0·055	0·26	0·056	0·28	0·062	½ ,,

In the above table, the values of the measures are given according to three estimates, viz. (1) log=Babylonian unit of 0.505 litre ; (2) ephah=65 pints ; (3) log=sextarius of 0.99 pint.

Foreign measures of capacity mentioned in NT.—Setting aside words which strictly denote a measure of capacity, but are used loosely to mean simply a vessel (*e.g.* 'cup' in Mk 7[4]), the following, among others, have been noted. **Bushel** (Mt 5[15]) is the translation of *modius*, which represents seah. **Firkin** is used (Jn 2[6]) to represent the Greek *metrētēs*, the rough equivalent of the *bath*. **Measure** in Rev 6[6] represents the Greek *choinix* of about 2 pints.

III. Measure of Weight.

The root š-ḳ-l, common to all Semitic languages, signifies the action of weighing. It then expressed, appropriately, the counting and paying of money ; and so the noun **shekel** became the unit of weight *par excellence*, and later, the fundamental unit of money. Weights were generally of stone (Pr 16[11]). The two bronze plates of a balance (*mōz^{e}nayim*), together with six stones have been found at Râs Shamra. Its small size suggests that it was normally used for weighing precious objects like gold, silver, perfumes, or spices.

The main denominations in Palestine were as follows : The **talent** (Gr. *talanton*, Heb. *kikkār*, meaning apparently a round, cake-like object). The **mina** : Akkadian *manû*, Hebrew *māneh*, Greek *mna* (cf 1 K 10[17] RSV ; AV, RV '**pound**'). The **shekel** : Akkadian *siglu*, Greek *siklos* or *siglos*. As a weight, this was quite unrelated to the money shekel (Gr. *didrachmon*), and references to shekels or other denominations of precious metal, in pre-exilic times, must therefore be to uncoined metal. The shekel was divided into twenty **gerahs** (Bab. *giru*). The Greek designation of the latter as *obolos* is only a rough equivalent, used because the obolus was the lightest unit of the hellenistic system.

The value of these units is difficult to establish. Ex 38[25f] equates 1 talent with 3000 shekels. According to the Babylonian system 60 minas=1 talent, in which case 1 mina=50 shekels. It is usually supposed that this was the rate in early Israel (cf 2 K 15[20], Dt 22[19]). It is highly probable that commercial rates did not always accord with the official scales of the Temple. Some (*e.g.* Barrois) interpret Ezk 45[12] to indicate that Ezekiel aimed to restore a sexagesimal system (the Mesopotamian) which had fallen out of use. But the probable translation of Ezk 45[12] is : 'The shekel shall be 20 gerahs ; 10 shekels are a fifth, and five shekels a tenth ; 50 shekels shall be your mina.' If this is right, Ezekiel was resisting a change to the Mesopotamian standard (also Syrian) of 1 mina to 60 shekels. In this case also, there would be nothing unusual about the '200 shekels after the royal weight' in 2 S 14^{26}. There is, in fact, no evidence of the Babylonian system of weights being adopted in Palestine. The Palestine scale would thus be :

kikkar . .	1				
mina . .	60	1			
shekel . .	3000	50	1		
beka . .	6000	100	2	1	
gerah . .	60,000	1000	20	10	1

The evidence of actual weights found in Palestine is as follows : **1.** Weights marked by a conventional sign, followed by a number, presumably indicating the scale of the system. These are usually numbered 2, 4, 8, or 16, and it may be assumed that they are based on the shekel. They offer an average weight of 11·424 grams for the shekel. **2.** Seven weights marked **pîm** (or perhaps *payim*). The meaning of *pîm* is obscure, but it is generally agreed that its value is **1** shekel. On the average the shekel turns out to be 11·14 grams. The discovery of the pîm settles the meaning of 1 S 13^{21}. See Pim. **3.** Seven weights marked **beka'**. This is ½ shekel (cf Gn 24^{22}, Ex 38^{26}), and the average weight of 6·112 grams gives a shekel of 12·224 grams. **4.** Two small bronze weights in the form of a turtle, have been found, but the interpretation of them is doubtful. The one would give a shekel of 21·04 grams, the other 12·495 grams. **5.** Nearly half the inscribed weights are marked **neṣeph** (which etymologically ought to mean 'a half'). The average weight of these is 9·84 grams, half, it has been suggested, of a heavy shekel of 19·7 grams.

Foreign weights in the NT.—The 'pound' of pure nard (Jn 12^{3}) or of myrrh and aloes (19^{39}) is best explained as the Roman *libra* (*litra* in the papyri) of 327·45 grams. The 'pound' in Lk 19^{13f} is the money-*mina* (see Money, 7).

For further information see especially K. Galling, *Biblisches Reallexikon*, 1937, pp. 186 f, 366 f, A.-G. Barrois, article 'La métrologie dans la Bible,' in *RB*, 1931, pp. 185–213 ; 1932, pp. 50–76 ; *Manuel d'Archéologie biblique* ii, 1953, pp. 243–258 ; D. Diringer, article 'Weights' in *Documents from Old Testament Times*, ed. D. Winton Thomas, 1958, pp. 227–230.

G. F. H.—**D. R. J.**

WELL.—See Cistern, Fountain, Water.

WEN.—Lk 22^{22} (AV, RV ; RSV 'discharge') ; see Medicine.

WENCH.—This word, once good English, was used in the Bishop's Bible of 1568, and was transferred to AV at 2 S 17^{17} (RV and RSV 'maidservant'). So Wycliffe at Mt 9^{24}, 'Go ye away, for the wenche is not dead, but slepith.'

WESTERN SEA.—See Sea.

WHALE.—**1.** Hebrew *tannîn* ; see Dragon, **4.** **2.** Hebrew *dāgh gādhôl*, the 'great fish' of Jon 1^{17}, is in the LXX and in Mt 12^{40} rendered in Greek by *kētos* and translated 'whale,' though the Greek word has a much wider significance. It is impossible to say what kind of fish is intended in the narrative. See, further, Jonah.

WHEAT.—Hebrew *ḥiṭṭāh*, Gn 30^{14}, Ex 34^{32} etc. ; Greek *sitos*, Mt 3^{12} 13$^{25, 29}$, Lk 3^{17} 16^{7} 22^{31} etc. The wheat of Palestine is mostly of the bearded varieties ; it is not only eaten as bread, but also boiled, unground, to make the peasant's dish *burghul*, which is in turn pounded with meat in a mortar (cf Pr 27^{22}) to make the festive delicacy *kibbeh*. Wheat is grown all over the valleys and plains of W. Palestine, though to a less extent than barley, but it is cultivated in the largest quantities in the *Nuqrah* or plain of the Hauran, one of the finest grain-growing countries in the world. The wheat harvest occurs from April to June ; its time was looked upon as one of the divisions of the year, Ex 34^{22}, Jg 15^{1}, 1 S 12^{17}. The expression 'fat of wheat' (AVm and RVm in Ps 81^{16}, 147^{14}) and 'the fat of kidneys of wheat' (Dt 32^{14}) refer to the finest flour of wheat. E. W. G. M.

WHEEL.—The various parts of a cart or chariot wheel are enumerated in connexion with the bronze wheels of Solomon's lavers, 1 K 7$^{30, 32f}$. In RSV v.^{33} reads : 'The wheels were much like a chariot wheel ; their axles, their rims, their spokes, and their hubs were all cast' (cf AV and RV). The rims were made in segments and dowelled together. One of the finest specimens of a Roman chariot wheel yet found has the rim, 'which is formed of a single piece of wood bent,' and the hub shod with iron, the latter being also 'bushed with iron' (Scott, *Hist. Rev.*, October 1905, p. 123, with illustrations). For the potter's wheel, see Potter. Wells and cisterns were also furnished with wheels, over which the rope passed for drawing up the water-bucket, Ec 12^{6}. See also Cart, Chariot. A. R. S. K.

WHIRLWIND represents two Hebrew words—*sūphāh* (Job 37^{9}, Pr 1^{27} etc., also translated '**storm**' in Job 21^{18}, Ps 83^{15}, Is 29^{6} etc.), and *sa'ar* or *s'ārāh* (2 K 2^{1}, Job 38^{1}, Jer 23^{19} etc., also translated '**tempest**' and 'stormy wind,' Ps 55^{8} 83^{15} 107^{25}, Ezk 13^{13} etc.). The words do not necessarily mean 'whirlwind,' and are applied to any furious storm. From the context, however, in certain passages, we gather that whirlwind is intended—a violent wind moving in a circle round its axis (2 K 2$^{1, 11}$, Job 38^{1} etc.). It often works great havoc in its path, as it sweeps across the country. Drawing up sand, dust, straw, and other light articles as it gyrates, it presents the appearance of a great pillar—an object of fear to travellers and dwellers in the desert. Passing over the sea, it draws up the water, and the bursting of the column causes the waterspout. God spake to Job from the whirlwind (Job 40^{6}) ; the modern Arabian regards it with superstitious dread, as the residence of demons. W. E.

WHITE.—See Colours, **1.**

WHITE OF AN EGG.—See Purslane.

WHORE.—This term is replaced generally in RV by **harlot** (q.v.), and does not appear in RSV.

WICK.—See Flax, Tow.

WIDOW.—Widows, from their poverty and unprotectedness, are regarded in OT as under the special guardianship of God (Ps 68^{5} 146^{9}, Pr 15^{25}, Dt 10^{18}, Jer 49^{11}) ; and consequently due regard for their wants was looked upon as a mark of true religion, ensuring a blessing on those who showed it (Job 29^{13} 31^{16}, Is 1^{17}, Jer 7^{6f} 22^{3f}) ; while neglect of, cruelty or injustice towards, them were considered marks of wickedness meriting punishment from God (Job 22^{9f} 24^{20f}, Ps 94^{6}, Is 1^{23} 10^{2}, Zec 7$^{10, 14}$, Mal 3^{5}). The Book of Deuteronomy is especially rich in such counsels, insisting that widows be granted full justice (24^{17} 27^{19}), that they be received as guests at sacrificial meals (14^{29} 16$^{11, 14}$ 26^{12f}), and that they be suffered to glean unmolested in field, oliveyard, and vineyard (24^{19f}). See, further, Inheritance, i. **2** (*c*) ; Marriage, **6.**

The earliest mention of widows in the history of the Christian Church is found in Ac 6^{1}, where the Hellenists murmured 'against the Hebrews because their widows were neglected' in the daily distribution of alms or food. In course of time these pensioners became an excessive burden on the finances of the Church. We thus find St. Paul dealing with the matter in 1 Ti 5$^{3-16}$, where he charges relatives and Christian friends to relieve those widows with whom they are personally connected (vv.$^{4, 8, 16}$), so that the Church might be the more able to relieve those who were 'widows indeed' (*i.e.* widows in actual poverty and without any one responsible for their support) (vv.$^{3, 5, 16}$). He further directs that 'none be enrolled as widows' except those who were sixty years of age, of unimpeachable character, and full of good works ; and he adds that 'the younger widows' should be 'refused' (*i.e.* not enrolled); for experience had shown that they 'grow wanton against Christ' and, re-marrying, 'rejected their first faith' (so RV; RSV renders 'violate their first pledge'). Since it could not have been the Apostle's intention that only widows over sixty should receive pecuniary help from the Church (for many young widows might be in great poverty), and since he could not describe the re-marriage of such a widow-pensioner as a rejection of her faith, it follows that the list of widows, from which the younger widows were to be excluded, was not the list of those who were in receipt of Church relief, but rather a list of those, from among the pensioner-widows, who were considered suitable by age and character to engage officially in Church work. Therefore we may see in this passage a proof of the existence thus early in the history of the Church of that ecclesiastical order of 'Widows' which we find mentioned frequently in post-Apostolic times.

C. T. P. G.

WIFE.—See Family, 2; Marriage.

WILD OLIVE.—See Grafting; Olive.

WILD OX.—See Unicorn.

WILDERNESS, DESERT.—These terms stand for several Hebrew and Greek words, with different shades of meaning. Generally, 'desert' is the more descriptive rendering, since the terms do not refer to heavily forested regions but to arid, unfertile, barren terrain. However, modern English translations continue to employ both terms, doubtless due to the fact that even 'desert' is not a perfect description; the regions referred to are sometimes mountainous in nature, plains where pastures exist after the rains, and settled regions such as that part of the Wilderness of Judah (see Judaea) near the Dead Sea where the Qumrân monastery and the Dead Sea Scrolls have been found.

1. *midhbār* (from *dābhar*, 'to drive') means properly the land to which the cattle were driven, and is used of dry pasture land where scanty grazing was to be found. It occurs about 280 times in OT and is usually translated 'wilderness' in the AV, and about a dozen times 'desert.' The RSV shows a preference for 'desert' in many places where AV translates 'wilderness' (1 Ch 5^{9}, Job 38^{26}, Ps 78^{17}, Is 42^{11}, Mt 15^{33} etc.). It is the place where wild animals roam: pelicans or vultures (Ps 102^{6}), wild asses (Job 24^{5}, Jer 2^{24}), ostriches (La 4^{3}), jackals (Mal 1^{3}); it is without settled inhabitants, though towns or settlements of nomadic tribes may be found (Jos 15^{61f}, Is 42^{11}). This term is usually applied to the **Wilderness of the Wanderings** or the Arabian desert, but may refer to any other waste. Special waste tracts are distinguished: wilderness of Shur, Zin, Paran, Kadesh, Maon, Ziph, Tekoa, Moab, Edom, etc.

2. *ʿᵃrābhāh* (probably from a word meaning 'dry') signifies a dry, desolate, unfertile tract of land, 'steppe,' or 'desert plain.' As a proper name, 'Arabah' (see Dt 1^{1}, Jos 11^{16} etc.) is applied to the great plain, including the Jordan Valley and extending S. to the Gulf of ʿAqaba, but is applied also to steppes in general, and translated 'wilderness,' 'desert,' and sometimes in plural 'plains,' *e.g.* of Moab, of Jericho.

3. *ḥorbāh* (from a root 'to be waste *or* desolate') is properly applied to cities or districts once inhabited now lying waste (whether or not in the desert, see Lv 26^{33}); it is variously translated as 'wastes,' 'deserts,' 'desolations,' although it is once used of the Wilderness of the Wanderings (Is 48^{21}, RSV 'deserts').

4. *ṣiyyāh* meaning 'dry' or 'parched' when used as an adjective (Is 41^{18}, Jer 51^{43}) is twice translated 'wilderness' in AV: Job 30^{3} (RV, RSV 'dry ground'), Ps 78^{17} (RV, RSV 'desert,' RVm 'a dry land'). It is used with *midhbār* and *ʿᵃrābhāh* (Jer 50^{12}, Is 35^{1}) and like them refers to arid, desert regions.

5. *tōhû* has the special meaning of a 'wild desolate expanse.' In Job 6^{18} it is the waste where the caravans perish. It is applied to the primeval chaos without form (Gn 1^{2}), also to the Wilderness of the Wandering (Dt 32^{10} 'howling *waste* of the wilderness').

6. *yᵉshīmôn* is variously translated as 'wilderness' or 'desert' (Dt 32^{10}, Is 43$^{19-20}$, Ps 68^{7} 78^{40} 106^{14} 107^{4}). When the word is used with the Hebrew article it is a place name 'Jeshimon' (q.v.) and as such may refer to a place near Ziph and Maon (1 S 23^{19} 26$^{1, 3}$) or to the region in the Jordan Valley N. of the Dead Sea (Nu 21^{20} 23^{28}).

7. The NT terms (cf LXX) are *erēmos* and *erēmia*, the former being used either as noun or as adjective, with 'place' or 'country' understood. The terms are generally translated 'wilderness' or 'desert' and as such may refer to the wilderness of Judaea (Mt 3^{1}) or to desert regions that are not specified (Mt 15^{33}). The RSV translates as 'lonely (place)' occasionally, and takes account of the possibility that the terms could be used for uninhabited areas not technically desert or wilderness in nature (Mt 14$^{13, 15}$, Mk 1^{35}, Lk 9^{12} etc.).

On deserts in NT see articles on respective names.

W. F. B.—W. L. R.

WILL.—'Will' and 'would' are often independent verbs in AV, and being now merely auxiliaries, their force is liable to be missed by the English reader. Thus, Mt 11^{14}, 'if ye will receive it' (RSV 'If you are willing to accept it'; cf RV); Jn 1^{43} 'Jesus would go forth into Galilee' (RV 'was minded to go forth,' RSV 'decided to go').

WILL.—See Predestination, Testament.

WILLOW.—Hebrew *ʿᵃrābhîm* (cf Arabic *gharab* 'willow' or 'poplar'), Lv 23^{40}, Job 40^{22}, Ps 137^{2}, Is 15^{7} 44^{4}; *ṣaphṣāphāh* (cf Arabic *ṣafṣâf*), Ezk 17^{5}. Most of the references are to a tree growing beside water, and apply well to the willow, of which two varieties, *Salix fragilis* and *S. alba*, occur plentifully by watercourses in the Holy Land. Some travellers consider the **poplar**, especially the willow-like *Populus euphratica*, of the same Nat. Ord. (*Salicaceae*) as the willows, more probable. Tristram, without much evidence, considered that *ṣaphṣāphāh* might be the *oleander*, which covers the banks of so many streams.

E. W. G. M.

WILLOWS, BROOK OF THE.—A wady in Moab, Is 15^{7}; perhaps the same as the Valley of **Zered** (q.v.).

WIMPLE.—Is 3^{22} AV (RV **shawls**, RSV **cloaks**).—The precise article of dress intended is unknown.

WIND.—The common Hebrew word for wind is *rûaḥ*, which must be variously translated 'spirit' and 'breath,' according to the context. It signifies that mysterious, incalculable energy which may be regarded as characteristic of God. Wind, for the Israelites, was not merely a meteorological phenomenon; it was divine energy in the world of nature. The oscillation of thought between spirit, breath, and wind (all of divine origin) may be clearly seen in Ezk 37$^{1-14}$ (cf RSVm) and in the remarkable use of 'pneuma' in Jn 3^{8}. The winds in Hebrew are designated by the four cardinal points of the compass. 'South wind,' *e.g.* may be either S., SW., or SE.; and so with the others. Cool winds come from the N., moist winds from the western sea, warm winds from the S., and dry winds often laden with fine sand, from the eastern deserts. Warmth and moisture, therefore, depend much upon the direction of the winds. During the dry season from May till October, the prevailing winds are from the N. and NW.; they do much to temper the heat of summer (Ca 4^{16}, Job 37^{9}). In September and October E. and SE. winds are frequent; blowing from the deserts, their dry heat causes the furniture to crack, and makes life a burden (Hos 13^{15}). Later, the winds from the S. prolong the warmth of summer (Lk 12^{55}); then the W. and SW. winds bring the rain (1 K 18^{44}, Lk 12^{54}). East winds earlier in the year often work great destruction on vegetation (Ezk 17^{10}). Under their influence strong plants droop, and flowers quickly wither (Ps 103^{16}).

Of the greatest value for all living things is the perpetual interchange of land and sea breezes. At sunrise a gentle air stirs from the sea, crosses the plain, and creeps up the mountains. At sunset the cooling air begins to slip down seaward again, while the upper strata move landward from the sea. The moisture thus carried ashore is precipitated in refreshing dew.

The 'tempestuous wind' (Ac 27^{14}), called Euroclydon or **Euraquilo** (q.v.) was the E.-NE. wind so prevalent in the eastern Mediterranean, called by sailors to-day 'the Levanter.' W. E.—**A. S. H.**

WINDOW.—See House, 7.

WINE AND STRONG DRINK.—Taken together in this order the two terms 'wine' and 'strong drink' are continually used in the OT as an exhaustive classification of the fermented beverages then in use (Lv 10^{9}, 1 S 1^{15}, Pr 20^{1} *et passim*). The all but universal usage in the OT—in NT 'strong drink' occurs only in Lk 1^{15}—is to restrict 'wine' (*yayin*) to the beverage prepared from the juice of the grape, and to denote by 'strong drink' (*shēkhār*) every other sort of intoxicating liquor.

1. Before proceeding to describe the methods by which wine in particular was made in the period covered by the canonical writings it is advisable to examine briefly the more frequently used terms for wine and strong drink. The examination of the term *shēkhār* and its root-meaning shows that it always means intoxicating drink. Among the early Semites a name similar to *shēkhār* and the Babylonian *shikaru* was given to the fermented juice of the date and later it was extended to signify all other fermented liquor (Kennedy, *EBi* iv, 5309 f). At a later period when the ancestors of the Hebrews became acquainted with the vine and its culture the Indo-Germanic term represented by the Greek *oinos* (with digamma, *woinos*) and the Latin *vinum* was borrowed, in the form *yayin*, to denote the fermented juice of the grape. The older term *shēkhār* then became restricted, as we have seen, to intoxicants other than grape wine.

Another term, of uncertain etymology, which occurs thirty-eight times is *tîrôsh*, rendered in the AV variously by 'wine' and 'new wine.' The ARV renders consistently with '**new wine**' but the RSV in thirty-four instances renders by 'wine' while in the remaining four cases (Hos 4^{11} 9^{2}, Hag 1^{11}, Zec 9^{17}) it gives 'new wine.' Strictly speaking *tîrôsh* is the freshly expressed grape juice, before and during fermentation, technically known as 'must' (from Lat. *mustum*). In this sense it is frequently named as a valued product of the soil with fresh oil (Dt 7^{13} 11^{14}, *et passim*)—that is to say, the raw, unclarified oil as it flows from the oil-press, to which it exactly corresponds. In some passages of the OT, however, and notably Hos 4^{11} where *tîrôsh* is associated with *yayin* and whoredom, as taking away the understanding (AV 'heart'), it evidently denotes the product of fermentation. Hence it may be said that *tîrôsh* is applied not only to the 'must' in the wine vat (v.^{3}) but to the 'new wine' before it has fully matured and become *yayin*, or, as Driver suggests (*Joel and Amos*, pp. 79 f) 'to a light kind of wine such as we know, from the classical writers, that the ancients were in the habit of making by checking the fermentation of the grape juice before it had run its full course' (cf *EBi* iv, 5307 f).

Of the rarer words for 'wine' mention may be made of *ḥemer* (Dt 32^{14}, and, in cognate form, Ezr 6^{9}, Dn 5^{1f}), which denotes wine as a result of fermentation, from a root signifying 'to ferment,' and *'āsîs*, a poetical synonym of *tîrōsh*, and like it used both of the fresh juice and of the fermented liquor (Jl 1^{5}, Is 49^{26}): in Am 9^{13} (AV), Is 49^{26} (AV) it is rendered 'sweet wine' while in the Joel passage (AV) 'new wine' is given. RSV varies with 'wine' in the Isaiah passage and 'sweet wine' in the other two. 'Sweet wine' suggests the *gleukos* ('new wine') of Ac 2^{13} (AV, RV, RSV). Reference may also be made to such poetical expressions as 'the blood of the grape' (Gn 49^{11}, Dt 32^{14}) and to the later 'fruit of the vine' (Mt 26^{29} and parallels) of the Gospels and the Mishnah.

2. The Promised Land was pre-eminently 'a land of wine . . . and vineyards' (2 K 18^{32}), as is attested by the widely scattered remains of the ancient presses. A normal winepress consisted of three parts, two rock-hewn troughs at different levels with a connecting channel between them. The upper trough or **press-vat** (*gath*) had a larger superficial area but was much shallower than the lower trough or **wine-vat** (*yeḳebh*; AV, RV 'wine-fat'). A typical press might have the upper trough about 8 feet square and 15 inches deep while the lower was 4 feet square and 3 feet deep (cf Miller, *Encyc. of Bible Life*, 407 f; Heaton, *Everyday Life in OT Times*, pp. 105 f); Dalman, *Arbeit u. Sitte in Palästina*, pp. 354 f). The distinction between the two is entirely obscured in the AV and is not always preserved clearly in the original.

The grapes were brought from the adjoining vineyard in baskets and were either spread out for a few days, with a view to increase the amount of sugar and diminish the amount of water in the grapes, or were thrown into the press-vat right away. There they were thoroughly trodden with the bare feet, the juice flowing through the conducting channel to the lower wine-vat. The next process consisted in piling the husks and stalks into a heap in the middle of the vat and subjecting the mass to mechanical pressure by means of a wooden press-beam, one end of which was fixed into a socket in the wall of the vat or adjacent rock, while the other end was weighted with stones.

While this may be considered the normal construction of a Hebrew winepress it is evident, both from archaeological discoveries and from the detailed references to wine-making in the Mishnah (see Danby, *The Mishnah*), that the number of troughs or vats might be as high as four (see illustrations in Dalman, *Arbeit u. Sitte* iv, 453 f) or as low as one. The object of a third vat was to allow the 'must' to settle and clarify in the second before running it off into the third. When only one vat was used it may have served either as a press-vat, in which case the 'must' was immediately transferred to earthen jars, or as a wine-vat to receive the 'must,' the grapes having been pressed in a large wooden trough such as the Egyptians used (cf Wilkinson, *Anc. Egyp.* i. 385, with illustrations). This arrangement would obviously be required where a suitable rock surface was not available. In such a case, indeed, a rock-hewn trough of any sort was dispensed with, a vat for the wooden press being supplied by a large stone hollowed out for the purpose, an excellent specimen of which from *Tell eṣ-Ṣâfi* is figured in Bliss and Macalister's *Excavations*, etc., p. 24.

Returning to the normal press-system we find that the 'must' was usually left in the wine-vat to undergo the first or 'tumultuous' fermentation after which it was drawn off (Hag 2^{16}, literally 'baled out') or, where the vat had a spout, simply run off into large jars or into wineskins (Mt 9^{17} and parallels) for the 'after-fermentation.' The modern Syrian wines are said to complete their first fermentation in from four to seven days and to be ready for use at the end of two to four months. In the Mishnah it is ordained that 'new wine' cannot be presented at the sanctuary for the drink-offering until it has stood for at least forty days in the fermenting jars.

When the fermentation had run its full course the wine was racked off into smaller jars and skins, the latter being preferred by travellers (Jos 9$^{4, 13}$). At the same time the liquor was *strained* (Mt 23^{24}; cf Is 25^{6}) through a metal or earthenware strainer, or through a linen cloth. In the further course of maturing, in order to prevent the wine from thickening on the **lees** (Zeph 1^{12}) it was from time to time decanted from one vessel to another. The even tenor of Moabite history is compared to wine which has not undergone this process (Jer 48^{11}). When sufficiently refined the wine was poured into jars lined with pitch which were carefully closed, sealed, and stored in the wine cellars (1 Ch 27^{27}). The Lebanon (Hos 14^{7}) and Helbon (Ezk 27^{18}) to the NW. of Damascus were localities specially celebrated for their wines.

No trace is found in the multitude of Mishnah references of any means employed to preserve wine in the unfermented state. It is improbable that with the means at their disposal the Jews could have done so even had they so desired. **Unfermented wine** was not known in that ancient time.

4. Of all the fermented liquors, other than wine, with which the Hebrews seem to have been familiar, the oldest historically was almost certainly that made from dates (cf **1**). These, according to Pliny, were steeped in water before being sent to the press, where they were probably treated as olives were treated in the oil-press (see OIL). **Date wine** was greatly prized by the Babylonians and is said by Herodotus to have been the principal article of Assyrian commerce.

In the Mishnah there is frequent mention of **cider** or ' apple ' wine, made from the quince or whatever other fruit the ' apple ' of the Hebrews may signify. The only other wine other than ' the fruit of the vine ' mentioned by name in the OT is the ' sweet **wine of pomegranates** ' (Ca 8^{2} RVm), ' the juice of my pomegranates ' (RV, RSV). Like the dates these fruits were first crushed in the oil-mill, after which the juice was allowed to ferment. In the Mishnah we find reference to various fermented liquors imported from abroad, among them the beer for which Egypt was framed. But it is doubtful if **beer** was used by the Israelites though the discovery of innumerable beer-mugs with strainer spouts shows it to have been a favourite drink of the Philistines (Albright, *Arch. of Palestine*, p. 115). A striking witness of the extent to which the wines of the West were imported has been revealed by the discovery of handles of wine jars, especially of *amphorae* from Rhodes : these have been excavated in large numbers from the cities in Southern Palestine.

5. The Hebrew wines were light, and in early times were probably taken without dilution. At all events, the first clear reference to diluting with water is found in 2 Mac 15^{39} : ' it is harmful to drink wine by itself or again to drink water by itself, while wine mixed with water is delicious ' and in NT times the practice of dilution seems to have been usual. The wine of Sharon, it is said, was mixed with two parts of water, being a lighter wine than most. With other wines, according to the Talmud, the proportion was one part of wine to three of water.

The ' mingling ' or mixing of strong drink denounced by Isaiah (5^{22}) has reference to the ancient practice of adding aromatic herbs and spices to the wine in order to add to its flavour and increase its ' headiness.' Such was the **spiced wine** of Ca 8^{2}. Jesus on the cross was offered ' wine mingled with myrrh ' (Mt 15^{23} ; cf Mt 27^{34} RV, RSV).

6. The use of wine was universal among all classes with the exception of those who had taken a vow of abstinence, such as Nazirites and Rechabites. The priests also had to abstain but only when on duty in the sanctuary (Lv 10^{9}). A libation of wine formed the necessary accompaniment of the daily burnt-offering and of numerous other offerings (cf Sir 50^{15} ; ' He reached out his hand to the cup, and poured a libation of the blood of the grape ; he poured it out at the foot of the altar '.

The attitude of the prophets and other teachers of Israel, including our Lord Himself, to the ordinary use of wine as a beverage is no doubt accurately reflected in the saying of Jesus ben-Sira : ' Wine drunk in season and temperately is rejoicing of heart and gladness of soul. Wine drunk to excess is bitterness of soul, with provocation and stumbling ' (31^{28f}). The Hebrews were aware of the danger and unsparingly denounced the sin of excessive indulgence (Is 5^{11f} 28$^{1-3}$, Hos 4^{11}, Pr 20^{1} 23$^{39-32}$, *et passim*). In the altered conditions of our own day it must be admitted that the rule of conduct formulated by Paul (1 Co 8$^{8-13}$; cf Ro 14$^{13-21}$) appeals to the individual conscience with greater urgency and insistence than ever before in the experience of Jew or Christian.

A. R. S. K.—**J. Pn.**

WINEFAT, WINEPRESS, WINE-VAT.—See WINE AND STRONG DRINK, **2.**

WINK.—To ' wink at,' *i.e.* pass over, is used of God in Ac 17^{30} ' The times of this ignorance God winked at ' (RV ; RSV ' overlooked '), and Wis 11^{23} ' Thou . . . winkest at the sins of men ' (RSV ' dost overlook men's sins ' ; cf RV). It is a good example of the colloquial language of the English Versions.

WINNOW.—See AGRICULTURE, **3.**

WISDOM.—The saying in Pr 3^{19f} (cf Ps 104^{24}) draws attention to two features of ' wisdom ' as that was understood in Israel. It is essentially practical in character ; and it is, like righteousness and life itself, primarily divine in origin. Man may partake of this wisdom—indeed if he is to make a success of life, he must ; but he will do so only in terms of reverence and piety (Ps 111^{10}, Pr 1^{7} 9^{10}, Sir 1^{14}). He will, however, never comprehend the fulness of ' wisdom ' (Job 28, Ps 139^{6}, Is 40$^{13f, 28}$). Further, there are close parallels between the forms of Israel's wisdom literature and that of the ancient world as that is preserved in the literature of Egypt and Mesopotamia.

Wisdom is that ability required for the good administration of a country's affairs Gn 41^{32}, Dt 1^{13}, for good craftsmanship Ex 28^{3}, Is 40^{20} ; for the ability of a general, Is 10^{13} ; for a mariner's skill, Ps 107^{27b} (literally ' all their wisdom is swallowed up ') ; it may correspond to what we should call ' shrewdness ' 2 S 13^{3} or ' sagacity ' 1 K 16^{28}. Thus it signifies that ability to distinguish between what is advantageous and what is harmful, rightly to assess a situation and to act in such a way as to bring intention to fulfilment. In the Wisdom Literature it becomes an ethical term, implicitly or explicitly related to the will of God. Under the monarchy, **the wise** formed a class comparable to the priests and the prophets. The references to them in the earlier records are scanty, but in Jer 18^{18} they are clearly a well recognized group ; cf Is 29^{14}, Ezk 7^{26}. Among them traditional wisdom was conserved and it was their function to guide the royal policy. Under David, we hear of wise women of Tekoa (2 S 14^{1ff}) and Abel-beth-Maacah (2 S 20^{14ff}) ; these do not form members of a guild but the latter town appears to have been noted as a place where wisdom was conserved. Jer 8^{8f} would suggest that from the sages were drawn the scribes, *i.e.* keepers of the royal archives (from whose records much of the historical material of Kings was derived) and royal advisers. If this be so, we may trace the official activity of the sages to an early period in the monarchy, 2 S 8^{17} 20^{25} and frequently thereafter. When in the post-exilic era prophecy had vanished or was rare, the Torah was complete and the priests were concerned with the conduct of the developed ritual, the functions of the sages was still to give counsel. But now their work was democratized, at least to the extent that they taught their wisdom to those who had leisure to attend a ' house of instruction,' (Sir 51^{23}) ; they also published their collections of wisdom sayings and reflections. Characteristic of these wisdom writers are such quasi-technical terms as discipline (*mûsār*), prudence (*'ormāh*), discretion (*m^ezimmāh*), learning (*leḳaḥ*), guidance (*taḥbûlôth*), parable (*māshāl*), riddle (*ḥîdhāh*).

The literary expression of Israel's sages is to be found in the books of Proverbs, Job, Ecclesiastes, Ecclesiasticus, Wisdom of Solomon, 1 Esdras 3^{1}–4^{63}, Tobit, Baruch 3^{9}–4^{4}, 4 Maccabees, and the Mishnaic ' Sayings of the Fathers ' ; Daniel may well be the product of this school in the peculiar circumstances of persecution ; the Joseph story of Gn 39–48 should probably be included here ; and the influence of the sages is to be found in the Psalter (cf Ps 1, 32, 37, 94) and in James. Some would include Song of Songs ; but, unless this collection of love poems was intended from the first as an allegory, it hardly comes into this category. The Wisdom books in their present form come from the post-exilic era ; but they contain within them material of much greater antiquity. The pursuit of ' wisdom ' had a long history, and derived much from extra-Israelite sources. That Israel knew and valued this international wisdom is evident from 1 K 4^{30}, Jer 49^{7} 50^{35} 51^{57}, Ezk 28$^{2-5}$, Ob ^{8}, Bar 3^{22f}. Comparison can now be made with the wisdom literature of Sumeria,

Babylonia, Egypt and Ugarit, some of which dates from the 3rd millennium B.C. There are two main types, (1) prudential wisdom, usually expressed in brief sentences; (2) reflective essays on the significance of life, often of a pessimistic character. The *forms* of Israel's sapiential writing correspond to the literary types of international wisdom. The closest parallels are to be found with the Teaching of Amen-em-ope (1000–600 B.C.), part of which is reproduced in Pr 22^{17}–24^{22}, and with the Proverbs of Aḥiḳar, a copy of which in Aramaic from an Akkadian original was found among the literature of the Jews of Elephantine. Parallels to Job and Ecclesiastes, though not of the same quality, have also been found in Mesopotamian and Egyptian literature. There are no literary survivals of the wisdom of Edom, but it is evident from its prologue that the Hebrew Job was a development of an original Edomite wisdom story. Apparently also two sections of Proverbs, 30$^{1-14}$ 31$^{1-9}$, are of Arabian origin since Massa was an Arabian tribe (Gn 25^{14}). The impact of international wisdom upon Israelite thought appears to have come in the reign of Solomon, apparently as the result of his international relationships and trading ventures. In that sense, Solomon is the father of Israel's wisdom literature, so that even as late as 100 B.C. and among the Jews of Alexandria a book of wisdom could be associated with his name. It is by no means impossible that Pr 10^{1}–22^{16} and 25–27 derive from the early monarchy.

It may be noted that in the OT wisdom books there is a striking absence of distinctively Israelite religious terminology; there are few allusions to the covenant, the work of God in history, election, the Messiah, and the Day of Yahweh. In their treatment of righteousness and justice, they commonly speak the same language as the extra-Israelite sages. Apart from the replacement of Ea, Shamash, Re, and Horus with Yahweh, it might almost appear that Israel's wisdom was one with that of the extra-Israelite world; it should be noted however, that the Apocryphal wisdom literature is explicitly integrated into Jewish faith and practice. Yet this 'aloofness' from Israel's distinctive faith is more apparent than real, even in the 'utilitarian' Proverbs. The influence of the teaching of Deuteronomy is apparent throughout, and the use of the name Yahweh, although comparatively rare, could not but create a faith and an attitude to life that the names of Shamash and Horus could not do. It is for this reason that the challenge that confronts the author of Job is of greater urgency than it could be to the pagan. Certainly the Jewish scholars of the 2nd cent. B.C. were not aware of any incongruity. It would seem that in Israel's wisdom literature we have an example of a bold, even exclusive faith, able to assimilate the best of human reflection on life so long as it was recognized that 'the fear of Yahweh is the beginning of wisdom.'

Finally we may notice the remarkable presentation of Wisdom in Pr 8^{22ff}, Wis 7^{22ff}. In the former passage we find a poetic personification of Wisdom; in the latter a presentation which closely resembles what later Christian thinkers would call a hypostasis. This conception of Wisdom as the divine agency (but hardly agent) in the work of creation, would seem to have been used in the NT in some of the finest Christological passages; cf Jn 1$^{1-18}$, Col 1^{15ff}, He 1^{3}. Wisdom in Sir 24$^{1-23}$ is identified with the Torah in which God revealed Himself as Creator and Saviour; it is in these terms that the Christian finds the appropriate language to speak of Jesus Christ. A. S. H.

WISDOM, BOOK OF.—See preceding article and APOCRYPHA, 6.

WISE MEN.—See MAGI; and, for **'the Wise,'** WISDOM.

WIST.—See WIT.

WIT.—The verb 'to wit,' which means 'to know,' is used in AV in most of its parts. The present tense is '***I* wot,** thou *wottest, he wots*, or *wotteth, we wot*; the past tense ***I* wist,** *he wist, ye wist*; the infinitive 'to wit.' In 2 Co 8^{1} occurs the phrase *do to wit*, i.e. *make to know*—'we do you to wit of the grace of God' (RV 'we make known to you,' RSV 'we want you to know'). The substantive **wit** means in AV 'knowledge'; it occurs only in Ps 107^{27} 'at their wits' end.' **Witty,** which is found in AV in Pr 8^{12}, Jth 11^{23}, Wis 8^{19} (retained in Jth 11^{23} in RV; cf RSV in all cases), has the sense of 'knowing,' 'skilful'; and **wittingly** (Gn 48^{14}; so RV; RVm and RSV 'crossing his hands') is 'knowingly.'

WITCH, WITCHCRAFT.—See MAGIC, DIVINATION, AND SORCERY.

WITHERED HAND.—See MEDICINE.

WITH(E)S.—Jg 16^{7} (AV and RV). This represents a term which probably means 'bow-strings of "green" gut'; cf RSV 'fresh bow-strings.' The English word means a supple twig from a willow (see also CORD).

WITNESS.—This is the rendering of Hebrew *'ēdh* and *'ēdhāh* and of the Greek *martys, martyria*, and *martyreō*, and compounds of this root. The original meaning of the Hebrew root was 'to return,' 'to repeat,' and the noun 'witness' denotes one who can repeat what he has seen or heard. By extension it was used to denote such things as stones erected as memorials of an agreement or event. Hence 'witness' may be:

1. *The person who can testify* to an agreement, to ensure its fulfilment, or to an event, or vouch for parties in debate, *e.g.* Gn 21^{30} (Abimelech as witness to Abraham's digging of a well), Is 8^{2} (Uriah as witness to Isaiah's act). Frequently God is invoked as such a witness, *e.g.* Gn 31^{50} (between Jacob and Laban); cf Job 16^{19}, 1 S 12^{5ff}, Jer 29^{23} 42^{5}. In the NT Paul calls on God to witness to his truth and the purity of his motives (Ro 1^{9}, 2 Co 1^{23} etc.).

2. *The witness in a legal sense*, witnessing an act of conveyancing (Jer 32^{10}) or a betrothal (Ru 4^{9f}), or giving testimony in a lawsuit, where two or more witnesses were required in a capital case (Nu 35^{30}, Dt 17^{6}, He 10^{28}), and in case of conviction the witnesses had to begin the carrying out of the sentence (Dt 17^{7}; cf Ac 7^{58}). Warnings against false witness are frequent (Ex 20^{16}, Pr 12^{17} 19$^{5-9}$ 21^{28} 25^{18} etc.), and one proved to have given false witness suffered the penalty his testimony would have brought on another (Dt 19^{16ff}). See also JUSTICE, II.

3. The person who testifies to what he has experienced by recounting it and making it known. The Israelite people is described as God's witnesses (Is 43$^{10, 12}$ 44^{8}). In the NT the Apostles frequently appear as witnesses (*martyres*) of the life, death, and resurrection of Jesus (Lk 24^{48}, Ac 1^{8} 2^{32} 3^{15} etc.), and so also Paul (Ac 22^{14f} 26^{12ff}). The heroes of faith are called 'the cloud of witnesses' (He 12^{1}), John the Baptist witnesses by his preaching (Jn 1$^{7f, 15, 32}$), and Jesus Himself is 'the faithful witness' in Rev 1^{5} 3^{14} (cf 1 Ti 6^{13}). *Martys* developed the meaning of *martyr*, and it is so rendered in AV in Ac 22^{20}, Rev 2^{13} 17^{6} and in RV and RSV in Rev 17^{6}.

4. *An inanimate reminder or memorial, e.g.* a heap of stones (Gn 31^{44}), an altar (Jos 22$^{26f, 34}$, Is 19^{19f}), the stone set up by Joshua (Jos 24^{27}), the Song of Moses (Dt 31^{26}), Job's disease (Job 16^{8}), or heaven and earth (Dt 30^{19} 31^{28}). In the NT the dust shaken off the disciples' feet is a witness against those who reject them (Mk 6^{11}). See also ARK, 1, TABERNACLE, 7. W. F. B.—**H. H. R.**

WITTY.—See WIT.

WIZARD.—See MAGIC, DIVINATION, AND SORCERY.

WOLF.—In AV and RV in the OT 'wolf' is always translation of *z^{e}'ēbh* (cf Arab. *dhi'b*), Gn 49^{27}, Is 11^{6} 65^{25}, Jer 5^{6}, Ezk 22^{27}, Hab 1^{8}, Zeph 3^{3}. Cf also the proper name Zeeb, Jg 7^{25}. In RV *'iyyîm* is translated 'wolves' in Is 13^{22} 34^{14} (AV 'wild beasts of the islands,' RSV 'hyenas'), Jer 50^{39} (AV 'wild beasts of the islands,' RSV 'jackals'); see JACKAL. The NT term is *lykos*, Mt 7^{15} 10^{16}, Lk 10^{3}, Jn 10^{12}, Ac 20^{39}.

The wolf of Palestine is a variety of *Canis lupus*, somewhat lighter in colour and larger than that of N. Europe. It is seldom seen to-day, and never goes in packs, though commonly in couples; it commits its ravages at night, hence the expression 'wolf of the evenings,' Jer 5^{6} (AV, RV; RSV 'from the desert'), Zeph 3^{3}; it was one of the greatest terrors of the lonely shepherd, Jn 10^{12}; persecutors are compared to wolves in Mt 10^{16}, Ac 20^{29}. E. W. G. M.

WOMAN.—1. In OT (*'ishshāh*, 'woman,' 'wife'; *nᵉḳēbhāh* [Lv 15^{33}, Nu 31^{15}, Jer 31^{22}], 'female') woman's position is one of inferiority and subjection to man (Gn 3^{16}); and yet, in keeping with the view that ideally she is his companion and 'help meet' (2^{18-24}), she never sinks into a mere drudge or plaything. In patriarchal times, Sarah, Rebekah, and Rachel stand side by side with their husbands. In the era of the deliverance from Egypt, Miriam is ranked with Moses and Aaron (cf Mic 6^{4}). In the days of the Judges, Deborah is not only a prophetess (q.v.), as other women in Israel were, but is herself a Judge (Jg 4^{4}). Under the monarchy, Jezebel in the Northern Kingdom and Athaliah in the Southern, afford illustrations of the political power and influence that a woman might wield. In religious matters, we find women attending the Feasts along with men (1 S 1^{1ff} etc.), taking part with them in acts of sacrifice (Jg $13^{20, 23}$ etc.), combined with them in the choral service of the Temple (Ezr 2^{65} etc.). And though in the Deuteronomy code woman's position is one of complete subordination, her rights are recognized and safeguarded in a way that prepares the soil for the growth of those higher conceptions which find utterance in Malachi's declaration that divorce is hateful to Yahweh (2^{16}), and in the picture of the virtuous wife with which the Book of Proverbs concludes (ch. 31). See, further, FAMILY, MARRIAGE.

2. In NT (*gynē*, 'woman,' 'wife'; *thēleia* [Ro 1^{26ff}], 'female'; *gynaikarion* [diminutive from *gynē*, 2 Ti 3^{6}], RSV 'weak women').—Owing to the influence of Rabbinism, Jewish women had lost some of their freedom (cf with the scene at the well of Haran [Gn 24^{10ff}]) the surprise of the disciples by the well of Sychar when they found Jesus 'speaking with a woman' [Jn 4^{27}]). But Jesus wrought a wonderful change. He did this not only by His teaching about adultery (Mt 5^{27f}) and marriage and divorce (vv.^{31f} 19^{3ff}), but still more by His personal attitude to women, whether good and pure like His own mother (there is nothing harsh or discourteous in the 'Woman' of Jn 2^{4}; cf 19^{26}) and the sisters of Bethany, or sinful and outcast as some women of the Gospels were (Lk 7^{37ff} 8^{2}, Jn 4). The work of emancipation was continued in the Apostolic Church. Women formed an integral part of the earliest Christian community (Ac 1^{14}), shared in the gifts of Pentecost (2^{1ff}, cf v.^{17}), engaged in tasks of unofficial ministry (Ro 16^{1f}, Ph 4^{2f}), and by and by appear (1 Ti 3^{11}) as holding the office of the **deaconess** (q.v.), and possibly (5^{3}) that of the **'widow'** (q.v., and cf TIMOTHY [EPISTLES TO], **5**). St. Paul's conception of woman and of man's relation to her is difficult (1 Co 7), but may be explained partly by his expectation of the Parousia (vv.$^{29-31}$), and partly by the exigencies of an era of persecution (v.^{26}). In a later Pauline Epistle marriage becomes a type of the union between Christ and the Church (Eph 5^{22-33}). And if by his injunction as to the silence of women in the Church (1 Co 14^{34ff}) the Apostle appears to limit the prophetic freedom of the first Christian days (Ac $2^{4, 17}$), we must remember that he is writing to a Church set in the midst of a dissolute Greek city, where Christian women had special reasons for caution in the exercise of their new privileges. Elsewhere he announces the far-reaching principle that in Christ Jesus 'there is neither male nor female' (Gal 3^{28}). J. C. L.

WONDERS (Heb. *mōphēth*; Gr. *teras, dynamis, ergon, sēmeion*).—Usually an awe-inspiring, terrifying act manifesting Divine power. In the OT it is often associated with *'ōth*, sign, especially in the idiom *signs and wonders* used of miraculous events of the Exodus (Dt 4^{34} 6^{22} 7^{19} 26^{8} 28^{46} 29^{3} 34^{11}, Ex $7^{3, 9}$ 11^{9f} etc.). The phrase came over into Greek translations of the OT as *sēmeia kai terata*, signs and wonders, an idiom known in Hellenistic Greek. It appears frequently in the NT with reference to the life and works of Jesus or the apostles and the end of the world (Mk 13^{22}, Mt 24^{24}, Jn 4^{48}, Ac $2^{22, 43}$ 4^{30} 5^{12} 6^{8} 7^{36} 14^{3} 15^{12}, Ro 15^{19}, 2 Co 12^{12}, He 2^{4}). Mk 13^{22} refers these phenomena to false Christs; 2 Th 2^{9} ascribes them to Satan; Rev 19^{20}, to a false prophet, reminiscent of Dt 13^{1-3}. Wonders are regarded as confirmation of claims of prophets, apostles, and other messengers of God. Such omens, portents, and prodigies were characteristic of Near Eastern and Hellenistic religions. Cf SIGNS, MIRACLES. S. V. McC.

WOOD.—See FOREST; also WRITING, **8.**

WOOF.—See SPINNING AND WEAVING.

WOOL.—Woollen stuffs were much used for clothes (Lv 13^{47ff}, Pr 31^{13} etc.); mainly, however, for outer garments. For underwear, linen was preferred, as being cooler and cleaner. Wool, falling swiftly a prey to moths and larvae (Is 51^{8} etc.), was not used for wrapping the dead. A garment of mingled wool and linen might not be worn (Lv 19^{19}, Dt 22^{11}). Josephus says this was reserved exclusively for the priests (*Ant.* IV. viii. 11 [208]). Dyed wool is referred to (He 9^{19}, cf Lv 14^{4f}), but its natural colour, white, makes it the criterion of whiteness and purity (Ps 147^{16}, Is 1^{18}, Dn 7^{9}, Rev 1^{14}). Wool was a valuable article of commerce (Ezk 27^{18}), and it figures in the tribute paid by king Mesha (2 K 3^{4}). W. E.

WORD.—Apart from the personal use of 'Word' as a title of Christ (see LOGOS), its Biblical interpretation presents few difficulties. Both in the OT and in the NT the original terms employed may pass from the meaning 'speech' to signify 'the subject matter of speech.' In some passages there is uncertainty as to whether the translation should be 'word' or 'thing.' For example, 1 K 11^{41} RVm has 'or *words*, or *matters*' as alternatives to 'the acts of Solomon.' In Ac 8^{21} 'you have neither part nor lot in this matter' probably means 'in the matter in dispute,' which was the coveted power of imparting the gifts of the Holy Spirit; but the RVm 'word' is preferred by some expositors, who think that the reference is to the word preached by the Apostles and its attendant blessings (cf Mk 1^{45}, Lk 1^{2}). The AV and RV retain 'word' in Mt 18^{16} and 2 Co 13^{1} (RSV 'charge'), although Dt 19^{15} reads: 'At the mouth of two witnesses, or at the mouth of three witnesses, shall every matter be established' (RSV 'charge'). J. G. T.

WORK.—In the Bible work is represented as appointed for man at the creation (Gn 2^{15}), ordained for six days of the week (Ex 20^{9}), and part of the normal lot of man (Ps 104^{23}). Warnings against **slothfulness** are frequent in Proverbs (*e.g.* 6^{6-11} 15^{19} 18^{9} 19^{15} 26^{14}). The Rabbis were not ashamed to earn their living, and Paul earned his as a tentmaker (Ac 18^{3}; cf 2 Th 3^{7f}). He says 'If any one will not work, let him not eat' (2 Th 3^{10}; cf Ps 128^{2}, Pr 20^{4}, 1 Th 4^{11}), though he maintained that he himself was entitled to support from those to whom he ministered (2 Co 9^{4-7}). Ben Sira, however, says that wisdom 'depends on the opportunity of leisure' (Sir 38^{24}), and deprecates the drudgery of labour (38^{25ff}), though he warns against scorning manual labour (7^{15}) and recognizes its necessity (38^{32}).

God's co-operation in man's work is recognized (Ps 127^{1}), and skill in workmanship is declared to be His gift (Ex 35^{30}–36^{2}); without His blessing labour is unavailing (Ps 127^{2}).

The law of the **sabbath** (q.v.) provided for a weekly rest, not merely for the free man, but also for slaves and animals (Ex 20^{10}), since work is not the whole of life. Christ calls men to labour for more than the meat which perishes (Jn 6^{27}), and Paul commends labour in the work of God, *i.e.* in the service of the Church of Christ (1 Co 16^{10}; cf Ac 13^{2}, Ph 2^{30}). He calls converts his workmanship (1 Co 9^{1}), though he recognizes that here, as in other spheres, man is but the co-worker with God (2 Co 6^{1}), without whose blessing toil is fruitless (1 Co

3$^{7-9}$). The author of Hebrews holds before the faithful believer the promise of a sabbath rest (He 4^{11}). H. H. R.

WORLD.—1. In OT.—In general it may be said that the normal expression for such conception of the universe as the Hebrews had reached is 'the heavens and the earth' (Gn 1^{1}, Ps 89^{11}, 1 Ch 16^{31}), and that 'world' is an equivalent expression for '**earth.**' So far as there is a difference, the 'world' is rather the fruitful, habitable earth, *e.g.* 'the earth is the Lord's, and the fulness thereof; the world, and those who dwell therein' (Ps 24^{1}; cf 50^{12} 90^{2}, Is 34^{1}). The religious sentiments awakened by the contemplation of Nature appear also in references to the heavens and the sea (*e.g.* Ps 8, 19, Job 38, 39). But of the ethical depreciation of the world, so prominent in some NT writings, there are in the OT few traces. The 'world' is to be judged in righteousness (Ps 9^{8} 96^{13} 98^{9}), and punished for its evil (Is 13^{11}). The transient character of its riches and pleasures, with the consequent folly of absorption in them, is perhaps indicated by another Hebrew word (meaning 'duration'; cf '*aeon*' below) rendered 'world' at Ps 17^{14} ('men whose portion in life is of the world'); also by the same word at Ps 49^{1} (see the whole Psalm). A word of similar meaning is rendered 'world' in AV at Ps 73^{12}, Ec 3^{11}, but RSV gives quite another turn to the sense.

The ethical aspect of the 'world' does not receive any fresh emphasis in the Apocrypha, though in the Book of Wisdom both the scientific interest in regard to the world and the impulses of natural religion are notably quickened (7$^{17-22}$ 9^{9} 11$^{17, 22}$ 13$^{1-9}$, cf Sir 17, 18). There is ample contrast between the stability of the righteous and the vanity of ungodly prosperity (*e.g.* Wis 1–5), but the latter is not identified with the 'world.' It is noticeable that in the Apocrypha the word *kosmos*, which in the LXX means 'adornment,' has reached its sense of 'world,' conceived as a beautiful order; in the NT this becomes the prevalent word.

2. In NT.—(1) The word 'Aion' (*Aeon*) is sometimes used in the meaning of world. But the original sense of *aiōn* refers to time. Thus *aiōn* means a long stretch of time, and in some cases eternity (as in Greek since Plato and in LXX since Deuteronomy–Joshua); it may be referred to as in the past or in the future. In the former sense, *e.g.* Lk 1^{70}, Ac 3^{21} (RSV 'from of old,' AV 'since the world began'). The eternal purpose of God is a purpose 'before the ages' (RSV), 1 Co 2^{7} (AV 'before the world'); similarly Col 1^{26}, Eph 3^{9}, Jd ^{25}. With negation: 'never since the world began,' Jn 9^{32}. In the latter sense *aiōn* means the never-ending future, the coming eternity. So the phrase 'unto the *aion*,' *i.e.* 'up to eternal (life),' Jn 4^{14}, '(life) for ever,' Jn 6^{51}, or with a negation 'never' in Jn 11^{26}. Such phrases occur especially in John and Revelation and in doxologies (*e.g.* Ro 1^{25} 9^{4}), often redoubled 'unto the *aions* of the *aions*,' *i.e.* 'for ever and ever' (Ph 4^{20}, Eph 3^{21}, 1 Ti 1^{17}) or 'unto all *aions*' (Jd ^{25}).

The time as 'aion' is always conceived as the time of the world, either the present world or the future. Hence the conception of 'aion' comes closer to the conception of world, just as in the Hebrew *'ôlām* the significations of time and world are combined. Therefore the translation of *aiōn* is sometimes '**age**' and sometimes 'world,' according to the context. Thus God is called the 'King of ages' (1 Ti 1^{17}), and we find expressions such as the creation of the *aiōns* (He 1^{2} 11^{3}) or 'the close of the age' (Mt 13^{39f}) and 'the end of the world' (He 9^{26}).

The conceptions of age and world are combined, especially in the apocalyptic literature. Here the distinction between the present age and the coming age is not only a formal chronological distinction, but the present age means the present world with all the conditions which make it provisional and perishable, declining into all evils and ruled by the demons and Satan. Correspondingly, the coming age is the coming world of eternity with all the splendour and bliss for which the eschatological hope looked forward.

The 'sons of this world' or 'of this age' (Lk 16^{8} 20^{34}) are the people who are obsessed with the 'cares of the world' (Mk 4^{19}, Mt 13^{22}), who are leading a sinful life (Eph 2^{2}; cf 1 Ti 6^{17}, 2 Ti 4^{10}). The 'debater of this age' is proud of the 'wisdom of the world' which God has 'made foolish' (1 Co 1^{20}; cf 3^{18}). The present world is controlled by 'the rulers of this age who are doomed to pass away' (1 Co 2^{6}; cf v.^{8}). St. Paul can even speak of the 'god of this age' (2 Co 4^{4}), as St. John speaks of the 'ruler of this world' (Jn 12^{31}; cf 14^{30}). But Christ is made the Lord over all worldly powers, 'not only in this age but also in that which is to come' (Eph 1^{21}). Christ has delivered the believers 'from the present evil age' (Gal 1^{4}); God will show them 'the immeasurable riches of his grace in the coming ages' (Eph 2^{7}; note the plural form); they have already 'tasted the powers of the age to come' (He 6^{5}). But now they must be admonished, 'Do not be conformed to this world' (Ro 12^{2}), and bidden to 'live sober, upright, and godly lives in this world' (Tit 2^{12}). They shall receive 'in the age to come eternal life' (Mk 10^{30}, Lk 18^{30}). 'Those who are accounted worthy to attain to that age . . . are equal to angels and are sons of God . . .' (Lk 20^{35}).

(2) But the most frequent term for 'world' is *kosmos*, which is sometimes extended in meaning to the material universe, as in the phrases 'from the beginning (' foundation,' 'creation') of the world' (*e.g.* Mt 24^{21} 25^{34}, He 4^{3}, Ro 1^{20}; for the implied thought of Divine creation cf Ac 14^{17} 17^{24}). More commonly, however, the word is used of **the earth**, and especially the earth as the abode of man. To 'gain the whole world' is to become possessed of all possible material wealth and earthly power (Mt 16^{26}, Mk 8^{36}, Lk 9^{25}). Because 'sin came into the world' (Ro 5^{12}), it is become the scene of the Incarnation and the object of Redemption (2 Co 5^{19}, 1 Ti 1^{15}, He 10^{5}, Jn 1$^{9f, 29}$ 3^{16f} 12^{47}), the scene also, alien but inevitable, of the Christian disciple's life and discipline, mission and victory (Mt 5^{14} 13^{38} 26^{13}, Jn 17^{15}, Ro 1^{8}, 1 Co 3^{22} 4^{9} 5^{10} 7^{31}, 2 Co 1^{12}, Ph 2^{15}, Col 1^{6}, 1 P 5^{9}, Rev 11^{15}). From this virtual identification of the 'world' with mankind, and mankind as separated from and hostile to God, there comes the ethical signification of the word specially developed in the writings of St. Paul and St. John. In this sense St. Paul and St. John like to use the phrase 'this world' (1 Co 3^{19} 5^{10} 7^{31}, Eph 2^{2}, Jn 8^{23} 12^{31} 16^{11} 18^{36}, 1 Jn 4^{17} etc.).

(*a*) *The Epistles of St. Paul.* To the Galatians St. Paul describes the pre-Christian life as slavery to 'the elemental spirits of the universe' (4^{3}, cf v.^{9}); through Christ the world is crucified to him and he to the world (6^{14}). Both thoughts recur in Colossians (2$^{8, 20}$). In writing to the Corinthians he condemns the wisdom, the passing fashion, the care, the sorrow of the world (1 Co 1^{20f} 3^{19} 7$^{31, 33f}$, 2 Co 7^{10}; cf *aiōn* above), and declares the Divine choice to rest upon all that the world least esteems (1 Co 1^{27f}, cf Ja 2^{5}). This perception of the true worth of things is granted to those who 'received not the spirit of the world, but the spirit which is from God' (1 Co 2^{12}); hence the saints shall 'judge the world' (1 Co 6^{2}; cf 11^{32}). In the argument of Romans the thought of the Divine judgment of the 'world' has incidental place, but in the climax St. Paul conceives of the 'trespass' of Israel as leading to 'riches for the Gentiles,' and of the 'rejection' of them as the 'reconcilation of the world' (11$^{12, 15}$; cf v.^{32} and 5$^{12-21}$). What St. Paul condemns, then, is hardly the world as essentially evil, but the world-spirit which leads to evil by its neglect of the unseen and eternal, and by its blindness to the true scale of values revealed in the gospel of Christ crucified.

(*b*) *The Gospel and First Epistle of St. John.* In these two writings occur more than half the NT instances of the word we are considering. That is, the term *kosmos* is *characteristic* of St. John, and, setting aside his frequent use of it in the non-ethical sense, especially as the sphere of the incarnation and saving work of Christ, we find an ethical conception of the 'world' deeper in its shadows than that of St. Paul. It is true that Jesus is the Light of the world (Jn 1^{9} 3^{19} 8^{12} 9^{5} 12^{46}), its Life-giver ($6^{33, 51}$), its Saviour (3^{17} 4^{42} 12^{47}); yet 'the world knew him not' (1^{10}), and the Fourth Gospel sets out its story of His persistent rejection by the world in language which at times seems to pass beyond a mere record of contemporary unbelief, and almost to assert an essential dualism of good and evil (7^{7} 8^{23} 9^{39} 12^{31} $14^{17, 30}$ $16^{11, 20}$). Here the 'world' is not simply the worldly spirit, but the great mass of mankind in deadly hostility to Christ and His teaching. In contrast stand His disciples, 'his own who were in the world' (13^{1}), chosen out of the world (15^{19}; cf 17^{6}), but not of it, and therefore hated as He was hated (15^{18f} $17^{14, 16}$). For them He intercedes as He does not for the world (17^{9}). In the 1st Epistle of St. John the same sharp contrasts meet us. The world lies within the scope of God's redemptive purpose in Jesus Christ (2^{2} 4^{14}), yet it stands opposed to His followers as a thing wholly evil, with which they may hold no traffic (2^{15-17}; cf Ja 4^{4}), knowing them not and hating them ($3^{1, 13}$). It is conceived as under the sway of a power essentially hostile to God,—the antichrist ($2^{18, 22}$ 4^{3}; cf 'the ruler of this world' Jn 12^{31} 14^{30} 16^{11})—and is therefore not to be entreated and persuaded, but fought and overcome by the 'greater' one who is in the disciple of Christ (4^{4} 5^{4f}). Faith 'overcomes the world,' but St. John reserves for his closing words his darkest expression of a persistent dualism of good and evil, light and darkness: 'We know that we are of God, and the whole world is in the power of the evil one' (5^{19}).

The idiomatic uses of the term 'world' in Jn 7^{4} 12^{19}, 1 Jn 3^{17} are sufficiently obvious. For the difficult expression 'an unrighteous world' applied to the tongue (Ja 3^{6}), see the Commentaries. S. W. G.—**R. B.**

WORM.—**1.** Hebrew *sās*, Is 51^{8}, the larva of a clothes-moth. See Moth. **2.** Hebrew *rimmāh*, Ex 16^{24}, Job 25^{6}, Is 14^{11} (RSV **'maggot'** in the last two of these passages). **3.** Hebrew *tôlā'îm*, *tôlē'āh*, *tôla'ath*, Ex 16^{20}, Job 25^{6}, Is 14^{11} 66^{24}, Jon 4^{7} etc. Both **2** and **3** are used to describe the same kind of worms (cf Ex $16^{20, 24}$), and most references are to maggots and other insect larvae which breed on putrid organic matter. These are very common in Palestine, occurring even on neglected sores and, of course, on dead bodies (Job 19^{26} 21^{26}). Jonah's worm (*tôlē'āh*) was probably some larva which attacks the roots, or perhaps a centipede. The 'worms' of Dt 28^{39} were probably caterpillars. **4.** Hebrew *rāḳābh*, Hos 5^{12} (AVm; AV, RV 'rottenness,' RSV 'dry rot'). In Pr 12^{4} where the same word is also translated 'rottenness,' it is rendered in LXX *skōlēx*, 'wood-worm,' which seems appropriate to the context. **5.** *zōḥᵃlê 'āreṣ*, Mic 7^{17} (AV 'worms of the earth'; RV, RSV 'crawling things of the earth'), may possibly refer to true earth-worms (which are comparatively rare in Palestine), but more probably to serpents. See Serpents, **10.** **6.** Greek *skōlēx*, Mk 9^{44} etc. The expression **'eaten of worms,'** used in describing (Ac 12^{23}) the death of Herod Agrippa I., would seem to refer to a death accompanied by violent abdominal pains, such symptoms being commonly ascribed in the Holy Land to-day to abdominal worms (*Lumbricoides*)—a belief often revived by the evacuation of such worms near the time of death. E. W. G. M.

WORMWOOD.—Hebrew *la'ᵃnāh*, Dt 29^{18} (AV, RV; RSV 'bitter fruit'), Pr 5^{4}, Jer 9^{15} 23^{15}, La $3^{15, 19}$, Am 5^{7} 6^{12} (in the last AV **hemlock**); Greek *apsinthos*, Rev 8^{11}. *la'ᵃnāh* was some bitter substance usually associated with **gall** (q.v.); it is used metaphorically for calamity and sorrow. Tradition favours some species of *Artemisia* (wormwood), of which several kinds are found in Palestine. E. W. G. M.

WORSHIP.—I. **In OT.**—**1.** In RSV the term 'worship' and its derivatives occur 112 times, as the translation of six Hebrew and Aramaic verb forms. The most important of these is the Hebrew *hishtaḥᵃweh*, 'to prostrate oneself,' which occurs 86 times. This term for worship is not only predominant in a statistical sense; it expresses the act and the attitude appropriate to the worship of a sovereign deity whose exclusive claim upon Israel is a central OT theme. The remaining terms are: *'ābhadh* 'to serve' (11 times); *yārē'* 'to fear' (Jos 22^{25}); *shārath* 'to minister or do service,' especially of a cultic sort (Ezk 20^{32}); *dārash* 'to seek or inquire (of the deity)' (Ezr 4^{2} 6^{21}); and the Aramaic *sᵉghadh* 'to pay homage to' (11 times, all in Dn 3). Numerous additional terms are employed to describe the acts and attitudes of worship, prominent among which are those referring to praise, rejoicing, prayer, sacrifice, making and payment of vows, etc.

2. Little is known of the earliest forms of worship in Israel. In Genesis, the patriarchs are reported to have built altars to Yahweh and there to have called on His name (Gn 12^{7-8} 13^{18} J, etc.). The slaughter of animals in connexion with the making of contracts or covenants is attested in this period (Gn 15; see also Jer 34^{18}) and may reflect similar customs known from the ancient Mesopotamian city of Mari. The worship of the God (or gods) of the patriarchs (the God[s] of the Fathers, Gn 31^{42} etc.) apparently required no elaborate priesthood or cult, since the deity was conceived to be almost a member of the tribe, one who accompanied the people in their wanderings, bound neither to a particular land nor to specific cult centres. The God of the patriarchs is reported to have chosen the places and the modes of His appearance to His people.

3. With the appearance of the deity to Moses and the subsequent deliverance of the slaves from Egypt, the foundation of Israelite worship is laid. Israel's God here appears under the name 'Yahweh,' a name for which no etymology or explanation is provided (Ex 3^{14-15} is best understood as the refusal to provide an etymological explanation of the name). He is a jealous God, who brooks no rivals. He will not permit any representations of Himself to be fashioned, nor may His name be used in conjuring or other forms of magic (Ex 20^{3-7}). The worship of such a deity will (or should) depend upon an understanding of his nature and purpose. The Israelite community of the time of Moses (or shortly thereafter) understood the nature and purpose of Yahweh to be disclosed in His dealings with His people in the concrete events of history. Specifically, the Exodus from Egypt, the covenant at Sinai and the guidance of Yahweh during the wilderness period are understood to be the central revelatory acts by means of which Yahweh's nature and purpose have been made known, and in the light of which He is to be worshipped. Moses is credited with having established the form of Israelite worship and cultic practice (Ex 25–31, 35–40), although numerous innovations are reported and have occurred in subsequent ages. The wilderness period, nonetheless, remains the norm for authentic worship in Israel (Am 5^{25}, Jer 7^{21-23}).

4. The confrontation of Canaanite worship after the Conquest brought many changes into the worship of Israel. Yahweh is conceived to have taken over the powers exercised by the Canaanite high god and his local manifestations, as well as all other numinous and demonic powers. Hence the way is prepared for the adoption of literary and cultic forms which had formerly been associated with the worship of the fertility deities (Jg 5, Pss 29, 68, Hab 3, etc.). The festivals connected with the barley harvest (Passover-Unleavened Bread), the wheat harvest (Pentecost) and the fruit harvest (Tabernacles) are marked by the Yahwistic covenant faith and are transformed into occasions upon which Yahweh's saving deeds are commemorated and the covenant renewed (Ex 12–13, Dt 26^{5-9}, Jos 24, etc.). The sacrificial rites also take on particular significance under the influence of the covenant faith. Their fundamental meaning is expiatory: the community and the individual acknowledge, through the shedding of blood and the offering of a portion of the produce of the ground, that life belongs to Yahweh its creator. In face of the faithlessness of Israel, Yahweh is understood to have the life of His people fully at His disposal. It is only His love and graciousness which lead Him to accept the sacrificial offerings in place of the lives of those who worship Him.

5. The establishment of the Monarchy was accompanied by an elaborate development in the forms and practices of Israelite worship. The extent of the influence of the 'divine kingship' ideology of the surrounding peoples upon Israelite kingship may be debated, but such influence to some degree is apparent. Yahweh is the king of Israel (Is 6^{5}); earthly kings rule only at His pleasure or sufferance. Yet as the agents of the deity, the kings were of central importance for Israelite life and worship. David's innovations in the area of worship were considerable, it appears. He appointed his own sons as priests (2 S 8^{18}). He established, or reinstituted. a processional ceremony in which the Ark of the Covenant was brought into Jerusalem on one of the great festivals (probably the autumn festival, 2 S 6; see Pss 24, 132). He is credited with having been the author of many psalms and of having introduced instrumental accompaniment to the music of Israel (Am 6^{5}). It seems likely that he introduced into Israel a new priesthood, that of the old Jebusite city, Jerusalem, the first incumbent being Zadok.

6. The periods of relative prosperity under subsequent kings were marked by further elaboration of the forms and practices of Israelite worship. Solomon's Temple became the centre for the community's worship and also became a stumbling block for Israelite faith. The close relationship between king and cult tended not only to give too great a place to the king and his family and court in the conduct of worship; it also prepared the way for an understanding of worship as a means of securing or even coercing the favour of Yahweh. Against this and similar corruptions of Israelite worship, including all forms of idolatry, the great prophets inveighed (Am 4^{4-5} $5^{4-5, 21-24}$, Hos 4 f, 8 f, Is 1^{10-20} etc.).

7. With the fall of the Temple, already predicted by Micah (3^{12}) and Jeremiah (chs. 7, 26), one of the most significant developments in Israelite worship occurred. Israel learned that true worship of Yahweh was not dependent upon the existence of one sacred centre, the dwelling-place (or place of appearance) of the deity. Individual **prayer,** by no means absent in the pre-Exilic community, is given a new impetus and status. Much of the psalmody of Israel is produced, or at the least elaborated, during the Exile. The priestly tradition is recorded in detail and set within the framework of the narrative and poetic materials of the Pentateuch. Local gatherings in the houses of exiles prepare the way for the establishment of the synagogues of the post-Exilic period (Ezk 33^{30-33}). The Law of Yahweh itself becomes an object of veneration, especially in the period after the Exile (Pss 1, 119). The restoration of the Temple was indeed of great significance for the post-Exilic community. It was the centre of the earth (Ezk 38^{12}), the place of gathering for Israel on the feast days, the particular site from which came judgment and direction for the life of man (Is 2^{3}, Mic 4^{2}). But the restored Temple was never to assume the importance which it formerly had; the **synagogue,** despite the simplicity of its forms of worship and the emphasis upon the study and application of the Law, became the real centre of Jewish life and worship. Hence the fall of Jerusalem in A.D. 70 was in itself no profound threat to the worship of the community of Israel.

8. The basic meaning of Israelite worship is to be found in the quality of the relationship which it both affirmed and established between God and man. OT worship displays a remarkable openness on the part of the community and the individual in their dealings with Yahweh. This is particularly true of the prayers. Unable to make images of the deity, Israel was free to praise the works of God in nature and in history. Since Israel was convinced of Yahweh's sole authority in the assembly of heaven, on earth, and under the earth, she had no recourse but to attribute to Yahweh the misfortunes and calamities which befell her. Yet, convinced also of Yahweh's involvement in the very details of human existence, Israelite worshippers developed a type of prayer which has few parallels in the prayers and liturgical literature of their neighbours. Yahweh may even be accused of deception (Jer 15^{18} $20^{7-8, 14-18}$), or of having forsaken His people (Ps 22^{1} etc.). These prayers, scattered throughout the entire OT, reveal how the Israelite man of faith stood ready to wrestle with God for a blessing (Gn 32^{24-32}).

The **Sabbath** (q.v.) was also of decisive significance in the worship of Israel. Although its historical origins remain obscure, it was a well-established part of the worship of Israel by the middle of the 8th cent. (Am 8^{5}) and is traditionally associated with the wilderness period (Ex 16^{22-30}). The remarkable fact is that nowhere in OT is a prescribed ritual for Sabbath observance to be found: the Sabbath is depicted as a day of rest and rejoicing in the goodness and faithfulness of Yahweh. The Sabbath provided time for reflection; it provided order for the common life of Israel; and it was thus one of the primary occasions for the development of that experience of communion with the living God which is reflected in OT literature and life.

In the act of worship the entire range of communication with the deity was opened. The saving deeds of Yahweh in the past were rehearsed and became an inescapable part of present experience, and the coming triumph of Yahweh's purpose for Israel—and for all mankind—was also, by anticipation, a part of the present. But all worship in Israel was required to find its issue and its authentication in service (Am 5^{24} etc.). Both worship and service were, at their best and truest, theocentric: they were human responses to the prior and determinative action and purpose of Yahweh.

See ADORATION, PRAISE, PRAYER, PREACHING, SABBATH, SACRIFICE, SYNAGOGUE, TEMPLE.

II. In NT.—The words most commonly translated 'worship' in NT are *proskuneō* ('to prostrate oneself before the diety or a ruler,' 52 times), *sebomai* ('to show reverence or respect,' 10 times), and *latreuō* ('to serve or carry out relitious duties, particularly of a cultic nature,' 11 times). The nouns *proskunētēs* ('worshipper,' Jn 4^{23}), *latreia* ('worship or service of God,' Ro 9^{4} 12^{1}, He 9^{1}), *eidōlolatreia* ('idol worship,' 1 Co 10^{14}), *thrēskeia* ('worship of God, religion, especially in cult,' Col 2^{18}), *leitourgia* ('service in temple or Christian service,' He 9^{21}), and *sebasma* ('object of worship,' 2 Th 2^{4}) occur sparingly in the sense of 'worship.' The adjective *theosebēs* ('god-fearing, devout,' Jn 9^{31}) and the verb *sebazomai* ('to show reverence, to worship,' Ro 1^{25}) complete the list of words translated in RSV by 'worship.'

Neither the form nor the content of worship in NT can be fully reconstructed from available sources. It is evident that Christian worship arose out of Jewish practices at both synagogue and Temple. Equally evident is the fact that early Christian worship was fixed upon God's saving work in Jesus Christ. The Jewish Sabbath is quickly replaced in Christian worship by the first day of the week (1 Co 16^{2}, Ac 20^{7}), the Lord's Day (Rev 1^{10}), although in the immediate period after Pentecost the community gathered daily (Ac 2^{46}). The Lord's Day is the occasion for celebration of the Resurrection of Jesus, His Resurrection having occurred on the first day of the week (Mk 16^{2} etc.). It is also the occasion for confrontation with the living Christ through the Spirit, present with His people, and for anticipation 6f His return in glory at the Last Day.

In Ac $2^{42, 46-47}$ and 1 Co 12, 14 (see also Col 3^{16-17}) are found the most explicit NT statements concerning the content of early Christian worship. Such worship included the following elements, at the least: proclamation and teaching, prayers, acts of communion (*koinōnia*), especially the Lord's Supper, prophetic discourses, ecstatic speech and its interpretation, and various benedictions and congregational responses. On particular (and probably distinct) occasions the rite of baptism was performed, almost certainly within a setting of Christian worship, although NT contains no more than fragments of liturgical formulas which accompanied the rite of baptism (Mt 28^{19} etc.). The distinction between the Service of the Word and the Lord's Supper must not be overdrawn. In NT references a *single* service is attested, which probably had its culmination in the Supper (Ac 2[42], 1 Co 11[28–29]). Public proclamation of the gospel is quite distinct from the worship of the Christian community, although a proper and necessary corollary of the worship, indeed of the very life, of the community (Ro 1[9]).

NT worship was concentrated upon the saving acts of God. Large place was given, it is believed, to lessons from OT (particularly the prophets), to the words and deeds of Jesus, and to the apostolic teaching. Paul's letters were probably read in connexion with the worship of the communities to which they were addressed and were also circulated among the congregations. In addition, the prophets were encouraged to speak that which the Spirit summoned them to speak, thus making concretely relevant the apostolic tradition and teaching. Outsiders were admitted to attend, and even to participate in, Christian worship (1 Co 14[16, 22–25]), although the Supper was reserved for believers (1 Co 11[27–30]). The arrangement of the Christian Church at Dura Europos (early 3rd cent. A.D.) indicates that the Supper and the rite of Baptism were celebrated in a different room from that in which the Service of the Word was held.

The *Didache* (9, 10, 14) and the letter of Pliny the Younger to the emperor Trajan (*Epp.* xcvi) contain additional information bearing upon the form and content of early Christian worship. It is impossible to determine, however, the extent to which these sources may properly be employed in the reconstruction of the form and content of worship in the NT period.

The prominence of prayer in NT worship is apparent throughout the entire NT. In the Gospels, Jesus is reported to have withdrawn from the crowds and from the disciples for private prayer (Mk 6[46] etc.). He taught His disciples how to pray (Mt 6[5–13], Lk 11[2–4]), even summoning them to pray for those who persecuted them (Mt 5[44]). The letters of Paul regularly open with the apostle's references to his prayers for his fellow-Christians, who are also instructed to 'pray constantly' (1 Th 5[17], Ro 12[12]). Intercessory prayers occupy a much larger place in Christian worship than was the case in OT or in Jewish worship. Prayers are generally addressed to God, through Jesus Christ, in the power of the Spirit (Eph 6[18], Col 3[17] etc.). The Spirit of God (the Holy Spirit, the Spirit of Christ) gives power and direction to the Christian and to the Church in order that their prayers may be appropriate (Ro 8[26], 1 Co 14[13–19]).

The dominant note in NT worship is that of joy and thanksgiving in face of God's gracious redemption of mankind in Jesus Christ. Having the 'first fruits of the Spirit' (Ro 8[23]), the Christian community rejoices in God's fulfilment of His promise to the fathers of old and waits with eager longing for the culmination of His work at the Last Day. Past, present, and future are united, but not dissolved, in the act of worship. He 'who was and is and is to come' (Rev 4[8]) is present with His people in worship—and He will come soon (Rev 22[12, 20]). The NT response to this hope and affirmation is: 'Amen. Come, Lord Jesus!' (Rev 22[20], 1 Co 16[22]). W. J. Ha.

WOT.—See Wit.

WOULD.—See Will.

WRATH.—See Anger, Anger of God.

WREATH.—See Crown.

WREATHEN WORK, Ex 28[14, 22] (AV, RV).—See Cord.

WRESTLING.—See Games.

WRITING.—1. Origin of writing.—The Bible has nothing to say of the origin of writing, which seems to have been invented early in the 4th millennium B.C. by the Sumerians and almost at the same time by the Egyptians. The cumbersome clay-tablets, which required special clay not easily found in the west, and the complicated ideographic and syllabic cuneiform systems of writing were confined to the east. The beginnings of an alphabetic script have been found in a group of pseudo-hieroglyphic inscriptions, which cannot yet be read, on stone and metal from Gebal (Byblos), contemporary with the Egyptian Middle Kingdom (*c* 2100–1700 B.C.) and in as yet imperfectly deciphered inscriptions from the turquoise-mines at Sinai dated *c* 1850–1600 B.C.; this proto-alphabet was based on the hieroglyphic system of the Egyptians, who had devised a kind of pseudo-alphabet for spelling out proper names and foreign words which could not be represented by pictographs. The famous cuneiform tablets from Ugarit (see Râs Shamra) on the Syrian coast were copied *c* 1400–1350 B.C.; they are written on clay-tablets but in an alphabet with special signs for three vowels (*a, i, u*) with *'āleph*, the glottal stop. The earliest inscriptions in a completely legible and intelligible purely Semitic script are those of several Phoenician kinglets from the same Gebal, dated from *c* 1500 B.C. (?) to 900 B.C. (Byblos I.–IV.). Neither the Ugaritic nor the Phoenician 'alphabets,' however, were true alphabets; it was not till *c* 850 B.C. that the Greeks invented separate symbols to represent vowels pure and simple, thereby creating a true alphabet.

2. Early writing in Israel.—Although cuneiform tablets were in use all round Palestine and even in it, as the Babylonian tablets found at Tell el-Amârna (Tall-al-'Amârinah) show (*c* 1400 B.C.), there is no evidence that the Israelites ever used this system. Whence the Hebrews can have learnt the art of writing is not known; for the OT has nothing to say on the subject and it is not mentioned in the stories of the patriarchs. Their ancestors may have known of the Sumerian and Babylonian systems, especially if they were immigrants from the east, but these never became acclimatized in the west, where they were used only for relatively short periods of time, though long enough for the idea to become well known. The historic Hebrews may have obtained the alphabetic system directly from its Sinaitic inventors or their successors or perhaps rather have learnt it at second hand from the Phoenicians who, if they did not invent it, had at an early age developed its use and did much to diffuse the knowledge of it. The earliest Hebrew inscription is the Calendar of Gezer (*c* 1000 B.C.), which is written to all intents and purposes in the Biblical language; and the oldest written documents mentioned in the OT are the Tablets of the Law (Ex 24[12–13] 31[18] E; cf Hos 8[12]), *c* 850 B.C. The writing on these was 'the writing of God' (Ex 32[16] E), *i.e.* engraved in lapidary or 'uncial' style, as distinct from that which was scratched 'with the pen of a man' (Is 8[1]) *c* 735 B.C., *i.e.* cursive script on a potsherd.

3. Character of writing.—The so-called Phoenician alphabet, which the Israelites adopted, consisted of twenty-two signs representing only consonants; the ambiguity thus created came to be partly mitigated by the use of the symbols for several weak sounds as vowel-signs to indicate the long vowels (*'āleph* and *h* for *â*; *w* for *ô, û*; *y* for *ê, î*); but it was not till long afterwards that signs for the short vowels were devised. The OT perhaps mentions two, and only two, of these letters by name; these are *ṣāw* for *ṣ* (emphatic *s*) and *ḳāw* for *ḳ* (Is 28[10, 13]). These suggest that the sound of the letter itself with a helping vowel was originally enough for its name, as it remained approximately ever afterwards for one (*hē'* for *h*). Otherwise, the Hebrews turned the sound into a common noun by adding a normal afformative to it (*ḥēth* for *ḥ*, *ṭēth* for *ṭ*, *bēth* for *b*), when it might be assimilated to a known word (so *bêth*, 'house'), or took a noun beginning with the same letter as its name (*wāw* 'peg' for *w*, *tāw* 'cross' for *t*); in these cases the name arose naturally out of the sound and preceded the sign, which was designed to fit the name (for example, the sign of a hand for *kaph* 'hand,' the name for the letter *k*). When the letter represented a compound sign, it received the name of a common object which seemed to resemble that sign (for example, the sign for *ṣ* being a strengthened form of that for *z*, they dropped *ṣāw* and called it *ṣādhê* 'grasshopper,' which the symbol had come roughly to resemble). The names then passed through an Aramaic dialect, as their forms show, into the Greek language. The order of the alphabet as given in modern grammars is already found in various acrostic passages in the OT (Na 1^{2-14}, Ps 9–10, 25, 34, 37, 111, 112, 119, 145, La 1–4, Pr 31^{10-31}, Sir 51^{13-29}), although there are a few variations in some passages, and this is confirmed by lists of letters, more or less complete, which archaeologists have discovered engraved in the same order; but the supposed inverted cyphers (Jer 25^{26} 51^{1}) are nothing but Rabbinic fictions. The neighbouring Phoenicians and Aramaeans, as also the Jews who spoke Aramaic in Egypt in the 5th cent. B.C., used quite different signs for numbers; but the divergent interpretations of the LXX prove conclusively that the letters of the alphabet served for the same purpose in the manuscripts before them. Direct evidence of this practice comes with the Maccabaean coins on which the number of the year of the revolt is indicated by the letters of the alphabet. The practice known as 'gematria,' whereby pseudo-historical information is extracted from the numerical value of the letters, like Nero's name from the number of the beast (Rev 13^{18}; cf Gn 14^{14} with 15^{2}, Ezk 4^{4-5}), affords evidence of the pre-Septuagintal use of the letters for numbers. Lastly, the letters were commonly used as abbreviations, not only by Jews in private documents or on coins (for example, *š* (=*sh*) for *sheḳel* 'shekel,' or *shānāh* 'year') but also in Biblical MSS, where this practice easily accounts for many variant readings, especially of the Divine name and of numbers (for example *š* for *shᵉnayim* 'two,' *shēsh* 'six,' *shebhaʿ* 'seven,' and *shᵉmōneh* 'eight').

4. The Script.—The script in the pre-exilic period was, as revealed by archaeology, largely lapidary and formal; but *ostraca* from Samaria (*c* 770 B.C.) and Lachish (*c* 586 B.C.) and *papyri* written by Jews in Egypt (5th cent. B.C.) have revealed cursive forms for use with brush and ink. After the exile the so-called 'Assyrian' or 'square character,' *i.e.* an Aramaic form of the script, displaced the old writing; the ascription of this change to Ezra was but pious fancy, based on a desire to bring a novelty under the sanction of a venerable name. The old style was revived on Maccabaean coins and on those of the First and Second Revolts, evidently as propaganda on behalf of the nationalist cause. The allusion, however, to *iōta* (*yôdh*) as the smallest letter (Mt 5^{18}) is only intelligible in reference to the new square script, which must then have been in ordinary use in the 1st cent. A.D. The most noticeable difference between the two scripts is in the use of five final forms in the new script, of which four are nearer to the corresponding forms in the old script; these were in fact the original forms, while the non-final forms were created by bending up the downward stroke leftwards, *i.e.* towards the following letter, and were due to the growth of the habit of running a letter into or joining it with the following letter in cursive writing. These five final forms also came to be used for the hundreds from 500 to 900, which were beyond the resources of the ordinary alphabet of twenty-two letters, since 400 was the last number which this could reach. What the 'tittle' of the NT is (Mt 5^{18}) remains uncertain; it may have been the projecting point or tip distinguishing some letters in the square alphabet (for example *b* from *k* or *d* from *r*) or the fanciful strokes called *tâghin* 'crowns' in elaborated calligraphy. To what extent words were divided or stops were used in ancient Hebrew MSS is not clear. They are divided by a stroke in most Phoenician inscriptions from Gebal or by a stroke or a point in early Aramaic inscriptions; words are separated by points and clauses by a stroke on the Moabite stone (*c* 9th cent. B.C.), which is unique in this respect. The Hebrew Calendar from Gezer has some strokes separating words but drops them after the first two lines; the Samaritan *ostraca* and the inscriptions from the Pool of Siloam (*c* 700 B.C.) regularly use points, while the *ostraca* from Lachish fluctuate in their use of them, to divide words; inscriptions and *papyri* of the Persian period begin to leave spaces between words. The practice of Jewish scribes is not directly known; but the frequency with which the LXX divides words wrongly suggest that they were not generally separated in the MSS which they used. In the Scroll of Isaiah (A) from Qumrân the words are clearly separated by spaces; and by this time the use of final letters was beginning to assist the reader to distinguish them.

5. Post-biblical Hebrew writing.—In Biblical times erasure was described as 'wiping out' (Ex 32^{32}, J; cf Col 2^{14}) apparently with water (Nu 5^{23}, P), which was of course only possible when non-metallic ink was used; when metallic ink, which eats into leather and can only be scratched out, came into use, the process was called scratching out by the Rabbis, and this term became general whatever ink was used. Occasionally a line was drawn through anything incorrect. Soon, however, erasures came to be disapproved in the Scriptures, especially the Law, and already in the Qumrân Scrolls dots are put above and below a letter or word which has been miscopied; in the same way Biblical MSS show *puncta extraordinaria* over letters or words (*e.g.* over 'and he kissed them' in Gn 33^{4}) to indicate that they should be disregarded though not expunged. Another device indicating that the scribes suspected a mistake in the text was the insertion of a vertical stroke called *pāsēḳ* in the text, usually in the middle of a suspected phrase or after a suspected word. Some of the Scrolls have marks in the margin intended apparently to indicate Messianic passages; and legal documents of the 2nd cent. A.D. from the Wilderness of Judah have crosses at the ends of short lines to prevent forged insertions. Between the fall of Jerusalem in A.D. 70 and the completion of the traditional or Massoretic text (Heb. *massōreth* 'tradition') a number of rules were invented for the guidance of scribes copying the Law; these have been collected in the tractate called *Massēkheth Sôphᵉrîm* 'tractate for scribes' attached to the Babylonian Talmud. They included the perpetuation even of accidental peculiarities of the archetype and the insertion of signs, whose meaning had sometimes been forgotten, in the text. The most important addition to the text, posterior to the completion of the Talmud, was the insertion of vowel-points. Only the signs of the Assyro-Babylonian cuneiform syllabary had included the vowels in themselves and *'āleph* at Ugarit had three forms according to the vowel with it, while a script without such signs was obviously in danger of misunderstanding (for example *zāraḳ* 'he sprinkled' might be read *zôraḳ* 'it was sprinkled'). All the other Semitic languages originally suffered from this difficulty, which the Ethiopians were apparently the first to try to eliminate by varying the form of the sign for the consonant according to the following vowel. The Syrians first put dots above or below to distinguish otherwise identical words (for example, above for *malkhâ* 'king' but below for *melkhâ* 'counsel'); then they placed the Greek signs for the principal vowels (*a*, *ā*/*ō*, *e*, *ī*, *u*) above or below the consonantal signs and finally developed a more elaborate system of dots to distinguish the finer points of pronunciation. After them the Arabs, imitating the Syrians *c* A.D. 700, punctuated texts of the Qur'ân with three signs for the three fundamental short vowels (*a*, *i*, *u*). Jewish scholars, faced with the same difficulties and knowing something of the earlier if not of the later of these methods of vocalization, tried out various devices, of which fragmentary specimens have survived the vicissitudes of transmission, until they hit on two which they finally adopted: the Palestinian or Tiberian in which the signs are put for the most part under, and the Babylonian in which they are put uniformly above, the line. The former is that found principally in the OT, the latter has survived principally in MSS of the Targumim. The Tiberian method, intended to standardize the reading and intonement of the Scriptures in the synagogue, is especially elaborate; for besides the vowel-signs it has an elaborate system of accents indicating whether words were to be read together or with a pause between them. There is some evidence that the use of these signs was sometimes disapproved, *e.g.* among the Qara'ites for Biblical texts and in other circles for profane texts; but their convenience was such that opposition to them was very slight and soon ceased.

Footnotes had not yet been invented, and the Massoretes adopted an ingenious device for recording variant readings. The familiar series of variants known as *k^{e}thîbh* 'written' and *k^{e}rê* '(what is) to be read' represent an attempt to preserve two readings known to them: the 'written' text contained the traditional consonants while the 'read' text presented the reader with the vowels of some totally different word which he was expected to substitute for it. This process sometimes yields surprising forms over which grammarians have wasted much ink. Unfortunately, no record has been preserved of the process whereby the text has been vocalized, and this can now only be reconstructed by analogy, *e.g.* by that of the Syriac Scriptures and the Qur'ân, which is entirely unsatisfactory. Clearly there must have been an immense mass of divergent readings between which the Massoretes were forced to make a choice; the LXX is a clear witness to this fact, since it is often demonstrably translating a text which is not the Massoretic text. The Biblical texts and fragments from the caves round Qumrân further illustrate this fact, though some of them are nearer to the Septuagintal and others to the Massoretic text. Unfortunately the Massoretes destroyed all the old MSS on which they had constructed their standardized text, so that their methods cannot be properly studied.

6. Character of writers.—The OT gives little information on such subjects as the methods of instruction and education. It contains only one passing allusion to the monotony of the pedagogue's instruction by endlessly repeating the letters of the alphabet to his pupils (Is $28^{10, 12}$). Quite early, however, even ordinary people may have been able to write (Jg 8^{14}, where the boy comes from a tribe on the Phoenician border; or is 'ticking-off' on a tally-stick meant?); and the numerous alphabetic masons' marks of the Israelite period support this statement. Yet at other times 'one knowing writing' had to be found if anything required to be read (Is 29^{11}); but this statement by no means contradicts that just made. The word *sôphēr*, however, though usually translated 'scribe' in the period of the kingdom (2 S 8^{17} 20^{25} *et al.*), probably meant 'musterer,' *i.e.* the officer responsible for calling up the levy (2 K 25^{19}; cf Jg 5^{14}). Jezebel could write a letter (if indeed she wrote it herself) to the elders of Jezreel and some one of them could read it (1 K 21^{8-11}); and Hezekiah read a letter (2 K 19^{14}). Similarly the author of Deuteronomy fancifully pictured not only Moses as writing down the Law (Dt 31^{24}) but also the king as making a copy of it for himself (Dt 17^{18}); but a personal act on the part of the king or queen must not necessarily be assumed, even though Ashurbanipal boasts of his skill in the 'difficult cuneiform script,' and another king (Cyrus or Nabonidus) is taunted with not knowing it. There are likely too, to have been professional **scribes** attached to the court (2 K 12^{11}; cf Es 3^{12}) and the local centres of government, as also to the headquarters of the army, as the letters from Lachish suggest; but Baruch seems to have been the first named member of this class (Jer (36^{26}). There will probably have been also persons plying such a craft, like the Muslim *kâtib* 'writer (of letters and legal documents),' for the benefit of private people wishing to employ them for such purposes (Ezk 9^{2-3}). After the Exile *sôphēr* came to denote a professional scribe, when Ezra became 'the scribe' *par excellence* (Neh $8^{4, 9, 13}$ 12^{36}); and such a name as Hassophereth (Ezr 2^{55}, Neh 7^{57}) belonging to a family of returned exiles proves that the business had become hereditary in certain families. Ezra, however, was scribe as well as priest (Ezr 7^{11}, Neh 12^{26}), thus testifying to the fact that the scribal profession was compatible, and might indeed be combined, with that of a priest. The combination of offices, however, is likely to have been accidental; for the Gospels clearly distinguish scribes from priests. The word will probably have already included the work of editing as well as copying the Law and comes soon afterwards to mean something like scholar or *savant* (1 Ch 27^{32}), such as the scribes of the Gospels must have been.

7. Use of writing.—The early history of Israel and Judah must have been transmitted, as Arab records seem to have been, for some period of time by word of mouth (Ps 44^{1}), being thus transmitted from father to son (Ex 13^{8} J); so Solomon's wisdom was spoken, not written (1 K 4^{32f}), and subsequently transferred from one collection to another (Pr 25^{1}). Only notes were apparently taken of Isaiah's utterances (Is 8^{16}; cf 8^{1}) and, when Jeremiah's prophecies were written down, the practice was a novelty which required description (Jer 36^{17-18}); but Habakkuk not long afterwards could speak of writing his words down as a familiar process (Hab 2^{2}). Apart from the tradition of the Tables of the Law there was no formal written Law before the 9th or 8th cent., when written decrees might be issued (Hos 8^{12}, Is 10^{1}) and the 7th cent., when 'the book of the law' was discovered (2 K 22^{8}–23^{3}), and written legal documents began to appear about the same time (Jer 3^{8} 32^{9-14}); but the practice must be older than the first mention of it. Job, too, wished that his indictment might be published in writing for all men to see (Job 31^{35}; cf 13^{26}). When official historical records may have been begun to be written down is not known; but some form of written record must have come into use fairly early in the history of the kingdom. The *mazkîr* or so-called 'recorder' found at the court of David and of subsequent kings (2 S 8^{16} *et al.*),however, was not the keeper of the records but the *nominator* or usher who introduced applicants to the royal presence; he cannot therefore be cited as evidence of the keeping of written archives at so early a date. Otherwise, the references to the keeping of written records (Is 34^{16}, Ps 139^{16}) are too vague to prove anything much; but the practice of book-keeping seems to have been well established by the 2nd cent. B.C. (Sir 42^{7}), and the writing of 'cheques' is mentioned in the NT (Lk 16^{6-7}). Genealogical rolls make their appearance after the Exile (1 Ch 9^{1}), but the archetypes on which they are based must already have been old, so faulty are they (1 Ch 4^{22}; cf 1 Ch 7^{12}, where 'Aher' is not a personal name but means 'another,' indicating a name lost in the archetype); but Arab practice shows that immense genealogies can be memorized, and errors may often therefore be due to failure of memory as much as to defective archetypes. In this period, too, references occur to official documents written in Aramaic and translated into Hebrew (Ezr 4^{7}) and to foreign scripts being learnt by Jews (Dn 1^{4}). In it, too, the complaint is made that 'of making books there is no end' (Ec 12^{12}). Soon afterwards the whole Scriptures are described generally as 'books,' *i.e.* as a library of books (Dn 9^{2}); but no library is mentioned before that which was supposed to have been made by Nehemiah and that actually made by the Maccabees (2 Mac 2^{13}).

Although three written documents in the form of inscriptions can be proved for the 10th cent. B.C. or thereabouts, writing for ordinary purposes such as letters and seals can hardly be proved before the 9th cent. and is not in any sense common before the beginning of the 6th cent. B.C. The purpose of writing, however, in the classical period must have been rather that of keeping a record than the diffusion of knowledge. No objection can then be raised *a priori* to the story that the tables of the Law were put away in the Ark (unlike the Babylonian, Greek, and Roman codes of laws, which were erected in public places); for their contents were supposed to be graven on the memory (Jer 31^{33}), while the written copy was kept merely as an authentic text ready to be consulted in case of doubt (Dt 31^{26}; cf 1 S 10^{25}). The conception of the Law as a book to be read through began after the Exile with Ezra (Neh 8^{1-8}; cf 8^{14} 13^{1}), whence it passed into the practice of the synagogue, where this use of it was fully developed (Lk 10^{26}). Finally, copies of the Scriptures normally belonged to the community, although occasionally highly placed or wealthy persons might possess books (Jos. *c. Ap.* i. 9 [51]).

8. Writing materials.—The earliest Semitic writings were impressed in clay or incised on stone (Ex 32^{16} E; cf Job $19^{23\text{f}}$). Consequently, all words describing writing denote primarily scratching, pricking or cutting: such are Assyrian *maḫāṣu,* 'to jab,' the Hebrew *ḥāḳaḳ* 'hewed,' incised' a text on a tablet (Is 10^{1}) and then 'wrote' on a scroll (Is 30^{8}, Job 19^{23}), and *kāthabh* 'wrote,' whose original sense may be seen in the Arabic *kataba* '[pricked], sewed, wrote': and the Assyrian-Babylonian *šaṭāru* 'to write' must once have meant something similar, as shown by the Arabic *saṭara* 'cut, inscribed, lined, wrote' (cf Gr. *graphein* 'to scratch, delineate, write'), a root from which the Hebrew *shōṭēr* 'officer' is derived. The material in Israel was normally stone for public inscriptions such as the Tables of the Law (Ex 24^{12} 31^{18} E 34^{2}, Jos 8^{32} D), sometimes covered with a hard plaster to give a good surface (Dt $27^{2-4,\,8}$); and stone was of course regularly used for seals. There is also perhaps a solitary reference to an inscription on lead (Job 19^{24}), like those bearing Hittite inscriptions which have been found by archaeologists; but incised letters, filled with lead, such as Darius I. had for his name at Behistun, are probably meant. Occasionally a brick might be used, as in the Babylonian fashion, *e.g.* for a plan (Ezk 4^{1}); and potsherds, though not mentioned in the OT, were commonly used for correspondence, as the letters from Lachish prove. Whether Isaiah's *gillāyôn* was a plain board of some sort of metal or wood (Is 8^{1}) is unknown. **Wooden staves** inscribed with the names of the participating persons are mentioned twice in connexion with a form of drawing lots (Nu 17^{2-3} P, Ezk 37^{16}). Skins or leather, which were commonly used in the ancient world from an early date, as classical writers and surviving texts on them prove, are not mentioned in the OT; but the letter of the Assyrian king which Hezekiah 'spread' before the Lord (Is 37^{14}) will have been written on something soft, such as the Assyrians also occasionally used; and **parchment** is mentioned as the material for notes in the NT (2 Ti 4^{13}). Already, too, in the 10th cent. B.C. **papyrus** had been imported from Egypt to Phoenician centres and in the 5th cent. B.C. it was used by the Jewish colony in Egypt for correspondence and legal documents; because of its relative cheapness it ultimately ousted skins for these purposes. It is not mentioned in the OT but is named as the material of an apostolic letter in the NT (2 Jn ^{12}). The instruments for writing were a graving tool or chisel for inscriptions on bricks or tablets (Is 8^{1}), and one called *'ēṭ* for use with leather (Jer 8^{8}, Ps 45^{1}). This seems to have been a **reed-pen** (cf 3 Jn ^{13}) or brush-like tool, since the cognate Syrian word means 'grass' (Wutz); so the Hebrew term, like the Latin *pinna* 'feather,' from which the English 'quill-pen' is derived, came to denote also one of metal (Jer 17^{1}, Job 19^{24}). The **ink-horn** and palette, for which an Egyptian term was used, became almost the badge of the professional scribe (Ezk $9^{2-3,\,11}$). The **ink** was black, as its Greek name signifies (2 Jn 1^{2}, 3 Jn ^{13}; cf Jer 36^{18}). That on the letters from Lachish is said to be metallic, while that on the Judaean Scrolls is non-metallic. So that generally used by Jewish scribes in the 2nd cent. A.D., was non-metallic, being made of soot mixed with oil and gum of balsam, and thus was easily washed off with a sponge; when R. Meir tried sometime after A.D. 100 to introduce a metallic ink, which was more durable and could only be erased with a pen-knife, R. Ishmael condemned the practice, whether as a pagan innovation or as involving damage to the scroll in case of erasure. Lastly, two ink-wells, one of bronze and one of earthernware have been found at Qumrân; and one contained traces of dried non-metallic ink.

An inscription was called simply a 'stone' (Jos 8^{32} EJ^{B}) or 'tablet' (Ex 24^{12} JE). The Hebrew *sēpher* 'writing' may occasionally have denoted an inscription, especially when it is said to be engraved (Is 30^{8}, Job 19^{23}), like the cognate Phoenician and South-Arabian words; but it soon became the ordinary word for any written document and finally for a **book**. When meaning a letter, the plural form was occasionally used (2 K 20^{12}); cf 19^{14} where, however, skin may be the material, possibly because letters might be written on double or folding **waxed tablets** such as both Assyrians and Romans had and such as Zechariah used to write down the name of his son, since he had been struck dumb and could not speak (Lk 1^{63}); but the singular form was usual. The book was in the form of a **roll** or **scroll** of leather, for which *papyrus* might also have been employed when it came into use (Jer 36^{1-32}, Ezk 3^{1-3}, Zec 5^{1-2}; cf Ps 40^{7}). The scroll might occasionally be written on both sides (Ezk 2^{9-10}, Rev 5^{1}); so Aramaic letters on leather, dated 411/10–408 B.C., from the Persian governors to their subordinate officers in Egypt have a summary of their contents and the address on the back or outside. The size of the scroll depended on that of the skin, but several skins could be sewn together to make a long roll, as the Judaean Scrolls show. The ultimate length was further controlled by the need to handle the scroll conveniently; it might contain one long work such as one of the Major Prophets (sixty-six, fifty-two, or forty-eight chapters) or several short works, such as the twelve Minor Prophets (sixty-four chapters). The writing was on the hairy side, which had been rendered smooth by pumice-stone, arranged in columns (Jer 36^{23}); and by the 1st cent. A.D. vertical and horizontal lines were impressed on the leather to obtain a proper alignment of the script, as on the Judaean Scrolls. The scroll was wound up in such a way that the end of the text was at the inside and the beginning at the outside; holding the bulk of the scroll in his left hand and the beginning in his right hand, the reader unwound it as he read the columns from right to left and wound it up again when he came to the end (Lk $4^{17,\,20}$). The book-form, arranged by quires or pages, hardly came into use before the 2nd cent. A.D.; and only parchment, never *papyrus*, was made up into books. **Paper,** which superseded parchment in books, was not introduced till imported by Moslems in the 7th cent. A.D. from the Far East.

9. Reading.—Readers in the ancient world normally read aloud, even to themselves; and St. Augustine tells how St. Ambrose surprised onlookers by reading to himself, saying *cum legebat, oculi ducebantur per paginas et cor intellectum rimabatur, vox autem et lingua quiescebant.* Hence the Babylonians and Assyrians said 'to proclaim' and 'to hear' or 'to see,' the Hebrews said 'proclaimed' (*ḳārā'*) and the Greeks 'to hear' (*akouein*); so Hezekiah, when reading a letter 'proclaimed' it (2 K 19^{14}), and Jehoiakim and the princes '**heard**' Jeremiah's book being read to them (Jer 36^{10-23}).

10. Writing as affecting the text of the Bible.—Accuracy in the modern sense was scarcely known in ancient times, and writers freely adapted what they were quoting to their own purpose; so late Assyrian scribes, copying old Babylonian texts, had no hesitation in adapting the spelling and idiom of these to the practice of their own times. The sense, not the form, was to them the essential thing. In the same way parallel texts in the OT freely diverge from one another. The scribes also made other arbitrary alterations to suit their own preconceived notions, *e.g.* to avoid anthropomorphisms or blasphemy: so 'cursed' is changed into 'blessed' when God is the object (1 K $21^{10,\,13}$, Job $1^{5,\,11}$ $2^{5,\,9}$). Other alterations of the text are sheer errors; for there must have been innumerable gaps or illegible passages in an archetype which have been disregarded or wrongly filled in, and errors in it have been perpetuated or miscorrected. Letters, many of which are in the Hebrew alphabet misleadingly alike, and words, often rare or unknown, have been miscopied; abbreviations have been misunderstood and incorrectly filled in; lines have been omitted or wrongly inserted from a neighbouring column, words inserted from the line above or below through the wandering of the scribe's eye (cf Gn 4⁷, where a clause is repeated from 3¹⁶). Accidental omissions, duly recorded in the margin, have been copied by a subsequent copyist into the wrong place (cf 2 K 20⁷⁻⁸ with Is 38²¹⁻²², where the prescription for Hezekiah's boil is given after his recovery from it); and variant readings, originally recorded in the margin, have sometimes crept into the text. Other insertions, which have been introduced from the margins, are liturgical instructions and glosses on rare words as well as the comments, pious or shocked, of the readers; in fact, glosses of every conceivable kind have made their way into the text and must be eliminated if the author's original meaning is to be recovered (see *L'Ancien Testament et L'Orient* [1957], 123–161). The Scrolls from Qumrân show a text which differs often in detail if rarely in substance from the Massoretic text, and therefore represents one which has not yet been standardized by the Massoretes, thereby proving the antiquity of many of these corruptions; and even after its standardization an immense number of divergent readings, of which the majority are trivial matters of orthography, has been preserved from the earlier period or has even crept into texts of a later period, as the collections of Kennicott and De Rossi abundantly prove. However this may be, an end was finally put to all these processes by the Massoretes who, having established the text to their own satisfaction (though on entirely unscientific principles), recorded letters and words, grammatical forms and every sort of peculiarity, in the *massôrāh* 'tradition,' a register of which the origin (like that of everything else in Hebrew literary history) is obscure but which can only have been perfected by meticulous toil during the course of many generations of scholars. Yet even so, the copyists of the Jewish Scriptures do not seem to have been nearly so accurate as the copyists of the Qur'ân; but the problems confronting them were very different. G. R. D.

WRITING CASE.—See INKHORN.

WYCLIFFE'S VERSION.—See ENGLISH VERSIONS, **7** ff.

X

XANTHICUS.—See TIME.

XERXES.—See AHASUERUS.

Y

YAHWEH.—See GOD, **4** (*c*).

YARN.—**1.** This is probably the correct translation of *'ēṭûn*, Pr 7¹⁶ (RV; AV, RSV **linen**). The word is of doubtful etymology and meaning. **2.** Hebrew *mᵉ'ûzzāl*, Ezk 27¹⁹ (RV). This is a very doubtful meaning; cf UZAL. **3.** *miḳwēh*, 1 K 10²⁸ (AV), *miḳwē'*, 2 Ch 1¹⁶ (AV). This is also very doubtful, as is RV 'drove.' RSV reads 'from **Kue**'; see KUE. See also SPINNING AND WEAVING; TRADE AND COMMERCE, **4.**

YEAR.—See TIME.

YEAST.—Found only in RSV in Gal 5⁹ for AV and RV '**leaven**' (q.v.).

YELLOW.—See COLOURS, **1.**

YIRON.—A city of Naphtali, in the mountains, Jos 19³⁸ (AV, RV **Iron**); probably modern *Yārûn*.

YODH.—See JOD.

YOKE.—See AGRICULTURE, **1**; WEIGHTS AND MEASURES, I.

YOKEFELLOW.—See SYNZYGUS.

Z

ZAANAN.—A place mentioned in Mic 1¹¹, where there is a characteristic word-play: 'The inhabitress of *Ṣa'ᵃnān* went [*yāṣᵉ'āh*] not out' (for fear of the enemy). Zaanan is generally considered to be the same as **Zenan** (q.v.).

ZAANAIM, Jg 4¹¹ (AV).—See ZAANANNIM.

ZAANANNIM.—The border of the tribe of Naphtali passed through 'the oak in Zaanannim,' Jos 19³³ (AV 'from **Allon** to Zaanannim'), and the tent of Heber the Kenite was at 'the oak in Zaanannim, which is near Kedesh, Jg 4¹¹ (AV 'the plain of **Zaanaim**'). RVm takes the preposition 'in' (Heb. *b*) as part of the name, and so reads *Bezaanannim*. The site is unknown.

ZAAVAN.—A descendant of Seir, Gn 36²⁷, 1 Ch 1⁴² (AV **Zavan**).

ZABAD ('he hath bestowed' or 'a gift').—Many names are derived from this root, both in OT and in Palmyrene and Nabataean inscriptions. About thirty-six are reckoned in OT—twenty-three in Chronicles, and nearly all in post-exilic books. In Gn 30²⁰ᵃ it is the first explanation of 'Zebulun.' The fuller form is **Zabdiel** or **Zebadiah** ('my gift is Y″'). **1.** A descendant of Judah, 1 Ch 2³⁶ᶠ; perhaps the same as **Zabud** in 1 K 4⁵. **2.** An Ephraimite, 1 Ch 7²¹. **3.** One of David's heroes, 1 Ch 11⁴¹; perhaps the same as **1.** **4.** One of the murderers of Joash, **2** Ch 24²⁶; called **Jozacar** in 2 K 12²¹. See also SHIMEATH. **5. 6. 7.** Laymen who married foreign wives, Ezr 10²⁷, 1 Es 9²⁸ (AV **Sabatus,** RV **Sabathus**); Ezr 10³³, 1 Es 9³³ (AV **Bannaia,** RV **Sabanneus**); Ezr 10⁴³ 1 Es 9³⁵ (AV **Zabadaias,** RV **Zabadeas**).

C. W. E.—**H. H. R.**

ZABADAEANS.—The name of an Arabian tribe defeated by Jonathan Maccabaeus in 144 B.C., 1 Mac 12³⁰ᶠᶠ. Its home was NW. of Damascus, and is probably to be identified with *Zebedâni*, near which is the village of *Kefr Zebâd* (cf *RB* xxxv, 1926, 216 f).

ZABADAIAS, 1 Es 9^{35} (AV).—See Zabad, **7.**

ZABADEAS, 1 Es 9^{35} (RV).—See Zabad, **7.**

ZABBAI.—1. One of the descendants of Bebai who had married a foreign wife, Ezr 10^{28}, 1 Es 9^{29} (AV **Josabad,** RV **Jozabdus**). **2.** Father of Baruch who assisted in the rebuilding of the wall, Neh 3^{20}. The *Ḳᵉrê* has, perhaps rightly, **Zaccai,** a name which occurs in Ezr 2^{9}, Neh 7^{14}, and is the origin of the name **Zacchaeus** (2 Mac 10^{19} and NT).

ZABBUD, Ezr 8^{14} (AV, RV).—See Zakkur.

ZABDEUS, 1 Es 9^{21} (AV, RV).—See Zebadiah, **6.**

ZABDI (? 'gift of Y″'; cf **Zebedee**).—**1.** The grandfather of Achan, Jos 7$^{1, 17f}$; called **Zimri** in 1 Ch 2^{6}. **2.** A Benjamite, 1 Ch 8^{19}. **3.** An officer of David, 1 Ch 27^{27}. **4.** A Levite, Neh 11^{17}; called **Zichri** in 1 Ch 9^{15}.

ZABDIEL ('my gift is El').—**1.** Father of one of David's officers, 1 Ch 27^{2}. **2.** A prominent official in Nehemiah's time, Neh 11^{14}. **3.** An Arabian who put Alexander Balas to death and sent his head to Ptolemy, 1 Mac 11^{17}.

ZABUD.—The son of Nathan, 1 K 4^{5}; perhaps the same as **Zabad, 1.**

ZABULON, Mt 4$^{13, 15}$, Rev 7^{8} (AV) = **Zebulun** (q.v.).

ZACCAI.—1. The eponym of a family of returning exiles, Ezr 2^{9}, Neh 7^{14}; called **Chorbe** in 1 Es 5^{12} (AV **Corbe**). **2.** Neh 3^{20} (*Ḳᵉrê*); see Zabbai, **2.**

ZACCHAEUS (= **Zaccai,** Ezr 2^{9}, Neh 7^{14}, literally 'pure').—**1.** An officer put to death by Judas Maccabaeus for treachery (2 Mac 10$^{18-22}$). **2.** According to Lk 19$^{1-10}$, a chief tax collector of Jericho who was attracted to Jesus. He is mentioned only by Luke. W. R. S.

ZACCHUR, 1 Ch 4^{26} (AV).—See Zaccur, **2.**

ZACCUR.—1. A Reubenite, Nu 13^{4}. **2.** A Simeonite, 1 Ch 4^{26} (AV **Zacchur**). **3.** A Merarite, 1 Ch 24^{27}. **4.** An Asaphite, 1 Ch 25$^{2, 10}$, Neh 12^{35}. **5.** One of those who helped to rebuild the wall, Neh 3^{2}. **6.** One of those who sealed the covenant, Neh 10^{12}; probably the same as mentioned in 13^{13}. **7.** A singer who put away his foreign wife, 1 Es 9^{24} (AV, RV **Bacchurus**).

ZACHARIAH.—1. 2 K 14^{29} 15$^{8, 11}$ (AV); see Zechariah, **13. 2.** 2 K 18^{2} (AV); see Zechariah, **15. 3.** Lk 11^{51} (RV); see Zechariah, **35.**

ZACHARIAS.—1. 1 Es 1^{8} (AV, RV); see Zechariah, **19. 2.** 1 Es 6^{1} 7^{3} (AV, RV); see Zechariah, **20. 3.** 1 Es 8^{30} (AV, RV); see Zechariah, **21. 4.** 1 Es 8^{37} (AV, RV); see Zechariah, **22. 5.** 1 Es 8^{44} (AV, RV); see Zechariah, **23. 6.** 1 Es 9^{27} (AV, RV); see Zechariah, **24. 7.** 1 Es 9^{44} (AV, RV); see Zechariah, **25. 8.** 1 Es 1^{15} (AV, RV); see Zechariah, **32. 9.** 1 Mac 5$^{18, 56}$ (AV, RV); see Zechariah, **33. 10.** Lk 1^{5} (AV, RV); see Zechariah, **34. 11.** Lk 11^{51} (AV); see Zechariah, **35. 12.** 1 Es 5^{8} (AV); see Seraiah, **6.**

ZACHARY, 2 Es 1^{40} (AV, RV).—See Zechariah, **20.**

ZACHER, 1 Ch 8^{31} (AV).—See Zechariah, **1.**

ZADOK.—1. Founder of an important branch of the Jerusalem priesthood. Traditionally (1 Ch 24$^{3, 6}$) his descent was traced from Eleazar the son of Aaron. He lived during the reigns of David and Solomon (2 S 8^{17}, 1 K 1^{8}) as high priest, being associated in that office during the former reign with **Abiathar** (instead of with Ahimelech his son as 2 S 8^{17}). Under Solomon Abiathar was deposed and Zadok made sole high priest, Abiathar having unwisely joined Adonijah's attempt at a *coup d'état* (1 K 2$^{26f, 35}$). Apparently the high priestly office remained in the hands of the Zadokites until Maccabaean times. To Ezekiel (as well as to the Qumrân sectarians in the time of Christ) the Zadokites were the only legitimate priests (Ezk 40^{46} 43^{19} 44^{15} 48^{11}). **2.** One of David's warriors, an Aaronite, who pledged allegiance to David at Hebron at his coronation (1 Ch 12^{28}). **3.** The father of Jerusha the mother of king Jotham (2 K 15^{33}, 2 Ch 27^{1}). **4.** Son of Baanah (see Ezr 2^{2}; Neh 7^{7}), a helper of Nehemiah in rebuilding the wall (Neh 3^{4}); possibly also one of 'those who set their seal' on the covenant (10^{21}). **5.** Son of Immer, who helped Nehemiah rebuild a portion of the wall (Neh 3^{29}). Perhaps the same as the scribe who was appointed by Nehemiah as one of the treasurers over the storehouses (13^{13}). **6.** Son of Ahitub and father of Shallum, a priest in the high priestly line (1 Ch 6^{12}; cf Ezr 7^{2}, Neh 11^{11}, 1 Es 8^{2} [AV **Sadduc,** RV **Sadduk**], 2 Es 1^{1} [AV, RV **Sadoc**]). **7.** An ancestor of Joseph the husband of Mary (Mt 1^{14} [AV, RV **Sadoc**]).
G. R. B.—**J. W. W.**

ZADOKITE FRAGMENTS.—See Dead Sea Scrolls.

ZAHAM.—A son of Rehoboam, 2 Ch 11^{19}.

ZAIN or **ZAYIN.**—Seventh letter of the Hebrew alphabet, and so used to introduce the seventh part of Ps 119, every verse of which begins with this letter.

ZAIR.—A place mentioned in 2 K 8^{21}. The parallel passage, 2 Ch 21^{9}, has 'with his princes' for 'to Zair,' but this is probably a corruption of the text in Kings. Zair is unknown, unless it is the same as **Zior** (q.v.).

ZAKKUR.—An exile who returned, Ezr 8^{14} (RSV, with *Ḳᵉrê*; AV, RV **Zabbud** with *Kᵉthîbh*); called **Istalcurus** in 1 Es 8^{40}.

ZALAPH.—The father of Hanun, Neh 3^{30}.

ZALMON.—1. The hill near Shechem where Abimelech and his followers cut wood for the burning down of the stronghold of Baal-berith, Jg 9^{45}. Possibly the same mountain is meant in Ps 68^{14} (AV **Salmon**), where a snowstorm is apparently referred to as contributing to the scattering of 'kings' opposed to the people of Yahweh. **2.** See Ilai.

ZALMONAH.—A stopping-place in the wilderness, Nu 33^{41f}. It is possibly modern *Bîr Madhkûr.*

ZALMUNNA.—See Zebah.

ZAMBIS, 1 Es 9^{34} (AV).—See Amariah, **8.**

ZAMBRI.—1. 1 Mac 2^{26} (AV); see Zimri, **1. 2.** 1 Es 9^{34} (RV); see Amariah, **8.**

ZAMOTH, 1 Es 9^{28} (AV, RV).—See Zattu.

ZAMZUMMIM.—A name given by the conquering Ammonites to the Rephaim, the original inhabitants of the land, Dt 2^{20}. They are described as a people 'great and many and tall like the Anakim' (see Rephaim). The name Zamzummim has been connected with Arabic *zamzam* 'to talk gibberish.' They may be the same as the **Zuzim** of Gn 14^{5}, in which case there is probably textual corruption in one of the passages. No secure identification can be suggested.

ZAMZUMMIMS, Dt 2^{20} (AV) = **Zamzummim** (q.v.).

ZANOAH.—1. A town in the Shephelah, Jos 15^{34}, Neh 3^{13} 11^{30}; it is personified in 1 Ch 4^{18}. It is the modern *Kh. Zānûʿ*, SE. of Zoreah. **2.** A place in the hill country of Judah, Jos 15^{56}; possibly modern *Kh. Beit ʿAmrah*, in the *Wâdī Abū Zenaḥ*, which preserves the ancient name.

ZAPHENATH-PANEAH.—The name given by Pharaoh to Joseph, Gn 41^{45} (AV **Zaphnath-paaneah**). It is explained by Egyptian *Ze-p-net-e-f-ʿonkh*, 'God speaks and he (the newly-born) lives'—a common type of Egyptian name in late times.

ZAPHNATH-PAANEAH, Gn 41^{45} (AV).—See Zaphenath-paneah.

ZAPHON ('north').—A city E. of Jordan, assigned to Gad, Jos 13^{27}; mentioned also in Jg 12^{1} (so RVm and RSV, for AV and RV 'northward'). It is possibly modern *Tell el-Qôs.*

ZARA, Mt 1^{3} (AV).—See Zerah, **2.**

ZARACES, 1 Es 1^{38} (AV).—See Zarius.

ZARAH, Gn 38^{30} 46^{12} (AV).—See Zerah, **2.**

ZARAIAS.—1. 1 Es 5^{8} (RV; AV **Zacharias,** RSV **Seraiah**); called **Seraiah** in Ezr 2^{2} and **Azariah** in Neh 7^{7}. **2.** An ancestor of Ezra, 1 Es 8^{2} (AV, RV; RSV omits); called **Zerahiah** in Ezr 7^{4}, and **Arna** in 2 Es 1^{2}. **3.** 1 Es 8^{31} (AV, RV; RSV **Zerahiah**); called

Zerahiah in Ezr 8^{4}. **4.** 1 Es 8^{34} (AV, RV; RSV **Zeraiah**); called **Zebadiah** in Ezr 8^{8}.

ZARAKES, 1 Es 1^{38} (RV).—See ZARIUS.

ZARDEUS, 1 Es 9^{28} (RV).—See ZERDAIAH.

ZAREAH, Neh 11^{29} (AV).—See ZORAH.

ZARED, Nu 21^{22} (AV).—See ZERED.

ZAREPHATH.—The Arab village of *Ṣarafand* lies on a promontory about 8 miles S. of Sidon. On the shore in front of it are the scattered remains of what must have been a considerable town, the Zarephath or **Sarepta** (Lk 2^{46} AV) of the Bible. Zarephath originally belonged to Sidon (1 K 17^{9}), but passed into the possession of Tyre after the assistance rendered by the fleet of Sidon to Shalmaneser IV. in 722 B.C. in his abortive attempt to capture insular Tyre. In Lk 4^{26} it is again called a city of Sidon. Zarephath is included in the list of towns captured by Sennacherib when he invaded Phoenicia in 701 B.C. It was the town in which Elijah lodged during the years of famine, 1 K 17^{8-24}; it is also mentioned in Ob ^{20}.

ZARETAN, Jos 3^{16} (AV).—See ZARETHAN.

ZARETHAN.—A town in the Jordan valley, Jos 3^{16} (AV **Zaretan**); it lay opposite Succoth, 1 K 7^{46} (AV **Zarthan**). It is mentioned also in the obscure text, 1 K 4^{12} (AV **Zartanah**). It is possibly modern *Qarn Ṣarṭabeh,* though some prefer *Tell es-Saʿidîyeh.* See also ZEREDAH and ZERERAH.

ZARETH-SHAHAR, Jos 13^{19} (AV).—See ZERETH-SHAHAR.

ZARHITES.—AV form of **Zerahites.** See ZERAH and IZRAHITES.

ZARIUS.—Called in 1 Es 1^{38} (AV **Zaraces,** RV **Zarakes**) the brother of Jehoiakim (AV **Joacim,** RV **Joakim**), King of Judah, and said to have been brought up out of Egypt by him. The name apparently is a corruption, through confusion of Hebrew *d* and *r,* of Zedekiah, who was a brother of Jehoiakim (2 K 24^{17}). The verse of 1 Esdras is entirely different from the corresponding passage in 2 Ch 36^{4b}.

ZARTANAH, 1 K 4^{12} (AV).—See ZARETHAN.

ZARTHAN, 1 K 7^{46} (AV).—See ZARETHAN.

ZATHOE(S), 1 Es 8^{32} (AV, RV).—See ZATTU.

ZATHUI, 1 Es 5^{12} (AV, RV).—See ZATTU.

ZATTHU, Neh 10^{14} (AV).—See ZATTU.

ZATTU.—A family of exiles that returned, Ezr 2^{8} 8^{5} (not in AV, RV; but supplied in RSV from 1 Es 8^{32}), Neh 7^{13}, 1 Es 5^{12} (AV, RV **Zathui**) 8^{32} (AV **Zathoe,** RV **Zathoes**). Several members of this family had married foreign wives, Ezr 10^{27}, 1 Es 9^{28} (AV, RV **Zamoth**); its head sealed the covenant, Neh 10^{14} (AV **Zatthu**).

ZAVAN, 1 Ch 1^{42} (AV).—See ZAAVAN.

ZAYIN.—See ZAIN.

ZAZA.—A Jerahmeelite, 1 Ch 2^{33}.

ZEALOT occurs in Lk 6^{15} and Ac 1^{13} as a designation of Simon, one of the disciples of Jesus. The Greek *Zēlōtēs* is derived from the Hebrew *ḳannā'*='jealous.' (The Hebrew has been preserved by transliteration into Greek in Mk 3^{18} and Mt 10^{4}, 'Simon the **Cananaean.**') The 'zealot' gave himself over to God to be an agent of Divine wrath and judgment against idolatry, apostasy, or any transgression of the Law which excited God's jealousy (jealousy and zeal both having the same Hebrew root).

For Jews in the Graeco-Roman period, the scriptural prototypes of 'zeal' were: (1) Simeon and Levi (Gn 34; cf Jth 9, Jub. 30); (2) Phinehas (Nu 25; cf Sir 45^{23}, 1 Mac $2^{26, 54}$, 4 Mac 18^{12}); and (3) Elijah (1 K 18^{40} $19^{10, 14}$; cf 1 Mac 2^{58}, Sir 48^{1-12}). Of these Phineas was the most important, for his zeal had been redemptive: 'And the Lord said to Moses, Phinehas . . . has turned back my wrath from the people of Israel, in that he was jealous with my jealousy among them . . . and made atonement for the people of Israel' (Nu 25^{10-13}). The zealous act of Phinehas had been 'reckoned for him for righteousness from generation to generation for ever' (Ps 106^{30-31}). In the 1st cent. A.D., Phinehas was actually referred to as 'the zealot' (4 Mac 18^{12}).

The theology of redemption through zeal for the Law became popular in the Maccabaean period (1 Mac 2^{15-28}, Jth 9, Jubilees 30). One of the main revolutionary parties in the war with Rome (A.D. 66–70) used the self-designation 'zealots' (*BJ* iv. iii. 9 [160–161]). Jesus was remembered by His disciples to have been motivated by zeal when he drove the money-changers out of the Temple (Jn 2^{17}). Paul's persecution of the Church was rooted in zeal for the Law (cf Gal 1^{13-14}, Ph 3^{6}, Ac 22^{3-4}). It is impossible to connect the Zealots of Josephus with his Fourth sect of Philosophy, since he himself makes no such connexion but rather suggests that the *sicarii* originated in that sect. The question is a complicated one, and we can only state the facts as they are preserved in the sources. It is not improbable that there was a large number of 'zealot' groups constituting the organized resistance to Rome from the time of Pompey onward. Simon, the 'Cananaean,' had probably been a member of one such group before he became a disciple of Jesus—whose opposition to their views, principles, and methods is clear from all the Gospels. W. R. F.

ZEBAIM, Ezr 2^{57}, Neh 7^{59} (AV).—See POCHERETH-HAZZEBAIM.

ZEBADIAH.—1, 2. Two Benjamites, 1 Ch $8^{15, 17}$. **3.** One of those who joined David at Ziklag, 1 Ch 12^{7}. **4.** One of David's officers, 1 Ch 27^{7}. **5.** An exile who returned with Ezra's second caravan, Ezr 8^{8}; called **Zeraiah** in 1 Es 8^{34} (AV, RV **Zaraias**). **6.** A priest who had married a foreign wife, Ezr 10^{20}, 1 Es 9^{21} (AV, RV **Zabdeus**). **7.** A Korahite, 1 Ch 26^{2}. **8.** One of the Levites sent by Jehoshaphat to teach in the cities of Judah, 2 Ch 17^{8}. **9.** An officer of king Jehoshaphat, 2 Ch 19^{11}.

ZEBAH ('victim').—A Midianite king, mentioned together with **Zalmunna,** who was killed by Gideon as the result of blood-revenge (Jg 8^{18-21}); both kings had, however, been previously overcome in battle by Gideon, who championed the Israelites against their Midianite oppressors. This victory must have been of vital and far-reaching consequences to the Israelites, for it is more than once commemorated long after as a landmark in the nation's history (Is 9^{4} 10^{26}, Ps 83^{11}). The death of Zebah and Zalmunna is very graphically described. Gideon commands Jether, his eldest son, to slay them, but being only a youth he is afraid; so the kings ask Gideon himself to kill them; he does so, and takes the crescents from the necks of their camels. This last action may conceivably imply a kindly remembrance of the kings on the part of Gideon, for from 8^{19} it would seem that it was only reluctantly, and from a sense of duty, that he slew them. W. O. E. O.

ZEBEDEE.—Father of James and John, husband of **Salome**; a comparatively rich fisherman, for he had 'hired servants' (see, *e.g.* Mk 1^{20} 15^{40}; cf Mt 27^{56}).

ZEBIDAH.—Mother of Jehoiakim, 2 K 23^{36} (so RV, RSV with *Kᵉthîbh*; AV **Zebudah** with *Ḳᵉrê*).

ZEBINA.—One of the sons of Nebo who had married a foreign wife, Ezr 10^{43}.

ZEBOIIM.—One of the five cities of the plain, Gn 10^{19} (AV **Zeboim**) $14^{2, 8}$, Dt 29^{33} (AV **Zeboim**), Hos 11^{5} (AV, RV **Zeboim**). The site has not been identified. See, further, PLAIN [CITIES OF THE].

ZEBOIM.—1. A city of Judah, Neh 11^{34}. Its location is unknown. **2.** A valley named in 1 S 13^{18} in describing the route followed by the Philistine marauders. The name means 'the valley of hyenas.' It is probably modern *Wâdī Abū Dabāʿ*, a branch of the *Wâdī Qelṭ*. **3.** See ZEBOIIM.

ZEBUDAH, 2 K 23^{36} (AV).—See ZEBIDAH.

ZEBUL.—A lieutenant of **Abimelech** (q.v.), who was left by him as governor of Shechem. He cleverly assisted his master in suppressing the revolt of **Gaal** (Jg 9^{26-41}). The episode is obscure, but he apparently acted loyally from the first; having no force at his command, he was obliged to use craft. This is clear, if vv.^{42ff} belong to a different narrative. C. W. E.

ZEBULUN.—According to OT tradition, the tenth son of Jacob, and the sixth of Leah (Gn 30^{20} E).

The original form of the name is uncertain, there being some evidence in favour of *Zebulon*, and even *Zebul* (*i.e.* without the old nunation). Gn 30^{20} presents a double explanation. One of these (apparently E's) connects it with the verb *zābhad*, 'to endow'; the other (J's) derives it from *zābhal*, 'to dwell,'—because Leah said, 'Now will my husband *dwell* with me.' The Râs Shamra texts attest a noun *zbl*, parallels suggesting quite certainly the meaning 'prince,' doubtless connected with the Assyrian verb *zabālu*, 'to carry, exalt.' Hence Zebulun may be the divine title of the tribal god (cf Asher, Gad). A similar name *Zi-ib-la-an-um*, is found as that of an individual in a text of the early 2nd millennium B.C. at Larsa, and the Egyptian Execration Texts from Luxor, from the 19th cent., refer to *Zblnw* among the Asiatic enemies of the Pharaoh, the name, however, referring not to a tribe but to a chief of the *Sutu*, or Bedouin. Tribes, however, are occasionally named after their chief, and this may be the earliest reference to the Hebrew tribe of Zebulun. It is a pity that the precise locality is not noted in the Execration Texts.

According to Gn 46^{14}, Zebulun is the progenitor of three tribal families through his three sons Sered, Elon, and Yahleel, who went down into Egypt with the other sons and grandsons of Jacob. The first and last of these names are notably like the town names Sarid and Nahalal, which were allotted to Zebulun according to Jos 19^{10f}.

At the time of the Sinai census the male **Zebulunites** from twenty years and upwards are given as 57,400, and their lot on the march was cast on the E. of the Tabernacle with Judah and Issachar (Nu 1^{31f} P). In the census in the Plains of Moab their number is given as 60,500 (Nu $26^{27, 64}$ P).

When the Râs Shamra legends (Keret) were first translated it was thought that there was a reference to Zebulun as a people in Galilee, but that view is now happily exploded.

The boundary line in Jos 19^{10-24} gives only the S. and E. boundaries, and is difficult to follow. Starting on the S. with Sarid (probably *Tell Shudūd*), about five miles SW. of Nazareth, it reached Jokneam, eight miles due W., on the further side of the Plain of Esdraelon. It extended about the same distance E., reaching, at the W. of Tabor, Daberath (which, however, in 21^{28} fell to Issachar), and then apparently turned sharply W. again to Japhia (*Jaffa* by Nazareth), thence NE. to Gath-hepher (probably *el-Meshhed*), N. to Rimmon (*Rummâneh*, overlooking the Plain of the Baṭṭûf from the S.), then W. to Hannathon (the impressive tell of *Khirbet el-Beidawîyyeh* at the W. end of the Plain of the Baṭṭûf), *Hinnatuni* of the Amarna Tablets. The remaining statement that 'the goings out thereof were at the Valley of Iphtahel' (*Wâdī el-Melek*) indicates a SW. direction, though no locality is noted. The N. border (with Naphtali) is not defined, and, as Asher reached Carmel, and marched with Zebulun at the valley of Iphtahel (vv.^{26f}), there is no room left for the access of Zebulun to the sea. The Blessing of Jacob, however, apparently extends Zebulun's territory to the sea (Gn 49^{13}), marching even with Sidon. In the Blessing of Moses (Dt 33^{19}) Zebulun is associated with Issachar in the traffic from the sea, which their occupation of Esdraelon and the Wâdi el-Melek enabled them to exploit, and in the worship at a mountain shrine, surely Tabor (cf Hos 5^{1}). This may well have been the amphictyonic shrine of these two tribes and perhaps others of the older Jacob (Leah) tribes, possibly the 'Israel' mentioned in this locality on the stele of Merneptah (1223 B.C.).

Zebulun shared in the great natural richness and fertility of the rest of Galilee, and the great 'way of the sea' (*via maris*), which ran through its territory from Acco to Damascus, brought it into touch with the outer world and its products.

In the war against Sisera 10,000 men of Zebulun and Naphtali went with Barak, and in the battle, whose issues were of decisive importance to the tribes of Israel, they immortalized themselves by their bravery (Jg 4^{10} 5^{18}). They, like the other tribes, however, could not dislodge the Canaanites from their urban settlements. One of the minor judges, Elon, came from Zebulun (Jg 12^{11}). In later history Zebulun, like the other northern tribes, played an unimportant rôle. According to 2 K 15^{29}, it would appear that Zebulun suffered depopulation when the country was incorporated in the Assyrian Empire as the province of Megiddo. See also TRIBES.

J. A. C.—**J. Gr.**

ZECHARIAH (Yahweh remembers).—**1.** Brother of Ner and uncle of Saul (1 Ch 9^{37}); called **Zecher** (AV **Zacher**) in 1 Ch 8^{31}. **2.** Son of Meshelemiah, keeper of the N. gate of the tent of meeting (1 Ch 9^{21} $26^{2, 14}$). **3.** A Levite musician (1 Ch $15^{18, 20}$). **4.** A priest in the time of David (1 Ch 15^{24} 16^{5}). **5.** A Levite, of the family of Kohath (1 Ch 24^{25}). **6.** A Levite, of the family of Merari (1 Ch 26^{11}). **7.** Father of Iddo, chief officer of Manasseh in Gilead (1 Ch 27^{21}). **8.** A prince of Judah in the days of Jehoshaphat (2 Ch 17^{7}). **9.** A Levite of the family of Asaph (2 Ch 20^{14}). **10.** Son of Jehoshaphat (2 Ch 21^{2}). **11.** Son of Jehoiada the priest, who after his father's death pronounced judgment upon the people for idolatry. By king Joash's command, he was stoned in the Temple court. As he died he said 'May Yahweh see and avenge' (2 Ch 24^{20-22}. See also **35**). **12.** A prophet, living in the earlier part of Uzziah's reign (2 Ch 26^{5}). **13.** Son of Jeroboam II. (2 K 14^{29} $15^{8, 11}$ AV **Zachariah**). See next article. **14.** A man of Isaiah's day, chosen with Uriah the priest as a reliable witness to the tablet containing the name of Maher-shalal-hashbaz (Is 8^{2}). He is described as son of Jeberechiah and might be identical with **16.** **15.** The father of Abi or Abijah, mother of king Hezekiah (2 K 18^{2} [AV **Zachariah**], 2 Ch 29^{1}. **16.** A reforming Asaphite under Hezekiah (2 Ch 29^{13}). Perhaps = **14.** **17.** Head of a Reubenite family (1 Ch 5^{7}). **18.** A Kohathite, an overseer of Temple repair under Josiah (2 Ch 34^{12}). **19.** A chief officer of the Temple under Josiah (2 Ch 35^{8} = 1 Es 1^{8} AV, RV **Zacharias**). **20.** The prophet (see ZECHARIAH [BOOK OF]). **21.** One of the family of Parosh (Ezr 8^{3} = 1 Es 8^{30} AV, RV **Zacharias**). **22.** Son of Bebai (Ezr 8^{11} = 1 Es 8^{37} AV, RV **Zacharias**). **23.** A leader sent by Ezra to Casiphia to fetch Levites (Ezr 8^{16f} = 1 Es 8^{44} AV, RV **Zacharias**). Perhaps = **21** or **22.** **24.** A descendant of Elam, married to a foreign wife (Ezr $10^{26, 44}$ = 1 Es 9^{27} AV, RV **Zacharias**). **25.** One of those who stood by Ezra at the reading of the Law (Neh 8^{4} = 1 Es 9^{44} AV, RV **Zacharias**); omitted in AV 1 Es). **26.** A descendant of Perez (Neh 11^{4}). **27.** A Shilonite (Neh 11^{5}). **28.** Son of Pashhur (Neh 11^{12}). **29.** A priest of the family of Iddo in the time of Joiakim (Neh 12^{16}). Perhaps = **20.** **30.** An Asaphite (Neh 12^{35}). **31.** A priest (Neh 12^{41}). Perhaps = **30.** **32.** 1 Es 1^{15} (AV, RV **Zacharias**) = **Heman** of 2 Ch 35^{15}. See HEMAN, **4.** **33.** Father of Joseph, an officer of Judas Maccabaeus (1 Mac $5^{18, 56}$ AV, RV **Zacharias**). **34.** A priest of the division of Abijah, husband of Elizabeth (Lk 1^{5} AV, RV **Zacharias**), and father of John the Baptist (Lk 1 and 3^{2}). As he was ministering in his turn in the Temple, the angel Gabriel appeared to him and predicted the birth and future work of his son. His disbelief was punished by dumbness, which was only cured when the child was brought to be circumcised and named, when, in obedience to Gabriel's command, he and Elizabeth insisted that he should be called John. Filled with the Holy Spirit he prophesied and spoke the *Benedictus* (Lk 1^{68-79}). **35.** The martyr mentioned by Jesus in Mt 23^{35}, Lk 11^{51} (AV **Zacharias**, RV **Zachariah**). The reference appears to be to the death of Zechariah, son of Jehoiada (**11**); and as Chronicles stands last in the Hebrew Bible, the phrase 'from Abel to Zechariah' would indicate the first and last victims of murder in the OT. In Matthew, however, Zechariah is called 'son of Barachiah,' which suggests confusion with Zechariah the prophet, son of Berechiah (**20**). No tradition that he died a martyr's death is known. The evangelist or a later copyist may have introduced the father's name, thinking either of the prophet or of a Zacharias son of Baruch mentioned by Josephus as murdered in the Temple by the Zealots (*BJ* IV. v. 4 [342]). Origen's identification of him with the father of John the Baptist (**34**) is most improbable.

ZECHARIAH (AV **Zachariah**), King of Israel, son of Jeroboam II. and last member of the house of Jehu to come to the throne. He reigned only six months, before being assassinated by Shallum ben Jabesh (2 K 14^{29} 15^{8-12}) who in his turn was killed by Menahem.

H. P. S.—**P. R. A.**

ZECHARIAH, BOOK OF.—The first eight chapters contain the genuine prophecies of Zechariah. Chs. 9–14 are sharply distinguished from these in form, language, and thought. They are generally regarded as anonymous prophecies (the name of the prophet does not appear) which became attached to the original book, and are often spoken of as Deutero-Zechariah.

I. CHAPTERS 1–8. **1. The Prophet (Zacharias** in 1 Es 6^{1} 7^{3} AV, RV; **Zachary** in 2 Es 1^{40} AV, RV), son of Berechiah, grandson of Iddo (1^{1}), is mentioned only in the book which bears his name and in Ezr 5^{1} 6^{14}, together with Haggai, as concerned in stirring up Zerubbabel and Joshua to rebuild the Temple. The work prospered through their activity.

2. Historical occasion and date.—The dates given in the book itself assign the prophecies to the second and fourth years of the reign of Darius I. The first message (1^{1-6}) is dated in the eighth month of Darius' second year (October–November, 520 B.C.); the section 1^{7}–6^{15} is assigned to the twenty-fourth day of the eleventh month (January–February, 519 B.C.); while chs. 7–8 are dated in the fourth year of Darius, on the fourth day of the ninth month (November–December, 518 B.C.). The prophecies are thus associated with the period of the rebuilding of the Temple (completed according to Ezr 6^{15} in 516 B.C.), though some sayings (*e.g.* 6^{14} 7^{2f}) may be later, and others (*e.g.* 2^{6f}) may be earlier.

3. Contents.—The book opens with an exhortation to return to Yahweh (1^{1-6}), based upon the sad experience of the fathers who had not heeded the word of the former prophets to turn from their evil ways. Zechariah, familiar with the teaching of his predecessors, builds upon the lessons which may be drawn from past experience.

The main body of the book (1^{7}–6^{15}) is made up of a series of eight visions and a symbolic action, together with other prophetic teaching. In the first vision (1^{7-17}), the prophet sees at night in a myrtle-shaded glen, horses and riders who are indicated by the angel who talks with him as being messengers of Yahweh. They report that all is quiet in the earth. The angel calls upon Yahweh: 'How long wilt thou have no mercy on Jerusalem and the cities of Judah, against which thou hast had indignation these seventy years?' In response, assurance comes that Yahweh is displeased with the nations which are at ease. He has returned to Jerusalem, His Temple is to be built, His cities are to overflow with prosperity. Zion shall be comforted and Jerusalem chosen. The second vision (1^{18-21}) is of four horns—the nations which have scattered the holy people—and four smiths who are to terrify them (*i.e.* the nations). In the third (2^{1-5}), the prophet sees a man setting out to measure Jerusalem; but Jerusalem is to be 'open villages,' spreading far and wide, and protected by Yahweh as by a wall of fire. A song follows, calling on the exiles to return; the nations which plundered are to be plundered themselves, and as Yahweh comes to dwell in Zion the nations shall be gathered to Him.

The fourth vision (ch. 3) shows Joshua the high priest standing before the angel of Yahweh. He is clothed in filthy garments and accused by the Satan, but the Satan is rebuked, the garments are removed, and Joshua is clothed in rich apparel with a clean turban on his head. This symbolizes the removal of guilt and Joshua is promised the full exercise of his priestly functions if he walks in Yahweh's ways. The further promise is made that he and his associates are a sign that Yahweh will bring His servant the Branch (cf 6^{12} and Is 4^{2}, Jer 23^{5} 33^{15}), *i.e.* Zerubbabel. The fifth vision (ch. 4) is of a seven-fold lamp, with an olive tree on either side. If the promise to Zerubbabel (vv.$^{6b-10a}$) is transferred to the end of the chapter, it becomes clear that the seven-fold lamp is interpreted as the eyes of Yahweh which run to and fro through the earth. The olive trees are explained as the two sons of oil, standing by the Lord of the whole earth, *i.e.* Zerubbabel and Joshua, governor and priest. It appears in 4^{12} that they actually feed the lamp with oil. The promise to Zerubbabel is that he will complete the Temple, not by might nor by power, but by Yahweh's spirit. The prominent place given in chs. 3 and 4 to governor and priest, secular and sacred leaders, as essential to the national well-being, is significant.

The sixth vision (5^{1-4}) is of a scroll which effects the curse of Yahweh upon thieves and perjurers. The seventh (5^{5-11}) depicts Wickedness, *i.e.* Idolatry, represented as a woman in an ephah, carried away from the land to Babylonia and worshipped there. The land is thus cleansed from sin of all kinds. The last vision (6^{1-8}) shows four chariots going out from between two mountains. The greatest interest is in the one which goes to the north country, *i.e.* Babylonia, to set Yahweh's Spirit at rest there. This may mean both the pouring out of His wrath and the stirring up of His people.

Ch. 6^{9-15} links closely with this last idea in describing a symbolic action, the crowning of Joshua (perhaps originally Zerubbabel). The assurance of the rebuilding of the Temple, and of peace between governor and priest, leads up to a call for help in the rebuilding by returned exiles, and a promise that these things will come about if men obey the voice of Yahweh. The whole series of visions culminates in a restored Jerusalem and a renewed people.

This theme is continued in the third section (chs. 7, 8), where a question concerning fasting leads to a renewed exhortation to obedience (7^{4-14}), and a series of promises of the glory, peace, and prosperity of restored Zion (8^{1-8}). Further words of encouragement and warning (8^{9-17}) are followed by a promise that fasts will be turned into rejoicing, and that many peoples shall come to seek Yahweh, knowing that He may be found with His people (8^{18-23}).

4. Significance.—The historical importance of Zechariah in connexion with the rebuilding of the Temple has already been noted. This rebuilding Zechariah, like Haggai, sees to be central to the hopes of the future. Drawing on the language of earlier prophecy, he warns the people of the disasters which come upon disobedience, but at the same time gives the assurance of Yahweh's willingness to return to His people. The new age can indeed only follow upon Yahweh's presence, and its manifestation in Jerusalem will lead to recognition throughout the nations.

These chapters have often been recognized as an important link between prophecy and apocalyptic. But although some of the symbols reappear later in apocalyptic, and there is at times less of directness in the presentation of the material than in earlier prophecy, and perhaps rather more of literary device, yet the prophetic experience is real and largely, though not entirely, associated with natural phenomena. The interpreting angel appears as in later apocalyptic; but angelic messengers are much older than Zechariah. There is little or no deliberate allegorizing of the visionary experiences; details are not given precise application. What may well be direct prophetic experience is in part concealed within a skilful literary structure, with visions and oracular material interwoven. The stress on prophetic authority and on the reality of the Divine call (cf 2^{9} 4^{9} 6^{15}) places Zechariah firmly within the great line of OT prophecy.

II. CHAPTERS 9–14.—**1. Critical analysis.**—The fact that Mt 27^{9} quotes from Zec 11^{12f} as a prophecy of Jeremiah led to the adoption of the view that the section 9–11 was by the earlier prophet, and 12–14 was also regarded as by Jeremiah by some scholars. The recognition of a division between these two sections led on to the view that they were independent, and various dates were proposed, for example 9–11 in the period of Hosea, and 12–14 shortly after the death of Josiah, these dates being based upon the interpretation of allusions in the text. But the suggestion that 9–14 was later than Zechariah was also put forward, and although the Zecharian authorship is still maintained in some circles, it is generally recognized to-day that the whole section is later than Zechariah in its present form. Difference of opinion remains as to whether some much earlier material has been incorporated in the later collection, and as to the occasion or occasions to which the oracles are to be assigned. The division into 9–11 and 12–14 is not altogether satisfactory, though it is indicated by the use of the heading 'Oracle' at 9^{1} and 12^{1} (as also at the beginning of the Book of Malachi which immediately follows), for 13^{7-9} may well be thought to belong with 11^{4-17}, and it hardly can be believed that $12–13^{6}$ is by the same author as 14.

2. Dating and interpretation.—It is not possible to connect 9–14 with certainty with any known events in the post-exilic period. The possibility that earlier material has here in some measure been re-interpreted makes it reasonable to suppose that allusions may be present to more than one period of history. The history of the post-exilic period is at some points so little known that dating of the oracles then is hazardous; equally fraught with uncertainty is dating in a well-known period like that of the Maccabees. If a choice must be made, the period following on the conquests of Alexander might well be preferred, but it may be that there has been application of earlier oracles to such a period, and the significance of the material may perhaps be better sought in its stress on the woes and distresses which usher in the new age, and on the establishment of final Divine rule, than in tracing exact allusions to events.

3. Contents.—$9^{1}–11^{3}$ contains mainly oracles of doom upon Israel's neighbours, with promises of dominion and prosperity for Israel, restored to her land. The opening oracle (9^{1-8}) depicts disaster upon Syria, Phoenicia and Philistia, but v.^{7} suggests the purifying of Philistia and its incorporation into Judah as a new clan. Yahweh returns to His house and protects His people (v.^{8}). The prediction of the coming king (vv.^{9f}) stresses the Divine empowering of the ruler, and the ending of warfare as in Ps 46, Is 2, Mic 4. An oracle of restoration from exile and of victory over the enemies in the power of Yahweh follows (vv.$^{11-16}$: the mention of Greece in v.^{13} might be a later application). Yahweh appears as giver of life ($9^{17}–10^{2}$), and there is a renewed promise of deliverance and return of the exiles (10^{3-12}), with the two kingdoms reunited and occupying the whole land. 11^{1-3} contains a triumphant oracle of disaster. 11^{4-17}, with which many scholars associate 13^{7-9}, contains a complicated allegory of shepherds. Yahweh's beneficent purpose is shown to be frustrated by the obstinacy of His people, as well as by the evil character of their rulers. The 'three shepherds' of v.^{8} presumably contains a specific allusion but appears to be intrusive and to represent a later reapplication of the original allegory. The significance of the symbolism, *e.g.* in vv.$^{12-13}$ is now very difficult to gauge.

The second main division of chs. 9–14, beginning at ch. 12, brings a familiar concept of the nations assembled against Jerusalem, but there to be consumed through the power of Yahweh. The reiterated 'on that day' in $12^{1}–13^{6}$ suggests the grouping of various sayings on similar topics. The picture is reminiscent of Zephaniah, Ezekiel, and Joel, and of psalm passages such as Ps 2. The 'day of the Lord' is visualized in terms of the overthrow of the nations to be accompanied—so 13^{1-6}—by the purification of God's own people. There is obscurity in the references to the house of David, perhaps suggestive of a realization of its inadequacy for the tasks to which it is called; and also in the allusions of 12^{10f} which refer to some ritual mourning. The strictures on the failure of prophecy in 13^{2-6} are also strange and difficult to interpret. 13^{7-9} speaks of the overthrow of the shepherds and of the purification of a remnant of the people. Ch. 14 gives another series of apocalyptic pictures of the siege of Jerusalem and the ushering in of the new age. It is to be a day of natural disaster as well as of battle (vv.$^{1-5}$); but the new age will be of light (v.^{6}), of new life for the land and security for the city (vv.$^{7-11}$). The nations are judged (vv.$^{12-15}$), but there is hope for the survivors of disaster to share in the worship of Yahweh. Blessing will be upon those who worship him, and all in Judah and Jerusalem will be sanctified.

4. Significance.—The much more strongly apocalyptic tone of chs. 9–14 contrasts with chs. 1–8; yet both sections are concerned with Yahweh's judgment and deliverance, and emphasis lies in chs. 9–14 upon the new age, and the fulfilment of men's hopes in times of distress and uncertainty. Its triumphant note perhaps accounts for its frequent quotation in the NT.

H. T. F.—**P. R. A.**

ZECHER.—See ZECHARIAH, **1.**

ZECHRIAS, 1 Es 8^{1} (RV).—See AZARIAH, **9.**

ZEDAD.—One of the points mentioned in defining the northern border of the Promised Land in Nu 34^{8}, and again in Ezekiel's ideal picture, Ezk 47^{15}. It is probably *Ṣedâd*, SE. of *Ḥomṣ*.

ZEDECHIAS, 1 Es 1^{46} (AV) = **Zedekiah, 6** (q.v.).

ZEDEKIAH.—1. Son of Chenaanah, and one of Ahab's four hundred court prophets, 1 K $22^{11, 24}$, 2 Ch $18^{10, 23}$. **2.** A prophet deported to Babylon with Jehoiachin, Jer 29^{21ff}. He and another, named **Ahab,** are denounced by Jeremiah for gross immortality as well as for falsely prophesying a speedy restoration from Babylon. It was probably their action as political agitators that brought on them the cruel punishment of being roasted in the fire by order of Nebuchadrezzar. **3.** Son of Hananiah, Jer 36^{12}. **4.** A signatory to the covenant, Neh 10^{1} (AV **Zidkijah**). **5.** An ancestor of Baruch, Bar 1^{1} (AV **Sedecias,** RV **Sedekias**). **6.** See next article.

ZEDEKIAH, the last king of Judah before its fall at the hands of the Babylonians, is known to us not only from the historical books, but also from references in the Book of Jeremiah. He was the third son of Josiah to assume the royal title. Jehoahaz was deposed by the Pharaoh; Jehoiakim had a troubled reign of eleven years, and escaped the vengeance of Nebuchadrezzar by dying just before the Babylonian reached Jerusalem. The young Jehoiachin suffered for the sin of his father, being carried into captivity after three months of barren kingship. With him were carried away the chief men of Judah to the number of eight thousand—Nebuchadrezzar thinking thus to break the seditious temper of the people. Over the remnant left behind Zedekiah was made king. His earlier name, **Mattaniah,** was changed to *Zedekiah* (meaning 'righteousness of Yahweh'), to indicate that the Babylonian monarch, in punishing the treachery of Jehoiakim, had the God of Judah on his side (2 K 24^{17}). We are told by Ezekiel ($17^{13, 19}$) that Zedekiah took an oath of allegiance to his suzerain. For **Zarius** of 1 Es 1^{38} see ZARIUS.

Nebuchadrezzar's confidence that the people would be submissive after the severe lesson they had received was disappointed. The new men who came to the front were as headstrong as, and even more foolish than, their predecessors. They were blind to the ludicrous insufficiency of their resources, and determined to play the game of politics against the great nations of the world. The court of Zedekiah was the centre of intrigues against the Babylonian power, and the plotters were fed with promises from Egypt. Zedekiah showed himself a weak man, unable to cope with the situation. In his fourth year ambassadors appeared at Jerusalem from the surrounding nations, to concert common measures against the oppressor. The majority of the prophets encouraged the movement; only Jeremiah saw the madness of the undertaking, and declared against it. His bold declaration of the truth brought upon him the enmity of the courtiers. Zedekiah seems to have been called to account by the great king, to whom he made some explanation which satisfied him, or at least lulled suspicion for a time. The movement itself came to nothing at this time. But in Zedekiah's ninth year renewed promises from Egypt induced the Jerusalemites to revolt, and Zedekiah was too weak to restrain them. Nebuchadrezzar replied promptly by marching in person against the rebels. Jerusalem was a stronghold in which the people had confidence, and they seem also to have believed fanatically that Yahweh would intervene to protect His Temple. This faith was raised to a high pitch by the approach of an Egyptian army under Pharaoh Hophra; for Nebuchadrezzar was compelled to raise the siege to meet the new enemy. The expression of the people's confidence that they had got from Yahweh all that they desired is seen in the indecent haste with which they reduced again to slavery the servants whom they had set free in order to obtain His favour (Jer 34[8ff]).

The joy was short lived. The Egyptians were hardly a serious problem to Nebuchadrezzar, and soon left him free to resume the siege, which he did with energy. The strongly fortified city was defended by its inhabitants with the courage of despair, and held out a year and a half. During this time they suffered all the horrors of siege, famine, and pestilence. Jeremiah, who still predicted disaster, was arrested, and would have perished in his dungeon had it not been for the compassion of one of the king's slaves (Jer 38). Zedekiah, who believed in him, consulted him by stealth, but could not nerve himself to follow the advice he received. When at last the wall was breached, the king attempted to escape to the Jordan valley, hoping thus to gain the eastern desert. But he was overtaken and carried to Nebuchadrezzar. The victor, considering that forbearance had ceased to be a virtue, slew the captive king's children before his eyes, then blinded the king himself and carried him away in chains to Babylon. The kingdom of Judah had come to an end (2 K 25[4ff]). H. P. S.

ZEEB.—See OREB AND ZEEB.

ZELA.—A town of Benjamin, Jos 18[28] (AV, RV **Zelah**); perhaps this name should be joined to the following name, as in LXX, giving **Zela-ha-eleph**. Saul and Jonathan were buried in Zela, 2 S 21[14] (AV **Zelah**). It is perhaps modern, *Kh Ṣalaḥ*, NW. of Jerusalem.

ZELAH, Jos 18[28] (AV, RV), 2 S 21[14] (AV).—See ZELA.

ZELA-HA-ELEPH.—See ZELA.

ZELEK.—One of David's heroes, 2 S 23[37], 1 Ch 11[39].

ZELOPHEHAD.—A Manassite who died during the wilderness journeyings, leaving no male issue. His five daughters successfully asserted their claim to the inheritance of their father, Nu 26[33] 27[1-7] 36[2-12], Jos 17[3], 1 Ch 7[15].

ZELOTES, Lk 6[15], Ac 1[13] (AV)=RV and RSV **Zealot** (q.v.).

ZELZAH.—A place in Benjamite territory, mentioned only in 1 S 10[2] as the site of Rachel's tomb. This stood in the neighbourhood of Bethlehem, Gn 35[19f]. Zelzah is quite unknown, and neither LXX nor Vulgate understood it as a place-name, though neither knew what it meant.

ZEMAR.—A Phoenician city mentioned with Sidon and Arvad in Ezk 27[8] (so RSV, conjecturally emending the Heb., which reads 'Thy wise men, O Tyre,' as AV, RV). From this city the **Zemarites** (q.v.) were named. Abel identifies it with *Tell Kazel*, while others have suggested *Ṭabbat el-Ḥammām*, slightly more to the N.

ZEMARAIM.—A city of Benjamin, near Bethel, Jos 18[22]. It probably gave its name to Mount Zemaraim, 2 Ch 13[4]. It is probably modern *Râs ez-Zeimarah*, near Ophrah.

ZEMARITE, THE.—A collective designation of one of the Canaanite communities in Gn 10[18], 1 Ch 1[16], named along with the Arvadite, and therefore presumably Northern Phoenicia. They lived in the city of **Zemar** (q.v.), Ezk 27[8].

ZEMIRA, 1 Ch 7[8] (AV).—See ZEMIRAH.

ZEMIRAH.—A son of Becher, 1 Ch 7[8] (AV **Zemira**).

ZENAN.—A town of Judah in the lowland, Jos 15[27]. It is possibly *'Araq el-Kharba*, W. of Lachish.

ZENAS.—A lawyer whom St. Paul asks Titus to send to him from Crete, with Apollos (Tit 3[13]). The name is perhaps a contraction from *Zenodorus*.

ZEPHANIAH.—**1.** The prophet (see next article). **2.** A Kohathite, 1 Ch 6[36]. **3.** Son of Maaseiah the priest in Jerusalem in the time of Zedekiah the king and Jeremiah the prophet, Jer 21[1] 29[25, 29] 37[3]. As next in rank to Seraiah, grandson of Hilkiah (1 Ch 6[14]), Zephaniah is called *second priest*, 2 K 25[18]. On the occasion of the final overthrow of Jerusalem he was put to death at Riblah, Jer 52[24ff]. **4.** The father of one Josiah in Babylon, Zec 6[10, 14].

ZEPHANIAH is the title of the ninth section of the Hebrew collection of the prophetic literature, entitled 'The Twelve Prophets,' which was probably compiled in the 3rd cent. B.C. Like other sections of this work it contains both earlier and later materials, though these cannot always be separated from one another with certainty. In the main the Book of Zephaniah consists of a prophecy of judgment delivered by Zephaniah about 627 B.C.

1. The prophet.—According to the title (1[1]) Zephaniah prophesied in the reign of Josiah (639–608 B.C.). Since the allusions in ch 1 point to the continuance unchecked of false worships such as those of 'the host of the heavens' which had prevailed under the previous kings Manasseh and Amon we may infer that Zephaniah prophesied before the Reformation of 621 B.C. Two further inferences with regard to Zephaniah are justifiable if, as is probable, the great-great-grandfather of Zephaniah was *king* Hezekiah (1[1]; cf *Expositor*, July 1900, pp. 76–80): (1) Zephaniah was of royal descent; (2) Like Jeremiah (Jer 1[6]) Zephaniah when he began to prophesy was a young man—say of some twenty-five years.

2. The Book.—The book of Zephaniah ought not to be read as a continuous whole. 1[2]–2[3] may be regarded as a genuine prophecy of Zephaniah save for minor additions, but 2[4-15] appears to be an insertion formed according to the usual scheme of setting oracles against the nations between oracles of judgment and promise to the prophet's own people. In its present form 1[2]–2[3] predicts as near at hand a judgment that is to affect the whole world (in v.[18] 'the whole land' [AV] is to be translated 'the whole earth' [so RSV]) and it describes in detail how it will affect Judah and summons that people to a solemn repentance (2[1-3]). The ground of judgment in the case of Judah is found in the prevalence of false worship (1[4-6]), of foreign fashions (1[8f]), and disregard of Yahweh (1[12]). According to the general opinion Zephaniah, like Jeremiah, who was prophesying at the same time, expected the Scythians to be the instruments of this judgment: at this time these hordes of barbarians were pouring down from the highlands of Asia.

Ch. 3 contains (1) a description of the sins of Jerusalem (vv.[1-7]), parallel to ch. 1 and particularizing rather different sins, or a prophetic description of Jerusalem at a later date: (2) a description of a universal judgment from which only the godly remnant of Judah will escape (vv.[11-13]); (3) a description of the glory of the Jews after Yahweh has delivered them from captivity (vv.[14-20]). Pfeiffer holds little if anything in this chapter can be from Zephaniah. Sellin, on the other hand, accepts almost the whole chapter. Eissfeldt judges vv.$^{1-13}$ with the exception of vv.$^{8-10}$ to be by the prophet while vv.$^{14-17}$ may also be genuine. Vv.$^{18-20}$ must be assigned to the post-exilic period.

It seems clear that Zephaniah, like the prophets of the 8th cent. and his own contemporary Jeremiah, was primarily a prophet of judgment to come upon his own people. In this respect he differed from two prophets of approximately the same period, Nahum and Habakkuk, both of whom probably prophesied after the Reformation of 621 B.C. Nahum is concerned entirely with judgment on Assyria while Habakkuk is perplexed by what to Zephaniah might have appeared the fulfillment of his prophecy—the present troubles of Judah. Zephaniah marks no new departure in prophetic activity or thought, but by his moral earnestness, and his insistence on the need for single-hearted devotion to the demands of Yahweh for righteousness, he performed for his own generation the service rendered a century earlier by Isaiah, whose influence on his thought and teaching is obvious (cf 1^{14-17} with Is 2^{12f}). G. B. G.—**J. Pn.**

ZEPHATH.—See HORMAH.

ZEPHATHAH.—A valley near Mareshah, mentioned in 2 Ch 14^{10}. But LXX reads ' north of ' for this word, in which case the valley ' north of Mareshah ' would be the valley of Elah (q.v.). Zephathah is otherwise unknown.

ZEPHI.—A son of Eliphaz, one of the dukes of Edom, 1 Ch 1^{36}; called **Zepho** in Gn $36^{11, 15}$.

ZEPHO.—See ZEPHI.

ZEPHON.—A Gadite, Nu 26^{15}; called **Ziphion** in Gn 46^{16}. The gentilic **Zephonites** occurs in Nu 26^{15}.

ZER.—A fortified city of Naphtali, Jos 19^{35}. Its location is unknown.

ZERAH (' shining ').—**1.** One of the sons of Reuel, Gn $36^{13, 17}$, 1 Ch 1^{37}. The name appears again as that of the father of Jobab, one of the early kings of Edom, Gn 36^{33}, 1 Ch 1^{44}. **2.** The younger-born of the twin sons of Judah by Tamar, his daughter-in-law, Gn 38^{30} (AV **Zarah**). He gives his name to the **Zerahites**, Nu 26^{20} (AV **Zarhites**). Of this family was Achan the son of Zabdi, Jos 7^{1}, or Zimri, 1 Ch 2^{6}. Zerah's sons are mentioned in 1 Ch 9^{6}, and Pethahiah (Neh 11^{24}) is one of his descendants. He finds a place in the genealogy of our Lord, Mt 1^{3} (AV **Zara**). **3.** A son of Simeon, and the founder of a family of **Zerahites** (AV **Zarhites**) within that tribe, Nu 26^{13}; also called **Zohar**, Gn 46^{10}, Ex 6^{15}. **4.** A Levite name, borne by a Gershonite, 1 Ch 6^{21}, and by a Kohathite, 1 Ch 6^{41}. **5.** The name of an Ethiopian—or, more probably N. Arabian—who invaded Judah in the reign of Asa (2 Ch 14^{9-15}). The story of this invasion is unknown to secular history, and rests solely on the authority of the Chronicler. There has been much controversy as to its historicity, and the question is still involved in obscurity. In any case the numbers in the text of Chronicles (580,000 men in Asa's army, 1,000,000 in Zerah's) are incredibly large.

ZERAHIAH.—**1.** An ancestor of Ezra, Ezr 7^{4}; in 1 Es 8^{2} (AV, RV; RSV omits) he is called **Zaraias**, and in 2 Es 1^{2} **Arna**. **2.** The father of Eliehoenai, one of the returned exiles, Ezr 8^{4}, 1 Es 8^{31} (RSV; AV, RV **Zaraias**).

ZERAIAH.—One who returned with Ezra, 1 Es 8^{34} (AV, RV **Zaraias**); called **Zebadiah** in Ezr 8^{8}.

ZERDAIAH.—A Jew who had married a foreign wife, 1 Es 9^{28} (AV **Sardeus**, RV **Zardeus**); in Ezr 10^{27} he is called **Aziza**.

ZERED.—The torrent-valley (*naḥal*) of Zered is named in the itinerary of Israel's journeyings, Nu 21^{12} (AV **Zared**), immediately prior to their crossing of the Arnon, and in Dt 2^{13} as the point that marked the close of the thirty-eight years' wanderings. It is the modern *Wâdī el-Ḥesâ*.

ZEREDA, 1 K 11^{26} (AV).—See ZEREDAH, **1.**

ZEREDAH.—**1.** The Ephraimite city in which Jeroboam was born, 1 K 11^{26} (AV **Zereda**); probably modern *Deir Ghassâreh*. **2.** A city mentioned in 2 Ch 4^{17} (AV **Zeredathah**). The parallel passage in 1 K 7^{46} has **Zarethan**, which is probably correct.

ZEREDATHAH, 2 Ch 4^{17} (AV).—See ZEREDAH, **2.**

ZERERAH.—A place mentioned in Jg 7^{22} (AV **Zererath**). It is probable that this is the same as **Zeredah, 2** (q.v.), and that both should be identified with **Zarethan** (q.v.).

ZERERATH, Jg 7^{22} (AV).—See ZERERAH.

ZERESH.—The wife of Haman, Est 5^{10-14} 6^{13}.

ZERETH.—A Judahite, 1 Ch 4^{7}.

ZERETH-SHAHAR.—A Reubenite town, Jos 13^{19} (AV **Zareth-shahar**). It is probably modern *Zārât*.

ZERI.—See IZRI.

ZEROR.—An ancestor of Saul, 1 S 9^{1}.

ZERUAH.—The mother of Jeroboam, 1 K 11^{26}.

ZERUBBABEL (probably = ' shoot of Babylon ': also **Zorobabel** in Apocrypha AV, RV and NT AV).—The son of Shealtiel (1 Ch 3^{17} Pedaiah), grandson of Jehoiachin, king of Judah, and appearing in the genealogies of Jesus as a direct ancestor (Mt 1^{12f}, Lk 3^{27}). He was the leader of one of the bands that returned from the Exile (Ezr 2^{2}, Neh 7^{7}) and was at one time governor (*peḥāh* of Judah (Hag 1^{1} etc.). On the question of his relationship to **Sheshbazzar,** see SHESHBAZZAR.

He was exhorted, with Joshua the high priest, to rebuild the Temple (Hag 1^{1ff} 2^{1ff}; cf Ezr 5^{1ff}) and particularly marked out for this task by Zechariah (4^{6-10} 6^{12f}). The Book of Ezra records the difficulties which met the builders from those who questioned their authority to build (Ezr 5^{3ff}), but appeal to Darius revealed that Cyrus had issued a decree authorizing the building, and the work was then brought to a successful conclusion (5^{6}–6). The name of Zerubbabel does not appear in the narrative of the completion of the Temple; nor does that of Joshua, though Haggai and Zechariah are both mentioned (Ezr 6^{13-15}). This silence has led to much speculation about Zerubbabel's fate, and not a few scholars have concluded that he was involved in an act of rebellion which led to his removal or death. Zec 6, however, strongly suggests that he did complete the work. Alternative explanations may be simply that his term of office expired, or that he died before the Temple was completed: his age at the time is unknown, but as grandson of Jehoiachin (who was 18 years of age in 597 B.C.), he could have been nearly sixty years of age. The Biblical record contains many examples of such sudden disappearances, leaving the reader uninformed concerning the outcome of events.

The view that Zerubbabel was engaged in rebellion has been thought to find support in Hag 2^{20-23}, which designates him as the ' servant of the LORD ' and as a ' signet,' *i.e.* executive officer, in a time of upheaval. In Zec 3^{8} and 6^{12ff}, he is clearly designated ' the Branch ' (see BRANCH), and reference to a crown might also imply political aspirations. The text in Zec 6 has probably been adapted subsequently to give greater prominence to the high priest. The functions of ' the Branch ' are described in terms which indicate hope of an age of peace and well-being, with guilt removed from the land. Nothing in the two prophetic books exhorts to political action, and indeed Zec 4^{6} definitely indicates that the deliverance is to be a Divine action (cf Hag 2), not the result of human rebellion.

Ezr 3^{8} appears to place Zerubbabel's activity in the early years of the reign of Cyrus. But it is not easy to reconcile this with 5^{2}. If both are regarded as historical, then presumably Zerubbabel on the early occasion was in a subordinate position to Sheshbazzar, but it seems more probable that the Chronicler has ascribed to Zerubbabel the earlier stage of the activity which should actually have belonged to Sheshbazzar (cf Ezr 5^{16}).

In 1 Es 3–5, Zerubbabel plays an important part in a contest of wits at the court of Darius I., but it seems very probable that the identification of the hero with

Zerubbabel is not original to the tale, which appears to have been taken over from the earlier sources, given a decided Jewish slant, and then applied to this situation. The mission of Zerubbabel to Jerusalem is here made the sequel to his winning the king's favour in this contest. W. O. E. O.—**P. R. A.**

ZERUIAH.—The mother of David's officers Abishai, Joab, and Asahel, who are always referred to as 'sons of Zeruiah.' The father's name is never mentioned, and he may have died early; or the mother may have been so remarkable a woman that her husband's name was not preserved; or we have a survival of the ancient custom of tracing kinship through the female line.

In 1 Ch 2^{16} Zeruiah and Abigail are called 'sisters of the sons of Jesse,' but in 2 S 17^{25} Abigail is called the daughter of Nahash. It seems more probable that for *Nahash* in 2 S 17^{25} we ought to read *Jesse*, than that Jesse's wife had previously been married to Nahash the Ammonite. According to this view, Zeruiah would be the daughter of Jesse and sister of David. W. F. B.

ZETHAM.—A Gershonite Levite, 1 Ch 23^{8} 26^{22}.

ZETHAN.—A Benjamite, 1 Ch 7^{10}.

ZETHAR.—A eunuch of king Ahasuerus, Est 1^{10}.

ZEUS, the ancient Greek 'god of the bright blue sky'—and also of the dark thunder clouds—the 'father of gods and men,' as often in Homer, is the only Greek god whose Indo-European origin is unquestioned. He was not the Creator of the world, but its sovereign ruler. The Roman god *Iuppiter* (*Diou-pater*, 'sky father') was thought by the Romans to correspond in attributes with the Greek god Zeus, and hence the two were identified. In modern times the name Zeus has been translated rather loosely as 'Jupiter' (*e.g.* 2 Mac 6^{2}); the RSV correctly uses the Greek word. The name *Zeus* in fact corresponds with the first syllable of Jupiter, and suggests the ruler of the celestial firmament, the one who gives light and causes rain, thunder, lightning, and other natural phenomena in the sky.

He was imagined to have usurped the authority of his father Kronos and thus to have become the chief and ruler of all other gods. As such he was worshipped all over the Greek world. The case of Ac 14^{12f} may be further complicated, if it was not the Greek Zeus who was referred to but the native supreme god of the Lycaonians—who was assumed by the author of Acts to correspond, as their chief god, to the Greek Zeus. But at least Luke did not hesitate to accept the identity, and we can scarcely go behind his narrative. All we know of this god is that his temple at Lystra was outside the city wall (Ac 14^{13}), and that Barnabas, as the big silent man, was taken for him. In Ac 19^{35} the term rendered 'from Jupiter' in AV and RV means simply 'from the sky' (so RSV). A. So.—**F. C. G.**

ZIA.—A Gadite, 1 Ch 5^{13}.

ZIBA.—A servant, probably a freedman, of Saul. He appears before David (2 S 9$^{1-11}$), possessing fifteen sons and twenty servants, and is consulted as to the existence of any members of the house of Saul. He informs David of the retreat of **Mephibosheth,** to whom David restores the lands of his father and appoints Ziba steward. On David's flight from Jerusalem (2 S 16$^{1-4}$) Ziba followed him with provisions, and accused Mephibosheth of treachery. He received a grant of his master's lands, but on David's return Mephibosheth was able to clear himself and was allowed to retain a half (2 S 19$^{24-30}$). W. F. B.

ZIBEON.—See Anah.

ZIBIA.—A Benjamite, 1 Ch 8^{9}.

ZIBIAH.—The mother of Joash of Judah, 2 K 12^{1}, 2 Ch 24^{1}.

ZICHRI.—**1.** A grandson of Kohath, Ex 6^{21}. **2, 3, 4, 5.** Four Benjamites, 1 Ch 8$^{19, 23, 27}$, Neh 11^{9}. **6.** An Asaphite, 1 Ch 9^{15}; called **Zabdi** in Neh 11^{17}. **7.** A descendant of Eliezer, 1 Ch 26^{25}. **8.** A Reubenite, 1 Ch 27^{16}. **9.** A Judahite, 2 Ch 17^{16}. **10.** Father of a captain in Jehoiada's time, 2 Ch 23^{1}. **11.** A mighty man of Ephraim, 2 Ch 28^{7}. **12.** A priest, Neh 12^{17}.

ZIDDIM.—A fortified city of Naphtali, Jos 19^{35}. It is possibly *Ḥaṭṭîn el-Qadîm*, now *Kefar Ḥiṭṭîm*.

ZIDKIJAH, Neh 10^{1} (AV).—See Zedekiah, **4.**

ZIDON.—See Sidon.

ZIF, 1 K 6$^{1, 37}$ (AV) = **Ziv** (see Time).

ZIHA.—A family of Nethinim (q.v.), Ezr 2^{43}, Neh 7^{46} 11^{21}, 1 Es 5^{29} (AV, RV **Esau**).

ZIKLAG.—A town given by Achish king of Gath to the outlawed David, 1 S 27^{6} 30^{1ff}, 2 S 1^{1} 4^{10}, 1 Ch 12$^{1, 20}$. In the national register of cities it is assigned to Judah (Jos 15^{31}) or to Simeon (19^{5}), and is mentioned also in the post-exilic list (Neh 11^{28}). It is possibly modern *Tell el-Khuweilfeh*.

ZILLAH.—See Adah.

ZILLETHAI.—**1.** A Benjamite family, 1 Ch 8^{20} (AV **Zilthai**). **2.** A Manassite who joined David at Ziklag, 1 Ch 12^{20} (AV **Zilthai**).

ZILPAH.—A slave-girl given to Leah by Laban, Gn 29^{24}, and by her to Jacob as a concubine, 30^{9}; she was the mother of Gad and Asher, vv.$^{10-13}$ 35^{26} 37^{2} 46^{18}. Cf Tribes of Israel.

ZILTHAI.—AV form of Zillethai (q.v.).

ZIMMAH.—A family of Gershonite Levites, 1 Ch 6$^{20, 42}$, 2 Ch 29^{12}.

ZIMRAN.—A son of Abraham and Keturah, Gn 25^{2}, 1 Ch 1^{32}.

ZIMRI.—**1.** A prince of the tribe of Simeon, slain by Phinehas, Nu 25$^{6-14}$, 1 Mac 2^{26} (AV **Zambri**). **2.** Son of Zerah, and grandfather or ancestor of Achan, 1 Ch 2^{6}; called **Zabdi** in Jos 7$^{1, 17f}$. **3.** A Benjamite, 1 Ch 8^{36} 9^{42}. **4.** See next article. **5.** 'All the kings of Zimri' are mentioned in the same verse, Jer 25^{25}, with those of Elam and the Medes as among those who were to drink the cup of the fury of the Lord. There is considerable doubt as to what place is meant, or even as to the genuineness of the phrase. It has been suggested that it may stand for **Elam** by Atbash (see Sheshach).

ZIMRI seized the throne of Israel by the murder of his king Elah, but held it only seven days before **Omri,** another general of the army, asserted himself as claimant. Omri, as is well known, was the stronger, and established himself after disposing of two opponents. The characterization of Zimri, as one who caused Israel to sin by following in the ways of Jeroboam, is due to the author's desire to pronounce judgment on all the kings of the Northern Kingdom, 1 K 16$^{9-20}$. Jezebel scornfully addressed Jehu as 'thou Zimri' (2 K 9^{31}), perhaps with the suggestion that his claim to the throne would be no more lasting.

ZIN (Nu 13^{21} 20^{1} 27^{14} 33^{36} 34^{3f}, Dt 32^{51}, Jos 15$^{1, 3}$).—A region traversed by the Israelites in their desert wandering after the Exodus and before and after the Sinai episode. In Nu 13^{21} 'the wilderness of Zin' is named as the southern limit from which the spies set out to explore Palestine. In Nu 33^{36} it is given as one of the stations in the desert wandering. The brief note 'the same is Kadesh' serves to explain the following verse ('And they journeyed from Kadesh'). Nu 20^{1} records the arrival of the children of Israel 'in the wilderness of Zin' in the first month (the year is not stated), and the following vv.$^{2-13}$ relate the events which took place at Meribah. The remaining two passages, Nu 27 and Dt 32, which are duplicates, refer to the punishment of Moses for his offence at 'the waters of Meribah of Kadesh in the wilderness of Zin.' Hence it may be inferred that the wilderness of Zin was the region round Kadesh, though the later sources in Nu 34^{3f} and Jos 15$^{1-3}$, describing the S. boundary of Canaan and Judah respectively, obviously include the W. escarpment of the *Wâdī ʿArabah*.

The close similarity between the events recorded in Ex 17 and Nu 20, and other points of resemblance between occurrences before and after Sinai suggest the question whether Sin and Zin respectively of the pre-Sinai and post-Sinai narrative may be variations developed in the course of tradition. Cf Paran.

ZINA.—See Zizah.

ZION (AV **Sion** in NT).—The name of the fortress of the pre-Israelite city of Jerusalem (2 S 5^{7}), which was conquered by David and made his capital. The name is frequently used in the Psalms and the Prophets as a synonym for Jerusalem. For the location of David's city see Jerusalem, I, **4**.

ZIOR.—A town in the hill-country of Judah, Jos 15^{54}, probably modern *Sa'îr*, NNE. of Hebron.

ZIPH.—**1.** A Calebite, 1 Ch 2^{42}. **2.** A son of Jehallelel, 1 Ch 4^{16}. **3.** A city of Southern Judah, Jos 15^{24}; probably modern *Kh. ez-Zeifeh*. **4.** A city in the hill-country of Judah, Jos 15^{55}; fortified by Rehoboam, 2 Ch 11^{8}. The wilderness of Ziph was one of the refuges of David when fleeing from Saul, 1 S 23$^{14f, 24}$ 26^{2}. The gentilic name **Ziphites** occurs in 1 S 23^{19} 26^{1}, Ps 54 Heading. Ziph is modern *Tell Zîf*, SE. of Hebron.

ZIPHAH.—A son of Jehallelel, 1 Ch 4^{16}.

ZIPHIMS, Ps 54 Heading (AV) = **Ziphites** (see Ziph, **4**).

ZIPHION.—See Zephon.

ZIPHRON.—An unknown place on the northern frontier of Canaan, Nu 34^{9}.

ZIPPOR (' sparrow '). — Father of Balak, Nu 22$^{2, 4, 10, 16}$ 23^{18}, Jos 24^{9}, Jg 11^{25}.

ZIPPORAH (' bird ').—One of the daughters of the priest of Midian, Ex 2^{21f}, wife of Moses and mother of Gershom. According to 18^{3} she had another son. For the incident of Ex 4^{24ff} see Moses.

ZITHRI, Ex 6^{22} (AV).—See Sithri.

ZIV.—See Time.

ZIZ.—The ascent of Ziz is mentioned in 2 Ch 20^{16} as the way by which the allied Moabites, Ammonites and Meunim made their way up from En-gedi to attack Jehoshaphat at Jerusalem. It is modern *Wâdī Ḥaṣāṣah*, SE. of Bethlehem.

ZIZA.—**1.** A Simeonite chief, 1 Ch 4^{37}. **2.** A son of Rehoboam, 2 Ch 11^{20}.

ZIZAH.—A Gershonite Levite, 1 Ch 23^{11}; called **Zina** in v.^{9}, probably by a copyist's slip.

ZOAN.—A city in the NE. of Lower Egypt. It is not mentioned in Genesis, but in Nu 13^{22} we are told that Hebron was built seven years before Zoan. In Ps 78$^{12, 43}$ ' the fields of Zoan ' are named as the place where the miracles associated with the deliverance from Egypt took place. In Is 19$^{11, 13}$ 30^{4}, Ezk 30^{14} it is referred to almost as the capital of Egypt, perhaps as being the royal city nearest the frontier. Zoan corresponds to an Egyptian form which became **Tanis** in Greek. It is now *Ṣân el-Ḥagar*, which has been excavated by Montet. It was once known as *Avaris* (Egypt. *Ḥa-w'rt*), which was the Hyksos capital. In the Ramesside period, in the reign of Seti i., it was refortified, and throughout the reign of Rameses ii. it continued to be a royal residence and bore the name *Per-Ramesse* (cf **Raamses** in Ex 1^{11}). Rameses ii. placed in the temple there a colossus of himself in granite, the greatest known, which Petrie calculated from the fragments to have measured 92 feet in height.

ZOAR.—See Plain [Cities of the], Lot.

ZOBA, 2 S 10^{6ff} (AV).—See Zobah.

ZOBAH.—An Aramaean state, the most powerful of the coalition of ' Syrian ' states which made war upon David while he was engaged with the Ammonites, 2 S 8^{3ff} 10^{6ff} (AV **Zoba** in latter), 1 Ch 18^{3ff} 19^{6ff}. In the time of Solomon, Rezon, a fugitive from the king of Zobah, established himself as king in Damascus. In 1 S 14^{47} it is said that Saul fought against Zobah, but this is probably a reflection back to Saul from David's campaign. The exact location of Zobah is not known, but it may have lain between Hamath and Damascus.

ZOBEBAH.—A Judahite, 1 Ch 4^{8}.

ZOHAR (' tawny ').—**1.** Father of Ephron the Hittite, Gn 23^{8} 25^{9}. **2.** A Simeonite family, Gn 46^{10}, Ex 6^{15}; in Nu 26^{13} and 1 Ch 4^{24} called **Zerah** (q.v.). **3.** A Judahite family, according to the *Ḳ^{e}rê* of 1 Ch 4^{7} (so AV of 1611). The *K^{e}thîbh* is incorrectly reproduced in modern editions of AV as **Jezoar**; RV, RSV have **Izhar** (q.v.).

ZOHELETH, STONE OF.—An object mentioned in connexion with the attempt of Adonijah upon the throne of Israel, 1 K 1^{9}. It was near the spring **En-rogel**, which is supposed to be the ' Virgin's Fountain,' in the Kidron valley. It was evidently a sacred rock or stone, and in its neighbourhood was a shrine. The name is usually taken to mean ' Serpent's stone ' (so RSV), and while this is not certain there is some reason to think it is sound. The shrine was closely connected with the shrine in Jerusalem where Zadok was priest (cf 2 S 17^{17ff}, from which it appears that when Zadok's sons were missed in Jerusalem, it was at once thought they might have gone to En-rogel). The **Brazen Serpent** later destroyed by Hezekiah (2 K 18^{4}), popularly supposed to date back to Moses, was probably a Jebusite sacred object before David captured Jerusalem, and it may well be that Zoheleth was a natural serpent-like stone near En-rogel, which was venerated as sacred, while the Brazen Serpent served to represent the deity it stood for in the associated shrine inside the city.

H. L. W.—**H. H. R.**

ZOHETH.—A descendant of Judah, 1 Ch 4^{20}.

ZOPHAH.—An Asherite, 1 Ch 7^{35f}.

ZOPHAI.—An ancestor of Samuel, 1 Ch 6^{26}; called **Zuph** in v.^{35} and 1 S 1^{1}.

ZOPHAR.—The third in order of Job's three friends, described as a **Naamathite,** Job 2^{11} etc. The LXX calls him ' king of the Minaeans.' He may have been the chief of a tribe on the borders of Idumaea; cf Job.

ZOPHIM.—The field of Zophim ' was one of the spots to which Balak took Balaam to view Israel, Nu 23^{14}. It is questionable whether we have here a proper name; the Hebrew expression means literally ' field of viewers *or* lookers out.' Such ' places of watching ' were naturally situated frequently on the tops of hills. The location must have been somewhere in the neighbourhood of Mount Pisgah. For **Ramathaim-zophim** see Ramah, **4.**

ZORAH.—A town allotted to Judah, according to Jos 15^{33} (AV **Zoreah**); but elsewhere spoken of as Danite, 19^{41}, Jg 18$^{2, 8, 11}$. It is usually mentioned with Eshtaol. It was the birthplace of Samson, Jg 13$^{2, 25}$, and he was buried between Zorah and Eshtaol, 16^{31}. It was fortified by Rehoboam, 2 Ch 11^{10}; it was later repeopled after the exile, Neh 11^{29} (AV **Zareah**). The gentilic name **Zorathites** occurs in 1 Ch 2^{53} 4^{2} (on 2^{54} see Zorites). Zorah is the modern *Ṣar'ah*, on the northern side of the **Valley of Sorek** (q.v.), opposite **Beth-shemeth** (q.v.), which lies on the southern side.

ZOREAH, Jos 15^{33} (AV).—See Zorah.

ZORITES.—A gentilic found only in 1 Ch 2^{54}, where it should probably be corrected to **Zorathite.** See Zorah.

ZOROASTRIANISM.—See Magi.

ZOROBABEL.—AV and RV form of Zerubbabel in the Apocrypha, and AV form in NT.

ZORZELLEUS.—See Barzillai, **1.**

ZUAR.—Father of Nethanel the head of the tribe of Issachar, Nu 1^{8} 2^{5} 7$^{18, 23}$ 10^{15}.

ZUPH.—**1.** An ancestor of Samuel, 1 S 1^{1}, 1 Ch 6^{35}; called **Zophai** in 1 Ch 6^{26}. **2.** The land of Zuph, 1 S 9^{5}; it probably derived its name from having been originally settled by the family of Zuph. The gentilic name **Zuphite**

probably underlies the name **Ramathaim-zophim** (q.v.) of 1 S 1^{1}. No known site can be said to contain any certain trace of the name Zuph.

ZUR (' rock ').—**1.** A Midianite prince slain by the Israelites, Nu 25^{15} 31^{8}, Jos 13^{21}. **2.** A Gibeonite family settled at Jerusalem, 1 Ch 8^{30} 9^{36}.

ZURIEL (' El is my rock ').—A Merarite chief, Nu 3^{35}.

ZURISHADDAI.—Father of Shelumiel, the chief of the tribe of Simeon, Nu 1^{6} 2^{12} $7^{36, 41}$ 10^{19}.

ZUZIM.—One of the nations defeated by Chedorlaomer and his allies when they went against the cities of the plain, Gn 14^{5}. It is described as being in **Ham** (q.v.). It is possible that they are the same as the **Zamzummim** (q.v.), but this does not help much, since they can no more be identified than the Zuzim.

ZUZIMS, Gn 14^{5} (AV)=**Zuzim** (q.v.).